DOMI MINA
NVS TIO
ILLV MEA
P9-AFP-910

THE OXFORD ENGLISH DICTIONARY

SECOND EDITION

THE OXFORD ENGLISH DICTIONARY

First Edited by

JAMES A. H. MURRAY, HENRY BRADLEY, W. A. CRAIGIE
and C. T. ONIONS

COMBINED WITH

A SUPPLEMENT TO THE OXFORD ENGLISH DICTIONARY

Edited by

R. W. BURCHFIELD

AND RESET WITH CORRECTIONS, REVISIONS
AND ADDITIONAL VOCABULARY

THE OXFORD ENGLISH DICTIONARY

SECOND EDITION

Prepared by
J. A. SIMPSON *and* E. S. C. WEINER

VOLUME I
A–Bazouki

CLARENDON PRESS · OXFORD
1989

Oxford University Press, Walton Street, Oxford OX2 6DP
Oxford New York Toronto
Delhi Bombay Calcutta Madras Karachi
Petaling Jaya Singapore Hong Kong Tokyo
Nairobi Dar es Salaam Cape Town
Melbourne Auckland
and associated companies in
Berlin Ibadan

Oxford is a trade mark of Oxford University Press

British Library Cataloguing in Publication Data
Oxford English dictionary.—2nd ed.
1. English language-Dictionaries
I. Simpson, J. A. (John Andrew), 1953-
II. Weiner, Edmund S. C., 1950-
423
ISBN 0-19-861213-3 (vol. I)
ISBN 0-19-861186-2 (set)

Library of Congress Cataloging-in-Publication Data
The Oxford English dictionary.—2nd ed.
prepared by J. A. Simpson and E. S. C. Weiner
Bibliography: p.
ISBN 0-19-861213-3 (vol. I)
ISBN 0-19-861186-2 (set)
1. English language—Dictionaries. I. Simpson, J. A.
II. Weiner, E. S. C. III. Oxford University Press.
PE1625.087 1989
423—dc19 88-5330

Data capture by ICC, Fort Washington, Pa.
Text-processing by Oxford University Press
Typesetting by Filmtype Services Ltd., Scarborough, N. Yorks.
Manufactured in the United States of America by
Rand McNally & Company, Taunton, Mass.

CONTENTS

This second edition of the Oxford English Dictionary

is respectfully dedicated to

HER MAJESTY THE QUEEN

by her gracious permission

PREFACE

THIS second edition of the *Oxford English Dictionary* amalgamates the text of the first edition, published in twelve volumes in 1933, the *Supplement*, published in four volumes between 1972 and 1986, and approximately five thousand new words, or new senses of existing words, which have gained currency since the relevant volume of the *Supplement* was published. The editorial policies which informed each of the constituent parts of this edition are detailed in the Introduction, which also includes information on the way in which the task of bringing the parts together was accomplished.

The University of Oxford has the honour, with Her Majesty's gracious permission, of dedicating this edition of the Dictionary to Her Majesty Queen Elizabeth the Second. In 1897 'this historical dictionary of the English language' was dutifully dedicated by the University to Her Majesty Queen Victoria, and on the completion of the first edition in 1928 it was presented to His Majesty King George the Fifth.

The aim of this Dictionary is to present in alphabetical series the words that have formed the English vocabulary from the time of the earliest records down to the present day, with all the relevant facts concerning their form, sense-history, pronunciation, and etymology. It embraces not only the standard language of literature and conversation, whether current at the moment, or obsolete, or archaic, but also the main technical vocabulary, and a large measure of dialectal usage and slang. Its basis is a collection of several millions of excerpts from literature of every period amassed by an army of readers and the editorial staff. Such a collection of evidence—it is represented by a selection of about 2,400,000 quotations actually printed—could form the only possible foundation for the historical treatment of every word and idiom which is the *raison d'être* of the work. It is generally recognized that the consistent pursuit of this method has worked a revolution in the art of lexicography. In 1891 a great English philologist wrote of the 'debt' which 'English grammar will some day owe to the *New English Dictionary*'; and the debt has been mounting up ever since. There is no aspect of English linguistic history that the Dictionary has not illuminated; its findings have called for the revision of many philological statements and the reconsideration of many judgements on textual matters. So wide is its scope and so intensive its treatment that it has served for students, both native and foreign, as a lexicon of many languages, and, though it deals primarily with words, it is virtually an encyclopaedic treasury of information about things. It has provided a ready quarry of material for many authors of treatises and dissertations. Abridgements and adaptations of it in several forms have been produced by the Oxford University Press: the *Shorter Oxford English Dictionary*, the *Concise Oxford Dictionary of Current English*, the *Pocket Oxford Dictionary*, the *Little Oxford Dictionary*, and numerous dictionaries for the use of students, children, and foreign learners.

In preparing this new edition of the *Oxford English Dictionary*, we have received help and support from a wide range of individuals and organizations. Foremost among these were IBM United Kingdom Limited, which donated the equipment on which the text was held and manipulated, made available to us proprietary software, seconded three computer experts to assist in the development of the computer system, and maintained throughout a close involvement in the management of the project; the University of Waterloo, in Canada, which provided valuable help in the structuring of the text and was an ever-ready source of technical advice; and the Department of Trade and Industry, which provided a grant—from its Support for Innovation Fund—to help cover the cost of lexicographical research. The very professional service provided by International Computaprint

Corporation in converting the text of the *Oxford English Dictionary* and *Supplement* into machine-readable form was of crucial importance.

The successful completion of the project is attributable in very large measure to the application and dedication of all those who were involved: lexicographers, computer staff, consultants, readers, library researchers, keyboarders, and proof-readers; and to the support and encouragement of the Advisory Council and Editorial Board (listed below), and of the Delegates and senior management of the Oxford University Press.

THE NEW OXFORD ENGLISH DICTIONARY PROJECT

1984–1989

STAFF

Project Director: T. J. BENBOW

Editorial

Co-Editors: J. A. SIMPSON, E. S. C. WEINER

Editorial Co-ordinators: J. C. SWANNELL, Y. L. WARBURTON

Senior Editor (Science): A. M. HUGHES (part-time)

Senior Assistant Editor: S. K. TULLOCH

Assistant Editors: E. BONNER (part-time), E. C. DANN, P. M. GILLIVER, J. PATERSON, B. T. PATON

Editorial Assistants (freelance): V. BROUGHTON, M. HARRINGTON, V. HURST, P. E. ROOKE, J. R. SPENCER

Integration Assistants: S. CHAPMAN, H. Y. CLARKE, L. C. ELLIOTT, A. GIBSON, C. GOODRICK-CLARKE, M. E. HAGUE, S. C. RENNIE, J. S. SIDDLE, I. C. WATSON

Administrative

Administration Manager: C. S. BENNETT

Secretary: S. ENJILY (1984–6), S. GARRARD (1986), K. C. E. VINES (1986–7), K. R. MANVILLE (1987–)

Computer Group

Manager: A. R. PRESCOTT (IBM) (1984–6), R. V. SABIDO (1986–7), R. S. HAWI (1987–)

Chief Designer: J. P. HOWES

D. B. HARRISON (IBM), J. J. CAHILL, M. F. COWLISHAW (IBM), J. M. A. FEW, F. R. KAZMAN (University of Waterloo), R. B. MACHIN, A. M. WEBB

L. V. ANADA, M. DITE, E. F. ERBES, C. T. MIDGLEY, J. A. N. MOSTYN, P. OSMAN, R. PRYCE

COLLABORATORS

The following assisted with library research:

G. M. Briggs (Oxford)
G. Chowdharay-Best (London)
D. Gilbert-Carter (Washington)
D. T. Hanks (Washington)
S. Hinkle (Boston)
D. D. Honoré (Oxford)
R. Keckeissen (New York)
M. Y. Offord (Oxford)
A. P. Orr (Washington)

The following gave valuable editorial assistance:

V. Donaghy
A. Dubin
M. Dunkley
D. J. Edmonds
A. Emmans
C. Hart
R. Temple
J. Waller-Vintar
C. M. Weiner
A. Whear
L. Yeates

During the span of the project, the files of the Oxford Dictionaries Department continued to benefit from the labours of the directed readers, the material submitted by voluntary readers, and the resources of independently compiled collections. In particular, it received from Mrs M. Moe a gift of a large collection of quotations relating to American English, compiled by her husband, the late Colonel A. F. Moe. Significant help was received from Mr D. Barnhart, Mr R. Barnhart, and Mr B. Garner. Notable contributors included Mr S. C. Boorman, Mr G. Charters, Mr G. Chowdharay-Best, Mr C. Collier, Mrs S. Fleming, Mr F. D. Hayes, Miss C. Graves Taylor, Miss R. Mateer, Miss V. Painting, Sir Edward Playfair, Miss G. Rathbone, Mr F. R. Shapiro, Mrs K. Shock, Mr David Shulman, Mr E. Trehern, Dr P. J. Wexler, and Mrs J. K. Williams.

It is with the greatest sadness that the Co-editors record the death, in February 1988, of Miss Marghanita Laski, a steadfast friend of the *OED* and its *Supplement* over some thirty years; especially as she did not live to see the results of her work incorporated into the *OED* itself. The exact size of her written contribution will never be known, but has been estimated at a quarter of a million quotations.

The following consultants and critical readers assisted with the new vocabulary:

Dr M. J. Aitken
Dr R. E. Allen
Dr P. W. Atkins
Mr A. J. Augarde
Dr S. Bradbury
Dr J. Branford
Mr S. Brooks
Dr M. R. Bryce
Dr R. W. Burchfield
Mr P. Burnett
Miss P. Byrde
Sir Alec Cairncross
Dr R. Cammack
Professor F. G. Cassidy
Dr P. A. Charles
Dr D. Clark
Dr F. Close
Dr J. Clutton-Brock
Professor J. Cortés
Mr J. M. Cottis
Mr M. Cowlishaw
Professor G. N. C. Crawford
Dr D. S. Davies
Dr P. D. Dennis
Dr G. Furniss
Mr P. G. W. Glare
Mr C. Gillett
Dr I. Goddard
Mrs J. Gray
Mr M. W. Grose
Mr P. S. Green
Mr R. Hall
Mr P. R. Hardie
Dr R. Hardie
Mr A. Hawke
Mr R. E. Hawkins
Mr M. T. Heydeman
Mr T. F. Hoad
Mr A. G. Hodgkin
Mrs D. D. Honoré
Dr D. M. Jackson
Mr P. Jarrett
Dr Ann Jefferson
Dr R. Jones
Professor T. Kaufman
Dr W. J. Kirwin
Dr H. E. M. Klein
Professor K. Koike
Miss M. Laski
Professor J. D. Latham
Professor J. Leech
Professor B. Lennox
Dr G. Lewis
Mr A. Louth
Dr R. S. McGregor
Ms. I. MacLeod
Professor J. B. McMillan
Dr L. V. Malakhovski
Dr F. H. C. Marriott
Dr K. Morgan
Dr C. Nic Phaidin
Mrs I. Opie
Dr W. S. Ramson
Mrs V. M. Richardson
Professor R. H. Robins
Dr D. A. Roe
Dr H. M. Rosenberg
Professor J. M. Rosenberg
Mr R. Russell
Professor N. G. Sabbagha
Mr R. Scruton
Mr D. L. F. Sealy
Mrs P. Simpson
Ms J. Smith
Dr J. R. Spencer
Professor E. G. Stanley
Mr A. J. Stevens
Dr J. Stubbs
Dr J. B. Sykes
Professor J. Tao
Professor G. Treitel
Dr W. R. Trumble
Mr G. W. Turner
Professor J. O. Urmson
Professor T. G. Vallance
Dr M. Weitzmann
Mr D. Willand
Mr J. Wilson
Mrs H. C. Wright
Mr B. Zephaniah
Dr R. D. Zorc

In addition to the members of the Advisory Council and the Editorial Board, the following gave valuable advice and help at various stages in the project:

Mr R. Beale
Mr E. Bodger
Dr L. Burnard
Mr R. Corwin
Mr E. O. V. Fletcher
Mr T. Hunt
Mr P. F. J. Luna
Mr J. Mackay
Mr A. Rosenheim
Dr W. R. Trumble
Mr L. Urdang
Mr N. S. Wedd
Mr R. Zich

The assistance of the following organizations was instrumental in the completion of this work:

The management of IBM UK Ltd., especially Mr J. W. Fairclough, Dr G. W. Robinson, Mr P. D. Wright.

The University of Waterloo Centre for the New OED, especially Professor G. Gonnet, G. Johannesen, Professor J. Stubbs, Professor F. W. Tompa.

The University of Oxford Phonetics Laboratory, especially its acting head, Dr I. Watson.

INTRODUCTION

THIS new edition of the *Oxford English Dictionary* contains the whole text, unaltered in all essentials, of the twelve-volume first edition, which appeared in 1933 as a reprint of the ten-volume *New English Dictionary on Historical Principles*, itself originally published in parts between 1884 and 1928. It also contains the complete text of the four-volume *Supplement to the Oxford English Dictionary*, published between 1972 and 1986; this superseded the previous *Supplement*, which was issued in 1933 as a companion to the main work.

The main purpose of this second edition is to present a version of the Dictionary in which these two parts, the twelve volumes and the four volumes, are amalgamated into a continuous, seamless text. Accordingly, every article from the *Supplement* has been either added in its proper alphabetical position (if a wholly new entry) or merged with its corresponding *OED* entry (following directions which the *Supplement* gives but the present edition omits, as now redundant). Instead of the sixteen volumes of large but unequal size in which the previous works were issued, it has been published in twenty slimmer and evenly sized volumes, which it is hoped will prove more convenient to use.

Although the *raison d'être* of this new edition is the integration of the two texts, and adherence to the instructions of the *Supplement*, whether explicitly stated or contextually implied, is the guiding principle of the work, the material brought over from the *Supplement* is by no means the only feature that differentiates the second edition from the first. New vocabulary has been added, certain important general revisions, and numerous local corrections, have been made, and the whole text has been given an entirely new typographical format. It is estimated that these changes, fuller details of which are given below, have affected (in different ways) the majority of the 290,500 entries contained in this edition, including virtually all articles on the commonest words. Together they have made this edition significantly richer in information, and more modern in aspect, than its distinguished predecessors.

Whereas the *Supplement* can be regarded for practical purposes as up to date, it is a matter of common knowledge that many elements of the original *OED* require revision. That is the very purpose for which the New OED Project, of which the present work is the first printed product, was initiated. Several of these requirements have been addressed in this edition. But the full revision and updating of the Dictionary (an outline agenda for which is given in the *History* section below) must be regarded as a long-term goal, demanding considerable resources, and therefore to be approached in stages. This new edition represents the first, and almost certainly the most arduous, step towards that goal.

The fundamental difference between this edition and its predecessors is, by its nature, quite invisible to the user of the Dictionary. Before the compilation of this edition, the *OED* and *Supplement*, which had only ever been typeset in hot metal, were computerized. The machine-readable version of the Dictionary resulting from computerization is now the master copy from which the present printed edition has been made. It is the version to which further modifications to the Dictionary will be applied, and from which new editions and offspring works of reference will be generated in the future.

But the machine-readable text is not distinct from the printed one merely by virtue of existing in a different physical medium, electronic instead of paper, or tape rather than type; or even by its priority in the production process. Much more important, it carries a whole new world of information. This has nothing to do with supplementary text. In addition to the conventional natural-language text taken over from the printed *OED* and *Supplement*, there is another layer of information: the 'mark-up language' or tagging system. The different categories of information into which the text can be partitioned, such as headword, pronunciation, variant form, quotation, or date of quotation, are each identified accurately and unambiguously by computer tags. These tags consist of short sequences of letters, mainly mnemonic in form (e.g. 'quot' for 'quotation'), set off by delimiting characters from the conventional text which they mark. They do not appear on the printed page, but are there translated into various features of layout, typography, and punctuation. Unlike the tags, most of the latter, viewed logically, are to some degree ambiguous and redundant, though familiar and convenient to the user of the Dictionary. Thus, the tags that signify 'headword' and 'date of quotation' accompany these elements, but no instruction to print them in bold type appears in the machine-readable text; they could as easily be printed in capitals or sanserif if desired. The typographical realization of an element is relative, being determined by the requirements of the particular published form; accordingly, information of this kind has been largely, though not absolutely, purged from the electronic master text.

Only the presence of this structural information within the text has made it possible to integrate the *OED* and *Supplement*, and to perform the other systematic changes listed below, with so small a staff and in so short a time, and only because of it is the further revision and updating of the Dictionary feasible at all. It is also the prerequisite for the conversion of the *OED* into a publicly available electronic database. The project team believes the addition of this information to have been, without doubt, their chief contribution to the future of the *Oxford English Dictionary*.

SPECIAL FEATURES OF THE SECOND EDITION

The distinctive features of this edition may be described under four headings: supplementary text, general revisions, local corrections, and typographical format. These will be explained in turn.

A. SUPPLEMENTARY TEXT

1. The 69,372 entries of the four-volume *Supplement* have been amalgamated with the 252,259 entries of the *OED*, first edition. 41,752 of these entries are new and independent; the remaining 27,620 have been integrated with the corresponding *OED* entries. The principles that guided this process of integration are explained below.

2. Entirely new articles dealing with an additional 5,000 words, combinations, and senses, have been included and integrated; these are located chiefly in the first third of the alphabet, where the work done for the *Supplement* is now twenty years or more old. The policy and history of this part of the project are set out below.

3. The 260 addenda and 83 spurious entries appended to Volume XII of the first edition have here been merged with the main text.

4. 560 corrections, being chiefly earlier illustrative examples, which were prepared for Volumes I and II of the *Supplement* but not inserted there, have been included here.

5. The process of integration has from time to time required that a lexical item, treated as a subordinate part of an entry in the *OED* or *Supplement*, should be elevated to the status of a main entry, and this has naturally entailed the writing of new text.

B. GENERAL REVISIONS

1. *IPA and stress-marked headwords.* The system devised by Sir James Murray for representing pronunciation, used in both the first edition of the *OED* and the *Supplement*, has now been replaced

throughout the text by the International Phonetic Alphabet. Many headwords and lexical items in the two parent works had their stress-pattern marked by symbols placed within them, instead of being followed by a phonetic transcription; these marks, which are placed *after* the stressed vowel, have been replaced by IPA stress-marks, which are placed *before* the stressed syllable. The principles of transcription and translation followed here are described below, pp. xxxiii–xxxiv.

2. *Foreign script*. In its etymological material, the first edition regularly cited foreign words in non-roman scripts; besides Greek, cited forms in Arabic script, the Cyrillic alphabet, Devanagari, the square Hebrew alphabet, and the Syriac script are quite usual. These were normally, but not universally, accompanied by transliterations. Except when citing Greek, the *Supplement* abandoned this practice, giving only transliterations. It was decided to follow the latter's practice in the present edition, considering that the dropping of the scripts would be more straightforward than the furnishing of accurate new non-roman forms, and that the first edition itself frequently neglected to supply the non-roman forms. Transcriptions have been supplied wherever they were missing in the first edition.

In quotations the presence of foreign script is, of course, an intrinsic feature; it has been preserved as far as possible, subject to the constraints upon 'artwork' and special characters in general (see below).

3. *Illustration and special characters*. The parent texts resort from time to time to the inclusion of what amount to pictorial illustrations, mainly diagrammatic or typographic in style. In the first edition a number of names for typefaces are typographically illustrated, and a few other concepts are conveyed diagrammatically. These have been omitted. Other more modest forms of illustration, which involve the use of individual special characters such as occur or might reasonably be expected to occur in the Dictionary, have been retained.

Between them, the two parent texts make use of approximately 660 characters apart from the ninety or so available on the typical keyboard. Virtually all of these have been retained, and some previously wrong have been corrected.

4. *Ordering of entries*. The alphabetical arrangement of entries in the *OED* and *Supplement* is to some extent affected by the presence of special characters, accents, punctuation, and capitalization within the headword. The principles which prevail, but are not universally followed, in the parent texts have been standardized throughout the present edition. As a result, certain details in the identification of some entries differ from their counterparts in the parent texts, and a few of these have consequently been removed some distance from their former position.

5. *Ordering of senses*. The sense-divisions of most entries in the first edition and its *Supplement* follow a very clear system of structural organization, as described below, p. xxxiii. The system has been extended to the few scattered entries which were (usually for no special reason) irregular in structure.

Entries in which a series of senses skips or duplicates a number, owing to simple editorial or typographical oversight, have been corrected.

6. *Cross-references*. Cross-references whose targets were changed as a result of the integration of *OED* and *Supplement* entries have been emended as far as possible. These changes reflect the changes to the identifying structure of an entry, listed below, p. xviii.

Many of the 580,000 cross-references in the Dictionary are imprecise, citing headwords without parts of speech and homonym numbers, for example. It was impossible for the automatic cross-referencing system to determine which of two or more possible targets was the one proper to an ambiguous cross-reference of this sort, and so, on the whole, these have not been made more precise; in many cases, the intended target is obvious to the reader, and amplification would merely be fussy. There were also a fair number of cross-references which, as printed, did not match any existing headword; this was nearly always because of a slight difference in spelling. Most of these have been emended in the present edition.

C. LOCAL CORRECTIONS

1. *The spelling of vocabulary items.* Certain conventions of spelling, as also of capitalization, hyphenation, and punctuation, have changed since the publication of the first edition; indeed the occurrence of some such changes is evidenced within the Dictionary itself. Harmonization of the whole text with currently acceptable style would have been impossible within the limits of this new edition. The *Supplement*, however, indicated many changes to the spelling of headwords, which have, of course, been effected; and an attempt has been made to carry such changes through into derivatives and combinations of the main words and into contiguous definitions. Other such updatings, overlooked by the *Supplement*, are carried out wherever possible.

2. *The main text of Dictionary entries.* Innumerable small misprints and slips have naturally been encountered, during editing, in the definitions, etymologies, and notes which form the core of the Dictionary text. These have been corrected.

3. *Quotations.* The text of quotations has been carefully protected from corruption. The working assumption was that it always correctly reproduces the original source, however strangely it may read. Nevertheless, an appreciable number of quotations came under suspicion of inaccuracy, or could be clearly seen to have suffered mutilation at the hands of compositors, and were checked and corrected from the sources.

It was a basic, and not unreasonable, requirement of our automatic processing that quotations (with certain regular exceptions, such as those from *Beowulf*) must begin with a date. Dates (sometimes only approximate) were supplied by means of bibliographical investigation to the small number of quotations that were found to lack them.

D. TYPOGRAPHICAL CHANGES

1. *Entry spacing.* In the first edition, no spacing separates entries one from another. This edition follows the *Supplement* in placing space between entries. Series of entries for variant and obsolete forms are treated in the same way, not run on as they often are in the first edition.

2. *Distinction between main and subordinate entries.* The typographical distinction in the first edition between main words and subordinate words, by which the latter were printed in a lighter bold type, has been given up in this edition, as it had already in the *Supplement*. Such a distinction is difficult to draw absolutely and is, in any case, of doubtful utility.

3. *Distinction between headword and other bold elements.* Besides the distinction between two kinds of headword just described, the first edition used other varieties of bold type to identify derivatives, combinations, and variant forms of the headword, when cited within the same entry. Derivatives were usually printed in dark bold similar to, but smaller than, that of the headword, while combinations and variant forms were printed in a lighter bold. The *Supplement* used only a single typeface to distinguish all three from the headword. In this edition derivatives and combinations are printed in a dark bold, smaller than the headword, and variant spellings are printed in a light bold. It seemed

logical to symbolize in the same way what are, in effect, subordinated headwords, but to differentiate them from the variant spellings of the main headword.

4. *Italicized vocabulary items.* The text of a Dictionary definition contains numerous elements printed in italics, which fall into several different categories of information: chiefly usage label, cross-reference, cited linguistic form, and lexical item (such as phrase or minor combination). This last element is of particular importance since, like the headword, derivative, or bold combination, it constitutes one of the keys by which the reader finds the information which he or she is seeking. Since this kind of element is specially marked by tags in the electronic version of the text, it seemed helpful to print it in this edition in a special bold italic typeface, clearly setting it off from all other italicized text.

5. *Capitalization of headwords.* In the first edition of the *OED*, every main headword was given a capital initial, regardless of whether the word was normally so written. Most derivatives, and many combinations, were also capitalized. The *Supplement*, in accord with modern lexicographical practice, abandoned this convention, giving a capital only where that is the normal spelling. This edition follows the *Supplement*'s practice.

For many words capitalization varies, either at different dates or in different senses. Because its convention disguised the problem, the *OED* often did not indicate the prevailing or preferred style. Where the intentions of the first edition were not deducible, as often with rare and obsolete words, decisions about capitalization were made on the basis of the printed quotations or analogy with similar and related words, or both.

6. *Abbreviations in initial letter entries.* Only a small number of abbreviations (i.e. initialisms) were listed under the entries for initial letters in the first edition. In line with recent linguistic developments, these lists were greatly augmented by the *Supplement*. But though these abbreviations have definitions, they are not picked out typographically in the parent texts. In this edition they are printed in bold type for easy identification.

7. *Asterisks in quotation paragraphs and cross-references.* In the Dictionary, quotations illustrating a series of combinations can be listed either in one chronological sequence, or (as is usual when the combinations are defined) in a series of chronological sequences, each illustrating one combination and all arranged in the alphabetical order of the combinations. In the first edition, an asterisk was placed in the first quotation of each sequence, marking the combination being illustrated. In the *Supplement*, this convention was not followed, because asterisks were used to mark two other features: sense numbers that were to be intercalated into the *OED* sequence, and cross-references to entries in the *Supplement*. As a result of integration, the latter conventions have disappeared; but also, many quotation series without asterisks from the *Supplement* have been merged with series with asterisks from the *OED*. In these cases, the asterisking convention has been carried through the whole merged quotation paragraph. It has not, however, been introduced into every paragraph of this kind originating in the *Supplement* alone.

8. *Hyphenation.* Unlike its parent texts, this edition has been printed without regular line-end hyphenation. Most of the hyphens printed are true ('hard') hyphens. This has the advantage that no extraneous hyphens are introduced into lexical items, variant forms, or other linguistic forms cited in the text. It also means that virtually no merely line-end ('soft') hyphens have been introduced into the text of quotations. Though this results in a less even layout of text on the page than in the parent texts, it is felt that the advantages outweigh this drawback.

When the text of quotations from the Dictionary was keyboarded, hyphens occurring at line endings had to be either dropped or retained (as 'hard' hyphens). Without consulting the original works from which the quotations were drawn, it was sometimes impossible to decide which would be correct, even after considering the date of the quotation, the evidence of the other quotations from the same work, and so on. In order to avoid a misleading decision, a special symbol (-) has been used to replace the hyphen of the parent text. This symbol indicates nothing more than the ambiguity of the hyphen in the parent text. It is also occasionally used to split a bold or italic combination, a derivative, or a word employed in a definition, for the sake of a line-break: in such cases, it is to be understood to indicate that the word is *not* normally written with a hyphen.

PRINCIPLES OF INTEGRATION

The integration of the text of the *Supplement* into that of the first edition of the *OED* (referred to below as 'the *OED*' for brevity's sake) was carried out in two stages. The major processes were performed automatically by computer programs specifically developed for the purpose. Printouts of the resulting merged entries were then edited by lexicographers, and the emendations marked on them were entered by keyboarders into the computer.

The guiding principle of both stages of the integration process was that the intentions of the *Supplement* should be faithfully followed unless there were very good reasons for departing from them.

INDEPENDENT ENTRIES

About 42,000 main entries in the *Supplement* were new and independent. They were put into their appropriate place in the alphabetical sequence.

A new entry having a headword with the same spelling and part of speech as one or more in the *OED* already had a different homonym number: it was placed after its *OED* homonym(s). If there was only one homonym in the *OED*, this was given the homonym number 1. A new entry having a headword with the same spelling but a different part of speech was placed in an appropriate position among the pre-existing entries, usually towards the end of the sequence (see the principles of entry ordering, p. xxxii below); where only a noun ('substantive') or nouns occurred in the *OED*, they had no explicit part of speech: the part of speech '*sb.*' was supplied.

Many combinations and derivatives treated, in the first edition, within the entries for the main words on which they are formed were elevated to the status of main words in the *Supplement*. The usual reason for this was a significant increase in the complexity of the senses of the word or its general acceptance as more than a casual or obvious compound of the root word. A certain number of forms treated as graphic or spoken variants of a main word in the first edition were similarly registered as separate, independent words in the *Supplement*. When such upgrading occurred, the material relating to the word in the first edition was not reprinted in full in the new entry; instead, cross-references were used to direct the reader to the definition, etymology, or quotation in question, implying that it was now part of the new entry. Accordingly, in the integrated text this original material has been moved (with appropriate editing) to the new position. Much effort has been devoted to detecting overlapping entries of this sort, many of which are extremely well disguised, especially when linked by only a single, inconspicuous quotation.

A certain number of *Supplement* entries directed the reader to delete the existing Dictionary entry and substitute a new one, the text of which then follows. Not infrequently, these entries also borrowed snatches of text from the former entry, especially the quotations given there. Before the original entries were discarded, the borrowed text was transferred to the new entries.

There were also entries in the *Supplement* which added further information to a different main word in the first edition, but nevertheless did not require a new entry to be created. There were two principal kinds. First, where the entry for a main word in the first edition had a derivative listed under it and the only addition to that entry in the *Supplement* related to the derivative, the latter was given, as it were, the temporary status of a main word solely for the purposes of supplementation. In such cases, the new material has been accommodated within the framework of the original main entry and the supplementary one has been discarded. Secondly, a variant form of a main word could be treated in a separate entry with illustrative quotations, because the variant in question either had not been listed and illustrated under the principal form, or had recently become recognized as the predominant spelling. In both cases the intention was that the two entries should be merged, in the latter with a change of spelling in the headword. Again, detecting such pairs of entries (and some forming larger groups) has been very difficult, especially as the spelling variation can bridge widely separated parts of the Dictionary (C and K, or E and Œ, for example), a factor which has occasionally frustrated the fulfilment of the *Supplement*'s intentions.

MATCHING ENTRIES

The remaining 28,000 entries in the *Supplement* had counterparts in the *OED* with which they were integrated. Four basic procedures were followed, in line with the main instructions to the user included in each entry: *addition*, *deletion*, *transference*, and *substitution*. Naturally not every one of the thousands of occasions when any of these changes was made is explicitly indicated in the text, but the intentions are nearly always quite clear.

In the headword section of the entry (the *identification*), the usual supplementary material consisted of a pronunciation or one or more variant forms or inflexions. Deletions were mainly of status labels (especially 'obsolete'). Transference of labels into a sense section was common. Substitution of a different spelling of the headword or a modified label occurred from time to time.

Etymologies were occasionally added or modified by deletion or substitution.

In the *signification*, additions made up the bulk of the changes occasioned by the *Supplement*. Where a complete new sense section was added, its numbering normally indicated the correct position. If the first edition had only one sense section at that level in the hierarchy, the absent sense number or letter (the first in the series: **A**, **1**, **a**, or (*a*)) was supplied. *Supplement* sense sections introduced by starred numbers were added at the appropriate point in the sequence, and the ensuing sense divisions were renumbered to accommodate them. When a section division (headed by a capital letter), covering the use of a word in a new grammatical category, was added at the end of an entry, the identification was altered to include the new part of speech. Sections containing derivatives were added at the end of the entry.

Supplementary material was frequently added to definitions; this was commonly made plain by the introductory word 'also', which sometimes became superfluous and was edited out. Occasions when the new material could merely be added, without modification, at the end of the existing definition were relatively rare. Often the new material had to be inserted within the old, or the whole rewritten into one definition. The domain of a label had sometimes to be restricted to cover only the intended portion of the definition. So multifarious were the modifications that the results can scarcely be distinguished from the deletions, transferences, and substitutions indicated from time to time by the *Supplement*.

The parts of the Dictionary which the *Supplement* especially augmented are the sections in which defined and undefined combinations are listed. Considerable labour was required to merge the corresponding lists (usually in alphabetical order). The defined combinations, resembling as they do complete entries in miniature, were susceptible to supplementation, deletion, modification, and substitution in any of their constituent parts. Their alphabetical sorting and rough merging was achieved automatically, but much work remained for editorial attention.

The addition of *quotations* was very frequent: when an entirely new sense-division was added, with its own group of quotations, when a sense section was supplemented, and as the sole modification to a sense section. In most cases this was a straightforward operation. Paragraphs of quotations that illustrate combinations, however, usually consist of a series, arranged alphabetically to correspond with the combinations, of short chronological sequences of quotations; the accurate fusing of parallel series of these was a complicated operation, requiring careful editing, both on paper and at the screen.

CROSS-REFERENCES

Integration of the *Supplement* with the main Dictionary text involved an enormous number of changes to the 'addresses' at which sections of text were located: namely, to the form of the headword, the part of speech associated with it, the homonym number distinguishing otherwise identical main words, or the number or letter identifying the sense-division under which a definition, combination, or quotation could be found. As a result, there was a danger that many cross-references would become invalid, since the elements to which they pointed would now be differently identified. This was countered by a twofold strategy. A computer program caused every change to the 'address' of an element brought about by the process of automatic integration to be applied to the cross-references which cited that address. Editorial staff subsequently ensured that changes made by them were logged and then applied to the corresponding cross-references. Inevitably, a few cross-references escaped both systems, including those in early volumes which were already passed for press before editorial changes that would affect them had been made in later volumes. There are around 600,000 cross-references in the *OED*, of which well over 20,000 have been adjusted in response to integration, and many more have been corrected or rendered more precise.

THE TRANSLATION OF THE PHONETIC SYSTEM

The system of phonetic transcription devised by Sir James Murray for use in the first edition and followed, for the sake of consistency, in the *Supplement* is a subtle and flexible means of recording English pronunciation. But many of the effects for which Murray strove in the design of his system were realized, not long afterwards, in the International Phonetic Alphabet (IPA). It seems very possible that, if the IPA had already achieved full development and widespread acceptance at the time that Murray was beginning work on the Dictionary, he would have adopted it instead of a system of his own. It was therefore logical to consider replacing Murray's system with IPA throughout the Dictionary. IPA has the advantage that it is very widely accepted and understood, and can be used to represent the sounds as well of regional and dialect English and foreign languages as of standard English. Indeed its introduction was regarded by many whom the project team consulted as among the highest priorities. It was decided that the change should be made for the present edition, rather than left until a future revision phase. But for reasons of historical interest, the Murray transcriptions have been retained in the electronic version alongside the IPA ones, the latter only having been printed.

A notable feature of the Dictionary is that obsolete main words, derivatives, and certain variant forms and combinations are not given phonetic transcriptions but have their stress-pattern indicated: the stress-dots (which are placed *after* the accented *vowel*, just as they are within the transcriptions) are printed within the body of the word or form. Naturally consistency required that the stress-dots within these forms should also be altered to IPA stress-marks (which are placed *before* the beginning of the accented *syllable*).

The short time available meant that there had to be rather strict limitations on the extent of the changes made. For native English words the variety of pronunciation represented is, broadly speaking, educated standard southern British, or 'Received Pronunciation' (RP). There could be no question, at this stage, of systematically registering non-RP (i.e. other British and non-British) pronunciations; although of course those already included in the Dictionary have remained and have been augmented by a few analogous cases. Again, pronunciation variants within RP, apart from those already registered in the Dictionary, could not be researched and documented, except as the evident need to include them arose in the course of the other editing. The adding of up-to-date pronunciations, except when prescribed by the *Supplement*, had to be kept to a minimum, for the same reasons. Essentially, a straightforward literal translation from the Murray system to IPA has been attempted, accompanied by correction of the errors inevitably arising from that process.

The method by which the translation of the Murray system to IPA was performed can be briefly summarized. As much of the translation as possible was carried out automatically by computer. The computer had to operate on two kinds of material: sequences of phonetic characters, and normal English words containing dots indicating the position of the stress accent. First, the program identified the strings of characters which it was required to process. It used the mark-up tags to do this. Then the actual translation was run. The program referred to three tables, one giving IPA equivalents for Murray's phonetic symbols (or groups of them); one giving rules that showed whether each IPA symbol is a vowel, a consonant, or a consonant cluster; and one giving similar rules for ordinary English spelling. The second and third table enabled the computer to deduce the correct position for an IPA stress-mark from the existing stress-dot in the text. Certain characters and groups were known in advance to have more than one possible IPA equivalent. These were printed out on a special report, as were all pronunciations in which the conversion failed; and from these, corrections were made at the keyboard. Altogether, 137,152 phonetic transcriptions and 137,274 stress-marked words were automatically translated.

A considerable number of phonetic transcriptions are found in other parts of an entry than the pronunciation key. These were not originally identified by the computer, and so a separate program was run in order to register them on a list for editorial transcription.

The conversion of Murray's phonetic system to IPA was not entirely straightforward. The peculiar nature of the system, the way in which it is applied both in general and in particular cases, and the historical variety of English speech which it was employed to record, all presented obstacles to the smooth application of the scheme of translation.

The peculiarities of Murray's phonetic alphabet can be ascribed to the time and circumstances of its devising.[1] It must here suffice to enumerate a few of its characteristics. It is used indiscriminately both for *phonetic* and *phonemic* transcription: that is, it is a set of symbols employed to represent both the members of the particular set of sounds that constitute the phonology of English, and the much larger set of infinitesimally differing sounds from all other phonologies to which reference is made in the Dictionary. As a means of representing standard English pronunciation, Murray's system is sensitive and generally lucid. It is less well-adapted for the transcription of dialectal and foreign words. Shift had often to be made with the limited range of typographical shapes that Murray had devised at the outset in order to transcribe unexpected foreign sounds. Symbols not listed in the original pronunciation key appeared during the progress of the Dictionary. Uncommon foreign sounds were handled differently on widely separated occasions.

With regard to consonants, there are few drawbacks to Murray's system, apart from the dearth of symbols for foreign sounds. Indeed, all but one of the primary consonant symbols correspond exactly to the set employed for English in the IPA. A fundamental feature of the vowel system that does not

[1] For a full discussion, the reader is referred to M. K. C. MacMahon, 'James Murray and the Phonetic Notation in the *New English Dictionary*', *Transactions of the Philological Society*, 1985, pp. 72–112.

translate easily into IPA is its analysis into 'ordinary', 'long', and 'obscure' vowels. Broadly, the same list of symbols appears under each heading, but (respectively) without a diacritical accent, accented with a macron (long mark), and accented with a breve (short mark). The implication is that the same underlying vowel manifests itself in three guises; and, further, that these guises are determined at least partly by its relationship to the stress accent of the word. The theory underlying the obscure vowels is that, *if* they were accorded stress, as they sometimes are in song or very careful enunciation, they would resemble their ordinary equivalents. This principle, though something like it is encountered in phonological theories, is not usually embodied in the standard IPA transcriptions used in dictionaries. If, as has here been done, it is set aside, then most of the obscure vowels are equivalent to the IPA ə ('schwa'; the sound of *a* in *sofa, particular*); while a few are translated into ɪ (the sound of *e* in *hatchet*). The main peculiarity of the long vowel series is that diphthongs are included in it; but this is an oddity of phonetic theory—the analysis of English diphthongs as long vowels followed by 'glides'—rather than an obstacle to translation.

The major problem arises in the 'ordinary' vowel series, which contains both vowels universally recognized as lacking length—the *i* of *pin*, for example—and vowels now normally transcribed as long vowels. These, in fact, are the members of the long series in another guise: a guise apparently taken on in a syllable under low stress. So, for example, the vowel of the second syllable of *Matthew* is an ordinary vowel, while that of *few* is long. Most classifications would treat them as identical. This would not pose a major problem of translation, if it were not that the same symbols employed for the second vowel of *Matthew* and its parallels throughout the vowel system (her*o*, Psych*e*, etc.) are also used to represent the principal vowels of the European languages—roughly speaking, the so-called 'cardinal vowels'. The two sets of vowels are not phonetically identical, or even close, and were not in Murray's time. Such symbols as these (along with some others) were straightforwardly ambiguous, and could not be translated correctly in every case by the computer.

Because Murray's system uses many of the same symbols for English and foreign vowel sounds, it was necessary to depart from certain conventions that are common in the transcription adopted by English dictionaries. A notable example is the use of (ɛ) for the vowel of *bed* in place of the more usual (e), because the English vowel is, for most English ears, closer to the cardinal open vowel of French *faire* or German *Bär* than to the cardinal narrow vowel of French *bébé* or German *Schnee*.

The variety of English pronunciation recorded by the Murray transcription is extremely 'precise', conservative, and (in present-day terms) old-fashioned. Most of its peculiar characteristics are systematic (they permeate the phonology) rather than occasional (features of the pronunciation of particular words, or groups of words). They are systematic enough for a phonetician to predict the way in which individual words will be transcribed, but not enough to make it easy for a computer to efface them all automatically. This is one reason why they have largely been retained in this edition. A second reason is that they constitute a useful record of one variety of English pronunciation in a particular period; and a third is that, for the general user, most of them are merely small nuances for which one can make allowance.

The chief phonological features that set the pronunciation represented in the Dictionary apart from most present-day phonetic descriptions of English are the following:

1. The stressed close vowels (iː, uː) are maintained in words like *idea*, *realize*, *museum*, *skua*, in contrast with the diphthongs (ɪə, ʊə) of *dear*, *rear*, *secure*.
2. The close vowels (iː, uː) are maintained in unstressed syllables in words like *delineate*, *creation*, *perpetual*, *graduate*, in contrast with the open vowels (ɪ, ʊ) of *genius*, *demonic*, *circulate*.

   It is in such syllables that the Murray transcription uses 'ordinary' vowels, not long ones. It is quite likely, therefore, that Murray was aware of no distinction in duration between these vowels, but it is also clear from the consistency with which the distinction is observed that he was aware of, or believed in, a distinction of vowel quality (specifically, of tension). The conventional IPA transcription, however, observes only a phonemic distinction between open vowels, which are treated as 'short', and narrow vowels, which are accorded symbols of length as well. The IPA transcriptions therefore convey the misleading implication that such vowels have, or had, greater duration.

3. Diphthongs (e.g., əʊ) are maintained in unstressed syllables in words like *homographic*, *protocol*, in contrast with the obscure vowel 'schwa' in words like *homonym*, *melody*.
4. Unstressed medial obscure vowels are not represented as having been elided, e.g. in *veterinary*.
5. A distinction is maintained between syllabic consonants and a sequence of obscure vowel and consonant, so that words like *principle* and *principal* are distinguished.
6. A distinction is drawn between a diphthong (ɔə) in words like *glory*, *boarder*, *mourning*, and a long vowel (ɔː) in words like *saurian*, *border*, and *morning*. This is not generally maintained in present-day IPA.
7. The nineteenth-century lengthening of the rounded low back vowel of words like *soft*, *cloth*, and *cross* is recorded (in this edition, as a separate variant; in the first edition, by a special symbol indicating the possibility of either pronunciation).

NEW VOCABULARY

HISTORICAL BACKGROUND

The decision to include in this edition some five thousand new items of vocabulary was taken in the light of several considerations. First, the pace of lexical innovation is rapid, and every dictionary must be continually enlarged or revised to accommodate the many new words and senses which become part of the language each year. Secondly, the compilation of new entries is a discrete editorial activity on which work could start straight away, independent of the revision which is envisaged as the business of subsequent phases of the project. Thirdly, as work on the *Supplement* came to an end, staff who were skilled in the compilation of *OED* entries, and a research base, in the form of a large quotation file, library researchers, consultants, etc., became available. Fourthly, other Oxford dictionaries, notably the *Shorter OED*, the *Concise Oxford Dictionary*, and the *Oxford Advanced Learner's Dictionary*, then in the process of revision, needed a selection of fully-researched new entries; this could be produced most efficiently by a central unit supplying material both to the New OED project and to other dictionaries.

Editorial work on new vocabulary began in 1983. It was recognized at the outset that the bulk of the material would lie in the early section of the alphabet. The lexical changes of the period (between ten and twenty years) since this part of the *Supplement* was prepared were yet to be recorded; moreover, the *Supplement*'s coverage of the vocabulary already in use at that period was limited both by the relatively modest scale on which the work was initially planned and by the extent of the collections, which were inevitably small in the early stages. In this it resembled, though for different reasons, the earlier *Supplement* of 1933, of which R. W. Chapman wrote: 'We projected accordingly . . . a wedge-shaped Supplement, designed to bring the work to an even date; it is, so to speak, all ABC and no XYZ.' But this asymmetry was a condition of the material being treated; there was no constraint on the editorial operation that confined it to one part of the alphabet. On the contrary, the storage of the material on the *New OED* database meant that very recent coinages from any point in the alphabet could as readily be accommodated.

SELECTION AND EDITING OF NEW MATERIAL

The large quotation file maintained by the Oxford English Dictionaries Department was the basis for selecting items for inclusion in this edition, as it had been both for the first edition and for the *Supplement*. It offered, as before, the most comprehensive and objective basis for the selection of vocabulary items and the provision of supporting evidence. The file was growing at the rate of some 120,000 quotations per year, collected predominantly by means of a reading programme covering books, magazines, etc., representing the main varieties of English used throughout the world, but enhanced by scholarly contributions of specific new information, earlier illustrative quotations, and other lexicographical material.

But new resources had become available to lexicographers during the previous decade. Perhaps the most important were the large computer databases containing research abstracts, newspaper and periodical texts, and legal reports. At first, computer-readable texts were used mainly to generate concordances. By the 1980s it was also possible, by rapidly searching the extensive text held on these databases, to pin down specific uses of individual words or phrases. These databases proved invaluable in tracing early uses of terms, in providing examples to complete the lexicographical record, and in supplying etymological information.

The databases of the 1980s rarely helped in the actual selection of new words for inclusion in the Dictionary. Inclusion was normally suggested by other means (such as evidence in the quotation file); the databases were used subsequently to provide additional information and to confirm the currency of the word or sense. It should also be stressed that these resources had to be used with some caution, as they might contain only recent text, or examples of English from only one area (notably North America), and they lacked the ability to identify the meaning in which a word was used in a given context or to distinguish it from the other meanings of that word. They did not, therefore, always provide a foundation for generalized, objective judgements on a particular linguistic or lexicographical point, but rather offered subsidiary evidence.

During the preparation of this edition, there was a general increase in interest in new words among lexicographers and their readers, particularly in North America and Great Britain. The two Barnhart Dictionaries of New English and their quarterly Companion presented well-researched material on neologisms. The Merriam-Webster Dictionaries published their record of new vocabulary in book form. Advance publicity for new dictionaries appearing throughout the world provided lists of the neologisms included in them. These were all valuable pointers to items that need to be included in the *OED*. And as ever, personal observation by members of the Dictionary Department and other contributors (the historical dictionary's own style of 'oral evidence') was a prolific source of further suggestions.

The selection of new words now included in the Dictionary is not intended to represent simply the emergent vocabulary of the last few years. To have selected solely according to this criterion would have highlighted terms which might not have achieved an established footing in the language, at the expense of other, older words. Indeed, one of the engaging aspects of historical lexicography is that terms which are held to be of recent origin often turn out to have existed for many years, though without achieving general currency. Recent neologisms have not been excluded, but have had to compete for their places alongside other candidates. In general, terms from most of the varieties of English are added, though the majority are current in American or British English, or in both. The vocabularies of modern computer technology, medicine, politics, economics, and popular culture are well represented, though not at the cost of terms from less obtrusive realms. Omission should not be equated with exclusion; a simple practical limit had to be set in accordance with the number of items that could be prepared in time for this edition.

There is no major difference between the editorial policy of the *Supplement* and that followed in the preparation of the further new entries; they are no more than an extension of the *Supplement* on a smaller scale, integrated, like the latter, into the main text of the Dictionary. In so far as these new entries have been compiled in accordance with the overall editorial policy of the second edition, they naturally embody a certain number of differences from the style of the *Supplement*. The stylistic changes have been described above, pp. xii–xvi. It was the policy of the *Supplement* to include earlier, further, and later examples of words and senses already in the Dictionary. This provision, being quite distinct from the addition of new entries, was not continued after the completion of the *Supplement*, but was deferred until such time as the full revision of the Dictionary may begin.

STATISTICS

This edition of the *Oxford English Dictionary* contains about 290,500 main entries, or about 38,000 (15 per cent) more than in the first edition. The extent of the text, however, has grown from around 44 million words to around 59 million, which represents an increase of 34 per cent. There are 350 million printed characters in this work. In addition to the headwords of main entries, the Dictionary contains 157,000 combinations and derivatives in bold type, and 169,000 phrases and combinations in bold italic type, making a total of 616,500 word-forms. There are 137,000 pronunciations, 249,300 etymologies, 577,000 cross-references, and 2,412,400 illustrative quotations.

GENERAL EXPLANATIONS

THE VOCABULARY

THE vocabulary of a widely diffused and highly cultivated living language is not a fixed quantity circumscribed by definite limits. That vast aggregate of words and phrases which constitutes the vocabulary of English-speaking people presents, to the mind that endeavours to grasp it as a definite whole, the aspect of one of those nebulous masses familiar to the astronomer, in which a clear and unmistakable nucleus shades off on all sides, through zones of decreasing brightness, to a dim marginal film that seems to end nowhere, but to lose itself imperceptibly in the surrounding darkness. In its constitution it may be compared to one of those natural groups of the zoologist or botanist, wherein typical species forming the characteristic nucleus of the order, are linked on every side to other species, in which the typical character is less and less distinctly apparent, till it fades away in an outer fringe of aberrant forms, which merge imperceptibly in various surrounding orders, and whose own position is ambiguous and uncertain. For the convenience of classification, the naturalist may draw the line which bounds a class or order outside or inside of a particular form; but Nature has drawn it nowhere. So the English vocabulary contains a nucleus or central mass of many thousand words whose 'Anglicity' is unquestioned; some of them only literary, some of them only colloquial, the great majority at once literary and colloquial—they are the *common words* of the language. But they are linked on every side with other words which are less and less entitled to this appellation, and which pertain ever more and more distinctly to the domain of local dialect, of the slang and cant of 'sets' and classes, of the peculiar technicalities of trades and processes, of the scientific terminology common to all civilized nations, and of the actual languages of other lands and peoples. And there is absolutely no defining line in any direction: the circle of the English language has a well-defined centre but no discernible circumference.[1] Yet practical utility has some bounds, and a dictionary has definite limits: lexicographers must, like naturalists, 'draw the line somewhere', in each diverging direction. They must include all the 'common words' of literature and conversation, and such of the scientific, technical, slang, dialectal, and foreign words as are passing into common use and approach the position or standing of 'common words', well knowing that the line which they draw will not satisfy all their critics. For the domain of 'common words' widens out in the direction of one's own reading, research, business, provincial or foreign residence, and contracts in the direction with which one has no practical connection: no one's English is *all* English. The lexicographer must be satisfied to exhibit the greater part of the vocabulary of *each* one, which will be immensely more than the whole vocabulary of *any* one.

In addition to, and behind, the common vocabulary, in all its diverging lines, lies an infinite number of *proper* or merely *denotative* names, outside the province of lexicography, yet touching it in thousands of points, at which these names, and still more the adjectives and verbs formed upon them, acquire more or less of connotative value. Here also limits more or less arbitrary must be assumed.

The language presents yet another undefined frontier, when it is viewed in relation to *time*. The living vocabulary is no more permanent in its constitution than definite in its extent. It is not today what it was a century ago, still less what it will be a century hence. Its constituent elements are in a state of slow but incessant dissolution and renovation. 'Old words' are ever becoming obsolete and dying out; 'new words' are continually pressing in. And the death of a word is not an event of which the date can be readily determined. It is a vanishing process, extending over a lengthened period, of which contemporaries never see the end. Our own words never become obsolete: it is always the words of our grandfathers that have died with them. Even after we cease to use a word, the memory of it survives, and the word itself survives as a possibility;

[1] The above diagram will explain itself, as an attempt to express to the eye the aspect in which the vocabulary is here presented, and also some of the relations of its elements typical and aberrant. The centre is occupied by the 'common' words, in which literary and colloquial usage meet. 'Scientific' and 'foreign' words enter the common language mainly through literature; 'slang' words ascend through colloquial use; the 'technical' terms of crafts and processes, and the 'dialect' words, blend with the common language both in speech and literature. Slang also touches on one side the technical terminology of trades and occupations, as in 'nautical slang', 'Public School slang', 'the slang of the Stock Exchange', and on another passes into true dialect. Dialects similarly pass into foreign languages. Scientific terminology passes on one side into purely foreign words, on another it blends with the technical vocabulary of art and manufactures. It is not possible to fix the point at which the 'English language' stops, along any of these diverging lines.

it is only when no one is left to whom its use is still possible, that the word is wholly dead. Hence, there are many words of which it is doubtful whether they are still to be considered as part of the living language; they are alive to some speakers, and dead to others. And, on the other hand, there are many claimants to admission into the recognized vocabulary (where some of them will certainly one day be received), that are already current coin with some speakers and writers, and not yet 'good English', or even not English at all, to others.

If we treat the division of words into current and obsolete as a subordinate one, and extend our idea of the language so as to include all that has been English from the beginning, or from any particular epoch, we enter upon a department of the subject of which, from the nature of the case, our exhibition must be imperfect. For the vocabulary of past times is known to us solely from its preservation in written records; the extent of our knowledge of it depends entirely upon the completeness of the records, and the completeness of our acquaintance with them. And the farther back we go, the more imperfect are the records, the smaller is the fragment of the actual vocabulary that we can recover.

Subject to the conditions which thus encompass every attempt to construct a complete English Dictionary, the present work aims at exhibiting the history and signification of the English words now in use, or known to have been in use since the middle of the twelfth century. This date has been adopted as the only natural halting-place, short of going back to the beginning, so as to include the entire Old English or 'Anglo-Saxon' vocabulary. To do this would have involved the inclusion of an immense number of words, not merely long obsolete but also having obsolete inflexions, and thus requiring, if dealt with at all, a treatment different from that adapted to the words which survived the twelfth century. For not only was the stream of English literature then reduced to the tiniest thread (the slender annals of the Old English or Anglo-Saxon Chronicle being for nearly a century its sole representative), but the vast majority of the ancient words that were destined not to live into modern English, comprising the entire scientific, philosophical, and poetical vocabulary of Old English, had already disappeared, and the old inflexional and grammatical system had been levelled to one so essentially modern as to require no special treatment in the Dictionary. Hence, we exclude all words that had become obsolete by 1150. But to words actually included this date has no application; their history is exhibited from their first appearance, however early.

Within these chronological limits, it is the aim of the Dictionary to deal with all the common words of speech and literature, and with all words which approach these in character; the limits being extended farther in the domain of science and philosophy, which naturally passes into that of literature, than in that of slang or cant, which touches the colloquial. In scientific and technical terminology, the aim of the first edition was to include *all words English in form,* except those of which an explanation would be unintelligible to any but the specialist; and such words, not English in form, as either were in general use, like *hippopotamus, geranium, aluminium, focus, stratum, bronchitis,* or belonged to the more familiar language of science, as *Mammalia, Lepidoptera, Invertebrata.* The policy governing the selection of the scientific terms included in the *Supplement* and added to this edition is considerably broader:

> Lexicographers are now confronted with the problem of treating the vocabularies of subjects that are changing at a rate and on a scale not hitherto known. The complexity of many scientific subjects is such too that it is no longer possible to define all the terms in a manner that is comprehensible to the educated layman.[2]

The inclusion of Latin generic names of plants or animals depends on the quantity of evidence found for the use of the word in an English context as the name of an individual and not as the name of a genus. Names of groups above generic level are included only in their anglicized forms, when sufficient evidence for these forms could be traced: thus *dytiscid* has an entry but *Dytiscidae* has not.

Down to the fifteenth century the language existed only in dialects, all of which had a literary standing: during this period, therefore, words and forms of all dialects are admitted on an equal footing into the Dictionary. Dialectal words and forms which occur since 1500 are not admitted, except when they continue the history of a word or sense once in general use, illustrate the history of a literary word, or have themselves a certain literary currency, as is the case with many modern Scottish words.

CLASSIFICATION OF THE VOCABULARY

For the purposes of treatment in this Dictionary, words and phrases are classed as: (1) main words, (2) subordinate words, (3) combinations, (4) derivatives. **Main words** comprise (1) single words, radical or derivative (e.g. *an, amphitheatrically*), (2) all those compound words (and phrases) which, from their meaning, history, or importance claim to be treated in separate articles (e.g. *afternoon, almighty, almsman, air-pump, aitch-bone, ale-house, forget-me-not, Adam's apple, all fours*), (3) important prefixes, suffixes, and combining forms which may give rise to large numbers of derivatives and compound words. The articles in which these are treated constitute the *main articles.* **Subordinate words** include variant and obsolete forms of main words, and such words of bad formation, doubtful existence, or alleged use, as it is deemed proper, on any ground, to record. The *main* and *subordinate* words are arranged in a single alphabetic series, distinguished simply by the treatment accorded them within the article; but articles dealing with spurious words are enclosed within square brackets. **Combinations,** when so simple as either to require no explanation, or to be capable of being briefly explained in connection with their cognates, are dealt with under the main words which form their first element, their treatment forming the concluding part of the main article. Similarly, such **derivatives** of a main word as do not by their frequency or complexity warrant a separate article are normally treated in an unnumbered paragraph following all the numbered sense sections of the main word, introduced by 'Hence', 'So', or 'Also'. Occasionally these will be found appended to an individual, num-

[2] 'Scientific terms', *Supplement,* Volume I, p. xix.

bered sense section and treated as part of that section for the purposes of exemplification.

MAIN WORDS

Every main word is treated, once for all, under its modern current or most usual spelling; or, if obsolete, under the most typical of its latest spellings; the form or spelling thus chosen being considered the *main form* of the word.

Occasionally a form or spelling of an obsolete word has been assumed, which is not actually found in the quotations adduced, but is in accordance with the usual analogies of the language, as seen in kindred words. Thus *annoyously* is given as the main form, on the analogy of *annoy, annoyous,* although only *anoyously* has actually been found.

Other important forms of each word, current or obsolete, are entered in their alphabetical order, as *subordinate words,* and are there concisely referred to the *main form* under which they are treated.

When a word which is historically one has different grammatical relations, it is treated as one word only, and the different relations are indicated by the division of the article into sections (marked **A, B, C**). This refers especially to substantives used also *attributively* (or *adjectivally*), as in 'an ounce of *gold,* a *gold* watch, *gold*-coloured scales'; to adjectives used *substantively* or *pronominally,* as in 'the *catholic* church, a good *catholic*; *that* book, *that* is mine, the words *that* he spoke'; to adjectives used adverbially, as in 'the *according* voice of national wisdom', 'he acted *according* to orders'; to adverbs, prepositions, and conjunctions, originally the same word, as ABOUT, AFTER, SINCE, AS; and of course *a fortiori* to verbs used *transitively* and *intransitively,* as 'to abide battle, to abide at home', which, in some dictionaries, are reckoned as two distinct words.

In this Dictionary, *transitive* and *intransitive* seldom appear even as leading divisions of a verb, but, in accordance with the actual history of the word, in most cases only as varying and often temporary constructions, subordinate to the different senses, and liable to pass one into the other in the development of the language. Thus a verb at one time intransitive finally takes a simple object, through the phonetic decay of a dative or genitive ending, or the elision of a preposition, and is accounted transitive, without any change either in form or meaning (e.g. ANSWER); and a verb used transitively, likewise without change of meaning and form, at length becomes intransitive, through the regular modern English suppression of the reflexive pronoun (e.g. Ezek. 20:22 I *withdrew* mine hand; Mark 3:7 Jesus *withdrew* himself to the sea; *Revised Version,* Jesus *withdrew* to the sea). The history of ANSWER or WITHDRAW would be misrepresented by splitting them each into two words, or even by classifying their senses in a manner which would conceal these historical relations.

But verbs uniform in their stems with substantives or adjectives, as LAND, to LAND, DRY, to DRY, ABSTRACT, to ABSTRACT, are, of course, distinct words; as are adjectives and adverbs which, through 'levelling' of terminations, have become identical in form, though originally distinct, as ALIKE *a.*, ALIKE *adv.*; and substantives and adjectives which have always been identical in form, but were of separate introduction into the language, and have separate histories, as ANIMAL *sb.*, ANIMAL *a.* Where a word originally one has been, in the course of its history, split into two, whether with distinction of sense, as ALSO, AS, or merely as synonyms, as ANT, EMMET; APPRENTICE, PRENTICE, both modern forms are treated as separate words, and there is a reference from one article to the other. Where two original words of identical or similar form have coalesced into one, the modern word is treated as one or two, according to practical utility. When they are treated as two words, these come, of course, immediately together: see ALLAY, ALLOW, AMICE.

The treatment of a Main Word comprises:

I. The **identification,** II. The **etymology,** III. The **signification,** IV. The **illustrative quotations.**

I. The **identification** includes:

1. The *main form,* i.e. the usual or typical spelling, as already described. (In certain cases where two spellings are in current use, both are given in the main form, as ANALYSE -YZE, COLOUR COLOR, INFLECTION INFLEXION.) Words believed to be *obsolete* are distinguished by prefixing †; *non-naturalized* or *partially naturalized* words, by ‖.

In the case of rare words, especially those adopted or formed from Latin equivalents, it is often difficult to say whether they are or are not obsolete. They are permanent possibilities, rarely needed, but capable of being used whenever they are needed, rather than actually discarded terms. To these and other words, of which the obsoleteness is doubtful, the † is not prefixed.

As to their citizenship in the language, words may be classed as *naturals, denizens, aliens,* and *casuals.* NATURALS include all *native* words like *father,* and all fully *naturalized* words like *street, rose, knapsack, gas, parasol.* DENIZENS are words fully naturalized as to use, but not as to *form, inflexion,* or *pronunciation,* as *aide-de-camp, locus, carte-de-visite, table d'hôte.* ALIENS are names of foreign objects, titles, etc., which we require often to use, and for which we have no native equivalents, as *shah, geyser, cicerone, targum, backsheesh, sepoy.* CASUALS are foreign words of the same class, not in habitual use, which for special and temporary purposes occur in books of foreign travel, letters of foreign correspondents, and the like. There are no fixed limits between these classes, and the constant tendency is for words to pass upwards from the last to the first. But, while casuals and aliens from unfamiliar languages are readily and quickly naturalized, words from French and the learned languages, especially Latin, which are assumed to be known to all the polite, are often kept in the position of denizens for centuries: we still treat *phenomenon* as Greek, *genus* as Latin, *aide-de-camp* as French. The words marked with ‖ in the Dictionary comprise *denizens* and *aliens,* and such *casuals* as approach, or formerly approached, the position of these. Opinions will differ as to the claims of some that are included and some that are excluded, and also as to the line dividing *denizens* from *naturals,* and the position assigned to some words on either side of it. If we are to distinguish these classes at all, a line must be drawn somewhere.

2. (Within parentheses) the *pronunciation* or symbolization of the actual existing form of the word, as explained below. A recognized difference of pronunciation is also shown, with occasional notes on the diversity. Of obsolete words usually no pronunciation is given, but the place of the stress or accent, when ascertained, is indicated by a stress mark (') before the stressed syllable, as **al'feres, 'anredly.** In partially naturalized words two pronunciations are often given, viz. the native (or what passes for the native), and one conformed more or less to English analogies; in actual use many intermediate varieties may be heard, cf. *rendezvous, envelope, environs, prestige, chignon, recitative, Koran, caviare*, and the like.

Being the delimiters both of phonetic notation and of notes about usage and variation, the parentheses are not strictly equivalent to the pairs of oblique strokes conventionally used in technical works to mark off phonetic transcriptions.

3. The *grammatical designation,* i.e. the part of speech, or subdivision of the same, as *pers. pron., vbl. sb.* See the list of abbreviations. Words having no grammatical designation are normally *substantives*: the letters *sb.* are employed only where required to avoid ambiguity.

4. (*a*) In words of more or less specific use, the *specification* or subject label, as *Mus.* (in Music), *Bot.* (in Botany), etc.

(*b*) The *variety* of English, when the word is not current in the standard English of Great Britain, as *U.S., N. Amer., Austral.*, etc.

(*c*) The *status*, where there is any peculiarity, as *Obs.* (obsolete), *arch.* (archaic or obsolescent), *colloq.* (colloquial), *dial.* Here also is added, when applicable, the epithet *rare*, with $^{-1}$, or $^{-0}$, indicating that only *one*, or *no* actual instance of the use of the word in context is known to us. Words apparently employed only *for the nonce*, are, when inserted in the Dictionary, marked *nonce-wd.*

5. (*a*) The principal earlier *forms* or spellings, with their chronological range indicated by the unit figure of the century, thus 3–6 = 13th to 16th cent.; 1 standing for all centuries down to 1100.

These figures also correspond broadly to distinct periods of the language; viz. 1 *Old English* or 'Anglo-Saxon'; 2 (12th c.) *Old English Transition* ('semi-Saxon'); 3 (13th c.) *Early Middle English*; 4 (14th c.) *Late Middle English*; 5 (15th c.) *Middle English Transition*; 6 (16th c.) *Early Modern* or Tudor *English*; 7 (17th c.) *Middle Modern English*; 8, 9, 20 (18th, 19th, and 20th c.) *Recent English.*

(*b*) The *inflexions,* i.e. plural of substantives, and principal parts of verbs, when other than the ordinary *-s, -ed.*

II. The **etymology** and *form-history* [within heavy square brackets] includes: 1. The *derivation,* showing the actual origin of the word, when ascertained. In some cases, this section also contains: 2. The *subsequent form-history* in English, when this presents special features, as phonetic change, contraction, corruption, perversion by popular etymology or erroneous association. 3. *Miscellaneous facts* as to the history of the word, its age, obsolescence, revival, refashioning, change of pronunciation, confusion with other words.

In the light of *historical* etymology, an English word is (1) the extant formal representative, or direct phonetic descendant, of an earlier word; that is to say, it is the earlier word itself, in a later or more recent form, as it has been unconsciously changed in the mouths of the successive generations that have used it. For example, ACRE (now really 'eɪkə(r)), formerly *aker,* is the extant form of Old English *æcer,* this the later form of prehistoric *æcr,* the special English form of *acr, akr,* this of West Germanic *akra,* this, through earlier *akra-z,* or Original Germanic *akro-z,* this of original Aryan or Indo-European *agro-s;* and *agros, akroz, akraz, akra, akr, æcr, æcer, aker, āker, acre* ('eɪkə(r)), are all merely successive and temporary forms of one and the same word, as employed during successive periods. The word has never died; no year, no day probably, has passed without its being uttered by many: but this constant use has so worn it down and modified its form, that we commonly look upon *acre* as a distinct word from *agros,* with which it is connected by many intermediate forms, of which only a few have been discriminated in writing, while the finer and more intimately connecting links have never been written. This *phonetic descent* is symbolized by (:—); thus ACRE:—OE. *æcer.*

If not the extant formal representative of an original Germanic word, an English word has been (2) *adopted* (a.), or (3) *adapted* (ad.), from some foreign language; i.e. it is a word once foreign, but now, without or with intentional change of form, used as English; or it has been (4) *formed* on or from (f.) native or foreign elements, or from a combination of them. *Adoption* is essentially a popular process, at work whenever the speakers of one language come into contact with the speakers of another, from whom they acquire foreign things, or foreign ideas, with their foreign names. It has prevailed in English at all periods from the earliest to the latest times: *inch, pound, street, rose, cat, prison, algebra, antic, orange, tobacco, tea, canoe, focus, meerschaum,* are adopted words. *Adaptation* is essentially a learned or literary process; it consists in adapting a foreign word to the 'analogies of the language', and so depriving it of its foreign termination. Examples are Latin or Greek words reduced to their stem form, or receiving recognized English endings. Latin words which lived on in Gaul there underwent regular phonetic changes, whereby they at length became 'French'; in this living French form they were adopted in Middle English; but in more recent times numerous Latin words have been taken into English directly, yet modified, in their terminations, in the same way as if they had lived on in French and been thence adopted into English.[3] Such

[3] The French words adopted before 1400 were generally taken from the Anglo-French, or French spoken for several centuries in England, where they had undergone further phonetic change. It was in strict conformity with linguistic facts that Chaucer told of his *Prioresse*:

> ... Frenssh she spak ful faire and fetisly,
> After the scole of Stratford atte Bowe,
> For Frenssh of Parys was to hire vnknowe:

for the Anglo-French dialect of the fourteenth century was

English words originate in an *adaptation* of the Latin original, not in an adoption of its French (or other Romance) extant representative. *Formation* consists in the combination of existing words or parts of words with each other, or with *living formatives*, i.e. syllables which no longer exist as separate words, but yet have an appreciable *signification* which they impart to the new product. Formation is the chief natural process by which the vocabulary of a language is increased. It is both popular and learned: in its popular application, it gives such words as *black-bird, shep-herd, work-er, high-ness, grand-ly, a-swim, be-moan, after-noon*; in learned application, such as *con-caten-ation, mono-petal-ous, chloro-phyl, tele-phone;* in a mixture of the two, such as *acknowledge-ment, lion-ize, starv-ation, betroth-al*.

Much of the terminology of modern science is identical, or as nearly so as the forms of the languages permit, in English and French, in English, French, and German, or sometimes even in most of the European languages. It would often be as difficult as useless to ascertain in which language a particular scientific term first appeared in print, this being, linguistically, a mere accident: the word was accepted as common property from the beginning. In such cases, *modern formation* (mod. f.) is frequently employed to intimate that it is uncertain in what modern language, English or continental, the word was first used; it may indeed have occurred first in some modern Latin work, either of English or foreign authorship. In the supplementary scientific articles added to this edition, the first use has been ascertained whenever possible and appears as the first example in the set of illustrative quotations. If a word was first coined in some other language before being adopted into English, details of the foreign coinage (when traceable) are provided in the etymology. All such foreign coinages have been verified at source since it sometimes happens that the details provided in specialized bibliographies and reference works are inaccurate. Details of the coinages of plant and animal names are provided in the normal way. When, however, the first use of a term preceded the date accepted as the starting-point for the valid nomenclature of the group involved, a reference to the first valid use is added in the etymology.

Phonetic descent (:—), *adoption* (a.), *adaptation* (ad.), word-*formation* (f.) are usually combined under the term *derivation*; but, until we know in which of them, singly or in combination, a word has originated, we do not know its etymology.

In this Dictionary, words originally native are traced to their earliest known English, and, when possible, to their earliest Germanic form, authenticated and illustrated by the cognate words in other Germanic languages and dialects; those of foreign origin are referred to the foreign word or elements whence they were immediately adopted or formed. In certain cases these foreign words, especially the French, are themselves traced to their antecedent forms or component elements; but these antecedents are considered only with a view to the clearer comprehension of the history and use of the word in English. To trace the remoter history of these words, and determine their Indo-European or other 'roots', is no part of their English history.

Of many words it has to be stated that their origin is either doubtful or altogether unknown. In such cases the historical facts are given, as far as they go, and their bearing occasionally indicated. But *conjectural etymologies* are rarely referred to, except to point out their agreement or disagreement with the historical facts; for these, and the full discussion which they require, the reader is referred to special treatises on etymology.

III. The **signification,** or *senses*. Some words have only one invariable signification; but most words that have been used for any length of time in a language have acquired a long and sometimes intricate series of significations, as the primitive sense has been gradually extended to include allied or associated ideas, or transferred boldly to figurative and analogical uses. This happens to a greater extent with *relational* words, as prepositions (cf. *about, after, against, and, anent*) than with *notional* words, as verbs and nouns; of these, also, it affects verbs and adjectives more than substantives; of substantives, it influences those which express actions, qualities, and mental conceptions (cf. *account*), more than those which name, and are, as it were, fixed to material objects. Yet even these latter have often acquired many different senses. Thus, *board* names a material object; yet compare: a thin *board,* a frugal *board,* a card-*board, board* and lodgings, passengers on *board,* to fall over *board,* to sit at the council *board,* a *board* school, the *Board* of Trade, to tread the *boards,* a sea-*board* parish.

The order in which these senses were developed is one of the most important facts in the history of the word; to discover and exhibit it are among the most difficult duties of a dictionary which aims at giving this history. If the historical record were complete, that is, if we possessed written examples of all the uses of each word from the beginning, the simple exhibition of these would display a rational or logical development. The

not only from Parisian, but from all dialects of continental French. In its origin a mixture of various Norman and other Northern French dialects, afterwards mixed with and greatly modified by Angevin, Parisian, Poitevin, and other elements, and more and more exposed to the overpowering influence of literary French, it had yet received, on this side of the Channel, a distinct and independent development, following, in its phonology especially, English and not continental tendencies. As the natural speech of the higher and educated classes, it died out in the fourteenth century; but it maintained a kind of artificial existence for a longer period, and was used (in an increasingly debased form) for writing law-reports down to the seventeenth century, in which stage it still influenced the spelling of English words. Its forms survive in many of our terminations: *armour, colour, glorious, gracious, envious, perilous, arrival, espousal, language, enjoy, benefit, gaoler, caitif,* are the actual Anglo-French forms, as distinct from those of continental Old and Modern French. As a rule, it may be assumed that the original form of every Middle English word of French origin was *identical* with the Anglo-French form; and that, where a gap appears between the earliest known English form of a word and its Old French equivalent, that gap would be filled up by the recovery of the Anglo-French and earliest English form. It was not until the fifteenth century, and chiefly at the hands of Caxton, that continental French forms and spellings began directly to influence our language.

historical record is not complete enough to do this, but it is usually sufficient to enable us to infer the actual order. In exhibiting this in the Dictionary, that sense is placed first which was actually the earliest in the language: the others follow in the order in which they appear to have arisen. As, however, the development often proceeded in *many* branching lines, sometimes parallel, often divergent, it is evident that it cannot be adequately represented in a single linear series. Hence, while the senses are numbered straight on 1, 2, 3, etc., they are also grouped under branches marked **I, II, III**, etc., in each of which the historical order begins afresh. Subdivisions of the senses, varieties of construction, etc., are marked **a, b, c**, etc.; subdivisions of these, used especially for sense-divisions under combinations and derivatives, (*a*), (*b*), (*c*), or (i), (ii), (iii), etc.

So far for words of which the senses have been developed in English itself. But in adopted or adapted words which had already acquired various significations in the language (e.g. Latin) from which they were taken, it often happens that the order in which the senses appeared in English does not agree with the natural order in which they were developed in the original language. The English order is in fact accidental. For it was not in the primary sense that the word was first taken into English, but in a figurative, transferred, or specialized use, as an ecclesiastical, legal, grammatical, or medical term, which perhaps took root in our language, and here received a development of its own. Subsequently, however, familiarity with the Latin language and literature sometimes led to a fresh adoption of the word in the primary sense, or to a sudden extension of English usage, so as to include the primary sense, which thus appears as of quite late origin in English. In such a case it is not possible to make the historical order of the senses in English agree with the logical order in which they arose in Latin or other previous language; and every such word must be treated in the way which seems best suited to exhibit the facts of its own history and use. Instances of such words are afforded by ADVENT, AGONY, ANNUNCIATION, APPEND.

Obsolete senses, like obsolete words, have † prefixed, so as to be at once distinguished from those now in use. Under ¶ are included *catachrestic* and erroneous uses, confusions, and the like.

To a great extent the *explanations* of the meanings, or definitions, have been framed anew upon a study of all the quotations for each word collected for this work, of which those printed form only a small part. But the labours of other scholars in this, the most successfully cultivated department of English lexicography, have not been neglected. In particular, the explanations of Dr Johnson and of his editor Archdeacon Todd have often been adopted unchanged (within inverted commas and marked J. or T.), as have those of N. Bailey, and other early lexicographers, to whom it is only right to give credit for original work which has become the common property of all their successors.

IV. The **quotations** illustrate the forms and uses of the word, showing the age of the word generally, and of its various senses particularly; the earliest and, in obsolete words or senses, the latest, known instances of its occurrence being always quoted. Except in special cases, where the letters of the Greek alphabet, α, β, γ, etc. are used to separate parallel forms, the illustration of the *forms* is subordinated to that of the *senses*: the quotations illustrating each sense immediately follow the explanation. They are arranged chronologically so as to give about one for each century, though various considerations often render a larger number necessary. The original spelling is retained, as an essential part of the history of the language. But merely graphical or typographical devices, such as contractions, erratic presence of capitals, and (in seventeenth-century books) employment of italics to emphasize words, phrases, or whole passages, are not reproduced; and simple blunders, which would mislead the reader, are tacitly corrected. The recent use of italics, to indicate a doubt about the status of a word, is retained as being often of historical importance.

As to letter, the Old and Middle English 'thorn' (þ = *th*) and Old English 'divided *d*' or 'edh' (ð; usually only a variant of 'þ', though sometimes distinguished) are retained; also ME. 'open-tailed *g*', or 'yogh' (ȝ = *y* initially, *gh* finally). In Old English, the letter *g* had the form 'ᵹ, ᵹ' (a peculiar British development of the Roman G). Besides the original sound in *go*, *gild*, this letter had also (at least in later Old English) a fricative sound as in Dutch da*g*, or Irish lou*gh*, (or both), and a palatalized sound, approximately = *y* in *ye*, *yes*. After the Norman Conquest the modern forms 'g, *g*', were introduced (from French) for the sound in *go*, and the new sound in *g*inger; but the OE. form (in process of time slightly modified) was retained for the sounds in lou*gh*, *y*es, till the introduction of printing. In printing Old English modern scholars sometimes reproduce the contemporary 'ᵹ, ᵹ' (as is done by Sievers, in his *Angelsachsische Grammatik*), but more commonly substitute modern 'g, *g*'. The adoption of either course exclusively in this work would have broken the historical continuity of the forms; in the one case, we should have had the same word appearing in the eleventh century as 'ᵹold', and in the twelfth century as 'gold'; in the other, the same word written in the eleventh century 'ge' and in twelfth century 'ȝe'. To avoid this, both forms are here used in Old English, in accordance with the Middle English distinction in their use; thus, 'gold', 'ᵹe', 'dæᵹ'. The reader will understand that 'g' and 'ᵹ' represent the same Old English letter, and that the distinction made between them is purely editorial (though certainly corresponding to a distinction of sound in OE.). For ME. the form 'ȝ' commonly used in reprints is employed, so that OE. 'ᵹe' becomes ME. 'ȝe', modern 'ye'; OE. 'ᵹenoᵹ, ᵹenoh', ME. 'ynoȝ, inouȝ', mod. 'enough'.

It is to be distinctly borne in mind that the quotations are not merely examples of the fully developed use of the word or special sense under which they are cited: they have also to illustrate its origin, its gradual separation from allied words or senses, or even, by negative evidence, its non-existence at the given date. It would often have been desirable to annotate the quotations, explaining the purpose for which they are adduced; but the exigencies of space render this impossible, and they are therefore left to speak for themselves. Some help has been offered by enclosing within [. . .] quotations given for what may be called subsidiary purposes.

The need to keep the Dictionary within practicable limits has also rendered it necessary to give only a minimum of quotations selected from the material available, and to make those given as brief as possible. It is to be observed that in their abridged form they simply illustrate the word, phrase, or construction, for which they are given, and do not necessarily express the sentiments of their authors, though in no case have they been intentionally curtailed in such a way as to misrepresent their original meaning. This, however, may always be ascertained, and the full context recovered, by help of the *exact reference* to author, work, and passage, which it is a special feature of this work to give. Here also the utmost conciseness has been indispensable; the exact date renders the surnames only of authors in many cases sufficient; the titles of books are so abbreviated as to be recognizable by those who know them, or to be adequate for the purpose of reference to a library or bibliographical catalogue. The reader is referred to the List of Abbreviations (p. lxvi) for the expansion of those most commonly used in citing book titles; details of many of the works cited may be found in the Select Bibliography at the end of the Dictionary.

In order to allow consistent reference to cited works, an approximately uniform value has been given to different forms of numerals. Thus, in all works, roman capitals (IV.) stand for *volume*; small capitals (IV.) for *book, part,* or other larger division; lower-case letters (iv.) for *chapter* or its equivalent; and arabic numerals (42/1) for *page* and, where relevant, column. Other divisions, as *marginal section*—the most useful of references, since it is not dependent on the paging of a particular edition—are indicated by special marks. In the Essayists of the eighteenth century (*Spectator,* etc.), of which the editions are innumerable, the reference is to the paragraphs of each essay or number, counted for this purpose. In *poetry,* the reference IV. iv. 42 means *act, scene, line*; or *canto, stanza, line,* (rarely *book, canto, stanza*), as the work may be divided. In *Shakespeare* (where the reading is that of the First Folio, 1623) the lines of the Globe edition are referred to. In dramatic works, or other long poems, of which the lines are not numbered, the arabic numerals mean the *page* of the edition quoted. Single poems are, whenever possible, cited by *name* and *line;* in Chaucer's *Canterbury Tales,* every edition of which has its own order and numbering, the only useful mode of reference was to number the lines of each piece, tale, or prologue, separately. As neither manuscripts nor editions agree as to the junction of the *Canon's Yeoman's Prologue* and *Tale,* the two have been reckoned as one piece. *Melibeus* and the *Parson's Tale* are referred to by the versicles as divided in the Six-text edition, but numbered separately. In many works, both prose and verse, the only available reference has been to the *volume* and *page* of a *specified edition,* which is thus indicated, 'Wks. 1802, III. 178'.

Whenever practicable, a work is dated and quoted from its first edition: if the reference is to a later edition (as has been often unavoidable), the date of this is added (within parentheses) to the reference.[4] It is necessary to be precise on this point, for later editions often change the spelling: hence, a quotation from them is valid for the use of the word, but not for its spelling, at the date assigned. In the first edition of this Dictionary, reasonable accuracy was attained in dates and references: in the former, absolute accuracy was in many cases impossible, and, for the purposes of this work, was not considered essential; in the latter, errors were inevitable in the work of so many years and so many readers.

The policy governing the supplementary quotations added to this edition is more rigorous with regard to the dating and verification of quotations; the bibliographical conventions stated here may stand for the ideal principles of the Dictionary as a whole. Quotations are normally taken from the earliest available printing of a work; where a later text has been used its date is given in parentheses after the title. Intentional exceptions can be found in often-quoted works whose first editions are rare; fuller details are shown in the Bibliography. Unverified quotations from secondary sources have an attribution in parentheses after the citation (e.g. Morris, Pettman, etc.).

The bold-face *date* is the date of first printing except for posthumous works. It is sometimes qualified by *c* (*circa*) or *a* (*ante* = before, not later than). The date of delivery of a lecture or production of a play is not normally accepted: the spoken word is dated by its first appearance in print. The date of composition is accepted, however, for dated letters, journals, and the like (of those which have not been written up for publication), but only exceptionally in other cases and only when there is good evidence for the date. Items in collections (e.g. of short stories) which were published earlier elsewhere are given this earlier date when it is known. It should be noted that these criteria are more severe and produce more conservative datings than those of many other reference works.

Author and title. This part of the citation is used first to identify the user of the quoted word, and secondly to identify the work from which a quotation is taken. Usually there is no conflict, but where there is the identification of the work takes precedence. Monographs are cited either by author and title or by title alone. Corporate authorship is not recognized: the names of institutions, business firms, etc., are not used in place of a personal name, but are added in parentheses at the end of titles. Periodicals and serials are cited by title (usually in abbreviated form); the authors of articles in periodicals are not usually named unless the quotation contains the first use of a word. The information given should be enough to identify the work, but occasionally it is not possible to give an unambiguous indication in the space available; in these cases the Bibliography gives a fuller account.

Form of name. Some frequently quoted authors are cited by surname alone; for most others the title-page of each work is the main authority, with deviations to allow for the standardization of initials where an author's own practice varies or for the purpose of avoiding ambiguity. Pseudonyms are indicated by single quotation marks (except that a few well-known pseudonyms like Geo. Eliot stand without the quotation marks), and authors who have changed their names are cited by the

[4] In the case of some well-known and often-quoted works, where the reference is always to a standard edition or modern literal reprint, it was not thought necessary by the first edition's editors to insert the date of it. Owing to the continual growth of literary and historical scholarship during and after their time, many of these are now no longer the most recent standard edition.

appropriate name for each work. Anonymous works are cited by title, but by author where the authorship has been established and is recognized in common practice. Small capitals usually denote the author of the quotation. The name of an editor of a work, who is not also the author of the actual quotation given, is normally printed in lower case. But quotations from many composite works have been attributed to the editors alone. Illustrative examples embodying typical recent usage of a word or sense, but not attributable to any exterior source, are introduced by the abbreviation '*Mod.*', preceded, where necessary, by a date, which is that of the fascicle of the first edition in which they were first printed.

SUBORDINATE WORDS

Under this head are here included: 1. (and mainly) *Obsolete* and *variant forms* of words, when these are so far removed in spelling as not to come closely before or after the regular forms, or readily to suggest them. These words are concisely referred to the main form to which they belong, with an explanatory synonym when the latter is itself obsolete; as **almacantar, -urie,** obs. ff. (= obsolete forms of) ALMUCANTAR; **abugge,** obs. w. and s.w.f. (= obsolete western and south-western form of) ABYE *v.*; **almoise, -moyse,** var. (= variant of) ALMOSE, *Obs.*, alms. To economize space, variant forms which differ from the regular form only in the doubling of a single consonant or the converse, as *appert* for APERT, *aple* for APPLE, or in the interchange of *u, v* or *i, j*, are not usually inserted. 2. *Irregular* or *peculiar inflexions* of Main Words. 3. Spurious or erroneous forms found in Dictionaries, or cited from single passages in authors, but having little or no claim to recognition as genuine constituents of the English vocabulary: their character is pointed, and their history briefly given. Entries for spurious words are enclosed in square brackets.

COMBINATIONS

Under this term are included all collocations of simple words in which the separate spelling of each word is retained, whether they are formally connected by the hyphen, or virtually by the unity of their signification. The formal union and the actual by no means coincide: not only is the use of the hyphen a matter of indifference in an immense number of cases, but in many where it is habitually used, the combination implies no unity of signification; while others, in which there is a distinct unity or specialization of meaning, are not hyphenated. The primary use of the hyphen is *grammatical*: it implies either that the syntactic relation between two words is closer than if they stood side by side without it, or that the relation is a *less usual* one than that which would at first sight suggest itself to us, if we saw the two words standing unconnected. Thus, in the three sentences, '*After consideration* had been given to the proposal, it was duly accepted', '*After consideration* the proposal was accepted', '*After-consideration* had shown him his mistake', we have *first* no immediate syntactic relation between *after* (conjunctive adverb) and *consideration*; *secondly,* the relation of preposition and object; *thirdly,* the relation of attribute and substantive, closer than the first, less usual than the second (since *after* is more commonly a preposition than an adjective). But *after-consideration* is not really a single word, any more than *subsequent consideration, fuller consideration*; the hyphen being merely a convenient help to the sense, which would be clearly expressed in speech by the different phrase-accentuation of *ˌafter considerˈation* and *ˈafter consideˌration*. And as this 'help to the sense' is not always equally necessary, nor its need equally appreciated in the same place, it is impossible that its use should be uniform. Nevertheless *after-consideration,* as used above, is on the way to becoming a single word, which *reconsideration* (chiefly because *re-* is not a separate word, but also because we have *reconsider*) is reckoned to be; and indeed *close grammatical relation* constantly accompanies close union of sense, so that in many combinations the hyphen becomes an expression of this unification of sense. When this unification and specialization has proceeded so far that we no longer analyse the combination into its elements, but take it in as a whole, as in *blackberry, postman, newspaper,* pronouncing it in speech with a single accent, the hyphen is usually omitted, and the fully developed compound is written as a single word. But as this also is a question of degree, there are necessarily many compounds as to which usage has not yet determined whether they are to be written with the hyphen or as single words. Many specialized combinations, indeed, are often not even hyphenated: especially is this the case with *descriptive names,* formed of a substantive preceded by an adjective or possessive case, or followed by a phrase, as *Aaron's rod, all fours, Black Jack, Jack of all trades, Jew's harp, sea anemone.*

There is thus considerable difficulty in determining to what extent combinations are matters for the lexicographer, and to what extent they are merely grammatical. While no attempt is made fully to solve this difficulty, combinations formal and virtual are, for practical purposes, divided into three classes: *First*: those in which each word retains its full meaning, the relation between them falling under one or other of the ordinary grammatical categories. Of these, specimens merely are given, at the end of each article, which are printed in heavy italics, and illustrated collectively by a few quotations. *Second*: Combinations of which the signification is somewhat specialized, but still capable of being briefly explained in a few words, in connection with their cognates. These also are concisely treated at the end of the main article, where they are printed in small, dark bold type in an alphabetical series, and illustrated by quotations arranged in the same order. When these are very numerous the first usage of the word illustrated is typically distinguished in the quotation by prefixing *, in order that it may catch the eye more readily. *Third*: Combinations which attain in specialization of sense to the position of full compounds or which are used in various senses, or have a long history, and thus require to be dealt with more at large. These are often enumerated (in SMALL CAPITALS) at the end of the main article, and thence referred to their alphabetical place, where they are treated in all respects as main words.

All compounds and combinations of interest or importance will thus be found either in their alphabetical order, or under the word which constitutes their first element. But phrases are treated under their leading word, as *on account of,* under ACCOUNT; and specific names, like *sea anemone, black alder,* under their generic names ANEMONE, ALDER, etc. *Sea anemone* is considered (linguistically) as a kind of *anemone,* but *Adam's needle* not as a kind of *needle,* nor *mouse-ear* as a kind of *ear.*

DERIVATIVES

This term is used for any word which has been formed by the addition of a suffix to a main word also treated in this Dictionary (also, more rarely, by the alteration or removal of the suffix of a main word). Derivatives may be regarded as occupying a half-way position between, on the one hand, combinations (arising out of syntactical relationships between words determined chiefly by their semantic reference) and, on the other, inflected forms (whose existence and form, with the exception in English of a limited set of irregular inflexions, are predetermined by the system of grammar). In other words, a very considerable number of the derivatives recorded are predictable and transparent: as, for example, the many adverbs formed by the addition of *-ly* from adjectives, the similarly derived abstract nouns in *-ness*, and the agent-nouns in *-er,* most of which are thrown up by syntactic transformations. So 'he is insufficiently motivated', 'a fashioner of sonnets', 'the coolness of our reception' are closely linked with 'his motivation is insufficient', 'to fashion sonnets', 'we had a cool reception'. On the very borderline with the inflexional system lie the verbal substantives and participial adjectives, ending in *-ing* and *-ed,* which are indistinguishable in form, and often in function also, from the corresponding gerunds and participles. At the other end of the scale there are small groups of derivatives incorporating uncommon suffixes, which have emerged or have been coined in much the same way as combinations (with which, indeed, they may be interchangeable). At the extreme, we find slang and journalistic formations such as those ending in *-ville* (*Squaresville*) or *-aholic* (*workaholic*), which resemble combinations in their *raison d'être.*

The necessity for the separate treatment of those derivatives which are actually homomorphic with regular inflected forms, such as the verbal substantives and participial adjectives, or whose incidence is so regular and natural as to amount almost to the status of inflexion, such as the adverbs formed with *-ly* or agent-nouns in *-er,* might almost be denied, on the grounds that the senses of the derivative are deducible from those of the parent word. But in fact the occurrence of even the obviously formed derivatives, and the relationships of their senses with the root words, is very often unpredictable and complex; and the suffixes by which they are formed cannot be tidily separated into two groups, according to whether their application is transparent and regular or not. It is, therefore, the practice of the Dictionary to register every recorded derivative, and to accord it such treatment as its own meaning and use necessitate. The majority of derivatives entered in the Dictionary will be found as main words in their own right, but linked through the cross-references employed in their etymologies, and frequently also in their definitions, to the main words on which they are formed.

Derivatives which are of infrequent occurrence, or which have only one sense, or only a few senses straightforwardly related to those of the root word, are usually treated in a separate paragraph at the end of the article for the parent word. They are printed in the same small, dark bold type as combinations, and are usually introduced by 'Hence' (signifying formation on, and chronological succession to, the root word), 'So' (implying derivation but not posteriority), or 'Also' (occasionally used to connect parallel derivatives when no parent word has been traced). This arrangement has the great merit that whatever information about the pronunciation, variations in form, and etymology is common to the derivative and its parent word need not be repeated. Further conciseness is sometimes achieved by the appending of derivatives at the end of the definition of the root word in an article that has only one sense-division. From time to time, a derivative that has arisen in only one sense of a complex main word is treated under that sense-division.

ORDERING OF ENTRIES

Entries are arranged in the Dictionary in the alphabetical order of their headwords. Alphabetization is based strictly upon the twenty-six letters of the standard English alphabet. An initial capital letter is treated as in no way distinct from a small one. The spacing within a headword consisting of two or more written words is disregarded. Hence, for example, the sequence of headwords *all-rounder, All Saints, allseed, All Souls, allspice.*

In a similar way, all characters and symbols that are not among the twenty-six letters are either disregarded, or treated like the alphabetical letters or combinations to which they are most nearly equivalent. Apostrophes, full points, hyphens, and spaces occurring anywhere within the headword are disregarded: hence, for the sake of ordering, *p'an* is equivalent to *pan, met.* to *met,* and *co-op* to *coop.* Diacritical accents are also ignored: so *cañon* is equivalent to *canon, korin* to *kōrin.* The ligatures æ and œ, naturally enough, are alphabetized as if written *ae, oe*; ø as simple *o*; 'thorn' (þ) and 'edh' (ð) are treated as equivalent to *th;* and 'yogh' (ȝ) as equivalent to *gh.*

Pairs of parentheses, enclosing optional letters, are ignored. A single opening parenthesis, marking off the last letter or letters of a word, functions in a way that is counter to the general rule: the letters following the opening parenthesis are disregarded for the purpose of ordering. So *anachoret(e* precedes *anachoretal.* The most typical function of this convention is to mark off a final silent *-e* that has little historical significance.

Headwords with the same spelling (*homographs*), including those rendered equivalent by the conventions just described, are normally ordered according to grammatical category. Prefixes and suffixes are labelled as such and treated as separate grammatical categories. Combining forms, though lacking a special label, are similarly treated. Variant and obsolete forms (subordinate words), and written or spoken abbreviations entered as main words, have likewise no special label, but are commonly treated as members of separate grammatical categories.

There is no absolutely fixed order in which grammatical categories are arranged. All other things being equal, the major grammatical categories of noun (*substantive* in the Dictionary's terminology), adjective, verb, and adverb, precede, in that order, the minor ones; but the ordering very frequently departs from this general principle, especially where a group of etymologically related homographs is arranged in an order that reflects the historical development.

Identically spelt headwords that also belong to the same grammatical category are distinguished by following superior numbers ('*homonym numbers*') and are usually arranged in the order of their earliest occurrence. Entries that are not explicitly labelled with a part of speech, but are treated as distinct grammatical categories (such as variant forms and abbreviations), are distinguished by superior numbering from others of the same kind, and not necessarily from unlabelled entries of other kinds.

ORDERING OF SENSES

Eight kinds of serial symbol are employed to mark the sense-divisions of an entry, and less commonly, to classify the written variants of the headword, and each is, generally speaking, identified with particular functions. At the highest level, bold capital letters (**A, B, C,** etc.) divide into sections an entry treating a word that is used in more than one grammatical relation. The main senses of a word are identified by bold arabic numerals (**1, 2, 3**). Important subdivisions of these, reflecting either semantic, grammatical, or phraseological extensions of the sense, are identified by bold small letters (**a, b, c**). Italic letters within parentheses (*a*), (*b*), (*c*), are employed either to subdivide the last level of sense-distinction still more finely, or to categorize the senses of combinations, derivatives, and phrases. Very occasionally it is necessary to subdivide a definition introduced by an italic letter, and then lower-case roman numerals in parentheses (i), (ii), (iii), are introduced.

The main sense-divisions, and any subdivisions they may have, proceed in a single sequence within the entry, or one grammatical section of it; so the appearance of **B** will start a new sequence **1, 2, 3** or **a, b, c.** But senses which have developed along several different and parallel branches are arranged into groups headed by bold capital roman numerals (**I, II, III**) and these do not interrupt the numerical sequence of the main sense-divisions. If a lower level of branching needs to be recognized (in the arrangement of a particularly large and complicated word, for example), an increasing series of asterisks (*, **, ***) is used. These sometimes also occur as a means of grouping the uses of phrasal verbs.

Greek letters (α, β, γ) are used primarily to classify variant forms at the head of an entry. Sometimes the illustrative quotations are grouped according to the variant forms they illustrate, and in this case each group of quotations is introduced by the corresponding Greek letter. Certain words with an exceptionally complicated form-history are divided into sections, of which the first, headed **A,** illustrates the forms. This section has the usual framework, but with the numeral and lower-case roman letter sequences indicating the major and minor grammatical divisions and the Greek letters indicating the main form-variations within each of them. If the word also has more than one grammatical relation, the signification (headed **B**) is divided into sections, headed (the capital letter series having already been appropriated) by bold capital roman numerals, each containing separate series of main senses introduced by arabic numerals.

PRONUNCIATION

The pronunciation is the actual living form or forms of a word, that is, *the word itself,* of which the current spelling is only a symbolization—generally, indeed, only the traditionally-preserved symbolization of an earlier form, sometimes imperfect to begin with, still oftener corrupted in its passage to our time. This living form is the *latest fact* in the form-history of the word, the starting-point of all investigations into its previous history, the only fact in its form-history to which the lexicographer can personally witness. For all his statements as to its previous history are only reproductions of the evidence of former witnesses, or deductions drawn from earlier modes of symbolizing the forms of the word then current, checked and regulated by the ascertained laws and principles of phonology. To register the current pronunciation is therefore essential, in a dictionary which deals with the language on historical principles. It would be manifestly absurd, for example, to trace the form-history of the first numeral from the Old Germanic *ain,* through the Old English *án,* to the Middle English *oan, on, oon, one,* and to stop short at the last of these, without recognizing the modern English (wʌn), which represents a greater change within the last three and a half centuries than had previously taken place in 1500 years. The fact that the *written* history, as embodied in the spelling, accidentally stops short at the Middle English *one,* makes it all the more necessary to give the modern history and current form of the living word, since of these no hint is otherwise conveyed.

The system of transcription employed in this edition is the International Phonetic Alphabet (IPA). It follows, in the main, the principles for transcribing English pronunciation used in other Oxford Dictionaries. The minor differences in style have been adopted in order to accommodate the phonetic representation of unassimilated foreign words, dialect and regional forms, and the reconstructed pronunciation of earlier English.

A list of the symbols employed in the transcription is provided in the Key to the Pronunciation (below, p. lxv). The following features deserve special notice:

Consonants. The breathed (voiceless) pronunciation of the combination *wh,* used by many speakers of English, is represented by (hw). The possibility that 'linking *r*' may occur at the end of a word in which a final *r* is written, when the following word begins with a vowel-sound, is symbolized by ((r)), e.g. *her* (hɜː(r)). Parentheses around other consonants, for example (j) in words like *suit,* (p) in words like *impromptu,* or (t) in words like *bench,* indicate that the enclosed sounds may or may not be heard in the context. A hyphen is used between (t) and (ʃ) belonging to separate word elements (e.g. in *courtship*) in contradistinction to the affricative group (tʃ) that is usually written *ch*. Double consonants are shown by the doubling of the symbol.

Vowels and Diphthongs. The symbolization of the vowels of the principal foreign languages cited generally corresponds to the system of so-called 'cardinal vowels'. English 'short e' (as in *bet*) is treated as approximately equivalent to cardinal no. 3, and therefore symbolized by (ɛ). Following the first edition, the long open vowel (ɔː) (as in *border*) is distinguished from the centring diphthong (ɔə) (as in *boarder*) which is of a different origin but has become identical with it in most varieties of southern British pronunciation. Length (symbolized by (ː)) is shown in English words, in accordance with general present-day custom, even though most 'long' and 'short' vowels are identified and distinguished more by their place of articulation than by their duration, which varies in accordance with context. The distinction observed in this Dictionary between the 'long' close vowels (iː) and (uː) and the 'short' open vowels (ɪ) and (ʊ) in syllables with low stress should be understood in the light of this. Length is marked in words from foreign languages in which this is conventional. It is occasionally marked in French words (in which it is not strictly necessary) when these are felt to have become somewhat Anglicized. Nasalization is shown by the tilde (˜). Parenthesized 'schwa' (ə) preceding the consonants (l), (m), or (n) indicates that these are, or may be pronounced as, syllabic consonants. Parentheses around any other vowel symbol indicate that it may or may not be heard in that context.

Alternative pronunciations. Alternative pronunciations for a word are listed, set off by commas, and where necessary labelled. Parallels (‖) indicate the non-naturalized pronunciation of the word. Older pronunciations are sometimes distinguished by 'formerly'; but no exhaustive analysis of the currency, frequency, or distribution of alternative pronunciations is implied by their ordering. An alternative pronunciation may be indicated simply by a transcription of that part of the word which is phonetically different, indicated by leading or following hyphens. The existence of a variant pronunciation with (æ) in many words which contain *a* (pronounced ɑː) is indicated by adding -æ- (or æ-) after the main transcription. The (now fairly rare) variant pronunciation of *o* (usually ɒ) as (ɔː) is indicated by a parallel convention.

Stress. The main stress is shown by a superior stress mark (ˈ) preceding the stressed syllable. Secondary stress is shown by an inferior stress mark (ˌ). Syllables can begin with a vowel, a single consonant, or as large a consonant group as would be articulable at the beginning of a word, but in certain words speakers actually make a syllable-division at a later point. Where stress is marked in ordinary graphic forms, the same general principles are observed, with certain allowances for English spelling. Any consonant combinations that make up only a single sound are treated as unbreakable (so *oˈccur, paraˈpsychic* but *acˈcede, resigˈnation*); single letters symbolizing consonant combinations are perforce unbreakable (so *eˈxistence*). Sometimes the function of the stress-mark is to show that a word is a disyllable rather than the monosyllable it might otherwise appear to be, e.g. *higher* (ˈhaɪə(r)) but *hire* (haɪə(r)); *ˈcreat* but *treat*.

THE HISTORY OF THE OXFORD ENGLISH DICTIONARY

THE FIRST EDITION 1857–1928[1]

If there is any truth in the old Greek maxim that a large book is a great evil, English dictionaries have been steadily growing worse ever since their inception nearly four centuries ago. To set Cawdrey's slim small volume of 1604 beside the completed Oxford English Dictionary is like placing the original acorn beside the oak that has grown out of it.

The immensity of this growth is explained by the successive introduction of three new principles in lexicography. The earlier dictionary-makers followed in the line of the old glossaries, and directed their attention to such words as were likely to be unfamiliar to the ordinary person. The widening of this narrow range during the seventeenth century is made obvious by the steady increase in size through Bullokar, Cockeram, Blount, and Phillips, until in the eighteenth the principle of general inclusion was practically accepted by Kersey and Bailey. The next stage is marked by Johnson's systematic use of quotations to illustrate and justify the definitions, the many omissions still existing in the vocabulary being partly filled by later supplementary works on the same lines. When to all this was superadded the principle of historical illustration, introduced by Richardson, it became inevitable that any adequate dictionary of English must be one of the larger books of the world.

It is remarkable that Richardson's dictionary, perhaps through certain defects in his method, did not at once attract the attention it deserved. From the appearance of the first instalment in the *Encyclopaedia Metropolitana* in 1819 to the full acceptance of the historical principle by the Philological Society almost forty years had passed, and the separate publication of his dictionary in 1836–7 did not affect to any appreciable extent the work of those lexicographers who followed in the wake of Johnson or Webster. Even his wealth of quotations remained unutilized, although they formed a natural storehouse for any who cared to search in it and bring forth 'treasures new and old' to add to those already available in the works of Johnson and his successors.

That a forward step was made towards the end of these forty years was due to the action taken by the Philological Society in the summer of 1857, apparently as the result of a suggestion made by F. J. Furnivall to Dean Trench in May. At the meeting held on 18 June 'the appointment of Messrs. Herbert Coleridge and Furnivall and Dean Trench by the Council, as a committee to collect unregistered words in English, was announced, and that they would report to the next Meeting of the Society in November'. At this stage the idea was to prepare and publish a volume supplementary to the later editions of Johnson, or to Richardson, and containing all words omitted in either of these dictionaries.

The committee did not report in November, but on the fifth of that month one of its members, Dean Trench, read the first part of a paper 'On some Deficiencies in our English Dictionaries', while the report was postponed till 3 December. This interval allowed the second part of the paper to be read on 19 November, when the Society showed its appreciation by resolving 'That The Dean of Westminster be requested to publish his interesting and valuable Paper. To this request he kindly acceded.' Publication followed almost immediately, the first edition bearing the date 1857 and the title 'On some Deficiencies in our English Dictionaries, being the substance of two papers read before the Philological Society, Nov. 5 and Nov. 19, 1857. By Richard Chenevix Trench, D.D., Dean of Westminster.'

Even at this day, after the lapse of a hundred and fifty years and the advance in English studies which has taken place during that time, Dean Trench's paper retains its value as a statement of what an English dictionary ought to be. No one who reads it can fail to see how clearly he anticipated the lines on which the Society's dictionary was ultimately compiled—all of them, indeed, a necessary result from the historical principle which he laid down as the only sound basis for the work.

At the meeting of 3 December 1857, a report from the 'Unregistered Words Committee was read by the Secretary to that Committee, Mr. H. Coleridge'. This was followed by the resolution 'That for the present this Report be received and laid on the table. This resolution was passed in consequence of a statement that a larger scheme, for a completely new English Dictionary, might shortly be submitted to the Society.' The Dean's paper had clearly convinced the Society of the inadequacy of its proposals, and had shown that nothing short of a 'completely new' work would suffice. In this natural way arose the epithet *New* which appeared on the title-page of the Dictionary when the time for publication arrived.

The Society lost no time in following up the new idea, little suspecting the magnitude of the task which lay before it, and the many years that would elapse before it would be completed, or even properly begun. On 7 January 1858, 'the following resolutions were passed relating to the undertaking of a New English Dictionary.

I. That instead of the Supplement to the Standard English Dictionaries now in course of preparation by the order of the Society, a New Dictionary of the English Language be prepared under the Authority of the Philological Society.

[1] This account is reproduced, with only minor modifications, from the 'Historical Introduction' to the *OED* published in 1933.

II. That the work be placed in the hands of two Committees, the one, Literary and Historical, consisting of The very Rev. The Dean of Westminster, F. J. Furnivall, Esq., and Herbert Coleridge, Esq. (Secretary), the other, Etymological, consisting of Hensleigh Wedgwood, Esq., and Prof. Malden, and that in questions of doubt as to the form which any article shall assume, the decision of the Literary and Historical Committee shall be final.

III. That the Society desires to express its thanks to the contributors who have kindly given their assistance to its Unregistered Words Committee, and to invite their assistance, and that of fresh volunteers, in the new undertaking.

IV. That Messrs. Furnivall and Coleridge be empowered to enter into such conditional agreement with Messrs. Nutt of London and Asher of Berlin, or such other Publishers as they think fit, to publish the Dictionary on such terms as they think fit.

V. That the Subscriptions of all Members who have joined or shall join the Society through the Unregistered Words Committee or the New Dictionary Committee, shall be placed, so far as required, at the disposal of the Committees now appointed, to defray their printing and other expenses.

VI. That the Philological Society will afford every assistance in its power to enable its Committees to make a Dictionary worthy of the English Language.'

As is indicated in the third of these resolutions, the Unregistered Words Committee had been remarkably successful, during its brief existence, in arousing interest in the Society's undertaking, and in enlisting willing helpers to aid in carrying it out. Towards the close of his paper as printed, Dean Trench had been able to make an encouraging statement on this head. 'Let me mention here that seventy-six volunteers have already come forward, claiming their shares in the task. A hundred and twenty-one works of English authors, in most cases the whole works of each author, have been taken in hand by them; and I may add that thirty-one contributions have already been sent in.' In this way began the system of voluntary readers, without whose help the material for the Society's dictionary could never have been collected at all, except at a prohibitive cost of time and money.

At the meeting on 21 January 1858, 'Mr. Furnivall read a circular which the New Dictionary Committee proposed to issue, stating the plan of the Dictionary and asking for help in carrying it out'. It does not appear whether the circular was actually issued, and further notices in the *Transactions* for that year are brief and unimportant. A glimpse of the progress that was being made is afforded by a passage in Coleridge's letter to Dean Trench (30 May 1860), which was printed in the second edition of the Dean's paper. 'More than a year passed away in combating various difficulties, and it was not till August 1858, that we felt ourselves in a position to announce the plan of a New Dictionary as a certainty, and to invite contributors to furnish us with assistance.' Negotiations with publishers had been carried on during the year, first with John Murray, and then with David Nutt; finally on 4 November, Furnivall 'stated that Messrs. Trübner & Co. had agreed to publish the Society's New English Dictionary'. The young co-workers, for both Furnivall and Coleridge were still in early manhood, had not only all the optimism of youth, but were embarking on an uncharted sea, quite unwitting of the long course which had to be sailed before the farther shore could even come into sight.

By 1859 the Committee was able to publish full details of the undertaking in the form of a 'Proposal for the Publication of a New English Dictionary by the Philological Society'. This document is a proof of the thoroughness and sound judgement with which the whole question had been considered. Opening with a review of the steps by which the idea of a 'new' dictionary had been reached, the authors of the Proposal went on to lay down certain principles as a basis for the work, of which the two most important are the first and fourth, viz.

I. The first requirement of every lexicon is that it should contain every word occurring in the literature of the language it professes to illustrate.

IV. In the treatment of individual words the historical principle will be uniformly adopted.

Other contents of the Proposal are 'Rules and Directions for Collectors' as agreed upon by the Literary, Historical, and Etymological Committees, and 'Mechanical and Practical Regulations'. These are 1. 'A list of the printed literature of England belonging to the period 1250–1526', with the added note, 'Those works marked with an asterisk are already undertaken'. 2. 'A list of works of the Second Period (1526–1674) already undertaken'. 3. A similar list of 'works of the Third Period (1674–1858) already undertaken'. This division of the literature into three periods, which originated with Coleridge and was maintained for some time as a basis of collecting, has a real foundation in fact. Although the dates 1526 and 1674 were chosen because the former was that of the first printed English New Testament, and the latter the year of Milton's death, they correspond very closely with significant epochs in the development of the English vocabulary. If arrived at by accident, they at the same time show a sound instinct for detecting the periods of essential change.

The volunteers were also beginning to play their part, and to provide the Committee with material to work upon. 'In April 1859 a paper containing queries respecting etymologies and several difficult passages from Early English books was circulated among members of the Society and contributors to the Dictionary, and conjectures in answer were invited ... So much of the results of this appeal as the Dictionary Committee consider sufficiently valuable, and sufficiently certain to be worth printing' was reported to the Society by Coleridge in a paper entitled 'Hints towards the explanation of some hard words and passages in English writers'. On 10 November of the same year, Coleridge, now formally appointed as editor, presented a 'report on the Society's proposed Dictionary'.

The following month saw another forward step, when on 8 December the Society resolved:

I. That a Committee be appointed to draw up a set of Rules for the guidance of the Editor of the Society's new English Dictionary.

II. That the Committee consist of:

The Very Rev. The Dean of Westminster	Thomas Watts, Esq.
	F. Pulszky, Esq.
Professor Key.	H. Wedgwood, Esq.
F. J. Furnivall, Esq.	Professor Goldstücker.

III. That the Committee be authorized to print the Rules drawn up by them, to circulate the printed Copies among all the Members of the Society, and to appoint one of the Society's nights of Meeting for a special discussion of the Rules by Members.

The Committee, or Coleridge himself on its behalf, set to work at once and prepared a draft of the rules, which was discussed, enlarged, and modified, at meetings held in December 1859 and January 1860, further considered and revised in April and May, and finally printed with the title of 'Canones Lexicographici, or rules to be observed in editing the New English Dictionary of the Philological Society'. Continued interest in the work is also shown by a paper read on 10 May, 'Observations on the plan of the Society's proposed new English Dictionary, by the Revd Derwent Coleridge', and by the appearance of a second edition of Dean Trench's two papers 'revised and enlarged. To which is added a letter to the author from Herbert Coleridge, Esq., on the progress and prospects of the Society's New English Dictionary.'

This letter is interesting as a survey of what had so far been accomplished, and closes on a confident note. 'I believe that the scheme is now firmly established, and I confidently expect ... that in about two years we shall be able to give our first number to the world. Indeed, were it not for the dilatoriness of many contributors ... I should not hesitate to name an earlier period.' Here also comes the first mention of co-operation from the English-speaking nation on the other side of the Atlantic. 'The Hon. G. P. Marsh of Burlington, Vermont, having kindly offered to act as secretary in America, I at once suggested that the Americans should make themselves responsible for the whole of the eighteenth-century literature, which probably would have a less chance of finding as many readers in England. This was agreed to, ... and contributors are, as I understand, coming in, but no results of their labours have reached us yet.' The suggestion was not a fortunate one, and was never seriously taken up.

By this time, on the basis of the material already sent in by contributors and of the existing dictionaries, Coleridge was hard at work preparing word-lists to serve as a guide in further collecting. The 'Third Period' was selected for this purpose, and by 14 February 1861, he was able to lay before the Society the first part of this 'Basis of Comparison', covering the letters A to D. The preliminary notice to this in its printed form is signed by Coleridge, and its publication was unfortunately the last of his valuable contributions to the progress of the work. On Thursday, 25 April, 'Mr. Furnivall announced the death on the preceding Tuesday of Herbert Coleridge, Esq., the Editor of the Society's New English Dictionary'. When the second part of the 'Basis of Comparison' (E to L) appeared later in the year, the prefatory note, dated 25 September, and signed by Furnivall, opened with these words: 'Since the publication of the First Part of this Basis, our proposed Dictionary has received a severe blow by the death of its first Editor, the able and accomplished Herbert Coleridge. In its service he caught the cold which resulted in his death. All through his illness he worked for it whenever leisure and strength allowed; and his last attempt at work—two days before he died—was to arrange some of its papers.'

The death of Coleridge at the age of 31 deprived the Dictionary, almost at the outset, of an editor of great promise. In addition to the activities already mentioned, he had compiled and published a Glossarial Index to the printed literature of the thirteenth century, rightly estimating the value of this as a basis for the early history of the language. He had also faced the problem of editing, and 'had prepared a few of the A words for printing, so far as the material sent in to him allowed'; this had been carried as far as the printing of a specimen page containing *affect–affection*. If this was premature, as it proved to be, it was because the magnitude of the work had not yet become apparent. Clear evidence of this is furnished by the set of specially made pigeon-holes which he considered would be large enough to contain the materials required at the outset. These provide about 260 inches of linear space, which would take no more than about 85,000 'slips'. As many as this were ultimately required for even one of the minor letters of the alphabet. Specimens of the articles prepared by Coleridge were printed in 1862, at the end of Part III of the 'Basis of Comparison', and extracts from others were read at a meeting of the Society on 24 April of the same year.

With Coleridge's death, the editorship passed to Furnivall, then in his thirty-sixth year. He immediately took up the duties, and on 23 May 'made a statement as to the present condition of the collections for the Society's Dictionary, and the course he proposed to pursue with regard to the scheme'. The lines of that course are clearly indicated in the 'Preliminary Notice' mentioned above. He was convinced that the time for editing was still at a distance. 'I have determined to put aside all idea of printing the first part of the Dictionary for four or five years unless some great unexpected help is forthcoming; and I propose, if all go well, to finish this Third-Period Basis early next year; then to compile Two Concise Dictionaries of Early and Middle English, which shall include severally all the materials sent in for the First and Second Periods.'

The magnitude of the task was thus becoming clearer, but in some points its extent was still underrated. 'Meantime,' Furnivall wrote, 'the etymological material will, I trust, be ready.' This was to be done by Dr Carl Lottner on the basis of Worcester's Dictionary, with the precaution that 'his work will be submitted to the Etymological Committee, perhaps before it is printed'. It had not yet become obvious that in many instances only the accumulation of material for the particular word could enable the editor to suggest or establish its real origin.

Another of Furnivall's first tasks was the compilation of a 'List of Books already read, or now (12 July 1861) being read for the Philological Society's New English Dictionary', covering 24 pages and published as an appendix to the *Transactions* for 1860–1. The numbers given here are: First Period, 143 Works and Authors; Second Period, 486; Third Period, 81. Among the principal readers are Furnivall and Coleridge, Revd J. Eastwood, H. H. Gibbs, E. S. Jackson, Revd Dr Stocker, W. C. Hazlitt, Mr Sprange, etc. The last page contains an intimation 'that the reading of any books not named in the foregoing List will be of service to the Dictionary. A list of those specially recommended to the notice of contributors is in preparation.'

Meanwhile, the Third Part of the 'Basis of Comparison', containing the letters M to Z, was on the way, and was issued in the third week of March 1862. Shortly before its appearance, on 27 February, Furnivall proposed the following resolutions, which were accepted by the Society.

1. That a concise Dictionary be prepared as a preliminary to the Society's proposed new English Dictionary and as a new basis of comparison for all the other periods.

2. That the concise Dictionary shall be as far as possible an abstract of what the large Dictionary should be, and shall contain—the Pronunciation, Critical marks, Etymologies, Roots, Prefixes, Suffixes, Definitions, and Homonyms of the words registered in it, with short quotations (a few words long) and the date and name of the Author for all words for which passages have been sent in to the Editor, and that all words, senses of words, idioms &c. known to exist, but for which authority has not yet been sent to the Editor, be supplied from any other available source and be marked with a * or other sign to denote the want of an authority.

3. That the Editor be authorised to entrust the quotations in his possession, and the sub-editing of any parts of the concise Dictionary to such of the contributors to the Dictionary or other Volunteers as he shall think fit.

It was also resolved:

That Mr. Furnivall be authorised to announce his plan to the contributors in the next part of the Third Period basis to sort the contributions and entrust them to the care of such sub-editors as he thinks fit, and that he be requested to print off at the expense of the Society a specimen of the concise dictionary which he proposes, and to lay it before the Society for their final decision before proceeding further with the printing of such dictionary.

In accordance with this the Third Part of the 'Basis' announced that 'the next step to be taken is to get out the Concise Dictionary hinted at in Part II'. Even this, it was clear, would take time, and 'nothing but the continuous labour of many years can make our Book anything like complete.—Let us then persevere.'

The idea of compiling a concise dictionary as a preliminary to the greater task was adopted by Furnivall on practical grounds; the agreement made with Trübner in 1858 had lapsed in course of time, and he saw no chance of finding another publisher for the larger work. In the expectation that the smaller task could be accomplished in a few years, he even entered into a personal contract with John Murray to have the manuscript ready for the press by the end of 1865. This view of the situation was natural while the material was still comparatively limited in amount. It became more and more unpractical as this continued to accumulate, for it involved the handling and arranging of all the slips for each word before the 'concise' article could be written, and consequently would have taken almost as much time as the preparation of the work on a more ample scale. This must, in time, have become obvious to the few volunteers who actually prepared portions of the Concise Dictionary, and it is not surprising that in the end the idea had to be given up, at considerable pecuniary loss to its originator. Apart from this, the employment of sub-editors was an idea which proved of great value for the later progress of the Dictionary, and to Dr Furnivall belongs the credit of originating the scheme and of issuing instructions for the guidance of these helpers in printed form, on 15 September 1862. Within the next year or two several of them prepared lists of the words coming under the letters which they had undertaken to sub-edit, and these were printed separately when ready, beginning in 1863 with that for B, 'compiled by W. Gee, Esq., sub-editor of the B words for the Concise Dictionary'. This contained no less than 93 pages in triple columns, giving the date of the earliest example of each word in the material, and the latest date for obsolete words, while each word is provided with numbers to indicate the periods (1, 2, and 3) for which there were quotations. Similar lists for N and U–V were issued in 1865. The latter contains a prefatory notice by Furnivall on the progress made in sub-editing, and lists of 'books now in hand for cutting up'. These words indicate a method of collecting material extensively employed from this time onward, by which the reader for the Dictionary was saved much time and labour by being freed from copying the quotations, while the Editor had the advantages of the original print and a fuller context. The defects of the method were that two copies of each book were required to give the full text, and that many early printed works were dealt with in this way which would have been of greater value in the hands of the editors.

From 1862 to 1872 the progress of the Dictionary in Furnivall's hands can be clearly traced in the annual circulars which he sent out to the members of the Philological Society. Portions of these are quoted in the 'Appeal to the English-Speaking Public on behalf of a New English Dictionary', issued by the Revd G. Wheelwright in 1875. A study of them shows considerable activity on the part of readers and sub-editors for the first three or four years, followed by a gradual slackening off, partly due to Furnivall's own increasing absorption in other interests. That for 1872 admitted that 'the progress in the Dictionary work has been so slight that no fresh report in detail is needed'.

These circulars were not included in the printed *Transactions* of the Philological Society, and in the pages of these there is remarkably little mention of the Dictionary during this period. On 6 November 1868, 'the Hon. Secretary [i.e. Furnivall] made a statement as to the progress of the Society's proposed new English Dictionary, together with a calculation by the Rev. G. Wheelwright, showing that about one-third of the work had been sub-edited'. A still briefer mention occurs under the date of 21 May 1869, and after this the subject does not recur until, in the annual presidential address by Alexander J. Ellis on 15 May 1874, it is included in a survey of the Society's work:

One of our works, for which great collections have been already made, remains, and may for some time remain, merely one of the things we have tried to do,—of course I allude to our projected dictionary. Several things, indeed, make me inclined to think that a Society is less fitted to compile a dictionary than to get the materials collected.

In the words that follow on this, Ellis clearly indicates that in his opinion the scholar best qualified to edit the Dictionary was Henry Sweet. The Revd Mr Wheelwright's 'Appeal' of the following year is in a more hopeful tone, and indicated the richness of the Dictionary material by giving a specimen of the letter F, which he had sub-edited; this extends to eight pages in triple columns and contains the words from *fa* to *face*.

During these years, Furnivall had of course not been idle. Not only had he continued to direct the collecting and sub-editing, but he had immensely increased the possibilities of the Dictionary by the foundation of the Early English Text Society in 1864, and the Chaucer Society in 1868. Without the former of these, the collecting of sufficient Middle English material would have presented almost insuperable difficulties, and in consequence the historical basis for many words would have been defective or altogether lacking. Although he took no part in the actual editing of the Dictionary in its ultimate form, he never ceased to contribute liberally to its stores, both from the publications of these societies and from other sources, including his daily morning and evening paper. If the Dictionary at one period quotes the *Daily News* and at another the *Daily Chronicle*, it is because Furnivall had changed his paper in the meanwhile. Through his early organization of the collecting and sub-editing, and his lifelong contributions, the work of Furnivall pervades every page of the Dictionary, and has helped in a great degree to make it what it is. He was fortunate in living long enough to see assured the completion of the work to which he had given so much of his busy life. Almost down to the time of his death in 1910 he still gave evidence of the unremitting activity, and interest in English studies, which had enabled him to achieve so much, while his genial disposition and constant readiness for new friendships explained his success in enlisting the help of others.

II

Before the Dictionary again becomes prominent in the *Transactions* of the Philological Society, a new and important element had entered into its history. James A. H. Murray, who had been a master at Mill Hill School from 1870, and had already made his mark in philological studies, had been approached in April 1876 by the firm of Macmillan with regard to a new dictionary. The idea of this, a dictionary to rival those of Webster and Worcester, had originated with Harper and Brothers of New York, who wished Macmillan to take part in the enterprise. Acting on the advice of Dr Richard Morris, who had consulted Furnivall in the matter, Macmillan proposed to Murray that he should undertake the editorship. Murray was not prepared to agree to this, unless the new dictionary was to be a great advance on the existing ones in respect of scholarship. Macmillan had heard of the intentions of the Philological Society, and asked whether the material already collected for it might not be available. Having, as the result of this suggestion, obtained some portions of the material, Murray prepared specimens of the kind of dictionary which he considered would be worth doing, and these were put into type. His ideas went far beyond those of the publishers, and a considerable time was spent in trying various modifications, till these reached the lowest point which in his opinion would have any real value. The divergent views of the publishers on this head were capable of adjustment, but difficulties arose in connection with the terms for the use of the Society's materials, and the negotiations came to an end.

The exhibition of the specimens produced from the material already collected, however, had the effect of again interesting the Philological Society in its old project. By May 1877 matters had begun to move; a letter from Furnivall written in that month tells where the various letters of the alphabet were to be found in the hands of the sub-editors. It was fortunate that the scattered material was, with the exception of one small portion, actually recoverable; one sub-editor, sending part of what he had, promised 'to search for the rest, which had been disposed by his wife in a lumber-room'.

Encouraged by these signs of new life, the Society again began to look round for a publisher, but at first without result, for with its small membership and limited funds the Society itself had nothing to offer but the material for the Dictionary, and no publisher was prepared to face the expenditure that would be required. Early in 1877, however, there were already foreshadowings of the ultimate connection with the Oxford University Press. Details of the scheme were submitted on behalf of the Society, and at the request of the Delegates a specimen of the proposed work was prepared by Murray. This was ultimately approved to such an extent that 'in the Spring of 1878, the then President of the Society, Mr H. Sweet, was authorized to open negotiations with the Delegates for the publication of the Dictionary'. As the prime mover in this new development, Murray also had a meeting with the Delegates at Oxford on 26 April, and 'thought there was good hope that the issue would be favourable'. This impression was confirmed by a letter (communicated to the Society on May 17) 'from the Secretary of the Delegates of the Clarendon Press, Prof. Bartholomew Price, saying that the Delegates had authorized him to enter into negotiations with the Society for the publication of the Dictionary on the basis of the terms submitted by the President to the Delegacy. The Council had accordingly directed the Dictionary Committee to meet Prof. Price, and try to come to terms with him.' Two such meetings were held before 21 June, and a basis of agreement was arrived at in the following October.

'The substance of the proposals' made by the Society as a basis for negotiation 'was, that the Delegates should advance the capital required for completing and publishing the work, that the gross profits should in the first place be applied exclusively to repaying their advances with interest, the net profits being then divided equally between the Delegates and the Society, that Dr J. A. H. Murray should be the Editor, and that he should be allowed ten years to complete the work in'. Various alterations were made in these proposals before the terms were finally embodied in two contracts, one between the Delegates and the Society, and the other between them and Dr Murray. In order to enter into this contract the Society had to be incorporated on a legal basis, and was registered in proper form on 2 January 1879. The contract, which is dated 1 March 1879, is printed in an Appendix to the Society's *Transactions* for 1877–9, where it occupies ten pages, with the addition of a specimen page of the proposed Dictionary, containing the words *castle* and *persuade*, and some subordinate entries based on these. At that stage the Dictionary contemplated was one estimated 'to occupy not less than 6,000 nor more than 7,000 pages, . . . and the said Dictionary shall be edited and prepared on the same principles and on the same lines of historical and linguistic evidence as to the forms and meanings of its words, as are shown in the Specimen page, and shall contain on its title page "Founded mainly on the materials collected by the Philological Society" '. This work is referred to in the contract as the 'principal dictionary', but provision was made for either party at a later date proceeding to compile and publish 'a larger dictionary containing not fewer than ten volumes, each containing not less than 1,600 pages of the size of the said Specimen page'. This was, in fact, a pretty close estimate of the size to which the Dictionary ultimately grew, and as early as November 1881 there was some anticipation of this growth, when the Delegates agreed to an increase in the number of pages from 6,400 to 8,400.

There are many other details in the contract which are interesting in themselves, or in the light of the later fortunes of the Dictionary, but on which it is not necessary to enlarge. The great facts which it embodied were that the Society had at last found its publisher, the Delegates had undertaken a task more magnificent than they knew of, and the Dictionary had found an editor capable of converting its latent possibilities into a great reality.

During the earlier part of these negotiations, however, Dr Murray had not definitely contemplated undertaking the editorship of the Dictionary, although he had taken a leading part in furthering the idea that it was something to be done. It was only when the necessity for a decision was forced upon him, by his being assured that the fate of the Dictionary depended on his acceptance, that he reluctantly agreed to assume the responsibility for a task which was even then formidable enough, though its full weight was not yet apparent. Several serious questions had to be faced in making this decision. It would be necessary to do the editing in addition to his work at Mill Hill School, even if he might be relieved of part of this. The housing of so great a mass of material could be satisfactorily accomplished only by providing special accommodation for it, and this and other necessary aids to the work involved at the outset the expenditure of private means in addition to the provision made by the Delegates. In spite of all these deterrents, he boldly faced the task, and set about providing the Dictionary with a home, and making it possible for himself to work at it. By the middle of February (he told the Society in May 1879) 'I had commenced the erection of an iron building, detached from my dwelling-house, to serve as a *Scriptorium*, and to accommodate safely and conveniently the materials. This has been fitted with blocks of pigeon-holes, 1,029 in number, for the reception of the alphabetically arranged slips, and with writing desks, reference desks, and other conveniences for the extensive apparatus required. On Lady Day . . . I received from Mr. Furnivall some ton and three-quarters of materials which had accumulated under his roof as sub-editor after sub-editor fell off in his labours. With a considerable body of assistants I have been engaged since that date, as to all appearance I must be for many months to come, in turning out, examining, sorting, and bestowing these materials.'

By the tenth of May, with a few exceptions, all the material in the hands of the sub-editors had either been sent in, or satisfactorily accounted for. It had, indeed, been widely scattered, and not only in Britain; the letter H came back all the way from Florence. Although so much of it was still in an undigested state, it was soon obvious that even all this mass was inadequate for the production of a satisfactory Dictionary on the lines that had been laid down. The material for many words, especially the commoner words, was obviously defective, and required to be augmented as rapidly as possible. A fresh appeal was made for voluntary readers, and even in April 1879 a number had come forward to help. At the end of that month, the Clarendon Press printed a thousand copies of 'An Appeal to the English-speaking and English-reading public to read books and make extracts for the Philological Society's *New English Dictionary*'. This appeal covers four pages, of which the first two summarize the history of the Dictionary from 1857 to 1879, the third explains the reading still required, and the fourth contains the statement 'A thousand readers are wanted, and confidently asked for, to complete the work as far as possible within the next three years'. To this are added four pages of book lists, and a set of directions to readers. This appeal, of which another five hundred copies were issued later, met with a gratifying response, and enabled the compilation of the Dictionary to be undertaken with confidence in the result.

The arranging of the old material in the Scriptorium, the organizing of the fresh collecting, and extensive correspondence with readers and sub-editors, were tasks which at first left but little time for the actual preparation of the Dictionary, or even for consideration of the many points which had to be settled before a real beginning could be made. For many of these there was no model which could be followed; they involved totally new principles in English lexicography, and required both scholarship and practical judgement to solve them satisfactorily. Coleridge and Furnivall had shown a sound understanding of what was necessary as a foundation for the Dictionary; to Murray belongs the credit of giving it, at the outset, a form which proved to be adequate to the end, standing the test of fifty years without requiring any essential modification to adapt it to the steady advance of English scholarship or the accession of new material.

III

At this point it will be well, both for the sake of greater clearness and of giving credit where credit is due, to give some account of the method of collecting the material for the Dictionary and of the work done by the voluntary readers and sub-editors. Each member of these two classes stood to the final editors in a relation similar to that which Socrates in the *Ion* compares to the magnet and the suspended rings, each depending on and operating through the other, although in the case of the Dictionary the order of their sequence was reversed.

The example of Johnson and Richardson had shown clearly that the citation of authority for a word was one of the essentials for establishing its meaning and tracing its history. It was therefore obvious that the first step towards the building up of a new dictionary must be the assembling of such authority, in the form of quotations from English writings throughout the various periods of the language. Johnson and Richardson had been selective in the material they assembled, and obviously some kind of selection would be imposed by practical limits, however wide the actual range might be. This was a point on which control was difficult; the one safeguard was that the care and judgement of some readers would make up for the possible deficiencies of others.

By the directions which were issued to intending readers in 1858, and again in 1879, uniformity in the method of presenting the quotations was attained. Each was written on a separate slip of paper, at first of the size of a half-sheet of note-paper, latterly of a quarter of a sheet of foolscap, except when readers who supplied their own paper (such as Dr Furnivall, Dr Fitzedward Hall, and the Revd W. B. R. Wilson) wrote on pieces of any size or quality that came to hand. This difference in size makes it easy to distinguish the slips belonging to the two periods of collecting. When completed, the normal slip presented three things, (1) the word for which it was selected, written in the upper left-hand corner, (2) the date, author, title, page, etc., of the work cited, and (3) the quotation itself, either in full, or in an adequate form. A typical slip therefore presented something like the following appearance:

Britisher

1883 Freeman Impressions U.S. iv. 29

I always told my American friends that I had rather be called a Britisher than an Englishman, if by calling me an Englishman they meant to imply that they were not Englishmen themselves.

To obviate the tedium of repeating item (2) over and over again on hundreds of slips, it was in a large number of instances printed on each, in accordance with an estimate of the number that would be required for the particular book, or was supplied by stamping after the quotations themselves had been written. In this way, too, it was easier to make the references to page, chapter, line, etc., conform to general rules.

How the readers were to be guided in their selection of words was thus explained in the directions issued in 1879:

> Make a quotation for *every* word that strikes you as rare, obsolete, old-fashioned, new, peculiar, or used in a peculiar way.
>
> Take special note of passages which show or imply that a word is either new and tentative, or needing explanation as obsolete or archaic, and which thus help to fix the date of its introduction or disuse.
>
> Make as *many* quotations *as you can* for ordinary words, especially when they are used significantly, and tend by the context to explain or suggest their own meaning.

It is obvious that these rules would apply in very varying degrees to different books, and that the task of some readers would be much more difficult and extensive than that of others in books of the same size. The amount undertaken or done by the different readers also varied enormously. In both periods of collecting there were a number who were marvels of industry and whose mark is plain on almost every page of the Dictionary to those who can recognize it. With these on the one hand, and the large army of lesser, but often important, contributors on the other, it is not surprising that the piles of quotations grew into the interminable series that filled to overflowing the pigeon-holes of the Scriptorium. How rapidly the material increased in the periods of greatest activity will best be realized by a few of the passages relating to this phase of the work. In May 1879, in response to the appeal issued at the end of April, '165 readers have offered themselves, 128 of these have chosen their books, been supplied with slips, and are now at work for us. The number of books actually undertaken and entered against readers is 234; arrangements are in progress for perhaps as many more.' A year later the number of readers had risen to 754. 'Altogether 1,568 books have been undertaken, of which 924 have been finished', and 'the total number of printed slips supplied to readers now amounts to 625,035, while the quotations returned are 361,670'. Of these readers some had sent in a large number of slips varying from 4,500 to 11,000. By another year (1881) 'the number of readers has now risen to upwards of 800, of whom 510 are still at work. The slips issued now number 817,625, and the quotations returned 656,900.' The total number of authors then represented in the Reference Index was 2,700, and the titles numbered some 4,500.

Many of the particulars of this remarkable activity were given in the preface to the first volume of the Dictionary, and a full list of the readers and the books read by them between 1879 and 1884, with the approximate number of quotations supplied by each, forms an appendix of 32 pages to the Presidential Address for 1884 (pp. 101–42).

On looking over this list, the observant reader will notice that the interest in the Dictionary which at its first beginning had been manifested in the United States had been maintained, though not on the lines suggested by Coleridge. The interest, and the results it produced, are specially referred to by Dr Murray in his Presidential Address for 1880 in these words:

> In connexion with the Reading, I cannot sufficiently express my appreciation of the kindness of our friends in the United States, where the interest taken in our scheme, springing from a genuine love of our common language, its history, and a warm desire to make the Dictionary worthy of that language, has impressed me very deeply. I do not hesitate to say that I find in Americans an ideal love for the English language as a glorious heritage, and a pride in being intimate with its grand memories, such as one does find sometimes in a classical scholar in regard to Greek, but which is rare indeed in Englishmen towards their own tongue; and from this I draw the most certain inferences as to the lead which Americans must at no distant date take in English scholarship.

Dr Murray then specially refers to the services rendered by Prof. Francis A. March of Lafayette College in directing the reading done in the United States at that time, and adds:

> There is another feature of American help to which I must allude, because it contrasts with that we have obtained in England—I refer to that offered to the Dictionary by men of Academic standing in the States. The number of Professors in American Universities and Colleges included among our

readers is very large; and in several instances a professor has put himself down for a dozen works, which he has undertaken to read personally, and with the help of his students. We have had no such help from any college or university in Great Britain; only one or two Professors of English in this country have thought the matter of sufficient importance to talk to their students about it, and advise them to help us.

By far the greater part of the material supplied by these American readers, it may be noted, was of the same type as that furnished by the British contributors, that is, it was mainly drawn from literary or scientific works written in standard English, or without noticeable American features in vocabulary or idiom. It was thus very serviceable in supplementing the English evidence, but failed to a very large extent to bring out the special developments of the language in the American colonies and the United States. Much of the material for these was specially supplied during the progress of the Dictionary by one or two workers, notably by Mr Albert Matthews of Boston.

In addition to the quotations supplied by all this new reading, a few collections of Dictionary material, which had already been made by various persons, were by them generously handed over for use in the new work. If the Dictionary as it stands is a monument of scholarship, it is also one of unselfish giving on the part of a great number of men and women whose nameless contributions form the foundation of almost every article it contains.

Only second in value to the work done by the voluntary readers was that of the volunteer sub-editors. Without these, the mere handling and reducing to alphabetical order of three and a half millions of slips would have formed a task sufficiently heavy to delay for some years the actual preparation of the Dictionary. Even those who did no more than this rendered good service, but most of them went much farther, and so arranged and subdivided the words they dealt with, and defined their various senses, that their work was of real value in the final editing. It is with good reason, therefore, that the portions done by each were carefully recorded in the various reports on the Dictionary presented to the Philological Society and in the Preface to each letter in the Dictionary itself.

IV

Amid all the turmoil of assembling the old material, collecting the new, and reducing both to some kind of orderly arrangement, Dr Murray was working out the lines on which the editing of the Dictionary was to proceed. The problem of the best means of indicating the pronunciation, for example, was under consideration for a long time, and was decided only after the views of various authorities had been duly taken into account. Correspondence on this subject with Isaac Pitman, James Lecky, and W. R. Evans, was still in progress in the summer and autumn of 1881 and the spring of 1882, and the notation finally adopted was submitted to, and accepted by, the Council of the Society on 17 March of that year.

Meanwhile the preparation of the letter A was making progress with the material then available. As early as 16 May 1879 this had advanced as far as *aby*, covering 557 words, and providing enough copy to make 36 pages of the Dictionary. A year later this had increased to 160 pages, going as far as *al*. By May 1881 the question of typography was being discussed, and there is mention of a specimen page in June. About the same time, the desire to settle down definitely to the real work of editing becomes obvious in the statement that 'the general amassing of quotations must cease with the present year'.

It had been estimated that three years would be required for all this preparatory work, and the estimate proved to be correct. On 19 April 1882, the first batch of copy went to the printer, and in his report to the Philological Society on 19 May, Dr Murray had the satisfaction of being able to announce 'the great fact ... that the Dictionary is now at last really launched, and that some forty pages are in type, of which 48 columns have reached me in proof'. To fill the first part, however, extending from *A* to *ant*, more than a thousand columns were necessary, and the task of providing these occupied the remainder of that year, and the greater part of the next. Finally, on 18 January 1884, advance copies of Part I were exhibited at a meeting of the Society, publication took place on 1 February, and the 'New English Dictionary' at once took its place as an incomparable record of the English tongue, far surpassing all that had as yet been accomplished or even dreamt of in the field of lexicography.

The beginning had been made; how to continue the work rapidly was the next question that called for solution. Simple arithmetic indicated that there was need for an increased rate of production, though it was not clear how this was to be attained. In May 1884 Dr Murray thought that with six good assistants 'it might be possible to produce two parts in the year, and thus finish the work in 11 years from next March'. This suggestion was no doubt justified by the facts as they were at that time. That it failed to work out was certainly due in great part to the fact that A was not a good letter on which to base the calculation, and to a steady increase in the material which could not at that time be foreseen.

All the work necessary to produce the first part had been done in the original Scriptorium at Mill Hill. It was clear that greater progress could be made if the editor could devote all his time to the work and be in closer touch with the printing at the Clarendon Press. As early as 1882 the idea of removal to Oxford had been suggested, but it was only towards the end of 1884 that the proposals began to take definite shape. The practical aspects of the question having been settled, the removal took place in 1885; a new Scriptorium was erected in the garden of the house at 78 Banbury Road, and here Dr Murray and his staff carried on their work for the next thirty years. The Scriptorium was not in itself lacking in space, but when into it were packed all the accumulated material, the necessary works of reference, and the tables, desks, and chairs required by the editor and six or seven assistants, it presented a crowded scene to the eye of the visitor. If John Baret had been able to look into it, he would have hailed it as another *Alvearie*, with a swarm of workers as busy as those who helped him to compile his own volume.

In the new quarters the Dictionary continued to make progress, and Part II, containing the words from

Ant to *Batten*, appeared in 1885. By that time it had become plain that some editorial co-operation was necessary to increase the rate at which successive parts could be produced. Here again the Dictionary was fortunate, as it had already been in rising, in Dr Murray's hands, out of the apparent impasse into which it had fallen ten years before. When Part I was published, the editor of the *Academy* handed it for review to Henry Bradley, who had but lately arrived in London, and was yet comparatively unknown in the world of scholarship. His review, which appeared in two parts, on 16 February and 1 March, at once marked him out as one of the few who were competent either to appreciate the Dictionary at its proper value, or to offer useful criticism. So clear an indication of possible help was not overlooked, and by July Bradley was assisting in the preparation of the latter part of B. From January 1888 he was independently editing the letter E, and continued with this and F while still engaged in other work in London. In 1896 he also moved to Oxford, and with his staff found quarters in the Clarendon Press itself.

From 1888 there were thus two distinct sections of the Dictionary simultaneously in progress, Dr Murray doing the whole volume occupied by C, and the half volume containing D, while Bradley completed that volume with E, and began the next (Vol. IV) with F. Down to 1900 the letters published, with the respective dates of the preparation of each, stand as follows:

A B	1882–8		
C	1888–93	E	1888–93
D	1893–7	F	1893–7
H	1897–9	G	1897–1900

In all this work the part played by the assistants who formed the staff of each editor was of the greatest importance. While considerable training and experience are required by every one, however well qualified, it is also true that the real dictionary worker is born and not made, and that no application or diligence will ever make up for the lack of natural aptitude for the work. The two earlier editors, and those who came later, were fortunate in having the services of a number of such assistants, some of whom (and those among the best) became connected with the Dictionary in its earlier stages and remained faithful to it for periods of twenty, thirty, and even forty years. Without their unflagging and efficient aid, no editor could have coped with the task without so much expenditure of his own time that the end of it would have been beyond all calculation. If those who read the original prefaces to the various letters will note the names that occur time after time at the end of these, they will do right to recognize that the bearers of these names have throughout many years borne the greater share of the labour by which the Dictionary was made possible.

Among these assistants a natural subdivision of labour readily established itself according to the special interests of each. Some became experts in preparing copy for the printer, drafting articles which required only a few editorial changes, or actually writing them in a form which admitted little or no improvement. To these fell the task of taking up the work already done by the sub-editors, of incorporating new material, of making fresh additions that were obviously required, of distinguishing senses and sub-senses, of writing the definitions, and of reconciling the historical order of the senses with their logical development from the original meaning of the word. This became a highly complicated task in the case of common words with a long history, such as the most frequently used verbs, adverbs, or prepositions. The difficulty of these had become apparent even in the early period of the work, and formed the subject of comment by Dr Murray in 1881:

> In returning to me his last batch, Mr. Jacob mentioned to me that the division of the meanings of the verb *Set*, and the attempt to put them in satisfactory order, had occupied him over 40 hours. In examining his results, with 51 senses of the simple verb, and 83 of phrases like *set-out*, *set-off*, *set-down*,—134 divisions in all—I do not wonder at the time. I suspect that the Editor will have to give 40 more to it, for the language seems not to contain a more perplexing word that *Set*, which occupies more than two columns of Webster, and will probably fill three of our large quarto pages.

When *set* finally came to be done, more than thirty years later, it took nearer 40 days than 40 hours to digest the mass of examples which had accumulated by that time; the word occupies a column more than 18 pages of the Dictionary, and extends to 154 main divisions, the last of which (*set up*) has so many subdivisions that it exhausts the alphabet and repeats the letters down to *rr*. Other words like *get*, *give*, *go*, *put*, *take*, may not rival this, but each of them required a vast amount of preliminary labour on the part of some assistant, which was of the greatest value in saving the time of the editor and giving him a clear basis on which to work.

Other assistants developed special ability in checking and verifying references readily and correctly, in finding earlier or desirable examples of words or uses, or in reading proofs and making additions to the material at that stage. When a staff had all these elements properly represented and distributed in it, and certain preliminaries to the work on each letter (such as the copying of glossaries, concordances, and indexes) had been fully carried out, steady progress could be made, and was made to an extent which seemed marvellous to foreign scholars acquainted with the difficulties of lexicography, but unfamiliar with the practical methods of overcoming them.

For the obtaining of full or accurate information on special points, it was frequently necessary to apply to outside authorities of the most varied kind. The services rendered by these were partly acknowledged on the title-page of the earlier parts and volumes in the words 'With the assistance of many scholars and men of science'. How many these were may be seen at large in the original prefaces to the various letters, but it should also be noted that there were many in those lists who would not have claimed to belong to either of these learned classes, but who could and did supply the information wanted with a clearness and fullness which made the editor's task easy, and gave him confidence in the correctness of his statements. If various errors to be found in standard works are not repeated in the Dictionary, it is frequently because someone with a practical knowledge of the subject had been specially consulted on the point, and had freely given the information required.

When the Dictionary had reached the stage of the

first proof (regularly supplied in sets of eight columns), it was found to be of much value to send these to various readers deeply interested in the work, to receive the benefit of their criticisms, suggestions, and additions. In this way many improvements were made, errors and misprints eliminated, and the history of words and senses more fully illustrated. In the latter respect the contributions of Dr Fitzedward Hall were of special value by reason of his own collection of material. His regular reading of the proofs extended over some twenty years, and after his death his collections for the later letters were placed at the service of the editors. Among nearly a score of others who reviewed the proofs for shorter or longer periods special mention should be made of Mr Henry Hucks Gibbs (Lord Aldenham), who also in other ways gave valuable help and encouragement in the early stages of the work; of Miss Edith Thompson of Bath, Canon Fowler of Durham, and Mr A. Caland of Wageningen in Holland, who not only supplied many fresh quotations, but as a foreign student of English frequently noticed points which did not so readily strike the native eye.

V

Although two editors and their staffs had been working separately from 1888, it was still considered by the Delegates of the Clarendon Press that the rate of progress ought to be increased, and it was clear that this could only be done by the appointment of a third editor. With this in view, William Alexander Craigie, then a lecturer at the University of St Andrews, was invited to Oxford in the summer of 1897, and after assisting Dr Bradley with the letter G, and Dr Murray with I and K, began separate editing with Q in 1901. From that date two sections of the Dictionary had their home in the Old Ashmolean Building in Broad Street, which had been left vacant by the removal of the Museum some years before. To these a third was added in 1914, when Charles Talbut Onions, who had at Dr Murray's invitation joined the staff in 1895, and had between 1906 and 1913 prepared special portions of M, N, R, and S, began with a separate staff to edit the later portion of that letter (Su–Sz).

With four editors and their staffs concurrently at work prospects for an early conclusion to the whole seemed brighter than they had ever been since the full magnitude of the undertaking became apparent. Unfortunately it was not long before various events began to mar these prospects, and bring unwelcome delays. The outbreak of the Great War soon began to reduce the staffs by withdrawing from them their younger members, and in time even some of those more mature in years. The loss of these trained workers for three or four years was naturally a serious handicap for those that remained. The next severe blow was the death of Sir James Murray (he had been knighted in 1908) on 26 July 1915, after more than thirty-eight years of connection with the Dictionary and thirty-three during which he had supplied copy to the printer without intermission. The transference of his staff to the Old Ashmolean, or to quarters near it, helped greatly to strengthen the three remaining sections, but there was no possibility of compensating for the loss that the work had sustained. If his wish had been fulfilled to the extent of seeing his eightieth birthday in 1917, it would not have coincided with the end of the Dictionary, as he had hoped, but those two years would have brought the completion of the work appreciably nearer in spite of the difficulties of the time.

With the end of the war, some of the assistants returned to their posts, and for some four years the work went on steadily (although the two younger editors were not continuously engaged on it nor able to give their whole time to it), until the death of Dr Bradley on 23 May 1923 removed another of its mainstays. By that time it was clearly too late to think of finding another editor; the best that could be done was to make full use of the more experienced assistants in the preparation of special sections of the letters that still remained. By this means it was possible for Dr Craigie, in spite of his removal to the University of Chicago in 1925, to take part with Dr Onions in the editing of W, and so enable the work to be finished in the beginning of 1928, almost exactly seventy years from the date on which the Philological Society had decided to make 'a completely new English Dictionary'.

With work on three or four letters going on simultaneously, and publication of each taking place as soon as the sections were ready, the sequence of the various parts of the Dictionary became more irregular after 1900, as will be seen from the following table:

Murray	*Bradley*	*Craigie*	*Onions*
I J K 1899–1901			
	L 1901–3		
O 1902–4		Q 1902	
		R–Re 1903–5	
P 1904–9	M 1904–8	N 1906–7	
		Re–Ry 1907–10	
	S–Sh 1908–14		
T 1909–15	St 1914–19	Si–Sq 1910–15	
		V 1916–20	Su–Sz 1914–19
	W–We 1920–3	U 1921–6	X Y Z 1920–1
		Wo–Wy 1927	Wh–Wo 1922–7

The total number of pages in the first edition was 15,487; of these no less than 7,207, or nearly half of the entire work were edited by Sir James Murray.

The early volumes of the Dictionary were as a rule published in parts of 352 pages at a price of twelve shillings and sixpence each, with three smaller sections introduced to make the divisions coincide with the end of the letters B, C, and E. The size of these parts necessarily involved a considerable time in the preparation of each, and a corresponding interval between the dates of publication. Towards the end of 1894 it was decided that a shortening of these intervals was desirable, and the new arrangement explained in the following announcement was adopted.

The Letters, A, B, C, and E of this great undertaking having been already published, the Delegates of the Clarendon Press have been urged from many quarters to consider the more frequent publication of the subsequent portions of the work, in smaller instalments, as each is completed by the Editors, so as to supply students of the English Language and Literature more promptly with the results of the latest researches.

In response to this demand, the Delegates have arranged for the punctual issue of the letters D and F in Quarterly Sections. The new issue will begin with the simultaneous publication of the opening part of each letter on November 15, and further instalments of the Editors' work will be regularly published thereafter on the first day of each Quarter, in such alternation as may seem desirable. The Delegates have no reason to fear any interruption in the continuous publication of the Dictionary on this plan.

This expectation was realized, and quarterly sections of 64 pages, or double sections of 128 (occasionally even a triple section of 192) were steadily issued for the next twenty years, until the reduction of staffs caused by the war, and other losses, made it impossible to continue with the same regularity. For the convenience of those who preferred them, however, the larger twelve-and-sixpenny parts were still issued whenever a sufficient number of consecutive single or double sections were available to make one.

At the time this change was made, a new name for the Dictionary was also introduced, though no change was made on the title-page. On the cover of the section containing *Deceit* to *Deject*, published on 1 January 1895, above the title, appeared for the first time the designation 'The Oxford English Dictionary', which was repeated on every section and part issued after 1 July of that year. The new name, being more distinctive than the old, steadily came more and more into use, and the abbreviation *OED* tended to supplant *NED*, although the latter was frequently employed for many years. A third abbreviation, *HED* (with H for Historical), though employed for a number of year in *Notes and Queries*, never attained general currency. Popularly the work was often referred to as Murray's, and the Philological Society by a natural tradition has continued to call it 'the Society's Dictionary'.

VI

During all these years of work, in addition to the growing appreciation which it steadily received, the progress of the Dictionary was diversified by a few extraneous events. On 12 October 1897, a large number of the readers, sub-editors, assistants, and other helpers were enabled to meet each other at Oxford by the generosity of the Provost and Fellows of The Queen's College, who on that date gave a complimentary dinner to 'Dr. Murray, Mr. Bradley, and some others who have helped in the production of the Historical English Dictionary'. The time was a fortunate one, for in that year it was still possible for some of the early workers to shake hands with those who were just beginning to take up the task which they had already carried on so long. Only a small number of the company which met that evening lived long enough to see the completion of the work.

In the same year the Dictionary was by permission dedicated to Her Majesty Queen Victoria, as intimated on a special page inserted in the part for January 1898.

Up to 1905 the whole expense of preparing and printing the Dictionary was borne by the Oxford University Press. In that year, however, a contribution was made towards the cost of the sixth volume, which was also recorded on a separate page in these words:

> This sixth volume is a memorial of the munificence of the Worshipful Company of Goldsmiths, who have generously contributed five thousand pounds towards its production.

When the completed dictionary was published in April 1928, the first copies were presented to His Majesty King George, and to Calvin Coolidge, President of the United States, as the highest representatives of the two great English-speaking nations.

On 6 June of the same year the Goldsmiths' Company celebrated the completion of the work by a dinner in the Company's hall in London, at which contributors and workers again had an opportunity of meeting, and of hearing the Prime Minister, Mr Stanley Baldwin, commend the results of their labours in eloquent and graceful terms.

During the progress of the work academic honours were from time to time conferred upon the editors by various universities, and at its completion the University of Oxford marked the occasion by conferring the honorary degree of D.Litt. on the two surviving editors, the Secretary to the Delegates of the Press, the Publisher to the University, and the Printer to the University.

Sir James Murray, as already mentioned, had in recognition of his services to scholarship received the honour of knighthood in 1908, the announcement being made in the Birthday list of 26 June, and the same distinction was bestowed on the third editor in the Birthday list of 3 June, 1928.

After the completion of the Dictionary in 1928, editorial work did not immediately cease. Since the *OED* had been published over a period of forty-four years, it was inevitable that many later additions to the language, both of new words and of new senses, should be lacking in the earlier volumes, and that even the later should to some extent present similar deficiencies. To remedy this as far as possible, the succeeding five years were devoted to the preparation of a supplementary volume, the scope of which is explained in the next section. After this work had been finished the original ten-volume *New English Dictionary on Historical Principles* was, in August 1933, reissued as *The Oxford English Dictionary* in twelve volumes. An additional volume was issued at the same time, containing the Supplement of new words and meanings, the Additions and Emendations prefixed to the original volumes, revised and amplified, a List of Spurious Words, and a List of Books quoted in the principal work; this last forming, as the 1933 Preface has it, 'a bibliography of English literature such as does not exist elsewhere'.

THE FIRST SUPPLEMENT, 1928–1933

From the earliest days of the publication of the Dictionary it had been envisaged that a Supplement or Supplements might be necessary, in order to keep the historical record of the language up to date, and to take account of subsequent research into the vocabulary already covered by the Dictionary. This possibility had been kept in view not only by members of the Dictionary staff but also by a certain number of the regular 'readers' who maintained a continuous flow of contributions to the material from which the work was being compiled; moreover, communications of corrections and additions were constantly sent in by many interested users of the published work. Consequently, when the original Dictionary was completed in 1928, a great body of quotations had been amassed with a view to a Supplement on a grand scale, which should not only treat the new words and new meanings that had come into being during the publications of the successive sections of the Dictionary, but should also correct and amplify the evidence for what was already in print. It was soon discovered, however, that such a Supplement, if it were to be at all a worthy and adequate addition to the main work, would demand intensive research by experienced workers extending over many years. This course could not be contemplated when the possibility of preparing a Supplement was considered as work drew to an end on the original Dictionary.

It was therefore resolved to produce a supplementary volume, the scope of which would in the main be restricted to the treatment of those accessions of words and senses which had taken place during the preceding fifty years. To this limitation there were to be two principal exceptions: items of modern origin and contemporary currency that had been either intentionally or accidentally omitted from the Dictionary would be included, and account would be taken of earlier evidence for American uses, which Sir William Craigie, at that time editing the *Dictionary of American English* in Chicago, was in a position to supply. Temporary or casual uses were recognized only in so far as they marked stages in the recent history of scientific discovery, invention, or fashion, or illustrated the progress of thought, usage, or custom during the half-century then under review. A few important corrections or amplifications of existing definitions were introduced under the necessity of bringing the work into line with recent research. The details of this policy were established by Dr C. T. Onions, under whose editorship the first *Supplement to the OED* was published in 1933.

The chief characteristics of the vocabulary set forth in the 1933 Supplement can be summarized briefly: on the technical side, it exhibited the great enlargement of the terminology of the arts and sciences at the close of the nineteenth century and in the early years of the twentieth—biochemistry, radio telegraphy and telephony, mechanical transport on land, at sea, and in the air, psychoanalysis, the cinema, to name a few outstanding subjects; on the purely linguistic side, the varied development of colloquial idiom and slang, to which the United States of America had made a large contribution, but in which the British dominions and dependencies of the time also contributed a conspicuous share. As in the main work, there was continually present the problem of the inclusion or omission of the more esoteric scientific terms and of the many foreign words reflecting the widened interest in the conditions and customs of distant countries; it was acknowledged that the problem had not been satisfactorily and comprehensively solved in every instance, as the material from which the Supplement was compiled had been collected principally while the original Dictionary was still in preparation, and following the same guidelines in operation during that work. In one respect the 1933 Supplement went somewhat beyond the limits of the main Dictionary, in its more generous inclusion of proper names; but even so, these were not admitted unless they had some allusive interest or were important for some linguistic, literary, or historical reason.

The result was a Supplement of over 800 pages which went far towards completing the documentation of the English language up to the end of the first quarter of the twentieth century and just beyond. However, extensive though it was, it still represented only a restricted selection from a large collection of material from which a much larger volume might have been produced. Once it had been completed, the *OED* team dispersed, and the editorial staff, including the last surviving Editor of the original Dictionary still in Oxford, Dr C. T. Onions, turned to other work. The *OED* library in Oxford was broken up, and quotation slips that had not been used were stored away, some later to be dispatched to other historical dictionary projects, notably for use in the preparation of the *Middle English Dictionary* at Ann Arbor, Michigan and the projected dictionary of Early Modern English.

A SUPPLEMENT TO THE OXFORD ENGLISH DICTIONARY, 1957–1986[1]

After the Second World War the Delegates of the University Press decided to re-establish a headquarters for the Dictionary in Oxford, and to prepare a revised version of the 1933 Supplement. In the end, this proved to be an even greater work than that which circumstances had forbidden in 1928, an addition to the main Dictionary of one-third of its size, taking almost thirty years to prepare. But this was not foreseen at the time. The original intention was simply to amplify the existing Supplement in a single-volume work of some 1,275 pages which would take account of the lexical development in English throughout the first half of the twentieth century. In 1957, R. W. Burchfield, a New Zealander who was then Lecturer in English Language and Literature at Christ Church, Oxford, and formerly a Rhodes Scholar at the University, accepted the invitation of the Delegates to edit the *Supplement*. It was envisaged that this new *Supplement* would take about seven years to complete.

At this stage, the editorial office of the Dictionary was located on one floor of a private house, No. 40 Walton Crescent, adjacent to the University Press's printing works and to the Clarendon Press itself. The presence in Oxford of Dr C. T. Onions provided valuable continuity between the *OED* and the projected new *Supplement,* and at the time it was still possible for the editor to receive the advice and encouragement of a small number of people who had worked on or for the

[1] The Editor's own account of this project may be read in the prefatory sections of the four volumes of the *Supplement,* especially the Introduction to Volume I (A–G), on which the present narrative has drawn.

Dictionary in other capacities. However, the lapse of some twenty years since the disbanding of the original *OED* staff meant that one of the first duties incumbent on the new editor was the selection and training of new assistants. In the days of the Dictionary itself, Sir James Murray had often found the recruitment of suitable staff to be a problematic and uncertain affair, and so it proved again. Gradually, though, the initial difficulties began to subside, and early work in the preparation of the new *Supplement* began to take a steadier course.

The raw material for a dictionary on historical principles—a file of quotations excerpted from the literature of the period treated—was almost entirely lacking. Among the material left behind after work on the 1933 Supplement there was indeed a collection of quotations numbering about 140,000, few of which had appeared in the Supplement itself, which included illustrative examples of words excluded in 1933 because they were not fully established at the time. Though useful, these materials fell far short of what was needed, both in quantity and range: the whole literature of the eventful quarter-century since 1933 had to be sifted from scratch. In 1957 an extensive reading programme was inaugurated, covering printed sources of all kinds relating to late nineteenth- and twentieth-century English. The sources included all the important literary works, as well as many hundreds of popular titles, a wide range of scientific books and journals, and large numbers of newspapers and periodicals, ranging from the national press to the publications of the 'underground'. Numerous works containing lexicographical information, such as *Notes and Queries, American Speech,* and many dictionaries of regionalisms, slang, jargon, and technical language, were converted into the form of dictionary slips. In addition, several valuable private collections were submitted to the Press, and these were also added to the quotation files. Thanks to these and subsequent valuable donations, to the comprehensiveness of the reading programme, to the alertness of the departmental staff in their private reading, and to the regular contributions of scholars and voluntary readers, the quotation file grew to contain at least two million, and possibly three million, slips by the time of the completion of the *Supplement,* and proved an excellent resource from which to make the initial selection of items for inclusion in the dictionary and from which to document the history of each term up to the present day.

At the same time it was necessary to build up a reference library of books in the department to which staff could turn for additional information about items for which entries were being prepared. Some volumes from the 1933 Supplement library were brought together again, and a further 7,000 or so books, especially dictionaries, were gradually acquired by the department. These consisted of books and periodicals dealing with the development of English in Great Britain, America, the Commonwealth, and elsewhere; a large collection of dictionaries (both English and bilingual), volumes on slang, dialect, etymology, and as many of the subject areas treated by the dictionary as it was convenient to house in the editorial offices, besides many of the novels, plays, and collections of published diaries and letters, which had been 'read' for the dictionary's quotation file and were at hand when quotations included in the dictionary needed checking.

By the early 1960s, it was clear that the development of the English language throughout the world had been much more rapid than either the Delegates of the Press or the Editor of the *Supplement* had at that time considered, and that the *Supplement* would occupy many more pages than had been originally intended. The paramount importance of reassessing the projected size of the *Supplement* had been highlighted by the publication in 1961 of *Webster's Third New International Dictionary,* which illustrated dramatically the proliferation of new vocabulary in North America and Great Britain in the early and mid-twentieth century. *Webster's Second* had appeared just one year after the earlier *OED* Supplement, in 1934, and offered a perfect basis for comparison in terms of the rate of change in the language, bringing home sharply to the Editor and his staff the necessity of improving considerably the *OED*'s own coverage of American English, and, *pari passu,* other overseas varieties of English. The original plans were revised to allow for a *Supplement* spanning three (and eventually four) volumes, concentrating much more extensively on the vocabulary of North America, the West Indies, Australia, and the other English-speaking countries of the world. The Editor drew a parallel between the current state of affairs on the *Supplement* and Dryden's remarks in the *Preface to the Fables* (1700):

> 'Tis with a Poet, as with a Man who designs to build, and is very exact, as he supposes, in casting up the Cost beforehand: But, generally speaking, he is mistaken in his Account, and reckons short of the Expence he first intended: He alters his Mind as the work proceeds, and will have this or that Convenience more, of which he had not thought when he began.[1]

A substantial research base had been built up by the mid-1960s. Besides assistant editors and researchers in Oxford, the *Supplement* soon had permanent members of staff working as researchers in the major libraries in London and Washington, and links with language centres and with other libraries throughout the world. A panel of specialist consultants was established to read and comment on individual entries in galley proof, and another panel of scholars and writers to read through continuous sections of galley proof with a critical eye. A radical departure from the policy adopted by the editors of the original Dictionary was the appointment from 1968 of graduates in scientific subjects, who took general responsibility for the drafting of entries in these disciplines. The necessity of taking this step had been impressed on the Editor as a result of his visit to the editorial offices of Merriam-Webster in 1967. Editorial work on the *Supplement* began in earnest in 1964, and the first instalment of copy (*A–alpha*) was delivered to the University Printer on 27 May 1965. From this point until the completion of the *Supplement* editorial staff were involved simultaneously in the preparation of copy for press, and in dealing with proofs. At first the University Printer, and subsequently (with considerable overlap) Messrs. William Clowes and Son Ltd., of Colchester, and, in the final stages, Latimer Trend

[1] *Supplement*, Volume II, p. vii.

Ltd., of Plymouth, were engaged in the typesetting of the *Supplement*.

The first volume of the *Supplement* (*A–G*) was published in 1972, and immediately established itself as a worthy sequel to the original Dictionary. Soon after its publication the Editor was honoured with the title of Commander of the British Empire for his services to scholarship. The dictionary was fortunate in attracting the interest of several scholars who began by reviewing the work in the academic press, and then became valuable consultants to the dictionary itself. Gradually more staff were appointed to the work of completing the *Supplement*, and by the mid-seventies some twenty-five people were involved in one or other editorial task, drafting the initial entries, reviewing the work of assistants, verifying bibliographical information, or conducting essential library research. The second volume (*H–N*), in which was included a dedication of the whole work to Her Majesty the Queen, appeared in 1976; by this time the editorial offices of the Dictionary were no longer large enough to contain the expanding number of staff, quotations, and research materials necessary for its preparation. Furthermore, the scope of the Dictionary department had expanded under the Chief Editorship of Dr Burchfield to include not simply work on the *Supplement*, but also the compilation and revision of the other Oxford Dictionaries, and for a time, a number of bilingual dictionaries as well. The department removed, therefore, to more extensive offices in St Giles', Oxford, in 1978; 1982 saw the publication of the third volume (*O–Scz*); and the *Supplement* was completed after twenty-nine years of editorial effort with the publication of the final volume in 1986.

Policy

Ian Hay's *First Hundred Thousand* (1915) contains the observation that 'the Oxford Dictionary of the English Language will have to be revised and enlarged when this war is over'. This fact had not escaped the notice of the Dictionary's editors, and they made ironic use of the quotation as evidence for the use of the adverb *when* (sense 4b).

The Delegates of the University Press had taken the decision in the 1920s to produce a Supplement which would concentrate on new vocabulary (embracing new words, new meanings of existing words, collocations and combinations, phrases, etc.); as plans were laid for the new *Supplement* in the 1950s to supersede the 1933 volume, it was again thought that the scope of the work should be restricted primarily to neologisms, thus leaving open the possibility of revising the main dictionary for the future.

Within this context, the principles by which entries for the new *Supplement* were prepared were inherited in most particulars from the original dictionary: the selection of material was based primarily upon a large quotation file collected as a result of reading an extensive range of sources; the style of definition, along with the critical apparatus (in the form of semantic and syntactic labelling, sense division, etc.) was derived closely from that employed in the parent work. However, although it did concern itself almost exclusively with additions to the language in the late nineteenth and twentieth centuries, many antedatings of material in the *OED* had been collected in the Dictionary's files over the years, and it was decided that, since the work was intended to update the historical record for the modern period in general, the new *Supplement* should include as many as possible of those antedatings which related to this period (for which 1820 was at first taken as the notional beginning, later 1750). Important though these predatings were, they still represented only a small fraction of the dictionary, which was primarily concerned with new lexical items.

The principal objective of the *Supplement* was to include all those standard words and senses which were new to the language in Britain since the period of the Dictionary. This objective was soon expanded to include as many of the standard terms from other varieties of English (notably North American English) as could be identified by the reading programme or by other resources. In the event, the broadening of the reading programme to encompass a much greater proportion of the written English of North America, Australia, New Zealand, South Africa, India, Pakistan, and other regions than had been the case for the *OED* itself had a profound effect upon the eventual coverage of these areas which the *Supplement* was able to achieve. In earlier years, Sir William Craigie had advocated the preparation of historical dictionaries treating specific varieties of English around the world. Largely as a result of his pioneering work in this field, a number of scholarly historical dictionaries, such as the *Dictionary of American English*, the *Scottish National Dictionary*, and the *Dictionary of Canadian English*, had been compiled, which assisted the preparation of the *Supplement* in two ways. First, they provided additional (often very detailed) evidence for items selected for the *Supplement*; secondly, their existence allowed the *Supplement* to omit many purely local items, on the grounds that entering them would simply duplicate material that was readily available elsewhere.

The standard vocabulary of British English was already well covered by the existing Dictionary. As well as recent additions to this, and wider coverage of common terms from the other varieties of English, much of the material prepared for the *Supplement* consisted of the scientific, technical, slang, dialectal, and other words which had passed into common use in the academic or technical fields, or in the social culture or geographical area, to which they belonged. This simply extended the policy of the 1933 Supplement into the age of computing, space technology, popular music, and the other areas of innovation and development by which the second and third quarters of the twentieth century had been characterized. Furthermore, whereas the *OED* had included nearly all the vocabulary, including *hapax legomena*, of important medieval and Renaissance authors such as Chaucer, Gower, and Shakespeare, the *Supplement* followed the more limited policy of presenting liberally, but not exhaustively, the occasional vocabulary of a wide range of major modern authors.

There is sometimes opposition to the appearance in dictionaries of words which are considered either generally offensive or opprobrious to a particular group. The arguments run, on the one hand, that to allow such usages into a dictionary is equivalent to sanctioning their use, and may even bring them to the notice of a wider public than would otherwise have been the case; and on the other hand, that to exclude such items would be tantamount to corrupting the historical record of the language, and would represent the first stage in a process of regulating the dictionary to fit the ethos of the times rather than the facts of the language. After very careful consideration of the matter, it was decided to admit to the *Supplement* the sexually taboo words formerly thought too gross and vulgar to be given countenance within the covers of a dictionary. This was done long after such vocabulary had been admitted to areas of general literature, and on the understanding that inclusion of these terms in a scholarly dictionary did not necessarily free dictionary editors to add them to dictionaries prepared for other audiences. Two of the most notorious of these terms happened to fall in the alphabetical range covered by the first volume of the *Supplement* (1972), where they appeared with a wide range of other colloquial and coarse expressions referring to sexual and excretory functions.

A second major area which involved the treatment of potentially offensive vocabulary concerned racial and religious terms. Consideration of this led to the formulation of certain general lexicographical guidelines for the *Supplement*: namely, that (*a*) offensiveness to a particular group was inadequate as the only ground for the exclusion of any word or class of words from the *OED*; (*b*) it was therefore desirable to enter new racial and religious terms however opprobrious they might seem to those to whom they were applied and often to those who had to use them, or however controversial the set of beliefs professed by the members of such groups; (*c*) it was also desirable, in order to avoid misunderstanding and consequent hostility, that the antiquated historical records of some words in this category already treated in the *OED* should be brought up to date.

Similarly, on the question of proprietary terminology, the *Supplement* endeavoured to follow a policy which safeguarded scholarly standards while not doing anything to imperil the proprietary rights of the owners of such terms. The proprietary status of each term likely to fall into this category was investigated thoroughly in Patent Office records in Britain and America, and elsewhere if this seemed to be necessary. If a term was found to be proprietary this was stated in the definition, and the earliest reference to the application or registration of the name in the official literature was cited as one of the illustrative quotations in the completed entry. It was sometimes found that a proprietary name had passed into general use: this fact was also related in the entry.

The editorial process

A brief description of the various processes involved in the preparation of entries for the first volume of the *Supplement* (1972) may be found on pp. xvi–xvii of the Introduction to that work. For subsequent volumes a broadly similar method was followed, but as the scope of the work expanded to encompass more diverse material and as the size of the *Supplement*'s staff grew to accommodate this, certain modifications were introduced to ensure that the work was conducted in the most efficient manner. The following account contains a slightly more detailed description of the practices that prevailed at the completion of the *Supplement*.

i. *Collection of material*. The raw material serving as a basis for the selection and preparation of entries in the *Supplement* consisted of the quotations which were collected as a result of a programme of directed reading established in 1957. Many illustrative quotations were also supplied by contributors outside the confines of the reading programme. All quotations were filed alphabetically according to catchword, and were available to staff working on the *Supplement*, to those working on other departmental projects, and to other interested scholars.

ii. *Sorting*. In order to establish which entries should be prepared for the *Supplement*, the entire quotation file was inspected section by section—in the early years by the editor; subsequently by his senior colleagues. Cards illustrating words and meanings selected for inclusion in the *Supplement* were extracted from the file, and grouped into 'bundles' (each consisting of between thirty and fifty items), ready for drafting. The primary selection was made by comparing the contents of the file with the relevant section of the *OED*, along with that of the 1933 Supplement which the new *Supplement* was to supersede. In addition, note was taken of terms not recorded (or sparsely attested) in the quotation file, but which seemed to deserve inclusion in the *Supplement* on the basis of their appearance in other dictionaries. Cards representing items already covered by the *OED*, as well as items considered too ephemeral or otherwise irrelevant to the *Supplement*, and pre-datings from before the modern period, were refiled in a separate sequence for possible later use. 'Bundles' of material were then handed to editorial assistants for drafting.

iii. *Drafting*. This process involved the preparation of a first draft of a dictionary entry for all of the items in a 'bundle'. Each assistant editor was expected to prepare complete entries, i.e. to ascertain the pronunciation and etymology of each new term where appropriate, to compose a definition, and to select and verify the quotations used. Clearly, the better an entry was prepared at this stage, the less work was needed in revising and editing it later. During this process the material available from the quotation file was augmented by further quotations found in the department's library of dictionaries, concordances, and other reference works. Often it was necessary for additional research work to be done in other libraries, such as the Bodleian Library in Oxford, the British Library in London, the Library of Congress in Washington, and elsewhere, in order to trace earlier and further quotations and to provide more detailed information for the definition. This work was normally conducted by library researchers appointed for the purpose. The library researchers were also responsible for verifying quotations from sources not available in the departmental library. All general items were drafted by non-specialist assistant editors; scientific, natural history, and social science terms were passed to specialist staff for drafting. Dictionary entries were prepared in handwritten form on 6 × 4 in. slips; a drafted entry would typically consist of head-cards containing the relevant headword, pronunciation and etymology where appropriate, the definition, and other information, followed by other cards bearing the quotations selected to illustrate the entry. When the entries were complete (and all outstanding library research had been returned) they were filed in the main alphabetical sequence of copy in readiness for subsequent review by senior staff.

iv. *Revision.* In order to allow the Editor to proceed at an efficient pace through the material it was necessary to interpose a revision stage between the initial drafting and the final editing. At first, this involved the incorporation by senior editors of scientific and technical drafting into the main sequence of entries (with concomitant adjustments to sense ordering, etc.), and revising long and complex entries. Subsequently this was extended to the inspection (and, if necessary, revision) of each entry. Quotations recently added to the quotation file were considered, and alterations made to entries in the light of these; occasionally new entries were prepared if the fresh material warranted this.

v. *Editing.* The final stage of entry preparation was, naturally, the sole responsibility of the Editor. Every entry was inspected minutely, further revisions were carried out, and delicate decisions (as in the treatment of 'sensitive' items, the balance in size between entries from different disciplines, etc.) were made in order to impose an editorial uniformity on the published work.

vi. *Bibliographical collation.* In the course of drafting, editorial staff endeavoured to ensure that the bibliographical details of works cited were correct. But at this stage it was the task of the bibliographer to establish consistency in respect of the date of publication, 'short title', and other matters. For this purpose an index of verified citation styles, consisting of the majority of the works cited in the *Supplement*, was maintained throughout the compilation of the work. From it, a bibliography of the works most frequently cited in the *Supplement* was published at the end of Volume IV.

Bibliographical verification was carried out either on the edited slips or, when publication schedules dictated, on corrected galley proofs.

vii. *Proofs and the use of specialist consultants.* Copy for the *Supplement* was sent in regular instalments to the printer, from whom multiple sets of galley proof for each range were received in corresponding instalments for further review.

Up to this point, the entries had been compiled entirely by the departmental staff; at this stage, they were submitted to outside scrutiny. Entries relating to particular disciplines or geographical regions were examined by consultants with specialist knowledge: they were often able to suggest modifications or to supply earlier or more appropriate attestations of the term under consideration. Furthermore, several complete sets of each batch of galley proofs were sent to critical readers for general comments. The improvements suggested by such independent experts were vital in maintaining the standard of Dictionary entries. These comments and suggestions were incorporated by the Editor or by his senior colleagues, along with the routine proof corrections. Quotations which had gathered in the files since the preparation of the copy were inspected, and in the light of them further alterations and additions were made. The corrected galleys were then reviewed by the Editor, and returned to the printer for setting in pages.

One last important process was carried out in page proof: the verification of cross-references. Every cross-reference in the batch of page proofs was checked against its target in the *OED*, the published volumes of the *Supplement*, the material in proof, or the manuscript copy. After the second round of page proof, the material was finally passed for press. By the time that the last pages of Volume IV were undergoing these final procedures, the preparation of the second edition of the *Oxford English Dictionary* had begun.

THE NEW OXFORD ENGLISH DICTIONARY PROJECT

Beginnings

Early in 1982, when the editing of the third and fourth volumes of *A Supplement to the Oxford English Dictionary* had reached an advanced stage, the Oxford University Press set itself to consider the future of the *OED*. The two questions of whether any further amplification or revision of the Dictionary should be undertaken, and whether an attempt should be made to combine the main *OED* with the four volumes of the *Supplement*, were recognized to be complementary. Publishing a supplement to the *Supplement*, or adding further material to it, had to be rejected as unsatisfactory expedients. The *OED* and *Supplement* should be combined before any further development was possible.

How should this amalgamation be performed? The two portions of the Dictionary had been typeset in hot metal. A new edition, whatever it might entail, would have to be typeset by computer. Conversion of the text into electronic form could be carried out either before or after the amalgamation. The option of creating copy for typesetting from the existing printed texts by means of cutting and pasting, or the marking-up of insertions and deletions, was dismissed. The technology of textual processing by computer was now at a stage of development that made it a highly appropriate tool for the task that OUP contemplated. The *OED* in machine-readable form, structured for use in a database management system, would be relatively easy to revise and, moreover, would be susceptible of a number of other applications, especially as a publicly available computer database. Indeed, the conversion of the Dictionary into electronic form, for just such a purpose, had already been suggested by parties both inside and outside the Press. It was therefore decided that the data conversion should be the first step taken, not only to lead into and facilitate the amalgamation, and subsequent editing, of the two parts of the Dictionary, but also to open up the possibility of its future development in electronic form.

A preliminary study, carried out by the Oxford English Dictionaries Department in March 1982 under the supervision of Dr R. W. Burchfield, concluded that both the conversion of the texts by manual keyboarding and their integration by experienced editors were feasible;[1] the report also listed the main aspects of the *OED* which were ripe for revision and correction. The Senior Officers of the Press determined at once to pursue the idea. Since the *OED* could be regarded as a kind of national monument, it was felt to be quite proper to solicit assistance, whether financial or technical, from Government departments, research institutions, or industrial companies. Accordingly, Mr Richard Charkin, the then Head of Reference Publishing, initiated a large number of approaches in various quarters, and in the meantime assembled the elements of an appeal brochure. By the end of the year the first outlines had emerged of a project that would involve computerizing and merging the two parts of the Dictionary, revising and updating the merged text, and publishing it in both a new printed and an electronic form.

The Identification of Partners

In March 1983 a small team was set up within the Press to begin the planning of the project. Its first task was to write the appeal booklet. It was decided that this should combine two aims. The first part, a clear explanation of the background and purpose of the project, was intended both for general information and more specifically to arouse the interest of any institutions or individuals who might wish to enter into some kind of partnership in the project. The second part, giving detailed technical specifications, was to be used by firms wishing to tender for the work of computerizing and merging the text.

By June, the brochure, entitled *A Future for the OED*, was complete. Copies were sent to computer companies, data conversion firms, on-line database proprietors, universities, libraries, and the British Government. A deadline of 1 August was set, by which time four firms had submitted tenders. The project team, evaluating these, quickly found that, while each tender had its own particular strengths, none furnished the Press with grounds for confidence that one tenderer, alone, could carry out the entire task to the required standard.

The initial idea had been that the chosen supplier would convert the text into electronic form, merge the *OED* and *Supplement*, and supply the resulting computer database to OUP; then, using the text editing system newly installed at OUP, lexicographical staff would revise and correct the Dictionary interactively and pass it on for composition and filmsetting. It now became evident that to carry out integration, to create a fully searchable database system, and to revise the bulk of the text in a single step would be impracticable, and it would be far too long before any new edition of the Dictionary could be published. A revised approach was needed. The project had to be broken down into smaller components; a number of different project partners were required, each responsible for what it could do best; and OUP should act as overall manager of the whole process, co-ordinating the separate components centrally. By the end of 1983, partnerships had been established with three contrasting institutions. These were as yet on an informal basis, but during the succeeding months of joint exploration they rapidly crystallized into formal agreements.

A data conversion firm of great experience and capacity, International Computaprint Corporation (ICC), a subsidiary of Reed International situated in Fort Washington, Pennsylvania, was selected to carry out the conversion of the two texts into electronic form. IBM United Kingdom Ltd. undertook to supply computer hardware and software, and to second a group of experts as the nucleus of a team of system designers: their task would be to build a computer system that would facilitate the integration of the two electronic texts into one. Early in 1984 it was confirmed that this assistance would take the form of a donation under the auspices of IBM's Academic Programme. The University of Waterloo in Ontario, Canada, had expressed great interest in the research aspects of the project as early as 1982. They undertook the task of designing a database system suitable for the dissemination of the *OED* in electronic form and for the phase of updating and editing which would follow integration. The geographical distribution of this partnership was felt by OUP to symbolize quite suitably the international significance of the *OED*.

Recognition of the national importance of the project followed soon afterwards. A copy of the brochure had been favourably received by the British Government, and as a result a subvention towards the cost of the lexicographical research was announced by the Department of Trade and Industry in May 1984.

There was one other development of great importance towards the end of 1983. Fifty years before, the remainder of the team responsible for the *OED*, having completed the original Supplement, dispersed, and there followed an interval of a whole generation during which no original historical lexicography was carried on at OUP. Because of this, the new *Supplement* had to be started virtually from scratch, and needed many years to make up the lost ground. It was imperative to avoid the repetition of such a hiatus at the completion of the *Supplement*. Accordingly, a small editorial group who had been engaged in the drafting of entries in Volume IV was set to continue the work of compiling new entries, starting again from A, but also taking in new words and senses anywhere in the alphabet for which entries were clearly needed. This new series of entries was called by the convenient acronym 'NEWS', standing for the 'New English Word Series'. It immediately became a valuable source of information for the other Oxford Dictionaries. Although a complete updating of the Dictionary was now postponed to a second phase of the project, it was decided during 1984 that approximately 5,000 items from this series should be included in the new edition of the *OED*, in order to

[1] The feasibility of using an optical scanner to convert the text of the Dictionary into machine-readable form was also investigated by OUP at this point, as also by others later. It was generally agreed that the complexity of the structure and the irregularity of the type would require an excessively large amount of editorial intervention in the scanning process; and it was not clear how an adequate framework of structural mark-up could be introduced into the text alongside this method of data conversion.

compensate for the temporal gap between the earlier and later volumes of the *Supplement*. The selection and editing of these articles was set in motion, and their text converted to machine-readable form at the end of 1986. This subject is treated more fully in the foregoing Introduction.

Planning

In January 1984 a department was established within OUP to manage the project. It was now possible to establish the objectives of the project, as follows: the conversion of the *Oxford English Dictionary* and *Supplement* to machine-readable form, ensuring that all information contained in the one form was carried over into the other; the integration of the two texts into one; the addition of articles on a selection of new words and senses; and the publication of the integrated version of the Dictionary within an acceptable time. These objectives constituted the first phase of the New Oxford English Dictionary Project. The revision, updating, and enhancement of the Dictionary (of which more is said below) would be the business of a subsequent phase.

Detailed planning was essential to the attainment of these objectives. An overall plan (known as the 'Plan of Record') was drawn up that identified all the major activities within the project, their interrelationships, the time each would take, and the resources of staff, equipment, and finance each required. These were: conversion of the data (or 'data capture'), initial proof-reading, computer development, automatic processing of the machine-readable text, editing of entries on the screen, composition of galley proofs, final proof-reading, and final page composition. For each of these a detailed plan was made. In July 1985, when the outline design of the computer system was complete, it became possible to estimate the times required by the process of building and using that system; these times were added into the plan, and a firm Plan of Record was established. Thereafter, the target dates for the completion of each main activity were fixed.

Proprietary software designed for project planning and spreadsheet operations was of vital help in developing and monitoring each of the interlocking detailed plans which made up the overall Plan of Record. This computer assistance immediately revealed the effects on that plan of changing any value (number of staff, amount of time, or cost). Hence it was possible to project time and cost quite accurately and to monitor progress against these projections. The use of such technically sophisticated methods, more redolent of engineering than lexicography, and unprecedented in the history of the Oxford Dictionaries, was necessitated by the scope and scale of the project. The latter may be roughly illustrated by some figures for the resources used in each main activity. Data capture, the keying of about 350,000,000 characters over 18 months, took 120 person-years; computer development took 14 person-years; automatic processing of the text took 10 months; interactive integration took 7 person-years; the two rounds of proof-reading, undertaken by over 50 people, each took 60 person-years; and final composition of the integrated text involved the setting of approximately 20,000,000 characters per week. The adoption of rigorous planning and adherence to strict monitoring of progress contributed significantly to the work's completion in full accordance with the schedule and expenditure forecast which had been established four years previously.

Data structure

Once firm plans had been made, it was intended that the conversion of the text into electronic form should begin as soon as possible. Preparations at ICC were by now well advanced. But for data capture to begin, a system for structuring the text had to be agreed upon. It was resolved that the tagging language inserted into the electronic version should do more than simply express the typographical features—layout, typeface, type size, font—of the printed text. It must, as its primary function, identify the structural elements which combine to form a dictionary entry. This was a prerequisite both for the development of the database in the future, and, as it turned out, for the automatic processes applied to the text in the course of integration.

Several months were devoted to the analysis of the structure of the *OED* and its *Supplement*, resulting in an inventory of the most important structural elements (amounting to between forty and fifty) and their current typographical realizations. The translation of this scheme into a system of tags, though not without its difficulties, was straightforward compared to the immense task of ensuring that each element of Dictionary text was supplied with the correct tag. It emerged from discussions with ICC that a tagging scheme of such size and complexity would be very hard to insert accurately into the text at the stage of initial data capture. It would require so much knowledge that the training of keyboarders would be very long and the typing very slow. It would also require extensive pre-editing of the text, which again would take an excessively long time and require much training. On the other hand, a more modest scheme would be manageable. Accordingly, a compromise mark-up scheme was devised. The fifteen or so most prominent textual elements received tags with structural meaning, while all other features of the text were coded with tags that had a conventional typographical meaning. Further coding was deferred to a later stage. Even with this scheme, ICC found it necessary to carry out a considerable amount of preliminary mark-up, conduct lengthy training sessions, and undertake several proof-reading cycles, before the text was ready to be shipped to Oxford.

On 15 May 1984, at a press conference in the premises of the Royal Society in London, a formal announcement of the launching of the New Oxford English Dictionary Project was made, including the news that IBM UK Ltd. would be making a substantial donation to the first phase of the project. Meanwhile, work on the means of carrying out the integration of the text was continuing in collaboration with IBM. Matters needing development were identified as: the database management system for holding and protecting the electronic text, the software tool by which it might be edited, and a means of correcting cross-references affected by integration. There was also the problem of enhancing the system of tagging introduced by ICC so that it should be an entirely 'generalized' mark-up language, that is to say, one having structural, not typographical, signification. At first this planning was conducted by means of a regular meeting between staff from OUP and IBM, but at length, in mid-July, the first secondee from IBM arrived at OUP as the project's computer group manager, and began to build up his team. From then on, the main instrument by which progress was monitored and problems were identified was a formal system of meetings, some at half-yearly and monthly intervals, at which representatives of the management of IBM were present, others occurring weekly and dealing with the minutiae of the project team's work.

During the following autumn the project gathered momentum. In September the University of Waterloo was granted Canadian Government funding with which to establish a Centre for the New OED as a focus for database research, from the point of view of both the academic user and the computer scientist. Early sketches of a potential database structure had already been made, and, more importantly, the project had attracted the interest of several researchers who might be able to provide parsing software which would facilitate the enhancement of the mark-up language. After some months of experimentation at the University of Waterloo, work was begun on this part of the system by the project's computer group, a vital contribution at the start being made by a secondee from Waterloo.

Also in September 1984, ICC sent to Oxford test data consisting of 100 pages of Dictionary text on magnetic tape. This not only proved the feasibility of the scheme for data capture but also made it possible to try out methods of proof-reading.

In October the project team drew up a formal Statement of User Requirements, which set out the aims of the first phase and the operations which the computer system would be required to perform. This gave the computer group a basis on which to develop their detailed design of the system, an activity which occupied their attention over the two succeeding years. An Editorial Board was constituted, consisting of about forty scholars in a wide range of disciplines; the idea being that they should give advice to the project team especially when the revision, updating, and enhancement of the dictionary were planned.

Data Capture

At the beginning of November 1984 the computer equipment from IBM was installed. At the same time, ICC began data capture in earnest. A team of ICC copy editors, based in Fort Washington, Pennsylvania, began to insert structural mark-up on enlarged copies of the Dictionary pages. These were passed to the data conversion personnel (both on the same site and in Tampa, Florida) for keyboarding. Data-validation routines and sample proof-reading were carried out by ICC before the proofs were shipped to Oxford. It was stipulated that the rate of errors should be no more than 7 in 10,000 keystrokes; and this requirement was met.

The first batch of magnetic tapes and proofs arrived in January 1985, and proof-reading immediately got under way. From then until June 1986 a regular cycle of data capture, proof-reading, and data correction was maintained. A team of some fifty freelance proof-readers was directed from Oxford. They were required to check not only the accuracy of the text but also the selection and positioning of the computer codes. They were provided with a detailed manual describing the structure of the Dictionary and the correct application of the tagging system. Double proof-reading—the reading of the same section of text by two people independently, followed by cross-collation—was employed for a trial period. It proved, owing mainly to the very low error rate maintained by ICC, not to reveal a markedly higher number of errors than a single reading; certainly not enough to justify the double outlay of expense and editorial effort. A single reading was therefore conducted, but experienced staff checked, emended, and supplemented all the corrections before the proofs were returned to ICC. In addition, a system of monitoring the proof-readers' work by detailed rechecking of random samples was carried out until satisfactory standards had been achieved. During the same stage, a prototype of the parsing program was run on most of the electronic text to validate its structure: this functioned rather like an additional (and, within certain limits, infallible) proof-reader.

When ICC returned the corrected tapes, these were subjected to a further check, on the screen, to ensure that the corrections had been carried out within the agreed margins. This left the text with an estimated residual error-rate of only 1 in 235,000 characters. Since most of these were minor errors of punctuation and spacing, and the text would subsequently be proof-read a second time, this was felt to be an acceptable level at which the data could proceed to automatic processing by computer.

Computer Development

In July 1985 the computer group issued an Outline System Design, describing the essential components and features of the New OED computer system. Over the following eighteen months, in close consultation with the lexicographers, the group built a unique dictionary system tailored to the special needs of the project.

Once the text had been captured, it was loaded on to the project's IBM 4341 mainframe at OUP. It was important that it should be stored in a database system that would allow the necessary access and processing facilities. The operating system used was IBM's VM 370; the database management system was SQL/DS. Every new version of the data created by each successive stage of processing and editing was retained in the database; no older version was overwritten, and the whole was regularly archived on to magnetic tape and stored at a remote site for safety.

The structure devised by Sir James Murray and used by him and all his successors for writing Dictionary entries was so regular that it was possible to analyse them as if they were sentences of a language with a definite syntax and grammar. They could therefore be parsed, and this was the next process to which the text was submitted. The objective of parsing, as already mentioned, was to transform the text into a version categorized by a system of generalized mark-up, known as SGML (Standard Generalized Mark-up Language), in which each element is identified by its function, not its printed appearance. The programs used for parsing were written by staff of the University of Waterloo. The 'grammar' of the Dictionary text with which they operated was written at Oxford. It was developed by running a postulated grammar against the Dictionary text to establish whether the latter could be transformed without rejection of the input or ambiguity in the output. Revised versions of the grammar were run repeatedly until the closest possible approximation was achieved. The grammar had to be descriptive, not prescriptive, since the computer could not be allowed to override lexicographical judgement, and only the most minor rewriting of the text to accommodate computerization was acceptable.

A particularly important proposal in the outline design was that the computer system should automatically carry out as much as possible of the integration of corresponding *OED* and *Supplement* entries, leaving the lexicographical team the task of correcting errors, harmonizing adjacent text, and coping with difficult cases. The integration routines used the mark-up to create a single sequence of text from the two component parts, following the main structural cues (headwords and sense divisions) and the instructions in the *Supplement* that were identified as 'integration instructions' during parsing. Subsequent analysis of the integration program's performance showed that it successfully handled about 80 per cent of the text, and spared the lexicographers and keyboarders between 50 per cent and 60 per cent of the number of tasks which they would otherwise have been obliged to perform interactively at the computer screen.

Integration caused the targets of thousands of cross-references to be changed, rendering the cross-references inaccurate. To cope with this problem, every cross-reference identified by the parser was numbered and copied; after integration, the stored copies were automatically matched with their targets, changed wherever necessary, and returned to the text. In a similar way the pronunciations were copied, translated into the International Phonetic Alphabet, and restored.

The problem arose of finding editorial software suitable for emending and integrating entries interactively at the computer terminal. Failing to discover any proprietary software that was adequate, the team resolved to develop its own. The product of this development was a new kind of text editor, designed for structured text, and originally known as LEXX. The initial work was carried out by an IBM secondee, and then taken over and extended by the OUP staff. This highly versatile editorial tool was designed to interface with a number of programs that controlled access to the Dictionary data held on the computer, allowed entries to be proofed for immediate checking, and provided a complete working environment with checks and controls to protect the integrity of the text. The combined sub-system was eventually named the OED Integration, Proofing, and Updating System (OEDIPUS).

Once editing was complete, the text was to be transferred for composition of galley and page proofs. It was decided that this part of the process should be performed by an outside supplier.

During 1986 data capture of the main *OED* and *Supplement* text was completed (the remaining text—the entirely new entries and the bibliography—was keyboarded during the following half-year). The last of the eighteen monthly batches of proofs was returned, corrected, to ICC in mid-August. A month later the automatic processing of the Dictionary data on the computer system began. First the text was read on to the system and validated. Next the parser was run. Structural errors encountered by the parser were corrected on-line by the editorial group. During the three months that elapsed, 5,711 corrections were made. Automatic integration itself begain in March 1987, and the automatic processing of the whole text of the Dictionary was completed at the end of May.

The Editing of the Integrated Text

After subjecting OEDIPUS to acceptance trials, the editorial group was given access to the system at the end of June 1987. The most efficient working method had already been determined by experimentation. Proofs, or more strictly speaking, printouts, of all entries that were subject to integration and the modifications resulting from it were run off by the computer system. The lexicographical group would work through these, examining the results of automatic integration and making corrections and other emendations. These alterations would be entered into the text on-line by a separate group of keyboarders. Galley proofs of the complete integrated text would then be produced by an outside supplier. Accordingly, editing of the printouts began in June, and, at the same time, a team of keyboard operators was engaged, trained, and assigned to the task of 'interactive integration'.

After the first few months, during which no galley proofs were composed, the editorial group found itself occupied on several fronts simultaneously. On account of its huge size, the text was handled by the computer in forty alphabetical ranges or 'tables'. At any one time, the group would be editing up to half a dozen text tables. Each of these would be undergoing one of four consecutive editorial processes. The first was the editing by lexicographers of proofs of all entries that had in any way been modified by the integration and cross-referencing programs. Next, these marked-up proofs were passed to the keyboard operators, who made the necessary emendations to the electronic text. At this stage, a number of other corrections had also to be made, some unconnected with the action of integration; also, many complicated problems of integration came to light (including entries that had wrongly eluded automatic integration) and had to be resolved, at the keyboard, by the lexicographical staff. Once the integration of a table had been approved, a magnetic tape was produced and sent to the composition suppliers, Filmtype Services Ltd., of Scarborough, North Yorkshire.

Galley proofs of the entire Dictionary text for each text table were produced and distributed to the team of proof-readers (now increased to more than sixty). On their return, the third stage began. The editorial group checked all proof-readers' corrections, and carried out many additional systematic checks, some facilitated by specific computer scans. Cross-references were dealt with at this stage. Once approved, the table was again put on tape and sent for composition. This time fully formatted page proofs were produced, and the breaks between volumes were inserted. The fourth stage consisted of the checking of these proofs to ensure that all galley proof corrections appeared correctly on them, and that no errors had crept into the text for any other reason, such as malfunctioning of the composition programs. The final corrections to the page proofs were again keyboarded into the database at Oxford; they were applied to the printed version by Filmtype Services either by the processing of a new magnetic tape copy or by simple keyboarding. When the final proof pages for a volume were deemed acceptable, the volume was passed for press.

Editorial Processes

During the course of the project, the text of the Dictionary was emended in numerous ways, over and above the central activity of integrating the matter from the *Supplement* into the main *OED*. Many classes of change were logically necessitated by integration; others, notably the adoption of the International Phonetic Alphabet and the addition of new words, were undertaken in order to increase the usefulness of the Dictionary. These alterations (a detailed explanation of which is given in the foregoing Introduction) were made during the three main stages by which the new edition was produced: initial data capture, automatic text processing, and interactive editing.

During initial data capture the chief amendments to the text were: the provision of transliteration for foreign script where the source text lacked it; the resolution of hyphenation problems; research on quotations with questionable text or imperfect citations; and the regularization of individual aberrantly structured entries. Before automatic text processing began, every main headword and bold subordinate headword in the *OED* that required an initial capital was marked by editorial staff and this information keyed into the computer, enabling the text and cross-references to be automatically emended. The system itself automatically carried out the conversion of the ICC tagging system to the generalized mark-up language; the translation of the Murray phonetic symbols and stress-marks into their IPA equivalents; the addition of a part of speech or homonym number to headwords no longer unique after integration; and the adjustment of cross-reference details affected by integration. The correction (by editors at the screen) of irregularities encountered by the parser was made at this stage, but corrections to capitalization, cross-references, and the phonetic transcriptions were made during the third stage. Many problems with the five hundred or so rarely occurring special characters, detected in the middle stage, were dealt with then too.

During the stage of interactive integration, galley-proof reading, and correction checking, the lexicographical group was notably assisted by a wide range of computer searches, the results of which were furnished on printed reports which could be tailored into formats of maximum usefulness. Among other matters, these reports covered unresolved cross-references, erroneous or ambiguous phonetic transcriptions, italicized phrases with initial capital letters, stray pronunciations that had not been converted to IPA, and entries with abnormal sense orders and structures. In addition, it was at this stage that the editorial group entered the addenda and spurious entries from Volume XII of the *OED*; the corrections which had been prepared for Volumes I and II of the *Supplement* but not inserted in them; and a host of minor corrections assembled on slips before and during the previous stages of the project. The entries for the twenty-six letters of the alphabet, and for certain similar two-letter groups, were also given special attention at this stage, as were many main entries from the *Supplement* which, for completeness' sake, required the transfer of portions of text from other (originally *OED*) entries. It may be said without exaggeration that the apparently straightforward task of amalgamating the two texts turned out to have ramifications and implications so multifarious, protean, and unpredictable that the project team occasionally despaired of detecting them all; and it is also freely acknowledged that resources sometimes did not permit them to carry out changes prescribed in the *Supplement* to quite the extent or degree implied by the latter. No effort was spared, however, in the attempt to carry out faithfully both the overt instructions and the implied purport of every one of the 69,372 entries in the *Supplement*.

The Future of the OED

It was recognized at the start of the project that no enhancements of the Dictionary could be carried out before the texts of the *Supplement* and the first edition of the *OED* had been combined. This amalgamation has been achieved, and the *OED* now exists in a second edition. But the English language continues to develop, the requirements of lexicography continue to change, and, accordingly, work on the *OED* continues too. The most important way in which the *OED* can be updated is by the addition of new words and senses, and this task is well in hand. Already 5,000 new items have been added to the second edition, and these can be regarded as an earnest of many more that are in the course of compilation. It has become very clear to the editors of this edition that virtually no new item can be added to the Dictionary without repercussions upon the entries already there. Purely as a result of integration, therefore, many changes have been made to the text which fall into the category of revision. Then, outside this sphere, the most important global revision of the text—the replacement of Murray's phonetic transcription with IPA—has already been achieved (though it could helpfully be extended, for example by the coverage of non-RP varieties). In short, the revision and updating of the *OED* is already well under way.

Much, however, remains to be done. Indeed some parts of the task could never be completed once for all, but that should be no deterrent from making a start. There is much in the style of the Dictionary, the punctuation, the capitalization, the definitional terminology, and the spelling (within entries and even of some headwords) that calls for modernization. In the cross-reference system, many improvements are desirable, notably in the citation of variant spellings as headwords and in the more precise specification of parts of speech, homonym numbers, and sense numbers. In the etymologies, the varying systems of transcription should be harmonized, the linguistic nomenclature should be brought up to date, and the results of recent research should be added. The organization of senses within many entries needs to be rethought. Numerous scientific and technical definitions need to be brought into line with present-day knowledge (though the *Supplement* amended the treatment of many of the most important terms). Many of the definitions of general vocabulary need to be reworked to take account of recent technological and social changes. There are a number of references to countries, currency values, institutions, and persons, which are now anachronistic; and there are still a few definitions which enshrine social attitudes that are now alien. The usage and subject labels should be made fully consistent and modernized.

Many current words are illustrated by a latest quotation from the first half of the nineteenth century, or even earlier, and it is difficult to distinguish them from words or senses that are now, in fact, disused. Recent examples ought to be supplied for every sense that is still current. The citation style of many quotations from the original *OED* could well be brought up to the standard of consistency of the *Supplement* (although improving it would require the rechecking of many thousands of quotations). Earlier examples exist (in various places) for thousands of words and senses, and these should be added. The coverage of English before 1700, and at least as far back as 1500, could be markedly improved. Last, but certainly not least, the coverage of English outside the United Kingdom needs to be greatly expanded, especially the English of North America, which is the greatest source of linguistic change, but not neglecting the English of the many other parts of the world where it is a first or important second language.

Other improvements could be mentioned, but these are the principal aspects of the *OED* on which there is work to be done, as most regular users of the Dictionary will recognize, however greatly they admire it. To these improvements the New OED project team hope to address their efforts in the coming years, so that the *Oxford English Dictionary* may continue to be an accurate and comprehensive register of the whole vocabulary of English.

THE FIRST EDITION: STAFF AND CONTRIBUTORS

1. *Contributors*

A. This list contains the names of the principal readers before 1884; many of these began reading as early as 1858. The material which they contributed formed a great part of the main foundation on which the Dictionary was based. Under some of the names the number of quotations sent in is given, as an indication of the time and labour expended by many of these readers.

J. Amphlett, MA
W. J. Anderson (of Fife)
G. L. Apperson (of Wimbledon, SW; 11,000)
Col. R. D. Ardagh
Thomas Austin (165,000)
Miss E. E. Barry (of London)
Revd E. M. Barry
Mrs Bathoe (of London)
A. Beazeley, CE (of Thornton Heath)
Revd W. H. Beckett
Revd W. C. Boulter
Revd G. B. R. Bousfield, BA
The Misses B. M. and L. Bousfield
Revd S. J. Bowles
William Boyd (of USA)
E. L. Brandreth
Prof. and Mrs Brandt (of USA)
James Britten, FLS
The Misses E. and J. E. A. Brown (of Cirencester)
Mrs Walter Browne (of Worcester)
Dr T. N. Brushfield (50,000)
R. K. Buehrle (of USA)
Miss E. F. Burton (of Carlisle; 11,400)
A. Caland (of Holland)
Mrs G. M. E. Campbell (of Peckham)
Dr R. S. Charnock
The Ven. Archdeacon Cheetham
(Dean) R. W. Church
Herbert Coleridge
Prof. A. S. Cook (of USA)
J. M. Cowper (of Canterbury)
Revd T. Lewis O. Davies, MA
Revd Cecil Deedes, MA
H. Dixon (of London)
C. E. Doble, MA
William Douglas (of London; 136,000)
Edward Dowden
Revd J. Eastwood
Miss Eisdell (of Colchester)
Prof. Robinson Ellis
Mr and Mrs F. T. Elworthy
The Misses Elworthy
A. Erlebach, BA
H. A. Erlebach, BA
Revd J. T. Fowler, DCL
W. Warde Fowler, MA
Miss A. Foxall (of Birmingham; 11,250)
Dr F. J. Furnivall (30,000)
W. Gee, jun. (of Boston, USA)
H. Hucks Gibbs, MA (Lord Aldenham)
The Hon. and Revd Kenneth F. Gibbs
Hon. Vicary Gibbs
W. F. Grahame (of Madras)
C. Gray (of Wimbledon, SW; 29,000)
Mrs C. Gray
Mrs T. H. Green
Revd W. Gregor, MA
Revd A. B. Grosart
Miss M. Haig (Mrs A. Stuart, of Edinburgh)
Fitzedward Hall, DCL
W. C. Hazlitt
Dr H. R. Helwich (of Vienna; 50,000)
T. Henderson, MA (48,000)
S. J. Herrtage
James Hooper (of Norwich)
J. D. Howell (of London)
E. C. Hulme (of London)
E. Wyndham Hulme (late of HM Patent Office)
Miss Jennett Humphreys (of Cricklewood; 18,700)
C. Mansfield Ingleby
Revd Aiken Irvine (of Ireland)
Miss Eva Jackson (of Bishop's Waltham)
E. S. Jackson, MA (of Plymouth)
P. W. Jacob (of Guildford)
W. W. Jenkinson (of London)
Revd J. B. Johnston, BD
Revd W. M. Kingsmill, MA
Revd E. H. Knowles
Revd W. Lees, MA (18,500)
Miss Lees (of Reigate)
Dr J. Wickham Legg
Dr R. J. Lloyd
Prof. A. Lodeman (of USA)
W. S. Logeman (of Cheshire)
Revd W. J. Löwenberg, MA
A. Lyall (of Manchester)
Falconer Madan, MA
S. D. Major (of Bath; 16,000)
Revd A. L. Mayhew, MA
Dr W. C. Minor
Mrs Moore (of Addlestone)
W. Moore (of London)
Dr Richard Morris
Horace Moule
Revd C. B. Mount, MA
Mrs J. A. H. Murray (Lady Murray)
H. J. R. Murray, MA (27,000)
E. T. R. Murray
J. M. Norman (of Crawley, Sussex)
Cornelius Paine (of Brighton)
E. Peacock (of Brigg)
H. S. Pearson (of Birmingham)
Revd C. W. Penny

J. Peto (of London)
(Sir) W. M. Flinders Petrie
Prof. G. M. Philips (of USA)
H. Phillips, Jun., Ph.D. (of USA)
B. W. Pierson (of USA)
Revd J. Pierson, DD (of USA; 46,000)
(Sir) Frederick Pollock, LL D
Mr and Mrs G. H. Pope (formerly of Clifton)
Revd C. Y. Potts
Dr R. C. A. Prior (11,700)
Sir John Richardson, KCB
W. M. Rossetti
Mr and Mrs H. F. P. Ruthven
The Misses E. and G. E. Saunders (of Addlestone)
G. A. Schrumpf, BA (of London)
Adrian Scott (of USA)
Miss F. E. Scott (of Leamington)
G. R. Scott, MA
(Sir) Owen Seaman
A. Shackleton (of Birkenhead)
Revd T. H. Sheppard
Prof. W. W. Skeat, LL D
Revd J. Smallpeice
Dr G. C. Moore Smith
Miss L. Toulmin Smith
T. C. Snow, MA
A. B. Sprange (of London)
W. Barclay Squire (of London)
(Sir) Leslie Stephen
Revd Dr C. W. Stocker
C. Stoffel (of Amsterdam)
(Dr) E. H. Sugden
Revd W. D. Sweeting
Dr W. Sykes
Revd B. Talbot (of USA; 16,600)
George Tansley (of London)
The Misses Edith and E. Perronet Thompson (15,000)
Alderman Joseph Thompson (of Manchester)
Hon. Mrs L. Tollemache
Mrs Toogood (of Kirkby, Yorkshire)
Revd J. T. Toye (of Exeter)
Paget Toynbee, D.Litt.
Richard Chenevix Trench
Revd Kirby Trimmer, MA
Mrs L. J. Walkey (of Leamington)
Miss P. Walter (of Somerset)
J. L. Ward, MA (of Burnley)
T. Ward (of Northwich)
Dr W. W. Webb
Miss M. Westmacott (of London)
Dr R. F. Weymouth
The Misses B.M. and R. Weymouth
Revd G. Wheelwright
Revd F. Gilbert White
G. H. White (of Torquay; 13,000)
R. Grant White (of USA)
R. J. Whitwell, B.Litt. (33,000)
Miss J. E. Wilkinson and Miss Gunning (of Cambridge)
R. D. Wilson (of London)
T. Wilson, MA (of St. Albans)
Revd W. B. R. Wilson, MA (of Dollar)
Miss Charlotte M. Yonge

B. A large number of those included in the above list continued to supply quotations for many years while the Dictionary was in progress. The readers given below began their work after 1884.

F. J. Amours (of Glasgow)
Revd J. Bell, DD (of Auchtermuchty, NB)
F. H. Butler (of London)
W. J. Bryan (of Oxford)
P. M. Campbell
C. H. Chadwick (of London)
Miss Ellen Channon
Prof. Albert H. Chester (of USA)
Revd Andrew Clark, MA
Miss Susan Cunnington
Miss Ada Dewick
B. W. Dexter
James M. Dixon (of Japan)
Edward S. Dodgson, MA
John Dormer (of London)
R. Duncan (of Crowthorne, Berks.)
Revd Henry Ellershaw (of Durham)
Miss Ellis (of Oxford)
J. H. Everett
Miss E. Fowler (of Doncaster)
Wendell P. Garrison (of USA)
I. R. Gillespie (of Newcastle-on-Tyne)
Miss Geraldine H. Gosselin (of London)
Miss Hellier R. H. Gosselin (of London)
Col. C. Gray (of London)
H. F. Hall (of Oxford)
J. D. Hamilton
R. Oliver Heslop (of Northumberland)
Revd J. W. Hooper, MA
Alfred H. Huth (of Oxford)
Miss Ingall (of Manchester)
Albert Jacka
Miss Constance Jacob
George Joicey (of Gateshead-on-Tyne)
(Sir) J. K. Laughton
R. E. Leader
Halkett Lord (of USA)
L. Marcan
Albert Matthews (of USA)
H. A. W. Millar (of Oxford)
W. Payne (of Hayward's Heath)
Miss C. Pemberton (of Austria)
James Platt, jun.
Revd C. Plummer, MA
Miss H. M. Poynter (of Oxford)
Richard B. Prosser (of London)
Mrs Rackham (of Cambridge)
John Randall (of London)
Dr W. H. D. Rouse
Abrm. Shackleton (of Birkenhead)
H. F. M. Simpson (of Edinburgh)
J. Challenor Smith (of London)
Miss L. M. Snow
E. V. Stocks (of Durham)
Miss E. H. Taylor (of Suffolk)
John J. Thompson
Miss S. M. Unwin
C. R. Wilkins
Miss Wilson (of London)
Edward S. Wilson (of Hull)
C. B. Winchester
W. N. Woods, BA (of London)

2. *Sub-editors*

The sub-editing of the material falls into two periods, viz. that done under the direction of Dr Furnivall between 1862 and 1879, and that carried on during the years while the Dictionary was in course of publication. The following list gives the sub-editors of the later period, but it should be noted that some of these (e.g. H. H. Gibbs, W. M. Rossetti, Revd T. H. Sheppard, Revd J. Smallpeice) were also at work during the earlier years. For the earlier period mention should further be made of Revd W. P. Bailey, Revd S. J. Bowles, Edward Dowen, W. Gee, jun. (of Boston, USA), W. F. Grahame, J. D. Howell, Revd Aiken Irvine, E. S. Jackson, Revd E. H. Knowles, Revd J. E. Middleton, Richard Morris, Horace Moule, Revd A. S. Palmer, Revd Ralph Proud, C. W. Staunton, Dr W. Woodham Webb, Revd G. Wheelwright, G. A. White, Miss Charlotte M. Yonge. Most of these were also readers in the early history of the Dictionary.

W. J. Anderson, portions of M and P (1880–1900)
Revd G. B. R. Bousfield, BA, portions of F, G, and R, large part of W (1880–96)
Walter Browne, portion of S (1881)
Samuel Taylor, portion of H (1881–2)
A. W. Longden, portion of H (1881–4)
A. Lyall, portion of T (1881–5)
Revd T. H. Sheppard, BD, portion of M, the whole of U and V (1881–5)
P. W. Jacob, portions of D, E, P, Q, R, and S (1881–6)
T. Henderson, MA, portions of B and C (1881–7)
T. Wilson, portions of I and T (1881–7)
E. C. Hulme, portions of C and L (1881–90)
Mrs L. J. Walkey, portions of D and W (1881–92)
Revd W. B. R. Wilson, MA, portions of C., revised former sub-editing of T, most of V, and part of W (1881–1919)
Charles Gray, portion of S (1882)
Revd C. Y. Potts, portion of L (1882)
W. Welch, portion of T (1882)
F. T. Elworthy, portion of D (1882–3)
Revd J. J. Smith, MA, portion of M (1882–3)

Miss M. Westmacott, portion of T (1882–3)
James Britten, FLS, portion of P (1882–4)
H. H. Gibbs (Lord Aldenham), portions of C, the whole of K and Q (1882–4)
H. M. Fitz-Gibbon, portion of H (1882–5)
Revd W. Gregor, MA, the whole of J (1882–5)
E. Warner, portion of L (1882–5)
G. A. Schrumpf, portion of H (1882–6)
H. S. Tabor, portions of I and W (1882–9)
G. L. Apperson, portions of B and C (1882–91)
Revd A. P. Fayers, BA, portions of B and N (1882–91)
Mrs G. H. Pope, portions of C and N (1882–91)
Revd J. Smallpeice, MA, portion of M, and X, Y, Z (1882–94)
A. Sweeting, portion of T (1882–96)
Revd W. H. Beckett, portion of W (1882–1901)
Miss J. E. A. Brown, portions of B, C, D, and P, the whole of I (1882–1907)
J. W. W. Tyndale, portion of D (1883–4)
R. F. Green, portion of N (1883–8)
A. Hailstone, portions of C and N (1883–90)
Revd W. J. Löwenberg, MA, portions of O and P (1883–96)
E. L. Brandreth, portions of G, H, and N, the whole of K (1883–1900)
(Prof.) F. E. Bumby, portion of N (1884)
W. M. Rossetti, portions of B and L (1884)
Revd Prof. W. W. Skeat, portion of R (1884)
Revd W. E. Smith, portion of D (1884)
Dr Brackebusch, portions of B (1884–5)
E. Gunthorpe, portions of A and B (1884–5)
The Hon. and Revd S. W. Lawley, MA, portion of M (1884–5)
Dr R. J. Lloyd, portion of H (1884–93)
Revd C. B. Mount, MA, portions of A, B, C, D, and V, revised former sub-editing of J and the large part of P (1884–1908)
Joseph Brown, MA, portion of M, revised former sub-editing of portions of S and U (1884–1914)
Revd C. G. Duffield, portion of T (1885)
Revd T. D. Morris, MA, portion of G (1885)
Revd (Dr) E. H. Sugden, portion of I (1885–7)
J. Peto, portions of C, F, and H (1885–92)
Mr and Mrs W. Noel Woods, BA, portions of B, C, and H (1885–92)
Miss M. Haig (Mrs A. Stuart), portion of O (1885–93)
R. M. M'Lintock, portion of P (1885–96)
James Bartlett, BA, revised former sub-editing of G and portions of M, O, R, and S (1888–1908)
Revd Canon R. Morris, DD, portion of I (1889–92)
John Dormer, portions of D and S (1890–1906)
Miss Edith Thompson, portion of C (1891)
H. A. Nesbitt, BA, portions of N and O (1893–5)
C. B. Winchester, revised former sub-editing of P, S, and V (1905–8)
Mrs W. A. Craigie (Lady Craigie), revised arrangement of U (1917–18)

3. *Assistants*

The names of these are here divided into three groups, indicative of the relative length of time during which they were engaged on the work. As will be seen from the dates given, those included in the first group were for many years members of their respective staffs, and by their knowledge and experience contributed immensely to the progress of the work. The staff to which each was attached is indicated by the initial letter of the editor's name (M. = Murray; etc.).

John Mitchell (1883–94; M.)
Walter Worrall, BA (1885–1933; M., B., O.)
A. T. Maling, MA (1886–1927; M., O.)
C. G. Balk (1885–1913; M.)
G. F. H. Sykes, BA (1885–1903; M., B.)
W. J. Lewis (1889–1933; B., O.)
F. J. Sweatman, MA (1890–1933; M., O.)
H. J. Bayliss (1891–1932; B., C.)
C. T. Onions, MA, D.Litt. (1895–1914; M., B.; 1914–Editor)
L. F. Powell, MA (1901–21; C.)
J. W. Birt (1906–33; O.)
George Watson, Hon. MA (1907–27; C.)
Miss E.R. Steane (Mrs L. F. Powell) (1901–32; C., O.)
Miss Rosfrith N. R. Murray (1902–29; M., C., O.)
Miss Elsie M. R. Murray (Mrs R. A. Barling) (1899–1920; M, O.)
Miss E. S. Bradley (1897–1932; B., O.)

G. R. Carline (B.)
P. T. J. Dadley (O.)
James Dallas (B., O.)
Alfred Erlebach, BA (M.)
(Dr) G. F. S. Friedrichsen (M.)
R. Girvan, MA (C.)
Dr A. B. Gough (M.)
Miss I. B. Hutchen (C.)
(Revd) A. H. Mann, MA (M.)
(Dr) Hereward T. Price (M.)
J. M. Ramsay, MA (C.)
F. R. Ray (C.)
(Revd) H. E. G. Rope, MA (M., C.)
H. F. P. Ruthven (M.)
A. R. Sewell (M., B.)
J. H. Smithwhite, BA (C.)
(Dr) E. J. Thomas (C.)
Charlton Walker, BA (B.)
F. A. Yockney (M., O.)

Revd Dr P. H. Aitken (M.)
F. S. Arnold, MA (B.)
T. Z. D. Babington, BA (M.)
Dr E. Brenner (M.)
W. J. Bryan (M.)
(Prof.) F. E. Bumby (M.)
C. G. Crump, BA (M.)
W. J. Fortune (O.)
G. G. R. Greene, MA (M.)
E. Gunthorpe (B.)
Miss M. D. Harris (M.)
S. J. Herrtage (M.)
Revd J. B. Johnston, BD (M.)
W. Landells (M.)
Revd R. H. Lord, MA (M.)
E. N. Martin (C., O.)
G. F. Maxwell (C.)
Revd George H. Morrison, DD (M.)
Miss Hilda Murray, MA (M.)
George Parker (M.)
P. J. Philip (M.)
M. L. Rouse (M.)
Miss Scott (M.)
H. R. Simpson (O.)
K. Sisam, B.Litt., MA (B)
Miss Skipper (M.)
E. E. Speight, BA (M.)
S. A. Strong, MA (B)
(Prof.) J. R. R. Tolkien (B.)
Miss A. M. Turner (B.)

4. *Proof Readers*

The following lists give the names of those who, outside of the regular staffs, rendered valuable help by regularly reading the proofs and making suggestions and additions. Those in the first list continued this important service for many years, in some cases from the beginning, and in all cases down to the year of their death or to the completion of the work.

Dr Fitzedward Hall († 1901)
H. Hucks Gibbs (Lord Aldenham) († 1907)
Revd J. B. Johnston, BD
Revd J. T. Fowler, DCL († 1924)
Miss Edith Thompson († 1929) and Miss E. Perronet Thompson
R. J. Whitwell, B. Litt. († 1928)
Dr W. Sykes († 1906)
F. J. Amours († 1910)
A. Caland († 1910).

Prof. F. E. Bumby
G. R. Carline
Dr G. F. S. Friedrichsen
H. Chichester Hart
W. W. Jenkinson
Dr G. Ch. van Langenhove
Revd J. A. Milne
Russell Martineau, MA
Revd C. B. Mount, MA
L. Pearsall Smith, MA
H. F. Rutter, M.Inst. C.E.
Prof. W. W. Skeat
W. H. Stevenson, MA
Revd W. B. R. Wilson, MA

5. *Other Helpers*

It would require several pages to give even a partial list of those who contributed separate items of information, either of their own accord or in reply to queries addressed to them. Special mention, however, should be made of a few authorities who, especially in the earlier years of the work, freely gave the editors the benefit of their special knowledge in their respective fields, e.g. Prof. Paul Meyer in Romanic Philology, Prof. E. Sievers in Germanic, Profs. W. W. Skeat and A. Napier in English, Prof. Sir John Rhŷs in Celtic, Sir Frederick Pollock in Law, and Prof. F. W. Maitland in History. For many years Mr James Platt supplied most of the material for the etymology of words from remote languages, with the dictionaries of which he had an unrivalled acquaintance.

Valuable service was also rendered by a succession of voluntary workers who verified doubtful quotations or references, and searched for special information, at the British Museum; prominent among these were Mr E. L. Brandreth, down to his death in 1907, his immediate successor in the field, Mr W. W. Jenkinson, and Mr R. J. Whitwell, who also did verification and research in the Public Record Office and for many years contributed much material of special value.

While similar verification and research in the Bodleian Library was done by several of the regular members of the Dictionary staffs, their work was greatly aided by the generous co-operation of the Librarian and staff of that institution, on which the constant demand for the requisite books has imposed a heavy burden for many years. The share of 'Bodley' in furthering the progress, and increasing the value, of the Dictionary is one that deserves to be gratefully remembered, and adds one more reason to those which have given the name of 'Oxford' to a work that can no longer be described as 'New'.

1933 SUPPLEMENT: STAFF AND CONTRIBUTORS

Editorial Staff

Dr C. T. Onions
Sir William Craigie

H. J. Bayliss
J. W. Birt
Miss E. S. Bradley
Miss E. V. V. Clark
Mrs Heseltine
Miss E. A. Lee
W. J. Lewis
A. T. Maling
Miss D. E. Marshall
M. M. Matthews
Miss R. A. N. R. Murray
J. L. N. O'Loughlin
Mrs L. F. Powell
Mrs A. S. C. Ross
F. J. Sweatman
G. Watson
W. Worrall
J. M. Wyllie

Contributors, Proof-readers, and Researchers

C. W. Adams
Dr F. A. Bather
H. Bayles
Dr Max Born (Berlin)
E. S. Brown
Dr R. W. Chapman
Mrs E. A. Coulson
Miss M. B. Cruickshank
Revd Dr W. Cruickshank
Revd F. G. Ellerton
C. A. Exley (Chicago)
A. J. Fowler
D. Freeman
L. N. Feipel (Brooklyn)
K. Foster
E. V. Gatenby (Fukushima, Japan)
Edvard Giese (Copenhagen)
H. W. Horwill
E. W. Hulme
Mrs A. J. Jenkinson
Revd J. B. Johnston
Dr E. H. Lendon
A. Lewis
G. G. Loane
Professor W. S. Mackie (Capetown)
F. Madan
A. Matthews
H. J. R. Murray
Revd T. G. Phillips (Isle of Man)
H. F. Rutter
Professor H. L. Savage (Princeton)
Dr A. B. A. Scott
W. B. Shaw
K. Sisam
Dr L. J. Spencer
E. V. Stocks (Durham)
L. R. M. Strachan
Dr E. H. Sugden
Dr A. E. H. Swaen (Amsterdam)
M. Venkanah (Vizianagram, India)
J. M. Watt
Miss E. G. Withycombe

Consultants

Sir Richard Burn
L. G. Carr Laughton
Dr J. Chadwick
R. P. Dewhurst
G. R. Driver
Sir Arthur Eddington
Professor A. Findlay
Professor N. Forbes
Dr J. K. Fotheringham
Dr A. E. M. Geddes
R. F. Harrod
N. B. Jopson
Dr J. G. Milne
Lord Passfield
Lord Riddell
M. Shaw
Dr N. V. Sidgwick
Professor F. Soddy
Col. H. R. H. Southam
M. H. Spielmann
D. Subotić
Sir Ernest Swinton
Professor F. W. Thomas
Dr J. F. Tocher
Dr N. T. Walker
The Librarian of the India Office
The Superintendent of the Kew Observatory
The Directors and staffs of the Natural History Museum and the Royal Botanic Gardens
The Printer to the University of Oxford
The Secretary of the Zoological Society
The Editors of *The Evening News, The Field, The Sketch,* and *The Stock Exchange Gazette*

A SUPPLEMENT TO THE OXFORD ENGLISH DICTIONARY STAFF AND CONTRIBUTORS

Editorial

Dr R. W. Burchfield

R. E. Allen
Wendy H. Archer
A. J. Augarde
J. P. Barnes
R. C. Beatty
D. B. W. Birk
Edith Bonner
Lesley S. Burnett
A. B. Buxton
Jill Cotter
E. C. Dann
Alana G. Dickinson
D. J. Edmonds
L. B. Firnberg
M. W. Grose
P. R. Hardie
G. D. Hargreaves
Joyce M. Hawkins
F. D. Hayes
A. Hodgson
Deborah D. Honoré
D. R. Howlett
A. M. Hughes
Betty Jennison
Elizabeth M. Knowles
M. A. Mabe
Deirdre McKenna
Rosamund E. Moon
G. Murray
R. C. Palmer
J. Paterson
Joan E. Pusey
Sandra Raphael
Rosemary J. Sansome
J. A. Simpson
Valerie Smith
Julia C. Swannell
J. B. Sykes
Della J. Thompson
W. R. Trumble
Anne Wallace-Hadrill
Yvonne L. Warburton
W. H. C. Waterfield
N. S. Wedd
E. S. C. Weiner
Frances M. Williams
Jelly K. Williams

Research Staff

P. J. Broadhead
Elizabeth Brommer
Jean H. Buchanan
Amanda J. Burrell
Katherine H. Emms
Joyce L. Harley
Peggy E. Kay
C. F. Kemp
Claire J. Nicholls
Adriana P. Orr
Gillian A. Rathbone
Veronica M. Salusbury
J. S. Wood

Other Assistants

N. van Blerk
Gillian Bradshaw
P. E. Davenport
Jennifer Dawson
R. J. Dixon
Juliet Field
R. C. Goffin
Sally Hilton
E. A. Horsman
L. M. Matheson
Elizabeth Price
Marjorie Purdon
Phyllis Trapp

Clerical and Secretarial Staff

D. Ann Baker
Pamela Bendall
Joan Blackler
Beta Cotmore
Kathleen Johnston
Katherine A. Shock
Afra E. Singer
Karin C. E. Vines
Caroline Webb
Anne Whear

Outside Researchers and Assistants

Grace M. Briggs
G. Chowdharay-Best
Daphne Gilbert-Carter
R. Hall
Sally Hinkle
Rita G. Keckeissen
Betsy Livingstone
Marguerite Y. Offord
N. C. Sainsbury

OTHER CONTRIBUTORS

Readers and contributors from collections

Mrs J. M. Addenbrooke
N. S. Angus
R. A. Auty
Professor W. S. Avis
Dr E. de B. Barnett
C. L. Barnhart
D. J. Barr
Dr E. H. Bateman
G. Bennett
R. Bowen
Mrs R. C. L. Boxall
Professor W. R. G. Branford
Dr D. S. Brewer
P. J. N. Bury
Professor F. G. Cassidy
The Revd R. M. Catling
G. Charters
R. L. Cherry
G. Chowdharay-Best
C. Collier
G. A. Coulson
P. T. J. Dadley
Mrs N. Day
G. W. Dennis
A. H. Douglas
Professor Sir Godfrey Driver
Mrs E. Duncan-Jones
Professor M. Eccles
E. H. Fathers
P. Ferriday
Mrs A. S. R. Gell
Mrs M. Gordon
W. Granville
D. Gray
Miss M. Gregory
G. Griffith
R. Hall
Mrs J. Harker
Mrs G. Hatton
Miss J. M. Hawkins
R. E. Hawkins
F. D. Hayes
Professor A. L. Hench
F. M. Henry
T. F. Hoad
Dom Sylvester Houédard
Dr M. D. W. Jeffreys
E. Jones
H. L. Jones
V. W. Jones
W. Kings
Miss M. Laski
Dr D. Leechman
Mrs J. Lindley
J. P. Lloyd
Dr J. Lyman
Mrs D. McColl
R. H. T. Mackenzie
W. S. Mackie
Professor J. B. McMillan
Mrs J. M. Marson
E. H. Mart
J. C. Maxwell
Miss A. Megroz
Dr F. Mish (G. & C. Merriam Co.)
Mrs J. Morgan
J. L. Nayler
Mrs P. Norton
Mrs M. Y. Offord
G. B. Onions
Mrs E. Owen
M. B. Parkes
Miss E. Penwarden
W. S. Pierpoint
Sir Edward Playfair
W. S. Ramson
Mrs C. Record
Miss A. Redmayne
Miss F. E. Richardson
The Revd H. E. G. Rope
Miss L. L. Ross
Mrs S. Ross
Professor N. G. Sabbagha
Miss R. C. Salzberger
D. Scott
F. R. Shapiro
J. C. Sharp
Professor G. Shepherd
David Shulman
Mrs V. Sillery
Mrs B. M. D. Smith
Mrs M. W. Smith
Mrs V. Smith

Mrs G. M. Spriggs
C. N. Stewart
C. P. Swart
Miss E. Symons
D. H. Thomson
Dr T. R. Thomson
The Revd A. F. Thorpe
F. J. Tidd Pratt
Sir St. Vincent Troubridge
N. van Blerk
J. Walker
Mrs C. Walton
Dr M. West
E. W. Whittle
J. D. A. Widdowson
Professor G. A. Wilkes
H. W. B. Wilson
Miss E. G. Withycombe
Dr L. S. Wittenberg
A. M. Wood
Dr H. B. Woolf (G. & C. Merriam Co.)

Outside Consultants

Dr G. E. H. Abraham
Dr G. C. Ainsworth
Professor A. J. Aitken
A. D. Alderson
Dr R. E. Allen
Dr P. W. Atkins
A. J. Augarde
Professor W. S. Avis
Professor J. R. Baines
Dr R. P. Beckinsale
Professor G. E. Blackman
Professor A. J. Bliss
Dr E. J. Bowen
Dr S. Bradbury
Dr J. Branford
Dr W. H. Brock
Professor T. Burrow
Dr R. S. Cahn
Sir Alexander Cairncross
Dr B. G. Campbell
H. Carter
J. Carter
Professor F. G. Cassidy
Miss Chan Yin-Ling
Dr P. A. Charles
M. J. E. Coode
Miss P. Cooray
Dr J. Cortés
Mrs J. Coulson
Dr S. T. Cowan
Professor G. N. C. Crawford
Professor C. D. Darlington
Professor N. Davis
Professor S. Deas
Professor E. J. Dobson
Miss J. Dobson
N. S. Doniach
Mrs U. Dronke
Professor A. R. Duckert
Dr R. D. Eagleson
P. G. Embrey
D. F. Foxon
Dr B. J. Freedman
R. B. Freeman
G. W. S. Friedrichsen
P. Fryer
M. P. Furmston
W. K. V. Gale
P. G. W. Glare
Dr I. Goddard
Professor G. H. Gonnet
W. Granville
P. S. Green
B. Greenhill
J. S. Gunn
Professor O. R. Gurney
Professor M. Guthrie
R. G. Haggar
R. Hall
Professor C. Hart
Dr R. M. Hartwell
Dr D. Hawkes
R. E. Hawkins
P. A Hayward
Dr W. A. Heflin
Dr M. H. Hey
M. T. Heydeman
Professor E. (Carr) Holmes
Dr A. K. Huggins
Dr R. Hunter
Dr K. Islam
Dr D. M. Jackson
P. Jarrett
Dr Russell Jones
Dr D. Julier
D. Kahn
Dr N. R. Ker
Dr W. J. Kirwin
Professor K. Koike
Dr D. Lack
Professor J. D. Latham
Professor J. Leech
Dr D. Leechman
Professor B. Lennox
Dr G. Lewis
R. P. W. Lewis
J. P. Lloyd
Dr A. Loveless
Dr D. J. Mabberley
Professor R. I. McDavid, Jr.
Dr R. S. McGregor
Professor J. B. McMillan
Dr C. I. McMorran
Dr T. Magay
Dr L. V. Malakhovski
Dr F. H. C. Marriott
R. D. Meikle
E. Mendelson
Professor G. B. Milner
P. A. Mulgan
D. D. Murison
P. H. Nye
Dr K. P. Oakley
Mrs I. Opie
P. Opie
M. B. Parkes
Dr A. B. Paterson
N. W. Pirie
Professor Dr I. Poldauf
N. G. Phillips
Capt. J. L. Pritchard
Professor C. Rabin
Mrs V. Richardson
Professor R. H. Robins
Dr D. A. Roe
Dr H. M. Rosenberg
Professor J. M. Rosenberg
Professor N. G. Sabbagha
K. S. Sandford
Dr H. G. A. V. Schenk
R. Scruton
J. S. G. Simmons
F. H. Smith
A. J. Stevens
Dr I. N. Stewart
Dr S. Stubelius
Dr W. C. Sturtevant
Dr C. H. V. Sutherland
Dr J. B. Sykes
P. Tamony
Associate Professor Tao Jie
Dr D. J. Thompson
J. B. Trapp
Professor G. Treitel
G. W. Turner
J. O. Urmson
Professor T. G. Vallance
N. van Blerk
Professor R. L. Venezky
Professor E. A. Vincent
Dr M. Weitzmann
The Revd Canon Professor M. F. Wiles
Dr D. R. Woodall
Dr D. Zorc

Critical proof-readers

Professor A. R. Duckert
Dr B. Foster
Professor A. L. Hench
M. W. Grose
T. F. Hoad
Mrs D. D. Honoré
Miss M. Laski
Mrs M. Y. Offord
Mrs L. W. Pauson
Mrs S. Ross
Professor E. G. Stanley
Dr K. Stubbs
Mrs H. C. Wright

KEY TO THE CONVENTIONS OF THE DICTIONARY

Abbreviations

For a list of abbreviations used in the Dictionary, see p. lxvi.

Abbreviations may be entered in the Dictionary either as *main words:*

ABTA, Abta (ˈæbtə). [Acronym f. the initial letters of the association.] The Association of British Travel Agents, established in 1950.

1950 *Travel Topics* Nov. 64/1 We can even hope that one day..membership of the A.B.T.A. will be accepted as sufficient evidence by the operating companies. **1963** *Times* 11 Jan. 6/5 The council of the Abta (the Association of British Travel Agents) in effect warned its members not to sell the scheme to the public, on the grounds that it contravened the association's code of conduct. **1981** *Economist* 24 Jan. 78/3 Competing operators argue that the customer gets less protection, since Travel Bazaar's four shops do not belong to the Association of British Travel Agents (Abta). **1984** *Daily Tel.* 12 Mar. 3/3 ABTA..is asking members to point out the dangers to tourists.

or in the final section of the entry for the corresponding *initial letter*, as at A III:

ASL, American Sign Language; **A.S.M.**, air-to-surface missile; **A.S.M.**, assistant stage-manager; **A/S.R.S.**, Air-Sea Rescue Service; **A.S.T.M.S.** (also with pronunc. ˈæstəmz), Association of Scientific, Technical, and Managerial Staffs; **A.S.V.**, air(craft) to surface vessel; **A.T.A.**, Air Transport Auxiliary;

Alphabetical order

The alphabetical order of the main entries in the Dictionary is strictly *letter-by-letter,* i.e. ignoring capitalization, punctuation, and spaces between words:

Athoan
athodyd
at-hold
Athole brose
at home, at-home
-athon

Note that headwords in which a final letter is *bracketed* with an opening bracket only appear where they would if the letter(s) after the bracket were not there:

air
air(e
airable

whereas those with both opening and closing brackets appear where they would if the brackets were not present:

amarant(h)ine
amarant(h)oid
amarantite

Where two words are identical in spelling, they are differentiated by *part of speech:*

aid (eɪd), *v.*
aid (eɪd), *sb.*

If two words of the same part of speech have distinct etymologies, they are differentiated by *superior numbers:*

†**aire,** *sb.*[1] *Obs.*; also 6 aare. [a. OFr. *aire*:—L. *āra* altar.] An altar.

†**aire,** *sb.*[2] *Obs.* Forms: 4 air, 5 eyre, 7 ayre, 4–7 aire. [a. OFr. *aire*: see AERIE.] The earlier equivalent of AERIE.

Combinations

Combinations of words, and compound words, may be entered in their normal alphabetical sequence as main words:

ˈair-ˌchamber. [AIR- 7.]

1. a. Any chamber or cavity filled with air in an animal or plant, *esp.* those in a 'chambered-shell.'

1847 ANSTED *Anc. World* iii. 43 In the Nautilus..we find a large, powerful, and complicated shell, composed of a number of separate compartments or air-chambers. **1855** OWEN *Vertebr.* I. ii. (L.) These air-chambers between the outer table and the immediate covering of the brain.

b. A chamber filled with air in a boat, airship, etc., to provide or assist buoyancy.

1881 W. D. HAY *300 Years Hence* vii. 133 In the upper part [of the boat] was the entrance and air-chamber. **1882** *Encycl. Brit.* XIV. 570/2 The buoyancy of the institution's lifeboat..is secured chiefly by means of a watertight deck..and two large air-chambers, one in the bow, the other in the stern. **1908** H. G. WELLS *War in Air* viii. §1 The airship was remarkably simple to construct: given the air-chamber material, the engines, [etc.]..it was really not more complicated..than an ordinary wooden boat had been..before.

2. In a pump or other hydraulic machine, a receptacle containing air, the elasticity of which, when condensed, maintains a constant pressure upon the water; an air-vessel.

1873 ATKINSON tr. *Ganot's Physics* §206 The fire engine is a force pump in which a steady jet is obtained by the aid of an air-chamber.

ˈair-ˌchambered, *a.* [f. prec. + -ED.] Furnished with air-chambers.

1856 KANE *Arct. Explor.* I. v. 49 It [boat] was air-chambered and buoyant.

If they are less complex, they are normally entered in the concluding section of the entry for the *first word,* as at AID:

8. *Comb.* and *attrib.*, chiefly in sense 7, as ***aid-band, -cohort, -force, -soldier***; or in sense 5, as ***aid-money***: (all *obs.*). Also **aid-major** *obs.* an adjutant; **aid-post**, a post at which wounded soldiers receive first medical attention; **aid-prayer** in *Law*: see 2.

or under the *combining form* which is their first element, as at AERO-:

ˌaerotheraˈpeutics (*Syd. Soc. Lex.*, 1881), **-ˈtherapy** = PNEUMATOTHERAPEUTICS; **aeˈrotropism** *Bot.* [ad. G. *aërotropismus* (H. Molisch 1885, in *Wiener Akad. Sitzungsber.* XC. I. 137), f. Gr. τροπή turning (τρέπειν to turn): see -ISM], the property, exhibited esp. by the growing roots of plants, of bending or turning towards a source of air; hence **aeroˈtropic** *a.*

Cross-references

Cross-reference to another main word (or derivative) is made in small Roman capitals:

ˈair-balloon. [AIR- 7.] †**1.** = **BALLOON** *sb.*[1] 3. *Obs.*

1753 *Publ. Advertiser* 25 May, A cascade, and shower of fire, and grand air-balloons, were most magnificently displayed.

2. A globose bag filled with gas so as to ascend in the air. cf. **BALLOON** *sb.*[1] 6.

1783 [see **BALLOON** *sb.*[1] 6]. **1783** *Morning Chron.* 8 Sept. 3/4 The first air-balloon he made was filled with fumous particles. **1784** JOHNSON in *Boswell* III. 626 On one day I, [etc.]

Where the entry referred to is for a proper noun, the cross-reference appears in small capitals with a full capital initial:

> ‖ **bengaline** (ˈbɛŋgəliːn). [mod.F.; so called from similarity to the fabric mentioned under BENGAL 1.] A (French) name for poplin, a mixed fabric of silk and worsted.
> **1884** *Pall Mall G.* 20 Sept. 4/1 Autumn Fashions, Bengaline (a superior substitute for Irish poplin).

Cross-reference to a phrase or word combination in another entry is made in italic type:

> A.C.V., air-cushion vehicle (see ***air-cushion*** (b) s.v. AIR *sb.*[1] B. II); A.C.W., aircraftwoman; A.D.C., aide-de-camp;

Some cross-references mix italic and small capitals; in these, the word in small capitals indicates the entry in which the phrase will be found:

> ‖ **absurdum** (æbˈsɜːdəm). [L. neuter of *absurdus* adj., used substantively as a scholastic term in med.L.] An absurd or illogical conclusion or condition. See **REDUCTIO *ad absurdum*.**
> *a* **1834** LAMB *Spec. fr. Fuller* 537 *note*, Setting up an *absurdum* on purpose to hunt it down. **1877** KINGLAKE *Crimea* (ed. 6) I. xv. 342 Reducing the theory of Representative Government to the *absurdum*.

Cross-reference entries are entered in the same alphabetical sequence as other main words:

> **absychitical,** erroneous form of APSYCHICAL.
>
> **ahwene,** variant of AWHENE *v. Obs.*, to vex.
>
> **ai, aie,** obs. forms of AY, AYE, and of EGG.

Derivatives

Derivatives of the main word may be treated as main words in their own right, or be placed in a section at the end of the entry for the word on which they are formed, introduced by 'Hence', 'Also', or 'So':

> **aeronautic** (ˌɛərəʊˈnɔːtɪk, ˌɛərəʊ-), *a.* [f. prec. + -IC; cf. Gr. *ναυτικ-ός* pertaining to sailing.] Of or pertaining to aeronauts, or to aerial navigation; sailing the air.
> **1784** *Hibernian Mag.* Sept. 489/2, I shall..attempt a description of his [*sc.* Richard Crosbie's] Aeronautic Chariot. **1826** MISS MITFORD *Our Village* Ser. II. (1863) 402 The announcement of the aeronautic expedition drew at least ten thousand gazers into the good town. **1876** M. COLLINS *Blacksm. & Scholar* I. viii. 197 The aeronautic art will not be perfected until the flight of birds is more carefully studied. **1878** *Daily News* 24 Oct. 6/4 The threads of the gossamer or aeronautic spider may be now seen. **1908** H. G. WELLS *War in Air* iv. §1 The Emperor forgave him and placed him in control of the new aeronautic arm of the German forces. *Ibid.* xi. §2 None of these countries had prepared for aeronautic warfare on the magnificent scale of the Germans. **1918** E. S. FARROW *Dict. Mil. Terms* 9 *Aëronautic Maps*, maps showing the contours and configuration of the land as closely as possible to the way it looks to the aviator from the air.
> Hence **ˌaeroˈnautica** *sb. pl.* [mod.L., see AERONAUTICS], matters or facts of aeronautics.
> **1753** [see AERONAUTICS]. **1838** T. M. MASON (*title*) Aeronautica. **1883** *Catal. Pat. Off. Libr.* II. 4 (*title*) Aëronautica Illustrata. A complete Cabinet of Aërial Ascents and Descents from the earliest period.

In some cases, the main word and derivative(s) are treated together:

> **asynapsis** (æ-, eɪsɪˈnæpsɪs). *Biol.* [f. A- *pref.* 14 + SYNAPSIS.] Absence of synapsis; failure of chromosomes to pair in meiosis. Hence **asyˈnaptic** *a.*
> **1930** G. W. BEADLE in *Cornell Univ. Agr. Exp. Sta. Mem.* CXXIX. (*title*) Genetical and Cytological Studies of Mendelian Asynapsis in *Zea mays.* **1937** C. D. DARLINGTON *Rec. Adv. Cytol.* (ed. 2) vii. 291 In 'asynaptic' maize which has as a rule no pairing of chromosomes at meiosis, the progeny nevertheless show the results of normal crossing-over. **1949** DARLINGTON & MATHER *Elem. Genetics* v. 110 A so-called asynaptic gene often..produces a general reduction in the crossing-over of all the chromosome pairs when homozygous.

Division into senses

Large Roman capital letters are used principally for division of an entry into different parts of speech:

> **annelid(e** (ˈænəlɪd), *sb.* and *a. Zool.* [a. mod.Fr. *annélide*, f. as next: see -ID.]
> **A.** ***sb.*** A member of the division of *Annelida*; a red-blooded worm.
> **1834** SIR C. BELL *Hand* 263 These annelides can creep and turn in every direction. **1857** WOOD *Obj. Sea-shore* 94 The commonest of the terrestrial annelids is the earth-worm.
> **B.** ***adj.*** Of or pertaining to the *Annelida*.
> **1855** KINGSLEY *Glaucus* (1878) 113 Long Annelid worms of quaintest forms and colours. **1865** BRISTOW *Figuier's World bef. Del.* iv. [No] indications of life, except annelide-tracks, and burrows.

Large Roman capital numerals are used to indicate the 'branches' or main historical divisions of the sense development: see General Explanations, p. xxix. The distinct senses of a word are numbered **1**, **2**, **3**, etc.; each of these senses may be further subdivided **a**, **b**, **c**, etc., and a further subdivision (*a*), (*b*), (*c*), or (i), (ii), (iii), etc. is also possible: for further explanation, see p. xxxiii.

Etymology

The etymology and form history are introduced by bold *square brackets*. In the main entry, these are placed after the variant forms:

> **annates** (ˈæneɪts, -əts). Also 6 **annatys**, 6–8 **annats**. **[**a. Fr. *annate* (15th c.), ad. med. and late L. *annāta* a year's space, work, proceeds, the same word which in its primary sense became in Fr. *année*. See -ATA.**]**.

Etymologies, or etymological information, may also occur in other places within an entry, still enclosed in square brackets:

> **airbrasive** *a.* and *sb.* **[**(A)BRASIVE ***a.*]** *Dentistry* (see quots.); **air-break**, (*a*) **[**BREAK ***sb.***[1] **5]** *Cricket*, a 'twist' or deviation in the air, of the ball when bowled; (*b*) **[**BREAK ***sb.***[1] **17 b]** *Electr. Engin.*, *attrib.* (see quot. 1910);

Labels

Labels normally appear in italic type, and are used to indicate the *status* or *usage* of a word or sense. Usage labels include indications of register (*colloq.*, *slang*), geographical area (*U.S.*, *Austral.*), or subject specialization (*Law*, *Linguistics*). For further explanation, see p. xxvii.

The *part of speech*, or grammatical category of a word, is normally given in italic type after the headword or subordinate word(s):

> **anneal** (əˈniːl), ***v.*** Forms: 1 **onælan** (**anælan**), 2
>
> **air-dammed *a.***, furnished with an air dam;

Where the subordinate words are given in bold italic type, the part of speech may follow in Roman:

> **air-dried** *a.*, dried by the action of the air; so ***air-dry*** v. trans.; **air-driven** *a.*, actuated by means of compressed air;

Where no part of speech is given, the entry is for a noun (substantive).

Pronunciation

The pronunciation, transcribed according to the International Phonetic Alphabet, is enclosed in *round brackets*:

aerobic (ɛə'rəʊbɪk), *a.* [f. AEROBE + -IC.]

‖ **aide-de-camp** (ɛddəkɑ̃, 'eɪddə,kɒŋ). *Mil.*

The pronunciation normally appears immediately after the headword or subordinate word, but may be given elsewhere, for example when different senses have distinct pronunciations:

adjoint ('ædʒɔɪnt), *sb.*[2] and *a.* [mod.Fr. *adjoint*, pa. pple. of *adjoindre* to ADJOIN, used as an appellative. Mod.Fr. form of prec.]

‖ **A.** *sb.*[2] (with pronunc. **adʒwɛ̃**). Official title of a French civil officer who assists the maire; also, an assistant professor in a French college.

For a detailed description of the IPA transcription used, see pp. xxiii–xxxiv; a key to the symbols is given on p. lxv.

In some cases, it is unnecessary to give a full phonetic transcription; instead, the word is printed with a stress mark (') before the stressed syllable:

aero'nautical, *a.* [f. prec. + -AL[1].] Of or belonging to aeronautics; connected with the navigation of the air.

Secondary stress is indicated by an inferior stress mark (,):

'air-con,ditioning, *vbl. sb.* [cf. CONDITION *v.* 9.] The process of cleaning air and controlling its temperature and humidity before it enters a room, building, etc., and in certain

Quotations

The quotations illustrate the use of the word in a given sense, and are normally arranged in *chronological* order, starting with the earliest available printed example of the sense:

aircraft ('ɛəkrɑːft, -æ-). [f. AIR- III. + CRAFT *sb.* 9.] Flying-machines collectively; a flying-machine.

Since the 1930s commonly restricted to denote an aeroplane (as distinct from a balloon or airship) or aeroplanes collectively. The nineteenth-century examples refer to balloons and airships.

1850 J. WISE *System of Aeronautics* xvi. 102 The aircraft has but one medium, the water-craft has two. **1876** C. B. MANSFIELD *Aerial Navig.* 2 Air-craft seems an appropriate term for the whole apparatus, including boat and gas vessel, or car and balloon. *Ibid.* 11. viii. 323 The inventors of air-crafts. **1903** *Aeronaut. Jrnl.* VII. 81/1 His world-famed aircrafts. **1909** *Daily Chron.* 26 Feb. 1/2 The vast commercial possibilities that the manufacture and world-wide use of air craft offer. **1910** ROTCH in *Epitome Aeronaut. Ann.*, [Suppose] an aircraft to possess the very moderate speed of 9 metres per second. **1910** *Daily Mail* 27 May 6/1 The three types of aircraft—the balloon, the airship, and the aeroplane. **1912** F. T. JANE *All the World's Air-craft* III. 7/1 It has .. been deemed advisable gradually to change the title of this annual to *All the World's Air-craft*, in order to avoid

A quotation in square brackets, usually preceding the first example, indicates a use which helps to illustrate the development of the sense, while not strictly exemplifying it:

Hence ,**aeromagne'tometer**, an instrument for making aeromagnetic measurements.

[1946 R. BALSLEY in *Petroleum Engineer* Aug. 108/1 The obvious advantages of the air-magnetometer are its speed .. and the fact that it can be used where ground methods are .. unpracticable.] **1948** *World Oil* CXXVIII. 223 (*heading*) Aeromagnetometer profile flown from Venezuela to Texas. **1969** *New Scientist* 9 Jan. 58/2 An aeromagnetometer survey to last several months will be started shortly.

Where many combinations are treated together, the quotations illustrating each are grouped chronologically and the groups are arranged in the alphabetical order of the combinations. Asterisks are sometimes used to mark the first quotation for each combination:

1889 *Cent. Dict.*, ***Air-blast.** **1902** *Encycl. Brit.* XXXIII. 422/1 In .. air-blast transformers, apertures are left in the core by means of which the cooling air can reach the interior portions. **1946** H. P. YOUNG *Electr. Power Syst. Control* (ed. 2) vii. 194 Air-blast breakers can be classified into three main types depending upon the manner in which the compressed air is directed at the arc. **1845** *North Brit. Rev.* IV. 128 An ***air-bloomery** .. was dependent, for its blast, upon the varying currents of air that played around the hill on which it was placed. **1860** W. FORDYCE *Hist. Coal* 110 The first smelting furnace .. was undoubtedly the Air-Bloomery, a low conical structure, with small openings at the bottom for the admission of air, and a larger orifice at the top for carrying off the gaseous products of combustion. **1855** OWEN *Skel. & Teeth* 7 The extremities of such ***air-bones** present a light, open net-work. **1872** *Rep. Comm. Patents 1871* I. 253 Westinghouse, George, Jr., .. Valve device for steam-power ***air-brake** couplings. **1945** R. B. BLACK in *Jrnl. Amer. Dental Assoc.* XXXII. 956/2 The ***airbrasive** process employs for its action a very fine—almost pinpoint—stream of compressed air into which a suitable finely divided abrasive agent has been introduced. **1953** I. GLICKMAN *Clin. Periodontology* xxxix. 665 *Airbrasive* which consists of fine abrasive powder (Dolemite in a stream of carbon dioxide) is used for removing surface deposits from the teeth. **1900** *Cricket* 29 Mar. 41/3 There is no necessity to mention Noble's ***air-breaks** any more.

For an explanation of the typographical conventions used in quotations, see p. xxx.

Superior numbers

Superior numbers are used to distinguish homonyms (see alphabetical order above) and after the labels *Obs.* and *rare* to indicate words or senses for which only one ($^{-1}$) or no ($^{-0}$) contextual example from a printed source was available to the editors.

Variant forms

Variant forms of a word are printed in light bold type, and are introduced by 'Also' or 'Forms':

‖ **abaca** ('æbəkə). **Also abaka.** The native name of the palm (*Musa textilis*) which furnishes what is commonly known as Manilla Hemp; [etc.]

aback (ə'bæk), *adv.* Forms: **1 on bæc; 2 a bec; 2–3 on bak, o bak; 2–5 a bak, abak; 4–8 a-back(e, abacke; 6- aback.** [OE. *on* prep. *bæc* sb. = unto [etc.]

Numerals are used before variant forms to indicate the century during which a particular form is recorded: see p. xxvii.

KEY TO THE PRONUNCIATION

THE pronunciations given are those in use in the educated speech of southern England (the so-called 'Received Standard'), and the keywords given are to be understood as pronounced in such speech.

I. *Consonants*

b, d, f, k, l, m, n, p, t, v, z *have their usual English values*

g as in *go* (gəʊ)
h ... *ho!* (həʊ)
r ... *run* (rʌn), te*rr*ier ('tɛrɪə(r))
(r) ... he*r* (hɜː(r))
s ... *see* (siː), *success* (sək'sɛs)
w ... *wear* (wɛə(r))
hw ... *wh*en (hwɛn)
j ... *yes* (jɛs)

θ as in *th*in (θɪn), ba*th* (bɑːθ)
ð ... *then* (ðɛn), ba*the* (beɪð)
ʃ ... *sh*op (ʃɒp), di*sh* (dɪʃ)
tʃ ... *ch*op (tʃɒp), di*tch* (dɪtʃ)
ʒ ... vi*s*ion ('vɪʒən), dé*j*euner (deʒøne)
dʒ ... *judge* (dʒʌdʒ)
ŋ ... si*ng*i*ng* ('sɪŋɪŋ), thi*n*k (θiŋk)
ŋg ... fi*ng*er ('fɪŋgə(r))

(FOREIGN AND NON-SOUTHERN)
ʎ as in It. serra*gl*io (ser'raʎo)
ɲ ... Fr. co*gn*ac (kɔɲak)
x ... Ger. a*ch* (ax), Sc. lo*ch* (lɒx), Sp. fri*j*oles (fri'xoles)
ç ... Ger. i*ch* (ɪç), Sc. ni*ch*t (nɪçt)
ɣ ... North Ger. sa*g*en ('zaːɣən)
c ... Afrikaans baardmanne*tj*ie ('baːrtmanəci)
ɥ ... Fr. c*u*isine (kɥizin)

Symbols in parentheses are used to denote elements that may be omitted either by individual speakers or in particular phonetic contexts: e.g. *bottle* ('bɒt(ə)l), *Mercian* ('mɜːʃ(ɪ)ən), *suit* (s(j)uːt), *impromptu* (ɪm'prɒm(p)tjuː), *father* ('fɑːðə(r)).

II. *Vowels and Diphthongs*

SHORT
ɪ as in p*i*t (pɪt), -n*e*ss, (-nɪs)
ɛ ... p*e*t (pɛt), Fr. *sept* (sɛt)
æ ... p*a*t (pæt)
ʌ ... p*u*tt (pʌt)
ɒ ... p*o*t (pɒt)
ʊ ... p*u*t (pʊt)
ə ... *a*nother (ə'nʌðə(r))
(ə) ... beat*e*n ('biːt(ə)n)
i ... Fr. s*i* (si)
e ... Fr. b*é*b*é* (bebe)
a ... Fr. m*a*ri (mari)
ɑ ... Fr. b*â*timent (bɑtimɑ̃)
ɔ ... Fr. h*o*mme (ɔm)
o ... Fr. *eau* (o)
ø ... Fr. p*eu* (pø)
œ ... Fr. b*oeu*f (bœf) c*oeu*r (kœr)
u ... Fr. d*ou*ce (dus)
ʏ ... Ger. M*ü*ller ('mʏlər)
y ... Fr. d*u* (dy)

LONG
iː as in b*ea*n (biːn)
ɑː ... b*a*rn (bɑːn)
ɔː ... b*o*rn (bɔːn)
uː ... b*oo*n (buːn)
ɜː ... b*u*rn (bɜːn)
eː ... Ger. Schn*ee* (ʃneː)
ɛː ... Ger. F*ä*hre ('fɛːrə)
aː ... Ger. T*a*g (taːk)
oː ... Ger. S*oh*n (zoːn)
øː ... Ger. G*oe*the ('gøːtə)
yː ... Ger. gr*ü*n (gryːn)

NASAL
ɛ̃, æ̃ as in Fr. f*in* (fɛ̃, fæ̃)
ɑ̃ ... Fr. fr*an*c (frɑ̃)
ɔ̃ ... Fr. b*on* (bɔ̃)
œ̃ ... Fr. *un* (œ̃)

DIPHTHONGS, etc.
eɪ as in b*ay* (beɪ)
aɪ ... b*uy* (baɪ)
ɔɪ ... b*oy* (bɔɪ)
əʊ ... n*o* (nəʊ)
aʊ ... n*ow* (naʊ)
ɪə ... p*ee*r (pɪə(r))
ɛə ... p*ai*r (pɛə(r))
ʊə ... t*ou*r (tʊə(r))
ɔə ... b*oa*r (bɔə(r))

aɪə as in f*ie*ry ('faɪərɪ)
aʊə ... s*ou*r (saʊə(r))

The incidence of main stress is shown by a superior stress mark (') preceding the stressed syllable, and a secondary stress by an inferior stress mark (ˌ), e.g. *pronunciation* (prəˌnʌnsɪ'eɪʃ(ə)n).

For further explanation of the transcription used, see *General Explanations*, Volume I.

LIST OF ABBREVIATIONS, SIGNS, ETC.

Some abbreviations listed here in italics are also in certain cases printed in roman type, and vice versa.

a. (in Etym.)	adoption of, adopted from
a (as *a* 1850)	*ante*, 'before', 'not later than'
a.	adjective
abbrev.	abbreviation (of)
abl.	ablative
absol.	absolute, -ly
Abstr.	(in titles) *Abstract, -s*
acc.	accusative
Acct.	(in titles) *Account*
A.D.	*Anno Domini*
ad. (in Etym.)	adaptation of
Add.	Addenda
adj.	adjective
Adv.	(in titles) *Advance, -d, -s*
adv.	adverb
advb.	adverbial, -ly
Advt.	advertisement
Aeronaut.	(as label) in Aeronautics; (in titles) *Aeronautic, -al, -s*
AF., AFr.	Anglo-French
Afr.	Africa, -n
Agric.	(as label) in Agriculture; (in titles) *Agriculture, -al*
Alb.	Albanian
Amer.	American
Amer. Ind.	American Indian
Anat.	(as label) in Anatomy; (in titles) *Anatomy, -ical*
Anc.	(in titles) *Ancient*
Anglo-Ind.	Anglo-Indian
Anglo-Ir.	Anglo-Irish
Ann.	Annals
Anthrop., Anthropol.	(as label) in Anthropology; (in titles) *Anthropology, -ical*
Antiq.	(as label) in Antiquities; (in titles) *Antiquity*
aphet.	aphetic, aphetized
app.	apparently
Appl.	(in titles) *Applied*
Applic.	(in titles) *Application, -s*
appos.	appositive, -ly
Arab.	Arabic
Aram.	Aramaic
Arch.	in Architecture
arch.	archaic
Archæol.	in Archæology
Archit.	(as label) in Architecture; (in titles) *Architecture, -al*
Arm.	Armenian
assoc.	association
Astr.	in Astronomy
Astrol.	in Astrology
Astron.	(in titles) *Astronomy, -ical*
Astronaut.	(in titles) *Astronautic, -s*
attrib.	attributive, -ly
Austral.	Australian
Autobiogr.	(in titles) *Autobiography, -ical*
A.V.	Authorized Version
B.C.	Before Christ
B.C.	(in titles) British Columbia
bef.	before
Bibliogr.	(as label) in Bibliography; (in titles) *Bibliography, -ical*
Biochem.	(as label) in Biochemistry; (in titles) *Biochemistry, -ical*
Biol.	(as label) in Biology; (in titles) *Biology, -ical*
Bk.	*Book*
Bot.	(as label) in Botany; (in titles) *Botany, -ical*
Bp.	Bishop
Brit.	(in titles) *Britain, British*
Bulg.	Bulgarian
Bull.	(in titles) *Bulletin*
c (as *c* 1700)	*circa*, 'about'
c. (as 19th c.)	century
Cal.	(in titles) *Calendar*
Cambr.	(in titles) *Cambridge*
Canad.	Canadian
Cat.	Catalan
catachr.	catachrestically
Catal.	(in titles) *Catalogue*
Celt.	Celtic
Cent.	(in titles) *Century, Central*
Cent. Dict.	*Century Dictionary*
Cf., cf.	*confer*, 'compare'
Ch.	Church
Chem.	(as label) in Chemistry; (in titles) *Chemistry, -ical*
Chr.	(in titles) *Christian*
Chron.	(in titles) *Chronicle*
Chronol.	(in titles) *Chronology, -ical*
Cinemat., Cinematogr.	in Cinematography
Clin.	(in titles) *Clinical*
cl. L.	classical Latin
cogn. w.	cognate with
Col.	(in titles) *Colonel, Colony*
Coll.	(in titles) *Collection*
collect.	collective, -ly
colloq.	colloquial, -ly
comb.	combined, -ing
Comb.	Combinations
Comm.	in Commercial usage
Communic.	in Communications
comp.	compound, composition
Compan.	(in titles) *Companion*
compar.	comparative
compl.	complement
Compl.	(in titles) *Complete*
Conc.	(in titles) *Concise*
Conch.	in Conchology
concr.	concrete, -ly
Conf.	(in titles) *Conference*
Congr.	(in titles) *Congress*
conj.	conjunction
cons.	consonant
const.	construction, construed with
contr.	contrast (with)
Contrib.	(in titles) *Contribution*
Corr.	(in titles) *Correspondence*
corresp.	corresponding (to)
Cotgr.	R. Cotgrave, *Dictionarie of the French and English Tongues*
cpd.	compound
Crit.	(in titles) *Criticism, Critical*
Cryst.	in Crystallography
Cycl.	(in titles) *Cyclopædia, -ic*
Cytol.	(in titles) *Cytology, -ical*
Da.	Danish
D.A.	*Dictionary of Americanisms*
D.A.E.	*Dictionary of American English*
dat.	dative
D.C.	District of Columbia
Deb.	(in titles) *Debate, -s*
def.	definite, -ition
dem.	demonstrative
deriv.	derivative, -ation
derog.	derogatory
Descr.	(in titles) *Description, -tive*
Devel.	(in titles) *Development, -al*
Diagn.	(in titles) *Diagnosis, Diagnostic*
dial.	dialect, -al
Dict.	Dictionary; *spec.*, the *Oxford English Dictionary*
dim.	diminutive
Dis.	(in titles) *Disease*
Diss.	(in titles) *Dissertation*
D.O.S.T.	*Dictionary of the Older Scottish Tongue*
Du.	Dutch
E.	East
Eccl.	(as label) in Ecclesiastical usage; (in titles) *Ecclesiastical*
Ecol.	in Ecology
Econ.	(as label) in Economics; (in titles) *Economy, -ics*
ed.	edition
E.D.D.	*English Dialect Dictionary*
Edin.	(in titles) *Edinburgh*
Educ.	(as label) in Education; (in titles) *Education, -al*
EE.	Early English
e.g.	*exempli gratia*, 'for example'
Electr.	(as label) in Electricity; (in titles) *Electricity, -ical*
Electron.	(in titles) *Electronic, -s*
Elem.	(in titles) *Element, -ary*
ellipt.	elliptical, -ly
Embryol.	in Embryology
e.midl.	east midland (dialect)
Encycl.	(in titles) *Encyclopædia, -ic*
Eng.	England, English
Engin.	in Engineering
Ent.	in Entomology
Entomol.	(in titles) *Entomology, -logical*
erron.	erroneous, -ly
esp.	especially
Ess.	(in titles) *Essay, -s*
et al.	*et alii*, 'and others'
etc.	et cetera
Ethnol.	in Ethnology
etym.	etymology
euphem.	euphemistically
Exam.	(in titles) *Examination*
exc.	except
Exerc.	(in titles) *Exercise, -s*
Exper.	(in titles) *Experiment, -al*
Explor.	(in titles) *Exploration, -s*
f.	feminine
f. (in Etym.)	formed on
f. (in subordinate entries)	form of
F.	French
fem. (*rarely* f.)	feminine
fig.	figurative, -ly
Finn.	Finnish
fl.	*floruit*, 'flourished'
Found.	(in titles) *Foundation, -s*
Fr.	French
freq.	frequent, -ly
Fris.	Frisian
Fund.	(in titles) *Fundamental, -s*
Funk or *Funk's Stand. Dict.*	*Funk and Wagnalls Standard Dictionary*
G.	German
Gael.	Gaelic
Gaz.	(in titles) *Gazette*
gen.	genitive
gen.	general, -ly
Geogr.	(as label) in Geography; (in titles) *Geography, -ical*

Geol.	(as label) in Geology; (in titles) *Geology, -ical*
Geom.	in Geometry
Geomorphol.	in Geomorphology
Ger.	German
Gloss.	Glossary
Gmc.	Germanic
Godef.	F. Godefroy, *Dictionnaire de l'ancienne langue française*
Goth.	Gothic
Govt.	(in titles) *Government*
Gr.	Greek
Gram.	(as label) in Grammar; (in titles) *Grammar, -tical*
Gt.	Great
Heb.	Hebrew
Her.	in Heraldry
Herb.	among herbalists
Hind.	Hindustani
Hist.	(as label) in History; (in titles) *History, -ical*
hist.	historical
Histol.	(in titles) *Histology, -ical*
Hort.	in Horticulture
Househ.	(in titles) *Household*
Housek.	(in titles) *Housekeeping*
Ibid.	*Ibidem*, 'in the same book or passage'
Icel.	Icelandic
Ichthyol.	in Ichthyology
id.	*idem*, 'the same'
i.e.	*id est*, 'that is'
IE.	Indo-European
Illustr.	(in titles) *Illustration, -ted*
imit.	imitative
Immunol.	in Immunology
imp.	imperative
impers.	impersonal
impf.	imperfect
ind.	indicative
indef.	indefinite
Industr.	(in titles) *Industry, -ial*
inf.	infinitive
infl.	influenced
Inorg.	(in titles) *Inorganic*
Ins.	(in titles) *Insurance*
Inst.	(in titles) *Institute, -tion*
int.	interjection
intr.	intransitive
Introd.	(in titles) *Introduction*
Ir.	Irish
irreg.	irregular, -ly
It.	Italian
J., (J.)	(quoted from) Johnson's *Dictionary*
(Jam.)	Jamieson, *Scottish Dict.*
Jap.	Japanese
joc.	jocular, -ly
Jrnl.	(in titles) *Journal*
Jun.	(in titles) *Junior*
Knowl.	(in titles) *Knowledge*
l.	line
L.	Latin
lang.	language
Lect.	(in titles) *Lecture, -s*
Less.	(in titles) *Lesson, -s*
Let., Lett.	letter, letters
LG.	Low German
lit.	literal, -ly
Lit.	Literary
Lith.	Lithuanian
LXX	Septuagint
m.	masculine
Mag.	(in titles) *Magazine*
Magn.	(in titles) *Magnetic, -ism*
Mal.	Malay, Malayan
Man.	(in titles) *Manual*
Managem.	(in titles) *Management*
Manch.	(in titles) *Manchester*
Manuf.	in Manufacture, -ing
Mar.	(in titles) *Marine*
masc. (*rarely* m.)	masculine
Math.	(as label) in Mathematics; (in titles) *Mathematics, -al*
MDu.	Middle Dutch
ME.	Middle English
Mech.	(as label) in Mechanics; (in titles) *Mechanics, -al*
Med.	(as label) in Medicine; (in titles) *Medicine, -ical*
med.L.	medieval Latin
Mem.	(in titles) *Memoir, -s*
Metaph.	in Metaphysics
Meteorol.	(as label) in Meteorology; (in titles) *Meteorology, -ical*
MHG.	Middle High German
midl.	midland (dialect)
Mil.	in military usage
Min.	(as label) in Mineralogy; (in titles) *Ministry*
Mineral.	(in titles) *Mineralogy, -ical*
MLG.	Middle Low German
Misc.	(in titles) *Miscellany, -eous*
mod.	modern
mod.L	modern Latin
(Morris),	(quoted from) E. E. Morris's *Austral English*
Mus.	(as label) in Music; (in titles) *Music, -al; Museum*
Myst.	(in titles) *Mystery*
Mythol.	in Mythology
N.	North
n.	neuter
N. Amer.	North America, -n
N. & Q.	*Notes and Queries*
Narr.	(in titles) *Narrative*
Nat.	(in titles) *Natural*
Nat. Hist.	in Natural History
Naut.	in nautical language
N.E.	North East
N.E.D.	*New English Dictionary*, original title of the *Oxford English Dictionary* (first edition)
Neurol.	in Neurology
neut. (*rarely* n.)	neuter
NF., NFr.	Northern French
No.	Number
nom.	nominative
north.	northern (dialect)
Norw.	Norwegian
n.q.	no quotations
N.T.	New Testament
Nucl.	Nuclear
Numism.	in Numismatics
N.W.	North West
N.Z.	New Zealand
obj.	object
obl.	oblique
Obs., obs.	obsolete
Obstetr.	(in titles) *Obstetrics*
occas.	occasionally
OE.	Old English (= Anglo-Saxon)
OF., OFr.	Old French
OFris.	Old Frisian
OHG.	Old High German
OIr.	Old Irish
ON.	Old Norse
ONF.	Old Northern French
Ophthalm.	in Ophthalmology
opp.	opposed (to), the opposite (of)
Opt.	in Optics
Org.	(in titles) *Organic*
orig.	origin, -al, -ally
Ornith.	(as label) in Ornithology; (in titles) *Ornithology, -ical*
OS.	Old Saxon
OSl.	Old (Church) Slavonic
O.T.	Old Testament
Outl.	(in titles) *Outline*
Oxf.	(in titles) *Oxford*
p.	page
Palæogr.	in Palæography
Palæont.	(as label) in Palæontology; (in titles) *Palæontology, -ical*
pa. pple.	passive participle, past participle
(Partridge),	(quoted from) E. Partridge's *Dictionary of Slang and Unconventional English*
pass.	passive, -ly
pa.t.	past tense
Path.	(as label) in Pathology; (in titles) *Pathology, -ical*
perh.	perhaps
Pers.	Persian
pers.	person, -al
Petrogr.	in Petrography
Petrol.	(as label) in Petrology; (in titles) *Petrology, -ical*
(Pettman),	(quoted from) C. Pettman's *Africanderisms*
pf.	perfect
Pg.	Portuguese
Pharm.	in Pharmacology
Philol.	(as label) in Philology; (in titles) *Philology, -ical*
Philos.	(as label) in Philosophy; (in titles) *Philosophy, -ic*
phonet.	phonetic, -ally
Photogr.	(as label) in Photography; (in titles) *Photography, -ical*
phr.	phrase
Phys.	physical; (*rarely*) in Physiology
Physiol.	(as label) in Physiology; (in titles) *Physiology, -ical*
Pict.	(in titles) *Picture, Pictorial*
pl., plur.	plural
poet.	poetic, -al
Pol.	Polish
Pol.	(as label) in Politics; (in titles) *Politics, -al*
Pol. Econ.	in Political Economy
Polit.	(in titles) *Politics, -al*
pop.	popular, -ly
Porc.	(in titles) *Porcelain*
poss.	possessive
Pott.	(in titles) *Pottery*
ppl. a., pple. adj.	participial adjective
pple.	participle
Pr.	Provençal
pr.	present
Pract.	(in titles) *Practice, -al*
prec.	preceding (word or article)
pred.	predicative
pref.	prefix
pref., Pref.	preface
prep.	preposition
pres.	present
Princ.	(in titles) *Principle, -s*
priv.	privative
prob.	probably
Probl.	(in titles) *Problem*
Proc.	(in titles) *Proceedings*
pron.	pronoun
pronunc.	pronunciation
prop.	properly
Pros.	in Prosody
Prov.	Provençal
pr. pple.	present participle
Psych.	in Psychology
Psychol.	(as label) in Psychology; (in titles) *Psychology, -ical*
Publ.	(in titles) *Publications*
Q.	(in titles) *Quarterly*
quot(s).	quotation(s)
q.v.	*quod vide*, 'which see'
R.	(in titles) *Royal*
Radiol.	in Radiology
R.C.Ch.	Roman Catholic Church
Rec.	(in titles) *Record*
redupl.	reduplicating
Ref.	(in titles) *Reference*
refash.	refashioned, -ing
refl.	reflexive
Reg.	(in titles) *Register*

reg. regular
rel. related to
Reminisc. (in titles) *Reminiscence, -s*
Rep. (in titles) *Report, -s*
repr. representative, representing
Res. (in titles) *Research*
Rev. (in titles) *Review*
rev. revised
Rhet. in Rhetoric
Rom. Roman, -ce, -ic
Rum. Rumanian
Russ. Russian

S. South
S.Afr. South Africa, -n
sb. substantive
sc. *scilicet*, 'understand' or 'supply'
Sc., Scot. Scottish
Scand. (in titles) *Scandinavia, -n*
Sch. (in titles) *School*
Sc. Nat. Dict. *Scottish National Dictionary*
Scotl. (in titles) *Scotland*
Sel. (in titles) *Selection, -s*
Ser. Series
sing. singular
Sk. (in titles) *Sketch*
Skr. Sanskrit
Slav. Slavonic
S.N.D. *Scottish National Dictionary*
Soc. (in titles) *Society*
Sociol. (as label) in Sociology; (in titles) *Sociology, -ical*
Sp. Spanish
Sp. (in titles) *Speech, -es*
sp. spelling
spec. specifically
Spec. (in titles) *Specimen*
St. Saint
Stand. (in titles) *Standard*
Stanf. (quoted from) *Stanford Dictionary of Anglicised Words & Phrases*
str. strong
Struct. (in titles) *Structure, -al*
Stud. (in titles) *Studies*
subj. subject
subord. cl. subordinate clause
subseq. subsequent, -ly
subst. substantively
suff. suffix
superl. superlative
Suppl. Supplement
Surg. (as label) in Surgery; (in titles) *Surgery, Surgical*
s.v. *sub voce*, 'under the word'
Sw. Swedish
s.w. south-western (dialect)
Syd. Soc. Lex. Sydenham Society, *Lexicon of Medicine & Allied Sciences*
syll. syllable
Syr. Syrian
Syst. (in titles) *System, -atic*

Taxon. (in titles) *Taxonomy, -ical*
techn. technical, -ly
Technol. (in titles) *Technology, -ical*
Telegr. in Telegraphy
Teleph. in Telephony
(Th.), (quoted from) Thornton's *American Glossary*
Theatr. in the Theatre, theatrical
Theol. (as label) in Theology; (in titles) *Theology, -ical*
Theoret. (in titles) *Theoretical*
Tokh. Tokharian
tr., transl. translated, translation
Trans. (in titles) *Transactions*
trans. transitive
transf. transferred sense
Trav. (in titles) *Travel(s)*
Treas. (in titles) *Treasury*
Treat. (in titles) *Treatise*
Treatm. (in titles) *Treatment*
Trig. in Trigonometry
Trop. (in titles) *Tropical*
Turk. Turkish
Typog., Typogr. in Typography

ult. ultimately
Univ. (in titles) *University*
unkn. unknown
U.S. United States
U.S.S.R. Union of Soviet Socialist Republics
usu. usually

v., vb. verb
var(r)., vars. variant(s) of
vbl. sb. verbal substantive
Vertebr. (in titles) *Vertebrate, -s*
Vet. (as label) in Veterinary Science; (in titles) *Veterinary*
Vet. Sci. in Veterinary Science
viz. *videlicet*, 'namely'
Voy. (in titles) *Voyage, -s*
v.str. strong verb
vulg. vulgar
v.w. weak verb

W. Welsh; West
wd. word
Webster *Webster's (New International) Dictionary*
Westm. (in titles) *Westminster*
WGmc. West Germanic
Wks. (in titles) *Works*
w.midl. west midland (dialect)
WS. West Saxon

(Y.), (quoted from) Yule & Burnell's *Hobson-Jobson*
Yrs. (in titles) *Years*

Zoogeogr. in Zoogeography
Zool. (as label) in Zoology; (in titles) *Zoology, -ical*

Signs and Other Conventions

Before a word or sense
† = obsolete
‖ = not naturalized, alien
¶ = catachrestic and erroneous uses

In the listing of Forms
1 = before 1100
2 = 12th c. (1100 to 1200)
3 = 13th c. (1200 to 1300), etc.
5–7 = 15th to 17th century
20 = 20th century

In the etymologies
* indicates a word or form not actually found, but of which the existence is inferred
:— = normal development of

The printing of a word in SMALL CAPITALS indicates that further information will be found under the word so referred to.

.. indicates an omitted part of a quotation.

- (in a quotation) indicates a hyphen doubtfully present in the original; (in other text) indicates a hyphen inserted only for the sake of a line-break.

PROPRIETARY NAMES

THIS Dictionary includes some words which are or are asserted to be proprietary names or trade marks. Their inclusion does not imply that they have acquired for legal purposes a non-proprietary or general significance nor any other judgement concerning their legal status. In cases where the editorial staff have established in the records of the Patent Offices of the United Kingdom and of the United States that a word is registered as a proprietary name or trade mark this is indicated, but no judgement concerning the legal status of such words is made or implied thereby.

THE OXFORD ENGLISH DICTIONARY

A (eɪ), the first letter of the Roman Alphabet, and of its various subsequent modifications (as were its prototypes Alpha of the Greek, and Aleph of the Phœnician and old Hebrew); representing originally in English, as in Latin, the 'low-back-wide' vowel, formed with the widest opening of jaws, pharynx, and lips. The plural has been written *aes*, A's, *As. **from A to Z***: see Z 3.

c **1340** Hampole *Pr. Consc.* 481 And by þat cry men knaw þan Whether it be man or weman, For when it es born it cryes swa. If it be man it says a! a! That þe first letter is of þe nam Of our forme-fader Adam. *c* **1386** Chaucer *Prol.* 161 On which was first i-write a crowned A, And after, Amor vincit omnia. **1401** *Pol. Poems* II. 57 I know not an *a* [Ā] from the wynd-mylne, ne a *b* [B] from a bole-foot. **1678** Butler *Hudib.* III. i. 1006 And loue your Loues with *A*'s and *B*'s. **1765** Tucker *Light of Nat.* II. 89 Tully tells us, a hog has been known to make a perfect letter A with his snout upon the ground; but nobody ever saw, or thought it possible to see, the whole poem of Ennius scratched out in that manner: and I believe he might have added safely, that no man ever saw a single A written by a hog, without a multitude of other irregular scratches round about it. *a* **1842** Tennyson *The Epic* 50 Mouthing out his hollow oes and aes, Deep-chested music.

The sounds now represented by A are thus symbolized in this work:—

(1) (eɪ) in n*a*me (neɪm) (4) (ɑː) in f*a*ther (ˈfɑːðə(r))
(2) (ɛə) in b*a*re (bɛə(r)) (5) (ɔː) in w*a*ter (ˈwɔːtə(r))
(3) (æ) in m*a*n (mæn) (6) (ɒ) in w*a*nt (wɒnt)

The vowel in ch*a*nt, p*a*st, varies with different speakers from 3 to 4.

1 and 2 are also commonly represented by the digraphs *ai*, *ay*, as in p*ai*n, p*ay*, p*ai*r (peɪn, peɪ, pɛə(r)); and 5 by *au*, *aw*, as in *laud*, *law* (lɔːd, lɔː). *Ai*, *ay* rarely represent a diphthong (aɪ), as in *ay*, Is*ai*ah (aɪ, aɪˈzaɪə); *au* is a diphthong (aʊ) only in foreign words.

In unaccented syllables these vowels are modified, and obscured; thus:—

(7) ɪ in vill*a*ge, marri*a*ge (ˈvɪlɪdʒ, ˈmærɪdʒ)
(8) ɪ/ə in separ*a*te, *adj.* (ˈsɛpərət, -ɪt)
(9) ə in lun*a*r, *a*mœb*a* (ˈluːnə(r), əˈmiːbə)

In rapid utterance the ə may become a mere voice glide, or entirely disappear, as sep*a*rate *adj.* ˈsɛpərət, ˈsɛp(ə)rət, ˈsɛprət. These phonetic variations in actual speech are reflected in variant spellings like mack*a*rel, mack*e*rel, mackrel; ab*a*net, abnet; car*a*vel, carvel; Cath*a*rine, Cath*e*rine, Cathrine; depend*a*nt, depend*e*nt; and common 'mistakes' in spelling, such as sep*e*rate.

II. The letters of the alphabet, or some of them, are also used to indicate serial order and distinguish things in a series, as the notes of the musical scale, the 'quires' or sheets of a book, classes of ships, propositions in logic, quantities in algebra, points, and hence lines and figures in geometry. As the order is in some cases fixed, *A* or *a* has some specialized uses:

1. In *Music*: The 6th note of the diatonic scale of C major, or the first note of the relative minor scale of C, corresponding to *la* in the Tonic Sol-fa notation. Also, the scale of a composition with A as its key-note; as 'a symphony in A'.

1609 Douland Ornithoparcus *Micrologus* 22 In the first part set *A* Base, in the third *D sol re*, in the fifth *A lamire.* **1806** Callcott *Gramm. of Music* The notes of Music are named from the first seven letters of the alphabet, A, B, C, D, E, F, G. When the Melody, or Tune, exceeds these seven, the same series of letters must be repeated. **1880** Grove *Dict. Mus.* I. 192 The beautiful and passionate Sonata in A which was inspired by and dedicated to his [Beethoven's] friend Madame Ertmann.

2. In *Nautical language*: see *A1* below.

3. In *Logic*: a universal affirmative.

1866 Mansel (in Bowen *Logic* 201) *A* is declared by Aristotle to be the most difficult proposition to establish, and the easiest to overthrow.

4. In *Abstract reasoning*, *hypothetical argumentation*, *Law*, etc. A means *any one* thing or person, B another, C a third, etc.; as, A becomes surety to B for C; C fails in his engagements, on which B, etc.

1870 Bowen *Logic* iii. 49 Every conceivable thing is either *A* or *not-A*. Of course *A* and *not-A*, taken together, include the universe.

5. In *Algebra*: *a*, *b*, *c*, and other *early* letters of the alphabet are used to express known quantities, as *x*, *y*, *z* are to express the unknown.

6. Designating a first-class road.

1921 *Autocar* 29 Oct. 829/2 Those roads, however, which have already received numbers are all of the first, or A, category and it is by no means probable that their numbers will suffer any change after once being fixed... Six boundary roads radiating from London are taken as the basis. Road A1 is that from London to Edinburgh; A2 runs from London to Dover; A3 London to Portsmouth.

7. Used of a type of blood.

1927 *Jrnl. Amer. Med. Assoc.* LXXXVIII. 1422/1 Dr. Karl Landsteiner has suggested the substitution of the well known letters O, A, B and AB for the Jansky numbers I, II, III and IV and the Moss numbers IV, II, III and I. The letters will..express the actual constitution of the blood corpuscles with respect to iso-agglutination, as far as it concerns the separation of the groups. **1928** *Jrnl. Exper. Med.* XLVII. 757 They separate the human bloods into four sharply defined groups designated as O, A, B, and AB.

8. *Sociol.* Designating the highest (or †lowest) of a series of social classes; now *spec.* the higher managerial, administrative, or professional class; a member of this. ***AB*** (Sociol.): *pl.*, the membership of the two highest social classes A and B; also in *sing.* and as *adj.*

1889 C. Booth *Life & Labour* I. I. ii. 33 The 8 classes into which I have divided these people are: A. The lowest class of occasional labourers, and semi-criminals. B. Casual earnings—'very poor' [etc.]. **1910** F. G. D'Aeth in *Sociol. Rev.* III. 270 The present class structure is based upon different standards of life... These varying standards tend to fall into seven groups..A. The Loafer..B. Low-skilled labour..C. Artizan..D. Smaller Shopkeeper and clerk..E. Smaller Business Class..F. Professional and Administrative Class..G. The Rich. **1936** Harrison & Mitchell *Home Market* xii. 59 Blue Symbols represent A grade—where chief income earner receives £10 per week or more. **1950** D. C. Jones in *Brit. Jrnl. Sociol.* I. 51 It will simplify both our analysis and your classification if you begin by thinking in terms of five main social classes, which we have lettered in descending order A, B, C, D, E. **1968** M. Abrams in J. A. Jackson *Social Stratification* vi. 135 In the middle 1950's,..the National Readership Survey came under the direction of the Institute of Practitioners in Advertising (I.P.A.)... Interviewers recorded the occupation of each respondent... The stratification of respondents into six grades—A, B, C_1, C_2, D and E—was based exclusively on occupation. **1984** *Social Trends* (Central Statistical Office) No. 14. x. 142 Almost every household in social classes A and B possessed a dictionary in May 1982. **1966** *Punch* 10 Aug. 212/1 We have shown..that the ABs watch the same kind of programmes as everybody else. **1969** *Listener* 31 July 164 Such trusts appeal primarily to AB readers. **1976** *New Society* 1 Jan. 5/1 Upper middle class ABs living in the prosperous southern counties. **1986** *Age* (Melbourne) 18 Jan. 8/4 The social niceties..are very A, B. When I say 'dick', Liz pounces.

9. Designating a range of international standard paper sizes (as *A0*, *A1*, *A2*, etc.), based on a proportion of 1: √2, with each size in the series having half the surface area of the previous one (see quot. 1937). Cf. B II. 2(v), C II. 4.

1932 *Industr. Standardization* III. 203/2 The European main or A-series of paper sizes... The basic sheet with an area of one square meter is designated A0 (A zero); the next smaller sheet by A1; half of this by A2, etc. **1937** E. J. Labarre *Dict. Paper* 277/1 The basic sizes are therefore: A-series = A0 = 841 × 1189 mm; B-series = B0 = 1000 × 1414 mm; C-series = C0 = 917 × 1297 mm. **1958** *B.S.I. News* Nov. 17/2 Another manufacturer..has laid down stocks of its 'Wove Writing' paper in three sizes from which the 'A' sizes can..be cut. **1962** F. T. Day *Introd. Paper* vii. 71 At present there is much discussion of the advantages of what are termed A and B paper sizes. **1982** *Financial Times* 25 Oct. I. 12/7 The new chassis..is about the size of an A4 sheet of paper. **1983** *Electronics* 1 Dec. 3E (*heading*) Linear CCD array senses images on A3-size pages.

10. ***A-side***, of a single-playing gramophone record: (the music recorded on) the side that is being promoted; contr. with *B-side* s.v. B II 2 b(vi).

1962 *Melody Maker* 7 July 10/1 No doubt the A side will get plenty of spins. **1968** *Guardian* 5 Jan. 18/4 The seven-man band arrived at the London recording studio to make the 'A' side of a new 'single'. **1970** J. Lennon in J. Wenner *Lennon Remembers* (1971) 49 Maybe if he was feeling guilty that he had most of the A-sides or something he'd give me a solo. **1984** *Sounds* 1 Dec. 6/5 The A-side features the inimitable talents of Jim Thirlwell on lead vocal.

III. *Abbreviations.* (Many abbreviations given here with the full stop are frequently used without it.)

A., a., *a.*, stands for: (1) *anno*, in the year, as A.D. *anno domini*, in the year of our Lord; A.M. *anno mundi*, in the year of the world; A.U.C. *anno urbis conditæ*, in the year of the city (Rome) having been founded; (2) *ante*, as 'a.m.' *ante meridiem*, before noon; a. 1600 or *a* 1600, before 1600; (3) *adjective*; *active* (verb); (4) *artium*, as A.B. *artium baccalaureus*; A.M. *artium magister*; which in England are now written B.A., M.A., Bachelor, and Master, of Arts; (5) *alto*; (6) *accepted* (of bills); (7) *Associate*, as A.L.S. Associate of the Linnæan Society; (8) R.A. Royal Artillery, Royal Academy or Academician; F.S.A. Fellow of the Society of Antiquaries; F.R.A.S. Fellow of the Royal Astronomical Society, and many similar titles; (9) A.B. able-bodied seaman; (10) *a* or *aa* in Med. ana, q.v.; **A**, adult, designating films suitable for exhibition to adult audiences; **A., a.**, ampere; **A**, atom(ic); **A**, in £A, Australian; **Å.**, Ångström; **A.A.**, Alcoholics Anonymous (orig. *U.S.*); also, a member of this organization; **A.A.**, **A.-A.**, anti-aircraft; **A.A.**, Automobile Association; **A.A.A.**, Amateur Athletic Association; **A.A.A.**, American Automobile Association; **A.A.F.**, Auxiliary Air Force; **A.A.M.**, air-to-air missile; **A. and R.** (see quots.); **A.B.**, Bachelor of Arts; **A.B.C.**, Aerated Bread Company; **A.B.C.**, Australian Broadcasting Corporation (formerly Commission); also, † Australian Broadcasting Company; **A.B.C.A.**, Army Bureau of Current Affairs, an organization which provided troops with information about current affairs during the 1939–45 war; **ABM**, anti-ballistic missile (orig. *U.S.*); cf. *I.C.B.M.* s.v. I III; **ABS**, acrylonitrile-butadiene-styrene; freq. *attrib.*, esp. designating a group of metallizable plastics consisting of a rubbery phase dispersed in a hard phase and with uses that include tubing, parts of car bodies, and domestic articles; **A.C.**, **A/C**, aircraftman; **A.C.**, **a.c.**, alternating current; **A.C.C.**, anodal (or anodic) closure contraction; **A.C.C.M.**, (also with pronunc. ˈækəm), Advisory Council for the Church's Ministry; **AC/DC**, **AC-DC** [humorously after A.C. and D.C. (alternating and direct electrical current): see above and D III. 3] *slang* (orig. *U.S.*), of a person: bisexual; **A.C.L.U.**, American Civil Liberties Union; **A.C.P.**, African, Caribbean, and Pacific (countries), *spec.* the signatories to the Lomé Convention (see quot. 1975[2]); **A.C.S.**, antireticular cytotoxic serum; **A.C.T.**, Australian Capital Territory; **A.C.T.H.**, *a*dreno*c*ortico*t*rop(h)ic *h*ormone; **A.C.T.T.**, Association of Cinematograph, Television, and Allied Technicians; **A.C.T.U.**, Australian (formerly also Australasian) Council of Trade Unions; **A.C.V.**, air-cushion vehicle (see *air-cushion* (b) s.v. AIR *sb.*[1] B. II); **A.C.W.**, aircraftwoman; **A.D.C.**, aide-de-camp, hence ***A.D.C.-ship***, aide-de-campship; **A.D.F.**, automatic direction finder; **A.D.G.B.**, Air Defence of Great Britain; **ADH**, antidiuretic hormone; **A.D.P.**, automatic data processing; **A.D.(S.)**, autograph document (signed); **A.E.F.**, American Expeditionary Forces; cf. *B.E.F.* s.v. B III. 1; **A.E.U.**, Amalgamated Engineering Union; **A.F., a.f.**, audio frequency; **A.F.C.**, Air Force Cross; **A.F.M.**, Air Force Medal; **A.F.S.**, Auxiliary Fire Service; **A.F.V.**, armoured fighting vehicle; **A.G.**, Adjutant-General; **A.G.**, Attorney-General; **A.G.M.**, annual general meeting; **A.G.R.**, advanced gas-cooled reactor; **A.H.**, *Anno Hegiræ* (see HEGIRA); **A.I.**, Air Interception; **A.I., A.I.D., A.I.H.**, artificial insemination (by donor, husband); **AI**, artificial intelligence; **A.I.D.**, Aeronautical Inspection Directorate (in quot. 1918 Department); **A.I.D.** (pron. eɪd) (*U.S.*), Agency for International Development, established in 1961 to give economic aid to underdeveloped countries; **A.I.F.**, Australian Imperial Force; **AIM** (pron. eɪm) (*U.S.*), American Indian Movement; **a.k.a.** (*colloq.*, orig. *U.S.*), also known as; **A.K.C.**, American Kennel Club; **A level**, Advanced level (of the General Certificate of Education examination); **A.L.P.**, Australian Labour Party; **A.L.(S.)**, autograph letter (signed); **ALU** (*Computing*), arithmetic and logic(al) unit; **A.M.**, Albert Medal; **A.M.**, amplitude modulation; cf. *F.M.* s.v. F III. 3 a; **A.M.A.**, American Medical Association; **A.M.D.G.** [L. *ad maiorem Dei gloriam*], to the greater glory of God (esp. as a motto of the Jesuits); **A.M.G.**, Allied Military Government; **A.N.C.**, African National Congress; **A.N.(S.)**, autograph note (signed); **A.O.N.B.**, area of outstanding natural beauty; cf. *S.S.S.I.* s.v. S I. 4 a; **A.P.**, Associated Press; **APB** (*U.S.*), all-points bulletin (see ALL III); **A.P.C.** (*Austral.* and *U.S.*), aspirin (= acetylsalicylic acid), phenacetin, and caffeine, used as an analgesic or antipyretic; a mixture, tablet, or capsule containing these; **A.P.I.**, American Petroleum Institute (used *spec.* with reference to a scale for expressing the relative density of oil, developed by the Institute, in which higher values correspond to lower densities); **APL** [now usu. expanded as 'a programming language', but see quot. 1966], a high-level computer programming language developed by IBM in the mid-1960s; **APR**, annual(ized) percentage rate (of interest on money lent on credit); **A.P.T.**, advanced passenger train; **ARC**, AIDS-related complex; **A.R.P.** (see AIR-RAID); **ASA** (also with pronunc. 'eɪsə), American Standards Association (used *spec.* in *Photogr.* with reference to a standard scale for rating film speed); **A.S.A.P., a.s.a.p.** (also with pronunc. 'eɪsæp), as soon as possible; **A.S.B.**, Alternative Service Book; **A.S.C.**, Army Service Corps; **ASEAN, Asean** (pron. 'eɪsɪən), Association of South-East Asian Nations; **ASH** (pron. æʃ), Action on Smoking and Health; **ASL**, American Sign Language; **A.S.M.**, air-to-surface missile; **A.S.M.**, assistant stage-manager; **A/S.R.S.**, Air-Sea Rescue Service; **A.S.T.M.S.** (also with pronunc. 'æstəmz), Association of Scientific, Technical, and Managerial Staffs; **A.S.V.**, air(craft) to surface vessel; **A.T.A.**, Air Transport Auxiliary; **A.T.&T.** (*U.S.*), American Telephone and Telegraph Company; **A.T.C.**, Air Traffic Control; **A.T.C.**, Air Training Corps; **A.T.C.**, Automatic Train Control; **ATM** (*Banking*, orig. *U.S.*), automated (orig. automatic) teller machine; **A.T.S.**, animal tub-sized; **ATV**, all-terrain vehicle; **A.T.V.**, Associated Television; **Å.U., A.U.**, Ångström Unit; **A.U.** = *astronomical unit* s.v. ASTRONOMICAL *a.* 3; **AUEW**, Amalgamated Union of Engineering Workers; **AV**, alternative vote; **A.V.**, Authorized Version (of the Bible); **A.V.H.**, initials of Hungarian secret police, also **A.V.O.**; **A.V.M.**, Air Vice-Marshal; **A.W.O.L.**, absent without leave (orig. *U.S.*); **A.W.U.**, Australian Workers' Union; **AZT**, azidothymidine.

See also (as main entries) ABTA, ACAS, ADAS, AIDS, A-OK, APEX *sb.*[2,3], APRA, ASCII, A.S.L.E.F., AWACS.

1914 *Times* 16 Feb. 6/2 Since the inception of the board [British Board of Film Censors]..627 have been passed for 'public' exhibition with the '*A' certificate. **1935** LD. MACMILLAN *Local Govt. Law & Admin.* III. 166 It is the practice of the Board of Film Censors to distinguish between films suitable for universal exhibition ('U' films) and films suitable for exhibition to adult audiences ('A' films) which by implication are unsuitable for children. **1936** *Sunday Express* 13 Dec. 14/1 Cinema Theatres. Academy, Ox.-st. Finnish Epic 'Fredlos' (A). **1889** S. R. BOTTONE *Electric Bells* ii. 56 Or if we like to use the initials of volts, ampères, and ohms..we may write $\frac{V}{R}$ = *A, or $\frac{\text{Volts}}{\text{Ohms}}$ = Ampères. **1937** *Rep. Joint Comm. Chem. Soc. Faraday Soc. etc.* 11 Ampère (in sub-units) = a. **1945** *Daily Mirror* 8 Aug. 1 (*headline*) Jap Radio says Evacuate—'Ware *A-Bombs. **1954** *Britannica Bk. of Year* 637/2 *A-test*, a test explosion of an atomic bomb. **1936** *Whitaker's Alman. 1937* 810/2 Total imports, 1935–36..£*A104,687,000. **1941** *Sat. Even. Post* 1 Mar. 10/3 The city editor, the assistant city editor and a nationally known reporter were *A.A.'s. **1943** *A.A.* (Alcoholic Foundation) 1 As an active member of A.A. since 1939, I feel myself a useful member of the human race at last. **1955** M. MCCARTHY *Charmed Life* i. 13 Drink..was one of the chief local dangers... In a village of four hundred souls, there was..a branch of A.A., with regular Wednesday meetings. **1977** M. FRENCH *Women's Room* (1978) ii. 117, I keep thinking I just have to get through today, you know? Like an AA. **1914** *Times Book of Navy* 145 The abbreviations used in the lists are as follows:..*A.A., Anti-air-craft guns. **1917** 'CONTACT' *Airman's Outings* 157 The A.-A. batteries have only worried us to the extent of half a dozen shells. **1943** *N. & Q.* CLXXXIV. 107/2 A.-A. barrage was audible from twenty miles away. **1905** *Autocar* 14 Oct. 443/1 Commonsense precautions taken with regard to villages, and at dangerous points, do not concern the *A.A., for therein it is considered lies the duty of the policeman. **1937** *Discovery* July liv/2 (Advt.), Victoria Hotel, A.A. H. & C. Electricity. **1882** *Amateur Athl. Assoc.: Rules*, Laws to be observed at every Athletic Meeting held under the sanction of the *A.A.A. **1955** *Times* 20 July 3/5 B. S. Hewson, the A.A.A. mile champion. **1902** *Automobile* May 1945/1 (*heading*) Constitution and by-laws of the *A.A.A. **1955** *Times* 4 Aug. 10/2 Colonel Hallington, the chairman of the A.A.A. contest board, said that the decision had been prompted by the accident at Le Mans. **1973** C. W. GEAR *Introd. Computer Sci.* vii. 311 Suppose that you have to design an online system for the AAA. It must store the road map of the United States. **1982** *Financial Times* 6 Dec. 1 The AAA contract..constitutes the major portion of Cook's U.S. travellers' cheque business. **1925** *Flight* 15 Jan. 32/2 The designating numbers of the *A.A.F. units will start with 600. **1958** *Aero-Space Terms* 1/1 *AAM, Air-to-air missile. **1958** *Times* 26 May 7/6 *A and R men, dee-jays, pluggers—to use the abbreviated titles by which artists and recording managers, disc jockeys and exploitation men are known. **1959** *TV Times* 14 Aug. 11/1 It all revolves around someone known as an 'A and R man'. The common translation of 'A and R' is Artists and Repertoire—and it is for these two items that the A and R man is responsible. **1773** *Boston News-Let.* 29 Apr. 2/2 Last Friday departed this life..John Alden, *A.B., aged 22. **1842** *Knickerbocker* XIX. 429 A man may..write A.B. after his name, and even A.M., and be no great things either. **1895** *Rep. to Harvard Club of Chicago* 2 (D.A.E.), Educational qualifications equivalent to the Harvard A.B. **1894** *Punch* 15 Dec. 285/1, I pass an *A.B.C., Where I purchase two or three Cakes and scones. **1941** E. BLUNDEN *Thomas Hardy* 120 Afterwards we went to a Lyons tea-shop, at which he [Hardy] was a little alarmed, being used only to an A.B.C. **1931** *Austral. Broadcasting Co. Ltd. Year Bk. 1930* 24 (*heading*) The widespread ramifications of the *A.B.C. **1933** *1st Ann. Rep. Austral. Broadcasting Commission* 9 A.B.C. (Sydney) Symphony Orchestra. **1957** 'N. SHUTE' *On Beach* iv. 132 The A.B.C.'s been doing a good job in telling people just the way things are. **1959** *New Statesman* 31 Jan. 151/1 The Australian Broadcasting Commission..is subject to constant pressure, much of it is organised, and ABC officials need remarkable stamina to resist political and sectarian attack. **1984** *Daily Tel.* 7 May 17/4 Air hostesses will become flight attendants and newsmen on the ABC will be journalists. **1942** *Rep. Comm. on Amenities in Women's Services (Cmd.* 6384) 44 *ABCA came into existence in September, 1941, to remedy this ignorance and to mitigate boredom. **1963** *Missiles & Rockets* 16 Sept. 14 (*heading*) Soviets may have ultimate *ABM. **1984** *Daily Tel.* 2 Feb. 18/6 The Air Vice-Marshal claims that Russia has violated the SALT and ABM treaties. **1964** *Brit. Plastics Year Bk.* (ed. 34) IV. 229/1 *A.B.S. Fabricators. **1967** *Times Rev. Industry* June 76/2 Familiar uses include..PVC or ABS..for decorative use in fascia boards. **1983** *McGraw-Hill Encycl. Chem.* 792/1 Ease of fabrication by a variety of methods, including typical metalworking methods such as cold stamping, has led to the development of new uses for ABS resins. **1889** E. J. HOUSTON *Dict. Electr. Words* 8 *A.C.C.—An abbreviation used in medical electricity for *Anodic Closure Contraction*, or the contraction observed on closing the circuit when the anode is lying over the muscle. **1893** DUNGLISON *Dict. Med. Sci.* (ed. 21) p. vii, A.C.C., anodal closure contraction. **1967** *Church of England Yearbk.* 177 Candidates for courses..are specially selected by *ACCM. **1984** *Oxf. Diocesan Mag.* Feb. 15/2 Calls for dis-establishment from Evangelicals, and some Catholics, for an 'all members ministry' (to quote ACCM). **1960** WENTWORTH & FLEXNER *Dict. Amer. Slang* 1/2 **ac-dc*, *ac/dc*,..bisexual. Some jocular use since *c*1940. **1972** D. LEES *Zodiac* 115 Being suspected of being AC/DC isn't going to ruin anyone these days. **1974** K. MILLETT *Flying* (1975) I. 91 You can also tell *Time* Magazine you're bisexual, be AC-DC in the international edition. **1983** *Him* May 7/2 I'm, well, a bit that way myself, if you follow... You know, AC/DC..half and half. **1936** *Amer. Mercury* Dec. 385/2 The fiction of the 'Liberalism' of the *ACLU has been firmly implanted in the popular mind. **1980** *Economist* 21 June 28/3 The ACLU may have a strong case. **1975** *Ann. Reg. 1974* 381 Jamaica's Minister of Trade..led the *ACP group. **1975** *Keesing's Contemp. Archives* 27050/1 A five-year convention establishing an overall trading and economic co-operation relationship between the European Economic Community and 46 developing African, Caribbean and Pacific (ACP) countries was signed in Lomé (the capital of Togo) on Feb. 28. **1983** *Financial Times* 4 Oct. 14 It offers some protection against declining prices for a range of ACP commodities through the Stabex mechanism; and it is committed to buying 1.3m tons of ACP sugar a year. **1938** *Official Year Bk. Australia* 390 *A.C.T. **1945** S. J. BAKER *Austral. Lang.* x. 187 We use *A.C.T.* or *F.C.T.* to denote the Australian or Federal Capital Territory where Canberra is situated. **1957** *Film & TV Technician* XXIII. 5/3 The new *A.C.T.T. badges and brooches can be obtained from Head Office. **1974** *Socialist Worker* 26 Oct. 11/2 The ACTT..organise more than 18,000 film and TV workers. **1985** *Listener* 28 Feb. 13/3 The ACTT has taken a strong interest in the development of the independent sector. **1928** *Econ. Rec.* May 108 The 1927 Congress..set itself to construct machinery that might act adequately in the field of Interstate industrial disputes. Hence the new Australasian Council of Trades Unions (*A.C.T.U.). **1972** J. BELFRAGE in G. W. Turner *Good Austral. Eng.* vi. 108 This is another local reference..to the active pro-labour work of the new President of the ACTU. **1986** *Courier-Mail* (Brisbane) 3 July 4/1 The acting Opposition Leader..said the commission should..not give in to ACTU and Government blackmail tactics. **1962** *Flight Internat.* LXXXI. 113 Free-moving *ACVs will be going into business also, together with hydrofoil craft. **1975** *Aviation Week & Space Technol.* 1 Sept. 17 Slightly smaller and considerably smaller versions of the Russian ACV craft are shown at top and bottom. **1837** EMILY EDEN *Let.* 28 Oct. in *Up the Country* (1866) I. i. 9 The *A.D.C.'s are very apt to assemble over our cabins at night. **1888** KIPLING *Plain Tales fr. Hills* 10 The A.-D.-C. in Waiting. **1896** *Punch* 4 Jan. 5/2 Permitted to retain his A.D.C.-ship after promotion from field-rank. **1948** *Shell Aviation News* No. 123, 10/2 When homing on a ground station with the *ADF the passage of the aircraft over the station is indicated by a 180° reversal of bearing within a few seconds. **1926** *Flight* 6 May 272/2 The Fighting and Wessex Bombing Areas are under the A.O.C.-in-C., *A.D.G.B. **1944** *Times* 1 Mar. 4/5 Sir Archibald Sinclair disclosed for the first time that the organization responsible for the air defence of this country is now known as A.D.G.B. (Air Defence of Great Britain). **1951** H. W. SMITH *Kidney* x. 245 It is only in birds and mammals that *ADH increases the tubular reabsorption of water. **1983** *Oxf. Textbk. Med.* II. XVIII. 20/2 Reliable assays for ADH in plasma or urine are now available. **1958** *Engineering* 4 Apr. 424/1 Automatic data processing (or *ADP) is the modern nervous system of corporate bodies. **1861** *Sotheby & Wilkinson Catal.* 1 July Tenison Mss. 36 A. signifies *Autograph* S. signifies *Signed* L. signifies *Letter* D. signifies *Document*. *Ibid.* 50 *Colbert*, A.L.S. to *Cavalier Bernino*, 1665—*Perrault* (the architect of the Louvre), *A.D.S. with portrait. **1912** F. K. WALTER *Abbrev. & Techn. Terms Book Catal.* 1 A.D., Autograph document. A.D.S., Autograph document signed. **1917** *U.S. Army A.E.F. Gen. Staff Press Rev.* 12 Dec. 1/1 Issued by the Second Section General Staff, G.H.Q.*A.E.F. **1977** H. FAST *Immigrants* III. 177 He joined in the singing of 'Smiles'..one of the theme songs of the AEF. **1921** *Justice* 24 Feb. 6/2 (*heading*) The N.U.R. and the *A.E.U. and also the R.C.A. *a* **1974** R. CROSSMAN *Diaries* (1976) II. 497, I spent the morning with the old A.E.U. members who have A.E.U. pensions. **1919** *Whitaker's Alman.* 144/1 *The Air Force Cross.* 1918—*A.F.C.—Instituted..for acts of courage or devotion to duty when flying, although not in active operations against the enemy. **1919** *London Gaz.* (Suppl. 5) 19 Dec. 15840/2 Actg. Serjeant Elmo O'Neal Bearden, *A.F.M. (South Russia). **1921** S. C. JOHNSON *Medal Collector* 237 A.F.M.—As for the A.F.C., but the width of the stripes is $\frac{1}{16}$ of an inch... The D.F.M. and A.F.M. ribbon will show at the top corner nearest to the left arm a triangle of white. **1939** *War Weekly* 1 Dec. 166/2 Flying Officer R. C. Graveley, O.B.E., receiving congratulations from members of a Leytonstone *A.F.S. station. **1940** *New Statesman* 21 Dec. 642 Most of its best workers are busy on A.R.P., or A.F.S., or evacuation, or some other emergency job. **1939** *War Illustr.* 18 Nov. p. iii/1 Wartime Abbreviations:..*A.F.V., Armoured Fighting Vehicle. **1942** *Wardens' Bulletin* (*City of Oxford Civil Defence*) No. 53, 18 June 3 Vehicles. Very dark dull grey with dark brown disruptive design. A.F.V.'s have black cross outlined in white. **1913** W. T. ROGERS *Dict. Abbrev.* 7/1 **A.G.*, Adjutant-General. **1914** W. S. CHURCHILL in M. Gilbert *Winston S. Churchill* (1972) III. Compan. I. 185 A.G., R.M. will make arrangements for their reception in the camps. **1957** H. H. JENKINS *Diction of 'Yank'* vi. 55 Many official and quasi-official abbreviations were used in GI speech the world over. The most widely known ones included..'A.G.' (the adjutant general, or his office, or a member of his staff). **1889** A. J. BALFOUR *Let.* 11 Apr. (Br. Libr. Add. MSS 49827 f. 845), My dear *A.G. *a* **1912** W. T. ROGERS *Dict. Abbrev.* (1913) 7/2 **A.G.M.* (gen.), Annual General Meeting. **1952** *Secretaries Jrnl.* 2 Aug. 99/2 It is surely not the intention to enable even private companies to hold their A.G.M.'s on paper with the members in various different places. **1961** *Architect & Building News* 21 June 814/1 Mr. Henry Brooke..spoke up for the need for better architecture when addressing the AGM of the Council for Visual Education recently. **1984** *National Trust* Spring 23/3 The present inordinately long period between June and the AGM caused unnecessary barriers. **1960** *Gloss. Atomic Terms* (H.M.S.O.) 2 **A.G.R.*, advanced gas-cooled reactor. **1961** *Ann. Reg. 1960* 405 The most advanced of the two schemes was the Advanced Gas-Cooled Reactor (AGR), the prototype of which was under construction at Windscale. **1983** *Listener* 14 July 6/1 The American reactor will produce five times as much intermediate waste as the AGR. **1788** GIBBON *Decl. & F.* V. lii. 418 The foundations of Bagdad were laid *A.H. 145, A.D. 762. **1940** F. STARK *Winter in Arabia* iv. 25 It [*sc.* the wooden minbar] belonged to the year A.H. 693 (1293 A.D.). **1945** *Electronic Engin.* XVII. 683 With the Battle of Britain by night must be associated the use of *A.I. or Air Interception. **1945** *Flight* 21 June 664/2 Later on came airborne interception equipment (A.I.), which comprised a radar set in the aircraft by means of which the target objective could be registered, stalked and attacked. **1971** *New Scientist* 2 Sept. 525 The first major effort of the *AI scientists was directed towards writing computer programs to translate automatically between languages. **1985** *Business Week* 1 July 78 Sales for AI technology will top £719 million this year. **1918** C. BRIGHT *Telegr., Aeronaut. & War* xix. 291 Steps should be taken..to introduce into the Aeronautical Inspection Department (*A.I.D.) more who have had a training that would especially fit them for the work in a technical sense. **1931** *Flight* 16 Jan. 56/2 Those who occupy those front offices such as the A.I.D. and the Meteorological Office staff. **1961** J. F. KENNEDY in *N.Y. Times* 27 May 2/5 Responsibility..will be assigned to a single agency—the Agency for International Development... The new agency—*A.I.D.—will be headed by an administrator of Under Secretary rank. **1983** *N.Y. Times* 11 Dec. 15/1 The inquiries

..involve a £14 million A.I.D.-financed contract. **1918** *Official Year Bk. Australia* XI. 1019 Little difficulty was experienced..in..obtaining and training horses for the mounted units of the *A.I.F. **1940** *War Illustr.* 16 Feb. 121 The Second A.I.F.—Australian Imperial Force—consisting of men who have volunteered for service either at home or abroad. **1971** *Minneapolis Tribune* 16 Aug. 12/2 The occupation began..when 25 Indians, most of them members of the American Indian Movement (*AIM) broke a window. **1983** *N.Y. Times* 11 Dec. 33/1 Whether or not the AIM Indians were involved, it was over quickly. **1955** R. J. Schwartz *Compl. Dict. Abbrev.* 8/1 **aka*, also known as. **1970** *New Yorker* 5 Dec. 142/1 (Advt.), Cassius Clay, a.k.a. Muhammud Ali. **1982** *Times* 8 Nov. 11/1 He is perhaps a shade too comfortable and not enough of a cad as Johnson, aka Ramirez, the outlaw. **1902** *Dog Fancier* Jan. 3/2 The dog show will be under *A.K.C. rules. **1983** *Christian Science Monitor* 18 Aug. B 22 It [*sc.* the Dog Museum of America] is located in the same building where the AKC has its headquarters. **1951** *Joint Matric. Board Gen. Cert. Exam. Reg.* 6 If a language is to be specially approved at the *A level. **1952** *Jrnl. Educ.* May 220/2 The award of an 'O' level pass on the 'A' level papers. **1922** *Round Table* Mar. 409 The federal conference of the *A.L.P., held at Perth in June, 1918. **1973** *Nation Rev.* (Melbourne) 31 Aug. 1434/1 Will the ALP grow a new set of wings? **1851** *Puttick & Simpson Catal.* 29 July, Autograph Letters 1, Letters autograph and signed are thus marked '*A.L.s.' **1962** *Automatic Data Processing Gloss.* (U.S. Bureau of Budget) 2/2 *ALU. **1984** *Byte* Jan. 135/1 A basic operation of the ALU will be to accept two 16-bit inputs and to produce a 32-bit product. **1918** *Times* 6 Sept. 3/2 It is notified in Army Orders that officers.. who have been awarded the Albert Medal are now entitled to add the distinctive letters '*A.M.' after their names. **1944** *A.M. [see amplitude 6 d]. **1962** E. Snow *Other Side of River* (1963) xlvi. 352 The hi-fi set and typewriter have already been stolen and only a worthless AM set remains. **1982** *Giant Bk. Electronics Projects* i. 27 Reduce hash picked up on AM broadcast sets. **1911** *Sunset* Sept. 284/1 Now and then the ducks left their pond and waddled pompously across the lawn, as if to let the *A.M.A. know that the 'quacks' had a right to membership, too. **1959** *New Statesman* 13 June 833/3 One cannot help wondering whether obstruction by the AMA has played any part in preventing Eckstein's book from being published earlier. **1984** *N.Y. Times* 24 Feb. 1A/6 (*heading*) A.M.A. bids doctors voluntarily freeze their fees for a year. [**1870** *Catholic Times* 13 Aug 1/3 (*heading*) A.M.G.D.] **1877** E. S. Dallas *Kettner's Bk. of Table* 279 Another liqueur, Bénédictine..is consecrated with the letters *A.M.D.G. (Ad majorem Dei gloriam). **1965** N. Freeling *Criminal Conversation* II. xiii. 148 We had to write at the top of the page..the Jesuit motto A.M.D.G. **1985** *Church Times* 29 Nov. 13/1 Men and women must be freed from oppression. But freed for what? By way of answer it is always possible to fall back on the Jesuits' formula AMDG. **1953** *Keesing's Contemp. Archives* 13006/1 Mr. Albert Luthuli (president-general of the *A.N.C.). **1959** *New Statesman* 6 June 779/1 The ensuing ban on Luthuli was timed to prevent him.. from presiding..at a special national ANC conference in Johannesburg. **1984** *Daily Tel.* 24 Mar. 16/1 For many years the ANC was a peaceful organisation dedicated to changing South Africa through non-violent means. **1912** F. K. Walter *Abbrev. & Techn. Terms Book Catal.* 1 *A.N.S. Autograph note signed. **1957** *Ann. Rep. Council Preservation of Rural Eng. 1956–7* 32/1 The Breckland area of Norfolk and Suffolk has also been considered..for designation as an *A.O.N.B. but rejected as unsuitable. **1973** *Times* 21 Apr. 14/5 Official AONB status allows government grants to be paid for tree-planting and removal of eyesores and enhancement. **1981** *Economist* 24 Jan. 72/2 Together national parks, AONBs and SSIs cover some 21% of the land area of England and Wales. **1879** *Chicago Tribune* 4 Mar. 5/4 Now, the *A.P. may be a very wicked institution, but a 'Monopoly' it is not. **1947** *Mem. Evidence Subm. to Royal Comm. on Press* I. 14 The full A.P. service is provided to Press Association and a selection of items is distributed to subscribers in this country. **1960** *Acronyms Dict.* (Gale Research Co.) 38 **APB*, all points bulletin. (Police call.) **1973** A. Burton *Police Telecommunications* viii. 255 The necessity occurs..to broadcast to all listening ears and stations a variety of general information broadcasts... These involve..robberies, burglaries..and general informational broadcasts. It is for this reason that the term 'all points bulletin (APB)' was adopted as being more descriptive of the intended use than 'general alarm'. **1979** A. Hailey *Overload* IV. xvii. 382 A man..drove away in a Volkswagen van half an hour before the place was raided. The police have issued an APB for the van. **1943** W. G. Sears *Materia Medica for Nurses* xi. 134 Tablets containing aspirin mixed with other drugs are..commonly used, e.g. Compound aspirin tablet... Tab. *A.P.C., containing aspirin.., phenacetin.., caffeine. **1970** G. Jackson *Let.* 30 Mar. in *Soledad Brother* (1971) 200 When I ask for medication the M.T.A. gives me an APC or two. **1924** *Circular U.S. Bureau of Standards* No. 154. 2 The American Petroleum Institute, the U.S. Bureau of Mines, and the U.S. Bureau of Standards in December, 1921, agreed to recommend that in the future only the scale based on the modulus 141.5 be used in the petroleum-oil industry, and that it be known as the *A.P.I. scale. **1958** *Times Rev. Industry* June 59/1 Crude oil prices are usually quoted on a scale..the heavier oil commanding..say 2 cents a barrel for each degree A.P.I. more than the lighter. **1984** *N.Y. Times* 26 Feb. II. 39/2 Check the product's specific gravity (density and viscosity). It should have an API range between 30 and 40 degrees. **1966** *AFIPS Conf. Proc.* XXIX. 677/2 *APL was conceived at the General Motors Research Laboratories to satisfy the need for convenient data handling techniques in a high-level language. Standing for *associative programming language*, it is designed to be embedded in PL/I as an aid to the user dealing with data structures in which associations are expressed. **1979** *Sci. Amer.* Dec. 90/1 An even more highly developed language in terms of the manipulation of arrays, indeed the most sophisticated of any of the programming languages in this respect, is APL. **1984** *N.Y. Times* 8 Jan. XII. 7/3 He taught himself how to program by sitting at a terminal with a book on APL. **1979** *Money Which?* Sept. 502/2 There are plans to make all lenders quote an *annual percentage rate of charge* (**APR*) worked out in a set way. **1983** *Which?* Oct. 450/3 Ask for written details about payment—find out the difference between cash and credit prices, the terms of any loans you're offered, and what the APR is. **1986** *Oxford Times* 15 Aug. 19/1 (Advt.), Fiat Uno 45... Total credit price £4,432.63. 0% APR. **1969** *Railway Mag.* Jan. 22/2 To overcome the lateral forces on passengers when such a fast train negotiates a curve, the *A.P.T. will incorporate a hydraulically-operated vehicle-body tilting mechanism which would be capable of 'banking' the bodies of the vehicles by up to 9 deg. to either side. **1971** *New Scientist* 10 June 624/2 The APT is going to be the common or garden inter-city train of the future. **1976** P. R. White *Planning for Public Transport* viii. 173 The first APTs to enter service will probably work the London-Glasgow run. **1984** *Time* 5 Nov. 91/3 Some individuals will develop the full-blown syndrome, others will simply manifest the flulike symptoms of AIDS-related complex (*ARC). *Ibid.*, Some ARC patients do get better. **1986** *N.Y. Rev. Bks.* 16 Jan. 43/1 It was also held to be the cause of the milder form of the illness known as AIDS-related complex (ARC) — a group of symptoms including swollen lymph glands in several parts of the body, night sweating, substantial weight loss, and recurrent diarrhea. **1929** *Amer. Standards Assoc. Year Bk.* 7/2 The *ASA limits itself strictly to those fields in which engineering methods apply. **1943** *Jrnl. Optical Soc. Amer.* XXXIII. 479/2 For general civilian use it would be more satisfactory to employ a name indicating that this value was related to speed. The term *American Standard Speed Number* was..chosen... The initials ASA may be used in connection with numerical values of Speed Number when determined in accordance with the complete method. **1976** *Early Music* Oct. 451/1 All films have a speed number on the carton—an ASA number —which indicates how sensitive the film is to light. **1955** R. J. Schwartz *Compl. Dict. Abbrev.* 16/3 **ASAP*,..as soon as possible (US Army). **1977** *Times Educ. Suppl.* 21 Oct. 51/5 (Advt.), Required A.S.A.P.: Young enthusiastic teacher to take P.E. **1977** *Daily Tel.* 7 Dec. 25 (Advt.), Do it a.s.a.p. He will be happy to talk to you. **1985** *Washington Post* 11 Aug. G4/3 It is selfish and inconsiderate for a guest [at a party] to conclude that he/she will not be entertained adequately and must therefore bail out ASAP. **1978** *Church Times* 14 July 4/4 To exclude the psalms from the *ASB would be to hasten their [*sc.* hymns'] decline. **1984** *Daily Tel.* 8 Mar. 18/5 There are parishes who have welcomed the freshness of ASB services. **1906** *Army & Navy Gaz.* 2 June 510/2 C.S.M. Yates, *A.S.C., Dublin. **1941** W. Fortescue *Trampled Lilies* xxviii. 267 She continued to cope throughout the day, marshalling her men like a General of the A.S.C. [**1963** F. D. Fawcett *Cycl. Initials & Abbrev.* 13/2 *ASEA*, Assocn. of S.E. Asia.] **1967** *Times* 9 Aug. 4/1 Leaders of five Asian countries today called for collective action to prevent outside interference in the region..after signing the joint declaration setting up the new Association of South-East Asian Nations (*A.S.E.A.N.). **1968** *Economist* 23 Mar. 33/1 We must not think that Asean is a common market. **1968** *Ann. Reg. 1967* 91 Early in August, Malaysia and Singapore participated together with Thailand, the Philippines, and Indonesia in the establishment in Bangkok of the Association of South East Asian Nations (ASEAN). **1977** *Bangladesh Times* 19 Jan. 11/6 The meeting would mark the first anniversary of the ASEAN summit meeting in Bali last year. **1983** *Listener* 2 June 16/1 Hanoi said it was pulling out an unspecified number of these as a gesture of good will towards Vietnam's non-Communist neighbours in ASEAN. **1968** *Christian Science Monitor* 30 Jan. 5/1 Most recently there is the formation of the brand new Action on Smoking and Health (*ASH) to act as a legal arm of the antismoking forces. **1971** C. Fletcher in R. G. Richardson *Proc. Second World Conf. Smoking & Health* (1972) 6 As chairman of ASH I also wish to express our thanks..for..financial support to help voluntary agencies to collaborate in action with the effects of legislative measures. **1983** *Listener* 30 June 36/1 After talking to ASH..I use the word 'lethal' advisedly. **1965** W. C. Stokoe et al. *Dict. Amer. Sign Lang.* 293 Some 'signs' for numbers in *ASL are simply configurations shown as letters are. **1983** A. Neisser *Other Side of Silence* i. 16 They..had spent five years trying to teach ASL to Washoe. **1958** *Aero-Space Terms* 4/1 *ASM, air-to-surface missile. **1926** J. Saville *Let.* (unpubl.) 12 May, Mr. Denville wants you to do *A.S.M. **1949** K. S. Allen *A.B.C. of Stagecraft for Amateurs* iv. 30 The A.S.M. often combines the duties of a stage-hand with that of 'props' or stage-carpenter, or for any useful purpose around the stage. **1982** S. Brett *Murder Unprompted* xviii. 156 He had a word with the A.S.M. before the show. **1967** in Hughes & Pollins *Trade Unions in Gt. Brit.* (1973) xliii. 200 A new body—the Association of Scientific, Technical and Managerial Staffs—would be established. The Executive Council of the *ASTMS would consist of six members each from the Executives of the present unions. **1979** Jenkins & Sherman *White-Collar Unionism* ii. 31 ASTMS..has over 440,000 members and is a general union. **1944** *U.S. War Dept. Techn. Man., TM 11–467* 364 *A.S.V. **1945** *Flight* 23 Aug. 210/1 A centimetric A.S.V., the device carried in Coastal Command aircraft which directed them to the surfaced U-boat. **1921** *Harper's Mag.* Oct. 632/2 Organized in 1885 for long-lines construction, the '*A. T. & T.' had grown steadily more powerful. **1965** J. A. Michener *Source* (1966) 884 Until the day when A.T. and T. drops to forty and you have an economic crisis. **1976** *Washington Post* 19 Apr. A6/2 AT&T ..owns most intercity long distance lines. **1949** *Jrnl. R. Aeronaut. Soc.* LIII. 959/2 The inefficiency of *A.T.C. (Air Traffic Control) procedures and patterns. **1934** *Railway Mag.* Apr. 290 (*caption*) Diagram of Signum *A.T.C. system. **1958** *Engineering* 14 Mar. 336/1 Before the Second World War..in general, the Great Western Railway had A.T.C. and the other British railways did not. **1976** *Business Week* 28 June 45 On the basis of the trial the average cost of a transaction with 60 *ATMs would be $1.25 vs. 40 cents using a live teller. **1979** *Good Housekeeping* Aug. 215/1 To use an ATM you need a plastic bank card. *a* **1912** *Spalding & Hodge's Paper Terminol.* ii. 1 Animal Tub-sized, or *A.T.S., is a term employed to denote the more costly method of passing the manufactured sheet through a bath or 'tub' of animal size. **1970** *Time* 23 Nov. 41 Marauders on *ATVs or snowmobiles occasionally strip hunters' shacks or loot vacation homes. **1987** *Washington Post* 21 Apr. A3/1 The rockhounds, the ranchers.., the All Terrain Vehicle (ATV) enthusiasts, all are resolved to..try to stop the idea. **1957** *Daily Mail* 4 Sept. 12/8 *ATV announce *The £4,000 Question* on September 14. **1927** H. N. Russell et al. *Astron.* I. App. p.i., 1 astronomical unit (*A.U.) = 1·4945 × 10^8 km. **1975** Kaye & Laby *Tables Physical & Chem. Constants* (ed. 14) i. 129 Primary constants. Measure of 1 AU... 1·49600 × 10^{11}m. **1984** *Aviation Week & Space Technol.* 2 Jan. 48/3 Halley will be..0·97 AU from Earth at the time of the Giotto encounter. **1971** *Times* 9 Nov. 19/7 The 1.4 m member *AUEW—the most important craft union in the country. **1986** *Financial Times* 13 Aug. 10/3 In the days of the joint GEC-Hitachi there were a number of unions recognised at the plant—the EETPU (716 members), AUEW (223), ASTMS (87), [etc.]. **1965** *New Statesman* 6 Aug. 174/1 His colleagues would happily settle for the single-member-constituency *AV system. **1983** *Financial Times* 2 Nov. 15 It is most unlikely in Australia, where the alternative vote (AV) system applies in the most important elections. **1868** B. F. Westcott *Gen. View Hist. Eng. Bible* iii. 334 In the later (Irish) editions of the 'Rhemes and Doway' Bible and New Testament there are considerable alterations, and the text is far nearer to that in the *A.V. **1982** G. Hammond *Making of Eng. Bible* 237 The same phrase occurs twice in Genesis... Tyndale renders both as 'speak kindly'. The AV follows his rendering. **1953** *N.Y. Times* 29 Mar. §vi. 9/3 The structure of terror in Hungary consists of many overlapping..agencies: It is a pyramid with the *Allam Vedelmi Hasotag* (State Security Authority, or secret police), at the apex. *A.V.H., which has 50,000 men and women in its force, is..the party's harsh punitive arm. **1956** *New Statesman* 22 Dec. 818/1 The.. lynching of many persons, A.V.H. men and Party members in particular. **1929** T. E. Lawrence *Let.* 22 Jan. (1938) v. 640, I could do nothing, with the *A.V.M., of what I'd hoped. **1956** *Times* 29 Nov. 10/5 The Kadar Government is also concerned..at the treatment being meted out by the population to former members of the *A.V.O. (secret police). **1921** *Outing* (U.S.) June 137/1, I was surprised to find one day that unless I left the following morning to rejoin my regiment I would be an '*a-w-o-l'. **1929** *Amer. Speech* IV. 351 Absence without leave is a military offense designated by the abbreviation awol, usually written without periods and sometimes with small letters, in the pronunciation of which each letter is pronounced. **1949** Wodehouse *Mating Season* x. 98 Nothing sticks the gaff into your chatelaine more than a guest being constantly a.w.o.l. **1957** B. & C. Evans *Dict. Contemp. Amer. Usage* 9/2 awol ..in World War I..was pronounced as four letters; in World War II, it was pronounced as a word. **1911** C. E. W. Bean '*Dreadnought' of Darling* xxxviii. 337 The situation, however, was supposed to be solved when the *A.W.U... issued instructions that the train must not be interfered with. **1983** *Financial Times* 25 Nov. 6/1 Mr. Frank Mitchell, federal secretary of the..Australian Workers' Union (AWU), issued an immediate rebuff to Mr. Dolan, saying work would proceed. **1985** *Business Week* 2 Dec. 86/2 Technically known as azidothymidine (*AZT), the drug has been tested on only 20 patients at the National Cancer Institute and Duke University. **1987** *Daily Tel.* 19 Jan. 4/8 Researchers said patients tested with AZT had benefitted in many ways, including improved neurological functions and reduced instances of opportunistic infections. **1987** *Sci. Amer.* Apr. 75/1 The prospect of long-term use has.. heightened concerns about AZT's considerable toxicity to bone-marrow cells, the precursors of blood cells.

IV. *Phrases.* **1. A per se**: the letter A when standing by itself, especially when making a word.

The word *a* was formerly spelt 'a-per-se, *a*,' that is, '*a* by itself makes the word *a*,' whence also the letter itself was sometimes called *A-per-se-A*. So also *I per se, O per se, &-per-se* (*and-per-se, an-per-se, ampersee*).

Hence **b.** *fig.* (also formerly **Apersie, Apersey, A per C**) the first, chief, most excellent, most distinguished, or unique person or thing; one who is *facile princeps*, or in modern phrase, *A 1*.

1475 Henryson *Test. of Cresseide* 78 (Speght's Chaucer) The floure and A per se of Troie and Grece. *a* **1500** *MS. Cantab.* Ff. ii. 38 f. 51 Thow schalt be an apersey, my sone, In mylys ij, or thre. **1501** Dunbar *Poems, Supplt.* (1865) 277 London, thowe arte of townes A per se. **1567** Drant *Horace Epist.* II. i If they make them A per se Aes that none are like to them. **1578** *Gude and Godlie Ballates* 128 Christ Jesus is ane A per C, And peirlesse Prince of all mercy. **1602** Middleton *Blurt* III. iii Who that is the a-per-se of all, the very cream of all.

2. A 1. Applied in Lloyd's Register to ships in first-class condition, as to hull and stores alike. 'The character A denotes New ships, or Ships Renewed or Restored. The Stores of Vessels are designated by the figures 1 and 2; 1 signifying that the Vessel is well and sufficiently found.' —*Key to the Register.* Added to the names of ships, as 'the fast-sailing ship "Sea-breeze", A 1 at Lloyd's', or used attributively, 'the splendid A 1 clipper-built ship "Miranda".'

Hence, *fig.* (familiar and savouring of commercial phraseology), ***A 1***, or in U.S. ***A No. 1***, is used adjectively for 'prime, first-class'.

1837 Dickens *Pickwick* 341 (1847) 'He must be a first-rater,' said Sam. 'A 1,' replied Mr. Roker. **1851** Mrs. Stowe *Dred* I. 313 An A number one cook, and no mistake. **1861** Col. G. Wolseley (*Reynolds' Newsp.* Nov. 24) The Chinese police are certainly A 1 at such work.

† **a**, *a.*[1] (*definite numeral*). *Obs.* or *dial.* [OE. *án*, one, of which the *n* began to disappear before a cons. about 1150. In the definite numeral sense, *án* and *á*, following the ordinary course of OE. long *á*, became in the south bef. 1300, *on* (*oon, one*), *o* (*oo*); and eventually *o* became obs., leaving *one* as the form in all positions; while *an* and *a*, pronounced lightly and indistinctly, became the 'indefinite article.' See next word. But in the north *an* (or *ane*) and *a* were written in both senses, the stress or emphasis alone distinguishing the numeral from the article.]

Apocopate form of *an*, *ane*, used only before a consonant. See AN(E, O *a.*, and ONE.

c **1200** *Trin. Coll. Hom.* 39 Ure drihten drof fele deules togedere ut of á man, þe was of his wit. c **1300** *K. Alis.* 5955 An eighe he had in his vys, And a foot, and no moo Iwys. c **1350** HAMPOLE *Prose Tr.* 32 Some ere of a tre and some er of anoþer. **1483** CAXTON, *Geoffroi de la Tour*, lf. iiii b, They satte att dyner in a hall and the quene in another.

A in the various forms *a, ae, eae, eea, yea, yà*, is still the regular form of the numeral *one* when used adjectively, in the northern dialects, the absolute form being *an, ane, ean, yen, yàn*, etc.

a (toneless ə; emph. eɪ), *a.*[2] (*'indefinite article'*). Before a vowel-sound **an** (ən, emph. æn). [A weakening of OE. *án*, 'one', already by 1150 reduced before a cons. to *a*. About the same time the numeral began to be used in a weakened sense (usually unexpressed in OE. as *he wæs gód man*, 'he was a good man'; cf. Chron. 1137 'he wæs god munec & god man,' and 1140 'he wæs *an* yuel man'); becoming in this sense proclitic and toneless, *ăn, ă*, while as a numeral it remained long, *ān, ā*, and passed regularly during the next cent. into *ōn, ō*; see the prec. word. Though *an* began to sink to *a* in midl. dial. by 1150, it often remained bef. a cons. to 1300; bef. sounded *h*, *an* was retained after 1600, and somet. after 1700, as *an house, an heifer, an hermitage*. The present rule is to use *an* bef. a vowel-sound (incl. *h* mute, as *an hour*); *a* bef. a consonant-sound (including *h* sounded, and *eu-, u-* with sound of *yū-*, as *a host, a one, a eunuch, a unit*). But in *unaccented* syllables, many, perhaps most, writers still retain *an* bef. sounded *h*, some even bef. *eu, u*, as *an historian, an euphonic vowel, an united appeal*, though this is all but obsolete in speech, and in writing *a* becomes increasingly common in this position. *A, an* has been indeclinable in midl. and north. dial. since 1150, but vestiges of the OE. declension (as nom. f. *ane*, gen. m. *anes*, gen. & dat. f. *are*, acc. m. *anne*) remained much later in southern. In north. *an* was frequently written *ane* (with *e* mute), the use of *a* and *an(e* being as elsewhere; but about 1475 Scottish writers began to use *ane* in all positions, a practice which prevailed till the disuse of literary Scotch after 1600. Quotations illustrating the history of the forms:—

c **1131** *O.E. Chron.* (Laud. MS.) anno 1125 Se man ðe hafde an pund he ne mihte cysten ænne peni at anne market. c **1150** *Ibid.* anno 1137, Wel þu myhtes faren all a dæis fare, sculdest þu neure finden man in tune sittende. c **1175** *Lamb. Hom.* 221 God þa ȝeworhte aenne man óf láme. a **1200** *Trin. Coll. Hom.* 47 ȝif hie was riche wimman, a lomb. 1205 LAYAMON I. 3 A [*masc.*] Frenchis clerc, Wace wes ihoten, þa luuede he a [*fem.*] maide, þeo was Lauine mawe. 1483 CAXTON *Geoffroi de la Tour* E 4 A baronnesse, ryght a hyghe and noble lady of lygnage. 1532 MORE *Conf. Tyndale* Wks. 1557 447/2 We haue two articles in english, *a & the*: *a* or *an* (for bothe is one article, the tone before a consonant the tother before a vowell) is commen to euery thinge almost. 1611 BIBLE *Acts* vii. 47 But Solomon built him an house [1881 *Revised* a house]. *Ibid.* vii. 27 An eunuch of great authority [*Revised* a eunuch]. 1732 POPE *Essay Man* iv. 78 Nor in an hermitage set Dr. Clarke. 1763 JOHNSON *Ascham* Wks. 1816 XII. 306 An yearly pension. 1823 LINGARD *Hist. Eng.* VI. 219 An eulogium on his talents. 1850 MRS. JAMESON *Sac. & Leg. Art* 206 A eulogium of Mary Magdalene. 1857 LEVER *Tom Burke* xxxix. 387 A eulogium on their conduct. 1843 *Penny Cycl.* XXVI. 25/2 In November [1835] the great seal was put to a charter creating a University of London. 1847 TENNYSON *Princess* i. 149 All wild to found an University For maidens.

About the 15th cent. *a* or *an* was commonly written in comb. with the following sb. as *aman, anoke, anele*. When they were separated, much uncertainty prevailed as to the division; thus we find *a nend, a noke, a nadder, an adder, an est*. In some words a mistaken division has passed into usage: see ADDER, NEWT.

c **1420** *Chron. Vilod.* 515 And ryȝt with þat worde he made a nend.]

A is strictly *adjective* and can only be used with a substantive following. Meanings:—

1. One, some, any: the oneness, or indefiniteness, being implied rather than asserted. It is especially used in first introducing an object to notice, which object, after being introduced by *a*, is kept in view by *the*; as 'I plucked *a* flower; this is *the* flower.' Used before a noun singular, and its attributes.

a. Ordinarily before the name of an individual object or notion, or of a substance, quality or state *individualized*, and before a collective noun, as *a tree, a wish, an ice, a beauty, a new ink, a greater strength, a second youth, a legion, a hundred, a pair*.

c **1175** *Lamb. Hom.* 121 Vre drihten wes iled to sleȝe al swa me dede a scep. **1297** R. GLOUC. 78 He hadde a gret ost in a lutel stonde. **1847** LONGF. *Ev.* I. i. 59 A celestial brightness—a more ethereal beauty. *Mod.* An ink that will retain its fluidity; a permanent black. Is it a red wheat? What kind of a wine is this? To walk out in a pouring rain. There was a something—of that we may be sure. Oh, a mere nothing.

b. Also before proper names, used connotatively, with reference to the qualities of the individual; or figuratively as the type of a class.

1596 SHAKS. *Merch. Ven.* IV. i. 223 A Daniel come to iudgement, yea a Daniel! **1665–9** BOYLE *Occ. Refl.* IV. xii. 245 (1675) Our own History affords us a Henry the Fifth. **1683** D. A. *Art of Converse* 53 Cannot ye praise a philosopher unless ye say he is an Aristotle. c **1830** *A Fable* (in *4th Irish Schbk.* 50) He whom his party deems a hero, His foes a Judas or a Nero. **1855** TENNYSON *Maud* I. iv. 46 Shall I weep if a Poland fall? shall I shriek if a Hungary fail?

c. *A* follows the adj. in *many a, such a, what a!* and the obs. or dial. *each a, which a*; it follows any adj. preceded by *how, so, as, too*, as *how large a sum*; and in earlier Eng. the genit. phrases *what manner, no manner, whatkins, nakins, what sort*, etc., as *what manner a man* = cujusmodi homo? (See these words.)

In none of these was the *a* found in Old English.

Many a is not to be confused with the approximative *a many* (see 2). *Such a* was earlier (2–3) *a such*. *Each a* and *which a* survive in the north, as *ilk a, whilk a*. *What manner a*, and its likes soon became corrupted to *what manner of*. See A *prep.*[2] = of.

1593 SHAKS. *3 Hen. VI*, v. iv. 12 Ah, what a shame! ah, what a fault were this! **1611** —— *Wint. T.* v. iii. 140 And haue (in vaine) said many A prayer vpon her graue. **1611** BIBLE *Ruth* iv. 1 Ho, such a one! [*Later reprints*, such *an* one.] —— *James* iii. 5 Behold, how great a matter a little fire kindleth [**1881** *Revised* Behold, how much wood is kindled by how small a fire.] *Mod.* Too high a price for so small an advantage. As fine a child as you will see.

d. With nouns of multitude, after which the gen. sign, or prep. *of*, has been omitted, *a* comes apparently before pl. nouns. Compare *a score of men, a dozen (of) men, hundreds of men, a hundred men, a thousand miles*; and the obs. *a certain of men* or *a certain men*, now *certain men*. (See under these words.)

c **1225** *Sawles Warde* 251 þah ich hefde a þusent tungen of stele. **1523** LD. BERNERS *Froissart* I. lxxx. 101 A certayne of varlettes and boyes, who ran away. *Ibid.* xiv. 13 A certayne noble knightis.. she kept. **1600** SHAKS. *A.Y.L.* I. i. 2 It was upon this fashion bequeathed me by will but poore a thousand crownes. **1653** HOLCROFT *Procopius* I. 32 Belisarius commanded Bessas with a 1000. selected men to charge them. **1860** TYNDALL *Glaciers* II. §11. 290 He had to retreat more than a dozen times.

2. *A* with numeral adjectives removes their definiteness, or expresses an approximate estimate: *some, a matter of, about*; as *a sixty fathom, a six years, a two hundred spears*; so also *a many men, a few retainers*, the latter already in OE. *áne feawa* (*áne* plural = some). An exceedingly common use of *a* in 14–16th c. Now obs. except in *a few, a great many, a good many* (*a many, a good few, a small few*, dialectal). See also under these words.

c **1000** *Gosp. Nicod.* (1698) 5 Ane feawa worda. **1297** R. GLOUC. 18 Þe kyng with a fewe men hymself flew. **1366** MAUNDEV. 57 That See is wel a 6 myle of largenesse in bredth. c **1386** CHAUCER *Squyres T.* 275 And up they risen, a ten other a twelve. **1523** LD. BERNERS *Froissart* I. xxxvii. 50 A ii hundred speres. *Ibid.* xxxviii. 51, A xx. M. Almaynes. **1551** TURNER *Herbal* II. 7 Stepe them a fiue or sixe dayes in vineger. **1595** DRAKE *Voyage* (Hakl. Soc.) 5 He had a three hundred men more in his squadron. **1600** SHAKS. *A.Y.L.* I. i. 121 And a many merry men with him. **1611** BIBLE *Luke* ix. 28 An eight days after these sayings. **1684** BUNYAN *Pilg. Prog.* II *Introd.* Have also overcome a many evils. **1833** TENNYSON *Miller's Dau.* 221 They have not shed a many tears. c **1860** H. BONAR *Hymn* A few more struggles here, A few more partings o'er, A few more toils, a few more tears, And we shall weep no more. *Mod.* A great many acquaintances, a good many well-wishers, a few tried friends.

3. In a more definite sense: One, a certain, a particular; the same. Now only used in a few phrases like *once on a day; two at a time; two, three, all of a sort, a size, a price, an age*.

c **1220** *St. Katherine* (Abb. Cl.) 1 Constantin & Maxence weren on a time.. hehest in Rome. **1523** LD. BERNERS *Froissart* I. cx. 132 In his dayes, ther was at a tyme, a great tournayeng before Cambray. **1551** ROBINSON *More's Utopia* 45 The killing of a man or the takyng of his money... were both a matter. **1553–87** FOXE *A. & M.* 695/1 (1596) Whether the christians yeeld to them, or yeeld not, all is a matter. **1601** SHAKS. *All's Well* I. iii. 244 He and his Phisitions Are of a minde. **1602** —— *Haml.* v. ii. 277 These Foyles haue all a length. **1694** BP. TENISON in Evelyn *Mem.* (1857) III. 344 Six little pieces of coin (all of a sort) found in an urn by a ploughman. **1701** SWIFT Wks. (1755) II. I. 25 The power of these princes.. was much of a size with that of the kings in Sparta. *Mod. Provb.* Fowls of a feather flock together.

4. 'Denoting the proportion of one thing to another.' J.; chiefly of rate or price: *in each, to* or *for each*; as a hundred *a* year, twenty pounds *a* man, thirty shillings *a* head, sixpence *an* ounce, a penny *a* line. This was originally the preposition *a*, OE. *an, on*, defining time, as in twice *a* day; whence by slight extension, a penny *a* day (*par* jour, *per* diem). Then, being formally identified with the indef. art., *a, an* was extended analogically from time, to space, measure, weight, number, as a penny *a* mile, sixpence *a* pound (*la* livre), tenpence *a* hundred, so much *a* head. See A *prep.*[1] 8 b.

c **1000** *Ags. Gosp.* Luke xvii. 4 Seofon siðum on dæȝ. a **1200** *Trin. Coll. Hom.* 67 Enes o dai. *Ibid.* 109 Anes á dái. **1382** WYCLIF *Matt.* xx. 2 A peny for the day. **1526** TINDALE *ib.* A peny a daye. **1584** W. E(LDERTON) *A new Yorkshire song* [Yorke, Yorke, for my Monie, etc.] *Yorksh. Anth.* (1851) 2 And they shot for twentie poundes a bowe. **1725** DE FOE *Voyage round the World* (1840) 50 His men to whom I gave four pieces of eight a man. **1794** SOUTHEY *Botany Bay Ecl.* 3 Wks. II. 82 To be popt at like pigeons for sixpence a day. **1849** MACAULAY *Hist. Eng.* I. 305 Three hundred and eighty thousand pounds a year.

a, also **a'** (ɔː), *a.*[3] [from ALL; *l* lost as in *alms, talk*. *A* occurs rarely and doubtfully in ME. north. or n. midl.; *a'* is the current spelling in modern literary Scotch.] = ALL.

1280 *Havelok* 610 He sal hauen in his hand A denemark and england. **1795** BURNS III. 234 For a' that, an' a' that, His ribbond, star, an' a' that, The man o' independent mind He looks an' laughs at a' that.

†**a** (ə), *pron. Obs.* or *dial.* [for *ha* = HE, HEO, HI, *he, she, (it), they*, when stressless; chiefly in southern and western writers. *A* for *he* (*ha* in the *Ayenbit*) is common from 3 to 5; in the dramatists of 6, 7, it is frequent in representations of familiar speech. *A* for *ha, heo*, = *she, they*, is rarer and somewhat doubtful in Layamon, but common in Trevisa; not found after 1450. Owing to the persistence of grammatical gender in the south, Trevisa also uses *a* = *he* of inanimate objects, and so apparently = *it*, which takes its place when rationality and sex are substituted for gender in the concord of the pronouns. The s.w. dialects still apply *he* to inanimate objects. See further under HE.]

1. He.

1250 LAYAMON (*later text*) I. 59 þat a lond a verde sechinge ware he mihte wonie [**1205** he ferde sechinde]. c **1315** SHOREHAM *Poems* 3 Ac a deythe and he not [i.e. wots not] wanne. **1387** TREVISA *Higden* (*Norm. Inv.* in Morris *Specim.* 341) Kyng Edward hadde byhote duc William þat a scholde be kyng after hym if he dyede wyþoute chyldern. c **1440** *Arthur* 370 He went ouer to þe hulle syde, And þere a fonde a wommane byde. **1553** SIR T. GRESHAM (in Froude *Hist. Eng.* V. xxix. 472/2) For that the retailer doth sell.. a doth not only take away the living of the Merchant. **1584** PEELE *Arraign. Paris* II. i. 22 Tut, Mars hath horns to butt withal, although no bull 'a shows, 'A never needs to mask in nets, 'a fears no jealous foes. **1604** SHAKS. *Haml.* III. iii. 74 Now might I doe it, but now a is a praying, And now Ile doo't, and so a goes to heauen. **1610** *Histriomastix* i. 157 A speaks to you players: I am the poet.

2. She.

1205 LAYAMON III. 127 Ne beo ich nauere bliðe, þa wile a [the queen] beoð aliue. c **1220** *St. Katherine* (Abb. Cl.) 136 þus hwil a wiste hire & þohte ai to witen hire meiden in meidenhad. **1387** TREVISA *MS. Cott. Vesp.* D. vii. 29 b, He ran home to uore & prayede hys wyf þat hue wolde helpe for to saue hym,.. bote a dude þe contrary.

3. It (for he).

1387 TREVISA (in Morris *Specim.* 334) Yn þis ylond groweþ a ston þat hatte gagates; ȝef me axeþ hys feyrnesse—a ys blak as gemmes buþ.. a brenneþ yn water & quencheþ in oyle.. ȝif a ys yfroted & yhat, a holdeþ what hym neyȝheþ; ȝef me axeþ hys goodnes, hyt heeleþ þe dropesy & hyt be ydrongke, etc. c **1500** *Spirit. Rem.* (in *Nugæ Poeticæ* 67) Cordys contrycio ys the too [= second] A wasshyth the woundes as doth a welle.

4. They.

1205 LAYAMON I. 149 Ouer se a icomen; hauene sone a nomen [**1250** Ouer see hii comen, and hauene hi nomen]. **1387** TREVISA *Higden* (*Descr. Brit.* in Morris *Specim.* 340) Þe kinges of Engelond woneþ alwey fer fram þat contray, for a buþ more yturnd to þe souþ contray; & ȝef a goþ to þe norþ contray, a goþ wiþ gret help & strengthe.

¶ *A* still retains all these meanings, and especially that of *he*, in southern and western dialects, where it appears as (ə, ə(r)). See Elworthy *Gramm. of West Somerset Dial.* 33, and Halliwell.

1853 AKERMAN *Wiltshire Tales* 169 One night a was coming whoame vrom market, and vell off's hos into the rood, a was zo drunk. **1864** TENNYSON *Northern Farmer* But Parson a comes an' a goos, an' a says it eäsy an' freeä. *Ibid.* Doctors, they knaws nowt, for a says what's nawways true: Naw soort o' koind o' use to saäy the things that a do.

In mod. north. dialects *a*, also *aa, ah, aw* (ɑː, ɔː) = I, being the first half of the diphthong (aɪ, ɔɪ).

1864 T. CLARKE *Jonny Shippard* (Westm. dial.) Let ma git theear, an a's mebbie preeave a bit aaldther ner tha tak ma ta be.

a, *v.* For *ha, ha'*, a worn-down form of HAVE (cf. French *a* from *habet*) when unaccented or obscure in compound verbal forms, or where the independent meaning is sunk in a phrase, as *might a been, would a said, should a thought, a done!* = have done, *a mind!* = have a mind. Exceedingly frequent in 13–17th c.; in later times chiefly in representations of colloquial or familiar speech, in which it is still often said, though infrequently written, except in specimens of local dialects, where also, under literary influence, it is generally spelt *ha*, *ha'*, although no *h* is pronounced.

1350 *Will. Palerne* 1177 A mynde on me lord, for þi moder love help me. **1366** Maundev. viii. 86 The Iewes wolde a stoned him. *c* **1400** *Apol. for Lollards*, I knowlech to a felid & seid þus. **1468** *Cov. Myst.* 38 (1841) Ha don; and answere me as tyght. **1477** Earl Rivers *Dictes* (Caxton) 13, & might a made you as euil as he. **1543** *Supp. to Hardyng* 105 Richard might..a saved hymself, if he would a fled awaie. **1556** *Chron. Grey Friars* 28 The byshoppe shulde a come agayne to Powlles, & a preched agayne. **1684** Bunyan *Pilg.* II. 84, I might a had Husbands afore now, tho' I spake not of it. **1864** Tennyson *Northern Farmer*, I done my duty by un, as I 'a done by the lond. **1864** Mrs. Lloyd *Ladies of Polcarrow* 149 We would a-had 'hurrahs' and a tar-barrel, Miss Loveday, ma'am. **1866** Mayne Reid *Headless Horseman* lxvii. 334 If 't hedn't a been for the savin' o' her, I'd a let 'em come on down the gully. **1952** E. Wilson *Tuesday & Wednesday* i, in *Equations of Love* 11 If I'd a known there was a luncheon party on I'd a stayed home. **1968** E. Gaines in E. Chapman *New Black Voices* (1972) 97 If I wasn't hungry, I wouldn't 'a' ate it at all.

b. In mod. use, repr. colloq. or dial. pronunc. of *have* in *could* (*must*, *should*, etc.) *have*: see COULDA, MUSTA, SHOULDA, etc.

†**a**, *adv. Obs.* Also **aa**, **o**, **oo**. [OE. *á*, *áwa*, cognate with ON. *æ̋*, OHG. *eo*, *io*, Goth. *aiw*, cf. *aiws* an age, L. *aevum*, Gr. αἰών and adv. αἰεί. This word became obs. in 13th c., being replaced by the cognate Norse word *aȝ*, *ai*, *ei*, *ay*, *aye*, still used. See AYE, and O.] Ever, aye, always.

a **1000** *Beowulf* 915 Gæð á wyrd swá hió sceal. *Ibid.* 1914 þæt þin [dóm] lyfað · áwa tó aldre. *c* **1175** *Lamb. Hom.* 183 Te engles .a. biholdeþ þé. **1205** Layamon II. 54 And a [**1250** euere] to ure liue · witen ure leoden. *c* **1220** *St. Kath.* 279 þat ha schulen lasten a. **1230** *Ancren Riwle* 36 World a buten ende. **1230** *Hali Meid.* 15 þer is a feht & mot beon aa nede.

a (ə), *prep.*[1] Also **o**. [A worn-down proclitic form of OE. preposition *an*, *on*. In compounds and common phrases this became *a* even in OE., as *abútan*, *a timan*. The separate *an* was labialized to *on*, which form also (in West Saxon) absorbed the prep. *in*, and so had the meanings *on*, *in*; *unto*, *into*, *to*. In 11th c., *on* began to be reduced before consonants to *o*, which from its tonelessness soon sank to *a* (ə). Before a vowel *an* was occasionally used; when emphatic *on* remained. The separate *a* is now rarely used, being replaced by the full *on*, *in*, or the various prepositions which represent them in modern idiom; except in a few verbal constructions, as *to go a begging*, *to set a going*; and in temporal distributive phrases, as *twice a day*, *once a year*, where it has been confused with the 'indefinite article.' See A *a.*[2] 4. But the preposition *a* really remains in a large number of combinations, where present spelling treats it as a prefix to the governed word, and the whole as a compound adverb, as *abed*, *afoot*, *aback*, *around*, *atop*, *afloat*, *asleep*, *alive*. As these combinations are now viewed as individual words, they will be found in their alphabetical places. The separate uses of *a*, treated here, are very numerous, but all included in those of OE. *on*.]

1. Superposition: on; as *a the ground*, *a water and a land*, *a the book*, *a the rood*, *a bed*, *a bench*, *a shipboard*, *a wheels*, *a foot*, *a horseback*. Obs. except in a few combinations, *abed*, *aboard*, *ashore*, *afield*, *afoot*, etc.

a **1200** *Moral Ode* in *Lamb. Hom.* 173 Wise men..a boken hit writen, þer [me] mei hit reden. **1205** Layamon III. 7 þa folc..þat þe eoden a uoten [**1250** afote]. **1230** *Ancren Riwle* 430 Ase ofte ase ȝe readeð out [= aught] o þisse boc. *c* **1420** Lydgate *Stor. Thebes* 1561 (Skeat) But he, allas! was mad light a foote. **1523** Ld. Berners *Froissart* I. xvii. 18 They are all a horsbacke. **1599** Shaks. *Hen. V*, IV. iii. 42 He..will stand a tip-toe. **1611** Chapman *May-Day* (*Plays* 1873) II. 328 Let her meditate a my late motion. **1616** Purchas *Pilg.*, *Desc. Ind.* (1864) 157 He almost first starued a ship-boord. **1645** Howell *Engl. Tears* 173/1 All my neighbour Countreys were a fire. **1861** *All Y. Round* V. 13 And made him trot, barefooted, on before Himself, who rode a horse-back.

2. Motion: on, upon, on to; as *a the ground*, *a the folk*, *a the stead*, *a field*, *a bed*. Obs. exc. as in prec. as *go a-shore*.

1205 Layamon I. 97 Moni eotend ic leide dead a þene grund. *c* **1305** *E.E. Poems*, *St. Katherine* 92 [Thou] þus fole maistres of clergie: bringest and settest a benche. **1523** Ld. Berners *Froissart* I. cxlvii. 176 The quene was brought a bedde of a fayre lady named Margarete.

3. Juxtaposition: on, at; chiefly in the phrases *a right* (or *left*) *half*, *a this* (or *that*) *side*, *a God's half* = on God's side or behalf; and *a-to-side* = a t' o side, on (the) one side, aside. Obs. exc. in comb.

c **1175** *Lamb. Hom.* 141 And þer stod a richt halue and a leeft: alse an castel wal. *c* **1380** *Sir Ferumbras* 1680 A þes half Mantrible þe grete Citee: ys þe brigge y-set. **1449** Pecock *Repressor* 336 In the daies of Princis A this side the Emperour Constantyn. **1477** Earl Rivers *Dictes* (Caxton) 1 To sette a parte alle ingratitude. **1483** Caxton *Geoffroi de la Tour* E. v, And bothe..wente and leyd them self abothe his sydes. **1600** Holland *Livy* xxxvii. xi. 950 Those vessels which lay atone side upon the land. **1684** Bunyan *Pilg.* II. 67 I thought he gave you something, because he called you a to-side.

†**4.** Position or situation: in; as *a thy hand*, *a the world*, *a the folk*, *a the shroud*, *a water*, *a blood*, *a Rome*. Obs.

c **1000** *Blickl. Hom.* 89 On bendum & o wope. *c* **1066** *O.E. Chron.* (Cott. MS.) an. 1011 Man nolde him átiman gafol beodon. **1205** Layamon I. 49 A þon heðene lawen [**1250** In þan heþene lawe]. *a* **1300** *Judas*, in *Reliq. Ant.* I. 144 Al it lavede a blode. **1401** *Pol. Poems* II. 43 Liȝtly a lewid man maye leyen hem a water. **1525** Ld. Berners *Froissart* II. ccxxxii. 721 So the bysshoppe returned and came into Almaygne, and founde the kyng a Conualence. **1608** Tourneur *Reveng. Tragœdie* v. i. 129 That's enow a' conscience! **1660** Harrington *Prerog. of Pop. Sov.* (1700) II. v. 362 Which is enough, a conscience!

5. General direction or position: in the direction of, towards; as, *a back*, *a fore*, *a far*, *a head*, *a side*. Still used in comb. *aback*, etc.

c **1420** Lydgate *Stor. Thebes* 1170 (Skeat *Spec. Eng. Lit.*) And the remnaunt amased drogh a bak.

6. Partition: in, into; as *a two*, *a three*, *a twelve*, *a pieces*. Obs. except in comb. *asunder*, *apart*.

c **1175** *Lamb. Hom.* 141 And þa fouwer weren ideled a twelue. *c* **1280** *E.E. Poems*, *Fall & Passion* 14 Hir þoȝt hir hert wol a two. **1398** Trevisa *Barth. De Pr. R.* III. xii. The vertu sensible þat meueþ is departid a thre [ed. **1535** on thre, **1582** in three]. **1509** Fisher *Wks.* (1876) 55 An other sawed a two. **1535** Coverdale *Acts* i. 18, & brast a sunder in the myddes. **1613** Shaks. *Hen. VIII*, v. iv. 80 Being torne a pieces. **1623** Bingham *Hist. Xenophon* 75 Their legs and sides crushed, and broken a peeces.

†**7.** Position in a series: at, in; as *a first*, *a last*, *a the(n) end*. Obs.

1205 Layamon III. 106 þ he com a þan ende. **1230** *Ancr. R.* 46 A last schal siggen, hwo se con: *Oremus*.

8. Time: in, on, by; as *a day*, *a night*, *an eve*, *a morrow*, *a Monday*, *a doom's day*. Occ. prefixed to OE. adverbial genitives *dæȝes* and *nihtes*, giving *a nights*, *now-a-days*. Obs. exc. in a few archaic phrases.

c **1000** *Ags. Gospels* Mark iv. 27, & sawe & arise daeȝes & nihtes [*Lindisf.* & slepeð & arisað on næht and on daeȝ. *Hatton*, & sawe & arise daiȝes & nihtes]. *Ibid.* Luke xxi. 37 He was on dæȝ on þam temple lærende . & on niht he eode & wunode on þam munte. **1205** Layamon II. 401 ȝif mon mihte mid crafte · a dæi oðer a nihte [**1250** Bi daiȝe oþer bi nihte]. *a* **1200** *Cotton Hom.* 239 A domes deie. **1362** Langland *P. Pl.* A i. 99 And not to faste a Friday. *c* **1430** *Syr Generides* 1797 Sith yesterday a eve, This sekenes first did him greve. **1525** Ld. Berners *Froissart* II. xxvii. 77 He had not thanne this vsage to ryn a nyghtes, as he doeth nowe. **1575** Laneham *Letter* 20 (1871) A Sunday, opportunely, the weather brake vp again. **1601** Shaks. *Jul. Cæs.* I. ii. 193 Let me haue men about me, that are fat, Sleekeheaded men, and such as sleepe a-nights. **1669** Digby *Closet Opened* (1677) 134 Monsieur de Bourdeaux used to take a mornings a broth thus made. **1688** Bunyan *Holy War* 336 The bold villain... lurks in the Diabolonian dens a days and haunts like a ghost honest men's houses a nights. **1721** Swift *Epist. Corr.* II. 557 Why did you not set out a Monday, like a true country parson?

b. Especially, with adverbs of repetition: *once*, *twice*, *many times*, *oft a day* (OE. *on dæȝe*), *twice a week*, *thrice a year*.

In this construction *a* is now generally explained as the 'indefinite article'; and it has, through such phrases as *a penny a day*, *fourteen shillings a weeks*, led to the use of *a* to express *rate*, or *proportion*, as in *a penny a mile*, *tenpence a pound*. Comp. French *deux francs par jour*, and *deux francs la livre*. See A *a.*[2] 4.

c **1000** *Ags. Gospels* Luke xx. 4 Seofan siþun on dæȝ [*Lindisf.* Seofa siðe on dæȝe]. *c* **1150** *Hatton Gosp.*, *ibid.* Seofen syðan on daiȝ. *a* **1200** *Trin. Coll. Hom.* 67 Ete nu leinte mete, and enes o day. *Ibid.* 109 Hie arist anes á dái. *c* **1305** *St. Edmund* 72 And werede here þrie a wyke, oþer tueye atte leste. **1382** Wyclif *Exod.* xxiii. 17 Thries a ȝeer [**1388** in the ȝeer] shal apere al thi maal child before the Lord thi God. *c* **1386** Chaucer *Knight's T.* 498 Ful ofte a day he swelte and seyde alas! **1611** Bible *Ps.* cxix. 164 Seuen times a day doe I praise thee. **1878** Huxley *Physiogr.* 174 It moves at the rate of between four and five miles an hour.

†**9.** Manner: in, with, etc.; as *a this wise*, *a some wise*, *a gram* = in wrath, *a scorn*, *a blisse*; *a French*, *a Latin*; *a great speed*, *a purpose* = on purpose, *a colour* = under colour, in the pretence, *a that'n* = in that way. Cf. OE. *on þisre wisan*, *on Englisc*, mod. *on this wise*, *in English*. Obs.

1230 *Ancren Riwle* 100 þis is a cruel word, & a grim word mid alle, þ vre Louerd seið ase a grome & a scorn. *c* **1305** *E.E. Poems*, *St. Kath.* 92 For ich wole bet þat ȝe hire ouercome: mid resouns a somme wise. **1387** Trevisa *Higden Polychr.* (in Morris *Specim.* 338) To construe here lessons & here þingis a Freynsch. *c* **1400** *Apol. for Lollards* 49 A color of takyng of almis. **1533** More *Answ. to Poysoned Boke* (Wks. 1557) 1117/2 Els may he neuer make himself so sure, and face it out a this fashion. **1590** Marlowe *Jew of Malta* IV. iii. 312 Stands here a purpose. **1601** Shaks. *All's Well* II. iii. 265 Why dooest thou garter vp thy armes a this fashion? **1695** Congreve *Love for Love* III. vii. 218 (1866) [A sailor says] An' you stand astern a that'n we two will never grapple together.

†**10.** Capacity: in any one's name; esp. *a God's name*. Obs.

c **1300** *Life of Beket* 146 And wende forth a Godes name: to the holi londe. *c* **1386** Chaucer *Doctor's T.* 250 Do with your child your wille, a goddes name! **1523** Ld. Berners *Froissart* I. cxix. 142 Let them depart whyder they woll a goddes name. *a* **1577** Northbrooke *Against Dicing* (1843) 152 Daunce a God's name. **1577** Vautroullier *Luther's Ep. to Galathians* 129 Worke on a Gods blessing. **1600** Holland *Livy* IX. iv. 315/2 Go then, Consuls, a gods name, redeem the cittie. **1702** Pope *Chaucer's Wife of Bath* 48 Let such (a God's name) with fine wheat be fed.

11. State: in; as *a live*, *a sleep*, *a work*, *a jar*, *a thirst*, *a blaze*, *a fright*, *a float*, *a stare*. In these the word governed by *a* was originally a noun, e.g. *life*, *sleep*, *work*, *float* ('on the Mediterranean flote,' Shaks. *Temp.* I. ii. 234), but being often the verbal sb. of state or act, it has been in modern times erroneously taken as a verb, and used as a model for forming such adverbial phrases from any verb, as *a-wash*, *a-blaze*, *a-bask*, *a-swim*, *a-flaunt*, *a-blow*, *a-dance*, *a-run*, *a-stare*, *a-gaze*, *a-howl*, *a-tremble*, *a-shake*, *a-jump*. These are purely modern and analogical.

1205 Layamon I. 59 Wel wes him on liue. [**1250** Wel was him aliue.] *c* **1225** *Sawles Warde* 249 Lest sum for-truste him, ant feole o slepe. **1533** More *Answ. to Poysoned Boke* Wks. (1557) 1119/1 Al the while that al those holy folke were a worke therwith. **1556** *Chron. Grey Friars* 47 And [they] sette it alle a fyer, and went their wayes agayne. **1611** Cotgr. *Estre au dessus du vent*, To flourish, live in prosperitie, be al a flaunt, or a hoight. **1611** Bible *2 Chron.* ii. 18 Three thousand and sixe hundred ouerseers to set the people a worke. **1616** R. C. *Times' Whistle* v. 1843 One straight falles a sleep. **1663** Spalding *Troubles in reign of Chas. I* (1829) 44 The soldiers sleeping carelessly in the bottom of the ship upon heather, were all a-swim, through the water that came in at the holes and leaks of the ship. **1868** *Morning Star* 18 June, Rocks which are a-wash at low tide.

12. Process; with a verbal sb. taken passively: in process of, in course of, undergoing. Varying with *in*: 'forty and six years was this temple in building.' *arch.* or *dial.*

(In modern language the *a* is omitted and the verbal sb. treated as a participle, passive in sense; as *the house was a building*, *the house was building*. In still more modern speech a formal participle passive appears: *the house was being built*.)

1393 Langland *P. Pl.* C iv. 51 We haue a wyndow a worchyng. **1489** Caxton *Faytes of Armes* I. xiv. 37 Suche fortyfycacyons are in dooyng. **1523** Ld. Berners *Froissart* I. cxx. 143 Ther they brake all [the bridge] to peaces that had been longe a makynge. **1598** Stow *Survay of London* i. 3 (1603) Whilst these things were a doing. **1611** Bible *1 Peter* iii. 20 In the dayes of Noah while the Arke was a preparing. **1662** H. More *Ant. ag. Atheism* (1712) III. xiii. 130 The shrieks of men while they are a murthering. **1692** Bentley *B.L.* 211 The state or condition of matter before the world was a-making, which is compendiously exprest by the word chaos. **1727** Wodrow *Corresp.* (1843) III. 296 Tomorrow, all day, papers will be a-reading.

13. Action; with a verbal sb. taken actively.

a. with *be*: engaged in. *arch.* or *dial.*

(In literary Eng. the *a* is omitted, and the verbal sb. treated as a participle agreeing with the subject, and governing its case, to *be fishing*, *fighting*, *making anything*. But most of the southern dialects, and the vulgar speech both in England and America, retain the earlier usage.)

1523 Ld. Berners *Froissart* I. xviii. 20 They had ben a fyghtyng with theyr ennemies. *c* **1590** Horsey *Travels* (Hakl. Soc.) 163 His enyme..that was a preparinge to invade his countrys. **1683** tr. Erasmus *Moriae Encomium* 18 She imitates me in being always a laughing. **1684** Bunyan *Pilg.* II. (1862) 209 She is a taking of her last farewell of her Country. **1716–18** Lady M. W. Montagu *Letters* I. xxvii. 88 Orders...which may possibly be a month a-coming. **1769** Robertson *Charles V*, III. VIII. 65 The tempest which had been so long a gathering was ready to break forth. **1815** Leigh Hunt *Feast of the Poets* 11 You'd have thought 'twas the Bishops or Judges a coming. **1845** Disraeli *Sybil* 296 (Routl.) 'A-dropping wages, and a-raising tommy like fun,' said Master Waghorn.

b. with verb of motion: to, into; to *go a fishing*, *come a wooing*, *fall a laughing*, *crying*, *fighting*, to *set the bells a ringing*, to *send children a begging*. *Arch.* or *dial.* save in a few phrases, as *to go a begging* (mostly of offices); and with *set*, as to *set the clock a going*, *the bells a ringing*, *folk a thinking*, where also *a* is often omitted.

1526 Tindale *John* xxi. 3 Simon Peter sayde vnto them: I goo a fysshynge. **1551** Robinson *More's Utopia* 43 Whither, I pray you, but a beggynge or elles a stealing. **1621** Burton *Anat. Mel.* (1651) III. 4. i. 3. 667 ..he would burst out a laughing. **1692** Bentley *B.L.* 61 Watches must be wound up to set them a going. **1715** Burnet *Hist. own Time* II. 207 (1766) As soon as he was taken he fell a crying. **1788** Th. Jefferson *Writings* II. 373 (1859) We were able to set the loan a going again. *Mod.* Such positions rarely go a begging.

a (ə), *prep.*[2] *Obs.* [worn down from *of*, *f* being dropped bef. a cons., and the toneless *o* sunk into the neutral ə, which being the ordinary sound of toneless *a*, as in *a man*, *ămain*, *Americă*, was here also written *a*. It was once the ordinary representative of *of* in certain phrases, as *men a war*, *cloth a gold*, *inns a court*, *time a day*, *fustian a Napes*, *out a doors* (where apparently confused with *at*, cf. *in a doores*) and familiarly in many others. In mod. spelling, *of* when contracted is written *o'*, but the familiar pronunciation is still (ə) as in *man o'*(ə) *war*.]

1. Of. Usu. repr. colloq., popular, or dial. pronunc., esp. in American and Black English. Freq. appended to the preceding word (sometimes with reduplication of final consonant), as CUPPA, KINDA, LOTSA, LOTTA, etc.

?**1500** *Chevy Chase* (*MS. Ashmole* 48) 84 He spendyd A spere a trusti tre. **1523** LD. BERNERS *Froissart* I. xxxviii. 52 The cyty was strong, and well furnysshed of men a warr. **1532** MORE *Conf. Dr. Barnes* VIII. (Wks. 1557) 804/2, Ye shall beare no part of that flesh foorth a dores. **1593** SHAKS. *Rich. II*, I. iii. 76 The name of John a Gaunt. **1599** —— *Much Ado* III. iv. 19 Cloth a gold and cut, and lac'd with siluer. **1599** CHAPMAN *An humerous dayes myrth* (Plays, 1873) I. 63 Theeues, Puritanes, murderers, in adoores, I say. **1631** LENTON *Leasures* char. 29 A young innes a court gentleman. **1673** J. JANEWAY *Heaven upon Earth* (1847) 286 'Tis not time-a-day for you to be sleeping or playing. **1800** M. EDGEWORTH *Castle Rackrent* 78 'Judy's out a luck,' said I, striving to laugh—'I'm out a luck,' said he. **1928** [see BULLSHIT 1]. **1965** C. COLTER in A. Chapman *New Black Voices* (1972) 72 See that squad car?—up in fronta the drug store. **1976** *CRC Jrnl.* July 14/1 All a we is one, all a we not the same. **1981** *Westindian World* 31 July 4/1 Who should I buck up last Saturday night but man about town and boss man a Root Magazine Godfrey Hope.

†**2.** Especially common in the phrase ***a clock*** = of the clock, o'clock. *Obs.*

c **1450** *Wills and Inv. Bury St. Edm.* 17 At vii of the clokke. **1480** *Plumpton Corr.* 40 Uppon Munday by viii a clocke. **1593** T. FALE *Art of Dialling* A. 3. The Meridian and twelve a clock line are all one. **1598** B. JONSON *Ev. Man in Hum.* (1616) I. iv. 14 It's sixe a clocke: I should ha' carried two turnes, by this. **1665** BOYLE *Occ. Refl.* VI. xv. 254 (1675) To know what a Clock it was. **1713** DERHAM *Physico-Theol.* 18 *note*, Sea-Breezes commonly rise in the Morning about Nine a Clock. **1741** AMHERST *Terræ Filius* I. 3 Coming into college at ten or eleven a clock at night.

†**3.** After *manner*, *kind*, *sort*, etc. *a*, orig. the 'indef. article,' was taken as = of. Orig. *what manner* was in the genitive relation, thus: what manner a man? *cujusmodi homo?* what manner men? *cujusmodi homines?* By being taken as = of, *a* was first extended to the plural, as 'what manner a men?' and then changed to *of*, as in the mod. 'what manner of men?' which no longer answers to *cujusmodi homines?* but to *qui modus hominum?* The dialects retain the original 'kind a' as *kinda*, *kinder*. *Obs.* See further s.v. MANNER *sb.*[1] 9.

1388 WYCLIF *Judg.* viii. 18 What maner men weren thei [**1382** What weren the men] that ȝe killiden in Thabor [**1611** What maner of men were they whom ye slew at Tabor?]. **1523** LD. BERNERS *Froissart* I. lxxv. 96 Ther abode alyue no maner a person. **1583** GOLDING *Calvin on Deut.* VI. 33. 17 a, We know what maner a one that is. **1592** RD. HYRDE tr. *Vives' Instr. Christ. Woman* G iij, What maner a ones they shoulde be, S. Peter, & S. Paule,.. teach.

†**a**, *prep.*[3] *Obs.* In phr. ***a þe***, a later form of OE. *oððe* = *oð* until + *þe* that, whereby *a* came to represent OE. *oð* till.

c **1175** *Lamb. Hom.* 5 Þus ha hine hereden a þe he rad in et þan est ȝete. *Ibid.* 45 Ic ham ȝeue reste... from non on saterdei a þa cume monedeis lihting.

†**a**, *conj. Obs.* A form apparently occurring occasionally before a consonant for *an* = and, if. In some cases, if not all, the correct MS. reading may be *ā*, compendium for *an*.

1. = And.

c **1280** *Fall & Passion* in *E.E. Poems* (1862) 13 Seue daies a seue niȝt . vte of heuen hi aliȝt . . an in to hellë wer iþrow. *c* **1400** *Apol. for Lollards* 56 He þat lettiþ not silk ȝeuing, wen he is holden a may, is strenid by þe same gilt. *c* **1450** *Morte Arth.* (Roxb. Cl.) 91 Wendyth home a leue youre werryeng.

2. = *and, an'*, if.

c **1450** *Morte Arth.* (Roxb. Cl.) 91 And yit a thow woldyst nyghe me nye, Thow shalt wele wete I am not slayn.

†**a**, *int. Obs.* or *dial.* form of O *int.* and AH *int.*

1. (In northern and early southern Eng.) O! (for which *ā! eh!* (ɛː, eː) is still the ordinary northern form) of invocation, surprise, admiration.

c **1175** *Lamb. Hom.* 45 A! hwi wepest þou, Paul? *c* **1340** HAMPOLE *Pr. Tr.* 1 A, a! that wondyrful name! A! that delittable name! —— *Pr. Consc.* 481 For when it es born it cryes swa: If it be man it says 'a.a.' And if þe child a woman be, When it es born it says 'e.e.' *c* **1460** TOWNLEY *Myst.* 109 A, Gylle! what chere?

2. (In later southern Eng.) Ah! of pain, grief, aversion.

c **1305** *E.E. Poems* 58 A beau frere quaþ þis oþer: strong is þi misdede. **1340** *Ayenb.* 92 A God hou hi byeþ foles and more þanne a best. *c* **1386** CHAUCER *Knight's T.* 220 He bleynte and cryed, a! As that he stongen were vnto the herte. *c* **1400** *Apol. for Lollards* 30 A ȝe vniust prestis, þorow ȝour bidding þe prest of God stintiþ þe office of blessing. **1485** CAXTON *Paris & Vienne* (1868) 28 A Veray God! I am wel dyscomforted.

3. Prefixed to proper names as a war-cry, as *A Warwick!* Modern writers treat it as the 'indefinite article'.

c **1450** *Merlin* (1866) II. 287 Than thei cried a Clarance with a lowde voyse. **1808** SCOTT *Marmion* VI. xxvii. The Border slogan rent the sky: A Home! a Gordon! was the cry.

4. Appended to lines 'in burlesque poetry, to lengthen out a syllable, without adding to the sense.' J. Not originally burlesque, but probably originating in the necessary retention of the ME. final *-e* where wanted for measure, the origin of which being forgotten, it was treated as an addition of *ă*. Thus ME. *sonne—yronne*, would be treated as *sun a!—run a!* Hence prob. the modern ballad and lyrical *O!* (which is not burlesque) as in 'My Nannie, O.'

1567 *Triall of Treasure* (1850) 33 Wherein I doe delight, a; ... To liue still in such plighte, a. **1611** SHAKS. *Wint. T.* IV. iii. 133 And merrily hent the Stile-a.. Your sad tyres in a Mile-a.

†**a, a-** (ə) *particle*, prefixed to the pa. pple. and occasionally to other parts of the verb, = earlier ȝe- [Ger. *ge-*, Goth. *ga-*, together, altogether, completely], which in OE. was sparingly used as a prefix to the pple. (more commonly making a compound verb), but in 2–4 became, as *ȝe-*, *y-*, *i-*, the regular sign of the pa. pple. in the south, as *y-come*, *i-don*, *i-sen*, *y-ben*, *i-ben*, *i-be*, etc. The toneless (ɪ) afterwards sank into (ə), as it is still pronounced in the south-western dialects, and was frequently written *a* distinct, or *a-* joined, in 14–16th c. As many verbs had also a derivative form in *a-* in OE. (as *wake awake*, *rise arise*), and many others were formed after them in ME., it is not always easy to say whether a pa. pple. in *a-* is to be referred to the simple verb, or to a derivative verb in *a-*, of which no other part is known. So in mod. G. *ge-standen* may be pa. pple. of *stehen*, or of *ge-stehen*. See I-, Y-.

c **1270** *Owl & Night.* 1602, Ah thu me havest sore i-gramed That min heorte is wel neh a-lamed. *c* **1400** *Tundale's Vis.* 700 Then seyd Tundale ablissyd be thou. **1458** *Domest. Arch.* (Abingdon MS.) III. 42 Chees & chekenes clerelych a dyght. **1684** BUNYAN *Pilg.* II. 70 The Highways have a been un-occupied heretofore. **1859** W. BARNES *Hwomely Rhymes* (Dorset dial.) 61 An' we have all a-left the spot, To teäke, a-scatter'd, each his lot.

a-, *prefix*, from various sources.

1. OE. *a-*, originally *ar-* (rarely preserved, as in *ar-æfnan*), OHG. *ar-*, *ir- ur-* (mod. G. *er-*), Goth. *us- ur-*, implying motion onward or away from a position, hence *away*, *on*, *up*, *out*, and thus with verbs of motion adding *intensity*; as in *a-bide*, *a-go*, *a-rise*, *a-wake*, and many obs. verbs; after the analogy of which it was subsequently prefixed to other vbs., not found with it in OE., as *a-curse*. In some words this *a-* has been formally confused with OFr. *a-*:—L. *ad-*, *ac-*, *af-*, etc. (No. 7), and, like this, refashioned after assumed L. analogies, as in *a(c)-curse*, for *a-curse*, *a(l)-lay* for *a-lay*, *a(f)-fright* for *a-fright*, etc.

2. ME. **a-**:—OE. *an*, *on*, prep. See A *prep.*[1] above. With nouns, *in*, *on*, *engaged in*, *at*, in loose combinations, which are really two words; as *abed*, *ashore*, *afield*, *asleep*, *alive*. With verbs, adverbs, and prepositions, more closely combined both in form and sense, as *aknow*, *ashame*, *afore*, *among*, *across*.

3. ME. **a-**:—OE. *of* prep. (see A *prep.*[2]) meaning *off*, *from*, in *a-down*, *a-thirst*; *of*, in *akin*, *anew*, *afresh*, *a-clock*.

4. ME. **a-**:—OE. *and-* against, opposite, as in *a-long*.

5. ME. **a-** for AT *prep.*, Norse *at* prep. 'to,' used in the north as sign of the infinitive = *to*. In *ado*, early northern Eng. *at do*. See also A-DOORS.

6. ME. **a-** for *i-*, *y-*:—*ȝe-*, as in *a(f)-ford*, *along* = owing to, and in southern pa. pples. as *a-done*, etc. See A *particle* above.

7. ME. **a-** = Fr. pref. *a-*:—L. *ad-*, to, at, hence sometimes expressing addition or increase, sometimes bringing *into* a state; as in *abandon*, *abase*, *abate*, *abut*, *achieve*, *adroit*, *agree*, *alarm*, *amass*, *amaze*, *ameliorate*, *amerce*, *amount*, *amuse*, *apropos*, *avail*, *avenge*, *avenue*, *aver*, *avouch*, *avow*. In 14th cent. a practice arose among French scribes of refashioning words originally having this prefix, after L. *ad-* and its phonetic variants *ac-*, *af-*, *ag-*, *al-*, *an-*, *ap-*, *ar-*, *as-*, *at-*; this extended in 15th c. to Eng., where the great majority of words from OFr. were so treated, so as to simulate a direct formation from L. Cf. *a(d)dress*, *a(c)count*, *a(f)fect*, *a(g)grieve*, *a(l)lege*, *a(n)noy*, *a(p)pear*, *a(c)quit*, *a(r)rive*, *a(s)sent*, *a(t)tain*, *a(d)venture*, *a(d)vertise*, *a(d)vise*, *a(d)vocate*, *a(d)vowson*, where etymological spelling would have simple *a-*. It was even extended to words not derived from L. *ad-*, as *a(d)vance*, Fr. *avancer*, L. *ab-anteāre*; *a(c)knowledge*, OE. *on-* + *knowledge*; *a(c)curse*, OE. *a-* + *curse*.

8. ME. **a-** = Fr. *a-*:—L. *ab* off, away, from; as in *a-bridge* (ab-breviāre), *a-steyne*, *a-soil*. Sometimes afterwards refashioned, as *ab-stain*, or confused with the prec. and erroneously respelt, as *as-soil*.

9. ME. **a-** = Anglo-Fr. *a-* for OFr. *e-*, *es-*:—L. *ex-* out, utterly; as in *a-mend* (L. emendare) *abash* (OFr. esbahiss-), *afforce* (esforcer), *affray* (esfrei), and many forms, now obs. or refashioned, as *a-may*, *as-aumple*, *as-cape*, *a-move*; or where the *a-* has been lost by aphesis, as *scapement*, *sample*, *spenser*; or has been confused with No. 10 and refashioned with *en-*, as *ex-emplum*, *es-emple*, *a-saumple*, *an-sample*, *en-sample*; or with *ad-* as *admerveille*.

10. ME. **a-**:—earlier Eng. and Anglo-Fr. *an-*, OFr. *en-*. This Anglo-Fr. *an-* was formally confused with OE. *an-* (see No. 2), and like it reduced bef. a cons. to *a-*, as in *abushment*, *acloy*, *acumber*, *alumine*, *apeach*, *apair*, *apoison*. In most cases these words are now obs. or refashioned, as *ambushment*, *encumber*, *enlumine*, *impeach*; or have been aphetized, as *peach*, *cloy*, *limn*; or have been further confused with words in *a-*:—L. *ad-* (No. 7), and erroneously respelt accordingly, as *accloy*, *accumber*, *allumine*, *appair*, *appeach*.

11. Many words with **a-** in one or other of the preceding senses have *aphetic* forms with the *a-* lost, as *adown down*, *amid mid*, *alive live*, *amend mend*, *abate bate*. In others the force of the prefix is so little apparent, that the derivatives in *a-* hardly differ in sense from their primitives, as in *rise arise*, *wake awake*, *grieve a(g)grieve*, *cumber acumber*, *done adone*. Hence, it naturally happened that all these *a-* prefixes were at length confusedly lumped together in idea, and the resultant *a-* looked upon as vaguely intensive, rhetorical, euphonic, or even archaic, and wholly otiose. With this vague feeling, *a-* was often prefixed by Spenser and other artificial archaists of the 16th cent. to words both of OE. and Romance origin, where it had no historical or etymological basis and can only be explained as due to vague form-association. This also was often treated like *a*:—L. *ad* (No. 7), and spelt *ad-*, *ac-*, *af-*, *ag-*, etc. accordingly.

12. **a-**, from L. *a* = *ad* prefix and preposition, *to*; reduced in late Latin to *a-* before *sc-*, *sp-*, *st-*; as in *a-scend*, *a-spirate*, *a-scribe*, *a-spect*, *a-spersion*, *a-spire*, *a-spirate*, *a-strict*, *a-stringent*. See AD-.

13. **a-**, from L. *a* = *ab*, prefix and preposition *from*, *off*, *away*; only before *v*, as in *avert*. See AB-.

14. **a-**, from Gr. ἀ-, used bef. a cons. for ἀν-, pref. of privation or negation = *without*, *not*, *-less*, in words introd. into Eng. through L. and Fr. as *abysm*, *adamant*, *amethyst*; or through L. as *acatalectic*, *adiaphorous*, *apetalous*; or from Gr. direct (or through a mod. lang.) as *amorphous*, *adipsy*; or formed on Gr. elements, as *abiogenetic*, *agnostic*. In the latter case, *a-* has become a living prefix of negation = *un-*, *non-*, applied not only to words from Gr., as *a-cotyledonous*, *a-chromatic*, *a-philanthropy*, but also to technical words from L., as *a-caulous*, *a-sexual*.

15. **a-**, from Gr. ἀ- intensive, as in *a-bolla*, *a-maurosis*, *a-tlas*.

-a, *suffix*, from various sources.

1. OE. **-a** (:—early Teut. *-o*) nom. ending of masc. *-n* stem nouns, and foreign words associated with them, as *ox-a*, *ass-a* (L. *asinō-*), *drac-a* (L. *dracōn-*). This *-a* became in ME. *-e*, as *ox-e*, *ass-e*, *drak-e*; in mod. E. dropped, or preserved only as a spelling expedient, *ox*, *ass*, *drake* (= *dreik*). Hence a com. ending of OE. names and titles of men, as in *Ida*, *Ella*, *Offa*, *Ceadda* (Chad), *Bæda* (Bede), *Bretwalda*.

2. Gr. and L. **-a**, nom. ending of fem. nouns of first decl., some of which have been adopted unchanged, as *idea*, *chimæra*, *basilica*, *area*, *arena*, *camera*, *corolla*, *formula*, *lamina*, *peninsula*; and esp. Nat. Hist. terms (often med. or mod.L.) as *alumina*, *ammonia*, *soda*; *alga*, *asafœtida*, *calceolaria*, *campanula*, *dahlia*, *fuchsia*, *lobelia*; *hyæna*, *boa*, *cicada*, *salpa*, *amœba*; and geog. as *Africa*, *Asia*, *Corsica*, *Malta*. Also proper names of women, as *Diana*, *Lydia*, *Julia*, *Maria*, *Aurora*, *Anna*, *Ada*, *Sophia*, *Victoria*; latinized forms of OE. names, as *Hilda* (Hild), *Godiva* (Godȝifu), *Elfrida* (Ælfþryð), *Ethelburga* (Æðelburȝ); med. or mod. female names formed on male names, as *Louis-a*, *Joann-a*, *Albert-a*, *Alexandr-a*, *Robin-a*, *Carol-in-a*, *Georg-in-a*, *Henri-ett-a*. (L. names of women and places remain unchanged, except when the Fr. form has been adopted, as Maria, Marie, *Mary*; Italia, Italie, *Italy*; Diana, Diane, *Dian* (arch.); Eurōpa, *Europe*; Africa, Afrique, *Afric* (arch.); Græcia, Grèce, *Greece*;

India, Inde, *Ind* (arch.); Hispania, Espayne, *Spain.*)

3. Mod. Rom. (It., Sp., Pg.) **-a**, ending of fem. nouns, as *lava, opera, piazza, regatta, sonata, stanza, tufa, umbrella*; *armada, flotilla, mantilla, peseta, vanilla*; hence in proper names of women, as *Isabella, Berengaria, Eva*; and occasionally a sex-suffix, as *don, donn-a, duenn-a*; *signor, -a*; *amoros-o, -a*; *infant-e, -a*; *sultan, -a*; *czar, czar-in-a*.

4. Gr. and L. **-a**, plural ending of neuter nouns, some of which have been adopted unchanged, as *phenomen-on, -a*; *strat-um, -a*; *dat-um, -a*; *miasma, -ta*; *genus, gener-a*; hence frequent in (mod.) L. plural names of classes of animals, as *Mammali-a, Amphibi-a, Crustace-a, Mollusc-a, Protozo-a, Quadruman-a, Cetace-a, Macrur-a*, of which the sing. is variously supplied by *Mammal, Mollusc, Quadruman, Crustacean, Amphibian*, etc.

5. Repr. colloq. or dial. pronunc. of: **a.** *do*, as *whatta you want?* (see WHADD(A)YA), etc.; **b.** *have* (see A *v.* b); **c.** *of* (see A *prep.*[2] 1); **d.** *to*, as GOTTA, OUGHTA, WANNA, etc.

aa, an occasional mode of spelling long *a*, now obs. or dial., as in **aage, aal, aale, aand(e, aare**. See AGE, ALL, ALE, AND(E, ARE.

†**aa**[1]. *Obs.* [prob. a. ON. *á*, cogn. w. OE. *éa*, Goth. *ahwa*, L. *aqua*; see also Æ, and EA.] A stream, a water-course.

1430 *Munim. Magd. Coll. Oxf.* No. 7 A. (Saltfleetby, Linc.) Communis sewere vocat' *le Seventowne Aa*.

‖**aa**[2] ('ɑːɑː). *Geol.* [Hawaiian *'a-'ā*.] A rough, scoriaceous lava, one of the two chief forms of lava emitted from volcanoes of the Hawaiian type, the other being PAHOEHOE.

1859 R. C. HASKELL in *Amer. Jrnl. Sci. & Arts* 2 Ser. XXVIII. 70 We..saw '*pahoihoi*' or solid lava forming, and also '*aa*' or clinkers. **1880** *Encycl. Brit.* XI. 531/2 The *a-a* or spongy lava, which, on account of its extreme roughness and hardness, is carefully avoided by all travellers. **1883** C. E. DUTTON in *U.S. Geol. Surv. 4th Ann. Rep.* 95 The second form of the lavas is called by the natives a-a, and its contrast with pahoehoe is about the greatest imaginable. It consists mainly of clinkers sometimes detached, sometimes partially agglutinated together with a bristling array of sharp, jagged, angular fragments. **1914, 1920** [see BLOCK *sb.* 23, *block lava*]. **1944** C. A. COTTON *Volcanoes* iv. 27 Cooling and solidification frequently takes a different course..in lava flows, producing the clinker-like 'aa' lava.

aa, variant of A, *adv. Obs.*, ever.

aac, aak, aakin; obs. forms of OAK, OAKEN.

‖**aal** (ɑːl) [The Bengali and Hind. name.] A plant, a species of *Morinda* allied to the madder, the roots of which yield a red dye; also the dye itself, used in India to colour cotton fabrics.

1875 URE *Dict. Arts* I. 1 Has obtained from the aal root a pale yellow substance which he calls morindin.

aald, obs. form of OLD.

Aalenian (ɑːˈlɛnɪən), *a. Geol.* [ad. F. *aalenien* (C. D. W. Mayer-Eymar 1864, in *Tableau Synchronistique des Terrains Jurassiques* (Zurich)), f. *Aalen*, name of a town in Baden-Württemberg, W. Germany: see -IAN.] Of, pertaining to, or designating a European stage at the bottom of the Middle Jurassic (or the top of the Lower Jurassic), next below the Bajocian; (see also quot. 1982). Also *absol.*

1896 *Q. Jrnl. Geol. Soc.* LII. 708 (*heading*) The strata of Aalenian age. **1903** [see PLIENSBACHIAN *a.*]. **1957** *Encycl. Brit.* XIII. 195/1 The Aalenian includes at the base the upper part both of the Bridport Sands of Dorset, and of the Northampton Sands. **1963** D. W. & E. E. HUMPHRIES tr. *Termier's Erosion & Sedimentation* xvi. 331 The Aalenian limestone..has an irregular surface whose hollows have been filled with 'paper' shale. **1982** W. B. HARLAND et al. *Geologic Time Scale* ii. 27/2 Some workers have regarded Aalenian as Early Bajocian in a three-fold division... We have accepted Aalenian as a distinct age.

‖**aam** (ɑːm, ɔːm). Forms: 5–7 **alm(e**; 7 **awme, aume**; 7–8 **ame, awm, aum.** [Du. *aam* (pl. *amen*); cogn. w. mod.G. *ahm, ohm*; MHG. *âme, ôme*; OHG. *âma, ôma* a cask; ON. *âma* a tub; a. L. *ăma, hăma*; ad. Gr. *ἄμη* a water-bucket. *Aam* is the mod.Du. spelling, the Eng. forms being only historical.] A Dutch and German liquid measure, formerly used in England for Rhenish wine; a cask. It varied in different continental cities from 37 to 41 gallons.

1526 *Ord. for Royal Househ. Henry VIII*, 195 Renish wine 4 fatts, every fat containing 3 Almez, at 30s. the Alme. **1604** *Act 1 James I*, c. xxxii (*granting Tonnage and Poundage*), Of euery Awme of Rhenish Wine, that is, or shall so come in, twelue pence. **1696** PHILLIPS, *Auln* or Aum of Renish Wine, a measure containing 40 Gallons, and as many pints over and above. **1717** BLOUNT *Law Dict.*, I find in a very old printed Book thus:—The Rood of Rhenish-wine of Dordreight is ten Awames, and every Awame is fifty Gallons; item the Rood of Antwarp is xliij Awames, and every Awame is xxxv Gallons. **1721** BAILEY, *Aulne* Of Rhenish Wine, a Vessel that contains 40 Gallons. **1731** *Ibid.* vol. II Ame (of Antwerp) a vessel containing 50 stoops, each stoop 7 pints English measure.

aan, -e, obs. forms of ON, and ONE.

‖**aandblom** ('ɑːntblɔm). *S. Afr.* Also 9 **aantblom, avondbloem.** [Afrikaans, f. *aand* evening + *blom* flower; cf. Du. *avondbloem*.] Any of several sweet-scented iridaceous wild flowers, esp. *Hesperantha falcata*. Also dim. ‖**aandblommetjie** (-əcɪ) (earlier often written in Du. form *avondbloemetje*).

1822 BURCHELL *Trav.* I. 273, I here met with a remarkable species of *Avond-bloem* (*Hesperanthera*). **1870** *Cape Monthly Mag.* Aug. 108 The scent of the 'avond bloemetjies' is fragrant in the air. **1890** A. MARTIN *Home Life Ostrich Farm* 21 Another of our favourites was the *aantblom*, a kind of ixia. **1915** R. MARLOTH *Flora S. Afr.* IV. 145 *H. falcata* (*Avond bloemetje*, generally pronounced '*aandbloem*'). **1927** *Chambers's Jrnl.* Mar. 190/1 Wild flowers, from the stately arum lily..to the modest *avondbloem*, which at night perfumed the whole veld with its fragrance. **1927** *Farming S. Afr.* 171 How often does one see..the beautiful 'painted ladies' or 'aandblommetjies' adding scent to the garden in the evening. **1953** V. BUCHANAN-GOULD *Vast Heritage* v. 80 Here the flowers had no perfume except for the rare aandblom.

aane, obs. form of AWN.

aar, obs. northern form of ERE.

‖**aard-vark** ('ɑːdvɑːk). [Adopted from the Dutch Colonists in South Africa, who have so named it from Du. *aarde*, in comp. *aard-* earth + *vark* = OE. *fearh*, OHG. *farh*, L. *porc-us* pig.] A South-African quadruped (*Orycterŏpus capensis* Cuv.), about the size of the badger, belonging to the insectivorous division of the Edentata, where it occupies an intermediate position between the Armadillos and Ant-eaters.

1833 *Penny Cyc.* I. 3 The aard-vark is in all respects admirably fitted for the station which Nature has assigned to it. **1834** PRINGLE *African Sketches* iv. 176 Such ant-hills as have been broken up and plundered by the aard-vark, or ant-eater. **1847** CARPENTER *Zoology* 281 The Aard-vark.. forms very extensive burrows at a little distance beneath the surface of the ground, which are sometimes so numerous, as to become sources of danger to horses and waggons traversing the country.

‖**aard-wolf** ('ɑːdwʊlf). [a. Du. *aard-wolf*, applied to this animal in S. Africa, f. *aarde* earth + WOLF.] A South-African carnivorous quadruped (*Proteles Lalandii* St. Hil.), of the size of a fox, occupying an intermediate position between the dogs, hyenas, and civets.

1833 *Penny Cyc.* I. 4 The genus Proteles contains but a single species, the Aard-wolf or earth-wolf, so called by the European colonists in the neighbourhood of Algoa Bay in South Africa. **1847** CARPENTER *Zool.* 198 The Aard-wolf (earth-wolf) is evidently the connecting link between the Hyænas and the Civets.

aare, variant of AIRE, *Obs.* altar.

Aaron[1] ('ɛərən). Proper name of the patriarch of the Jewish priesthood; hence used of a leader of the church. (*Rare*, and perh. only in loc. cit.)

1607 TOPSELL *Four-footed Beasts, Ep. Dedic.*, Aarons, and such as sit at the Helme of the Church, or are worthily advanced for their knowledge in Learning and State, I mean both Bishops and Doctors.

aaron[2] ('ɛərən). *Herb.* [a. Gr. *ἄρον*, corruptly spelt like the prec. word.] The herb Arum, Wake Robin, or Cuckoo Pint.

1611 COTGR., *Jarrus*; Wake-robin, Starch-wort, Rampe, Aaron, Calues-foot, Cuckoe-Pint. **1741** *Compl. Family-Piece* I. iv. 248 Take..Aaron Root 2 Pounds,..Nutmegs 1 Ounce.

Aaronic (ɛəˈrɒnɪk), *a.* [f. AARON[1] + -IC.] Of or belonging to Aaron, Levitical.

1874 REYNOLDS *John the Baptist* III. i. 142 John..one of the last representatives of the Aaronic priesthood. **1879** C. G. ROSSETTI *Seek and Find* 307 Yet has the Aaronic priesthood, no less recognisably than the other, both a real and a typical majesty of its own.

Aaronical (ɛəˈrɒnɪkəl), *a.* [f. prec. + -AL[1].] **a.** = AARONIC. **b.** High-priestly, pontifical.

1618 FEATLY *Clavis Myst.* ii. (1636) 14 S. Gregory by smoaking flaxe understandeth the Aaronical Priesthood. **1628** BP. HALL *Maried Clergie* I. xviii. 759 Our archbishops and bishops have wanted some Aaronicall accoutrements,—gloues, rings, sandals, miters and pall, and such other trash.

Aaron's-beard ('ɛərənzˈbɪəd), *Herb.* [Ref. to *Psalm* cxxxiii. 2.] A name popularly applied to several plants; especially the Great St. John's wort (*Hypericum calycinum*), from its prominent tufts of hair-like stamens; a cultivated species of Saxifrage (*S. sarmentosa*) from S. Africa, and the Ivy-leaved Toadflax (*Linaria Cymbalaria*), from the long dependent runners which they throw over the edge of a flowerpot; also, a shrub (*Spiraea salicifolia*), from its dense racemes of hairy-looking flowers; and locally to other plants. Prior *Dict. Eng. Plant Names*, s.v.

1549 *Complaynt of Scotl.* vi. 67 (1872) I sau ane erb callit barba aaron, quhilk vas gude remeid for emoroyades of the fundament. **1878** R. THOMPSON *Gardener's Assist.* 656/2 H[ypericum] calycinum, rose of Sharon or Aaron's beard.

Aaron's Rod. [Ref. to *Numbers* xvii. 8.]

1. *Herb.* A name popularly applied to different plants with tall flowering stems; especially the Great Mullein or Hag-taper (*Verbascum Thapsus*), and the Golden Rod (*Solidago Virgaurea*), or a cultivated Canadian species of the latter.

1834 MARY HOWITT *The Garden* (Sketches of Nat. Hist. 1851) 108 I'd Jacob's Ladder, Aaron's Rod, And the Peacock Gentianella.

2. *Arch.* 'An ornamental figure representing a rod with a serpent entwined about it; improperly called the *caduceus* of Mercury.' Weale *Dict. of Terms* 1849, and other mod. Dict. —Not in Gwilt or Parker.

aas, obs. form of ACE *sb.*

‖**aasvogel** ('ɑːsfəʊgəl). Also **aasvoël**. [S. African Du., f. *aas* carrion (cf. EES) + *vogel* bird, FOWL *sb.*; Afrikaans *aasvoël*.] A South African vulture, esp. *Gyps kolbii*.

1838 W. C. HARRIS *Exped. S. Afr.* xix. 186 *note*, *Vultus Fulvus*, and *Vultus Auricularis*: White and Black Aasvogel of the Cape Colonist. **1887** RIDER HAGGARD *Jess* xxvi, They would not be found till the aasvögels had picked them clean. **1903** KIPLING *Five Nations* 94 Well the keen *aas-vogels* know it. **1910** J. BUCHAN *Prester John* iv. 73, I thought it was an aasvogel, but another thought it was a baboon. **1924** R. CAMPBELL *Flaming Terrapin* vi. 90 Great aasvogels, like beetles on a pond, Veered in slow circles. **1939** S. CLOETE *Watch for Dawn* xii. 154 'What are you looking for up there?' .. 'Aasvöels, brother. Where there is death there are vultures.'

aat, obs. form of OAT.

†**ab**[1], *Obs. rare*[−1]. [Etym. unknown; only in loc. cit. Perhaps a misprint.] Sap.

1577 W. HARRISON in Holinshed *Desc. Engl.* II. xxii. 213 Yet diverse have assaied to deale without [*read* with our] okes to that end, but not with so good successe as they have hoped, bicause the ab or juice will not so soone be removed and cleane drawne out.

‖**Ab**[2] (æb). [cf. Chald. *'bb* to bring forth the first or early fruit; Heb. *ēb* verdure.] The fifth month of the Hebrew ancient sacred year, but the eleventh of the civil year. Also the twelfth month of the Syrian year, answering to August.

1833 *Penny Cyc.* I. 5 On the 1st day of Ab a fast is held in commemoration of the death of Aaron..The month of Ab may begin in some years as early as the 10th July, in others as late as the 7th August.

ab-, *pref.* repr. L. *ab*, prep. 'off, away, from,' cogn. w. Gr. *ἀπό*, Skr. *apa*, OTeut. *af*, OE. *of*, mod.E. *of, off*, mod.G. *ab*. In L. it was reduced to *a-* before *p-*, *m-*, and *v-*, became *au-* before *f-*, and *abs-* before *c-* and *t-*. The form *ab-* was in OFr. generally retained as in *abusum, abus*; sometimes changed to *av-* as in *abortionem, avortion*; sometimes reduced to *a-* as in *abbreviāre, abregier, abridge*. *Ab-* appears in Eng. in words that have lived on through OFr. as *abuse*; that have been adapted or formed in later Fr. as *absorb*; or have been adapted or formed in Eng. as *ablaqueate, abhominal, abarticulation*. Quite recent, and apparently suggested by *ab-normal*, are formations like *ab-oral, ab-actinal*, in which *ab-* is used for 'position away from.'

aba[1] ('æbə). An altazimuth instrument, specially designed by M. Antoine d'Abbadie [from whom it is said to be named] for determining the latitude without the use of the artificial horizon required by the sextant on land, and also for determining small angular heights and true bearings of terrestrial objects, without the trouble occasioned by the sextant.

1876 *S. Kens. Loan Coll. Catal.* (ed. 3) 747 A person familiar with the use of the sextant only, on observing circum-meridian altitudes for his first attempt with the aba, obtained his latitude to within 4″. **1879** *Daily News* 23 Aug. 4/4 The chief instrument he [an African explorer] used was the sextant, but he also used the aba.

aba[2], **abba**[2] ('æbə). [Arab. *'abā'*.] A sleeveless outer garment, resembling a sack with openings for the head and arms, worn by Arabs.

1811 tr. *Niebuhr's Trav. Arab.* cxxii, in Pinkerton *Voy.* X. 156 A blind tailor at Basra, who earned his bread by making Abbas. **1833** A. CRICHTON *Hist. Arabia* II. v. 193 A silk gown, over which is thrown a white abba of the finest manufacture of El Hassa. *Ibid.* viii. 350 The common abba is without sleeves, resembling a sack, with openings for the head and arms. **1880** L. WALLACE *Ben-Hur* VIII. iv. 496 Galileans in his league, carrying short swords under their long abbas. **1934** F. STARK *Valleys Assassins* ii. 74, I enveloped myself in the brown *abba*, tightly pinned under the chin. **1942** M. HOME *House of Shade* iii. 54 Over it was an *aba*, or sleeveless coat of fine linen.

abac ('eɪbæk). [ad. Fr. *abaque*, ad. L. *abacus*; cf. ABACK *sb.*] An alignment chart, a type of nomogram, by means of which the value required is read off by placing a ruler or other straight edge across points representing known values.

F. *abaque* in this sense is used by L. Lalanne, *Description et Usage de l' Abaque* (1845); in an 1846 Eng. tr. of Lalanne, *abaque* is rendered by *abacus*.

1930 R. T. BEATTY *Radio Data Charts* 12/1 We have two variable quantities which we multiply together to obtain the third variable, that is, we have to draw scales for three quantities, a, b, c, so that a.b = c... Having thus ascertained the relative sizes of the scales, we can proceed to construct the abac. **1934** *Jrnl. R. Aeronaut. Soc.* XXXVIII. 545 An abac is constructed to give rapid determination of exposure time in reference to time of year, state of sky, colour of subject. **1956** *Electronic Engin.* XXVIII. 533 A rapid method of circuit and transformer design is given in which a series of 'abacs' is used to evaluate the design constants.

‖**abaca** ('æbəkə). Also **abaka**. The native name of the palm (*Musa textilis*) which furnishes what is commonly known as Manilla Hemp; occasionally applied in commerce to the fibre, whence 'the most exquisite textile fabrics, and the elegant Manilla hats are manufactured.' Lindley & Moore *Treas. Bot.*, and Yeats *Nat. Hist. Comm.*

1818 *Blackw. Mag.* III. 579 Fine timber is to be found in all the islands [Philippines]; also..abacca, a kind of hemp. **1909** *Teachers' Assembly Herald* ii. 43/1 Weaving with the fine threads of abaka. **1925** in J. A. Hammerton *Countries of World* V. 3238/2 The staple abaca, or hemp, the product which first made the name of Manila known all over the world.

abacinate (ə'bæsɪneɪt), *v. rare*$^{-0}$. [f. med.L. *abacināre*, It. *abbacināre*; f. *ab* off + *bacin-us* a BASIN or cup.] To blind by placing hot irons, or metal plates, in front of the eyes.

abacination (əbæsɪ'neɪʃən). [n. of action f. prec.] (See quotation.)

1866 *Chambers' Jour.* 261 Rendered the delinquent liable to abacination—blinding by means of red-hot irons held before the eyes.

‖**abaciscus** (æbə'sɪskəs). *Arch.* [L., a. Gr. ἀβακίσκος, dim. of ἄβαξ a slab.]

1. 'A square compartment enclosing a part or the entire pattern or design of a Mosaic pavement.' Gwilt.

†**2.** 'Sometimes used as synonymous with abacus.' Gwilt. *Obs.*

abacist ('æbəsɪst). [ad. late L. *abacista*, f. *abacus*: see -IST.] 'One who uses an abacus in casting accounts; a calculator.' T.

1387 TREVISA *Higden's Polychr.* (Rolls Ser.) VII. 69 He [Gerebertus] was þe firste þat took abacus of Sarsyns, and ȝaf rules þer ynne, þat mowe unneþe be understonde of þe kunnyngeste men of þe craft, þe whiche craftes men beþ cleped abaciste. [*Vix ab acutis abacistis intelliguntur.*] **1872** WHARTON *Law Lex.* Abacist or Abacista, a caster of accounts, an arithmetician.

†**aback**, *sb. Obs. rare*$^{-1}$. [ad. Fr. *abaque*, ad. L. *abacus.*] A square tablet or compartment.

1603 BEN JONSON *James I's Enter.* Wks. 1838 529/1 In the centre, or midst of the pegne, there was an aback or square, wherein this elegy was written.

aback (ə'bæk), *adv.* Forms: 1 **on bæc**; 2 **a bec**; 2–3 **on bak, o bak**; 2–5 **a bak, abak**; 4–8 **a-back(e, abacke**; 6– **aback**. [OE. *on* prep. *bæc* sb. = unto *or* in the rear, backward. The prep. and sb., long written separate, were at length treated as one word; already in 3 the prefix began to be dropped, leaving BACK as the ordinary modern form of the word, *aback* being confined chiefly to nautical language. Cf. *adown* and *down*, *around* and *round*, etc.]

1. Motion: in a direction backwards, to the rear, towards that which is behind; back. *Fig.* From the front, or scene of action, off, away, to a distance. ***to draw, go, come a-back***: to retreat; ***to drive a-back***: to repulse; ***to put a-back***: to repel, reject.

c **1000** *Ags. Gospels* Matt. iv. 10 Gang þu sceocca on bæc! *John* vi. 66 Maneȝa his learning-cnihtas cyrdon on-bæc, & ne eodun mid him. *c* **1175** *Lamb. Hom.* 239 Mid al þan þe þer middenarde for his lufe werpeð abéc. **1297** R. GLOUC. 131 So þat þ e white was aboue, as þe folk y seye, And drof þe rede al abak out of þe put ney. *c* **1400** *Apol. for Lollards* 56 He [Christ] turnid & seid to Peter, Go o bak after Me, Sathanas. **1449** PECOCK *Repressor* III. iii. 290 Certis this seiyng may be at fulle Putt Abak and be rebukid. **1483** CAXTON *Gold. Leg.* 117/2 O ye right noble knyghtes which ben comen to the victorye & now goo abacke! **1490** —— *Eneydos* xxiii. 87 The sterres also and all the fyrmamente she maketh to retorne abacke. **1500** *Partenay* 5080 Neuer put A-bake, manly was of myght. *c* **1505** DUNBAR *Goldin Terge* xxi, Syne went abak, rebutit of the prey. **1552** LYNDESAY *Tragedy* 134 Than was I put abak frome my purpose, And suddantlie caste in captyuitie. **1554** *Interl. of Youth* (in Hazlitt's *Dodsley* II. 6) Aback, fellows, and give me room. *c* **1596** *King and Barkur* 46 (in Hazlitt's *E.P.P.* I. 6) The tanner lokyd a bake tho, The heydes began to fall. *a* **1834** COLERIDGE *The Two Founts* (Poems 340) To shrink aback and cower upon his urn. **1865** CARLYLE *Fredk. Gr.* VI. xv. v. 10 Alas, Belleisle had his accident in the Harz; and all went aback, from that time.

2. Rest, or resistance to motion: in a position to the rear, in that which is behind, in a backward position; in the rear, behind. *Fig.* Away from the front or scene of action, at a distance, aloof, in retirement. ***to hold aback***, to restrain, hinder; ***to stand aback from***, to stand aloof, to avoid, or eschew.

c **1120** *O.E. Chron.* (Laud MS.) anno 1110, And furðor nihtes syððan he ufor astah, he wæs ȝesewen on bæc on þæt norðwest gangende. *c* **1430** LYDGATE *Bochas* I. ix. (1544 lf. 16 b), But aback winter can somer undermine And al his freshnes sodeinly decline. *c* **1525** SKELTON *On Tyme* 22 And when tyme is, to put thyselfe in prease, And when tyme is, to holde thyself abacke. **1637** RUTHERFORD *Letters* xciv. (1862) I. 242 Keep yourself in the love of Christ and stand far aback from the pollutions of the world. **1870** MORRIS *Earthly Par.* I. I. 87 A temple fair We came to, set aback midst towering trees. **1878** JOAQUIN MILLER *Songs of Italy* 122 Front and aback there is nothing but flood.

3. *Naut.* Said of the sails of a ship, when laid back against the mast, with the wind bearing against their front surfaces. Also, of the ship, when her sails are so laid.

1697 JUMPER in *Lond. Gaz.* mmmccxcv. 1, I braced my main topsails aback. **1762** FALCONER *Shipwreck* ii. 427 Away there! lower the mizen yard on deck, He calls, and brace the foremost yards aback! **1790** R. BEATSON *Nav. and Mil. Mem.* II. 58 The Revenge was necessitated to throw her sails all aback. **1847** ROSS *Voyage to South Pole* II. 217 We instantly hove all aback to diminish the violence of the shock.

b. Hence the nautical phrase **to be taken aback**, 'when through a shift of wind or bad steerage, the wind comes in front of the square sails and lays them back against the masts, instantly staying the ship's onward course and giving her stern way; an accident exceedingly dangerous in a strong gale.' Sir John Richardson.

1754 EELES *Let.* 2, in *Phil. Trans.* XLIX. 144 If they luff up, they will be taken aback, and run the hazard of being dismasted. **1870** *Daily News* Sept. 16 This proves to my mind that the Captain was taken as flat aback as could be by a squall striking her from starboard.

c. *fig.* Of persons. ***to take aback***: to surprise or discomfit by a sudden and unlooked-for check.

1840 HOOD *Up the Rhine* 21 The boy, in sea phrase, was taken all aback. **1842** DICKENS *Amer. Notes* 52 I don't think I was ever so taken aback in all my life. **1878** BOSWORTH SMITH *Carthage* 95 They were for the moment taken aback by the strange appearance of the vessels coming into battle with their masts left standing.

4. ***aback of, aback o'***: at the back of, on the back of, behind (cf. *back of*, BACK *adv.* 15). *arch.*, *dial.* (see *E.D.D.* and *Sc. Nat. Dict.*), and *U.S.* (where *Obs.* or *dial.*).

1783 W. FLEMING *Jrnl. in Kentucky* 8 Jan. in Mereness *Trav. Amer. Col.* (1916) 663 Fern Creek is lost in ponds and low flat land a back of the Falls. **1836** EDWARD *Hist. Texas* v. 79 Those districts..aback of the older settled ones. **1849** *Gloss. Prov. Words Teesdale* 1 Aback, prep. Behind; as, stand aback o' me. **1876** MORRIS *Sigurd* II. 150 So he leapeth aback of Greyfell, and rideth the desert bare. **1894** HALL CAINE *Manxman* I. xi. 50 Just aback of the lighthouse. **1908** J. LUMSDEN *Doun i' th' Loudons* 80 Be aff, ye limmer, unman men nae mair, A-back o' granny, is the post for you!

†**abackstays** (ə'bæksteɪz), *adv. Obs. Naut.* [A *prep.*[1] on, and BACK-STAYS.] Having the more important sails hauled round so as to lie in the plane of the wind's direction, and thus to present no surface to it. (Done when a square-rigged vessel is sailing in a wind more or less astern, and it is desired to stop or slacken her speed temporarily; or in lying 'hove to.' The stays or stay-ropes lie permanently in this plane, whence the sail was said to be *abackstays*, now *backed.*)

1628 SIR K. DIGBY *Voyage into Medit.* 75 (1868) I, lying with my foresaile abackestayes, could not fill time enough to stretch out a head of her till shee was gott abord me vpon the bowe. **1630** J. TAYLOR (Water P.) *A Braue Sea-fight* Wks. III. 39/2 The James got betweene one of their fleet, and singled her out, lying by her sides with foresaile and foretopsaile abackstayes, so neere as a man might quoit a Bisket cake into her. **1694** *Lond. Gaz.* mmdcccclxxviii. 1 Captain Teissere remained a back stays several hours.

†**abackward**, *adv. Obs.* [ABACK *adv.* + -WARD.] The earlier form of BACKWARD.

1205 LAYAMON 20086 Arthur thehte hine a bacward. *c* **1374** CHAUCER *Boethius* 108 Orpheus loked[e] abakwarde on Erudice his wijf and lost[e] hir and was deed.

[**abacot**, a spurious word found in many dictionaries, originating in a misprint of BYCOKET.]

abactinal (,æbæk'taɪnəl, ,æb'æktɪnəl), *a. Zool.* [f. L. *ab* away from + ACTINAL.] Remote from the actinal area; pertaining to that part of the surface of a radiated animal which is opposite to the mouth, e.g. the apex of a sea-urchin, or upper surface of a star-fish. See ACTINAL.

1857 L. AGASSIZ *Contrib. Nat. Hist. America* IV. 376 I have called this side..the oral or actinal area, and the opposite side the aboral or abactinal area. **1864** A. AGASSIZ in *Reader* No. 85, 204/2 The spines on the abactinal area. **1881** MACKINTOSH in *Nature* No. 628, 41 The abactinal system and ambulacral plates of a Cidarid combined with the thin test and hollow spines of a Diadema.

abaction (æ'bækʃən). *rare.* [ad. assumed L. *abactiōn-em*, n. of action, f. *abigere* to drive away; see next.] A driving away, as of cattle. (In Cockeram 1626, and some mod. Dict., but perhaps never in general use.)

1949 C. FRY *Lady's not for Burning* 11 He says he has also committed petty larceny, Abaction, peculation and incendiarism.

†**abactor** (æ'bæktə(r), -ɔː(r)), *Obs.* [a. late L. *abactor*, n. of agent f. *abig-ĕre*, sup. *abact-um*, to drive off, esp. in late L. to drive away cattle; f. *ab* off, away + *ag-ĕre* to drive.] 'One who drives away or steals cattle in herds, or great numbers at once, in distinction from those that steal only a sheep or two.' J.

1659 HAMMOND *On Psalms* cxliv. 14, 696 The safety of their herds, not only from straying, but in time of warr, from invaders and abactors, whose breaking in..is attended with the cattels passing through or going out. **1691** BLOUNT *Law Dict.* Abactors (*abactores*) were stealers of Cattle or Beasts, by Herds or great numbers; and were distinguished from *Fures.* **1829** LAMB *Lett.* II. 66 (1841) The Abactor or Abactor's wife (vide Ainsworth) would suppose she had heard something.

‖**abaculus** (ə'bækjʊləs), *Arch.* [L. dim. of *abacus*: see next.] = ABACISCUS.—Fairholt.

abacus ('æbəkəs). Pl. **abaci** ('æbəsaɪ). [a. L. *abacus*, f. Gr. ἄβαξ a board or slab, a draught-board, a calculating table, a sideboard, a plate, &c. Used in Eng. in several of the Gr. and L. meanings.]

†**1.** A board or tray strewn with sand, for the delineation of figures, geometrical diagrams, etc. *Obs.*

1387 TREVISA *Higden's Polychr.* (Rolls Ser.) VII. 69 Abacus is a table wiþ þe whiche schappes beþ portrayed and ipeynt in powdre, and abacus is a craft of geometrie. [Not in the original Higden.]

2. A calculating table, or frame; *spec.* one in which balls slide upon wires, and *gen.* any arrangement for the mechanical solution of arithmetical problems.

1686 *Obs. conc. Chinese Char.* in *Misc. Cur.* III. 216 Their Abacus or counting Board, for performing the Operations of Arithmetick, which I find pretty near to agree with that of the antient Romans. **1861** T. WRIGHT *Ess. on Archæol.* II. xv. 67 The system of the abacus appears to have continued in use..till late in the twelfth century. **1871** EARLE *Philol. Eng. Tongue* 353 The science of calculation by nine figures and zero, which was gradually superseding the abacus or ball-frame, with its counters. **1881** *Nature* No. 625, 593 M. Gariel has thus arrived at a kind of abacus by which the various problems that arise may be geometrically solved by simple inspection.

3. *Arch.* The upper member of the capital of a column, supporting the architrave; in the Tuscan, Doric, and ancient Ionic orders, a square flat plate, but in the Corinthian and Composite, variously cut and ornamented.

1563 SHUTE *Architecture* iv. 2a The Abacus, that lieth upon Voluta, is iust .4. square flat like to a trencher. **1664** EVELYN tr. *Freart, Parallel of Arch.* 129 The Abacus..is that quadrangular piece..serving instead of a Corona or drip to the Capitel. **1760** RAPER in *Phil. Trans.* LI. 797 The pointed abacus shews the architecture to be Greek. **1879** SCOTT *Lect. on Archit.* I. 127 The crochet capital, which is magnificently developed beneath round abaci.

†**4.** = ABACK, *sb. Obs.* (perh. never used in Eng.)

5. *Gr. & Rom. Antiq.* A side-board.

1853 SOYER *Pantroph.* 264 The most precious plate is arranged before the arrival of the guests, on the abacus, or sideboard.

abad, abade, obs. forms of ABODE *sb.* and *v.*

†**abada**. *Obs.* Also **abda, abath**. [a. Pg. *abada*, the female rhinoceros; 'perh. Malay; Favre gives *bādak* (*k* mute) as rhinoceros, Batta *badak*, Macassar *bāda*, Javan. *wadak*.' (Col. Yule.) Cf. Arab. *abadat*, 'animal fugax, pavidum, immansuetum; fera.' Freyt.] An early name for the Rhinoceros.

a **1599** BARKER in *Hakluyt* II. 591 (1812) We sent commodities to their king to barter for Amber-griese and for the hornes of Abath..Now this Abath is a beast which hath one horne onely in his forehead and is thought to be the female Vnicorne, and is highly esteemed of all the Moores in those parts as a most soverayne remedie against poyson. **1613** PURCHAS *Pilgr.* I. v. ii. 387 Full of Elephants and Abada's (this Beast is the Rhinoceros). *Ibid.* (1864) 2 In Bengala are found great numbers of Abdas or Rhinocerotes, whose horne (growing up from his snowt,) is good against poyson, and is much accounted of throughout all India. **1625** —— *His Pilgrimes* II. 1773 The Abada or Rhinoceros is not in India, but only in Bengala and Patane.

Abaddon (ə'bædən). [Heb. *ăbaddōn*, transl. in *Prov.* xv. 11, *destruction*, from *ābad* he perished.] Used in *Rev.* ix. 11 as equivalent to the Gr. 'Απολλύων, destroyer, as the name of 'the angel of the bottomless pit.' Hence applied by

Milton to the bottomless pit, or abyss of hell, itself.

c 1382 WYCLIF *Rev.* ix. 11 The aungel of depnesse, to whom the name bi Ebru Labadon [*v.r.* Abbadon, Laabadon, Abadon], forsothe bi Greke Appolion, and bi Latyn hauynge the name Destrier. **1526** TINDALE *ibid.* The angell of the bottomlesse pytt, whose name in the hebrew tonge is Abadon. **1611** *Ibid.* Whose name in the Hebrew tongue is Abaddon. **1671** MILTON *Par. R.* IV. 624 In all her gates Abaddon rues Thy bold attempt. **1842** TENNYSON *St. Simon Styl.* 169 Abaddon and Asmodeus caught at me. **1850** NEALE *Med. Hymns* 27 Michael, who in princely virtue Cast Abaddon from on high.

abade, obs. form of ABODE *sb.* and *v.*

†**abæili-en**, *v. Obs.* OE. **abæliȝ-an.** [Perh. cogn. w. ABELȜ-AN.] To offend, vex.

a 1000 *Chr. & Satan* 195 Ðæt he ne abæliȝe bearn wealdendes. **1205** LAYAMON II. 3 Bruttes weoren bisie, & often hine a-bæileden.

a-baffled, a-bafelled, s.w. dial. f. BAFFLED.

abaft (əˈbɑːft, -æ-), *adv.* and *prep.* Also 4 obaft. [A *prep.*[1] on, at, + *baft*, *bæft*, *bi-æften*, OE. *be-æftan*, itself a combination of *be*, *bi*, prep. about + *æftan*, adv. behind, back. See BAFT and AFT.]

A. *adv.*

†1. Of direction: backwards. *Obs.*

c 1275 *Cursor Mundi* 22150 *Gött. MS.* The watris for to rin on baft. *Cotton MS.* The burn[i]s for to rin obaft. (*Other MSS.* of baft, on bafte.)

2. Of position: *literally*, back, behind, in the rear. From an early period, it seems to have been confined to a ship (in reference to which its immediate source *baft* is also found in the 14th c.); the bows are the foremost, and the stern the *aft*ermost part, hence *abaft* means 'In the after part or stern half of the ship.'

1628 DIGBY *Voyage to Medit.* 46 She was in excellent trimme (drawing 15 foote abaft and 14 and 3 inches before). **1677** *London Gazette* mcxciv. 4 The St. Mary of Ostend with 22 Men,..having two Guns, one afore, and the other abaft. **1748** ANSON *Voyage* II. iv. (ed. 4) 220 Her upper works were rotten abaft. **1833** MARRYAT *Peter Simple* (1863) 256 I hove the log, marked the board, and then sat down abaft on the signal chest. **1863** KINGSLEY *Water Babies* vii. 271 But Tom and the petrels never cared, for the gale was right abaft, and away they went over the crests of the billows.

3. By extension from the nautical term.

1797 THOS. BRYDGES *Homer Travestie* II. 237 Two heads are twice as good as one; When one stands forward, one abaft, They spy all matters fore and aft.

B. *prep.* [The adv. defined by an object.]

In the rear of, behind. Only in nautical lang., with reference to a ship or any specified part of her.

1594 DAVIS *Seamens Secrets* (1607) 6, I may say in the Seaman's phrase..in the time of her separation she is abaft the Sunne. **1599** RD. HAKLUYT *Voyages* II. I. 187 The Boteswaine of the Galley walked abaft the maste, and his Mate afore the maste. **1757** ROBERTSON *Portsm. Docky.* in *Phil. Trans.* I. 292 Beside, the mawls worked at several shoars set up abaft the said 64 feet. **1825** H. B. GASCOIGNE *Path to Naval Fame* 53 Abaft the Beam impelling breezes blow. **1857** SHERARD OSBORN *Quedah* ii. 31 A little cabin, which I saw abaft the mainmast. **1860** MAURY *Phys. Geog. Sea* xv. 642 The wind is aft, through the north-east just abaft the beam.

abaht (əˈbɑːt), repr. dial. and colloq. pronunc. of ABOUT *adv.* and *prep.*

1860 'T. TREDDLEHOYLE' *Bairnsla Ann.* (*E.D.D.*) 39 Ah wor rairly off abaght it. **1898** *Eng. Dial. Dict.* I. 9/1 Ah've all abaht eniff apple-trees i' t'gardin. **1901** G. B. SHAW *Capt. Brassbound's Conversion* I. 217 *Rankin.* Well, what about them? *Drinkwater.* Wot abaht them! Waw, theyre eah. **1937** D. L. SAYERS *Busman's Honeymoon* i. 54 'E 've a right to knock me abaht. **1968** *Listener* 6 June 742/2 These moved.. among the crowd crying 'Speshul! Speshul! Royal Wedding speshul... Read all abaht it.' **1977** *Melody Maker* 26 Mar. 10/5 'Splitting notes', what's all that abaht?

abaid, obs. form of ABODE *sb.* and *v.*

abaie, abaye, obs. forms of ABYE *v.*

†**abail**, *v. Obs. rare*[−1] [f. BAIL *v.*, with pref. A-, in what sense doubtful.] ? To give bail for, liberate on bail, or from bail.

? **1450** *Copy of a Paper Roll. temp. Hen. VI* (in 3rd Rep. of Hist. MSS. Comm. (1872) 279) He [the Duke] therfor conspired..to labour the delivraunce of the seid Duke of Orliaunce, & so to h[ave the] seid seale ayen, the which he complesshed withoute other payements of Fynaunce, raunceoun, or depance, & toke grate sommes of gy[ftes], & rewarde beside forth, & the kynge ne the lands never abailled.

†**abaisance** (əˈbeɪsəns). *Obs.* [a. OFr. *abaissance* abasement, humility, n. of action f. *abaissant* pr. pple. of *abaisser* to lower: see ABASE. From the earliest period confused in Eng. with *obeisance*, Fr. *obéissance*, obedience, n. of action f. *obéir* to obey. A few writers in 7–8 tried in vain to restore the etymological distinction.] The bending of the body as a mark of respect; a bow.

[**1393** GOWER *Conf.* III. VI. iii. 75 And ate last he gan to lout And obeisaunce unto her make.] **1671** SKINNER *Etymol. Ling. Ang.* To make a low abaissance. **1675** *Art of Contentment* IV. xv. 199 Haman can find no gust in all the sensualities of the Persian court, because a poor despicable Jew denies his abaisance. **1721** BAILEY An Abaisance, a low Conge or Bow, a stooping down. **1755** JOHNSON Obeysance is considered by Skinner as a corruption of abaisance, but is now universally used. [**1838** DICKENS *Nich. Nick.* (C.D. ed.) xxiv. 193 Miss Snevellicci made a graceful obeisance.]

abaisch, abaish, abaisse, obs. forms ABASH.

abaise, obs. form of ABASE.

abaiser (əˈbeɪsə(r)), 'Burnt ivory or ivory black.' Weale *Dict. Terms* (1849), and mod. Dict.

†**abait**, *v. Obs.* Also **abate, abeyte.** [f. A- *pref.* 1 on + BAIT.]

†1. To set on (a dog), to hound on, bait.

1485 MALORY *Morte d' Arthur* XVIII. xxi. (1817) II. 355 This lady the huntresse had abated her dogge for the bowe at a barayne hynde.

†2. *fig.* To excite, stimulate (the appetites).

1303 R. BRUNNE *Handlyng Synne* 181 Hys flesshe on here was so abeytede, þat þyke womman he coveytyde.

abait, -ment, obs. forms of ABATE, -MENT.

abak, obs. form of ABACK *adv.*

†**abalienate** (æbˈeɪlɪəneɪt), *v. Obs.* [f. L. *abaliēnāt-um*, pa. pple. of *abaliēnā-re* to estrange; f. *ab* off, away, + *aliēnā-re* to estrange; f. *aliēn-us* belonging to another; see ALIEN.]

1. 'To make that another's which was our own before. A term of the civil law not much used in common speech.' J. (Only used as a technical equivalent of *Abaliēnāre* in Rom. Law.)

2. To remove; to estrange in feeling.

1554 JN. PHILPOT *Exam. & Writ.* (Parker Soc.) 328 No distances of places, no chance, no perversity of men, shall abalienate me from your clemency and faithfulness. **1652** GAULE *Mag-astro-mancer* 202 God may be pleased..so to abalienate, or suspend, corruptions for the present.

3. To cause loss or aberration of (intellect).

1585 ABP. SANDYS *Sermons* (1841) 300 The devil and his deceitful angels do so..abalienate their minds, and trouble their memory, that they cannot tell what is said. **1652** GAULE *Mag-astro-mancer* 195 Extasies of prophets did not so abalienate their mindes as that they apprehended not what they did or said.

abalienation (æbˌeɪlɪəˈneɪʃən), [ad. L. *abaliēnātiōn-em*, n. of action, f. *abaliēnā-re*: see prec.]

1. 'The act of giving up one's right to another person; or a making over an estate, goods, or chattels by sale, or due course of law.' J. (A technical use of the word to translate *Abalienatio* in Rom. Law.) Also *fig.*

1828 KIRBY & SPENCE *Intr. to Ent.* III. xxxii. 307 The most entire abalienation of shape already known is in female Coccus.

†2. Removal or transference of feeling; estrangement. *Obs.*

1656 J. TRAPP *Expos. Matt.* vii. 1 (1868) The not giving vent to our hearts, by a wise and plain reproof, causeth abalienation of affection. **1683** S. CLARK *Lives, S. Fairclough* 191 Neither difference of Opinion, nor distance of place, nor seldomness of Converse, nor any worldly respects, did cause the least ab-alienation from a person so unworth.

†3. Loss or failure of the mental faculties. *Obs.*

1652 GAULE *Mag-astro-mancer* 90 When reason is most suspended, obscured, and debarred, as in sleeps, dreams, abalienations, distractions, etc. **1853** MAYNE *Exp. Lex. Abalienation*: A term formerly used for decay, either of the whole or part of the body; also for loss or failing of the senses or mental faculties, according to Scribonius Largus.

abalone (æbəˈləʊnɪ). *U.S.* Also **abelone, avalone,** etc. [Amer. Sp. *abulón* (f. Monterey Indian *aulun*) in same sense.] A gastropod mollusc of the genus *Haliotis*, used for food; an ear-shell or sea-ear. Also *attrib.*

1850 B. TAYLOR *Eldorado* I. xvii. 174 The avelone, which is a univalve, found clinging to the sides of rocks, furnishes the finest mother-of-pearl. **1870** *Amer. Naturalist* III. 250 These shells are popularly called Sea-ears... In California the people call them *Abalones*. *Ibid.* 256 Haliotis or Abalone shells. **1882** *Harper's Mag.* Oct. 728 They [*sc.* Chinamen in S. California] prepare..the avallonia meat and avallonia shells for their home market. **1910** *Encycl. Brit.* I. 6 The abalone shell is found..on the southern California coast, and when polished makes a beautiful ornament. **1936** RUSSELL & YONGE *Seas* (ed. 2) xvi. 350 Among the many shells used for decorative purposes we..mention one, known in the Channel Islands as the Ormer and on the Pacific coast of North America as the Abalone.

†**aband** (əˈbænd), *v. Obs.* [An artificial contraction of ABANDON, used by Spenser and other of the Elizabethan affecters of archaism; prob. in imitation of pairs like *open, ope.*]

1. To abandon, forsake.

1559 *Mirror for Mag., Albanact* xx. 27 Let us therefore both cruelty abande, And prudent seeke both gods and men to please. **1590** SPENSER *F.Q.* II. x. 65 And Vortiger enforst the kingdome to aband.

2. To banish.

1559 *Mirr. Mag.* 119 Tis better far the enemies t' aband Quite from thy borders, to a forren soile.

A band (eɪ bænd). *Histology.* [Named *A* (in place of *Q*) by K. Hürthle 1909, in *Arch. f. die ges. Physiol.* CXXVI. 23, repr. G. *anisotrop* anisotropic (in allusion to its optical properties).] Each of the transverse bands which alternate with I bands in fibrils of striated muscle, appearing dark under polarized light and composed of longitudinal filaments of myosin (and actin).

[**1937** J. D. BERNAL in Needham & Green *Perspectives in Biochem.* 47 The individual myofibril..consists alternately of two portions... The anisotropic portion (*A*), has a markedly stronger positive double refraction than the other. .. A certain amount of evidence points to the greater thickness of the *A* portions.] **1939** *Physiol. Rev.* XIX. 287 The A (for anisotropic, also called Q in the older literature) and the I..bands, respectively. **1966** C. R. & T. S. LEESON *Histol.* ix. 163/1 During contraction the A band remains constant in length but the H band and I band diminish. **1974** D. & M. WEBSTER *Compar. Vertebr. Morphol.* vi. 114 These actin filaments are not only in the I band but also extend into the A band, running between myosin filaments.

‖**abandeˈrado.** *Obs.* [Sp. *abanderado* or *banderado*, 'an Ensignes seruant which carrieth the ensigne for his master' Minsheu 1623, f. *bandera* a banner.]

1598 BARRET *Theorike of Warres* ii. i. 21 If he deliuereth his [Ensign] vnto his Abanderado,..the rest are to do the like. *Ibid.* The Abanderados are vsed to be souldiers, and some do set their owne seruants to that office.

†**abanˈdon, -ˈdoun**, *adv. Obs.* 3–4. Also **abandun, abaundune.** [a. OFr. phr. *à bandon, à bandun*, f. *à* at, to, *bandon, -un* 'ban, proscription, authoritative order, jurisdiction, control, disposal, discretion,' as in *avoir à* (or *en*) *bandon*, to have in one's jurisdiction, at one's disposal, under one's control; *à son bandon* at his pleasure; *courir à bandon* to run at one's own discretion, without restraint, impetuously. See also BANDON *sb.* and cf. the phrases *at his bandoun, in hir bandoun*, etc.]

1. Under jurisdiction, control, authority; at (one's) free disposal.

c 1225 *Ureisun of God Almihti* 203 To beon moder of swich sune..& habben him so abaundune [*Lamb. MS.* abandun] ðet he wulle ðet þin wille oueral beo i-uorðed.

2. At one's own discretion, at one's will, without interference or interruption from others. Hence, **a.** Unrestrictedly, freely, recklessly, with all one's might, in full career. **b.** Unstintedly, entirely, wholly. **c.** Without bounds, to the fullest extent. (Cf. OFr. *une porte overte a bandon.*)

a 1320 *Guy of Warw.* (Turnb.) 181 Ther com an hundred knightes of gret might, Alle thai folwed him abandoun, And he mett with hem als a lyoun. c 1320 *Arthour & Merlin* 6016 His ribbes and scholder fel adoun Men might se the liuer abandon. **1423** JAMES I *King's Quair* II. vi Quhare as in strayte ward, and in strong prison, Without confort, in sorowe abandoune.

abandon (əˈbændən), *v.* Also 4–6 **abandoun(e, abandune, habandone, habandoune.** [a. OFr. *abandune-r, abandone-r*, f. phr. *à bandon*: see ABANDON *adv.*; = *mettre à bandon* in its various senses; to put under any one's jurisdiction, to leave to any one's mercy or discretion; to leave one to his own discretion, let loose, let go; to put under public jurisdiction or ban, proscribe, banish.]

I. To subjugate absolutely.

†1. To reduce under absolute control or authority; to subjugate, subject, subdue. (Chiefly *northern.*) *Obs.*

1375 BARBOUR *Bruce* xxxii. 8 And sa the land abandonit he That none durst warn him do his will. c **1425** WYNTOWN *Cron.* II. ix. 36 þai dowtyd at [= that] hys senyhowrey, Suld þame abawndown halyly. c **1525** SKELTON *Magnif.* 1477 I have welthe at wylle Fortune to her law cannot abandune me. **1533** BELLENDENE *Livy* II. 141 The majeste of consulis micht nocht abandoun the instant furie of pepill.

II. To give up absolutely.

2. To give up to the control or discretion of another; to leave to his disposal or mercy; to yield, cede, or surrender absolutely a thing *to* a person or agent.

c 1386 CHAUCER *Persones T. De Luxuria* 800 Avoutrie.. thurgh whiche tho, that somtime were on fleshe, abandone hir bodies to other persons. **1477** EARL RIVERS *Dictes* 87 (Caxton) If thou wol habandone to thy body al his wil thou shalt be the worse. **1667** DRYDEN *Ann. Mir.* 224 He sigh'd, abandoning his charge to fate. **1761** HUME *Hist. Eng.* I. *init.* To abandon that place to the merciless fury of the enemy. **1849** MACAULAY *Hist. Eng.* I. 303 Those who completely abandoned to others the direction of the vessels.

†3. To sacrifice, devote, surrender. *Obs.*

c 1450 *Merlin* (1877) xx. 334 When he his bodye thus abandoneth for us welle ought we oures for to abandon for hym. **1523** LD. BERNERS *Froissart* I. ccxv. 272 All those that wolde take on them this croysey, and that wolde abandon their bodyes willyngly to distroy these yuell people and their companyons. **1642** ROGERS *Naaman* 163 He will abandon all his worth, and gage his credit too, but hee will haue it. **1718** LADY M. W. MONTAGU *Letters* lxxix. 131 I abandon all things to the care of pleasing you.

4. *refl.* To give oneself up without resistance, to yield oneself unrestrainedly—as *to* the mastery of a passion or unreasoning impulse.

1564 HAWARD *Eutropius* vii. 68 [Nero] at laste, did habondone hymselfe whollye over to so great disworship, that he woulde daunce and singe openly in the apparaile of common mynstrelles. **1601** SHAKS. *Twel. N.* I. iv. 19 If she be so abandon'd to her sorrow As it is spoke, she never will admit me. **1722** DE FOE *Hist. Plague* 165 They gaue themselves up, and abandoned themselves to their despair. **1762** KAMES *Elem. Crit.* II. 26 (1833) Has nothing left but to abandon himself to chance. **1879** MCCARTHY *Hist. Own Time* II. xxix. 379 He seldom abandons himself altogether to the inspiration of the poet.

†**5.** *intr.* (by omission of refl. pron.) and *pass.* To give oneself up, devote oneself *to* a pursuit or course. *Obs.*

1393 GOWER *Conf.* II. 1603 (I. 213) Which so ferforth was abandouned To Cristis feith. *Ibid.* III. 253 Lucrece his wife all environed With women, which were abandoned To werche. **1483** CAXTON *G. Leg.* 144/2 After he abandonned to lede an holy lyf.

6. *trans.* To relinquish to underwriters all claim to property insured, or to any part of it which may be recovered, after a loss. (Often used *absol.*)

1755 N. MAGENS *Essay on Insurances* I. 89 When a ship.. shall not be heard of in three months beyond the usual time for such a voyage, she may be considered as lost, and the Insured is permitted to abandon Ship and Cargo to the Insurers, and to demand payment of the sums they have respectively underwrote. **1809** TOMLINS *Law Dict.* s.v. Insurance II. 7 As soon as the Insured receive accounts of such a loss as entitles them to abandon, they must, in the first instance, make their election whether they will abandon or not; and if they abandon, they must give the Underwriters notice in a reasonable time, otherwise they waive their right to abandon. **1848** ARNOULD *Law of Mar. Ins.* (1866) II. III. vi. 855 If the assured, by mortgaging his ship, has parted with the power of conveying an absolute title, he cannot abandon to the underwriters on ship.

7. To let go, give up, renounce, leave off (a possession, habit, practice, pursuit); to cease to hold, use, or practise.

1393 GOWER *Conf.* prol. 766 (I. 29) Thus was abandoned Thempire, which came never ayeine Into the hands of no Romaine. **1460** *Pol. Rel. & Love Poems* 70 For suche yefte is Abandounyng expresse That [= what] with worship a-yein may not be take. **1577** tr. Bullinger *Decades* 111 The commaundement for abandoning and not worshipping of images. **1777** BURKE *Lett. to Bristol Sheriffs* Wks. III. 173 The sense of the nation obliged the court of Charles the second to abandon the Dutch war. **1856** KANE *Arctic Explor.* II. xvi. 172 Our fine theodolite we were forced to abandon. **1879** LUBBOCK *Scient. Lect.* v. 152 It is a great mistake to suppose that implements of stone were abandoned directly metal was discovered.

8. To forsake, leave, or desert (a place, person, or cause); to leave without one's presence, help, or support.

1490 CAXTON *Eneydos* vi. 29 To habandoune and leue the swete countrey of theyr natiuyte. **1588** ALLEN *Admonition* 57 The like vsurper Richard the third, being.. abandoned of the nobility and people. **1671** MILTON *Sams.* 118 As one past hope, abandoned, And by himself given over. **1722** DE FOE *Hist. Plague* 105 How can you abandon your own flesh and blood? **1792** *Anecd. of W. Pitt* II. xxii. 3 King Frederick's good fortune did not abandon him. **1879** MISS BRADDON *Vixen* III. 215 I felt myself abandoned and alone in the world.

¶ In many expressions, as to abandon a ship, fortress, post of duty, etc., the idea partakes of both 7 and 8.

1790 BURKE *Reg. Peace* Let. IV. Wks. V. 98 The helm of justice is abandoned. **1849** MACAULAY *Hist. Eng.* I. 633 When Tangier was abandoned, Kirke returned to England. **1860** MAURY *Phys. Geog. Sea* xix. 807 That ship was made a complete wreck in a few moments, and she was abandoned by the survivors.

III. To let loose.

†**9.** *refl.* To let oneself loose, give oneself up impetuously or recklessly, rush headlong, risk oneself. *Obs.*

1375 BARBOUR *Bruce* XVII. 393 Thar mycht men assailȝeouris se Abandoune thame richt hardely. *Ibid.* III. 48 And the King him abandonyt ay To defend behind his mengȝe. *c* **1530** LD. BERNERS *Arthur of Lytell Bryt.* (1814) 120 Hector.. spurred hys horse, and habandoned hymselfe amonge his enemyes.

†**10.** To let loose, set free, liberate. *Obs. rare.*

1583 STANYHURST *Virgil* II. 41 Thow soon of holye godesse, from flame thy carcas abandon Thee foes haue conquer'd, Troy towne is fyred of al sides.

IV. To banish.

†**11.** To put to the ban, interdict, proscribe, banish: *fig.* to expel, cast out, reject. *Obs.*

1548 UDALL etc. *Erasm. Paraph.* Matt. xi. 2 Abandone them from him and deliuer them to Jesus. **1567** R. MULCASTER *Fortescue* (1672) 98 To abandon sin out of the Realme, & to advance vertue. **1570** LEVINS *Manipulus*, To Abandon, *Exterminare.* **1581** JOHN STUDLEY *Seneca's Tragedies, Hippolytus* 58b, Craggy crested Taurus mount whose hoary and frosty face With numming cold abandons all inhabitors the place. **1582** *Rheims Bible* Luke vi. 22 Blessed shall ye be when men shall hate you and abandon [*ejecerint*] your name as evil. **1596** SHAKS. *Tam. Shr.* Ind. ii. 112 Being all this time abandoned from thy bed. **1649** BP. HALL *Cases of Consc.* II. vii. 134 (1654) Whipt them in the publique Amphitheater, and abandoned them out of their dominions. **1660** CIMELGUS BONDE *Scutum Regale* 137 Flatterers will he abandon from his Court, and those who keep other mens estates will he banish from his Realm.

†**b.** *refl.*

1577 VAUTROULLIER *Luther's Ep. to Galat.* lf. 6 Thus I abandone my selfe from all actiue righteousness, both of mine owne and of Gods law.

†**aban'don, -'doun(e,** *sb.*[1] *Obs.* [a. OFr. *abandon*, f. vb. *abandoner*; but in form confused with the adv. ABANDON, so that both in OFr. *à abandon*, and in ME. *at, in abandoun*, take the place of the simple *à bandon*, and *at, in bandoun.*] = BANDON.

1. Complete control; mostly in phr. *to put* or *take in* (= into) ***abandoun, to have in abandoun, to give in abandoun***: to give into the absolute control of another, give up absolutely.

1475 CAXTON *Jason* 62, I haue nothing of valeur but that ye shall haue at your abandon and will. **1523** LD. BERNERS *Froissart* I. ix. 8, I and my sonne shall be to you for euer bounde, and wyll put all the realme of Ingland in your abandon.

2. To do a thing *in* or *at abandoun*: recklessly, impetuously, unreservedly, lavishly. (*Northern.*)

1375 BARBOUR *Bruce* xv. 59 The Scottis men dang on so fast, And schot on thame at abandoune. *c* **1400** *Rom. Rose* 2342 Aftir this swiffte, it is good resoun, He yeve his good in abandoun.

abandon (əˈbændən), *sb.*[2] ? *Obs.* [f. ABANDON *v.*] The act of abandoning; abandonment, relinquishment; *spec.* of property insured to the underwriters.

1755 N. MAGENS *Essay on Insur.* I. 89 The Insurers shall be obliged to pay 92 per cent. within two months from and after the Time such Abandon was notified to them. ?**1776** LD. KAMES (T.) These heavy exactions have occasioned an abandon of all mines but what are of the richer sort.

¶ Cited by Todd from Sandys as 'a forsaker; he who has abandoned or left anything': so in succeeding dictionaries; but Sandys's word is *Abandoner.*

abandon (əˈbændən, formerly ‖abɑ̃ːˈdɔ̃, æbənˈdɒŋ), *sb.*[3] [mod.Fr. *abandon*, f. vb. *abandonner* to ABANDON. See ABANDONMENT 5.] *Lit.* a letting loose, abandonment or surrender to natural impulses; hence entire freedom from artificial constraint or from conventional trammels, unconstrainedness of manner, careless freedom, dash.

1822 L. SIMOND *Switzerland* I. 285 There was more *abandon* in what she [*sc.* Mme de Staël] said, than in what she wrote. **1831** *Fraser's Mag.* III. 358/1 It is the heart alone which is surrendered to its 'abandon'. **1850** M. F. OSSOLI *Woman in 19th Cent.* (1862) 228 I love 'abandon' only when natures are capable of the extreme reverse. **1850** MRS. JAMESON *Sacred and Leg. Art* 210 Flung in all the abandon of solitude amid the depth of leafy recesses. **1851** RUSKIN *Mod. Paint.* I. II. v. ii. 4. 345 The magnificent *abandon* of Harding's brush. **1879** DOWDEN *Southey* iii. 75 He had not yet come out from the glow and the noble *abandon* of the South. **1922** JOYCE *Ulysses* 636 She also was Spanish or half so, types that wouldn't do things by halves, passionate abandon of the south. **1930** W. S. MAUGHAM *Gent. in Parlour* xxxix. 223 There was no abandon in their dance.

abandonable (əˈbændənəb(ə)l), *a.* [f. ABANDON *v.* + -ABLE.] Capable of being abandoned.

1611 COTGR., *Cessible*: yeeldable, resignable, abandonnable.

†**a'bandonate,** *v. Obs. rare*[−1]. [Prob. f. It. *abbandonāre* to abandon; the orig. in loc. cit. is *non abbandonate.* But cf. *perturb* and *perturbate*, *determine* and *determinate*, *extirp* and *extirpate*, *invoke* and *invocate*, etc.] = ABANDON *v.*

1654 SIR A. COKAINE tr. *Dianea* of F. Loredano iv. 365 Friend, abandonate not Dianea, for Dianea will not forsake thee alive or dead.

abandoned (əˈbændənd), *ppl. a.* [f. ABANDON *v.* + -ED.]

1. Given up, relinquished, forsaken, cast off.

1477 CAXTON *Jason* 916 I pray you that ye will haue regarde to myn offre abandonned. **1578** GEFF. FENTON *Hist. Guicciardin* (Contents) The Pope being abandoned of all hope, accordeth with the Imperials. **1600** SHAKS. *A.Y.L.* v. iv. 202 I'll stay to know at your abandon'd cave. **1704** ROWE *Ulysses* III. i. 1093 A poor, forlorn, abandon'd woman. **1820** SHELLEY *Prom. Unbd.* I. i. 217 As rainy wind thro' the abandoned gate Of a fallen palace. **1878** LEVER *Jack Hunter* vii. 46 A waiting-maid in the abandoned finery of her mistress.

2. Self-given up *to* any influence or pursuit; devoted. Now always to things evil or opposed to reason.

1393 GOWER *Conf.* II. 1603 (I. 213) Which so ferforth was abandouned To Cristis feith. **1474** CAXTON *The Chesse* 104 Lecherye corupted and apayred the corages of tho men that ben abandoned to the same delyte. **1601** SHAKS. *Twel. N.* I. iv. 19 If she be so abandoned to her sorrow. **1692** BENTLEY *Boyle Lect.* i. 13 Abandon'd to a callousness and numbness of Soul. **1722** DE FOE *Hist. Plague* 163 The people sat still .. quite abandoned to despair. **1830** SCOTT *Demonol.* Let. x. Profligate, worthless, sharking cheats, abandoned to vice.

3. Hence (without *to*): Given up unrestrainedly to evil influences; utterly bad, immoral, profligate. Of men and their actions.

1692 PRIOR *Ode in imit. Hor.* III. 2 Where our abandon'd youth she sees Shipwreck'd in luxury, and lost in ease. **1705** STANHOPE *Paraph.* XI. 476 That treacherous Kiss of an abandoned Disciple. **1711** STEELE *Spectator* VI. 1 Abandoned writings of men of wit. **1769** *Junius Lett.* xxxiv. 150 Have you a single friend.. so shameless, so thoroughly abandoned, as to undertake your defence? **1834** COLERIDGE *Table Talk* 316 An abandoned woman who had been notoriously treacherous to us. **1880** SPALDING *Eliz. Demonology* 39 The abandoned impudence of the man!

abandonedly (əˈbændəndlı), *adv.* [f. prec. + -LY[2].]

1. In an abandoned manner; unrestrainedly, profligately, shamelessly.

1714 B. MANDEVILLE *The Bees* (1725) I. 65 The more he wallows in lust and strains every faculty to be abandondly voluptuous. **1788** BURKE *Sp. agt. Warren Hastings* Wks. XIII. 301 If there had been one more desperately and abandonedly corrupt.. to be found in India.

2. In ABANDON (*sb.*[3]), free from conventional restraint. *rare.*

1855 THOREAU *Letters* (1865) 126 True, it is well to live abandonedly from time to time.

abandonee (ə,bændəˈniː). [f. ABANDON *v.* + -EE; repr. Fr. *abandonné.*] The person to whom anything is formally or legally abandoned; *spec.* the underwriter to whom the salvage of a wrecked vessel is abandoned. See ABANDON *v.* 6.

1848 ARNOULD *Law. of Mar. Ins.* (1866) II. III. vi. 869 It is a question, whether, upon abandonment to the underwriter on goods, the abandonee takes the salvage subject to Ship-owner's claim for freight. **1880** MACLACHLAN *Merch. Shipp.* (ed. 3) x. 507 If, upon the completion of a voyage, the abandonee may withhold the goods until the freight is paid, he must have acquired an indefeasible title to it.

abandoner (əˈbændənə(r)). [f. ABANDON *v.* + -ER[1].] One who abandons or forsakes; a forsaker. (Gen. followed by *of.*)

1599 SANDYS *Europæ Speculum* 64 (1632) Yet they onely can sufficiently perhaps esteeme, who have seene a Frier an abandoner of the world. *c* **1613** BEAUM. & FL. or ? SHAKS. *Two Nob. Kins.* v. i. 138 Oh sacred, shadowie, cold, and constant queene, Abandoner of revells, mute, contemplatiue. **1664** H. MORE *Myst. of Iniq.* 558 (Apology) Their Reverend Predecessours, who were so judicious and zealous Abandoners of the Church of Rome.

abandoning (əˈbændənıŋ), *vbl. sb.* [f. ABANDON *v.* + -ING[1].] Used in various senses of the verb.

1. The action of giving up, forsaking, deserting.

1640 BP. HALL *Christian Mod.* 32 (Ward's rep.) It is more profitable to endure a scandal than an abandoning of truth. **1651** *Sir W. Rawleigh's Ghost* 217 The Israelites returned again to their old vomit by abandoning of God. **1790** BURKE *Reg. Peace* Let. IV. Wks. V. 98 When thus the helm of justice is abandoned, an universal abandoning of all other posts will succeed.

†**2.** The action of banishing, casting out, expulsion. *Obs.*

1611 SPEED *Hist. of Gr. Brit.* VII. xxxvi. 332 For the better ordering and administring of iustice, and for the abandoning of theeues. **1660** MILTON *Free Commw.* 449 The abandoning of all those whom they call Sectaries, for the detected Falshood and Ambition of som.

†**a'bandonly,** *adv. Obs.* [f. ABANDON *sb.*[1] + -LY[2]. Hence = *in* or *at abandoun*, and, like that, northern.] Recklessly, impetuously, unguardedly.

1375 BARBOUR *Bruce* VIII. 461 Thai yschit all abandounly And prikket furth sa willfully. **1375** *Ibid.* XI. 629 The Erll abaundonly Tuk the playn feld. *c* **1470** HENRY *Wallace* iv. 670 He tuk the strenth magre thar fayis will; Abandonly in bargan baid thar still.

abandonment (əˈbændənmənt). [a. Fr. *abandonnement*, f. *abandonner* to ABANDON: see -MENT.] The action or process of abandoning; the condition of being abandoned.

1. The action of relinquishing to another, of giving up, letting go, forsaking.

1611 COTGR., *Abandon* The quitting, abandonment, or prostitution of a thing vnto others. **1788** BURKE *Sp. agt. Hastings* Wks. XIII. 468 Mr. Hastings's abandonment of all his own pretences. **1818** BYRON *Ch. Harold* IV. cxxvii 'Tis a base Abandonment of reason to resign Our right of thought. **1856** KANE *Arctic Explor.* II. xvii. 179 I regard the abandonment of the brig as inevitable.

2. *Comm. Law.* The relinquishment of an interest or claim; esp. in *Marine Insurance.*

1809 TOMLINS *Law Dict.* Insurance II. 7 Abandonment is as ancient as the Contract of Insurance itself. **1848** ARNOULD *Law of Mar. Ins.* (1866) II. III. vi. 852 Abandonment therefore is the act of cession, by which.. the assured, on condition of receiving at once the whole amount of the insurance, relinquishes to the underwriters all his property and interest in the thing insured.

3. Self-abandonment; the surrender of oneself to an influence, of one's presence of mind, pretensions, etc.

1860 R. A. VAUGHAN *Ho. w. Mystics* (ed. 2) I. 153 Then understood this Master that true Abandonment, with utter Abasement, was the nearest way to God. **1870** EMERSON *Soc. & Solit.* iv. 69 Where heats and panics and abandonments are quite out of the system.

4. The condition of being abandoned.

1839 DE QUINCEY *Recoll. Lakes* Wks. 1862 II. 1 Fortitude which could face an occasion of sudden mysterious abandonment.

5. Freedom from restraint of manner, careless freedom, abandon.

1831 CARLYLE *Sartor Res.* 87 (1858) Gaily in light, graceful abandonment, the friendly talk played round that circle. **1842** MRS. BROWNING *Grk. Chr. Poets* 158 (1863) The elasticity and abandonment of Shakespeare. **1844**

DISRAELI *Coningsby* III. i. 88 His manner was frank even to abandonment.

‖**abandum.** *Law.* [med.L. *abandum*, and *abando-nis* = OFr. *abandon*. See ABANDON *sb.*[1]] 'Anything sequestered, proscribed, or abandoned.' Tomlins *Law Dict.* 1809.

‖**abanet, abnet** ('æbənət, 'æbnət). [Heb. *abnēt*, a belt, *Lev.* viii. 13.] **1.** *Jewish Antiq.* 'A band made of fine linen, and used to bind as a girdle about the body of persons in authority, especially the Jewish priests.' Kitto *Cycl. Bib. Lit.* (1849) 19.

1707 PHILLIPS, *Abanet* or *Abnet* (Heb.) a sort of Girdle that Priests wore among the Jews.

†**2.** Hence, *Surg.* A girdle-like bandage. *Obs.* **1802** TURTON *Med. Gloss.* **1853** MAYNE *Exp. Lex.*

‖**abangan** (ə'baŋgən), *sb. pl.* [Javanese, f. *abang* red (see quot. 1959).] Syncretistic or nominal Muslims of Indonesia, esp. Java. Also *attrib.*

[**1927** A. W. NIEUWENHUIS in *Encycl. Islam* II. 498/2 The observance of the five daily *ṣalāt's* varies considerably... In Central Java and Atjeh they are neglected by the majority and those who observe them faithfully..are given special names (*wong putihan, lebe, santri*) and distinguished from the great mass of the people (*wong abangan, bangsat*).] **1956** C. GEERTZ in *Econ. Devel. & Cultural Change* IV. 138 The *abangan*, whose main adherence is to what is often miscalled 'the Javanese religion' (*agama djawa*). **1958** H. J. BENDA *Crescent & Rising Sun* i. 14 The *abangan* tradition of the Javanese peasant—rooted in age-old pre-Hindu mysticism with accretions from later, including Muslim, religious elements. **1959** W. F. WERTHEIM *Indonesian Soc. in Transition* (ed. 2) viii. 224 There was a clear distinction between..those considered pious Moslems, who followed meticulously the precepts of Islam..and (probably because of the white garments they preferred to wear while praying) were called the *putihan*, the 'white ones', and..the mass of the Javanese who were less strict in the observance of the duties prescribed by religion and were called *abangan*, the 'red ones'. **1976** C. A. COPPEL in J.A.C. Mackie *Chinese in Indonesia* ii. 71 President Suharto and his ruling group of *abangan* generals.

†**a'bann(e,** *v. Obs.* [OE. *abann-an* f. A- *pref.* 1, + *bann-an* to summon, and cogn. with ON. *banna* to interdict: see BAN; on which in sense 2 the word seems to be re-formed.]

1. To summon by proclamation. (only OE.)

1006 *O.E. Chron.* (Laud. MS.) Ðá hét se cyng abannan út ealne þeódscipe of Westseaxum.

2. To put under the ban of the church, anathematize.

1562 JEWEL *Apol.* II. 697 How durst the Bishops in this present council of Trident so solemnly to abanne and accurse all them that dare to find fault with the same.

abannation. *Obs.* var. of the following.

†**aba'nnition.** *Obs.*—[0] [expl. as f. *ab* away + *ann-us* year; but evidently n. of action f. med. Lat. *abannīre* (cf. Fr. *bannir* and Eng. *abann*) to banish.] 'A Banishment for one or two years for manslaughter.' J. from Blount *Glossogr.* 1656, and Bailey 1721. So *abannatio* in Du Cange, but evidently a mere guess from a false etymology, the meaning being simply 'banishment.'

1656 BLOUNT *Glossogr.*, *Abannition*, a banishing for a year, properly among the Greeks, for man-slaughter.

‖**abap'tiston.** *Obs.*—[0] [Gr. ἀβάπτιστον, not immersed, f. ἀ priv. + βαπτίζ-ειν to dip.] 'The crown of the old trepan, which was conical, or had some contrivance to prevent it from penetrating the cranium too suddenly, and so injuring the brain.' *Syd. Soc. Lex.* (So called by Galen, and inserted in early Dictionaries as the Greek name, but having apparently no claim to be English.)

1696 PHILLIPS, *Abaptiston* or *Anabaptiston*, a Surgeon's instrument. **1847** in CRAIG, etc.

†**a'bar,** *v. Obs. rare*—[1]. [f. A- *pref.* intensive + BAR *v. Abarrer* also occurs in late Anglo-Fr. Littleton *Inst.* 410.] To bar, debar.

1586 J. HOOKER *Giraldus' Hist. Irel.* in *Holinsh.* II. 17/2 They were thus abarred from approching to assaile the citie.

[**abarcy.** [ad. med.L. *abartia* 'insatiabilitas' Du Cange.] 'Insatiableness' Bailey vol. II. 1731. The L. and Eng. seem alike fictions.]

†**abare,** *v. Obs.*—[0] [OE. *abari-an.*] 'To make bare, uncover, or disclose,' Bailey, vol. II. 1731; whence in J., etc., but purely OE., obs. bef. 1100.

[**abarstic -ke,** *a.* 'Insatiable,' Cockeram 1626. Du Cange connects it with *abartia*; Blount 1712 with *berstan* to burst: 'who has so large a Belly that tho' 'tis full it will not burst.' Some error.]

abarticulation (,æbɑːtɪkjuː'leɪʃən). *Anat.* [ad. mod.L. *ab-articulātio*, a word for word rendering of Gr. ἀπ-άρθρωσις used by Galen, f. *ab* off, from, + *articulātio* a jointing, n. of action f. *artĭcŭl-āre* to join: see ARTICLE.] A kind of articulation admitting of free motion in the joint.

1751 CHAMBERS *Cycl.* s.v., *Abarticulation*, in Anatomy, the same with diarthrosis. **1853** MAYNE.

‖**abas.** *Obs.*—[0] 'A Persian weight, used in weighing pearls; one eighth less than the European caract.' Chambers *Cycl. Supp.* 1753, whence in subseq. Dicts. but without quotations.

abase (ə'beɪs), *v.* Forms: 4 **abesse**; 5 **abasse**; 6 **abace, adbass, abbase**; 6– **abase**. [ad. OFr. *abaiss-ier, abeiss-ier, abess-ier, abes-ier* (mod.Fr. *abaisser*), f. *à* to + *baissier* to lower:—late L. **bassāre* f. *bass-us* 'short or low of stature' (in Papias = *curtus, humilis*, but in Isidore = *crassus, pinguis*); also a surname in early Lat. The regular mod. repr. of OFr. *abaissier, abessier*, ME. *abesse*, would be *abease, abeace* (cf. *ease, lease, grease, peace*); the actual *abase* is due to the influence of *base* adj. Must be distinguished from early and northern forms of ABASH; of which *abayss, abaisse, abasse* became by phonetic change *abash*, before *abesse* (by influence of *base*) became *abase*; but in the north, where *s* was not changed to *sh*, *abaisse, abase*, = *abash* are found contemporary with southern *abase* the present vb.]

1. To lower (physically), depress, bring or cast down. *arch.*

1477 CAXTON *Jason* 10 And peleus..began to abasse and hange doun his heed. **1589** PUTTENHAM *Engl. Poesie* (1811) III. xxiv. 246 Their seruitours, speaking or being spoken vnto, abbase their eyes in token of lowlines. **1594** SHAKS. *Rich. III*, I. ii. 247 And will she yet abase her eyes on me? **1596** SPENSER *F.Q.* II. ii. 26 Suddeinly that warriour gan abace His threatned speare. **1671** SALMON *Syn. Medic.* III. xxii. 405 It abaseth inflamations and Feavers wonderfully. **1676** *Phil. Trans.* XI. 680 A Pump..whose Sucker..is raised and abased by two Levers. **1870** J. R. LOWELL *Am. my Books* Ser. II (1873) 323 Its delectable mountains which night shall utterly abase and destroy.

2. To lower in rank, office, condition, or character; to humble, humiliate; often with the sense of *degrade, make base.*

1393 GOWER *Conf.* I. 111 Our king hath do this thing amis, So to abesse his roialte. **1539** BP. TONSTALL *Sermon on Palme sondaye* (1823) 1 He dyd abase hym selfe, takynge vpon hym the fourme of a seruant. **1605** BACON *Adv. Learn.* I. 16 The grosse and palpable flatterie, whereunto many have abassed & abused their wits and pens. *a* **1762** LADY M. W. MONTAGU *Letters* lix. 79 Heaven..you know delights in abasing the proud. **1834** DISRAELI *Rev. Epick* I. xl. 44 (1864) Their end To level not to raise: where equal all All are abased. **1876** FREEMAN *Norm. Conq.* I. App. 620 This famous refusal of Rolf to abase himself.

†**3.** To lower in price or value, to depreciate, debase (coin). *Obs.*

1569 GRAFTON *Chron. Ed. VI* an. 5, 1316 The peece of ix pence was abaced to sixpence. *a* **1656** HALES *Golden Remains* Ser. I (1673) 14 If He that abases the prince's coin deserves to die. **1669** CHILD *Disc. Trade* 244 (ed. 4) The charge of mending our land would be doubled, and the land abased to seven or eight years purchase. **1736** CARTE *Life of Ormonde* I. 12 The standard of it [the coin] which had been much abased in the time of her father Henry VIII.

†**abase,** *adv. Obs. rare* [a. Fr. *à bas* down: see BASE.] Down, lower; back.

1542 BOORDE *Dyetary* iv. 238 (1870) The seller vnder the pantry, sette somwhat abase; the kychen set somwhat a base from the buttry and pantry.

abased (ə'beɪst), *ppl. a.* [f. ABASE *v.* + -ED.]

1. Lowered, cast down, downcast. *arch.*

1652 CRASHAW *Sacred Poems* 164 Now by abasèd lids shall learn to be Eagles, and shut our eyes that we may see. **1801** SOUTHEY *Thal.* xii. 19 With head abased, he laid An arrow in its rest.

2. *Her.* = Fr. *Abaissé*: Turned downwards, as the wings of an eagle. Also, said of a charge when placed lower than its customary position; opposed to *enhanced.*

1741 CHAMBERS *Cycl.*

3. Lowered, humbled, in rank, condition, character, feelings, etc.

1611 BIBLE *Phil.* iv. 12 I know both how to be abased, and I knowe how to abound [*Wyclif* lowid, *Tindale* cast doune]. **1782** COWPER *Retiremt.* 94 I shrink abas'd, and yet aspire to Thee. **1823** SCOTT *Peveril* 255 (1865) It is well he is abased; but if it lies with me, I may humble his pride, but will never ruin his house. **1863** MRS. JAMESON *Leg. of Monast. Orders* 348 He knew not how to deal with ruffians so abased.

†**4.** Debased, depreciated, as coinage. *Obs.*

abasedly (ə'beɪsɪdlɪ), *adv.* [f. ABASED + -LY[2].] In an abased or humbled manner; humbly, abjectly, downcastly.

1571 HENRYSON *Fables* 42 The sheepe againe before the Wolfe arenȝied, But (= without) Advocate, abasedly could (= did) stand. **1859** MASSON *Milton's Youth* in *Essays* 42 Those other passages..which exhibit the poet as..looking about abasedly among his literary contemporaries.

abasement (ə'beɪsmənt). [f. ABASE *v.* after Fr. *abaissement*: see -MENT.]

1. The action of abasing, lowering, casting down, or humbling, in rank or character; humiliation.

1561 T. N[ORTON] *Calvin's Inst.* I. xiii. 47 (1634) The time was not yet come of his abasement. **1589** PUTTENHAM *Eng. Poesie* 266 (1869) And almost speak vntruly and iniuriously by way of abbasement. **1748** RICHARDSON *Clarissa* II. ii. 12 (1811) Pride in ourselves must, and forever will, provoke contempt, and bring down upon us abasement from others. **1857** BUCKLE *Civil.* I. viii. 549 The abasement of the clergy preceded the humiliation of the crown.

2. The condition of being abased; humiliation, degradation.

1611 BIBLE *Ecclus.* xx. 11 There is an abasement because of glory; and there is that lifteth vp his head from a low estate. **1747** HERVEY *Medit.* II. 136 The deepest Degrees of possible Abasement. **1828** CARLYLE *Misc.* I. 231 (1857) Conscious of its errors and abasement. **1860** R. A. VAUGHAN *Ho. w. Mystics* (ed. 2) I. 153 True Abandonment, with utter Abasement, was the nearest way to God.

abaser (ə'beɪsə(r)). [f. ABASE *v.* + -ER[1].]

1. He who, or that which, abases.

1650 J. WEEKES *Truth's Confl.* iii. 76 Yours will be found the great exaltress of free-will, and the great abaser of free-grace. **1656** J. TRAPP *Expos.* Rom. iv. 16 Paul was a great advancer of the grace of God, and abaser of man.

†**2.** *Rhet.* The figure *Tapinosis*; depreciatory phraseology. *Obs.*

1589 PUTTENHAM *Eng. Poesie* 266 (1869) These and such other base wordes do greatly disgrace the thing, and the speaker or writer: the Greekes call it *Tapinosis*, we the *Abaser.*

abash (ə'bæʃ), *v.* Forms: 4 **abayss, abaisse, abasse**; 4–5 **abaisshe, -aische, -asche, -assche**; 5–6 **abasshe, -asche, -aszshe**; 4–6 **abashe**; 6– **abash**. Northern: 4–6 **abaiss(e, abase**. [ad. Anglo-Fr. *abaïss-* = OFr. *ebaïss-*, *esbaïss-*, lengthened stem (occurring in pple. *abaïss-ant*, 3 pl. *abaïss-ent*, subj. *abaïsse*, etc.) of *ésb-aïr*, mod.Fr. *ébahir*; f. *es*:—Lat. *ex* 'out, utterly' + *baïr, bahir* = Ital. *baïre* to astound, regarded as formed on *bah!* a natural exclamation of astonishment. The OFr. *-iss* here became *-ish*, as in *perish, finish, punish*, and the *i* was absorbed, as in *punch*; in the north the *-s* remained, as in *cheriss, fluriss, punyss*; hence a formal confusion between northern forms of *abash*, and the distinct vb. ABASE, q.v.]

1. To destroy the self-possession or confidence of (any one), to put out of countenance, confound, discomfit, or check with a sudden consciousness of shame, presumption, error, or the like. **a.** *active.*

1375 BARBOUR *Bruce* VIII. 247 And thouch that thai be ma than we, That suld abaiss ws litill thing. **1430** *Pilg. Lyf of Man* 117 It is thilke bi whiche I abashe alle the bestes of the cuntre. **1496** W. DE WORDE *Dives & Pauper* XIV. viii. 340/1 The lyon with his crye abassheth all other bestes. **1570** LEVINS *Manipulus*, To Abashe *Stupefacere.* **1574** tr. *Marlorats Apocalips* 26 For although lightning be bright, yet is it not chærefull, but rather abasheth men. **1600** HEYWOOD *1st Edw. IV*, IV. 27 To weaken and abash their fortitude. **1751** FIELDING *Amelia* III. ix. Wks. 1784 VIII. 304 A man whom no denial, no scorn could abash. **1863** H. ROGERS *Life of J. Howe* iii. 83 If not to convince, to silence and abash the gainsayer.

†**b.** *refl.* [mod.Fr. has only the refl. form *s'ébahir.*] To gape with surprise, to stand confounded. *Obs.*

c **1450** LONELICH *Holy Grail* xxi. 291 Thanne the Kyng Abasched him sore For þe wordes he herde thore. **1485** CAXTON *Paris & Vienne* 62 Abasshe you not for thys derkenes.

c. Most common in the *passive*: to be, stand, or feel abashed; *at* an occasion, *of* (*obs.*), *by* a cause.

c **1325** *E.E. Allit. Poems* 42. 149 Þat oþer burne watȝ abayst of his broþe wordeȝ. **1366** MAUNDEV. xxix. 295 Alisandre was gretly astoneyed and abayst. **1382** WYCLIF *Mark* v. 42 And thei weren abaischt [**1388** abaischid] with greet stoneying. *c* **1386** CHAUCER *Clerkes T.* 955 Right nought was sche abaissht of her clothing [*v.r.* abayst[-2], abast, abayssht, abasshed, abasscheḍ]. **1483** CAXTON *G. Leg.* 70/3 Whan Dauid herd this he was sore abasshed. **1535** COVERDALE *Is.* xiii. 8 One shall euer be abaszshed of another. **1667** MILTON *P.L.* i. 331 They heard, and were abasht, and up they sprung. **1807** CRABBE *Village* ii. 79 And while she stands abash'd, with conscious eye. **1876** GLADSTONE *Homeric Synch.* 72 I might have been abashed by their authority.

†**2.** *intr.* (by omission of refl. pron.) To stand dumb with confusion or astonishment; to lose self-possession or confidence; to flinch or recoil with surprise, shame, or sense of humiliation. *Obs.*

1391 CHAUCER *Boethius* 146 (1868) No strong man ne semeþ nat to abassen or disdaigner as ofte tyme as he hereþ þe noise of þe bataile. **1477** CAXTON *Jason* 45 b, The herte of man sholde not abasshe in no thing. **1530** PALSGR. I abasshe, or am amazed of any thing, *Je me esbahis.* **1577–87** HOLINSH. *Chron.* III. 1098/2 For she, notwithstanding all the fearefull newes that were brought to hir that daie, neuer abashed. **1585** JAMES I *Essayes in Poesie* 44 She did shame The Sunne himself, her coulour was so bright, Till he abashit beholding such a light.

† **a'bash**, *sb. Obs. rare*$^{-1}$. [f. the vb.] Loss of self-possession, confusion from surprise, shame, or the like. = ABASHMENT.

1393 GOWER *Conf.* II. 46 The kynges doughter, which this sigh, For pure abasshe drewe hir adrigh.

† **abashance**. *Obs. rare*$^{-1}$. [a. OFr. *abaïssance*, = *esbaïssance*, *ébahissance*, n. of action, f. *abaïssant* pr. pple. of *abaïr*, *esbahir*: see ABASH and -ANCE.] Abashment, dismay.

c **1430** *Syr Generides* 5515 Sampson beheld [Generides], And saw that he noo colour lese, Nor noo maner abasshaunce, But bare him bold of countynaunce.

abashed (ə'bæʃt), *ppl. a.* Forms: 4 **abayst, abaist**; 4–5 **abaissht, -aisscht, -assht**; 5–6 **abasshed**; 6 **abaszshed**; 6– **abasht, abashed**; also aphetic BASHED. [ABASH *v.* + -ED.] Put out of self-possession, stricken with surprise; confounded, discomfited, disconcerted; checked with a sense of shame, presumption, or error.

1340 HAMPOLE *Pr. Consc.* 1431 Swa þat man suld mare drede and be abayste, Over mykel in þe world here to trayste. **1534** LD. BERNERS *Golden Bk. of Marc. Aurel.* (1546) O iiii b, We holdyng downe our heddes abashed. **1718** POPE *Iliad* viii. 540 The pensive goddesses, abash'd, controll'd. **1859** TENNYSON *Enid* 765 Enid, all abash'd she knew not why, Dared not to glance at her good mother's face.

abashedly (ə'bæʃɪdlɪ), *adv.* [f. prec. + -LY[2].] In an abashed manner; with confusion of face.

c **1817** HOGG *Tales & Sketches* IV. 26 George at length came forward abashedly.

† **a'bashedness**. *Obs. rare* [f. as prec. + -NESS.] The quality or state of being abashed; abashment.

1530 PALSG. 193 Abasshednesse, *fraievr*, s.f.

abashing (ə'bæʃɪŋ), *vbl. sb.* Also 4 **abasshyng**; and in Northern writers, 5– **abaysing, abaisyng, abasing**; not to be confounded with ABASING. [f. ABASH *v.* + -ING[1].] The act of confounding, or putting to dismay; the state of confusion, dismay, or astonishment; abashment. Now mostly gerundial.

c **1374** CHAUCER *Boethius* IV. 1 Certes, quoth she, that were a great maruayle, and an abashinge without end. **1375** BARBOUR *Bruce* XVII. 573 Thre sper-lynth, I trow weill mycht be Betuix thame, quhen sic abasing Tuk thame. **1404** H. SHARISBROOK, in Ellis *Orig. Lett.* II. 10. I. 30 A gret abayschynge to oure enmyes. *c* **1425** WYNTOWN *Cron.* VIII. xxxvii. 77 Ðai suld noucht have had abaysyng. *Ibid.* IX. I. 66 Rycht airly in til þe dawing He stoutly come but abaisyng And til the Castelle set a stale, And syne gert bryn wp þe Town hale. *a* **1564** BECON *Demands of Script.* in *Prayers*, etc. (1844) 604 The amazing, dread, and abashing of the mind that the wicked men have of the wrath of God. **1580** HOLLYBAND *Treas. French Tong.*, *Effray*, or *effroy*, feare, astonying, abashing, amasing.

abashless (ə'bæʃlɪs), *a. rare.* [f. ABASH *sb.* + -LESS.] Unabashed, shameless; the reverse of *bashful*.

1868 BROWNING *Ring & Book* i. 127 Words as ready and as big As the part he played, the bold abashless one. *Ibid.* i. 203 This else abashless mouth.

abashment (ə'bæʃmənt). Forms: 5 **abaysshment, abaschement**; 6 **abasshement, abashement**; 6– **abashment**. [ad. OFr. *abaïssement* = *esbahissement*, *ébahissement*, n. of action f. *abaïr*, *esbahir*. see ABASH and -MENT.] Confusion from surprise, shame, or sudden check; confusion of face.

c **1410** LOVE *Bonaventura's Spec. V. Chr.* iii. (Gibbs MS.) As þe perfyte meke may not here his praysynge wyth owten abaschment and schame fastnesse. **1489** CAXTON *Faytes of Armes* I. xv. 43 They were dysconfyted more by abaysshment than by armes. **1523** *State Papers Hen. VIII*, IV. 36 An abashment and grete discorage to all those that be of the Frenche faccion. **1600** ABBOT *Jonah* 423 That speech of the great abashment of his people should be brought to the King. **1749** WALPOLE *Lett. to H. Mann* No. 200 (1834) II. 271 To the great abashment of the Jacobites. **1837** CARLYLE *Fr. Rev.* III. IV. vii. 168 (1871) On her countenance there was visible neither abashment nor pride.

abasia (ə'beɪsɪə). *Med.* [mod.L., ad. F. *abasie*, f. A- *pref.* 14 + Gr. βάσις step: see -IA.] Inability to walk, caused by lack of coordination of the muscles. Hence **a'basic** *a.* Cf. ASTASIA.

1890 [see ASTASIA]. **1891** P. C. KNAPP in *Jrnl. Nerv. & Ment. Dis.* XVI. 673 (*title*) Astasia-abasia, with the report of a case of paroxysmal trepidant abasia associated with paralysis agitans. **1909** *Cent. Dict.* Suppl., Abasia, abasic. **1918** A. A. BRILL tr. *Freud's Totem & Taboo* 159 A motor inhibition, an abasia or an agoraphobia, becomes perfected and detailed.

abasing (ə'beɪsɪŋ), *vbl. sb.* [f. ABASE *v.* + -ING[1].] The action of lowering or depressing, **a.** physically. **b.** in mind or feeling. **c.** of debasing or depreciating the currency (*obs.*). Now mostly gerundial.

1555 HARPSFIELD *Divorce Hen. VIII* (1878) 298 The inestimable loss it [England] suffered by the decay and abasing of money. **1569** GRAFTON *Chron. Ed. VI*, an. 5, 1315–6 At this tyme also the kinges maiestie, with the aduice of his priuye counsaile, did now purpose not onely the abacyng of the sayd copper moneys, but also ment wholly to reduce them into bollion. **1608** HIERON *Wks.* I. 745/1 To the abasing& humbling of my hart. **1611** BIBLE *2 Cor.* xi. 7 Haue I committed an offence in abasing my selfe, that you might be exalted. **1625** BACON *Essays* xxii (1862) 92 This would be done, with a demure Abasing of your Eye.. as the Iesuites also doe use. **1642** ROGERS *Naaman* 30 Gods purpose towards him in this abasing of his stout heart.

abasing, obs. north. form of ABASHING *vbl. sb.*

abasing (ə'beɪsɪŋ), *ppl. a.* [f. ABASE *v.* + -ING[2].] Lowering, depressing, humbling.

a **1665** GOODWIN *A being filled with the Spirit* (1867) 116 The bodies of the saints, which now in the state of mortality are vile, that is, of an abasing and humbling complexion and frame.

abask (ə'bɑːsk, -æ-), *adv.* [A *prep.* of state + BASK *v.*: see A *prep.*[1] 11.] In a basking condition, basking.

1866 NEALE *Sequ. & Hymns* 144 Ephesus lies all abask in Mediterranean noonday.

‖ **abassi, -s**. *Obs.* 'A silver coin current in Persia,.. somewhat less than an English shilling.' Chambers *Cycl. Supp.* 1753.

Ibid. The Abassi took its denomination from Schah Abas II, king of Persia, under whom it was struck.

† **a'bastard**, *v. Obs.* [ad. Fr. *abastardir* (as old as 12th c.) from *à* prep. + *bastard*. Cf. OSp. *abastardar*.] *prop.* To make or declare bastard or illegitimate: hence, to make spurious or degenerate; to debase, corrupt, deteriorate.

1610 DONNE *Pseudo-Martyr* 226. §6 In some of the meane Parents by the way there may be fallacies which may corrupt & Abastard it. **1651** *Life of Father Sarpi* 86 (1676) They further insinuated that the Roman Religion was insensibly abastarded.

† **abastardize, -ise** (ə'bɑːstədaɪz, -æ-), *v.* ? *Obs.* [f. Fr. *abastard-ir*, *-iss-ant*: see prec. The term. *-ise* representing the *-iss-* of the extended stem in Fr. has been refashioned after vbs. in -IZE. Cf. AMORTIZE.] To render bastard, spurious, or degenerate; to debase, or deteriorate.

1580 HOLLYBAND *Treas. French Tong.*, *Abastardir*.. to corrupt, or abastardise, to counterfait. **1605** DANIELL *Queen's Arcadia* v. iv. (Wks. 1717) I. 224 And being our selves Corrupted, and abastardized thus. **1610** DONNE *Sermon* xcvi. IV. 258 An insinuating of false and adulterous blood, in abastardizing a race, by supposititious children. **1653** BULWER *Artificiall Changeling* (quoting Donne) Doe not abastardise that noble kind, that noble nature, that God hath imparted to thee.

† **abastardized**, *ppl. a. Obs.* [f. prec. + -ED.] Degenerate, debased, spurious.

1653 URQUHART *Rabelais* (1727) ii. viii. The soule, by which our name continues blessed amongst men would be degenerate and abastardised.

† **a'basure**. *Obs.* [f. ABASE *v.* + -URE; of Eng. formation, after words like *eras-ure*, *seiz-ure*.] The action of abasing; the condition of being abased; humiliation.

1653 MANTON *Ep. James* ii. 1 Wks. 1871 IV. 181 They offered injury and contumely to them, because of their outward abasure and despicableness. **1671** FLAVEL *Fount. of Life* xix. 55 And it was no small Abasure of Christ to bind himself to the Law as a Subject made under.

abatable (ə'beɪtəb(ə)l), *a.* [a. OFr. *abatable* (Britton), f. *abatre*: see ABATE *v.*[1] and -ABLE.] Capable of being abated.

1821, 1 and 2 *Geo. IV* c. 41, §1 By law, every such nuisance, being of a public nature, is abateable as such by indictment. **1865** NICHOLS *Britton* II. xviii. 9 The writ is thereby abatable [Fr. *si est le bref abatable*].

† **abatayl**, *v. Obs. rare.* [for *anbatayl* = *enbatayl*, a. OFr. *enbataille-r*: see EMBATTLE.] To embattle.

c **1380** *Sir Ferumbras* 4310 Mantrible þe Citee ys y-called, Wyþ marbre fyn ys he walled, & abatayled with toures hye.

† **abataylment**. *Obs. rare* [see prec.] Battlement.

c **1325** *Gaw. and Gr. Kn.* 790 Enbaned vnder þe abataylment, in þe best lawe.

abate (ə'beɪt), *v.*[1] [a. OFr. *abat-re*, *abat-tre*, f. *à* prep. to + *batre*, *battre* to beat:—late L. *battĕre*, *batĕre*, from cl. L. *batuĕre*. In the technical senses 18, 19, the identity of the prefix is uncertain, and the relation to the other senses undetermined.]

I. To beat down, demolish, destroy.

1. *trans.* To beat down, throw down, demolish, level with the ground. *Obs.* exc. in Law.

1366 MAUNDEV. viii. 95 (1839) Jerusalem hath often tyme ben distroyed, & the Walles abated & beten doun. *c* **1420** *Palladius on Husb.* II. 5 Hem to desolate Of erthe, and all from every roote abate. **1494** FABYAN vii. 490 Yᵉ gates of Bruges, of Ipre, of Courtray, and of other townes were abated and throwyn downe. **1576** LAMBARDE *Peramb. Kent* 185 (1826) Bycause Apultre was not of sufficient strength for their defence and coverture they abated it to the ground. **1643** PRYNNE *Doom of Cowardice & Treach.* 4 And that night came a great party of them, and by fine force made an assault and abated the Baracadoes. **1664** EVELYN *Kal. Hort.* 13 (1729) During the hottest months carefully abate the weeds. **1809** TOMLINS *Law Dict.* s.v., *To abate*; to prostrate, break down, or destroy. In law to abate a castle or fort is to beat it down. **1864** *Wandsw. Br. Act* 44 If any work made by the Company in, over, or across the River Thames.. be abandoned or suffered to fall into disuse or decay, the Conservators of the River Thames may abate and remove the same.

† **2.** *fig.* To put down, put an end to, do away with (any state or condition of things). *Obs.*

c **1270** *E.E. Poems, Old Age* 149 When eld blowid he is blode. his ble is sone abatid. **1340** HAMPOLE *Pr. Consc.* 1672 Ded [= death], of al þat it comes to, abates And chaunges all myghtes and states. *c* **1350** *Will. Palerne* 1141 To abate þe bost of þat breme duke. **1413** LYDGATE *Pylg. Sowle* v. xii. 103 (1843) And fynally abatid is the strif. **1585** ABP. SANDYS *Serm.* 79 (1841) St. Paul abateth this opinion. *Ibid.* 293 To abate the haughty conceit which naturally we have of ourselves.

3. Esp. *Law.* **a.** To put an end to, do away with (as a nuisance, or an action).

1297 R. GLOUC. 447 And oþer monye luþer lawes, þat hys elderne adde ywroȝt, He behet, þat he wolde abate. **1768** BLACKSTONE *Comm.* III. 168 The primitive sense is that of abating or beating down a nusance. **1780** BURKE *Sp. on Econ. Ref.* Wks. III. 247 They abate the nuisance, they pull down the house. **1844** H. ROGERS *Essays* I. ii. 88 He has not lived in vain who has successfully endeavoured to abate the nuisances of his own time. **1859** DE QUINCEY *The Cæsars* Wks. X. 104 To put him down and abate him as a monster.

b. To render null and void (a writ).

1580 BARET *Alvearie*, His accusation or writte is abated or ouerthrowne when the Attorney by ignorance declareth not the processe in due forme, or the writte abateth. **1621** SANDERSON *Serm.* Ad. Cl. II. xxii. 30 (1674) And any one short Clause or Proviso, not legal, is sufficient to abate the whole Writ or Instrument. **1726** AYLIFFE *Parergon* 266 This only suspends but does not abate the action. **1741** ROBINSON *Gavelkind* vi. 109 The Writ was abated by the Court. **1809** TOMLINS *Law Dict.* s.v., *To abate a nuisance* is to destroy, remove, or put an end to it.. *To abate a writ* is to defeat or overthrow it by shewing some error or exception.

4. *intr.* (through *refl.*) To be at an end, to become null or void; *esp.* of writs, actions, appeals.

1602 W. FULBECKE *First Part of Parallele* 62 In the summons A. was omitted, wherefore the writte abated. **1745** DE FOE *Eng. Tradesm.* I. xvi. 148 Commissions shall not abate by the death of his majesty. **1768** BLACKSTONE *Comm.* III. 247 The suit is of no effect, and the writ shall abate. **1809** TOMLINS *Law Dict.* s.v. It is said an appeal shall abate, and be defeated by reason of covin or deceit. **1860** MASSEY *Hist. Engl.* III. xxxi. 437 The Committee of Privileges resolved, that impeachments stood on the same footing as appeals and writs of error; consequently they did not abate.

II. To bring down, lower, depress.

† **5.** To bring down (a person) physically, socially, or mentally; to depress, humble, degrade; to cast down, deject. *Obs.*

c **1325** GROSSETESTE *Castel of Loue* 1334 He was abated of his tour [= in his turn]. *c* **1386** CHAUCER *Persones T.* 118 The heyher that they were in this present lif, the more schuln thay ben abatid and defouled in helle. **1470–85** MALORY *Morte Arthur* (1634 repr. 1816) I. 241 Then sir Beaumains abated his countenance. **1564** BAULDWIN *Moral Phil.* (ed. Palfr.) iii. 4 Hee is to be honoured among them that be honoured, that fortune abateth without fault. **1618** RALEIGH *Remains* (1644) 27 If any great person to be abated, not to deal with him by calumniation or forged matter. **1651** JER. TAYLOR *Sermons* I. ix. 104 They were abated with humane infirmities and not at all heightened by the Spirit.

† **6.** *intr.* To fall, be dejected, humbled. *Obs.*

1306 *Political Songs* (Camd. S.) 216 Ys continaunce abated eny bost to make. **1387** TREVISA *Higden* Rolls Ser. II. 185 þe bolde nolle abateþ [*cervix deprimitur*]. *c* **1460** *Urbanitatis* in *Babees Book* (1868) 16 Lette not þy contynaunce also abate. **1642** ROGERS *Naaman* 30 The naturall spirit of the hautiest.. will abate and come downe.

† **7.** To abate *of*; to bring down (a person) from; hence to deprive of, curtail of. *Obs.*

c **1430** *Octouian Imperator* 1316 (Weber III. 212) He was abated of all hys hete. *c* **1530** LD. BERNERS *Arthur of Lytell Bryt.* 105 (1814) That she be not thereby abbated of her noblenesse and estate. **1605** SHAKS. *Lear* II. iv. 161 She hath abated me of halfe my Traine. **1637** LISLE tr. *Du Bartas* 30 Mens bodies were abated of their bignesse.

III. To bring down in size, amount, value, force.

† **8.** To beat back the edge or point of anything; to turn the edge; to blunt. *lit.* and *fig.* *Obs.*

1548 HALL *Chron.* 689 Such wepons as the capitain of the Castle shall occupie, that is, Morrice pike sworde target, the poynt and edge abated. **1594** SHAKS. *Rich. III*, v. v. 35 Abate the edge of Traitors, gracious Lord. **1613** W. BROWNE *Brit. Past.* I. iv. (1772) 107 With plaints which might abate a tyrant's knife. **1625** BACON *Essays* ix, To abate the edge of envy. **1634** HEYWOOD *Maidenh. lost* xi. 120 The name of Childe Abates my Swords keene edge. **1699** EVELYN *Acetaria* 145 (1729) Such as abate and take off the keeness.

9. To bring down in size; lower, lessen or diminish (things tangible). *arch.*

1398 TREVISA *Barth. De Pr. Rerum* (1495) XVII. lxxviii. 652 Gutta abatyth all swellynge and bolnynge. **1611** BIBLE *Gen.* viii. 3 After the end of the hundred and fiftie dayes, the waters were abated. **1612** WOODALL *Surgeon's Mate* Wks. (1653) 11 Small Files are used.. to abate any end of a bone ..which is fractured. **1662** EVELYN *Chalcog.* (1769) 59 In wood, which is a graving much more difficult; because all the work is to be abated and cut hollow. **1823** SCOTT *Peveril* (1865) 241 A lucky accident had abated Chiffinch's party to their own number.

10. *intr.* To decrease in size or bulk. *arch.*

1587 GOLDING *Mornay's Chr. Relig.* xiv. 220 (1617) The more that the body abateth in flesh, the more workfull is the mind. **1597** WARNER *Albion's Eng.* III. xviii. 86 Their poyson, growing when it seemeth to abate. **1726** De Foe *Hist. Devil* I. x. 121 (1840) The arke rested, the waters abating.

11. *trans.* To bring down in value, price, or estimation. *arch.*

1340 *Ayenb.* 28 Vor þe guode los to abatye, and hire guodes to loȝy, þe envious agrayþeþ alle his gynnes. *c* **1400** *Rom. Rose* 286 She ne might all abate his prise. *c* **1460** Fortescue *Absol. & Lim. Mon.* (1714) 116 Hou the Pricys of Merchaundises, growyn in this Lond, may be holdyn up, and encreasyd, and the Prycys of Merchaundise, brought into this Lond abatyd. **1651** Hobbes *Leviathan* II. xxii. 119 They raise the price of those, and abate the price of these. **1670** R. Coke *Disc. of Trade* 33 If the Importation of Irish Cattel had abated the Rents of England one half.

12. *intr.* To fall in amount, value, or price, suffer reduction, be reduced. *arch.* exc. in *Law.*

1745 De Foe *Eng. Tradesm.* II. xxxii. 101 As wages abate to the poor, provisions must abate in the market, and rents must sink and abate to the landlords. **1768** Blackstone *Comm.* II. 512 And in case of a deficiency of assets, all the general legacies must abate proportionably, in order to pay the debts.

13. *trans.* To lessen or lower in force or intensity (a quality, feeling, action, etc.); to diminish, lessen, lighten, relieve, mitigate.

1330 R. Brunne *Chron.* 269 His moder Helianore abated þer grete bale. **1340** Hampole *Pr. Consc.* 2840 For na thyng may abate þair pyne. **1574** tr. *Marlorats Apocalips* 33 Charitie is lyke fyre, whyche is easyly put oute if it be abated. **1593** T. Hyll *Profitable Arte of Gard.* 137 The sauor of them [garlic] wilbe greatly abated. **1599** Shaks. *Hen. V*, III. ii. 24 Abate thy Rage, abate thy manly Rage. **1611** Bible *Deut.* xxxiv. 7 His eye was not dimme, nor his naturall force abated. **1670** Walton *Lives* IV. 288 Lord, abate my great affliction, or increase my patience. **1759** Robertson *Hist. Scot.* I. II. 156 She shook the fidelity, or abated the ardour of some. **1859** Mill *Liberty* ii. 68 To abate the force of these considerations.

14. *intr.* To fall off in force or intensity; grow less, calm down.

c **1400** *Destr. Troy* XI. 4665 Sesit the wyndis; The bremnes abated. **1599** Shaks. *Hen. V*, IV. iv. 50 My fury shall abate, and I The Crownes will take. **1697** Dryden *Virg. Georg.* I. 463 (1721) When Winter's Rage abates, when chearful Hours Awake the Spring. **1720** De Foe *Capt. Singleton* xvi. 274 Towards morning the wind abated a little. **1837** Carlyle *Fr. Rev.* I. VI. iii. 322 This conflagration of the South-East will abate. **1869** *Echo* Oct. 9 The Foot and Mouth Disease which has been raging with some virulence is now beginning to abate.

IV. To strike off, deduct.

15. *trans.* To strike off or take away a part, to deduct, subtract.

a. with *of* (*out of, from* obs.).

c **1391** Chaucer *Astrolabe* 34 Abate thanne thees degrees And minutes owt of 90. **1413** Lydgate *Pylgr. Sowle* IV. viii. 62 (1483) He nele noo thynge abaten of the prys. **1551** Recorde *Pathway to Knowl.* II. Introd., And if you abate euen portions from things that are equal, those partes that remain shall be equall also. **1570** Dee *Math. Praef.* 9 If from 4. ye abate 1. there resteth 3. **1611** Bible *Lev.* xxvii. 18 It shall be abated from thy estimation. **1679–88** *Secret Service Moneys of Chas. & Jas. II*, 126 (Camd. S. 1851) To be abated out of the moneys that are or shall be due to him for work. **1741** *Complete Family-Piece* I. ii. 192 Take..9 eggs, abating 4 whites. **1745** De Foe *Eng. Tradesm.* I. xix. 178 Rather than abate a farthing of the price they had asked. **1866** Rogers *Agric. & Prices* I. xx. 506 The merchant abating something of his morning price.

b. with *obj.* (orig. *dative*) of the person.

1465 *Manners & Househ. Exps.* 465 Roberd Thrope lente me l.s... and herof he moste a bate me [= to me] .xiiij.s. **1647** Sanderson *Sermons* Ad Aul. xv. 1 (1673) 209 He therefore sendeth for his Master's Debtors forthwith; abateth them of their several Sums, and makes the Books agree. **1671** Flavel *Fount. of Life* iii. 6 When the Payment was making, he will not abate him one Farthing. **1771** Franklin *Autobiog.* Wks. 1840 I. 61 She would abate me two shillings a week for the future.

c. *absol.* To make an abatement.

1530 Palsgr. 420, I alowe or abate upon a reckenyng or accompte made. **1745** De Foe *Eng. Tradesm.* I. xix. 179 He cannot abate without underselling the market, or underrating the value of his goods. **1817** Jas. Mill *Brit. India* II. IV. iv. 134 Lacey offered to abate in his pecuniary demand.

16. *fig.* To omit, leave out of count; to bar or except.

1588 Shaks. *L.L.L.* v. ii. 547 Abate [a] throw at Novum, and the whole world againe, Cannot pricke out five such. **1700** Law *Council of Trade* 253 (1751) Abating accidents which happen but seldom. **1772** Johnson in *Boswell* (1816) II. 149 Abating his brutality, he was a very good master. **1865** Sala *Diary in America* I. 307 Abating the gold and silver plate.

17. To abate *of* (a thing): to deduct something from, make an abatement from; to lower, or lessen in amount. *arch.*

1644 Bulwer *Chirologia* 144 It falls short and abates of the perfection of the thing. **1645** Bp. Hall *Remedy of Discontent.* 27 Their fading condition justly abates of their value. **1653** Izaak Walton *Compl. Angler* 2 [I shall] either abate of my pace, or mend it, to enjoy such a companion. **1765** Tucker *Lt. of Nat.* II. 635 Their own experience and the world they converse with will abate of this excess. **1810** Scott *Lady of Lake* v. iii. 22 The guide abating of his pace Led slowly through the pass's jaws.

V. Technical.

†**18.** *Falconry.* To beat with the wings, flutter. More commonly aphetized to bate. *Obs.*

c **1430** *Bk. of Hawkyng* in *Rel. Antiq.* I. 297 If that she [the hawk] abate, let her flee, but be war that thou constreyne her not to flee. **1575** Turberville *Booke of Falc.* 135 You shall keepe hir alwayes in best plighte and leaste daunger to abate.

†**19.** In *Horsemanship.* 'A Horse is said to Abate, when working upon Curvets, he puts his two hind Legs to the Ground, both at once, and observes the same Exactness at all Times.' Bailey 1721; whence in J. and subseq. Dicts. *Obs.*

abate (əˈbeɪt), *v.*[2] *Law* [a. Anglo-Fr. *abat-re,* earlier *enbatre, embatre* (see a- *pref.* 10), in the legal phr. *se enbatre* or *abatre en* (Britton) to thrust oneself forcibly into, f. *en* in, into + *batre* to beat; see abate *v.*[1] Subseq. confused with the prec. both in Anglo-Fr. and Eng.; the law-books treat it as the same word.] To intrude or thrust oneself forcibly or tortiously into a tenement between the death of the owner and the accession of the legal heir. **a.** *refl.* (early instances are wanting).

1865 Nichols tr. *Britton* III. i. 2, II. 2 Because a person that has no right may immediately after the death of any one abate himself into the inheritance of the right heir, and keep out the heir and chief lord of the fee [Fr. *sei enbatre en le heritage*]. *Ibid.* II. xx. 4. I. 336 He by his own force abated himself into the tenement [Fr. *se abaty en cel tenement*].

b. *intr.* (by omission of refl. pron. in late Anglo-Fr., or ME. The ordinary construction since 6.)

1528 Perkins *Profitable Booke* v. §325. 144 If a man seised of three acres in fee taketh a wife and dyeth and a stranger abate in one of the acres. **1629** Coke *First Pt. of Inst.* 277 Betweene the death and the entry of the heire, an estranger doth interpose himselfe, and abate [Fr. *et un estraunge abate*]. **1809** Tomlins *Law Dict.* s.v., He that steps in between the former possessor and his heir is said to abate; he is called an abator, and this act of intrusion or interposition is termed an abatement.

†**aˈbate,** *sb. Obs.* [f. abate *v.*[1]] Abatement.

1. Depression, casting down.

1423 James I *King's Quair* II. xxi. For quhich sodayne abate, anon astert The blude of all my body to my hert.

2. The lowering of a quality; diminution.

1646 H. Lawrence *Com. & Warre with Angels, Ep. Ded.* The abate of power & strength which sinne had caus'd.

3. Deduction, subtraction.

1646 Sir T. Browne *Pseud. Ep.* IV. vii. 195 Nor will the difference be sensible in the abate of scruples or dragmes.

abated (əˈbeɪtɪd), *ppl. a.* [f. abate *v.*[1] + -ed.]

†**1.** Beaten, subdued, cast down. *Obs.*

1534 More *Comf. agaynste tribul.* III. (Wks. 1557) 1258/1 That oure fleshlye affeccions, be more abated and refrayned by the dreade and terroure of hell. **1548** in Strype *Eccl. Mem.* VI. 351 The weakness of his often abated enemies. **1610** Shaks. *Coriol.* III. iii. 132 Deliver you As most abated Captiues, to some Nation That wonne you without blowes. **1661** *Parismus* I. 89 Which so revived the abated hearts of the Thessalins.

2. Diminished, reduced, lowered in quality or amount.

1594 R. C[arew] *Huarte's Exam. of Wits* (1616) 45 And those in whom this abated heat approcheth least. **1607** Topsell *Serpents* (1673) 629 By fasting it hath made his flesh low and abated. **1855** I. Taylor *Restor. Belief.* 100 An abated Christianity. **1859** —— *Logic in Theol.* 312 To establish an abated, or a contrary belief.

abatement[1] (əˈbeɪtmənt). [a. OFr. *abatement, abattement,* f. *abattre*; see abate *v.*[1] and -ment.] The action of abating, or state of being abated, with most of the senses of the vb.

1. The act of overthrowing, putting down, or doing away with; the state of being overthrown, quashed or annulled. *Obs.* exc. as a Law term: the abatement of a nuisance, action, writ, or claim. 'In its present most general signification it relates to writs or plaints, and means the quashing or destroying the plaintiff's writ or plaint.' Tomlins.

1528 Perkins *Profitable Booke* v. §385. 167 (1642) A plea which goeth meerely in abatement of the writ. **1599** Marston *Scourge of Villanie* II. vii. 205 Their only skill rests in Collusions, Abatements, stoppels, inhibitions. **1768** Blackstone *Comm.* III. 5 A fourth species of remedy..is the abatement, or removal, of Nusances. **1809** Tomlins *Law Dict.* s.v., A Plea in Abatement is a plea put in by the defendant, in which he shows cause to the court why he should not be impleaded or sued. **1860** Massey *Hist. Engl.* III. xxxi. 438 The opinion in Westminster Hall was in favour of the abatement.

2. The act of lowering, lessening, or lightening; the state of depreciation, diminution, or decrease; the subsidence (of action); alleviation or mitigation (of evils).

1517 Hawes *Past. Pleas.* xliii. 14 And in like wise without abatement I shall cause for to be memoriall The famus actes. **1601** Shaks. *Twel. N.* I. i. 13 Nought enters there..But falls into abatement, and low price. **1655** Cromwell (Carlyle) *Sp.* iv., I had much abatement of my hopes; though not a total frustration. **1675** Baxter *Catholick Theologie* II. viii. 141 A delay of their future misery, and hopes of its abatement. **1794** Sullivan *View of Nat.* I. 67 Like a high sea on the abatement of a storm. **1878** Gladstone *Prim. Homer* 108 A sense of depression and disappointment, and abatement of the higher energies.

†**b.** Something which lightens toil; relaxation, recreation. *Obs.*

1513 Douglas *Æneid* v. prol. 45 For quha sa list sere gladsum gamis lere, Ful mony mery abaitmentis followis here.

3. The result of abating or lessening; the amount by which anything is abated; decrease, deduction, drawback. *lit.* and *fig.* and as a technical term in *Comm.*

1624 John Gee in *Shaks. Cent. Pr.* 160 The third abatement of the honor and continuance of this Scenicall company is, that they make their spectators pay to deare for their Income. **1625** Bacon *Essays* viii. 267 He hath a great Charge of Children: As if it were an Abatement to his Riches. **1722** De Foe *Hist. Plague* (1756) 183 All the Abatement I could get was only, that..I should be obliged to hold it but three Weeks. **1858** Ld. St. Leonards *Hbk. on Property Law* ii. 7 Equity will compel him to take it, and will allow him a proper abatement out of the purchase-money. **1866** Rogers *Agric. & Prices* I. xxviii. 677 The farmer obtained for the three years an abatement of two marks.

4. *Heraldry.* A supposed mark of depreciation.

1610 Guillim *Display of Heraldrie* viii. §1. 31 (1611) An Abatement is an accidentall mark annexed to coat-armour denoting some vngentleman-like, dishonorable, or disloiall demeanour qualitie or staine in the bearer whereby the dignitie of the coate-armour is greatly abased. **1751** Chambers *Cycl.* s.v., It is a little controverted among authors, whether heraldry allows of any such things as regular abatements..The last editor of Guillim discards the whole notion of Abatements as a chimaera.

abatement[2] (əˈbeɪtmənt). [a. Anglo-Fr. *abatement,* earlier *enbatement* (both in Britton), f. *abatre = enbatre*; see abate *v.*[2] and -ment.] The action of abating in a heritage, usurpation of a tenement; intrusion, tortious entry. See abate *v.*[2]

1330 R. Brunne *Chron.* 278 For þat mischance of Blanche mariage, For þat abatement he chalenges it þorgh right. **1528** Perkins *Profitable Booke* v. §325. 144 (1642) If the heire of him after whose death the abatement was, recover the acre of land in which the abatement was. **1586** Hooker *Giraldus's Hist. Ireland* in Holinshed II. 83/2 After the decease of the earle James, a bastard Butler had by abatement intruded. **1717** Blount *Law Dict., Abatement* (Fr.) is sometimes used for the Act of the Abator; as the Abatement of the Heir into the Land, before he has agreed with the Lord. **1865** Nichols *Britton* III. i. 3. II. 3 Intrusion is a wrongful abatement during the vacancy of the soil [Fr. *intrusioun est torcenous abatement*]. *Ibid.* III. i. 4 By reason of the abatement [Fr. *pur l'embatement*]. *Ibid.* VI. ix. II. 354 Those impleaded of hamsoken, or of fresh force, or of abatement [Fr. *ou de enbatement*].

abater[1] (əˈbeɪtə(r)). [f. abate *v.*[1] + -er[1].] He who or that which abates, lowers, or mitigates.

1609 W. M. *Man in the Moone* sig. C1v, He [the Tobackonist, i.e. a smoker] is his owne strengths enfeebler ..his appetites abater. **1683** Lady R. Russell *Lett.* (1773) x. 14 Time, or necessity, the ordinary abater of all violent passions. **1732** Arbuthnot *Rules of Diet* 263 Abaters of Acrimony or Sharpness. **1839** *New Monthly Mag.* LVII. 538 It is not..with the remotest intention of reflecting on the abaters of the dog-cart nuisance.

aˈbater[2]. [f. abate *v.*[1] + -er[2], in imitation of *misnom-er, rejoind-er, remind-er.*] An abating, a plea in abatement.

1660 H. More *Myst. Godliness* I. vi. 17 It being a great abater to our zeal and fervency in Religion to think that in the end of our life we shall be dodged and put off by a long senseless and comfortless Sleepe of the Soul under the sods of the Grave. **1662** —— *Ant. agst. Ath.* I. viii. 2, 22 Our fancy can shuffle in this abater, viz. that, etc.

abating (əˈbeɪtɪŋ), *vbl. sb.* [f. abate *v.*[1] + -ing[1].] The action or process of bringing down or lowering.

1. The action of casting down or overthrowing; and *fig.* of doing away with, or putting an end to. *Obs.* except in *Law.*

c **1460** Fortescue *Abs. & Lim. Mon.* (1714) 34 What Dishonour is this, and abatyng the Glory of a Kyng. **1768** Blackstone *Comm.* III. 168 This expression, of abating, which is derived from the French and signifies to quash, beat down, or destroy, is used by our law in three senses. The first, which seems to be the primitive sense, is that of abating or beating down a nuisance..and in a like sense..of abating a castle or fortress.

2. A lowering, lessening, diminution, decrease.

c **1460** Fortescue *Abs. & Lim. Mon.* (714) 37 Pensions without grete abatyng of the Kyngs Revenues. **1548** W. Thomas *Ital. Gram.* (1567) *Diminumento,* the abatyng or decrease. **1674** Playford *Skill of Musick* I. xi. 38 Those excellent Graces and Ornaments..which we call Trills, Grupps, Exclamations of Increasing or Abating of the Voice. **1699** Evelyn *Acetaria* 12 (1729) Nor ought it to be over-oyl'd, too much abating of its grateful acidity. **1861** Trench *Seven Ch. in Asia* 77 The abating of any other love but that to God and Christ.

3. A deducting, or subtracting.

1557 Recorde *Whetst.* S iij b, Subtraction doeth depend onely of the signe of abatemente, which is this—, and signifieth lesse, or abatyng. *c* **1620** A. Hume *Orthog. Brit. Tongue* 23 In abating from the word following, we, in the north, use a mervelouse libertie.

abating (əˈbeɪtɪŋ), *ppl. a.* [f. abate *v.*[1] + -ing[2].] Decreasing, subsiding.

1727 De Foe *Hist. Apparitions* xi. 218 The abating force of the water. **1801** Southey *Thalaba* ii. 26 Wks. IV. 58 To deluge o'er with no abating flood Our consummated World.

abatis (ˈæbətɪs). *Milit.* Also **abattis, abbatis, abbattis.** [a. Fr. *abatis* mass of things thrown down:—OFr. *abateïs*:—late L. **abatetīci-us* arising from throwing down; cf. vb. *abatre*. See ABATE.]

A defence constructed by placing felled trees lengthwise one over the other with their branches towards the enemy's line, and piling them up until a shelter for workmen is obtained.

1766 SMOLLETT *Hist. Eng.* (1828) II. 391 The ground before it [was] covered with an abbatis, or felled trees, with their boughs pointing outwards, and projecting in such a manner as to render the intrenchment almost inaccessible. **1795** NELSON in *Nicolas's Dispatches* (ed. 2) I. 380 The Seamen and Carpenters were all night employed in cutting down trees to form an abbatis. **1810** WELLINGTON in *Gurwood's Despatches* VI. 504 The first is loop-holed and there is an Abbatis in its front. **1847** GLEIG *Battle of Waterloo* 152 The riflemen attended to their own security by throwing an abattis across the chaussée. **1863** *Life in the South* II. 160 An abbatis still surrounded the stone bridge. **1865** *Morning Star* Mar. 30 At about twenty paces in front of this earthwork is what is termed the abatis.

abatised ('æbətɪst), *ppl. a.* [f. prec. + -ED[2].] Provided with an abatis.

1859 WORCESTER cites *Sat. Rev.*

‖**abat-jour** (aba'ʒuːr). *Arch.* [mod. Fr. = ce qui *abat* le *jour*, what throws down the daylight.] **a.** A sky-light. (Hardly in Eng. use; not in Gwilt.) **b.** A device for reflecting light downwards.

1830 in BRITTON *Dict. Archit.* **1853** J. W. CROKER in *Q. Rev.* XCIII. 413 He was confined to a single room..it had one window, closely barred and blinded by an *abat-jour*, which admitted only a small degree of oblique light. **1936** *Burlington Mag.* July 31/2 Two candlesticks behind are formed of leaves; between them is a vertical metal post bearing on the upper part a movable canopy serving as *abat-jour*.

‖**abaton** ('æbətən). *Greek Antiq.* [a. Gr. ἄβατον, neut. sing. of ἄβατος not to be trodden, f. ἀ- priv. + βατός accessible (βαίνειν to walk, go).] An enclosure attached to a temple of Asclepios, where patients slept.

1884 A. C. MERRIAM in *Amer. Antiquarian* VI. 304 Thereupon sleep fell upon him, and a serpent issuing from the Abaton, healed his toe with his tongue, and when he had done this he glided back again into the Abaton. **1885** *Q. Rev.* Apr. 302 The patients were sleeping in the sacred enclosure or *abaton* of the temple. **1925** *Lancet* 3 Oct. 689/1 In nearly all cases the patient comes to the shrine of Asclepios, sleeps in the 'abaton', has a vision or a dream.

abator[1] (ə'beɪtə(r), -,tɔː(r)). [late Anglo-Fr. *abator* *-tour*, n. of agent f. *abatre*; see ABATE *v.*[1] and -OR. Used for ABATER in legal senses.]

1. One who abates or overthrows a nuisance, etc.

2. = ABATER.

1592 S. DANIELL *Compl. of Rosam.* (1717) 41 Impiety of Times, Chastity's Abator. **1606** *Sir Gyles Goosecappe* sig. H, That painting is pure chastities abator.

abator[2] (ə'beɪtə(r), -,tɔː(r)). *Law* [a. late Anglo-Fr. *abator*, *-tour* agent n. f. *abatre* = *enbatre*: see ABATE[2] and -OR.] One who abates, or without right seizes upon the possession of a freehold between the death of its owner and the entry of the heir or devisee.

1531 *Dial. on Laws of Eng.* II. xii. 81 (1638) The abators were bounden in conscience to restore to the executors..the profits. **1629** COKE *First Pt. of Inst.* 194 Where there bee two joynt Abators or Intruders which come in merely by wrong. **1768** BLACKSTONE *Comm.* III. 168 This entry of him is called an abatement, and he himself is denominated an abator. **1832** *Edin. Rev.* LV. 324 The abator, or wrongful occupier ..had entered upon the lands.

abattoir ('æbətwɑː(r)). [mod.Fr. f. *abattre* to strike down. See ABATE.] A slaughter house for cattle.

1820 M. STARKE *Trav. on Continent* i. 5 Among the most prominent improvements..during the late reign are..the five Slaughter-houses, called *Abattoirs*. **1833** *Penny Cycl.* I. 8/2 The abattoirs of Paris are five in number; three being on the right bank of the Seine, and two on the left. **1840** PERRONET THOMPSON *Exercises* (1842) V. 340 As the sacrifice of one little pig compared with the massive slaughters that decorate a Parisian abattoir. **1866** *Cycl. Useful Arts* I. 2/2 Abattoirs have recently been erected in London. **1958** *Times Rev. Industry* Sept. 75/2 Economy installations in Sheffield Corporation abattoir's boiler plant will save the ratepayers £700 a year.

[**abatude**, given by Bailey, etc. as = diminished, and in subseq. Dicts. as sb., is merely a dictionary travesty of med. Lat. *abatuda* = *abatuta*, in *pecunia abatuda*, clipped money. See Wharton *Law Lex.* (1872) 6.]

abature ('æbətjʊə(r)). [a. Fr. *abatture*, *abature*, throwing down.] The traces left by a stag in the underwood through which he has passed.

1575 G. TURBERVILE *Booke of Venerie* 68 Of the iudgement of the Abatures and beating downe of the lowe twigges and the foyles. **1630** TAYLOR (Water P.) *Wks.* I. 93 What Necromanticke spells are Rut, Vault, Slot, Pores, and Entryes, Abatures, and Foyles, Frayenstockes, Frith and Fell, Layres, Dewclawes, and Dowlcets, drawing the Covert, Blemishes, Jewelling, Avaunt-laye, Allaye, Relaye, Foreloyning, Huntcownter, Hunt-change, Quarry, Reward, and a thousand more such Utopian fragments of confused Gibberish. **1751** CHAMBERS *Cycl.* s.v. *Age*, The huntsmen have several other marks whereby to know an old hart without seeing him: as the clot, entries, abatures, etc.

abaundon, see ABANDON.

†**a'bave**, *v. Obs.* Also **abaue**, **abaw(e**. [Prob. a. OFr. *abaub-ir*, *abab-ir* to astonish, confound, frighten, disconcert, repr. L. *ad* to + *balb-um* stammering. No Fr. form *abavir* is cited by Godef., but its rise from *ababir* would be regular. The derivation from Fr. *esbah-ir*, sometimes proposed, does not account for the final *-ave*, *-aue*, *-awe*.] *trans.* To put to confusion, discomfit; also *intr.* (*rare*) to be confounded (Fr. *s'abaubir*).

1303 R. BRUNNE *Handlyng Synne* 9536 Loke how ȝe mow be a-bawede þat seye þat þe Jewe ys sauede. *c* **1375** CHAUCER *Dethe of Bl.* (Fairf. MS.) 614 And al abawed where so I be My pees in pledynge and in werre. *c* **1430** LYDGATE *Bochas* (1554) IV. i. 101 a, They were abaued [*rhymes with* saued]. —— *Minor Poems* 144 To fynde a mene the sowle for to save. Of this terrible doolful inspeccioun The peeplis hertys gretly gan abave.

abaxial (æb'æksɪəl), *a. Bot.* [mod. f. L. *ab* away from + *axi-s* axle + -AL[1]; less analogically formed than the following.] **a.** = ABAXILE.

1857 HENFREY *Elem. Botany* 303 It [the embryo] may be abaxial or excentric, when the layer of endosperm is thickest on one side.

b. Of, pertaining to, or designating the surface (usu. the underside) of a leaf, etc., which during development initially faces away from the main axis or stem; opp. ADAXIAL *a.* Cf. DORSAL *a.* 2 b.

1900 B. D. JACKSON *Gloss. Bot. Terms* 1/2 *Abaxial*, .. the side of a lateral organ away from the axis. **1914** M. DRUMMOND tr. *Haberlandt's Physiol. Plant Anat.* vi. 289 The presence of the last-mentioned layer [in the leaf] illustrates a tendency on the part of the plant to extend the photosynthetic system beyond its ordinary limits, wherever illumination provides an opportunity. Such an abaxial palisade-layer..constitutes, as it were, a miniature copy of the principal adaxial system. **1960** W. B. CROW *Synopsis of Biol.* xxi. 152 The leaf is..often clearly differentiated into an adaxial or ventral surface turned towards the stem, and an abaxial or dorsal surface away from it. **1979** *Nature* 22 Nov. 425/2 Abaxial and adaxial patterns of stomatal response to light.

abaxile (æb'æksaɪl), *a. Bot.* [mod. f. L. *ab* away from + *axi-s* axle + -ILE.] Off the axis or central line; eccentric.

1854 BALFOUR *Outl. Bot.* 265 When the embryo is not in the centre of the seed it is abaxile or eccentric.

†**abay** (ə'beɪ). *Obs.* [a. OFr. *abai* barking, f. vb. *abayer* to bark; cf. mod. Fr. *aboi* in phrase *être aux abois*, *mettre aux abois* (found in 15 c.): to be or put *at bay*, said of the stag etc. in the moment of extremity, when closed in by the dogs which are *barking* after him. See BAY *sb.*[3]]

1. Barking, baying of dogs upon their prey; especially when they have run it down, and are closing round it. ***to stand at abay***, said of the dogs: to stand barking round.

1580 BARET *Alvearie*, Abbay is a French woorde, and signifieth barking against something..For when the Dere is utterly wearied and out of breath, then is he faine (setting himselfe to some hedge, tree, etc.) to stande at defiance against all the houndes barking rounde about him, and to defende himselfe with his hornes, as it were at the sworde poynt, as long as he is able. Hereupon we say commonly of men at variance: He will holde or keepe him at abbay. **1616** SURFL. & MARKH. *Countrey Farme* 700 At such times as foxes and brocks haue young ones, you must take all your old earth dogs, and let them take the earth, afterward when they shal begin to stand at an abbaie, then must the young ones be brought vnto the mouth of the hole one by one and there cause them to heare the abbaie.

2. ***to be at abay***, said of the hunted animal when the dogs 'stand at abay' round him, or have reduced him to desperation; hence, to be in extremities, to be in straits so as to have nowhere to turn, to be in desperation. (Now *at bay*.)

c **1350** *Will. Palerne* 46 And euere the dogge at the hole held it at a-baye. *c* **1400** *Sir Degrevant* 238 Hertus bade at abey One a launde by a ley. *c* **1430** *Hymns to Virg.* etc. (1867) 70 Y am huntid as an herte to a-bay, I not whidir y may me turne. **1430** LYDGATE *Chron. Troy* I. vi. She was at abay yset Amyd hope and fearfull dreade also. **1580** SIDNEY *Arcadia* (1622) 34 The Stagge..turning his head, made the hounds, with change of speech, to testifie that he was at a bay; as if from hot pursuit of their enemie, they were suddenly come to a parley. **1596** SPENSER *State Irel.* Wks. 1862, 536/1 All former purposes were blancked (and) the Governour at a bay. **1670** MILTON *Hist. Eng.* Wks. 1851, v. 229 Who like a wild Beast at abbay, seeing himself surrounded, desperately laid about him, wounding some in his fall.

abaya (ə'beɪjə). Also **abeih, abbai, abaiya, abeya, abaye**, etc. [Arab. *'abāya*.] = ABA[2].

1836 LANE *Mod. Egypt.* I. i. 35 A kind of black woollen cloak, called *'abbáyeh*. **1855** J. L. PORTER 5 *Yrs. Damascus* I. iv. 195 The ample folds of an abeih. **1884** S. W. BAKER *Heart Africa* iii. 36 (Stanford), A white cashmere abbai. **1922** *Blackw. Mag.* Sept. 358/1 A dazzling yellow 'jibba' covered by a red 'abaiya'. **1942** F. STARK *Lett. from Syria* iv. 172 A man in a black 'abeya galloped past. **1946** A. KOESTLER *Thieves in Night* II. iii. 144 Issa came in, his abaye hurriedly thrown over his underclothes.

†**a-baye**, *adv. Obs. rare*[−1]. [properly phrase: A *prep.*[1] at + BAY *sb.* short. f. ABAY. OFr. has both *bayer* and *abayer*. See BAY.] At bay.

c **1300** *Kyng Alis.* 3882 Wher hy hym myghte, so hound abaye [= as hound at bay], Othir bygile othir bytreye.

†**abayle**, *v. Obs. rare*[−1]. [ad. OFr. *abailli-er* to overtake, gain, reach.] To reach, get to.

1430 LYDGATE *Chron. Troy* v. xxxvi. Or that he the cytye myght abayle, Horestes Knyhtes unwarely haue him mette.

Abaza (ə'bɑːzə), *sb.* (and *a.*). Also **Abas, Abazah**, etc. [Native name of the people for themselves; cf. Russ. *abazinskiy*.] **a.** A member of a north-west Caucasian people, inhabiting mainly the Karachaev-Cherkess Autonomous Region of the U.S.S.R. **b.** The language of this people, classified with Abkhaz in the Abkhaz-Adygey sub-group of north-west Caucasian languages. Also *attrib.* or as *adj.*

1814 [see CHECHEN]. **1838** [see ABKHAZ]. **1845** *Encycl. Metrop.* XV. 609/1 The Abkhasians or Abázahs. *Ibid.* XIX. 532/2 An Abázah chief. **1956** *Trans. Philol. Soc. 1955* 128 The Abaza language has experienced a succession of orthographies, based on Arabic, Roman, and Cyrillic letters. *Ibid.* 138 Abaza displays no such clear distinction as that of Noun and Verb in most Indo-European languages. **1964** R. H. ROBINS *Gen. Linguistics* viii. 331 Abaza, a Caucasian language, has been cited as an extreme case of a verb-centred language in which the verb form represents in itself a sort of small-scale model of the structure of the whole sentence. **1977** *Language* LIII. 450 An excellent sketch of some areas of Abaza phonology and morphology..exists. **1979** *Trans. Philol. Soc.* 232 According to the 1970 census there were 96,331 speakers of Adyche, 311,078 of E. Circassian in the USSR. This contrasts with 24,449 speakers of Abaza and 79,835 of Abkhaz.

abb- is often found in older spelling where *ab-* is now used. Thus **abbase, abbatis, abbet, abbettor, abbay, abbortive, abbredge, abbut, abbuttal**, which see under their ordinary spelling with one *b*.

abb (æb). Forms: 1 **áwebb, óweb, áb**; 8–9 **abb**. [f. A- *pref.* 1 + WEB; cf. OE. *awefan* = OHG. *arweban*, mod.G. *erweben* to weave, f. *a* up + *wefan* to weave. (Ettmüller suggests for *an-web*, comparing mod.G. *anweben* to weave on *or* to.) Another OE. form was *áwef*, *ówef* whence WOOF.] The woof or weft in a web. Also *attrib.*

a **1000** ÆLFRIC etc. in Wright's *Vocabularies* I. 282/1 *Stamen* wearp. *Subtimen* aweb. *Ibid.* 66/1 *Subtegmen* awebb. *Ibid.* 59/2 *Trama* vel *subtemen* oweb *vel* ab. *Ibid.* 40/1 *Tramasericum* seolcen ab..*Linostema* linen wearp, *vel* wyllen ab. **1757** LISLE *Husbandry* 500 What is on the back and ribs is somewhat finer, and makes, in druggets, the thread called abb. **1774** *Act 14 Geo. III.* c. xxv, Frauds are frequently committed by persons employed in the woollen manufactory..by the weavers withholding part of the woof or abb yarn delivered to them. **1835** PARTINGTON *Brit. Cycl.* s.v. Abb, the yarn of a weaver's warp, whence the wool of which it is made is termed abb-wool.

‖**Abba**[1] (æbə). [An Aramaic word, Chal. *abbâ*, Syr. *abbâ* or *abbô*, the father, or O father.] Being retained in the Greek text of the N.T., and the versions, along with its transl. *father*, the combination *Abba father* is used by devotional writers as a title of invocation to the first person of the Trinity. Also a title given in the Syriac and Coptic churches to bishops, and by bishops to the patriarch: father, religious superior.

1382 WYCLIF *Rom.* viii. 16 The spirit of adopcioun of sones..in which we cryen, Abba, fadir. **1557** *Genevan, ibid.* The Sprite of adoption, whereby we crye Abba, that is to say, Father. **1611** BIBLE *Mark* xiv. 36 And he said, Abba, father, all things are possible vnto thee. **1652** J. SMITH *Sel. Disc.* 525 Abba is a word of honour and glory, even as Rabbi: whence the Latin *Abbas*, and our English Abbot, have been derived to denote the greatest person in a society. **1719** WATTS *Hymn* 'Behold what wondrous grace' (556), My faith shall Abba, Father, cry And thou the kindred own.

abba[2], see ABA[2].

abba, obs. form of ABBEY.

abbace, obs. form of ABBESS.

abbacination, variant of ABACINATION.

abbacy ('æbəsɪ). Also 5–6 **abbasy**, 6–7 **abbacie**. [A modification of the earlier ABBATIE, assimilated to forms like *prelacy*, med.L. *-acia*, *-atia*. It appears to have been originally a Scotch form.]

1. The dignity, estate, or jurisdiction of an abbot.

c **1425** WYNTOWN *Cron.* VII. v. 123 Of byschaprykis, or abbasyis, Or ony kyrkis benefyis. **1552** LYNDESAY *Tragedie* 53 At Arbroith I began,—Ane Abasie of gret ryches and rent. **1580** BARET *Alvearie*, An Abbasie or the office of an Abbot, *Antistitium*. **1634–46** J. ROW (the father) *Kirk of Scot.* (1842) 55 That almes be given out of abbacies, as of before. **1651** BAXTER *Inf. Bapt.* 322 Who knoweth not, that a Canonship, Abbacy, Bishoprick, are but relations? **1691** BLOUNT *Law Dict.*, Abbacy (*abbatia*) is the same to an Abbot, as Bishoprick to a Bishop: We may call it his Paternity. **1776** ADAM SMITH *Wealth of Nat.* II. v. i. 385 (1869) The abbot..was elected by the monks of the monastery, at least in the greater part of abbacies. **1872** W.

F. SKENE *Fordun's Chron.* II. 413 The word 'Abthania' has no connection whatever with the word 'Thanus.' It is a Latin form of the Gaelic word Abdhaine, which is the equivalent of the Latin 'Abbatia' and signifies both the office of Abbot and the territory belonging to an Abbacy. **1873** BURTON *Hist. of Scot.* I. xii. 399 He is called the lord of the Abbacy.

2. The period during which any one is abbot. **1794** W. TINDAL *Hist. Evesham* 26 In the second year of Randulf's Abbacy Thomas, then dean, went with him to Rome. **1877** R. J. KING in *Academy* 3 Nov. 438 The east window of Bristol is the work of Edmund Knowle, whose long abbacy ranged from 1306 to 1332.

abbad, OE. form of ABBOT.

abbadisse, OE. form of ABBATESS, *Obs.*, abbess.

‖**abbas** ('æbəs). The L. original of ABBOT, formerly sometimes used as a title in English. **1377** LANGLAND *P. Pl.* B. v. 171 Bothe Priour and suppriour, And oure *pater abbas*. **1844** LINGARD *Hist. Anglo-Saxon Ch.* (1858) I. iv. 135 He became their Abbas or spiritual father.

abbas, -se, obs. form of ABBESS.

Abbassid, -ide (ə'bæsɪd, 'æbəsɪd, -aɪd), *a.* and *sb.* Also **Abbasid, -ide.** [f. name of *al- 'Abbās* (566–652) + patronymic suff. *-id(e.)*] **A.** *adj.* Of or pertaining to the dynasty (750–1258) of caliphs of Baghdad claiming descent from Abbas, uncle of Mohammed. **B.** *sb.* A member of this dynasty.

1788 GIBBON *Decl. & F.* V. lii. 431 The bloody conflict of the Ommiades and Abbassides. **1872** H. A. RAWES *God in His Works* iii. 54 The Ommiad Caliphate of Damascus and the Abbasside Caliphate of Bagdad began and ended. When the thirty-seven Abbasides began to reign, Zacharias was in the Chair of Peter. **1920** H. G. WELLS *Outline Hist.* VI. xxxii. 332/2 Another great Arab family, the Abbas family, the Abbasids..had long been scheming for power. **1923** *Ibid.* VII. xxxiii. 357/2 There was still an Abbasid Caliphate in Bagdad. **1963** *Listener* 14 Mar. 471/1 Under the Abbasid and Umayyad dynasties, Arab and Jew served as transmitters of arts and skills.

abbat, variant of ABBOT.

‖**abbate** (ab'ba:te). [Ital.:—L. *abbāt-em*, ABBOT.] An Italian abbot; the same as the French *abbé*.

1822 W. TAYLOR in *Monthly Mag.* LIII. 334 The abbate obtained a catalogue of a library extant in the Seraglio. **1860** HAWTHORNE *Marble Farm* (1879) II. xxiv. 241 An abbate.. was sitting there.

†'**abbatess, 'abbotess.** *Obs.* Forms: 1 abbadisse, abbudisse, abbodisse; 1–4 abbodesse; 2–7 abbatisse, abbatesse; 5 abatyse. [a. *abbadissa*, late L. and early Rom. pronunc. of L. *abbātissa* (cf. Pr. and It. *abbadessa*) fem. of *abbas*, *abbāt-em*, ABBOT; introduced into Eng. at or soon after the Conversion; afterwards assimilated to the literary L. spelling as *abbatisse*. In 2 or 3 the Fr. *abbesse* was introduced, but the earlier form continued to exist beside it as *abbatesse, abbotess* till 7.] = ABBESS.

c **855** *O.E. Chron.* an. 680 And þy ylcan ȝeare forþferde Hild abbodesse on Streonesheale. *c* **885** K. ÆLFRED *Bæda* iv. 24 On Hilde mynstre þære abbudissan wæs sum bróðor Cædmon ȝeháten. *a* **1000** *A.S. Inst. Polity* in *Anc. Laws* II. 320 Riht is þæt abbodas & huru abbadissan fæste on mynstrum singallice wunian. **1002** *Will of Wulfric, Cod. Dip.* VI. 147 And ælcon abbode and æalcon abbatissan .v. mancusas goldes. **1393** LANGLAND *P.Pl.* C. VII. 128 Ich haue an Aunte to a nunne · and to an abbodesse [*v.r.* abbesse, abbasse]. *c* **1450** in Wright's *Vocab.* 215 *Hec abatissa*, a abatyse. **1538** LELAND *It.* II. 67. §6 Bertane was the first Abbatisse therof. **1580** HOLLYBAND *Treas. Fr. Tong.*, *Abbesse*, an Abbatesse. **1633** HANMER *Chron. Irel.* 60 This Saint Yta was an Abbatesse, whose originall was of Meth. **1647** N. BACON *Hist. Disc.* xiii. 87 Abbatisses were present, & attested the acts of that Synod. **1649** SELDEN *Laws of Eng.* I. vii. 15 (1739) To govern, chuse, appoint, confirm, and remove Abbots, Abbotesses, Presbyters, and Deacons. **1685** R. MORDEN *Geogr. Rectified* Germany 132 The Abbey Quedelnburg, whose Abbatess was sometimes Princess of the Empire.

abbathie, variant of ABBATIE, *Obs.*, abbacy.

abbatial (ə'beɪʃ(ɪ)əl), *a.* [a. Fr. *abbatial* (16th cent. in Litt.), ad. late L. *abbātiāl-is* f. *abbātia*. See ABBATIE and -AL[1].] Of or pertaining to an abbacy, abbot, or abbess.

a **1642** URQUHART *Rabelais* IV. xiv. (1855) He was a public person, a servant to the monking tribe, apparitor to the abbatial mitre. **1747** CARTE *Hist. Eng.* I. 420 The King became entitled to the profits of the lands of bishopricks and abbatial manses. **1851** PALGRAVE *Norm. & Eng.* I. 366 This is not the Cathedral but an Abbatial Church. **1876** FREEMAN *Norm. Conq.* II. x. 445 He bestowed the abbatial benediction on Wulfstan.

†**abbatical** (ə'bætɪkəl), *a.* *Obs.* [f. L. *abbāt-em* ABBOT + -ICAL; apparently by form-assoc. with *sabbatical*.] = ABBATIAL.

1655 FULLER *Ch. Hist.* Let others dispute, whether Ceolwolphus thus dispensed with them by his new Abbatical, or old Regal Power. **1774** T. WEST *Antiq. of Furness* (1805) 75 Notwithstanding his abbatical dignity.

†'**abbatie.** *Obs.* Forms: 3 abboddie; 6 abbatie, ab(b)athie. [ad. late L. *abbatia, abbathia, abbadia* (cf. Pr. *abadia*), n. of state, f. *abbāt-em* ABBOT. Afterwards changed to ABBACY, after words in *-cy*, ad. L. *-cia, -tia.*] = ABBACY.

c **1270** *An Old English Miscellany* 145 On willames dayeþe yonger kynges wes þat Abboddie by-numen. **1561** T. N[ORTON] *Calvin's Inst.* IV. 28b, Abbaties and priories are geuen to very boyes, by priuilege, that is to say, by common and vsuall custome. **1655** FULLER *Ch. Hist.* IV. 147 No Bishoprick, Abathie, Dignitie, or Rectorie, of value in England was likely to fall, but a successour in reversion was by the Popes provisions fore-appointed for the same.

a'bbaye. An archaic form of ABBEY, sometimes found in modern writers.

1805 SCOTT *Lay of L.M.* II. xxiv. Glad when he passed the tombstones grey, Which girdle round the fair Abbaye.

‖**abbé** ('æbeɪ). [mod.Fr. *abbé*:—OFr. *abe, abet*: —L. *abbāt-em*; see ABBOT.] The French title answering to Eng. *abbot*, but extended to 'every one who wears an ecclesiastical dress,' Littré; and specially applied to one having no assigned ecclesiastical duty, but acting as a professor, private tutor, or master of a household; in which sense the word is simply transferred into Eng. instead of being translated. Thus, 'Anselm, abbot of Bec,' 'the Abbé Montmorency.' Cf. Ital. ABBATE.

1530 PALSGRAVE *Lesclarcissement* 11 f. lvi[r], For to the abbe ..they say *a làbbe*. **1701** T. MARWOOD *Diary* in *Cath. Rec. Soc. Publ.* (1909) VII. 100, I walkt out to ye Abbé's a League & ½ off. *Ibid.* 108 And [we had] Abbé Villebreuille with us. **1712** SWIFT *Jrnl. to Stella* 13 Dec. (1948) II. 581, I must see the Abbè Gautier. **1719** GAY *Let.* 8 Sept. in *Lett. Henrietta, C'tess of Suffolk* (1824) I. 34 A French marquis drove an abbé from the table by railing against the vast riches of the church. **1780** COWPER *Prog. Error* 385 Ere long some bowing, smirking, smart Abbé Remarks two loiterers that have lost their way. **1885** LORD R. GOWER *Old Diaries* 10 Apr. (1902) 20 Monsieur Floquet..is a grey-haired, abbé-like man. **1955** *Times* 8 July 11/4 A strange, weird, little man, looking something between an actor and an *abbé*.

abbe, *v.* = *habbe*, common for HAVE in 2–3.

abbed, abbeod, obs. forms of ABBOT.

abbeit, abbet, abbite, obs. forms of HABIT.

abbess ('æbɪs) Forms: 3–7 **abbesse**; 4 **abbes(e, abbeys**; 4–5 **abbas**; 4–6 **abbasse**; 5–6 **abbace**; 7– **abbess.** [a. OFr. *abbesse, abesse*, earlier *abeësse, abaësse* (Pr. *abadessa*):—late L. *abbadissa, -tissa*, fem. of *abbāt-em* ABBOT; see -ESS. This OFr. form appears beside the earlier ABBATESS in 2–3, and has superseded it since 7.] **a.** The female superior of a nunnery or convent of women, having the same authority over nuns that an abbot has over monks.

1297 R. GLOUC. 370 Þe eldeste, þat was at Came nonne & abbese. *c* **1300** *Met. Hom.* 164 That was abbes of a nunrye. **1393** GOWER *Conf.* III. 337 His wife..that was abbesse there, Unto his tale hath laid her ere. *c* **1400** *Rom. Rose* 6352 Somtyme am I prioresse, And now a nonne, & now abbesse. *c* **1420** *Chron. Vilod.* 155 Bot Radgunde was first sacryd Abbas þere. **1482** *Monk of Evesham* 91 A certen worschipful abbas was ther. **1513** *Lyfe of St. Werburge* 78 And dyd electe to them · an other abbace. **1590** SHAKS. *Com. Err.* V. i. 166 Go some of you, knocke at the Abbey gate, And bid the Lady Abbesse come to me. **1859** TENNYSON *Guinevere* 688 And likewise for the high rank she had borne, Was chosen Abbess, there, an Abbess, lived For three brief years, and there, an Abbess, past To where beyond these voices there is peace.

†**b.** *transf.* (See quot. 1785.) *Obs.* (See also Farmer *Slang* (1890) I. 3/2.)

1749 J. CLELAND *Mem. Woman Pleasure* I. 59 Who should come in but the venerable mother Abbess herself! handed in by a tall, brawny young horse-grenadier. **1770** [see NUN *sb.*[1] I c]. **1785** GROSE *Dict. Vulg. Tongue*, Abbess, or Lady Abbess, a bawd, the mistress of a brothel. **1793** 'PETER PINDAR' *Poet. Epistle to the Pope* 33 So an old Abbess for the rattling Rakes, A tempting dish of human nature makes. **1837** W. KIDD *London & its Dangers* 36 The Infernal wretches, who traffic in the souls and bodies of their helpless victims, are called—Lady Abbesses.

abbest, obs. form of ASBESTOS.

Abbevillian (æbə'vɪlɪən), *a.* Also **Abbevillean.** [ad. Fr. *Abbevillien* (H. Breuil 1932, in *Préhistoire* I. 125), f. the place-name *Abbeville* (Somme), France.] = CHELLEAN *a.* Also *absol.*

[**1928** G. B. BROWN *Art of Cave Dweller* ii. 36 The so-called early 'drift' period is generally called the 'Chelles' period..though in honour to Boucher de Perthes it might well have been named after Abbeville.] **1934** L. S. B. LEAKEY *Adam's Ancestors* v. 101 L' Abbé Breuil..has suggested the substitution of the name Abbevillian for Chellean, since Chelles from which the latter name is derived is not a Chellean site. **1937** *Discovery* June 179/2 The Sinanthropus [industry]..belongs to the Lower Pleistocene and is attributed to the Abbevillean in the French palæolithic sequence. **1947** J. & C. HAWKES *Prehist. Brit.* i. 12 Contemporary with the earliest Abbevillian was the Cromer flake culture.

abbey ('æbɪ). Forms: 3–5 **abbeye**; 3–8 **abbaye**; 3 **abbei**; 4 **abey**; 4–7 **abbay**; 6 **abba, abee, abbie, abbeie**; 6–8 **abby**; 3– **abbey.** [a. OFr. *abaïe, abeïe, abbaïe, abbeïe* (mod. *abbaye*), Pr. *abadia*:—late L. *abbādia, abbāthia, abbātia*, n. of state, f. *abbātem* ABBOT. *Abbey, abbathie, abbacy*, all represent the same L. word, but English has differentiated *abbacy* and *abbey*, which are both included in L. *abbatia*, and Fr. *abbaye.*]

1. A monastery of religious persons secluded from the world, and under vows of celibacy, consisting of *monks* governed by an *abbot*, or of *nuns* under an *abbess*. The development of meaning was—**a.** the jurisdiction or benefice of an abbot, abbacy. **b.** the religious establishment or corporation. **c.** the monastic buildings. But these senses cannot always be separated.

1250 LAYAMON III. 191 At Bangor was on abbey [**1205** munuclif] ifulled with monekes. *Ibid.* III. 192 He hadde in soue abbayes [**1205** on seuen hepen] sixtene hundred monakes. **1297** R. GLOUC. 369 Þere, as þe batayle was, an abbey he let rere..þat ys ycluped in Engelond, abbey of þe batayle. *c* **1300** *St. Brandan* 263 Into meni o stede, and siththe into an Abbei. **1375** BARBOUR *Bruce* xx. 599 The Erll of Murreff..hass gert bery The kyngis hert at the abbay of melross. *c* **1450** LONELICH *Grail* liv. 154 In Abbey [Iosephe] was buryed ful Solempne, Whech Abbey of Glaystyngbery now men hald. **1534** LD. BERNERS *Golden Boke of Marcus Aurel.* [1546] C vi. If ye gyue an abbaye to a foole. **1536** *Exhortacyon to the North* in Furnivall's *Ballads from MSS.* Abbas to suppresse we haue lytyll nede. **1548** HALL *Chron.* (1809) 729 With great triumph rode these ij Cardinalls together to the Abee. **1590** SHAKS. *Com. Err.* V. i. 155 Then they fled Into this Abbey, whether we pursu'd them. **1595** —— *John* I. i. 48 Our Abbies and our Priories shall pay This expeditions charge. **1605** CAMDEN *Remaines* 191 William Rufus loved wel to keep vacant Bishopriks and Abbies in his handes. **1639** DRUMM. OF HAWTH. *Consid. to Parlt.* Wks. 1711, 186 That all bishops houses, concierges, abbays, and nunries, be made places to entertain soldiers. **1651** W. G. tr. *Cowel's Inst.* 204 Had monies owing to them in the name of their Abbies. **1759** ROBERTSON *Hist. of Scot.* (1817) 276 The Scottish monarchs had the sole right of nomination to vacant bishoprics and abbeys. **1772** PENNANT *Tours in Scotland* 255 (1774) All the monks of this abby. **1861** WADE *Melrose Abbey* 251 The estates of the abbey were granted by Queen Mary to the earl of Bothwell.

2. Since the dissolution of the monasteries, popularly applied to the Abbey Church, as *Westminster Abbey* (in London, *the Abbey*); entering also into the names of private residences, which were formerly abbatial houses, as *Battle Abbey, Newbattle Abbey.*

1557 MORE *Richard III*, 192 (1641) Entred the Abbie at the West end. **1584** POWEL *Lloyd's Cambria* 142 The toombe of Gerald Sitfylt in the Abbeie of Dore. **1624** BEAUM. & FL. (Bell's ed.) *Rule a wife* IV. i. 45 This would do rarely in an abby window to cozen pilgrims. *a* **1674** CLARENDON *Hist. Reb.* I. IV. 265 The Abby at Westminster. **1712** ADDISON *Spectator* No. 329. 1 He had been reading my paper upon Westminster Abbey. **1849** MACAULAY *Hist. Eng.* xi. All the steeples from the Abbey to the Tower, sent forth a joyous din. **1882** *Daily News* 27 April 4/7 In the presence of a large and representative gathering the remains of the late Mr. Darwin were yesterday interred in Westminster Abbey.

3. *Scotl.* The precincts of the Abbey of Holyrood, as a sanctuary for insolvent debtors.

1709 FOUNTAINHALL *Decisions* II. 518 If he offered to go back to the Abbey, and was enticed to stay and hindered to go. *a* **1776** *Cock Laird* (Herd's *Ballads* II. 36) When broken, frae care The fools are set free, When we make them lairds In the Abbey, quoth she.

4. *Attrib.* and *Comb.*; as ***abbey-church, abbey gate, vault, wall, window.*** Also **abbey-counter** (see COUNTER *sb.*[3] 1 a), a medal presented to a pilgrim as a token of his having visited a shrine (cf. PILGRIM's *sign*); **abbey-labourer**, a labourer in the service of an abbey; **abbey-lands**, estates of an abbey; **abbey man**, a member of a monastery, a monk; **abbey-monger**; **abbey-stead**, a monastic settlement; the site of an abbey. Also ABBEY-LAIRD, ABBEY-LIKE, ABBEY-LUBBER, q.v.

1649 DRUMM. OF HAWTH. *Hist. James V*, Wks. 1711, 105 She was crowned queen of Scotland in the abby-church of Holyrood-house. **1839–42** C. KNIGHT *Pict. Edition Works Shakspere. Comedies* II. 231/1 Jettons..were commonly used for purposes of calculation, in abbeys and other places. .. From their being found among the ruins of English abbeys they are usually termed abbey-counters. **1868** STEPHENS *Runic Mon.* II. 535 There was also a class of Jettons commonly called Abbey-counters, with similar or cognate instructive stamps. **1590** SHAKS. *Com. Err.* V. i. 165 Go some of you, knocke at the Abbey gate. **1655** FULLER *Ch. Hist.* I. v. 28 Abbey-labourers, not Abbey-lubbers, like their Successours in after-Ages. **1679** PRANCE *Add. Narrative* 30 To secure abbey-lands to their owners. *c* **1550** BALE *K. Iohan* 27 Thou art styll an abbeman. **1679** PRANCE *Add. Narrative* 30 It is almost incredible, what a Qualm..came over the Hearts of the stoutest abby-mongers in England. **1819** SCOTT *Ivanhoe* II. x. 175 It is a rich abbey-stede, and they do live upon the fat. **1845** HIRST *Poems* 43 'Till in abbey-vault I sleep. **1590** SHAKS. *Com. Err.* V. i. 265 I neuer came within these abbey wals.

abbeyed ('æbɪd), *a.* [f. ABBEY + -ED[2].] Provided with an abbey or abbeys.

1828 [see MANSIONED *ppl. a.*]. **1864** A. JEFFREY *Hist. Roxburghshire* IV. i. 56 Bonny Teviotdale, abbeyed, towered and castled. **1864** E. CASWALL *May Pageant* III. 30 Now ancient Shrewsbury appears in sight..Fair-abbey'd formerly ere Faith's decline.

abbey-ˈlaird. [See ABBEY 3.] An insolvent debtor sheltering in the precincts of Holyrood Abbey. (Humorous.)

1861 R. CHAMBERS *Dom. Ann. Scot.* III. 349 It being part of the law of Scotland that diligence cannot be proceeded with on Sunday, the Abbey Lairds, as they were jocularly called, were enabled to come forth on that day, and mingle in their wonted society.

†**ˈabbey-like,** *a.* Like an abbey; monastic, monkish. *Obs.*

1553–87 FOXE *A. & M.* 80/2 (1596) The admixture of all these abbeielike additions of moonkish miracles. **1644** R. CULMER *Cathedr. Newes*, An Abbey-Like, Corrupt and rotten condition.

†**abbey-lubber** (,æbɪˈlʌbə(r)). A lazy monk; a reproachful name in regular use after the Reformation.

1538 STARKEY *England* 131 (1871) The nuryschyng also of a grete sorte of idul abbey-lubbarys wych are apte to no thyng but as the byschoppys and abbotys be, only to ete and drynke. **1589** THOMAS NASHE *Anat. Absur.* 7 Those exiled Abbie-lubbers, from whose idle pens, proceeded those worne out impressions of the feyned no where acts, of Arthur of the rounde table. **1611** COTGR., *Archimarmitonerastique*, an Abbey-lubber, or Arch-frequenter of the Cloyster beefe-pot, or beefe-boyler. **1655** MOFFETT & BENNET *Health's Improv.* (1746) 365 Maximinus the Emperor, who, like our old Abbay-lubbers, did eat till he sweat. **1693** W. ROBERTSON *Phras. Gen.* 446 A porridge-belly Friar, an abbey lubber. **1705** HICKERINGILL *Priest-Cr.* II. iv. 45 The Dissolutions of Monasteries, that fed Abbey-Lubbers and wanton Nuns.

Comb. **abbey-lubber-like.**

1570 BARNABE GOOGE *Popish Kingdome* II. 23 So abby lubber lyke they liue, & Lordes they called bee.

abbiliment, see ABILIMENT, HABILIMENT.

abbod, early form of ABBOT.

abboddie, early form of ABBATIE, *Obs.*, abbacy.

abbodisse, OE. form of ABBATESS, *Obs.*, abbess.

abbot (ˈæbət). Forms: 1 **abbad, abbud**; 1–3 **abbod**; 2–3 **abbeod**; 3–4 **abbed**; 2– **abbot.** By-form 2–7 **abbat.** [a. *abbād-em*, late L. and early Rom. pronunc. of L. *abbăt-em*, in nom. *abbas* (4th c.), a. Gr. ἀββάς, ad. Syriac *abbā*, father (see ABBA), an appellation given originally in the East to all monks (cf. Ital. and Sp. *padre*, Fr. *père*), but restricted at length in the West to the superior of a monastery. Adopted in Eng. at or soon after the English Conversion; the original *abbad* became by assimilation to the native ending *-ud*, *-od*, *abbud*, *abbod*, whence the 13th c. *abbed*; the mod. representative would have been *abd* (cf. Ger. *abt*), but in 12th c. the L. *abbăt-em* gave a new literary form *abbat*, under the influence of which OE. *abbod* became *abbot*, found as early as 1123. *Abbat* continued as a by-form till 1700, and was especially affected by the ecclesiastical writers of 5–7. The difference is merely graphical, the atonic *-ot* and *-at* being alike (-ət).]

1. The head or superior of an abbey. After the dissolution of the monasteries, sometimes applied to the layman to whom the revenues of an abbacy were impropriated.

†**a.** Early form *abbod*, *-ed*.

c **880** K. ÆLFRED *Bæda* v. 13 On þam mynstre wæs.. Abbad and messepreost Æðelwold haten. **905** *O.E. Chron.* (*Parker MS.*) Eadwold cynȝes ðeȝen, and Cenulf abbod. *c* **1175** *Lamb. Hom.* 93 Bi heore abbodes iwissunge. **1205** LAYAMON II. 125 þe abbed an horse leop..þus seide þe abbed [**1250** þe abbod vppe his horse leop..þus spac þe abbod]. *c* **1230** *Ancren Riwle* 314 þuruh þen abbodes gropunge. **1297** R. GLOUC. 447 ȝyf byssop, oþer abbed, in þys lond ded were.

†**b.** By-form *abbat*.

c **1130** *O.E. Chron.* (*Laud. MS.*) anno 1123 And bed his biscopes and his abbates and his þeiȝnes. **1297** R. GLOUC. 376 Byssopes and abbates to hys wylle echon. *c* **1400** *Rom. Rose* 2694 Fatter than abbatis or priours. **1571** BP. JEWEL *On 1 Thessal.* (1611) 116 Ioachimus an Abbat hath told vs Antichrist shall be called, holy Lord, and most holy Pope. **1598** HAKLUYT *Eng. Voyages* I. 71 Confirming likewise al things..by their Abbate. **1614–25** JN. BOYS (Wks. 1630) 130 The begging Frier would be Prior: the Prior, an Abbat. **1691** BLOUNT *Law Dict.*, *Abbat* or *Abbot*, A Spiritual Lord, that has the rule and preheminence over a Religious House.

c. Current form *abbot*.

c **1123** *O.E. Chron.* (*Laud. MS.*) anno 963 [He] halȝode him þa abbot. *Ibid.* anno 1123 Ansealm abbot of S. Ædmund. *c* **1377** LANGL. *P. Pl.* B. x. 326 þe abbot of Abyndoun And alle [his] issu for euere. *c* **1489** *Plumpton Corr.* 84 My servant John Tomlynson hath taken a farmehold of the abut of Fountayns..which the abott wyll record the taking. **1611** COTGR., *Il iure comme vn Abbé* He sweares like an Abbot, viz. extreamly. **1613** SHAKS. *Hen. VIII*, IV. ii. 20 O Father Abbot! An old man, broken with the storms of State, Is come to lay his weary bones among ye. **1641** *Les Termes de la Ley* 2 Abbot, was the soveraigne head, or chiefe of those houses, which when they stood were called Abbies, and this Abbot together with the Monks of the same House, who were called the Convent, made a Corporation. **1751** CHAMBERS *Cycl.* Mitred Abbots were those privileged to wear the mitre; and allowed, withal, a full episcopal authority within their precincts..and were lords of parliament. Of these Sir Edward Coke reckons 27 in England. **1845** DISRAELI *Sybil* (1863) 13 The lay abbot of Marney, also in this instance like the other whig lords, was careful to maintain..a very loyal and dutiful though secret correspondence with the court of St. Germains. **1861** MOTLEY *Dutch Rep.* I. 270, *Provb.* When the Abbot has dice in his pocket, the convent will play.

†**2.** 'Also a title borne by several magistrates, and other lay persons. Among the Genoese, one of their principal magistrates was called the Abbat of the people.' Chambers *Cycl.* 1741. *Obs.*

†**3.** Applied ironically to the leader of certain disorderly festivities, as the ***Abbot of Misrule, Abbot of Unreason.*** *Obs.*

4. *Comb.* **abbot-presbyter.**

1772 PENNANT *Tours in Scotland* 255 (1774) The island always had for a governor an Abbot-Presbyter.

abbotcy (ˈæbətsɪ). *rare.* [f. ABBOT + -CY; of which ABBACY is the ordinary derivative.] = ABBACY, ABBOTSHIP.

1844 LINGARD *Hist. Anglo-Saxon Ch.* (1858) II. xiii. 269 The abbotcy of St. Alban's.

abbotess, variant of ABBATESS, *Obs.*, abbess.

†**abbotric** (ˈæbətrɪk). *Obs.* Forms: 1 **abbodrice,** 2 **abbotrice,** 3 **abbodryche,** 6 **abbatrik,** 7 **abbotrick.** [f. ABBOT + -RIC = OE. *rice* kingdom, realm, rule.] The benefice or jurisdiction of an abbot; an abbacy.

c **1120** *O.E. Chron.* (Laud. MS.) anno 656, On his time wæx þet abbodrice..swiðe rice. *Ibid.* anno 963, He macode þær twá abbotrice. **1127** *Ibid.* þæt he ne mihte hafen twa abbotrices on hande. *c* **1200** *Charter of Eadweard* (1067) *Cod. Diplom.* IV. 225 Ic habbe unnen Baldewine abbot ðe abbotríche intó seint Eádmundes biri. *a* **1300** *O.E. Misc.* 145 And Baþe wes Abbodryche. **1553–87** FOXE *A. & M.* (1596) 189/2 He had had diverse bishopriks and abbatriks in his hand which were vacant. **1711** MADOX *Hist. Excheq.* 7 He filled up a great many vacant Bishopriks and Abbotricks.

abbotship (ˈæbət-ʃɪp). Also 7 **abbatship.** [f. ABBOT + -SHIP.] The office or rule of an abbot; abbacy; abbatial term of office.

1495 *Vitas Patrum* (W. de Worde) I. clviii. 163 b, All the Religious that so besily desyred her to take upon her the auctorytee of the abbotshypp. **1560** J. DAUS tr. *Sleidane's Comm.* 348 a, In steade of one bishoppricke, which they left, they had of them again many abbotships, or such other like promotions. **1691** WOOD *Ath. Oxon.* II. 114 Richlieu..confer'd upon him the abbatship of Charroux. **1872** *Spectator* 6 April 444 The last years of John of Whethamstede's first abbotship were not passed without the accustomed miscellaneous litigations.

abbozzo (aˈbɒtsəʊ). Also **abozzo.** [It.] A rough drawing or sketch (for a portrait, etc.); an outline or draft (of a speech, essay, etc.).

1849 [see ALLA PRIMA]. **1890** MORLEY *Diary* 20 Nov. in *Recoll.* (1917) I. 256 A letter from Mr. G. containing an 'abozzo', as he headed it, of what it would be well for us to say. **1905** W. HOLMAN HUNT *Pre-Raphaelitism* I. xiii. 361 Another dashing abozzo, said to be a portrait.

†**aˈbbreviarist.** *Obs. rare*⁻¹. [f. L. *breviārium* abridgement, epitome + -IST; whence regularly *breviarist*; expanded into *abbreviarist* after *abbreviate.*] One who makes an epitome or compendium.

1679 PRANCE *Add. Narrative* 18 The Dying Speeches of all the Criminals are punctually set down by him, by our Abbreviarist.

abbreviate (əˈbriːvɪət), *ppl. a.* [ad. L. *abbrĕviātus* shortened, pa. pple. of *abbreviā-re*, f. *ab* off, or ? *ad* to + *breviā-re* to shorten, f. *brevi-s* short.] Abridged, shortened, cut short. At first used both as pple. and adj., but afterwards superseded in most senses by the normal pple. ABBREVIATED. Now used chiefly = ABBREVIATED 2.

1530 *A proper Dyaloge* 19 (1863) At seynt Edmundesbury ..the famous prince duke Humfray of his lyfe was abbreuiate. **1677** GALE *Ct. Gentiles* II. III. 146 I shal give an abbreviate Idea or character of his spirit & zele for God. **1852** J. D. DANA *Crustacea* II. 1078 Penult [joint] abbreviate. **1860** GOSSE *Romance Nat. Hist.* 357 The muzzle in the latter is more abbreviate.

†**aˈbbreviate, -at,** *sb. Obs.* [The adj. used elliptically, like L. *abbreviātum* that which is abridged.] An abridgement, short sketch, abstract, epitome.

1531 ELYOT *Governor* (1580) 205 An abbreuiate, called of ye Greekes and Latins, Epitoma. **1674** BREVINT *Saul at Endor* 104 To pick and chuse out of every Creature, as it came out, the very best of it for this true Pandora and true Abbreviate of all his works. **1686** SIR S. MORELAND in *Pepys' Diary* VI. 153 An unfortunate and fatall accident has lately befallen me, of which I shall give you an abbreviat. **1708** CHAMBERLAYNE *State of Gr. Brit.* I. II. xi. 91 (1743) The Speaker taking the Bill in his hand, reads the Abbreviate or Abstract of the said Bill. **1716** WODROW *Corresp.* (1843) II. 155 This is an abbreviate of this attempt.

abbreviate (əˈbriːvɪeɪt), *v.* Also 5–7 **abreviate.** [f. ABBREVIATE *ppl. a.*; or on the analogy of vbs. so formed; see -ATE. A direct representative of L. *abbreviāre*; as ABRIDGE, and the obs. ABBREVY(E, represent it indirectly, through OFr. *abregier* and mid.Fr. *abrévier*. Like the latter, *abbreviate*, was often spelt *a-breviate* in 5–7.] To make shorter, shorten, cut short in any way.

1530 PALSGR., I abrevyate: I make a thynge shorte, *Je abrege.* **1625** BACON *Essays* xxiv. 99 (1862) But it is one Thing to Abbreviate by Contracting, Another by Cutting off.

†**1.** *trans.* To make a discourse shorter by omitting details and preserving the substance; to abridge, condense. *Obs.*

a **1450** *Chester Pl.* I. 2 (Sh. Soc.) This matter he abbrevited into playes twenty-foure. **1592** GREENE *Conny catching* III. 16 The queane abreuiated her discourse. **1637** RALEIGH *Mahomet* 34 Abreviated out of two Arabique writers translated into Spanish. **1672** MANLEY *Interpreter* pref., I have omitted several Matters..contracted and abbreviated Others.

†**b.** To make an abstract or brief of, to epitomize. *Obs.*

c **1450** TREVISA *Higden's Polychr.* I. 21 (Rolls Ser.) Trogus Pompeius, in hys xl[ti] iiij. bookes, allemoste of alle the storyes of the worlde, whom Iustinus his disciple did abbreuiate. **1603** FLORIO *Montaigne* (1634) 627 To reade, to note, and to abbreviate Polibius. **1648–9** *The Kingdomes Weekly Intelligencer* Jan. 16 to 23 The high court of Justice did this day sit again concerning the triall of the King. The charge was brought in and abreviated.

†**c.** *Math.* To reduce (a fraction) to lower terms. *Obs.*

1796 *Mathem. Dict.* I. 2 To abbreviate fractions in arithmetic and algebra, is to lessen proportionally their terms, or the numerator and denominator.

†**2.** *intr.* To speak or write briefly, to be brief. *Obs.*

1597 WARNER *Albion's Eng.* XII. lxxiv. 302 But new Rome left, of old Rome now abreuiat we will. **1622** MALYNES *Anc. Law-Merch.* 233 To abbreuiate, I do referre the desirous Reader hereof to Master Hill his booke of Husbandrie.

3. *trans.* To shorten by cutting off a part; to cut short. **a.** Of time. *arch.*

1529 WHITINTON *Vulgaria* 56 Ryot..abbreviateth and shorteneth many a mannes lyfe. **1621** BURTON *Anat. Mel.* I. ii. 3. xv. 130 (1651) That adventure themselves and abbreviate their lives for the publike good. **1646** SIR T. BROWNE *Pseud. Ep.* 300 Against this we might very well set the length of their lives before the flood, which were abbreviated after.

b. Of any operation occupying time.

1494 FABYAN VI. 333 If it sounde any thynge to theyr dishonoure, than shall it be abreuyatyd or hyd that the trouthe shall not be known. **1655** FULLER *Ch. Hist.* II. ix. 116 King Ethelbert was at his Devotions, which he would not omit, nor abbreviate for all their Clamour. **1865** E. B. TYLOR *Early Hist. Man.* iii. 48 The ancient Egyptian may be seen in the sculptures abbreviating the gesture.

c. Of things material; mostly *fig. arch.*

1552 LATIMER *Serm. for 3rd Sund. in Adv.* Wks. II. 287 His hand is not abbreuiated, or his power diminished. **1599** A. M. *Gabelhouer's Boock of Physicke* 178/2 Abbreviate as then the bagge, because it may gentlelye, & easilye exulcerate. **1661** MILTON *Accedence* (Wks. 1738) I. 607 The long way is much abbreviated, and the labour of understanding much more easy.

d. Of words spoken or written, or symbols of any kind: To contract, so that a part stands for the whole. *The common mod. use.*

1588 SHAKS. *L.L.L.* v. i. 26 He clepeth a Calf, Caufe: Halfe, Haufe, neighbour vocatur nebour; neigh abreuiated ne: this is abhominable. **1724** DE FOE etc. *A Tour* I. 364 (1769) The Exancester of the Saxons, which was afterwards abbreviated to Excester and Exeter. **1880** GEIKIE *Phys. Geog.* I. iv. 27 Paris is situated two degrees, twenty minutes, and nine seconds east from Greenwich, which is abbreviated thus: 2° 20′ 9″E.

e. Of sounds: To make (a vowel or syllable) short.

1699 BENTLEY *Phalaris* 136 The Dorians abbreviate even ας in the Accusative Plural. **1727** SWIFT *Let. on Eng. Tongue* Wks. 1755 II. I. 188 That barbarous custom of abbreviating words to fit them to the measure of their verses.

abbreviated (əˈbriːvɪeɪtɪd), *ppl. a.* [f. prec. + -ED. It takes the place, to some extent, of ABBREVIATE *ppl. a.*]

1. Shortened, cut short, in the various senses of the vb.

1552 LATIMER *Serm. 3rd S. in Adv.* Wks. II. 287 His hand is not abbreuiated, or his power diminished. **1870** BOWEN *Logic* vii. 221 The syllogism constituting a chain may be partly complete and partly abbreviated. **1881** H. JAMES jun. *Portrait of a Lady* liv. (in *Macm. Mag.* XLV. 7) The two ladies faced each other at an abbreviated table.

2. *Nat. Hist.* Relatively short; shorter than the ordinary type, or than the adjoining parts.

1870 HOOKER *Stud. Flora* 62 Spergula.. Leaves opposite, with abbreviated leaf-buds in their axils.

†**aˈbbreviately,** *adv. Obs. rare.* [f. ABBREVIATE *a.* + -LY².] Shortly, briefly, concisely.

1599 NASHE *Lenten Stuffe* 31 Abbreuiately and meetely according to my old Sarum plaine song I haue harpt vpon.

abbreviating (əˈbriːvɪeɪtɪŋ), *vbl. sb.* [f. ABBREVIATE *v.* + -ING¹.] The act or process of shortening; abbreviation, compression.

1668 WILKINS *Real Char.* 343 Both these [prefixes] may contribute to the abbreviating of language.

abbreviation (ə,briːvɪˈeɪʃən). Also 5–7 **abreviacioun, -ation.** [a. Fr. *abréviation*, ad. L. *abbreviātiōn-em*, n. of action, f. *abbreviā-re*: see ABBREVIATE. The prefix in Fr. *a-* has been refashioned, after L., to *ab-*.]

1. The act of shortening, reducing in length.

1530 PALSGR. 193 Abrevyation, *abreviation.* **1576** LAMBARDE *Peramb. Kent* 233 (1826) Neither hath this our manner of abbreviation, corrupted the names of townes and places onely. *c* **1590** HORSEY *Travels* (Hakl. Soc.) 156 With som small abreviacion and pronunciacion it [the Russian language] coms near the Polish. **1605** TIMME *Quersitanus* III. 164 We come..to the causes of the conseruation, prolongation, destruction, and abreuiation of our life. **1824** SOUTHEY *Book of the Church* I. 311 They might purchase a free passage through Purgatory, or at least, an abbreviation of the term.

2. The result of abbreviating; an abbreviated or reduced form; short summary, abridgement.
1460 CAPGRAVE *Chron.* 17 Of these thre sones grew al mankynde in this world, and be what order here schul ȝe have abreviacioun. **1589** NASHE *Dedic. to Brune's Menaphon* (1880) 12 And heere could I enter into a large fielde of invective against our abiect Abbreviations of Artes. **1791** BOSWELL *Johnson* (1831) I. 180 Johnson's abbreviations are all distinct and applicable to each subject. **1865** E. B. TYLOR *Early Hist. Man.* iii. 52 To make a sort of abbreviation of this movement.

3. *esp.* A shortened form of a spoken word, or written symbol; a part of a word or symbol standing for the whole.
1727 SWIFT *Letter on Eng.* Wks. 1755 II. I. 188 Most of the books we see now-a-days are full of those manglings and abbreviations. **1855** THACKERAY *Newcomes* (1872) iv. 35 Smiffle, it must be explained, is a fond abbreviation for Smithfield. **1876** FREEMAN *Norm. Conq.* I. App. 547 The latter form is clearly a mere abbreviation.

abbreviator (əˈbriːvɪeɪtə(r)). Also 7 -er. [a. L. *abbreviātor*, n. of agent f. *abbreviā-re* to shorten; cf. Fr. *abréviateur*.]
1. One who abbreviates, abridges, or shortens.
1615 HELKIAH CROOKE *Body of Man* 206 Oribasius, the great abreuiater of antiquity. **1779** GIBBON *Misc. Wks.* (1814) IV. 565 The opinion which attributes the last-mentioned passage to the abbreviator, rather than to the original historian. **1860** ADLER *Prov. Poet.* xiii. 286 Outlines in which the arid hand of the abbreviator does not become apparent.

2. *spec.* 'An officer in the court of Rome, appointed as assistant to the vice-chancellor for drawing up the pope's briefs, and reducing petitions, when granted, into proper form for being converted into bulls.' Chambers 1751.
1532 *Addr. from Convoc.* in STRYPE *Mem. Ref.* v. 481 The writers, abbreviators, and registers of the letters, minutes, and bulls. **1611** COTGR., *Abbreuiateur*, An abbreuiator; a maker of breefs, or of writs. **1751** CHAMBERS *Cycl.* The earliest mention made of abbreviators in the papal court is in one of the *extravagantes* of John XXII in 1317..The abbreviators at present make a college of 72 persons, divided into two parks or ranks.

†**3.** A school of physicians so named. *Obs.*
1605 TIMME *Quersitanus* Pref. v, Among Physitians there are Empericks, Dogmaticks, Methodici or Abbreviators, and Paracelsians.

abbreviatory (əˈbriːvɪətərɪ), *a.* [f. L. *abbreviāt-* ppl. stem of *abbreviāre*: see ABBREVIATE + -ORY.] Tending to abbreviate or shorten.
1847 In CRAIG. **1935** G. K. ZIPF *Psycho-Biol. of Lang.* (1936) iii. 93 These abbreviatory phonetic changes may be 'spontaneous', or accentual, or assimilatory, or dissimilatory. **1943** *Mind* LII. 268 In his notation for proofs, Quine uses ingenious abbreviatory devices.

abbreviature (əˈbriːvɪətjʊə(r), -tʃə(r)). [f. L. *abbreviāt-* (see prec.) + -URE.]
†**1.** The process of abbreviating; abbreviation, shortening. *Obs.*
1659 HAMMOND *On Psalms* iii. 7. 26 The abbreviature or apocope hath no example. **1673** JER. TAYLOR *Suppl. to Serm. for Year* (1678) 131 I must be forced to use summaries and arts of abbreviature in the enumerating those things.

†**2.** An abbreviated or shortened state, condition, or form; shortness. *Obs.*
1614 SELDEN *Titles of Honor* 114 Cultus alienus siue extraneus, or Idolatrie, which they commonly express by עז in abbreviature. **1650** JER. TAYLOR *Holy Dying* i. §3. 27 (1727) God in pity..hath reduced our misery to an abbreviature.

3. An abbreviated or abridged copy; an abridgement, compendium, epitome, or abstract.
1650 JER. TAYLOR *Holy Dying* iii. §9. 4 There are certain compendiums or abbreviatures and shortenings of religion, fitted to several states. **1755** CARTE *Hist. Eng.* IV. 55 To bestow their time in the fathers and councils rather than on compendiums and abbreviatures. **1812** COLERIDGE *The Friend* v. vii. 316 (1867) It is indeed little more than an abbreviature of the preceding observation and the deductions therefrom.

4. An abbreviated or contracted form of a word or phrase; a contraction, an abbreviation.
c **1630** JACKSON *Creed* viii. 27 Wks. VIII. 116 From mistake of letters or abbreviatures by the transcribers. **1682** SIR T. BROWNE *Chr. Mor.* (1756) 35 The hand of Providence writes often by abbreviatures. **1724** WODROW *Corresp.* (1843) III. 149 The reading was easy to me, though some abbreviatures stopped me a little.

†**abbrevy(e, abrevye,** *v. Obs. rare.* [a. mid. Fr. *abrévie-r, abb-*, (14th c.) ad.L. *abbreviāre* to shorten: see ABBREVIATE, the modern form from L., and ABRIDGE, the earlier equivalent from OFr. *abregier*.] = ABBREVIATE, ABRIDGE.
1483 CAXTON *G. Leg.* 424/4 Which hystorye Saint Justyn abreuyed or shorted.

abbroche, obs. form of ABROACH *v.*

†**a'bbrochment,** *Obs.* Also abrochement. [A Dictionary rendering of med.L. *abrocamentum*, used in the Acts of Parlt. of Edw. III., and formed apparently on the stem of BROK-ER, BROK-AGE.]
1672 T. MANLEY *Interpreter*, Abbrochment (*abbrocamentum*) is a forestalling of a market or fair, by buying up the wares before they are exposed to sale in the market or fair, and then vending them again by retail. **1691** BLOUNT, &c.

abbud, OE. form of ABBOT.

abbudisse, OE. form of ABBATESS, *Obs.*, abbess.

abbuttal, obs. form of ABUTTAL.

abby, obs. form of ABBEY.

abbyt(e, obs. form of HABIT.

ABC (ˌeɪbiːˈsiː), *sb.* 4–; also written as a word: 3–6 abece; 5 **apece, apecy, apsie;** 6 **apcie, absee, absie, absey, abeesee;** 5–7 **abce;** 6–7 **abcie;** 7 **abcee, a-bee-cee.** (These *names* were most frequent in sense 3.) The first three letters of the alphabet; hence
1. The alphabet itself. [So in OFr. *A B C, abece.*]
1297 R. GLOUC. 266 He was more þan ten ȝer old, ar he couþe ys abece. **1356** WYCLIF *Last Age* 28 Euery lettre in þe abece may be souned wiþ opyn mouþ save .m. lettre one. **1387** TREVISA *Higden* VI. 259 (Rolls Ser.) He founded as meny abbayes as beþ lettres in þe A B C [*in alphabeto*]. *c* **1394** *Piers Pl. Crede* 9 A and all myn A B C After have I lerned. **1440** *Prompt. Parv.* A-pece apecy [**1499** abce] *alphabetum, abecedarium.* *a* **1520** *Myrroure of Our Ladye* 139 There is xxii letters in the Abce of hebrew. **1573** COOPER *Thesaurus, Abecedarium, -rii* An Absee. **1611** FLORIO, *Abecè* the A B C or Criscrosse-row. **1653** URQUHART *Rabelais* I. xiv, Master Tubal Holophernes, who taught him his A B C, so well that he could say it by heart backwards. **1781** COWPER *Convers.* 14 Sorting and puzzling with a deal of glee Those seeds of science called his A B C. *a* **1845** HOOD *Huggins & Duggins* 5 I'd carve her name on every tree, But I don't know my A B C.

†**2.** An alphabetical acrostic; a poem of which the successive stanzas, or lines, begin with the letters of the alphabet in order. *Obs.*
c **1382** WYCLIF *Jeremiah, Prologue* 10 In Jewere onli and Beniamyn he profeciede, and of his citee the fallingus with fourfold abece he weilede. *c* **1430** *The A B C of Aristotle* (1868) Whoso wilneþ to be wiys, & worschip desiriþ, Lerne he oo lettir, & looke on anoþir Of þe a b c of Aristotill: argue not aȝen þat. **1597** SPEGHT *Edn. of Chaucer* (title) Chaucers A B C, called La Priére de Nostre Dame. **1855** *Bell's Chaucer* VI. 125 The A B C is a prayer to the Blessed Virgin somewhat in the manner of an acrostic. It consists of twenty-three stanzas, each of which begins with one of the letters of the alphabet, arranged in their order. [It is a transl. of the French hymn in *Pilgr. of the Lyfe of Man.*]

3. A spelling-book, or primer, teaching the alphabet and first elements of reading (*Obs.*); hence *fig.* the first principles, most elementary part, or simplest rudiments (of any subject).
c **1400** *Poem* in *Reliq. Antiq.* I. 63 Quan a chyld to scole xal set be, A bok hym is browt, Naylyd on a brede of tre, That men callyt an abece. **1571** *Wills & Inv. North. Count.* (Surtees Soc.) II. 362, xiiij doss' papr latten abeesees iijs vjd —iiij doss' abeesees in p'chment ijs. **1579** TOMSON *Calvin's Sermons* 22/1 When he gaue vs his worde, hee did not giue vs an A. b. c. onely, but hee taught vs with open mouth. **1583** GOLDING *Calvin on Deuteron.* Serm. xix. 110. 27 a, Wee abide still at our Absie, and wot not what rule or doctrine meaneth. *a* **1593** H. SMITH *Sermons* 252 This is the Abce, and Primmer, and Grammar, the first lesson and last lesson of a Christian. **1637** *Decree of Star Chamb.* §10 (Arber's *Areop.* 14) Any Bibles, Testaments..Primers, Abcees, or other booke or books. **1641** MILTON *Animadv.* (1851) 204 To tutor their unsoundnesse with the Abcie of a Liturgy. **1879** FARRAR *St. Paul* II. 152 *note*, The notion may be that ritualism is only the elementary teaching, the A B C of religion.

4. *Attrib.*, as in **ABC-book** or **abcee-book, absey-book,** primer, horn-book; an introductory book to any subject, often in catechism or dialogue form. So ***ABC-scholar, ABC-learner, ABC-teacher; ABC*** (= Alphabetical) ***Railway Guide*** (also *absol.*).
1595 SHAKS. *John* I. i. 196 I begin 'I shall beseech you'; that is question now, And then comes answer like an Absey booke: 'O sir,' sayes answer, 'at your best command.' **1611** FLORIO, *Abecedario*, a teacher or learner of A B C; also a horne-booke, or A-bee-cee-booke. **1440** *Prompt. Parv.* Apece lerner, or he þat lernythe þe abece. *Alphabeticus, abecedarius.* **1580–95** MUNDAY *John à Kent* etc. 60 Which a meere abce scholler in the arte Can doo it with the least facilitie. **1632** SHERWOOD, An Abcee-learner or teacher, *Abecedaire* (Fr.) **1853** (*title*) A.B.C. or Alphabetical Railway Guide. **1917** W. PETT RIDGE *Amazing Years* iii. 41, I found an A.B.C. and selected a train. **1936** A. CHRISTIE *ABC Murders* iv. 31 A railway guide, you say. A Bradshaw—*or an ABC*?

ABC, or abee-cee is even found as a vb. 'to say the alphabet.'
1611 FLORIO, *Abecedáre*, to alphabet or abee-cee. *a* **1845** HOOD *My Son & Heir* 12 A coppersmith I can't endure—Nor petty usher A B C-ing.

ABC. A process in making artificial manure.
1879 E. G. BARTHOLOMEW in *Cassell's Tech. Educ.* I. 115 The A B C is a patented process, and obtains its name from the three initial letters of the three principal ingredients..alum, blood, and clay.

abcaree, *sb.* (Anglo-Ind.) See ABKARI.

ABC-darian, obs. form of ABECEDARIAN.

abda, var. of ABADA, *Obs.* rhinoceros.

‖**abdest** (ˈɑːbdɛst). [Pers. *ābdast*, f. *āb* water + *dast* hand.] The Mohammedan rite of washing the hands before prayer.
1847 In CRAIG.

abdicable (ˈæbdɪkəb(ə)l), *a.* [f. L. *abdicā-re* + -BLE, repr. a possible L. **abdicābilis*.] Capable of being abdicated.
Mod. Such responsibilities are not abdicable at will.

abdicant (ˈæbdɪkənt), *a.* and *sb. rare.* [ad. L. *abdicant-em* pr. pple. of *abdicāre*, to abdicate; cf. Fr. *abdiquant*.]
A. *adj.* Abdicating, renouncing, who abdicates.
1654 WHITLOCK *Manners of the Engl.* 93 (T.) Wicked Jews, murtherers of Christians, monks abdicant of their orders.
B. *sb.* One who abdicates.

abdicate (ˈæbdɪkeɪt), *v.* [f. L. *abdicāt-*, ppl. stem of *abdicā-re* to renounce, disown, reject; f. *ab* off, away + *dicā-re* to proclaim, make known.]
1. *trans.* To proclaim or declare to be no longer one's own, to disclaim, disown, cast off; *esp.* to disown or disinherit children. Now only as a tech. term of Rom. Law (L. *abdicare filium*, also *patrem*).
1541 ELYOT *Im. Gov.* 149 The father..doeth abdicate nowe and then one, that is to saie, putteth them out of his familie. **1644** MILTON *Jus Populi* 34 Parents may not causelessly abdicate or disinherit children. **1697** POTTER *Antiq. Greece* IV. xv. 351 (1715) Parents were allow'd to be reconcil'd to their children, but after that could never abdicate them again. *a* **1763** SHENSTONE *Essays* 117 Wherever I disesteemed, I would abdicate my first cousin. **1828** SEWELL *Oxf. Pr. Essay* 70 Sons were exposed, abdicated, and sold by the laws of Solon.

†**2.** To depose (from an office or dignity). *Obs.*
1621 BURTON *Anat. Mel.* I. 2. III. xv. 127 (1651) The Turks abdicated Cernutus, the next heir, from the empire.

†**3.** *refl.* To formally cut oneself off, sever, or separate oneself from anything; *esp.* to divest oneself of an office (L. *abdicare se magistratu*). *Obs.*
1548 HALL *Chron.* Introd. Hist. Hen. IV. 11 (1809) To perswade a man..to Abdicate himselfe from his empire and imperiall preheminence. **1689** EVELYN *Mem.* (1857) II. 299 The great convention..resolved that King James..had by demise abdicated himself and wholly vacated his right. **1689** H. MORE *Myst. Iniq.* 28 A Prince..who, by transgressing against the Laws of the Constitution, hath abdicated himself from the Government, and stands virtually Deposed.

†**4.** *trans.* To put away, cast off, discard (anything). *Obs.*
1553–87 FOXE *A. & M.* (1596) 333/2 The King our soueraigne lord and maister cannot abdicate from himselfe this right. **1633** BP. HALL *Hard Texts* 343 Neither hast thou, O Cyrus, so well known me as to abdicate thine Idolatry. **1642** ROGERS *Naaman* 527 If the Lord Jesus purposely would defile and abdicate the seventh day Sabbath of the Jew. **1688–9** LADY R. RUSSELL *Letters* No. 84. II. 11 Accidents may abdicate your opinion.

5. To formally give up (a right, trust, office, or dignity); to renounce, lay down, surrender, abandon; at first implying voluntary renunciation, but now including the idea of abandonment by default. See the parliamentary discussions of 1688.
1633 BP. HALL *Hard Texts* 41 Abdicating our just privileges. **1688** LD. SOMERS *Speech on the Vacation of the Throne* The word abdicate doth naturally and properly signify, entirely to renounce, to throw off, disown, relinquish any thing or person, so as to have no further to do with it; and that whether it be done by express words or in writing (which is the sense your Lordships put upon it, and which is properly called resignation or cession), or by doing such acts as are inconsistent with the holding and retaining of the thing, which the Commons take to be the present case. **1726** DE FOE *Hist. Devil* (1840) I. i. 14 The thrones which the Devil and his followers abdicated and were deposed from. **1783** JOHNSON *Club Rules* in *Boswell* (1816) IV. 277 Whoever shall for three months together omit to attend..shall be considered as having abdicated the club. **1805** FOSTER *Essays* I. vii. 90 To have abdicated the dignity of reason. **1857** PRESCOTT *Philip* I. i. 10 The Regent Mary formally abdicated her authority. **1857** RUSKIN *Pol. Ec. Art*, 5 A power not indeed to be envied..but still less to be abdicated or despised.

6. *Comm. Law.* Said of the insurer surrendering his rights of ownership to the underwriters.
1755 N. MAGENS *Ess. Insur.* II. 36 The Owners of such Gold, Silver, or Pearls, cannot renounce or abdicate them to the Underwriters.

7. *absol.* (by ellipsis of the thing resigned, usually the *throne* or *crown*). To renounce or relinquish sovereignty, or its equivalent.
a **1704** T. BROWN *Epigr.* Wks. 1730 I. 121 Either he must abdicate or thou. **1726** DE FOE *Hist. Devil* (1840) II. i. 181 The Devil abdicated for awhile. **1837** CARLYLE *French Rev.* I. VII. xi. 399 Is it not strange so few kings abdicate; and none yet heard of has been known to commit suicide? **1879** GLADSTONE *Gleanings* III. i. 5 The Majority have in virtue

and effect abdicated, and their opponents are the true and genuine corporation.

abdicated ('æbdɪkeɪtɪd), *ppl. a.* [f. prec. + -ED.]
1. Formally renounced, resigned, or given up. Used especially of a possession, right, or function.
1688 LD. SOMERS *Speech*, It is an entire alienation of the thing abdicated, and so stands in opposition to *dicare*. **1689** *Apol. Fail. Walker's Acc.* 25 A Head Abdicated of Reason and Five Senses. **1713** ADDISON *To Sir Godf. Kneller* Old Saturn too, with up-cast eyes, Beheld his abdicated skies. **1728** G. CARLETON *Mem. Eng. Officer* 233 The Siege thus abdicated (if I may use a modern Phrase). **1852** COCKBURN *Life of Jeffrey* I. 26 Some new obstacle to my belief, which might return me to my abdicated opinion.
2. Deposed from an office, function, or dignity. In 17th c. including deposition by others (see ABDICATE 2), but now always, self-deposed, having formally laid down or divested himself of a dignity or trust. (See the ambiguity of its application to James II.)
1691 *New Disc. Old Intreague* xviii. 15. So found too late their abdicated James. **1714** SWIFT *State of Affairs* Wks. II. I. 215 Those who wish to see the son of the abdicated prince upon the throne. **1781** GIBBON *D. & F.* II. xli. 531 The abdicated monarch fled from the justice of his country. **1825** SOUTHEY in *Q. Rev.* XXXII. 368 That strange personage, Christina, the abdicated Queen of Scotland. **1866** HOWELL *Venetian Life* xx. 349 The abdicated Emperor of Austria.

abdicating ('æbdɪkeɪtɪŋ), *vbl. sb.* [f. ABDICATE *v.* + -ING[1].] The act of formally resigning, renouncing, or abandoning. (Now mostly gerundial.)
1673 *Lady's Calling* I. §2. 7. 14 If the abdicating a child be a thing so unnatural. **1689** LD. SOMERS *Speech*, For Abdicating a thing it is sufficient to do an act which is inconsistent with retaining it. **1809** TOMLINS *Law Dict.* s.v., On King James II's leaving the kingdom, and abdicating the government. **1875** H. E. MANNING *Mission of Holy Ghost* iii. 87 It is not content with abdicating the powers of reason.

abdication (æbdɪ'keɪʃən). [ad. L. *abdicātiōn-em*, n. of action, from *abdĭcāre*: see ABDICATE and -ION[1].] The act of abdicating, in various senses of vb.
1. The action of formally renouncing, disowning, or casting off. Now only applied to the disowning of a son in Roman Law.
1552 R. HULOET *Abcedarium*, Abdication, as when the father doth wyllyngly exclude the sonne from his inheritaunce, *Abdicatio.* **1615** BP. HALL *Contemp.* III. 66 A just abdication from thy favour and protection, and an interminable seisure by satan. **1651** HOBBES *Gov. & Soc.* ix. §7. 139 A son also is freed from subjection in the same manner as a subject and servant are. For emancipation is the same thing with manumission, and abdication with banishment.
†**2.** Deposition from sovereignty. *Obs.*
1660 R. COKE *Elem. of Power & Subj.* 57 Who..had they been able, would have advanced the power of the Senate to the abdication of Cæsars.
3. Resignation, surrender, renunciation (generally). Const. *of.*
1618 BP. HALL *Righteous Mammon* 719 Both in preparation of mind, and (when need is) in a charitable abdication, hearken to the duties which God layes upon you. **1668** J. HOWE *Blessedness of the Righteous* (Wks. 1834) 261/2 Which abdication of the earth, as none of their country. **1695** *Anc. Const. Eng.* 61 The doing of any act that is utterly inconsistent with the being or end of the thing for which it is ordained, is as true a renouncing, or abdication of that thing as if it were made in express words. **1786** BURKE *Articles agt. Hastings* Wks. XII. 323 He recommends an entire abdication for ever,..of all power and authority. **1848** LYTTON *Harold* IV. i. 78 He implored the Earl to aid his abdication of the throne.
4. *esp.* Resignation or abandonment, either formal or virtual, of sovereignty or other high trust.
'It is used when there is only an implicit Renunciation, as when a Person does Actions that are altogether inconsistent with his Trust.' BAILEY 1721.
1688 in *Somers's Tracts* I. 441 They pitched upon Dereliction or Abdication, not that either of these were commensurate to the state of the business. **1726** DE FOE *Hist. Devil* (1840) I. i. 14 The abdication and expulsion of the Devil and his angels. **1781** GIBBON *Decl. & Fall* II. 2 After the defeat and abdication of Licinius, his victorious rival proceeded to lay the foundations of a city. **1809** TOMLINS *Law Dict.* s.v. Abdication, in general, is where a magistrate or person in office, renounces and gives up the same before the term of service is expired. **1843** LYTTON *Last of Barons* III. v. 173 What suicide is to a man, abdication is to a king.
5. *Comm. Law.* Formal renunciation or relinquishment of the ownership of goods by an insurer to the underwriters; abandonment.
1755 N. MAGENS *Ess. Insur.* II. 38 A Ship is unfit to prosecute her Voyage, when an Abdication is made before the justice and Leave given to discharge her.

abdicative ('æbdɪ,keɪtɪv), *a.* *rare*$^{-0}$. [f. L. *abdicātīv-us*, f. *abdicāt-us*: see ABDICATE and -IVE.] 'Causing or implying abdication.' J.
1731 BAILEY, whence in JOHNSON 1755, etc.

abdicator ('æbdɪ,keɪtə(r)). [L. n. of agent from *abdĭcāre*; see ABDICATE and -OR.] One who abdicates.
1864 *Daily Telegraph* Nov. 16 It is hard to lose a crown where the civil list can never be; it is painful to abdicate when the abdicator has no pension for his abdication.

Abdim ('æbdɪm). *Ornith.* [Name of an early 19th-c. governor of Nubia.] ***Abdim's stork***: a small stork, *Ciconia abdimii* (family Ciconiidæ), native to tropical Africa, with glossy black head, neck, and back and a white belly. Also *ellipt.*
1872 ANDERSSON & GURNEY *Birds of Damara Land* 280 Abdim's Stork. **1930** G. L. BATES *Handbk. Birds W. Afr.* 109 One year, in February, a large company of Abdims remained on my land for days. **1963** A. SMITH *Throw out two Hands* (1966) xvi. 155 Abdim's storks treading their way through the long grass looking for frogs.

†'**abdite,** *a. Obs. rare*$^{-1}$. [ad. L. *abdit-us* hidden away, pa. pple. of *abd-ĕre* to put away, hide; f. *ab* off, away + *dă-re* to give, put. Cf. *reconditus* recondite.] Hidden away, put out of the way.
1635 HEYWOOD *Hierarchie* VIII. 561 Things supernaturall we finde The depth whereof we cannot well conceive To [= too] Abdite and retruse from man's weake minde.

†**abditive** ('æbdɪtɪv), *a. Obs.*$^{-0}$ [f. L. *abditīv-us*, f. *abdit-us*: see prec. and -IVE.] 'Having the power or quality of hiding.' J.
1731 BAILEY, whence in JOHNSON 1755, etc.

abditory ('æbdɪtərɪ). [ad. L. *abditōri-um* a hiding-place, f. *abdit-*, ppl. stem of *abdĕre*: see prec. and -ORY.] A hidden or withdrawn place, a concealed repository.
1658 DR. ROBINSON *Eudoxa* 162 In the center of the kernel of grain, as the safest abditory, is the source of germination. **1809** TOMLINS *Law Dict.* s.v., *Abditorium*, An abditory or hiding-place, to hide and preserve goods, plate, or money.

abdomen ('æbdəmən, æb'dəʊmən). [a. L. *abdōmen*, of unknown etymology; it has been suggested from *abd-ĕre* to stow away, conceal, cover; and from *adeps, adip-em*, fat, as if for **adipomen*. Occurs first in transl. from French.]
†**1.** *orig.* Fat deposited round the belly; the fleshy parts of the belly or paunch. *Obs.*
1541 COPLAND tr. *Galyen's Terapeutyke* 2 Gij, The membrane y[t] is stretched vnder labdomen [= *l'abdomen*]. **1601** HOLLAND *Pliny* (1634) I. 344 In old time they called this morcell in Latine Abdomen. **1607** TOPSELL *Four-footed Beasts* (1673) 300 *Acites* is a swelling in the covering of the belly, called of the Physitians Abdomen, comprehending both the skin, the fat, eight muscles, and the film or panicle called Peritoneum. **1692** COLES, Abdomen, the Fat which is about the Belly.
2. *Anat.* The belly; the lower cavity of the body, from the diaphragm downwards, which contains the stomach, bowels, and other organs of nutrition; sometimes used as including, and sometimes as excluding, the pelvic cavity; and often in *Nat. Hist.* used of the outer surface of the belly.
1615 H. CROOKE *Body of Man* 796 There bee tenne Muscles which couer the nether Belly, on either side fiue, called the Muscles of the Abdomen. **1656** RIDGLEY *Pract. of Physick* 94 It floweth down into the cavity of the Abdomen. **1751** CHAMBERS *Cycl.* The abdomen is lined internally with a thin soft membrane..called the peritonæum. **1847** CARPENTER *Zool.* §74 The skin of the abdomen, in front of the mammary glands, forms a pouch which contains and protects the young [of Kangaroos, etc.]. **1872** HUXLEY *Physiology* I. 5 The trunk is naturally divided into the chest or thorax, and the belly or abdomen.
3. *Zool.* In the higher *Arthropoda* (as insects, spiders, and crabs), the posterior division of the body, usually distinctly marked off from the anterior part containing the thorax and head.
1788–9 HOWARD *New Royal Cycl.* 1230 In insects of the third order..the head, thorax, and abdomen are wholly different from those of the other orders. **1847** CARPENTER *Zool.* §739 The body [of Spiders] is composed of two principal parts nearly always distinct:—one called the *cephalo-thorax*..the other termed the *abdomen*. **1855** GOSSE *Marine Zool.* I. 157 [The crabs have the] abdomen little developed, bent under the body, with no trace of a swimming tail. **1868** DUNCAN *Insect World* Intr. 9 In the perfect insect the abdomen does not carry either the wings or the legs.

abdominal (æb'dɒmɪnəl), *a.* and *sb.* [ad. mod.L. *abdōmināl-is*, f. *abdōmen, abdōmin-*; see -AL[1].]
A. *adj.*
1. *Anat.* Of or pertaining to the abdomen; ventral. ***abdominal belt.***
1746 DR. R. JAMES *Introd. to Moffet's Health's Impr.* 8 The perpetual Compressure of the Stomach, and all the abdominal Viscera. **1836** TODD *Cycl. An. & Ph.* I. 16 A degree of antagonism exists between the diaphragm and the abdominal muscles. **1870** ROLLESTON *Animal Life* 7 The walls of the abdominal and pelvic cavities. **1874** WOOD *Nat. Hist.* 553 That which is found on the under surface and in front of the vent is called the abdominal fin. **1879** *Syd. Soc. Lex.* 8 In man the respiration is said to be abdominal, in woman thoracic. **1907** H. C. BEECHING *Let.* in E. V. Lucas *Post-Bag Diversions* (1934) 25, I have become once more erect and acquisitive. I attribute the change to an abdominal belt. **1909** H. G. WELLS *Tono-Bungay* III. ii. 334 Going about making love indeed!—in abdominal belts!—at his time of life!
2. *Zool.* Belonging or attached to the abdomen of insects and crustacea.
1874 LUBBOCK *Orig. Metam. Insects* I. 7 Like caterpillars, having three pairs of legs and in the former case abdominal pro-legs as well. **1877** HUXLEY *Anat. Inv. An.* vi. 346 Cynthia has its branchial appendages attached to the abdominal members.
3. *Zool.* Epithet of an order of fishes, a division of the soft-finned group of the Osseous fishes, having the ventral fins under the belly, as in the common carp, salmon, herring, etc.
1835 KIRBY *Hab. & Inst. An.* I. ii. 113 The herring.. belongs to the tribe called abdominal fishes, or those whose ventral fins are behind the pectoral. **1847** CARPENTER *Zool.* 573 [These] have greater facility of ascending and descending than the abdominal fishes. **1854** BADHAM *Prose Halieutics* 235 That grand ichthyological section called abdominal, of which the leading feature is to have the belly-fins suspended behind the pectorals or side-fins.
B. *sb.* **1.** An abdominal fish; in *pl.* **abdominals,** more commonly L. ‖**Abdominales** (-'eɪliːz), the order of soft-finned Osseous fishes, which have the ventral fins under the abdomen and behind the pectorals.
2. An abdominal operation.
1932 KIPLING *Limits & Renewals* 358 It was the trephining work that had stuck on his mental retina. (Odd! It used to be abdominals with *me.*)

‖**Abdominalia** (æb,dɒmɪ'neɪlɪə). *Zool.* [mod.L. pl. neut. of *abdōmĭnālis*; see ABDOMINAL: sc. *animalia* animals.] An order of the Cirripedes or barnacles, having the body composed of one cephalic, seven thoracic, and three abdominal segments, the latter bearing three pairs of cirri.
1876 BENEDEN *An. Parasites* 55 The whole family of the Abdominalia, a name proposed by Darwin, if I am not mistaken, have the sexes separate.

abdominally (æb'dɒmɪnəlɪ), *adv.* [f. ABDOMINAL *a.* + -LY[2].] In or with reference to the abdomen.
1889 in *Cent. Dict.* **1897** M. H. KINGSLEY *Trav. W. Africa* xxvi. 581, I am not thinking of starting a sanatorium for abdominally-afflicted Africans. **1907** *Practitioner* Dec. 845 Nothing definite was ever felt abdominally.

abdomino- (æb'dɒmɪnəʊ), used as comb. form of ABDOMEN, as in ***abdomino-anterior, -perineal, -posterior*** adjs. (see quots.).
1890 BILLINGS *Med. Dict.*, *Abdomino-vesical pouch*, depression in peritoneum as it passes from apex of bladder to the anterior abdominal wall. **1893** DUNGLISON *Dict. Med. Sci.* (ed. 21), *Abdomino-anterior*, term given to position of fœtus in utero with abdomen presenting anteriorly. *Abdomino-posterior*, term given to position of fœtus with abdomen presenting posteriorly. **1949** *New Gould Med. Dict.* 2/1 *Abdominoperineal*, relating to the abdominal and perineal regions. **1962** *Lancet* 1 Dec. 1172/2 Abdomino-perineal excision of the rectum.

abdominoscopy (æb,dɒmɪ'nɒskəpɪ). *Med.* [mod. f. L. *abdōmen, abdōmin-*, + Gr. -σκοπία looking at, viewing; see -SCOPY.] 'Term for the operation or mode of ascertaining the existence of abdominal disease by percussion mediate or immediate, by inspection, measurement, and manual examination.' Mayne 1851.
Not in CRAIG 1847.

abdominous (æb'dɒmɪnəs), *a.* [f. L. *abdōmen, abdomin-*, + -OUS, as if from a L. **abdōminōsus*.] Having a paunch, or big belly; corpulent.
1651 CLEVELAND *Dial. Two Zealots* 44 (Wks. 1677) 34 It's so abdominous [*1st ed.* abominous]. The Trojan Nag was not so fully lin'd. **1655** FULLER *Ch. Hist.* x. xvii. 10 He was ..somewhat abdominous, and corpulent in his body. *a* **1782** COWPER *Pr. Error* 217 Gorgonius sits, abdominous and wan, Like a fat squab upon a Chinese fan. **1878** H. M. STANLEY *Dark Cont.* I. xv. 3 To see him surrounded by fat wives and abdominous brats.

abduce (æb'djuːs), *v. arch.* [ad. L. *abdūc-ĕre* to lead away; f. *ab* off, away + *dūc-ĕre* to lead. Now generally replaced by ABDUCT.]
1. To lead or draw away by act or persuasion; to abduct.
1537 *State Papers Hen. VIII*, I. 557 From the whych opinion I colde not abduce them with all my endevor. **1863** *N. & Q.* 3rd Ser. III. 284 Sir Henry Hayes, a gallant Corcagian knight, abduced a Quaker damsel.
†**2.** To draw away, as by an abducent or abductor muscle. *Obs.*
1646 SIR T. BROWNE *Pseud. Ep.* III. xx. 156 If we abduce the eye into either corner, the object will not duplicate.

abducent (æb'djuːsənt), *ppl. a.* [ad. L. *abdūcent-em* pr. pple. of *abdūc-ĕre*: see ABDUCE.] Drawing away or out. Used chiefly in anatomy, as the opposite of *adducent*.
1713 DERHAM *Physico-Theol.* IV. ii, [This] is the case of the adducent and abducent muscles [of the eye]. **1751** CHAMBERS *Cycl.* s.v. Abductor, *Abductor* or *Abducent* in anatomy, a name common to several muscles whose action is the withdrawing, opening, or pulling back, the parts they are fixed to. **1875** *Encyc. Brit.* (ed. 9) I. 881 The Abducent or sixth nerve springs out of the groove between the lower border of the pons and the anterior pyramid of the medulla oblongata.

abduct (æb'dʌkt), *v.* [f. L. *abduct-um*, pa. pple. of *abdūc-ere*; see ABDUCE. Cf. *conduct*, *induct*.] Not in Craig 1847; the earlier word was ABDUCE.

1. To lead or take away improperly, whether by force or fraud; to carry off, to kidnap. Applied especially to the illegal carrying off of a woman or child.

1834 LANDOR *Imag. Conv., Exam. of Shaksp.* (Sir Thos. Lucy *loq.*) That a goose on the common.. may be seized, bagged, and abducted, with far less offence to the laws. **1837** CARLYLE *Fr. Rev.* II. IV. 227 His Majesty has been abducted, or spirited away, 'enlevé,' by some person or persons unknown. **1848** LEIGH HUNT *Jar of Honey* v. 63 Two foxes, one of whom is meditating to abduct his breakfast. **1861** *Sat. Rev.* No. 286. 400 The dairymaid.. is courted by her master's son, and afterwards forcibly abducted by the same villain. **1877** STEPHEN *Crim. Law* XXX. 179 A and B, two girls under 16, run away from home together. Neither abducts the other.

2. To draw away (any member of the body) from its natural or ordinary position.

1836 TODD *Cycl. An. & Ph.* I. 297/1 The second [muscle] goes to the base of the first toe, and abducts it. **1846** J. MILLER *Pract. of Surg.* xl. 639 Dislocation [of the Hip] downwards.. The thigh is much abducted, and cannot be brought near its fellow.

abducted (æb'dʌktɪd), *ppl. a.* [f. prec. + -ED.]

1. Led or carried away improperly, kidnapped.

1878 J. BEERBOHM *Wanderings in Patagonia* His wrongs avenged, and his abducted wives restored to his affectionate keeping. **1882** J. HAWTHORNE *Fortune's Fool* I. xii. (in *Macm. Mag.* XLV. 273) By to-morrow morning Madeleine would have lived out her character of the abducted heiress.

2. Of a member of the body: Drawn away.

1872 HUXLEY *Physiology* VII. 174 A limb is.. abducted when it is drawn away from the middle line.

abductee (æbdʌk'tiː). [f. ABDUCT *v.* + -EE[1].] A person who has been abducted.

1975 *Facts on File World News Digest* 17 May 333/3 Another abductee had been set free May 13. **1979** *Daily Tel.* 19 Jan. 4/4 Mozambique, which was short of food, had ordered recruits and abductees back across the border. **1983** *Human* Sept./Oct. 13/2 Alleged abductees.

abduction (æb'dʌkʃən). [ad. L. *abductiōn-em* n. of action f. *abdūcĕre*; cf. Fr. *abduction*: see ABDUCE.] A leading or drawing away, in var. senses of vbs. *abduce* and *abduct*. In Johnson 1773, with no quot., but much earlier in *Anatomy* and *Logic*.

1. A leading away.

1626 COCKERAM, *Abduction*: a leading away. **1873** *Times* Sept. 9 Increased abduction of the stream by the water companies.

2. The act of illegally carrying off or leading away anyone, such as a wife, child, ward, voter. Applied to any leading away of a minor under the age of sixteen, without the consent of the parent or guardian; and the *forcible* carrying off of any one above that age.

1768 BLACKST. *Comm.* IV. IV. xv. §9. 218 The other offence, that of kidnapping, being the forcible abduction or stealing away of a man, woman, or child from their own country, and sending them into another, was capital by the Jewish law. **1833** *Penny Cycl.* I. 19/1 The forcible abduction and marriage of women is a felony. **1835** THIRLWALL *Greece* I. v. 153 In the abduction of Helen, Paris repeats an exploit attributed to Theseus.

3. The muscular withdrawal of a limb or other part of the body outward from the medial line.

1666 J. SMITH *Solomon's Portr. Old Age* (1676) 62 If we consider how they [the muscles] can stir the limb inward and outward, they can perform adduction, abduction. **1787** A. FYFE *Compend. of Anat.* (1815) I. II. 294 *Pyriformis* [Muscle] .. *Action*: To assist in the Abduction of the Thigh, and in its rotation outwards. **1836** TODD *Cycl. An. & Ph.* I. 156/1 Those motions of inclination of the foot known under the names of adduction and abduction.. take place in the joints of the tarsus.

4. *Surg.* The separation of contiguous parts after a transverse fracture, causing the gaping of a wound, the recession of the two parts of a broken bone, etc.

1753 CHAMBERS *Cyc. Supp.* s.v., This Abduction is the same with what Greek writers call ἄπαγμα or ἀπόκλασμα.. some Latin writers call it *abruptio*. **1879** *Syd. Soc. Lex.* s.v.

5. *Logic.* A syllogism, of which the major premiss is certain, and the minor only probable, so that the conclusion has only the probability of the minor; apagoge.

1696 PHILLIPS, Abduction is an Argument which leads from the conclusion to the demonstrations of the hidden and not signified Proposition. **1766** SCOTT *Dict. Arts. & Science* Abduction, in logic a form of reasoning called by the Greeks apagoge, in which the greater extreme is evidently contained in the medium, but the medium not so evidently in the lesser extreme. **1872** GROTE *Aristotle* I. vi. 290 After adverting to another variety of ratiocinative procedure, which he calls Apagoge or Abduction.. Aristotle goes on to treat of Objection generally.

abductor (æb'dʌktə(r)). [a. mod.L. *abductor*, n. of agent, f. *abdūc-ĕre*: see ABDUCE and -OR. Adopted in Eng. from the language of anatomy.]

1. *Anat.* A muscle which serves to draw any part of the body from its normal position, or from the median line of the body. (Often treated as Lat. with pl. *abductōr-es*.) Also *attrib.* with *muscle*.

1615 H. CROOKE *Body of Man* 743 For euery Muscle almost hath set vnto him another, whose action is contrary to his as.. to an adductor is set an abductor. **1713** DERHAM *Physico-Theol.* v. ii. 327 By being inserted into one of the Sesamoid Bones of the great Toe, diverts the Power of the Abductor Muscle. **1787** HUNTER in *Phil. Trans.* LXXVII. 439 The muscles that open the eyelids.. may be called the elevator, depressor, adductor, and abductor. **1828** QUAIN *Elem. of Anat.* (1848) I. II. 412 The abductor of the great toe is placed horizontally along the inner side of the sole of the foot. **1872** MIVART *Anatomy* viii. 282 Some muscles move a bone away from a given axis, and are therefore termed abductors.

2. One who abducts or illegally leads away. (A modern use, not in Todd 1818.)

1847 CRAIG, *Abductor*, one guilty of abduction. **1872** *Daily News* Nov. 6 The women themselves, most interested in the immunities of their sex, usually gave their sympathy to the abductors.

a-be, *Sc.* [Prob. for *at be*, early northern infinitive = to be.] In phr. *let a be*: let be, let alone; not to mention.

1818 SCOTT *Br. of Lamm.* I hate fords at a' times, let abe when there's thousands of armed men on the other side. **1822** —— *Pirate* xxxvii. 288 (1859) I am for let-a-be for let-a-be, as the boys say.

abe, obs. form of ABYE *v.*

abeal, obs. form of ABELE.

abeam (ə'biːm), *adv.* or *pred. a.*, prop. *phrase. Naut.* [f. A *prep.*[1] of general direction + BEAM *sb.* The 'beams' of a ship lie at right angles to the keel.] In a line at right angles to the ship's length, opposite to the centre of her side; *abreast* of her actual position, as dist. from *afore* or *ahead*, *abaft* or *astern*. Const. *of*. Also of aircraft.

c **1836** M. SCOTT *Cruise of the Midge* (1863) 23 What is that abeam of us? said Mr. Sprawl, who had now come on deck. **1853** KANE *Grinnell Exped.* (1856) XII. 29 Cape Farewell was on our starboard quarter, and the Land of Desolation nearly abeam. **1875** 'STONEHENGE' *Brit. Sports* II. VIII. i. §5. 619 When he has brought N. to bear exactly a-beam eight points from the direction of the vessel's head. **1941** J. A. HAMMERTON *ABC of RAF* 119/1 Abeam (on the Beam). Directly at right angles to the fore and aft line.

abear (ə'bɛə(r)), *v. str.* Past and pple., as in BEAR, but now obs. [OE. *aberan*, f. A- *pref.* 1 + *beran* BEAR.]

†**1.** To bear, carry. *Obs.*

a **1000** *Ags. Gosp.* Matt. xxiii. 4 Hefiȝe byrðyna þe man aberan ne mæȝ. *c* **1160** *Hatt. Gosp.* ibid. Hefiȝe byrdene þe man abere ne mæȝ. *a* **1200** *Cotton Hom.* 225 þat flod wex and aber up þan arc.

2. To endure, suffer; now always with *cannot*. A word of honorable antiquity, widely diffused in the dialects; in London reckoned as a vulgarism.

c **885** K. ÆLFRED *Boeth.* xxxix. 10 Hi ne maȝon nán earfoða aberan. *c* **1175** *Lamb. Hom.* 35 Heo [þe saule] ne mei abeoren alla þa sunne þe þe mon uppon hire deð. *c* **1230** *Ancren Riwle* 158 þolemod is þe þet þuldeliche abereð wouh þet me deð him. **1836-7** DICKENS *Sketches* (1850) 151/2 The young lady denied having formed any such engagements at all—she couldn't abear the men, they were such deceivers. **1855** ATKINSON *Whitby Glossary* s.v. She cannot abear that man, very much dislikes him. **1861** DICKENS *Great Expec.* I. vii. 96 He couldn't abear to be without us. **1864** TENNYSON *Northern Farmer* 64 I couldn abear to see it.

†**3.** *refl.* To comport or demean oneself. *Obs.*

1596 SPENSER *F.Q.* v. xii. 19 So did the faerie knight himselfe abeare, And stouped oft his head from shame to shield. *Ibid.* VI. ix. 45 Thus did the gentle knight himselfe abeare.

†**a'bear**, *sb. Obs. rare.* [f. the vb.] Bearing, gesture, action, behaviour.

c **1315** SHOREHAM *Poems* 60 And ȝef the man other that wyf By cheaunce doumbe were, ȝef may wyten hare assent By soum other abere. **1655** H. VAUGHAN *Silex Scint* (1858) II. 149 I met with a dead man, Who, noting well my vain abear, Thus unto me began.

abearance (ə'bɛərəns). [f. ABEAR *v.* + -ANCE, being a synonym of ABEARING, on the analogy of the pairs *appearing*, *appearance*, *abhorring*, *abhorrence*, etc., formed on vbs. of Romance origin.] Behaviour; always in phr. ***good abearance***.

1568 WATSON *Polybius* 93 a, Of their confederates and mates they would cut of, and keep the lands, for good abearance. *c* **1630** JACKSON *Creed* II. xxxi. Wks. II. 144 The supreme magistrate might bind their tongues and pens to good abearance. **1683** *Col. Rec. Pennsylv.* I. 88 To finde good security for thy good abearance. **1768** BLACKST. *Comm.* IV. 256 The other species of recognizance with sureties is for the good abearance or good behaviour.

†**a'bearing** (ə'bɛərɪŋ), *vbl. sb. Obs.* [f. ABEAR *v.* + -ING[1].] The action of comporting or behaving oneself; behaviour, conduct. Nearly always in the legal phr. ***good abearing***, which early passed into popular use. Supplanted by the hybrid synonym ABEARANCE.

1494 FABYAN VI. cliv. 141 That there after he shulde be of good aberynge to warde the kyng. **1534** MORE *Vpon the Passion* Wks. 1557, 1289/1 Man should.. haue standen styl vpon the wynning or loosing of heauen after his abearing. **1625** FINCH *Law* (1636) 338 Sufficient suretie and mainprise for their good abearing towards the king, and towards his people. **1708** *Les Termes de la Ley* 371 Good abearing (*Bonus gestus*) signifies, the exact carriage or behaviour of a subject to a king and his liege-people, to which men sometimes for their loose demeanour are bound.

†**a'beat**, *v. Obs.* [f. A- *pref.* 1, intensive + BEAT. In ME. sometimes confused with ABATE, which it closely approached in form and sense.] To beat, strike.

a **1000** *Christ* (Grein) 941 Steorran streðað of heofone stormum abeátne. *c* **1400** *Destr. Troy* XIV. 5686 There was no Greke so grym, ne of so gret wille, Durst abate on þo buernes, ne to þonke stride.

abece, a-bee-cee, abeesee, obs. forms of ABC.

abecedarian (ˌeɪbɪsiː'dɛərɪən), *a.* and *sb.* Also 7 ABCDarian; 8 abcedarian. [f. med.L. *abecedāri-us* (see ABECEDARY) + -AN.]

A. *adj.*

1. Of or pertaining to the alphabet; marked with the alphabet; arranged in alphabetical order, as *abecedarian* psalms, like the 119th.

1665 GLANVILLE *Scepsis Scientifica* xxiv. §2. 150 The letter which is most distant in the Abecedarian circle from that which the needle turns to. **1668** BP. WILKINS *Real Character* 45 The first and more simple ingredients required to the framing of Discourse or Language are stiled Elements Abecedarian. **1751** CHAMBERS *Cycl.* We meet with Abecedarian psalms, lamentations, prayers, and the like, chiefly among Hebrew writers. **1864** G. MACVICAR in *Reader* 16 July, 78 The earlier chemists, who, under the charm of the moment, adopted an abecedarian method which.. can be made to yield nothing more than the most ambiguous syllables. **1881** *Athenæum* No. 2801. 10/1 Abecedarian requirements have rendered the present volume the least interesting.

2. Occupied in learning the alphabet, or pertaining to one so occupied.

1651 NOAH BIGGS *New Disp.* §170. 130 Those ABCdarian Nuntii. **1685** COTTON *Montaigne* I. 606 There is an abecedarian ignorance that precedes knowledge, and a doctoral ignorance that comes after it. **1819** SOUTHEY *Letters* (1856) III. 148 When she heard my abecedarian interpretation of your abominableness.

B. *sb.* [The adj. used elliptically.]

1. One occupied in learning the alphabet. In U.S. the regular school term.

1603 FLORIO *Montaigne* II. xxviii. 394 O fond-foolish for an old man to be ever an Abecedarian. **1851** S. JUDD *Margaret* (1871) II. i. 168 The goal of every breathless whip-fearing abcd-arian's valorous strife. **1880** *New Engl. Journal of Educ.* 20 May, 325/1 (Time-table) 9 to 9.15 Opening Exercise; 9.15 to 9.25 Abecedarians, &c. &c.. Abecedarians should have at least four recitations per day.

2. One engaged in teaching the alphabet and merest rudiments of instruction.

1691 WOOD *Athenæ Oxon.* (1817) iii. 213 (*Thos. Farnabie*) His distresses made him stoop so low, as to be an abcdarian, and several were taught their horn-books by him. **1714** WALKER *Sufferings of Clergy* II. 405 He had a wife and six children, whom he made a shift to maintain, by submitting to be an ABC-darian at Williton in this county. **1803** HAY *Wexford Insurrection* 65 He therefore commenced abecedarian. **1836** HOR. SMITH *Tin Trumpet* I ABCdarian seems to have been an ancient term for a pedagogue.

abecedary (ˌeɪbɪ'siːdərɪ), *a.* and *sb.*[1] Also ABCDary, abcedary, abscedarie. [ad. med.L. *abecedāri-us* alphabetical, also sb. masc. a learner of the alphabet; f. the names of the letters A B C D. See also next word.]

A. *adj.*

1. Of or according to the alphabet; alphabetic; marked with the alphabet; arranged in alphabetical order.

1580 FLEMING in Baret's *Alvearie* Nnnn 2 Such Prouerbes as we have collected and reduced into an Abecedarie Index or Table. **1646** SIR T. BROWNE *Pseud. Ep.* (1650) 76 Two Abecedary circles, or rings with letters described round about them. **1803** W. TAYLOR in *Ann. Rev.* I. 431 The French are very fond of abecdary instruction.

2. Engaged with or needing to learn the alphabet; illiterate.

1589 NASHE *Anat. Absurd.* 20 Thanking God with that abscedarie Priest in Lincolnshire, that he neuer knewe what that Romish popish Latine meant. **1603** FLORIO *Montaigne* I. lv. 170 There is a kind of Abecedarie ignorance preceding science: another doctorall following science.

B. *sb.*

An abecedary scholar or teacher. (Cf. Florio 1611, *Abecedário*, a teacher or learner of A B C.)

1607 SIR T. BODELEY *Let. to Ld. Bacon* in Bacon's Wks. (1730) 578 Being now become again as it were abecedarii by the frequent spelling of particulars, to come to the notice of the true generals. **1623** MINSHEU, An Abecedarie, or teacher of petties, vide *Abecedario. Abecedario*, a teacher to spell, reade, and the vse of the a b c, &c.

†**abe'cedary**, *sb.*[2] *Obs.* Also 5 abscedary; 6 absedary; 7 abcedarie. [ad. med.L. *abecedārium* an alphabet or primer; cf. *Prom. Parv.* 1440 Apece, *alphabetum*, *abecedarium*, and Cooper *Thesaurus* 1573, *Abecedarium*, an absee; see prec. and -ARIUM, -ARY.] A table or book containing the alphabet; a primer; the first rudiments of anything.

1432-50 *Harl. Tr. of Higden* (Rolls Ser.) VII. 333 Lanfrancus toke to hym an abscedary [**1387** TREVISA, A þing wiþ letters for to spel]. **1575** *A Brieff Discours* 35 (1846)

Therfore, it was lawfull to begin off suche rudimentes or absedaries. **1615** BYFIELD *On Colossians* ii. 8 (1869) 198/1 But it is most likely they [the laws] are called so [rudiments or elements] by a grammatical relation to the abcedaries. **1623** MINSHEU, An Abecedarie or alphabet, vide *Abece. Abece*, the crosse rowe or alphabet of all the letters. **1660** HY. HEXHAM *Engl. & Nether-Duytch Dict.*, *Een A B C*, an Abecedarie or an alphabet. *Een A B C Meester*, a Schoole-master that teacheth the Abecedarie.

† **a'beche**, *v. Obs. rare.* Also **abeshe**. [a. OFr. *abechier*, *abeschier*, to feed (young birds) with the beak; f. *à* to + *bec* beak.] To feed.

1393 GOWER *Conf.* III. 25 Yet should I somdele ben abeshed, And for the time well refreshed. **1731** BAILEY, *Abeched*, fed, satisfied.

abed (ə'bɛd), *adv.* Forms: 1–2 **on bedde**, 2–3 **o bede**, 3 **a bedde**, 5 **a-bed**, 7– **abed**. [A *prep.*[1] of position = OE. *on* + BED *sb.* It is only within the last three centuries that the two words have been written as one.]

1. In bed. Somewhat *arch.*

c **1000** *Ags. Gosp.* Luke xvii. 34 On þære nihte beoð tweʒen on bedde. **1205** LAYAMON 15706 Ich wæs on bedde. [*later text* Ich was abedde.] **1297** R. GLOUC. 547 To habbe inome hom vnarmed, & some abedde aslepe. **1377** LANGL. *P. Pl.* B. v. 417 And ligge abedde in lenten, and my lemman in myn armes. **1556** *Chron. Grey Friars* 20 They came sodeinly to Sandwych in the mornynge, when men wære a bede. **1604** SHAKS. *Oth.* III. i. 33 You haue not bin a-bed then? **1605** —— *Macb.* II. i. 12 The King's a bed. **1684** BUNYAN *Pilg.* II. 77 We need not, when a-bed, lie awake. **1762** HUME *Hist. Eng.* IV. lix. 573 (1806) The princess Henrietta was obliged to lie a-bed for want of a fire to warm her. **1876** SMILES *Scotch Naturalist* ii. 30 (ed. 4) The lights were out, and all were thought to be abed.

2. Confined to bed (by illness); laid up.

1660 PEPYS *Diary* (1879) I. 151 Our wench very lame, abed these two days. **1761** SMOLLETT *Gil Blas* I. I. x. 51 (1802) A violent fit of the gout and rheumatism, that kept him a-bed. **1873** W. H. DIXON *Two Queens* III. xv. ix. 182 Louis being abed with gout, and otherwise broken in his health.

†**3. to bring a-bed**: to deliver of a child; gen. in passive, ***to be brought a-bed***, now *to bed*. Also *fig.* to deliver one of a subject, draw out. *Obs.*

1523 LD. BERNERS *Froissart* I. cxlvii. 176 The quene was brought a bedde of a fayre lady named Margarete. **1572** BARNABE GOOGE *Husbandrie* (1586) 43b, The recording hereof is my great joye; for in talking of these matters you bring me a bedde. **1580** NORTH *Plutarch* (1676) 34 To go her full time, and to be brought abed in good order. **1610** G. FLETCHER *Christ's Vict.* I. 50 Upon her breast Delight doth softly sleep, And of Eternal joy is brought abed.

abed(e, obs. past tense of ABIDE.

† **a'bede**, *v. Obs.* Forms: 1–2 **abeódan**, 3–4 **abede(n**. *Pa. t.* 1 **abeád**, 3 **abed**, 4 **abode**. *Pa. pple.* **aboden**. [f. *a*-away, back, + *beód-an* to announce: see BID *v.*] To announce, deliver (a message).

c **885** K. ÆLFRED *Oros.* IV. vi, Ðæt he wolde ðæt ærende abeodan. **1205** LAYAMON 4423 þa spec Brennus, and his ærnde abed. *c* **1380** *Sir Ferumb.* 1540 Me selue þy message y wil abede. *Ibid.* 1780 Y schal be þe furste of alle: þat our message schal a-bede. *Ibid.* 1924 He comeþ by-fore þe Amyrel: & ys message abed him þere. *Ibid* 1985 Hure message þay abode dispitously: & schamede me ful sore.

abedge, obs. form of ABYE *v.*

abeere, obs. form of ABIER, on a bier.

† **a-before, abefoir**, *adv. Sc.* Of before, of former times (Fr. *d'avant*).

1609 *Acts Parl. Jas. VI* (1814) 457 (JAM.) The landis.. quhilkis wer abefoir vnite, creat, and incorporat in ane hail and frie tennendrie.

abege(n, abeʒen, abeie, variants of ABEY *v.*[1] *Obs.*, to bow.

abegge, abeie, obs. forms of ABYE *v.*

abeigh (ə'biːx, əbɛ'ɪx), *adv. Sc.* [OF uncert. deriv.; possibly f. A *prep.*[1] in + Norse *beig*, *beyg*, fear. In any etym. the final guttural must be accounted for.] 'At a shy distance, aloof.' Jamieson.

c **1707** *Auld Gray Mare* in *Jacob. Relics* I. 69 Whene'er her tail play'd whisk, Or when her look grew skeigh, It's then the wise auld man Was blythe to stand abeigh. **1787** BURNS III. 142 Town's bodies ran, an' stood abeigh, An' ca't thee mad.

abeisance, obs. f. ABAISANCE, OBEISANCE.

† **a'belde**, *v. Obs. rare*[−1]. [f. A- *pref.* 1, away, onward + BELDE, OE. *bealdian* to be bold; f. *beald* WS. form of *bald* bold.] To wax bold, become bolder.

c **1300** *K. Alis.* 2442 Weber I. 103 So they weore cowardes alle,.. Theo folk of Perce gan abelde.

abele (ə'biːl, 'eɪbəl). Also 7–8 **abeele, abeal, abeile**. [a. Du. *abeel* (*abeel-boom*), a. OFr. *abel*, earlier *aubel* (*albel*), north Fr. *aubiel*:—late L. *albell-us* (found in 12th c., applied to this tree), dim. of *alb-us*, white. (See Diez 351, and Grimm *Dict.* I. 22.).] The white poplar tree (*Populus alba*).

1681 *Lond. Gaz.* mdclxii. 4 If any Person desire to be furnished with young Abeele Plants.. they may be furnished with what quantity they please,.. at 10s. a hundred. **1681** WORLIDGE *Syst. Agric.* 96 The Abele-tree is a finer kind of white Poplar, and is best propagated of Slips from the Roots. **1703** *Art's Improvement* I. 33 The whitest Wood, and such as the Grain is least visible in, is fitest for this purpose; as Aspen, Abel, Sycamore, Maple or good white Beech. **1725** BRADLEY *Fam. Dist.* s.v. *Poplar*, There is a finer sort of white Poplar, which the Dutch call Abele, and is transported hither from Holland. *Ibid.* s.v. *Garden-fences*, Lime-trees or Horse Chesnuts, whose Roots do less harm than those of Elms, Abeals, or almost any other Tree. **1730** SWIFT *Wks.* II. 636 You have cut down more plantations of willows and abeles than would purchase a dozen such islands. **1850** MRS. BROWNING *Poems* II. 49 Six abeles i'the kirkyard grow, on the north-side in a row. **1859** KINGSLEY *Plays & Puritans* (1873) 76 The one great abele tossing its sheets of silver in the dying gusts.

† **a'belʒe-n**, *v. Obs.* Forms: 1 **abelʒan**, 2–4 **abelʒe(n**. *Pa. t.* 1 **abealh**, 2–4 **abelh, abalh**. *Pa. pple.* 1 **abolʒen**, 2–3 **abolʒe(n**, 3 **abolwe(n**, 4 **abolke**. [f. A- *pref.* 1 + *belʒan* to swell with anger.]

1. *trans.* To anger, enrage.

a **1000** *Solom. & Sat.* 328 Ne sceal ic ðe abelʒan. *c* **1175** *Lamb. Hom.* 111 ʒif he miltsað þan men þe hine abelh. **1205** LAYAMON I. 67 þe bearn was abolʒen [*l.t.* abolʒe]. *Ibid.* I. 273 Morpidus þe balde . iwærð him abolwen [*l.t.* a-bolwe]. *c* **1315** SHOREHAM 22 That hy ne be abolke In prede.

2. *intr.* To become angry.

1250 LAYAMON III. 47 þo abalh ʒaweyn, and wreþþede him swiþe [*e.t.* an-bælh].

A'belian, 'Abelite, Abe'lonian, *Eccl. Hist.* [f. *Abel*, Gen. iv. 8.] A member of a small sect of ancient heretics in the north of Africa, stated by Augustine to have lived in continence after marriage, after the alleged example of 'the righteous Abel.'

1751 CHAMBERS *Cyc.* s.v. Who in this footing should have been called Adamites rather than Abelians.

Abelian (ə'biːlɪən), *a. Math.* Also **abelian**. [f. the name of Niels Henrik *Abel* (1802–29), Norwegian mathematician + -IAN.] Of, pertaining to, or designating certain mathematical concepts to which Abel's research contributed; *spec.* (*a*) an integral of a function of two variables which are related to one another by an algebraic equation; (*b*) an equation all of whose roots are rational functions of one of them; (*c*) [after F. *groupe abélien* (C. Jordan *Traité des Substitutions* (1870) II. ii. 172)], a group whose binary operation is commutative.

1847 *Rep. Brit. Assoc. Adv. Sci. 1846* I. 75 What are the corresponding functions to which the hyper-elliptic or Abelian integrals are inverse, and how by means of them can Abel's theorem be stated? **1861** *Ibid. 1860* I. 126 This equation is of the kind called Abelian; that is to say, each of the *e* periods is a rational function of any other. **1897** [see INTEGRAND]. **1898** *Q. Jrnl. Math.* XXIX. 169 This paper generalizes to the Galois Field the work of Jordan.. on the decomposition of the Abelian group, studied earlier by Hermite in connection with the transformation of Abelian functions. **1972** M. KLINE *Math. Thought* xxvii. 655 Work on the inversion of hyperelliptic and Abelian integrals up to the entry of Riemann on the scene was hampered by the limited methods of handling multiple-valued functions. *Ibid.* xxxi. 755 The cyclotomic equation.. is an example of an Abelian equation. **1976** *Sci. Amer.* Nov. 55/1 Maxwell's theory is an Abelian gauge theory; non-Abelian gauge theories are distinguished from it by the fact that the fields themselves carry quantum numbers. **1982** W. S. HATCHER *Logical Found. Math.* viii. 241 Other examples of systems we will wish to call categories are the following.. the class of abelian groups as objects with group homomorphisms as mappings.

abeliche, -liche, -yche, obs. forms of ABLY.

Abelmosk ('eɪb(ə)lmɒsk). [ad. mod.L. *abelmoschus*, ad. Arab. *abu'l-misk* father, *i.e.* source, of musk.] A genus of plants of the order *Malvaceae*, of which one species (*A. esculentus*) is cultivated in the south of France for its pods.

abel-whackets: see ABLE-WHACKETS.

Abenaki (ɑːbɪ'nɑːkɪ, æbɪ'nækɪ), *a.* and *sb.* Also 8–9 **Abnaquis**, etc.; **Abnaki**. [ad. F. *abénaqui*, ad. E. Abenaki *wapánahki*, lit. 'person of the dawn land'.] **A.** *adj.* Of, pertaining to, or belonging to any of several Algonquian-speaking Indian peoples of northern New England and the Maritime provinces; some or all of these peoples collectively. **B.** *sb.* **a.** (A member of) any of these peoples, distinguished by specialists as the Western Abenaki, the Eastern Abenaki, and the Abenaki (or Wabanaki) Confederacy (whose core members were the W. and E. Abenaki, the Maliseet-Passamaquoddy, and the Micmac). **b.** Either of the Eastern Algonquian languages of the W. and E. Abenaki, or both taken as a subgroup or undifferentiated.

1721 *Jrnl. House of Representatives Mass.* (1922) III. 110 My people.. Summons thee to retire from off the Land of the *Abnaquis*. *Ibid.* 111 The Signature of the Nations of the Abnaquoise. **1827** *Spirit of Seventy-Six* (Frankfort, Ky.) 8 Nov. 1/3 Wabanocky Indians squatting about in groups. **1833** J. PICKERING in *Mem. Amer. Acad. Arts & Sci.* I. xv 569 The reader will.. pronounce the Abnaki words as a Frenchman would. **1884** 'J. LAURENT' *New Familiar Abenakis & Eng. Dialogues* 5 It is.. intended to preserve the *uncultivated* Abenakis language from the gradual alterations which are continually occurring. **1902** [see ANIMATE *a.* 4b] **1907** F. W. HODGE *Handbk. Amer. Indians* I. 2 Abnaki... A name used by the English and French of the colonial period to designate an Algonquian confederacy centering in the present state of Maine, and by the Algonquian tribes to include all those of their own stock resident on the Atlantic seaboard, more particularly the 'Abnaki' in the N. and the Delawares in the S. **1912** T. MICHELSON in *28th Ann. Rep. U.S. Bureau Amer. Ethnol. 1906–7* 280 The existing dialects.. are Micmac,.. Passamaquoddy,.. and Abnaki. **1927** L. BLOOMFIELD in C.F. Hockett *Leonard Bloomfield Anthol.* (1970) 145 He transcribes the same word as Abnaki *segankw*. **1947** R. P. T. COFFIN *Yankee Coast* 226 These Abenakis painted their faces the colors of death.. when they went on the warpath and slew the Mohawks. **1970** R. LOWELL *Notebk.* 84 We saw the burial ground of the Abenaki. **1976** K. V. TEETER in T. A. Sebeok *Native Lang. Amer.* I. 506 The splitting of Abnaki into Eastern and Western branches follows the current practice of the principal workers in the field, Day and Siebert. **1984** *Christian Science Monitor* 27 Apr. 30 Worumbo was a sachem of the Abenaki Indians.

† **a'bequitate**, *v. Obs.*[−0] [f. L. *abequitāre*, *-āt-um* to ride off.] 'To ride away.' Minsheu 1627.

aberand, north. var. ABERRING, *Obs.* See ABERR.

Aberdeen (æbə'diːn). The name of a city and county in Scotland.

1. ***Aberdeen Angus***, one of a breed of polled black beef cattle, originally from Scotland but now widely distributed and exported; also ANGUS.

1862 E. RAVENSCROFT (*title*) The Polled Herd Book containing Pedigrees of Animals of the Polled Aberdeen Angus and Galloway Breeds. **1891** R. WALLACE *Rural Econ. Aust. & N.Z.* xxxii. 413 The Aberdeen-Angus Polled cattle are slowly but surely working their way to the front in the Colonies. **1953** E. SMITH *English Traditions* 3 Some breeds of cattle.. e.g. the Aberdeen Angus, [are reared] for beef.

2. ***Aberdeen terrier***, a rough variety of Scotch terrier; also *Aberdeen* ellipt.

1880 H. DALZIEL *Brit. Dogs* xxiv. 362 Those selected for prizes.. were not *the* old hard-haired Scotch terrier, but a well-known distinct variety yclept the Aberdeen terrier. **1889** *Ibid.* (ed. 2) II. xxiv. 363 Such are the Dandie Dinmont, the Skye, and the Aberdeen Terrier, the latter now merged in the class recognised at our shows as the Scotch Terrier. **1907** B. M. CROKER *Company's Servant* xxxiii. 337 Two prim Aberdeens, and a pink-eyed bull terrier. **1922** V. WOOLF *Jacob's Room* xiii. 270 The Aberdeen terrier must be exercised.

3. A type of fishing-hook: see quot.

1893 *Outing* (U.S.) XXII. 123/1 Of all the makes and shapes of hooks the 'Aberdeen', of very fine steel-wire, with long, straight shank and a broad, even bend, terminating in a short, barbed point, is the surest shape for large-mouthed trout.

4. Other *attrib.* uses.

1756 A. BUTLER *Lives Saints* I. 50/1 The Aberdeen Breviary.. was printed at Edinburgh, by Walter Chapman, in 1509. **1866** *Illustr. London News* 14 Apr. 366/2 The columns and cornice.. are of polished Aberdeen granite. **1904** GOODCHILD & TWENEY *Technol. & Sci. Dict.* 74/2 *Aberdeen Granite*, a grey granite, extremely hard and durable.

aberdevine (ˌæbədə'vaɪn). Also 8 **abadavine, aberdavine**. [Etym. unascertained.] A bird-fanciers' name of the siskin (*Carduelis spinus*), a small bird, closely related to the goldfinch.

1735 ALBIN *Nat. Hist. Birds, Suppl.* Plate 76 The Abadavine. *Ibid.* p. 71 *text* (dated 1740) The Aberduvine. **1768** PENNANT *Brit. Zool.* II. 310 It [the siskin] is to be met with in the bird shops in London, and.. sells at a higher price than the merit of its song deserves: it is known there by the name of the Aberdavine. *c* **1850** W. C. L. MARTIN *Our Song Birds*, The siskin or Aberdevine.. this pretty little bird can be scarcely considered as a native of the British islands, but it visits us during the winter.

Aberdonian (æbə'dəʊnɪən). [f. med.L. *Aberdonia*: see -IAN.] A native or inhabitant of Aberdeen in Scotland.

a **1670** SPALDING *Troub. Chas. I* (1850) I. 181 To convoy our Abredonianis in thair Kirkcaldie bark. **1773** BOSWELL *Jrnl. Tour Hebr.* 23 Aug. (1785) 99 That the Aberdonians had not started a single *mawkin* (the Scottish word for hare) for us to pursue. **1791** NEWTE *Tour Eng. & Scot.* 191 A striking difference between the Moravians and Aberdonians. **1861** *Two Cosmos* III. iii, The pettifogging Aberdonian had been at first disappointed. **1906** *Westm. Gaz.* 24 Apr. 10/1 A miller on the Don, an Aberdonian.

abere, obs. form of ABEAR *v.*

† **'abere**, *a. Obs.* OE. *ǽbere*, 'Clear and evident by proof, manifest, notorious,' Bosworth; as *Se ǽbera þeóf* the notorious thief, Laws of Edgar, ii. 7; *ǽbere morð* manifest murder. Hence **abere-murder**. *Obs.* 'Plain or downright murder, as distinguished from manslaughter and chancemedley.' Phillips 1706. [Only a dictionary transformation of Law-Latin *aberemurdrum*, for OE. *ǽbere morð*.]

aberne, obs. form of AUBURN.

Abernethy ('æbəˌniːθɪ, -ˌnɛθɪ). [Prob. f. name of John *Abernethy*, surgeon (1764–1831).] A kind of hard biscuit flavoured with caraway seeds.
1836 DICKENS *Sk. Boz* II. 107 Eating Abernethy biscuits. **1845** DODD *Brit. Manuf.* 22 'Abernethy', 'butter', 'fancy', or 'sponge' biscuit. **1860** JEAFFRESON *Bk. Doctors* I. 198 The hard biscuits, known as Abernethies. **1886** *Bakers' Guide* 84.

†**a'berr**, *v. Obs.* [ad. L. *aberrā-re* to go astray, f. *ab* off, away + *errā-re* to wander.] To wander off, go astray, diverge from a recognized path. *fig.*
1536 BELLENDENE *Boece* (1821) II. 50 Thay..usit the cursit ritis of Paganis, aberand fra the Cristin faith. **1646** SIR T. BROWNE *Pseud. Ep.* 189 We may aberre from the proper acception, mistaking one side for another. *Ibid.* 217 Others might be out in their account, aberring severall waies from the true and just compute. **1658** DR. ROBINSON *Eudoxa* 143 When we follow the steps of dubious guides, we may soon aberre from the way of truth.

aberrance (ə'bɛrəns). [f. ABERRANT, on the type of nouns in -NCE, a. OFr. *-nce*:—L. *-ntia*.] The action of straying or diverging from a recognized course; vagary.
1665 GLANVILLE *Sceps. Scient.* xvi, This..would alter the crasis of his understanding, and render it as obnoxious to aberrances as now. **1865** W. M. ROSSETTI *Fine Art* (1867) 276 The two remaining contributions..are Japanese subjects, unsurpassed in delicate aberrances and intricate hap-hazards of colour. **1874** JONES & SIEV. *Path. Anat.* 4 The perversion or aberrance of a natural function.

aberrancy (ə'bɛrənsɪ). [f. ABERRANT, on the type of nouns in -NCY, ad. L. *-ntia*.] The quality or condition of being aberrant; divergency from the standard of usage, propriety, reason, truth, etc.
1646 SIR T. BROWNE *Pseud. Ep.* I. iii. 9 Thus they commonly affect no man any farther then hee deserts his reason, or complies with their aberrancies. **1863** G. C. GELDART in *Macm. Mag.* May, 63 What is that monstrous shape of many-headed absurdity, or what that grotesque misconception of some aberrancy?

aberrant (ə'bɛrənt), *a.* [ad. L. *aberrant-em*, pr. pple. of *aberrā-re*. See ABERR.]
1. *lit.* Wandering away or straying from a defined path; hence *fig.* diverging or deviating from any moral standard.
1848 KINGSLEY *Saint's Trag.* (1878) IV. ii. 123 Such a choice must argue Aberrant senses, or degenerate blood. **1864** COCKRAN tr. *Pressensé's Reply to Renan* 83 People see in it the signs of a diseased, aberrant genius.
2. Deviating widely from the ordinary or natural type, exceptional, irregular, abnormal; especially in *Nat. Hist.*
1830 LYELL *Princ. Geol.* (1875) II. III. xxxvii. 322 If there be such proneness in each aberrant form to merge into the normal type. **1835** KIRBY *Habits & Inst. An.* II. xvi. 74 The usual oral organs, though a little aberrant in their structure. **1839** HALLAM *Lit. Eur.* I. viii. §28 These aberrant lines are much more common in the dramatic blank verse of the seventeenth century. **1857** H. MILLER *Sch. & Schoolm.* viii. 167 His mother, though of a devout family of the old Scottish type, was an aberrant specimen. **1878** M. FOSTER *Physiology* IV. v. 560 The events are much more characteristic in the typical female than in the aberrant male. **1881** WESTCOTT & HORT *N.T. in Greek* II. 240 It would be ..difficult to derive the neutral reading from any coalescence of the aberrant readings.
Hence **a'berrantly** *adv.*
a **1878** GEO. G. SCOTT *Recoll.* (1879) vii. 291 Skidmore followed my design, but somewhat aberrantly. **1929** *New Statesman* 31 Aug. 614/1 Most unfortunately we have aberrantly accepted a mandate for Palestine.

aberrate ('æbəreɪt), *v.* [f. L. *aberrāt-* ppl. stem of *aberrā-re*: see ABERR.] To diverge or deviate from the straight path; to produce aberration, as in optics. Also *fig.*
1765 DOLLOND *Telescopes* in *Phil. Trans.* LV. 55 The surfaces of the concave lens may be so proportioned as to aberrate exactly equal to the convex lens, near the axis. **1818** *Blackw. Mag.* III. 274, I love occasionally to aberrate from routine. **1951** W. FAULKNER *Requiem for Nun* (1975) II. iii. 202 The Governor..has got to try to act like he regrets having to aberrate from being a gentleman.
Hence **'aberrated** *ppl. a.* (chiefly *U.S.*), characterized by aberration; abnormal, distorted; mistaken.
1893 F. ADAMS *New Egypt* II. vii. 208 Men..could argue with him over what they took to be aberrated or mistaken points. **1970** *N.Y. Times Mag.* 5 July 20/4 We've been living in a kind of aberrated period since World War II. **1976** *Sci. Amer.* Aug. 81/2 A lens..converts a parallel beam of light into an intentionally distorted, or aberrated, wave front. **1982** *Washington Post* 28 Jan. D7 DeJesus, a .193 hitter last, aberrated season.

aberrating ('æbəreɪtɪŋ), *ppl. a.* [f. prec. + -ING[2].] Going astray, subject to aberration.
a **1854** DE QUINCEY (in Webster), The product of their own defective and aberrating vision.

aberration (æbə'reɪʃən). [ad. L. *aberrātiōn-em*, n. of action, from *aberrāre*: see ABERR. The Fr. *aberration* seems to be later.] The action of wandering away or straying; the state of error or irregularity thence resulting.
1. *lit.* A wandering away, a straying; a deviation or divergence from the straight or recognized path.
1615 H. CROOKE *Body of Man* 42 These vessels do not directly passe vnto the braine, but after diuers contortions and aberrations from a right & direct progresse. **1794** SULLIVAN *View of Nature* II. 83 The aberration of the common center of all these currents from the north point. **1827** SCOTT *Surg. Daugh.* i. 23 The slightest aberration would plunge him into a morass, or throw him over a precipice. **1827** CARLYLE *Misc., Richter* (1869) 18 A comet with long aberrations. **1830** LYELL *Princ. Geol.* II. 81 The aberration of plants to great distances from their native countries. **1878** LADY HERBERT tr. *Hübner's Round the World* II. viii. 433 We hope that something useful will come out of their aberrations.
2. *fig.* A deviation or divergence from a direct, prescribed, or ordinary course or mode of action.
1610–31 DONNE *Selections* (1840) 206 Though thy heart have some variations, some deviations, some aberrations from that direct point, upon which it should be bent. **1646** SIR T. BROWNE *Pseud. Ep.* 262 Where the real works of Nature, or veritable acts of story are to be described, digressions are aberrations. **1648** HERRICK *Hesperides* I. 42 If thou chance t'espie Some abberrations in my poetry. **1750** JOHNSON *Rambler* No. 86. ¶13 More than one aberration from the rule in any single verse. **1817** JAS. MILL *Brit. India* II. IV. i. 10 Promoted according to the rule of seniority, unless where directions from home prescribed aberration. **1861** GEO. ELIOT *Silas Marner* 80 The very pins on her pincushion were stuck in after a pattern from which she was careful to allow no aberration. **1881** WESTCOTT & HORT *N.T. in Greek* II. 249 Such singular readings of ℵ would be nothing more than examples of early aberration early extinguished.
3. A wandering from the path of rectitude, or standard of morality; moral irregularity.
1594 T. B[EARD] tr. *La Primaudaye's Fr. Acad.* 2 *Ep. to Reader*, Error in religion and aberration in manners. **1656** BP. HALL *Occ. Med.* (1851) 103 The distractions of my thoughts, and the aberrations of my life. **1813** SISMONDI *Lit. Europe* (1846) II. xxi. 28 Deep pity for her mother's aberration. **1840** H. ROGERS *Essays* II. v. 221 The infallible standard by which each man measures the aberrations of his neighbour. **1869** LECKY *Europ. Morals* II. i. 5 Habitually measuring character by its aberrations.
4. A wandering of the intellect, an abnormal state of any intellectual faculty; deficiency or partial alienation of reason.
1823 LINGARD *Hist. Eng.* VI. 312 Her affliction seemed to produce occasional aberrations of intellect. **1829** SCOTT *Demonology* x. 354 Shades of mental aberration have afterwards occurred. **1878** SEELEY *Stein* II. 554 The slightest aberration in his [Napoleon's] mind, might be represented by the complete transformation of Europe.
5. Deviation from the ordinary or normal type of any natural production; abnormal structure or development.
1846 LYTTON *Lucretia* (1853) Pref., And the phenomena that seemed aberrations from nature were explained. **1869** BUCKLE *Civ.* II. vii. 403 The apparent aberrations presented by minerals are strictly regular. *Ibid.* III. v. 444 He studied the aberrations of structure and of function.
6. *Optics.* The non-convergence of rays of light, reflected or refracted, to one focus.
That due to the failure of a spherical mirror or lens to cause all the rays to meet in a single point (as is effected by a parabolic mirror or lens) is called *spherical aberration*; the distance of any ray from the geometrical focus, when measured along the axis, is its *longitudinal* aberration, and when measured at right angles to the axis, its *lateral* aberration. *Chromatic aberration* is an additional irregularity in the refraction of light through lenses, due to the different refrangibilities of the different coloured constituents of white light, whereby these diverge from one another, fringing the images of objects with the prismatic colours.
1753 CHAMBERS *Cycl. Supp.* There are two species of the aberrations of rays..one arising from the figure of the glass or speculum, the other from the unequal refrangibility of the rays of light. **1868** LOCKYER *Elem. Less. Astron.* No. 466. 217 If such an achromatic lens be truly made, and its curves properly regulated, it is said to have its spherical aberration corrected as well as its chromatic one, and the image of a star will form a nearly colourless point at its focus.
7. *Astron.* The displacement of the true position of a heavenly body to an observer on the earth, occasioned by the joint effect of the earth's motion, and the non-instantaneous transmission of light; hence also called ***aberration of light***.
As the earth has two motions, there is a *diurnal* as well as an *annual* aberration, the amount of the former being, for a star, very minute. *Planetary* aberration is effected by the additional element of the motion of the planet itself, during the time occupied by the passage of its light to the earth.
1856 LARDNER *Astron.* §2448 The apparent displacement produced by aberration is always in the direction of the earth's motion. **1867** E. B. DENISON *Astron. without Math.* 193 We may explain aberration thus: If you are running when the rain comes down straight without any wind, you get wet in front and not behind, and the rain beats against you as it would if you were standing still, and the wind blowing in your face. And if you carry an empty telescope tube pointed straight up, the rain will not fall through it, but will strike against the back inside: if you want the rain to fall through, you must slope the tube forwards, more or less according to your velocity forwards compared with that of the rain downwards. Then for rain substitute light, and the motion of the earth for your own running, and you know what aberration is. **1869** DUNKIN *Midnight Sky* 157 Dr. Bradley..made the important discovery of the aberration of light.

aberrational (ˌæbə'reɪʃənəl), *a.* [f. prec. + -AL[1].] Of, pertaining to, or characterized by aberration; eccentric, irrational, or unsound. Also, diverging from the normal, abnormal.
1866 *Reader* No. 164. 170/1 The aberrational myths of early ages. **1909** W. BATESON *Mendel's Princ. Heredity* I. x. 178 It is probable that the various aberrational forms of mammals and birds so often recorded by systematists as 'isabelline' are all similar cases of the replacement of black by chocolate. **1923** GLAZEBROOK *Dict. Appl. Physics* IV. 314/2 The differences between the cosines and unity occur as a small correcting factor in the aberrational expression. **1975** *Church Times* 7 Nov. 11/1 There is much more to the current upsurge of intuitivism that is positive and healthy than is aberrational. **1978** R. STEVENS *Law & Politics* (1979) 69 There were at least two aberrational years before 1900 when Scottish appeals exceeded English.

†**abe'runcate**, *v. Obs.*[–0] [f. *aberuncāre*, erroneous form of L. *averruncāre* to avert, remove anything sinister.] 'To pull up by the roots; to extirpate utterly.' J.
1731 BAILEY, vol. II, *Aberuncated*, pulled up by the roots, weeded.

aberuncator, incorrect form of AVERRUNCATOR, an instrument for lopping trees.

abeshe, variant of ABECHE, *Obs.*, to feed.

†**a'besse**, *Obs.* [a. Fr. *abaisse*; f. vb. *abaisser* to reduce.] In cookery or confectionery, a piece of paste rolled very thin.
1725 BRADLEY *Fam. Dict.* s.v. *Casse-museau*, Dress a small abesse of puff paste very thin, garnish one of the ends with a bit of marrow of an inch long.

abesse, obs. form of ABASE *v.*

abessive (æ'bɛsɪv), *a.* Chiefly *Finnish Gram.* [f. L. *abesse* to be distant + -IVE.] Applied to the case which denotes absence.
1890 C. N. E. ELIOT *Finnish Gram.* 132 The comitative and abessive express respectively the presence and absence of an object. **1930** F. R. BLAKE in *Curme Vol. Ling. Studies* 37 The immaterial adnominal cases are..abessive—coffee *without sugar*.

abeston, obs. form of ASBESTOS.

abet (ə'bɛt), *v.* Also 4 **abette**, 6 **abbet**. [a. OFr. *abeter*, f. *à* to + *beter* to bait, hound on; prob. ad. Norse *beita* to cause to bite, hence to 'bait,' to hound on dogs, etc.; causal of *bíta* to bite.]
†**1.** To urge on, stimulate (a person *to* do something). *Obs.*
c **1380** *Sir Ferumb.* 5816 Bot if he þanne wold take fulloȝt, As he hym wolde abette. **1587** FLEMING *Cont. of Holinsh.* III. 1579/2 The Scottish queene did not onelie advise them, but also direct, comfort, and abbet them, with persuasion, counsell, promise of reward, and earnest obtestation.
2. *esp.* in a bad sense: To incite, instigate, or encourage (a person, *to* commit an offence (*obs.*), or *in* a crime or offence). In legal and general use.
1590 SHAKS. *Com. Err.* II. ii. 172 Abetting him to thwart me in my moode. *a* **1593** H. SMITH *Wks.* (1867) II. 429 He will not only pardon without exception, but he will abet them in their damnable courses. **1658–9** MR. SCOTT in *Burton's Diary* (1828) IV. 36 Are those fit to have a parliamentary authority, that will undertake to abet the single person to levy taxes without you? **1770** BURKE *Pres. Discon.* Wks. II. 259 He abets a faction that is driving hard to the ruin of his country. **1809** TOMLINS *Law Dict.* s.v. To abet..in our law signifies to encourage or set on. **1866** KINGSLEY *Hereward* xviii. 219 The two regents abetted the ill-doers. **1876** FREEMAN *Norm. Conq.* III. xii. 113 To abet them against their sovereign.
†**3.** To support, countenance, maintain, uphold, any cause, opinion, or action. *Obs.* in a good sense.
1596 SPENSER *F.Q.* I. x. 64 Then shall I soone..abett that virgins cause disconsolate. **1603** DRAYTON *Heroical Epist.* (1619) xvi. 29 Who moves the Norman to abet our Warre? **1646** SIR T. BROWNE *Pseud. Ep.* 26 No farther to abet their opinions then as they are supported by solid reason. **1649** MILTON *Eikon.* Wks. 1738, I. 387 The Parlament..had more confidence to abet and own what Sir John Hotham had done. **1725** WOLLASTON *Relig. Nat.* §2. 31 That which demands next to be considered..as abetting the cause of truth.
4. *esp.* in a bad sense: To encourage, instigate, countenance a *crime* or *offence*, or anything disapproved of.
1779 JOHNSON *L.P.* Dryden II. 367 He abetted vice and vanity only with his pen. **1786** BURKE *Warren Hastings*, Wks. 1842, II. 214 To abet, encourage, and support the dangerous projects of the presidency of Bombay. **1849** MACAULAY *Hist. Eng.* II. 36 Having abetted the western insurrection. **1876** FREEMAN *Norm. Conq.* I. v. 286 The invasion was aided and abetted by Richard's subjects.
†**5.** To back up one's forecast of a doubtful issue, by staking money, etc., to BET. *Obs.*
1630 TAYLOR (Water P.) *Travels, Ded.* Wks. III. 76 I doe (out of mine own cognition) auerre and abett that he is senselesse.

†**abet**, *sb. Obs.* [a. OFr. *abet* instigation, wile, trickery; f. *abeter*: see ABET *v.* Cf. med. law L. *abettum*, f. Fr. *abet*.]
1. Fraud, cunning, wiles.
c **1315** SHOREHAM 58 Hyt was God self that spousynge ferst · In Paradys sette; The fend hyt was that schente hyt all

· Myd gyle and hys abette. **1460** *Pol. Rel. & Love Poems* (1866) 63 Loue is subtille, and hath a grete abaite.

2. Instigation, aid, encouragement (of an offence); abetment.

c **1374** CHAUCER *Troyl.* II. 356 I am thyn eme, the shame were to me, As wel as thee, if I shold assent, Thurgh myn abet, that he thine honour shent. **1596** SPENSER *F.Q.* IV. iii. 11 Lo! faitour, there thy meede unto thee take, The meede of thy mischalenge and abet.

abetment (əˈbɛtmənt). [ad. Anglo-Fr. *abetement, abettement* (not found in continental Fr.), n. of action, f. *abeter*: see ABET. The var. *anbetment* arose from conf. of the prefix with Eng. *a-*:—*an-*.]

1. The action or fact of abetting; instigation, encouragement.

a. *Usually* of an offence.

c **1380** *Sir Ferumb.* 2364 þanne schal heo beo for-brent, For hure couyne to-ward þat route: & hure anbettyment. **1461** *Paston Lett.* 430, II. 76 The abbettement and steryng of sum ille dysposed persones. **1538** FITZHERBERT *Just. Pea.* (1538) 136 b, Found gyltie of any abbetment, counsaylynge, helpinge or maynteyninge of or to any suche felonies. **1768** BLACKSTONE *Comm.* IV. 36 The very advice and abetment amount to principal treason. **1816** SCOTT *Old Mort.* 65 The recusancy of Cuddie Headrigg the ploughman, and the abetment which he had received from his mother. **1878** *Daily News* 26 Sept. 6/1 When I say fomented, I mean that the abetment is of an indirect character, passive rather than active.

†**b.** *Formerly* in a more general sense: encouragement, countenance, aid. *Obs.*

c **1535** SIR T. MORE *Debellacion of Salem & Byzance* Wks. (1557) 1019/1 He neither seeth nor assigneth so much as any assembly about them, or promise or abetment to procure and pursue them. *a* **1677** BARROW *Sermons* II. xx. 279 (1683) Never hardly any eminent Person appeared with a pretence of coming from God.. without God's visible interposal and abetment.

†**2.** Deception. Cf. ABET *sb. Obs.*

1586 FERNE *Blazon of Gentrie* 330 Such men which by fraude or abetment shall go about to stop or rather to preuent the ordinance of lawes.

†**3.** A bet, betting. *Obs.*

1615 BP. HALL *Contemp.* VIII. (1628) 975 As some skilfull player loses on purpose.. to draw on the more abetments.

abettal (əˈbɛtəl). *rare.* [f. ABET *v.* + -AL[2].] The action of abetting; encouragement (of an offence).

[Not in CRAIG, 1847. In WORCESTER, 1859.] **1861** *Sat. Rev.* 23 Nov. 528 No limit is imposed upon their discretion, either in respect to the nature of the abettal or the extent of proof required.

abettance (əˈbɛtəns). = ABETMENT 1. *rare.*

1829 SCOTT *Anne of G.* III. v. 128 The affray at La Ferette ..had no origin or abettance from us. **1835** *Fraser's Mag.* XI. 347/1 In the Roman Catholic Church of Ireland, the rewards are..for connivance, if not absolute abettance, of the foulest and most atrocious crimes.

abetter (əˈbɛtər). [f. ABET *v.* + -ER[1]. Formed on *abet* as an Eng. verb, as in *speak-er, begett-er*, etc.: see ABETTOR.] One who abets; an instigator, supporter, or promoter (*usually* of an offence, or of the offender).

1611 SPEED *Hist. Gr. Brit.* IX. ii. 426 [He] shewed the like measure of crueltie upon the Scotish Abetters, as they had done against the English. **1664** H. MORE *Myst. Iniq.* i. 3 So far forth as they are Teachers, Abetters, or Obtruders of such Practices or Principles. **1681** DRYDEN *Hind and Panther* iii. 353 But let th' abetters of the panther's crime Learn to make fairer wars another time. **1735-8** LD. BOLINGBROKE *Diss. upon Parties* 78 The Dissenters.. became Abetters of his Usurpations. **1825** *Brother Jonathan* I. 308 Aiders and abetters of my rebellion.

abetting (əˈbɛtɪŋ), *vbl. sb.* [f. ABET *v.* + -ING[1].] The encouragement, promoting, or instigation (*usually* of anything culpable). Now mostly gerundial.

c **1374** CHAUCER *Troylus* II. 356 If I shold assent, Thurgh myn abettyng [*v.r.* abet], that he thine honour shent. **1629** SIR H. LYNDE *Via tuta* 26 A great abetting to their whole doctrine. **1634** BP. SANDERSON *30 Serm.* (1681) II. 292 The abetting, countenancing, or strengthening of any injurious act. **1821** SCOTT *Kenilw.* (1867) 96 You suppose my Lord of Leicester capable of abetting, perhaps of giving aim and authority, to the base proceedings.

abettor (əˈbɛtə(r), -ɔː(r)). Also 6 **abettour.** [a. Anglo-Fr. *abettour* (OFr. *abetere, abetiere*), f. *abeter*: see ABET, and -OR, -OUR.] This is the constant form of the word as a legal term, and the more frequent even in the general sense; though in the latter, ABETTER, formed on Eng. analogies, is also common.

1. *Law* and *gen.* One who abets, instigates, or encourages to the committing of any offence.

1514 FITZHERBERT *Just. Pea.* (1538) 142 Every suche person so offendinge, theyr ayders..and abbettours..shall runne in the daunger. **1589** PUTTENHAM *Eng. Poesie* (1869) 153 The simple woman is not so much to blame as her lewde abbettours. **1660** R. COKE *Elem. Power & Subj.* 250 Every such person, their Aiders, Counsellors and Abettors shall be adjudged Traitors. **1768** BLACKSTONE *Comm.* I. 138 The person committing, and all his aiders, advisers and abettors. **1856** MRS. STOWE *Dred* (1856) II. v. 60 To be your abettor in any treason you might meditate.

2. *gen.* One who encourages, countenances, or supports another in any proceeding; one who supports or advocates an opinion or principle; a supporter, adherent, advocate. (Prob. never now used in a distinctly *good* sense, as in 17th c.)

1580 LYLY *Euphues & his Engl.* 270 Foes, which by thy well doing thou mayst cause to be earnest abettors of thee. **1640** BP. HALL *Episcop. by divine Right* II. §17. 184 Julius, Bishop of Rome, the great Abbettor of Athanasius. **1651** BAXTER *Inf. Bapt.* 227 An opinion that hath learned and godly abettors. **1756** BURKE *Vind. Nat. Soc.*, Wks. 1842, I. 17 A very material difference between my manner of reasoning and that which is in use amongst the abettors of artificial society. **1782** PRIESTLEY *Matter & Spirit* I. §3. 36 The abettors of that hypothesis..object to mine. **1855** SINGLETON *Virgil* I. 18 Pref., The abettors of such a system must forget that in good authors, etc.

abevacuation (ˌæbɪˌvækjuːˈeɪʃən), *Med.* [f. L. *ab* off, from + EVACUATION; cf. *ab-articulation*.] 'A partial or incomplete evacuation, whether naturally or artificially produced.' Mayne 1851. Also 'Evacuation which is effected by the passage of matter from one organ into another.' *Syd. Soc. Lex.* 1879.

‖**ab extra** (æb ˈɛkstrə), *phr.* [late L., f. L. *ab* from + *extrā* adv., without, outside.] From outside, from without.

1642 T. GOODWIN *Encouragements to Faith* (1650) 7 There are many Demonstrations of his will herein, that may be taken *ab extra* from his [*sc.* God's] Oath. **1652** N. CULVERWEL *Light of Nat.* xi. 115 The divine understanding never receives the least tincture from an object, no species *ab extra*, but views all things in the pure Crystal of his own essence. **1672-1859** [see AB INTRA]. **1864** MRS. GASKELL *Wives & Daughters* (1866) I. ix. 101 It was a great relief to her to have Mr. Gibson to decide for her... Such decisions *ab extra*, are sometimes a wonderful relief. **1941** W. TEMPLE *Citizen & Churchman* iv. 65 They were no longer to be apart from the world, bringing to it *ab extra* the divine act of redemption.

†**abey(e, abeiȝ(e,** *v.*[1] *Obs.* Forms: *Inf.* 1 **abéȝan,** 2 **abeȝen,** 3 **abeiȝe(n,** 4 **abeye.** [A- *pref.* 1 + *béȝ-an* to bend (trans.), f. *búȝan, beáȝ*, to bow: see BEY *v.*] To bend, bow, subject, make obedient.

1073 *O.E. Chron.* (Laud. MS.) anno 1073 [Hi] þet land amyrdon, and hit eall abeȝdon. *c* **1380** *Sir Ferumb.* 5657 þow ne wolt þyn herte ab[e]ye To Char[lis] þat ys so gret. *c* **1420** *Chron. Vilod.* 97 Ni þei abeiȝedoun hem no þing to þe king hest.

abey (əˈbeɪ), *v.*[2] *rare.* [Modern formation deduced from *abeyance*, as said of the possession; not a. OFr. *abeer*, 'to gape for, aspire to,' said of the claimant.] To put in abeyance, waive.

1868 BUCHANAN *Trag. Dram.* Wallace I. ii. All right of rank and place abeyed, I'll follow any of the three.

abey(e, obs. form of ABYE *v.*

abeyance (əˈbeɪəns). Also 7 **abeiance, abbayance.** [a. Anglo-Fr. *abeiance, abeyance* (Littleton), = OFr. *abeance, abaence*, n. of condition, f. *abeer, abaher*, to gape or aspire after; f. *à* to + *beer, baer, bader*, mod. *bayer*, to open wide (the mouth), gape = Pr. and Sp. *badar*, It. *badare*:—late L. *badāre* (in Isidore = *oscitare*, 'to open the mouth wide, gape'); origin undetermined: see conjectures in Diez and Littré. In OFr. the condition of the heir or other aspirant, in whose *abeance*, aspiration, or appetence a title or property stood; hence in Eng. law applied to the condition of the property, the ownership of which is thus claimed, or merely liable to be claimed by some one.]

1. *Law.* Expectation or contemplation of law; the position of waiting for or being without a claimant or owner.

1528 PERKINS *Profitable Booke* (1642) xi. §708. 308 The fee is in abeyance. **1574** tr. *Littleton, Tenures* 119 a, The righte of fee simple is in abeiance, that is to say alonely in the remembrance, entendemente and consideration of the lawe. **1649** SELDEN *Laws of Eng.* (1739) I. lxvi. 145 The right was vanished into the Clouds, or, as the Lawyers term it, in Abeyance. **1691** BLOUNT *Law Dict.* s.v. And it is a Principle in the Law, That of every Land there is a Fee-simple in some man, or it is in Abeyance. **1763** LD. BARRINGTON in Ellis *Orig. Lett.* II. 449. IV. 462 Sir Francis Dashwood called to the House of Lords as Baron Dispenser (in abeyance since Lord Westmoreland's death). **1863** COX *Inst. of Eng. Gov.* I. vii. 67 There are several instances of a barony revived after an abeyance of several centuries. **1864** BOUTELL *Heraldry Hist. & Pop.* xiii. 90 The Peerage that is in Abeyance is dormant only, and not dead.

2. A state of suspension, temporary non-existence or inactivity; dormant or latent condition liable to be at any time revived.

1660 R. COKE *Elem. Power & Subj.* 61 And this monarchy not a thing in abeiance, an aiery title, but an absolute free and independent monarchy. **1794** BURKE *Sp. agst. Hastings* Wks. XV. 13 His honour is in abeyance; his estimation is suspended, and he stands as it were a doubtful person. **1829** SCOTT *Demonology* vi. 181 The belief was fallen into abeyance. **1868** MILMAN *St. Paul's* xvii. 419 In the abeyance of the Cathedral services. **1878** TAIT & STEWART *Unseen Univ.* vii. §204. 203 That the soul may remain veiled or in abeyance until the resurrection.

abeyancy (əˈbeɪənsɪ). *rare.* [f. ABEYANCE, with ending -NCY, more specially expressing quality or state.] A condition or state of abeyance.

1872 HAWTHORNE *Septimius* (ed. 2) 247 There seemed to be some pretentions to a title, too, from a barony which was floating about, and occasionally moving out of abeyancy.

abeyant (əˈbeɪənt), *a.* [A mod. form deduced from ABEYANCE. Not a. OFr. *abeant*, which was said of the person aspiring, not of the thing that was the object of aspiration.] Existing in a state of abeyance or suspension; dormant; latent.

[Not in CRAIG 1847.] **1866** BURKE *Dorm. & Ext. Peerage, Contents*, Peerages, dormant, extinct, forfeited and abeyant.

abeyd, obs. form of ABIDE.

abeysance, obs. f. ABAISANCE, OBEISANCE.

abeyte, variant of ABAIT *v. Obs.*, to bait.

abgect, obs. form of ABJECT.

†ˈ**abgregate,** *v. Obs.*[—0] [f. L. *abgregāt-* ppl. stem of *abgregā-re*, f. *ab* from + *greg-em* (nom. *grex*) flock.] 'To disperse, as it were to lead out of the flock.' Cockeram 1612, Phillips 1678. App. never used.

†**abgreˈgation.** *Obs.*[—0] [n. of action f. L. *abgregāre*.] 'A separation from the flock,' Bailey, vol. II. 1731. App. never used.

abholish, obs. form of ABOLISH.

abhominable, abhomination, etc., the regular spelling of ABOMINABLE, ABOMINATION, etc. in OFr., and in Eng. from their first use to 17th c., due to an assumed derivation from *ab homine*, 'away from man, inhuman, beastly,' which influenced their early use, and has coloured the whole meaning of the words to the present day.

†**abhominal,** *a. Obs.* [f. L. *ab* away from + *homin-e* man + -AL[1], in imitation of the reputed etymology of ABOMINABLE (see prec.)] Unworthy of a man, inhuman, unmanly.

1550 CROWLEY *Epigr.* 480 So boeth sortes commit Moste abhominal blasphemie. **1659** FULLER *Appeal of Inj. Innoc.* (1840) 517 What could I have written more fully and freely in the cordial detestation of such abhominal libels?

†**abhominalty.** *Obs. rare*[—1]. [f. prec. + -TY.] An inhuman deed.

1483 CAXTON *Geoffroi de la Tour* vii, The grete crueltees and abhomynaltees that she had done.

abhor (æbˈhɔː(r)), *v.* Also 5-7 **abhorre.** [ad. L. *abhorrē-re* to shrink back in dread, to be far from, to be inconsistent with; f. *ab* away from + *horrē-re*, to bristle, to stand with, or as, hair on end, to stand aghast, to shudder with fright, etc. Cf. Fr. *abhorrer* which may have given the trans. sense; the intr. ones are clearly from L.]

†**1.** *trans. lit.* To shrink back from with shuddering, to view with horror or dread. *Obs. rare.*

1513 DOUGLAS *Æneid* XIII. x. 47 Abhor thou not the fyre and flambis bricht, From thy dere spousis hede glaid to the hicht.

2. *fig.* To regard with horror, extreme repugnance or disgust; to hate utterly, loathe, abominate.

a. Obj. a noun or noun-phrase.

1449 PECOCK *Repr.* 563 Thei abhorren aboue alle othere.. the Sacrament of the auter, the preciose bodi and blood of Crist. **1494** FABYAN I. xxvi. 19 (1542) The Brytons abhorred the lynage of Gorbodio. **1535** COVERDALE *Ecclus.* l. 25 There be two maner of people, that I abhorre fro my hert. **1542** BOORDE *Dyetary* (1870) viii. 247 To slepe on the backe vpryght is utterly to be abhorred. **1601** SHAKS. *Twel. N.* II. v. 219 He will come to her in yellow stockings, and 'tis a colour she abhorres. **1611** BIBLE *Ps.* cvii. 18 Their soule abhorreth all manner of meate. **1726** W. PENN *Life* Wks. I. 137 I always abhorr'd discounting private favours at the Publick cost. **1793** BURKE *Let. to Comte D'Artois*, Wks. 1844, IV. 186 Abhor intrigue, and you will have the benefit of counsel. **1860** TRENCH *Serm. in Westm. Abbey* xxvi. 297 How many shun evil as inconvenient, who do not abhor it as hateful... To abhor evil is to have it in a moral detestation; to shrink back from it with a shuddering horror, as one would shrink back from a hissing, stinging serpent.

b. Obj. an infinitive phr.

1555 *Fardle of Facions* II. x. 216 This people so despiseth al other men,..that thei abhor to speake to theim. **1611** SHAKS. *Cymb.* IV. ii. 357 Nature doth abhorre to make his bed With the defunct. **1644** MILTON *Areop.* 53 Which I know ye abhorre to doe. **1718** POPE *Iliad* XIII. 331 Inglorious here, my soul abhors to stay. **1799** W. TAYLOR in Robberds' *Memoirs* I. 306, I abhor to exceed my income.

†**3.** *causally.* To make one shudder, to horrify; to cause horror or disgust. Mostly *impers. Obs.*

1536 LD. BERNERS *Golden Boke of Marcus Aurel.* (1546) J v. b, Flesshe oughte not to be so leane, that it abhorre, nor so fatte that it cloie the stomacke. **1541** ELYOT *Image of Gov.* 7 It abhorreth me to expresse his beastly lyuyng. **1565** J. HALLE *Hist. Expost.* (1844) 18 It would abhorre any honest mans eares to heare of it. **1604** SHAKS. *Oth.* IV. ii. 162 I cannot say Whore; It do's abhorre me, now I speake the word.

†**4.** *intr. lit.* To shudder, feel horror or dismay. *Obs. rare.*

1535 W. STEWART *Cron. Scot.* I. 358 Quhen thai saw the greit Montanis thay abhorrit with thame.

†**5.** *fig.* To shrink with horror, repugnance, disgust, or dislike *from*. *Obs.*

1538 STARKEY *England* 21 Wych [thing] hath causyd many grete, wyse, and polytyke men to abhorre from commyn welys. **1548** UDALL etc. *Erasm. Paraph.* Matt. xvii. 23 Theyr mynd abhorred so muche from the remembrance of death. **1617** FYNES MORYSON I. 3. i. 208 Most part of the Mariners are Greekes, the Italians abhorring from being sea men. **1651** R. WITTIE tr. *Primrose's Popular Errours* III. i. 133 Some doe so much abhorre from the use thereof, that they think it almost present poyson. *a* **1656** HALES *Golden Rem.* (1688) 423 They abhorr'd from the conceit of many men who would believe nothing but what they were able to give a reason for.

†**6.** To be repugnant, be at variance, be inconsistent, differ entirely *from*. *Obs.*

1553–87 FOXE *A. & M.* II. 357 It did nothing at all abhor from nature. **1650** F. G[REGORY] *Maps and Charts, Posthuma* 324 Our own Island useth to bee likened to a Triangle, and it doth not much abhor from that Figure. **1671** EVELYN *Memoirs* (1857) III. 234 This new-minted transubstantiation, abhorring from the genuine and rational sense of the text.

†**ab'horfulness.** *Obs. rare*⁻¹. [Formed on apparent analogy with *fearfulness*, *carefulness*, *cheerfulness*, in which the basis is the sb. *fear*, *care*, *cheer*, not the vb. *Abhorful* is not cited.] Abhorrence.

1556 RECORDE *The Castle of Knowledge* 114 Natures abhorfulness to permitte any emptines.

†**ab'horment.** *Obs.* [f. ABHOR *v.* + -MENT.] The action of abhorring; the condition of abhorrence, detestation.

1576 BAKER tr. *Gesner's Jewell of Health* 77/2 Which water ..was delectable and without abhorrement to the pacients. **1648** SYMMONS *Vindication* 122 Our abhorment of the cruelties of the Irish, and how they are out-gone by the English rebels. **1651** *Life of Father Sarpi* (1676) 73 Might be believed to have had the baseness of Flatterers in abhorment.

abhorred (æb'hɔːd), *ppl. a.* [f. ABHOR *v.* + -ED.]

1. Regarded with horror or disgust, detested.

1605 SHAKS. *Lear* I. ii. 81 Abhorred Villaine, vnnaturall, detested, bruitish Villaine. **1723** DE FOE *Col. Jack* (1840) 177 The abhorred crimes he had committed. **1832** GEN. P. THOMPSON *Exercises* (1842) II. 320 The abhorred thing which weighed on our fathers like an incubus. **1846** KEBLE *Lyra Innoc.* (1873) 141 Thy right arm shall wield his sword, Wield, and take his head abhorred.

†**2.** Filled with horror, horrified. *Obs.*

1602 SHAKS. *Haml.* V. i. 206 How abhorred my Imagination is; my gorge rises at it.

abhorrence (æb'hɒrəns). [f. ABHORRENT *a.* after nouns from Fr. in *-nce*:—L. *-ntia*: see -NCE. Cf. also the rather earlier ABHORRENCY. By analogy *abhorrence* is strictly the *action* or fact of abhorring, and *abhorrency* the *quality* of being abhorrent; but in this as in other words which express a continuous action or lasting state of feeling, the distinction disappears, and after a period, during which the two forms were used synonymously, *abhorrency* was dropped, and *abhorrence* alone retained.]

1. The action of abhorring or shrinking from with horror; the feeling of detestation, repugnance, or utter dislike.

1660 R. COKE *Elem. Power & Subj.* 64 By a general abhorrence, democracy hath been exploded upon the face of the earth for above 1700 years. **1680** *Address to Chas. II* in Somers's *Tracts* I. 106 The Premises considered, We your Majesty's Petitioners, out of a just Abhorrence of such a dangerous and pernicious Council, etc. **1704** RAY *Creation* I. 83 Nature's abhorrence of a Vacuity or empty space. *c* **1746** HERVEY *Med. & Contemp.* (1818) 75 The Prince of Peace rejects them with abhorrence. **1759** ROBERTSON *Hist. Scotl.* I. IV. 324 The Scots were held in abhorrence all over Europe. **1765** TUCKER *Lt. of Nat.* II. 659 Our abhorrences and tormenting passions, as well as the soothing, were designed for our benefit. **1809** W. TAYLOR in *Monthly Mag.* XXVII. 458 A proof..of abhorrence against vice. **1860** TYNDALL *Glaciers* I. §19. 134 A wrench, for which I entertain considerable abhorrence. **1866** KINGSLEY *Hereward* xvii. 215 A woman's instinctive abhorrence of wrong.

2. An expression of abhorrence; in *Eng. Hist.* specially applied to certain addresses presented to Charles II. (see quotation in prec. dated 1680).

1678 MARVELL *Growth of Popery* Wks. 1875 IV. 305 The members of Parliament were under a penalty to take the oath, and make the declaration and abhorrence insuing. **1735–8** LD. BOLINGBROKE *Dissn. upon Parties* 81 Their Brethren refused to sign an Abhorrence of this Invitation. **1740** NORTH *Exam.* III. vii. §60. 548 A World of such Flowers went to the adorning these returns of the People's Duty to the King, and scarce in any one of them the Word Abhor was wanted; which gave the Faction, in their Turn, Occasion to fall upon the Loyallists with that Term, in Manner as I shall shew; and thence the Addresses on this Occasion [anno 1680] were called Abhorrences.

3. The object of abhorrence; what excites repugnance and detestation.

1752 YOUNG *The Brothers* V. i. Wks. 1757 II. 287 His father's rebel! Brother's murderer! Nature's abhorrence, and—thy lawful Lord! **1783** COWPER *Letters* Nov. 23 Wks. 1876, 148 Politics are my abhorrence.

†**abhorrency** (æb'hɒrənsɪ). *Obs.* [f. ABHORRENT, after nouns in *-ncy*, ad. L. *-ntia*; see -NCY. Cf. ABHORRENCE.]

1. The quality, state, or feeling of being abhorrent of, or of holding a thing in hatred and disgust; extreme repugnance or dislike.

1605 BACON *Adv. Learn.* 157 Motions simple are..lastly, Motion of Rest or abhorrency of Motion, which is the Cause of many things. **1627** FELTHAM *Resolves* II. lxv. (1677) 297 A vast Prerogative, that man hath over the rest of the Creatures, by only knowing their Inclinations and Abhorrencies. **1659** JER. TAYLOR *Ductor Dubit.* I. i. 21 (2) A natural abhorrency against unnatural lusts. **1660** BOYLE *New Experim. Phys.-Mech.* ii. 41 Nature's abhorrency of a Vacuum. **1661** *Origen his Opinions* in *Phœnix* (1721) I. 24 Out of an abhorrency to such Blasphemy. **1690** LOCKE *Educ.* Wks. 1812 IX. 100 The first tendency to any injustice.. must be suppressed with a shew of wonder and abhorrency, in the parents and governors. **1709** STRYPE *Ann. Ref.* xli. 416 The lay people were growing into an abhorrency of those that wore them.

2. That which excites abhorrence; a thing abhorrent to one; = ABHORRENCE 3.

1729 BURKITT *On New Test.* Heb. x. 38 Backsliders from the gospel are, in a peculiar manner, the abhorrency of the soul of God.

abhorrent (æb'hɒrənt), *ppl. a.* [ad. L. *abhorrent-em*, pr. pple. of *abhorr-ēre*: see ABHOR.]

1. Abhorring, shrinking with horror; having or showing abhorrence, repugnance, or detestation (*of*).

1749 SMOLLETT *Regicide* IV. iii. 79 (1777) No! let me wipe thee..From my abhorrent thoughts! **1810** SOUTHEY *Kehama* viii. 9 Whiten the lip, and make the abhorrent eye Roll back and close. **1835** I. TAYLOR *Spirit. Despotism* iv. 155 The two principles..are abhorrent the one of the other. **1869** GLADSTONE *Juv. Mundi* xv. §5. 533 The Greek of the heroic age was eminently temperate and abhorrent of excess.

2. In a position of recoil or dissent *from*; strongly opposed to; at variance *subjectively*.

a. Of persons, which is the original use.

1619 SANDERSON *Serm. I. ad Clerum* §21 They (the Puritans) jumpe with the Papists, whom they would seeme above all others most abhorrent from. **1664** H. MORE *Apology* 498 Which I must confess Calvin seems abhorrent from. **1678** CUDWORTH *Intell. Syst.* 71 These Philosophers fall unawares into that very thing which they are so abhorrent from. **1790** BURKE *French Rev.* 199 The persons most abhorrent from blood, and treason, and arbitrary confiscation.

b. Of things: So far removed *from* as to be repugnant or inconsistent.

1720 ROWE *Tamerlane* V. i. 71 It is a manner Abhorrent from the softness of thy Sex. **1794** BURKE *Rep. of Committee on Lords' Journ.* Wks. XIV. 379 Two stages of proof, both of them contrary to the law, and both abhorrent from its principles. **1822** T. TAYLOR *Metam. of Apuleius* 364 For similars are not abhorrent from similars. **1845** STEPHEN *Laws of Eng.* I. 113 An act abhorrent from Hindoo superstition. **1864** MERIVALE *Boyle Lect.* 37 The simple theory of the Gospel..was strange and abhorrent from the prejudices of the heathen.

3. Repugnant in nature or character (*to*); at variance *objectively*.

1660 R. COKE *Elem. Power & Subj.* 64 It is abhorrent and impossible to frame a Commonwealth in England from the example of the Romans and Athenians. *Ibid.* 49 Anarchy is like a vacuum in Nature; so abhorrent, that the World will rather return into Chaos, then suffer it. **1677** HALE *Prim. Orig. Mankind* 2 I think Atheism so unreasonable a thing, so abhorrent to the Light of Nature. **1685** BURNET *More's Utopia* 9 In a Way so abhorrent to my Genius. **1796** BURKE *Regicide Peace* Wks. 1842 II. 323 A guilty race, to whose frame..order, peace, religion, and virtue, are alien and abhorrent. **1863** KEMBLE *Residence in Georgia* 15 They are not abhorrent to nature.

4. Hence, through influence of 1: Viewed with repugnance and aversion; hateful, detestable, abhorred.

1833 I. TAYLOR *Fanaticism* §1. 3 Pride, abhorrent as it is. **1852** MISS YONGE *Cameos* (1877) III. xiii. 114 These of course were abhorrent to the English, who were delighted when Edward and Warwick hurried to the north. **1874** R. CONGREVE *Essays* 166 The case becomes almost infinitely more abhorrent, when their acts..expose others to suspicion.

abhorrently (æb'hɒrəntlɪ), *adv.* [f. ABHORRENT *a.* + -LY².] In an abhorrent manner, with abhorrence.

1813 JAMES MONTGOMERY *World bef. Flood* IX. 14 Still on the youth, his eye, wherever cast, Abhorrently return'd, and fix'd at last.

abhorrer (æb'hɔːrə(r)). [f. ABHOR *v.* + -ER¹.]

1. One who abhors.

1611 COTGR., *Haineur*, a hater, loather, detester, abhorrer. *c* **1660** JER. TAYLOR *Artif. Hands* 134 Those things, whereof they sometimes were great abhorrers. **1705** HICKERINGILL *Priest-Craft* II. viii. 89 A Protestant Succession, of which the Highflyers are generally Abhorrers. **1827** HALLAM *Const. Hist.* (1876) I. iv. 195 Every abhorrer of ceremonies..might be trusted as protestant to the heart's core.

2. *Eng. Hist.* A nickname given in 1680 to those who signed addresses of ABHORRENCE.

1680 *Political Ballads* (1860) I. 214 This makes abhorrers, makes lords protest, They know not why nor wherefore. **1682** *Second Plea for Nonconf.* 78 Abhorrers of Addresses, and Non-Addresses. **1757** TINDAL *Rapin* anno 1679–80 As soon as the parliament was prorogued, and the duke of York at court, many addresses were presented in abhorrence of the former, so that two parties were formed, called the petitioners and abhorrers. **1849** MACAULAY *Hist. Eng.* I. ii. 256 Opponents of the Court were called Birminghams, Petitioners, and Exclusionists. Those who took the King's side were Antibirminghams, Abhorrers, and Tantivies. **1870** CURTIS *Hist. Eng.* anno 1680 The factions were known by the names of petitioners and abhorrers, terms which soon became superseded by whig and tory.

ab'horrible, *a.* Now *rare.* [f. L. *abhorrē-re* (see ABHOR), on the type of *horrible*, L. *horribilis* f. the simple *horrēre*.] To be abhorred, detestable.

1633 T. ADAMS *Exp. 2 Pet.* ii. 7 (1865) 364a, How abhorrible is that vice, which shall rob a man of himself, and lay a beast in his room! **1822** J. SCOTT *Life Rev. T. Scott* (ed. 5, 1823) xvi. 531 O Lord, abhor me not—though I be indeed *abhorrible*, and abhor myself! **1849** *Blackw. Mag.* Nov. 646 Hamlet's uncle, Claudius, seems to me to be the most that can be borne of one purely abhorrible. **1862** *Illustr. Times* 17 May 46/3 The relief consists..in being fed upon detestable gruel, and such other abhorrible viands as poor-law guardians may consider economical and proper.

abhorring (æb'hɔːrɪŋ), *vbl. sb.* [f. ABHOR *v.* + -ING¹.]

1. The action of shrinking from with horror; detestation, repugnance, disgust; = ABHORRENCE 1.

1530 PALSGR. 193 Abhorryng, *horrevr* s.f. **1607** HIERON *Wks.* I. 269 An vtter disliking and abhorring of the things which before they tooke pleasure in. **1607** SHAKS *Coriol.* I. i. 172 He that will give good words to thee, wil flatter Beneath abhorring. **1643** MILTON *Divorce* viii. 38 (1851) A certain religious aversation and abhorring, which can no way sort with marriage. **1860** TRENCH *Serm. in Westm. Abbey* v. 53 That state may be one in itself sufficient to provoke abhorring.

2. That which causes abhorrence or horror; an object of disgust; = ABHORRENCE 3.

1606 SHAKS. *Ant. & Cl.* V. ii. 60 Lay me starke-naked, and let the water-Flies Blow me into abhorring. **1611** BIBLE *Is.* lxvi. 24 They shall be an abhorring vnto all flesh. **1862** TRENCH *Miracles* xxix. 414 When it was become an abhorring even to them that had loved it best.

†**abhorring** (æb'hɔːrɪŋ), *ppl. a. Obs.* [f. ABHOR *v.* + -ING².] Abhorrent, repulsive, repugnant. Const. *from*, which is occ. omitted.

1611 *Troublesome Raigne of K. John* II. 85 An act Abhorring in the eares of Christian men. **1643** MILTON *Divorce* II. vii. 79 (1851) Which is utterly abhorring from the end of all Law. **1649** SELDEN *Laws of Eng.* I. xli. 68 (1739) A matter quite abhorring the custom of all the Grecians. **1678** MARVELL *Growth of Popery* 4 There was..nothing so Monstrous to Reason, so abhorring from Morality.

†**abho'rrition.** *Obs. rare*⁻¹. [f. L. *abhorrē-re* after nouns in *-ition*, repr. L. *-itiōnem*, f. pa. pple., wanting in this vb. in L.] The action of abhorring, abhorrence.

1656 HEN. EARL OF MONMOUTH *Advert. fr. Parnassus* 222 Whose damn'd writings many forbore to read, out of meer abhorition of such things.

abhyme, variant of ABIME, *Obs.*, abyss.

‖**Abib** ('eɪbɪb). [Heb. *ābīb*, lit. a spike of corn.] The first month of the Jewish ecclesiastical, the seventh of the civil year, afterwards called Nisan.

1535 COVERDALE *Exod.* xiii. 4 This daye are ye gone out, euen in yᵉ moneth of Abib. **1833** *Penny Cycl.* I. 29 In the calendar of the modern Jews, Abib is no longer the beginning of the year, its place being usurped by Tisri, which was anciently the seventh month. Abib contains thirty days, and must not begin on Monday, Wednesday, or Friday.

abichite ('æbɪkaɪt), *Min.* [Named after Dr. Abich of Tiflis.] A synonym of CLINOCLASITE. Dana. A native arsenate of copper, found chiefly associated with other copper ores and veins in Cornwall and elsewhere.

abidal (ə'baɪdəl). *rare.* [f. ABIDE *v.* + -AL². After analogy of Romance words like *removal*, etc.] The act of abiding; abode, stay.

1850 BLACKIE *Æschylus* I. 199 I will drag thee alive..To the dens of the damned For thy lasting abidal.

abidance (ə'baɪdəns). [f. ABIDE *v.* + -ANCE. An instance of the Romance vb.-affix *-ance*:—L. *-antia*, added to an Eng. vb. in imitation of such words as *subsidence*, *observance*, *continuance*, which are adoptions of actual or possible Fr. words.]

1. Abiding, dwelling, continuance.

1647 FULLER *Hy. War* v. xi. 249 The Christians had no longer abidance in the holy hill of Palestine. **1668** CULPEPER & COLE tr. *Bartholinus Anat.* II. vi. 101 From its abidance there, the blood would not be perfected but become adust. **1755** S. WALKER *Sermons* vi, The Days of Man are shrunk into the Abidance of a Moment. **1837** J. H. NEWMAN *Prophetical Office* 102 It considers doubt incompatible with practical abidance in the truth.

2. Continuance in a submissive or docile manner *by*; conformity to.

1875 HELPS *Essays* 179 A judicious abidance by rules, and holding to the results of experience, are good.

abide (ə'baɪd), *v. str.* Pa. t. abode (ə'bəʊd), also **abided.** Pa. pple. **abode,** also **abided, abidden.**

Forms: *Inf.* 1 abíd-an, 2–4 abid-en, 4–5 abyden, 3–6 abyde, 3– abide. *Ind. pres.* 3rd sing. 1 abídeð, 1–4 abit, 4– abideth, 6– abides; (*north.* 3– abydes, -ys -is). *Pa. t.* 1 abád, 2–3 abad (3 abed, abeod), 3–5 abod (abot), 3–6 abood, 5 abode; also 6–7 abidd, abid, 8– abided; (*north.* 3–6 abade, 5–6 abaid(e;) *pl.* 1 abidon, 2–5 abiden, 5 abydyn, abide, aboden, 5–6 aboode, 5– abode. *Pa. pple.* 1 abiden, 2–7 abiden, 3–6 abyden, 6 abydden, 6–7 abidd, abid, 6– abidden; also 6 aboded, 7 abode, 8 abided. [1. OE. *abídan*, cogn. w. Goth. *us-beidan* to remain on; f. A- *pref.* 1, of onward motion + *bídan*: see BIDE. 2. The historical conj. is *abide, abode, abidden*, but pa. t. and pa. pple. have been variously assimilated to each other, and to the weak conjugation. As early as 6, *abidden* was shortened to *abid(d*, and this form occ. used for the past (cf. *writ, bit*). On the other hand, *abidden* was in 6 assimilated to pa. t. as *aboden* and *abode*; the latter is now the common form, though *abidden* occurs in 19th c. writers, and some make a weak pa. t. and pa. pple. *abided*. 3. Orig. *intrans.* but in OE. as in Gothic taking a genitive of the object that was the occasion of the abiding, as *we abidon his*, we waited *on account of* or *for* him: this was subsequently replaced by a dative or accusative, the simple object of later times, whereby the vb. became *transitive*.]

I. *intr.* To wait, stay, remain.

†1. To remain in expectation, wait. *Obs.*

c **1120** *O.E. Chron.* (Laud. MS.) anno 1091 He [cyng Melcolm] for mid his fyrde ut of Scotlande into Loðene on Englaland and pær abad. *c* **1175** *Lamb. Hom.* 103 His wite abideð on þere oðre weorlde. *c* **1250** *Genesis & Ex.* 1638 Ðre flockes of sep ðor-bi, Ðat ðor abiden al for-ði. *c* **1374** CHAUCER *Boethius* (1868) 63 I abood til þat thow haddest swych habyte of thy thowght as thow hast now. *c* **1450** *Merlin* xviii. 290 Thei abode stille in the town, and sojourned to abide to here tidinges of Kynge Arthur. **1611** SPEED *Hist. G. Brit.* IX. xii. 108 Hee had almost abidden in leaguer before it one whole year. **1611** BIBLE *Gen.* xxii. 5 Abide you here with the asse, and I and the lad will goe yonder. **1634** *Modern. of Malory's Prince Arthur* (1816) II. 249 Sir Percivale had abidden there till mid-day.

†**b.** Const. *on, upon, for. Obs.*

c **1430** LYDGATE *Minor Poems* (1840) 223 Wheron was wrytyn a resoun fulle ryghte, And alle was: 'For the better abyde.' *c* **1450** LONELICH *Graal* II. 329 The steward Of the kynge that Abod vppon hise lord. **1483** CAXTON *G. Legend* 215/3 The Gates of heuen were opene and abode for her. *Ibid.* 99/3 They that were there abode upon thende of the thyng. **1533** BELLENDENE *Livy* v. 418 The Faderis.. determit to abide on the returning of thare legatis. **1548** UDALL *Erasm. Paraph.* Matt. viii. 12 We know what misery and wretchednes abydeth for us.

†**2.** To wait before proceeding further; to pause, delay, stop. *Obs.*

c **1230** *Ancren Riwle* 338 Moni mon abit to schriuen him uort þe nede tippe. **1297** R. GLOUC. 382 He nolde noȝt abyde vorte hys fader dep. *c* **1386** CHAUCER *Knight's T.* 2124 Theseus abyden hadde a space Or eny word cam fro his wyse brest. *c* **1420** *Palladius on Husb.* I. 118 In places cold thyne hervest sede betyme Is best to haast; in springyng seed to abyde. **1496** W. DE WORDE *Dives & Pauper* VI. xxv. 275/1 God abode of punysshynge tyll he had undernomen Eue. **1513** DOUGLAS *Æneid* XI. ii. 91 Eneas tho gan styntyn and abaide, And wyth ane pietuous regret thus he sayd. **1528** MORE *Dial. Heresyes* IV. Wks. 1557, 251/1. Abide ye quod I, and ye shal heare worse yet. **1535** COVERDALE *Judg.* xvi. 2 Abyde, tomorrow whan it is lighte, we wyll slaye him.

†**b.** To tarry over a work. *Obs.*

1531 ELYOT *Governour* (1580) 137 That incomparable treasure called amitie, in the declaration wher-off I haue aboden the longer.

†**3.** To stop (absolutely); to come to a halt. *Obs.*

c **1305** *E. Eng. Poems & Saints' Lives* 58 Aȝen þe deuel he com adoun: & bad þe schrewe abide. **1430** *Syr Generides* (1865) 122 Here horses that thei on ride, Were so werie that thei abide. *c* **1480** *Robert the Deuyll* (Thom's Romances I. 54) Abyde, thou false traytour. **1634** *Modern. of Malory's Pr. Arthur* (1816) I. 103 I was so furious in my quest that I would not abide.

†**4.** To stay behind, to remain (after others have gone). *Obs.*

1375 BARBOUR *Bruce* XII. 73 Than thai with-drew thaim euirilkane, And durst nocht than abyde to ficht. *c* **1450** *Reliq. Antiq.* I. 309 Fy on a false hert that dar not abyde. **1523** LD. BERNERS *Froissart* I. ii. 3 All such as in cruel batels haue ben seen abyding to [=till] the discomfeture. **1565** GOLDING *Cæsar* 243 Suche as had abidden behinde to tyll the grounde.

5. To remain after other things are taken; to remain over, be left. *arch.*

c **1399** *Pol. Poems* II. 12 (1859) Here fame abit, bot al is vanite. **1535** COVERDALE *Amos* ii. 15 The archer shall not abyde, and the swifte off fote shall not escape. *a* **1842** TENNYSON *Ulysses* 65 Tho' much is taken, much abides.

6. To remain without going away, to stay.

1205 LAYAMON 13135 Vortiger þer abed [**1250** þar abod]. *c* **1386** CHAUCER *Clerkes T.* 1050 Hem that stooden hir bisyde, Unnethe aboute hir mighte thay abyde. *c* **1420** *Chron. Vilod.* 1087 Thre dayes and thre nyȝt he þer abodde. **1574** tr. *Marlorats Apocalips* 37 You are they that haue abidden by me in al my temptations. **1605** SHAKS. *Macb.* III. i. 140 Ile call vpon you straight: abide within. **1791** COWPER *Iliad* ix. 407 He within his ships Abode the while. **1820** SCOTT *Monast.* (1867) 459 Had I abidden with him. *a* **1842** TENNYSON *Two Voices* 158 While thou abodest in the bud, It was the stirring of the blood. *a* **1845** LYTE *Hymn* Abide with me! fast falls the eventide, The darkness thickens, Lord, with me abide.

7. Of things: To remain, continue (in a place).

c **1450** LONELICH *Grail* xxix. 32 The braunch in hire hond was Abydinge. **1598** SYLVESTER *Du Bartas* (1641) I. ii. 11/2. 48 Aire clung to Aire, and Earth with Earth abid. **1652** CULPEPER *Eng. Phys.* 42 Before the stalk with the flowers have abidden a month above ground. **1732** LAW *Serious Call* xxiii. 464 (ed. 2) Their guilt still abides upon you. **1876** FREEMAN *Norm. Conq.* IV. xviii. 185 Whose name abode on Northumbrian tongues as the embodiment of good and just government.

8. To remain in residence; to sojourn, reside, dwell.

1461–82 *Ord. for Royal Househ.* Edw. IV. 24 A Prince.. abyding at sojourne in this court, he hathe been accustomed to pay for his diettes. *Ibid.* 25 If the prince be so abyding in a household at a certayne.. then the Thesaurere to be charged. **1577** *St. Augustine's Manuell* Pref., Thou [God] art in me, because thou abydest in my mynde. **1611** BIBLE *Luke* viii. 27 And ware no clothes, neither abode in any house, but in the tombes. **1686** DRYDEN *Hind & P.* III. 634 No Martin there in winter shall abide. **1862** MISS MULOCH *Domestic Stories* 243 I had abided for a brief space at that paradise of cockneys, Southend. **1875** HELPS *Anim. & Masters* vi. 136 I thought of the mean hovels in which many of our peasantry abide.

9. To remain or continue in some state or action, to continue to be *something*.

c **1250** *Genesis & Ex.* 422 An hundred ȝer after is dead, Adam fro eue in srifte abead. **1366** MAUNDEV. (1839) xxviii. 289 The Coles will duellen and abyden alle quyk. **1388** WYCLIF *John* viii. 7 Whanne thei abiden [*v.r.* abideden, abedin, **1382** lastiden or contynuede] axynge hym. **1477** EARL RIVERS (Caxton) *Dictes* 14 b, If thou wilt the loue of thy frend shal abyde ferme unto the, be curteise to him. *a* **1520** *Myrroure of Our Ladye* 298 After the byrthe, thou haste abyden vyrgyn vndefowled. **1523** LD. BERNERS *Froissart* I. cxcviii. 2 The towne abode frenche. **1611** BIBLE *John* xv. 10 If ye keepe my commandements, ye shal abide in my loue, euen as I haue kept my Father's commandements, and abide in his loue [*Wyclif* dwelle, *Tindale, Coverd. Cranm. Geneva* byde, *Rheims* abide]. **1881** *Globe* 21 Sept. (leader) One of the few Southerners in public life who abided faithful to the Constitution when the battle of secession began.

10. To abide *by*: *lit.* to remain with; hence, to stand firm by, to hold to, remain true to.

1509 FISHER *Wks.* I. 221 His commaundement must nedes be obeyed and abyden by. **1528** MORE *Dial. Heresyes* II. Wks. 1557, 183/1 The verye churche hath euer had some that hath abidden by theyr faith. **1772** *Letters of Junius* No. lxviii. 337 You will abide by the authority of this great man. **1813** MAR. EDGEWORTH *Patronage* (1833) I. xix. 333 Lord Oldborough abided not only by his own measures, but by his own instruments. **1855** TENNYSON *Maud* I. xvi. 25 Dare I bid her abide by her word? **1860** TYNDALL *Glaciers* I. §24. 171 The rules were fixed, and I must abide by them.

11. To continue in existence, endure, stand firm or sure.

1398 TREVISA *Barth. De P.R.* XIV. xxxiv. 480 The cyte in mount Segor sholde haue stonde stronge and abyde, yf they had not synned. *c* **1460** FORTESCUE *Abs. & Lim. Mon.* (1714) 86 Hys Highness woll establish the same Lyvelood than remayning, to abyde perpetually to his Crowne. **1535** COVERDALE *Ps.* xci. 7 But thou Lorde o most hyest, abydest worlde without ende. **1611** BIBLE *Ps.* cxix. 90 Thou hast established the earth, and it abideth. **1876** FREEMAN *Norm. Conq.* I. iv. 153 The Norman.. abides in his lineage and in his works, but he is Norman no longer. **1878** JOAQUIN MILLER *Songs of Italy* 123 Nothing has been that abideth now.. Nothing shall be that shall abide.

II. *trans.* To wait for, await the issue of, endure.

12. To wait for, await; remain ready for, watch for, expect. (The object was orig. a *genitive*.)

a. *lit.* of persons awaiting persons or things. *arch.*

c **1000** *O.E. Gosp.* Matt. xi. 3 Eart þu þe to cumenne eart, oððe we oþres sceolon abidan? (*Lindisf.* Oðer we bidas.) *c* **1160** *Hatt. Gosp.* Luke i. 21 And þæt folc wæs zacharium ȝe-abyddende. **1205** LAYAMON III. 226 Þer heo abiden wederes, For þe wind heom stod toȝæines. *c* **1230** *Ancren Riwle* 358 Menske & reste abit us et hom, in ure owune londe. *c* **1280** *Owl & Night.* 1700 Ȝef ȝe abideth mine [= wait for me] here, ȝe schule on other wise singe. *c* **1305** *E.E. Poems, Life of Pilate* 113 Ech schrewe wole abide his tyme. *a* **1315** *Northern Psalter* xxxix. 2 Abidand Laverd abade I. **1382** WYCLIF *Luke* ii. 25 To alle þat abiden þe redempcion of israel. *c* **1400** *Syr Perecyvelle* 1278 My lady, lele Lufamour, Habyddis the in hir chambour. **1423** JAMES I *King's Quair* IV. x, Wele is him that his tyme will abit. **1449** PECOCK *Repr.* 206 Whom alle holi men fro the bigynnyng of the world Aboden. **1483** CAXTON *G. Leg.* 21/1 We have abyden the every day. **1520–41** WYATT *Poet. Works* (1861) 17 I abide, and abide; and better abide, After the old proverb, the happy day. **1541** ELYOT *Image Gov.* 41 He abode an answer thereof. **1605** STOW *Annales* 676, 500 men ..abiding the wind in the port of Sandwich. **1722** DE FOE *Hist. Plague* 21 The generality stayed and seemed to abide the worst. **1829** SCOTT *Antiq.* xxi. 143 'I wad e'en streek mysell out here, and abide my removal.' **1859** TENNYSON *Enid* 980 I will abide the coming of my lord.

b. *fig.* of things (as fate, surprise, punishment) awaiting persons. *arch.*

1340 *Ayenb.* 128 Þe wrechche ne þengþ of þe gibet þet him abit. **1382** WYCLIF *Acts* xx. 23 Bondis and tribulaciouns at Jerusalem dwellen to me [*one MS.* abyden me; *text of* **1388** abiden me]. **1526** TINDALE *ibid.* Bondes and trouble abyde me. **1549** COVERDALE *Erasm. Paraphr. 1 Pet.* ii. 10 As long as we were the sonnes of the synful Adam, an infortunate enheritaunce abode us. **1619** T. TAYLOR *Titus* i. 13. 260 He knewe that bands and imprisonment did abide him in euerie citie. **1640** *Homilies* I. II. III. 88 Those most grieuous and intolerable torments, which abide all uncleane persons. **1826** E. IRVING *Babylon* II. VI. 142 A foretaste of the fiery lake which abideth him.

†**13.** To wait till the end of, hear through. *Obs.*

c **1450** LONELICH *Grail* xv. 769 And Iosephes Abod Alle hire Answere Evene to the Ende that sche seide þere. *Ibid.* xxiii. 5 And the Kyng Alle his tales wel Abod, & ful wel hem likede.

14. To await defiantly, to face, to encounter, withstand, or sustain.

1297 R. GLOUC. 302 Dreduol he was to ys fon, þat hym durste vewe abyde. **1375** BARBOUR *Bruce* III. 14 He bauldly thaim abaid. *c* **1435** *Torrent of Portugal* 1470 He wold not the geaunt abyde. *c* **1440** *Gesta Rom.* II. lvii. 421 A man or a woman may abide the conflicte of all vices, but [lechery] he moste flee. **1570–87** HOLINSH. *Scot. Chron.* (1806) I. 378 The other cast themselves about and manlie abode their enemies. **1623** J. BINGHAM *Hist. Xenophon* 47 They had not the heart to abide you; why should you be afraid of them. **1649** CROMWELL *Lett. & Sp.* (Carl.) Let. 67 Those gentlemen who have abid the brunt of the service. **1816** SCOTT *Old Mort.* (1868) xv. 724 The.. insurgents appeared to be drawn up with the purpose of abiding battle. **1858** H. MILLER *Sch. & Schoolm.* 133 He soon learned to abide.. terrors which most of my bolder companions shrank from encountering.

15. To await submissively, await the disposal of, submit to.

c **1360** CHAUCER *A B C* 131 My faderes chastisinge þat dar I nouht abiden in no wise. **1400** *Gamelyn* 24 On his deep bed to a-bide Goddes wille. **1480** CAXTON *Chron. Englond* ccxlii. 277 He founde suffisaunt suerte to abyde the lawe. **1523** LD. BERNERS *Froissart* I. xxv. 36 To abyde the ordynaunce of the Kyng of Fraunce. **1594** SHAKS. *Rich. II*, V. vi. 23 Heere is Carlile, liuing to abide Thy Kingly doome, and sentence. **1705** PERRY *Hist. Coll. Am. Col. Ch.* I. 163 Having abiden her Majesty's just determination. **1791** T. PAINE *Rights of Man* (ed. 4) 158 The creditors ought to have abided the fate of the Government. **1821** JOANNA BAILLIE *Met. Leg.* Wallace xcv. 4 He must abide his fatal doom. **1859** TENNYSON *Enid* 584 [Thou shalt] Crave pardon for that insult done the Queen, And shalt abide her judgment on it.

†**16.** To endure, suffer, bear, undergo, sustain. *Obs.*

1205 LAYAMON 15565 He þeos dundes abad [*later text*: And he his dunt a-bod]. **1465** M. PASTON in *Paston Lett.* 503 II. 190 He wold noth abyde the sorow and trobell that ye have abyden to wyn all Sir John Fastolf ys gode. **1526** TINDALE *Hebr.* xii. 2 For the ioye that was set before hym abode the crosse. **1584** POWEL *Lloyd's Cambria* 199 The castele Abood diuerse assaults. **1588** A. KING *Canisius' Catech.* 125 Christ our lord.. abaid ye schame of ye croce. **1601** HOLLAND *Pliny* (1634) I. 59 The other name.. Valerius Soranus blurted out and soone after abid the smart for it. **1606** —— *Suetonius* 239 Domitian abidd condigne punishment for his avarice and crueltie. **1616** SURFL. & MARKH. *Countrey Farme* 412 The best and sweetest, though not alwaies stronger than that which hath abode the presse. **1638** SANDERSON *Serm.* II. 96 Service so hard that it might not be abiden. **1703** MOXON *Mech. Exerc.* 103 It will not be strong enough to abide tough Work.

17. To bear, endure, tolerate, put up with; rarely (now never) in a simple affirmative sentence, but in such as 'I cannot abide, I can scarcely abide, who can abide?'

1526 TINDALE *John* viii. 43 Ye cannot abyde the hearynge off my wordes. **1535** COVERDALE *Job* xix. 17 Myne owne wyfe maye not abyde my breth. *c* **1585** *Faire Em.* II. 591 Of all things, I cannot abide physic. **1618** RALEIGH *Remains* (1644) 128 Oyntment is pleasing to Man; but Beetles and Bees cannot abide it. **1622** BABINGTON *Wks.* III. 121 If Saint Iohn should haue done so, no man would haue abid him. **1627** DRAYTON *Agincourt*, etc. 121 He would not haue aboad it. **1676** ETHEREDGE *Man of Mode* II. i. 15 (1684) He calls me Rogue, tells me he can't abide me. **1727** DE FOE *Hist. Apparitions* xv. 370 He could not abide an ass. **1833** HT. MARTINEAU *Three Ages* III. 84 She could not abide the country, and would not be tempted to leave dear London. **1875** HELPS *Anim. & Masters* i. 6 People can't abide pamphlets in these days.

b. With an infinitive object: To endure, bear.

c **1460** *Poem agt. Friars* in *Rel. Antiq.* I. 322 To serve to that same frer, the Pope mot abyde. **1551** ROBINSON *More's Utopia* 162 [I] was not sure whether he coulde abyde that anye thynge shoulde be sayde. **1561** T. N[ORTON] *Calvin's Instit.* I. 36 Who can abyde to say, that then the Sonn entred into the bosome of the Father. *a* **1593** H. SMITH *Serm.* 97 Nature cannot abide that any place should be empty. **1603** DRAYTON *Barons Warres* II. 2 Could not abide to heare the name of Peace. **1607** TOPSELL *Four-footed Beasts* (1673) 244 A horse cannot abide to look upon a camel. **1611** BIBLE *Transl. Pref.* 2 They cannot abide to heare of altering. **1642** FULLER *Holy & Prof. State* V. viii. 389 Painted faces cannot abide to come nigh the fire. **1773** GOLDSMITH *She Stoops to Conq.* I. i. 50 I can't abide to disappoint myself. **1840** GEN. THOMPSON *Exercises* (1842) V. 323 One or two lords cannot abide to see a Pasha set up his back against his 'legitimate master.'

¶ Through confusion of form with ABYE, q.v., when that vb. was becoming archaic, and through association of sense between *abye* (pay for) *a deed*, and *abide the consequences of a deed*, *abide* has been erroneously used for *abye* = pay for, atone for, suffer for.

1586–93 MARLOWE *Edw. II*, II. ii. 882 Dear shall you both abide this riotous deed. **1607** SHAKS. *Jul. Caes.* III. ii. 119 If it be found so, some will deere abide it. **1719** YOUNG *Revenge* III. i. Wks. 1757 II. 148 O sacred faith! How dearly I abide thy violation!

†**abide**, *sb. Obs. rare*$^{-1}$. [f. the vb.] An abode or stay.

1640–1 *Kirkcudbr. War-Comm. Minute Book* (1855) 46 That Kilquhennady be Captaine of Kirkpatrick-Durham, and Glaisteres liberated of that charge during Kilquhennady's abyde at hame.

†**abideable**, *a. Obs. rare*$^{-1}$. [f. ABIDE *v.* + -ABLE.] Able to be borne or endured.
1611 COTGR., *Soustenable*, sustainable, supportable, abideable.

abider (ə'baɪdə(r)) [f. ABIDE *v.* + -ER[1].] One who abides; in various senses of the vb. Esp.
†**1.** One who waits or awaits. *Obs.*
1543–63 BECON *New Catechism* (1844) 143 Such patient abider of the Lord's leisure was Job. **1548** W. THOMAS *Ital. Gram.* (1567) *Dimorante*, the abider or tarier.
†**2.** One who sustains an attack or stands his ground. *Obs.*
1581 SIDNEY *Def. Poesie* (1622) 503 Maisters of warre, and ornaments of peace, speedie goers, and strong abiders, triumphers both in Campes and Courts. **1614** RALEIGH *Hist. World* (1736) III. xii. §7. 126 The Lacedæmonians, being very firme abiders, might seem the more likely to prevaile.
3. One who dwells; a dweller, a resident.
1611 COTGR., *Habitant*, a dweller, or abider in a place. **1627** SPEED *Eng. etc. abridged* xi. §4 What [land] is worst for the Rider, is best for the Abider. **1816** SCOTT *Old Mort.* 59 The scattered remnant, who, for His name's sake, were abiders in the wilderness.

abiding (ə'baɪdɪŋ) *vbl. sb.* Also abidyng(e, abydyng(e, -ing(e. [f. ABIDE *v.* + -ING[1].] The action or state of one who abides.
†**1.** An awaiting, expecting, looking-for, lying-in-wait-for; expectation, waiting. *Obs.*
a **1300** *Northern Psalter* xxxviii. 8 And now, whilk es min abiding dai? Noght ne Laverd? (Vulg. *Et nunc quae est expectatio mea?*) **1382** WYCLIF *ibid.* And now what is myn abiding? whether not the Lord? *c* **1430** *Syr Generides* 234 And that is al his abiding, For to be wedded as a king. *c* **1450** LONELICH *Graal* II. 381 As thowgh nothing that they wyste of owre abydyng. **1599** HAKLUYT *Voyages* II. i. 67 Thus in abiding for the Duke of Berrie, and for the Constable, who were behind.
†**2.** A waiting at a point, stopping, cessation, pausing; pause, delay. *Obs.*
c **1400** TUNDALE *Circumc.* 86 All abowet the rede blode can gon, Withowt abydyng. *c* **1450** *Merlin* (1877) xv. 256 Thei made no lenger abidinge but mette togeder fiercely. **1480** CAXTON *Chron. Engl.* ccxxi. 213 They shold smyte of syr edmondes hede.. withoute any maner of abydyng or respyte.
†**3.** A bearing or enduring; endurance, patience, long-suffering. *Obs.*
c **1325** *E.E. Allit. Poems* C. 419 þy long abydyng wyth lur [= loss], þy late vengaunce. **1535** COVERDALE *Ps.* ix. 18 The pacient abydinge of soch as be in trouble shall not perish for euer. **1580** HOLLYBAND *Treas. Fr. Tong.*, *Patience*, patience, abiding.
4. An enduring, continuing, or remaining; continuance, duration, permanence. *arch.*
1535 COVERDALE *1 Chron.* xxix. 15 Our life vpon earthe is as a shadowe, and here is no abydinge. **1611** BIBLE *ibid.* And there is none abiding. **1674** N. FAIRFAX *Bulk & Selvedge* 26 It cannot be thought that two abidings or durations, to wit, time and everlastingness, should be together and not be the same abiding.
5. A remaining, tarrying, staying, residing, or dwelling at a place.
c **1440** *Generydes* (1873) 131 The wordis that she sayde of his abiding there. **1616** SURFL. & MARKH. *Countrey Farme* 719 Her quiet and peaceable abiding in her cage. **1808** SCOTT *Marm.* II. xiv. Nor long was his abiding there.
†**6.** A place where one stops; a station or position. *Obs.*
1571 DIGGES *Geomet. Pract.* I. xxviii. sig. I i, The seconde station M, where ye shal now set the centre of your instrument, the diameter lying right agaynst your first abyding.
†**7.** A place where one habitually remains or resides; abode, habitation, dwelling. *Obs.*
1382 WYCLIF *1 Esdras* ix. 37 The sonus of Irael weren in ther abidingus [**1388** abidyngis]. **1587** FLEMING *Contin. Holinshed* III. 1406/2 Neereness and commoditie of mens abidings. **1607** DEKKER *Knight coniuring* (1842) 87 Get leaue for thy ghost to come from her abiding.
8. *Attrib.* as in *abiding house, city*, and esp. **abiding-place**, place of abode.
1571 DIGGES *Geomet. Pract.* I. xxviii. A B C are the markes in the fielde to be measured, D the first abyding or standing place. **1580** HOLLYBAND *Treas. Fr. Tong.*, *Lieu de Demeure*, dwelling, abiding place. **1597–8** *Stat. 39 Eliz.* v. An Acte for erecting of Hospitalles, or abiding and working Howses for the poor. **1805** SOUTHEY *Madoc in Azt.* Wks. 1853 V. 206 Here had the chief Chosen his abiding place. **1876** FREEMAN *Norm. Conq.* I. vi. 424 Next year Cnut came back to England as his real home and abiding place. **1879** DOWDEN *Southey* iii. 52 But his heart needed an abiding-place.

abiding (ə'baɪdɪŋ), *ppl. a.* [f. ABIDE *v.* + -ING[2].]
†**1.** Enduring, standing firm. *Obs.*
1377 LANGL. *P. Pl.* B. xix. 289 Bolde and abidynge bismeres to suffre.
2. Lasting, permanent.
1851 MAURICE *Proph. & Kings* 81 The ark.. was there as an abiding witness of an invisible presence. **1876** FREEMAN *Norm. Conq.* I. vi. 462 Witness to the abiding connexion between Normandy and the North. **1878** A. J. CHURCH *Stories from Virgil* v. 45 The abiding love of her that was once Hector's wife.
3. *Comb.* **law-abiding**, adhering to the law.
1876 FREEMAN *Norm. Conq.* I. vi. 501 An English patriot who on every other occasion appears as conciliatory and law-abiding. **1879** T. H. ESCOTT *Eng.* ii. 498 The colonists are law-abiding and law-loving people.

abidingly (ə'baɪdɪŋlɪ), *adv.* [f. prec. + -LY[2].] In an abiding manner.
†**1.** Assiduously, patiently. *Obs.*
a **1520** *Myrroure of Our Ladye* 64 Thys gostly study.. muste be contynued ful besely and abydyngly euery day.
2. Enduringly, permanently.
1840 CARLYLE *Heroes* (1858) iii. 258 The noblest idea.. is sung, and emblemed forth abidingly, by one of the noblest men. **1881** *Contemp. Rev.* Feb. 174 We have clutched some good lawlessly, and found it abidingly precious.

abidingness (ə'baɪdɪŋnɪs). [f. ABIDING *ppl. a.* + -NESS.] Permanence, lastingness.
1857 NEWMAN *Serm. Var. Occas.* ix. 163 The world.. discerns and recognizes her abidingness, her unchangeableness. **1860** PUSEY *Min. Proph.* 503/2 His [Zechariah's] book opens.. contrasting the transitoriness of all human things.. with the abidingness of the word of God. **1920** E. I. WATKIN in Hess *God & Supernatural* v. 142 The abidingness in another form of the positive value of noble pain.

abie, obs. form of ABYE *v.*

†**a-bier, abeere**, *adv.*, prop. *phrase. Obs.* [See A *prep.*[1]] On, upon, or to a bier; into the coffin.
c **1450** *Pol. Poems* II. 229 Hit is a shrewde pole, pounde, or a welle, That drownythe the dowghty, and bryngethe hem abeere.

abietate ('æbɪəteɪt). *Chem.* [mod. f. L. *abiet-em* fir-tree + -ATE[4].] A salt of abietic acid.

abietene ('æbɪəti:n). [mod. f. L. *abiet-em* fir-tree + -ENE, repr. Gr. -ηνη, female descendant.] A hydro-carbon obtained by distillation of the resin or balsam of the nut-pine of California (*Pinus sabiniana*), analogous to oil of turpentine.
1875 URE *Dict. of Arts* I. 2 The commercial article is used under different names, abietene, crasine, theoline, &c. for the removal of paint from clothing and woven fabrics.. The vapour of abietene is a powerful anæsthetic when inhaled.

abietic (æbɪ'ɛtɪk), *a. Chem.* [f. L. *abiet-em* fir-tree + -IC.] Of or pertaining to fir. *abietic acid*, a monobasic acid, $C_{20}H_{30}O_2$, which is the essential constituent of resin.
1864 *Reader* No. 86. 239/3.

abietin(e ('æbɪətɪn). *Chem.* [f. L. *abiet-em* fir + -IN(E, repr. Gr. -ινη, female descendant.] A neutral resin extracted from Strasburg turpentine or Canada balsam, products of two species of *abies*, or fir.

abietinic (æbɪə'tɪnɪk), *a. Chem.* [ABIETIN + -IC.] Of or pertaining to abietin. *abietinic acid*, a bibasic resinous acid, $C_{44}H_{64}O_5$, obtained from species of fir.

abietite ('æbɪətaɪt). *Chem.* [mod. f. L. *abiet-em* fir + -ITE, chem. formative.] A saccharine substance $C_6H_8O_3$, obtained from the needles of the silver-fir, analogous to mannite.

abigail ('æbɪgeɪl). [From the name of the 'waiting gentlewoman' in Beaumont and Fletcher's popular play of *The Scornful Lady*; so named possibly in allusion to the expression 'thine handmaid' so frequently applied to herself by Abigail the Carmelitess, *1 Sam.* xxv. 24–31; but Bible names were common at this date without any special allusion.] A waiting-woman; a lady's-maid.
1666 PEPYS *Diary* IV. 195 By coach to the King's play-house, and there saw 'The Scornful Lady' well acted; Doll Common doing Abigail most excellently, and Knipp the widow very well. **1693** CONGREVE *Old Bachelor* III. vi. (1866) 157 Thou art some forsaken Abigail we have dallied with heretofore. **1771** SMOLLETT *Humphry Clinker* (1815) 57 An antiquated Abigail, dressed in her lady's cast clothes. **1849** LYTTON *Caxtons* XIV. vi. 370 (1875) The woman was dressed with a quiet neatness that seemed to stamp her profession as that of an abigail—black cloak with long cape, of that peculiar silk which seems spun on purpose for ladies' maids. **1864** DUKE OF MANCHESTER *Court & Soc. Eliz. to Anne* I. 81 Her house remained full of dons and pages, ladies and abigails.

abigailship ('æbɪgeɪlʃɪp). [f. prec. + -SHIP.] The estate or condition of a waiting-woman.
1803 JANE PORTER *Thaddeus* (Warne) 72 The appellation 'Mistress' put her in mind of her *ci-devant* abigailship.

†'**abigate**, *v. Obs. rare*$^{-1}$. [Irreg. f. L. *abig-ĕre* (f. *ab* off, away + *agĕre* to drive) + -ATE[3].] To drive away.
1657 TOMLINSON *Renou's Dispens.* 282 Whose faculties are inferiour to no medicament in abigating diseases.

abigge, obs. form of ABYE *v.*

†**abiliment.** Also 5 **ablement**, 7 **abillement**; Sc. 5– **abulȝement, abuilyment.** Obs. form of HABILIMENT, used in all the senses, but esp. in those of warlike munitions and accoutrements, things which fitted out or made able for war. See ABLE.
1422 *Surrender of Market of Meaux* in Rymer *Fœdera* (1710) X. 212 All the ablements of Werre. **1557** MORE *Richard III* (1641) 414 K. Richard being furnished with men and all abiliments of war. **1589** K. JAMES VI in Ellis *Orig. Lett.* II. 228. II. 29 Havinge directit the beraris.. marchandis of Edinburgh, toward London for bying and provision of certaine abulȝementis. **1605** CAMDEN *Remaines* 171 With harnesse and abillements of warre. **1830** SCOTT *Leg. Montrose* vi. 181 I must go down, look after my war-saddle and abuilziements [*z printed for* ȝ].

†**abilitate**, *v.* [obs. f. HABILITATE, q.v., the *h* being dropped, as in ABILITY.] To give ability or fitness; to enable. See ABLE.
1627 SIR J. COOK in Rushworth's *Hist. Coll.* (1659) I. 502 Necessity hath no law, you must abilitate the state to do.

†**abilitation** [obs. f. HABILITATION, q.v., the *h* being dropped, as in prec.] A rendering fit or able, a communication of ability. See ABLE.
c **1656** BP. HALL *Soliloquies* 47 Thou.. vouchsafest to give me an abilitation to the work.

ability (ə'bɪlɪtɪ). Forms: 4 **ablete**, 5 **abilite, habylite**, 5–6 **abletee, abilte, habilite**, 6 **habilitye, abilite, -ti, abylyte, abilyte, abylite**, 6–7 **habilitie, hability, abilitie**, 7– **ability.** [a. OFr. *ableté*:—L. *habilitāt-em*, n. of quality f. *habilis*: see ABLE and -TY. The Fr. was in 4–5 refashioned after L., as *habilité, habileté*, and was followed by the Eng., though the initial *h* was probably never sounded, and after a long struggle on the part of scholars like More, Ascham, Sidney, Hooker, Bacon, Browne, etc., to preserve this written link with L., it finally disappeared before 1700.]
†**1.** Suitableness, fitness, aptitude. *Obs.*
c **1380** WYCLIF *Of Confessions* Wks. 1880, 331 If his ablete shulde be proued.. before he were accepted. **1430** LYDGATE *Chron. Troy* II. xvii, She entre maye the relegyon Of myghty Bachus for habylite. **1509** FISHER *Eng. Wks.* 290 Grete abletees of nature to noble dedes. **1570** DEE *Math. Præf.* 18 Skillfull habilitу, also, for any occasion or purpose. **1622** FOTHERBY *Atheomastix* II. i. §6. 181 The habilitie and capacitie of the matter. **1678** MARVELL *Def. John Howe* Wks. 1875 IV. 187 A faculty conserved.. includes no such hability and present promptitude in itself to action.
2. The quality in an agent which makes an action possible; suitable or sufficient power (generally); faculty, capacity (*to do* or *of doing* something).
c **1391** CHAUCER *Astrolabe* I, I have perceived well by certeyne evidinces thine abilite to lerne sciences. *c* **1535** MORE *Debell. Salem & Byzance* Wks. 1557, 1000/1 Yf the onely power and habilitie to fain, wer a cause sufficient. **1551** ROBINSON *More's Utopia* 13 Though I be of muche lesse habilitie to do any thinge. **1570–87** HOLINSH. *Scot. Chron.* (1806) II. 340 We are not of habilitie.. to indure sa greit and intollerabil panis. **1594–1600** HOOKER *Serm.* iii. Wks. 1617, 729 Furnished with habilitie to annoy. **1605** TIMME *Quersitanus* I. iv. 13 The which habilitie of taking forme is in the subject. **1636** HEALEY *Cebes* 156 A better Hability to have goodnesse infused into them. **1651** *Life of Father Sarpi* (1676) 19 The fame of his prudence and hability of government. **1711** F. FULLER *Medic. Gymn.* 11 The Body of Man.. acquires by frequent Motion an Ability to last the longer. **1860** TYNDALL *Glaciers* II. §17. 323 The glacier of the Rhone.. its ability to expand laterally is increased.
b. The action itself, a thing within one's ability.
1602 SHAKS. *Oth.* III. iii. 2 Be thou assur'd, good Cassio, I will do All my abilities in thy behalfe.
c. Power to do a thing of legal validity; capacity in law.
1528 PERKINS *Prof. Booke* (1642) iii. §193. 86 Such persons are of ability in law to take liverie of seisin by force of feoffments of other men of abilities in law to make feoffments. **1649** SELDEN *Laws of Eng.* (1739) I. xxxvi. 55 The Canonists had in those days brought into custom other ages of ability in matters concerning Marriage.
3. Bodily power; strength. (Still common in Scotland.)
1549 J. OLDE tr. *Erasmus on Ephes.* II. 6, I being (as concerning myne owne habilitie) feble and weake. **1576** LAMBARDE *Peramb. Kent* (1826) 211 To lift a great stone easily Which before divers Lay persons could not stirre with all their strength and abilitie. **1607** TOPSELL *Four-footed Beasts* (1673) 137 Impudently begging and complaining of bodily weakness where is no want of ability. **1622** WITHER *Motto 'Nec Habeo'* (1633) 520 I have not found ability so much To carry milstones.
4. Pecuniary power; wealth, estate, means. *Obs.* exc. in a few phrases in which 'to give' is perhaps always mentally added.
1502 ARNOLD *Chron.* 84 Where as diuers periured fremen of smale abylite haue vsed and daily vse, to bye clothe and other marchaundises of England. **1526** TINDALE *Acts* xi. 29 Every man accordinge to his habilite. **1580** BARET *Alvearie* To be of abilitie: to liue like a gentleman. What abilitie or liuing is he of? or what may he dispende a yeere? **1601** SHAKS. *Twel. N.* III. iv. 378 Out of my leane and low ability Ile lend you something: my having is not much. **1665** MANLEY tr. *Grotius's Low Countrey Warres* 817 Upon most the fine exceeded their ability. **1729** BURKITT *On New Test.* Luke ii. 24 She was to bring a lamb of a year old for a burnt offering, in case she was a person of ability. **1766** GOLDSMITH *Vicar* xiv. A draught upon my neighbour was to me the same as money; for I was sufficiently convinced of his ability.
5. Mental power or capacity; talent, cleverness.
1604 SHAKS. *Oth.* III. iii. 247 Though it be fit that Cassio haue his Place For, sure, he fills it vp with great Ability. **1604** T. WRIGHT *Passions of the Mind* v. iii. 177 If a man haue not a good naturall habilitie, it is impossible by art to come to any perfection. **1650** BULWER *Anthropomet.* i. 6 The brain is not so figur'd as is requisite for wit and hability. **1794** SULLIVAN *View of Nat.* II. 154 A late ingenious writer, who has evidently studied his subject with ability and precision. **1858** BUCKLE *Civiliz.* I. vii. 427 La Fayette was no doubt inferior to Condorcet in point of ability. **1878** M. L.

HOLBROOK *Hygiene of the Brain* 3 The comparative ability of men is also an interesting subject.

6. A special power of the mind, a faculty. (Usually in *plural*.)

1587 GOLDING *De Mornay* xv. 237 Euery abilitie thereof is in . . the body, as much in one part as in another, as a whole soule in euery part; notwithstanding that euery seueral abilitie thereof seeme to be seuerally in some particuler member . . as the sensitiue ability seemeth to rest in the head, the irefull in the heart, and [the] quickning in the liuer. **1606** SHAKS. *Tr. & Cr.* I. iii. 179 All our abilities, gifts, natures, shapes. **1651** HOBBES *Leviathan* I. viii. 32 Such abilityes of the mind, as men praise. **1776** GIBBON *Decl. & Fall* I. xiii. 267 His abilities were useful rather than splendid. **1879** *Cassell's Techn. Educ.* IV. 130/1 Their natural abilities, combined with excellent taste.

†**a'bime.** *Obs.* The earliest form of ABYSM.

a **1300** *Cursor Mundi* 22678 Right unto þe abime fra heþen. **1616** DRUMM. OF HAWTH. *Wks.* 1711, 13/2 Feel such a case as one whom some abime [*other edd.* abisme] In the deep ocean kept had all his time.

‖**ab initio** (æb ɪˈnɪʃɪəʊ), *phr.* [L.] From the beginning; hence, as quasi-*adj.* = INITIAL *a.* A. 1.

1600 B. JONSON *Ev. Man out of Hum.* Prol., If those lawes . . had beene deliuered vs, *ab Initio*; and in their present vertue and perfection. **1767** H. WALPOLE *Lett.* (1843) Ser. I. let. cv. 344 It ought to have been declared null *ab initio*. **1817** COLERIDGE *Biog. Lit.* ix. 138 Assuming as a postulate, that both [*sc.* Truth and Being] are ab initio, identical and co-inherent. **1838** J. S. MILL *Diss. & Disc.* (1859) I. 349 He [*sc.* Bentham] begins all his inquiries by supposing nothing to be known on the subject, and reconstructs all philosophy *ab initio*. **1906** *Harmsworth Encycl.* VIII. 6011/2 If such legal right is abused, the act of trespass becomes an *ab initio* one. **1937** KIPLING *Something of Myself* viii. 207, I found that when, to save trouble, I 'wrote short' *ab initio* much salt went out of the work. **1943** T. HORSLEY *Find, Fix & Strike* 21 The Swordfish was used as an *ab-initio* trainer.

‖**ab intra** (æb ˈɪntrə), *phr.* [mod.L.] From within.

1672 T. JACOMB *Romans* v. 186 When 'tis [*sc.* sin] committed with little opposition *ab intra* and in spight of all opposition *ab extra*, I assure you then it hath a great power. **1805** COLERIDGE *Notebks.* (1962) II. 2444 The difference therefore between Fabrication and Generation becomes clearly indicable/the Form of the latter is ab intra, *evolved*, the other ab extra, *impressed*. **1859** J. MARTINEAU *Ess., Rev. & Addresses* (1891) III. 526 If we neither add anything to our premisses *ab extra*, nor draw anything *ab intra*, that was not comprised in them before, no new thing ever can appear.

abiogenesis (ˌæbɪəʊˈdʒɛnɪsɪs), *Biol.* [f. Gr. ἄβιος without life (f. ἀ priv. + βίος life) + γένεσις birth: see GENESIS.] The (supposed) origination or evolution of living organisms from lifeless matter without the action of living parents; 'spontaneous generation.' (Introduced by Prof. Huxley in addressing Brit. Assoc. at Liverpool, Sept. 1870.)

1870 HUXLEY in *Brit. Assoc. Rep.* lxxvi. To save circumlocution, I shall call . . the doctrine that living matter may be produced by not-living matter, the hypothesis of Abiogenesis. **1875** *Encyc. Brit.* (ed. 9) s.v., Abiogenesis, as a name for the production of living by not-living matter, has of late been superseding the less accurate phrase 'Spontaneous Generation.'

abiogenetic (ˌæbɪəʊdʒəˈnɛtɪk), *a.* *Biol.* [f. Gr. ἄβιος without life + γενητ-ός originated + -IC.] Of or pertaining to abiogenesis.

abiogenetically (ˌæbɪəʊdʒəˈnɛtɪkəlɪ), *adv.* *Biol.* [f. prec. + -AL[1] + -LY[2].] In an abiogenetic manner; by way of abiogenesis.

1875 HUXLEY in *Encycl. Brit.* (ed. 9) s.v. *Biology* 688 (also *Anat. Inv. An.* i. 36) Therefore they have been formed abiogenetically.

abiogenic (ˌeɪbaɪəʊˈdʒɛnɪk), *a.* [f. as ABIOGENESIS: see -GENIC.] Not derived from living organisms; occurring independently of life or life processes, but perhaps preceding or leading to them. Opp. BIOGENIC *a.* 2.

1891 *19th Cent.* Jan. 18 This method of creation may . . have been repeated . . with abiogenic germs. **1957** A. SYNGE tr. *Oparin's Orig. Life on Earth* (ed. 3) v. 153 During . . those many millions of years which separate the time of the formation of the Earth from the appearance of life on it, there took place the abiogenic, organic-chemical evolution of carbon compounds. **1968** *Proc. R. Soc.* B. CLXXI. 54 The land surface . . may have provided ideal conditions for the abiogenic synthesis of organic compounds. **1973** B. J. WILLIAMS *Evolution & Human Origins* vii. 94/1 The abiogenic production of organic molecules. **1983** *Precambrian Res.* XXIII. 1 (*heading*) Ancient microspheres: abiogenic, protobiogenic, or biogenic?

Hence **abioˈgenically** *adv.* = ABIOGENETICALLY *adv.*, ABIOTICALLY *adv.*

1965 *Proc. R. Soc.* A. CCLXXXVIII. 441 Many of the present-day biologically important molecules have been constructed abiogenically from the primeval atmosphere. **1971** *Nature* 10 Sept. 136/2 When life started, the principal mode of metabolism is thought to have been anaerobic fermentation of organic compounds which had formed abiogenically in the primaeval environment.

abiogenist (ˌæbɪˈɒdʒənɪst). *Biol.* [f. Gr. ἄβιος without life + -γεν-ής born, produced + -IST.] One who holds the hypothesis of abiogenesis.

1870 HUXLEY *Crit. & Addr.* (1873) x. 233 It has been a common objection of Abiogenists that, if the doctrine of Biogeny is true, the air must be thick with germs. **1877** *Echo* 22 Oct. 4/1 Except to the Abiogenists, or believers in spontaneous generation, the origin of the first protoplasmic mass is just as much a problem, whether it is fashioned from ordinary matter, or originates from matter infused and organised by a spiritual substance.

abiogenous (ˌæbɪˈɒdʒənəs), *a.* *Biol.* [f. Gr. ἄβιος without life + -γεν-ής born + -OUS.] Coming into existence without springing from antecedent living beings; produced by 'spontaneous generation.'

abiogeny (ˌæbɪˈɒdʒənɪ). [f. Gr. ἄβιος without life + -γένεια birth.] = ABIOGENESIS.

abiological (ˌæbɪəˈlɒdʒɪkəl, ˌeɪbaɪəʊ-), *a.* [f. Gr. ἀ not + BIOLOGICAL; cf. Gr. βίος life + λόγ-ος discourse + -ICAL.] Not pertaining to biology; pertaining to the study of inanimate things. Also, abiotic, inanimate.

1868 H. B. JONES *Croonian Lect.* ii. 63 In the abiological sciences the earliest ideas of matter were quite separate from the ideas of force. **1877** HUXLEY *Anat. Inv. An.* i. 1 The biological sciences are sharply marked off from the abiological, or those which treat of the phenomena manifested by not-living matter. **1970** *Nature* 14 Mar. 1029/1 Glycine and alanine are amino-acids most commonly synthesized in simulated primitive Earth (abiological) environments. **1981** G. PORTER in W. Palz et al. *Energy from Biomass* 672 We may seek to construct an abiological photosynthetic system.

abiotic (eɪbaɪˈɒtɪk), *a.* [f. A- *pref.* 14 + BIOTIC *a.*; cf. Gr. ἄβιος without life.] **a.** Characterized by the absence of life; inanimate. **b.** That is harmful to or destructive of living organisms.

1893 in DUNGLISON *Dict. Med. Sci.* **1950** F. D. HOWITT in *Brit. Encycl. Med. Practice* (ed. 2) I. 158 Ultra-violet rays between 1,894 Å and 2,900 Å are called abiotic rays, for they are inimical to life. **1952** *New Biol.* XII. 99 In abiotic times, such molecules, rich in free energy, might survive for long periods. **1961** J. KEOSIAN in *Encycl. Biol. Sciences* 672/2 Abiotic synthesis of organic compounds, first simple then complex, preceded the origin of life on earth.

Hence ˌ**abiˈotically** *adv.*, in an abiotic manner; without the involvement of living cells or organisms.

1952 *New Biol.* XIII. 125 N. H. Horowitz . . attributes the evolution of enzyme chains and cycles to an adaptive response to the using up of the limited stock of abiotically formed energy-rich molecules. **1970** *Nature* 5 Dec. 924/2 The discovery . . supports the hypothesis that the whole collection of amino-acids was produced abiotically. **1982** *Geol. Rundschau* LXXI. 1 (*heading*) Organic compounds in the early atmosphere formed abiotically from atomic carbon.

abirritant (æbˈɪrɪtənt), *a.* and *sb.* *Med.* [f. L. *ab* off, away + IRRITANT.] Any soothing agent which causes diminution of irritation.

1879 *Syd. Soc. Lex.*

abirritate (æbˈɪrɪteɪt), *v.* *Med.* [f. L. *ab* off, away + IRRITATE.] To cause diminution of irritation.

abirritation (æbˌɪrɪˈteɪʃən). *Med.* [f. L. *ab* off, away + IRRITATION.] A condition of the system opposite to that of irritation; a depressed condition of the various tissues.

1879 *Syd. Soc. Lex.*

abirritative (æbˈɪrɪteɪtɪv), *a.* *Med.* [f. L. *ab* off, away + IRRITATIVE.] Characterized by or due to abirritation.

[**abishering, abishersing** (Rastall), according to Spelman an error for *mishering, mishersing, miskering*, 'vox forensis, forensibus ipsis ænigmatica.' (Some confusion; a correspondent suggests MISKENNING, a flaw in pleading.)

1579 RASTELL *Expos. Termes Lawes, Abishersing* (and in some copyes Mishersing,) that is to be quite of amercementes before whom soeuer of transumption [ed. 1598 transgression] proued. **1610** FOLKINGHAM *Art of Survey* III. iv. 71 Abishersing, alias Mishersing, implies both forfaitures and Amerciaments of all transgressions within the Fee, and also the immunity from like penalties. **1672** MANLEY *Interpreter, Abishersing* (as *Rastal* in his *Abridgment* expounds it) is to be quit of Amerciaments before whomsoever of transgression proved. It is called in the *New Termes of Law, Mishersing*. **1696** PHILLIPS, Abishershing. **1706** PHILLPS, Abisherifing.]

Abissian, var. ABYSSINIAN.

abiston, abistos, obs. forms of ASBESTOS.

abit, obs. variant of OBIT *sb.*

abit, obs. 3rd sing. of ABIDE *v.*

abit(e, obs. form of HABIT.

abitacioun, obs. form of HABITATION.

†**a'bite**, *v.* *Obs.* [f. A- *pref.* 1 + BITE.] To bite, nip, taste.

c **1000** ÆLFRIC *Deut.* xxviii. 31 Man sliþþ þinne oxon beforan þé, and þú his ne abitst. **1205** LAYAMON III. 75 His cnihtes . . uuenon þan Brutten, Swulc heo heom wolden abiten. *a* **1250** *Owl & Night.* 77 Thu starest so thu wille abiten Al that thu miȝt mid clivre smiten. *c* **1300** *K. Alis.* 7096 (Weber I. 291) Broune lyons, and eke white, That wolden fayn his folk abyte. **1377** LANGL. *P. Pl.* B. xvi. 26 Windes . . in blowyng-tyme abite þe floures. *a* **1450** *Vox & Wolf* 203 (Hazl. *E.P.P.* I. 64) A thousent shep ich habbe abiten.

¶ Confused with ABYE.

c **1460** *Towneley Myst.* 15 We, yei, that shal thou sore abite.

†**a'bition.** *Obs.* [ad. L. *abitiōn-em* departure, death.] 'A going away or dying.' Blount 1656.

‖**Abitur** (æbiˈtuːr, -ˈʊə(r)). [Ger., abbrev. of *abiturium* (1881), f. mod.L. *abiturīre*: see ABITURIENT.] In Germany, an examination in a wide range of subjects taken in the final year of secondary school.

Successful candidates were formerly entitled to a university place; the examination now forms part of the selection process for universities and other centres of higher education.

[**1863**: see ABITURIENT. **1868** M. ARNOLD *Sch. & Univ. Cont.* xvii. 177 Leaving the public schools without undergoing the *Abiturientenexamen* there.] **1933** *Granta* 19 Apr. 358/1 Germany . . has a host of *Handelshochschulen*, *Technische Hochschulen* and others, which I have classed together as universities and as forming—with the *Abitur*-forms of the *Gymnasien* and *Realgymnasien*—a mainstay of active National Socialism. **1957** *Encycl. Brit.* X. 297/2 Various types of secondary school . . prepared pupils for entry to the universities or technical colleges by means of the *Abitur* examination taken at the age of 18 or 19. **1968** *Listener* 30 May 699/1 The *Abitur* (A-level) automatically entitles its holders to enter university. **1979** *Nature* 15 Nov. 231/1 Georg Wittig was born on 16 June, 1897 in Berlin and after his *Abitur* hesitated between chemistry or music. **1980** *Economist* 23 Aug. 41 Until the late 1960s the Abitur . . was a passport to automatic admission to university to study any subject.

abiturient (æbɪˈtjʊərɪənt). [G., ad. mod.L. *abiturient-*, pr. pple. of *abiturīre*, desiderative of *abīre* to go away.] In Germany, a pupil who is leaving a 'gymnasium' or high-school to enter a university. Also *attrib.*

1863 *Chambers's Encycl.* V. 168/2 The boys attend . . till they reach the age of 18, when, after a special examination (the abiturient or maturity examination), they are transferred to the university. **1868** M. ARNOLD *Sch. & Univ. Cont.* xvii. 179 The *Abiturient*, or leaving boy, must have been two years in *prima*. *Ibid.* 181 These *externi*, as they are called, are not examined along with the *Abiturienten* of the gymnasium. **1917** JEVONS in *Times Educ. Suppl.* 7 June 215 Examinations for which abiturient pupils may have to be prepared.

abject (ˈæbdʒɪkt), *ppl. a.* [ad. L. *abject-us*, pa. pple. of *abjĭcĕre* to cast off, throw away, f. *ab* off, away + *-jic-ĕre* = *jac-ĕre* to throw, cast. At first, like its L. original, a pple. and adj., accented *ab'ject*. After the formation of the vb. *abject*, it was gradually superseded in the ppl. use, by the regular form *abjected*, but remained as an adj. with shifted accent *'abject*, also from an early period used substantively.]

A. *pple.* and *adj.*

†**1.** *pple.* Cast off, cast out, rejected. *Obs.*

c **1430** LYDGATE *Bochas* (1554) II. i. 43 a, Thus was Saul . . Abiect from his royal see. **1509** BARCLAY *Shyp of Folys* I. 72 The Holy Bybyll grounde of trouthe and of lawe Is now of many abiect and nought set by. *c* **1585** *Faire Em* II. 388 I am abiect in those gracious eyes, That with remorse erst saw into my grief. **1614** W. BROWNE *Shepherd's Pipe* Wks. 1772 III. 16 Well worthy were it me to been abiect From all good company.

2. *adj.* Cast down, downcast, brought low in position, condition or estate, low-lying.

a **1520** *Myrroure of our Ladye* 52 And hir outwarde apparell was nat after the condicion of hir persone, but moch meke and abiecte. **1526** TINDALE *2 Cor.* vii. 6 He thatt comfortith the abiecte. **1671** MILTON *Samson* 169 To lowest pitch of abject fortune thou art fall'n. **1729** R. SAVAGE *The Wanderer* I. 399 Rains redundant flood the abject ground. **1742** WALPOLE *Lett. to H. Mann* 26 (1834) I. 112 I hope his state will grow more abject every day. **1840** MACAULAY *Essays, Clive* II. 502 Nothing more than a nominal dignity was left to the abject heirs of an illustrious name. **1854** S. DOBELL *Balder* xiii. 56 Lying most humbly weary and abject On the immoveable earth.

3. Down in spirit or hope; low in regard or estimation, degraded, mean-spirited, despicable.

1548 UDALL, etc. *Erasm. Paraph.* Matt. x. 19 Unlearned and abiecte men. **1593** SHAKS. *2 Hen. VI*, IV. i. 105 These paltry, seruile, abiect Drudges. **1642** SIR T. BROWNE *Relig. Med.* 163 I repute my self the most abjectest piece of mortality. **1771** SMOLLETT *Humphry Clinker* (1815) 91 I know nothing so abject as the behaviour of a man canvassing for a seat in parliament. **1849** MACAULAY *Hist. Eng.* I. 527 *note*, Howard was an abject liar. **1879** O'CONNOR *Ld. Beaconsfield* 554 Those who in adversity are the most abject, are in prosperity the most insolent.

B. *sb.* One cast off; a castaway, an outcast; a degraded person.

1534 MORE *Comforte agt. Tribulacyon* I. Wks. 1557, 1145/1 He is not an abiect, cast out of god's gracious fauour. **1582** T. BENTLEY *Monumt. Matrones* iii. 328 O almightie God: which raisest vp the abiects, and exaltest the miserable from the dunghill. **1611** BIBLE *Ps.* xxxv. 15 The abiects gathered themselues together against me. **1631** G. HERBERT *Temple, Sacrifice* 36 Servants and abjects flout me, they are witty. **1818** SHELLEY *Prom. Unbd.* III. iv, The subject of a tyrant's will Became, worse fate! the abject of his own. **1867** H. BUSHNELL *Dark Things* 57 What wonder that men have been deified and set up as idols of religious worship, when souls are only abjects to themselves.

†**abject** (æb'dʒɛkt), *v. Obs.* [f. prec., like *content* vb. from *content* adj. ABJECT continued to be used for some time as its pa. pple. but was gradually superseded by *abjected.*]

1. To cast off, throw off or away, cast out, exclude, reject, *lit.* and *fig.*; generally, though not always, as inferior, unworthy, or vile, and hence passing into the idea of casting down, degrading.

*c***1475** HENRYSON *Moral Fables* 42 Arguments they reuolue, some abiecting, and some can hald. **1509** BARCLAY *Ship of Fooles* (1570) 217 To learne the wayes his vices to abiect. **1534** *Polyd. Verg., Eng. Hist.* I. 89 The Brittaines.. abiecting the Romaine yoke, created him kinge. **1587** GASCOIGNE *Workes*; *Hearbes, Weedes* 287 A Lover being disdainfully abiected by a dame of high calling. **1611** SPEED *Hist. Gt. Brit.* IX. xxiv. 104 Dauid durst not touch Saul, though he was abiected by God. **1650** VENNER *Via Recta* 111 The Spawn of them is to be abjected.

2. To cast or throw down; hence *fig.* to lower, degrade, abase, debase.

1553 FOXE *A. & M.* (1596) 167/2 Such of the cleargie as abjected themselues to be underlings or servants. **1557** *Geneva N.T.* 1 Cor. iv. 10 *note*, In abiecting him selfe and exalting the Corinthians he maketh them ashamed of their vayne glorie. **1563** *Homilies* II. (1859) 445 A gross carnal feeding, basely abjecting and binding ourselves to the elements and creatures. **1604** T. WRIGHT *Passions of the Mind* v. §3. 181 The eye.. may be grauely eleuated vp to heuen or abiected to earth. **1630-40** DONNE *Serm.* ix. 22 What phrases of abjecting themselves in respect of the Prince, can exceed David's humble expressing of himself to Saul?

†**abjectate,** *v. Obs.* In Bailey vol. II. 1731, as a synonym of ABJECT *v.* Probably never used.

†**abjected** (æb'dʒɛktɪd), *ppl. a. Obs.* [f. ABJECT *v.* + -ED.] Cast off, rejected; cast down, dispirited.

1633 LD. BROOKE *Mustapha* Chorus 5. v. 158 Lift up the hopes of thy abjected Prophets. **1647** LILLY *Christian Astrology* lxxxiii. 449 The abjected [obtains] a Command or Office in some other Country.

†**ab'jectedness.** *Obs.* [f. prec. + -NESS.] Downcast condition; abasement, abject state or condition.

1660 BOYLE *Seraphic Love* 69 [Christ] from the height of Glory.. sunk Himself to the bottom of Abjectedness, to exalt our condition to the contrary extreme. **1694** LD. DELAMER *Wks.* 56 [James II] courted and even humbled himself to those very people whom before he would not admit into his presence, and with so much abjectedness made an offer of their Charter and Franchises of the City of London and other Corporations.

abjection (æb'dʒɛkʃən). [a. Fr. *abjection*, ad. L. *abjectiōn-em*, noun of action, f. *abject-* ppl. stem of *abjicĕre*: see ABJECT *a.*]

†**1.** The action of casting down; abasement, humiliation, degradation. *Obs.*

*c***1525** MORE *De quat. Nouiss.* Wks. 1557, 87/2 Suche humility contempt and abieccion of our self. **1608** CHAPMAN *Byrons Tragedie* Plays 1873 II. 312 He would be the death Of him he should die by, ere he sufferd Such an abiection. **1653** JER. TAYLOR *Serm.* xv. II. *Growth in Grace*, He reckons it no abjection to be abased in the face of man.

2. The condition or estate of one cast down; abasement, humiliation, degradation; downcastness, abjectness, low estate.

*c***1410** LOVE *Bonaventura's Speculum* (Gibbs MS.) viii. Ffor he wold þat his lownes and abieccioune were knowen. **1548** UDALL etc. *Erasm. Paraph.* S. Luke ix. 58 His lowe state of abjection in this world. **1576** LAMBARDE *Peramb. Kent* (1826) 362 Somewhat releeved from this penurie, nakednes, and abiection. **1594** HOOKER *Eccl. Pol.* (1632) v. 278 Basenesse, abjection of mind, or seruilitie. **1675** *Art of Contentment* III. §19. 191 Tho Christ seem the same to us in his glory which he did in his abjection. **1741** MIDDLETON *Cicero* (ed. 3) I. iv. 250 A base remissness and abjection of mind. **1879** M. ARNOLD *Equality* (Mixed Essays) 93 Who that has seen it can ever forget.. the abjection and uncivilisedness of Glasgow? **1881** F. P. COBBE *Duties of Women* 9 The women of Europe have never sunk to the abjection of the women of the East.

†**3.** The action of casting off or away; rejection.

1607 ROGERS *39 Articles* 62 The torments of hell, the second death, abjection from God. **1652** J. MAYER *Comment. on the Prophets* 63 The abjection of the Jews, [and] the receiving of the Gentiles. **1655** W. GOUGE *Comm. on the Hebrews* x. 2 The Arminian errour of excision or abscission, and abjection from Christ.

†**4.** That which is cast off or away; refuse, scum, dregs. Usually *fig.* of persons.

1447 BOKENHAM *Lyvys of Seyntys* (Roxb. Cl.) 124 Thou shalt of comoun bordel be the abjeccyoun. *c***1510** *Bonaventura's Myrrour* (Pynson) xiii. E ij, I am a worme and natte a man; reprefe of men and abjection of people. **1534** *Polyd. Verg., Eng. Hist.* I. 195 These dregges and abjection of all menn.

abjective (æb'dʒɛktɪv), *a. rare.* [f. L. *abject-* (see ABJECTION) + -IVE, as if from a L. **abjectīvus*, not found.] Tending to lower or demoralize.

1865 MAJ. NICHOLLS in *Pall Mall Gaz.* 23 Sept. 11/2 We saw then.. how abjective, in a moral sense, had been the terrible influence of these campaigns.

abjectly ('æbdʒɪktlɪ), *adv.* [f. ABJECT *a.* + -LY[2].] In an abject, mean, or degrading manner; basely.

1588 SHAKS. *Tit. And.* II. iii. 4 Him that thinks of me so abiectly. **1622** FOTHERBY *Atheomastix* II. xi.§6. 324 No man can be so abiectly minded, but he must needs know God to be the Governour of all things. **1851** HELPS *Friends in Council* I. 28 We must not abjectly bow down before rules and usages. **1859** DE QUINCEY *Caesars* Wks. X. 24 No mob could be more abjectly servile than was that of Rome.

abjectness ('æbdʒɪktnɪs). [f. ABJECT *a.* + -NESS.] Abject or downcast condition; depression, abasement, degradation, humiliation, servility.

1599 SANDYS *Europæ Speculum* (1632) 160 A timorous very base mindednesse and abjectnesse. **1682** BURNET *Rights of Princes* Pref. 96 By the abjectness of their stile. **1788** BURKE *Sp. agt. Warr. Hast.* Wks. XIII. 271 In this humiliation and abjectness of guilt, he comes here. **1870** LOWELL *Study Windows* 229 He could look to God without abjectness, and on man without contempt.

abjoint (æb'dʒɔɪnt), *v. Biol.* [f. AB- + JOINT *v.*] *trans.* To separate by formation of a joint or partition, as the cells and spores in certain fungi. So **ab'junction**, the process of such separation.

1887 GARNSEY tr. *K. Goebel's Outl. Classif. Plants* 83 The non-motile cells are the result of abjunction. *Ibid.*, The extremity of which [sterigmata].. enlarges, and is then abjointed as a gonidium. **1889** E. S. BASTIN *College Botany* 313 Conidia.. formed from hyphae by the separation of cells in succession from their free ends—a process called abjunction.

abjudge (æb'dʒʌdʒ), *v. rare.* [f. L. *ab* away + JUDGE *v.*; representing L. *abjūdicāre* in its classical sense: see ABJUDICATE.] To take away from any one by judicial decision; the opposite of *adjudge*.

1855 I. TAYLOR *Restoration of Belief* 155 Even if one of the three [pastoral Epistles of St. Paul] were abjudged it would still keep its place in argument as a good imitation of the apostolic manner.

†**abjudicate** (æb'dʒ(j)uːdɪkeɪt), *v. Obs.* [f. L. *abjūdicāt-* ppl. stem of *abjūdicā-re* to deprive one of a thing by judicial sentence; but taken in the sense of 'to decide against a thing.']

1. To pass judgment against; reject as illegal.

1602 FULBECKE *Pandectes* 27 Of the Emperour Constantine furtiue and priuy mariages are vtterly condemned and abiudicated: because it is against Christianitie. —— *The Second Part of the Parallele* 21 Our [canon] law doth not refuse or abiudicate the kinds of improper contractes.

2. = ABJUDGE *v.*

1775 ASH and subseq. Dicts.: n.q.

abjudication (æbˌdʒ(j)uːdɪ'keɪʃən). [n. of action f. ABJUDICATE: see -ION[1].] The action of abjudicating; rejection by judicial sentence.

1676 In BULLOKAR. **1818** In TODD. WORCESTER cites C. J. FOX; WEBSTER cites KNOWLES.

†'**abjugate,** *v. Obs.*—[0] [f. L. *abjugāt-* ppl. stem of *abjugā-re* to unyoke; f. *ab* off, from + *jugā-re* to yoke, f. *jug-um* a yoke.] 'To unyoke, to uncouple.' Bailey vol. II. 1731, whence in J.

†**ab'junct,** *ppl. a. Obs. rare*—[1]. [ad. L. *abjunct-us* unyoked, separated, pa. pple. of *abjungĕre*, f. *ab* off, from + *jung-ĕre* to yoke, join.] Disjoined, disconnected, severed.

1610 *Histrio-mastix* I. 89 That knowledge (that considers things) Abjunct from sencive matter, is exacter Then that which joynes it selfe with elements.

abjunctive (æb'dʒʌŋktɪv), *a. rare.* [f. L. *abjunct-* ppl. stem (see above) + -IVE; as if from a L. **abjunctīv-us*, analogous to *conjunctīv-us*, *adjunctīv-us*, but not found.] Of a disconnected or isolated character; exceptional.

1832 I. TAYLOR *Saturday Evg.* (1833) 270 It is this power which leads on always from the less perfect, towards the more perfect;—from the accidental and abjunctive, to the universal.

abjuration (ˌæbdʒ(j)ʊ'reɪʃən). [ad. L. *abjūrātiōn-em*, n. of action f. *abjūrā-re*: see ABJURE.]

1. Renunciation on oath; forswearing (particularly of heretical opinions).

1514 FITZHERBERT *Justyce of Pea.* (1538) 106 Yf any person hereafter arrayned.. alledge.. upon abjuracyon made.. the issue shall be tried furthwith before the same justices. **1532** MORE *Confut. of Barnes* VIII. Wks. 1557, 789/2 Now frere Barns in one of the articles which was layed agaynste hym at his abiurasion. **1655** FULLER *Ch. Hist.* IX. 176 Iohn Hilton Priest, made a solemn Abjuration of his blasphemous heresies. **1661** PAGITT *Heresiog.* 106 The abjuration of certain Familists at Pauls Crosse. **1839** W. IRVING *Chron. Wolfert's Roost* (1855) 129 To avoid the sneers and jests of the Parisian public, the ceremony of abjuration took place at Melun. **1856** FROUDE *Hist. Eng.* II. 21 Prisoners who refused to abjure their errors, who persisted in heresy, or relapsed into it after abjuration, were sentenced to be burnt at the stake.

2. *fig.* Solemn or formal renunciation or giving up of anything.

1669 *Survey of Napthali* II. 113 An abjuration of part of the Churches Christian liberty. **1842** H. ROGERS *Introd. to Burke's Wks.* 71 To demand an abjuration of all friendship with those who in any measure favoured it.

3. An official repudiation upon oath of any principle ecclesiastical or political, as the supremacy of the pope, the claims of the house of Stuart.

1650 JOHN ROW (son) *Hist. Kirk Scot.* (1842) 540 Supposing that Episcopacie were indifferent in itselfe to be used or refused yet I am sworne against it, and my abjuration of it will be called a sin or a dutie. *a***1674** CLARENDON *Hist. Reb.* III. XVI. 558 That no person whatsoever might be admitted to the exercise of any Office or Function in the State or in the Church, who did not first take the Oath of Abjuration of the King, and of all his Family. **1726** AYLIFFE *Parergon* 15 An abjuration of some Doctrines of the Church of Rome.

Hence ***Oath of Abjuration***, i.e. disclaiming any right to the crown of England on the part of descendants of the Pretender: imposed by 13 William III. c. 6; 1 Geo. I. c. 13; 6 Geo. III. c. 53: now superseded by a new form of the Oath of Allegiance.

1708 SWIFT *Sacram. Test.* II. I. 137 Leading teachers in the north, who having refused the abjuration oath, yet continue their preaching. **1726** AYLIFFE *Parergon* 15 There is likewise another Oath of Abjuration, which Laymen and Clergymen are both oblig'd to take; and that is to abjure the Pretender. **1863** COX *Inst. of Eng. Gov.* I. viii. 128 Three oaths were required to be taken by members of Parliament. These oaths were—the oath of allegiance, of supremacy, and abjuration. **1878** LECKY *Eng. in 18th Cent.* II. vii. 403 Who refused to take the abjuration oath.

4. ***abjuration of the realm, a town***, etc.: an oath taken to leave it for ever.

1592-3 *Act 35 Eliz. cap.* 1 Euery such offender.. shall departe out of this Realme at such Hauen or Port.. as shall be assigned and appointed by the sayd Justices before whom such abiuration shall be made. **1622** R. CALLIS *Statute of Sewers* (1647) 188 Butchers are to be abjured the Town, if they offend the fourth time in selling measled flesh; and this is a special Abjuration. **1691** BLOUNT *Law Dict.*, Abjuration, a forswearing or renouncing by Oath; a sworn banishment, or an Oath taken to forsake the Realm for ever. **1726** AYLIFFE *Parergon* 15 In the 8th of Edward II. an Abjuration is a Divorce between Husband and Wife. **1768** BLACKSTONE *Comm.* IV. 370 Some punishments consist in exile or banishment, by abjuration of the realm, or transportation to the American colonies.

abjure (æb'dʒ(j)ʊə(r)), *v.* Also 6 **abjowre.** [a. Fr. *abjure-r* (in Palsgr.), ad. L. *abjūrā-re* to deny on oath, f. *ab* away + *jūrā-re* to swear.]

1. To renounce on oath; to retract, recant, or abnegate (a position or opinion formerly held).

a. *trans.*

1501 *Will of John Bawde* in *Bury Wills* 83 (1850) Alle tho wyllys abieured and revokyd byfor thys day mad. **1528** MORE *Dial. Heres.* I. Wks. 1557, 108/2 He was forced to forswere and abiure certaine heresyes. **1610** SHAKS. *Temp.* v. i. 51 But this rough Magicke I heere abjure. **1774** BURKE *Sp. on Amer. Tax.* Wks. II. 379 The principle which lord Hillsborough had abjured. **1829** SOUTHEY *Young Dragon* iii. Wks. VI. 274 My pagan faith I put away, Abjure it and abhor it. **1871** R. W. DALE *Ten Commandts.* vi. 155 I must die rather than abjure a single article of my creed.

b. *absol.*

1528 MORE *Dial. Heres.* IV. Wks. 1557, 282/1 Nor neuer yet found I ani. j. but he would once abiure, though he neuer intended to kepe his othe. **1531** *Dial. on Laws of Eng.* II. xxix. 115 (1638) If a man be convict of heresy and abjure, hee hath forfeit no goods. **1538** BALE *Thre Lawes* 1773 Wylt thu here abiure or no? I wyll neyther abiure, nor yet recant Gods glorye.

†**2.** *causally.* To cause to forswear or recant (heresies, etc.). *Obs.*

1480 CAXTON *Chron. Eng.* VII. 159b/2 (1520) Reynold Pecoke bysshop of Chestre was founde an herytyke, and the thyrde daye of Decembre was abjured at Lambeth. **1494** FABYAN VII. ccxliv. 286 Almaricus, a studyent of Parys, helde sertayne opynyons of heresy, of y[e] which whan he was abiured, he tooke suche thought y[t] he dyed shortly after. **1528** MORE *Dial. Heres.* III. Wks. 1557, 216/2 Considering that they might, as in conclusion they did, abiure him otherwise. **1536-42** THYNNE *Animadv.* App. I And then all such must be burned, or ellis ab-Iuryd.

3. To disclaim solemnly or formally; to repudiate or reject upon oath (a claim or claimant).

1597 DANIEL *Civ. War* IV. xxix, The foule report Of that assasinate: which utterly He doth abjure. **1665** MANLEY tr. *Grotius's Low-Countrey-Warrs* 183 To abjure all Authority over the Netherlands. **1667** MILTON *P.L.* VIII. 480 To find her, or for ever to deplore Her loss, and other pleasures all abjure. **1799** T. JEFFERSON *Writings* IV. 301 (1859) I sincerely join you in abjuring all political connection with every foreign power. **1851** MACAULAY *Essays, Milton* I. 15 While they abjured the innocent badges of popery. **1863** COX *Inst. Eng. Govt.* I. viii. 128 The oath prescribed for abjuring the Pretender and his descendants. **1876** FREEMAN *Norm. Conq.* I. v. 381 The assembly abjured the whole house of Æthelred. **1877** MOZLEY *Univ. Serm.* i. 3 [The Christianity of the Gospel] abjures force, it throws itself upon moral influence for its propagation and maintenance.

b. *absol.*

1671 MILTON *P.R.* I. 473 Say and unsay, feign, flatter, and abjure.

4. ***to abjure the realm, town, commonwealth***, etc.: to swear to abandon it for ever.

1530 PALSGR. 415 I abjowre, I forsake myne errours, as an heretyke dothe, or forswere the kynges landes; *Je abjure.* **1576** LAMBARDE *Peramb. Kent* (1826) 497 If he take Sanctuarie, and do abiure the Realme. **1609** SIR J. SKENE *Reg. Mag.* 155 Gif any man hes abjured the towne (sworne to passe forth of the burgh) and is returned agaime. **1651** W. G. tr. *Cowel's Inst.* 274 He who kills Deere, and cannot finde security to put in for the payment of the Fine imposed, is compelled to abjure the Common-wealth. **1677** HOBBES *Dial. on Com. Laws Eng.* 183 When a Clerk heretofore was convicted of Felony, he might have saved his life by abjuring the Realm; that is, by departing the Realm within a certain time appointed, and taking an Oath never to return. **1768** BLACKSTONE *Comm.* IV. 399 Even while abjurations were in force, such a criminal was not allowed to take sanctuary and abjure the realm.

b. *absol.*

1726 AYLIFFE *Parergon* 14 Whoever was not capable of this Sanctuary, could not have the Benefit of Abjuration: and therefore, he that committed Sacrilege could not abjure.

†**5.** *causally.* To cause one to forswear the realm, to banish. *Obs.*

1603 DRAYTON *Barons Warres* I. xv, T' abjure those false Lords from the troubled Land. **1655** FULLER *Ch. Hist.* III. 90 He was onely abjured the Realm for ever. **1709** STRYPE *Ann. Ref.* xxvi. 269 His life was pardoned; notwithstanding he was abjured the realm.

abjured (æb'dʒ(j)ʊəd), *ppl. a.* [f. prec. + -ED.]

†**1.** *actively.* That has abjured or renounced heresy, etc.; recanted. *Obs.*

1533 MORE *Apology* xxxv. Wks. 1557, 899/1 Bayfielde the monke and apostata, that was an abiured, and after periured and relapsed heretyke, [was] well and woorthelye burned in Smithfielde.

2. *passively.* Sworn against; repudiated on oath.

c **1746** HERVEY *Meditations* (1818) 203 If an abjured pretender had cut his way to our throne.

†**ab'jurement.** *Obs. rare*⁻¹. [f. ABJURE *v.* + -MENT.] The process of abjuring; abjuration, renunciation.

1646 J. HALL *Poems* Pref., Such sinnes as these are veniall in youth; especially if expiated with timely abjurement.

abjurer (æb'dʒ(j)ʊərə(r)). [f. ABJURE *v.* + -ER¹.] One who abjures or forswears; one who solemnly repudiates or gives up.

1777 SHERIDAN *Sch. Scand.* III. iii, What man can pretend to be a believer in love, who is an abjurer of wine?

‖**abkari** (ɑːb'kɑːrɪ). Also **abkary, abcaree, aubkaury.** [a. Pers. *āb-kār* water (liquor)-business, a distillery, with connecting particle *-i-*.] The manufacture or sale of spirituous liquors; hence in Anglo-Indian, the excise duty levied upon such manufacture and sale. (Col. Yule.)

1797 *Bengal Regulations* x. 33 The stamps are to have the words 'Abcaree licenses' inscribed in the Persian and Hindee languages and character. **1857** *Calcutta Rev.* Dec. 282 The Abkari settlement is made..in the following manner.

Abkhasian (æb'keɪʃ(ɪ)ən; also -zɪən, -ʒən), *a.* and *sb.* Also **Abkhazian.** [f. *Abkhasia* (see def.) + -AN.] **A.** *adj.* Of or pertaining to the U.S.S.R. territory of Abkhasia in the Caucasus. **B.** *sb.* One of the Abkhasian people; also, the language of this people.

1845 *Encycl. Metrop.* XV. 609/1 The whole of the north-eastern coast from the mouths of the Kúban to the Sokhúm, the boundary of Mingrelia, is occupied by the Abkhasians. **1867** *Cornhill Mag.* Oct. 504 Of the early history of the Abkhasian race little is known...Records are wanting among a people who have never committed their vocal sounds to writing; they know that they are Abkhasians, and nothing more. **1876** *Encycl. Brit.* V. 258/2 Petty expeditions against the Circassian and Abkhasian tribes. **1879** *Ibid.* X. 433/1 Uslar's 'Caucasian Family' comprises the following three great divisions: 1. Western Group. Typical races: Tcherkessians and Abkhasians. **1959** E. H. CARR *Socialism in One Country* II. IV. xx. 265 The constitutional anomaly of the region was the Abkhazian republic occupying a small coastal strip on the Black Sea.

Abkhaz (æb'hɑːz, ‖ap'xas), *sb.* (and *a.*) Also **Abkhas.** [Prob. ad. Russ. *abkhazskiĭ*, perh. ult. f. Arab.; the people's name for themselves is *apshua.*] (A member of) the Abkhasian people; their language. Also *attrib.* or as *adj.*

1838 *Penny Cycl.* XI. 177/2 The *Abases*, or Abkhases, occupy Abasia proper. **1845** *Encycl. Metrop.* XIX. 532/1 The territory of the Abkhasses. **1956** J. LOTZ in Saporta & Bastian *Psycholinguistics* (1961) 5/1 Abkhaz, a language of the Caucasus, uses both tongue-raising and lip-rounding in its impressive array of palatalized, labialized, and labio-palatalized consonants. **1957** *Encycl. Brit.* I. 48/2 Abkhazia ..was the home of the Abkhaz (Apkhaz) tribe (in Abkhaz *Apsua*, in Greek *Abasgoi*). **1960** *Encycl. Islam* (ed. 2) I. 100/2 The Abḵhāz are mentioned in ancient times as *Abasgoi* (by Arrian) or *Abasgi* (by Pliny). **1972** *Language* XLVIII. 845 He attributes such systems to Caucasian languages, viz. Abkhaz and Adyge. **1975** *Nature* 6 Nov. 41/3 The environment but not the diet resembles that of Abkhasia, where longevity is reportedly geographic rather than specifically ethnic, affecting Russians, Abkhases and Jews who live in the area.

†**ablactate** (æb'lækteɪt), *v. Obs. rare*⁻⁰. [f. L. *ablactāt-* ppl. stem of *ablactā-re* to wean; f. *ab* off + *lactāre* to suckle; f. *lac, lact-*, milk.] 'To wean from the breast.' J.

ablactation (ˌæblæk'teɪʃən). [ad. L. *ablactātiōn-em*, n. of action f. *ablactāre*; see ABLACTATE.]

1. The weaning of a child, or the young of quadrupeds, from the mother.

1656 BLOUNT *Glossog.*, *Ablactation*, a weaning, as children from the Mother's Teat. **1666** J. SMITH *Solomon's Portr. Old Age* (1752) 74 The time of ablactation of the child is indicated by the beginning of the use of the teeth. **1841** COCKBURN *Jeffrey* II. Let. 157 The consequences of too sudden and peremptory an ablactation. **1863** BURTON *Abeokuta* I. 45 In Northern Europe ablactation begins when the milk teeth appear.

2. *Hort.* The process of grafting (trees), also called inarching.

1676 J. REA *Flora* 195 Called grafting by Approach, by some Ablactation. **1681** WORLIDGE *Syst. Agric.* 321 Ablactation is one of the ways of Grafting; that is, weaning the Cion by degrees from its mother. **1763** MILLER *Gard. Dict. Abridged* s.v. *Grafting*, Grafting by approach or ablactation..is to be performed in the month of April. **1802** W. FORSYTH *Fruit Trees* xxii. 311 (1824) Grafting by approach, or ablactation when the stock..and the tree from which you take your graft, stand so near together that they may be joined.

†**a'blacted,** *ppl. a. Obs.*⁻⁰. 'Weaned.' Cockeram 1612.

abland, *ppl. a. Obs.* See ABLIND.

†**a'blandishment.** *Obs. rare*⁻¹. [The prefix *a-* is prob. suggested by Sp. *ablandar* to blandish.] Blandishment.

1728 MORGAN *Hist. Algiers* II. iv. 283 He began to call by their names some of his favourite Renegadoes, intreating them to give admittance to him. All these ablandishments little availed.

†**a'blaqueate,** *v. Obs. rare*⁻¹. [f. L. *ablaqueāt-* ppl. stem of *ablaqueā-re* to disentangle, loosen (the earth round roots); f. *ab* off, away + *laqueā-re* to entangle, f. *laqueus* a noose.] To loosen or remove the soil round the roots of trees, so as to let their fibres spread out. A term of Roman husbandry.

c **1420** *Palladius on Husb.* IV. 91 A better way for hem I wol declare: Ablaquiate hem deep or make hem bare. **1721** BAILEY, *Ablaqueate*, To uncover the roots of trees. [So in later Dicts.]

†**a'blaqueation.** *Obs.* [ad. L. *ablaqueātiōn-em*, n. of action f. *ablaqueā-re*: see prec.] The breaking up or removal of the soil around the roots of trees; the laying bare of roots.

c **1420** *Palladius on Husb.* II. 1 Alle Januerie ablaqueacion The vynes axe in places temporate. *a* **1600** ? LAMBARDE *Office of Alienations*, If it be suffered to starve by want of ablaqueation and other good husbandry. **1664** EVELYN *Kal. Hort.* (1729) 190 Dig borders, &c. Uncover, as yet, roots of trees where ablaqueation is requisite. **1725** BRADLEY *Fam. Dict.* s.v. *Fir tree*, They abhor all stercoration, nor will they endure much to have the earth opened about their roots for ablaqueation. [JOHNSON 1755 and in later Dicts.]

†**a'blast,** *v. Obs.* [OE. *onblæst-an*, f. *on* on, in + *blæst-an* to blast, blow.] To blow upon or at.

1393 GOWER *Conf. Am.* II. 251 Venim and fire togider he cast, That he Iason so sore ablast.

ablastemic (ˌæblæ'stɛmɪk), *a.* [f. Gr. ἀ priv. + βλάστημ-ος growth + -IC.] Not connected with germination; non-germinal.

1881 *Nature* XXIII. 277 There exists in the almond tribe ..another form [of asparagin] apparently not having any physiological connection with the other [blastemic asparagin], which may be referred to as ablastemic.

ablastous (ə'blæstəs), *a. rare*⁻⁰. [f. Gr. ἀ priv. + βλαστ-ός sprout, offspring + -OUS. Cf. mod.Fr. *ablaste.*] Without germ or bud; unfruitful.

1879 *Syd. Soc. Lex.*

a'blate, *v.* [f. L. *ablāt-* ppl. stem of *aufer-re* to carry away; f. *ab* off, away + *fer-re*, pa. pple. *lāt-um*, to bear.] **a.** To take away, remove. In mod. use *spec.* by ablation. *Obs.* in general sense; in modern use as back-formation from ABLATION.

1542 BOORDE *Dyetary* (1870) xxi. 284 Althoughe the skynnes or huskes be ablated, or cast away. **1606** WARNER *Albion's Eng.* XV. xcv. 379 A conquest though it much addes, alters, and ablates. **1902** *Encycl. Brit.* XXXI. 744 When the cerebral hemispheres have been ablated. **1923** *Times Lit. Suppl.* 16 Aug. 541/1 The low sun..evaporates or 'ablates' the ice continually. **1974** *Nature* 8 Nov. 94/1 Rockets can only pick up the micrometeroids after they have been retarded by the atmosphere and contaminated by meteoric dust ablated from larger meteoroids.

b. *Astr.* and *Astronautics. trans.* To erode by ablation.

1952 *Astrophys. Jrnl.* CXVI. 203 In the meteor work.. only the parameter (where Γ is the retardation coefficient and ζ the energy to ablate unit mass of meteor material).. could be determined from the observations. **1959** *Dublin Evening Press* 8 June 5/6 The nose cone is covered with several layers of tough plastic highly resistant to temperature. As the cone falls back through the atmosphere, the layers of plastic are eroded, or 'ablated', off in turn, but they achieve their ultimate object of protecting the cone's main substance. **1978** *Sci. Amer.* Mar. 84/2 Even though the atmosphere of Mars is thin, it is dense enough to ablate and break up small incoming meteoroids before they reach the surface.

c. *intr.* To undergo ablation; to lose mass as a result of heating produced by friction.

1960 *Jrnl. Aero/Space Sci.* XXVII. 539/1 The total radiation..was measured as the model ablated in the arc tunnel. **1963** *Jrnl. Geophysical Res.* LXVIII. 4329/1 At sufficiently low pressures, tektite glass ablates without producing any ring waves. **1974** *Nature* 26 Apr. 811/2 Some australites starting quite spherical ablate to characteristic button-like shapes.

Hence **a'blating** *vbl. sb.* and *ppl. a.*; **a'blated** *ppl. a.*

1959 W. A. HEFLIN *Aerospace Gloss.* 1/1 For hypersonic reentry bodies, ablating materials must handle temperatures in surrounding air up to 15,000° F. *Ibid.*, *Ablating nose cone*, a nose cone designed to prevent heat transfer to its internal structure by the use of an ablating material. **1961** J. F. VEDDER in F. S. Johnson *Satellite Environment Handbk.* v. 97 Most meteoritic material, by the time it reaches the Earth's surface, has been reduced to dust or to spherules of ablated material in its passage through the atmosphere. **1980** *Nature* 1 May 12/2 Excited atoms and molecules emit radiation and the luminous power so produced has been found to be proportional to the rate of loss of kinetic energy of the ablated atoms.

ablation (æ'bleɪʃən). [ad. L. *ablātiōn-em* a carrying away, n. of action, f. *ablāt-* ppl. stem of *aufer-re*: see prec. Cf. Fr. *ablation* used in sense 2.]

1. The action or process of carrying away or removing; removal. *spec.* Gradual removal *of* superficial material (cf. senses 4, 5).

1577–87 HARRISON *England* I. II. i. 37 (1877) The decaies and ablations seene and practised at this present. **1598** HAKLUYT *Voyages* I. 148 Marchants haue sustained sundry damages and ablations of their goods. **1677** GALE *Court of Gent.* II. IV. 261 Physic mutation is by Addition or Ablation and Substraction of some real Entitie. **1687** H. MORE *App. to Antidote* (1712) 227 In the real ablations of Witches and Magicians, when they happen. **1981** *N.Y. Times* 26 Apr. VI. 86/1 It is this ablation of incandescent material from such a meteorite that leaves the traditional fiery trail across the night sky.

†**2.** *Med.* The removal or subsidence of the acute symptoms of a disease; cessation, remission. *Obs.*

1651 NOAH BIGGS *New Dispens.* 76. §120 It doth naturally betoken the ablation of it. **1671** SALMON *Syn. Medic.* III. xxxvi. 514 If in the ablation of the disease, there be not a.. reparation of the strength, the sick may dye. **1831** HOOPER *Med. Dict.* 4 *Ablation*, in some old writings, expresses the interval betwixt two fits of a fever, or the time of remission.

3. *Surg.* The removing or taking away of any part of the body by mechanical means.

1846 J. MILLER *Pract. of Surg.* xxvi. 350 There is safety in nothing short of summary ablation—not only of the nipple itself, but of the mamma also. **1872** COHEN *Dis. of the Throat* 207 [He] succeeded in the ablation of one of these polyps by means of a metallic nail attached to a thimble.

4. a. [In this sense a. F. *ablation* (L. Agassiz 1842, in *Compt. Rend.* XV. 285).] *Geol.* The wearing away or superficial waste of a glacier by surface melting, or of a rock by the action of water. In mod. use, the surface loss of snow or ice as a result of melting and evaporation.

1842 *Edin. New Philos. Jrnl.* XXXIII. 400 M. Agassiz then notices his observations relative to the glacier itself... The ablation of the surface, resulting from the melting and the evaporation, has also been more considerable at the centre than at the edges. **1860** TYNDALL *Glaciers* II. §32. 418 The ablation of the ice must be less than what is generally supposed. **1863** J. BALL *Guide to West. Alps* Introd. 70 The vast amount of ablation, or loss, which a glacier annually undergoes through the melting of the surface. **1942** C. A. COTTON *Climatic Accidents in Landscape-Making* xi. 138 'Ice falls'.., often with crowded ridges and pinnacles sharpened by ablation. **1960** B. W. SPARKS *Geomorphol.* xii. 267 In these marginal regions, there must be a constant struggle between the tendency of the ice sheet to advance as it is slowly supplied with ice from the highlands, and the tendency for ablation to cause the ice front to recede. **1978** *Nature* 5 Jan. 50/1 An iceberg's underwater shape clearly affects its stability, with most of an iceberg's ablation occurring beneath the waterline.

b. The removal of sand or salt from a surface by the action of the wind.

1961 L. D. STAMP *Gloss. Geogr. Terms* 1/2 Some recent writers refer to ablation of sandy areas by wind. **1962** *Special Stud. Utah Geol. & Mineral. Survey* II. 3 At the time that the salt reposed in the central part of the basin, the eastern side had risen to the point that it began to suffer wind ablation. **1965** A. HOLMES *Princ. Physical Geol.* (ed. 2) xxii. 751 The base-level for wind action is that of the water table, which may be far below sea-level. The 'pans' of S. Africa.. and the depressions of the N. African and Mongolian deserts, have all been excavated by ablation.

5. *Astr.* and *Astronautics.* The loss of surface material from a body as a result of frictional heating as it passes through an atmosphere.

1951 *Astrophys. Jrnl.* CXIV. 460 More direct methods of determining actual surface losses by ablation should be developed. **1958** in *Amer. Speech* (1960) XXXV. 283 *Ablation*, melting of nose cone materials during reentry of space ships or vehicles into the earth's atmosphere at hypersonic speeds. **1960** *Nature* 29 Oct. 353 Baker has concluded that the australites entered the atmosphere as cold, independent bodies, most of which neither tumbled nor rotated during ablation. **1961** *New Scientist* 4 May 241 The blunt end [of the space capsule] acts as an 'ablation shield' for re-entry. **1972** *Q. Jrnl. R. Astron. Soc.* XIII. 88 The abundance of sodium in the high atmosphere—thought to be the result of meteoric ablation. **1977** A. HALLAM *Planet Earth* 24 Ablation entirely destroys a high proportion..of a meteoroid entering the atmosphere.

6. Special Combs.: **ablation moraine** *Geol.*, rock debris which has accumulated as a result of the ablation of the glacier in which it was previously embedded; †a deposit of this; **ablation till** *Geol.*, ablation moraine.

1909 R. S. TARR in *Zeitschr. f. Gletscherkunde* III. 85 (*heading*) The *ablation moraines. *Ibid.*, The material in the ablation moraines does not have an even distribution over the ice surface. **1942** C. A. COTTON *Climatic Accidents in Landscape-Making* xi. 145 Much rock debris that falls on to the surface [of the glacier]..reappears as 'ablation moraine'. **1970** R. J. SMALL *Study of Landforms* xi. 383 Towards the margins of the ice..englacial debris will be exposed in large quantities on the surface, thus forming 'ablation moraine'. ..With the ultimate disappearance of the ice, a layer of structureless detritus ('ablation till') will be left. **1968** EMBLETON & KING *Glacial & Periglacial Geomorphol.* xiii. 301 Lodgement till is sometimes referred to as ground moraine,..and *ablation till as ablation moraine. The use of the term 'moraine' is particularly confusing. **1974** H. F. GARNER *Origin of Landscapes* viii. 488/2 Ablation till is lowered rather gently to the ground by wasting ice and is generally loose.

ablatitious (æblə'tɪʃəs), *a.* [f. L. *ablāt-us* taken away, removed (see ABLATE) + -ITIOUS, L. *-īcius*; cf. *addit-itious*.] Having the quality or character of a withdrawal or deduction. ***ablatitious force*** (in *Astr.*) that which diminishes the gravitation of a satellite towards its planet, esp. of the moon towards the earth.

The moon being sometimes nearer to, and sometimes farther from, the sun than the earth, the attraction of the sun on the moon will sometimes be greater, and sometimes less, than his attraction on the earth. The difference estimated along the tangent to the moon's orbit and along the radius drawn from her position to the earth is called the *tangential* and *central disturbing force* respectively. The central disturbing force is ablatitious when it lessens the gravitation of the moon towards the earth. It is ablatitious in syzygies and addititious in quadratures.

1833 SIR J. HERSCHEL *Astron.* xi. 352 This..is termed the ablatitious force, because it tends to diminish the gravity. *Ibid.* 365 The average effect..gives the preponderance to the ablatitious or enfeebling power.

ablatival (æblə'taɪvəl), *a. Gram.* [f. ABLATIVE + -AL.] Pertaining to the ablative case.

1854 ELLICOTT *Comm. Gal.* v. *1*, 81 *ȝ*..The usual ablatival explanation, 'quâ nos liberavit'. **1884** *Trans. Amer. Philol. Assoc.* XV. 5 The ablatival uses of the genitive will be shown to be more numerous,..in Sophokles at least, than the grammars would lead one to suppose.

ablative ('æblətɪv), *a.* and *sb.* [a. Fr. *ablatif, -ive*, ad. L. *ablātīv-us*, lit. of or pertaining to removal from, f. *ablāt-* ppl. stem of *auferre* to carry away (see ABLATE and -IVE); applied by Cæsar to a case of the noun found in L. but not in Gr. In Latin only used in the grammatical sense.]

1. Name of one of the cases of the noun in Latin and some other Aryan languages, the proper function of which was to express *direction from* a place, or *time*. In Latin it was extended to the *source* whence an action proceeds, the *cause* or ideal source of an event, the *instrument* and *agent* or material sources of an action, the *manner* in which, and sometimes the *place* and *time* at which anything is done. Often used substantively, *case* being understood.

The ablative was one of the original Aryan cases. In Greek, Teutonic, and Slavonic, it was lost or formally confounded with other cases; but it survived in Latin, where it had absorbed the Instrumental, and in part the Locative of earlier Aryan (whence its extension in L. to other than ablative senses). The case, not occurring in Greek, was without a name, till the appropriate one of *Cāsus Ablātīvus* was given to it, from its primary function, by Julius Caesar. Since the rise of Comparative Philology the name has been applied to the same case wherever found existing, as well as to the relation properly expressed by it, however this may be formally shown.

ablative absolute, in Latin Grammar, an ablative case of a noun with a participle in concord, expressing the time, occasion, or circumstance of a fact stated, as *sole oriente, tenebrae aufugiunt*, at, upon, or through the sun rising, darkness flees away.

c **1440** *Gesta Rom.* (1879) 418 The vjᵗ. case is ablatif case, and are they that stelyn and leuyn on oþer mennes goodes. **1527** WHITINTON *Vulgaria* 3 Somtyme it is put in the ablatyue case absolute. **1589** *Pappe with an Hatchet* 25 (1844) We haue brought Martin to the ablatiue case, that is, to be taken away with a Bulls voyder. *c* **1620** HUME *Orthogr. Brit. Tong.* (1865) 29 The ablative is noated with prepositiones in, with, be, and sik lyke. **1861** MAX MÜLLER *Sci. Lang.* 100 We learn from a fragment of Cæsar's work, *De Analogia*, that he was the inventor of the term ablative in Latin. **1879** WHITNEY *Sanscrit Gr.* §289 The ablative is the 'from'-case, in the various senses of that preposition: it is used to express removal, separation, distinction, issue, and the like.

†**2.** (From the etymol. meaning). Of or pertaining to taking away or removing; ablatitious. *Obs.*

1567–9 HARDING *On Iewell's Defense of the Apology* (1611) 508 Such is the Logicke, such are the topicks of this new negatiue and ablatiue Divinity..taking away many good things pertaining to the maintenance of Christian Religion and God's honour. **1622** BP. HALL *Sermon bef. His Maiestie* 15 Sept. 489 Ablatiue directions are first needfull to vnteach error ere wee can learne truth. **1713** FLAMSTEED *Letter to Mr. Sharp* in Bailey's *Acc. of Flamsteed* 304 D (1835) [Sir Isaac Newton] has lately published his *Principia* anew, wherein he makes this equation ablative where it was formerly to be added, and to be added where it was subductive.

3. *Astronautics.* Of or pertaining to something which ablates (ABLATE *v.* b).

1959 *N.Y. Times* 30 Aug. 42/4 Special ablative material on the capsule's nose would burn away from the heat of friction as the gradually thickening atmosphere slowed the vehicle.

4. *Surg.* Involving the removal or destruction of an organ or tissue.

1962 *Lancet* 27 Jan. 180/2 In the 2 operable cases chemotherapy was followed within a month by ablative surgery. **1977** *Ibid.* 29 Oct. 899/2 The natural history of the disease may be interrupted by ablative therapy (subtotal thyroidectomy or the use of radioiodine). **1984** *Amer. Jrnl. Surg. Path.* VIII. 183/1 All nine patients were treated by ablative surgery.

ablator (ə'bleɪtə(r)). *Astronautics.* [f. ABLATE *v.* + -OR.] An outer layer, as in a rocket engine, designed to ablate readily when heated and so reduce the transfer of heat to the underlying material.

1963 L. E. HOOKS in *AIAA Jrnl.* I. 2640/2 The noses of superorbital re-entry vehicles will receive significant radiant heating pulses during deceleration. Designers..must prevent this energy..penetrating... This may be done by using opaque heat shields, charring ablators, or ablators that have opaque vapor states. **1970** N. ARMSTRONG et al. *First on Moon* xiii. 307 Thirty-four pounds had been trimmed from the engine's weight by replacing the thrust chamber's asbestos lining with a light, glass-reinforced ablator. **1983** *Aviation Week & Space Technol.* 5 Dec. 22/3 The carbon phenolic ablator in the throat of one of the Mission 8 boosters was within 9 sec. of burning through.

ablaut ('ablaʊt). *Philol.* [mod. Germ., f. *ab* off + *laut* sound.] Vowel permutation; systematic passage of the root vowel into others in derivation, as in *sing, sang, song, sung*, apart from the phonetic influence of a succeeding vowel as in *umlaut*.

1849 E. THOMSON *Select Monuments* p. xxxi, As if it took its meaning from 'roar'; which in reality is the *ablaut*-form of 'rear'. **1871** EARLE *Philol. Eng. Tong.* §124 (1880) But it was in the verbal conjugation that the Ablaut found its peculiar home, and there it took formal and methodical possession. **1886** *Athenæum* 4 Sept. 302/3 The Gothic word differs in ablaut-grade from its Teutonic cognates. **1923** J. K. WALLENBERG *Ayen. of Inwyt* 145 Franck, 'leuk' derives the Continental forms from a Teut. basis *hlū-* which he considers to stand in ablaut-relation to Du. *lauw.* **1935** *Mod. Lang. Notes* L. 533 The ablaut-patterns of the strong verbs in the ME dialects of the east and central midlands. **1963** in A. Brown & P. Foote *Early Eng. & Norse Studies* 73 On *-hæfi* and *-hæfi* as ablaut variations, see A. Noreen.

ablaze (ə'bleɪz), *adv.* and *pred. a.* Properly phrase **a blaze**; older form **on blaze**. [f. A *prep.*[1] + BLAZE.]

1. In a blaze, in a flame.

1393 GOWER *Conf. Am.* v. 3510. II. 244 That casten fire and flame aboute So that they setten all on blase. **1801** SOUTHEY *Thalaba* XII. 15 All ablaze, as if infernal fires Illum'd the world beneath. **1863** TYNDALL *Heat* i. 11 Forests are sometimes set ablaze by lightning. **1876** FREEMAN *Norm. Conq.* III. xi. 71 The sky was ablaze with a mighty mass of flame.

2. *fig.* **a.** In flashing or brilliant colours, gleaming.

1851 LONGF. *Gold. Leg.* IV. iii, What treasures of heart these pages hold, All ablaze with silver and gold. **1878** BLACK *Green Past. & Picc.* ii. 12 A wilderness of sandy heath and dark-green common now all ablaze with gorse and broom.

b. In the full glow of excitement.

c **1840** CARLYLE, The young Cambridge democrats were all ablaze to assist Torrijos. **1859** LYTTON *What will he do?* I. 93 The London season was still ablaze. **1879** J. D. LONG *Æneid* IX. 961 Ablaze with anger at his brother's death.

able (eɪb(ə)l), *a.* Forms: 4–6 **abill(e**, 5 **abyl, abylle, abel,** 5–6 **abul,** 5–7 **hable,** 6–8 **habil,** 7–8 **habile,** 4– **able;** [a. OFr. *hable, able* (mod.Fr. *habile*):—L. *habil-em*, verbal adj., f. *habē-re* to hold; lit. 'easy to be held or handled, handy,' hence 'pliant, suitable, fit for a purpose.' The initial silent *h* has been generally dropped in Eng. from the first, though many classical scholars tried to restore it in 6–7. In 5 the Fr. *hable, able* was refashioned after L. as *abille, habil, habile*, and spellings imitating either these or L. *habil-em* occur in Eng. and Sc. writers in 6–7, of which *habile* has come down to the present day, as a differentiated form, *able* leaning in mod. use to the sense of *power*, *habile* to that of *skill*. Of the derivatives *ability* has lost the *h*, but *habilitate, habilitation, habiliment* retain it, through being narrowed down to senses which connect themselves with mod.Fr. *habit, habiller*. In earlier senses, which clearly connected themselves with *able* and *ability*, we find *abiliment, abilitate*, and *abilitation*.]

I. *passively.*

†**1.** Easy to handle or use. *Obs.*

a. Of persons: Facile, complaisant.

1382 WYCLIF *Nahum* iii. 3 The fornycaciouns of the hoore fair and able. *a* **1423** JAMES I *King's Quair* III. xxxvi, By vertew pure of zour aspectis hable.

b. Of things: Manageable, handy, convenient.

1710 T. BETTERTON in Oldys *Hist. Eng. Stage* v. 67 The Hands are the most habil members of the Body.

†**2. a.** Suitable, fit, appropriate; suited, adapted, fitted. Const. *to, for. Obs.*

1398 TREVISA *Barth. de P.R.* xiv. 49 A felde oþer lyeþ leye ..or is able to pasture..or bereþ floures and is able to been. *c* **1430** *Freemasonry* 125 He may not ben able To lordys profyt. **1583** STUBBES *Anat. of Abuses* 103 (1877) A good peece of beef was thought than good meat, and able for the best. **1659** BROME *Queen* v. vii. 118 To the next able Tree with him, and hang him presently. **1717** WODROW *Correspondence* (1843) II. 335 An ecclesiastical judicatory are most habile judges of what is necessary.

†**b.** Seemly, proper. *Obs.*

a **1480** in *Babees Book* 44 Ne spitte þow not over the tabylle, Ne therupon, for that is no þing abylle.

†**3.** Liable, apt, subject, likely, fit. Const. *to. Obs.* exc. in *dial.*

1413 LYDGATE *Pilgr. of Sowle* II. lx. (1859) 57 Thyne was the action, and I nought but abyl for to suffre. *a* **1423** JAMES I *King's Quair* I. xiv, To fortune both and to infortune hable. **1536** BELLENDENE *Boece's Croniklis* (1821) I. 11 Becaus thay knew al pepil but successioun abill to perische, thay send thair ambassatouris to the Scottis, desiring to have thair dochteris in mariage. **1656** EARL MONM. *Advert. Parnassus* etc. 40 A spectacle able to make a man die for anger. **1866** MRS. LINTON *Lizzie Lorton* III. 116 [He] is noo yeble to be beggared if folks hev a mind.

II. *actively.*

4. a. Having the qualifications for, and means of, doing anything; having sufficient *power* (of whatever kind is needed); in such a position that the thing is possible for one; qualified, competent, capable. Const. *for, to.*

c **1325** *E. Eng. Allit. Poems, Pearl* 598 (1864) 18 Þenne þe lasse in werke to take more able. *c* **1400** *Tale of Beryn* 3237 (1876) Tyll it [the child] be abill of prentyse to craft of tanery. *c* **1440** *Gesta Rom.* 269 (1879) To be abill to wed hure. *c* **1450** MYRC 1231 For he was more abeler þen þow To alle manere gode and prow. **1489** CAXTON *Faytes of Armes* II. v. 99 Whan they see the ost so lessed they thought to be able for theym. **1535** COVERDALE *1 Kings* xxii. 22 Thou shalt disceaue him, and shalt be able. *c* **1538** STARKEY *England* II. i. 150 Grettur nombur of men than he ys Abul to promote. **1596** SHAKS. *Tam. Shr.* v. i. 79 I thank my good Father, I am able to maintaine it. **1611** BIBLE *Matt.* xxii. 46 No man was able to answere him a word. **1627** FELTHAM *Resolves* I. xxxiv. Wks. 1677, 59 Worth without wealth, is like an able servant out of imployment. **1758** S. HAYWARD *Sermons* iv. 108 Christ is thus a compleat and able saviour. **1850** KINGLAKE *Crimea* VI. ix. 228 Abler..than others to bring their country new strength. **1860** TYNDALL *Glaciers* I. §16. 105 He finally concluded that I was able to take care of myself. **1867** SMYTH *Sailor's Wd.-Bk.* s.v. *Able seaman*, a thorough or regular bred sailor.

b. Legally qualified.

1708 KERSEY, Admission, or Admittance..in Law is when a presentation to a void Benefice being made by the Patron, the Bishop allows the Clerk to be able. **1751** CHAMBERS *Cyc.* s.v. *Admission*, A bishop..allows a clerk to be able, or competently qualified for the office; which is done by the formula *Admitto te habilem.*

†**5.** Having general physical or material strength; strong, vigorous, powerful. *Obs.*

c **1375** *Morte Arthure* 2636 He wille be Alexander ayre,.. Abillere þane ever was syr Ector of Troye. **1514** BARCLAY *Cyt. & Uplandyshman* 71 His shoulders large, for burthen strong and able. **1601** SHAKS. *All's Well* IV. v. 86 His Highnesse comes post..of as able bodie as when he number'd thirty. **1607** ROWLANDS *Diog. Lanth.* 30 But in thy youth and able strength, Giue prouidence thy hand. **1642** R. CARPENTER *Experience* I. xv. 108 Dores strengthened with able barres. **1690** PETTY *Polit. Arith.* (1691) ii. 37 So many able Men, whose lives are taken away, for the crimes which ill Discipline doth occasion. **1863** ATKINSON *Whitby Gloss.* A yabble kind of a man, a strong stout person.

†**6.** Having material resources; influential, powerful, wealthy. *Obs.*

1578 *Ps.* cxxviii. in *Scot. Poems of 16th cent.* II. 122 So will the Lord make thee abill. **1665** PEPYS *Corresp.* (1879) VI. 103 It was the child of a very able citizen in Gracious Street. **1863** MRS. TOOGOOD *Spec. Yorkshire Dialect* He's an able man, he has a good bit o' land hereabouts.

7. Having or showing general mental power or skill; talented, clever. Said of men and their achievements. When applied to the cleverness of *tact* or *dexterity*, it is now commonly differentiated as *habile* after mod.Fr.

1577–87 HARRISON *England* I. II. i. 29 (1877) Such number of able pastours as may suffice for everie parish to haue one. **1611** BIBLE *Ex.* xviii. 21 Thou shalt prouide out of all the people able men. **1686** DRYDEN *Hind & P.* II. 432 Those able heads expound a wiser way. **1734** tr. *Rollin, Anc. Hist.* III. VII. 449 Much more able with his tongue than his sword. **1792** *Anecd. of W. Pitt* III. xliv. 197 General Washington proved himself..an abler general. **1802** MAR. EDGEWORTH *Moral Tales* I. xiii. 107 (1816) F...was by no means so able a boxer as his opponent. **1840** GEN. THOMPSON *Exercises* (1842) V. 211 The ablest exposure of..the Factory fraud, which it has been my fortune to see. **1876** FREEMAN *Norm. Conq.* I. iii. 114 An able king is practically absolute.

8. *Comb.* ***able-minded, -souled.*** ABLE-BODIED, ABLE-WHACKETS, q.v.

1849 THOREAU *Week on Concord* 81 Let not the apprehension..discourage the cheerful labors of the able-souled man. **1934** G. B. SHAW *On the Rocks* Pref. 151 Every able-bodied and able-minded and able-souled person.

9. Used for the letter 'A' in transmitting messages (first adopted by services signalling units in Dec. 1942). Cf. ACK.

1943 *Signal Training (All Arms)* No. 5, p. 7 The letters will be spoken in the following form A ABLE B BAKER C CHARLIE.

¶ Used by Sc. writers adverbially = ABLES, ABLINS. Possibly, perhaps.

c **1528** LYNDESAY *Dreme* 893 Quho wyll go sers amang sic heirdis scheip, May, habyll, find mony pure scabbit crok. **1651** D. CALDERWOOD *Hist. Kirk* (1843) II. 523 Both write and say he is evill spokin of..and able he will give credite.

†**able,** *v. Obs.* For forms see ABLE *a.* [f. ABLE *a.* Cf. Fr. *habiller*, used in all the senses of this verb, from which a by-form, *habyle, habylle*, Sc. *abilȝe, abulȝe*, is also found in senses 1 and 2. In sense 3 replaced by ENABLE.]

1. *trans.* To fit, adapt; to prepare, make ready. (Const. *to, into, unto.*)

c **1340** HAMPOLE *Prose Tr.* (1866) 20 Tille oure soule be somwhat..abiled to gostely werke. *c* **1430** in *Babees Book* (1868) 27 First þi silf able with al þin herte to vertuose discipline. **1449** PECOCK *Repr.* III. viii. 324 Deedis..disposing and Abling into the grettist Unpitee. **1471** RIPLEY *Comp. Alch.* v. iii. (1652) 148 Unto Regeneratyon them ablyng. **1553–87** FOXE *A. & M.* I. 601/2 There are but few in number, that do able them thus faithfully to grace. **1583** STANYHURST *Poems* 140. §2 This new strange passadge winter his hoarnes habled.

2. To fit out or prepare the person; to attire, to dress. (Cf. ordinary mod. sense of Fr. *habiller.*)

a **1450** *Knt. de la Tour* 159 He abled hym selff in an other gowne.

3. To endow with fitting power or strength; to make capable; to capacitate, or enable (*to do* anything).

1506 W. DE WORDE *Ordinary of Crysten Men* IV. iv. 172 It hym dysposeth & ableth to contynue in good werkes. **1617** HIERON *Wks.* II. 249 Indowments..whereby the hauer of them is abled of God to performe & to discharge the seruices of that calling. **1693** EVELYN *Mem.* (1857) III. 335 If God shall me able.

4. To endow with general power or skill (of body or mind); to make strong or powerful; to empower, strengthen, confirm, or fortify.

1483 CAXTON *Cato* h vi b, In lyke wyse by ofte studyeng..men able them in whatsomeuer scyence that it be. **1550** BALE *Im. of Both Ch.* B. v, The Apostle of bothe testamentes, abled both by the lawe and the gospell. **1592** WYRLEY *Armorie* ii. 115 Ioue abled much our might. **1631** J. DONNE *Resurrection* in Farr's *S.P.* (1848) 14 And life, by this death abled, shall controule Death.

b. To empower legally, to make competent.

c **1470** *E.E. Gilds* 316 And, whan he is abelled, to give a brekefast to the Maister and Wardons, or he bee admytted. *c* **1600** STRYPE *Ann. Ref.* xxvii. 284 (1709) That none be abled in law to receive any benefice..unless he be a preacher.

c. To warrant, vouch for.

1605 SHAKS. *Lear* IV. vi. 172 None do's offend, none, I say, none, I'll able 'em.

-able, a. Fr. *-able*:—L. *-ābilem*, adj. suffix, the special form taken by the suffix *-bili-* (see -BLE) when added to vbs. in *-āre*, Fr. *-er*. Extended in Fr. to vbs. of all conjugations, *-ble* taking the place of *-nt* in pr. pple., thus *périss-able, recev-able, vend-able, défend-able, mouv-able*. Originally found in Eng. only in words from OFr. but soon by analysis of such instances as *pass-able, agree-able, amend-able*, treated as a living suffix, and freely employed to form analogous adjectives, not only on vbs. from Fr., but at length on native words, as *bearable, speakable, breakable, wearable*. This extension seems to be largely due to form-association with the adj. ABLE (to which the suffix is not related), so that *eatable*, e.g. is taken as *eat + able*, able to be eaten. The vb. has often a sb. of the same form, as in *debat-able, rat(e)-able*; these lead the way to such as *carriageable, clubbable*, where the sb. seems to be the source, and *saleable*, in which no vb. exists. Recent usage adds *-able* even to a verbal phrase as *get-'at-able, come-'at-able*. Now always with passive sense, but in early words often active, as in *comfortable, suitable*, able to comfort, suit.

able-bodied (ˌeɪb(ə)l'bɒdɪd), *a.* [f. *able body* (see quot. from Shaksp. under ABLE *a.* 5) + -ED².] Having an able body, i.e. one free from physical disability, and capable of the physical exertions required of it; in bodily health; robust.

a **1622** MASSINGER etc. *Old Laws* v. i, A lusty woman, able-bodied, and well-blooded cheeks. **1690** PETTY *Polit. Arith.* v. 90 In New-England, there are vast numbers of able bodyed Englishmen, employed chiefly in Husbandry. **1800** COLQUHOUN *Comm. & Pol. Thames* xvi. 511 Encouraged able-bodied Landsmen to betake themselves to the Sea-service. **1851** SPENCER *Soc. Statics* xxviii. §6 The Poor-Law Commissioners were to have eradicated able-bodied pauperism. **1876** FAWCETT *Polit. Econ.* I. iv. 29 Able-bodied labourers were in full employment.

able-bodiedness. [f. prec. + -NESS.] Soundness of bodily health; ability to work; robustness.

1870 *Daily News* 8 Sept. 6 The bulk of these gentry are dismissed, and told to make their able-bodiedness available for defending the ramparts.

†**a'blectick,** *a. Obs.*—⁰ [? f. *ablect-us* separated, selected; a word of doubtful existence in L.] 'Any thing garnished for sale.' Cockeram 1612, Cole 1708, etc. Only in old Dict.

ablegate ('æblɪgeɪt), *sb.* [ad. mod.Fr. *ablégat* or L. *ablegāt-us*, prop. one dispatched, pa. pple. of *ablegā-re*; see next.] An envoy of the papal see, who brings to a newly-appointed cardinal his insignia of office.

[**1651** W. MACDONNELL *Anglia Liberata* ii. 37 In the beginning of his pretended Answer, nick-names them *Ab-Legats* in the *Diminutive*, and calls them *pretended Ambassadors*, as if they merited not the title of true Legats or Ambassadors.] **1890** W. M. BRADY *Anglo-Roman Papers* iii. 239 In 1778, when he [*sc.* Card. Braschi] went as Ablegate to carry the Berretta to the two Cardinals, De la Rochefoucauld and De Rohan. **1927** *Month* Sept. 256 The central interest of the evening was the anticipated arrival of the Apostolic Ablegate, the high ecclesiastic sent by the Pope to bring the red biretta to the new Cardinal.

†**'ablegate,** *v. Obs. rare.* [f. L. *ablegāt-* ppl. stem of *ablegā-re* to dismiss; f. *ab* off, away + *legāre* to send on a message.] To send abroad or to a distance.

1657 *Physical Dict., Ablegate*, remove, turn out, send forth or out of the way. *c* **1665** R. CARPENTER *Prag. Jesuit* 64 Thou hellish Dog, Depart, or I will amand, ablegate, and send thee to some vast and horrid Desert.

†**able'gation.** *Obs.* [a. L. *ablegātiōn-em* a dismissing, n. of action f. *ablegāre*: see prec.] 'The act of sending abroad.' J. Dispatch, dismissal.

1615 CROOKE *Body of Man* 462 The ablegation of excrements. **1649** JER. TAYLOR *Gt. Exemp.* xv. §4 Punished with ablegation and confinement in outer darkness. **1662** H. MORE *Antid. agt. Ath.* I. xi. 35 (1712) An Arbitrarious Ablegation of the Spirits into this or that determinate part of the body.

ablement. *Obs.* See ABILIMENT, HABILIMENT.

†**ablemost,** *a. Obs.* [A factitious superl. of ABLE, imitating *foremost, hindmost*, etc. though not analogous; see -MOST.] Ablest, most able.

1614 SYLVESTER *Bethulian's Rescue* i. 108 (D.) All the Coverts of the Able-most For Pate, Prowesse, Purse.

ablen, a dialect form of ABLET (according to Ash and Craig).

†**a'blend,** *v. Obs.* Forms: *Inf.* 1 ablendan, 2–4 ablende(n, 4 ablynde(n. *Ind. pres. 3rd sing.* 1–4 ablendeð, ablent, 4 ablyndeþ. *Pa. t.* 1–3 ablende, ableynte. *Pa. pple.* 1 ablænd, 2–4 ablent, 4 abland. [f. A- *pref.* 1 + *blend-an* to blind. Cf. Ger. *erblenden*. See also ABLIND, with which it was in later times confused.] To dazzle, to take away the sight (temporarily); to blind the moral vision.

c **1000** ÆLFRIC *Pastoral Ep.* in *Anc. Laws* II. 372 He[Arius] wæs ablænd on his mode. **1205** LAYAMON 14659 He heom walde ufel don: Baðe ablenden and anhon. *c* **1230** *Ancren Riwle* 86 Ualse uikelare ablendeð þeo þe ham hercneð. **1297** R. GLOUC. 208 Ac þet blod adoun wende So vaste, in eye, and in face, þat hym ney ablende. *c* **1320** *Seuyn Sages* (W.) 2462 The walmes han the abland. *a* **1327** *Pol. Songs* 345 And so is al this world ablent, that no man douteth sinne. **1340** *Ayenb.* 16 Þis ȝenne of prede..ablent men ȝuo þet hi ham-ȝelve ne knaweþ. **1377** LANGL. *P. Pl.* B. x. 264 A beem in þine owne [eye] A-blyndeth þi-selue. *Ibid.* XVIII. 323 Lucifer loke ne myȝte So lyȝte him ableynte. **1393** —— C. XXI. 142 Þis light and þis leom · shal Lucifer a-blende.

†**'ableness.** *Obs.* Forms: 4 abilnesse, 4–7 ableness(e, 5 ablynesse, 5–6 ablenes, 6 hablenes(se. [f. ABLE *a.* + -NESS.] The quality of being able; ability.

c **1390** CHAUCER *Test. Love* II. 284/2 (1560) I wist well thine ablenes my service to further. **1398** TREVISA *Barth. De P.R.* (1495) XVIII. xxv. 797 The wylde gote hath ablynesse and lyghtnesse to renne. **1489** CAXTON *Faytes of Armes* I. x. 28 They saw hem with theyre ablenes of body. **1535** COVERDALE *2 Cor.* iii. 5 Oure ablenesse commeth of God. **1548** GESTE *Preuee Masse* 72 More or less, according to his hablenes. **1610** HEALEY *Augustine's City of God* I. x. 17 It taught them a sparing dyet and ablenesse to faste. **1642** ROGERS *Naaman* 440 The Prophets ablenesse to heale him.

ableow, ableu, ablewe, pa. t. of ABLOW *v. Obs.*

†**ablepsy.** *Obs. rare*—¹. [ad. L. *ablepsia*; a. Gr. ἀβλεψία blindness; f. ἀ not + βλέπω, fut. βλέψω, I see.] Blindness, physical or mental.

1652 URQUHART *Jewel* (Wks. 1834) 279 Who doubteth, that is not blinded with the ablepsie of an implicite zeal?

†**ablesse.** *Obs. rare*—¹. [f. ABLE *a.* + -ESSE Fr. formative of state, not used in Fr. with this word, but apparently employed by Chapman after the analogy of *noblesse* = *nobleness* and Spenser's *idlesse*.]

1596 CHAPMAN *Iliad* v. 248 And then preferr'd his ablesse and his mind to all his ancestors in fight.

ablet ('æblɪt). Also **ablette, ablen.** [a. Fr. *ablette* 'a little blay or bleak' Cotgr., dim. of *able*:—late L. *abula* for *albula* dim. of *alba* white.] 'A name given in some parts of England to the Bleak, a small fresh-water fish, *Leuciscus alburnus*.' Ash 1775, Craig 1847.

1885 *Encycl. Brit.* XVIII. 448/2 Spheres of thin glass are filled with a preparation known as 'essence d'orient', made from the silvery scales of the bleak or 'ablette'. **1936** RUSSELL & YONGE *Seas* (ed. 2) xvi. 351 On the Continent the little fresh-water 'ablette' is the main source of pearl essence.

ablety, abletee, obsolete forms of ABILITY.

able-whackets [f. WHACK.] 'A popular sea-game with cards, wherein the loser is beaten over the palms of the hands with a handkerchief tightly twisted like a rope. Very popular with horny-fisted sailors.' Smyth *Sailor's Word-Bk.*

abliche, obsolete form of ABLY.

†**'abligate,** *v. Obs.*—⁰ [f. L. *ab* from + *ligāt-* ppl. stem of *ligare* to bind.] 'To bind or tye up from,' Bailey, vol. II. 1731, whence in Johnson 1755.

†**abli'gation.** *Obs.*—⁰ [n. of action f. prec.] 'A tying up from,' Smart 1849, whence in Webster, etc.

[**abligurie.** *Obs.*—⁰ 'Spending in belly-cheere,' Cockeram 1612 and Minsheu 1626. Bailey 1742 corrects the form to ABLIGURITION with same def.]

†**abligu'rition.** *Obs.* [ad. L. *abligūrītiōn-em* n. of action f. *abligūrī-re* to squander on dainties; f. *ab* away + *ligūrī-re* to eat delicately, to be fond of dainties; desider. f. *ling-ĕre* to lick.] 'Prodigal expense on meat and drink.' J.

1742 BAILEY, *Abligurition*, a prodigal spending in Belly-Cheere.

†**a'blind,** *v. Obs.* [f. A- *pref.* 1 + BLIND *v.* Cf. Ger. *er-blinden* and the trans. form ABLEND, for which in later times *ablind* was sometimes put.] To grow blind.

c **1175** *Lamb. Hom.* 109 Gif þe eȝe ablindað. *c* **1230** *Ancren Riwle* 92 Heo ablindeð in þe inre eien. *Ibid.* 62 Ablinde þe heorte, heo is eð ouercumen.

†**'abling** ('eɪblɪŋ), *vbl. sb. Obs.* [f. ABLE *v.* + -ING¹.] The act of fitting or empowering.

1489 CAXTON *Faytes of Armes* I. ix. 24 Al this was by cause they shuld bere trauailles and be vsed in ablyng of them self.

ablings, -ins ('eɪblɪnz), *adv.* properly northern. [f. ABLE *a.* + -LINGS.] In a manner that is able to be; possibly, perhaps.

1597–1605 A. MONTGOMERIE *Poems* (1821) 42 The man may ablens tyne a stot That cannot count his kinsch. **1768** ROSS *Helenore* 101 I've ablins said that I sall tak you with me. **1863** ATKINSON *Whitby Gloss.* s.v. As for walking sae far and nae farther, I think I aiblins might.

†**'ablocate,** *v. Obs.*—⁰ [f. L. *ablocāt-* ppl. stem of *ablocāre* to lease; f. *ab* away + *locāre* to place, set.] 'To set, or let out to hire.' Cockeram 1612; whence in Bailey 1721, Johnson 1755, etc.

†**ablo'cation.** *Obs.*—⁰ [n. of action f. prec.] 'A letting out for money.' Bullokar 1676; whence in Bailey 1731, and Johnson 1755.

abloom (ə'blu:m), *adv.* and *pred. a.*, properly *phrase.* [A *prep.*¹ + BLOOM.] In or into bloom.

1855 BROWNING *Men & Women* II. *Saul* 128 The fern-branches all round..Broke a-bloom. **1863** *Macm. Mag.* Jan. 164 The whole hollow was abloom with the yellow gorse. **1876** MISS BRADDON *Josh. Hagg. Dau.* I. v. 168 Sweet wild flowers abloom under their feet.

†**a'blow,** *v. Obs.* [f. A- *pref.* 1 intensive + *blaw-an* to BLOW.]

1. To blow or breathe upon or into. *lit.* and *fig.*

c **1000** ÆLFRIC *Gen.* ii. 7 God..on ableow on his ansine lifes orðunge. *c* **1175** *Lamb. Hom.* 99 Crist ableow þana halȝa gast ofer þa apostlas..þe helende ableu his gast on his apostlas. *c* **1320** *Arthour & Merlin* 8546 Aswon tho sche ouer threwe Wawain sone hir ablewe.

2. *intr.* and *trans.* To puff up, swell. *lit.* and *fig.*

c **1000** *Saxon Leechdoms* II. 250 Eft, þonne se milte ablawen wyrð, sona he aheardian. *Ibid.* 168 Ablawunge & aheardunge þæs blodes on þam milte. *c* **1315** SHOREHAM *Poems* 160 Thos he [the devil] gan hyre herte ablowe, And hy sey that frut..Was fayr and god. *Ibid.* 166 Þet was ablowe þorȝ þe fenim of þe fende.

ablow (ə'bləʊ), *adv.* or *pred. a.* [A *prep.*¹ + BLOW *v.*¹ or *v.*²] Blooming; blowing.

1893 W. B. YEATS *Poems* (1957) 743 For dreams are the flowers ablow. **1912** COMPTON MACKENZIE *Carnival* xxiv. 268 A black mushroom hat a-blow with rosebuds. **1921** W. DE LA MARE *Crossings* 12 The tide's aflow, the wind ablow.

†**a'bloy.** *Obs.*—¹ [perh. ad. OFr. *ablo!* 'vive! courage! allons! ferme!' Godefroi.]

c **1340** *Gawayne & Gr. Knt.* 1173 (1864) 37 Þe lorde for blys abloy Ful oft con launce & lyȝt, & drof þat day with joy, Thus to þe dark nyȝt.

†**a'blude,** *v. Obs. rare.* [ad. L. *ablūd-ĕre* to be unharmonious, differ from; f. *ab* away from + *lūd-ere* to play e.g. on an instrument.] To differ, be out of keeping. Const. *from.*

1612–15 BP. HALL *Contemp.* IV. ix. 265 (1863) The occasion, the place, abludes not much. **1650** —— *Balm of Gilead* 183 The wise advice of our Seneca (not much abluding from the counsell of that blessed Apostle). **1655**

L'ESTRANGE *Charles I*, 4 It will not be amisse nor ablude from the usuall ceremony.

abluent ('æblu:ənt), *a.* and *sb.* [ad. L. *abluent-em*, pr. pple. of *ablu-ĕre* to wash off or away; f. *ab* off + *lu-ĕre* to wash.] Washing away; carrying off impurities; abstergent. Used chiefly, if not entirely, in *Med.*; where also *sb.* an abstergent.

1751 CHAMBERS *Cycl., Abluents, Abluentia*, in medicine, a name which some authors give to a sort of remedies, better known by the name of *abstergents*. **1853** MAYNE *Expos. Lex., Abluent*, washing away; that which washes away or carries off impurities.

a-blush (ə'blʌʃ), *adv.* and *pred. a.*, properly *phrase.* [A *prep.*[1] + BLUSH.] Blushing, ruddy.

1852 THOS. AIRD *Mem. of Moir* 128 The bank, all a-blush with roses.

ablute (æ'bl(j)u:t), *v. colloq.* [Back-formation f. ABLUTION.] *trans.* and *intr.* To wash (oneself).

1892 *Judy* 9 Mar. 110/2 She went off to.. wash her face... I'd previously abluted mine. **1924** *Blackw. Mag.* Nov. 691/1 Postal work would have been sadly disorganised if Father Moti had kept the postal staff abluting. **1959** C. MACINNES *Absolute Beginners* 183, I put on some music and abluted, then made two Nescafés.

a'bluted, *ppl. a.* [pa. pple. of vb. *ablute* (ABLUTE *v.*), not found until later (cf. *dilute, diluted*); f. L. *ablu-ĕre, ablūt-um*; f. *ab* off + *lu-ĕre* to wash.] Washed away; washed clean.

1650 VENNER *Via Recta* 307 Excorticated Barley well mundified and abluted. **1754** GARDNER *Hist. Dunwich* The shingle & sand were so abluted in some places, by the vehemence of the furious waves. **1922** JOYCE *Ulysses* 695 He scratched.. his partly exposed, wholly abluted skin.

ablution (æ'bl(j)u:ʃən). [ad. L. *ablūtiōn-em*, n. of action from *ab-luĕre* to wash off.]

1. The act or process of washing clean.

†**a.** In early usage in alchemy and chemistry, the purification of bodies by the use of suitable liquids.

c **1386** CHAUCER *Chan. Yem. Prol.* 303 Oyles ablucioun, and metal fusible. **1477** NORTON *Ordin. Alch.* (1652) v. 59 Water clenseth with ablution blive. **1594** PLAT *Jewell-house* II. 40 A soft or slimie substance, which you may after cleanse by ablution. **1610** B. JONSON *Alchemist* II. v. 632 (1616) The martyrizations Of mettalls, in the worke... Putrefaction, Solution, Ablution, Sublimation, etc. **1612** WOODALL *Surgeon's Mate* (Wks. 1653) 268 Ablution is exaltation, cleansing unclean things by often infusion. **1754** HUXHAM *Antimony* in *Phil. Trans.* XLVIII. 853 Great care should be taken therefore in the ablution of the sulphur auratum.

†**b.** 'The rinsing of chymical preparations in water, to dissolve and wash away any acrimonious particles.' J. *Obs.*

1751 CHAMBERS *Cycl., Ablution* is sometimes used.. for the washing or infusing certain medicines in water to freshen them, and dissolve their salts; otherwise called *dulcifying*.

c. The washing of the body as a religious rite.

1533 MORE *Apology* viii. (Wks. 1557) 861/1 Obedience on the mannes part in submytting hymselfe to that ablucion [baptism]. **1781** COWPER *Conversation* 566 A Jordan for the ablution of our woes. **1786** BURKE *Art. agst. Hastings* Wks. II. 442 The Rajah desired leave to perform his ablutions. **1856** STANLEY *Sinai & Pal.* vii. 306 Ablutions, in the East, have always been more or less a part of religious worship.

By extension (later, not in Chambers 1751):—

d. The washing or cleansing of one's person.

1748 SMOLLETT *Rod. Rand.* lxiv. 466 (1804) Having performed the ceremony of ablution I shifted. **1835** THIRLWALL *Greece* I. vi. 179 An ablution.. uniformly preceded the repast. **1859** JEPHSON *Brittany* iv. 38 I made up for the necessarily scanty ablutions of the morning.

e. In Rom. and Angl. Churches: the washing of chalice and paten after the celebration. In Rom. Ch., the washing of the priest's hands before assuming the sacred vestments, and during the celebration.

2. a. The water etc. with which anything has been washed; *spec.* in Catholic Ritual, the wine and water used to rinse the chalice, and wash the fingers of the celebrant after the communion.

1718 POPE *Iliad* I. 413 Wash'd by the briny wave, the pious train Are cleansed, and cast the ablutions in the main. **1846** MASKELL *Mon. Rit. Eccl. Ang.* I. 239 The ablution in other instances, if not cast into the fire, was to be carried into the sacrarium, doubtless in order to be thrown away through the piscina. **1866** LEE *Direct. Anglic.* (ed. 3) 351 The wine poured into the chalice and also the wine and water poured into the same and over the priest's fingers.. is drunk by the celebrant and called the ablution.

†**b.** A lotion. *Obs.*

1671 SALMON *Syn. Medic.* III. lxxxiv. 733 Cured by washing with the ablution of Turpethum Minerale.

3. *pl.* A building containing facilities for washing oneself. Chiefly *Mil.*

1958 B. BEHAN *Borstal Boy* III. 264, I went down to the ablutions and there were fellows washing and shaving. **1964** J. HALE *Grudge Fight* v. 74 Get him out to the ablutions. Bring some soap.

4. *attrib.* and *Comb.*, as ***ablution bench, block, cabinet, place, trough.***

1911 *R. Army Med. Corps Training* (War Office) xii. 75 The ablution places need to be located conveniently near the men's tents. *Ibid.*, Ordinary ablution-benches with foot-gratings. **1921** *Jrnl. R. Naval Med. Service* VII. 242 The ablution cabinet in the after inboard corner. **1967** *Gloss. Sanitation Terms* (*B.S.I.*) 6 *Ablution trough*, a wash basin of elongated rectangular shape in plan, at which more than one person can wash at the same time. **1971** *Sunday Times* (Johannesburg) 28 Mar. 29/7 (Advt.), Heated swimming pool, caravan park and ablution block. **1985** *Daily Tel.* 23 Feb. 36/5 The fire began in an ablution block [at an airport].

ablutionary (æ'bl(j)u:ʃənərı), *a.* [f. prec. + -ARY.] Of or pertaining to washing the body, or parts of it.

1864 HAWTHORNE *Pansie* (quoted in *Reader*) Those tonsorial, ablutionary, and personally decorative labours.

†**a'bluvion.** *Obs.*—[0] [ad. med.L. *ablūviōn-em* for *ablūvium*, f. *ab* away + *luĕre* to wash. Cf. ALLUVION.] That which is washed away.

WEBSTER and WORCESTER cite DWIGHT.

ably ('eıblı), *adv.* 5–; also 4 **abelyche, abilly,** 5–6 **ablie** [f. ABLE *a.* + -LY[2].] In an able manner; with fitness, power, or cleverness.

1398 TREVISA *Barth. De P.R.* (1495) XII. xvii. 425 In fyghtynge the cocke meuyth the fethers of his tayle.. that he maye soo the more ably come to the batayle. *c* **1430** *Freemasonry* 243 That he the craft abelyche may conne. **1592** WYRLEY *Armorie* iv. 89 Thinking it against our power sure Ablie well, one yeare strong to indure. **1855** MACAULAY *Hist. Eng.* III. 525 He had.. done his duty ably, honestly, and fearlessly. **1876** FREEMAN *Norm. Conq.* II. x. 477 Never was a campaign more ably planned.

-ably, compd. suffix, f. -ABLE + -LY (early *-abelliche*) supplying adverbs to the adjectives in *-able* of all ages, as *passably, unspeakably, rateably.*

ablynd, variant of ABLEND *v. Obs.*

abmigration (ˌæbmaı'greıʃən). *Ornith.* [f. AB- *pref.* + MIGRATION.] (See quots.) Hence **'abmigrate** *v. intr.*

1923 A. L. THOMSON in *Brit. Birds* XVI. 276 Some such term as 'abmigration' might perhaps be used to describe the northward departure in spring, for a new summer area, on the part of birds which had made no corresponding southward journey in the previous autumn. **1929** E. M. NICHOLSON *Study of Birds* v. 54 Birds which are native to one country, may 'abmigrate', and be found breeding in another, up to thousands of miles away. **1953** *New Biol.* XV. 54 Abmigration occurs when a bird (usually a young one), bred in this country and wintering here, accompanies foreigners which have also wintered here to *their* home countries in the Spring, instead of returning to its own British nesting grounds.

Abnaki, var. ABENAKI.

abnegate ('æbnıgeıt), *v.* [f. L. *abnegāt-* ppl. stem of *abnegā-re* to refuse, to deny, f. *ab* off, away + *negā-re* to deny.]

1. To deny oneself (anything), to renounce or surrender (a right or privilege).

1657 *Deuine Louer* 12 The which will of ours I meane is lesse abnegated or mortified in or by matter of abstaynings or restreignings then in or by those of suffering. **1846** GROTE *Greece* II. II. vi. 534 Voluntarily abnegating their temporal advantages. **1861** MILL *Utilit.* ii. 23 All honour to those who can abnegate for themselves the personal enjoyment of life. **1870** *Pall Mall G.* 7 Sept. 1 To do so would be to abnegate the one claim they have on the popular allegiance.

2. To renounce or abjure, as a tenet; 'to deny,' J. (The only meaning given by him.)

1755 JOHNSON *Dict., Abjure*: to retract, recant, or abnegate a position upon oath. **1775** DE LOLME *Eng. Const.* (T.) They have abnegated the idea of independent rights of the people. **1858** CARLYLE *Heroes* 312 (1858) The very possibility of Heroism had been, as it were, formally abnegated in the minds of all. **1875** FARRAR *Silence & Voices* iii. 52 Man when he abnegates his God is a creature so petty, so foolish.

abnegation (ˌæbnı'geıʃən). [ad. L. *abnegātiōn-em* refusal, denial, n. of action from *abnegāre*: see ABNEGATE, and cf. Fr. *abnégation* (16th c.) in Littré, which has only meaning 2.]

1. Denial, negation; refusal, formal rejection (of a doctrine, etc.).

1554 KNOX *Godly Letter* C. vj. b. What is in Asya? ignoraunce of God, what in Affrika? abnegation of Christe. **1633** ADAMS *Exp. 2 Peter* ii. 2. (1865) 235 Let us follow Peter's confession, not his abnegation. **1646** GAULE *Cases Consc.* 148 That hath brought us to an Abnegation of the Sacred Trinity. **1825** SOUTHEY in *Q. Rev.* XXXIII. 155 On Easter.. he was to eat animal food, in abnegation of the opinion imputed to the heretics on that subject. **1875** MCLAREN *Serm.* Ser. II. xiv. 253 It is no cowardly abnegation of the responsibility of choice which is here enjoined.

2. Denial (of anything) to oneself; self-denial; renunciation (of rights, claims, or things esteemed).

1639 ROUSE *Heav. Univ.* vi. 91 (1702) The abnegation of all humane wisdom in a passive childlike resignation of the soul to the Divine Spirit. **1853** MRS. JAMESON *Leg. Monast. Ord.* 242 He set forth to preach.. humility, abnegation of the world. **1866** MOTLEY *Dutch Rep.* III. ix. 519 His abnegation of an authority which he had not dared to assume.

3. Self-abnegation; renunciation of oneself; self-sacrifice.

1657 REEVE *God's Plea* 304 So much humility, so much abnegation.. do not these discover a true mortified spirit? **1679** PENN *Addr. Prot.* (1692) II. v. 146 The Pretences of Romanists to Abnegation, to a Mortified and Self-denying Life. **1858** CARLYLE *Heroes* 237 Difficulty, abnegation, martyrdom, death are the allurements that act on the heart of man. **1878** BOSW. SMITH *Carthage* 399 That alternation.. of sordid selfishness and sublime abnegation.

b. *Self* is now often expressed.

1847 YEOWELL *Anc. Brit. Ch.* viii. 77 The principal reason, however, which rendered the monastic orders so powerful.. was the total abnegation of self. **1870** BOWEN *Logic* xiii. 446 That earnestness of inquiring purpose which leads not so much to an abnegation as to the entire forgetfulness of self.

abnegative ('æbnıˌgeıtıv), *a. rare.* [f. *abnegāt-* ppl. stem of *abnegāre* (see ABNEGATE) + -IVE, as if ad. L. **abnegātīvus*.] Of or belonging to abnegation; denying; renouncing; negative.

Not in CRAIG 1847; WEBSTER cites CLARKE, and WORCESTER cites *Monthly Rev.*

abnegator ('æbnıˌgeıtə(r)). [a. L. *abnegātor*, agent-noun from *abnegāre*: see ABNEGATE.] One who abnegates; one who denies, or renounces.

1637 SANDYS *State of Relig.* 96 Fighters against the light, protectors of darkenesses.. abnegators and dispensers against the Lawes of God. **1834** GEN. THOMPSON *Exercises* (1842) III. 415 Habitual abnegators of the principles of public and private morality.

abnet, variant of ABANET.

Abney ('æbnı). The surname of Sir William de Wiveleslie *Abney* (1844–1920) in ***Abney level*** (LEVEL *sb.* 1), a small hand instrument used by surveyors for measuring slopes and angles above the horizon. Also ***Abney clinometer.***

1889 G. W. USILL *Pract. Surveying* iii. 33 The Abney Level.—This portable and neat little instrument is a reflecting level and clinometer combined... It was invented by Captain Abney (of photographic renown). **1946** R. J. C. ATKINSON *Field Archaeol.* II. iii. 136 *Abney Clinometer*.. The instrument consists of a sighting tube fitted with a pin-hole aperture, [etc.]. **1955** *Oxf. Jun. Encycl.* VIII. 429/1 The Abney level or clinometer, which consists of a sighting tube fixed to a semicircular vertical plate marked in degrees, with a spirit level attached to its index, is.. used to measure vertical angles.

†**'abnodate,** *v. Obs.*—[0] [f. L. *abnōdāt-* ppl. stem of *abnōdā-re* 'to clear trees of knots'; f. *ab* off + (*g*)*nōd-us* knot.] 'To prune trees, etc.' Bailey 1721, whence in Ash, and mod. Dicts.

†**abno'dation.** *Obs.*—[0] [ad. late L. *abnōdātiōn-em*, n. of action f. prec.] 'The act of cutting away knots from trees; a term of gardening.' J.

1678 PHILLIPS, *Abnodation*, An untying, or cutting off of knots, also pruning of Trees. [So BAILEY 1721, BRADLEY 1724, JOHNSON 1755, etc.]

abnormal (æb'nɔ:məl), *a.* [A refashioning of the earlier ANORMAL (a. Fr. *anormal*, ad. med.L. *anormal-us* for *anōmal-us*, a Gr. ἀνώμαλ-ος: see ANOMALOUS) after L. *abnormis* (see ABNORMOUS). Few words show such a series of pseudo-etymological perversions; Gr. ἀνώμαλ-ος, L. *anōmal-us*, having been altered in late L. after *norma* to *anormālus*, later *anormālis*, whence Fr. *anormal* (13th c.) and Eng. *anormal*; the latter referred to L. *abnorm-is*, and altered to *abnormal*. It has displaced the earlier *abnormous*.] Deviating from the ordinary rule or type; contrary to rule or system; irregular, unusual, aberrant.

[**1835** HOBLYN *Dict. of Medicine, Anormal* (Lat. *anormis*) without rule [*Abnormal* not in]. **1853** MAYNE, *Anormal*, departing from the natural condition, the same as *Abnormal*.] **1835–6** TODD *Cycl. Anat. & Ph.* I. 19 The relative positions of the contents of the abdomen, and the abnormal states of that cavity. **1836** *Pen. Cycl.* s.v. Botany, *Abnormal*, contrary to general rules. **1840** HAMBLE *Dict. Geol. & Min.* Abnormal, Abnormous (*abnormis* Lat.) Irregular, unwonted, unnatural. **1841** MYERS *Cath. Thoughts* iv. §25. 302 The Mosaic system must always be considered as an abnormal, exceptional Dispensation. **1842** FERGUSSON *Pract. Surg.* xxiii. 105 In false joints, as in most other abnormal conditions. **1859** DARWIN *Orig. Species* v. 119 (1873) The wing of a bat is a most abnormal structure. **1871** BLACKIE *Four Phases* I. 121 The strange and abnormal habits of certain savage tribes. **1877** ROBERTS *Handbk. Med.* I. 77 (ed. 3) Abnormal ingredients may be present. **1878** E. WHITE *Life in Christ* v. xxxi. 533 Special mercy and abnormal compassion.

abnormalism (æb'nɔ:məlız(ə)m). [f. ABNORMAL *a.* + -ISM.] The condition of being or tendency to be abnormal; also, an abnormal thing. So **ab'normalist,** one who is characterized by abnormalism (Funk, 1893).

1894 *Thinker* V. 536 If it were so [i.e. that the organism was nothing more than the creature of environment] one would have expected.. that abnormalism would be more frequent. **1907** *Daily Chron.* 24 Dec. 5/2 Specialist on Abnormalism.

abnormality (æbnɔ:'mælıtı). [f. ABNORMAL + -ITY; cf. *formality*, etc.] It wants the depreciatory force which generally attaches to ABNORMITY.

1. The quality or state of being abnormal; irregularity of constitution.

1854 BALFOUR *Outl. Bot.* 213 In cases in which the stamens are not equal in number to the petals the abnormality may be traced to suppression of a certain number. **1874** CARPENTER *Ment. Phys.* (1879) II. x. 459 That remarkable abnormality known as Double Consciousness.

1880 DR. RICHARDSON in *Fraser's Mag.* Nov. 675 The back, abnormally bent, retains its abnormality.

2. An instance or embodiment of such irregularity; an abnormal or unusual feature or act.

1859 TODD *Cycl. Anat. & Phys.* V. 208/1 Other congenital abnormalities of the pelvic bones are mentioned. **1868** *Sat. Rev.* 26 Dec. 828/2 The abnormalities of his position would thus be considerably mitigated. **1879** SPENCER *Ethics* xi. §74. 98 Such abnormalities of conduct as are instanced above. **1880** C. & F. DARWIN *Movem. Plants* 157 Such abnormalities would probably never..occur with forms developed in a state of nature.

abnormalize (æbˈnɔːməlaɪz), *v.* [f. ABNORMAL *a.* + -IZE.] *trans.* To render abnormal. Also *absol.*

a **1871** DE MORGAN *Budget Parad.* (1872) 339 The toe-bone might have been abnormalised by therian..malady. **1890** *Sat. Rev.* 4 Jan. 16/1 The Romantic turned Realist, who tries to avoid Classicality and *das Gemeine*, not merely by individualizing, but by abnormalizing, if we may say so. **1895** *Arena* (Boston) Aug. App. p. vi, The excessive use of alcohol, which abnormalizes (if I may so express it) man's entire being.

abnormally (æbˈnɔːməlɪ), *adv.* [f. ABNORMAL + -LY[2].] In an abnormal or irregular manner; irregularly; extraordinarily.

1845 *Vest. Creat.* (ed. 3) 340 Such abnormally constituted beings [not in ed. 1844]. **1859** DARWIN *Orig. Spec.* v. 154 The most abnormally developed organs may be made constant. **1870** *Pall Mall G.* 7 Oct. 4 In time of war imagination is apt to be abnormally prolific. **1871** STEWART *Heat* 45 The bulb is therefore abnormally dilated.

[**abnormeth**, quoted from Chaucer, *Troylus* I. 327, a misreading of *vnourneth*: see UNORN *v.*]

abnormity (æbˈnɔːmɪtɪ). [ad. L. *abnormitas*, noun of quality from *abnormis*; see next.]

1. The quality of being abnormal or irregular; contrariety to the ordinary rule or type; irregularity, deformity, monstrosity.

1731 BAILEY, *Abnormity*, mishapeness, hugeness. [Not in PHILLIPS 1706, nor in JOHNSON 1755.]

2. A special instance or embodiment of such irregularity; an abnormal or irregular form; a monstrosity or malformation.

1859 *Westm. Rev.* XXXI. 91 [The baby] rivalled that physiological abnormity by coming into the world with a file and hammer in his hand. **1865** C. C. BLAKE in *Reader* No. 145. 409/2 Such an abnormity as the Neanderthal skull. **1871** MRS. WHITNEY *Real Folks* (1872) xix. 258 An abnormity..like a calf born with two heads.

abnormous (æbˈnɔːməs), *a.* [f. L. *abnorm-is* irregular (f. *ab* away from + *norma* rule) + -OUS. Cf. *enormous.*] 'Irregular, misshapen.' J. (no quot.) Hence **abˈnormously** *adv. rare.*

[Not in PHILLIPS 1706.] **1742** BAILEY, *Abnormous*, mishapen, vast, huge. **1771** *Antiq. Sarisb.* 240 Sir Toby Matthews was a character equally if not of a more abnormous cast than his suspected coadjutor. **1838–9** HALLAM *Hist. Lit.* IV. IV. v. §48. 251 The general structure of the couplet through the seventh century may be called abnormous. **1846** GROTE *Greece* I. i. 3 (1862) The former [divine myths] being often the more extravagant and abnormous in their incidents. **1878** TROLLOPE *Is he Popenjoy?* II. ii. 26 A brat so abnormously distasteful and abominable.

†**abnoxious**, *a.*, incorrect form of OBNOXIOUS.

1649 BP. HALL *Cases Consc.* (1654) IV. iii. 321 Of ill report, and abnoxious to various censures.

†**abˈnutive**, *a. Obs. rare*$^{-1}$. [f. late L. *abnūtīvus* (Pandects) adj. f. *abnūt-* ppl. stem of *abnu-ĕre* to decline (f. *ab* away + *nu-ĕre* to nod or beckon).] Negative; implying denial or refusal.

a **1682** W. EVATS *Grotius' War & Peace* 189 For such an act, hath the force of a positive act, and is not to be ranked among those which are barely Abnutive [L. *nec manet intra fines nude abnutivos*].

Abo, abo (ˈæbəʊ), *a.* and *sb. Australian slang.* [Shortened f. ABORIGINAL (see note below).] Aboriginal.

The currency of *Abo* was assisted by its use in the Sydney *Bulletin* feature entitled 'Aboriginality' (first number 21 Apr. 1888): see quots. [1906–1933].

[**1906** *Bulletin* (Sydney) 5 Apr. 14/3 Can any aboliar state definitely how long sheep can do without water? *Ibid.* 2 Aug. 16/4 Have read the 'Abo.'s' on it. *Ibid.* 18 Oct. 17/3 Remarkable the number of 'Abo' writers who have been chased by snakes. **1907** *Ibid.* 17 Jan. 14/2 [He] says Chinese extract the gall-juice of crows for physic. All Abo-shine. **1933** *Ibid.* 1 Nov. 20/4 Would any Aboliar like to enter for the oldest-kangaroo stakes?] **1922** 'TE WHARE' *Bush Cinema* 38 An 'abo' legend attaches to the great bluff between Bermagni and Tathra. *Ibid.* 91 Fires were lighted, and the 'abos' feasted royally on fish broiled on live coals. **1933** *Bulletin* (Sydney) 25 Jan. 20 The idea of better housing for the abos. **1950** 'N. SHUTE' *Town like Alice* iii. 82 Black boys—black stockmen. Abos.

aboad, aboade. See ABODE and ABIDE.

aboard (əˈbɔəd, əˈbɔːd), *adv.* and *prep.* Also 5–7 abord(e, 6 abrode, aburd, 6–7 aboord(e, 7 abourd, and incorr. abroad. [f. A *prep.*[1] + BOARD, and Fr. *à bord*, to which apparently the modern use of *aboard*, *on board*, is chiefly due. *Board* is orig. Teutonic: in OE., *bord* a plank, table, shield, and poetically a ship, whence *on borde* in ship. But this poetic form seems to have died out with OE., the ordinary ME. prose being *within shippes borde*, within the ship's boarding or sides. Meanwhile the Teut. *bord*, OHG. *bort*, had been adopted in Fr. as 1. board, plank, whence the boarding or sides of a vessel; hence, 2. the vessel itself, and, 3. the side or border of anything, edge, coast, shore. *À bord*, in or on a ship; *bord à bord*, board to board, side by side, hard aboard, touching; *venir à bord*, to come a-shore, to land; *aborder* to come to the side of; *abord*, approach, accosting. These uses and phrases were adopted in Eng. where also from the use of *board* in *within shippes borde*, etc., *a-board* was very soon regarded as the Eng. prep. *a* + *board*, and expanded passim into *on board.*]

A. *adv.*

1. On board, within the boards (of a ship); **a.** (position) in or on a ship or other floating vessel.

1587 TURBERVILE *Trag. Tales* (1837) 174 The men aboord that see them come Prepare them selves to fight. **1610** SHAKS. *Temp.* I. i. 21 Good, yet remember whom thou hast aboord. **1675** HOBBES *Odyssey* 171 Then I my fellows bad aboard to stay And guard the ships. **1805** SOUTHEY *Madoc* xvii. (1853) V. 128 Now all is done. Stores, beeves and flocks and water all aboard.

b. (motion) on to or into the ship.

1509 BARCLAY *Ship of Fooles* (1570) ¶¶ vj. There is great number that fayne would aborde..our ship can holde no more. **1600** HOLLAND *Livy* XLIII. lvi. 1148 h, C. Lucretius..himself went abourd unto a trireme galley. **1602** SHAKS. *Haml.* I. iii. 56 Yet heere Laertes? Aboord, aboord for shame, The winde sits in the shoulder of your saile. **1611** BIBLE *Acts* xxi. 2 And finding a ship sailing ouer vnto Phenicea, wee went abroad [*sic*], and set foorth. **1725** POPE *Odyssey* II. 332 The Mariners by my command Shall speed aboard. **1849** GROTE *Greece* V. lvii. 118 (1862) The Syracusans got aboard, and rowed close along-shore.

c. *all aboard*, the call to warn passengers to get aboard a vessel about to start. Also used (chiefly *U.S.*) in connexion with coaches and trains.

1838 J. C. NEAL *Charcoal Sk.* 76 He..gave himself a gentle impulse, crying 'All aboard!' and slid slowly but majestically down. **1871** BARNUM *Struggles & Triumphs* 363, I should have expected..to have seen him dressed in a pea jacket, blowing off steam, and crying out 'all aboard that's going'. **1873** J. H. BEADLE *Undevel. West* xv. 251 All aboard for Yosemite and the Big Trees. **1903** A. D. MCFAUL *Ike Glidden* xxxi. 297 He and his bride boarded the train, and the conductor announced, 'All aboard'.

transf. **1878** I. L. BIRD *Rocky Mts.* (1879) 148 'Head them [*sc.* cattle] off, boys!' our leader shouted; 'all aboard! hark away!' and..away we all went at a hand-gallop. *c* **1890** MCK. WRIGHT in A. E. Woodhouse *N.Z. Farm & Station Verse* (1950) 33 All aboard! all aboard! is the cry They're a ripping lot of shearers in the shed. **1911** W. H. KOEBEL *Maoriland Bush* viii. 122 Then comes the..signal to commence work [*sc.* shearing]—the stentorian cry of 'All Aboard'. **1928** A. E. ANDREWS *C. C. Andrews: Recoll. 1829–1922* 169 At dusk a non-commissioned officer of the guard would call out 'All aboard', and upstairs we promptly would go.

d. On, or into, a train, aircraft, etc. Freq. *U.S.* Cf. BOARD *sb.* 14 c.

1856 M. J. HOLMES *L. Rivers* iv. 33 She..told him that 'the trunks..were every one on 'em left!' 'No, they are not ..I saw them aboard myself.' **1905** KIPLING *Actions & Reactions* (1909) 112 Our coach will lock on when..the clerks are aboard. **1931** W. G. MCADOO *Crowded Years* i. 7 When the..train..rattled up to the..station..the McAdoo family..climbed aboard. **1961** *Newsweek* 14 Aug. 13/1 Hardly anyone of the crew of six [etc.]..paid any attention to the man and teen-age boy who had come aboard. **1976** *Daily Tel.* 30 June 1/4 An advance on the 83 originally presumed to be aboard.

2. a. Alongside, on one side (of a ship or shore). Modified by *hard, close.* See also BOARD *sb.* 12 d.

1494 FABYAN VII. 373 The Turkes..ordeyned .iiii. barges or suche lyke vessayles, &..sodaynly brought them a bord where ye Cristen host lay. **1772–84** COOK *Voyages* (1790) V. 1782 He was desirous of keeping the coast of America aboard. **1881** *Daily Tel.* Jan. 28 The proximity of the coast which the education of his skipper obliges him, if possible, to keep close aboard.

b. *fig.*

1758 DYCHE & PARDON s.v. *Aboard*, In sports and games this phrase signifies, that the person or side in the game that was either none, or but few, has now got to be as many as the other.

c. to lay (a ship) **aboard**: to place one's own ship alongside of (it) for the purpose of fighting.

1593 SHAKS. *2 Hen. VI*, IV. i. 25 I lost mine eye in laying the prize aboord. **1655** HEYWOOD *Fortune by Land* etc. IV. 416 Shall we grapple, and lay their Ship aboard? **1815** SCOTT *Lord of the Isles* v. xxiv. A bark from Lorn Laid them aboard that very morn.

d. to fall aboard. *lit.* *of* a ship; to strike its side, fall foul of it. †*fig.* *with* or *of* a person or thing: to come to words, to quarrel; to attack, fall upon. The *of* is sometimes omitted.

1604 F. T. *Case is Altered* in Thynne's *Animadv.* (1865) 140 He falls aboord with him for her, to have her for his seruant. **1630** HOWELL *Letters* (1650) I. 387 I have sent your Lordship this small survey of the Latin..in my next I shall fall aboard of her three daughters, viz. the Italian, the Spanish, and the French. **1697** RAY in *Phil. Trans.* XIX. 636 The Horse again refused the Grass, and fell aboard the Hemlock, greedily eating it up. **1816** 'QUIZ' *Grand Master* i. 16 Why, are you blind?..steer large, You'll get aboard of that coal barge.

†**e. to bring aboard**: to bring to land. **to come to aboard** (Fr. *venir, arriver à bord*): to arrive at the shore, to land. *Obs.*

1550 NICOLLS *Thucydides* 53 They came to aborde in the porte of Philie. *a* **1600** *Mar. of Wit & Wisd.* Prol. (Shaks. Soc. 1846) 6 Then Fancy frames effects to bring his braine aborde, And shelue his ship in hauens mouth.

f. to haul the tacks aboard: 'to bring their weather clues down to the chess-tree, or literally, to set the courses.' Smyth *Sailor's Wd.-Bk.*

1549 *Compl. of Scotlande* vi. 40 (1873) Hail doune the steir burde lufe harde a burde.

¶ Used by Spenser *catachr.* for ?abroad, adrift.

1591 SPENSER *M. Hubberd's Tale* 324 They were in doubt, and flatly set abord. **1591** ? —— *Ruins of Rome* Wks. 1862 433/1 The foord..with his tumbling streames doth beare aboord The ploughmans hope.

B. *prep.* [by omission of *of*, after the adv.]

1. On board of, within the boards or sides of; **a.** (position) in or on (a ship).

1607 CAPT. KEELING in *Shaks. Cent. of Praise* 79 I envited Captain Hawkins to a ffishe dinner, and had Hamlet acted abord me. **1805** SOUTHEY *Madoc* xvii. (1853) V. 131 Is he aboard the fleet?

b. (motion) on to or into (a ship).

1466 *Manners & Househ. Exp. Eng.* 383 My mastyr paid fore botes to set them a bord the barge. **1606** SHAKS. *Ant. & Cl.* II. vi. 83 Aboord my Gally, I inuite you all. **1608** —— *Peric.* v. iii. 11 Her fortunes brought the maid aboord us. **1628** DIGBY *Voy. to Medit.* 1 (1868) Sent some of my men abord her. **1720** DE FOE *Capt. Singleton* xii. 205 He came aboard my ship. **1878** G. MACDONALD *Ann. Quiet Neighb.* xxiv. 429 Don't think I want to get aboard your ship.

c. In, or into (a train). Also on or in(to) an aircraft, etc. Freq. *U.S.*

1855 *Knickerbocker* XLV. 561, I..put myself 'a-board' the six-o'clock Train. **1869** 'MARK TWAIN' *Innoc. Abr.* xii. 79 We..stepped aboard the train. **1972** L. B. JOHNSON *Vantage Point* iii. 53 The next day, May 9, Mrs. Johnson and I left Washington aboard a Presidential jet. **1985** *Aviation Week & Space Technol.* 21 Jan. 134/3 Why not preserve the fixture used to initially transport the satellite aboard the shuttle?

†**2.** Along, by the side of. To fall aboard anything = fall aboard *of* it: see A 2 d. *Obs.*

1506 GUYLFORDE *Pylgr.* 62, §3 (Cam. Soc.) [We] laye amost harde abrode the grete vggly rokkes. **1602** CAREW *Cornwall* 29 b, Vail'd with nights robe, they stalke the shore aboord. **1642** FULLER *Holy & Prof. State* II. xxi. 134 They came hard aboard the shore. **1677** *Lond. Gaz.* mccxxxvi. 4 The Channel close aboard the Main at Winterton-ness.

¶ Used by Spenser *catachr.* for ?abroad, across the breadth or surface of.

1591 SPENSER *Virgil's Gnat* 46 Nor yron bands abord The Pontick sea by their huge Navy cast.

aboard, obsolete form of ABORD *v.*, to approach, board, land on.

aboard, obsolete form of ABORD *sb.*, approach.

†**aˈboast**, *v. Obs. rare*$^{-1}$. [f. A- *pref.* 11 (here with trans. force) + BOAST.] To address boastfully or haughtily.

1377 LANGL. *P. Pl.* B. VI. 156 A Brytonere, a · braggere a-bosted pieres als.

†**aˈbob**, *v. Obs. rare*$^{-1}$. [a. OFr. *abobe-r*, *abaube-r*, also *abaubier*, *abaubir* to astonish, astound, frighten:—L. **adbalbā-re* to strike speechless, f. *ad* to + *balbus* stammering.] To astonish, confound.

c **1330** *Arthour & Merlin* (1838) 1969 The messangers were abobbed tho, Thai nisten what thai mighten do.

abococket. See BYCOKET.

†**aˈbodance.** *Obs. rare*$^{-1}$. [f. ABODE *v.* + -ANCE, a Romance affix added to a native word.] A foretelling, prefiguring, portending, omen.

c **1630** JACKSON *Creed* VII. xvii. (1844) VII. 133 It had been 'verbum male ominatum,' an ill abodance, if the first of these five Egyptian cities..should be called the City of destruction.

abode (əˈbəʊd), past tense of ABIDE.

abode (əˈbəʊd), *sb.*[1] Forms: 1–3 abád, 3–5 abod, 4–7 abood, 5 aboode, 6 aboade, 6–7 aboad, 5– abode. Northern 3–6 abade, 5–7 abaid(e. [vbl. sb. of ABIDE, with same stem-vowel as the pa. t.; cf. *ride, rode, road.*]

†**1.** The action of waiting; delay. *esp.* in phrase **without abode**, without delay, immediately. *Obs.*

a **1250** *Juliana* (Bodl. MS.) 73 A! stalewurðe men doð hire biliue to-deað buten abade. **1314** *Guy Warw.* 46 Thurch the bodi his swerd glod Ded he fel withouten abod. **1375** BARBOUR *Bruce* i. 142 He buskyt hym, but mar abad. *c* **1386** CHAUCER *Knt. T.* 107 And right anoon, withoute eny abood His baner he desplayeth. *c* **1430** LYDGATE *Bochas* (1554) I. xv. 31 Whateuer he sayd, as longeth to Echo, Without abode, she sayd the same also. **1485** TREVISA *Higden* (1527) I. xxxviii. 406 And made no more abood But ran anone into the wood. *c* **1500** *Lancelot of the Laik* (1865) 3259 Kyng clamedyus makith non abaid. **1577** HOLINSHED *Chron.* III. 918/1 Without anie abode he entered the barge. **1596** SHAKS. *Merch. Ven.* II. vi. 21 Sweete friends, your patience for my long abode, Not I, but my affairs haue made you wait.

†**2.** A temporary remaining; a stay. *Obs.*

c **1384** CHAUCER *H. Fame* III. 942 Of restes, of labour, of viages, Of abood, of deeth, of lyfe. *c* **1460** FORTESCUE *Abs. & Lim. Mon.* (1714) 49 Their long or schorte Abode. **1599** HAKLUYT *Voyages* II. I. 143 In any of their abodes or passages by sea or land. **1607** HIERON *Wks.* I. 452 Wee are wont to describe a short abood by lodging in an inne. **1651** HOBBES *Leviathan* III. xli. 263 There are two parts of our Saviour's Office during his aboad upon the Earth. **1749** FIELDING *Tom Jones* VI. ix. 76 (1840) He waxeth wroth at your abode here.

†**3.** Used by Puttenham for the rhetorical practice of 'dwelling upon a point.' *Obs.*

1589 PUTTENHAM *Eng. Poesie* 240 (1869) The perswader.. should dwell vpon that point longer then vpon any other, and as it were to make his chief aboad thereupon, for which cause I name him the figure of aboad, according to the Latine name.

4. Habitual residence, dwelling.

1576 LAMBARDE *Peramb. Kent* 201 (1826) During his aboade in Kent, he had so incroched upon the lands. **1591** SHAKS. *1 Hen. VI*, V. iv. 88 The Countrey where you make abode. **1611** BIBLE *John* xiv. 23 We will come unto him, and make our abode with him. **1718** POPE *Iliad* V. 101 The brave Dolopian's mighty line, Who near adored Scamander made abode. **1860** R. A. VAUGHAN *Ho. w. Mystics* (ed. 2) I. 206 To dwell on the union of Christians with Christ; on His abode in us, and our abiding in Him.

5. An abiding-place, a dwelling-place, place of ordinary habitation; house or home. ***abode of love***: see AGAPEMONE; ***(of) no fixed abode***: a conventional *phr.* used of a person without a settled habitation.

1614 RALEIGH *Hist. World* II. 499 Her aboad was about the River Liris. **1633** G. HERBERT *Temple* 167, Ps. xxiii. 4 In deaths shadie black abode Well may I walk. **1667** MILTON *P.L.* III. 734 That spot to which I point is Paradise, Adam's abode. **1767** FORDYCE *Serm. to Yng. Wom.* II. xii. 207 Visits to the abodes of misfortune and pain. **1849** MACAULAY *Hist. Eng.* I. 320 He troubled himself little about decorating his abode.

1852 *Roget's Thes.* 223/1 Abode of love, agapemone. **1931** G. B. SHAW *Let.* 24 Nov. in *To a Young Actress* (1960) 156 If the customer wants to decorate a bedroom in an Abode of Love he (or she) may require something quite different from the keeper of a boarding house in Tunbridge Wells.

1883 *Times* 9 Jan. 4/6 At the Guildhall, yesterday, Charles M'Manes, who said he was a labourer but had no fixed abode, was charged on remand. **1922** JOYCE *Ulysses* 447 Henry Flower. No fixed abode. Unlawfully watching and besetting. **1962** *Oxford Mail* 20 Jan. 3/7 Two labourers of no fixed abode, who pleaded 'Guilty' to robbing——with violence at Stone.

†**abode**, *sb.*[2] *Obs.* [f. A-BEDE *v.*, OE. *abeód-an*, pa. pple. *a-boden*, 'to announce'; on the analogy of the simple sb. BODE, and its relation to the primitive *beódan, boden*: see next word.] An announcement, prediction, prognostication.

c **1600** CHAPMAN *Iliad* (1857) XIII. 146 If even the best of Gods, High thund'ring Juno's husband, stirs my spirit with true abodes. **1667** *Decay of Chr. Piety* §5. 196 That great unsensibleness many of us shew of what others groan under, is a very ominous abode. **1696** OVINGTON *Voyage to Surat* A superstitious fancy that mending old clothes in a morning is of very ill abode.

†**abode**, *v. Obs.* 6–7 also aboad(e. [f. ABODE *sb.*[2], on the analogy of the simple vb. *bode* (OE. *bodian*) f. the sb. *bode* (OE. *bod*). OE. had the primitive vb. *beódan*, ME. BEDE, pa. pple. *boden*, the sb. *bod*, ME. BODE, and its deriv. vb. *bod-ian*, mod.E. to BODE; also the deriv. vb. *abeódan*, ME. ABEDE, pa. pple. *aboden*; whence at a later time the prec. sb. and this vb.]

1. *trans.* To presage, prognosticate, be ominous of, BODE, FOREBODE.

1593 SHAKS. *3 Hen. VI*, V. vi. 45 The Owle shriek'd at thy birth, an euill signe, The Night-Crow cry'de, aboding lucklesse time. **1603** —— *Henry VIII*, I. i. 93 This tempest Dashing the Garment of this Peace, aboaded The sodaine breach on't. **1603** GREENWEY *Tacitus, Ann.* (1622) III. ii. 67 The which when Piso perceiued, to aboade his vtter destruction. **1665** J. SPENCER *Prodigies* 83 Lest it should abode the running of that Vessel upon rocks.

2. *intr.* To be ominous.

1659 HAMMOND *On Psalm* lix. 5 This abodes most sadly to Saul at this time. **1673** *Lady's Calling* II. §4. 16. 30 No night raven or screech-owl can abode half so dismally as these domestic birds of prey.

†**abodement**[1]. *Obs.* [f. ABODE *v.* + -MENT, an early instance of a native vb. with this suffix.] A foreboding, presage, or omen.

1593 SHAKS. *3 Hen. VI*, IV. vii. 13 Tush man, aboadments must not now affright vs. **1651** *Reliquiæ Wottonianæ* 119 The Lord Bishop.. took the freedom to ask whether he had never any secret abodement in his minde. **1665** J. SPENCER *Prodigies* 179 But where matters ungrateful fall before us, we usually serve our little hatreds, by deriving upon them the Opinion of being ill abodements.

†**abodement**[2]. *Obs.* [An irreg. formation on ABODE *sb.*[1], perh. due to form-assoc. with prec.] Abode, abiding.

1592 WYRLEY *Armorie* i. 131 Making abodement with the loued Prince. **1616** DRUMM. OF HAWTH. *Poems* 174 Nor time nor Place Of thy abodement shadows any Trace, But there to me Thou shin'st.

†**aboding**, *vbl. sb. Obs.* [f. ABODE *v.* + -ING[1].] Boding or foreboding.

a **1710** BP. BULL *Wks.* II. 489 What strange ominous abodings and fears do many times on a sudden seize upon men of certain approaching evils.

†**aboding**, *ppl. a. Obs.* [f. ABODE *v.* + -ING[2].] Foreboding, portending, ominous.

c **1630** JACKSON *Creed* VIII. xxvii. (1844) VIII. 107 This unreasonable, ill aboding desire did displease the Lord.

abof, aboffe, obsolete forms of ABOVE.

aboȝe, *adv. Obs.* dial. f. aboue, abowe, ABOVE.

c **1380** *Sir Ferumbras* 2972 By þat was Gyoun vp a-stoȝe; oppoun þe laddre an heȝ, And þe rop y-knyt þe tree aboȝe. *Ibid.* 4319 Amydde þe brigge þar stent a tour y-buld aboȝe wyþ gret honour.

aboȝen, *pa. pple.* of ABOW *v. Obs.*

aboȝt(e, aboht(e, obs. *past t.* of ABYE *v.*

‖**aboideau, aboiteau** ('æbədəʊ, -təʊ; Fr. abwado, -to). *Canadian.* 9 ab(b)atteau. Pl. -eaux, -s. [Canadian Fr.] In Nova Scotia and New Brunswick, a sluice-gate in a dike. Hence as *v.* (*rare*), to provide with such a sluice-gate.

1825 *Novascotian* (Halifax) 9 Mar. 86/1 Before half an hour the violence of the water washed away.. the complete side of the abatteau. *Ibid.* 16 Mar. 99/2 Heretofore Abbateaus have been constructed in too narrow a base. **1830** MOORSOM *Lett. N.S.* 187 The *aboiteau* is provided with a floodgate which opens and closes with the preponderating water. **1876** J. R. CAMPBELL *Hist. Yarmouth Co., N.S.* 5 The abatteau was protected by a long pier running out seaward. **1903** *Bot. Gaz.* Sept. 180 (Cent. D. Suppl.), At first sight it might seem wise to aboideau all rivers at their mouths. **1905** CROSSKILL *Prince Edward Is.* 85 As a result of such legislation, Aboideaux.. have been constructed at the undermentioned places. **1955** in *Jrnl. Canad. Ling. Assoc.* (1958) IV. 9 Bulldozers and all types of modern machinery .. are constructing an aboiteau to provide protection to a considerable marsh body.

aboil (ə'bɔɪl), *adv.* [f. A *prep.*[1] on, in + BOIL.] In or into a boiling state; a-boiling.

1858 HUGH MILLER *Schools and Schoolm.* vi. 127 Scenes of cruelty and spoliation of which the recollection.. had still power enough to set his Scotch blood aboil.

†**abolete.** *Obs. rare*$^{-1}$. [ad. L. *abolēt-us*, pa. pple. of *abolēre*: see ABOLISH.] Obsolete, out of use.

c **1525** SKELTON *Why come ye not* 710 And dare use this experiens To practyse such abolete sciens.

abolish (ə'bɒlɪʃ), *v.* Also 5–6 **abolyssh**, 6 **abholish**; Sc. 7 **abolliss.** [a. Fr. *aboliss-*, lengthened stem of *abolir*:—L. *abolēsc-ĕre*, inceptive of *abolē-re* to grow out of use, and trans. to destroy, do away with; f. *ab* off, away + obs. *olē-re* to grow. In Eng. as in French always trans.] To put an end to, to do away with; to annul or make void; to demolish, destroy or annihilate. Its application to persons or concrete objects is nearly obsolete; it is usually said of institutions, customs or practices. Formerly often followed by *from, out of*; now usually without complement.

1490 CAXTON *Eneydos* xxvi. 94 Thou hast abolysshed my fraunchise. **1542** *Contn.* FABYAN VII. 700 This yere was the bishop of Rome.. abholished quit out of this realme. **1542** BRINKLOW *Compl.* (1874) xix. 44 How can wickydnesse abolyssh wyckednesse, but rather increase it? **1596** SPENSER *F.Q.* II. iv. 45 And with thy blood abolish so reprochfull blott. **1607** TOPSELL *Four-footed Beasts* (1673) 371 He doth craftily dissemble and abolish his foot-steps to deceive the Hunters. **1609** SKENE *Reg. Maj.* 4 The fourtie dayes, or thrie sunnes, granted to the persewer.. is discharged and abollissed. **1611** BIBLE *Is.* ii. 18 And the idoles hee shall vtterly abolish. **1718** LADY M. W. MONTAGU *Lett.* No. 49 II. 56 The adventure.. abolished that heathenish ceremony. **1837** CARLYLE *Fr. Rev.* I. v. ix. 291 Thus in any case, with what rule soever, shall the Bastille be abolished from our Earth. **1854** KINGSLEY *Lett.* (1878) I. 415 Some dislike the notion of its being possible to abolish pestilence by sanitary reform. **1877** *Daily News* 5 Nov. 5/1 We know that the best way to abolish darkness is to give light, that the best way to abolish folly is to spread wisdom.

abolishable (ə'bɒlɪʃəb(ə)l), *a.* [f. ABOLISH *v.* + -ABLE. Cf. mod.Fr. *abolissable.*] Capable of being abolished, or put an end to; liable to abolition.

1660 HOWELL, Abolishable, *Amortissable, abrogable.* **1837** CARLYLE *Fr. Rev.* I. II. viii. 83 Hope is but deferred; not abolished, not abolishable. **1860** RUSKIN *Mod. Painters* V. VIII. iii. §4. 180 This Leonidas shall.. abolish—so far as abolishable—his own spirit.

abolished (ə'bɒlɪʃt), *ppl. a.* [f. ABOLISH *v.* + -ED.] Put an end to, done away with, suppressed.

1869 A. S. AYRTON in H. of Comm. *Daily News* June 19 This was an abolished office, and there was no contract binding Government to give the officers of an abolished office their full salaries for life.

abolisher (ə'bɒlɪʃə(r)). [f. ABOLISH *v.* + -ER[1].] One who abolishes, puts an end to, or abrogates.

1742 MIDDLETON *Cicero* III. xi. 264 (ed. 3) The abolisher of a tyranny. **1806** W. TAYLOR in *Ann. Rev.* IV. 208 The abolisher of the political equality of religious sects. **1858** GLADSTONE *Hom. Age* II. 132 The Conqueror and Disarmer but not yet Abolisher of Death.

abolishing (ə'bɒlɪʃɪŋ), *vbl. sb.* [f. ABOLISH *v.* + -ING[1].] The act or process of putting an end to, or doing away with; a suppression, destruction, or annihilation; abolition. (Now mostly gerundial.)

1549 J. PONET (*title*) Ochinus, Bernard, of Siena. A Tragedie or Dialoge of the uniuste vsurped Primacie of the Bishop of Rome, and of the iust Abolishyng of the same, etc. **1653** MILTON *Cons. Hirelings* Wks. 1851, 353 To have prov'd in general the abolishing of Tithes. *a* **1665** GOODWIN *A being filled with the Spirit* (1867) 299 The abolishing or cessation of the deeds of the flesh.

abolishment (ə'bɒlɪʃmənt). *arch.* [f. ABOLISH *v.* + -MENT. Cf. Fr. *abolissement* 16th c. (which may be the direct source).]

1. The process of abolishing, putting an end to, or doing away with; annulment, or destruction. (It scarcely differs from ABOLISHING *sb.* on the one hand, or ABOLITION on the other: the latter is now generally used instead.)

1542–60 BECON *Potation for Lent* Wks. 1843, 119 Remember that he offered himself.. for the abolishment of all your sins. **1563** FOXE *A. & M.* 835/2 The Kynges supremacie, and thabolyshement of the byshop of Rome's author[it]ie. **1611** SPEED *Hist. Brit.* VII. xxxii. 322 Abolishment of the peruerse law of the West-Saxons. **1626** *Rawleigh's Ghost* (1651) 200 Decreeing the abolishment and death of mankind in revenge of their sinnes. **1812** SOUTHEY in *Q. Rev.* VIII. 328 By abolishing that system in the countries which he has subjected, and by necessitating its abolishment in others. **1881** *Journ. Educ.* 1 Feb. 25/2 The main points urged in the memorial were—1. the abolishment of payment for pass.

2. The result of abolishing; a state of annihilation, or cessation of existence.

1868 BROWNING *Ring & Bk.* III. IX. 1499 Abolishment is nothingness, And nothingness has neither head nor tail.

abolition (æbə'lɪʃən). [a. Fr. *abolition*, or ? ad. L. *abolitiōn-em* annulling, amnesty, n. of action from *abolēre*: see ABOLISH.]

1. The act of abolishing, or putting an end to; the fact of being abolished, or done away with; annulling, destruction, or annihilation.

1529 MORE *Suppl. Soules* Wks. 1557, 311/2 They by the distruccion of the clergy, meane the clere abolycion of Christes faith. **1533** ELYOT *Castel of Helth* 55 (1541) It signifieth a short abolicion or dissolution of nature. *a* **1638** MEDE *Par. 2 Pet.* iii. Wks. 1672, III. 617 We look for a New heaven and a New earth to precede this abolition. **1651** JER. TAYLOR *Serm.* I. xxii. 286 Requiring onely contrition, even at the last for the abolition of eternal guilt. **1763** LD. BARRINGTON in Ellis *Orig. Lett.* II. 505 IV. 474 He recommended Union and Abolition of party Distinctions. **1792** GOV. MORRIS *Spark's Life & Wr.* (1832) III. 29 The abolition of the slave trade is disagreeable to them. **1862** H. SPENCER *First Prin.* I. v. §29. (1875) 103 The abolition of an imaginable agency, and the substitution of an unimaginable one. **1875** WOOD *Therap.* 375 (1879) The paralysis or quietness must have been due to an abolition of sensation.

b. *spec.* The abolition of the slave-trade, which, in the end of the 18th and during the 19th centuries, both in the European colonies, and still more in the United States of America, became a great political question, so as to be spoken of familiarly as 'abolition.' Hence *attrib.* as the 'abolition movement,' an 'abolition speech,' etc.

1788 T. CLARKSON (*title*) Essay on the comparative Efficiency of Regulation or Abolition as applied to the Slave-trade. **1808** —— *Hist. of the Abolition* II. ii. 118 The author travels to Paris to promote the abolition in France. **1863** W. PHILLIPS *Speeches* vi. 132 Dr. Channing has thanked the Abolition party. **1863** KEMBLE *Resid. in Georgia* 57 Until the late abolition movement.

†**2.** A putting out of memory; a final overlooking or condoning, an amnesty. Also (in *Law*) permission to condone an offence, or withdraw from its prosecution.

1606 HOLLAND *Suetonius* 89 After that Cæsar was slaine.. all men for feare of troubles and uprores decreed a finall abolition and oblivion of that fact. **1691** BLOUNT *Law Dict.*, *Abolition*, A destroying or putting out of memory; the leave given by the King or Judges to a criminal accuser to desist from further prosecution. **1809** TOMLINS *Law Dict.*, *Abolition*, a destroying or effacing or putting out of memory.

abolitionary (æbə'lɪʃənərɪ), *a.* [f. ABOLITION + -ARY.] Dealing with abolition or annihilation; destructive.

1868 AUG. BOBORUIKIN *Nih. in Russia* in *Fortn. Rev.* IV. (N.S.) 133 If he is a Nihilist, he should profess exclusively negative and abolitionary doctrines.

abolitionism (æbə'lɪʃənɪz(ə)m). [f. ABOLITION 1 b. + -ISM.] The principles or measures of abolitionists; opposition to negro slavery.

1808 WILBERFORCE *Let. to Wm. Smith* in *Life* (1838) III. xxii. 385 With a view to having the Spanish deputies well impregnated with Abolitionism. **1853** M. HOWITT tr. *Bremer's Homes of New World* III. 344 Violent abolitionism is more and more giving place to a nobler and calmer spirit. **1860** *Sat. Rev.* No. 255. 340/2 Even in the Free States Abolitionism is not quite safe.

abolitionist (æbə'lɪʃənɪst). [f. ABOLITION + -IST.] **a.** One who aims at or advocates the abolition of any institution or custom.

1836–7 DICKENS *Sketches* (1850) 144 The abolitionist of the national debt, the unflinching opponent of pensions. **1871** *Daily News* Nov. 1 Who, indeed, among the abolitionists of Purchase has ever denied that English gentlemen.. have served their country on the battle-field?

b. Applied specially, and probably originally, to persons seeking the abolition of negro slavery. Used also *attrib.*

1790 CLARKSON in *Slave-trade* II. 212 Many looked upon the abolitionists as monsters. **1842** DICKENS *Lett.* I. 61 (ed. 2) I speak of..all parties—Slave Upholders and Abolitionists. **1859** *Times* 28 Dec. 6/4 The vagaries of the Abolitionists would cause a revulsion of feeling in favour of the South. *Ibid.* The doings of their Abolitionist brethren.

c. Applied to one who advocates the abolition of capital punishment. Used also *attrib.*, esp. of countries, states, which have abolished capital punishment.

1927 E. R. CALVERT *Cap. Punishment in 20th Cent.* ii. 23 The abolitionist recognises..the need to protect society against murder, but he realises that the problem cannot be solved by the mere infliction of unpleasant consequences. *Ibid.* iii. 48 The relative culture and ethical standards in the abolitionist and non-abolitionist states. **1930** *Times* 3 Apr. 7/7 The cumulative experience of abolitionist countries demonstrated beyond reasonable doubt that the death penalty is not necessarily a deterrent. **1956** *Times* 10 July 6/3 There was no evidence to show that the police in abolitionist countries were any less safe than they were in retentionist countries.

abolitionize (æbəˈlɪʃənaɪz), *v.* [f. ABOLITION + -IZE.] To imbue with the principles of abolitionism; to render opposed to slavery. Chiefly in U.S.

1848 BARTLETT, To *abolitionize*: to convert to the doctrines of the abolitionists. **1863** S. L. J. 'A Blockaded Brit. Subj.' *Life in the South* I. i. 3 Scheme of abolitionizing Virginia.

abolke, ? for *abolȝe(n*, pa. pple of ABELȜEN.

‖**abolla** (əˈbɒlə). [referred to a Gr. ἀμβολή for ἀναβολή a throwing back and around; but very doubtful.] A woollen cloak worn chiefly by the soldiers and lower classes of ancient Rome.

1868 SMITH *Dict. Ant.* s.v. The abolla was used by the lower classes at Rome, and consequently by the philosophers who affected severity of manners and life. Hence the expression of Juvenal, *facinus majoris abollae*—a crime committed by a very deep philosopher.

‖**aboma** (əˈbəʊmə). 'A large species of serpent, which inhabits the morasses and fens of South America, *Epicratis Cenchria*.' *Penny Cycl.* 1836.

‖**abomasum, -us** (æbəʊˈmeɪsəm, -əs). [mod.L., f. L. *ab* away from + *omās-um* or *omass-um* (a Gallic word) bullock's tripe, *hence* a fat paunch.] The fourth, and true digestive, stomach of ruminants.

1706 PHILLIPS, *Abomasum*, the Paunch of a Beast, the Tripes; in Anatomy, one of the four Stomachs of Ruminant Animals. **1741** CHAMBERS *Cycl.* It is in the Abomasus of calves and lambs that the rennet, or earning is found, wherewith housewives turn or curdle their milk. **1875** BLAKE *Zool.* 32 In the 4th division, abomasus, or rennet, the lining membrane is filled with gastric tubular glands.

A-bomb: see A III.

abominable (əˈbɒmɪnəb(ə)l), *a.* (and *adv.*) Also 4–7 **abhominable.** [a. Fr. *abominable, abhominable* ad. L. *abōminābil-is* deserving imprecation or abhorrence; f. *abōminā-ri* to deprecate as an ill omen; f. *ab* off, away + *ōmen*; cf. the exclamation '*ab-sit ōmen!*' In med.L. and OFr., and in Eng. from Wyclif to 17th c., regularly spelt *abhominable*, and explained as *ab homine*, quasi 'away from man, inhuman, beastly,' a derivation which influenced the use and has permanently affected the meaning of the word. No other spelling occurs in the first folio of Shaks., which has the word 18 times; and in *L.L.L.* v. i. 27, Holophernes abhors the 'rackers of ortagriphie,' who were beginning to write *abominable* for the time-honoured *abhominable*.]

A. *adj.* **1.** Exciting disgust and hatred, generally by evident ill qualities, physical or moral; offensive, loathsome; odious, execrable, detestable.

a. Of things.

1366 MAUNDEV. (1839) ix. 101 The abhomynable Synne of Sodomye. **1382** WYCLIF *1 Mac.* i. 57 Kyng Antiochus beeldide the abominable [**1388** abhominable] ydol of desolacioun. **1398** TREVISA *Barth. De P.R.* XVIII. xci. 840 The frogge is venemouse and abhomynable therefore to men. **1535** FISHER *Wks.* (1876) 373 Askyng of him mercy for your abhominable offences. **1588** SHAKS. *L.L.L.* v. i. 27 Neighbour vocatur nebour; neigh abreuiated ne: this is abhominable, which he would call abbominable. **1603** —— *Meas. for Meas.* III. ii. 25 From their abhominable and beastly touches. **1611** BIBLE *Lev.* vii. 21 Any vncleane beast, or any abominable vncleane thing. **1661** PAGITT *Heresiog.* 91 The authors of this opinion that set Prayers are abhominable. **1667** MILTON *P.L.* x. 465 This infernal pit, Abominable, accursed, the house of woe. **1756** BURKE *Vind. Nat. Soc.* Wks. I. 76 Shall we pass by this monstrous heap of absurd notions, and abominable practices? **1876** HUMPHREY *Coin Coll. Man.* xxiv. 337 The abominable profligacy of her character did not prevent a servile senate from conferring divine honours upon her.

b. Of persons.

1382 WYCLIF *Titus* i. 16 Thei ben abomynable [**1388** abhominable] and vnbyleveful, and reprouable to al good werk. **1535** COVERDALE *Wisd.* xiv. 9 For the vngodly & his vngodlynes are both like abhominable vnto God. **1610** SHAKS. *Temp.* II. ii. 163 The poore Monster's in drinke: An abhominable Monster. **1619** T. TAYLOR *Titus* i. 16. 324 The miserable condition of the hypocrite; Hee is an abhominable person. **1668** CULPEPER & COLE tr. *Bartholinus Anat.* I. xxviii. 70 A young woman the Wife of an abominable Taylor. **1878** B. TAYLOR *Deukalion* I. iv. 36 Distinct, abominable, I see ourselves before the Titans were.

c. ***Abominable Snowman***, name applied to a creature alleged to exist in the Himalayas. (Cf. YETI.)

1921 *Times* 31 Oct. 10/6 The men were never seen..but footprints were found which were suspected of being those made by these men, who are apparently known to the Tibetans as Meetoh Kangmi, or 'Abominable Snowmen', and small colonies of these people are believed to exist on the slopes of Everest, Chumalhari, and Karola. **1955** *Ann. Reg.* 1954 A British party which set out to investigate the Abominable Snowman or Yeti found that legendary creature most elusive and returned with only a few more photographs of footprints.

2. *loosely.* Very unpleasant or distasteful.

1860 TYNDALL *Glaciers* I. §27. 218 The rain was pitiless and the road abominable. **1874** BLACK *Pr. of Thule* 37 Sheila had nothing to do with the introduction of this abominable decoration.

B. as *adv.*

1477 NORTON *Ordin. Alch.* (1652) v. 73 For they maie be abhominable sower, Over-sharpe, too bitter.

¶ ABOMINABLE has occasionally been used, like *terrible, prodigious*, as a simple intensive. Juliana Berners (15th c.) writes of 'a bomynable syght of monks,' i.e. a large company. Cf. ABOMINATION 5 and ABOMINATIONLY.

abominableness (əˈbɒmɪnəb(ə)lnɪs). Also 6–7 **abhominablenesse.** [f. ABOMINABLE + -NESS.] The quality or state of being very offensive; loathsomeness, odiousness.

1530 PALSGR., Abhomynablenesse, *abhominableté*. **1541** R. BARNES *Wks.* (1573) 329 Yet men had rather here this abhominablenes, then for to release a litle of theyr own will. **1649** CROMWELL *Let.* 72 (Carl.) The propositions enclosed;—which for their abominableness, manifesting also the impudency of the men, I thought fit to present to your view. **1692** BENTLEY *Boyle Lect.* i. 3 We must forbear to urge atheists with the..Abominableness of their Principles. **1819** SOUTHEY *Lett.* (1856) III. 148 My abecedarian interpretation of your abominableness.

abominably (əˈbɒmɪnəblɪ), *adv.* Also 6–7 **abhominably.** [f. ABOMINABLE + -LY².]

1. So as to cause disgust and hatred; offensively, loathsomely; odiously.

a **1520** *Myrroure of Our Ladye* 194 They..ledde theyr lyues abhomynably in fylthe of flesshely luste. **1535** COVERDALE *Wisd.* xix. 12 They dealt so abhominably & churlishly with straungers. **1602** SHAKS. *Ham.* III. ii. 39 I haue thought some of Natures Iouerney-men had made men, and not made them well, they imitated Humanity so abhominably. **1611** BIBLE *1 Kings* xxi. 26 And hee did very abominably in following Idoles. **1791** BURKE *Reg. Peace* Wks. IX. 46 The Committee for foreign Affairs [Sansculottes] were such slovens, and stunk so abominably, that no Muscadin Ambassadour..could come within ten yards of them. **1881** SALA *Illus. Lond. News* 19 Feb. 171 The abominably despotic government of the kingdom of the Two Sicilies.

2. *loosely.* Very badly, unpleasantly, or distastefully.

1643 TREVOR *Let.* in Carte's *Collect.* (1735) 259 The King wants armes and money abominably. **1743** WALPOLE *Lett. to H. Mann* 87 (1834) I. 303 My dear child she brags abominably. **1853** KANE *Grinnell Exped.* i. 486 (1856) The abominably iterated accordions, with their kindred Jews-harps.

abominate (əˈbɒmɪneɪt), *v.* [f. L. *abōmināt-* ppl. stem of *abōminā-ri*: see ABOMINABLE and -ATE³.]

1. To feel extreme disgust and hatred towards; to regard with intense aversion; to abhor, loathe.

1644 BULWER *Chironomia* 53 Who refuse, abhor, detest or abominate some execrable thing. **1649** MILTON *Eikonokl.* i. 339 (1851) A Scotch Warr, condemn'd and abominated by the whole kingdom. **1706** DE FOE *Jure Divino* Pref. 4 Those who Swore to him when he was King..are all Perjur'd Rebels; abominable, and to be abominated by all good Men. **1728** NEWTON *Chronol. Amended* 9 The Egyptians..lived only on the fruits of the earth, and abominated flesh-eaters. **1866** MOTLEY *Dutch Rep.* III. v. 437 Influential persons in Madrid had openly abominated the cruel form of amnesty which had been decreed.

2. *loosely.* To dislike strongly.

1880 V. LEE *Italy* IV. iii. 170 Steele..had no musical sense, and abominated operas. **1881** A. TROLLOPE *Ayala's Angel* III. xlvi. 37 Then he spake again 'I do abominate a perverse young woman.'

abominate (əˈbɒmɪnət), *ppl. a.* [ad. L. *abōmināt-us* pa. pple. of *abōminā-ri*: see ABOMINABLE.] Held in abomination, detested.

1850 BLACKIE *Æschylus* I. 194 These are the horrid feasts, Of gods abominate. **1852** KINGSLEY *Andromeda* 58 Grieving the eyes of their pride, abominate, doomed to their anger.

abominated (əˈbɒmɪneɪtɪd), *ppl. a.* [f. ABOMINATE *v.* + -ED.] Held in abomination, detested.

1721 AUBREY *Misc.* I. 97 So certainly does the Revenge of God pursue the abominated Murderer.

abomination (əˌbɒmɪˈneɪʃən). Also 4–7 **abhominacioun, abhomynacion.** [a. Fr. *abomination* (13th c. in Litt.) ad. L. *abōminātiōn-em* n. of action f. *abōminā-ri*: see ABOMINABLE.]

1. The feeling or state of mind of combined disgust and hatred; abhorrence, detestation, loathing.

1395 PURVEY *Remonstr.* (1851) 7 Alle resonable men have greet abhominacioun of bodili sodomie. **1483** CAXTON *G. Leg.* 431 [He] vysyted the hospytalles..wythout abhomynacion of dyfformyte ne of ordure or fylthe of somme pacyente. **1525–30** MORE *De quat. Nouis.* Wks. 1557, 96 We se gret cause to haue it in hatred & abominacion. **1611** BIBLE *1 Sam.* xiii. 4 Israel also was had in abomination with the Philistines. *Mod.* To regard smoking with abomination.

†**b.** Physical disgust, nausea. [So in early Fr.] *Obs.*

1398 TREVISA *Barth. De P.R.* (1495) VII. viii. 228 Yf gedynes comyth of the stomak the pacyent felyth abhomynacion and wamlynge.

†**2.** A state or condition giving rise to intense disgust; defilement, pollution, abominableness. *Obs.*

1413 LYDGATE *Pylg. Sowle* (1483) III. i. 49 What stynke and corrupcion what fylthe and abhomynacion is there withynne the helle. **1480** *Rob. the Devyll* 31 I desyre youe to heare my confession Of my greate synnes the abhomynacon.

3. An action, or custom, abominable, detestable, odious, shamefully wicked or vile; a degrading vice.

c **1325** *E.E. Allit. Poems* B. 1173 (1864) 73 He vsed abominaciones of idolatrye. *c* **1386** CHAUCER *Man of Lawes T.* 88 He..Wolde never wryte in non of his sermouns Of such unkynde abhominaciouns. **1494** FABYAN VI. clxxxi. 180 Yᵉ great abhomynacion of thyse tyranous Danys, that beat, robbed, and slewe yᵉ innosent people without mercy. **1549** LATIMER *7 Serm. bef. Edw. VI* (1869) 207 What an abhominacion is it? the foulest that euer was to attribute to mans worke oure saluacion. **1606** SHAKS. *Ant. & Cl.* III. vi. 94 Th' adulterous Anthony, most large In his abhominations. **1611** BIBLE *Mal.* ii. 11 An abomination is committed in Israel. **1682** BURNET *Rts. of Princes* v. 159 He was not guilty of these monstrous Abominations. **1852** MISS YONGE *Cameos* (1877) III. xxiii. 355 Ninety-five theses, many of which were directed against the special abominations of Tetzel.

4. An object that excites disgust and hatred; a thing detested or detestable. (Followed by *unto, to.*) *esp.* in the Bible, a cause of pollution, an idol.

1366 MAUNDEV. (1839) xxviii. 282 Fro him comethe out smoke and stynk and fuyr, and so moche Abhomynacioun, that unethe no man may there endure. **1382** WYCLIF *Matt.* xxiv. 15 Ȝe schulen se the abhomynacioun of discomfort that is seid of Danyel, the prophete. **1535** COVERDALE *2 Kings* xxiii. 13 Malcom the abhominacion of the children of Ammon. **1611** BIBLE *Prov.* xii. 22 Lying lippes are abomination to the Lord. **1794** SULLIVAN *View of Nat.* II. Nor was it until the days of Hezekiah..that this abomination [the brazen serpent] was torn from the land. **1856** KANE *Arctic Explor.* II. v. 59 Brewed up flax-seed and lime-juice and quinine and willow-stems into an abomination which was dignified as beer.

†**5.** *loosely.* An unpleasant or disgusting amount, etc. *Obs.*

1604 DEKKER *Honest Wh.* (1873) 8, I ha spent an abomination this voyage.

†**abomiˈnationly,** *adv. Obs.* [f. ABOMINATION + -LY².] Abominably; hatefully; to an extent which is an abomination to the speaker.

1593 G. HARVEY *Pierces Supererog.* 180 Deriding dunsically, banging abominationly. **1716** MRS. BEHN *Young King* v. iii. 365 Let me see a little; my wife loves Newalties abominationly, and I must tell her something about the King.

abominator (əˈbɒmɪneɪtə(r)). [f. ABOMINATE *v.* + -OR, as if a L. **abōminātor* agent noun f. *abōminārī*.] One who abominates or detests; an abhorrer or extreme hater.

1816 SCOTT *Old Mort.* i. More than one non-juring bishop, whose authority and income were upon as apostolical a scale as the greatest abominator of Episcopacy could well desire.

†**aˈbomine,** *v. Obs.* [a. Fr. *abomine-r*, 14th c., ad. L. *abōminārī*.] = ABOMINATE *v.*

1683 HAMMOND *Wks.* IV. xii. 643 The Primitive Christians were branded and abomined by them for three special faults. *a* **1745** SWIFT (L.) By topics which though I abomine 'em May serve as arguments *ad hominem*.

†**abone,** *v. Obs.*⁻⁰ [See quot. Never used.]

1656 BLOUNT *Gloss.*, *Abone* (from the Italian *abonare* or *abbonare*) to make good or seasonable, to ripen.

‖**abonné** (abɔne). [Fr., f. pa. pple. of *abonner* to enrol as a subscriber.] One who subscribes to a periodical, etc.; also, a season-ticket holder at the theatre. See next.

[**1896** E. DOWSON *Let.* (1967) 343 Write to me soon, mon vieux, & *send me an occasional* 'Daily Chronicle'. I am abonné to the 'Journal'—but otherwise more literatureless.] **1909** BEERBOHM *Around Theatres* (1924) II. 417 He came forth into the sunshine—sunshine than which he was more dazzling to the abonnés. **1938** P. LÉON in *Lett. J. Joyce* (1966) III. 414 The abonnés..rather astonished, one of them saying: Il va un peu fort celui-là. **1954** *Ballet Ann.* IX. 86 Encouraged by the patronage of *abonnés* who have inherited their fathers' seats in the stalls. **1959** *Listener* 8 Jan. 73/1 Mr. O'Brien's anthology is not exactly the selection an old *abonné* to the *NRF* [sc. *Nouvelle Revue Française*] would make for his own pleasure.

‖**abonnement** (əbɒnəmɑ̃). [Fr.: see prec.] A subscription for a season ticket at a theatre (ski-school, etc.); the ticket itself. Freq. *attrib.*

1894 W. ARCHER *Theatr.* '*World*' *1893* 148 A series of twelve Ibsen performances at the Opera Comique Theatre was subsidised by a subscription in the nature of an abonnement. **1897** —— *Theatr.* '*World*' *1896* p. li, The abonnement system, which obtains at all the great theatres of the Continent, but which the long run renders impossible, should be introduced and carefully fostered. **1963** *Times* 20 Feb. 16/7 For example, the *stagione* and *abonnement* system (necessitating unvaried programmes on a subscription throughout the season), while working well for opera, is hard on the ballet. **1964** *Harper's Bazaar* Nov. 118 New *abonnement* ski passes will be issued..entitling bearers to use any..of the uphill transport. **1970** N. FLEMING *Czech Point* i. 7 A man..came out, compared my face with its scowling likeness on my *abonnement*, trapped a T-bar and launched me off on a trip up a thousand feet of mountain.

abood, obsolete form of ABODE.

a'boon, *adv.* and *prep.* Northern form of ABOVE; also used as a poetic form.

1875 B. TAYLOR *Faust.* I. i. 4 Dazzling light & fainter sparkles Gleam in cloudless dark aboon.

aboord, obsolete form of ABOARD.

aboral (æ'bɔərəl), *a. Zool.* [f. L. *ab* away from + -ORAL, f. L. *ōr-* mouth.] Pertaining to the region of the animal body at the opposite extremity from the mouth. Used especially of those types of animal structure in which the mouth occupies one of the poles.

1857 L. AGASSIZ *Contrib. Nat. Hist. N. America* IV. 376 I have called this side [of radiate animals] the oral or actinal area, and the opposite side the aboral or abactinal area. **1878** MACALISTER *Invertebr.* 56 The intestine..ends in a small aboral sac or cloaca.

aborcement, var. ABORSEMENT, *Obs.*, abortion.

abord (ə'bɔəd), *v. arch.* Also 6–7 **aboard, abord(e, abourd, abboord.** [a. Fr. *aborde-r* to come to the side of, approach, land, f. *à bord* to the side of; see ABOARD *adv.* Cf. ACCOST *v.*]

†**1.** To approach, come close to; to enter, land on, gain a footing upon. *Obs.*

1509 HAWES *Past. Pleas.* xxxvi. 20 And the royall shyppe, yclipped Perfitenes, They dyd aborde. **1530** PALSGR. 415 I aborde: as one shyppe doth another, *Jaborde.* I aborde a shyppe, *Je aborde.* **1589** IVE *Fortif.* 5 That an enemie may bee the more troubled to abourd the Fort. *Ibid.* 38 Approched, aborded, and surprised. **1611** COTGR., *Confiner*, to abboord, adioyn, lye neere vnto. **1691** RAY *Wisd. God* (1714) 201 The first Spaniards that aborded America.

2. To accost. *Obs.* or *arch.*

1611 COTGR., *Aborder*, to approach, accoast, abboord. *a* **1628** F. GREVILLE *Life of Sidney* 74 (1652) To abbord, either with question, familiarity, or scorn. **1841** THACKERAY *Professor* ii. 176 He..aborded the two ladies with easy eloquence.

†**a'bord**, *sb. Obs.* Also **aboard.** [a. Fr. *abord* approach; f. *aborde-r*: see prec.]

1. The act of approaching; approach; manner of approach. Cf. Fr. *au premier abord.*

1611 COTGR., *Arrivée*, an arriuall, accesse, abboord, or comming to. **1645** DIGBY *Nat. Bodies* 253 (L.) He [a blind man] would at the first aboard of a stranger..frame a right apprehension of his stature. **1655** JENNINGS *Elise* 116 This, at first aboard, astonish'd Cyrilla. **1774** CHESTERFIELD *Let.* 186 (R.) Whether your first abord made that advantageous impression. **1854** P. G. PATMORE *Friends & Acq.* III. xviii. 100 Such were the impressions produced on me by the first *abord* of John Hunt, as I saw him within his prison walls. **1884** *Edin. Rev.* Oct. 557 Her granddaughter has a vivid recollection of Mrs. Merivale in her later days, with a slightly formal and old-fashioned 'abord'.

2. Way of approach.

1670 LASSELS *Voy. Italy* I. 82 I never saw a more stately abord to any Citty then to this [Genoa].

abord, obs. form of ABOARD *adv.*

†**a'bordage.** *Obs.* [a. Fr. *abordage.*] An attack upon a ship by boarding it.

c **1550** SIR J. BALFOUR *Practicks* (1754) 640 The master farther gettis of the ship takin be him and the companie, the best cabill and anchor for his abordage.

†**abordering,** *ppl. a. Obs. rare.* [implies a vb. *aborder*, apparently due to confusion between BORDER *v.* and ABORD *v.*, Fr. *aborder*, in Cotgr. 'to lye neere vnto.'] Bordering, neighbouring, contiguous.

1566 DRANT *Horace, Sat.* II. i. Leste people nygh aborderyng, myght wyn the same. **1567** *Ibid. Ep.* I. iii. Twixt towers, abordringe next [Lat. *vicinas*].

abore, obs. pa. pple. of ABEAR *v.*

aborigen, aborigin (æ'bɒrɪdʒɪn). [a form occasionally occurring as a singular to ABORIGINES (which had no sing. in L.); ad. Fr. *aborigène*, or following the analogy of the simple ORIGIN, L. *orīgo*, *orīgin-em*, pl. *orīgin-es.* But the tendency is to treat ABORIGINES as a purely Eng. word, and make the singular *aborigin-e.*]

1606 WARNER *Albion's Eng.* xv. xciii. 374 For Welsh and Scots, so far-forth we *Aborigens* may name. **1832** I. TAYLOR *Sat. Even.* (1834) 349 He is then aborigin of all spheres of thought, & finds himself at home & at ease in every region. **1859** R. F. BURTON *Lake Reg. Cent. Afr.* in Journ. R.G.S. XXIX. 135. §7 The Cimex lectularius..is apparently an aborigen of the country.

aboriginal (æbə'rɪdʒɪnəl), *a.* and *sb.* [f. L. *ab origine* (see ABORIGINES) + -AL[1].]

A. *adj.*

1. First or earliest so far as history or science gives record; primitive; strictly native, indigenous. Used both of the races and natural features of various lands.

1667 WATERHOUSE *Fire of Lond.* 70 Mr. Spencer, the trusty and Aboriginal Librarier. **1830** LYELL *Princ. Geol.* (1875) II. III. xliv. 507 The very sites of the aboriginal forests. **1845** FORD *Handbk. Spain* i. 31 *n.* The wild habits and early condition of the aboriginal Iberians. **1874** LYELL *Elem. Geol.* vi. 77 The pebbles therefore in the older gravels are exclusively constituted of granite and other aboriginal rocks. **1875** STUBBS *Const. Hist.* I. i. 2 The English are not aboriginal, that is, they are not identical with the race that occupied their home at the dawn of history.

2. *spec.* Dwelling in any country before the arrival of later (European) colonists.

1788 BURKE *Sp. agt. W. Hastings* Wks. XIII. 64 This aboriginal people of India. **1866** LIVINGSTONE *Journ.* (1873) I. x. 252 Munongo..would apply to these aboriginal chiefs for it.

3. a. Of or pertaining to aborigines, to the earliest known inhabitants, or to native races.

1851 D. WILSON *Preh. Annals* (1863) I. ii. 57 The aboriginal fleets of Ancient Caledonia. **1864** *Social Sci. Rev.* I. 299 By putting fire-arms into their hands the English doubled the aboriginal power. **1874** SAYCE *Comp. Philol.* v. 175 The chances are that a modern Hindoo will be altogether, or in great part, of aboriginal blood, unless he be a Brahmin.

b. *spec.* (freq. with capital initial) of or pertaining to the aboriginal inhabitants of Australia.

1820 *N.S.W. Pocket Almanack* 74 Institution for the Children of the aboriginal Natives of this Colony. **1896** MORRIS *Austral English* p. xiv, In several books statements will be found that such and such a word is not Aboriginal, when it really has an aboriginal source but in a different part of the Continent. **1929** K. S. PRICHARD *Coonardoo* ii. 25 All aboriginal babies are honey-coloured when they are born. **1944** F. CLUNE *Red Heart* 16 The region is an Aboriginal Reserve, closed to white men. **1969** *Northern Territory News* (Darwin) 11 July 9/7 Many Aboriginal groups in full tribal regalia will compete for the coveted shield tonight. **1980** *Age* (Melbourne) 1 May 1/1 The chief teachers are Aboriginal 'aunts'—herbal specialists..whose traditional role was as backstop to the male nunkari.

B. *sb.* **a.** (with *pl.*) [The adj. used elliptically.] An original inhabitant of any land, now usually as distinguished from subsequent European colonists. Also *spec.* one of the aboriginal inhabitants of Australia.

1767 T. HUTCHINSON *Hist. Prov. Mass. Bay* iii. 269 A good friend to the aboriginals of every tribe. **1828** *Hobart Town Courier* 19 Apr. 1/2 Nothing herein contained shall authorize..any Settler..to make use of force (except for necessary self-defence) against any Aboriginal. **1845** DARWIN *Voy. of Nat.* (1879) xix. 441 The thoughtless aboriginal..is delighted at the approach of the white man. **1873** A. TROLLOPE *Australia* i. 60 It will be as well to call the race by the name officially given to it. The government styles them 'aboriginals'..the word 'native' is almost universally applied to white colonists born in Australia. **1911** E. M. CLOWES *On Wallaby* xi. 299 In all matters connected with hunting the aboriginal, in the hard school of necessity, has brought his powers of observation to a fine point. **1938** X. HERBERT *Capricornia* (1939) xi. 144 He did not mind trying a nameless prisoner if he were an Aboriginal. **1943** K. TENNANT *Ride on Stranger* xvi. 180 Four aboriginals have a death sentence for shoving a spear through a policeman. **1969** *Sun-Herald* (Sydney) 13 July 52/1 An Aboriginal is not a white man and he does not want to be.

b. *fig.* Of words.

1858 MARSH *Lect. Engl. Lang.* xxiv. 539 The mischief it [poetry] has done to the language by employing aliens as substitutes for worthier aboriginals.

aboriginalism (æbə'rɪdʒɪnəlɪz(ə)m). [f. ABORIGINAL + -ISM.] The due recognition of native races.

1868 *New Zealand paper* quoted in *Daily News* Sept. 3 But England has become troubled with qualms of conscience, or it may be a sentiment, about aboriginalism.

aboriginality (,æbə,rɪdʒɪ'nælɪtɪ). [f. ABORIGINAL + -ITY.] The quality of being aboriginal; existence in or possession of a land at the earliest stage of its history.

1851 *Archæol. Cambr.* (N.S.) II. 254 M. Worsaae denies the aboriginality of the Celts. **1860** *Westm. Rev.* (N.S.) No. 36. 432 The presumption..is in favour of immigration rather than aboriginality.

aboriginally (,æbə'rɪdʒɪnəlɪ), *adv.* [f. ABORIGINAL + -LY[2].] From the very beginning; from the origin of a race; in the earliest times or conditions known to history or science.

1821 W. TAYLOR in *Month. Rev.* XCV. 428 The eastern shore had certainly been peopled, aboriginally, with Saxon settlers. **1845** DARWIN *Voy. of Nat.* (1879) xviii. 424 The land having been aboriginally covered with forest trees. **1875** —— *Insectiv. Plants* xv. 359 It seems scarcely possible that each tentacle could have aboriginally existed as a prolongation of the leaf.

aboriginary (,æbə'rɪdʒɪnərɪ). [f. ABORIGINE; the termination formed on L. *orīgināri-us* an original inhabitant: see -ARY.] An aboriginal inhabitant.

1868 BROWNING *Ring & Bk.* IV. xi. 1918 Name me, a primitive religionist—As should the aboriginary be, I boast myself.

‖**ab origine** (æb ɒ'rɪdʒɪnɪ), *adv. phr.* [Lat. phr., f. *ab* from + *origine* abl. sing. of *orīgo* ORIGIN, source: cf. ABORIGINES.] From the beginning; from the conception (of an idea, etc.).

1537 LATIMER *Let.* 6 Sept. in *Rem.* (1845) II. 382 As I can affirm unto you with certain and sure arguments, as you shall hereafter know all together *ab origine.* *a* **1706** EVELYN *Diary* an. 1700 (1955) III. 449 We found the maine building to receede outward: 'It was Mr. Chichleys & Prats opinion that it had been so built ab origine for an effect in Perspective, in reguard of the height. *a* **1734** R. NORTH *Examen* (1740) I. ii. 117 [*sc.* 125] A proper Mover or Informer of the Matter *ab origine.* **1847–9** R. B. TODD *Cycl. Anat. & Physiol.* IV. I. 102/1 It would appear probable, then,..that chemical change is in some measure worked out by (and, inferentially, that chemical differences exist *ab origine* in) blastemata themselves.

aborigines (æbə'rɪdʒɪniːz, -ɪz). *sing.* **aborigine** (see etym.). [A purely L. word, applied to those who were believed to have been the inhabitants of a country *ab origine*, i.e. from the beginning (see ORIGIN). At first only in the pl.; for the sing. ABORIGINAL has been used, also ABORIGEN, ABORIGIN; and *aborigine* (,æbə'rɪdʒɪniː), which, seeming to be more in accordance with ordinary Eng. analogies, is the usual form, though etymologically as indefensible as *serië* or *indicè* as a sing. of *series, indices.*]

1. a. The original inhabitants of a country; originally, the race of the first possessors of Italy and of Greece, afterwards extended to races supposed to be the first or original occupants of other countries.

a **1547** J. HARRISON *Exhort. to Scottes* (1873) 214 The old latins..callyng themselfes Aborigines, that is to saie: a people from the beginnyng. **1610** HOLLAND *Camden's Brit.* I. 9 Diodorus and others..would have the Britans to be.. meere Aborigines; that is, Homelings and not forren brought in. **1735–8** LD. BOLINGBROKE *Dissn. upon Parties* 141 The antient Britons are to us the Aborigines of our Island. **1841** SPALDING *Italy* I. 44 The Umbrians are said to have been the aborigines of Italy. **1879** B. TAYLOR *Germ. Lit.* 3 The aborigines of Germany had their bards, their battle-songs and their sacrificial hymns.

β **1864** R. F. BURTON *Miss. to Dahome* 19 The Bube, as may be proved by his language, is an aborigine of the mainland.

b. *fig.*

1655 FULLER *Ch. Hist.* II. 119 The Aborigines and the Advenae, the old Stock of Students, and the new Store brought in by St. Grimball. **1704** SWIFT *Battle of Bks.* (1711) 224 As to their own Seat, they were Aborigines of it.

2. *spec.* The natives found in possession of a country by Europeans who have gone thither as colonists.

aborigine is now common esp. in Australia.

a **1789–96** J. MORSE *Amer. Geog.* I. 594 Calvert, their leader, purchased the rights of the aborigines. **1845** DARWIN *Voy. of Nat.* xix. 435 (1873) A score of the black aborigines passed by. **1868** GRANT DUFF *Polit. Surv.* 112 From 300,000 to 400,000 aborigines reside within the territory of Liberia.

β **1858** VIELÉ *Following Drum* 216 The aborigine was inclined to dispute the point. **1864** *Spectator* 31 Dec. 1689 It seems probable that in half a century there will not be one aborigine left in Australia. **1876** J. BURROUGHS *Winter Sunshine* (1883) vi. 133 If the red aborigine ever had his summer of fulness and contentment. **1922** *Times* 8 Aug. 5/4 (*headline*) The Australian Aborigine: His Future Welfare. **1959** *Chambers's Encycl.* I. 804/2 The aborigine's social and spiritual feeling for his own land means that he does not covet the land of other people.

3. Occas. used also of animals and plants.

1677 HALE *Prim. Orig. Man.* II. vii. 199 Whereby it appears that the Brutes were not Aborigines. **1845** DARWIN *Voy. of Nat.* vi. 119 (1879) I doubt whether any case is on record of an invasion on so grand a scale of one plant over the aborigines.

aborne, obsolete form of AUBURN.

aborning (ə'bɔːnɪŋ), *adv.* and *pred. a.* Chiefly *U.S.* [f. A *prep.*[1] 12 + *borning*, f. BORN.] (While) being born or produced.

1934 in WEBSTER. **1943** H. A. WALLACE *Century of Common Man* (1944) 87 A future which..will save and share the culture past and now aborning. **1957** D. W. BROGAN *French Nation* v. 189 The Franco-Russian alliance was a long time aborning. **1961** F. G. CASSIDY *Jamaica Talk* xiv. 297 Some names are obsolete; some died aborning. **1961** *Woman's Own* 16 Dec. 9/1 A home for a child aborning.

†**a'borsement.** *Obs.* Also 6 **aborcement.** [A variant of ABORTMENT due to the fluctuation between *abort-us* and *abors-us* in L. See next.] Abortion, premature expulsion of the fœtus, miscarriage.

1540 T. RAYNOLDE *Birth of mankynde* (1654) 82 Aborcement or vntimely birth is, when the woman is delyuered before due season. **1650** BP. HALL *Cases of Consc.* 91 To give any such expelling or destructive medicine, with a direct intention to work an aborsement.

†**a'borsive,** *a. Obs. rare*$^{-1}$. [f. L. *aborsus*, variant of *abortus*, pa. pple. of *aborīri*: see ABORT. Nonius (c. 5, n. 506) makes a distinction between *abortus* and *aborsus*, evidently

connecting the latter with *ordiri* to begin; and this was probably also the meaning of Fuller.] Abortive from the first; checked before even a beginning had been made.

1639 FULLER *Holy War* v. xxv. 287 (1840) Most of these designs were abortive, or aborsive rather.

abort (əˈbɔːt), *v.* [f. L. *abort-* ppl. stem of *aborī-ri* to miscarry, disappear, f. *ab* off, away + *orī-ri* to arise, appear, come into being. Cf. Fr. *avorte-r*:—late L. **abortā-re*, f. *abort-us.*]

1. a. *intr.* To miscarry, to have a premature delivery of a child.

1580 HOLLYBAND *Treas. Fr. Tong., Avorter,* to abort, or when a woman goeth not hir full time. **1655** LESTRANGE *Charles I,* 104 This Spring the Queen.. aborted of a son. **1859** TODD *Cycl. An. & Ph.* V. 615/2 A woman who aborted at the sixth month.

b. *trans. fig.* To bring to a premature or fruitless termination. *spec.* in *Aeronautics.* Also *lit.*, to terminate (a pregnancy).

1614 *Reliq. Wotton.* (1672) 431 It [the Parliament] is aborted before it was born. **1880** *Contemp. Rev.* XXXVII. 248 Lord Brougham did write a novel, but it was rather aborted than produced. **1962** J. GLENN in *Into Orbit* 41 A bright red light at the very top of this panel is labelled 'Abort'... You could be aborted automatically..or by a command from the ground. **1963** *Amer. Speech* XXXVIII. 118 We lost an engine, so we aborted the mission. **1966** *Listener* 6 Oct. 503/2 In rats..after a female has successfully mated with a male, the presence of another male a little distance away immediately aborts the pregnancy. **1977** *Lancet* 5 Feb. 271/1 Several parents who would have had their pregnancies aborted, had prenatal diagnosis not been available, have allowed them to continue to term. **1977** E. J. TRIMMER et al. *Visual Dict. Sex* (1978) xxii. 247 In 1938, a British gynecologist was tried for aborting the pregnancy in a girl of fourteen who had been raped.

c. *intr.* use of prec. *U.S.*

1946 *Britannica Bk. of Year* 832/1 *Abort,* to fail to complete a mission or flight; said of an aeroplane. **1963** *Amer. Speech* XXXVIII. 118 A specified point on the runway..used as a decision point for aborting. If trouble develops on the take-off roll before go-no-go, it is possible to abort and stop the aircraft on the remaining runway.

d. *trans.* To cause (a woman) to abort; to perform an abortion on. Also *absol.* and *refl.*

[**1933** G. R. SCOTT *Mod. Birth Control Methods* ix. 118 The pregnant uterus is not easily aborted by a sound or similar instrument.] **1934** D. D. BROMLEY *Birth Control* xi. 143 Abortionists.., as a rule, avoid trouble by refusing to abort a patient who is more than two and a half months along. **1967** *Listener* 30 Nov. 686/3 Wretched little dramas of scruffy girls in jeans being aborted after men with sideburns..had got them in the family way. **1969** *Daily Tel.* 28 Apr. 14 National Health surgeons on the whole remain disinclined to abort frivolously. **1973** *Nation Rev.* (Melbourne) 31 Aug. III. 1450/3 This person has signed a statement to the effect that his girlfriend was aborted here. **1977** *Lancet* 3 Sept. 496/1 Perhaps the most disturbing result was the response to the statement 'A physician has the responsibility to inform the husband or parents of any female he aborts.' **1980** *Daily Tel.* 25 Jan. 15/6 We want them to come to the doctor first, not go off and damage themselves, abort themselves or see an illegal abortionist.

e. *trans.* To prevent the further development of (a fœtus or embryo in the womb) by removing it or causing its expulsion; to remove in the course of an abortion.

1974 *Daily Tel.* 7 Sept. 2/7 A woman carrying a test-tube baby would be monitored so carefully..that any abnormalities would be discovered and the foetus aborted. **1976** *Church Times* 2 Jan. 14/5 A silent march of witness in memory of the 800,000 unborn children aborted under the 1967 Abortion Act was held. **1979** *Daily Tel.* 28 Apr. 2 The baby was aborted at a Barnsley hospital..after it was discovered her 20-year-old mother had been infected with German measles. **1986** *Guardian* 3 Nov. 17/1 They argued for some sex education in schools so that teenage girls could learn how to have babies rather than to be forced to abort them.

2. *Biol.* To become sterile or nugatory; to undergo arrestment of development, so as to remain in a merely rudimentary condition, or to shrink away entirely; said either of the development of an individual, or of a race of plants or animals.

1862 DARWIN *Fertiliz. Orchids* 70 If the discs had been small..we might have concluded that they had begun to abort. **1877** MIVART *Elem. Anat.* iii. 112 They [the turbinal bones] may, on the contrary, abort altogether, as is the case in the probably smell-less Porpoises.

abort (əˈbɔːt), *sb.* [ad. L. *abort-us* an untimely birth, f. *aborī-ri*: see ABORT *v.*]

1. A miscarriage, an untimely birth: *lit.* and *fig. Obs.*

1621 BURTON *Anat. Mel.* (1651) I. ii. IV. vi. 160 In Japonia 'tis a common thing to stifle their children if they be poor, or to make an abort. **1651** *Reliq. Wotton.* 241 Julia, a little before dying of an abort in childbed. **1656** J. TRAPP *Expos.* 2 Tim. i. 15 (1868) 651/2 These stars fell from heaven, as fast as the fig-tree makes abort, with any never so light and gentle a wind.

2. The imperfect offspring of an untimely birth. *Obs.*

1603 HOLLAND *Plutarch's Morals* 140 False births, unkinde or strange aborts. **1671** SALMON *Syn. Medic.* II. xlv. 306 Lest the Child, for want of Nutriment, prove an Abort.

3. *Aeronaut.* An abortive flight by an aeroplane, etc.; an aeroplane, etc., that so fails. (See also quot. 1962.) *U.S.*

1958 *Aero-Space Terms, Abort* 1. An instance of a rocket missile or vehicle failing to function effectively and not achieving the objective plotted for it. 2. A rocket missile or vehicle that so fails. **1960** *Times* 18 Oct. 13/6 A thing which detects errors in the interiors of missiles is now known as 'abort sensory equipment'. **1962** *Into Orbit* Glossary 243 *Abort,* an escape; in spacecraft terms an emergency separation of the capsule from the booster—or even the emergency exit of the Astronaut from the capsule. **1963** *Amer. Speech* XXXVIII. 118 The control room had to classify our flight as an air abort.

aborted (əˈbɔːtɪd), *ppl. a.* [f. ABORT *v.* + -ED. Cf. mod.Fr. *aborté.*]

1. Born before its time; hence, imperfect, undeveloped.

1604 T. WRIGHT *Pass. of Mind, Ep. Ded.* [I] could not tell whether to reioyce to see mine aborted infant revived.

2. *Biol.* Rendered abortive or sterile; reduced to a state of imperfect development, checked in normal development. Applied in Morphology to the rudimentary or imperfect appendages which, in some species, represent the perfect organs of what may be considered the archetype or ancestral form. Thus spines are aborted branches, the breasts of male beings are aborted teats, etc.

1859 DARWIN *Orig. Spec.* (1873) v. 116 When this occurs, the adherent nectary is quite aborted. **1867** J. HOGG *Microsc.* II. i. 324 Thorns, such as those of the rose, are aborted branches. **1870** ROLLESTON *An. Life* Introd. 109 This rudimentary or aborted condition of the hepatic organ.

abortient (əˈbɔːʃ(ɪ)ənt), *a.* *rare*$^{-0}$. [ad. L. *abortient-em* pr. pple. of *abortī-re* (in Vulgate), f. *abort-us*; see ABORT *sb.*] '*Bot.* Miscarrying; sterile.' Craig 1847, and later Dicts.

abortifacient (əˌbɔːtɪˈfeɪʃ(ɪ)ənt), *a.* and *sb.* [f. L. *abortus*: see ABORT + *facient-em* making: see -FACIENT.]

A. *adj.* Productive of abortion, causing premature delivery.

1875 WOOD *Therap.* (1879) 70 It seems to me incredible that..doses of quinia are abortifacient. **1877** WOODMAN & TIDY *Forensic Med.* 755 Savine..has often proved abortifacient.

B. *sb.* [sc. drug.]

1875 WOOD *Therap.* 537 (1879) Its use as an abortifacient is accompanied by the gravest dangers to life. **1877** WOODMAN & TIDY *Forensic Med.* 760 Dry herbs, reputed abortifacients.

aborting (əˈbɔːtɪŋ), *vbl. sb.* [f. ABORT *v.* + -ING[1].] A miscarrying; a failure to produce perfect progeny or fruit.

1580 HOLLYBAND *Treas. Fr. Tong., Avortement,* aborting.

aborting (əˈbɔːtɪŋ), *ppl. a.* [f. ABORT *v.* + -ING[2].] Producing abortions; miscarrying.

1632 BP. M. SMYTH *Serm.* 256 What wilt thou giue them? barren wombes (or aborting wombs).

abortion (əˈbɔːʃən) Also 6 **abhorsion.** [ad. L. *abortiōn-em* n. of action f. *aborī-ri*: see ABORT.]

1. The act of giving untimely birth to offspring, premature delivery, miscarriage; the procuring of premature delivery so as to destroy offspring. (In *Med.* abortion is limited to a delivery so premature that the offspring cannot live, i.e. in the case of the human fœtus before the sixth month.)

1547 BOORDE *Brev. Health* iii. 8 Abhorsion is when a woman is delyvered of her chylde before her tyme. **1646** SIR T. BROWNE *Pseud. Ep.* 67 Physitions..promise therein a vertue against abortion. **1778** ROBERTSON *America* I. IV. 297 The women by the use of certain herbs procure frequent abortions. **1869** LECKY *Europ. Morals* II. i. 22 The practice of abortion was one to which few persons in antiquity attached any deep feeling of condemnation.

b. *fig.* Failure (of aim or promise).

1710 in *Somers's Tracts* I. 10 All the Fruit of his Labour ends in Sterility and Abortion. **1797** GODWIN *Enquirer* I. v. 35 Genius [may] terminate in an abortion. **1814** MISS BURNEY *Wanderer* IV. 58 The abortion of my purpose may have made me appear a mere female mountebank.

2. *Biol.* Arrestment of development of any organ, so that it either remains a mere rudiment, or is entirely shrivelled up or absorbed.

1842 ASA GRAY *Struct. Bot.* (1880) vi. §3. 179 Non-appearance of some parts which are supposed in the type = Abortion or Suppression. **1859** DARWIN *Orig. Spec.* (1873) v. 116 The partial or complete abortion of the reproductive organs. **1870** ROLLESTON *An. Life* 25 The skull of the Common Fowl differs in the abortion of the posterior crus.

3. The imperfect offspring of an untimely birth, or any dwarfed and misshapen product of generation; hence *fig.* the nugatory or empty result of any action.

1640 BP. HALL *Christ. Mod.* (Ward) 15/1 Those bodily delights..alas! what poor abortions they are, dead in the very conception. **1858** HAWTHORNE *Fr. & It. Journ.* I. 171 A little abortion of a man..hastened before us. **1872** O. W. HOLMES *Poet. Breakf. Tab.* x. 315 The doctrine of man's being a blighted abortion, a miserable disappointment to his Creator. **1878** H. M. STANLEY *Dark. Cont.* II. iii. 74 His feet are monstrous abortions.

abortional (əˈbɔːʃənəl), *a.* [f. ABORTION + -AL[1]. Cf. *nation-al.*] Of or pertaining to abortion; of the nature of a miscarriage or failure.

1865 CARLYLE *Fredk. Gt.* VI. xv. vi. 22 The Treaty.. proved abortional, and never came to fulfilment.

abortionist (əˈbɔːʃənɪst). [f. ABORTION + -IST.] One who procures abortion or miscarriage.

1872 THOMAS *Dis. of Women* 63 Professional abortionists —men and women who make a business of infantile murder.

†**aˈbortivate,** *v.* *Obs.* *rare*$^{-1}$. [f. L. *abortīv-us,* ABORTIVE, after anal. of *captiv-ate, activ-ate,* etc. See -ATE[3].] To render abortive; = ABORTIVE *v.*

*c***1630** JACKSON *Creed* v. vii. Wks. 1844 IV. 62 Atheists may so far abortivate or dead the seeds of religion sown in their souls.

†**aˈbortivate,** *ppl. a.* *Obs.* *rare*$^{-1}$. [f. ABORTIVATE *v.* for *abortivated*: after analogy of ppl. adj. like *separate* of identical form with the vb. See -ATE[2].] Imperfect, defective.

*c***1630** JACKSON *Creed* x. xxiii. Wks. 1844 IX. 150 They were a kind of abortivate or ill thriven seed, no true sons or children.

abortive (əˈbɔːtɪv), *a.* and *sb.* [ad. L. *abortīv-us,* f. *abort-us*: see ABORT and -IVE.]

A. *adj.*

†**1.** Of or pertaining to abortion. **a.** Produced by abortion, born prematurely; also, derived from a still-born animal, as ***abortive parchment.*** *Obs.*

1394 *P. Ploughm. Crede* 485 Fy on his pilche! He is but abortiif, Eked with cloutes. **1594** SHAKS. *Rich. III,* I. ii. 21 If euer he haue Childe, Abortiue be it. **1614** B. RICH *Honestie of this Age* (1844) 6 These abortiue brates that are thus hastely brought into the world. **1663** COWLEY *Verses & Ess.* (1669) 3 Th' abortive Issue never liv'd. **1664** EVELYN *Diary* (1827) II. 217 A sort of paper very broad thin & fine like abortiue parchment.

†**b.** Causing abortion, rendering fruitless. *Obs.*

1611 HEYWOOD *Gold. Age* v. i. (1874) 74 We but saue Our Innocent bodies from th' abortiue graue. **1667** MILTON *P.L.* II. 441 With utter loss of being Threatens him, plunged in that abortive gulf. **1753** CHAMBERS *Cycl. Supp.* s.v. *Abortion,* Roman authors speak of the ***poculum abortionis*** or abortive draught.

†**c.** Failing to produce offspring, miscarrying. *Obs.*

1621 BURTON *Anat. Mel.* (1651) I. ii. I. iii. 55 Witches.. make Women abortive not to conceive. **1662** R. MATHEW *Unl. Alch.* §87. 121 It..then brought from her an abortive or false conception.

2. Failing of the intended effect, coming to nought; fruitless, useless, unsuccessful.

1593 SHAKS. *2 Hen. VI,* IV. i. 60 Let it make thee Crest-falne, I, and alay this thy abortiue Pride. **1665** in *Phil. Trans.* I. 43 This also proved abortive, though there was great appearance of success at first. **1713** ADDISON *Cato* III. vii. Our first design, my friend, has prov'd abortive. **1778** ROBERTSON *America* I. III. 213 Though this attempt proved abortive it was not without benefit. **1827** SCOTT *Surg. Dau.* II. 35 Two slips of ground, half arable, half overrun with an abortive attempt at shrubbery. **1876** FREEMAN *Norm. Conq.* II. ix. 420 He would rather have laboured to hinder Ealdred's mission, or to make it abortive.

3. *Biol.* Arrested in development; defective, imperfect; sterile, barren.

1794 MARTYN tr. *Rousseau's Bot.* x. 103 The florets..of the ray are imperfect, and therefore abortive or frustrate. **1834** GOOD *Bk. of Nat.* I. 177 The thorns of plants are abortive branches. **1866** LIVINGSTONE *Journ.* (1873) I. iii. 60 He had an abortive toe. **1879** DE QUATREFAGES *Hum. Spec.* 74 Datura seeds, which he observed to become abortive or devoid of embryo.

B. *sb.* [The adj. used *absol.*]

†**1.** An abortive progeny; a still-born child; a calf or other young animal dropped prematurely. (Sometimes used derisively.)

a **1300** *Cursor Mundi* 22. 849 þe childir þat es abortiues þaa þat er not born o-liues. **1382** WYCLIF *Job* iii. 16 Or as abortif hid I shulde not abide, or that conceyved seȝen not liȝt. **1413** LYDGATE *Pylg. Sowle* (1483) IV. xxiv. 70 Wherof seith the appostel seynt Powle that our lord had shewed hym self to hym as to an abortyue. *c* **1605** ? ROWLEY *Birth of Merlin* IV. i. 335 Bearded abortive, thou foretell my danger? **1634** PEACHAM *Gentlem. Exerc.* I. xxv. 88/2 Take the fine skin of an Abortive which you may buy in Paternoster-row. **1760** T. W. *Human Life* in *Phil. Trans.* LII. 48 From hence abortives and stilborn are included in the burials.

†**b.** A fine kind of vellum, being the skin of an abortive calf.

1519 W. HORMAN *Vulgaria* 80 b, §9 That stouffe that we wrytte vpon..is somtyme called parchement, somtyme velem, somtyme abortyue.

†**2.** An abortive delivery; a miscarriage.

1587 LD. MASCAL *Govern. of Cattle* (*Sheepe*) (1627) 246 Also abortiues come when they giue them in some place nothing but akornes for their meate.

†**3.** The fruitless, imperfect, or unsuccessful result of an endeavour.

1610 HOLLAND *Camden's Brit.* I. 391 Yet giue me leave.. to cast forth my conjecture (although it is an abortive) concerning this point. **1654** FULLER *Two Sermons* 75 Whether this will ever be really effected, whether it will prove an Abortive..Time will tell. **1706** DE FOE *Jure Divino* IX. 209 It [the Work] scarce out-liv'd The hated Birth: The wild Abortive dy'd.

†**4.** An abortive drug.

1647 STAPYLTON *Juvenal* 19 Whil'st with abortives the poore Julia marr'd Her fruitefull wombe.

†**a'bortive**, *v.* *Obs.* [f. ABORTIVE *a.* Cf. to *negative*.]

1. *trans.* To cause abortion; to render ineffectual or fruitless.

1615 *Albumazar* I. iii. (D.) One of your bold thunders may abortive And cause that birth miscarry. **1627** FELTHAM *Resolves* (1677) II. lxxxiv. 341 In War, the vexed Earth abortives all her fruitfulness. **1699** EVELYN *Acetaria* 118 (1729) This is that which abortives the Perfection of the most glorious and useful Undertakings.

2. *intr.* To miscarry; prove abortive.

1692 HACKET *Life of Williams* II. 147 (D.) When peace came so near to the birth, how it abortived..comes now to be remembered.

abortively (ə'bɔːtɪvlɪ), *adv.* [f. ABORTIVE *a.* + -LY².] In an abortive manner; by untimely birth; by premature arrestment; ineffectually.

1598 FLORIO, *Abbortare*, to be deliuered abortiuely. **1633** HEYWOOD *Eng. Trav.* (1874) III. 48 I thus abortiuely, before my time, Fall headlong to my Graue. **1742** YOUNG *Night Th.* (1757) VII. 96 If abortively poor man must die.

abortiveness (ə'bɔːtɪvnɪs). [f. ABORTIVE *a.* + -NESS.] The quality of being abortive; unproductiveness, fruitlessness, state of failure.

1657 WINTHORPE in *Burton's Diary* (1828) II. 268 We were well warned by the abortiveness of another Bill as good. **1674** R. GODFREY *Inj. & Abuses in Phys.* 52 At the Abortiveness and irrationality of which Recipe who is able enough to admire? **1865** W. G. PALGRAVE *Centr. Arabia* I. 314 Plans and schemes..destined to lasting abortiveness.

†**a'bortment.** *Obs.* [f. ABORT *v.* + -MENT; cf. Fr. *avortement*, f. *avorter* to abort. See also ABORSEMENT.] The action of aborting; premature expulsion of the fœtus.

1607 TOPSELL *Four-footed Beasts* (1673) 18 The Mare shall suffer abortment. **1652** CULPEPER *Eng. Phys.* 86 They are dangerous for women with childe..they cause abortment.

abortorium (æbɔː'tɔərɪəm). Pl. **abortoria.** [f. *abort-*, as in ABORT *v.*, ABORTION, + -ORIUM.] A hospital or a hospital department that specializes in performing abortions.

1934 *Lancet* 3 Nov. 1027/2 The abortorium which I visited in Leningrad was part of a general hospital... There were four such hospitals in Leningrad, and the number of abortions performed in this one alone approached 1000 a month. **1973** A. F. GUTTMACHER in Walbert & Butler *Abortion, Society & Law* 71 In recognition of the financial potential, several proprietary hospitals were converted into abortoria.

abortus (ə'bɔːtəs). Pl. **abortuses.** [mod.L., f. L. *abortus* premature birth: see ABORT *v.*] An aborted fœtus.

1910 in *Lippincott's New Med. Dict.* **1957** C. T. CALVERT *Spontaneous & Habitual Abortion* xviii. 391 Knowledge regarding abortuses..is one of the most neglected branches of pathology in most hospitals. **1970** *Sci. Jrnl.* June 78/3 A tetraploid ovum is capable of a little further development and abortuses have been found with 92 chromosomes in all their cells. **1974** *Nature* 15 Feb. 422/1 Anyone experimenting with an abortus at any age near to viability does so at his peril.

a'bortus 'fever. [L. *abortus* miscarriage.] An infection caused by *Brucella abortus bovinus* or by other species of the genus *Brucella*, and transmitted to man in milk or meat products; undulant fever. Cf. BRUCELLOSIS.

1927 *Lancet* 31 Dec. 1414/2 *(title)* Is it Undulant or Abortus Fever in Great Britain? **1932** *Ibid.* 28 May 1152/2 Attempts to induce abortus fever experimentally in volunteers. **1936** *Nature* 21 Nov. 889/1 Well-recognized generic names..the diptheroids..and the organisms of undulant and abortus fevers (*Brucella*).

†**abote**, *ppl. a.* (? for *abeaten* or *abated*) a factitious form in one of the later poems attrib. to Chaucer.

a **1597** *'Chaucer's Dreme'* 1292 Of whiche sight glade, God it wote, Sche was abasched & abote.

abought, obs. pa. t. and pple. of ABYE.

abought, abowght, obs. forms of ABOUT.

aboulia, abulia (ə'buːlɪə, ə'bjuːlɪə). [mod.L., f. Gr. ἀ- priv. + βουλή will; cf. Gr. ἀβουλία thoughtlessness.] Loss of will-power, as a mental disorder. Hence **a'boulic, a'bulic** *a.* (and *sb.*). Also **aboulo'mania** = ABOULIA.

1848 DUNGLISON *Med. Lex.* (ed. 7), *Abulia*, loss of the will, or of volition. **1878** tr. *von Ziemssen's Cycl. Med.* XIV. 542 In some cases this abulia reaches such a degree that the patients..abandon almost every movement, do not leave their bed [etc.]. **1889** *Buck's Handbk. Med. Sci.* VII. 687/2 Desire exists, resolution is formed, but no action, or only feeble action, follows. This would..be a form of *aboulia*. **1890** BILLINGS *Med. Dict.*, *Aboulomania*, a form of insanity characterized by inability to exert the will. **1893** DUNGLISON *Dict. Med. Sci.* (ed. 21), *Abulic*, one who has lost power of will. **1894** GOULD *Dict. Med.*, *Abulic*, characterized by or affected with abulia; of defective will-power. **1899** W. JAMES *Talks to Teachers* xv. 179 A condition of perfect 'abulia', or inability to will or act. **1900** J. ROYCE *Let.* 12 Sept. in R. B. Perry *Tht. & Char. of W. James* (1935) I. 815 That left me ..morally tired,—mildly aboulic, so to speak. **1940** *Brit. Jrnl. Psychol.* Jan. 235 When the individual is in a dither of indecision, or when he suffers from temporary *aboulia*.

†**abound**, *a.* *Obs.* [a. Fr. *abonde*:—L. *abund-um* abundant; f. same elements as vb. *abundā-re*: see ABOUND *v.*] Overflowing; plentiful; abundant.

c **1400** TUNDALE *Circumcision* 92 The streme of sapience Of whyche the flod most joly is habownd. *c* **1430** *Syr Generides* (1865) 311 Of plentie thus he was abound To hem al that he his frendes found.

abound (ə'baʊnd), *v.*¹ Forms: 4–5 **habunde**, 4–6 **habound(e**, 4– **abound(e.** *Pr. pple.*: 4 **abundende**, 5 **abowndand.** [a. OFr. *abunde-r*, *abonde-r*, *habonde-r*:—L. *abundā-re* to overflow; f. *ab* from + *undā-re* to flow in waves; f. *unda* a wave. Afterwards erroneously connected with *habē-re* to have, and spelt with an initial *h* both in Fr. and Eng.] To overflow as water does from a vessel; or as a vessel does with water.

1. To be present in overflowing measure; to be plentiful; to prevail widely.

1382 WYCLIF *2 Cor.* ix. 8 Forsoþe god is myȝty for to make al grace abounde in ȝou. **1481** CAXTON *Myrrour* I. v. 22 By the helpe of our Lorde of whom all science groweth and haboundeth. **1523** LD. BERNERS *Froissart* I. cccxci. 672 Bycause of the great plenty and welthe that haboundeth in those parties, the people are all ydell. **1590** SHAKS. *Mid. N.* II. i. 105 Rheumaticke diseases doe abound. **1611** BIBLE *Phil.* iv. 17, I desire fruit that may abound to your account. **1667** MILTON *P.L.* III. 312 In thee Love hath abounded more than glory abounds. **1845** FORD *Handbk. of Spain* i. 48 The trial becomes greater in proportion as hardships abound. **1850** MCCOSH *Div. Govt.* (1874) III. ii. 395 The discontent which abounds in the world.

†**2.** To be full, to be rich or wealthy; to have to overflowing. (Of persons.) *Obs.*

1382 WYCLIF *1 Mac.* iii. 30 And he aboundide [**1388** was riche] ouer kyngus that weren bifore hym. *c* **1400** *Apol. for Lollards* 51 Þat he life lustili, or habunde after hienes of the world. **1611** BIBLE *Phil.* iv. 18 But I have all and abound. **1613** SHAKS. *Hen. VIII*, I. i. 83 Kinsmen of mine..that haue By this, so sicken'd their Estates, that neuer They shall abound as formerly. **1713** STEELE *Englishm.* No. 21. 137 He cannot bear to see any man want whilst he abounds. **1765** HARRIS *Three Treat.* III. i. 153 Each supply where he is deficient by exchanging where he abounds.

3. To abound *in*: To be plentiful, wealthy, or copious in; to possess to a marked extent, so as to be characterized by; to have wealth of. (Used of persons and things, in reference to inherent qualities, characteristic attributes, or things whereby the subject is made wealthy, eminent, or distinguished.)

1382 WYCLIF *2 Cor.* vii. 4, I abounde (or am plenteuous) in ioye in al oure tribulacioun. *c* **1449** PECOCK *Repr.* III. x. 337 These haboundiden in greet doctrine. **1535** COVERDALE *Jer.* vi. 6 Like as a condyte aboundeth in water, euen so this cite aboundeth in wickednesse. **1611** SHAKS. *Wint. T.* II. i. 120 When you shall know your Mistris Has deseru'd Prison, then abound in Teares. **1676** CLARENDON *Surv. Leviathan* 21 In which kind of Illustrations..his whole Book abounds. **1798** FERRIAR *Illustr. of Sterne* iv. 101 Some languages.. abound in figurative expressions. **1869** BUCKLE *Civil.* III. iv. 259 At the christening..the Scotch were accustomed to assemble their relations,..in whom, then as now, they much abounded.

4. To abound *with* (*of* obs., cf. Fr. *abonder de*): To be filled with, teem or swarm with, to be rife with, to possess in great numbers. (Used chiefly of things, in reference to accidental or unessential properties, or such as do not essentially add to the 'abundance' of the subject. 'The ship abounds in conveniences, but it abounds with rats.')

¶A place abounds *with* all those things, which abound *in* it; it abounds *in* those things only which by their abundance give it a character, or add to its resources.

c **1374** CHAUCER *Boethius* (1868) 82 Whiche water habundeþ most of rede purpre. Þat is to seyen of a maner shelfisshe. **1375** BARBOUR *Bruce* XIII. 716 Hys cuntre Haboundyt weill off corne. *c* **1425** WYNTOUN *Cron.* VIII. xxii. 34 Elizabeth Qwene of England Of gret Tresore abowndand. **1513** DOUGLAS *Virgil's Æneis* (1710) VII. 46 Hir figure sa grisly grete haboundis, Wyth glourand ene. **1583** STANYHURST *Æneis* (1880) II. 62 Thee shoars of Dardan for her oft with bloodshed abounded. **1611** BIBLE *Prov.* xxviii. 20 A faithfull man shall abound with blessings. **1705** ADDISON *Rem. on Italy* (pref.) It abounds with Cabinets of Curiosities. **1756** BURKE *Vind. Nat. Soc.* Wks. I. 38 The palaces of all princes abound with such courtly philosophers. **1846** T. WRIGHT *Mid. Ages* II. xix. 256 Warton's history is very incomplete, and abounds with inaccuracies.

†**5.** To go at large, be at liberty, revel, expatiate: in the phr. **to abound in one's own sense** (late L. *abundare in suo sensu*, Fr. *abonder dans son sens*): to follow one's own opinion, use one's liberty of judgment.

1382 WYCLIF *Rom.* xiv. 5 Ech man habunde or be plenteuous in his witt (Vulg. *Unusquisque in suo sensu abundet*). **1552** TAUERNER *Proverbes* 14 For the excludynge of contencyon we suffre euery man to abounde in his owne sence. **1601** HOLLAND *Pliny* (1634) I. 145, I wil not greatly busie my head thereabout, but suffer euery man to abound in his own sence. **1642** ROGERS *Naaman, to Reader* 4 How abounding in their owne sense, and stiffe in their owne conceit. **1651** CARTWRIGHT *Cert. Relig.* I. 42 In those points ..the Church leaves every man to abound in his own sense. **1775** BURKE *Sp. Concil. with Am.* Wks. III. 95, I was resolved..to let others abound in their own sense, and carefully to abstain from all expressions of my own.

†**6.** *trans.* To overflow with, to pour forth.

1591 *Troubles. Raigne of K. John* 62 [He] foretelleth famine, aboundeth plentie forth. **1631** A. CRAIGE *Pilgrime and Heremite* An hoarse hoarie Heremite..Whose boyling Breast nought but blacke baile abounded.

¶ In the following, *abaundon* = devote, is the true reading:

c **1386** CHAUCER *Pars. T.* 639 He that lovith God, wol.. abounde himself, with alle his might, wel for to dóon. [3 *MSS.* abunden, habunden; 2 abaundone, abawndone; 1 enforce.]

†**abound**, *v.*² *Obs.* [? f. A- *pref.* 11 + BOUND *v.*; but only known in pa. pple., so that the *a-* may be for I-, Y-. See A *particle*.] To set limits to, to restrain.

1398 TREVISA *Barth. De P.R.* (1495) IV. iii. 81 A fletynge thynge..dryeth · puttyth itselfe as it were abounded, and to lette the fletynge. **1627** SPEED *England descr. & abridged* i. §9 The old names of whose Nations as also the knowledge of their seuerall abodes..haue of late with infinite labours.. beene probably restored and abounded.

abound, obs. past pple. of BIND *v.*

†**aboundable**, *a.* *Obs.* [f. ABOUND *v.*¹ + -ABLE.] Fully sufficient, abundant.

c **1420** *Palladius on Husb.* XII. 19 And for an acre fatte is hable Sex strike to sowe, and lesse is aboundable In mene lande.

aboundance, -ant, -ly, obs. ff. ABUNDANCE, etc.

abounder (ə'baʊndə(r)). [f. ABOUND *v.*¹ + -ER¹.] One who abounds, has plenty, or is wealthy.

1755 YOUNG *Centaur* iii. Wks. 1757 IV. 184 Say, ye strangers to care, and abounders in mirth! **1876** BROWNING *Pacchiarotto* v. 81 Wanters, abounders, March in gay mixture.

abounding (ə'baʊndɪŋ), *vbl. sb.* [f. ABOUND *v.*¹ + -ING¹.] Overflowing or plentiful supply.

1690 PENN *Rise & Progr. Quakers* (1834) 12 The aboundings of grace. [Now gerundial.]

abounding (ə'baʊndɪŋ), *ppl. a.* [f. ABOUND *v.*¹ + -ING².]

1. Overflowing; flowing in a full stream.

1684 tr. *Bonet, Merc. Compil.* III. 64 We must consider the quantity of the abounding bloud. **1816** BYRON *Childe Harold* III. 50 But Thou, exulting and abounding river. **1826** DISRAELI *Viv. Grey* IV. vi. 162 The beautiful and abounding Rhine.

2. Plentiful; abundant.

1697 *Snake in the Grass* (ed. 2) 80 The surest Method..for a Young Man to step into an abounding Trade. **1866** *Standard* 15 Sept. 4/5 The abounding cases of hardship which continually occur under certain obnoxious statutes.

†**3.** Affluent.

1631 DONNE *Biathanatos* (1644) 91 For every labourer is miserable and beastlike in respect of the idle abounding men.

abourne, obs. form of AUBURN.

about (ə'baʊt), *adv.* and *prep.* Forms: 1–2 **onbútan, a-bútan, a-buton**; 2–3 **a-buten, abuuten**; 3 **abute**; (4 **abote**;) 4–5 **abouten, abowten**; 4–6 **aboute**; 5 (**abought, abowght**); 6– **about.** North.: 3 **abut**; 4 **about, obout, abowt** (with final *e* already dropped). By-form, 5 **abowtes, abouts**, with genitival ending. [OE. *on-bútan* (cf. OFries. *abûta*), f. *on* in, on + *bútan* without, outside of (itself an earlier comb. of *be* by, near, + *útan* properly locative of *út* out, used adjectively or substantively; cf. *be northan*, etc.) The primary meaning of *on-bútan* was thus, *on* or *by the outside of*, hence *around*, wholly or partially. The idea of *round*, *about*, was originally expressed in OE. by *ymbe*, and its compound *ymb-útan*; the latter scarcely survived the 11th c., and the former became obs. in the 13th, *about* taking the place of both. The weakening to *a-bútan* began in the 10th c. Mod. poets have sometimes *'bout*. The word was from the first used without (adv.) or with (prep.) an object; the latter in the accus. or dat. The adverbial and prepositional uses are here separated, but the distinction is one of construction rather than of meaning, and it often melts away: see A 3, B 9.]

A. (without obj. expressed) *adv.* **I.** Position.

1. a. Around the outside, around; on every side.

c **1120** *O.E. Chron.* (Laud. MS.) an. 1090 [Hi] besæton þonne castel abuton. *c* **1230** *Ancren Riwle* 246 Kastel þet haueð deope dich abuten, & water beo iðe dich, þe Kastel is wel kareleas aȝean his unwines. **1387** TREVISA *Higden* (Rolls Ser.) I. 245 Þe Frensche men and Hannibal byseged hem [the Romans] all aboute. **1430** LYDGATE *Story of Thebes* 1339 in Skeat's *Spec.* 37 A bed ryȝt softe, Rychly abouten apparayled With clothe of golde. **1610** SHAKS. *Temp.* v. i. 180 Now all the blessings Of a glad father, compasse thee about. **1673** RAY *Journey thro' Low Countries* 2 Dunkerk is ..strongly fortified all about. **1873** BROWNING *Red Cott. N.-Cap Country* 109 The haschisch-man..Then shows him how to smoke himself about With Paradise.

b. Towards every side, in every or any direction from a point, all round; *fig.* in *cast about, look about.*

1205 LAYAMON III. 26 Þa bi-sæh þat wif abuten [**1250** aboute]. **1380** *Sir Ferumb.* 159 Behold aboute now y praye, ouer and on euery helue. *c* **1400** *Cokes Tale of Gamelyn* 550 The scherref aboute cast Gamelyn for to take. **1591** SHAKS.

Rom. & Jul. III. v. 40 The day is broke, be wary, looke about. **1697** DRYDEN *Virgil's Georg.* I. 447 By fits he deals his fiery Bolts about.

2. Less definitely: on any side; near, in the neighbourhood, without defining the exact direction.

1205 LAYAMON 12577 Arwen fluȝen ouer wal · al abuten ouer al. **1377** LANGL. *P. Pl.* B. II. 158 Sompne alle segges in schires aboute. *c* **1385** CHAUCER *Leg. G. Wom.* 720 Wemen that were neigheboris a-boute. **1388** WYCLIF *Ecclus.* xlvi. 16 The enemyes stondynge aboute on ech side. **1480** CAXTON *Chron. Eng.* ccxliv. 304 They caught a gyde that knewe al the countreye aboute. **1859** JEPHSON *Brittany* vi. 71 Lying about was what seemed to me to be the old altar-stone. **1877** MRS. OLIPHANT *Makers of Flor.* Introd. 12 The tocsins.. were sounding all about. *Mod.* Better to earn a little than hang about doing nothing.

3. Nearly, approximately; not many more or less;—used with numbers or quantities. (Almost prepositional: about a hundred men were there = men, *about a hundred in number*, were there. See B 9.)

1055 *O.E. Chron.* (Cotton MS.) Man slóh ðær mycel wæl, abutan feower hund manna, oððe fife. *c* **1131** —— (Laud. MS.) an. 1127 þær mihte wel ben abuton twente oðer þritti horn blaweres. **1297** R. GLOUC. 247 Þys was in þe ȝer of grace syx hondred ȝer ywys, And aboute an foure & þrytty. **1535** COVERDALE *Josh.* iv. 13 Aboute a fortye thousande men ready harnessed to the warre, wente before the Lorde. **1611** BIBLE *Ex.* xxxii. 28 There fell of the people that day about three thousand men. **1802** MAR. EDGEWORTH *Moral Tales* (1816) I. iv. 20 A girl of about seven years old. **1849** MACAULAY *Hist. Eng.* I. 348 In 1685 London had been, during about half a century, the most populous capital in Europe. **1879** LOCKYER *Elem. Astron.* vi. 36. 208 Light travels about 186,000 miles a second.

4. Hence, in familiar language, of degrees of quality: nearly, almost, all but. ***much about***: very nearly.

1614 OVERBURY *A Wife*, etc. (1638) 94 Much about Gentlemanlike. **1832-6** COBBETT *Prospectus of his Wks.* (aff. to *Eng. Gramm.*) In about every one of these works I have pleaded the cause of the working people. **1842** E. MIALL *Nonconf.* II. 335 The money-Moloch of our country..is about the grimmest, fiercest, most implacable god. **1850** E. P. WHIPPLE *Ess. & Rev.* I. 299 The difference between duty and conduct..about measures the difference between the real and the actual. **1852** DICKENS *Bleak Ho.* II. 102 You're about right respecting the bond. **1880** HAWLEY SMART *Social Sinners* I. ix. 182 The first two are about the nicest girls in all London. **1882** SIR W. HARCOURT in *Times* 13 June 10/2 This amendment was about as relevant to the clause as it would be if it related to sheep-stealing. *Mod. colloq.* I am about tired of this. Is your work about finished? Near about.

II. Motion.

5. a. Round, in rotation or revolution. Hence, *fig.* **to come about**: to revolve (as time), to complete a revolution, to be fulfilled; to come to pass, turn out, or happen. **to bring about**: to cause to revolve; bring to pass, accomplish.

c **1000** ÆLFRIC *Manual of Astron.* 10 Seo firmament tyrnð symle onbutan us..& ealle ða steorran..turniað onbutan mid hyre. **1340** HAMPOLE *Pr. Consc.* 7712 Bot þe planetes er noght led swa, Ffor in þair cercles obout þai ga. *c* **1450** *Merlin* 7 The devell was right gladde that he hadde brought this a-bouten. **1535** COVERDALE *1 Chron.* xxi. 1 And whan yͤ yeare came aboute, what tyme as yͤ kynges vse to go forth, Ioab..layed sege vnto Rabba. **1580** TUSSER *Husbandry* x. 45 To make thee repent it ere year about go. **1602** SHAKS. *Haml.* v. ii. 391 And let me speake to th' yet vnknowing world How these things came about. **1607** —— *Coriol.* IV. v. 160 What an Arme he has, he turn'd me about with his finger and his thumbe, as one would set vp a Top. **1681** WORLIDGE *Syst. Agric.* 29 Ere the year be about it may yield you three such Crops. **1707** FREIND *Peterboro's Cond. in Spain* 200 A revolt had been brought about in the city of Valencia. **1768** STERNE *Sent. Journey* (1778) II. 36 Let the heralds officers twist his neck about if they will. **1876** FREEMAN *Norm. Conq.* I. iv. 239 An accommodation was hardly brought about when Lewis died.

b. In rotation, in succession; alternately, whether of *many* or *two*.

1393 LANGLAND *P. Pl.* C. III. 232 And ȝaf pardon for pans · pound-meel a-boute. **1801** STRUTT *Sports & Past.* II. i. 50 Butts..at which the inhabitants were to shoot, up and down, (called in the poetical legends 'shooting about') upon all feast days. *c* **1817** J. HOGG *Tales & Sketches* III. 199 We have often sat together..reading verse about with our children in the Bible. **1851** MAYHEW *Lond. Lab.* III. 145 Turn and turn about's fair play. Billy, now it's your turn.

6. a. In partial rotation; half round; from front to back or *vice versa*;—usually with *turn*, *face*. Less usually, a short way round; to one side, aside, away. To send one ***to the right about***: right off in the opposite direction, away with a vengeance. To get a thing ***the wrong way about***: by the wrong end or side. To tell a story ***the other way about***: quite oppositely; ***to bring one about*** (or round), i.e. from illness or insensibility.

1535 COVERDALE *Prov.* xii. 7 Or euer thou canst turne the aboute, the vngodly shal be ouerthrowne. **1596** SHAKS. *Merch. V.* II. vi. 64 The winde is come about, Bassanio presently will goe aboord. **1709** STRYPE *Ann. Ref.* xlv. 456 He had been a very zealous protestant, but under Q. Mary came about, and was as hot the other way. **1859** TENNYSON *Elaine* 605 Saying that she checked And sharply turned about to hide her face.

b. *Naut.* On or to the opposite tack, as to ***make, put, go about***, to ***go about ship***.

1588 *Orders for the Span. Fleet* in *Harl. Misc.* (Malh.) II. 45 If he [the admiral] change her course, or make about. Before he goeth about, he will shoot off a piece; and being about, will put forth another light upon the poop. **1633** *Stafford Pac. Hib.* xvi. 337 (1821) They tacked about, and made for Kinsale. **1690** *Lond. Gaz.* mmdlxx. 3 The French Admiral fired a Gun and went about Ship, and stood to the Westward. **1836** MARRYAT *Midsh. Easy* xxvi. 103 Don't you think we had better go about? *Ibid.* xxx. 117 The Aurora was put about. **1867** SMYTH *Sailor's Wd.-Bk.*, *Ready about!* and *About-ship!* are orders to the company to prepare for tacking.

7. Round, in circumference; in circuit. *lit.* and *fig.*

1598 SHAKS. *Merry Wives* I. ii. 44 Indeede I am in the waste two yards about. **1600** HAKLUYT *Voyages* (1810) III. 429 A more easie way though it were farther about. **1626** BACON *Sylva* §328. (1650) 73 The sure way (though most about) to make gold. **1651** tr. *Bacon, Life & Death* 62 The Operation..is slow, and as it were about. **1705** ADDISON *Italy* (1767) 181, I have seen old Roman rings so very thick about, and with such large stones in them. **1728** MORGAN *Hist. Algiers* II. i. 212 Algiers..measures barely one league about.

8. In a circuitous or winding course; with frequent turnings; hither and thither; to and fro; up and down. Also, of the position of things so scattered irregularly on a surface: here and there, up and down.

a **1123** *O.E. Chron.* (Laud. MS.) an. 1001 And þanon wendon in Wiht-land, and þær him ferdon on buton swa swa hi sylf woldon. *c* **1200** *Trin. Coll. Hom.* 37 He bereð abuten here senil hakel. **1205** LAYAMON 25756 Arður eode abute · & his cnihtes bi his siden. **1340** HAMPOLE *Pr. Consc.* 2361 Bot if a synful myght se with-oute, How foul þe syn es, þat he bers oboute. *c* **1450** LONELICH *Grail* xiii. 201 Thanne Kyng Eualach Abowtes gan sende Aftyr his barowns. **1611** BIBLE *Deut.* xxxii. 10 Hee ledde him about, he instructed him. **1751** EARL CHATHAM *Lett. to Nephew* ii. 5, I have been moving about from place to place. *c* **1817** J. HOGG *Tales & Sketches* V. 150 He bustled about & about, speaking to every one. **1855** MACAULAY *Hist. Eng.* III. 373 He had been willing to be the right hand of Dundee: but he would not be ordered about by Cannon. *Mod.* To move furniture about; scatter seeds about; find plants growing about; insects crawling about.

9. Hence: On the move, afoot, astir: going, moving; going on, acting, in action; prevailing (as a disease).

1297 R. GLOUC. 246 Enfryd, Edwyne's broþer, þo he sey þys wo aboute, To Cadwal he wende, & mercy cryde vor doute. *c* **1360** *Song of Yesterday* in *E. Eng. Poems* (1862) 136 Bisi aboute . þei [children] han ben . To cacchen hit with al heore miht. **1598** SHAKS. *Merry Wiv.* v. v. 59 About, about, Search Windsor Castle (Elues) within, and out. **1602** —— *Haml.* II. ii. 617 Fye vpon't! Foh! About, my Braine! **1663** PEPYS *Diary* (1876) II. 309 The building of St. James's by my Lord St. Albans, which is now about. **1815** BIRKBECK *Jrny. through France* 62 The wife of one of the labourers was about, and seemed perfectly hearty. *Mod.* At present, when small-pox is about.

†10. ***to go about to do anything***: to bestir oneself, to busy oneself, to endeavour; to form designs, to contrive, conspire. *Obs.*

c **1380** *Sir Ferumbras* 5821 Al ys for noȝt, ȝe A-boute goes: ȝe ne bringeþ him neuere to ȝoure purpos. *c* **1400** *Apol. for Loll.* 113 [þei] gredyly gon abowt to geyt al þat þey may. **1599** SHAKS. *Much Ado* I. iii. 12 Thou goest about to apply a morall medicine, to a mortifying mischiefe. **1611** BIBLE *John* vii. 19 Why goe ye about to kill me? **1635** N. R. tr. *Camden's Elizabeth* I. 56 Cardinall Granvill..went about to set the English and the Netherlanders..at variance. **1690** LOCKE *Hum. Underst.* I. IV. vii. §1. 276 No Body..ever went about to show the Reason of their Clearness.

†11. ***to be about (for) to do***: to be engaged in, to be busied in preparation for, to be scheming, preparing, or intending. *Obs.* Cf. B 6.

c **1230** *Ancren Riwle* 234 Satan is ȝeorne abuten uorto ridlen þe ut of mine corne! *c* **1386** CHAUCER *Knt. T.* 284 Thou woldest falsly ben aboute To love my lady. **1541** R. BARNES *Wks.* 1573, 325/2 The deuell hath beene of long tyme aboute to bring in this snare for priests. **1634** *Modern. of* MALORY *Pr. Arthur* (1816) I. 125 'You will never be about to do such deeds.' 'Nay, son,' said she, 'and thereto I make you assurance.'

12. Hence, it forms (with the infinitive) a future participle: On the point of, going; as *scripturus*, about to write, going to write, on the point of writing.

1535 COVERDALE *Josh.* xviii. 8 They were aboute to go for to descrybe the londe. **1580** BARET *Alvearie*, To be about or ready to flie awaye. **1611** BIBLE *Rev.* x. 4 And when the seuen thunders had vttered their voices, I was about to write. **1665** MANLEY tr. *Grotius's Low-Countrey-Warrs* 289 Prince Maurice..shews his Army in Battel-Array, as if about to storm. **1816** J. WILSON *City of the Plague* I. iv. 186 The wounded soldier rests his head About to die upon the dead. **1871** SMILES *Character* (1876) iii. 74 A Catholic money-lender, when about to cheat, was wont to draw a veil over the picture of his favourite saint.

b. In neg. contexts ***not about to*** (do something): not intending to or on the point of. *colloq.* (chiefly *N. Amer.*).

1959 M. RUSS *Half Moon Haven* I. 96, I ain't about to work that hard for no reason. **1975** [see TRASHER 2]. **1982** *Record Mirror* 13 Feb. 18/1 I'm not about to foist something on the public just for the sake of releasing something.

In this use it passes from the *adv.* to the *prep.*, which becomes still more distinct in 13. See B 6.

13. By further extension it is used with the verbal sb. in the same sense.

1793 SMEATON *Edystone Lighth.* §254 The season we were then about concluding. **1865** CARLYLE *Fredk. Gt.* ix. 169 (1873) England seems about deserting him. *Ibid.* 88 The celestial sign of the balance just about canting.

B. (with object expressed) *prep.* **I.** Position.

1. a. On the outside, on the outer surface of; on every side of, all round; around, surrounding.

c **880** K. ÆLFRED *Pastoral Care* xxi. (Sweet, *Reader* 14) Ond suǽ suǽ he sceolde bion ȝetrymed onbútan Hierusalem. *c* **1000** ÆLFRIC *Exod.* xix. 12 Þu tæcst ȝemæro abutan þone munt. *c* **1120** *O.E. Chron.* (Laud. MS.) an. 1104 Feower circulas to þam mid dæȝe onbutan þære sunnan. **1154** *Ibid.* 1137 Me dide cnotted strenges abuton here hæued, & diden an scærp iren abuton þa mannes throte. *Ibid.* 1135 An sterres abuten him at middæi. *a* **1200** *Cotton. Hom.* 239 Under him helle muð open. abuuten him all folc. *c* **1250** *Gen. & Ex.* 3455 Abute ðis munt ðu merke make. *c* **1300** *Early Engl. Ps.* (1844) lxxvii. 28 Obout þar teldes þar þai lai. *c* **1386** CHAUCER *Prol.* 158 Of smal coral aboute hire arme sche baar A peire of bedes. *c* **1450** LONELICH *Grail* xiv. 216 [He] beheld the hepes that Abowten him were. **1535** COVERDALE *Ps.* cxxxviii. 3 Thou art aboute my path and aboute my bedd. **1611** BIBLE *Mark* xii. 1 A certaine man planted a vineyard, and set an hedge about it. **1655-60** T. STANLEY *Hist. of Philos.* (1701) 9/2 Of equiangle triangles, the sides that are about equal angles are proportional. **1830** TENNYSON *Fair Women* 162 The Roman soldier found Me lying dead, my crown about my brows. **1873** BROWNING *Red Cott. N.-Cap Country* 239 The balustrade About the tower.

b. Towards every side of oneself; in every direction; all round.

1340 *Ayenb.* 150 Vor hi zyeþ briȝtliche and ine hare herten, and al abote ham. *c* **1380** *Sir Ferumbras* 126 Þanne þe kyng gan waxe wroþ; & aboute him gan be-holde. **1535** COVERDALE *Tob.* xi. 5 The mother of Tobias sat daylie.. vpon yͤ toppe of an hill, from whence she might se farre aboute her. **1607** HIERON *Wks.* I. 397 Many a coward layeth about him for a bout or two. **1625** tr. *Gonsalvius, Span. Inquis.* 12 Vnlesse he look well about him, and be circumspect in his dealing. **1863** LONGF. *Falcon of Ser Federigo* 190 He looked about him for some means or way To keep this unexpected holiday.

2. (Position) around less definitely: around any part of, somewhere near, on some side of (not excluding the *inside*), in or near. (Shading into 11.)

1366 MAUNDEV. iii. 15 Abouten Grece there ben many Iles. **1470** *Paston Lett.* 641 (1874) II. 399 I wold passyngly fayne that ye wer in London..or nye abowght London. **1535** COVERDALE *1 Chron.* x. 27 In the nighte season also remayned they aboute the house of God. **1601** SHAKS. *Twel. N.* II. iv. 13 He is about the house. **1653** WALTON *Angler* i. 20 Creatures inhabiting both in and about that element. **1771** *Antiq. Sarisbur.* 7 Carausius was born of mean parentage about Cleves in Germany. *Mod.* The Snake's-head grows in meadows about Oxford. The idlers hanging about the door of the public-house.

3. With persons, the literal sense of around soon passed into those of holding a position beside, being in common intercourse with, habitually connected with, in attendance on, in the suite of.

c **1175** *Lamb. Hom.* 55 Pater Noster 13 Abuten us he [beelzebub] is for to blenchen. **1366** MAUNDEV. xxii. 242 Tho lordes only that ben aboute him. **1483** CAXTON *G. de la Tour* ii. b, The fend that euer is incessauntly aboute the synnar. **1550** THOMAS *Ital. Dict.*, *Excubitore*, the chamberer that watcheth as it is used aboutes great Personages. **1598** SHAKS. *Merry Wives* II. ii. 17 Hang no more about mee, I am no gibbet for you. **1611** —— *Wint. T.* II. i. 59 Beare the Boy hence, he shall not come about her. **1723** BP. BLACKALL *Wks.* I. 46 They become ten times more uneasy to themselves than to those who are about them. **1837** J. H. NEWMAN *Par. Serm.* (ed. 3) I. xxv. 384 We get used to the things about us. **1876** FREEMAN *Norm. Conq.* II. ix. 365 The king was allowed to have about him his Norman stallers.

4. a. Somewhere on or near the person; in one's pockets or other receptacles; with, at hand.

1567 MAPLET *A greene Forest* 12b, It [Kabiates] is thought being borne about one to make a man eloquent. **1590** SHAKS. *Com. Err.* III. ii. 146 [She] told me what priuie marks I had about mee. **1598** —— *Merry Wives* I. i. 209 You haue not the booke of Riddles about you, haue you? **1637** MILTON *Comus* 647 If you have this [herb] about you..you may Boldly assault the necromancer's hall. **1801** STRUTT *Sports & Past.* II. iii. 86 When they had lost all they had about them, they would sometimes pledge a part of their wearing apparel.

b. *fig.* in reference to mental faculties, etc.: ***about one***, at command, in readiness for use.

1622, 1809 [see WIT *sb.* 3 c]. **1747** CHESTERFIELD *Let.* 30 Oct. (1774), Wherever you are, have (as the low, vulgar expression is) your ears and your eyes about you. **1779** *Mirror* 20 Apr. 99 Things were not a bit mended by my wife's sollicitude (who, to do her justice, had all her eyes about her) to correct them. **1873** NEWMAN *Idea Univ.* (ed. 3) vi. 128 He has his eyes ever about him. **1923** *Times Lit. Suppl.* 18 Jan. 33/2 We shall need to have our best wits about us if we are to avoid confusion.

5. Attributive connexion: Appertaining to; attached to as an attribute or attendant circumstance.

1603 SHAKS. *Meas. for M.* II. i. 163 His face is the worst thing about him. **1793** SMEATON *Edystone Lighth.* §254 Leaving every thing about the work, up to the entry door, ready to go to sea. **1859** JEPHSON *Brittany* v. 56 There was a look about it..which seemed to me to be foreign. **1876** FREEMAN *Norm. Conq.* II. vii. 124 There must have been something specially hateful about this tax.

6. Practical connexion: Near so as to meddle with; concerned or occupied with; dealing with, attending to, interfering with; prosecuting, trying to do or to make. The early quot. show the transition in 'busy about,' from the literal busy *round*, to busy *interfering with*. (To send one ***about his business***: off, away, *i.e.* to attend to his own affairs. See BUSINESS.) Closely connected with A 10-13, of which the two latter are indeed in modern use prepositional.

c **1175** *Lamb. Hom.* 175 Þa þe weren eure abuten þisse worldes echte. *c* **1220** *S. Marherete* 16 Ant am in hare beddes so bisi ham a buten. *c* **1385** CHAUCER *Leg. Good W.* 1610 This thinge the whiche ye ben aboute. *c* **1400** *Apol. for Lollards* 23 Þe souereynes of þe kirke howun not to curse for temporal þingis, ne bisy a bowt hem. *c* **1440** *Generydes* 1173 (1873) Ffor this iv yere we haue ben it abought. **1605** SHAKS. *Wint. T.* IV. iv. 693 The Prince himselfe is about a peece of Iniquitie. **1611** BIBLE *Luke* ii. 49 Wist yee not that I must bee about my fathers businesse? **1642** ROGERS *Naaman* 436 The worke which himselfe and Paul went about. **1751** HARRIS *Hermes* (1841) 225 These machines . . must be the work of one who knew what he was about. **1801** STRUTT *Sports & Past.* Introd. 44 Neither might they . . prevent any one from passing peaceably about his business. **1878** G. MACDONALD *Ann. Quiet Neighb.* iv. 44 Whoever made it has taken long enough about it. *Mod.* What are you about there?

7. a. Abstract connexion: Touching, concerning; in the matter of, in reference or regard to. The regular preposition employed to define the subject-matter of verbal activity, as in to speak, think, ask, dream, hear, know *about*; to be sorry, pleased, perplexed *about*; to give orders, instructions, information *about*; to form plans, have doubts, feel sure *about*.

1230 *Ancren Riwle* 344 Hu hire stont abuten vleschliche tentaciuns, ȝif heo ham haueð. *c* **1449** PECOCK *Repr.* I. xix. (Skeat, *Specim.* 51) Defautis doon aboute ymagis & pilgrimagis ben myche liȝter & esier to be amendid. **1590** SHAKS. *Two Gent.* III. i. 2 We haue some secrets to confer about. **1596** —— *Merch. V.* I. iii. 109 In the Ryalto you haue rated me About my monies and my vsances. **1599** —— (*Title*) Much Adoe about Nothing. **1611** BIBLE *Lev.* vi. 5 All that about which hee hath sworne falsly. **1777** HUME *Ess. & Treat.* I. 193 Shall we be indifferent about what happens? **1854** KINGSLEY *Alexandria* ii. 50 It is better to know one thing than to know about ten thousand things. **1855** MACAULAY *Hist. Eng.* IV. 13 Twenty governments, divided by quarrels about precedence, quarrels about territory, quarrels about trade, quarrels about religion.

b. This passes occasionally into the sense, on account of, because of.

1597 SHAKS. *2 Hen. IV*, v. i. 25 Doe you meane to stoppe any of Williams wages, about the Sacke he lost the other day? **1598** —— *Merry Wives* IV. i. 5 He is very couragious mad, about his throwing into the water.

c. In colloq. phr. ***to be (all) about***, (of an abstract subject) to be primarily concerned with; to have as a central theme or essential truth. Freq. used without a named subject, as ***what it's all about***, the reality of a situation.

1937 P. TOMLIN *Love Bug will bite You* (*song*) 2 That's what love is all about. **1943** [see HOKEY-COKEY]. **1962** *Listener* 20 Dec. 1046/2 This immense transition—from being a slave to being a friend—is what Christianity is all about. **1971** A. SHAFFER *Sleuth* I. 39 Poor blighter, he had no idea what it was all about... Sitting there every night hunched up over those watches. **1976** *Listener* 20 May 637/3 After all, this is what the concept of a tolerant multi-cultural, multi-racial society is all about. **1982** A. PRICE *Old 'Vengeful'* 247 Love and war were about winning, not fair play. **1984** A. BROOKNER *Hotel du Lac* 166 They like the feeling that they have had to fight other men for possession. That is what it is all about, really.

8. Of a point of time: Near, nigh; close to, not far from; in giving an approximative date or hour.

1154 *O.E. Chron.* (Laud. MS.) an. 1140 Abuton non tid dæies, þa men eten. *c* **1230** *Ancren Riwle* 24 Abute swuch time alse me singeð messe. **1297** R. GLOUC. 431 He deyde aboute þulke tyme. *c* **1386** CHAUCER *Knight's T.* 1331 Þise lordes al and some Bene on the sonday to þe cite come Aboute prime. **1534** tr. *Polyd. Verg., Eng. Hist.* I. 56 Cæsar abowte the æquinoctiall time of harveste, retourned into Fraunce. **1598** SHAKS. *Merry Wives* v. i. 12 Bee you in the Parke about midnight. **1611** BIBLE *John* vii. 14 Now about the middest of the feast Jesus went vp into the Temple, and taught. **1756** BURKE *Vind. Nat. Soc.* Wks. I. 27 About this time, another torrent of barbarians . . poured out of the south. **1882** *Daily News* 22 Mar. 2/8 They returned to their quarters about three o'clock.

9. Of a point in a scale of quantity: Near, close to, not much above or below; in giving an approximate weight, measure, or point on any scale.

1590 SHAKS. *Two Gent.* IV. iv. 163 *Sil.* How tall was she? *Jul.* About my stature. **1768** GOLDSM. *Good Nat. M.* III. He's much about my size and figure. *Mod.* Its boiling point is about 150° Fahr. About the same elevation as the top of Primrose Hill.

¶ These two last are closely connected with the adverbial senses A 3, 4; cf. Come about six o'clock; stay about an hour; to weigh about a pound; to be about right.

II. Motion.

10. Round the outside of; round (in opposition to across, over, or into). *arch.* (To beat ***about the bush***. See BUSH.)

c **1000** ÆLFRIC *Manual of Astronomy* 8 Læssan ymbgang hæfð se man þe gæð abútan án hús, þonne se ðe eall ða burh be-gæð. *c* **1075** *O.E. Chron.* (Laud. MS.) an. 1000 And his scipu wendon út abuton Leȝceastre. **1205** LAYAMON 26065 And Arður aneouste þat treo bieorn abute. *a* **1300** *Fragm.* in Wright *Pop. Science* 132 Hevene goth aboute the wordle. **1598** SHAKS. *Merry Wives* IV. iv. 31 Herne the Hunter . . Doth all the winter time, at still midnight Walke round about an Oake. **1655–60** T. STANLEY *Hist. of Philos.* (1701) 86/2 He sent two Companies of Horse secretly about the Hill. **1697** DAMPIER *Voyages* (1729) I. 257 They could not get about the Cape. **1722** WOLLASTON *Relig. of Nat.* v. 79 The revolution of a planet about the sun.

11. a. Round or over the parts of; in circuit over the surface of; to and fro in; across or over in any direction. Used also of the position of things scattered over the surface of anything: here and there in or on. (Shading into 2.)

1534 MORE *Upon the Passion* Wks. 1557, 1318/1 Do my message in preching my woorde about the worlde. **1596** SPENSER *F.Q.* I. i. 11 That path they take, that beaten seem'd most bare, And like to lead the labyrinth about. *c* **1605** *Ratseis Ghost* B 1 Players were never so thriftie as they are now about London. **1610** SHAKS. *Temp.* I. ii. 220 In troops I haue dispers'd them 'bout the Isle. **1878** G. MACDONALD *Ann. Quiet Neighb.* iv. 43, I was wandering about the place, making some acquaintance with it. **1879** TENNYSON *Lover's T.* Friends . . who lived scatteringly about that lonely land. *Mod.* The cowslips dotted about the field.

b. Frequenting, mingling in the pursuits of; esp. in the common phrase ***about town***.

1593 NASHE *Foure Lett. Confuted* 83 Since I first knew him about town. **1848** THACKERAY *Vanity F.* I. 131 A perfect and celebrated 'blood' or dandy about town. *Ibid.* 192 He was not very wise; but he was a man about town, and had seen several seasons. **1849** MACAULAY *Hist. Eng.* II. 153 Some Roman Catholics about the court had, indiscreetly or artfully, told all.

C. *Comb.* When used as a verb-complement, *about* was occasionally, like separable prefixes in German, prefixed to the verb, as in ***about go***, ***about run***, ***about stand***; these have sometimes been connected by hyphens, but are scarcely compounds. Also **about-speech** *obs.*, a roundabout phrase, circumlocution; **about-standing** (cf. Germ. *Umstand*) *obs.*, a circumstance; **about-writing** *obs.*, the legend round the head stamped on a coin. Also ABOUT-SLEDGE, ABOUTWARD, q.v.

1340 HAMPOLE *Pr. Consc.* 7583 Þir twa hevens ay obout-rynnes, Both day and nyght, and never blynnes; þe erth, þat þa hevens obout-gase, Es bot als a poynt Imyddes a compase. **1382** WYCLIF *Ecclus.* xlvi. 16 He inwardly clepide the almiȝty Lord, in aȝenfiȝting the enemys aboute stondende. **1513** DOUGLAS *Virgil's Æneis* I. 12 (1710) Rycht so by about-speich often tymes And semblabill wordis we compyle our rymes. **1340** *Ayenb.* 174 Vor he ssel zigge alle his zennes . . and þe aboutestondinges of þe zennes. *Ibid.* 175 Ac þe aboutestondinges alle þet moreþ þe zennes. *c* **1449** PECOCK *Repr.* II. ii. 140 And thei seiden, It is the ymage and the Aboute-writing of Cæsar, the Emperour.

about (ə'baʊt), *v.*[1] *Naut.* [f. phr. *about-ship* see ABOUT *adv.* 6 b.] To change the course (of a ship) to the other tack.

1688 I. CLAYTON *Virginia* Let. 4 in *Phil. Trans.* XVII. 984 Generally when they About the Ship as they call it, they are so nigh the Shoar, that, etc.

† **about,** *v.*[2] *Obs.* [a. Fr. *abouter* said of a tumour, f. *à bout* to a head: *bouter* of buds.]

1725 BRADLEY *Fam. Dict.*, *Abouting*, a term used by the French gardeners to denote that the Trees are budded; as it signifies, in regard to Animals, the making a kind of a Head or Abscess. **1731** BAILEY, *Abouted*, budded. [In ASH 1775.]

about-face, *v. intr.* and *sb.* orig. and chiefly *U.S.* [Shortening of *right about face* (RIGHT ABOUT B. 1, 2).] = ABOUT-TURN. (Cf. FACE *v.* 9 b.)

1861 *Harper's Mag.* Aug. 364/2 'About-Face!' was the next command. **1918** FARROW *Dict. Mil. Terms* 1 *About Face*, one of the facings in the school of the soldier, executed by facing to the rear, turning to the right. **1924** *Scribner's Mag.* July 36/1 Morrow got very white—about-faced, and marched out of the room. **1930** *Liberty* 6 Sept. 33/2 That's enough to make us do an about face and give it [*sc.* a car] the gas. **1934** *Baltimore Sun* 20 Sept. 2/1 (*headline*) Backers [of Cotton Act] Do An About Face. **1959** *Times* 20 Feb. 8/2 If he did not mislead the Prime-Minister, his abrupt about-face was certainly disconcerting.

aboutie, obs. form of ABUT *v.*

† **abouts, aboutes,** *adv.* and *prep.*, a genitival form of ABOUT used in 5–6; still preserved in certain compound adverbs as HEREABOUTS, THEREABOUTS, WHEREABOUTS, and the obs. THENABOUTS. [prob. of northern origin, with *-es* for *-en*, as in northern genitives, plurals, possessive pronouns, and vbl. inflections.]

A. *adv.*

c **1450** LONELICH *Grail* II. 27 In his herte hadde he gret thowht howh this mater abowtes schold ben browht.

B. *prep.*

c **1450** LONELICH *Grail* xxv. 215 Al and some abowtes him ganne to drawen. **1552–3** *Inv. Church Goods, Stafford*, 29 Abouts iiij yeres paste [they] solde xlix shepe & vi kie. **1596** SPENSER *F.Q.* I. ix. 36 His garment, nought but many ragged clouts . . The which his naked sides he wrapt abouts.

a'bout-sledge. [ABOUT + SLEDGE.] The largest hammer used by smiths.

1703 MOXON *Mech. Exer.* 4 The About Sledge is the biggest Hammer of all, and . . they hold the farther end of the Handle in both their Hands, and swinging the Sledge above their Heads, they . . let fall as heavy a Blow as they can upon the Work. **1849** WEALE *Dict. Terms.*

about-turn. [Shortening of *right about turn* (RIGHT ABOUT B. 1, 2).] ***about turn!*** a military command (cf. TURN *v.* 22 c). Hence as *sb.*, a reversal of position (lit. and fig.), point of view, etc. (cf. TURN *sb.* 8). So as *v. intr.*, to execute an about-turn.

1893 *Infantry Drill* 11. 59 The instructor will then give the command About—Turn. By the Right. Quick—March. **1937** J. A. LEE *Civilian into Soldier* 32 This is the army, not the Salvation Army. About Turn! **1942** C. S. LEWIS *Broadc. Talks* I. v. 29 If you're on the wrong road, progress means doing an about-turn and walking back to the right road. **1959** *Times* 3 June 8/1 Congregation to-day executed a graceful about-turn on the question of retaining the classical languages as compulsory subjects for candidates taking Responsions. **1960** *Guardian* 7 July 7/6 The whole party about-turned on the steps.

† **a'boutward, -s,** *adv. Obs.* 4–7. [ABOUT A 11 and B 6 + -WARD.] Striving, trying, contriving, tending towards;—shading off, as it became obsolete, into the mere idea of being about to, going.

c **1400** *Sir Tryam.* 65 Syr Marrok . . Was faste aboutewarde To do hys lady gyle. *a* **1440** *Sir Eglamour* 658 Thou art abouteward, Y undurstonde To wynne alle Artas of myn honde. **1524** *State Papers Hen. VIII*, IV. 257 Suche Counsaillours . . wolde be aboutewarde to distroy and putte doune noble men. **1534** tr. *Pol. Verg., Eng. Hist.* II. 128 The earle of Warweke . . was than at hys owne towne aboutward to come very shortly unto the camp. **1611** SPEED *Hist. Brit.* IX. xxi. 96 All those that shall bee aboutwards to stop vs in the said pilgrimage.

above (ə'bʌv), *adv.* and *prep.* Forms: 1–2 (**bufan, bufon**); 2 (**bufen, buven, buuen, buuenne**), **abufan**; 3 (**buven, buve**), **abuuen, abuue**; 3–4 (**boven**), **aboven**; 4–5 **abouen, abowen(e**; 4–7 **aboue**; 5 **abouyn, aboun**; 6 **abowe (abuffe, aboufe, abofe, aboif)**; 4– **above**. North.: 4 **abouen, obowen**; 4–6 **abown(e, aboun, abone**; 6– **abune, abuin, aboon**. [f. A *prep.*[1], on, + *bufan* above, atop (cf. ODu. and MLGerm. *boven*), itself an earlier comb. of *be* 'by, near, about' + *ufan* adv. 'up, above' (cf. Germ. *oben*), properly locative case of *uf-* (Goth. *uf*) up, upward. The simple *ufan* originally expressed the whole idea of its successive expansions *b(e)ufan*, *a-b(e)ufan*. *A-bufan* did not appear till the 12th c., and was evidently a northern formation, being rarely found out of northern or north-eastern writers before the end of the 13th, when it generally replaced *bufan*, which as *bove* became obs. in the 14th. *'Bove* is also an occasional aphetism of *above* in modern poets. For the illustration of the senses, *bove* and *above* are here taken together, though *formally* distinct words. A parallel compound of *bufan* was *bibufen* = BEBOVE; cf. *a-fore*, *be-fore*; of *ufan*, *an-ufan*, ANOVE(N. *Bufan* was used in OE. without (adv.) or with (prep.) an object; the latter in the dative. *A-bufan* was at first adverbial, but soon acquired the prepositional use of *bufan*. The adverbial and prepositional constructions are here separated, though in the development of meaning they form historically only a single series; and, as in ABOUT, in certain modern uses, the grammatical distinction melts away; see B 8.]

A. (without object expressed) *adv.*

1. a. Overhead; in a place vertically up; on high; upstairs.

c **1000** ÆLFRIC *Manual of Astron.* 2 Seo sunne gæð . . eall swa feorr adune on nihtlicre tide under þære eorþan swa heo on dæȝ bufan up astihð. **1340** HAMPOLE *Pr. Consc.* 612 Bathe fra aboven and fra benethe. **1413** LYDGATE *Pylg. Sowle* (1859) v. i. 68 Angels also I sawe fleen to and fro, . . by see and land, and in the eyer abouen. **1598** SHAKS. *Merry Wives* IV. ii. 78 My Maids Aunt the fat woman of Brainford, has a gown aboue. **1611** BIBLE *Prov.* viii. 28 When hee prepared the heauens, I was there . . when he established the cloudes aboue. **1799** WORDSWORTH *Prel.* I. 14 (1850) Far above Was nothing but the stars and the grey sky. **1865** DICKENS *Our Mut. Fr.* iii. 13 In another corner a wooden stair leading above.

b. In heaven. Also elliptically *to* heaven; and ***from above***, from heaven.

c **1250** *Gen. & Exod.* 10 Đan sal him almightin luuen, Her bi-neðen and ðund abuuen. **1460** *Pol. Rel. & Love Poems* (1866) 430 From here sone þat ys a-bouen. **1611** BIBLE *James* i. 17 Euery good gift and euery perfect gift is from aboue. **1647** H. MORE *Song of Soul* I. ii. 40 And ever naming God, he lookd aboven. **1814** SOUTHEY *Roderick* vii. (1853) IX. 71 That vow hath been pronounced and register'd Above. **1861** TENNYSON *In Mem.* lxxxiv. 10 And whether trust in things above Be dimm'd of sorrow, or sustain'd.

2. On the surface; on the outside; covering, binding down, or over all. ? *Obs.* or *dial.*

c **1305** *Life of Beket* 266 Thabyt of monek he nom, And siththe clerkes robe above. **1340** *Ayenb.* 236 Þe linene kertel betokneþ chastete of herte. Þe gerdel above betocneþ chastete of bodie. *c* **1440** *Ancient Cookery* in *Housh. Ord.* (1790) 468 Make a drage . . of pouder of ginger mynced, and strewe aboven theron. **1611** BIBLE *Numb.* iv. 25 The couering of the badgers skinnes that is aboue upon it.

3. In a higher place; farther up a mountain or river; farther from the sea; hence (*obs.*) on shore, whence men 'go down to the sea in ships.'

c **1270** *Assumpcioun de N. Dame* 22 Þenkeþ on my sorwe nowe, How I hange here abowe, How I hange apon a tre. *c* **1325** *E.E. Allit. Poems* A. 1022 Þe cyte stod abof ful sware. **1366** MAUNDEV. xxv. 262 It hath aboven toward Inde, the Kyngdom of Caldee. *c* **1435** *Tor. of Portugal* 1462 Ffast from land row they began, Above they left that gentilman, With wyld bestis to have byde. **1611** BIBLE *Josh.* ii. 13 The waters of Jordan shall be cut off from the waters that come down from above. *Mod.* Below were the silvery lakes, above were the snowy peaks.

4. Higher on a written sheet or page; and hence, in an earlier part of a writing or book; before in order. (Often used as *a.* and *sb.*; see C 1: and in *comb.*; see D, and ABOVE-SAID.)

c **1120** *O.E. Chron.* (Laud. MS.) an. 1090 Eall swa wæ ǽr abufan sædan be þam cynge. **1340** *Ayenb.* 247 Þe bysye lyue huerof we habbeþ aboue y-speke. **1574** *Wills & Inv. North. Count.* II. 405 The Rest of all my Land I gyf and leiff to my sone..except that aboun is exceptet. *Mod.* Several examples of this construction are given in the exercise above.

†5. *fig.* (From the idea of two wrestlers or combatants.) In superiority; having the upper hand in a struggle; victorious. *Obs.*

1205 LAYAMON 3764 Ofte heo fuhten. ofte heo weren buuenne [*later text* bofe] and ofte bi-neoðen. **1330** R. BRUNNE *Chron.* 32 If he wild praie him..He wild do þe bataile, and þei suld be aboue. **1375** BARBOUR *Bruce* IX. 94 Vencust is he, And gerris his fayis abovin be. **1611** BIBLE *Deut.* xxviii. 13 And the Lord shall make thee the head and not the tail; and thou shalt be aboue only and shalt not be beneath.

6. *fig.* In a higher rank, position, or station. Also, *ellipt.* a higher court, etc.

1340 HAMPOLE *Pr. Consc.* 1467 Now er we aboven, and now doun broght. *c* **1400** *Apol. for Lollards* 9 He may not do þis, but in as mykil as it soundiþ to þe hed of þe kirk abouyn. **1465** MARG. PASTON *Past. Lett.* 502. II. 185 Ye shuld fynde a mene to have a wrytte from above. ?**1530** SIR R. CONSTABLE in *Plumpton Corr.* 228 Make me a letter of atturney unto some of your frinds aboufe to clame your arrearegеs.

7. In addition, *esp.* in the phrase **over and above**.

1596 SHAKS. *Merch. V.* IV. i. 413 And stand indebted ouer and aboue In loue and seruice to you euermore. **1602** —— *Haml.* II. ii. 126 This..hath my daughter shew'd me: And more aboue hath his soliciting As they fell out..All given to mine eare. **1850** MRS. STOWE *Uncle Tom's C.* vi. 35 'Old lady don't like your humble servant, over and above,' said Haley.

8. More than, fully: see B 8, in which *above* hovers between an adv. and prep.

B. (with obj.) *prep.*

1. Directly over, vertically up from; on or over the upper surface; on the top of, upon, over.

c **1000** ÆLFRIC *Gen.* i. 7 And to-twæmde þa wateru þe wæron under þære fæstnisse fram þam þe wæron bufan þære fæstnisse. —— *Homl.* (Sweet *A.S. Reader* 86) Æteowode heofonlic leoht bufon ðam apostole. *c* **1175** *Lamb. Hom.* 95 Þe halia gast wes iseȝen on fures heowe bufan þam apostlas. *a* **1200** *Moral Ode* (*Lamb. Hom.*) 87 He is buuen us and binoþen, biforen and bihinden. *c* **1230** *Ancren Riwle* 362 And we..wulleð mid eie stien to heouene þet is so heih buuen us. *c* **1315** SHOREHAM 117 Al that hys bove and under molde. **1340** HAMPOLE *Pr. Consc.* 2794 Þat place es neghest aboven hel pitte, Bytwen purgatory and itte. *c* **1450** *Merlin* 134 So eche bar other to the erthe, and theire horse a-bouen hem. **1595** SHAKS. *John* II. i. 397 Now by the sky that hangs aboue our heads, I like it well. **1611** BIBLE *Gen.* i. 7 And God ..diuided the waters, which were vnder the firmament, from the waters, which were aboue the firmament. **1833** WORDSWORTH *Sonnets* xxxii. Hell opens, and the heavens in vengeance crack Above his head.

2. Relatively over, covering; farther from the centre of a solid body; on the outer surface of; on the top of; outside of, over. ?*Obs.* or *dial.*

1375 BARBOUR *Bruce* XVI. 581 A chemeyr, for till heill his veid, Abone his armyng had he then. **1523** LD. BERNERS *Froissart* I. ccxvii. 275 The sayd lordes toke on them to weare aboue all theyr garmentes, the redde crosse.

3. Higher up a slope, nearer the source of a river, or summit of a mountain, than; farther from the sea than. Also, of time: earlier than. (*Occasionally* higher on a map, farther north than.)

c **896** *O.E. Chron.* Be Lygan xx mila bufan Lunden-byriȝ. **1330** R. BRUNNE *Chron.* 42 Bot in þe ȝere after, obowen Grimsby Eft þei gan aryue. **1375** BARBOUR *Bruce* x. 31 Thar Iohne of lorne gert his menȝhe Enbuschit be abooyn the vay. **1564** KNOX *Let.* quoted in P. F. TYTLER'S *Hist. Scot.* (1864) III. 402 Two barges..came in our Firth, abone the Inch. **1789–96** MORSE *Amer. Geog.* I. 1 The greatest part of Europe being situated above the 45th degree of Northern latitude. **1855** HT. MARTINEAU *Guide to Eng. Lakes* 36 Behind and above it the vale head rises into grandeur. **1862** STANLEY *Jewish Ch.* (1877) I. ii. 33 We are still above the point of separation between the various tribes.

4. Higher in absolute elevation than; rising or appearing beyond the level or reach of. ***above ground***: out of the grave, alive. *fig.* Of sounds.

1205 LAYAMON 26051 Ah Arður bræid heȝe his sceld buuen [*later text* boue] his hælme. *c* **1230** *Ancren Riwle* 46 Mid te þume up buue þe uorheaued. **1340** HAMPOLE *Pr. Consc.* 4760 Þe se sal ryse..Abowen þe heght of ilka mountayne. **1552** LYNDESAY *Monarche* 5463 Ierome sayis, it sall ryse on heycht Abone montanis, to mennis sycht. **1653** WALTON *Angler* ii. 43 The Otter which you may now see above water at vent. **1711** F. FULLER *Med. Gym.* 79 Legions of the dead might have been above ground. **1855** KINGSLEY *Heroes, Theseus* II. 212 The citadel of Corinth towering high above all the land. **1878** H. TAYLOR *Notes f. Life* in *Wks.* IV. 139 The poetry of those from whom he borrowed will..thus ..be embalmed when the body of their works is no longer aboveground. *a* **1884** *Mod.* His voice was heard clear above the din. **1913** A. G. BRADLEY *Other Days* iii. 90 Marlburians of the sixties are still numerous above-ground.

5. *fig.* Superior to (the influence of); out of reach of; not exposed or liable to be affected by; not condescending to.

c **1340** HAMPOLE *Prose Treat.* 13 Cristes lufe..lyftes abowne layery lustes and vile couaytes. **1653** WALTON *Angler* 6 We enjoy a contentedness above the reach of such dispositions. **1782** PRIESTLEY *Corr. of Christianity* I. I. 61 It was not pretended that the subject was above human comprehension. **1819** WORDSWORTH *Poems of Sent.* xxviii. 4 My spirit seems to mount above The anxieties of human love. **1832** HT. MARTINEAU *Life in Wilds* iii. 42 [He] was quite above owing his meal to the request of a little girl.

b. ***above*** (***the head of***) (someone): = *over* (one's) *head* s.v. HEAD *sb.*[1] 37 f. *colloq.*

1867 J. BLACKWOOD *Let.* 11 Dec. in *Geo. Eliot Lett.* (1956) IV. 406, I inclose revise of Felix Holt's Address... The only fear is its being too much above your audience. **1914** JOYCE *Dubliners* 221 He was undecided about the lines from Robert Browning for he feared they would be above the heads of his hearers. **1926** G. B. SHAW *Translations & Tomfooleries* 67 You could understand him when he was talking right above my head. You could talk about his work to him. I couldnt. **1979** A. MCCOWEN *Young Gemini* 49 See Rep. Comp. do 'Candida' bit above me but very good.

6. *fig.* Higher in rank or position than; over in authority.

c **1200** *Ormulum* 17970 Forr he þatt fra bibufenn comm Iss ane abufenn alle. **1340** HAMPOLE *Pr. Consc.* 4120 And heghen hym..Aboven al þat er paens goddes calde. **1607** SHAKS. *Timon* III. ii. 94 Men must learne now with pitty to dispence, For Policy sits aboue Conscience. **1611** BIBLE *1 Chron.* xxvii. 6 This is that Benaiah, who was mightie among the thirtie, and aboue the thirtie. **1697** DRYDEN *Virgil, Georgics* IV. 602 (1721) He breath'd of Heav'n, and look'd above a Man. **1718** *Free-thinker* No. 57. 13 You dress, not only above your circumstances, but above your condition. **1829** SCOTT *Antiq.* xxxii. 223 'She brought me up abune my station.' **1850** MC COSH *Div. Govt.* (1874) III. i. 299 The conscience looks to a law above it.

7. Higher in degree; surpassing in quality; in excess of, beyond; more than. ***above all***: beyond everything; first of all; chiefly. ***above measure***: beyond or more than what is meet; in excess of moderation; excessively.

1377 LANGL. *P. Pl.* B. x. 357 Þat is—loue þi lorde god · leuest aboue alle. *c* **1400** *Apol. for Lollards* 64 & þan he schal vnderstond a boun his enemies, & ouer his techars. **1535** COVERDALE *Ps.* xliv. 7 God hath anoynted the with the oyle of gladnes aboue thy felowes. **1610** SHAKS. *Temp.* I. ii. 168 He furnish'd me..with volumes, that I prize aboue my Dukedome. **1611** BIBLE *James* v. 12 But aboue all things, my brethren, sweare not. —— *2 Cor.* xii. 7 Least I should bee exalted aboue measure. **1829** WORDSWORTH *Poems of Sent.* xxxvii. Taught to prize Above all grandeur, a pure life uncrossed By cares.

8. Surpassing in quantity, amount, or number; more than. (Here the prep. passes again into the adv., at least the numeral following may be the nominative of a sentence, or the object of a vb. or of another prep. Cf. *nearly* a hundred, *above* a hundred were present.)

1509 HAWES *Past. of Pl.* xvi. 59 She is not yet in al above xviii. yere. **1610** SHAKS. *Haml.* II. ii. 455 It was neuer Acted: or if it was, not aboue once. **1713** STEELE *Englishm.* No. 11. 71 These Motions are performed by Wheels, which are above fifty in Number. **1849** MACAULAY *Hist. Eng.* I. 335 Above a sixth part of the nation is crowded into provincial towns of more than thirty thousand inhabitants.

9. In addition to, besides (in ***over and above***).

1581 MARBECK *Bk. of Comm. Places* 1138 To looke for a good turne againe, or anything else, over and above the principall. **1618** BOLTON tr. *Florus*, Putting in a sword over and above their bargaine, into the false balances. **1866** GEO. ELIOT *Felix Holt* xlvii. 406 Over and above the stings of conscience..he had the powerful motive of desiring to do what would satisfy Esther. *Mod.* He earns a large sum over and above his salary by commissions.

10. Phr. ***above oneself***: in a state above the normal; out of hand. Also said of horses when they are overfed and under-exercised, or have not undergone the full training for a race.

1890 KIPLING *From Sea to Sea* (1899) I. 455, I have..seen more decent men above or below themselves with drink, than I care to think about. **1893** *Punch* 23 Sept. 137 Lest the spirits of the travelling tourist should rise so high that he might run the chance of 'getting a bit above hisself', as horsedealers graphically express it. **1897** *Daily News* 7 Nov. 7/3 Horses run best when they are above themselves. **1937** V. WOOLF *The Years* 282 He was a little flushed, a little, as nurses used to say, 'above himself'.

C. Elliptically (quasi- *a.* and *sb.*).

1. By *ellipsis* of a pple. as *said*, *written*, *mentioned*, *above* stands attributively, as 'the above explanation'; or the noun also may be suppressed and *above* used absolutely, as 'the above will show,' etc. Hence of a paragraph, etc.: preceding, previous.

1779 W. RUSSELL *View of Soc.* II. xcvi. 437 Just as I was concluding the above, I received yours. **1831** *Ipswich Jrnl.* 23 July 3/4 The above Estate is Freehold. **1847** THACKERAY *Van. Fair* (1848) xiv. 126 Some short period after the above events..one more hatchment might have been seen in Great Gaunt Street. **1851** F. W. ROBERTSON *Serm.* Ser. IV. (1863) I. vi. 33 In God's world there is not one monotony of plains without hills... There is an above and there is a below. **1864** G. W. MOON *Dean's English* (ed. 2) 34 You have so confusedly used your pronouns in the above paragraph, that it may be construed in ten thousand different ways. **1873** BANISTER *Music* iii. 11 The above signs for the Breve measure being omitted. **1919** CONRAD *Arrow of Gold* IV. ii. 157 The above sequence of thoughts was entirely unsympathetic and it was followed by a feeling of satisfaction that I, at any rate, was not suffering from insomnia. **1976** T. STOPPARD *Dirty Linen* 51 During the above speech French is becoming increasingly agitated, and Maddie increasingly angry.

†2. With a possessive case, ***at, to mine*** (***thine, his***, etc.) ***above***: something above what I am (thou art, he is). **to bring one to his above**: to bring him to a superior position or condition; **to come to**, or **be at the above of**: to attain the superiority or mastery of, to surmount, overcome, or master. *Obs.* 3–5.

1330 R. BRUNNE *Chron.* I. i. 253 (Rolls Ser.) Mykel I ȝow love, I have ȝow holpen to ȝoure above. **1387** TREVISA *Higden* (Rolls Ser.) II. 29 [They] schal have þe better ende and be at here aboue [Lat. *praevalere*]. *c* **1420** *Palladius on Husb.* I. 199 And vynes..By processe may be brought to thair above. **1475** CAXTON *Jason* xx b, I hope to come to thaboue of myn enterpryse. **1484** CAXTON *Ord. Chyualry* 72 [He] cometh to the aboue of his enemyes.

D. *Comb. above* was occasionally, when used as a verb-complement by early writers, prefixed to the verb, as is still the case with similar adverbs in German; thus we have ***above build***, ***above rise***, etc., which however are scarcely compounds. But when *above* in sense A 4, 'higher on a page or document,' was prefixed to pa. pples., many regular compound adjs. were formed, such as ***above-cited***, ***above-mentioned***, ***above-named***, ***above-written***, which see under ABOVE-SAID. Also ***above-average*** adj.; **above-ground**, a techn. term in dancing; above the ground (cf. B.4); **above-hand**, overhand; **above-head**, *obs.*, overhead; **above-seated**, *obs.*; **above-stairs**, *obs.*, upstairs; **above-wonderful**, *obs.*, more than wonderful. Also ABOVE-BOARD, ABOVE-SAID, q.v.

1952 C. P. BLACKER *Eugenics* xi. 306 Children..who make an impression of being promising and above-average in abilities and character. **1960** K. AMIS *New Maps of Hell* (1961) v. 127 The required above-average score for articulateness. **1382** WYCLIF *Jude* ii. 20 Aboue byldinge ȝou silf to ȝoure moost hooly feith. **1622** MASSINGER, etc. *Old Law* III. ii. [Dancing-master *loq.*] Now here's your in-turn, and your trick above ground. **1892** *Daily News* 19 Feb. 5/4 In the whole hamlet there were only three above-ground dwellings. **1940** G. GREENE *Power & Glory* I. iii. 37 A big above-ground tomb. **1674** PLAYFORD *Skill of Musick* II. 114 The violin is usually plaid abovehand. **1793** SMEATON *Edystone Lightho.* §253 The weather..above-head had remained..much the same. **1382** WYCLIF *James* ii. 13 Forsothe mersy aboue reisith doom. **1683** tr. *Erasmus, Moriae Enc.* 78 The above-seated Gods in Heaven. **1758** JOHNSON *Idler* No. 28. ¶5, I cannot be above stairs and below at the same time. **1625** A. GILL *Sacred Philos.* II. 171 Nothing of this was in that above-wonderfull generation.

above-board (ə'bʌvbɔəd), *adv. phr.* often used adjectively. [f. ABOVE *prep.* + BOARD *sb.*]

1. 'In open sight; without artifice or trick. A figurative expression, borrowed from gamesters, who, when they put their hands under the table, are changing their cards.' J. (He adds, 'It is used only in familiar language'; but see the quotations.)

a. In orig. use.

1616 BEAUM. & FL. *Cust. Country* I. i. Yet if you play not fair play, and above-board too, I have a foolish gin here.

b. *fig.* Openly, freely; without dissimulation or concealment; also, publicly exhibited.

1628 EARLE *Microcosm.* lxxvi. 157 One that..does it fair and above-board without legerdemain, and neither sharks for a cup or a reckoning. **1648** SYMMONS *Vind.* 46 Such a disloyal, hypocritical, unchristian, and bloody faction as this now above-board. **1664** H. MORE *Myst. Iniq.* ix. 27 They would have dealt above-board, and like honest men. **1788** BURKE *Sp. agst. Hastings* Wks. XIII. 293 All that is in this transaction is fair and above-board. **1871** FREEMAN *Histor. Ess.* Ser. I. iii. 69 Edward's conduct was throughout honest and aboveboard.

aboven, obs. form of ABOVE.

abovesaid (ə'bʌv,sɛd), *ppl. a. arch.* [ABOVE *adv.* A 4 + SAID.] Mentioned higher up on a document or page; previously mentioned; aforesaid (which is the ordinary modern equivalent).

1366 MAUNDEV. iv. 26 Alle the contreyes and Iles aboveseyd. **1494** FABYAN, v. xciii. 68 After the abouesayd victory..he sped hym towarde Yorke. **1680** H. MORE *Apocalypsis Apoc.* 355 The wicked suggestions of the abovesaid Jezebel. **1790** COWPER *Lett.* June 17 Wks. 1876, 332 This, and more of the same sort passed in my mind on seeing the old woman abovesaid.

Similarly, **above-bounden, -cited, -found, -given, -mentioned, -named, -written.**

1755 N. MAGENS *Ess. Ins.* II. 393 Whereas the abovenamed CD hath advanced and lent unto the abovebounden A & B the sum of £500, etc. **1653** MILTON *Consid. Hirelings* Wks. 1851, 378 By that command to Peter, and by this to all Ministers abovecited. **1765** FERGUSON in *Phil. Trans.* LV. 68 Multiplying the above-found quantities by the square of the diameter. **1865** LUBBOCK *Preh. Times* 325 He refers to the above-given calculation. **1707** FREIND *Peterboro's Cond. in Spain* 26 We are willing to comply with the King's desire for the above-mention'd attempts. **1865** LUBBOCK *Preh. Times* 336 The above-mentioned facts prove only that it will not always do so. **1601** HOLLAND *Pliny* (1634) II. 604 Xenocrates mine authour aboue-named affirmeth that, etc. **1674** PLAYFORD *Skill of Musick* I. xi. 45 Tryal may be made in the above-written Notes.

‖**ab ovo** (æb 'əʊvəʊ), *phr.* [a. L. *ab* from + *ōvō*, abl. of *ōvum* egg.] From the (very) beginning.

Cf. Hor. *Sat.* i. 3. 6 *ab ouo usque ad mala* 'from the egg to the apples', alluding to the Roman custom of beginning a meal with eggs and ending it with apples; and Hor. *A.P.* 147 *Nec gemino bellum Troianum orditur ab ouo*, in allusion to the twin egg from which Helen of Troy was born.

a **1586** SIDNEY *Apol. Poet.* (1595) Sig. K1v, If they [dramatic poets] wil represent an history, they must not (as *Horace* saith) beginne *Ab ouo*: but they must come to the principall poynt of that one action, which they wil represent. **1623** J. CHAMBERLAIN in *Court & Times of Jas. I* (1848) II. 389, I spoke with one yesterday, that on Tuesday heard the king relate the whole story, *ab ovo*, from point to point, with great contentment. **1862** THACKERAY *Philip* I. i. 11 Shall we begin *ab ovo*, sir? *c* **1879** W. JAMES in R. B. PERRY *Tht. & Char. of W.J.* (1935) I. 480 Cognition would have to be evolved again almost *ab ovo*. **1927** D. H. LAWRENCE *Mornings in Mexico* 12 Is it possible that we are so absolutely, so innocently, so *ab ovo* ridiculous?

†**abow**, *v. str. Obs.* 1–5. Forms: *Inf.* 1 abúȝan; 2–3 abuȝe(n, abue(n, abouwe(n, abue(n, aboue; 3–4 abowe. *Pa. t.* 1 abeáȝ; 1–2 beáh, *pl.* abuȝon; 2–3 abeh; 3 (*trans.*) abuyde; 4 (*intr.*) aboȝede, abowȝ. *Pa. pple.* 1 aboȝen. [OE. *abúȝan*, f. A- *pref.* 1 + *búȝan*; cogn. w. OHG. *arbiugan*, NHG. *er-biegen*, Goth. *us-biugan*.]

1. *intr.* To bend, incline, bow, stoop; *fig.* to do homage or reverence, to submit.

c **1000** *Beowulf* 1555 þær fram sylle abeaȝ medu-benc moniȝ. **1086** *O.E. Chron.* (Laud. MS.) Ealle þa men on Englalande him to abugon. *c* **1175** *Lamb. Hom.* 227 þe nefer ne abeah to nane deofel ȝyld. **1250** LAYAMON 4049 þat mak[ede a]lle þe oþer mid strengþ ȝam a-bouwe. **1297** R. GLOUC. 193 þe noble steede, þat al þe world abueþ to. *Ibid.* 302 So þat noþer of þys kynges abouynde to oþer nere. *c* **1380** *Sir Ferumbras* 2070 Wel corteysly þanne aboȝede she. *Ibid.* 3390 Ac Roland þanne til hym a-bowȝ.

2. *trans.* To cause to bend; to bend or incline (a thing); also *refl.* See ABEYE (? whence *abuyde*).

c **1175** *Lamb. Hom.* 45 Sancte paul.. abeh him redliche to his lauerdes fet. **1297** R. GLOUC. 476 An other him smot tho, That he abuyde is face adown, vort ther com mo. *c* **1430** *Hymns to Virgin* 59 (1867) 97 Woldist þou god knowe.. And to him meekeli þee abowe, þan schal neuere myscheef in þee falle. **1480** CAXTON *Chron. Eng.* cxxiii. 103 Yf the englysshmen had not abowed doune hir hedes.. vnto the danoys they shold haue ben bete.

abow, abowyn, obs. forms of ABOVE.

abowten, abowght, obs. forms of ABOUT.

abox, a-box (əˈbɒks), *adv. Naut.* [f. A- *pref.* 2 + BOX *v.*[1] (sense 13).] Applied to the position of the head-yards when only the head-sails are laid aback.

1801 CAPT. FERRIS in *Naval Chron.* VI. 245 With an intent.. to brace the head yards a-box. **1867** [see BRACE *v.*[2]]. **1867** SMYTH *Sailor's Word-bk.* s.v., To lay the head-yards square, or abox. **1922** *Blackw. Mag.* Dec. 803/2 Her sides were flaked with rust, her yards all a-box. **1961** F. H. BURGESS *Dict. Sailing* 7 *Abox*, term applied to yards of a mast that are braced in opposite direction to those on a neighbouring mast; a handy practice to retain a vessel under control.

abracadabra (ˌæbrəkəˈdæbrə). [L.; origin unknown. Occurs first in a poem by Q. Severus Sammonicus, 2nd c.] A cabalistic word, formerly used as a charm, and believed to have the power, when written in a triangular arrangement, and worn round the neck, to cure agues, etc. Now often used in the general sense of a spell, or pretended conjuring word; a meaningless word of mysterious sound; jargon, gibberish.

1696 AUBREY *Misc.* 105 Abracadabra, a Mysterious Word, to which the Superstitious in former times attributed a Magical power to expel Diseases, especially the Tertian-Ague, worn about their neck. **1810** BENTHAM *Art of Packing* (1821) 124 Thereby, in legal abracadabra, like man and wife, but one person. **1824** COLERIDGE *Aids to Refl.* (1848) I. 130 Leave him.. to retaliate the nonsense of blasphemy with the abracadabra of presumption. **1860** T. A. G. BALFOUR *Typ. Charac. Nat.* 118 Abrá, which is here twice repeated, is composed of the first letters of the Hebrew words signifying Father, Son, and Holy Spirit, viz. Ab, Ben, Ruach, Acadosch. **1879** *Lit. World* 5 Dec. 358/2 The new abracadabra of science, 'organic evolution.'

abracock, obs. form of APRICOT.

†**abrad**, *Obs. rare*[−1]. Perhaps = OE. *abrǽdde*, pa. t. of *abrǽdan* (Germ. *erbreiten*) to make broad or wide, open widely.

1300 *Owl & Nightingale* 1042 The hule.. Mid thisse worde hire eȝen a-brad.

†**abrad**, *ppl. a. Obs. rare*[−1]. [A doubtful form of uncertain origin and meaning.]

c **1320** *Seuyn Sages* (W.) 610 Fair i-woxe and fair i-sprad, But the old tre was abrad.

abradant (əˈbreɪdənt), *a.* and *sb. U.S.* [f. ABRADE *v.* + -ANT[1].] **A.** *adj.* = ABRADING *ppl. a.* (Cent. Dict. 1889). **B.** *sb.* An abradant substance.

a **1877** KNIGHT *Dict. Mech.* 247/1 *Bath-brick*, a fine silicious material, found in the vicinity of Bath, England, compacted into the form of bricks, and used as an abradant.

abrade (əˈbreɪd), *v.* [ad. L. *abrādĕre* to scrape off, f. *ab* off + *rād-ĕre* to scrape.]

1. To rub or wear off (a part *from* anything).

1677 HALE *Prim. Orig. Man.* 95 What is successively abraded from them [mountains] by decursion of Waters.

2. To wear down by rubbing, to rub away; *lit.* and *fig.*

1748 *Phil. Trans.* XLV. 47 They.. are capable of enlarging their room as they grow bigger, by abrading the sides of their cells. **1804** W. TAYLOR in *Ann. Rev.* II. 336 A hackneyed clamouring for religion and order will not abrade the popularity.. of a French government. **1856** KANE *Arctic Explor.* II. i. 11 To dogs famishing.. frozen food often proves fatal, abrading the stomach and œsophagus. **1863** LYELL *Antiq. of Man* xv. 293 Stones which lie underneath the glaciers.. abrade, groove, and polish the rock.

3. *intr.* To wear or rub away.

1890 C. DIXON *Stray Feathers* xvi, Birds which assume many nuptial ornaments in spring, gorgets, plumes, and crests, which drop out or abrade as soon as the pairing season has passed.

abraded (əˈbreɪdɪd), *ppl. a.* [f. ABRADE + -ED.]

1. Rubbed off, removed by friction.

1677 [See ABRADE 1]. **1862** *Sat. Rev.* 8 Feb. 155 Those youthful martyrs.. cannot have restored to them the abraded cuticle they have lost. **1871** TYNDALL *Frag. of Sc.* (ed. 6) I. xii. 362 Composed of the broken and abraded particles of older rocks.

2. Worn by friction, rubbed; *lit.* and *fig.*

1792 *Phil. Trans.* LXXXII. 45 Part of its mass is worn away; but a larger portion, lying just above the abraded part, is heated to redness. **1877** E. CONDER *Basis of Faith* iv. 138 What is every word but a condensed fragment of history, on whose abraded surface is still legible the handwriting of countless generations of minds? **1878** M. FOSTER *Physiol.* II. iii. 316 But absorption takes place very readily from abraded surfaces.

abrader (əˈbreɪdə(r)). [f. ABRADE + -ER[1].] That which rubs or wears down a surface.

1881 *Metal World* I. 4. The file is essentially a cutting tool, not a mere abrader.

abrading (əˈbreɪdɪŋ), *ppl. a.* [f. ABRADE + -ING[2].] Wearing down, wasting by friction.

1830 LYELL *Princ. Geol.* I. 13 The abrading power of floods, torrents, and rivers. **1860** MAURY *Phys. Geog. Sea* i. §55 Protected from the abrading action of its currents.

†**Abraham, Abram**, *a. Obs.* [Corruption of AUBURN, formerly often written *abern, abron*.]

1599 *Solim. & Pers.* (Hazlitt's *Dodsley* V. 363) Where is the eldest son of Priam, That Abraham-colour'd Trojan? Dead. **1607** SHAKS. *Coriol.* II. iii. 21 Our heads are some browne, some blacke, some Abram, some bald [*fol. of* 1685 *alters to* auburn]. **1627** PEACHAM *Compl. Gent.* 155 (1661) I shall passe to the exposition of certain colours.—Abram-colour, i.e. brown. Auburne or Abborne, i.e. brown or brown-black.

Abrahamic (eɪbrəˈhæmɪk), *a.* [f. the name of *Abraham*, the first of the Hebrew Patriarchs (Gen. xi. 26–xxv. 18), + -IC.] Of, pertaining to, or characteristic of Abraham.

1807 W. BENTLEY *Diary* 10 May (1911) III. 293 Mr. Worcester who, upon the ground of the Abrahamic Covenant, attacked the Baptists has been answered by Baldwin & Merril. **1865** F. H. LAING in H. E. Manning *Ess. Relig. & Lit.* 1st Ser. 185 The Mosaic dispensation.. contains.. what had been already made covenant matter before—as the precepts of Noah and the Abrahamic rite of circumcision. **1908** G. S. GORDON *Let.* 17 Jan. (1943) 33 The young men are arriving... I feel positively Abrahamic towards them—as if they were the sons of Isaac or something of the sort. **1974** *Anderson* (S. Carolina) *Independent* 23 Apr. 2B/4 Funeral services for Mrs. Emmie Pack Stone.. will be conducted Tuesday at 4 p.m. at Guthrie Grove Church of God of Abrahamic Faith.

Abraham-man, Abram-man. [Possibly in allusion to the parable of the beggar Lazarus in *Luke* xvii.] One of 'a set of vagabonds, who wandered about the country, soon after the dissolution of the religious houses; the provision of the poor in those places being cut off, and no other substituted.' Nares.

1561 AWDELAY *Frat. Vacaboundes* 3 An Abraham man is he that walketh bare-armed and bare-legged and fayneth hymselfe mad. **1633** MASSINGER *New Way to Pay* II. i. Are they padders, or Abram-men, that are your consorts? **1813** *Q. Rev.* IX. 167 Pretended maniacs who wandered over England, under the name of Abram-men.

Hence, **to sham Abraham**: to feign sickness, a phrase in use among sailors; also used substantively.

1780 O. GOLDSMITH *Misc. Works* Essay xxiv. p. 154, I shammed Abraham, merely to be idle. *c* **1805** *Astonishing Abraham Newland* 7 I've heard people say, sham Abraham you may, But you mus'nt sham Abraham Newland. **1835** *Court Mag.* vi. 234/1 Now, all this is sheer nonsense—all sham Abraham, pretty one. **1860** J. C. HOTTEN *Dict. Slang*, When Abraham Newland was Cashier of the Bank of England, and signed their notes, it was sung: 'I have heard people say that sham Abraham you may, but you mustn't sham Abraham Newland.' **1863** C. READE *Hard Cash* II. xix. 284 'Look out,' he cried in some alarm; 'he's shamming Abraham.'

†**Abraham's Balm.** *Herb.* An old name of the chaste tree (*Vitex Agnus castus*), a native of the shores of the Mediterranean.

1676 BULLOKAR *Expositor*, Abraham's Baum.. hath a singular property to procure chastity, for which cause physicians have named it Agnus castus.

†**a'braid**, *v. str. Obs.* Forms: *Inf.* 1 abreȝdan, abrédan, 3 abreiden, 4–5 abreyde, 5 abrayde, abraide, 6 erroneous abray. *Pa. t.* 1 abræȝd, abræd(de, 2 abred, abræid, 3 abraid, abreid, 4 abreyde, 4–5 abrayde, abraide, 5–6 abraid, abrayed. *Pa. pple.* 1 abroȝden, abroden, 2 abroiden, abroden, abruden. [f. A- *pref.* 1 + BRAID, OE. *breȝdan* to twist, cogn. w. OSax. *bregdan*, OFries. *breida*, OIcel. *bregða*; hence primarily to twist or wrench back, *retorquēre*. In the primary *trans.* meaning the vb. became early obs. The *intransitive* sense, 'to spring, start,' was prob. also obs. bef. 1600, when Spenser gave it the false form *abray*, taken from the past *abraid*. In the sense of 'to ejaculate' *abraid* remained in the 16th c., and was provided with a weak past *abraided*.]

1. *trans.* To wrench or pull out, to snatch, withdraw, draw (a sword).

c **1000** *O.E. Gosp.* Matt. xxvi. 51 Witudlice án þæra.. abræd hys sweord. *c* **1150** *Hatton Gosp.*, *ibid.* Witodlice an þara.. abred hys sweord. *a* **1200** *Cotton Hom.* 239 Alles goddes fend simle fram his ȝeseсðe abroden bienn. *c* **1200** *Trin. Coll. Hom.* 209 Ure soule is abroiden of þe hunte grune. **1205** LAYAMON 26534 Sone his sweord he ut abræid [*later text* vp breid].

2. *intr.* To start, usually out of sleep, a swoon, or fit; to awake; occ. also, to start or burst into motion; to spring or dart.

c **1230** *Ancren Riwle* 214 He schal a domesdei grimliche abreiden mid te dredful dreame of þe englene bemen. *Ibid.* 238 And te holi mon abreid. *c* **1250** *Genesis & Ex.* 2111 Ðe king abraid and woc in ðhogt. *c* **1386** CHAUCER *Clerkes T.* 1005 Til sche out of hir masidnesse abrayde. —— *Squyres T.* 469 And after that sche gan of swown abreyde. *c* **1430** LYDG. *Bochas* (1554) IV. i. 101 Marcus in his bed lying Gan tabrayde. **1501** DOUGLAS *Palice of Hon.* (1787) III. iii. 55 Be not affrayit scho said.. And with that word up the strait rod abraid. *c* **1570** THYNNE *Pride & Lowlines* (1841) 65, I sodenly out of my sleepe abraid. **1596** SPENSER *F.Q.* IV. vi. 36 But, whenas I did out of sleepe abray, I found her not. *Ibid.* IV. iv. 22 And now by this Sir Satyrane abraid Out of the swowne. **1600** FAIRFAX *Tasso* XIII. l. 244 But from his studie he at last abraid, Call'd by the Hermit old.

b. *trans.* To arouse, startle.

1596 SPENSER *F.Q.* III. i. 61 For feare lest her unwares she should abrayd. *Ibid.* III. xi. 8 The braue maid would not for courtesie, Out of his quiet slumber him abrade.

3. *intr.* To break forth abruptly into speech; to burst into a cry; to shout out.

c **1430** LYDGATE *Bochas* (1544) I. i. 1 a, Our fader Adam sodeynly abrayde, And to mine autour, euen thus he sayde. *Ibid.* I. i. 5 b, In their working, as thei gan abrayde No man wist what that other sayd. *c* **1440** *Ipomydon* (W.) 1149 Ipomydon with that stroke abrayde, And to the kynge thus he sayde. **1531** ELYOT *Governour* (1580) 102 Holding his eyes and handes up towards heaven [he] abrayded with a loud voyce. **1541** —— *Image Gov.* (1556) 145 After that he had sette a good space without speakyng, he abraided out at the last. **1566** DRANT *Horace, Sat.* II. B, Who.. doth not abrade, and crye, Uppon the greateste God of all?

b. *trans.* To ejaculate.

1578 T. PROCTER in *Heliconia* I. 172 Wherwith distrest, with wood-like rage the wordes he out Abrade.

4. *intr.* To rise nauseously in the stomach.

1533 ELYOT *Castel of Helth* (1541) 33 An appetite to eate or drynke mylke, to the extent that it shal not arise or abraied in the stomake.

5. *refl.* To exert oneself.

1530 PALSGR. 415/1, I abrayde, I inforce me to do a thinge, *Je mefforce*. He dyd abrayde him to reche it.

6. (In Lydgate.) To resort *to*, frequent.

c **1430** LYDGATE *Bochas* (1554) III. v. 75 a, O thou princesse of worldly goodes veyne, To thy flatterers I never did abrayde. *Ibid.* VI. xv. 161 b, Plato, To whose cradle Bees dyd abrayde.

†**a'braid**, *sb. Obs.* [f. ABRAID *v.*] A start.

1570 LEVINS, *Manipulus*, An Abrayd, *impetus*.

†**abraid**, *v.* and *sb.*, **abraiding**, *vbl. sb.*, 15th c. forms of UPBRAID, -ING due to phonetic confusion with prec.

c **1430** *Babees Book* 28 Of old surfaytes abrayde nat thy felawe. *c* **1430** LYDGATE *Bochas* (1554) VII. iv. 167 b, If the famous prudent olde Caton Had agein me in such caas made abrayd. *c* **1430** *Syr Generides* 9335 The king seid.. Goo hens for drede of more care. [Generides] for that abraiding Waxed wroth toward the king. **1530** PALSGR. 415/1, I abrayde one, I caste one in the tethe of a matter. **1599** GREENE *Alphonsus* (1861) 231 That thou da'rst thus abraid me in my land.

abraid, obs. form of ABROAD.

abranchial (əˈbræŋkɪəl), *a. Zool.* [f. Gr. ἀ priv. + βράγχια gills + -AL[1].] = ABRANCHIATE. Hence **a'branchialism**, abranchial condition.

1839 TODD *Cycl. Anat.* II. 732/1 The Abranchial Annelida.. are naturally hermaphrodite. **1861** HULME tr. *Moquin-Tandon's Med. Zool.* II. III. iv. 137 Leeches are abranchial annelida. **1902** *Encycl. Brit.* XXX. 796/1 The Pterotracheidæ [have] no shell and opisthobranchialism, or even abranchialism in Firoloida.

abranchiate (əˈbræŋkɪət), *a. Zool.* [Same deriv. + -ATE[2].] Having no gills.

1855 OWEN *Comp. Anat. Invert. An.* 667 Abranchiate.. when an animal is devoid of gills.

†**abrase** (əˈbreɪs), *ppl. a. Obs.* [ad. L. *abrās-us*, pa. pple. of *abrādĕre*: see ABRADE.] Rubbed smooth; rubbed clear from all markings; unoccupied, clean, blank. (Cf. L. *tabula rasa*.)

1600 B. JONSON *Cynthia's Revels* V. vii. 42 A nymph as pure and simple as the Soule, or as an abrase Table. **1688** R. HOLME *Acad. Armory* I. 12 But we must hold such things [blank shields] as Plato did his abrase tables, to be fit and capable of any form.

abrase (ə'breɪs), *v.* [f. L. *abrās-* ppl. stem of *abrād-ĕre*; see prec. Cf. *erase* and Fr. *raser*.] To rub off or away; to wear down by friction; to abrade (which is the ordinary form of the word).

1593 NASHE *Christ's Teares* 37 b, Thy habitation is quite abrased and plowed vppe. **1612** COCKERAM, Abrase, to shaue. **1859** W. H. GREGORY *Egypt in 1855–6*, I. 253 Sufficient skin has been abrased from thy shins. **1867** SMYTH *Sailor's Wd.-Bk.* s.v. *Abrase*, to dubb or smooth planks.

†**a'brasing,** *vbl. sb. Obs.* [f. ABRASE *v.* + -ING[1].] The act of scraping or rubbing off; abrading.

1482 *Monk of Evesham* (1869) 83, I sawe suche persons by full ofte betyngys and abrasyng of naylys alto toryn.

abrasion (ə'breɪʒən). [ad. L. *abrāsiōn-em*, n. of action from *abrādĕre* to ABRADE. Cf. Fr. *abrasion*, a recent word only used in sense 3.]

1. The act or process of rubbing off or away, wearing down by friction. *lit.* and *fig.* ***abrasion platform***, a flat surface at the edge of the sea produced by the abrading action of the waves.

1656 BLOUNT *Glossogr.*, *Abrasion*, a shaving away. **1837** BABBAGE *Bridgw. Treat.* K 250 Let us suppose, that from the abrasion of the channel, the later tide arrives.. earlier than before. **1858** J. G. HOLLAND *Titcomb's Lett.* iii. 32 To speak pleasantly when irritated.. to avoid abrasion and collision. **1866** CRUMP *Banking* i. 4 All coins will, by wear or abrasion, become thinner. **1878** H. M. STANLEY *Dark Cont.* II. xii. 361 The least abrasion of the skin was likely to result in an ulcer. **1922** FLATTELY & WALTON *Biol. Sea-Shore* ii. 36 Lastly we have the more extensive, nearly horizontal plane produced by long-continued wave erosion, and commonly called the abrasion platform. **1937** WOOLDRIDGE & MORGAN *Physical Basis Geogr.* xxi. 322 In other cases it [*sc.* the wave-cut beach-bench] is continued seaward in a flatter surface, the abrasion platform, over which a thin offshore 'veneer' of finer material may be spread.

2. The result of rubbing off. †**a.** The substance rubbed off, débris. *Obs.* **b.** A rubbed or abraded place.

1740 DR. CHEYNE *Ess. Regimen* 5 Earth.. being probably the Ramenta or abrasions of the other elements. **1853** KANE *Grinnell Exped.* (1856) xxxiv. 305 Costing only a smart pull and a bleeding abrasion afterwards. **1878** BRYANT *Pract. Surg.* I. 34 A bed-sore may appear as a simple abrasion.

3. 'Abrasion is sometimes used ... for the act of wearing away the natural mucus which covers the membranes, and particularly those of the stomach and intestines, by sharp corrosive medicines.' Chambers *Cycl.* 1751; also in *Syd. Soc. Lex.* 1879.

abrasive (ə'breɪsɪv), *a.* and *sb.* [f. L. *abrās-us*: see ABRASE + -IVE; as if from a L. **abrāsīvus*.] **A.** *adj.* **a.** Having the property of abrading.

1875 URE *Dict. Arts* s.v. *Abrasion*, The abrasive tool or grinder is exactly a counterpart of the form to be produced. **1880** G. C. WALLICH in *Athen.* 6 Mar. 316 To dispose of the supposition that the shape of the Pyrospores is due to any rolling or abrasive action at the sea bed.

b. *fig.*

1925 T. DREISER *Amer. Trag.* (1926) I. II. xxxiv. 387 His mind was troubled with hard, abrasive thoughts. **1963** EDMUND WILSON in *New Statesman* 8 Feb. 198/3 Abrasive is coming in, in application to literary qualities.

B. *sb.* An abrasive substance or body.

1853 O. BYRNE *Artisan's Handbk.* 17 To polish the tool upon the oil-stone, or other fine abrasive for setting the edge. **1951** *Good Housek. Home Encycl.* 11/1 Abrasives are useful for heavily soiled surfaces, when soap and water or detergents are unsuccessful and some gentle friction is required. **1960** *Jrnl. Iron & Steel Inst.* CXIV. 406/1 A study of bonded abrasives.

‖**Abraum Salts** ('abraʊm sɒlts). [ad. Germ. *Abraum-salze* salts to be removed.] Mixed salts found above the pure rock-salt at Stassfurt in Prussia, and also in the Isle of Wight, once thought useless, now used for producing chloride of potassium.

1753 CHAMBERS *Cycl. Suppl.* s.v. Abraum.. a species of red clay, used in England.. to give a red colour to new mahogany-wood. **1875** URE *Dict. Arts* s.v. Abraum Salts.. are employed on a very large scale for the production of chloride of potassium.

‖**abraxas.** Also **abrasax.** A cabalistic word used as a charm and sometimes inscribed on gems for that purpose.

1738 WARBURTON *Div. Legat.* II. 153 These Gems called Abraxas. **1828** R. WALSH *Anc. Coins* (ed. 2) 39 The word Abrasax, sometimes spelled Abraxas, was the great mystery of the Gnostics. **1898** T. WATTS-DUNTON *Aylwin* i. §6. 37 He had a large collection of amulets, Gnostic gems and abraxas stones. **1905** FARNELL *Evol. Relig.* iv. 188 In certain Egyptian papyri containing Abraxas prayers, we find the prayer coupled with the reminder that the petitioner knows the divine mystic name.

abray, a false form of ABRAID *v.* found in Spenser; deduced from the pa. t. *abraid*, *abrayde*, quasi *abrayed*.

abrazite ('æbrəzaɪt), *Min.* [f. Gr. ἀ ? intensive + βράζ-ειν to boil + -ITE mineral formative.] 'A mineral which effervesces when melted before the blowpipe.' Craig 1847. According to Dana a synonym of Gismondite.

abrazitic (æbrə'zɪtɪk), *a. Min.* [Same deriv. but with ἀ privative.] 'Not effervescing when melted before the blow-pipe.' Craig 1847.

‖**abrazo** (a'braθo, -so). [Sp.] An embrace or hug, used as a salutation on meeting or parting in Spain and Latin America.

1928 *Spectator* 7 Jan. 10/2 No match.. begins without an exchange of bouquets of flowers and affectionate *abrazos* between the rival captains. **1962** N. MAXWELL *Witch-Doctor's Apprentice* iii. 29 Each of the women put a limp hand on my shoulder in the old-fashioned *abrazo* and greeted me politely with 'Adiós, señorita, I have much pleasure.' **1977** *Time* 19 Sept. 19/3 The *abrazo*, of course, does not clinch the treaty, which faces a months-long scrap in the U.S. Senate and a plebiscite in Panama as well. **1984** *New Yorker* 24 Dec. 31/1 Why, bless us, yes, and here are kisses For Garry Trudeau and the missus,.. Plus *abrazos* meant to convey our Love to Sr. Pérez de Cuéllar.

abreaction (æbrɪ'ækʃən). *Psychiatry.* [f. AB- + REACTION, after G. *abreagierung*.] The liberation by revival and expression of the emotion associated with forgotten or repressed ideas of the event that first caused it. Hence **abre'act** *v.*, to eliminate by abreaction; **abre'active** *a.*, of this kind of treatment.

[**1895** J. BREUER & S. FREUD *Studien über Hysterie* iv. 223 Heilung hysterischer Symptome durch.. Abreagiren.] **1912** A. A. BRILL tr. *Freud's Sel. Papers Hysteria* (ed. 2) 6 The abreaction (abreagiren).. is not the only form of discharge at the disposal of the normal psychic mechanism of the healthy person who has experienced a psychic trauma. The memory of the trauma even where it has not been abreacted enters into the great complex of the association. **1916** C. E. LONG tr. *Jung's Anal. Psychol.* 242 When the abreaction takes place under hypnotism, or with other magical accessories. *Ibid.*, The neurosis is caused by trauma. The trauma is abreacted. **1926** W. MCDOUGALL *Outl. Abnormal Psychol.* 451 The assumption underlying the practice of Abreaction was that the forgotten or repressed 'ideas' were beset (*besetzt*) by a charge of emotional energy or *libido*; and that the process of Abreaction discharges this energy from the system. **1926** *Contemp. Rev.* Aug. 191 It is claimed that they [*sc.* early memories] can be traced down through links of emotion—called 'ab-reaction'—from the conscious mind into the so-called unconscious stratum. **1944** BRENMAN & GILL *Hypnotherapy* (1947) iv. 72 Although the 'abreactive method' has been used extensively in World War II, the alteration in consciousness which is necessary for such a 're-living' has usually been brought about by drugs. **1958** A. HUXLEY *Brave New World Revisited* (1959) 107 The process known in England as 'abreaction therapy', in America as 'narcosynthesis'.

†**abreak,** *v. Obs.* For forms see BREAK. [OE. *a-brecan* f. A- *pref.* 1 + *brecan* to break.]

1. *trans.* To break in pieces.

1205 LAYAMON 25929 Nu hafeð be [? he] mine ban alle! ladliche a-brokene.

2. *intr.* To break forth, burst out.

1205 LAYAMON 722 Ich am mid ærmðen abroken vt of þon benden. *c* **1320** *Arthour and Merlin* 7903 And gif we may owhai abreke Fle we hem with gret reke.

abreast (ə'brɛst), *adv.* prop. *phrase.* Also 5–6 **abrest.** [f. A *prep.*[1] in + BREAST *sb.*]

1. With breasts in a line, or with fronts in a line so as to compose as it were one breast of a wave when in motion; side by side (in advancing).

1599 SHAKS. *Hen. V*, IV. vi. 17 My soule shall thine keepe company to heauen: Tarry (sweet soule) for mine, then flye a-brest. **1675** *Lond. Gaz.* mi. 2 The Mines succeeded very well, and made a breach, that 16 Men might enter a-breast. **1879** FROUDE *Cæsar* xiv. 205 A pass.. so narrow that but two carts could go abreast along it.

†**b.** Also written variously as ***on a breast, of breast, in a breast, breast-a-breast.***

c **1450** LONELICH *Grail* xx. 271 Owt they Comen Al On Abrest. **1567** MAPLET *Greene Forest* 68 Another goeth and taketh vpon him his [the leading crane's] office.. and that other commeth to their place which be of breast. **1728** G. CARLETON *Mem. Eng. Officer* 40 We could but very rarely go two on a Breast. *Ibid.* 69 At the End of our March all our Powder-Waggons were plac'd breast a-breast. **1801** R. GALL *Tint Quey* 179 Then a' at ance (it is nae jest) Moved slowly forit in a breast.

2. *Naut.* With the ships equally distant, and parallel to each other, so that each is at right angles to the line of the squadron.

1697 POTTER *Antiq. Greece* (1715) III. xx. 150 If the winds were high.. sailing one by one; but at other Times they went Three or more in a Breast. **1817** JAS. MILL *Brit. India* II. IV. iv. 144 The English, having the wind, came down a-breast.

3. *Naut.* '*Abreast*, within-board, signifies on a parallel with the beam.' Smyth *Sailor's Wd.-Bk.*

4. ***abreast of***: in a position parallel to, or alongside of something stationary; also *fig.* (In nautical lang. *of* is frequently omitted.)

1748 ANSON *Voyage* (ed. 4) III. vi. 466 We were a-breast of a chain of Islands. **1833** MARRYAT *Jac. Faithf.* vi. 22 The tide was about three quarters ebb, when the barge arrived abreast of Millbank. **1845** LOWELL *Crisis* Wks. 1879, 671 They must upward still, and onward, Who would keep abreast of truth. **1857** TOMES *Amer. in Japan* xv. 356 The Island of Ohosima, about two miles distant abreast the ships.

5. ***abreast with***: advancing on or to a level with, keeping up with; often *fig.* as, to keep abreast with the thought of the age. In naut. lang. *with* is sometimes omitted.

1655 FULLER *Ch. Hist.* VII. 397 My Observations, as printed, goe abreast in parallel columes with those of His Highnesse. **1833** MARRYAT *Jac. Faithf.* xxvii. 96 [We] were soon abreast and close to the wherry, pulling with us down the stream. **1860** SMILES *Self-Help* iii. 59 Nothing else could have enabled him to keep abreast with the flood of communications that poured in.

†**abreathe,** *v. Obs. rare.* [f. A- *pref.* 1 + BREATHE.] To give time to recover breath.

c **1450** *Merlin* 335 And made hem refressh and girde hir horse and a-brethe hem.

†**abreid** (ə'bri:d), *adv. Obs.* or *dial.* [OE. *on brede* in breadth, Chaucer *on brede*, mod. Scotch *a breid, abreed.*] Apart, widely. (Cf. ABROAD, a later formation which took the place of *a brede* in Eng.)

c **1400** *Destr. Troy* XXIX. 11877 Bothe obreade& aboue [þai] brekyn the yates. **1787** BURNS III. 143 Spread abreed thy weel-fill'd brisket.

†**abre'nounce,** *v. Obs.* [f. L. *ab* off, away + RENOUNCE, after med.L. *abrenunciā-re* to repudiate; f. *ab* away, off + *renuntiā-re* to unsay, retract; f. *re* back + *nuntiā-re* often corrupted to *nunciā-re* to tell.] To renounce, repudiate; to contradict.

1537 LATIMER *Serm. before Convoc.* 6 Many of these.. will no better acknowledge and recognise theyr parentes.. but abrenounce and cast them of. **1553–87** FOXE *A. & M.* (1596) 159/1 Commanding all the clergie.. either to abrenounce their wiues, or their livings. **1566** KNOX *Hist. Ref. Scotl.* Wks. 1846 I. 300 Many began opinly to abrenounce thare ald idolatrie. **1656** J. TRAPP *Exp.* Matt. xvi. 24 (1868) 202/1 Let him deny himself.. let him abrenounce himself flatly.

†**abre'nouncing,** *vbl. sb. Obs.* [f. prec. + -ING[1].] Repudiation, rejection.

c **1550** COVERDALE *Carrying of Christ's Cross* ii. Wks. II. 234 Where is our abrenouncing and forsaking of the world?

†**abre'nunciate,** *v. Obs. rare* [f. med.L. *abrenunciāt-us* for *abrenuntiāt-us*, pa. pple. of *abrenuntiā-re*; see ABRENOUNCE. Cf. *announce* and *enuntiate*.] = ABRENOUNCE.

1618 *Chron. of S. Francis.* Dedic., It sauored of the world which ye have abrenunciated.

abrenunciation (ˌæbrɪnʌnsɪ'eɪʃən), *arch.* [ad. med.L. *abrenunciātiōn-em*, n. of action from *abrenunciāre*; see prec. Mod.Eng. in all the derivatives of *nuntiāre* follows the incorrect late L. spelling *nunciāre*.] Renunciation: retractation, repudiation.

1641 *Life of Cheeke* in *Hurt of Sedit.* iii b, An abrenuntiation of that truth which he had so long professed. **1655** FULLER *Ch. Hist.* VIII. 37 Hard usage in prison.. drew from his mouth an abrenuntiation of that Truth. **1720** WATERLAND *8 Serm.* 318 A Profession of Faith in.. God the Father, Son, and Holy Ghost, immediately followed upon the Abrenuntiation of the Devil. **1842** H. E. MANNING *Unity of the Ch.* 20 The catechumen.. turned to the West for the abrenunciation of Satan.

†**a'breption.** *Obs.* [n. of action, f. L. *abrept-* ppl. stem of *abrip-ĕre*, f. *ab* off, away + *rap-ĕre* to snatch: see -ION[1].] Snatching away; complete separation.

1681 HALLYWELL *Melampronæa* 73 (T) Cardan relates of himself that he could when he pleased fall into this ἀφαίρεσις, disjunction, or abreption of his soul from his body. **1686** *Reg. Privy C. Scotland* (1932) XIII. 76 In this case his Majestie was not to be considered in his royal capacity as giving gifts or grants, in which case there is place for abreption and subreption. **1828** *Blackw. Mag.* XXIV. 157/2 This earliest Abreption of this famous Fleece. **1872** MCCLINTOCK & STRONG *Bibl., Eccles. Cycl.* IV. 623/2 Such an abreption of bodily functions is calculated to enhance the perceptions of celestial verities.

‖**abreuvoir** (abrœv'war). [mod.Fr., f. *abreuver* to cause to drink:—OFr. *abeuvrer*:—late L. *abeverāre*, for *adbiberā-re*, f. *bibĕre* to drink.]

1. A watering place for animals. (? Not Eng.)

2. 'In masonry, the joint between two stones, or the interstice to be filled up with mortar or cement.' Gwilt.

abrevye, abreviate: see ABBREVYE, -IATE.

abri (ə'bri:). [a. Fr.] A shelter; *spec.* in *Archæol.*, a shallow cave which affords protection, a rock-shelter.

1802 C. JAMES *New Mil. Dict.* **1887** T. MCK. HUGHES in *Trans. Vict. Inst.* XXI. 91 The most interesting caves.. are only rock-shelters—abris—such as are seen in the Dordogne district. **1931** *Antiquity* V. 428 They [*sc.* human teeth] have been found in one of the abri in France. **1949** K. P. OAKLEY *Man the Toolmaker* vi. 38 (*caption*) Diagrammatic section of ideal rock-shelter (shallow cave or *abri*). **1982** *N.Y. Times* 21 Nov. x. 12/4 Living sites were the fronts of caves or under a shelf of overhanging rock—called an abri.

abricock, -coct, -cot, obs. forms of APRICOT.

abricotine (æ'brɪkəʊti:n, -ɪn). [a. Fr., f. *abricot* APRICOT + -INE[4].]

1. (With capital initial.) A proprietary name for a variety of apricot brandy liqueur.

No longer proprietary in the U.S.

1906 *Official Gaz.* (U.S. Patent Office) 11 Sept. 607/1 A. Garnier, Enghien-les-Bains, France... *Abricotine*...

Cordials. **1921** *Trade Marks Jrnl.* 8 June 1170 *Abricotine*.. User claimed from 31st January, 1895. 410,417. A liqueur. Caroline Henriette Garnier trading as Veuve A. Garnier and .. as P. Garnier,.. Enghien-les-Bains. **1951** *Good Housek. Home Encycl.* 339/1 The kernels and the fresh or dried fruit are used to flavour apricot brandy (or abricotine). **1980** P. V. PRICE *Dict. Wines & Spirits* 12 Well-known brands are Marie Brizard's *Apry*, Garnier's Abricotine, but most *liqueur* establishments make an apricot liqueur.

2. An apricot plum. (So in Fr.) *nonce-use*.

1930 E. SITWELL *Coll. Poems* 124 Shone.. apricots so ripe their kernels seem Gemmed amethysts,—the rose abricotine, And one who wears a blond lace pelerine.

abridgable, -geable (əˈbrɪdʒəb(ə)l), *a.* [f. ABRIDGE *v.* + -ABLE.] Capable of being abridged; liable to abridgment.

1864 CARLYLE *Fredk. Gt.* IV. 338 Abridgable in a high degree.

abridge (əˈbrɪdʒ), *v.* Forms: 4 abrege, 4–5 **abregge, abrigge,** 4–6 **abrydge,** 6 **abbredge,** 6– **abridge.** [a. OFr. *abregie-r, abrege-r* (Pr. *abrevjar*):—L. *abbreviā-re*, f. *ab* off or ? *ad* to + *breviā-re* to shorten, f. *brevis* short.] Always *trans.*

1. To shorten; to make shorter, to cut short in its duration, to lessen the duration of. Originally of *time*, or things occupying time.

1340 HAMPOLE *Pr. Consc.* 4571 þan sal God abrege his [Anticrist's] days Als Mathew in þe Godspel says. *Ibid.* 4575 'Bote his days war abreged,' says he, 'Fone men fra þan sal save be.' Bot his tyme God abrege sal þan. *c* **1386** CHAUCER *Merch. T.* 370 (E. 1614) He wolde abregge hir labour alle and some [*MS. Lansd.* a-brigge]. *c* **1440** MYRC *Instr. to P.P.* 1629 ȝef he be sory for hys synne.. A-bregge hys penaunce þen by myche. **1534** MORE *Comforte agst. Tribul.* III. Wks. 1557, 1213/2 He shall for the loue of hys electes.. abbredge those daies. **1590** SHAKS. *Two Gent.* III. i. 245 Besides, thy staying will abridge thy life. **1751** SMOLLETT *Per. Pickle* (1779) IV. lxxxvi. 17 The bridegroom.. abridged his visit. **1834** HT. MARTINEAU *Moral* I. 17 To make a greater quantity with the same capital; in other words, to abridge the labour.

2. **a.** To make shorter in words, whilst retaining the sense and substance; to condense, epitomize.

1393 *Wills & Inv. North. Count.* IV. 186 And in kase be that this wytword will noght perfurnysche, I will it be abrydged. **1494** FABYAN V. cxv. 89 I passe ouer in abrydgynge and shortynge somedeale of this Storye. **1611** BIBLE *Transl. Pref.* 5 Efnard (is reported) to haue abridged the French Psalter. **1849** MACAULAY *Hist. Eng.* I. 474 James had ordered Sancroft to abridge the ritual. **1863** MAX MÜLLER *Chips* (1880) II. xxvi. 294 This work was abridged in the first half of the ninth century.

b. To produce by shortening *from* or abridging (a larger work); to condense *from*.

1782 PRIESTLEY *Corr. Christ.* I. Pref. 19 Some things will be found.. abridged from other works. **1810** (*title*) A vocabulary Persian, Arabic and English abridged from the quarto edition of Richardson's dictionary as edited by Charles Wilkins. **1889** in Watson & Burbury *Math. Theory Electricity & Magnetism* II. (Final advt. section) 1 *An Intermediate Greek-English Lexicon*, abridged from the above. Small 4to. **1971** *Nature* 9 July 81/1 The following account is abridged from a thesis by George L. Small, professor of geography at the City University of New York.

3. *Law.* 'To make a declaration or count shorter, by subtracting or severing some of the substance from it.' Blount 1691, Tomlins 1809.

4. To cut off, cut short; to reduce to a small size. Now *rare* of things material.

c **1420** LYDGATE *Minor Poems* (1840) 5 Alle myscheffes from him to abrigge. **1605** *Play of Stucley* (1878) 186 But 'tis not thou, nor any power but his.. That can abridge my purpose. **1639** FULLER *Holy War* (1840) II. xxxi. 91 She retired herself to Sebaste, and abridged her train from state to necessity. **1748** SMOLLETT *Rod. Rand.* (1804) xxv. 172 Spoons.. two of which were curtailed in the handles, and the other abridged in the lip. **1822** SCOTT *Nigel* vi. Sir Mungo.. laid on his hilt his hand, or rather his claw, (for Sir Rullion's broadsword had abridged it into that form).

5. To curtail, to lessen, to diminish (rights, privileges, advantages, or authority).

1393 GOWER *Conf.* III. 152 Largesse it is, whose privilege There may non avarice abrege. **1534** MORE *On Passion* Wks. 1557, 1356/2 His former feare shall no whit abridge his rewarde. **1651** HOBBES *Leviathan* II. xxvi. 138 The naturall Liberty of man may by the Civill Law be abridged. **1702** POPE *Jan. and May* 489 He watch'd her night and day, Abridg'd her pleasures, and confin'd her sway. **1761** HUME *Hist. Eng.* I. viii. 178 A tribunal whose authority he had himself attempted to abridge. **1853** F. W. ROBERTSON *Serm.* Ser. III. xvi. 207 The Apostle Paul counsels these men to abridge their Christian liberty.

6. With a person:—Const. *of*, rarely *from, in.* To stint, to curtail in; to deprive of; to debar from.

1303 R. BRUNNE *Handl. Synne* 11950 Whan of synne þou art abreggede. **1523** FITZHERBERT *Surveying* (1539) iv. 8 It were agayne reason to abrydge a man of his owne righte. **1596** SHAKS. *Merch. Ven.* I. i. 126 Nor do I now make mone to be abridg'd From such a noble rate. **1692** SOUTH *12 Serm.* (1697) I. 33 Much tied and abridged in his freedom. **1768** BLACKSTONE *Comm.* I. 154 The legislative therefore cannot abridge the executive power of any rights which it now has by law, without it's own consent. **1839** H. ROGERS *Essays* II. iii. 147 The language, abridged of its native power, needed this transfusion of fresh blood.

†**aˈbridge**, *sb. Obs. rare*⁻¹. [f. the vb.] A condensed form, an epitome, a compendium.

1634 T. HERBERT *Travaile* 2 Great Brittaine.. contains the summe and abridge of all sorts of excellencies.

abridged (əˈbrɪdʒd), *ppl. a.* [f. ABRIDGE *v.* + -ED.] Shortened, cut short; contracted, condensed.

c **1370** WYCLIF *Rule of St. Francis* Wks. 1880, 41 þei may haue breuyaries, þat is small sauteris or abreggid. **1490** CAXTON *How to Die* 23 Thus endeth the trayttye abredged of the arte to lerne well to deye. **1646** SIR T. BROWNE *Pseud. Ep.* 298 In our abridged and septuagesimall ages, it is very rare.. to behold the fourth generation. **1819** SCOTT *Ivanh.* xiv. (1820 I. 291) In heaven's name, said he, to what purpose serve these abridged cloaks? **1876** FREEMAN *Norm. Conq.* I. App. 651 This account appears in an abridged form.

abridgedly (əˈbrɪdʒɪdlɪ), *adv.* [f. prec. + -LY².] In a shortened or concise form.

1801 WOODHOUSE in *Phil. Trans.* XCI. 98 A method of abridgedly representing the sine etc. of an arc. *Ibid.* 100 Which series is abridgedly expressed by the symbol.

abridger (əˈbrɪdʒə(r)). [f. ABRIDGE *v.* + -ER¹.] One who or that which abridges, shortens, or makes abridgments; a summarizer, synoptist, or compiler.

1555 *Fardle of Facions* II. iv. 137 I rather fansie.. to folowe the founteines of the first Authours, then the brokes of abredgers. **1651** tr. *Bacon, Life and Death* 21 The Great Abridger of Age was the Floud. **1699** BURNET 39 *Articles* (1700) xxii. 222 He was an Abridger of a larger Work. **1858** H. MILLER *Sch. & Schoolm.* 451 A concocter of paragraphs, or an abridger of Parliamentary debates.

abridging (aˈbrɪdʒɪŋ), *vbl. sb.* [f. ABRIDGE *v.* + -ING¹.] The act or process of shortening the duration of any thing, or lessening it; or of making a short compendium or abstract of a larger work.

c **1386** CHAUCER *Pars. T.* 168 Yit avaylen thay to abrigging of the peyne of helle. **1475** *Boke of Noblesse* 31 The said chieftein must pay his men.. bethout any defalking [or] abbregging of here wagis. **1611** BIBLE *2 Macc.* ii. 26 This paineful labour of abridging.. was not easie, but a matter of sweat. **1676** CLARENDON *Surv. Leviathan* 297 The abridging his universal jurisdiction.

abridgment, abridgement (əˈbrɪdʒmənt). Also 6 **abrygement.** Spelt *abridgment* as early as 7. [a. OFr. *abregement* f. *abréger* + -MENT as if from a L. **abbreviāmentum*.]

1. The act or process of abridging or shortening; a shortening of time or labour; a curtailment of privileges.

1494 FABYAN VI. clxi. 154 His sayde sone.. was a cause of the abrygement, or shortynge of his dayes. **1599** SHAKS. *Hen. V*, v. Cho. 44 Then brooke abridgement; and your eyes aduance After your thoughts, straight backe againe to France. *c* **1660** SOUTH *Serm.* (1715) I. 5 Wilt thou demonstrate, that there is any Delight in a Cross, any Comfort in violent Abridgments. **1774** BRYANT *Mythol.* I. 80 The name of Cyrus seems to have suffered an abridgment of this nature. **1855** MACAULAY *Hist. Eng.* III. 48 Irregular vindications of public liberty.. are almost always followed by some temporary abridgments of that very liberty.

b. (?) *fig.* A means of shortening or whiling away. (The sense may be 3.)

1590 SHAKS. *Mids. N.D.* v. i. 39 Say, what abridgement haue you for this euening? What maske? What musicke?

2. An abridged state or condition; a shortened form; abbreviation.

1797 GODWIN *Enquirer* I. vi. 41 We must not.. read them in abridgment. **1876** FREEMAN *Norm. Conq.* I. App. 751 The account given is essentially the same, with some abridgements and verbal differences.

3. A compendium of a larger work, with the details abridged, and less important things omitted, but retaining the sense and substance; an epitome, or abstract.

1523 FITZHERBERT *Surueying* 30 He wyll cause his audytoure to make a value in maner of a bridgement of all the sayd minystre accomptes. **1611** BIBLE *Transl. Pref.* 2 One that extinguished worthy whole volumes to bring his abridgements into request. **1734** tr. *Rollin's Anc. Hist.* (1827) I. 163 I shall in the first place give the principal events of it in a chronological abridgment. **1876** FREEMAN *Norm. Conq.* I. App. 694 His narrative is a mere meagre abridgement.

b. An epitome or compendium of any subject, which might be treated much more fully; a concise record, or instance; a synopsis; a representation in miniature.

1609 SKENE *Reg. Majest.* 4 The Crowner, or the Schiref.. sall take inspection of his wounds, quha is slane, & sall cause their Clerk make ane abrigement of them. **1625** BACON *Essays* (1862) 128 To be Master of the Sea, is an Abridgement of a Monarchy. **1655** FULLER *Ch. Hist.* VI. 327 Ingratitude is the abridgement of all basenesse. **1702** ADDISON *Medals* III. 154 You represented your ancient coins as abridgements of history. **1774** GOLDSMITH *Retal.* 94 Here lies David Garrick, describe me who can; An abridgment of all that was pleasant in man. **1826** SCOTT *Mal. Malagr.* Let. i. 4, A filthy little abridgement of a crocodile.

4. *Law.* The leaving out of certain parts of a plaintiff's demand, in which case the writ still holds good for the remainder.

1641 *Termes de la Ley* 4 Abridgement of a plaint or demaund.

abrim (əˈbrɪm), *adv.* or *pred. a.* [f. A *prep.*¹ + BRIM *sb.*²] Full to the brim; brimming.

1896 KIPLING *Seven Seas* 114 Weed ye trample underfoot Floods his heart abrim. **1920** A. E. W. MASON *Summons* ii. 16 Partly because of her vivid colouring and because she was abrim with life. **1934** D. L. SAYERS *Nine Tailors* IV. i. 330 Dyke and drain were everywhere abrim. **1951** W. DE LA MARE *Winged Chariot* 55 Abject with misery or with bliss a-brim.

abrin (ˈeɪbrɪn). *Chem.* [f. mod.L. *Abrus* (see def.) + -IN¹.] A highly poisonous proteid contained in the jequirity bean (*Abrus precatorius*).

1884 KLEIN *Micro-org. & Disease* 165 Messrs. Warden and Waddell published in Calcutta during the present year .. a large number of observations on the jequirity poison... They have.. proved, that the active principle is a proteid —*abrin*—closely allied to native albumen. **1897** [see PHYTALBUMOSE].

†**abriped**, [irreg. f. *abrip-ĕre*.] 'Ravished.' Cockeram 1626.

abristle (əˈbrɪs(ə)l), *adv.* or *pred. a.* [f. A *prep.*¹ + BRISTLE *v.*¹] Bristling.

1916 E. POUND *Lustra* 97 A-bristle with antennae to feel roads. **1919** M. BEERBOHM *Seven Men* 180 So a-bristle am I with memories of the meetings I had with its author. **1927** *Chambers's Jrnl.* May 345/2 Stripes sprang to his feet with a growl, every hair abristle.

abroach (əˈbrəʊtʃ), *adv.* prop. *phrase.* Also 4–5 **abroche, abroache.** [f. A *prep.*¹ in state of + BROACH.]

1. Broached; pierced; in a condition for letting out or yielding liquor. **to set abroach**: to broach, to pierce and leave running.

1393 GOWER *Conf.* II. 183 Right as who set a toune abroche, He percede the harde roche. *c* **1450** J. RUSSELL *Nurture* in *Babees Book* 121 So when þow settyst a pipe abroche good [sone,] do aftur my lore. **1594** PLAT *Jewell-house* II. 15 There is none [of the fatts of wine] worth the tasting, but that onlie which is abroach. **1697** DRYDEN *Virgil* Wks. 1806 II. 218 The jars of gen'rous wine.. He set abroach, and for the feast prepar'd. **1751** SMOLLETT *Per. Pickle* (1779) II. lxvi. 226 There was a butt of strong beer abroach in the yard. **1855** MACAULAY *Hist. Eng.* IV. xvii. 67 Hogsheads of ale and claret were set abroach in the streets.

b. *fig.*

1533 MORE *Debel. Salem* v. Wks. 1557, 39/2 They [the new brotherhood] be a barel of poyson, yᵗ the dyuel hath late set abroche. **1633** G. HERBERT *Temple* 29, *Agonie* 15 That juice, which on the crosse a pike Did set again abroach. **1662** H. MORE *Antid. agst. Ath.* (1712) II. vii. 59 There was a general Provision of Water, by setting the Mountains and Hills abroach.

2. Hence, In a state to be diffused or propagated; afloat; afoot; astir. **to set abroach**: to broach, to set a-foot, to publish or diffuse.

1528 MORE *Heresyes* IV. Wks. 1557, 284/2 Ascribing al our dedes to destenie.. they.. set al wretchednes abroche. **1591** SHAKS. *Rom. & Jul.* I. i. 111 Who set this auncient quarrell new abroach? **1611** SPEED *Hist. Brit.* (1632) IX. xxiii. 1130 These stirres thus abroach, the Earle was sent into those parts. **1638** WILKINS *Discov. New World* (1684) II. 2 Let but some upstart Heresie be set abroach. **1742** YOUNG *Night Th.* II. 465 Hast thou no friend to set thy mind abroach? **1835** BROWNING *Paracel.* 31 But 'twas not my desire to set abroach Such memories and forebodings.

†**aˈbroach**, *v. Obs.* Also 4–5 **abroche.** [a. OFr. *abrochie-r, abroche-r*, f. *à* prep. to + *brocher* to prick, pierce; see BROACH.]

1. To pierce (a cask, etc.) so as to let the liquor flow out.

c **1386** CHAUCER *Wyf of Bathes Prol.* 177 Whethir thou wilt sippe Of thilke tonne, that I schal abroche. **1440** *Prompt. Parv.* Abbrochyn or attamyn a vesselle of drynke, *Attamino.* **1530** PALSGR. 425/2 I abroche, I set abroche a vessell, *Je broche*.. Abroche our wyne of Beaune.

2. *fig.* To give vent or utterance to.

c **1325** *E.E. Allit. Poems* A. 1122 þen glory & gle watȝ nwe abroched. **1430** LYDGATE *Chron. Troy* II. x. Thus she.. After swete the bitter can a broche.

abroad (əˈbrɔːd), *adv.* and *prep.* and *sb.* Forms: 3–4 **a brod,** 4 **a-brood,** 5 **on brode,** 5–6 **a-brode,** 6 **abroade,** 6– **abroad.** [f. A *prep.*¹ on, in, at + BROAD *a.* Cf. *a-long, at large,* and A-BREDE, OE. *on brede*, mod.Sc. *a breid.*]

A. *adv.*

1. **a.** Broadly, widely, at large, over a broad or wide surface.

1297 R. GLOUC. 542 That win orn abrod so, That it was pite gret of so much harm ido. **1483** CAXTON *G. de la Tour.* g viij b, Plenty of sylke and clothe of gold was there abrode. **1611** BIBLE *Rom.* v. 5 The loue of God is shed abroad in our hearts. **1796** MRS. GLASSE *Cookery* xiv. 216 Pour it on it and spread it abroad with a rolling-pin. **1839** CARLYLE *Chartism* (1858) iii. 14 Would to Heaven one could preach it abroad into the hearts of all sons and daughters of Adam.

b. Widely asunder, with the fragments or portions widely scattered.

c **1260** *E.E. Poems* (1862) 6 Al þat þou wan here wiþ pine, a-bro[d] þin eir sal wast it al. *c* **1400** *Apol. for Lollards* 73 He þat gedreþ not wiþ Me, he sckateriþ a brod. **1483** CAXTON *Golden Leg.* 165/2 A man in that companye.. smote hym on the heed that his brayne fyl alle abrode. **1588** SHAKS. *Tit. A.* IV. i. 106 The angry Northerne winde Will blowe these sands like Sibels leaues abroad. **1654** G. GODDARD in *Burton's Diary* (1828) I. 79 The Parliament had already taken the Government abroad, (in pieces was meant,) and had altered and changed it. **1875** B. TAYLOR *Faust* I. x. 127 Then a chance will come, a holiday, When, piece by piece, can one abroad the things display.

c. Widely apart, with the parts or limbs wide spread.

c **1430** *Syr Generides* 4487 With his armes spred on brode To Ismael his brodre he rode. *c* **1440** *Lay-Folks Mass-Bk.* C. 242 He wille sprede his armes on brade [**1450** abrade]. **1535**

COVERDALE *2 Kings* xix. 14 Whan Ezechias had receaued the letters..[he] layed them abrode before the Lorde. **1598** GERARDE *Herball* I. xxxv. §5. 50 But the leaues be more spred abroad. **1627** BACON *New Atlantis* 6 At his coming he did bend to us a little, and put his arms abroad. **1769–90** SIR J. REYNOLDS *Disc.* (1876) x. 15 The locks of the hair are flying abroad in all directions. **1847** LONGF. *Evan.* I. v. 116 Stretched abroad on the seashore motionless lay his form.

†**d.** Hence, *Naut.* 'An old word for *spread* pa. pple.; as all sail *abroad*.' Smyth *Sailor's Word-Bk.*

1667 *Lond. Gaz.* cxxxvi/1 The Dragon Fregat appearing with Dutch Colours abroad, the Captain..remanded his Men. **1790** BEATSON *Nav. & Mil. Mem.* I. 187 The Admiral made the signal..for those who were to lead, to do so with the starboard tacks abroad by a wind.

2. *lit.* At large; freely moving about; and *fig.* current in the outside world.

c **1500** *Robin Hood* II. vii. 11 Sad news I hear there is abroad, I fear all is not well. **1538** STARKEY *England* 148 For I wot not whether I may speke thys a-brode. **1588** SHAKS. *L.L.L.* I. i. 190 Ther's villanie abroad, this letter will tell you more. **1699** BENTLEY *Phalaris* 364 In the interval of time between them..these pretended Laws of Charondas came abroad. **1704** RAY *Creation* II. 288 What is abroad round about us in this aspectable World. **1849** MACAULAY *Hist. Eng.* II. 365 He was perfectly aware of the suspicions which were abroad.

3. Out of one's house or abode; out of doors; out in the open air.

1377 LANGL. *P. Pl.* B. II. 176 To bere bischopes aboute, abrode in visytynge. **1553** UDALL *Roister Doister* (1869) 42 I bid him keepe him warme at home For if he come abroade, he shall cough me a mome. **1597** SHAKS. *2 Hen. IV*, I. ii. 107 I am glad to see your Lordship abroad: I heard say your Lordship was sicke. I hope your Lordship goes abroad by aduise. **1663** GERBIER *Counsel* 101 Any floor level with the ground receives more dirt from abroad. **1728** YOUNG *Love of Fame* (1757) v. 127 Tho' sick to death, abroad they safely roam. **1841** BORROW *Zincali* I. iv. 296 He found me not, as I was abroad dining with a friend. **1859** JEPHSON *Brittany* iii. 23 The whole population was abroad, either reaping or threshing. *Mod.* The badger ventures abroad only after dusk.

4. Out of the home country; in or into foreign lands. ***from abroad***: from foreign lands.

c **1450** LONELICH *Grail* xxxvii. 679 Estward ayens the sonne lokeden they there Ful fer abrod into the Se. **1559** *Myrroure for Mag. Salisbury* xv. 7 The one at home, the other abrode in Fraunce. **1605** SHAKS. *Macb.* v. viii. 66 Calling home our exil'd Friends abroad. **1719** DE FOE *Crusoe* I. 5, I resolv'd not to think of going Abroad any more, but to settle at Home. **1832** HT. MARTINEAU *Hill & Valley* vi. 85 The Welsh iron-masters had now rivals abroad. **1849** MACAULAY *Hist. Eng.* I. 317 At the close of the reign of Charles the Second, great part of the iron which was used in the country was imported from abroad. **1866** GEO. ELIOT *Felix Holt* Epil. 429 He was understood to have gone to reside at a great distance; some said 'abroad,' that large home of ruined reputations.

5. Wide of the mark or the truth; 'out,' astray.

1806 J. BERESFORD *Miseries* I. i. 5 Unless I am quite abroad still; and if so, I will humbly wait, while you..clarify my understanding. *a* **1828** J. BERNARD *Retrosp. Stage* (1830) I. ix. 283 The actors appearing to be all abroad when they were at home. **1838** DICKENS *Nich. Nick.* (C.D. ed.) vi. 33 I'm only a little abroad, that's all. **1842** THACKERAY *Van. Fair* I. 5 At the twelfth round the latter champion was all abroad, as the saying is, and had lost all presence of mind. **1876** M. ARNOLD *Lit. & Dogma* 244 The first deals successfully with nearly the whole of life, while the second is all abroad in it.

B. *prep.* [The adv. with place expressed]. Out, over, throughout. *Obs.* or *arch.*

1523 LD. BERNERS *Froissart* I. ccxxxv. 330 So then the prince's host spred abrode that countre. **1653** BAXTER *Peace of Consc.* 51 [They] will proclaim abroad the world that our Ministers are Legalists. **1662** STILLINGFLEET *Orig. Sacr.* (ed. 3) I. vi. §5. 99 And walk abroad the world.

¶ Used as adj.; and elliptically for ***go abroad***.

1550 LEVER *Sermons* 29 Their riches muste abrode in the countrey, to bie fermes. **1615** CHAPMAN *Odyssey* xvi. 551 Then to the queen was come The Wooers' plot, to kill her son at home, Since their abroad design had miss'd success. **1676** COTTERELL tr. *Cassandra* VI. 97 We must abroad again.

C. *sb.* [cf. *adv.* sense 4 and quot. 1866.] Any region outside one's homeland.

1895 K. GRAHAME *Golden Age* 98 She was somewhere over in that beastly abroad. **1925** R. MACAULAY *Casual Commentary* 138 Restaurants and hotels are getting fuller. Abroad is getting fuller. **1934** H. G. WELLS *Exper. Autobiog.* II. 565 'Abroad' was a slightly terrifying world of adventure. **1945** N. MITFORD *Pursuit of Love* xv. 114 'Frogs,' he would say, 'are slightly better than Huns or Wops, but abroad is unutterably bloody and foreigners are fiends.' **1958** K. AMIS *I like it Here* iii. 40 Why was abroad occupied exclusively by the Romance-speaking family of nations?

¶ Examples of a comparative form.

1923 E. SIDGWICK *Restoration* i. 16 Henry was abroad; he had meant to go abroad, and he had gone abroader than anybody less happily-guided than himself had ever dreamed of. **1939** A. THIRKELL *Before Lunch* vii. 190, I never can think why when people say abroad they mean France as a rule, and yet most other places are much abroader than France.

abroad, occ. by confusion for ABOARD, ABROOD.

†**abrodietical**, *a.* or *sb. Obs.*$^{-0}$ [f. Gr. ἁβροδίαιτος living delicately + -ICAL.] 'A delicate person.' Cockeram 1612. 'Feeding daintily, delicate, luxurious,' Minsheu 1627. Prob. never used.

abrogable (ˈæbrəgəb(ə)l), *a.* [f. L. *abrogā-re*: see ABROGATE + -BLE; as if ad. L. **abrōgābilis*.] Capable of being abrogated or done away with.

1599 SANDYS *Europæ Spec.* (1632) 40 It is cleerly contrarie to such a positive Law of God,..no way abrogable or dispensable with. *a* **1718** PENN *Tracts* in Wks. 1726 I. 686 But those Things that are abrogable, or abrogated in the Great Charter, were neuer a Part of the Fundamentals.

abrogate (ˈæbrəgət), *a.* and *pple. arch.* Also 5–7 **abrogat.** [ad. L. *abrogāt-us* pa. pple. of *abrogāre* to repeal, cancel (f. *ab* off, away, + *rogāre* to propose a law). In earlier use than the verb to ABROGATE, whence also a new participle *abrogated*, now more generally used.] Repealed, annulled, cancelled, abolished by authority.

1460 CAPGRAVE *Chron.* 181 So that statute was abrogat, and no lenger kept. **1538** STARKEY *England* 102 Ther be few lawys and statutys, in parlyamentys ordeynyd, but, by placardys and lycence..they are broken and abrogate. **1552–5** LATIMER *Serm. & Rem.* (1845) 244 That no curate command the even to be fasted of an abrogate holiday. **1609** SKENE *Reg. Majest.* Pref. A 7 Some of them are abrogat, be posteriour lawes, or be desuetude, are obscured. **1635** N. R. tr. *Camden's Eliz.* Introd., Lawes made by King Henry the eight against the Protestants are repealed..the Masse is abrogate. *a* **1845** SOUTHEY *Inscriptions* xlv. Wks. III. 177 The promise on the Mount vouchsafed, Nor abrogate by any later law.

abrogate (ˈæbrəgeɪt), *v.* Pa. pple. 5–7 **abrogat, abrogate;** 6– **abrogated.** [f. prec., or on analogy of vbs. so formed.]

1. To repeal (a law, or established usage), to annul, to abolish authoritatively or formally, to cancel.

1526 TINDALE *Heb.* viii. 13 In that he sayth a new testament he hath abrogat the olde. **1553** WILSON *Rhetorique* 24 b, They abrogate suche vowes as were proclaimed to be kept. **1649** MILTON *Eikonokl.* 46 Doubtless it repented him to have establish'd that by Law, which he went about so soon to abrogate by the Sword. **1666** FULLER *Hist. Cambr.* (1840) 157 Thus was the pope's power fully abrogated out of England. **1775** BURKE *Sp. Concil. with Amer.* Wks. III. 60 We wholly abrogated the ancient government of Massachuset. **1841** MYERS *Cath. Thoughts* IV. §26. 305 The Law of the Jews..was not rejected nor contradicted by the Gospel..but simply abrogated by being absorbed. **1862** LD. BROUGHAM *Brit. Constitn.* i. 22 But the same power which formed these rules may abrogate or suspend them.

2. To do away with, put an end to.

1588 SHAKS. *L.L.L.* IV. ii. 55 Perge, good M. Holofernes, perge, so it shall please you to abrogate scurilitie. **1634** T. HERBERT *Travaile* 141 Others say all the world was a paradice till sinne abrogated its glory. **1851** MRS. BROWNING *Casa Guidi Wind.* 95 Pay certified, yet payers abrogated. **1855** OWEN *Skel. & Teeth* 86 In the whales the movements of these vertebræ upon one another are abrogated.

abrogated (ˈæbrəgeɪtɪd), *ppl. a.* [f. prec. + -ED.] Abolished by authority, annulled.

1709 STRYPE *Ann. Ref.* xxvii. 283 The open observers of abrogated [fasting-]days to be punished. **1879** FARRAR *St. Paul* I. 3 The heavy corpse of an abrogated Levitism.

abrogating (ˈæbrəgeɪtɪŋ), *vbl. sb.* [f. ABROGATE *v.* + -ING[1].] The act or process of repealing, annulling, or authoritatively abolishing; abrogation. (Now mostly gerundial.)

1577 tr. *Bullinger, Decades* (1592) 410 The abrogating of the lawe consisteth in this that followeth. **1643** MILTON *Divorce* (1851) Introd. 9 We have an expresse law of God.. whereof our Saviour with a solemn threat forbid the abrogating. **1664** H. MORE *Myst. Iniq.* 103 The nulling of the Authority of S. Paul's writings were the abrogating of the very Law of Christ. *Mod.* Before abrogating the law.

abrogation (æbrəˈgeɪʃən). [ad. L. *abrogātiōn-em* repeal, n. of action, from *abrogāre*: see ABROGATE *a.* Perhaps immed. from Fr. *abrogation* 16th c. in Littré.] The act of abrogating; repeal or abolition by authority. (Not now used of persons or things concrete.)

1535 COVERDALE *Mal.* iii. Contents, Off the abrogacion of the olde leuiticall presthode. **1617** *Janua Ling.* 1041 To repeale a statute is as much as an abrogation. **1651** HOBBES *Leviathan* II. xxvii. 157 The Command, as to that particular fact, is an abrogation of the Law. **1692** S. JOHNSON *(title)* An Argument proving, that the Abrogation of King James by the People..was according to the Constitution. **1734** tr. *Rollin's Anc. Hist.* (1827) I. Pref. 48 The universal sorrow which the abrogation of that feast would occasion. **1866** ROGERS *Agric. & Prices* I. iv. 83 The act would be oppressive..and the abrogation of a settled right.

abrogative (ˈæbrəgeɪtɪv), *a.* [f. L. *abrogāt-* ppl. stem of *abrogāre* + -IVE.] Having the quality of abrogating.

Mod. A statute abrogative of these privileges.

abrogator (ˈæbrəgeɪtə(r)). [f. ABROGATE *v.* + -OR, -ER[1].] One who abrogates or authoritatively repeals.

1599 SANDYS *Europæ Spec.* (1632) 96 Abrogators and dispensers against the Lawes of God. **1633** T. ADAMS *Exp. 2 Pet.* ii. 7 (1865) 359 Not an abrogater of the ceremonial, but a filler of the law moral.

†**a'broge**, *v. Obs. rare.* [a. Fr. *abroge-r*:—L. *abrogā-re*: see ABROGATE.] = ABROGATE.

c **1450** in HALLAM *Middle Ages* (1872) III. 188 Nor might by his last will nor otherwise altre, change, nor abroge.

abroken, obs. pa. pple. of ABREAK and BREAK.

abron, abroun, abrun(e, obs. ff. AUBURN.

abrood (aˈbruːd), *adv.* prop. *phr.* Also 3–4 **abrode.** [A *prep.*[1] + BROOD *sb.*] On its brood or eggs; hatching eggs; breeding young, mischief, etc.

a **1250** *Owl & Nightingale* 518 So sone so thu sittest abrode, Thu for-lost al thine wise. **1398** TREVISA *Barth. De P.R.* (1495) XII. ii. 409 The egle is a foule that selde syttyth abrood and selde hath byrdes. **1586** HOOKER *Giraldus's Hist. Irel.* II. 153/2 That Romish cockatrice, which a long time had set abrood vpon hir egs, had now hatched hir chickins. **1656** J. TRAPP *Exp. Matt.* v. 8 (1868) 48 b, The natural heart is Satan's throne..he sits abrood upon it. **1694** ABP. SANCROFT *Serm.* 135 The Spirit of God sate abrood upon the whole rude Mass, as Birds upon their Eggs.

†**a'brook**, *v. Obs. rare*$^{-1}$. [f. A- *pref.* 11 + BROOK *v.*] To brook, endure, bear.

1592 SHAKS. *2 Hen. VI*, II. iv. 10 Sweet Nell, ill can thy Noble Minde abrooke The abiect People, gazing on thy face.

abrupt (əˈbrʌpt), *a.* and *sb.* [ad. L. *abrupt-us* broken off, precipitous, disconnected, pa. pple. of *abrump-ĕre*, f. *ab* off + *rump-ĕre* to break.]

A. *adj.* **1.** Broken away (from restraint). *Obs.*

1583 STUBBES *Anat. Abuses* (1877) 23 There is not a people more abrupte, wicked, or perverse, liuing upon the face of the Earth.

2. Broken off, terminating in a break. ? *Obs.*

1607 TOPSELL *Serpents* (1653) 603 The voyce of Serpents ..differeth from all other Beasts hissing, in the length thereof: for the hissing of a Tortoise is shorter and more abrupt. **1611** SPEED *Hist. Brit.* III. xxxix. §5. 344 The Circle of their liues are oftentimes abrupt before it be drawn to the full round. **1634** CHILLINGWORTH *Charity by Cath.* I. ii. §9 Of Ecclesiastes he (Luther) saith, 'This book is not full, there are in it many abrupt things.' **1753** CHAMBERS *Cycl. Suppl.* s.v. *Amianthus*, The bodies of it are flexile and elastic, and composed of short and abrupt filaments.

3. a. Characterized by sudden interruption or change; unannounced and unexpected; sudden, hasty.

1591 SHAKS. *1 Hen. VI*, II. iii. 30 My lady craues, To know the cause of your abrupt departure? *a* **1725** POPE *Odyssey* I. 413 Abrupt, with eagle speed she cut the sky, Instant invisible to mortal eye. **1834** H. MILLER *Sc. & Leg.* (1857) xxviii. 420 The motions of the vessel were so fearfully abrupt and violent. **1871** BROWNING *Balaustion* 2135 Nor, of that harsh, abrupt resolve of thine, Any relenting is there!

b. Of literary style: Passing suddenly from thought to thought or phrase to phrase.

1636 B. JONSON *Discovery* (J.) The abrupt stile, which hath many breaches, and doth not seem to end but fall. **1763** J. BROWN *Poetry & Music* §5. 84 His [Æschylus'] Imagery and Sentiments are great; his Style rugged and abrupt. **1877** SPARROW *Serm.* vii. 93 In short, he is abrupt, in order to awake attention, and give it a right direction.

4. Precipitous, steep.

1618 BOLTON *Florus* II. xii. 126 [He] walled Macedonia every where in..by planting Castles in abrupt places. **1726** THOMSON *Winter* 99 Tumbling thro' rocks abrupt, and sounding far. **1823** RUTTER *Fonthill* 2 Across this valley is an abrupt ridge. *c* **1854** STANLEY *Sinai & Palest.* (1858) iii. 167, I do not mean that the ravines of Jerusalem are so deep and abrupt as those of Luxembourg.

5. a. *Bot.* Coming to a sudden termination; not tapering off, truncated. **b.** *Geol.* Of strata: Suddenly cropping out and presenting their edges.

1833 LYELL *Princ. Geol.* III. 197 The Meerfelder Maar is a cavity of far greater size..the sides presenting some abrupt sections of inclined secondary rocks. **1854** BALFOUR *Bot.* 395 The Tulip-tree, remarkable for its abrupt or truncated leaves.

B. *sb.* An abrupt place; a precipice, chasm, or abyss.

1667 MILTON *P.L.* II. 409 Upborn with indefatigable wings Over the vast abrupt, ere he arrive The happy Ile. **1735** THOMSON *Liberty* I. 314 Whole stately Cities in the dark Abrupt Swallow'd at once. *Ibid.* III. 525 When the whole loaded Heaven Descends in Snow, lost in one white Abrupt. **1887** W. C. RUSSELL *Frozen Pirate* I. vi. 73 It was like the face of a cliff, a sheer abrupt.

a'brupt (əˈbrʌpt), *v.* [f. prec., or on analogy of vbs. so formed. Cf. *cor-rupt, dis-rupt*.] To break off, sever; to interrupt suddenly.

1643 SIR T. BROWNE *Relig. Med.* (1656) I. §13 Buzzing thy praises which shal never die, Till death abrupts them. **1646** —— *Pseud. Ep.* 323 The effects of whose activity are not precipitously abrupted, but gradually proceed to their cessations. **1682** —— *Chr. Morals* (1756) 100 The insecurity of their enjoyments abrupteth our tranquillities. **1819** *Blackw. Mag.* V. 737/2 This gas obtains in greatest abundance in the vicinity of dykes which abrupt the coal. **1949** 'M. INNES' *Journeying Boy* xi. 130 But to abrupt his journey in a strange town..was a procedure..unnecessarily drastic. **1958** *Observer* 29 June 15/6 The film version of 'The Brothers Karamazov'..does not deliberately distort the novel or abrupt it.

abrupted (əˈbrʌptɪd), *ppl. a. rare.* [f. ABRUPT *v.* + -ED.] Suddenly broken off; abrupt.

1633 FORD *Love's Suc.* III. iii. (1811) 409 Did not I note your dark abrupted ends Of words half spoke; your 'wells, if all were known'?

abruptedly (əˈbrʌptɪdlɪ), *adv.* [f. prec. + -LY[2].] In an abrupt or hurried manner; abruptly.

1847 GROTE *Hist. Greece* IV. II. l. 380 (1862) Abruptedly and unexpectedly.

abruption (əˈbrʌpʃən). [ad. L. *abruptiōn-em* breaking off, n. of action f. *abrump-ĕre*. See ABRUPT.]

1. A breaking off, an interruption, a sudden break (in a narrative, etc.). *arch.*

1606 SHAKS. *Tr. & Cr.* III. ii. 69 *Tr.* O Cressida, how often haue I wisht me thus? *Cr.* Wisht my Lord? the gods grant? O my Lord. *Tr.* What should they grant? what makes this pretty abruption? *a* **1652** J. SMITH *Sel. Disc.* vi. 211 The pseudo-prophetical spirit..is also conjoined with alienations and abruptions of mind. **1779** JOHNSON *L.P.*, *Cowley* (1816) 40 Thoughts, which to a reader of less skill seem thrown together by chance are concatenated without any abruption. **1868** MILMAN *St. Paul's* ii. 40 Sudden and total abruption of all intercourse.

2. A sudden snapping or breaking; the breaking away of portions of a mass.

1657 TOMLINSON *Renou's Disp.* 145 Effused by the abruption of the glasses. **1860** J. P. KENNEDY *Horse Shoe Robinson* viii. 97 A cleft, which suggested the idea of some sudden abruption of the earth. **1866** *Reader* 1 Sept. 767 The work of abruption, or hollowing out, during the embryonic state is little less active than that of secretion or building up. **1879** BRYANT *Pract. Surg.* II. 8 The removal of the softer kinds of polypi should always be by abruption.

abruptly (əˈbrʌptlɪ), *adv.* [f. ABRUPT *a.* + -LY[2].] In an abrupt manner. Hence,

1. With a sudden break off, without warning or preparation, suddenly.

1590 GREENE *Neuer too late* (1600) 18 And so as I begun passionately, I breake off abruptly. Farewell. **1670** MILTON *P.R.* II. 10 Now missing him their joy so lately found, So lately found, and so abruptly gone. **1783** COWPER *Lett.* Nov. 24 Wks. 1876, 149 Your mother wants room for a postscript so my lecture must conclude abruptly. **1838** DICKENS *Nich. Nick.* (C.D. ed.) xxii. 171 'Will you let me take the bundle now?' asked Nicholas, abruptly changing the theme. **1862** ANSTED *Channel Isl.* (ed. 2) I. i. 3 Fifty miles more to the east ..the French coast abruptly bends round to the north.

2. Interruptedly, with sudden breaks.

1607 TOPSELL *Four-footed Beasts* (1673) 586 The body [of the Civet-cat]..having divers & sundry black spots scattered abruptly throughout. **1618** BOLTON *Florus* Pref., The varietie of matter makes the minde abruptly flit from one thing to another. **1850** LYNCH *Theoph. Trinal.* ix. 162 The generations do not succed each other abruptly, but pass one into the other like the pictures in dissolving views.

3. Precipitously.

1623 BINGHAM *Xenophon* 59 The Carduchan Mountaines being abruptly steepe, lay directly hanging ouer the same Riuer. **1877** KINGLAKE *Crimea* (ed. 6) III. i. 3 It is the high land nearest to the shore which falls most abruptly.

4. *Bot.* With a sudden termination; as *abruptly pinnate*, when several pairs of leaflets are formed without an intermediate one at the end.

1870 HOOKER *Stud. Flora* 183 *Scabiosa succisa*.. Rootstock short, abruptly truncate. *Ibid.* 18 *Fumaria densiflora*..lower petal abruptly dilated at the tip.

abruptness (əˈbrʌptnɪs). [f. ABRUPT *a.* + -NESS.] The state or quality of being abrupt. Hence,

1. Suddenness, unexpectedness of action.

1603 B. JONSON *Pt. of King's Entert'mt.* Wks. 1846, 533 Pardon, if my abruptnesse breed disease. **1751** JOHNSON *Rambler* No. 139 ¶7 The beginning [of Samson Agonistes] is undoubtedly beautiful and proper, opening with a graceful abruptness. **1838** DICKENS *Nich. Nick.* (C.D. ed.) xxii. 176 Nicholas could not refrain from smiling at the abruptness of the question.

2. The presence of sudden breaks; the roughness or interruption thereby caused; *esp.* ruggedness in literary style or social manner.

1642 HOWELL *For. Trav.* (1869) §12. 58 Some other languages..as having no abruptnesse of Consonants, have some advantage of the English. **1695** WOODWARD *Nat. Hist.* IV. 173 Crystallized Bodies found in the perpendicular Intervalls have always..Abruptness at the end of the Body whereby it adhered to the Stone..which Abruptness is caused by its being broke off from it. **1772** J. WARTON *Ess. on Pope* I. 10 Pope lengthened the abruptness of Waller, and at the same time contracted the exuberance of Dryden. *Ibid.* ii. 27 The abruptness and brevity of the sentences are much in character. **1865** MRS. WHITNEY *Gayworthys* (1879) xxiii. 214 Full of little merry sarcasms and abruptnesses. **1874** *Athenæum* May 2, A certain abruptness in his manner, and ..scant appreciation of her society, at once repel her and pique her curiosity.

3. Precipitousness, ruggedness, steepness.

1620 HOWELL *Lett.* (1650) I. 38 I had much ado to reach hither; for besides the monstruous abruptness of the way, these parts of the Pyreneys..are never without thieves. **1876** PAGE *Adv. Text-Book Geol.* ii. 40 Breadth or abruptness of its valleys.

abrutalize, *v. rare*[−1]. [f. A- *pref.* 11, intensive + BRUTALIZE; cf. *a-bastardize*.] = BRUTALIZE.

1795 J. WALKER *Elem. Geog.* Pref., To re-apply the abrutalizing scourge.

abrygge, obs. form of ABRIDGE *v.*

abs- *pref.*, repr. L. *abs-* the form of AB- off, away, from, used before *c- q-* and *t-*, as in *abscessus*, *abs-condere*, *abs-tractus*, *abs-tinens*. In words that survived into OFr. reduced to *as-*, as *as-traire*, *as-tenir*; subseq. refashioned after L. as *abs-traire*, *abs-tenir*. In words taken directly from L. into later Fr. and Eng. *abs-* from the first.

†**abˈscede**, *v. Obs. rare*[−1]. [ad. L. *abscēd-ere* to depart; f. *abs* away + *cēde-ere* to go.] To move away, to lose contact.

1650 BULWER *Anthropomet.* xvi. 164 By reason of the motion of the right Arm, the Scapula is distracted & abscedes.

†**abˈscedent**, *a. Obs.* [ad. L. *abscēdent-em* pr. pple. of *abscēd-ĕre*: see prec.] 'Applied formerly to those parts which, when the body is in its natural condition, are either united or contiguous to other parts, but when diseased no longer maintain their union or contact, as the bones, etc., in ulceration.' Mayne 1851; *Syd. Soc. Lex.* 1879.

abscess (ˈæbsɪs). [ad. L. *abscēss-us* a going away, an abscess (Celsus), f. *abscēdĕre*: see ABSCEDE.] A collection of pus or purulent matter formed by a morbid process in a cavity of the body.

1543 TRAHERON tr. *Vigo's Chirurg.* (Interpretn. Strange Wordes) Aposteme..In latyne it is called *abscissus*. **1615** H. CROOKE *Body of Man* 415 The purulent matter of the Chest is by Nature euacuated..lastly by Apostemation or abcesse. **1836** TODD *Cycl. An. & Ph.* I. 604/2 Few or no abscesses granulate till they are exposed. **1860** SMILES *Self-help* iv. 89 It was averred that vaccinated children became 'ox-faced,' that abscesses broke out to 'indicate sprouting horns.'

abscessed (ˈæbsɪst), *ppl. a.* [f. prec. + -ED[2].] Diseased with abscesses.

1856 KANE *Arctic Explor.* II. i. 17 Our sick have finished the bear's head, and are now eating the condemned abscessed liver of the animal.

†**abˈscession.** *Obs. rare.* [ad. L. *abscēssiōn-em* going away, separation, n. of action f. *abscēdĕre*: see ABSCEDE.]

1. Departure, removal; cessation of a pain, etc.

1599 A. M. *Gabelhouer's Bk. of Phys.* 98/2 Administre heerof to the Patient after the abscessione of the stitch. **1659** GAUDEN *Tears of Ch.* 3 (D.) [Not] excommunicating himself by voluntary Schisme, declared abscession, separation, or apostasie.

2. = ABSCESS.

1610 BARROUGH *Meth. Physik.* (Nares) If truly it doth turne into abscessions..it shall be lawfull to use medicines which can both matter, open, and cleanse the ulcer.

†**abˈscessional.** *Obs. rare*[−1]. [f. ABSCESSION + -AL[2]; cf. *processional*. Prop. adj. *sc.* 'order, decree.'] A permission or command to depart.

1656 J. TRAPP *Exp. Matt.* xix. 7 (1868) 216/1 It was true that Moses commanded..that he should give her an abscessionale, a bill of divorcement.

abscind (æbˈsɪnd), *v. arch.* [ad. L. *abscind-ĕre* to tear or cut off, f. *ab* off, away + *scindĕre* to tear, rend.] To cut off. *lit.* and *fig.*

1657 *Phys. Dict.*, Abscinded, cut off. **1731** BAILEY, Abscind, to cut off. **1750** JOHNSON *Rambler* No. 90 ¶9 When two syllables likewise are abscinded from the rest, they evidently want some associate sounds to make them harmonious. **1861** HOOK *Lives of Archbps.* I. iii. 145 The flowing locks at the back of his head were abscinded.

abˈscinded, *ppl. a.* [f. prec. + -ED.] Cut off.

a **1733** R. NORTH *Lives of Norths* III. 125 The worst grievance [of the shrievalty] was the executioner coming to him for orders touching the abscinded members, and to know where to dispose of them.

abˈscise, *v.* [f. L. *abscīs-* ppl. stem of *abscīd-ĕre* to cut off; f. *abs* off + *cædĕre* to cut. Cf. *excise*, *incise*.] To cut off or away. Also *Bot.*, *intr.* to fall off, to separate by abscission.

1612 WOODALL *Surgeon's Mate* Wks. 1653, 90 If the nerve shall be wholly abscised, lesser symptomes..ensue. **1879** *St. George's Hosp. Rep.* IX. ix. 473 This eye was abscised.. and she is now able to admirably manage an artificial substitute. **1909** WEBSTER, *Abscise* (*Bot.*), to separate by abscission. **1940** MEYER & ANDERSON *Plant Physiol.* xxxvi. 651 Leaves, however, are not the only organs or parts of plants which abscise. **1964** S. DUKE-ELDER *Parsons' Diseases of Eye* (ed. 14) xvi. 197 If prolapse of iris has occurred it should usually be abscised.

abscisic (æbˈsɪsɪk), *a. Biochem.* [f. ABSCIS(IN + -IC.] *abscisic acid*: a plant hormone, $C_{15}H_{20}O_4$, which promotes seed and bud dormancy and inhibits germination.

1968 F. T. ADDICOTT et al. in *Science* 29 Mar. 1493/3 Abscisin II was the name given to the second of two abscission-accelerating substances isolated from cotton fruit... Some confusion has developed from the use of the two names, abscisin II and dormin... We now propose the term abscisic acid. **1969** *New Scientist* 10 Apr. 71/1 Abscisic acid..is now believed to be the principal plant hormone controlling dormancy. **1978** *Sci. Amer.* Aug. 75/3 Sprouting of the seeds within the ripe fruit, for which the temperature and moisture conditions are ideal, is inhibited by abscisic acid and unidentified substances that are normally present. **1978** *Nature* 12 Oct. 571/2 The known and accepted hormonal regulators of plant growth and development comprise the auxins, the gibberellins, the cytokinins, abscisic acid and (perhaps) ethylene.

abscisin (æbˈsɪsɪn, ˈæbsɪsɪn). *Biochem.* [f. ABSCIS(SION + -IN[1].] A substance isolated from cotton bolls that promotes leaf abscission; *abscisin II*, the plant hormone now called abscisic acid.

1961 LIU & CARNS in *Science* 11 Aug. 384/2 A crystalline substance, designated abscisin, which accelerates abscission of excised debladed petioles.., has been isolated from cotton burs. **1963** K. OHKUMA et al. in *Science* 20 Dec. 1592 Crystalline abscisin II, with a tentative molecular formula of $C_{15}H_{20}O_4$, has been isolated from young cotton fruit. It accelerates abscission when applied in amounts as low as 0.01 μg per abscission zone. **1965** *Nature* 27 Mar. 1269/1 We have isolated the dormin from sycamore..and have established its identity with abscisin II. **1968** *New Scientist* 25 Jan. 187/1 Plant hormones such as..auxin, gibberellin, and abscisin have special roles in controlling growth. **1968** [see ABSCISIC *a.*]. **1972** GOODWIN & MERCER *Introd. Plant Biochem.* xv. 328 Abscisic acid.., also previously known as abscisin II and dormin,..is now known to be widely if not ubiquitously distributed in plants.

abscision (æbˈsɪʒən). [ad. L. *abscīsiōn-em* n. of action f. *abscīd-ĕre* to cut off or away: see ABSCISE. *Abscīsio* and *abscissio* were confused in L., and *abscision* can scarcely be separated from ABSCISSION in Eng.] A cutting off or away.

1594 HOOKER *Eccl. Pol.* (1617) v. 351 [They] cure wilfully by abscision that which they might both preserue and heale. **1767** A. CAMPBELL *Lexiphanes* (1774) 105 An abscision of vowels, a detruncation of syllables.

absciss, abscisse (ˈæbsɪs), *sb.* Pl. -es; more commonly in the L. form **abscissa** (æbˈsɪsə), pl. **abscissae**; also Eng. **abscissas.** [L. *abscissa* (sc. *linea* a line) cut off; pa. pple. of *abscindere*: see ABSCIND.] **1.** *Geom. Literally*, a line or distance cut off; *spec.* the portion of a given line intercepted between a fixed point within it, and an ordinate drawn to it from a given point without it.

In *Conic Sections*: the segment (or segments) of a diameter (or in a hyperbola, a diameter produced), intercepted between the point where it is cut by an ordinate, and the bounding curve. In *Rectilineal Coördinates*, the segment of a given line, *x*, intercepted between the point where it is cut by another line, *y*, and that in which it is cut by a line parallel to the latter drawn from a given point without it, and called the *ordinate*.

1698 DE MOIVRE in *Phil. Trans.* XX. 192 The Abscisse corresponding to a certain Area in any Curve. **1748** HARTLEY *Observ. on Man* I. iii. §2. 339 The Ordinates & Points of the Absciss being given, in the unknown Curve. **1798** in *Phil. Trans.* LXXXVIII. 7 It was found to be a very accurate parabola, the abscissa of which was 13·85 in. **1841** YOUNG *Math. Dissert.* I. 10 In what directions the positive abscissas and the positive ordinates are usually taken. **1871** B. STEWART *Heat* §141 Let us..reckon the temperatures along a line of abscissae after the manner represented in the figure.

2. *Bot.* **absciss layer**, a layer of cells across the base of the petiole in deciduous leaves.

1893 in *Funk's Stand. Dict.* **1898** H. C. PORTER tr. *Strasburger's Text-bk. Bot.* I. §1. 143 Preparatory to the falling of leaves an absciss layer is formed, by means of which the separation of the leaves from the stem is effected. **1924** HOLMAN & ROBBINS *Textbk. Gen. Bot.* vi. 180 The conditions which favor leaf fall cause the cells near the lower end of the leaf stalk to become meristematic and to give rise to a zone of delicate, thin-walled cells extending clear across the base of the petiole. This is called the *absciss layer* (ed. 3, 1934, vi. 198 *abscission layer*). **1940** *Bot. Gaz.* CII. 323 (*title*) Effect of growth substances on the absciss layer in leaves of *Coleus*.

abˈsciss, *v.* [Back-formation f. ABSCISSION.] *trans.* and *intr.* To cut off; to abscind; to abscise. Hence **abˈscissed** *ppl. a.*

1869 G. LAWSON *Dis. & Injuries of Eye* ii. 51 The Staphyloma may be abscissed. *Ibid.* 52 Another way of abscissing the staphyloma is to transfix its base with a Beer's knife. **1918** *Bot. Gaz.* LXVI. 36 The numbers refer to the total number of abscissed petioles at the corresponding dates. *Ibid.* 41 The lower leaves began to absciss. **1938** PRIESTLEY & SCOTT *Introd. Bot* x. 140 (*caption*) Naturally abscissed branches of oak. *Ibid.* xxxviii. 554 These twigs.. may be abscissed after many years of growth.

abscission (æbˈsɪʃən). [ad. L. *abscissiōn-em* n. of action f. *abscindĕre*; see ABSCIND. *Lit.* 'a tearing away,' but confused with ABSCISION, q.v.]

1. The action or process of abscinding; a cutting off or violent separation. *lit.* and *fig.*

1612 WOODALL *Surgeon's Mate* Wks. 1653, 387 This abscission is not done without great danger of death. **1655** FULLER *Church Hist.* VI. 290 Abscission is the onely plaster for such an incurable Gangrene. **1750** JOHNSON *Rambler* No. 88 ¶12 The abscission of a vowel is undoubtedly vicious when it is strongly sounded. **1878** BRYANT *Pract. Surg.* I. 375 Abscission is the removal of that portion of the eyeball situated in front of the attachments of the recti muscles.

†**2.** The state of being cut off; separation and removal. *Obs.*

1633 T. ADAMS *Comm. 2 Pet.* i. 8. (1865) 97 Bearing no fruit, they are cut away from the vine; incision is blessed, but abscission most wretched. **1649** JER. TAYLOR *Great Exemp.* I. §8. 114 He denounced judgement & great severities to.. impenitents, even abscission and fire unquenchable.

3. *Bot.* The natural separation of parts following the disorganization of the cells in the absciss layer. Hence, *abscission layer* = *absciss layer*.

1889 E. S. BASTIN *College Bot.* 403 *Abscision* [*sic*], a term applied to that mode of the detachment of spores in Fungi which consists in the disorganization of the zone connecting the spores with the hypha. **1916** *Bot. Gaz.* LXI. 225 That this separation of walls actually obtains can be proved by taking rather thick sections of suitable material and.. pulling the portions separated by the abscission layer apart on the slide. **1934** [see ABSCISS *sb.* 2]. **1946** *Nature* 3 Aug. 147/2 Abscission in shot-hole disease of peach. **1950** METCALFE & CHALK *Anat. of Dicotyledons* I. 545 Before flowers or fruits fall off, a definite abscission layer is formed.

†**ab'scissor.** *Obs. rare*⁻¹. [f. L. *absciss-* ppl. stem of *abscind-ĕre* + -OR; as if a. L. **abscissor*.] One that tears or rends asunder.

1647 LILLY *Christian Astr.* xxviii. 184 We may justly call him Strong, Hurtfull, Destroyer, Abscissor, because he onely destroys and perverts the nature of the Question.

†**ab'sconce,** *v. Obs. rare*⁻¹. [a. MFr. *absconse-r* to hide, f. L. *abscons-us* a late pa. pple. for *abscondit-us*.] To hide, to conceal.

1572 *Lament. of Lady Scotland* (Scottish Poems of 16th cent. II. 241) With ȝour murning weid absconce my face.

absconce (æb'skɒns), *sb.* [ad. med.L. *absconsa* a dark lantern, f. *abscondĕre*; see prec.] A dark lantern used in monasteries (see Du Cange), and at lauds and matins in the Roman Catholic church.

abscond (æb'skɒnd), *v.* [ad. L. *abscond-ĕre* to hide or stow away, f. *abs* off, away + *condĕre* to put together, to stow, f. *con* together + *dăre* to put.]

† **1.** *trans.* To hide away, to conceal (anything). *Obs.* or *arch.*

1612 WOODALL *Surgeon's Mate* Wks. 1653, 388 I advise it to be privately absconded for the reputation sake. **1669** FLAMSTEAD in *Phil. Trans.* IV. 1105 The Moon approaching them (Stars of the 5th and 6th Magnitude) within 4 or 5 degrees, absconds them to the naked eye. **1699–1703** J. POMFRET *Poet. Wks.* (1833) 99 The trembling Alps abscond their aged heads In mighty pillars of infernal smoke. **1868** CUSSANS *Handbk. Heraldry* xi. 146 The first is absconded, or covered, by the Canton.

2. *refl.* (*Obs.* or *arch.*)

1673 in *Phil. Trans.* VIII. 5180 Before Saturn did abscond himself in the beams of the Sun. **1681** WORLIDGE *Syst. Agric.* 258 After a dark night.. the little Fish will then bite best, having absconded themselves all night for fear of the greater. **1721** STRYPE *Eccl. Mem.* (1822) I. 315 The poor man fled from place to place absconding himself.

3. *intr.* (by omission of the refl. pron.) 'To hide oneself; to retire from the public view: generally used of persons in debt, or criminals eluding the law.' J.; to go away hurriedly and secretly.

1565–78 CHURCHYARD *Chippes* (1817) 20 He was obliged to abscond, & to make his escape, in priest's attire. **1694** FALLE *Jersey* i. 34 The King.. was forced to abscond with great danger of his Person, till he found a passage into France. **1726** DE FOE *Hist. Devil* (1840) II. vii. 267 He did his devilish endeavour, and stayed till he was forced to abscond again. **1782** PRIESTLEY *Matter & Spirit* I. xvii. 197 The villain who had absconded for a year would not escape punishment. **1865** CARLYLE *Fredk. Gt.* VIII. XVIII. xi. 5 Some few absconded, leaving their property as spoil. **1870** J. R. LOWELL *My Study Windows* 4 In the coldest weather ever known the mercury basely absconded into the bulb.

†**ab'scond,** *a. Obs. rare*⁻¹. [? for ABSCONDED.] Hidden from view.

1719 D'URFEY *Pills* (1872) II. 12 Pleased with the thought he should sit abscond and see them.

absconded (æb'skɒndɪd), *ppl. a.* [f. ABSCOND + -ED.] Concealed, hidden away; secluded, secret.

1691 WOOD *Ath. Oxon.* I. col. 83 The Author was living in an absconded Condition in Fifteen hundred fifty & six. **1710** SHAFTESBURY *Charact.* (1737) II. III. ii. 402 I am now oblig'd to go far in the pursuit of Beauty; which lies very absconded and deep. **1834** R. M. MILNES (Lord Houghton) *Mem. of Many Sc.* 42 The eager heart was wont To lead us to the boar's absconded rest, Unwearied.

abscondedly (æb'skɒndɪdlɪ), *adv.* [f. prec. + -LY².] In a concealed manner; in concealment; in retirement.

1691 WOOD *Ath. Oxon.* I. col. 537 He [Thomas Fitzherbert] would now and then hear a sermon.. by an old Roman priest that then lived abscondedly in Oxon.

abscondence (æb'skɒndəns). [f. L. *abscond-ĕre* to ABSCOND + -ENCE; after words a. Fr. *-ence*:—L. *-entia*.] The action or condition of absconding; fugitive concealment, seclusion.

1880 MASSON *Milton* VI. I. ii. 162 The place of his retirement and abscondence was a friend's house in Bartholomew Close. **1881** *Sat. Rev.* 5 Mar. 299 Mr. Parnell, though he has since returned, has been in abscondence.

absconder (æb'skɒndə(r)). [f. ABSCOND + -ER¹.] One who absconds; a runaway from justice.

1751 SMOLLETT *Per. Pickle* (1779) IV. xc. 87 Eternal war against the absconder & the rigid creditor. **1864** *Realm* 24 Feb. 4 Atrocities perpetrated by Van Diemen's Land absconders in the early days of the gold discovery.

absconding (æb'skɒndɪŋ), *vbl. sb.* [f. ABSCOND + -ING¹.] The act of self-concealment; a secret running away from public gaze, or from justice.

1684 LUTTRELL *Brief. Rel.* (1857) I. 298 The coming over of these Scotchmen.. and their absconding at the first breaking out of the plott. **1715** BURNET *Hist. own Time* (1766) II. 211 His going out of the way might incline the Jury to believe the evidence the more for his absconding. **1849** MACAULAY *Hist. Eng.* II. 552 Still, however, the king concealed his intention of absconding even from his chief ministers.

absconding (æb'skɒndɪŋ), *ppl. a.* [f. ABSCOND + -ING².] Concealing itself, or hiding; retiring, secretive; runaway.

1692 *Brit. Victrix* 3 In proud Procession how they go, To meet the Lurking and Absconding Foe. **1709** J. COLLIER *Ess. Mor. Subj.* (ed. 6) II. 127 When they see.. a remote and absconding kind of Countenance, they conclude it Cain's Mark. **1879** W. H. DIXON *Royal Windsor* II. iii. 29 No person was allowed to shelter and employ absconding men.

†**ab'scondment.** *Obs. rare*⁻¹. [f. ABSCOND *v.* + -MENT.] State of concealment; hiding.

1658 R. FRANCK *North. Mem.* (1821) 336 You may observe him in holes or hollow banks.. out of which abscondments any man may angle him, that contrives but a worm neatly on the end of a wand.

†**ab'sconsion.** *Obs.*⁻⁰ [ad. L. *absconsiōn-em*, doubtful n. of action f. *abscondĕre*, attributed to Pliny: see ABSCOND.] Hiding, concealment.

In PHILLIPS 1658, BAILEY 1742.

absee, absey, absie, obs. forms of ABC.

‖**abseil** ('æbzaɪl, 'æbseɪl). *Mountaineering.* [G. *abseilen*, f. *ab* down, *seil* rope.] The technique of descent of a steep face by means of a doubled rope fixed above the climber. So as *v. intr.*, to use the abseil or 'rope down' technique in descent. Hence **'abseiling** *vbl. sb.*

1933 G. D. ABRAHAM *Mod. Mountaineering* x. 184 To help in the *abseil* or descent of steep, almost holdless places. **1941** C. F. KIRKUS *Let's Go Climbing!* v. 76 To abseil you must be unroped. Hang the rope over a higher bough, so that it hangs down on either side and both ends are resting on the ground. You thus have a double rope to slide down. *Ibid.* 78 In the Alps a great deal of abseiling is done. **1954** *Oxf. Mountaineering 1954* 59 One member of the party ascended the first pitch of Brant, and was then forced to abseil off, for nobody would, or could, follow him. **1955** M. BANKS *Commando Climber* v. 80, I had to untie for the last abseil down to the glacier. **1956** R. C. EVANS *On Climbing* xii. 170 He had been *abseiling*, and the rock over which he had looped his doubled rope had come away.

absence ('æbsəns). Also 4 **absens.** [a. Fr. *absence*, refash. from OFr. *ausence*:—L. *absentia* n. of state f. *absent-em* ABSENT.]

1. The state of being absent or away (from any place); also the time of duration of such state.

c **1374** CHAUCER *Troyl. & Cres.* IV. 427 Absens of hire shal dryve hire out of herte. **1393** GOWER *Conf.* I. 203 He made Edwin his lieutenaunt.. That he the lond in his absence Shall reule. *c* **1440** *Gesta Rom.* I. i. 3 The knyȝt.. told him howe his wife hadde don in his absence. **1526** TINDALE *Phil.* ii. 12 Not when I was present only, but now moche more in myne absence. **1660** DRYDEN *Astræa Redux* 21 For his [Charles II's] long absence Church and State did groan. **1719** YOUNG *Busiris* II. i. (1757) 29 Methinks Absence has plac'd her in a fairer light. **1754** RICHARDSON *Grandison* V. iii. 21 She was very variable all that time in her absences. **1859** LD. J. RUSSELL *Addr. to Electors of Lond.*, Among the defects of the Bill, which were numerous, one provision was conspicuous by its presence, and one by its absence. **1862** TRENCH *Miracles* xxviii. 380 Our Lord.. was now returning to Capernaum, after one of his usual absences. **1864** TENNYSON *En. Arden* 246 She mourn'd his absence as his grave. **1882** *Daily News* 3 July 2/1 Other usually prominent members were for several hours conspicuous by their absence.

b. *poet.* An absent form or face. Cf. *presence*.

1866 W. D. HOWELL *Venetian Life* 118 The balconies are full of the Absences of gay cavaliers and gentle dames. **1873** HIGGINSON *Oldport Days* i. 14 What graceful Absences (to borrow a certain poet's phrase) are haunting those windows.

2. Of things: Want, failure, withdrawal.

1398 TREVISA *Barth. De P.R.* (1495) IX. xxii. 361 Floures that open ayenst the sonne closen in the euen for absence of the sonne. **1765** HARRIS *Three Treat.* I. 24 Was it not the Absence of Health, which excited Men to cultivate the Art of Medicine. **1847** CARPENTER *Zool.* I. §239 They [the Edentata] all agree in the absence of teeth in the front of the jaws. **1863** KEMBLE *Resid. in Georgia* 24 A total absence of self-respect.

3. Absence (*of mind*): inattention to what is going on; failure to receive impressions of what is present, through preoccupation with other matters; involuntary abstraction.

1710 ADDISON *Spectator* No. 77 I continued my walk, reflecting on the little absences and distractions of mankind. **1728** YOUNG *Love of Fame* (1757) III. 103 Absence of mind Brabantio turns to fame, Learns to mistake, nor knows his brother's name. **1782** PRIESTLEY *Matter & Spirit* I. x. 129 Absence of mind is altogether an involuntary thing. **1837** CARLYLE *Fr. Rev.* I. VII. vi. 366 Disquietude, absence of mind is on every face; Members whisper, uneasily come and go.

4. At Eton College, calling of the roll to ascertain if all the boys are present, or who are absent.

1856 W. N. LETTSOM *Song of Floggawaya* 6 So the Lord of Puggawaugun Laid on them an extra absence; E'en at that they snapp'd their fingers. **1865** *Pall Mall Gaz.* 8 June, 10 Absence, as it is called at Eton, requiring the presence of the boys to answer their names.

†**'absency.** *Obs. rare*⁻¹. [ad. L. *absentia*; see ABSENCE, the ordinary form, taken from Fr., while *absency* is a direct adaptation of L.] = ABSENCE.

1599 BUTTES in Arber's Introd. to *James I's Counterblast* 93 Or Plinies Nosemen (mouthles men) surnam'd, Whose breathing nose supply'd Mouths absency.

absent ('æbsənt), *a.* and *sb.* [a. Fr. *absent*, refashioned from OFr. *ausent*:—L. *absent-em* pr. pple. of *ab-sum*, *ab-esse* to be away.]

A. *adj.*

1. Being away, withdrawn from, or not present (at a place).

1382 WYCLIF *Deut.* xxix. 15 Ne to ȝou alone I this covenaunt smyte, and thes oothes conferme, but to all present & absent. *c* **1440** *Gesta Rom.* I. vii. 16 And while (the serpent) was absent, ther com a toode, and entrid into the nest. **1601** SHAKS. *Jul. C.* IV. iii. 156 With this she fell distract, And (her Attendants absent) swallow'd fire. **1716–18** LADY M. W. MONTAGU *Lett.* I. xi. 37 I know that you can think of an absent friend even in the midst of a court. **1751** JOHNSON *Rambler* No. 152 ¶13 Letters are written.. to preserve in the minds of the absent either love or esteem. **1817** JAS. MILL *Brit. India* II. v. v. 485 Absent officers were summoned to join their corps.

2. Of things: Withdrawn; wanting, not existing.

1718 POPE *Iliad* VIII. 633 Let numerous fires the absent sun supply. **1810** COLERIDGE *Friend* (1865) 94 The reason is either lost or not lost, that is, wholly present or wholly absent. **1847** CARPENTER *Zool.* II. §523 In fishes the ribs are sometimes entirely absent. **1860** TYNDALL *Glaciers* II. §17. 324 Crevasses.. are almost totally absent at the opposite side of the glacier.

3. Of time: Not present, distant, afar off.

1535 COVERDALE *Is.* xiii. 21 And as for Babilons tyme, it is at honde, & hir dayes maye not be longe absent.

4. Absent-minded; paying no attention to, and receiving no impression from, present objects or events.

1710 STEELE *Spectator* No. 30 ¶4 The whole assembly is made up of absent men, that is, of such persons as have lost their locality, & whose minds and bodies never keep company with one another. **1761** SMOLLETT *Gil Blas* (1802) III. VIII. xiii. 39, I lost all my gaiety, became absent and thoughtful; in a word, a miserable animal. **1875** P. G. HAMERTON *Intell. Life* XI. v. 429 Deep thinkers are notoriously absent, for thought requires abstraction from what surrounds us.

†**B.** *sb.* One who is absent, an absentee. *Obs.*

c **1425** WYNTOWN *Cronykyl* VII. viii. 200 Þe Byschapys þat þare ware, Of þa Absentis had na poware For til mak awnser. **1535–75** ABP. PARKER *Corresp.* 308 How many be resident .. & in what place and calling the Absents do dwell. **1699** BURNET 39 *Articles* (1700) xxviii. 341 Some parts of the Elements were sent to the absents, to those in Prison, and particularly to the sick. **1702** EDMUND GIBSON *Schedule Review'd* 27 The Absents lose their Right of Voting.

C. *Comb.* **absent healing**, the healing of sickness by a spiritualist medium who is not present with the patient; contrasted with *contact healing* s.v. CONTACT *sb.* 6 a; **absent-minded**, *a.* pre-occupied, = ABSENT *a.* 4; **absent-mindedly**, *adv.* in a pre-occupied manner, without active attention, = ABSENTLY; **absent-mindedness**, pre-occupation, = ABSENCE 3; **absent voter**, one authorized because of special circumstances to vote (by post, etc.) at a general election though absent at the time from the ordinary place of voting; hence ***absent vote***, a vote so authorized (cf. ABSENTEE 1 b).

1906 H. W. DRESSER *Health & Inner Life* ix. 218 Oftentimes *absent healing is very effective,—occasionally more successful than present treatment. **1945**, **1956** [see *contact healing* s.v. CONTACT *sb.* 6 a]. **1973** *Spiritualist News* Dec. 2/4 (Advt.), Nerves, ulcers... All complaints. Absent Healing. **1854** THOREAU *Walden* 184 Dreaming and *absent-minded all the way. **1890** W. JAMES *Princ. Psychol.* I. iv. 115 Very absent-minded persons in going to their bedroom to dress for dinner have been known to take off one garment after another and finally to get into bed. **1881** H. JAMES, jun. *Portrait of a Lady* xxxvi. in *Macm. Mag.* XLIV. 91 'Do you believe him?' Osmond asked, *absent-mindedly. **1879** CALDERWOOD *Mind & Brain* 274 When so occupied a person is readily charged with *absent-mindedness, and his look conveys the impression of remoteness from present influences. **1925** *Hansard Commons* Ser. 5, CLXXXIII. 1355, I do not see any need for imposing as a condition for receiving the benefit of an *absent vote the necessity of being habitually engaged in an employment which compels a man to be away from his place of residence for a period of not less than 10 days in each month. **1918** *Act 8 Geo. V* c. 64, sched. 1, §16 The registration officer, if satisfied that there is a probability that the claimant, by reason of the nature of his occupation, service, or employment, may be debarred from voting at a poll at parliamentary elections held during the time the register is in force, shall place the claimant (if registered) on the *absent voters list.

absent (æb'sɛnt), *v.* [a. Fr. *absente-r*, ad. L. *absentā-re* to keep away; f. *absent-em*; see ABSENT *a.*]

†**1.** *trans.* To keep away, detain or withhold from being present. *Obs.*

1530 PALSGR. 415, I absente farre out of presence, *Je esloyngne*; I absent or kepe out of sight, *Je absente.* **1557** SURREY *Aeneid* IV. 908 And cruel so absentest me from thy death. **1580** SIDNEY *Arcadia* I. 5 They absented his eyes from beholding the issue. **1678** MARVELL *Growth of Popery* 28 The other, the honester Fellow it seems of the two, only was absented.

b. *refl.* To keep or withdraw (oneself) away.

a **1420** OCCLEVE *De Reg. Princ.* 1434 From his cure he hym absentethe. **1480** CAXTON *Chron. Eng.* ccxlii. 342 The quene with the prynce was in the north, and absented her from the kynge. **1602** SHAKS. *Haml.* v. ii. 358 If thou did'st euer hold me in thy heart, Absent thee from felicitie awhile. **1786** T. JEFFERSON *Writings* (1859) II. 47, I..hope that I may be permitted at times to absent myself from this place. **1855** MACAULAY *Hist. Eng.* III. 378 The Club attempted to induce the advocates to absent themselves from the bar.

†**2.** *intr.* To be or stay away; to withdraw.

c **1400** *Rom. Rose* 4914 Though for a tyme his herte absente, It may not fayle, he shal repente. **1681** R. KNOX *Hist. Rel. Ceylon* 137 Then we were bidden to absent, while they returned our answers to the King. **1709** in Strype's *Ann. Ref.* xxix. 300 Many absented this afternoon, appearing neither in person nor proxy.

†**3.** *trans.* (by omission of *from*; cf. *avoid*). To leave. *Obs. rare.*

1695 LUTTRELL *Brief Rel.* (1857) III. 520 Bills of high treason are found at the sessions against 23 persons, most Romanists, who have absented the kingdom.

absent (ˈæbsənt), quasi-*prep.* *U.S.* (chiefly *Law*). [f. prec.] In the absence of, without.

1944 *Rep. Supreme Court S. Dakota* (1948) LXX. 191 We think it clear that under this definition, absent any other facts, there arises an implied contract that the patient will pay. **1953** *Federal Suppl.* CVII. 527/2 Absent federal legislation upon the subject, states may, within limits of reasonableness, regulate the use of their highways. **1960** *Cases Decided* (U.S. Court of Claims) (1962) CXLVIII. 354 It is inevitable another gorge and flood will occur at this point, absent a recreation of conditions exactly as they appeared previously. **1965** R. FLESCH *ABC of Style* 6 *Absence.* Don't use *in the absence of* as a preposition instead of *without*... Some lawyers use the word *absent* in the same ugly way. **1972** *N.Y. Law Jrnl.* 24 Oct. 5/3 Absent such an appeal, the constitutional issues were conclusively determined against Ender. **1976** *N.Y. Times* 20 Dec. 23A/2 Absent such a direct threat, Mr. Carter professes to feel no pressure. **1983** *National Law Jrnl.* (U.S.) 15 Aug. 34 Absent federal regulation, an Indian tribe possesses exclusive jurisdiction to regulate the hunting and fishing activities of tribal members on reservation land taken for government dam and reservoir projects.

†**absen'taneous**, *a.* *Obs*—⁰. [f. ABSENT + -ANEOUS, analogous to *instant-aneous*, cf. L. *momentāneus.*] Done in absence, pertaining to absence.

In BAILEY 1721, ASH 1775, etc.

absentation (æbsənˈteɪʃən). [ad. med.L. *absentātiōn-em* n. of action f. *absentā-re* to make absent; f. *absent-em* ABSENT. Cf. *presentation.*] The action of absenting oneself.

1800 WAKEFIELD *Let. to Fox* Mar. 13 Your absentation from the house is a measure which always had my most entire concurrence. **1852** SIR W. HAMILTON *Discussions* 229 His absentation at that juncture becomes significant.

absented (æbˈsɛntɪd), *ppl. a.* [f. ABSENT *v.* + -ED.] Withdrawn; retired; absent.

1548 GESTE *Priv. Masse* 83 He meanethe not that Christes body is absented from hys supper. **1580** SIDNEY *Arcadia* (1622) 201 Imboldned by your absented maner of living. **1646** QUARLES *Shepherds Eclog.* i. But tell me Gallio..to whose keep Hast thou committed thy absented sheep.

absentee (æbsənˈtiː). [f. ABSENT *v.* + -EE.]

1. a. One who is absent, or away, on any occasion.

1537 in (1691) BLOUNT *Law Dict.*, *Absentees* or *des Absentees*, was a Parliament so called, held at Dublin, 10 May, 28 H. 8. **1724** SWIFT *Drapier's Lett.* vii. Wks. 1761 III. 134 The occasional absentees, for business, health, or diversion. **1850** in *Pro. Am. Phil. Soc.* V. 160 Sir John Ross, an absentee of four winters. **1872** *Daily News* Apr. 6 Cabinet Council..was attended by thirteen of the Ministers, the absentees having been Lord Halifax and the Marquis of Hartington.

b. = *absent voter.* Also (chiefly *U.S.*) ***absentee vote, voter, voting.***

1925 *Hansard Commons* Ser. 5, CLXXXIII. 1362 The Territorial Soldier is mentioned [in the Bill] but not the regular soldier, I presume because the regular soldier will come into the class of general absentee. **1932** *N.Y. Times*, 10 Oct. 2/5 Uniform laws governing absentee voting in the United States were urged today by John F. Costello. *Ibid.* 29 Oct. 17/2 (*headline*) Grandmother's 'Duty' to Child Wins Fight for Absentee Vote. **1936** *Daily Oklahoman* (Okla. City) 4 Nov. 12/6 Iowa was the first state to adopt the absentee voter idea. **1957** *N.Z. Offic. Year-Bk.* 1957 29 An elector may, however, vote as a 'special voter'... These latter conditions replace the former classes of absentee, postal, and declaration voters.

2. One who systematically stays away from his country or home; a landlord who lives abroad. (Often used *attrib.*, as an ***absentee king.***)

1605 CAMDEN *Remains* (1637) 189 King Henry the eight.. enriched himselfe by the spoyles of Abbayes, by first fruits, tenths, exactions, and absenties in Ireland. **1723** SWIFT *Argt. agst. Bishops* Wks. 1761 III. 265 The farmer would be screwed up to the utmost penny by the agents and stewards of absentees. **1838–9** HALLAM *Hist. Lit.* III. III. iv. §55. 166 The coin of Naples was exhausted by the revenues of absentee proprietors. **1851** HT. MARTINEAU *Hist. of Peace* (1877) III. IV. ix. 36 In 157 benefices, no service was performed, the incumbent being an absentee. **1876** FREEMAN *Norm. Conq.* I. vi. 454 The Norwegians preferred a foreign and absentee king.

absenteeism (æbsənˈtiːɪz(ə)m). [f. ABSENTEE + -ISM.] **a.** The practice of being an absentee, or of absenting oneself from duty or station. *esp.* The habit of landlords who live away, or in a foreign country, or otherwise at a distance from their estates.

1829 GEN. THOMPSON *Absenteeism* in *Westm. Rev.* Jan. *Exerc.* (1842) I. 55 The only permanent effect of any given quantity of absenteeism, is to make Ireland a smaller Ireland. **1852** MISS YONGE *Cameos* (1877) IV. III. 34 There was a talk of forbidding absenteeism of clergy from their benefices. **1877** WALLACE *Russia* vii. 109 The prevailing absenteeism among the landlords.

b. *spec.*, in industry, the repeated absence of employees; in schools, of the pupils.

1922 J. D. HACKETT in *Management Engineering* Feb. 1 (*sub-heading*) Absenteeism. **1941** *Punch* 3 Sept. 201 Committee on National Production..we shall do our best to decrease absenteeism during the coming winter. **1957** *Observer* 8 Sept. 1/7 Absenteeism was a factor with such a direct and devastating effect on performance that it could destroy the fruits of the technical advance into which the industry [coalmining] was putting so much effort. **1957** *Oxford Mail* 25 Sept. 1/9 Schools in Oxford City have so far been unaffected, and it was stated today that there is no undue absenteeism for this time of year.

absenteeship (æbsənˈtiːʃɪp). [f. ABSENTEE + -SHIP.] = ABSENTEEISM.

1778 *Philos. Surv. South Irel.* 364 Absenteeship would no otherwise affect Ireland, than it does the distant parts of England. **1824** W. COBBETT *Hist. Protestant 'Reformation'* V. §150 The great cause of the miseries of Ireland, at this moment, is '*absenteeship*'.

absenter (æbˈsɛntə(r)). [f. ABSENT *v.* + -ER¹.] One who absents himself; who does not attend.

1678 MARVELL *Corresp.* Let. 86 Wks. 1872–5 II. 233 The House was calld on Thursday, and ordered that the absenters should each be fined 40*l.* **1705** STANHOPE *Paraphr.* III. 207 Had not these Absenters from the Feast before us, all this to alledge in their own Vindication? **1829** SOUTHEY in *Q. Rev.* XXXIX. 143 The dissenters and the absenters..will properly encourage the college in which any religion may be taught, or none.

absenting (æbˈsɛntɪŋ), *vbl. sb.* [f. ABSENT *v.* + -ING¹.] The act of being or of going away; absence, withdrawal. (Now mostly gerundial.)

1593–1620 SIR R. HAWKINS *Voiage into South Sea* (1847) 104 These absentings and escapes are made most times onely to pilfer and steale. *a* **1709** SIR R. ATKINS *Parl. & Polit. Tracts* (1734) 123 The Offence of absenting from the Parliament. *Mod.* Accused of absenting himself wilfully from his employment.

absently (ˈæbsəntlɪ), *adv.* [f. ABSENT *a.* + -LY².] In an absent manner; with absence of mind.

1873 BLACK *Pr. of Thule* xxii. 369 Absently thinking of all the strange possibilities now opening before him. **1881** W. COLLINS *Black Robe* I. viii. 240 Romayne looked up and answered absently, 'I don't know yet.'

†**absentment** (æbˈsɛntmənt). *Obs.* [f. ABSENT *v.* + -MENT.] The act of absenting oneself; a withdrawal, or staying away.

1600 ABBOT *On Jonah* 357 Separations and absentments from the Sacraments. *a* **1677** BARROW *Serm.* (1683) II. xxvii. 383 Humane death is..a peregrination, or absentment from the body.

absentness (ˈæbsəntnɪs). [f. ABSENT *a.* 4 + -NESS.] The quality of being absent in mind; absentmindedness; involuntary abstraction.

1858 H. MILLER *Sch. & Schoolm.* 386 He has..more than the average absentness of the great scholar about him.

absey, *Obs.* See ABC.

absidal, variant of APSIDAL.

†**absimilation.** *Obs. rare*⁻¹. [f. L. *absimil-is* unlike + -ATION; cf. *assimilation, dissimilation.*] The act or process of making or becoming unlike.

c **1630** JACKSON *Creed* XIII. ix. Wks. 1844 VIII. 232 The absimilation of this man..from himself that he might be like the Son of God.

absinthe, absinth (ˈæbsɪnθ; Fr. absɛ̃t). Also 9 absanth. [a. mod.Fr. *absinthe*, the plant wormwood, and hence the liqueur; ad. L. *absinthium.*]

1. a. The plant *Absinthium* or wormwood.

1612 BENVENUTO *Passenger's Dialogues* (Nares) Absinth and poyson be my sustenaunce. **1657** TOMLINSON *De Renou's Dispens.* xxxvii. 316 Though Absynth be an herb of vulgar dignotion, yet scarce two agree in..describing its species. **1860** PIESSE *Lab. Chem. Wonders* 172 The principal bitter used in England is..derived from the hop plant.. in Italy it is from absinth.

b. The prairie-sage, sage-brush. *U.S.*

1843 FRÉMONT *Explor. Rocky Mts.* in *Narrative* (1846) 14 The artemesia, absinthe, or prairie sage, as it is variously called. *Ibid.* 56 Absinthe bushes..grew in many thick patches. **1846** SAGE *Scenes Rocky Mts.* iv. 31 Countries abounding with *absinthe* or wild sage. **1849** PARKMAN *Oregon Trail* 146 Multitudes of strange medicinal herbs, more especially the absanth, which covered every declivity.

2. Essence of wormwood; also *fig.*

1865 CARLYLE *Fredk. Gt.* III. IX. iv. 115 What a drop of concentrated absinth follows next.

3. An alcoholic liqueur originally distilled from wine mixed with wormwood, but said now often to contain none. Also used of a colour resembling the green of absinthe.

1842 *Blackw. Mag.* LII. 494/2 We took a glass of *absinthe* to compose our nerves. **1854** THACKERAY *Newcomes* I. 63 Barnes orders absinthe-and-water. **1861** *Times* 25 Mar. 8/6 Algeria..imports great quantities of Burgundy wines and absinth. **1869** *Pall Mall G.* 24 Sept. 12 Every man taking his coffee or his absinthe. **1872** *Young Englishwoman* Dec. 644/1 Absinthe, pale green. **1938** J. CARY *Castle Corner* 33 A sunray was turning the rollers from hawthorn to absinthe. **1963** *Harper's Bazaar* May 41 An absinthe suit with a deep draped armhole.

absinthial (æbˈsɪnθɪəl), *a.* [f. L. *absinthi-um* wormwood + -AL¹.] Of or pertaining to wormwood; hence bitter.

c **1525** SKELTON *Image Hypoc.* II. 309 Doctors that take all. By lawes absynthyall. And labyrinthiall. **1860** R. A. VAUGHAN *Ho. w. Mystics* (ed. 2) I. 110 It was once called the Valley of Wormwood..Bernard and his monks come..lo! the absinthial reputation vanishes—the valley smiles—is called, and made, Clairvaux, or Brightdale.

absinthian (æbˈsɪnθɪən), *a.* [f. L. *absinthi-um* + -AN.] Of or pertaining to wormwood; absinthial.

1638 T. RANDOLPH *Poems* (1652) 60 Best Physick then when gaul with suger meets Temp'ring Absinthian bitternesse with Sweets. **1833** W. E. WALL in *Fraser's Mag.* VIII. 659/1 Despair presents her cup Apsinthian. **1843** T. CARLYLE in *Foreign Q. Rev.* XXXI. 570 Huge temporary Pumpkin, saccharine, absinthian.

absinthiate (æbˈsɪnθɪeɪt), *v.* [f. L. *absinthi-um* + -ATE³.] To impregnate with wormwood.

absinthiated (æbˈsɪnθɪeɪtɪd), *ppl. a.* [f. prec. + ED.] Impregnated with wormwood.

1661 R. LOVELL *Animals & Min.* 363 The diseases of the ventricle..are cured..[by] red wine absinthiated, and exercise. **1808** MACDONALD *Telegr. Comm.* 59 The adscititious part of an absinthiated preparation. *Mod.* Absinthe properly so called is a spirit distilled from absinthiated wine.

absinthic (æbˈsɪnθɪk), *a.* *Chem.* [f. ABSINTH + -IC.] Of or belonging to absinth, as ***absinthic acid.***

1879 *Syd. Soc. Lex.*

absinthin (æbˈsɪnθɪn). *Chem.* [f. L. *absinthi-um* + -IN(E⁴.] The bitter principle of wormwood or *Artemisia Absinthium.*

1853 MAYNE. **1879** *Syd. Soc. Lex.*

absinthine (æbˈsɪnθaɪn, -ɪn). [f. L. *absinthi-um* + -INE¹.] Having the characteristics of absinth; bitter.

1865 CARLYLE *Fredk. Gt.* IV. XI. ix. 111 We must add two notes, two small absinthine drops, bitter but wholesome.

absinthism (ˈæbsɪnθɪz(ə)m). [f. ABSINTH + -ISM.] A disease resembling alcoholism, arising from the abuse of absinthe.

1879 *Syd. Soc. Lex.*

absinthium (æbˈsɪnθɪəm). *Bot.* [L.] The wormwood, *Artemisia Absinthium* of Linnæus, distinguished by its intensely bitter aromatic taste.

1398 TREVISA *Barth. De P.R.* (1495) XVII. xii. 610 Abscintiuȝ: wormode is a full sharpe herbe. **1748** *Phil. Trans.* XLV. 299 For baking and roasting they make use of Abrotanum, Absynthium, and such-like. **1792** A. YOUNG *Trav. in France* 366 Some of the absinthium and lavender, so low and poor, as hardly to be recognized.

absinthole (æbˈsɪnθəʊl). *Chem.* [f. ABSINTH + -OLE.] $C_{10}H_{16}O$. A liquid camphor obtained from the oil of wormwood.

1879 *Syd. Soc. Lex.*

absis, obs. form of APSIS.

absist, absistos, obs. forms of ASBESTOS.

†**ab'sist** (æbˈsɪst), *v.* *Obs. rare*⁻¹. [ad. L. *absistĕre* to stand off, withdraw, f. *ab* off, away, + *sist-ĕre* to stand, redupl. deriv. of *sta-re* to stand.] To withdraw, desist.

1614 RALEIGH *Hist. World* III. 74 They promised to absist from their purpose of making a war. **1731** BAILEY, Absist, to cease, leave off. **1755** JOHNSON, Absist, to stand off, to leave off.

†**ab'sistence.** *Obs.*—⁰ [f. ABSIST + -ENCE, cf. *persistence.*] 'A standing off.' Mod. Dicts.

‖**absit** (ˈæbsɪt). [L. *absit* let (him) be absent, 3rd pers. sing. pres. subj. of *abesse* to be absent.] Permission given to a student to be absent. (Cf. EXEAT.)

1884 DICKENS *Dict. Univ. Cambridge* 3/1 *Absit*, every Undergraduate wishing to leave Cambridge for a whole day, whether including a night or not, must obtain an 'absit' from his Tutor. **1920** 'TWO OF 'EM' *Guide to Camb. Univ. Life* 7 Exeats (for one night or more) and absits (for one day) may be obtained from College Tutors on producing a sufficient reason.

‖**absit omen** (ˈæbsɪt ˈəʊmən). [L., may this omen be absent, i.e. void.] May no ominous significance attach to the words.

1594 JAMES VI OF SCOTLAND *Let.* 5 June in *Lett. Eliz. & Jas. VI* (Camden Soc., 1849) 107 Quhich shall neuer be, except ye constraine me unto it, but *absit omen.* **1854** THACKERAY *Newcomes* II. xxvi. 292 *Absit omen!* I will say again. I like not the going down of yonder little yacht. **1886** *Athenæum* 20 Feb. 260/1 He says that if the Queen herself were to shoot Mr. Gladstone through the head (*absit omen!*) no court in England could take cognizance of the act. **1944**

A. L. ROWSE *English Spirit* xxix. 209 We lost the American Colonies, and had to redeem the situation by a twenty-year struggle with Revolutionary and Napoleonic France. *Absit omen!*

†**absoil, absoyle,** *v. Obs.* [a. 14 c. Fr. *absolir, absollir, absoillir*, a refashioning of OFr. *asollir, asoillir*, also *assoiler, asolier, asoler*, to ASSOIL, after L. *absolvĕre*.] = ASSOIL; to absolve.

c **1450** *Merlin* 11 He seyde unto hir, quod he, 'Thow art fulle of the deuell; how sholde I absoyle the.' **1537** *Instit. Chr. Man* 8 b, To loose and absoyle from synne all persons whiche be dewly penitent. **1548** UDAL, etc. *Erasm. Paraphr.* John viii. 11 He deliuered the aduoutresse oute of the stonecasters handes and yet did not clerely absoyle her as fautlesse.

†**absolent, absolete,** erroneous forms due to a confusion between ABSOLUTE and OBSOLETE, which latter frequently appears as *absolute* even in good writers of 6–7, while *absolute* was similarly transformed into *obsolute*. The confusion was partly due to form, partly to sense 4 of ABSOLUTE, *completed, finished*; hence, by easy transition, *done with*.

a **1550** *Sq. of Lowe Degre* 630 in Hazl. *E.P.P.* II. 47 They called hym knyght absolent. **1621** BURTON *Anat. Mel.* II. iv. I. i Their medicines absolete, and now most part rejected. **1640** WILKINS *Disc. concg. New Planet* (1684) II. 3 To think everything that is antient to be absolute. **1642** HOWELL *For. Trav.* 44 Or they are some absolet peeces reflecting happily upon the times of Cosmo de Medici. **1660** STILLINGFLEET *Irenicum* (1662) I. vi. §6. 121 Either in reviving absolete customes, or imposing new. **1679** OATES *Myst. Iniq.* 10 These..labour to reduce their Society to an obsolute Monarchy. **1687** SETTLE *Reflect. on Dryden's Plays* 7 How many times he uses that damn'd canting absolete word [Host] for Army in one Play.

absolute (ˈæbsəljuːt), *a.* [a. mid. Fr. *absolut* (mod. *absolu*), a 14th c. latinizing of OFr. *asolu, assolu*:—L. *absolūt-um* loosened, free, separate, acquitted, completed, etc.; pa. pple. of *absolvĕre*: see ABSOLVE. The senses were largely taken in 6–7 direct from L., in which the development of meaning had already taken place, so that they do not form a historical series in Eng.] Originally a *pple.* absolved, disengaged: then *adj.* disengaged or free from imperfection or qualification; from interference, connexion, relation, comparison, dependence; from condition, conditional forms of knowledge or thought. Formerly compared *absoluter, -est*.

I. Detached, disengaged, unfettered.

†**1.** *pple.* Absolved, loosened, detached, disengaged (*from*). *Obs.*

c **1374** CHAUCER *Boethius* 175 Men sen it vtterly fre and absolut from alle necessite.

†**2.** Disengaged from all interrupting causes, untrammelled; hence, completely absorbed *in* any occupation. *Obs.*

1483 CAXTON *G. Leg.* 197/1 She abode there as recluse.. absolute in wakyng, in prayers, in fastynges and orysons.

†**3.** Disengaged from all accidental or special circumstances; essential, general. *Obs.*

1398 TREVISA *Barth. de Pr. R.* (1495) I. 5 The fader, the son, the holy ghost be thre persones by personall proprytees, but thabsolute propritees be comune to all thre persones.

II. Absolute in quality or degree; perfect.

4. Free from all imperfection or deficiency; complete, finished; perfect, consummate.

c **1374** CHAUCER *Boethius* 89 For þe nature of þinges ne token nat her bygynnyng of þinges amenused and inperfit, but it procediþ of þingus þat ben al hool, and absolut. **1550** BULLINGER in Strype's *Eccl. Mem.* II. 407 The most wise and absolute counsils. **1579** LYLY *Euphues* 123 A young man so absolute, as yat nothing may be added to his further perfection. **1602** CAREW *Cornwall* 62 Captaine Hender, the absolutest man of war for precise obseruing martiall rules. **1603** SHAKS. *Meas. for M.* v. i. 44 As shie, as graue, as iust, as absolute: As Angelo. **1615** SANDYS *Travels* 207 Where mariners be English: who are the absolutest vnder heauen in their profession. **1627** FELTHAM *Resolves* (1677) I. xxvi. 46 It is not to any man given, absolutely to be absolute. **1643** PRYNNE *Sov. Pow. Parl.* Ded. A ii. b, One person of the exquisitest judgement,..deepest Policy, absolutest abilities. **1705** STANHOPE *Paraph.* I. 49 The most absolute and perfect of all examples. **1875** RUSKIN *Lect. on Art* III. 69 Two great masters of the absolute art of language, Virgil and Pope.

5. a. Of degree: Complete, entire; in the fullest sense.

1574 tr. *Marlorat's Apocalips* 40 From whence should we fetch the rule of absolute perfection. **1592** GREENE in *Shaksp. Cent. Praise* 2 Being an absolute *Johannes fac totum*. **1641** MILTON *Ch. Discip.* (1851) I. 32 The honour of its absolute sufficiency. **1664** DR. H. POWER *Exp. Philos.* I. 3 These holes were not absolute perforations, but onley dimples. **1678** CUDWORTH *Intell. Syst.* 897 Which yet is an Absolute Impossibility. **1792** *Anec. of Pitt* III. xliii. 154 The absolute necessity for making peace with America. **1862** A. TROLLOPE *Orley Farm* xvi. 127 This may with absolute strictness be the case. **1878** G. MACDONALD *Ann. Quiet Neighb.* xviii. 356 Leaving me in absolute ignorance of how to interpret her.

†**b.** *spec.* Of numbers, parts: complete. (Cf. Plin. *Ep.* 9. 38 *liber numeris omnibus absolutus*, a book complete in all its parts.) *Obs.*

1623 HEMINGE & CONDELL *Pref. Shakesp.*, All the rest, absolute in their numbers, as he conceiued them. **1667** MILTON *P.L.* VIII. 421 And through all numbers absolute, though One.

c. Of a decree or rule: see DECREE *sb.* 4 b, RULE *sb.* 4 a.

1836, 1860 [see NISI]. **1922** JOYCE *Ulysses* 638 Then the decree *nisi* and the King's Proctor to show cause why and, he failing to quash it, *nisi* was made absolute.

6. Pure and simple, mere; in the strictest sense. ***absolute alcohol***, *i.e.* perfectly free from water.

1563 *Homilies* (1640) II. xxi. II. 286 David was no common or absolute subject. **1677** HALES *Prim. Orig. Man.* I. vi. 118 Duration without a thing that dureth..is the veriest, the absolutest Nothing that can be. **1688** CLAYTON in *Phil. Trans.* XVII. 989 The Fishing Hauk is an absolute Species of a Kings-fisher. **1693** —— in *Misc. Cur.* (1708) III. 340 Musk-Rats, an absolute Species of Water-Rats, only having a curious Musky scent. **1834** E. TURNER *Elem. Chem.* 877 The strongest alcohol..is called absolute alcohol, to denote its entire freedom from water. **1847** L. HUNT *Men, Wom. & Bks.* II. I. 8 The absolutest, and sometimes loathsomest, trash. **1871** B. STEWART *Heat* §26 To register still lower temperatures..a thermometer filled with Absolute Alcohol is employed.

III. Absolute or detached in position or relation; independent.

7. Of ownership, authority: Free from all external restraint or interference; unrestricted, unlimited, independent. ***absolute prize***, one which becomes the absolute property of the winner, as distinguished from a *challenge* cup, etc. held till competed for anew.

1533 TINDALE *Sup. of the Lord* 30 To dispute of God's almighty absolute power,..is great folly and no less presumption. **1576** LAMBARDE *Peramb. Kent* (1826) 263 The Bishops were never absolute owners heereof, till the time of King William Rufus. **1630** PRYNNE *Anti-Arm.* 115 It makes man an absolute, an independent creature. **1695** *Anct. Const. Eng.* 19 As for the King..he hath not absolute unlimited power of doing whatever he will. **1738** WESLEY *Psalms* (1765) 89 Possest of absolute Command, Thou Truth and Mercy dost maintain. **1861** *Times*, 10 July, Lord Spencer offered an absolute prize cup worth 20*l.*, to be competed for at 500 yards by the best shot of each of the three schools. **1862** H. SPENCER *First Princ.* (1875) I. ii.§12. 38 Thus the first cause must be in every sense perfect, complete, total: including within itself all power, and transcending all law, Or to use the established word, it must be absolute.

8. Hence, having absolute power, governing absolutely; unlimited by a constitution or the concurrent authority of a parliament; arbitrary, despotic.

1612 DRAYTON *Poly-olbion* xi. 178 Nor could time euer bring In all the seauen-fold rule an absoluter King. **1625** BACON *Ess.* xix. 80 To depresse them [nobles] may make a King more Absolute, but less safe. **1735–8** LD. BOLINGBROKE *Dissn. on Parties* 160 Absolute Monarchy is Tyranny; but absolute Democracy is Tyranny and Anarchy both. **1756** BURKE *Vind. Nat. Soc.* Wks. I. 46 Republicks have many things in the spirit of absolute monarchy. **1775** SHERIDAN *Reading* 353 Our constitution is made up of a due mixture of the three species of government, being partly monarchical, partly republican, and partly absolute. **1876** FREEMAN *Norm. Conq.* I. iii. 114 An able king is practically absolute.

9. Standing out of (the usual) grammatical relation or syntactic construction with other words, as in the ***ablative absolute***. The ***absolute form*** of a word: that in which it is not inflected to indicate relation to other words in a sentence. Also ***absolute clause, comparative, construction, superlative***.

¶The absolute case in English was formerly the Dative or Instrumental: it is now the Nominative.

1527 WHITINTON *Vulg.* 3 Somtyme it is put in the case of the ablatyue case absolute. **1594** BLUNDEVIL *Exerc.* (ed. 7) I. xvi. 41 The Absolute [Numbers] are simply pronounced without having any relation to any other number, measure, or quantity, as 2, 3, 4, &c. **1612** BRINSLEY *Pos. Parts* (1669) 77 The Ablative case absolute. What mean you by absolute? A. Without other government. **1751** HARRIS *Hermes* (1841) 142 All existence is either absolute or qualified: absolute, as when we say, B is; qualified, as when we say, B is an animal. **1859** SIR W. HAMILTON *Metaphysic* II. xxxvi. 330 The child commences, like the savage, by employing only isolated words in place of phrases; he commences by taking verbs and nouns only in their absolute state. **1862** E. ADAMS *Elements Eng. Lang.* (ed. 2) 178 This A.S. dative was the origin of the *absolute* construction in English. **1889** M. CALLAWAY *Absol. Pple. in Anglo-Saxon* vii. 51 The notions usually expressed by an absolute clause in Latin are habitually denoted otherwise in Anglo-Saxon. *Ibid.* The absolute construction is not an organic idiom of the Anglo-Saxon language. **1904** ONIONS *Adv. Eng. Syntax* §61a, Absolute Clauses are clauses in which the Predicate is formed with a Participle instead of a Finite Verb, and which are equivalent in meaning to Adverb Clauses of Time, Reason, Condition, or Concession, or to an Adverbial Phrase expressing Attendant Circumstance. *Ibid.* §61b, The Absolute construction seems in all periods to have been felt to be foreign to the genius of English. **1931** CURME *Syntax* 508 The absolute comparative is not as common as the absolute superlative..*higher* education; a *better*-class café.

10. Viewed without relation to, or comparison with, other things of the same kind; considered only in its relation to space or existence as a whole, or to some permanent standard; real, actual; opposed to *relative* and *comparative*.

¶***Superlative absolute***, that which expresses a *very high* degree of quality, as distinct from stating that it is the highest of a set compared together (*Superlative relative*).

1666 BOYLE in *Phil. Trans.* I. 239 The Absolute or Comparative height of mountains. **1753** JOHNSON *Adventurer* No. 3 Wks. 1787 IX. 110 We find in it absolute misery, but happiness only comparative. **1785** REID *Intell. Pow. Man* 293 This space therefore which is unlimited and immoveable, is called by Philosophers absolute space. **1822** IMISON *Sci. & Art* I. 447 Absolute motion is the actual motion that bodies have, independent of each other, and only with regard to the parts of space. **1878** HUXLEY *Physiogr.* 68 It is not so much the absolute quantity of moisture in the air as its relative humidity.

IV. Free from condition or mental limitation; unconditioned.

†**11.** Of persons and things: Free from all doubt or uncertainty; positive, perfectly certain, decided. Sometimes *adv.* positively. *Obs.*

1603 SHAKS. *Meas. for M.* III. i. 5 Be absolute for death. **1604** ROWLANDS *Looke to It* 14 Thou that wilt vow most absolute to know, That which thy conscience knowes thou neuer knew. **1611** SHAKS. *Cymb.* IV. ii. 106 I am absolute 'Twas very Cloten. **1662** R. MATHEW *Unl. Alch.*§92. 160 He would warrant my recovery..he commended it as one of the most absolute things in the World. **1676** COTTRELL *Cassandra* VI. 561 'Twill suffice to confirm me absolute in the opinion I have of thy Vertue.

12. a. Of statements: Free from conditions or reservations; unreserved, unqualified, unconditional.

1625–49 CHARLES I. *Wks.* 294 My thoughts were sincere and absolute without any sinister ends. **1664** H. MORE *Myst. Iniq.* 89 That it is not an Absolute, Inconditionate Promise to the Whole is plain. **1736** BUTLER *Anal.* II. vii. 363 Some of these promises are conditional, some are as absolute, as anything can be expressed. **1832** J. AUSTIN *Lect. Jurispr.* (1879) I. xii. 357 Where an obligation is absolute there is no right with which it correlates.

b. *esp.* in *Logic.*

1736 BUTLER *Anal.* I. vi. 104 The Question..is not absolute,..but hypothetical. **1860** THOMSON *Laws of Thought* 297 With the exception of the last case it would be impossible to frame an absolute proposition. **1870** BOWEN *Logic* V. 127 In respect to the Relation of the Predicate to the Subject, Judgments are divided into simple or absolute, and conditional.

13. *Metaph.* Existing without relation to any other being; self-existent; self-sufficing.

1858 MANSEL *Bamp. Lect.* (ed. 4) ii. 30 By the Absolute is meant that which exists in and by itself, having no necessary relation to any other being. **1869** J. MARTINEAU *Ess.* II. 269 Schelling has vindicated the possibility of knowing the absolute. **1875** H. E. MANNING *Holy Ghost* xii. 325 There has sprung up..a school of men who tell us that the Absolute is unknowable, and that we can therefore know nothing of God.

14. *Metaph.* Capable of being thought or conceived by itself alone; unconditioned.

1853 SIR W. HAMILTON *Discuss.* App. I. To Cusa we can indeed articulately trace, word and thing, the recent philosophy of the Absolute. **1856** FERRIER *Inst. Metaph.* 370 Whatever can be known (or conceived) out of relation, that is to say, without any correlative being necessarily known (or conceived) along with it, is the known Absolute. *Ibid.* (ed. 2) 10 Another phantom is a mask, or rather a whole toy-shop of masks, which philosophers have been pleased to call the 'Absolute'; but what they exactly mean by this name—what it is that is under these trappings,—neither those who run down the incognito, nor those who speak it fair, have ever condescended to inform us.

15. *Metaphys.* Considered independently of its being subjective or objective.

1809–10 COLERIDGE *Friend* (ed. 3) III. 212 The absolute is neither singly that which affirms, nor that which is affirmed; but the identity and living copula of both. **1858** R. A. VAUGHAN *Ess. & Rev.* I. 57 Schelling pronounced the subject and object identical in the absolute. **1860** —— *Ho. w. Myst.* (ed. 2) I. 213 Shake off that dream of personality, and you will see that good and evil are identical in the Absolute.

¶In the last three uses the word approaches the character of a substantive, as the name of a metaphysical conception: ***the Absolute***, i.e. that which is absolute.

16. In specific combinations with sbs., as ***absolute contraband, drought, initials, majority, zero***, etc. (see the sbs.); also **absolute address** *Computing*, an actual address, as determined by the hardware of a computer; an address expressed in machine language; cf. *relative address* s.v. RELATIVE *a.* 9; **absolute altitude** *Aeronaut.*, the altitude of an aircraft above the surface of the earth over which it is flying; hence ***absolute altimeter, height***; **absolute ceiling** *Aeronaut.* (see quot. 1950; cf. CEILING *vbl. sb.* 6 b); **absolute error**, the difference between the actual value of a measurement or other quantity and the number that is assigned to it; **absolute humidity** (see quot. 1946); **absolute magnitude** *Astr.*, the magnitude of a star if at a standard distance of 10 parsecs; **absolute music**, self-dependent instrumental music without literary or other extraneous suggestions (opp. *programme music*); hence ***absolute musician***; **absolute pitch** *Mus.*, (*a*) a fixed standard of pitch determined by the rate of vibration (see PITCH *sb.*[2] 23); (*b*) used of the ability to recognize or reproduce the pitch of a note; **absolute temperature** *Physics*, temperature calculated from the scale associated with the thermodynamic experiments of Lord Kelvin (1824–1907), and based on an absolute zero (see ZERO *sb.* 3) of approx. −273·16°C.; hence ***absolute (temperature) scale***; **absolute unit** (see quot. 1940); **absolute value** *Math.*, (*a*) of a real number, its value irrespective of its sign

—called also *numerical value*, or *modulus*; (*b*) of any complex number $x + iy$, the positive square root of $x^2 + y^2$—called also *modulus* (Webster, 1934) (see MODULUS 2c).

[**1949** *Math. Tables & other Aids Computation* III. 541 The provision of extra binary digits in the coding as an indication of whether the corresponding address is to be taken as an absolute location in the memory [etc.].] **1951** *Ibid.* V. 234 An *absolute address is interpreted in the usual sense merely as a number identifying a specific memory location. **1956** Absolute address [see *relative address* s.v. RELATIVE *a.* 9]. **1970** O. DOPPING *Computers & Data Processing* xix. 308 In an object program, every data cell is identified by means of its absolute address which is irrelevant to the problem and difficult for the programmer to remember. **1983** *Your Computer* (Austral.) Aug. 25/1 If a program is edited, all the absolute addresses are changed. **1941** *Aeronautics* Mar. 65/2 **Absolute altimeter*. The instrument operates through a radio transmitter which.. sends out a radio wave so that it is reflected back from the earth... The elapsed time for the circuit of the wave is converted into absolute altitude. **1934** *Aircraft Engin.* June 162/2 '*Absolute altitude' seems a curiously pretentious, and indeed misleading, term for the height of an aircraft above the earth. **1920** *Flight* 9 Sept. 980/2 Characteristics of the Martin torpedo 'plane are: *Absolute ceiling.. 10,000 ft. **1950** *Gloss. Aeronaut. Terms* (*B.S.I.*) I. 25 *Absolute ceiling*, the height at which the rate of climb of an aircraft would be zero in standard atmosphere under specified conditions. **1923** GLAZEBROOK *Dict. Appl. Physics* IV. 580/2 (*heading*) *Absolute, relative, and proportional errors. **1968** FOX & MAYERS *Computing Methods for Scientists & Engineers* iii. 45 It is *not*, however, connected with the corresponding *growth* of absolute *error* in the trial solutions. **1980** C. S. FRENCH *Computer Sci.* xxi. 127 Relative error = Absolute error/True Value. **1936** *Aircraft Engin.* Nov. 298/2 We cannot help wishing it were possible to define an *absolute height akin to absolute temperature. **1867** A. BUCHAN *Handy Bk. Meteorol.* 93 It may also be termed the *absolute humidity of the atmosphere. **1946** *Humidity of the Air* (*B.S.I.*) 3 *Absolute humidity*, the weight of water vapour present in unit volume of moist air, i.e. grains per cubic foot or grams per cubic metre. **1902** J. C. KAPTEYN in *Pbns. Kapteyn Astron. Lab.* No. 11, p. 12 We further define the **absolute magnitude* (*M*) of a star..as the apparent magnitude which that star would have if it was transferred to a distance from the sun corresponding to a parallax of 0″·1. **1914** A. S. EDDINGTON *Stellar Movements* viii. 170 Absolute magnitudes (magnitude at a distance of 10 parsecs). **1890** G. B. SHAW *London Music 1888–89* (1937) 329 The first sign of a reaction in favor of abstract or '*absolute' music against the great Wagnerian cult of tone poetry and music drama. **1895** —— *Sanity of Art* (1908) 28 Instrumental music.. designed to affect the hearer solely by its beauty of sound and grace and ingenuity of pattern. This is the art which Wagner called absolute music. **1946** BACHARACH *Brit. Mus.* iii. 53 All the same *The Planets* are in no sense programme music. One must accept them as seven pieces of 'absolute' music. **1880** GROVE *Dict. Mus.* II. 129/2 Instances of a similar kind from the works even of the most '*absolute' musicians might be multiplied *ad libitum*. **1864** A. J. ELLIS in *Proc. R. Soc.* XIII. 394 A compound tone will be represented by the *absolute pitch of its primary and the relative pitches of its partial tones. **1903** R. HUGHES *Mus. Guide* I. 239/2 The vibration-number of a tone also gives it an absolute pitch according to the particular pitch accepted as the standard. **1914** A. EAGLEFIELD HULL *Mod. Harmony* iv. 51 If the possession of the sense of absolute pitch is a *sine quâ non* for the proper reception of such music, then the circle of appreciation at present is narrowed down almost to vanishing-point. **1938** *Oxf. Compan. Mus.* 2/2 Sir Frederick Ouseley.. was all his life remarkable for his sense of absolute pitch. At five he was able to remark, 'Only think, papa blows his nose in G'. **1848** W. THOMSON [LORD KELVIN] in *Phil. Mag.* XXXIII. 316 The characteristic property of the scale which I now propose is, that all degrees have the same value; that is, that a unit of heat descending from a body A at the temperature T° of this scale, to a body B at the temperature (T − 1)°, would give out the same mechanical effect, whatever be the number T. This may justly be termed an *absolute scale, since its characteristic is quite independent of the physical properties of any specific substance. **1852** J. P. JOULE in *Phil. Trans. R. Soc.* I. 67, I take.. a case in which the receiver C contains air of the atmospheric density, and of which the *absolute temperature is 849°·464 Fahr. or 390°·464 on the scale of Fahrenheit's thermometer. **1857** W. THOMSON in *Trans. R. Soc. Edin. 1854* XXI. 125 The determination of the absolute temperatures of the fixed points is then to be effected by means of observations indicating the economy of a perfect thermo-dynamic engine, with the higher and the lower respectively as the temperatures of its source and refrigerator. **1884** Absolute temperature [see LAW *sb.*[1] 17c(*b*)]. **1958** MANSFIELD *Element. Nucl. Physics* I. 2 The absolute temperature scale.. is related to the speed *c* of the molecules such that at absolute zero.. all molecules are at rest. **1857** *Proc. R. Soc. Edin. 1851* 97 Taking ·02 as the electro-chemical equivalent of water in British *absolute units, the author has thus found 16300 as the electromotive force of an element of copper and bismuth. **1873** *First Rep. Brit. Assoc. Comm. Selection Dynam. & Electr. Units* §7, We accordingly recommend the general adoption of the *Centimetre*, the *Gramme* and the *Second* as the three fundamental units; and.. that they be distinguished from 'absolute' units otherwise derived, by the letters 'C.G.S.' prefixed. **1940** *Chambers's Techn. Dict.* 3/1 *Absolute unit*, a unit which may be defined directly in terms of the fundamental units of length, mass, and time. **1907** O. VEBLEN *Introd. Infinites. Analysis* 14 The symbol $|x|$ .. indicates the 'numerical' or '*absolute' value of x. **1909** *Cent. Dict.* Suppl. (s.v. *number*), *Absolute value of a complex number*, $x = a + bi$, is $+ (a^2 + b^2)^{\frac{1}{2}}$: denoted by $|x|$. *Absolute value of a real number*, *a*, its value taken positively: denoted by $|a|$. **1930** DURELL & ROBSON *Adv. Trigonom.* 145, *r* is called the modulus, or sometimes the *absolute value*, of the complex number $x + yi$ and is denoted by $|x + yi|$ or by mod $(x + yi)$. **1931** P. DIENES *Taylor Series* 48 We call the positive number $|\sqrt{a^2 + b^2}| = |a + bi|$ the absolute value or modulus of $a + bi$.

absolutely ('æbsəlju:tlɪ), *adv.* [f. prec. + -LY[2].] In an absolute position, manner, or degree.

I. Separately, independently.

1. In a manner detached from other things; without the existence or presence of anything else; separately, independently.

1532 MORE *Confut. Tindale* Wks. 1557, 450/2 Yf he speke of hym absolutly, without mencion of any speache before hadde wyth hym. **1603** HOLLAND *Plutarch's Mor.* 67 Of all things then that be in the world, some have their essence and being of themselves absolutely and simply. **1618** BP. HALL *Serm.* v. 121 Nothing is, nothing lives absolutely, but he; all other things, by participation from him. **1736** BUTLER *Anal.* (1807) Introd. 3 It cannot but be discerned absolutely as it is in itself. **1877** E. CONDER *Bas. Faith* iv. 146 We may say that God exists absolutely, or is the Absolute Being, if we are careful to explain that we oppose 'absolute' to 'dependent.' God alone has being in Himself. But 'absolute existence,' if we do not explain what kind of existence we are speaking of, is a phrase absolutely without meaning.

†**2.** Essentially. *Obs.*

1661 BRAMHALL *Just. Vind.* ii. 9 If one part of the Universall Church do separate itself from another part, not absolutely, or in Essentials, but respectively.

3. With unrestricted or unlimited ownership or authority; despotically.

1612 DRAYTON *Poly-olbion* v. 75 Now Sabrine, as a Queene, miraculouslie faire Is absolutelie plac't in her Emperiall Chaire. **1660** *Trial of the Reg.* 11 It is one.. thing to have an Imperial Crown and another thing to govern absolutely. **1875** MAINE *Hist. Inst.* ix. 254 The spear [was] the symbol of property held absolutely and against the world.

4. Without the addition of any qualification, logical or grammatical. *Gram.* Without the usual construction, as when an adjective is used without a substantive, or a transitive verb without an object expressed.

1656 tr. *Hobbes's Elem. Phil.* (1839) 113 As magnitude is by philosophers taken absolutely for extension, so also velocity or swiftness may be put absolutely for motion according to length. **1668** CULPEPER & COLE *Bartholinus' Anat.* II. Introd. 85 The middle Venter or Belly termed Thorax the Chest, and by some absolutely Venter. **1766** BOSWELL *Johnson* (1816) II. 21 You seem to use genus absolutely, for what we call family. *Mod.* In 'the public are informed,' 'the young are invited,' *public* and *young* are adjectives used absolutely.

5. Viewed by itself, without reference to, or comparison with, others. Opposed to *comparatively* or *relatively*.

1635 N. CARPENTER *Geog. Del.* I. v. 117 The Globe of the Earth may bee considered either Absolutely in it selfe, or Comparatively in respect of the Heauenly Bodyes. **1651** BAXTER *Inf. Bapt.* 11 Though none be small absolutely, yet many are very small in comparison of greater. **1874** MOTLEY *Barneveld* I. i. 8 Somewhat larger resources absolutely, though not relatively, than the Seven Provinces.

II. Without doubt or condition.

†**6.** Certainly, positively. *Obs.*

1489 CAXTON *Fayt of Armes* IV. x. 257 Noon oughte to swere absolutly for a thinge but that by his owne eyen he be sure and certeyn that it is soo. **1612** BRINSLEY *Lud. Lit.* (1627) xxi. 249 This helpes memory.. to have the text most absolutely.

7. Without condition or limitation; unconditionally, unreservedly.

1644 QUARLES *Judgm. & Mercy* 276 Though life be not absolutely granted, yet death is but conditionally threatened. **1724** A. COLLINS *Gr. Chr. Relig.* 69 Tho' absolutely speaking, the promise of the Messias might be fulfilled without it, yet hypothetically it could not. **1876** GROTE *Eth. Frag.* 162 Absolutely—not under limitation.

8. Actually, positively, as a simple fact. (Qualifying the truth of the statement rather than the fact stated.)

1851 HELPS *Friends in C.* I. 3 He was absolutely endeavouring to invent some new method for proving something that had been proved before in a hundred ways. **1853** KANE *Grinnell Exped.* (1856) xlvii. 432 Three young ladies of the half-breed, absolutely with frocks on. **1863** KEMBLE *Resid. Georgia* 59 She absolutely embraced him.

III. Of manner and degree: Completely, perfectly.

9. In a way that clears off everything; conclusively, finally, completely, unreservedly.

1597 SHAKS. *2 Hen. IV*, IV. i. 164 To heare, and absolutely to determine. **1603** —— *Meas. for M.* IV. ii. 225 This shall absolutely resolue you. **1656** BRAMHALL *Replic.* v. 194 They refused absolutely to submit. **1667** MILTON *P.L.* IX. 1159 Why didst not thou, the head, Command me absolutely not to go. **1758** S. HAYWARD *Serm.* v. 141 Many absolutely deny Deity to the Son. **1817** JAS. MILL *Brit. India* II. v. iv. 448 Absolutely to strip them of their dominions.

†**10.** Perfectly; in the most excellent manner. *Obs.*

1601 HOLLAND *Pliny* (1634) I. 222 Most elegantly and absolutely described by the Poet Virgill.

11. a. To the fullest extent, in the highest or utmost degree; entirely, wholly, altogether, quite.

1570 DEE *Math. Praef.* That they may be very absolutely skillfull. **1602** WARNER *Albion's Eng.* Epit. 390 (1612) A Prince absolutely valorous and vertuous. **1635** N. CARPENTER *Geog. Delin.* I. ii. 37 The earth is not absolutely and geometrically round. **1676** EARL ORRERY *Parth.* 24 Which I have now as absolutely forgotten. **a 1704** T. BROWN *1st Sat. Persius* (1730) I. 52 Surely, Jack, thou'rt absolutely mad. **1790** BURKE *Fr. Rev.* Wks. V. 117 Rendering our whole government absolutely illegitimate. **1820** SCOTT *Monast.* ii. 409 The glen.. was not absolutely void of beauty. **1834** MISS MITFORD in L'Estrange's *Life* III. ii. 14 My going to town to spend money is absolutely out of the question. **1855** MACAULAY *Hist. Eng.* III. 55 It was absolutely necessary that he should quit London. **1860** TYNDALL *Glaciers* I. §10. 66 Escape seemed absolutely impossible. **1862** STANLEY *Jewish Ch.* (1877) I. vii. 131 He was to come absolutely alone.

b. with a *sb.* In the strictest sense.

1649 MILTON *Eikonokl.* 145 To be absolutely a tyrant. **1879** DAVIDSON in *Cassell's Tech. Educ.* I. 163 Not professors in name only, but absolutely professional men of the highest position.

c. emphasizing *no*, *nothing*.

1726 BUTLER *Serm. Rolls Chap.* II. 43 There is absolutely no bound at all to prophaneness. **1849** MACAULAY *Hist. Eng.* II. 195 A man who had absolutely no claim to high place except that he was a Papist. **1865** MILL *Liberty* iii. 33/2 That people should do absolutely nothing but copy one another. **1876** FREEMAN *Norm. Conq.* I. iii. 106 The King could do absolutely nothing without the consent of his Wise Men. **1878** HUXLEY *Physiogr.* 40 You would see absolutely nothing in the space above the boiling water.

d. Also *ellipt.*; *colloq.* (orig. *U.S.*), used as an emphatic affirmative: yes, quite so. (Stressed *abso'lutely*.)

1892 'MARK TWAIN' *Amer. Claimant* xxiv. 154 'Do you mean to say that if he was all right and proper otherwise you'd be indifferent about the earl part of the business?' 'Absolutely.' **1917** A. WAUGH *Loom of Youth* III. i. 154 'But, sir, was it true to Harrow life?' 'Absolutely; and it's as true to the life of any other Public School.' **1922** JOYCE *Ulysses* 720 Was the narration otherwise unaltered by modifications? Absolutely. **1937** R. STOUT *Red Box* ix. 136 'I trust that we are still brothers-in-arms?—' 'Absolutely. Pals.'

¶ For additional emphasis, *bally* and similar words are sometimes inserted medially in slang use, as *abso-bally-lutely*.

1914 W. L. GEORGE *Making of an Englishman* III. v. 299 Oh, don'tcher care, it's all over, absoballylutely. **1924** C. HAMILTON *Prisoners of Hope* ii. 56 All I ask is that you'll.. let me go on to hit the sheets. I'm absoballylootly all in. **1929** KIPLING *Limits & Renewals* (1932) 367 'Did it cure him?' I asked.. 'Ab-so-bally-lutely,' said Keede. **1935** E. WEEKLEY *Something about Words* i. 24 This natural tendency to add body and content to words is possibly prehistoric... A crude example of this persisting instinct is offered by the contemporary *abso-bloody-lutely*.

absoluteness ('æbsəlju:tnɪs). [f. ABSOLUTE + -NESS.] The quality of being absolute (in various senses of the adj.).

†**1.** The quality of being complete or finished; completeness, perfection. *Obs.*

1570 DEE *Math. Præf.* 16 The puritie, absolutenes.. of Principall Geometrie. **1574** ABP. WHITGIFT *Def. Answ.* Tract i. Wks. 1851 I. 173 The canonical scriptures are of that absoluteness and perfection that nothing may be taken away from them, nothing added to them. **1633** BP. HALL *Hard T.* 137 He findes not any such stability or absoluteness in his very Angels. **1692** BP. SOUTH *12 Serm.* (1697) I. 36 There is nothing that can raise a man to that generous absoluteness of condition.

†**2.** Independence. *Obs.*

1605 BACON *Adv. Learn.* II. 35 He pretended not to make any newe Philosophie, yet did vse the absolutenesse of his owne sense vpon the olde. **1652** P. STERRY *Eng. Deliv. North. Presb.* Pref., Giving them a more Excellent Being in this Relative State and Subordination, than they had in their absolutenesse.

3. Unlimited or unrestrained authority; arbitrary rule.

1614 RALEIGH *Hist. World.* II. 439 Monarches need not to feare any curbing of their absoluteness by mighty subjects, as long as by wisedome they keepe the heartes of the people. **1633** BP. HALL *Hard T.* 513 Alexander of Macedon.. shall rule very powerfully and with great freedom and absoluteness. **1728** MORGAN *Hist. Algiers* I. vi. 195 His brother and predecessor laid the foundation of that absoluteness. **1854** KINGSLEY *Alexandria* iv. 158 Their belief in God's omnipotence and absoluteness dwindled into the most dark, and slavish, and benumbing fatalism.

4. Freedom from conditions; unconditional quality; unreservedness.

1651 BAXTER *Inf. Bapt* 299 The excellency of the mercy promised, rather than any absoluteness in the promise. **1674** HICKMAN *Hist. Quinquart.* (ed. 2) 31 God's Decree, and the absoluteness or conditionality thereof. **1699** BURNET *39 Articles* (1700) xvii. 149 In the main points, the Absoluteness of the Decree, the Extent of Christ's Death, the Efficacy of Grace, and the Certainty of Perseverance, their opinions are the same.

5. Unconditioned or independent existence.

1864 KINGSLEY *Rom. & Teut.* (1875) iii. 68 Thus denying the absoluteness.. the illimitability, by any category of quantity, of that one Eternal.

6. Positiveness, actuality; independent or objective reality.

1678 CUDWORTH *Intell. Syst.* 719 Sense considered alone by itself doth not reach to the Absoluteness either of the Natures, or of the Existence of things without us, it being as such, nothing but Seeming, Appearance, and Phancy. **1856** R. A. VAUGHAN *Ho. w. Myst.* I. v. ii. 169 To gaze on the Divine Nature in its absoluteness and abstraction, apart from the manifestation of it to our intellect, our heart, and our imagination.

¶ Catachr. for *obsoleteness*. (See ABSOLENT.)

1612 BREREWOOD *Ess. Lang. & Rel.* vi. 52 The Verses of the Salii.. could hardly be understood.. in the latter time of the Commonwealth, for the absoluteness of the Speech.

absolution (æbsə'lju:ʃən). Also 3 **absoluciun**, 3–6 **-cion**, 4–5 **-cioun**, **-coun**, **-tioun**, 5 **-tyoun**, 5–6 **-cyon**, **-tyon**, 6– **-tion**. [a. Fr. *absolution*, ad. L. *absolūtiōn-em* n. of action, f. *absolv-ere* to absolve. In its ecclesiastical sense, in early popular use in Fr. and Eng.]

1. *gen.* An absolving, discharging, or formal setting free (*from* guilt, sentence, or obligation); remission (*of* sin or penance).

c **1400** *Apol. for Lollards* 19 Schakyng a wey synne from him be absolucoun of sacrament, and mekly taking a noþer absolucoun of iurisdiccoun of him þat cursid. **1447** *Lyvys of Seyntys* (1835) 49 Whan thou hast get an absolucyon Of this curs and hast fecundyte. **1538** STARKEY *England* 124 Hys powar..extendyth only to the absolutyon of syn. **1638** KNOLLES *Hist. Turkes* (ed. 5) 50 He..procured of the bishops a general absolution for them all, from the oath of obedience which they had before giuen unto the Emperor. *c* **1850** FABER *Hymn* 'Sweet Saviour bless us,' Grant us, dear Lord, from evil ways True absolution and release. **1875** STUBBS *Const. Hist.* II. xiv. 155 He..applied for a bull of absolution from the oaths so lately taken.

2. *spec.* Remission or forgiveness of sins declared by ecclesiastical authority. (*The earliest use.*)

c **1200** *Trin. Coll. Hom.* 95 Shereðuresdaies absolucion þe liðe þe sinne bendes. *Ibid.* 99 Cumen..a palm sunedai to procession, a shereðursdai to absoluciun, a lange-fridai to holi cruche. *a* **1384** WYCLIF *Antecrist and his Meynee* 153 False absoluciouns bouȝt at þe court of Roome. *c* **1400** *Rom. Rose* 7700 Kneele doune anon, And you shal have absolucioun. *a* **1520** *Myrroure of Our Lady* 39 Trew shryfte of mouthe with absolucion folowyng lyghtyth moche a soulle. **1558** BP. WATSON *Seven Sacr.* xxx. 192 Fyrst to confesse hym selfe and receyue the Sacrament of Absolution. **1638** *Penit. Conf.* (1657) vii. 128 Without Confession to a Priest no absolution. **1704** NELSON *Festiv. & Fasts* (1739) II. iv. 494 The Priest..with a loud voice did proclaim publick Absolution. **1809** BRYDONE *Sicily* xxxiv. 330 This is the first mortal sin, for which there is neither atonement nor absolution, 'to lie with a nun, and yet not be in orders.' **1851** LONGF. *Gol. Leg.* VI. i. After confession, after absolution, When my whole soul was white I prayed for them. **1852** F. W. ROBERTSON *Serm.* (Ser. IV. 1863) xxxvii. 281 Absolution is the authoritative declaration of forgiveness.

b. The formula declaring sins to be remitted.

a **1520** *Myrroure of Our Ladye* 101 After Pater Noster foloweth an Absolucyon, that is as moche to say as a losynge fro or a fredome. **1660** R. COKE *Power & Subj.* 90 But a Deacon cannot consecrate the Sacrament, pronounce absolution nor benediction. **1662** *Bk. of Comm. Prayer* (Rubric) The Absolution or Remission of Sins, To be pronounced by the Priest alone, standing.

3. Remission of penance or other ecclesiastical sentence.

a **1674** CLARENDON'S *Hist. Rebel.* I. II. 86 To restrain any Excommunication from being pronounced, or Absolution from being given, without the approbation of the Bishop. **1726** AYLIFFE *Parergon* 18 The word Absolution..in the Canon-Law, and among Divines, is not only used to denote an Acquittal or Discharge of a man..but it likewise signifies a Relaxation of him from the obligation of some sentence pronounced either in a Court of Law, or else in Foro Pœnitentiali. And thus there is in this Law one kind of Absolution, which is term'd Judicial; and another, which is styled a Declaratory or Extra-Judicial Absolution.

4. Forgiveness of offences generally.

1330 R. BRUNNE *Chron.* 215 þou may fulle lightly haf absolutioun, For it was a gilery, þou knew not þer tresoun. *c* **1340** *Gawayne & Gr. Knt.* 1882 And of absolucioun he on þe segge calles. **1393** GOWER *Conf.* III. 372 Touchende my confession, I axe an absolution Of Genius, er that I go. **1480** CAXTON *Chron. Eng.* (1520) v. 59/2 Then themperour meked hymselfe and fell downe to the grounde and asked mercy and absolucyon. **1612** DEKKER *Diuell is in it* Wks. 1873 III. 282 I absolution beg on both my knees, For what my tongue offended in. **1856** FROUDE *Hist. Eng.* I. 276 The government, while granting absolution to the nation, determined to make some exceptions. **1876** FREEMAN *Norm. Conq.* III. xii. 92 In the hope that an absolution after the fact might be won.

†**5.** *Rom. Law.* A legal acquittal, a declaration of not guilty. *Obs.*

c **1600** HOLYDAY *Juv.* 244 In one [waxen table] being written the letter A, to signifie the acquittal or absolution of the defendant. **1631** PRESTON *Effect. Faith* 79 The sentence of absolution was given by white stones, as the sentence of condemnation was by black stones. **1651** HOBBES *Leviathan* II. xix. 97 Condemnation, than absolution more resembles Justice. **1726** AYLIFFE *Parergon* 18 The word Absolution..in the Civil Law imports a full and entire acquittal of a person by some final Sentence of Law, upon hearing the Merits of a Cause. **1741** MIDDLETON *Cicero* (ed. 3) II. vi. 120 It was all charged to the absolution of Gabinius after his daring violation of religion. **1875** POSTE *Gaius* IV. §114. 590 The grounds effectual for the absolution of the defendant.

†**6.** Dismissal, getting quit of. *Obs. rare.*

1655 FULLER *Ch. Hist.* XI. x. §8 (1845) VI. 315 But grant it true, not a total absolution, but a reformation thereof [of the liturgy] may hence be inferred.

†**7.** The act of delivering words; delivery. *Obs.*

a **1637** B. JONSON *Discoveries* Wks. 1846, 759 Some language is high and great..the composition full, the absolution plenteous, and poured out, all grave, sinewy, and strong.

absolutism ('æbsəlju:tɪz(ə)m). [f. ABSOLUTE *a.* + -ISM; after mod.Fr. *absolutisme.*] The practice of, or adherence to, the absolute, in theology, politics, or metaphysics.

1. *Theol.* 'The dogma of God's acting absolutely in the affair of salvation, and not being guided in his willing, or nilling, by any reason.' Scott *Suppl. to Chambers.*

1753 CHAMBERS *Cycl. Supp.* s.v. Absolutism is one of those doctrines charged on the Calvinists, for which the Lutherans refuse all union with them. **1775** ASH, *Absolutism*, the doctrine of predestination.

2. *Polit.* The practice of absolute government; despotism; an absolute state. (First used, together with ABSOLUTIST, by Gen. Perronet Thompson.)

1830 GEN. THOMPSON *Exerc.* (1842) I. 295 The experiment of trying to have an agent of the foreigner upon the throne, with leave to bring back the old absolutism. **1840** *Ibid.* V. 148 The old flag of absolutism, which it might be well enough to hoist two centuries ago, but is all too late now. **1841** SPALDING *Italy* I. 24 Our dislike of absolutism in government..tempts us to overcharge all its evils. **1862** M. HOPKINS *Hawaii* 253 The king's power was absolute; and as is usually the case with absolutisms, his chiefs in their separate spheres were smaller despots. **1878** SEELEY *Stein* II. 231 Standing armies ushered in a period of absolutism over the whole Continent.

3. = ABSOLUTENESS; positiveness.

1854 FARADAY *Lect. on Educ.* 72/2 The mind naturally desires to settle upon one thing or another; to rest upon an affirmative or a negative; and that with a degree of absolutism which is irrational and improper.

4. *Philos.* The philosophy of the Absolute (see ABSOLUTE *a.* 13, 14, 15, and ABSOLUTIST *sb.* and *a.* 2).

1878 S. H. HODGSON *Philos. Reflection* I. 121 The same school of objective, or non-Idealist, absolutism. **1884** W. JAMES *Ess. Rad. Empir.* (1912) xii. 279 The one *fundamental* quarrel Empiricism has with Absolutism is over this repudiation by Absolutism of the personal and aesthetic factor in the construction of philosophy. **1890** —— *Princ. Psychol.* I. x. 353 In demanding a more 'real' connection than this obvious and verifiable likeness and continuity, Hume seeks 'the world behind the looking-glass', and gives a striking example of that Absolutism which is the great disease of philosophic Thought.

absolutist ('æbsəlju:tɪst), *sb.* and *a.* [f. ABSOLUTE *a.* + -IST; after mod.Fr. *absolutiste.*]

A. *sb.* An adherent or partisan of absolutism.

1. *Polit.* One who is in favour of an absolute government.

1830 GEN. THOMPSON *Exerc.* (1842) I. 300 Absolutists and priests may rail. **1866** MOTLEY *Dutch Rep.* II. i. 127 [Cardinal Granvelle] was a strict absolutist..His deference to arbitrary power was profound and slavish. **1879** tr. *Busch's Bismarck* II. 286 A kindly, upright, and sensibly conducted absolutism is the best form of government..But we have no longer any thorough-going Absolutists.

2. a. *Metaph.* One who maintains the absolute identity of subject and object.

1856 FERRIER *Inst. Metaph.* 169 Out of this question.. came the whole philosophy of the Alexandrian absolutists. **1859** SIR W. HAMILTON *Lect. Metaph.* II. xxiii. 79 The materialist may now derive the subject from the object, the idealist derive the object from the subject, the absolutist sublimate both into indifference. **1862** H. SPENCER *First Princ.* (1875) I. iii. §20. 65 On this 'primitive dualism of consciousness'..Mr. Mansel founds his refutation of the German absolutists.

b. *Philos.* One who maintains that absolute certainty, or some other absolute, is attainable.

1896 W. JAMES *Will to Bel.* (1897) 12 The absolutists in this matter say that we not only can attain to knowing truth, but we can *know when* we have attained to knowing it. *Ibid.* 14 We are all such absolutists by instinct.

B. *adj.* **1.** [The *sb.* used attributively.] Practising or supporting absolutism in government; despotic.

1837 GEN. THOMPSON *Exerc.* (1842) IV. 241 Imagine that the Tories had undertaken to conduct an interference in favour of absolutist principles. **1838** *Ibid.* IV. 337 The absolutist powers will take it up next. **1850** MAZZINI *Royalty & Repub.* 182 A pretext for the machinations of absolutist governments. **1880** E. PEACOCK in *Academy* 28 Aug. 145 This absolutist tradition derived from the flatterers of Henry VIII.

2. *Philos.* Of or pertaining to absolutism or absolutists.

1884 W. JAMES *Ess. Rad. Empir.* (1912) xii. 273 Fact holds out blankly, brutally and blindly, against that universal deliquescence of everything into logical relations which the Absolutist Logic demands. **1896** —— *Will to Bel.* (1897) 12 We may talk of the *empiricist* way and of the *absolutist* way of believing in truth. **1936** A. J. AYER *Lang., Truth & Logic* vi. 106 The 'absolutist' view of ethics—that is, the view that statements of value are not controlled by observation..but only by a mysterious 'intellectual intuition'.

absolutistic (æbsəlju:'tɪstɪk), *a.* [f. prec. + -IC; cf. *Calvinistic.*] Of or pertaining to absolutists or absolutism; = ABSOLUTIST *a.*; as 'absolutistic principles.'

1854 *Tait's Mag.* XXI. 352 [It] attempted to reconcile the self-government of the nation with the domination of thirty-four absolutistic princes! **1905** W. JAMES *Meaning of Truth* (1909) iii. 57 It means..a break with absolutistic hopes, when one takes up this inductive view of the conditions of belief. **1940** *Mind* XLIX. 426 Hegel..used his principle of the identity of reason and reality..to defend the idea of the absolutistic state (an idea called, today, 'totalitarianism').

Hence **absolu'tistically** *adv.*

1909 W. JAMES *Pluralistic Universe* 365 An *ipse dixit* of Mr. Bradley's absolutistically tempered 'understanding'.

absolutive ('æbsəlju:tɪv, æbsə'lu:tɪv), *sb.* and *a.* *Gram.* [f. ABSOLUTE *a.* + -IVE.] (Pertaining to or being) an absolute form of a word. See ABSOLUTE *a.* 9.

1948 G. V. TAGARE *Historical Gram. Apabhraṁśa* 324 In Prakrits we find the following terminations of the Absolutives. **1965** A. MASTER tr. *J. Bloch's Indo-Aryan from Vedas to Mod. Times* 281 Contrariwise, Sanskrit has actually created a category of absolutive or gerund. **1972** R. S. MCGREGOR *Outline Hindi Grammar* 174 Note the frequency of unrelated absolutives in passive constructions. **1975** *Language* LI. 805 One exponent of this construction in Luiseño involves the suffix sequence *-i-č*, where *-č* is an absolutive suffix otherwise found on non-possessed nouns. **1979** *Trans. Philol. Soc.* 221 In place of the past indefinite in the above examples we may substitute the so-called absolutive. **1985** *Canad. Jrnl. Linguistics* XXX. 208 In a number of Mayan languages..absolutives but not ergatives relativize.

,absoluti'zation. [cf. next.] The process of making absolute; the action of the verb ABSOLUTIZE.

1863 D. W. SIMON tr. *Dorner's Person of Christ* Div. II, vol. III. 7 Herein, therefore, is already involved the germ of the absolutization of subjectivity. **1939** *Theology* XXXIX. 454 The Nazi..his dethronement of reason and his absolutization of uncontrolled racial or group impulse. **1951** *Scottish Jrnl. Theol.* IV. 288 The Old Church..deliberately set itself apart from the rest of Christendom by demanding rigid conformity to its own absolutisations of tradition.

'absolutize, *v.* [f. ABSOLUTE *a.* + -IZE.] To make absolute; to convert into an absolute. Hence **'absolutizing** *vbl. sb.*

1936 *Mind* XLV. 74 Modes of absolutising what is merely relative. **1952** *Theology* LV. 282 Study of typical answers given in the past can..prevent us from absolutizing our own or any one else's solutions. **1952** *Essays in Crit.* II. 371 Death as the 'absolutizing' of the real experience of sleep. **1958** W. STARK *Sociol. of Knowl.* iii. 118 Philosophers have even tended to absolutize the relative.

absolutory (æb'sɒlju:tərɪ), *a.* [ad. L. *absolūtōri-us*, Sueton., serving for acquittal: see ABSOLUTE and -ORY.] Of or pertaining to absolution; absolving.

1640 FULLER *Abel Rediv.* (1867) I. 329 Bertelerius prevailed with the senate; and he granted unto him his absolutory letters. **1726** AYLIFFE *Parergon* 491 Though an absolutory sentence should be pronounced in favour of the persons.

absolvable (æb'sɒlvəb(ə)l, æbz-) *a.* [f. ABSOLVE *v.* + -ABLE.] Capable of being absolved, deserving acquittal.

1865 CARLYLE *Fredk. Gt.* V. XIX. v. 526 Tried by the standard of common practice, Schmettau is clearly absolvable.

†**absolvant.** *Obs.* [a. Fr. *absolvant*, pr. pple. of *absoudre*:—L. *absolventem*, whence the modern ABSOLVENT.] He who absolves.

1506 W. DE WORDE *Ordinary of Crysten Men* IV. viii. [190] After the jugement and dyscrecyon of the absoluant.

†**absolvatory,** *a. Obs.* [Irregularly formed on ABSOLVE, in imitation of *consolatory*, etc., the true form being ABSOLUTORY, q.v.]

1611 COTGR., *Absolutoire*: Absoluatorie, pardoning, forgiving. **1706** PHILLIPS, *Absolvatorie*, Belonging to a discharge or acquittal. [In BAILEY 1721. Not recognized by JOHNSON, but in TODD, WORCESTER, and WEBSTER.]

absolve (æb'sɒlv, æb'zɒlv), *v.* [ad. L. *absolvĕre* to loosen, free, acquit, complete; f. *ab* off, from, + *solv-ĕre* to loose. Cf. Fr. *absoudre*, *absolv-ant*. Bef. its employment the main senses were expressed by ASSOIL. In the pronunciation of this word and its derivatives, usage, as well as the opinion of orthoepists, is divided between ǎbs- and ǎbz-; cf. *absorb*, *solve*, *dissolve*, *resolve*.] Always *trans.*

1. To set free, pronounce free (*from* blame, guilt, moral burden; *from the penalties and consequences of* crime or sin).

c **1538** STARKEY *England* iv. 124 To declayre penytent heartys contryte for ther syn to be absoluyd from the faute therof. **1579** LYLY *Euphues* 174 Who absolued Mary Magdalen from hir sinnes but Christ? **1619** T. TAYLOR *Titus* ii. 14. 317 Absoluing vs both from the guilt and punishment of them. *a* **1674** CLARENDON *Hist. Rebel.* I. 20 Notwithstanding..that he was absolved from any notorious crime..he was at last condemned in a great Fine. **1832** HT. MARTINEAU *Ireland* ii. 17 Father Glenny had readily absolved her from the sin of mistrusting heaven. **1868** *Ecce Homo* (ed. 8) I. i. 5 Absolved from all anxieties by the sense of his protection. **1870** R. W. DALE *Weekd. Serm.* i. 17 This does not absolve him from moral blame.

2. *spec.* To pronounce (one) acquitted of sin, to give absolution or remission of sins to.

a. simply, or *for* some offence.

1535 COVERDALE *Jere.* xi. 15 As though that holy flesh might absolue the. *a* **1570** BECON *Wks.* 560, Neither did the apostles absolve any otherwise than by the preaching of God's word. **1596** SHAKS. *Rom. & Jul.* III. v. 233 To make confession, and to be absolu'd. **1638** *Penit. Conf.* (1657) xi. 307 The Frier absolved him, but kept not his counsel. **1719** YOUNG *The Revenge* IV. i. (1757) II. 167 And yet (For which the saints absolve my soul!) did wed. **1817** MISS MITFORD in L'Estrange's *Life* II. i. 11 One's conscience may be pretty well absolved for not admiring this man. **1865** F. PARKMAN *Champlain* (1875) vi. 265 Biard..gained his pardon, received his confession, and absolved him.

b. *of* the sin.

1651 HOBBES *Leviathan* III. xxxviii. 241 With them that were absolved of their sinnes. **1866** KINGSLEY *Hereward* iii. 80 But I dare not absolve him of robbing a priest.

3. To remit, give absolution for (a sin or crime).

1592 WARNER *Albion's England* (1612) VIII. xli. 198 The Pope for pay absolueth euery thing. **1647** COWLEY *Mistress, Dial.* viii. (1669) 77 The Cause absolves the Crime. **1662** DRYDEN *To Hyde* 60 Not to increase, but to absolve, our crimes. **1845** FORD *Handb. Spain* i. 67 He was a good Roman Catholic canon who believed everything, absolved everything, drank everything, ate everything, and digested everything.

4. To acquit (a person) of a criminal charge, to pronounce not guilty. *esp.* in Roman law.

1628 HOBBES *Thucydides* (1822) 62 Pausanias..having been calld in question by them (the Spartans) was absolvd. **1651** —— *Leviathan* I. xvi. 83 In condemning, or absolving, equality of votes, even in that they condemne not, do absolve. **1665–9** BOYLE *Occ. Refl.* Ep. Ded. (1675) Divers of the Criticks will chuse rather to Absolve my Writings, than Condemn Your Judgment. *a* **1725** POPE *Odyssey* XI. 702 Absolves the just, and dooms the guilty souls. **1741** MIDDLETON *Cicero* (ed. 3) II. vi. 156 Cato, who absolved him, chose to give his vote openly. **1880** MUIRHEAD *Gaius* IV. §47 Words are introduced empowering the judge to condemn or absolve. *Ibid.* 163 He does so without incurring any penalty, and is at once absolved.

5. To set free, discharge (*from*, formerly *of*, obligations, liabilities).

1649 MILTON *Eikonokl.* 137 To be..his own Pope and to absolve himselfe of those ties. **1761** HUME *Hist. Eng.* I. viii. 176 The Popes authority..had absolved them from all oaths which they had taken. **1862** LD. BROUGHAM *Brit. Const.* xii. 172 He also appealed to the Pope to be absolved from the obligations which he had contracted. **1876** FREEMAN *Norm. Conq.* III. xii. 150 So many wrongs had at last absolved him from every duty of a vassal.

†**6.** To clear up, solve, or resolve; to explain (i.e. to unloose the knot of doubt or difficulty). *Obs.*

1577 HELLOWES *Gueuara's Fam. Ep.* 195 Some high mysterie, which if it be facil to demaund, is very difficil to absolue. **1590** RECORDE, etc. *Gr. of Arts* (1646) 118 It maketh just 700 pounds, and so is the question truly absolved. **1612** FLETCHER *Women Pleas'd* v. i. 43 If I absolve the words? **1667** EVELYN *Mem.* (1857) III. 195 The inventions, and phenomena already absolved, improved, or opened.

†**7.** To clear off, discharge, acquit oneself of (a task, etc.); to perform completely, accomplish, finish. *Obs.*

1577 tr. *Bullinger, Decades* (1592) 194 In these fewe wordes are comprehended al that which profound Philosophers doe scarsely absolue in infinite bookes. **1619** T. TAYLOR *Titus* ii. 15. 538 Thus by the assistance of God, haue wee absolued this second Chapter. **1621** BURTON *Anat. Mel.* (1676) II. ii. III. 160/2 Saturn in 30 years absolves his sole and proper motion. **1652** GAULE *Mag-astro-mancer* 144 'Tis their own task; and, till they absolve it, they must give us leave to tell them. **1667** MILTON *P.L.* VII. 94 The work begun, how soon Absolved. **1718** PRIOR *Poems* 300 She conscious of the Grace, absolv'd her Trust, Not unrewarded. **1744** AKENSIDE *Pleas. Imag.* I. 194 Bend the reluctant planets to absolve The fated rounds of time. *a* **1801** E. DARWIN *Zoonomia* III. 363 The frequent swallowing of weak broth..relieves the patient, and absolves the cure.

absolved (æbˈsɒlvd, æbz-), *ppl. a.* [f. prec. + -ED.]

1. Set free, delivered, cleared.

1535 COVERDALE *Jer.* vii. 9 Tush, we are absolued quyte, though we haue done all these abhominacions. **1651** HOBBES *Leviathan* III. xlii. 275 In case the absolved have but a feigned Repentance. **1815** SCOTT *Ld. of Is.* VI. xxix. Even if now He stood absolved of spousal vow. **1876** FREEMAN *Norm. Conq.* I. v. 375 He may have thought himself absolved from his duty.

†**2.** Cleared up, solved; completed. *Obs.*

1577 HELLOWES *Gueuara's Fam. Ep.* 171 Beholde your doubt absolued. **1615** CROOKE *Body of Man.* 301 When the Infant is perfected and absolued the vitall heate floweth onely from the heart as from a most plentifull fountaine.

absolvent (æbˈsɒlvənt, æbz-), *ppl. a.* and *sb.* [ad. L. *absolvent-em*, pr. pple. of *absolvĕre* to absolve. Preceded in use by the Fr. form ABSOLVANT.]

A. *ppl. a.* Absolving, acquitting.

1837 CARLYLE *Fr. Rev.* II. VI. vi. 394 Patriotism..insults many leading Deputies of the absolvent Right-side.

B. *sb.* One who absolves.

1651 HOBBES *Leviathan* III. xlii. 275 This Forgiveness..is thereby without other act, or sentence of the Absolvent, made void.

absolver (æbˈsɒlvə(r), æbz-). [f. ABSOLVE *v.* + -ER[1].] One who absolves, pronounces absolution, or acquits.

1663 BLAIR *Autobiogr.* (1818) ii. 26 He is made to us..righteousness as our justifier and absolver. **1669** H. MORE *Antid. ag. Idolatry* i, They that take upon them to be the only absolvers of sin, are themselves held fast in the snares of eternal death. **1827** KEBLE *Chr. Year*, 6 Sund. aft. Trin., The absolver saw the mighty grief And hastened with relief. **1855** MACAULAY *Hist. Eng.* IV. 681 The public feeling was strongly against the three absolvers.

absolving (æbˈsɒlvɪŋ, æbz-), *vbl. sb.* [f. ABSOLVE *v.* + -ING[1].] The process of setting free; acquitting. Also (*obs.*) solving; completing.

1757 BURKE *Abr. Eng. Hist.* Wks. X. 125 It is changing the nature of his crime; it is absolving.

absolving (æbˈsɒlvɪŋ, æbz-), *ppl. a.* [f. ABSOLVE *v.* + -ING[2].] That absolves or sets free; acquitting.

1696 LUTTRELL *Brief Rel.* (1857) IV. 46 One of the absolving parsons has privately printed his vindication. **1862** TRENCH *Miracles* ix. 206 The absolving words are not to be regarded as optative merely,..but as declaratory.

absolvitor (æbˈsɒlvɪtɔː(r)). *Sc. Law.* Also 6 -ure, 6–7 -our(e, 7–9 -ur. [L. *absolvitor* 'let him (her) be absolved', 3rd pers. sing. imperative pass. of *absolvere* to ABSOLVE.] A decision of the court in favour of the defender.

1547 *Burgh Rec. Aberdeen* I. 250 Maister Thomas Dauesoun..protestit that the said freris haue any absoluitour of the said Johnis clame. **1586** *Protest of A. Hunter* in De Foe *Mem. Ch. Scot.* (1717) Add. 196 The Person excommunicated declaring no Signs of true Repentance, nor craving the said Absolviture by himself, nor by his Procurators. **1609** SKENE *Reg. Maj., Form of Proces* 122 They will pronunce sentence absolvitor, or condemnatour, in the principal cause conform to these rules. **1859** in J. F. Macqueen *Rep. Cases Ho. Lords* (1861) III. 760 If the absolvitor had been a general absolvitor on the merits of the cause. **1910** *Encycl. Brit.* I. 76 s.v. *Absolution.*

absonant (ˈæbsənənt), *a.* [f. L. *ab* off, away from + *sonant-em* sounding, pr. pple. of *sonāre* to sound; on the analogy of *con-sonant, dis-sonant*, and L. *absonus.*] Harsh, inharmonious; *fig.* discordant or abhorrent to reason, nature, etc.; unreasonable, unnatural. Const. *to, from.*

1564 HAWARD *Eutropius* To Reader 7, It is very absonant that anye one who hath the perfect use of corn and grain..woulde refuse the same to be fed wyth acornes. **1600** HOLLAND *Livy* XLI. xviii. 1107 *note*, I mervell much therefore, why it [the word Osse]..should be condemned as absonant, and not pleasing to the ear. **1657** M. HAWKE *Killing is Murder* 42 Absonant from the harmony of the Scriptures. **1864** R. F. BURTON *Mission to K. of Dahome* II. 176, I must again refer to a curious fixed idea in England, absonant withal, touching human sacrifice at Dahome.

†ˈ**absonate**, *v. Obs.*[—0] '(*A law term.*) To avoid, to detest.' Ash 1775. [Apparently merely his adaptation of med.L. *absoniāre*, rendering *ascunian* in Anglo-Saxon Laws.]

†ˈ**absonism**. *Obs. rare*[—1]. [f. L. *abson-us* ABSONOUS + -ISM.] Something absonous or discordant in the use of language; solecism.

1593 NASHE 4 *Lett. Confuted* 68 Euerie third line hath some of this ouer-rackt absonisme.

†**absonous** (ˈæbsənəs), *a. Obs.* [f. L. *abson-us* out of tune + -OUS.] *lit.* Out of tune, inharmonious; *fig.* incongruous, absurd, unreasonable. Const. *to.*

1622 FOTHERBY *Atheom.* II. xi. §4. 318 That noise, as Macrobius truly inferreth, must be of necessity either sweet and melodious, or harsh and absonous. **1664** H. MORE *Myst. Iniq.* How absonous and ridiculous it is not to interpret Prophetick Figures according to the approved meaning and observable use of the Prophetick style. **1681** GLANVILLE *Sad. Trium.* (1726) I. 67 Which Distribution, notwithstanding, is as absonous and absurd as if he had distributed Animal into Sensitive and Rational.

absorb (əbˈsɔːb), *v.* Pa. pple. **absorbed**, formerly **absorpt**. [a. mod.Fr. *absorbe-r*, a refashioning, after L., of OFr. *asorber*, more commonly *asorbir, assorbir*:—L. *absorbē-re* to swallow up, f. *ab* off, away + *sorbē-re* to suck in; pa. pple. *absorpt-us*, whence ABSORPT, formerly used as pa. pple. In no Dict. bef. Blount 1656; Cockeram 1626 has ABSORBEATE; Cotgr. 1611 has Fr. '*Absorbé*, supped or drunk wholly up; devoured, swallowed, consumed.']

I. To swallow up.

†**1.** To swallow up; as water, mire, an earthquake; also *fig. Obs.*

1490 CAXTON *Eneydos* xxvii. 160 Take my sowle and delyuere her..from these sorowfulle peynes in whiche I am absorbed in the grete viage of heuynes. **1548** UDALL, etc. *Erasm. Paraph.* Matt. xvii. 5 A bryghte cloude ouershadowed thapostles, lest they should be absorpte and ouercummed with the highnesse of the sighte. **1684** T. BURNET *Th. of Earth* 85 As to Rome, there is..a more dreadful fate that will attend it; namely, to be absorpt or swallowed up in a lake of fire and brimstone. **1725** POPE *Odyssey* XII. 130 Beneath, Charybdis holds her boist'rous reign 'Midst roaring whirl-pools, and absorbs the main. *a* **1800** COWPER *On names in Biogr. Britann.* Dark oblivion soon absorbs them all.

2. Hence, To swallow up, to include or take a thing in to the loss of its separate existence; to incorporate. ***to be absorbed***, to be swallowed up, or comprised in, so as no longer to exist apart.

1553–87 FOXE *A. & M.* III. 17 The substance of the bread is absorpt..into the human body of Christ. **1659** PEARSON *On Creed* (1839) 231 That old conceit of Eutyches..that the humanity was absorbed and wholly turned into the Divinity. **1820** W. IRVING *Sketch Bk.* I. 120 In some countries, the large cities absorb the wealth and fashion of the nation. **1866** ROGERS *Agric. & Prices* I. iv. 65 The purchase of a pound of candles would have almost absorbed a workman's daily wages. **1876** FREEMAN *Norm. Conq.* I. ii. 9 Into the English nation his own followers were gradually absorbed.

3. To engross, or completely engage the attention or faculties.

1830 BARONESS BUNSEN in Hare's *Life* I. ix. 353 [It] could not so far absorb me as to prevent my often turning my back upon it. **1853** KANE *Grinnell Exped.* (1856) xliii. 403 [I] only postponed it because I happened to get absorbed in a book. **1875** FARRAR *Silence & Voices* iii. 52 Let us absorb our entire beings in this one aim.

II. To drink in.

4. To suck in, drink in (a fluid); to imbibe.

a **1626** BACON (J.) The evils that come of exercise are that it doth absorb and attenuate the moisture of the body. **1814** SIR H. DAVY *Agricult. Chem.* 15 Animal and vegetable matters deposited in soils are absorbed by plants. **1878** HUXLEY *Physiogr.* 24 The clay refuses to absorb the water.

5. To take up (imponderable agents) by chemical or molecular action.

1707 in *Phil. Trans.* XXV. 2374 Whether the Muslin absorps the Effluvium,..I cannot tell. **1794** SULLIVAN *View of Nat.* I. xiv. 140 Some reflect the rays without producing any change, and those are white; others absorb them all, and cause absolute blackness. *c* **1860** FARADAY *Forces of Nat.* iii. 78 Whenever a solid body loses some of that force of attraction by means of which it remains solid, heat is absorbed. **1869** ROSCOE *Chem.* 186 It is found possible to absorb hydrogen in certain metals. **1899** RUTHERFORD in *Phil. Mag.* XLVII. 123 The α radiation from uranium and its compounds is rapidly absorbed in its passage through gases. **1923** GLAZEBROOK *Dict. Appl. Physics* IV. 582/1 The rays are absorbed according to an exponential law. **1942** STRANATHAN *Particles* xii. 470 The atmosphere..acted merely as an absorbing blanket, absorbing radiation coming from above.

absorbability (əbˌsɔːbəˈbɪlɪtɪ). [f. ABSORBABLE + -ITY.] The state or quality of being absorbable; capability of being absorbed.

1812 SIR H. DAVY *Chem. Philos.* 241 The weight of chlorine, its absorbability by water. **1875** WOOD *Therap.* (1879) 409 This absorbability depends largely upon the presence of free fatty acids in the oil.

absorbable (əbˈsɔːbəb(ə)l), *a.* [f. ABSORB + -ABLE.] Capable of being absorbed or imbibed.

1779 INGENHOUSZ *Inflamm. Air* in *Phil. Trans.* LXIX. 385 Which..might more properly be called vapour, as it is absorbable by water. **1859** LEWES *Physiol. of Com. Life* I. iii. 208 Liquid albumen is very slightly absorbable and not at all assimilable; but when acted on in the stomach, it becomes readily absorbable and assimilable.

absorbance (əbs-, əbˈzɔːbəns). [f. ABSORB *v.* + -ANCE.] The logarithm of the ratio of the luminous flux entering a sample or object to that transmitted by it; = *optical density* s.v. OPTICAL *a.* 2 a.

1947 *Nat. Bureau Standards Let. Circular* No. 857. 4 Those in the Bureau most concerned with the matter have formulated the terminology given below... $A_i = -\log_{10} T_i = \log_{10} 1/T_i = \log_{10} I_0/I$ = absorbance of the sample. **1971** *Nature* 4 June p. x/1 (Advt.), A high performance double-beam instrument designed for linear transmittance and linear absorbance measurements in the 190–800 nm wavelength range providing a resolution of 0·2 nm. **1978** *Ibid.* 3 Aug. 447/2 (*caption*) Ordinate: optical absorbance was taken as a measure of cell dissociation. **1982** *SynFuels* 15 Oct. 6 The HPLC apparatus consists of two dual-piston pumps, an injection valve, a chromatographic column, and an ultraviolet (UV) absorbance detector.

absorbancy (əbs-, əbˈzɔːbənsɪ). [f. ABSORB *v.* + -ANCY.] **1.** The ratio of the optical density (absorbance) of a solution to that of a similar body of the solvent alone.

[**1934** WEBSTER, *Absorbency, absorbancy*, one measure of the degree to which a solution absorbs radiant energy.] **1947** *Nat. Bureau Standards Let. Circular* No. 857. 4 Those in the Bureau most concerned with the matter have formulated the terminology given below... $T_s = T_{soln}/T_{solv}$ = transmittancy of the sample... $A_s = -\log_{10} T_s = \log_{10} 1/T_s$ = absorbancy of the sample. **1972** *Science* 2 June 1038/3 This indicates that photoconversion is first order in either direction and supports the conclusion..that the reversible absorbancy changes are the result of mutual photointerconversion of two different forms. **1976** *Nature* 22 Jan. 236/1 Vitamin E content of the filtrate was quantitated by absorbancy at 292 nm.

2. = ABSORBENCY 2. Also *fig.*

1974 *Saturday* (Charleston, S. Carolina) 20 Apr. 10A/5 Apparently the critic doesn't 'hear' the golden silence and complete absorbancy the audience has been enthralled into. **1977** *Washington Post* 6 May D13/3 Its medieval woodcuts..are here to teach us something about absorbancies and textures, washes, bleaching, dyes. **1982** *Financial Times* 19 July 6/2 The company..has a development contract for cloth of enhanced absorbancy for the new service respirator.

absorbative (əbˈsɔːbətɪv), *a.* [f. ABSORB *v.* + -ATIVE.] = ABSORPTIVE *a.*

1893 *Longman's Mag.* Mar. 481 He had enjoyed the life with the peculiar appropriative, assimilative, absorbative gust of the typical schoolboy. **1920** GALSWORTHY *In Chancery* I. vii. 66 The two young ones having been supplied with food, the process went on silent and absorbative.

†**abˈsorbeate**, *v. Obs.* [Irreg. f. L. *absorbē-re* + -ATE.] 'To swallow up.' Cockeram 1626. Prob. nowhere else.

absorbed (əbˈsɔːbd), *ppl. a.* [f. ABSORB + -ED.] *lit.* Swallowed up; imbibed. *fig.* Engrossed or entirely occupied.

1763 H. WALPOLE *Corresp.* (1837) II. 198 Monsieur de Nivernois had been absorbed all day..translating my verses. **1862** *Lond. Rev.* 23 Aug. 156 Large sums are paid..to the officers of the absorbed company. **1865** DICKENS *Our Mut. Fr.* I. 2 He eyed the coming tide with an absorbed attention. **1871** B. STEWART *Heat* Introd., The laws which regulate the distribution of absorbed heat. **1876** FREEMAN *Norm. Conq.* II. x. 518 Absorbed in his own meditations.

absorbedly (əbˈsɔːbɪdlɪ), *adv.* [f. prec. + -LY[2].] In an absorbed manner; with engrossed attention.

1868 *Daily News* 15 July, The next man's credentials being favourably and absorbedly affirmed. **1880** MARK TWAIN *Tramp Aboard* ii. 230, I saw young men gaze long and absorbedly at her.

absorbedness (əb'sɔːbɪdnɪs). [f. ABSORBED *a.* + -NESS.] Engrossed attention, mental concentration.

1881 W. ROBERTSON in *Sunday Mag.* Apr. 245 The passionate absorbedness with which again and again intellect has plumbed its way forward in search for God.

absorbefacient (æbˌsɔːbɪ'feɪʃ(ɪ)ənt, -ʃənt), *a.* and *sb.* [f. L. *absorbē-re*: see ABSORB + *facient-em* pr. pple. of *facĕre* to make; on analogy of such adj. as *rubefacient*, f. L. *rubefacĕre*: see -FACIENT.]

A. *adj.* Causing absorption, drying up.

B. *sb.* [sc. agent, substance.]

1875 WOOD *Therap.* (1879) 406 Dr. J. Moleschott praises it [Iodoform] most highly as an absorbefacient, affirming that by its use he has obtained absorption of various lymphatic tumors.

absorbency (əb'sɔːbənsɪ). [n. of state f. L. *absorbent-em*: see ABSORBENT and -NCY.]

†1. The action of absorbing (which would be properly *absorbence*); absorption. *Obs. rare.*

1762 DUNN *Size of Sun* in *Phil. Trans.* LII. 469 Whether this effect arises from.. absorbency of the rays, seems to me to deserve a proper enquiry.

2. The quality of being absorbent; absorptiveness.

1859 GULLICK & TIMBS *Painting* 106 Ivory and enamel being quite smooth, and without texture or absorbency. **1975** *Chem. Week* 9 July 34/3 All-cotton shirts.. are making a comeback and at premium prices. Selling point:.. cotton's absorbency. **1984** *N.Y. Times* 28 Oct. VI. 86/2 According to cosmetic chemists, the ideal powders should have five characteristics: covering power, absorbency, adhesiveness, slip and bloom.

absorbent (əb'sɔːbənt), *a.* and *sb.* [ad. L. *absorbent-em*, pr. pple. of *ab-sorbēre*: see ABSORB.]

A. *adj.* Absorbing, imbibing, swallowing; absorptive. *absorbent system*, see B 3. **absorbent cotton** *U.S.*, cotton wool.

1718 QUINCY *Compl. Disp.* 81 It is both detergent and absorbent. **1752** BROOKE *Inoculation* in *Phil. Trans.* XLVII. 471 The absorbent vessels.. will always take in a sufficient quantity of the matter to contaminate the whole mass of the circulating fluids. **1869** PHILLIPS *Vesuvius* v. 140 Rain sinks in some considerable proportion into the absorbent soil. **1889** in *Cent. Dict.* **1890** BILLINGS *Med. Dict.* I. 7/1 *A[bsorbent] cotton*, L. gossypium... Cotton freed from adhering impurities, and deprived of oily matter by boiling in a dilute alkaline solution and thorough washing; absorbent and protective; used as a surgical dressing. **1947** *Hygeia* Oct. 767/2 The thermometer should be kept in a small tumbler, one-quarter filled with antiseptic solution, with a little absorbent cotton in the bottom of the glass.

B. *sb.* An absorbing substance or apparatus.

1. Any substance which absorbs fluids through its sensible or insensible porosity; applied in a special sense in *Med.* to such substances as chalk, magnesia, which absorb the acidity of the stomach.

1718 QUINCY *Compl. Disp.* 79 Dryers, or Absorbents,.. prevent those superfluous Moistures, which the Nerves are frequently overcharg'd with. **1769** BUCHAN *Dom. Med.* (1826) xlii. 175 But the best and safest absorbent is magnesia alba. **1845** DARWIN *Voy. of Nat.* xi. 249 (1879) The clouded sky seldom allows the sun to warm the ocean, itself a bad absorbent of heat. **1875** WOOD *Therap.* (1879) 611 *Absorbents*, This class contains remedies which are used for the purpose of absorbing acrid and deleterious materials,.. on the exterior of the body, and.. in the alimentary canal.

2. *fig.*

1821-30 LD. COCKBURN *Mem. own Time* 220 The country gentlemen, the absorbents of every prejudice. **1875** HELPS *Ess., Org. Daily Life* 174 A persecution, which pinches, but does not suppress, is merely an irritant, and not an absorbent.

3. *Physiol.* (in *plural.*) The vessels through which the process of absorption is carried on in animals and plants, such as the lacteals in the former, the extremities of the roots in the latter. *Attrib.* in **absorbent system**.

1753 CHAMBERS *Cycl. Suppl.* Naturalists speak of the like Absorbents in plants; the fibrous or hairy roots of which are considered as a kind of *vasa Absorbentia*. **1795** ABERNETHY *Anat. of Whale* in *Phil. Trans.* LXXXVI. 29, Absorbents.. which terminated by open orifices. **1836** TODD *Cycl. An. & Ph.* I. 20/1 The absorbents.. were among the organs which were the latest in being discovered by anatomists. **1847** YOUATT *Horse* vi. 110 Much of the cartilage is taken away by vessels called absorbents. **1856** WOODWARD *Fossil Shells* 30 The mollusca have no distinct absorbent system.

absorber (əb'sɔːbə(r)). [f. ABSORB + -ER[1].] One who, or something which, absorbs. Chiefly *techn.* Cf. SHOCK-*absorber*.

1792 A. YOUNG *Trav. France* 153 He has a pair of scales made at Paris,.. an air pump,.. an absorber,.. a respirator. **1861** *Sat. Rev.* No. 279. 222/1 Nitrogen and oxygen.. are feeble absorbers and radiators. **1873** SYMONDS *Gk. Poets* I. 29 Aristotle was the absorber of all previous and contemporary knowledge into one coherent system. **1922** GLAZEBROOK *Dict. Appl. Physics* I. 689/2 A low pressure is maintained in the evaporator by causing the evaporated vapour to pass into another vessel, called the absorber, where it comes into contact with cold water in which it becomes dissolved. **1933** *Discovery* Aug. 260/1 The wheel and tyre are sprung in conjunction with absorbers. **1949** *Gloss. Terms Refrigeration (B.S.I.)* 4 *Absorber*, the vessel, used in an absorption system, in which the refrigerant vapour is absorbed. **1958** *Chambers's Techn. Dict.* 952/1 *Absorber*, material for capturing neutrons without generating more neutrons, e.g., boron and cadmium, much used for controlling and shielding reactors. **1962** A. NISBETT *Technique Sound Studio* 239 Soft absorbers depend for their action on such things as the friction of air particles in the interstices of the material.

absorbing (əb'sɔːbɪŋ), *ppl. a.* [f. ABSORB + -ING[2].] **a.** *lit.* Swallowing, imbibing; hence, incorporating, taking into itself; *fig.* engrossing, all-engaging.

1754 *Phil. Trans.* XLVIII. 582 The absorbing and exhaling vessels, and the cuticle. **1860** TYNDALL *Glaciers* II. §3. 246 Radiant heat is allowed to fall upon an absorbing substance. **1862** *Lond. Rev.* 23 Aug. 156 An amalgamation, under such circumstances, is a positive fraud on the proprietors of the absorbing office. **1876** FREEMAN *Norm. Conq.* II. ix. 330 He must have been engaged at this time in some such absorbing pursuit.

b. *spec.* in *Physics*.

1904 RUTHERFORD *Radio-Activity* iv. 113 Leonard.. has shown that the absorption of cathode rays is nearly proportional to the density of the absorbing matter. **1913** —— *Radioactive Substances* iv. 148 If an absorbing screen is placed in the path of the rays, the velocities of the α particles .. should all be diminished by the same amount. **1923** [see ABSORPTION 4 b].

absorbingly (əb'sɔːbɪŋlɪ), *adv.* [f. prec. + -LY[2].] In an absorbing manner; engrossingly, entirely.

1836 *Blackw. Mag.* XL. 13/1 Mr. Hillary was at that eventful moment absorbingly engaged with a letter. **1868** *Athenæum* 25 July 105/1 The sole idea which absorbingly possessed him[Edward] was that of erecting a great Norman Abbey in Westminster. **1872** LIDDON *Elem. of Relig.* v. 173 Any common act of prayer keeps.. the understanding occupied earnestly, absorbingly, under the guidance of faith.

†**absor'bition.** *Obs.* [Irregularly formed, as if from a L. **absorbitus*, instead of *absorptus*, whence regularly ABSORPTION.] = ABSORPTION.

c **1680** SIR T. BROWNE *Tracts* 165 Where to place that concurrence of waters or place of its absorbition there is no authentick decision.

absorp, obs. form of ABSORB.

absorpt (æb'sɔːpt), *ppl. a. arch.* [ad. L. *absorpt-us* pa. pple. of *absorbē-re*: see ABSORB.] The earlier equivalent of ABSORBED: swallowed up; *rarely fig.* engrossed.

1528 MORE *Dial. conc. Heresyes* IV. Wks. 1557, 267/1 For all other synnes (if belief and faith stand fast) be quite absorpt and supped vp he sayth in that fayth. **1626** T. H. tr. *Caussin's Holy Court* 89 To raigne in heauen for euer, and there to remayne absorpt, in an ocean of pleasures. **1736** J. H. BROWNE *Pipe of Tob.* (1768) 119 Absorpt in yellow care, And at each puff imagination burns. **1839** BAILEY *Festus* (1848) xix. 210 Their souls absorpt of darkness.

†**ab'sorpted**, *ppl. a. Obs.* [f. L. *absorpt-us* (see prec.) + -ED: cf. *corrupt, corrupted, abrupt, abrupted.*] = ABSORPT, ABSORBED.

a **1631** DONNE *Serm.* IV. xcvi. 242 Absorpted & swallowed up into the nature and essence of God himself.

absorpti'ometer. [f. L. *absorpt-um* or ? *absorptiōn-em* (see next) + -METER = Gr. μέτρον measure, measurer.] **1.** An instrument for measuring the amount of absorption of gases in various liquids.

1879 WROBLEWSKI in *Nature* XXI. 191 The absorptiometer which I have constructed for the determination of the co-efficients of absorption, consists of glass throughout.

2. An apparatus for measuring colour-absorption by means of a photo-electric device.

1939 *Thorpe's Dict. Appl. Chem.* III. 305/2 Moll, Burger and Reichert.. have devised a 'spectroscopic absorptiometer' which can be used at any part of the photographable spectrum. **1947** *Nature* 11 Jan. 50/2 Applications of the spectrograph and the photo-electric absorptiometer. **1953** *Electronic Engin.* XXV. 212 The continuous flow self-balancing absorptiometer is an instrument for detecting and giving continuous indication of small changes in colour density of a liquor.

Hence **abˌsorptio'metric** *a.*, of, pertaining to or involving an absorptiometer.

1909 in *Cent. Dict.* Suppl. **1950** *Engineering* 3 Mar. 240/2 The determination of silicon in plain carbon steels.. by the absorptiometric method. **1956** *Nature* 24 Mar. 550/2 Conventional absorptiometric methods of gas analysis.

absorption (əb'sɔːpʃən). [ad. L. *absorptiōn-em* a swallowing, n. of action f. *absorpt-us*: see ABSORPT.] The act or process of swallowing up or sucking in. Hence,

I. Swallowing up.

†**1.** The swallowing up or engulfing of bodies. *Obs.*

1597 J. KING *Jonah* (1864) xxii. 139 The absorption or burial. *a* **1656** BP. HALL *Rem.* 24 (1808) The aversion of God's face is confusion.. but his whole fury is the utter absorption of the creature. **1753** CHAMBERS *Cycl. Suppl.* Absorptions of the Earth, a term used by Kircher and others, for the sinking in of large tracts of land, by means of subterranean commotions.

2. a. The swallowing up or disappearance of things through their inclusion in or assimilation to something else; incorporation in something else.

1741 WARBURTON *Alliance Ch. and St.* 165 (T.) Of the ancient Greek philosophy.. its gradual decay, and total absorption in the schools. **1834** GEN. THOMPSON *Exerc.* (1842) III. 201 But at the same time that copyists were being thrown out of employ, printers must have been in demand; here then was one way for the absorption of at least a portion of the copyists. **1860** *All Y. Round* No. 68, 418 The absorption of dialects by the Latin.. gave a great impulse to civilisation. **1878** SEELEY *Stein* III. 415 A provision expressly intended to prevent the absorption of peasant-holdings.

b. *Med.* and *Path.* Removal of tissues or deposits by natural process, or by the use of medicines.

1804 ABERNETHY *Surg. Observ.* 16 Another curative indication naturally arises which is to promote the absorption of the new formed substance. **1881** MIVART *Cat* 20 Spaces are then formed in this substance by absorption.

3. Entire engrossment or engagement of the mind or faculties.

1855 DICKENS *Lett.* (1880) I. 379 The absorption of the English mind in the war. **1859** GEO. ELIOT *Adam Bede* 26 It was an expression of unconscious placid gravity of absorption in thoughts that had no connection with the present moment. **1875** FARRAR *Silence & Voices* ix. 164 Blind, groping, illiberal absorption in some mechanical routine.

II. Drinking in.

4. a. The sucking in of fluid or of particles dissolved therein; the taking up of imponderable agents, such as light.

1744 WARRICK *Injection* in *Phil. Trans.* XLIX. 489 Wherein the power of absorption seemed very considerable. **1794** J. HUTTON *Philos. Light, Heat, & Fire* 89 Such are the laws observed in the various absorption and reflection of light. **1794** SULLIVAN *View of Nat.* V. 329 The Arena, so called from its being covered with sand for the absorption of the blood. **1854** BALFOUR *Outl. Bot.* 133 When liquids are brought into contact with the leaves of plants, absorption takes place. **1871** TYNDALL *Fragm. Sci.* (ed. 6) I. ii. 35 In this transfer.. consists the absorption of radiant heat.

b. *spec.* in (*a*) *Electr.* (See quots.)

1884 O. HEAVISIDE in *Electrician* 2 Feb. 270/1 If we pass an electric current.. across the junction, there will be, by elementary principles, a continuous absorption of energy. *Ibid.* 271/2 The absorption of energy is at the zinc surface where the current goes with the E.M.F. **1904** GOODCHILD & TWENEY *Technol. & Sci. Dict.* 2/1 *Electrical Absorption*, the storing up of a part of the electrical energy of a charged condenser by the dielectric.

(*b*) *Nucl. Physics* and *Radiology*. The reduction in intensity of a beam of radiation during its passage through matter. Also *attrib.*

1899 RUTHERFORD in *Phil. Mag.* XLVII. 128 The absorption coefficient for the α radiation is 1·6, or 160 times as great. **1923** GLAZEBROOK *Dict. Appl. Physics* IV. 582/1 The absorption of β rays is investigated by placing thin sheets of the absorbing material in the path of the rays and measuring the activity through different thicknesses. **1926** R. W. LAWSON tr. *Hevesy & Paneth's Man. Radioactivity* vii. 77 We can detect the increased absorption... Such 'absorption edges' enable us to determine the 'levels' of a series. **1943** *Gloss. Terms Electr. Engin. (B.S.I.)* 143 *Absorption-coefficient*, of a homogeneous substance, for X-rays of a given wavelength, the ratio of the linear rate of change of intensity at any point to the intensity at that point. **1947** G. THOMSON *Atom* (ed. 3) xi. 99. Experiments show that these discontinuities in absorption, or Absorption Edges as they are called, are extremely well marked. **1958** *Optima* Mar. 36/1 Neutron absorption converts uranium 238 into element 94—plutonium.

(*c*) *Acoustics.* (See quot. 1900.)

1900 W. C. SABINE in *Amer. Architect* 7 Apr. 4/2 Sound, being energy, once produced in a confined space, will continue until it is either transmitted by the boundary walls, or is transformed into some other kind of energy, generally heat. This process of decay is called absorption. *Ibid.* 12 May 44/1 An attempt to connect the rate of decay.. with the absolute co-efficient of absorption of the wall. **1958** *B.S.I. News* Aug. 8/2 Measurement of the absorption coefficient in a reverberation room.

(*d*) *Radio.* Loss of power in the transmission of radio waves. Also *attrib.* Hence also in *Radar*.

1914 *Rep. Brit. Assoc. Adv. Sci. 1913* 607 (*title*) Atmospheric Refraction and Absorption as affecting Transmission in Wireless Telegraphy. **1931** *B.B.C. Year-Bk.* 435/1 Absorption Control. A method of 'controlling' the high-frequency oscillations delivered to the aerial in a wireless telephone transmitter, so that they vary in amplitude at the low frequency of modulation. *Ibid.*, Absorption Wavemeter. A wavemeter consisting of a low-loss oscillatory circuit which is tuned to the transmission to be measured. **1948** TAYLOR & WESTCOTT *Princ. Radar* iii. 26 The related concept of effective absorption area A_a of an aerial.

(*e*) *Refrigeration.* (See quots.)

1922 GLAZEBROOK *Dict. Appl. Physics* I. 689/2 Absorption Machines.. act by the absorption of one substance by another, to form a solution or compound, and the subsequent separation of the constituents by the agency of heat. **1949** *Gloss. Terms Refrigeration (B.S.I.)* 4 *Absorption system*, a system in which the variation of solubility with temperature or pressure is employed to produce refrigeration.

5. *Physiol.* The imbibing of fluids by the vessels or tissues of the body; *esp.* the reception of nutritive material by the lacteals of the intestine.

1753 CHAMBERS *Cycl. Supp.* s.v., Absorption in the animal economy is used for that power whereby the small open orifices of vessels imbibe liquors. **1848** CARPENTER *Anim. Phys.* 37 It is by means of the membrane lining the digestive cavity, that the functions of digestion & absorption are performed. **1881** MIVART *Cat* 167 Another process, which is ancillary to nutrition and secretion, is termed Absorption.

III. 6. *Comb.* **absorption band**, 'a region of darkness produced in the spectrum of white light which has passed through an absorbing medium' (*Brit. Med. Dict.* 1961) (cf. *spectrum-band*); **absorption coefficient**, a numerical quantity expressing the degree to which a substance absorbs something; *spec.* = ABSORBANCE; **absorption factor** *Optics* and *Photometry* (see quot. 1940); **absorption lines**, the dark lines of an absorption spectrum (cf. *spectrum-line*, and FRAUNHOFER); **absorption spectrum** (see quot. 1940).

1867 J. HOGG *Microsc.* I. ii. 121 For most *absorption-bands particularly if faint the prism would be used in the first position. **1905** GOODCHILD & TWENEY *Technol. & Sci. Dict.* XI. 698/2 An examination of the transmitted light in the spectroscope will show dark bands in its spectrum corresponding to the wave length of the light absorbed by the substance. The bands are called *absorption bands*, and their nature, position, and extent..serve to identify the substance. **1899** RUTHERFORD in *Phil. Mag.* XLVII. 141 The results given in the previous table allow us to determine the *absorption coefficient of air at various pressures. **1947** *Radiology* XLIX. 320/2 The total amount of energy absorbed as beta rays to produce the same effect is given by the product of the median lethal dose in rep times the surface area of the animal..divided by the absorption coefficient of the particular beta emission used. **1950** *Chambers's Encycl.* XII. 699/2 The solubility of a gas is sometimes expressed by its absorption coefficient, which is the number of volumes of gas..which dissolve in unit volume of liquid. **1963** R. W. DITCHBURN *Light* (ed. 2) xv. 551 Observations on the transmission in a homogeneous medium which absorbs, but does not scatter, the light are summarized in Lambert's law... $L(z) = L_0e^{-2\alpha z}$. The constant 2α is called the absorption coefficient. **1932** *Gloss. Terms Illum. & Photom.* (*B.S.I.*), *Absorption factor. **1940** *Chambers's Techn. Dict.* 3/2 *Absorption factor*, the ratio of the difference between the total luminous flux falling on a surface and the sum of the fluxes transmitted through and reflected from the surface, to the total luminous flux falling on the surface. **1889** *Cent. Dict.* (s.v. *absorption*), (*caption*) Part of Solar Spectrum, showing *Absorption-lines. **1928** D. BRUNT *Meteorol.* v. 39 This effect is shown in the spectrum by..a number of narrow dark lines running across the spectrum in definitely fixed positions, marking the absence of the light absorbed. Each element in the absorbing medium produces its own set of dark absorption lines. **1879** HARTLEY & HUNTINGTON in *Proc. R. Soc.* 235 In order to ascertain whether isomeric bodies exhibited similar or identical *absorption spectra a series of benzene derivatives was examined. **1940** *Chambers's Tech. Dict.* 4/1 *Absorption spectrum*, the system of absorption bands, or lines, seen when a selectively absorbing substance is placed between a source of white light and a spectroscope. **1950** *Sci. News* XV. 89 Oxyhæmoglobin and oxychlorocruorin have each their characteristic absorption spectrum.

absorptive (əb'sɔːptɪv), *a.* [f. L. *absorpt-*, ppl. stem of *absorbēre* to ABSORB + -IVE, as if ad. L. **absorptīvus*.] Having the quality of absorbing, swallowing, or imbibing. *fig.* Engrossing.

1664 H. MORE *Myst. Iniq.* viii. 132 There being no Ark left to take Sanctuary in, and to be safe from the working and absorptive waves. **1667** WATERHOUSE *Fire of Lond.* 32 This harrass of Fire and that so generally absorptive of the city. **1831** BREWSTER *Optics* xvi. 137 The absorptive power of air is finely displayed in the colour of the morning and evening clouds. **1870** ROLLESTON *Anim. Life* 34 Absorptive as well as secreting glands exist in great abundance in the walls of the digestive tube. **1881** W. J. ROLFE Pref. to *Coriol.* 6 His lazy, somnolent, stupidly absorptive satisfaction.

absorptiveness (əb'sɔːptɪvnɪs). [f. prec. + -NESS.] The quality of being absorptive.

absorptivity (ˌæbsɔːp'tɪvɪtɪ). [f. ABSORPTIVE *a.* + -ITY.] = ABSORPTIVENESS.

WEBSTER cites DANA.

absoyle, obs. var. of ASSOIL *v.*: see ABSOIL.

absquatulate (æb'skwɒtjuːleɪt), *v.* Also **absquotilate**. [A factitious word, simulating a L. form (cf. *abscond*, *gratulate*) of American origin, and jocular use.] To make off, decamp.

1837-40 HALIBURTON *Clockmaker* (1862) 363 Absquotilate it in style, you old skunk,..and show the gentlemen what you can do. **1858** DOW *Serm.* I. 309 in Bartlett *Dict. Amer.*, Hope's brightest visions absquatulate. **1861** J. LAMONT *Seahorses* xi. 179 He [an old bull-walrus] heard us, and lazily awaking, raised his head and prepared to absquatulate.

absquatulation (æbskwɒtjuː'leɪʃən). [f. ABSQUATULATE *v.*: see -ATION.] The action of 'absquatulating' or decamping.

1847 H. N. MOORE *Fitzgerald & Hopkins* 164 Artaxerxes and Euphrosyne, after the absquatulation of their pet daughter with the Irish nobleman incog.,..were completely confounded. *a* **1884** M. PATTISON *Mem.* (1885) vi. 213 M[anuel] Johnson jocularly proposed to write the history of Absquatulation. **1901** 'LINESMAN' *Words by Eyewitness* (1902) 248 The enclosing and utter absquatulation of the commando.

[**abstable**, sometimes quoted from Gower *Conf.* I. 211. II. 1553, is a misreading for *obstacle*.]

abstain (æb'steɪn), *v.* Forms: 4-5 **abstene**, 4-6 **absteyn(e**, **-ein(e**, 6 **asteine**, 6-7 **abstayne**, **abstaine**, 7- **abstain**. [a. Fr. *absteni-r*, a 14th c. refashioning of OFr. *asteni-r* (whence occ. Eng. *asteine*):—L. *abstinē-re* to withhold, f. *abs* = *ab* off, away from + *tenē-re* to hold. The Fr. (like the Eng. originally) is only reflexive, *s'abstenir*, L. *se abstinēre* to keep oneself from, refrain from.]

†**1.** *refl.* To keep or withhold *oneself*. Const. *of*, *from*. *Obs.*

c **1380** *Sir Ferumbras* 3761 In herte hur gan to greue. of wepyng ne miȝt sche abstene hur noȝt. **1382** WYCLIF *1 Cor.* ix. 25 Ech man that stryueth in fyȝt, absteyneth him fro alle thingis. **1483** CAXTON *G. de la Tour* ij. b, To kepe trewly her maryage and also absteyne her of synne. *c* **1500** *Lancelot of the Laik* 1261 My consell is, therfore, you to absten. **1535** COVERDALE *Acts* xv. 20 Wryte vnto them that they absteyne them selues from fylthynesse of Idols.

2. *intr.* (by gradual suppression of the pron. object.) To keep or withhold oneself, to refrain. Const. *from* (*of* obs.)

1382 WYCLIF *Num.* vi. 3 Fro al that may make dronkun, thei shulen absteyne. *c* **1449** PECOCK *Repr.* I. xiv. 78 Y must here therof abstene and forber. **1538** STARKEY *England.* 17 To absteyn from flesch apon the Fryday..ys now reputyd a certayn vertue. **1598** BARRET *Theor. of War.* V. v. 165 To absteine from committing these excesses. **1667** MILTON *P.L.* IV. 748 Our Maker bids increase; who bids abstain But our destroyer, foe to God and man? **1746** *Col. Records Penn.* V. 50 That they do abstain from all servile Labour on that Day. **1798** FERRIAR *Illustr. of Sterne* ii. 38 D'Aubigné was so fond of writing epigrams, that he could not abstain from them. **1860** TYNDALL *Glaciers* I. §3. 26 I therefore abstained from mentioning it subsequently.

b. To refrain *from* voting. Hence without const., not to use one's vote.

1885 A. W. PEEL in *Hansard Commons* 12 May 342, I should recommend each Member to be guided by his own feelings in the matter, and to vote or abstain from voting as he thinks fit. **1931** *Daily Mirror* 9 Sept. 3/1 Three Socialists abstained—Miss Picton Turberville, Mr. Strauss and Sir Norman Angell. **1931** *Economist* 12 Sept. 466/2 Sir Oswald and the small group which supports him abstained from the lobby. **1946** W. S. CHURCHILL *Victory* 93 You felt it necessary on account of your convictions to abstain from the division about Poland. **1959** P. G. RICHARDS *Honourable Members* vi. 147 In November, 1954, the Parliamentary Labour Party decided to abstain on the vote ratifying the London and Paris agreements. **1965** A. J. P. TAYLOR *Eng. Hist. 1914-45* viii. 281 Time and again, the Liberals split three ways—some voting with the government, some against, the rest abstaining. **1984** *Times* 11 July 1/1 About 25 Conservative MPs abstained at the end of a Commons debate last night.

3. *esp.* (being used most frequently in reference to eating and drinking). To refrain from food, to fast (*obs.*); to refrain from the use of alcoholic beverages, to be a 'total-abstainer.'

1534 LD. BERNERS *Gold. Bk. of M. Aurel.* (1546) D. iij, If he be temperate and moderate, all wil absteyne. **1547** BOORDE *Brev. of Health* i. 7 Many men wolde eate meate if they had it, and therfor nolens volens, they do asteine. **1867** B. NICOLS in *Cleric. Testy. to Tot. Abs.* 98 Several have told me..that while they had abstained, some for weeks or months, they were far better in every respect than while they drank.

†**4.** *trans.* (later and rare, and probably a literary imitation of the trans. use of L. *abstinere*). To keep back, keep off.

1509 BARCLAY *Shyp of Folys* (1874) II. 275 From outwarde thynges his mynde doth he abstayne. **1534** LD. BERNERS *Gold. Bk. M. Aurel.* (1546) H ij *b*, For a small season the louer maie absteyne his loue. **1645** MILTON *Tetrach.* (1851) 154 For what difference at all whether he abstain men from marying, or restraine them in a mariage hapning totally discommodious. **1644-58** J. CLEVELAND *Gen. Poems* (1677) 140 My Lord doth justly abstain his hand from his Dispatch.

abstainer (æb'steɪnə(r)). [f. ABSTAIN + -ER[1].] One who abstains; *esp.* one who abstains from eating or drinking particular things; in older writers a Nazarite, in modern use an abstainer from alcoholic beverages, a 'total abstainer.'

1535 COVERDALE *Amos* ii. 12 But ye gaue the absteyners wyne and drynke [WYCLIF Naȝareys: **1611** Nazarites]. —— *Lam.* iv. 7 Hir absteyners (or Nazarees) were whyter then ye snowe or mylke. **1683** TRYON *Way to Health* 407 The holy Men and Prophets..were strict Abstainers, and separated themselves from the Uncleannesses, Oppressions and Violencies that the superfluous worldly Belly-Gods do subject themselves unto. **1862** *Sat. Rev.* XIII. 617/2 This observation supplies an answer to some of the usual arguments of the total-abstainers. **1879** BLACK *Macleod of Dare* xxxvi. 322 If they ever put up an asylum in Mull, it will be a lunatic asylum for incurable abstainers.

abstaining (æb'steɪnɪŋ), *vbl. sb.* [f. ABSTAIN + -ING[1].] The act or practice of keeping oneself, or refraining, *from* anything. (Now mostly gerundial, the sb. being supplied by ABSTINENCE.)

c **1440** *Gesta Rom.* (1879) 423 This wille of abstenyng from synne ledithe here to heuyn. **1660** R. COKE *Elem. Power & Subj.* 133 It is not alwaies the doing, or abstaining from what is commanded or forbidden, which is virtue, but only the ingenuous and upright doing or abstaining. **1744** HARRIS *Three Treat.* (1841) 86 It prescribes no abstainings, no forbearances out of nature. **1850** CLOUGH *Dipsychus* II. ii. 74 But for perfection attaining is one method only, abstaining.

abstaining (æb'steɪnɪŋ), *ppl. a.* [f. ABSTAIN + -ING[2].] Practising abstinence (from alcoholic beverages).

1867 J. W. BARDSLEY in *Cleric. Testy. to Tot. Abst.* 30 The bride was the daughter of an abstaining clergyman.

abstainment (æb'steɪnmənt). *rare.* [f. ABSTAIN + -MENT; cf. *attainment*.] The act or condition of keeping from or refraining.

1859 DUKE OF BUCKINGHAM *Mem. Crt. of George IV*, I. ii. 418 The abstainment on his part from all intrigue.

absteinous, abstenious, by-forms due to confusion of ABSTAIN, older absteine, w. ABSTEMIOUS.

abstemious (æb'stiːmɪəs), *a.* Also 6 **abstenious**, **absteinous**. [f. L. *abstēmi-us* + -OUS. *Abstemius* was considered by L. writers to be f. *abs* away from + *tēmētum* intoxicating liquor; but even in L. was extended to temperance in living generally. The verbal resemblance to *abstain*, *absteine*, has in Eng. given it a still wider use, and also produced the forms *absteinous*, *abstenious*.]

1. Dispensing with wine and rich food; temperate or sparing in food; characterized by or belonging to such temperance; sparing.

a. Of persons, their lives, or habits.

1624 HEYWOOD *Gunaikeion* v. 226 To this absteinous life shee added the strict vow of chastitie. **1718** POPE *Iliad* XIX. 328 Let me pay To grief and anguish one abstemious day. **1832** CARLYLE *Remin.* I. 26 Mother and father were assiduous, abstemious, frugal without stinginess. **1878** BLACK *Green Past. and Picc.* xxix. 234 They were remarkably abstemious at breakfast.

b. Of the food.

1776-88 GIBBON *Decl. & Fall* lviii, His [Peter the Hermit's] diet was abstemious, his prayers long and fervent. **1832** SCOTT *Talism.* ii. 26 The meal of the Saracen was abstemious.

2. Abstinent, refraining, sparing (with regard to other things than food). *rare.*

1610 SHAKS. *Temp.* IV. i. 53 Be more abstemious, Or else good night your vow. **1632** MASSINGER *Maid of Hon.* II. ii. The king..Is good and gracious..Abstemious from base and goatish looseness. **1823** LAMB *Elia* (1865) I. xxi. 163 You advised an abstemious introduction of literary topics.

abstemiously (æb'stiːmɪəslɪ), *adv.* [f. prec. + -LY[2].] In an abstemious manner; sparingly, temperately.

1725 BRADLEY *Fam. Dict.* s.v. *Spleen*, If the obstruction of the Spleen proceeds from..having lived a little abstemiously. **1794** SULLIVAN *View of Nat.* II. 358 There are many monastical persons, who live abstemiously all their lives.

abstemiousness (æb'stiːmɪəsnɪs). [f. ABSTEMIOUS + -NESS.] The quality of being abstemious, or sparing in the use of strong drink and delicacies.

1626 DONNE *Serm.* V. cxxxix. 486 As if God required such a forbearing, such an abstemiousness in man as that being set to rule and govern the creatures he might not use and enjoy them. **1655** FULLER *Ch. Hist.* II. x. 130 He could digest a Bishoprick, which his abstemiousness formerly refused. **1827** SCOTT *Surg. Dau.* i. 23 Four years, or so, of abstemiousness enable them to stand an election dinner.

abstenance, obs. form of ABSTINENCE.

abstention (æb'stɛnʃən). [a. Fr. *abstention* (OFr. *astension*), n. of action f. L. *abstent-* ppl. stem of *abstinēre*: see ABSTAIN.]

†**1.** The act of keeping back or restraining. *Obs.*

1521 WOLSEY in Strype's *Eccl. Mem.* I. 50 The abstention of war, which may be as soon broken..as all the other assurance, cannot then prevail. **1653** GAUDEN *Hieraspistes* 103 Which present denial, or abstention of such an one from receiving the holy Sacrament, might afterwards be examined by publick and lawful authority.

2. The act of keeping oneself back, abstaining or refraining; the state of refraining or of being kept back.

1624-47 BP. HALL *Rem. Wks.* (1660) 303 Many sighes and teares which now he bestowed upon his abstention from that dearly affected devotion. **1865** M. ARNOLD *Ess. in Critic.* (1875) x. 267 In them the character of abstention and renouncement, which we have noticed in Ali himself, was marked yet more strongly. **1870** *Daily News* 23 Apr., M. Picard..justifies his abstention from signing the manifesto of the Left.

3. *spec.* The act of refraining from voting; an instance of this. Also *transf.*

1880 *Illust. Lond. News* 21 Feb. 178 The votes given were —for Mr. Clarke 7683..There were over 7000 abstentions. **1922** *Encycl. Brit.* II. 562/2 The extremist group proposed abstention from the polls and an armed rising. **1948** *Bull.* (U.S. Dept. of State) 4 July 3/2 If a permanent member of the Security Council abstains from voting on a nonprocedural decision of the Council, such abstention is not considered to be a veto. **1955** G. GORER *Exploring Eng. Character* iv. 64 An eighth of the people interviewed (12 per cent) refused to commit themselves in any way, much the highest figure of abstentions on any question in the field survey. **1979** H. KISSINGER *White House Years* xix. 771 In 1969 the Important Question resolution had passed by a wide margin of 71 in favor, 48 against, and 4 abstentions.

ab'stentionism. [f. ABSTENTION + -ISM; cf. ABSTENTIONIST.] The policy of refusing to use one's vote. Also generally, non-participation in the established political process.

1902 F. CLARKE tr. *Ostrogorski's Democracy & Organiz. Polit. Parties* II. 759/1 (Index) Abstentionism, political, of the English middle class. **1960** *New Left Rev.* Nov.-Dec. 4/2

We must take account of the high degree of political 'abstention' by many activists of CND... 'Abstentionism' was..a fairly representative feeling. **1973** J. Biggs-Davison *Hand is Red* ix. 113 Abstentionism by the minority plagued the early years of the state. **1974** J. White tr. *Poulantzas's Fascism & Dictatorship* iv. iii. 209 As early as 1919, the communist faction of the Socialist Party..proposed 'abstentionism', i.e. non-participation in elections and in parliament. **1982** *N.Y. Times* 6 July A3/4 He added that there had been a record turnout and that abstentionism had been 'defeated'.

abstentionist (æbˈstɛnʃənɪst). [f. ABSTENTION + -IST.] One who practises or approves abstention.
1880 *Blackw. Mag.* June 810 We may expect other Conservative abstentionists to imitate the good example set by Lord Carnarvon.
Also *attrib.* (passing into *adj.*).
1927 *Glasgow Herald* 10 Aug. 10/2 The exhilarating risks of a forward, as distinct from a cautious and abstentionist, policy. **1955** *Times* 14 July 6/4 The break-away 'abstentionist' group of the Argentine Conservative..Party has issued a declaration demanding the resignation of President Perón.

abstentious (æbˈstɛnʃəs). [f. ABSTENTI-ON + -OUS, analogously to *contention, contentious*, L. *contentiōn-em, contentiōs-us*.] Characterized by abstinence; self-restraining or refraining.
1879 Farrar *St. Paul* II. 447 The Colossian teachers were trying to supplement Christianity, theoretically by a deeper wisdom, practically by a more abstentious holiness.

†**abˈster**, *v. Obs. rare.* [ad. L. *absterrēre* to frighten from, f. *abs* from + *terrēre* to frighten.] To deter. (Perhaps only used by Becon.)
1542 Becon *Christmas Banq.* Wks. 1843, 63 This in like manner should abster and fear me and mine from doing evil. —— *Pleas. New Nosegay* Wks. 1843, 198 Unfeigned Humility..also absterreth and frayeth us from all arrogancy, pride, and elation of mind.

absterge (æbˈstɜːdʒ), *v.* [? a. Fr. *absterge-r* (16th c. in Littré), ad. L. *abstergēre* to wipe away, f. *abs* off + *tergēre* to wipe. Perhaps directly from the Latin.] To wipe away; to wipe clean; to cleanse; also *fig.* to purge.
1541 R. Copland *Galyen's Terap.* 2 Hj b, But yf ye wyll clense the vlcere ye must chuse thynges yᵗ absterge or wasshe moderatly, as rawe hony. **1621** Burton *Anat. of Mel.* (1651) II. ii. II. 238 Baths..are still frequented..all over Greece, and those hot countries; to absterge belike that fulsomeness of sweat, to which they are there subject. **1718** Quincy *Compl. Disp.* 98 [It] absterges the mucus from the stomach and other parts. **1817** Coleridge *Ess. on Own Times* (1850) III. 957 It was left for the Kraulmen, from whose errors they [some converts from 'Hottentotism'] absterged themselves, to insult and abuse them as apostates and renegades.

abstergent (æbˈstɜːdʒənt), *a.* and *sb.* [? a. Fr. *abstergent* (16th c.), ad. L. *abstergent-em* pr. pple. of *abstergēre*; see prec. Perhaps f. the Lat. direct.]
A. *adj.* Cleansing, scouring, having a cleansing quality.
1612 Woodall *Surg. Mate* Wks. 1653, 37 Honey..hath an abstergent or cleansing force. **1830** Lindley *Nat. Syst. Bot.* 162 Abstergent properties, mixed sometimes with a good deal of acridity, distinguish them [the house-leek tribe]. **1860** J. P. Kennedy *Life of W. Wirt* II. ix. 149 The abstergent, bracing, exhilarating touch of a sea-bath after a hot day.
B. *sb.* [sc. agent or substance.]
1751 Chambers *Cyc.* Abstergents or Abstersive medicines ..abrade and wipe away such mucous particles as they meet in their passage, and thus cleanse the parts from viscid, or impure adhesions. **1859** R. F. Burton in *Jrnl. R.G.S.* XXIX. 323/3 One reason perhaps which causes them to avoid heavy and close-fitting clothing is their want of abstergents.

†**abstergify**, *v. Obs. rare*⁻¹. [irreg. f. L. *abstergē-re*, + -FY.] 'To cleanse.'
1612 Benvenuto *Passenger's Dialogues, Ital. & Eng.* (Nares) Specially, when wee would abstergifie, and that the huske remaine behind in the boyling of it.

†**abˈsterse**, *v. Obs. rare*⁻¹. [f. L. *absters-us*, pa. pple. of *abstergēre*, cf. *asperse*.] = ABSTERGE.
1646 Sir T. Browne *Pseud. Epid.* 164 Some attrition from an acide and vitriolous humidity in the stomack..may absterse, and shave the scorious parts thereof.

abstersion (æbˈstɜːʃən). Also 6 **abstertion, abstarcion.** [a. Fr. *abstersion* (16th c.), n. of action f. L. *absters-* ppl. stem of *abstergēre*: see ABSTERGE and -ION¹.] The act or process of wiping clean, cleansing, scouring, or purging. *lit.* and *fig.*
1543 Traheron *Vigo's Chirurg* II. xvii. 28 Incarne [the place] wyth thys incarnative, whych dothe bothe incarne and mundifye with some abstertion. **1562** Bulleyn *Dial. betw. Sorenes* 16 a, Use the maner of digestion, and abstarcion in maner as I haue said. **1649** Jer. Taylor *Great Exemp.* I. ix. 135 The Messias..needed not the abstersions of repentance, or the washings of baptisme. **1814** Scott *Wav.* (1829) xx. 153 The task of ablution and abstersion being performed..by a smoke-dried skinny old Highland woman. **1850** Merivale *Hist. Rom. Emp.* (1865) VIII. lxvi. 218 No great city was ever so badly placed for due abstersion by natural outfall.

abstersive (æbˈstɜːsɪv), *a.* and *sb.* [a. Fr. *abstersif, -ive*, f. L. *absters-* ppl. stem of *abstergēre*: see ABSTERSE and -IVE.]
A. *adj.* Having the quality of purging, cleansing, scouring, or washing away impurities.
1533 Elyot *Castel of Helth* (1541) 27 White betes are also abstersive, and lowseth the bealye. **1603** Holland *Plutarch's Morals* 656 These almonds have an abstersive propertie to bite, to clense and scoure the flesh. *a* **1680** Butler *Rem.* (1759) I. 111 Has an abstersive Virtue to make clean Whatever Nature made in Man obscene. **1725** Pope *Odyss.* xx. 189 And let th' abstersive sponge the board renew. **1845** Ford *Hdbk. Spain* 124 *Aqua bendita* which the devil is said to hate even worse than monks did the common abstersive fluid.
B. *sb.* [sc. medicine or agent.] Also *fig.*
1563 T. Gale *Antid.* I. iii. 3 Such medicines as do mundifie, and clense wounds or filthy vlcers, are called abstersiues. **1645** Milton *Tetrach.* (1851) 159 The lowest lees of a canonicall infection livergrown to their sides, which perhaps will never uncling, without the strong abstersive of som heroick magistrat. **1702** Petty in Sprat's *Hist. R. Soc.* 295 Abstersives are Fuller's earth, Soap, Linseed-oyl, and Oxgall. **1727** Swift *Gulliver* III. vi. 216 Administer to each of them..abstersives.

abstersiveness (æbˈstɜːsɪvnɪs). [f. prec. + -NESS.] The quality of being cleansing or purgative.
1657 G. Starkey *Helmont's Vind.* 327 The Abstersivenesse of the Saline Elixir promotes the cure for the Nephritis. **1662** Fuller *Worthies* (1840) III. 203 The abstersiveness of this water, keeping a wound clean, till the balsam of nature doth recover it. **1759** Martin *Nat. Hist.* I. co. Surrey 144 It [Epsom water] was at first applied to sores, which from its Abstersiveness [*pr.* Abstensiveness] it soon healed.

abstersory (æbˈstɜːsərɪ), *a.* ? *Obs. rare.* [f. L. *absters-*, ppl. stem of *abstergēre* + -ORY.] Cleansing, purgative; abstersive.
1673 C. Butler *Fem. Mon.* (1634) 170 Being boiled it [honey] is..lesse laxative, also lesse sharpe and abstersory. **1650** Venner *Via Recta* 55 It hath also a very speciall abstersory property.

abstinence (ˈæbstɪnəns). [a. Fr. *abstinence*, refashioned on OFr. *astenance, astinence*:—L. *abstinentia*, n. of quality f. *abstinent-em*, pr. pple. of *abstinē-re*. See ABSTAIN.]
1. a. The action or practice of abstaining or refraining; forbearance. Const. *from* (*of* obs.).
1382 Wyclif *Num.* xxx. 14 That bi fastynge and abstynens of other thingis she traueyl hir soul. *c* **1440** *Gesta Rom.* (1838) I. ii. 7 Goode werkis of kyndnesse, abstinence fro synne, and almysdede. **1594** Hooker *Eccl. Pol.* (1632) v. 388 Jewish Abstinence from certaine kinds of meates. **1692** Dryden *St. Eurem. Ess.* 343 The true Devout Person breaks with Nature..to take pleasure in the abstinence of pleasures. **1732** Arbuthnot *Rules of Diet* 397 There are no better rules than Abstinence from those things which occasion it. **1862** Trench *Miracles* xv. 260 Abstinence from an outward work is not essential to the observance of a Sabbath.
b. *spec.* A forbearance from hostilities, an armistice or truce.
1419 Sir W. Bardolph in Ellis *Orig. Lett.* II. 23. I. 75 Duryng the abstinence of werr of viij dayys. **1469** *Paston Lett.* 624 II. 379 I sent you a bill which concludith an abstinence of werre to be had unto Fryday last was. **1577–87** Holinshed *Chron.* III. 1192/1 Mondaie the seuenteenth of June about eight of the clocke, an abstinence of warre was concluded. **1873** Burton *Hist. Scot.* V. lvi. 116 The truce or abstinence..was continued by short additions to the end of the year.
2. *absol.* Forbearance of any indulgence of appetite, self-restraint: **a.** continence (the oldest sense); **b.** fasting; **c.** the practice of abstaining from alcoholic beverages, also known as ***total abstinence.***
c **1300** *St. Brandan* (1844) 35 There he ladde a full strayte and holi lyfe in grete penaunce and abstynence. **1340** *Ayenb.* 236 Þet chastete ssel bi straytliche y-loked and wel wyþ-draȝe be abstinence [uorberinge]. *c* **1386** Chaucer *Pers. T.* 757 Agayns glotonye the remedie is abstinence. **1494** Fabyan (1542) v. cxxxv. 120 She remeued to Ely, and there was abbesse, and lyued in great penaunce and abstynence. **1526** Tindale *Acts* xxvii. 21 Then after longe abstinence, Paul stode forth in the myddes of them. **1588** Shaks. *L.L.L.* iv. iii. 259 Say, Can you fast? your stomacks are too young: And abstinence ingenders maladies. **1611** Bible *2 Esdras* vii. 55 The faces of them which haue vsed abstinence, shall shine aboue the starres. **1704** Nelson *Festivals & Fasts* (1739) 434 No Abstinence can partake of the Nature of Fasting except there be something in it that afflicts us. **1837** J. H. Newman *Par. Serm.* (ed. 2) III. xv. 231 Such light abstinences as come in our way. **1843** Lytton *Last of Bar.* III. v. 163 His table was supplied more abundantly and daintily than his habitual abstinence required. **1853** Kingsley *Hypatia* Pref. 14 The passionate Eastern character, like all weak ones, found total abstinence easier than temperance.
3. *Pol. Econ.* The practice of abstaining from expenditure in order to accumulate capital.
[**1848** Mill *Pol. Econ.* I. I. v. 83 Suppose that every capitalist came to be of opinion that not being more meritorious than a well-conducted labourer, he ought not to fare better; and accordingly laid by, from conscientious motives, the surplus of his profits; or suppose this abstinence not spontaneous, but imposed by law or opinion upon all capitalists.] **1867** J. Laing *Theory of Business* ii. 25 Cost..is resolvable into prior outlay, on account of labour, and 'abstinence'. **1890** A. Marshall *Princ. Economics* IV. vii. I. 289 That sacrifice of present pleasure for the sake of future, which is the chief cause of the accumulation of wealth, has been called abstinence by economists. **1899** J. B. Clark *Distrib. Wealth* ix. 126 Abstinence is nothing more than electing to take out income in the form of wealth-creating goods, instead of that of pleasure-giving goods.
4. Special Comb.: **abstinence syndrome** *Med.*, the group of physical symptoms that appear when a person who is addicted to a drug suddenly stops taking it; cf. *withdrawal symptoms* s.v. WITHDRAWAL 7.
[**1929** *Jrnl. Pharmacol. & Exper. Therap.* XXXVI. 473 Abstinence symptoms are..due to the fact that stimulation of the nervous system, or increased irritability, outlasts the depression.] **1934** *Jrnl. Amer. Med. Assoc.* 10 Nov. 1420/2 These observations included the presence and degree of the signs..which are pertinent to the *abstinence syndrome. **1955** *Publ. Amer. Dial. Soc.* xxiv. 34 Addicts..are more likely to talk when faced with the terrible abstinence syndrome in jail. **1974** M. C. Gerald *Pharmacol.* xi. 197 The abstinence syndrome [of chloral hydrate] resembles that seen after chronic alcohol usage.

abstinency (ˈæbstɪnənsɪ). [ad. L. *abstinentia*: see ABSTINENCE.] The quality of being abstinent; the habit or practice of abstaining, especially from food; fasting; a fast. (Not always kept distinct from ABSTINENCE, the action of refraining, but never used with *from*.)
1576 Woolton *Chr. Manual* (1851) 46 Ignorant people undoubtedly, if they see any men lean with abstinency.. conceive an especial conceit of their sanctimony and holiness. **1649** Selden *Laws of Eng.* (1739) II. xxxiv. 153 She wanted a mind to that course of life [marriage] from natural abstinency. **1683** Tryon *Way to Health* 76 Abstinency is the only Physitian that a man can make use of..also, Abstinency is the most skilfullest cook. **1874** Reynolds *John Bapt.* iii. §2. 165 John the Nazarite, in..his duties and abstinencies.

abstinent (ˈæbstɪnənt), *a.* and *sb.* [a. Fr. *abstinent*, refashioned on OFr. *astenant*:—L. *abstinent-em*, pr. pple. of *abstinē-re*: see ABSTAIN.]
A. *adj.* Holding back or refraining; *esp.* from indulgence of appetite; continent, abstemious, temperate.
c **1386** Chaucer *Pers. T.* 873 Abstinent in etyng and drynkyng, in speche and in dede. *c* **1440** *Prompt. Parv.* Abstynent, or absteynynge. **1588** A. King *Canisius' Catech.* 132 b, Bot he, quha is abstinent, sal prolonge his lyf. **1603** Holland *Plutarch's Morals* 651 And he agaïne, who is too too sober, and abstinent altogether, becommeth unpleasant and unsociable. **1713** *Guardian* (1756) I. 16 She has passed several years in widowhood with that abstinent enjoyment of life, which has done honour to her deceased husband. **1867** J. Martineau *Chr. Life* (ed. 4) 84 What abstinent integrity is..demanded by many a master.
B. *sb.* One who abstains, an abstainer, a faster. In *Eccl. Hist.* the *Abstinents* were a sect who appeared in the 3rd century.
c **1440** *Prompt. Parv.* Abstynent..or he that dothe abstynence. **1615** Chapman *Odyssey* xvii. 381 And this same harmful belly by no mean The greatest abstinent can ever wean. **1669** J. Reynolds *Disc.* in *Harl. Misc.* (1745) iv. 48 Some of these Abstinents were of melancholick complexions. **1753** Chambers *Cyc. Suppl.* s.v., Some represent the *Abstinentes*..that they particularly enjoined abstinence from the use of marriage; others say, from flesh; and others, from wine. **1860** *All Y. Round* No. 64. 322 There is also [in China] a female sect called the Abstinents ..who make a vow to abstain from everything that has enjoyed life, and to eat nothing but vegetables.

†**abstiˈnential**, *a. Obs. rare*⁻¹. [f. L. *abstinentia* + -AL¹. Cf. *penitential*.] Of or pertaining to abstinence.
1681 *Religio Clerici* 120 Granting we have arrived at some proficiency in the Abstinential vertues.

abstinently (ˈæbstɪnəntlɪ), *adv.* [f. ABSTINENT + -LY².] In an abstinent manner, with abstinence.
1626 Donne *Devotions* 582 O if thou hadst euer re-admitted Adam into Paradise, how abstinently would he haue walked by that tree. **1788** Johnson *Lett.* 230. II. 109 Mr. Thrale never will live abstinently till he can persuade himself to abstain by rule.

†**abˈstorted,** *ppl. a. Obs.* [f. L. *abs* away + *tort-us* twisted + -ED.] 'Forced away, wrung from another by violence,' J., (from Phillips 1662, Bailey 1721). Cockeram 1626 has 'Abstorqued, wrested away by force'.

abstract (ˈæbstrækt), *ppl. a.* and *sb.* [ad. L. *abstract-us* drawn away, f. *abs* off, away + *tractus*, pa. pple. of *trahĕre* to draw.] At first, like its L. orig., a participle and adjective, accented *abˈstract*; after the formation of the vb. *abstract*, ABSTRACTED gradually took its place as a participle, leaving ˈ*abstract* with a new accent as an adjective only.
A. *pple.* and *adj.*
†**1.** Drawn, derived, extracted. *Obs.*
1387 Trevisa *Higden* (Rolls Ser.) I. 21 The names of the auctores been rehersede here, of whom thys presente cronicle is abstracte. **1496** *Bk. of St. Albans* (1810) 6 The fyve perfyte [coats of arms] ben thise, Termynall: Collattrall: Abstrakte: Fyxall: & Bastarde.
†**2.** Withdrawn, drawn away, removed, separate; = ABSTRACTED 1. Const. *from. Obs.*

1690 J. Norris *Beatitudes* (1694) I. 171 The more abstract therefore we are from the body..the more fit we shall be both to behold, and to indure the Rays of the Divine Light. **1726** *Let.* in *Wodrow's Corresp.* (1843) III. 237 As to the other query about Mr. Simson, I believe you know I kept myself abstract in his former process. **1765** Harris *Three Treat.* II. iv. 80 There is an eminent Delight in this very Recognition itself, abstract from anything pleasing in the Subject recognized.

3. Withdrawn from the contemplation of present objects; = abstracted 2. *arch.*

1509 Barclay *Ship of Fooles* (1570) 51 Their minde abstract, not knowing what they say. **1860** R. A. Vaughan *Ho. w. Mystics* I. VI. i. 153 Master Eckart ceased, and went on his way again..with his steady step and abstract air.

4. a. Withdrawn or separated from matter, from material embodiment, from practice, or from particular examples. Opposed to *concrete*.

1557 Recorde *Whetst.* A ii, Abstracte nombers are those, whiche have no denomination annexed vnto them. **1651** Hobbes *Leviathan* I. iv. 16 Called names Abstract; because severed (not from Matter, but) from the account of Matter. **1678** Cudworth *Intell. Syst.* 806 These Demons or Angels, are not Pure, Abstract, Incorporeal Substances. **1810** Coleridge *Friend* (1865) 121 Luther lived long enough to see the consequences of the doctrines into which indignant pity and abstract ideas of right had hurried him. **1846** Mill *Logic* I. ii. §4. 33 An abstract name is a name which stands for an attribute of a thing. **1851** Sir J. Herschel *Study of Nat. Phil.* I. ii. 18 Abstract science is independent of a system of nature,—of a creation,—of everything, in short, except memory, thought, and reason. **1870** Yeats *Nat. Hist. Comm.* 5 No amount of abstract reasoning would have led us to discover the properties and uses of iron. **1873** Gladstone in *Daily News* Feb. 19 What I understand by an abstract resolution is a resolution which does not carry with it an operative principle likely to produce within a reasonable time particular consequences.

b. Ideal.

1736 Butler *Analogy* II. viii. 399 That the three angles of a triangle are equal to two right ones is an abstract truth. **1775** Burke *Sp. on Concil. w. Am.* Wks. III. 51 Abstract liberty, like other mere abstractions, is not to be found. Liberty inheres in some sensible object. **1828** Sewell *Oxf. Prize Ess.* 10 [They] never placed the perfection of human excellence, as Lycurgus, in the abstract soldier. **1840** Thirlwall *Greece* VII. lv. 110 It is not to be supposed, that ..he was animated..by abstract philanthropy.

c. Abstruse.

1725 Wodrow *Corresp.* (1843) III. 173, I was extremely pleased with some of his reasonings; but in some places he was so abstract and out of my dull way of thinking, that I could not reach him. **1794** Sullivan *View of Nat.* I. iv. 21 [He] will tremblingly..repose upon abstract speculations, and incomprehensible mysteries.

d. In the fine arts, characterized by lack of or freedom from representational qualities.

1915 *Forum* (N.Y.) Dec. 665 This painter no doubt has tried to be significantly abstract. *Ibid.* 670 Dore shows an uninteresting abstract canvas. **1921** A. Huxley *Crome Yellow* xii. 116 His work..[is] frightfully abstract now—frightfully abstract and frightfully intellectual. **1929** C. Day Lewis *Transitional Poem* I. 16 The intellectual Quixotes of the age Prattling of abstract art. **1948** H. Read *Art Now* 134 In practice we call 'abstract' all works of art which, though they may start from the artist's awareness of an object in the external world, proceed to make a self-consistent and independent aesthetic unity in no sense relying on an objective equivalence. **1948** R. O. Dunlop *Understanding Pictures* iv. 42 The pure abstract picture in which all representation of objects, all extraneous subject-matter, was finally eliminated and the canvas contained only shapes, spaces, colours.

e. Of other art forms.

1877 G. B. Shaw *How to become Musical Critic* (1960) 14 Detailed programs seem to be a complete mistake. They may impart a certain interest to a composition for those who are incapable of appreciating abstract music. **1890** ——[see absolute *music*]. **1957** *Listener* 19 Dec. 1041/2 In poetry, as in painting, it is perhaps the abstract which is nowadays the easiest to do passably... Mr. Roy Fuller's competence and self-confidence as an abstract poet in the Auden manner are unquestionable. **1958** *Oxford Mail* 23 Aug. 6/5 The music is thin, the ballet abstract in form and inventive in choreography. **1962** *Times* 15 Jan. 14/5 Of all the common errors to do with ballet, none is now more common, or more erroneous, than that implied by the comparatively recent term 'abstract ballet'.

5. *absol.* 'The abstract,' that which is abstract, the abstract consideration of things; the ideal.

1615 Crooke *Body of Man* 45 They adde indeed a perfection, not to life, that is, to the concreate as we say, but to liuing, that is, to the abstract. **1628** T. Spencer *Logic* 141 Justice in the abstract, is nothing. **1820** W. Irving *Sk. Bk.* I. 47 She has no idea of poverty but in the abstract: she has only read of it in poetry.

6. *Comb.* **abstract-concrete** *a.*, concerning both abstract and concrete aspects; **abstract expressionism** (orig. *U.S.*) (cf. sense A. 4 d) = action *painting*; hence ***abstract expressionist*** a. and sb.; **abstract impressionism** (orig. *U.S.*), a form of painting which combines the characteristics of abstract art and impressionism; hence ***abstract impressionist*** a. and sb.

1874 J. Fiske *Cosmic Philos.* I. I. viii. 215 Molar physics, molecular physics, and chemistry, dealing with abstract laws of motion and force that are gained from experience of concrete phenomena, and appealing at every step to the concrete processes of observation and experiment, may be distinguished as abstract-concrete sciences. **1959** *Listener* 2 July 26/2 The international idioms of pure Abstract, Abstract-Concrete, Tâchiste, Automatist, and all the rest. **1964** *Language* XL. 249 The opposition 'abstract-concrete' as it is customarily used to characterize aphasic speech. **1952** *Amer. Artist* Apr. 26 (*title*) From abstract expressionism to new objectivity. **1957** B. S. Myers *Art & Civiliz.* 656 The New York school of Abstract Expressionism led by such artists as Jackson Pollock (1912–1956) and Willem de Kooning (b. 1904). **1958** *Observer* 3 Aug. 11/7 William Johnstone's method has an increasing air of abstract-expressionist improvisation. **1957** D. Cooper in *Monet* (Edin. Festival Catal.) 6 We..find the last works of Monet described as 'abstract impressionism', a label which serves the convenient purpose of immediately linking them with that tendency in contemporary painting for which the term 'abstract expressionism' has already been coined. **1958** L. Alloway in *Abstract Impressionism* (Arts Council G.B.) 4/1 The term Abstract Impressionism seems to have been coined by Elaine De Kooning in 1951 at the Arts Club, 8th Street, New York. **1958** *Observer* 15 June 15 Joan Mitchell's ..painting..might indeed be called 'abstract impressionist'. **1958** *Listener* 9 Oct. 570/3 Humphrey Spender comes out as an accomplished abstract impressionist.

B. *sb.* Something abstracted or drawn from others; hence,

1. 'A smaller quantity containing the virtue or power of a greater' (J.), or one thing concentrating in itself the virtues of several; a compendium.

1561 T. N[orton] tr. *Calvin's Inst.* (1634) I. xiii. 57 So shall the Godhead of the Sonne bee an abstract from the essence of God, or a derivation out of a part of the whole. **1606** Shaks. *Ant. & Cl.* I. iv. 9 You shall finde there a man, who is th' abstracts of all faults, That all men follow. **1677** Hale *Prim. Orig. Man.* IV. viii. 362 He is an Abstract or Compendium of the greater World. **1836** Gen. Thompson *Exerc.* IV. 127 The Peers are not an abstract, or at all events not a fair abstract, of the upper classes.

2. *spec.* A summary or epitome of a statement or document. Also *attrib.*

1528 Gardiner in Pocock *Rec. of Ref.* I. I. 117 We send herein enclosed, abstracts of such letters as hath been sent to the pope's holiness. **1715** Burnet *Hist. own Time* (1766) II. 82 I will give you here a short abstract of all that was said. **1799** Wellington *Lett.* (G.D.) I. 34 In the abstracts, it appears that the strength of the..forces consisted of 48,000 men. **1863** Cox *Inst. of Eng. Govt.* Pref. 8 Copies or abstracts of State papers and records. **1867** Smyth *Sailors' Word-Bk.* s.v. An abstract log contains the most important subjects of a ship's log. **1927** [see abstractor]. **1959** L. M. Harrod *Librar. Gloss.* (ed. 2) 12 *Abstract.* I. A form of current bibliography in which contributions to periodicals are summarized... When published in periodical form they are known as journals of abstracts. 2. The individual entry. **1962** *Lancet* 19 May 1068/1 Have you ever tried doing abstracts? I once did—for about a year. It was the American articles that caused me the most anguish.

b. abstract of title (*Law*): An epitome of the evidences of ownership.

1858 Ld. St. Leonards *Property Law* viii. 57 One great complaint at the present day, is the necessity of carrying back abstracts of title for sixty years.

3. An abstraction, an abstract term.

1530 Palsgr. 50 All suche substantives..especially if they be suche as the logicians call abstractes. *a* **1638** Mede *Apost. of latter Times* 100 The Hebrewes use Abstracts for Concretes..as *justitia pro justis*: captivity for captives. **1765** Tucker *Lt. of Nat.* I. 498 Our abstracts derive all originally from the concrete.

4. A work of art in the abstract style (see sense A. 4 d).

1950 in Webster Add. **1958** 'N. Blake' *Penknife in Heart* ii. 30 The great mainsail curved up into the darkness, like a sculptured abstract. **1959** *House & Garden* July 72 A whole lot of modern designs..included mechanically produced abstracts.

abstract (æb'strækt), *v.* [f. abstract *ppl. a.*, like *content* vb. f. *content* adj. After the appearance of the vb., *abstract* was used for some time as its pa. pple. till superseded by the normal *abstracted.*]

1. *trans.* To withdraw, deduct, remove, or take away (something); *euphem.* to take away secretly, slyly, or dishonestly; to purloin.

1542 Boorde *Dyetary* (1870) xi. 258 The brande abstracted and abjected. **1549** *Compl. of Scotl.* xv. 127 Thou suld abstrak thy inuectiue reprocha. **1588** A. King *P. Canisius' Catech.* h vij, Giff ȝe sowld abstract vair fra 30. **1834** Ht. Martineau *Moral* II. 42 The public burdens, which at present abstract a large proportion of profits and wages. **1852** Layard *Nineveh* ix. 233 The principal public quarrels related to property abstracted by the Arabs from one another's tents. **1872** W. Black *Adv. Phaeton* vi. 72 Von Rosen had quietly abstracted the bearing-reins from the harness. **1880** Geikie *Phys. Geog.* ii. 10. 68 When evaporation takes place, heat is abstracted by the vapour from the surface which evaporates.

b. *absol.* To deduct; to derogate; to take away.

1825–45 Carlyle *Schiller* (ed. 2) II. 97 There is throughout a certain air of stiffness and effort which abstracts from the theatrical illusion.

†**c.** *Chem.* To separate an essence or chemical principle by distillation, etc.; to extract. *Obs.*

? **1685** Boyle (J.) Having dephlegmed spirit of salt, and gently abstracted the whole spirit, there remaineth in the retort a styptical substance. **1725** Bradley *Fam. Dict.* s.v. *Scurvy*, From the fresh gather'd tops of Fir a little bruised, Abstract spirit of Wine or at least good Nants Brandy.

2. *trans.* To draw off or apart; to separate, withdraw, disengage *from.*

1557 Paynell *Barclay's Jugurtha* 28 b, His mynde was abstract..from the defence of goodness and honesty vnto his olde vice. **1649** Selden *Laws of Eng.* (1739) I. lv. 97 To abstract the mixed people each from other. **1663** Cowley *Of Solitude* Wks. 1710 II. 696 The Importunities of Company or Business, which would abstract him from his Beloved [Poetry]. **1692** Bentley *Boyle Lect.* vi. 212 They ought to abstract their Imagination from that false Infinite Extension, and conceive one Particle of Matter. **1756** Burke *Subl. & B.* Wks. I. 262 Campanella..could so abstract his attention from any sufferings of his body that he was able to endure the rack itself without much pain.

b. *absol.* To withdraw (the attention), divert.

1823 Lamb *Elia* (1865) Ser. II. ii. 250 The healing influence of studious pursuits was upon him, to soothe and to abstract.

3. *refl.*, and *intr.* with *refl.* meaning. To withdraw oneself, to retire *from. lit.* and *fig.*

1671 *True Non-Conformist* 17 Desirous..that private men abstract from officious meddling. **1690** Locke *Hum. Underst.* IV. iv. 8 Wks. 1727 I. 263 The Truth and Certainty of Moral Discourses abstracts from the Lives of Men. **1722** Steele *Consc. Lover* II. i. When I abstract myself from my own Interest in the thing.

b. ***abstracting from***: withdrawing in thought from, leaving out of consideration, apart from. *Obs.* or *arch.*

1655 Marq. Worcester *Cent. Inv.* Dedic. II. 16, Yet, abstracting from any Interest of my own, but as a Fellow-subject and Compatriot will I ever labour. **1667** *Decay of Chr. Piety* v. §26. 240 Take her as mere Paynim, abstracting from the expectation of reward or punishment. **1679** Jenison *Narr. Pop. Plot* 24 His Person (abstracting from his Crimes) having been always..dear to me. **1711** C. M. *Let. to Curat* 95 Abstracting from..what was needful for humouring the thing, the Curat seldom speaks but in the words of the First-rate Divines. **1847** De Quincey *Secret Soc.* Wks. 1863 VI. 254 Abstracting, however, from the violent disturbances of those stormy times..we may collect that the scheme of the Farrers was, etc.

4. To separate in mental conception; to consider apart from the material embodiment, or from particular instances.

1612 Drayton *Poly-olbion* A 2 The verse oft..so infolds, that suddaine conceipt cannot abstract a forme of the clothed truth. *c* **1690** South *Serm.* (1715) I. 163 For the Vulgar have not such Logical Heads, as to be able to Abstract such subtile Conceptions. **1776** Gibbon *Decl. & F.* I. xxi. 575 We may strive to abstract the notions of time, of space, and of matter. **1870** Jevons *Elem. Logic* xxxii. 285 To abstract is to separate the qualities common to all individuals of a group from the peculiarities of each individual.

†**5.** To derive, to claim extraction for. Cf. abstract *a.* 1. *Obs.*

1610 Gwillim *Displ. Her.* (1660) I. vi. 38 Our understanding is informed from what Line of Consanguinity the Bearer of such difference doth abstract himselfe.

6. To make an abstract of; to summarize, epitomize; to abridge.

1678 Quarles *Arg. & Parth.* I There dwelt that Virgin, that Arcadian glory, Whose rare composure did abstract the story Of true Perfection. **1743** Franklin *Let.* Wks. 1840 VI. 17 That the business and duty of the Secretary be..to abstract, correct, and methodize such papers as require it. **1795** Gibbon *Auto-Biog.* 46 This system I studied, and meditated, and abstracted. **1882** *Pall Mall G.* 10 May 5/1 We cannot attempt to abstract the article here, but some salient points can be given.

abstractable (æb'stræktəb(ə)l), *a.* Also -ible. [f. abstract *v.* + -able.] Capable of being abstracted, in the senses of the verb.

1893 W. James in *Mind* II. 509 There must be *some* things whose resemblance is *not* based on such discernible and abstractable identity. **1943** A. M. Farrer *Finite & Infinite* viii. 94 The only common properly abstractible form is that of mere numerability. **1958** D. J. Furley in A. D. Booth et al. *Aspects of Transl.* 64 A poem has meaning in very many different ways..some may be abstractable only at the cost of others.

abstracted (æb'stræktɪd), *ppl. a.* [f. abstract *v.* + -ed.]

1. Drawn off, withdrawn, removed; separate, apart *from.*

1660 R. Coke *Just. Vind.* 3 The whole body of Geometry is of all Sciences most intelligible, and yet abstracted from all sensible matter. **1667** Milton *P.L.* IX. 463 The Evil one abstracted stood From his own evil, and for the time remained Stupidly good. **1736** Butler *Analogy* II. vii. 374, [A] single event, taken alone and abstracted from all such correspondence. **1870** Lowell *Study Wind.* 237 The Provençal love-poetry was as abstracted from all sensuality as that of Petrarca.

2. Withdrawn from the contemplation of present objects; absent in mind.

1643 Sir T. Browne *Relig. Med.* (1656) II. §11 Our grosser memories have then [in our dreams] so little hold of our abstracted understandings, that they forget the story. **1731** A. Hill *Adv. to Poets* ix, For a Great Poet is, naturally, an abstracted thinker. **1824** Scott *St. Ron. Well* (1868) xxx. 712 He walked on, sucking his cigar, and apparently in as abstracted a mood as Mr. Cargill himself. **1864** Skeat tr. *Uhland's Poems* 170 And therefore let yon maiden take my place, Who sits so silent and abstracted there.

†**3.** Separated from matter or from concrete embodiment, ideal; hence, abstruse, difficult. (*Obs.* replaced by abstract *a.* 4.)

1615 Crooke *Body of Man* 30 The Faculties..are but abstracted Notions. **1648** Wilkins *Math. Mag.* I. i. 4 The ancient Mathematicians did place all their learning in abstracted speculations. **1750** Johnson *Rambler* No. 76 ⁋2 It is natural to mean well, when only abstracted ideas of virtue are proposed to the mind. **1794** Sullivan *View of Nat.* I. 111 The actual divisibility of matter, indeed, is a subject so very intricate and abstracted, that it can only be conjectured upon. **1801** Strutt *Sp. & Past.* Introd. §9. 11 The abstracted love of glory. **1823** Lamb *Elia* (1865) Ser. I. i. 7 A newspaper was thought too refined and abstracted.

4. Presented in abstract; concentrated, epitomized. ? *Obs.*

1633 MASSINGER *Guardian* III. vi. The subtlety of all wantons, tho' abstracted, Can show no seeming colour of excuse To plead in my defence.

abstractedly (æb'stræktɪdlɪ), *adv.* [f. prec. + -LY[2].] In an abstracted or abstract manner.

1. Separately, distinctly, independently *from.*

1637 SANDERSON *21 Serm.* Ad Aul. vi. (1673) 90 We consider it abstractedly from those discommodiousnesses and incumbrances which yet inseparably cleave thereunto. **1741** MIDDLETON *Cicero* II. vii. 84 If we consider this famous passage of the Rubicon, abstractedly from the event, it seems to have been..hazardous & desperate. **1865** MILL *Repr. Gov.* 24/2 Abstractedly from religious considerations, a passive character..may not indeed be very useful to others.

2. With absence of mind.

1836 DICKENS *Nich. Nick.* (C.D. ed.) 57 'Where indeed!' said Nicholas abstractedly. **1866** GEO. ELIOT *Felix Holt* III. xxxvii. 47 The minister paused, and seemed to be abstractedly gazing at some memory.

3. From an abstract point of view; in the abstract; abstractly.

1649 JER. TAYLOR *Great Exemp.* III. §17, If we consider a spiritual life abstractedly, and in itself. **1790** BURKE *Fr. Revol.* Wks. V. 36 Abstractedly speaking, government, as well as liberty, is good. **1826** DISRAELI *Viv. Grey* VI. iv. 330 A constitutional freedom the absence of which they only abstractedly feel.

abstractedness (æb'stræktɪdnɪs). [f. ABSTRACTED + -NESS.] The state of being abstracted or withdrawn. Hence,

†**1.** = ABSTRACTNESS. *Obs.*

1665 GLANVILLE *Scepsis Scient.* 63 It was not only the abstractedness of the matter, that rendered Aristotle's physiology so difficult of comprehension.

†**2.** Withdrawal of self, disinterestedness. *Obs.*

1748 RICHARDSON *Clarissa* (1811) I. xx. 148 Your abstractedness, child, savours, let me tell you, of greater particularity, than what we aim to carry.

3. Withdrawal from the contemplation of present things; absence (of mind).

1705 STANHOPE *Paraphr.* III. 209 Not that we are to like or love nothing but Him; for of such Abstractedness our Condition is not capable. **1844** PHILLIPS *Mem. of Smith* 109 A certain abstractedness of mind..continually broke the symmetry of Mr. Smith's lectures.

4. Ideality.

1878 DOWDEN *Studies* 425 He..can value the abstractedness, the aspiration, the Druidic nature-worship of Laprade.

abstracter (æb'stræktə(r)). [f. ABSTRACT *v.* + -ER[1].] One who abstracts, separates, or makes an abstract.

1681 MANNYNGHAM *Disc.* 58 A very judicious abstracter would find it a hard task to be anything copious. **1732** BERKELEY *Minute Philos.* (1732) II. 126 An Abstracter or Refiner shall so analyse the most simple instantaneous Act of the Mind, as to distinguish therein divers Faculties and Tendencies. **1878** J. THOMSON *Plenip. Key* 8 For what did our great High Pontiff call himself? was it not the Abstracter of the Quintessence?

abstracting (æb'stræktɪŋ), *vbl. sb.* [f. ABSTRACT *v.* + -ING[1].] The act or process of withdrawing, separating, taking away, or forming abstract notions. (Now mostly gerundial.)

1690 LOCKE *Hum. Underst.* (ed. 3) II. xi. 76 The power of Abstracting is not at all in them [the beasts]. **1879** J. WRIGHTSON *Farming* etc. in *Cassell's Techn. Educ.* IV. 108/2 We conclude..by abstracting a sentence or two from Mr. H. N. Jenkins's report.

abstraction (æb'strækʃən). [a. Fr. *abstraction* (14th c. in Littré), ad. L. *abstractiōn-em*, n. of action f. *abstract-us*, pa. pple. of *abstrahĕre*; see ABSTRACT.]

1. The act of withdrawing; withdrawal, separation or removal; in modern usage *euphem.* secret or dishonest removal; pilfering, purloining.

1549 *Compl. of Scotl.* (1873) i. 19 He dois chestee them be the abstraction of..superfluite. **1660** R. COKE *Power & Subj.* 122 I say, Justice must have..abstraction from all affections of love, hate, or self-interest. **1794** PALEY *Evid.* (1817) II. ii. 65 Amongst the negative qualities of our religion..we may reckon its complete abstraction from all views of ecclesiastical or civil policy. **1818** FARADAY *Exp. Res.* vi. 13 He there states its production to be dependent on the abstraction of ammonia by the atmosphere. **1823** LAMB *Elia* (1865) Ser. II. vii. 284 He robs nothing but the revenue, —an abstraction I never greatly cared about. **1848** MILL *Pol. Econ.* 5 (1876) A wrongful abstraction of wealth from certain members of the community.

†**2.** 'Abstraction, in chemistry, denotes the drawing off, or exhaling away, a menstruum from the subject it had been put to dissolve. Some also use the word as synonymous with distillation or even cohobation.' Chambers *Cyc. Suppl.* 1753.

3. The act or process of separating in thought, of considering a thing independently of its associations; or a substance independently of its attributes; or an attribute or quality independently of the substance to which it belongs.

1647 H. MORE *Poems* 126 Next argument let be abstraction, When as the soul with notion precise Keeps off the corporal condition. **1710** BERKELEY *Hum. Knowl.* I. §5 Can there be a nicer strain of abstraction than to distinguish the existence of sensible objects from their being perceived. **1782** PRIESTLEY *Mat. & Spir.* I. x. 113 Mr. Locke.. observed..that abstraction is nothing more than leaving out of a number of resembling ideas what is peculiar to each. **1855** BAIN *Senses & Intell.* (1864) III. iv. §17. 606 The first in order of the scientific processes is Abstraction, or the generalizing of some property, so as to present it to the mind, apart from the other properties that usually go along with it in nature. **1859** SIR W. HAMILTON *Lect. on Metaph.* II. xxxiv. 285 Abstraction is thus not a positive act of mind, as it is often erroneously described in philosophical treatises, —it is merely a negation to one or more objects, in consequence of its concentration on another.

4. The result of abstracting: the idea of something which has no independent existence; a thing which exists only in idea; something visionary.

1644 MILTON *Educ.* (1738) 136 They present their young unmatriculated novices at first coming with the most intellective abstractions of logic and metaphysics. **1818** HAZLITT *Eng. Poets* (1870) ii. 44 Death is a mighty abstraction, like Night, or Space, or Time. **1850** GLADSTONE *Gleanings* V. lxxvi. 218 Laws are abstractions until they are put into execution. **1851** MARIOTTI *Italy in 1848*, i. 4 They can see nothing in it, save only an idle, chimerical abstraction. **1878** G. A. SIMCOX in *Academy* 605/3 Science, strictly speaking, is an abstraction, and is not and never can be adequate to the whole, even of our experience.

5. A state of withdrawal or seclusion from worldly things or things of sense.

1649 JER. TAYLOR *Great Exemp.* (1653) 124 Lifted up by the abstractions of this first degree of mortification. *a* **1744** POPE *Let.* (J.) A hermit wishes to be praised for his abstraction.

6. The state of mental withdrawal; inattention to things present; absence of mind.

1790 BOSWELL *Johnson* (Rtldg.) xxiv. 215 As he [Johnson] could neither see nor hear at such a distance from the stage, he was wrapped up in grave abstraction. **1848** L. HUNT *Jar of Honey* iii. 31 Sir Isaac Newton carried abstraction far enough, when he used a lady's finger for a tobacco-stopper.

7. In the fine arts, the practice or state of freedom from representational qualities; a work of art with these characteristics.

1915 *Forum* (N.Y.) Dec. 662 Sheeler..fears to take the final leap into abstraction, not feeling sufficiently sure of his desires. **1921** A. HUXLEY *Crome Yellow* xii. 117 Soon, he says, there'll be just the blank canvas. That's the logical conclusion. Complete abstraction. **1948** R. O. DUNLOP *Understanding Pictures* iv. 44 Cubism was a half-way house on the road to pure abstraction. **1954** WYNDHAM LEWIS *Demon of Progress in Arts* I. vii. 29 It is usually those of very little talent who furnish the little crowds of people painting empty abstractions.

8. *Comb.* **abstraction-monger**, one who deals with visionary ideas.

1860 R. A. VAUGHAN *Ho. w. Mystics* (2 ed.) II. 95 His philosophy is never that of the abstraction-monger.

abstractional (æb'strækʃənəl), *a.* [f. prec. + -AL[1].] Of or pertaining to abstraction.

1865 MILL *Comte* 10 Instead of the Theological we should prefer to speak of the Personal..; instead of Metaphysical, the Abstractional or Ontological. **1867** H. BUSHNELL *Dark Things* 300 A result of this abstractional process. **1907** W. JAMES *Meaning of Truth* (1909) vi. 153 Reduced to a bare abstractional scheme. **1942** *Mind* LI. 241 Spinoza's constant use of '*quatenus*' rather than '*qua*' is no mere stylism, but is closely bound up with his rejection of the abstractional view of knowledge.

abstractionism (æb'strækʃənɪz(ə)m). [f. ABSTRACTION + -ISM.] **1.** The pursuit or cult of abstractions.

1909 W. JAMES *Meaning of Truth* xiv. 284 Abstractionism of the worst sort dogs Mr. Russell in his own trials to tell positively what the word 'truth' means. **1914** F. H. BRADLEY *Ess. Truth & Reality* 143 Prof. James, in *Pragmatism*.. insists..on taking the crime in its abstraction as absolutely real. And then he goes on (Hegel would have smiled) to denounce 'abstractionism'.

2. *spec.* The cult or practice of abstract art.

1926 *Lit. Digest* 30 Oct. 28/2 Expressionismus, expressionism..abstractionism, are being tried. **1937** H. READ *Art & Society* ii. 49 Generally a high degree of naturalism excludes a co-existent abstractionism. **1952** *Lit. Guide* Apr. 60/1 Ours is the age of atomic energy..of psycho-analysis and abstractionism in the arts.

abstractionist (æb'strækʃənɪst). [f. ABSTRACTION + -IST.] **1.** One who occupies himself with abstractions; an idealist. Also as *adj.*

1841 *Kendall's Expositor* I. 373 There are two sorts of Abstractionists in our country... The Virginia Abstractionist is one who recognizes the obligations of oaths, the duty of obeying the Constitution [etc.]... The Kentucky Abstractionist is one who looks chiefly to abstracting money from the people's pockets for the purpose of building up a Nobility. **1844** EMERSON *Ess.* Ser. II. viii. 158 She [*sc.* Nature] punishes abstractionists. **1863** B. TAYLOR *H. Thurston* I. 37 'And your fanatical abstractionists never look at anything in a practical way!' rejoined the Hon. Zeno. **1930** *Time & Tide* 24 May 670 Shall I sum up my criticism of Lady Rhondda's attitude.. by calling it too 'abstractionist'? **1945** A. A. LUCE *Berkeley's Immaterialism* II. 32 Abstractionists are inveterately disposed to think that matter exists.

2. One who practises or advocates the principles of abstract art.

1925 *Internat. Studio* June 229/2 The extremes are held by those who advocate 'innocence of the eye' and the 'pure abstractionists'. **1934** *Burlington Mag.* Aug. 94/1 'The Evolution of Abstract Art' is an intelligent statement by one of the most uncompromising of the younger abstractionists. **1950** A. HUXLEY *Themes & Variations* iv. 184 The pure abstractionist will come forward with a question. Seeing that the non-representational passages in representational works are so expressive, why should anyone bother with representation?

†**abstractitious** (,æbstræk'tɪʃəs), *a. Obs.* [f. L. *abstract-us*: see ABSTRACT + -ITIOUS.] Resulting from abstraction.

1742 BAILEY, Abstractitious [in Pharmacy], a term used to distinguish that Spirit which is drawn from Plants naturally abounding with it. **1853** MAYNE *Exp. Lex.*, *Abstractitious*, old term applied to spirits obtained from plants by distillation, as opposed to that produced by fermentation.

abstractive (æb'stræktɪv), *a.* and *sb.* [ad. assumed L. **abstractīvus*, f. *abstract-us*: see ABSTRACT and -IVE.]

A. *adj.* Of abstracting character or tendency. **a.** Drawing back, withdrawing. **b.** Having the power of abstraction; performing the mental operation of abstraction. **c.** Epitomizing.

1490 CAXTON *Eneydos* xii. 47 Elysse was esprysed with brennyng loue towarde Enee, leuynge by dyspense abstractyue her first vowes of chastyte promysed. **1610** HEALEY *Aug. City of God* IX. xvi. 336 The wisest men in their greatest height of abstractiue speculation. **1668** HOWE *Bl. of Righteous* (1825) 92 How can we divide, in our most abstractive thoughts, the highest pleasures..from this dependence. **1859** SIR W. HAMILTON *Lect. on Metaph.* II. xxxiv. 284 The human body..is thus itself a kind of abstractive machine. The senses cannot but abstract. **1862** *Athenæum* 559/2 We should like to see Mr. Mill's abstractive descriptions reprinted.

B. *sb.* Anything abstractive; *spec.* an abstractive writing, an abstract.

1611 SPEED *Hist. Gt. Brit.* IX. xxi. 67 These are the abstractiues taken out of larger discourses, whereof you may reade if you please, more in Hollinshead.

abstractively (æb'stræktɪvlɪ), *adv.* ? *Obs.* [f. prec. + -LY[2].] In an abstractive or abstract manner; in the abstract, abstractly; separately.

1611 SPEED *Hist. Gt. Brit.* (1632) IX. xvi. 862 They who abstractiuely disputed these highest questions. **1627** FELTHAM *Resolves* Wks. 1677, II. xii. 186 So that life which abstractively is good, by Accidents and Adherencies may become unfortunate. **1677** HALES *Prim. Orig. Mankind* Pref., Yea when I make use of the Sacred and Infallible Scriptures, I do use them abstractively from their Divine and Infallible Authority.

abstractiveness (æb'stræktɪvnɪs). *rare.* [f. ABSTRACTIVE + -NESS.] The quality of being abstractive; the property of drawing away or separating.

1818 BENTHAM *Ch.-of-Engl.* 274 Abstractiveness, the property of drawing a man out of the meritorious course to which he should be attached.

abstractly ('æbstræktlɪ), *adv.* [f. ABSTRACT *a.* + -LY[2].] In an abstract manner. **a.** In an abstract or epitome. **b.** In the abstract; absolutely; without reference to circumstances external.

a **1638** MEDE *Wks.* 1672, I. ii. 5 *Nomen tuum*, God's name ..or His sacred Deity, to wit abstractly expressed. **1717** BENTLEY *Boyle Lect.* (1735) ii. 392 Death, abstractly consider'd, is nothing but Privation. **1852** MCCULLOCH *Tax. & Fund.* (ed. 2) I. iv. 125 Abstractly considered, nothing could be fairer than this proposal.

abstractness ('æbstræktnɪs). [f. ABSTRACT *a.* + -NESS.] The quality of being abstract, or of being withdrawn and separate from the actual, the concrete, or the common; subtilty.

1690 LOCKE *Hum. Underst.* (T.) Truths which established prejudice, or the abstractness of the ideas themselves, might render difficult. **1862** H. SPENCER *First Princ.* (1875) I. ii. §14. 44 The truth we have arrived at is one exceeding in abstractness the most abstract religious doctrines.

ab'stractor. [a. L. *abstractor*, n. of agent f. *abstract-us*: see ABSTRACT.] = ABSTRACTER. (Analogically the more regular form.) One who makes abstracts; *spec.* as the title of a grade of clerks in the Civil Service. Also *attrib.*

The office of abstractor arose from the requirements of Section 6 of the Births and Deaths Registration Act of 1836, according to which the Registrar General was to prepare 'a general abstract of the number of births, deaths and marriages'. Before 1855 the members of the staff at Somerset House engaged on this work were designated 'task-workers'. From 1890 onwards the term has been applied to a new class of 'assistant clerks' in various departments. The spelling *abstracter* gave place to *abstractor* between 1859 and 1866.

1646 QUARLES *Sheph. Or.* ix. If each abstraction draws A curse upon the abstractor from those laws, How can your Councels scape this judgment then? **1855** (Aug.) Statistical abstracter [appointed at the General Register Office, Somerset House]. **1897** *Westm. Gaz.* 3 Sept. 1/2 The old writers or copyists are to be done away with; and in their stead an army of 'abstractors' substituted. **1901** *Daily Chron.* 5 Oct. 6/5 Two abstractor clerks in the War Office. **1927** BALBI *Deafness Expl.* title-p., Appointed by the Institution of Electrical Engineers as Abstractor to Science Abstracts in Electro Acoustics. **1964** *Times Lit. Suppl.* 2 Jan. 16/1 (Advt.), [We] require an abstractor..for our new Research and Development Centre at Harlow.

‖**abstractum** (æb'stræktəm). *Philos.* Usu. in pl. **-ta.** [mod.L., neut. of L. *abstractus* ABSTRACT *ppl. a.*] = ABSTRACT *sb.* 3.

[**1620** BACON *Instauratio Magna* II. bk. i. §51, p. 63 Intellectus humanus fertur ad abstracta propter naturam propriam.] **1865** Farrar *Lang.* 69 In this sense all words are Abstracta. **1865** J. H. Stirling *Secret of Hegel* II. iii. ii. 136 Such despairing contemplation is a result of our occupying only the *abstractum* of the Ansichseyn. **1868** N. Porter *Hum. Intell.* iv. viii. 650 The infinite, etc., may stand for the infinitude, the unconditionedness, the absoluteness of some being—*i.e.*, as an *abstractum* or property of a being. *Ibid.* 651 If they [*sc.* the terms] are used only in the sense of *abstracta*, then the question..is, Can they *be conceived* by the mind? **1932** G. D. Hicks *Berkeley* 159 The *abstracta* in question failed to satisfy this test. **1942** *Mind* LI. 247 The common man would probably hold that the abstracta in all or at any rate in most of these senses are somehow or other 'unreal'.

abstrict (æb'strɪkt), *v. Biol.* [f. L. *ab* off + *strict-*, ppl. stem of *stringĕre* to bind.] *trans.* and *intr.* To separate by constriction: see abstriction.

1893 Tuckey *Amphioxus* 41 Part of the embryo..was abstricted by the egg membrane. *Ibid.* 149 They both abstrict completely from the alimentary canal. **1895** [see abstriction 2].

†**ab'stricted**, *ppl. a. Obs.*$^{-0}$ [f. L. *ab* off + *strict-us* bound (on anal. of *adstrictus*) + -ed.] 'Loosened, unbound.' Bailey 1731, whence in J.

ab'striction. [f. L. *ab* off + *strictiōn-em*, n. of action, f. *stringĕre* to bind, on anal. of *adstrictionem*.] †**1.** A loosening or unbinding. *Obs. rare*$^{-1}$.

1650 H. Brooke *Conserv. of Health* 192 Disease which upon an unadvised abstriction would be riveted into the Body.

2. *Biol.* Separation by constriction.

1893 Tuckey *Amphioxus* 141 An abstriction of the fold formation of the dorsal wall. **1895** Oliver tr. *Kerner's Nat. Hist. Plants* II. 20 Spores which arise..by abstriction and abjunction..the effect..is as though the end of the sac had been tied off or abstricted.

†**ab'stringe**, *v. Obs.*$^{-0}$ [f. L. *ab* off + *string-ĕre* to tie, on anal. of *adstringĕre*.] 'To unbind or loosen.' Bailey 1731, whence in J.

†**ab'strude**, *v. Obs.* Less correctly **abtrude**. [ad. L. *abstrūd-ĕre* to thrust away, conceal, f. *abs* away + *trūd-ĕre* to thrust.] To thrust away.

1627 Feltham *Resolves* (1677) i. xii. 18 Those that are perfect men..must as well know bad, that they may abtrude it. **1662** Phillips, *Abstrude*, to thrust away from. [Thence in Bailey, Johnson, etc.]

abstruse (æb'stru:s), *a.* Also 6–7 **abstruce**. [ad. L. *abstrūs-us* thrust away, concealed, pa. pple. of *abstrūd-ĕre*: see prec. Mentioned by P. Heylin as an 'uncouth and unusual word' in 1656.]

†**1.** Concealed, hidden, secret. *Obs.*

1602 Thynne *Chaucer* (1865) 107 The Abstruse skill, the artificiall veine; By true Annalogie I ryhtly find. **1620** Shelton *Don Quixote* (1746) II. iv. xv. 194 Hidden in the most abstruse dungeons of Barbary. **1667** Milton *P.L.* v. 712 The eternal eye, whose sight discerns Abstrusest thoughts. **1762** B. Stillingfleet *Linn. Or.* in *Misc. Tracts* 9 That the abstruse forces of the elements, which otherwise would escape our senses, may be made manifest.

2. Remote from apprehension or conception; difficult, recondite.

1599 Thynne *Animadv.* (1865) 36 That abstruce scyence whiche Chaucer knewe full well. **1671** Milton *Sams. Ag.* 1064 Be less abstruse, my riddling days are past. **1704** Swift *Tale of a Tub* Wks. 1760 I. 13 Readers, who cannot enter into the abstruser parts of the discourse. **1751** Watts *Improv. Mind* (1801) 107 Let not young students apply themselves to search out deep, dark, and abstruse matters, far above their reach. **1848** H. Miller *First Impr.* (1857) xix. 340 Men who had wrought their way..into some of the abstrusest questions of the schools. **1855** Milman *Lat. Chr.* (1864) V. ix. viii. 380 But these were solitary abstruse thinkers or minds which formed a close esoteric school.

†**abstrused**, *ppl. a. Obs. rare*$^{-1}$. [f. L. *abstrūs-us*: see abstruse + -ed. Cf. *diffuse*, *diffused*.] Concealed, hidden, remote.

1607 Topsell *Serpents* 762 This plague the hollow breast, and every vital part Abstrused..Did open unto Death.

abstrusely (æb'stru:slɪ), *adv.* [f. abstruse + -ly^{2}.] In an abstruse manner; secretly; obscurely.

1611 Cotgr., *Secrettement*..hiddenly, duskely, abstrusely, mystically. **1686** *Basil Valentine, His Last Will & Test.* xxii. Be acquainted with its [the Fire-Rod's] friendlinesse..which is abstrusely hid, and goeth invisibly. *Mod.* The subject is treated too abstrusely to be of interest to the general reader.

abstruseness (æb'stru:snɪs). [f. abstruse + -ness.] The quality of being abstruse; obscurity, difficulty of apprehension.

a **1691** Boyle *Wks.* II. 267 (R.) It is the abstruseness of what is taught in them that makes them almost inevitably so [obscure]. **1754** Edwards *Fr. of Will* (ed. 4) ii. vii. 90 Not to insist any longer on the abstruseness of this distinction. **1810** Coleridge *Friend* I. iii. 18 You hear *The Friend* complained of for its abstruseness and obscurity.

abstrusion (æb'stru:ʒən), *rare*$^{-0}$. [ad. L. *abstrusiōn-em*, n. of action from *abstrūs-us*: see abstruse.] The action of thrusting away.

[Not in Craig 1847. In Ogilvie 1861].

abstrusity (æb'stru:sɪtɪ), *arch.* Also 7 **abstrucity**. [ad. assumed L. **abstrūsitas*, n. of state f. *abstrūs-us*; see -ity.] **a.** Abstruseness; obscurity. **b.** Anything abstruse; an obscure or recondite matter or point.

1632 H. R[eynolds] *Mythomystes* 42 Those secreter Mysteries, and abstrusities of most high diuinity. **1646** Sir T. Browne *Pseud. Epid.* i. viii. 34 Those authors are also suspicious, nor greedily to be swallowed, who pretend to write of..the occult abstrucities of things. **1658** —— *Gard. of Cyrus* II. 560 He may meet with abstrusities of no ready resolution. **1755** B. Martin *Mag. of Arts & Sci.* viii. 165 Reason, Nature, and Analogy here are but blind Guides; they conduct us with Certainty but a little Way in the Abstrusities of infinite Creation. **1839** M. Tupper *Proverb. Philos.* (ed. 3) 285 All will again be for abstrusity. **1925** Dreiser *Amer. Trag.* (1926) II. iii. xiii. 179 There were criminal lawyers deeply versed in the abstrusities and tricks of the criminal law.

†**ab'strusive**, *a. Obs. rare*$^{-1}$. [ad. assumed L. **abstrūsīvus*, f. *abstrūs-ūs*: see -ive.] Of abstruse quality or tendency; abstruse, recondite.

1655–60 T. Stanley *Hist. of Philos.* (1701) 65/2 Pericles could easily reduce the exercise of his mind from secret abstrusive things to publick popular causes.

†**ab'sume**, *v. Obs.* [ad. L. *absūm-ĕre* to take away, f. *ab* away + *sūmĕre* to take.] To consume gradually, to waste away, to carry off.

1596 Barlow 3 *Serm.* i. 45 A Famine..lasting three full yeares, absuming many men. **1677** Hales *Prim. Orig. Man.* i. iii. 85 For if it had burned part after part, the whole must needs be absumed in a portion of time. **1756** C. Lucas *Ess. on Waters* III. 310 The humidity is absumed to about one sixteenth.

†**absumption.** *Obs.* [ad. L. *absūmptiōn-em*, n. of action f. *absūmpt-us*, pa. pple. of *absūm-ere*: see absume.] The process of wasting away, gradual destruction.

1651 tr. *Bacon, Life and Death* 53 Dead Bodies, if they be not intercepted by Putrefaction, will subsist a long time, without any notable Absumption. **1661** R. Lovell *Anim. & Min.* 334 Trembling..is cured, if from the absumption and dissolution of spirits, by analepticks, moderate sleepe, and wine.

absurd (æb'sɜ:d), *a.* and *sb.* [a. Fr. *absurde*, ad. L. *absurd-us* inharmonious, tasteless, foolish, f. *ab* off, here intensive + *surdus* deaf, inaudible, insufferable to the ear.]

A. *adj.*

†**1.** *Mus.* Inharmonious, jarring, out-of-tune. *Obs. rare.*

1617 *Janua Ling.* 773 A harpe maketh not an absurd sound.

2. Out of harmony with reason or propriety; incongruous, unreasonable, illogical. In modern use, *esp.* plainly opposed to reason, and *hence*, ridiculous, silly.

a. Of things.

1557 Recorde *Whetst.* Bb iij b, 8 − 12 is an Absurde nomber. For it betokeneth lesse then nought by 4. **1602** Shaks. *Haml.* i. ii. 103 Fye, 'tis a fault to Heauen, A fault against the Dead, a fault to Nature, To reason most absurd. **1671** J. Webster *Metallogr.* i. 5 That they had no other skill but onely to embalm, were absurd to imagine. **1781** Cowper *Hope* 65 'Tis grave philosophy's absurdest dream, That heaven's intentions are not what they seem. **1855** Macaulay *Hist. Eng.* III. 249 That such reverence may be carried to an absurd extreme is true. **1878** Jevons *Prim. Pol. Econ.* 36 It would be quite absurd if a dozen travellers in one party were to light a dozen separate fires, and cook a dozen separate meals.

b. Of persons.

1597 Bacon *Ess., Negociating* (1862) 196 Use also, such Persons, as affect the Businesse, wherin they are Employed..Froward and Absurd Men for Businesse that doth not well beare out it Selfe. *a* **1674** Clarendon *Hist. Rebel.* I. iii. 178 The next day after that Argument, Sir Arthur Haslerig, an absurd, bold man..preferr'd a Bill in the House of Commons. **1765** Harris *Three Treat.* iii. i. 161 Is not Education capable of..making us greatly Wise or greatly Absurd. **1874** Black *Pr. Thule* 16 'My dear fellow,' said Ingram at last, 'don't be absurd.'

†**B.** *sb.* An unreasonable thing, act, or statement. *Obs.* exc. as a rendering of Fr. *l'absurde* (Camus).

1610 *Histrio-mastix* ii. 264 Our heavenly poesie, That sacred off-spring from the braine of Jove, Thus to be mangled with prophane absurds. **1635** Heywood *Hierarch.* v. 292 Of which Absurds, I'le make no more narration. **1954** H. Read *Anarchy & Order* 13 He [Albert Camus] suggested a philosophy of the absurd, and his subsequent work..has been an affirmation of 'absurdism' in politics and ethics, as well as in metaphysics. **1962** *Listener* 13 Dec. 1027/1 The theatre of the absurd, whose master remains Camus.

ab'surdism. [ad. Fr. *absurdisme* (Camus).] (See quots.) Hence **ab'surdist** *a.*; as *sb.*, one who writes or admires absurdist drama. See *theatre of the absurd* s.v. theatre *sb.* 3 c.

1954 [see absurd B. *sb.*]. **1959** *N. & Q.* CCIV. 380/1 The absurdist dilemma. **1960** *20th Cent.* Apr. 321 The absurdist ethic does not recommend either..virtue or..crime. **1965** *Listener* 13 May 705/1 The American absurdist..resorts to strategies of overstatement, rather than a single suggestive scene. **1974** J. I. M. Stewart *Gaudy* iii. 40 Beckett led the field, backed by Ionesco, Adamov, and other absurdists. **1983** *N. & Q.* Dec. 573/1 The absurdists sneered at the didacticism of the Brechtians.

absurdity (æb'sɜ:dɪtɪ). [a. Fr. *absurdité*, f. L. *absurditāt-em*, n. of state f. *absurd-us*: see absurd and -ity.]

†**1.** *Mus.* Lack of harmony, untunefulness.

1674 Playford *Musick* iii. 37 In the last disallowance, which is when the upper part stands, and the lower part falls from a lesser third to a fifth, many have been deceived, their ears not finding the absurdity of it.

2. The state or quality of being absurd; opposition to obvious reason or truth; folly.

1528 More *Heresyes* ii. Wks. 1557, 184/2 Which argument hath..much inconuenience and absurdite folowyng therupon. **1615** Crooke *Body of Man* 507 In that he [Aristotle] hath written concerning the vse of the brain.. he cannot be redeemed from palpable absurdity. **1750** Johnson *Rambler* No. 71 ¶13 Divines have shewn the absurdity of delaying reformation. **1798** Ferriar *Eng. Histor.* 248 Caprice..prefers absurdity of invention to correct imitation. **1840** Carlyle *Heroes* (1858) 269 His Koran has become a stupid piece of prolix absurdity.

3. Anything absurd; a statement, action, or custom opposed to obvious truth or sound reason; a logical contradiction; a foolish error.

1528 More *Heresyes* i. Wks. 1557, 138/2 All whiche absurdities & vnreasonable folyes appeareth as well in the worshippe of our ymages, as in the Painims ydolles. **1570** Billingsley *Euclid.* i. i. 10 Of a demonstration leading to an ..absurditie, you may haue an example in the fourth proposition. **1643** Sir T. Browne *Relig. Med.* (1656) i. §49 Moses..committed a grosse absurdity in Philosophy, when with these eyes of flesh he desired to see God. **1727** Swift *Gulliver* ii. viii. 168 The captain hearing me utter these absurdities concluded I was raving. **1846** Mill *Logic* (1868) i. iv. §3. 89 At first sight this division has the air of an absurdity. **1879** McCarthy *Hist. own Times* I. ii. 10 It is not that the demands of the Chartists were anachronisms or absurdities.

absurdly (æb'sɜ:dlɪ), *adv.* [f. absurd + -ly^{2}.] In an absurd or foolish manner; in a manner obviously opposed to what is reasonable or appropriate; illogically.

1561 T. N[orton] *Calvin's Inst.* i. 22 They imagined God to haue many natures although they thought somwhat lesse absurdely than the rude people did of Jupiter, Mercurie, Uenus, Minerua and other. **1660** R. Coke *Just. Vind.* Pref. 4 Mr. Hobbs..therefore most absurdly makes *jus naturæ* to be contrary to *lex naturæ*. **1784** Cowper *Task* ii. 548 The pastor..taught To gaze at his own splendour, and to exalt Absurdly, not his office, but himself. **1878** Jevons *Prim. Pol. Econ.* 34 Anyone who has tried to..play the piano, without having learned to do it, knows how absurdly he fails.

absurdness (æb'sɜ:dnɪs). [f. absurd + -ness.] The quality or state of being absurd; absurdity.

1587 Golding *Mornay's Chr. Relig.* (1617) xxvi. 458 The absurdnesse which we suppose to be there [in Scripture], is but a seeming so to our ignorance. **1612** Brinsley *Gram. Sch.* 212 What they cannot vtter well in Latine, cause them first to do it naturally and liuely in English, and shew them your selfe the absurdnesse of their pronuntiation, by pronouncing foolishly or childishly, as they do. **1674** N. Fairfax *Bulk and Selv.* Cont., To make the best he can of the scurvy recoil of his absurdness and impossibility.

‖**absurdum** (æb'sɜ:dəm). [L. neuter of *absurdus* adj., used substantively as a scholastic term in med.L.] An absurd or illogical conclusion or condition. See reductio *ad absurdum*.

a **1834** Lamb *Spec. fr. Fuller* 537 *note*, Setting up an *absurdum* on purpose to hunt it down. **1877** Kinglake *Crimea* (ed. 6) I. xv. 342 Reducing the theory of Representative Government to the *absurdum*.

absychitical, erroneous form of apsychical.

ABTA, Abta ('æbtə). [Acronym f. the initial letters of the association.] The Association of British Travel Agents, established in 1950.

1950 *Travel Topics* Nov. 64/1 We can even hope that one day..membership of the A.B.T.A. will be accepted as sufficient evidence by the operating companies. **1963** *Times* 11 Jan. 6/5 The council of the Abta (the Association of British Travel Agents) in effect warned its members not to sell the scheme to the public, on the grounds that it contravened the association's code of conduct. **1981** *Economist* 24 Jan. 78/3 Competing operators argue that the customer gets less protection, since Travel Bazaar's four shops do not belong to the Association of British Travel Agents (Abta). **1984** *Daily Tel.* 12 Mar. 3/3 ABTA..is asking members to point out the dangers to tourists.

abthain, abthane ('æbθeɪn). [An Eng. or rather Lowland Sc. formation on med.L. *abthania*, for Gaelic *Abdhaine*, abbacy or abbotrick, *abbatia*, variously written in the charters *Abthen*, *Abthein*, *Abbathain*, *Abbethayne*. The meaning of *Abthania* being lost, it was supposed to be some ancient dignity, for the holder of which the imaginary title of *Abthanus* was invented by Fordun (*Scotochron.* iv. xxxix.), and explained by him from a false etymology as *Father* (*abbas*) or *Superior of the Thanes*. Thenceforward the imaginary *Abthane* flourished in Scottish History, till the recent explanation of the word by Dr. W. F. Skene in *Historians of Scotland* IV, *Fordun* II. 413.]

1. Erroneous use: a 'Superior Thane.'

1535 Stewart *Cron. Scot.* II. 620 Duncane his oy succeidit to his ring, His dochteris sone..Quhilk weddit wes with the Abthan of Dow. **1614** Selden *Titles of Honor* 285 Som interpret their Thane by..Steward; and deliuer that the chief Steward of Scotland was called Abthan. **1872** SKENE transl. *Fordun* IV. xxxix, Abthane is the superior of the Thanes, or their lord under the king.

2. Correct use: an abbacy (of the early Scottish church).

1872 SKENE *Fordun* II. 413 In the Chartulary of Arbroath we have a grant of the 'Ecclesia Sancta Mariae de veteri Munros, cum terra ejusdem ecclesiae, quae Scotice Abthen vocatur,' and in the confirmation by William the Lion it is called 'terra Abbatiae de Munros.' These notices are sufficient to show that the word Abthain was the equivalent *Scottice* of Abbatia.

¶ If a representative of Gael. *abdhaine, abthaine*, med.L. *abthania*, is retained as a special term for 'the territory of those churches called Monasteria, which were founded by the Columban clergy' in ancient Celtic Scotland, the best form would be *Abthany*, as distinct from the equivocal *Abthane* and his supposed jurisdiction *Abthanry* or *Abthanage*.

abthainry, abthanrie ('æbθənrɪ). *Scot. Hist.* [f. prec. + -RY.] An abbacy; the territory and jurisdiction of an abbot; also the secular jurisdiction of what were previously abbatial lands. (Erroneously used as the jurisdiction of the imaginary ABTHANE. As the office itself was the *Abthaine*, the words ABTHAINRY and ABTHANAGE are unnecessary, and should be disused. See note to prec.)

1872 SKENE *Fordun* II. 413 The following Abthainries appear in the Chartularies and Records: *Dull*, Abthania, etc. *Ibid.* 414 The owners of an Abbatia or Abthanrie appear to have occasionally borne the title of Abbe or Abbot.

abthanage ('æbθənɪdʒ). [f. ABTHANE + -AGE.] The jurisdiction of the imaginary ABTHANE. See prec.

1872 E. W. ROBERTSON *Hist. Essays* 127 A grant..in which the ecclesiastical and temporal prerogatives over a district were alike vested in an abbot, seems to have been often known in early days as an Abthanage.

abtrude, variant of ABSTRUDE *v. Obs.*

a'bubble, *adv.* and *pred. a.* [f. A *prep.*[1] + BUBBLE.] Of persons, etc.: bubbling over (with merriment, etc.); full of excited activity.

1936 M. FRANKLIN *All that Swagger* xliv. 412 He remembered..the budding woman in a frilly gown, abubble with high spirits. **1962** *Times* 24 Jan. 13/5 Miss Holm's Marie..was all abubble with girlish glee. **1976** *New Yorker* 12 Jan. 55/3 Broadway is abubble with revivals. **1983** *N.Y. Times* 14 Sept. D22/5 John Emmerling..was all abubble with new-business news yesterday.

†**abuccinate**, *v. Obs. rare*⁻¹; more corr. abbucinate. [f. L. *a, ab* from + *buccinā-re*, properly *būcinā-re* to trumpet, publish abroad (f. *būcina* a trumpet) + -ATE³.] To proclaim as with a trumpet.

1569 T. NEWTON *Cicero, Of olde Age* 8 a, But all men can not bee Scipiones nor Maximi to abuccinate and recompt what Cityes they have sacked.

abuchment, abuchyment, variants of ABUSHMENT, *Obs.*, ambush.

abue, abuȝe, var. of ABOW, *v. Obs.*, to bow.

abuf, obs. form of ABOVE.

abugge, obs. w. and s.w. form of ABYE *v.*

abuilding (ə'bɪldɪŋ), *adv.* and *pred. a.* (prop. *phr.*) Now chiefly *U.S.* [f. A *prep.*[1] 12 (= on) + BUILDING *vbl. sb.*; often construed as quasi-*pr. pple.*] Being built.

1535, *a* **1665** [see BUILD *v.* 7]. **1888** [in *N.E.D.*, s.v. A *prep.*[1] 12]. **1939** V. WOOLF *Diary* 15 Apr. (1984) V. 215 Noises & houses abuilding oppress. **1946** K. TENNANT *Lost Haven* (1947) viii. 111 The *Fortune* had been eighteen months abuilding already. **1972** *Newsweek* 10 Jan. 22/3 Muskie organizations are functioning full-throttle in eleven states and abuilding in 22 more. **1981** *Sci. Amer.* Dec. 61/1 A comprehensive theory of cancer causation was abuilding last spring.

†**abuilyeit, abulȝeit**, *ppl. a. Obs.* [Sc. form of HABILLED, f. vb. *habille*, Sc. *abulȝe*, a. Fr. *habille-r* to fit out, array, attire.] Arrayed, attired.

1513 DOUGLAS *Æn.* XII. Prol. 34 Abulȝeit in his lemand fresche array, Furth of his palice riall ischit Phebus. **1762** ANDERSON in Lecky *Rationalism* (1878) II. 286 *note*, The wives and daughters of merchants should be abuilzied [*z for* ȝ].

abuilyement, abulȝement, obs. Sc. forms of ABILIMENT, HABILIMENT.

abulia, abulic: see ABOULIA.

abumbral (,æb'ʌmbrəl), *a. Zool.* A shortened equivalent of the following word.

1881 E. R. LANKESTER in *Jrnl. Microsc. Sc.* Jan. 124 The cells of the adumbral wall are like those of the ring-canal. The cells of the abumbral wall are modified by the deposit of block-like masses of a dense substance within them.

abumbrellar (,æbʌm'brɛlə(r)), *a. Zool.* [mod. f. L. *ab* away from + UMBRELLA, applied to the disk of *Acalepha*: cf. *abactinal, aboral.*] In sea-blubbers: pertaining to that surface of the *velum* or marginal ridge, which is turned away from the 'umbrella' or disc, in opposition to the *adumbrellar* surface which faces the 'umbrella.'

‖**Abuna** (ə'bu:nə). [Eth. and Arab. *Abu-na*, pater noster, our father.] The Patriarch of the Abyssinian Church.

1635 PAGITT *Christianogr.* 40 They are subject to a Patriarch of their owne, whom they call Abunna. *c* **1870** W. STAUNTON *Eccles. Dict.* (ed. 4) Add. 2, *Abuna*, the native name for..the chief bishop of the Abyssinian church.

abund, obs. north. form of ABOUND *v.*

abund, *pple. pass. Obs.* OE. *ȝe-bund-en*, bound. See BIND.

c **1280** *Seven Sins* in *E. Eng. Poems* (1862) 18 Nas neuer non so fule ilimp . as he in helle liþ abund.

abundance (ə'bʌndəns). Forms: 4-6 **abundaunce, habundaunce, -ance**; 5-6 **boundance, haboundaunce, -ance**; 4-7 **aboundaunce, -ance**; 4- **abundance.** [a. OFr. *abundance, abondance, hab-*:— L. *abundantia*, n. of state f. *abundant-em*, ABUNDANT. The spelling *habundance* frequent in Fr. and Eng. from the 14th c. was due to the word being mistakenly supposed to be a derivative of *habēre* to have. An aphetic *boundance*, 5-6, was due to initial *a* being taken as the indef. art. quasi *a boundance.*]

1. Overflowing state or condition, overflow; superfluity; enough and more than enough: hence in a looser sense, plentifulness, copiousness.

1366 MAUNDEV. (1839) xiv. 152 There ben hilles where men geten gret plentee of manna, in gretter habundance than in any other contree. **1382** WYCLIF *Mal.* iii. 10 ȝif y shal not opne to ȝou the gutters of heuen, and schal sheede out to ȝou blessyng vnto aboundaunce. **1446** HENRY *Wallace* IV. 347 A land of gret boundance. **1535** FISHER *Wks.* (1876) 382 You shall be partener to the more plentuous aboundance of his loue. **1611** BIBLE *Ps.* cv. 30 The land brought foorth frogs in abundance. **1796** BP. WATSON *Apol. for Bible* 190 There were false prophets in abundance amongst the Jews. **1823** DE QUINCEY *Lett. on Educ.* (1860) i. 10 My thoughts on that matter are from the abundance of my heart.

2. a. An overflowing quantity or amount; a large quantity, plenty.

1340 *Ayenb.* 261 Abundance and plenté of alle guode. **1483** CAXTON *G. de la Tour* (1868) 135 They shalle yeue accompte of thaire habundance of the worldely goodes that they haue had. **1595** SHAKS. *John* II. i. 148 What cracker is this same that deafes our eares With this abundance of superfluous breath? **1722** DE FOE *Moll. Fl.* (1840) 346 I ordered abundance of good things for our comfort in the voyage. **1824** DIBDIN *Lib. Comp.* 112 Abundance of valuable information.

b. Less correctly: A large number, very many.

1375 BARBOUR *Bruce* x. 110 Quhar men mycht se So gret aboundance cum off fe, That it war voundir till behald. **1687** T. BROWN *Saints in an Uproar* Wks. 1730 I. 82 Abundance of worthless and fabulous scoundrels. **1751** FIELDING *Amelia* Wks. 1784 IX. XI. ii. 254 There are abundance..who want a morsel of bread for themselves and their families.

3. Plentifulness, or plentiful supply, of the good things of life; superfluity, affluence, wealth.

1382 WYCLIF *Luke* xii. 15 (Lea Wilson's MS.) Be war fro al coueytise, for not in þe aboundaunce of any man is his liif. **1535** COVERDALE *1 Chron.* xxx. 16 O Lorde oure God, all this abundaunce..came of thy hande. **1611** BIBLE *Eccl.* v. 12 But the abundance of the rich will not suffer him to sleepe. **1653** HOLCROFT *Procopious* I. 17 Victory brings all to that side it enclines to. In your swords therefore consists your safety, and aboundance. **1857** Bohn's *Handbk. of Prov.* 305 Abundance, like want, ruins many.

†**4. a.** Added to nouns: In abundance, in large quantity, or number. (Probably after the analogy of *wine enough, ships enow.*) *Obs.* **b.** Adverbially before adj.: Very much, a great deal. *Obs.*

1675 HOBBES *Iliad* 106 For ships abundance laden were come in. *Ibid.* 164 While spears abundance at him hurled were. —— *Odyssey* 103 Sheep & goats there lay Abundance sleeping. *Ibid.* 167 And wine abundance drink. **1710** SWIFT *Baucis & Phil.* Wks. 1755 III. II. 35 The ballads pasted on the wall..Now seem'd to look abundance better, Improv'd in picture, size, and letter.

5. In solo whist, a declaration by a player that he will take nine tricks single-handed. Also in Fr. form *abondance.*

1888 WILKS & PARDON *How to Play Solo Whist* 8 *Abondance.* (Abundance.) An independent call to make nine tricks. **1890** R. F. GREEN *Solo Whist* i. 3 *Abondance*, in which case the declaring player engages to make nine out of the thirteen tricks. **1911** *Encycl. Brit.* XXV. 362/1 Abundance in the turn-up suit takes precedence over abundance in other suits. **1961** MERVYN JONES *Potbank* xiii. 53, I went solo and was..criticized for my timidity. 'You could have gone abundance with that lot.'

6. *Ecology.* (See quots.)

1905 F. E. CLEMENTS *Research Methods in Ecol.* 314 *Abundance*, the total number of individuals in an area. **1932** FULLER & CONARD tr. *Braun-Blanquet's Plant Sociol.* iii. 30 Abundance is intended to express the plentifulness (number of individuals) of each species. **1957** P. GREIG-SMITH *Quant. Plant Ecol.* iii. 61 Abundance (defined as mean density within occupied quadrats).

7. *Physics.* (See quots.)

1922 F. W. ASTON *Isotopes* ix. 111 In discussing the nuclear structure of elements the question of their relative abundance in nature is one of great interest. **1955** *Gloss. Terms Radiology (B.S.I.)* 13 *Relative abundance*, the proportion of a given isotope in a particular specimen of an element, usually expressed as a percentage. **1962** *Nature* 19 May 621/2 Although the masses of individual nuclides that constitute an element can be measured very accurately, their abundances in an element cannot be determined.

a'bundancy. [ad. L. *abundantia*; see prec. and -NCY.] The quality or state of being abundant; abundantness, plentifulness.

1620 SHELTON *Don Quixote* III. xxix. 202 The Clearness of the Water, the gentle Current, and the Abundancy of the liquid Crystal. **1654** SIR A. COKAINE *Loredano's Dianea* I. 6 She breathed out most hot sighs..accompanied with an abundancy of teares. **1893** *Illustr. Lond. News* 7 Jan. 22/2 The abundancy of detail that folk-lore delights in. **1959** *New Scientist* 19 Mar. 625/2 Relative abundancies of barley mutants.

abundant (ə'bʌndənt), *a.* For forms cf. ABUNDANCE. [a. OFr. *abundant, abondant, hab-*:—L. *abundant-em* overflowing, pres. pple. of *abundā-re*, f. *ab* away from + *undā-re* to flow in waves, f. *unda* a wave. For initial *h-* see ABUNDANCE.]

1. Overflowing, more than sufficient; existing in great plenty, plentiful, ample; (properly of fluids, but transferred to other substances and to qualities).

c **1450** TREVISA *Higden* (Rolls Ser.) I. 367 The water was so habundante that hit pereschede þe woman with here childe. **1509** FISHER *Wks.* (1876) 120 Where synne is haboundant charity waxeth colde. **1535** COVERDALE *Dan.* v. 11 Because that soch an abundaunt sprete, knowlege & wisdome was founde in him. **1611** BIBLE *1 Tim.* i. 14 And the grace of our Lord was exceeding abundant, with faith, and loue. **1783** COWPER *Let.* Nov. 24 Wks. 1876, 148 A treatment which I had abundant reason to expect. **1874** HELPS *Soc. Press.* iii. 46 The larger the town the more abundant and varied is the noise in it.

2. Possessing in excess or superfluity; hence, having great plenty, wealthy, abounding. Const. *in* (*of* obs.)

1366 MAUNDEV. (1839) xxi. 230 To defend the and thi contree that art so habundant of Tresore. *c* **1400** *Destr. Troy* XIII. 5205 The same yle I said you, Cicill is calt, Ay abundand of blisse. *Ibid.* v. 1695 All abundaunt in blisse. *c* **1450** TREVISA *Higden* (Rolls Ser.) I. 108 Also that londe of Juda is..habundaunt in hony & mylke. **1526** TINDALE *2 Cor.* xi. 23 They are the ministers of Christ..I am moare; in labours moare aboundant. **1611** BIBLE *Isa.* lvi. 12 To morrow shal be as this day, and much more abundant. **1789–96** MORSE *Amer. Geog.* II. 42 The river Motala..is very abundant in salmon. *c* **1854** STANLEY *Sinai & Palest.* (1858) vii. 313 The one river of Palestine..abundant in its waters.

3. *quasi-adv.*

a **1725** POPE *Odyssey* XVI. 237 They wept abundant and they wept aloud.

4. *Math.* [tr. Gr. ὑπερτέλειος beyond completeness or perfection (Theon Smyrnæus, 2nd c. A.D.).] Designating a number whose divisors (including 1) add up to more than the number. Cf. DEFICIENT *a.* 1 c, PERFECT *a.* 8.

1557 R. RECORD *Whetstone of Witte* sig. A. ivᵛ, Imperfecte nombers be suche, whose partes added together, doe make either more or lesse, then the whole nomber it self... And if the partes make more then the whole nomber, then is that nomber called superfluouse, or abundaunt. **1709** V. MANDEY *System. Math.* 5 There are found but few Perfect Numbers... All the rest are abundant or deficient. **1966** OGILVY & ANDERSON *Excursions in Number Theory* ii. 23, The problem has been completely solved for even numbers: 26, 28, 34, and 46 are the only even numbers greater than 24 that are not the sum of two abundant numbers. **1983** *Austral. Personal Computer* Nov. 136/1 *Problem.* Submit a program..to determine if a given integer is perfect, abundant or deficient.

abundantly (ə'bʌndəntlɪ), *adv.* For forms cf. ABUNDANCE. [f. prec. + -LY².] Overflowingly, exceedingly, enough and to spare; hence, in large measure, plentifully, copiously, amply, sufficiently for all purposes. (Formerly compared *abundantlier, abundantliest.*)

1382 WYCLIF *Tob.* iv. 9 If myche were to thee, abundauntli ȝif [**1388** ȝyue thou plenteuousli]. *c* **1460** SIR J. FORTESCUE *Abs. & Lim. Mon.* (1714) 31 It is verey necessary ..that the Kyng have aboundantly, wherewith his astate may be honorably kepte. **1533** ELYOT *Castel of Helth* (1541) 34 Mylke taken to purge melancoly wold be drunke in the morning abundantly. **1603** *Eng. Mourning Garment* in *Harl. Misc.* (Malh.) II. 497 Her table was the abundantliest furnished of any princes in the world. **1611** BIBLE *Gen.* ix. 7 Be ye fruitfull, and multiply, bring foorth abundantly in the earth. **1786** BURKE *Art. agst. W. Hastings* Wks. 1842 II. 131 The evil designs of the said Hyder Beg were abundantly known. **1817** JAS. MILL *Brit. India* III. v. iv. 432 They began now to feel their situation abundantly uneasy. **1880** GEIKIE *Phys. Geog.* ii. 8. 54 The vapour which rises so abundantly from sea and land into the atmosphere diffuses itself through the air.

†**abundary.** *Obs. rare*⁻¹. [f. L. *abund-us* 'abundant,' after the analogy of *luminary, granary*, and other forms in -ARY = L. *-arium.*] An overflowing source, a fountain-head.

1622 DONNE *Serm.* (1839) VI. 215 And to these [the catechisms, homilies etc.] as to Heads and Abundaries, from whence all Knowledge necessary to Salvation may

Abundantly be Derived, he directs the Meditations of Preachers.

abune, obs. north. form of ABOVE.

abura (ə'b(j)u:rə). [Yoruba.] A tree of tropical West Africa, *Mitragyna ciliata*, from which a soft pale wood is obtained; also, the wood of this tree.

1926 *Imp. Inst. Bull.* XXIV. 2 *Abura*..A fairly soft, fine and close-grained wood, of moderate weight and plain appearance, with light reddish-brown heartwood and slightly paler sapwood. *Ibid.* 3 Abura wood should be useful locally for light constructional and other work. **1954** *Archit. Rev.* May 332/2 To relieve the large areas of plastic sheeting internally, there is wall panelling in places in abura and iroba.

†**a'burden**, *v. Obs. rare*$^{-1}$. [f. A- *pref.* 11, intensive + BURDEN *v.*] To burden, oppress.

1620 SHELTON *Don Quixote* I. III. viii. 187 From whence I have no hope ever to return, my years do so aburden me.

aburn, aburne, obs. forms of AUBURN.

aburst (ə'bɜ:st), *adv.*, prop. *phrase.* [A *prep.*[1] of state + BURST *sb.* The modern use of the word is not descended from the old, but analogous to ABLOOM, etc.]

†**1.** In a burst (of rage, etc.).

1205 LAYAMON II. 639 Cnihtes an burste weoren. **1250** Cnihtes a borst weren.

2. In a bursting condition; bursting.

1876 MRS. WHITNEY *Sights & Ins.* II. xxxvi. 650 Country like this,—all alive, and aburst, and teeming.

a-burton: see BURTON b.

abusable (ə'bju:zəb(ə)l), *a.* [f. ABUSE *v.* + -ABLE.]

†**1.** Of abusing or deceiving character; deceptive. *Obs.*

1660 H. MORE *Myst. of Godl.* 25 As for that abusable Opinion of Imputative Righteousness..I have shewn my dissatisfaction touching that point.

2. Capable of being abused.

1667 H. MORE *Div. Dial.* (1713) III. xxxix. 288 Whose Humor is to abuse in me whatever is or is not abuseable. **1826** *Edin. Rev.* Sept. 445 What an..abusable power is this to confide to any body of men! **1892** *Sat. Rev.* 4 June 641/1 The venerable but abusable principle of grievance first, Supply afterwards. **1904** G. B. SHAW *Commonsense Munic. Trading* ix. 86 Readjusting the burden of the rates by an obviously abusable method.

†**a'busage.** *Obs.* [f. ABUSE *v.* + -AGE.] Abuse, misuse, perversion; defilement. Revived in Partridge's title (quot. 1942).

1548 GESTE *Preuee Masse* 133 He commaunded only y[e] ryght usage and not y[e] abusage..of y[e] premisses..He doth ..detest y[e] abusers with there abusage of hys commaunded service. **1617** WITHER *Fidelia* in *Juven.* 1633, 453 But grant I had been guilty of abusage, Of thee I'm sure I ne'er deserved such usage. **1649** W. BLITH *Eng. Impr.* (1653) 192 Many good Ploughs are utterly spoyled in the usage or abusage.

1942 E. PARTRIDGE (*title*) Usage and Abusage. A guide to good English.

abuse (ə'bju:z), *v.* [a. Fr. *abuse-r* (cf. Pr. and Sp. *abusar*, It. *abusare*), pointing to a popular L. **abūsā-re*, f. *abūs-us*, pa. pple. of *abūt-i*, 1. to use up, 2. to misuse, 3. (late L.) to disuse, f. *ab* away + *ūti*, *ūsus* to USE.]

†**1.** *Sc.* To disuse, give up. *Obs.*

1471 *Parl. Jas. III* (1814) 100 (Jam.) At [= That] the futbal and golf be abusit in tym cummyng, & the buttis maid up, & schuting usit.

2. a. To use improperly, to misuse; to make a bad use of, to pervert, or misemploy; to take a bad advantage of. *spec.* To take (a drug) for a purpose other than a therapeutic one.

1413 LYDGATE *Pylg. Sowle* (1859) I. xv. 12 Wel thou wost who that me hath abused, myn enemy, that hath me now accused. **1483** CAXTON *Cato* g viij, Thou oughtest to dyspende thy goodes by mesure..to thende that men sayen not that thou abusest them. **1581** LYLY *Euphues* (1636) E. x, How wantonly, yea and how willingly haue we abused our golden time. **1611** BIBLE *1 Cor.* ix. 18 That I abuse not my power in the Gospel. **1663** GERBIER *Counsel* C vj. *a*, With more I shall not presume to abuse your Lordships patience. **1771** *Junius Lett.* lxi. 317 The liberty of the press may be abused. **1829** SCOTT *Rob Roy* i. 64 I dare not promise that I may not abuse the opportunity so temptingly offered me. **1876** FREEMAN *Norm. Conq.* II. x. 503 Restoring his brother to the authority which he had so abused. **1968** *Jrnl. Health, Physical Educ. & Recreation* XXXIX. 27/1 Any substance capable of altering man's mood has abuse capability... The specific substance abused is of less direct importance to the user than the end result. **1972** E. H. ELLINWOOD in Ellinwood & Cohen *Current Concepts on Amphetamine Abuse* xiv. 146/1 The greatest increase in libido was often noted in women, especially those who had been relatively frigid prior to abusing amphetamines. **1984** *Brit. Med. Jrnl.* 8 Sept. 612/2 He abused a wide variety of drugs.

†**b.** To use in error, to mistake. *Obs.*

1548 TURNER *Names of Herbes* 29 Cholchicum is abused of some Poticaries for Hermodactylus. **1551** —— *Herbal* (1568) I. 41 Some have abused long smallage for persely, wherein they have been deceived.

†**3.** To misrepresent, colour falsely; to adulterate. *refl.* To show oneself in false colours, to make false pretensions. *Obs.*

c **1430** LYDGATE *Bochas* (1554) IX. iii. 197 b, With litle grayn, your chaffe ye can abuse. **1509** HAWES *Past. of Pleas.* xviii. 84 O goodd madame! though that they abused Them to theyr ladyes in theyr great deceyte, Yet am I true. **1697** *View of Penal Laws* 243 None selling Wines in Gross shall abuse or mix any of them with other Ingredients. **1702** *Eng. Theophr.* Pref. 4 How miserably that noble author has been abused by his Translators. **1749** FIELDING *Tom Jones* (1840) XVII. ii. 243/2 He hath been abused, grossly abused to you.

†**4. a.** To make a wrong use of any one's confidence; to impose upon, cheat, or deceive (a person). *Obs.* but preserved in the negative *disabuse*.

1481 CAXTON *Myrrour* II. ix. 87 Wherof..the maronners sayling by this see ben gretely deceyued and abused. **1553** LYNDESAY *Mon.* I. 1004 Rychtso the woman hir excusit, And said: 'the serpent me abusit.' **1649** JER. TAYLOR *Great Exemp.* III. xvii. 65 He was abused into the act by a Prophet. **1702** *Eng. Theophr.* 248 A Prince that desires by means of his Ambassador to deceive any other Prince, must first abuse his own Ambassador, to the end he should speak with the more earnestness. **1776** WESLEY *Wks.* 1830 IV. 39 Many saw how miserably they had been abused by those vulgarly called Gospel Preachers.

†**b.** *refl.* and *pass.* To be deceived, mistaken. *to be abused upon* or *in*: to form a mistaken idea of, to fall into error about. *Obs.*

1477 CAXTON *Jason* 41 b, If ye juge the disposition of my body after the colour of my face ye be gretly abused. **1525** LD. BERNERS *Froissart* II. ccxxiv. [ccxx.] 703 The Christen men were abused vpon ii. popes..some beleuyng on the one pope, and some vpon the other. *Ibid.* ccxxv. [ccxxi.] 704 [He] had great dout that he was sore abused in those two popes. **1605** BACON *Adv. Learn.* I. 41 You are much abused if you think your vertue can withstand the Kings power. **1660** HOWELL, Thou dost abuse thyself grossly: *Tu t' abuses tout a fait.* *a* **1718** PENN *Tracts* Wks. 1726 I. 766 That so we may not profane the name of God..nor abuse our selues unto Eternal Perdition. **1734** tr. *Rollin's Anc. Hist.* (1827) VII. XVII. 305 To see themselves abused in the hopes they had entertained.

5. To ill-use or maltreat; to injure, wrong, or hurt.

1556 W. LAUDER *Tractate* 331 And, geue thay haue the floke abusit, ȝe, Kyngs, sall be for that accusit. **1611** BIBLE *2 Mac.* xiv. 42 Chusing rather to die manfully, then to come into the hands of the wicked to be abused otherwise then beseemed his noble birth. **1662** FULLER *Worthies* 117 He that abuseth his servants, giving them too little food or sleep. **1691** LUTTRELL *Brief Rel.* (1857) II. 315 The duke of Norfolke was abused in the fray at the playhouse. **1756** BURKE *Vind. Nat. Soc.* Wks. I. 39 In this kind of government human nature is not only abused and insulted, but it is actually degraded. *Mod.* It is the characteristic of the English drunkard to abuse his wife and family.

6. To violate, ravish, defile. ? *Obs.*

1553 LYNDESAY *Monarche* I. 1236 Quhow men and wemen schamefullye Abusit thame selfis vnnaturallye. **1611** BIBLE *Judg.* xix. 25 And abused her all the night vntil the morning. **1767** FORDYCE *Serm. to Yng. Women* I. i. 9 He that abuses you dishonours his mother.

7. To wrong with words; to speak injuriously of or to; to malign, revile. **a.** *trans.*

1604 SHAKS. *Oth.* V. i. 123 I am no Strumpet, but of life as honest, As you that thus abuse me. **1705** OTWAY *Orphan* II. iv. 564 What have I done? and why do you abuse me? **1839** KEIGHTLEY *Hist. Eng.* II. 52 A preface in which the Pope was abused in the most virulent terms.

b. *intr.*

1468 *Coventry Myst.* (1841) 73 Whow durste thou amonge fruteful presume and abuse?

abuse (ə'bju:s), *sb.* [a. Fr. *abus*:—L. *abūsus*, 1. wearing out, 2. misuse; n. of completed action from *abūt-i*. See ABUSE *v.*]

†**1.** The process of using up or wearing out. *Obs.*

1539 CRANMER *Col.* ii. 22 Touch not, tast not, handell not: whych all peryeshe thorow the very abuse [WYCLIF vse. TINDALE & **1611** vsinge].

2. a. Wrong or improper use, misuse, misapplication, perversion. *spec.* The non-therapeutic or excessive use of a drug; the misuse of any substance, esp. for its stimulant effects. Cf. *drug-abuse* s.v. DRUG *sb.*[1] 1 b; *solvent abuse* s.v. SOLVENT *sb.* 5.

1538 BALE *Thre Lawes* 709 These two wyll hym so vse Ichone in their abuse. **1602** WARNER *Albion's England* (1612) IX. lii. 236 Yet things, that of themselues be good, abuse brings out of square. **1756** C. LUCAS *On Waters* I. 29 I have observed the same from the abuse of Spa water. **1846** MILL *Logic* (1868) I. ii. §4. 29 Imitating him in this abuse of language. **1862** LD. BROUGHAM *Brit. Const.* i. 18 It would be a great abuse of terms to call the Venetian a Mixed Aristocracy. **1879** G. C. HARLAN *Eyesight* vi. 78 It [tendency to short sight] may sometimes originate in later life from abuse of the eyes. **1961** *Drug Addiction* (Rep. Interdepartmental Comm., Min. Health & Dept. of Health, Scotl.) 15 The abuse of stimulant drugs such as the amphetamines and phenmetrazine has led to some publicity and concern. **1969** R. R. LINGEMAN *Drugs from A to Z* p. vii, The fact that in recent years drug use, or more correctly abuse, has radically changed is..the *raison d'être* of this book. **1970** (*title*) Alcohol abuse. (Office of Health.) **1974** M. C. GERALD *Pharmacol.* vi. 124 Whereas..amphetamine-like drugs may be useful in the early stages of dieting, the development of tolerance and their abuse potential limit their long-term value as appetite-suppressants. **1984** *Sunday Times* 9 Dec. 3/6 This is a setback for the campaign against increasing heroin abuse among the young in all parts of the country.

b. *Rhet.* Improper use of words, catachresis.

1589 PUTTENHAM *Eng. Poesie* (1869) 190, Catachresis, or the Figure of abuse..if for lack of naturall and proper terme or worde we take another, neither naturall nor proper and do vntruly applie it to the thing which we would seeme to expresse. *a* **1716** SOUTH *12 Serm.* (1744) II. 93 The acception of the word amongst the Greeks and Latines..is through abuse and degeneration.

3. A bad or improper usage (*i.e.* a use which has become chronic), a corrupt practice.

1486 CAXTON *Curial* 3 The abuses of the courte..ben suche that a man is neuer suffred tenhaunce hymself. **1550** CROWLEY *Last Trumpet* 615 Thou learned man, do not disdayne..Thy greate abuses to refrayne, And in thy callyng to go ryght. **1699** DR. TANNER in *Pepys' Diary* VI. 186 Some letters about the abuses of Christ's Hospital. *a* **1745** SWIFT *Adv. of Relig.* Wks. 1824 VIII. 107 The nature of things is such, that, if abuses be not remedied, they will certainly increase. **1780** BURKE *Sp. on Econ. Ref.* Wks. III. 247 There is a time, when the hoary head of inveterate abuse will neither draw reverence, nor obtain protection. **1855** MACAULAY *Hist. Eng.* IV. 121 It seemed perfectly natural that he should defend abuses by which he profited.

†**4.** Imposture, deceit; delusion. *Obs.*

1555 *Fardle of Facions*, Pref. 15 Some he [the deuell] reuersed into their former abuses and errours. **1602** SHAKS. *Ham.* IV. vii. 51 Or is it some abuse? Or no such thing? **1605** —— *Macb.* III. iv. 142 My strange and self-abuse Is the initiate feare, that wants hard vse. **1653** URQUHART *Rabelais* I. xlv, Do the false prophets teach you such abuses?

†**5.** Injury, wrong, ill-usage. *Obs.*

1593 SHAKS. *3 Hen. VI*, III. iii. 188 Did I let passe th' abuse done to my Neece? **1598** —— *Merry Wives* V. iii. 8 My husband will not reioyce so much at the abuse of Falstaffe, as he will chafe at the Doctors marrying my daughter. **1682** LUTTRELL *Brief Rel.* (1857) I. 224 Lieutenant Colonel Quiney..offered an abuse to Sir John Lawrence by pulling him down off the hustings.

6. Violation, defilement (now only in *self-abuse*).

1580 SIDNEY *Arc.* II. (T.), Was it not enough for him to have deceived me, and through the deceit abused me, and after the abuse forsaken me? **1751** CHAMBERS *Cycl.* s.v. *Abuse*, Self-Abuse is a phrase used by some late writers for the crime of self-pollution.

7. Injurious speech, reviling, execration; abusive language.

1559 *Myrroure for Mag.* i. 4 Blowen up the blast of all abuse. **1603** SHAKS. *Meas. for M.* V. i. 347 Harke how the villaine would close now, after his treasonable abuses. **1759** DILWORTH *Life of Pope* 77 Mr. Pope bore for a long time the gross abuses thrown out by his adversaries. **1780** HARRIS *Philol. Enq.* (1841) 534 For every past age, when present, has been the object of abuse. *a* **1859** MACAULAY *Hist. Eng.* (1861) V. xxiv. 128 The two parties, after exchanging a good deal of abuse, came to blows.

abused (ə'bju:zd), *ppl. a.* [f. ABUSE *v.* + -ED.]

†**1.** Worn out, consumed by use; hence, disused, obsolete. *Obs.*

1494 FABYAN VI, Whiche made theyr prayers to goddes abused, As Jupiter and Mars. **1536** BELLENDENE *Boece's Cron. Scotl.* (1821) I. 260 Thay convenit in Argyle..to lerne thair pepill the art of chevalry; for thay war mony yeris abusit, but ony exercition thairof.

2. Misused; wronged, done violence to, violated.

1592 SHAKS. *Rom. & Jul.* IV. i. 29 Poore soule thy face is much abus'd with teares. **1605** —— *Lear* IV. vii. 15 O you kind Gods! cure this great breach in his abused Nature! **1645** USSHER *Body of Divin.* (1647) 226 For the brazen Serpent abused, was worthily broken in pieces. **1719** DE FOE *Rob. Crusoe* I. 42 Abus'd Prosperity is oftentimes made the very Means of our greatest Adversity.

3. Imposed upon, deceived, mistaken, misguided.

1473 WARKWORTH *Chron.* 13 Sere Jhon Westerdale, whiche aftyrward for his abused disposycion was casten in presone. **1549** *Compl. Scotl.* (1872) viii. 72 O ignorant, abusit, ande dissaitful pepil. **1660** MILTON *Free Commw.* 454 The general defection of a misguided and abus'd Multitude. **1706** ADDISON *Rosamd.* II. vi. Misc. Wks. 1726 I. 123 The bower turns round, my brain's abus'd, The Labyrinth grows more confus'd. **1801** SOUTHEY *Thalaba* iv. 9 Wks. IV. 140 Things view'd at distance through the mist of fear, By their distortion terrify and shock, The abused sight.

†**abusedly** (ə'bju:zɪdlɪ), *adv. Obs. rare*$^{-1}$. [f. prec. + -LY[2].] Mistakenly, improperly; by abuse of language.

1625 J. WODROEPHE *Marrow of Fr. Tongue* x. 180 The Inhabitants and trades-men are (abusedly) called 'Monsieur and Madame.'

abusee (ə,bju:'zi:). [f. ABUSE *v.* + -EE.] One who is abused; correl. to ABUSER.

1836 HOR. SMITH *Tin Trumpet* I. 9 Abuse, intemperate, excites our sympathies, not for the abuser but the abusee.

†**a'buseful**, *a. Obs.* [f. ABUSE *sb.* + -FUL.] Abounding in abuse; using or practising abuse; abusive, reproachful.

1642 *Caval. Adv. to his Maj.* 7 The abusefull termes he spoke. **1660** HOWELL, An Abusefull fellow: *Fascheux, abuseur.* **1693** T. BARLOW *Remains* 397 He scurrilously Reviles the King and Parliament by the abuseful Names of Hereticks and Schismaticks.

a'busefully, *adv. rare.* [f. prec. + -LY[2].] In an abuseful or abusive manner; abusively; improperly. *dial.* and *colloq.*

1656 EARL OF MONM. *Advert. fr. Parn.* 239 Maintaining promise both to God and man, which most commonly is so abusefully measured by the compass of interest. **1672** R. TAYLOR *Cromwell, or Flagel.* 22 Most abusefully employed in hyring Wagons for the Earl of Essex's Army. **1875** W. D. PARISH *Dict. Sussex Dial.* 12 He treated her most abusefully, and threw abroad all her shop-goods. **1914** KIPLING *Divers. of Creatures* (1917) 53 Talkin' most abusefully.

ab-usefulness. *rare.* Used by Ruskin for, Capability of improper use.

1862 RUSKIN *Unto this Last* 124 And it depends on the person, much more than on the article, whether its usefulness or ab-usefulness will be the quality developed in it.

†**a'busement.** *Obs.* [a. Fr. *abusement* 'an abusing, or misusing, mockery, beguiling,' Cotgr., f. *abuser*: see ABUSE *v.* and -MENT.] An abusing or misleading.

1819 'R. RABELAIS' *Abeillard & Heloisa* 333 Amusements which Abeillard had prov'd abusements.

abuser[1] (ə'bjuːzə(r)). [f. ABUSE *v.* + -ER[1].] One who abuses: hence,

1. One who uses improperly, misuses, misapplies or perverts; a perverter.

c **1450** *Moral Play* in *Le Bibliophile*, 1 May 1863, 55 An abuser of Justice hateth my syght. **1638** WILKINS *New World* (1707) ix. 67 There being not any Absurdity.. for which these Abusers of the Text will not find out an argument. **1746** J. HERVEY *Medit. & Contempl.* (1818) 42 God.. may swear in his wrath, that such abusers of his long-suffering 'shall never enter into his rest.' **1860** *Westm. Rev.* (N.S.) No. 35. 66 The abusers of power received a merited amount of censure.

†2. One who perverts truth or abuses confidence; a deceiver or impostor. *Obs.*

1579 TOMSON *Calvin's Serm. Timothy* 826/2 All they which giue themselues to wickednesse.. are false varlets & abusers, in pretending at this day the name of Christians. **1604** SHAKS. *Othello* I. ii. 78, I therefore apprehend and do attach thee, For an abuser of the World, a practiser Of Arts inhibited. **1614** ROWLANDS *Fooles Bolt* For so doth Sathan, soules abuser, First tempt to ill, then turne accuser. **1667** DENHAM *Sophy* (J.) Next thou, the abuser of thy prince's ear.

3. One who uses badly or injures; an ill-user, violator; one who seduces, a ravisher.

c **1608** FLETCHER *Faithf. Sheph.* I. 230 Retire awhile Behind this Bush, till we have known that vile Abuser of young Maidens. **1611** BIBLE *1 Cor.* vi. 9 Nor adulterers, nor effeminate, nor abusers of themselues with mankine. **1665** J. SPENCER *Prodigies* 127 (T.) That day of vengeance, wherein God will destroy the murderers and abusers of his servants.

4. One who reviles, or decries; a reviler.

1836 HOR. SMITH *Tin Trumpet* I. 9 Abuse, intemperate, excites our sympathies, not for the abuser but the abusee. **1861** FLOR. NIGHTINGALE *Nursing* 53 I should be very glad if any of the abusers of tea would point out what to give to an English patient after a sleepless night, instead of tea.

†**abuser**[2] (ə'bjuːzə(r)). *Obs.* [a. Fr. *abuser* inf. used subst.: see ABUSE *v.*] Illegal or wrongful use.

1646 in Rushworth's *Hist. Coll.* I. IV. 316 That an act be passed for granting and confirming of the charters.. of the City of London, notwithstanding any Nonuser, Misuser or Abuser. *a* **1734** NORTH *Examen* III. viii. §60. 630 The Corporation.. for every unlawful Act done by the Body was seisable, for the Abuser, as forfeited.

†**a'bush(e, a'busse, a'busche,** *v. Obs.* [Reduced form of AMBUSH *v.*, 3-4 *en-bush, anbush*, a. OFr. *em-busche-r*; the toneless Fr. *en-*, phonetically treated in Eng. as toneless OE. *an-*, became *ă-*, and then often disappeared; hence the series, *en-'bush, an-'bush* (now *'ambush*), *a-'bush, 'bush.*] To ambush.

c **1300** *Life of Beket* 1382 In huding as it were.. for he him abussed there. **1330** R. BRUNNE *Chron.* 187 Saladyn priuely was bussed beside þe flom. *Ibid.* Sarazins.. enbussed þorgh þe feld. *c* **1350** *Will. Palerne* 3634 A fersche ost.. a-buschid þer bi-side, in a brent greue.

†**a'bushment.** *Obs.* Forms: 4 **abusse-, abuche-, abuchy-ment,** 4-6 **abusshe-, abuschement,** 5-6 **abuschment,** 6 **abushment.** [Reduced form of AM-BUSHMENT, in 3-4 *an-'bushment, en'bushment*, a. OFr. *embuschement* (see prec.); whence the series *en'bushment, an-'bushment, a-'bushment, 'bushment.*] Ambushment, ambush.

1380 *Sir Ferumb.* 1380 Of ys enbuschyment þan brak he out. 812 Of þys anbuschymentis þan brek out. 798 And leued ȝond on a-buchyment. 2898 Noȝt fer fro þen buchyment þere. **1485** CAXTON *Charles the Grete* 133 Your peple that shal be hydde in the busshement shal come out on them. **1489** —— *Faytes of Armes* I. xxviii. 83 To putte abusshement where as they shal passe fore-by. **1592** WYRLEY *Armorie* ii. 45 Vs to intrap abushment one they plast.

†**a'bushmently,** *adv. Obs.* [f. prec. + -LY[2].] In ambush, by way of ambuscade.

1552 HULOET *Abcedarium*, s.v., Abushmently, or in Abushment, *Confertim*.

abusing (ə'bjuːzɪŋ), *vbl. sb.* [f. ABUSE *v.* + -ING[1].]

†1. The action or process of using up. *Obs.*

1554 J. PHILPOT *Exam. & Writings* (1842) 419 Touch not, taste not, handle not, which all perish with the abusing of them.

2. The action or process of misusing, perverting, spoiling, injuring, reviling. (Now mostly gerundial.)

c **1530** *Lett. on Supp. of Mon.* (1843) 12 Hys [Latimer's] mynde ys myche more agenst the abusyng off thynges then agenst the thynge hytt selfe. **1598** SHAKS. *Merry Wives* I. iv. 4 Here will be an old abusing of God's patience, and the King's English. **1617** HIERON *Wks.* 1619-20 II. 125 What specialties are ripped vp, both of Gods fauours to their state, & of their abusings of His goodnesse. **1678** *Trans. at Ct. of Spain* 24 The abusing of Money that I have been speaking of. *Mod.* To try the old device of abusing the plaintiff's attorney.

†**a'busion.** *Obs.* [a. OFr. *abusion*, ad. L. *abūsiōn-em*, n. of action f. *abūti, abūsus*: see ABUSE *v.* Exceedingly common from 4 to 6; but not in Bible 1611, and rare after.]

1. Misuse, misapplication, perversion.

c **1450** LONELICH *Grail* xxx. 389 To putten so foul a thing in Abvcioun To so riche a thing with-outen Comparison. **1528** MORE *Heresyes* III. Wks. 1557 245/1 I would not for my mynde witholde the profite that one good deuoute vnlerned ley man might take by the reading, not for the harme that an hundred heretikes would fall in by theyr own wilful abusion. **1549** CHALONER tr. *Erasmus, Moriæ Enc.* What is madnesse else, savyng a general errour and abusion of the mynde? **1558** KENNEDY *Compend. Tract.* in *Miscell. Wod. Soc.* (1844) 152 To mak up thair housis be abusioun of the patrimony of the Kirk.

2. Perversion of the truth; deceit, deception, imposture; also an instance of such perversion or deception.

c **1386** CHAUCER *Man of Lawes T.* 116 Many a subtyl resoun forth they leyden; They spekyn of magike, and of abusioun. **1485** CAXTON *Chas. the Grete* 53 Leue the creaunce of thy god Mahon & of other ydolles, whyche ben but abusyon and decepcyon. **1542** HALL *Chron.* (1809) 844 Indulgencies and Pardons graunted.. to the Abusion of the people and the deceivyng of our Soules. **1596** SPENSER *F.Q.* II. xi. 11 Foolish Delights and fond Abusions, Which doe that sence besiege with fond illusions. **1640** YORKE *Vnion of Honour* 48 This intoxication, and abusion of the World, was wonderfully encreased by the secret revolt of Sir Robert Clifford, Knight.

3. *Rhet.* Misapplication or perversion of terms, catachresis. (Cf. L. *abūsio* in Cicero and Quintil.)

1553 WILSON *Rhet.* 93 Abusion, called of the Grecians Catachresis, is when for a proper certaine woorde we use that which is most nighe unto it. **1636** B. JONSON *Eng. Gram.* (1692) I. xi. 680 Many Diminutives there are, which rather be abusions of Speech, than any proper English words.

4. Violation of law or right, outrage, wrong; anything opposed to propriety; bad or improper usage; corrupt or shameful fact or practice.

c **1374** CHAUCER *Troylus* IV. 991 And certes that were an abusion, That God shuld haue no perfyt clere weting More than we men. *a* **1420** OCCLEVE *De Reg. Princ.* 40 Fy! it is to grete an abusioun, To see a man, that is but wormes mete, Desire richesse & grete possessioun. **1482** *Monk of Evesham* (1869) 58 Grete bestys onnaturally schapyne.. in a fowle damnable abusion compellyd hem to medylle with hem. **1557** MORE *Edward V* (1641) 72 Howbeit much of this great abusion might be amended. **1547** *Homilies* (1640) I. x. III. 76 Usurped power full of enormities, abusions, and blasphemies. *a* **1718** PENN *Tracts* Wks. 1726 I. 519 The Ancient Common Law of England.. declares, That all Restraints of Jurors are Abusions of the Law.

5. Contemptuous or reproachful language; reviling, insult.

1382 WYCLIF *Ps.* xxxi. 18 Trecherous lippis, That speken aȝen the riȝtwis wickidnes, in pride and in abusioun [**1611** contemptuously]. **1529** RASTELL *Pastyme, Hist. Brit.* (1811) 292 With many sclaunderous wordes, to the great abusyon of all the audyence. **1553-87** FOXE *A. & M.* (1596) 1018/1 I will leaue out Christes answere, least I should be thought ouer free and plaine in.. uttering of abusions.

†**abusious,** *a. Obs. rare*[−1]. [f. ABUSION on analogy of pairs like *vexation, vexatious*; cf. Fr. *abuseux* 'full of abuses' (Cotgr.) See -OUS.] Given to abuse, abusive.

1594 *Taming of a Shrew* iv. Marrie, my timber shall tell the trustie message of his maister even on the very forehead of thee, thou abusious villaine.

abusive (ə'bjuːsɪv), *a.* [a. Fr. *abusif -ive*:—L. *abūsīv-us*, f. *abūsus*: see ABUSE and -IVE. Some of the meanings are direct from L.] Characterized by abuse or abusing: hence

1. Wrongly used, perverted, misapplied, improper: in *Rhetoric*, catachrestic.

1583 FULKE *Def.* vi. 253 You are driven to seek a silly shadow for it [sacrificial power] in the abusive acception and sounding of the English word 'priest.' **1603** FLORIO *Montaigne* (1632) I. xxii. 48 Notwithstanding this abusive custome, loyaltie in married women is highly regarded. **1651** BAXTER *Inf. Bapt.* 89 Therefore it is sinfull to prefer before it an abusive sence, wherein Scripture never useth the word. **1710** SHAFTESBURY *Charact.* I. §2 (1737) II. 192 [Thou] didst mock Heaven's Countenance, and in abusive Likeness of the Immortals mad'st the Compound Man. **1859** SIR W. HAMILTON *Lect. Metaph.* II. xxxiii. 262 The Reproductive Imagination (or Conception, in the abusive language of the Scottish philosophers) is not a simple faculty.

2. Full of abuses; corrupt. *arch.*

1589 NASHE *Anat. Absurd.* 5 The abusive enormities of these our times. **1628** WITHER *Brit. Rememb.* IV. 281 If our Lawyers will In their abusive wayes continue still. **1780** BURKE *Sp. on Econ. Ref.* Wks. 1842 I. 238 First.. is the royal household. This establishment, in my opinion, is exceedingly abusive in its constitution. **1838** HALLAM *Hist. Lit.* I. I. iv. §55. 299 The determination of Leo to persevere in defending all the abusive prerogatives of his see.

†3. Deceitful, cheating. *Obs.*

1602 DANIELL *Civ. Wars* IV. lxxxv. (1718) II. 136 When as th' illighten'd Soul discovers clear Th' abusive Shews of Sense. **1624** BACON *Consid. on War with Spain* Wks. 1740 III. 515 Whatsoever is gained by an abusive treaty, ought to be restored *in integrum.* **1667** *Decay of Chr. Piety* iv. §3. 222 He dazles their eyes with the glorious, but abusive proposal of becoming like Gods.

†4. Given to misusing, ill-using, perverting. *Obs.*

1652 J. BURROUGHES *Exp. Hosea* vii. 276 Most are abusive in their desires after, and use of the creature. **1669** PENN *No Cross* xiv. §8 Wks. 1726 I. 351 The Fashions and Recreations now in Repute are very abusive of the End of Man's Creation.

5. Employing or containing bad language or insult; scurrilous, reproachful.

1621 HOWELL *Lett.* (1650) I. 62 Some years since, there was a very abusive satire in verse brought to our King. **1702** POPE *Jan. & May* 71 Abusive Nabal ow'd his forfeit life To the wise conduct of a prudent wife. **1710** in Somers' *Tracts* III. 1 The Subject is nice, the Age abusive, the Town full of Observers and Reviewers. **1865** DICKENS *Our Mut. Friend* xv. 381 You're an.. abusive.. bad old creature.

abusively (ə'bjuːsɪvlɪ), *adv.* [f. prec. + -LY[2].] In an abusive manner: hence,

1. In a wrong use, improperly, incorrectly. *Rhet.* By improper use of language or terms; catachrestically.

1531 ELYOT *Governour* (1875) 16 Athenes and other citees of Grece.. concluded to lyue as it were in a comminaltee, which abusiuely they called equalitee. **1664** EVELYN tr. *Freart, Paral. of Archit.* vii. 24 The Ionic fluting which is abusively employ'd in this place. **1678** CUDWORTH *Intellect. Syst.* 229 Goodness and Providence, Personated, are sometimes also Abusively, called Gods and Goddesses. **1728** MORGAN *Hist. Algiers* II. i. 213 The Spaniards, most corruptly & most abusively murder & confound several Letters. **1836** LANDOR *Per. & Asp.* Wks. 1846 II. 378 Her malignity alone could influence so abusively the generous mind of Agapenthe. **1874** TRENCH *Sacr. Lat. Poetry* (ed. 3) Introd. 18 *Numeri* is only abusively applied to verses which rest on music and time, and not on the number of the syllables.

2. With abusive language; reproachfully, foully.

1755 JOHNSON *Dict.*, *Abusively*, reproachfully. *a* **1797** H. WALPOLE *George II* (1847) I. xii. 408 Delaval had spoken pompously and abusively against the petitioner. **1878** LECKY *Eng. in 18th Cent.* II. ix. 579 Who were often themselves abusively attacked by ignorant lay preachers.

abusiveness (ə'bjuːsɪvnɪs). [f. ABUSIVE + -NESS.] The quality of being abusive: hence,

†1. Wrongness of use, perversion, perversity. *Obs.*

a **1677** BARROW ii. 328 (L.) This point doth clearly demonstrate.. the abusiveness of evacuating all his [Our Lord's] laborious and expensive designs in acquiring us.

2. Foulness or rudeness of language.

1633 G. HERBERT *Church Porch* 236 Pick out of mirth, like stones out of thy ground, Profanenesse, filthinesse, abusivenesse. **1683** WYCHERLY *Country Wife* III. i. (R.) I can no longer suffer his scurrilous abusiveness to you. *Mod.* The abusiveness of their language passes description.

abusse, variant of ABUSH, to ambush. *Obs.*

abut (ə'bʌt), *v.* [appears to represent two Fr. vbs. of cognate origin; OFr. *abouter* 'toucher par un bout,' *abouter à, sur*, to border on (countries, estates), mod.Fr. *abouter*, techn. to join two things end to end, f. *à* to + *bout* end; and OFr. *abuter*, 'toucher au but,' f. *à* to + *but* end, mod.Fr. *abuter*, 16th c. *abutter*, to put end to end, touch with an end, as 'toutes les rues qui abuttoient à la maison de ville' (Littré); in la Vendée they use *abutter* to signify 'mettre un support à un mur' (Godefroi). Cf. also mod.Fr. *aboutir* to touch with an end, terminate in or on. In reference to boundaries *abut* represents *abouter*; architecturally it = *abuter, abutter*. The position of sense 1 is uncertain.]

†1. *intr.* To stick out, lean forward (as in looking out at a window or over a battlement). *Obs.*

c **1230** *Ancren Riwle* 62 Ne aboutie heo nout vt et ham,[the battlements] leste heo þes deofles quarreaus habbe amidden þen eien.

2. To end at, march with, border *on*, as contiguous lands or estates do.

1463 *Manners & Househ. Exps. of Eng.* 461 A pece of pastor.. abuttynge to Hogge medew on the northe. **1650** FULLER *Pisgah Sight* IV. ii. 22 The land allotted him [Ishmael] ranged out so far, that the bounds and borders thereof abutted on all his kindred. **1793** WHITE *Nat. Hist. Selb.* (1853) i. 11 Being very large and extensive it [Selborne parish] abuts on twelve parishes. **1837** W. HOWITT *Rur. Life* (1862) III. iii. 229 Such is the region which abuts upon the Yorkshire dales.

b. *trans.* (*on* omitted.)

1871 *Athenæum* 25 Mar. 374 We discovered a hole in the pavement abutting the wall. **1882** *Pall Mall G.* 31 May 2/2 The Rotherhithe Baths, abutting Southwark Park.

3. To end *on* or *against*, to touch with a projecting end or point; to lean *upon* at one end. Properly said of the end or corner of anything projecting so as to touch or lean on the side of another.

1578 T. N. tr. *Conq. of W. India* 201 It is made of stone, with foure dores that abutteth upon the three calseys. **1589** PUTTENHAM *Eng. Poesie* (1869) 133 If their last syllables abut not vpon the consonant in the beginning of another word. **1833** LYELL *Princ. Geol.* III. 348 Tertiary strata of the older Pliocene epoch abut against vertical mica-schist. **1836** TODD *Cycl. An. & Ph.* I. 281/2 In the Ostrich the last rib abuts against the ilium. **1868** MILMAN *St. Paul's* viii. 190 The Chapter House abutted on the south aisle of the Cathedral.

b. *trans.* (*on* omitted.)
1864 *Athenæum* No. 1929, 505/3 The arches are abutted by outstanding structures.

4. *trans.* To cause to end *against*; to project.
1802 J. PLAYFAIR *Illustr. Huttonian Th.* 378 Such a face.. can have been produced only by having been abutted against some stratified rock.

abute(n, obs. form of ABOUT.

†**abuten,** *prep. Obs.* 2–3. The adv. *á* aye, ever, and prep. *buten*, OE. *bútan*, without; orig. and prop. written separate, but afterwards, from the frequency with which they came together in certain phrases, as *á buten ende*, written as one word, in which at length the meaning of *á* was often sunk, and the whole used as = *without*. Not found after 13th c.
c **1175** *Lamb. Hom.* 181 þer is blisse abuten treȝe, and lif abuten deaþe. *c* **1230** *Ancren Riwle* 396 World a buten ende. *c* **1250** *Moral Ode* (1862) 33 He is soð sunne & briht . & dai a-buten nihte.

¶ Occ. the two words are written as one in other connexions, as in the following, which should be printed *á, bute* 'always, unless.'
c **1175** *Lamb. Hom.* 23 He wunet þer-on abute þu hit bete.

abutilon (əˈbjuːtɪlɒn). *Bot.* [mod.L. ad. Arab. *aubūtīlūn* applied to this or an allied genus by Avicenna.] A genus of plants (N.O. *Malvaceæ*) with handsome yellow or white flowers veined with red.
1731 BAILEY, Abuttillon [with Botanists] yellow mallows. **1865** *Gayworthys* II. 202 Some tender abutilons like drops of redder gold.. and little English violets.

abutment (əˈbʌtmənt). [f. ABUT *v.* + -MENT. Cf. OFr. *aboutement*, 'borne, limite, extrémité qui confine avec une autre.' Godefroi.]

1. The meeting end to end; the place where projecting ends meet each other; junction.
1644 EVELYN *Mem.* (1857) I. 118 The four fountains of Lepidus, built at the abutments of four stately ways. **1674** N. FAIRFAX *Bulk & Selv.* 26 Two rooms cannot be within one abutment, unless they be thereby clapt into one.

2. The action of abutting, or terminating upon.
1870 ROLLESTON *An. Life* 43 Separated into a lumbar and a sacral division, by the abutment of the iliac bones upon the vertebrae.

3. *Arch.* The solid part of a pier or wall, etc., against which an arch abuts, or from which it immediately springs, acting as a support to the thrust or lateral pressure. In a bridge, the masonry (or rock) at either end supporting the arches.
1793 SMEATON *Edystone Lightho.* §274 The sloping abutments of an arch [*now* skewback]. **1823** NICHOLSON *Pract. Builder* 328 In masonry, the abutments of a bridge mean the walls adjoining to the land. **1879** *Building Constr.* in *Cassell's Techn. Educ.* I. 197 Piers imply supports which receive vertical pressure, whilst abutments are such as resist outward thrust.

4. By extension, That upon which anything abuts or leans, or from which it receives firm support.
a **1734** NORTH *Examen* II. v. §81. 365 The whole Scheme and Abutment of the rebellious Project was founded upon them. **1793** HOLCROFT *Lavater's Physiog.* ix. 54 I have generally considered the Nose as the foundation or abutment of the brain. **1850** MERIVALE *Hist. Rom. Emp.* (1865) VIII. lxiii. 30 The no less rugged abutments of the northern spurs of the Balkans. **1860** TYNDALL *Glaciers* I. §25. 187 Long clear icicles, tapering from their abutments. **1873** MIVART *Elem. Anat.* ii. 64 Its [the sternum's] human condition of serving as a ventral abutment to ribs though general is not constant.

abuttal (əˈbʌtəl). [f. ABUT *v.* (in sense 2) + -AL^2.] Abutment; *pl.* the extremities or bounds of land; the parts in which it abuts upon neighbouring lands.
1630 BACON *Maxims Com. Law* xxv. 89 The land is set forth by bounds and abuttals. **1780** MARSHAM in *Phil. Trans.* LXXI. 451 *note*, I have the deed between my ancestor.. and the Copyhold Tenants of his Manor.. and the abuttal is clear. **1809** TOMLINS *Law Dict.* s.v. The boundaries and abuttals of corporation and church land.. are preserved by an annual procession. **1876** GWILT, *Abuttals*: the buttings or boundings of land.

†**abuttalling** (əˈbʌtəlɪŋ), *vbl. sb.* ? *Obs.* [f. ABUTTAL *sb.* used as *v.* + -ING^1.] The marking or declaration of abuttals or terminations of lands.
a **1641** SPELMAN *Antient Deeds & Charters* v. (R.) The particular manner of abuttalling, with the term itself, arose from the Normans, as appeareth in the Customary of Normandy, cap. 556, where it is said, that the declaration must be made *par bouts et costes destites terres saisies*, of the abuttals and sides of the said lands seized.

abutter (əˈbʌtə(r)). [f. ABUT + -ER^1.] One who, or that which, abuts. *spec.* The owner of contiguous property.
1874 *Fitchburg City Docum.* (1874) 220 The concrete walks on Depot Court and Pleasant Street have been wholly paid for by the abutters. **1877** W. H. BURROUGHS *Taxation* 430 The expense of the work to be borne by the abutters.

abutting (əˈbʌtɪŋ), *ppl. a.* [f. ABUT + -ING^2.] Projecting towards; terminating upon or against; coming into contact, touching.
1599 SHAKS. *Hen. V*, I Prol. 21 Whose high, vp-reared, and abutting Fronts, The perillous narrow Ocean parts asunder. **1674** N. FAIRFAX *Bulk & Selv.* 88 Those bodies or beings that cannot have a placely respect, cannot have an abutting or touching respect. **1848** LYTTON *Harold* iv. 313 She crept.. into the shade of abutting walls.

abuzz (əˈbʌz), *adv.* or *pred. a.* [f. A *prep.*^{1} + BUZZ *sb.*^{1} and *v.*^{1}] In a buzz; filled with buzzing.
1859 DICKENS *T. Two Cities* III. ix, The court was all astir and a-buzz. **1859** GEO. ELIOT *A. Bede* I. xxi, I hate the sound of women's voices; they're always either a-buzz or a-squeak. **1926** J. G. KERR in *Rep. Brit. Assoc. 1926* 111 The whole air is abuzz with discussions on sex.

abversion, obs. irreg. form of AVERSION.
1638 *Reliq. Wotton.* (1672) 481 Rather an obduration then an abversion.

†**'abvolate,** *v. Obs.*$^{-0}$ [irreg. form of AVOLATE.] 'To fly away.' Cockeram 1626, Blount 1656, Phillips 1662. Not in Bailey. 'Not used,' Ash 1775.

†**abvo'lation.** *Obs.*$^{-0}$ [n. of action f. prec.] 'A flying away.' Bullokar 1676. 'Not used,' Ash 1775.

aby, abye (əˈbaɪ), *v. arch.* Forms: *Inf.* 1 abycg-an, abicg-an; 2 abug-en, 2–4 abuggen, abigg-en; 3–4 abugg-e, abigg-e; 4 abegg-e, abedge; abey-e(n, abei-e, abé; aby-en, abi-en; 4–5 abaye, abaie; 4–6 abie; 5 (abyche); 6 (abygge), 4–9 aby, abye. *Pa. t.* 1–3 abohte; 3–4 aboȝte, abouȝte; 4–5 aboughte; 5– abought. *Pa. pple.* 1–3 aboht; 3–4 aboȝt, abouȝt; 4– abought. *Abugge* (*ü*) was s.w.; *abegge, abedge* s.e.; *abeye, abye, abie* mdld. and nor. [f. A- *pref.* 1 away, out, back + BUY, OE. *bycgan*]; cogn. w. Goth. *usbugjan* to redeem: see BUY.]

†1. *trans.* To buy, purchase, pay for. *Obs.*
c **1175** *Lamb. Hom.* 185 Nis nan blisse soþes in an þing þet is utewið · þet ne beo to bitter aboht. *c* **1200** *Moral Ode* in *Trin. Coll. Hom.* 224 Swines brade is wel swete.. Ac al to diere he hit abuið þe ȝiefð þar-fore his swiere. *c* **1300** in Wright's *Lyr. Poetry* xxxvii. 103 A thyng that is ful precious, ful duere hit ys aboht. *c* **1374** CHAUCER *Compl. Mars & Venus* 334 Thus dere abought is Love in yevynge. **1503** *Stat. 19 Hen. VII*, vi. §1 Theves.. bryng such stolen vessell unto theym.. to sell.. and abought they bryng it to pryve places.. and ther sell much part of hit to straungers.

2. *trans.* To pay the penalty for (an offence), to redeem, atone for, suffer for, make amends for, expiate: commonly with *sore, dearly*, etc. *arch.*
c **1175** *Lamb. Hom.* 35 þa wrecche saule hit scal abuggen. **1205** LAYAMON 8158 þu me smite bi þon rugge, Ah sare þu hit salt abuggen. *c* **1230** *Ancren Riwle* 306 Bute ȝif he abugge þe sunne þet he wrouhte. *c* **1270** *King Horn* 110 Wiþ swerd oþer wiþ kniue, We scholden alle deie And þi fader deþ abeie. *c* **1314** *Guy Warw.* (1840) 49 His deth thou schalt wel sore abigge. *c* **1380** *Sir Ferumb.* 2848 Abigge þow schalt þis wronge: þat þov ous hast y-don. *Ibid.* 3404 þilke companye þo ful dere aboȝte: þat þay come þare. **1393** LANGL. *P. Pl.* C. XI. 233 Here abouȝte þe barn · hus belsires gultes. **1393** GOWER *Conf.* I. 261 Thy false body shall abie And suffre, that it hath deserved. *Ibid.* II. 386 He wolde done his sacrilegge That many a man shulde it abegge [*some edd.* abedge]. *c* **1400** *Gamelyn* 810 He schal it abegge that broughte him thertoo. *c* **1430** *Hymns to Virg.* 118 Now lete my flesche my synnis abie! **1560** *Thersites* (Hazl. *Dodsl.* I. 406) They shall aby bitterly the coming of such a guest. **1613** BEAUM. & FL. *Knt. of Burning Pestle* III. iv. 26 Foolhardy knight, full soon thou shalt aby This fond reproach, thy body will I bang. **1815** SCOTT *Lord of Isles* v. xxvii. By Heaven, they lead the page to die.. They shall abye it! **1876** BANCROFT *Hist. U.S.* V. ix. 432 Dearly did the Cherokees aby their rising.

3. *trans.* To pay (as a penalty); suffer, endure. *arch.*
1374 CHAUCER *Boethius* 39 þou quod she abaist þus þe tourment of þi fals[e] opinioun. *c* **1386** —— *Knight's T.* 1445 Keep me fro the vengans of thilk yre, That Atheon aboughte trewely. **1596** SPENSER *F.Q.* III. iv. 38 Who dyes, the utmost dolor doth abye; But who that lives, is lefte to waile his losse. **1870** MORRIS *Earthly Par.* III. IV. 339 Certes thou wouldst abye A heavy fate if thou shouldst lie herein.

†4. *absol.* To pay the penalty, to make restitution, to atone, to suffer. *Obs.*
c **1300** *Vox & Wolf* 208 ȝe, quad the vox, al thou most sugge, Other elles-wer thou most abugge. *c* **1386** CHAUCER *Doctor's T.* 100 For I dar wel seye, If that thay doon, ye schul ful sore abeye. **1393** LANGL. *P. Pl.* C. XXI. 448 Ac for þe lesynge þat þow, lucifer · lowe til eue, þow shalt abygge bitere. **1400** *Pol. Rel. & Love Poems* (1866) 256 I am gylty & þou abeyst. *c* **1449** PECOCK *Repr.* III. viii. 331 Lete it Abie which is gilti. **1548** UDALL etc. *Erasm. Par.* Luke xii. 47 He shall abye with many a sore strype. **1596** SPENSER *F.Q.* III. vi. 24 If I catch him in this company.. he dearly shall abye: Ile clip his wanton wings that he no more shall flye.

†5. *absol.* To endure, remain; or *trans.* to endure, experience. In this sense ABY came to be identical with senses of ABIDE, and was formally confused with it: see Note ¶ under ABIDE. *Obs.*
1450 *Past. Lett.* 134 I. 179 Knowlage of myche more thyng than he myth have.. because of short abyng. **1591** SPENSER *Ruines of Time* 101 For warlike power, and peoples store, In Britannie was none to match with mee, That manie often did abie full sore. **1596** —— *F.Q.* III. vii. 3 But nought that wanteth rest can long aby.

abye, rare variant of ABEYE *v.* to bend. *Obs.*

abylement, abyliment, obs. f. HABILIMENT.

abylite, obs. form of ABILITY.

abysm (əˈbɪz(ə)m). Also 3–7 abime, abyme 5–7 abysme; 6–7 abisme, abism. [a. OFr. *abisme, abime* (cogn. w. Pr. *abisme*, Sp. *abismo*):—late pop. L. **abyssimus*, a superlative of *abyssus*, lit. the profoundest depth; see ABYSS. *Abime*, which appears earlier in Eng., represents the Fr. pronunciation from 10th c., now also the mod.Fr. spelling *abîme*. Probably *abisme* was at first merely an artificial spelling, in imitation of the Fr.; we find *abisme* rhyming with *time* as late as 1616; the modern pronunciation follows the spelling.]

1. *prop.* The great deep, the bottomless gulf, believed in the old cosmogony to lie beneath the earth, and supposed to be, *specifically*: b. an imaginary subterraneous reservoir of waters; c. hell, or the 'bottomless pit,' the 'infernal regions.'
c **1300** *Cursor Mundi* 22678 (Cotton MS.) Aboue þe erth and beneþen Right unto þe abime fra heþen [*other MSS.* abyme]. **1490** CAXTON *Eneydos* xi. 43 I desire and wysshe that erste thabysme of thobscure erthe swalowe me. *c* **1530** LD. BERNERS *Arthur of Lytell Bryt.* (1814) 43 The abysme and swalowe of the earth. **1632** HEYWOOD *Iron Age* II. Wks. 1874 III. 409 Yet here's a hand can rayse you, deeper cast Then to the lowest Abisme.
b. *c* **1325** *E.E. Allit. Poems* B. 363 þen bolned þe abyme & bonkeȝ con ryse. **1483** CAXTON *Gold. Leg.* 39/4 The welles of the abysmes were broken and the cataractes of heven were opened. *a* **1834** COLERIDGE *Dest. Nations* Poems 76 Or if the Greenland wizard in strange trance Pierces the untravelled realms of Ocean's bed Over the abysm.
c. **1509** BARCLAY *Shyp of Folys* (1874) I. 135 Sometime he punyssheth with infernall abhyme. **1606** SHAKS. *Ant. & Cl.* III. xiii. 147 When my good Starres.. Haue empty left their Orbes, and shot their Fires Into th' Abisme of hell. **1663** COGAN tr. *Pinto's Voy. & Adv.* xli. 162 The gluttonous Serpent that lived in the profound Obism of the house of smoak. **1857–69** HEAVYSEGE *Saul* (ed. 3) 418 Roll, roll away, thou Stygian smoke, And let me into the abysm look.

2. Any deep immeasurable space, a profound chasm or gulf. *lit.* and *fig.*
1495 CAXTON *Vitas Patrum* (W. de Worde) II. 291 aa, His Jugemens be as a grete & a depe abysme. **1610** SHAKS. *Temp.* I. ii. 50 What seest thou els In the dark-backward and Abysme of Time? **1616** DRUMM. OF HAWTH. *Poems* 59 Feele such a case, as one whom some Abisme, In the deep Ocean kept had all his Time [in Wks. 1711, 13 *printed* Abime]. **1653** COGAN *Diod. Siculus* 95 This river.. is swallowed up in an abysme or overture of the earth. **1818** KEATS *Endymion* II. 379 And down some swart abysm he had gone, Had not a heavenly guide benignant led. **1873** MASSON *Drumm. of Hawth.* xi. 223 He flung himself bodily into the abysm.

3. *Attrib.*
1818 KEATS *Endym.* III. 28 The abysm-birth of elements.

†**a'bysm,** *v. Obs.* [a. Fr. *abysme-r*, earlier spelling of *abîmer*, f. *abysme* sb.] To engulf.
1611 COTGR., *Abysmer*, to Abisme or ingulph.

abysmal (əˈbɪzməl), *a.* [f. ABYSM *sb.* + -AL^1.]

1. Of, pertaining to, or resembling an abyss; fathomless; deep-sunken. *lit.* and *fig.*
[**1656** BLOUNT *Glossogr.* **1721** BAILEY. Not in JOHNSON.] **1817** COLERIDGE *Biogr. Lit.* 83 'Only fourpence,' (O! how I felt the anti-climax, the abysmal bathos of that fourpence)! **1850** MRS. BROWNING *Poems* I. 7 Countless angel-faces, still and stern, Pressed out upon me from the level heavens, Adown the abysmal spaces. **1865** *Sat. Rev.* 4 Feb. 146/1 Madame had carious teeth, abysmal eyes, and a wide wet grin. **1879** FARRAR *St. Paul* II. 546 The government of Nero .. at this moment presented a spectacle of awful cruelty and abysmal degradation.

2. In weakened sense: of an exceptionally poor standard or quality; extremely bad.
1904 H. JAMES *Golden Bowl* II. xxviii. 345 She had.. told her maid, a new woman, whom she had lately found herself thinking of as abysmal, that she didn't want her. **1933** DYLAN THOMAS *Let.* ?15 Oct. (1985) 25, I always said his taste was abysmal. **1965** G. MELLY *Owning-Up* vi. 59, I can still remember some of the abysmal patter which he delivered. **1984** *N.Y. Times* 10 July A23/1 Guatemala's abysmal human rights record.

abysmally (əˈbɪzməlɪ), *adv.* [f. prec. + -LY^2.] After the manner of an abyss; with unfathomable depths; unfathomably.
1879 GEO. ELIOT *Theo. Such* xviii. 314 The prejudiced, the puerile, the spiteful, and the abysmally ignorant.

†**a'bysming,** *ppl. a. Obs.* [f. ABYSM *v.* + -ING^2.] Sinking into or forming an abyss; engulfing.
1644 DIGBY *On the Soul* 464 To ayme att the discouery of these abisming depths.

†**a'bysmus.** *Obs.* [late L., occ. used in Eng. instead of ABYSM.] An abysm or abyss.
1611 COTGR., *Abysme*: An Abysmus; a bottomlesse hole or pit.

abyss (əˈbɪs). Also 4–7 abyssus, abissus. [ad. L. *abyss-us*, a. Gr. ἄβυσσος bottomless, sb. the deep.]The older forms in Eng. were ABIME, ABYSM from the Fr. The L. *abyssus* was adopted as a more learned word in 4, and in course of 6, englished as *abyss*. Thus the word has had five variants, *abime*, *abysm*, *abysmus*, *abyssus*, *abyss*; of which *abyss* remains as the ordinary form, and ABYSM as archaic or poetic.

1. The great deep, the primal chaos; the bowels of the earth, the supposed cavity of the lower world; the infernal pit. (See ABYSM.)

1398 TREVISA *Barth. De P.R.* (1495) XIII. xx. 449 The primordiall and fyrste matere in the begynnynge of the worlde not dystinguyd by certayn fourme is callyd Abyssus .. Abyssus is depnesse of water vnseen and therof come and springe welles and ryuers. **1413** LYDGATE *Pylgr. Sowle* (1483) III. x. 56 This pytte is the chyef and the manoyr of helle that is clepid Abissus. **1534** *Polyd. Verg., Eng. Hist.* II. xii. 56 a, For the desire hereof [gold] they have dygged in the depe bottomlesse abisse of the yerth. **1649** LOVELACE *Poems* (1659) 155 Ye blew flam'd daughters oth' Abysse, Bring all your Snakes, here let them hisse. **1704** RAY *Creation* I. 93 Bring up Springs & Rivers from the great Abyss. **1753** CHAMBERS *Cycl. Suppl.* s.v. The existence of an Abyss, or receptacle of subterraneous waters is .. defended by Dr. Woodward. **1835** THIRLWALL *Greece* I. vi. 198 The abyss of Tartarus, fast secured with iron gates, and a brazen floor.

2. A bottomless gulf; any unfathomable or apparently unfathomable cavity or void space; a profound gulf, chasm, or void extending beneath.

1639 MASSINGER *Unnat. Combat* II. i. Were I condemned .. to fill up .. A bottomless abyss, or charge thro' fire, It could not so much shake me. **1667** MILTON *P.L.* VII. 212 They viewed the vast immeasurable abyss Outrageous as a sea, dark, wasteful, wild. **1794** SULLIVAN *View of Nat.* I. 30 How striking the profundity of the abysses! the frightful elevation of the rocks! **1831** SCOTT *A. Geierst.* ii. 25 I can see the part of the path lying down in the abyss. **1873** SIR J. HERSCHEL *Pop. Lect.* ii. §4. 50 That awful abyss which separates us from the stars.

3. *fig.*

1619 H. HUTTON *Follie's Anat.* (1842) 18 And in th' abysse of vintners chalked score, Shipwrack good fortune. **1620** SHELTON *Don Quixote* IV. xxi. 167 You have flung it into the Abissus of Silence. **1621** BACON in *Four Cents. Eng. Lett.* (1881) 43 Your majesty's heart, which is an abyssus of goodness, as I am an abyssus of misery. **1632** SANDERSON 21 *Serm.* Ad. Mag. (1673) 280 There is an abyssus, a depth in thy heart which thou canst not fathom with all the line thou hast. **1686** DRYDEN *Hind & Panther* 66 Thy throne is darkness in the abyss of light, A blaze of glory that forbids the sight. **1796** BURKE *Reg. Peace* i. Wks. VIII. 80 Some of them seemed plunged in unfathomable abysses of disgrace. **1871** F. T. PALGRAVE *Lyr. Poems* 101 Into the dismal abysses Where outworn centuries lie.

4. 'Abyss is also used in heraldry, to denote the centre of an escutcheon.' Chambers *Cycl. Suppl.* 1753. (Fr. *une fleur de lis en abîme*, Littré.)

abyss (ə'bɪs), *v.* [f. ABYSS *sb.*] To swallow up in an abyss, to engulf.

c **1860** LOWELL *Poet. Wks.* 1879, 381 The drooping sea-weed hears, in night abyssed .. the wave's receding shock.

abyssal (ə'bɪsəl), *a.* [ad. late L. *abyssāl-is* of or belonging to an abyss, f. *abyss-us*; see ABYSS and -AL[1].] Of unsearchable depth, unfathomable; belonging to the lowest depths of ocean. ***abyssal zone***, the bottom strata of the sea, the belt of water below 300 fathoms.

1691 BEHMEN *Theosoph. Philos.* 42 Whose immensity is Abyssal. **1752** W. LAW *Spir. of Love* (1816) II. 66 God is an abyssal infinity of love, wisdom, & goodness. **1830** LYELL *Princ. Geol.* (1875) II. III. xlix. 589 The Coral fauna of the deep and abyssal sea. **1872** NICHOLSON *Palæont.* 23 The abyssal mud of the Atlantic is to a very large extent composed of the microscopic shells of Foraminifera.

Abyssinia (æbɪ'sɪnɪə). *slang.* The name of the country (see ABYSSINIAN *a.* and *sb.*) used to represent a colloq. pronunc. of 'I'll be seeing you!': a jocular catch-word at parting.

1934 M. H. WESEEN *Dict. Amer. Slang* xiii. 173 [College slang] *Abyssinia*, I'll be seeing you. **1939** M. HARRISON *Vernal Equinox* 237 'Coming, young Figg?' .. 'Well, I'll be back.' 'Abyssinia!' said Mr. Flowerdew. **1949** L. P. HARTLEY *Boat* i. 4 Good-bye, dear, cheerio, Abyssinia. **1960** J. MITFORD *Hons & Rebels* xxii. 159 You'll find people generally say, 'I'll be seeing you' instead of 'goodbye'... You may be able to raise a laugh by saying, 'Abyssinia'. **1983** *N.Y. Times* 27 Feb. II. 25/1 'Abyssinia, Henry'—'Abyssinia', .. the 1920's expression for 'I'll be seeing you'.

Abyssinian (æbɪ'sɪnɪən), *a.* and *sb.* Also 7 **Abissian**, 7–8 **Abassin**, 7–9 **Abyssin(e)**. [f. *Abyssinia*, the name of a country in East Africa (now officially called Ethiopia) + -IAN.] **A.** *adj.* Of or pertaining to Abyssinia, its Christian church, its inhabitants or their language. Also *transf.*

1638 W. CHILLINGWORTH *Relig. Protestants* Answ. 2. 105 This therefore we deny both to your and all other Churches of any one denomination, as the Greek, the Roman, the Abyssine. *a* **1666** J. EVELYN *Diary* 18 Jan. an. 1645 (1955) II. 301 Divers China, Meerian, Samaritan, Abyssin & other Oriental books. **1686** [W. WAKE] *Def. of Exposition of Doctr. Ch. Eng.* 78 The Grecian, Armenian, Abassine Churches .. have .. differed from the Church of Rome. **1781** GIBBON *Decl. & F.* III. xxxiii. 351 Their names are honourably inscribed in the Roman, the Habyssinian, and the Russian calendar. *a* **1806** WORDSWORTH *Prel.* VI. 592 Como, .. a darling bosom'd up In Abyssinian privacy. **1816** COLERIDGE *Kubla Khan* in *Christabel* etc. p. 57 It was an Abyssinian maid And on her dulcimer she play'd. **1928** E. SITWELL *Five Poems* 16 Rich trees And Abyssinian glooms have fostered these.

b. Abyssinian cat, a breed of domestic cat having long ears and short brown hair ticked with grey; also *ellipt.*; **Abyssinian gold** = TALMI.

1876 W. G. STABLES *Cats*, *(caption)* Abissinian .. brought from Abissinia at the conclusion of the war. **1893** J. JENNINGS *Domestic or Fancy Cats* ii. 16 In size, the Abyssinian resembles the self-coloured English cat. **1959** *Chambers's Encycl.* III. 168/2 Abyssinians .. are speckled black and grey, differing from tabbies in having no pattern on the body... There is no ground for supposing that this breed originated in the country after which it is named. **1890** Abyssinian gold [see TALMI]. **1933** E. A. SMITH *Working Prec. Met.* xx. 381 Copper Zinc Alloys .. Abyssinian Gold.

B. *sb.* **a.** An inhabitant of Abyssinia. **b.** A member of the Abyssinian Christian church.

1621 T. MUN *Discourse Trade* 16 The great quantitie of gold & some siluer .. yearely brought thither from the Abissians countrie in Ethiopia. **1671** A. WOODHEAD *Consid. Counc. Trent* xvi. 294 Ethiopians, or Abyssines, agreeing in this Point with the Roman. **1735** S. JOHNSON tr. *Lobo's Voy. to Abyssinia* Pref. p. ix, He neither exaggerates overmuch the Merits of the Jesuits .. nor aggravates the Vices of the Abyssins. **1737** R. CHALLONER *Cath. Chr. Instr.* viii. 109 'Tis the Practice .. of the Cophts or Egyptians, and of the Abassins or Ethiopians, who all use in their Liturgies their ancient Languages. **1753** E. CHAMBERS *Cycl.* Suppl., The Abyssinians are a branch of the Copts, or Jacobites; with whom they agree in admitting only one nature in Jesus Christ, and rejecting the council of Chalcedon. **1845** J. C. PRICHARD *Nat. Hist. Man* (ed. 2) xi. 103 Hairs of a Negro .. and of some Abyssinians .. were .. viewed both as transparent and opaque bodies. **1936** *Discovery* June 170/1 The Abyssinians—essentially Hamitic in origin—are nowadays much mixed with Semites and Negroes. **1957** *Encycl. Brit.* I. 73/1 Although the country is now officially described as Ethiopia, the terms 'Abyssinia' and 'Abyssinians' have been retained as being more properly descriptive of the land and people whether from the ethnological, historical or geographical points of view.

‖**abyssus** (ə'bɪsəs). [L.; see ABYSS.] The form in which the word ABYSS was first used.

abyt, obs. f. HABIT = clothing, Fr. *habit*.

ac, obs. early form of OAK.

†**ac**, *conj. Obs.* 1–6 (only north. in 6), also **ak(e** *passim*; 2–4 **oc, ok**, 1–3 **ah, ach, auch, auȝ, auh.** [OE. *ac*, cogn. w. OSax. *ac*, Goth. *ak*, OHG. *oh.*] But.

a **1000** CYNEWULF *Andreas* 2420 Ne míþ ðu, ah ðinne módsefan staðola. *c* **1000** *Ags. Gosp.* Matt. v. 17 Ne com ic ná to towurpan, ac ȝefyllan. **1145** *O.E. Chron.* (Laud. MS.) an. 1140 God wimman scæ wæs, oc scæ hedde litel blisse mid him. *c* **1175** *Lamb. Hom.* 145 Alle we beoð in monifald wawe .. ach god almihtin us freureð. *Ibid.* 211 Ich liuie nout ich : auh crist liueð in me. *c* **1200** *Trin. Coll. Hom.* 258 Inne þe nis lac ne lest . auȝ alle holinesse. *c* **1200** *Orm.* 1891 Þatt wass i Marrch, acc Marrch wass þa Neh all gan ut till ende. *c* **1270** *K. Horn* 116 Ofte hadde Horn beo wo Ac neure wurs þan him was þo. **1340** *Ayenb.* 18 Þe guodes .. ne byeþ naȝt his, ake byeþ his lhordes guodes. *c* **1380** *Sir Ferumb.* 4413 Buþ noȝt agast, Ac holdeþ forþ ȝour way an hast. *a* **1400** *E.E. Saints Lives* III. 8 Hit nas noȝt for is owen gilt Ok hit was .. for sin þine. **1535** STEWART *Cron. of Scotl.* II. 630 Amang the aill gart tume thame in the fat; Ac leit it stand at greit laser and lenth.

ac-, *pref.* assimilated form of L. *ad-* to, bef. *c-(k-)* and *qu-*, as in *ac-cumulāre*, *ac-cēdĕre*, *ac-quiescĕre*. Reduced in OFr. to *a-*, and so entered Eng. in 3–4. But in 4–5 the spelling *ac-* was artificially restored in Fr. in imitation of L., and in 4–5 this extended to Eng. as in *ac-count*, *ac-quit*, EE. *a-cunte*, *a-cwite*, *a-quite*. In all modern words from L., *ac-* is written, though *a-* only is pronounced. While the refashioning of the OFr. words was going on, *ac-* was ignorantly extended to some words having *a-* = OFr. *an-en-*:—*in-*, or *es-*:—*ex-*, as *a(c)cloy*, *a(c)cumber*, *a(c)coup*, EE. *acloye*, *acumbre*, *acoupe*, OFr. *encloer*, *encombrer*, *encoulper* = L. *inculpare*, and even to some words with *a-* = OE. *a-* or *on-*, as *a(c)curse*, *a(c)know*, *a(c)knowledge*.

ac-, the earlier spelling of many words, which in consequence of the refashioning mentioned in the prec. are now spelt **acc-**, under which they will be found.

-ac, *suffix* formerly **-aque**, **-ak(e**, **-ack**, primarily adj., whence also sb. formative, repr. Gr. *-ακός*, *-ακή*, *-ακόν*, the form of the adj. suffix *-κός*, in comb. w. sb. in *-ια*, *-ιος*, *-ιον*, as *καρδιακ-ός cardiac*, of the heart, *ἡλιακ-ός heliac*, of the sun, *δαιμονιακ-ός demoniac*, belonging to a demon. Some of these were adopted in L. as *cardiăc-us*, *dæmoniăc-us*, *elegiăc-us*, *aphrodīsiăc-us*, on the model of which others as *maniac-us*, *iliac-us* have been formed in med. or mod.L. Thence they have been adopted in Fr. as learned words in *-aque*, partly from which, as in *demoniac*, partly from L. or Gr. they have been adopted in Eng. e.g. *ammoniac*, *aphrodisiac*, *cardiac*, *celiac*, *elegiac*, *demoniac*, *hypochondriac*, *iliac*, *maniac*, *prosodiac*, *zodiac*. See also -ACAL.

acacia[1] (ə'keɪʃ(ɪ)ə). [a. Lat. *acacia*, a. Gr. *ἀκακία*, of uncertain origin; perh. containing *ἀκή* a point, in reference to its thorns.]

1. *Bot.* A genus of Leguminous shrubs or trees, of the *Mimosa* tribe, found in the warmer regions of the Old World; several species of which yield Gum Acacia or Gum Arabic, Catechu, and other products; they form in Australia thickets called scrubs.

1543 TRAHERON *Vigo* (1586) 429 Acacia is a thorny tree growing in Egipte. **1712** POMET *Hist. of Drugs* I. 17 He raised several Acacias, which are very prickly. *c* **1854** STANLEY *Sinai & Palest.* (1858) i. 20 The wild Acacia (*Mimosa Nilotica*) everywhere represents the 'seneh' or 'senna' of the Burning Bush. **1866** LINDLEY & MOORE *Treas. Bot.* 5 The aspect of an Acacia scrub, which is one of the characteristic features of Australian vegetation.

2. *pop.* The North-American Locust-tree, called also False-Acacia (*Robinia pseud-Acacia*), with sweet-scented white flowers, grown as an ornamental tree in England.

1664 EVELYN *Sylva* (1776) II. iv. 358 The Acacia .. deserves a place among our Avenue Trees. **1816** SHELLEY *Alastor* 437 The ash and the acacia floating hang Tremulous and pale. **1855** TENNYSON *Maud* I. xxii. 45 The slender acacia would not shake One long milk-bloom on the tree.

3. *Med.* The inspissated juice of the unripe fruit of species of *Acacia* and *Mimosa*, used as a drug.

1601 HOLLAND *Pliny* (1634) II. 194 There is a kind of Thorne, whereof commeth Acacia .. found in Egypt. **1769** HILL *Fam. Herbal.* (1812) 2 German acacia is the juice of unripe sloes evaporated. **1853** MAYNE *Exp. Lex.* s.v. Acacia .. the pharmacopœial name for gum-Arabic .. the concrete juice of *Acacia vera*, etc.

†**acacia**[2]. *Obs.* 'Something resembling a kind of roll or bag, seen on medals in the hands of several of the consuls and emperors, from the time of Anastatius.' Chambers *Cycl.* 1751. 'Filled with earth ... to remind him of his frailty and mortality.' Chambers *Suppl.*

acacine ('ækəsɪn). [f. ACACIA[1] + -INE[4] chem. form.] Pure gum arabic.

†**acacio.** [Apparently for Fr. *acajou* mahogany.] 'A heavy, durable wood of the red mahogany character, but darker and plainer; it is highly esteemed in ship-building.' Weale 1849.

†**'acacy.** *Obs.*—[0] [ad. Gr. *ἀκακία* guilelessness, f. *ἀ* priv. + *κακός* evil.] 'Innocence, a being free from malice.' Bailey 1731. ('Not much used') Ash 1775. Prob. never used.

Academe ('ækədi:m). Also **Achademe.** [f. L. *Acadēmīa*; perhaps erroneously (in Milton correctly) from *Acadēmus*: *Atque inter silvas Academi quærere verum*, Hor. *Ep.* II. ii. 45.]

1. a. *poetic* = ACADEMY 1, 3.

1588 SHAKS. *L.L.L.* I. i. 13 Our Court shall be a little Achademe. *Ibid.* IV. iii. 352 The Books, the Arts, the Achademes. *a* **1642** PEACHAM *Emblems*, *Rura mihi* etc. Thy solitary Academe should be Some shady grove upon the Thames' fair side. **1671** MILTON *P.R.* IV. 244 See there the olive grove of Academe, Plato's retirement. **1847** TENNYSON *Princess* ii. 180 The softer Adams of your Academe. **1870** LOWELL *Cathed.* Poet. Wks. 1879, 448 That best academe, a mother's knee.

b. = ACADEMIC B. 2 a.

1938 *Mod. Lang. Rev.* XXXIII. 560 The principal secular cultural influence at work in the seventeenth century is the late, rather jaded Humanism of a bureaucracy, and its bearers are not courtiers, but academes and officials. **1955** *Times Lit. Suppl.* 9 Dec. 733/3 Here .. are values put upon things in human life by defence chiefs, airmen, soldiers, security officers, academes, scientists.

2. The academic community; the world of university scholarship. Formerly only in (poet.) phr. ***the groves of Academe*** (tr. Horace's *silvas Academi*: see etym.).

[**1671**: see GROVE 1 b.] **1849** THACKERAY *Pendennis* I. xviii. 166 Into this certainly not the least snugly sheltered arbour among the groves of Academe, Pen now found his way. **1950** C. FRY *Venus Observed* I. 10 But how I longed As a boy for the groves and grooves of Academe. **1964** *Word Study* Feb. 1/1 The lexicographical donnybrook provoked .. in the journalistic world (with some minor flurries in the darker nooks of academe) can now be surveyed conveniently. **1970** *Daily Colonist* (Victoria, B.C.) 25 Dec. 9/2 For all his preoccupation with the microscope and academe, Rothschild is obviously a genuine tough guy. **1976** *Nature* 29 Jan. 257/1 Mr Fred Mulley, .. has been urging students to think more of industrial careers and less of academe or the civil service. **1977** I. SHAW *Beggarman, Thief* I. i. 2 A profession not held in particularly high esteem in the Halls of Academe. **1979** *Maledicta* III. 17 People of my kind are as unpopular in the Austrian groves of Academe as in the American ones. **1983** *Times Lit. Suppl.* 1093/3 His frequent jolly trips to London .. are the social highlight of his entire life and of his contacts with the world outside academe.

academese (æ,kædə'mi:z). [f. L. *Acadēm-* (see ACADEME, etc.) + -ESE.] The style or language of academic scholarship; dry academicalism.

1959 I. POOL in Saporta & Bastian *Psycholinguistics* (1961) 328/1 The fact that we discuss content analysis in academese indicates the class of things to which we conceive of it as belonging. **1965** *Times Lit. Suppl.* 25 Nov. 1043/1 The swing and mocking beat he can weave into a *Harlem Nocturne* here congeals into a parody of hermetic academese. **1976** *Ibid.* 2 July 818/5 Passages of high seriousness clump along in ponderous academese. **1985** W. SAFIRE in *N.Y. Times Mag.* 21 July 9/2 You're sure you grasped the full import of the academese in the sentence before this parenthetical aside?

academia (ækə'diːmɪə). Also **Academia.** [mod.L.: see L. *Acadēmia* and -IA¹.] The academic world or community; scholastic life; = ACADEME 2.

1956 W. H. WHYTE *Organization Man* (1957) xvii. 217 Let's turn now from the corporation to academia... If the academic scientist is seduced, it cannot be explained away as ..the pressures of commercialism. **1967** MRS. L. B. JOHNSON *White House Diary* 9 Oct. (1970) 582 If I had to capsule these two days in Academia, how would I? **1969** R. NEUSTADT in A. King *Brit. Prime Minister* 137 'In-and-outers' from the law firms, banking, business, academia, foundations, or occasionally journalism. **1971** A. SAMPSON *New Anat. Brit.* viii. 156 Businessmen liked to adopt the language of academia, and any conference of second-rate salesmen is now liable to be called a seminar..and any report a thesis. **1983** *Times* 17 Jan. 8/8 Has the Falklands inquiry been his last lapse from Academia?

academial (ækə'diːmɪəl), *a.* [f. L. *acadēmia* + -AL¹.] 'Relating to an academy, belonging to an academy.' J.; academic.

[**1755** in JOHNSON. n.q.] **1852** SIR W. HAMILTON *Discuss.* 411 The right of Academial Instruction was deputed to a limited number of 'famous colleges.'

†**Academian** (ækə'diːmɪən). *Obs.* [f. L. *acadēmia* academy + -AN.]

1. A disciple of Plato.

1534 LD. BERNERS *Golden Boke of M. Aurel.* (1546) B. ij. Peripateciens, Academiens and Epicuriens.

2. A member of an academy; an academic or academician.

1599 MARSTON *Sc. of Villanie* II. vi. 201 Then straight comes Friscus, that neat Gentleman, That newe discarded Academian. **1611** SPEED *Hist. Gt. Brit.* (1632) IX. xix. 931 Reuerence of the man..moued so the affection of the Oxford Academians. **1661** K. W. *Conf. Charact.* (1860) 69 The cook, and the bedmaker..are the necessary evils of an accademian. **1691** WOOD *Ath. Oxon.* I. col. 22 He went to Loraine..reading the Hebrew Lecture to the Academians of that place.

academic (ækə'dɛmɪk), *a.* and *sb.* [ad. med.L. *acadēmic-us*, Fr. *académique.*]

A. *adj.*

1. Belonging to the Academy, the school or philosophy of Plato; sceptical.

1610 HEALEY *St. Aug., City of God* (1620) XI. xxvi. 408 I fear not the Academike arguments..that say: what if you erre? **1777** HUME *Ess. & Treat.* II. 134 The wise lend a very academic faith to every report which favours the passion of the reporter. **1756** BURKE *Subl. & B.* Pref., Wks. I. 87 Cicero true as he was to the academick philosophy.

2. a. Of or belonging to an academy or institution for higher learning; hence, collegiate, scholarly.

c **1588** GREENE *Friar Bacon* ii. 6 Masters of our academic state That rule in Oxford. **1599** BP. HALL *Virgidem* IV. vi. 83 Oh let me lead an academicke life. **1633** G. HERBERT *Temple* 39, *Affliction* 45 Thou often didst with Academick praise Melt and dissolve my rage. **1750** JOHNSON *Rambler* No. 163 ¶4 Which my academick rudeness made me unable to repay. **1831** CARLYLE *Sart. Res.* (1858) 17 It betokens in the Author a rusticity and academic seclusion. **1875** B. TAYLOR *Faust* II. i. II. 9 See hitherward your grateful scholar wending Outgrown the academic rods of old.

b. *academic freedom*, the freedom of a teacher to state his opinions openly without censorship, or without the fear of losing his position, etc. (cf. G. *akademische Freiheit*); see also quot. 1963.

1901 *World's Work* July 920/2 Every right-thinking man will stand firmly for academic freedom of thought. **1930** *Jrnl. Abnormal Psychol.* XXV. 156 Academic Freedom... University instructors should have the greatest possible freedom in discussing their opinions with their students. **1963** *Times* 9 Mar. 8/4 The Chancellor of the University of Natal..unveiled a plaque..to commemorate 'the death of academic freedom' through the imposition of racial segregation in South African universities.

3. Of or belonging to a learned society, or association for the promotion of art or science; of or belonging to an Academician.

1879 *Daily Tel.* May 23 Each successively forced the heavy portals of Somerset House and Trafalgar-square to.. admit them..to Academic rank.

4. Not leading to a decision; unpractical; theoretical, formal, or conventional.

1886 *Times* 31 Mar. 7/2 This discussion partook of an academic character, for it was well understood that, whatever the result of the discussions might be, no practical step would be taken in the present Parliament. **1888** H. JAMES in *Scribner's Mag.* IV. 73/1 Mr. Wendover asked her if she liked English society and if it was superior to American ..; she thought his questions 'academic'—the term she used to see applied in the *Times* to certain speeches in Parliament. **1897** D. G. HOGARTH *Philip & Alex. of Macedon* I. 85 Since the references..to the Olynthian war are in the last degree meagre and vague, and those to Philip merely general, the Olynthiacs would possess for the historian only an academic interest. **1901** C. ELIOT in *Foreign Office Confid. Print Ser., E. Africa* LXVIII. xi (30 Nov.) 7 North of Mount Elgon..the frontier should proceed in a straight line.., but at present the point seems to be of purely academic interest, as we are not likely to extend our effective Administration to this district. **1929** H. G. WELLS *King who was King* vi. §2. 198 All this discussion, Sirs, is— academic. The war has begun already. **1931** *Economist* 21 Nov. 961/2 The results of the elections can only be of academic interest, as there were no Opposition candidates. **1957** *Times* 19 Nov. 11/2 If Russia's rockets can do what Mr. Khrushchev claims they can the blocking of American ports would surely be academic.

5. Conforming too rigidly to the principles (in painting, etc.) of an academy; excessively formal.

1889 *Cent. Dict.* (s.v. *academic*), *Figure of academic proportions*, in painting, a figure of a little less than half the natural size, such as it is the custom for pupils to draw from the antique and from life..hence, an *academic figure, composition*, etc., is one which appears conventional or unspontaneous, and smacks of practice-work or adherence to formulas and traditions. **1934** HASKELL *Balletomania* xv. 310 It did not take long for the new movement to become solidly and immovably academic. **1941** *Manchester Guard. Wkly.* 17 Jan. 51 As an artist he was never too revolutionary to be easily understood, yet never academic enough to be dull. **1961** *Times* 22 Mar. 16/1 The figure-studies by Puvis are complacent and academic in the worst sense.

B. *sb.* [The adj. used *absol.*]

1. An ancient philosopher of the Academy, an adherent of the philosophical school of Plato; a Platonist.

1586 B[EARD] tr. *La Primaudaye's Fr. Acad.* 9 Plato, Xenophon..& manie other excellent personages, afterward called Academikes. **1671** MILTON *P.R.* IV. 277 Mellifluous streames that watered all the schools Of academics old and new. **1751** CHAMBERS *Cycl.* s.v. They who embraced the system of Plato, among the ancients, were called *academici*, Academics; whereas those who did the same since the restoration of learning, have assumed the denomination of Platonists. **1830** SIR J. MACINTOSH *Progr. of Eth. Philos.* Wks. 1846 I. 28 His [Cleanthes'] most formidable opponent, Arcesilaus the academic.

2. a. A member of a college or university; a collegian. Now *spec.* a senior member of a university; a member of the academic staff of a university or college; also *loosely*, an academically-gifted person.

It is unclear even from the full context of quot. 1894 whether a student or faculty member is referred to by 'academic'.

1587 FLEMING *Contn. Holinshed* III. 1379/1 At hir being in Cambridge..thus did an academike write in praise of the forenamed earle. **1611** CORYAT *Crudities* 438 All the men generally doe weare it, both citizens and Academicks. **1750** JOHNSON *Rambler* No. 29 ¶13 The academick hopes to divert the ladies. **1795** GIBBON *Auto-Biog.* 26 The uniform habit of the academics, the square cap and black gown. **1838** *Fraser's Mag.* XVII. 468 He annoyed tutors, proctors, *et hoc genus omne*;..but was, on the whole, a not indecorous young academic. [**1894** *Univ. Chicago Weekly* 4 Oct. 4/1 One student, a member of the graduate school,..was heard one day soliciting an 'Academic' to set him right on the question of credits.] **1954** A. S. C. ROSS in *Neuphilologische Mitteilungen* LV. 32 People who use them are either non-U (very often, commercial travellers) or, if U, are elderly academics. **1955** J. WAIN *Interpretations* p. xv, The contributors are mainly either academics—men who draw salaries from Universities—..or..members of the 'literary world'. **1965** W. GOLDING *Hot Gates* 26 It is a fact that academics seldom wear academic dress. **1976** J. ARCHER *Not Penny More* ii. 26 He had never been a brilliant scholar, and he envied the natural academics among his classmates. **1981** V. GLENDINNING *Edith Sitwell* 3 The second man too was an academic, though not a specialist in English literature.

b. = ACADEMICAL B, which is the more usual term.

1823 LOCKHART *Reg. Dalton* (1842) 144 Dressed in the full academics of a gentleman Commoner—one of the most graceful, certainly, of all European costumes.

3. A member of a society for promoting art or science; = ACADEMIST 2, ACADEMICIAN. *rare.*

1751 CHAMBERS *Cycl.* s.v., *Academics* or rather *Academists* is also used among us for the members of the modern Academies, or instituted societies of learned persons. **1868** SWINBURNE *Ess. & Stud.* (1875) 372 Like Coriolanus, the painter [Sandys] might say..it is his to banish the judges, his to reject the 'Common cry' of academics.

4. pl. *Academics*, Eng. name of the *Academica*, one of the writings of Cicero.

5. *pl.* Academic studies. *U.S.*

1974 *Anderson* (S. Carolina) *Independent* 18 Apr. 4B/1 'They must be good in academics as well as coordination,' she said. **1977** *Time* 10 Oct. 39/3 Their report cited such cadet slang terms as 'cool on academics' and 'cooperate and graduate' as indicative of the attitude of a large majority of a typical class. **1981** *Underground Grammarian* Sept. 2 When the community appeals to higher standards of academics, that always kills spiritual values.

academical (ækə'dɛmɪkəl), *a.* and *sb.* [f. ACADEMIC *a.* and *sb.* + -AL¹.]

A. *adj.*

1. = ACADEMIC A 1. *rare.*

1666 J. SMITH *Old Age* 256 With Devotion to admire that Academical Inscription ἀγνώστῳ θεῷ [to an unknown God].

2. a. = ACADEMIC A 2, for which it is now more commonly used.

1587 FLEMING *Contn. Holinshed* III. 1321/2 As the academicall poet sometime said at the gratious entering of hir maiestie into Cambridge. **1769** *Lett. of Junius* vii. 30 An academical education has given you an unlimited command ..of speech. **1853** FELTON *Fam. Lett.* (1865) iii. 22 He came punctually in his academical costume. **1868** M. PATTISON *Academ. Organ.* 83 Academical life within college walls is a more valuable moral and social discipline than a solitary lodging.

b. *academical clerk*: at certain colleges of Oxford University, a junior member of a college who receives an emolument in return for undertaking duties (esp. singing) in chapel. Hence *academical clerkship*.

1873 *Oxf. Univ. Cal.* 260 Academical clerks. **1948** *Ibid.* 501 Academical Clerkships, Scholarships, and Exhibitions ..have been added at different times by various benefactors. **1972** *Ann. Rep. Christ Church* (Oxford) *1971* 19 Scholars numbered 94, Exhibitioners 84, Rhodes Scholars 4, and Academical Clerks 3 (a new category; the name conceals their main function—to be song-birds in the groves of Academe). **1984** *Oxf. Univ. Cal.* 229 [New College] The choir consists of a chaplain, eight academical clerks, six lay clerks, and sixteen choristers.

3. Of or belonging to an academy for the cultivation of *belles lettres*, arts, or sciences; of or pertaining to an academician.

1879 *Athenæum* 17 May 639 Academical in the sense that Couture's art was academical, the other work of the venerable member of the Institute pleases us more.

B. *sb. pl.* Academical robes; the articles of dress usually worn by the students, graduates, or officials of a college or university.

1823 LOCKHART *Reg. Dalton* (1842) 130 *Proctor.* 'Who are you? Are you gownsmen? Young man, how dare you be without your academicals?' **1861** T. HUGHES *T. Brown at Oxf.* xix. At first he caught up his cap and gown..On second thoughts, however, he threw his academicals back on to the sofa.

academicalism (ækə'dɛmɪkəlɪz(ə)m). [f. ACADEMICAL *a.* + -ISM.] Academical style (in a derogatory sense).

1890 *Athenæum* 14 May 640/1 The execution is marred by conventional coldness and obsolete academicalism.

academically (ækə'dɛmɪkəlɪ), *adv.* [f. ACADEMICAL *a.* + -LY².] In academic or academical manner. **a.** Platonically; sceptically. **b.** In relation to an academy or seat of learning.

1591 HORSEY *Travels* (1857) 237 [We] toke Cambridge.. one our waye..and wee wear verie accademicallie enterteyned. **1682** *Cabalistical Dial.* 17 (T.) These doctrines I propose academically, and for experiment sake. **1876** EMERSON *Ess.* Ser. I. x. 245 There are degrees in idealism. We learn first to play with it academically. **1879** *Standard* 1 July 4 Academically, Ireland is worse off than England.

academician (ə,kædə'mɪʃən). [a. Fr. *académicien*, f. med.L. *acadēmic-us*: see -IAN.]

1. A member of an academy, or society for promoting arts and sciences; first used of the members of the French Academies, and in England of the Royal Academy; now much more widely. It has taken the place of ACADEMIST.

1748 B. FRANKLIN *Let.* 7 Nov. in *Wks.* (1840) VII. 40 If you have the journal of the French Academicians to Lapland, I should be glad to see it. **1755** JOHNSON *Plan of Dict.* Wks. 1787 IX. 169 The academicians of France rejected terms of science in their first essay. **1818** J. NORTHCOTE *Sir J. Reynolds* II. 146 Invective and satire against the principal Academicians, and most pointedly against Sir Joshua. **1830** LYELL *Princ. Geol.* (1875) II. II. xxix. 119 The Academicians described derangements in some of the buildings of Calabria. **1963** *Oxf. Univ. Gaz.* 30 May 1337/1 The Degree of Doctor of Letters, *honoris causa*, ..will be conferred upon Academician Mikhail Pavlovich Alexeyev.

2. A collegian; = ACADEMIC B 2. *rare.*

1749 CHESTERFIELD *Lett.* 196 (1792) II. 237 As for Turin ..you cannot conveniently reside there as an academician. **1873** C. A. BRISTEDS *Five Yrs. in Eng. Univ.* (ed. 3) 34 The ignorance of the popular mind has often represented academicians riding, travelling, etc. in cap and gown.

academicism (ækə'dɛmɪsɪz(ə)m). [f. ACADEMIC + -ISM.] **1.** A tenet or opinion of the Academic philosophy.

1610 HEALEY *St. Aug., City of God* 753 In these new Academicismes..the question medleth not with the nature of that which we are to attaine. **1880** J. S. REID *Cicero's Acad.* 93 Varro was a follower of the Stoicised Academicism of Antiochus.

2. = ACADEMISM 2.

1887 *Century Mag.* Nov. 30 The inroad of academicism and all the subsequent degradation of art. **1905** W. JAMES *Mem. & Stud.* (1911) v. 84 He denounced me for the musty and mouldy and generally ignoble academicism of my character. **1948** BOASE in *Jrnl. Warburg & Courtauld Inst.* X. 99 It is dry academicism at its worst, but was admired at the time.

academicize (ækə'dɛmɪsaɪz), *v.* [f. ACADEMIC *a.* + -IZE.] *trans.* To render academic (sometimes with the implication of losing touch with the everyday world). So **aca'demicized, aca'demicizing** *ppl. adjs.*

1968 S. ROSEN in *Man & World* Feb. 80 The logicist ideology leads so quickly to boredom that it is easily absorbed by the ideology of the academicized marketplace. **1969** NAIRN & SINGH-SANDHU in Cockburn & Blackburn *Student Power* 109 They [*sc.* art colleges] have been academicized in the way described. **1972** P. COVENEY *Geo. Eliot's Felix Holt* 20 The question of the correct dating of 'five-and-thirty years ago' is no academicizing quibble. **1978** *Fortune* Dec. 50 The modern corporation, wrongly thinking that larger size and rapid change require special managerial methods, now runs the risk of academicizing and ruining itself.

Academism (ə'kædəmɪz(ə)m). [f. ACADEMY + -ISM.]

†**1.** 'The doctrine of the Academic philosophy.' J. *Obs. rare.*

c **1730** A. Baxter *Enq. into Nat. Soul* (1745) II. 254 This is the great principle of Academism and Scepticism, That Truth cannot be perceived.

2. The state or quality of being academic (see esp. ACADEMIC *a.* 5).

1926 R. Fry *Transformations* 114 The academism of the 'Mannerists', whose ideal consisted in the exaggeration of the manner of Michelangelo and Raphael. **1947** *Horizon* Jan. 19 The atmosphere of academism and late romanticism. **1953** *Ballet Ann. 1954* 63 Thus was born Academic Dancing; and soon the term 'academism' became synonymous with 'routine'.

†**Academist** (əˈkædəmɪst). *Obs.* [a. Fr. *académiste*: see ACADEMY and -IST.]

1. An Academic philosopher; a sceptic.

c **1730** A. Baxter *Enq. into Nat. Soul* (1745) II. 255 Sometimes a Dogmatist..and sometimes a regular and precise Academist. **1691** Ray *Creation* (1704) II. 386 These Academists (Aristotle and Pliny) do not refer merely to the lightness of this Creature's Body.

2. A member of an academy for the promotion of arts or sciences. In this sense it is now supplanted by ACADEMICIAN.

1691 Ray *Creation* (1704) II. 384 The Parisian Academists observe of the Sea-Tortoise, that the Cleft of the Glottis was strait and close. **1782** J. Warton *Ess. on Pope* II. ix. 70 Such is the Commentary of the academist on these famous lines.

3. A pupil in a school for riding, etc. See ACADEMY 5.

1651 Evelyn *Diary* Sept. 7 Chevalier Paul..had never been an Academist, and yet govern'd a very unruly horse.

†**A'cademite.** *Obs.* ? A follower of Plato: see ACADEMY 1, 2.

1574 Whitgift *Defence* 39 Infected with the rustic sect of Academites.

academize (aˈkædəmaɪz), *v. rare.* [f. ACADEMY + -IZE.] To form into an academy.

1868 *Daily Tel.* May 4 English literature indeed made up its mind long since not to be inregimented or academised.

Academy (əˈkædəmɪ). Also 5 **achadomye**, 6 **achademya**. [a. Fr. *académie*, ad. L. *acadēmīa*, a. Gr. ἀκαδημία, more properly ἀκαδήμεια adj., f. Ἀκάδημος name of a man; cf. Horace's *silvas Academi*, the 'groves of Academus.']

1. Proper name of a garden near Athens where Plato taught.

1474 Caxton *The Chesse* 86 Plato..chose his mansion and dwellyng in achadomye. **1603** Holland *Plutarch* 275 The Academy, a little pingle or plot of ground, was the habitation of Plato. **1807** Robinson *Archæol. Græca* I. i. 16 Academy.. was a large enclosure of ground which was once the property of a citizen at Athens named Academus..Some however say that it received its name from an ancient hero.

2. The philosophical school or system of Plato.

1677 Gale *Crt. of Gentiles* II. III. 132 From the Philosophers Scholes, specially from Plato's Academie. **1751** Chambers *Cycl.* s.v. The ancient academy doubted of everything, and went so far as to make it a doubt, whether or no they ought to doubt. **1871** Farrar *Witness of Hist.* iii. 100 Without eloquence she silenced the subtle dialectics of the Academy.

3. a. A place where the arts and sciences are taught; an institution for the study of higher learning; in the general sense including a university, but in popular usage restricted to an educational institution claiming to hold a rank between a university or college and a school. In England the word has been abused, and is now in discredit in this sense. Since the 18th cent. (chiefly *Sc.*), an institution of higher secondary education; more recently in Scotland, applied to many state secondary schools.

1549 *Compl. of Scot.* (1872) 13 Thir tua princis be chance entrit in the achademya, to heir ane lesson of philosophie. c **1588** Greene *Friar Bacon* ii. 37 Joying that our academy yields A man suppos'd the wonder of the world. **1758** Johnson *Idler* No. 33 ⁋27 The fashionable academies of our metropolis. **1785** in A. Warder *Burgh Laws Dundee* (1872) 196 The Dean reported to the assessors that the Town Council proposed to institute an academy in the town. **1838** Dickens *Nickleby* iii. 20 At Mr. Wackford Squeers's Academy, Dotheboys Hall, at the delightful village of Dotheboys, near Greta Bridge in Yorkshire. **1849** Macaulay *Hist. Eng.* I. 532 He had been master of an academy which the Dissenters had set up at Islington. **1868** *Rep. Schools Inquiry Comm.* VI. 38 All these four schools have been converted from ancient grammar schools into 'academies'. This is a term which has apparently a peculiar force in Scotland, and seems frequently to imply that at some period a *proprietary* element has been added to the ancient burgh institution. **1876** Grant *Burgh Schools Scotl.* II. ii. 115 The oldest Academy in Scotland is that of Perth. **1960** *3rd Statistical Acct. Scotl.* (*Aberdeenshire*) 482 The status and designation of 'Academy' was granted to Ellon Secondary School, and that of 'Rector' to the headmaster, only a few years ago. **1980** *Logophile* III. III. 18/1 Although there are Rectors of some episcopal churches in Scotland, a Rector is normally the (non-clergyman) headmaster of an academy (senior secondary school, usually founded over 100 years ago).

†**b.** *fig.* The arts, or circle of knowledge, taught in an academy, or a treatise comprehending them. *Obs.*

1636 Healey tr. *Theophrastus' Char.* 10 Whatsoever belongeth to the womens Academie, as paintings, preservings, needle-workes, and such-like. a **1667** Cowley *Elegy on Littleton* Wks. 1711 III. 50 He that had only talk'd with him, might find A little Academy in his Mind. **1675** A. Browne (*title*) Ars pictoria: or an Academy treating of Drawing, Painting, etc. **1754** H. Walpole *Lett. to H. Mann* 257 (1834) III. 74 That living academy of love-lore my Lady Vane.

4. Hence, a place of training.

1570 Sir H. Gilbert *Qu. Elizabethes Achademy* 12 Wherby your Maiesties and Successors courtes shalbe for euer..becomen a most noble Achademy of chiuallrie, pollicy and philosophie. **1677** R. Gilpin *Dæmon. Sacra* (1867) 67 Evil company is sin's nursery & Satan's academy. **1761** Hume *Hist. Eng.* II. xli. 425 The assemblies of the zealots in private houses which..had become so many academies of fanaticism. **1847** L. Hunt *Men, Women, & Bks.* II. xii. 310 The graces and good qualities which she retained..rendered her house a sort of academy of good breeding.

5. A place of training in some special art, as a Riding Academy, the Royal Military Academy, etc.

1734 tr. *Rollin's Anc. Hist.* IV. x. 411 They called the places..Gymnasia, which answers very near to our academies. **1751** Chambers *Cycl.* s.v., *Academy* is particularly understood of a riding-school. **1882** *Daily News* 5 May 2/1 The Professor of Chemistry and Physics at the Royal Military Academy at Woolwich..The Officer who was placed in charge of the Academy.

6. A society or institution for the cultivation and promotion of literature, of arts and sciences, or of some particular art or science, as the French Academy, the Imperial Academy of St. Petersburg, the Royal Academy of Painting, Sculpture and Architecture, which latter is commonly called in England 'the Academy.' *Familiarly* the name is extended to the *Annual exhibition* of the Society.

1691 Ray *Creation* (1704) II. 390 Several Creatures dissected by the Royal Academy of Sciences at Paris. **1769** Sir J. Reynolds *Disc. at Opening of Royal Academy* An Academy, in which the polite Arts may be regularly cultivated, is at last opened among us by Royal Munificence. **1858** Max Müller *Chips* (1880) III. i. 34 After the model of the literary academies in Italy, academies were founded at the small courts of Germany. **1873** Black *Pr. of Thule* (1875) xii. 190 We were at the Academy all the morning, and mamma is not a bit tired.

7. *Attrib.*, as in ***Academy-board***, ***Academy Dinner***, ***Academy-figure***, ***Academy Lectures***, etc. An ***Academy-figure*** is usually drawn half-life-size in crayon or pencil from a nude model. ***Academy award***: an award of the Academy of Motion Picture Arts and Sciences (Hollywood, U.S.A.) for success in a field connected with cinematographic entertainment; ***academy blue*** (see quot. 1926).

1941 B. Schulberg *What makes Sammy Run?* x. 190, I know we're going to knock them for a row of Academy Awards. **1950** *Amer. Speech* XXV. 3 *Johnny Belinda*, an Academy award motion picture of 1948. **1926** A. S. Jennings *Paint & Colour Mixing* (ed. 7) xxviii. 301 *Academy Blue*, a mixture of French ultramarine and viridian, ground only in oil and used by artists. **1859** Gullick& Timbs *Painting* 217 Academy board is a thin millboard, on which most of the studies made at the Academy are painted. **1769** Sir J. Reynolds *Disc.* i, I have seen also Academy figures by Annibale Caracci..drawn with all the peculiarities of an individual model. **1859** Gullick & Timbs *Painting* 313 When a painter introduces a figure wanting in repose or in its parts inharmonious..it is at once called 'Academic,' or an 'Academy Figure.'

acadialite (əˈkeɪdɪəlaɪt). *Min.* [f. *Acadie*, Fr. name of Nova Scotia + -LITE repr. Gr. λίθος stone.] '*Acadialite*, from Nova Scotia, is only a reddish chabazite.' Dana.

Acadian (əˈkeɪdɪən), *sb.* and *a.* [f. *Acadia* (Fr. *Acadie*), the name of a former French colony on the Atlantic seaboard of N. America, which included the present Maritime Provinces of Canada (Nova Scotia, New Brunswick, and Prince Edward Island) + -AN: see CAJAN.]

A. *sb.* **1. a.** A native or inhabitant of Acadia or of the Maritime Provinces; *spec.* a French-speaking descendant of French settlers in Acadia.

1705 *Boston News-Let.* 14 May, At break of day..our harbour was beset with..some Accadians at Pessemaquaddy and Port Royall, and Cannadians. **1757** *Mem. Principal Trans. Last War* 12 The French inhabitants (whom for Distinction-sake I shall call Acadians)..were by the treaty allowed their option either to retire..or to remain there. **1790** R. Beatson *Naval & Mil. Mem.* I. 306 They were joined by as many Canadians, Acadians and Indians. **1832** W. D. Williamson *Hist. State Maine* II. 264 The energetic efforts of its government to bring the Acadians or French Neutrals, into obedience. **1959** W. R. Bird *Maritimes* iii. 85 The Acadians are a careful people, dealing shrewdly, saving, working hard, and the farms are without mortgages. **1974** P. Gzowski *Bk. about this Country* 11/1 Edith Butler, a tall, shy, graceful Acadian who may have the most beautiful eyes in Canada—she certainly writes and sings some of the most beautiful songs. **1984** *Daily Tel.* 29 Dec. 15/4 A government plan to spend £75,000 to put up the flag of the Acadians..on key government buildings has annoyed many.

b. A native or inhabitant of Louisiana descended from inhabitants of Acadia (see quot. 1931); also *loosely*, any poor French-speaking Louisianian.

1803 T. Jefferson in *Deb. Congress U.S.* (1852) 8th Congress 2 Sess. App. 1506/2 The three succeeding settlements, up to Baton Rouge, contain mostly Acadians. **1878**, **1880** [see CAJAN]. **1931** W. A. Read *Louisiana-French* p. xviii, The Acadians of Louisiana are the descendants of the French who were formally expelled by the English from Acadie, or Nova Scotia, on Friday, September 5, 1755. **1947** *Amer. N. & Q.* VI. 173/1 The Cajuns—south-west Louisiana Acadians of Norman and Breton ancestry—were seemingly very resourceful in this art.

B. *adj.* **1. a.** Of or pertaining to Acadia or the Acadians.

1826 T. Flint *Recoll.* 322 The inhabitants [of Louisiana] are principally French.. and the very Arcadian [*sic*] race, about which so much has been said and sung. **1847** Longfellow *Evangeline* I. 1 In the Acadian land, on the shores of the Basin of Minas. **1876** G. Bancroft *Hist. U.S.* III. x. 417 He sent De Pontleroy..to travel throughout America..in the guise of an Acadian wanderer. **1888** G. W. Cable (*title*) Bonaventure, a prose pastoral of Acadian Louisiana. **1922** P. A. Taverner *Birds of E. Canad.* (rev. ed.) 138 There are several subspecies of the Saw-whet Owl in Canada; but only one, the Acadian Owl, the type form, is ever found in the east. **1970** M. Orkin *Canadian Eng.* i. 13 On the east coast..had settled the 'Acadian Loyalists', largely from the New England states.

b. ***Acadian French.*** (*a*) The French who inhabited Acadia; their descendants, esp. those living in the Maritime Provinces; (*b*) the dialect of French spoken in the Maritime Provinces or in Louisiana.

1806 J. Stewart *Acct. Prince Edward Island* 153 It is not denied by the Acadian French still resident on the Island, that they were very partial to this savage practice of their neighbours. **1891** A. Fortier in *PMLA* VI. 77 The lower class speak the Acadian French mixed with the Creole patois and a little English. **1970** M. Orkin *Canadian Eng.* i. 14 Excepted from the Bluenose country were Cape Breton and Pictou County, almost wholly settled by..Highlanders, along with a few thousand 'Associated Loyalists' and a few 'Acadian French'. **1976** *Language* LII. 251 L[ucci] examines the status of Acadian French within the context of French Canada, and the main lines of the history of the Acadian settlement.

2. *Geol.* **a.** Of, pertaining to, or designating the Middle Cambrian in (esp. eastern) North America. Also *absol.* See quot. 1982.

[**1855** J. W. Dawson *Acadian Geol.* i. 2 The Acadian provinces form a well-marked geological district, distinguished from all the neighbouring parts of America by the enormous and remarkable development within it of rocks of the Carboniferous and New Red Sandstone systems.] **1868** —— in *Proc. Amer. Assoc. Advancement Sci.* XVI. 118 These rocks..having been ascertained to be Devonian, there still remained an immense thickness of underlying rocks of uncertain age... It is proposed to call this series, represented in New Brunswick by the St. John slates, the Acadian Series. **1880** J. D. Dana *Man. Geol.* (ed. 3) III. ii. 166 The Primordial or Cambrian Period in North America includes two subdivisions... (1.) The Acadian Epoch; (2.) The Potsdam Epoch. **1917** *Jrnl. Geol.* XXV. 148 In the Lockport the time..marked the close of the Niagaran; in the Eldon it marks the close of the Middle Cambrian or Acadian. **1982** W. B. Harland et al. *Geologic Time Scale* ii. 11/2 In North America..names have had regional significance often contrasted between Appalachian and Cordilleran usage, i.e. Georgian, Acadian and Potsdam ..in the east..and somewhat later, in the west, Waucoban, Albertan and Croixian. Usage now tends to favour the western nomenclature.

b. Of, pertaining to, or designating an orogenic era in Late Devonian and Mississippian times that affected esp. the Appalachians and the east coast of Canada.

1895 H. S. Williams *Geological Biol.* ii. 42 A geological revolution is expressed by unconformity and more or less disturbance and displacement of the strata... Elevation and unconformity terminating the Devonian formations of Maine, New Brunswick, and Nova Scotia..may..be called the Acadian revolution. **1933** Schuchert & Dunbar *Textbk. Geol.* (ed. 3) II. xi. 208 The Acadian orogeny.. produced the strong folding now seen in the Devonian and older rocks of New Hampshire, Maine, and northern New Brunswick. **1980** *Sci. Amer.* Oct. 136/1 The southern Appalachians have evolved in a series of collisions of fragments of continental or island-arc material at the eastern edge of North America in the Taconic, the Acadian and the Alleghenian orogenies.

acajou (ˈakaʒu). [Fr. word: see CASHEW.]

1. The Cashew or Cashew-nut.

1725 Bradley *Fam. Dict.* s.v. The Nut or Chestnut of Acajou, a Fruit that is almost as big as a Chestnut. **1794** Martyn *Rousseau's Bot.* xix. 262 Acajou or Cashew we know chiefly by the nut, which grows at the end of a fleshy body as large as an orange, and full of an acid juice.

2. A medicinal preparation yielded by the mahogany tree (Fr. *acajou*).

1879 *Syd. Soc. Lex.*

-acal, compound *suffix*; consisting of -AL[1] repr. L. *-ālis*, *-āle* 'of the nature of, belonging to,' added to -AC (q.v.), which although strictly an adj. ending was so often used substantively, e.g. *demoniac*, *maniac*, *ammoniac*, *aphrodisiac*, that it became usual to make the adj. in *-acal* even when no sb. occurs, as *heliacal*. As in the cogn. -IC, -ICAL, adjectives in *-ac* are primary objective attributes, *of* or *pertaining to* the *thing*, while adjectives in *-acal* are only secondary, *of the nature of* or *connected with* the *attribute* in *-ac*, or its embodiment, hence more remotely and subjectively relating to the *thing*; e.g. the *cardiac* arteries, a *cardiac* (medicine), *cardiacal* qualities of a herb. But this distinction is not always observed. Examples: *ammoniacal*, *aphrodisiacal*, *cardiacal, demoniacal, heliacal, hypochondriacal, maniacal, paradisiacal, prosodiacal, theriacal.*

acalculia (eɪkælˈkjuːlɪə). *Med.* [mod.L., f. A- *pref.* 14 + CALCUL(ATE *v.*[1] + -IA[1].] = DYSCALCULIA.
1926 *Brain* XLIX. 120 Lesions that cause acalculia, or impossibility of calculation, are often very large and associated with word-blindness and agraphia or severe visual disturbance. **1974** H. SCHUELL *Aphasia Theory* i. 57 Nielsen has identified 87 specific defects, including various types of aphasia..and acalculia, which are produced by lesions in a specified site.

†**acale, akale,** *ppl. a. Obs.* [contr. for fuller *acalen; probably:—OE. *of-calen* pa. pple. of vb. *of-calan, -cól, -calen,* f. *of* + *calan* to be cold; but possibly:—a lost OE. *acalen,* f. *a-* pref. intensive, off, away + *calan. Acale* is parallel to *awake* ppl. adj. for *awaken*:—OE. *awac-en* pa. pple. See also the later *acold.*] Cold, frozen.
c **1320** *Seuyn Sages* (W.) 1512 What helpeth hit lenger tale? That night he sat wel sore akale And his wif lai warme abedde. **1377** LANGL. *P. Pl.* B. XVIII. 392 Bothe hungry and akale. **1393** *Ibid.* C. XXI. 439 For blod may seo blood · boþe a-þurst and a-cale, Ac blod may nat seo blod · blede, bote hym rewe. **1393** GOWER *Conf.* III. 296 He was so sore a cale, That the wiste of him self no bote.

acaleph (ˈækəlɛf), **acalephe** (ˈækəliːf). *Zool.* Also **acaliphe.** An animal of the class ACALEPHA.
1706 PHILLIPS, *Acaliphe,* the great stinging nettle, or the Sea-nettle, a sensible Plant. **1835** KIRBY *Habits & Inst. of An.* I. vi. 195 The Gelatines which some consider as a distinct class under the name of Acalephes. **1872** DANA *Corals* App. II. 375 Acalephs, or Jelly-fishes, or Medusæ as many of them are called.

‖**Acalepha** (ækəˈliːfa), *sb. pl. Zool.* [mod.L. sb. pl. (prop. adj. sc. *animalia*) f. Gr. ἀκαλήφη a nettle; also used in the form *Acalephæ* fem. pl.] A class of Radiate marine animals, embracing the Jelly fishes and Medusas, of pellucid gelatinous substance; so called from possessing the power of stinging or tingling anything which they touch, whence some of them are also known as sea-nettles. The *sing.* is supplied by *Acaleph, Acalephan.*
1846 PATTERSON *Zoology* 39 The various functions performed by the Acalephae. **1855** GOSSE *Marine Zool.* I. 37, Class 11 *Acalepha* (Sea Blubbers), The most common form of these animals is that of an umbrella or a mushroom; a broad circular convex disk of jelly, usually clear and colourless.

acalephan (ækəˈliːfən), *a.* and *sb. Zool.* [f. prec. + -AN.]
A. *adj.* Of or belonging to the class Acalepha.
Mod. Its structure shows an approach to the Acalephan type.
B. *sb.* An Acaleph, or animal of the class Acalepha.
1843 OWEN *Anat. Invert. An.* 111 The form described and figured by M. Sars in 1829 as a new genus of Acalephan. **1854** *Knight's Eng. Cycl.* I. 24 The general opinion seems to be that touch is the only sense possessed by the Acalephans.

acalephoid (ækəˈliːfɔɪd), *a. Zool.* [f. ACALEPHA + -OID repr. Gr. -οειδ-ής like.] Resembling the Acalepha or jelly-fishes.
WEBSTER cites DANA, WORCESTER cites OWEN.

acalycal (əˈkælɪkəl), *a. Bot.* [f. Gr. ἀ priv. + κάλυκ-α cup + -AL[1].] Of stamens: Inserted on the receptacle without adhesion to the calyx.

acalycine (əˈkælɪsaɪn), *a. Bot.* [ad. mod.L. *acalycin-us* f. Gr. ἀ not + κάλυξ, -ῦκ-α flower-cup: see -INE[1].] Having no calyx or flower-cup.
1858 GRAY.

acalycinous (ækəˈlɪsɪnəs), *a. Bot.* [f. mod.L. *acalycin-us* + -OUS.] = ACALYCINE.
1858 GRAY.

acalyculate (ækəˈlɪkjuːlət), *a. Bot.* [f. Gr. ἀ priv. + mod.L. *calycul-us* dim. of *calyx* cup + -ATE[2].] Having no calyculus or accessory calyx.

a-camp (əˈkæmp), *adv.* prop. *phrase. rare.* [f. after *a-field.*] To the camp.
1809 J. BARLOW *Columbiad* VI. 637 Some carmen, as acamp they drove, Had seen her coursing for the western grove.

†**a'cang(en,** *v. Obs.* [f. A- *pref.* 1, intensive + CANGEN.] ? To grow foolish or mad.
c **1220** *St. Kath.* (Abb. Cl.) 2045 Þe Keiser, al acanget, hefde ilosed mon dream. *Ibid.* 2112 Hu nu, dame, dotes tu? Cwen, acanges tu nu?

†**aca'nonical,** *a. Obs.* [f. late L. *acanonic-us* a. Gr. ἀκανόνικος + -AL[1].] Not belonging to the canon (of Scripture); uncanonical.
1753 CHAMBERS *Cycl. Supp.* The Apocryphal books are also called Acanonical.

acanth (əˈkænθ). *Bot.* Also 7 **acante.** [a. Fr. *acanthe*; ad. L. ACANTHUS.] = ACANTHUS.
1662 GERBIER *Principles* 5 The Corinthian Heads to represent a Basket with Acante Leaves. **1866** LINDLEY & MOORE *Treas. Bot.* 6 The genuine acanths, formerly called Brancursines, are emollient.

acanthaceous (ˌækænˈθeɪʃəs), *a. Bot.* [f. L. ACANTH-US + -ACEOUS.] Of the type of the Acanthus; epithet of the natural order *Acanthaceæ* of which the Acanthus is the typical genus.
1751 CHAMBERS *Cyc.* s.v. *Acanthus,* Acanthus..the representation of the leaves of an acanthaceous plant. **1880** J. S. COOPER *Coral Lands* I. xvii. 197 An acanthaceous herb, inhabiting swamps.

acanthine (əˈkænθɪn, -aɪn), *a.* [f. L. ACANTHUS + -INE.] Of, or pertaining to, the Acanthus.
1753 CHAMBERS *Cycl. Supp.* s.v., Acanthine garments..a kind of embroidery, wrought in imitation of the Egyptian acanthus or thorn. **1823** NICHOLSON *Pract. Builder* 579 Acanthine means ornamented with leaves of the acanthus.

acanthite (əˈkænθaɪt). *Min.* [f. Gr. ἄκανθα a thorn + -ITE formative of names of minerals.] 'A native sulphide of silver, found at Freiberg, etc.; crystals usually slender-pointed prisms; color iron-black or like argentite.' Dana.

acantho- ad. Gr. ἀκανθο- combining form of ἄκανθα thorn, as in ἀκανθο-φόρος thorn-bearing; hence in many modern compounds with sense of 'thorn, thorny.' **acan'thodian** (-ˈəʊd-), earlier also **-ean,** *a.* and *sb.,* (of) a small spiny-finned, shark-like fossil fish of the genus *Acanthodes* found esp. in rocks of the Devonian period.
1852 D. T. ANSTED in *Man. Geogr. Sci.* I. xii. 380 The Acanthodians and Dipterians (two families of Ganoids, nearly allied to the Lepidoids). **1861** P. DE M. G. EGERTON in *Geol. Survey U.K., Memoirs, Organic Remains* Dec. X. 67 The scales..resemble those of the other Acanthodean fishes. **1869** J. POWRIE in *Trans. Edin. Geol. Soc.* 286 None of our Old Sandstone Acanthodeans have yet been found of large size. **1894** R. H. TRAQUAIR in *Geol. Mag.* Dec. IV. I. 256 We may also, in the series of Acanthodian genera, trace every gradation from the most to the least claviculoid shape. **1937** *Phil. Trans. R. Soc.* B. CCXXVIII. 58 The whole fish is covered with the customary square Acanthodian scales.

acanthocephalous (əˌkænθəʊˈsɛfələs), *a. Physiol.* [mod. f. Gr. ἀκανθο- thorn + κεφαλ-ή head + -OUS.] Having a spiny head.
1839–47 TODD *Cycl. Anat. & Phys.* III. 534/1 In many of the Acanthocephalous Sterelmintha..the skin..becomes more coriaceous.

acanthocladous (ækænˈθɒklədəs), *a. Bot.* [f. Gr. ἀκανθο- thorn + κλάδ-ος shoot + -OUS.] 'Having spiny branches.' Gray *Bot. Text-bk.*

acanthological (əˌkænθəˈlɒdʒɪkəl), *a. Zool.* [f. Gr. ἀκανθο- thorn + -LOGICAL.] Pertaining to the study of the nature and functions of spines, founded on the study of spines.
1881 MACINTOSH in *Nature* No. 628. 41 The systematic value of acanthological characters.

acanthophorous (ækænˈθɒfərəs), *a. Bot.* [f. Gr. ἀκανθοφόρ-ος bearing thorns, prickly + -OUS.] 'Spine-bearing.' Gray *Bot. Text-bk.*

acanthopterous (ækænˈθɒptərəs), *a.* [f. Gr. ἀκανθο- thorn + πτερ-όν wing + -OUS.] *prop.* Spiny-winged, as the Cassowary; but used also as spiny-finned = ACANTHOPTERYGIOUS.
1870 ROLLESTON *An. Life* 42 The perch, and indeed the entire Acanthopterous order to which it belongs.

acanthopterygian (əˌkænθɒptəˈrɪdʒ(ɪ)ən), *a.* and *sb. Zool.* [f. ACANTHOPTERYGII + -AN.] Belonging to the spiny-finned fishes; *substantively,* a spiny-finned fish.
1835 KIRBY *Habits & Inst. of An.* II. xxi. 393 The Acanthopterygians, or spiny-rayed Fishes. **1855** OWEN *Skel. & Teeth* 23 Those fishes which have one or more of the hard spines at the beginning of the pectoral, ventral, dorsal, and anal fins are called 'acanthopterygian,' or spiny-finned fishes. **1863** BURTON *Book Hunter,* If you speak of an Acanthopterygian, it is plain that you are not discussing perch in reference to its roasting or boiling merits.

‖**Acanthopterygii** (əˌkænθɒptəˈrɪdʒɪaɪ), *sb. pl. Zool.* [mod.L., prop. adj. plur. masc. (sc. *pisces*), f. Gr. ἀκανθο- thorn + πτερύγι-ον a fin, dimin. of πτέρυξ a wing.] An order of Fishes, forming the first group of the Osseous sub-division, distinguished by having hard and spiny rays in the dorsal fins, as in the common perch and stickleback; spiny-finned fishes.
1833 *Pen. Cycl.* [See next.] **1847** CARPENTER *Zool.* II. §551 The Acanthopterygii cannot be easily subdivided, except into families.

acanthopterygious (əˌkænθɒptəˈrɪdʒəs), *a. Zool.* [f. ACANTHOPTERYGII + -OUS.] Having spine-like rays in the dorsal fin; spiny-finned:—an epithet of a group of fishes.
1833 *Pen. Cycl.* s.v. *Acanthopterygii,* M. Cuvier divided the Acanthopterygious Fishes into fifteen families.

acanthus (əˈkænθəs). [L., a. Gr. ἄκανθος, f. ἄκανθα thorn, f. ἀκή a sharp point.]
1. *Bot.* A genus of herbaceous plants (monopetalous exogens, N.O. *Acanthaceæ*). In popular use, the name is chiefly applied to the species *A. spinosus,* Bear's Breech or Brank-Ursine, native to the shores of the Mediterranean, and cultivated in England, celebrated among the Greeks and Romans for the elegance of its leaves.
1616 SURFLET & MARKHAM *Countrey Farme* 203 Beares-breech, called of the Latines Acanthus. **1667** MILTON *P.L.* IV. 696 On either side Acanthus, and each odorous bushy shrub, Fenced up the verdant wall. **1842** TENNYSON *Lotos-E.* 142 The emerald-colour'd water falling Thro' many a wov'n acanthus-wreath divine!
2. *Arch.* A conventionalized representation of the leaf of *Acanthus spinosus,* used in the decoration of the Corinthian and Composite capitals; said to have been modelled after the plant by Callimachus.
1751 CHAMBERS *Cycl.* s.v., *Acanthus,* in architecture, an ornament of the Corinthian and Composite orders. **1879** SCOTT *Lect. on Archit.* I. 81 They assume an almost Classic form—the acanthus being freely used.

a'canticone. *Min.* [mod. f. Gr. ἀκή point + ἀντί against, opposite + κῶνος cone.] A synonym of Arendalite, a kind of epidote. (Not used by Dana.)
1804 *Edin. Rev.* III. 308 Epidote..comprehends thallite and the acanticone of d'Andrada.

‖**a capella, a cappella.** [It. *cappella* chapel.] = ALLA CAPELLA; also see quots.
1876 in STAINER & BARRETT *Dict. Mus. Terms.* **1901** *Daily News* 3 Jan. 6/3 'The 100th Psalm', which is written for eight voices—a capella style. **1938** *Oxf. Compan. Mus.* 4/1 *A cappella* or *a capella*... This refers to the period up to and including the sixteenth century when church music was written for unaccompanied voices... Hence nowadays often used of choral music as a synonym for 'unaccompanied'. **1947** A. EINSTEIN *Mus. Romantic Era* iv. 36 A succession of delicate and refined *a cappella* composers, such as Mendelssohn and Brahms.

acapnia (eɪˈkæpnɪə, æ-). *Path.* [mod.L., f. Gr. ἄκαπνος without smoke, f. ἀ- priv. + καπνός smoke; see -IA[1]. Cf. F. *acapnie.*] Diminution or deficiency of carbon dioxide in the blood.
1907 *Amer. Jrnl. Physiol.* XIX. p. xv, This condition of acapnia lowers the tonus of the peripheral blood vessels. **1911** *Encycl. Brit.* XXIII. 190/1 Professor Angelo Mosso was led..to attribute mountain sickness to lack of carbon dioxide, a condition which he designated by the word 'acapnia'. **1913** *Lancet* 23 Aug. 557/2 Many of the deaths under anæsthetics are due to the condition termed acapnia, that is a depreciation of the carbon dioxide tension in the blood.

acapsular (əˈkæpsjuːlə(r)), *a. Bot.* [f. A- *pref.* 14, not + L. *capsula* CAPSULE + -AR.] Not having a capsule.
1879 *Syd. Soc. Lex.*

Acapulco (ækəˈpʊlkəʊ). The name of the popular resort of *Acapulco* (*de Juárez*), in Guerrero state on the west coast of Mexico, used *attrib.* in ***Acapulco gold*** to designate a variety of marijuana grown locally (see quot. 1965). Also *ellipt.* as ***Acapulco.***
1965 *Marijuana Newslet.* 30 Jan. in R. R. Lingeman *Drugs from A to Z* (1969) 1 *Acapulco gold.* This is a special grade of pot growing only in the vicinity of Acapulco. The color is either brownish gold or a mixture of gold and green. This grade has a potency surpassed by few of the green varieties and usually comes at slightly higher prices or in short weights. **1968–70** *Current Slang* (Univ. S. Dakota) III–IV. 1 *Acapulco,* best grade of marijuana.—Watts. **1974** M. C. GERALD *Pharmacol.* i. 13 He has been enticed by 'notes from the underground', exalting the wonders of 'acid' and 'Acapulco gold'. **1981** *Amer. N. & Q.* XX. 21/2 A number of names refer to the place of origin of a particular type: *Acapulco gold, Canadian black, Chicago green,* [etc.].

acardiac (əkɑːˈdɪək), *a. Physiol.* [mod. f. Gr. ἀκάρδι-ος without a heart (f. ἀ not + καρδία heart) + -AC; after Gr. καρδιακ-ός of the heart.] Without a heart.
1879 *Syd. Soc. Lex.*

acarian (əˈkɛərɪən), *a.* [f. Gr. ἀκαρι or mod.L. ACARUS + -(I)AN.] Pertaining to, caused by, or of the nature of an acarus or mite.
1877 W. T. FOX *Atlas Skin Dis.* 16 The absence of acarian furrows and interdigital vesiculations. **1902** *Encycl. Brit.* XXV. 197 *Sheep-scab,* a loathsome skin disease due to an acarian parasite.

‖**acariasis** (ækəˈraɪəsɪs). *Path.* [mod.L., f. Gr. ἄκαρι a mite + -ASIS.] A species of skin-disease, caused by parasites of the mite kind.
1828 KIRBY & SPENCE *Entomol. Lett.* I. iv. 97 The term Acariasis by which I propose to distinguish generically all acarine diseases.

acaricide (ˈækərɪsaɪd). [f. mod.L. ACAR-US + *-cīda* -killer; f. *cædere* in comp. *-cīdĕre* to kill.] A preparation for destroying *Acari.*
1879 *Syd. Soc. Lex.* **1947** *Nature* 4 Jan. 32/1 The use of a highly refined petroleum oil for application to orchard trees

as an insecticide and acaricide is firmly established as a valuable pest-control treatment with citrus.

Hence **acari'cidal** *a.*

1946 *Ann. Reg. 1945* 349 Only the 'gamma' isomer.. is actively insecticidal and possesses in addition acaricidal properties.

acarid ('ækərɪd). [ad. mod.L. ACARIDÆ.] An arachnid of the family *Acaridæ*; a mite. So **aca'ridian**.

1875 *Encycl. Brit.* II. 275 Acaridians.. are to be found under stones, dead leaves, [etc.]. **1881** A. LESLIE tr. *Nordenskiöld's Voy. Vega* I. iii. 147 Arachnids, acarids, and podurids occur most plentifully [in the Arctic regions]. **1910** E. RAY LANKESTER *Sci. fr. Easy Chair* xiv. 317 Red-spider is a small mite or acarid.

‖**Acaridæ** (ə'kærɪdiː), *sb. pl. Zool.* [mod.L., f. ACAR-US + -IDÆ.] A family of small Arachnida, breathing by pores like insects; comprising mites and ticks. (For the sing. *Acaridan* is used.)

1847 CARPENTER *Zool.* II. §766 The Acaridae are very widely, in fact universally, distributed.

acaridan (ə'kærɪdən), *a.* and *sb. Zool.* [f. ACARID-Æ + -AN.] Of or belonging to the *Acaridæ* or mites. *sb.* A member of the mite family.

1835 KIRBY *Habits & Inst. of An.* II. xix. 306 The bat is infested by another parasite, placed by Dr. Leach at the end of the Acaridans.

acarine ('ækəraɪn), *a.* and *sb.* [f. mod.L. ACARUS + -INE[1].] **A.** *adj.* Of, belonging, or due, to *Acari* or mites.

1828 KIRBY & SPENCE *Entomol. Lett.* I. iv. 98 The cause of either the pedicular or acarine disease.

B. *sb.* = ACARID.

1891 *Athenæum* 19 Dec. 837/2 Association.. between certain acarines of the family Gamasidæ and certain species of ants.

acaroid ('ækərɔɪd), *a. Zool.* [f. mod.L. ACAR-US + -OID.] Having the form of, or allied to, an *Acarus* or mite; mite-like.

1880 F. W. BURBIDGE *Gard. of Sun* xiv. 293 My skin.. was covered with irritable red eruptions, caused by a minute red parasite of acaroid nature.

acaroid, see ACCAROID.

acarologist (ækə'rɒlədʒɪst). [f. *acaro-*, used as comb. form of mod.L. ACARUS + -OLOGIST.] One who studies or treats of the *Acari*.

1890 *Proc. Zool. Soc.* 416 Almost all the members of the genus [Damæus] have a.. globular abdomen, or else one which is discoidal, the latter being considered a separate genus by some Acarologists. **1902** *Ann. & Mag. Nat. Hist.* IX. 311 The sense in which acarologists use the genus *Oribata*.

acarophilous (ækə'rɒfɪləs), *a. Bot.* [f. as prec. + -PHILOUS, after *entomophilous* adj.] Applied to plants that are fertilized by the agency of mites. So **acarophily** (-'ɒfɪlɪ), acarophilous character.

1898 *Nature* 3 Nov. 15/1 A number of cases of acarophily among ferns.

acarpellous (ækɑː'pɛləs), *a. Bot.* [f. Gr. ἀ not + mod.L. *carpell-us* CARPEL + -OUS.] Having no carpels.

1879 *Syd. Soc. Lex.*

acarpous (əkɑː'pəs), *a. Bot.* [f. Gr. ἀ not + κάρπ-ος fruit + -OUS.] Not producing fruit; unfruitful; sterile.

‖**Acarus** ('ækərəs). *Zool.* Pl. Acari (-aɪ). [mod.L. f. Gr. ἄκαρι a mite, f. ἀκαρής minute, too short for cutting, f. ἀ not + καρ- aorist stem of κείρειν to cut.] A genus of minute Arachnida, or spider-like animals, embracing the cheese-mite and its congeners; a mite.

1658 SIR T. BROWNE *Gard. of Cyrus* iv. 179 [Boiled water] affording neither uliginous coats, gnatworms, Acari, etc., like crude and common water. **1847** CARPENTER *Zool.* II. §766 Some of the Acari have the power of spinning webs.. one of these is well-known as the Red Spider in hothouses. **1862** MRS. SPEID *Last Years in India* 140 The fowls have been exterminated by small-pox, and by the assaults of a little blue acarus.

ACAS ('eɪkæs). Also **Acas**. [Acronym f. the initial letters of the organization.] The Advisory, Conciliation, and Arbitration Service, set up by the British Government (in 1974 as CAS and renamed in 1975) to mediate in industrial disputes.

[**1974** E. WIGHAM in *Times* 3 Dec. 19/4 The Conciliation and Arbitration Service (CAS) has now been operating for three months.] **1975** *Times* 16 Jan. 27/5 The body set up to deal with labour disputes and related industrial issues was yesterday retitled the Advisory Conciliation and Arbitration Service (ACAS). The new name simply prefixes the word Advisory to the old name. **1977** *Time Out* 17 June 6/2 The compromise also involved bringing in the government's Advisory, Conciliation and Arbitration Service (ACAS), whose job is to implement the Employment Protection Act. **1984** *Daily Tel.* 10 Mar. 36/3 A senior industrial relations official of Acas.. has been seconded to GCHQ.. to advise on relations between management and staff.

†**acas**, *adv. Obs.* [a. OFr. *à cas*, by chance, accidentally; see CASE.]

c **1300** *Sir Tristrem* (1811) So it bifel acas.

†**acast**, *v. Obs.* 3–4, also **akast**. *Pa. t.* **acaste**. *Pa. pple.* **a-casten, acast, akest**. [f. A- *pref.* 1 away + CAST.] To cast down, throw down, cast away or off.

c **1220** *Seinte Marherete* 1 [Ha] overcomen ant akasten hare þreo cunne fan. *c* **1220** *Leg. St. Katherine* 1127 Deað ne acaste nawt Crist, ah Crist ouercom deað. *c* **1225** *Hali Meidenhad* 5 Warpeð eauer toward tis tur for to kasten hit adun.. And nis ha witerliche akast, & in to þeowdom idrahen. *c* **1230** *Ancren Riwle* 318 Ich was sone ouerkumen: and þereuore þe sunne is more þen ȝif ich hefde ibeon akest mid strencðe. *c* **1320** *Seuyn Sages* (W.) 600 The olde tre his vertu gan acast. **1394** *Creed of Pierce Pl.* 197 Now is my comfort a-cast.

acat, obs. form of ACHATE and AGATE.

acatalectic (əkætə'lɛktɪk), *a. Pros.* [ad. late L. *acatalēctic-us* ad. Gr. ἀκατάληκτ-ος (negat. of καταληκτος: see CATALECTIC).] Not catalectic; not wanting a syllable in the last foot; complete in its syllables: also *subst.* 'A verse, which has the complete number of syllables, without defect or superfluity.' J.

1589 PUTTENHAM *Eng. Poesie* (1869) 142 The Greekes and Latines vsed verses.. which they called Catalecticke and Acatalecticke. **1751** CHAMBERS *Cycl.* s.v. *Catalectic*, The antients called *Catalectic Verses*, those which wanted either feet or syllables; in opposition to *Acatalectics*, which are complete verses, wanting nothing. **1859** DONALDSON *Gr. Gram.* §656 The most important, and perhaps the oldest species of iambic verse, was the *Trimeter Acatalectic*.

acatalepsy (ə'kætəlɛpsɪ). [ad. med.L. *acatalēpsia*, a. Gr. ἀκαταληψία incomprehensibleness, f. ἀ not + κατά thoroughly + λῆψις a seizing.] Incomprehensibility:—a term of the Sceptic philosophers; the correlative of agnosticism, which is said of the mental faculty, while acatalepsy is the property of the unknowable object.

1605 BACON *Adv. of Learning* (1640) Pref. 37 Those very schooles of Philosophers, who downe-right maintained Acatalepsie or Incomprehensibility. **1676** in *Phil. Trans.* XI. 791 The Academicks, who professing an Acatalepsy, affirmed this one thing only to be certain, *Nihil certi sciri posse*. **1847** LEWES *Hist. Philos.* (1871) I. 369 Arcesilaus could from Plato's works deduce his own theory of the incomprehensibility of all things: the acatalepsy.

acataleptic (əkætə'lɛptɪk), *a.* and *sb. rare.* [f. scholastic L. *acatalēpticus* (Fr. *acataleptique*) f. Gr. ἀκατάληπτ-ος incomprehensible + *-icus*, see -IC.] **A.** *adj.* Relating to acatalepsy; incapable of being certainly comprehended or ascertained.

[**1731** in BAILEY.] **1847** LEWES *Hist. Philos.* (1871) I. 369 According to the Academicians all Perceptions were acataleptic, i.e. bore no conformity to the objects perceived.

B. *sb.* An adherent of the doctrine of acatalepsy.

1878 C. P. KRAUTH *Vocab. Philos. Sci.* 11 All sceptics and Pyrrhonians were called acataleptics.

acatallactic (əkætə'læktɪk), *a. rare.* [f. Gr. ἀ not + CATALLACTIC.] Opposed to catallactics or political economy.

1865 *Pall Mall G.* 12 Dec. 23 Communism and socialism, in all their forms.. I utterly adjure—Christian or un-Christian; catallactic or acatallactic.

‖**acatastasis** (ækə'tæstəsɪs). *rare*[−1]. [f. Gr. ἀ not + κατάστασις settlement; the compound does not occur in cl. Gr.] An unsettling, or confusing.

1683 DR. E. HOOKER *Pref. Pordage's Myst. Div.* 89, O the Metempsychosis of our Souls! It is not a mere Acatastasis of our minds that marreth all the Beutie and Glorie of our Religion.

†**acate**. *Obs.* 4–7, also **acat, achat, achate**. [a. early OFr. (11th c.) and Norman *acat* (later OFr., 12th c., *achat*) purchase; stem of *acater*, *achater* (mod.Fr. *acheter*) to buy:—late L. *accaptā-re* to acquire, f. *ac-* = *ad-* to + *captāre* to seize, catch at. The original Eng. form *acat*, *acate*, under later Fr. influence varied with *achat*, ACHATE, which, in the original sense of *purchase*, became at length the regular form. But in the sense of *provisions, dainties*, the Norman form *acates* predominated, and was finally aphetized to CATES.]

1. Buying, purchasing, purchase.

c **1386** CHAUCER *Prologue* 571 Algate he wayted so in his acate, That he was ay biforn and in good state [*later MSS.* achaat, achate].

2. *pl.* or *coll. sing.* Things purchased; such provisions as were not made in the house, but had to be purchased fresh when wanted, as meat, fish, etc. Hence, all provisions except the home produce of the baker and brewer; foreign viands, dainties, delicacies. Aphetized as early as 1460 to CATES.

1465 *Manners & Househ. Exps. Eng.* (1841) 511 My master paid to Braham.. that he toke John Kooke for freshe acates. **1526** *Househ. Ord. of Hen. VIII* (1790) 139 To make provision of fresh acate, as well for flesh as fish. **1611** COTGR. s.v. *Ver*, *Tout estat est viande aux vers*: All States are wormes acates. *a* **1637** B. JONSON *Sad Shepherd* I. iii. 19, I, and all choise that plenty can send in; Bread, wine, acates, fowl, feather, fish, or fin. **1692** HACKET *Life of Williams* I. 33 To which accates he [Abp. Spalato].. never put his hand towards them, but liked our venison and English dishes a great deal better.

acategorical (əkætɪ'gɒrɪkəl), *a. rare*[−1]. [f. A- *pref.* 14, not + CATEGORICAL.] Not categorical, or according to the categories; loose, or inexact, in reasoning.

1661 K. W. *Conf. Charact.* (1860) 84 [They] fill up their sermon with the riff-raff of their own nodles.. and a multitude of illogicall acatagoricall reasons and arguments.

†**a'cater, a'catour.** *Obs.* Also **achatour, achator**. [a. Anglo-Norm. *acatour*, early OFr. *acateor* (later OFr. *achatour*, mod.Fr. *acheteur*) a buyer:—late L. *accaptātōrem*, n. of agent f. *accaptāre*: see ACATE. ACHATOUR came to be restricted more to the official title of an officer of the Royal Household; *acatour*, *acater*, passed into common use, and was aphetized to *catour*, CATER.] A purchaser of provisions, a purveyor; a provider or preparer of cates or delicacies; a cater or caterer.

c **1386** CHAUCER *Prol.* 568 (Camb. MS.) A gentyl Maunciple was þere of a temple, Of whiche acatouris myȝte take exsaumple (*Harl. MS.* achatours). *a* **1637** B. JONSON *Devil is an Ass* I. ii. (? iii.) He is my wardrobe man, my acater, cook, Butler, and steward.

†**a'catery.** *Obs.* Also **acatry, accatre, accatry, achatry.** [f. ACATER + -Y.] Provisions purchased; also, 'the room or place allotted to the keeping of all such provisions as the purveyors purchased for the King.' Halliwell.

a **1377** *Househ. Ord. of Edw. III* (1790) 4 Buttery, Achatry, Chandery, etc. **1522** *Visit of Charles V to Eng.* in *Rutl. Pap.* (1842) 78 Item, placardes to be hadd for the purveors of the pultre, accatre, and other. **1526** *Househ. Ord. of Hen. VIII*, 142 The serjeant of the acatry.. shall see that.. as well flesh as fish, be good & of the best. **1551** *MS.* in *Macm. Mag.* XLV. 447 The Acatrye, or purchases made of flesh meat, 579*l.*, includes veals, lamb, muttons, hogs of bacon. **1751** CHAMBERS *Cycl.* s.v., The officers of the Acatery, are a serjeant, two joint-clerks, and a yeoman of the salt-stores.

acatharsy ('ækəθɑːsɪ). *Med.* [ad. Gr. ἀκαθαρσία f. ἀ priv. + καθάρσι-ος purging; f. καθαίρ-ειν to cleanse.] Filth, impurity; lack of purging.

WORCESTER cites BUCHANAN.

acathisia, var. AKATHISIA.

acatholic (æ'kæθəlɪk, eɪ-), *a.* and *sb.* [A- *pref.* 14.] Non-Catholic. Hence **aca'tholicism**.

1809 F. PLOWDEN *Hist. Irel.* I. 120 Not a single writer.. foreign or native, catholic or acatholic. *c* **1815** W. POYNTER *Let.* in B. Ward *Eve Cath. Emanc.* (1911) II. xxiii. 124 Their call.. was supported by the practice of other countries, a-Catholic as well as Catholic. **1820** J. MILNER *Suppl. Mem. Eng. Cath.* II. 132 To prevent the virtual choice of a Catholic Bishop by an A-Catholic Ministry. **1891** A. J. HARRISON *Probl. Christianity & Scepticism* xiv. 269 If Christians were never enamoured of Acatholic or even Anti-catholic interpretations, the Freethinker would have little success. *Ibid.* xv. 272 (*heading*) Acatholicism. **1902** *Encycl. Brit.* XXX. 525/1 The fourth provincial synod of Westminster, which legislated on 'acatholic' universities. **1934** F. ROLFE *Desire & Pursuit of Whole* 142 It is possible.. for acatholics to pray with catholics catholically.

acaudal (ə'kɔːdəl), *a.* [f. A- *pref.* 14, not + CAUDAL.] = ACAUDATE, the more correct form.

1859 TODD *Cycl. Anat. & Phys.* v. 121/2 The several stages of development of the peculiar acaudal.. spermatic corpuscles.

acaudate (ə'kɔːdeɪt), *a.* [f. A- *pref.* 14 + CAUDATE.] Tailless.

1879 *Syd. Soc. Lex.*

acaulescent (ˌækɔː'lɛsənt), *a. Bot.* [f. A- *pref.* 14, not + CAULESCENT.] Apparently stemless, having a very short stem, or having the stem concealed in the ground.

1854 BALFOUR *Outl. Bot.* 49 The stem is so short in some plants, as the Primrose, Cowslip.. that they are called stemless or acaulescent. **1869** M. T. MASTERS *Veg. Teratol.* Absolute suppression of the main axis is tantamount to the non-existence of the plant, so that the terms 'acaulescent,' 'acaulosia,' etc., must be considered relatively only.

acauline (ə'kɔːlɪn, -aɪn), *a. Bot.* [f. mod.L. *acaul-is* stemless (f. Gr. ἀ priv. + L. *caulis* stem) + -INE. Cf. mod. Fr. *acaule*.] = ACAULESCENT.

1847 in CRAIG.

acaulose (ækɔː'ləʊs), *a. Bot.* [f. mod.L. *acaul-is* (see prec.) + -OSE.] = ACAULESCENT.

1686 in *Phil. Trans.* XVI. 284 Capillary or Acaulose Herbs. **1845** BRANDE *Dict. Sc.* s.v., Acaulose.. a term used for those plants which have no stem.

acaulous (ə'kɔːləs), *a. Bot.* [f. mod.L. *acaulis*, Fr. *acaule* + -OUS.] = ACAULESCENT.

1847 In CRAIG.

¶ Of the three preceding attempts to english Linnæus's *acaulis*, Jussieu's *acaule*, this is most in accordance with Eng. analogies.

acausal (eɪ'kɔːzəl), *a.* Chiefly *Philos.* [A- *pref.* 14.] Not causal; independent of or not involving the relationship of cause and effect.

1936 [see *micro-process* s.v. MICRO- 1]. **1955** R. F. C. HULL tr. C. G. Jung (*title*) Synchronicity: an acausal connecting principle. **1972** KOESTLER *Roots of Coincidence* iii. 86 Kammerer develops his central idea that coexistent with causality there is an a-causal principle active in the universe, which tends towards unity. **1981** *Nature* 2 Apr. 363/2 Blandford, McKee and Rees reviewed the possibilities for the expansion of extragalactic radio sources... The range of possibilities is large. There are the 'acausal' models such as the 'Christmas tree' version involving independent sources whose unrelated eruptions mimic expansion.

Hence **acau'sality; a'causally** *adv.*

1953 *Scottish Jrnl. Theol.* VI. 374 Physics, it seems, has been forced to become more philosophical by its successive reduction of matter to an indeterminate element, of space and time to relativity, and of mechanical necessity to acausality. **1962** J. JACOBI *Psychol. C. G. Jung* (ed. 6) iii. 63 Jung..has devoted a number of studies to the problem of acausality. **1974** *Sci. Amer.* Jan. 113/2 They are 'acausally' related in the Eastern metaphysical sense of being parts of a vast cosmic design that lies beyond the reach of science but is partially accessible to the subconscious mind of the person who casts the sticks. **1975** J. TAYLOR *Superminds* vi. 105 The absence of any natural limitation on the amount of acausality which could be achieved.

†**a'ccable,** *v. Obs. rare*⁻¹. [a. Fr. *accable-r.*] To overwhelm, crush.

a **1626** BACON vi. 272 Ord. MS. (L.) Honours have no burden but thankfulness, which doth rather raise men's spirits, than accable them or press them down.

Accadian, var. of AKKADIAN *a.* and *sb.*

accaroid, acaroid ('ækərɔɪd). Also 'accroid. [Etym. unkn.; appar. not related to ACAROID *a.*] The name given to a resinous gum obtained from various Australian trees, esp. the blackboy or grass-tree, used for preparing varnish, paper size, etc. Usu. *attrib.*, as ***accaroid gum, resin,*** etc.

The blackboy gum and Botany Bay gum yield red and yellow varieties respectively.

1857 DUNGLISON *Dict. Med. Sci.* (ed. 12) 987/1 *Xanthorrhœa*, Grass Tree. A genus of trees in Australia... Two resins are obtained from them, one the yellow resin of *Xanthorrhœa* or of New Holland,..Botany Bay resin, Acaroid resin or gum. **1937** R. S. MORRELL et al. *Synthet. Resins* xiii. 307 *Gum Accroides.* This resin possesses various names, acaroid resin, grass tree gum, black boy gum, &c. There are two varieties, red and yellow. The red variety.. dissolves in methylated spirit and gives varnishes which possess high finish very resistant to oil. **1959** *Chambers's Encycl.* II. 84/1 Xanthorrhœa balsams are the accaroid resins from *Xanthorrhœa* species, particularly *X. australis*. .. The accaroids are varnish resins.

accede (æk'siːd), *v.* [ad. L. *accēd-ĕre*, f. *ac-* = *ad-* to + *cēdĕre* to move on, go, come. Cf. Fr. *accéder* (14th c.)]

I. *intr.* To come to a place, state or dignity; to come into an opinion, to agree.

1. To come forward, approach, or arrive (at a place or state).

1677 GALE *Crt. of Gentiles* II. iv. 239 As soon as it existes it perisheth: it recedes as soon as it accedes. **1759** WILSON *Tourmalin* in *Phil. Trans.* LI. 317 One body electrified *plus* and another body electrified *minus*..accede, or move towards each other. **1862** F. HALL *Refut. Hindu Philos. Syst.* 258 A property, acceding, or seceding, changes its subject.

2. To arrive at, or enter upon an office or dignity. Const. *to.*

1756 C. LUCAS *Ess. on Waters* I. Dedn., That Chosen Family..acceded to the thrones of these Redeemed Realms. **1799** S. TURNER *Anglo-Sax.* (1828) I. 440 A petty prince in the southern parts of Scandinavia who acceded in 862. **1867** BURTON *Hist. Scot.* I. 43 The Emperor Julian..had just acceded to the purple. **1879** THE PRINCE OF WALES in *Daily News* 28 Apr. 2/5, I acceded to this post after the death of my lamented father.

3. To join oneself, become a party, give one's adhesion; hence, to assent, agree *to* (*unto* obs.).

1432–50 TREVISA *Higden* (Rolls Ser.) I. 51 Alle thynges lyffenge or groenge accede moore tollerably to the hieste colde then to the hieste heete. **1726** AYLIFFE *Parergon* 21 An Accessory is said to be that, which does accede unto some Principal Fact or Thing in Law. **1774** BRYANT *Mythol.* II. 191 We may accede to the account given of them by Zonaras. **1838** THIRLWALL *Greece* V. xxxvii. 12 Potidæa had already acceded to the confederacy. **1867** LADY HERBERT *Cradle Lands* viii. 217 In an evil hour this proposal was acceded to.

II. *trans.*

4. (Only in pa. pple.) To assign or award (an office or dignity).

1818 COLERIDGE *Friend* I. xii. 134 A most puissent military chieftain of low birth, who will have acceded to him a fellowship with the other Sovereigns of the earth. **1875** A. TROLLOPE *Prime Min.* I. i. 5 And this most precious rank was acceded to him.

accedence (æk'siːdəns). [a. Fr. *accédence*, f. *accéder*; see ACCEDE *v.*, and -ENCE.] The action of acceding; entering upon or agreeing to.

1597 DANIEL *Civile Wares* iv. 69 Thus were they entred in the first degree (and accedence) of action. **1859** D. OF BUCKINGHAM *Mem. Crt. George IV*, I. iv. 167 You are to waive the accedence to a junction till you are enabled to satisfy the theories and calculations of your uncles.

accedence, by confusion for ACCIDENCE.

acceder (æk'siːdə(r)). *rare.* [f. ACCEDE *v.* + -ER¹.] One who accedes, joins, or enters upon (a dignity).

1821–30 LD. COCKBURN *Mem. own Time* 464 The original members of the Academy objected to be swamped by a gush of so many acceders all at once.

acceding (æk'siːdɪŋ), *vbl. sb.* [f. ACCEDE *v.* + -ING¹.] Approaching, coming; adhering, assenting.

1759 WILSON *Tourmalin* in *Phil. Trans.* LI. 323 In this state they were electrified *plus*, as appeared by their acceding towards amber when it was rubbed and brought near them.

‖**accelerando** (æksɛlə'rændəʊ), *adv. Music.* [It. pr. pple. of *accelerāre* to accelerate.] With gradual increase of speed. (Used as an instruction in music.) Also as *sb.*: a gradual increase of speed or a passage where this occurs.

1842 J. F. WARNER *Dict. Mus. Terms* 5/1 *Accelerando*, hastening, moving faster and faster, increasing the quickness of the time. **1889** G. B. SHAW *London Music 1888–9* (1937) 210 It [*sc.* an orchestrion]..made pauses and ritardandos and accelerandos in the most natural manner. **1938** *Oxf. Compan. Mus.* 816/1 It is difficult to find performances where there are no rallentandos and accelerandos over longer stretches, superposed on the tempo rubato of the shorter ones. **1962** *Listener* 31 May 969/3 Emphasis is placed on the growth and decay of phrases by accelerandi or ritardandi.

†**ac'celerate,** *ppl. a. Obs. rare*⁻¹. [ad. L. *accelerāt-us* pa. pple. of *accelerā-re* to quicken; f. *ac-* = *ad-* to + *celer* swift.] Quickened, hastened.

1527 GARDINER in Pocock's *Rec. Ref.* I. xxxviii. 73 Whose expedition we desire your grace may be the more accelerate.

accelerate (æk'sɛləreɪt), *v.* [f. prec. or on analogy of vbs. so formed; see -ATE³.]

1. *trans.* **a.** To quicken, or add to the speed of (a motion or process).

1601 SIR A. SHERLEY *Trav. into Persia* (1613) 4 My iourney was under-taken in the dead of winter, and I left no paines untaken to accelerat it. **1771** *Junius Lett.* xlii. 223 Every step accelerates the rapidity of the descent. **1791** HAMILTON tr. *Berthollet's Art of Dyeing* I. I. §1. iii. 57 Light greatly accelerates the combustion of colouring matter. **1873** BUCKLE *Civilis.* III. v. 319 The selfishness of the individual accelerates the progress of the community.

b. To quicken (anything) in motion or process. To increase the speed of (a railway train, motor-car, motor-engine, etc.); also *absol.* (cf. sense 3).

1631 BRAITHWAIT *Whimzies* 62 Elevate that tripode; sublimate that pipkin..accelerate your crucible. **1797** *Encycl. Brit.* II. 492/1 After conjunction Jupiter will again accelerate Saturn. **1888** *Boy's Own Paper* (Summer No.) 43/2 He made..imperceptible changes in the speed of the train, accelerated it or diminished it so steadily. **1902** HARMSWORTH et al. *Motors* xv. 328 To accelerate a little when wishing to change...will assist very materially in accomplishing the change of speed successfully. **1919** B. H. DAVIES *Motor Driving* 52 The expansion of the cushions of compressed air accelerates them on their downward strokes. **1924** *Motor* 21 Oct. 578/1 Everybody accelerating all they knew to reach the corner first.

c. *Physics.* To impart high velocities to charged particles (as electrons) by electrical or magnetic means.

1931 *Physical Rev.* XXXVIII. 2021 The electric field between tubes is always in a direction to accelerate the ions as they pass from..one tube to..the next.

2. a. To hasten the occurrence of (an event); to bring it nearer, by quickening intervening processes, or by shortening the interval.

1525–30 MORE *De quat. Nouiss.* Wks. 1557, 101 Their maner of liuing must nedes accelerate this dredfull day, & drawe it shortly to them. **1662** FULLER *Worthies* (1840) III. 68 Change of air and diet..are conceived to have accelerated his death. **1772–84** COOK *Voyages* (1790) VI. 2216 The intelligence we had gained..rendered us the more anxious to accelerate our departure. **1875** STUBBS *Const. Hist.* III. xviii. 87 The commons accelerated the grant of a tenth..due at Martinmas.

b. To place earlier in point of time, to antedate.

1855 MILMAN *Lat. Christ.* (1864) I. I. ii. 72 Deliberate invention..in defiance of history, accelerated the baptism of Constantine.

3. *intr.* To add to one's speed, to increase in speed, or become swifter.

1646 SIR T. BROWNE *Pseud. Ep.* 194 Putrefaction..shall retard or accelerate according to the subject and season of the year. **1868** W. R. GREG *Lit. & Soc. Judg.* 419 This deterioration still continues, if even it does not accelerate.

accelerated (æk'sɛləreɪtɪd), *ppl. a.* [f. prec. + -ED.] Hastened, quickened. ***accelerated motion,*** in *Physics*: motion continually increased in velocity.

1803 WOOD *Mech.* §1. 11 When the successive portions of space, described in equal times, continually increase, the motion is said to be accelerated. **1850** MᶜCOSH *Div. Govt.* (1874) II. iii. 243 The stone loosened from the brow of the mountain, and descending with an ever accelerated speed. **1903** *Proc. Physical Soc.* XVIII. 598 The radiating power of an accelerated electric charge. **1942** STRANATHAN *Particles* vii. 295 On the classical theory of radiation from an accelerated electron it can be shown that the energy distribution should approach zero asymptotically at short wave lengths.

acceleratedly (æk'sɛləreɪtɪdlɪ), *adv.* [f. prec. + -LY².] In an accelerated manner; with ever increasing speed.

1751 BLAKE *Steam-Eng. Cyl.* in *Phil. Trans.* XLVII. 198 A weight on the piston, driving it to a depth of five feet.. within the cavity of the cylinder; acceleratedly, till friction and an impediment from the steam..shall equal the accelerative force.

accelerating (æk'sɛləreɪtɪŋ), *vbl. sb.* [f. ACCELERATE *v.* + -ING¹.] The action or process of quickening, hastening, or causing to happen more speedily. (Now mostly gerundial.) Also *attrib.*, as ***accelerating chamber, field, tube*** (see ACCELERATE *v.* 1 c).

1591 SIR H. UNTON *Corresp.* (1847) 49 For the accelerating of bothe theise matters, I praie you, faile not to presse the King. **1665** GLANVILLE *Sceps. Sci.* Addr. 17 The accelerating and bettering of Fruits. **1932** *Physical Rev.* XL. 23 The method for the multiple acceleration of ions to high speeds..is so arranged that as an ion travels from the interior of one tube to the interior of the next there is always an accelerating field. *Ibid.* XLII. 902 Charged atoms are accelerated..at each passage through an accelerating chamber. **1942** STRANATHAN *Particles* xi. 431 The accelerating tube, including a source of ions at one end and the target to be bombarded at the other, must have sufficient length to prevent spark-over along the outside of the tube.

accelerating (æk'sɛləreɪtɪŋ), *ppl. a.* [f. ACCELERATE *v.* + -ING².] Quickening, hastening, or tending to quicken or hasten. ***accelerating force***: a force that produces continually increased motion.

1829 U. K. S. *Nat. Philos.* I. I. iii. §25. 9 This peculiar species of motion is therefore called accelerated motion, and the force which produces it is called an accelerating force. **1878** SEELEY *Stein* iii. 524 England's rapidly accelerating decline, he [Niebuhr in 1828] writes, is a very remarkable and mournful phenomenon.

acceleration (æksɛlə'reɪʃən). [ad. L. *accelerātiōn-em*, n. of action f. *accelerā-re*: see ACCELERATE *a.* and -ION¹. Cf. mod.Fr. *accélération.*]

1. a. The action or process of accelerating, quickening or hastening. Also *spec.* of charged particles (cf. ACCELERATE *v.* 1 c).

1531 ELYOT *Governour* (1834) 117 Who beholding..the acceleration or haste to his [Cæsar's] confusion, caused by his own edict or decree, will not commend affability. **1663** COWLEY *Verses & Essays* (1669) 45 A Garden, destined to the tryal of all manner of Experiments concerning Plants, as their Melioration, Acceleration, Retardation, Conservation. **1732** ARBUTHNOT *Rules of Diet* 266 Those things which take off the Causes of Acceleration retard the Motion of the Blood. **1822** IMISON *Sc. & Art* I. 84 But the friction of the teeth and the resistance of the air check this acceleration. **1909** H. A. LORENTZ *Theory of Electrons* 120 The radiation from a single electron..is determined by the acceleration. **1932** [see ACCELERATING *vbl.sb.*]. **1942** STRANATHAN *Particles* vii. 294 The negative linear accelerations suffered by the electrons as they strike the target.

b. The process of increasing the speed of a motor-engine or -vehicle; hence, capacity of being accelerated, as an attribute of the vehicle itself.

1901 *Motor-Car World* II. 238/1 Instantaneous acceleration when the clutch is once more engaged. **1926** *Daily News* 18 May 4/5 There are many British cars with fine acceleration.

2. The condition of being accelerated or hastened; increased speed.

1534 LD. BERNERS *G. Boke of M. Aurel.* (1546) F. viij. b, Gret acceleracion in busynesses nowe presente maketh greate inconueniences in tyme to come. **1784** JOHNSON in *Boswell* (1816) IV. 455 No, sir; you cannot conceive with what acceleration I advance towards death.

3. The extent to which anything is accelerated; in *Nat. Phil.* the rate of increase of velocity per unit of time. ***uniform*** or ***constant acceleration***: the unvarying amount per second added to the velocity or rate at which a body is moving, *e.g.* under the influence of gravity.

1656 tr. *Hobbes's Elem. of Philos.* (1839) 232 The body will be carried through the same strait line..provided it have like acceleration. **1677** HALE *Prim. Orig. Man.* 5 There be many things touching Matters Physical..as concerning the degrees of acceleration of Motion. **1794** G. ADAMS *Nat. & Exper. Phil.* III. xxvii. 118 The law of acceleration, in falling bodies, was not discovered till the time of Galileo. **1876** TAIT *Rec. Adv. in Phys. Sc.* xiv. 352 Rate of change of velocity is called in kinematics, acceleration. **1879** THOMSON & TAIT *Nat. Phil.* I. I. §28 The velocity of a point is said to be accelerated or retarded according as it increases or diminishes, but the word acceleration is generally used in either sense, on the understanding that we may regard its quantity as either positive or negative.

4. *Astr.* and *Physics.* Acceleration of the *fixed stars*; the time (3′ 55·9″) which the stars gain upon the sun in passing the meridian each day, or by which the sidereal day is shorter than the solar, due to the advance of the earth in her orbit while revolving on her axis. Of the *planets*, the increased velocity with which they advance from aphelion to perihelion. Of the *moon*, an increase (of about 11" in the century) in the rapidity of the moon's mean motion, discovered by Halley. Of the *tides*, the amount by which from special causes, high or low water occurs at any place before the calculated time.

1849 Mrs. Somerville *Connex. of Phys. Sc.* §5. 43 This secular increase in the moon's velocity is called the Acceleration.

accelerative (æk'sɛlərətɪv), *a.* [f. accelerate *v.* + -ive; as if ad. L. **accelerātīvus*.] Pertaining or tending to acceleration; quickening; adding to velocity.

1751 Blake *Steam-Eng. Cyl.* in *Phil. Trans.* XLVII. 198 Till friction..shall equal the accelerative force. **1839** Carlyle *Chartism* vi. 145 Democracy makes rapid progress ..in a perilous accelerative ratio. **1862** Mrs. Speid *Last Years in India* 14 Three second-class passengers, to whose minds the firing of the signal gun had carried no accelerative convictions, were left behind.

accelerator (æk'sɛləreɪtə(r)). [f. accelerate *v.* + -or, as if a. L. **accelerātor*, n. of agent f. *accelerāre*; see accelerate. *Accelerater* is less in accordance with the usual formation of agent nouns from -ate.] **a.** He who or that which accelerates or quickens. *Specifically* applied to the nerves and muscles that increase the speed of certain organic functions; and also to a light vehicle to convey letter-carriers to their districts, and accelerate the delivery of letters.

1611 Cotgr., *Avanceur*: a forwarder, aduancer, hastener, accelerater. **1841** Hor. Smith *Moneyed Man* III. xi. 325 Steam..that stupendous power which has since become the great accelerator of mind and matter. **1861** G. M. Musgrave *By-Roads* 124 Our red-coated postmen drop out of the accelerators. **1875** Wood *Therap.* (1879) 115 The accelerators of the heart..are of course paralyzed by spinal section.

b. *Photogr.* A substance used to shorten the duration of development of a negative.

1858 Sutton & Worden *Dict. Photogr.* 3 *Accelerators*. This name is given to any substances used in photographic processes, with a view to shorten the time of exposure, either in the camera or the printing-frame. *c* **1865** *J. Wylde's Circ. Sci.* I. 157/1 By using the above solutions as accelerators, a rich red rose-colour is produced on the plate. **1898** *Barnet Bk. Photogr.* 24 The alkali sets the reducer in action and is called the accelerator. **1932** Hardy & Perrin *Princ. Optics* xi. 223 The developer usually contains four components: a reducing agent, an accelerator, a preservative, and a restrainer.

c. An apparatus for regulating the speed of the engine in a motor-vehicle, esp. for increasing speed; also *attrib.* as ***accelerator pedal***, the pedal that controls the 'throttle'; **accelerator valve** (see quot. 1901).

1900 W. W. Beaumont *Motor Vehicles* viii. 147 The other governor control is known as the accelerator. **1901** *Motor-Car World* Oct. 272/1 A by-pass throttle or 'accelerator' valve, by opening which a full charge of mixture can be admitted at any speed of the engine. **1902** Harmsworth et al. *Motors* vii. 129 If the driver wishes to slow down..he does not necessarily change his gear, but operates the accelerator. **1904** A. B. F. Young *Complete Motorist* ix. 219 The accelerator pedal..has its uses, notably in changing to a higher speed. **1959** *Chambers's Encycl.* IX. 576/2 The driver moves off by depressing the accelerator having first shifted a miniature gear lever..into the normal operating position. *Ibid.*, The..speeds at which such changes occur are partially dependent upon the use..of the accelerator pedal.

d. A substance used to increase the speed of a chemical or organic process, *spec.* in the vulcanization of rubber or the curing of a plastic.

1908 *Proc. Chem. Soc.* XXIV. 132 (*title*) Acids as accelerators in the acetylation of amino-groups. **1912** H. E. Potts *Chem. Rubber Ind.* 91 Calcined magnesia is useful.. as an accelerator of vulcanization, particularly for resinous rubbers. **1936** *Ann. Reg. 1935* II. 56 In controlling the span and speed of life in fruits in store, ethylene is now used as an accelerator of ripening. **1943** R. S. Morrell et al. *Synthet. Resins* (ed. 2) iv. 180 Reduction in curing time of urea-formaldehyde moulding powders can be obtained by using 'latent' accelerators. **1956** *Gloss. Terms Concrete* (*B.S.I.*) 5 *Accelerators*, additives which, when added to concrete during mixing, will appreciably quicken setting and/or hardening.

e. *Physics.* An apparatus which imparts high velocities to free electrons or other atomic particles by electrical or magnetic means, esp. ***linear accelerator*** (see quot. 1962). Cf. cyclotron.

1931 *Science* XXXVIII. 2030 Focusing occurs along the accelerators and is accomplished quite automatically by the curved electric fields between adjacent cylindrical accelerators. **1935** *Physical Rev.* XLVIII. 495/2 The term 'magnetic resonance accelerator' is suggested... The first word is added to distinguish it from the apparatus of Sloane and Lawrence which can be called a 'linear resonance accelerator'. **1942** Pollard & Davidson *Appl. Nucl. Physics* 55 The simplest type of apparatus utilizing this method is the linear multiple accelerator. **1947** L. W. Alvarez et al. in *Science* CVI. 506/2 (*title*) Initial Performance of a 32-Mev Proton Linear Accelerator. **1953** *Lancet* 17 Oct. 840/2 An 8-million-volt linear accelerator..the first machine of its kind to be built for X-ray therapy. **1958** *Engineering* 7 Feb. 174/3 The accelerator provides a..source of high-energy electrons. **1962** *Gloss. Terms Nucl. Sci.* (*B.S.I.*) 6 Among the multiple accelerators distinction is made between linear, in which the particles move in a straight line, and cyclic, in which they move in a circular or spiral orbit.

acceleratory (æk'sɛlərətərɪ), *a.* *rare*$^{-0}$. [f. accelerate *v.* + -ory as if ad. L. **accelerātōrius*.] = accelerative. In Craig 1847.

accelerogram (æk'sɛlərəʊgræm). [f. *accelero-* (see accelerometer) + -gram.] A tracing produced by an accelerograph.

1937 *Bull. Seismol. Soc. Amer.* XXVI. 325 The degree of accuracy with which accelerograms of earthquake motions may be interpreted. **1971** *Nature* 10 Sept. 99/1 Much of the energy recorded in the accelerograms was at periods less than 1 s, and the shaking lasted for a few seconds.

accelerograph (æk'sɛlərəʊgrɑːf, -æ-). [f. *accelero-* (see next) + -graph.] An apparatus for recording the succession of pressures developed in a power-chamber by the combustion of a charge; also, an instrument for recording the acceleration of earth-tremors.

1909 in *Cent. Dict.* Suppl. **1950** *Engineering* 10 Feb. 159/3 An accelerograph..gives a distant record of acceleration. **1956** *Atlantic* 19 Dec. 19/1 A device called the Accelerograph, something like a baby seismograph, is turning this art into a science.

accelerometer (æksɛlə'rɒmɪtə(r)). [f. *accelero-* irreg. combining form repr. accelerate *v.*, etc. + -meter.] An instrument for ascertaining the acceleration of a moving body or for measuring mechanical vibrations.

1904 *Amer. Inventor* 15 July 312 (Cent. Dict. Suppl.), Accelerometer... This instrument consists of two glass vessels connected by a tube, one containing a liquid such as mercury and the other red alcohol. **1910** *Westm. Gaz.* 22 Mar. 5/2 Measuring B.H.P. on the Road, by an Accelerometer. **1932** *Discovery* Apr. 114/2 Accelerometers have been carried [in aircraft] to measure the resultant forces experienced in flight. **1946** *Nature* 14 Sept. 361/2 A vibrograph and accelerometer..much used to obtain vibration records on ships at sea.

†**accend** (æk'sɛnd), *v.* *Obs.* 5–8. [ad. L. *accendĕre* to kindle, set on fire; f. *ac-* = *ad-* to + *-cendĕre* = **candĕre* to set a-light.] To kindle; to set light to, set on fire. *lit.* and *fig.*

1432–50 Trevisa *Higden* (Rolls Ser.) I. 187 In this cuntre is a ston callede Asbeston, whiche accendede oonys is neuer extincte. *a* **1468** *Cov. Myst.* (1841) 214 Ageyn hym wrathe if thou accende The same in happ wylle falle on the. **1524** *State Papers, Hen. VIII*, VI. 367 Makyng suche persuasyons unto the Pope, as may accende and kindle hym therunto. **1622** Fotherby *Atheomastix* Pref. 18 He must needes..be greatly accended vnto true deuotion. **1729** Shelvocke *Artillery* IV. 279 Accended by the Wind, or Rain, or Dew, it must consequently take fire.

accendibility (æk,sɛndɪ'bɪlɪtɪ). [f. accendible: see -ity.] Capacity of being kindled, set on fire, or inflamed; inflammability.

1859 Worcester cites *Edin. Rev.*

accendible (æk'sɛndɪb(ə)l), *a.* ? *Obs.* *rare*$^{-1}$. [f. accend + -ible as if ad. L. **accendibilis*.] Capable of being kindled, or set on fire.

1630 H. Lord *Relig. of Persees* 44 Such fire as is occasioned by lightning falling on some tree or thing accendible.

†**ac'cending**, *ppl. a.* *Obs.* [f. accend *v.* + -ing².] Kindling.

1646 Sir T. Browne *Pseud. Ep.* 90 Small-coale, Salt-peter and Camphire made into powder will bee of little force, wherein notwithstanding there wants not the accending ingredient.

†**accensed** (æk'sɛnst), *ppl. a.* *Obs.* [f. L. pa. pple. *accens-us* kindled + -ed. Analogous to *incensed*, but no vb. to *accense* is cited.] Kindled, set on fire, inflamed.

1573 T. Twyne *Æneid* XII. L l3b, The valient brothers band with griefe accensit in ire [L. *accensi*]. **1613** T. Adams *Pract. Wks.* in Nichol's *Purit. Div.* (1861) I. 458 Candles once accensed are not to be thrust into abstruse corners. **1760** Stiles *Erupt. Vesuv.* in *Phil. Trans.* LII. 41 The flames, and the accensed stones thrown up, were very terrible.

accension (æk'sɛnʃən). *Obs.* or *arch.* [ad. L. *accensiōn-em*, n. of action, f. *accend-ere*, *accens-us*: see accend.] The action of kindling or the state of being kindled; ignition; inflammation; heat.

1646 Sir T. Browne *Pseud. Ep.* 88 From Small-coal ensueth the black colour and quick accension. **1673** *Phil. Trans.* VIII. 6170 What remedies are proper for the Blood, to mend..its defective or excessive accension. **1729** Shelvocke *Artillery* III. 148 The great quantity of windy Exhalation, produced by the accension of the Salpeter. **1801** W. Taylor in *Monthly Mag.* II. 645 This machine may facilitate the admixture and accension of the airs.

accent ('æksənt), *sb.* [a. Fr. *accent*, OFr. *acent*:—L. *accent-um* f. *ad* to + *cantus* singing, a literal rendering of Gr. *προσῳδία*, f. *πρός* to + *ᾠδή* song, lit. 'song added to' sc. speech: see note under sense 1.]

1. A prominence given to one syllable in a word, or in a phrase, over the adjacent syllables, independently of the mode in which this prominence is produced.

Accent in Gr. (*προσῳδία*) is explained by Dion. Hal. *περὶ συνθέσεως ὀνομάτων* ch. xi. as a distinct difference of musical pitch in pronouncing the syllables of a word, those having the *grave* or heavy accent (*βαρεῖα gravis*) being spoken at a comparatively low pitch, those having the *acute* or sharp accent (*ὀξεῖα acūtus*) being spoken as nearly as possible a musical Fifth higher (*διὰ πέντε*), and those having the *circumflex* accent (*περισπωμένη circumflexus*) beginning in the high pitch and descending a Fifth during the pronunciation of the same syllable. The same three varieties occurred in Latin, but their positions in a word followed very different laws. This variety of pitch disappeared for both Latin and Greek towards the end of the Third Century A.D. when the feeling of quantity was lost, and the high pitch in Greek and Latin became merely greater force, and this stress accent has remained the substitute for musical accent in modern Greek, in Italian and Spanish, and is also found in German and English. In Swedish and Norwegian a musical syllabic accent remains in use; in Danish it is replaced in some circumstances by a peculiar catch, and in others by stress, as in English. In French, where probably stress was at one time strongly marked, the difference for at least three centuries has been so slight that writers have disputed as to its nature and the position of the stress syllable. In all languages having the stress, a variable alteration of pitch and quality of tone always prevails, and is used to express varieties of feeling. This expression belongs to rhetoric. The grammatical varieties of accent in English are great, but are all varieties of stress. The position is fixed in words of more than one syllable. Monosyllables have various degrees of stress according to circumstances. Hence the distinction of *syllabic* accent for the first, and *verbal* accent, *phrase* accent, or *emphasis* for the second. (A. J. Ellis.)

1581 Sidney *Def. Poesie* (1622) 529 Though we doe not obserue quantitie, yet wee obserue the accent very precisely. **1589** Puttenham *Eng. Poesie* (1811) II. vi. 65 To that which was highest lift vp and most eleuate or shrillest in the eare, they gaue the name of the sharpe accent, to the lowest and most base because it seemed to fall downe rather than to rise vp, they gaue the name of the heauy accent, and that other which seemed in part to lift vp and in part to fall downe, they called the circumflex, or compast accent: and if new termes were not odious, we might very properly call him the (windabout) for so is the Greek word. *a* **1637** B. Jonson *Eng. Gramm.* (1696) All our vowels are sounded doubtfully. In quantity (which is time) long or short. Or, in accent (which is tune) sharp or flat. **1748** J. Mason *Elocution* 26 When we distinguish any particular syllable in a word with a strong Voice, it is called Accent; and when we thus distinguish any particular Word in a Sentence it is called Emphasis. **1871** Earle *Philol. Eng. Tongue* xii. 525 Accent is the elevation of the voice which distinguishes one part of a word from another.

2. a. The marks by which the nature and position of the spoken accent were indicated in a word.

The old Latin forms (´) *acūtus*, (\`) *gravis*, (ˆ) *circumflexus*, are retained, but each one now represents mere stress, except in works on elocution where (´) now generally represents a *rising* (not a fixed high) pitch; (\`) a *falling* pitch (the ancient circumflex), and (ˆ) a rising followed by a falling pitch, not used in ancient Latin and Greek. Some writers use (ˆ) for length only, the same as (¯). The old meanings are quite lost. (A. J. E.)

b. Marks used to distinguish the different qualities of sound indicated by a letter, called diacritical accents.

The old ´ \` ˆ are mostly used, as French *e é è ê* in *je*, *été*, *tiède*, *même*, but a great variety of other signs have also been introduced. These diacritical accents sometimes distinguish meaning only, as French *a à*, *la là*. These marks are not used in English orthography. But sometimes \` is used to shew that *-ed* is to be pronounced as a distinct syllable, as *learnèd*, *hallowèd*, and some write *é* for a final *e* pronounced, as *Hallé* (properly German *Halle*). (A. J. E.)

1596 Spenser *State of Irel.* 30 Being likewise distinguished with pricke and accent, as theirs aunciently. **1611** Florio, *Accento*: an accent or point ouer anie letter to giue it a due sound. **1611** Cotgr., *Accent aigu*: a sharp accent marked thus ´, and much used. *Accentuer*: to marke, note, or pronounce, with an Accent. *c* **1620** Hume *Orthogr. Brit. Tongue* (1865) 22 The grave accent is never noated, but onelie understood in al syllabes quherin the acute and circumflex is not. **1807** Robinson *Archæol. Græca* V. xiii. 470 The ancient Greeks used no accents, which are supposed to have been invented and introduced about two hundred years before Jesus Christ. After the Greek language became the favourite study of foreigners, it was necessary to facilitate the pronunciation of it by applying marks of accent for that purpose: and this, very probably, induced Aristophanes of Byzantium to invent and introduce those accentual virgulae.

c. Marks of various kinds placed over and under the consonants in Hebrew, serving as signs of tone and of interpunctuation; hence *fig.* the minutest particular (of the Mosaic law).

1610 Holland *Camden's Brit.* I. 443 That we, who sift every pricke and accent of the law, may see the upright simplicity of that age. **1659** B. Walton *Considerator Considered* 264 The Masorites..invented the names and figures of the vowels and accents, which they have left to posterity; though the later Grammarians herein differ from the ancienter about the names, nature, number, and use.

3. The mode of utterance peculiar to an individual, locality, or nation, as 'he has a slight accent, a strong provincial accent, an indisputably Irish, Scotch, American, French or German accent.' Without defining word: of a regional English accent.

This utterance consists mainly in a prevailing quality of tone, or in a peculiar alteration of pitch, but may include mispronunciation of vowels or consonants, misplacing of stress, and misinflection of a sentence. The locality of a speaker is generally clearly marked by this kind of accent. (A. J. E.)

1600 Shaks. *A.Y.L.* III. ii. 359 Your accent is something finer, then you could purchase in so remoued a dwelling. **1602** Daniel *Musoph.* st. cli. Our accent's equal to the best. *c* **1620** Hume *Orthogr. Brit. Tongue* (1865) 27 We fynd the south and north to differ more in accent then symbol. **1711** Addison *Spect.* No. 29 ¶4 The Tone, or (as the French call it) the Accent of every Nation in their ordinary Speech is altogether different from that of every other People.. By the Tone or Accent I do not mean the Pronunciation of each particular Word, but the Sound of the whole Sentence. **1772** Johnson in Boswell's *Life* II. 14 I have been correcting several Scotch accents in my friend Boswell. **1789** T. Jefferson *Wks.* 1859 II. 559 He spoke French without the least foreign accent. **1840** Carlyle *Heroes* (1858) 247 Accent is a kind of chanting; all men have accent of their own,—though they only notice that of others. **1860** Hawthorne *Marble Faun* (1868) I. xii. 128 There is Anglo-Saxon blood in her veins.. and a right English accent on her tongue. **1930** H. G. Wells *Autocr. Mr. Parham* II. i. 74 Underbred contradictory people with accents and most preposterous views. **1934** —— *Exp. Autobiogr.* II. viii. 522 He spoke with an accent. **1956** D. Abercrombie *Prob. & Princ.* iv. 42 *Accent*.. is a word which, in its popular use, carries a stigma: speaking *without* an accent is considered preferable to speaking *with* an accent... The popular, pejorative, use of the word begs an important question by its assumption that an accent is something which is added to, or in some other way distorts, an accepted norm. **1962** *Guardian* 5 Oct. 9/2 They were poor, they had 'accents', the children went to State schools.

4. The way in which anything is said; pronunciation, utterance, tone, voice; sound, modulation or modification of the voice expressing feeling.

1538 Bp. Bonner in Foxe *A. & M.* (Catley) V. 155 He said with a sharp accent. **1604** Shaks. *Oth.* I. i. 75 *Rod.* Ile call aloud. *Iago.* Doe, with like timerous accent, and dire yell. **1644** Milton *Education* Wks. 1738, 138 And solemnly pronounced with right accent & grace. **1699** Dryden *Tales from Chaucer, Good Parson* 16 Mild was his accent, and his action free. With eloquence innate his tongue was arm'd. **1725** Pope *Odyssey* x. 402 Transform'd to beasts, with accents not their own. **1727** Swift *Poisoning of Curll* Wks. 1755 III. I. 151 What this poor unfortunate man spoke, was so indistinct, and in such broken accents. **1768** Sterne *Sent. Journey* (1778) I. 123 I thought by the accent, it had been an apostrophe to his child. **1820** W. Irving *Sketch Book* I. 43 The accents of those we love soften the harshest tidings. **1831** Scott *Abbot* ii. 20 Echoing the question with a strong accent of displeasure and surprise. **1847** Hamilton *Rewards & Punishm.* (1853) iii. 120 The very accents of consultation are heard.

5. *poet.* A significant tone or sound; a word; in *pl.* speech, language; including both the tones and their meaning.

1595 Shaks. *K. John* v. vi. 95 Pardon me, That any accent breaking from thy tongue, Should scape.. mine eare. **1601** —— *Jul. C.* III. i. 113 How many Ages hence Shall this our lofty Scene be acted ouer, In State[s] vnborne, and Accents yet vnknowne? **1663** Butler *Hudibras* I. iii. 186 Forcing the Vallies to repeat The Accents of his sad regret. **1718** Pope *Iliad* III. 285 The copious accents fall, with easy art. **1777** Sir W. Jones *An Ode of Petrarch* 66 Soft-breathing gales, my dying accents hear. **1817** Byron *Manf.* III. iv. (1868) 312 In thy gasping throat The accents rattle. **1857** Emerson *Poems* 16 One accent of the Holy Ghost The heedless world hath never lost.

6. *Prosody.* The stress laid at more or less fixed intervals on certain syllables of a verse, the succession of which constitutes the rhythm or measure of the verse.

English verse is theoretically marked by a periodical recurrence of *strong* syllables, having a loud stress, a certain number of times in a line, separated by one or two weak or unaccented syllables. The habits of poets do not however carry out this theoretical law. Thus in 'to err is human, *to* forgive divine,' theory would require *to* to be strong; similarly in 'for the poor *craven* bride*groom said* never *a* word,' theory would require the first syllable in *craven* to be weak and both *groom* and *said* to be as weak as the *-ver* and *a* which follow. They are not so. Hence has arisen the conception of rhythmically or metrically accented and unaccented syllables, as distinguished from the grammatically or verbally accented syllables. Thus, in the above examples, *to* has the rhythmical and not the verbal or phrase accent, and *craven* has the syllabic but not the rhythmical accent; *err* has both verbal and rhythmical accent, *divine* has both syllabic and rhythmical accent. (A. J. E.)

1588 Shaks. *L.L.L.* IV. ii. 124 You finde not the apostraphas, and so misse the accent. **1589** Puttenham *Eng. Poesie* (1811) II. iii. 59 Your ordinarie rimers vse very much their measures in the odde as nine and eleuen, and the sharpe accent vpon the last sillable, which therefore makes him go ill fauouredly. **1871** Abbott & Seeley *Eng. Lessons for Eng. People* 152 Accent in Metre if it fall on any syllable in a word, *must* fall on the principal Word-accent. Accent in Metre *may* fall on syllables that have not a distinct word-accent. We can never have three consecutive clearly pronounced syllables without a Metrical Accent.

7. *Music. Anciently*: the marks placed over words to shew the various notes or turns or phrases to which they were to be sung, these generated the *neumes* and the latter the *notes*. *In modern music*: stress recurring at intervals of time which are generally fixed, but may be varied by syncopation and cross accentuation.

1609 J. Douland *Ornithop. Microl.* 69 Accent (as it belonged to Church-men) is a melody, pronouncing regularly the syllables of any words, according as the naturall accent of them requires. **1795** Mason *Ch. Music* i. 11 In respect to Accent, Rhythm and Cadence, Music becomes an object of criticism which supersedes what is purely harmonical. **1809** Callcott *Mus. Gram.* 41 The bars of music are not only useful for dividing the Movement into equal Measures, but also for shewing the Notes upon which the Accent is to be laid... In the course of this work the accented will be termed the strong parts, and the unaccented the weak parts of a measure. **1867** Macfarren *Harmony* i. 4 The sense comprising rhythm, accent, and numberless delicate gradations.

8. *fig.* Distinctive stress, force, sharpness, or intensity; a distinction, or distinguishing mark, character or tone. Now esp. with *on*: emphasis.

1639 Fuller *Holy War* (1840) v. xxi. 278 Now these are the several accents of honour in the German Service. **1647** Ward *Simple Cobler* (1843) 37 The accent of the blow shall fall there. **1655** Gurnal *Christian in Arm.* I. 27 That which gave accent to Abraham's Faith, was that he was 'fully perswaded, that what God had promised, he was able to perform.' **1662** Fuller *Worthies* II. 108 Marsh made amends for all these failings with his final constancy, being both burnt and scalded to death (having a barrel of pitch placed over his head, an accent of cruelty peculiar to him alone). **1863** A. Gilchrist *Life of W. Blake* I. 41 The interior, with its galleries.. and elaborately decorated apsidal dwarf-chancel, has an imposing effect and a strongly marked characteristic accent (of its day) already historical and interesting. **1947** F. Meynell in E. Barker *Char. England* xviii. 389 The design of the components—the type, paper, and binding—will show local accents. Since the difference between good and bad design.. may be a question of millimetres in the thickness of a part of a letter.. even these slight national accents are of great importance to the bibliophile. **1955** *Financ. Times* 5 Nov. 4/3 The accent in exports is likely to shift away from ready-made products to the sulphonates which are necessary for their manufacture. **1958** *Times* 15 July 7/7 Inside the accent is on comfort, with deeply upholstered seats which reduce fatigue to the minimum on long journeys. **1959** *Observer* 29 Mar. 12/8 The accent was on poverty, squalor and ugliness, but the balance was kept with comments on the good old days which never were.

9. a. *Art.* A touch of colour or light which serves to bring the features of a structure into relief or furnishes a contrast in a scheme of colour.

1849 Ruskin *Seven Lamps Archit.* iii. 79 The Greek workman cared for shadow only as a dark field wherefrom his light figure or design might be intelligibly detached: his attention was concentrated on the one aim at readableness, and clearness of accent. **1888** *Contemp. Rev.* May 712 A few stronger touches, and an accent of light on the neck. **1900** *Westm. Gaz.* 17 Mar. 3/2 A trained eye which discerned at a glance where the accents of a building lay.

b. Something that emphasizes or highlights (esp. by contrast) a decorative style. Freq. *attrib.* Chiefly *U.S.*

1972 *Times* 15 Dec. 27/3 Lighting in general is indirect, with much use of spots, floods and accent lights. **1974** *State* (Columbia, S. Carolina) 15 Feb. 6-A/2 A beautiful Mediterranean credenza cabinet with double speakers, a perfect accent to any room decor. **1977** *New Yorker* 12 Sept. 87/2 It [*sc.* a purse] will fit in beautifully with its superb leather, accent stripe and stitching. **1984** *Tampa* (Florida) *Tribune* 28 Mar. 3B/3 (Advt.), *Drexel*, wicker accent chair in rich tobacco finish.

10. *attrib.*, as ***accent-shift***, ***-shifting***.

1935 D. L. Sayers *Gaudy Night* xviii. 382 How *dared* he pick up her word 'sleep' and use it four times in as many lines, and each time in a different foot, as though juggling with the accent-shift were child's play? **1940** *Amer. Speech* XV. 200/2 Experimental study of the origin of secondary intonation (accent) in the Slavic languages. Accent shift has been accompanied by the introduction of rising inflection. **1926** Fowler *Mod. Eng. Usage* 386/2 Words in which accent-shifting is tentative only:—construe' v. (doubtful), co'nstrue n.

accent (æk'sɛnt), *v.* [a. Fr. *accente-r*, OFr. *acenter*, f. *accent* sb.]

1. To pronounce, utter, or distinguish with accent or stress, to lay the vocal stress upon; to emphasize.

1530 Palsgr. 415 I can nat accent aryght in the latyn tonge. **1589** Puttenham *Eng. Poesie* II. xiii. 110 *Gŏd graūnt thīs peāce māy lōng ĕndūre*—Where the sharpe accent falles more tunably vpon [*graunt*] [*peace*] [*long*] [*dure*] then it would by conuersion, as to accent them thus: *Gōd graŭnt-thīs peăce-māy lŏng-ēndūre*. **1790** Blair *Rhetoric* I. ix. 225 In Greek and Latin, no word is accented farther back than the third syllable from the end. **1795** Mason *Ch. Music* Wks. 1811 III. 291 For the preservation of this Rhythm in Music it is necessary that at least one note in every bar should be accented. **1868** *Pall Mall G.* 23 July 4 The probability is.. in favour of these words having been accented in his [Milton's] day as they now are.

2. To mark with a (written) accent.

Mod. He accented his exercise very carelessly, making more than twenty mistakes.

3. To pronounce, utter, intone.

a **1639** Wotton (J.) And now congeal'd with grief, can scarce implore Strength to accent, Here my Albertus lies! **1656** W. Coles *Art of Simpling* 93 The warbling notes, which the charming birds accent forth from amongst the murmuring leaves. **1816** Scott *Old Mort.* xv. (1830) II. 116 These solemn sounds, accented by a thousand voices, were prolonged among the waste hills.

4. *fig.* To mark emphatically or distinctly; to heighten, sharpen, or intensify; to make conspicuous.

1655 Gurnal *Christian in Arm.* I. 67 The remembrance of his sin in hell thus accented will adde to his torment. **1725** Wodrow *Corr.* (1843) III. 207, I were an ungrateful wretch, if this royal favour did not quicken and accent my concern in them. **1876** Miss Braddon *Josh. Hagg. Daughter* II. 10 'Of course I'm not eluding to ladies like you,' said the farmer ..accenting his speech by a slap on Priscilla's spare shoulder. **1877** R. J. King in *Academy* 3 Nov. 438/2 The great piers, of Doulting stone, are accented at the cardinal points by shafts of dark lias.

accented (æk'sɛntɪd), *ppl. a.* [f. ACCENT *v.* + -ED.] Distinguished by or marked with accent or stress; emphasized. Hence **ac'centedly** *adv.*

1837 Hallam *Hist. Lit.* (1847) I. i. §34. 29 The accented, or if we choose rather to call them so, emphatic syllables, being regulated by a very different though uniform law. **1856** *Titan* July 64 An elderly man.. made me a bow; And accentedly said, 'Sir, I have not the pleasure?' **1873** Miss Broughton *Nancy* II. 120 'Algy!' repeat I, in a tone of the profoundest, accentedest surprise. *c* **1905** F. Rolfe *N. Crabbe* (1958) xx. 132 He tore off to Crabbe's friend Neddy: thus accentedly putting his fat foot further into everything. **1934** —— *Desire & Pursuit of Whole* viii. 70 She was accentedly hearty.

accenting (æk'sɛntɪŋ), *vbl. sb.* [f. ACCENT *v.* + -ING[1].]

1. A pronouncing with accent or stress.

1633 P. Fletcher *Purple Isl.* v. xli. [It] perfects the sound and gives more sharp accenting. **1653** Walton *Angler* 106 The ill pronunciation or ill accenting of a word in a Sermon spoiles it.

2. The marking of the written accent.

1661 Boyle *Style of H. Script.* 129 The strange Mysteries they fancy in the strange Accenting of the Ten Commandments in the Original.

3. Uttering or pronouncing; intoning.

1552 Huloet *Abcedarium*, Accenting or trew pronouncyng or readyng: *Accentus.* **1657** T. May *The Life of a Satyrical Puppy called Nim* 41 O how he weigh'd each word to the very poyse of Accenting.

accentless ('æksəntlɪs), *a.* [f. ACCENT *sb.* + -LESS.] Unmarked by accent or emphasis.

1879 Max Müller in *Academy* 5 July 11/1 The Svarita, an excellent expedient to break through the ekasruti or monotonous and accentless recitation prescribed for the Sûtras.

accen'tology. *Linguistics.* [f. ACCENT *sb.* + -OLOGY.] The study of accentuation or stress in speech; a system or systems of accentuation.

1971 M. Halle in *Linguistic Inquiry* II. 1 (*title*) Remarks on Slavic accentology. **1984** *Times Lit. Suppl.* 2 Mar. 228/4 A full account would also have to include his work on such subjects as comparative Slavonic accentology.

accentor (æk'sɛntə(r)). *Ornith.* [Late L. *accentor* one who sings with another (Isidore), f. L. *ad* to + *cantor* singer, f. *canĕre* to sing.] A genus of passerine singing birds (Bechstein), including the hedge-sparrow or hedge accentor, *A. modularis*; a bird of this genus.

a **1825** [see HEDGE 9]. **1890** [see ROBIN[1] 4c]. **1909** W. Verner *Life among Wild Birds in Spain* VI. iii. 305 One of the few species met with in these stony wastes is the Alpine Accentor (*Accentor collaris*). **1920** *Edin. Rev.* Jan. 72 The hedge sparrow and golden-crested wren, the former of which is.. an accentor, and the latter a regulus. **1954** R. Peterson et al. *Field Guide Birds Brit.* 302 Mountain Accentor. *Prunella montanella.*

b. The golden-crowned thrush or oven-bird, *Siurus auricapillus* of the United States.

1884 Coues *N. Amer. Birds* (ed. 2) 308.

accentual (æk'sɛntjuːəl), *a.* [f. L. *accentu-s* accent + -AL[1], as if ad. L. **accentuālis* analogous to *manuālis*, *visuālis*. First in Todd 1818.] Of or belonging to accent; formed by accent, as distinct from quantity, as in *accentual iambics*, etc., verses in which the ancient alternation of long and short syllables, is replaced by an alternation of strong and weak syllables, as in the versification of English, and other modern languages.

1610 E. Bolton in *Shaks. Cent. Praise* 91 Our tongue hath not received dialects or accentuall notes as the Greeke. **1775** Tyrwhitt *Lang. of Chaucer* I. §10. 83 To form any judgment of the versificaton of Chaucer, it is necessary that we should know the syllabic value of his words and the accentual value of his syllables. **1837** Hallam *Hist. Lit.* (ed. 3) I. 27 The latter [poem] is in accentual iambics with a sort of monotonous termination in the nature of rhyme. **1870** Lowell *Am. my Books* Ser. II (1873) 292 Our prosody is accentual merely. **1875** Whitney *Life of Lang.* iv. 53 The Germanic languages are all characterized by a pretty strong accentual stress.

accentualist (æk'sɛntjuːəlɪst). [f. ACCENTUAL *a.* + -IST.] One who advocates a particular theory of accent, *spec.* concerning the interpretation of plainsong (see quot. 1954).

1909 in *Cent. Dict.* Suppl. **1937** *Downside Rev.* LV. 349 Father Robertson allows himself occasionally to enunciate rhythmic principles which run directly counter both to the theory and the practice of the accentualists. **1940** G. Reese *Music in Middle Ages* v. 141 The accentualists.. consider the accent the principal—according to some, the only—rhythmical determinant of its melodies. **1954** *Grove's Dict. Mus.* (ed. 5) VI. 820/1 The Accentualists hold that the change from quantity to accent in both Greek and Latin in about the 5th century caused the longs and shorts in the chant to change to notes of equal value and that the principal and secondary accents of particular syllables in particular words.. determine the rhythm of that phrase.

accentuality (æk͵sɛntjuː'ælɪtɪ). *rare*$^{-1}$. [*nonce-wd.* f. ACCENTUAL *a.* + -ITY.] The quality of being accentual; also in *pl.* accentual particulars or characteristics.

a **1834** LAMB *Misc. Wks.* 1871, 451 With an insight into the accentualities and punctualities of modern Saxon.

accentually (æk'sɛntju:əlɪ), *adv.* [f. ACCENTUAL + -LY².] In an accentual manner; with due attention to accent.

1837 HALLAM *Hist. Lit.* I. I. i. §34. 31 The stress falling on the penultimate, as is the usual case in a Latin pentameter verse, accentually read, in our present mode.

accentuate (æk'sɛntju:eɪt), *v.* [f. med.L. *accentuā-re, -ātum*, f. *accentus*: see ACCENT, and -ATE³. Cf. Fr. *accentuer*.]

1. To pronounce, or distinguish with an accent.

1731 BAILEY, *Accentuate*: to pronounce in reading or speaking according to the accent. **1827** HARE *Guesses at Truth* II. 212 They [the French] never accentuate their words or their feelings: all is in the same key; a cap is *charmant*, so is Raphael's Transfiguration. **1880** *Paper & Printing Trades Journ.* xxx. 7 You will find that he accentuates his words..quite naturally.

2. To mark with the written accent.

1846 T. WRIGHT *Ess. on Mid. Ages* I. I. 9 The [Anglo-Saxon] scribes not only omitted accents, but they often accentuated words wrongly.

3. *fig.* To mark strongly, emphasize.

1865 LECKY *Rationalism* I. 371 To accentuate strongly the antagonism by which human nature is convulsed. **1875** HAMERTON *Intellect. Life* VII. v. 254 His marriage would strongly accentuate the amateur character of his position.

accentuated (æk'sɛntju:eɪtɪd), *ppl. a.* [f. prec. + -ED.] *lit.* Pronounced with or distinguished by accent; furnished with written accents. *fig.* Emphasized, strongly marked.

1873 A. FLINT *Physiol. of Man* i. 20 If the nerves be examined..their anatomical elements appear in the form of simple fibres with strongly accentuated borders. **1873** SYMONDS *Grk. Poets* xii. 403 The olive stem retains in youth and middle and old age the distinction of finely accentuated form.

accentuation (æk,sɛntju:'eɪʃən). [ad. med.L. *accentuātiōn-em* intoning, chanting, n. of action f. *accentuare*: see ACCENTUATE.]

1. The marking of accent or stress in speech; the use or application of accent.

1827 HARE *Guesses at Truth* II. 208 The Latin..has substituted a stately monotonousness for the ever flexible rhythm and changing accentuation of the Greek. **1859** DE QUINCEY *Wks.* XII. 189 The accentuation of Milton's age was, in many words, entirely different from ours. **1866** FELTON *Anc. & Mod. Greece* I. iii. 37 It has been recently placed beyond a doubt that the Sanscrit system of accentuation is identical with that of the Greek.

2. The notation of accents in writing.

1846 T. WRIGHT *Ess. on Mid. Ages* I. i. 10 In every [Anglo-Saxon] word we ought to know the accentuation. *Mod.* Two Greek words which differ only in accentuation.

3. Mode of pronunciation; vocal modulation.

1818 SCOTT *Rob Roy* 347 There was a strong provincial accentuation, but, otherwise, the language..was graceful, flowing and declamatory. **1879** A. TROLLOPE *Cousin Henry* xiv. 161 Read them one after another..slowly, but with clear accentuation so that every point..might be understood.

4. *fig.* Emphasizing, laying stress or dwelling upon, bringing into prominence.

1875 STUBBS *Const. Hist.* III. xxi. 501 The constant 'accentuation,' as it is called, of principles in historical writing, invariably marks a narrow view of truth.

accentuator (æk'sɛntju:eɪtə(r)). [agent-n. in L. form f. ACCENTUATE *v.*] One who or that which accentuates; spec. (*a*) one who marks words with written accents; (*b*) a device for marking the accent in musical performance.

1876 J. MARTIN tr. *C. F. Keil's Comm. Ezek.* xxvi. 19–21 I. 382 We should then have to take the clause as independent and affirmative, as the accentuators and the Targum have done. **1923** *Daily Mail* 10 Jan. 2 (Advt.), Auteola Player Piano... Automatic Accentuator and Sustaining Pedal.

†**accenty.** *Obs. rare*⁻¹. Irreg. var. of ACCENT.

1600 TOURNEUR *Trans. Metamorph.* (1878) 175 Still tumbles forth half-breathed accenties.

†**accept** (æk'sɛpt), *ppl. a. Obs.* [ad. L. *accept-us*, pa. pple. of *accip-ĕre* to receive, take what is offered, f. *ac-* = *ad-* to + *-cipĕre* = *capĕre* to take.] = ACCEPTED.

1382 WYCLIF *2 Cor.* vi. 2 In tyme accept, or wel plesynge, I haue herd thee. **1432–50** TREVISA *Higden* (Rolls Ser.) I. 108 Thapostle testifienge, that 'thei diedde alle, the promissiones not accepte.' *c* **1510** BARCLAY *Mir. of Good Manners* (1570) E ij. Suche maners shall thee make..before all other accept and amiable. **1526** TINDALE *Luke* i. 75 In suche holynes and ryghtewesnes that are accept before him. **1599** SHAKS. *Hen. V*, v. ii. 82 We will suddenly Passe our accept and peremptorie answer.

accept (æk'sɛpt), *v.* Pa. pple. at first **accept**, now **accepted**. [? a. Fr. *accepte-r* (14th c. *accepter*), ad. L. *acceptā-re*, freq. of *accip-ĕre*: see prec. (Wyclif may have taken it directly from L.)] *gen.* To take or receive what is offered. Hence,

1. a. To take or receive (a thing offered) willingly, or with consenting mind; to receive (a thing or person) with favour or approval, *e.g.* to receive as a prospective husband. Also, to take or receive with patience or resignation, to tolerate.

c **1380** WYCLIF *Eng. Wks.* (1879) 257 þes foure witnessis weren acceptid of þe holy gost. **1461–83** *Ord. for Royal Househ.* 54 Wardes..take..allwey lyveres of mete & drinke & other by the Thesaurere of houshold tyll they be accepted to theyre landes or elles solde by the Kinge. **1494** FABYAN III. lvii. 37 They made humble request to the kynge that he wolde accept theym vnto his grace. **1525** LD. BERNERS *Froissart* II. lxxxvii. 257 He sente letters of defyaunce.. whiche were nothynge pleasaunt accepted of the Kynge. **1535** COVERDALE *Mal.* i. 13 Ye haue brought me in a meatofferynge, shulde I accepte it of youre honde? **1596** SHAKS. *Merch. Ven.* I. ii. 109 You should refuse to performe your Father's will, if you should refuse to accept him. *Ibid.* IV. ii. 9 His ring I doe accept most thankfully. **1719** YOUNG *Busiris* II. i. (1757) 32 My lord, I want the courage to accept What far transcends my merit. **1782** COWPER *Let.* 18 Nov. Wks. 1876, 121 Accept, therefore, your share of their gratitude. **1802** SOUTHEY *Thalaba* v. 39 Hear me, Angels! so may Heaven Accept, and mitigate your penitence. **1859** GEO. ELIOT *Adam Bede* II. xvii. 3 These fellow-mortals, every one, must be accepted as they are. **1862** WILKIE COLLINS *No Name* I. I. ii. 26 Accept the situation—as the French say. **1880** M. PATTISON *Milton* 55 The girl herself conceived an equal repugnance to the husband she had thoughtlessly accepted. **1882** *Daily Tel.* 17 May, (*Cricket.*) Leslie gave an easy chance to M'Donnell at slip, which was not accepted. **1934** *Punch* 3 Jan. 6/1 There are not going to be fewer cars, but more, so you'll be wise to accept them.

b. Of a female animal: to permit (copulation).

1931 PICKARD & CREW *Rabbit Breeding* ii. 10 The period of 'season' or 'heat' is the time when a doe accepts coitus. **1933** E. F. DAGLISH *Dog Owner's Guide* viii. 199 Some bitches will accept the dog earlier, but about the tenth day is usually the ideal.

2. to accept the person or **face of**: To receive any one's advances with favour, to treat him as a *persōna grāta*, to favour him (*esp.* on corrupt grounds, as personal attractions, rank, influence, power to bribe). Hence **to accept persons**: To show (corrupt) partiality or favouritism. [A Hebraism *nāsā' phānīm* 'to accept the face,' literally rendered in N. T. Gr. προσωποληπτεῖν, and in Vulgate *acceptāre persōnam, -as*, whence it has passed into Eng. theological language.]

c **1360** WYCLIF *De Dotacione Eccl.* 104 For Crist may not of his ryȝtwisnes þus accepte persones. **1535** COVERDALE *1 Esd.* iv. 39 The trueth accepteth no personnes, it putteth no difference betwixte rych or poore. **1611** BIBLE *Job* xiii. 10 He will surely reproue you, if yee doe secretly accept persons. —— *Gal.* ii. 6 God accepteth no mans person. [WYCLIF, God takith not the persoone of man. TINDALE, God loketh on no man's person. COVERDALE, God loketh not on the outwarde appearaunce of men. CRANMER, God loketh on the outward appearaunce of no man. GENEVA, God loketh on no man's person. RHEIMS, God accepteth not the person of man.]

3. To receive as sufficient or adequate; hence, to admit, agree to, believe.

1530 PALSGR. 416, I accepte, or take in worthe, or alowe: I accepte all his commaundementes in good worthe. **1534** WHITTINTON *Tully's Off.* (1540) III. 167 These thre bokes shall be accept and taken as straungers or gestes amonge the commentaryes and workes of Cratippus. **1651** HOBBES *Leviathan* II. xxi. 114 He hath Libertie to accept the condition. **1729** BURKITT *On New Test.* Mark xii. 44 God Almighty accepts the will of those that give cheerfully. **1876** FREEMAN *Norm. Conq.* II. App. 530 A fact which we may surely accept on the authority of the Biographer. *Mod.* His apology was not accepted. To accept the Calvinistic doctrine of the atonement, the evolution theory, etc.

b. *Law.* **to accept service of a writ**: to agree to consider as valid its informal delivery.

4. To take formally (what is offered) with contemplation of its consequences and obligations; to take upon oneself, to undertake as a responsibility.

1524 WOLSEY in Strype's *Eccl. Mem.* (1721) I. 81 They shall have little leisure either to mind or accept the seige of Calais. **1530** PALSGR. 416, I accepte, or take in hande. **1728** POPE *Dunc.* II. 167 Osborne and Curl accept the glorious strife. **1869** HOOK *Lives of Archbps.* I. vii. 368 His disinclination to accept the office was real and sincere. **1880** M. PATTISON *Milton* 94 The post was offered him, but would he accept it?

¶ In the preceding senses *accept* is frequently followed by *of*.

1580 NORTH *Plutarch* (1676) 22 They sent defiance to each other..Both of them accepted of it. **1611** BIBLE *2 Macc.* xiii. 24 And [the King] accepted well of Maccabeus, made him principall gouernor. **1722** DE FOE *Hist. Plague* 71 If he would accept of that lodging he might haue it. **1792** T. JEFFERSON *Writings* (1859) III. 456 There are some hopes they will accept of peace. **1818** *Q. Rev.* XVIII. 459 He will not accept of the text as adopted by his predecessors.

5. a. *Comm.* To accept a bill or draft (said of the person to whom the bill or letter of exchange is addressed, or one who takes his place, or accepts 'for the honour' of the drawer or endorser): to acknowledge formally its receipt or presentation, and undertake the liability or obligation to meet it when due; to agree or promise to pay.

The acceptor usually writes the word 'Accepted' with his signature on the face of the document; adding the date, when the latter affects the date of payment.

1665 S. BING in Ellis *Orig. Lett.* II. 310, IV. 24 Trading strangely ceaseth, and bills of Exchange are not accepted. **1848** MILL *Pol. Econ.* (1876) III. xi. §3. 312 A bill of exchange..when accepted by the debtor, that is authenticated by his signature, becomes an acknowledgment of debt.

b. *absol.*

a **1845** HOOD *Sniffing a Birthday* vii, I'm free to give my IOU, Sign, draw, accept, as majors do.

acceptability (æk,sɛptə'bɪlɪtɪ). [ad. late L. *acceptābilitāt-em* (used in scholastic theology, Du Cange), n. of state f. *acceptābilis*. See ACCEPTABLE.] The quality of being acceptable; = ACCEPTABLENESS, which is the commoner form.

1660 JER. TAYLOR *Worthy Comm.* i. §3. 48 For the obtaining the grace and acceptability of repentance. —— *Wks.* III. Serm. 10 Praying with his heart and with the acceptabilities of a good life. **1850** W. IRVING *Goldsmith* xxv. 253 Endeavouring by the aid of dress to acquire that personal acceptability..which nature had denied him.

acceptable (æk'sɛptəb(ə)l, 'æksɪptəb(ə)l), *a.* [a. Fr. *acceptable*, ad. L. *acceptābil-is*, vbl. adj. f. *acceptāre*. See ACCEPT and -ABLE. Orig. pronounced, according to the analogy of words in *-ble* from Fr. and L., '*acceptable*, and so in all poets to the present day; but from the tendency to treat it as a direct derivative from the vb. *ac'cept*, as in *ad'visable*, *mi'stakable*, *de'niable*, *under'standable*, the pronunciation *ac'ceptable* is now more prevalent. So with the derivatives *acceptably*, *-ableness*. Sometimes compared *acceptabler*, *-est*.] Capable, worthy, or likely to be accepted or gladly received; hence, pleasing, agreeable, gratifying, or welcome.

c **1386** CHAUCER *Sompn. T.* 205 Oure prayeres..Ben to the hihe God mor acceptable Than youres. **1447** BOKENHAM *Lyvys of Seyntys* (1835) 280 That the acceptabyllere the sacryfyse of hyr preyers to God myht alwey be. **1535** COVERDALE *Mic.* vi. 6 What acceptable thynge shal I offre vnto the Lorde? **1611** BIBLE *Deut.* xxxiii. 24 And of Asher hee said,..Let him be acceptable to his brethren. **1667** MILTON *P.L.* x. 139 This woman, whom thou mad'st to be my help..So fit, so acceptable, so divine. **1738** WESLEY *Psalms* (1765) cxviii. x. Now, send us now thy saving Grace, Make this the acceptable Hour. **1850** W. IRVING *Goldsmith* xxix. 283 He was becoming more and more acceptable in ladies' eyes. **1850** MRS. BROWNING *Drama of Exile* I. 74 Found acceptable to the world instead Of others of that name. **1861** DICKENS *Gt. Expec.* viii. 36 The bread and meat were acceptable, and the beer was warming.

acceptableness (æk'sɛptəb(ə)lnɪs, see prec.). [f. prec. + -NESS.] The quality of being acceptable, or agreeable to a receiver, entertainer, hearer, etc.

1611 COTGR., *Agreableté*, Agreeablenesse, acceptablenesse. **1648** *Eikon Basilike* 120 A greater Blessing & acceptableness attends those Duties which are rightly performed. **1865** *Sat. Rev.* 4 Nov. 573 Announcing his own acceptableness by repeating the churchwarden's praises of his last Sunday's homily. **1877** MOZLEY *Univ. Serm.* ii. 29 Love..is what gives the character of acceptableness to all our actions.

acceptably (æk'sɛptəblɪ), *adv.* [f. ACCEPTABLE + -LY². The accent varies, as in ACCEPTABLE; Southey has *ac'ceptably*.] In an acceptable or agreeable manner; so as to be accepted; so as to give satisfaction.

1535 COVERDALE *Ecclus.* xliv. 16 Enoch walked right & acceptably before the Lorde. **1611** BIBLE *Heb.* xii. 28 Let vs haue grace, whereby wee may serue God acceptably. **1829** SOUTHEY *All for Love* i. Wks. VII. 153 And Heaven acceptably receive His costliest sacrifice. **1859** REEVE *Brittany* 87 The glare of the sun being acceptably veiled at intervals.

acceptance (æk'sɛptəns). [a. OFr. *acceptance*, f. *accepter*; see ACCEPT and -ANCE.]

1. a. The act or fact of accepting, or taking what is offered, whether as a pleasure, a satisfaction of claim, or a duty.

1596 SPENSER *State of Irel.* (J.) By the acceptance of his sovereignty, they also accepted of his laws. **1607** SHAKS. *Coriol.* II. iii. 9 If he tel vs his Noble deeds, we must also tell him our Noble acceptance of them. **1667** MILTON *P.L.* v. 531 Our voluntarie service he requires, Not our necessitated, such with him Findes no acceptance. *a* **1764** R. LLOYD *The Poet* Wks. 1774 II. 21 The mob his kind acceptance begs Of dirt, and stones, and addle-eggs. **1876** FREEMAN *Norm. Conq.* II. App. 531 William or his advisers may..have pressed the acceptance of the crown on Eadward.

b. The accepting of copulation by a female animal.

1925 F. A. E. CREW *Animal Genetics* x. 297 The sexual season is divided into..*procestrum*..*œstrum*, the phase of desire and acceptance of the male.

2. *esp.* Favourable reception. **a.** Of persons.

1596 SHAKS. *Merch. Ven.* IV. i. 164, I neuer knewe so yong a body, with so old a head. I leaue him to your gracious acceptance. **1611** COTGR., *Malgrace*..bad acceptance, ill opinion. **1814** SOUTHEY *Roderick* vii. Wks. IX. 71 That vow hath been pronounced..whereby we stand For condemnation or acceptance. **1882** *Daily Tel.* Mar. 9 The vocalist..sang with marked acceptance.

b. Of things: Favourable consideration, approval; and hence, of statements, theories, etc.: Mental assent, belief.

1669 PEPYS *Diary* (1877) V. 452 It did meet with the Duke of York's acceptance & well-liking. **1779** NEWTON *Bk. of Praise* (Gold. Tr. Ser.) 52 By Thee my prayers acceptance gain Although with sin defiled. **1794** SULLIVAN *View of Nat.* II. 230 Recommend them to the belief and acceptance of all reasonable persons. **1854** FARADAY *Exp. Res.* lv. 470 The assertion finds acceptance in every rank of society. **1880** CARPENTER in *19th Cent.* No. 38. 602 The probability of their volcanic origin seems so strong as to justify its full acceptance.

c. ***acceptance of persons***: undue favour on personal grounds, partiality. See ACCEPT 2, ACCEPTION 2.

1855 MACAULAY *Hist. Eng.* IV. 580 A Sovereign who had sworn that he..would do justice, without acceptance of persons.

3. The state or condition of being accepted.

1649 SELDEN *Laws of Eng.* (1739) I. v. 12 She first brought Austin into acceptance with the King. **1714** T. ELLWOOD *Life* (1765) 72, I found acceptance with the Lord. **1745** WESLEY *Answ. to Church* 17 Can we deny, That Holiness is a Condition of Final Acceptance?

4. The sense in which a word or expression is accepted or taken; understood signification. *rare.* (More usually ACCEPTATION 4.)

a **1716** SOUTH (J.) An assertion, most certainly true, though, under the common acceptance of it, not only false but odious. **1857** S. OSBORN *Quedah* xvii. 237 Neither Jadee nor I were sportsmen in the proper acceptance of the word.

5. The quality of being accepted or acceptable; acceptableness, agreeableness.

1593 MARLOWE *Dido* III. iii. 926 Love and duty led him on perhaps To press beyond acceptance to your sight. **1666** SOUTH *Serm.* Tit. ii. 15 Wks. 1715 I. 197 Some Men cannot be Fools with so good Acceptance as others. **1868** BROWNING *Ring & Bk.* 837 The Canon! We caress him..A man of such acceptance.

6. *Comm.* (See ACCEPT *v.* 5.) **a.** The act of formally accepting the liability to pay a bill of exchange when due; the formal engagement to pay it. Also *attrib.*, as ***acceptance bank, credit, house***. Cf. ACCEPTING *vbl. sb.* 2. **b.** The bill itself when 'accepted' by A.B. is termed *A.B.'s acceptance*.

1682 J. SCARLETT *Stile of Exch.* 59 Acceptance must be demanded of him only, to whom the Bill is directed. **1865** TRAFFORD *G. Geith* II. ii. 30 There is scarcely a business man..the aim and object of whose life is not to get his acceptances into circulation. **1866** CRUMP *Banking* v. 117 Acceptance..signifies an engagement on the part of the drawee to meet the bill in money when it falls due. **1923** *Crowell's Dict. Bus. & Finance*, Acceptance Bank. **1927** G. G. MUNN *Encycl. Bank. & Finance*, Acceptance Houses. **1948** G. CROWTHER *Outl. Money* (ed. 2) ii. 70 Usually..the merchant agrees with one of the London banks..to 'accept' the bill for him, and the presence on the bill of the name of a bank or of an 'acceptance house' immediately makes the bill a 'prime' bill. **1958** *Spectator* 6 June 720/1 Fresh information about the sterling balances, and about acceptance credits, an important method by which international trade is financed in the City of London.

c. ***acceptance world***: used by A. Powell in the ordinary *Comm.* sense and also *transf.*, of life 'accepted' as a debt which must eventually be repaid.

1955 A. POWELL (*title*) The Acceptance World.

7. *Law.* An agreeing to the act or contract of another (as a predecessor in office or agent) by some act which amounts to a recognition or approval of the same, and binds the person in law.

1574 tr. *Littleton's Tenures* 99 b, A man shal have none advantage by suche release that shalbe againste his owne propre acceptance. **1691** BLOUNT *Law Dict.* s.v. *Acceptance* is..a tacite kind of agreeing to some former Act done by another, which might have been undone or avoided.

8. The paper or card on which an invitation is accepted.

1873 J. H. BEADLE *Undevel. West* xviii. 342 The 'nervous-hystericky Italian hand' resumed its beautiful regularity on pink-tinted 'acceptances'. **1957** R. CARRINGTON *Mermaids & Mastodons* ix. 136 Twenty-one acceptances were received and..the guests arrived at the appointed hour.

9. *Racing.* A horse accepted for a race (freq. in *pl.*).

1923 *Daily Mail* 1 Feb. 9/1 The acceptances..are satisfactory for the 'Lincoln'. **1928** *Ibid.* 25 July 14/5, I expect to find him among the acceptances for the Chesterfield Cup at Goodwood. **1946** F. SARGESON *That Summer* 69, I wrapped it in a sheet of newspaper I was keeping because of the acceptances.

10. Special Comb. **acceptance trials**, the trial or trials which a new ship, etc., undergoes before being accepted into service; cf. *trial-trip* s.v. TRIAL *sb.*[1] 13.

1958 *Weekly Law Rep.* 28 Nov. 1127 Upon completion of the craft, the builders will notify the buyer in writing that the craft is ready for *acceptance trials to be run. **1971** *Daily Tel.* 18 Feb. 2/3 Formal acceptance trials with the 1906A will begin on Monday. The computer is due to be in full operation by the end of next month. **1976** *Islander* (Victoria, B.C.) 7 Mar. 6/2 She was launched Oct. 6..and her acceptance trials were held on May 11. **1978** R. V. JONES *Most Secret War* v. 45 Occasionally, I had something practical to do such as the acceptance trials of the first airborne television equipment for the R.A.F.

acceptancy (æk'sɛptənsɪ). [f. ACCEPT, as if ad. L. **acceptantia*. See -NCY.] Willingness to receive, receptiveness.

1856 MRS. BROWNING *Aur. Leigh* ii. 1057 Here's a proof of gift, But here's no proof, sir, of acceptancy.

acceptant (æk'sɛptənt), *a.* and *sb.* [a. Fr. *acceptant* adj. and sb., properly pr. pple. of *accepter* to accept.]

A. *adj.* Willingly receiving (what is offered), receptive. Const. *of.*

1851 RUSKIN *Mod. Painters* II. III. 2. iii. §18 Too painful to be endured even by the most acceptant mind. **1866** —— *Eth. of Dust* 152 Angelico merely takes his share of this inheritance, and applies it in the tenderest way to subjects that are peculiarly acceptant of it.

†**B.** *sb.* One who accepts, or takes what is offered; an accepter. *spec.* The acceptor of a bill. *Obs.*

1596 CHAPMAN *Iliad* VII. Argt. 3 Nine Greeks stand up acceptants every one, But lot selects strong Ajax Telamon. **1682** J. SCARLETT *Stile of Exch.* 41 If the Draught be for the account of the Drawer..it is not necessary that he advise the Acceptant of the course.

acceptation (ˌæksɪp'teɪʃən). [a. Fr. *acceptation* (14th c. in Littré) ad. late L. *acceptātiōn-em*, n. of action f. *acceptāre*; see ACCEPT.]

†**1.** *gen.* The action of taking, or receiving, what is offered, whether by way of favour, satisfaction, or duty; reception; = ACCEPTANCE 1. *Obs.*

1426 *Past. Lett.* 7 I. 25 By this acceptacion of this bysshopricke, he hath pryved hym self of the title that he claymed. **1528** GARDINER in Pocock's *Rec. Ref.* I. li. 133 Temper it so as might further the acceptation of this Commission. **1635** J. HAYWARD *Banish'd Virg.* 219 Upon acceptation of this last courteous proffer, they mount up. **1692** BENTLEY *Boyle Lect.* ix. 326 Without his Satisfaction there is no Remission of Sins nor Acceptation of Repentance.

2. *esp.* Favourable reception; = ACCEPTANCE 2, which is now in this sense the usual word.

†**a.** Of persons. *Obs.*

1567 *Trial of Treasure* (1850) 5 Though the style be barbarous..our author desireth your gentle acceptation. **1658** *Wh. Duty of Man* III. xii. 31 You cannot deceive God, nor gain acceptation from him by anything which is not perfectly hearty and unfeigned.

b. Of things: Favourable reception, approval; hence, assent, acquiescence, belief.

1611 BIBLE *1 Tim.* i. 15 This is a faithfull saying, and worthy of all acceptation. **1651** HOBBES *Leviathan* I. xiv. 69 Without mutuall acceptation, there is no Covenant. **1803** MAR. EDGEWORTH *Manufact.* (1831) i. 73 Their cards of acceptation were shewn in triumph. **1855** H. REED *Lect. Eng. Lit.* (1878) x. 318 What else can explain the large acceptation, which a poem like 'Gray's Elegy' found at once? **1881** J. A. BROWN in *Nature* XXIII. 559 That hypothesis will have a better claim to acceptation.

†**c.** ***acceptation of persons***: = ACCEPTION 2. *Obs.*

1565 JEWEL *Repl. to Harding* (1611) 387 God..hath no acceptation, or choice of persons.

3. The state of being accepted or acceptable; acceptableness, regard. *arch.* = ACCEPTANCE 3.

1594 HOOKER *Eccl. Pol.* II. (T.) Some things..are notwithstanding of so great dignity and acceptation with God. **1642** ROGERS *Naaman* 110 Elbow roome in the world, acceptation with our betters. *c* **1800** KIRKE WHITE *Lett.* (1837) 248 Not only to secure your own acceptation.

4. The sense in which a word or sentence is accepted or received; the received meaning.

1614 RALEIGH *Hist. World* II. 243 Which Nationall Law, according to divers acceptations..may be sometime taken for a Species of the Naturall, sometime of the Humane. **1690** LOCKE *Hum. Underst.* (1695) IV. i. 302 It is necessary first, to consider the different acceptations of the word Knowledge. *a* **1754** FIELDING *Remedy of Affl.* Wks. 1775 IX. 254 In its common and vulgar acceptation it [Philosophy] signifies, the search after Wisdom. **1830** GEN. P. THOMPSON *Exerc.* (1842) I. 286 War, in the acceptation of modern publicists, is self-defence against reform.

†**5.** *Acceptation* of a bill of exchange = ACCEPTANCE 6. *Obs.*

1622 G. MALYNES *Anc. Law-Merch.* 400 [He] doth come to him vpon whom the said Bill was directed, and desireth his promise of acceptation.

ac'ceptativeness, *rare*$^{-0}$. [f. *acceptative* (not cited), f. L. *acceptāt-* ppl. stem of *acceptā-re*; see ACCEPT and -IVE.] Tendency to give acceptance to statements. Prob. only in loc. cit.

1870 SMITH *Syn. & Antonyms*, *Credulity*, *Syn.* Gullibility, Simplicity, Acceptativeness.

accepted (æk'sɛptɪd), *ppl. a.* [f. ACCEPT *v.* + -ED.]

1. Received as offered; well-received; approved.

1493 *Petronylla* 26 She was acceptyd so in the lordys sight To be noumbryd one of the maydyns fyue Afore Jhesu that bare their laumpys light. **1611** BIBLE *1 Sam.* xviii. 5 And he [David] was accepted in the sight of all the people. **1814** SOUTHEY *Roderick* vii. Wks. IX. 73 The royal Goth Had offer'd his accepted sacrifice. **1879** TOURGEE *Fool's Errand* xxii. 129 Ideas at variance with the accepted creed.

†**2.** Hence, satisfactory, acceptable. *Obs.*

a **1500** *Songs on Costume* (1849) 54 Humylyté..Most accepted was onto the Deyté. **1611** BIBLE *2 Cor.* vi. 2 Beholde, now is the accepted time. **1677** HALE *Contempl.* II. 49 And surely, the first fruits of our Lives..are best accepted to him.

acceptedly (æk'sɛptɪdlɪ), *adv.* [f. prec. + -LY[2].] In the accepted manner: hence, †**a.** acceptably, welcome (*obs.*); **b.** according to common acceptation, admittedly.

1599 JONSON *Ev. Man out of Hum.* I. ii. 92 It [payment] comes more acceptedly, than if you gave 'hem a new-yeeres gift. **1872** in *Athenæum* 5 Oct. 435/3 No statesman..would dare to use a sentence out of their acceptedly divine Revelation, as having now a literal authority over them.

accepter (æk'sɛptə(r)). [f. ACCEPT *v.* + -ER[1]. Now the general word; ACCEPTOR the older form is retained in special senses.] One who accepts, or receives what is offered or presented. ***accepter of persons*** or ***faces***, a judge who is influenced by the personal acceptableness of individuals, one who shows partiality on personal grounds. See ACCEPTION 2.

1585 ABP. SANDYS *Serm.* (1841) 226 God is no accepter of persons. **1748** RICHARDSON *Clarissa* (1811) I. xlv. 349 The giver and accepter are principally answerable in an unjust donation. **1860** TRENCH *Serm. in Westm. Abbey* xv. 176 He now is..the justifier and accepter of the ungodly.

acceptilate (æk'sɛptɪleɪt), *v.* [f. ACCEPTILATION, as if this originated in a L. vb. *acceptilā-re*, *acceptilāt-um*, which had no existence.] A technical phrase in writers on Rom. law, for discharging an obligation by *acceptilatio*.

1880 MUIRHEAD *Gaius* 441 Whether a debt could be partially acceptilated was matter of dispute.

acceptilation (ækˌsɛptɪ'leɪʃən). [ad. L. *acceptilātiōn-em*, properly *accepti lātio* an accounting of a thing as received.] A technical term in Roman law, 'importing the remission of a debt by an acquittance from the creditor testifying the receipt of money which has never been paid.' J. Also *fig.* in a theological sense, free remission.

1562-3 FOXE *A. & M.* (1596) 993/2, I neither am, neither shall be able to requite this your lordships most special kindnesse..unlesse I shoulde use that ciuill remedie called in law acceptilation. **1656** JER. TAYLOR *Answ. to Bp. of Rochester* (R.) Our justification which comes by Christ is by imputation and acceptilation, by grace and favour. **1880** MUIRHEAD *Gaius* 241 An obligation is also extinguished by acceptilation, which is as it were an imaginary payment.

accepting (æk'sɛptɪŋ), *vbl. sb.* [f. ACCEPT *v.* + -ING[1].] **1.** The action of taking or receiving what is offered or presented; acceptance, reception. ***accepting of faces*** or ***persons*** of men: partiality, undue favour; see ACCEPT 2, ACCEPTION 2.

1577 tr. *Bullinger, Decades* (1592) 193 One of these two vices, which so infecteth the mindes of Judges..is the accepting of faces, or respect of persons. *a* **1649** DRUMM. OF HAWTH. *Fam. Ep.* Wks. 1711, 156 Your chearful accepting of such like essays heretofore. *Mod.* John's accepting of the appointment.

2. *attrib.*, as ***accepting house***. Cf. ACCEPTANCE, sense 6.

1919 R. G. HAWTREY *Currency & Credit* vii. 105 Accepting houses authorise merchants to draw bills, on condition that the necessary funds are provided to meet the bills when due. **1962** *Times* 13 Sept. 11/5 Rothschilds have remained..the only accepting house in the City to have avoided turning itself into a legal company.

accepting (æk'sɛptɪŋ), *ppl. a.* [f. ACCEPT *v.* + -ING[2].] That accepts or has accepted.

1718 POPE *Iliad* XV. 438 Presumptuous Troy mistook the accepting sign. **1861** GÖSCHEN *For. Exch.* 55 The value of money in the accepting country.

acception (æk'sɛpʃən). *rare.* [ad. L. *acceptiōn-em*, n. of action f. *accept-* ppl. stem of *accipĕre*; see ACCEPT. Used by Wyclif to translate the Vulg. *acceptio persōnārum* (*Rom.* ii. 11, etc.) *acception of persons*, a phrase occurring hundreds of times down to 1700, when it was supplanted by ACCEPTING, ACCEPTANCE. In the general sense of ACCEPTANCE = *reception*, the word is rather rare; but in that of ACCEPTATION = *signification*, in regular use from 6 till the beginning of 8. Cf. Fr. *acception*, which has likewise yielded to *acceptation* in the general sense, but still remains in senses 2 and 3, *acception de personne*, *acception d'un mot*.]

1. The act of accepting; the receiving or taking of anything presented; acceptance, reception.

1483 CAXTON *Gold. Leg.* 427/1 To euerichone [he] rendryd his owne by right withoute ony accepcion or takyng of money. **1578** LYTE *Niewe Herball* Pref. 2 Most humbly craving a favourable acception hereof. **1624** J. SMITH *Virginia* v. 194 Acknowledgement and acception of all resident Gouernours. **1662** H. STUBBE *Indian Nectar* i. 5 The universal acception of this drink amongst the most sober. **1921** *Glasgow Herald* 7 Apr. 6/3 Acception of the Premier's proposal followed by its rejection.

2. ***acception of persons*** or ***faces***. [A Hebrew phrase *massō phānīm*, 'accepting of the face,' verbally rendered in Gr. προσωποληψία, L. *acceptio personæ*, *-ārum*, the latter simply adapted in Fr. and Eng.] The receiving of the personal advances of any one with favour; *hence*, corrupt acceptance, or favouritism, due to a person's rank, relationship, influence, power to bribe, etc. See ACCEPT 2. (The earliest sense in Eng.)

1382 WYCLIF *Rom.* ii. 11 For accepciouns of persoones, that is, to putte oon bifore another withoute desert, is not anentis God. [TINDALE parcialyte, CRANMER and **1611** respect, *Rheims* acception.] **1494** FABYAN VI. clxi. 154 He shuld purpose the sothe & trowthe withoute accepcion of parsonys, and ponysshe mysdoers, as well the ryche as the poore. **1677** GALE *Crt. of Gentiles* II. IV. 372 Acception of persons has place only where..any favors one more than another.

3. The accepted or received meaning or signification of a word or phrase; = ACCEPTATION 4.

1543 *Necessary Doctrine* B, Faythe in the fyrst acception, is consydered as it is a seuerall gifte of God by it selfe. **1612** T. TAYLOR *Titus* i. 7. (1619) 121 The Apostle's argument and context can admit no other acception. **1651** BAXTER *Inf. Bapt.* 186 That is the common acception, in six hundred places it is so taken. **1711** J. GREENWOOD *Eng. Gram.* 86 This Acception of the term. **1850** E. W. GRINFIELD *Apol. Septuag.* 179 To use Greek words, in such peculiar acceptions. **1937** *Nature* 20 Nov. 866/2 These initial restrictions on the meaning and acception of experience.

¶ **acception** is frequently found for EXCEPTION, with which it was phonetically confounded.

acceptive (æk'sɛptɪv), *a.* [f. ACCEPT *v.* + -IVE, as if ad. L. **acceptīvus*. Cf. *deceptive*.]

1. *passively*. Fit or suitable for acceptance; appropriate.

1596 CHAPMAN *Iliad* VII. 85 Myself will use acceptive darts, And arm against him. *c* **1851** MRS. BROWNING *Loved Once* And yet that word of 'Once' Is humanly acceptive.

2. *actively*. Having a tendency to accept, ready to accept; receptive of things offered.

1601 JONSON *Poëtaster* III. iv. 74 Please you to be acceptive ..Yes sir, feare not; I shall accept. **1609** —— *Case is Alt.* II. vii. 76 The people generally are very acceptive, and apt to applaud any meritable work. **1653** BROME *City Wit* IV. iii. 350 *Jo.* Received they my Jewells? *Cra.* Yes, they prov'd acceptive. **1883** W. WHITMAN *Specimen Days* 84 Returning to the naked source-life of us all—to the breast of the great silent savage all-acceptive Mother. **1920** *Edin. Rev.* Jan. 46 Reverently acceptive of every Victorian formula.

Hence **accep'tivity**, the quality or condition of being acceptive.

1920 E. & C. PAUL tr. *Baudouin's Suggestion & Auto-suggestion* Gloss., *Acceptivity*, the readiness with which the subconscious accepts an idea.

acceptor (æk'sɛptə(r), -ˌtɔː(r)). Also 4-6 acceptour. [a. Anglo-Fr. *acceptour*, ad. L. *acceptōr-em* n. of agent, f. *accept-* ppl. stem of *accipĕre* to receive; see ACCEPT. This is the older form of the word, found in Wyclif, afterwards replaced by or refashioned as ACCEPTER; in recent times it has been restored in a special sense, and is sometimes also, after the L., used in the general sense.]

1. One who accepts; = ACCEPTER.

1382 WYCLIF *Acts* x. 34 For god is not acceptour of persones. **1865** *Athenæum* No. 1979. 434/1 The interpretation..has found innumerable acceptors.

2. He who accepts a bill of exchange, or formally undertakes its payment when due.

1776 A. SMITH *Wealth of Nat.* I. II. ii. 309 If, when the bill becomes due, the acceptor does not pay it. **1868** ROGERS *Pol. Econ.* (ed. 3) xi. 150 The Bill of Exchange..is an order written by the drawer and addressed to the acceptor.

3. An atom or molecule capable of receiving an electron and so combining with another atom or molecule; *spec.* in a semi-conducting material (see quot. 1950). Cf. DONOR 2.

1907 *Chem. Abstr.* 2342 It should be possible to substitute the anode of an electrolytic cell in place of the acceptor in an oxidation process. **1927** N. V. SIDGWICK *Electronic Theory of Valency* vii. 116 When a co-ordinate link is formed between two atoms, one of them gives the other a share in two of its own (previously unshared) electrons... We may call the atom which lends the two electrons..the *donor*, and the one which receives them..the *acceptor*. **1940** S. GLASSTONE *Text-Bk. Physical Chem.* (1941) i. 99 The terms donor and acceptor are often employed to describe the two atoms, or the molecules in which they are present, involved in a dative bond. **1949** *Physical Rev.* LXXV. 865/2 The ionization energy of donors is less than that of acceptors, probably because conduction electrons have a smaller effective mass than holes. **1950** W. SHOCKLEY *Electrons & Holes in Semi-conductors* (1951) i. 14 Impurities with a valence of five are called 'donor impurities' because they donate an excess electron to the crystal; those with a valence of three are called 'acceptor impurities', since they accept an electron from somewhere else in the crystal to complete the structure of the valence bonds with their neighbors, thus leaving a hole to conduct.

4. An apparatus designed to accept; also *attrib.*, as ***acceptor circuit***. Cf. REJECTOR.

1923 *Harmsworth's Wireless Encycl.* I. 9/2 Any circuit which comprises an inductance and capacity in series, which is in resonance with the frequency applied to it, is said to be an acceptor circuit for that frequency. **1931** *B.B.C. Year-Bk.* 435/1 *Acceptor Circuit*, a tuned oscillatory circuit, having the opposite characteristics of a rejector circuit. **1946** *Electronic Engin.* XVIII. 45 It is better to tune the acceptor well below 25 c/s.

†**ac'cerse**, *v. Obs. rare*$^{-1}$. [ad. L. *accers-ĕre* to summon; perh. only in loc. cit.] To summon.

1548 HALL *Chron. Edw. IV*, an. 10 (R.) The Erle of Warwicke..thereupon accersed and called together his army.

†**accer'sited**, *pa. pple. Obs. rare*$^{-1}$. [f. L. *accersīt-us*, pa. pple. of *accersĕre* to summon + -ED; perh. only used in loc. cit.] Summoned, sent for.

1548 HALL *Chron.* (1809) 475 Your realme to the whiche you be..by your people accercited & vocated unto.

access ('æksɪs, æk'sɛs), *sb.* Forms: 4 **acces**; 4-7 **accesse**; 5- **access**; and in the special sense IV: 4 **axcesse, axcess**; 5 **axces, axesse, axez, aksis**; 5-6 **axes, axis**; 6 **axys, acceys.** [In sense IV, the earliest in Eng., a. Fr. *accès*, OFr. *aces, aceis*:—L. *accēss-us*, a coming unto, vbl. sb. f. *accēd-ĕre* to come to: see ACCEDE *v.* In this sense the word soon received the Eng. accent '*access*, whence the spellings *axes, axis*, etc., above. In its more general senses app. taken direct from L. *accēss-us* chiefly after 1500, and retaining the pronunc. *ac'cess* in all the poets of 6-8; but '*access* is given by Sheridan 1789, rejected by Smart 1857, used by Tennyson 1864, and is now apparently the more usual, as more distinct from *ex'cess*. Cf. *re'cess, suc'cess*; '*abscess*, '*process*. Like variety of usage prevails as to *access-ary, -ory*, and their derivatives, though in these it is more common to accent the first syllable.]

I. Coming to or towards; approaching.

†**1.** The action of going or coming to or into; coming into the presence of, or into contact with; approach, entrance. (Const. *into, unto, to.*) *Obs.*

1528 GARDINER in Pocock *Rec. Ref.* I. xlvii. 90 How to use and order ourself at our access to the pope's presence. **1682** GREW *Anat. Plants* 10 Lest its new access into the ayr should shrivel it. **1699** GARTH *Dispensary* I. (1706) 2 The Goddess ..shuns the great access of vulgar eyes. **1718** POPE *Iliad* XIV. 195 Safe from access of each intruding power. **1721** STRYPE *Eccl. Mem.* I. 138 He kept an honourable post here: and had great access of gentlemen to him.

2. a. The habit or power of getting near or into contact with; entrance, admittance, admission (*to* the presence or use of). Also *attrib.*, as ***access-time***, the time taken to reach 'information' stored in a computer.

1382 WYCLIF *Rom.* v. 2 By whom we han accesse, or nyȝ goynge to. **1534** *Polyd. Verg., Eng. Hist.* (1846) I. 23 Thus crowse have free accesse to these highe trees. **1579** GOSSON *Sch. of Abuse* (Arb.) 39 How many times hath access to Theaters beene restrayned. **1600** SHAKS. *A. Y. L.* I. i. 98 He is heere at the doore, and importunes accesse to you. **1772-84** COOK *Voyages* (1790) IV. 1192 These voyages have facilitated the access of ships into the Pacific Ocean. **1864** TENNYSON *Aylm. F.* 503 Those at home..Then closed her access to the wealthier farms. **1876** FREEMAN *Norm. Conq.* II. viii. 180 Some office which..gave him close access to the person of his princely nephew. **1879** LUBBOCK *Sc. Lect.* xi. 39 This prevents the access of ants and other small creeping insects. **1950** W. W. STIFLER *High-Speed Computing Devices* xiv. 304 We define the access time of a system as the time required to withdraw a number from storage. **1960** E. DELAVENAY *Introd. Machine Trans.* ii. 20 Access to data..is very rapid, the average access time being of the order of a few millionths of a second.

b. *Broadcasting.* The practice of giving broadcasting time to individuals and groups who wish to present programmes of their own devising, free of management by the broadcasting organization. Usu. *attrib.* Cf. *public-access* s.v. PUBLIC *a.* 5 g.

[**1972** *Times* 12 Feb. 2/4 Broadcasting organizations should operate under some system of workers' self-management or industrial democracy, should be free from government control, and should provide regular access for individuals and groups to express specialist and minority views, according to Mr Anthony Wedgwood Benn.] **1972** *Ibid.* 14 July 16/6 Recently David Attenborough, controller of BBC TV programmes asked Rowan Ayres, who runs [*Late Night*] *Line-Up* to explore the possibilities of 'access television'..where groups can use air time on their own terms. **1973** *Ibid.* 22 Sept. 14/4 Where will Access end? It is unlikely that..professional broadcasters will be ousted from their seats by amateurs. **1977** *Rep. Comm. Future of Broadcasting* 24 in *Parl. Papers* 1976-7 (Cmnd. 6753) VI.1 Working a 24 hour-a-day 7 day a week access channel, Government would be able to offer every adult a second a year. **1983** *Listener* 10 Feb. 11/1 Radios 4, 3 and 2..could be extended through a much greater use of access radio: allow individuals to have more control in the making and compiling of programmes.

3. The state or faculty of being approached; accessibility.

c **1425** WYNTOUN *Cron.* v. iii. 21 He gret repayre amang þaim mád; Be sic access he kend wele. **1559** *Myrroure for Mag.* (ed. 2) xiii. 1 Disdayne not prynces easye accesse. **1662** GERBIER *Princ.* 13 The Staires..are..of so easie an Accesse, as that Travellers do ascend them on Horse-back. **1791** BOSWELL *Johnson* (1816) I. 244 He insisted on Lord Chesterfield's general affability and easiness of access. **1870** YEATS *Nat. Hist. Comm.* 89 Markets are so difficult of access, that much wealth is wasted.

4. The action of coming towards, coming, approach, advance. Contrasted with *recess*.

1610 HEALEY *Aug. City of God* (1620) v. vi. 193 We see the alteration of the year by the Sunnes accesse and departure. **1695** WOODWARD *Nat. Hist. of Earth* (1723) VI. 279 The Sea, by this Access and Recess, shuffling the empty Shells. **1843** J. MARTINEAU *Endeav. after Chr. Life* (1876) 506 The Rainbow interpreted by the prism..painting the access and recess of his thought.

†**5.** A coming to work or business, an assembling or meeting of a body. The *access* and *recess* of Parliament. *Obs.*

1587 FLEMING *Contn. Holinshed* III. 1584/1 A briefe report of the second accesse..and of the answer made in the name of the lords of the parlement. **1647** MAY *Hist. Parl.* II. i. 3 Before the Accesse and meeting again of the Parliament.

†**6.** A coming to office, dignity, or sovereignty; arrival at the throne; = ACCESSION 3. *Obs.*

1641 CHARLES I *Let. to Judges* 5 July 3 Our Accesse to the Crowne. **1650** J. HALL *Paradoxes* 25 Many Princes have sweetened and disguised the memory of their accesse to Government. **1759** MARTIN *Nat. Hist.* I. 247 Their first Access to their Dignity.

II. A way or means of approach.

7. a. An entrance, channel, passage, or doorway. Also *attrib.*

1642 HOWELL *For. Trav.* 14 They..have not those obvious accesses and contiguity of situation. **1670** MILTON *Hist. Brit.* II. Wks. 1847, 484 The Accesses of the Island were wondrously fortify'd. **1725** POPE *Odyssey* VIII. 51 Now all accesses to the dome are fill'd. **1831** SCOTT *Anne of Gei.* ii. 25 If there be actually such a pass, there must be an access to it somewhere. **1943** J. S. HUXLEY *TVA* 78 (*caption*) Access Road. **1959** JOHN, DUKE OF BEDFORD *Silver-Plated Spoon* x. 202 The new access roads were nearly ready. **1962** *Listener* 10 May 800/2 The East German regime's agreement was needed for use of the access routes to the city. *Ibid.* 24 May 902/1 The motor vehicle is demanding completely novel arrangements of buildings and access ways.

b. *fig.*

1605 BACON *Adv. Learn.* (1640) Pref. 17 We doe heere, in the Accesse to this work, Poure forth humblest and most ardent supplications to God. **1720** ROWE *Amb. Step-Mother* Prol. 7 The Poet does his Art employ, The soft Accesses of your Souls to try. **1878** R. W. DALE *On Preaching* vii. 216 We ought to try..every possible access to the conscience.

III. A coming as an addition.

8. The coming of anything as an addition; adherence, addition, increase, growth. Now almost obs. and replaced by ACCESSION.

1576 LAMBARDE *Peramb. Kent* (1826) 272 The death of this one man [Becket]..brought thereunto more accesse of estimation and reverence. **1610** GWILLIM *Displ. Herald.* (1660) III. xxvi. 258 They had in them neither accesse nor defect. **1667** MILTON *P.L.* IX. 310, I from the influence of thy looks receive Access in every virtue. **1728** NEWTON *Chronol. Amended* 10 The Philistims, strengthned by the access of the Shepherds, conquer Israel. **1869** PHILLIPS *Vesuv.* ix. 261 The liquid mass of rock is always ready to be poured out upon the access of adequate pressure. **1881** BROADHOUSE *Mus. Acoustics* 270 Their varying rates bring about, at regular intervals, an access of tone, which the crests of the waves correspond, and a diminution of tone when the crest of one coincides with the trough of the other.

IV. A coming on or attack of illness, anger, etc.

9. A coming on of illness or disease, especially of sudden illness; an attack or fit.

c **1325** *E.E. Allit. Poems* C. 325 Þacces of anguych watȝ hid in my sawle. **1423** JAMES I *King's Quair* II. xlviii, Bot tho began myn axis and turment. *a* **1597** '*Chaucer's Dreme*' Wks. 1855, 56 The peyne, and the plesaunce, Which was to me axes and hele. **1656** RIDGLEY *Pract. Phys.* 139 Let meat be given at the time of the least accesse. **1678** BUTLER *Hudibras* III. ii. 822 Relapses make Diseases More desp'rate than their first Accesses. **1748** HARTLEY *Observ. on Man* I. i. §1. 7. 55 In the Access of most Fevers the Patient is listless & sleepy. **1821** G. TICKNOR *Life, Lett. & Journ.* I. xvii. 334 He had had an access of paralysis the afternoon previous. **1862** TRENCH *Miracles* xxvii. 368 These accesses of his disorder might come upon him at any moment.

†**10.** *spec.* An ague fit; ague, intermitting fever. *Obs.*

c **1374** CHAUCER *Troylus* II. 1316 A charme..The whiche can helen the of thyn accesse. **1398** TREVISA *Barth. De P.R.* (1495) VII. xxxviii. 252 Fyrste the cold and therafter the heete and euery daye axes, yet worse, for some daye comith double axes. **1459** *Paston Lett.* 970 III. 426, I was falle seek with an axeȝ. **1475** AUDELAY *Poems* 47 A seke man, That is y-schakyd and schent with the aksis. **1493** *Petronylla* 45 And Petronilla quaketh in hir accesse. *a* **1500** *Lancelot of the Laik* (1865) 2 So be the morow set I was a-fyre In felinge of the access hot and colde. **1527** L. ANDREW tr. *Brunswyke's Distyll. Waters* A ij, The same water..is good for the dayly axces or febres. **1751** CHAMBERS *Cycl.* s.v. *Ague*, The cure [of Ague] is usually begun with an emetic of ipecacuanha, an hour before the access.

11. *fig.* An outburst; a sudden fit of anger or other passion. (Modern, after Fr. *accès*.)

1781 J. MOORE *Italy* (1790) II. lxi. 214 These accesses and intervals [of thunder and explosion] continued with varied force. **1815** SOUTHEY in *Q. Rev.* XIII. 10 In a fresh access of jealousy, [he] plunged a dagger into her heart. **1878** BOSW. SMITH *Carthage* 56 He gave him [his brother] over, in an access of sublime patriotism, to the death he had deserved.

¶ **access** is frequently found written for EXCESS *sb.*, chiefly by phonetic confusion; but the senses also approach in 8 above; see quot. of date 1610.

access ('æksɛs), *v.* [f. the sb. or (in sense 2) back-formation from ACCESSION *v.*] **1.** *trans.* **a.** To gain access to (data, etc., held in a computer or computer-based system, or the system itself).

1962 A. M. ANGEL in M. C. Yovits *Large-Capacity Memory Techniques for Computing Systems* 150 Through a system of binary-coded addresses notched into each card, a particular card may be accessed for read and write operations. **1965** *New Scientist* 27 May 585/2 Each user, and each user's programme, must be restricted so that he and it can never 'access' (read, write, or execute) unauthorized portions of the high-speed store. **1971** J. B. CARROLL et al. *Word Frequency Bk.* p. xix, The citation records are accessed by a citation-select control deck. **1977** *Sci. Amer.* May 90/1

(Advt.), Design engineers can now access the computer directly through terminals in their offices. **1983** *Times* 8 Jan. 13/6 The library's statistical section uses its Polis terminal to access various statistical databases. **1983** R. ALLASON *Branch* xii. 168 By accessing the information relating to a person's contributions it is possible to learn his place of work.

b. *gen.*

1978 *Verbatim* Feb. 1/2 The University of California at Berkeley.. announces the hours during which its business office 'may be accessed'. **1986** *Daily Tel.* 5 Feb. 11 It is these markets that Sikorsky want to access through their 'Trojan Horse' tactics.

2. = ACCESSION *v. rare.*

1975 *Language for Life* (Dept. Educ. & Sci.) xv. 232 There is the handling of existing or purchased material: ordering, receiving, accessing, issuing, stock-checking, and progress-chasing. **1978** *Times Lit. Suppl.* 1 Dec. 1392/2 That awful day the Assistant Keeper had flu, the central heating leaked, and the Lowestoft Hoard had to be accessed.

accessarily (ˈæksɪsərɪlɪ, ækˈsɛsərɪlɪ), *adv.* [f. ACCESSARY *a.* + -LY².] After the manner of an accessary; also (less correctly) for ACCESSORILY.

1623 MINSHEU, *Accessoriaménte*, accessarily, consentingly.

accessariness (ˈæksɪsərɪnɪs, ækˈsɛsərɪnɪs). [f. ACCESSARY *a.* + -NESS.] The state or quality of being accessary; concurrence, privity.

1654 GAYTON *Festiv. Notes* II. vi. 60 Shee.. doth vindicate all refractory damosels, from the least accessarinesse or lyablenesse of guilt from the ends (violent or melancholy) of their puling.. Servants. **1667** *Decay of Chr. Piety* xix. §18. 370 Perhaps this consideration will draw us.. into the guilt of a negative accessariness to the present mischiefs.

accessary (ˈæksɪsərɪ, ækˈsɛsərɪ), *sb.* and *a.* [f. ACCESS *sb.* + -ARY, as if ad. L. **accēssāri-us*, an analogical formation on *accēssus*, cf. *emissary*, *commissary*, *adversary*, *notary*. The sb. is etymologically *accessary* and the adj. *accessory*, cf. emiss*ary* sb., promiss*ory* adj., but as the adj. was first taken directly from the sb. it was naturally spelt *accessary*. Being afterwards 'rectified' by scholars to *accessory*, after the L. *accessōrius*, it drew the noun after it, so that this also is now often spelt ACCESSORY. In the legal sense the word is commonly *accessary* (though Blackstone wrote *accessory*), and Webster recommends that it be so preserved, and spelt *accessory* in other senses. But as it is often used of things *fig.* from the legal sense, as in *accessary* and *principal*, it is doubtful if the distinction is practicable. The historical and etymological pronunc. is ˈ*accessary*, but *ac*ˈ*cessary* (cf. *inter*ˈ*cessory*) is also in use. So with its derivatives.]

A. *sb.*

1. One who accedes, or gives his accession (formerly *access*) to any act or undertaking; an adherent, assistant, or helper. In *Law*: 'He who is not the chief actor in the offence, nor present at its performance, but in some way concerned therein, either before or after the fact committed.' 1768 Blackstone *Comment.* IV. 35.

1480 CAXTON *Chron. Eng.* (1520) VII. 157 b/1 To take and brynge hym and his accessaryes to the kynge. **1594** NASHE *Unfort. Trav.* 40 To prison was I sent as principal, and my master as accessarie. **1660** H. FINCH *Regicides* (1679) 158 He knows very well there are no accessaries in Treason. **1859** MILL *Liberty* iv. 129 The moral anomaly of punishing the accessary.

2. Of things. (Partly *fig.* from the last, partly from ACCESSORY *a.*) Anything assisting or contributory; anything subordinate; an adjunct, or accompaniment. (See ACCESSORY, B. 1.)

1534 LD. BERNERS *Gold. Bk. of M. Aurel.* (1546) Hh. ij, The auctoritie of his office.. ought to be his accessarie, and his good lyfe for principall. **1699** BENTLEY *Phalaris* 424 It shews no great reverence to those Sacred Writings, to bring them, though it be but as Accessaries, into Farce and Ridicule. **1850** MRS. JAMESON *Sacred & Leg. Art* 355 The attention.. is distracted by the accessaries.

B. *adj.*

1. Of persons: Acceding or adhering *to*; assisting as a subordinate. In *Law*: Participating or sharing in a crime, though not the chief actor; participant, privy.

1594 SHAKS. *Rich. III*, I. ii. 192 To both their deaths shalt thou be accessary. **1698** DRYDEN *Æneid* IV. 543 A God's command he pleads, And makes Heav'n accessary to his Deeds. **1741** RICHARDSON *Pamela* (1824) I. xix. 30 Don't imagine that I would be accessary to your ruin for the world. **1827** HALLAM *Const. Hist.* (1876) I. i. 31 Both houses of parliament were commonly made accessary to the legal murders of this [Henry VIII's] reign.

†**2.** Of things: Subordinate, additional, accompanying, non-essential, adventitious; = ACCESSORY, A. 1 (which is now alone used in this sense). *Obs.*

1552–5 LATIMER *Serm. & Rem.* (1845) 37 Hawking and hunting is but an accessary thing. **1661** BRAMHALL *Just Vind.* iii. 38 Foundations which were good in their original institution ought not to be destroyed for accessary abuses. **1691** *Case of Exeter Coll.* 29 The Oath being accessary to the Statutes.

accessibility (æk,sɛsɪˈbɪlɪtɪ). [f. ACCESSIBLE + -ITY. Cf. Fr. *accessibilité* also quite modern.] The quality of being accessible, or of admitting approach. *fig.* Openness to influence.

[WEBSTER cites LANGHORNE 1766–1802. Not in CRAIG 1847; In WORCESTER 1859.] **1810** COLERIDGE *Friend* (1865) 362 Accessibility to the sentiments of others.. often accompanies feeble minds. **1842** MRS. BROWNING *Grk. Chr. Poets* (1863) 10 The greater accessibility of Latin literature. **1850** MERIVALE *Hist. Rom. Emp.* IV. xxxviii. 323 The accessibility of Italy upon this side.. was at all times a matter of anxiety to her rulers. **1865** M. ARNOLD *Ess. in Crit.* (1875) v. 190 The French.. have shown more accessibility to ideas than any other people.

accessible (ækˈsɛsɪb(ə)l), *a.* [a. Fr. *accessible* (in Cotgr.), ad. L. *accēssibil-em*, vbl. adj. f. *accēss-* ppl. stem of *accēd-ĕre*; see ACCEDE *v.* and -BLE.]

1. Capable of being used as an access; affording entrance; open, practicable. Const. *to.*

1610 SHAKS. *Cymb.* III. ii. 84 Accessible is none but Milford way. **1667** MILTON *P.L.* IV. 546 With one ascent Accessible from Earth. **1835** J. HARRIS *Gt. Teacher* (1837) 347 All the paths of human ambition were open and accessible to him.

2. a. Capable of being entered or reached; easy of access; such as one can go to, come into the presence of, reach, or lay hold of; get-at-able. Const. *to.*

1642 HOWELL *For. Trav.* 45 She [Spain] hath bold accessible coasts. **1670** G. H., *Hist. Cardinals* II. ii. 149 He is accessible enough, but not too liberal to the poor. **1776** GIBBON *Decl. & Fall* I. xix. 537 The town was accessible only by two wooden bridges. **1850** MERIVALE *Hist. Rom. Emp.* (1871) V. xli. 89 The ear of the public was accessible perhaps by no other means. **1855** PRESCOTT *Philip II*, I. I. iv. 52 He was.. as accessible as any one could desire, and gave patient audience to all who asked it. **1861** MAY *Const. Hist. Eng.* (1863) I. i. 44 Evidence, not accessible to contemporaries, has since made his statement indisputable.

b. *fig.* Accessible *to*: open to the influence of.

1818 SCOTT *Hrt. of Midl.* 185 He had shewn himself in a certain degree accessible to touches of humanity. **1881** *Rep. of Elect. Comm.* in *Daily Tel.* 31 Jan. 500 or 600 [voters] are at all times accessible to bribery.

c. Able to be (readily) understood or appreciated. Freq. applied to academic or creative work.

1961 *Athene* Autumn 6/2 Serious art is not easily accessible to the untutored. **1968** *Listener* 29 Feb. 280/2 Shostakovich's music since 1938.. being a good deal more emotionally accessible than his early work. **1980** *Amer. Speech* LV. 37 All three terms are semantically accessible and productive in the speech of the areas where they occur. **1984** *N.Y. Times* 8 July x. 9/1 At the Science Center almost every exhibit demands action and the sometimes-forbidding world of science becomes accessible.

Hence **ac'cessibly** *adv.*

1889 in *Cent. Dict.* **1909** in WEBSTER. **1978** *Nature* 27 Apr. 776/1 Those familiar with eighteenth-century Scottish verse or, more accessibly, with the Oxford English Dictionary, will know that a tappit hen can be either a chicken with a crest on its head or a jug. **1984** *Financial Times* 12 June IV. p. xiii, The council has 30 offices scattered accessibly throughout the shires.

ac'cessibleness. [f. ACCESSIBLE *a.*] Accessibility.

1829 *Examiner* 13 Dec. 793/1 The security against oppression, which his accessibleness gives to his subjects. **1845** J. B. MOZLEY *Essays* (1878) I. 203 His accessibleness, affability, openness, and all those features of the genuine public character. **1857** W. R. ALGER *Genius of America* 15 This.. universal accessibleness of honors.

ac'cession (ækˈsɛʃən). [a. Fr. *accession* (14th c. in Godef.), ad. L. *accēssiōn-em* a going to, joining, increase, n. of action f. *accēdĕre*, *accēssum*: see ACCEDE *v.* It has partly occupied the ground of the earlier ACCESS.] Generally, the action of going to, joining oneself to, and its result. Hence,

I. A coming to.

1. The action of coming near, approach; a coming into the presence of any one, or into contact with any thing; admittance, admission; = ACCESS 1.

1652 GAULE *Mag-astro-mancer* 160 The rationall creatures are the more noble in themselves, and of more neer accession to the divine similitude. **1655** FULLER *Ch. Hist.* IX. 100 There is moreover granted leave of accession unto him. **1677** HALE *Prim. Orig. Man.* 19 Now there may be many things in Nature unto which we can have neither of these accessions of Sense. **1691** RAY *Creation* (1714) 198 For want of Accession of the Sun. **1812** SIR H. DAVY *Chem. Philos.* 395 Two of the oxides of lead may be formed by heat, with accession of air. **1853** KANE *Grinnell Exped.* (1856) xxxv. 312 It might be supposed.. that the accession of solar light would be accompanied by increase of temperature.

†**2.** The action of coming to (a point) by forward or onward motion; advance, coming, arrival. *Obs.*

1646 SIR T. BROWNE *Pseud. Ep.* 57 Not varying at all by the accession of bodyes upon, or secession thereof, from its surface. **1655–60** T. STANLEY *Hist. Philos.* (1701) 9/2 He first found out the accession of the Sun from Tropick to Tropick. **1656** tr. *Hobbes, Elem. Philos.* (1839) 471 Now this expansion of the air upon the superficies of the earth, from east to west, doth, by reason of the sun's perpetual accession to the places which are successively under it, make it cold at the time of the sun's rising and setting.

3. The act of coming or attaining to a dignity, office, or position of honour, *esp.* the throne.

1769 BURKE *State of Nation* Wks. II. 15 That the only good minister.. since his Majesty's accession, is the Earl of Bute. **1876** FREEMAN *Norm. Conq.* I. iv. 232 Hugh, on his accession to manhood, did homage to the King.

II. A coming to as an addition.

4. The act of coming to so as to join, or of joining oneself to; joining, addition.

1633 T. ADAMS *Comm. 2 Pet.* i. 6 (1865) 79 Necessary therefore is the accession of piety to patience. **1675** BARCLAY *Apol. for Quakers* xiv. §4. 498 The Church can be no ways bettered by the Accession of Hypocrites. **1876** FREEMAN *Norm. Conq.* I. v. 356 England had gained greatly by the accession of the valiant Thurkhill.

5. The act of acceding or agreeing to an opinion, plan, or proceeding; adherence, assent.

1603–5 SIR J. MELVIL *Mem.* (1735) 130 The King repented himself of his Accession to that affair. **1794** S. WILLIAMS *Hist. Vermont* 283 Declaring their acquiescence in, and accession to the determination made by Congress. **1828** SCOTT *F.M. Perth* II. 251 The Prince had no accession to this second aggression upon the citizens of Perth.

b. *Deed of Accession*, in Scotch Law, a deed by the creditors of a bankrupt, by which they accede to a trust executed by their debtor for the general behoof, and bind themselves to concur in the arrangement.

6. a. That which adds itself, or is added to anything; that whereby it is increased; addition, augmentation, increase. Applied also to persons.

1588 LAMBARDE *Eirenarcha* I. ix. 47 The forme of this Commission hath varied with the time, and received sundrie accessions. **1592** W. WEST *Symbolæogr.* B iiij. 37 A, Accessions.. to contracts be these things which be required beside the principall things themselves. **1692** WASHINGTON tr. *Milton, Def. Pop.* (1851) v. 139 And Egypt became an Accession to the kingdom of Ethiopia. **1778** JOHNSON in *Boswell* III. 159 Mr. Banks desires to be admitted [to the club]; he will be a very honourable accession. **1798** WELLESLEY *Desp.* 25 He has not yet obtained any formidable accession of strength from his alliance with France. **1838** HALLAM *Hist. Lit.* I. Pref. 10 This volume.. is a very convenient accession to any scholar's library. **1855** PRESCOTT *Philip II*, I. IV. ii. 409 Every year the fraternity received fresh accessions of princes and nobles.

b. *attrib.*; **accession(s book**, a book in which are entered the accessions to a library: so ***accessions list***; ***accession number***, ***stamp***. Hence **ac'cession** *v. trans.*, to enter in the accessions register of a library (orig. *U.S.*); so **ac'cessioning** *vbl. sb.*

1876 W. F. POOLE in *Publ. Libr. U.S.* I. 489 The books must then be entered in the 'accession catalogue'. *Ibid.*, Every work entered has its accession number. **1877** *Library Jrnl.* May 316/1 The accession-book properly kept up is the librarian's official indicator for his whole collection. **1882** Accessions-List 3 Chief older works [Bodl., L.P. Access. lists b. 5]. **1892** G. M. JONES *Salem* (Mass.) *Public Library Rep.* 9 The new books have been promptly accessioned. **1896** *Library Jrnl.* Dec. 129/2 Accessioning, classifying, and cataloguing. **1900** *Library* 1 Mar. 153 The Mitchell Library. Rough Accessions Book. *Ibid.* 154 The books are stamped with an 'accession stamp' on the back of the title-page. **1920** W. C. B. SAYERS *Brown's Man. Libr. Econ.* xxxv. 479 Accessioning is done the ordinary way. **1928** *Armstrong Coll. Rep. 1927–8* 73, 5,000 volumes and 3,050 pamphlets have been classified and accessioned but not fully catalogued. **1961** T. LANDAU *Encycl. Librarianship* (ed. 2) 2/1 The accession number also serves to link the book with the catalogue (or shelf register) and the charging system, and distinguishes between copies of a book when there is more than one.

7. *Law.* Addition to property by natural growth or artificial improvement; which becomes the property of the owner of that which receives the addition, who is said to acquire the proprietorship thereof by Accession.

1768 BLACKSTONE *Comm.* II. 404 The doctrine of property arising from accession is also grounded on the right of occupancy. **1832** J. AUSTIN *Jurispr.* (1879) II. liv. 904 The acquisition of 'jus in rem' by accession.. as land washed away and joined to one's own land, or the fruits of one's own land. **1847** CRAIG, s.v. Artificial accession is that addition which is the result of human industry, called likewise industrial accession, as trees planted, or a house built on the property of another, which belongs to the proprietor of the ground, and not to the planter or builder.

†**III.** A coming on or invasion of disease; an attack, fit, or paroxysm; also a visitation, or fit of folly, etc. = ACCESS 9. *Obs.*

1655 H. VAUGHAN *Silex Scint.* I. 105 Pills that change Thy sick Accessions into setled health. **1771** SMOLLETT *Humphry Cl.* (1815) 162 Some of our family have had very uncommon accessions.. [and] sometimes speak as if they were really inspired. **1827** SOUTHEY *Lett.* (1856) IV. 54 Those accessions of folly to which men are sometimes subject.

accessional (ækˈsɛʃənəl), *a.* [f. prec. + -AL¹.] Pertaining to or due to accession; of the nature of an increase, additional, accessory.

1646 SIR T. BROWNE *Pseud. Ep.* 196 This accessionall preponderancy is rather in appearance then reality. **1784** J. BARRY *Lect. on Art* (1848) v. 187 Almost all compositions afford these accessional advantages. **1805** FOSTER *Ess.* IV. viii. 253 You will find various accessional suggestions.

‖**accessit** (ækˈsɛsɪt). [L. *accessit*, 3 sing. pa. t. of *accēdĕre* to approach.] **1.** With reference to French examinations: = PROXIME ACCESSIT.

1884 *Harper's Mag.* Mar. 597/2 In the competition for the.. prize medal.. he gained the *accessit.* **1898** *Daily News* 20 Jan. 8/5 He became a student at the Paris Conservatoire, where, however, he did not take very high honours, gaining only a second accessit in comic opera.

2. A secondary vote given in the election of a Pope: see quots.

1877 *Encycl. Brit.* VI. 240/1 After each scrutiny an 'accessit' takes place; i.e.,..it is open to every voter to declare that he 'accedes' to such or such a candidate. **1882** SCHAFF *Relig. Encycl.* I. 521 Every morning a ballot is cast, followed in the evening by an 'accessit'.

†**accessive** (æk'sɛsɪv), *a. Obs.* [a. Fr. *accessif, -ive*; ad. late L. *accēssīv-us*, f. *accēssus*; see ACCESS, and -IVE.]

1. Pertaining to access or approach; seeking to approach, pressing in, aggressive. *rare.*

[**1611** FLORIO has the adv. in this sense: see ACCESSIVELY.] **1641** SIR R. NAUNTON *Fragm. Reg.* in *Phenix* VII. I. 206 My Lord of Essex..then grew accessive in the appetite of her favour.

2. Fitted for, or capable of, access; accessible.

1609 HEYWOOD *Brytaine's Troy* VI. x. 137, I haue stopt up each Accessive way. **1611** COTGR., *Accessif,* Accessible, accessiue, easie to come vnto.

¶ **accessive** also by confusion for EXCESSIVE.

†**ac'cessively,** *adv. Obs.* [f. prec. + -LY².] In an accessive manner; pressingly, aggressively.

1611 FLORIO, *Accessoriaménte,* accessiuelie, by his own seeking.

accessless (æk'sɛslɪs), *a. poet.* [f. ACCESS + -LESS.] Without access; inaccessible.

1615 CHAPMAN *Odyss.* VII. 387 A ruthless billow smit Against huge rocks, and an accessless shore, My mangl'd body. *a* **1750** AARON HILL *Works* (1753) IV. 296 Th' accessless wilds Of bleak-brow'd mountains. **1852** *Fraser's Mag.* XLV. 452 The corpse of him most dear to me is left, To rot, unwashed, amid accessless rocks.

accessor, Sc. form of ACCESSORY, B.

accessorial (æksɪ'səʊrɪəl), *a.* [f. L. *accessōrius,* see ACCESSORY + -AL¹.] Of the nature of an accessory or accompaniment; associated in a secondary yet useful manner; auxiliary, supplementary.

1726 AYLIFFE *Parergon* 490 A sentence pray'd or mov'd for..on Accessorial matters..may be uncertain. **1860** WHITESIDE *Italy in 19th Cent.* xli. 431 Lastly, there are accessorial punishments. The pillory, public acknowledgment of guilt, etc.

accessorily ('æksɪsərɪlɪ, æk'sɛsərɪlɪ), *adv.* [f. ACCESSORY *a.* + -LY².] In an accessory or supplementary manner, additionally; also (less correctly) for ACCESSARILY.

c **1400** *Apol. for Lollards* 22 Neþeles it is not to deme þat ne it is leful to curse accessorily. [**1755** In JOHNSON, etc.]

accessoriness. [f. ACCESSORY *a.* + -NESS.] The quality of being accessory; secondary character, subordinate association. Sometimes used less correctly for ACCESSARINESS.

a **1655** VINES *Lord's Sup.* (1677) 386 Allowance & content defiles by accessoriness unto the sin. **1668** WILKINS *Real Char.* 35 Relations of quality at large..4. *Accessoriness,* Abet, adherent, second, Companion.

accessorize (æk'sɛsəraɪz), *v.* orig. *U.S.* [f. ACCESSORY *sb.* + -IZE.] *trans.* To provide or furnish with an accessory or accessories. Also *intr.* So **ac'cessorizing** *vbl. sb.* (Chiefly in *Advertising.*)

1939 *Amer. Speech* XIV. 316 A hankie to accessorize a costume. **1947** in *Amer. Speech* (1948) XXIII. 69/1 A sign I saw in [a] show-window in Connecticut avenue: Our staff is especially trained to accessorize your home. **1951** *Word Study* Oct. 3/1 Advertising men love to invent words, as in this piece: '..It is a flattering color to almost every man and the easiest to *accessorize*.' **1958** *Vogue* Apr. 142 Cotton in town needs strict accessorizing to avoid any hint of a holiday look. **1961** *Sunday Times* 29 Oct. 37/3 Do accessorise simply, pick plain colours for bag and shoes.

accessory ('æksɪsərɪ, æk'sɛsərɪ), *a.* and *sb.* [ad. late L. *accēssōri-us* adj., f. *accēssōr,* agent noun f. *accēd-ĕre*; see ACCEDE *v.*, and -ORY.] For the variant pronunciations, of which '*accessory* is historical and etymological (cf. '*promissory*), see ACCESSARY.

A. *adj.*

1. a. Of things: Coming as an accession; contributing in an additional and hence subordinate degree; additional, extra, adventitious. spec. *accessory (food) factor.*

1618 BOLTON *Florus* II. ix. 122 The Iles in that Sea.. accessory members of the Ætolian Warre. **1726** AYLIFFE *Parergon* 21 A Principal obligation extinguishes an Accessory obligation if they do both concur in one and the same Person. **1842** A. GRAY *Struct. Bot.* (1880) iii. §2. 44 Accessory Buds. These are..multiplications of the regular axillary bud. **1872** HUXLEY *Physiol.* VI. 139 To distinguish the essential food-stuffs or proteids from the accessory food-stuffs or fats and amyloids. **1875** OUSELEY *Mus. Form* v. 38 Accessory passages may be added to either, or both, of the principal themes. **1912** F. G. HOPKINS in *Jrnl. Physiol.* XLIV. 425 (*title*) Feeding Experiments Illustrating the Importance of Accessory Factors in Normal Dietaries. **1919** *Lancet* 23 Aug. 338/1 The kind and degree of accessory factors in the common dietary. *Ibid.*, It would be interesting to discover whether they [*sc.* pickles] fill a gap also by supplying accessory food factors.

b. *accessory nerve,* the eleventh cranial nerve.

1842 DUNGLISON *Dict. Med. Sci.* (ed. 3) 15/2 Accessory ligament, muscle, nerve, &c. **1858** GRAY *Anatomy* 496 The Spinal Accessory Nerve consists of two parts. **1950** R.-M. S. HEFFNER *Gen. Phonetics* 41 The velum and uvula are controlled, in part at least, by fibers from the accessory, or eleventh cranial nerve.

c. *accessory chromosome* = *sex chromosome* (SEX *sb.*).

1902 C. E. MCCLUNG in *Biol. Bull.* III. 43 (*title*) The Accessory Chromosome—Sex Determinant? *Ibid.* 72 My conception of the function exercised by the accessory chromosome is that it is the bearer of..the faculty of producing sex cells.

2. Aiding in a crime, privy; = ACCESSARY B 1 (the better spelling in this sense).

1607 *Mis. Enforced Marriage* II. in Hazl. *Dodsl.* IX. 506 Thyself a murderer, thy wife accessory. **1751** SMOLLETT *Per. Pickle* (1779) II. xlvi. 86 We shall be accessory to the ruin of this enslaved people. **1818** SCOTT *Rob Roy* 121 He charged me with being accessory to the felony.

B. *sb.* [The Scotch form **accessor** is adopted directly from Fr. *accessoire*: *L'accessoire suit le principal.* Littré.]

1. An accessory thing; something contributing in a subordinate degree to a general result or effect; an adjunct, or accompaniment. *spec.* (in *pl.*): the smaller articles of (esp. a woman's) dress, as shoes, gloves, etc.; minor fittings or attachments for a motor-car, etc. Occas. in *sing.*

1549 *Compl. of Scot.* (1872) xiii. 112 ȝour particular veil is bot ane accessor of ȝour comont veil [= common weal] ande the accessor followis the natur of the prencipal. **1603** HOLLAND *Plutarch's Mor.* 70 All pleasures else, I Accessories call. **1726** AYLIFFE *Parergon* 21 If a Man sells a House, the Glass-Windows thereunto belonging are said to be sold as an Accessory. **1847** DICKENS *Haunted Man* (C.D. ed.) 222 Seasoning..is an accessory dreamily suggesting pork. **1859** GULLICK & TIMBS *Painting* 129 Accessories are those objects in a picture, auxiliary or accessorial to the general effect, but apart from the principal subject or figure. **1882** *Daily Tel.* 16 May 2 No mansion in Belgravia is better provided in all the accessories of luxurious ease. **1896** M. BEERBOHM *Dandies & Dandies* in *Wks.* 4 The many little golden chains..would have seemed vulgar to Mr. Brummell. For is it not to his fine scorn of accessories that we may trace that first aim of dandyism, the production of the supreme effect through means the least extravagant? **1902** [see *chicken-brooding,* CHICKEN *sb.*¹ 7]. **1958** *Woman's Own* 5 Nov. 10/1 She was wearing a pastel green suit with white accessories. **1961** *John O' London's* 23 Feb. 212/4 Writing about a woman's 'accessories' (gloves, handbag, umbrella, shoes). **1962** *Observer* 2 Dec. 31/1 *Most important accessories*..Heater..screen-washers..fog-lights..loose covers..cigar-lighter.

2. Of persons: = ACCESSARY A 1 (the more usual and better spelling in this sense).

1602 *Choose a Good Wife* V. iii. in Hazlitt's *Dodsley* IX. 93 For justifiers are all accessories, And accessories have deserv'd to die. **1667** MILTON *P.L.* X. 520 Transformed Alike, to serpents all, as accessories To his bold riot. **1726** AYLIFFE *Parergon* 21 A man that gives Aid, Counsel, or Assistance unto any Crime, is..an Accessory thereunto. **1855** MACAULAY *Hist. Eng.* IV. 288 But that he was an accessory after the fact no human being could doubt.

accessour, obs. form of ASSESSOR.

acceys, obs. form of ACCESS, attack, coming on (of disease).

1541 R. COPLAND *Galyen's Terapeutyke* 2 D i b, Vlceres that come to cycatryce, and open agayne shall be healed in the acceys and vlceracyon.

acchymosis, obs. form of ECCHYMOSIS.

‖**acciaccatura** (at,tʃakkə'tuːrə). *Mus.* [Italian, f. *acciaccāre* to crush, pound.] An ornament or 'grace' in Music, consisting of a small note (or two at a distance of not more than a minor third from each other) performed as quickly as possible before an essential note of a melody, the single small note (or first of the two) being a semitone below the essential note; a 'crush-note.'

1876 TROUTB. & DALE *Music Primer* 47 The *beat* is a short acciaccatura, consisting of its first note only, a semitone below any note to which it gives special force. The *twitch* is a short acciaccatura consisting of its latter note only.

accide, variant of ACCIDIE, *Obs.* sloth.

†'**accidence**¹. *Obs.* [a. Fr. *accidence,* ad. L. *accidentia* sb. chance; f. *accident-em,* pr. pple. of *accid-ĕre* to fall, happen: see -NCE.] Hap, mishap, chance; fortuitous circumstance.

1393 GOWER *Conf.* II. 153 And ofte of accidence..They ben corrupt by sondry way. **1513** DOUGLAS *Æneis* X. Prol. 23 Thy maist supreme indiuisibil substance..Rengand eterne, ressauis na accidence. **1604** DEKKER *King's Entert.* Wks. 1873 I. 300 Summon each Sence To tell the cause of this strange accidence. **1811** J. PINKERTON *Petralogy* Introd. 4 Petralogy..divided into twelve domains..six being distinguished by circumstances or accidences of various kinds.

accidence² ('æksɪdəns). [Apparently a corruption of *accidents* (ACCIDENT *sb.* 9), Fr. *accidens,* transl. L. *accidentia* pl. neut., but perhaps a direct formation on the latter treated as a sb. fem. See quot. dated 1751.]

1. That part of Grammar which treats of the Accidents or inflections of words; a book of the rudiments of grammar.

1509 HAWES *Past. Pleas.* (1845) V. ix. 23 Dame Gramer.. taught me ryght well Fyrst my Donet and then my accidence. **1598** SHAKS. *Merry Wives* IV. i. 16, I pray you aske him some questions in his Accidence. **1612** BRINSLEY *Lud. Lit.* (1627) iv. 40 Let us begin with the rudiments of the Grammar, I meane the Accedence. **1751** CHAMBERS *Cycl.*, *Accidence, Accidentia,* a name chiefly used for a little book, containing the first elements, or rudiments of the Latin tongue. **1840** DE QUINCEY *Style* Wks. XI. 198 With two or three exceptions..we have never seen the writer..who has not sometimes violated the accidence or the syntax of English grammar.

2. Hence, by extension: The rudiments or first principles of any subject.

1562 G. LEIGH (*title*) The Accedence of Armorie. **1664** BUTLER *Hudibras* II. ii. 221 Their Gospel is an Accidence By which they construe Conscience. **1870** LOWELL *Among my Books* Ser. II. (1873) 162 The poets who were just then learning the accidence of their art.

accidency ('æksɪdənsɪ). ? *Obs. rare*⁻¹. [ad. L. *accidentia* sb. chance: see ACCIDENCE, which represents the Fr. form of the same word, and -NCY.] A fortuitous circumstance or acquisition; a chance; a windfall.

1864 BURTON *Scot Abroad* II. ii. 202 That country, where quarters, accidencies and shifts are the greatest part of their subsistence.

accident ('æksɪdənt), *sb.* [a. Fr. *accident*:—L. *accidens, -ent-,* sb. properly pr. pple. of *accid-ĕre* to fall, to happen.] As in many other adopted words, the historical order in which the senses appear in Eng. does not correspond to their logical development, a fact still more noticeable in the derivatives.

I. Anything that happens.

1. †a. An occurrence, incident, event. *Obs.* b. Anything that happens without foresight or expectation; an unusual event, which proceeds from some unknown cause, or is an unusual effect of a known cause; a casualty, a contingency. ***the chapter of accidents***: the unforeseen course of events. c. *esp.* An unfortunate event, a disaster, a mishap.

c **1374** CHAUCER *Troylus* III. 918 This accident so petous was to here. **1483** CAXTON *Cato* k vi, By some accidentes and wantynges of nature thauncyent retournen and becomen as chyldren. **1571** Q. ELIZABETH in Ellis's *Orig. Lett.* II. 189. III. 1 You maie well gesse, by the accidentes of the time, whie I have not made anie answer. **1604** SHAKS. *Oth.* I. iii. 135 I spoke..Of mouing Accidents by Flood and Field. **1650** FULLER *Pisgah Sight* II. 63 The most memorable Accident in this place, was the Idolatry of the Israelites to Baal-peor. **1688** DRYDEN *Brit. Rediv.* 183 No future ills nor accidents appear, To sully and pollute the sacred infant's year. **1702** *Eng. Theophrastus* 230 The wisest councils may be discomposed by the smallest accidents. **1793** SMEATON *Edystone Lightho.* §117 In the progress of the work we should lie so widely open to accidents. **1824-8** LANDOR *Imag. Conv.* (1846) 453 Him I would call the powerful one, who..turns to good account the worst accidents of his fortune. **1871** H. LEE *Miss Barrington* I. xxi. 299 Leaving time to fight for them and putting their trust in the chapter of accidents. **1879** CARPENTER *Ment. Phys.* II. xii. 504 He was led to the discovery..by a series of happy accidents. **1882** *Daily News* 10 July 3/6 Serious railway accident: thirty persons injured. *Mod.* 'Insure your life against accidents.'

d. *colloq.* An accidental or untimely call of nature.

1899 *Allbutt's Syst. Med.* VIII. 244 The wearing of india-rubber urinals, and other means of avoiding 'accidents'. **1926** *Nation* 9 Jan. 517/2 Then a new child had, as Mabel calls it, 'an accident'. She may have been afraid of asking to go out. **1959** A. WESKER *Roots* II. i. 38 Jimmy Beales give him a real dowsin' down..'cause he had an accident.

e. A child conceived or born as a result of an unintended pregnancy; (an event which leads to) an unplanned pregnancy. Cf. MISTAKE *sb.* 1 d. *colloq.*

1932 D. L. SAYERS *Have his Carcase* xxv. 322 Jenny Moggeridge's Baby Charles what was a accident what Mrs Moggeridge was looking after. **1967** M. DRABBLE *Jerusalem the Golden* v. 110, I had two, and then Gabriel was an accident. **1978** F. WELDON *Praxis* xx. 173 'You could always have an accident,' observed Praxis, 'and simply find yourself pregnant.' **1986** *Sunday Tel.* 16 Mar. 10/6 A survey in Australia showed that working women had fewer accidents ..on the Pill.

2. *abstractly,* Chance, fortune. (By accident = Fr. *par accident* (14th c.), L. *per accidens.*)

1490 CAXTON *Eneydos* xxviii. 110 Hir deth naturalle oughte not to hauen comen yet of longe tyme, but by acydente and harde fortune. **1611** SHAKS. *Cymb.* v. v. 278 Consider Sir, the chance of Warre, the day Was yours by accident. **1756** C. LUCAS *On Waters* III. 141 The good or ill they do depend alike upon accident. **1788** JOHNSON *Lett.* I. cxiv. 239 Nature probably has some part in human characters and accident has some part. **1876** FREEMAN *Norm. Conq.* I. App. 628 William, whether by accident or by design, was not admitted.

†3. *Med.* An occurring symptom; *esp.* an unfavourable symptom. *Obs.*

1563 T. GALE *Antidotarie* II. 23 Thys Vnguent..dothe.. remoue diuers accidentes and sicknesses. **1622** BACON *Henry VII,* 9 There began..a disease then new: which of the Accidents and manner thereof they called the Sweating-sicknesse. **1671** MILTON *Samson* 612 Oh, that torment.. must secret passage find To the inmost mind, There exercise all his fierce accidents.

†**4.** A casual appearance or effect, a phenomenon. *Obs.*

c **1386** CHAUCER *Clerkes T.* 551 Non accident for noon adversité Was seyn in hir. **1635** N. CARPENTER *Geogr. Del.* I. x. 220 The Inhabitants of a Right Spheare in respect of the heauens haue the same accidents. **1695** WOODWARD *Nat. Hist. Earth* i. (1723) 24 These Fossil Shells are attended with the ordinary accidents of the marine ones, ex. gr. they sometimes grow to one another. **1765** HARRIS *Three Treat.* II. ii. 66 Music may imitate the Glidings, Murmurings, Tossings, Roarings, and other Accidents of water.

5. An irregular feature in a landscape; an undulation.

c **1870** LOWELL *Poet. Wks.* (1879) 391 Accidents of open green, Sprinkled with loose slabs square and gray. **1878** in *19th Cent.* 42 Taking advantage of every accident of the ground to conceal himself.

II. That which is present by chance, and therefore non-essential.

6. a. *Logic.* A property or quality not essential to our conception of a substance; an attribute. Applied especially in Scholastic Theology to the material qualities remaining in the sacramental bread and wine after transubstantiation; the essence being alleged to be changed, though the accidents remained the same.

c **1380** WYCLIF *Eng. Wks.* (1880) 466 No man durste seye til nou þat accident is goddis body, for þis newe word may haue no ground. **1413** LYDGATE *Pylg. Sowle* (1483) IV. xxvi. 71 Quantite is an accident only appropred to bodyly thynges. **1483** CAXTON *Gold. Leg.* 439/3 Whan the breed is conuerted into the precious body of our lord the accidentes abyden..whytnesse, roundenesse and sauoure. **1561** T. N[ORTON] *Calvin's Inst.* (1634) I. xiii. 56 Hee sticketh not to faigne new accidents in God. **1656** tr. *Hobbes's Elem. Philos.* (1839) 104 Wherefore, I define an accident to be the manner of our conception of body. **1664** H. MORE *Myst. Iniq.* xiii. 45 But I demand, Whether is it less Idolatry to adore the Accidents of the Bread..or the Bread it self? **1765** TUCKER *Lt. of Nat.* I. 17 Disposition, configuration, and motion, are ..accidents in ancient dialect, or modifications according to modern philosophers. **1846** MILL *Logic* I. vii. §8. 181 Inseparable accidents are properties which are universal to the species but not necessary to it..Separable Accidents are those which are found in point of fact to be sometimes absent from the species. **1872** O. SHIPLEY *Gloss. Eccl. Terms* 179 *Elements*, the English equivalent term for the accidents after consecration.

b. *Textual Criticism.* = ACCIDENTAL B. *sb.* d.

1942 W. W. GREG *Edit. Probl. Shakes.* p. 1, What may conveniently be called the 'accidents' of presentation, namely the spelling, punctuation, and other scribal or typographical details. *Ibid.* p. liii, The only other accident we need consider is line division.

7. Hence, by extension, Any accidental or non-essential accompaniment, quality, or property; an accessory, a non-essential.

1621 BURTON *Anat. Mel.* (1651) I. i. III. ii. 31 Old age, from which natural melancholy is almost an inseparable accident. **1725** DE FOE *Voy. round World* (1840) 6 We had also a third design in our voyage, though it may be esteemed an accident to the rest. **1837** DISRAELI *Venetia* (1871) I. i. 2 With all the brilliant accidents of birth, and beauty, and fortune. **1843** KINGSLEY *Lett.* (1878) I. 104 Eternity is really his home, and Time but an accident to him.

8. *Heraldry.* An additional point or mark that may be retained or omitted in a coat of arms.

1610 GWILLIM *Heraldry* (1660) I. iii. 15 I call those notes or marks, Accidents of Armes, that..may be annexed unto them, or taken from them, their substance still remaining.

†**9.** *Grammar. pl.* (L. *accidentia*, Quintil.) The changes to which words are subject, in accordance with the relations in which they are used; the expression of the phenomena of gender, number, case, mood, tense, etc. *Obs.* replaced by ACCIDENCE.

1589 PUTTENHAM *Eng. Poesie* (1869) 182 Not changing one word for another, by their accidents or cases. **1612** BRINSLEY *Posing of the Parts* (1669) 1 The Accidents; that is, the things belonging to the parts of speech.

10. a. *attrib.* and *Comb.*

1866 *Boston Directory* 565/2 The Pioneer Accident Insurance Company in America. **1892** A. PINERO *Magistrate* III, p. 135 Tell Sergeant Lugg to look over the Accident-Book, this morning's Hospital Returns. **1899** *Westm. Gaz.* 2 Mar. 8/3 Last year we paid about 5,000 accident claims. **1899** *Daily Chron.* 10 Aug. 5/7 They were manning the accident boat. **1905** *Ibid.* 19 Sept. 4/4 Life-saving and accident-preventing machinery. **1906** *Ibid.* 15 June 5/5 The accident rate was considered..low. **1918** W. HUTCHINSON *Doctor in War* (1919) xxii. 231 There seemed to be no even approximately 'accident-proof' type of airman. **1964** *Economist* 4 Jan. 34/2 Motorists..with their accident-potentiality enhanced by alcohol.

b. accident neurosis, a neurosis caused or precipitated by an accident; **accident-prone** *a.*, predisposed or likely to cause or attract an accident; also *absol.*; so **accident-proneness**, such predisposition or likelihood.

1901 in DORLAND *Med. Dict.* 442/2 Accident neurosis. **1932** J. H. HUDDLESON *Accidents, Neuroses & Compensation* iv. 59 Accident neuroses make up the most discussed group. **1961** *Listener* 28 Sept. 459/1 The term 'accident neurosis' refers to a disabling complaint of nervous origin: the symptoms are subjective, and there is usually no bodily sign of any emotional disturbance. **1926** FARMER & CHAMBERS *Psychol. Study Accident Rates* 3 'Accident proneness' implies the possession of those qualities which have been found to lead to an undue number of accidents. *Ibid.*, A person can be said to be accident prone without any knowledge of the number of accidents he has sustained. **1951** *Sci. Amer.* Aug. 68/3 A pushed conveyance such as a wheelbarrow..is..less accident-prone than the pulled four-wheel truck. **1952** *Lancet* 28 June 1296/1 Flanders Dunbar made a study of the accident-prone which bears out reasonable expectations. **1954** A. KOESTLER *Invis. Writing* xv. 167 Their accident-proneness was entirely due to the hazard of a Jewish origin.

†**'accident**, *a. Obs.* [ad. L. *accident-em* falling, happening, pr. pple. of *accid-ĕre*. See ACCIDENT *sb.*] Accidental, contingent, incidental.

1509 HAWES *Past. Pleas.* (1845) XXVII. xx. 123 Desteny is a thyng accydent. **1610** HEALEY *St. Aug., City of God* XI. iv. 389 They can neuer shew how that misery befalleth it anew, that was neuer accident to it before.

†**accident**, *v. Obs. rare*$^{-1}$. [f. ACCIDENT *sb.*] To endow with accidents or sensible attributes; to materialize or inform.

1548 GESTE *Pr. Masse* 86 Christes body is adjudged of no man to be accidented, notwythstanding it is presented in the accidentes of the bread.

accidental (æksɪˈdɛntəl), *a.* and *sb.* [? a. Fr. *accidental, -el*, 16th c. in Littré (cf. Pr. and Sp. *accidental*, It. *accidentale*), ad. med. or late L. *accidentāl-is* f. *accidens, -ent-*, sb. (see ACCIDENT *sb.*); cf. *occidentāl-is, parentāl-is*. The regular L. form would probably have been *accidentiāl-is* f. *accidentia*, cf. *essential, substantial.*] Earliest occurrence in senses 3, 4.

A. *adj.*

I. Coming by chance, or on a chance occasion.

1. Happening by chance, undesignedly, or unexpectedly; produced by accident; fortuitous.

1578 TIMME *Calvin on Gen.* 84 As though all the crookedness of our disposition were not accidental. **1607** TOPSELL *Four-footed Beasts* (1673) 267 Accidentall diseases be those that come by chance, as by surfetting, of cold, heat, and such like thing. **1653** WALTON *Compl. Angler* i. 14, I made an accidental mention of it. **1765** TUCKER *Lt. of Nat.* II. 88 A man shoots at a rat in his yard, and kills a chicken which he did not intend, therefore we call this accidental. **1830** LYELL *Princ. Geol.* I. 256 They are causes, therefore, as constant as the tides themselves, and, like them, depend on no temporary or accidental circumstances. **1882** *Pall Mall G.* 10 May 3/1 The jury..deciding after some hesitation to find only accidental death.

2. Of or pertaining to a chance occasion or chance circumstances; casual, occasional.

1506 W. DE WORDE *Ordinary of Crysten Men* V. vii. [415] The prayse of the good dedes done in the estate of mortall synne is a Joye accidentalle. **1533** ELYOT *Castel of Helth* (1541) 39 Some accidentall cause, as syckenes, or moche studye. **1603** SHAKS. *Meas. for M.* III. i. 149 Oh fie, fie, fie: Thy sinn's not accidentall, but a Trade. **1772** PENNANT *Tours in Scotl.* (1774) 341 Discovered by the accidental digging of peat. **1825** WATERTON *Wanderings* I. i. 109 The accidental traveller..can merely mark the outlines of the path he has trodden. **1836** TODD *Cycl. An. & Ph.* I. 497/1 Accidental Cartilage..the cartilaginous concretions.. found in situations where they do not ordinarily exist.

II. Present by chance; non-essential.

3. *Logic.* Pertaining to logical accidents; not essential to the conception of a substance; not of the nature of its essence; non-essential.

1553-87 FOX *A. & M.* III. 251 Pendleton saith that the colour [of bread] was the earthly thing, and called it an accidental substance. **1628** T. SPENCER *Logick* 277 The second, and third [figures] haue perfection essentiall, but not accidentall. **1788** REID *Active Powers* I. i. 513 There are other relative notions that are not taken from accidental relations. **1846** MILL *Logic* I. vi. §2. 147 All properties, not of the essence of the thing, were called its accidents..and the propositions in which any of these were predicated of it were called Accidental Propositions.

4. Non-essential to the existence of a thing, not necessarily present, incidental, subsidiary.

c **1386** CHAUCER *Melibœus* 432 The cause accidental was hate; the cause material, ben the five woundes of thy doughter. **1670** BAXTER *Cure of Ch. Div.* 18 If in any integral or accidental point you think that you are wiser. **1750** JOHNSON *Rambler* No. 150. ¶4 Those accidental benefits which prudence may confer on every state. **1858** F. W. ROBERTSON *Lect.* ii. 148 Poetry is a something to which words are the accidental, not by any means the essential form.

5. *Music. Accidental* sharps, flats, naturals: signs of chromatic alteration, raising or lowering notes a tone or semitone, strictly so called only when they occur before particular notes, and not in the *signature* of the various keys.

1806 CALLCOTT *Mus. Gram.* Accidental Sharps and Flats only affect the Notes which they immediately precede. **1867** MACFARREN *Harmony* i. 23 The employment in the minor of an accidental sharp or natural.

6. *Optics. Accidental* colours: complementary colours not actually caused by light, but due to subjective sensation.

1849 MRS. SOMERVILLE *Connex. of Phys. Sc.* §19. 184 After looking steadily for a short time at a coloured object, such as a red wafer, on turning the eyes to a white substance, a green image of the wafer appears, which is called the accidental colour of red. All tints have their accidental colours.

7. *Painting. Accidental* lights: 'secondary lights; effects of light other than ordinary daylight.' Fairholt.

8. *Perspective. Accidental* point: 'A point in the horizontal line, where lines parallel among themselves, though not perpendicular to the picture, do meet.' Phillips 1706.

¶ Also used *adverbially*.

1622 ROWLANDS *Good Newes* 13 Two canting rogues, that old consorts had bin, Did accidentall at an alehouse meet.

B. *sb.* **a.** A casual or subsidiary property, see A 3; **b.** *Music.* A sharp, flat, or natural, occurring not at the commencement of a piece of music in the signature, but before a particular note, see A 5; **c.** *Painting. pl.* 'Those unusual effects of strong light and shade in a picture produced by the introduction of the representations of artificial light, such as those proceeding from a fire, candle, or the like.' Fairholt. **d.** *Textual Criticism.* [cf. *adj.* 3.] Applied to any feature that is non-essential to the author's meaning. Cf. ACCIDENT *sb.* 6 b.

1651 BAXTER *Inf. Bapt.* 31 You must distinguish between the Essentials and some Accidentals of the Jewish Church. **1726** AYLIFFE *Parergon* 75 Altho' a Custom introduc'd against the Substantials of an Appeal be not valid..yet a Custom may be introduc'd against the Accidentals of an Appeal. **1868** OUSELEY *Harmony* (1875) i. 6 The use of them [sharps, flats, etc.] both as accidentals and in the signature. **1942** W. W. GREG *Edit. Probl. Shakes.* p. liv, It is desirable that the preservation of accidentals should be seen in proper perspective. **1959** *N. & Q.* CCIV. 119/2 If no long s was available in his fount, it would surely have been better to have substituted the modern s for this 'accidental' of early script and typography. **1964** *Ibid.* CCIX. 179/1 Such variants as & for *and* throughout suggest that Fischer is more faithful than Clark to accidentals.

accidentalism (æksɪˈdɛntəlɪz(ə)m). [f. ACCIDENTAL *a.* and *sb.* + -ISM.]

1. Accidental manner. In *Painting*, The effect produced by accidental lights.

1851 RUSKIN *Mod. Painters* I. II. 4. iii. §4. 287 The constant habit of nature to..make the symmetry and beauty of her laws the more felt by the grace and accidentalism with which they are carried out.

2. *Med.* A system of medicine which regards disease as an accidental modification of health and preventible by the arrestment of external causes.

1879 *Syd. Soc. Lex.*

accidentalist (æksɪˈdɛntəlɪst). [f. ACCIDENTAL + -IST.] One who believes in or practises ACCIDENTALISM 2.

1879 *Syd. Soc. Lex.*

accidentality (ˌæksɪdənˈtælɪtɪ). [f. ACCIDENTAL + ITY.] Accidental state or quality, casualness; = ACCIDENTALNESS.

1651 N. BIGGS *New Dispens.* 168 In this only supposed Accidentality. **1831** COLERIDGE *Table Talk* 147 I wish..to take from history it's accidentality, and from science it's fatalism.

accidentally (æksɪˈdɛntəlɪ), *adv.* [f. ACCIDENTAL + -LY².] Sense 2 was the earlier in use; see ACCIDENT *sb.*

1. a. In an accidental manner; by accident, by chance, unintentionally, casually.

1588 SHAKS. *L.L.L.* IV. ii. 143 A Letter..which accidentally..hath miscarried. **1607** —— *Coriol.* IV. iii. 40 I am most fortunate, thus accidentally to encounter you. **1639** FULLER *Holy War* (1840) II. xxi. 77 Being accidentally poisoned by one of his own arrows. **1771** *Junius Lett.* xlvi. 246 A great authority..I accidentally met with this morning. **1823** LAMB *Elia*. Ser. II. xxiii. 393 (1865) Accidentally their acquaintance has proved pernicious to me.

b. joc. phr., ***accidentally on purpose***: with the appearance of an accident although actually on purpose or by pre-arrangement.

1862 LADY MORGAN *Mem.* x. 91 Dermody neglected the order—perhaps 'accidentally on purpose'. **1916** R. FROST *Let.* 14 Nov. (1964) 45 My not meeting De la Mare in England was rather accidentally on purpose. **1946** R. LEHMANN *Gipsy's Baby* 137 The other one chiming in all wrong every time accidentally on purpose to spoil the effect.

†**2.** Non-essentially, incidentally, as a secondary or subsidiary effect. *Obs.*

1398 TREVISA *Barth. De P.R.* (1495) XVII. i. 593 Drye essencialli and moyst accidentally. **1541** R. COPLAND *Guydon's Quest. of Cyrurg.* Suppose that holly they do nat contrary, neuerthelesse they contrary accydentally. **1651** HOBBES *Gov. & Soc.* iii. §21. 50 Every man is presumed to seek what is good for himselfe naturally, and what is just, only for Peaces sake, and accidentally. **1781** GIBBON *Decl. & Fall.* III. 139 The invasion of the Goths..contributed, at least accidentally, to extirpate the last remains of Paganism.

accidentalness (æksɪˈdɛntəlnɪs). [f. ACCIDENTAL + -NESS.] The quality or fact of being accidental; casualness, fortuitousness.

1684 CHARNOCK *Attrib. of God* (1834) I. 557 The necessity of their meeting in regard of their master's order and the accidentalness of it in regard of themselves. *Mod.* The alleged accidentalness of the explosion.

†**acci'dentarily**, *adv. Obs.* [f. ACCIDENTARY + -LY².] By way of accident; casually, incidentally.

1651 HOBBES *Leviathan* II. xxv. 133 Directed principally to his own benefit, and but accidentarily to the good of him that is counselled.

† **accidentary** (æksɪˈdɛntərɪ), *a. Obs.* [f. ACCIDENT *sb.* + -ARY; as if ad. L. **accidentārius.*] Sense 2 was the earlier in use; see ACCIDENT *sb.*

1. Fortuitous, casual; = ACCIDENTAL 1, 2.

1607 WALKINGTON *Opt. Glasse of Hum.* 34 For this accidentary death instance mote be given of many. **1655** CULPEPER *Riverius* v. iv. 127 In some an accidentary Stammering cometh by a Catarrh. **1678** *Cathol. Cause* in *Harl. Misc.* (Malh.) II. 134 Those that erroneously refer all things unto . . fortune, or such like accidentary events.

2. Having the nature of a logical accident, not affecting the essence, non-essential; = ACCIDENTAL 3, 4.

c **1555** HARPSFIELD *Div. of Hen. VIII* (1878) 246 The second perfection . . is not essential but accidentary. **1656** HOBBES *Six Less.* Wks. 1845 VII. 218 Is not the circumduction of a semicircle accidentary to a sphere?

accidented (ˈæksɪdəntɪd), *ppl. a.* [f. ACCIDENT *sb.* (see I. 5) + -ED². Cf. Fr. *accidenté.*] Characterized by accidents. (Cf. ACCIDENT *sb.* 5.)

1878 R. L. STEVENSON *New Arab. Nights* ii. 27 The highest and most accidented of the sandhills immediately adjoined: and from these I could overlook Northmour. **1879** *Daily News* 16 Apr. 3/2 A reckless headlong steeple-chase over a violently accidented ploughed field. **1925** *Blackw. Mag.* May 670/2 Owing to the echoes and the accidented nature of the ground, it was not quite certain where the sounds came from.

accidential (æksɪˈdɛnʃəl), *a. rare.* [f. L. *accidentia*, see ACCIDENCE¹ + -AL¹. Cf. *essential.*] Characterized by non-essential qualities.

1811 J. PINKERTON *Petralogy* Introd. 4 Petralogy . . divided into twelve domains . . six being distinguished by circumstances or accidences of various kinds, may be called circumstantial, or accidential. **1814** *Edin. Rev.* XXIII. 67 The last [six domains] . . are denoted by the ingenious appellation of Accidential.

accidentiality (æksɪˌdɛnʃɪˈælɪtɪ). [f. ACCIDENTIAL + -ITY.] An accidential quality.

1814 *Edin. Rev.* XXIII. 66 We are assailed, at every step, by . . accidentialities, and all the ineffable appellations. *Ibid.* 67 While the last six are . . on account of their 'accidentiality,' subdivided.

† **acciˈdentiary,** *a. Obs. rare*⁻¹. [f. L. *accidentia* ACCIDENCE² + -ARY.] Engaged on the accidence (in Grammar).

1633 BP. MORTON *Discharge* 186 You know the word Sacerdotes to signifie Priests, and not the Lay-people, which every Accedentiarie boy in schooles knoweth as well as you.

† **ˈaccidently,** *adv. Obs.* [f. ACCIDENT *a.* + -LY².] Sense 2 was the earlier in use; see ACCIDENT *sb.*, -AL¹.

1. Accidentally, casually, by chance.

1611 SPEED *Hist. Gt. Brit.* (1632) IX. vii. 530 Which Act was accidently hanseld. **1782** J. FLETCHER *Let.* Wks. 1795 VII. 239, I broke my shin accidently against a bench. **1864** E. SARGENT *Peculiar* III. 87 Accidently attending an auction he buys an infant slave.

2. Non-essentially, incidentally, as a subsidiary or secondary effect.

1506 W. DE WORDE *Ordinary of Crysten Men* v. v. [400] They haue glorye not to haue done them [sins] . . but accydently for as moche as they haue done penaunce. **1533** ELYOT *Castel of Helth* (1541) 13 Age [is] . . accidently moist, but naturally cold and dry. **1616** SURFLET & MARKH. *Countrey Farme* VI. xxii. 626 But and if it [wine] be yet so drunke immoderately . . accidently it cooleth . . and quite undoeth the prouocations and acts of lust.

‖ **accidia.** [a. med.L. *accīdia* (see ACCIDIE).] = ACCIDIE.

1930 *Time & Tide* 28 Mar. 414/2 Half of them suffer from the deadly spiritual disease of accidia. **1947** C. GRAY *Contingencies* iii. 89 The combination of medieval *accidia* and modern *weltschmerz*, which we find in his [Liszt's] *Hamlet*.

accidie. Forms: 3–4 acˈcide, acˈcyde; 3–5 acˈcidie, acˈcydye, ˈaccidye; 5–6 acˈcydye. [a. OFr. *acˈcide, aˈcide*, ONormFr. *acˈcidie, aˈcidie*; ad. med.L. *accīdia*, corrupt. of late L. *acēdia*, a. Gr. ἀκηδία heedlessness, torpor (in Cicero, *Att.* xii. 45) n. of state f. ἀ not + κῆδ-ος care, κήδ-ομαι I care, lit. *non-caring-state*. *Acēdia* became a favourite ecclesiastical word, applied primarily to the mental prostration of recluses, induced by fasting, and other physical causes; afterwards the proper term for the 4th cardinal sin, *sloth, sluggishness*. (See Chaucer, *Persones T.* 603.) Its Greek origin being forgotten, the word was variously 'derived' from *acidum* sour (see *Cæsarius* quoted in Du Cange, and Roquefort '*Acide*: Ennui, tristesse, dégoût: d'*acidum*'); and from *accidĕre* to come upon one as an *accident* or *access*, whence the med.L. corruption, *accidia*, and OFr. and Eng. *acˈcide, acˈcidie*. The latter is Norman, the former Parisian; the later Eng. accentuation was *ˈaccidie*. With the restoration of Gr. learning, the L. became again *acedia*, whence a rare ACEDY in 17th c.] Sloth, torpor.

c **1230** *Ancren Riwle* 208 Under accidie, þet ich cleopede slouhðe. **1303** R. BRUNNE *Handl. Synne* 4784 Swych synne men kalle accyde Yn Goddes seruyse slogh betyde. *Ibid.* 5326 Hyt ys sloghnes and kalled accyde, Fro goddys seruyse so long þe hyde. *c* **1340** HAMPOLE *Pr. Treat.* 21 Breke doune also as þou may flesshely likyngis oþer in accidie or in bodili ease, or glotonie, or licherye. **1377** LANGL. *P. Pl.* B. v. 366 And after al þis excesse He hadde an accidie þat he slepte saterday and sonday. *c* **1386** CHAUCER *Persones T.* 603 After the synne of Enuye and of Ire, now wol I speken of the synne of Accidie [*Lansd. MS.* accide]. **1393** GOWER *Conf.* II. 19 To serve accidie in his office, There is of slouth an other vice. **1484** CAXTON *Ordre of Chyualry* 81 A man that hath accydye or slouthe hath sorowe and angre the whyle that he knoweth that an other man doth wel. **1484** —— *Ryall Book* A 5 The fourth heed of the beest of hell is slouthe, whyche is callyd of clerkys accidye. **1520** W. DE WORDE *Treatise of this Galaunt* (Furnivall's *Ball. fr. MSS.* I. 448) Abhomynable accydye accuseth all our nacyon Our aungelyke abstynence is nowe refused. **1891** F. PAGET (*title*) The Spirit of Discipline . . with an . . essay concerning Accidie. **1923** J. M. MURRY *Pencillings* 21 The worst attack of accidie . . gives way before them. **1936** H. G. WELLS *Anat. Frust.* vi. 54 There is nothing before you but sloth and apathy, accidie, which is a lingering suicide.

acˈcidious, *a. rare.* [ad. med.L. *accidiōsus* wearisome, f. *accidia*: see prec.] 'Slothful.' Bailey 1731. '*rather bombastic.*' Ash 1775.

a **1400** *Pore Caitiff* (MS. Harl. 2335) lf. 17, þe accidious man haþ ydilnesse sleuþe & sleep for his god. **1912** PAGET & CRUM *Francis Paget* 136 Men who would not go there might . . be thought . . accidious.

† **acˈcidity.** *Obs.*⁻⁰ [ad. med.L. *acciditas*, irreg. f. *accidia*: see ACCIDIE.] 'Slothfulness.' Bailey 1731. Ash 1775.

† **ˈaccinate,** *v. Obs. rare*⁻¹. [improp. f. L. *accinĕre* + -ATE³.] = To ACCENT.

1652 URQUHART *Jewel* Wks. 1834, 233 Conforme to the matter's variety, elevating or depressing, flat or sharply accinating it [the elocution], with that proportion of tone that was most consonant with the purpose.

† **acˈcinct,** *ppl. a. Obs.*⁻⁰ [ad. L. *accinct-us* pa. pple. of *accing-ĕre* to gird.] 'Girded, prepared, ready.' Bailey 1731. Ash 1775.

acˈcinge, *v. rare.* [ad. L. *accing-ĕre* to gird, *refl.* to undertake.] To 'gird up one's loins,' apply oneself.

1657 TOMLINSON *Renou's Dispens.* 219 Æschylus never accinged himself to write tragedies unless he were first madefied with wine. **1829** T. L. PEACOCK *Misfort. Elphin* xiv, This task, to which I have accinged myself, is arduous. **1886** *Oxf. Mag.* 12 May, When Mr. Jesse Collings accinges himself to constructive legislation. **1888** 'Q' *Troy Town* xiv. 166 Peter, instead of adjuring Miss Limpenny to fear no more the heat o' the sun, accinged himself to the practical difficulty.

accipenser, see ACIPENSER.

† **accipient** (ækˈsɪpɪənt), *ppl. a. Obs.*⁻⁰ [ad. L. *accipient-em* pr. pple. of *accip-ĕre* to take to oneself.] 'One who receives.' J.

1731 In BAILEY, whence in Johnson etc. n.q.

‖ **accipiter** (ækˈsɪpɪtə(r)). [a. L. *accipiter*, f. *accipĕre* to take to oneself: see ACCEPT.]

1. *Zool.* A bird of prey, a member of the order *Accipitres*, or *Raptores*, including the eagles, falcons, etc.

1874 WOOD *Nat. Hist.* 275 The genus *Accipiter* finds representatives in every quarter of the globe.

2. *Surg.* 'A bandage applied over the nose, resembling the claw of a hawk.' *Syd. Soc. Lex.*

accipitral (ækˈsɪpɪtrəl), *a.* [f. ACCIPITER + -AL¹ as if ad. L. **accipitrālis.*] Of the nature of a falcon or hawk; rapacious; keen-sighted.

1841 CARLYLE *Miscell.* (1857) IV. 245 Of temper most accipitral. **1881** LOWELL in *Harper's Mag.* Jan. 271 That Hawthorne's eyes were sometimes accipitral we can readily believe.

† **acˈcipitrary.** *Obs.* [ad. med.L. *accipitrārius* a keeper and tamer of hawks.] 'One who catches birds of prey.' Craig 1847.

? *a* **1600** HALLIWELL cites NASHE.

accipitrine (ækˈsɪpɪtraɪn), *a. Zool.* [a. Fr. *accipitrin-e*, f. L. *accipiter*: see -INE¹. Cf. *aquiline.*] Of the falcon kind; hawk-like.

1838 *Pen. Cycl.* XI. 513/2 M. Latreille places the Secretary in his second family of the Diurnal tribe of Rapacious birds, viz. the Accipitrine. **1872** RUSKIN *Eagle's Nest* §11 The difference between man and man is in the quickness and quality, the accipitrine intensity, the olfactory choice, of his νοῦς.

accise, an earlier form of the word now corruptly written EXCISE, orig. *asise, assise, acise*: see ASSIZE *sb.*

1645 HOWELL *Fam. Lett.* §1. 14 The monstrous Accises which are impos'd upon all sorts of Commodities.

‖ **accismus** (ækˈsɪzməs). *Rhet.* [med. or mod.L., a. Gr. ἀκκισμός coyness, affectation.] A feigned refusal of that which is earnestly desired.

1753 CHAMBERS *Cycl. Supp.* s.v., Cromwell's refusal of the crown . . may be brought as an instance of an Accismus. **1876** tr. *Richter's Levana* IV. iv. 89. 243 A woman uses no figure of eloquence—her own, at most, excepted—so often as that of accismus.

† **acˈcite,** *v. Obs.* 6–7, also 6 **acite, acyte, assite.** [ad. late L. *accitāre*, f. *ac-* = *ad-* to + *cit-āre* to summon; see CITE. The earlier forms seem to represent an OFr. derivative **aciter* (not in Godef.).]

1. To summon, to call, to cite.

1506 W. DE WORDE *Ordinary of Crysten Men* IV. xxix. [328] We be now acyted for to appere unto suche and soo meruayllous Iugement. **1524** S. FISH *Suppl. for Beggers* 3 Howe muche money get the somners . . by assityng the people to the commissaryes court, and afterward releasing thapparaunce for money? **1600** CHAPMAN *Iliad* XI. 595 Our heralds now accited all that were Endamag'd by the Elians. **1674** MILTON *Declaration etc.* Wks. 1851, 465 His most noble Uncle Stanislaus . . whom . . Valour and youthful Heat accited at his own expence and private forces into the Tauric fields.

2. To cite (in writing), to quote.

a **1631** DONNE *Ess.* (1651) 23 And Beasts who have often the honour to be our Reproach, accited for examples of vertue & wisdome in the Scriptures.

3. To arouse, to excite (with which word it was probably sometimes confounded).

1597 SHAKS. *2 Hen. IV*, II. ii. 64 And what accites your most worshipful thought to thinke so? *a* **1637** B. JONSON *Underwoods* (1692) 563 What was there to accite So ravenous and vast an Appetite?

acclaim (əˈkleɪm), *v.* Also 4 **acleim,** 5 **acleyme,** 6–7 **acclame.** [Strictly there are two verbs: the current ACCLAIM ad. cl. L. *acclāmā-re* f. *ac-* = *ad-* to, at + *clāmā-re* to shout (cf. mod.Fr. *acclamer*), the spelling assimilated to CLAIM; and an earlier northern *acleim, acclame*, ad. med.L. *acclāmā-re* to claim (see many instances in Du Cange); the form of the latter suggests an OFr. **aclame-r, aclaime-r*, but this is unknown to Littré and Godef.]

I. From med.L. *acclāmāre* = *vindicāre, asserere.*

† **1.** To lay claim to, to claim. (In Scotch and northern writers.) *Obs.*

c **1320** *Syr Bevis* 1344 Ech yer [he] . . Acleimede his eritage. **1535** STEWART *Cron. Scot.* III. 495 How Donald of the Ylis come in Ros and acclamit the Erldome thairof. **1609** SKENE *Reg. Majest.* 12 That it may be knawin . . quhilk of them hes maist richt, to the lands acclamed. **1717** WODROW *Corresp.* (1843) II. 326 Other Protestant Churches where this power is acclaimed.

II. From the classical L. senses.

2. *trans.* To applaud, extol; welcome with acclamation.

1633 BP. HALL *Hard Texts* 243 A magnificent Prince that is honord & acclaimed of all his subjects. **1865** *Cornh. Mag.* Aug. 246 Beatrice . . acclaimed by angels . . descends to accompany him in his visit to Paradise. **1879** MCCARTHY *Hist. own Times* II. 165 An immense amount of national enthusiasm accompanied and acclaimed the formation of the volunteer army. **1881** *Times* Feb. 24 The spirit which acclaimed the speeches of Mr. Bright.

b. (With complement.) To name with acclamation as; to proclaim or announce with applause.

1749 SMOLLETT *Regicide* v. ix. (1777) 121 The shouting crowd Acclaims thee king of traitors. **1876** SWINBURNE *Erechtheus* 462 The twelve most high Gods judging with one mouth Acclaimed her victress.

c. *intr.* To shout applause.

1652 STAPYLTON *Herodian* 16 The Romans did this brave young Emp'rour crown . . Acclaiming from their steeples and their towers. **1857** CARLYLE *Fr. Rev.* II. VI. vii. 343 And all men accuse, and uproar, and impetuously acclaim.

3. *trans.* To shout; to call out; *spec.* to utter an ACCLAMATION 3.

1690 LESTRANGE *Alliance of Div. Off.* (1846) vi. §3. 247 We presently all rise up acclaiming, 'Glory be to Thee, O Lord.' **1850** MRS. BROWNING *Poems* I. 166 Who art thou, victim, thou—who dost acclaim Mine anguish in true words, on the wide air?

acclaim (əˈkleɪm). [f. the vb.] The act of acclaiming; acclamation, applause; a shout of applause. (Mostly poetic.)

1667 MILTON *P.L.* XI. 519 All the host of Hell With deafening shout returned them loud acclaim. **1699** DRYDEN *Pal. & Arcite* 525 The vaulted firmament With loud acclaims and vast applause is rent. **1810** SCOTT *Lady of L.* II. xxi. Echoing back with shrill acclaim, And chorus wild the chieftain's name. **1859** TENNENT *Ceylon* II. x. ii. 600 Universal acclaim pronounces Minery . . the most charming sylvan spot in Ceylon.

acclaimable (əˈkleɪməb(ə)l), *a. rare*⁻¹. [f. ACCLAIM *v.* 1 + -ABLE.] Capable of being claimed; liable to be claimed.

1704 *Rymer's Fœdera* II. 551 in C. Macfarlane's *Hist. Eng.* (1845) IV. 42 He meant not to relinquish his right of property in the kingdom of Scotland, acclaimable hereafter.

acclaimer (əˈkleɪmə(r)). [f. ACCLAIM *v.* + -ER¹.] One who acclaims, or applauds; an applauder.

1869 *Daily News* 28 Apr., Public opinion . . was beginning to tell upon these indefatigable acclaimers and accomplices of every folly.

acclaiming (əˈkleɪmɪŋ), *ppl. a.* [f. ACCLAIM *v.* + -ING².] Loudly approving or applauding.

1868 MILMAN *St. Paul's* xvii. 446 Unhesitating and acclaiming gratitude for his inappreciable services.

†'**acclamate**, *v. Obs. rare*$^{-1}$. [f. L. *acclāmāt-*, ppl. stem of *acclāmā-re*: see ACCLAIM and -ATE[3].] = ACCLAIM *v.*

1667 WATERHOUSE *Fire of Lond.* 49 Which causes that axiom to be so acclamated among Politicians.

acclamation (æklə'meɪʃɛn). [ad. L. *acclāmātiōn-em* a shouting at or to, n. of action f. *acclāmāre*: see ACCLAIM. Cf. Fr. *acclamation*, also 16th c. in Littré.]

1. The action of acclaiming. †**a.** Calling to, appealing. *Obs.* **b.** Loud or eager expression of assent or approval, as to vote a motion ***by acclamation***. Also, to elect a candidate ***by*** (also †***with***) ***acclamation***: unanimously (or overwhelmingly) and without a ballot; *N. Amer.* (orig. *Canada*). **c.** Shouting in honour of any one.

1585 ABP. SANDYS *Serm.* (1841) 56 The people of Israel.. sang with joyful acclamation unto the Lord. **1612** T. TAYLOR *Titus* (1619) iii. 8. 679 Giuing consent and acclamation vnto the most weighty and necessarie doctrine of free iustification. **1750** JOHNSON *Rambler* No. 91. ¶3 With the general acclamation of all the powers. **1827** *Gore Gaz.* (Ancaster, Ontario) 8 Dec. 161/2 The friends of Mr. Papineau intended that the election should be carried unanimously, and by acclamation, in his favor. **1844** *Examiner* (Toronto) 23 Oct. 3/1 Yesterday, the election was held for this County, when Jacob de Witt..was returned with acclamation. **1849** MACAULAY *Hist. Eng.* I. 408 Dryden ..joined his voice to the general acclamation. **1860** FROUDE *Hist. Eng.* VI. xxxi. 196 The spirit which thirty years before had passed the Six Articles Bill by acclamation. **1868** PEARD *Water-farming* v. 51 Crowned long ago by acclamation king of fish, learning has done him [the salmon] homage. **1912** J. SANDILANDS *Western Canad. Dict. & Phrase-Bk.* s.v., *Acclamation*, a candidate who is unanimously elected to office without the trouble of going to the poll is said to be elected by acclamation. **1964** *Daily Colonist* (Victoria, B.C.) 8 Oct. 20/1 Stephen Juba..became the first mayor from this city to be elected by acclamation in nearly a quarter of a century. **1984** *Congress. Q. Weekly Rep.* 23 June 1506/1 Boschwitz was nominated by acclamation at the GOP state convention.

2. An act of acclaiming; an exclamation, or phrase addressed to anyone in a loud voice, †**a.** (as in early L.) in expression of dislike; †**b.** (as in later L.) of approbation or applause. Hence **c.** Loud applause or approbation however expressed.

1541 ELYOT *Image of Gov.* 172 With these and other moste ioyouse acclamations, the emperour issued out of the Theatre. **1606** HOLLAND *Suetonius* 39 Acclamations must be restrained heere to the worse sense..of Curses and Detestations. **1611** BIBLE *1 Macc.* v. 64 The people assembled vnto them with ioyfull acclamations. **1611** SPEED *Theatre Gt. Brit.* 121/1 The cruell tyrant, to stop her cries and acclamations, slew her. **1664** H. MORE *Myst. Iniq.* 361 That auspicious Acclamation of the Senate to their Cæsars, *Felicior Augusto, Melior Trajano.* **1673** *Lady's Calling* II. §2. 75 To force their unhappy mothers to that sad acclamation, Blessed are the wombs which bare not. **1718** POPE *Iliad* xv. 872 This happy day with acclamations greet. **1776** GIBBON *Decl. & Fall* I. x. 196 The acclamations of the soldiers proclaimed him emperor. **1862** LD. BROUGHAM *Brit. Constitn.* x. 136 The assembled people..by their acclamations gave an affirmative answer.

d. An election by acclamation: see sense 1 b above. *Canada.*

1958 *Citizen* (N. Vancouver) 4 Dec. 1/7 Strange there's a shortage of Board candidates in the District but an acclamation is not unusual in the City. **1964** *Martlet* (Univ. Victoria, B.C.) 8 Oct. 1/1 Acclamations have filled all students' council positions vacated through resignations but one.

†**3.** *Rhet.* A brief isolated sentence in a discourse, emphasizing what precedes it. *Obs.*

1561 J. DAUS tr. *Bullinger on Apocal.* (1573) 8 b, He finisheth the title With an acclamation [*Rev.* i. 3]. *Ibid.* 56 b, Hereunto is annexed the wonted acclamation..Let hym that hath eares, heare etc. [*Rev.* ii. 7 etc.] **1641** MILTON *Animadv.* (1851) 202 This ancient Father mentions no antiphonies, or responsories of the people heer, but the only plain acclamation of Amen. **1657** J. SMITH *Myst. Rhet. Unv.* 143 Acclamation is a figure, when after a thing is done or declared, a clause or part of a sentence is added, briefly purporting some Emphasis.

†**acclamator.** *Obs. rare*$^{-1}$. [n. of action, L. in form, f. L. *acclāmā-re* (see ACCLAIM), on the analogy of *clāmātor* f. *clāmāre*.] One who joins in acclamation; an acclaimer, an applauder.

1651 EVELYN *Diary* (1827) II. 38 He went almost the whole way with his hat in hand, saluting the ladys & acclamators, who had filled the windows with their beauty and the air with 'Vive le Roi.'

acclamatory (ə'klæmətərɪ), *a.* [f. L. *acclāmāt-* ppl. stem of *acclāmāre*, see ACCLAIM + -ORY as if ad. Lat. **acclāmātōrius*.] Relating to or expressing acclamation.

1675 T. BROOKS *Gold. Key* Wks. 1867 V. 488 Christ's justice hath two acclamatory notes, 'Higgajon, Selah.' **1864** R. CHAMBERS *Bk. of Days* II. 199 He..was sent out again by the acclamatory voice of the nation.

†**a'cclearment.** *Obs. rare*$^{-1}$. [f. CLEARMENT: see A- *pref.* 11 as if f. a vb. ACCLEAR; cf. OFr. *aclarir, aclairir.*] Clearing, exculpation.

1692 HACKET *Life of Williams* I. 148 The accused Lord protested upon his salvation he was not the discoverer. The acclearment is fair, and the proof nothing.

acclimatable (ə'klaɪmətəb(ə)l), *a.* [f. ACCLIMATE + -ABLE.] Capable of being acclimatized, suitable for acclimatization.

1880 *Echo* 18 Sept. 2/6 Dr. Ricoux defines what he calls an 'acclimatable zone.'

acclimatation (əklaɪmə'teɪʃɛn). [a. Fr. *acclimatation*, n. of action f. *acclimater* to ACCLIMATE.] = ACCLIMATIZATION.

1859 *Sat. Rev.* 3 Sept. 281 The true Pheasants..are all capable of the most perfect acclimatation in Western Europe. **1863** *All Year Round* 11 July 467/1 Experiments have proved how possible is the acclimatation of the ailanthe silkworm on the northern side of the English Channel.

acclimate (ə'klaɪmət), *v.* [a. mod.Fr. *acclimate-r* (Acad. Dict. 1798) f. *à* to + *climat* CLIMATE.]

1. To habituate to a new climate; = ACCLIMATIZE, now much more common. *lit.* and *fig.* Now chiefly *U.S.*

1792 A. YOUNG *Trav. in France* 296 Kerry, where the arbutus is so ac-climated, that it seems indigenous. **1859** *Sat. Rev.* 12 Feb. 183/2 The idea of acclimating the eland in England is due to the late Earl of Derby. **1872** O. W. HOLMES *Poet at Breakf. T.* iii. 75, I have not been long enough at this table to get well acclimated. **1934** F. SCOTT FITZGERALD *Tender is Night* II. viii. 196 'I'll drop in after dinner,' Dick promised. 'First I must get acclimated.' **1937** S. CHENEY *World Hist. Art* (1938) xiii. 400 The Byzantine style, which had been acclimated there during the rule of the Western exarchs.

2. *intr.* = ACCLIMATIZE *v.* 2.

1861 WINTHROP *C. Dreeme* 174 Until I acclimate to the atmosphere of work. **1864** *Good Words* 228/2 They.. acclimated easily, and they prospered.

acclimated (ə'klaɪmətɪd), *ppl. a.* [f. ACCLIMATE + -ED.] Habituated to a new or strange climate. *lit.* and *fig.*

1849 in J. R. COMMONS *Doc. Hist.* (1910) I. 253 The proprietor of several thousand arpents of land..is desirous to dispose of 45 acclimated negroes. **1856** LEVER *Martins of Cro' M.* 592 Acclimated, as I may say, to such incidents. **1862** *Times* 18 Apr. 8/6 Even among the acclimated New Orleanists the annual mortality is, etc. **1921** B. MATTHEWS in *S.P.E. Tract* V. 8, I have asked why these thoroughly acclimated French words should not be made to wear our English livery. **1961** *Times* 24 Feb. 3/6 Shivering ceases in the acclimated animal.

acclimatement (ə'klaɪmətmənt). *rare.* [a. mod.Fr. *acclimatement*: see ACCLIMATE and -MENT.] The condition of being acclimatized; habituation or adaptation to climate.

1823 COLERIDGE *Notes Theol. & Polit.* 401 The multitude of genera of animals and their several exclusive acclimatements at the present period.

acclimation (æklɪ'meɪʃən). [f. ACCLIMATE, by form-assoc. with words like *narrate, narration*, in which *-ate* is a vbl. ending: in *acclimate* it is part of the stem.] = ACCLIMATATION or ACCLIMATIZATION; but see last quot.

1826 FLINT *Recoll.* 132 The gradual process of *acclimation.* **1837** T. BACON *First Imp. Hindostan* I. p. vii, English residents in India imbibe peculiarities in the process of *acclimation.* **1853** KANE *Grinnell Exped.* (1856) iii. 26 [I] could temper down at pleasure the abruptness of my acclimation. **1859** *Sat. Rev.* 12 Feb. 183/2 With such animals as these [American deer] acclimation is comparatively easy. **1878** BARTLEY tr. *Topinard's Anthrop.* II. viii. 393 The words acclimation and acclimatization are not synonymous. The former is understood of the spontaneous and natural accommodation to new climatic conditions, the latter of the intervention of man in this accommodation.

acclimatizable (ə'klaɪmə,taɪzəb(ə)l), *a.* [f. ACCLIMATIZE + -ABLE.] Capable of being acclimatized.

1860 *Sat. Rev.* 14 Apr. 466/2 Supposed exhaustion of the series of acclimatizable animals.

acclimatization (ə,klaɪmətaɪ'zeɪʃɛn). [f. ACCLIMATIZE + -ATION.] The process of acclimatizing, or of being acclimatized, or habituated to a new climate. Also *attrib.*, as 'the Acclimatization Society.'

1830 LYELL *Princ. of Geol.* (1875) II. III. xxxvii. 320 This acclimatization has been the result of Natural Selection during thousands of generations. **1878** J. BULLER *New Zealand* I. Introd. 17 In the acclimatization gardens our British song-birds..are now finding a home. **1880** GUNTHER *Fishes* 185 The first successful attempts of acclimatisation were made with domestic species.

2. An example of acclimatization; a thing which has been acclimatized.

1864 OWEN *Power of God* 43 The bird which we call turkey..was one of our best acclimatisations after the discovery of the New World.

acclimatize (ə'klaɪmətaɪz), *v.* [f. Fr. *acclimater*: see ACCLIMATE + -IZE. A more recent and more common adaptation of Fr. *acclimater* than *acclimate.*]

1. *trans.* To habituate or inure to a new climate, or to one not natural. *lit.* and *fig.*

1836 MACGILLIVRAY *Trav. of Humboldt* xi. 128 Having in some measure become acclimatized. **1876** M. DAVIES *Unorth. Lond.* 289, I have long since learned to get readily acclimatized to unfamiliar ecclesiastical surroundings. **1880** GUNTHER *Fishes* 185 Attempts to acclimatise particularly useful species in countries in which they were not indigenous.

2. *refl.* and *intr.* To grow or become habituated to a new climate.

1862 M. HOPKINS *Hawaii* 63 The settlers acclimatise to the new locality. **1877** DOWDEN *Shaks. Prim.* vi. 144 He cannot acclimatise himself, as Alcibiades can, to the harsh and polluted air of the world.

acclimatized (ə'klaɪmətaɪzd), *ppl. a.* [f. prec. + -ED.] Habituated or inured to a particular climate.

1855 W. H. RUSSELL *The War* II. xiv, The Sardinians, now acclimatized..form a fine corps. **1881** DR. GREENE in *Sc. Gossip* No. 202. 223 An acclimatised grey parrot is very hardy.

acclimatizer (ə'klaɪmə,taɪzə(r)). [f. ACCLIMATIZE + -ER[1].] One who acclimatizes, or naturalizes foreign species in a new country. *lit.* and *fig.*

1864 DR. J. E. GRAY in *Athenæum* No. 1926. 407/2 The schemes of the would-be acclimatizers. **1869** DILKE *Greater Brit.* xiv. 391 We English are great acclimatisers: we have carried trial by jury to Bengal, tenant-right to Oude, and caps and gowns to..Calcutta University.

acclimatizing (ə'klaɪmətaɪzɪŋ), *vbl. sb.* [f. ACCLIMATIZE + -ING[1].] = ACCLIMATIZATION.

1881 COXWELL in *Standard* 3 Feb., Skill, judgment, and a certain amount of acclimatising were indispensable for that kind of work [ballooning].

acclimature (ə'klaɪmətjʊə(r)), *rare.* [f. ACCLIMATE + -URE, on apparent analogy of *legislat-ure*, etc. See ACCLIMATION.] = ACCLIMATIZATION.

1847 In CRAIG. WEBSTER and WORCESTER cite CALDWELL.

acclime (ə'klaɪm), *v. rare*$^{-1}$. [Apparently short for ACCLIMATE; as *clime* for *climate.*] ?To acclimate, habituate.

1843 E. JONES *Sensation & Event* 22 And now to acclime His gasping life to the heaven it nears.

†**a'ccline,** *v. Obs. rare*$^{-1}$. [ad. L. *acclīnā-re* to lean towards; f. *ac-* = *ad-* to + *clīnā-re* to bend.] To incline, or slope towards.

c **1420** *Palladius on Husb.* I. 250 Eke cornes best wol thryve In open lande solute acclyned blyve Uppon the sonne.

†**a'cclive,** *a. Obs. rare*$^{-1}$. [ad. L. *acclīv-is, acclīv-us* steep, f. *ad* to, towards + *clīvus* a rising ground.] Rising with a slope, sloping upward, steep; = ACCLIVOUS, ACCLIVITOUS.

a **1697** AUBREY *Acc. Verulam* in *Lett.* II. 231 (T.) From hence to Gorhambery is about a little mile, the way easily ascending, hardly so acclive as a desk.

acclivitous (ə'klɪvɪtəs), *a.* [f. ACCLIVIT-Y + -OUS; cf. *calamity, calamit-ous.* See -ITOUS, -OUS.] Of the nature of, or characterized by an acclivity; having an upward slope.

1815 PAULSON in Henderson's *Iceland* 203 We continued our route up the S.E. side of the Yökul, where it was least acclivitous. **1879** *Contemp. Rev.* 507 Herds of agile creatures abounding in the acclivitous glades of the woods.

acclivity (ə'klɪvɪtɪ). [ad. L. *acclīvitāt-em* steepness; f. *acclīv-is, acclīv-us*; see ACCLIVE and -ITY.] The upward slope of a hill; an ascending slope.

[Not in COTGRAVE or FLORIO 1611 or MINSHEU 1623.] **1614** PURCHAS *Pilgr.* v. xiii. 511 These bottomes of the sea haue also their..hillocks, mountaines, valleyes, with the Acclivities and Decliuities of places. **1692** BENTLEY *Boyle Lect.* viii. 290 The additional Acclivity would be imperceptible. **1789–96** J. MORSE *Amer. Geog.* XI. 319 The ascent to the upper story is not by steps but a paved acclivity. **1850** MERIVALE *Hist. Rom. Emp.* (1865) I. viii. 323 The acclivity was studded with the pleasure-houses of the noble families of Rome.

acclivous (ə'klaɪvəs), *a.* [f. L. *acclīv-us* + -OUS.] Rising with a slope, sloping upward, ascending.

1731 BAILEY [not in 1721]. **1771** SHERIDAN *Aristænetus' Love Ep.* III. 21 The bank acclivous rose, and swelled above. **1850** J. LEITCH *Müller's Anc. Art* §294. 329 The tombs at Chalcis..are hewn out in the gently acclivous rocky ground.

accloy (ə'klɔɪ), *v. Obs.* or *arch.* Also 5 **encloy**, 8 **ancloy**, 5–6 **acloy**. [a. OFr. *encloye-r*, earlier *encloër* (mod. *enclouer*):—late L. *inclāvā-re* to drive in a nail, f. *in* in + *clāvāre* to nail, f. *clāv-us* nail. The Anglo-Fr. *en-*, *an-*, being formally associated with OE. *an-*, *on-*, was worn down to *a-*, by aphesis of which came the later *cloy*. By further confusion with *a*:—L. *ad*, *acloy* became in the literary spelling of 6–7 *ac-cloy*, as *a-cuse* became *ac-cuse*. Hence the series *en-cloy, an-cloy, a-cloy* (*cloy*), *ac-cloy*.] The development of meaning is fully seen under CLOY.

1. To drive a nail into a horse's foot when shoeing; hence, to lame. *lit.* and *fig.*

c **1325** *Polit. Songs.* 335 Thus knihtshipe [is] acloied and waxen al fot lame. **1393** LANGL. *P. Pl.* C. XXI. 296 With crokes and with kalketrappes · a-cloye we hem echone. *c* **1440** *Prompt. Parv.* A-cloyed, *Acclaudicatus, inclavatus*, Acloyȝen (acloyin), *Acclaudico, acclavo, inclavo.* **1530** PALSGR. 416 I a cloye with a nayle as an yuell smythe dothe an horse foote, *Je encloue.* I wolde ryde further but my horse is a cloyed..*est encloué.* **1607** TOPSELL *Four-footed Beasts* (1673) 323 *Of Accloyd or Prickt*, Accloyd is a hurt that cometh of shooing, when a Smith driveth a nail in the quick, which will make him to halt. **1725** BRADLEY *Fam. Dict.* s.v. *Prict*, Prict, otherwise call'd Ancloy'd, Cloy'd and Retraised, a Misfortune which befalls Horses, when by the Negligence, or Unskilfulness of the Farrier, they are prick'd in driving the Nails.

2. To pierce, stab. *rare.*
1470 HARDING *Chron.* lxx. 5. 5 Of his people many [were] slain and foule acloyed.

3. To stop up an aperture as with a nail, peg, or other obstruction, to stop a passage. See CLOY. Hence,

4. To block, obstruct, clog, choke. *lit.* and *fig.*
c **1430** LYDGATE *Bochas* III. xxi. 92 a (1554) Wherby his purpose should be encloyed. **1555** *Fardle of Facions* II. viii. 172 Otherwise the housebande menne should in siede tyme ..be muche acloyed and hyndered by the fowels. **1596** SPENSER *F.Q.* II. vii. 15 But mucky filth his braunching armes annoyes, And with uncomely weedes the gentle wave accloyes. **1647** H. MORE *Song of the Soul* II. i. I. xii. They are ill accloy'd With cloddie earth, and with blind duskishnesse annoy'd. **1652** ASHMOLE *Theatr. Chem. Brit.* lv. 201 For with what Mettall soever that Mercury be joyned, Because of her Coldnes and Moistnes sche ys acloyd. **1676** CUDWORTH *Serm.* 1 John ii. 3. (ed. 3) 55 Heaven [is].. Holiness, freed from those encumbrances that did ever clog it and accloy it here. **1835** BROWNING *Paracel.* Wks. 1863 I. 29 Discovering the true laws by which the flesh Accloys the spirit.

5. To fill full. **a.** To fill to satiety. **b.** To overfill, overload, burden, oppress.
c **1374** CHAUCER *Assembly of Foules* 518 Whoso it doth, full foule himself acloyeth, For office uncommitted oft annoyeth. **1430** LYDGATE *Chron. Troy* I. x. The people in sorowe and wo acloyed. **1557** PAYNELL *Barclay's Jugurtha*, 28 b, Many other of his sect were corrupt and accloyed with bribes. **1567–9** JEWEL *Def. Apol.* (1611) 373 We are accloied with Examples in this behalfe. **1581** T. HOWELL *His Devises* (1879) 189 Whose wanton Fole by her sweete mylke acloyde Oft kicks the Nurse. **1610** G. FLETCHER *Christ's Vict.* in Farr's *S.P.* (1848) 72 Their brain sweet incense with fine breath accloyes. **1611** COTGR. To accloy: see, to cumber, to overcharge.

6. To overburden (the stomach); to nauseate.
1519 HORMAN *Vulgaria* xi. 32 b, My stomake is accloyed. **1530** PALSGR. 416 I acloye ones stomacke with excesse of meate and drinke, *Jengloutis.*

7. To disgust, weary, become offensive to.
1530 PALSGR. 416 I acloye, I forwery, *Je lasse.* He acloyeth me horrybly: *il me lasse horriblement.* **1593** G. HARVEY *Pierces Super.* 138 What honest mynde or civill disposition is not accloied with these noisome and nasty gargarismes. **1704** RAY *Creation* II. 230 They..would be accloyed with long Nights very tedious.

†**a'ccloy.** *Obs. rare*[−1]. [The vb. used subst.] *Farriery.* A stab or prick with a nail.
1725 BRADLEY *Fam. Dict.* s.v. *Halting*, Distemper..in the Sole from some Prick, Accloy, Nail, etc.

†**a'ccloying,** *vbl. sb. Obs.* [f. ACCLOY *v.* + -ING[1].] Filling up; overloading.
1557 PAYNELL *Barclay's Jugurtha* 112 The accloyeng of gyftes gyuen for rewardes..was vnknowen. **1598** FLORIO, *Fastidio*, tediousness, lothsomnes..a loathing of the stomack, an accloying.

accoast, *v.*; **accoasting,** *vbl. sb.* The older forms of ACCOST, ACCOSTING, while they retained the sense of to *coast*, *border upon*, or *join*.

accoie, variant of ACCOY *v. Obs.* to soothe.

†**a'ccoil,** *v. Obs.* [a. OFr. *acoillir* to gather, assemble (mod. *accueillir* to receive):—late L. *accolligĕre*, *adcolligere* to associate; f. *ad* to + *colligĕre* to gather. See COIL.] *intr.* To gather together, to collect. (Only in Spenser.)
1596 SPENSER *F.Q.* II. ix. 30 About the caudron many cookes accoyld With hookes and ladles.

a'ccoil, *sb. rare.* [a. OFr. *acoil* (mod. *accueil*) reception, welcome, f. *accueiller*, OFr. *acoillir*: see prec.] Reception, welcome.
1814 SOUTHEY *Rodk.* xvii. Wks. IX. 157 He had a secret trembling on his lips..he fear'd To have it chill'd in cold accoil.

accolade (ækəʊ'leɪd, akəʊ'lɑːd; now usu. 'ækəʊleɪd). [a. mod.Fr. *accolade*, ad. It. *accollata*, sb. f. pa. pple. of *accollare* to embrace about the neck; see ACCOLL, and -ADE. Introduced into Fr. in 16th c. superseding the OFr. cogn. *acolée*; it has similarly superseded the earlier ACOLEE in Eng.]

1. a. Properly, an embrace or clasping about the neck; technical name of the salutation marking the bestowal of knighthood, applied at different times to an embrace, a kiss, and a slap on the shoulders with the flat blade of a sword.
[Not in COTGRAVE 1611 who has *Accollade* (Fr.) a colling, clipping, imbracing about the necke; Hence, the dubbing of a Knight, or the ceremony used therein.] **1623** FAVINE *Theat. Honour* I. vi. 51 Giuing him also the Accollade, that is to say, Kissing him. **1706** PHILLIPS, *Accollade*, clipping and colling, embracing about the Neck. **1753** CHAMBERS *Cycl. Supp.* s.v. Antiquaries are not agreed, wherein the Accolade properly consisted. **1817** SCOTT *Waverley* I. x. 131 The quantities of Scotch snuff which his accolade communicated. **1852** MISS YONGE *Cameos* I. xvi. 122. (1877) Henry conferred on him the accolade, or sword blow, which was the chief part of the ceremony. **1858** WISEMAN *Last Four Popes* 511 Could he [the Pope] receive him [Czar Nicholas] with a bland smile and insincere accollade?

b. *fig.* A supreme honour; a mark of approval or admiration; a bestowal of praise, a plaudit; an acknowledgement of merit.
1852 P. J. BAILEY *Festus* (ed. 5) 250, I would knight you on the spot, But, really, I'm afraid, my sword's forgot. However, take my verbal accolade! **1906** 'O. HENRY' in *Munsey's Mag.* Aug. 559/2 All this meant that Curly had won his spurs, that he was receiving the puncher's accolade. **1940** W. FAULKNER *Hamlet* II. ii. 131 The impotent youths who..had conferred upon them likewise blindly and unearned the accolade of success. **1955** E. BLISHEN *Roaring Boys* I. 18 Improbable accolades. 'Good old sir!' 'You're a sport, sir!' **1961** M. BEADLE *These Ruins are Inhabited* (1963) ix. 113 A Nobel Prize is the top accolade a scientist can receive. **1974** 'J. HERRIOT' *Vet in Harness* xii. 89 Once the long process had been completed and the last piece of marzipan and icing applied she dearly loved to have the accolade from an expert. **1984** *Ann. Rep. Racal Electronics PLC* 7/1 The highest accolade in the engineering profession—election to the Fellowship of Engineering—was bestowed in April 1984 on Geoffrey Lomer.

2. *Music.* A vertical line or brace, used to couple together two or more staves. (Sometimes confined to a *straight* thick line so used, as distinguished from a *brace* or double curve; but in mod.Fr. *accollade* = the brace or double curve ⏟, used not merely in music but in ordinary printing, algebra, classification, etc.)
1882 ROCKSTRO in Grove's *Dict. Mus.* s.v. *Score*, In Scores ..the Staves are united, at the beginning of every page, either by a Brace, or by a thick line, drawn, like a bar, across the whole, and called the Accolade.

accoladed (ækəʊ'leɪdɪd), *ppl. a.* [f. prec. + -ED[2].] Having received the accolade; knighted, dubbed.
1863 *Daily Tel.* 17 Nov. 4/4 The sonorous cognomen of each of these accoladed Princes.

accolated ('ækəleɪtɪd), *ppl. a.* [f. mod.Fr. *accolé*, It. *accollato*, see prec.] = ACCOLLED 3.
1879 H. PHILLIPS *Notes upon Coins* 2 There are medals of ..Napoleon and Josephine accolated.

†**'accolent,** *a. Obs.*[−0] [ad. L. *accolent-em* pr. pple. of *accolĕre* to dwell near.] 'Dwelling hard by.' Bailey 1731, Ash 1775, Johnson, etc.

†**a'ccoll,** *v. Obs.* 4–5 **acole,** 5–6 **accoll.** [a. OFr. *acole-r*, f. *a* to + *col* neck. Spelling afterwards assimilated to mid. Fr. *accoller* (mod.Fr. *accoler*). Cf. It. *accollare*, suggesting a late L. or early Rom. *accollāre*, f. *ac-* = *ad-* to + *collum* neck).] To throw the arms round the neck of, embrace, clasp, hug.
1340 *Gawayne & Gr. K.* 1936 þen acoles he [þe] knyȝt, & kysses hym þryes. *Ibid.* 2472 þay acolen & kyssen, [bikennen] ayþer oþer. *c* **1450** *Merlin* xv. 234 And each acoled other in armes for grete love. **1557** SURREY *Aeneid* II. 1055 Thrise raught I with mine armes taccoll her neck.

a'ccolled, *ppl. a. Her.* [f. ACCOLL + -ED. The Fr. form *accollé* (mod.Fr. *accolé*) is more used.]

1. Wreathed about the neck, collared, gorged.
1723 ASHMOLE *Antiq. Berks.* III. 134 Accolled with a Ducal Coronet.

2. Intertwined; entwined, wreathed.

3. Conjoined, united; joined at the sides like two shields, or at the angles like two lozenges; placed side by side like two busts or heads on a coin; jugate; accolated. [In this sense sometimes referred to It. '*accolare* to glue vnto or together' Florio, f. *cola* (colla), Gr. *κόλλα* glue; but this seems only a plausible explanation of a use somewhat remote from the original sense of *accollé* and *accolled*.]

accomber, -bre; -braunce. See ACCUMBER.

accombi'nation. *rare.* [f. L. *ac-* = *ad-* to + COMBINATION.] The act of combining together.
WORCESTER cites *Q. Rev.*

accommodable (ə'kɒmədəb(ə)l), *a.* [a. Fr. *accomodable*, f. *accomoder* to suit: see ACCOMMODATE and -ABLE.] Capable of being accommodated; suitable.
1603 FLORIO *Montaigne* (1632) II. viii. 212 A fit and accommodable condition for such a dignitie. **1672** R. TAYLOR *O. Cromwell* 176 That the Title of the Protector might be made accomodable to the Laws. **1724** WATTS *Logic* v. §4 Wks. 1813 VII. 467 We must be furnished with such general rules as are accommodable to all this variety.

accommodableness (ə'kɒmədəb(ə)lnɪs). [f. prec. + -NESS.] Capability of becoming or being made suitable.
c **1760** CATH. TALBOT *Ess.* iii. Wks. 1809, 83 Let me be allowed to make a new word, and let that word be accommodableness.

†**accommodant,** *a. Obs. rare*[−1]. [a. Fr. *accomodant* pr. pple. of *accomoder* to suit: see ACCOMMODATE and -ANT.] Accommodating, self-accommodating, suiting oneself to circumstances.
1693 EVELYN *De la Quintinye's Compl. Gard.* 7 Be they Plants, or Trees, there is none of them, as to their Culture.. more Easie, Tractable, and (as I may say) Accommodant, then are Orange and Lemon-Trees.

†**a'ccommodate,** *ppl. a. Obs.* [ad. L. *accommodāt-us* suited, suitable, pa. pple. of *accommodā-re*, f. *ac-* = *ad-* to + *commodāre* to suit; f. *commod-us* suitable in measure, fitting; f. *com-* = *cum* together with + *modus* measure, manner.] Suited, adapted, fitted; hence suitable, fitting, fit.
1525 WOLSEY in Strype's *Eccl. Mem.* I. 95 Loving and kind words..meet and accommodate for the company present. **1531** ELYOT *Governor* I. x. 26 (1557) Moste accommodate to the aduancemente of some vertue. **1627** SPEED *Irel. descr. & abridged* iv. §4 Many accomodate and fit Bayes, Creekes, and nauigable Riuers. **1680** H. MORE *Apocalypsis* Pref. 15 Grotius..is now accounted the Chiefest Interpreter, and most accomodate to baffle the true and genuine meaning of those Prophecies. **1765** HARRIS *Three Treat.* III. i. 122 The Sovereign Good ought to be something..accommodate to all Places and Times. **1796** PEGGE *Anonym.* (1809) 186 Applications of passages in the Classics, when they are perfectly accommodate, always give pleasure.

accommodate (ə'kɒmədeɪt), *v.* [f. prec. or on anal. of vbs. so formed. See -ATE[3].] To fit or suit.

I. To fit one thing or person *to* another.

†**1.** To apply fittingly (a thing to a person); to attribute or ascribe, by way of explanation, or from inherent fitness. *Obs.*
1531 ELYOT *Governor* (1834) 174 This sentence is.. supposed to have been first spoken by Chilo. Others do accommodate it to Apollo. **1676** J. OWEN *Wor. God* 133 Many names..are equally accommodated unto all that are partakers of it, as Elders, Bishops.

2. a. To adapt, fit, suit, or adjust (one thing or person *to* another) either actually or in idea.
1588 WHITEHORNE *Machiauels Arte of Warre* 104 b, [He] must accommodate himselfe with the situation. **1692** BENTLEY *Boyle Lect.* ix. 335 The Political Institutions of Moses were accommodated to the circumstances of Affairs. **1725** DE FOE *Voy. round World* (1840) 210 Accommodate himself to the men on board. **1831** SCOTT *Peveril* iv. 60 I would fain accommodate myself to your scruples. **1856** BREWSTER *Mart. of Sc.* III. ii. (ed. 3) 184 Kepler likewise observed the power of accommodating the eye to different distances.

b. *spec.* in *Philol.*
1933 *O.E.D. Suppl.*, *Shin*.., accommodated pronunciation of *sinh.* **1939** R. W. CHAPMAN *Adjs. fr. Proper Names* 59 *Persien* or *Percien* is in English of the fourteenth century. This in the sixteenth century was accommodated to the regular *-ian.* **1962** E. S. OLSZEWSKA in Davis& Wrenn *Eng. & Medieval Stud.* 120 The alliterative formula is borrowed from a Norse coupling of the two synonyms.. with the second noun accommodated in form to the native cognate.

†**3.** *intr.* (by omission of refl. pron.) To adapt oneself *to*. *Obs.*
1597 BACON *Coulers of Good & Evill* x. 153 Keepe the minde in suspence from settling and accomodating in patience and resolution. **1677** *Governm. Venice* 72 Cato.. knew not how to accommodate to the propensity of the age.

4. To show the adaptation or correspondence of one thing to another; to make a statement fit with facts or *vice versâ*; to make consistent, to harmonize; to adapt by analogy, or by 'humouring' an account or statement. (Often used in the sense of producing an artificial or surface harmony.) Const. *to*, (*with*, *unto* obs.).
1603 HOLLAND *Plutarch's Morals* 17 Ponder well the intention of Poëts, unto which they addresse & accommodate their verses. **1655–60** T. STANLEY *Hist. Philos.* (1701) 75 To accommodate this time with our account is neither easie nor certain. **1760** JORTIN *Life of Erasmus* II. 226 Erasmus suspected that this MS. had been accommodated by the Transcriber to the Latin Version. **1860** TRENCH *Serm. in Westm. Abbey* ix. 93 The words.. were not accommodated to Christ, but were most truly fulfilled in Him.

II. To fit things (*sc.* to each other).

5. To adjust, reconcile (things or persons that differ), and hence, to compose, settle (their difference); to bring to harmony or agreement.
1597 DANIEL *Civile Wares* VIII. lxv. Repaire to us, who will accomodate this businesse. **1677** *Governm. Venice* 53 The Senat found some way or other of interposing, under colour of accommodating their Quarrel. **1753** CHAMBERS *Cycl. Supp.* s.v. *Galenist*, At present, the Galenists and chemists are pretty well accommodated. **1786** T. JEFFERSON *Writings* (1859) I. 562 It is uncertain how far we should have been able to accommodate our opinions. **1849** MACAULAY *Hist. Eng.* II. 667 At length the dispute had been accommodated.

6. Hence (with obj. indefinitely represented by *it*), *to accommodate it*: to settle or compromise matters.
1667 PEPYS *Diary* 30 Nov. The King will accommodate it by committing my Lord Clarendon himself.

7. *intr.* (by entire suppression of object) To settle differences, to come to terms.
1648 EVELYN *Mem.* (1857) III. 12 Either they must accommodate with His Majesty, or resolve to despatch with monarchy. **1748** RICHARDSON *Clarissa* (1811) IV. 60 I hardly expect that we can accommodate. **1801** T. FREEMANTLE in Dk. of Buckingham's *Crt. George III*, III. 154/2 I hope we shall accommodate with the Danes.

†**III.** To fit a thing (*sc.* for its proper uses). *Obs.*

†**8.** To fit or equip (a thing for use); to put in order; hence, to repair, refit, mend. (Fr. *raccommoder.*) *Obs.*

1624 CAPT. SMITH *Virginia* (1629) 61 The rest of the day we spent in accommodating our boat. **1763–5** SMOLLETT *Travels* 311 One of the irons of the coach gave way.. we were detained two hours before it could be accommodated. **1812** HENRY *Camp. agst. Quebec* 143 We found it well accommodated for our lodgment.

†**9.** To fit (a person, for any duty or position); to meeten. *Obs.*

1658 SIR H. SLINGSBY *Diary* (1836) 211 You shall every day get by heart some new lesson, that may season and accommodate you.

†**10.** To minister convenience to; to aid, speed, facilitate. *Obs.*

1634 MASSINGER *Very Woman* IV. ii. One o' the slaves he lately bought.. To accommodate his cure. **1690** LOCKE *Hum. Underst.* (1727) I. II. xxiii. §12. 129 We are able.. several ways to accommodate the Exigencies of this Life. **1703** MAUNDRELL *Journ. Jerus.* (1732) 36 To accomodate the passage you have a path.

IV. To fit (a person with the understood requisites of the occasion).

11. To furnish (a person *with* (*of* obs.) something requisite or convenient); to equip, supply, provide. Now usually with the sense of doing it to suit a person's felt requirements. (An *obs.* and *rare* const. is to accommodate a thing *to* a person.)

1597 SHAKS. *2 Hen. IV*, III. ii. 72 A Souldier is better accommodated, then with a Wife. **1598** B. JONSON *Ev. Man in Hum.* (1616) I. x. 17 Hostesse, accommodate vs with another bed-staffe. —— *Poetaster* iii. 4 (Nares) Will you present and accomodate it to the gentleman. **1627** *Lisander & Calista* III. 43 To goe unto Paris to accommodate him there of such things as were most necessary. **1672** JORDAN *Lond. Triumph.* in Heath's *Grocers' Comp.* (1869) 489 Three score and six poor men, pensioners, accommodated with Gowns and Caps. **1725** DE FOE *Voy. round World* (1840) 269 We had wax candles brought in to accomodate us with light. **1794** S. WILLIAMS *Hist. Vermont* 94 His hind feet are accommodated with webs. *Mod.* Can you accommodate me with cash for a cheque?

12. *simply.* To suit, oblige, convenience. Also *absol.*

1663 COGAN *Voy. & Adv. of Pinto* lxxix. 321 If it were such as would accommodate us, he would desire us to buy it. **1784** COWPER *Task* I. 73 Ingenious fancy, never better pleas'd Than when employ'd t' accomodate the fair. **1861** GEORGE ELIOT *Silas M.* 24 I was willing to accommodate you by undertaking to sell the horse. **1881** MRS. RIDDELL *Senior Partner* xxxi, A common money-lender willin' to accommodate. **1888** GUNTER *Mr. Potter of Texas* xiv, 'Won't you be seated?'.. 'Certainly! Anything to accommodate!'

13. *esp.* To furnish or supply with suitable room and entertainment; to make room for, entertain suitably; to receive as an inmate.

1715 BURNET *Hist. own Time* (1766) I. 81 How the King would be accommodated if he came among them. **1772** *Hist. Rochester* 17 The honour of accommodating her (the Queen) at his house. **1840** DICKENS *Barn. Rud.* (C.D. ed.) lviii. 273 The cell.. having recently accommodated a drunken deserter, was by no means clean.

accommodated (ə'kɒmədeɪtɪd), *ppl. a.* [f. prec. + -ED.] Made fit or suitable; fitting, fit; adapted, suited.

1611 COTGR., *Propre*.. seemlie, comelie, well accommodated. **1630** JN. TAYLOR *Gt. Eater of Kent* 13 After some accomodated salutations, I asked him if he could eate any Thing? *a* **1674** CLARENDON *Hist. Rebell.* III. XIII. 286 He had a little House well enough accommodated. **1829** I. TAYLOR *Enthus.* iii. 61 An accommodated yet legitimate sense of the word.

†**a'ccommodately,** *adv. Obs.* [f. ACCOMMODATE *a.* + -LY².] In a manner suited or adapted *to.*

1681 GLANVILLE *Sad. Trium.* (1726) I. 73 We do not speak properly, tho more accomodately to the vulgar Apprehension. **1687** H. MORE *Conjec. Cab.* (1713) 68 Of all these, Moses his wisdom held fit to give an account accommodately to the capacity of the people.

†**a'ccommodateness.** *Obs.* [f. ACCOMMODATE *a.* + -NESS.] The quality of being accommodate or suited; suitableness.

1660 H. MORE *Myst. Godliness* VI. vi. 228 The fitness and accommodateness of so ample a Reward. **1677** HALLYWELL *Sav. of Souls* 80 (T.) Its [the Gospel's] aptness and accomodateness to the great purpose of men's salvation.

accommodating (ə'kɒmədeɪtɪŋ), *vbl. sb.* [f. ACCOMMODATE *v.* + -ING¹.] The action of adapting, suiting, fitting, adjusting, furnishing, obliging, or making room for. (Now mostly gerundial.)

1619 SIR T. EDMONDES *Let.* in *Eng. & Germ.* (1865) 57 His journey to Germany for the accommodating of the broyles in Bohemia. **1625** MEADE in Ellis *Orig. Lett.* I. 318. III. 210 [The] Students at Oxford are by Letters of the Council commanded away for the better accommodating the parliament. *Mod.* They have no means of accommodating so many visitors.

accommodating (ə'kɒmədeɪtɪŋ), *ppl. a.* [f. ACCOMMODATE *v.* + -ING².] As a *pple.* Fitting, suiting, giving accommodation. Hence, *adj.* Affording, or disposed to afford accommodation; obliging, pliant, conciliatory; easy to deal with; in an evil sense, pliable, accessible to corruption.

1775 BURKE *Conc. Amer.* Wks. III. 59 Perhaps a more smooth and accomodating spirit of freedom in them would be more acceptable to us. **1850** MRS. STOWE *Unc. T. Cab.* xxxix. 342 Cassy had been unusually gracious and accommodating in her humours. **1855** PRESCOTT *Philip II*, I. I. ii. 18 The accommodating spirit of the good ecclesiastic had doubtless some influence in his rapid advancement.

accommodatingly (ə'kɒmədeɪtɪŋlɪ), *adv.* [f. prec. + -LY².] In an accommodating manner; so as to suit or convenience; conveniently, obligingly.

1847 A. SMITH *Stuck-up People* (ed. 4) 39 Mr. Lacquer drops it into the plate so accommodatingly presented to him. **1873** G. C. DAVIES *Mount. Mead. & Mere* xi. 88 Griffith guided the worm accommodatingly to the noses of the largest [fish].

accommodation (ə,kɒmə'deɪʃən). [a. Fr. *accommodation* (Cotgr. 1611), ad. L. *accommodātiōn-em*, n. of action f. *accommodā-re* to ACCOMMODATE.]

1. a. The action of accommodating, or process of being accommodated; of fitting, adapting, adjusting, suiting; adaptation, adjustment.

1644 BULWER *Chironomia* 58 Gestures and motions must come in with their accommodation. **1665** GLANVILLE *Scepsis Sc.* Addr. 6 That disputing physiology is of no accommodation to your designs. **1769–90** SIR J. REYNOLDS *Disc.* (1876) v. 372 Skilful accommodation of other men's conceptions to his own purpose. **1841** MYERS *Cath. Thoughts* III. §4. 12 What was Judaism itself.. but a great system of accommodation?

b. *spec.* The action or power of adapting the eyes to view objects at various distances.

1833 BREWSTER *Nat. Magic* iii. 53 The accommodation of the eye to the distinct vision of external objects. **1875** WOOD *Therap.* (1879) 358 Local application of gelsemia to the eye produces.. paralysis of accommodation.

c. *spec.* in *Psychol.*

1875 A. BAIN *Emotions & Will* (ed. 3) 83 Under a fresh shock this accommodation operates by diminishing the interval of transition. **1895** J. M. BALDWIN *Mental Development* vii. 217 Accommodation as it is best to call it in psychology, adaptation in biology. **1901** —— *Dict. Philos. & Psychol.* I. 8/1 As habit is the principle of mental 'conservation of type', so accommodation is the principle of modification of type. **1937** R. M. MACIVER *Society* vi. 106 To his complex changeful world man can achieve only a partial adjustment, a compound of conflict and accommodation (by the latter term we mean the process in which the person or the group comes to fit into a given situation and to feel 'at home' within it).

2. a. Adaptation of a word, expression, or system to something different from its original purpose.

1724 A. COLLINS *Gr. Chr. Relig.* 212 The frequent accommodation of the Septuagint Version to the later Hebrew. **1860** TRENCH *Serm. in Westm.* ix. 92 The adaptation or accommodation of a prophecy.. having properly no allusion to Him at all. **1865** MOZLEY *Miracles* vii. 282 Some intermediate religion being preached first as an accommodation.

b. *Philol.* The action of accommodating or fact of being accommodated (cf. ACCOMMODATE *v.* 2 b); adaptation; assimilation.

1871 KENNEDY *Pub. Sch. Lat. Gram.* 18 Incomplete Assimilation or Accommodation takes place when the former Consonant is changed, not to the latter, but to one more akin to this in sound. **1925** P. RADIN tr. *Vendryès's Language* I. iii. 59 In the first case accommodation takes place, in the second case epenthesis. **1932** GORDON & ONIONS in *Medium Ævum* I. 127 It is necessary to suppose an English accommodation of the Scandinavian word to account for the forms that the word presents in our dialects.

3. Self-adaptation; conformity to circumstance; conciliatory disposition or conduct: obligingness.

1768 STERNE *Sent. Journey* (1778) I. 4 When I had.. drank the King of France's health, to satisfy my mind that I bore him no spleen.. I rose up an inch taller for the accomodation. **1827** HALLAM *Const. Hist.* (1876) II. viii. 66 His object in these accommodations was to draw over the more moderate Romanists. **1830** SIR J. MACINTOSH *Eth. Philos.* Wks. 1846 I. 186 Accommodation, without which society would be painful, and arduous affairs would become impracticable.

4. An arrangement of a dispute; a settlement, composition, treaty, or compromise.

1645 *Liberty of Consc.* 36 By accommodation I understand an agreement of dissenters with the rest of the Church in practicall conclusions. **1689** SELDEN *Table Talk* 62 'Tis hard to make an accommodation between the King and the Parliament. **1745** DE FOE *Eng. Tradesm.* II. xxxix. 119 He will bring all differences to a friendly accommodation. **1855** PRESCOTT *Philip II*, I. I. vi. 81 Negotiations were now opened for an accommodation between the belligerents.

5. The supplying with what is suitable or requisite.

1737 JOHNSON *Rambler* 145. ¶1 The meanest artisan or manufacturer contributes more to the accommodation of life, than the profound scholar and argumentative theorist.

6. a. Anything which supplies a want, or affords aid or refreshment, or ministers to one's comfort; a convenience, an appliance.

1616 SURFL. & MARKH. *Countrey Farme* 539 When a man liueth farre from his necessarie accommodations, as from his fuell, his fencing, his timber. **1662** FULLER *Worthies* (1840) III. 731 Wilton is the stateliest and pleasantest for gardens, fountains and other accommodations. **1769–90** SIR J. REYNOLDS *Disc.* (1876) 301 The regular progress of cultivated life is from necessaries to accommodations, from accommodations to ornaments. **1866** GEO. ELIOT *Felix Holt* 4 They probably thought of the coach with some contempt, as an accommodation for people who had not their own gigs.

b. *attrib.* ***accommodation address***, an address used solely or primarily for convenience of correspondence; freq. one adopted to conceal the whereabouts of the addressee; ***accommodation bridge*** (see quot. 1954); ***accommodation ladder*** (see quot. 1867); ***accommodation road***, a road constructed to give access to a property or piece of land not adjoining a public road; ***accommodation stage, train***, one stopping at all (or nearly all) the points or stations on the route (*U.S.*).

1894 LITTLECHILD *Reminisc.* vii. 69 One of their number arranged, on some plausible story, for letters to be received for him at an 'accommodation address'—generally a small shop. **1914** 'I. HAY' *Knight on Wheels* I. i. 13 A small greengrocer's shop—an 'accommodation address' of the most ordinary type—whose proprietor admitted that he was in the habit of taking in letters on behalf of some of his customers. **1958** *Economist* 16 Aug. 552/2 A *pied-à-terre* for meetings and an accommodation address and telephone, linked by private line with their main premises. **1813** MAR. GRAHAM *Jrnl. in India* 128 A particular police regulates the catamarans, accommodation-boats and bar-boats. *a* **1809** A. REES *Cycl.* VI. s.v. *Canal*, For *occupation*, or accommodation bridges.. a kind of swing or swivel bridge has.. been adopted. **1954** *Highway Engin. Terms* (*B.S.I.*) 24 *Accommodation bridge*, a bridge serving an accommodation road. **1769** W. FALCONER *Dict. Marine* §Z1 Accommodation-*Ladder*, is a sort of light stair-case, occasionally fixed on the gangway of the admiral.. of a fleet. **1839** G. W. M. REYNOLDS *Pickwick Abroad* i. 7 That faithful domestic descended the accommodation-ladder, and once more stood upon the deck of the vessel. **1847** DISRAELI *Tancred* (1871) IV. xi. 327 From the door of the house were some temporary steps, like an accommodation ladder. **1867** SMYTH *Sailors' Wd.-Bk.* s.v. *Accommodation ladder*, a convenient flight of steps fixed at the gang-way, by which officers and visitors enter the ship. **1881** MISS BRADDON *Asphodel* I. 289 Goring Lane was an accommodation road, leading down from the home farm to the meadows. **1909** KIPLING *Actions & Reactions* 36 No better than accommodation-roads. **1811** *Columbian Centinel* (Boston) 25 Sept. 3/1 Accomodation stage[-coach]. **1843** 'R. CARLTON' *New Purchase* 19 So remarkably accommodating were the old-fashioned accommodation stages and stage owners. **1838** *Boston Almanac* 49 Depots on the Providence Rail Road. Accommodation Train. **1860** O. W. HOLMES *Prof. Breakf.-t.* iii. 80 Accomodation train. A good many stops, but will get to the station by and by.

c. *ellipt.* for ***accommodation stage, train.*** *U.S.*

1829 A. ROYALL *Pennsylvania* II. 9, I.. intended to take the Accommodation in the morning. **1877** 'E. W. MARTIN' *Hist. Great Riots* 117 The Sharpsville 'accommodation'.. had been lying for two hours without an engine. **1891** C. ROBERTS *Adrift in America* ii. 33 We went on what is called an 'accommodation', that is, a freight train with a passenger car at the end of it.

7. a. *esp.* Room and suitable provision for the reception of people; entertainment; lodgings. (Formerly, and still *U.S.*, mostly in *pl.*)

1604 SHAKS. *Oth.* I. iii. 239 Such Accomodation and besort As leuels with her breeding. **1650** CROMWELL *Let.* 92 (Carlyle) The having of a garrison there would furnish us with accommodation for our sick men. **1722** DE FOE *Moll Fl.* (1840) 343 These had accommodations assigned them in the great cabin. **1803** PORTER *Thad. Warsaw* (1831) xi. 100 The Hummums, Covent Garden, has as good accommodations as any in town. **1804** G. T. HOPKINS *Diary* 24 Feb. in *Maryland Hist. Mag.* (1909) IV. 3 We rode to the house of.. a neighbouring farmer, where we found good accomodations. **1856** KANE *Arctic Explor.* I. xvi. 192 Our sole accommodation a tent barely able to contain eight persons. **1937** C. S. JOHNSON *Negro in Amer. Civ.* xxiv. 338 The wastefulness of exactly dual accommodations [for Negroes and for whites in railway trains].

b. *attrib.* ***accommodation house***, a lodging house for travellers (freq. derog.); ***accommodation paddock*** (Austral. and N.Z.), see quot. 1933; ***accommodation unit***, for purposes of official enumeration: a single place of residence.

1823 'JON BEE' *Slang 2 Accommodation-house.* The Reader had better consult 'Fubbs' than we explain the minute difference that exists between these and a 'Dress-house' or a 'Bodikin'. **1857** H. W. HARPER *Let. fr. N.Z.* 1 Sept. (1914) 17 There I found what is known as an accommodation house. **1861** MAYHEW *London Labour* (Extra vol.) (1862) 249/1 Those who gain their living by keeping accommodation houses.. are of course to be placed in the category of the people who are dependant on prostitutes. **1933** *Bulletin* (Sydney) 1 Nov. 21/3 An accommodation-house that has never received its due meed of notoriety. **1933** L. ACLAND in *Press* (Christchurch, N.Z.) 9 Sept. 15/7 *Accommodation Paddocks*, paddocks kept by publicans and others for the use of travelling stock.. unknown, of course, until the roads were fenced in the 'seventies. **1947** C. B. BRERETON *No Roll of Drums* xvi. 143, I know your accommodation paddock is eaten out. **1950** D. MAXWELL FYFE in *Hansard Commons* 5th Ser. CDLXXII. 853 One million 'accommodation units' have been built since the war. **1951** *Evening Stand.* 17 Aug. 4/1 The Ministry of Health's classic 'accommodation unit', which Mr. Churchill killed stone-dead by singing the phrase to the tune of Home, Sweet Home.

8. a. Pecuniary aid in an emergency; a loan. ***Accommodation Bill***, a bill not representing or originating in an actual commercial transaction, but for the purpose of raising money on credit.

1790 HAMILTON in *Ann. 1st Congress* II. 2058 The accommodations which they might derive in the way of their business, at a low rate. **1803** *Edin. Rev.* II. 102 All accommodation bills are iniquitous. **1807** SCOTT *Lett.*

(1932) I. 411 With respect to accomodations in my opinion we ought to get rid of all that floating balance which . . has hitherto kept us in poverty. **1824** SCOTT *Ronan's Well* (1868) xv. 653 There is maybe an accommodation bill discounted now and then, Mr. Touchwood; but men must have accommodation, or the world would stand still—accommodation is the grease that makes the wheels go. **1826** —— in Lockhart's *Life* (1839) VIII. 336 Having obtained an accommodation of £100 from Ballantyne. **1868** ROGERS *Polit. Econ.* (ed. 3) xi. 142 Persons pay highly for accommodation, because they have no security, or no good security, to offer. **1882** *Daily News* July 3 (Advt.) *Cash Accommodation.*—Respectable Householders in town or country supplied with money at moderate interest.

b. *attrib.* as ***accommodation note, paper.***

1797 *Deb. Congress* 27 June (1851) 395 Many of such notes were what was called 'accommodation notes'; all acknowledgments of debt, and therefore no proof of wealth. *Ibid.* 28 June 401 Being able to raise money by accommodation notes to pay duties. **1829** SHERWOOD *Gaz. Georgia* (ed. 2) 75 The Bank to collect the debts due the State, and debtors to be allowed to renew their notes . . as persons borrowing money on accommodation paper.

accommodative (ə'kɒmədeɪtɪv), *a.* [f. *accommodāt-* ppl. stem of *accommodā-re* + -IVE; as if ad. L. **accommodātivus*.] Tending to accommodate; accommodating.

1841 MYERS *Cath. Thoughts* III. §26. 97 This peculiarity of its accommodative character. **1880** BURTON *Reign of Q. Anne* III. xix. 211 In the strifes, religious and secular, that had shaken Scotland, no such accommodative adjustment had been permitted to grow.

accommodativeness (ə'kɒmə,deɪtɪvnɪs). [f. prec. + -NESS.] The quality of being accommodative; adaptability, pliableness; tendency to give or show accommodation.

1860 *Times* 4 July 10/2 Mere accommodativeness to the irresistible tide of events. **1868** MERIVALE in *Fortn. Rev.* Nov. 472 [They] are apt to learn much of forbearance and civility, and kindness and accommodativeness.

accommodator (ə'kɒmədeɪtə(r)). [a. L. *accommodātor*, n. of agent f. *accommodāre*: see ACCOMMODATE.] **a.** He who, or that which, accommodates (in various senses of the vb.).

c **1630** W. ROBINSON in *Lett. Sci. Men* (1841) I. 11 At the most he is but the accommodator, (an easy trifle,) not the inventor. **1662** FULLER *Worthies* (1840) III. 125 These [Nails] are the accommodators generally to unite solid bodies. **1762** WARBURTON *Doct. of Grace* II. 331 (T.) Mahomet wanted the refinement of our modern accommodators.

b. A temporary domestic help. *U.S.*

1948 F. P. KEYES *Dinner at Antoine's* (1949) ii. 32 Tossie was in great demand as an 'accommodator' at débutante parties. **1959** *Encounter* Nov. 43/2 In the evenings, the old 'accommodators' dart about the city, carrying their black uniforms and white aprons in a paper bag. They . . go anywhere to cook and serve dinners.

†**acco'mmode**, *v.* *Obs. rare*$^{-1}$. [a. Fr. *accommode-r*, ad. L. *accommodā-re* to ACCOMMODATE. Cf. *incommode*.] A by-form of ACCOMMODATE.

1671 VINES *Lord's Sup.* 90 In reason did Christ accomode his blessing to the occasion.

†**acco'mmodement.** *Obs. rare*$^{-1}$. [a. Fr. *accommodement*, f. *accommoder*; see prec. and MENT.] An arrangement, settlement, or accommodation.

1678 GALE *Crt. Gentiles* III. 123 They required the Jansenists to conforme in those points controverted, in order to an accommodement.

accompactment. ?A compactment; a compact.

a **1500** *Merlin* 249 in Percy's *Folio MS., Bal. & Rom.* I. 430 Vortiger the traitor bold lett make accompackement of erles & barrons that were gent.

†**a'ccompanable, -iable**, *a. Obs.* [a. Fr. *accompagnable* f. *accompagner* + -ABLE.] Sociable, companionable.

1548 GESTE *Preuee Masse* 135 Sequestering him selve from hys accompanable parrishioners. **1580** NORTH *Plutarch* (1676) 871 Cecinna was neither for person nor manners accompaniable for the people. **1580** SIDNEY *Arcadia* (1622) 6 A shew, as it were, of an accompanable solitarinesse, and of a ciuill wildenes. [Not in COTGR. or FLORIO 1611. The former has Fr. *accompagnable*, companable, sociable.]

accompanier (ə'kʌmpənɪə(r)). [f. ACCOMPANY + -ER[1].] He who, or that which, accompanies.

[**1755** In JOHNSON as a 'Dictionary word.'] **1823** LAMB *Elia* 436 Dear, cracked spinnet of dearer Louisa! . . thou thin accompanier of her thinner warble. **1834** PERRONET THOMPSON *Exerc.* (1842) III. 33 He would then be prepared to come out as an accompanier of the voice.

accompaniment (ə'kʌmpənɪmənt). Also 8 accompanyment. [a. Fr. *accompagnement* (13th c. in Littré) f. *accompagner* + -MENT.] **1.** Anything that accompanies; 'something attending or added as a circumstance to another, either by way of ornament, or for the sake of symmetry or the like.' Bailey 1731. Not in Johnson.

1756–82 J. WARTON *Ess. Pope* (ed. 4) I. §2. 77 The magnificent spectacle . . which is, if I may be allowed the expression, the accompanyment of the picture. **1782** GILPIN *Wye* 4 None of these landscapes however are perfect, as they want the accompaniments of foregrounds. **1875** BRYCE *Holy Rom. Emp.* (ed. 5) xvi. 286 A Roman sedition was the all but invariable accompaniment of a Roman coronation.

2. *Music.* The subsidiary part or parts, instrumental or vocal, added for the sake of effect to a melody or musical composition; chiefly applied to the instrumental part which sustains the voice. Hence **accompani'mental** *a.*

1744 DYCHE, *Accompaniment*, the instrumental part playing or moving while the voice is singing. **1754** GRAY *Progr. Poetry* I. i, Pindar styles his own poetry with its musical accompaniments *Αἰοληῒς μολπή*. **1795** MASON *Ch. Mus.* Wks. 1811 III. 318 The former [Purcell] adding Violin accompaniments to some of his anthems and services. **1859** JEPHSON *Brittany* v. 60 Sung in unison with a modest organ-accompaniment. **1917** C. SCOTT *Philos. of Modernism* ix. 71 There are two ways of treating old airs from an accompanimental point of view. **1959** *Times* 18 May 9/7 There is nothing subordinate . . in Schubert's accompanimental patterns.

3. *Heraldry.* 'Such things as are applied about the shield, by way of ornament, as the belt, mantlings, supporters, etc.' Bailey, vol. II. 1731.

accompanist, accompanyist (ə'kʌmpənɪst, ə'kʌmpənɪɪst). [f. ACCOMPANY + -IST.] One who, or that which, accompanies; *esp.* the performer who takes the accompanying part in music.

1833 *Pen. Cycl.* I. 74 *Est modus in rebus*—and sensible accompanists well know this medium. **1837–9** DICKENS *Oliv. Tw.* II. iv. 143 The accompanyist played the melody. **1871** *Athenæum* 15 July 89 Mr. Emanuel and Signor Fiori, accompanists. **1872** *Daily News* 7 Aug., A fleet of friendly accompanyists [yachts] brought up the rear. **1878** HUEFFER in Grove's *Dict. Music* I. 28 From which post he soon advanced to that of accompanyist at the same theatre.

accompany (ə'kʌmpənɪ), *v.* [a. Fr. *accompagne-r* f. *à* prep. to + *compagne* COMPANION.] To make any one, to make oneself, become or act as a companion.

I. To accompany one thing to or with another.

†**1.** To accompany (a person or thing) *to* (another): to add as companion; to associate; to add or conjoin to. *Obs.*

1483 CAXTON *Gold. Leg.* 174/1 As many as ye can conuerte to your feythe . . ye shal haue lycence to baptyse them and to accompanye them to your lawe. **1553–87** FOXE *A. & M.* (1596) 127/2 The King againe gathered his men . . & with fresh souldiours to them accompanied, met the Danes.

2. To accompany (a person (*obs.*) or thing) *with* (another): to send it with (or give it) the accompaniment or addition of; to supplement it by; to join to it. (Rare and less correct const. *by*.)

1629 HOWELL *Fam. Lett.* (1650) 163, I thought it a good correspondence with you to accompagne it with what follows. **1655** LD. BURGHLEY in Fuller's *Ch. Hist.* IX. 167, I have thought good to accompany him with these my letters. **1810** W. TAYLOR in Robberds' *Mem.* II. 285 Accompanying my letter by a copy of the 'Tales of Yore.' *Mod.* He accompanied the word with a blow.

†**3.** *refl.* To associate or unite oneself *with*. *Obs.*

1477 EARL RIVERS (Caxton) *Dictes* 119 Accompanye the with good peple and thou shalt be one of them. **1650** SIR A. WELDON *Crt. & Char. K. James* 62 And did accompany himselfe with none but men . . by whom he might be bettered.

†**II.** To accompany (*sc.* oneself) with others. *Obs.*

†**4.** *intr.* (by omission of refl. pron.) To accompany *with*: to associate, consort, or keep company with; *euphem.* to cohabit with. *Obs.*

1534 LD. BERNERS *Gold. Bk. M. Aurel.* (1546) G ij b, Suche as accompanyeth with man-killers and murtherers. **1577** *Test. of 12 Patr.* When Anan was marriageable, I gaue Thamar unto him, & he likewise of a spite accompanied not with her. **1676** CLARENDON *Surv. Leviath.* 257 Those men who had accompanied with them all the time. **1760** T. HUTCHINSON *Hist. Col. Mass. Bay* (1765) v. 461 A young woman was not less esteemed for having accompanied with a man.

†**5.** *absol.* To associate in a company; to congregate; to meet, to unite or combine. *Obs.*

1540 WHITTINTON *Tully's Off.* I. 70 Swarmes of bees do accompany . . for as moch as they be companable by nature. **1577** HELLOWES tr. *Gueuara's Fam. Ep.* 27 Noblenesse and contention did neuer accompanie in one generous personage.

III. *trans.* (from 4, by omission of *with*.) To accompany persons or things.

†**6.** To remain or stay with; to keep company with; *euphem.* to cohabit with. *Obs.*

c **1500** *Remedie of Loue* in Speght's *Chaucer* (1602) 308 b/1 If she sit idle . . not accompanide . . with maidens I meane, or women. **1580** SIDNEY *Arcadia* (1622) 195 Shee vsed no harder wordes to her, then to bid her go home, and accompanie her solitarie father. **1660** R. COKE *Power & Subj.* 161 We teach, that upon Festival and Fasting times every man forbear to accompany his wife.

†**7.** *fig.* To tenant or fill (a place) with company. *Obs. rare.*

1631 *Celestina* XXI. 201 What hast thou done with my daughter? where hast thou bestow'd her? who shall accompany my disaccompanied habitation?

8. To go in company with, to go along with; to convoy; to escort (for safety), to attend (as a retinue). (The passive formerly took *with*, now *by*.)

c **1460** FORTESCUE *Abs. & Lim. Mon.* (1714) 48 Which Ambassatours . . schal nede to be honorably accompanyd. **1494** FABYAN I. ii. 8 Accompanyed with a great Nombre of Troyans . . [he] landed in the countre of Italye. **1588** SHAKS. *Tit. A.* I. i. 333 Panthean Lords, accompany Your Noble Emperour and his louely Bride. **1659** RUSHWORTH *Hist. Collect.* I. 76 The Marquiss went privately accompanied with the Earl of Bristol. **1722** DE FOE *Hist. Plague* 43 That no neighbours nor friends be suffered to accompany the corpse to church. **1801** STRUTT *Sports & Past.* I. i. 11 The ladies often accompanied the gentlemen in hunting parties. **1876** FREEMAN *Norm. Conq.* III. x. 462 The Earl went as a pilgrim, accompanied by his wife.

b. *fig.* Of things personified or viewed as companions.

1477 EARL RIVERS (Caxton) *Dictes* 91 Couetise hath accompaigned them from their childehode. *a* **1541** WYATT *Complaint* (1831) 161 So shall mine eyes in pain accompany my heart. **1611** BIBLE *Heb.* vi. 9 Wee are perswaded better things of you, and things that accompany saluation. **1645** FULLER *Good Thoughts* (1841) 23 Lord, I read how Jacob (then only accompanied with his staff) vowed at Bethel, that . . he would make that place thy house. **1856** MILL *Logic* (1868) I. v. §4. 109 One attribute always accompanies another attribute. **1875** HAMERTON *Intell. Life* I. iii. 14 His adviser prescribed a well-cooked little *déjeuner à la fourchette*, accompanied by half a bottle of sound Bordeaux.

9. To go along with, or characterize, as an attribute or attendant phenomenon. (The passive still takes *with*, but *by* is sometimes found.)

1731 SWIFT *Pref. to Sir W. Temple's Wks.* I. 254 To prevent him from finding them in other Places very faulty, and perhaps accompanied with many spurious Additions. **1751** JORTIN *Serm.* (1771) I. IV. 62 Their faith was accompanied with greater degrees of fervour. **1794** SULLIVAN *View of Nat.* I. 179 The sparkling flame and vivid heat which accompany the rapid combustion produced by that air [oxygen]. **1869** PHILLIPS *Vesuvius* iv. 112 The ejections of scoriæ were accompanied by bellowings. **1878** GLADSTONE *Prim. Homer* 148 The wisdom of Nestor is amusingly accompanied with self-complacent reflection.

10. *Music.* To join a singer or player, by singing or playing on any instrument an additional part or parts. (The player is said also to accompany the singing or piece sung, as well as the singer; and to accompany, *with* music, *on* the instrument.)

1583 GOLDING *Calvin's Deut.* xliii. 255 A gratious and pleasaunt melody wherein wee be accompanied with the Angels of heauen. *c* **1680** SIR T. BROWNE *Tracts* 124 This hymn accompanied with instrumental musick. **1753** RICHARDSON *Grandison* (1781) VI. liv. 351 After breakfast, Lucy gave us a lesson on the harpsichord. Sir Charles accompanied her finger, at the desire of the company. **1845** E. HOLMES *Mozart* 26 A lady asked him if he could accompany by ear an Italian Cavatina . . [he] accompanied it with the bass without the least embarrassment. **1869** OUSELEY *Counterpoint* xx. 162 The counter-subject is a supplementary melody, intended to accompany the subject and answer.

¶ The preposition used after the passive *accompanied* is still somewhat unsettled. As in passives generally, it was formerly *with*; but *by* is now always said of personal agents, and, it appears, of things personified or viewed as active agents: 'He was accompanied *by* two policemen,' 'a ship accompanied *by* several native junks.' When *accompany* is used causally, *with* introduces the secondary agent or instrument, as 'he accompanied the word *with* a blow;' and this is of course retained in the passive, 'the word was accompanied *with* a blow (by him).' Hence *with* is used in the passive whenever the agency may be looked upon as merely secondary, or as an *accompaniment* rather than a *companion*, even though no primary agent is expressed, 'The operation was accompanied *with* much pain.' Cf. *associated, combined* with; *attended* with *pain*, by *satellites*; *followed* by unpleasant *symptoms*.

accompanying (ə'kʌmpənɪɪŋ), *vbl. sb.* [f. ACCOMPANY + ING[1].] The action of being a companion, associating, going or acting with; or of giving anything an accompaniment. *spec.* The act of playing an additional part on an instrument in support of a singer. (Now mostly gerundial.)

1581 SIDNEY *Def. Poesie* (1622) 515 Heraclitus . . is to be praised for compassionate accompanying iust causes of lamentations. **1649** DRUMM. OF HAWTH. *Hist. James III* Wks. 1711, 56 Acts were made that no convention of friends should be suffered for the accompanying & defence of criminal persons. *Mod.* May I have the pleasure of accompanying you?

accompanying (ə'kʌmpənɪɪŋ), *ppl. a.* [f. ACCOMPANY + -ING[2].] Acting as a companion; going along with; attending; attached, appended.

1850 McCOSH *Div. Govt.* (1874) III. iii. 428 The moral good or the evil lies not in the affection itself, but in its accompanying desire or volition. **1880** HAUGHTON *Phys. Geogr.* iii. 134 The Gulf Stream is shewn in the accompanying map.

†**a'ccompass**, *v. Obs. rare*$^{-1}$. [f. L. *ac-* = *ad-* + COMPASS *v.*: see A- *pref.* 11.] To compass; to go about, to contrive.

1692 HACKET *Life of Williams* I. 189 The Prince . . was privy to the undertakings of his [Lord Cranfeild's] adversaries and accompassed suffrages to condemn him.

†**a'ccomplement.** *Obs.* 6–7. [f. late L. *accomplē-re* (f. *ac-* = *ad-* to + *complēre* to fill, see COMPLETE) + -MENT. Formed directly from L.

like *complement, supplement*, whereas the more common ACCOMPLISHMENT was adopted from Fr.] Anything that completes or perfects; that adds grace or ornament to body or mind. See ACCOMPLISHMENT, 3.

1587 FLEMING *Contn. Holinshed* III. 1579 Accompanied with all princelie and gracefull accomplements. **1596** ? SHAKS. *Edw. III*, IV. vi. 66 A puissant host of men Array'd & fenc'd in all accomplements. **1634** PEACHAM *Gent. Exerc.* to Rdr. 1 Those things of accomplement required in a Scholler or Gentleman. **1642** BIRD *Mag. Honour* 107 b, Vertue and riches.. (as Ecclesiastes teacheth) maketh a good accomplement.

†**accomplet(e**, *ppl. a. Obs. rare*$^{-1}$. [ad. late L. *accomplēt-us* pa. pple. of *accomplēre*; see ACCOMPLISH.] Filled up, complete.

a **1450** *Knt. de la Tour* 110 The fest was fulfelled and a complet in eueri wise.

a'ccompletive, *a. rare.* [f. L. *accomplēt-* ppl. stem of *accomplēre* (see ACCOMPLISH) + -IVE.] Having the property of fulfilling; tending to accomplish.

1839 BAILEY *Festus* (1848) xiv. 216 Full of inborn virtue more than known, Accompletive of destiny divine.

accomplice (ə'kɒmplɪs, ə'kʌmplɪs). [f. the earlier COMPLICE. The prefixed *ac-* is not accounted for; it may have arisen from the indef. art. *a complice*, or by assimilation to *accomplish*; there is no analogous form in L. or Fr.] An associate in guilt, a partner in crime. Const. *of*; also *with* the criminal, *in* (*to* obs.) the crime.

1485 CAXTON *Chas. the Grete* (1880) 164, I shal make thadmyral to dye, and al hys complyces. **1589** NASHE *Alm. for Parrat* 5 d, Call to minde the badde practise of your brother the Booke-binder and his accomplishes at Burie. **1596** SPENSER *State Irel.* 20 And many the like of others his accomplices and fellow-traytors. **1692** DRYDEN *St. Euremont's Ess.* 319 He was a friend of Cataline's and a secret accomplice of his Crime. **1732** LEDIARD *Life of Sethos* II. VII. 43 Thou who has been accomplice with the thieves and murtherers. **1735-8** LD. BOLINGBROKE *Diss. on Parties* 152 We cannot lose..our Constitution, unless We are Accomplices to the Violations of it. **1853** H. ROGERS *Ecl. Faith* 158 To permit any evils which we can prevent is in like manner to be accomplices in the crime. **1860** W. COLLINS *Wom. in White* II. ii. 181 English society is as often the accomplice as it is the enemy of crime.

2. *rare.* and perh. *only playfully*, in a sense not bad.

1591 SHAKS. *1 Hen. VI*, v. 2. 9 Successe vnto our valiant Generall, And happinesse to his accomplices. *c* **1860** WRAXALL tr. *R. Houdin* vii. 96 In the mean while be kind anough to act as my accomplice.

a'ccompliceship. *rare.* [f. prec. + -SHIP.] = ACCOMPLICITY.

1834 SIR H. TAYLOR *Ph. v. Artevelde* I. v. ix. Wks. 1864 I. 136 This craven cowardly companion—Of whose accompliceship to do the deed, And not the deed itself, I speak with shame.

accom'plicity. *rare.* [f. as prec. + -ITY.] The state of being an accomplice; criminal assistance.

WORCESTER cites *Q. Rev.*

†**accompliment**, *sb. Obs. rare*$^{-1}$. [f. AC- = A- *pref.* 11 + COMPLIMENT.] = COMPLIMENT *sb.*

1601 CORNWALLYES *Ess.* (1631) II. xxviii. 27 This is the most poysonous qualitie in accomplements, the pretyest are those that meane neither well nor ill.

†**accompliment**, *v. Obs. rare*$^{-1}$. [f. as prec.] = COMPLIMENT *v.*

1601 CORNWALLYES *Ess.* (1631) II. xxviii. 23 Wee accomplement, and..kisse the hand.

accomplish , (ə'kʌmplɪʃ, ə'kɒmplɪʃ), *v.* Also accomplice, -ise, -isse, -yshe, -ysshe, -issh(e. [a. OFr. *acompliss-* extended stem of *acomplir, acumplir*, now *accomplir* (as in pr. pple. *accompliss-ant*):—late L. *accomplēre* (f. *ac-* = *ad-* to + *complēre* to fill up, complete): see -ISH. The historical pronunc. is (ə'kʌmplɪʃ); said in 1884 (*N.E.D.*) to have 'recently given way' to a pronunciation (ə'kɒmplɪʃ) founded on the spelling, but nonetheless widely current during the 20th cent.]

1. *trans.* To fulfil, perform, or carry out (an undertaking, design, desire, promise, etc.).

c **1386** CHAUCER *Melibeus* 199 Grete thinges ben not ay accompliced by strengthe, ne by delyvernes of body, but by good counseil. *c* **1450** *Merlin* 61 It shall not be in thy tyme; ne he that shall a-complesshen it, is not yet be-geten. **1480** CAXTON *Chron. Eng.* ccxlvi. 311 He spared no thyng of his lustes ne desyres, but accomplysshed them after his lykyng. **1593** SHAKS. *Rich. II*, III. iii. 124 And all the number of his faire demands Shall be accomplish'd without contradiction. **1611** BIBLE *Prov.* xiii. 19 The desire accomplished is sweet to the soule. **1769** BURKE *State Nat.* Wks. II. 43 The original great purposes of the war were more than accomplished by the treaty. **1878** SEELEY *Stein* II. 511 What is here proposed, was, we know, actually accomplished..under the leadership of Alexander.

†**2.** *intr.* To carry out a design. *Obs. rare.*

1490 CAXTON *Eneydos* v. 26 Thenne Eneas and alle his sequele (having) made theym redy for to accomplysshe and leve the sayd countrey..mounted upon the see. **1509** HAWES *Past. Pleas.* XI. xxix. (1845) 44 It is ever the grounde of sapience, Before that thou accomplysh outwardly, For to revolve understandyng and prepence All in thy selfe full often inwardly.

3. To bring to an end, complete, or finish (a work).

1447 BOKENHAM *Lyv. Seyntys* Introd. 1 (1835) The auctour..after hys cunnyng doth his labour To a complyse the begunne matere. **1577-87** HOLINSHED *Chron.* I. 161/2 The abbeie of Abington also he accomplished and set in good order. **1605** THYNNE *Advoc.* in *Animadv.* (1865) 112 Therby to accomplish the quadrat number, the number of all perfection. **1855** PRESCOTT *Philip II*, I. II. i. 154 The work of the reformer was never accomplished so long as anything remained to reform.

b. To complete (a portion of time).

1574 tr. *Littleton's Tenures* 22 b, After that shee had accomplished the age of xiiij. **1611** BIBLE *Dan.* ix. 2 The word of the Lord came to Ieremiah the Prophet, that he would accomplish seuentie yeeres in the desolations of Ierusalem. **1809** KENDALL *Trav.* I. vi. 46 All such inhabitants in this state as have accomplished the age of twenty-one years.

c. To complete (a distance).

1855 PRESCOTT *Philip II* (1857) I. 120 Rising ground which lay between him and the French prevented him from seeing the enemy until he had accomplished half a league or more. **1860** TYNDALL *Glaciers* I. §11. 86 We had accomplished our journey just in time.

4. To complete with external appurtenances; to equip perfectly.

1588 LAMBARDE *Eirenarcha* I. xii. 65 Our Justices of the Peace..are accomplished with double power, the one of Jurisdiction, and the other of Coertion. **1599** SHAKS. *Hen. V*, IV. Chor. 12 The Armourers accomplishing the Knights, With busie Hammers closing Riuets vp. **1662** FULLER *Worthies* (1840) I. 367 The garden on the back side, with an artificial rock and wilderness, accomplisheth the place with all pleasure. **1673** JORDAN *London in Splend.* in Heath *Grocers' Comp.* (1869) 509 Thus accomplish'd they march from their place of meeting to Clothworkers' Hall. **1813** SCOTT *Rokeby* v. iv, Those arms, those ensigns, borne away, Accomplished Rokeby's brave array.

5. To perfect in mental acquirements and personal graces; to polish, to finish off.

1475 CAXTON *Jason* 32 Jason was more and more in the graces of the ladyes, for the best born, the most fayre, the best accomplished..fyxed their loue in him. **1591** SHAKS. *Two Gent.* IV. iii. 13 Thou art a Gentleman: Valiant, wise, remorse-full, well-accomplish'd. **1639** FULLER *Holy War* (1840) Ep. Ded. 6 Next religion, there is nothing accomplisheth a man more than learning. **1726** VANBRUGH *Journ. Lond.* III. (1730) 246 Every thing that accomplishes a fine Lady is practised, to the last perfection. **1842** MRS. BROWNING *Gr. Chr. Poets* 176 From the Italian poets as well as the classical sources and the elder English ones, did Milton accomplish his soul. **1863** COWDEN CLARKE *Shaksp. Char.* xvi. 401 These qualities adorn the character of Portia, and these go to accomplish a perfect woman.

accomplishable (ə'kɒmplɪʃəb(ə)l), *a.* [f. prec. + -ABLE.] Capable of being accomplished; attainable; practicable.

1792 T. PAINE *Rights Man* II. Ded., That which you suppose accomplishable in fourteen or fifteen years. **1846** CARLYLE quoted in *Manch. Guard.* 10 Feb. 1881 This.. seems to me the most accomplishable and by no means the least needful.

accomplished (ə'kɒmplɪʃt), *ppl. a.* [f. ACCOMPLISH + -ED.]

1. Fulfilled, completed, finished, perfected.

1577-87 HOLINSHED *Chron.* III. 886/1 The little children of the king, of whom the eldest had not yet run eight yeares accomplished. **1726** VANBRUGH *Relapse* I. iii. (1730) 17, I have brought your Lordship as accomplish'd a suit of clothes as ever Peer of England trod the stage in. **1784** COWPER *Task* I. 88 Convenience next suggested elbow chairs, And luxury th' accomplished sofa last. **1801** SOUTHEY *Thalaba* VII. xxix. IV. 263 With its rewards and blessings strews my path Thus for the accomplish'd service. **1882** *Bill of Lading*, In Witness whereof the Master or Agent of the said Ship hath signed Bills of Lading, all of this Tenor and Date, one of which being accomplished the others to be void.

2. Complete, perfect; *esp.* in acquirements, or as the result of training.

1475 CAXTON *Jason* 32 The best accomplished and the most speciall [ladies] fyxed their loue in him. **1581** SIDNEY *Def. Poesie* (1622) 524 That Realme neuer brought forth a more accomplished iudgement, more firmely builded vpon vertue. **1611** SHAKS. *Cymb.* I. v. 103 Your Italy containes none so accomplish'd a courtier to conuince the honour of my mistris. **1786** COWPER *Lett.* 19 Feb. (Wks. 1876) 227 An accomplished person moves gracefully without thinking of it. **1833** MISS AUSTEN *Pride & Prej.* 33 No one can be really esteemed accomplished who does not greatly surpass what is usually met with. **1874** BLACKIE *Self-Culture* 25 Accomplished speaking, like marching or dancing, is an art.

†**3.** Completely versed (*in*), fully informed. *Obs.*

1603 FLORIO *Montaigne* (1634) 497 Finding him so faire, so young and strong, she, who was perfectly accomplished in all his qualities, aduised him to lye with her.

accomplisher (ə'kɒmplɪʃə(r)). [f. ACCOMPLISH + -ER[1].] One who accomplishes; who carries out, completes, perfects; a finisher or perfecter.

1611 COTGR., *Parfaiseur*, a perfecter, accomplisher, finisher. **1687** H. MORE *Conject. Cabbal.* (1713) Pref. 2 Such inspiration as this is no distracter from, but an accomplisher and an enlarger of the humane faculties.

accomplishing (ə'kɒmplɪʃɪŋ), *vbl. sb.* [f. ACCOMPLISH + -ING[1].] The action of fulfilling, completing, perfecting, or finishing. (Used both as sb. and gerund.)

1581 MARBECK *Bk. Notes & Com. Pl.* 307 The Jewes.. supposed that the hearing and vnderstanding of the lawe was sufficient to the accomplishing of the same. **1649** DRUMM. OF HAWTH. *Fam. Ep.* Wks. 1711, 161 All the qualities requisite for the accomplishing of a perfect creature. **1855** MACAULAY *Hist. Eng.* IV. 536 Scarcely any step was taken towards the accomplishing of her favourite design. **1858** J. G. HOLLAND *Titcomb's Lett.* viii. 76 It is a divine contrivance or plan for accomplishing this purpose.

accomplishment (ə'kɒmplɪʃmənt). [a. Fr. *accomplissement* action of accomplishing. See ACCOMPLISH and -MENT.]

1. The action of accomplishing, or state of being accomplished; fulfilment, completion, consummation.

c **1460** FORTESCUE *Abs. & Lim. Mon.* (1714) 8 He would not have it governyd..but by his own Will; by which and for th'accomplishment thereof he made it. **1561** T. N[ORTON] *Calvin's Inst.* (1634) II. xvi. 244 We have in his death a full accomplishment of salvation. **1612** T. TAYLOR *Titus* i. 9. (1619) 183 Such divine prophecies, and predictions, together with the exact accomplishments. **1779** JOHNSON *L.P., Granville* Wks. 1787 III. 217 He wrote the poem to the earl of Peterborough, upon his Accomplishment of the duke of York's marriage with the princess of Modena. **1860** FROUDE *Hist. Eng.* V. xxiv. 3 He saw England, as he believed, ripe for mighty changes easy of accomplishment.

2. The act of perfecting, or state of being perfected; perfection, completion.

1561 J. DAUS tr. *Bullinger on Apocal.* (1573) 91 b, The Saints..are commaunded patiently to abyde, vntyll the accomplishement of their brethren. **1646** SIR T. BROWNE *Pseud. Ep.* 9 Mahomet..set out the felicitie of his heaven, by the contentments of flesh..slightly passing over the accomplishment of the soule. **1666** FULLER *Hist. Cambridge* (1840) 158 Robert Wakefield..who, for his better accomplishment, travelled most parts of Christendom. **1710** SHAFTESBURY *Charact.* (1737) II. II. §2. 251 Is not this the sum of all?—the finishing stroke and very Accomplishment of Virtue?

3. Anything accomplished or performed; anything achieved by study or practice; a performance, achievement, or attainment.

1599 SHAKS. *Hen. V*, Prol. 30 Turning th' accomplishment of many yeares Into an Howre-glasse. **1664** POWER *Exp. Philos.* III. 124 It has been held accomplishment enough to graduate a student, if he could but stiffly wrangle out a vexatious dispute. **1797** MRS. RADCLIFFE *The Italian* (1824) xxv. 665 A harmony, not the effect of torpid feelings, but the accomplishment of correct and vigilant judgement. **1881** A. HERSCHEL in *Nature* No. 622. 508, I have here ventured to disown, and to disclaim for myself some of the major accomplishments of meteor-spectroscopy.

4. Anything that completes, finishes off, or completely equips. **a.** Formerly including bodily equipment, accoutrement; **b.** now, a faculty or quality that completes or perfects a person for society—that adds delicacy of taste and elegance of manners to accuracy of knowledge and correctness of thought. As such faculties, besides accomplishing or *perfecting* their possessor, are usually also accomplished or *attained* by study and practice, as in sense 3, the common modern use of the word combines the two senses in that of 'an ornamental attainment or acquirement,' *i.e.* some study accomplished which accomplishes the student. The word is also abused to mean 'superficial acquirements,' embellishments that pretend to perfect or complete an education which does not exist.

1605 BACON *Advanc. Learn.* II. 2 Conduits, Cesternes, and Pooles..men haue accustomed..to beautifie and adorne with accomplishments of Magnificence and State, as well as of vse and necessitie. **1641** MILTON *Ch. Discip.* (1851) II. 50 The externall Accomplishments of kingly prosperity, the love of the people, their multitude, their valour, their wealth. **1672** JORDAN *Lond. Triumph.* in Heath *Grocers' Comp.* (1869) 491 The company of Artillerymen..being in all their accomplishments of gallantry, some in Buff, with Head pieces, many of massy silver. **1774** *Advt. to Chesterfield's Letters* 8 Hence we find him induced to lay so great a stress on what are generally called Accomplishments, as most indispensably requisite to finish the amiable and brilliant part of a complete character. *a* **1830** TENNYSON *Sonnets* viii. 4 To dance and sing, be gaily drest, And win all eyes with all accomplishment. **1853** DE QUINCEY *Sp. Mil. Nun.* §5. 9 To fold and seal a letter adroitly is not the lowest of accomplishments.

5. ***accomplishment quotient*** U.S. = ACHIEVEMENT *quotient*.

1924 BAGLEY & KEITH *Introd. Teaching* 192 The accomplishment quotient. **1934, 1957** [see ACHIEVEMENT 4].

accompt, *v.* and *sb.*, arch. form of ACCOUNT; still occas. written for the *sb.* in the sense of money reckoning.

accomptant, arch. form of ACCOUNTANT.

accompter, obs. form of ACCOUNTER.

†**accompter, acompter.** *Obs.* [a. Fr. *acompter, acc-*, inf. used substantively: see ACCOUNT *v.* and -ER[2].] Account, reckoning.

1483 ARNOLD *Chron.* (1811) 271 The averagis of the last acompter.

†**accon'sent**, *v. Obs. rare*$^{-1}$. [perh. ad. It. *acconsentire* to consent unto (Florio 1598), f. *a*,

ad to + *consentire* to CONSENT.] *intr.* To consent to anything proposed, to give consent.

1560 J. DAUS tr. *Sleidane's Comm.* 350 a, The Emperour very hardly acconsented at the laste.

accorage, var. ACCOURAGE *v. Obs.* to encourage.

accord (ə'kɔːd), *v.* Also **acord(e**, and aphetically **cord(e**. [a. OFr. *acorde-r*:—late L. *accordā-re*, f. *ac-* = *ad-* to + *cor*, *cord-is* heart; cf. cl. L. *concordāre*. As in French the *c* began to be doubled in writing in 5 after the Latin spelling.] *Lit.* to bring heart to heart: hence, to reconcile, reconcile oneself, agree, agree to, agree to give.

I. *trans.* To cause to agree, to reconcile.

†**1.** To bring (persons) into agreement or harmony, to reconcile one *with* another. *Obs.*

1123 *O.E. Chron.* (Laud. MS.) an. 1120 An se arceb[iscop]..wearð þurh þone papan wið þone cyng acordad. **1297** R. GLOUC. 388 Þo wende vorþ Roberd Courtese & Edgar Aþelyng, And acordede Macolom, & Wyllam oure kyng. **1366** MAUNDEV. xviii. 195 (1839) ȝif 2 persones ben at debate, & peraventure ben accorded be here Frendes. **1461** *Past. Lett.* 421. II. 63 The parson hopyth verily to make yow acordyd when he comyth to London. **1523** LD. BERNERS *Froissart* cccxxvi. 335 We wolde gladly and we coude, acorde you and hym toguyder. **1613** PURCHAS *Pilgr.* II. xx. 223 Then shall be peace among men and beasts; if there arise any war among the Gentiles the Messias shall accord them. **1702** tr. *Le Clerc's Prim. Fathers* 102 To the end it might appear that he had accorded them more by persuasion than force.

†**2.** *refl.* and *pass.* To reconcile oneself, to agree, to come to an agreement. Const. *with*. *Obs.*

c **1340** *Gawayne & Gr. Knt.* 2380 Cowardyse me taȝt To acorde me with couetyse, my kynde to for-sake. **1366** MAUNDEV. 195 (1839) It behovethe that every of hem, that schulle ben accorded, drynke of otheres Blood. *c* **1450** *Merlin* 79 The kynge seide to this, 'I a-corde me well, and will that it be so as ye haue devised.' **1483** CAXTON *Gold. Leg.* 72/2 All the Royames fro the ryuer of the endes of the phylisteis unto thende of egypte were acorded with hym. **1619** W. SCLATER *Expos. Thessalns.* I. i. (1627) *Mentior*, if my soule accord him not. **1762–86** H. WALPOLE *Vertue's Anecd. Paint.* I. 179 (1786) Let but France and England once dispute which first used a hatchet, and they shall never be accorded 'till the chancery of learning accommodates the matter by pronouncing that each received that invaluable utensil from the Phoenicians.

3. To bring into agreement (things that differ); to reconcile (quarrels or differences); to compose, settle, arrange (a matter). *arch.*

c **1385** CHAUCER *Leg. Good W.* 2027 And whan these thynges ben a-cordit thus Adoun sit Thesyus up-on his kne. *c* **1400** *Apol. for Lollards* 1, I purpos to take & vndirstond her wordis..and so to acorde hem to gidir. **1481** CAXTON *Myrrour* I. xii. 37 Musyque accordeth alle thinges that dyscorde. **1580** *Proscr. agst. Pr. Orange* in *Phenix* (1721) I. 438 We sent the Baron—that he might accord the whole matter. **1615** SANDYS *Trav.* 239 To accord a dangerous sedition, they chose Gelon for their tyrant. **1655** FULLER *Ch. Hist.* I. iv. 19 Who will undertake to accord the Contradictions in Time and Place, between the severall Relations of this History. **1676** NEWTON in *Phil. Trans.* XI. 192 Mr. Lucas will be enabled to accord his tryals of the Experiment with mine. **1842** LONGF. *Sp. Stud.* II. vi. 14 Is there no way left open to accord this difference?

†**4.** To compose, sing, or play (something) in harmony; to attune. Const. *to*. *Obs.*

1580 SIDNEY *Arcadia* 72 (1622) The first sports the shepheards shewed, were full of such leaps and gambols, as being accorded to the pipe, made a right picture of their chiefe god Pan, and his companions the Satyres. *a* **1650** SHERBURNE *Sun-rise* v, But all those little birds..Accord their disagreeing throats. **1663** H. COGAN *Voy. & Adv. Pinto* xxiii. 84 Six girles..that very harmoniously accorded their voyces to certain Instruments of Music whereon they played.

II. *intr.* (by suppression of refl. pron.) To agree.

5. To come to an agreement or to terms; to be at one, to agree. **a.** *simply*. (Often emphasized by *together*, *in one*.)

1154 *O.E. Chron.* an. 1135 Siððan Balduin acordede. **1330** R. BRUNNE *Chron.* 48 In þe sex batailes was many a man slayn. At þe last þei acorded, þe lond was fulle fayn. *c* **1450** *Merlin* vi. 99 Than acorded alle the noble men and wise, and seide that he hadde seide soth. *c* **1500** *Reliq. Antiq.* I. 233 Two wymen in one howse, Two cattes and one mowce, Two dogges and one bone, Maye never accorde in one. **1667** *Decay of Chr. Piety* v. §8. 228 Herod and Pilate, Sadducees and Pharisees accord against Christ. **1809** J. BARLOW *Columbiad* IV. 241 Quell'd by his fame, the furious sects accord. **1817** SCOTT *Waverley* II. xix. 293 Proceed as we accorded before dinner, if you wish to remain longer in my service.

b. *with* (a person or opinion.)

1123 *O.E. Chron.* (Laud. MS.) an. 1120 Æfter heora sehte acordedan ealles þæs cynges Heanriȝes aȝene men wið hine. *c* **1360** CHAUCER *A.B.C.* 27 God vouched saf thoruh þee with us to accorde ffor certes crystes. **1387** TREVISA *Higden* (Rolls Ser.) VI. 369 Charles cordede with Rollo. **1653** HOLCROFT *Procopius* II. 45 We may repaire to the Emperour, and conclude and accord with him. **1865** CARLYLE *Fredk. Gt.* X. XXI. v. 57 The Queen accorded with this view of the matter.

†**c.** *in* (an opinion or course). *Obs.*

1377 LANGL. *P. Pl.* B. XVIII. 232 Alle þe wyse of þis worlde · in o witte acordeden, That such a barne was borne · in bethleem citee. **1449** PECOCK *Repr.* 243 And manye of these men Accordiden to gidere in chesing to hem oon & the same thing for her God. **1630** PRYNNE *Anti-Arm.* 182 The wheeles in a clocke..haue contrary motions, yet they sweetly concurre and accord in the same effect. **1677** HALE *Prim. Orig. Man.* 61 Mankind in general..seems to have those common sentiments in them, and to accord in them in a very great measure.

†**d.** *of* or *upon* (the matter in question). *Obs.*

c **1450** LONELICH *Graal* II. 140, & acorden they myhten not In non weye Of these .xij. loves Certeynlye. **1562** CECIL in Ellis *Orig. Lett.* II. 159 II. 266 The Quenes Majestie was contented in June to accord upon an Enterview in August with the Quene of Scottes. *a* **1593** H. SMITH *Wks.* (1867) II. 84 We have long purposed to serve God..but we cannot accord of the time when to begin. **1640** BP. HALL *Episc. by div. Right* I. §18. 71 Such a Kingdome upon earth..cannot yet be fully knowne and accorded upon.

†**e.** With *subord. cl. Obs.*

1297 R. GLOUC. 388 Hii acordede atte laste in suche fourme þere, þat woþer of hem tueye lenger alyue were, þat he ssolde be oþere's eyr. *c* **1385** CHAUCER *Leg. Good Wom.* Prol. 3, I acord wel that it ys so. **1483** CAXTON *Gold. Leg.* 169/1 They wold not accorde that he shold be amytted to be worshypped emonge the goddes. *a* **1593** H. SMITH *Wks.* (1867) I. 469 One despised another, because they did not accord what wisdom was. **1676** ROW *Suppl. Blair's Autobiog.* (1848) xi. 327 It was accorded that these mulcts should be divided.

†**6.** To agree *to* (something viewed as a standard, rule, aim, end in view, or course to be taken); to assent or consent *to*. *Obs.*

1340 HAMPOLE *Pr. Consc.* 2500 Here to acordes, als þe buk telles us, Ysidre þe grete clerk. **1366** MAUNDEV. (1839) v. 38 They were at gret discord for to make a Soudan, And fynally thei accordeden to Melechnasser. **1393** GOWER *Conf.* III. VI. 27 Her chinne accordeth to the face, All that he seeth is full of grace. *c* **1450** *Merlin* vi. 96 Thei acorded to the counseils of Merlyn. **1600** SHAKS. *A.Y.L.* v. iv. 139 You, to his loue must accord, Or haue a Woman to your Lord. **1633** STAFFORD *Pac. Hib.* (1821) xviii. 189 The Earle accorded both to time and place. *a* **1674** CLARENDON *Hist. Reb.* I. III. 193 These things so graciously accorded unto by your Majesty.

†**b.** With *inf. Obs.*

1366 MAUNDEV. (1839) xxviii. 282 Some of oure Fellowes accordeden to enter, and somme noght. *c* **1450** *Merlin* (1877) xii. 191 Thei acorded to go to logres in bretein, the chief Citee of kynge Arthur. **1578** T. N. tr. *Conq. W. India* 102 He did secretly accord with one of the maisters of his fleete in the night season to bore holes in them. **1605** VERSTEGAN *Dec. Intell.* (1628) vi. 173 Odo Bishop of Bayeux accorded to furnish him with forty ships.

7. Of things: To agree, be in harmony, be consistent. Const. *with*.

1393 LANGL. *P. Pl.* C. IV. 364 Ryht as adjectif and substantif A-cordeþ in alle kyndes · with his antecedent. **1477** EARL RIVERS (Caxton) *Dictes* 64 Moche wyne & sapience may not accorde. **1483** CAXTON *Gold. Leg.* 218/4 Other bokes of Josephus accorden ynough wyth the sayde storye. **1542** BOORDE *Dyetary* (1870) ix. 250 More meate than accordeth with nature. **1810** SCOTT *Lady of the L.* II. xxv. His form accorded with a mind Lively and ardent. **1839** KEIGHTLEY *Hist. Eng.* II. 56 Parliament met..and its acts perfectly accorded with the royal wishes. *Mod.* His principles and practice do not accord well together.

†**8.** *impers.* To agree with propriety; to be suitable or proper. (L. *convenit*.) *Obs.*

c **1374** CHAUCER *Troyl.* II. 1043 For if a peyntour wold peynt a pyke With assis feet, and heed it as an ape, Hit cordid not. *a* **1520** *Myrroure of Our Ladye* 66 Suche bokes of gostly fruyte as accordeth for you to rede or to here. **1556** W. LAUDER *Tractate* (1864) 410 So that he sall tyll euery wycht Do that thyng quhilk accords, of rycht.

III. *trans.* (by omission of the prep. in 5, 6).

†**9.** To agree upon, arrange. *Obs.*

c **1386** CHAUCER *Melibeus* 383 But now let us speke of the counseil that was accorded by youre neighebours. **1485** CAXTON *Paris & Vienne* 58 Whan therle of Flaunders had accorded the maryage. **1574** tr. *Littleton's Tenures* 12 b, After the number of yeres that is accorded betwene the lessor and the lessee. **1676** W. ROW *Suppl. Blair's Autobiog.* (1848) x. 193 All business being thus accorded and ordered.

10. To agree to, consent to, grant (a request); hence, in 19th c. To grant (a thing asked) *to* (a person), to give with full consent, to award.

1393 LANGL. *P. Pl.* C. IV. 275 Seriauntes for here seruice · mede þey asken, And taken mede of here maistres · as þei mow a-corde. *a* **1649** LD. HERBERT in Cobbett's *State Trials* I. 336 Who thereupon sends word of it to Charles and Ferdinand, intreating them to assist their aunt, which they accorded. **1718** POPE *Iliad* x. 352 The heroes pray'd, and Pallas from the skies Accords their vow. *c* **1820** WORDSWORTH *Sonnets* (Chandos) 143 Bright as the glimpses of eternity, To saints accorded in their mortal hour. **1861** TEMPLE & TREVOR *Tannhäuser* 22 Hell the horrid prayer Accorded with a curse. **1873** MAX MÜLLER *Sc. Relig.* 330 A kind of anticipated Christianity had been accorded to the ancient sages.

¶ Phonetically confused with RECORD.

1625 PURCHAS *Pilgrims* II. 1064 They have accorded in their old Bookes.

accord (ə'kɔːd), *sb.* For forms see prec. [a. OFr. *acord*, *acorde* agreement, f. *acorde-r*: see ACCORD *v.*]

1. Reconciliation, agreement, harmony; concurrence of opinion, will, or action; consent.

1297 R. GLOUC. 237 (R.) Some frend hym byþoȝte bet, & bytuene hem gonne ryde, And made acord bytuene hem. **1387** TREVISA *Higden* (Rolls Ser.) III. 247 Molimicius was i-buried by þe temple of Acord [*juxta templum Concordiæ*]. **1393** GOWER *Conf.* Prol. 1049 In heven is pees and al accorde But helle is full of such discorde. *c* **1450** *Merlin* i. 20 Thou purchasest a-corde be-twene the and thi husbonde. *a* **1520** *Myrroure of Our Ladye* 61 He behoteth that in eche lande where eny Monastrery of thys order ys founded, there shall be encresed peace and accorde. **1619** R. JONES *Recant. Serm.* in *Phenix* 1708 II. 495 True Accord is an Union of..the Will and Affections. **1784** COWPER *Task* VI. 380 Thus harmony and family accord Were driv'n from Paradise. **1800** WORDSWORTH *Brothers* Wks. I. 110 He fed the spindle of his youngest child, Who, in the open air, with due accord Of busy hands and back and forward steps, Her large round wheel was turning.

†**b.** To *fall at* or *of accord*: to be reconciled. *to be of, at accord* with: to agree with. *Obs.*

c **1386** CHAUCER *Doctor's T.* 25 And for my werke no thing wol I axe; My lord and I ben fully at accord. —— *Frankl. T.* 13 That pryuely she fil of his accord To take hym for hir housbonde and hir lord. *c* **1430** LYDG. *Bochas* (1554) I. viii. 12 a, Poetes make thereof no mencion..how they fell at accorde. **1523** LD. BERNERS *Froissart* I. viii. 6 They besought and requyred eche other among them selfe to be of a peasable accorde. *Ibid.* I. xiv. 14 That the sagis of the realme might..fall at acorde howe the realme shuld be gouerned. **1600** SHAKS. *A.Y.L.* I. i. 67 Sweet Masters bee patient, for your Fathers remembrance, be at accord. **1704** RAY *Creation* Ded. 3 I am of accord with him.

c. *with* (*of* obs.) *one accord*: with entire agreement, with one consent, with unanimity.

1375 *Lay-Folks Mass-Bk.* B. 541 Make þou, gode lorde, my body & my soule of one a-corde. **1393** GOWER *Conf.* III. VII. 269 And thus of one accorde upright To Rome at ones home ayein They torne. **1535** COVERDALE 1 *Kings* xxii. 13 Beholde, The wordes of yͤ prophetes are with one acorde good before the kynge. **1611** BIBLE *Acts* xix. 29 They rushed with one accord into the Theatre. **1878** M. A. BROWN *Nadeschda* 34 With one accord On castleyard and all around The people sink on bended knee.

2. A formal act of reconciliation, or agreement; a treaty of peace, a treaty generally.

1297 R. GLOUC. 388 Þys acord was vaste ymade þoru stronge treuþe ynou. Vaste yplyȝt in eyþer syde, þat non ne wyþ drou. *c* **1440** *Generydes* 6399 The corde is made, the mortuall werre is sese, Betwix hym and the Sowdon all is pece. **1480** CAXTON *Cron. Eng.* ccxxxi. 247 The pees and the acord y made bitwene the ij kynges. **1577–87** HOLINSHED *Chron.* III. 889/2 The pope, whom they named as conseruator of the accord. **1614** RALEIGH *Hist. World* II. 275 Thirdly the accord which Israel made with these crafty Canaanites, was without warrant. **1700** DRYDEN *Fables, Pal. & Arcite* 1034 If both are satisfy'd with this accord Swear by the laws of knighthood on my sword. **1860** MOTLEY *Netherlands* I. v. 240 (1868) Antwerp might perish, before a general accord with Holland and Zeeland could be made.

3. *Law.* A private or extrajudicial arrangement.

1625 SIR H. FINCH *Law* 181 (1636) Accord is an agreement betweene the parties themselues. **1768** BLACKSTONE *Comm.* III. 15 Accord is a satisfaction agreed upon between the party injuring and the party injured; which, when performed, is a bar of all actions upon this account.

4. Agreement or harmonious correspondence of things or their properties, as of colours or tints. *esp.* of sounds: Agreement in pitch and tone; harmony.

c **1384** CHAUCER *H. of Fame* 696 Mo loue dayes and acordes Then on Instrumentes be acordes. **1398** TREVISA *Barth. de P.R.* (1495) III. iv. 51 Pyctagoras callyth the soule Armony, acorde of melodye. **1483** CAXTON *G. Leg.* 412/1 Somtyme they sange psalmes aboute the aulter..by accorde to gyder. **1563** BARNABE GOOGE *Eglogs* (Arb.) 110 Or yf it were the sweete accorde that syngyng Byrdes dyd keepe. **1605** BACON *Adv. Learn.* I. 32 In that fayned relation of Orpheus Theater..all beasts and birds assembled..listening vnto the ayres and accords of the Harpe. **1659** HAMMOND *On Psalm* xxiv. 7. 138 That rendring can have no accord with the Hebrew. **1777** SIR W. JONES *Ess.* ii. 200 Our boasted harmony, with all its fine accords, and numerous parts, paints nothing, expresses nothing. **1826** SCOTT *Woodst.* (1832) I. i. 5 Bating an occasional temptation to warble along with the accord, he behaved himself as decorously as any of the congregation. **1867** MRS. OLIPHANT *Madonna Mary* (Tauchn.) I. xiii. 161 It was a strange sort of position and strangely out of accord with her character and habits. **1879** G. C. HARLAN *Eyesight* ii. 15 The color of the iris is usually in accord with the general coloring of the individual.

†**5.** Assent to a proposal or request; permission, grant. *Obs.*

1393 GOWER *Conf.* I. 102 Though it be nought with her accorde. **1483** CAXTON *G. Leg.* 301/1 Som monkes by thaccorde of Charles had impetred and goten of Nycholas the pope the body of Saynt Urban the pope. **1602** SHAKS. *Ham.* I. ii. 123 This gentle and vnforc'd accord of Hamlet Sits smiling to my heart.

b. *of* (*by*, *on* obs.) *one's own accord*: by one's unsolicited assent; of one's own spontaneous motion.

c **1450** LONELICH *Holy Grail* xiii. 102 And whanne king Eualach herd this word, Thus thanne dide he be his owne Acord. **1555** *Fardle of Facions* Pref. 9 Thenhabitours ouer all became milded and wittied, shaking of (euen of their owne accorde) the bruteshe outrages. **1611** SHAKS. *Wint. T.* II. iii. 63 On mine owne accord, Ile off, But first, Ile do my errand. **1611** BIBLE 2 *Cor.* viii. 17 But being more forward, of his owne accord he went vnto you. **1697** DRYDEN *Virgil, Past.* vii. 13 Your lowing Heifers, of their own accord, At wat'ring time will seek the neighb'ring Ford. **1862** A. TROLLOPE *Orley Farm* xiv. 109 She had no idea of giving up Felix of her own accord, if he were still willing to take her.

†**a'ccord**, *adv.* or *a. Obs.* [? for *a accord*; or shortened f. pple. *accorded*.] In accord, in agreement.

c **1374** CHAUCER *Troyl.* v. 446 Nor in this world ther is noon instrumente Delicious, thorugh wynde, or touche on corde,..But at that fest, it nas wel herde acorde. *a* **1440** *Sir Degrevant* 1767 Hyt is gode ye be a-corde And yowre wyllus ware. **1461** *Past. Lett.* 402. II. 28 I pray yow bryng hem to gedyr, and set hem acord.

accordable (ə'kɔːdəb(ə)l), *a.* Also 4–5 **acordable**. [a. OFr. *acordable*, f. *acorder*; see ACCORD *v.* and -ABLE.]

†**1.** Agreeing, consonant, harmonious, accordant; suitable, agreeable. *Obs.*

c **1374** CHAUCER *Boethius* 62 (1868) The fasoun of this worlde, the which they now leden in acordable feith by fayre moeuynges. **1393** GOWER *Conf.* II. 225 It is nought discordable Unto my word, but accordable. **1470** HARDING *Chron.* lxxviii. 14. 5 With all seruyce for the death accordable.

2. Capable of being accorded, harmonized, or reconciled; reconcilable.

1664 H. MORE *Apology* 486 Most easily accordable with the Attributes of God and the Phænomena of Providence. *Mod.* Things hardly accordable with our ordinary notions.

accordance (ə'kɔːdəns). Also 3–4 acordance, -auns. [a. OFr. *acordance* agreeing, n. of action f. *acorder*; see ACCORD *v.* and -ANCE.]

1. The action or state of agreeing; agreement; harmony; conformity.

1303 R. BRUNNE *Handlyng Synne* 2006 Se how þese wymmen a-cordaunce Plesyde God .wyþ lytyl penaunce. **1330** —— *Chron.* 180 þei parted þe oste in tuo, þorgh comon acordance. *c* **1400** *Rom. Rose* 498 Ful blisful was the accordaunce, Of swete and piteous songe thei made. **1596** SPENSER *F.Q.* v. viii. 14 So can they both themselves full eath perswade To faire accordaunce. **1633** BP. HALL *Hard T.* 605 I will draw my Church to a happie accordance so as both Jewes and Gentiles shall be linked together in the bonds of peace. *c* **1800** WORDSWORTH *To the Moon* Wks. 1849 V. 278 Touched by accordance of thy placid cheer, With some internal lights to memory dear. **1869** PHILLIPS *Vesuv.* vi. 164 If we place in parallel columns the number of earthquakes and the number of volcanic eruptions, the degree of accordance will be seen at a glance.

b. *esp.* in the modern phrase, ***in accordance with*** (rarely *to*): in agreement or harmony with; in conformity to.

1806–31 A. KNOX *Rem.* (1844) I. 44 Where religion is pursued..in accordance with the views of the New Testament some tastes of such happiness are soon perceived. **1861** GEO. ELIOT *Silas M.* 20 With which the look of gloomy vexation on Godfrey's blond face was in sad accordance. **1865** PUSEY *Truth & Off. Eng. Ch.* 212 This was in accordance to Du Pin's previous conviction. **1880** W. H. DIXON *Windsor* IV. xxviii 262 His deeds were never in accordance with his votes.

2. The action of granting.

1881 *Times* 20 Aug. 9/2 The scheme..includes, among other matters, the accordance to Ireland of the rights both of taxing herself and of spending the taxes as she pleases.

accordancy (ə'kɔːdənsɪ). [f. ACCORD *v.*, as if ad. L. **accordantia*: see -NCY.] A condition or state of agreement; harmony.

1790 PALEY *Hor. Paul.* Rom. i. 10 This..brings the narrative in the Acts nearer to an accordancy with the epistle. **1826** E. IRVING *Babylon* II. VII. 234 Mercy and justice in sweetest accordancy.

accordant (ə'kɔːdənt), *a.* Also acordant. [a. OFr. *acordant*, pr. pple. of *acorder*: see ACCORD *v.* and -ANT.]

1. Agreeing, consonant, conformable. Const. *to*, *with*; the latter is now the more common; perhaps a distinction should be observed between ***accordant to*** a rigid standard, ***accordant with*** a parallel circumstance.

c **1315** SHOREHAM 89 Acordaunt to thy trauayl, Lord, graunte me thy coroune. *c* **1374** CHAUCER *Parlt. Foules* 203 Therwith a wynd..Made in the leuys grene a noyse softe Acordaunt to the bryddis song a lofte. **1393** GOWER *Conf.* III. 163 So thy prince for to queme Is nought to reson accordaunt. **1494** FABYAN cxlvii. 133 (1811) An excedynge nombre, to be accordaunt with reason. **1579** *News from North* in Thynne's *Animadv.* (1865) Pref. 135 As neer accordant to the truth as I could. **1776** BOSWELL *Johnson* (1816) II. 486, I went to the Cathedral, where I was very much delighted with the music, finding it to be peculiarly solemn, and accordant with the words of the service. **1822** BARRY CORNWALL *Miscell. Poems, Autumn*, Man's bounding spirit ebbs and swells more high Accordant to the billow's loftier roll. **1852** MISS YONGE *Cameos* II. xxxi. 327 (1877) The motto must have been more accordant with the pride of London than with Henry's good sense.

2. *absol.* †a. Agreeing or concurring in mind, agreeable. *Obs.* b. Agreeing in external action or motion; *esp.* of sounds: harmonious.

1599 SHAKS. *Much Ado* I. i. 14 Hee loued my niece your daughter, and meant to acknowledge it this night in a dance, and if hee found her accordant, hee meant to..instantly breake with you of it. *a* **1764** R. LLOYD *Poet. Wks.* 1774 I. 151 While eager genius plumes her infant wings, And with bold impulse strikes th' accordant strings. **1830** LYELL *Princ. Geol.* (1875) II. II. xxxiii. 233 These data..are not as yet sufficiently extensive or accordant in different regions. **1850** BLACKIE *Æschylus* II. 100 Thy tale with mine accordant chimes. **1877** KINGLAKE *Crimea* (ed. 6) III. iv. 357 That kind of understanding which leads to..accordant action.

†3. Agreeing with any one's character, or with circumstances; suitable, fitting, appropriate. *Obs.*

1413 LYDGATE *Pylgr. Sowle* II. lviii. 56 (1859) Sothly, this lykenes is accordaunt. **1477** CAXTON *Dictes* 149 It is acordaunt that his [Socrates'] dyctes and sayengis shold be had as well as others. **1574** tr. *Littleton's Tenures* 136 *a*, Yf tenaunt by the curteyse had aliened in fee with warrantie accordaunt.

accordantly (ə'kɔːdəntlɪ), *adv.* [f. prec + -LY².] In a manner accordant or agreeing; agreeably, conformably (*to*, *with*); suitably, fitly, properly.

c **1400** *Apol. for Lollards* 55 Are þei not, a cordantly to þe wordis of þe prophets, werr, & abhominabler þan carnal sodomists. **1621** T. ADAMS *White Devill* (1629) 60 If any be worthy to beare the usurer company, let it be the rioter, though of contrary dispositions, yet in this journey fitly and accordantly met. **1858** H. BUSHNELL *Nat. & Supernat.* xii. 394 (1864) Accordantly also with such a conception of God, the divine unity is reproduced as trinity. **1875** B. TAYLOR *Faust* II. III. 176 The echo of his orders then returns no more Accordantly to him in swiftly finished acts.

accorded (ə'kɔːdɪd), *ppl. a.* [f. ACCORD *v.* + -ED.] Reconciled; harmonized; agreed to, granted.

1581 SIDNEY *Def. Poetrie* (Arb.) 46 The Liricke, who with his tuned Lyre, and wel accorded voyce, giueth praise, the reward of vertue, to vertuous acts. **1806** WORDSWORTH *Sonnets to Lib.* xxviii. 44 Nations wanting virtue to be strong Up to the measure of accorded might.

accorder (ə'kɔːdə(r)). [f. ACCORD *v.* + -ER¹.] One who accords; one who agrees; one who cordially grants or bestows.

1860 L. HUNT *Autobiog.* ix. 174 Hearty accorders with the dictum of the apostle, who said.. **1861** *Cornhill Mag.* III. 543 There is only one modern instance of a sovereign raising an unmarried lady to a place in the peerage out of pure gallantry, and with attendant increase of respect and honour both to the accorder and to the recipient.

according (ə'kɔːdɪŋ), *vbl. sb.* [f. ACCORD *v.* + -ING¹.] The action of reconciling, harmonizing, or granting. (Now mostly gerundial.)

1530 PALSGR. 193 Accordyng, *Acordance.* **1709** STRYPE *Ann. Ref.* ii. 54 Laws for the according and uniting of the people into an uniform order of religion. *Mod.* I cannot think of according you such unusual privileges.

according (ə'kɔːdɪŋ), *ppl. a.* and *adv.* Also 4 accordend, 5–6 cording. [f. ACCORD *v.* + -ING².]

A. *adj.*

†1. Agreeing, corresponding *to*; matching. *Obs.*

1398 TREVISA *Barth. De P.R.* (1495) XVII. ii. 595 Some trees haue humour proporcyonall and acordynge eyther to other, so that the humour of that one be acordynge to nourysshe and to fede that other. *c* **1460** *Household Stat.* in *Babees Book* (1868) 329 Not oolde robis and not cordyng to the lyuerey. **1480** *Robert the Devyll* 2 I se well yt ys youre wyll that I shoulde be maryed, But yet woulde I have one to myne estate Accordynge. *a* **1520** *Myrroure of Our Ladye* 7 For there ys many wordes in Latyn that we haue no propre englyssh acordynge therto. **1532** THYNNE *Dedic. Chaucer* in *Animadv.* (1865) 24 Frutefulnesse in wordes wel accordynge to the matter and purpose.

2. *absol.* Agreeing in nature or action; consentient, harmonious.

c **1450** *Merlin* 52 He is but a fole, that hath tolde these two dethes, whiche may not be acordinge. **1626** W. SANDYS *Ovid's Metamorph.* II. 216 An other hurles a stone; this, as it flew, His voice and harps according tunes subdue. **1780** BURKE *Sp. at Bristol* Wks. 1842, III. 395 This according voice of national wisdom ought to be listened to with reverence. **1864** TENNYSON *Aylmer's F.* 453 Harder the times were and the hands of power Were bloodier, and the according hearts of men Seemed harder too.

†3. Agreeing with what is right or due; becoming, proper, appropriate, fitting. *Obs.*

1449 PECOCK *Repr.* III. viii. 324 It is not semeli.. conuenient and according. **1483** CAXTON *Gold. Leg.* 399/3 A clerke..sayd it was not honest ne accordyng, to mysentrete the holy body by vyolente hondes. **1526** TINDALE *Rom.* i. 27 And receaved in them selves the rewarde of their errour as it was accordynge [**1611** meete]. **1577–87** HOLINSHED *Chron.* III. 1190/1 The whole armie should be readie armed with their weapon and furniture according by midnight. **1674** PLAYFORD *Skill of Mus.* II. 101 A bass-viol for divisions must be of a less size, and the strings according.

B. *adv.*

†1. *absol.* In a manner logically agreeing with the premises; = ACCORDINGLY 4. *Obs.*

? **1495** *Plumpton Corr.* 110 Send me word by wrytting how he wilbe demeaned, & therafter I shall entreat him according. **1523** FITZHERBERT *Bk. Surueying* 2 Wherfore the acres are to be praysed [= appraised] accordynge. **1603** SHAKS. *Meas. for M.* v. i. 487 Sirha, thou art said to haue a stubborne soule That apprehends no further then this world, And squar'st thy life according—Thou'rt condemn'd.

†2. According *after*, according *at*: In accordance or agreement with. *Obs.*

1523 LD. BERNERS *Froissart* I. cccxxix 515 The kynge of Nauer [was] to pay them their wages..acordyng after the same rate that the kynge of Englande was wonte to paye his men of warre. *Ibid.* ccccvi. 705 Acordyng at the kynges desyre [he] dyde beare him ouer all the great wodes and trees.

3. According *as*: Consistently as, exactly or just as, in a manner corresponding to the way in which...(Now confined to an accordance with one of two or more alternatives.)

1509 HAWES *Pastime of Pleas.* (1845) 48 Wyth humble voyce and also moderate Accordynge as by hym is audyence. **1591** SHAKS. *1 Hen. VI*, II. iii. 12 Madame, according as your Ladyship desir'd, By message crau'd, so is Lord Talbot come. **1678** BUTLER *Hudibras* III. i. 912 Like Musick, that proves bad or good According as 'tis understood. **1785** REID *Ess.* I. iv. 82 (1803) Analogical reasoning..may afford a greater or less degree of probability, according as the things compared are more or less similar in their nature. **1855** BAIN *Senses & Intell.* II. ii. §1 (1864) 233 According as bodies become transparent they cease to be visible.

4. According *to.* a. In a manner agreeing with, consistent with, or answering to; agreeably to.

a **1450** *Chester Plays* I. 3 (1843) Of the drapers you the wealthy companye The creation of the worlde, Adam and Eve, Accordinge to your wealth, set out wealthilye. **1535** COVERDALE *Ps.* ciii. 10 He hath not dealt with vs after oure synnes, ner rewarded vs acordinge to oure wickednesses. **1579** LYLY *Euphues* 430 (1868) Cut thy coat according to thy cloth. **1593** T. WATSON *Poems* (1870) 208 To paint thy glories cording their desart. **1602** SHAKS. *Haml.* II. i. 47 Good sir, or fo, or friend, or Gentleman, According to the Phrase. **1780** BURKE *Sp. Econ. Ref.* Wks. III. 295 According to the present course of the office, and according to the present mode of accounting there, this bank must necessarily exist somewhere. **1876** FREEMAN *Norm. Conq.* II. vii. 153 This, according to our ideas, seems the worst action of his life.

†b. Suitably to, with respect or reference to. *Obs.*

1549 LATIMER 7 *Serm. bef. Edw. VI* (1869) 133 Calling to remembraunce..that I must preach, and preach afore ye kyngs maiesti I thought it mete to frame my preching according to a king. **1611** BIBLE *Rom.* i. 3 His Sonne Iesus Christ our Lord, which was made of the seed of Dauid according to the flesh. **1647** J. SALTMARSH *Sparkles of Glory* 21 (1847) I must decrease, but he must increase, which surely was spoken not according to the persons of John and Christ, but according to their ministration.

c. [Cf. F. *c'est selon.*] *absol.* (elliptically) in colloq. use, as in ***that's according*** (i.e. to circumstances), 'that depends'.

1863 H. E. PRESCOTT *Amber Gods* 57 'Don't be angry', she pleaded... 'I only want to know if you will make him happy.' 'That's according,' said I. **1937** PARTRIDGE *Dict. Slang* s.v. **1971** *Caribbean Q.* June 15, I do take a drink, but it is according.

accordingly (ə'kɔːdɪŋlɪ), *adv.* [f. ACCORDING *ppl. a.* + -LY².] †1. Harmoniously, agreeably; correspondingly. *Obs.*

c **1449** PECOCK *Repr.* I. xvii Into the same vnderstondingis to gidere accordingli thei fallen. **1481** CAXTON *Myrrour* II. vi. 76 The olyfauntes goo moche symply and accordyngly to gydre. **1514** in Strype's *Eccl. Mem.* (1822) I. II. iv. 9 The king's most gracious coin is not accepted here [Tournay] and in England accordingly.

†2. In accordance with what is proper or due; suitably, becomingly, duly, properly. *Obs.*

1528 GARDINER in Pocock *Rec. Ref.* I. xliii. 83 We shall not fail to signify the same unto your highness by our letters accordingly. **1567** DRANT *Horace's Ep.* A. vj. To shape oute things accordyngly besetes a Poet's arte. **1634** FORD *P. Warbuck* III. ii. (1811) 57 Enter at one door four Scotch Anticks, accordingly habited; at another Warbeck's followers disguised as four Wild Irish in trowses, long-haired, and accordingly habited.

†3. In accordance with the order specified; respectively. *Obs.*

1603 HOLLAND *Plutarch's Mor.* 842 Empedocles supposeth that Males and Females are begotten by the meanes of heat and cold accordingly.

4. In accordance with the logical premises; agreeably, correspondingly.

1599 SHAKS. *Much Ado* III. ii. 125 When you haue seene more, & heard more, proceed accordingly. **1655** FULLER *Ch. Hist.* VI. 314 He was..adjudged to ride with his face to the Horse-tale at Windsor and Ockingham with papers about his head, which was done accordingly. **1792** *Anecd. W. Pitt* III. xxxix. 31 He is the receiver of stolen goods, and ought to be treated accordingly. **1848** C. BRONTË *Jane Eyre* (ed. 3) v. 36 She told me to remember that she had always been my best friend, and to speak of her and be grateful to her accordingly.

5. In accordance with the sequence of ideas; agreeably or conformably to what might be expected; in natural sequence, in due course; so.

1688 *Col. Rec. Pennsylv.* I. 235 He answered he would read it himselfe to yᵉ board, and accordingly read the same. **1772** PENNANT *Tours in Scotl.* 261 (1774) Accordingly having put up two days provisions—we put off. **1860** TYNDALL *Glaciers* I. §13. 92 The summer..was accordingly devoted to this purpose.

†6. Accordingly *to*; agreeably or conformably to; according to. *Obs.*

1500 H. SWINBURN *Testaments* 98 The value of the mariage..is commonlie rated accordinglie to the profites of his landes. *a* **1520** *Myrroure of Our Ladye* 69 When ye rede these bokes ye oughte to laboure in your selfe inwardly, to sturre vp your affecyons accordingly to the matter that ye rede.

7. Accordingly *as* = just as, according as. See ACCORDING *adv.* 3.

1618 tr. *Barneveld's Apology* G *b*, Questions were moued accordingly as order required, in these Prouinces. **1880** CYPLES *Hum. Exp.* v. 109 And accordingly as the simultaneity repeats.

accordion (ə'kɔːdɪən). [f. It. *accord-are* to attune an instrument, to play in unison: the termination imitates words like *clarion.*] a. A portable musical hand-instrument invented in 1829 by Damian at Vienna (Grove), consisting of a small pair of bellows and a range of keys, which on being pressed admit wind to metal reeds. Now also ***piano accordion***, an improved type of accordion, with a piano-keyboard instead of buttons for producing the notes.

1831 *Harmonicon* Mar. 56/1 The Accordion is about nine inches long, four wide, and about the same in depth; not unlike a small tea-caddy in appearance. It is made after the manner of a bellows, and the tone is produced by raising and lowering the upper part, at the same time pressing one of the ivory keys, of which there are five on those commonly used. **1839** *Inventors' Advocate* 17 Aug. 12/2 A daily musical performance on Reisner's Improved Accordion. **1842** DICKENS in Forster's *Life* III. iv. 105 I have bought another accordion. The steward lent me one on the passage out and I regaled the ladies' cabin with my performances. **1860** DICKENS *Uncomm. Trav.* in *All Year Round* 10 Mar. 464/1 It was real talent!..a kind of piano-accordion, played by a young girl. **1864** ENGEL *Music Anc. Nat.* 18 Each of these tubes contains a small metallic tongue, like the so-called free-reed stops of our organ, or like our accordion. **1878** PROUT in Grove *Dict. Music.* I. 40 The æolina may be regarded as the first germ of the Accordion and Concertina. **1938** *Oxf. Compan. Mus.* 788/1 The application of the.. piano keyboard (hence the term 'Piano Accordion') was made by Bouton, of Paris, in 1852. **1958** *Listener* 25 Sept. 484/3 The unexpected and ingenious completion of the wind ensemble of the Nonet with a piano-accordion.

b. *attrib.* and *Comb.*, having a series of folds like those of the bellows of an accordion, as ***accordion door, pleat, pleating, skirt, wall, window; accordion-plaited, -pleated*** adjs.

1885 *Catal. Cookery & Food Exhib.* x, The Permanent Accordion Pleating Manufacturing Company. **1888** *Daily News* 25 Oct. 2/6 The sleeves..are made of..nun's-veiling, arranged in accordion pleats. **1895** [see PLEATED *ppl. a.*]. **1899** HOWELLS *Ragged Lady* xvii, She had on an accordion skirt. **1905** *Smart Set* Oct. 29/1 A portly front, an accordeon-plaited chin, a thick, oily forehead. **1936** *Times* 18 Jan. 9/5 The skilful use of different planes at the corner accordion windows and fluting on the tower. **1959** 'S. RANSOME' *I'll die for You* i. 17 Through the wide-open accordion door..he saw her. **1959** I. ROSS *Image Merchants* (1960) iv. 67 The accordion wall was always open between their two..offices. **1962** *Times* 22 Jan. 13/3 Accordion-pleated chiffons.

accordionist (əˈkɔːdɪənɪst). [f. prec. + -IST.] A player on the accordion.

accordment (əˈkɔːdmənt). Also 4 **acordement**, 4–5 **accordement**. [a. OFr. *acordement* act of agreeing, f. *acorder*; see ACCORD *v.* and -MENT. The old word seems to have become obsolete in 5; and to have been formed anew in 8 either from mod. Fr. *accordement*, or independently from ACCORD *v.*] Agreement, reconciliation; reconcilement.

c **1330** *Arthour & Merlin* 2604 Long therafterward, verrament Was y-made acordement Bitvene Ygerne and the king. **1393** GOWER *Conf.* III. 90 To make melodie By vois and soune of instrument Through notes of accordement. **1480** CAXTON *Chron. Eng.* (1520) II. 17 b/1 Accordement was made bytwene Brenne and Belyn through Cornewen that was theyr moder. **1790** CATH. GRAHAM *Lett. on Educ.* 466 Such determinations are construed by the stoics to be a proper accordment of their volitions to the will of the Deity.

†**a'ccorporate**, *v.* *Obs.* *rare*⁻¹. Also **adcorporate** in Dict. [f. late L. *accorporāre* to unite in one body; f. *ac-* = *ad-* to + *corpus, corpor-is* a body.] To unite, to INCORPORATE.

1612 COCKERAM, *Adcorporated*, married. **1643** MILTON *Divorce* (1851) Introd. 4 Custome..rests not in her unaccomplishment, until by secret inclination she accorporat herself with error. **1732** BAILEY, *Adcorporate*, to join Body to Body.

accost (əˈkɒst), *v.* Also 6–7 **acoast, accoast**. [a. Fr. *accoste-r*, OFr. *acoster*:—late L. *accostāre* to be side to side, f. *ac-* = *ad-* to + *costa* rib, in late L. side. While still consciously connected with COAST it remained *accoast*, but since the idea of *to address* has become the leading one, it has been pronounced and written *accost*. Cf. ABORD, *aboard*.]

†**1.** *intr.* (as in late L. *accostare cum*). To lie alongside, to coast, border; keep close. *Obs.*

1596 SPENSER *F.Q.* v. xi. 42 All the shores, which to the sea accoste, He day and night doth ward both farre and wide. *Ibid.* VI. ii. 32 Ne is there hauke which mantleth her on pearch, Whether high towring or accoasting low. **1611** COTGR., *Accoster*: To accoast, or joyne side to side; to approach, or draw neere unto.

†**2.** *trans.* To border on, adjoin. *Obs.*

1610 HOLLAND *Camden's Brit.* I. 641 On the south side it is accosted with the Severn sea. **1642** FULLER *Holy & Prof. State* IV. xix. 338 If his land accosteth the sea, he considereth what havens therein are barr'd. **1662** —— *Worthies, Derbyshire* 235 Lapland hath since been often surrounded (so much as accosts the sea) by the English.

†**3.** To go alongside of; to keep by the side of, to sail along the coast or side of. *Obs.* Cf. COAST *v.*

1578 G. FENTON *Hist. Guicciardin* (1618) 346 The French ..after they had accoasted the enemie to the mount Argentaro, returned againe to Genes. **1603** FLORIO *Montaigne* (1634) 463 This [society of books] accosteth and secondeth all my course, and everywhere assisteth me.

†**4.** *refl.* To accost oneself *with*: To keep beside, keep company with. *Obs. rare.*

1633 J. DONE tr. *Aristeas* 92 Those that custome and acost themselves with men wise and prudent..change from good to better.

†**5.** *intr.* To approach, draw near *to*. *Obs. rare.*

1635 J. HAYWARD *Banish'd Virgin* 54 If, leaving naturall considerations, we accost to the supernaturall.

6. *trans.* To go close to, to approach, for any purpose; to assail, to face; to make up to. *arch.*

1599 BP. HALL *Virgidem, Def. to Envie* 29 That Envie should accoast my muse and me. **1601** SHAKS. *Tw. Night* I. iii. 52 T. Accost Sir Andrew, accost..*A.* Good mistris Mary, accost. *T.* Accost, is front her, boord her, woe her, assayle her. **1611** COTGR., *Aborder*: To approach, accoast, abboord, or draw neer unto. **1641** LD. BROOKE *Episcopacy* 22 Iron when accoasted by two load-stones of equall vertue on either side, not daring to embrace either, hovereth in medio between both. **1645** QUARLES *Sol. Recant.* x. 72 Rebell not thou, nor in a hostile way Accoast thy Prince; or suffer, or obey. **1704** SWIFT *Ta. Tub* Wks. 1760 I. 100 How fading and insipid do all objects accost us that are not conveyed in the vehicle of delusion. **1765** TUCKER *Lt. of Nat.* II. 382 Incapable of resisting the first temptation that should accost him. **1874** J. H. NEWMAN *Dream of Geront.* 16 All around Over the surface of my subtle being, As though I were a sphere, and capable To be accosted thus.

7. a. To make up to and speak to; to address.

1612 CHAPMAN *Widdowe's Teares* Plays 1873 III. 10 Ile a-coast her Countesship. **1630** LORD *Banians* 20 Shuddery at length accoasted her, whose approach she received doubtfully. **1667** MILTON *P.L.* IV. 822 [They] thus, unmoved with fear, accost him soon. **1718** POPE *Iliad* x. 224 Nestor with joy the wakeful band survey'd, And thus accosted through the gloomy shade. **1785** COWPER *Gilpin* 56 The Callender..Laid down his pipe, flew to the gate, And thus accosted him. **1794** PALEY *Evid.* (1817) II. ix. 216 The first epistle of Peter accosts the Christians dispersed throughout Pontus, Galatia, Cappadocia, Asia, and Bithynia. **1833** BREWSTER *Nat. Magic* i. 4 The vocal statue of Memnon, which began at the break of day to accost the rising sun. **1839** W. IRVING *Wolfert's Roost* (1855) 101 Accosting the commander with an air of coolness and unconcern.

b. Of a woman: to solicit in the street for an improper purpose.

1887 *Times* 12 July 11/5 The police-constable said she was in company with a second female, and that they had accosted gentlemen. **1927** *Daily Mail* 29 Sept. 10/1 The Cass case of 40 years ago, in which a young woman of irreproachable character was arrested..and charged..with accosting.

accost (əˈkɒst), *sb.* [f. the vb.] Address, salutation, greeting.

1616 B. JONSON *Cynth. Revels* v. iii, They act their accost severally to the lady that stands forth. **1650** A. B. *Mutatus Polemo* 27 At the first accost there was nothing but dumb shews. **1807** J. BERESFORD *Miseries* II. xviii. 170 Shooting your affectionate accosts, enquiries, and details, at each other. **1854** MRS. GASKELL *North & S.* viii. in *Househ. Wds.* No. 236. 159/1 She shrunk with fastidious pride from their hail-fellow accost, and severely resented their unconcealed curiosity. **1859** RAMSAY *Scot. Life & Char.* 60, I recollect her accost to me as well as if it were yesterday. **1877** J. MORLEY *Crit. Misc.* Ser. II. 248 The warm kindliness of his accost.

accostable (əˈkɒstəb(ə)l), *a.* [a. Fr. *accostable* (16th c. in Litt.): see ACCOST and -ABLE.]

†**1.** *actively.* Ready to accost, courteous. *Obs.*

1622 HOWELL *Lett.* (1650) I. 92 The Walloon is quick and sprightful, accostable and full of compliment. **1634** *Ibid.* II. 24 The French are a free and debonnaire acostable people: ..at first entrance one may have acquaintance.

2. *passively.* Capable of being accosted or approached; approachable, accessible, affable.

1655 LESTRANGE *K. Charles* 92 Seeing God is accostable by inorganicall and inaudible ejaculations. **1863** N. HAWTHORNE *Old Home* (1879) *Up the Thames* 285 Old soldiers, I know not why, seem to be more accostable than old sailors.

accosted (əˈkɒstɪd), *ppl. a. Her.* [f. ACCOST *v.* + -ED.] Placed side by side.

1610 GWILLIM *Disp. Heraldry* (1660) III. xv. 177 He beareth..a chevron between 6 Rams accosted, counter-tripping, two, two, and two.

accosting (əˈkɒstɪŋ), *vbl. sb.* Also 7 **accoasting**. [f. ACCOST *v.* + -ING¹.] Now only gerundial.

†**1.** A coming alongside. *Obs.*

1635 J. HAYWARD *Banish'd Virgin* 80 The accoasting of the six to one of the sides [of the ship] afforded our knights the commodity to tell our oaremen that the ship was by us taken.

2. Approach or advance (towards intercourse).

1603 FLORIO *Montaigne* (1632) I. xiii, The..first accoastings of society and familiarity. **1736** HERVEY *Mem.* II. 114 This prostration was known to be so acceptable an accosting to his Majesty's pride.

†**a'ccostment.** *Obs.* *rare*⁻¹. [f. ACCOST *v.* + -MENT.] The action of accosting; salutation, assault, accost.

1652 ? SIR A. COCKAYNE *Cassandra* I. 34 Infinitely surprised by an accostement and usage so extraordinary.

‖**accouche** (əˈkuːʃ, əˈkaʊtʃ), *v.* [a. Fr. *accouche-r*, f. *à* to + *coucher* to put to bed:—OFr. *culcher*:—L. *collocā-re* to lay together. See COUCH. Recognized as French, and, like the three following, used to avoid vernacular words.] To assist or deliver women in child-birth; to act as a midwife or accoucheur.

1867 *Lancet* March 23 (Advt.) A Gentleman, aged 26, long accustomed to Visit, Accouche, Dispense, and having good references.

‖**accouchement** (akuʃmɑ̃, əˈkuʃmənt, əˈkaʊtʃmənt). [Fr., n. of action f. *accoucher*: see prec. and -MENT.] Delivery in child-bed.

1803 ELIZ. WYNNE in *Wynne Diaries* 2 Sept. (1940) III. iv. 89 Mrs. Otway's accouchement which is daily expected. **1809** *Q. Rev.* I. 340 She receives the necessary attendance in her premature accouchement. **1843** *Pict. Times* 102 Until her Majesty's accouchement took place. **1853** ALISON *Hist. Europe* (Am. ed.) I. iv. 109 The direct line of succession depended on the success of her accouchement. **1859** TENNENT *Ceylon* II. IX. vi. 546 Their accouchements were assisted by women retained for their knowledge of midwifery. **1955** *Times* 23 Aug. 9/4 Feelings of relief at a safe accouchement.

‖**accoucheur** (akuˈʃœːr). [Fr., n. of agent f. *accoucher*: see ACCOUCHE *v.*] *Properly* a man who assists women in child-birth, a man-midwife; but until the very recent adoption of the Fr. *accoucheuse*, used of both sexes. Also *fig.*

1759 STERNE *Trist. Shandy* (1802) II. xii. 181 Nothing will serve you but to carry off the man-midwife.—*Accoucheur*, —if you please, quoth Dr. Slop. **1775** in *Phil. Trans.* LXV. 312 To an experienced *accoucheur* will be a sufficient index. **1810** *Edin. Rev.* XVII. 147 A violent philippic against accoucheurs in general. **1845** DISRAELI *Sybil* (1863) 43 His father was only an accoucheur. **1847** LEWES *Hist. Philos.* (1867) I. 127 He [Socrates] was an accoucheur of ideas. He assisted ideas in their birth, and, having brought them into light, he examined them, to see if they were fit to live; if true, they were welcomed; if false, destroyed. **1848** H. ROGERS *Ess.* I. VI. 328 All the progeny of poor Theatetus..expire as soon as they see the light, under the rude hand of this logical accoucheur. **1859** *Edin. Rev.* CIX. 332/1 Mrs. Hockley was a professional *accoucheur* for many years.

‖**accoucheuse** (akuˈʃœːz). [Fr., fem. of ACCOUCHEUR. Of very recent use in Eng.] A mid-wife.

[**1847** In CRAIG.] **1867** *Pall Mall G.* 26 July, 10 Mdme. Siebold, the accoucheuse here mentioned, had only three months before attended the Duchess of Kent at the birth of the Princess Victoria.

†**accounsel**, *v.* *Obs.* Also 5 **accounsayl**. [a. OFr. *aconseillie-r*, f. *à* to + *conseillier* to COUNSEL.] To counsel, advise.

c **1420** *Richd. Cœur de Lion* 2140 (Weber I. 82) And called him without fail, and said he wold him accounsayl. **1649** SELDEN *Laws of Eng.* (1739) II. iii. 18 They shall not accounsel the King in decreasing the Rights of the Crown.

account (əˈkaʊnt) *v.* Forms: 3 **acunte(n**, 4 **acounte**, 5–6 **acompte, acownte, accompte, accounte**, 6–7 **accompt**, 6– **account**. [a. OFr. *acunte-r, aconte-r* (Pr. *acontar, acomtar*):—late L. *accomptā-re* for **accomputā-re*, f. *ac-* = *ad-* to + *computā-re* to calculate (f. *com-* together + *putā-re* to reckon). In 14th c. *conter*, in the original sense of *computāre* 'count,' began to be artificially respelt *conpter, compter*, after the Lat., the natural spelling *conter* remaining in the sense of *narrāre* 'tell'; the variant spellings passed to *aconter* and Eng. *account, accompt*, though here with no corresponding division of meaning. The doubled *-c-* is part of the same refashioning.]

I. To count, reckon. Mostly *Obs.*

†**1. a.** *trans.* To count, count up, enumerate. *Obs.*

1303 R. BRUNNE *Handlyng Synne* 6392 þe katel was acountede More þan þe testament amountede. **1387** TREVISA *Higden* (Rolls Ser.) I. 9, I schulde also write þe famous stories and acounte þe ȝeres from þe bygynnynge of þe world anon to oure tyme. **1393** GOWER *Conf.* III. 78 He sigh The sterres such as he accompteth. **1430** LYDG. *Chron. Troy* I. vi, She gan acounte and caste well the tyme. **1483** CAXTON *Gold. Leg.* 78/4, I knowe wel that my fader and my moder acompte the dayes. **1582** BENTLEY *Monumt. Matrones* II. 1 My sinnes..in number are so manie..that I cannot account them.

†**b.** *absol.* To count, perform the act of counting. *Obs.*

1393 GOWER *Conf.* III. 89 The wise man accompteth After the formal proprete Of algorismes a be, ce. **1631** PRESTON *Breastp. Love* 198 When men have knowledge onely to know, as they have money to account with, and not to buy and sell with. **1660** T. STANLEY *Hist. Philos.* (1701) 56/2 He said, the Greeks made no other use of Money but to account with it. **1776** ADAM SMITH *Wealth of Nat.* I. I. x. 117 He [a grocer] must be able to read, write, and account.

†**2. a.** *trans.* To calculate, reckon, compute. *Obs.*

1398 TREVISA *Barth. De P.R.* (1495) IX. iv. 349 The Grekes acounte tyme and yeres fro the fyrst Olympias. **1547** J. HARRISON *Exhort. Scottes* 214 Wee accompt nobilitie by auncientie of yeres. **1571** DIGGES *Geom. Pract.* I. xvii, It is also to be wayed how this difference of highnesse and lownesse is to be accompted. **1635** N. CARPENTER *Geogr. Delin.* II. xiv. 224 The second is accompted from the pole, the other is conceiued to lye betwixt both. **1692** RAY *Dissol. of World* 25 I suppose that the Deity doth account days of a thousand years long. **1766** CHALKLEY *Wks.* 71 Which were to the Number of Forty-five, thus accounted. **1788** MARSDEN in *Phil. Trans.* LXXVIII. 414 The era of the Mahometans, called by them the Hejera, or Departure, is accounted from the year of the flight of Mahomet..from Mecca.

†**b.** To reckon in, count in; to include in an enumeration or reckoning. *Obs.*

1481 CAXTON *Myrrour* I. vi. 29 The philosophres that thenne were..acompted but thre maner of peple in the world. **1586** T. COGAN *Haven of Health* (1636) 159 Accounting the Lent season, and all fasting dayes in the yeare, together with Wednesday, Friday, and Saturday. **1614** RALEIGH *Hist. World* II. 372 By accounting of some part of the yeares of affliction..we have the just number of three hundred yeares. **1826** SOUTHEY in *Q. Rev.* XXXIV. 335 They argued that Wales, Scotland, and Ireland ought to be accounted with England.

c. To reckon *to*, put to the credit of. *rare.*

1577–87 HOLINSHED *Chron.* I. 115/1 Some account that yeare vnto his reigne, in the which his predecessors Osrike and Eaufride reigned. **1675** T. BROOKS *Golden Key* Wks. 1867 V. 226 The imputation of Christ's righteousness to us is a gracious act of God the Father, whereby as a judge he accounts believers' sins unto the surety, as if he had committed the same. **1846** D. JERROLD *Chron. Clovernook* Wks. 1864 IV. 408 You have all sorts of graces accounted to you.

†**d.** To reckon or count *on*, expect. *Obs.*

1587 TURBERVILLE *Trag. Ta.* (1837) 108 And selfe same day that he accompted on, to make Returne unto his mother's house at Boline.

†**e.** To reckon or calculate *that*, to conclude. *Obs.*

1570 BARNABE GOOGE *Popish Kingd.* I. 2 *b*, For every man accompted sure, that after losse of life They should receyve eternall blisse, and heaven voyde of stryfe. **1667** PRIMATT *City & Country Builder* 32 It may be accompted that a yard of Earth square will make seven or eight hundred of Bricks.

II. To render a reckoning.

3. a. *intr.* To reckon for moneys given or received, to render or receive an account.

1393 LANGL. *P. Pl.* C. XII. 298 þe reyue oþer þe conterroller. þat rekene mot and acounte Of al þat þei hauen had. *c* **1550** CHEKE *Matt.* xviii. 23 Lijk vnto a man which is a king which wold come to accompt with his servants. **1687** *Royal Order* 27 Nov. in *Lond. Gaz.* mmccxcviii/1 And that they do likewise Accompt every two Months with each Soldier for Six-Pence per Week more. **1714** ELLWOOD *Autobiog.* 260 To take a journey into Kent and Sussex, to Accompt with their Tenants, and overlook their Estates. **1780** BURKE *Sp. Econ. Ref.* Wks. III. 296 We have a long succession of paymasters and their representatives, who have never been admitted to account, although perfectly ready to do so. **1817** JAS. MILL *Brit. India* II. IV. v. 189 Both insisted upon the fact, that Ramnaramin was ready to account fairly.

b. *trans.* To render account of.

1614 SELDEN *Titl. Honor* 243 Before him as Chief Justice were all suits determined, crimes examined, the Crown-reuenue accompted, and whatsoeuer done, which, to so great iurisdiction was competent. **1868** M. PATTISON *Academ. Organ.* §2. 42 All receipts should be accounted to a finance committee.

4. To account *for*: **a.** *lit.* To render an account or reckoning of money held in trust; *hence*, **b.** to answer *for* discharge of duty or conduct.

1679 PENN *Addr. Prot.* I. §8. 41 (1692) If every poor Soul must Account for the Employment of the small Talent he has received from God. *a* **1700** DRYDEN *Juv. Sat.* xiii. At once accounting for his deep arrears. *a* **1710** ATTERBURY *Sermons* (R.) A future reckoning, wherein the pleasures they now taste must be accounted for.

c. To give a satisfactory reason *for*, to explain.

1768 STERNE *Sent. Journey* (1778) I. 190 Mr. Shandy.. accounted for nothing like anybody else. **1770** *Junius Lett.* xli. 214 How will you account for the conclusion? **1794** SULLIVAN *View of Nat.* I. 209 In accounting for the monsoons, however, it is necessary to mark the peculiar circumstances which obtain in the Indian Ocean. **1800** MRS. R. TRENCH *Rem.* 86 I dined also again with the Arnsteins, who I see hate the Austrian government. She is a Prussian, and according to the late cant phrase 'That accounts for it.' **1860** TYNDALL *Glaciers* II. §4. 248 Having thus accounted for the greater cold of the higher atmospheric regions.

d. *in sporting phrase*: To answer for the fate of, be the death of, make away with. Also, to beat in a contest.

1842 THACKERAY *Van. Fair* II. xx, The persecuted animals bolted above ground: the terrier accounted for one, the keeper for another. **1858** *Let. fr. Lahore* 28 Sept. in *Times*, 19 Nov., In the course of one week they were hunted up and accounted for; and you know that in Punjab phraseology 'accounting for' means the extreme fate due to mutineers. **1928** *Daily Mail* 25 July 14/1 The filly should account for Pure Gem, Falakeh, and company.

III. To estimate, consider.

†**5.** *trans.* To take into account, or consideration; to consider. *Obs.*

?**1400** *Roberd of Cysilee* 26, in Hazl. *E.P.P.* I. 270 The kynge thoght he had no pere For to acownte, nodur far nor nere. **1486** CAXTON *Curial* 7 They acompte not the pryckkyng that he hath felt in the pourchassyng of it.

6. *trans.* To reckon, estimate, value, hold (a thing to be so and so). **a.** with simple complement.

1377 LANGL. *P. Pl.* B. XI. 15 And bad me for my contenaunce Acounten clergie light. *Ibid.* XIX. 410 Neuere man.. þat acounted conscience at a cokkes fether or a hennes. **1470** MALORY *Morte d'Arthur* (1817) II. iv. That ony shold be accounted more hardy or more of prowesse. **1563** *Myrroure for Mag.* (ed. 2) *Blacksm.* xxxiv. 4 Which of all wreckes we should accompt the worst. **1579** LYLY *Euphues* 80 In the meane season accompt me thy friend. **1596** SHAKS. *Merch. V.* IV. i. 417 And I deliuering you, am satisfied, And therein doe account my selfe well paid. **1621** BURTON *Anat. Mel.* Democr. to Reader 36 We accompt Germanes heavy dull fellowes. **1653** WALTON *Angler* 86 A Trout.. that is accounted rare meat. **1728** NEWTON *Chronol. Amended* i. 123 Chronologers.. account Phidon the seventh from Temenus. **1827** SCOTT *Highl. Widow* I. 169 The Lowland herds and harvests they accounted their own. **1837** CARLYLE *Fr. Revol.* (1872) I. I. i. 2 Fortune was ever accounted inconstant. **1865** MILL *Liberty* ii. 24/1 By Christianity I here mean what is accounted such by all churches and sects—the maxims and precepts contained in the New Testament.

†**b.** with *as*, *for*. *Obs.*

1480 CAXTON *Descr. Ireland* (1520) 6/1 [It] is acounted for a myracle that lechery reygnethe not there as wyne reygneth. **1558** BP. WATSON *Seven Sacr.* i. 5 [He] would the holle church shoulde accompt him as a faythful soldiour. **1566** ADLINGTON tr. *Apuleius* 9 Milo is called an elder man and accompted as chiefe of those whiche dwel without the walles of the Citie. **1586** T. COGAN *Haven of Health* (1636) 170 It may seeme to be flesh, except you would account it as a Syren or Mermayden, that is halfe fish and halfe flesh. **1611** BIBLE *Rom.* viii. 36 Wee are accounted as sheepe for the slaughter. **1630** PRYNNE *Anti-Arm.* 118 Accounting it for a slaue, whereas it is a Lord, a King. **1660** FULLER *Mixt. Contempl.* (1841) 211 To contest and contend who shall be accounted for the greatest. **1674** PLAYFORD *Musick* III. 1 Unison, Eighth, Fifteenth, are accounted as one, for every Eighth is the same.

c. with *inf.* or *subord. cl.*

1558 BP. WATSON *Seven Sacr.* i. 4 He shall be of all the armie accompted to haue bene a faithfull soldiour. *a* **1593** H. SMITH *Wks.* (1867) II. 65 She accounted the glory of God to be taken from Israel. **1611** BIBLE *2 Peter* iii. 15 Account that the long suffering of the Lord is saluation. *a* **1626** BACON *Use Com. Law* 42 The Father shall there bee accompted to die without heire. **1669** BUNYAN *Holy Citie* 165 Those precious Stones, Paul accounts to be those that are converted by the Word. **1864** J. H. NEWMAN *Apologia*, App. 22 I account no man to be a philosopher who attempts to do more.

†**d.** rarely with *on*. *Obs.*

1614 B. RICH *Honestie of this Age* (1844) 57 I think bribery is no sinne at all; or if it be, it is but veniall, a light offence, a matter of no reckoning to account on. **1646** J. G[REGORY] *Notes & Obs.* (1650) 5 It is plainly void and supernumerary, and an escape not fit to be accounted upon the Sagenesse of that translation.

7. To account *of*: To estimate, value, esteem; to think *much*, *little*, *nothing*, etc. of a thing. (Now only in the *passive*.)

c **1369** CHAUCER *Dethe of Blaunche* 1237 God wote she acounted nat a stree Of al my tale, so thoght me. **1587** HARRISON *England* (1877) I. 2. ii. 38 The see of Canturburie ..whose archbishop.. is most accompted of commonlie. **1589** BEARD tr. La Primaudaye's *Fr. Acad.* 334 For everie beast is accounted of according to his vertue. **1611** BIBLE *1 Kings* x. 21 None were of siluer, it was nothing accounted of in the dayes of Solomon. **1649** SELDEN *Laws of Eng.* (1739) I. xvi. 32 [They] thereby taught Princes to account of Canons but as Notions. **1684** R. WALLER *Ess. Nat. Exper.* 45 This Experiment is not to be much accounted of. **1829** I. TAYLOR *Enthus.* (1867) §4. 76 They are nothing to be accounted of. **1853** LYNCH *Self-Impr.* v. 104 Let him not be accounted of, unless he has a backbone of character. **1863** CANON ROBINSON in *Macm. Mag.* March, 410 Never was preaching more accounted of than in the sixteenth century.

†**IV.** To recount, narrate. *Obs.*

†**8.** To recount, relate. *Obs.* **a.** *trans.*

c **1386** CHAUCER *Monkes T.* 715 Why schuld thyn infortune I nought acounte, Syn in astaat thou clombe were so hye. **1483** CAXTON *G. de la Tour* b i Thensample of the doughters of the king of denmarke which I shall acompte to yow. **1485** CAXTON *Charles the Gr.* (1880) 175 A messager departed.. for tacompte and telle the tydynges. **1563** FOXE *A. & M.* 762 b, I was bolde to accompte vnto them mery tales of my mysery in pryson. **1596** SPENSER *F.Q.* III. vi. 30 Long worke it were Here to account the endlesse progeny Of all the weeds that bud and blossome there.

†**b.** *intr.*

1393 GOWER *Conf.* III. 160 To accompte Of hem was tho the grete fame. *c* **1400** *Destr. Troy* XIII. 5443 To acounte of þe kynges,—Caras was on, And Nestor another.

account (əˈkaʊnt), *sb.* Forms: 3–4 **acunt**, 4 **acont**, 4–6 **acount(e**, 5–6 **acompt(e**, **accownt(e**, 5–**accompt**, 6– **account**. [a. OFr. *acunt*, *acont*, later *acompt* 'account', f. *à* to + *cont*:—late L. *compt-um*, cl. L. *comput-um* a calculation, f. *computā-re* to calculate: see prec. Cf. also OFr. *acunte*, *aconte*, later *aconpte*, *accompte* 'account', f. vb. *acunter*, *accompter*, to account; see prec. The senses of both are found in the Eng. word. The refashioned Fr. spelling *accompt* of 15th c. also passed into Eng., was favoured in 6–7, and is even now sometimes met with in the arithmetical sense.]

I. Counting, reckoning.

1. Counting, reckoning, enumeration, computation, calculation. Now chiefly in a few phrases: ***to cast accounts***, to revolve or make calculations, to calculate; ***money of account***, denominations of money used in reckoning, but not current as coins.

c **1305** *E.E. Poems* (1862) 50 Eiȝte hondred ȝer & neoȝentene: bi acountes riȝte. *a* **1360** *A Song of Yesterday* 66 in *E.E. Poems* 135 And in vr hertes acountes cast Day bi day. **1477** NORTON *Ordin. Alch.* (Ashm. 1652) v. 84 Twenty-six Weekes proved by accompt. **1570** BILLINGSLEY *Euclid* v. Introd. 126, *Arithmetique*, the arte of accomptes and reckoning. **1597** MORLEY *Introd. Musicke* 86 It is twentie miles by account from London to Ware. **1601** HOLLAND *Pliny* (1634) I. 74 The Greekes and Chaldeans account of yeares. **1611** BIBLE *Eccl.* vii. 27 Counting one by one to finde out the account. **1612** BREREWOOD *Lang. & Relig.* xiii. 140 Five miles of descent in perpendicular account. **1616** SURFLET & MARKH. *Countrey Farme* 397 Women with child, and neere their accompts. **1632** MASSINGER *Maid of Hon.* II. ii, You are in a wrong account still. **1662** H. MORE *Antid. ag. Ath.* (1712) I. ii. 12 When he has cast up his account. **1664** G. M. in Marvell's *Corr.* Wks. 1872–5 II. 103 Which according to the Moscovite accompt was the third hour of the day. **1691** LOCKE *Money* Wks. 1727 II. 72, I have spoke of Silver Coin alone, because that makes the Money of Account. **1711** ADDISON *Spect.* No. 25. ¶2 As for the remaining Parts of the Pound, I keep no accompt of them. **1741** RICHARDSON *Pamela* (1824) I. i. 17 My lady's goodness had put me to write and cast accompts. **1742** POPE *Poet. Wks.* (Tauchn. 1848) 286 This day Tom's fair account has run.. to eighty one. **1844** LINGARD *Hist. Anglo-Saxon Ch.* (1858) II. 391 From the coinage we now proceed to moneys of account. **1871** DAVIES *Metric System* III. 204 The weights for account are different from the weights for trade. *Mod.* Writing good, dictation very good, quick at accounts.

II. Reckoning of money received and paid.

2. a. A reckoning as to money, a statement of moneys received and expended, with calculation of the balance; a detailed statement of money due. Hence, ***to open*** or ***close an account with one***. ***to render*** or ***send in an account***: to give any one a statement of money due by him. ***to pay*** or ***settle an account***: to pay the amount therein shown to be due. ***account current***: a continuous account in which sums paid and received are entered in detail. ***joint account***: a transaction or speculation entered into by two parties not otherwise in partnership. In the general sense commonly in the plural, as, ***to keep accounts***. ***to balance*** or ***square accounts with any one***: to pay or receive the balance shown by a statement of account. Also **b.** One of the heads or subdivisions under which accounts are kept in a ledger, as a ***cash account***, ***general goods account***, ***bills receivable account***, the ***profit and loss account***, ***personal accounts***, a ***suspense account***. *transf.* (as *sb. pl.*). The department of a firm or organization whose job is to deal with accounts. In full, ***accounts department***.

c **1300** *Life Of Beket* 164 This child.. Servede a burgeys of the toun, and his acountes wrot. *c* **1386** CHAUCER *Shipm. T.* 87 Wolde no man schold him lette Of his accomptes. **1413** LYDG. *Pylgr. Sowle* (1483) IV. xxxiv. 83 The Shirreue muste yeue rekkenynge soo that the ende of his offyce is acountes of money. **1523** FITZHERBERT *Surveying* (1539) xvii. 35 The accomptes of euery bayly or reue and other acomptance. **1593** SHAKS. *Rich. II*, I. i. 130 My Soueraigne Liege was in my debt, Vpon remainder of a deere Accompt. **1607** —— *Timon* II. ii. 142 At many times I brought in my accompts, Laid them before you. *a* **1618** RALEIGH *Mahomet* 42 Reckoning made without an hoste is subject to a reare accompt. **1636** HEALEY *Theophrastus' Characters* xxiv. 84 If hee cleare an accompt with any, hee commands his boy to cast away the Compters. **1652** BROME *Joviall Crew* I. 358 The ballance of the several Accompts, Which shews you what remains in Cash. **1682** J. SCARLETT *Stile of Exch.* 39 The account currant.. should alwayes be clear and demonstrative, and show how the account stands with the Correspondent at all times. **1685** R. MORDEN *Geogr. Rectified* 275 They keep their Accompts by Livers, Solds, and Deniers. **1719** W. WOOD *Surv. Trade* 88 The Commissioners of the Publick Accompts. **1727** ARBUTHNOT *Hist. John Bull* (1755) 16 Bless me, what immense sums are at the bottom of the accompt! **1771** FRANKLIN *Autobiog.* Wks. 1840 I. 68, I attended the business diligently, studied accounts, and grew expert at selling. **1779** JOHNSON *L.P.*, *Fenton* Wks. 1787 III. 198 Detained him with her as the auditor of her accompts. **1823** SCOTT *Peveril* II. ix. 195 The shot has balanced all accompts. **1839** G. P. R. JAMES *Gent. Old Sch.* v. 51 You are running up a long account against us. **1841** MACAULAY *W. Hastings* (1851) I. 7 After two years passed in keeping accounts in Calcutta, Hastings went up the country. **1852** THACKERAY *Esmond* (1876) I. ix. 79 Besides writing my lord's letters, and arranging his accompts for him. **1853** LYTTON *My Novel* I. x. xx. 175 When you have squared your account with 'delicacy,' come to me. **1878** MRS. H. WOOD *Pomeroy Ab.* II. iii. 282 (Tauchn.) I told him I should take the accounts into my own hands. **1928** L. URWICK et al. *Organizing Sales Office* vii. 144 The Accounts Department was responsible that the sales manager was notified if a salesman was unable to balance his payments with his receipts. **1960** L. F. URWICK *Department Store* 2 (Chart) Accounts. **1963** 'J. LE CARRÉ' *Spy who came in from Cold* xxiii. 197 We got Elsie in Accounts to help with the gossip. **1986** *Sunday Tel.* (Colour Suppl.) 12 Jan. 34/4 On Mondays,.. the books are 'tapped off', or checked over with one of the girls from accounts.

c. *On Stock Exchange.* The fortnightly or monthly settlement of transactions between buyers and sellers, or the transactions to be then settled. A sale ***for the account***, as distinguished from a sale for cash, is an engagement on the part of the seller to deliver, and on the part of the buyer to receive and pay for the stock sold, at the ensuing settlement. ***account day***, on the stock exchange, the last day of the account, on which stock is delivered and paid for and differences are paid; also called ***pay day***.

1879 MELSHEIMER & LAURENCE *Lond. Stock Exch.* 8 The account days for English and India stocks, &c... are always fixed at least five weeks beforehand. *Ibid.* 18 On the third and last day of the settlement (called the 'account day' or 'pay day') the delivery of securities commences at ten o'clock. **1880** *Daily Tel.* April 30 A large amount of business was done for the new account. **1928** *Morn. Post* 19 Nov., A contract setting out that these 50 shares have been sold for the account November 22—next Thursday, that is—and bought for the following account day, December 6.

d. An arrangement to keep money in a bank, etc.; a sum of money so kept, a bank account; ***current account***, ***deposit account***, etc.: see under first element. Also, a credit arrangement with a firm, shop, etc.

1833 H. MARTINEAU *Berkeley Banker* I. i. 7 He waited in some impatience the opportunity of learning with what bank this great merchant meant to open an account. **1850** THACKERAY *Pendennis* xli. 351 Pen thought of opening an account with a banker. **1874** MRS. RIDDELL *Mortomley's Est.* II. ii. 24 To have an account at an old banking establishment. **1931** C. L. BOLLING *Retail Management* xiii. 275 Where customers ask for goods to be charged to credit accounts, precautions must be taken.. to see that the name and address.. and particulars.. are correctly recorded, as a basis for the charge to her [sc. the customer's] account. **1944** W. S. MAUGHAM *Razor's Edge* iv. 123 We know the manager of the bank in Chicago where Larry has his account. **1971** A. SHAFFER *Sleuth* I. 23 Cancelling the account at Harrods.

e. *transf.* A customer or client having an account with a firm. Chiefly *U.S.*

1937 *Time* 8 Mar. 83/1 Adding to the impressive list of Erickson accounts such majors as the Standard Oil group, California Packing, Zonite, Beech-Nut. **1962** H. O. BEECHENO *Introd. Business Stud.* x. 90 Advertising agencies refer to each of their clients as an 'account'. **1985** *Church Times* 8 Feb. 17/4 Collins have a vacancy for a Representative to sell their Bibles and Liturgical publications to established accounts in the North of England.

3. ***in account with***: in business relations requiring the keeping of an account *with*. ***to place*** or ***pass to account***: to debit or credit a person's account *with* an amount. ***for account of***: to be sold or realized for, to be accounted for to.

1647 J. Saltmarsh *Sparkles of Glory* (1847) 109 I left my adversary still upon some account with me. **1678** Lestrange *Seneca's Morals* 4 (1702) For there are, that reckon it an Obligation.. and place it to Accompt. **1690** Locke *Hum. Unders.* (ed. 3) III. x. 279 A man in his Accompts with another. **1711** Steele *Spectator* No. 87. ¶2 Beauty is thrown in to the accompt in matters of sale. **1732** Law *Serious Call* (ed. 2) i. 12 Placed to her account at the last day. **1823** Scott *Quent. D.* (1871) xxviii. 365 Oh! do not reckon that old debt to my account. **1826** T. Tooke *Currency* 102 A very considerable proportion are shipped for account of the manufacturers. **1882** *Daily Tel.* 4 May, A large portion of the gold recently advised as having been shipped from Australia has been landed at Galle for Indian account.

4. a. ***on account***: as an item to be accounted for at the final settlement, in anticipation of or as a contribution to final payment, as an interim payment on account of something in process. ***on one's account***: so that it shall be charged or entered to his account; in his behalf and at his expense. ***on one's own account***: for one's own interest, and at one's own risk.

1611 Bible *Philemon* 18 If hee oweth thee ought, put that on mine account. **1678** Butler *Hudibras* III. ii. 1158 Resolution Charg'd on th' account of Persecution. **1691** Petty *Polit. Arith.* x. 114 All Commodities, bought and sold upon the accompt of that Universal Trade. **1698** Luttrell *Brief Rel.* (1857) IV. 333 The summ of £250,000 be allowed upon account towards defraying the charge of disbanding the private troopers. **1801** Jane Austen *Let.* 14 Jan. (1952) 109 She.. desired me to ask you to purchase for her two bottles of.. Lavender Water.. provided you should go to the Shop on your own account. **1826** Disraeli *Vivian Grey* v. vi. 199 Shall I throw down a couple of Napoleons on joint account? **1852** McCulloch *Taxation* (ed. 2) III. i. 420 Going into the money-market and borrowing 1000*l.* on his account. **1853** Lytton *My Novel* I. III. xiii. 129 [She] was sometimes austere and brusque enough on her own account, and in such business as might especially be transacted between herself and the cottagers. **1855** Prescott *Philip II* (1857) I. I. vii. 124 The sum offered by the constable on his own account and that of his son. **1879** J. Grant in *Cassell's Techn. Educ.* IV. 62/2 He started in business on his own account.

b. Hence, ***upon*** (obs. since 1750), ***on account of***: (*a*) In consideration of, for the sake of, by reason of, because of.

1647 J. Saltmarsh *Sparkles of Glory* (1847) 86 Upon this account those offices have been thought ordinary which were upon the mere and pure account of the Holy Ghost. **1652** M. Needham tr. *Selden's Mare Cl.* 82 The Customs out of this Sea were very great, onely upon the accompt of Fishing. **1694** Lestrange *Fables* No. 444 (ed. 6) 481 She'll never Trouble herself farther upon any Accompt of mine. **1727** Swift *Gulliver* III. iv. 199, I was far their inferior, and upon that account very little regarded. **1759** Robertson *Hist. Scot.* I. VI. 400 On many accounts she did not think it prudent. **1792** Burke in *Corr.* (1844) III. 367 It is a matter on which I am doubly anxious,—on its own account, and on account of your concern in it. **1832** Ht. Martineau *Demerara* i. 10 He keeps at home now, on account of his great age.

†(*b*) In the matter of, with regard to, concerning. *Obs.*

1657 Cromwell *Lett. & Sp.* (Carl.) IV. 270 The arguments were upon these three accounts. **1657** Austen *Fruit Trees* I. 5 Men are generally mistaken upon this accompt. **1679** Penn *Address to Prot.* (1692) II. iv. 123 He hath said so well on this Account, that there is little need I should say any more. **1743** N. Appleton *Serm.* 34 Should he be never so poor and low upon outward Accounts. **1749** Fielding *Tom Jones* (1840) XIII. iv. 190 I am satisfied on the account of my cousin.

(*c*) ***on account***; ***account of***: *ellipt.* for 'on account of (the fact that)'. *slang.*

1936 E. Waugh *Mr. Loveday's Outing* 44 The purser who's different on account he leads a very cynical life. **1936** Wodehouse *Laughing Gas* xi. 117, I was feeling kind of down, on account that tooth of mine was giving me the devil. **1942** *Horizon* July 62 Fred's five foot ten.. but I tell him he's still a shrimp, account of I'm so tall. **1948** E. Waugh *Loved One* 52 Take your three days off, Mr. Barlow, only don't expect to be paid for them on account you're thinking up some fancy ideas.

(*d*) ***on no account***, certainly not, in no circumstances.

1855 Prescott *Philip II* (1857) I. II. vii. 280 He recommends the king on no account to remove Granvelle from the administration. **1918** B. Webb *Diary* 24 Jan. (1952) I. II. 107 The British Trade Union representative will, on no account, be late for his meals or early for his meetings. **1945** E. Waugh *Brideshead Revisited* I. i. 23 Three hundred a year; on no account give him more. **1969** J. Orton *What Butler Saw* I. 24 She's under strong sedation and on no account to be disturbed. **1973** E. F. Schumacher *Small is Beautiful* I. ii. 31 If a man can normally earn, say, $5000 a year, the average cost of establishing his workplace should on no account be in excess of $5000.

5. A reckoning in one's favour; interest, profit, advantage: esp. in ***find one's account in***; ***turn it to one's account***.

1611 Bible *Phil.* iv. 17 I desire fruit that may abound to your account. **1701** Swift *Wks.* 1755 II. I. 34 Wherein they expected best to find their own account. **1727** —— *Modest Prop.* II. II. 61 They will not yield above three pounds.. which cannot turn to account either to the parents or kingdom. **1788** Priestley *Lect. on Hist.* v. lxvi. 545 Gaul manifestly found its account in being conquered by the Romans. **1832** Ht. Martineau *Hill and Valley* iv. 52 A kind, too, which cannot be turned to any other account. **1860** Thoreau *Lett.* 192 (1865) However, he found his account in it as well as I. **1863** Cowden Clarke *Shaks. Char.* ii. 286 To make the best account of everything they encounter. **1878** Bosw. Smith *Carthage* 329 But the inactivity which was forced upon him.. he turned to good account.

6. The preparing or making up a statement of money transactions.

1646 Recorde etc. *Ground of Arts* 258 Now for the Accompt of Auditors, take this example. **1781** Gibbon *Decline & Fall* II. 55 The actual account employed several hundred persons. **1827** Hallam *Const. Hist.* (1876) II. xi. 377 Hence the bill appointing commissioners of public account.

III. The rendering of a reckoning.

7. A particular statement of the administration of money in trust: *esp. in phrases*; To give, yield, *or* render an account; to ask an account; to call *or* bring to account.

1513 Ld. Dacre in Ellis *Orig. Letters* I. 34. I. 97 Alwey I shall be redy to gif accompt of the same at your pleasure. **1528** Perkins *Profitable Bk.* (1642) viii. §504. 221 The ordinary cannot demand accompt for them. **1535** Coverdale *Luke* xvi. 2 Geue accompte of thy stewardshipe. *c* **1538** Starkey *England* II. ii. (1871) 186 To make a rekenyng and count before a juge. **1603** in *Shaksp. Cent. Praise* 103 The Accompte of the right honourable the Lord Stanhope of Harrington for all such somes of money as have beine receaved and paied. **1653** Holcroft *Procopius* III. 76 Calling the Italians to accompt, who never toucht the Emperour monies. **1738** *Hist. View of Crt. Excheq.* ii. 18 The Sheriff was upon his Account, and shewed the Book of the Clerk of the Pells in his Discharge. **1866** Mrs. Gaskell *Wives & Daughters* (Tauchn.) I. xvii. 285 The money for which he will give no account.

8. Hence **a.** A statement as to the discharge of responsibilities generally; answering for conduct.

c **1340** Hampole *Pr. Consc.* 3986 Þe Acunt and þe rekennyng þat þai sal yheld of alle þair lyfyng. *Ibid.* 5613 Alle þat sal com byfor Crist þat day, Sal strayt acounte yhelde. *a* **1450** *Knight de la Tour* 59 Of the which God wille axse hem acompte at the dredfulle day. **1563** *Homilies* II. xv. II. (1640) 204 Let us call ourselves to an accompt. **1579** Tomson *Calvin's Serm. on Tim.* 116/1 Will not God aske vs an accompt? **1599** Shaks. *Much Ado* IV. i. 338 Claudio shall render me a deere account. **1601** Barlow *Serm. at Paules Crosse* Pref. 1 Heaven is not liable to any accompt. **1654** E. Johnson *Wonder-working Prov.* 183 Being questioned how he came by it, could give no good accompt. **1732** Law *Serious Call* (ed. 2) ii. 21 Whether we shall be call'd to account at the last day. **1824** Scott *St. Ron. Well* (1868) xiii. 643 Obliged to bring somebody or other to account for the general credit of the Well. **1876** Freeman *Norm. Conq.* III. xii. 89 Theobald of Chartres was also called to account.

b. The final account at the judgment-seat of God, on the 'great day of accounts.'

1743 J. Morris *Serm.* ii. 52 In this awful account they, who are set on the left hand, are supposed to believe in Christ. **1822** S. Rogers *Italy* (1852) 107 Many a transgressor sent to his account. **1848** Marryat *Childr. N. Forest* (Tauchn.) xx. 248 He has gone to his account! God forgive him.

c. ***to give account of***: to give an explanation, account for.

1775 Johnson *Lett.* No. 126 (1788) I. 274, I am so much disordered by indigestion, of which I can give no account, that it is difficult to write more.

d. ***to give a good account of***: to be successful with; do his duty by.

1617 F. Moryson *Itinerary* II. II. i. 109 We doe hope to giue her Maiestie a very good account of her Kingdome, and of our selues, vntill wee shall haue cause to sue for more reliefe. **1684** *Scanderbeg Redivivus* iv. 81 Offering that with an Army of 60 thousand.. he did not doubt but to give a good account of this Summers Campaign. **1779** J. Wesley *Jrnl.* 29 Dec. (1786) XIX. 16 We have a musket and a fusee. If you load one, as fast as I discharge the other, I will give a good account of them all. **1809** B. H. Malkin tr. *Lesage's Gil Blas* I. I. ii. 24 Those said eggs of which he had given so good an account. **1883** R. L. Stevenson *Treas. Isl.* xvi. 133 We flattered ourselves we should be able to give a good account of a half-dozen [*sc.* mutineers] at least. **1928** *Daily Mail* 7 Aug. 8/3 They are likely to give a very good account of themselves in the big fight.

†**9.** In the prec. sense the pl. *accounts* was formerly used collectively, or as a singular. **a.** of money.

1398 Trevisa *Barth. De P.R.* (1495) VI. xvii. 202 Wyse and waar and cunnynge to ȝeue acomptes and rekenynge. **1461** *Paston Lett.* No. 395. II. 19 That I may have xx[ti] *li*, I xall ȝeve ȝow acompts ther of. **1591** Lambarde *Archeion* (1635) 30 He talketh of Accompts to be made to the King there. **1611** Bible *Dan.* vi. 2 That the Princes might giue accompts vnto them, and the King should haue no damage. **1704** *Col. Records Penn* XI. 128 And return accompts thereof. **1762** Goldsmith *Beau Nash* 14 To giue in his accompts to the masters of the temple.

b. of responsibility or conduct.

c **1260** *A Sarmun* 24 in *E.E. Poems* 3 Ȝe sulle we ȝiue acuntis Of al þat we habbiþ ibe here. *c* **1300** *Seyn Julian* (Ashm.) 98 Biuore our maister wende, Oure acountes uorte yelde. *c* **1460** *How a Marchande &c.* 248 in *E.P.P.* (1864) 207 I wyll neuyr aske yow accowntys. **1526** Tindale *Matt.* xviii. 23 They shall geve acountes at the daye off judgement. **1549** Coverdale *Paraph. Erasm. on Hebrues* 6 Unto whom we must geue an accomptes of our lyfe. **1549** Latimer 7 *Serm. bef. Edw. VI* (1869) 50 Before whom thou shalt appere one day to rendre a strayght accomptes, for the dedes done in thy flesh. **1564** Becon *Gen. Pref.* Wks. 1843, 25 We shall render an accompts for the lives of them all.

c. ***to hand in one's accounts***, to die. *U.S.*

1873 Aldrich *Marj. Daw* 150 The hotel remains to-day pretty much the same as when Jonathan Bayley handed in his accounts in 1840.

10. *Law.* A writ or action against a bailiff or receiver, or others, who, by reason of their offices or business, are to render accompt but refuse to do it. Tomlins *Law Dict.* 1809.

1622 Malynes *Anc. Law-Merch.* 468 The trial of an Action of Account at the common-law is tedious. **1641** *Termes de la Ley* Acompt is a Writ, and it lyeth where a Bayliffe or a receiver to any Lord or other man, which ought to render accompt, will not giue his account. **1809** Tomlins *Law Dict.* s.v. One merchant may have accompt against another where they occupy their trade together.. Account does not lie against an infant, but it lies against a man or woman that is guardian, bailiff, or receiver, being of age and dis-covert.

IV. Estimation, consideration.

11. Estimation, consideration, esteem, worth, importance in the eyes of others; esp. in the phrases: a person or thing *of* some *account*; to be held *in* some *account*.

1393 Gower *Conf.* I. 217 That he his fader in disdeigne Hath take and sette at none accompte. **1587** Fleming *Contn. Holinshed's Chron.* III. 1375/1 To view Sussex and the havens, and as he thought, to tast the best of account there. **1598** B. Jonson *Ev. Man in his Hum.* I. i. 11 A Scholler.. of good accompt, in both our Universities. **1599** Greene *Alphonsus* 44 (1861) 244 Rich Pactolus, that river of account. **1613** Purchas *Pilg.* (1864) 3 Wild goats, whose hornes are in account against venome. **1645** Pagitt *Heresiogr* (1662) 208 More ancient and of so special accompt. **1667** Primatt *City and Country Builder* 3 Decent Houses made for the dwelling of gentry or citizens of accompt. **1680** W. Allen *Peace & Unity* 11 To appear considerable in the account of others. **1681** Dryden *Abs. & Ach.* I. 628 Moses' laws he held in more account, For forty days of fasting in the mount. **1767** Fordyce *Serm. to Y. Wom.* I. iii. 95 Are all these of no account? **1876** Freeman *Norm. Conq.* IV. xviii. 222 The town of Huntingdon was, then as now, one of much less account than Cambridge.

12. ***to make account of***: to hold in estimation, regard as important; to value, esteem.

1393 Gower *Conf.* III. 267 A leon in his rage, Which of no drede set accompt. **1490** Caxton *Eneydos* xvi. 62 Therof she made none acompte. **1578** Lyte *Dodoens* 735 This kind of Nut is a wild fruite, whereof men make none accompt. **1580** North *Plutarch* (1676) 4 She was not a beast to be made light account of. **1611** Bible *Ps.* cxliv. 3 Or the sonne of man, that thou makest account of him? **1616** Surflet & Markh. *Country Farme* 581 At Rome this kind of bread is made no account of. **1855** Prescott *Philip II* (1857) II. vii. 276 They were indignant that so little account should be made of their representations. **1860** Dickens *Uncom. Trav.* (1866) vi. 37/1 Of the page I make no account, for he is a boy. **1866** Mrs. Gaskell *Wives & Daughters* (Tauchn.) I. xviii. 329 The little account she made of her own beauty pleased Mr. Gibson.

†**13.** Reckoning, estimate, consideration, thought. *esp.* in phrase ***to make account*** (***that, to do***): to reckon, calculate, resolve, expect. *Obs.*

1583 Golding *Calvin's Deut.* xix. 110 Wee haue made our Account to rest simply vppon his Word. **1586** G. Whitney in Farr's *S.P.* (1845) I. 206 And make accompte that honor to be theires. **1600** Holland *Livy* XLI. xix. 1108 h, Making full account [*haud dubie*], that the next day the enemies would yield. **1611** Bible *1 Macc.* vi. 9 He made account that he should die. **1623** Bingham *Xenophon* 41 Wife and Children, which he made account neuer to see again. **1633** Bp. Hall *Hard T.* 52 That yee may know where to make account of my presence. **1642** Howell *For. Trav.* 37 Make accoump for matters of fertility of soyle. **1662** H. More *Antid. agt. Ath.* (1712) Pref. Gen. 5, I make account I began then to adorn my Function. **1697** Patrick *On Exodus* i. 17 They made account the things of God were to be preferr'd before those of Men. **1729** Burkitt *On N.T., Mark* vi. 35 No pastors in the sight of God and in the account of Christ. **1784** Cowper *Task* IV. 356 Oh happy! and in my account, denied That sensibility of pain.

14. ***to take into account***, ***take account of***: to take into consideration as an existing element, to notice; so, ***to leave out of account***.

1681 Chetham *Angler's Vade-mecum* xl. §30 (1689) 304 Some Rivulets are taken into the accompt **1844** Ld. Brougham *Alb. Lunel* (1872) I will.. take the royal training into my account. **1868** Kingsley *Heroes* IV. 129 Do you take no account of my rule? **1871** Smiles *Character* (1876) i. 25 It is not great men only that have to be taken into account. **1880** Gen. Adye in *19th Cent.* No. 38. 702 Any system must be bad which leaves out of account the first principle of regimental efficiency.

15. ***to lay one's account with*** (***on, for***): to reckon upon, anticipate, expect. (*orig. Scotch.*)

1746 *Rep. on Cond. Sir J. Cope* 189 These are fixed Resolutions, on which your Royal Highness may lay your account. **1748** Smollett *R. Random* (1812) I. 176 I must lay my account with such interruption every morning. **1799** Dundas in *Wellesley Desp.* 644 We must lay our account with being at all times obstructed in our views. **1827** Hallam *Const. Hist.* (1876) I. v. 233 The jurors must have laid their account with appearing before the star-chamber. **1844** Ld. Brougham *Alb. Lunel* (1872) II. v. 167 You may lay your account with increasing rather than stemming the mischief. **1845** Hamilton *Pop. Educ.* (ed. 2) ii. 17 We as Christians need not lay our account for any other state of society. **1852** McCulloch *Taxation* III. ii. 456 (ed. 2) We may lay our account with being again involved in war.

V. Narration, relation.

16. A particular statement or narrative of an event or thing; a relation, report, or description. phr. ***by all accounts***.

1614 Raleigh *Hist. World* III. 5 To this accompt agreeing with the Scriptures.. I have sometimes subscribed. **1633** Campion *Hist. Ireland* Ep. Ded. II. 1 An accompt of my poore voyage. **1715** Steele *Addison's Drummer* Pref., Having recommended this Play.. I feel myself obliged to give some Account of it. **1762** GOLDSMITH *Cit. World* (1837) cxix. 464 Though I gave a very long account, the justice said, I could give no account of myself. **1792** *Anec. W. Pitt* I. ii. 29, A dark, confused, and scarcely intelligible accompt. **1793** SMEATON *Edystone Lightho.* §313 Edwards gave account that they lighted the house, as they were directed. **1798** MRS. INCHBALD *Lovers' Vows* (ed. 3) II. i, By all accounts the Baroness was very haughty. **1804** MISS AUSTEN *Watsons* (1879) 335 Begin and give me an account of everything as it happened. **1825** J. NEAL *Bro. Jonathan* I. i. 10 [She was] the prettiest one, though, 'by all accounts'. **1860** DICKENS *Uncom. Trav.* (1866) v. 31/2 When he heard of talent, trusted nobody's account of it. **1872** FREEMAN *Hist. Ess.* (ed. 2) 14 The whole Norman account of Godwine is one of the best specimens of the growth of legend.

b. An interpretation or rendering of a piece of music.

1961 in WEBSTER. **1963** *Listener* 28 Mar. 571/1 The best things in his five concerts were 'his noble account of Mendelssohn's *Ruy Blas* Overture [etc.]. **1969** *Ibid.* 31 July 161/2 These performances are backed by another gramophone 'classic': Lisa Della Casa's account of Strauss's *Four Last Songs*. **1983** *Classical Music* Nov. 21/4 Roger Norrington conducted a fizzing account of Offenbach's score.

17. *Attrib.* and *Comb.* **account-book**, a book prepared for the keeping of accounts. **account day**, day of reckoning. **account(s) executive**, in an advertising agency: one whose job is to manage the interests of particular clients. **account sales**, a detailed account of the sale of a parcel or cargo of goods.

1699 BENTLEY *Phalaris* 535 He represents the Account-Book of some of the wealthy Men of that Age. **1838** CARLYLE *Sart. Res.* II. iii. 124 My Teachers were hide-bound Pedants, without knowledge of man's nature or of boy's; or of aught save their lexicons and quarterly account-books. **1853** LYTTON *My Novel* II. VIII. xii. 51 Never kept the money; and never looked into the account books! **1860** FROUDE *Hist. Eng.* V. xxix. 460 If the account-books of twenty years of confusion.. were not forthcoming and in order, they were to be proceeded against without mercy. **1580** HOLLYBRAND *Treas. Fr. Tong.*, *Dresseur de compte*, an accompte caster. **1837** CARLYLE *Fr. Rev.* I. II. viii. 83 Now the account day has come. **1931** F. B. LANE *Advertising Admin.* xii. 141 The accounts executive.. is usually an executive member of the agency organization and a widely-experienced advertising man. **1962** H. O. BEECHENO *Introd. Business Stud.* x. 90 An Account Director or Account Executive is the administrative officer who looks after particular clients' interests. **1986** *Daily Tel.* 20 Jan. 6/5 Account executives are the co-ordinating link with the client.

☞*Phrase-key.* Balance *a* 2, bring to *a* 7, call to *a* 7, cast *a* 1, close *a* 2, *a* current 2, find *a* in 5, for *a* of 3, for the *a* 2 c, give *a* of 8 c, d, hold in *a* 11, in *a* with 3, joint *a* 2, keep *a* 2, lay *a* with 15, leave out of *a* 14, make *a* of, that 12, 13, of *a* 11, on *a* 4, open *a* 2, pass, place to *a* 3, render *a* 2, 7, settle *a* 2, square *a* 2, take into *a*, take *a* of 14, turn to *a* 5, upon *a* 4.

†**a'ccount**, *ppl. Obs.* Also **accompte**. [Contr. for ACCOUNTED *account'd*, as *lit* for *lighted*.] = ACCOUNTED.

1548 CRANMER *Catechismus* 100 b, Yet verely (all thynges accompte) theyr losse is greater then theyr gaynes. **1608** SHAKS. *Pericles* I. i. 30 Was with long use account'd [*Globe ed.* account] no sin.

accountability (ə,kaʊntə'bɪlɪtɪ). [f. ACCOUNTABLE: see -BILITY.] The quality of being accountable; liability to give account of, and answer for, discharge of duties or conduct; responsibility, amenableness. = ACCOUNTABLENESS.

1794 S. WILLIAMS *Hist. Vermont* 140 No mutual checks and ballances, accountability and responsibility. **1808** *Mem. Dr. J. Cadman* (1853) 75 To affect the accountability of man. **1837** J. HARRIS *Grt. Teacher* 170 The perception of your new accountability might well impress you with an awful concern. **1849** GROTE *Greece* V. II. xlvi. 475 Individual magistrates exposed to annual accountability. **1859** MILL *Dissert.* I. 467 Pushing to its utmost extent the accountability of governments to the people.

accountable (ə'kaʊntəb(ə)l), *a.*; also 6–7 **accomptable**. [f. ACCOUNT *v.* + -ABLE.]

1. Liable to be called to account, or to answer for responsibilities and conduct; answerable, responsible. Chiefly of persons. **a.** (*to* a person, *for* a thing).

1583 T. WATSON *Poems* (1870) 134 He setteth them downe in this next page following, but not as accomptable for one of the hundreth passions of this booke. **1603** DRAYTON *Heroical Ep.* (1619) Pref., I ought to be accountable of my private meaning. **1623** SANDERSON *Serm.* Ad. Mag. I. 10 (1674) 86 They stand accountable to him from whom they have received it; and woe unto them if the accounts they bring in be not.. answerable to the receipts. **1688** *King's Decl.* 14/2 I am nevertheless Accomptable for all Things that I openly and voluntarily.. do or say. **1713** STEELE *Englishm.* No. 1. 9 I am accountable to no Man, but the greatest Man in England is accountable to me. **1812** WELLINGTON in *G.D.* IX. 153 The officer commanding the company must be accountable to the volunteer for the residue of the sum. **1873** W. COLLINS *New Magd.* (Tauchn.) I. xiv. 222 She is not accountable for her actions.

b. Also without *to* or *for*.

1642 *Declar. Lords and Comm.* 9 Jan., 4 The Lord Lieutenant and Committee shall be accomptable. **1736** BUTLER *Anal.* I. vi. 152 That he was in fact an accountable child. **1742** MIDDLETON *Cicero* I. Pref. 36 (ed. 3) The Consuls, whose reign was but annual and accountable, could have no opportunity of.. erecting themselves into Tyrants. **1788** REID *Active Powers* I. v. 523 It is of the highest importance to us, as moral and accountable creatures. **1836** J. GILBERT *Chr. Atonem.* (1852) viii. 222 God has chosen also to sustain the character of a governor of accountable agents.

†**2.** To be counted or reckoned on. *Obs.*

1603–5 SIR J. MELVIL *Mem.* (1735) 286, I could do him accountable Pleasure and good Service. **1709** J. COLLIER *Ess. on Sev. Mor. Subj.* I. 39 (ed. 6) Those who have not, must be Curates.. or else lay by the use of their Priesthood; which I am afraid is not very accountable.

†**3.** Able to be reckoned or computed. *Obs.*

1589 PUTTENHAM *Eng. Poesie* (1869) 90 There is an accomptable number which we call arithmeticall (*arithmos*) as one, two, three.

†**4.** To be reckoned or charged; chargeable, attributable *to*. *Obs.*

1681 EVELYN in *Pepys Corr.* 311 That I did not proceed with the rest is accountable to his successor.

5. Able to be accounted for or explained; explicable. (Cf. *unaccountable*.)

1665 GLANVILLE *Scepsis Sci.* 34 The proposed Instances are far more accountable then this before us. **1684** T. BURNET *Theo. Earth* i. 20 A way of making the deluge fairly intelligible, and accountable without the creation of new waters. **1834** HT. MARTINEAU *Moral* III. 124 The progress of freedom has been continuous and accountable. **1869** SWINBURNE *Ess. & Stud.* (1875) 207 There is another omission after verse 165, more accountable than this. **1876** GEO. ELIOT *D. Deronda* III. xxxvi. 59 By George—it was a very accountable obstinacy.

b. With *for*.

1745 WESLEY *Answ. Church* 45 Every thing, which is not strictly accountable for, by the Ordinary Course of Natural Causes. **1862** F. HALL *Refut. Hindu Philos. Syst.* 81 The phraseology.. is accountable for only by the identity, under one aspect, of a property and that which is propertied.

accountableness (ə'kaʊntəb(ə)lnɪs). [f. prec. + -NESS.] The quality or fact of being accountable or liable to give account and answer for conduct; responsibility, amenableness (*to* a person, *for* a thing).

1668 HONYMAN *Surv. Naphtali* (1669) II. 64 Subordination to the Prince, as to direction, accountableness, or censurableness. **1680** MATHER *Irenicum* 11 The lawfulness and usefulness of Synods in the Church of God, and the accountableness of particular Congregations thereunto. **1788** REID *Active Powers* IV. vii. 622 His accountableness has the same extent and the same limitations. **1858** DE QUINCEY *Whiggism* Wks. VI. 65 The same disdain of accountableness to his party leaders. **1868** MISS BRADDON *Dead Sea Fr.* (Tauchn.) II. xiv. 198 The.. ideas of man's accountableness for the soul of his weaker partner.

accountably (ə'kaʊntəblɪ), *adv.* [f. ACCOUNTABLE *a.* + -LY[2].] In a manner accountable, that can be reckoned, or that can be accounted for.

1646 SIR T. BROWNE *Pseud. Ep.* 307 The Sunne ariseth unto the one sooner then the other, and so accountably unto any Nation subjected unto the same parallell. **1665** J. SPENCER *Prophecies* 122 He acts so accountably and consonantly to our Notions in the Works of his Providence. **1713** *Guardian* No. 55 (1756) I. 244 If a christian forgoes some present advantage for the sake of his conscience, he acts accountably.

accountance, occ. found for *accountants* (Fr. *accomptans*), pl. of ACCOUNTANT *a.* or *sb.*

accountancy (ə'kaʊntənsɪ). [f. ACCOUNTANT: see -CY.] The art or practice of an accountant.

1854 *Illus. Lond. News* 22 Apr. 378 The practical adaptation of the decimal system to our money and accountancy. **1872** MISS BRADDON *Rob. Ainsleigh* I. xvi. 287 His task of cleansing this Augean stable of foul accountancy. **1879** *Standard* 7 Apr. [Advt.] Accountancy Pupil.—An Opening for a Young Gentleman in an Accountant's Office.

accountant (ə'kaʊntənt), *a.* and *sb.*; also **accomptant**. [a. (15th c.) Fr. *accomptant* (OFr. *acuntant*), pr. pple. of *accompter*, *acunter*: see ACCOUNT *v.*]

†**A.** *adj.* Giving or liable to give an account; accountable, responsible. (In early usage with plural *-s*.) *Obs.*

1494 FABYAN VII. 366 He admytted to that offyce William de Hadestok & Anketyll de Aluerun, and sware theym to be accomptauntes, as theyr predecessours were. **1603** SHAKS. *Meas. for M.* II. iv. 86 His offence is so, as it appeares Accountant to the Law, vpon that paine. **1604** —— *Oth.* II. i. 231 Peraduenture I stand accomptant for as great a sin. **1611** SPEED *Hist. Gt. Brit.* (1632) IX. ix. 605 [It] was no reason why he should not stand accountant to the Son. **1622** DONNE *Serm.* cxxiv. V. 225 He.. that is accomptant for their souls. **1649** SELDEN *Laws Eng.* I. lxvii. 176 (1739) The Guardian in Socage remaineth accomptant to the Heir, for all profits both of Land and Marriage.

B. *sb.*

1. One who renders or is liable to render account; one accountable or responsible. In *Law*, the defendant in action of Account. (In earliest instances not separable from prec. adj.; afterwards a true sb. The pl. was sometimes corruptly *accomptance*, Fr. *accomptans*; cf. *accidents*, *-nce*, *acquaintants*, *-nce*.)

1453 LD. LE SCROPE in *Test. Eborac.* (1855) II. 192 Acquyt and discharged of ony dett yat yei, or ony of yaime, owe me, except foreyne accomptaunts and seruaunts accomptaunts. **1523** FITZHERBERT *Surveying* 30 a, All the mynistre and partyculer accomptes of euery baylye or reue and other accomptance. *Ibid.* 30 b, If the accomptance bring him perfyte rentals and court roles. **1613** *Life Wm. Conq.* in *Sel. fr. Harl. Misc.* (1793) 23 Committed to prison; not as bishop of Bayonne, but as earl of Kent, and as an accomptant to the king. **1630** R. BRATHWAIT *Eng. Gent.* (1641) 223 They must be accomptants in that great assize where neither greatnesse shall bee a subterfuge to guiltinesse, nor their descent plead priviledge for those many houres they have mis-spent. **1649** SELDEN *Laws Eng.* II. xx. 98 (1739) He took away the course of farming of Sheriff-wicks, and make the Sheriffs bare accountants for the Annual profits. **1708** CHAMBERLAYNE *Grt. Brit.* (1743) I. II. ii. 46 All accomptants to him for any of his Revenues. **1745** FLEETWOOD *Chron. Precios.* App. 17 The said accomptant chargeth himself with arrearages. **1809** TOMLINS *Law Dict.* s.v. *Account*, It is no plea by an accomptant that he was robbed. **1844** WILLIAMS *Real Prop. Law* (1877) 91 Any crown debtor, or accountant to the crown. **1865** *Times* 17 Aug., An 'imprest' means an advance of public money to enable the person to whom it may be made to carry on some public service; and the person to whom the advance is made is called the 'imprest accountant.'

2. One who counts or can count or reckon; a reckoner, calculator.

1646 H. LAWRENCE *Comm. & Warre w. Angels* 31 In matters of numbring and account, an accountant will tell you that in a quarter of an hower. **1697** DAMPIER *Voyages* (1729) I. 360 The Mindanaians are no good Accomptants; therefore the Chinese that live here, do cast up their Accompts for them. **1710** STEELE *Tatler* No. 228. ¶ 10 He is an excellent Penman and Accomptant. **1742** YOUNG *Night Thoughts* IX. 1307 O ye Dividers of my Time! Ye bright Accomptants of my days, and months, and years. *c* **1817** J. HOGG *Ta. & Sk.* V. 21 The best grammarian, the best reader, writer and accountant in the various classes that he attended. **1828** MISS MITFORD *Our Village* Ser. III. 7 (1863) A false accomptant, a stupid arithmetician, would put her out of humour.

3. One who professionally makes up or takes charge of accounts; an officer in a public office who has charge of the accounts. ***accountant-general***, the chief or superintending accountant in various public offices.

1539 *Househ. Ord.* in *Thynne's Animadv.* (1865) 33 And the said Books shall be examined with the Accomptants and particular Clerkes for the perfecting of the same. **1605** CAMDEN *Rem.* 18 To admonish accontants to be circumspect in entring. **1655** FULLER *Ch. Hist.* VI. 353 Herein the Dean and Chapter of Paul's, were both their own Accomptants and Auditors. **1679–88** *Secr. Serv. Mon. Chas. II & Jas. II*, 121 (1851) To Katherine, the widow and relict of Dr Robert Wood, dec'ed, late accomptant generall of the Revenue in Ireland. **1719** D'URFEY *Pills* (1872) VI. 329 A British accountant that's frolic and free, Who does wondrous Feats by the Rule of Three. **1753** SMOLLETT *Ct. Fathom* 142/1 (1784) A third was the issue of an accomptant, and a fourth the offspring of a woollen-draper. **1829** I. TAYLOR *Enthus.* (1867) ii. 32 Note particularly and with the scrupulosity of an accomptant. **1878** JEVONS *Prim. Polit. Econ.* 82 Skilful accountants should examine the books at the end of the year, and certify the amount of profits due to the men.

†**4.** A narrator. *Obs. rare.*

1655 FULLER *Ch. Hist.* Cent XII. i. §70 The same accomptant, when coming to set down, what then, and there was offered to Christ's, or the High-Altar, dispatcheth all with a blanke, *Summo Altari nil*.

accountantship (ə'kaʊntənt-ʃɪp). [f. prec. + -SHIP.] The office or employment of an accountant.

1824 R. WATTS *Bibliotheca* III (*Heading*) Accounts, Accompts, and Accomptantship. **1858** H. MILLER *Sch. & Schoolm.* 507, I was not a little surprised.. to be offered by him the accountantship of the branch bank.

accounted (ə'kaʊntɪd), *ppl. a.*, also **acounted**, **accompted**. [f. ACCOUNT *v.* + -ED.] Counted, reckoned, considered.

1362 LANGL. *P. Pl.* A. I. 88 He is a-counted to þe gospel ..And eke I-liknet to vr lord. **1385–6** In Rymer *Fœdera* XII. 479 To serue the King in his warres beyond see an hole yere with two speres, himself accompted. **1550** CROWLEY *Epigr.* 111 Men accompted wyse and honeste do so. **1585** ABP. SANDYS *Serm.* (1841) 297 This is the acceptable and only accounted time. **1653** HOLCROFT *Procopius* I. 21 Beyond which it is called Dalmatia, accompted of the western Empire.

†**accounter** (ə'kaʊntə(r)). *Obs.* Forms: 4 **acountour**, **acounter**; 6–7 **accompter**, **accounter**. [Prob. a. OFr. *acuntour*, *acontour* (not in Godefr.), n. of agent f. *acunter*: see ACCOUNT *v.* and -OUR.]

1. One who accounts, reckons, calculates, renders an account.

1303 R. BRUNNE *Handl. Synne* 5410 Lordynges cunseylours Wykkede legystrys or fals acountours. **1540** WHITTINTON *Tullyes Off.* I. 27 That we may be as good accompters of our offyces and dutyes. **1587** GOLDING *De Mornay* viii. 92 It is not for me to stand here disprouoing the doubts of the Accounters of times. **1591** PERCIVALL *Sp. Dict.*, *Contador*, an accounter, a receiuer of the exchequer, computator, quæstor. **1601** CORNWALLYES *Ess.* (1631) II. li. 328 Hee that can make so even a reckoning is none of the worst Accompters. **1633** STAFFORD *Pac. Hib.* (1821) x. 343 The Accounter, the Steward of the artillery remayning.

2. A narrator.

1356 WYCLIF *Last Age* 26 Þis also [he] schewiþ openly bi discripcioun of tyme, of Eusebi, Bede, and Haymound, most preued of acounteris, or talkeris.

accounting (ə'kaʊntɪŋ), *vbl. sb.* [f. ACCOUNT *v.* + -ING[1].]

1. The action or process of reckoning, counting, or computing; numeration, computation. Now esp. the management of financial affairs, e.g. those of a business enterprise; = ACCOUNTANCY. Cf. BOOK-KEEPING.

1387 TREVISA *Higden* (Rolls Ser.) I. 39 Dionysius Exiguus acordeþ nouȝt with þe Gospel in acountynge of ȝeres. *c* **1400** TUNDALE *Circumcis.* 85 By just a countyng in the kalendere The fyrst day of the new yere. **1494** FABYAN I. 2 Thus endyth thaccomptynge of the yeres of the worlde from the Creacion of Adam vnto the Incarnacion of Christ. *a* **1716** SOUTH 12 *Serm.* (1717) III. 407 Running behind-hand in his Spiritual Estate, which, without frequent Accountings, he will hardly be able to prevent. **1855** in *Accountant* (1874) 24 Dec. 5/1 Accountants are frequently employed by courts of law..to aid those courts in their investigations of matters of accounting. **1885** F. H. CARTER (*title*) Practical book-keeping adapted to commercial and judicial accounting. **1892** in J. Isaac *Sci. of Accounts* p. ii, The Indian method of Double Entry classification represents a New Method of Accounting. **1913, 1924** [see *cost accounting* s.v. COST *sb.*[2] 6]. **1957** *Encycl. Brit.* I. 102/2 The subject matter of accounting embraces every aspect of an enterprise which can be expressed in terms of money. **1962** H. O. BEECHENO *Introd. Business Stud.* vii. 62 The form of accounting most generally used..is called financial accounting. **1978** P. MATTHIESSEN *Snow Leopard* (1979) iv. 285, I pay wages to the sherpas for their months of faithful work, having Tukten explain to Dawa the when, where, and why of the accounting.

b. *Attrib.* or *Comb.* †**accounting-book**, *Obs.* account-book; †**accounting-house**, *Obs.* counting-house; **accounting machine**, a machine for performing book-keeping operations such as addition, dating, and tabulating; †**accounting-table**, *Obs.* counter, desk.

1552-5 LATIMER *Serm. & Rem.* (1845) 206 Christ is the accounting book, and register of God. **1812** CRABBE *Tales* 16, Wks. 1834 V. 168 This trader view'd a huge accompting-book. **1788** V. KNOX *Winter Evgs.* III. VIII. i. 105 Your souls are..confined in their flight to the regions of Change Alley and your accompting-houses. **1916** *Office Appliances* July 22/1 The new Remington accounting machine..confers all the benefits of mechanized ledger posting. **1957** *Economist* 2 Nov. 418 An extremely versatile accounting machine, especially designed for the small and medium sized business. Sales, purchase, and general ledgers, stock records, cost records, payroll—it will do them all! **1978** J. KELLOCK *Elements of Accounting* xii. 214 The punched-card method reduced the cost of processing information and at the same time accelerated the speed of producing data compared with manual and accounting machine systems. **1649** JER. TAYLOR *Gt. Exemp.* II. xi. 21 Jesus drave the beasts out of the Temple and overthrew the accounting tables.

2. Accounting *for* (gerundially): Answering for, giving a satisfactory explanation of. Proverbial phr. ***there is no accounting for tastes*** [cf. L. *de gustibus non est disputandum*].

1823 J. GALT *Entail* xxix. 277 But you know..that there is no accounting for tastes. **1855** PRESCOTT *Philip II* (1857) I. viii. 144 One obvious way of accounting for this, doubtless, is by the spirit of persecution which hung like a dark cloud over her reign. **1867** A. TROLLOPE *Last Chron. Barset* I. xxxi. 263 He had not the slightest objection to recognizing in Major Grantly a suitor for his cousin's hand... There was..no accounting for tastes. **1903** G. B. SHAW *Man & Superman* III. 101, I don't admire the heavenly temperament..but it takes all sorts to make a universe. There is no accounting for tastes: there are people who like it.

accounting (əˈkaʊntɪŋ), *ppl. a.* Also **accompting**. [f. ACCOUNT *v.* + -ING[2].]

†**1.** Counting, reckoning. *Obs.*

1551 RECORDE *Pathw. Knowl.* II. 42 That is to saye D. E. K. H, which was at no tyme accompting as percell of any one of them. *a* **1628** F. GREVILLE *Life of Sidney* (1652) 28 The ill-accompting hand of war.

2. That keeps accounts. *arch.*

1810 CRABBE *Borough* xxi. 6 A kind merchant hired his useful pen, And made him happiest of accompting men.

†**a'ccountless**, *a. Obs.* [f. ACCOUNT *sb.* + -LESS.]

1. Beyond count or reckoning, countless.

? **1650** *Don Bellianis of Greece* 54 Yielding the accountless thanks of dutiful servitors at your command.

2. Free from accountableness; irresponsible.

1655 J. SHIRLEY *Politician* I. i, Accountless liberty Is ruin of whole families.

accountment (əˈkaʊntmənt). *rare.* [f. ACCOUNT *v.* + -MENT.] The work of accounting or reckoning for, responsibility.

1857 HEAVYSEGE *Saul* (1869) 404 On Samuel may the feud's accountment fall, And the blood be on the fiend that stirred my gall.

accoup, variant of ACOUP *v. Obs.* to blame.

†**a'ccouple**, *v. Obs.* 6-7. Also 6 **acople, acouple**. [a. OFr. *acople-r*, later *acouple-r*, to join in a couple, f. *à* to + *cople, couple*, COUPLE. Refashioned Fr. spelling *accoupler* (see AC-) also followed in Eng.] To join one thing to another, to couple.

1486 *Plumpton Corr.* 50 Ye be acopled as brether and sisters. **1605** BACON *Adv. Learn.* II. 14 That application which he accoupleth it withal. **1613** SIR H. FINCH *Law* (1636) 369 They were never accoupled in lawfull matrimonie. **1622** BACON *Henry VII*, 81 Accoupling it with an Article in the nature of a Request. **1635** D. PERSON *Varieties* II. ix, Fire being accoupled to a matter contrary to its owne nature..this terrestriall matter draweth the fire perforce with it.

accouplement (əˈkʌp(ə)lmənt). [a. Fr. *accouplement* (16th c. in Littré), n. of action f. *accoupler*: see ACCOUPLE and -MENT.]

†**1.** The action of coupling one thing to another; union, pairing; marriage union. *Obs.*

1483 CAXTON *Gold. Leg.* 347/4 This excellence that virgynyte had as to the respect of thaccouplement of mariage appiereth by manyfold comparacion. **1576** LAMBARDE *Peramb. Kent* (1826) 339 The lawe of God maketh the accouplement honorable amongst all men. **1594** R. C[AREW] *Huarte's Exam. Men's Wits* (1616) 318 If the father be wise in the works of the imagination, and..take to wife a woman cold and moist in the third degree, the sonne borne of such an accouplement, shalbe most vntoward.

2. (In carpentry.)

1823 NICHOLSON *Pract. Builder* 579 Accouplement, in carpentry; a tie or brace, or the entire work when framed.

†**a'ccoupling**, *vbl. sb. Obs.* [f. ACCOUPLE + -ING[1].] The act of joining two things into a couple or pair; coupling; esp. union in marriage.

1525 MORE *Richard III* Wks. 1557, 63/2 For lack of which lawfull accoupling, & also of other thinges, which the said worshipful doctor rather signified then fully explaned.

accoupment, var. ACOUPEMENT, *Obs.* blame.

†**a'ccourage**, *v. Obs.* Also **acco'rage**. [a. Fr. *accourage-r* to hearten, encourage, imbolden, OFr. *acorager*, f. *à* to + *corage*, mod.Fr. *courage*, COURAGE.] To encourage, hearten.

1596 SPENSER *F.Q.* II. ii. 38 But that same froward twaine would accorage, And of her plenty adde unto their need. *Ibid.* III. viii. 34 But he endevored with speaches milde Her to recomfort, and accourage bold.

†**a'ccourse.** *Obs. rare*[−1]. [a. Fr. *accourse* = It. *accorso*:—L. *accursus* a running to, f. *ac-* = *ad-* to + *cursus* running, f. *curr-ĕre* to run.] A running up, a hastening forward.

1635 J. HAYWARD *Banish'd Virgin* 215 Hee call'd for water, which came (but too late), with the accourse of all that were above, to helpe her.

†**a'ccourt**, *v. Obs. rare*[−1]. [f. COURT *v.*, with *ac-* = *ad-* to, here intensive or expletive: see A- *prep.* 11. A Spenserian artificial form.] To court.

1596 SPENSER *F.Q.* II. ii. 16 Her other sisters..were at their wanton rest, Accourting each her frend with lavish fest.

accoustics, obs. bad spelling of ACOUSTICS.

accoustre, -trament, obs. f. ACCOUTRE, -MENT.

accoutre (əˈkuːtə(r)), *v.* Also 7 **accoustre, acoutre**. [a. MFr. *accoustre-r* (mod. *accoutrer*), of uncertain origin; prob. f. *à* to + *coustre, coutre*, a sacristan or vestry keeper, who robed the clergyman: see Littré and Skeat. The Fr. *accoustrer* was in 16th c. pronounced *accoutrer* (Cotgr. 1611 has both spellings), whence *accoutre* is the ordinary Eng. form; *accoustre* occurs less commonly in 17th c.] To attire, equip, array. (Rare except in the pa. pple. ACCOUTRED.)

1606 DEKKER *Seven Sins* II. (Arb.) 19 Another therefore of the Broode..aptly accoustred, and armed Cap-a-pe. **1659** *Lady Alimony* II. vi. in Hazl. Dodsl. XIV. 322 But hark you, madam; what be those brave blades That thus accoutre you. **1682** BUNYAN *Holy War* 55 So gallant a company so bravely accoutred. **1686** *Lond. Gaz.* No. 2182/4 There could not be a finer body of men, nor better accoutred. **1706** PHILLIPS, *To accouter*, to dress, attire, or trim. **1727** SWIFT *Gulliver* IV. xi. 335 He accoutred me with other necessaries, all new. **1755** CROKER *Ariosto's Orl. Fur.* XLVI. xlvi. II. 407 Leon his 'squires commanded, him to take, Accoutre him, and fit for Ruggier make. **1849** DICKENS *B. Rudge* i. 3 (C.D. ed.) He.. was accoutred in a riding dress. **1869** *Pall Mall G.* 13 Oct. 4 The new system of accoutring the soldier can only be introduced gradually.

accoutred (əˈkuːtəd), *ppl. a.* Also 7 **accoustred**. [f. prec. + -ED. The first part of the verb to be used, and the only one in common use.] Attired, dressed, equipped, arrayed; generally with the idea of being specially attired for some purpose.

1596 SHAKS. *Merch. Ven.* III. iv. 63 When we are both accoutered like yong men. **1601** —— *Jul. C.* I. ii. 105 Vpon the word, Accoutred as I was, I plunged in. **1652** BENLOWE *Theophila* XL. lvi. At length shee's built up with accoutred grace. **1663** H. COGAN *Voy. & Adv. Pinto* 200 All mounted on horses, very richly accoustred. **1713** DERHAM *Physico-Theol.* 225 The helpless well accoutered and provided for. **1795** SOUTHEY *Joan of Arc* iv. 87 Wks. I. 54 Trimly accoutred court-habiliments **1858** MOTLEY *Dutch Rep.* XI. 57/1 It was a very triumphant thing to see them thus richly dressed and accoutred.

accoutrement (əˈkuːtəmənt). Also 6 **accoustrament**, 6-7 **accustre-, accutre-, accoustrement**. [a. mid. Fr. *accoustrement* (mod. *accoutrement*), n. of action f. *accoustrer*: see ACCOUTRE *v.* and -MENT.]

1. Apparel, outfit, equipment. *Almost always in the pl.*, clothes, trappings, equipments. *Milit.* The equipments of a soldier other than arms and dress.

1549 *Compl. of Scotl.* (1872) vii. 68 The acoutrementis ande clethyng of this dolorus lady, vas ane syde mantil. **1586** FERNE *Blazon of Gentrie* 29 Let al men embrodure, depaint, engraue and stampe vpon their hanginges, walles, windowes, and other domesticall *accoustrammentes* these glorious and commendable ensignes. **1596** SHAKS. *Tam. Shr.* III. ii. 121 To me she's married, not vnto my cloathes: Could I repaire what she will weare in me, As I can change these poore accoutrements, 'Twere well for Kate, and better for my selfe. **1600** —— *A.Y.L.* III. ii. 402 You are rather point deuice in your accoustrements. **1641** SANDERSON *Serm.* II. 6/1 What are all our crossings, and kneelings, and duckings? What surplice, and ring, and all those other rites and accoutrements that are used in or about the publick worship; but so many commandments of men? **1649** W. BLITHE *Eng. Improver Impr.* (1652) 195 Having his Plough and all its Accutrements compleated. **1751** WATTS *Improv. Mind* (1801) 365 Rich and glittering accoutrements wherewith the Church of Rome hath surrounded her devotions. **1813** WELLINGTON in Gurwood's *Desp.* X. 495 In order to collect the wounded and their arms and accoutrements. **1850** MERIVALE *Rom. under Emp.* III. xxviii. 329 There was no camp filled with plate, jewels, and splendid accoutrements to be devoted to plunder. **1858** GEN. P. THOMPSON *Audi Alt. Part.* I. lxii. 241 Without sacrificing everything to the game of the war-contractor and the accoutrement-maker.

2. The process of accoutring or being accoutred.

1598 SHAKS. *Merry Wives* IV. ii. 5 Not onely in the simple office of loue, but in all the accustrement, complement, and ceremony of it. **1850** LEITCH *Muller's Anc. Art* §409. 552 Youthful representations, with slight indication of accoutrement.

†**a'ccoward**, *v. Obs.* [a. mid. Fr. *accouard-ir*, f. *à* to + *couard* coward.] To render cowardly; to intimidate, cow, or make faint-hearted.

1530 PALSGR. 416 I accowarde, I make one faynte herted, *Je accouardys*: I thought that all the wordes in the world shuld not have accowarded the.

†**a'ccowardize**, *v. Obs.* Also 5 **acowardyse**. [f. Fr. *accouardis(s-)* extended stem of *accouardir*: see prec.; assimilated to vbs. in -IZE.] = ACCOWARD.

1480 CAXTON *Ovid's Metam.* XII. xiii, [Patroclus] assayled the Troyans whom he greved moche and acowardysed and mad them torne to flyghte. **1611** COTGR., *Acouhardir*: To accowardize, effiminate, make faint-hearted.

accownt(e, obs. form of ACCOUNT.

†**accoy**, *v. Obs.* Also 4-5 **acoy(e, acoie**, 6-7 **accoy(e**. [a. OFr. *acoie-r, acoye-r* to calm, appease, f. *à* to + *coi* quiet, calm:—L. *quiēt-um* QUIET.] To still, calm, quiet, or appease; *hence*, to soothe or coax (the alarmed or shy), to tame, silence, or daunt (the forward or bold).

c **1350** *Wm. of Palerne* 56 Þe cherl..chastised his dogge, bad him blinne of his berking, & to þe barne talked, acoyed it to come to him, & clepud hit oft. *c* **1374** CHAUCER *Troylus* V. 782 He nyst how best hire herte for t' acoie. *c* **1400** *Rom. Rose* 3564 Bialacoil, his most joye, Which alle hise peynes myght acoye. **1430** LYDG. *Chron. Troy* II. xiv, Brother a whyle do acoye The cruel tourment that byndeth you so sore. **1530** PALSGR. 416 I acoye, I styll, *Je apaise*, or *je rens quoy*: Be he never so angrye, I can accoye hym: *tout soyt il courroucé, je le puis apayser* or *accoyser*. **1557** *Tottell's Misc.* (Arb.) 197 Transmuted thus sometime a swan is he, Leda taccoye, and eft Europe to please. **1567** TURBERVILLE *Louer abused*, A loving wight For to accoy, accoy, And breede my joy. **1579** SPENSER *Sheph. Cal.* Feb., Then is your careless courage accoyed. **1596** —— *F.Q.* IV. viii. 59 I received was, And oft imbrast..And with kind words accoyd. **1598** B. YONG tr. *Diana* That sweete gracious smile,..wherewith I sawe thee not accoyd. *a* **1600** PEELE *Eclogue* III. 152 How soon may here thy courage be accoy'd? **1647** H. MORE *Poems* 76 The voice these solemn sages nought at all accoyes. **1706** PHILLIPS, *To Accoy* (old word): To assuage.

accoynt, early form of ACQUAINT.

accrase, accraze, variants of ACRAZE *v. Obs.*

†**accrease** (əˈkriːs), *v. Obs.* Also 5 **acrese**, 6-7 **accress(e**, 6 **accreace**. [a. OFr. *accreistre, accreiss-ant*:—L. *accrēsc-ĕre*, f. *ac-* = *ad-* to + *crēsc-ĕre* to grow. See also ACCRESCE, later, f. L. In sense 2, probably for earlier *encrese*, INCREASE; see A- *pref.* 10.]

†**1.** *intr.* To increase or grow by addition. *Obs.*

1535 W. STEWART *Cron. Scotl.* II. 529 Malice and invy, With greit fervour accressand to sic feid. **1598** FLORIO, *Accrescere*, to increase, to accrease, to add vnto, to augment, to growe, to multiplie, to spring, to accrew, to eeke. **1635** D. PERSON *Varieties* I. §6. 24 Such as aske, why the sea doth never debord nor accreace a whit, notwithstanding that all other waters doe degorge themselves into her bosome.

2. *trans.* To increase. *Obs.*

1401 *Pol. Poems* II. 105 (1859) Mo fyngris on myn hond than foure and the thombe amenusith my worching more than it acresith.

†**a'ccrease**, *sb. Obs.* [f. the vb.] Increase.

1598 FLORIO, *Accrescimento*, Encrease, accrease, profit, advancement, accrew, eeking. **1603** —— *Montaigne* (1634) 93 The friendship I beare unto my selfe, admits no accrease, by any succour I give my selfe in any time of need. *Ibid.* (1632) I. xix. 34 For then we shall have worke sufficient, without any more accrease.

accredit (əˈkrɛdɪt), *v.* Also 7 **acredit**. [a. Fr. *accrédite-r*, earlier *accréditer* Cotgr. = *mettre à crédit*, f. *à* to + *crédit* CREDIT. Occurs in 7, but not in general use till late in 8. In no Dict. bef. Todd 1818.]

1. To put or bring into credit, to set forth as credible; to vouch for, sanction, or countenance.
1620 SHELTON *Don Quixote* II. IV. vi. 65 As well by these reasons as by many other.. which acredit and fortifie mine opinion. *c* **1775** COWPER *Let.* 43 (T.) His censure will (to use the new diplomatic phrase) accredit his praises. **1802** HOWARD in *Phil. Trans.* 175 The exhibition of this stone.. did not tend to accredit the account of its descent. **1822** SOUTHEY in *Q. Rev.* XXVIII. 29 The prediction of calamities for France accredited these dreams. **1850** MRS. JAMESON *Sacr. & Leg. Art* 223 It was not sufficiently accredited for a church legend. **1879** GLADSTONE *Sp. at Glasgow* 6 Dec. [His] mode of action at the Cape of Good Hope does not tend to accredit his advice in Affghanistan.

2. To send forth with credentials, to furnish with letters of credit; to recommend by documents as an envoy or messenger. Const. *to*, *at*.
c **1794** MATHIAS *Pursuits of Lit.* 320 (1798) He represents the opinions of a very large portion of their body by whom he is accredited. **1852** GLADSTONE *Gleanings* IV. vi. 144 There are representatives of Portugal and Spain, accredited from Sovereigns themselves symbols of the popular principle. **1860** MOTLEY *Netherlands* II. xviii. 432 (1868) The sovereign to whom I am accredited. **1863** KINGLAKE *Crimea* I. vi. 89 (1876) There was a prospect of his being accredited at St. Petersburg.

3. a. To accredit *one* with *something*: To accredit it as his, to vouch for his being the owner or author of it; to ascribe or attribute it to him.
1864 *Morning Star* 13 June 4 Whenever topics fail them these worthy gentlemen fall back upon his Royal Highness and accredit him with the most wonderful sayings and doings. **1880** MCCARTHY *Hist. own Times* III. 208 Mr. Bright himself was accredited with having said that his own effort to arouse a reforming spirit.. was like flogging a dead horse.

b. To attribute (a thing) *to* a person. *U.S.*
1876 A. WILDER in R. P. Knight *Symb. Lang.* p. xxvii, To the fanatical hordes of Islam.. is to be accredited the extinction of the Mystic Orgies of the East. **1900** *N. & Q.* 9th Ser. 22 Dec. 487/1 The introduction of the name [Columbia] as a poetic title for the United States is to be accredited to Dr. Timothy Dwight.

†**a'ccreditate**, *v. Obs.* [f. Fr. *accrédite-r* or It. *accreditā-re* + -ATE³, as if f. L. **accrēditā-re*, *accrēditāt-us*, assumed as their source.] A by-form of ACCREDIT.
1654 SIR A. COKAINE tr. *Loredano, Dianea* IV. §3. 306 She bowed, kissing the Thracians hands, who would not resist it, to accreditate the beginnings of his Love to be of estimation. **1660** HOWELL *Lexicon Tetragl.* To Philol., It will be an occasion hereby to accreditat her the more.

accreditation (əkrɛdɪ'teɪʃən). [n. of action f. prec.: see -TION.] The action of accrediting; the fact of being accredited; recommendation to credit or to official recognition.
1806 *Mem. of R. Cumberland* I. 417 Having received my instructions and letters of accreditation from the earl of Hillsborough on the 17th day of April 1780. **1814** SIR R. WILSON *Pr. Diary* II. 291 Obtaining my letters of accreditation, etc., I set off at one o'clock in the morning.

accredited (ə'krɛdɪtɪd), *ppl. a.* [f. ACCREDIT + -ED. Cf. Fr. *accrédité* used in the same sense.] **a.** Furnished with credentials, publicly or officially recognized; given forth as worthy of belief, authoritatively sanctioned.
1634 J. CANNE *Necess. Separ.* (1849) 3. Those accredited believers for whom it was appointed. **1804** SOUTHEY in *Ann. Rev.* II. 4 Columbus persevered, and his discoveries received the name of India from his accredited error. **1810** —— *Lett.* II. 201 Colonel Burke is there as an accredited spy. **1831** GEN. P. THOMPSON *Exerc.* (1842) I. 436 The latest accredited rumour is, that the Lords are determined to resist the reformation of the House of Commons. **1837** WHEWELL *Hist. Induct. Sc.* I. 238 (1857) They sought their philosophy in accredited treatises. **1863** *Conf. Ticket of Leave Man* 4 To reward long-accredited service in a confidential situation. **1870** *Illustr. Lond. News* 29 Oct. 438 The diplomatic body accredited at Madrid.

b. Used of a grade of milk. (Term disused as official designation since 1954.)
1932 *Min. Agric. & Fish. Pubn.* (*title*) Scheme for the introduction of county registers of accredited milk producers. **1933** *E. Angl. Inst. Agric. Rep. 14th County Clean Milk Comp., 1933* 13 Members of the County Registers of Accredited Milk Producers will be in a very strong position. This Register.. was inaugurated in Essex in 1931. **1934** *Milk Marketing Board's Scheme of Accred. Producers* ser. P.B. 3, p. 2 What will the term 'Accredited Milk' stand for? It will be milk from cows that have been clinically tested; from farms where scrupulously clean methods are practised—and itself a product subject to bacteriological tests.

accrediting (ə'krɛdɪtɪŋ), *vbl. sb.* [f. ACCREDIT + -ING¹.] The action of vouching for or furnishing with credentials. (Mostly gerundial.)
1834 SOUTHEY *Doctor* cxvii. 285 (1862) I have wronged Job's wife by accrediting a received calumny. **1850** ALISON *Hist. Europe* VIII. lv. §10. 566 The effects.. appeared in the accrediting of Russian ambassadors to the courts of these infant sovereigns. **1872** W. MINTO *Eng. Lit.* Introd. 24 There is not so much unanimity in accrediting him with dignity.

accrediting (ə'krɛdɪtɪŋ), *ppl. a.* [f. ACCREDIT + -ING².] Giving credit, furnishing with credentials.
1865 *Cornh. Mag.* Nov. 608 Having negotiated bills and obtained money for a considerable amount, the 'honourable traveller' had taken himself off before notices of protest had come from the accrediting bankers.

accrementitial (,ækrɪmən'tɪʃəl), *a. Biol.* [f. L. **accrēment-um* addition (f. *accrēsc-ĕre*, see ACCRESCE; cf. *excrēment-um* f. *excrēsc-ĕre*) + *īci-us* + -AL¹; see -ITIAL.] Pertaining to accrementition.
1879 *Syd. Soc. Lex.*

accrementition ('ækrɪmən'tɪʃən). *Biol.* [Improperly formed by form-assoc. with prec. The regular word would be *accrementation*; cf. *fer-ment-ation*.] Organic growth, by development of blastema, or by fission of cells, in which the new formation is exactly like that from which it proceeds; = ACCRETION.
1879 *Syd. Soc. Lex.*

accresce (ə'krɛs), *v.* Also 7 access. [ad. L. *accrēsc-ĕre* to grow to, grow on, f. *ac-* = *ad-* to + *crēscĕre* to grow. Substituted for, or refashioned on, earlier ACCREASE from Fr., the form *access* being intermediate.]

1. To accrue. *Obs.* exc. as rendering *accrēscere* in Rom. law; see ACCRETION 8 b.
1634-46 J. ROW (the father) *Hist. Kirk Scotl.* (1842) 84 Prebendaries founded upon tithes to access to the ministers liveing, and the rest for schoolls. **1661** *Laws & Acts 1st Parlt. Chas. II. of Scotl.* 3 Considering the great advantages [that] do accress to the publick good of His Subjects, by the due observance of such ancient and well grounded Customs and Constitutions. *a* **1685** *Househ. of Chas. II* in *Househ. Ord.* (1790) 378 [It] accresses only to theire chamber keeper, to the ruyne of the waiters table. **1753** *Stewart's Trial* 161 These lands were the best farms on the estate, and most of the benefits accresced from them. **1880** MUIRHEAD *Gaius* II. §199 The share of any one who fails accresces to his co-legatee.

†**2.** *intr.* To increase, grow up. *Obs.*
1637 GILLESPIE *Eng. Pop. Cerem.* II. iii. 19 How little moates have accresced to Mountains.

†**3.** *trans.* To increase, add to. *Obs.*
1652 URQUHART *Jewel* Wks. 1834, 247 Having repaired to the great city of Vienne to accresce his reputation in some more degrees.

accrescence (ə'krɛsəns). [f. (as if through Fr.) on late L. *accrēscentia*, n. of quality f. *accrēscent-em* pr. pple. of *accrēsc-ĕre*; see prec. and -NCE.]

1. The process of growing continuously, continuous growth.
1839 COLERIDGE *Statesm Man.* App. B 296 The silent accrescence of belief from the unwatched depositions of a general, never-contradicted hearsay.

2. Something which grows on a thing from without; an accretion.
1649 JER. TAYLOR *Gt. Exemp.* xvii. §6 The primitive Christians.. when they had washed off the accrescences of Gentile superstition, they chose such rites which their neighbours used. *c* **1819** COLERIDGE in *Rem.* (1836) II. 220 This accrescence of objectivity in a ghost that yet retains all its ghostly attributes and fearful subjectivity is truly wonderful.

accrescency (ə'krɛsənsɪ), *Obs. rare*⁻¹. [ad. late L. *accrēscentia*; see prec. and -NCY.] *prop.* The quality of being accrescent or of growing on; *hence*, an accrescence or accretion.
1649 JER. TAYLOR *Gt. Exemp.* I. iv. 124 We shall have more of human infirmities to be ashamed of than can be excused by the accrescencies and condition of our nature.

accrescent (ə'krɛsənt), *a.* [ad. L. *accrēscent-em* pr. pple. of *accrēscĕre*: see ACCRESCE.]

1. Growing continuously, ever increasing.
1753 SHUCKFORD *Creation & Fall* 90 (R.) New appearances of accrescent variety and alteration. **1891** *Temple Bar* June 222 Accrescent layers of instruction sandwiched in between patches of narrative.

2. *Bot.* Continuing to grow, growing larger after flowering; applied to those parts of the flower which normally fall off or wither after fertilization.
1857 HENFREY *Botany* 102 Occasionally [the calyx] grows during the maturation of the fruit, and is accrescent, forming.. a vesicular envelope to the fruit. **1876** OLIVER *Elem. Bot.* 231 Observe the two accrescent (enlarging after flowering) bracteoles, replacing the perianth in the pistillate flowers of Orache.

‖**accrescimento** (ak,kreʃɪ'mento), *sb. Mus.* [mod. Ital., n. of action, f. *accrēscere* to increase.] The increase of the length of a note by one half, indicated by placing a dot after it. (Little used.)
1847 In CRAIG.

accrete (ə'kriːt), *v.* [f. L. *accrēt-*, ppl. stem of *accrēsc-ĕre*; see ACCRESCE.]

1. *intr.* To grow together by adhesion, to combine.
1784 J. TWAMLEY *Dairying* 175 How the different parts accrete to bring on Fermentation, or cause the Intestine motion excited in Vegetables. **1875** WHITNEY *Life of Lang.* xii. 248 The variously accreted formative elements.

2. *intr.* To grow to, adhere, attach itself *to*.
1869 *Spectator* 1 May 532 An instrument of power too long neglected and disused, the loyalty which accretes to the impartial, impassive, all-protecting State. **1880** *Ibid.* 3 Jan. 11/2 In this country, popularity, no less than power, tends to accrete to the old.

3. a. *trans.* To cause (a thing) to grow or unite *to*.
1871 EARLE *Philol. Eng. Tongue* vii. 262 We must assume that the reader has thoroughly accreted and assimilated this distinction to his habits of mind. **1881** MYERS *Wordsworth* 95 Its arguments and theories have lain long in Wordsworth's mind, and have accreted to themselves a rich investiture of observation and feeling.

b. To draw or attract to oneself or itself. Hence **a'ccreted** *ppl. a.*
1901 H. B. GEORGE *Relat. Geogr. & Hist.* 260 It became the seat of one of the small principalities which happened to accrete other dominions. **1914** G. B. SHAW *Common Sense about War* 11 He, too, accreted fools and knaves, and ended defeated in St. Helena. **1921** *Chambers's Jrnl.* 10 Sept. 648/1 The accreted and reclaimed land.

accrete (ə'kriːt), *ppl. a.* [ad. L. *accrēt-us*, pa. pple. of *accrēscĕre*; see ACCRESCE.]

1. Formed by accretion; made up, factitious.
1824 LANDOR *Imag. Conv.* Wks. 1846 I. xxvii. 152 Milton is no factitious or accrete man; no pleader, no rhetorician. **1859** TODD *Cycl. Anat. & Phys.* V. 411/1 Masses of accrete .. colouring matter.

2. *Bot.* Grown together by adhesion of external parts; said of organs normally separate.
1847 LINDLEY *Introd. Bot.* (1848) II. 379, *Accrete*; fastened to another body, and growing with it (De Cand.). **1880** A. GRAY *Bot. Text-Bk.* 393, *Accrete*, Grown together, consolidated with some contiguous body.

accretion (ə'kriːʃən). [ad. L. *accrētiōn-em*, n. of action, f. *accrēt-* ppl. stem of *accrēsc-ĕre*; see ACCRESCE.]

1. The process of growing by organic enlargement; continued growth.
1615 CROOKE *Body of Man* 430 The action of the Increasing faculty we call Accretion, that is, when the whole body encreaseth in all his dimensions. **1684** LEIGHTON on *1 Peter* ii. 1 (1817) To desire the word for the increase of knowledge.. is necessary and commendable and being rightly qualified is a part of spiritual accretion. *c* **1720** GIBSON *Diet of Horses* v. 78 (ed. 3) Young Horses require a greater quantity of food, as that is necessary for the Accretion and Growth of their Bodies. **1828** KIRBY & SPENCE *Introd. Entom.* IV. xxxix. 82 The blood is the principal instrument of accretion. **1859** HELPS *Friends in C.* II. x. 232 The tendency of all power is to accretion, and indeed, to very rapid accretion.

2. The growing together or coherence of separate particles, or of parts normally distinct; continuous coherence; concretion.
1655-60 T. STANLEY *Hist. Philos.* 183/2 (1701) After the second accretion followeth this contemplation which holdeth the third room. **1656** tr. *Hobbes's Elem. Philos.* 479 (1839) As for stones, seeing they are made by the accretion of many hard particles within the earth. **1794** SULLIVAN *View of Nat.* I. 94 Compounded indurated matters which are, formed by the accretion of particles, accumulated and deposited by water. **1853** PHILLIPS *Rivers of Yorksh.* iii. 43 The drop, gathered by accretion of minute particles, may be snow, ice, or water. **1866** FELTON *Anc. & Mod. Greece* I. ii. 24 They [languages] agree, with a single doubtful exception, in the agglutinating or synthetic method, called by Humboldt incorporation, by Cass, coalescence, and by Schoolcraft, accretion.

3. Anything formed by the preceding process.
1873 H. ROGERS *Orig. Bible* (ed. 3) iv. 171 That the Bible is an accretion of casual writings arbitrarily linked together.

4. The process of growth by external addition.
1626 BACON *Sylva* VII. §602 (1651) 125 Plants doe nourish; Inanimate Bodies doe not: They have an Accretion, but no Alimentation. **1627** HAKEWILL *Apol.* I. iv. §1. 40 The losse of Elements is recovered by compensation, of mixt Bodies without life by accretion, of living Bodies by succession. **1678** HOBBES *Decam. Physiol.* viii. 94 They may by accretion become greater in the Mine, or perhaps by generation, though we know not how. **1836** TODD *Cycl. Anat. & Phys.* I. 33/1 An organized part increases in its dimensions.. not by mere accretion, nor by simple distention. **1869** NICHOLSON *Zool.* 2 When unorganised bodies increase in size, as crystals do, the increase is produced simply by what is called 'accretion,' that is to say, by the addition of fresh particles from the outside. **1871** FARRAR *Witn. Hist.* I. 39 The presumptuous arrogance which can measure its [a crystal's] angles, but throw no light on the laws of its accretion.

†**5.** The assimilation of external matter by a growing body. *Obs.*
1633 T. ADAMS *Exp. 2 Pet.* iii. 18 (1865) 819 I must lay to your charge.. the acquisition [of grace], and the accretion of it.

6. The adhesion of external matter or things to anything so as to increase it.
1713 STEELE *Englishman* No. 2, 12 A false Appearance of Wealth within, but no Accretion of Riches from abroad. **1765** DELAVAL in *Phil. Trans.* LV. 38 Augmented by the accretion of the oily and earthy parts of that moisture. **1873** GOULBURN *Pers. Relig.* ii. 12 This constant discharge of old particles, or accretion of new ones.. is a sign of the vitality of the body. **1876** DOUSE *Grimm's Law* §61. 151 The accretion after *K* pure, of the palatal semivowel *y*. **1881** *Daily Tel.* 8 Mar. To the fund estimated to be produced by the accretion of new subscribers must be added the large percentage of renewed subscriptions.

7. That which has grown upon or been gradually added from without; an extraneous addition.

1653 A. WILSON *James I.* Proem 4 To remove the accretion of bad Humors. **1677** HALE *Prim. Orig. Man.* 96 Those places..have buried the fallen Trees three, four, or five foot deep in the ground, by an accretion or cover of Earth. **1774** BRYANT *Mythol.* I. 164 This accretion will be in every age enlarged; till there will at last remain some few outlines only of the original occurrence. **1853** MERIVALE *Rom. Rep.* v. 150 (1867) He strove to pare away the accretions of age. **1878** GLADSTONE in *19th Cent.* 752 Professor Geddes divides the Iliad into a primary work and a later secondary addition or accretion.

8. *Law.* **a.** The increase of property by the adherence of something to it, as of land by the formation of alluvium; = ACCESSION. **b.** The increase of an inheritance or legacy by the addition of the share of a failing co-heir or co-legatee.

1830 LYELL *Princ. Geol.* I. 308 To this source the rapid accretions of land on parts of the Syrian shores where rivers do not enter, may be attributed. **1880** MUIRHEAD *Gaius* II. §124 If a man have instituted say his three sons as his heirs, but have passed over his daughter, she by accretion becomes heir to the extent of a fourth of the inheritance. *Ibid.* 447 Where there were several agnates of the same degree, and some declined the inheritance, their shares went by accretion to those who took.

accretional (əˈkriːʃənəl), *a.* [f. ACCRETION + -AL[1].] = ACCRETIONARY *a.*

1957 G. E. HUTCHINSON *Treat. Limnol.* I. vii. 529 They [*sc.* slush balls] may become connected by thin ice, giving a dynamic accretional ice sheet. **1971** *Nature* 9 Apr. 362/1 An accretional model..suggests that the lunar core is composed of primordial matter, never melted, and that the interior temperature is rising.

accretionary (əˈkriːʃənərɪ), *a.* [f. ACCRETION + -ARY.] Characterized or formed by accretion.

a **1835** J. PHILLIPS *Geol.* in *Encycl. Metrop.* (1845) VI. 674/2 An accretionary rock, formed by the cementation of coralline reliquiæ. **1872** D. BROWN *Life John Duncan* 409 The 'real' [body], he says, shrinks at the amputation of a limb, the 'accretionary' part only being cut off. **1932** J. S. HUXLEY *Prob. Relat. Growth* v. 149 The most familiar examples of organs growing by the accretionary method are shells.

accretive (əˈkriːtɪv), *a.* [f. L. *accrēt-*, ppl. stem of *accrēscĕre* (see ACCRESCE) + -IVE, as if ad. L. **accrētīvus*.] Belonging to accretion or continuous growth.

1665 GLANVILLE *Scepsis Sci.* ix. 81 We can no more discern their accretive motion, than we can their most hidden cause. *Ibid.* xi. 60 We have no sense of the accretive motion of Plants or Animals. **1852** *Tait's Mag.* XVI. 667 The constitution of the mind is not accretive, but fixed and unalterable. **1889** E. CARPENTER *Civilisation* 137 If we take the external view of Variation..modification or race-growth appears as an unconscious or accretive process. **1912** O. ELTON *Surv. Eng. Lit.* I. 249 He likes a complex rather than a merely coordinate or accretive structure.

accrew(e, obs. form of ACCRUE *sb.* and *v.*

†**a'ccriminate**, *v. Obs. rare*[−1]. [f. L. *ac-* = *ad-* to + *crimina-ri* to accuse of crime.] To accuse of a crime.

1655 LESTRANGE *Charles I*, 146 Being accriminated in the Star-chamber for this corrupting of witnesse.

†**accrimi'nation**, *Obs. rare*[−1]. [n. of action, f. prec.] Accusation of crime.

1655 LESTRANGE *Charles I*, 54 King Charles..did not discern any thing in the accriminations, of so horrid import as might blemish his owning him [Buckingham].

accroach (əˈkrəʊtʃ), *v.* Also 4–6 **acroche, accroche.** [a. OFr. *acroche-r* (later *accrocher*, see AC-) to hook in, draw with a hook; cf. *acroc* sb.; f. *à* prep. *to* + *croc* crook, hook; an adoption of a word common to Scandinavian, German, and Celtic,—OIcel. *krók-r*, ODu. *croke*, Breton *krôk*, Welsh *crwg*, Gaelic *croc-an*. See CROOK.] *prop.* To draw with a hook or grapple; hence,

1. To draw to oneself, catch, attract, acquire.

c **1325** *E.E. Allit. Poems* A. 1068 Þe mone may þer of acroche no myȝte To spotty. **1393** GOWER *Conf.* II. 315 And fire, whan it to tow approcheth, To him anon the strength accrocheth Till with his hete it be devoured. *Ibid.* I. 314 The ship, which wend his helpe accroche, Draf all to pieces on the roche. *c* **1430** LYDG. *Bochas* III. v. 73 a (1554) Ambitious t'accroche great richesse. **1530** PALSGR. 416 I acroche, as a man dothe that wynneth goodes or landes off another by sleyght, *Jaccroche*.

2. With *to oneself*: To grasp or lay hold on what is not one's own; to usurp (authority or jurisdiction).

1520 RASTALL, *Stat.* 25 Ed. III. viii. §3 For that the secular Justices doe accroche to them conisance of voidance of benefices or right. —— *25 Edw. III.* 6 (anno 1350) The Bishop of Rome accroching to him the Seigniories of such possessions and Benefices, doth giue and graunt the same Benefices to Aliens. **1643** PRYNNE *Sov. Power Parl.* III. 34 The said Sir Hughes had accroached to them the royall power in divers manner. **1750** CARTE *Hist. Eng.* II. 595 Aiding and abetting the five appealed and attainted persons, in their accroaching to them the royal power. **1875** STUBBS *Const. Hist.* II. xvi. 374 They had attempted to accroach to themselves royal power.

3. *intr.* To encroach. [See A- *pref.* 7.]

1530 PALSGR. 417 The mighty men accroche ever upon their poore neyghbours: *les puissans accrochent tousjours sur leurs poures voysyns.*

accroaching (əˈkrəʊtʃɪŋ), *vbl. sb.* [f. prec. + -ING[1].] (Now mostly gerundial.)

1. The act of drawing to oneself.

c **1430** LYDG. *Bochas* III. xix. 91 a (1554), Their accroching of temporal riches Whan thei be tirantes.

2. The seizing or usurping of sovereign power.

1768 BLACKSTONE *Comm.* IV. 76 The accroaching, or attempting to exercise, royal power (a very uncertain charge) was in the 21 Edw. III. held to be treason in a knight of Hertfordshire, who forcibly assaulted and detained one of the king's subjects till he paid him 90*l.* **1874** CURTIS *Hist. Eng.* 126 They had been guilty of accroaching to themselves the royal authority.

accroachment (əˈkrəʊtʃmənt). [a. Fr. *accrochement*, n. of action, f. *accrocher*; see ACCROACH and -MENT.] The action of accroaching; usurpation; encroachment.

In PHILLIPS 1706, BAILEY, JOHNSON, etc.

accroid, var. ACCAROID.

accrual (əˈkruːəl). [f. ACCRUE *v.* + -AL[1].] **a.** Accruement; *spec.* in *Law*, = ACCRETION 8 b. Also in *Book-keeping* (see quot. 1949).

1880 MUIRHEAD *Gaius* 447 *Adcretio*, accretion or accrual. **1883** ADDISON *Contracts* (ed. 8) II. ii. 430 The subject-matter of the bailment was lost in the lifetime of the devisor, and has not been in the possession of the bailee since the accrual of the title of the devisee. **1913** *Rep. N.Y. & Hudson R. Railroad Co.* 11 The amount of taxes on railroad property ..was £462,550.00 larger than the accruals in 1912. **1929** C. I. LEWIS *Mind & World-Order* vi. 194, I can safely predict the accrual of *something* the particular nature of which I cannot now determine. **1949** NORTHCOTT & FORSYTH *Pract. Book-Keeping* vii. 105 An accrual [is]..the proportionate part of a liability that will not fall due for payment until after the Balance Sheet date.

b. *attrib.*, as ***accrual basis*** (see quot. 1960).

1934 in WEBSTER. **1941** BANGS & HANSELMAN *Accounting for Engineers* II. ix. 135 Natural outgrowths of the fundamental characteristics of keeping business records are two bases of operation, namely, the cash basis and the accrual basis. **1960** NANASSY & SELDEN *Business Dict.* 3 *Accrual basis*, a method of keeping the books of account by which expenses and income are charged to periods to which they are applicable, regardless of when payments for such expenses and income are made.

†**accrue** (əˈkruː), *sb. Obs.* Also 6–7 **accrewe.** [a. Fr. *accrue*, OFr. *acreue*, *acrewe* growth, increase, orig. pa. pple. of *ac-croître*, OFr. *acreistre*:—L. *accrēscĕre*: see ACCREASE.]

1. Accession, reinforcement. (Cf. CREW.)

1577–87 HOLINSHED *Chron.* III. 1135/1 The towne of Calis and the forts thereabouts were not supplied with anie new accrewes of soldiors. **1630** M. GODWYN *Annals Eng.* III. 283 Should be able..to oppose the French by the accrue of Scotland. **1641** *Pref. to Cheke's Hurt of Sedition*, c 2 This accrue of honour to her sonne made his learned mother the Vniversity a suiter to him.

2. Advantage accruing.

1625 SIR H. FINCH *Law* To Reader (1636) Witnesse the very phrase, the termes of Art, excluding all hope of accrue to Lay-conceited opinions.

3. A stitch increasing the size of network.

1725 BRADLEY *Fam. Dict.* s.v. *Casting-net*, As you work, cast some Accrues from six Meshes to six Meshes, even to the second Range from the Lever, and make the third without Accrues; then cast the Accrues again to the fourth Range, and work the fifth without Accrues, and do so by all the rest, until the Net is eight or nine Foot in Heighth.

accrue (əˈkruː), *v.* Also 5 **acrewe**, 6–7 **accrew.** [App. f. the sb. in early sense of OFr. *acrewe* 'that which grows up, to the profit of the owner, on the earth or in a wood,' though early instances of this in Eng. are wanting. It translates L. *accrēscĕre* and OFr. *acreistre* in the law-books.]

1. To fall (*to* any one) as a natural growth or increment; to come by way of addition or increase, or as an accession or advantage. Const. *unto, to.*

1470 HARDING *Chron.* Proem. xii. 7 So by your mother the right to you acrewes. **1579** SPENSER *Sheph. Cal.* Ded., That, by the basenes of such parts, more excellencie may accrew to the principall. **1602** WARNER *Albion's Eng.* (1612) IX. xlv. 213 To him by law-Descents, the Scepter did accrew. **1622** HEYLYN *Cosmogr.* (1682) I. 140 Such lesser parcels and additaments, as have accrewed to their Estate. **1622** R. CALLIS *On Stat. Sewers* (1647) 30 Lands left to the shore by great quantities..accrew wholly to the King. **1642** SIR T. BROWNE *Relig. Med.* 59 There are, I confess, some new additions, yet small to those which accrew to our Adversaries. *a* **1680** BUTLER *Rem.* (1759) I. 234 More Proselites and Converts use t'accrue To false Persuasions, than the right and true. **1691** RAY *Wisd. God* (1714) 204 Several advantages which accrue to us. **1768** BLACKSTONE *Comm.* II. 269 The forfeiture for such alienations accrued in the first place to the immediate lord of the fee. **1856** MISS MULOCH *John Halifax* (ed. 17) 223 Pay over to your order all moneys, principal and interest, accruing to her.

2. To arise or spring as a natural growth or result. Const. *from* (*by*, *of* obs.). *Esp.* of interest: To grow or arise as the produce of money invested.

1589 HORSEY *Trav.* App. 302 (1857) The costomes that acrewe by traffycke manye kyndes of wayes. **1592** W. WEST *Symbolæogr.* I. i. §21 B, Obligations accrewing of these are said to bee contracted by consent. *c* **1620** H. ANDERSON *Law of Christ* in Farr's *S.P.* 306 From innocence a native joy accrues. **1635** QUARLES *Emblems* (1718) I. i. 6 What danger can accrue from such blest food. **1672–5** COMBER *Comp. Temple* (1702) 202 The comfort and credit that will accrue from such admissions. **1710** PRIDEAUX *Orig. Tithes* ii. 34 A Divine Right is that which accrueth from a Divine Law. **1766** [C. ANSTEY] *New Bath Guide* xv. 66 Do the Ills of Mankind from Religion accrue? **1774** BRYANT *Mythol.* I. 14 Great light..will accrue from examining this abuse. **1852** MᶜCULLOCH *Taxation* III. ii. 451 Interest begins to accrue from the moment that the loan is bargained for.

†**3.** To grow, grow up. *Obs.* (See ACCRESCE.)

1604 C. EDMONDS *Cæsars Com.* 116 They would haue accrewed to such a multitude of people, as could not haue bene contained within the rules of gouernement. **1612** WARNER *Albion's Eng.* II. xi. 50 But sight and talke accrew to loue. **1633** P. FLETCHER *Purple Is.* I. i. 1 The world more aged by new youths accrewing. **1682** GLANVILLE *Saducismus* (ed. 2) I. 126 Body is a substance material coalescent or accruing together into one.

4. †**a.** *trans.* To gather up, collect. *Obs.*

1594 R. C[AREW] *Huarte's Trial of Wits* (1596) i. 7 When our nature hath accrued al the forces that she can haue. *Ibid.* iv. 41 A man..at one instant..accrues more wit and abilitie than he had before. **1665** MANLEY *Grotius's Low-Countrey-Warrs* 656 The United States, to whom but newly redeem'd from Servitude was accrewed an Ample Dominion. [The last example is perhaps *intr.* Cf. the sun *was* risen.]

b. More recently, to gain by increment, to accumulate.

1929 F. C. BOWEN *Sea Slang* 1 *Accrue chocolate, to*, in the Navy, to make oneself popular with the officers. **1961** in WEBSTER. **1975** *Facts on File* 1 Nov. 800/1 Officials said that at the end of May, $589.5 million, or 70% of the trust's total loans and investments, were not accruing interest. **1980** K. CROSSLEY-HOLLAND *Norse Myths* p. xvii, It was only as the monarchy accrued greater power and significance that it became hereditary.

accrued (əˈkruːd), *ppl. a.* [f. prec. + -ED.]

1. Accumulated by growth.

1780 KIRWAN in *Phil. Trans.* LXXI. 18 To determine.. the real specific gravity of this acid..the quantity of accrued density must be found, and subtracted. **1881** *Times* 19 Feb. 9/5 With an accrued surplus of revenue over expenditure and an augmenting income.

2. *Her.* Grown up, full grown, as a tree.

1864 BOUTELL *Heraldry Hist. & Pop.* xi. 70 Trees..if grown to maturity, are *accrued*.

accruement (əˈkruːmənt). [f. ACCRUE *v.* + -MENT.] The process or work of accruing; hence,

1. The action of falling to any one, as a natural growth or accession; the coming into existence or becoming due of *interest* on money.

1611 SPEED *Hist. Gt. Brit.* (1632) IX. vii. 530 He did unquestionably vpon the first accruement of the interest.. exercise all the offices of the royall power. **1672** R. TAYLOR *Cromwell* 10 The glory and grandeur of that renowned succession to, and accrument of, Dominion.

2. That which accrues or has accrued; an addition or accession by natural growth; an increment.

1607 WALKINGTON *Opt. Glasse of Hum.* Ep. Ded. 2 It brings a great accrument unto wisdome and learning. **1622** HEYLYN *Cosmogr.* (1682) II. 73 Much impoverished in their Estates by Marriages and other accruments. **1649** JER. TAYLOR *Gt. Exemp.* II. 95 We shall not finde any great affluence of temporall accruements. **1662** FULLER *Worthies* III. 164 The Knight calmly gave in the unquestionable particulars of the Bottom he began on, the accrewment by his Marriage, and what was advanced by his industry and frugality. **1678** JER. TAYLOR *Suppl. Serm.* 245 For ever receiving new Additions and fresh Accruments.

accruer (əˈkruːə(r)). *Law.* [f. ACCRUE *v.* + -ER[2], by form-imitation of *misnom-er, us-er*, etc., where the termination is that of Fr. infin.] The action of accruing; = ACCRETION 8 b.

1865 NICHOLS *Britton* II. ii. 9, I. 219 There is also a kind of title which has some resemblance to succession, namely title by accruer [*siccum par accres*]. This is where, by the death of one parcener without heir, his share accrues to the other parcener. *Ibid.* VI. ii. 7, II. 316 If one of them dies, the shares of the rest shall be thereby increased..by a kind of right called that of accruer [*apelé dreit de accres*].

accruing (əˈkruːɪŋ), *vbl. sb.* [f. ACCRUE *v.* + -ING[1].] Natural growth. (Now mostly gerundial.)

Mod. On the accruing of the interest.

accruing (əˈkruːɪŋ), *ppl. a.* [f. ACCRUE *v.* + -ING[2].] Coming as a natural accession or result; arising in due course.

1683 *Brit. Speculum* 234 The Inestimable and unspeakable Blessings accrewing from the Union of England and Scotland. **1704** SWIFT *Ta. Tub* ix. (1709) 117 A mighty advantage accruing to the public. **1817** JAS. MILL *Brit. India* II. v. viii. 670 The accruing demands of the current year. **1877** H. A. PAGE *De Quincey* II. xix. 172 To set forth even the accruing disadvantages in humorous self-irony.

accrust (əˈkrʌst), *v. rare*[−1]. [f. L. *ac-* = *ad-* to + *crusta* hard surface.] ? To stiffen or harden.

1881 BLACKMORE *Christowell* in *Gd. Wds.* Mar. 148 Her name accrusted finally to the positive form of 'Spotty.'

accuate, obs. var. ACUATE *v.*

†**accub.** 'The print of any creature's foot.' Cockeram 1626.

accu'bation (ˌækjuːˈbeɪʃən). [ad. L. *accubātiōn-em*, var. of *accubitiōn-em*, n. of action, f. *accubā-re* to lie near to, f. *ac-* = *ad-* to + *cubāre* to lie.]

†1. The posture of reclining at table, practised by many ancient nations.

1646 Sir T. Browne *Pseud. Ep.* 241 Accubation, or lying downe at meales was a gesture used by very many nations. *Ibid.* 244 Now there was leaning on Jesus bosome one of his disciples whom Jesus loved; which gesture will not so well agree unto the position of sitting, but is naturall..in the Laws of accubation. **1656** Cowley *Davideis* (1669) ii. 71 The words of Session and Accubation are often confounded, both being in practice at several Times, and in several Nations.

2. *Med.* Lying in; = accouchement.

1879 *Syd. Soc. Lex.*

acculturation (əkʌltjʊəˈreɪʃən). Chiefly *U.S.* [f. ac- *pref.* + culture *sb.* + -ation.] The adoption and assimilation of an alien culture. Also *transf.* So **a'ccultural** *a.*, involving or produced by acculturation; **a'cculturative** *a.*, involving or producing acculturation; **a'culture**, cultural elements acquired by acculturation; **a'cculturate**, **a'cculturize** *vbs. trans.* and *intr.*, to cause to change or to become changed through acculturation.

1880 J. W. Powell *Study Ind. Lang.* (ed. 2) 46 The force of acculturation under the overwhelming presence of millions has wrought great changes. **1895** *Smithsonian Rep.* 44 The arts and industries of the partially acculturized Papago Indians. **1900** *Rep. Bur. Amer. Ethnol. 1897–8* i. p. xxi, When an invention is accepted and used by others it is acccultural. **1904** G. S. Hall *Adolescence* II. 726 There is little acculture [among American Indians]. **1934** Webster, Acculturate, v. **1936** *Amer. Anthropologist* XXXVIII. 149 Acculturation comprehends those phenomena which result when groups of individuals having different cultures come into continuous first-hand contact, with subsequent changes in the original culture patterns of either or both groups. *Note*: Under this definition, acculturation is to be distinguished from *culture-change*, of which it is but one aspect, and *assimilation*, which is at times a phase of acculturation. **1950** F. Eggan *Soc. Org. W. Pueblos* v. 248 Change from a lineage to a 'bilateral' system, under acculturative influences. **1950** *Mind* LIX. 195 A primitive community that is in the process of being acculturated to the West. **1951** R. Firth *Elem. Soc. Org.* iii. 81 Terms such as ..'acculturation' were introduced to express the way in which new patterns of behaviour or types of relationship were acquired and incorporated into a primitive system. **1959** V. Packard *Status Seekers* (1960) xvi. 232 They [*sc.* the private schools] acculturate 'the members of the younger generation..into an upper-class style of life'. **1963** *Time & Tide* Oct. 5/3 Many of the Indians have become a[c]culturised.

†**a'ccumb**, *v.* *Obs. rare*$^{-1}$. [ad. L. *accumb-ĕre* to lay oneself down, *esp.* at table, f. *ac-* = *ad-* to + *-cumbere* to stoop, lie down.] To recline at meals, like the Greeks and later Romans.

1646 Sir T. Browne *Pseud. Ep.* 241 Now of their accumbing places, the one was called Stibadion and Sigma, carrying the figure of an halfe Moone, and of an uncertaine capacity.

†**a'ccumbency.** *Obs. rare*$^{-1}$. [f. accumbent, as if ad. L. **accumbentia*: see -ncy.] The state of being accumbent; the reclining position at table.

1658 J. Robinson *Eudoxa* v. 142 They dare not seem to worship the bread, by kneeling before it; yet will they reverence it with their head bare; which is no gesture befitting familiar accumbency, and fraternal communion.

accumbent (əˈkʌmbənt), *ppl. a.* and *sb.* [ad. L. *accumbent-em*, pr. pple. of *accumb-ĕre*: see accumb.]

A. *adj.*

1. Lying up to, or reclining at table.

1727 C. Arbuthnot *Anct. Coins, etc.* 134 The Roman recumbent or (more properly) accumbent posture in eating was introduc'd after the first Punick War.

2. *Bot.* Lying against anything; used in opposition to *incumbent*, or lying upon something. A term applied to the embryo of crucifers, when the cotyledons have their edges longitudinally applied to the folded radicle.

1835 Hooker *Brit. Flora* 294 *Thlaspi*: *Pouch* laterally compressed, emarginate; *valves* winged at the back, many-seeded. *Cotyledons* accumbent (O=).

B. *sb.* One who reclines at table according to the ancient manner. Hence *generally*, One who is at table (without regard to posture).

1656 Bp. Hall *Occas. Medit.* (1851) 91 What a penance must be done by every accumbent, in sitting out the passage through all these dishes.

†**a'ccumber**, *v.* *Obs.* Forms: 4–5 acombre, acumbre; 4–6 acomber, acumber; 5–6 acomer, accombre; 6 accumbre, accoumbre, accomber, accumber. [for earlier *encombre* (see a- *pref.* 10), a. OFr. *encombre-r*, f. *en* in, on + *combrer*, *cumbrer*; see cumber. Subseq. confused with words in *a-* :—L. *ad-*, and refashioned as accumber. For this the original *encumber* and simple *cumber* have again been substituted, *accumber* not appearing after 1600.] To encumber, overload, oppress, overwhelm, crush.

*c***1314** *Guy Warw.* 118 Mete we hem ther on the doune, Acumbre hem and legge hem doune. **1377** Langl. *P. Pl.* B. ii. 50 And lat no conscience acombre þe. **1399** *Dep. Rich. II*, 9 Ffor they a-combrede the contre, and many curse servid, And carped to the comounes with the kyngys mouthe. **1460** Capgr. *Chron.* 122 Ethelthredus..was so acomered with the Danes, that he..acorded with them to pay hem ȝerly X thousand pound. **1470** Harding *Chron.* lxvii. [A] greate whereafter it received the name of Hexaclinon, Octoclinon. multitude of paiens..accombred all the realme. **1477** *Past. Lett.* 793 III. 183, I wote not whether that the length of mater acumbred you. **1481** Caxton *Reynard* (1844) 43 I make my confession openly..that my soul be not acombred. **1535** Fisher *Wks.* 416 She was sore accombred with that open shame. **1544** Phayer *Of the Pestilence* ii. ii. Oftentimes accombred with manye naughtye sycknesses. **1561** T. N[orton] *Calvin's Inst.* i. 53 Vnlesse we listed to accomber our selues in thinges trifling and vnprofitable. **1563** *Homilies* ii. xv. ii. (1859) 449 Yea, being accombred with the cloaked hatred of Cain, with the long covered malice of Esau. **1580** Campion *Hist. Irel.* (1633) ix. 28 Unable any longer to dwell in their ships, accumbred with carriage of women and children.

†**a'ccumbered**, *ppl. a.* *Obs.* Also 4 acombred, 5–6 accombred. [f. prec. + -ed.] Overwhelmed, embarrassed, entangled, encumbered.

*c***1300** *K. Alis.* 8025 Acombred buth theo lymes alle. *c***1386** Chaucer *C.T. Prol.* 508 (Ellesm. & Hengw.) He sette nat his benefice to hyre And leet his sheepe encombred in the myre [*other MSS.* acombred, acumbret, acumbrede]. **1520–41** Wyatt *Poet. Wks.* (1861) 147 As doth th' accumbred sprite the thoughtful throes discover, Of fierce delight, of fervent love, that in our hearts we cover. **1562** Sternh. & H. *Ps.* cxliii. 4 (1619) Within me in perplexitie Was mine accombred sprite. **1577–87** Holinshed *Chron.* III. 907/2 My conscience was incontinentlie accombred, vexed, and disquieted.

†**a'ccumbering**, *vbl. sb.* *Obs.* Also 4 accombring. [f. accumber + -ing^{1}.] The action of encumbering, overloading, or overwhelming.

1340 *Ayenb.* 182 Vor ine þe ende liþ ofte þe accombringe and nyxt þe havene spilþ ofte þet ssip þet geþ zikerliche ine þe heȝe ze.

†**a'ccumbing**, *vbl. sb.* *Obs.* [f. accumb + -ing^{1}.] A reclining at table.

1646 [See under accumb].

†**a'ccumbrance.** *Obs.* Also 5 acombraunce, 6 acc-. [for earlier *encombraunce*, a. OFr. *encombrance*, f. *encombre-r*: see accumber and -nce.] The act of encumbering, impeding, overwhelming; molestation, injury.

1489 Caxton *Faytes of Armes* i. xvii. 49 Which thyng is grete acombraunce and full of parel. *a***1521** *Helyas* in Thoms' *E.E. Pr. Rom.* (1858) III. 67 To noye and do accombraunce to them.

†**a'ccumbrous**, *a.* *Obs.* Also 5 acombrous [for earlier *encomberous*: see accumber and -ous; cf. cumbrous.] Cumbrous, oppressive, troublesome.

*c***1392** Chaucer *Compl. Venus* 42 (Tanner MS.) A litill tyme his gifte is agreable But ful acombrous is the vsynge [*other MSS.* encoumberouse, encumbrous, encomberous].

accuminate, obs. variant of acuminate.

†**accumul(e**, **accumyl(e**, *v.* *Obs. rare*$^{-1}$. [a. Fr. *accumule-r*, ad. L. *accumulā-re*: see next.] The early form of accumulate.

1490 Caxton *Eneydos* iii. 17 In whiche place there hadde be accumyled or heped of sonde a lytyl hylle or mountycle.

accumulate (əˈkjuːmjʊlət), *ppl. a.* Also 6 accumulat, accumilate. [ad. L. *accumulāt-us*, pa. pple. of *accumulā-re* to heap up; f. *ac-* = *ad-* to + *cumulā-re* to heap; f. *cumul-us* a heap.] Heaped up by additions; aggregate. Formerly both *adj.* and *pple.*; as pple. now replaced by accumulated.

1533 More *To Henry VIII*, Wks. 1557, 1424/1 Of your mere abundant goodnes heped and accumilate vpon me. **1605** Bacon *Adv. Learn.* i. 11 Socrates..was made a person heroycall, and his memorie accumulate with honors diuine and humane. **1667** H. More *Div. Dial.* (1713) v. xxix. 498 A very accumulate Completion of that Prediction. **1704** T. Hearne *Duct. Hist.* (ed. 3) I. 223 It was an accumulate Number, or Council of Priests, to whom ordinary appeals came. **1821** Southey *Vis. Judgm.* Wks. X. 225 The blast with lightning and thunder Vollying aright and aleft amid the accumulate blackness. **1878** B. Taylor *Pr. Deukalion* ii. iv. 80 The accumulate store saved from the wrecks of Time.

accumulate (əˈkjuːmjʊleɪt), *v.* [f. prec. (or on analogy of vbs. so formed); with pple. *accumulated*, in presence of which the earlier participial use of *accumulate* went out.]

1. *trans.* To heap up in a mass, to pile up; to amass or collect. a. Usually *fig.*

1529 Wolsey in Ellis *Orig. Lett.* i. 105. II. 11 I desyre nat thys for any mynde, God ys my jugge, that I have to accumulat good. **1541** Elyot *Im. Gouern.* 8 This Zoticus..solde all the saiynges and doynges of the Emperour, intendynge to accumilate abundance of richesse. **1604** Shaks. *Oth.* iii. iii. 370 Neuer pray more: Abandon all remorse On Horrors head, Horrors accumulate. **1613** —— *Hen. VIII*, iii. ii. 107 What piles of wealth hath he accumulated? **1692** Ray *Dissol. World* 41 I might accumulate places out of the Ancients and moderns to this purpose. **1769** Burke *State Nat.* Wks. II. 82 She borrowed large sums in every year; and has thereby accumulated an immense debt. **1798** Ferriar *Cert. Var. Man* 199 Pliny exerted surprising industry in accumulating authorities. **1840** Macaulay *Clive* 7 Those who lived to rise to the top of the service often accumulated considerable fortunes. **1875** Gladstone *Gleanings* VI. xxxvi. 128 To accumulate observances of ritual is to accumulate responsibility.

b. *lit.* (*after Lat.*) *rare.*

1809 J. Barlow *Columbiad* iii. 662 Soon the young captive prince shall roll in fire, And all his race accumulate the pyre. **1880** Stanley in *Evening Standard* 24 Feb. 8/5 Had either of them fallen in that arduous struggle, their graves would have been accumulated with all the honours which the American Republic could bestow.

c. *absol.* (in fig. sense).

1858 J. G. Holland *Titcomb's Lett.* vii. 237 We strive to accumulate beyond our wants and beyond the wants of our families.

2. To take (*degrees*) by accumulation, to take a higher degree at the same time with a lower, or at a shorter interval than is usual; as permitted at some of the English Universities; also *absol.*

1691 Wood *Ath. Oxon.* I. col. 862 He accumulated the degrees in Physick, and was afterwards honorary Fellow of the Coll. of Phys. at Lond. *Ibid.* I. col. 819 Rob. Moor of New Coll. who accumulated, was admitted. **1721** Amherst *Terr. Fil.* Ded. 7 Doctor Wills..was strenuously opposed in taking his degree..and was by many persons denied the common favour of accumulating. **1753** Chambers *Cycl.* Wood gives numerous instances of Accumulators, i.e. persons who accumulated or took degrees by Accumulation, at Oxford.

3. *intr.* (from reflexive). To grow into a mass, quantity or number; to go on increasing. (Not in J.)

1759 Symmer in Ellis *Orig. Lett.* ii. 477 IV. 413 Setting aside the debt that must accumulate upon it. **1769** Goldsmith *Deserted Vill.* 52 Ill fares the land, to hast'ning ills a prey, Where wealth accumulates, and men decay. **1796** J. Morse *Amer. Geog.* I. 417 These funds..are fast accumulating by interest. **1816** Shelley *Alastor* 431 More dark And dark the shades accumulate. **1856** Kane *Arctic Explor.* I. xx. 250 On the 26th disasters accumulated. **1866** Motley *Dutch Rep.* iv. v. 627 Events were rapidly rolling together from every quarter, and accumulating to a crisis. **1868** Peard *Water-farming* xv. 157 Mud is apt to accumulate in such places.

accumulated (əˈkjuːmjʊleɪtɪd), *ppl. a.* [f. prec. + -ed.] Heaped up, collected. Also ***accumulated temperature*** (see quots.).

1692 C. O'Kelly *Macariæ Excidium* in T. C. Croker *Narr. Contests in Ireland* (1841) 97 His good fortune to have retired before such accumulated misfortunes happened to his country. **1762** Falconer *Shipw.* ii. 263 Accumulated perils thus arise. **1764** Reid *Inq. Hum. Mind.* v. §1. 119 They make heat a particular element diffused through nature, and accumulated in the heated body. **1781** Gibbon *Decl. & F.* III. 144 To enrich his army with the accumulated spoils of three hundred triumphs. **1850** D. Thomas *Crisis of Being* i. 2 The past has given to you its accumulated experiences to study. **1860** Dickens *Lett.* (1880) II. 121 Yesterday I burnt ..the accumulated letters and papers of twenty years. **1884** *Meteorol. Off. Wkly. Weather Rep.* p. iv, The Accumulated Temperature is expressed in 'Day-degrees',—a Day-degree signifying 1° F. of excess or defect of temperature above or below 42° F. continued for 24 hours, or other number of degrees for an inversely proportional number of hours. **1952** *Jrnl. Ecol.* XL. 376 Most attempts at measuring the effects of temperature on plant growth have involved the summation of daily, weekly or monthly mean temperatures above a certain base-line... Such a use of summed mean temperatures or 'accumulated temperatures' assumes that growth ceases below the base-line employed.

accumulating (əˈkjuːmjʊleɪtɪŋ), *vbl. sb.* [f. as prec. + -ing^{1}.] The action of heaping up, of gathering, or growing into a heap. Also gerundially.

1794 Sullivan *View Nat.* I. 76 These different matters, in accumulating, form a cone, the necessary shape given by accumulated substances falling from the same given point. **1861** Geo. Eliot *Silas M.* 15 How the love of accumulating money grows an absorbing passion.

attrib.

1852 McCulloch *Taxation* (ed. 2) iii. i. 419 By giving additional force to the accumulating principle, and by stimulating individuals to maintain themselves.

accumulating (əˌkjuːmjʊleɪtɪŋ), *ppl. a.* [f. as prec. + -ing^{2}.] Growing into a heap or stock; increasing.

1824 Southey *Bk. of the Ch.* I. 309 A large and accumulating fund of good works, which though supererogatory in the Saints were nevertheless not to be lost.

accumulation (əˌkjuːmjʊˈleɪʃən). [ad. L. *accumulātiōn-em*, n. of action, f. *accumulāre*: see accumulate.]

1. The action of accumulating; heaping up, amassing, collecting. *lit.* and *fig.*

1606 Shaks. *Ant. & Cl.* iii. i. 19 His lieutenant, For quicke accumulation of renowne, Which he atchiu'd by' th' minute, lost his fauour. **1612** Brerewood *Lang. & Relig.* xiii. 136 That gathering of waters & discovery of the Earth, was made, not by any mutation in the Earth, but by a violent accumulation of the waters, or heaping them up on high. **1750** Johnson *Rambler* No. 147 ¶1 Little things grow by continual accumulation. **1825** McCulloch *Pol. Econ.* iv. 415 In all tolerably well governed countries, the principle of accumulation has uniformly had a marked ascendancy over the principle of expence. **1875** Hamerton *Intell. Life* v. ii. 185 There are a hundred rules for getting rich, but the instinct of accumulation is worth all such rules put together.

2. The action or process of growing into a heap, or large amount. *spec.* The growth of a

sum of money by the continuous addition of the interest to the principal.

1490 CAXTON *Eneydos* xviii. 68 Merueyllouse sorowe, wherof her herte was surprysed in gret accumylacyon of extreme dysplaysur. **1828** LD. GRENVILLE *Sinking Fund* 9 The principle of unlimited accumulation was expressly excluded from that law, by a provision which limited to four millions the sinking fund then established. *c* **1854** STANLEY *Sinai & Palest.* (1858) iii. 172 The accumulation of ruins and rubbish from above must have raised its ancient level. **1878** HUXLEY *Physiogr.* 189 They form, by their accumulation, a cone-shaped mound or hill.

3. The combination of several distinct acts or exercises into one, so that they are performed at a single exercise, or without the usual interval. *spec.* The taking of several degrees together, and in such a way that the exercises for the lower count as part work for the higher.

1753 CHAMBERS *Cycl. Supp.* s.v., Accumulation of degrees, in an university, is used for the taking of several degrees together, and with fewer exercises, or nearer to each other, than the ordinary rules allow of. **1865** *Monastic Life in Mid. Ages* in *Englishm. Mag.* Feb. 139 It would not appear that the divine offices were said then as now by accumulation, i.e. by joining several of the services together at convenient times.

4. a. An accumulated mass; a heap, pile, or quantity formed by successive additions.

1490 CAXTON *Eneydos* xv. 61 He was therof vtterly dysplaysed wherby a grete acumulacyon of yre and wrathe he begate wythin the roote of hys herte. **1665** MANLEY *Grotius's Low-Countrey-Warrs* 6 This great Accumulation of Fortune, being transposed unto the Austrian Family.. augmented their Power. **1760** JOHNSON in *Boswell* (Routl.) 225 You [Dr. Burney] are an honest man to have formed so great an accumulation of knowledge. **1843** CARLYLE *Past & Pres.* (1858) 242 The Ant lays up accumulation of capital. **1876** FREEMAN *Norm. Conq.* I. 656 The nickname evidently alludes to his great accumulations of property. **1878** HUXLEY *Physiogr.* 64 The winter's accumulation of snow is never completely melted by the summer sun.

b. ***mountain of accumulation***; also ***accumulation mountain*** (see quot. 1956).

1886 *Sc. Geogr. Mag.* II. 150 Mountains of Accumulation.—Volcanoes may be taken as the type of this class of mountains. **1898** J. GEIKIE *Earth Sculpt.* xvi. 272 Some of these have been piled or heaped up at the surface—they have grown into heights by gradual accumulation, and may therefore be termed *accumulation-mountains.* **1956** J. C. SWAYNE *Conc. Gloss. Geogr. Terms* 9 *Accumulation mountain*, a mountain the growth of which has taken place by accretion from outside, usually due to volcanic, though in some cases to epigenic, action.

accumulative (əˈkjuːmjʊlətɪv), *a.* [f. L. *accumulāt-* ppl. stem of *accumulāre*: see ACCUMULATE + -IVE.] Characterized by accumulation.

1. Arising from accumulation or successive additions of particulars; cumulative, collective.

a **1651** CLEVELAND *Rupertismus* 167 Scatter th' accumulative King; untruss That five-fold Fiend the State's Smectymnuus. **1652** MILTON *Lett. of State* Wks. 1847, 596/2 For more ample and accumulative satisfaction, and to remove all Scruples from your Excellency. **1662** FULLER *Worthies* II. 211 The Distinction of Accumulative and Constructive Treason was coyned, and caused his Destruction. **1766** *Hist. Europe* in *Ann. Reg.* 9/1 No particular crime was specified in the sentence against Sully, but a general accumulative charge in which treason was comprehended. **1862** WHATELEY in *Life & Corr.* (1866) II. 392 Such persons cannot understand the force of accumulative proof.

2. Of things: So constituted as to accumulate or increase in amount; as money does by the continuous addition of the interest to the principal.

1857 RUSKIN *Pol. Econ. Art.* ii. 96 Thus the science of nations is to be accumulative from father to son: each learning a little more and a little more; each receiving all that was known, and adding its own gain: the history and poetry of nations are to be accumulative; each generation treasuring the history and songs of its ancestors, adding its own history and its own songs: and the art of nations is to be accumulative, just as science and history are; the work of living men not superseding, but building itself upon the work of the past. **1863** *Morning Star* 7 Jan. 6 The sinking fund is accumulative.

3. Of persons: Given to accumulate or amass.

1817 COLERIDGE *Poems* 139 Taylor is eminently discursive, accumulative, and (to use one of his own words) agglomerative.

accumulatively (əˈkjuːmjʊlətɪvlɪ), *adv.* [f. prec. + -LY².] In an accumulative manner; collectively.

1657 REEVE *God's Plea for Nineveh* 144 We cry cunningly, artificially, disjunctively, by parts, by halfes, rather then cry really, accumulatively, mightily. **1870** SMITH *Syn. & Antonyms, Apiece*, adv. *Ant.* Collectively, Accumulatively.

accumulativeness (əˈkjuːmjʊlətɪvnɪs). [f. as prec. + -NESS.] The quality of being accumulative; tendency to amass.

1862 THORNBURY *Turner* I. 363 That greedy accumulativeness that made Turner amass money, made him also, in its intellectual tendency, accumulate facts.

accumulator (əˈkjuːmjʊleɪtə(r)). [a. L. *accumulātor*, n. of agent f. *accumulāre*; see ACCUMULATE and -OR.]

1. One who heaps up, amasses, or collects.

1748 RICHARDSON *Clarissa* I. 62 (1811) To go on heaping up, till Death, as greedy an accumulator as themselves, gathers them into his garner. **1870** *Athenæum* 23 July 111/1 The contemptible insignificance of the sordid accumulator ..whose wealth becomes much less his own property than the possession of society.

2. One who takes degrees by accumulation.

1691 WOOD *Ath. Oxon.* I. col. 851 Charles Croke of the same house, an Accumulator and Compounder. **1753** CHAMBERS *Cycl. Supp.* Wood gives numerous instances of Accumulators; i.e. persons who accumulated, or took degrees by Accumulation at Oxford.

3. a. Anything that accumulates. *spec.* An apparatus or arrangement for collecting and storing electricity. In various specific uses: see quots. In a computing machine: that part which collects and compounds the units of 'information' that it receives.

1833 *Brit. Pat.* 6357, I claim generally the use of compressed air as an accumulator of power to be made use of when required. **1856** *Engineer* 23 May 284 The cranes are worked by means of water pressure stored up in a cylinder termed an accumulator. **1877** W. THOMSON *Voy. of Challenger* II. iii. 43 These accumulators are india-rubber bands, ¾ inch in diameter and 3 feet in length. **1878** *Engineering* XXVI. 271 (*title*) Hydraulic Accumulator and Pumps. **1879** R. S. BALL in Cassell's *Techn. Educ.* I. 241/2 This energy is stored up by the engine in what is called an accumulator. **1881** *Standard* 30 Dec. 5/3 The Faure, Planté, and Meriten's accumulators.. are assuredly among the great factors of the future. **1881** SIR W. THOMSON in *Nature* No. 619, 434 However convenient and non-wasteful the accumulator—whether Faure's electric accumulator, or other accumulators of energy hitherto invented. **1883** GLADSTONE & TRIBE *Chem. Secondary Batteries*, p. ix, It is somewhat unfortunate that they have been called 'accumulators' or 'storage batteries'. **1911** *Encycl. Brit.* XXII. 227/2 A hydraulic accumulator ordinarily consists of a hydraulic cylinder and ram, the ram being loaded with sufficient weight to give the pressure required in the hydraulic mains. **1946** *Electronics* Apr. 310/2 The arithmetic elements include 20 accumulators, 1 multiplier and 1 combination divider and square rooter. **1947** D. R. HARTREE *Calculating Machines* 17 An accumulator..has a number of channels for the reception and transmission of numerical information. **1949** *Gloss. Aeronaut. Terms* (*B.S.I.*) II. 15 *Fuel accumulator*, a device for storing fuel, during a portion of the starting cycle, in order to augment the flow momentarily when a predetermined fuel pressure has been reached. **1949** *Gloss. Terms Refrigeration* (*B.S.I.*) 4 *Accumulator*, a liquid refrigerant container in the low-pressure side of the system.

b. *attrib.* and *Comb.*

1883 *Daily News* 10 Sept. 2/1 This installation is by the International Electric Company, and combines seven series of accumulator stations. **1898** *Engineering Mag.* XVI. 164/1 In Europe..accumulator traction has a decidedly better outlook. **1946** *Electronics* Apr. 310/2 (*caption*) Rear view of two of the accumulator racks. **1946** *Nature* 13 July 54/2 Adequate control of accumulator-charging current.

4. In betting: one who carries forward the amount won on one event and stakes it on a subsequent event; a bet of this kind. Also *attrib.*

1889 BARRÈRE & LELAND *Dict. Slang* I. 14/1 *Accumulator* (racing), a person who backs one horse, and then if it wins results (sometimes including original stakes) goes on to some other horse. **1923** *Turf Guardian Yr. Bk.* 12 In accumulators or commissions subject to contingencies, no further investments can be made after an objection is lodged or a dead heat occurs. **1951** E. RICKMAN *Come Racing* xviii. 182 Doubles, trebles and accumulators are popular among those backers who are particularly attracted by the possibility of winning a substantial sum for a small outlay. **1961** *New Statesman* 15 Sept. 336/1 A professional racing man..felt impelled to have an accumulator bet on every race on the day's card.

†**accur(re**, *v. Obs.* [ad. L. *accurr-ĕre* to run to, f. *ac-* = *ad-* to + *curr-ĕre* to run. Cf. Fr. *accourir.*] To run to, to run together; to meet (*intr.* and *trans.*).

c **1555** HARPSFIELD *Divorce of Hen. VIII* (1878) 30 Both these impediments accurre in this marriage. **1603** DRAYTON *Heroical Ep.* v. 118 Thus all accurre, to put backe all excuse. **1651** *Rawleigh's Ghost* 340 When we vehemently apply our minde to understand, and apprehend any thing, we scarcely observe and note such things, as do accurre our sense.

¶ Often for OCCUR, through confusion of *ŏ* and *ă*.

accuracy (ˈækjʊrəsɪ). [f. ACCUR-ATE; see -ACY.] The state of being accurate; precision or exactness resulting from care; hence, precision, nicety, exactness, correctness.

1662 H. MORE *Antid. ag. Ath.* II. x. 70 (1712) Which perfect artifice and accuracy might have been omitted. **1684** R. WALLER *Ess. Nat. Exper.* 12 Experiments that require a greater acuracy. **1765** HARRIS *Three Treat.* III. II. 186 But why then, said I, such Accuracy about Externals. **1814** SCOTT *Waverley* (1817) I. ix. 114 The garden..seemed to be kept with great accuracy. **1824** DIBDIN *Libr. Comp.* 90 This edition is executed with particular attention to accuracy. **1869** HUXLEY *Physiol.* vii. 204 (ed. 3) Accuracy of singing depends upon the precision with which the singer can voluntarily adjust the contractions of the thyro-arytenoid and crico-thyroid muscles.

†**accurance.** *Obs. rare*⁻¹. [f. L. *accūrā-re* to take care of (see ACCURATE) + -NCE.] A taking care, care, solicitude.

1677 HALE *Contempl.* II. 23 Can a woman..forget a Child, a piece of her self, her sucking child..when her natural Love is heightened by a pitiful accurance.

accurate (ˈækjʊrət), *a.* [ad. L. *accūrāt-us* performed with care, exact, pa. pple. of *accūrā-re* to apply care to; f. *ac-* = *ad-* to + *cūrā-re* to care for; f. *cūra* care.] In Latin only said of things, but in Eng. extended in sense 2 to persons.

†**1.** Executed with care; careful. *Obs.* in the general sense.

1621 BURTON *Anat. Mel.* II. ii. IV. (1676) 176/1 Those acurat diaries of Portugals, Hollanders, etc. **1650** VENNER *Via Recta* 224 An Accurate Diet is that when a man taketh his meats in a certaine measure, order, and number. **1675** *Art of Contentm.* ix. §11. 228 Finally his [Christ's] life expiring amidst the full sense of these accurate torments. **1738** *Lond. & Country Brewer* III. (1743) 242 Such Drink always remains so, notwithstanding their most accurate Attempts to the contrary.

2. Of things and persons: Exact, precise, correct, as the result of care.

1612 BRINSLEY *Lud. Liter.* xx. 242 (1627) They might come in time to be as accurate in writing Greeke for the stile and composition, as in Latine. **1684-5** BOYLE *Hist. Min. Waters* 68 The accuratest way, I know, is by comparing the differing weights that the same sinking Body has in common Water, and in the Liquor propos'd. **1794** SULLIVAN *View of Nat.* I. 89 [He] discovers a very accurate knowledge of mineralogy. **1824** DIBDIN *Libr. Comp.* 110 Executed by one of the most accurate and learned printers of the age.

3. Of things, without special reference to the evidence of *care*: Exact, precise, correct, nice; in exact conformity to a standard or to truth.

1651 HOBBES *Gov. & Soc.* xvii. §12. 308 The accurate and proper signification (i.e.) the definition of those names. **1660** H. MORE *Myst. Godl.* VII. xvii. 359 By how much accurater their Predictions are, by so much the more cause of suspicion. **1756** BURKE *Introd. Subl. & B.* Wks. I. 97 The term taste, like all other figurative terms, is not extremely accurate. **1850** LYNCH *Theoph. Trinal* i. 17 Accurate thought on definite subjects can alone give freedom and variety to general meditations. *Mod.* I am afraid that the solution of the problem is not quite accurate.

accurately (ˈækjʊrətlɪ), *adv.* [f. prec. + -LY².] In an accurate manner.

†**1.** Of manner alone: Carefully. *Obs.*

1632 SHERWOOD Accurately, *soigneusement, exactement.* **1669** EVELYN *Vintage* 41 (1675) When the white is tunn'd, close it immediately and accurately.

2. Of manner and result: With careful exactness or nicety.

1611 BIBLE *Transl. Pref.* 7. It got credit with the Jewes, to be called κατὰ ἀκρίβειαν, that is, accurately done. *a* **1665** J. GOODWIN *A being filled w. the Spirit* 395 (1867) The apostle doth distinguish very accurately and carefully in that case. **1776** A. SMITH *Wealth of Nat.* I. I. viii. 81 The price of labour..cannot be ascertained very accurately anywhere. **1879** LOCKYER *Elem. Astron.* i. 16 All the constellations, and the positions of the principal stars, have been accurately laid down in Star-Maps.

3. Of result alone: Precisely, exactly, correctly; without error or defect.

1651 HOBBES *Gov. & Soc.* xv. §2. 238 Yet this, to speake properly, and accuratly, is not to reigne, for he is sayed to reigne, who rules..by precepts and threatnings. **1771** *Junius Lett.* lxii. 321 A man who has not read that argument, is not qualified to speak accurately upon the subject. **1817** MALTHUS *Population* I. 474 The average number of the births being for a period of 30 years almost accurately equal to the number of deaths. **1860** TYNDALL *Glaciers* I. §6. 42 The ridges upon its surface accurately resemble waves in shape.

accurateness (ˈækjʊrətnɪs), [f. ACCURATE *a.* + -NESS.] The quality of being accurate; careful exactness; precision, nicety. (More properly a quality of a person, while ACCURACY is a state of a thing; the accurateness of an observer; the accuracy of his results)

1644 EVELYN *Mem.* (1857) I. 55 Which being kept with all imaginable accurateness..seemed a Paradise. **1662** FULLER *Worthies* (1840) II. 289 Such his accurateness, as not only to tell the initial words in every of their books, but also to point at the place in each library where they are to be had. **1675** BAXTER *Cath. Theol.* II. viii. 168 He was not so wanting in accurateness, but that he knew how to have exprest himself, had that been his meaning. **1695** WOODWARD *Nat. Hist. Earth* (1723) i. 7 As to the Certainty and Accurateness of my Observations, thus much may..be said. **1871** *Standard* 1 Feb., Their shells were not fired with that accurateness upon which they so much pride themselves.

†**a'ccurrent**, *a. Obs. rare*⁻¹. [ad. L. *accurrent-em*, pr. pple. of *accurrĕre* to run toward; f. *ac-* = *ad-* to + *curr-ĕre* to run.] Running or flowing into; affluent, tributary.

1432-50 TREVISA *Higden* (Rolls Ser.) I. 57 That see [the Pontic] is moore swete..for floodes, accurrente on euery side.

accurse (əˈkɜːs), *v. Obs.* or *arch.* Forms: 2-5 **acurse**, 2-4 **acorse, acorsy**, 5- **accurse**. *Pa. pple.* **accursed**, also 6-8 **accurst**. [f. A- *pref.* + OE. *cursian* to CURSE. As *a-curse* is not found before the 12th c., the prefix does not here represent an older *ar-* or *an-*, but is imitated from the *a-* into which both of these had then sunk, and was apparently intensive, as in *wake, a-wake, rise, a-rise*. In 5, when the scribes latinized the Fr. prefix *a-* before *c* to *ac-*, they servilely did the same with *a-curse*, whence the false spelling *ac-curse.*] To pronounce or imprecate a curse upon, to anathematize; to devote to perdition, evil, or misery.

c **1175** *Lamb. Hom.* 31 þene preost he mot isechen þe hine acursede · þet he hine iblecie onȝein þet he hine acursede. *a* **1250** *Owl & Night.* 1701 (Cott. MS.) ȝe schule on oþer wise singe And acursi alle fiȝtinge [*Arch. MS.* cursi]. **1297** R. GLOUC. 474 He acorsede all thulke men, that he hadde uorth ibrouȝt. *Ibid.* 296 Hii myȝte acorsy þe fole quene, þat Seynt Edward slou. *a* **1320** *Guy Warw.* (Turnb.) 6 He acursed the time that hir say [= saw]. *c* **1360** WYCLIF *De Dot. Eccl.* 55 Popis..confermen and acursen men whanne hem likiþ and myslikiþ men. **1377** LANGL. *P. Pl.* B. Prol. 99 Lest crist in cons[is]torie · acorse ful manye. **1494** FABYAN VII. 361 She had also purchased a curse of the pope, to a curse all y^e said barons. **1532** MORE *Confut. Tindale* Wks. 1557, 710/1 Of Noe hys owne sonnes one ye wot wel was so bad, that hys owne father accursed him. **1649** JER. TAYLOR *Great Exemp.* III. xiv. 50 God can accurse the soul as well as punish the body. **1667** MILTON *P.L.* x. 175 Because thou hast done this, thou art accursed Above all cattle. **1868** MILMAN *St. Paul's* iii. 70 He had been Dean of St. Paul's, and in that office accursed at Paul's Cross all who had searched.

accursed, accurst (əˈkɜːsɪd, əˈkɜːst), *ppl. a.* Forms: 2–5 **accursed(e, acorsed;** 3 **akursid, akursede;** 4 **acursid;** 5–6 **accursed, accurst.** [f. *acurse*, later ACCURSE *v.* + -ED.]

1. Lying under a curse or anathema; anathematized; doomed to perdition or misery. *c* **1220** *S. Marherete* 10 þu ouercume..þene acursede gast. *c* **1230** *Ancren Riwle* 234 Efter þreottene ȝer com þe akursede gost þet hefde hire itented. **1388** WYCLIF *Gal.* i. 8 Be he acursid [**1526** TINDALE Holde him as a cursed]. **1611** Let him be accursed.] **1393** LANGL. *P. Pl.* C. XXI. 97 And calde hem 'caytifs a-corsed': for þis was a vil vilanye. *c* **1450** LONELICH *Grail* xxix. 453 Therfore acursed schalt thou be Thorwhowt alle the erthe ful sikerle, And the erthe, a-corsed I wel it be do. **1588** SHAKS. *Tit. A.* v. iii. 5 Take you in this barbarous Moore, This Rauenous Tiger, this accursed deuill. **1611** —— *Wint. T.* III. iii. 52 Most accurst am I To be by oath enioyn'd to this. **1611** BIBLE *Joshua* xxii. 20 Did not Achan the sonne of Zerah commit a trespasse in the accursed thing? **1718** POPE *Iliad* VI. 174 A wretch accurst and hated by the gods! **1829** HOOD *Eug. Aram* xxviii. [I] sought the black accursed pool With a wild misgiving eye. **1855** TENNYSON *The Letters* 36 Thro' you, my life will be accurst.

2. Worthy of the curse, or bringing a curse along with it; execrable, damnable; detestable, hateful. **1591** SHAKS. *Two Gent.* v. iv. 71 The priuate wound is deepest: oh time, most accurst: 'Mongst all foes that a friend should be the worst. **1713** STEELE *Englishm.* No. 48, 308 That accursed Quality..or Disorder of the Mind, called Ambition. **1858** O. W. HOLMES *Aut. Breakf. T.* xii. 119 I never saw the accursed trick performed. **1863** KEMBLE *Resid. in Georgia* 97 This accursed system of slavery.

3. *absol.* quasi-*sb.* **1611** BIBLE *Joshua* vii. 12 Neither will I bee with you any more, except yee destroy the accursed from amongst you. **1814** SOUTHEY *Roderick* xii. (1853) IX. 113 Swear that thy soul Will make no covenant with these accursed.

accursedly (əˈkɜːsɪdlɪ), *adv. arch.* [f. prec. + -LY^2.] In an accursed manner; damnably. **1607** TOURNEUR *Rev. Trag.* III. i. in Hazl. *Dodsl.* X. 69 *Sup.* Fell it out so accursedly? *Amb.* So damnedly? **1630** TAYLOR (Water P.) *Agt. Cursing* Wks. I. 48/1 How many of vs,..instead of giving God glory, praise, and thankes for all his benefits, doe most accursedly (or maliciously) sweare him ouer and ouer, from the head, to the foot.

accursedness (əˈkɜːsɪdnɪs). *arch.* [f. as prec. + -NESS.] The quality or state of being accursed. **1583** GOLDING *Calvin's Deuter.* cxx. 739 Shall wee mistrust that our Lorde Jesus Christ hath not sufficient power to doe away all our accursednesse? **1674** N. FAIRFAX *Bulk & Selv. World* 6 Blotting out of the Book of God would have been a good, and accursedness from Christ, a blessedness.

accursing (əˈkɜːrsɪŋ), *vbl. sb. arch.* [f. ACCURSE *v.* + -ING^1.] The act of pronouncing or imprecating a curse; anathematization, excommunication. **1574** tr. *Littleton, Tenures* 42 a, The Bishopes letters under hys seale, witnessing the accursynge. **1602** CAREW *Cornwall* 129 b, Some in Germany..who for a Semblable prophanation with dauncing, through the Priests accursing continued it on a whole yere together.

†**accurtation.** *Obs.* 6. [a. med.L. *accurtātiōn-em*, n. of action, f. late L. **accurtā-re* (It. *accortar*) to abbreviate; f. *ac-* = *ad-* to + *curtāre* to shorten; f. *curt-us* short.] Shortening, curtailment, abbreviation. **1583** STANYHURST *Virgil* To Reader 36 [M is] clipped if the next word beginne with a vocall: as *fame, name*; for albeit E be the last letter, that must not salue M from accurtation, because in the eare M is the last letter. **1594** PLAT *Jewell-house* I. 44 In the time whereof, some English wits..did offer to make a great and gainefull accurtation, and yet could not be heard.

accusable (əˈkjuːzəb(ə)l), *a.* [a. Fr. *accusable*, ad. L. *accūsābilis*, f. *accūsā-re*: see ACCUSE *v.* and -ABLE.] Liable to be accused or censured; blameworthy, reprehensible; liable to the charge (*of*). **1646** SIR T. BROWNE *Pseud. Ep.* 245 Wherein indeed the hand of the Painter is not accusable, but the judgement of the common Spectator. **1676** 'A. RIVETUS, JR.' *Mr. Smirke* 55 Yet those that were accusable were all very well satisfied. **1858** DE QUINCEY *Autobiog. Sk.* Wks. I. ii. 58 Thumping or trying to thump, somebody who is accused or accusable of being heterodox.

accusably (əˈkjuːzəblɪ), *adv.* [f. prec. + -LY^2.] In an accusable manner; with liability to accusation. **1879** G. MEREDITH *Egoist* III. x. 213 There is a probability of your being not less than the fount and origin of this division of father and daughter, though Willoughby in the drawing-room last night stands accuseably the agent.

accusal (əˈkjuːzəl). [f. ACCUSE *v.* + -AL^1.] The act of accusing; accusation. **1594** R. C[AREW] *Godfrey of Bulloigne* (1881) 54 Ech gainst himselfe doth this accusall lay. **1821** BYRON *Cain* III. i. Cain! clear thee from this horrible accusal. **1860** *Introd. Autobiog. Leigh Hunt* 9 To him the shocking part of these accusals lay in their uncharitableness. **1878** GEO. ELIOT *Coll. Breakf. Party* 707 Your accusal, Rosencranz, that art Shares in the dread and weakness of the time.

accusant (əˈkjuːzənt), *a.* and *sb.* [a. Fr. *accusant*, pr. pple. and sb.:—L. *accūsant-em*, pr. pple. of *accusā-re* to ACCUSE.]

†**A.** *adj.* Accusing. *Obs.* **1611** COTGR. *Accusant* (partic.) accusant, accusing.

B. *sb.* One who accuses; an accuser. **1611** COTGR. *Accusant*, An accusant, or accuser. **1635** SIR J. HARINGTON *Epigr.* II. 6 Surely one should be deemed a false accusant, That would appeach Leda for a Recusant. **1660** BP. HALL *Rem. Wks.* 54 The Accusant must hold him to the proof of the charge. **1832** GEN. P. THOMPSON *Exerc.* (1842) II. 66 He accuses the father of having only told half. He replies, he has told it all to the 'collége.' The accusant says, he knows that.

accusar, obs. form of ACCUSER.

accusation (ækjuːˈzeɪʃən), Also 5 **accusasiowne, accusacion.** [a. Fr. *accusation* ad. L. *accūsātiōnem*, n. of action, f. *accusā-re* to ACCUSE.]

1. The act of accusing or fact of being accused; arraignment. **1430** LYDGATE *Chron. Troy* III. xxv. His clauses for to rede That reswoned in conclusiowne Onely of malyce to accusasiowne. **1483** CAXTON *G. de la Tour* f v b, Mardocheus was accused of the accusacion of Amon and was nothynge gylty. **1599** SHAKS. *Much Ado* II. ii. 55 Be thou constant in the accusation, and my cunning shall not shame me. **1611** BIBLE *Luke* xix. 8 If I haue taken any thing from any man by false accusation, I restore him foure fold. **1667** MILTON *P.L.* IX. 1190 Thus they in mutual accusation spent The fruitless hours. **1794** BURKE *Sp. agst. Hastings* Wks. XV. 13 A man who is under the accusation of his country is under a very great misfortune. **1859** TENNYSON *Enid* 83 Then like a shadow past the people's talk And accusation of uxoriousness Across her mind.

2. The charge of an offence or crime, or the declaration containing it; an indictment. *c* **1425** WYNTOWN *Cron.* IX. Prol. 46 At a court I mon appeir Fell accusationis þare til here. *a* **1450** *Chester Plays* (1847) II. 44 Men of thyn owne nacion Shewen for thy damnacion With manye accusacion And all this daie have. **1603** SHAKS. *Meas. for M.* II. iv. 157 My vouch against you, and my place i'th State Will so your accusation ouer-weigh. **1759** ROBERTSON *Hist. Scotl.* I. II. 152 An accusation so improbable gained but little credit. **1855** MILMAN *Lat. Christ.* (1864) II. III. vii. 136 He is not content with repelling the accusation as false and alien to his humane disposition. **1862** A. TROLLOPE *Orley Farm* lviii. 421 (ed. 4) To this accusation I will not plead.

accusatival (əˌkjuːzəˈtaɪvəl), *a.* [f. L. *accūsātīv-um* + -AL^1.] Pertaining to the accusative case. **1874** SAYCE *Comp. Philol.* vii. 289 The so-called genitive termination in *i*, which the second substantive takes in Assyrian, is but a modification of the accusatival *-a*.

accusative (əˈkjuːzətɪv), *a.* [a. Fr. *accusatif, -ive*, ad. L. *accūsātīv-us*, lit. of the nature of accusation, a verbal rendering of the Gr. (πτῶσις) αἰτιατική (the case) 'of accusing,' but also 'of or pertaining to that which is caused or effected (τὸ αἰτιατόν)'; hence, *prop.* the case of the effect, or thing directly affected by verbal agency.]

1. *Grammar.* In inflected languages the name of the case whose primary function was to express destination or the goal of motion; hence the case which follows prepositions implying motion towards, and expresses the object of transitive verbs, i.e. the destination of the verbal action; sometimes applied, in uninflected languages, to the *relation* in which the object stands, as shown by its position alone. By omission of the word *case*, *accusative* is commonly used substantively. *c* **1440** *Gesta Rom.* (1879) 417 The fourte case is accusatif case. *a* **1535** MORE *Confut. Barnes* VIII. 742/1 (1557) Some vnlearned vse thys worde learne for thys worde teache, with his accusatyue case set oute, as Richarde learneth Robert. **1598** SHAKS. *Merry W.* IV. i. 45 *Evans.* Well, what is your Accusatiue case? *William.* Accusatiuo hinc. *c* **1620** A. HUME *Orthogr. Brit. Tong.* 29 (1865) The accusative hath noe other noat then the nominative; as, the head governes the bodie. **1751** HARRIS *Hermes* II. iv. 283 (1786) The Accusative is that Case, which to an efficient Nominative and a Verb of Action subjoins either the Effect or the passive Subject. **1879** J. A. H. MURRAY *Address to Philol. Soc.* 60 The use of the Accusative to supply a Nominative, originally wanting in neuter nouns, is probably connected with the appearance of the passive voice in the verb.

†**2.** (From ACCUSE *v.*) Pertaining, tending, or addicted to accusation; accusatory. *Obs. rare.* *a* **1400** *Cov. Myst.* 84 (1841) The elefnte [degree] is accusatyf confessyon of iniquite of whiche ful noyous is the noyis. *a* **1576** SIR E. DERING *Speeches* 112 (T.) This hath been a very accusative age. **1641** 'SMECTYMNUUS' *Vindic. Answ.* '*Humb. Remonst.*' §13, 168 Episcopacy and their Cathedrals, with whom it is now the Accusative age.

accusatively (əˈkjuːzətɪvlɪ), *adv. rare.* [f. prec. + -LY^2.] '1. In an accusative manner. 2. Relating to the accusative case, in grammar.' J. *a* **1884** *Mod.* In midland English the dative case *him* began to be used accusatively in the first quarter of the 12th century.

†**accusator, accusatour.** *Obs.* 4–5. [a. literary Fr. *accusateur*, which in 4–5 took the place of the pop. Fr. *acuseür*:—L. *accūsātōrem*.] An accuser. **1382** WYCLIF *Acts* xxiii. 30 I sente him to thee, denounsinge and to accusatours [**1388** accuseris] that thei seie at thee. *c* **1425** WYNTOWN *Cron.* VI. xiv. 22 All þai..þat he Hys accusatowris trowyd to be.

accusatorial (əˌkjuːzəˈtɔərɪəl), *a.* [f. L. *accūsātōri-us* belonging to an accuser + -AL^1.] Of or pertaining to an accuser. Applied to legal procedure, in which a distinct accuser or prosecutor appears. **1823** BENTHAM *Not Paul but Jesus* 350 In modern Rome-bred law, this mode of procedure, in which the parts of judge and prosecutor are performed by the same person, is styled the inquisitorial; in contradistinction to this, that in which the part of prosecutor is borne by a different person, is styled the accusatorial. **1847** *Secr. Soc. Middle Ages* 332 The Fehm-tribunals had three different modes of procedure; namely, that in case of the criminal being taken in the fact, the inquisitorial, and the purely accusatorial.

accusatorially (əˌkjuːzəˈtɔərɪəlɪ), *adv.* [f. prec. + -LY^2.] In an accusatorial manner; after the mode of, or by means of, a formal accuser. **1847** *Secr. Soc. Middle Ages* 333 When a crime had been committed, and the criminal had not been taken in the fact ..it was imperative that he should be proceeded against accusatorially.

accusatory (əˈkjuːzətərɪ), *a.* [ad. L. *accūsātōri-us* belonging to an accuser or accusation.] Of or belonging to accusing; of the nature of, tending to, or containing an accusation. **1601** HOLLAND *Pliny* (1634) I. 171 Æschines..at Rhodes rehearsed that accusatorie oration which he had made against Demosthenes. **1726** AYLIFFE *Parergon* 50 In a charge of adultery, the accuser ought to set forth in the accusatory libel..some certain and definite time. **1850** GROTE *Greece* VIII. II. lxii. 37 He represented the demagogic and accusatory eloquence of the democracy. **1861** DICKENS *Gt. Expect.* I. iii. 32 [He] moved his blunt head round in such an accusatory manner as I moved round, that I blubbered out to him, 'I couldn't help it, Sir!'

accusatrix. *rare.* [f. L. *accūsātrix*, fem. of *accūsātōr*: see -TRIX.] A female accuser. **1655** J. JENNINGS *Elise* 149 Isabel, the accusatrix, is in full liberty. **1897** MARY KINGSLEY *W. Africa* 25 Confronted with his accusatrix.

accuse (əˈkjuːz), *v.* Forms: 3–4 **acuse,** 4– **accuse.** [a. OFr. *acuse-r*:—L. *accūsā-re* to call to account; for *accausā-re*, f. *ac-* = *ad-* to + *causā-re*; f. *causa* cause, reason, account. In 14th c. the Fr. prefix *a-* began to be refashioned after L. as *ac-* in Fr. and Eng.]

1. To charge with a fault; to find fault with, blame, censure.

a. Of persons. **1297** R. GLOUC. 523 Sir Hubert de Boru..Acused was to the king of mani luther prise. **1340** HAMPOLE *Pr. Consc.* 5423 Many accusers þar sal be þan, To accuse þam byfor þat domesman. **1393** LANGLAND *P. Pl.* C. IV. 220 For conscience acuseþ the · to congie þe for euere. *c* **1440** *Gesta Rom.* (1879) 417 The wolfe had Envie, and began to accuse hym to the lyon. **1535** COVERDALE *2 Sam.* xix. 27 He hath accused thy seruaunt before my lorde ye kynge. **1611** BIBLE *Prov.* xxx. 10 Accuse not a seruant vnto his master. **1715** BURNET *Hist. Own Times* (1823) I. 366 He had accused him to the King. **1847** TENNYSON *Princess* iv. 220 She sent for Blanche to accuse her face to face.

b. Of things. *c* **1450** LONELICH *Grail* xxvii. 331 Why art thow so hardye & so fre The erthe to acvsen in ony degre? **1646** SIR T. BROWNE *Pseud. Ep.* I. iv. 16 The Pharisees..accused the Holinesse of Christ. **1681** DRYDEN *Abs. & Ach.* 622 Such frugal Virtue Malice may accuse. **1708** CHAMBERLAYNE *St. Gt. Britain* (1743) I. III. i. 140 Which being done accordingly, he accuseth their contumacy. **1781** GIBBON *Decl & F.* II. xxxi. 181 Popular clamour accused the dearness and scarcity of wine. **1857** Bohn's *Handbk. Prov.* 305 Accusing the times is but excusing ourselves.

2. (With the charge expressed.) To blame, charge, indict. **a.** with *as* (*for* obs.). **1513–4** R. PACE in Ellis *Orig. Lett.* I. 37 I. 108 For the punischement off suche as were accusidde as autors off the sayde poysonynge. **1538** STARKEY *England* 10 The socyety and company of man ys not to be accusyd as the cause of thys mysordur. **1593** SHAKS. *2 Hen. VI*, I. iii. 192 Doth any one accuse Yorke for a Traytor? **1655** FULLER *Ch. Hist.* v. 229 Many indeed accuse such payments, as Popish in their original. **1673** W. CAVE *Prim. Chr.* I. i. 6 Caecilius..accuses the Christians for a desperate undone and unlawful faction. *Mod.* He was accused as accessary to the crime.

†**b.** with *subord. cl.* or *inf. phr. Obs.* **1535** COVERDALE *2 Macc.* x. 21 Accusynge those personnes, that they had solde the brethren for money. **1577** HANMER *Anc. Eccl. Hist.* (1619) 46 Certaine of this sect and opinion, were accused to have come from the Ancestors of

Judas. **1611** Bible *Luke* xvi. 1 The same was accused vnto him that he had wasted his goods. **1690** Locke *Hum. Underst.* Wks. 1727 I. i. ii. §25. 11 That I may not be accused, to argue from the Thoughts of Infants, which are unknown to us, and to conclude, from what passes in their understandings.

3. To accuse (a person) *of*, (*for*, *in*, *upon* obs.): To charge with the crime or fault of.

1393 Gower *Conf.* III. 236 The world hath oft accused Full grete princes of this dede. *c* **1430** Lydgate *Bochas* (1544) i. ii. 22 a, Atreus accused himself of murdre, and his brother upon advoutrye. **1579** Gosson *Sch. Abuse* (Arb.) 17, I accuse my selfe of discourtesie too my friendes in keeping these abuses so long secret. **1598** Shaks. *Merry Wives* ii. i. 180 These that accuse him in his intent towards our wiues, are a yoake of his discarded men. **1602** —— *Haml.* iii. i. 124, I could accuse me of such things, that it were better my Mother had not borne me. **1655** Fuller *Ch. Hist.* ix. 163 As a Father of the Church, he is accused for too much conniving at the factious disturbers thereof. **1809** Southey in *Q. Rev.* I. 193 The Romanists accuse the Protestants for their indifference. **1878** Seeley *Stein* III. 476 They may accuse his admirers of claiming too much, but they can bring no such accusation against himself.

4. *absol.* (by omitting the personal object), as in 'Who is he that accuseth?' and hence, *intr.* To bring an accusation; to utter charges.

c **1380** Wyclif *Wycket* 18 Nowe a dayes they accusen falsely agaynste Chryste. **1579** Lyly *Euphues* (1636) E 4 Doth not Physicke destroy if it be not wel tempered? Doth not Law accuse if it be not rightly interpreted? **1868** George Eliot *Sp. Gypsy* 318 He accused no more, But dumbly shrank before accusing throngs Of thought.

5. To betray, disclose. Hence, *fig.* to reveal, display, indicate, show, or make known. (*Rare in mod. Eng.*, and when found, perhaps in imitation of mod.Fr., in which this is a common sense of *accuser*.)

c **1400** *Rom. Rose* 1591 Right so the cristalle stoon shynyng, Withouten ony disseyvyng, The entrees of the yerde accusith. **1477** Earl Rivers *Dictes* (Caxton) 29 Withoute he wolde accuse them that wer consenting to make werre ayenst the King. **1580** Sidney *Arcadia* ii. 124 The Princes did in their countenances accuse no points of fear. **1649** Milton *Eikonokl.* Wks. 1738 I. 376 This wording was above his known Stile and Orthography, and accuses the whole composure to be conscious of some other Author. **1658** *Reliq. Wotton.* (1672) 362, I cannot (according to the Italian phrase)..accuse the receit of any Letter from you. **1864** Crowe & Cavalcaselle *Painting in Italy* II. xxi. 523 The distribution of the scene accuses an absence of motive or thought.

†**a'ccuse**, *sb. Obs. rare.* [f. the vb.] The act of accusing or charging with crime; charge, accusation.

1593 Shaks. *2 Hen. VI*, iii. i. 160 And dogged Yorke..By false accuse doth leuell at my life. **1647** N. Bacon *Hist. Disc.* xxxvi. 86 In nature of positive accuse of one for a crime.

accused (əˈkjuːzd), *ppl. a.* [f. accuse *v.* + -ed.] Charged with a crime or fault. Commonly used subst., as ***the accused***: he or she who is accused in a court of justice, the prisoner at the bar.

1593 Shaks. *Rich. II*, i. i. 17 And frowning brow to brow, our selues will heare Th' accuser, and the accused. **1728** Pope *Dunc.* iv. 420 Th' accus'd stood forth, and thus address'd the Queen. **1855** Macaulay *Hist. Eng.* IV. 521 He and he alone..could save the accused from the gallows. **1876** Freeman *Norm. Conq.* II. vii. 144 Eustace and the other accused persons should not be given up.

†**accusement** (əˈkjuːzmənt). *Obs.* [a. MFr. *accusement*, vbl. sb., f. *accuser*: see accuse and -ment.] The action of accusing or charging with an offence; an accusing, an accusation, a charge.

c **1374** Chaucer *Troylus* iv. 557 Than thynke I, this were her accusemente, Syn wel I woot I may hire nought purchace. **1393** Gower *Conf.* I. 216 The gilteles was dampned there And deide upon accusement. **1509** Barclay *Ship of Fooles* (1570) 27 To her husbande she accused him falsly... Ipolitus was murdered for this accusement. **1596** Spenser *F.Q.* v. vii. 47 He gan t' efforce the evidence anew, And new accusements to produce. **1715** Burnet *Hist. Ref.* (1865) III. 34 The same justices shall..punish the offenders, according as their offences shall appear to them upon the accusement.

accuser (əˈkjuːzə(r)). Also 5–6 **accusar.** [f. accuse *v.* + -er[1]. See the parallel forms accusour from OFr. and accusatour from MFr. and L. *Accuser*, though Eng. in form, may have originated in an altered pronunciation of *accusour* with accent thrown back and final syllable obscured. Cf. *soldier*, *warder*, orig. *soldiour*, *wardour*.] One who accuses or blames; *esp.* one who accuses or prosecutes in a court of justice.

1340 Hampole *Pr. Consc.* 5422 Many accusers þar sal be þan..Fiften maneres of accusours sere. **1388** Wyclif *Acts* xxiii. 35 Y schal here thee he seide, whanne thin accuseris comen [**1526** Tindale, accusars]. **1489** Caxton *Fayt of Armes* iv. xi. 262 What shuld be doon of the accusar. **1535** Coverdale *2 Esd.* xvi. 65 Youre owne synnes shalbe youre accusers in that daye. **1605** Shaks. *Lear* iv. vi. 174 Take that of me my friend, who haue the power to seale th' accusers lips. **1667** Milton *P.L.* iv. 10 Satan, now first inflamed with rage, came down, The tempter ere the accuser of mankind. **1726** Ayliffe *Parergon* 4 Whatever Persons the Civil-Law forbids to be accusers, the Canon-Law does the self-same. **1876** Freeman *Norm. Conq.* I. vi. 499 Godwine's accuser was an Englishman of the highest rank.

Comb. ***accuser-general*** sb., ***accuser-like*** adj. or adv.

1561 T. N[orton] *Calvin's Inst.* iv. 88 Whosoeuer knoweth the thyng it selfe will confesse that there is nothyng spoken accuserlike. **1828** E. Irving *Last Days* 209 There is no accuser-general in any Christian state, nor in any Christian church.

accusing (əˈkjuːzɪŋ), *vbl. sb.* [f. accuse *v.* + -ing[1].] The action of charging with an offence; accusation. (Now mostly gerundial.)

c **1300** *K. Alisaunder* 3973 He is forth brought, and the kyng Geveth him acoysyng. *c* **1440** *Gesta Rom.* (1878) 241 Whenne the Emperoure had harde this accusynge, he was hili hevi. **1538** Starkey *England* 121 Ferther also in the accusyng of treson, ther ys, me semyth, over-grete lyberty. **1611** Cotgr., *Clabauderie*..an enuious accusing. *Mod.* Why are you so persistent in accusing me?

accusing (əˈkjuːzɪŋ), *ppl. a.* [f. accuse *v.* + -ing[2].] Charging with a fault, blaming; reproachful.

1580 Sidney *Arcadia* ii. 126 Accusing Sycophants of all men did best sort to his nature. **1709** Stanhope *Paraphr.* IV. 175 So bitter is the Reflection, so dismal is the Prospect of an accusing Mind. **1859** Geo. Eliot *Adam Bede* 17 So candid, so gravely loving, that no accusing scowl, no light sneer could help melting away before their glance.

accusingly (əˈkjuːzɪŋlɪ), *adv.* [f. prec. + -ly[2].] In an accusing manner; reproachfully.

1580 Hollyband *Treas. Fr. Tong.*, *Categoriquement*, accusingly. **1867** H. Bushnell *Dark Things* 224 Our moral nature recoils accusingly upon itself.

†**accusor, -our.** *Obs.* [a. Anglo-Fr. (14th c.) *a(c)cusour* (mod.Fr. *accuseur*):—OFr. *acusor*, *acuseor*:—L. *accusātōr-em*: see accusator. Subseq. supplanted by or altered to *accuser*, with native suffix -er: see -or, -our.] The early form of accuser.

1340 Hampole *Pr. Consc.* 5422 Many accusers þar sal be þan..Fiften maneres of accusours sere. *c* **1385** Chaucer *Leg. G.W.* Prol. 353 For in your court is many a losengeour, And many a queinte toteler accusour. **1413** Lydg. *Pylgr. Sowle* (1483) i. viii. 5 The accusours haue fyrst place and tyme of audyence. **1494** Fabyan vi. cxciii. 197 [He] shulde forfayte a certayne peny, wherof yᵉ one half shuld fall to the accusour.

accustom (əˈkʌstəm), *v.* Forms: 5 **acustum(e,** 5–6 **acustom(e,** 6 **accustome,** 6– **accustom.** [a. OFr. *acostume-r*, later *acoustumer*, *accoustumer* (mod.Fr. *accoutumer*) f. *à* to + *costume*, *coustume*:—late L. *cōstūma*:— earlier *cōstūdinem*:— cl. L. *consuetūdinem* custom. The vb. *accōstūmāre* was probably already in use in late pop. L. The prefix *a-* was refashioned as *ac-* after L. in 14th c.]

†**1.** *trans.* To make (a thing) customary, habitual, usual, or familiar; to practise habitually. Most common in the passive, ***to be accustomed***: to be made customary, to be practised habitually. *Obs.*

1477 Earl Rivers *Dictes* (Caxton) 74 Angre the not sodeynly, for if thou acustume it, it wolle tourne ones to thy harmes. **1523** Ld. Berners *Froissart* I. cliii. 182 [He] was made cardynall..by authoritie of a bull fro the pope, the which hadde nat be acustomed ther before. **1567** *Trial of Treasure* in Hazl. *Dodsl.* III. 265 Hypocrites accustom the like, day by day. **1593** Marlowe *Dido* iv. iii. (1700) 416 Such ceremonious thanks, As parting friends accustom on the shore. **1650** Venner *An Advert.* 370 It were much better to abate and attemper their bloud by fasting..than to accustome the opening of a vein. **1768** Blackstone *Comm.* III. 88 Whether such tithes be due and accustomed.. cannot be determined in the ecclesiastical court.

†**b.** To use (a thing) customarily or habitually; to frequent as a customer. *Obs. rare* exc. in pa. pple.

1690 [See under accustomed, 2.] **1852** Thackeray *Esmond* (1876) i. xiv. 126 An house used by the military in his time as a young man, and accustomed by his Lordship ever since.

†**2.** *intr.* (refl. pron. suppressed). To become familiar, go or act familiarly. To accustom *to*: to resort to, frequent; to accustom *with*: to consort or cohabit with. *Obs.*

1567 Maplet *Greene Forest* 101 All those sea fishes which accustome to Aquitania. **1670** Milton *Hist. Brit.* Wks. 1738 II. 33 We with the best man accustom openly; you with the basest commit private adulteries.

3. To habituate, familiarize (a person or thing *to* (*in*, *into*, *for*, *with* obs.) something, or *to do* something).

1478 *Liber Niger* in Pegge's *Curialia Misc.* 86 It [the office of Barber to the king] hath been much accustomed to one or two well known officers. **1490** Caxton *Eneydos* vii. 31 [They] dyd alle other thynges whiche is acustumed to be doon bytwene neyghbours and good frendes. **1509** Hawes *Past. Pleas.* xxxv. ii, Bulwarkes about accustomed for warre. **1535** Coverdale *Ecclus.* xxiii. 9 Let not thy mouth be accustomed with swearinge [**1611** Accustome not thy mouth to swearing]. **1586** *Let. to Earle of Leycester, etc.* 14, I haue not accustomed my tongue to be an instrument of untrueth. **1592** Hyrde tr. *Vives, Instr. Chr. Woman* B. iij. What thing soever they have beene accustomed in before, they doe the same afterward. **1664** Evelyn *Sylva* 19 The incomparable use of this noble Tree for shade and delight, into whatever Figure you will accustom them. **1756** Burke *Subl. & B.* Wks. I. 160 When we can accustom our eyes to it [danger], a great deal of the apprehension vanishes. **1851** Ruskin *Mod. Painters* I. ii. i. ii. §2. 50 The ear is not accustomed to exercise constantly its functions of hearing; it is accustomed to stillness.

b. *refl.*

1483 Caxton *G. de la Tour*, a vj. It shalle be to yow a lyght thyng yf ye accustomme yow therin. **1561** T. N[orton] *Calvin's Inst.* iii. 182 We should accustome vs with much abasing of our selues, reuerently to looke vp vnto the mightinesse of god. **1585** Abp. Sandys *Serm.* (1841) 172 If we accustom ourselves with sinning..our custom will wax to be our nature. **1718** Lady M. W. Montague *Lett.* I. xxxii. 112, I cannot enough accustom myself to this fashion to find any beauty in it. **1754** Earl of Chatham *Lett. to Nephew* v. 39 Towards servants, never accustom yourself to rough and passionate language. *Mod.* She soon accustomed herself to her new surroundings.

†**c.** *intr.* (from *refl.*) To be wont, to use, to have the habit *to do* something. *Obs.*

1571 Jewel on *1 Thess.* iv. 6 (1611) 78 The mouth that accustometh to lie slaieth the soule. **1602** Carew *Cornwall* 27 b, Some accustomed to burne it on heapes in pits at the cliffe side. **1649** Milton *Eikonokl.* Pref., Kings, who ever have accustom'd from the cradle to use thir will onely as thir right hand. **1668** Evelyn *Mem.* (1857) III. 209 Those, therefore, who..accustom to wash their heads, instead of powdering, would doubtless find the benefit of it.

d. *pass.* To be habituated, to be in the habit, to be wont or used.

1534 Ld. Berners *Gold. Bk. M. Aurel.* (1546) B 8 b, The auncient Romayn historiens were not accustomed to write the lyues of the Emperours fathers. **1611** Bible *Jer.* xiii. 23 Then may ye also doe good, that are accustomed to doe euill. **1788** Reid *Active Powers* i. vii. 530 We are accustomed to call the first the cause, and the last the effect. **1846** Mill *Logic* ii. v. §6 (1868) 269 Were we not well accustomed to see the sun and moon move.

†**a'ccustom**, *sb. Obs.* [f. the vb.] Custom, habit, habituation.

1523 Skelton *Garland of Laurel* 64 The accustome and usage Of auncient poetis. **1533** Bellendene *Livy* (1822) 66 And now, be lang accustum, [he] has perfitelie lernit all the Romane lawis. **1538** Leland *Itin.* V. §8. 56 Hoele..by auncient Accustume was wont to give the Bagge of the Sylver Harpe to the best Harper of North Walys. **1645** Milton *Tetrach.* (1851) 171 Tribonian defines Matrimony a conjunction of man and woman containing individual accustom of life.

†**a'ccustomable,** *a. Obs.* [f. accustom *v.* + -able.] Usually practising or practised; habitual, usual, customary, wonted.

1494 Fabyan vii. 375 He also made..punysshement for all accustomable great swerers. **1538** Latimer *Serm. & Rem.* (1845) 394 The rest I commit to your accustomable goodness. **1577–87** Harrison *Eng.* (1877) i. ii. xiii. 260 The prince dooth..loose nothing of his duties accustomable to be paid. **1625** tr. *Gonsalvius's Span. Inquis.* 65 The Jayler commeth to visite his prisoners at his accustomable houres. **1677** Hale *Prim. Orig. Man.* ii. vii. 201 Animals even of the same Original..be diversified by accustomable residence in one Climate. **1741** T. Robinson *Gavelkind* iv. 39 The accustomable and actual Partition.

accustomably (əˈkʌstəməblɪ), *adv. arch.* [f. prec. + -ly[2].] In a manner conformable to custom; customarily, habitually, usually, ordinarily.

c **1450** *Chester Pl.* i. 5 You, bowchers of this citie The storie of Sathan, that Christe woulde needes tempte, Set out as accostamablie have yee. **1494** Fabyan vii. 344 Excepte ii. tunne of wyne, which the Kyng accustomably had of euery shyp commynge from Burdeaux. *c* **1540** *Polyd. Verg., Eng. Hist.* (1846) I. 153 When the childe was not accustomablie seene the suspicion might easlie arrise. **1576** Lambarde *Peramb. Kent* (1826) 95 Pride is a fault that accustomably followeth prosperitie. **1655** Baily *Life of Fisher* xxii. 203 The shirt of haire (which accustomably he wore on his back). **1725** Cotes *Dupin's Eccl. Hist.* I. ii. iii. 45 To pay what was accustomably due for them. **1806** J. Pytches in *Monthly Mag.* XXII. 209 The word is accustomably written with a *d* by all authors.

†**a'ccustomance.** *Obs.* Also **ac(c)ustumaunce.** [a. OFr. *acostumance*, *acoustumaunce*, *acc-*, f. *acostumer*: see accustom and -ance.] Customary use or practice; custom, habit.

c **1384** Chaucer *Hous of Fame* 28 Or ellis by dysordynaunce Of naturell acustumaunce [*v.r.* accustumaunce, accustomaunce, accustomance]. **1483** Caxton *Cato* b iij b, Oftentymes they inclyne or bowen to such playes by acustumance. **1603** Holland *Plutarch's Mor.* 1213 Exercise and accustomance to sobriety, temperance and continency. **1660** Boyle *New Exp. Phys.-Mech.* Digr. 375 By accustomance, some Men may bring themselves to support the want of Air a pretty while. **1690** —— *Chr. Virtuoso* i. 103 An Accustomance of endeavouring to give Clear Explications of the Phænomena of Nature.

†**a'ccustomarily,** *adv. Obs.* [f. accustomary *a.* + -ly[2].] Usually, customarily.

1662 H. More *Antid. agt. Ath.* Pref. Gen. 11 (1712) A tenacious adhesion to what has accustomarily been received. *a* **1689** Cleveland (J.) Go on, rhetorick, and expose the peculiar eminency which you accustomarily marshal before logick to publick view.

accustomary (əˈkʌstəmərɪ), *a. arch.* [f. accustom *sb.* + -ary representing an analogically formed late L. **accōstūmārius*, whence also OFr. *acostumier.*] Usual, customary.

1541 Coverdale *The old Faith* Wks. 1844 I. Prol. 3 The accustomary goodness of God. **1654** Sir A. Cokaine tr. *Loredano, Dianea* i. i. 71 The Armenians..demanded the obedience accustomary to the Sea. **1662** H. More *Antid. agt. Ath.* (1712) i. i. 9 They that adhere to Religion in a mere superstitious and accustomary way..easily turn Atheists. **1755** Magens *Ess. Insur.* I. 428 The accustomary Methods of such dealings wherein we were respectively engaged.

1865 *Cornh. Mag.* Sept. 273 At length came bed-time, and the accustomary little speeches.

†**a'ccustomate,** *ppl. a. Obs.* [f. ACCUSTOM + -ATE[1] as if ad. late L. **accŏstŭmātus*, cf. It. *accostumato*, Pg. *acostumato*, OFr. *acostumé*.] Accustomed, habituated, wonted.

1494 FABYAN VII. 552 After noone were proclamacyons made in accustumat placis of the cytie. **1533** BELLENDENE *Livy* (1822) II. 108 Thair wes certane public sacrifices quhilkis war accustumate to be done alanerlie be kingis. *a* **1568** COVERDALE *Fruitful Less.* Wks. 1844 I. 205 Long accustomate doing of virtuous deeds.

†**accusto'mation.** *Obs. rare*[−1]. [n. of action f. OFr. *acostume-r*, late L. **accŏstŭmā-re*: see -ATION.] The action of rendering habitual; the habitual practice or use.

1605 *Narrat. Bloudy Murthers of Sir J. Fitz* (1860) 14 [He] stoutly persevered in the accustimation of his former breaches of all commendable carriage.

accustomed (ə'kʌstəmd), *ppl. a.* [f. ACCUSTOM *v.* + -ED.] The pple. has all the const. of the vb.

1. Made customary, practised habitually; wonted, used; customary, habitual, usual.

1483 CAXTON *G. de la Tour* a i b, They had neyther drede ne shame, so moche were they endurate and acustomed. **1483** —— *Gold. Leg.* 258/1 He sent an Aungel acustomed whiche shewed to her to fore the demonstraunce of hir departyng. **1585** ABP. SANDYS *Serm.* (1841) 349 He left them to be devoured with pestilence, with hunger, and with the sword, the accustomed instruments of his wrath. **1600** SHAKS. *A.Y.L.* III. v. 4 The common executioner Whose heart th' accustom'd sight of death makes hard. **1684** BUNYAN *Pilgrim* II. 75 They had prepared for them a Lamb, with the accustomed Sauce belonging thereto. **1776** GIBBON *Decl. & F.* I. 341 He used the victory with his accustomed moderation. **1819** SHELLEY *Ros. & Helen* 142 The accustomed nightingale still broods On her accustomed bough. **1876** MISS BRADDON *Josh. Hagg. Dau.* II. 28 They had both grown accustomed to the half light of the wood by this time, and saw each other's faces very clearly.

†**2.** Frequented by customers. *Obs.*

1690 *Lond. Gaz.* mmdcxi. 4 The Bull-Inn in Fenny-Stratford..a well Accustomed Inn, is to be Lett ready Furnished. **1761** SMOLLETT *Gil Blas* (1802) I. II. vii. 171 There I got a place..in a well accustomed shop, much frequented on account of the neighbourhood of the church. **1772** GRAVES *Spiritual Quixote* IX. vi. (D.) [He] observed to my landlord that his seemed to be a well-accustomed house.

accustomedly (ə'kʌstəmdlɪ), *adv.* [f. prec. + -LY[2].] In an accustomed manner; usually, customarily.

1615 SANDYS *Trav.* 248 About mid-day, when for certaine houres it accustomedly forbeareth to flame.

accustomedness (ə'kʌstəmdnɪs). [f. ACCUSTOMED *a.* + -NESS.] The quality or fact of being accustomed or customary; wontedness, habituation.

1661 K. W. *Conf. Charact.* (1860) 42 Through his continual use and accustomednesse to..coin new words he makes no conscience of breaking oaths. **1869** RUSKIN *Queen of the Air* §137 It is the habit of all modesty to love the constancy and 'solemnity,' or, literally, 'accustomedness,' of law. **1876** MRS. RIDDELL *Above Suspicion* II. xii. 283 His Lordship stepped, with an air of dignified accustomedness ..into the carriage.

†**accustomer.** *Obs.* [f. ACCUSTOM *v.* + -ER[1], or a. OFr. *acostumier*, *acustumier*:—late L. **accŏstŭmārius*, f. *cŏstŭma*: see ACCUSTOM *v.*] ? A collector of customs. (So in OFr.)

1538 LELAND *Itin.* II. §7. 97 The Accustumer of Bridgewater hath translatid this Place to a right goodly and pleasant dwelling house.

accustoming (a'kʌstəmɪŋ), *vbl. sb.* [f. ACCUSTOM *v.* + -ING[1].]

†**1.** The action of making oneself familiar with, using, practising, consorting. *Obs.*

1567 MAPLET *Greene Forest* 25 Brought to it by evill accustoming, [thou] giuest consent, and, so wonne, dost becken at it. **1599** SANDYS *Europæ Spec.* (1632) 235 Their people with small accostoming understand the Liturgies well enough. **1643** MILTON *Divorce* (1851) iii. 27 They who have liv'd most loosely by reason of their bold accustoming, prove most succesfull in their matches.

2. The action of habituating or familiarizing. Now always gerundial.

1617 HIERON *Wks.* II. 340 Now the accustoming of the tongue to euill speech is like the poysoning of the well. *Mod.* By accustoming one's eyes gradually to the light.

accustrement, obs. form of ACCOUTREMENT.

accyde, -ie, -ye, variants of ACCIDIE, *Obs.* sloth.

ace (eɪs), *sb.* Forms: 3–6 **as**, 4–6 **aas**, **ais**, **ase**, 6– ace, *Pl.* aces; in 4–5 **aas**. [a. Fr. *as*:—L. *as* unity, a unit, (said to be a. Tarentine ἄς, for Gr. εἷς one). In OFr. popularly restricted to the side of the dice marked with *one* pip.]

1. a. *One* at dice, or the side of the die marked with one pip or point, and counting as one; afterwards extended to cards, dominos, etc., and meaning the throw of *one*, or the card, etc. so reckoned. ***ambs ace***, the first connexion in which the word occurs in Eng. (OFr. 12th c. *ambes as*), both aces; ***deuce ace*** (OFr.) two aces, at one throw (now taken as *deux* + *ace* = 2 and 1; so ***trey ace, syce ace***, etc.)

c **1300** [See under 2.] **1566** UDALL *Royster Doyster* III. iii. (1847) 45, I wyll he here with them, ere ye can say trey ace. **1611** SHAKS. *Cymb.* II. iii. 3 Your Lordship is the most patient man in losse, the most coldest that euer turn'd vp Ace. **1650** SHERWOOD, To cast ambes-ace, *Faire ambezatz.* **1656** HOBBES *Lib. Necess. & Chance* (1841) 41 This will be yet clearer by considering his own instance of casting ambs-ace, though it partake more of contingency than of freedom. **1680** COTTON *Compl. Gamester* in Singer *Hist. Play. Cards* 336 If you put in your dice so that two fives or two fours lie a-top, you have in the bottom turned up two two's, or two treys; so if six and an ace a-top, a six and an ace at bottom. **1880** *Boy's Own Bk.* 619 The dice are perfect cubes, marked with dots from one to six..one is called *ace*, two *deuce*, three *tré* (or *trois*), four *quatre*, five *cinque*, and six *size*.

b. At cards.

1533 MORE *Debell. Salem & Byzance* Wks. 1557, 955/2, I am as sure of this game..as he that hath iii. aces in his hande. *c* **1590** HARRINGTON *Marcus at Primero* in Singer *Hist. Play. Cards* 253 For either Faustus prime is with three knaves, Or Marcus never can encounter right, Yet drew two aces. **1594** PLAT *Jewell-house* III. 42 Carefull schollers will find some of these helpes, as good as the Ace of heartes in their wrighting; heedelesse Drones will scarce make the Ace of Diamondes of the best meanes. **1676** ETHEREDGE *Man of Mode* II. i. (1684) 18 She loves nothing So well as a black Ace. **1741** RICHARDSON *Pamela* (1824) I. 187 By the ace [in whist] I have always thought the laws of the land denoted; and as the ace is above the king or queen, and wins them, I think the law should be thought so too. **1853** LYTTON *My Novel* I. xii. 47 The unfortunate adversary has led up to ace king knave—with two other trumps. Squire takes the Parson's ten with his knave, and plays out ace king.

c. In lawn tennis, badminton, etc.: an unreturnable stroke, esp. a service that the opponent fails to touch; a point thus scored.

1889 W. M. BROWNLEE *Lawn-Tennis* vi. 158 He was equal to scoring two aces against the fair wind. **1933** *Times* 18 Nov. 5/7 Six of his nine aces were given to him by his opponent failing to bring off his drop shots. **1955** *Times* 28 June 2/7 Against this the luckless Drobny simply could not conjure up the old magic of first service aces.

d. A point scored at racquets, badminton, etc.

1819 *Examiner* 7 Feb. in Hazlitt *Table-Talk* (1967) 88 In the three first games, which of course decided the match, Peru got only one ace. **1845** in *Appleton's Ann. Cycl.* (1886) 77/2 The game [*sc.* baseball] to consist of twenty-one counts or aces. **1875** *Encycl. Brit.* III. 228/2 His adversary scores one point towards game, called an *ace*. **1947** R. SMITH *Baseball* 40 A turn at bat was a 'hand' and a run was an 'ace'. **1974** MILLS & BUTLER *Tackle Badminton* ii. 26 A game consists of 15 points (or aces), except in ladies' singles.

e. *U.S. slang.* A dollar; a one-dollar bill.

[**1921** P. & T. CASEY *Gay-Cat* ix. 92 He fumbled..in his trousers pocket. 'It's not much—only an ace spot.'.. It was a dollar bill.] **1925** H. LEVERAGE in *Flynn's* 3 Jan. 690/1 *Ace*, a dollar. **1931** *Amer. Mercury* Nov. 351/1 *Ace*, a dollar. **1941** J. SMILEY *Hash House Lingo* 8 *Ace*, one dollar. **1955** D. W. MAURER in *Publ. Amer. Dial. Soc.* xxiv. 116 He comes up with a bundle of scratch as big as your fist, but it's a mish —all aces.

2. *fig.* **a.** As the *ace* at dice was the lowest or worst number, *ace* was frequently used for bad luck, misfortune, loss. *Esp.* in ***ambs ace*** and ***deuce ace*** the lowest possible throw, and hence, naught, worthlessness, nothing. **b.** But in some games at cards, the ace is the most valuable, and hence the 'ace of men' the perfection or highest. See also AMBS-ACE.

c **1300** *Harrowing of Hell* 21 Stille be thou, Sathanas! The ys fallen ambes aas. *c* **1386** CHAUCER *Monkes T.* 583 (*Six-t.* 670) Empoysoned of thin oughne folk thou were; Thyn sis fortune is torned into an aas. [*Lansd.* as.] *c* **1386** —— *Man of Lawes T.* 26 Youre bagges beth nat fuld with ambes aas, But with sys synk, that renneth on your chaunce. [*v.r.* as, ais.] **1481** CAXTON *Reynard the Foxe* 62 A pylgrym of deux aas. **1787** BURNS (Chamb.) 74 My heart-warm love to guid auld Glen, The ace and wale o'honest men.

c. [After F. *as.*] In the war of 1914–18, an airman who had brought down ten enemy machines; a crack airman.

1917 *Times* (weekly ed.) 14 Sept. 757 Second Lieutenant Lufbery, the 'ace' of the American Lafayette flying Squadron. **1918** E. SIDGWICK *Jamesie* III. 170 Gabriel is what they call an 'ace' here, a great adventurer of the air. **1921** *Punch* 12 Jan. 26/1 Airman, playwright, Empire-builder,..Ace of all the furious aces, slightly bald D'Annunzio! **1940** *War Illustr.* 12 Apr. 366 To be officially recognized as an air 'Ace' a pilot must have ten definitely established victories to his credit.

d. Chiefly *U.S.* A person outstanding in any activity or occupation; also *attrib.* Also (*U.S. slang*), in *pl.*, anything or anyone outstandingly good.

1919 WODEHOUSE *Damsel in Distress* ii. 35 Put it in your diary, Mac, and write it on your cuff, George Bevan's all right. He's an ace. **1931** G. IRWIN *Amer. Tramp & Underw. Slang* 17 *Aces*, anything or anyone considered to be the best or most desirable. **1932** WODEHOUSE *Hot Water* vi. 113 You're aces, boy. **1935** R. S. WOODWORTH *Psychol.* (ed. 10) x. 245 Any occupation in which master workmen, virtuosos, and 'aces' occur. **1936** *New Yorker* 15 Feb. 12/2 We found ourselves..talking with an ace pulp writer. **1937** *Daily Express* 20 Apr. 23/2 London's ace players [in an orchestra] —improvising hot numbers. **1943** *Amer. Speech* XVIII. 72/1 That broad (female) is aces with me. **1961** *Guardian* 30 Sept. 12/6 The ace byliners found their stories on the back page.

e. ***on one's ace***, on one's own. *Austral.* and *N.Z. slang.* Now *rare.*

1904 *Truth* (Sydney) 2 Oct. 3/1 As a burglar bold, Kelly works strictly on his ace, believing that comradeship in crime is dangerous. **1908** E. G. MURPHY *Jarrahland Jingles* 58 Brim's in London on his 'ace'. *c* **1926** 'MIXER' *Transport Workers' Song Bk.* 66 When men are picked around me, And I'm left upon my ace. **1934** A. RUSSELL *Tramp-Royal in Wild Austral.* 213 Send 'em out 'on their ace' and they'll probably 'go camp' under the first shady tree they come to.

f. Phr. ***ace in the hole***, an advantage so far concealed; a card up one's sleeve, a trump card. *slang* (chiefly *N. Amer.*).

1915 G. BRONSON-HOWARD *God's Man* VI. iii. 371 Ever hear of a gambler's ace in his sleeve—'ace in the hole', they call it. **1922** *Collier's* 23 Sept. 24/1, I got a millionaire for an ace in the hole. **1933** F. WILLOUGHBY *Alaskans All* 129 If she [*sc.* the Arctic] doesn't get you with trick currents and shifting ice, she tries smothering you with blizzards, or starving you. If these fail, her ace in the hole is the cold. **1952** 'E. BOX' *Death in Fifth Position* (1954) i. 3 We've had a bad season so far... Wilbur is our ace-in-the-hole. **1974** *Jrnl. Politics* XXXVI. 93 Reprogramming had been used as an 'ace in the hole' to resolve situations 'that have been allowed to deteriorate to the point of emergency'. **1984** *N.Y. Times* 6 May III. 6/1 In the long haul,..AM's ace in the hole may be the $213 million net operating loss carryforward it still has left from its 1981–82 losses.

3. *fig.* A single point, a minute portion, a jot, particle, or atom.

1528 MORE *Heresyes* I. Wks. 1557, 170/2, I will not muche sticke with you for one ace better. **1579** TOMSON *Calvin's Serm. on Tim.* 13/2 Such as did their best to be an ace above Timothie. **1586** J. HOOKER *Giraldus's Hist. Irel.* in *Holinshed* II. 95/1 [He] determined to go an ase beyond his fellows, in betraieng the castell to the gouernor. **1587** GASCOIGNE *Steele Glass* Epil. 42 Better looke off than looke an ace too farre. **1598** tr. *Terence, Eun.* III. i. Did I tell thee how I tooke a young man down an ace lower at Rhodes? **1621** BURTON *Anat. Mel.* Democr. (1651) 9, I may peradventure be an ace before thee. **1652** CULPEPPER *Engl. Phys. Enl.* (1809) 165 The root spreadeth like the other, neither will it yield to its fellow one ace of bitterness. **1737** *Dragon of Wantley* in *Aquar. Naturalist* (1858) 355 The Corporation worshipful He valued not an ace.

b. ***to bate an ace***: To abate a jot or tittle, to make the slightest abatement.

a **1600** *Proverb* in Camden *Rem.* (1623) 293 Bate me an ace, quoth Bolton. **1616** *Englishmen for my Money* II. ii. in Hazl. *Dodsl.* X. 504 Yet a man may want of his will, and bate an ace of his wish. *a* **1638** MEDE *Paraphr. on 2 Peter* iii. 9 God would not bate them an ace of the judgment they had merited. **1676** MARVELL *Mr. Smirke* Wks. 1875 IV. 60 The exposer has not bated him an ace. *a* **1733** NORTH *Lives of Norths* (1826) III. 323 Bating him that ace, he was truly a great man.

c. ***within an ace of***: On the very point of, within a hair's breadth of.

a **1704** T. BROWN *Lett.* Wks. 1730 I. 184, I was within an ace of being talked to death. **1711** POPE *Lett.* (1736) V. 112, I was within an ace of meeting you. **1824** W. IRVING *Tales of Trav.* II. 43, I came within an ace of making my fortune. **1880** *Manch. Guard.* Oct. 30, A conspiracy to restore the Throne, was within an ace of being carried into execution.

4. *Attrib.* **ace-high** *a.* *N Amer. colloq.*, valued or esteemed highly (orig. in Poker, used of a hand in which the highest card is an ace); **ace-point**: the first of the points or divisions of the tables in backgammon.

[**1878** F. H. HART *Sazerac Lying Club* 154 A discussion on the Russo-Turkish war relieved the tedium of 'ace-high' and single pairs.] **1901** S. E. WHITE *Westerners* xxii. 224 Your bull [terrier] wouldn't be ace high. **1906** 'O. HENRY' *Four Million* (1916) 123 From the very first dose he was ace high and everybody else looked like thirty cents to her. **1948** *Time* 12 Jan. 34/3 In one field, at least, the Russians were still ace-high with Americans last week. **1880** *Boy's Own Bk., Backg.* 619 The men move towards their ace-points.. white counts round from the ace-point of black, and black counts round from the ace-point of white.

¶ *ace* is in many dialects pronounced *yace*, *yas*, *yess*, whence in the following: ***O ace***, a curious spelling of OYEZ! or O yes! with plural *O's ace* for *Oyezes.*

1635 BRATHWAIT *Arcadian Princesse* ii. 196 Having first commanded Cletor, the Pretorian Cryer, with three O's ace to command silence.

ace (eɪs), *v.* [f. prec.]

1. [cf. prec., 1 d.] *trans.* To score an ace against (an opponent); to gain an ace by playing (the ball).

1923 *Glasgow Herald* 9 July 11 [*Tennis*] His breezy attack, in which the desire to 'ace' his adversary at every stroke was the dominating factor. **1927** *Daily Express* 21 May 9/2 Eight times Tilden aced his service ball.

2. [cf. prec., 2 d.] To achieve high marks in (an examination, etc.). Also *fig.* and ***to ace it.*** *U.S. slang.*

1959 *Amer. Speech* XXXIV. 156 To make a perfect score on a test is to *ace it*. **1962** C. L. BARNHART in Householder & Saporta *Probl. in Lexicogr.* 170 *Ace*... Informal. To achieve a high mark in: He aced the examination. **1966** MRS. L. B. JOHNSON *White House Diary* 18 Jan. (1970) 354 Luci walked in..happy as a lark, saying, 'Mama, I probably aced it!' (her zoology final). **1983** *Verbatim* Winter 4/1 Hall..was apparently *acing* his courses in Latin, Greek, and Rhetoric. **1986** *New Yorker* 10 Nov. 95/1, The flight was over almost before it started. 'Our tradition is 'Give us a few seconds and we'll ace it.'..But this time we had no chance.'

-ācea, L. suffix, pl. neut. of *-āceus*, comp. adj. formative (= *-āc-* + *e-us*) = belonging to, of the nature of: see -ACEOUS. The analogy of a few words in L., as *gallīnāceus*, has been followed in the extensive use of this ending (in neuter pl. agreeing with *animālia* understood) to form names of classes or orders of animals, like

Crustācea crusty or shell-coated animals, *Cētācea* animals of the nature of the whale (*cētus*). These are collective plurals; the sing. is supplied by *crustaceous animal*, *crustacean*.

-āceæ, L. suffix, pl. fem. of *-āceus*, as above. The analogy of L. words like *herbāceus*, *rosāceus*, *violāceus*, *hordeāceus* has been followed in the unlimited use of this ending (in fem. pl., sc. *plantae*) to form collective names of orders or families of plants, as *Rosaceae*, *Geraniaceae*, *Algaceae*, *Graminaceae*, etc.

-ācean, comp. adj. (or sb.) formative, f. L. *-āceus* + -AN. As an adj. = *-aceous*; as a sb. it supplies a sing. to collective plurals in *-acea*, as a *crustacean* = a crustaceous (animal), one of the *Crustacea*.

acebutolol (æsɪ'bju:təlɒl). *Pharm.* [f. ACE(TYL + BUT(YR- + -OL reduplicated.] A beta-blocking drug used in cases of hypertension, angina, and arrhythmia.

1972 *Approved Names* (Brit. Pharmacopœia Comm.) Suppl. IV. 3 *Acebutolol*, (±)-1-(2-Acetyl-4-butyramido phenoxy)-3-isopropylaminopropan-2-ol. **1975** *Daily Tel.* 21 Feb. 3/8 Acebutolol.. is taken orally so that it works on the central nervous system of those prone to heart attacks. **1983** *Brit. Med. Jrnl.* 22 Jan. 266/2 We describe a case in which hypersensitivity pneumonitis appeared to be related to administration of acebutolol.

acedia (ə'si:dɪə). [L.: see ACEDY.] Sloth, torpor, = ACCIDIE: esp. as a condition leading to listlessness and want of interest in life.

1607 R. PARKER *Schol. Disc. agst. Antichrist* II. 74 The ceremonies.. offende the ministers and the Pastors... Many of these are brought to an Acedia by them. **1922** W. R. INGE *Outspoken Ess.* 149 The medieval casuists classified acedia, which is just this temper, among the seven deadly sins. **1927** AUDEN & C. DAY LEWIS in *Oxf. Poetry*, p. v, That acedia and unabashed glorification of the subjective so prominent in the world since the Reformation. **1950** A. HUXLEY *Themes & Var.* 202 To *acedia* and confusion, to nightmare and *angst*, to incomprehension and panic bewilderment.

acediamine (ˌæsi:'daɪəmaɪn). *Chem.* [f. ACE(TIC + DIAMINE.] An amine of composition

$$C_2N_2H_6 = (H_3C)C \left\{ \begin{matrix} =NH \\ -NH_2 \end{matrix} \right. ,\text{ also called}$$

Ethenyl-diamine, or *Methyl-methenyl-diamine*, derived from two molecules of ammonia in one of which H, in the other H_2 are replaced collectively by the trivalent radical Ethenyl $(C_2H_3)'''$.

1877 WATTS *Fownes' Chem.* II. 225.

†**acedy.** *Obs. rare.* [ad. L. *acēdia*, a. Gr. ἀκηδία heedlessness, sluggishness, torpor, n. of state f. ἀ priv. + κῆδ-ος care, concern, κήδ-ομαι I heed. A later derivative of the word which gave the very common ME. ACCIDIE, q.v.] Torpor, stupor.

1623 BP. HALL *Serm.* v. 140 Though the mind be sufficiently convinced of the necessity or profit of a good act; yet for the tediousness annexed to it, in a dangerous spiritual acedy, it insensibly slips away from it.

Aceldama. [a. Ἀκελδαμά, the Gr. representation of an Aramaic phrase, Chal. *ḥᵃqēl dᵉmâ*, *Syr. ōkēl damō* the field of blood.] The name given to the field in the vicinity of Jerusalem, purchased with the blood-money received and relinquished by Judas Iscariot. Hence *fig.* A field of bloodshed, a scene of slaughter or butchery.

1382 WYCLIF *Acts* i. 19 Thilke feeld was clepid Achildemak [**1388** Acheldemak] in the langage of hem, that is the feeld of blood. **1611** *Ibid.* That field is called in their proper tongue, Aceldama, that is to say, The field of blood. *a* **1658** CLEVELAND *Content* (1687) 38 In this dark way Of Death, this Scarlet-streak'd Aceldama. **1658** R. FRANCK *North. Mem.* (1821) 20 Are not the nations about us like an acaldemy of blood, that darkens the air? **1742** YOUNG *Night Th.* VI. 103 Love Divine, Which lifts us.. From earth's aceldama, this field of blood. **1756** BURKE *Vind. Nat. Soc.* Wks. I. 22 What an Aceldama, what a field of blood Sicily has been in ancient times. **1859** DE QUINCEY *The Cæsars* Wks. X. 175 All brought their tributes of beauty or deformity to these vast aceldamas of Rome.

acele, variant of A-SEAL *v. Obs.* to seal.

acellular (eɪ'sɛljʊlə(r)), *a. Biol.* [f. A- 14 + CELLULAR *a.*] Having no cells, not consisting of or divided into cells; *spec.* (*a*) composed of a single cell, unicellular; (*b*) multinucleate, syncytial.

1940 L. H. HYMAN *Invertebrates* I. iii. 44 We prefer to refer to the Protozoa as acellular, rather than as unicellular animals, that is, animals whose body substance is not partitioned into cells. **1960** *Nature* 12 Mar. 780/1 (*heading*) A mating-type system in an acellular slime-mould. **1974** D. & M. WEBSTER *Compar. Vertebr. Morphol.* viii. 162 They [*sc.* most fish scales] are composed of two thin layers: a somewhat bonelike, but acellular osteoid layer and an inner, very dense fibrous layer. **1984** *Acta Cytol.* XXVIII. II. 118 (*heading*) Acellular bodies in sputum.

acenaphthene (ˌæsi:'næfθi:n). *Chem.* [f. ACE(TIC + NAPHTHENE.] A compound substance of the Naphthalene group,

$$C_{12}H_{10}, = C_{10}H_6\left\langle \begin{matrix} CH_2 \\ | \\ CH_2 \end{matrix} \right. \text{ or naphthalene with}$$

two atoms of H replaced by divalent ethene $(C_2H_4)''$.

1877 WATTS *Fownes' Chem.* II. 581 Acenaphthene.. crystallises from fusion in flat prisms, from alcohol in long needles.

acenaphthylene (ˌæsi:'næfθɪli:n). *Chem.* [f. ACE(TIC + NAPHTHA + -YL = base + -ENE = derivative.] A compound substance of the naphthalene group,

$$C_{12}H_8, = C_{10}H_6\left\langle \begin{matrix} CH \\ \| \\ CH \end{matrix} \right. \text{ having two atoms of H}$$

less than Acenaphthene, whence it is derived.

1877 WATTS *Fownes' Chem.* II. 582 Acenaphthylene is formed by passing the vapour of acenaphthene over gently heated lead oxide. It.. crystallises in yellow tables.. its picric acid compound forms yellow needles.

acenne, early f. AKENNE *v. Obs.* to bring forth.

acent, obsolete form of ASSENT *sb.* and *v.*

acentric (ə'sɛntrɪk), *a.*

1. *Geom.* [f. Gr. ἄκεντρ-ος without centre + -IC.] Destitute of a centre.

1852 GREGORY *Solid Geom.* (ed. 2) 77 Acentric Surfaces: the general equation to these may be put in the form..

2. *Biol.* [f. A- 14 + -CENTRIC.] Of a chromosome: having no centromere. Also as *sb.*

1937 C. D. DARLINGTON in *Nature* 30 Oct. 760/2 When the bivalent.. attempts to divide, the 'dicentric' chromatid forms a bridge between the daughter nuclei, and the 'acentric' one incapable of movement, is lost. **1939** STURTEVANT & BEADLE *Introd. Genetics* (1940) viii. 128 Acentric and dicentric chromosomes or chromosome fragments are not usually transmitted from one cell generation to another with any regularity. **1949** DARLINGTON & MATHER *Elem. Genetics* vi. 131 Any single crossing-over within this loop gives two new chromatids, one with two centromeres attached to it, a dicentric, the other with none, an acentric.

aceose, early form of ACHOOSE *v. Obs.* to select.

-aceous ('eɪʃəs), compd. adj. formative f. L. *-āce-us*, *-a*, *-um*, of the nature of, (f. *āc-* + *-e-us*, *-e-a*, *-e-um*, see -EOUS) + -OUS, favoured by the formal resemblance of the compd. Eng. *-ace-ous* to the simple L. *-āce-us* of the nom. masc. Of extensive use in Nat. Hist., where it supplies adjectives, Eng. in form, to the nouns in *-ācea*, *-āceae*, as *cetaceous*, *crustaceous*, *testaceous*, *rosaceous*, *ranunculaceous*, *papilionaceous*; also in other words, as *setaceous*, *cretaceous*, *carbonaceous*, *saponaceous*, *argillaceous*, *coriaceous*, *herbaceous*, *membranaceous*, etc. Only a few of these represent actual L. words in *-āceus*, the majority being purely modern and analogical.

†**acephal**, *a.* and *sb. Obs. rare* Also **asephal**. [a. Fr. *acéphale*, ad. late L. *acephal-us*: see ACEPHALI.]

A. *adj.* Having no head or chief; = ACEPHALOUS.

1549 *Compl. Scot.* xx. 167 There is ane vthir sort of veyris callit battellis asephales, that is, quhen the pepil gadris togiddir in ane grit conuentione but the autorite of the superior.

B. *sb.* A (supposed) headless animal; = ACEPHALAN.

1607 TOPSELL *Four-footed Beasts* (1673) 9 The West region of Lybia and Æthiopia have great store of Cynocephals, Babouns, and Acephals, beasts without a head, whose eyes and mouth are in their breasts.

‖**acephala** (ə'sɛfələ), *sb. pl. Zool.* [late L. *acephala*, a. Gr. ἀκέφαλα adj. neut. pl. = headless (sc. *animalia*).] Name given (by Lamarck) to one of the two great divisions of Molluscs. The sing. is supplied by ACEPHAL or more commonly ACEPHALAN.

1847 CARPENTER *Zool.* §876 The Conchiferous Acephala, with scarcely an exception, have bivalve shells. **1863** LYELL *Antiq. Man* xxii. 442 A greater number of acephala or lamellibranchiate bivalves could be identified with living species than of gasteropods.

acephalan (ə'sɛfələn), *a.* and *sb.* [f. prec. + -AN.]

1. *adj.* Of or pertaining to the ACEPHALA.

Mod. An animal of the acephalan type.. One skilled in acephalan zoology.

2. *sb.* An animal of the division ACEPHALA.

1856 WOODWARD *Man. Mollusca* 49 Viviparous reproduction.. appears to take place in the acephalans.

‖**Acephali** (ə'sɛfəlaɪ), *sb. pl.* [late L. (Isid.) pl. of *acephal-us* a. Gr. ἀκέφαλ-ος headless, f. ἀ priv. + κεφαλ-ή head.]

1. *Nat. Hist.* (Imaginary) men or animals without heads.

1600 ABP. ABBOT *Jonah* 209 Some such things were talked of, *Acephali*, men without heads, *Cynocephali*, men with heads like to dogs. **1753** CHAMBERS *Cycl. Supp.* s.v. Though the existence of a nation of Acephali be ill warranted.

2. *Eccl. Hist.* A name applied to various Christian sects or bodies, from the want of a chief or leader, from acknowledging no earthly head, or from rejection of episcopal jurisdiction.

1625 A. GILL *Sacr. Philos.* ii. 195 The heresies concerning the proprieties of the Mediator.. The Acephali or headlesse, because they had neither bishops, nor priests. **1642** JER. TAYLOR *Episcopacie* (1647) 333 Why are they called Acephali? Nicephorus gives this reason, and withall a very particular account of their heresy.. They refused to live under Bishops. **1707** PHILLIPS, *Acephali*, a sort of Hereticks, whose first Ring-leader is unknown. *Acephali Sacerdotes*, Priests that own no Bishop over them, Independent Ministers. **1751** CHAMBERS *Cycl.* s.v. The name Acephali is sometimes applied to such priests, or bishops, as are exempted from the discipline and jurisdiction of their ordinary bishop or patriarch.

†**3.** *Eng. Hist.* 'Certain Levellers that acknowledg'd no Head or Superiour, mention'd in the Laws of K. Henry I.' Phillips 1707.

1721 BAILEY [as in PHILLIPS]. *a* **1824** D'ISRAELI *Cur. Liter.* (1866) 448/2 That party which as far back as in the laws of our Henry I, are designated by the odd descriptive term of Acephali, a people without heads, the strange equality of levellers.

†**Ace'phalian**, *a.* and *sb. Obs.* [f. prec. + -AN.]

A. *adj.* Belonging to the ecclesiastical sect or party of the ACEPHALI.

B. *sb.* A member of this sect.

1586 T. ROGERS *39 Art.* (1607) 54 Detestable therefore is the error of the Acephalians, who denied the properties of the two natures in Christ.

acephalic (æsɪ'fælɪk), *a.* [f. Gr. ἀκέφαλος (see ACEPHALI) + -IC.] Headless, *lit.* and *fig.* So **acephalia** (æsɪ'feɪlɪə), absence of a head.

1656 BLOUNT *Glossogr.*, *Acephalick*.., without head, title, or beginning. *Ibid.* s.v. *Heresie*, The Acephalick Sects of Barcotabas, [etc.]. **1839-47** *Todd's Cycl. Anat.* III. 718/1 A total defect of the brain is found in that state in which the head is wanting (*Acephalia*)... The acephalic state is very frequent. It is always associated with complete or nearly complete absence of the cranial bones. **1924** *Glasgow Herald* 31 Dec., The acephalic creatures, with eyes in their breasts, of whom.. St. Augustine declared he had seen a specimen.

†**ace'phalisis, akephalisis**, *sb. Obs. rare*—¹. [Gr. in form, as if n. of action, f. a vb.* ἀκεφαλίζειν, f. ἀκέφαλ-ος headless.] Headlessness.

1611 SPEED *Hist. Gt. Brit.* IX. x. 20 King Edward.. would not neglect the aduantage of this Akephalisis, or want of a knowne head in Scotland.

†**A'cephalist.** *Obs. rare.* [f. ἀκέφαλ-ος + -IST.] One who professes the doctrines of the (Ecclesiastical) *Acephali*; one who acknowledges no head or superior.

1659 GAUDEN *Eccl. Angl. Susp.* 464, I ask these Acephalists, who will indure no head but that on their own shoulders, whether the City of London is worse governed, because it hath a Lord Maior among and above the Aldermen and Common Councel. **1696** PHILLIPS, *Acephalists*, a sort of Hereticks, whose first founder is unknown; also Vagabond Clergymen, having neither King nor Bishop for their Head.

a'cephalite. [f. med.L. *acephalīta* f. *acephalus*: see -ITE.] = ACEPHALIST. Applied to various sects in Eccl. Hist.

acephalocyst (ə'sɛfələʊsɪst). [ad. mod.L. *acephalocystis*, f. Gr. ἀκέφαλ-ος headless + κύστ-ις bladder.] A headless bladder-worm; a name applied by Laennec to the group of parasitic worms known as hydatids. They are now ascertained to be the immature form (*larva* or *scolex*) of one of the tapeworms (*Taeniadae*), which, when it has quitted the egg, finds its way from the intestine to the liver or other solid organ of its host, and there enlarges into a globular cyst, while the head is inverted so as not to appear externally.

1836 TODD *Cycl. Anat. & Phys.* II. 116/1 The Acephalocyst is an organized being, consisting of a globular bag.. The young Acephalocysts are developed between the layers of the parent cyst. **1839** *Ibid.* III. 196/1 The Entozoa met with in the human liver are hydatids or acephalocysts. **1862** FULLER *Dis. Lungs* 307 In all instances in which acephalocysts are met with in the lungs, the issue of the case is extremely doubtful.

acephalocystic (əˌsɛfələʊ'sɪstɪk), *a.* [f. prec. + -IC.] Belonging to, or of the nature of, acephalocysts.

1859 TODD *Cycl. Anat. & Phys.* V. 26/1 Every thing that is known of the acephalocystic productions seems to point to the view that they are all nearly allied.

acephalous (ə'sɛfələs), *a.* [f. Fr. *acéphale* or late L. *acephal-us* (a. Gr. ἀκέφαλος) + -OUS.]

1. Without the head, headless.

1731 BAILEY, vol. II, *Acephalous*, without a head. 1753 CHAMBERS *Cycl. Supp.* Some modern travellers still pretend to find Acephalous people in America. 1774 COOPER in *Phil. Trans.* LXV. 311, I take the liberty to remit you an account of the delivery of a very curious acephalous monster. 1836–9 TODD *Cycl. Anat. & Phys.* II. 219/2 In the true acephalous fœtus the bones of the face..are of course wanting. 1846 GROTE *Greece* I. I. xvi. 592 Without the ancestorial god the whole pedigree would have become not only acephalous, but also worthless and uninteresting. 1854 BADHAM *Prose Halieutics* 391 With so strong an inducement for fishmongers to decapitate congers, acephalous specimens would probably be..common.

2. Having or recognizing no governing head or chief.

1751 CHAMBERS *Cycl.* s.v., Acephalous, in a figurative sense is more frequently applied to persons destitute of a leader, or chief..We find a great number of canons of council..against Acephalous clerks. 1857 SIR F. PALGRAVE *Hist. Norm. & Eng.* II. 324 Regality was the organic element of the commonwealth..an acephalous body politic was inconceivable. 1858 GLADSTONE *Homer* I. 502 The acephalous state of the Elian division of the army. 1875 STUBBS *Const. Hist.* II. xv. 267 The tendency to division was strengthened by the acephalous condition of the Courts.

3. *Zool.* Having no part of the body specially organized as a head or seat of the brain and special senses. ***acephalous molluscs*** = ACEPHALA.

1741 CHAMBERS *Cycl.* s.v., Acephalous worms, or what are supposed such, are frequent. 1835 KIRBY *Hab. & Inst. Anim.* I. ix. 268 The acephalous or bivalve Molluscans. 1836 TODD *Cycl. Anat. & Phys.* I. 166/2 The mouth..in the acephalous annelida is directed forwards. 1879 CARPENTER *Mental Physiology* I. ii. §49. 49 The two primary divisions of the [Molluscous] series,—the cephalous and the acephalous.

4. *Bot.* Headless, with the natural head aborted or cut off.

1880 GRAY *Bot. Text-Bk.* 393.

5. Wanting the beginning, as an imperfect manuscript; wanting the first syllable or foot of the verse, said esp. of a hexameter beginning with a short syllable.

1753 CHAMBERS *Cycl. Supp.*, *Acephalus* is used in poetry for a verse which is lame or defective, by wanting a beginning. 1841 DE QUINCEY *Rhet.* 403 (1860) A false or acephalous structure of sentence.

acequia (əˈseɪkɪə). *U.S.* Also **azequia, zequia.** [Sp., ad. Arab. *sāqīah*.] A canal for irrigation; an open drain.

1844 GREGG *Commerce Prairies* I. 152 All the *acequias* for the valley..are conveyed from the main stream. 1857 MAYNE REID *War Trail* v, As the mustang sprang over the zequia. 1859 BARTLETT *Dict. Amer.* (ed. 2) s.v., The irrigating ditches used in Texas and New Mexico are called *Acequias*... The word is sometimes spelt *azequia* or *zequia*. 1921 *Chambers's Jrnl.* 14 May 382/2 He takes the ointments and flings them into the acequia—the open drain that still traverses some country houses, where the water dissolves and washes away the contents of the pots. 1958 *Amer. Speech* XXXIII. 106 When the Rocky Mountain Project is completed, it will show where..water ditches are called *irrigation ditches, government canals*, or *acequias* ('sequies').

acer (ˈeɪsə(r)). Also **Acer.** [a. L. *acer* maple.] A tree or shrub of the genus of this name: = MAPLE 1. Also, the wood of the maple.

1878 R. THOMPSON *Gardener's Assistant* (new ed.) 929/1 (Index), Acers for chalk soil. 1912 H. H. THOMAS *Compl. Gardener* xxv. 344 Among the Acers are some handsome trees and shrubs. 1958 *Listener* 18 Sept. 430/1, I have seen these flowers used for table decoration,..with coloured acer leaves—that is the Japanese maple—and ivy trails. 1977 *Early Music* July 453/2 (Advt.), Tonewoods for musical instrument makers. We specialise in acer (maple, sycamore), spruce, rosewood, etc. 1983 P. BALLARD *Oasis of Delight* i. 28/2 The collection of ornamental trees had a large group of acers.

aceramic (eɪsəˈræmɪk), *a.* *Archæol.* [f. A- 14 + CERAMIC *a.*] Lacking pottery; characterized by the absence of pottery remains. *spec.* applied to early (pre-pottery) Neolithic culture; also *absol.*

1961 J. MELLAART in *Anatolian Stud.* XI. 70 The top of this aceramic mound showed all the signs of prolonged denudation. *Ibid.* 73 A long early pottery-Neolithic must.. be intercalated between the beginning of Late Neolithic.. and the Aceramic. 1967 *Listener* 30 Mar. 426/3 The Sarakatsani might be described as aceramic Neolithic for they have domestic animals and no pottery. 1978 *Antiquaries Jrnl.* LVIII. 137 The earlier phases were virtually aceramic, despite prolific deposits of domestic debris. 1980 *Glasgow Archaeol. Jrnl.* vii. 32/1 The mainly aceramic material culture shows strong links with S Scotland.

acerate (ˈæsəreɪt). *Chem.* [mod. f. L. *acer* maple + -ATE[4].] A salt of aceric acid.

1847 CRAIG, Aceric acid exists in the juice of the maple tree, in the shape of an acerate of lime.

acerb (əˈsɜːb), *a.* [ad. L. *acerb-us* harsh to the taste; cf. mod.Fr. *acerbe*.] Sour, with an addition of bitterness or astringency, as unripe fruit; also *fig.* sharp and harsh.

1657 *Phys. Dict.*, *Acerb*, sowr or sharp. 1661 R. LOVELL *Anim. & Min.*, Some are austere and acerb..as rosted quinces, wardens, services. 1751 CHAMBERS *Cycl.* s.v., Physicians usually make Acerb an intermediate savour between acid, austere, and bitter. 1766 LEE in *Phil. Trans.* LVI. 96 Three drams of a gummy substance intensely bitter and acerb. 1873 MRS. WHITNEY *Other Girls* (1876) xviii. 241 A kindlier touch to her antitheses than pertained to those of that acerb damsel.

acerbate (əˈsɜːbət), *ppl. a.* [ad. L. *acerbāt-us* pa. pple. of *acerbā-re* to embitter; see prec. and -ATE[2].] Embittered, exasperated; severe.

1869 *Echo* 16 Sept. 1/3 The very faults of a fat man are less acerbate than those of other people.

acerbate (ˈæsəbeɪt), *v.* [f. L. *acerbāt-* ppl. stem of *acerbā-re* to embitter; f. *acerb-us* bitter, harsh.] To sour or embitter; usually *fig.* to exasperate.

[1731 In BAILEY, vol. II. 1818 In TODD n.q.] 1845 LYTTON *Zanoni* Ep. Ded., The ignoble jealousy and the sordid strife which degrade and acerbate the ambition of Genius. 1862 A. TROLLOPE *North Amer.* I. 86 The Canadians..have been vexed and acerbated by the braggadocio of the Northern States.

acerbic (əˈsɜːbɪk), *a.* [f. L. *acerb-us* + -IC.] Of a sour, harsh, or severe character. Freq. of speech, manner, or temper: sharp, cutting.

1865 *North Brit. Daily Mail* 4 Dec., Exaggerated notions are entertained now-a-days regarding the gloomy acerbic nature of Sabbath observance among the ancient Jews. 1971 *Times Lit. Suppl.* 21 May 582/1 The fury he aroused in the acerbic breast of Karl Marx. 1976 *Economist* 13 Mar. 33 As defeat in Florida came closer.., his speeches grew less polite and more acerbic. 1984 *Washington Post* 3 Aug. B7 Although they borrow from Tom Lehrer and Mark Russell.., they are far less acerbic—perhaps because they are part of what they lampoon.

†**aˈcerbitude.** *Obs.*—[0] [ad. L. *acerbitūdo* harshness, f. *acerbus*.] 'Sourness, harshness in taste, bitterness.' Bailey, vol. II, 1731, and in mod. Dicts.

acerbity (əˈsɜːbɪtɪ). [a. Fr. *acerbité*, ad. L. *acerbitāt-em*, n. of quality f. *acerb-us* ACERB.]

1. Sourness of taste, mingled with bitterness or astringency; harshness, roughness of taste.

1611 COTGR., *Acerbité*: Acerbitie, sharpnesse, sournesse. 1620 VENNER *Via Recta* vii. 113 By reason of their acerbity, they are soone offensiue to the teeth. *a* 1735 ARBUTHNOT *Aliments*, in *Philol. Anglic.*, Fruit, especially unripe fruit, has a degree of acerbity in it. 1814 *Edin. Rev.* XXIII. 118 Salt communicates an unpleasant acerbity to substances.

2. *fig.* Of men, their words and actions: Sharpness mingled with bitterness, keen harshness.

1572 G. BUCHANAN in *Knox's Wks.* (1846) I. 29 Thai ar in consultation to mitigat sum part the acerbite of certain wordis. 1626 T. H. tr. *Caussin's Holy Crt.* 411, I yet among so many acerbityes sucke some sweetnesse out of the world. *a* 1677 BARROW *Serm.* Wks. 1716 I. 339 We may imagine what acerbity of pain must be endured by our Lord. 1844 DISRAELI *Coningsby* I. ix. 35 A spell that can soften the acerbity of political warfare. 1877 MISS WORBOISE *Our New House* xiv. 214 There was an acerbity in her tone that made me feel extremely uncomfortable.

aceric (əˈsɛrɪk), *a.* [ad. mod.L. *aceric-us*, f. *acer* maple; see -IC.] Of the nature of, or pertaining to the maple. ***aceric acid***, an acid which exists in the sap of the maple.

1847 CRAIG. (See under ACERATE.)

acerose (ˌæsəˈrəʊs), *a.* [ad. L. *acerōs-us* chaffy, f. *acus*, *acer-is* chaff; apparently afterwards referred in error to *acus*, *acu-s* a needle or *acer* sharp; whence sense 2 in which it has been used by botanists since Linnæus. See *Phil. Botanices* pp. 42, 219.]

1. Chaffy; like, or mixed with chaff.

1721 BAILEY, vol. II. 1775 ASH, and mod. Dicts.

2. *Bot.* Needleshaped and rigid; as in the leaves of heaths and pines.

1785 MARTYN *Rousseau's Bot.* (1794) xxviii. 445 The leaves of all these are linear and permanent; Linnæus calls this sort of leaf acerose. 1870 BENTLEY *Bot.* 159 When a linear leaf terminates in a sharp rigid point like a needle, it is acerose or needle-shaped.

acerote, *a.* [? mispr. for ACEROSE in sense 1.]

1612 COCKERAM, *Acerote bread*, Browne bread.

acerous (ˈæsərəs), *a.* *Bot.* [f. L. *acerōs-us*, as if ad. Fr. *acéreux*.] = ACEROSE.

1847 In CRAIG; and in mod. Dicts.

†**acerseˈcomic.** *Obs.*—[0] [f. L. *acersecom-ēs* in Juv., a. Gr. ἀκερσεκόμης with unshorn hair, + -IC.]

1612 COCKERAM, *Acersecomicke*, One whose hair was never cut.

acertain, obs. form of ASCERTAIN.

†**acerval,** *a.* *Obs.*—[0] [ad. L. *acervālis* adj. f. *acervus* a heap; see -AL[1].] 'Belonging to a heap.' Bailey 1731, and subseq. Dicts.

acervate (ˈæsəveɪt), *v.* *rare*—[0]. [f. L. *acervāt-* ppl. stem of *acervāre* to heap up, f. *acerv-us* a heap.] 'To heap up.' J. (no quot.)

1612 COCKERAM, *Aceruate*, To mough up. 1847 CRAIG, *Acervate*, To heap together.

acervate (əˈsɜːvət), *ppl. a.* [ad. L. *acervāt-us*, pa. pple. of *acervā-re* to heap.] Heaped, growing in heaps, or in closely compacted clusters.

1848 DANA *Zoophytes* 293 The spines, in adult specimens, often acervate. 1867 J. HOGG *Microsc.* II. ii. 400 Bundles of acervate spiculæ of the flesh.

acervately (əˈsɜːvətlɪ), *adv.* [f. prec. + -LY[2].] In an acervate manner; in heaps or clusters.

1848 DANA *Zoophytes* 358 Cells at summit acervately proliferous.

acervation (ˌæsəˈveɪʃən). *rare.* [ad. L. *acervātiōn-em*, n. of action f. *acervā-re* to heap up.] The action of heaping up, accumulation.

1676 BULLOKAR, *Acervation*, A gathering into heaps. 1755 JOHNSON, s.v. *Aggregate*, The complex or collective result of the conjunction or acervation of many particulars. 1794 SULLIVAN *View of Nat.* II. 106 The deposition and acervation of oily, greasy parts of marine substances. 1823 CONYBEARE in *Buckland's Reliq. Diluv.* 196 These accumulations..sometimes by their acervation constitute decided hills.

acervative (əˈsɜːvətɪv), *a.* [f. L. *acervāt-* ppl. stem of *acervāre* + -IVE.] Pertaining or tending to heaping up; piled or heaped up.

1865 CARPENTER in *Intell. Observer* No. 40. 289 Piled together irregularly, or in an acervative manner.

acervose (ˌæsəˈvəʊs), *a.* *rare.* [f. L. *acerv-us* heap + -OSE, as if ad. L. **acervōsus*.] 'Full of heaps.' Bailey 1731, Johnson, etc.

acervuline (əˈsɜːvjʊlaɪn), *a.* [f. L. *acervul-us* a little heap + -INE[1].] Of the form or appearance of little heaps.

1875 J. W. DAWSON *Dawn of Life* iv. 66 The cells became a mass of rounded chambers, irregularly piled up in..an acervuline manner. 1876 PAGE *Advd. Text-book of Geology* x. 192 Weathered specimen of Eozoon..with acervuline portion above and laminated below.

acervulus (əˈsɜːvjʊləs). [mod.L. (S. T. Soemmerring 1793, in C. F. Ludwig *Scriptores Neurologici Minores* III. 323), dim. of L. *acervus* heap: see -ULOUS.] †**1.** *Anat.* In full ***acervulus cerebri***: = *brain-sand* s.v. BRAIN *sb.* 6. *Obs.*

1806 A. FYFE *Anat. Human Body* (ed. 2) II. 15/1 Near, or in the Substance of the Pineal Gland, small Calcareous Concretions are sometimes found, called, by Soemmerring, *Acervulus Cerebri*, from their being generally found collected in a heap. 1882 *Quain's Elem. Anat.* (ed. 9) II. 327 The follicles [of the pineal]..often contain..much gritty calcareous matter (acervulus cerebri, brain sand), composed of microscopic particles.

2. *Bot.* A flat mass of fungal conidiophores embedded in the tissue of the host plant.

1872 W. A. LEIGHTON *Lichen-Flora Gt. Brit.* (ed. 2) p. xvi, *Acervuli*, little heaps or clusters. 1931 CLEMENTS & SHEAR *Genera of Fungi* 196 Melanconiaceae..Strata typically bearing simple or ramose basidia upon which the conidia arise, forming acervuli or masses, which are immersed or erumpent. 1947 C. E. SKINNER et al. *Henrici's Molds, Yeasts, & Actinomycetes* (ed. 2) v. 96 The third order, the Moniliales.., contains the remaining forms, whose conidiophores are produced neither in pycnidia nor upon acervuli, but are formed from superficial hyphae over the entire surface of the fungus colony. 1972 E. MOORE-LANDECKER *Fundamentals of Fungi* v. 139 Conidiophores may be produced as part of a distinct nonsexual fructification that resembles an ascocarp. These include the acervulus, an open mass of closely packed conidiophores which may form a flat discoid cushion of spores.

acescence (əˈsɛsəns). [a. mod.Fr. *acescence*, f. *acescent*, after nouns in *-nce*:—L. *-ntia*: see ACESCENT and -NCE.] The action of becoming acid or sour; the process of acetous fermentation. (Not in Johnson's Dict., though used by him.)

1765 JOHNSON *Note on Shaks.*, *Timon* III. i, Alluding to the *turning*, or acescence of milk. 1791 *Edin. New Disp.* 39 Glutinous matter seems to run into putrefaction, without shewing any previous acescence.

acescency (əˈsɛsənsɪ). [f. ACESCENT, after nouns in -NCY, ad. L. *-ntia*; see -NCY.] The quality or state of being acescent, or of turning sour; tendency to sourness; incipient or slight acidity.

1756 C. LUCAS *Ess. on Waters* III. 333 [It is] from an acrimony, not acescency, of the juices. 1776 WITHERING *Arrangem. Brit. Plants* (1796) III. 710 The leaves, put into sour beer, soon destroy the acescency. ?1838 *Life of Wilberforce* 465 All sweetness without the slightest acescency.

acescent (əˈsɛsənt), *a.* and *sb.* [a. mod.Fr. *acescent*, or ad. L. *acēscent-em* pr. pple. of *acēscĕre* to grow sour, inceptive of *acē-re* to be sour; stem *ac-* sharp, as in *ac-id*, *ac-ute*.]

A. *adj.* Turning sour; or having the tendency to turn acid, or to undergo acetous fermentation, as milk, etc.; hence, slightly sour, 'turned.' *lit.* and *fig.*

1731 ARBUTHNOT *Aliments*, *Chem. Terms* 29 Substances, which are not perfectly Acid, but naturally turn so, I call Acescent. 1746 R. JAMES *Introd. Moffet's Health's Impr.* 30 The Milk of the Ass, Goat, Cow, Mare, and Sheep, are acescent, that is, turn sour upon Putrefaction, like acescent Vegetable Juices, from whence it is prepared. *c* 1816 WILBERFORCE in *Life* (1838) IV. xxxi. 305 Their feelings cannot but be wounded and acescent. 1826 FARADAY *Exp.*

Resear. xxxi. 174 A disagreeable acescent odour something resembling that of putrescent milk.

B. *sb.* An acescent substance; one liable to undergo acetous fermentation.

1731 ARBUTHNOT *Aliments* viii. 213 Animal Diet qualify'd with a sufficient Quantity of Acescents, as Bread, Vinegar, and fermented Liquors.

acet-. *Chem.* In comb. = ACETIC, ACETYL before a vowel, as in *acet-amide, acet-anilide, acet-uric.*

acetable ('æsɪtəb(ə)l). [ad. L. *acētābulum*, now commonly used in the L. form, q.v.]

1. An ancient Roman, and old medical, fluid measure; a saucerful; usually reckoned at 2½ fluid ounces, or one-eighth of a pint.

1551 TURNER *Herbal* II. 78 An acetable holdeth two vnces and an half. **1601** HOLLAND *Pliny* XX. xiii, Take a saucer full or acetable of the juice and so drink it with wine.

2. = ACETABULUM 2 b.

1684 tr. *Bonet's Merc. Compit.* IX. 340 If the Humour run into the Acetable, and force the head of the thigh-bone out.

acetabular (æsɪ'tæbju:lə(r)), *a.* [f. L. *acētābulum* + -AR, as if ad. L. **acētābulār-is*.] Cup-like, cup-shaped; sucker-shaped.

1849 MURCHISON *Siluria* App. 544 The acetabular hooklets of Cephalopods. **1856** WOODWARD *Mollusca* I. 76 The specimens.. show the large acetabular bases of the hooks.

acetabuliferous (æsɪ,tæbju:'lɪfərəs), *a. Zool.* [f. L. *acētābul-um* + -FEROUS = bearing.] Bearing acetabula; furnished with fleshy cups or suckers for adhering to bodies.

1836 TODD *Cycl. Anat. & Phys.* I. 550/1 The nerves are continued of a simple structure as far as the acetabuliferous extremities. **1851** RICHARDSON *Geol.* viii. 253 There are ten of these acetabuliferous arms. **1877** HUXLEY *Anat. Inv. An.* viii. 507 Two acetabuliferous tentacles take their origin on the inner side of a cup-like hood.

acetabuliform (æsɪ'tæbju:lɪfɔ:m), *a. Bot.* [ad. mod.L. *acētābuliformis* saucer-shaped; see ACETABULUM, and -FORM.] Shaped like a saucer, or shallow cup, as the calyx or corolla of many flowers.

1835 LINDLEY *Introd. Bot.* II. 352 (1848) *Acetabuliform*: concave, depressed, round, with a border a little turned inwards; as the fruit of some lichens. **1880** GRAY *Bot. Text-bk.* 394.

‖**acetabulum** (æsɪ'tæbjʊləm). [L. *acētābulum* a vinegar cup or saucer, also a saucerful, a liquid measure, and *fig.* a cup or saucer-shaped cavity; f. *acētum* vinegar + *-abulum* dim. of *-abrum* = a holder or receptacle. Used in Eng. both as the proper name of the ancient vessel and measure, and as a technical term in various sciences.]

1. *Rom. Antiq.* **a.** A vessel of porcelain or metal for holding vinegar at table; a cup or cup-shaped vessel. **b.** A liquid measure of the capacity of this vessel, about half a gill or 2½ fluid ounces.

1398 TREVISA *Barth. De P.R.* (1495) XIX. cxxiii. 933 The vessel in the whyche was soure wyne and corrupte was callyd Acetabulum. **1601** HOLLAND *Pliny* (1634) s.v., Acetabulum, or Acetable, a measure among the Romans, of liquor especially, but yet of dry things also, the same that oxybaphon in Greeke. **1857** BIRCH *Anc. Pottery* (1858) II. 335 A small vase for oil or vinegar, acetabulum. *Ibid.* II. 317 Small vases called acetabula, or vinegar cups.

2. *Animal Physiol.* Applied to various cup-shaped cavities and organs: as, **a.** A sucker of the cuttlefish, or other cephalopod, by which it adheres to bodies. **b.** The socket of the thigh-bone. (Both of these uses in Pliny); *Hence*, by analogy, **c.** The socket or cavity of any joint in insects. **d.** A lobe or cotyledon of the placenta, in ruminating quadrupeds.

a. **1661** R. LOVELL *Hist. Anim. & Min.* Amongst Fishes.. The Mollusca, or soft.. some have acetabula, and two long trunks. **1835** KIRBY *Habits & Inst. Anim.* I. App. 357 Two oval plates, or disks, containing four oblong acetabula or suckers. **1851** RICHARDSON *Geol.* viii. 252 The arms are provided with acetabula or sucking discs, for adhesion to bodies. **1877** HUXLEY *Anat. Inv. An.* viii. 532 In Nautilus, the brachial processes are short, and possess no acetabula. **b.** **1709** BLAIR *Osteogr. Eleph.* in *Phil. Trans.* XXVII. 150 The Acetabulum was perforated in the bottom. **1872** HUXLEY *Physiol.* vii. 173 In one joint of the body, the hip, the socket or acetabulum fits.. closely to the head of the femur. **1873** MIVART *Elem. Anat.* v. 180 The socket for the thigh-bone is called the acetabulum or cotyloid cavity. **c.** **1828** KIRBY & SPENCE *Entomol.* III. xxxv. 537 The base is a spherical boss moving in an acetabulum of the thoracic shield. **1835** —— *Habits & Inst. Anim.* II. xxii. 432 The lower [jaw] extends beyond the skull, a condyle of which acts in an acetabulum of that jaw. **d.** *a* **1859** WORCESTER cites DUNGLISON.

3. *Bot.* **a.** 'The receptacle of certain fungals.' Lindley & Moore. **b.** 'An obsolete name of the herb Navelwort.' Bailey 1731.

acetal ('æsɪ,tæl). *Chem.* [f. ACET(IC) + AL(COHOL).] **1.** A colourless liquid with alcoholic smell, found among the first portions of the distillate in preparing spirit of wine; a derivative of aldehyde, converted by oxidizing agents into acetic acid. It is the *diethylate of ethylidene or ethidene* $CH_3—CH(OC_2H_5)_2$.

1853 URE *Dict. Arts* (ed. 4) I. 1 Acetal, is the subacetate of ether, having for its chemical symbol 3AcO + AcO₃. It is a light colourless ethereous liquid. **1869** ROSCOE *Elem. Chem.* 250 Acetal is isomeric with diethyl glycol.

2. Sometimes extended to analogous ethidene derivatives in other series of the hydrocarbons, as ***dimethyl acetal***, found in crude wood-spirit; also called *ethidene dimethylate*, $CH_3—CH(OCH_3)_2$. In this nomenclature, the preceding substance is distinguished as ***diethyl acetal***.

acetaldehyde (,æsɪ'tældɪhaɪd). *Chem.* [contr. for *acetic aldehyde*.] Common or Ethyl aldehyde, viewed as the special aldehyde of the acetic series.

1877 WATTS *Fownes' Chem.* II. 249 Acetic aldehyde, or Acetaldehyde, also called Ethyl aldehyde, but more generally by the simple name aldehyde.

acetamide ('æsɪtə,maɪd, ə'sɛtəmaɪd). *Chem.* [f. ACET- + AMIDE.]

1. The primary AMIDE in which the replacing acid radical is ACETYL; $C_2H_3O.NH_2$; a white crystalline solid of nearly neutral properties.

1873 WILLIAMSON *Chem.* §282 Products formed like acetamide by the replacement of hydrogen in ammonia by a radical of chlorous properties are called amides. **1874** ROSCOE *Elem. Chem.* 354 Acetamide is a colourless solid, fusing at 78°, and boiling at 222°. **1877** WATTS *Fownes' Chem.* II. 379 Acetamide.. crystallizes in long needles.

2. A series of analogous compounds, in which two or all three hydrogen atoms in ammonia NH_3, are replaced by the radical acetyl (*diacetamide, triacetamide*), or in which one or two are replaced by acetyl, and one or two by other radicals, as *ethyl-acetamide, ethyl-diacetamide*, etc.

acetaminophen (,æsɛtə'mi:nəʊfɛn, əsi:tə'mi:nəʊfɛn). *Pharm.* [f. ACET- + AMINO- + PHEN-.] (The official U.S. name for) the drug paracetamol.

1960 *National Formulary XI* (U.S.) 10/2 Acetaminophen Tablets. **1964** *Jrnl. Pharmaceutical Sci.* LIII. 1280/1 There are many formulations containing aspirin, caffeine, and acetaminophen (APAP). **1974** M. C. GERALD *Pharmacol.* xiv. 272 When aspirin cannot be tolerated, acetaminophen is probably the safest and most effective analgesic-antipyretic substitute. **1978** *Detroit Free Press* 16 Apr. (Parade) 27/1 People who drink heavily should not take sleeping pills or large amounts of acetaminophen, an aspirin substitute.

acetanilide (,æsɪ'tænɪlaɪd). *Chem.* [f. ACET(YL) + ANILIDE.] A compound of aniline in union with the radical acetyl, forming an acetamide with the radical phenyl. $C_6H_5.NH.C_2H_3O$. Less correctly *acetaniline*. Used esp. as an analgesic and antipyretic.

1864 ROSCOE *Elem. Chem.* 411. **1877** FOWNES *Man. Chem.* II. 453 Acetanilide, or Phenylacetamide, produced by heating aniline and glacial acetic acid for several hours.. forms colourless, shining, laminar crystals, melting at 112°–113°. **1882** *Athenæum* 2859, 211 Acetaniline acted on by chloride of lime at a temperature of 270 Cent. produces a beautiful yellow to which the name of flavaniline is given. **1897** *Trans. Amer. Pediatr. Soc.* IX. 41, I have collected several cases of acetanilide poisoning in children where the drug was used externally as an antiseptic. **1956** *Lancet* 24 Mar. 339/1 Acetanilide is a dangerous drug because the body de-acetylates part of it into aniline.

acetarious (æsɪ'tɛərɪəs), *a.* [f. L. *acētāri-a* see next + -OUS.] Used in salads, as lettuce, cress, etc.

1822 J. C. LOUDON *Encycl. Gardening* (1835) III. i. viii. §7. 856 The acetarious vegetables are.. all articles of comparative luxury, or condiments rather than food. **1832** *Veg. Subst. Food of Man* 299 Vegetables.. eaten raw.. in their natural state, or blanched, are.. termed acetarious, or salad plants. **1835** J. C. LOUDON in *L. Hunt's Journal* No. 70. 261 Those.. would not readily reconcile themselves to the acetarious productions of Dublin and Glasgow during that season.

†**'acetars, 'acetaries**, *sb. pl. Obs.* [ad. L. *acētāri-a* salad plants, prop. adj., neut. pl. of *acētāri-s*, pertaining to *acēt-um* vinegar.]

1612 COCKERAM, *Acetarr*, a salad of smal hearbes. **1657** *Phys. Dict.*, *Acetaries*, sallets, or herbs mixed with vinegar to stir up appetite. **1676** BULLOKAR, *Acetar*, a sallad of raw herbs eaten with vineger. **1775** ASH, *Acetars*, salads and vinegar.

acetary ('æsɪtərɪ). [ad. mod.L. *acetārium*, f. *acēt-um* vinegar + *-arium* receptacle; see -ARY.] 'An acid pulpy substance in certain fruits, as the pear, inclosed in a congeries of small calculous bodies towards the base of the fruit.' Craig 1847.

1674 GREW *Anat. Plants* I. vi. (1682) 41 Within this lies the Acetary; 'tis allways sour, and by the bounding of the Calculary of a Globular Figure. *Ibid.* IV. ii. §5. 183 I have taken leave to name it the Acetary. **1753** CHAMBERS *Cycl. Supp.* s.v., The quince also has an Acetary, resembling, tho' less than, that of a pear.

acetate ('æsɪteɪt). *Chem.* [f. ACET-IC + -ATE[4].]

1. A salt formed by the combination of acetic acid with an alkaline, earthy, or metallic base; as ***acetate of lead***, called also *sugar of lead*.

1827 FARADAY *Chem. Manip.* §10. 253 Nitrate of mercury, acetate of lead. **1869** ROSCOE *Elem. Chem.* 94 Marsh gas may .. be artificially prepared by heating sodium acetate. **1872** WILLIAMSON *Chem.* §278 The metallic acetates are, for the most part, very soluble in water. **1876** HARLEY *Mat. Med.* 143 Acetate of potash was known in the 13th cent., and probably earlier.

2. A synthetic material in the manufacture of which acetic acid is used, esp. *attrib.*, as ***acetate rayon***, rayon made from cellulose acetate (see CELLULOSE B. c), ***acetate silk***, etc.

1920 C. SALTER tr. *Georgievics' Textile Fibres* 11 Acetate Silks. **1925** *Good Housekeeping* Apr. 142/3 Acetate silk.. being made out of.. cotton or wood-pulp.. with acetic acid. **1926** A. L. WYKES *Working Viscose Silk* 34 Acetate rayons burn more slowly than other rayons. **1932** A. HUXLEY *Brave New World* iii. 58 Her jacket was made of bottle-green acetate cloth. **1940** *Chambers's Techn. Dict.* 6/2 *Acetate film*, positive or negative film consisting of emulsion carried on a base of cellulose acetate. **1964** *Which?* Aug. 252/2 *Acetate*, made from cellulose by chemical treatment of wood-pulp or cotton linters... Used for a wide range of woven fabrics such as satins, taffetas, brocades and moirés for dress and furnishing.

3. Orig., a disc made of glass coated with cellulose acetate, used for direct recording by a cutting stylus; hence, any direct-cut disc (of whatever material), as opposed to a pressing.

[**1940** *How to make Good Recording* (Audio Devices, Inc.) 9 'Acetate' recording discs have.. made possible high-fidelity recording with simple and inexpensive equipment.] **1962** A. NISBETT *Technique Sound Studio* iv. 87 'Acetates' are particularly fragile, and under heavy playing weights the groove rapidly breaks up. **1967** *Crescendo* May 22/3, I just got the acetate of the new album, which comes out May 1st in the States. **1975** *Gramophone* Dec. 1001/3 The Halcyon has twenty-one tracks, from privately-made acetates. **1980** *Musicians Only* 26 Apr. 12/3, I must have cut 40 acetates.

acetated ('æsɪteɪtɪd), *ppl. a.* [formally pa. pple. of *acetate* vb., apparently not otherwise used.] Treated or combined with acetic acid, formed into an acetate.

1791 HAMILTON tr. *Berthollet, Art of Dyeing* I. I. §1. v. 86 The precipitate obtained from acetated lead. **1794** G. ADAMS *Nat. & Exper. Phil.* I. xi. 450 Acetated mercury. **1804** ABERNETHY *Surgical Observ.* 127 Bathing it with a solution of acetated lead.

acetation (æsɪ'teɪʃən). [n. of action f. ACETATE; see prec. and -TION.] = ACETIFICATION.

1863 H. ROGERS *Life of J. Howe* v. 155 *note*, As though.. it had, by some magical process of acetation, been all at once turned into verjuice.

acetazolamide (,æsɪtə'zɒləmaɪd). Also **acetazoleamide** (-'zəʊl-). [f. ACET- + AZO- + AMIDE.] A drug used as a diuretic, an anticonvulsant, and in the treatment of glaucoma.

1954 T. H. MAREN et al. in *Bull. Johns Hopkins Hosp.* XCV. 200 Acetazoleamide.. is a specific inhibitor of the widely distributed animal enzyme, carbonic anhydrase. **1955** *Lancet* 2 Apr. 706/2 Acetazoleamide has theoretical pharmacological qualifications as an oral diuretic. **1961** *Lancet* 29 July 240/1 When admitted she was having seizures... She was immediately given.. 750 mg. of primidone, 1 g. of acetazolamide. **1962** *Lancet* 28 Apr. 900/2 In such cases [of acute congestive glaucoma] acetazolamide has proved a useful adjunct to intensive miotic therapy.

acetenyl ('æsɪtɪnɪl). *Chem.* [short for *acetylenyl*, f. ACETYLENE + -YL.] A name for the univalent group C_2H; = $C \equiv CH$, = ACETYLENE minus one atom of hydrogen; as in ***acetenyl-benzene*** $C_6H_5 - C \equiv CH$.

1877 WATTS *Fownes' Chem.* II. 434 Acetenyl-benzene or Phenyl-acetylene.. is an aromatic liquid, boiling at 140°.

acetic (ə'si:tɪk, ə'sɛtɪk), *a.* [mod. f. L. *acēt-um* vinegar (f. *acē-re* to be sour) + -IC.] Of the nature of vinegar; pertaining to vinegar. Hence,

1. acetic acid: The special acid of which vinegar is a diluted or crude form, produced by the acetous fermentation of alcohol. *Chemically*, the monatomic monobasic acid of the ethyl or dicarbon series, $C_2H_4O_2 = C_2H_3O(OH)$, derived from ethyl alcohol $C_2H_5(OH)$ by the substitution of an atom of oxygen for two of the hydrogen of the ethyl. ***anhydrous acetic acid***, a synonym of ***acetic anhydride***; see 2.

1808 HENRY *Epit. Chem.* (ed. 5) 302 It appears that acetic acid differs from the acetous, only in containing less water and no mucilage. **1814** SIR H. DAVY *Agric. Chem.* 108 Acetic acid, or vinegar, may be obtained from the sap of different trees. **1827** FARADAY *Chem. Manip.* §12. 280 Acetic acid.. is much in use in the arts in an impure state. **1860** PIESSE *Lab. Chem. Wonders* 97 Concentrated acetic acid is also a powerful disinfectant.

2. ***acetic series***: The series of compound bodies related to acetic acid, or containing the radical ACETYL C_2H_3O; as ***acetic ether*** or ***ethyl acetate*** $C_2H_5.C_2H_3O_2$, a fragrant liquid; ***acetic oxide*** or ***anhydride*** $(C_2H_3O)_2O$, a heavy oil gradually converted by water into acetic acid.

1871 TYNDALL *Frag. of Science* I. ii. 56 (ed. 6) Reducing dry air to the pressure of the acetic ether. **1872** WILLIAMSON

Chem. §279 Acetic ether has an agreeable odour, by which its presence can be detected. **1875** DARWIN *Insectiv. Plants* vi. 88 The acid belongs to the acetic or fatty series. **1876** HARLEY *Mat. Med.* 349 Acetic anhydride may be isolated by several processes.

acetification (əˌsɛtɪfɪˈkeɪʃən). **acetifaction** in Ash. [f. L. *acēt-um* vinegar + -FICATION = -making.] The action of converting into vinegar; the chemical reaction which converts alcohol into acetic acid.

1753 CHAMBERS *Cycl. Supp.* s.v., Acetification is a branch or species of fermentation, arising by exposing vinous liquors in open vessels, and a warm place, which turns them acid. **1863** WATTS *Dict. Chem.* I. 8 Mother of vinegar.. is a nitrogenised body, which has the power of exciting the acetification of pure alcohol in the presence of atmospheric air. **1871** *Echo* July 27 In countries where wine and cyder prevail, domestic vinegar is obtained by the acetification of these beverages.

acetifier (əˈsɛtɪfaɪə(r)). [f. ACETIFY *v.* + -ER[1].] An apparatus for conducting acetous fermentation, and producing vinegar.

1863 *Sarson & Son's Circular*, This Vinegar is pure as when first drawn from the Acetifiers.

acetify (əˈsɛtɪfaɪ), *v.* [f. L. *acēt-um* vinegar + -FY = make.]

1. *trans.* To subject to acetous fermentation; to convert into vinegar; to make sour.

1872 WILLIAMSON *Chem.* §277 A stream of wash either fresh or partially acetified.

2. *intr.* To become sour, to undergo acetous fermentation. Cf. ACETIZE.

a **1864** WEBSTER cites *Encyc. Dom. Econ.*

acetimeter (ˌæsɪˈtɪmɪtə(r)). [a. Fr. *acétimètre*, f. L. *acēt-um* vinegar + *mètre* ad. Gr. μέτρον a measure.] An instrument for measuring the strength of vinegar or other acids.

1875 URE *Dict. Arts* I. 16 Acid which contains 40 per cent. of real acetic acid, is in the language of the Revenue, 35 per cent. over proof; it is the strongest acid on which duty is charged by the Acetimeter.

acetimetrical (ˌæsɪtɪˈmɛtrɪkəl), *a.* [f. prec. + -ICAL.] Of or pertaining to acetimetry; used in the measurement of the strength of vinegar.

1875 URE *Dict. Arts* I. 16, 1000 grains of the above proof [acid] would require 50 measures of the acetimetrical alkaline solution.

acetimetry (ˌæsɪˈtɪmɪtrɪ). [f. L. *acēt-um* vinegar + -METRY = Gr. -μετρία measuring.] The determination of the strength of vinegar, or the ascertaining of the degree of sourness or proportion of acetic acid in any substance.

1875 URE *Dict. Arts* I. 15 (Title of Article).

acetin (ˈæsɪtɪn). *Chem.* [f. ACET- + -IN(E = Gr. -ίνη daughter, derivative, here used to form a term matching *glycerin.*] Acetic glycerin; class name of a series of thick oily liquids, formed (by Berthelot) by the action of acetic acid upon glycerin; they consist of glycerin $C_3H_5(OH)_3$ in which one, two, or all the three hydrogen atoms are replaced by the radical acetyl C_2H_3O, the result being *mono-*, *di-*, or *tri-acetin*; the formula of the last is $C_3H_5(OC_2H_3O)_3$.

1874 ROSCOE *Elem. Chem.* xxxvi. 386. **1877** WATTS *Fownes' Chem.* II. 285.

†**'acetite** (ˈæsɪtaɪt). *Chem. Obs.* [f. L. *acēt-um* vinegar + -ITE.] A salt of the supposed acetous acid; the substances formerly so named are ACETATES.

1791 HAMILTON tr. *Berthollet, Art of Dyeing* I. I. §1 ii. 29 One pound of acetite of lead, or sugar of lead. **1802** CHEVENIX in *Phil. Trans.* XCII. 135, I sent a current of oxygenized muriatic acid through a solution of acetite of potash. **1812** SIR H. DAVY *Chem. Philos.* 394 A solution of acetite of lead, i.e. sugar of lead, may be used. **1822** IMISON *Science & Art* II. 61 A piece of paper, dipped in a solution of acetite of lead.

acetize (ˈæsɪtaɪz), *v. rare.* [f. L. *acēt-um* vinegar + -IZE.] = ACETIFY.

1859 R. F. BURTON in *Jrnl. R.G.S.* XXIX. 185 The vinegar is also made of honey.. and water.. mixed, and poured in a calabash under the sun to ferment and acetize.

aceto-. *Chem.* In comb. = ACETIC, ACETYL before a consonant (cf. ACET-), as in ***aceto-chloride, aceto-nitril, acetophenone, aceto-sodacetate***, etc.

1880 tr. *Wurtz, Atom. Theory* 180 This is the case in the combinations described by Carius under the name of plumbic aceto-chlorhydrin, aceto-bromhydrin, and aceto-iodhydrin.

ˌacetoa'cetic, *a.* [f. ACETO- + ACETIC *a.*] **acetoacetic acid**, an unstable acid, present in traces in urine and in increased amount in the urine of diabetic patients; prepared from **acetoacetic ester**: a colourless liquid ester, ethyl acetoacetate.

1903 WALKER & MOTT tr. *Holleman's Org. Chem.* I. 291 Acetoacetic acid.. is not of much importance, but its ethyl ester, acetoacetic ester, is a very interesting compound. **1956** *Nature* 24 Mar. 545/1 The formation of large amounts of acetoacetic acid $CH_3-CO-CH_2-COOH$. **1957** *Technology* Aug. 226/2 Another [chapter] on.. synthetic reagents includes.. acetoacetic and malonic esters.

acetometer (æsɪˈtɒmɪtə(r)). [f. L. *acēt-um* vinegar + Gr. μέτρον a measure. See -OMETER.] Another form of ACETIMETER.

1855 STOCKHARDT *Experim. Chem.* §514. 409 Glass cylinders constructed for this purpose [ascertaining the strength of vinegar] and divided into degrees are called acetometers. **1863** WATTS *Dict. Chem.* I. 12 The determination of the strength of commercial acetic acid by the hydrometer or acetometer, as it is called when graduated for this purpose, is not much to be depended upon.

‖**acetonæmia** (ˌæsɪtəʊˈniːmɪə). *Med.* [f. ACETONE + Gr. αἷμα blood.] (See quot.)

1876 tr. *Wagner's Gen. Pathol.* 577 Acetonæmia is a morbid state.. characterized by the presence of acetone in the blood.

acetonamine (ˈæsɪtəʊnəˌmaɪn). *Chem.* [f. ACETONE + AMINE.] A compound amine, obtained by heating acetone with ammonia; two or three of the hydrogen atoms of which are replaced by molecules of acetone, which also lose sufficient oxygen to form water with the hydrogen from the ammonia. Hence *di-* and *tri-acetonamine*, with other more complicated compounds.

1877 WATTS *Fownes' Chem.* II. 263.

acetonate (ˈæsɪtəʊneɪt). *Chem.* [f. ACETONE + -ATE[4].] A salt of acetonic acid.

1873 WILLIAMSON *Chem.* 295 [Hydric] acetonate is in its composition homologous with lactate.

acetone (ˈæsɪtəʊn). *Chem.* [f. ACET(IC) + Gr. -ώνη female descendant; see -ONE.] A colourless limpid liquid related to acetic acid, but containing less oxygen; pyro-acetic spirit. It is the acetic member of the *ketones*, or ketone of the acetic series, and is also called *dimethyl ketone*, $CO(CH_3)_2$. Now widely used as an organic solvent and in the preparation of chloroform, etc.

1839 URE *Dict. Arts* 14 *Acetone*, the new chemical name of pyro-acetic spirit. **1858** THUDICHUM *The Urine* 314 Acetone is a colourless thin liquid. **1873** WILLIAMSON *Chem.* 289 Acetone is a neutral liquid of an agreeable odour. **1875** URE *Dict. Arts* I. 15 s.v. *Acetimetry*, The acetate of silver gives no acetone; whilst those of the alkaline earths yield chiefly acetone or marsh gas. **1876** tr. *Wagner's Gen. Pathol.* 577 Acetone.. is produced according to some in the stomach and intestines, according to others in the liver and thence is carried into the blood. **1877** FOWNES *Man. Chem.* II. 261 Acetone is very inflammable and burns with a bright flame. **1922** *Chambers's Encycl.* I. 33/2 Acetone.. is a solvent for gums and resins. **1957** V. J. KEHOE *Technique Film & T.V. Make-Up* iii. 31 *Acetone*, solvent used for cleaning spirit gum out of net and gauze hair goods and for various sealers. **1958** *Everyman's Encycl.* (ed. 4) 47/2 Acetone ($CH_3{\cdot}CO{\cdot}CH_3$), or Dimethyl Ketone.. is miscible with water, alcohol, and ether in all proportions... It is also used in the preparation of.. chloroform, iodoform, and viscose rayon.

attrib. **1928** A. B. CALLOW *Food & Health* ii. 21 In the absence of carbohydrates 'acetone bodies' are produced which give rise to biliousness. **1951** *Gloss. Terms Plastics Industry (B.S.I.)* 8 *Acetone resin*, a synthetic resin formed by the reaction of acetone with another compound, such as phenol or formaldehyde. **1961** *Brit. Med. Dict.* 12/2 *Acetone bodies*, aliphatic ketones and hydroxy ketones found in the blood and urine of severe diabetics as the result of the incomplete breakdown of fatty and amino acids, a condition known as ketosis.

acetonic (æsɪˈtɒnɪk), *a. Chem.* [f. ACETONE + -IC.] Of or derived from acetone, as in ***acetonic acid*** $C_4H_8O_3$.

1873 WILLIAMSON *Chem.* 295 Butylactic and oxybutyric acids are names given to acids of the same composition as acetonic acid.

acetonitril (ˌæsɪtəʊˈnaɪtrɪl). *Chem.* [f. ACETO- + NITRIL.] An alcoholic cyanide or hydrocyanic ether; the nitrogen compound, or *nitril*, of the acetic series, C_2H_3N, called also *ethenyl nitril*, and, as the cyanide of the methyl series, *methyl cyanide* $CH_3.CN$.

1869 ROSCOE *Elem. Chem.* 320. **1877** FOWNES *Man. Chem.* II. 92 The bodies obtained by these two processes are oily liquids.. Methyl cyanide, ethenyl-nitril, or acetonitril, boils at 77°.

acetonuria (ˌæsɪtəʊˈnjʊərɪə). *Path.* [f. ACETONE + URIA.] An excess of acetone bodies in the urine; ketonuria.

1894 GOULD *Illustr. Dict. Med.* 26/2 **1907** *Practitioner* Oct. 551 The feature of this disorder.. is the occurrence of acetonuria during the attack. **1961** *Lancet* 9 Sept. 566/2 Its hypoglycæmic action in diabetes is associated with an increased incidence of acetonuria.

acetophenetidin (ˌæsɪtəʊfɪˈnɛtɪdɪn). *Med.* Also **acetphe'netidin.** [f. ACETO- + PHENETIDIN.] A white crystalline compound used as an antipyretic and analgesic; phenacetin.

1910 *Practitioner* Apr. 552 Kephaldol is a yellowish-white powder.. containing the following percentage composition: Citric acid 6 per cent., Salicylic acid 33 per cent., Acetphenetidine 48 per cent. **1943** *Martindale's Extra Pharmacopœia* (ed. 21) II. 321 Tabellæ Acetophenetidini.. contain 90 to 110% of the labelled amounts of acetophenetidin. **1959** *Brit. Pharmaceut. Codex* 547 Phenacetin.. *Synonyms*: Acetophenetidin; Phenacetinum.

acetophenone (ˌæsɪtəʊfɪˈnəʊn). *Chem.* [f. ACETO- + PHEN(YL + -ONE.] Methyl phenyl ketone; HYPNONE; used esp. as a constituent of certain synthetic perfumes.

1871 *Jrnl. Chem. Soc.* XXIV. 258 Ethylbenzene alcohol.. is obtained.. by hydrogenising acetophenone in alcoholic solution. **1886** [see HYPNONE]. **1924** *Times Trade & Engin. Suppl.* 29 Nov. 243/2 Quite a number of changes have taken place among perfumery chemicals.. acetophenone.. and nerolin.. are all cheaper. **1944** J. GRANT *Hackh's Chem. Dict.* (ed. 3) 8/2 *Acetophenone*,.. used medicinally as a hypnotic, and also in perfumes (orange blossoms).

acetose (æsɪˈtəʊs), *a.* [ad. late L. *acētōs-us* sour, f. *acētum* vinegar: see -OSE.] Tasting like vinegar; sour. Chiefly applied to the natural sourness of unripe fruits, sorrel, etc.

1533 ELYOT *Castel of Helth* 36 (1541) With sugar and vyneger is made Sirupe Acetose. **1751** CHAMBERS *Cycl.* s.v., Acetous or Acetose, something relating to Vinegar. **1854** AINSWORTH *Flitch of Bacon* II. iii. 117 If acetose claret I happen to sip. **1868** PAXTON *Bot. Dict.*, *Acetose*, sour, tart, acid.

†**acetose, -ouse**, *sb. Obs.* [ad. mod.L. *Acetōsa* (f. *acētōs-us* sour), given to the plant by Tournefort as generic name.] The herb Sorrel or Sorrel Dock (*Rumex Acetosa*).

1547 BOORDE *Brev.* in *Dyetary* 102 (1870) Qualyfie the heate of the Lyuer and the stomake with the confection of Acetose. **1605** TIMME *Quersitanus* III. 177 The juice of lemons, the water Melissa, Acetouse, and of roses mingled with the sayd wine.

acetosity (æsɪˈtɒsɪtɪ). [ad. late L. *acētōsitas*, f. *acētōsus* sour: see ACETOSE and -ITY.] The quality of being acetose or sour; sourness, tartness.

1599 A. M. *Gabelhouer's Bk. of Phys.* 12/1 Throughe the acetositye of the Vineger the duricies of the Eggeshels wil be mitigated. **1612** WOODALL *Surgeon's Mate* Wks. 1653, 175 The juice or pulpe of Tamarinds hath a great acetositie. [**1731** in BAILEY, and subseq. Dicts.]

†**ace'tosous**, *a. Obs.* [f. L. *acētōs-us* + -OUS.] An early by-form of ACETOSE, ACETOUS.

1605 TIMME *Quersitanus* III. 189 Fermentation.. consisteth in a certaine acetosus liquor of nature. **1612** WOODALL *Surgeon's Mate* Wks. 1653, 174 Rather use Acetososus medicines.

acetous (ˈæsɪtəs), *a.* [ad. Fr. *acéteux, -euse*, ad. late L. *acētōs-us*; see ACETOSE.] **a.** Of or pertaining to vinegar; having the qualities of vinegar; sour. Also *fig.*

1778 BP. LOWTH *On Isaiah* (1778) 268 Unless further fermentation is promoted by their lying longer on their own lees, they will.. soon degenerate into a liquor of an acetous kind. **1837** CARLYLE *Fr. Rev.* I. IV. iv. 200 A man.. whose small soul, transparent wholesome-looking as small ale, could by no chance ferment into virulent alegar, the mother of ever new alegar, till all France were grown acetous, virulent. **1865** *Athenæum* No. 1942. 52/1 Stimulating unguents and acetous lotions.

b. ***acetous fermentation***: The chemical reaction by which sugar or alcohol is changed into vinegar; occurring naturally when bread, milk, or beer turns sour.

1794 SULLIVAN *View of Nat.* I. 148 This latter, modified by the various fermentations, produces.. the acid of vinegar, after having been anew modified by the acetous fermentation. **1822** IMISON *Science & Art* II. 159 The vinous fermentation must be checked in time, otherwise the acetous fermentation would begin. **1833** *Penny Cycl.* I. 237/2 Fermentation is of three kinds: the vinous, producing alcohol; the acetous, yielding vinegar; and the putrefactive. **1857** HAWTHORNE *Fr. & It. Journals* II. 236 The Romans like their bread.. in a state of acetous fermentation.

c. ***acetous acid***: A name formerly given to vinegar in the belief that it differed from acetic acid by containing one atom less of oxygen in its molecule. Since it has been ascertained that vinegar is only dilute acetic acid the name has become *obsolete*.

1791 HAMILTON tr. *Berthollet, Art of Dyeing* I. I. §1 ii. 30 [It] combines with the acetous acid and produces an acetite of alumine. **1796** PEARSON in *Phil. Trans.* LXXXVI. 398 It afforded no acetite of lead on digesting it in acetous acid. **1806** *Brit. Encycl.* I. 13 Acetous acid in that concentrated state in which it is called radical vinegar. **1828** MARCET *Conversations on Chemistry* II. 218 The acetous acid is developed by means of the acetous fermentation.

aceturic (ˌæsɪˈtjʊərɪk), *a. Chem.* [f. ACET- + URIC.] In ***aceturic acid***, $CH_2\begin{cases}NH.C_2H_3O\\CO_2H\end{cases}$ a secondary amide, consisting of glycocine with one H atom of the typical ammonia replaced by the radical acetyl; hence also called *acetyl-glycocine*.

1877 WATTS *Fownes' Chem.* II. 383.

acetyl (ˈæsɪtɪl). *Chem.* [f. ACET(IC) + Gr. ὕλη substance, stuff: see -YL(E. Hence 'radical of the acetic series.'] **a.** A monatomic organic radical

C_2H_3O, the oxidized radical of the dicarbon series, and the basis of the acetic series.

1864 *Athenæum* No. 1937. 788/3 The ethylate of acetyl. **1873** WILLIAMSON *Chem.* §281 Acetic acid is a molecule of water in which the two atoms of hydrogen are replaced by two atoms of acetyl. **1880** CLEMENSHAW *Wurtz's Atomic Theory* 277 Acetyl is ethyl modified by substitution.

b. Also *attrib.* and in *Comb.*, as ***acetyl-cellulose***, ***chloride*** (also acetic, acetylic chloride), ***-orthoamidobenzoic acid***, ***peroxide***, ***-salicylic acid***, ***silk***.

1879 WATTS *Dict. Chem.* VI. (Suppl.). 418 *Acetyl-cellulose. **1915** P. E. SPIELMANN tr. *von Richter's Org. Chem.* I. 665 Acetyl Cellulose is formed by the action of glacial acetic acid.. and a small quantity of concentrated sulphuric acid.. on cellulose. **1880** *Athenæum* 13 Nov. 645/2 The following papers were read: On *Acetylorthoamidobenzoic Acid. **1877** WATTS *Fownes' Chem.* II. 286 *Acetyl peroxide $(C_2H_3O)_2O_2$ is a viscid liquid, which explodes with violence when heated, and acts as a powerful oxidizing agent. **1897** *Jrnl. Chem. Soc.* LXXII. I. 531 *Acetyl salicylic acid.. is obtained by adding small quantities of ferric chloride (100 grams) to a mixture of salicylic acid (80 grams) and acetic chloride. **1899** Acetylsalicylic acid [see ASPIRIN]. **1921** *Jrnl. Soc. Dyers & Colourists* XXXVII. 294 Possibly dyed *Acetyl Silk yarn could be used for weaving with cotton.

acetylation (ə,sɛtɪ'leɪʃən). *Chem.* [f. ACETYL + -ATION.] The introduction of one or more acetyl groups into (a compound) by means of a chemical reaction. Hence **acetylate** (ə'sɛtɪleɪt), *v.*; **a'cetylated, a'cetylating** ***ppl. adjs.***

1895 *Jrnl. Chem. Soc.* LXVII. 447 Acetylation of Cellulose. **1908** *Ann. Rep. Chem. Soc.* V. 83 Many experiments on the.. acetylation of amino-groups have also been made. **1909** WEBSTER, Acetylate, v. **1927** T. WOODHOUSE *Artificial Silk* iv. 31 The raw material is almost invariably cotton which is acetylated by acetic anhydride in the presence of a catalyst, usually sulphuric acid... The cellulose acetate thus formed is precipitated by the addition of water, and freed from its acetylating solution. **1939** *Nature* 29 July 217/1 Modifications in the acetylation of cellulose for the production of acetate rayon include the use of special solvents. **1946** *Nature* 19 Oct. 553/2 Believing that the usual methods of acetylation give degraded products, Wassermann has attempted to acetylate alginic acid with ketene. **1959** *Times Rev. Industry* Sept. 4/1 Non-cellulosic fibres such as.. acetylated cellulose (Tricel).

acetylcholine ('æsɪtɪl'kɒlaɪn). *Biochem.* [f. ACETYL + CHOLINE.] The acetyl ester of choline, $C_7H_{17}O_3N$, a chemical secreted at the ends of many nerve-fibres.

1906 *Brit. Med. Jrnl.* 22 Dec. 1789/2 Acetyl-choline, the first of this series, is a substance of extraordinary physiological activity. **1933** *Jrnl. Physiol.* LXXIX. 255 The only choline ester which has hitherto been isolated in a chemically pure state from animal tissues is acetylcholine, which was found to be present in large quantities in the spleens of horses and oxen. **1944** *Ann. Reg. 1943* 353 The electrical and chemical theories of transmission of nerve impulses may be reconciled by the discovery that acetylcholine is an essential link in the generation of the electrical changes recorded during activity.

acetylene ('æsɪtɪ,liːn, now usu. ə'sɛtɪliːn). *Chem.* [f. ACETYL + Gr. -ηνη female descendant, weaker derivative: see -ENE.] **a.** A gaseous hydrocarbon C_2H_2, = $HC \equiv CH$, also called ethine, interesting as being producible by the direct combination of carbon and hydrogen at a high temperature, and of forming by further syntheses more complex carbon compounds, thus rendering possible the artificial preparation of organic substances from their simple elements.

1864 H. SPENCER *Biology* I. 8 With the exception of acetylene, the various hydro-carbons are not producible by directly combining their elements. **1869** ROSCOE *Elem. Chem.* 95 Acetylene is a colourless gas, which burns with a bright luminous flame, and possesses a disagreeable and very peculiar odour; it is produced in all cases of incomplete combustion, and its smell may be noticed when a candle burns with a smoky flame. **1873** WATTS *Fownes' Chem.* I. 559 Ethine or Acetylene is one of the constituents of coal gas. **1877** *Ibid.* II. 1 Recently it has been shown that ethine or acetylene, C_2H_2, can be produced by the direct combination of carbon and hydrogen; that this compound can be made to take up two additional atoms of hydrogen to form [olefiant gas, or] ethene C_2H_4; and that this.. can be converted into alcohol, C_2H_6O, a body formerly supposed to be producible only by the fermentation of sugar.

b. *attrib.* in ***acetylene gas***; hence ***acetylene (gas) lamp***.

1895 *Nation* 19 Dec. 447/2 Acetylene gas. **1897** *U.S. Patent* in W. E. Gibbs *Lighting by Acetylene* (1898) 139 Acetylene gas lamp. **1900** V. B. LEWES *Acetylene* 466 Acetylene lamps for signalling.

c. *ellipt.*

1915 W. S. MAUGHAM *Of Human Bondage* xlii. 198 The sea of faces, half seen in the glare of acetylene.

acetylenic (ə,sɛtɪ'lɛnɪk, -'iːnɪk), *a. Chem.* [f. ACETYLEN(E + -IC.] Made from, or involving the use of, acetylene.

1915 *Chem. Abstr.* 3221 (*title*) Preparation of acetylenic nitriles and of 1-halogenated acetylene derivatives. **1946** *Nature* 10 Aug. 205/1 (*title*) Acetylenic Ketones. *Ibid.* 14 Dec. 876/2 The fungistatic activity of a considerable number of ethylenic and acetylenic compounds.

acetylic (æsɪ'tɪlɪk), *a. Chem.* [f. ACETYL + -IC.] Of or belonging to acetyl; as in ***acetylic*** or ***acetyl chloride***.

1881 *Athenæum* 12 Nov. 634/3 Malic anhydride can be obtained directly from malic acid by heating with an excess of acetylic chloride.

acetylide (ə'sɛtɪlaɪd). *Chem.* [f. ACETYL(ENE + -IDE.] A carbide that can be regarded as formed from acetylene by the replacement of one or both hydrogen atoms by a metal atom; a carbide containing the C_2H^- or C_2^{2-} ion.

1863 *Chem. News* 3 Jan. 3/1 Acetylide of copper having the property of detonating by an elevation of the temperature or by a blow. **1902** *Encycl. Brit.* XXV. 36/2 It [*sc.* acetylene] had the power of combining with certain metals, more especially copper and silver, to form acetylides of a highly explosive character. **1951** I. L. FINAR *Org. Chem.* iv. 73 If acetylene is passed over heated sodium, both the monosodium and disodium acetylides are formed. **1965** PHILLIPS & WILLIAMS *Inorg. Chem.* I. xv. 565 An example is the formation of the acetylide ion C_2H^-, which in water reacts with H^+ to give the parent acid acetylene. **1984** *Tetrahedron Lett.* XXV. 2411 (*heading*) Nature of the intermediate from the reaction of lithium acetylide with boron trifluoride etherate.

‖**ach** (ɑːx), *int.* [Not Eng. unless meant for an emphatic and strongly aspirated form of *ah!* Used in German and Celtic.]

1865 E. CLAYTON *Cruel Fort.* III. 81 Ach! you irritate me.

ach, variant of AC, *conj. Obs.*, but.

ach, obs. form of OWE.

Achæan (ə'kiːən), *a.* and *sb.* Also **Achaian** (ə'kaɪən), **Achean.** [f. L. *Achæus*, a. Gr. Ἀχαιός, f. Ἀχαία Achæa.] **A.** *adj.* Of or belonging to Achæa, a name of varying application, in Homeric usage applied to Greece generally, later to a district of the northern Peloponnesus. **B.** *sb.* An inhabitant of Achæa (or Greece).

1567 G. TURBERVILLE tr. *Ovid's Her.* III. 71 In all the Achaian soyle. **1607** TOPSELL *Foure-footed Beastes* 126 The Achaian Harts are said to haue their gall in their tailes. *Ibid.* 315 The Achæans had this degre in high estimat. **1676** HOBBES tr. *Homer's Iliad* II. 28 The rest That in the Army of th' Achæans were. *Ibid.* 33 These were the Leaders of th' Achean forces. **1715** POPE *Iliad* II. 834 The Achaians, Myrmidons, Helleneans bear. **1797** *Encycl. Brit.* I. 63 Achaia was.. taken for all those countries that joined in the Achæan league, reduced by the Romans to a province. **1833** *Penny Cycl.* I. 82/1 The history of the Achæans forms an inconsiderable part of the general history of Greece till about B.C. 251. **1925** G. MURRAY *Eumenides* p. viii, That glorified Achaean chieftain who was King of gods and men in the ordinary Homeric tradition. **1956** J. FORSDYKE *Greece before Homer* iv. 83 There is not yet any reason beyond the resemblance in the place-name to connect the people of Ahhiyawa with the Achaians of Greece.

Achæmenian (ækiː'mɛnɪən), *a.* and *sb.* [f. L. *Achæmenius*, f. Gr. Ἀχαιμένης Achæmenes, said to have been the ancestor of Cyrus + -IAN.] Also **Achæmenid** (ə'kiːmənɪd), *a.* and *sb.* [-ID[3].] **A.** *adj.* Of or pertaining to a member of the dynasty that ruled in ancient Persia from the time of Cyrus the Great (d. 529 B.C.) until the death of Darius III in 330 B.C. **B.** *sb.* A member of this dynasty.

1717 G. SEWELL et al. tr. *Ovid's Metam.* I. IV. p. 122 The Vogue of Achæmenian Towns obtain'd. **1885** *Encycl. Brit.* XVIII. 565/1 It is far more likely that Anshan was a place in Persis, the proper family seat of the Achæmenians. **1886** *ibid.* XXI. 849/1 A residence of the Achæmenian kings. **1900** M. L. MCCLURE tr. *Maspero's Passing of Empires* vii. 736 Compare the tombs of the Achæmenids. **1931** *Times Lit. Suppl.* 8 Jan. 18/1 In the Achaemenid period the soil was rocky and muddy with the leavings of Babylonia and Assyria. **1939** A. J. TOYNBEE *Stud. Hist.* VI. 207 The Achaemenid Great King Artaxerxes Ochus. **1956** —— *Hist. Approach Relig.* iv. 51 This Macedonian Greek founder of an Egyptian successor-state to the Achaemenian Empire.

achæne, var. form of ACHENE.

achænocarp (ə'kiːnəʊkɑːp). *Bot.* [f. Gr. ἀ priv. + χαίν-ειν to gape + καρπ-ός fruit; cf. ACHENE. The Gr. for 'not gaping' is ἀχανής, whence an etymological derivative would be *achanocarp*.] A fruit which is an achene.

1880 GRAY *Bot. Text-Bk.* 394, *Achænocarp*, general name of a dry and indehiscent fruit.

achætous (ə'kiːtəs), *a.* [f. A- 14 + Gr. χαίτη hair + -OUS.] Having no setæ.

1896 BENHAM in *Cambr. Nat. Hist.* II. 263 The peristomium is achaetous in the adult.

†**a'chafe**, *v. Obs.* 4–5; also **eschaufe, achauf(fe**; esp. in pple. **achaufed, achauffed**. [:—earlier ESCHAUFE, a. OFr. *eschaufe-r* (mod. *échauffe-r*) to heat; f. *es*:—L. *ex* out, extremely + *chaufe-r*:—late L. **calefā-re* for *calefac-ĕre* to heat, warm, f. *calēre* to be hot + *facĕre* to make. See A- *pref.* 9.] To heat, to warm; also *fig.* to kindle anyone's wrath, to heat with passion, to chafe.

c **1325** *E.E. Allit. Poems* B. 1143 His wrath is achaufed. *c* **1340** *Gawayne & Gr. Knt.* 883 He sete in þat settel semlych ryche, & achaufed hym. *c* **1374** CHAUCER *Boethius* 22 Whan þe sterre sirius eschaufeþ hym. *c* **1450** LONELICH *Grail* xxiii. 507 Whanne cold thing a-chawfed is owht, Anon to red colour it is i-browht. **1480** CAXTON *Chron. Eng.* ccxxxiv 256 Prynce Edward was sore achafed and greued. *c* **1490** —— *Ovid, Metam.* X. vi. Grete hete, whereof the ground was sore achauffid.

achage ('eɪkɪdʒ). *rare.* [f. ACHE *v.* + -AGE; suggested by *break-age.*] Aching state. (Humorous.)

1878 TENNYSON *Q. Mary* I. i. O, the Pope could dispense with his Cardinalate, and his achage, and his breakage.

Achaian, var. ACHÆAN.

achalasia (ækə'leɪzɪə). *Path.* [mod.L., f. Gr. ἀ- priv. + χάλασις slackening, relaxation, f. χαλᾶν to relax + -IA[1].] Failure (of a muscle) to relax. Hence **acha'lasic** *a.*, of an organ, etc., affected by achalasia.

1914 A. F. HERTZ [= A. F. HURST] in *Q. Jrnl. Med.* VIII. 300 Achalasia of the Cardia (so-called.. Cardiospasm)... For the word 'achalasia' I am indebted to Sir Cooper Perry, who coined it for me, as it was obvious that the word 'cardiospasm' and the erroneous idea it conveys would never be discarded unless some less cumbersome expression.. was devised. **1927** *Lancet* 19 Mar. 618/2 Achalasia of the cardia is a condition in which the cardiac sphincter does not relax ..in the act of deglutition. **1939** *Brit. Med. Jrnl.* 23 Dec. 1225/2 Mega-oesophagus (Cardiospasm).. is now regarded as an achalasia, or failure of the cardio-oesophageal sphincter to relax. **1962** *Lancet* 12 May 1008/2 These receptors are present in both circular and longitudinal muscle from the body of the normal and the achalasic œsophagus.

†**a'change, a'chaunge.** *Obs. rare*$^{-1}$. [:—earlier *eschange, eschaunge* (afterwards refashioned to EX-CHANGE) a. OFr. *eschange, échange*. See A- *pref.* 9.]

1470 HARDING *Chron.* xiii. 1 So was the name of this ilke Albyon All sette on side in Kalender of achaunge.. And Briteyn hight so furth by newe eschaunge, After Brutus.

†**a'chape**, *v. Obs.* [A by-form of ESCAPE, adopted from later OFr. *échaper*, occas. *achaper* (mod. *échapper*):—early OFr. and Norm. *escaper*, whence the ordinary form. Scotch writers in 6 have *echap* as in Fr. Also aphetized in 5 to CHAPE. Cf. SCHAPE, SHAPE, and SCAPE.] = ESCAPE.

1250 LAYAMON II. 342 þe Alemains' þat a-chaped were [**1205** weoren awei idraȝene]. *c* **1325** *E.E. Allit. Poems* B. 970 þe wrake þat no wyȝe achaped. *c* **1350** *Will. Palerne* 2805 Whan þe hert & þe hind · were of so harde a-chaped. *Ibid.* 1248 Gretly y þonk god · þat gart me a-chape. **1588** A. KING *Canisius' Catech.* 143 Præsumption of gods mercie to echap for sinne vnpunished.

†**achaque.** *Obs.* [Sp. word.] Habitual indisposition, ailment.

1646 HOWELL *Fam. Lett.* (1650) I. 407, I am sorry to hear of your achaques, and so often indisposition there.

‖**achar** (ətʃɑː(r)), *Anglo-Ind.* Also **atchaar, attjar, achiar.** [a. Pers. *āchār* pickles, adopted in nearly all the vernaculars of India for acid or salt relishes, and extended by Europeans to pickles of every description. Mentioned by Garcia 1563. (Col. Yule.)]

1697 DAMPIER *Voy. round World* I. 391, *Achar* I presume signifies sauce. They make it in the East Indies. **1866** LINDLEY & MOORE *Treas. Bot.* 9, *Achiar*; an Eastern condiment, formed of the young shoots of *Bambusa arundinacea*.

†**a'charne**, *v. Obs. rare.* [a. Fr. *acharne-r* to flesh, bait; refl. *s'acharner* to thirst for blood, become cruel:—late L. **adcarnā-re* f. *ad* to + *carn-em* flesh.] To become greedy of flesh, to thirst for blood.

c **1400** *MS. Bodl.* 546, 35 b, þer ben somme [wolves] þat eten chyldren & men and eteþ noon oþer flesh fro þat tyme þat þei be a charm[? n]ed wiþ mannys flesh.. Whanne thei acharneth in a contre of werre, there as batayles haue ybe, there thei eteth of dede men.

acharne, obs. form of ACORN.

‖**acharnement** (aʃarnəmɑ̃, ə'tʃɑːnmənt). [Fr. n. of action, f. *acharne-r* to give a taste of flesh (to dogs, falcons, etc.) Included as a technical military term in James's *Mil. Dict.* 1816 which professed to give 'the explanation of military terms in English, with the admixture of French words.'] Eagerness for blood, bloodthirsty fury, ferocity.

1816 JAMES *Mil. Dict.* (ed. 4), *Acharnement*, Fr., the rage and frenzy to which soldiers are subjected in the heat of an engagement. **1830** *Caledonian Merc.* Sept. 30 The extraordinary acharnement of the Belgians against their Government. **1833** *Blackw. Mag.* XXXIII. 502 The dreadful *acharnement* which marked the war on both sides —the *acharnement* of long-hoarded vengeance and maddening remembrances. **1854** BADHAM *Prose Halieutics* 46 Leaping at it with all the acharnement of dogs on a boar's back. **1857** DEQUINCEY *Wks.* VII. 299 The Jewish *acharnement* against the Christians.. would be inflamed to a frantic excess.

†**a'chased**, *pple. Obs. rare*$^{-1}$. [Either from a vb. *achase*, f. A- *pref.* intensive + CHASE, or from the

simple CHASE with *a-* for *i-*, *y-*, in pa. pple. See A- *particle*.] Chased.

c **1440** *Partonope* 6888 But both a chased were ryght wele.

achate (ˈækət), *sb.*[1] *arch.* [a. OFr. *acate*, *achate*, ad. L. *achātes*, a. Gr. ἀχάτης. The unchanged L. *achates* was also in common use. In end of 6 the form AGATE, *agath* was adopted from the Fr., and is now the ordinary form.] An agate, a kind of precious stone. (It was occasionally confounded from similarity of name with the *gagates* or *jet*.)

c **1230** *Ancren Riwle* 134 Enne deorewurðe ȝimston þet hette achate. **1398** TREVISA *Barth. De P.R.* (1495) XVI. x. 557 Achates is a precyous stone, and is blacke wyth white veynes. **1430** LYDG. *Chron. Troy* I. vi. Which stone these prudent clerkes call Achates most vertuous of all. **1535** COVERDALE *Ex.* xxviii. 19 A Ligurios, an Achatt and an Ametyst [**1590** *Genevan* achate, **1611** agate]. **1648** SIR E. BACON in *Bury Wills* (1850) 216, I give him alsoe my achate with the picture of the butterfly in it. **1750** *Leonardus' Mirror of Stones* 64 Sicily gave the first Achates, which was found in the River Acheus. **1855** P. J. BAILEY *Mystic* 90 The achate, wealth adductive, and the mind Of the immortals gladdening.

†**aˈchate**, *sb.*[2] *Obs.* 4-7. Also **achat**. [a. OFr. (12th c.) *achat* purchase:—earlier OFr. and Norm. *acat*, whence the earlier Eng. form *acat*, *acate*, which became *achat*, *achate*, under later Fr. influence, and in the original sense of *purchase*. In the sense of *provisions*, the prevailing form remained ACATES, aphetized CATES.]

1. The act of purchasing or buying; purchase; contract, bargain.

c **1374** CHAUCER *Boethius* 15 Coempcioun þat is to seyn comune achat or bying to-gidere. *c* **1386** —— *Prol.* 570 For whethur that he payde, or took by taille, Algate he wayted so in his Acate [*later MSS.* achaat(e, achate]. *c* **1460** *Bk. Curtasye* in *Babees Bk.* (1868) 317 Of achatis and dispenses þen wrytes he. **1601** *Househ. Ord. Ed. II*, §43 (1876) 25 He must make the achates in due manner for the kinges best profet. **1691** BLOUNT *Law Dict.*, *Achat* is used for a Contract or Bargain.

2. *pl.* Things purchased; provisions that were not made in the house, by the baker or brewer, but had to be purchased as wanted. In this sense more commonly ACATES.

1469 *Ord. Royal Househ.* 93 Pieces of beefe, & moton, & all other acates. **1596** SPENSER *F.Q.* II. ix. 31 The kitchin clerke, that hight Digestion, Did order all th'achates in seemely wise. **1644** HEYLIN *Life of Laud* II. 300 Every Office in the Court had their several diets.. with great variety of Achates.

†**aˈchate**, *v. Obs. rare.* [a. OFr. *achate-r* (12th c.) older *acater* (11th c.) to purchase:—late L. *accaptā-re*, f. *ac-* = *ad-* to + *captā-re* to take, seize. Cf. mod.Fr. *acheter*.] To purchase, lay in provision of.

1601 *Househ. Ord. Ed. II*, 36 A serjant of the scullery who shal achate & puruey fuel, coale, etc.

†**aˈchatour**. *Obs.* Also **acatour**, **achator**, **achater**. [a. AngloFr. *achatour*, earlier *acatour* (mod.Fr. *acheteur*):—late L. *accaptātōr-em*, n. of agent f. *accaptāre*: see prec. Originally a variant of ACATOUR, ACATER.] A purchaser or buyer of provisions; esp. the officer who purchased provisions for the royal household; a purveyor.

c **1386** CHAUCER *Prol.* 568 A gentil Maunciple was ther of a temple Of which achatours mighten take exemple (*other MSS.* acatouris). *c* **1475** *Lib. Nig. Ed. IV* in *Househ. Ord.* (1790) 22 The officers, ministers, achatours, purveyours, sergeaunts. **1601** *Househ. Ord. Ed. II*, 33 The flesh and the fish which the achators shal send into the larder. **1751** CHAMBERS *Cycl.* s.v., *Pourveyor* became a term so odious in times past, that, by Stat. 36 Ed. III, the heinous name pourveyor was changed into that of *achator*, or *buyer*.

†**achatry**. *Obs.* [A variant of ACATERY.] The office or room of the Achatour.

a **1377** *Househ. Ord. Ed. III* (1790) 4.

a-ˈchatter. [f. A *prep.*[1] 11 + CHATTER *v.*] Chattering.

1828 WILSON in *Blackw. Mag.* XXIV. 277 Morning magpie, a-chatter at skreigh of day. **1876** EGAN tr. *Heine's Atta Troll* 89 Shivering and with teeth a-chatter. **1883** *Harper's Mag.* Jan. 166/1 Eyes blinking and teeth a-chatter.

achauf, **achauff**, var. ACHAFE *v. Obs.* to warm.

ache (eɪk), *v.* Pa. t. and pple. **ached**. Forms: *Inf.* 1 acan; 2-4 aken, -in, eken; 3-9 ake; 8-9 ache. *Ind. pres. 3rd sing.* 1 æcð; 2-4 **akþ**, **akeþ**. *Pa. t.* 1-2 óc; 2-4 ok; 3-4 ook; 4-5 oke; 4-5 akede, -ide; 5- aked; 8-9 **ached**. *Pa. pple.* 1 acen; 2-3 **aken**; soon obs. and repl. by **aked**; 8-9 **ached**. A late Sc. variant is **ȝaik**, **yak**(e. [Originally a strong vb. of same class as *take*, *shake*, but with weak inflections since 4. The current spelling *ache* is erroneous; the vb. being historically *ake*, and the sb. *ache*, as in *bake*, *batch*, *speak*, *speech*. About 1700 the sb. began to be confused in pronunciation with the vb., whence some confusion in spelling between *ache* and *ake*; and finally instead of both being written *ake*—the word that has survived,—both vb. and sb. are now written *ache*—the word that has become obsolete. That is, the word *ache* has become obs. and been replaced by the word *ake*, while the spelling *ake* has become obs. and been replaced by the spelling *ache*. For this paradoxical result, Dr. Johnson is mainly responsible: ignorant of the history of the words, and erroneously deriving them from the Gr. ἄχος (with which they have no connexion) he declared them 'more grammatically written *ache*.' See next word.]

1. a. To be in pain, to have the sensation of pain continuous or prolonged; to throb with pain.

c **1000** ÆLFRIC *Gram.* 36 (MS. D.) Acað míne eágan. *c* **1175** *Lamb. Hom.* 149 þenne wule his hearte ake alse his fet & his honde. *c* **1200** *Trin. Coll. Hom.* 21 Ðe time cam swo þat hire ne oc . ne ne smeart. *c* **1230** *Ancren Riwle* 360 Betere is finker offe þen he eke euer. *a* **1250** *Juliana* (R. MS.) 48 Ant bond.. ba twa his honden þat him eoc euch neil. **1297** R. GLOUC. 208 Ech lyme hym ok. *c* **1305** *St. Andrew*, in *E.E. Poems* (1862) 100 Him oke ech bon. **1377** LANGL. *P. Pl.* B. VI. 258 So owre wombe aketh. **1382** WYCLIF *1 Kings* xv. 23 In the tyme of his eelde he akide the feet. *c* **1385** CHAUCER *Leg. Good W.* 706, I preye God lat oure hedes never ake! **1393** LANGL. *P. Pl.* C. xx. 159 þauh alle my fyngres oken. *c* **1400** *Rom. Rose* 6910 Sadde burdons that men taken, Make folkes shuldris aken. **1413** LYDG. *Pylgr. Sowle* (1483) V. xiv. 105 When I the Appel took Hit sat so nyhe my sydes that they ook. *c* **1430** *Hymns to Virg.* (1867) 80 Oure body wole icche, oure bonis wole ake. *c* **1440** *Prom. Parv.*, Akyn: *doleo.* **1572** *Lament. Lady Scotland* (Scottish Poems 16th Cent.) II. 243 My heid dois wark and ȝaik. **1595** SHAKS. *John* IV. i. 41 When your head did but ake I knit my hand-kercher about your browes. **1664** BUTLER *Hudibras* II. ii. 797 Cramm'd 'em till their Guts did ake With Cawdle, Custard and Plum-cake. **1729** SAVAGE *Wanderer* i. 176 Now veers the wind full east; and keen, and sore, Its cutting influence aches in every pore! **1753** RICHARDSON *Grandison* (1781) I. xxx. 216 Does not your heart ake for your Harriet? **1821** KEATS *Isabella* xxviii. Ah! when a soul doth thus its freedom win It aches in loneliness. **1821** COMBE *Dr. Syntax, Consolation* iii. 187 Her death made many a bosom ake Upon the banks of Keswick Lake. **1850** MRS. BROWNING *Prom. Bound* Poems I. 153 Thy sorrow aches in me.

b. *fig.* Of a person: to suffer the pains of longing (*to* do something); to long or yearn *for*; to be impatient or anxious (in anticipation). orig. *U.S.*

1893 'MARK TWAIN' in *Cosmopolitan* Nov. 57/1, I saw she had been aching to have me ask it. **1922** S. ANDERSON *Triumph of Egg* 14 Gee! I ached to see that race and those two horses run, ached and dreaded it too. **1937** 'J. BELL' *Murder in Hospital* xi. 218 Rachel is simply aching to get back. **1948** L. A. G. STRONG *Trevannion* xvii. 315 Her beauty made me ache to have it with me always. **1967** J. BOWEN *After Rain* (1972) II. 52 But, love, I want to. We both want to. I ache for it. **1978** C. RAYNER *Long Acre* xvi. 160 Amy was aching to hurry him. **1985** D. LESSING *Good Terrorist* 44 Now she ached for tea, something to eat.

†**2.** *trans. causal.* To make to ache. *Obs. rare.*

1566 UDALL *R. Doyster* IV. vi. (1847) 68 Ill ake your heades bothe! I was never werier, Nor never more vexte, since the first day I was borne.

ache (eɪk), *sb.*[1] Forms: 1 ace, æce, ece; 2-3 eche; 2-9 **ache**; (4 hacche); 6 **atche**. [OE. *æce* is a primary deriv. of vb. *ac-an* to ACHE, in which, as in parallel forms, the *c* (k) was palatalized to *ch* (tʃ), while in the vb. it remained (k); cf. *make*, *match*; *bake*, *batch*; *wake*, *watch*; *break*, *breach*; *speak*, *speech*; *stick*, *stitch*. Occasional early instances of *ake* as sb. are northern, in which dialect *c* (k) was not palatalized, cf. *make* = match, *steik* = stitch, *kirk* = church. In 7 the sb. was still *atche* (ɑːtʃ, ɛːtʃ) pl. *atch-es* (ɑːtʃɪz, ɛːtʃɪz), but about 1700 it began to be confused with the vb. as (ɛːk). The spelling of the latter has in turn been changed to *ache*, so that though both vb. and sb. are now really *ake*, both are in current spelling written *ache*. See prec. The former pronunciation survives in the dialectal *eddage* = *head-ache*; cf. *Smallage* for *Small Ache* f. ACHE *sb.*[2] The 'O.P.' rioters, ignorant of the Shaksperian distinction of *ake* and *ache*, ridiculed the stage pronunciation of the sb. by giving it to the vb. in 'John Kemble's head *aitches*.'] A pain; in later usage, a continuous or abiding pain, in contrast to a sudden or sharp one. Used of both physical and mental sensations.

c **885** K. ÆLFRED *Bæda* v. iii. (1722) 616 Eal ðæt sár and se æce onwæȝ alæded wæs. *c* **940** *Sax. Leechd.* II. 32 Maniȝ man hæfþ micelne ece on his eaȝum. *c* **1200** *Trin. Coll. Hom.* 165 Eche and smertinge, sorinesse, werinesse. *c* **1230** *Ancren Riwle* 360 He þet naueð eche under so sor ekinde heaued. *c* **1350** *Will. Palerne* 826 So harde hacches of loue here hert hadde þirled. **1388** WYCLIF *1 Kings* xv. 23 Asa hadde ache in feet. *c* **1440** *Prom. Parv.* 8 Ake, or ache, or akynge: *Dolor.* **1568** TURNER *Herbal* 20 Catarres, runninges of the eyes and other aykes. **1592** H. CHETTLE *Kind-Harts Dr.* (1841) 22 These trauelers that, by incision, are able to ease all atches. **1599** SHAKS. *Much Ado* III. iv. 56 *Beat.* I am exceeding ill, hey ho. *Mar.* For a hauke, a horse, or a husband? *Beat.* For the letter that begins them all, H. **1610** —— *Temp.* I. ii. 370 Ile racke thee with old Crampes Fill all thy bones with Aches, make thee rore. **1674** J. B[RIAN] *Harvest-Home* §4. 23 Free from attaches Of sickness weakness, in no part feel aches. **1727** SWIFT *City Shower* Wks. 1755 III. ii. 38, A coming show'r your shooting corns presage, Old aches throb, your hollow tooth will rage. **1796-7** COLERIDGE *Poems* (1862) 22 All the thousand aches 'Which patient merit of the unworthy takes.' **1807** CRABBE *Village* I. 149 And hoard up aches and anguish for their age. **1862** B. TAYLOR *Poet's Journal* (1866) 21 The steady ache of strong desires restrained.

†**ache** (eɪtʃ), *sb.*[2] *Obs.* [a. Fr. *ache*:—L. *apium*, ad. Gr. ἄπιον parsley (or some allied plant). The intermed. stages between *apium* and *ache* were *apio*, *apje*, *apche*.] An umbelliferous plant; properly the Smallage (i.e. *Small-Ache*) or Wild Celery (*Apium graveolens*), but loosely applied also to other species of *Apium*, and allied genera, as *parsley*.

c **1300** in Wright *Lyric P.* 26 The primerole he passeth, the parvenke of pris, With alisaundre thare-to, ache ant anys. **1502** ARNOLD *Chron.* 172 Also ete fenel sede corny and ache. **1601** HOLLAND *Pliny* (1634) II. 24 As for the garden Ach, commonly called Parsly, there be many kinds thereof. **1865** *Pop. Sc. Rev.* IV. 199 Celery.. having been formerly called Ache in England which is in fact its true English name.

ache (eɪtʃ), *sb.*[3] Name of the letter H, q.v.

1599 SHAKS. [see quot. under ACHE *sb.*[1]]. **1623** MINSHEU *Span. Gram.* 6, H. This letter.. is called in the Spanish as in the English *Ache.*

ache, obs. form of AGE, and of ASH (tree).

†**aˈcheat, achete**, *v. Obs.* [Intermediate form between ESCHEAT and CHEAT, with A- *pref.* 9 = OFr. *es-*, *e-*.] To escheat, confiscate; do one out of.

c **1430** LYDG. *Bochas* II. xiii. 86 a, The treasour of them and of their line Acheted was. *c* **1440** *Prom. Parv.*, A-chetyn *Confiscor.* **1460** CAPGRAVE *Chron.* 192 The Kyng.. comaunded alle his temporal good to be achetid.

†**aˈcheck**, *v. Obs.* [f. A- *pref.* 11 + CHECK. Only found in *pa. pple.*, so that the prefix may be A- *particle*.] To check, bring to a sudden stop.

c **1384** CHAUCER *Hous of Fame* 2093 And when they metten in that place They wer a-cheked bothe two. [*MS. Bodl.* a-chekid, *Caxt.* a chekked, *Thynne* a checked.]

†**aˈcheer**, *v. Obs.* [f. A- *pref.* 11 + CHEER *v.* See also ENCHEER.] To cheer, to cheer up.

1607 HIERON *Wks.* I. 302 The soule is acheered and inwardly refreshed. **1617** *Ibid.* II. 191 Make vs to know that Thou art pacified towards us.. this one thing shall be able to acheere vs. **1660** A. SADLER *Subject's Joy* 2 She also [to acheer the King] doth.. præsagingly præact his just Inauguration.

acheilary (əˈkaɪlərɪ), *a. Bot.* [f. Gr. ἀ not + χεῖλ-ος lip + -ARY. Better spelt *achilary*.] Wanting the lip of the corolla.

1868 MASTERS *Veg. Teratology* 398 *Acheilary*, proposed.. to apply to the deficiency of the lip in certain Orchidaceæ.

acheilous (əˈkaɪləs), *a. Bot.* [f. Gr. ἀ not + χεῖλ-ος lip + -OUS. Better *achilous*.] Without a lip.

1879 *Syd. Soc. Lex.*

acheke, variant of ACHECK *v. Obs.* to check.

acheke, variant of ACHOKE *v. Obs.* to choke.

acheless (ˈeɪklɪs), *a.* [f. ACHE *sb.* + -LESS.] Without ache or throb.

1880 V. LEE *Belcaro* ii. 26 A vague, acheless pain.

achelor, obs. form of ASHLAR *sb.*

achement, acheament, ach'ment, intermediate forms between ACHIEVEMENT and HATCHMENT.

achene (əˈkiːn). *Bot.* Also **achæne**. [ad. mod.L. *achænium*, an anomalous formation on Gr. ἀ priv. + χαίν-ειν to gape (whence the true adj. form ἀχᾶν-ής not gaping); sometimes spelt *achenium*, and erroneously explained as f. Gr. ἀχήν poor, wanting, ἀχηνία want.] A small dry one-seeded fruit which does not open to liberate the seed.

1845 LINDLEY *Sch. Bot.* i. 18 (1858) The *achænium*.. is small, seedlike, dry. **1855** HENFREY *Sketch of Plants* 15 Ranunculaceæ, the carpels.. ripening into a hard seedlike indehiscent body (achene). **1876** OLIVER *Elem. Bot.* 98 They [the carpels or seeds scattered over the surface of a strawberry] are indehiscent, and therefore wholly agree with the achenes of buttercups. **1960** W. B. R. LAIDLAW *Guide Brit. Hardwoods* i. 19 Winged achenes are termed *samaras*, as in ash or elm.. . The small nutlets of alder and birch are also achenes. **1961** R. W. BUTCHER *Brit. Flora* I. 21 The achene is an indehiscent dry fruit with the single seed loosely enclosed in a dry, horny pericarp.

achenial (əˈkiːnɪəl), *a. Bot.* [f. L. *achæni-um*, see prec. + -AL[1].] Pertaining to an achene.

1881 G. MACLOSKIE in *Nature* XXV. 174 Observations on the achenial awns of *Erodium Moschatum*.

acher (ˈeɪkə(r)). [f. ACHE *v.* + ER[1].] He who, or that which, aches.

a **1845** HOOD *True Story* iii. (1871) 317 And this same tooth pursued their track By adding achers unto achers.

acher, obsolete form of USHER.

‖**Acheron** (ˈækərɒn). [L. *Acheron* a. Gr. Ἀχέρων.] A fabulous river of the Lower World; hence, the infernal regions.

1590 SHAKS. *Mids. N.D.* III. ii. 357 With drooping fogge as blacke as Acheron. **1637** MILTON *Comus* 604 Under the sooty flag of Acheron. **1667** —— *P.L.* II. 578 Sad Acheron of sorrow, black and deep. **1756** BURKE *Subl. & B.* Wks. I. 199 The poisonous exhalation of Acheron is not forgot.

Acherontic (ækəˈrɒntɪk), *a.* [ad. L. *acherontic-us* adj. f. *Acheron, -ontem.*] Of or belonging to Acheron, infernal; hence, dark, gloomy; also, waiting to cross the river of death, tottering on the brink of the grave, moribund.

1600 TOURNEUR *Metamorph.* xviii. 121 To shrowde her safe from Acherontícke mistes. **1621** BURTON *Anat. Mel.* III. iii. IV. ii. (1676) 379/2 An old acherontic dizzard, that hath one foot in the grave. **1860** *All Y. Round* No. 43. 404 At night they [owls] fill these Acherontic woods with demon hooting.

Acherontical (ækəˈrɒntɪkəl), *a. rare*⁻¹. [f. prec. + -AL¹.] Infernal.

1635 PAGITT *Christianogr.* 270 Our Acherontical powder treason for the heinousness thereof will seem incredible in all ages to come.

[**acherset** (Bailey). See CHERSET.]

†**aˈchesoun.** *Obs.* [a. OFr. *acheson, acheison, achaison, -un* occasion, cause, motive:—L. *occāsiōn-em* occasion, n. of action f. *occās-* ppl. stem of *occid-ĕre*, f. *oc-* = *ob-* in the way of + *cad-ĕre* to fall. Very early refashioned in Anglo-Fr. as *anchesoun, enchesoun*, by form-assoc. with words in which *a-* stood for earlier *en-, an-*: see A- *pref.* 10, so that ENCHESOUN, ENCHEASON, became a far more common form in Eng. Also as early as 3 aphetized to CHESOUN.] Occasion, reason, purpose, motive.

c **1330** *Arthour & Merlin* 132 And all he it dede for traisoun, King to be was his achesoun.

c **1230** *Ancren Riwle* 232 Six ancheisuns beoð hwi God.. wiðdrauhð him. **1297** R. GLOUC. 452 Wan ich am enchesun of such pereyl. *a* **1400** *Metr. Hom.* 38 Bot chesoun till him fand scho nan.

Acheulian (əˈʃ(j)uːlɪən), *a. Archæol.* Also **Acheulean**. [ad. F. *acheuléen* (G. de Mortillet 1873, in *Comptes Rendus du Congrès Préhist.* 436), f. the name of Saint-*Acheul* (Somme), France.] Of or belonging to the palæolithic period of Europe succeeding the Chellean, represented by the remains found at Saint-Acheul, near Amiens.

[**1894** DAWSON *Meeting-Place Geol. & Hist.* v. 69 Within the former [*sc.* the palæolithic period] he [Mortillet] believes that it is possible to separate different ages... Respectively the Achulienne, Chellienne, Mousterienne, [etc.].] **1909** in *Cent. Dict.* Suppl. **1921** R. A. S. MACALISTER *Text-Bk. Europ. Archæol.* I. ii. 56 Those [*sc.* terms] of the Lower Palaeolithic are the Pre-Chellean, Chellean, and Acheulean. **1939** *Ann. Reg. 1938* 368 The Swanscombe skull suggests that Acheulean man was not distinguishable morphologically from *Homo sapiens*. **1940** *Oxoniensia* V. 161 Two paleolithic hand-axes of Acheulian type have been discovered.

à cheval: see CHEVAL.

acheve, obs. form of ACHIEVE *v.*

†**achevisaunce.** *Obs.* [a. OFr. *achevis-, acheviss-ance* n. of action f. *achevir, achevissant*, by-form of *achever* to ACHIEVE. *Achevissance* is an early by-form of the more common *achevance*, Eng. ACHIEVANCE; it has also been aphetized to *chevisance*.] Achieving, accomplishment.

c **1430** LYDG. *Minor Poems* (1840) 77 And almesdede shal make achevisaunce, T'exclude by grace the rigour of vengeaunce.

achew, obs. by-form of ESCHEW. See ACHUE.

achievable (əˈtʃiːvəb(ə)l), *a.* [f. ACHIEVE *v.* + -ABLE.] Capable of being achieved.

c **1630** JACKSON *Creed* VII. iv. Wks. VII. 22 Whether the conversion of other metals or materials into gold be acheivable. **1851** H. SPENCER *Soc. Stat.* xxxii. §2 The degree of conformity achievable by one is not the same as that achievable by others.

†**aˈchievance.** *Obs.* Also 6–7 **atchievance.** [a. OFr. *achevance*, n. of action f. *achever* to ACHIEVE. See -ANCE.] Achievement, performance.

1531 ELYOT *Governor* 195 (1580) To them that will read his noble actes and atchieuances. **1599** HAKLUYT *Voy.* II. 26 Of all which his atchevances the sayd K. Richard sent his letters of certificate. **1633** T. N[EWTON] *Lemnie's Touchst. Complex.* 28 Their dexterity for the attainment of any notable atchievance surpasseth.

achieve (əˈtʃiːv), *v.* Forms: 4–6 **acheve**; 4 **achyve**; 5 **acheive, atcheve**; (6 **ascheve**); 6–7 **atchive**; 6–9 **atchieve**; 5– **achieve**. [a. Fr. *acheve-r*, formed from phrase *à chief (venir)*:—late L. *ad caput venire* to come to a head with, to bring to a head, to finish. An aphetic form, common in ME. but now obs., was CHIEVE. Northern writers had also ESCHEVE, with the prefix erroneously refashioned by form-assoc. with words in *a-* for original *es-*, as *achape* for *eschape, escape*.]

I. Of a process: To finish, complete.

1. *trans.* To bring to a successful issue, to carry out successfully (an enterprize); to accomplish, perform.

c **1325** *E.E. Allit. Poems* A. 474 What more-hond moȝte he a-cheue. *c* **1374** CHAUCER *Troylus* v. 785 He that nought nassayeth, nought nacheveth. **1475** CAXTON *Jason* 13 b, Myrro suffrid him tachieue alle his proposition. **1513** MORE *Edw. V*, 3 Appointed to atchieve a more abominable enterprise. **1587** HOLINSHED *Chron.* III. 808/1 Thus began the iusts, which was valiantlie atchiued by the king. **1664** H. MORE *Myst. Iniq.* 336 The strange Feats they say Antichrist is then to atchieve. **1725** POPE *Odyss.* I. 99 Let all combine to achieve his wish'd return. **1815** SOUTHEY *Roderick* XIX. 96 Much might Count Julian's sword achieve for Spain. **1853** C. BRONTE *Villette* xix. 188 (1876) He was achieving, amongst a very wretched population, a world of active good.

2. *absol.*

1607 SHAKS. *Coriol.* IV. vii. 23 [He] does atcheeue as soone As draw his sword. **1713** STEELE *Guardian* No. 13 ¶5 This youth has a mind prepared to achieve for the salvation of souls.

†**3.** *trans.* To bring to an end or termination; to finish, to terminate. *Obs.*

c **1385** CHAUCER *Leg. G. Wom.* 2111 For tacheve myn batayle I wolde nevere from this place fle. *c* **1400** *Rom. Rose* 4630 How is this quarelle yit acheved Of Loves side? *Ibid.* 1068 And yvel achyved mote they be, These losenger ful of envye! **1534** LD. BERNERS *Boke of M. Aurelius* B (1546) All these thynges tyme acheueth and burieth. **1599** SHAKS. *Hen. V*, IV. iii. 91 Bid them atchieue me, and then sell my bones.

†**4.** *intr.* To come to a natural end or conclusion; to end, result, turn out. *Obs.*

1393 GOWER *Conf.* III. 81 For it shall never well acheve, That stont nought right with the beleve. *a* **1440** *Sir Degrevant* 464 He shalle love that swet wyȝt, Acheve how hit wold. **1523** LD. BERNERS *Froissart* I. cccl xxvi. 626 Wherfore all your busynes shall acheue the better. **1534** —— *Boke of M. Aurelius* D d viii b (1546) Thei [gods] bee called immortall.. and we be called mortall.. thus acheuethe the persones: but the goddis neuer.

II. Of an end: To attain, gain.

5. *trans.* To succeed in gaining, to acquire by effort, to gain, win.

a. An abstract property or possession.

1393 GOWER *Conf.* II. 10 All though thou mightest love acheve. **1523** LD. BERNERS *Froissart* I. cxxxvi. 164 He achyued suche grace among them there, that, etc. **1601** SHAKS. *Twel. N.* v. i. 378 Some are borne great, some atchieue greatnesse. **1674** MILTON *P.L.* XI. 792 Having spilt much blood.. and achieved thereby Fame in the world. **1833** HT. MARTINEAU *Berkeley* I. vii. 151 Now is the time for you and me to try to achieve a truer independence. **1874** BLACK *Pr. Thule* 35 He had achieved a good reputation.

†**b.** A material acquisition. *Obs.*

1393 GOWER *Conf.* III. 170 Whan that he wenith best acheve His gode world, it is most fro. **1555** *Fardle of Facions* App. 315 What time then ye shall haue achieued the land of Chanaan. **1604** SHAKS. *Oth.* II. i. 61 He hath atchieu'd a Maid That paragons description. **1618** BOLTON *Florus* (1636) 325 Provinces are atchieved by the sword, but retayned by Iustice.

†**6.** *intr.* To arrive or attain successfully (*to* a point or position). *Obs.*

1495 CAXTON *Vitas Patrum* (W. de Worde) I. xlvii. 84 b, That this begynnynge maye achyeue fro good to better. **1553–87** FOXE *A. & M.* 17/1 (1596) By the means whereof, the archbishops of the Romish see haue atchiued to their great kingdome.

7. *trans.* To attain successfully, to reach (an end).

a **1569** KYNGESMILL *Man's Estate* xi. (1580) 77 By these means, in some hath he atchived the ende of his message. **1684** R. WALLER *Ess. Nat. Exper.* 70 Whether she Atchieves her End by Contracting, or Rarefying the Fluid. **1794** SULLIVAN *View of Nat.* I. 255 These able men strove to attain the same great end, and separately atchieved it. **1882** *Daily News* 17 July 4/6 Even though to achieve its [the policy's] necessary ends, it should lead to invasion and war.

8. [See OVER-ACHIEVER, UNDER-ACHIEVER.] *intr.* To be successful in attaining one's (educational) goals. See ACHIEVER b.

1953 [see OVER-ACHIEVER]. **1958** *School & Society* 7 June 269/2 To achieve requires considerable effort, but a child must learn.. pleasure in what one is doing. **1962** *Educ. Leadership* Oct. 15/2 They achieve in school by holding offices, being popular, and.. leading the crowd in materialistic displays. **1980** *Church Times* 11 July 4/3 He believed that there were intelligent people in the parish who had not achieved academically. **1984** *Ibid.* 31 Aug. 9/4 A report commissioned by the Inner London Education Authority concluded that the main ingredient of achievement was the desire to achieve.

achieved (əˈtʃiːvd), *ppl. a.* [f. prec. + -ED.] Completed, accomplished; attained, won.

1474 CAXTON *Chesse* 39 Goten and achyeued by force of money. **1648** COTTRELL tr. *Davila, Hist. France* 23 (1678) Their newly atchieved greatness. **1805** S. TURNER *Anglo-Saxons* I. vi. 81 (1828) The '*adjectis Britannis imperio*' of Horace is rather a poetical figure than an achieved fact.

achievement (əˈtʃiːvmənt). Also 6–9 **atchievement**, and see sense 3. [a. Fr. *achèvement* a finishing, completing, n. of action, f. *achever*. See ACHIEVE.]

1. The action of achieving, completing, or attaining by exertion; completion, accomplishment, successful performance.

1475 CAXTON *Jason* 110 b, With thachieuement of these deuises the king Oetes approched. *c* **1585** *Faire Em* I. 69 The bliss That hangs on quick achievement of my love. **1638** KNOLLES *Hist. Turkes* 182 (ed. 5) He would vndertake the atchieuement of that exployt. **1815** SOUTHEY *Roderick* IX. 19 So it be lawful, and within the bounds of possible atchievement. **1878** B. TAYLOR *Pr. Deukalion* I. vi. 46 What virtue lies More in achievement than its hot desire?

2. Anything achieved, accomplished, or won by exertion; a feat, a distinguished and successful action, a victory.

1593 R. HARVEY *Philad.* 106 Spending the might of it [the flesh] in contemplatiue assaults and atchiuements. **1602** WARNER *Albion's Eng.* XI. lxviii. 289 We intreate of great Achiuements done By English, in contrarie Clymes. **1678** JORDAN *Lond. Triumph.* in Heath *Grocer's Comp.* (1869) 522 You might see an hundred persons confusedly scrambling in the dirt for the frail atchievement of a bunch of raisins. **1794** SULLIVAN *View Nat.* II. 367 The many and great atchievements attributed to heroes of the first ages. **1824** DIBDIN *Libr. Comp.* 161 The achievements of Agincourt and Waterloo. **1855** BREWSTER *Newton* II. xxvii. 398 The achievements of genius, like the source from which they spring, are indestructible.

3. *Her.* An escutcheon or ensign armorial, granted in memory of some achievement, or distinguished feat. (In this sense variously contracted or corrupted to **atcheament, achement, atch'ment, ach'ment, achment, hachement, hatchment.**)

1548 HALL *Chronicle, Henry V*, 50 The Hachementes wer borne onely by capitaynes. **1586** FERNE *Blazon of Gentrie* 186 The creast, tymber, mantell, or worde, bee no part of the coat-armour; they be addicions called atcheaments. **1610** GWILLIM *Displ. Heraldry* VI. v. 394 An Atchievement, according to Leigh, is the Arms of every Gentleman, well marshalled with the supporters, Helmet, Wreath and Crests, etc. **1750** GRAY *Let.* in *Poems* (1775) 214 To raise the cieling's fretted height, Each pannel in achievements cloathing. **1809** W. TAYLOR in Robberds' *Memoir* II. 283 Let no motto be written upon its ach'ment but *Resurgam*. **1868** STANLEY *Westm. Abb.* iv. 201 Graves, piled with the standards and achievements of the noble families of Florence.

4. *Psychol.* Chiefly *U.S.* Performance in a standardized test (***achievement test***) or tests. So ***achievement age, quotient*** (abbrev. *A.Q.*): see quot. 1921.

1921 *Univ. Illin. Bur. Educ. Res. Bull.* VI. 5 Medians are the mental age norms, which are used as a basis for translating the point scores into achievement ages. *Ibid.*, Provision is made for comparing a pupil's achievement score ..with the norm corresponding to his mental age by dividing his achievement age by the standard score for his mental age. This quotient is called the Achievement Quotient. *Ibid.*, The plan consists of establishing for the achievement tests mental age norms which are used to supplement the usual grade norms. **1934** WARREN *Dict. Psychol.* 1/1 *AQ*, abbrev. for accomplishment (or achievement) quotient. **1957** *Encycl. Brit.* XVIII. 673/2 Tests of proficiencies, also called achievement tests, are intended to measure outcomes of systematic education and training in school or occupation toward a conventionally accepted pattern of skill or knowledge... Several subject tests may be combined into an achievement battery for measuring general school proficiency either in point scores or 'achievement ages' and perhaps 'accomplishment quotients' (AA/CA).

achiever (əˈtʃiːvə(r)). Also 6–8 **atchiever.** [f. ACHIEVE + -ER¹.] **a.** One who achieves; an accomplisher, or winner.

1594 J. KING *Jonah* (1864) 301 That notable achiever of the victories of God. **1599** SHAKS. *Much Ado* I. i. 8 A victorie is twice it selfe, when the atchieuer brings home full numbers. **1661** SYLV. MORGAN *Sph. Gentry* III. iv. 36 There was nothing which was gained by armes, but was born in armes and did carry a proportion to the Atchiever. **1860** FROUDE *Hist. Eng.* V. xxiv. 3 He saw.. himself as the achiever of the triumph.

b. One who is motivated and successful in the attainment of (educational) goals; also in extended use outside education. Cf. OVER-ACHIEVER, UNDER-ACHIEVER.

1960 *Jrnl. Educ. Res.* Jan. 172/2 Achiever was defined as a student in the top or first quartile of his class. **1962** M. ARGYLE in *Listener* 11 Jan. 62/2 Higher standards and stronger demands were made by the parents of achievers. **1970** I. L. HOROWITZ *Masses in Lat. Amer.* i. 3 Those who study development.. naturally tend to celebrate 'achievers' and denigrate 'ascribers'. **1983** *Fortune* 2 May 292/2 Achievers constitute the second-largest contingent... They are 'diverse, gifted, hard-working.. people who have built "the system" and are now at the helm'.

achieving (əˈtʃiːvɪŋ), *vbl. sb.* Also **achevyng, achiving, atchieving.** [f. ACHIEVE + -ING¹.] A completing, accomplishing or successful performing. (Now mostly gerundial.)

1539 TAUERNER *Prouerbes* (1552) 25 One daye or lytel tyme is not ynoughe for the acheuynge of a greate matter. **1625** BACON *Ess.* xxxix. (1862) 162 For the Atchieving of a desperate Conspiracie, a Man should not rest upon the Fiercenesse of any mans Nature.

achill (əˈtʃɪl), *adv.* and *pred. a.* prop. *phrase.* [A- *prep.*¹ + CHILL.] In a state of chill; chilly.

1870 MORRIS *Earthly Par.* III. IV. 391 Had the flowers shrunk, the warm breeze grown a-chill?

achillea (ækɪˈliːə, əˈkɪlɪə). *Bot.* Also **Achillea.** [a. L. *achillēa, achillēos* (Pliny), f. Gr. Ἀχίλλειος plant supposed to have been used medicinally by Achilles, f. Ἀχιλλεύς Achilles.] A plant of the genus of this name (family Compositæ), which comprises hardy perennial, usually aromatic plants with flower-heads usually in corymbs; *spec.* a common garden flower, *A. filipendulina*, having large, convex clusters of bright yellow flower-heads on tall, stiff stems. Cf. MILFOIL, SNEEZEWORT, YARROW *sb.*

[**1546**: see YARROW *sb.*] **1597** J. GERARDE *Herball* 916 This plant *Achillea* is thought to be the very same, wherewith *Achilles* cured the wounds of his soldiers. **1785** T. MARTIN tr. *Rousseau's Lett. Elem. Bot.* 400 Achillea or Milfoil has an oblong-ovate imbricate calyx. **1908** G. JEKYLL *Colour in Flower Garden* viii. 72 Groups of the clear white Achillea, The Pearl, and the round purple heads of Globe Thistle. **1955** A. G. L. HELLYER *Flowers in Colour* 11 Achilleas may be roughly divided into two groups, the taller kinds most suitable for herbaceous borders, and the dwarf and spreading kinds for rock gardens or walls. **1979** J. TAYLOR in I. Webb *Compl. Guide Flower Arrangement* xiii. 190 Orange and blue are complementary colours but the green foliage and the yellow achillea prevent it from being a direct complementary.

Achillean (ˌækɪˈliːən), *a.* [f. *Achille-s* prop. name of a Grecian hero + -AN.] Resembling Achilles; invulnerable, invincible.

1637 GILLESPIE *Eng. Popish Cer.* C 3 We are not well advised to enter into combate with such Achillean strength. **1849** W. FITZGERALD tr. *Whitaker, Disputation* 276 How well this reason deserves to be considered Achillean, will appear hereafter.

Achilles' heel, see HEEL *sb.*[1]

Achilles' tendon. = TENDON *of Achilles.*

1900 DORLAND *Med. Dict.* 674/2

†**Achillize**, *v. Obs. rare.* [f. *Achill-es*, see ACHILLEAN *a.* (cf. *to hector*) + -IZE, as in Gr. ποιητίζ-ειν to play the poet, and Eng. *tyrannize.*] To play Achilles with, to chase as Achilles did the Trojans.

1672 MARVELL *Rehearsal Transp.* I. 217 He Hectors and Achillizes all the Nonconformists. **1673** *Transpr. Rehears'd* 20 You would expect that he had Hector'd and Achilliz'd 'em all out of the pit.

achilous (əˈkaɪləs), *a. Bot.* [The same as ACHEILOUS, of which it is the more analogical spelling, Gr. -ει becoming in L. -ī and Eng. -*i*.] Without lips.

achime (əˈtʃaɪm), *adv.* and *pred. a.* prop. *phrase.* [A *prep.*[1] of state + CHIME.] Chiming, ringing.

1860 RUSKIN *Mod. Painters* V. VI. x. §18. 100 A little belfry of grain-bells, all a-chime.

aching (ˈeɪkɪŋ), *vbl. sb.* Forms: 2–4 **akyng**, 5–8 **aking**, 7–9 **aching**. [f. ACHE *v.* + -ING[1].] A painful throbbing; a feeling of continued pain.

c **1374** CHAUCER *Troylus* I. 1088 A man that hurt is sore, And is sumdel of akyng of his wound. **1398** TREVISA *Barth. De P.R.* (1495) XVII. clxxxv. 726 A dronklew mann feleth.. aking in his heed. **1580** HOLLYBAND *Treas. Fr. Tong.*, The aking of ones fingers endes with very cold. *c* **1690** SOUTH 12 *Serm.* II. 42 Painful Girds and Achings, which are at least called the Gout. **1842** WORDSWORTH *Borderers* IV. Wks. 1849 VI. 323 'Tis a strange aching that, when we would curse And cannot.

aching (ˈeɪkɪŋ), *ppl. a.* Forms: 3 **akende, ekinde**; 5–6 **akynge**; 6–8 **aking**; 8– **aching.** [f. ACHE *v.* + -ING[2].] Having the sensation of continuous or ever-recurring pain, throbbing painfully.

c **1230** *Ancren Riwle* 360 So sor ekinde heaued. **1398** TREVISA *Barth. De P.R.* (1495) V. xix. 124 Yf the mouth be reed.. and hote and akynge and brennynge. **1606** SHAKS. *Tr. & Cr.* V. x. 35 A goodly medcine for mine aking bones. **1702** ROWE *Tamerlane* II. i. 961 My aking sight hangs on thy parting beauties. **1870** MORRIS *Earthly Par.* I. I. 385 Yet is there in mine heart an aching pain.

†**b.** *fig.* in phr. ***an aching tooth.*** *Obs.*

1552 HULOET *Abcedarium*, Akynge tothe, *Rabidus dens.* **1674** W. ALLEN *Dang. Enthus.* 83 One would think you have an aking Tooth against outward teaching. **1721** SOUTHERNE *Maid's last prayer* II. I. i. 17 Thou hast such an aking tooth after that maidenhead of hers.

achingly (ˈeɪkɪŋlɪ), *adv.* [f. prec. + -LY[2].] In an abidingly painful manner; painfully.

1873 MISS BROUGHTON *Nancy* III. 216 My eyes—dry now, achingly dry—flashing a wretched hostility back into his. **1881** COXON *Basil Plant.* II. 106 He wanted it, craved for it acheingly.

‖**achi'ote, a'chote.** [Sp. *achiote*, ad. native Amer. *achiotl.*] A native name for the seeds of the Arnotto or Arnatto (*Bixa orellana*), and the red colouring matter obtained from their pulp.

1796 MRS. GLASSE *Cookery* xxi. 342 As much achiote as will make it the colour of brick. **1866** *Treas. Bot.* 10 Achote, the seeds of the Arnotto.

achiral (eɪˈkaɪərəl), *a. Chem.* [f. A- 14 + CHIRAL *a.*] Of a crystal or three-dimensional form: not chiral.

1966 *Angewandte Chem.* (Internat. ed.) V. 408/1 The trimethylene dihalide has two achiral forms and two enantiomeric pairs. **1971** *Sci. Amer.* July 120/1 The molecules of sodium chlorate are achiral but the crystal is chiral. **1983** *Jrnl. Org. Chem.* XLVIII. 3762/1 A three-step construction of optically active tetronic acids and butenolides from achiral allylic alcohols.

Hence **achi'rality**, the state or property of being achiral.

1983 WILLEM & BROCAS in J. Maruani *Symmetries & Properties Non-Rigid Molecules* 389 (*heading*) The relation between the double coset structures and the chirality or achirality of chemical pathways of degenerate rearrangements.

achirite (ˈækɪraɪt). *Min.* [See quot.] A synonym of DIOPTASE.

1837–80 DANA *Min.* 402 Named Achirite after Achir Mahméd, a Bucharian merchant.. who furnished the specimens that were taken in 1785.. to St. Petersburg.

achison, acheson (Scotch coin). See ATCHISON.

achkan (ˈætʃkən). Also **atchkan.** [Hindi *ackan.*] A long coat worn by men in India.

1911 *Encycl. Brit.* XIV. 419/1 Garments for outdoor wear are the.. *achkan* or *sherwāni*... The *achkan*.. is buttoned straight down the front. Both *angā* and *achkan* reach to a little below the knee. **1939** M. R. GODDEN *Black Narcissus* v. 52 He was plainly dressed in a dove-coloured achkan and white cotton pantaloons like jodhpurs. **1954** J. MASTERS *Bhowani Junct.* iii. 28 A chuprassi in a scarlet achkan. **1959** *20th Cent.* June 602 An old man in a plain atchkan... This was Jawaharlal Nehru.

achlamydate (əˈklæmɪdət), *a. Zool.* [f. Gr. ἀ not + χλαμύδ-α (χλαμύς) cloak, mantle + -ATE[2].] Of certain Molluscs: Having no mantle.

1877 HUXLEY *Anat. Inv. An.* viii. 510 In the achlamydate forms true gills are usually absent.

achlamydeous (æklәˈmɪdiːəs), *a. Bot.* [mod. f. Gr. ἀ priv. + χλαμύδ-α cloak + -EOUS.] Having no floral envelope; destitute of apparent calyx and corolla. Applied to a division of Exogens, named by De Candolle *Achlamydeæ.*

1830 LINDLEY *Nat. Syst. Bot.* Introd. 24 Its absence [that of the Calyx] implies the absence of the corolla also.. By its absence all the orders called Achlamydeous are characterised. **1876** OLIVER *Elem. Bot.* 40 Having therefore no envelope to the essential organs, they [the willow flowers] are called achlamydeous.

achlorhydria (æklɔəˈhaɪdrɪə, eɪ-). *Path.* [mod.L., f. Gr. ἀ- priv. + *chlorhydr(ic* (CHLOR-[2]) + -IA.] Lack of hydrochloric acid in the gastric secretions.

1898 *Allbutt's Syst. Med.* V. 529 The secretion is deficient in hydrochloric acid, in many cases it may be actually wanting (achlorhydria). **1907** *Practitioner* Apr. 558 Both the achlorhydria and the neoplastic process might have a common basis in an alteration of the alkalinity of the tissue fluids. **1930** *Q. Jrnl. Med.* XXIII. 175 Bennett proved that a secretion of hydrochloric acid could be evoked in many cases of apparent achlorhydria.

achma, achme, obs. forms of ACME.

achmatite (ˈækmətaɪt). *Min.* [See quot.]

1837–80 DANA *Min.* 282 Achmatite is ordinary Epidote, in crystals, from Achmatovsk, Ural.

achmit, variant of ACMITE.

†**a'choke,** *v. Obs.* Forms: 1 **aceocian,** 2 **acheke(n,** 4 **achoke(n.** [f. A- *pref.* 1 + CHOKE:—? OE. *ceocian.*] To choke, to suffocate.

c **1200** *Trin. Coll. Hom.* 181 Adam þar-offe bot, and wearð þar mide acheked . and þureh þat one snede wearð al his ofspring acheked. *c* **1374** CHAUCER *Boethius* 47 3if þou wilt achoken þe fulfillyng of nature wiþ superfluites. *c* **1385** —— *Leg. Good W.* 2004 Whan that Theseus seeth The beest acheked, he shall on him leepe.

Acholi (əˈtʃəʊlɪ), *sb.* and *a.* Also 9 **Shooli, Shuli.** [Native name.] **A.** *sb.* (A member of) a farming and pastoral people of northern Uganda; the Nilotic language of this people. **B.** *adj.* Of or pertaining to the Acholi or their language.

1874 S. W. BAKER *Ismailïa* II. iii. 94 Abou Saood.. had told the Shooli natives to attack me. *Ibid.* xii. 435 The chase supplies the great tribe of Shooli with clothing. **1888** MRS. R. W. FELKIN tr. *E. Schnitzer's Emin Pasha in Central Afr.* I. vi. 106 So early as Baker's time, Rocháma (Rot Yarma) was chief of all the Shuli. **1902** *Rep. on Protectorate of Uganda* 24 in *Parl. Papers* (Cd. 671) XLVIII. 569 The political organization of various native States.. has been carried out.. amongst the Masai of the Mau district,.. and to some extent.. the Acholi,.. and Bankole. **1902** *Encycl. Brit.* XXXIII. 541/2 The languages spoken in the Uganda Protectorate belong to the following stocks:—.. III. *Nilotic* (Acholi, Aluru, Jaluo, &c.). **1936** *Uganda Jrnl.* III. 175 (*heading*) Some notes on Acholi religious ceremonies. **1948** *Ibid.* XII. 82 The name by which the people are known is Acholi, originally written Shuli: but in the country itself they are called Ganyi, and the language is called Luganyi. **1964** C. WILLOCK *Enormous Zoo* i. 18 Justin's wife was about to have another baby. She called it Lyec, the Acholi for elephant. **1977** *Time* 7 Mar. 16/3 Amin [*sc.* President of Uganda] was determined to annihilate two tribes, the Acholi and the Langi, both of which are predominantly Christian. **1984** *N.Y. Times* 8 Aug. A1/1 Most army members are from the Langi and Acholi tribes, which support Mr. Obote.

acholia (æˈkɒlɪə, eɪ-). *Path.* [See ACHOLOUS *a.*; -IA.] A deficiency or an absence of bile. (In quot. 1903 *spec.* = cœliac disease.) Hence **a'cholic** *a.* = ACHOLOUS *a.*

1848 DUNGLISON *Dict. Med. Sci.* (ed. 7) 19/1. **1864** W. AITKEN *Pract. Med.* (ed. 3) II. 813 Occasionally death occurs under symptoms of acholia. **1893** *Funk's Stand. Dict.*, Acholic. **1903** W. B. CHEADLE in *Lancet* 30 May 1497/1 An affection of the digestive tract.. is that condition which I have ventured to term 'acholia'... Acholia is specially characterised, as the name implies, by the absence of bile. *Ibid.* 1497/2 Acholic stools occur usually in children under five years of age. **1963** E. D. PALMER *Clinical Gastroenterology* (ed. 2) xvii. 580/2 After the common duct has been obstructed for some time, acholia, or failure of bile production, may result.

acholithite, acholite, obs. forms of ACOLOUTHITE, ACOLYTE.

acholous (ˈækələs), *a.* [f. Gr. ἄχολ-ος lacking bile + -OUS.] Deficient in or without bile.

c **1850** WHEWELL quoted in Mozley *Miracles* ii. 232 The untrue, Aristotelian fact of the longevity of acholous animals.

acholuria (ækəˈl(j)ʊərɪə). *Path.* [mod.L., f. Gr. ἄχολ-ος lacking bile + -URIA.] Absence of bile pigment in the urine. Hence **acho'luric** *a.*, characterized by acholuria.

1902 *Lancet* 20 Dec. 1708/2 (*title*) Acholuric icterus. We are indebted entirely to French clinicians for the description of *ictère acholurique*—chronic jaundice of slight degree (subicterus) in which there is no bile in the urine. **1905** GOULD *Dict. New Med. Terms* 23/2 Acholuria. **1910** *Lancet* 22 Jan. 254/2 Four cases of congenital acholuric jaundice.. in one family are recorded. **1930** *Q. Jrnl. Med.* XXIII. 222 Panton and Valentine describe one severe case of acholuric family jaundice which did not respond to whole liver.

achondrite (æˈkɒndraɪt). *Min.* [f. A- 14 + CHONDRITE 2.] A meteorite containing no chondrules.

1904 *Proc. Amer. Philos. Soc.* XLIII. 232 *Achondrites.* Stones poor in Nickel-iron, essentially without round chondrules. **1944** C. PALACHE et al. *Dana's Syst. Min.* I. 121 The stony meteorites without chondri, named *achrondrites*, show porphyritic, ophitic, and granular textures resembling those found in some terrestrial rocks. **1957** *Encycl. Brit.* XV. 338/1 The comparatively few chondrule-free stone meteorites are called achondrites.

achondroplasia (æˌkɒndrəʊˈpleɪzɪə, eɪ-). *Path.* [mod.L., f. Gr. ἄχονδρο-ς without cartilage + πλάσ-ις moulding, conformation + -IA[1].] Abnormal formation of cartilage resulting in a form of dwarfism. Hence **achondro'plasiac,** one affected with this condition; also **achondro'plasiac, achondro'plasic, achondro'plastic** (prevailing form) *adjs.*, of, or affected with, achondroplasia.

[**1890** BILLINGS *Med. Dict.* I. 14/2 *Achondroplasie*, (F.). Want of normal cartilage development.] **1893** DUNGLISON *Dict. Med. Sci.* (ed. 21) 10/2 *Achondroplasia*, imperfect formation or development of cartilage. **1897** *Allbutt's Syst. Med.* III. 124 *Achondroplasia*, fœtal cretinism.. characterised chiefly by extreme and abnormal shortness of the long bones of the limbs. **1902** *Lancet* 5 Apr. 982/1 Achondroplasic workers in metal are represented on the Egyptian monuments, a circumstance which is interesting in connexion with the lameness and deformity of Hephaistos or Vulcan in classical mythology. **1906** *Lancet* 9 June 1598/1 An achondroplasiac dwarf. **1913** DORLAND *Med. Dict.* (ed. 7) 24/1 *Achondroplastic*, pertaining to or affected with achondroplasia. **1919** [see DWARFISM]. **1934** *Nature* 5 May 691/1 The dwarfism.. is not rachitic but achondroplastic. Five, and probably all six, of the representations of dwarfs at Amarna exhibit the inward turning feet due to talipes. **1951** *Lancet* 30 June 1418/1 (*heading*) Struts for Achondroplasiacs. Have you ever wondered what it would be like to be an achondroplastic dwarf?

†**achoose,** *v. Obs.* Forms as in CHOOSE. [f. A- *pref.* 1 + CHOOSE, OE. *ceósan.*] To choose out.

c **1150** *Cott. Hom.* 229 þa seðða aceas he him leorning-chnihtes, erest twelf, þa we hatað apostles.

‖**achor** (ˈeɪkɔː(r)). *Med.* [L. *achor*, Gr. ἀχώρ scald, scurf.] A scaly eruption in the hairy scalp, constituting the disease scald-head.

1585 H. LLOYD *Treas. Health* B iij, The Pustules called Achores or Tineae be engendred of a humore. **1678** PHILLIPS, *Achor*, a disease possessing the hairy scalp or musculous skin of the head, and eating therein like a moth; it is commonly called in English, the Scald. **1835** HOBLYN *Dict. Med. Terms, Achor*, a small acuminated pustule, which contains a straw coloured matter, and is succeeded by a thin brown or yellowish scab.

achorn(e, obs. form of ACORN.

†**a-christism.** ? *nonce-wd.* [f. Gr. ἀ priv. + χριστ-ός Christ; after *atheism.*] Disbelief in Christ.

1726 M. HENRY *Wks.* 1835 II. 722 But what do you think of such a thing as a-Christism?

achroite (ˈækrəʊaɪt). *Min.* [f. Gr. ἄχρο-ος colourless + -ITE min. formative.] 'Colorless tourmaline from Elba.' Dana.

achromat (ˈækrəʊmæt). [a. G. *achromat* (O. Lummer 1897, in *Zeitschr. f. Instrumentenkunde* Aug. 228), f. *achromatisch* ACHROMATIC *a.*] An achromatic lens. Also ***achromat lens.***

1900 S. P. THOMPSON tr. *O. Lummer's Contrib. Photogr. Optics* vii. 41 These two-lens combinations corrected in this sense achromatically and spherically we shall henceforth call achromats. **1902** BOLAS & BROWN *Lens* vii. 71 A 'new achromat'—to use again the designation of Professor Silvanus Thompson for a lens in which the positive member consists of glass of higher refraction with lower dispersion—has its cemented surface positive or converging. **1942** J. MITCHELL *Ilford Man. Photogr.* i. 20 The maximum aperture at which a single achromat can be used is about *f*/14. **1977** *Nature* 23 June 738/1 The flat-field objectives, both achromats and apochromats, are completely new designs, giving improved colour corrections over the widest 25 mm field of view. **1982** *N.Y. Times* 4 July II. 24/6 There are two types of telescopes suited to this kind of photography: refractors which use a two-element achromat lens, and reflectors, utilizing a highly polished precision ground mirror.

achromatic (ˌækrəʊˈmætɪk), *a.* [f. Gr. ἀχρώματ-ος colourless (f. ἀ priv. + χρῶματ- colour) + -IC.]

1. *Optics.* Free from colour; not showing colour from the decomposition of light in passing through a refracting medium; as an achromatic lens or telescope. (Sometimes used substantively by ellipsis of 'lens,' as 'a four-inch achromatic.')

1766 MATY (tr. from Fr.) in *Phil. Trans.* LVI. 57, I likewise made use of a very good achromatic telescope. **1784** HERSCHEL in *Phil. Trans.* LXXV. 44 One of Mr. Dollond's best 3½ feet achromatics. **1805** *Edin. Rev.* Apr. 34 The fact, that the eye is achromatic, cannot be doubted. **1831** BREWSTER *Optics* ix. §67. 83 They..will refract white light to a single focus free of colour. Such a lens is called achromatic. **1848** QUEKETT *Microscope* (1855) 37 In 1747.. Euler suggested the construction of achromatic object-glasses. **1859** PARKINSON *Optics* ix. 154 A combination of prisms or lenses is said to be achromatic when the dispersion of the pencils of light refracted through them is reduced within the narrowest possible limits. **1869** TYNDALL *Lect. on Light* 42 The human eye is not achromatic. It suffers from chromatic aberration. **1878** NEWCOMB *Pop. Astron.* II. i. 125 An achromatic of four inches aperture was then considered of extraordinary size.

2. *Biol.* Of tissue: Uncoloured, not absorbing colour from a fluid. See ACHROMATIN.

1882 J. T. CUNNINGHAM in *Jrnl. Microsc. Sc.* Jan. 41, Figs. 30 and 31, from the cranial cartilage of a toad, show the achromatic striæ more clearly.

achromatically (ˌækrəʊˈmætɪkəlɪ), *adv.* [f. prec. + -AL[1] + -LY[2].] In an achromatic manner; so as to produce freedom from colour.

1881 *Edin. Rev.* 540 The eye does not deal achromatically with the coloured constituents of light.

achromaticity (əˌkrəʊməˈtɪsɪtɪ). [f. ACHROMATIC + -ITY.] The quality of being achromatic; = ACHROMATISM.

1845 *Encycl. Metrop.* IV. 423 s.v. *Light*, The order in which they [lenses] are placed is of no consequence as far as Achromaticity is concerned. **1860** SIR J. HERSCHEL in *Encycl. Brit.* s.v. *Telescope*, This condition..furnishes the 'equation of achromaticity' of an eye-piece. **1876** WEBB in *Chambers' Astron.* 745 Errors due to the imperfect achromaticity of the object-glass.

achromatin (əˈkrəʊmətɪn). *Biol.* [f. Gr. ἀχρώματ-ος uncoloured + -IN, repr. Gr. -ινη female descendant, hence, derivative.] Tissue which is not stained by colouring matter when immersed in it.

1882 J. T. CUNNINGHAM in *Jrnl. Microsc. Sc.* Jan., 37 Flemming concludes from this that the nucleus is composed of two substances, of which one is stained by dyes, the other not, and he accordingly calls the former chromatin, the latter achromatin. **1882** GILBURT in *Jrnl. Quek. Cl.* Ser. II. No. I. 33 The two daughter nuclei now approach each other somewhat, the achromatin bulging out between them.

achromatism (əˈkrəʊmətɪz(ə)m). [mod. f. Gr. ἀχρώματ-ος uncoloured + -ISM.] The state or quality of being achromatic, or of transmitting only white light.

1797 *Encycl. Brit.* s.v. *Telescope*, Mr. Dollond was anxious to combine this achromatism of the eye-pieces with the advantages which he had found in the eye-pieces with five glasses. **1859** PARKINSON *Optics* ix. 167 The conditions of achromatism depend only on the focal lengths of the component lenses. **1881** G. R. PIGGOTT in *Nature* No. 622. 515 Achromatism is seldom attained without generating a whitish haze, the inevitable accompaniment of residuary spherical aberration.

achromaˈtistous, *a. rare.* [f. mod. Fr. *achromatiste* (see ACHROMATISM) + -OUS.] Colourless; achromatic.

1879 *Syd. Soc. Lex.*

achromatization (əˌkrəʊmətaɪˈzeɪʃən). [f. ACHROMATIZE + -ATION.] The action or process of achromatizing, or rendering achromatic.

achromatize (əˈkrəʊmətaɪz), *v.* [mod. f. Gr. ἀχρώματ-ος colourless + -IZE.] To deprive of colour; to render achromatic.

1845 *Encycl. Metrop.* IV. 423 s.v. *Light*, If we can achromatise each elementary prism, the whole system is achromatic. **1848** QUEKETT *Microscope* (1855) 38 In 1784 Æpinus made many fruitless trials to achromatize the microscope. **1872** EVERETT tr. *Deschanel's Nat. Phil.*, Two prisms..will achromatize one another if..the product of deviation by dispersive power is the same for both.

achromatized (əˈkrəʊmətaɪzd), *ppl. a.* [f. prec. + -ED.] Rendered achromatic.

1871 SIR J. HERSCHEL *Fam. Lect. on Sc.* 135 Looking at the comet through an achromatized doubly refracting prism.

achromatopsia (əkrəʊməˈtɒpsɪə). *Med.* Also 9 achromatopsy. [Mod.L., f. Gr. ἀχρωματ-ος without colour + -οψία seeing f. ὄψις sight.] Inability to distinguish colours; colour-blindness.

1849–52 TODD *Cycl. Anat. & Phys.* IV. 1452/2 Achromatopsy, or insensibility of the eye to colours, is an affection which has been recognised nearly two hundred years. **1853** R. G. MAYNE *Expos. Lex. Med. Sci.* (1860) 12/1 *Achromatopsia*, a faulty term intended to indicate inability to distinguish colours, but really meaning incapability of seeing them at all: achromatopsy. **1907** J. H. PARSONS *Dis. Eye* xx. 421 Colour Blindness or Achromatopsia may be congenital or acquired. **1932** S. DUKE-ELDER *Text-bk. Ophthalmol.* I. xxv. 982 Achromatopsia falls into a completely different category from dichromatic vision. **1978** *Nature* 28 Sept. 347/2 Any investigator who obtained access to..more than one case of cortical blindness or achromatopsia in a lifetime would count himself lucky indeed.

achromatopsy: see ACHROMATOPSIA.

†**aˈchromic**, *a. Obs.* [same deriv. as ACHROMATIC, but improperly formed.] = ACHROMATIC (of which it seems to have been the earlier form).

1761 SHORT in *Phil. Trans.* LII. 179 Reflector of 2 feet focus, with an achromic object-glass micrometer of 40 feet focus.

aˈchromous, *a. rare.* [same deriv. and formation.] Colourless; without colouring matter.

1879 *Syd. Soc. Lex.*

achromycin (ækrəʊˈmaɪsɪn). *Pharm.* [f. Gr. ἄχρο-ος (see ACHROOUS *a.*), from an absence of pigmentation + -MYCIN.] †**a.** = PUROMYCIN. *Obs. rare.*

1952 J. N. PORTER et al. in *Antibiotics & Chemotherapy* II. 409 A new species of actinomycete, *Streptomyces albo-niger*, was obtained which was capable of producing a hitherto undescribed antibiotic, possessing..activity against certain bacteria..*Trypanosoma* as well. Because the antibiotic is devoid of pigment in the crystalline state, it has been given the name Achromycin.

b. (Properly with capital initial.) A proprietary name for the antibiotic tetracycline.

1952 *Official Gaz.* (U.S. Patent Office) 23 Sept. 922/2 American Cyanamid Company, New York... *Achromycin.* For antibiotic. **1953** *Trade Marks Jrnl.* 30 Sept. 876/2 *Achromycin*... Antibiotics and antibiotic preparations, all being pharmaceutical preparations. American Cyanamid Company. **1964** S. DUKE-ELDER *Parsons' Dis. Eye* (ed. 14) xiv. 145 Tetracycline (achromycin),..and Neomycin are 'broad-spectrum' antibiotics with a considerable antibacterial action. **1976** P. PARISH *Medicines* xlii. 265 Since the fifties numerous tetracyclines have been produced and tested but only a few have proved to be of value. These include..tetracycline (Achromycin [etc.]). **1981** *Proc. Nat. Acad. Sci. India* B. LI. 38 Datta..shows that achromycin and aureofungin enhanced seed germination of black mustard only at 1 ppm, other concentrations being inhibitory.

achronical, -ly, incorr. forms of ACRONYCAL, -LY.

achronism (ˈækrənɪz(ə)m). *nonce-wd.* [f. Gr. ἄχρονος without time + -ISM.] The state of timelessness; deficiency of time.

1877 R. LOWE in *Daily News* 26 July 3/3 It [House of Commons] has not got the element of time. It is smitten, if I may coin a word, not with an anachronism, but an achronism—viz. the absence of time.

¶ Occ. for ANACHRONISM, as if *an achronism*.

1674 MARVELL *Rehearsall Transp.* II. 135, I speak not of stale Achronismes, but of things that really happen'd all since the writing of your Reproof. **1697** *Verdicts conc. Virgil & Homer* §3. 8 All Authors have observed two..Faults of Achronism and Slander in that Episod of Dido.

achroö-, combining form of ACHROOUS common in chemical nomenclature, as **achroödextrin** colourless dextrin, **achroöglycogen**, etc.

1879 *Academy* 35, *Science Notes.*

achroous (ˈækrəʊəs), *a.* [f. Gr. ἄχρο-ος colourless (f. ἀ priv. + χρόα, χροιά colour) + -OUS.] Colourless; achromatic.

1879 *Syd. Soc. Lex.*

acht, obs. form of AUGHT *sb.*, OUGHT *v.*

acht, obs. north. form of EIGHT.

†**achtande**, *a. Obs. rare*[−1]. [a. ONorse *áttand-i* eighth, f. *átta* eight; cogn. w. OE. *eahtoðe*, OHG. *ahtodo* (dialectally *ahtande*, *achtende*), Goth. *ahtuda*.] Eighth.

a **1400** *Metr. Hom.* 26 And al the erthe the achtande day Sal stir and quac and al folc slay.

achtaragdite (ɑːxtəˈrægdaɪt). *Min.* [f. *Achtaragda* a Russian river + -ITE min. formative.] An earthy hydrous aluminous silicate, considered by Dana a doubtful species, and placed in his appendix to clays.

†**achue**, *v. Obs.* [A by-form of *eschue*, ESCHEW: see A- *pref.* 9. So OFr. has occ. *achevir* for *eschevir* (*eschever*, *eschiver*, mod. *esquiver*).] = ESCHEW.

c **1440** *Promp. Parv.* 6 Achwyn or fleyn; *vito, devito.* Achuynge, or beyng ware (*v.r.* achewynge, achue): *precavens, vitans.*

achy (ˈeɪkɪ), *a.* [f. ACHE *sb.*[1] + -Y[1].] Full of aches; suffering from continuous or recurring pain.

1875 GEO. ELIOT *Let.* 4 Mar. (1909) 44, I will not write more now, because my head is achy. **1878** DISRAELI in Monypenny & Buckle *Life* (1920) VI. 260 I'm too ill and achy to be out later. **1882** W. HARCOURT in Gardiner *Life* (1923) I. 461, I was rather achy last night. **1926** *Chambers's Jrnl.* 31 July 552/2 His throat was rather achy.

achylia (əˈkaɪlɪə). *Path.* [mod.L., f. as ACHYL(OUS *a.* + -IA[1].] Lack of chyle. Also ***achylia gastrica***, absence of chyle from the gastric juices.

1894 GOULD *Illustr. Dict. Med.* 28/1 *Achylia*, absence or deficiency of juice, or of chyle. **1909** *Practitioner* Nov. 735 Iodized solutions of potassium iodide suit the stenotic forms of chronic gastritis and cases of total gastric achylia. **1962** *Lancet* 13 Jan. 107/2 Patients with Bilroth-II resection or other forms of achylia gastrica.

achylous (əˈkaɪləs), *a. Phys.* [f. Gr. ἄχυλ-ος without juice + -OUS.] Without chyle.

1879 *Syd. Soc. Lex.*

achymous (əˈkaɪməs), *a. Phys.* [f. Gr. ἄχυμ-ος without juice + -OUS.] Without chyme.

1879 *Syd. Soc. Lex.*

acicle (ˈæsɪk(ə)l). *Nat. Hist.* [ad. L. *acicula*, more commonly used; see next word.] = ACICULA.

1852 DANA *Crustacea* I. 434 The basal part of the outer antennæ furnished above with a moveable acicle.

‖**acicula** (əˈsɪkjʊlə). *Nat. Hist.* Pl. **aciculæ**. [L., dimin. of *acus* a needle. Incorrect variants are *aciculum*, *aciculus*.] A technical name for a slender needle-like body, such as the spines or prickles with which some animals and plants are furnished, or the needle-like crystals of certain minerals; 'the bristle-like abortive flower of a grass.' Lindley *Treas. Bot.*

1875 J. W. DAWSON *Dawn of Life* iv. 87 This fringe..is..made up of a multitude of extremely delicate aciculi, standing side by side like the fibres of asbestos. **1858** W. CLARK tr. *Van der Hoeven's Zool.* I. 231 Body round, with 4 rows of double aciculæ. **1877** HUXLEY *Anat. Inv. An.* v. 229 The neuropodial is very much longer than the notopodial aciculum.

acicular (əˈsɪkjʊlə(r)), *a.* [ad. mod.L. *aciculāris*, f. ACICULA a small needle. See -AR.] Needle-like; resembling a slender needle or bristle, as the leaves of pine-trees, and various crystals.

1794 PEARSON in *Phil. Trans.* LXXXIV. 396 Oxalic acid produced immediately a precipitation of white acicular crystals. **1836–9** TODD *Cycl. Anat. & Phys.* II. 234/2 The phosphate..of lime [forms] small acicular prisms. **1848** DANA *Zooph.* 449 With long acicular, and nearly naked branchlets. **1857** H. MILLER *Test. of Rocks* 496 Coniferous trees, that retain at all seasons their coverings of acicular spiky leaves. **1860** RUSKIN *Mod. Painters* V. VIII. iii. §5. 182 Their trees always had a tendency to congeal into little acicular thorn-hedges.

acicularly (əˈsɪkjʊləlɪ), *adv.* [f. prec. + -LY[2].] In an acicular manner; after the manner of needles or fine prickles.

1834 R. ALLAN *Mineral.* 147 *Actinolite* comprehends the green acicularly-crystallized varieties.

aciculate (əˈsɪkjʊlət), *a. Nat. Hist.* [ad. mod.L. *aciculāt-us*, f. ACICULA: cf. *caudat-us* f. *cauda*, and see -ATE[2].] *prop.* Furnished or clothed with aciculæ; marked as with needle-scratches; *improperly* = ACICULAR.

1836 *Penny Cycl.* V. 251 Aciculate, needle-shaped. **1870** HOOKER *Stud. Flora* 121 Calyx-tube densely aciculate.

aciculated (əˈsɪkjʊleɪtɪd), *ppl. a.* [f. mod.L. *aciculāt-us*, see prec. + -ED; cf. *striate -d*, *separate -d*.] Marked or striated with fine impressed lines, as if produced by the point of a needle. Lindley *Treas. Bot.*

aciculiform (əˈsɪkjʊlɪfɔːm), *a.* [ad. mod.L. *aciculiformis*, f. ACICULA + *-formis* = -shaped. See -FORM.] Needle-shaped, ACICULAR.

1847 In CRAIG.

aciculine (əˈsɪkjʊlaɪn), *a.* [ad. mod. L. *aciculinus*, f. ACICULA: see -INE[1].] = ACICULAR.

1847 In CRAIG.

aciculite (əˈsɪkjʊlaɪt). *Min.* [f. ACICULA + -ITE, mineral formative.] A synonym of AIKINITE, or Acicular Bismuth.

aciculum, -us, incorrect variants of ACICULA.

acid (ˈæsɪd), *a.* and *sb.* [a mod.Fr. *acide* (Cotgr. 1611) or ad. L. *acid-us* adj. of state, f. *acē-re* to be sour (root *ac-* sharp).]

A. *adj.*

1. a. Sour, tart, sharp to the taste; of the taste of vinegar.

1626 BACON *Sylva* VII. §672 It [sorrel] is a cold and acid herb. **1676** in *Phil. Trans.* XI. 614 These crystals are pure vitriol, acid-austere. *a* **1704** LOCKE *Cond. Underst.* §40 The acid oil of vitriol is found to be good in such a case. **1855** BAIN *Senses & Intell.* II. ii. §13. 162 (1864) The sour or acid taste is much more uniform in its nature than either the saline or the alkaline. **1866** J. T. SYME in *Treas. of Bot.* 830 This plant has a pleasant acid taste.

b. ***acid drop***, short for ACIDULATED *drop*: a sweet made of sugar strongly flavoured with tartaric acid. Also ***acid tablet*** (formerly *acidulated tablet*).

1836 *Mag. Dom. Econ.* July 28 Acid Drops.—Boil one pound of lump-sugar, one cupful of water, and one table spoonful of vinegar till it snaps like glass. **1889** *Pract. Confectioner* 1 May 5/1 Run through the small acid-drop rollers. **1902** *Boy's Realm* 29 Nov. 388/4 He should carry about him a few acid tablets, and slip one of these in his mouth when the desire for smoking is particularly strong upon him.

Also *fig.*

1869 *Porcupine* 17 July 149/3 *Saturday Review* Acid-drops may do for babes—strong men want sharper sauce. **1960** *Times* 27 Oct. 15/2 Her best characters are viewed satirically..but, even so, many of her acid-drops are soft-centred.

2. a. *fig.*

1775 BOSWELL *Johnson* II. 370 (1826) Beauclerk..said in his acid manner, 'He would cut a throat to fill his pockets, if it were not for the fear of being hanged.' **1826** DISRAELI *Viv. Grey* VI. vi. 346 A hale old woman, with rather an acid expression of countenance. **1851** RUSKIN *Stones of Venice* I. xxiii. 264 (1874) The mere dogtooth is an acid moulding, and can only be used in certain mingling with others, to give them piquancy; never alone.

b. Applied to an intense colour.

1916 H. G. WELLS *Mr. Britling sees it Through* I. v. 175 The dark turf at the wayside..became for a moment an acid green as the glare passed. **1923** D. H. LAWRENCE *Birds, Beasts & Flowers* 151 You acid-blue metallic bird. **1959** *Listener* 29 Jan. 209/1 The acid blues and beautifully placed creamy whites are not to be met with outside Russia.

3. a. *Chem.* Having the essential properties of an ACID. See B. (Not separable in early use from 1.)

a **1727** NEWTON quoted in *Chambers' Cycl.* s.v. *Acid*, In decompounding sulphur we get an Acid salt. **1747** BERKELEY *Siris* 124 The mild native acids are observed more kindly to work upon and more thoroughly to dissolve metallic bodies than the strongest acid spirits produced by a vehement fire. **1812** SIR H. DAVY *Chem. Philos.* 48 The analysis of mineral bodies..by the application of acid and alkaline menstrua. **1873** WILLIAMSON *Chem.* §58 The solution has a slightly acid reaction to litmus-paper.

b. Derived from an acid by partial exchange of the replaceable hydrogen, as ***acid radical, salt.***

1868 J. P. COOKE *Chem. Philos.* (1870) ix. 83 The metallic atoms are basic radicals, while the non-metallic atoms are acid radicals. **1869** [see ANHYDRIDE]. **1869** ROSCOE *Elem. Chem.* 132 Thus [from dibasic acids] two classes of salts are derived; the so-called *acid salts*, where only one atom of hydrogen has been replaced, and the *neutral salts*, where both atoms have been replaced by a metal. Hydrogen potassium sulphite $HKSO_3$ in an acid salt. **1870** [see ANION]. **1873** FOWNES *Chem.* I. 339 The acid sulphite is very soluble in water, and has an acid reaction. **1947** G. THOMSON *Atom* (ed. 3) xiv. 128 When the salt is formed, water is eliminated and takes with it the oxygen, from the metallic oxide, leaving the metal in combination with the residue of the acid, called the Acid Radical.

c. ***acid dye***, a dye used in an acid bath for dyeing textiles, etc.; also one used as a stain in certain kinds of microscopical and histological research. So ***acid colour***, the dyestuff itself or the resultant colour.

1888 *Jrnl. Soc. Dyers & Colourists* IV. 107 When wool is boiled in a neutral solution of these acid dyes it merely becomes tinted. **1888** A. SANSONE *Dyeing* vii. 140 There is no end to the shades that can now be produced by means of these acid colours. **1902** *Encycl. Brit.* XXVII. 557/1 *Acid Colours.* These dyestuffs are so called because they dye the animal fibres wool and silk in an acid bath; they do not dye cotton... The colouring matters themselves are of an acid character. **1942** G. BOURNE *Cytol. & Cell Physiol.* i. 2 Acid dyes cannot effectively be used supravitally in this way..to show pre-existing structures; but some of them can most profitably be injected into living animals, certain of whose cells will take them up in a characteristic way.

d. Of, pertaining to, or resulting from an ***acid process*** of steel manufacture in which the converter or furnace is lined with acid refractory, and acid slag is used for refining. (Cf. BASIC *a.* 2 c.)

1903 H. H. CAMPBELL *Manuf. & Prop. Iron & Steel* 8 The growth of the basic Bessemer practice made it necessary to have a distinguishing name for the old way, and it is therefore called the *acid* process. *Ibid.* 23 If acid steel does not follow exactly the same law as basic steel, then it is certain that they are not the same. **1944** *Jrnl. Iron & Steel Inst.* CL. 177 P, Comparing the 18 basic steels with the 30 acid steels, there is practically no difference in the mechanical-test results.

e. ***acid value***, a measure of the free acid content of a substance.

1911 *Jrnl. Soc. Chem. Ind.* 15 Apr. 409/1 Acid value of oils and fats. **1912** THORPE *Dict. Appl. Chem.* (ed. 2) III. 767/2 The acid value indicates the number of milligrams of potassium hydroxide required to saturate the free fatty acids in one gram of an oil or fat. **1931** CARLETON ELLIS *Hydrogenation Org. Subst.* lxi. 853 A method of utilizing the acid values of sodium acid sulphate or bisulphate is recommended by Becquevort and Deguide.

f. ***acid rain***: rain with significantly increased acidity as a result of atmospheric pollution.

1859 R. A. SMITH in *Q. Jrnl. Chem. Soc.* XI. 232 The stones and bricks of buildings..crumble more readily in large towns where much coal is burnt... I was led to attribute this effect to the slow, but constant, action of the acid rain. **1929** *Encycl. Brit.* XX. 841/1 Acid rain is also directly harmful to plant life, and affects adversely the soil. **1972** *N.Y. Times* 12 June 12/3 Sweden has presented to the United Nations Conference on the Human Environment a 'case study' of the effects in Sweden of acid rains generated largely by emissions from the industrial belt stretching from the Ruhr to the British Midlands. **1980** *Financial Rev.* (Sydney) 18 Apr. 30/2 Acid rain is generally caused by the release of oxides of sulphur and nitrogen into the atmosphere where they may combine with water to form sulphuric acid and nitric acid molecules which then fall to earth with rainwater. **1984** *Daily Tel.* 2 Jan. 8/6 Acid rain is moving up the protest charts.

4. *Min.* = ACIDIC 2.

1874 LYELL *Elem. Geol.* xxviii. 497 Rocks containing an excess of silica from 60 to 80 per cent. are termed by many petrologists 'acid' rocks.

B. *sb.*

1. a. *Popularly*, A sour substance. *Chem.* A substance belonging to a class of which the commonest and most typical members are sour, and have the property of neutralizing alkalis, and of changing vegetable blues to red; all of which are compounds of hydrogen with another element or elements (oxygen being generally the third element), and in the decomposition of a compound substance are relatively electro-negative, and borne to the positive pole.

1696 PHILLIPS [not in ed. 1678], Acid in Chymistry, that sharp Salt, or that potential and dissolving Fire which is in all mix'd Bodies, and gives 'em being. Of Acids, Vitriol is the chiefest, Sea-salt next to that. **1712** tr. *Pomet's Hist. Drugs* I. 57 The Edges or Points of the Acid penetrate the gustatory Nerve. *a* **1727** NEWTON quoted in *Chambers' Cycl.* (1751) s.v. *Acid*, The particles of Acids are of a size grosser than those of water. **1747** BERKELEY *Siris* 159 What the chemists say, of pure acids being never found alone, might as well be said of pure fire. **1791** HAMILTON *Berthollet, Art of Dyeing* Pref. 7 The improvement depends principally on the use of the acids. **1814** SIR H. DAVY *Agric. Chem.* 106 The acids found in the Vegetable kingdom are numerous. **1837** WHEWELL *Hist. Induct. Sc.* XIV. x, The whole fabric of chemistry rests, even at the present day, upon the opposition of acids and bases; an acid was certainly at first known by its sensible qualities, and how otherwise, even now, do we perceive its quality? **1871** TYNDALL *Frag. of Sc.* I. v. 161 (ed. 6) Neither acids nor alkalies had the power of rapid destruction. **1879** MᶜCARTHY *Hist. Own Times* I. 42 Lord John Russell..was especially effective in a cold irritating sarcasm, which penetrated the weakness of an opponent's argument like some dissolving acid.

b. ***acid test***, the testing for gold by means of nitric acid; *fig.* a crucial test.

1892 G. E. GEE *Jeweller's Assistant* 131 The old-fashioned platinum alloy, in imitation of the bright gold alloys of thirty years ago, can hardly be said to have any golden tinge in its appearance. It certainly withstood the acid test very well, and this will be the only point of resemblance worthy of comparison. **1912** L. J. VANCE *Destroying Angel* (1913) xi. 149 Few professional beauties could have stood, as this woman did, the acid test of that mercilessly brilliant morning. **1918** WOODROW WILSON in *Times* 9 Jan. 8/1 The treatment accorded Russia by her sister nations in the months to come will be the acid test of their good will. **1955** *Times* 27 July 8/6 The acid test, however, would come with the Foreign Ministers' meetings in October, when generalities had to be translated into specific agreements.

c. The hallucinogenic drug LSD. *slang* (orig. *U.S.*).

1966 ALPERT & COHEN *LSD* (inside cover), *Acid*, LSD-25, lysergic acid diethylamide. **1966** H. S. THOMPSON *Hell's Angels* (1967) xxi. 246 Contrary to all expectations, most of the Angels became oddly peaceful on acid. **1967** *Melody Maker* 2 Sept. 9 People were..trying to shove STP on me, and acid. **1968** J. D. MACDONALD *Pale Grey for Guilt* (1969) xii. 152 'Do you mean narcotics, girl?' 'That's the fuzz word. But all we had was acid and grass. Booze is a lot worse for you.' **1970** J. LENNON in J. Wenner *Lennon Remembers* (1971) 30, I was influenced by acid and got psychedelic, like the whole generation, but really, I like rock and roll and I express myself best in rock. **1973** *To Our Returned Prisoners of War* (U.S. Office of Secretary of Defense) 1 *Acid*, refers to the hallucinogenic drug, Lysergic Acid Diethylamide, (LSD). **1974** K. MILLETT *Flying* (1975) I. 41 Stoned on pot and acid all day long, he calls it indulgence if we drink whisky. **1976** M. MACHLIN *Pipeline* iv. 47 You're stoned out of your mind again. What're you on now? Reds? C? Acid?

2. ***to put the acid on*** (someone), to exert pressure on (a person) for a loan, a favour, etc. Also *to ply, try, the acid. Austral. slang.*

1906 *Bulletin* (Sydney) 15 Mar., Note 'to put the gas on'—a variant of 'to put the acid on',—the latter familiar slang from the mine-assayer's lexicon. **1935** *Ibid.* 3 Apr. 20/1 He was evidently applying the acid to ascertain if my tombstone was as good as ordered. **1938** J. MOSES *Nine Miles from Gundigai* 10 The barber's shop's a witness-box (They ply the acid there). **1945** BAKER *Austral. Lang.* vi. 124 *To put the hard word* (or *acid*) *on* a girl, to make a request to her for favours. **1947** J. MORRISON in *Coast to Coast 1946* 158 They want to shift the ship at seven. That puts the acid on us.

3. ***to come the acid*** (cf. A. *adj.* 2): to behave in an 'acid' manner, to be unpleasant or offensive, to speak in a caustic or sarcastic manner. *slang.*

1925 FRASER & GIBBONS *Soldier & Sailor Words* 3 *Coming the acid*, stretching the truth; making oneself unpleasant; trying to pass on a duty; exaggerating one's authority. **1936** J. CURTIS *Gilt Kid* vi. 61 If the queer fellow tried to come any acid he would get hit right on the razzo. **1939** H. HODGE *Cab, Sir?* xviii. 259 Any attempt to 'come the acid', so far from frightening the cabman, will probably result in the cabman's giving him a little fatherly advice. **1953** 'H. CECIL' *Nat. Causes* vii. 95 Why come the old acid? Not even a 'sit down, old man—'.

4. In numerous combs. in *Chem.* (see also A. 3), as ***acid-base***; **acid-embossing**, embossing (of glass) by treatment with acid; **acid-fast** [FAST *a.* 1 h] *a.*, resistant to decolorization by an acid when stained: said esp. of bacteria (hence ***acid-fastness***); **acid-forming** *a.*, producing or yielding an acid; **acid-free** *a.*, not containing an acid; **acid-proof** [PROOF *a.* 1 b], *a.*, (*a*) impervious to acid; capable of resisting the deleterious action of acid, (*b*) = ACID-*fast*.

1917 *Chem. Abstr.* 3050 (*caption*) Observations on acid-base equilibrium in the body. **1925** W. MORSE *Appl. Biochem.* 575 Modern biochemistry considers the mineral substances of the food..as participating in the acid-base metabolism of the body. **1937** MCGRATH & FROST *Glass in Arch. & Decoration* 405 The French artist-technicians, Paule and Max Ingrand, have demonstrated more delightfully than anybody else the possibilities of acid-embossing and sand-blasting. **1904** *Med. Ann.* 578 With regard to examination of sputum, it must be remembered that several observers have reported 'acid-fast' bacilli which were apparently non-tubercular. **1909** *Cent. Dict.* Suppl., Acid-fastness. **1925** C. H. BROWNING *Bacteriol.* viii. 175 Ehrlich showed, however, that tubercle bacilli possessed the remarkable property of acid-fastness, that is to say they withstood the decolorising action of strong acids..when once they had been stained. **1869** H. E. ROSCOE *Elem. Chem.* xvii. 175 Oxides may be divided into (1) Basic oxides; (2) Peroxides; (3) Acid-forming oxides. **1914** *Lancet* 28 Mar. 908/1 The air of New York schools was examined for the acid-forming streptococci. **1930** *Paper Terminol.* (*Spalding & Hodge*) 1 *Acid free*, paper free from any acid or other material likely to have deleterious effects. **1934** R. F. INNES *Causes & Prevention Decay in Leather* 1/2 Modern knowledge demands that leather should not only be 'Acid free' but 'Protected' as well. **1868** G. A. SALA *Notes & Sk. Paris Exhib.* xxvii. 387 They [*sc.* safes] are also stated to be acid proof. **1909** *Installation News* iii. 271 [Conduit] protected by an even *and not too thick* coating of acid proof, moisture resisting, flexible enamel. **1913** DORLAND *Med. Dict.* (ed. 7) 32/2 *Acid-proof*, same as acid-fast. **1937** E. J. LABARRE *Dict. Paper* 95/2 Acid proof paper is generally wood Manilla, Kraft or Rope Wrapping which has been treated to resist acids or acid fumes.

5. (In sense 1 c above). **a.** Special Combs. **acid freak**, [FREAK *sb.*[1] 4 c], **head** [HEAD *sb.* 7 e], one who habitually takes the drug LSD; **acid rock**, (see quots. 1971); **acid trip**, a hallucinatory experience induced by taking the drug LSD.

1969 *Acid freak [see FREAK *sb.*[1] 4 c]. **1966** *Acidhead [see PSYCHEDELIC *a.* 1 b]. **1968** A. DIMENT *Bang Bang Birds* viii. 142 Acid heads are such nice people they want to be friends with the whole world. **1974** M. C. GERALD *Pharmacol.* i. 13 With the realization that the..'acid head', and 'dope addict' also reside in 'good, middle-class homes', the public..has become increasingly concerned. **1966** *Acid rock [see PSYCHEDELICALLY *adv.*]. **1971** E. E. LANDY *Underground Dict.* 22 *Acid rock*, psychedelic music... It emphasizes electronic sounds; has a very prominent beat, repeated sounds. *Ibid.*, Acid rock is considered to be the musical equivalent of an LSD-induced state. **1977** *Zigzag* Aug. 24/2 The highlight was the closing 'Rock And Roll is Dead (And We Don't Care)', a guaranteed showstopper intro'd by Tommy's entirely vicious parody of an acid-rock axe hero. **1967** *Acid trip [see FREAKY *a.* 2]. **1974** K. MILLETT *Flying* (1975) III. 356 Today a day so beyond possibility that I am flowing through it like a fairy tale. Or an acid trip. **1982** T. GUNN *Occasions of Poetry* II. 182 The acid trip is unstructured, it opens you up to countless possibilities.

b. Simple attrib. and Comb. uses.

1966 *Life* 25 Mar. 30c/1 A bad trip—a sudden vision of horror or death which often grips LSD users when they take it without proper mental preparation—overtakes a teen-age girl at an 'acid party' near Hollywood's Sunset Strip. **1966** H. S. THOMPSON *Hell's Angels* (1967) xxi. 246 My own acid-eating experience is limited in terms of total consumption, but widely varied as to company and circumstances. **1969** *Listener* 24 Apr. 578/2 For these 'acid drop-outs' the frontier between reality and fantasy is blurred. **1970** A. TOFFLER *Future Shock* xiii. 260 Blending the blue jeans of the beats with the beads and bangles of the acid crowd, the hippies became the newest..subcult. **1976** *Time Out* 2 Apr. 51/5 Genuine acid-punk rockers. **1977** *Rolling Stone* 30 June 124/1 If they ever do play either the dark side or light side of the moon, rest assured they will bedeck those static craters with helium-filled pigs and acid-hued light shows.

acidæmia (æsɪˈdiːmɪə). *Path.* Also **-emia**. [mod.L. f. L. *acid-um* ACID + Gr. αἷμα blood.] A condition of excessive acidity in the blood.

1906 DORLAND *Med. Dict.* (ed. 4) 24/2 *Acidemia*, abnormal acidity of the blood. **1914** *N.Y. Med. Jrnl.* XCIX. 987/2 (*title*) Alcohol acidemia. **1965** [see ALKALÆMIA].

acidanthera (æsɪˈdænθərə). [mod.L. (C. F. Hochstetter 1844, in *Flora* 14 Jan. 25), f. Gr. ἀκιδ-, ἀκίς pointed object + mod.L. *anthēra* ANTHER, in allusion to the cuspate anthers.] A flowering plant of the genus of this name (family Iridaceæ), which comprises tender herbaceous perennials having corms and native to tropical and southern Africa.

1959 *Times* 13 June 1/7 Genuine end of season offer of the lovely *acidanthera*, beautiful *sparaxis*, [etc.]. **1962** *Amat. Gardening* 10 Mar. 5/1 Acidantheras from Abyssinia are gladiolus-like plants with white flowers. **1980** *Daily Tel.* 19 Apr. 29/1 Even those who really dislike gladioli are usually enchanted by their close relative, the acidanthera, whose white flowers are marked with maroon at the centre and which has a pronounced perfume.

acidic (əˈsɪdɪk), *a. Min.* [f. ACID + -IC.]
1. Applied by Dana to that element in a ternary compound mineral, which forms an oxygen, sulphur, or other salt, with a basic element; e.g. the silicon in silicate of lime. See quotation under ACIDIFIC.
1880 DANA *Mineral.* Introd. 16 In some classes of compounds only part of the oxygen serves to unite the acidic element to the basic.
2. Abounding in an acidic element, usually silicon.
1877 GREEN *Phys. Geol.* ii. §5. 47 So the Crystalline rocks can be divided..into the Highly Silicated or Acidic rocks. **1878** LAWRENCE tr. *Cotta, Rocks Classified* 120 The acidic rocks..are distinguished by a felspar richer in silica. **1879** RUTLEY *Study of Rocks* iv. 34 Both acidic and basic rocks are known in some instances to have emanated, etc.
3. Of, pertaining to, or of the nature of, an acid. Also *fig.*
1889 in *Cent. Dict.* **1905** *Harmsworth Encycl.* II. 1162/2 Though neutral to litmus, carbon disulphide exhibits some acidic properties, uniting with alkaline sulphides to form sulpho-carbonates. **1961** *John O'London's* 21 Dec. 678/3 Starkly etched portraits of immigrants in New York heat-wave, doom-laden acidic.

acidiferous (ˌæsɪˈdɪfərəs), *a. rare.* [f. L. *acidum*; see ACID + -FEROUS bearing.] Producing or yielding an acid.
1812 SIR H. DAVY *Chem. Philos.* 12 Of undecompounded inflammable or acidiferous substances not metallic.

acidifiable (əˈsɪdɪˌfaɪəb(ə)l), *a.* [f. ACIDIFY + -ABLE.] Capable of being converted into, or of combining so as to form, an acid.
1794 G. ADAMS *Nat. & Exper. Phil.* I. App. 531 Any simple substance which, by its combination with oxygen, becomes an acid, is termed the acidifyable base, or radical of that acid. **1808** HENRY *Epit. Chem.* 214 (ed. 5) The brittle and acidifiable [metals] include four species. **1812** SIR H. DAVY *Chem. Philos.* 482 Amongst the acidifiable bodies, sulphur, which is represented by 30, may be supposed to consist of 6 hydrogene, and 24 basis. **1853** CHAMBERS *Introd. to Sciences* 81 Those formed with the other acidifiable bases being generally of minor importance.

acidifiant (əˈsɪdɪfaɪənt), *a.* [a. Fr. *acidifiant* pr. pple. of *acidifier* to ACIDIFY; see -ANT.] Acidifying.
1879 *Syd. Soc. Lex.*

acidific (æsɪˈdɪfɪk), *a. Min.* [f. L. *acid-um* ACID + *-fic-us* making: see -FIC.] Applied by Dana to the oxygen, sulphur, selenium, or tellurium, in a mineral, which is an oxygen, sulphur, selenium, or tellurium salt of any basic element.
1880 DANA *Mineral.* Introd. 15 Ternary compounds (called also salts and double binaries) consist of elements of three kinds, (1) basic, (2) acidic, (3) acidific. Thus.. sulphate of lead contains (1) lead, (2) sulphur, (3) oxygen; the sulphantimonite, jamesonite, contains (1) lead and iron, (2) antimony, (3) sulphur..The replacing power of the elements is in proportion to their combining power, the combining power being reckoned in number of atoms of oxygen (or sulphur, or the acidific element, whatever it may be).

acidification (əˌsɪdɪfɪˈkeɪʃən). [n. of action f. ACIDIFY: see -FICATION. Also in mod.Fr.] The act or process of acidifying; conversion into an acid.
1794 G. ADAMS *Nat. & Exper. Phil.* II. xiv. 61 These operations, instead of furnishing us with an acidification, of which we have no conception, lead us only to consider these acids as liberated. **1804** in *Phil. Trans.* XCIV. 322 After the complete acidification of the sulphur. **1837** WHEWELL *Hist. Induct. Sc.* III. XIV. vii. 141 The leading generalisation of Lavoisier, that acidification was always combination with oxygen, was found untenable. **1847** *Rural Cycl.* I. 590 To prevent the too rapid acidification of the cream, and formation of the butter. **1863** FOWNES *Elem. Chem.* 481 (ed. 9) The best vinegar is made from wine by spontaneous acidification.

acidifier (əˈsɪdɪfaɪə(r)). [f. ACIDIFY + -ER¹.] Anything that acidifies, or generates an acid. The name was originally given (in error) to oxygen, as the supposed active agent in producing acids.
1847 In CRAIG. **1875** URE *Dict. Arts.* I. 18.

acidify (əˈsɪdɪfaɪ), *v.* [mod. f. L. *acid-um* ACID + -FY = to make. Cf. Fr. *acidifier.*]
1. To make acid or sour. *Chem.* To convert into an ACID by combination with any substance. Also *fig.*
1797 PEARSON in *Phil. Trans.* LXXXVIII. 29 The three acids (viz. the oxymuriatic, the nitro-muriatic, and the nitric) which can acidify oxides. **1808** HENRY *Epit. Chem.* 272 (ed. 5) Sugar is acidified by distillation with nitric acid. **1837** CARLYLE *Fr. Rev.* III. III. iii. 181 His thin existence all acidified into rage, and preternatural insight of suspicion. **1851** RICHARDSON *Geol.* v. 82 The name of the acid was derived from the substance acidified by the oxygen.
2. *intr.* (*refl.*) To become acid.

acidifying (əˈsɪdɪfaɪɪŋ), *ppl. a.* [f. ACIDIFY + -ING².] Forming an acid; that combines so as to form an acid.
1784 CAVENDISH in *Phil. Trans.* LXXIV. 152 Another thing which Mr. Lavoisier endeavours to prove is, that dephlogisticated air is the acidifying principle. **1794** G. ADAMS *Nat. & Exper. Phil.* I. IX. 360 Called by M. Lavoisier the oxygenous or acidifying principle. **1822** IMISON *Science & Art* II. 54 It has lately been discovered, that hydrogen, like oxygen, is an acidifying principle. **1830** LINDLEY *Nat. Syst. Bot.* 84 Malic acid..is also almost the sole acidifying principle of the berries of the Mountain Ash. **1851** RICHARDSON *Geol.* v. 83 The erroneous idea of oxygen being the general acidifying principle.

acidimeter (ˌæsɪˈdɪmɪtə(r)). [mod. f. L. *acid-um* ACID + Gr. μέτρον measure.] An instrument for measuring the strength of acids.
1839 REID *Elem. Chem.*, Such instruments are termed Acidimeters when charged with alkali for ascertaining the value of acids. **1875** URE *Dict. Arts* I. 21 Fill the acidimeter up to 0 (zero) with the solution of caustic lime. *Ibid.* I. 19 A standard liquor of ammonia of that strength (17 grains of ammonia in 1000) becomes therefore a universal acidimeter.

acidimetrical (ˌæsɪdɪˈmɛtrɪkəl), *a.* [f. L. *acid-um* ACID + Gr. μετρικ-ός pertaining to measure + -AL¹.] Of or pertaining to acidimetry.
1875 URE *Dict. Arts* I. 23 Acidimetrical operations may likewise be performed by determining the weight instead of the volumes of the carbonic acid expelled from bicarbonate of potash..by a given quantity of acid. *Ibid.* Liebig's acidimetrical method.

acidimetry (ˌæsɪˈdɪmɪtrɪ). [mod. f. L. *acid-um* ACID + Gr. μετρία a measuring. The form of the word is due to the previous existence of *alkalimetry*.] The chemical process of measuring the strength of acids, 'that is to say the quantity of pure free acid contained in a liquid.' Ure.
1839 REID *Elem. Chem.*, To ascertain the strength of any acid, an operation that is now termed Acidimetry. **1875** URE *Dict. Arts* I. 18 Acidimetry is exactly the reverse of alkalimetry, since in prinicple it depends on the number of volumes of a solution of a base diluted with water to a definite strength, which are required to neutralize a known weight or measure of the different samples of acids.

acidity (əˈsɪdɪtɪ). [a. Fr. *acidité* (16th c.); or of its prototype, L. *aciditāt-em*, n. of quality f. *acid-us* sour: see ACID.] **a.** The quality or state of being acid or sour; sourness, tartness, sharpness to the taste.
1620 VENNER *Via Recta* vi. 95 Sugar correcteth their acidity. **1656** *B. Valentine, Repet. Former Writings* 11 There is an acetum made of antimony, of an acidity as other acetums are. **1681** WORLIDGE *Syst. Agric.* 9 The heat of the fire evaporating, and consuming the Acidity of the Earth. **1732** ARBUTHNOT *Rules of Diet* 262 No animal Substance produceth Acidity, except Milk. **1748** HARTLEY *Observ. on Man* I. i. §3. 98 Acidities, and other Irritations in the Bowels. **1863** MITCHELL *Farm of Edgewood* 143, I count upon its brilliant colouring, and its piquant acidity, in the first days of August.
b. *fig.*
1711 P. H. *Two Late Parliam.* 130 He reflected on each mistake with unusual acidity. **1823** *Blackw. Mag.* May 567 The augmented acidity and more naked shallowness of Brougham. **1915** W. S. MAUGHAM *Of Human Bondage* lii. 266 The vicar answered with some acidity.

acidize (ˈæsɪdaɪz), *v.* [f. ACID *sb.* + -IZE.] To treat with acid, to acidify; *spec.* to apply acid to an oil (or other) well in order to neutralize the lime.
1909 *Cent. Dict.* Suppl., *Acidize*, to treat with an acid; render acid. **1936** B. M. KINGSTON *Acidizing Handbk.* 10 Since 1932, wells in practically every lime field of the United States have been acidized. **1958** *Times* 5 Nov. 16/7 Since yesterday's statement regarding the Puri well a formation.. has been acidized and further flow tests taken.

acidly (ˈæsɪdlɪ), *adv.* [f. ACID *a.* + -LY².] Sourly.
1880 MISS LAFFAN *Christy Carew* II. vi. 263 'Well,' retorted Mrs. Carew acidly, 'she only shows her ignorance.'

acidness (ˈæsɪdnɪs). [f. ACID *a.* + -NESS.] The quality of being acid, degree of acidity.

†**aciˈdoleous**, *a. Obs.* [f. L. *acid-us* sour + *ole-um* oil + -OUS.] An oily liquid of acid character, as vitriol.
1674 GREW *Anat. Plants* III. 2. iv. §15 A Rosin, is originally a Turpentine, or Acidoleous Liquor. **1676** *Ibid.* III. ii. (1682) 259 Rosin and Mastick seem to be more purely acidoleous gums.

acidophil, -phile (æˈsɪdəfɪl, -faɪl), *a.* and *sb.* [f. ACID *sb.* + -O- + -PHIL(E.] **A.** *adj.* Having an affinity for acids, staining readily with an acid dye. (Cf. OXYPHIL *a.*) **B.** *sb.* A cell or histological element readily stained by an acid dye. Hence **aˌcidoˈphilic, aciˈdophilous** *adjs.*
1900 DORLAND *Med. Dict.* 21/1 *Acidophil* 1. Easily stained by acid dyes. 2. An element or substance that is readily stained with acid dyes. *Acidophilic, Acidophilous*, readily stained with acid dyes. **1927** HENDERSON & GILLESPIE *Text-bk. Psychiatry* IX. 217 Dunlap was unable to demonstrate the occurrence of acidophile staining in the nuclei of nerve cells in any of his cases. **1932** FULLER & CONARD tr. *Braun-Blanquet's Plant Sociol.* xiii. 311 This concentration [of the soil solution] causes a speedy weeding out of the acidophilous species which are found in the first stages on raw siliceous soils and sands. **1951** G. BOURNE *Cytol. & Cell Physiol.* (ed. 2) ix. 400 Acidophil intranuclear inclusions resembling those produced by viruses have been reported in cells under such conditions that there is no reason to assume any relationship with a virus infection. **1958** *Immunology* I. 13 No carbohydrate-containing substance was demonstrable in the acidophils.

acidophilus (æsɪˈdɒfɪləs), *a.* [mod.L., esp. in *Lactobacillus acidophilus*, a species of bacteria causing fermentation in milk; cf. ACID *sb.*, -PHIL.] ***acidophilus milk***, milk fermented by any of several bacteria and used therapeutically.
1921 RETTGER & CHEPLIN *Intestinal Flora* iv. 112 Four strains of *B. acidophilus* have been employed for the production of acidophilus milk. **1929** *Lancet* 25 May 1126/2 Each block..contain[s] some 150 billion bacilli..the number usually present in a pint of comparable acidophilus milk.

acidosis (æsɪˈdəʊsɪs). *Path.* [irreg. f. ACID *sb.* + -OSIS.] An acid condition of the blood such as occurs in diabetes.
1900 E. KLEEN *Diabetes Mellitus* vii. 227 The acid diathesis, the acidosis, causes an increase of ammonia in the blood and the urine in cases of severe diabetes. **1905** HEWLETT tr. *Krehl's Clin. Path.* Index, Acidosis, in diabetic coma. **1913** PEMBREY & RITCHIE *Gen. Path.* 690 The term 'acidosis' is applied to the condition in which abnormal quantities of organic acids fail to be oxidized by the tissues.

‖**acidulæ** (əˈsɪdjʊliː), *sb. pl. Obs.* [L. *acidulus* adj. 'sourish,' in pl. fem. sc. *aquæ* waters.] A name formerly given to springs of *cold* mineral waters, from their sharp and pungent taste, then considered acid.
1681 PHILLIPS, *Acidulæ*; Any Medicinal or Spaw-waters that are not hot; in which respect they are oppos'd to Thermae. **1681** T. WILLIS *Rem. Med. Wks.* (Vocab.) *Acidulæ*. Medicinal waters running forth from veins of iron, copper, and such like, called Spaws from that famous place for mineral-waters, the Spaw in Germany. **1765** BROWNRIGG in *Phil. Trans.* LV. 242 The brisk and pungent taste of the acidulæ is also a further evidence that the mineral air which they contain is nearly related to the choak-damp.

acidulate (əˈsɪdjʊleɪt), *v.* [f. L. *acidul-us* sourish (dim. of *acid-us* ACID) + -ATE³, as if repr. a L. **acidulā-re*. Cf. mod. Fr. *aciduler.*] To make somewhat acid or sour; to flavour with an acid. Also *fig.* of the temper. (Rare exc. in pa. pple.)
1732 ARBUTHNOT *Rules of Diet* 311 Decoctions of mealy substances acidulated. **1747** WALL in *Phil. Trans.* XLIV. 588, I acidulated the Liquors with the Vitriolic Acid. **1844** T. J. GRAHAM *Dom. Med.* 91 [Vinegar] may be used to acidulate barley-water, or any other ordinary beverage of the patient. **1856** MACAULAY *Johnson* (1860) 99 Garrick.. could obtain from one morose cynic scarcely any compliment not acidulated with scorn.

acidulated (əˈsɪdjʊleɪtɪd), *ppl. a.* [f. prec. + -ED.] Rendered somewhat acid or sour; flavoured with acid. Also *fig.* Somewhat soured in temper. ***acidulated drop*** (***tablet***) = ACID *drop* (*tablet*).
1732 ARBUTHNOT *Rules of Diet* 245 Likewise all acidulated and chalybeat Waters. **1836** DICKENS *Astley's* in *Sk. Boz.* I. 305 Ma, in the openness of her heart, offered the governess an acidulated drop. **1837** BREWSTER *Magnetism* 156 Two ends of the wire were plunged in slightly acidulated water. **1838** *Mag. Dom. Econ.* Oct. 109 Acidulated drops.—Rasp some orange peel... Add..orange juice,..Dry..then drop. **1851** MAYHEW *Lond. Labour* I. 203/2 Barley-sugar and acidulated drops. **1853** SOYER *Pantropheon* 122 The pomegranate, whose acidulated flavour is so pleasing to the inhabitants of hot climates. **1889** *Pract. Confectioner* 1 May 4/1 Acidulated Raspberry Tablets. **1906** *Daily Chron.* 1 Oct. 6/5 He was not an 'acidulated drop curate'.

acidulation (əˌsɪdjʊˈleɪʃən). [f. ACIDULATE *v.* + -TION.] The action or process of acidulating; the state of being acidulated. Also *fig.*
1849 *Jrnl. R. Agric. Soc.* X. 395 The acidulation of the fermenting sap promotes their growth. **1919** L. STRACHEY *Let.* 27 Nov. in *V. Woolf & Strachey* (1956) 85, I have retired, probably permanently, into this acidulation of ice.

†**acidulcis**, *a.* [L. in form, f. *acid-us* sour + *dulcis* sweet.] Sour and sweet blended, *aigre-doux.*
1675 GREW *Anat. Plants* VI. i. §4 (1682) 280 The taste of a Peppin is Acidulcis.

acidulent (əˈsɪdjʊlənt), *a.* [a. Fr. *acidulant* pr. pple. of *aciduler* to sour slightly.] = ACIDULOUS.
1834 PRINGLE *Afr. Sk.* vi. 203 Being of such an acidulent quality that sheep..will not eat it. **1837** CARLYLE *Fr. Rev.* I. I. iv. 20 (1857) Abbé Moudon starts forward; with anxious acidulent face. **1865** —— *Fredk. Gt.* IX. xx. x. 179 Wrapt in despondency and black acidulent humours.

acidulous (əˈsɪdjʊləs), *a.* [f. L. *acidul-us* sourish + -OUS.] Slightly sour, sourish, sub-acid. Also *fig.* Sour-tempered.
1769 BUCHAN *Dom. Med.* liv. (1826) 265 Acidulous chalybeate waters. **1796** BURKE *Let. Noble Lord* Wks. VIII 44 Whatever in his pedigree has been dulcified by an exposure to the influence of heaven in a long flow of generations, from the hard acidulous, metallick tincture of the spring. **1830** LINDLEY *Nat. Syst. Bot.* 44 The fruit of a species of Sauranja is said to be acidulous, and to resemble Tomatoes in flavour. **1860** PIESSE *Lab. Chem. Wonders* 82 Gold is not easily acted upon by acidulous agents. **1865** CARLYLE *Fredk. Gt.* IX. xx. x. 179 Towards the middle of March, he becomes specially gloomy and acidulous.

†**acier.** *Obs.* Also asser. [OFr. *acer*, later *acier*:—low L. *aciārium* steel, properly adj. qualifying *ferrum*, f. *acies* point, edge + *-ārius* adj. affix = concerned with; hence *edging* or

pointing iron.] Steel (properly Fr., but occ. used in early Eng.).

1866 ROGERS *Agric. & Prices* I. xix. 470 Steel, sometimes called by its English name, but much more commonly known as asser or acier, is found even more frequently.

acierage (ˈæsɪərɪdʒ). [a. mod.Fr. *aciérage* f. *acier* steel + -AGE.] The process of depositing a layer of steel on the surface of another metal, to render it more durable, as is sometimes done with stereotype plates, and engraved copper-plates.

acierate (ˈæsɪəreɪt), *v.* [f. F. *aciérer* (f. *acier* steel) + -ATE³.] *trans.* To convert into steel. So **acieration** (æsɪəˈreɪʃən) [F. *aciération*], conversion into steel.

1866 *Phil. Trans.* CLVI. 439 The inquiry suggests itself whether acieration would not be promoted by alternation of temperature frequently repeated. **1880** *Encycl. Brit.* XIII. 342/1 This prevents the ready access of carbon and carbon oxide to the covered-up part, and hence hinders or entirely prevents acieration thereat. **1887** *Dublin Rev.* July 55 The beautiful mechanical contrivance of Sir Henry Bessemer by which crude iron..is acierated in half an hour. **1900** S. COLVIN in *Brit. Mus. Return* 51 Proof before the plate was acierated.

‖**acies.** *Obs.* [L. *acies* edge, keenness, sharpness.] The keen attention or aim, of the eye, ear, etc. when fully directed towards any object.

1646 SIR T. BROWNE *Pseud. Ep.* 181 A Frogge..seemes to behold a large part of the heavens, and the acies of his eye to ascend as high as the Tropick. **1677** HALE *Prim. Orig. Man.* 30 Though I do by the Empire of my Will direct the Motion or Acies of my Organ to this or that Object.

aciform (ˈæsɪfɔːm), *a.* [mod. f. L. *acu-s* needle + -FORM.] Needle-shaped.

1847 In CRAIG.

†**acin, acine** (ˈæsɪn). *Obs.* [a. Fr. *acine*, ad. L. *acin-us*: see ACINUS.] One of the small grains of which a blackberry or mulberry is composed.

1693 SIR H. SLOANE in *Phil. Trans.* XVII. 923 An Oval Berry, made up of two, three, or more Acins or little Berries. **1775** ASH, *Acine*, berries growing in bunches.

acinaceous (ˌæsɪˈneɪʃəs), *a.* [f. ACIN-US + -ACEOUS.] Consisting of acini; formed of a cluster of small berries or fleshy drupes, like a blackberry or raspberry.

1775 In ASH.

‖**acinaces** (əˈsɪnəsiːz, əˈkɪnəkiːz). [The L. spelling of Gr. ἀκινάκης, orig. a Persian word.] *Anc. Hist.* A short sword or scimitar.

acinacifolious (əˌsɪnəsɪˈfəʊlɪəs), *a.* *Bot.* [f. ACINACES + L. *foliōs-us* leafy.] Having acinaciform leaves. (See next.)

1879 *Syd. Soc. Lex.*

acinaciform (ˌæsɪˈnæsɪfɔːm, əˈsɪnəsɪfɔːm), *a.* [ad. mod.L. *acinaciform-is*, f. ACINACES; see -FORM.] Scimitar-shaped. In *Bot.* applied to leaves, etc., 'curved, rounded towards the point; thick on the straighter side, thin on the convexity.'

1774 in *Phil. Trans.* LXV. 104 The body..becomes of an acinaciform shape, to the point of the tail, which is rather blunt. **1836** *Penny Cycl.* V. 251 *Acinaciform*, scymitar-shaped. **1838** LOUDON *Encycl. Plants* (1855) 617 *Dolichos tetraspermus*..pods racemose acinaciform 4-seeded. **1876** *Encycl. Brit.* (ed. 9) IV. 112 When the veins (of a leaf) spread out in various planes, and there is a large development of cellular tissue, so as to produce a succulent leaf, such forms occur as..acinaciform, or scimitar-shaped.

acinar (ˈæsɪnə(r)), *a. Anat.* [f. ACIN(US + -AR¹.] Of or pertaining to an acinus.

1936 *Nature* 12 Dec. 1000/2 In an albino strain [of mice], the males treated with œstrone showed a more localized acinar development.

aci'nesic, *a. Med.* [improp. f. Gr. ἀκινησία or ἀκίνησις motionless + -IC.] = ACINETIC.

1879 *Syd. Soc. Lex.*, Acinesic remedies are those which are opposed to motion.

acinetic (æsɪˈnɛtɪk), *a. Med.* [f. Gr. ἀκίνητ-ος motionless + -IC.] Preventing motion.

1879 *Syd. Soc. Lex.*

acinetiform (æsɪˈniːtɪfɔːm), *a.* [f. mod.L. *acinēta* (f. Gr. ἀκίνητος motionless) + -FORM.] Having the form of *Acinetae*, a genus of parasitical infusorial animalcules, with spherical bodies furnished with radiating trumpet-shaped suckers, which are not in constant motion like the cilia or flagella of other infusoria.

1877 HUXLEY *Anat. Inv. An.* ii. 108 Balbiani figures all the stages by which the acinetiform embryo becomes a Paramœcium. **1878** MACALISTER *Invertebr.* 28 Other minute forms, called Acinetae, are small stalked masses whose surface is studded with radiating, retractile tubular suckers, through which they suck the juices of their prey.

aciniform (əˈsɪnɪfɔːm, ˈæsɪnɪfɔːm), *a.* [ad. mod.L. *aciniform-is* f. ACINUS. See -FORM.] **a.** Having the form of a cluster of grapes, consisting of closely packed berries or drupes. **b.** Full of small kernels like a grape.

1847 CRAIG, *Aciniform*, full of small kernels. **1853** MAYNE, *Aciniform*; having the form or appearance or colour of a grape; grape-like. **1877** HUXLEY *Anat. Inv. An.* vii. 381 These glands are divisible into five different kinds (aciniform, ampullate, aggregate, tubuliform, and tuberous).

acinose (ˌæsɪˈnəʊs), *a.* [ad. L. *acinōsus* full of grapes, grapelike, f. ACINUS.] Consisting of *acini*; composed of, or resembling, a cluster of small berries.

1873 WEALE *Dict.* 5 *Acinose*, a term applied to iron ore found in masses, and of several colors. **1874** ROOSA *Dis. of Ear* 210 The mucous membrane is made smooth by numerous acinose glands.

acinous (ˈæsɪnəs), *a.* [f. L. *acinōsus* (see prec.) as if ad. Fr. *acineux*.] = ACINOSE; applied especially to glands occurring in clusters.

1872 COHEN *Dis. of Throat* 179 This pouch is ordinarily enveloped by acinous glands. **1878** HABERSHON *Dis. Abdomen* 51 Some isolated submucous glands of an acinous character may still be found.

‖**acinus** (ˈæsɪnəs). Pl. acini. [L. *acinus*, a berry growing in a cluster, a grape; also a kernel occurring in a cluster, a grapestone.]

†**1.** A berry which grows in clusters, as grapes, currants, etc.; sometimes applied to the whole cluster. *Obs.*

1731 BAILEY, vol. II, *Acini*..small grains growing in bunches..of which the fruit of the Elder-tree, Privet, and other plants of the like kind are composed.

2. *Bot.* One of the small fleshy berries or drupes which make up such compound fruits as the blackberry; sometimes applied to the compound fruit which they compose.

1830 LINDLEY *Nat. Syst. Bot.* 81 Fruit either 1-seeded nuts, or acini, or follicles containing several seeds. **1834** GOOD *Bk. of Nat.* I. 164 The acinus or conglomerate berry, as in the rasp. **1837** MACCULLOCH *Attrib. of God* III. xlvi. 220 The acinus of botanists constitutes the basis of another class of fruits, and the Raspberry is a familiar example. **1880** GRAY *Bot. Text-Bk.* 394, *Acinus*..now sometimes applied to the separate carpels of an aggregate baccate fruit, or to the contained stone or seed.

3. The stones or seeds of grapes and berries.

1731 BAILEY, vol. II, *Acini* [with Physicians] the seed that is within a fruit, and thence they in their prescriptions frequently use *uva exacinata*, i.e. the Acini or seeds being taken out. **1880** [See under 2].

4. *Anat.* A racemose gland; a blind end of a duct of a secreting gland, which is divided into several lobes.

1751 CHAMBERS *Cycl.* s.v. *Acini*, Anatomists have called some glands of a similar formation [to bunches of grapes] *Acini Glandulosi*. **1877** HUXLEY *Anat. Inv. An.* vii. 410 The ducts which arise from these acini unite first into a single trunk on each side.

5. *Anat.* (See quot.)

1847 YOUATT *Horse* xiii. 297 There are, scattered through the substance of the liver, numerous little granules, called acini, from their resemblance to the small stones of certain berries.

-acious (-ˈeɪʃəs), *compd. suffix*, forming adjs. meaning 'given to, inclined to, abounding in'; f. L. *-āci-* (nom. *-ax*), adj. ending added chiefly to vb. stems (Fr. *-ace*) + -OUS; as L. *vīv-ere* to live, *vivāci-* lively (Fr. *vivace*), Eng. *vivaci-ous*; so *mendacious, voracious, fallacious, capacious*. Hence adv. in *-aciously*; sbs. of quality in *-acious-ness, -acity*; vbs. in *-acitate*.

‖**acipenser** (æsɪˈpɛnsə(r)). *Zool.* [L.] The sturgeon.

1853 SOYER *Pantropheon* 216 Some flatterers..with eyes fixed on the noble accipenser, compared its flesh to the ambrosia of the immortals.

acise, obs. form of ASSIZE *sb.*

-acitate (-ˈæsɪteɪt), *compd. suffix* = *-aci-* (see -ACIOUS) + *-t-* (see -TY) + -ATE, forming vbs. on adjs. in *-aci-ous* or sbs. in *-aci-ty*, according to the regular type of vbs. in -TATE (L. *-tāre, -tātum*) f. sbs. in -TY (L. *-tātem*). As *cap-acitate*, to produce the capacity.

acite, early form of ACCITE *v.* to summon.

-acity (-ˈæsɪtɪ), formerly -acite, -acitie, *compd. suffix.* a. Fr. *-acité*, ad. L. *-ācitāt-em* (nom. *-ācitās*), f. *-āci-* (see -ACIOUS) + *-tāt-* (see -TY), according to the regular type of sbs. of quality in *-tāt-em* f. 3rd decl. adjs. in *-i-*, as *celeri-tāt-em, vorāci-tāt-em, voracity*, the quality of being voracious. All the Fr. adjs. in *-acité* are literary adaptations of or formations on L. words; the Eng. are either adoptions of Fr. words, or analogous formations on L. adjs. Every adj. in -ACIOUS may have a sb. of quality in *-acity*, on some of which are formed vbs. in *-acitate*; as *cap-aci-ous, capaci-ty, capacit-ate*.

ack (æk) and vars., used for *a* in the oral transliteration of code messages and in telephone communications, as in ***ack emma***, for *a.m.* = ante meridiem; air mechanic. See ACK-ACK, EMMA. In military use replaced by *able* in Dec. 1942.

1898 *Signalling Instructions* (War Office) 86 The letters T, A, B, M,..will be called toc, ak [1904 *Signalling Regs.* ack], beer, emma. **1917** 'IAN HAY' *Carrying On* vi. 134 He [the Signaller] salutes the rosy dawn as 'Akk Emma', and eventide as 'Pip Emma'. **1918** *Signalling Simplified* 11 Special Names of Letters. (Semaphore and Morse.) A = Ack... Note that, in signalling, these Special Names must *always* be used, i.e. A is always Ack, M is always Emma, and so on. **1927** D. L. SAYERS *Unnatural Death* III. xxiii. 285 Some damned thing at the Yard, I suppose. At three ack emma! **1930** BROPHY & PARTRIDGE *Songs & Slang, 1914–18* 93 *Ack Emma*, Air Mechanic, in the Royal Air Force. Also a.m. = morning. **1934** V. M. YEATES *Winged Victory* 78 The Ak Emma went off in search of food. *a* **1935** T. E. LAWRENCE *Mint* (1955) xxii. 78 We shorten them [*sc.* our ranks] to LAC, AC I, AC II, and speak of ourselves as 'ack-emmas' (the air mechanic of the Great War) or 'urks'.

ack, occas. Sc. form of ACT *v.* and *sb.*

ack(e, variant of AC *conj. Obs.*, but.

-ack, earlier form of -AC, *suffix.*

ack-ack (ˈækˈæk), *a.* and *sb.* Also **Ack-Ack**. [Redupl. form of ACK, repr. *A.A.* (see A III).] **A.** *adj.* Anti-aircraft. **B.** *sb.* Anti-aircraft gun, gunfire, regiment, etc.

1939 *Collier's* 2 Dec. 19/1 One unscheduled move and the machine would have been blown from the air by those long, lean guns the British call Aak Aaks, signalers' code for anti-aircraft. **1940** R. WALKER *Flight to Victory* vii. 49 Engine failure due to ack-ack fire. **1943** E. BONE tr. *W. Wassilewska's Rainbow* vi. 105 'There are more guns under the limes...' 'Ack-ack perhaps?' **1944** *Amer. Speech* XIX. 293 Some fliers who, in their conversation, were careful to distinguish between the enemy's flak and our ack-ack. **1944** 'N. DREW' *Amat. Sailor* ix. 267 Occasionally, for extra special shows, an ack-ack cruiser was in attendance. **1945** *Daily Express* 20 Apr. 4/6 Captain Flack A.A.—Captain Flack, of the Ack-Ack, has been transferred to the Royal Engineers.

ackamarackus (ækəməˈrækəs). *slang* (orig. *U.S.*). Also **ackamaraka**. [Origin unknown.] In phr. ***the old ackamarackus***: a tale or explanation that seeks to convince through deception; a 'tall' story, a hackneyed tale; nonsense, malarkey.

1934 D. RUNYON in *Collier's* 3 Feb. 8/3 This is strictly the old ackamarackus, as the Lemon Drop Kid cannot even spell arthritis. **1950** P. TEMPEST *Lag's Lexicon* 1 'Don't give me the old ackamaraka' = don't tell me tall yarns, don't try to bluff me. **1954** D. POWELL in *Sunday Times* 16 May 11/8 The story is about an American circus in Germany, a spiv who picks up a German floozie, a high diver who marries her, and a dumb giant who brings her wayside flowers. In fact, it is the old circus ackamarackus.

ackee, akee (ˈækiː). [Native name.] The fruit of the tropical sapindaceous tree *Blighia sapida*; the tree itself.

1794 A. BROUGHTON *Hortus Eastensis* 11 The Akee [from] Africa [presented by] Dr. Tho. Clarke, 1778. **1866** *Treas. Bot. Blighia*..consists of only one species, *B. sapida*, which produces the Akee fruit. **1890** H. T. THOMAS *Untrodden Jamaica* 12 The scarlet blots of the ackee. **1916** *Nature* 1 June 286/1 Dr. Scott..concludes that vomiting sickness, so prevalent in that island [*sc.* Jamaica], is due to poisoning by ackee fruit, Blighia sapida. **1956** J. HEARNE *Stranger at Gate* xix. 151 He chewed the..salty, shredded fish and smooth, yellow gobbets of ackee.

ackele, variant of AKELE *v. Obs.*, to cool.

†**acker**¹. *Obs.* or *dial.* Also **aker, akyr, aiker.** [Of uncertain origin; probably a variant of EAGRE *sb.*, the 'bore' on tidal rivers, called by Lyly *agar*.]

†**1.** ? Flood tide; bore; strong current in the sea. *Obs.*

c **1440** *Prom. Parv.* 8 Akyr of the see flowynge [**1499** aker], *Impetus maris.* ? *a* **1500** *Knyghthode & Batayle* MS. Cott. Titus A xxiii. 49, quoted in *Prom. Parv.* 8 Wel know they the remue yf it a-ryse, An aker is it clept, I vnderstonde, Whos myght there may no shippe or wynd wyt stonde. This remue in th' occian of propre kynde Wyt oute wynde hathe his commotioun. **1552** HULOET *Abecedarium*, Aker of the sea, whiche preventeth [= precedes] the flowde or flowynge, *impetus maris.*

2. A ripple, furrow, or disturbance of the surface of water; a 'cat's-paw.' *dial.*

1808 JAMIESON *Scot. Dict.*, *Aiker*, the motion, break, or movement, made by a fish in the water, when swimming fast. **1865** WAY in *Prom. Parv.* 8 In Craven Dial., Acker is a ripple on the water. **1865** *Provincialism* in *Cornhill Mag.* July 34 Sailors at sea name it when seen on a larger scale by the expressive term 'cats-paw.' The North-country peasant, however, knows it by the name 'acker,' implying, as it were, a space ploughed up by the wind.

acker² (ˈækə) *slang.* (orig. *Services'*). Also **akka, akker.** [Prob. ad. Arab *fakka* small change, coins; app. first among British and allied troops in Egypt.] **1.** *Mil.* A piastre.

1937 PARTRIDGE *Dict. Slang* 7/2 *Akka*, an Egyptian piastre: Regular Army's: from ca. 1920. **1948** B. PEARSON in C. K. Stead *N.Z. Short Stories* (1966) 125 Well, the cheapest thing was twenty ackers, I had only ten till pay-day. *a* **1963** J. LUSBY in 'B. James' *Austral. Short Stories* (1963) 239 'See who it was?' 'No.' 'The long red guy—pounds to ackers,' said Rafe. **1976** G. TALBOT *Permission to Speak* iii. 39 Piastres were not suffering, except from the contemptuous slang of British troops who called them 'ackers'.

2. *gen.* Usu. in *pl.* Money, cash; coins or bank-notes.

1939 *Airman's Gaz.* Dec., Useful for drilling holes in the pay bobs when the ackers are short. **1946** J. IRVING *Royal Navalese* 21 *Akka*, money. **1958** M. K. JOSEPH *I'll soldier no More* ix. 166 'Ow 'bout this, Sarge?.. There's some akkers in it - francs. **1965** H. R. F. KEATING *Is Skin-deep, is Fatal* xix. 229, I can't offer a great deal in the way of ackers. Though you'd get your ten per cent, old man. **1977** D. CLARK *Gimmel Flask* ix. 166 Saves a few ackers, I suppose. **1980** R. ADAMS *Girl in Swing* (1981) xix. 243 These buggers, they're all into the ackers—swamp us tomorrow before we can make two bids.

acker, obs. form of ACRE.

ackerne, obs. form of ACORN.

ackerspyre, -sprit, obs. or dial. variants of ACROSPIRE.

acketon, obs. form of ACTON, HAQUETON.

†**a'cknow, aknow**, *v. Obs.* Forms: *Inf.* 1 **oncnáwan**; 3-5 **aknowe(n, aknowe**; 5-6 **aknow.** *Pa. t.* 1 **oncneaw**; 2- **aknew.** *Pa. pple.* 1 **oncnáwen, onknaun, oknaun**; 4 **oknowen**; 4-6 **aknowen, aknowe**; 5 **aknow**; 6 **aknown, aknowne, acknowen**; 6-7 **acknown(e, acknown.** [f. ON, in, on + *cnáwan* to know (by the senses), to recognize; the prefix afterwards reduced, as usual, to *o-*, *a-*, and at length corruptly written *ac-* in imitation of *ac-* before *c- k- q-* in words adopted from L. See A- *pref.* 2.] Very rare after OE. period exc. in pa. pple.

1. To come to know, recognize.

933 *Battle of Maldon* (Sweet 134) Man mihte oncnáwan ðæt se cniht nolde wácian æt ðām wīge. *c* **1330** *Arthour & Merlin* 1081 But gif Y do hir ben a-knawe With wild hors do me to drawe. *c* **1430** *Syr Generides* 6739 Tho [Generides] wold be a-know, Ful simplie he answerd.. It am I, hide it wol I noght.

2. To admit or show one's knowledge, acknowledge, confess.

c **1000** ÆLFRIC *On O. Test.* (Sweet 68) Ðæt he mihte oncnáwan his mánfullan dǣda. *a* **1500** *Merline* 901 (Percy Fol. MS. I. 450) To mee wold shee neuer aknow That any man for any meede Neighed her body. **1561** T. N[ORTON] *Calvin's Instit.* IV. 134 God will not be acknowen true in the receiuyng [of the bread] it selfe, but in the stedfastnesse of his owne goodnesse.

3. In pa. pple. Acquainted, apprized, informed (*of*).

1330 R. BRUNNE *Chron.* 69 If he wild not so, he suld mak him oknowen, He suld wynne it.. as for his owen. **1490** CAXTON *Eneydos* xviii. 68 To departe out of my land sodaynly wythout to make me a knowen thereof.

4. *to be acknown*: To be (self-)recognized or avowed in relation to anything; hence, to avow, confess, acknowledge (*to* a person).

a. *absol.*

c **1350** *Will. Palerne* 4391, I haue þe gretli a-gelt, to god ich am a-knowe. *c* **1430** LYDG. in *Mass Bk.* 390 (1879) I am aknowe, and wot ryght well I speke pleynly as I fel. *c* **1440** *Prom. Parv.* 280 Knowlechyn or ben a-knowe be constreynynge, *Fateor*. Knowlechyn or ben a-knowe wylfully, *Confiteor*. **1460** CAPGRAVE *Chron.* 266 The Erl of Warwick.. was a knowe, as thei seid. For which confession the King gave him lif, and exiled him.

b. with *subord. cl.*

c **1350** *Will. Palerne* 4788 þat we ar worþi to þe deth wel we be a-knowe. *c* **1440** *Gesta Rom.* 201 The first knyght was aknow that he slew the man. **1447** BOKENHAM *Lyvys of Seyntys* Introd. 14 Be not aknowe whom it comyth fro. *c* **1450** PECOCK *Repr.* 149 Neither he wolt be Aknowe that the ymage is his God. **1534** MORE *Treat. on the Passion* Wks. 1557, 1273/2 They.. will not be aknowen that it is his. **1535** COVERDALE *2 Macc.* vi. 6 There durst no man be a knowne that he was a Jewe. **1535-75** ABP. PARKER *Corr.* 441 To put you in remembrance not to be acknown to him that you have it from me. **1548** HALL *Chron.* (1809) 374 Menne must sometym for the maner sake not bee aknowen what they knowe. **1583** GOLDING *Calvin, Deut.* xxxiv. 202 In deede men will not be acknowen yt it is so. **1639** H. AINSWORTH *Annot. on Pentat.* Pref. 4 They will not bee a knowne that they pray or doe worship unto them.

c. with *simple obj.*

c **1374** CHAUCER *Boethius* 17 þat I confesse and am a-knowe. **1414** BRAMPTON *7 Penit. Ps.* lvii. 22, I am aknowe my synfull lyif. *c* **1430** *How the Good Wif, etc.* 159 in Hazl. *E.P.P.* 191 Tylle thei crye mercy, and be here gylte aknowe. *c* **1440** *Gesta Rom.* 395 She wolde haue more sharpe penaunce, and was a-knowe all here synnes to a wicked preste.

d. with *of*.

c **1430** *How the Good Wijf, etc.* 191 in *Babees Bk.* 46 Til þei crie mercy, & be of her gilt aknowe. *c* **1440** *Gesta Rom.* 201 It is better forto be aknow of my synne here openly, and take my penaunce. **1496** *Dives & Pauper* (W. de Worde) VI. xxiv. 272/2 He wolde not be aknowen of his synne, but put his synne on god, and excused hym by Eue. **1526** TINDALE *Rom.* i. 28 As it semed not good vnto them to be aknowen of God, even so God deliveryd them vppe vnto a leawde mynd. **1560** DAUS *Sleidane's Comm.* 390 b, Touching religion & doctrin, they will be acknowne of none error. **1589** PUTTENHAM *Eng. Poesie* (1811) III. xxii. 212 So would I not haue a translatour be ashamed to be acknowen of his translation. **1604** SHAKS. *Oth.* III. iii. 319 Be not acknowne on't: I haue vse for it. **1633** BP. HALL *Hard T.* 140 The very place where he grew shall not be acknowne of him.

†**acknowledge**, *sb. Obs.* [f. AKNOW, ACKNOW *v.* + -LEDGE, after the analogy of KNOWLEDGE from KNOW.] Admitted or communicated knowledge, recognition, cognizance.

1548 GESTE *Preuee Masse* 91 The Kynges Majestie.. hath enforced them to the outward acknowledge therof. *a* **1555** RIDLEY *Wks.* 332 Before I should make the king's majesty privy unto it and of acknowledge, before the collation of it.

acknowledge (æk'nɒlɪdʒ), *v.* [either from ACKNOWLEDGE *sb.*, like the earlier KNOWLEDGE *v.* f. KNOWLEDGE *sb.*; or formed on KNOWLEDGE *v.*, like AKNOW on KNOW. There was also an earlier *i-knowledge*. By 16th c. the earlier vbs. *knowledge* and *a(c)know* (exc. in pa. pple.) were obs., and *acknowledge* took their place. (In this and the kindred words, many pronounce ('nəʊlɪdʒ).]

1. To own the knowledge of; to confess; to recognize or admit as true.

1553 LATIMER in *Southey's C.P. Bk.* Ser. II. 55 One man took remorse of conscience, and acknowledged himself to me that he had deceived the king. **1599** SHAKS. *Much Ado* I. ii. 13 He loued my niece your daughter, and meant to acknowledge it this night in a dance. **1611** —— *Wint. T.* III. ii. 62 In name of Fault, I must not At all acknowledge. **1611** BIBLE *Jer.* iii. 13 Acknowledge thine iniquity that thou hast transgressed against the Lord thy God. **1756** BURKE *Vind. Nat. Soc.* Wks. I. 35, I acknowledge indeed, the necessity of such a proceeding. **1794** SULLIVAN *View of Nat.* I. 71 The sea, he must acknowledge, is always at the same level. **1850** MCCOSH *Div. Govt.* IV. i. (1874) 464 Their views of God are acknowledged to be miserably meagre.

2. To recognize or confess (a person or thing to be something); **a.** with *complement*. **b.** *simply*: To recognize (one) to be what he claims; to own the claims or authority of. ***acknowledge the corn*** (U.S.): see CORN *sb.*[1] 7.

1481 CAXTON *Myrrour* III. xxiv. 193 In whiche translacion I acknowleche myself symple, rude and ygnoraunt. **1590** SHAKS. *Com. Err.* V. i. 322 Thou sham'st to acknowledge me in miserie. **1597** —— *1 Hen. IV*, III. ii. 111 Through all the Kingdomes that acknowledge Christ. **1611** BIBLE *Wisd.* xii. 27 They acknowledged him to be the true God, whome before they denyed to know. —— *Prov.* iii. 6 In all thy wayes acknowledge him, and he shall direct thy pathes. **1651** HOBBES *Leviathan* I. x. 43 He acknowledgeth the power which others acknowledge. **1762** GOLDSM. *Cit. World* (1837) iv. 16 An Englishman is taught to acknowledge no other master than the laws which himself has contributed to enact. **1781** GIBBON *Decl. & F.* III. 65 The authority of Theodosius was cheerfully acknowledged by all the inhabitants of the Roman world. **1849** MACAULAY *Hist. Eng.* I. 532 A secret purse from which agents too vile to be acknowledged received hire. **1876** FREEMAN *Norm. Conq.* II. ix. 433 Harold was publicly acknowledged as.. the designated successor to the crown.

3. To own as genuine, or of legal force or validity; to own, avow, or assent, in legal form, to (an act, document, etc.) so as to give it validity.

1870 PINKERTON *Guide to Administr.* 48 A release should be acknowledged before proper authority and recorded in the office for recording deeds, etc.

4. To own with gratitude, or as an obligation (a gift, or service rendered). Hence, To acknowledge (the receipt of) a letter.

1667 MILTON *P.L.* XI. 612 But they his gifts acknowledg'd none. *Mod.* To acknowledge the divine goodness in our deliverance. I hope you have properly acknowledged their kindness. These letters have not been acknowledged.

5. To show recognition of (see quot. 1881).

1881 OGILVIE (Annandale), *Acknowledge*, to show recognition by some act, as by a bow, nod, smile, lifting the hat, &c., as a mark of friendship or respect; to salute; as, she met him in the street, but barely *acknowledged* him. **1886** 'MAXWELL GRAY' *Silence Dean Maitland* 163 He acknowledged this compliment with a slight bow. **1888** MRS. H. WARD *R. Elsmere* xx, He thought his greeting was acknowledged. *Ibid.* xxvi, Robert smiled slightly, acknowledged the bow, but did not speak.

acknowledgeable (æk'nɒlɪdʒəb(ə)l), *a.* [f. ACKNOWLEDGE *v.* + -ABLE.] Capable of being acknowledged or admitted; recognizable.

1856 RUSKIN *Mod. Painters* III. IV. x. §2 Of all painters [Turner] seemed to obtain least acknowledgeable resemblance to nature.

acknowledged (æk'nɒlɪdʒd), *ppl. a.* [f. as prec. + -ED.] Recognized, confessed, owned; admitted as true, valid, or authoritative.

1769 *Junius Lett.* iii. 19 The acknowledged care and abilities of the adjutant-general. **1781** GIBBON *Decl. & F.* II. 87 These five youths, the acknowledged successors of Constantine. **1810** COLERIDGE *Friend* (1865) 122 To do anything which the acknowledged laws of God have forbidden me to do. **1860** TYNDALL *Glaciers* I. §24. 168 Their pleasure is that of overcoming acknowledged difficulties. **1868** GEORGE ELIOT *Felix Holt* 14 To rule in virtue of acknowledged superiority.

acknowledgedly (æk'nɒlɪdʒdlɪ), *adv.* [f. ACKNOWLEDGED *a.* + -LY[2].] By general acknowledgement; admittedly, confessedly.

1685 *Gracian's Courtier's Manual* 95 Such as are acknowledgedly capable of being good judges. **1827** HARE *Guesses at Truth* (1847) Ser. I. 375 The historian's facts are true; the poet's are acknowledgedly fictitious. **1845** *Vestig. Creat.* (ed. 3) 150 Marsupialia, acknowledgedly low forms in their class.

acknowledger (æk'nɒlɪdʒə(r)). [f. ACKNOWLEDGE *v.* + -ER.] One who acknowledges or owns the claims of.

1535-75 ABP. PARKER *Corr.* 112 Ye his followers & acknowledgers partake of this sin also. *a* **1662** HERRICK *Poems* (1844) 31 And ever live a true acknowledger. **1678** CUDWORTH *Intell. Syst.* I. iv. 186 Aristotle [was] an acknowledger of many gods.

acknowledging (æk'nɒlɪdʒɪŋ), *vbl. sb.* [f. as prec. + -ING[1].] Recognizing or admitting as true or valid; owning, confessing, or avowing. (Now mostly gerundial.)

1561 T. N[ORTON] *Calvin's Instit.* III. 324 To come to the acknowledginge of the trueth. **1591** PERCIVALL *Sp. Dict.*, *Conocimiento*, knowledge, acknowledging, *Cognitio, agnitio, notitia*. **1611** BIBLE *Philemon* 6 The acknowledging of euery good thing. *Mod.* I should like to know the facts before acknowledging the letter.

†**acknowledging** (æk'nɒlɪdʒɪŋ), *ppl. a. Obs.* [f. as prec. + -ING[2].] Making known or expressing regard, esteem, gratitude; grateful. (Fr. *reconnaissant*.) Now only as participle.

1692 DRYDEN *St. Euremont's Ess.* 199 There are but few acknowledging Persons. *a* **1700** —— *Dram. Wks.* (1701) III. 8 Certainly, if ever Nation were oblig'd, either by the Conduct, the Personal Valour, or the good Fortune of a Leader, the English are acknowledging, in all of them, to your royal Highness. **1750-1** MRS. DELANY *Lett.* 9 She.. was.. so acknowledging that I should desire her acquaintance, that she overwhelmed me with her civilities.

acknowledgment (æk'nɒlɪdʒmənt). Also **acknowledgement** (a spelling more in accordance with Eng. values of letters). [f. ACKNOWLEDGE *v.* + -MENT. An early instance of *-ment* added to an orig. Eng. vb.]

1. The act of acknowledging, confessing, admitting, or owning; confession, avowal.

1594 HOOKER *Eccl. Pol.* (1632) V. 394 To require acknowledgement with more than daily and ordinarie testifications of grief. **1599** SHAKS. *Hen. V*, IV. viii. 124 Yes Captaine: but with this acknowledgement, That God fought for vs. **1684** MANTON *Serm.* Wks. 1872 IX. 325 Now the act of faith is an assent, not knowledge but acknowledgment. **1686** *Col. Rec. Pennsylv.* I. 185 In case he give not an acknowledgment of his great abuse. **1792** *Anecd. W. Pitt* III. xliv. 195 A formal acknowledgement of our errors.. must precede every attempt to conciliate. **1825** *Br. Jonathan* III. 301 By which he can escape any acknowledgement of subordination.

†**2.** Recognition, knowledge. *Obs.*

1616 SURFLET & MARKH. *Countrey Farme* 123 To take acknowledgement of the loue that one Horse beareth towards another, and accordingly to set them one by another in the Stable.

3. The act of recognizing the position or claims of; owning or recognition in a particular character.

1611 BIBLE *Coloss.* ii. 2 The acknowledgement of the mysterie of God, and of the Father, and of Christ. **1697** *Snake in the Grass* (ed. 2) 223 These Priests turned to every Power and every Government, as it turned; and made Addresses and Acknowledgements to every Change of Government. **1818** JAS. MILL *Hist. Brit. Ind.* (ed. 4) I. I. ii. 58 All such places as owe acknowledgment to the Dutch. **1849** MACAULAY *Hist. Eng.* I. 291 The king was, by.. the recent and solemn acknowledgment of both houses of parliament, the sole captain general of this large force.

4. A formal declaration or avowal of an act or document, so as to give it legal validity.

1651 W. G. tr. *Cowel's Instit.* 98 He payes a yearly Rent, by way of an acknowledgement of the Seigniorie. **1858** LD. ST. LEONARDS *Property Law* xiv. 93 The suit must be brought within twenty years next after the last of such acknowledgments, or the last of such payments (as the case may be). *Mod.* Has there been any acknowledgement of indebtedness? This was a virtual acknowledgement of the contract.

5. The owning of a gift or benefit received, or of a message; grateful, courteous, or due recognition.

1612 DEKKER in Wks. 1873, 261 Acknowledgement is part of payment sometimes. **1630** LORD *Banians* Ep. Ded., Let it be as an Attestate of my acknowledgments to you. **1747** W. GOULD *English Ants* Ded., I am, with all Acknowledgment, your most Obliged Humble Servant, William Gould. **1769** *Junius Lett.* v. 27 You.. may be satisfied with the warm acknowledgements he already owes you. **1775** TRUMBULL in Sparks' *Cor. Am. Rev.* (1853) I. 10 These instances of kindness claim my most grateful acknowledgments. *Mod.* After so public an acknowledgement of his friend's help.

6. Hence, The sensible sign, whereby anything received is acknowledged; something given or done in return for a favour or message, or a formal communication that we have received it.

1739 T. SHERIDAN *Persius* Ded. 3, I dedicate to you this Edition and Translation of Persius, as an Acknowledgment for the great Pleasure you gave me. **1802** MAR. EDGEWORTH *Moral T.* (1816) I. xvi. 133 To offer him some acknowledgement for his obliging conduct. **1881** *Daily Tel.* Dec. 27 The painter had to appear and bow his acknowledgments. *Mod.* Take this as a small acknowledgement of my gratitude.

7. *Comb.* **acknowledgment-money**.

1717 BLOUNT *Law Dict.* s.v., Acknowledgment-money is a Sum of Money paid by some Tenants, at the Death of their Landlord, in Acknowledgment of their new one.

acknown, pa. pple. of ACKNOW.

ackward, obs. form of AWKWARD.

aclastic (ə'klæstɪk), *a. Nat. Phil. rare.* [f. Gr. ἄκλαστ-ος unbroken + -IC.] Not refracting; applied to substances which do not refract the rays of light which pass through them.

1879 *Syd. Soc. Lex.*

†**a'cleave**, *v. Obs. rare*[−1]. [f. A- *pref.* 1 + CLEAVE. Not recorded in OE.] To cleave or split.

1460 in *Pol. Rel. & Love Poems* 252 And as þyn hert aclef atwynne With doleful deth on þe rode tre.

acleim, acleyme, early f. ACCLAIM *v.* to claim.

aclinic (ə'klɪnɪk), *a.* [f. Gr. ἀκλῖν-ής unbending (f. ἀ priv. + κλίν-ειν to bend) + -IC.] Without inclination. Applied to the magnetic equator, or line surrounding the earth and cutting the terrestrial equator, on which the magnetic needle has no dip but lies horizontal.

[Not in CRAIG 1847.] **1850** ANSTED *Elem. Geol.* 20 There is in the neighbourhood of the earth's equator, and cutting it at four points, an irregular curve called the magnetic equator or aclinic line. **1873** ATKINSON *Ganot's Phys.* (ed. 6) 565 The aclinic line is the line which joins all these places on the earth where..the dipping-needle is quite horizontal.

a-clock, earlier form of o'clock. See A *prep.*[2] and CLOCK.

†**a'close,** *v. Obs. rare.* [f. OFr. *aclos* closed up ? for *enclos*, or f. *a* to (see A- *pref.* 7) + *clos*:—L. *claus-um* shut.] To enclose, shut up.

c **1315** SHOREHAM, 145 God nys nauȝt in ther worldle aclosed Ac hy ys ine hym. *c* **1400** *Destr. Troy* XXVI. 10524 þan Paris and his pepull past to the temple Keppit hom in couert, aclosit hom þerin.

a-cloy, earlier and better f. ACCLOY *v. Obs.* to cloy.

†**a'clumsid,** *ppl. a. Obs. rare*[−1]. [? pa. pple. of **aclumsen*, f. A- *pref.* 1 + *clumsen* to be stiff or numb; or for *y-clumsed* pa. pple. of the simple vb. See A *particle*.] Benumbed, paralysed. Cf. ACUMBLE.

1388 WYCLIF *Jer.* vi. 24 Oure hondys ben aclumsid, tribulacioun hath take vs.

acme ('ækmiː). Also 7 **achme, achma,** 8–9 **acmé, acmè.** [a. Gr. ἀκμή point. Long consciously used as a Gr. word, and written in Gr. letters from Ascham 1570 to Goldsmith 1750, although spelt as Eng. by B. Jonson 1625, and commonly afterwards.]

1. *gen.* The highest point or pitch; the culmination, or point of perfection, in the career or development of anything.

1570 ASCHAM *Scholem.* (1863) 93 The Latin tong, euen whan it was, as the Grecians say, in ἀκμῇ, that is, at the hiest pitch of all perfitenesse. *a* **1637** B. JONSON *Discov.* So that he may be named, and stand as the mark and ἀκμή of our language. **1641** W. CARTWRIGHT *Lady Err.* II. iv. (1651) 23 I' th' heat and achme of devotion. **1655** FULLER *Ch. Hist.* III. 78 Date we from this day, the achme or vertical height of Abbeys, which henceforward began to stand still, & at last to decline. **1659** LESTRANGE *Alliance Div. Off.* ix. The Liturgy and ceremonie of our Church, drawing nigh to its ἀκμή. **1675** OGILBY *Brit.* Ded., In the Achma of the Three Last Empires of the World. **1765** GOLDSM. *Ess., Taste*, By the age of ten his genius was at the ἀκμή. **1790** BURKE *Fr. Revol.* Wks. V. 236 The growth of population in France was by no means at its *acmé* in that year. **1800** WEEMS *Washington* (1877) xi. 155 Having at length attained the acme of all his wishes. **1817** MALTHUS *Population* III. 57 No country has ever reached, or probably ever will reach, its highest possible acme of produce. **1835** I. TAYLOR *Spir. Despotism* §5. 188 A position whence the transition was easy to the acmé of unbounded despotism. **1868** GLADSTONE *Juv. Mundi* (1870) xi. 421 It is however in Achilles that courtesy reaches to its acmè. **1880** *Boy's Own Bk.* 240 The acme of bicycle riding.

†**2.** *esp.* **a.** The period of full growth, the flower or full-bloom of life. *Obs.*

1620 VENNER *Via Recta* viii. 174 They haue not attained vnto the Acme, or full height of their growing. **1625** B. JONSON *Staple of News* Prol. (1631) 5 He must be one that can instruct your youth, And keepe your Acme in the state of truth. **1650** BULWER *Anthropometam.* §22. 245 [It] may be either in the achma or declination of our age. **1660** T. STANLEY *Hist. Philos.* (1701) 259/2 Youth is the encrease of the first Refrigerative part, Age the decrease thereof, ἀκμη, the constant and perfect Life which is betwixt both. **1664** EVELYN *Sylva* 37 Every tree..after each seven years improving twelve pence in growth, till they arriv'd to their acme. **1844** STANLEY *Arnold's Life & Corr.* II. x. 314 The thought that the forty-ninth year, fixed by Aristotle as the acme of the human faculties, lay still some years before him.

b. The point of extreme violence of a disease, the crisis. *arch.*

c **1630** JACKSON *Creed* VIII. xiii. Wks. VII. 496 Christ Jesus ..in the very ἀκμή of his agony..did set the fairest copy of that obedience. **1676** GREW *Plants, Lect.* II. i. §26 (1682) 242 We may conceive the reason of the sudden access of an acute Disease, and of its Crisis..when the Cause is arrived unto such an ἀκμή. **1752** in *Phil. Trans.* XLVII. lxxiii. 586 From the beginning to the flatus or acme of the disease, they almost all die. **1837** CARLYLE *Fr. Revol.* (1872) I. v. vi. 167 Paris wholly has got to the acme of its frenzy.

Acmeism ('ækmiːɪzm). [ad. Russ. *akmeizm*, f. Gr. ἀκμή ACME: see -ISM.] An early twentieth-century movement in Russian poetry which rejected the values of Symbolism in favour of formal technique and clarity of exposition; the poetic theory represented by this movement.

1926 D. S. MIRSKY *Contemp. Russ. Lit.* vi. 253 Acmeism (the rather ridiculous word was suggested with a satirical intention by a hostile Symbolist and defiantly accepted by the new school..) had its centre in St. Petersburg. **1944** *Slavonic Rev.* Oct. 1 Gumilyov's place as the acknowledged leader and master of a new literary school—'Acmeism'—has not been evaluated as yet. **1949** L. I. STRAKHOVSKY *Craftsmen of Word* 2 'The year 1910 marks the crisis of Symbolism,' wrote Alexander Blok. 'In that year were manifested new movements, which adopted a hostile attitude both to Symbolism and to one another: Acmeism, Ego-Futurism, and the first beginnings of Futurism.' **1961** H. MUCHNIC *From Gorky to Pasternak* 10 This individualist attitude, variously manifested, not only in Symbolism itself but in its several offshoots—Acmeism, Futurism, Formalism, as well as in the entirely personal nightmares of such writers as Leonid Andreyev—was to clash most sharply with the dogma of Soviet art.

Also '**Acmeist**, a member or admirer of the Acmeist movement in poetry (usu. in *pl.*); also *attrib.* or as *adj.*

1922 *Slavonic Rev.* I. 221 They called themselves Acmeists, and their poetry is a return to more concrete and realistic modes of expression. **1942** G. SHELLEY *Mod. Poets from Russia* 9 Nikolai Gumilev was one of the founders of the Acmeist movement. **1949** L. I. STRAKHOVSKY *Craftsmen of Word* 2 Because the Acmeists set forth as their goal in poetry a chiseled verse, a precision of images, an exactness of epithets, detachment, a rational approach to creation, and, above all, craftsmanship and the proper use of the word in its exact and not its transitory meaning, they brought to Russian poetry a clarity and vigor which it had not known since the times of Pushkin. **1965** C. BROWN *Prose of Osip Mandelstam* 12 It was the mysticism of the Symbolists, their fascination with the occult and the other world, to which the Acmeists objected. **1974** T. P. WHITNEY tr. *Solzhenitsyn's Gulag Archipel.* I. I. ix. 336 The Acmeists and the Futurists ..had drunk Oldenborger's pure cold water. **1976** *Times Lit. Suppl.* 6 Aug. 988/3 Both in their textural thinness and their formal laxity, his poems are surely a long way from the Acmeist tradition to which Daniel Weissbort assigns them.

acmite ('ækmaɪt). *Min.* Also **akmite.** [f. Gr. ἀκμή point, from the shape of its crystals.] A brownish, brittle mineral belonging to the Amphibole group of Bisilicates.

1837–80 DANA *Min.* 224 Acmite..occurs near Kongsberg in Norway. **1910** *Encycl. Brit.* I. 149/1 *Acmite*, or Aegirite, a mineral of the pyroxene group... It was first discovered.. in the pegmatite veins of granite..near Kongsberg in Norway, and was named by F. Stromeyer in 1821.

acne, acneon, obs. forms of A-KNEE.

acne ('ækniː). *Path.* [mod.L., supposed to be a corruption of Gr. ἀκμή point.] (See quotations.)

1835 HOBLYN *Dict. of Med. Terms* 3, *Acne*, tubercular tumours slowly suppurating, chiefly occurring in the face. **1853** MAYNE, Acne..also called *Rosy-drop.* **1876** DUHRING *Dis. Skin.* 257 Acne is an inflammatory, usually chronic disease of the sebaceous glands, characterized by the formation either of papules, tubercles, or pustules, or a combination of these lesions, occurring for the most part about the face.

acned ('æknɪd), *a.* [f. ACNE + -ED[2].] Suffering from or exhibiting acne; pimply. Also *transf.*

1955 W. GADDIS *Recognitions* I. v. 200 He reared his acned chin. **1967** L. DEIGHTON *Expensive Place to Die* xviii. 128 The visitors had spread through Paris... Acned little girls in bumbag trousers, lithe Danes, fleshy Greeks... Paris had them all that summer. **1977** *Time Out* 17 June 18/1 'Tis a moral tale of two youths,..played by Richard Mottau and Patrick Murray with all the acned confusion and adolescent sullenness they can muster. **1981** *N.Y. Times* 15 Mar. VII. 13/3 Fat, ugly and acned, she lived in awe of her sister.

acneiform ('ækniːɪfɔːm), *a.* Also erron. **acneform.** [f. ACNE + -(*i*)FORM.] Of the nature of acne.

1877 W. T. FOX *Atlas Skin Dis.* 25 The acneiform spots do not make their appearance until the disease has been some time in existence. **1884** *Lancet* 31 May 978/2 A Dermatitis taking an acneform character.

acnestis (æk'niːstɪs). [mod.L., a. Gr. ἄκνηστις spine, backbone.] That part of the back between the shoulder-blade and the loins which an animal cannot reach to scratch.

1807 in *Edin. Med. & Phys. Dict.* II. Suppl. **1927** *Observer* 3 Apr., That spot known to crossword solvers as the acnestis.

acnodal (æk'nəʊdəl), *a. Geom.* [f. ACNODE + -AL[1].] Of or pertaining to acnodes.

1873 SALMON *Higher Plane Curves* 126 Nodal cubics may obviously be subdivided into crunodal and acnodal.

acnode ('æknəʊd). *Geom.* [f. L. *acus* needle + NODE.] = *conjugate point* (s.v. CONJUGATE *a.* 6 a).

1873 SALMON *Higher Plane Curves* 23 In this case no real point is consecutive to the origin, which is then called a conjugate point or acnode. **1961** C. C. T. BAKER *Dict. Math.* 3 *Acnode*, an isolated point or conjugate point of a curve. A point in whose neighbourhood there is no other point of the curve.

acoast, obs. form of ACCOST *v.*

†**a-coast,** *adv.* prop. *phrase. Obs.* Also 3–4 **acost.** [A *prep.*[1] + COAST. The earlier *a-cost* was a direct adoption of OFr. *à coste*, mod. *à côte*: see COAST.]

1. At one side, by the side, by the coast. See ACOST.

2. Ashore.

1599 HAKLUYT *Voy.* II. II. 100 After we had lost ancres, hoising vp the sailes for to get the ship a coast in some safer place.

acock (a'kɒk), *adv.* prop. *phr.* [A *prep.*[1] of state + COCK.] In cocked fashion; defiantly.

1846 JERROLD *Chron. Clovern.* Wks. 1864 IV. 379, A man, who, on his outstart in life, sets his hat acock at matrimony —a man who defies Hymen and all his wicked wiles.

a-cock-bill, *Naut.* Having the bills or tapering ends cocked or pointing upwards. Said of the anchor when it hangs from the cathead ready for dropping, and also of the yards of a vessel, when they are placed at an angle with the deck.

1708 *Sea Dict.* s.v. *Anchor*, The Anchor is a Cock-bell, when the Anchor hangs up and down by the Ship's Side. **1833** *Pen. Cycl.* I. 507/1 An anchor is said..to be 'a cock-bill,' when hanging vertically. **1867** SMYTH *Sailor's Word-bk.* 198 To put the yards a-cock-bill is to top them up by one lift to an angle with the deck. A sign of mourning.

a-cock-horse, *phrase*: see COCK-HORSE.

acœlomate (æ'siːləʊmeɪt, æsiː'ləʊ-), *a. Zool.* [f. A- 14 + CŒLOMATE *a.*] Having no cœlome or body-cavity; not cœlomate. Also **acœ'lomatous** *a.*

1879 tr. *Haeckel's Evol. of Man* II. xxv. 404 Although these acœlomatous Worms have no body-cavity, no blood, no vascular system, they always have a kidney system. **1889** *Cent. Dict.*, Acœlomate. **1921** J. A. THOMSON *Outl. Zool.* (ed. 7) ix. 137 The Cœlentera..form a very large series of Acœlomate Metazoa.

acoie, variant of ACCOY *v. Obs.* to calm.

Acol ('ækɒl). [f. *Acol* Road, Hampstead, London, the address of a house in which the system was devised.] The name given to a system of bidding in bridge.

1938 COHEN & REESE *Acol Syst. Contract Bridge* 2 The Acol system, deriving its name from the former Acol club where it was developed..first attracted attention in 1937. **1959** *Listener* 11 June 1042/1 Acol has two types of bid for strong hands. **1959** REESE & DORMER *Bridge Player's Dict.* 12 *Acol system*, this system is played by the majority of British tournament players and some of its ideas are reflected in modern American systems such as Stayman and Kaplan-Sheinwold.

†**aco'lastic(ke,** *a. Obs.*[−0] [f. Gr. ἀκόλαστ-ος, see next, + -IC.] 'A prodigall person.' Cockeram 1612. 'That liveth under no correction, riotous.' Blount 1656. 'Incorrigible, not better by chastisement.' Bullokar 1676.

†'**acolaust.** *Obs.* [? ad. Gr. ἀκόλαστ-ος unchastised, licentious.] One that revels in sensual pleasures (like the prodigal of the parable).

1633 T. ADAMS *Exp. 2 Pet.* ii. 19 (1865) 547/1 The acolaust loathes the service of that churl, that allowed him no better diet than husks.

acold (ə'kəʊld), *a. arch.* Forms: 3 **acoled** (?), 4 **acoold, acoild,** 5–6 **acolde,** 6–7, 9 **acold.** [prob. orig. *a-cólod, a-cóled*, pa. pple. of *acólian, acólen* (see ACOOL), which became regularly *acooled* in 16th c., but when used adjectively preserved the original *o* before two consonants, or by assimilation to adj. COLD.] Cooled, chilled, cold.

c **1314** *Guy Warw.* 20 Al to michel thou art afoild [= afoolèd], Now thi blod it is acoild. **1393** GOWER *Conf. Am.* III. 35 Thus lay this pouer in great distresse, Acolde and hongry at the gate. *c* **1400** *Rom. Rose* 2658 And waite without in woo and peyne, Full yvel a-coolde in wynde and reyne. **1461** *Past. Lett.* 421 II. 63 It begynyth to wax a cold abydyng her. **1474** CAXTON *Chesse* 52 He behelde where satte an olde knyght that was sore acolde. **1563** *Homilies* II. ii. III. (1859) 233 Who have need either of meat when we be hungry, or drink when we be thirsty, or clothing when we be acold. **1589** PUTTENHAM *Eng. Poesie* (1869) 236 Alwaies burning and euer chill a colde. **1605** SHAKS. *K. Lear* III. iv. 59 Tom's a-cold. **1608** TOURNEUR *Reveng. Trag.* II. i. 51 All thriues but chastity; she lyes a cold. **1821** KEATS *St. Agnes' Eve* i. 170 The owl for all his feathers was a-cold. *a* **1843** SOUTHEY *Compl. of Poor* Wks. II. 195 And we were wrapt and coated well, And yet we were a-cold. **1863** A. B. GROSART *Small Sins* (ed. 2) 90 Their a-cold breath blights the fragile blossoms. **1870** MORRIS *Earthly Par.* III. IV. 341 Before the sun of that day grew acold.

†**a'cold,** *v. Obs.* [OE. *acald-ian*, W. Sax. *acealdian* cogn. w. OHG. *irchalten*, mod.G. *erkalten*; f. A- *pref.* 1 + OE. *cald-ian, cealdian* to become cold.]

1. *intr.* To become cold.

c **880** K. ÆLFRED *Greg. Past.* lviii. 447 Swa eac ðæt wearme wlacað, ær hit eallunga acealdiȝe. **1388** *Wimbleton's Sermon* in Halliw., The syknesse of the world thou schalt knowe by charyté acoldyng. *c* **1440** *Gesta Rom.* 96 When this knyght þat was accolded,—& hit was grete froste.

2. *trans.* To make cold, cool.

c **1230** *Ancren Riwle* 404, O sond ne groweð no god, and bitocneð idel : and idel acoaldeð & acwencheð þis fur.

acole, earlier form of ACOOL *v.* and of ACCOLL *v.*

†**acolee.** *Obs.* [a. OFr. *acolee* embrace, hug; properly pa. pple. of *acoler*: see ACCOLL.] The embrace, or other greeting, by which knighthood was conferred: the earlier equivalent of ACCOLADE.

c **1450** *Merlin* xxi. 374 The kynge Arthur yaf hym the acolee, and bad god make hym a gode knyght.

a'cology. *Med. rare.* [f. Gr. ἄκος cure, remedy + -λογία treatise; see -LOGY.] 'The doctrine of therapeutic agents in general, or of the method of curing disease.' Craig 1847, etc.

†**acolouthite.** *Obs. rare.* Also 7 acholithite. [f. Gr. ἀκόλουθ-ος + -ITE.] By-form of ACOLYTE.

1599 Bp. Hall *Virgidem* iv. vii. 53 To see a lasie dumbe Acholithite, Armed against a devout flyes despight. **1642** Jer. Taylor *Episcopacie* (1647) 174 The office of an acolouthite, of an exorcist, of an ostiary, are no way dependent on the office of a deacon.

acoluteship, obs. form of ACOLYTESHIP.

acoluth, obs. but more correct f. ACOLYTE.

acoluthic, var. AKOLUTHIC *a.*

acolyctine (ækəʊ'lɪktaɪn). *Chem.* [f. the plant whence derived.] An organic base obtained from *Aconitum Lycoctonum*; supposed to be identical with aconine.

acolyte ('ækəlaɪt). Forms: 3-6 acolyt, 4 acolite, 6 acoluth(e, 6-9 acolyth(e, 8-9 acolyte. [ad. med.L. *acolitus, acolithus, acolythus*, corrupt forms of *acolūthus* a. Gr. ἀκόλουθος following, attending upon, subst. an attendant. The normal form is *acoluth*, as written by some of the 16th c. scholars. Occ. aphetized to COLET, and expanded to ACOLYTHIST, ACOLOUTHITE.]

1. *Eccl.* An inferior officer in the church who attended the priests and deacons, and performed subordinate duties, as lighting and bearing candles, etc.

c **1000** Ælfric *Past. Ep.* in *Anc. Laws* II. 378 *Acolitus* is se þe leoht berð æt Godes þenungum. *c* **1315** Shoreham 45 The ferthe [degree in orders] acolyt hys to segge y-wys Tapres to bere wel worthe. **1382** Wyclif *Coloss.* Prol., Therfore the apostle, thennis boundyn, writith to hem fro Effecie bi Tyte, a dekene, and Honesym, acolite. **1460** Capgrave *Chron.* 74 He that schuld be mad a Bischop schuld first be a benet..and then a colet; and then subdiacone, diacone, and prest. **1555** *Fardle of Facions* II. xii. 267 The Acholite, whiche we calle Benet or Cholet, occupieth the roume of Candle-bearer. **1561** T. N[orton] *Calvin's Inst.* (1634) iv. 155 They play yᵉ Philosophers about yᵉ name of Acoluth, calling him a *Ceroferar*, a taper bearer with a worde..wheras *Acoluthos* in Greke simply signifieth a folower. **1588** A. King *Canisius' Catech.* 109 Gif ony man deseruis to be ane Bishope lat him first be ostiar, secundlie lecteur, nixt ane Exorcist, efter ane Acolyt. **1594** Hooker *Eccl. Pol.* vii. xx. Wks. III. 347 The bishops attendants, his followers they were; in regard of which service the name of Acolythes seemeth plainly to have been given. **1637** Gillespie *Eng. Popish Cerem.* iii. viii. 161 Exorcists, Monkes, Eremits, Acoluths, and all the whole rabble of Popish orders. **1649** Selden *Laws of Eng.* i. x. (1739) 18 Acolites, which waited with the Taper ready lighted. **1824** Southey *Bk. of the Ch.* I. 353 The candlestick, taper and urceole were taken from him as acolyte. **1849** W. Fitzgerald tr. *Whitaker's Disput.* 505 The apostolic canons ..name only five orders,—the bishop, priest, deacon, reader, and chanter, omitting the exorcist, porter, and acolyth. **1855** tr. *Labarte's Arts Mid. Ages & Renaiss.* i. 15 Two acolythes carried the candlesticks. **1873** W. H. Dixon *Two Queens* I. vi. x. 369 At every porch a priest came out with acolyte and choir.

2. In other senses: **a.** An attendant or junior assistant in any ceremony or operation; a novice.

1829 Scott *Demonol.* vii. 213 Nor are such acolytes found to evade justice with less dexterity than the more advanced rogues. **1831** —— *Kenilw.* xxxii. (1853) 296 To awaken the bounty of the acolytes of chivalry. **1865** Dickens *Our Mut. Fr.* i. 137 It was the function of the acolyte to dart at sleeping infants.

b. An attendant insect or other animal.

1876 Beneden *An. Paras.* 4 Species at the mercy of others, and dependent on acolytes, which are in every respect inferior to themselves.

c. An attendant star.

1876 Chambers *Astron.* 910 *Acolyte*..sometimes used to designate the smaller of two stars placed in close contiguity.

acolyteship ('ækəlaɪt-ʃɪp). Also 6 **acoluteship.** [f. prec. + -SHIP.] The position or office of an acolyte.

1562 Foxe *A. & M.* I. 749/2 [Degrading] from Acoluteship, by taking from them the Cruet and Candlestick.

acolythist. *arch.*; also 8 **acolothist.** [f. med.L. *acolyth-us* + -IST.] By-form of ACOLYTE.

1726 Ayliffe *Parergon.* 96 To ordain the Acolothist, to keep the Sacred Vessels, etc. *Ibid.* 184 The word Clerk is confin'd to the Seven Degrees..viz. the Ostiarius..the Acolythist, Reader, Exorcist, Sub-deacon, Deacon, and Presbyter. **1751** Chambers *Cycl.* s.v. *Acoluth*, Among the ecclesiastical writers, the term *Acolythus* or *Acolythist*, is peculiarly applied to those young people, who in primitive times aspired to the ministry. **1811** Grant *Hist. Eng. Ch.* I. 158 Two candlesticks for the acolythists. **1844** Lingard *Hist. A.S. Ch.* (1858) I. iv. 133 Subordinate officers were required; and we soon meet..with..acolythists..these were ordained.

acomber, -bre, variants of ACCUMBER *v. Obs.*

acombraunce, -ous, var. ACCUMBRANCE, -OUS.

†**a'come,** *v. Obs.* Forms: *Inf.* 1 acuman, 3 acome(n. *Pa. pple.* 1 **acumen**, 5 **acomen.** [f. A- *pref.* 1 + *cum-an*; cf. OHG. *irqueman*, mod.G. *erkommen.*] To come to, attain, reach.

a **1000** Cædmon *Gen.* 1544 Wæs of fere acumen. **1297** R. Glouc. 126 Eldol..Hente a strong leuour þat him a-com at hand bi cas. *c* **1315** Shoreham 73 Ase ȝef hy hyȝt myȝt wel a-come To letten other wyle. *a* **1450** *Chester Pl.* (1843) I. 109 Though in thee be God vereye A-comen againste kinde.

acomer, var. ACCUMBER *v. Obs.* to encumber.

†**a-'compass,** *adv. Obs.* prop. *phrase.* [a. OFr. *à compas*, f. *compas* circle.] In a circle.

c **1385** Chaucer *Leg. Good W.* 301 And with that word, a-compas enviroun, They setten hem ful softely adoun.

acompte, obs. form of ACCOUNT *sb.* and *v.*

†**acompter.** *Obs.* [a. Fr. *acompter* to ACCOUNT, inf. used subst.] Account, reckoning.

1483 Arnold *Chron.* (1811) 271 The averagis of the last acompter.

acondylous (ə'kɒndɪləs), *a. Nat. Hist.* [f. Gr. ἀ priv. + κόνδυλ-ος a joint + -OUS.] Not jointed.

1853 In Mayne.

acone (ə'kəʊn, eɪ-), *a. Ent.* [f. A- 14 + CONE *sb.* 10.] Of the eyes of insects: without a cone.

1888 Rolleston & Jackson *Forms Animal Life* 502 In acone eyes one cell stands in the centre with the six others around, and the visual rods or rhabdomeres are contained one in each cell. **1957** A. D. Imms *Gen. Textbk. Ent.* (ed. 9) 105 In the acone eyes there is a group of elongate, transparent cone cells but the latter do not secrete any kind of cone whether crystalline or liquid.

aconelline (ækəʊ'nɛlaɪn). *Chem.* [dimin. f. ACONINE.] An organic base obtained from the root of the aconite; also called *Aconella.*

1876 Harley *Mat. Med.* 771 Messrs. T. & H. Smith have isolated another crystalline body identical with narcotia, and have called it aconella. **1879** *Syd. Soc. Lex.*, Aconellin.

aconic (ə'kɒnɪk), *a. Chem.* [Short. f. ACONITIC.]

1. In *aconic acid*: A non-saturated monobasic acid of formula $C_5H_4O_4$.

1877 Fownes *Man. Chem.* II. 355 By boiling with baryta-water, aconic acid is resolved into formic and succinic acids.

2. In comb. a group of isomeric non-saturated bibasic acids of formula $C_5H_6O_4 = C_3H_4.2(CO_2H)$, derived from aconitic acid by the loss of carbon dioxide in distillation. They are distinguished as *citraconic, itaconic, mesaconic*, and *paraconic.*

1877 Fownes *Man. Chem.* II. 353 Citraconic and itaconic acids are produced by the action of heat on citric acid.

aconicke, 'Poysonous.' Cockeram 1626. [? for *aconitic.*]

aconine ('ækənaɪn). *Chem.* [f. L. *aconītum.*] A substance obtained by the continued action of hot water on aconitine, supposed to be identical with napelline.

aconital (ækəʊ'naɪtəl), *a. rare.* [f. L. *aconīt-um* + -AL¹.] Of the character of aconite.

a **1642** Urquhart *Jewel* Wks. 1834, 281 Almost ready to choak with the aconital bitterness and venom thereof. **1834** H. Miller *Sc. & Leg.* vii. (1857) 98 The aconital bitterness of the preacher.

aconitate (ə'kɒnɪteɪt). *Chem.* [f. L. *aconīt-um* + -ATE⁴.] A salt of Aconitic acid.

1873 Williamson *Chemistry* §307 When the citrate is cautiously heated, it loses the elements of a molecule of water, forming aconitate ($C_6H_6O_6$).

aconite ('ækənaɪt). [a. Fr. *aconit*, ad. L. *aconītum*, ad. Gr. ἀκόνιτον of uncertain etymol. The L. form *aconitum* is also used unchanged, especially in sense 2.]

1. A genus of poisonous plants, belonging to the order *Ranunculaceæ. esp.* the common European species *Aconitum Napellus*, called also Monk's-hood and Wolf's-bane. Also applied loosely or erroneously to other poisonous plants.

1578 Lyte *Dodoens* 426 Aconit is of two sortes..the one is named..Aconit that baneth, or killeth Panthers. The other ..Aconit that killeth Woolfs. **1598** Sylvester *Du Bartas* i. iii. (1641) 27/1 Onely the touch of Choak-pard Aconite Bereaves the Scorpion both of sense and might. **1601** Holland *Pliny* II. 271 (1634) It groweth naturally vpon bare and naked rocks, which the Greeks cal Aconas: which is the reason (as some haue said) why it was named Aconitum. **1613** Heywood *Braz. Age* ii. ii. 215 With Aconitum that in Tartar springs. **1697** Dryden *Virgil's Georgic* ii. 209 Nor pois'nous Aconite is here produc'd, Or grows unknown, or is, when known, refus'd. **1794** Martyn *Rousseau's Bot.* xxi. 298 Aconite has the upper petal arched; and three or five capsules. **1860** Piesse *Lab. Chem. Wond.* 91 The accidental substitution of aconite root or monkshood for horse-radish.

2. An extract or preparation of this plant, used as a poison and in pharmacy. *poet.* Deadly poison.

1597 Shaks. *2 Hen. IV*, iv. iv. 48 Though it doe worke as strong As Aconitum, or rash Gun-powder. **1606** Dekker *Newes fr. Hell* (1842) 87 *note*, Ingenious, fluent, facetious T. Nash, from whose abundant pen hony flow'd to thy friends, and mortall aconite to thy enemies. **1656** Cowley *Anacreont.* i. (1669) 41 All the World's Mortal to 'em then, And Wine is Aconite to men. *a* **1735** Ld. Lansdowne *To Mira* 21 (1779) Despair, that aconite does prove, And certain death, to others' love. *a* **1868** H. Buck *Infant Life* (ed. 3) 124 *Aconite*..this remedy has been aptly styled 'The Homœopathic Lancet.' **1869** *Daily News* May 26 She and the deceased had eaten the root of a plant called wolf's-bane, the active poison of which is aconite.

3. winter aconite: Common name of another little plant of the same order, *Eranthis hyemalis*, having a yellow anemone-like flower springing from a whorl of leaves.

1741 *Compl. Fam. Piece* ii. iii. 379 Yellow Aconite, double scarlet and dwarf Lichnis. **1794** Martyn *Rousseau's Bot.* xxi. 299 The winter-flowering species commonly called Winter-Aconite, is the only one that drops its petals. **1879** *Spectator* 6 Sept. 1127/1 The small yellow winter-aconite is more cheery than the lingering rosebud born too late to bloom.

aconitia (ækəʊ'nɪʃɪə). *Chem.* [f. L. *aconīt-um*; ending as in *ammonia.*] = ACONITIN.

1835 Hoblyn *Dict. Med. Terms, Aconitia*, an alkaloid; the narcotic principle of *A. Napellus.* **1882** *Pall Mall G.* 13 Jan. 8/1 Aconitia caused death by paralyzing the heart.

aconitic (ækəʊ'nɪtɪk), *a. Chem.* [f. L. *aconīt-um*; see ACONITE + -IC.] Of or pertaining to aconite. *aconitic acid*, a basic triatomic acid $(C_6H_3O_3)'''(OH)_3$ existing in monkshood, larkspur, and other plants, and also obtained by heating citronic acid.

1873 Fownes *Chem.* 730 Aconitic Acid exists in Monkshood.

aconitine (ə'kɒnɪtaɪn). *Chem.* [f. L. *aconītum* + -IN(E.] The essential principle of aconite, an extremely poisonous vegetable alkaloid; a light white powder, without smell, with a bitter taste.

1847 Craig, Aconitine. **1853** Mayne, Aconitin. **1879** *Syd. Soc. Lex.* s.v. *Aconitia*, Aconitine resembles Curara in impairing the conducting power of the motor nerves. **1881** Wontner in *Standard* 30 Dec. 2/5 One of these pills, at all events, contained a sufficient dose of aconitine to cause death.

acont(e, early form of ACCOUNT *v.* and *sb.*

‖**à contre-cœur** (akɔ̃trkœːr). Also **à contre cœur, à contrecœur.** [Fr., lit. 'against one's heart'.] Against one's will, reluctantly.

1803 E. Wynne *Diary* 10 July (1940) III. iv. 83 He really goes to sea quite *à contre coeur* as he was now so comfortably settled here. **1856** Geo. Eliot *Jrnl.* 8 May-26 June in *Geo. Eliot Lett.* (1954) II. 244 My preoccupation with my article, which I worked at considerably *à contrecoeur*, despairing of its ever being worth anything. **1893** Yonge & Coleridge *Strolling Players* xxv. 220 Having agreed, it would be well not to go on *à contre cœur*. **1926** R. Firbank *Eccentricities Cardinal Pirelli* vii. 84 Dear child... She accepts him..but a little à contre-cœur. **1939** A. Toynbee *Study of Hist.* IV. 376 In the West the linguistic concessions which had been made, *à contre-cœur*, to the Slavonic tongue and to the Glagolitic script were never allowed to develop from being a local curiosity into becoming a general practice. **1979** 'J. le Carré' *Smiley's People* i. 22 She explained how she had assembled the two trivial reports that were the..price of her freedom. It was *à contre-cœur*, she said; invention and evasion, she said; a nothing.

†**a'cool,** *v. Obs.* Forms: *Inf.* 1 **acólian,** 2-3 **acolen,** 3-4 **acole,** 4-5 **acoole,** 5-6 **acoole.** *Pa. pple.* 1 **acólad, acólod,** 2-4 **acoled,** 5-6 **acooled.** See ACOLD for adj. forms of the pple. [f. A- *pref.* 1 intensive + *cólian* to cool or make cold. Cf. AKELE, OE. *acélan*, originally the transitive vb. while *acólian* was intr.]

1. *intr.* To wax cold, to cool.

a **1000** *Ags. Gosp.* Matt. xxiv. 12 Maneȝra lufu acolað. *a* **1200** *Cott. Hom.* 237 þes lare and laȝe swiðe acolede þurh manifead sénne. *a* **1250** *Owl & Night.* 1273 Nis nout so hot that hit nacoleth.

2. *trans.* To cool. (The first instance may be *intr.*)

a **1250** *Owl & Night.* 205 Ich wot he is nu suthe acoled. **1548** Udall, etc. *Erasm. Paraphr. John* 103 b, The Lorde Jesus dyd thus abate and acoole that arrogancie. **1540** Whittinton *Tully's Offyce* ii. 77 The greuance of heates be acooled and abated.

†**a'cop,** *adv. Obs. rare.* [A *prep.*¹ + COP top.] On the top; on high.

1610 B. Jonson *Alch.* ii. vi. 33 Marry, sh' is not in fashion yet; she weares A hood, but it stands acop.

acopic (ə'kɒpɪk), *a.* and *sb. Med.* [mod. f. Gr. ἄκοπ-ος removing fatigue (f. ἀ priv. + κόπος weariness) + -IC.] Remedying fatigue; anything which has the property of removing the feeling of fatigue.

acople, early form of ACCOUPLE *v. Obs.*

†**'acopon.** *Obs. Med.* [translit. of Gr. ἄκοπον adj. neut., sc. φάρμακον; see prec.] A soothing

salve; a poultice or plaster to relieve pain; an anodyne.

1661 R. LOVELL *Anim. & Min.* 82 Old oile boiled to the temper and thicknesse of an Acopon, helpeth all vices of the nerves, and paines.

‖**acor.** *Med.* [L. *acor* f. stem *ac-* sharp.] Sourness or acidity, as of the stomach.

1847 In CRAIG. **1853** In MAYNE.

acord, -ant, etc., earlier form of ACCORD, -ANT, etc.

†**a'core,** *v. Obs.* Forms: *Inf.* 2–3 acori-en, acory-en, acory-e; 4 acore. [f. A- *pref.* 1 intensive + *corian*, cogn. w. ODu. *coren*, OHG. *coron, choron*, to taste. Neither *corian* nor *acorian* has yet been found in OE., and the history of the word is a blank before its appearance in the 12th c. as below.] To taste, feel the smart of, suffer.

c **1200** *Trin. Coll. Hom.* 45 Oðer hadde the gult . and ure hlouerd ihesu crist hit acorede. *c* **1230** *Ancren Riwle* 60 þu schalt acorien þe rode: þat is acorien his sunne. *c* **1270** *Old Eng. Misc.* 75 In helle..Acoryen hit ful wraþe. **1297** R. GLOUC. 75 þat a corede al þis lond. *c* **1305** *E.E. Poems* 63 þu hit schalt acore sore. *c* **1330** *Florice & Bl.* 767 Thou ne aughtest nowght mi deth acore.

acorn ('eɪkɔːn). Forms: 1 æcern, æcirn, (2–3 ? akern); 4–7 akern, (4 hakern); 4 *pl.* acres, atcherne; 4–5 acharn(e; 4–6 achorn(e, 5 akerne, ackerne, accharne, acorun, accorne, hockorn; 5–7 acorne, oke-corne; 6 akecorne, okehorne, acquorn, eykorn; 6–7 akehorne, akorne, acron; 7 oke-corn, akorn; 6– acorn. [The formal history of this word has been much perverted by 'popular etymology.' OE. *æcern* neut., pl. *æcernu*, is cogn. w. ON. *akarn* neut. (Dan. *agern*, Norw. *aakorn*), Du. *aker* 'acorn,' OHG. *ackeran* masc. and neut. (mod.G. *ecker*, pl. *eckern*) 'oak or beech mast,' Goth. *akran* 'fruit,' prob. a deriv. of Goth. *akr-s*, ON. *akr*, OE. *æcer* 'field,' orig. 'open unenclosed country, the plain.' Hence *akran* appears to have been originally 'fruit of the unenclosed land, natural produce of the forest,' mast of oak, beech, etc., as in HG., extended in Gothic to 'fruit' generally, and gradually confined in Low G., Scand., and Eng., to the most important forest produce, the mast of the oak. (See Grimm, under *Ackeran* and *Ecker*.) In Ælfric's *Genesis* xliv. 11, it had perhaps still the wider sense, a reminiscence of which also remains in the ME. *akernes of okes*. Along with this restriction of application, there arose a tendency to find in the name some connexion with *oak*, OE. *ác*, north. *ake, aik*. Hence the 15th and 16th c. refashionings *ake-corn, oke-corn, ake-horn, oke-horn*, with many pseudo-etymological and imperfectly phonetic variants. Of these the 17th c. literary *acron* seems to simulate the Gr. ἄκρον top, point, peak. The normal mod. repr. of OE. *æcern* would be *akern, akren*, or ? *atchern* as already in 4; the actual *acorn* is due to the 16th c. fancy that the word *corn* formed part of the name.]

1. Fruit generally, or ? mast of trees. *Obs.*

c **1000** ÆLFRIC *Gen.* xliii. 11 Bringað þam men lac, somne dæl tyrwan & hunig and stor, and æcirnu & hnite. *c* **1374** CHAUCER *Boeth.* (1560) I. 201/1 (1868) 25 Let him gone, beguiled of trust that he had to his corne, to Achornes of Okes. *Ibid.* (1868) 50 To slaken her hunger at euene wiþ acornes of okes.

2. a. The fruit or seed of the oak-tree; an oval nut growing in a shallow woody cup or *cupule*.

c **1000** ÆLFRIC *Gloss.* in Wright's *Voc.* 33 & 80 *Glans*, æcern. *Ibid.* 284 *Glandix*, æceren. *c* **1350** *Will. Palerne* 1811 Hawes, hepus & hakernes, & þe hasel-notes. **1387** TREVISA *Higden* (Rolls. Ser.) I. 195 (The Athenians) tauȝte..ete acharns [*Caxton* acornes]. *Ibid.* II. 345 Toforehonde þey lyued by acres (= *cum ante glandibus sustentarentur*). **1388** *Inv. of Goods of Sir S. Burley* in *Prom. Parv.* 6 Deux pairs des pater nosters de aumbre blanc, l'un countrefait de Atchernes, l'autre rounde. **1398** TREVISA *Barth. De P.R.* (1495) IX. xix. 357 Nouembre is paynted as a chorle betyng okes and fedyng his swyne with maste and hockornes. *Ibid.* XVII. cxxxiv. 690 The hoke beeryth fruyte whyche hyghte Ackerne. *Ibid.* XVIII. lxxxvii. 837 Hogges bothe male and female haue lykynge to ete Akernes. *c* **1440** *Prom. Parv.* 361 Ocorn or acorn (**1499** occarne, or akorne) frute of an oke. *Ibid.* 6 Accorne or archarde, frute of the oke. *a* **1500** *Nominale* in Wright's *Voc.* 228 *Hec glans* a nacorun. **1500** *Ortus Voc.* Accharne, okecorne. **1509** FISHER *Wks.* 234 (1876) He coude not haue his fyll of pesen and oke cornes. **1523** FITZHERBERT *Surv.* xxix. 51 Ye must gather many akehornes. **1547** SALESBURY *Dict. Eng. & Welsh, Mesen* An oke corne. **1549** *Compl. Scotl.* xvii. 144 (1872) Acquorns, vyild berreis, green frutis, rutis & eirbis. **1551** TURNER *Herbal.* III. 109 (1568) The oke whose fruite we call an Acorn, or an Eykorn, that is the corn or fruit of an Eyke. **1552** HULOET, Woode bearynge maste or okehornes, *Glandaria sylua.* **1565** JEWEL *Repl. to M. Harding* 302 (1611) They fed of Akecornes, and dranke water. **1570** ASCHAM *Scholem.* 145 (1870) To eate ackornes with swyne, when we may freely eate wheate bread emonges men. **1572** J. BOSSEWELL *Armorie* II. 74b, To assuage theire hongre at euen with the Akecornes of Okes. **1580** TUSSER *Husbandry* 28 For feare of a mischiefe keep acorns from kine. **1580** NORTH *Plutarch* (1595) 236 The Arcadians..were in olde time called eaters of akornes. **1586** B[EARD] *La Primaudaye's Fr. Acad.* II. 117 (1594) The hogge, who with his snowte alwayes towardes the earth, feedeth upon the akornes that are underneath the Oakes. **1594** PLAT *Jewell-house* III. 13 You may feed Turkies with brused acrons. **1597** BACON *Ess.* 256 (1862) *Satis quercus*, Acornes were good till bread was found, etc. **1611** HEYWOOD *Gold. Age* I. i. 11 He hath taught his people—to skorne Akehornes with their heeles. **1611** COTGR., *Couppelettes de gland*, Akorne cups. **1613** W. BROWNE *Brit. Past.* II. II. iii. (1772) 96 Green boughs of trees with fat'ning acrones lade. **1627** MAY *Lucan* VI. (1631) 481 That famed Oake fruitfull in Akehornes. **1632** SANDERSON 12 *Serm.* 471 Vnder the Oakes we grouze vp the Akecorns. **1640** BROME *Sparagus Gard.* 113 Leekes, and Akornes here Are food for Critickes. **1649** LOVELACE *Grasshopper* 34 Thou dost retire To thy Carv'd Acron-bed to lye. **1651** HOBBES *Leviathan* IV. xlvi. 368 They fed on Akorns, and drank Water. **1664** EVELYN *Sylva* 15 (1679) Any Oak, provided it were a bearing Tree, and had Acorns upon it. **1674** GREW *Anat. Plants* I. i. (1682) 3 *Oak-Kernels*, which we call *Acorns. Ibid.* IV. II. iv. 186 An Akern, is the *Nut* of an Oak. *a* **1682** SIR T. BROWNE *Tracts* 27 Some oaks do grow and bear acrons under the sea. **1712** tr. *Pomet's Hist. Drugs* I. 81 The Acorn of the Cork is astringent. *c* **1821** KEATS *Fancy* 248 Acorns ripe down-pattering While the autumn breezes spring. **1859** COLEMAN *Woodl. Heaths & Hedges* 7 The young trees usually first produce acorns when about fifteen to eighteen years old.

b. An artificial object resembling an acorn in shape. Also in *Comb.* (see quots.)

1580 T. BAWDEWYN in E. Lodge *Illustr. Brit. Hist.* (1791) II. cliv. 243, I did send yowre Honor..a cup wᵗʰ a cover..two saltes, 11 acornes. **1795** *Ann. Reg. 1772* (ed. 5) Chron. 85/1 The lightning was attracted by the acorn on the top of the chapel. *a* **1884** KNIGHT *Dict. Mech.* Suppl. 3/2 *Acorn-headed Bolt*, a carriage-bolt with an ornamental head..in shape resembling an acorn. **1935** C. G. BURGE *Compl. Bk. Aviation* 85/1 *Acorn*, a device introduced at the intersection of bracing wires to prevent abrasion. **1935** *Burlington Mag.* LXVII. 150/2 The acorn-bulb [in a drinking-glass]..is exactly matched by a stem in the Thaurin Collection at Rouen. **1943** *Gen* 19 June 42/2 Acorn Tops are screwed on to the ends of brass curtain rods. **1960** H. HAYWARD *Antique Coll.* 9/2 *Acorn clock*, shelf or mantel clock..with the upper portion shaped somewhat like an acorn... *Acorn knop*, a knop or protuberance on the stem of a drinking glass, tooled in the form of an acorn.

3. *Naut.* 'A conical piece of wood fixed on the uppermost point of the spindle, above the vane, to keep it from being blown off from the mast-head.' Craig 1847.

1769 in W. FALCONER *Dict. Marine.*

4. sea-acorn = ACORN-SHELL.

1764 CROKER *Dict. Arts.* s.v., Acorn, a genus of shell-fish, of which there are several species.

5. *Attrib.* (in sense 2.) in *acorn-bread, crop, meal*, etc.; **acorn-cup**, the cupulate involucre in which the acorn grows; **acorn-barnacle** = ACORN-SHELL; **acorn squash** *N. Amer.*, a variety of squash having a longitudinally grooved and ridged surface; **acorn-sugar** = QUERCITE; **acorn tube, valve** *Radio*, a small acorn-shaped valve; **acorn-worm**, a worm-like animal of the class *Enteropneusta*, having an acorn-shaped anterior end to its body.

1882 J. HAWTHORNE *Fortune's Fool* I. xxiii. (in *Macm. Mag.* XLVI. 44) What I need now is a bellyful of venison and acorn-bread. **1859** COLEMAN *Woodl. Heaths & Hedges* 7 Swine took his place in the woods and to them the acorn crop..has for past years been resigned. **1590** SHAKS. *Mids. N.D.* II. i. 31 All there Elues for feare Creepe into Acorne cups, and hide them there. **1758** NEEDHAM in *Phil. Trans.* L. 783 Their shape..when they are extended resembles nearly that of an acorn-cup. **1836** PRAED *Poems* (1865) I. 412 She sent him forth to gather up Great Ganges in an acorn-cup. *a* **1845** HOOD *The Elm Tree* iii. 16 With many a fallen acorn-cup. **1937** A. H. VERRILL *Foods Amer. gave World* 84 There are the..scalloped squashes, vegetable marrows, Hubbard squashes and the little deeply-fluted diamond or acorn-squashes. **1981** *Farmstead Mag.* Winter 38/1 The type [of squash] most readily found on supermarket shelves is the acorn squash. **1899** *Syd. Soc. Lex.*, *Quercite*, the so-called acorn-sugar or oak-sugar. **1934** *Electronics* Sept. 282/1 The 'acorn' tubes which amplify, oscillate, and detect waves as short as 40 centimeters have now reached the stage of practical manufacture. **1937** *Nature* 2 Jan. 34/2 The very small 'acorn' valve for the transmission and reception of telephony on a wave-length of about one metre. **1889** *Cent. Dict.* Acorn-worm. **1955** *Sci. News Let.* 9 Apr. 232/1 Known popularly as the acorn worm, the balanoglossus is found throughout the sea-coasts of the world. **1959** A. HARDY *Fish & Fisheries* v. 116 The most primitive of all chordate animals, the acorn-worm *Balanoglossus* and its relatives.

acorned ('eɪkɔːnd), *a.* [f. ACORN + -ED².]

1. Furnished or provided with acorns; bearing acorns; *esp.* in *Her.*

1611 GUILLIM *Heraldrie* 105 He beareth Azure, a Cheueron Ermine, three Oken Slips, acorned proper.

2. Fed or filled with acorns.

1611 SHAKS. *Cymb.* II. v. 16 Like a full Acorn'd Boare, a Iarmen on[e] Cry'd oh, and mounted. **1855** BROWNING *Men & Women* II. 160, I liken his grace to an acorned hog.

acorn-shell. Popular name of a multivalve Cirriped (*Balanus*, Ellis), called also Sea-acorn, allied to the Barnacles, but without a flexible stalk, several species of which live sessile upon rocks, piles, iron pillars, and shells of other marine animals, between high and low water-mark.

1764 CROKER *Dict. Arts* s.v., The great furrowed Acorn-shell..is found sticking to the rocks in the East and West Indies. **1857** WOOD *Comm. Obj. Seashore* viii. 157 The entire surface of the limpet was covered with acorn-shells.

acorse, -y, obs. forms of ACCURSE *v.*

acorun, obs. form of ACORN.

‖**Acorus** ('ækərəs). [L., = Gr. ἄκορος, Dioscorides.] A genus of Endogenous plants (Nat. Ord. *Orontiaceae*), of which the native Eng. species is the Sweet Flag or Galingale (*Acorus Calamus*), formerly used, from its aromatic odour when bruised, for strewing on floors and in churches; and still employed to flavour beer, etc.

1714 *French Bk. of Rates* 88 Acorus per 100 Weight.

acosmic (ə'kɒzmɪk), *a.* [f. as ACOSM(ISM + -IC.] Of or pertaining to acosmism; not cosmic. So **a'cosmical** *a.*

1843 *Blackw. Mag.* LIV. 652/1 This man is an Idealist—or as we would term him,..an Acosmical Idealist; that is, an Idealist who absolutely denies the existence of an independent material world. **1904** G. S. HALL *Adolescence* II. xvi. 537 Some..despair of building up again the world they have lost out of its acosmic elements. **1937** A. HUXLEY *Ends & Means* xiv. 284 Pantheism in either its pancosmic or acosmic form. **1953** R. NIEBUHR *Christ. Realism & Polit. Probl.* (1954) xi. 169 Culture religions are..pantheistic in either the cosmic or the acosmic sense.

acosmism (ə'kɒzmɪz(ə)m). [mod. f. Gr. ἀ priv. + κόσμ-ος world + -ISM.] A denial of the existence of the universe, or of a universe as distinct from God.

1847 LEWES *Hist. Philos.* II. 176 (1867) Logically there is but a trivial distinction between his Acosmism, which makes God the one universal being, and Atheism, which makes the cosmos the one universal existence. **1866** J. MARTINEAU *Ess.* I. 223 The akosmism of Spinoza and the atheism of Comte.

acosmist (ə'kɒzmɪst). [mod. f. Gr. ἀ priv. + κόσμ-ος world + -IST.] One who denies the existence of the universe or its distinctness from God. So **aco'smistic** *a.*

1847 LEWES *Hist. Philos.* (1852) III. 145 Spinoza did not deny the existence of God; he denied the existence of the world; he was consequently an Acosmist, not an Atheist. **1866** D. W. SIMON tr. *Dorner's Person of Christ* Div. II, vol. II. 46 He did not make the negative acosmistic theology his final goal. **1899** W. R. INGE *Christ. Mysticism* iv. 138 This judgment followed the appearance of a strongly pantheistic or acosmistic school of mystics.

†**a'cosmy.** *Obs.* [ad. Gr. ἀκοσμία disorder, f. ἀ priv. + κόσμος order.] (See quot.)

1704 J. HARRIS *Lex. Techn.*, *Acosmy*, is an ill state of Health accompanied with the loss of the Natural Florid Colour of the Face.

†**a'cost,** *adv. Obs.* Also 6 **a-coast.** [a. OFr. *a coste* (mod.Fr. *à côte*), f. *a* to, at + *coste* side:—L. *costa* rib, in late L., side. Afterwards treated as if formed on Eng. A *prep.*¹ + COAST in its restricted sense of 'side of the land.']

1. On or by the side; beside; aside; at one side.

c **1300** *K. Alisaunder* 6485 On a grene wode acost Verrament, ther he fond Wymmen growing out of the ground. *Ibid.* 6028 Feorre about, and eke acost, He sente his messangers bet. *c* **1330** *Arthour & Merlin* 7613 Forth thai passeth this lond acost.

2. Ashore. See ACOAST.

acost, earlier form of ACCOST *v.* and *sb.*

acotyledon (ə,kɒtɪ'liːdən). *Bot.* [f. mod.L. *acotylēdones*, f. Gr. ἀ without + κοτυληδών a cup-shaped hollow, also the plant Navel-wort, and in *mod. Bot.* a seed-lobe, f. κοτύλη a hollow, cup. It provides a sing. for the L. word, which is often retained unchanged in the pl.] A plant which has no distinct cotyledons, or seed-lobes; as a fern, moss, fungus, or seaweed.

1819 *Pantologia* I. s.v., The distinction of vegetables into acotyledons, monocotyledons, dicotyledons..has been long made, and is the basis of Jussieu's natural arrangement. **1850** MᶜCOSH *Div. Govt.* II. i. 119 (1874) Acotyledons, without seed-lobes, such as lichens and fungi.

acotyledonous (əkɒtɪ'liːdənəs), *a. Bot.* [f. prec. + -OUS.] Having no distinct cotyledons or seed-lobes, attribute of one of Jussieu's three great divisions of the vegetable kingdom.

1819 *Pantologia* I. s.v., It is a doubt however, whether any plant be strictly acotyledonous. **1835** HOOKER *Brit. Flor.* 477 *Acotyledonous* or Cellular Plants: this class corresponds with the 24th *Cryptogamia* in the Linnæan System. **1880** GRAY *Bot. Text-Bk.* 394 *Acotyledonous*, without cotyledons ..Mostly applied to plants which have no proper seed nor embryo, and therefore no cotyledon.

‖**acouchi** (ə'kuʃɪ). *Bot.* [native name with Indians of Guiana.] *Acouchi* resin or balsam: the inspissated juice of *Icica heterophylla*, a forest tree of Guiana.

1866 A. SMITH in *Treas. of Bot.* 617 Balsam of Acouchi, yielded by *I. heterophylla*, is employed as a vulnerary.

acouchy (ə'kuʃɪ). *Zool.* [a. Fr. *acouchi, agouchi*, said to be adaptation of native name in Guiana.] A small rodent quadruped allied to the guinea-pig, and agouti, sometimes called the Surinam Rabbit.

1831 *Philos. Mag.* X. 147 A stuffed specimen and a skeleton of the Acouchy (*Dasyprocta Acuschy*, Illig.) having been laid on the table. **1833** *Pen. Cycl.* I. 214 The Acouchi is considerably smaller than either of the foregoing species, and is at once distinguished by the greater length of its tail . . In other respects it is of the same form as the Agoutis.

acoumeter (a'kaʊmɪtə(r)). [improp. f. Gr. ἀκούειν to hear + -METER = Gr. μέτρον measure.] An instrument, invented by Itard, for estimating the power or extent of the sense of hearing. Variant names in Dicts. **acouometer, acoemeter, acousmeter.** Also, **acou'metric** *a.*, of or pertaining to acoumetry.

1839 K. GRANT *Hooper's Med. Dict.* (ed. 7) 31 Acoumeter or Acumeter . . an instrument invented by Itard for estimating the extent of the sense of hearing. **1847** In CRAIG, and subseq. Dicts. **1890** *Cassell's Fam. Mag.* Feb. 188/1 It is proposed to form phonograms into an acoumetric scale for the examination of the hearing. **1911** S. S. COLVIN *Learning Process* vi. 94 Auditory acuity may also be determined . . with elaborate instruments such as Seashore's audiometer or Lehmann's acoumeter.

acoumetry (ə'kaʊmɪtrɪ). [f. as prec. + -METRY.] The measuring or estimation of the power or extent of the sense of hearing. Variant forms found in Dicts. are **acouometry, acoemetry, acousmetry.**

1879 *Syd. Soc. Lex.*

acount(e, early form of ACCOUNT *sb.* and *v.*

acounter, -our, early forms of ACCOUNTER.

† **a'counter,** *v. Obs.* Also 4 acuntre. [A reduced form of *encounter*, a. OFr. *encontrer, encountrer*; see A- *pref.* 10.] To encounter, meet.

c **1350** *Will. Palerne* 3602 So kenli þei a-cuntred at þe coupyng to gadere þat þe kniȝt spere . . alto-schiuered.

† **a'counter, acountre,** *sb. Obs.* [f. prec.: cf. ENCOUNTER *sb.*] An encounter.

c **1314** *Guy Warw.* 291 The acountre of hem was so strong, That mani dyed ther among. *c* **1440** *Morte Arthur* 49 In alle the batailles that Launcelot had bene With hard acountres hym agayne.

† **acountering,** *vbl. sb. Obs.* [f. ACOUNTER *v.* + -ING[1].] Encountering, jousting.

c **1420** *Avowynge of Arthur* xxxv, Of knyȝtus in a-cowunturinge This forward to fulfille.

† **a'coup(e,** *v.*[1] *Obs.* Forms: 3 acoup-en, 4 acope, acoupe, 5 acoulpe. [a. OFr. *acope-r, acolper, aculper, acoulper, acouper*, f. *à* to + *coulper, couper*, to blame:—L. *culpā-re*, f. *culpa* fault, blame; or ? for earlier *encolper, encouper*:—L. *inculpā-re*. *Adculpāre* is not found in L. Subseq. refashioned as *accoup*: see AC-.] To accuse.

1297 R. GLOUC. 544 Me acoupede hom harde inou, & suththe atte laste, As theues & traitors, in strong prison me hom caste. *c* **1300** *Life of Beket* 773 The King sat anheȝ on his cee, and acopede him faste. **1340** HAMPOLE *Pr. of Consc.* 2947 A man has drede bodily, When he es acouped of felony. **1377** LANGL. *P. Pl.* B. XIII. 459 Til conscience acouped hym þere-of · in a curteise manere. **1480** CAXTON *Chron.* cxcviii, And Syre Robert hym acoulped in thys maner. **1717** BLOUNT *Law Dict.*, *Accouped*, His conscience accouped him [quoted from *P. Pl.* as above]. So BAILEY 1731.

† **a'coup(e,** *v.*[2] *Obs.* [a. OFr. **acolpe-r, acoupe-r*, to strike on (not in Godef.); f. *à* to + *couper* to strike, cut; f. *coup*, OFr. *colp*, stroke, blow:—late L. *colpus*:—*colapus, colaphus*, a. Gr. κόλαφος a cuff.] To strike, shower blows.

c **1380** *Sir Ferumb.* 1594 So harde þay acoupede on hur scheldes: þat broke buþ boþe hure schafte.

† **a'coupement.** *Obs. rare*[—1]. [a. OFr. *acoupement*, n. of action, f. *acouper*; see ACOUPE *v.*[1]] Accusation.

a **1300** *Floriz & Bl.* 664 Hit nere noȝt elles riȝt iugement Biþuten ansuare to acupement. *c* **1330** (*later text*) 691 Hit ner nowt riȝt iugement Wiþouten answere to acoupement.

† **a'couping,** *vbl. sb. Obs.* [f. ACOUPE *v.*[2] + -ING[1].] A coming to blows; the shock of spear on shield.

c **1350** *Will. Palerne* 3438 At þe a-coupyng þe kniȝtes speres · eiþer brak on oþer.

acouple, variant of ACCOUPLE *v. Obs.*

‖ **acousmata,** *sb. pl. Obs.* [Gr. ἀκούσματα pl. of ἄκουσμα anything heard, n. of action f. ἀκού-ειν to hear.] Things received on authority: a technical word of a school of philosophy.

1655–60 T. STANLEY *Hist. Philos.* 374/1 (1701) They did esteem those amongst them the wisest, who had most of these Acousmata. Now all these Acousmata were divided into three kinds; some tell, what something is, others tell, what is most such a thing; the third sort tell, what is to be done, and what not.

† **acousmatic** (ækaʊz'mætɪk). *Obs.* [ad. L. *acousmatic-us* (of which the pl. *acousmatici* also occurs unchanged), a. Gr. ἀκουσματικός lit. one willing to hear.] A professed hearer, a class of scholars under Pythagoras, who listened to his teaching, without inquiring into its inner truths or bases.

1655–60 T. STANLEY *Hist. Philos.* 358/1 (1701) There were many Auditors called Acousmaticks, whereof he gained two thousand by one oration. *Ibid.* 373/1 The Acousmatici they, who heard only the chief heads of learning, without more exact explication.

acou'smetric, *a.* [improp. f. Gr. ἄκουσις hearing + μέτρ-ον measure + -IC.] Pertaining to acoumetry. (Also found in Dicts. as **acousmometric.**)

acoustic (ə'ku:stɪk, ə'kaʊstɪk), *a.* and *sb.* [a. Fr. *acoustique*, ad. Gr. ἀκουστικ-ός pertaining to hearing, f. ἀκού-ειν to hear. The reg. Eng. representative of the Gr. would be *acustic.*]

A. *adj.*

1. a. Pertaining to the sense of hearing, used in hearing, auditory; adapted to aid hearing; pertaining to the science of audible sounds. ***acoustic coupler*** (see COUPLER 2 e); ***acoustic impedance***, see IMPEDANCE; ***acoustic mine***, a submarine mine designed to be exploded by sound-waves transmitted under water; ***acoustic phonetics***, the study of sound-waves of speech; so ***acoustic-phonetic*** adj.

1605 BACON *Adv. Learn.* 135 This hath place . . in Acoustique Art; for the Instrument of hearing is like to the straits and winding within a Cave. **1743** tr. *Heister's Surg.* 435 An acoustic Instrument so small as to be concealed under one's Wig. **1822** IMISON *Sc. & Art* I. 230 A very useful contrivance, called *acoustic* or *speaking tubes*, which are now fixed up in houses for the purpose of speaking from one story to another. **1855** OWEN *Skel. & Teeth* 34 The acoustic capsule remains in great part cartilaginous. **1864** *Reader* 18 June 783/2 The two primary sounds, the co-existence of which gives rise to the acoustic figures, are not in absolute unison. **1865** *Pall Mall G.* 30 June 11 The drawing-room . . formed a very aristocratic but not very acoustic theatre for the display of their talents. **1867** *Under one Roof* 14 Mrs Clevedon's ears, though exquisitely shaped, were very sharp in the acoustic sense. **1871** TYNDALL *Frag. Science* I. x. 331 (ed. 6) There we had the acoustic opacity of the air. **1873** SIR J. HERSCHEL *Pop. Lect.* vii. § 102. 318 An evident acoustic shadow. **1878** FOSTER *Physiol.* III. i. 392 The olfactory, optic and acoustic nerves are purely sensory nerves. **1879** PRESCOTT *Sp. Telephone* 47 Already has the acoustic telegraph been invented. *Ibid.* 49 A perfect system of acoustic telegraphy. **1941** *Hansard Commons* 9 Sept. 5th Ser. CCCLXXIV. 67 [Mr. Churchill] The attack . . is now waged continually by the acoustic mine as well as the magnetic. **1941** C. P. R. GRAVES *Life Line* 23 Acoustic mines have been dealt with by our mine-sweepers for months. . . The sound vibrations of a ship's engines act . . in the same way as a finger placed on an ordinary electric bell-push, connecting two electrically alive points and causing current to flow and explode the mine. **1933** L. BLOOMFIELD *Language* v. 75 The phonetician can study either the sound-producing movements of the speaker (*physiological phonetics*) or the resulting sound-waves (*physical* or *acoustic phonetics*). **1948** M. JOOS *Acoustic Phonetics* 5 Acoustic phonetics is now in its infancy... Acoustic phonetics discussion, even when it is carried on by a linguist, must deal with sound as sound. **1960** *Amer. Speech* XXXV. 230 an acoustic-phonetic study of internal open juncture. **1964** *New Statesman* 1 May 705/1 (Advt.), University of Leeds. Applications are invented for the following posts... Lecturer in Acoustic Phonetics.

b. Of a gramophone or a musical instrument, esp. a guitar: designed so that the sound is recorded or reproduced by mechanical rather than by electrical or electronic means. Opp. ELECTRIC *a.* 2 b.

1932 G. WILSON *Gramophones* viii. 43 Ultimately the radio-gramophone . . will hold the field to the virtual exclusion of either acoustic gramophone or straight radio-receiver. **1943** *Gramophone* June 19/2 (*heading*) Acoustic and electrical reproduction. **1945** ROWE & WATSON *Junkshoppers' Discography* 2 Except for the M.C.B.B. and 'Hottentot' items, Aco are all pre-electric (acoustic) recordings. **1951** SACKVILLE-WEST & SHAWE-TAYLOR *Record Guide* 718 LPs cannot be played at all on an acoustic gramophone. **1966** *Exchange & Mart* 3 Feb. 74/3 (Advt.), The best ever bargain in acoustic guitars. **1978** *Gramophone* Jan. 1321/3 Two of my favourite musicians are involved: the tenor saxophonist Teddy Edwards . . and Cedar Walton (he is heard on both electric and acoustic pianos). **1979** *Arizona Daily Star* 22 July 1. 7/1 He plays acoustic guitar and harmonica.

2. Applied to any device or material designed to lessen sound or noise; sound-absorbent.

1924 *Sci. Amer.* Sept. 165/1 Professor Sabine invented an acoustic tile that is many times as absorbent as the usual masonry surfaces. **1931** STEWART & LINDSAY *Acoustics* vii. 175 The construction of an acoustic filter. **1937** *Discovery* Dec. 388/1 The new . . trains have both roof and sides covered with acoustic blankets made of asbestos. **1960** *House & Garden* Aug. 46/3 Acoustic board . . 1*s.* 3*d.* sq. ft. **1961** *Listener* 31 Aug. 310/2 We all know what a difference absorbent acoustic tiles on a ceiling . . make to the restful character and quality of a public space.

B. *sb.*

1. A medicine or appliance which assists hearing.

1704 J. HARRIS *Lex. Techn.*, *Acousticks*, Medicines or instruments which help the hearing. **1727** SWIFT *Gulliver* III. vi. 216 Administer to each of them . . accoustics. **1790** BAILEY (ed. Harwood) [as in Harris].

2. in *pl.*: see ACOUSTICS.

3. The acoustic quality or properties of a place or a sound, esp. as regards reverberation time. Cf. ACOUSTICS 3.

1961 [see DRY *a.* A. 18 b]. **1965** *Listener* 10 June 876/2 When in a [radio] thriller two voices stop and after a gap start again in the same acoustic, it takes conscious adjustment to realize . . that we are on the following morning. **1976** *Gramophone* Jan. 1266/3 Some readers may recall the way in which the acoustic of the old Queen's Hall came through clearly. **1981** I. MCEWAN *Comfort of Strangers* iv. 44 Far behind them they heard the children, their voices distorted by an acoustic which suggested a room of vast proportions, chanting a religious formula or an arithmetical table.

acoustical (ə'ku:-, ə'kaʊstɪkəl), *a.* [f. ACOUSTIC *a.* and *sb.* + -AL[1].] **1. a.** Of or pertaining to the science of acoustics. ***acoustical impedance***, see IMPEDANCE.

1831 FARADAY *Exp. Res.* xlvi. 314 On a peculiar class of acoustical figures: and on certain forms assumed by groups of particles upon vibrating elastic surfaces. **1859** DICKENS *T. of two Cit.* 65 Such a curious corner in its acoustical properties, such a peculiar Ear of a place. **1871** EARLE *Philol. Eng. Tongue* § 109 The acoustical study of the organs of speech. **1877** TYNDALL in *Daily News* 2 Oct. 2/5 Does it describe an optical and acoustical fact, a visible host, an audible song?

b. = ACOUSTIC A. 2.

1932 P. E. SABINE *Acoustics & Archit.* ix. 192 The application of one of the more highly absorbent of the acoustical plasters . . would have been a natural means of securing the desired reverberation time. *Ibid.* x. 228 A number of acoustical materials were investigated, both as to the viability of bacteria within them and as to the possibilities of adequately disinfecting them.

2. Promoting hearing.

a **1845** HOOD *T. of Trumpet* xxv, For the Aurist only took a mug, And pour'd in his ear some acoustical drug.

acoustically (ə'ku:-, ə'kaʊstɪkəlɪ), *adv.* [f. prec. + -LY[2].] In an acoustic manner; in relation to the hearing or appreciation of sounds.

1874 TYNDALL in *Contemp. Rev.* 826 The day was acoustically clear; at a distance of 10 miles the horn yielded a plain sound. **1880** H. SWEET in *Academy* 3 Apr. 254 Many phoneticians still confuse them acoustically.

acoustician (,æku:-, ,ækaʊ'stɪʃən). [f. ACOUSTIC, on analogy of *physic-ian*, etc.; see -ICIAN.] One versed in acoustics.

1859 *Nat. Mag.* V. 102/1 He had already been engaged specially, in his capacity of 'acoustician', to remedy some defect of the St. Petersburg Opera-house. **1879** A. J. HIPKINS in Grove *Dict. Mus.* II. 54 It is . . agreed, even by acousticians, that the piano had best remain with thirteen keys in the octave. **1879** *Spectator* 22 Feb. 241 Mr. A. J. Ellis, Mr. Sedley Taylor, and other acousticians. **1956** H. WHITEHALL in *Kenyon Rev.* XVIII. 422 The acousticians can measure minute variations in stress, pause and pitch. **1957** *Technology* Oct. 302/1 Acousticians may have largely silenced the famous echo [*sc.* in the Albert Hall].

acoustico-, combining form of ACOUSTIC.

1880 in *Nature* XXI. 359 An acoustico-electrical kaleidoscope . . consists of a microphone used in conjunction with an induction-coil and a Geissler tube, and is . . intended for the optical study of sounds. **1940** *Chambers's Techn. Dict.* 9/2 *Acousticolateral system*, in Vertebrates, afferent nerve-fibres related to the neuromast organs and to the ear, receptors in aquatic forms of relatively slow vibrations. **1946** S. ULLMANN in *Word* Aug. 118 The phoneme is defined as the smallest acoustico-phonetic unit of speech. **1949** R. JAKOBSON in A. Cohen *Phonemes of English* (1952) ii. 30 Among a multitude of acoustico-motor possibilities there is a restricted number upon which language chooses to set a value. **1951** G. HUMPHREY *Thinking* iii. 87 A subject might begin a reaction series by mentally repeating the letter E when that letter appeared. Gradually this 'acousticokinaesthetic presentation' disappeared. **1957** M. E. BROWN *Physiol. of Fishes* II. ii. 155 Phylogenetically the acoustico-lateralis system of sense organs is as old as the vertebrates. **1960** *Amer. Speech* XXXV. 234 Acoustico-cineradiographic analysis considerations.

acousticon (ə'kaʊstɪkən). [ad. Gr. ἀκουστικόν neut. sing. of ἀκουστικός ACOUSTIC.] An instrument for helping the deaf to hear.

1900 in DORLAND *Med. Dict.* (22/1). **1920** *Chambers's Jrnl.* 27 Nov. 831/2 An instrument known as 'The Acousticon', which we believe . . to be a real boon to those suffering from deafness.

acoustics (ə'ku:-, ə'kaʊstɪks). [pl. of ACOUSTIC *a.* used as sb., on analogy of *mathematics, politics*, etc.; see -ICS. Usually treated as a singular.]

1. The science of sound, and of the phenomena of hearing.

1683 in *Phil. Trans.* XIV. 473 Hearing may be divided into Direct, Refracted and Reflex'd, which are yet nameless unless we call them Acousticks, Diacousticks, Catacousticks. **1692** WOOD *Ath. Oxon.* IV. 499 (1820) An introductory Essay to the Doctrine of Sounds containing Some Proposals for the Improvement of Acoustics. **1805** CARLISLE in *Phil. Trans.* XCV. 198 A more intimate knowledge of the structure of the organs of hearing may illustrate the doctrines of acoustics. **1810** COLERIDGE *Friend* iii. 89 (1867) Which may easily impose on the soundest judgements, uninstructed in the optics and acoustics of the inner sense. **1830** SIR J. HERSCHEL *Nat. Phil.* 248 Acoustics, then, or the science of sound, is a very considerable branch of physics. **1833** BREWSTER *Nat. Magic* i. 3 The science of Acoustics furnished the ancient sorcerers with some of their best deceptions.

2. Also pl. of ACOUSTIC *sb.* an acoustic medicine.

3. The acoustic properties (of a building, etc.).

1885 H. W. LUCY in *Eng. Illustr. Mag.* Dec. 193/2 Whilst the vast majority of the peers are practically inaudible in the press gallery, I cannot call to mind any individual case in which the public interest materially suffers owing to the faulty acoustics of the chamber. **1895** D. F. Tovey *Let.* in M. Grierson *D. F. Tovey* (1952) iii. 37 The execrable acoustics of the Sheldonian.

acousto- (ə'kuːstəʊ), comb. form of ACOUSTIC *a.* and *sb.*, as in **acousto-e'lectric** *a.*, involving the interaction of sound and electricity, esp. the generation of a voltage by a sound wave or stress wave; **a,cousto-elec'tricity**, electricity produced by sound waves or stress waves; acousto-electric phenomena; **a,cousto-elec'tronics** *sb. pl.* (const. as *sing.*), a branch of electronics concerned with the application and use of acousto-electric phenomena; so **a,cousto-elec'tronic** *a.*; **acousto-'optic, -'optical** *adjs.*, involving the interaction of sound and light, esp. the modulation or control of light by means of sound waves; so **acousto-'optically** *adv.*; **acousto-'optics** *sb. pl.* (const. as *sing.*).

1953 R. H. Parmenter in *Physical Rev.* LXXXIX. 990/2 We discuss the effect on the conduction electrons of a crystal resulting from a single traveling longitudinal acoustic wave in the crystal... There are a few electrons..capable of being trapped by the moving electric field... Those having a maximum energy will..give rise to a net electric current... Such a generation of an electric current by a traveling acoustic wave may be called the *acousto-electric effect. **1968** *New Scientist* 23 May 402 Acousto-electric oscillators may also be useful for measuring changes in applied strain. **1984** *Aviation Week & Space Technol.* 3 Dec. 78 A joint program..is under way to develop further a phase-insensitive ultrasonic transducer design based on the acoustoelectric rather than the piezoelectric response. **1959** *New Scientist* 8 Jan. 86/2 (*heading*) *Acoustoelectricity. **1984** *Jrnl. Acoustical Soc. Amer.* LXXVI. 826 Creation of an *SH* magnetoacoustic surface mode akin to the Bleustein-Gulyaev mode of acoustoelectricity. **1970** *Sci. Jrnl.* May 46/3 At a minimum the *acousto-electronic elements must accommodate half a wavelength end to end to allow the coupling and amplifying function to take place between the two types of wave. **1984** *IEEE Trans. Sonics & Ultrasonics* XXXI. 77/1 In mass produced acoustoelectronic devices..the cost of packaging makes up a significant proportion of the total cost of the device. **1968** *Sendai Symposium on Acoustoelectronics* (Tohoku Univ.) 6 The term '*acoustoelectronics' which has been used here in this Institute means a science of intermediate field between electronics and acoustics. **1975** *Proc. Symp. Optical & Acoustical Microelectronics 1974* 625 The advantages of Gulyaev-Bleustein waves for acoustoelectronics are shown. **1967** *Jrnl. Appl. Physics* XXXVIII. 5152/1 An *acousto-optic device. **1970** *New Scientist* 7 May 285 The acousto-optic modulator is a prism of fused quartz..with an electro-acoustic transducer..on one end. **1971** *Nature* 9 July 111/1 The focused light beam is made to scan rapidly over a selected area of the mirror by means of two acousto-optic light deflector cells. **1973** *McGraw-Hill Yearbk. Sci. & Technol.* 143/2 Acoustooptic interaction..enables a tiny pencil-like laser beam to 'write' or make 'dots' of light in less than a millionth of a second. **1966** *Applied Optics* V. 1674/1 The high center frequency would require a solid *acoustooptical medium. **1970** *New Scientist* 21 May 377/1 Dr King has chosen rather to include an intermediate photographic recording stage and by doing so uses only one acousto-optical cell. **1982** *Defense Electronics* June 40/3 A 500-MHz bandwidth acousto-optical processor, wide IF bandwidth receiver..provides spectral surveillance. **1983** *Ibid.* Jan. 115/2 The *acousto-optically Q-switched Nd:YAG laser..provides high peak energies. **1969** *IEEE Jrnl. Quantum Electronics* V. 331/1 Acoustooptic laser modulators provide time-bandwidth products of more than 20000 and the theoretical feasibility of reaching even higher values has made *acoustooptics one of the most potent and versatile laser modulation methods available today. **1972** *Sci. News* 9 Dec. 381 Practical applications of acoustooptics are showing up in many areas where laser light may be used to gain or transmit information. **1983** *Washington Post* 2 May (Business Suppl.) 40/4 Isomet designs and manufactures products that control lasers by acousto-optics, a technology that uses ultrasonic signals that are capable of diffracting beams of light.

acoutre, obs. form of ACCOUTRE *v.*

†**a'cover**, *v. Obs.* Forms: 1 **a-cofri-an**, 2-4 **acover-en**. Subseq. aphetized to COVER *v.*², (not to be confused with *cover* = Fr. *couvrir*). [With OE. *a-cofrian* for *ar-covrian*, cf. OHG. *ir-koboron*, pointing to an OTeut. **er-cober-an*, ad. L. *re-cuperā-re*, in its popular form *re-coberā-re*, cf. Sp. *recobrar* and OFr. *recovrer*, *recouvrer*. See RECOVER.] *trans.* To recover, get back, regain. *intr.* To regain health, recover from illness.

a **1100** *Ags. Leechd.* iii. 184 Se þe lið raðe acofrað. *c* **1225** *Hali Meidenhad* 11 þat ilke þing þat ne mei neuer beon acouered..Ne schal tu neauer nan oðer al swuch acoueren. *c* **1230** *Ancren Riwle* 412 ȝe muwen akoueren hit þene nexte sunendei þerefter. *Ibid.* 364 Heo beoð boðe seke; þe on..drinkeð bitter sabraz uorto akoueren his heale. *c* **1330** *Arthour & Merlin* 8519 Belisent, withouten lesing Acouerd and vndede her eyin.

†**a'covering**, *vbl. sb. Obs.* [f. prec. + -ING¹.] Recovering.

c **1225** *Hali Meidenhad* 27 Of þis lure nis nan acoueringe.

acoward, earlier form of ACCOWARD *v. Obs.*

1485 Caxton *Chas. the Grete* 173 There is none so franke ne valyaunte that wyl acoward hymself.

acownte, obs. form of ACCOUNT.

†**a'coy**, *adv. Obs. rare*⁻¹. [f. A- *pref.* 11 + COY; or for *acoye*, *acoie*, a. OFr. *acoié*.] ? Calmed, subdued.

1567 Turberville *Compl. Absence of his Loue* If thou had'st ment (unhappie hap) Thus to have nipt my joy, Why didst thou show a smiling cheere That shouldst have looked acoy.

acoye, variant of ACCOY *v. Obs.* to calm, tame.

acquaint (ə'kweɪnt), *ppl. a.* and *sb. arch.* For forms see ACQUAINT *v.* [a. OFr. *acoint*, later *accoint*:—L. *accognit-um*, *ad-cognit-um*; f. *ad* to + *cognit-um* pa. pple. of *cognōsc-ĕre* to know, f. *co-* = *com* together + *gnōsc-ĕre* to come to the knowledge of, inceptive of **gno-ĕre* to know. Superseded in lit. Eng. by the pple. ACQUAINTED, but retained in northern Eng. and in lit. Scotch.]

A. *ppl. a.* = ACQUAINTED: personally known; mutually known; having personal or experimental knowledge of. Const. *with* (*to* obs.)

1297 R. Glouc. 465 He was a quointe muche to the quene of Fraunce. **1375** Barbour *Bruce* VII. 138 Forthir aquynt quhill that we be. *c* **1400** *Rom. Rose* 5203 With such love be no more aquente. *c* **1450** *Merlin* iv. 72, I shall make you aqueynte with a gode man. **1663** Blair *Autobiog.* (1848) v. 79 Desirous that I should be acquaint with him. **1720** Wodrow *Corr.* II. 471 (1843) Some coffee-houses you are acquaint with. **1794** Burns *Wks.* IV. 295 John Anderson my jo, John, When we were first acquent, Your locks were like the raven, Your bonnie brow was brent. **1867** J. Ingelow *Story of Doom* VII. 131 As men the less acquaint with deeds of blood.

†**B.** *sb.* An acquaintance. (Cf. OFr. *acoint* = *familier, ami.*) *Obs.*

c **1386** Chaucer *Sompn. T.* 283 Harl. MS., To thy subjects do noon oppressioun; Ne make thyn acqueyntis fro the fle [*Six-text MSS.* acqueyntance-s].

acquaint (ə'kweɪnt), *v.* Forms: 3-5 **acoint(e, akoint(e, acoynt(e**; 4-5 **aqueynt, aqweynt, acqueynt**; 6 **acquaynt**; 6- **acquaint**. *Aphet.* 4-6 **quaynt(e**. [a. OFr. *acointe-r*, also *acuintier*, *acointier*, *acoentier*:—late L. *adcognitā-re*, *accognitā-re* (c. 856) to make known, f. *adcognit-um*: see prec. Cf. mod.Fr. *s'accointer*.] Primary sig. To make known, but in Eng. reflexive from the first.

†**1.** *refl.* To make oneself known, introduce oneself, become known (*to* any one). *Obs.*

1297 R. Glouc. 15 Heo a coynted hym a non, and bi comen frendes gode. *c* **1314** *Guy Warw.* 35 To king Athelston thou schalt aqueynt the. *c* **1400** *Destr. of Troy* VII. 2931 Acoyntyng hom with kissyng and clippyng in armes. **1483** Caxton *G. de la Tour* C ij. He hym self also spente largely for to acqueynte hym att the festes.

†**2.** *intr.* (by omission of refl. pron.) To become acquainted, or familiar; to attain to a state of mutual knowledge. *Obs.*

c **1384** Chaucer *Hous of Fame* 250 To telle the manere How they aqueynteden in fere. **1509** Hawes *Past. Pl.* XI. xxi, But of rude people the wyttes are so faynt, That wyth theyr connyng they can not acquaynt. **1559** *Myrroure for Mag., Mortimers* xiii. 2 Well was the man that myght with me acquaynte. **1678** Bunyan *Pilg. Prog.* I. 156 He would that you should stay here a while to acquaint with us. **1774** H. Walpole *Corresp.* (1837) III. 111 Though the Choiseuls will not acquaint with you I hope their abbé Barthelemi is not put under the same quarantine.

3. *refl.* To make (oneself) to have knowledge of, to give, or gain for, oneself personal knowledge of, or acquaintance *with* (any one). Now only in passive 'To be acquainted (*with* anyone)'; the active is supplied by 'to become acquainted with,' 'to make the acquaintance of,' and *fam.* 'to get to know.'

1330 R. Brunne *Chron.* 225 þan went þis Ottobone þorghout þe cuntre, & quaynted him with ilkone. **1369** Chaucer *Dethe of Blaunche* 532 And I saw that, and gan me aqueynt With hym. *c* **1430** *How the Good Wijf tauȝte hir Douȝter* 88, in *Babees Bk.* 40 Aqweynte þee not with eche man þat gooþ bi þe strete. *c* **1450** Lonelich *Grail* lii. 931 Mochel desire I now trewelye..Aqweynted with him to be. **1483** Caxton *G. de la Tour* hv. b, It is good to acqueynt hymself with holy men. **1611** Bible *Job* xxii. 21 Acquaint now thy selfe with him, and be at peace. **1653** Marvell *Let.* I. Wks. 1875 II. 5 Most of this time..hath been spent in acquainting ourselves with him. **1798** Southey *Eng. Ecl.* i. Wks. III. 8 You did not know me, But we're acquainted now.

4. *refl.* and *trans.* To give (oneself or any one) experimental knowledge of, or acquaintance *with* (a thing).

1567 *Triall of Treasure* (1850) 15 Next here with Sturdiness you must you acquainte. **1611** Bible *Eccl.* ii. 3 Acquainting mine heart with wisedome. **1651** Hobbes *Leviathan* II. xxii. 120 Power to order the same; and be acquainted with their accounts. **1666** Fuller *Hist. Waltham Ab.* (1840) 268, I shall select thence some memorable items, to acquaint us with the general devotion of those days. **1683** Dryden *Life of Plutarch* 65 Where he may command all sorts of books, and be acquainted also with such particulars as have escap'd the pens of writers. **1863** Bright *Speeches, Amer.* (1876) 139 No man in America or in England is more acquainted with the facts of this case. *Mod.* Acquaint yourself with the duties of your new sphere.

†**5.** *trans.* To familiarize, accustom, or habituate. Const. *with*, or *inf. phrase. Obs.*

1586 B[eard] tr. *La Primaudaye's Fr. Acad.* II. 284 Acquainting our selves to love them that doe us good. **1599** Hakluyt *Voyages* II. II. 137 The recouerie of their diseases doeth acquaint their bodies with the aire of the countries where they be. **1612** Brinsley *Grammar-Sch.* 213 Acquaint them to pronounce some speciall examples. **1658** Evelyn *French Gard.* (1675) 144 You may take off the bells to acquaint them [plants] with the air.

6. *trans.* To inform (a person) of (a thing); to make cognizant or aware. Const. *with*, *that* (*of* obs.).

1559-66 *Hist. Estate Scotl.* in *Miscell. Wod. Soc.* (1844) 57 They sent a post to the Queene, acquainting her of the matter. **1586** James VI in Ellis *Orig. Lett.* I. 224. III. 21 Quho indeid are fullie aquentid thairwith. **1611** Shaks. *Wint. T.* IV. iv. 696 It were a peece of honestie to acquaint the King withall. **1703** Maundrell *Journ. Jerusalem* (1732) 66 To acquaint the Governour of our Arrival. **1742** Fielding *Jos. Andrews* IV. v. 115 He was acquainted that his worship would wait on him. **1818** Scott *Hrt. Midl.* 185 Jeanie..could scarce find voice to acquaint him, that she had an order from Bailie Middleburgh. **1855** Prescott *Philip II*, II. vii. (1857) 276 They had acquainted the regent with their intention.

b. *ellipt.* (with personal obj. only). To inform.

1590 Shaks. *Com. Err.* III. ii. 15 Be secret false; what need she be acquainted? **1749** Fielding *Tom Jones* VI. ii. (1840) 68/1 [He] begged her, if anything ailed his daughter, to acquaint him immediately. **1775** Sheridan *Duenna* I. iv. 196, I shall certainly acquaint your father.

†**c.** (with the thing only as obj.) To tell, make known. *Obs.* (In this sense the word comes round again to the original sense of *adcognitāre*.)

1607 Rowlands *Famous Hist.* 79 Acquaint thy name in private unto me. **1678** Butler *Hudibr.* III. i. 1390 And he knows nothing of the Saints, But what some treach'rous spy acquaints.

†**acquaintable** (ə'kweɪntəb(ə)l), *a. Obs.* Also **aqueyntable, acquayntable.** [a. Fr. *acointable*, f. *acoint-er*. See ACQUAINT and -ABLE.] Easy to be acquainted with, affable, familiar.

c **1400** *Rom. Rose* 2213 Wherfore be wise and aqueyntable, Goodly of word, and resonable. **1525** Ld. Berners *Froissart* II. xlii. 134, I founde hym ryght gracyous..courtoys, amyable, and acquayntable. **1611** Cotgr., *Accointable*, acquaintable, easie to be acquainted, or familiar, with.

acquaintance (ə'kweɪntəns). Forms: 3-4 **acoyntaunse**; 3-5 **acqueyntaunce, aquayntonce**; 4-5 **acqueintance, -aunce, acqueyntanse**; 6 **acoynt-, acquent-, acquayntaunce**; 6- **acquaintance.** North.: 4-5 **aquentance**; 5 **aqweyntans, -ance, acqueyntawns.** Aphet.: 3-4 **queyntance**; 5-6 **quayntaunce**; 6-7 **quentance.** [a. OFr. *acointance*, 15th c. *accointance*, n. of action, f. *acointer*. See ACQUAINT *v.* and -NCE.]

1. a. Personal knowledge; knowledge of a person or thing gained by intercourse or experience, which is more than mere recognition, and less than familiarity or intimacy. Const. *with* (*of* obs.). **to take acquaintance** *of*, *with*: to acquaint oneself with (*Obs.*); = *mod.* **to make the acquaintance of**, form an acquaintance with. **on acquaintance**, on becoming (or being) acquainted with.

1393 Gower *Conf.* I. 212 Deth comend er he besought Toke with this king such acqueintaunce. *c* **1400** *Destr. Troy* v. 1865 He has no knowlage, ne acoyntaunse of my cors. **1480** Caxton *Chron. Eng.* IV. (1520) 36/2 Vortiger..thought prevely in his herte thrughe quayntaunce for to be kynge hym selfe. **1595** Shaks. *John* V. vi. 15 Pardon me, That any accent breaking from thy tongue, Should scape the true acquaintance of mine eare. **1675** Crowne *Country Wit* IV. 61 What would this fellow have? who let him in without my acquaintance? **1756** Burke *Subl. & B.* Wks. I. 164 Knowledge and acquaintance make the most striking causes affect but little. **1875** Bryce *Holy Rom. Emp.* vii. (ed. 5) 116 An acquaintance with those works themselves such as only minute and long-continued study could give.

a **1450** *Knt. de la Tour* 55 Eue..toke aqueintaunce lightly of the serpent. **1490** Caxton *Eneydos* x. 40 He toke grete acqueyntaunce and ofte repayred vnto the palays. **1509** Hawes *Past. Pl.* XXX. xii, I toke acquayntaunce of her excellence. **1647** Crashaw *Poems* 208 For who so hard, but, passing by that way, Will take acquaintance of my woes. **1860** Tyndall *Glaciers* I. §6. 43 We spent a day or two in making the general acquaintance of the glacier.

1905 A. Burvenich *Eng. Idioms* 23 *Acquaintance*..to gain on—; *gagner à être connu.* **1912** 'Saki' *Unbearable Bassington* xiii. 240 One rode for sweltering miles for the chance of meeting a collector or police officer, with whom most likely on closer acquaintance one had hardly two ideas in common. **1922** E. O'Neill *Anna Christie* II. 150 Are you trying to kid me? Proposing—to me!—for Gawd's sake!—on such short acquaintance? **1983** *Economist* 2 July 90/3 Far more intelligent than most people thought on first acquaintance.

b. *Philos.* Knowledge of a person, thing, or other entity (e.g. sense-datum, universal) by direct experience of it, as opposed to knowing facts about it. So ***knowledge of, by, acquaintance*** (opp. *knowledge-about* or *by description*).

1865 Grote *Expl. Philos.* I. iv. 61 If by knowledge we mean acquaintance or familiarity, kenntniss, then we know the thing in itself. **1885** W. James in *Mind* X. 28 An interminable acquaintance, leading to no knowledge-*about*. **1890** —— *Princ. Psychol.* I. viii. 221 *There are two kinds of knowledge* broadly and practically distinguishable: we may call them respectively *knowledge of acquaintance* and *knowledge-about*. Most languages express the distinction; thus, γνῶναι, εἰδέναι; *noscere, scire*; kennen, wissen; connaitre, savoir. **1905** B. Russell in *Mind* XIV. 479 The distinction between *acquaintance* and *knowledge about* is the distinction between the things we have presentations of, and the things we only reach by means of denoting phrases. **1911** —— in *Proc. Aristot. Soc.* XI. 127 We began by distinguishing two sorts of knowledge of objects, namely, knowledge by *acquaintance* and knowledge by *description*. Of these it is only the former that brings the object itself before the mind. **1954** J. A. C. BROWN *Soc. Psychol. Industry* iii. 95 Two kinds of knowledge: 'knowledge-about', based on reflexion and abstract thinking, and 'knowledge-of-*acquaintance*', based on direct experience.

2. The state of being acquainted, or of knowing people and being known by them; mutual knowledge. Const. *with* (*of* obs.), *obj. gen.* as'her acquaintance'; *reciprocal gen.* as 'our acquaintance.'

c **1300** *K. Alis.* 6173 Queyntaunce of al men they schoneth. *Ibid.* 7259 For acqueyntaunce that hath beon.. heom bytweone. **1375** BARBOUR *Bruce* II. 167 Thusgat maid thai thar aquentance. *c* **1386** CHAUCER *Freres T.* 42 For here acqueintaunce was not come of newe. *c* **1400** *Rom. Rose* 6493, I love bettir the queyntaunce, Ten tyme, of the kyng of Fraunce. *c* **1425** WYNTOUN *Cron.* VI. xviii. 64 In swylk a-qweyntans swa þai fell. **1514** BARCLAY *Cytezen & Uplondyshm.* (1847) 62 For olde acquayntance betwene them erst had bene. **1530** RASTELL *Purgatory* Prol., Of old famylyer accoyntaunce. **1590** SHAKS. *Mids. N.* III. i. 185, I shall desire you of more acquaintance, good Master Cobweb. **1603** *Philotus* 41 To mak mair quentance vs betwene, I glaidly could agrie. **1611** BIBLE *2 Macc.* vi. 21 The olde acquaintance they had with the man. **1773** GOLDSM. *She Stoops to Conq.* II. i. (1854) 36 Give me leave to introduce Miss Neville to your acquaintance. **1822** BYRON *Werner* I i, Let's have some wine, and drink unto Our better acquaintance. **1838** DICKENS *Nich. Nick.* xxx. (C.D. ed.) 244 Those who had not the honour of his acquaintance.

3. A person or persons with whom one is acquainted. (Originally a collective noun, with both sing. and pl. sense, but now usually *singular*, with pl. *acquaintances*.)

c **1386** CHAUCER (6-text MSS.) *Sompn. T.* 283 Ne make thyne aqueyntance nat for to flee [3 *MSS.* acquaintances, *Harl. MS.* acqueyntis]. *c* **1525** SKELTON *Bowge of Courte* 45 There coude I none aquentaunce fynde. **1526** TINDALE *Luke* ii. 44 Sought him amonge their kynsfolke and acquayntaunce [WYCLIF knowleche]. **1532** MORE *Confut. Tindale* Wks. 1557, 702/2 He was his acquaintaunce and familyar. **1596** SHAKS. *1 Hen. IV*, v. iv. 102 What? Old Acquaintance? Could not all this flesh Keepe in a little life? **1663** COWLEY *Verses & Ess.* 89 (1669) Now meditate alone, now with Acquaintance talk. *a* **1794** GIBBON *Miscell. Wks.* 1814 II. 96 If among a crowd of acquaintances, one friend can afford you any comfort. **1816** MISS AUSTEN *Emma* I. iii. 17 The acquaintance she had already formed were unworthy of her. **1861** GEO. ELIOT *Silas Marner* 31 He might meet some acquaintance in whose eyes he would cut a pitiable figure.

acquaintanceship (əˈkweɪntənsʃɪp). [f. prec. + -SHIP. A modern formation due to the application of the simple *acquaintance* to a person; cf. *friend-ship*.] The standing or relation of an acquaintance or of mutual acquaintances; the state or position of having acquaintance or personal knowledge; = ACQUAINTANCE 2.

1803 SOUTHEY in Robberds' *Mem. W. Taylor* I. 440 A man with whom I have scarcely had any intercourse, not even of common acquaintanceship. **1881** MASSON *Carlyle* in *Macm. Mag.* XLV. 71 His acquaintanceships among his fellow-students do not appear to have been numerous.

acquaintancy (əˈkweɪntənsɪ). *rare.* [f. ACQUAINTANCE, by substituting the ending -NCY, which is distinctively one of state; cf. *coherence* and *coherency*.] = prec. (and due to same cause).

1859 MAHONEY *Rel. Father Prout* 567 But there came anon, As we journey'd on, Down the deep Garonne, An acquaintancy, Which we deem'd, I count, Of most high amount.

†**acquaintant** (əˈkweɪntənt). *Obs.* [a. Fr. *acointant*, later *accointant*, pr. pple. of *accointer*; see ACQUAINT *v.*] = ACQUAINTANCE 3; by which it has now been disadvantageously superseded; there has perhaps been some confusion between the pl. *acquaintants, -ans*, and the collective *acquaintance*.

1611 COTGR., *Rompre la paille avec*, To fall out with a friend, companion, or familiar acquaintant. **1627** FELTHAM *Resolves* II. v. Wks. 1677, 169 If not for his own sake, yet for that of his children and acquaintants. **1694** LESTRANGE *Fables* ccccliii. (ed. 6) 493 He finds his old Friend and Acquaintant. **1704** SWIFT *Tale of a Tub* I. 164 (1768) He and his readers are become old acquaintants.

†**acquainˈtation.** *Obs. rare*$^{-1}$. [n. of action f. ACQUAINT + -ATION. Not in Fr. though **acointation* would have been quite reg.] = ACQUAINTANCE.

1468 SIR J. PASTON in *Lett.* 588 II. 321, I as yet have govyn yow bot easy cause to remembyr me for leke of aqweyntacion.

acquainted (əˈkweɪntɪd), *ppl. a.* For forms see ACQUAINT *v.* [f. ACQUAINT *v.* + -ED.]

1. Personally known; familiar, through being known. Const. *to, unto. Obs.* of person; *arch.* of things.

c **1314** *Guy Warw.* 57 To an ermite he is y-go That he was ere aqueynted to. **1560** PHAËR *Eneid* IX. B b 3 The horsmen kest themselues in crokings knowen of quainted ground. **1565** JEWEL *Repl. M. Harding* (1611) 377 These authorities ..be also plaine and euident, and well acquainted and knowen vnto the World. **1597** SHAKS. *2 Hen. IV*, v. ii. 139 That Warre, or Peace, or both at once may be As things acquainted and familiar to vs. **1627** FELTHAM *Resolves* I. xxxv. Wks. 1677, 60 Fram'd so, in an acquainted shape, to advantage his deceit the more. **1805** SOUTHEY *Madoc in Aztl.* xiv. Wks. V. 297 With cautious strength did Madoc aim attack, Mastering each moment now with abler sway, The acquainted sword. **1823** LAMB *Elia* II. ix. (1865) 294 We are at home and upon acquainted ground.

2. Personally known (to any one) and having personal knowledge (of him); having mutual knowledge. Const. *with*.

c **1230** *Ancren Riwle* 218 þet he beo wel akointed mid ou. *c* **1400** *Rom. Rose* 600 Aqueynted am I & pryve With Myrthe, lord of this gardyne. **1494** FABYAN v. cxxxiii. 117 An holy man, named Felix, yᵉ which he was firste acqueynted with in Fraunce. **1509** HAWES *Past. Pl.* XIX. xiii, Tell me I pray you hertely..how were ye acquaynted? **1611** SHAKS. *Cymb.* I. iv. 132, I pray you be better acquainted. **1779** JOHNSON *L.P.*, *Gay* Wks. 1787 III. 204 [Pope] when he became acquainted with Gay..received him into his inmost confidence. **1882** *Daily News* 29 July 3/6 They had been some time acquainted, and walked out together.

3. Having personal or experimental knowledge; possessed of personal knowledge, more or less complete. Const. *with*, rarely *of* (men or things).

1480 *Ragman Roll* 190 in *Hazl. E.P.P.* 177 Your hert ys roted in humylyté, And aquented nothing wyth his contrarye. **1535** COVERDALE *Isa.* lxiii. 16 For Abraham knoweth vs not, nether is Israel acquainted with vs. **1611** BIBLE *Isa.* liii. 3 A man of sorrows, and acquainted with griefe. **1771** *Junius Lett.* xliv. 237 We have but one way left to make ourselves acquainted with it. **1836** WHATELY *Let.* in *Life* (1866) I. 346 Being sure of his being better acquainted than most people in England of the real state of Irish affairs. **1868** GEO. ELIOT *Felix Holt* 34 You have kept yourself.. thoroughly acquainted with English politics.

†**4.** Familiarized by experience *with*, accustomed *to*. *Obs.*

1533 BELLENDENE *Livy* I. 107 (1822) The swetnes of native cuntre, to quhilk men bene nocht haistelie acquentit. **1623** BINGHAM *Xenophon* 71 It was a strong drinke..very pleasant to them that were acquainted with it. *a* **1674** CLARENDON *Hist. Reb.* (1843) 692/2 A vulgar spirit, accustomed to no excesses, and acquainted only with a very moderate fortune. **1683** TRYON *Way to Health* 578 They'l be acquainted at Java and Japan..to understand their own Constitution.

B. *absol.* quasi-*sb.*

1577 HELLOWES *Gueuara's Fam. Ep.* 257, I take my leaue of your friendship, and also to call you my acquainted.

acquaintedness (əˈkweɪntɪdnɪs). [f. prec. + -NESS.] The state of being acquainted; the degree or amount of acquaintance.

1661 BOYLE *Style of H. Script.* 244 Afterwards by Acquaintednesse brought to Believe the Scripture upon its Own score. **1851** I. TAYLOR *Wesley & Method.* (1852) 222 A full ministerial acquaintedness with those inexhaustible treasures of thought.

acqueint, acquenche, var. AQUENCH *v. Obs.*

acquest (əˈkwɛst). [a. 16th c. Fr. *acquest*, mod. *acquêt*, OFr. *aquest*:—late L. *acquīst-um*, *acquīsit-um* for *acquīsīt-um*, pa. pple. (used subst.) of *acquīr-ĕre*, see ACQUIRE. The parallel form ACQUIST follows the med.L. *acquīstum*, It. *acquisto*, and has been more generally used for the action or process, while *acquest* is commonly used for the thing acquired, in which sense it is used in Fr. and in jurisprudence.]

1. A thing acquired, an acquisition.

1622 BACON *Hen. VII*, 97 New Acquests are more Burthen, then Strength. **1622** HEYLIN *Cosmogr.* (1682) I. 156 Being all (except Bretagne) the first acquests of the French. **1630** HOWELL *Lett.* (1650) I. 385 The Romans sent legions..partly to secure their new acquests. **1671** F. PHILIPPS *Reg. Necess.* 536 That Earthly Honor which his great Acquests in the Study and Practice of the Law had gained him. *a* **1734** NORTH *Examen* III. vi. §95. 494 Mentioning the French King's Acquests in Flanders. **1864** SIR F. PALGRAVE *Norm. & Eng.* IV. 11 England..was an acquest fully subject to the Conqueror's disposal.

†**2.** The action of acquiring. More commonly written ACQUIST. See also QUEST, to which this sense often approached. *Obs.*

1613 SIR A. SHERLEY *Trav. to Persia* 100 When if there be anything acquisited, the distribution of the members of that bodie is such, vpon whom the acquest is to be made, that there is no possible pretendence from one to the others getting. **1652** M. NEEDHAM tr. *Selden's Mare Cl.* 425 The detaining of the said people with their goods as also his suagement and award for the forfeiture and acquest of them, he hath justified before you. **1684** J. SCOTT *Chr. Life* (ed. 3) 173 We are in the Acquest, and they in the Possession of the heavenly Canaan. **1713** DERHAM *Physico-Theol.* IV. xi. 206 The peculiar structure of the principal Parts acting in the acquest of their Food. **1787** J. BARLOW *Oration* 4 July 16 He was..one of our principal supporters in the acquest of Independence.

3. *Law.* Property gained by purchase, or gift, or otherwise than by inheritance.

†**acquiˈescate**, *v. Obs. rare*$^{-1}$. [improp. f. Fr. *acquiesce-r* + -ATE³. Cf. *terminer, terminate, isoler, isolate*.] = ACQUIESCE.

a **1586** SIDNEY *Wanstead Play* Wks. 1674, 623 (D.) Do but acquiescate to my exhortation, and you shall extinguish him.

acquiesce (ækwɪˈɛs), *v.*, also 7 aquiess(e, acquiese. [a. MFr. *acquiesce-r* (16th c. in Littré), f. L. *acquiēsc-ĕre*; f. *ac-* = *ad-* to, at + *quiēsc-ĕre* to rest.]

†**1.** *intr.* To remain at rest, either physically or mentally; to rest satisfied (*in* a place or state). *Obs.*

c **1620** A. HUME *Orthogr. Brit. Tongue* (1865) 9 But as now we sound it in quies and quiesco, the judiciouse ear may discern tuae soundes. But because heer we differ not, I wil acquiess. **1642** HOWELL *For. Trav.* (1869) 88 Being safely returned to his Mother soile, he may very well acquiesse in her lap. **1756** BURKE *Subl. & B.* Wks. I. I. §9. 136 We were not made to acquiesce in life and health. **1788** PRIESTLEY *Lect. on Hist.* v. li. 386 No situation—in which he can entirely acquiesce, so as to look out for no farther improvements.

†**b.** To acquiesce *from*: To rest, or cease from. *Obs. rare.*

1659 LESTRANGE *Alliance Div. Off.* (1846) 12, I resolved totally to acquiesce from such contests.

†**c.** To acquiesce *under*: To remain in quiet subjection, to submit quietly, to remain submissive. *Obs.*

1680 in Somers's *Tracts* II. 90 For if he be innocent, and that the Right of Succession be his, all Men will quietly acquiesce under him. **1749** FIELDING *Tom Jones* IX. vii. (1840) 137/2 Our readers may not so easily acquiesce under the same ignorance. **1771** *Junius Lett.* xliv. 236 Privilege of parliament..has hitherto been acquiesced under. **1781** T. JEFFERSON *Corr.* Wks. 1859 I. 310 [It may] lead the minds of the people to acquiesce under those events which they see no human power prepared to ward off.

2. To agree tacitly to, concur *in*; to accept (the conclusions or arrangements of others).

1651 HOBBES *Leviathan* I. vii. 32 Our Beleefe..is in the Church; whose word we take, and acquiesce therein. **1672** MARVELL *Rehearsal Transp.* I. 52 You are bound to acquiesce in his judgment, whatsoever may be your private Opinion. **1690** LUTTRELL *Brief Rel.* (1857) II. 21 The said citty acquiesced, and wrote a submissive letter to the king. **1781** COWPER *Lett.* 4 Oct. Wks. 1876, 85, I perfectly acquiesce in the propriety of sending Johnson a copy of my productions. **1831** SCOTT *F.M. Perth* xi. (1874) 115 Douglas seemed to acquiesce in the necessity of patience for the time. **1877** MOZLEY *Univ. Serm.* iv. 76 They speak with an air of men whose claims have been acquiesced in by others.

†**b.** Const. *to, with*. *Obs.*

1651 HOBBES *Gov. & Soc.* xi. §6. 171 We must acquiese to their sayings, whom we have truly constituted to be Kings over us. **1685** LADY R. RUSSELL *Lett.* 24. I. 64 The great thing is to acquiesce with all one's heart to the good pleasure of God. **1703** DE FOE *Shortest way to Peace* in *Miscell.* I. 465 If they acquiesce with a Church of England Government. **1748** RICHARDSON *Clarissa* (1811) V. 33 Clarissa had a double inducement for acquiescing with the proposed method.

†**3.** *trans.* To bring to rest; to appease, satisfy, or harmonize. *Obs.*

1658-9 LOCKYER in Burton *Diary* (1628) IV. 114 This union did most acquiesce all interests.

†**acquiˈescement.** *Obs.*$^{-0}$ [a. Fr. *acquiescement*, n. of action f. *acquiescer*; see ACQUIESCE and -MENT.] = ACQUIESCENCE.

1721 BAILEY, *Acquiescence, Acquiescency, Acquiescement*, the Act of Acquiescing; Consent, Compliance.

acquiescence (ækwɪˈɛsəns). [a. Fr. *acquiescence*, n. of action f. *acquiescer*; see ACQUIESCE and -NCE.]

1. The action or condition of acquiescing; resting satisfied; rest, quiet satisfaction.

a **1631** DONNE *Selections* (1840) 49 In the spirit of contentment, and acquiescence, and thankfulness to God. *a* **1667** JER. TAYLOR *Serm.* xx. *On Chr. Prudence*, That is most eligible, and most to be pursued which is..the acquiescence, the satisfaction and proper rest of our most reasonable appetites. **1867** J. MARTINEAU *Chr. Life* (ed. 4) 88 A life of worldly acquiescence..will not do.

2. Silent or passive assent to, or compliance with, proposals or measures.

1661 BRAMHALL *Just Vind.* ii. 11 They confound obedience of acquiescence with obedience of conformity. **1775** JOHNSON *Tax. no Tyr.* 7 Terrifying the English hearer to tame acquiescence. **1817** JAS. MILL *Brit. India* II. v. viii. 678 His policy was..to excite opposition to those whose acquiescence he failed in acquiring. **1845** DARWIN *Voy. of Nat.* viii. (1879) 157 The Chief Justice smiled acquiescence. **1875** HAMERTON *Intell. Life* VII. vii. 261 Women live in an atmosphere of acquiescence which makes them intolerant of anything like bold and original thinking.

b. Const. *in* (*with, to* obs. or arch.).

1646 SIR T. BROWNE *Pseud. Ep.* 18 By a content and acquiescence in every species of truth we embrace the shadow thereof. **1763** WILKES *Corr.* (1805) I. 228 Necessity ..drove him to an entire acquiescence with every measure prescribed. **1794** SULLIVAN *View of Nat.* I. 401, I yet cannot ..implicitly yield an acquiescence to a superior faculty in the moon. **1856** MISS WINKWORTH tr. *Tauler's Serm.* xxii. 363 Free and full acquiescence to the will of God. **1866** ROGERS *Agric. & Prices* I. xxv. 624 Patient acquiescence in the enormous charges levied.

acquiescency (ækwɪˈɛsənsɪ). [f. L. *acquiēscent-em*: see -NCY, as if ad. L. **acquiēscentia*.] The quality of being acquiescent; a condition of peaceful agreement or submission.

1654 COTTON *Eccles.* (1860) 54 Which acquiescency in the creature is an idolatry which the Lord will curse. **1668** J. HOWE *Bless. Righteous* Wks. 1834, 217/2 Their former acquiescency, and sedate temper was hence, that they believed God would deal well with them at last. **1684**

MANTON *Expos. Lord's Prayer* Matt. vi. 13 Our faith, that is, our acquiescency in the mercy & power & wisdom of God.

acquiescent (ækwɪˈɛsənt), *a.* and *sb.* [ad. L. *acquiēscent-em*, pr. pple. of *acquiēsc-ĕre*; see ACQUIESCE, and -NT.]

A. *adj.* Acquiescing; disposed to acquiesce, quietly agree, or assent.

[**1697** *Acquiescent-ly* occurs: see next.] **1753** RICHARDSON *Grandison* xxiii. (1781) III. 236, I really think his Sisters are too acquiescent. **1863** KINGLAKE *Crimea* (1876) I. ii. 38 The acquiescent policy of 1829 would again be followed.

B. *sb.* One who acquiesces, who silently assents or submits.

1810 COLERIDGE *Friend* (ed. 3) II. 117 Such fear-ridden and thence angry believers, or rather acquiescents, would do well to re-peruse the book of Job.

acquiescently (ækwɪˈɛsəntlɪ), *adv.* [f. prec. + -LY².] In an acquiescent manner; with silent assent.

1697 HUMFREY *Right. of God* III. 37 Mr. Samuel Cradock ..falls in with Sir Charles, and acquiescently receives the same Notion from him. **1876** GEO. ELIOT *D. Deronda* VII. lii. 493 Mirah smiled acquiescently, but had nothing to say.

acquiescer (ækwɪˈɛsə(r)). [f. ACQUIESCE *v.* + -ER¹.] One who acquiesces.

a **1800** MRS. M. ROBINSON *Mem.* (1801) I. 122, I know too well that I have been sufficiently the victim of events, to become the tacit acquiescer where I have been grossly misrepresented. **1837** LOCKHART *Life of Scott* III. x. 329 An undoubting acquiescer in 'the decision of the public'.

acquiescing (ækwɪˈɛsɪŋ), *vbl. sb.* [f. ACQUIESCE + -ING¹.] Silently agreeing; assenting; giving a passive adherence. (Now mostly gerundial.)

1689 *Col. Rec. Penn.* I. 314 You declared your acquiesceing with my Government. *Mod.* Would anyone dream of acquiescing in such a decision?

acquiescing (ækwɪˈɛsɪŋ), *ppl. a.* [f. ACQUIESCE + -ING².] Assenting, silently compliant.

1842 H. E. MANNING *Serm.* (1848) I. vi. 86 Beware, then, of an easy, acquiescing temper, which lulls you to be secure.

acquiescingly (ækwɪˈɛsɪŋlɪ), *adv.* [f. prec. + -LY².] In an acquiescing manner; with silent assent; acquiescently.

1842 H. E. MANNING *Serm.* (1848) I. xi. 153 Even they that have higher yearnings, and pulses that beat for nobler deeds, sink back acquiescingly under the burdensome traditions of our easy life. **1855** BROWNING *Men. & Wom.* I. 136 Yet acquiescingly I did turn as he pointed.

†**aˈcquiet**, *v. Obs.* [f. late L. *acquiētā-re* to put at rest; f. *ac-* = *ad-* to + *quiētā-re* to QUIET.] To set at rest, quiet, or pacify.

1548 LD. SOMERSET *Epist. to Scots* 244 Is it not better to compose & acquiete al this calamitie and trouble by mariage? **1577** tr. *Bullinger, Decades* (1592) 666 They may acquiet themselues, and rest from their laboures. **1613** SIR A. SHERLEY *Trav. to Persia* 86 No fauour, grace, nor benefits from your Maiesty, can acquiet his mind.

†**aˈcquieting**, *vbl. sb. Obs.* [f. prec. + -ING¹.] A bringing to rest, quieting, or pacification.

1534 MORE *Comf. agt. Tribul.* II. Wks. 1557, 1209/2 For the acquyetinge of their conscience speake we now.

acquight, obs. form of ACQUIT.

acquirability (əkwaɪərəˈbɪlɪtɪ). [f. ACQUIRABLE + -ITY.] The quality of being acquirable; capability of being acquired or attained; attainableness.

1794 PALEY *Nat. Theol.* xxvi, The acquirability of civil advantages, ought, perhaps, in a considerable degree to lie at the mercy of chance.

acquirable (əˈkwaɪərəb(ə)l), *a.* [f. ACQUIRE *v.* + -ABLE.] Capable of being acquired; attainable.

1646 SIR T. BROWNE *Pseud. Ep.* 174 Wherein as yet mens enquiries are blinde, and satisfaction acquirable from no man. **1784** J. BARRY *Lect. on Art* ii. (1848) 112 Invention.. can hardly be considered as an acquirable quality. **1880** MUIRHEAD *Gaius* 598 In early times an *hereditas* was held acquirable by usucapion by one who had no title as heir.

acquire (əˈkwaɪə(r)), *v.* Forms: 5 aqwere, acquere, 6 acquyre. [a. OFr. *aquer-re, acquer-re*:—L. *acquīr-ĕre* to get in addition; f. *ac-* = *ad-* to + *quærĕre* to seek. Refashioned in 6 after L.]

1. a. To gain, obtain, or get as one's own, to gain the ownership of (by one's own exertions or qualities).

c **1435** *Seven Sages* (P.) 1080 Thanne the childe were gode of lore, ȝyt he wolde aqwere more. **1483** CAXTON *Cato* x viij. These fyue goodes acqueren the juste and good folke after their dethe. **1602** SHAKS. *Haml.* III. ii. 8 In the verie.. Whirle-winde of Passion, you must acquire, and beget a Temperance that may giue it Smoothnesse. *a* **1680** BUTLER *Rem.* (1759) I. 173 For what w'acquire by Pains and Art Is only due t'our own Desert. **1769** *Junius Lett.* iii. 17 He has acquired nothing but honour in the field. **1847** YEOWELL *Anc. Brit. Ch.* ix. 93 But if the clergy thus acquired riches, they applied them to the noblest purposes.

b. Const. *for* (*to* or *dative obj.* obs.).

1601 SHAKS. *All's Well* IV. iii. 80 The great dignitie that his valour hath here acquir'd for him. **1624** GATAKER *Transubst.* 144 Thereby to acquire judgement or condemnation to themselves. **1656** W. MONTAGUE *Accompl. Wom.* I Such a kind of wit acquires us a command as powerful as pleasing. **1759** ROBERTSON *Hist. Scot.* (1817) I. II. 382 Another circumstance contributed to acquire the Regent such considerable influence.

2. To receive, or get as one's own (without reference to the manner), to come into possession of.

1613 SHAKS. *Hen. VIII*, II. iii. 9 Pompe, the which To leaue, a thousand fold more bitter, then 'Tis sweet at first t'acquire. **1758** JOHNSON *Idler* No. 9 ⁋8 The Idler acquires weight by lying still. **1818** ACCUM *Chem. Tests* 167 The mixture will acquire an orange colour. **1862** RUSKIN *Unto this Last* 130 If, in the exchange, one man is able to give what cost him little labour for what has cost the other much, he acquires a certain quantity of the produce of the other's labour. And precisely what he acquires the other loses.

†**3.** 'To come to, to attain.' J. *Obs. rare.*

1665 GLANVILLE *Scepsis Sci.* xi. 60 Motion cannot be perceived without the perception of its terms, viz. the parts of space which it immediately left, and those which it next acquires.. Now the space left and acquir'd in such slow progressions is so inconsiderable that, etc.

4. Of radar or a radar operator: to begin receiving signals from; to locate.

1962 A. SHEPARD in *Into Orbit* 171 Once the spacecraft goes into orbit, the stations pass it on from one to the other. .. Their radar devices 'acquire' it first, then lock on to it and follow it until it leaves their area. **1970** N. ARMSTRONG et al. *First on Moon* iv. 78 Apollo 11 about to be acquired at the Tananarive (Malagasy Republic) station. **1975** D. G. FINK *Electronics Engineers' Handbk.* xxv. 58 Targets for high-resolution trackers must be designated with reasonable accuracy if they are to be acquired when near the threshold of sensitivity.

¶ Confused with ENQUIRE and REQUIRE. See AD- 2.

1624 HEYWOOD *Gunaikeion* II. 57 None at that age acquires after things unknown. **1553–87** FOXE *A. & M.* II. 48/2 (1684) The Cardinal hath acquired, at the commandment of the Pope, three things of me to be observed.

†**aˈcquire**, *sb. Obs. rare*⁻¹. Also 6 acquier. [f. the vb.] Acquirement or gain.

1592 WYRLEY *Armorie* iii. 116 An English squier Had tane Flauigni, cald John Dalison, Wherein prouision was of great acquier, With as good wine as need would well desier.

acquired (əˈkwaɪəd), *ppl. a.* [f. ACQUIRE *v.* + -ED.] Gained or obtained by one's own exertion; gained, in contradistinction to *innate* or *inherited*.

a. gen.

1606 SHAKS. *Tr. & Cr.* II. iii. 201 No, this thrice worthy and right valiant Lord Must not so staule his Palme, nobly acquir'd. **1651** HOBBES *Leviathan* I. viii. 35 Acquired Wit, I mean acquired by method and instruction. **1790** BURKE *Fr. Revol.* Wks. V. 96 Illustrious in rank, in descent, in hereditary and in acquired opulence. **1826** DISRAELI *Viv. Grey* VII. v. 415 His natural habits as a boy and his acquired habits as a courtier. **1873** SYMONDS *Grk. Poets* ii. 63 Empedocles possessed more acquired and original knowledge than any of his contemporaries.

b. In specific senses and phrs.: (*a*) *Med.* (See quots.) ***acquired immune deficiency syndrome***, a syndrome more commonly known as AIDS.

1842 DUNGLISON *Dict. Med. Sci.* (ed. 3) 20/1 *Acquired Diseases*, diseases which occur after birth, and which are not dependent upon hereditary predisposition. **1934** *Ann. Reg. 1933* 64 Salaman described what is apparently a clear case of acquired immunity to potato virus in tobacco plants. **1961** WEBSTER *Acquired*: of disease or abnormal states, developed after birth (acquired heart disease)—opposed to *congenital*. [**1980** T. MORITO et al. in Krakauer & Cathcart *Immunoregulation & Autoimmunity* 39 (*heading*) Suppressor cell activity in human cord blood and in acquired immune deficiency states.] **1982** *Morbidity & Mortality Weekly Rep.* 24 Sept. 507 Between June 1, 1981, and September 15, 1982, CDC received reports of 593 cases of acquired immune deficiency syndrome (AIDS). **1984** *McGraw-Hill Yearbk. Sci. & Technol. 1985* 66/2 The 1980s will be associated with the new acquired immune deficiency syndrome (AIDS), a far more devastating and mysterious disease.

(*b*) ***acquired taste***, a taste (for a food or drink) that is gained by experience; also *transf.* applied to any thing or person for which or for whom one has acquired a liking (as distinct from a natural or spontaneous taste).

1858 *Illustr. News of World* 24 July 55/3 A yielding to the acquired taste of tobacco cannot be gratified for any length of time without..affecting the breath. **1881** OGILVIE (Annandale) s.v., Abilities natural and acquired; an acquired taste. **1885** W. S. GILBERT *Mikado* II. 43 He would have loved me in time. I am an acquired taste.

(*c*) ***acquired character*** [CHARACTER *sb.* 8b], *characteristic*, *Bot.*, *Zool.*, a development in an individual plant or animal occurring during its lifetime through the influence of its environment. (Cf. LAMARCKIAN *a.*)

[**1794** E. DARWIN *Zoonomia* I. §xxxix. 503 Many of these acquired forms or properties are transmitted to their posterity.] **1876** E. R. LANKESTER tr. *Haeckel's Hist. Creation* I. ix. 204 We may first divide all the different phenomena of inheritance into two groups, which we may distinguish as the transmission of inherited characters, and the transmission of acquired characters. **1893** PARKER & RÖNNFELDT tr. *Weismann's Germ-Plasm* IV. xiii. 392 By acquired characters I mean those which are not preformed in the germ, but which arise only through special influences affecting the body or individual parts of it. **1899** W. Z. RIPLEY *Races of Europe* (1900) xiv. 382 Whether the short stature of the Jew is a case of an acquired characteristic which has become hereditary, we are content to leave an open question. **1926** J. S. HUXLEY *Essays Pop. Sci.* II. 22 So-called 'acquired characters', in other words modifications caused by the environment.. are not inherited at all, or else to such a slight degree as not to be of any great importance in heredity and evolution. **1945** B. RUSSELL *Hist. West. Philos.* (1946) xxi. 753 If, as Lamarck held,..acquired characteristics were inherited. **1958** *Times* 1 July 11/7 Since acquired characters are not inherited, the supply of heritable variation is indeterminate and blind.

acquirement (əˈkwaɪəmənt). [f. ACQUIRE *v.* + -MENT. Cf. 16th c. Fr. *acquerement*, OFr. *aquerrement*, f. *aquerre* to acquire.]

1. The action of acquiring (usually of personal enhancements).

1712 ADDISON *Spectator* No. 409 ⁋7 It is very difficult to lay down Rules for the Acquirement of such a Taste. **1818** MRS. SHELLEY *Frankenstein* iii. 59 (1865) Learn..how dangerous is the acquirement of knowledge. **1866** GEO. ELIOT *F. Holt* II. xviii. 51 That wisdom of the serpent which ..is only of hard acquirement to dove-like innocence.

2. That which is acquired; the result of acquiring for oneself; gain, or attainment. Usually a personal attainment of body or mind, as distinct from an *acquisition* or material and external gain, and opposed to a natural *gift* or *talent*.

1630 J. HAYWARD *Edw. VI* (J.) These his acquirements, by industry, were exceedingly both enriched and enlarged by many excellent endowments of nature. **1646** SIR T. BROWNE *Pseud. Ep.* 18 We embrace the shadow thereof [of truth], or so much as may palliate its just and substantiall acquirements. **1704** SWIFT *T. of Tub* (1709) 77 Every Branch of Knowledge has received wonderful Acquirements since his age. **1802** MAR. EDGEWORTH *Mor. Tales* I. 206 (1866) A woman of considerable information and literature; acquirements not common amongst..ladies. **1862** LD. BROUGHAM *Brit. Const.* xv. 218 His capacity was far from mean, and his acquirements were very considerable.

b. *collectively.*

1868 M. PATTISON *Academ. Organ.* §4. 95 The competition is not an examination in acquirement, but turns mainly on the performance of exercises. **1878** SEELEY *Stein* I. 149 A man of greater ability and acquirement than Stein.

acquirer (əˈkwaɪərə(r)). [f. ACQUIRE *v.* + -ER¹.] One who acquires, or obtains for himself.

1768 BLACKSTONE *Comm.* II. 221 He was not descended, nor derived his blood, from the first acquirer. **1865** CARLYLE *Fredk. Gt.* I. II. ix. 108 This is the third Hohenzollern whom we mark as a conspicuous acquirer.

acquiring (əˈkwaɪərɪŋ), *vbl. sb.* [f. ACQUIRE *v.* + -ING¹.]

1. The action of gaining or obtaining for oneself; gaining possession.

1656 tr. *Hobbes, Elem. Philos.* 14 (1839) For the acquiring of philosophy. **1660** R. COKE *Power & Subj.* 264 How fraile a mans reason and understanding is, even to the acquiring of things necessary for his preservation. **1878** M. L. HOLBROOK *Hygiene of the Brain* 41 There is a limit to our acquiring power.

2. The thing gained or obtained for oneself; acquirement, acquisition.

1630 NAUNTON *Fragm. Reg.* 27 (1870) The King in honour could doe no lesse, than give back to his Son..the acquirings of his Fathers profession. **1828** CARLYLE *Misc.* I. 205 (1857) Infinite longings and small acquirings.

†**aˈcquiry.** *Obs.* [f. ACQUIRE *v.* + -Y². Cf. *inquiry*, *expiry*.] The process of acquiring; acquirement, acquisition.

1549 CHALONER tr. *Erasmus, Moriæ Enc.* Iiij. b, How muche lesse costeth the acquirey of this felicitee. **1644** *Vindic. Treat. Monarchy* v. 35 This Title got the favour of a great party, and was a maine Meane facilitating his acquirie [of England]. *a* **1677** BARROW *Serm.* (1686) III. vi. 62 No art indeed requireth more hard study and pain toward the acquiry of it.

†**ˈacquisite**, *a. Obs.* 6–7. Also, acquysite, acquisit. [ad. L. *acquīsīt-us* pa. pple. of *acquīrĕre*. See ACQUIRE.] Acquired; gained, gotten, obtained for oneself. Used orig. also as pa. pple. of ACQUIRE.

1532 MORE *Confut. Tindale* Wks. 1557, 696/1 The faythe acquysite and gotten by gyuing credence to the reporte. **1621** BURTON *Anat. Mel.* I. i. II. ii, A Humor is a liquid or fluent part of the Body..either innate and borne with vs, or adventitious and acquisite. **1634** PRESTON *New Covenant* 323 It is not only put into the mind as acquisit habits are, but it is ingrafted as any naturall disposition is. **1660** MILTON *Free Commw.* 436 Good Education and acquisit Wisdom ought to correct the fluxible fault, if any such be. **1677** HALE *Prim. Orig. Man.* 63 Which could not be from any habit barely acquisite by the exercise of Faculties.

†**acquisited**, *ppl. a. Obs.* [app. due to formal confusion of ACQUISITE and ACQUISTED.] Acquired.

1613 SIR A. SHERLEY *Trav. to Persia* 100 If there be anything acquisited, the distribution of the members of that bodie is such, vpon whom the acquest is to be made, that there is no possible pretendence from one to the others getting.

acquisition (ækwɪˈzɪʃən). [ad. L. *acquīsītiōn-em* n. of action, f. *acquīsīt-*, ppl. stem of *acquīrĕre*. See ACQUIRE.]

1. The action of obtaining or getting for oneself, or by one's own exertion.

1387 TREVISA *Higden* Rolls Ser. I. 35 The adquisicion of a hollesom merite. **1651** HOBBES *Leviathan* II. xix. 96 Versed more in the acquisition of Wealth than of Knowledge. **1736** BUTLER *Anal.* I. iv. 110 Neither is it offered to our acceptance, but to our acquisition. **1842** H. ROGERS *Introd.*

Burke's Wks. (1842) I. 3 A tenacious memory, and an unrivalled facility of acquisition. **1876** HAMERTON *Intell. Life* II. ii. 61 Work involves the acquisition of new habits.

2. A thing acquired or gained; a gain or acquirement.

1477 EARL RIVERS (Caxton) *Dictes* 53 Trouble not thyself gretly with wordely acquisicions. **1610** SHAKS. *Temp.* IV. i. 13 Then as my guest [*v.r.* gift], and thine owne acquisition Worthily purchas'd, take my daughter. **1686** R. BURTON (*title*) View of the English Acquisitions in Guinea. **1750** JOHNSON *Rambl.* No. 77 ¶11 Writers whose powers & acquisitions place them high in the rank of literature. **1809** SYD. SMITH *Wks.* 1867 I. 174 A great classical scholar is an ornament and an important acquisition to his country. **1840** MACAULAY *Ess.*, *Clive* 89 Acquisitions made by the arms of the State belong to the State alone.

3. The initial location of a target by radar. Freq. *attrib.*

1958 *Aero-Space Terms* 1/1 *Acquisition and tracking radar*, a radar set that locks onto a strong signal and tracks the object reflecting the signal. **1962** A. SHEPARD in *Into Orbit* 167 They [*sc.* computers] prepare a series of predictions as to exactly when the capsule will appear over other tracking stations along the route and transmit this data, which we call 'acquisition messages', to each station in the form of readable, teletyped messages. **1975** D. G. FINK *Electronics Engineers' Handbk.* XXV. 58 A two-dimensional bank of acquisition cells is usually established (as in some search radars) and the region of angular uncertainty is scanned sequentially until the target is detected.

acquisi'titious, *a.* ? *Obs.* [f. *acquīsīt-* ppl. stem of *acquīrĕre*: see ACQUIRE + -ITIOUS.] Of the nature or character of an acquisition; gained by exertion; acquired, as opposed to *native* or *innate*.

1653 A. WILSON *James I*, His choler and fear.. drew him with most violence, because they were not acquisititious, but natural. **1673** H. MORE *App. to Antid.* i. §2. 181 That there is no such idea of God at all as we have describ'd, neither innate, nor acquisititious. **1684** tr. *Bonet's Merc. Compit.* VI. 244 Consider here the temperament natural and acquisititious.

acquisitive (əˈkwɪzɪtɪv), *a.* [f. *acquīsīt-* ppl. stem of *acquīrĕre* (see ACQUIRE) + -IVE, as if ad. L. **acquīsītīvus*.] Characterized by acquisition, Hence,

†**1.** Belonging to one by acquisition: that has been, or is liable to be, acquired; acquisititious. *Obs.*

1637 *Reliq. Wotton.* 106 (1672) He died not in his Acquisitive but in his Native Soil. **1642** FULLER *Holy & Prof. State* I. xv. 48 Neither doth an apprentiship extinguish native, nor disinable to acquisitive Gentry.

2. Able, or given, to make acquisitions; acquiring.

1846 GROTE *Greece* I. i. 51 (1862) The knavish, smooth-tongued, keen and acquisitive Hermês. **1865** CARLYLE *Fredk. Gt.* II. v. ii. 67 The sieging Turks, liberative Sobieskis, acquisitive Louis Fourteenths. **1870** BOWEN *Logic* x. 316 The beginning of all knowledge is in single acts of the Perceptive or Acquisitive Faculty.

acquisitively (əˈkwɪzɪtɪvlɪ), *adv.* [f. prec. + -LY[2].] In an acquisitive manner; in a manner expressing or tending to acquisition.

1591 PERCIVALL *Sp. Dict.* F. b, Verbes put acquisitiuely with the signe *for* will haue a datiue of the person, and a nominatiue or accusatiue of the thing [*e.g.* do this for me]. **1612** BRINSLEY *Posing of Parts* 74 (1669) All sorts of verbs which are put acquisitively.

acquisitiveness (əˈkwɪzɪtɪvnɪs). [f. ACQUISITIVE + -NESS.] The quality of being acquisitive; propensity to make acquisitions, or to make oneself possessor of things; desire of possession. (One of the faculties to which phrenologists have allotted a special 'organ' or region of the brain.)

1826 *Edin. Rev.* XLIV. 271 Because avarice is a vice of pretty common occurrence, it is raised into an original attribute of our nature, by the name of Acquisitiveness. **1827** HARE *Guesses at Truth* I. 143 Civilization takes the heart and sticks it beside the head, just where Spurzheim finds the organ of acquisitiveness. **1862** STANLEY *Jewish Ch.* I. ii. 31 (1877) The ear-ring or nose-ring.. the exact ornaments still so dear to Arab acquisitiveness.

acquisitor (əˈkwɪzɪtə(r)). *rare*[−0]. [f. *acquīsīt-* ppl. stem of *acquīrĕre* (see ACQUIRE) + -OR, as if a. L. **acquīsītor*.] One who acquires. (In mod. Dicts.)

acquist (əˈkwɪst). [a variant of ACQUEST, after L. *acquīsīt-um*, med.L. *acquīst-um*, It. *acquisto*. Commonly used for the action, while *acquest* is more common for the result.]

1. The action of acquiring, acquisition, gain.

1613 SIR A. SHERLEY *Trav. to Persia* 7 The profite which must needs follow from so great an acquist. **1629** BACON *War with Spain* in *Harl. Misc.* (Malh.) IV. 138 A nation, that is manifestly detected to aspire to monarchy and new acquists. **1650** JER. TAYLOR *Holy Liv.* (1727) Pref. 2 Assist their endeavours in the acquist of vertues. *a* **1677** BARROW *Serm.* (1683) II. iii. 53 Let us therefore be exhorted, if we do want it [faith], to endeavour the acquist of it by all proper means. **1850** BROWNING *Christmas Eve* 213 How gladly! if I made acquist, Through the brief minute's fierce annoy, Of God's eternity of joy. **1851** TRENCH *Poems* 177 In the acquist of what is life's true gage.

†**2.** A thing acquired, an acquisition. Commonly written ACQUEST. *Obs.*

1635 J. HAYWARD *Banish'd Virgin* 75 The parts neerest it were the Tingitans new acquists in Iberia. *a* **1677** BARROW in *Beauties of Barrow* (1846) 165 In the gifts of fortune, or in the acquists of industry.

†**a'cquist**, *v. Obs. rare*[−1]. [ad. It. *acquistare* or Sp. *aquistar* to acquire; f. med.L. *acquīst-um*:—cl. L. *acquīsīt-um*: see prec. and ACQUEST.] To gain for oneself, acquire.

1598 BARRET *Tehor. Warres* II. i. 28 He shall acquist and gaine the name.. of a.. vertuous and discreet Captaine.

†**a'cquisted**, *ppl. a. Obs.* [f. prec. + -ED; also written ACQUISITED, by assimilation to L.] = ACQUIRED.

1613 SIR A. SHERLEY *Trav. to Persia* 11 The preseruation of their States, so great and so many acquisted. *Ibid.* 100 If there be anything acquisited. **1635** J. HAYWARD *Banish'd Virgin* 178 He bestowes on them his acquisted crownes.

†**a'cquister.** *Obs. rare*[−1]. [f. ACQUIST *v.* + -ER[1].] = ACQUIRER.

1613 SIR A. SHERLEY *Trav. to Persia* 27 Learning of other, and exercitation.. are the acquisters of all Sciences.

acquit (əˈkwɪt), *v.* Forms: 3 **acwit-en, aquyte**; 3–4 **aquite**; 4 **aquytye**; 4–6 **acqwyte, acquyte**; 4–7 **acquite**, 6– **acquit.** *Pa. pple.* 3 **aquited, aquyted**; 4 **acquite**; 5 **aqwyt, aquytte**; 6 **acquyte**; 4–7 **acquit**; 7– **acquitted.** [a. OFr. *aquite-r*, *acuiter* (Pr. *aquitar*):—late L. **acquitāre*, f. *ac-* = *ad-* to + **quitāre*, = L. *quiētare* to settle; see QUIT. As in *quit*, the vowel was long, *aquīte*, to 16th and even 17th c. Cf. *requīte*.] *orig.* To quiet, appease, or satisfy a claim. Hence, To satisfy or settle the claimant or creditor; to clear or discharge the debtor.

I. To acquit a claim, debt, obligation.

1. To settle, clear off, discharge, pay (a claim, debt, or liability).

c **1230** *Ancren Riwle* 126 þet is ure raunsun þet we schulen areimen us mide, & acwiten ure dettes touward ure Louerd. **1297** R. GLOUC. 565 To & fifti þousund pound, al in one daye.. God wite in o dai wan it aquited be. **1393** LANGL. *P. Pl.* C. XVI. 12 Yf he quike by-quethe hem auht · oþer wolde helpe aquite here dettes. *c* **1400** *Rom. Rose* 6744 If his wynnyng be so lite, That his labour wole not acquyte Sufficiantly al his lyvyng. **1475** CAXTON *Jason* 67 It behoueth that I acquite myn avowe. **1598** B. YONG tr. *Diana* 51 The debt.. which.. we are neuer able to acquite. *a* **1642** QUARLES *Samson* in Farr's *S.P.* (1848) 126 The sweetness of the season does invite Your steps to visit Timnah, and acquite Your last night's promise. **1725** POPE *Odyss.* xx. 362 This gift acquits the dear respect I owe. **1770** *Junius Lett.* xl. 204 An obligation he was.. unable to acquit. **1829** I. TAYLOR *Enthus.* §7. 146 (1867) A responsibility that can never be absolutely acquitted. **1832** SISMONDI *Ital. Repub.* viii. 173 It was not till the month of April, 1370.. that they could acquit the enormous sum of 300,000 florins.

†**2.** To discharge the claims or duties of (an office), to perform, fulfil, accomplish, finish. *Obs.*

c **1530** LD. BERNERS *Arthur* (1814) 175 The whiche knyghte.. hath aquyted the Porte Noyre, and acheued all alone the aduentures of that place. **1592** DAVIES in Chalmers' *Eng. Poets* V. 86/2 Nor can a judge his office well acquit If he possess'd of either party be. *a* **1670** HACKET *Life of Williams* II. 42 Like Samuel, when he had acquitted his government, he liv'd in estimation like the chief of the prophets.

3. To discharge (a debt arising out of something done *to* or *for* us); to pay back, pay off, requite (a benefit or injury). *arch.*

c **1314** *Guy Warw.* 30 Here is thine hors, Y giue it te, When Ichaue nede, aquite it me. **1393** GOWER *Conf.* III. 352 Thus wolde I for my last word beseche, That thou my love aquite, as I deserve. *c* **1440** *Morte Arthur* 48 (1819) Welle acquyteste thou it me, That I haue worshipped any knyght. **1529** WOLSEY in Ellis *Orig. Lett.* I. 104. II. 9 And as my poore shal increase, so shal I not fayle to acquyte your kyndnes. **1535** *A Goodly Prymer* (1834) 60 Make us that we acquit not evil for evil. *c* **1630** JACKSON *Creed* VII. xviii. Wks. VII. 150 Some reward sufficient to acquit or countervail his pains. **1726** GAY *Fables* I. xv. 45 When services are thus acquitted, Be sure we pheasants must be spitted.

†**4.** To discharge (a debt arising out of something done *by* us); to pay for, atone for (an offence). *Obs.*

1593 SHAKS. *Lucr.* 1071 Till life to death acquit my forced offence. **1598** B. YONG tr. *Diana* 25 What haue I done, that I haue not acquitted, Or what excesse, that is not amply paied? **1600** HEYWOOD *1 Edw. IV*, 18 Vntil at Tyburn you acquit the fault.

†**5.** To cancel (a debt due *to* us), to surrender, give up (a claim or right). *Obs. rare.*

1649 SELDEN *Laws of Eng.* I. xix. 35 (1739) The Lord might acquit his own title of Bondage, but no man could be made free without the act of the whole body.

II. To acquit the claimant or creditor.

†**6.** To pay off (a person in respect *of* a debt due to him, a benefit or injury received of him); to repay, requite, be quits with. *Obs.*

c **1380** *Sir Ferumb.* 3084 þan schalt þov him acquyte wel: of al ys shrewidnesse. *Ibid.* 3298 Ofte sche doþ me gyle, Y hope to Mahoun þat ȝute y schel: ones a-quyte hur wyle. *c* **1425** WYNTOWN *Cron.* IX. x. 70 Thar-of I dare the welle acqwyte. *c* **1525** SKELTON *Poems* 180 Scrybbyl thou, scrybyll thou, rayle or wryght, Wright what thou wylte, I xall the aquyte. **1580** TUSSER *Husb.* vii. 16 So many as looue me, and vse me aright, With treasure and pleasure, I richly acquite. **1596** SHAKS. *Merch. Ven.* V. i. 138 *Por.* For as I heare he was much bound for you. *Ant.* No more then I am wel acquitted of. **1599** —— *Hen. V*, II. ii. 144 Their faults are open, Arrest them to the answer of the Law, And God acquit them of their practises.

†**7.** To discharge or dispossess (a person *of* something belonging or due to him); deprive of. *Obs.*

a **1300** *Floriz & Bl.* 208 þer nis non so riche king þat dorst entermeten of eni such þing And þe Admiral hit miȝte iwite þat he nere of his lif aquite. *c* **1300** *K. Alis.* (W.) 3868 Y am of Perce deschargid, Of Mede, and of Assyre aquyted.

III. To acquit the debtor, prisoner, person charged or responsible.

†**8.** To pay the debt for and free (a debtor or prisoner); to deliver, ransom. *Obs.*

c **1230** *Ancren Riwle* 394 Ne telleð me him god feolawe þet leið his wed ine Giwerie uorto acwiten ut his fere? *c* **1380** *Sir Ferumb.* 3453 He schal be kept, by swete iesous, For to aquytye on of ous, If he wer take there. **1596** SPENSER *F.Q.* I. vii. 52 For, till I have acquit your captive knight, Assure your selfe, I will you not forsake.

†**9.** To cancel the debt of and set free (one's own debtor or prisoner); to release, liberate. *Obs.*

1375 BARBOUR *Bruce* XIX. 237 He send and acquyt hym all planly, And gaf the trewis wp oppinly. *c* **1386** CHAUCER *Freres T.* 299 Pay anoon, let se, Twelf pens to me, and I the wil acquite. **1630** PRYNNE *God No Impostor* 32 A man who hath two just, two deepe ingaged Debtors, doth freely acquite the one.

10. To set free, release, liberate, deliver, rid (a person *of* or *from* a duty, obligation, or burden). *arch.*

1463 J. BARET in *Bury Wills* 21 (1850) To a qwyte the said Seynt Marie preest of the taske Abbott's cope, and alle maner charges. **1574** tr. *Littleton's Tenures* 26 a, Theye were acquited agaynste theire lorde of al manner of services. *c* **1627** BP. HALL *Dauids Ps. Metaphr.* vii, From bloody spight Of all my raging enemies Oh! let thy mercy me acquite. **1654** JER. TAYLOR *Real Pres.* 27 To acquit us from our search after this question in Scripture. **1696** in *Col. Rec. Penn.* I. 498 Desired of the Governor to be acquitted of his assistance-shipp. **1701** SWIFT *Cont. Nobles & Com.* Wks. 1755, II. I. 28 To be acquitted of all their debts. **1853** *Arabian Nights* 131 (Routl.) The liberty you grant me acquits you of all obligation towards me.

11. To set free or clear from a charge or accusation; to exculpate, exonerate, declare not guilty (*of*, formerly *from* the thing charged).

c **1386** CHAUCER *Persones T.* 105 A man may aquyte himself byforn God by penaunce. **1393** LANGL. *P. Pl.* C. XXI. 394 Ich.. Boþe aquyte and aquykye · þat was aqueynt þorw synne. *c* **1450** *Merlin* 87 Vlfyn is somewhat a-quytte of the synne that he hadde in the love makinge. **1528** MORE *Heresyes* III. Wks. 1557, 211/2 Than may the iudges acquite and assoyle the defendaunt. **1611** BIBLE *Job* x. 14 Thou wilt not acquite me from mine iniquitie. **1620** SANDERSON *Serm.*, *Ad Pop.* I. iii. (1674) 137, I hope.. to acquit his Holiness and Truth and Justice from all sinister imputations. **1759** ROBERTSON *Hist. Scotl.* I. IV. 311 The jury under these circumstances could do nothing else but acquit him. **1833** HT. MARTINEAU *Loom & Lugger* II. v. 108 To acquit him wholly of the charge. **1880** McCARTHY *Hist. Own Time* IV. liii. 149 Three others were acquitted after a long trial.

†**12.** *refl.* To discharge, free, deliver, rid, oneself (*of* any thing). *Obs.*

1375 BARBOUR *Bruce* XVIII. 74 Bot we acquyt vs vtirly, That nane of vs will stand to ficht. **1489** CAXTON *Fayt of Armes* III. xxiii. 222 He is lyke his seruant and in hys mercy, unto tyme that he haue acquytted hym self of hys raunson. **1616** SURFLET & MARKH. *Countrey Farme* 687 The Hart.. vvhen hee seeth himselfe neere pursued by the dogges, indeuoureth and bestirreth himselfe how to acquite and rid himselfe of them. **1671** MILTON *Samson* 896 Gods unable To acquit themselves, and prosecute their foes But by ungodly deeds. **1711** F. FULLER *Medic. Gymnast.* 5 Observe how Nature acquits her self of what we commonly call a Cold. **1753** RICHARDSON *Grandison* 22 (1781) III. 215 What shall I do to acquit myself of the addresses of this Count of Belvedere?

13. To discharge oneself (*of* duty or responsibility). Hence, *simply*, To discharge the duties of one's position, perform one's part on any occasion.

c **1386** CHAUCER *Clerkes T.* 880 Ther can no man in humblesse him acquite As woman can. *c* **1450** *Merlin* 39 Ye were foles in youre art, that wolde not a-quite you as trewe men. **1475** CAXTON *Jason* 116 The daye of thy promesse is passed thou acquitest the not. **1523** LD. BERNERS *Froissart* I. cxi. 133 Ye knowe right well howe I haue aquyt myselfe. **1594** SHAKS. *Rich. III*, V. v. 3 Couragious Richmond, Well hast thou acquit thee. **1662** FULLER *Worthies* II. 488 (1840) Those flowers carry it clearly, which acquit themselves to a double sense, sight and smell. **1776** GIBBON *Decl. & F.* I. x. 203 They acquitted themselves of their important charge with vigilance and success. **1863** THACKERAY *Pendennis* xlvii. 412 Lady Mirabel.. in a common note of invitation or acceptance acquitted herself very genteelly. **1878** SIMPSON *Sch. Shaks.* I. 94 He was present and acquitted himself like a man.

†**b.** With complement: To perform one's part as, prove oneself. *Obs.*

1642 FULLER *Holy & Prof. St.* II. xvi. 110 Hard, rugged and dull natures of youth acquit themselves afterwards the jewels of the countrey. **1655** —— *Ch. Hist.* IX. 174 The Queen.. acquitted herself more then Woman in her masculine resolutions.

acquit (əˈkwɪt), *ppl. a. arch.* [Short for *acquited*, *acquitted*, on analogy of pa. pples. like *hit*, *lit*, *hid*. See QUIT.] Acquitted, cleared, set free.

1393 GOWER *Conf.* I. 362 Nought as he wolde, it was acquit. **1460–4** *Past. Lett.* 434, II. 81, I am ryght ille aqwyt. **1551** ROBINSON *More's Utopia* 15, I am herin clerely acquytte and discharged of all blame. **1674** *Gov. of Tongue* §6, 137 We may then.. see him we censur'd acquit, and our selves doom'd. **1875** BLACKMORE *A. Lorraine* I. xi. 88 Hilary Lorraine was quite acquit of Oxford leading-strings.

† **a'cquit,** *sb. Obs.* [f. the vb.; cf. Fr. *acquit*, OFr. *acquit, acuit*, f. *aquiter* to ACQUIT.] The act of acquitting; discharge; guarantee; acquittance, acquittal.

1475 CAXTON *Jason* 33 Madame I haue seruid you as well as to me is possible..for thacquite of chiualerye. *a* **1521** HELYAS in Thoms' *E.E. Pr. Rom.* (1858) III. 135 The sayd abbot..demaunded of him familiarly the sauf conduyt and acquite for the countreys and landes of beyonde the sea. **1738** WARBURTON *Div. Legat.* I. 291 *note*, Faintly, and only by way of acquit.

acquitment (ə'kwɪtmənt). ? *Obs.* [a. OFr. *aquitement* action of acquitting. See ACQUIT *v.* and -MENT.] The action of acquitting, discharging, or releasing; acquittal, discharge, release.

1643 MILTON *Divorce* II. xiv. 98 (1851) The indulgent arrears which those judiciall acquitments had ingaged him in. **1645** —— *Tetrachordon* 191 On both sides the acquitment will be reasonable, if the bondage be intolerable. **1683** tr. *Erasmus, Moriæ Enc.* 27 Creditable acquitment of ovrselves in any one station of life. **1703** MANTON *Expos. Is.* liii. 6 Wks. 1871 III. 320 It is God that justifieth, the whole business of your acquitment is carried on by the Lord. **1810** BENTHAM *Art of Packing* (1821) 255 The judge's certificate of acquitment.

acquittal (ə'kwɪtəl). Also 5–6 **acquitayle, acquytaylle,** 6 **acquyghtall,** 6–8 **acquittall.** [f. ACQUIT *v.* + -AL[2]. Also in late Anglo-Fr. (Littleton).]

†**1.** Payment, repayment, requital, or retribution; an amends, set-off, or counter-consideration. *Obs.*

c **1430** LYDG. *Minor Poems* (1840) 89 To shewe how moche that konnyng may availe; And wey ageynwardes the froward acquitayle. **1440** J. SHIRLEY *Dethe of James I* (1818) 22 Thay were all takyn, and byhedid at Edynburghe. The Qwene did herselfe grete worship for here trew acquitalle [*printed* acquitable]. **1547** HEYWOOD *Wit & Folly* (1846) 5 The sotts pleaseure in this last acquyghtall Counterwayleth his payne. **1749** H. WALPOLE *Lett. to H. Mann* 200 (1834) II. 274, I have been long in arrears to you, but I trust you will take this huge letter as an acquittal.

2. Release or discharge from debt or obligation; = ACQUITTANCE 2. *Obs.* exc. in *Law.*

1463 J. BARET in *Bury Wills* (1850) 42 My executours.. shall make a clere declaracion and a trewe accountys yeerly ..for here trewe acquytaylle. **1641** *Termes de la Ley* 9 To acquit and discharge him of all rents, services, and such like: This discharge is called acquitall. **1809** TOMLINS *Law Dict.*, *Acquittal*..signifies in one sense to be free from entries and molestations of a superior lord for services issuing out of lands. **1815** SCOTT *Ld. of Isles* IV. xxvii, The ring and spousal contract both, And fair acquittal of his oath.

†**3.** A release, or deliverance, from liability or risk. Cf. ACQUITTANCE 4. *Obs. rare.*

1618 BOLTON *Florus* IV. ii. 292 Nor was the forbearance of him [Cæsar] an acquitall any longer; for Brutus, and Cassius ..conspired to assassinate him.

4. A setting free, or deliverance from the charge of an offence, by verdict, sentence, or other legal process.

a **1535** MORE *Wks.* 238 (R.) The chaunceler..neuer durst abyde the tryal of xii men for his acquitayle: but was fain by frendship to get a pardon. **1629** COKE *Instit.* 100a, Hereof cometh acquitall, and *quietus est*, (that is) that hee is discharged. **1772** *Junius Lett.* Pref. 15 The jury should bring in a verdict of acquittal. **1840** MACAULAY *Clive* 88 The sentence ought to be one, not merely of acquittal, but of approbation.

5. Discharge (of duty); performance.

1656 MILTON *Lett. of State* (1851) 344 His own deserts in the diligent acquittal of his trust. **1835** I. TAYLOR *Spirit. Despotism* §4. 154 For the acquittal of none of these perplexing duties does a church receive one word of guidance.

acquittance (ə'kwɪtəns), *sb.* Forms: 4 **aquitans, acquetaunce, acquitance,** 5 **aquetons,** 4–6 **acquitaunce,** 6– **acquittance.** [a. OFr. *aquitance* n. of action, f. *aquiter*. See ACQUIT *v.* and -ANCE. Cf. QUITTANCE.]

1. The action of settling or satisfying the legal demands of others, the clearing off of debt or obligation; satisfaction, settlement, repayment.

1330 R. BRUNNE *Chron.* 156 Tenþousand mark & mo, þat now er in balance..I salle bring him to stalle, bot he mak me acquitance. *c* **1460** *Curtasye* in *Babees Book* (1868) 319 Ofpe resayuer speke wylle I, þat fermys resayuys wyrturly Of grayuys, and hom aquetons makes. *c* **1550** *Everyman* in Hazl. *Dodsl.* I. 127 Knowledge, give me the scourge of penance, My flesh therewith shall give acquittance. **1769** *Junius Lett.* xiii. 57 This may be an acquittance of favours upon the turf.

2. Hence, putting the result (however attained) for the means: The act of releasing from a debt or obligation; release, discharge.

c **1360** CHAUCER *A.B.C.* 60 And with his blood he wrote that blisfull bill Upon the crosse as generall acquetaunce, To every penitent. *c* **1400** *Rom. Rose* 4707 Love it is an hatefulle pees, A free acquitaunce withoute relees. **1528** PERKINS *Prof. Bk.* ii. §148 (1642) 66 If a man bring an Action of debt against me..and I plead against him acquittance. **1574** tr. *Littleton, Tenures* 31 b, Service by homage auncestrel draweth to hym acquitance, that is to saye, the Lorde oughte to acquite hys tenante against al other lordes above him of everye manner of service. **1627** FELTHAM *Resolves* II. v. Wks. 1677, 168 The whole worlds wealth is a bribe too small to win him [Death] to acquittance. **1672** MARVELL *Rehearsal Transp.* I. 307 If a man be in the Churches debt once, 'tis very hard to get an acquittance. **1848** MILL *Pol. Econ.* II. 60 Payment in bank-notes is a complete acquittance to the payer.

3. A writing in evidence of a discharge; a release in writing; a receipt in full, which bars a further demand. Also *attrib.* as ***acquittance-roll.***

1377 LANGL. *P. Pl.* B. XIV. 189 He shulde take þe acquitance as quik and to þe qued schewe it. **1393** J. CROXTON in *Test. Eborac.* (1836) 186, I will that the same company sele Robyn another generall acquitans, and gif hym xls. **1531** *Dial. on Laws of Eng.* II. xlii. 138 (1638) The creditour had taken an acquittance of him without paying him his mony. **1588** SHAKS. *L.L.L.* II. i. 161 Boyet, you can produce acquittances For such a summe. **1684** *London Gaz.* mdcccxciv. 4 Lost..a File with Writings and Acquittances, supposed to be dropt not far off the Exchange, London. **1727** ARBUTHNOT *Hist. J. Bull* 61 The same man bought and sold to himself, paid the money, and gave the acquittance. **1844** *Queen's Regul. & Ord. Army* 137 An acquittance-roll, containing the names of the Men of each Troop, or Company, and showing the debts and credits, with the Signature of each Man. **1852** MCCULLOCH *Taxation* II. vi. 294 (ed. 2) The tax on receipts, or acquittances for money, was introduced into this country in 1783.

†**4.** Deliverance, release (from danger or trouble). Cf. ACQUITTAL 3. *Obs. rare.*

1610 HEALEY *St. Aug., City of God* VIII. xvi. 307 That perfection..that is promised vs after our acquittance from mortalitie. **1621–31** LAUD *Serm.* (1847) 55 Neither of these elements [fire and water] have any mercy, but the 'mercy of the Highest' was his acquittance from both.

5. Exoneration from a charge; remission of offences; discharge. = ACQUITTAL 4. *rare.*

1612 T. TAYLOR *Titus* iii. 3 (1619) 608 They rest herein as a sufficient acquittance from all their vnrighteousnes. **1783** BURKE *Sp. on Fox's E. Ind. Bill* Wks. 1842 I. 286 They gave him a full and complete acquittance from all charges of rebellion. **1860** C. INNES *Scotl. in Mid. Ages* 193 Purgation and acquittance according to ancient law.

6. Discharge (of a duty); = ACQUITTAL 4. *rare.*

1865 W. G. PALGRAVE *Centr. Arabia* I. 225 The precise exactitude required in the acquittance of religious duties.

† **a'cquittance,** *v. Obs. rare.* [f. the sb. Cf. to *receipt* an account, to *pension*, etc.] *trans.* To give an acquittance or discharge; to discharge.

1464 MARG. PASTON in *Past. Lett.* 490 II. 159 The sewtys wer wythdrawyn on bothe partyes, and iche of hem aquytauncyd othyr. **1590** GREENE *Neuer too late* (1600) 3 Nor am [I] a Pilgrime to acquittance sinne with penance. **1594** SHAKS. *Rich. III*, III. vii. 233 Your meere enforcement shall acquittance me From all the impure blots and staynes thereof.

acquitted (ə'kwɪtɪd), *ppl. a.* Formerly ACQUIT. [f. ACQUIT *v.* + -ED.] Discharged, released, set free, exonerated (from a charge or offence).

1679 MARG. MASON *Tickler Tickled* 8 But what have these acquitted Offenders got by this Excuse? **1780** BURKE *Sp. Econ. Ref.* Wks. III. 247 It is not possible to give a fair verdict by which he will not stand acquitted.

acquitter (ə'kwɪtə(r)). [f. ACQUIT *v.* + -ER[1].] One who acquits, or releases.

1748 RICHARDSON *Clarissa* (1811) VII. 101 He will be but a languid acquitter. **1859** *Times* 26 Dec. 8/4 If we are to maintain our position as the heirs of Bacon and the acquitters of Galileo.

acquitting (ə'kwɪtɪŋ), *vbl. sb.* [f. ACQUIT *v.* + -ING[1].] A discharging, setting free, or releasing. (Now mostly gerundial.)

1436 *Pol. Poems & Songs* II. 159 Ffor concyens and for myne acquytyng Ayenst God and ageyne abusyon. **1668** WILKINS *Real Char.* II. i. §5. 41 Relations of Action, IV Commerce, 9 Acquitting, Discharge, Quittance. *Mod.* The jury hesitated about acquitting the prisoner.

acraldehyde (ˌæ'krældɪhaɪd). *Chem.* [f. L. *acr-is*, acrid + ALDEHYDE.] One of the polymeric modifications of ALDEHYDE.

1869 ROSCOE *Elem. Chem.* 350 Aldehyde is capable of existing in three other peculiar states..a third modification termed Acraldehyde boils at 110°. The molecular formula appears to be $C_4H_8O_2$ or $2(C_2H_4O)$.

‖**acrania** (ə'kreɪnɪə). *Phys.* [mod.L. f. Gr. ἀ priv. + κρᾱνίον skull.] Defective development consisting in the absence partial or total of the skull.

1849–52 TODD *Cycl. Anat. & Phys.* IV. 956/2 Acrania does not seem to interfere with uterine life.

acranial (ə'kreɪnɪəl), *a.* [f. mod.L. *Acrania*, sb. pl., applied by Haeckel to the lowest type of *Vertebrata*, represented by the *Amphioxus* or *Lancelot*: see prec.]

1870 ROLLESTON *Anim. Life* 32 In all Vertebrata, with the exception of the *Amphioxus*, which is hence called 'Acranial,' the neural canal widens considerably in the anterior region of the body. **1878** BELL *Gegenbauer's Elem. Comp. Anat.* 444 The indifferent stage in which the head is found in the Acrania makes it impossible to distinguish any distinct cephalic skeleton.

a'crasial, *a. rare*[−1]. [f. ACRASY + -AL[1].] Ill-regulated, untempered, intemperate.

1851 S. JUDD *Margaret* II. xi. 321 (1871) 'Acrasial Philogamy? Brother Edward, what is that?' 'That,' replied Edward, 'is an incurable malady to which young persons are subject.'

acrasin ('ækrəsɪn). *Bot.* [f. mod.L. *Acras-is*, name of a genus of slime moulds (P. van Tieghem 1880, in *Bull. de la Soc. Bot. de France* XXVII. 318), f. Gr. ἀ- A- *pref.* 14 + κρᾶσις fusion: see -IN[1]. Cf. quot. 1969 and ACRASY.] A substance secreted by the cells of some slime moulds which acts as an attractant for them and causes their aggregation.

1947 J. T. BONNER in *Jrnl. Exper. Zool.* CVI. 22 We have deduced..that during the aggregation of Dictyostelium there is some type of chemical substance..produced continuously or at frequent intervals by the center, which freely diffuses, and the myxamoebae move..towards the point of its highest concentration... The term *acrasin* is suggested, and it can be defined..as a type of substance consisting either of one or numerous compounds which is responsible for stimulating and directing aggregation in certain members of the Acrasiales. **1969** —— in *Sci. Amer.* June 80/3, I gave the unidentified attractant the name acrasin because the proper name of the cellular slime molds is Acrasiales, and also because in Edmund Spenser's *Faerie Queene* there is a witch named Acrasia who attracted men and transformed them into beasts. **1970** *Nature* 26 Sept. 1365/2 Slime mould amoebae are attracted to a certain substance which they secrete themselves. (It is called acrasin, and has been identified in one species as cyclic-AMP[2].)

† **'acrasy.** *Obs.* [ad. med.L. *acrasia*, which seems to confuse Gr. ἀκρᾱσία ill-temperature, badly-mixed quality (f. ἄκρᾱτος unmixed, untempered, intemperate) applied by Hippocr. to meats, with ἀκρᾱσία impotence, want of self-command (f. ἀκρᾱτής powerless, without authority, without self-command, incontinent).] Irregularity, disorder, intemperance. In Spenser's *Faerie Queene*, intemperance or incontinence personified as an enchantress.

1596 SPENSER *F.Q.* II. xii, *motto*, Guyon..Doth overthrow the Bower of Blis, And Acrasy defeat. **1617** S. D[ANIEL] *Hist. Eng.* (1617) 156 A time [reign of Henry III] that hath yeelded notes of great varietie with many examples of acrasie, and diseased State, bred both by the inequality, of this Princes manners, and the impatience of a stubborne Nobility. **1707** PHILLIPS, *Acrasia*, Indisposition, Disorder. [Also as in BAILEY.] **1731** BAILEY, vol. II. *Acrasy* (with Physicians) the Excess or Predominancy of one Quality above another in Mixture, or in the Constitution of a Human Body. **1780** CORNISH *Life of Firmin* 84 (T.) A little prone to anger, but never excessive in it, either as to measure or time; which acrasies..occasion great uneasiness. **1818** TODD, *Acrasy*, Excess, irregularity.

† **'acratism.** *Obs.* [ad. Gr. ἀκράτισμα breakfast, f. ἄκρᾱτος neat (wine).] See quot.

1805 W. TAYLOR in *Monthly Mag.* XX. 34 An acratism was the old name for a whet, or cordial.

acrawl (ə'krɔːl), *adv.* or *pred. a.* [f. A *prep.*[1] 11 + CRAWL *sb.*[1] and *v.*[1]] Crawling (*with*).

1830 *Blackw. Mag.* XXVIII. 146 Mountain tops..a-crawl with insects, above a few acres of wet! **1834** *Ibid.* XXXV. 1003 Something a-crawl in the ditch. **1909** R. SABATINI *St. Martin's Summer* i. 14 He felt himself the meanest, vilest thing a-crawl upon this sinful earth. **1923** *Chambers's Jrnl.* 29 Dec. 73/1 The slime..seems acrawl with strange forms of life.

† **acraze** (ə'kreɪz), *v. Obs.* Also 6 **acrase,** 6–7 **accrase, accraise, accraze.** [Either formed on Eng. vb. CRAZE, with A- *pref.* 10, or a. Fr. *acrase-r* (Cotgr. *accrazer*) var. of *écraser* (see A- *pref.* 9) f. a simple **craser*, cogn. w. Eng. CRAZE, CRASH, f. Norse *kras-a, krasa*, to shiver, crash. A- refashioned as AC- in 6 after words f. L.] To weaken, impair, enfeeble.

1549 CHEKE *Hurt of Sedition* (1641) 38 With cold in the nights which acrazeth the body. **1577–87** HOLINSHED *Chron.* III. 1049/2 By glutting of meats which weakeneth the bodie, and with cold in the nights which accraseth the bodie.

† **acrazed** (ə'kreɪzd), *ppl. a. Obs.* [f. prec. + -ED.]

1. Weakened, enfeebled, diseased in body, affected with illness, indisposed; impaired.

1521 *State Pap. Hen. VIII*, VI. 83 The same day I spake with the King, my Lady was sumwhat accrased. **1540** WHITTINTON *Tullyes Off.* I. 37 The maner of phisycions is to be folowed, whiche with easy medicynes cure them that be a lytell acrased. **1565** JEWEL *Repl. to Harding* (1611) 183 Then is M. Hardings argument much acrased, and concludeth not so much, as is pretended. *a* **1670** HACKET *Life of Williams* II. 100 No good physician will try experiments upon an accrazed body.

2. Mentally affected; crazed.

1576 GASCOIGNE in Nichols's *Prog. Q. Eliz.* I. 496 A Porter? surely then He eyther was accrased, Or else, to see so many men His spirits were amased. **1634** SIR J. HARINGTON *Ariosto's Orl. Fur.* XLVI. xxi. 396 Don Leon with these newes was so accrazed, He seemed in a traunce.

acre ('eɪkə(r)). Forms: 1 (acer), **æcer, æcyr;** 2 **æker;** 2–7 **aker;** 5 **akere, akyre, hakere;** 5–6 **akir;** 6 **acer;** 4– **acre.** *Pl.* **acres:** in 1 **æceras, acras,** 2–5 **akres.** [OE. *æcer, acer*, cogn. w. Goth. *akr-s*, ON. *akr*, OSax. *accar*, OFris. *ekker*, OHG. *achar*; L. *ager*, Gr. ἀγρός; Skr. *ajras* plain; originally 'open country, untenanted land, forest'; cf. Gr. ἄγριος, L. *agrestis* wild, ἀγρεύς a hunter, *peragrāre* to rove; then, with advance in the agricultural state, pasture land, tilled land, an enclosed or defined piece of land, a piece of land of definite size, a land measure. Very early adopted in med.L. and OFr. as *acra*, *acre*, whence the mod. spelling for the regular *aker*.]

1. a. A piece of tilled or arable land, a field. *Obs.* exc. in *God's Acre* [from mod. Germ.] a churchyard, and prop. names as ***Long Acre***.

c **975** *Rushw. Gosp.* Matt. xii. 1 Eode se hælend þurh acras. c **1000** *Ags. Gosp., ibid.*, Se Hælend fór ofyr æceras [*MS. C.* æcyras]. c **1160** *Hatton Gosp., ibid.*, Se Hælend for ofer ækeres. c **1000** *Ags. Gosp.* Matt. xxvii. 8 Forþam is se æcer ȝehaten Acheldemagh, þæt is..blodes æcyr. c **1160** *Hatton Gosp., ibid.*, Forþam ys se aker ȝehaten Acheldemach, þæt ys ..blodes aker [*Lindisf.* & *Rushw.* lond blodes, blodes lond]. **1330** R. Brunne *Chron.* 115 Pople with alle þe recchesse, & akres, als þei wonnen, þorgh þer douhtinesse, þe lond þorgh þei ronnen. c **1425** Wyntown *Cron.* viii. xxvi. 70 Þe Mylnaris akyre it callyd wes, And men sayis, bath Hors and Man In þat-Akyre was lwgyd þan. **1483** Caxton *G. de la Tour* f vj, A good man..named Nabot which had an Aker of a Vine yerd. **1635** N. Carpenter *Geog. Delin.* ii. x. 179 Some parcels of ground should as pastures bee diuided from Woody acres. a **1700** Dryden *Ep., To Sir G. Etheredge* 33 Spite of all these fable-makers, He never sow'd on Almain acres. **1844** Longfellow *Misc. Poems, God's Acre*, I like that ancient Saxon phrase, which calls The burial ground God's Acre!.. This is the field and Acre of our God, This is the place where human harvests grow.

b. By modern writers the pl. *acres* is used rhetorically for *lands, fields, landed estates.* **broad acres**, extensive lands.

2. a. A definite measure of land, originally as much as a yoke of oxen could plough in a day; afterwards limited by statutes 5 Edw. I, 31 Edw. III, 24 Hen. VIII, to a piece 40 poles long by 4 broad (= 4840 sq. yds.), or its equivalent of any shape.

'Normally, it was understood to consist of thirty-two furrows of the plough, a furlong in length.' A. S. Ellis in *N. & Q.* 16 Sept. 1882, 230.

c **1000** Ælfric *Dial. in OE. & Lat.* (Thorpe *Anal.* 8) Ælce dæȝ ic sceal erian fulne æ cer oððe máre. **1038–44** *Charter of Eadweard, Cod. Dipl.* IV. 77 An mylen be doferware troce. & seofon æceras þarto. **1377** Langl. *P. Pl.* B. vi. 4, I have an half acre to erie. c **1420** *Palladius on Husb.* v. 15 Thre hors a yere an acre wel sufficeth. **1466** *Manners & Househ. Exps.* 326, I have ȝeven to John Hamondes wyffe iiij. hakeres of wete. **1494** Fabyan vii. ccxxii. 246 An acre conteyneth xl. perches in length, and iiii. in brede: & iiii. acres make a yerde, and v. yerdes make an hyde, and viij. hydes make a knyghtes fee, by the whiche reason, a knyghtes fee shuld welde clx. acres, & that is demed for a ploughe tyll in a yere. **1502** Arnold *Chron.* (1811) 173 Of what length soo euer they be, clx. perches make an akir. **1542** Recorde *Grounde of Artes* 208 (1575) A Rod of lande, whiche some call a roode, some a yarde lande, and some a Farthendele, 4 Farthendels make an Acre. **1581** Stafford *Exam. of Compl.* ii. 43 (1876) One Acer bearinge as much Corne as two most commonly were wont to do. **1602** Carew *Cornwall* 36 a, Commonly thirtie Acres make a farthing land, nine farthings a Cornish Acre, & foure Cornish Acres, a Knight's fee. **1610** Shaks. *Temp.* i. i. 70 Now would I give a thousand furlongs of sea for an acre of barren land. **1624** Capt. Smith *Virginia* iv. 126 English Wheat will yeeld but sixteene bushels an aker. **1669** J. W[orlidge] *Syst. Agric.* (1681) 321 An Acre is one hundred and sixty square Lug, or Pearch of Land, at sixteen foot and a half to the Perch; but of Coppice-wood eighteen foot to the Perch is the usual allowance. But an Acre sometimes is estimated by the proportion of Seed used on it; and so varies according to the Richness or sterility of the Land. **1691** Petty *Pol. Anat.* 52, 121 Irish Acres do make 196 English Statute Acres. **1790** Burke *Fr. Rev.* Wks. V. 212 Their estates were bound to the last acre. **1799** J. Robertson *Agric. in Perth*, A Scotch acre commonly = 6084 square yards. If the differences of inches were narrowly attended to in making the Scotch chain, a Scotch acre would be equal to 6150·7 square yards. **1807** Crabbe *Par. Reg.* ii. 248 He, for his acres few so duly paid, That yet more acres to his lot were laid.

b. *loosely* in *pl.* Large quantities, a wide expanse.

1830 Gen. P. Thompson *Exerc.* (1842) I. 317 If the King wants a yacht, or Her Majesty's Grace would like a few acres of real lace. **1865** Carlyle *Fredk. Gt.* II. v. vi. 111 He.. writes cunningly acres of despatches to Prince Eugene.

†3. As a lineal measure: an **acre length**, 40 poles or a furlong (*i.e.* furrow-length); an **acre breadth**, 4 poles or 22 yards. *Obs.* or *dial.*

c **1380** *Sir Ferumb.* 971 þe frensche men þai made reculle: wel an akers lengþe. *Ibid.* 2770 þay dryuen hem aȝen an aker lengþe. c **1425** Wyntown *Cron.* vii. iv. 162 And fra it a spere wes drawyn.. Large thre akyre leynth of Land. c **1440** *Morte Arthure* 3850 With þe lussche of þe launce he lyghte one hys schuldyrs, Ane akere lenghe one a launde, fulle lothely wondide. **1523** Fitzherbert *Husb.* (1534) C 2, xvi. fote and a halfe, to the perche or pole, foure perches to an acre in bredth, and fortye perches to an acre in lengthe. **1535** Coverdale *1 Sam.* xiv. 14 The first slaughter that Ionathas and his wapen bearer dyd, was..with in the length of halue an aker of londe. [**1611** An halfe acre of land. *Marg.* halfe a furrow of an acre of land.] a **1540** [K. James of Scotl.] *Christis Kirk of the Grene* viii, Be ane aikerbraid it cam not neir him. **1601** Holland *Pliny* (1634) I. 117 The length of the very demy Island..is not aboue 87 miles and a halfe, and the breadth in no place lesse than two acres of land. c **1805** Wordsworth *The Brothers* (Chandos ed.) 31/2 What a feast. To see an acre's breadth of that wide cliff One roaring cataract! **1809** Bawdwen *Domesday Bk.* 326 Four Villanes have there one plough, and an acre of wood in length and one acre in breadth.

4. *Comb.* **acre-foot** *Irrigation*, a unit of volume of water equal to one acre in area and one foot in depth; **acre-land**, *obs.*, ploughed or arable land; **acre-shot**, *obs.*, a payment or charge rated at so much per acre. Also acre-dale, acre-man, acre-staff, q.v.

a **1400** *Chron. Engl.* in Ritson's *Met. Rom.* II. 270 In thilke time, in al this londe, On aker-lond ther nes yfounde Ne toun ne houses never on Er then Bruyt from Troye com. **1479** R. Rokewoode in *Bury Wills* 53 (1850) Also an acre londe inclosed, late purchased of Water Dey. **1585** *Act 27 Eliz.* xxiv. §1. 3 Such of the said Sea-banks as are not maintained..at the charge of any Township or by Acre-shot or any other common charge. **1909** in *Cent. Dict.* Suppl., Acre-foot **1958** *New Scientist* 10 Apr. 8/1 It [the Kariba dam] will contain 140 million acre-feet of water.

¶ **acre** (or **acre-fight**), explained by Cowel as 'an old sort of duel fought by single combatants, English and Scotch, between the frontiers of their kingdoms, with sword and lance,' seems to be merely transliterated by him from a med.L. phrase *acram committere* in the Annals of Burton 1237, where *acram* (for *pugnam*) is a bad translation of OE. *camp* combat, confused with L. *campus*, Fr. *champ*, and so with Eng. *acre*. From Cowel it has found its way into mod. Dicts., outside of which 'to fight an acre' or 'acre-fight' has no existence.

acreable ('eɪkərəb(ə)l), *a. rare.* [f. acre + -able.] Of or proper to an acre; per acre.

1792 A. Young *Trav. in France* 341 As to..the acreable produce of corn land, the difference will be found very great indeed. **1880** Bence-Jones *Macm. Mag.* No. 246, 514 Reduction of the acreable rent for the number of wet acres taken.

acreage ('eɪkərɪdʒ). [f. acre + -age.] Extent or amount of acres; acres collectively or in the abstract. Also *attrib.* as ***acreage-rate***.

1859 Sir E. Tennent *Ceylon* II. 235 (ed. 2) Suitable lands yet to be brought under cultivation may add treble to the present acreage. **1860** *Times* 4 Jan. 10/6 The tenantry paying a small acreage rate. **1871** Smiles *Character* ii. 62 (1876) The cultivable acreage of our country.

acred ('eɪkəd), *a.* [f. acre + -ed[2].] Possessing acres, or landed estates; mostly in *comp.* as ***large-acred***.

1844 Disraeli *Coningsby* ii. iv. 74 It was from such materials..with great numbers, largely acred..but without knowledge, genius..or faith, that Sir Robert Peel was to form a great Conservative party. **1859** Geo. Eliot *Adam Bede* 51 If ever I live to be a large-acred man.

acre-dale. *dial.* [f. acre + *dale* = deal:—OE. *dæl* part share.] 'Lands in a common field, in which different proprietors held portions of greater or less quantities. *North.*' Halliwell.

acredit, obs. form of accredit *v.*

acreless ('eɪkəlɪs), *a.* [f. acre + -less.] Without acres or landed estates. Also *fig.*

1890 *Temple Bar* June 226 The lady had the bad taste to prefer the acreless to the acred. **1941** L. H. B. Lyon *Tomorrow Revealing* 14 A stealthy and mute fertility still moves The acreless heart.

†acreman. *Obs.* A cultivator of the ground, a husbandman, or ploughman.

c **1000** Ælfric *Gloss.* 5 Æcerman, *agricola*. **1389** R. Wimbledon *Serm.* in Helmingh. MS. (also in Foxe *A. & M.* (1562) I. 622) If þe laboreris were not, boþ prestis and kniȝtis mosten bicome acremen and heerdis. c **1400** *Lay le Freine* 176 Acre-men yede to the plough.

†acreme. *Obs.* [An entry copied from Dict. to Dict. since 17th c.; its source has not been ascertained; and as the form of the word does not admit of explanation, there is ground to suspect its origination in some error in the transcription of a L. or OFr. document. If the word existed, and is correctly explained, it would be a *square acre*, i.e. a piece of land a furlong square = 48,400 sq. yds.]

1669 J. W[orlidge] *Systema Agriculturæ* (1681) 321 An Acreme of Land is ten Acres. **1706** Phillips, *Acreme*, a law-word for ten Acres of Land. **1725** Bradley *Fam. Dict.* s.v., *Acreme* of Land, ten Acres of Land. **1751** Chambers *Cycl.*, and **1819** Rees *Cycl.* s.v., *Acreme*, a term sometimes used in antient law-books for ten acres.

acrese, early f. accrease *v. Obs.* to increase.

†acre-staff. *Obs.* (See quotations.)

1611 Cotgr., *Curette*, a plough-staffe, or Aker-staffe (wherewith the cutter is cleansed). **1616** Surflet & Mark. *Countrey Farme* 532 The acker-staffe to cleanse the plowe when it shall be loaden with earth or other vild matter. **1650** Fuller *Pisgah-Sight* ii. viii. 174 Let none turn their flailes, aker-staves, sheep-hooks, shuttles, needles, into swords, till first with Gedeon they have a warrant from God. **1866** Rogers *Agric. & Prices* I. xxi. 539 The ploughman was provided with a pole shod with a flat iron, and called in later times an aker-staff.

acrewe, early form of accrue *v.*

†'acrid, *sb. Obs.* [ad. Gr. ἀκρίδα (nom. ἀκρίς) locust.] A locust.

One of the terms introduced by Cheke in attempting to give a closer version of the Greek N.T. Used by no one else.

c **1550** Cheke *Matt.* iii. 4 His meat was acrids and wild honi.

acrid ('ækrɪd), *a.* [an irreg. and recent formation on L. *ācri-s* sharp, pungent (f. root *ac-*, in *acute, acid, acerb*) + -id, perh. in imitation of *acid*. Cf. Fr. *âcre* (in Cotgr. 1611). Preceded in 17th c. by *acrimonious*, also by *acris* unchanged, and the more regularly formed *acrious*.]

1. Bitter and hot or stinging to the taste, or having a similar effect upon the eyes, skin, and mucous membrane; bitterly pungent, irritating, corrosive.

1712 tr. *Pomet's Hist. Drugs* I. 221 Of an acrid astringent taste. **1732** Arbuthnot *Rules of Diet* 296 Stimulating Substances abounding with a pungent acrid Salt. **1764** Reid *Inq. Hum. Mind* vi. §21, 187 Gnawed and corroded by some acrid humour. **1784** Cowper *Task* i. 448 The mariner, his blood inflamed With acrid salts. **1830** Lindley *Nat. Syst. Bot.* 129 This resin is extremely acrid, causing excoriations and blisters if applied to the skin. **1856** Mrs. Browning *Aurora Leigh* 49 The sweat of labour in the early curse Has (turning acrid in six thousand years) Become the sweat of torture. **1868** Bain *Ment. & Mor. Sc.* 39 In the third class of tastes, there is present an element arising through the nerves of Touch..The acrid combines the fiery with the bitter.

2. Bitterly irritating to the feelings; of bitter and irritating temper or manner. (Stronger than *acrimonious*.)

[Not in Johnson 1773.] **1781** Cowper *Charity* 503 Their acrid temper turns, as soon as stirred, The milk of their good purpose all to curd. **1840** Carlyle *Heroes* 297 (1858) He was found, close at hand, to be no mean acrid man; but at heart a healthful, strong, sagacious man. **1850** Merivale *Hist. Rom. Emp.* VIII. lxiv. 129 (1865) Tacitus grows more acrid, more morbid in temper, even to the last.

acridian (ə'krɪdɪən), *a.* and *sb. Ent.* [f. Gr. ἀκρῖδ-, ἀκρίς locust + -ian; cf. F. *acridien*.] **A.** *adj.* Of or pertaining to an orthopterous insect of the family *Acridiidæ*, comprising certain locusts and grasshoppers. **B.** *sb.* An insect of this family.

1878 *Boston Soc. Nat. Hist. Proc.* XIX. 336 Mr. S. H. Scudder exhibited a number of western Acridians in illustration of one type of dimorphism. **1889** *Cent. Dict.*, Acridian, *a.* **1904** A. P. Morse *Res. N. Amer. Acridiidæ* 7 The Acridian fauna of the southeastern United States. **1930** T. S. Eliot tr. *St. John Perse's Anabasis* 49 My heart gives heed to a family of acridians.

Acridid ('ækrɪdɪd), *sb.* and *a. Ent.* Also **acridid**. [f. mod.L. *Acrididæ*, earlier *Acridiidæ*, family name f. *Acrida*, generic name f. Gr. ἀκρῖδ-, ἀκρίς locust: see -id[3].] **A.** *sb.* An orthopterous insect of the family Acrididæ, which includes locusts and short-horned grasshoppers. **B.** *adj.* Of or pertaining to this family. Also **A'cridiid** *sb.* and *a.*, in the same sense.

1923 H. M. LeFroy *Man. Entomol.* viii. 54 The Acridiids form the most important group of the Orthoptera and contain the true locusts. **1925** A. D. Imms *Gen. Textbk. Entomol.* 224 The Acridiid subfamily Œdipodinæ. **1941** *Ann. & Mag. Nat. Hist.* VIII. 511 No Acridid has been found in deposits of an age earlier than the Tertiary. *Ibid.* 519 The Recent Acridid genera. **1946** F. E. Zeuner *Dating Past* xii. 366 A second instance is that of the acridid grasshopper *Euchorthippus elegantulus* Znr., also from Jersey. **1967** M. J. Coe *Ecol. Alpine Zone Mt. Kenya* 94 The insect fauna of Mt. Kenya is very little known, but the author has observed flightless Acridids. **1968** H. Oldroyd *Elem. Entomol.* ix. 98 A few other Acridiids rub the fore- and hind-wings of the same side together. **1972** Swan & Papp *Common Insects N. Amer.* iii. 70 The acridids or grasshoppers—sometimes called shorthorn grasshoppers—may be differentiated from the tettigoniids or longhorn grasshoppers by their short antennae.

acridine ('ækrɪdaɪn). *Chem.* [? f. acrid *a.* + -ine = Gr. -ινη daughter, derivative.] A crystalline substance, $C_{12}H_9N$, of the diphenyl group, isomeric with carbazol, extracted from coal-tar oil.

1877 Fownes *Man. Chem.* II. 563.

acridity (ə'krɪdɪtɪ). [f. acrid *a.* + -ity; cf. *acid-ity*. A formation, having no prototype in Fr. or L., which has superseded the more regular *acritude* and *acrity*, and to a great extent the literal use of *acrimony*. Not in Todd 1818; in the quot. from Boorde it is probably an error.]

1. The quality of being acrid; a combination of bitterness to the taste with irritancy or corrosion to the mucous membrane; pungent, inflammatory, or corrosive bitterness.

1547 A. Boorde *Breuiary* cccxxxii. 107 b, This infirmitie [Strangury] may come thorowe acredite or sharpness of the water. **1803** *Edin. Rev.* III. 13 An acid, when combined with an alkali..destroys the acridity of the alkali. **1830** Lindley *Nat. Syst. Bot.* 7 Acridity, causticity, and poison, are the general characters of this suspicious order. **1876** Bartholow *Mat. Med. & Therap.* (1879) 259 When swallowed it leaves a sense of constriction and acridity in the throat.

2. Irritant bitterness of speech or temper.

1859 G. Meredith *R. Feverel* I. i. 17 The very acridity of the Aphorisms..sprang from wounded softness, not from hardness. **1861** Freer *Henry IV & M. de Med.* II. 215 Madame La Marquise revelled in well-aimed acridity of speech, inexpressibly provoking. **1881** *N.Y. Nation* XXXII. 367 The acridity which marks his speeches is quite absent from his private conversation.

acridly ('ækrɪdlɪ), *adv.* [f. ACRID *a.* + -LY².] In an acrid manner; with sharp or irritating bitterness: **a.** to the taste or bodily senses.

1793 ABERNETHY in *Phil. Trans.* LXXXIII. 61 Not so acridly or nauseously bitter as common bile.

b. to the feelings of others.

1837 CARLYLE *Fr. Rev.* I. VII. i. 340 Complimentary harangues, of which, as Loustalot acridly calculates, 'upwards of two thousand have been delivered within the last month.'

acridness ('ækrɪdnɪs). *rare.* [f. ACRID *a.* + -NESS.] The quality of being acrid; acridity.

1769 SIR J. HILL *Fam. Herbal.* (1812) 27 The water is a gentle carminative, without any heat or acridness.

acriflavine (ækrɪ'fleɪvɪn). *Med.* [irreg. f. ACRI(DINE + FLAVINE.] An orange-red, odourless powder, used as an antiseptic for wounds, cuts, etc.

1917 C. H. BROWNING et al. in *Brit. Med. Jrnl.* 21 July 71/1 The unsubstituted 3.6-diamino-10-methyl-acridium compound—'flavine', now called 'acriflavine'. **1918** *Lancet* 16 Feb. 257/1 Acriflavine has a very marked bactericidal inhibiting action on streptococci and a less marked on staphylococci. **1943** *Endeavour* Apr. 41/2 It had been shown that acriflavine or proflavine need not kill trout ova which they nevertheless sterilize. **1954** HEILBRON & BUNBURY *Dict. Org. Comp.* (rev. ed.) I. 28/2 *Acriflavine* (Trypaflavine) $C_{14}H_{15}N_3Cl_2$..commercial product usually contains a proportion of the unmethylated base (hydrochloride).

Acrilan ('ækrɪlæn). The proprietary name of a synthetic acrylic fibre.

1951 *U.S. Pat. Off., Official Gaz.* 8 May 387/2 The Chemstrand Corporation, Philadelphia. *Acrilan.* For Yarns, Threads, and Yarn and Thread Filaments. **1952** *N.Y. Times* 11 Sept. 52/1 The new synthetics such as Orlon, Dacron, Acrilan and Vicara will find their best use in apparel in blends with the older man-made fibers such as rayon and acetate. **1957** *Observer* 13 Oct. 11/5 Housewives will like the 100 per cent. Acrilan blankets which have newly come into our shops.

acrimonious (,ækrɪ'məʊnɪəs), *a.* [ad. Fr. *acrimonieux, -euse*, ad. med.L. *ācrimōniōs-us*, f. *ācrimōnia*; see ACRIMONY and -OUS.]

1. 1 = ACRID 1. *arch.*

1612 WOODALL *Surgeon's Mate* Wks. 1653, 180 If it proceed of an acrimonious fretting humor, etc. **1646** SIR T. BROWNE *Pseud. Ep.* 336 Artificiall copperose..is a rough and acrimonious kinde of salt. **1664** DR. H. POWER *Exp. Philos.* I. 63 A sharp and acrimonious vapour that strikes our nostrils. **1732** ARBUTHNOT *Rules of Diet* 298 All Substances that abound with an acrimonious Salt and Volatile Oil are hurtful. **1813** MARSHALL *Gardening* §19, 328 (ed. 5) The sap is very (even dangerously) acrimonious. **1856** MILL *Logic* IV. v. §4 (1868) II. 244 Natural substances which possessed strong and acrimonious properties.

2. Bitter and irritating in disposition or manner; bitter-tempered.

1775 JOHNSON *Tax. no Tyr.* 69 Malignity thus acrimonious. **1831** SCOTT *Abbot* i. 12 Engaged in a furious and acrimonious contest. **1833** I. TAYLOR *Fanaticism* §1, 2 If ..his feelings are petulant and acrimonious. **1849** MACAULAY *Hist. Eng.* I. 565 Only a single acrimonious expression escaped him. **1861** MAY *Const. Hist. Eng.* I. i. 54 (1863) Political hostility had been embittered by the most acrimonious disputes.

acrimoniously (,ækrɪ'məʊnɪəslɪ), *adv.* [f. prec. + -LY².] In an acrimonious manner; with irritating bitterness or severity.

1829 S. TURNER *Mod. Hist. Eng.* IV. II. xxvii. 173 Commencing and acrimoniously pursuing a personal and deadly warfare against the queen. **1866** C. C. FELTON *Greece* II. vii. 114 They often differed, sometimes acrimoniously.

acrimoniousness (,ækrɪ'məʊnɪəsnɪs). *rare*—⁰. [f. as prec. + -NESS.] The quality or habit of being acrimonious.

1818 In TODD, and subseq. Dicts.

acrimony ('ækrɪmənɪ). [ad. L. *ācrimōnia* pungency, f. *ācri-s* sharp; see -MONY. Cf. Fr. *acrimonie* ad. from the L. about the same time as the Eng. word, and possibly its actual model.]

1. Biting sharpness to the taste or other bodily sense; pungency; irritancy; acridity. *arch.*

1542 BECON *Christm. Banq.* 68 (1843) The acrimony and tartness of this dish shall so pierce your stomachs, that it shall minister to you an appetite and lust to devour the other the more greedily. **1578** LYTE *Dodoens* 55 Pimpernell is hoate and dry without any acrimonie, or byting sharpnesse. **1635** J. SWAN *Spec. Mundi* vi. §2, 195 (1643) Water strained through ashes is endued with a certain tart and salt kind of acrimonie. **1711** F. FULLER *Medic. Gymn.* 88 When the Blood of a Poor Consumptive Wretch is..loaded with Acrimony. **1804** ABERNETHY *Surg. Observ.* 227 The effect of the acrimony of the putrid blood. **1830** LINDLEY *Nat. Syst. Bot.* 214 [The milk-tree] is described..to yield a copious stream of thick, rich, milky fluid, destitute of all acrimony. **1876** GROSS *Dis. Urin. Org.* 23 To allay the acrimony of this fluid.

2. Sharp or irritating bitterness of disposition or manner.

1618 SIR H. MAY in *Fortescue Papers* 47 Which may stir up a fresh acrimony in your Lordship towardes me. **1630** NAUNTON *Fragm. Reg.* (1870) 16 Emulations, which are apt to rise and vent in obloquious acrimony (even against the Prince). *a* **1674** CLARENDON *Hist. Rebel.* I. I. 22 They who flattered him most Before, mentioned him Now with the greatest bitterness and acrimony. **1770** LANGHORNE *Plutarch's Lives* I. 195/2 (1879) Cleon attacked him with great acrimony. **1803** WELLINGTON *Gen. Disp.* II. 461 There is no occasion for interference or acrimony of expression. **1858** FROUDE *Hist. Eng.* III. xvi. 401 The acrimonies which the debate had kindled.

†**'acrious**, *a. Obs.* [f. L. *ācri-s* pungent (f. root *ac-* sharp, in *ac-id, ac-ute*) + -OUS, as in *alacri-ous, hilari-ous*, etc. The earliest adaptation of L. *acris*, mod.Fr. *âcre*, attempted in Eng. (Grew, in 1675, used the L. *acris* unchanged.) Superseded by the irregularly formed *acrid.*] = ACRID.

1675 GREW *Plants, Lect.* VI. i. (1682) 281 Acris is also compounded. For first, simply Hot, it is not; because there are many Hot Bodies which are not Acria..Nor secondly, it is simply Pungent. **1682** *Weekly Mem.* 238 Cattharticks, and whatsoever is acrious, being hurtful. **1689** in *Phil. Trans.* XVI. 552 In the Gout the humour likewise is of a different Nature; sometimes Acid, or Saline, and sometimes Acrious. **1694** *Ibid.* XVIII. 34 The Acrious Particles of which it consists.

†**'acrisy.** *Obs.*—⁰ [ad. med.L. *acrisia*, a. Gr. ἀκρισία want of judgment. Also used in the L. form (Phillips 1706, Kersey 1726, *Syd. Soc. Lex.* 1879).]

1. 'That of which no judgment is passed, or choice made; a matter in dispute; also want of Judiciousness, or Rashness in Judging.' Bailey 1721.

2. 'Such a State or Condition of a Disease, that no right Judgment can be made of it, or the Patient, whether he will recover, or not.' Bailey 1721.

‖**acrita** ('ækrɪtə), *sb. pl. Zool.* A singular form is ACRITAN. [mod.L., a. Gr. ἄκριτα, pl. neut. of ἄκριτος undistinguishable, sc. *animalia.*] A name given by MacLeay to a division of the animal kingdom, comprehending the Infusoria, the Polypes, and some of the Intestina; so called from the want of a distinct nervous system. Adopted in 1835 by Owen for a series of the Radiated animals.

1835 KIRBY *Habits & Inst. Anim.* I. iv. 149 [Infusories also called] Acrita or indiscernibles. **1835** OWEN in Todd *Cycl.* s.v., The Acrita have been termed Protozoa, as being on the first step of animal organization. **1837** WHEWELL *Induct. Sc.* III. XVII. vii. §2. 450 Some naturalists have doubted whether these zoophytes are not referrible to two types (acrita or polypes, and the true radiata), rather than to one. **1879** CHAMBERS *Encycl.* s.v. *Zoology*, The lowest animals, in which no trace of a nervous system has been discovered, have been formed into a separate division of the animal kingdom, under the names Acrita and Protozoa.

acritan ('ækrɪtən), *a.* and *sb. Zool.* [f. prec. + -AN.] *adj.* Belonging to the Acrita. *sb.* An individual of the Acrita (to which word it supplies a sing.).

acritarch ('ækrɪtɑːk). *Palæont.* [f. Gr. ἄκριτ-ος uncertain + ἀρχή origin.] Any of a group of unicellular microfossils of uncertain affinity having hollow, organic tests.

1963 W. R. EVITT in *Proc. Nat. Acad. Sci.* XLIX. 158 A proposal for a new informal group of microfossils of organic composition and unknown affinity to be known as acritarchs. *Ibid.* 300 Left behind by this transfer is a 'residue' of forms of unknown affinities for which the name Hystrichosphaerida is no longer appropriate. It is for this 'residue' that I propose the name *acritarchs*... The name chosen implies no affinity with any other organisms and is not derived from the name of any taxon included in the group. **1970** R. M. BLACK *Elements Palaeont.* xix. 299 Acritarchs are included here along with algae since they most nearly resemble cysts or vegetative stages in the life cycle of certain algae..; but there seems some possibility that a number will eventually be identified otherwise. **1979** *Nature* 8 Feb. 464/2 The first cycle was governed by organic-walled plankton (acritarchs, green and blue-green algae), whereas the second cycle was dominated by calcareous nannoplankton (coccolithophorids, dinoflagellates).

acrite ('ækrɪt), *a. Zool.* [ad. Gr. ἄκρῑτ-ος; see ACRITA.] Of or pertaining to the Acrita; acritan.

1835 OWEN in Todd *Cycl. Anim. Phys.* I. 48 The fissiparous and gemmiparous modes of reproduction are not, however, the exclusive modes by which the Acrite classes are perpetuated. **1847-9** TODD *Cycl. Anat. & Phys.* IV. 21/2 The Hydra..in its whole structure, is completely acrite.

acritical (ə'krɪtɪkəl), *a. Med.* [f. Gr. ἀ priv. + CRITICAL.] Not having or indicating a crisis; applied to a disease, symptoms, etc.

1864 in WEBSTER. **1879** in *Syd. Soc. Lex.*

acritochromacy (,ækrɪtəʊ'krəʊməsɪ). [mod. f. Gr. ἄκριτο-ς undistinguishing + χρωματ- colour: see -ACY.] Colour-blindness, achromatopsy.

1879 *Syd. Soc. Lex.* and mod. Dicts.

†**'acritude.** *Obs. rare.* [ad. L. *acritūdo* sharpness, f. *acri-s* sharp; see -TUDE.] Sharpness or pungency of taste; pungency mixed with heat or biting quality; = ACRIDITY.

1675 GREW *Plants, Lect.* VI. i. (1682) 281 Acritude is Pungency joyned with Heat. **1681** —— *Museum* III. 341 In green vitriol, with its astringent and sweetish Tasts, is joyn'd some Acritude. **1753** CHAMBERS *Cycl. Supp.* s.v. *Acrid*, The characteristic therefore of Acritude consists in pungency joined with heat. **1773** in JOHNSON.

†**'acrity.** *Obs. rare*—¹. [ad. mod.Fr. *âcreté*, ad. L. *acritas, -tātem* (Gell.) sharpness, f. *acri-s* sharp. Cf. *alacrity.*] Sharpness, keenness.

1619 A. GORGES tr. *Bacon, De Sap. Veter.* xviii, *Diomedes* 87 That is, by the acrity of prudence and severity of judgement [*prudentia quadam acri, et judicii severitate*]. **1721** BAILEY, *Acrity*, Sharpness in Taste, Tartness. [So in subseq. edd.]

acro-. Gr. ἀκρο- combining form of ἄκρος *a.* terminal, highest, topmost; *sb.* a tip, point, extremity, peak, summit; as in ἀκρό-λιθος stone-tipped, ACROLITH; ἀκρόπολις the highest city, ACROPOLIS; ἀκρόνυχ-ος happening at the point of night-fall, ACRONYCHAL. Largely used in its various senses to form modern technical terms.

‖**,acro'ama.** Pl. ,acro'amata. [Gr. ἀκρόᾱμα anything heard, f. ἀκροᾶσθαι to hear.]

1. A rhetorical declamation (as opposed to an argument).

1852 SIR W. HAMILTON *Disc.* 153 Facciolati expanded the argument of Pacius..into a special Acroama; but his eloquence was not more effective than the reasoning of his predecessors.

2. *Anc. Phil.* Oral teaching heard only by initiated disciples; *esoteric* doctrines, as distinguished from the *exoteric*, which might be committed to writing, and published to the world.

1580 NORTH *Plutarch* (1676) 561 Alexander did..learn of Aristotle..other more secret, hard, and grave Doctrine, which Aristotles Scholars do properly call *Acroamata.*

†**acroamare**, *a. Obs. rare*—¹. [improp. f. L. *acris* pungent + *amār-um* bitter.] Pungently bitter.

1657 TOMLINSON *Renou's Disp.* 273 Its roots [those of Acorus] are..of an acroamare sapour.

acroamatic (,ækrəʊə'mætɪk), *a.* and *sb.* [ad. Gr. ἀκροαματικός adj., f. ἀκρόᾱμα. See ACROAMA.]

A. *adj.* Of or pertaining to hearing; hence, privately communicated by oral teaching to chosen disciples only; esoteric, secret.

1632 T. RANDOLPH *Jealous Lovers* IV. (1652) 64 Noyse That with obstreperous cadence cracks the organs Acromatick. *a* **1656** J. HALES *Gold. Rem.* John xviii. 36, 148 Beloved, we read no Acroamatick lectures; the secrets of the Court of Heaven..lie open alike to all. **1656** BLOUNT *Glossogr.*, *Acromatick*, that hearkens or gives ear to anything, that requires much study and search; also musical, harmonious, or delightful to the ear. **1770** LANGHORNE *Plutarch's Lives* II. 716/1 (1879) You did wrong in publishing the acroamatic parts of science. **1819** REES *Cycl.* s.v. *Books*, Acroamatic Books—Books containing some secret and sublime matters, calculated for adepts and proficients on the subject.

B. *sb. pl.* [The adj. used ellipt. after Gr. τὰ ἀκροαματικά = acroamatic (matters).] Aristotle's lectures to intimate friends and scholars on the esoteric parts of his philosophy.

1660 HOWELL *Lex. Tetragl.*, The Peripatetic in his Acroamatiques, the Egyptians in their Hieroglyphics.. involve the choicest of their Knowledge (though obscurely). **1678** CUDWORTH *Intell. Syst.* 314 The Egyptians, besides their vulgar and fabulous theology..had another arcane and recondite theology; these two theologies of theirs differing as Aristotle's Exotericks and Acroamaticks.

†**acroa'matical**, *a. Obs.* [f. prec. + -AL¹; see -ICAL.] = ACROAMATIC.

1580 NORTH *Plutarch* (1676) 561 Alexander unto Aristotle greeting. Thou hast not done well to put forth the Acroamaticall Sciences. **1605** BACON *Adv. Learn.* (1640) 273 The one is an Exotericall or revealed; the other an Acroamaticall or concealed Method. *a* **1656** J. HALES *Gold. Rem.* 189 (1688) Divide his Lectures and Readings into Acroamatical and Exoterical.

‖**acroasis** (,ækrəʊ'eɪsɪs). Pl. acroases. [Gr. ἀκρόᾱσις a hearing, something listened to, f. ἀκροᾶσθαι to hear.] *Anc. Hist.* An oral discourse; a discourse listened to.

1655-60 T. STANLEY *Hist. Philos.* 358/1 (1701) Six hundred Persons..came to his nocturnal Acroasis, perhaps meaning the Lectures through a Skreen during their Probation. **1842** MRS. BROWNING *Gk. Chr. Poets* 64 [He] gave his admiring poems the appropriate and suggestive name of *acroases*—auscultations, things intended to be heard.

acroatic (,ækrəʊ'ætɪk), *a.* and *sb.* [ad. Gr. ἀκροατικ-ός, of or proper to hearing, f. ἀκροᾶσθαι to hear.] = ACROAMATIC.

1655-60 T. STANLEY *Hist. Philos.* 232/1 (1701) He called ..Acroatick those [discourses] in which more remote and subtile Philosophy was handled. **1847** CRAIG, *Acroatics*.. Aristotle's lectures on the abstruser points of philosophy.

acrobacy ('ækrəbæsɪ). [cf. Fr. *acrobatie.*] Acrobatics.

1918 *Observer* 17 Nov. 6/4 The 'D.H. 10'..loops the loop and performs any acrobacy which is usually only demanded of a fighting scout. **1923** A. HUXLEY *Antic Hay* xvi. 230 The *monster*..climbs up the runged back of his chair and stands, by a miraculous feat of acrobacy, on the topmost bar. **1928** A. HASKELL *Some Stud. in Ballet* 116 The line is not clearly and scientifically marked between dancing and acrobacy.

acrobat ('ækrəbæt). Also acrobate. [a. mod.Fr. *acrobate*; f. Gr. ἀκρόβατος walking on tiptoe, climbing aloft, f. ἄκρος point, or highest + -βατος vbl. adj., f. vb. stem βα- to go. Used in pl. *acrobates* as a term of Classical Antiq. before the adoption of the modern word from Fr.] A rope-dancer; a performer of daring gymnastic feats and evolutions; a tumbler. *lit.* and *fig.*

1825 FOSBROKE *Encycl. Antiq.* (1843) II. 673 *Acrobates*.. were Rope Dancers of which there were four kinds. **1845** [T. MARTIN] *Bon Gaultier Ballads* 99 And the Clown in haste arising from the footstool where he sat Notified the first appearance of the famous Acrobat. **1846** *Punch* 24 Jan. 52 We have no doubt that the performances at St. Stephen's during the coming session will be enlivened by feats of agility and strength on the part of the three great Political Acrobats. **1859** W. S. COLEMAN *Woodl. Heaths & Hedges* (1866) 98 Those little ornithological acrobats the Tit-mice. **1860** *Cornhill Mag.* Mar. 275 We can go and purchase Noah's arks and flexible acrobats for our children. **1879** *Daily Tel.* 30 May, The acrobat of to-day is a skilled professor of the trapeze and the parallel bars; he flies through the air, or comes careering from a hole in the ceiling.

acrobatic (,ækrə'bætɪk), *a.* and *sb. pl.* [f. prec. + -IC. Cf. mod.Fr. *acrobatique*.] **A.** *adj.* Of or pertaining to an acrobat, gymnastic performer, or tumbler.

1861 BP. G. SMITH *10 Weeks in Japan* xxvi. 373 One of the actors came forth before the crowd of holiday-makers and performed a variety of acrobatic evolutions. **1880** A. TROLLOPE *Duke's Children* III. x. 109 The acrobatic manœuvre which had carried Mr. Spooner over the peril.

B. *sb. pl.* Acrobatic performances or feats. Also *transf.* and *fig.*

1882 G. MACDONALD *Weighed & Wanting* II. iv. 28 There was not much popular receptivity for acrobatics in the streets. **1890** *Athenæum* 22 Feb. 239/1 The art and science of what may be called acrobatics have never yet received really adequate treatment. **1915** *Morn. Post* 20 Apr. 7/7 The German railway acrobatics. **1917** W. J. LOCKE *Red Planet* ix, A mind trained in the acrobatics of a Calvinistic Theology. **1922** *Daily Mail* 4 Dec. 11 Habton is a very fast chaser, but rather given to acrobatics.

acrobatically (,ækrə'bætɪkəlɪ), *adv.* [f. prec. + -AL[1] + -LY[2].] After the manner of an acrobat; with gymnastic skill.

1880 MISS BROUGHTON *Second Thoughts* I. I. xii. 206 Most of them are standing acrobatically on their heads.

acrobatism ('ækrəbætɪz(ə)m). [f. ACROBAT + -ISM.] The art or profession of the acrobat; the performance of gymnastic feats. *lit.* and *fig.*

1864 *Daily Tel.* 29 July, The course and its follies..its quacks and mountebanks, and its acrobatism. **1865** *Reader* No. 133. 76/1 Displays of vocal acrobatism. **1866** S. G. O[SBORNE] *Lett. on Educ.* 13 This infantine, mental acrobatism, is to me simply hateful. **1882** *Athenæum* 1 July 11 A certain amount of moral acrobatism will be practised on the line which divides the proper from the improper.

acroblast ('ækrəblɑːst, -æ-). *Biol.* [f. ACRO- + -BLAST.] A body in the spermatid from which arises the acrosome.

An earlier sense 'tissue of the germinal wall' (after G. *akroblast*, J. Kollmann) was short-lived.

1907 H. D. KING in *Amer. Jrnl. Anat.* VII. 348 This body is undoubtedly concerned in the formation of the acrosome of the spermatozoön, and therefore I suggest for it the name acroblast as somewhat more appropriate than 'chromatoid Nebenkörper'. **1958** *New Scientist* 13 Nov. 1272/2 The acroblasts..have an onion-like layered membrane structure. **1963** E. V. COWDRY et al. *Special Cytology* (ed. 2) III. 1758 The Golgi bodies and idiozome material have collected at one side of the nucleus to form the acroblast.

acrocarpous (,ækrəʊ'kɑːpəs), *a. Bot.* [mod. f. Gr. ἄκρο-, see ACRO- + καρπ-ός fruit + -OUS.] Having the fructification at the end or top of the primary axis; terminal-fruited. Said of some mosses.

1863 M. BERKELEY *Brit. Mosses* Gloss. 311 *Acrocarpus*, bearing fruit at the tip of the stem or branches. **1875** BENNETT & DYER *Sachs' Bot.* The flower of Mosses either terminates the growth of a primary axis (Acrocarpous Mosses), or the axis is indeterminate.

acrocentric (ækrəʊ'sɛntrɪk), *a. Cytology.* [f. ACRO- + -CENTRIC.] Of a chromosome: having the centromere close to the end. Hence as *sb.* Cf. METACENTRIC *a.*, TELOCENTRIC *a.*

1945 M. J. D. WHITE *Animal Cytol. & Evol.* ii. 20 A distinction still exists in practice between those [chromosomes] which have the centromere somewhere near the middle and those in which it is very close to the end. The former we shall call *metacentric*, the latter *acrocentric*. **1946** *Nature* 26 Oct. 587/2 The chromosome number of the parthenogenetic females generally amounted to 68, made up of six pairs of metacentric and twenty-eight pairs of acrocentric elements. **1949** I. F. & W. D. HENDERSON *Dict. Sci. Terms* (ed. 4), *Acrocentric*, a rod-shaped chromosome. **1962** *New Scientist* 22 Nov. 457 The chromosome involved is one of the four small acrocentrics—those having one arm much shorter than the other.

acrocephalic (,ækrəʊsɪ'fælɪk), *a. Phys.* [mod. f. Gr. ἄκρο-, see ACRO- + κεφαλ-ή head + -IC. A better form would be *acrocephalous*. Cf. Fr. *acrocéphale*.] Characterized by a lofty skull.

1878 BARTLEY tr. *Topinard, Anthrop.* v. 176 Acrocephalic, elevated skull.

acrocephaly (,ækrəʊ'sɛfəlɪ). *Phys.* [mod. f. Gr. ἄκρο-, see ACRO- + κεφαλ-ή head + -Y[3].] Loftiness of skull.

1878 BARTLEY tr. *Topinard, Anthrop.* II. xi. 483 The height of the vertical diameter or acrocephaly.

acroche, earlier form of ACCROACH *v. Obs.*

acrochord ('ækrəkɔːd). *Zool.* [see ACROCHORDON.] A snake of the genus *Acrochordus*, family *Hydridæ*, having a fusiform body covered with tricuspid scales.

1833 *Penny Cycl.* I. 98 The acrochord is covered with scales like all other serpents, though they are minute and separate from one another..When the skin is inflated, and apparent between the scales, these assume the granulated or warty appearance expressed by the name.

acrochordite, var. AKROCHORDITE.

‖**acrochordon** (,ækrəʊ'kɔːdən). *Path.* [a. Gr. ἀκροχορδών a wart with a thin neck, f. ἄκρο-, see ACRO- + χορδή cord.] A kind of hard and elongated wart, supposed to resemble the end of a string; a hanging wart.

1720 SHADWELL *Humourists* II. I. 153 O, sir, I should have fought better, but for..some Acrochordones upon my right shoulder. **1853** MAYNE *Exp. Lex.*, *Acrochordon*..a small wart, having a narrow base or pedicle.

a-crock (ə'krɒk). [Fr. *à croc*.] With a prop or support; in ***arquebus-a-crock***, ***musket-a-crock***.

1615 SANDYS *Travels* 153 Wherein are certaine harquebuses acrock for the safe-guard of the harbour. **1634** T. HERBERT *Travaile* 15 The Sentinell with his musquet acrocke was set to guard it.

†**acro'comic**. *Obs.*[—0] [f. Gr. ἀκρόκομ-ος having hair at the tip, like a goat's chin + -IC.] 'One having long hair.' Cockeram 1626. (Never used.)

acrodont ('ækrədɒnt), *sb.* and *a. Zool.* [f. Gr. ἄκρο-, see ACRO- + ὀδόντ-α tooth.] A name given by Owen to lizards whose teeth are firmly soldered to the ridge of the jaw-bones. Used also as adj.

1849-52 TODD *Cycl. Anat. & Phys.* IV. 884/1 In a few Iguanians..the teeth appear to be soldered to the margins of the jaws; these have been termed 'Acrodonts.' **1872** MIVART *Anat.* 256 We may have teeth which become anchylosed to the summit of the jaw, there being no bony wall developed on either the inner or the outer side of the teeth, as in certain Lizards termed Acrodont. **1872** NICHOLSON *Palæont.* 363 In its dentition Telerpeton seems to have been 'acrodont.'

acrogen ('ækrədʒɛn). *Bot.* [mod. f. Gr. ἄκρο-, see ACRO- + -γενης -born; see -GEN.] A cryptogamous plant of the higher division, including ferns and mosses, so called from having a distinct perennial stem with the growing point at its extremity, in contradistinction to *Thallogens*, as lichens and fungi, which have no permanent stem, but grow from a central rosette.

1845 LINDLEY *Sch. Bot.* ii. (1858) 22 *Acrogens* differ essentially from the two other classes, in having no flowers. **1857** H. MILLER *Test. Rocks* i. 12 In the Coal Measures.. both the Gymnogens and Acrogens are largely developed.

acrogenic (,ækrəʊ'dʒɛnɪk), *a. Bot.* [f. prec. + -IC.] Of or pertaining to acrogens.

1857 H. MILLER *Test. Rocks* i. 23 The Old Red flora seems to have been prevailingly an acrogenic flora.

acrogenous (æ'krɒdʒənəs), *a. Bot.* [f. ACROGEN + -OUS.] Of the nature of acrogens; increasing in growth from the extremity of a stem.

1848 DANA *Zoophytes* iv. §69. 68 Polyps have an acrogenous growth, and bud periodically as they grow upward. **1866** BERKELEY in *Treas. Bot.* 14 A few acrogenous Liverworts have the habit of Lichens, but differ totally in structure.

acrography (æ'krɒgrəfɪ). [mod. f. Gr. ἄκρο-, see ACRO- + -γραφία writing.] The art of making blocks in relief, as a substitute for wood-engraving.

acrolect ('ækrəlɛkt, 'ækrəʊ-). *Linguistics.* [f. ACRO- + -LECT.] In a post-creole community, the social dialect most closely resembling the standard language; also, in extended use: the most prestigious or 'highest' social dialect of any language. Cf. BASILECT, MESOLECT.

1965, etc. [see -LECT]. **1977** *Language* LIII. 330 Speakers in a post-creole community are triply pressured: to avoid the basilect, to acquire the acrolect, and to vary the mesolect. **1978** *Archivum Linguisticum* IX. 44 Women are far from being initiators of linguistic change in the direction of the acrolect. **1983** *Amer. Speech* LVIII. 49 The acrolect, West Indian standard English, is essential primarily for external relations.

Hence **acro'lectal** *a.*

1977 *Language* LIII. 334 There is very little discussion on Providence Island about acrolectal talk, but there is a tremendous amount of speculation about the basilect. **1980** *English World-Wide* I. I. 81 The use of acrolectal varieties is not denied in an appropriate environment. **1983** *Amer. Speech* LVIII. 272 *Nassauvian* for a native Bahamian is considered acrolectal in contrast to the basilectal *Nassau man*.

acrolein (ə'krəʊliːɪn). [f. L. *acr-is* sharp, pungent + *olē-re* to smell + -IN(E = Gr. -ινη daughter, derivative; here used to form a term analogous to *glycerin*.] A colourless acrid liquid, of pungent irritating odour, formed in the destructive distillation of glycerin (from which it is derived by the abstraction of two molecules of water, thus, Glycerin $C_3H_5(OH)_3$, Acrolein C_3H_4O''). It is the aldehyde of allyl, produced by the oxidation of allyl alcohol, and itself rapidly oxidizing to acrylic acid.

1857 MILLER *Elem. Chem.* III. vi. 385 *Acrolein*, or *Acrylic Aldehyd*..a substance which, from its intensely irritating effects upon the mucous membrane.., has received the name of *acrolein*. **1869** ROSCOE *Elem. Chem.* xxxvi. 388 *Allyl alcohol*..is oxidized in presence of air and platinum to acrolein and acrylic acid, which stand to this alcohol in the same relation as aldehyde and acetic acid stand to ethyl alcohol.

acrolith ('ækrəlɪθ). [ad. L. *acrolith-us*, a.Gr. ἀκρόλιθος having the ends of stone; f. ἄκρος extreme, end + λίθος stone.] 'A statue, with the head and extremities of stone, the trunk being usually made of wood, either gilt or draped.' *Encycl. Brit.* 1853. Used in early Grecian art.

1850 LEITCH tr. *Müller's Anc. Art* §119, 91 The extremities are of marble after the manner of acroliths.

acrolithan (æ'krɒlɪθən), *a.* [f. prec. + -AN.] Of, pertaining to, or of the nature of an acrolith.

1842 BRANDE *Dict. Sci.* 11 According to Vitruvius there was a temple at Halicarnassus dedicated to Mars wherein was an acrolithan statue of the God.

acrolithic (,ækrəʊ'lɪθɪc), *a.* [f. ACROLITH + -IC.] = prec.

1857 BIRCH *Anc. Pott.* (1858) II. 192 The acrolithic statues of Greece.

acrologic (,ækrəʊ'lɒdʒɪk), *a.* [mod. f. Gr. ἄκρο- (see ACRO-) + λόγ-ος word + -IC. Cf. Fr. *acrologique*.] Pertaining to, or founded on, initials.

1882 I. TAYLOR jun. in *Academy* 28 Jan. 68 This method of acrologic notation may have received a further extension; so that the ciphers 1, 2, and 3 may have been derived from the initial letters of *eka*, *dva*, and *tri*, to which they bear some resemblance.

acrological (,ækrəʊ'lɒdʒɪkəl), *a.* [f. as ACROLOGIC *a.* + -AL.] = ACROLOGIC *a.* Hence ,**acro'logically** *adv.*

1831 *Edin. Rev.* LIII. 383 A task for which his [M. Klaproth] Letters on Acrological Hieroglyphs prove him to be so eminently qualified. **1883** I. TAYLOR *Alphabet* I. i. 43 The symbol was used 'acrologically', to express simply the initial syllable of the word. **1932** J. JOYCE *Let.* 29 Aug. (1957) 324 Short verses for children, or fables or merely acrological rhymes.

acromatic, used erron. for ACHROMATIC and ACROAMATIC.

acromegaly (ækrəʊ'mɛgəlɪ). *Path.* [ad. Fr. *acromégalie* (P. Marie), f. Gr. ἄκρον extremity + μέγας, μεγαλ- great.] A disease characterized by hypertrophy and enlargement of the extremities. Hence **acromegalic** (-mɪ'gælɪk) *a.*, pertaining to or of the nature of acromegaly; *sb.*, one affected with acromegaly.

1889 *Brain* July 59 Acromegaly. By Pierre Marie, M.D. **1896** *Godey's Mag.* Feb. 125/1 A..very rare disease,.. acromegaly, or the enormous enlargement of the feet, hands, face, and chest. **1902** *Lancet* 27 Sept. 884/2 The historic and folklore record about acromegalic and giant. **1909** *Cent. Dict. Suppl.*, Acromegalic, a. and n. **1937** *Jrnl. R. Anthrop. Inst.* LXVII. 161 Acromegalic crania are not infrequently metopic. **1937** W. INGE *Modernism in Lit.* 3 A modernist sculptor will carve figures apparently suffering from elephantiasis or acromegaly. **1953** *Sci. News* XXX. 62 Acromegaly..is a condition caused by an excessive production of growth hormone in the adult. **1964** L. MARTIN *Clinical Endocrinol.* (ed. 4) i. 29 X-ray of an acromegalic's hand.

acromial (ə'krəʊmɪəl), *a. Phys.* [ad. mod.L. *acromiāl-is*; cf. Fr. *acromiale*. See ACROMION and -AL[1].] Of or pertaining to the ACROMION.

1836 TODD *Cycl. Anat. & Phys.* I. 363/2 The acromial artery arises from the anterior side of the axillary artery. **1855** HOLDEN *Hum. Osteol.* (1878) 140 The acromial end [of the clavicle] is broad and flattened.

acromio-clavicular (ə'krəʊmɪəʊklæ'vɪkjʊlə(r)), *a. Anat.* [f. ACROMIO(N + CLAVICULAR *a.*] (See quot. 1858.)

1858 GRAY *Anat.* 158 The *Superior Acromio-Clavicular Ligament* is a broad band of fibres, of a quadrilateral form, which covers the superior part of the articulation, extending between the upper part of the outer end of the clavicle, and the superior part of the acromion... The *Inferior Acromio-Clavicular Ligament*..covers the inferior part of the articulation. **1942** *Lancet* 10 Oct. 424/1 Only one example of congenital dislocation of the acromio-clavicular joint appears to have been recorded.

‖**acromion** (ə'krəʊmɪən). *Phys.* [a. Gr. ἀκρώμιον f. ἄκρο-ς extremity + ὦμος shoulder. Cf. Fr.

acromion, which may be the direct source of the Eng.] The outer extremity of the shoulder-blade; the apophysis forming the upper and posterior extremity of the shoulder-blade, which is articulated with the external extremity of the clavicle, and gives attachment to the trapezoid and deltoid muscles. Also *attrib.* as *acromion process*.

1615 Crooke *Body of Man* xii. xxvii. 985 The extremity of this Spine is commonly called ἀκρώμιον, albeit according to Hippocrates Acromion be the articulation of the clauicle with the vpper part of the blade. **1827** Abernethy *Surg. Wks.* II. 154 The patient complained of pain, extending towards the axilla and also towards the acromion. **1836** Todd *Cycl. Anat. & Phys.* I. 364/2 The branch of the supra-scapular.. descends under the root of the acromion process.

acron, obsolete form of acorn.

acronarcotic (ˌækrəʊnɑːˈkɒtɪk), *a.* [improp. f. L. *acris* sharp, pungent + narcotic.] Having both acrid and narcotic qualities.

1882 in *Med. Temp. Jrnl.* LI. 126 Its acronarcotic or corrosive effect upon the stomach and alimentary canal.

acronych (əˈkrɒnɪk), *a.* Also 7 acronick. [ad. Gr. ἀκρόνυχ-ος at nightfall, vespertine; f. ἄκρος tip, point + νύξ night. Cf. Fr. *acronyque.*] = acronychal.

1594 Davis *Seaman's Secrets* ii. (1609) 25 The triple rising and setting of the Starres, Cosmice, Acronyce, and Heliace. **1652** Urquhart *Jewel* Wks. 1834, 235 Her appearance was like the.. acronick rising of the most radient constellation of the firmament. **1833** Keightley *Ovid's Fasti* 15 The cosmic rising or setting was the true one in the morning: the acronych (ἀκρόνυχος) the true one in the evening.

acronychal, acronycal (əˈkrɒnɪkəl), *a.* Also acronical, achronical, achronycal, acronichal. [f. prec. + -al¹. Incorrectly spelt *achronical*, as if derived from χρόνος time; and with many intermediate forms.] Happening in the evening or at night-fall, vespertine, as the acronychal rising or setting of a star. (Sometimes used as if = Rising in the evening or at sunset *and* setting at sunrise; but this is not correct. When the rising is *acronychal*, the setting is *cosmical*, and *vice versâ*.)

1594 Blundeville *Exerc.* iv. 35 (ed. 7) 492 Now to know the Acronical rising of any star at any time, bring the starre to the East part of the Horizon. **1622** Heylin *Cosmogr.* iii. (1682) 109 The rising and setting of the Stars, whether Heliacal, Acronical, Matutine, or Vespertine. **1642** More *Poems* (1647) 173 At eventide when they rise Acronicall. **1697** Dryden *Virgil* (1806) II. 159 The achronical rising.. is when it appears at the close of day. **1751** Chambers *Cycl.* s.v., The *Achronychal* is one of the three poetical risings, and settings of the stars; and stands distinguished from *Cosmical* and *Heliacal*. **1837** Whewell *Hist. Induct. Sci.* (1857) I. 160 The acronycal and heliacal risings and settings of the stars. **1856** Burritt *Astron.* 60 [Incorrect use.] When a star rose at sun-setting, or set at sun-rising, it was called the Achronical rising or setting.

acronychally (əˈkrɒnɪkəlɪ), *adv.* [f. prec. + -ly².] In an acronychal manner; at the acronychal time; at sunset or nightfall.

1594 Blundeville *Exerc.* iv. 34 (ed. 7) 491 Turne the degree of the Sunne unto the West part of the Horizon, and .. marke what starres are ready to go downe with him, for those are said to set Acronically, and staying the Globe still there in the West, marke what starres at that present do rise in the East part of the Horizon, for those are said to rise Acronically. **1706** Phillips s.v. *Achronychal*, When a Star rises at Sunset, it is said to Rise achronychally, and when a Star sets with the Sun 'tis said to Set achronychally. **1876** Chambers *Astron.* 910 A heavenly body is said to rise or set acronically when it rises or sets at sunset.

acronyctous (ˌækrəʊˈnɪktəs). [f. Gr. ἀκρόνυκτ-ος, an occas. variant of ἀκρόνυχος; see acronych.] = acronychal. (In mod. Dicts.)

acronym (ˈækrənɪm). orig. *U.S.* [f. acr(o- + *-onym* after homonym.] A word formed from the initial letters of other words. Hence as *v. trans.*, to convert into an acronym (chiefly *pass.* and as *pa. pple.*). Also **acroˈnymic** *a.*; **acroˈnymically** *adv.*; **ˈacronyming** *vbl. sb.*; **ˈacronymize** *v. trans.*

1943 *Amer. N. & Q.* Feb. 167/1 Words made up of the initial letters or syllables of other words.. I have seen.. called by the name *acronym*. **1947** *Word Study* 6 (*title*) Acronym Talk, or 'Tomorrow's English'. **1947** *Word Study* May 6/2 Some new forms combine the initial syllables (resembling blends) instead of initial letters, as in the case of Amvets (American Veterans' Association).. but they still are in the spirit of acronyming. *Ibid.* 7/2 There has definitely been a speed-up in 'acronyming'. **1950** S. Potter *Our Language* 163 Acronyms or telescoped names like *nabisco* from *National Biscuit Company*. **1954** *Britannica Bk. of Yr.* *1954* 638/1 Typical of acronymic coinages, or words based on initials, were.. mash (Mobile Army Surgical Hospital). **1956** R. Wells in M. Halle et al. *For Roman Jakobson* 665 Take the WE counterpart of the SE expression to be acronymized (*North Atlantic Treaty Organization*), and select from each word the first one or two or three letters in such a way that the selected letters, assembled and regarded as one word, will have a normal, pronounceable SE counterpart. **1967** *Sci. News* 19 Aug. 177/1 The TacSatCom, as it is acronymed, is a small-scale system which should be in the field soon. **1971** *Daily Tel.* 3 Feb. 12 Has the Establishment realised, inquires an acronymically-minded reader, that if the Industrial Relations Bill becomes law, it will not be only Ireland that is saddled with an IRA? **1972** *Sat. Rev.* (U.S.) 3 June 30 Nitrogen oxide, acronymed NOx, is another of the plant's noxious by-products. **1981** *Amer. Speech* LVI. 65 *Byte* is a fairly far-fetched way of acronymizing *binary digit eight*. **1981** *Maledicta* V. 99 Who were the real 'ethnics', acronymically speaking? **1983** *Verbatim* Spring 2/2 Paulies play *puck* (ice hockey) or *hoop* (basketball, also acronymed to *b-ball*).

acrook (əˈkrʊk), *adv.*, prop. *phrase.* [A *prep.*¹ + crook.] In a bend or curve; awry, crookedly.

1480 Caxton *Descr. Brit.* 12 Humbre renneth fyrst a crook oute of the southside of York. *a* **1500** *Court of Love* liv, And truly els the matter is acrooke. **1553** Udall *Roister Doister* (1869) 62 This gear goth acrook. **1881** Miss Rossetti *A Pageant* 177 Our spirits immersed In wilfulness, our steps run all acrook.

acroparæsthesia (ˈækrəʊpærɪs-, -ɪsˈθiːsɪə, -z-). *Path.* [f. acro- + paræsthesia.] A disease marked by vasomotor changes in peripheral parts of the body.

1894 *Med. News* LXV. 178/2 (*title*) The Treatment of Acro-Paresthesia (Numbness of the Extremities). **1900** *Lancet* 23 June 1795/2 The affection called 'acroparæsthesia' has.. not been described as occurring in this country, though it undoubtedly does occur. **1908** *Practitioner* Aug. 298 Stengel discusses.. cases in which numbness, tingling, burning, and other symptoms.. known collectively as 'acroparaesthesia', occur in elderly persons who have different degrees of arterio-sclerosis.

acropetal (əˈkrɒpɪtəl), *a.* *Veg. Phys.* [mod. f. Gr. ἄκρο- (see acro-) + L. *pet-ĕre* to seek + -al¹, after analogy of *centripetal.*] Tending towards the summit or apex; said of the order in which the parts of a plant arise, when the course of development is from below upward.

1875 Bennett & Dyer *Sachs' Bot.* 149 Similar lateral members usually arise on the common axial structure in acropetal or basifugal order, *i.e.* the younger a member is, the nearer it is to the apex; counting from below upwards the members arise in the order of their age. **1882** *Nature* No. 636, 236 Is the ramification in plants everywhere and always acropetal? by M. Trécul. He is led to a negative.

acropetally (əˈkrɒpɪtəlɪ), *adv.* *Veg. Phys.* [f. prec. + -ly².] In an acropetal manner; with development from below upwards.

1878 M'Nab *Bot.* 66 Secondly, the root does not develope leaves acropetally.

acrophobe (ækrəʊˈfəʊb). [f. acro- + -phobe: see acrophobia.] One who suffers from a morbid dread of heights.

1955 M. McCarthy *Charmed Life* v. 105 She used to force herself.. like an acrophobe who makes himself look over a parapet. **1960** 'A. Burgess' *Doctor is Sick* i. 9 Edwin was an acrophobe. His head began to spin. **1972** L. Hancock *There's a Seal in my Sleeping Bag* v. 95 For acrophobes like me the height of the grass blotted out the long drop to the sea.

acrophobia (ækrəʊˈfəʊbɪə). [f. acro- + phobia.] Morbid dread of heights. Hence **acroˈphobic** *a.*

1892 D. H. Tuke *Dict. Psychol. Med.* 679 *Acrophobia*, described by Dr. Andrea Verga, means the dread of being in high places. **1899** *Allbutt's Syst. Med.* VII. 886 Both agoraphobia and acrophobia are common forms of imperative ideas. **1959** *New Yorker* 24 Oct. 34/3 We walked over to the winding parapet,.. took a shuddering, acrophobic look down the well.

acrophonetic (ˌækrəʊfəʊˈnɛtɪk), *a.* [mod. f. Gr. ἄκρο-, see acro- + φωνητ-ός to be uttered + -ic.] Pertaining to acrophony.

1866 Felton *Anc. & Mod. Greece* I. iii. 49 The principle of this alphabetic element has received the technical name of acrophonetic, or the principle of initial sounds.

acrophonic (ækrəʊˈfɒnɪk), *a.* [f. acrophon(y + -ic.] Pertaining to acrophony.

1909 in *Cent. Dict.* Suppl. **1932** *Times Lit. Suppl.* 7 Jan. 13/1 The Hittite pictographic script which he thought was acrophonic. **1959** A. G. Woodhead *Gr. Inscriptions* 18 The Greek names for the letters of the alphabet are acrophonic, the first letter of the name expressing the sound of the letter to which the name is given.

acrophony (æˈkrɒfənɪ). [mod. f. Gr. ἄκρο- (see acro-) + -φωνία voice, sound.] The sound of the initial; the use of what was originally a picture-symbol or hieroglyph of an object to represent phonetically the initial syllable or sound of the name of the object; *e.g.* employing the symbol of an *ox*, '*aleph*,' to represent the syllable or letter *a*.

1880 R. S. Poole in *Encycl. Brit.* IV. 808 The Phœnician letters had names indicating an origin from a hieroglyphic system on the same principle of acrophony.

Acropolis (əˈkrɒpəlɪs). [Gr. ἀκρόπολις, f. ἄκρο- (see acro-) + πόλις city. (The pl., rarely used, would be analogically *acropolēs*; we find the Gr. ἀκροπόλεις simply transliterated.)] The elevated part of the town, or the citadel, in a Grecian city; *esp.* that of Athens. Also *fig.*

1662 More *Antid. agst. Ath.* ii. xii. (1712) 79 As if Nature kept garrison in this *Acropolis* of Man's body, the Head. **1840** Arnold *Hist. Rome* II. 428 The Acropolis of Corinth was held by one Alexander. **1850** Leitch tr. *Müller's Anc. Art* §168, 146 Massive walls.. surround their cities, not merely their acropoleis. **1876** Humphrey *Coin Coll. Man.* vi. 65 In Athens the weights connected with the coinage were kept with great care in the Acropolis.

†**acrosaline**, *a.* *Obs.* [improp. f. L. *acris* sharp, pungent + saline.] Salt and acrid.

1761 *British Mag.* II. 117 The urine remarkably acrosaline.

acroscopic (ækrəʊˈskɒpɪk), *a.* *Bot.* [f. Gr. ἄκρον apex + -σκοπος viewing + -ic.] Looking, or on the side, towards the apex.

1882 Vines tr. *Sachs' Bot.* 450 In *Azolla*, the leaves of the one row all arise from one cell of the acroscopic part of the segment.

acrosome (ˈækrəsəʊm). *Zool.* [ad. G. *akrosoma* (M. von Lenhossék 1898, in *Archiv. Mikrosk. Anat.* LI. 282), f. acro- + *-some* (cf. Gr. σῶμα body).] A cap-like structure forming the anterior part of the head of a spermatozoon. Hence **acroˈsomal, acroˈsomic** *adjs.*

1899 J. H. McGregor in *Jrnl. Morphology* XV. Suppl. 91 For this body in mammals Lenhossek proposed the term 'Akrosom', and throughout the present paper I shall call it the *acrosome*. *Ibid.* 93 The attachment of acrosome to nucleus marks the anterior end of the spermatid from the start. **1940** *Chambers's Techn. Dict.* 10/1 Acrosomal. **1951** G. H. Bourne *Cytol. & Cell Physiol.* (ed. 2) vi. 271 There is evidence.. that the [Golgi] apparatus is associated with.. the formation of fatty yolk in eggs, and of the acrosome in spermatozoa. **1952** *Amer. Jrnl. Anat.* XC. 169 One to four granules.. coalesced, forming one larger structure, the acrosomic granule. **1960** L. Picken *Organization of Cells* vi. 231 The 'acrosomic system' (that is, acrosome, head-cap, and precursors). *Ibid.* 233 The acrosomal vesicle containing the acrosome.

acrospire (ˈækrəspaɪə(r)), *sb.* Also *Obs.* or *dial.* **ackerspyre, akerspire.** [f. Gr. ἄκρο- (see acro-) + σπεῖρ-α anything twisted, or σπείρ-ειν to sow.] 'The first leaf that appears when corn sprouts; it is a developed plumule.' Lindley *Treas. of Bot.*

1674 Grew *Anat. Plants* i. i. §13 (1682) 3 In corn, it is that Part, which after the Radicle is sprouted forth, or come, shoots towards the smaller end of the Grain, and by many Malsters, is called the Acrospire. **1858** Maunder *Scient. Treas.* 443 By the aid of moisture, the barley is made to germinate, that is to put forth roots and almost its acrospire or first sprout; and by the aid of fire, the roots are destroyed and the acrospire prevented from bursting the skin.

acrospire (ˈækrəspaɪə(r)), *v.* Also 7–8 **akerspire.** [f. prec.] To throw out the first leaf-sprout.

1616 Surflet & Mark. *Countrey Farme* 557 Turne the malt vpon the floore twice or thrice a day, least forbearing so to doe, the corne heat, and by that meanes aker-spire, which is, to sprout at both ends, and so loose the heart of the graine, and make the malt good for nothing. **1742** *Lond. & Country Brewer* i. (ed. 4) 6 Turning the Malt often, that it neither moulds nor aker-spires.

acrospired, *ppl. a.* [f. acrospire *v.* + -ed.] Furnished with an acrospire, having the first leaf-sprout.

a **1755** Mortimer (J.) For want of turning, when the malt is spread on the floor, it comes, and sprouts at both ends, which is called acrospired, and is fit only for swine.

acrospiring, *vbl. sb.* [f. acrospire *v.* + -ing¹.] Sprouting into leaf.

1725 Bradley *Fam. Dict.* s.v. *Malt*, If to prevent the acrospiring it be thrown thin, many of the Corns will dry.

acrospore (ˈækrəspɔə(r)). *Bot.* [f. Gr. ἄκρο- (see acro-) + σπόρ-ος fruit: see spore.] A spore produced at the apex of a hypha or cellular filament forming the structural element of fungi; a basidiospore.

1870 H. Macmillan *Bible Teachings* vi. 127 No less than four kinds of fructification—spores, acrospores, zoospores, oospores—have been discovered on the same plant.

acrosporous (æˈkrɒspərəs), *a.* *Bot.* [f. prec. + -ous.] Pertaining to or characterized by acrospores.

1870 Bentley *Bot.* 379 All Fungi which thus bear their spores on the outside of peculiar cells or basidia, have been called Basidiosporous or Acrosporous.

across (əˈkrɒs), *adv.*, *prep.* and *adj.* Also aphetically cross. [A *prep.*¹ in + cross. Cf. Fr. *encroix*, whence Caxton's *in cross*, perh. the earliest form.]

A. *adv.*

1. In the form of a cross, crosswise, crossing each other, crossed.

1480 Caxton *Chron. Eng.* cxciv. 170 Syr hugh spencer.. fell doune vpon the grounde by the see bank acros with his armes and thryes kist the grounde. **1485** —— *Chas. the Gt.* 239 He layed hys armes vpon hys body in maner of a crosse. *Ibid.* 240 He fonde Rolland expyred, hys hondes in crosse vpon hys vysage. **1590** Webbe *Trauailes* (1868) 25 Two kniues are layde acrosse vpon the loafe. **1646** H. Lawrence *Com. & Warre w. Angels* 117 Thinke not to goe to heaven with your armes acrosse. **1771** Foot *Penseroso* iii. 120 Yonder, tow'rds the east A warrior frowns in stone, his legs across. **1826** Wordsworth *Poems on Affec.* xi. Wks. 1849 I. 152 Pine not like them with arms across.

2. a. In a position or direction crossing the length-line of anything, transversely; hence, from side to side, or corner to corner, through.

1523 FITZHERBERT *Husb.* (1534) F 5 The whiche blyster must be slytte with a knyfe a-crosse. **1601** SHAKS. *Twel. N.* v. i. 178 H'as broke my head a-crosse, and has giuen Sir Toby a bloody Coxcombe too. **1774** *Phil. Trans.* LXIV. 355, I found it impossible to saw it directly a-cross. **1850** MRS. STOWE *Uncle Tom's C.* ix. 71, I jumped right on to the ice, and how I got across I don't know. *Mod.* Was the Channel rough when you came across?

b. *Naut.*

1633 STAFFORD *Pac. Hib.* viii. (1821) 325 And ride with their yards a crosse. **1794** NELSON in Nicolas's *Disp. & Lett.* (1845) I. 504 [Ships] of the Line, sails bent, some with top-gallant yards across.

c. *to come across* (*with*): to hand over, contribute (money, information, etc.). *slang* (orig. *U.S.*).

1910 *Sat. Even. Post* 13 Aug. 8/1, I knew pull was required ..but I hadn't learned that I'd have to come across with the price as well. **1915** J. LONDON *Jacket* viii. 62 You might as well come across now and save trouble. **1928** D. SAYERS *Lord Peter views Body* 16, I think you ought to come across with the rest of the story. **1938** WODEHOUSE *Summer Moonshine* ix. 99 He hinted that one had got to come across. **1948** M. ALLINGHAM *More Work for Undertaker* xxii. 253 'Did she admit it?' 'Yes... But she wouldn't come across till dawn.'

d. Of a crossword clue: relating to a word that is to be written in on a horizontal line of the puzzle; of the solution to such a clue or the spaces in which it is to be written: along a horizontal line of the puzzle. Often after the clue number. Cf. DOWN *adv.* 1 b.

1924 C. LAYNG *Cross-Word Puzzles* 7 We now have..the first two letters of No. 7 across. **1944** T. A. BOTT *How to make Crossword Puzzles* i. 5 Avoid two-letter spaces, either Across or Down. **1960** G. W. TARGET *Teachers* 47 'Good morning, Purnell,' said Woodgate from about seven across and nine down in his crossword, 'though it's really rather cold, isn't it?' **1971** R. RENDELL *One Across* iii. 30 He filled in 28 across, which completed his puzzle. **1986** *Times* 5 Sept. 12/2 His technique is to start at 1 across and then go to 1 down.

3. In a position actually or potentially the result of crossing anything; on the other side.

1816 SCOTT *Old Mort.* 146 Lord Evandale..was no sooner across than he was charged by the left body of the enemy's cavalry. *Mod.* At this rate we shall soon be across.

4. Not straight or directly; obliquely, athwart, awry, amiss. *Obs.* exc. *dial.* Cf. B. 1 c.

1559 *Mirr. for Mag.* 344 (T.) When king and queen saw things thus go across, To quiet all, a parliament they called. **1615** BP. HALL *Contempl.* III. vii. 64 The squint-eyed pharisees looke a-crosse at all the actions of Christ. **1687** R. LESTRANGE *Answ. Dissenter* 8 This Gentleman will needs set them on a-Cross, and then Exclayme against them as [the most Contrary Things in the World]. **1887** BARING-GOULD *Red Spider* I. vii. 110 When folks who look straight before them fall across. *Ibid.*, The two who have got across. **1891** S. WEYMAN *New Rector* ix. 173 Lindo must beware of getting across with him. **1892** *Cornh. Mag.* July 28 Matters were soon across again between the pair. **1897** *Daily News* 4 Mar. 6/1 He is getting across with the farmers now, for he roundly rates them on account of their apathy.

B. *prep.* [The adv. with obj. expressed.]

1. Direction: In a direction forming a cross with, or transverse to; **a.** at right angles with.

1634 BRERETON *Trav.* (1844) 45 A long table..placed length-ways in an aisle which stands over across the church. **1697** POTTER *Antiq. Greece* I. viii. (1715) 42 A Partition.. reaching quite cross the Theater. **1742** YOUNG *Night Th.* IV. 721 Faith builds a bridge across the gulph of death. **1816** J. WILSON *City of Plague* I. i. 77 How idly hangs that arch magnificent, Across the idle river. **1830** TENNYSON *Lady Clara Vere* 31 But there was that across his throat Which you had hardly cared to see. **1860** TYNDALL *Glaciers* I. §12, 88 A line set across the fissured portion [of the ice].

b. at any angle with; sideways or obliquely against. *to come across*: to come upon or meet obliquely, indirectly, or unintentionally.

a **1626** BACON (T.) The harp hath the concave not along the strings, but across the strings. **1747** COLLINS *The Passions* (1830) 61 When Cheerfulness, a nymph of healthiest hue, Her bow across her shoulder flung. **1816** J. WILSON *City of Plague* II. ii. 211 Across our gracious lady's bed A blast hath come as from the grave. **1860** DICKENS *Uncom. Trav.* vii. (1866) 49/2 A wind very like the March east wind of England, blew across me. **1876** FREEMAN *Norm. Conq.* III. xii. 191 We come across more than one incidental mention of those wars. *Mod.* I ran across him in the City yesterday.

c. *to get across*: to annoy, get on the wrong side of (someone). *slang*.

1926 D. SAYERS *Clouds of Witness* i. 30 One was always getting across Denver, but it never came to anything. **1960** M. STEWART *My Brother Michael* xiv. 183 He's got across that damned Greek.

2. a. Motion: From side to side of; quite through, over, in any direction except lengthwise. *across the country*: straight through between two points, without regard to the regular roads; not along the regular roads. *across lots* (U.S.): see LOT *sb.* 6 a.

1591 SHAKS. *1 Hen. VI*, IV. i. 114, I charge thee waft me safely crosse the Channell. **1611** —— *Wint. T.* IV. iv. 15 When my good Falcon made her flight a-crosse Thy Fathers ground. **1728** THOMSON *Spring* 439 You, now retiring, following now Across the stream, exhaust his idle rage. **1784** COWPER *Task* VI. 275 Pushing iv'ry balls Across a velvet level. **1832** TENNYSON *Miller's Dau.* 32 After dinner talk Across the walnuts and the wine. **1849** MACAULAY *Hist. Eng.* I. 573 He was directed to hasten thither across the country. **1866** GEO. ELIOT *Felix Holt* xlvi. 402 A sort of gleam seemed to shoot across his face. **1866** J. MARTINEAU *Ess.* I. 372 A footman will run your errand across the town. **1876** G. O. TREVELYAN *Life & Lett. Macaulay* II. i. 16 All its associations and its traditions swept at once across his memory. **1879** TENNYSON *Lover's T.* 9 Permit me, friend, I prythee To pass my hand across my brows.

b. Phr. *across the footlights*: from the performers to the audience; hence advb. (by ellipsis) in *to get* or *come across* (*to*), to reach the audience or the public, to make oneself or itself understood or appreciated; similarly *to get it across*. (For *to put it across* see PUT *v.*[1])

1894 G. B. SHAW *Let.* 11 June (1965) 443, I want to see how much of it they succeed in getting across the footlights. **1913** KIPLING *Diversity of Creatures* (1917) 190 Tell a fellow now, did I get it across? **1921** *Sat. Westm. Gaz.* 27 Aug. 14/2 Some vitality that may be as far away as you like from lifelikeness..but nevertheless gets across to the reader from the writer. **1923** SILBERRAD *Lett. Jean Armiter* vi. 148 Sorry —my fault—one fails to get across. **1923** *Westm. Gaz.* 27 Feb., It is very doubtful whether the play would get across the footlights in an ordinary run. *Ibid.* 26 Mar., 'Magda', dressed as a comedy of manners of a hundred years ago, would probably come across more satisfactorily than it does played as..contemporary tragedy. **1927** *Observer* 16 Oct. 15/3 The lower comedy is at present in the making, but Miss B. C., Mr. E. M. and Mr. L. H. are experts at getting it across. **1927** *Daily Tel.* 19 July 12/4 The Earl of Birkenhead ..said..he had never succeeded in projecting his personality across the footlights.

c. *across the board* (esp., with hyphens, as *attrib. phr.*). (See quot. 1950.) *U.S.*

1950 WEBSTER Addenda. *Across-the-board*, embracing all classes or categories without exception;—from placing a combination wager on a race horse to win, place, or show, that is, betting 'across the board'; as, an *across-the-board* tax cut. **1958** *Listener* 24 July 116/2 There is a common *cliché* among labour relations specialists in the United States that it is not the across-the-board wage increase..which is decisive. **1961** *Flight* LXXX. 134/2 There has been no across-the-board reduction since tourist fares were introduced eight years ago. **1964** R. D. HOPPER in I. L. Horowitz *New Sociology* xix. 317 Job displacement..is occurring right across the board.

d. Distribution: from one side of (a country, etc.) to the other; throughout. Chiefly *N. Amer.*

1950 [see sense 2 c]. **1961** L. HUGHES *Ask your Mama* 43 They know me, too, downtown, All across the country, Europe—Me who used to be nobody. **1968** *Globe & Mail* (Toronto) 17 Feb. 5/7 The teen-agers arrive with a petition that has been going around high schools across the province since the fall. **1978** *Times* 10 Mar. 16 The money raised in Oxfam shops across Britain goes to create employment opportunities..in poor countries throughout the world.

3. Position: On the other side of, beyond, over.

c **1750** *Jacobite Toast*, 'The King across the water!' **1855** TENNYSON *Daisy* 92 To lands of summer across the sea. *Mod.* The great republic across the Atlantic.

C. *adj.* Of a crossword clue: referring to a word that fills spaces along a horizontal line of the puzzle. See sense 2 c of the adv. Cf. DOWN *a.* 1 f.

1925 C. LAYNG *Layng's Junior Cross-word Puzzles* 8 Running slowly through the 'across' definitions. **1963** D. ST. P. BARNARD *Anat. Crossword* ii. 37 Some enthusiasts even went to the extent of making a duplicate pattern and working the Across clues on one, and the Down clues on the other. **1986** *Times* 5 Sept. 12/2, I believe that setters usually start with the Across clues... The Down clues..are usually easier.

†**acrossed** (əˈkrɒst), *ppl. a. Obs. rare*⁻¹. [Apparently a blending of ACROSS and CROSSED. See ACROSS A. 1.] Crosswise, crossed.

1548 W. THOMAS *It. Gram.* (1567) *Raccosciare*, to sit vpon the legges acrossed, as the taylours vse to doe.

acrost (əˈkrɒst), *adv.* and *prep. U.S. dial.* and *colloq.* [f. ACROSS *adv.* and *prep.* + inorganic *-t.*]

A. *adv.* Across; from side to side.

1779 W. MCKENDRY *Jrnl.* 6 Sept. in *Proc. Mass. Hist. Soc.* (1886) II. 467 The Lake..is..about 8 miles acrost. **1846** F. M. WHITCHER *Widow Bedott Papers* (1856) vii. 77 Kier said he heered her stretch her neck acrost and whisper. **1908** *Dial. Notes* (Boston, Mass.) III. 285.

B. *prep.* Across; *come acrost*, come upon.

1759 in *Essex Inst. Hist. Coll.* (1882) XIX. 145 Ye enemy fird at our men a Crost ye River. **1831** *Louisville* (Ky.) *Advertiser* 17 Oct., I came acrost a feller..fast asleep. **1852** STOWE *Uncle Tom* xxii, A good, round, school-boy hand, that Tom said might be read 'most acrost the room'. **1906** F. LYNDE *Quickening* 2 A-smashin' the whisky jug acrost the wagon tire.

acrostic (əˈkrɒstɪk), *sb.* and *a.*[1] Also 6-8 **acrostick(e, 7 achrostiche, acrostique, 7-8 acrostich.** [ad. L. *acrostichis*, a. Gr. ἀκροστιχίς, f. ἄκρο- (see ACRO-) + στίχος a row, order, line of verse. Occurs in the L. form as late as 1642. The etymological spelling is *acrostich*, as in *distich*. Cf. Fr. *acrostiche.*]

A. *sb.*

1. A short poem (or other composition) in which the initial letters of the lines, taken in order, spell a word, phrase, or sentence. Sometimes the last or middle letters of the lines, or all of them, are similarly arranged to spell words, etc., whence a distinction of *single*, *double*, or *triple* acrostics. See also TELESTICH.

1587 GOLDING *De Mornay* xxxii. 508 Cicero..maketh mention of Sybil's Acrosticke, that is to say, of certeine verses of hirs whose first letters made the name of that king. **1605** CAMDEN *Rem.* (1637) 340 Our Poets have their knacks as young Schollers call them, as Ecchos, Achrostiches, Serpentine verses. **1642** MONTAGU *Acts & Mon.* 220 The whole Poeme, or Passage of that *Acrostichis*, is a Description of the generale Judgement. **1656** COWLEY *Of Wit* vi. Wks. 1686, 2 In which who finds out Wit, the same may see In An'grams and Acrostiques, Poetry. **1711** ADDISON *Spectator* No. 60 ¶4 Besides these there are compound Acrosticks, where the principal Letters stand two or three deep. **1767** A. CAMPBELL *Lexiphanes* (1774) 98 Rhyme is fit for nothing but madrigals, epigrams and acrosticks. **1841** SPALDING *Italy* II. 25 Publius Optatianus Porphyrius composed, in 326, a poem, still extant, in praise of Constantine, the lines of which are acrostics. **1844** LINGARD *Hist. A.-S. Ch.* ii. (1858) II. 145 Acrostics were also admired, both single and double.

2. A Hebrew poem in which the consecutive lines or verses begin with the successive letters of the alphabet; an ABECEDARIAN poem.

1753 CHAMBERS *Cycl. Supp.* s.v., Some pretend to find Acrostics in the psalms, particularly in those called Abcdarian psalms. **1868** CHAMBERS *Encycl.* I. 33 It was customary at one time to compose verses on sacred subjects after the fashion of these Hebrew acrostics, the successive verses or lines beginning with the letters of the alphabet in their order.

†**3.** The beginning or end of a verse. *Obs.*

1614 SELDEN *Titles of Honor* (1614) 12 That Acrostich ..Κρῆτες ἀεὶ ψεῦσται. **1753** CHAMBERS *Cycl. Supp.* s.v., Tho' an *Acrostic* properly signifies the beginning of a verse, yet it is sometimes also used for the end or close of it; as by the author of the constitutions, when he orders one to sing the hymns of David, and the people to sing after him the *Acrostics* or ends of the verses.. This was called singing *Acrostics, Acrostichia*, which is a species of psalmody usual in the antient church.

B. *adj.* Pertaining to or characterized by acrostics (in senses A. 1, 2).

1682 DRYDEN *Macflecknoe* 206 Leave writing plays, and choose for thy command, Some peaceful province in Acrostic land. **1669** GALE *Crt. of Gentiles* I. I. xii. 78 That the Phenician order [of Letters]..was most ancient, appeares by the Acrostic verses of David. **1868** CHAMBERS *Encycl.* I. 33 The Acrostic poetry of the Hebrews.

acrostic (əˈkrɒstɪk), *a.*[2] [A factitious formation from ACROSS, or ACROSSED (= *acrost*).] Crossed, folded across; moving crosswise, erratic, zig-zag.

1602 MIDDLETON *Fam. of Love* IV. iv. Wks. II. 179 What melancholy sir, with acrostic arms, now comes? **1797** W. TAYLOR in *Monthly Rev.* XXIII. 566 The capricious skips of an acrostic itinerary.

acrostical (əˈkrɒstɪkəl), *a. rare.* Also **acrostichal** [f. ACROSTIC *a.*[1] + -AL[1].] Of the nature of, consisting of, or in the form of an acrostic.

1843 J. HOLLAND *Psalmists Brit.* I. 104 The whole Bible is abridged in a sort of scheme of acrostical mnemonics. **1887** LUPTON in *W. Smith's Dict. Chr. Biog.* IV. 648/1 The Eighth Book, in acrostichal verse. **1894** *Athenæum* 28 July 128/3 Chaucer's 'A B C', a curious acrostical prayer 'like Psalm cxviii'.

acrostically (əˈkrɒstɪkəlɪ), *adv.* [f. prec. + -LY[2].] After the manner of an acrostic.

1865 E. B. TYLOR *Early Hist. Man.* v. 103 Letters may be named..acrostically, by names chosen because they begin with the right letters.

acrostichal (əˈkrɒstɪkəl), *a.* (*sb.*) *Ent.* [a. G. *acrostichal* (J. Mik *Dipterolog. Untersuchungen*, 1878).] 'Situated in the highest rank or row —used of certain bristles on the mesonotum of muscoid flies' (Webster). Also *ellipt.* as *sb.*

1884 C. R. OSTEN-SACKEN in *Proc. Ent. Soc. Washington* 509 The intermediate pair of rows is represented by two, sometimes one..row of peculiar, minute bristles, which Prof. Mik calls the *acrostichal bristles.* **1925** IMMS *Textbk. Ent.* III. 601 Thoracic Bristles..*Acrostichal*: a row along each side of median line. **1939** WEBSTER *Acrostichal n.*, an acrostichal bristle. **1961** J. E. COLLIN *Empididae* I. 59 Very short biserial acrostichal bristles... There may, however, often be a distinct posthumeral bristle, and all except the acrostichals may be longer and stronger.

acrostichic (ækrəʊˈstɪkɪk), *a.* [f. Gr. ἀκροστιχ-ίς ACROSTIC + -IC.] Of or pertaining to acrostics.

1880 R. N. CUST *Ling. Ess.* 353 In assigning these names the Acrostichic principle was followed inversely.

acrostichoid (əˈkrɒstɪkɔɪd), *a. Bot.* [f. ACROSTIC(H + -OID.] Resembling the commencement of lines of poetry; an epithet of the genus of ferns *Acrostichum*, N.O. *Polypodiaceae*, so called from the peculiar distribution of the sori on the back of the fronds.

1882 T. MORE in *Gardeners' Chron.* No. 438 XVII. 672 The decurrent base, with light brown spore-cases, forming the usual universal acrostichoid fructification.

acrosticism (əˈkrɒstɪsɪz(ə)m). [f. ACROSTIC + -ISM, more correctly *acrostichism.*] The method of acrostics; acrostichal arrangement or character.

1842 MRS. BROWNING *Grk. Chr. Poets* 73 There is an earnestness in the poem, acrostic as it is,—a leaning to beauty's side,—which is above the acrosticism.

acrotch, variant of ACCROACH *v. Obs.* to grasp.

acroteleutic (ˌækrəʊtɪˈljuːtɪk). [f. Gr. ἀκροτελεύτι-ον the fag-end, hence the burden or chorus (f. ἄκρος extreme + τελευτ-ή end) + -IC.] 'Among Ecclesiastical writers, the end of a verse or psalm, or something added thereto to be sung by the people.' Chambers *Cycl. Suppl.*

1753 CHAMBERS *Cycl. Supp.* s.v., The *Gloria Patri* is by some writers called the *Acroteleutic* to the psalms; because always used to be repeated by the people at the end of each.

acroter (əˈkrəʊtə(r)). Also **acrotere.** [a. Fr. *acrotère*, ad. L. *acroterium*, ad. Gr. ἀκρωτήριον a summit or extremity, f. ἄκρος extreme, endmost, highest. The L. form *acroterium* (ˌækrəʊˈtɪərɪəm) and Gr. *acroterion* are more commonly used.]

1. *Arch.* In *pl.* **acroteria** or **acroters**, prop. 'The pedestals, often without bases, placed on the centre and sides of pediments for the reception of figures.' Gwilt. Sometimes applied less correctly to the statues on these pedestals.

1706 PHILLIPS, *Acroteres*, in *Architecture*, Pedestals upon the Corners and Middle of a Pedement to support Statues. **1708** *View of Lond.* I. 95/2 Over each Column, upon Acroters, is a Lamp. **1751** CHAMBERS *Cycl.*, *Acroteria* or *Acroters* in Architecture. **1857** BIRCH *Anc. Pottery* (1858) I. 292 The acroteria of tombs were coloured blue and green.

†**2.** 'The pinnacles or other ornaments standing in ranges on the horizontal coping or parapets of a building.' Gwilt. In this sense the pl. ***acroteria*** is found as a collective singular. *Obs.*

1678 PHILLIPS, *Acroteria*, in Architecture are those sharp and spiry Battlements or Pinnacles, that stand in ranges, with Rails and Balasters upon flat Buildings. **1720** STOW *London* (ed. Strype) III. viii. (1754) I. 650/1 At the west end is an Acroteria of the figures of the Apostles each about eleven feet high. **1759** MARTIN *Nat. Hist.* I. 295 The Cornish, on which is a kind of Acroteria, enriched with Roses.

†**3.** *Med.* The extremities of the body, as the hands, feet, and head. *Obs.*

1706 PHILLIPS, *Acroteria*, the utmost parts of a Man's Body, as his Fingers-ends. **1753** CHAMBERS *Cycl. Supp.*, The *Acroteria* growing cold in acute distempers, is held a prognostic of death.

acroterial (ˌækrəʊˈtɪərɪəl), *a.* [f. L. *acroteri-um* + -AL[1].] Pertaining to, or having the character of, an acroterium.

1708 *View of Lond.* I. 96/2 The Acroterial Pinnacles are of the Gothic order. **1833** *Pen. Cycl.* I. 100 The bases or pedestals on which the acroterial ornaments are placed.

†**acroˈteriasm.** *Obs.* [ad. Gr. ἀκρωτηρίασμα mutilation f. ἀκρωτηριάζειν to cut off the extremities.] Amputation of the extremities; 'The act of cutting off the extreme parts of the body, when putrefied, by a saw.' Chambers, *Cycl. Suppl.* 1753.

In BAILEY **1731**, ASH **1775**.

acroterion, acroterium, see ACROTER.

acrotic (əˈkrɒtɪk), *a. Path.* [improp. f. ἀκρότ-ης an extreme + -IC.] Of diseases: Pertaining to the surface or outside.

1853 MAYNE *Exp. Lex.*

acrotism (ˈækrətɪz(ə)m). *Med.* [mod. f. Gr. ἀ priv. + κρότ-ος sound of striking + -ISM.] Lack of pulsation.

1853 MAYNE *Exp. Lex.*

acrotomous (æˈkrɒtəməs), *a. Min.* [f. Gr. ἀκρότομ-ος having the top cut off + -OUS.] 'Having a cleavage parallel with the base.' Dana.

a-crow (əˈkrəʊ), *adv.* or *pred. a. poet.* [f. A *prep.*[1] + CROW *v.*] Crowing.

1898 G. MEREDITH *Poems* I. 141 Straight cocks a-crow. **1919** W. B. YEATS *Two Plays for Dancers* 16 The strong March birds a-crow, Stretch neck and clap the wing.

†**a-cry,** *adv.* or *phrase.* [A *prep.*[1] + CRY.] In a cry, crying.

1593 NASHE *4 Lett. Confut.* 80 He brides it and simpers it out a crie, No forsooth God dild you.

acryl (ˈækrɪl). *Chem.* [f. ACR(OLEIN + -YL(E = Gr. ὕλη substance, stuff.] The hypothetical oxidized radical of the allyl series, C_3H_3O, formed from allyl by the substitution of an atom of oxygen for two of hydrogen; a constituent of acrolein and acrylic acid.

acrylate (ˈækrɪleɪt). *Chem.* [f. ACRYL + -ATE.]

1. A salt of acrylic acid (which is hydrogen acrylate).

1873 WILLIAMSON *Chem.* §302 By its [acrolein's] oxidation, hydric acrylate is formed.

2. ***acrylate*** (***resin***), a synthetic resin made by polymerizing derivatives of acryl.

1935 C. ELLIS *Chem. Synthetic Resins* 1461 (*index*) Acrylates. **1936** *Industr. & Engin. Chem.* XXVIII. 271/1 The acrylate and methacrylate polymers are characterized by their excellent adhesion to most surfaces. **1938** *Jrnl. R. Aeronaut. Soc.* XLII. 100 The problem of choosing between cellulose acetate and acrylate resin plastics for aircraft windows. **1942** *Paint Technol.* VII. 205 (*title*) Acrylate Resins in Surface Coatings. **1953** *Encycl. Brit.* XVIII. 41I/2 Polymethyl acrylate is tough and rubbery; polyethyl acrylate is softer and more rubbery; polybutyl acrylate is sticky..polyoctyl acrylate..is almost liquid in consistency.

acrylic (əˈkrɪlɪk), *a. Chem.* [f. ACRYL + -IC.] Of or containing the radical acryl; as the ***acrylic series*** of compounds. ***acrylic acid***, $C_3H_3O.OH$, formed by the oxidation of acrolein. Also ***acrylic fibre***, ***plastic***, ***resin***, etc., synthetic substances prepared from acrylic acid or its derivatives. Also **acrylic** *sb.* (usu. *pl*).

1855 H. WATTS tr. *Gmelin's Handbk. Chem.* IX. 369 Acrylic acid. **1869** ROSCOE *Elem. Chem.* xxxvi. 389 Acrylic acid is the first term of a series of monobasic acids, [which] differ from the series of fatty acids in containing two atoms of hydrogen less. **1877** FOWNES *Man. Chem.* II. 304 Of the acids of the first group, called normal acrylic acids, some occur mostly as glycerides in vegetable and animal organisms. **1936** *Industr. & Engin. Chem.* XXVIII. 271/2 The acrylic resins show many unique physical, chemical, and mechanical properties. **1939** H. R. SIMONDS *Industr. Plastics* 69 The important trade names for the acrylic plastics..are: Plexiglas, Lucite, Crytalite, Acryloid. **1941** *Jrnl. R. Aeronaut. Soc.* XLV. 370 Transparent Acrylic Resins for Cockpit Enclosures. **1942** *Jrnl. Amer. Dent. Assoc.* XXIX. 640 Acrylics in Restorative Dentistry. **1945** H. D. WARD in V. E. Yarsley *Plastics Applied* 83/2 For coloured telephones acrylic plastics have been chosen. **1945** S. HOLT *Ibid.* 187/1 Acrylic teeth offer advantages in requiring no pin or diatoric anchorage..and do not break in processing or wear. **1947** *Lancet* 22 Mar. 379/1 The acrylic resins..have proved satisfactory for making artificial eyes. **1953** *Economist* 24 Oct. 275 Acrylic fibres (these, broadly speaking, are the fibres that can be given a wool-like 'feel', as distinct from the more silky texture of nylon or 'terylene'). **1960** *Which?* Jan. 19/2 The acrylics are easy to wash, do not shrink or stretch, and generally need no ironing.

acrylonitrile (ˌækrɪləʊˈnaɪtraɪl). *Chem.* [f. ACRYL(IC *a.* + -O- + NITRILE.] Vinyl cyanide, $CH_2{:}CH.CN$, a colourless liquid which is copolymerized in the manufacture of certain synthetic materials; the nitrile of acrylic acid.

1893 *Jrnl. Chem. Soc.* LXIV. I. 682, β-hydroxypropionitrile..yields acrylonitrile when distilled with phosphoric anhydride. **1947** MEE & DARKEN tr. *Karrer's Org. Chem.* (ed. 3) 180 Acrylonitrile..readily polymerises and therefore serves for the manufacture of plastics and artificial rubber. **1964** N. G. CLARK *Mod. Org. Chem.* vii. 121 Acrylonitrile: obtained from acetylene and hydrochloric acid by passing the mixed vapours at ordinary temperature and pressure into a suspension of cuprous chloride in dilute hydrochloric acid.

acse, acsi-en, early forms of ASK.

act (ækt), *sb.* [*orig.* a. Fr. *acte*, but in some of the senses referring directly to L. *actus* a doing, and *actum* a thing done (pl. *acta*).]

1. a. A thing done; a deed, a performance (of an intelligent being).

c **1384** CHAUCER *H. of Fame* 347 And al youre actes red and songe [*MS. Bodl.* actys]. *c* **1460** FORTESCUE *Abs. & Lim. Mon.* (1714) 99 Thay have no Hertys to do so terryble an Acte. **1535** COVERDALE *Ps.* lix. 12 Thorow God we shal do greate actes, for it is he that shal treade downe oure enemies. **1584** POWEL *Lloyd's Cambria* 99 The prowesse and worthie Actes of the ancient Brytaines. **1611** BIBLE *Transl. Pref.*, As worthy an acte as euer he did. **1678** BUTLER *Hudibras* III. i. 925 An act and deed that makes one heart Become another's Counter-part. **1807** CRABBE *Par. Reg.* III. 74 And snatch some portion of their acts from fate. **1832** J. AUSTIN *Lect. Jurispr.* xviii. (1879) I. 427 The only objects which can be called acts are the consequences of volitions..The involuntary movements which are the consequences of certain diseases are not acts.

b. A thing done as the result, practical outcome, or external manifestation of any state, and, whence the state may be inferred.

1751 JORTIN *Serm.* (1771) I. ii. 27 God required of him this act of obedience. **1768** BLACKSTONE *Comm.* II. 477 This hath been declared by the legislature to be an act of bankruptcy, upon which a commission may be sued out. *Mod.* It would be the act of a madman.

c. Any operation of the mind, as distinguished from the content or object of that operation. Also *attrib.*, as ***act psychology***, psychology regarded as the study of such acts; = INTENTIONALISM.

1694 LOCKE *Essay* (ed. 2) II. xxi. §30. p. 134 Desiring and willing are two distinct Acts of the mind. **1890** W. JAMES *Princ. Psychol.* II. xx. 168, I can[n]ot feel them by a pure mental act of attention unless they belong to quite distinct parts of the body. *a* **1927** E. B. TITCHENER *Systematic Psychol.* (1929) iii. 194 The importance of the 'act' in modern psychology derives from the work of Brentano. **1934** H. C. WARREN *Dict. Psychol.* 5/1 *Act psychology.* 1. A system of psychology which holds that every psychical phenomenon is characterized by the intentional inherence of an object. 2. A system..in which the data are psychic activities, usually of a subject upon an object. **1936** A. J. AYER *Lang., Truth & Logic* vii. 188 We do not accept the realist analysis of our sensations in terms of subject, act, and object.

d. *spec.* The act of procreation; sexual intercourse. With *the.*

1596 SHAKS. *Merch. Ven.* I. iii. 84 When the worke of generation was Betweene these woolly breeders in the act. **1611** BIBLE *John* viii. 4 This woman was taken in adultery, in the very act. **1923** H. CRANE *Let.* 9 May (1965) 133 They do everything but the Act itself right on the stage. **1930** D. H. LAWRENCE *A Propos of Lady Chatterley's Lover* 12 Balance up the consciousness of the act, and the act itself. **1959** N. MAILER *Advts. for Myself* (1961) 177 They do not talk about the act when it has failed to fire.

†**2.** A state of accomplished fact or reality, as distinguished from subjective existence, intention, possibility, etc. *Obs.*

1398 TREVISA *Barth. De P.R.* IV. i. (1495) 78 The noblest thynges of shappes of kynde and of crafte that be hydde comyth forth in acte and in dede. **1595** SHAKS. *John* IV. iii. 135 If I in act, consent, or sinne of thought Be guiltie. **1662** MORE *Antid. agst. Ath.* Ep. Ded. (1712) 2 Plato, if he were alive again, might find his timorous supposition brought into absolute Act. **1677** HALE *Prim. Orig. Man.* 109 They are only in possibility, and not in act.

†**3.** ? Activity, active principle. *Obs.*

1398 TREVISA *Barth. De P.R.* III. xxiv. (1495) 74 The soule is acte and perfeccion of the body. **1652** J. BURROUGHES *Exp. Hosea* v. 92 Grace is called the Divine nature, and God (we know) is a pure act, and it is called the life of God. **1694** LESTRANGE *Fables* clxv. (1714) 179 Nothing can be more contrary to God Himself, who is a Pure Act, then the Sleeping and Drowsing away of our Life and Reason. **1730** BEVERIDGE *Priv. Thoughts* I. 18 But my Reason tells me, God is a pure Act, and therefore How can He suffer any Punishments.

4. a. The process of doing; acting, action, operation. (L. *actus.*) *arch.* exc. in ***Act of God***: action of uncontrollable natural forces in causing an accident, as the burning of a ship by lightning.

1494 FABYAN VII. 579 The acte of Frenshmen standynge moche in ouer rydynge of theyr aduersaryes by force of speremen. **1594** DRAYTON *Idea* 860 Wise in Conceit, in Act a very sot. **1635** J. SWAN *Spec. Mundi* v. §2. (1643) 130 The Materiall cause [of the rainbow] is not water in act. **1732** POPE *Ess. on Man* ii. 105 The rising tempest puts in act the soul. **1784** COWPER *Task* VI. 340 To give such act and utt'rance as they may To extasy too big to be suppress'd. **1850** MRS. BROWNING *Poems* II. 193 And hear the flow of souls in act and speech. **1882** *Charter-party*: The Act of God, the Queen's Enemies, Fire, and all and every other Dangers and Accidents of the Seas..always excepted.

b. ***in the act***: in the process, in the very doing; in the interval, however momentary, between the inception and completion of the deed; on the point of. (L. *in actu.*)

1596, 1611 [see sense 1 d above]. **1678** BUTLER *Hudibras* III. i. 666 And off the loud oaths go, but, while They're in the very act, recoil. *c* **1746** J. HERVEY *Medit. & Contempl.* (1818) 220 It is in the very act to fly. **1826** SOUTHEY *Vind. Eccl. Angl.* 86 He was in the very act of death. **1874** BOUTELL *Arms & Armour* v. 78 When armour was in the act of ceasing to be worn.

5. Something transacted in council, or in a deliberative assembly; hence, a decree passed by a legislative body, a court of justice, etc. (L. *actum*, pl. *acta.*)

1458 in *Dom. Archit.* III. 43 This was preved acte also in the perlement. **1535** COVERDALE *Josh.* xxiv. 26 Iosua wrote this acte in the boke of the lawe of God. **1593** SHAKS. *3 Hen. VI*, II. ii. 91 You..Haue caus'd him by new act of Parliament, To blot out me, and put his owne Sonne in. **1640-1** *Kirkcudbright War-Com. Min. Bk.* (1855) 98 All fugitives must be apprehendit and punished conforme to the actes. **1693** *Mem. Count Teckely* II. 91 The Male-contents demanded a general Act of Indempnity. *a* **1704** T. BROWN *Praise of Wealth* Wks. 1730 I. 83 Before this proclamation passed into an irrevocable act. **1795** SEWEL tr. *Hist. Quakers* II. VII. 66 They asked him if he knew not of an act against meetings. **1839** KEIGHTLEY *Hist. Eng.* I. 373 An act of attainder was passed against York, Salisbury, their wives and children.

6. a. A record of transactions or decrees; any instrument in writing to verify facts. (L. *actum*, pl. *acta.*)

1535 COVERDALE *Ezra* vi. 2 A boke, & in it was there an acte wrytten after this maner. **1663** BUTLER *Hudibras* I. i. 143 He could reduce all things to Acts. **1704** NELSON *Festiv. & Fasts* (1739) 7 In the Acts of the Martyrdom of St. Ignatius we find. **1726** AYLIFFE *Parergon* 27 Judicial Acts are said to be all those Writings, and matters which relate to Judicial Proceedings, and are sped in open Court at the Instance of one of the Parties Litigant; and, being reduced into writing by a Publick Notary..are recorded by the Authority of the Judge. **1789** *Constit. U.S.* iv. §1 Full faith and credit shall be given in each state to the public acts, records and judicial proceedings of every other state. **1821** BYRON *M. Faliero* I. i. (1868) 315 The ducal table cover'd o'er With..petitions, Despatches, judgements, acts, reprieves, reports.

b. ***Acts*** (***of the Apostles***), name of one of the books of the N. Test.

1539 TONSTALL *Serm. on Palme sondaye* (1823) 55 It appereth playnly in the x. of the actes. **1549** COVERDALE *Erasm. Paraphr. Rom.* Argt., As Luke in the xxi chapiter of thactes reherseth. **1833** CRUSE tr. *Eusebius, Eccl. Hist.* II. x. 59 It is also recorded in the book of Acts.

c. ***act and deed***, part of a formula used when signing a legal instrument and putting a finger on the seal at the end of the transaction.

1756 D. GARRICK *Let.* in C. Oman *D. Garrick* (1958) 177 The act and deed of the wife, in such cases [*sc.* business matters], pass for nothing. **1827** BARNEWALL & CRESSWELL *Reports* V. 671 [He] produced the parchment, placed it on the table, signed his name, and then said, 'I deliver this as my act and deed', putting his finger at the same time on the seal. **1877** W. S. GILBERT *Sorcerer* I. p. 9 They deliver it—they deliver it As their Act and Deed! **1910** *Encycl. Brit.* I. 156/2 In law it means any instrument in writing, for declaring or justifying the truth of a bargain or transaction, as: 'I deliver this as my act and deed.'

7. a. A 'performance' of part of a play; *hence*, One of the main divisions of a dramatic work, in which a definite part of the whole action is completed. Also often *fig.* (L. *actus.*)

? **1520** *Terens in Englysh* (*Andria*) The furst scene of the furst Act. **1549** CHALONER tr. *Erasmus's Praise of Folie* sig. N iv *verso*, Resteth now the fifte acte or parte, wherein it behoueth them to shew foorth all their cunning and profunditie. **1565** NORTON & SACKV. *Gorboduc (title-p.)*, The Tragedie of Gorboduc Where of three Actes were wrytten by Thomas Nortone, and the two laste by Thomas Sackuyle. *Ibid.*, sig. A iiᵛ The Order of the dôme shewe before the firste Acte. **1613** SHAKS. *Hen. VIII*, Epil. 3 Some come to take their ease, And sleepe an act or two. *c* **1615** FLETCHER *Mad Lover* I. 21 Away then: our Act's ended. **1751** JOHNSON *Rambler* No. 156 ¶8 An act is only the representation of such a part of the business of the play as proceeds in an unbroken tenor, or without any intermediate pause. **1769** *Junius Lett.* xxiii. 112 Can age itself forget that you are now in the last act of life? **1858** DE QUINCEY *Grk. Trag.* in Wks. IX. 64 The very meaning of an act is, that in the intervals, the suspension of the acts, any possible time may elapse, and any possible action go on. **1876** FREEMAN *Norm. Conq.* II. x. 507 We are approaching the close of the first act of our great drama.

†**b.** An interval or interlude in a play. *Obs.*

1606 J. MARSTON *Parasitaster* Actus Quintus. Whilest the Act is a playing, Hercules and Tiberio enters, Tiberio climes the tree, and is received above by Dulcimel. **1611** COTGRAVE *Dict.*, *Acte*..an Act, or Pause in a Comedie, or Tragedie. **1623** SHAKES. *Mids. N.* III. ad fin., They sleepe all the Act. **1653** MIDDLETON & ROWLEY *Changeling* III. i (*stage-direction*) In the act-time De Flores hides a naked rapier behind a door.

c. One of a series of short performances in a variety programme, circus, etc. Also, the entertainer or entertainers (considered *collect.*) by whom an act is performed. Cf. *double act* s.v. DOUBLE *a.* 6.

1890 'BIFF' HALL *Turnover Club* vi. 63 The usual attraction was'Professor Etherio, the flying man', who did a rope-walking act. **1912** *Stage Year Bk. 1912* 39 The boom in bare flesh..Even those managers who..had refused to give engagements to this class of 'act', were soon tumbling over one another. **1933** P. GODFREY *Back-Stage* xviii. 228 Their act was booked for a tour by the African theatres. **1959** *Times* 16 Oct. 12/3 The team had completed their twists, loops and all the tricks of their acts which had been seen..in..other air shows.

1919 F. HURST *Humoresque* 300 Two specialty acts and a pair of whistling Pierrots. **1929** *Daily Express* 12 Jan. 3/5 New comedy acts are needed most. These, if found, will be helped to find better material and to buy attractive costumes. **1971** *Rolling Stone* 24 July 12/2 The customers.. aren't going to be able to take a chance on the unknown or lesser known acts if the record is priced too high.

d. *transf.* An imitation of a theatrical part, a piece of acting; a display of exaggerated behaviour; pretence (of being what one is not); esp. ***to put on an act*** (colloq.), to show off, to talk for display, to behave insincerely, to act a part.

Also in other phrases: ***to get into the act*** (*colloq.*, orig. *U.S.*), to become a participant; to involve oneself in some (successful, fashionable, etc.) venture or activity; also (***to be***) ***in on the act***; ***to get one's act together*** (*colloq.*, orig. *U.S.*), to (re-)organize effectively one's (muddled or disorganized) life, business, etc.

1928 BARRIE *Peter Pan* in *Plays* 20 We are doing an act; we are playing at being you and father. **1934** FAITH BALDWIN *Innocent Bystander* (1935) viii. 145 When he spoke of the theatre he wasn't putting on an act. He was himself. **1934** J. O'HARA *Appointment in Samarra* (1935) viii. 235 You put on some kind of an act with Caroline, and..she fell for it. **1939** A. HUXLEY *After Many a Summer* II. v. 220 It was such a relief not to have to put on that act with Pete for the benefit of uncle Jo. **1946** M. DICKENS *Happy Prisoner* viii. 158 This girl's not naturally like that. She's putting on an act. **1953** A. W. FIELDING *Stronghold* III. ii. 192 This might have been an act designed to impress us. **1959** *Times* 1 Apr. 8/3 Some men were injured and some were 'putting on an act'.

(*b*) **1947** *Current Biog. 1946* 168/1 The Durante quips ('I've got a million of 'em', 'Everybody wants to get into da act,'..) are 'timelessly colorful'. **1951** 'J. TEY' *Daughter of Time* viii. Morton had been very much 'in on the act'. **1958** *Spectator* 22 Aug. 239/1 President Chamoun got back into the act by announcing that they would not be asked to withdraw from the Lebanon. **1967** *Listener* 22 June 835/2 No one for a moment supposes that Friendly will not be in on the act. **1969** M. PUZO *Godfather* II. xiii. 188 The author ..came west on Johnny's invitation, to talk it over without agents or studios getting into the act.

(*c*) **1976** *Billings* (Montana) *Gaz.* 17 June 1-G/1 (*caption*) Winfield, after giving it careful consideration, I have decided to get my act together and split! **1977** C. MCFADDEN *Serial* (1978) iv. 15/1 Like, I can't get my act together... Leonard, I *need* you. I want you to help me get clear. **1984** *Times* 22 May 3/1 We need to get our act together... Users have been divided so far and are being picked off by the publishers one by one.

e. *attrib.* ***act-drop*** = DROP *sb.* 16.

1884 [see EXECUTE *v.* 2]. **1890** G. B. SHAW in *Star* 28 Apr. 2/3 She made a very marked impression which the audience gave vehement emphasis to after each descent of the act-drop. **1896** [see DROP *sb.* 16]. **1960** *Times* 29 Sept. 16/7 An act-drop is lowered to display a multicoloured abstract design.

8. In the Universities, a thesis publicly maintained by a candidate for a degree, or to show a student's proficiency.

At Oxford, the *Act* took place early in July. The graduates kept *Acts*, or discussed theses, on Saturday and Monday; on the intervening *Act Sunday*, two of the new Doctors of Divinity preached *Act Sermons* before the University. The Act was last held after long interruption in 1733; in 1856 the name, with all that related to the ceremony, was removed from the Statute-book, and only survives in the appellation *Act Term* sometimes given to Trinity Term. At Cambridge, the name is still given to the thesis and accompanying examination required for the obtainment of the doctor's degree in Divinity, Law, and Medicine.

1549 CHALONER tr. *Erasmus's Praise of Folie* sig. M iv *verso*, At their Actes and Comencements ye dooe see theim swadled in with so many cappes, coyues, and furde hoodes as they weare. **1592** T. NASHE *Strange News* I. 279 Acts are but idle wordes, and..Pumps and Pantofles...therefore do no Acts..onelie..to Oxford they trudge,..and there are confirmed in the same degree they took at Cambridge. **1607** [R. PARKER] *Scholas. Disc. agst. Antichrist* I. ii. 89 For proofe heereof, what need I goe further then to an Vniuersitie Acte, where before a confluence and concourse of people,..a Doctor incipient in Diuinitie publisheth these verses. **1641** LD. BROOKE *Disc. Nat. Episc.* II. vii. 118 They desire they may have leave (as Probationers) to exercise, or keepe Acts, before the Church; 'till the Church shall approve of them. **1654** GATAKER *Disc. Apol.* 42 At the time..were divers created Doctors without attendance to keep Acts. **1691** WOOD *Ath. Oxon.* II. 182 Upon Act Sunday the same year he preached the University Sermon at S. Maries. **1695** KENNETT *Paroch. Antiq.* II. 58 This method was first reflected on by Mr. Peter Heylin, in an Act sermon at St. Mary's in Oxon, July 11, 1630. **1713** *Guardian* No. 72 (1756) I. 320 This paper is written with a design to make my journey to Oxford agreeable to me, where I design to be at the Publick Act. **1733** BERKELEY in Fraser's *Life* vi. 207 The approaching Act at Oxford is much spoken of. **1877** *Camb. Univ. Calend.* 51 The Degree of Bachelor in Divinity, for which the requisite Exercises are, one Act, and an English Sermon. The Act is required to be kept in the following manner:..The Candidate shall read a thesis composed in Latin by himself on some subject approved by the Professor; the Professor or graduate presiding, shall bring forward arguments or objections in English for the Candidate to answer, etc.

†**9.** An *auto da fé*, or act of faith; a burning of heretics. *Obs.*

1709 STRYPE *Annals of Ref.* xx. 228 In this act also were burnt the bones and picture of D. Ægidio.

act (ækt), *v.* [f. L. *act-* ppl. stem of *ag-ĕre* to drive, carry on, do. Probably influenced in its development by ACT *sb.* More than a century intervened between the use of the word by the Sc. poet Henryson, and its first appearance in Eng.]

†**1.** *trans.* To put in motion, move to action, impel; to actuate, influence, animate. *Obs.*

1602 WARNER *Alb. Eng.* XIII. lxxvii. 316 Thy Senses fiue that acte thy life; thy Speache, whereby to many Thou doest communicate thy selfe, saue God disclameth any. **1605** TIMME *Quersitanus* ii. 8 All spirit..in the world is acted & gouerned by the spirit. **1642** ROGERS *Naaman* 453 There was a different principle that acted them. **1649** H. GUTHRY *Mem.* (1702) 54 The People of Scotland are much acted by their Ministers Doctrine. **1675** BARCLAY *Apol. Quakers* II. §1. 19 They are not acted nor led by God's Spirit. **1677** GALE *Crt. of Gentiles* II. IV. 235 Al his companions, who are acted by the same atheistic princepes. **1691** PETTY *Pol. Arith.* iii. 54 Ships, and Guns do not fight of themselves, but Men who act and manage them. **1712** ADDISON *Spec.* No. 287 ¶1 If I shall be told that I am acted by prejudice, I am sure it is an honest prejudice. **1732** POPE *Ess. on Man* ii. 59 Self-love, the spring of motion, acts the soul. **1748** RICHARDSON *Clarissa* (1811) III. 309 Mrs. Howe was acted by the springs I set at work.

†**2.** To bring into action, bring about, produce, perform, work, make, do (a thing or process). *Obs.*

1594 GREENE *Orl. Furioso* 17 Thus did I act as many brave attempts. **1611** SPEED *Hist. Gt. Brit.* VII. xliv. (1632) 414 Dunstan..who not onely did refuse to act his Coronation. **1649** SELDEN *Laws of Eng.* II. viii. (1739) 52 Whereby they did get power to act other enormities mentioned in the Charge. **1660** T. STANLEY *Hist. Philos.* (1701) 82/2, I do most act the business of the Commonwealth, if I practise it only. **1726** DE FOE *Hist. Devil* I. xi. (1840) 172 Had Satan been able to have acted anything by force. **1791** T. PAINE *Rights of Man* (ed. 4) 144 Measures which at other times it would censure, it now approves, and acts persuasion upon itself to suffocate its judgment.

3. To carry out in action, work out, perform (a project, command, purpose). *arch.*

1610 SHAKS. *Temp.* I. ii. 273 To act her earthy, and abhord commands. **1659** REYNOLDS in Burton's *Diary* (1828) IV. 302 Our enemies..take an advantage of a parliament sitting to act all their plots. **1693** *Mem. Count Teckely* Pref. 11, A formed Design, intended to be acted in one Place after another, throughout Europe. **1718** POPE *Iliad* I. 426 The unwilling heralds act their lord's commands. *a* **1842** TENNYSON *Œnone* 146 To live by law, Acting the law we live by without fear.

4. To carry out or represent in mimic action (an ideal, incident, or story); to perform (a play). Hence *fig.* in a bad sense: To simulate, counterfeit.

1594 M. DRAYTON in *Shaks. Cent. of Praise* 13 Acting her passions on our stately stage. **1601** *Returne fr. Parnass.*, *Ibid.* 48 Let me see you act a little of it. **1602** SHAKS. *Haml.* II. ii. 455 It was neuer acted: or if it was, not aboue once, for the Play I remember pleas'd not the Million. **1812** J. & H. SMITH *Rejec. Addr.* v. (1873) 40 It is built to act English plays in. **1823** LAMB *Elia* Ser. I. xx. (1865) 149 A present sense of the blessing, which can be but feebly acted by the rich. **1849** MACAULAY *Hist. Eng.* II. 474 Sunderland acted calumniated virtue to perfection. **1858** DICKENS *Lett.* (1880) II. 43 It is extremely well acted by all concerned.

5. With various complemental phrases, esp. ***to act out***; now *spec.* in *Psychiatry*, to represent (one's unconscious impulses, desires, etc.) in action; also *absol.* or *intr.*, esp. to misbehave, to behave anti-socially (orig. *U.S.*). Cf. ACTING *vbl. sb.* 3 c.

1611 W. GODDARD *Sat. Dial.* E b, Oh, her that well cann acte-out such sweete partes. **1646** SIR T. BROWNE *Pseud. Ep.* I. vi. 23 To act the Fable into a reality. **1659** SOUTH *Serm.* Matt. x. 33 I. 83 It has been still preached up, but acted down. **1715** BURNET *Hist. Own Time* II. 237 Lord Tweedale saw, that..he would act over his former extravagances. **1790** BURKE *Fr. Rev.* Wks. V. 36 This would be to act over again the scene of the criminals condemned to the gallies. **1840** CARLYLE *Heroes* vi. (1858) 354 To speak-out, to act-out what Nature has laid in him. **1860** E. G. WHITE *Spiritual Gifts* II. 45 Said Bro. H., 'If I was well I should partake of this food, and I believe GOD has healed me, and shall act out my faith.' **1913** *Dialect Notes* IV. 3 *Act out*, to misbehave, of children in school, etc. Orono [Maine]. **1934** A. TATE in *New Republic* 14 Mar. 128/1 The characters.. suffer no dramatic alteration; an episode ends when they have acted out enough of the moral to please the poet. **1945** [see ACTING *vbl. sb.* 3 c]. **1949** M. MEAD *Male & Female* ix. 197 Some societies permit periods of licence in which those who feel that they are able to cope with more members of the other sex than are normally permitted to them have a chance to act out their day-dreams without disrupting the social order. **1951** G. HUMPHREY *Thinking* 310 While a human being thinks his problem out, an animal acts it out. **1965** G. MCINNES *Road to Gundagai* xi. 192 He persuaded the boys to act out episodes from the *Odyssey* and the *Aeneid*. **1974** H. L. FOSTER *Ribbin'* ii. 46 The child with a learning or physical problem or disability may act-out to divert attention from, for example, his inability to read. **1983** N. HUMPHREY *Consciousness Regained* vii. 75 Human ancestors were acting out the physiological states of fear or jealousy long before they were in a position to have insight into them.

6. ***to act a part***, or ***the part of***: *orig.* To sustain the part of one of the characters in a play, *hence* to simulate. *fig.* To fulfil the character or duties of.

1611 SHAKS. *Cymb.* III. iv. 26 That part, thou (Pisanio) must acte for me. **1684** T. BURNET *Theo. Earth* 185 Our life now is so short..by that time we begin to understand our selves a little, and to know where we are, and how to act our part, we must leave the stage, and give place to others. **1769** *Junius Lett.* xxxv. 167 You have still an honourable part to act. **1794** PALEY *Evid.* II. ix. (1817) 211 Those who had acted and were acting the chief parts in the transaction. **1876** FREEMAN *Norm. Conq.* III. xii. 121 He acted something like the part of a deserter.

7. To act (anyone): To personate, assume the character of, to play; *orig.* on the stage; *fig.* in real life; *dial.* it passes into the sense of mimicking, mocking.

1651 HOBBES *Leviathan* I. xvi. 80 He that acteth another, is said to beare his Person, or act in his name. **1670** COTTON *Espernon* III. IX. 470 Why should *I* take that ill from you, which I suffer from Marais, who every day acts me in your presence? This Marais was..a Buffoon, that had a marvellous faculty of imitation. **1727** SWIFT *To Yng. Lady* Wks. 1755 II. II. 41 A wise man..soon grows weary of acting the lover and treating his wife like a mistress. **1742** YOUNG *Night Th.* IV. 556 She gives the soul a soul that acts a god. **1796** GOV. MORRIS *Sparks' Life & Writ.* (1832) III. 98 It is to act, not to be, the monarch, and he suits better the theatre than the throne. **1837** J. H. NEWMAN *Par. Serm.* xxvi. (ed. 3) I. 390 What was it but to act the child, to ask how many times a fellow-Christian should offend against us.

8. a. *intr.* (object suppressed). To perform on the stage.

1598 J. MARSTON in *Shaks. Cent. of Praise* 27 Say who acts best? Drusus or Roscio? **1611** CORYAT *Crudities* 247, I saw women acte, a thing that I neuer saw before, though I haue heard that it hath beene sometimes used in London. *a* **1625** FLETCHER *Mad Lover* II. i. 8 Plague act yee, I'le act no more. **1718** LADY M. W. MONTAGUE *Lett.* I. xxi. 64 No women are suffered to act on the stage.

b. Of a play: to be susceptible of being performed (well or otherwise).

1668, 1789 [see READ *v.* 18 a, b]. **1821** BYRON in Trelawny *Recoll. Shelley & Byron* (1858) 29 My plays won't act..my poesy won't sell. **1916** S. KAYE-SMITH *John Galsworthy* 17 Galsworthy's plays have the advantage of acting well—unlike much literary drama.

9. To perform on the stage of existence; to perform actions, to do things, in the widest sense. **a.** With special reference to the reality of the doing, as opposed to *think*, *speak*, etc. **b.** With reference to the manner or mode of action, and hence = behave, comport, or demean oneself.

1684 *Scanderbeg Rediv.* vi. 133 The Emperour obliged himself to Act with an Army of Sixty Thousand Men against the Turks. **1742** YOUNG *Night Th.* II. 92 Who does the best his circumstance allows Does well, acts nobly; angels could no more. **1751** JORTIN *Serm.* (1771) VII. i. 13 Who beleeve in Christ, with a resolution to act suitably to this persuasion. **1756** BURKE *Vind. Nat. Soc.* Wks. I. 14 We begin to think and to act from reason and from nature alone. **1833** HT. MARTINEAU *Loom & Lug.* I. iv. 54, I never could act for myself in my life. **1846** SIR R. PEEL *Sp. on resigning* 28 June, Acting..from pure and disinterested motives. **1865** MILL *Repr. Gov.* 8/2 It is what men think, that determines how they act. **1876** FREEMAN *Norm. Conq.* IV. xviii. 145 In overcoming the hostility of the West, William acted as he always did act.

c. To do the duties of an office temporarily, without being the regular officer; to act *for*, or in the absence of another. To act *as*: To perform in the character of, to do the work of, to serve as. (Also of things.)

1804 [See under ACTING *vbl. sb.* 5 a.] **1849** MACAULAY *Hist. Eng.* I. 490 He had no scruple about acting as chaplain. **1857** LIVINGSTONE *Trav.* vi. 114 A person who acted as interpreter. **1879** G. C. HARLAN *Eyesight* ii. 25 They [the eye-lashes] are delicately sensitive to the slightest touch, and act as feelers to warn the eye of the approach of any small object. *Mod.* Is any one empowered to act in the manager's absence? *Mod.* I am here to act for my brother; to act in behalf of the children.

d. To act *on, upon*: To regulate one's conduct according to.

1814 JANE AUSTEN *Mansf. Park* III. x. 201 It was somehow or other ascertained, or inferred, or at least acted upon, that they were not at all afraid. **1847** TENNYSON *Princess* II. 211 If more there be, If more and acted on, what follows? *Mod.* I wish the maxim were more generally acted upon in all cases.

e. To act *up to*: To come up in practice to an assumed standard, to fulfil or carry out in practice.

1747 in *Col. Rec. Penn.* V. 149 As long as you shall act up to your Engagements. **1829** LANDOR *Imag. Convers.* (1842) II. 99 Your lordship acts up to your tenets. **1849** MACAULAY *Hist. Eng.* II. 63 That..the members of the Church of England would act up to their principles.

f. ***to act up***: to act in an abnormal or unexpected manner; to 'put on an act'; to become unruly, to 'play up'. *colloq.*

1903 A. ADAMS *Log Cowboy* xviii. 275 The horse of some peeler..acted up one morning. **1929** D. H. LAWRENCE *My Skirmish with Jolly Roger* 8 When people act in sex, nowadays they are half the time acting up. **1956** J. HEARNE *Stranger at Gate* xxxvii. 282 'I'm sorry,' he said, 'I'm acting up a bit. I feel pretty tight inside.' **1964** *New Statesman* 20 Nov. 786/2 She would have to 'act up' to convince anyone that her mental health is in danger.

10. a. Of things: To put forth energy, produce effects, exert influence, fulfil functions.

1751 JOHNSON *Rambler* No. 141 ¶2, A combination of inconsiderable circumstances, acting when his imagination was unoccupied. **1812** W. TAYLOR in *Month. Rev.* LXIX. 384 Rapid composition acts best. **1870** JEVONS *Elem. Logic* xxix. 251 When several causes act at once. **1878** HUXLEY *Physiogr.* 63 A fall of snow thus acts like a mantle of fur thrown over the earth. *Mod.* The brake refused to act.

b. To act *on*: To exert influence on; to influence, affect. (Here *act on* comes round nearly to the earliest transitive sense of *act*; see 1.)

1810 COLERIDGE *Friend* (1865) 124 Reason to act on man must be impersonated. **1812** SIR H. DAVY *Chem. Philos.* 437 The clear liquor..is acted on by a rod of zinc. **1855** BREWSTER *Life of Newton* I. xii. 322 One sphere will act upon another with a force directly proportional to their quantities of matter. **1855** BAIN *Senses & Intell.* II. ii. §2 (1864) 177 Gases do not act on the touch.

actability (æktə'bɪlɪtɪ). Also irreg. -ibility. [f. ACTABLE *a.*: see -BILITY.] Of a play: capability of being acted.

1836 *Fraser's Mag.* Apr. 451 Opinions..as to the actibility of certain unacted plays. **1925** *Glasgow Herald* 9 Apr. 4 When Hugh M'Diarmid's Braid Scots play, 'The Purple Patch', appeared,..doubts were expressed as to its actability.

actable ('æktəb(ə)l), *a.* [f. ACT *v.* + -ABLE.]

1. Capable of being acted (on the stage).

1849 *Eclec. Rev.* XXVI. 212 If not actable, to what end the acting form? **1881** M. THOMAS in *Dram. Ref. Jrnl.* Nov. 216/2 He first learnt how to write a fairly actable comedy.

2. Capable of being acted or carried out in practice.

1878 TENNYSON *Harold* III. i. 72 Is naked truth actable in true life?

†**actæon** (æk'tiːən), *v. Obs.* [f. *Actæon*, the mythological hunter turned into a stag by Diana, with a play upon his becoming 'horned.'] To cuckold.

1615 NICHOLS *Disc. Marriage* xi. in *Harl. Misc.* (Malh.) III. 274 There are of opinion, that there is, in marriage, an inevitable destiny..which is either to be actæoned, or not to be. *a* **1658** CLEVELAND *Vit. Uxoris* x, And thou'lt Actæon'd be.

†**'actative.** *Obs. rare*⁻¹. [f. ACT *v.*, by form-assoc. with words like *purgative*, *restorative*, *provocative*, of which the basis is not the Eng. *purge*, *restore*, *provoke*, but L. *purgāre*, etc.; see -ATIVE.] ? A thing that animates or energizes. See ACT *v.* 1.

1605 TIMME *Quersitanus* I. xiii. 53 A certaine red ocre..an asswager of things and a right actative and a great mitigator of all griefes and paines.

acted ('æktɪd), *ppl. a.* [f. ACT *v.* + -ED.] **a.** Carried out in action; performed (esp. dramatically); feigned.

1597 DANIEL *Civile Wares* V. lxxiii. Envie had been unable to reprove His acted life unless shee did him wrong. **1648** MILTON *Tenure of Kings* Wks. 1738 I. 322 All the acted zeal that for these many years hath fill'd their bellies. **1855** TENNYSON *Will* 12 But ill for him who..ever weaker grows thro' acted crime. **1859** JEPHSON *Brittany* vii. 86 The acted drama cannot long survive among a reading people.

b. *acted-out* (Psychiatry): see ACT *v.* 5.

1949 M. MEAD *Male & Female* xiv. 290 The first rule of petting is the need for keeping complete control of just how far the physical behaviour is to go; one sweeping impulse, one acted-out desire for complete possession or complete surrender, and the game is lost.

‖**acte gratuit** (akt gratɥi). [Fr. (A. Gide).] A gratuitous or inconsequent action performed on impulse.

1933 'REBECCA WEST' *St. Augustine* iii. 40 It was simply a demonstration against order..; in fact, it was an *acte gratuit* of the sort that fills M. André Gide with such ecstasy. **1949** 'N. BLAKE' *Head of Traveller* I. i. 25 I'm an Artist. I should only be interested in murder as an *acte gratuit*. **1950** W. H. AUDEN *Enchafèd Flood* (1951) iii. 96 His criminal *acte gratuit* of shooting the Albatross.

actin ('æktɪn). *Biochem.* [f. Gr. ἀκτίς ray + -IN¹.] A protein which with myosin plays an important part in the contraction and relaxation of muscle (see ACTOMYOSIN).

1942 A. SZENT-GYÖRGYI in *Stud. Inst. Med. Chem. Univ. Szeged* I. 67 Myosin B is a stoichiometric compound of myosin A and another substance. We will call this other substance 'actin'. **1944** —— *Stud. on Muscle* II. 29 This property of actin, that it is capable of existing in two forms, in globular and fibrous form, which can be reversibly transformed into each other, is striking and unique. **1962** *Gray's Anat.* (ed. 33) 40 The thinner filaments believed to be largely composed of actin.

actinal (æk'taɪnəl, 'æktɪnəl), *a. Zool.* [f. Gr. ἀκτίς, ἀκτῖν-α ray + -AL¹.] Pertaining to that part or surface of a radiate animal which contains the mouth and surrounding organs, as the lower side of a starfish; a term introduced by L. Agassiz in connexion with his view that the body of a radiate animal is essentially a sphere, with the mouth or actinostome at one of the poles.

1857 L. AGASSIZ *Contrib. Nat. Hist. N. Amer.* IV. 376 The so-called mouth is always placed at one of these poles, and from it radiate the most prominent organs, in consequence of which I have called this side of the body the oral or actinal area, and the opposite side the aboral or abactinal area. **1872** DANA *Corals* i. 22 The upper extremity (of an actinia) is called the actinal end, since it bears the tentacles or rays.

actine ('æktɪn). [ad. Gr. ἀκτῖν- ray.] **1.** (See quot.)

1849 SIR J. HERSCHEL in *Adm. Man. Sci. Enq.* 295 The abstract unit of solar radiation to be adopted in the ultimate reduction of the actinometric observations is the actine.

2. A 'ray' or radiating part of a sponge-spicule.

1887 SOLLAS in *Encycl. Brit.* XXII. 416/2 Two actines soldered together by intervening silica.

acting ('æktɪŋ), *vbl. sb.* [f. ACT *v.* + -ING¹.]

1. The process of carrying out into action; performance, execution.

1601 SHAKS. *Jul. C.* II. i. 63 Betweene the acting of a dreadfull thing, And the first motion. **1853** F. ROBERTSON *Serm.* Ser. I. viii. 124 Let impression pass on at once to acting.

2. The performance of deeds, doing, continued action, practice; in *pl.* doings, practices, proceedings, conduct. Usually with reference to the manner or character of what is done.

1603–5 SIR J. MELVIL *Mem.* (1735) 267 So to direct my Actings as they might tend to his Glory. **1649** CROMWELL in Southey's *Common-Pl. Bk.* Ser. II. (1849) 128 It's easie to object to the glorious actinges of God—if we look too much upon instruments. **1722** DE FOE *Hist. Plague* (1754) 10 Rather for a Direction to themselves to act by, than a History of my Actings. **1825** LD. COCKBURN *Mem. own Time* iii. 164 The past actings of Courts ought not to be merely stated, but criticised and appreciated. **1826** SCOTT *Woodst.* viii. (1846) 88 The great actings which are now on foot in these nations.

3. a. The performing of plays or other fictitious scenes and incidents, playing, dramatic performance; feigning a character not one's own, simulation.

1664 PEPYS *Diary* (1879) III. 80 The play not good, nor anything but the good actings of Betterton and his Wife and Harris. **1761** CHURCHILL *Rosciad* Poems 1763 I. 31 Whose Acting's hard, affected, and constrain'd. **1779** SHERIDAN *Critic* I. i. 450, I speak only with reference to the usual length of acting plays. **1856** FROUDE *Hist. Eng.* I. 61 Acting was the especial amusement of the English, from the palace to the village green.

b. ***acting over***: A re-enacting, repetition.

1646 SIR T. BROWNE *Pseud. Ep.* 171 Making the creatures of one Element, but an acting over those of an other.

c. ***acting out*** (esp. in *Psychiatry*): (abnormal behaviour caused by) the representation of unconscious impulses, desires, etc., in (often anti-social) action. See ACT *v.* 5.

1945 O. FENICHEL in *Psychoanal. Rev.* XXXII. 197 'Acting out', as distinguished from the other phenomena, is an acting, not a mere feeling, not a mere thinking, not a mere mimic expression, not a mere single movement. This.. distinguishes it from symptom formation. **1955** T. H. PEAR *Eng. Social Differences* 27 The conscious identification of an individual with a social class, and the acting-out of this identification with organizational participation. **1963** *New Society* 7 Nov. 22/2 A group of bright boys who have acting-out problems that prevent them from following a formal programme. **1975** *Christian* II. 228 The third such mechanism is testing out the bonds that are developing between the patient and therapist... Frequently this involves 'acting-out behaviour', as we [*sc.* psychotherapists] call it, asserting a spurious independence through behaviour obviously ill-advised, usually thoroughly unwise.

4. The putting forth of energy or activity, working, operation.

1647 SPRIGG *Angl. Rediv.* I. i. 2 This did but put nature upon more vigorous and industrious actings to defend itself. **1754** EDWARDS *Freed. Will* I. §1, 2 There is nothing else in the Actings of my Mind, that I am conscious of while I walk. **1833** CHALMERS *Constit. Man* iv (1835) I. 173 The actings and reactings that take place between man and man. **1846** H. E. MANNING *Serm.* (1848) II. ii. 30 The continual actings of the desires, lusts, imaginations, leave soils and stains.

5. a. *Comb.* **acting-order**, i.e. order for acting in a certain capacity; *spec.* A temporary appointment to a vacant position made by one entitled to do so, but which may or may not be confirmed by the superior authority. **acting manager**, a person responsible for arranging the scenery, costumes and acting of a play (often himself an actor); producer; hence ***acting management***.

1733 B. VICTOR *Mem. Life B. Booth* 7 And the part of Cato was given to Mr. Booth by two of his Masters, who were Acting Managers. **1804** NELSON in Nicolas's *Despatches* VI. 199, I..have appointed Mr. Edward Flin, of the Victory, to act in the Bittern..a copy of whose Acting-Order is also herewith transmitted..I therefore hope their Lordships will confirm the appointment. **1829** H. FOOTE *Compan. Theatres* 30 In 1795, a share was purchased by John Grubb, Esq. to whom Mr. Kemble resigned the acting management. **1836** MARRYAT *Midship. Easy* (1863) 213, I really think that an acting order would do more than the doctor can. **1860** *Players* I. 138 He has also had the acting management during the summer months of the Surrey Gardens. **1879** C. E. PASCOE *Dram. List* 237/1 Acting and Stage Manager: George Bartley.

b. Suitable for dramatic performance; *spec.* susceptible of being performed well (cf. ACT *v.* 8 b).

1768 D. GARRICK *Let.* 26 Mar. (1831) I. 295 Also five copies of all the acting plays and farces half-bound. **1825** P. EGAN *Life of Actor* 203 The *School of Adversity*..is one of the best acting plays in the whole catalogue of the drama. **1827** J. BOADEN *Mem. Mrs. Siddons* II. 244 The Cleopatra of Dryden..did not range among her acting parts. **1829** *Harlequin* 20 June 43 The third act—the finest portion of our acting drama—was consequently inefficient. **1854** A. C. MOWATT *Autobiogr. of Actress* 203, I designed the play wholly as an *acting* comedy. **1898** L. MERRICK *Actor-Manager* 234 It was a finer acting-scene for Blanche than for himself. **1901** CLARA MORRIS *Life on Stage* 142 It was an excellent acting part, very sweet and tenderly pathetic in the first act.

c. Applied to versions of plays specially prepared for actors' use (provided with full stage-directions, etc.), as ***acting copy***, ***edition***, ***version***.

1844 J. COWELL *Thirty Years among Players* (1845) I. vii. 19/2, I went home and read Ross and Lennox from the acting copy. **1850** [see COPY *sb.* 6]. **1850** (*title*) Lacy's acting edition of plays. **1855** W. B. WOOD *Pers. Recoll. Stage* 185, I could not, however, but regret that he had not adopted the acting version which we formerly used. **1910** W. W. GREG *Shaks. Merry W.* Introd. 31 These four scenes cannot have been altogether omitted in the acting version. **1942** G. MITCHELL *Laurels are Poison* xiv. 162 An 'acting copy' of *Richard of Bordeaux*.

acting ('æktɪŋ), *ppl. a.* [f. ACT *v.* + -ING².]

1. Performing (dramatically). **b.** ***acting-out*** (esp. in *Psychiatry*): that acts out an unconscious impulse, repressed desire, etc., often through anti-social behaviour. See ACT *v.* 5.

1945 O. FENICHEL in *Psychoanal. Rev.* XXXII. 201 The 'acting out-neurotic characters', who otherwise are comparable to addicts. **1974** H. L. FOSTER *Ribbin'* i. 15 There also happen to be quite a number of seriously disturbed and aggressive acting-out youngsters as well as physically handicapped children inhabiting our schools.

2. Performing functions, putting forth activity.

1597 DANIEL *Civile Wares* VII. xxxiv, The acting spirits up and awake doe keepe.

3. Performing temporary or special duties; on temporary service. As a qualifying adj.

1797 NELSON in Nicolas's *Despatches* VII. 133 The Gunner of the Peterell not having joined, I shall put John Brady acting into the Peterell. **1836** MARRYAT *Midsh. Easy* xxv, He..served his time, was acting lieutenant for two years and then somehow or other he bore up for the Church. **1873** *Porcupine* 24 May 124/1 The proud position of acting editor of the *Mail* is a far higher honour than that of any collector of Customs, acting or inactive. **1946** J. IRVING *Royal Navalese* 19 *Acting Unpaid*. A rating who is granted permission by his Captain to wear some badge or mark of rank..although, by regulation, he is not entitled to it and cannot therefore be paid accordingly.

¶In senses 2 and 3 it is used esp. as a qualifying adj. to official titles, meaning either doing duty temporarily, as ***acting-captain***; or doing duty solely, though nominally associated with another or others who take no practical share in the work, as ***acting-manager***, ***-secretary***, ***-trustees***, ***-executors***, etc.

1801 NELSON in Nicolas's *Despatches* IV. 287 Our friend Troubridge will tell you his opinion of the present Acting-Captain of the San Josef. **1832** HT. MARTINEAU *Hill & Valley* ii. 19 He resolved..to be an acting partner.

‖**Actinia** (æk'tɪnɪə). *Zool.* Pl. actiniæ, actinias. [mod.L. f. (by Linn.) Gr. ἀκτῖν- ray.] *prop.* A genus of *Zoophytes* belonging to the family *Actiniadæ*; *pop.* extended to any animal of the family, whether of the genus *Actinia* or one of its congeners; a Sea-Anemone, or animal of the Sea-Anemone group.

1748 SIR J. HILL *Nat. Hist.* 94 The body of the actinia is of a naturally cylindrick, but variable figure. **1767** ELLIS *Actinia* in *Phil. Trans.* LVII. 428 The Actinia, called by old authors..*Urtica marina*, from its supposed property of stinging, is now more properly called by some late English authors the Animal flower. **1850** DANA *Geol.* i. 10 The waters abound in..asterias or star-fish, and the variously coloured actinias or sea-flowers. **1855** KINGSLEY *Glaucus* (1878) 112 Beautiful Actiniæ filled the tiny caverns with living flowers.

actinian (æk'tɪnɪən). *Zool.* [f. ACTINIA + -AN.] A sea-anemone belonging to the genus *Actinia*.

1888 *Athenæum* 30 June 830 A tube-forming actinian (*Cerianthus membranaceus*). **1902** *Fortn. Rev.* June 1012 The actinian..merely responds mechanically to a chemical stimulus.

actinic (æk'tɪnɪk), *a.* [f. Gr. ἀκτῖν- ray + -IC.] Of or pertaining to actinism.

1844 SIR J. HERSCHEL *Brit. Assoc. Report* 13 While the actinic influence is still fresh upon the face (i.e. as soon as it is removed from the light). **1845** *Pen. Cycl.* I. 167/2 A beam of solar light is made up of three distinct sets of rays—the luminous, the calorific, and the chemical or actinic rays. **1859** *Bentley's Q. Rev.* No. 3, 157 The actinic force, or that of the violet end of the spectrum, quickens germination much more than the luminous. **1870** PROCTOR *Other Worlds* x. 246 Besides light and heat, the stars emit actinic rays. **1871** H. MACMILLAN *True Vine* 124 We produce photographs by a power in the sunbeam called the chemical, or actinic power. **1874** HARTWIG *Aer. World* vi. 68 These ultra violet, actinic, or Ritterian rays, as they have been named, after their discoverer Ritter.

actinide ('æktɪnaɪd). *Chem.* [f. ACTIN(IUM 2 + *-ide* as in LANTHANIDE.] One of the elements with an atomic number of 89 (actinium) or higher. Also *attrib.*, as ***actinide series.***

1945 G. T. SEABORG in *Chem. & Engin. News* XXIII. 2192/1 This rare-earth-like series begins with actinium in the same sense that the 'lanthanide' series begins with lanthanum. On this basis it might be termed the 'actinide' series. **1950** F. GAYNOR *Encycl. Atomic Energy* 14 Recently the discovery of two new actinide elements, *berkelium* and *californium* has been announced. *Ibid.*, The actinides and the rare earth elements show a striking similarity of extra-nuclear electron structure. **1958** R. D. CONNOR in O. R. Frisch *Nucl. Handbk.* iv. §21 The second 'rare earth' series starts at actinium and is called the *actinide series* just as the original series starting at lanthanum is termed the *lanthanide series*.

actiniform (æk'tɪnɪfɔːm), *a.* [f. Gr. ἀκτῖν- ray + -FORM.] Having a radiated form; of the form of a sea-anemone, as the coralline polypes.

1843 OWEN *Anat. Inv. Anim.* 87 Many of the large actiniform polypes of the tropical seas combine with a structure which is essentially similar to our sea-anemonies, an internal calcareous axis or skeleton. **1855** KNIGHT *Eng. Cycl.* III. 587 *Madrepora*, Animals actiniform, rather short, with twelve simple tentacula.

actinism ('æktɪnɪz(ə)m). [f. Gr. ἀκτῖν- ray + -ISM.]

†**1.** 'The radiation of heat or light, or that branch of Philosophy which treats of it.' Craig 1847. *Obs.*

2. That property or force in the sun's rays by which chemical changes are produced, as in photography.

1844 R. HUNT *Brit. Assoc. Report* 30 By a most careful prismatic analysis of the rays..I have ascertained the relative quantity of the active chemical principle (Actinism). **1849** LINDLEY *Elem. Bot.* 56 Mr. Hunt believes that the germination of seeds in the spring..is dependent upon the variations in the amount of actinism—or chemical influence—of light and of heat in the solar beam. **1862** R. H. PATTERSON *Ess. Hist. & Art* 13 The electro-positive and electro-negative rays, of which Heat and Actinism are the representatives.

actinium (æk'tɪnɪəm). *Chem.* [mod.L. in form, f. Gr. ἀκτῖν- ray + -IUM, as in *sodium, potassium,* etc.] **1.** A supposed chemical element, a metal discovered in 1881 in association with zinc; so called because of the action of light upon its salts.

1881 *Nature* XXIV. 428 The existence of a new metallic element, actinium, in the zinc of commerce. *Ibid.* No. 620, 470 *On the New Metal Actinium*, by J. L. Phipson. The sulphide of actinium is described as a pale yellow canary-coloured substance.

2. A radioactive metallic element found, associated with thorium, in pitchblende. Symbol Ac; atomic weight 227; atomic number 89.

[**1900** A. DEBIERNE in *Compt. Rend.* CXXX. 906.] **1900** *Jrnl. Chem. Soc.* LXXVIII. II. 350 (*title*) Actinium: A New Radio-active Element. *Ibid.* 351 The rays emitted by actinium produce the same effects as those from radium and polonium. **1906** RUTHERFORD in *Phil. Mag.* XII. 362 In order to obtain a homogeneous source of α rays, the active deposit of actinium was used... This active deposit consists of two products, actinium A and B, the former of which is rayless. **1958** R. D. CONNOR in O. R. Frisch *Nucl. Handbk.* iv. §4 It gradually became clear that there existed three naturally-occurring families of radio-active substances, called the *Uranium-Radium Series*, the *Thorium Series* and the *Actinium Series. Ibid.* iv. §24 Actinium..can be produced artificially by bombarding radium (Ra^{226}) with neutrons.

actino-, a. Gr. ἀκτῖνο- combining form of ἀκτίς (gen. ἀκτῖν-ος) a ray, a beam, as in ἀκτῖνοβόλος darting rays. Entering into numerous derivatives, chiefly connected (1) with ACTINISM, (2) with animals related to the ACTINIA. **actinodermatitis**, dermatitis arising from the action of actinic rays; **actinomorphic** *a.* = ACTINOMORPHOUS *a.*

1906 DORLAND *Med. Dict.* (ed. 4) 27/1 *Actinodermatitis*.. X-ray dermatitis. **1898** H. C. PORTER tr. *Strasburger's Textbk. Bot.* I. i. 16 Such parts of plants as may be divided by each of three or more longitudinal planes into like halves are termed either..Radial, or Actinomorphic.

actinobacillosis (,æktɪnəʊbæsɪ'ləʊsɪs). [ad. F. *actinobacillose* (Lignières & Spitz 1902, in *Bull. Soc. Méd. Vét.* XX. 487), f. *Actinobacillus* (see def.) + -OSIS.] A disease affecting cattle and other animals and sometimes man, caused by the bacterium *Actinobacillus lignieresi.*

1903 *Vet. Jrnl.* VII. 110 In actinobacillosis the lymphatic glands are always involved. **1934** ZINSSER & BAYNE-JONES *Textbk. Bacteriol.* (ed. 7) lv. 867 Actinobacillosis..is primarily a disease of cattle, occurring chiefly in Argentina, with lesions like those of actinomycosis. **1955** GAIGER & DAVIES *Vet. Path. & Bact.* (ed. 4) xv. 307 Actinobacillosis is chiefly a disease of cattle; it is occasionally met with in sheep.

†**acti'nobolism.** *Obs.* [f. Gr. ἀκτινοβόλ-ος ray-darting (f. ἀκτινο- ray + βολή throwing) + -ISM.]

1681 T. WILLIS *Rem. Med. Wks.* (Vocab.), *Actinobolism*, an irradiation of beams, or shooting forth of the spirits like beams of the sun.

'actino-'chemistry. [See ACTINO-.] The chemistry of actinism; that branch of chemistry, which treats of the chemical energies existing in the solar rays.

1844 SIR J. HERSCHEL *Brit. Assoc. Report* 12, A contribution to the newly created science of actino-chemistry. **1853** R. HUNT *Man. Photog.* 116 Proceeding only to the more delicate processes when he has mastered the rudimentary details of the more simple forms of actino-chemistry. **1875** URE *Dict. Arts* I. 28 Actino-chemistry was a term first applied by Sir John Herschel, and has been generally adopted.

actinograph (æk'tɪnəgrɑːf, -æ-). [f. ACTINO- + γράφ-ος writing. Cf. Gr. ἀκτῖνογραφία.] **a.** An instrument, invented by Sir J. Herschel in 1838, for recording the variations in the power of the solar rays.

1840 SIR J. HERSCHEL *Phil. Trans.* I. 46 Description of an Actinograph, or self-registering Photometer for meteorological purposes. **1853** R. HUNT *Man. Photog.* 154 The instrument constructed by Sir John Herschel, which he has named an actinograph, not only registers the direct effect of solar chemical radiation, but also the amount of general actinic power in the visible hemisphere.

b. *spec. Photogr.* An instrument (of which there are various kinds) used for recording the actinic power of the light, to determine the correct time of exposure for a photographic plate. (*Disused.*)

1890 *Anthony's Photogr. Bull.* III. 432 The actinograph [before us] is..an ingenious application of the slide rule for the purpose of determining photographic exposures. **1902** *Encycl. Brit.* XXX. 702/1 In Hurter & Driffield's 'Actinograph', the light coefficient is given by a printed card showing the curves for every day in the year.

actinoid ('æktɪnɔɪd), *a.* [f. ACTINO- + -ειδ-ής -form.] Having the form of rays, radiated; said of a division of Zoophytes or Polypes, having the internal cavity divided by radiated partitions, as in the coral zoophytes.

1848 DANA *Zoophytes* iv. §37, 43 Other actinoid polyps. **1860** *Actinolog. Brit.* Introd. 22 The *cnidæ*, in the Actinoid Zoophytes, are not confined to one organ or set of organs.

actinolite (æk'tɪnəlaɪt). *Min.* Incorrectly **actynolite.** [f. ACTINO- ray + λίθος stone.] A bright green variety of Hornblende, occurring usually in fasciculated crystals.

1833 LYELL *Elem. Geol.* (1865) 592 Hornblende and Actinolite may be united. **1835** KIRBY *Habits & Inst. Anim.* I. vi. 193 Actinolites, Pyrites, and other substances exhibit it [a tendency to radiation] in the former [the mineral kingdom]. **1876** PAGE *Advd. Text-bk. Geol.* v. 104 Asbestos or amianthus..may be regarded as a variety of actynolite.

actinolitic (æk,tɪnə'lɪtɪk), *a. Min.* [f. prec. + -IC.] Of the nature of actinolite.

1878 LAWRENCE tr. *Cotta, Rocks Class.* 149 The diorite at Klausen contains actinolitic hornblende with oligoclase.

actinology (æktɪ'nɒlədʒɪ). [f. ACTINO- + -LOGY.] The science of the chemical action of light.

1860 in MAYNE *Expos. Lex.* Add.

actinomere (æk'tɪnəmɪə(r)), *Zool.* [f. ACTINO- + μέρ-ος part.] A portion of the surface of a radiated animal cut off by any two meridional lines reaching from pole to pole. See ACTINAL.

1869 NICHOLSON *Zool.* 111 Eight meridional bands, or 'ctenophores,' bearing the comb-like fringes, or characteristic organs of locomotion, traverse at definite intervals the interpolar region, which they divide into an equal number of lune-like lobes, termed the 'actinomeres.'

actinometer (,æktɪ'nɒmɪtə(r)). [f. ACTINO- + μέτρον measure.] **1.** An instrument for measuring the intensity of the sun's heating rays; first invented by Sir John Herschel, and described in Edinb. Journal of Science for 1825.

1833 SIR J. HERSCHEL *Brit. Assoc. Report* 379 The actinometer is an instrument..for measuring at any instant the direct heating power of the solar rays. **1879** *Photogr.* in *Cassell's Techn. Educ.* III. 326 The consequent progress of the printing may be most accurately determined by means of the actinometer. **1880** RADCLIFFE in *Contemp. Rev.* Feb. 210 In interplanetary space, if the experiments with the actinometer are to be trusted, the temperature is not less than 256° Fahrenheit below the freezing point of fresh water.

2. *Photogr.* (See quots.)

1866 J. W. SWAN in *Brit. Jrnl. Photogr.* 16 Mar. 125/2, I name the instrument the 'photographic Actinometer', because it is exclusively designed for regulating the exposure in photographic printing. **1926** TANSLEY & CHIPP *Aims & Methods in Study of Vegetation* 93 The ordinary photographic 'actinometer' or 'exposure meter' is a very useful instrument for roughly measuring the relative light intensities of different habitats. **1958** M. L. HALL et al. *Newnes Compl. Amat. Photogr.* vii. 94 *Actinometers.* Used for many years, but now obsolete, these measured the light intensity falling on the subject by the time taken by a printing-out paper to darken to match a standard tint.

actinometric (,æktɪnəʊ'mɛtrɪk), *a.* [f. ACTINO- + μετρικός measuring.] Of or pertaining to the measurement of the intensity of the sun's heat.

1849 SIR J. HERSCHEL *Admiralty Man. Sci. Enq.* 295 The ultimate reduction of the actinometric observations. **1881** *Eng. Mech.* 27 May 280/1 Some actinometric measurements were made last autumn at different heights in the Alps, by M. Puiseux.. The activity of this [vegetation] at Montsouris was proved to be in direct proportion to the actinometric degree.

actinometrical (,æktɪnəʊ'mɛtrɪkəl), *a.* [f. prec. + -AL[1].] = ACTINOMETRIC.

1873 ATKINSON tr. *Ganot's Physics* 345 The absorptive action which the aqueous vapour in the atmosphere exerts on the sun's heat has been established by a series of actinometrical observations made by Sorel at Geneva.

actinometry (,æktɪ'nɒmɪtrɪ). [f. ACTINO- + -μετρια measurement.] The measurement or estimation of the radiation of heat from surfaces.

1860 MAURY *Phys. Geog. Sea* vii. §367 We have in the land and sea-breezes a natural index to the actinometry of sea and land, which shows that the radiating forces of the two are very different.

actinomorphous (,æktɪnəʊ'mɔːfəs), *a. Bot.* [f. ACTINO- ray + μορφ-ή form + -OUS.] Of radiated shape.

1858 GRAY *Bot. Text-bk.* 394 *Actinomorphous*, capable of bisection through two or more planes into similar halves, as is a regular flower.

actinomyces (,æktɪnəʊ'maɪsiːz). [mod.L., f. Gr. ἀκτίς, -ιν- ray (see ACTINO-) + μύκης fungus.] The ray-fungus, the presence of which, in cattle, constitutes the disease **,actinomy'cosis**, forms of which are known as *lumpy jaw* (LUMPY *a.* 1 c) and *wooden tongue* (WOODEN *a.* 9). Also *attrib.* Hence **,actinomy'cotic** *a.*, resembling, related to, or caused by actinomyces.

1882 *Times* 8 Nov. 5/6 From the peculiar manner in which the fungus grows..it has received the name of Actinomyces, and it is consequently proposed to designate the disease Actinomykosis. **1884** KLEIN *Micro-org.* xvi. 148 In the centre of the nodules lie dense groups of peculiar club-shaped corpuscles—*actinomyces*... Each of these actinomyces-corpuscles appears homogeneous. **1885** *Lancet* 2 May 808/1 The first genuine instance of Actinomycosis in this country. **1900** *Jrnl. Exper. Med.* V. 179 The actinomycotic form of the tubercle bacillus. **1949** H. W. FLOREY et al. *Antibiotics* I. i. 53 The lysate was a good antigen and they employed it for the treatment of three cases of actinomycosis.

actinomycetes ('æktɪnəʊmaɪ'siːtiːz, sometimes anglicized to -'maɪsiːts). *Biol.* [f. ACTINO- + MYCETES.] A group of minute organisms of the order Actinomycetales, commonly held to be filamentous bacteria; treated as sing. (of less common occurrence) **actinomycete.**

1916 *Jrnl. Bacteriol.* I. 197 (*title*) Possible Function of Actinomycetes in Soil. **1919** S. A. WAKSMAN in *Jrnl. Bacteriol.* IV. 189 Studies in the metabolism of the actinomycetes. **1935** *Lancet* 2 Nov. 1014/2 (*title*) Pathogenic Actinomycetes. **1947** C. E. SKINNER et al. *Henrici's Molds, Yeasts, & Actinomycetes* (ed. 2) 351 The term actinomycete we write in the lower case to indicate that it is not used in a taxonomic sense but somewhat in the manner we would use yeast or mold. **1950** *Lancet* 22 July 138/1 The actinomycetes, a heterogeneous group comprising many thousands of species, are found in soil (in which they may represent nearly a quarter of the cultivable micro-organisms), in dust, fresh water, and lake bottoms, in decaying plant and animal residues, and on vegetation.

actinomycin ('æktɪnəʊ'maɪsɪn). *Biochem.* [f. ACTINO- + Gr. μύκης fungus + -IN[1].] An antibiotic substance of the actinomycetes group originally isolated by S. A. Waksman and H. B. Woodruff from certain micro-organisms found in soil.

1940 *Proc. Soc. Exper. Biol.* XLV. 610 The active substance was tentatively designated as 'actinomycin'. It is proposed here to designate the above two preparations as 'actinomycin A' and 'actinomycin B'. **1944** *Ann. Reg. 1943* 359 Actinomycin is bactericidal but lethal to animals. **1946** *Lancet* 20 Apr. 582/1 Other fungus-products—streptomycin, streptothricin, actinomycin, and clavacin.

actinophage (æk'tɪnəʊfeɪdʒ). *Biochem.* [f. ACTINO(MYCETES + PHAGE.] A virus that attacks actinomycetes.

1947 H. C. REILLY et al. in *Jrnl. Bacteriol.* LIV. 451 The term 'bacteriophage' is usually applied to the virus or phage of bacteria, and the term 'mycophage' to that of fungi. By analogy, the term 'actinophage' may be used to designate the phage of actinomycetes. **1951** *Bacteriol. Proc.* 48 An actinophage has been isolated from cultures and fermenter mashes of *S. aureofaciens.* **1961** *Nature* 18 Feb. 603/2 The possible utility of actinophage susceptibility as a criterion for species differentiation in the genus *Streptomyces* has been the subject of much discussion.

actinophone (æk'tɪnəfəʊn). [f. ACTINO- + -φων-ος sounding, vocal.] (See quot.)

1881 A. G. BELL in *Nature* 12 May 44 We have decided to ..limit the word..actinophone..to apparatus for the production of sound..by actinic rays.

actinophonic (æk,tɪnəʊ'fɒnɪk), *a.* [f. prec. + -IC, after Gr. -φωνικ-ός pertaining to voice.] Pertaining to sound produced by chemical action.

1881 in *Nature* No. 622, 528 When exposed in dark to a copper plate gradually heated with an oxyhydrogen blow-pipe, no sound is heard in the telephone till the plate is raised to a dull red; then it gradually increases in intensity. The author is disposed to consider the phenomenon photophonic rather than actinophonic.

actinophorous (,æktɪ'nɒfərəs), *a.* [f. Gr. ἀκτῑνοφόρ-ος (f. ἀκτῑνο- ray + -φορος- bearing) + -OUS.] Bearing straight projecting spines; spiny.

1863 H. J. CARTER in *Ann. Nat. Hist.* XII. 32 The actinophorous rays of..Rhizopods.

actinopterygian (,æktɪnəʊtə'rɪdʒɪən), *a.* and *sb.* *Ichthyol.* Also **Actino-**. [f. mod.L. *Actinopterygia*, name of a group of fishes (E. D. Cope 1889, in *Amer. Naturalist* XXIII. 855), earlier *-pteri* (Cope 1872): see ACTINO-, PTERYGIUM.] **A.** *adj.* Of, pertaining to, or designating the group of ray-finned fishes, one of the three main groups of bony fishes, and containing most of the present-day varieties as well as many fossil kinds. **B.** *sb.* A fish of this group.

1891 A. S. WOODWARD *Catal. Fossil Fishes in Brit. Mus. (Nat. Hist.)* II. p. xxii, The great group of Actinopterygian Teleostomi is that concerning which palæontology affords most extensive information. **1898** —— *Outl. Vertebrate Palæontol.* 81 This was the only type of Actinopterygian existing until the Permian period. **1977** A. HALLAM *Planet Earth* 240 (*caption*) An example of evolutionary trends in a group of animals is seen here in the evolution of actinopterygian fishes. **1979** *Nature* 18 Jan. 176/2 The mutual relations of salmon (an actinopterygian), lungfish (a dipnoan) and cow (a mammal, a class which can be traced back to rhipidistian crossopterygians by way of reptiles and amphibians) are certainly worthy of serious consideration.

actinostome (æk'tɪnəstəʊm). *Zool.* [f. ACTINO- + στόμα mouth.] L. Agassiz's name for the mouth of radiated animals, considered by him as essentially different from that of Vertebrates.

1857 L. AGASSIZ *Contrib. Nat. Hist. N. Amer.* IV. 376. **1880** BELL in *Zool. Jrnl. Lin. Soc.* XV. No. 82, 127 The actinostome has been pushed forwards and to the left.

†**'actinote.** *Min. Obs.* [f. Gr. ἀκτῑνωτ-ός rayed; f. ἀκτινο- ray.] A synonym of ACTINOLITE.

1804 *Edin. Rev.* III. 308 Some of the common and glassy strahlsteins correspond to actinote. **1852** T. ROSS tr. *Humboldt's Trav.* II. xxiv. 434 Rock-crystals..coloured by chlorite or blended with actinote.

actinotherapy (,æktɪnəʊ'θerəpɪ). [f. ACTINO- + THERAPY.] Treatment of disease by means of light rays. Hence **,actinothera'peutic** *a.*, **,actinothera'peutics** *sb. pl.*

1903 DORLAND *Med. Dict.* (ed. 3) 26/1 Actinotherapy. **1908** *Practitioner* June 818 Various methods of treatment other than actinotherapy and X-ray therapy. **1913** DORLAND *Med. Dict.* (ed. 7) 35/2 Actinotherapeutics. **1925** E. H. & W. K. RUSSELL (*title*) Ultra-Violet Radiation and Actinotherapy. **1931** *Times Lit. Suppl.* 1 Jan. 14/4 Surgeon-in-Charge, Actino-Therapeutic Department, Guy's Hospital. **1942** *Archit. Rev.* XCII. 5 The central corridor, either side of which the X-ray and actinotherapy rooms are planned. **1943** *Gloss. Terms Electr. Engin.* (*B.S.I.*) 144 *Ultra-violet therapy* (*actino-therapy*), the treatment of diseases by ultra-violet radiation of wavelengths between 4000 Ångström units and 2500 Ångström units.

actino-uranium (,æktɪnəʊjʊ'reɪnɪəm). [f. ACTINO- + URANIUM.] The radioactive isotope of uranium of mass 235.

1929 RUTHERFORD in *Nature* 2 Mar. 313/2 The probable mass of this new isotope, which for convenience will be called actino-uranium. **1958** H. J. GRAY *Dict. Physics* 14/1 Actino-uranium..is explosive when in sufficiently high concentration, owing to nuclear fission, and was used in the first atomic bomb.

‖**Actinozoa** (,æktɪnəʊ'zəʊə), *sb. pl.* *Zool.* [mod.L. f. ACTINO- + Gr. ζῷα pl. of ζῷον animal.] A class of Radiated animals, comprising part of the *Cœlenterata* of Huxley, and of the *Zoophytes* of other naturalists, containing the sea-anemones and coral polypes. The sing. *Actinozoon* is rare.

1872 NICHOLSON *Palæont.* 85 Of the living groups of the Actinozoa, the Ctenophora and the Sea-anemones from their absence of hard parts, are unknown in a fossil condition. **1878** M. FOSTER *Physiol.* II. i. §2, 224 Why the gastric membrane of the bloodless actinozoon or hydrozoon does not digest itself.

actino'zoal, *a. Zool.* [f. prec. + -AL¹.] Of or belonging to the Actinozoa.

1872 *Monogr. Gymnoblastic Hydroids* 199 Used as an argument for the actinozoal nature of the *Ctenophora*.

‖**actio in distans** (,æktɪəʊ ɪn 'dɪstænz). Also **actio ad distans.** [L., = 'action upon a thing standing apart'.] The exertion of force by one body upon another separated from it by space, as in some theories of gravitation; action at a distance. Also *fig.*

1846 W. HAMILTON in *Reid's Wks.* 852/1 Repulsion.. remains, as apparently an *actio in distans*,..inconceivable as a possibility [for inclusion among the primary qualities of body]. **1890** W. JAMES *Princ. Psychol.* I. ii. 47 In these cases it seems probable that it [*sc.* hemiopia] is due to an *actio in distans*, probably to the interruption of fibres proceeding from the occipital lobe. **1901** BALDWIN *Dict. Philos.* I. 421/2 Intimately associated with gravitation is the question whether it is really an *actio ad distans*—whether it takes place without any intervening medium or other agency. **1909** W. JAMES *Meaning of Truth* x. 221 By a sort of *actio in distans* my statement had taken direct hold of the other fact. **1937** A. H. MURRAY *Philos. of James Ward* iv. 78 The monads or 'psychoids' are qualitatively distinct and are capable of what in scholastic philosophy was called *actio in distans*.

action ('ækʃən), *sb.* Also 4-5 **accion, -oun.** [a. Fr. *action* ad. L. *actiōn-em* a doing, performance, f. *act-* ppl. stem of *ag-ĕre* to do: see -ION¹.]

I. *Generally.*

1. The process or condition of acting or doing (in the widest sense), the exertion of energy or influence; working, agency, operation.

a. Of persons. (Distinguished from *passion*, from *thought* or *contemplation*, from *speaking* or *writing*.)

1393 LANGL. *P. Pl.* C. II. 94 And holde with hym and with hure · þat han trewe accion. **1413** LYDG. *Pylgr. Sowle* II. lx. (1859) 57 Thyne was the action, and I nought but abyl for to suffre. *c* **1425** WYNTOWN *Cron.* VI. xix. 32 He gave up all hys actyown. **1586** *Let. to Earl of Leycester* 26 In case he failed in the action of her deliuery. **1597** SHAKS. *2 Hen. IV*, II. iv. 406 The vndeseruer may sleepe, when the man of Action is call'd on. **1600** —— *A. Y. L.* IV. i. 141 Certainely a Womans thought runs before her action. **1653** WALTON *Angler* i. 15 Is not yet resolved whether contemplation or Action be the chiefest thing. **1692** BENTLEY *Boyle Lect.* ix. 309 The human Soul is vitally united to the Body by a reciprocal commerce of Action and Passion. **1750** JOHNSON *Rambler* No. 184 ¶10 It is necessary to act, but impossible to know the consequences of action. **1754** EDWARDS *Freed. Will* II. §4, 48 The exercise of his Activity is Action. **1756** BURKE *Vind. Nat. Soc.* Wks. I. 19 Millions, who know no common principle of action. **1828** D. STEWART *Wks.* VI. 121 The word action is properly applied to those exertions which are consequent on volition. **1846** MILL *Logic* I. iii. §5, 71 What is an action? Not one thing, but a series of two things: the state of mind called a volition, followed by an effect. **1855** BAIN *Senses & Intell.* I. i. §3 (1864) 5 Volition is separated from Feeling, by superadding the characteristic of action, or the putting forth of energy to serve an end.

b. Of things. (Distinguished from *inaction*, *repose*.) ***quantity of action***, in *Physics*: The momentum of a body multiplied into the time.

c **1386** CHAUCER *Persone's T.* (Ellesmere) 82 In how manye maneres been the acciouns or werkynges of Penitence [4 *MSS.* accions *of* worchyng]. **1775** HARRIS *Philos. Arrangem.* (1841) 329 Another mode of action may be found in the following instances. A lamb acts upon the senses of a wolf —that sensation acts upon his appetite—that appetite acts upon his corporeal organs. By the action of these organs he runs, he seizes, and he devours the lamb. **1833** BREWSTER *Nat. Magic* xi. 293 To avoid all risk of two opposite actions arriving at the same instant at any part of the engine. **1842** GROVE *Corr. Phys. Forces* 77 If gold be immersed in hydrochloric acid, no chemical action takes place. **1869** PHILLIPS *Vesuv.* iv. 124 The intervals of action and repose were irregular. **1869** OUSELEY *Counterpoint* xiv. 83 Until the additional parts recommence their action. **1879** THOMSON & TAIT *Nat. Phil.* I. I. §326 Taking it, however, as we find it, now universally used by writers on dynamics, we define the Action of a Moving System as proportional to the average kinetic energy, which the system has possessed during the time from any convenient epoch of reckoning, multiplied by the time.

c. ***in action***: In a condition of activity, at work, in practical or effective operation. Conversely, ***out of action***.

1652 M. NEEDHAM tr. *Selden's Mare Cl.* To Reader, The Republick maintein's continually in action a great number of ships, gallies and galliots. **1714** SWIFT *State of Affairs* Wks. 1755 II. I. 216 The bulk of those who are now most in action either at court, in parliament, or publick offices, were then boys at school. **1827** HALLAM *Const. Hist.* iii. (1876) I. 154 Schemes..were put in action against her life. **1919** G. B. SHAW *Heartbreak House* Pref. p. xxxix, The Higher Drama put out of action. The effect of the war on the London theatres may now be imagined. **1961** T. COFFIN *Not to Swift* (1962) xviii. 201 Trig and a very black colored boy from Detroit had killed or put out of action ten guerrillas by grenades and hand-to-hand fighting.

d. ***action of a verb, verbal action***: The action expressed by a verb; properly of verbs which assert *acting*, but conveniently extended to *the thing asserted by a verb*, whether action, state, or mere existence, as I *strike*, I *stand*, I *live*, I *am*.

e. Activity considered noteworthy or important; freq. with *the. spec.* in gambling or betting, esp. in phr. ***where the action is*** (freq. *transf.*, i.e. the centre of some activity); also in drug-trafficking, etc. ***a piece*** (***share***, etc.) ***of the action***, involvement in this. *slang* (orig. *U.S.*).

1933 D. RUNYON in *Collier's* 28 Jan. 8/1 And he is well established as a high player in New Orleans, and Chicago, and Los Angeles, and wherever else there is any action in the way of card-playing, or crap-shooting. **1944** D. BURLEY *Orig. Handbk. Harlem Jive* 107 Well, the Davy Crocketts at the trap knock their wigs and come on the double deuce action with the F Behind. *a* **1953** E. O'NEILL *Hughie* (1959) 36 Hell, I once win twenty grand on a single race. That's action! A good crap game is action, too. **1962** 'K. ORVIS' *Damned & Destroyed* xiv. 90 'What happens then?.. Pal, I got to get action some place.'.. 'Action is the magic word. At six bucks a cap, ten caps a day, a guy has to hustle some.' **1964** *Amer. Speech* XXXIX. 117, I was an undergraduate before I became aware of the special application for the phrase used in speaking of dates, *to get action*. **1964** *Look* 15 Dec. 37/1 Nightclub proprietors, by installing record players to replace live bands and adopting the French name 'discothèque', have created the legend that this is where the action is. **1966** *Maclean's Mag.* 4 June 1 And last year mink breeders from Scandinavia to California were falling over themselves to buy a piece of the action. **1973** C. SAGAN *Cosmic Connection* (1974) vii. 52 We [sc. mankind] are in the galactic boondocks, where the action isn't. **1978** S. BRILL *Teamsters* vi. 213 The real action for Dorfman at the pension fund didn't come until March 1967. **1982** *Times Lit. Suppl.* 2 Apr. 373/2 Not that the activity should be suppressed, but that the aggrieved party should get a share in the action.

2. The exertion of force by one body upon another; influence.

c **1360** CHAUCER *A.B.C.* 20 Myn sinne and myn confusioun..Han taken on me a grevous accioun. **1692** BENTLEY *Boyle Lect.* iv. 134 He exposed them to the action of the Sun. **1748** HARTLEY *Observ. Man* I. i. §1, 15 The subtle Actions of the Small Particles of Bodies over each other. **1812** WOODHOUSE *Astron.* xv. 149 The action, or the attractive force, of the Sun and Moon, on such protuberance. **1822** FARADAY *Exp. Res.* xvi. 75 With similar acid the action on the pure steel was hardly perceptible. **1846** MILL *Logic* III. xxi. §4 (1868) II. 107 Implicitly obedient to the action of fixed causes. **1853** SOYER *Pantropheon* 117 Submit the whole to the action of a slow fire. **1860** TYNDALL *Glaciers* I. §2, 17 Observed upon the rocks and mountains the action of ancient glaciers. **1878** HUXLEY *Physiogr.* 62 By submitting a block of ice to the action of a sunbeam.

3. a. A thing done, a deed. Not always distinguished from ACT, but usually viewed as occupying some time in doing, and in *pl.* referred to habitual or ordinary deeds, the sum of which constitutes *conduct*.

1600 SIR W. CORNWALLIS in *Shaks. Cent. Praise* 41 His lawes and actions. **1602** SHAKS. *Haml.* III. i. 87 And enterprizes of great pith and moment, With this regard their Currants turne away [*v.r.* awry], And loose the name of action. **1605** —— *Macb.* IV. ii. 3 When our Actions do not, Our feares do make vs Traitors. **1611** BIBLE *1 Sam.* ii. 3 The Lord is a God of knowledge, and by him actions are weighed. **1690** LOCKE *Hum. Underst.* I. iii. (1695) 16, I have always thought the Actions of Men the best Interpreters of their thoughts. **1769** ROBERTSON *Charles V*, V. II. 252 The manner in which he justified this action was still more offensive than the action itself. **1837** CARLYLE *Fr. Rev.* (1872) II. III. i. 86 An action, the product and expression of exerted force. **1859** DE QUINCEY *Lessing* Wks. XIII. 289 Successional objects, or of which the parts are in succession, we call actions: consequently actions compose the proper object of poetry.

b. Proverb: ***actions speak louder than words***.

1845 *Knickerbocker* XXV. 106 He had heard that 'actions speak louder than words', and he acted. **1856** ABRAHAM LINCOLN *Coll. Wks.* (1953) II. 352 'Actions speak louder than words' is the maxim. **1906** F. MCCULLAGH *With Cossacks* 178 The gallant foreigner, who could not tell them how he sympathized with them, but whose actions spoke louder than words.

4. The thing represented as done in a drama; the event or series of events, real or imaginary, forming the subject of a fable, poem, or other composition.

1712 ADDISON *Spec.* No. 267 ¶2 This Action [of an Epic] should have three Qualifications in it. First, It should be but One Action. Secondly, It should be an entire Action; and, Thirdly, It should be a great Action. *Ibid.* No. 273 ¶1 Having examined the Action of Paradise Lost, let us in the next place consider the Actors. **1751** CHAMBERS *Cycl.* s.v., The action of the Iliad holds but forty-seven days.

†**5.** *pl.* The transactions, acts, or records of a court or deliberative body. (Fr.) *Obs. rare.*

1612 BREREWOOD *Lang. & Relig.* xxi. 187 As we read in the actions of that Councel. **1635** PAGITT *Christianogr.* I. iii. (1636) 197 The 3 tome of the sixt action of the second Councell of Nice.

6. Mode of acting. **a.** Of persons: Gesture, oratorical management of the body and features in harmony with the subject described; in *Sculpt.* and *Painting*: Gesture or attitude as expressive of the sentiment or passion depicted.

1579 GOSSON *Sch. of Abuse* 68 Players action doeth answere to their partes. **1603** HOLLAND *Plutarch's Mor.* 55 The phrase, utterance, and action of those that exercise to make speeches. **1602** SHAKS. *Haml.* III. ii. 19 Sute the Action to the Word, the Word to the Action. **1605** —— *Macb.* V. i. 32 It is an accustom'd action with her, to seeme thus washing her hands. **1748** J. MASON *Elocution* 38 Under the Word Pronunciation the Antients comprehended Action as well as Elocution. **1758** JOHNSON *Idler* No. 90 ¶8 In the pulpit little action can be proper. **1801** STRUTT *Sports & Past.* II. i. 64 The representation of an archer with his bow in the action of shooting. **1850** MERIVALE *Hist. Rom. Emp.* liv. (1865) VI. 403 It was not the mere trick of action, or knack of speaking, that he was to acquire. **1856** PATMORE *Angel in Ho.* I. II. ii. (1879) 162 She spoke this speech, and marked its sense By action.

b. Of animals. *esp.* The trained management of the body or limbs by domesticated animals.

1599 SHAKS. *Hen. V*, III. i. 6 Imitate the action of the Tyger. **1882** *Daily News* 30 May 3/1 The judges considered as a prime essential the action of the competing horses, and this of course would be action according to the behests of English park fashion. *Mod.* The roan has good knee-action.

c. The way in which an instrument acts; also *concretely*, the arrangement or mechanism by which this is effected.

1845 *Lond. Univ. Calend. Exam. Papers* 219 Explain the action (1) of the siphon, (2) of the air-pump. **1865** Dickens *Our Mut. Fr.* ii. (C.D. ed.) 4 The grand pianoforte with the new action. **1881** Greener *Gun* 195 This lever is secured in position by the screw and washer to a pivot passing through the lever, the said pivot being solid with the action.

d. Used as a film director's word of command.

[**1914** J. B. Rathbun *Motion Picture Making* iii. 68 At the word 'Ready', given by the producer, the camera man starts cranking the machine and the actors stand alert... An instant after follows the order, 'Start your action'.] **1923** F. A. Talbot *Moving Pictures* xiv. 218 Ready! Action! Camera!!! Go!!!! **1959** *Elizabethan* June 26/1 If there is a cameraman then the director calls out 'Action' to the actors, then 'Roll 'em' and the cameraman starts the camera.

II. *Specifically.*

7. a. The taking of legal steps to establish a claim or obtain judicial remedy; legal process; the right to raise such process. ***to take action***: to institute legal proceedings; hence *gen.* to take steps in regard to any matter, to act. ***property in action***, i.e. not in possession, but recoverable by legal process. (The earliest sense in Eng.)

1330 R. Brunne *Chron.* 196 Whilk of vs is doun, & mad is recreant, Cleyme & accioun he lese. *c* **1440** *Gesta Rom.* I. xxxix. 129, I may have noone accione ayenst the. **1594** R. Parsons *Next Succession* Cont., Such as may have clayme or action to the crowne of England at this day. **1641** *Termes de la Ley* 59 The King himselfe cannot grant his thing in Action, which is uncertain. **1660** T. Stanley *Hist. Philos.* (1701) 22/1 Liable to the action of every Man. **1768** Blackstone *Comm.* II. 396 We will proceed next to take a short view of the nature of property in action, or such where a man hath not the occupation, but merely a bare right to occupy the thing in question; the possession whereof may however be recovered by a suit or action at law: from whence the thing so recoverable is called a thing, or *chose*, in action. **1769** *Junius Lett.* Pref., A double remedy is open to them by action and indictment. **1809** Tomlins *Law Dict.* I. D/2 If one calls a merchant bankrupt, action lies. **1865** G. W. Lyttelton *Ephemera* I. 174 In the whole.. Session the only 'action taken'—according to the vile modern Yankeeism—by Lord Derby.. was to move for a Committee on Noxious Vapours. **1880** F. G. Lee *Church under Q. Eliz.* I. v. 279 Her Majesty's advisers, therefore, lost no time in taking fresh action consequent upon the publication of this Bull. *a* **1884** *Mod.* He took prompt action to defend his rights. **1922** Joyce *Ulysses* 309 So Joe starts telling the citizen about.. taking action in the matter. **1961** *Times* 12 May 21/1 Did anybody, or a friendly Power, at any time.. suggest that this man was a suspect,.. and if so, what action was taken?

†**b.** Legal ground. ***action of battle*** = '*casus belli*.' *Obs.*

1536 Bellendene *Cron. Scot.* (1821) II. 374 The Paip.. decernit the Scottis to have just action of battal, in defence of thair liberteis, aganis King Edward.

8. A legal process or suit.

1483 Caxton *Gold. Leg.* 431/3 Doubtyng that the stryf accions and pletynges of the poure shold come onely to the presence and knowlege of hys counceyllours. **1523** Fitzherbert *Surveying* 7 The lorde maye haue an actyon of Trespace agaynst any man. **1591** Lambarde *Archeion* (1635) 99 In all other Actions personalls or realls, we have power to yeeld such Iudgements as doe appertaine. **1597** Shaks. *2 Hen. IV*, II. i. 2 Mr. Fang, haue you entred the Action? **1641** *Termes de la Ley* 6 Actions personals be such actions whereby a man claimeth debt, or other goods and chattels.. for wrong done to his person. **1690** W. Walker *Idiom. Anglo-Lat.* 9 I'le clap an action on your back. **1768** Blackstone *Comm.* II. 393 While they thus continue my qualified or defeasible property.. an action will lie against any man that detains them from me, or unlawfully destroys them. **1794** S. Williams *Hist. Vermont* 216 Actions of ejectment were commenced in the courts at Albany. **1809** Tomlins *Law Dict.* I. D/1 A man attainted of treason.. cannot bring an action. **1849** Macaulay *Hist. Eng.* I. 179 All actions for mesne profits were effectually barred by the general amnesty.

†**9.** A proposition, motion, or question for discussion. (L. *actio*.) *Obs. rare.*

1533 Bellendene *Livy* II. (1822) 154 Valerius dictator.. afore ony accioun wes discussit be the senate, proponit the accioun of the victorius pepill.

10. Active operation against, or engaging an enemy, fighting.

1604 Shaks. *Oth.* II. iii. 186 Would in Action glorious I had lost Those legges. **1606** —— *Tr. & Cr.* IV. v. 113 They are in action. **1684** *Scanderbeg Rediv.* v. 115 His Majesty with a Natural Air of Gallantry usual to him in time of Action. **1761** Smollett *Humphry Cl.* (1815) 95 Retire into a peasant's house, near the scene of action. **1805** in Nicolas's *Dispatches* VII. 167 Bore up, and made all sail, forming in two divisions—cleared Ship for Action. **1861** J. H. Macdonald *Evol. of Battalion* 7 Column formations again, in the British army, are for motion, and not for action, understanding the word action to mean, as in military parlance, engaging the enemy.

11. a. An engagement with the enemy, a fight.

1599 Shaks. *Much Ado* I. i. 6 How many Gentlemen haue you lost in this action? **1665** Pepys *Diary* (1879) III. 175 His serviceablenesse in this late great action. **1684** *Life of John III of Poland* v. 116 In this great Action the most Memorable Victory that has been Atchieved in our Age, or indeed almost in any other. **1769** Robertson *Charles V*, v. iii. 330 They defeated the nobility in several actions. **1798** Nelson in Nicolas's *Dispatches* III. 95 During their march they had some actions with the Mamelukes. **1799** Wellington *Gen. Disp.* I. 22 More troops being sent to their aid, a general action took place. **1855** Macaulay *Hist. Eng.* III. 437 Between the army of Waldeck and the army of Humieres no general action took place.

b. ***action front!, action rear!***, military commands in artillery regiments to prepare for action against the enemy in front of, behind, the line of guns.

1860 *Man. Artill. Exerc.* I. 30 Unlimbering or coming into Action... At the word *Action front*, each number repairs to his post as in limbering up. **1875** *Man. Field Artill. Exerc.* VI. 205 Guns.. in heavy ground.. should be brought into action in the required direction by the word '*Action rear*'. **1892** Kipling *Barrack-r. Ballads* 37 But 'e swung 'is 'orses 'andsome when it came to 'Action Front!' **1902** *Field Artill. Training* v. 161 Guns.. may be brought into action.. by the command '*Action rear*', so as to save unnecessary labour and delay. *Ibid.* v. 167 On the command '*Action front*' the guns are brought into action.. and.. officers go to their places in action.

12. Histrionic personation; acting of plays, performance. ? *Obs.*

1626 Massinger *Rom. Actor* IV. ii, As thou didst live Rome's bravest actor, 'twas my plot that thou Shouldst die in action. **1710** Steele *Tatler* No. 3 ¶1 This Evening the Comedy.. was acted for the Benefit of Mrs. Bignall.. Through the whole Action, she made a very pretty Figure.

†**13.** A theatrical performance, a play. *Obs.*

1679 *Trials of White & Other Jesuits* 47 [Parry *loq.*] He was at an Action of ours, a Latine Play.

14. A devotional or religious performance or exercise; a solemn 'function.' ***Action Sermon*** (Scotch), a Sacramental or Communion discourse.

1825 E. Irving in Mrs. Oliphant's *Life* I. xi. 368, I returned home about seven, and addressed myself to write my action sermon. **1855** F. Procter *Bk. of Comm. Prayer* 353 The Lord's Prayer also begins the action of thanksgiving [*actio gratiarum*]. **1863** *Glasgow Her.* 15 Apr., An interval is now allowed in some congregations between the 'action sermon' and the sacramental service.

†**15.** A share in a joint-stock company (as if the amount of *action* or *operation* which one takes in it). (Fr.) *Obs.*

1641–1706 Evelyn *Diary* (1819) II. 40 African Actions fell to £30, and the India to £80. **1683** *Lond. Gaz.* mdcccxv. 4 The Actions of our East-India Company are very much fallen. **1715** Burnet *Hist. own Times* I. 573 The actions sinking on the sudden on the breaking out of a new war. **1750** Chambers *Cycl.* s.v., To melt or liquidate an Action, is to sell, or turn it into money. **1758** *Ann. Reg.* 235 An English lady being possessed of Actions shares in the Embden company. **1864** Burton *Scot Abroad* II. 264 The impetuosity with which the actions rose.

16. *Comb.* **action committee, group**, etc., one chosen to take active steps, esp. in local or national politics; **action current** *Biol.*, the electrical current produced in living tissue during activity; **action-noun**, a substantive expressing action; **action-packed** *a.*, full of action or excitement; **action painting** (orig. *U.S.*), the theory or practice of the action school in art; a form of abstract art in which the paint is placed in strokes or splashes on the canvas by the spontaneous or random action of the artist; hence ***action painter, school***, etc.; **action-photography**, photography representing the subject in action; hence ***action-photograph***; also ***action picture, shot*** (shot *sb.*[1]), etc.; **action point**, a specific proposal for action, arising from a meeting, discussion, conference, etc.; an issue on which it is agreed that some action should be taken; **action potential** *Biol.*, the difference in electrical potential between the excited and unexcited parts of a nerve or muscle; **action replay**, a playback (at normal speed or in slow motion) of a recorded incident in a sports match, esp. immediately after the action occurs; also *transf.*; cf. replay *sb.* 2; **action research** chiefly *Sociol.*, research which leads to the establishment and implementation by project researchers of methods designed to alleviate the (esp. social) problems under review; hence **action researcher**; **action song** (see quot. 1938); **action station** (action 10, 11), a position assigned to someone going into action; (*pl.*) the signal to proceed to such a position; **action-taking** *a.*, litigious; **action-time** *Psychol.*, the period between the application of a stimulus and (the resulting) reaction; reaction-time.

1949 *Britannica Bk. of Yr. 1949* 686/1 *Action committee, a Communist committee appointed to purge societies and organizations of all non-Communist elements, as a means of consolidating a communistic revolution. **1952** *Ann. Reg. 1951* 105 [In S. Africa] the 'Commando' started as a small body of ex-servicemen calling itself the War Veterans Action Committee. **1958** *Oxf. Mail* 30 Dec. 1/4 The programme also calls for a scientific action committee to organise research. **1883** J. B. Sanderson in *Phil. Trans. R. Soc. 1882* CLXXIII. 55 Of the nature of this preliminary disturbance (to which alone the term excitatory variation ought to be applied, it alone being the analogue of the '*action current' of animal physiology) we know nothing. **1914** *Amer. Jrnl. Physiol.* XXXIV. 425 The action-current is the only known change accompanying excitation in nerve which is competent to stimulate an adjoining nerve. **1955** *Ann. Reg. 1954* 121 Dr. Awolowo's party [in Nigeria], the *Action Group, lost ground except in the territory of the Yorubas. **1958** *Observer* 21 Dec. 2/5 Pacifist Youth Action Group. **1879** Whitney *Sanskrit Gram.* 374 There is hardly a suffix by which *action-nouns are formed which does not also make agent-nouns or adjectives. **1953** K. Reisz *Technique Film Editing* ii. 76 The final chase was best presented as a 'battle of wits', instead of a wild *action-packed shooting-match. **1983** *Listener* 10 Feb. 40/1 (Advt.), An action-packed novel by John Brasow linked with the BBC 1 serial. **1952** H. Rosenberg in *Art News* 22 (*title*) The American *action painters. *Ibid.* 49/1 Action painting is painting in the medium of difficulties. **1958** *Times* 24 June 6/4 As an Action painter his contemplation results in an eruption of black and scarlet blunt-edged squares. **1958** D. Lewis *Alan Davie* [Exhib. catal.] 1 The action painter does not begin a canvas with a preconceived idea. *Ibid.*, Other terms given to it have been 'tachism', 'abstract expressionism', etc., but *action painting is the best of these terms because it does not characterise the end-result.. so much as the process. **1904** G. W. Beldam *Great Golfers* (title-p.), Illustrated by 268 *action-photographs. **1905** Beldam & Fry *Great Batsmen* p. xi, The book is founded upon *Action-Photography and Actual Experience. **1915** N. V. Lindsay *Art of Moving Picture* ii. 9 Many *Action Pictures are indoors. **1925** *Kodak Mag.* Dec. 203 With a 'Graflex' camera fitted with a focal plane shutter it is possible to take all sorts of action pictures at a Rugby match. **1982** *Industry Week* 22 Feb. 52 His predecessor.. relied on a decentralized style of management that delegated responsibility to the 'lowest possible level where *action points resided'. **1984** *Washington Post* 23 Apr. (Business Suppl.) 30/2 What the District gets in Coopers & Lybrand's compilation of 'Action Points' is a rehash of most every form of welfare for the rich ever proposed in the name of 'economic development'. **1986** *Financial Times* 18 June 9/5 The action points agreed at a previous seminar in January fall into four broad areas: auto-crime, residential burglary, violent crime and crime at the workplace. **1926** *Amer. Jrnl. Physiol.* LXXVIII. 635 When the nerve at the anode is depressed sufficiently to reduce the amplitude at the anode to about normal, the supernormal effect beyond, toward the cathode, seems to be due to recovery of the *action potential from the depression, to the usual anodal maximum. **1939** W. B. Yapp *Introd. Animal Physiol.* 187 The action potential and the conduction rate both vary approximately as the area of cross-section of the fibre. **1973** *Listener* 22 Nov. 720 To see only the *action replays of the Royal Wedding, that long-drawn-out Match of the Day, was no doubt to miss the cumulative effect of an occasion. **1977** J. Laker *One-Day Cricket* 115 The action replay can be of great help.. in showing the reason for a batsman's dismissal. **1961** *Economist* 25 Feb. 741/1 A preliminary report on their project of '*action-research' has now been prepared. **1964** *Listener* 2 Apr. 563/2 The invasion of a big city by a team of action researchers is something of an enterprise. **1975** *Language for Life* (Dept. Educ. & Sci.) xxvi. 552 Educational research in this country takes three main forms: survey, fundamental analytical research, and action-research. **1957** *Observer* 22 Sept. 13/6 The exhibition of these cunning daubs [by chimpanzees], in a gallery which has hitherto striven to remove misgivings about the '*action' or *tachiste* school, is scarcely calculated to win fresh converts. **1936** *Amat. Photographer* 1 July 23/2 With quick-*action shots, such as the high dive, care will be necessary in correctly 'panning' the camera to cover the swift movement. **1958** *Listener* 23 Oct. 662/3 The action-shots in this absorbing film seemed to me as remarkable as Disney's 'Living Desert'. **1908** M. Steele (*title*) Children's *Action Songs. **1938** *Oxf. Compan. Music* 15/1 The English Action Song, a children's song with some measure of dramatic movement on the part of the singers. **1947** 'A. P. Gaskell' *Big Game* 95 The [Maori] girls.. sang an action song... The small girls moved stiffly, but the bigger ones were relaxed, their hands fluttered delicately, moving easily and clapping exactly in time. **1914** B. Ramsay *Diary* 25 Aug. in W. S. Chalmers *Full Cycle* (1959) 20 On being asked why he was not at his *action station, the marine replied.. that he was 'duty servant'. **1916** *Times* 12 June 4/3 At 3.45 on May 31 action stations were sounded off by the buglers. **1917** 'Taffrail' *Sub* xi. 256 Long before daylight the next morning our men.. had mustered at their action stations. **1923** *Man. Seamanship (H.M.S.O.)* II. 46 The custom is—Mondays—Fleet, squadron or ship drill.. Fridays—Action stations. **1943** C. S. Forester *Ship* 7 When H.M.S. *Artemis* was at action stations the wardroom ceased to be the officers' mess. **1605** Shaks. *Lear* II. ii. 18, A lily-liver'd *action-taking knave. **1906** *Academy* 21 July 60/1 Investigations.. into the *action-time of stimulus upon visual sensation.

action (ˈækʃən), *v.* [f. the sb. Cf. Fr. *actionner*.]

1. To institute a legal action against.

1733 Fielding *Don Quix.* Wks. 1861, 999, I don't question but to action him out on't. **1881** *Echo* 1 July 2/4 To prove his innocence, he took the only course open to him—actioned his enemy for libel.

2. To take action on (a request, etc.), to process; to put into effect. Used *esp.* in business jargon.

1962 L. Deighton *Ipcress File* xxxii. 209 The E.M.P... promised to action it for me if I let his A.D.C. have details in writing. **1981** *Daily Tel.* 22 Jan. 2/7 Dismissal will be actioned when the balance of probabilities suggests that an employee has committed a criminal act or another of gross misconduct. **1985** *Rescue News* Summer 8/1 Concern has been expressed at the manner in which the whole operation has been put together and actioned.

actionability (ˌækʃənəˈbɪlɪtɪ). [f. actionable *a.*: see -bility.] Liability to action at law.

1883 Moyle *Institut. Justinian* I. 46 Actionability is only one of such usual incidents.

actionable (ˈækʃənəb(ə)l), *a.* [f. action *sb.* 8 + -able.] Subject or liable to an action at law; of such a character that an action on account of it will lie.

1591 Lambarde *Archeion* (1635) 90 Baited, and bitten with libells and slanders that be not actionable. **1691** Shadwell *Scowrers* II. Wks. IV. 331 Have a care what you say, Sir, your words will be actionable. **1768** Blackstone *Comm.* III. 217 This.. is no injury to the sufferer, and is therefore not an actionable nusance. **1778** Miss Burney *Evelina* ix. (1784) II. 71 Everybody agreed that the illusage the Captain had given her was actionable. **1848** Arnould *Mar. Insur.* I. iv. (1866) I. 160 Guilty of actionable negligence.

actionably ('ækʃənəblı), *adv.* [f. prec. + -LY².] 'In a manner subject to a process of law.' Todd.

actional ('ækʃənəl), *a.* [f. ACTION *sb.* + -AL¹. Cf. *rational, fractional,* etc.] Of or pertaining to action or actions.

1731 In BAILEY. **1870** J. GROTE *Exam. Util. Philos.* xviii. 307 The actional principle of conservatism. **1935** G. O. CURME *Gram. Eng. Lang.* II. 218 The common actional form is employed also as a statal passive... 'The door *was shut* (state) at six, but I don't know when it *was shut* (act)'. **1958** PRIEBSCH & COLLINSON *Germ. Lang.* (ed. 4) I. iii. 106 A dative singular in *-anne* (with doubling caused by *j* on the analogy of neuter actional *ja*-stems like *gikōsi* 'chatter').

†'**actionary.** *Obs.* [f. ACTION *sb.* 15 + -ARY, after Fr. *actionnaire*; cf. *missionary.*] A shareholder in a joint-stock company.

1731 BAILEY [see ACTIONIST 1]. **1751** CHAMBERS *Cycl.*, *Actionary* or *Actionist*, a term frequent in foreign newspapers; denoting the proprietor of an action or share in a company's stock. **1755** JOHNSON, *Actionary*, one that has a share in actions or stocks.

actioned ('ækʃənd), *ppl. a.* [f. ACTION *sb.* 6b.] Having an action of a specified kind. Usu. preceded by a defining word.

1837 *Times* 20 June 1 (Advt.), Twenty remarkably fine, powerful, young, fresh, good-actioned, short-legged Horses, in beautiful condition. **1875** [see BAR *sb.*¹ 29a]. **1928** *Daily Tel.* 30 Oct. 17/7 Quick-actioned, weight-shifting Shires, Clydesdales, Suffolks, or Percheron horses. **1949** E. JENKINS *Six Criminal Women* 186 She drove herself in a phaeton with two 'handsome actioned' cobs.

actioner ('ækʃənə(r)). [f. ACTION *sb.* 6 + -ER¹.] An artisan who makes the action of an instrument, as of a gun, piano, etc.

1881 *Daily Tel.* 12 Dec. Advt., To Gunmakers only.—Wanted, a few good, steady hands. No actioners, lockmakers, barrelmakers, or military workmen need apply.

actionist ('ækʃənıst). [f. ACTION *sb.* + -IST.]

†1. = ACTIONARY; a shareholder. *Obs.*

1731 BAILEY, *Actionary* or *Actionist*, a Person who owns or is possessed of Actions, Shares, or Stock, in a Company. **1755** In JOHNSON.

2. One who professes, practises, or lays great stress on (oratorical) action.

1812 *Religionism* 32, *Actionists* (title), Some taught by thee, Demosthenes, are bent, On action, action, action, ne'er content With emphasis of utterance (fault absurd!) Unless pronounced, and acted too, each word.

actionize ('ækʃənaız), *v. rare.* [f. ACTION *sb.* 8 + -IZE. Cf. Fr. *actionner.*] To bring a legal action against.

1872 COMP. READE *Take Care* 291 'My dear sir,' replied the lawyer, 'you have the power of actionising these people for conspiracy.'

actionless ('ækʃənlıs), *a.* [f. ACTION *sb.* + -LESS.] Void of action, inactive, inert.

c **1817** J. HOGG *Tales & Sk.* (1837) IV. 199 With regard to the natural affection of this animal [sheep], stupid and actionless as it is, the instances that might be mentioned are without number.

†'**actious,** *a. Obs.* [ad. L. *actiōsus* officious, turbulent; f. *actiōn-em* ACTION *sb.*: see -OUS.] Abounding in, or giving rise to action, active, energetic.

1592 WARNER *Albion's Eng.* VIII. xliii. (1612) 207 The fourth and fifth of Henries were as actious as the rest. **1607** DEKKER *Hist. Wyatt* 114 He knowes you to be eager men, martiall men..verie actious for valour. **1613** *Uncasing of Machiavel's Instr.* 22 Be rich, I say; nay, boy, be rich and wise! Gold is an actious mettle for the eyes.

†**acti'tation.** *Obs.*—⁰ [n. of action f. L. *actitā-re* to act much, freq. of *ag-ĕre* to act.] 'Debating of lawsuits.' Bailey 1742. 'Action quick and frequent.' J.

'**activate,** *v.* [f. ACTIVE *a.* + -ATE³. Cf. *captivate*, and mod.Fr. *activer.*] **a.** To make active, move to activity. Cf. ACTUATE. Hence '**activated** *ppl. a.*, '**activating** *ppl. a.* and *vbl. sb.*

1626 BACON *Sylva* §83 For as Snow and Ice especially, being holpen and their cold Activated by nitre or salt, will turn water into Ice and that in a few hours. **1642** BP. MONTAGU *Acts & Mon.* 190, I cannot see that he would consent with Ambrose, that they [the Sibyls] were activated by the Deuill. **1673** O. WALKER *Education* (1677) 124 This warms and activates the spirit in the search of truth. **1858** BENNET *Nutrition* ii. 42 Increased muscular vigour.. activates respiration. **1905** *Sat. Westm. Gaz.* 15 July 13 The young English dramatist has very few opportunities of making the hair of the Philistine stand on end or activating his digestion. **1926** J. A. THOMSON *Man in Light of Evol.* 10 The rarely activated muscles of our ear-trumpet. **1926** *Public Opinion* 22 Oct. 408/3 The planet and its activating sun. **1940** H. G. WELLS *Babes in Darkling Wood* II. iii. 195 She wanted 'activating'. She had recently acquired that word. **1961** *Essays & Stud.* XIV. 76 The motives of self-appointed moralists... Are they activated by concern for public morality? **1962** *Amer. Speech* XXXVII. 271 A flat plate set in the pavement to detect traffic in order to activate traffic lights.

b. *spec.*: (*a*) *Chem.*, to render active, reactive, excited (of carbon, molecules, etc.); ***activated carbon***, carbon, esp. charcoal, which has been treated to increase its adsorptive power; (*b*) *Physics*, to make radioactive; (*c*) to aerate (sewage) as a means of purification; ***activated sludge***, aerated sewage containing aerobic bacteria.

1902 *Jrnl. Soc. Chem. Industry* XXI. 1102/2 Schönbein.. found that sulphurous acid had a remarkable 'activating' (*activirende*) effect on various oxidising substances, *i.e.*, they were considerably more active in the presence of small quantities of sulphurous acid. **1903** *Electr. World & Engineer* 10 Jan. 86 (C.D. Suppl.), Underground air is not like activated air. **1903** *Sci. Amer.* Suppl. 18 Apr. 22815/1 In these measurements it is necessary to maintain the body to be 'activated' for several hours at a negative potential of several thousand volts. **1907** *Med. Record* 3 Aug. 171 The former [ferment, viz. enterokinase] activates the pancreatic juice. **1919** *Jrnl. Industr. & Engin. Chem.* XI. 282 The development of activated charcoal as a canister filler was largely the work of two Cleveland organizations. **1921** *Glasgow Herald* 13 Aug. 5 The new process of producing activated sludge by which complete purification of the sewage is achieved. **1921** *Jrnl. Soc. Chem. Industry* XL. (Trans.) 230/2 (*title*) Activated Carbon. **1934** *Jrnl. Inst. Sanit. Engin.* Sept. 252 The sewage is settled, treated by the activated sludge process, by sand filters and by chlorination. **1937** A. M. PRENTISS *Chemicals in War* xix. 549 The filter [in a gas-mask canister] consists of an oval-shaped perforated sheet-metal container filled with a mixture of 80 per cent activated charcoal and 20 per cent soda lime. **1938** R. W. LAWSON tr. *Hevesy & Paneth's Man. Radioactivity* (ed. 2) xi. 133 We find that the wire now shows no initial α-activity after its removal from the activating vessel. *Ibid.* x. 119 Most of the elements situated between boron and calcium have been activated under the influence of α-rays. **1956** A. H. COMPTON *Atomic Quest* 71 Pulling the last activated slugs from the Hanford piles.

Hence **activation** (æktı'veıʃən), the action of activating; the state of being activated; in specific uses corresp. to those of the vb.; ***activation analysis*** = RADIOACTIVATION *analysis.*

1906 *Practitioner* Dec. 747 Mixed sera from several animals might be used, in the hope of finding one suitable for activation with human serum. **1919** *Science* L. 568/1 (*title*) Charcoal activation. **1927** HALDANE & HUXLEY *Animal Biol.* ii. 54 Activation, or the starting-off of the egg on development. **1930** *Engineering* 21 Feb. 257/3 At least one of the molecules concerned must be 'activated' and this 'activation' may well be due to the absorption of radiation. **1931** J. W. MCBAIN *Sorption of Gases by Solids* iv. 59 Methods of activation always involve heating to more or less elevated temperatures which may range from 350° C to 1,150° C. **1940** *Ann. Reg. 1939* 371 Gene mutations were generally regarded as due to individual atomic activations. **1949** *Atomics* Nov. 106/2 Tracers are only rarely radioactive. To overcome this difficulty, the sample may be irradiated either with high energy charged particles or thermal neutrons... This method is known as activation analysis. **1960** *Nature* CLXXXV. 196 Neutron activation analysis of ancient Roman potsherds.

Also '**activator,** one who (*rare*) or a thing which activates (in various technical senses); a catalyst.

1911 R. C. PUNNETT *Mendelism* (ed. 3) 45 A ferment which behaves as an activator of the chromogen. **1913** DORLAND *Med. Dict.* (ed. 7) 36/1 *Activator*, a substance which renders some other substance active: especially an inorganic substance which combines with an inactive enzyme to render it capable of effecting its proper reaction. **1948** *Electronic Engin.* XX. 225 The inclusion of activators such as zinc, copper, antimony..in calcium oxide caused speedy and violent ion-burning. **1958** *Spectator* 4 July 9/3 They chose Maurice Buckmaster, who later became famous as an activator of the French Resistance. **1962** *Lancet* 27 Jan. 192/1 The defect in fibrinolytic activity is associated with 'unavailability' rather than with an absolute deficiency of tissue activator. **1963** B. FOZARD *Instrumentation Nucl. Reactors* vi. 63 In scintillation phosphors these impurities are known as activators.

active ('æktıv), *a.* and *sb.* Also 4–5 **actif.** [prob. a. Fr. *actif*, fem. *active*, ad. L. *actīv-us.* But it may be a direct adoption of the L., in the theological phrase *vita actīva*, which is the earliest application of the word in Fr. and Eng. alike.] *gen.* Characterized by action. Hence

A. *adj.* **1. a.** Opposed to *contemplative* or *speculative*: Given to outward action rather than inward contemplation or speculation; practical; *esp.* with 'life.' (Also formerly *absol.* in *pl.* sc. virtues, faculties.)

1340 *Ayenb.* 199 Holy writ ous tekþ tuo maneres of liue ..þe verste is yhote workvol [active] vor þet hi is ine zuynch of guode workes. **1340** HAMPOLE *Prose Tr.* 24 Vnto thes men itt longith som tyme to vsene werkis of mercy in actife liffe. **1362** LANGL. *P. Pl.* A VII. 236 Actyf lyf or contemplatyf · Crist wolde hit alse. *c* **1400** *Apol. for Loll.* 23 Also þei tokun actifis & contemplatifis; þat sterun to vertewe be þer two maneris. **1401** *Pol. Poems* II. 63 There is maad mencion of two perfit lyves, that actif and contemplatif comounli ben callid, ffulli figurid by Marie and Martha hir sister. **1538** STARKEY *England* 4 But wether hyt [i.e. perfection] stond in the actyve lyfe.. or els in the contemplative..hyt ys not al sure. **1604** SHAKS. *Oth.* I. iii. 271 My speculative and active [1623 offic'd] instruments. **1609** TOURNEUR *Fun. Poeme* 355 All his industries (As well in actives as contemplatives). **1660** T. STANLEY *Hist. Philos.* (1701) 161/1 Philosophy concerns either action or contemplation (thence assuming two names, Contemplative and Active) the Active consisting in practice of moral Actions, the Contemplative, in penetration of abstruse Phisical causes, and the nature of the Divinity. **1828** D. STEWART *Wks.* VI. 122 As the operations in the minds of other men escape our notice we can judge of their activity only from the sensible effects it produces; thence we are led to apply the character of activity to those whose bodily activity is the most remarkable, and to distinguish mankind into two classes, the Active and the Speculative.

†**b.** Practical, as opposed to *theoretical. Obs.*

1609 DOULAND *Orinthop. Microl.* 2 Active Musicke, which also they call Practick, is..the knowledge of singing well.

2. Opposed to *passive*: Originating or communicating action, exerting action upon others; acting of its own accord, spontaneous. In 17th c. often *absol.* in *pl.* sc. qualities, forces.

c **1400** *Apol. for Loll.* 14 God may not autorise þat actyfe cursyng..But passyue cursyng..is just. **1413** LYDGATE *Pylg. Sowle* II. lx. (1859) 57 Quod the body..thou were in me actyf as fire is in the wood, and I in to the passyf as woode is in the fyre. **1477** NORTON *Ordin. Alch.* v. (Ashmole 1652) 54 Heate, and Cold, be qualities Active, Moisture, and Drines, be qualityes Passive. **1592** W. WEST *Symbolæogr.* I. 48 G. The actiue person in Instrumentes is he which maketh the Instruments. **1677** HALE *Prim. Orig. Man.* IV. v. 332 If it should be in the power of an Angel by applying actives to passives to produce an Insect. **1736** BUTLER *Analogy* I. v. 117 Perception of danger is a natural Excitement of passive fear and active caution. **1846** MILL *Logic* III. iii. §9 (1868) 292 Objects which they first believed to be intelligent and active are really lifeless and passive. **1876** FREEMAN *Norm. Conq.* II. x. 492 The treasons of Eadwine were often passive rather than active.

3. *Grammar.* **a.** *properly*, An epithet of Voice in verbs used transitively; opposed to *Passive* (and, in some languages, to *Reflexive* or *Middle*). That form of the verb in which the action asserted by it is viewed as a characteristic or attribute of the thing whence it issues, as opposed to the *Passive* Voice in which the action is viewed as an attribute of the thing towards which it is directed; or, that form of the verb in which the logical subject of the action is made by the speaker the grammatical subject of his assertion, as shown by the verb's agreement with it in inflections, by position, or otherwise. This being (in Aryan Languages) the simple or original form, verbs used intransitively naturally have no other, and are said to have the Active Voice only.

b. *Less correctly*, said of verbs themselves; in two senses. 1. Applied to verbs which assert that the subject *acts upon* or affects something else, as distinguished from *Passive* Verbs, or such as assert of the subject that it is acted on by something or *suffers* the action, and *Neuter* Verbs which assert an action or state that has neither character. 2. Applied to all verbs that assert *action* as distinct from mere *existence* or *state*; in this sense Active Verbs are divided into *Active Transitive*, in which the action passes over to or affects an object, as *kill* (corresponding to the *Active* of 1), and *Active Intransitive*, in which the action does not affect an object, as *rise* (forming part of the *Neuter* verbs of 1), *Neuter* in this nomenclature being restricted to verbs of existence or state, as *be, sit.*

Both of these uses of the word are etymologically defensible, but both are inconvenient: the distinction between *action* and *state* is not always clear, and above all is one of *things*, not of *assertions* about them; that of *action* and *passion* is merely that of two ways of viewing and asserting the *same* action; while the passing over of an action to an object or the contrary is better expressed by *Transitive* and *Intransitive*, and is moreover not a division of verbs, but of the constructions of each verb separately, the great majority of verbs in Eng. having both constructions.

1530 PALSGR. 4 The thyrde parsonnes plurelles of verbes actyves in the frenche tonge..ende in *ent.* **1591** PERCIVALL *Span. Dict.* C b, Of Uerbs personals there be three kinds, Actiue, Passiue and Neuter. **1765** W. WARD *Ess. Gram.* 59, A verb in the active voice very frequently denotes a state which implies no real action, as for instance *to suffer*; and so, a verb in the passive voice frequently denotes a state which implies no real suffering, as *to be found.* **1876** MASON *Eng. Gram.* 59 We may speak of one and the same action by means either of a verb in the active voice, or of a verb in the passive voice.

4. a. Opposed to *quiescent* or *extinct*: Existing in action, working, effective, having practical operation or results. ***active list*** (see LIST *sb.*⁶); also *transf.*; ***active service***, war service in the field, at sea, or in the air.

1640–4 CAPT. MERVIN in Rushworth's *Hist. Coll.* III. (1692) I. 214 The Gray-headed Common Laws Funeral; and the Active Statutes death and Obsequies. **1790** BOSWELL *Johnson* xxiv. (Rtldg.) 215 Here was one of the many, many instances of his active benevolence. **1790** BURKE *Fr. Rev.* 39 The whole government would be under the constant inspection and active controul of the popular representative and of the magnates of the kingdom. **1829** [see SERVICE *sb.*¹ 12]. **1830** LYELL *Princ. Geol.* I. 317 Kamtschatka, where there are seven active volcanos. **1838** *Navy List* 20 Sept. 118 Alphabetical List of Masters. Those in Italics are unfit for active Service. **1852** *Ibid.* 20 Dec. 327 The number of Captains on the Active List will be reduced to a number not permanently exceeding 350. **1857** LIVINGSTONE *Travels* vi. 113 It contains an active poison. **1876** FREEMAN *Norm. Conq.* II. vii. 102 Weary of tarrying where there was no chance of active service. **1878** HUXLEY *Physiogr.* 79 It is the oxygen which is the active agent. **1899** KIPLING *Absent-Minded Beggar* i, He is out on active service, wiping something off a slate. **1906** *Harmsworth Encycl.* VII. 576/2 No officer on the active list is allowed to leave the United Kingdom without special permission. **1907** *Jrnl. Soc. Arts* LV. 429/1 Of these only the Remington and the Hammond are to-day on the active list.

b. *spec.* in *Physics*, = RADIOACTIVE *a.*

1900 RUTHERFORD in *Phil. Mag.* XLIX. 163 The top layer of paper over the thorium was found to be active on its upper side. **1905** [see *active deposit*]. **1938** R. W. LAWSON tr. *Hevesy & Paneth's Man. Radioactivity* (ed. 2) x. 120 Active isotopes that are lighter than the stable types disintegrate with emission of positrons.

5. Opposed to *sluggish* or *inert*: Abounding in action; energetic, lively, agile, nimble; diligent, busy, brisk. (Of persons and things.)

1597 SHAKS. *2 Hen. IV*, IV. iii. 24, I were simply the most actiue fellow in Europe. **1609** *Man in the Moone* (1849) 31 It maketh her unfitte to performe any agill or active thing. **1666** PEPYS *Diary* (1879) III. 485 He being the activest man in the World. **1718** POPE *Iliad* XV. 683 So strong to fight, so active to pursue. **1786** COWPER *Lett.* 31 Jan. Wks. 1876 224 Infirmities.. which make him less active than he was. **1857** BUCKLE *Civil.* iii. 142 Now, the richest Countries are those in which man is most active. **1863** FAWCETT *Pol. Econ.* III. vi. 371 An active demand for any other commodity is characterised by a rise in its price or value. **1866** ROGERS *Agric. & Prices* I. xxiii. 599 The most active seat of the trade. **1880** *Manch. Guard.* 16 Dec., The market to-day has been more active than for a considerable time.

6. On the credit side of the balance-sheet, of the nature of an asset; as opposed to *passive*, i.e. of the nature of a liability. (Common in Fr., but hardly English.)

1875 POSTE *Gaius* III. 350 Selling the active and passive universality of the insolvent's estate.. to a purchaser who became liable to the insolvent's creditors.

7. Used as the first element in such obv. *Comb.* as ***active-bodied***, ***active-limbed***, ***active-minded***.

1870 BRYANT *Homer* I. v. 152 There the active-limbed, Fleet Iris stayed them. **1837** WHEWELL *Induct. Sc.* (1857) I. 121 The pleasure which.. active-minded men feel in exercising the process of deduction. **1878** SEELEY *Stein* III. 547 The more active-minded among his contemporaries.

8. *Comb.* **active carbon, charcoal** = activated carbon, charcoal (see ACTIVATE *v.* b); **active current** *Electr.* (see quot. 1926); **active deposit** *Physics* (see quot. 1955); **active layer** *Geomorphol.*, a surface layer of soil, overlying permafrost, that freezes in winter and thaws in summer; **active mass** *Chem.*, the molecular concentration of a substance (see *mass-action* (*b*) s.v. MASS *sb.*[2]).

1918 *Jrnl. Industr. & Engin. Chem.* X. 813/2 If our object is to make an active carbon, none of the mineral matter must be removed before heating. **1921** *Jrnl. Soc. Chem. Industry* XL. (Trans.) 231/1 All the secret process active carbons come upon the market in the form of a fine powder. **1938** *Thorpe's Dict. Appl. Chem.* II. 319/2 Active charcoal is widely used in industry for the recovery of valuable products which exist as attenuated vapours in unadsorbable gases. **1924** S. R. ROGET *Dict. Electr. Terms* 2 Active current. **1926** *Gloss. Terms Electr. Engin.* (*B.S.I.*) 30 *Active current*, that component of an alternating current (regarded as a vector quantity) which is in phase with the voltage. **1905** RUTHERFORD in *Phil. Trans. R. Soc. 1904* A. CCIV. 172 In speaking generally of the active matter, which causes excited activity, without regard to its constituents, I have used the term 'active deposit'. **1906** —— *Radioactive Transformations* iv. 95 All bodies surrounded by the radium emanation become coated with an invisible active deposit, possessing physical and chemical properties which sharply distinguish it from the emanation. **1955** *Gloss. Terms Radiology* (*B.S.I.*) 6 *Active deposit*, solid radioactive deposit formed by the decay of a radioactive emanation. **1943** S. W. MULLER *Permafrost* 5 Above the permafrost is a layer of ground that thaws in the summer and freezes again in the winter. This layer represents the seasonally frozen ground and is called the active layer. **1977** A. HALLAM *Planet Earth* 89 The churning of the active layer by freezing and thawing prevents the development of a stable soil structure. **1909** *Cent. Dict.* Suppl., Active mass. **1910** *Encycl. Brit.* VII. 27/1 These spatial concentrations are often called the 'active masses' of the reacting components. **1932** PHILBRICK & HOLMYARD *Text Bk. Theoret. & Inorg. Chem.* II. iii. 110 This law was first enunciated in 1864 [in *Forhandl. i Vidensk.-Selsk. i Christiania*, p. 92] by Guldberg and Waage, who stated that *the rate at which a substance reacted was proportional to its active mass.*

B. *sb.* **1.** A person devoted to the active life. (Cf. *adj.* I and CONTEMPLATIVE *sb.* I.)

c **1380** [see CONTEMPLATIVE B. *sb.* 1]. *a* **1425** *Cloud of Unknowing* (1944) 5/18 Into þis day alle actyues pleynen hem of contemplatyues, as Martha did on Mary. **1671** PHILLIPS *New World of Words*, *Actifs*, an order of Fryars, that feed on Roots, and wear tawny habits. **1946** E. A. PEERS *Fool of Love* vii. 118 It is as an active that Ramon [Lull] appeals to the present age most widely. **1950** A. HUXLEY *Themes & Variations* 154 Were there not then, as always, a few ardent contemplatives and actives?

2. [Elliptical uses of the adj.] **a.** See ACTIVE *a.* 1, 2.

b. *Gram.* The active voice; an active verb. Cf. PASSIVE *sb.* 2.

1530 PALSGR. Introd., The actyves have but the pronowne or substantyve before the verbe. **1582** G. MARTIN *Discoverie Manifold Corruptions* i. 13 If passives must be turned into actives, and actives into passives, participles disagree in case from their substantives..: who would so presume in the text of holy Scripture, to haue al grammar.. at his commaundement, but Beza & his lik? **1611** BRINSLEY *Pos. Parts.* (1669) 29 Cannot a Verb Neuter take *r*, to make it a Passive, as Actives do? *c* **1620** A. HUME *Orthogr. Brit. Tongue* (1865) 32 Verbes of doing are actives or passives. The active verb adheres to the person of the agent; as, Christ hath conquered hel and death. **1669** MILTON *Accedence* 20 The Active Signifieth to *do*, and always endeth in *o*, as *Doceo*, I teach. **1818** E. V. BLOMFIELD tr. *Matthiæ's Gr. Gram.* II. 710 The effect of the active consists in determining the case which it governs. **1879** W. W. GOODWIN *Elem. Greek Gram.* (new ed.) 110 The uncontracted forms of the future active and middle of φαίνω.. are found in Homer and Herodotus. **1933** O. JESPERSEN *Essent. Eng. Gram.* xii. 121 The subject of a passive verb is what in the active would be an object. But if in the active there are two objects, only one of them can be made the subject. **1973** N. S. SMITH tr. *Ruwet's Introd. Generative Gram.* vi. 114 This solution.. still does not allow the formal indication of the relation between the passive (3) and the active (4). **1985** R. QUIRK et al. *Comprehensive Gram. Eng. Lang.* 163 In English, prepositional verbs.. can often occur in the passive, but not so freely in the active.

activeable, perhaps = 'excitable,' f. stem of *activ-ate* (cf. *separate*, *separable*): but probably to be read as two words *active able*.

In Hazlitt's *Dodsley* spelt *activable*.

1602 *Return fr. Parn.* IV. 5 (Arb.) 62 To thinke so many actiueable wits, That might contend with proudest birds of Po, Sits now immur'd within their priuate cells.

actively ('æktɪvlɪ), *adv.* [f. ACTIVE *a.* + -LY[2].] In an active manner; hence

†**1.** In action, as opposed to contemplation; practically, in practical life. *Obs.*

c **1400** *Apol. for Loll.* 22 Neþeles it is not to deme þat ne it is leful to curse accessorily; for þat tendiþ but to men lifing actifly.

2. In originating action; by one's own action; voluntarily, spontaneously. (Opposed to *passively*.)

1590 H. SWINBURN *Testaments* 203 He that is condemned for a famous libell is intestable, both actiuely and passiuely: that is to say, he can neither make a testament, nor receiue anie benefite by a testament. **1649** BP. HALL *Cases of Consc.* (1654) 38 Is the fraud actively yours, done by you to another? **1849** MACAULAY *Hist. Eng.* II. 635 The king was at least passive. He could not actively counterwork the regent. **1858** MOTLEY *Dutch Repub.* Introd. v. 19 His son Poppo.. did not actively oppose the introduction of Christianity.

3. *Grammar.* In the manner or with the construction of an active verb; **a.** in a manner asserting action; **b.** transitively.

1612 BRINSLEY *Pos. Parts* (1669) 30 Deponents.. signifying Actively, that is, when they are construed like Actives.. Active Verbs or Verbs signifying Actively govern the Accusative. *Ibid.* 37 Rehearse them Actively and Passively together. **1661** *Grand Debate* 88, *Nulla salus in nobis* is spoken actively and not possessively or passively.

4. With effective or vigorous action; energetically, busily; briskly, nimbly.

1602 SHAKS. *Haml.* III. iv. 87 Since Frost itselfe as actiuely doth burne, And Reason panders Will. **1605** STOW *Ann.* 1429, 9 Trumpets and a kettle drome did very actiuely sound the Danish march. **1646** SIR T. BROWNE *Pseud. Ep.* 189 Some most actively use the contrary arme and leg. **1816** SCOTT *Old Mort.* 217 Actively engaged in his military duties. **1869** PHILLIPS *Vesuv.* iii. 79 Within the crater was found a round and small actively eruptive cone.

activeness ('æktɪvnɪs). [f. ACTIVE *a.* + -NESS.] The quality of being active; agility, nimbleness, energy, diligence; = ACTIVITY 2.

1601 R. CHESTER *Love's Martyr* lxvi. (1878) 96 Because in activenesse she much excelled. **1612** WARNER *Albion's England* I. iv. 12 Yea yet a Lad, for Actiuenes The world did lack his like. **1754** EDWARDS *Freed. Will.* IV. §3, 203 Action, when set properly in Opposition to Passive or Passivenesse is.. a meer Relation; 'tis the Activeness of something on another thing. **1878** *N. Amer. Rev.* CXXVI. 307 Activeness in religious practices, and soundness in ethical teachings.

activism ('æktɪvɪz(ə)m). [f. ACTIVE *a.* + -ISM.]

1. A philosophical theory which assumes the objective reality and active existence of everything.

1907 W. R. B. GIBSON *Eucken's Philos. of Life* (ed. 2) App. 170 Activism has affinities with Pragmatism, especially on its negative side. **1920** H. L. ENO *Activism* x. 176 Activism is.. essentially realistic. It assumes the 'objective' validity and 'real' being of entities and relations, as well as the fundamental relational complexes of space, time, number, and change.

2. A doctrine or policy of advocating energetic action.

1920 *Glasgow Herald* 12 Aug. 7 It is a question of repelling the fateful activism of the Entente just as it was necessary in 1916 to stand against German activism. **1933** V. A. DEMANT *God, Man & Society* iii. 93 The major conflict in modern society between technique to save effort, and the moral philosophy of economic 'activism' which is embodied in economic theory and practice. **1960** *Spectator* 19 Aug. 272 The sizzling flame of activism is visible in both the agricultural and pastoral districts.

Hence **activist** ('æktɪvɪst), an advocate of activism in either sense; also *attrib.* (passing into *a.*) = **acti'vistic** *a.*

1907 W. R. B. GIBSON *Eucken's Philos. of Life* (ed. 2) App. 170 Eucken deliberately adopts the activistic label as a distinctive philosophical badge. **1909** *Athenæum* 17 Apr. 469/3 Pragmatism.. is tainted with the characteristic activist fallacy of making process as active account for the structural form of process which it implies. **1913** E. UNDERHILL *Mystic Way* 31 The positive and activistic mysticism of the West. **1915** *Times* 7 Aug. 7/6 For some, neutrality simply means a passive aloofness. For others, neutrality should be active, and these are divided, in the current jargon, with active and passive 'activists'. **1949** *Theology* LII. 363 American Christianity has tended traditionally to express itself in an activist form. **1954** KOESTLER *Invisible Writing* 206 He was not a politician but a propagandist, not a 'theoretician' but an 'activist'.

activity (æk'tɪvɪtɪ). [a. Fr. *activité*, ad. med.L. *activitātem*, a word of the Scholastic Philosophy, = *vis agendi*, f. L. *actīvus*; see ACTIVE.]

1. a. The state of being active; the exertion of energy, action.

1549 COVERDALE *Erasm. Paraphr. 1 Cor.* 33 There is of al men but one god, of whome the power and actiuitie of al thinges.. haue theyr begynnynges. **1648** BP. REYNOLDS *Lord's Supper* xi, All manner of activity requiring a contact and immediateness between the agents and the subject. **1664** POWER *Exp. Philos.* Pref. 13 The supreme Being (who is Activity itself). **1665** *Phil. Trans.* I. 50 What is the Sphere of Activity of Cold? **1703** MOXON *Mech. Exerc.* 98 The Saw is designed to cut only in its Progress forwards; Man having in that Activity more strength. **1764** REID *Inq. Hum. Mind.* ii. §10, 115 No man would attribute great activity to the paper I write upon. **1782** PRIESTLEY *Matter & Spirit* I §16, 189 We have no experience of.. primary activity, in any respect. **1876** MOZLEY *Univ. Serm.* iii. 49 Activity is naturally at first sight our one test of faith. **1879** THOMSON & TAIT *Nat. Phil.* I. I. §263 If the Activity of an agent be measured by its amount and its velocity conjointly; and if, similarly, the Counter-activity of the resistance be measured by the velocities of its several parts and their several amounts conjointly, whether these arise from friction, cohesion, weight, or acceleration;—Activity and Counter-activity, in all combinations of machines, will be equal and opposite.

b. *spec.* in *Physics*, = RADIOACTIVITY; the disintegration rate of a radioactive substance.

1903 RUTHERFORD in *Phil. Mag.* V. 446 The excited activity from radium decays much faster than that produced from thorium. **1926** R. W. LAWSON tr. *Hevesy & Paneth's Man. Radioactivity* xxiv. 174 The α-activity of uranium in equilibrium with all its transformation products is 4·73 times as large as that of the uranium itself. **1958** W. K. MANSFIELD *Elem. Nucl. Physics* iii. 21 The disintegration rate.. is known as the *activity* of the sample... The unit of activity is the *curie*, which is the rate at which 1 g of radium decays.

c. The degree to which a substance, *spec.* an enzyme, exhibits its characteristic property.

1898 B. MOORE in E. A. Schäfer *Text-bk. Physiol.* I. 322 The activity of a diastatic enzyme can be most accurately estimated by determining the amount of sugar (maltose) formed under given conditions in a given time by a given volume of the solution, acting on a measured volume of a standard solution of starch mucilage. **1921** *Jrnl. Soc. Chem. Industry* (*Trans.*) XL. 230/2 In the first half of the nineteenth century.. French chemists had succeeded in increasing the activity of animal and vegetable chars. **1929** *Proc. R. Soc.* B. CIV. 218 The results.. clearly demonstrate the inhibitory effect of CO upon the oxidase activity of yeast cells. **1938** *Thorpe's Dict. Appl. Chem.* (ed. 4) II. 317/1 The outstanding property of active charcoals is their adsorptive activity towards vapours, gases, and dissolved substances... Activity is expressed in terms of adsorptive capacity which is measured for any given substance by the quantity absorbed under specified conditions. **1969** T. E. BARMAN *Enzyme Handbk.* I. 5 There are various ways of expressing the catalytic efficiency of an enzyme. Of these molecular activity (the number of molecules of substrate transformed per minute per molecule of enzyme) requires an accurate knowledge of the molecular weight of the enzyme and catalytic centre activity (the number of molecules of substrate transformed per minute per catalytic centre) an accurate knowledge of active site concentrations. The quantity specific activity, however, merely requires the weight of enzyme required to produce a certain activity. Thus, the specific activity of an enzyme is defined as units per mg of enzyme protein. One unit.. is that amount of enzyme which will catalyze the transformation of one micromole of substrate per minute under standard conditions. **1976** *Nature* 16 Sept. 251/1 The enzyme had a specific activity of about 17 μmol ATP hydrolysed per mg protein min^{-1} at 37° C.

d. *Physical Chem.* A thermodynamic quantity which is a measure of the effective concentration of a substance in a system which departs from ideal behaviour, being defined as an exponential function of chemical potential and reciprocal temperature.

1907 G. N. LEWIS in *Proc. Amer. Acad. Arts & Sci.* XLIII. 262 We shall find it desirable to introduce besides the fugacity.. another quantity which has the dimensions of concentration. This quantity we will call the activity. **1948** GLASSTONE *Textbk. Physical Chem.* (ed. 2) ix. 687 The simplest method for evaluating the activity of a solvent is by determination of vapour pressure. **1975** *Nature* 2 Oct. 398/1 Most microorganisms.. are often able to grow.. in the presence of environmental solutes sufficiently high to reduce the water activity to values as low as 0·86. **1978** P. W. ATKINS *Physical Chem.* 20 As the concentration increases positive cations tend to congregate in the vicinity of the negative anions, and vice versa... Instead of talking in terms of the concentration of ions it then becomes more significant to talk in terms of their effective concentration, or activity.

2. The state or quality of being abundantly active; brisk or vigorous action; energy, diligence, nimbleness, liveliness.

1530 PALSGR. 193 Activyte, quickenesse, *actiuite* (Fr.). **1535** COVERDALE *Gen.* xlvii. 6 Yf thou knowest that there be men of actiuyte amonge them, make them rulers of my catell. **1606** SHAKS. *Tr. & Cr.* III. ii. 60, If shee call your actiuity in question. *a* **1704** T. BROWN *Table Talk* Wks. 1730 I. 144 Laziness and want of activity. **1775** BURKE *Sp. Conc. Amer.* Wks. III. 46 Neither the perseverance of Holland, nor the activity of France. **1832** SCOTT *Woodst.* 183 The latter stepped back with activity. **1854** ALISON *Hist. Eur.* IV. xxvii. 255 The sieges of these places.. were now pressed with activity. **1869** PHILLIPS *Vesuv.* iii. 51 The volcano continued to manifest activity till November. **1882** *Daily News* 5 Mar., There is not quite so much activity in the iron market.

†**3.** Physical exercise, gymnastics, athletics. Also *attrib.* *Obs.*

1552 HULOET *Abcedarium*, Master whyche teacheth actiuitie, *Gymnastes*. *c* **1595** J. NORDEN *Spec. Brit.*, *Cornwall*

(1728) 29 Especially Wrastling and Hurling, sharpe and seuere actiuities. **1624** BOLTON *Nero Cæsar* 61 The antient Greeke Gymnasium was diuided into three chiefe spaces, or actiuitie-yards. **1710** STEELE *Tatler* No. 51 ¶3, A great deal of good Company of us were this Day to see or rather to hear an artful Person do several Feats of Activity.

4. a. Anything active; an active force or operation.

1646 SIR T. BROWNE *Pseud. Ep.* 307 Some..to salve the effect have recurred unto the influence of the starres, making their activities Nationall. **1677** HALE *Prim. Orig. Man.* 348 Christ and his Apostles, did wonderful things, beyond the reach and power of created Agents or Activities. **1823** LAMB *Elia* II. ix. (1865) 294 An endless string of activities without purpose, of purposes destitute of motive. **1869** HUXLEY in *Scient. Opinion* 28 Apr. 486/1 The study of the activities of the living being is called its physiology. **1876** GEO. ELIOT *D. Deronda* v. xxxvii. 353 Still more he wanted to escape standing as a critic outside the activities of men.

b. *spec.* (esp. in *pl.*) The parts of a school curriculum devoted to projects carried out by the pupils; also applied *attrib.* to a system or method of teaching involving such projects. orig. *U.S.*

1923 E. COLLINGS *Exp. with Project Curriculum* vii. 325 Curriculum Principles... A series of concrete and practical activities directed toward some foreseen end. **1934** *Nat. Soc. Study Educ. 33rd Yearbk.*, (*title*) The Activity Movement. **1938** *Amer. Speech* XIII. 204 She suggests that classes organized for 'activities' can get more out of radio than others. **1960** C. W. HARRIS *Encycl. Educ. Research* 852/1 The project and activity methods were commonly used..in the twenties and thirties..as a general approach to teaching.

5. *attrib.* and *Comb.*

1905 W. JAMES *Ess. Radic. Empir.* (1912) vi. 185 An activity-process is the form of a whole 'field of consciousness'. **1905** —— *Notebk.* 17 Dec. in R. B. Perry *Tht. & Char. of W.J.* (1935) II. 757 Purely on the plane of the analysis of what experience *is*, the *co*-ness of content there is but the intellectual preliminary to *activity*-experience. *a* **1910** —— *Some Probl. Philos.* (1911) xiii. 210 Where now is the typical experience [of causation] originally got? Evidently it is got in our own personal activity-situations. **1940** R. S. WOODWORTH *Psychol.* (ed. 12) xi. 364 In one type of experiment, energy output is measured by use of the *activity cage*, which is like a squirrel cage... A mechanical counter shows the number of times the animal's running has turned the wheel round.

6. Special Comb. **activity coefficient** *Physical Chem.*, the ratio of the activity of a substance to its actual concentration (a measure of deviation from ideality); **activity sampling** *Work Study* (see quot. 1959); **activity wheel**, a tread-wheel on which the activity of small mammals is measured; also used for exercising pets.

1911 NOYES & BRAY in *Jrnl. Amer. Chem. Soc.* XXXIII. 1646 For each substance in solution, as the concentration is decreased, the ratio of activity to concentration, the **activity coefficient* (*A/C*) approaches a constant value, which in aqueous solutions may for convenience be assumed to be unity at infinite dilution. **1921** *Jrnl. Amer. Chem. Soc.* XLIII. 1114 The term activity coefficient has been used in two senses, sometimes to mean the ion activity divided by the assumed ion molality, and sometimes to express the ion activity divided by the gross molality of the electrolyte. This latter usage..is more expressly designated..the *stoichiometrical* activity coefficient. **1978** P. W. ATKINS *Physical Chem.* xii. 357 Once the standard electrode potential of a cell is known, the activity coefficient can be determined for any ionic strength simply by measuring the e.m.f. of the cell. [**1949** *Amer. Psychologist* IV. 306/2 (*heading*) The sampling method of activity analysis.] **1959** *Gloss. Terms Work Study* (B.S.I.) 17 **Activity sampling*,..a technique in which a large number of instantaneous observations are made over a period of time of a group of machines, processes or workers. Each observation records what is happening at that instant and the percentage of observations recorded for a particular activity or delay is a measure of the percentage of time during which that activity or delay occurs. **1979** *Steel Times Internat.* Sept. 9/2 Activity sampling could also be used to study the movement of rail traffic. **1950** N. L. MUNN *Handbk. Psychol. Res. on Rat* iii. 53/2 The usual *activity wheel provides a measure of the total number of revolutions..traveled in a given period. **1981** *New Scientist* 13 Aug. 407/1 An activity wheel seems to be an obligatory feature of any complete hamster cage.

actless ('æktlɪs), *a. rare.* [f. ACT *sb.* + -LESS.] Without action, inactive.

1682 T. SOUTHERNE *Loyal Brother* I. i. Wks. I. 21, A poor, young, actless, indigested thing, Whose utmost pride can only boast of youth And innocence. **1765** LAW *Behmen's Expl. 4th Table* 18 This Idea, or Spirit of the Soul, dumb and actless.

actograph ('æktəʊgrɑːf, -æ-). [f. ACT(IVITY + -O + -GRAPH.] A device enabling the amount of movement of an animal placed inside it to be recorded.

1956 *Psychol. Abstr.* XXX. 40/1 The construction and performance of an actograph are described. **1965** B. E. FREEMAN tr. *Vandel's Biospeleol.* xxiii. 379 An actograph, of which there are many types, can be used to measure overall activity. **1975** *Sci. Amer.* Feb. 70/3 The boxes are balanced on a knife-edge fulcrum, and as the incarcerated crab moves between ends of this improvised actograph the box teeters, closing a microswitch that causes a deflection of a pen on a chart recorder.

actomyosin (ˌæktə'maɪəsɪn). *Biochem.* [irreg. f. Gr. ἀκτίς + MYOSIN.] A complex of actin and myosin.

1942 A. SZENT-GYÖRGYI in *Stud. Inst. Med. Chem. Univ. Szeged* I. 67 The myosin-actin complex will be called 'actomyosin'. **1944** —— *Stud. on Muscle* III. 39 The formation of actomyosin is reversible and the complex readily dissociates under different conditions into its components, actin and myosin. **1957** *Lancet* 21 Dec. 1288/2 The contractile element of muscle is actomyosin.

acton ('æktən). Forms 3–5 **aketoun**; 4 **acketton**; 4–9 **aketon**; 5 **akatown, aktone, actone, -oun(e, -owne, hacton**; 6 **hocqueton, hocton**; 6–7 **haketon**; 6–9 **hacqueton**; 5–9 **acketon, haqueton**; 4– **acton**. [a. OFr. (12th c.) *auqueton*, later (15th, 16th c.) *hocqueton, hocton*, mod. Fr. *hoqueton*, cotton wool, padding, whence, a padded and quilted jacket; a. Sp. *alcoton, algodon* 'cotton, bombast,' ad. Arab. *alqūtun, al-qūtn* the cotton. Obsol. since 16th c. exc. as a historical term. *Acton* is the lineal descendant of the ME. forms; in Fr. the word has since received an initial *h*, which has also influenced English since Caxton's time in the forms HAQUETON, *hacqueton, haketon, hacton*, some of which also are still in historical use. *Hoqueton, hocqueton, hocton*, are later Fr. forms, not now used.] A stuffed jacket or jerkin, at first of quilted cotton, worn under the mail; also, in later times, a jacket of leather or other material plated with mail.

c **1300** *K. Alis.* 5150 Withouten cotoned aketoun, Oither plate, oither gaumbisoun. *c* **1386** CHAUCER *Sir Thopas* 149 And next his schert an aketoun, And over that an haberjoun. *c* **1400** *Sege off Melayne* 917 Ther oon he keste an acton syne. *a* **1450** *Syr Perecyvelle* 1102 Blode rede was his stede, His aktone and his other wede. *c* **1450** LONELICH *Graal* II. 199 Here hors, here armures, here akatowns. **1475** CAXTON *Jason* 16 He percid hit and the hauberk and the haqueton. **1496** *Dives & Pauper* (W. de Worde) x. vi. 380/1 We muste do aboue the Jacke or acton of charyte. **1523** LD. BERNERS *Froissart* I. ccccxxx. 756 With pauesons and cootes of steele, hoctons, shapeaux, and bassinettes. **1576** HOLINSHED *Chron.* II. 581 The bishop had upon him a certeine cote of defense, which was called an aketon. **1599** THYNNE *Animadver.* 31 Aketon or Haketone you [Speght] expounde a jackett withoute sleves..But haketon is a slevelesse jackett of plate for the warre, couered with anye other stuffe; at this day also called a jackett of plate. **1609** SIR J. SKENE *Reg. Maj.* 25 That ilk laick landed man haueand ten punds in gudes and geir, sall haue for his bodie, and for defence of the Realme, ane sufficient Acton, ane basnet, and ane gloue of plate. **1623** CAMDEN *Rem.* (1637) 196 They had also about this time..a jacket without sleeves called a Haketon. **1805** SCOTT *Lay L. Minst.* III. vi. But Cranstoun's lance, of more avail..Through shield, and jack, and acton past. **1828** —— *F.M. Perth* III. 341 His rich acton, and all his other vestments, looked as if they had been lately drenched in water.

actor ('æktə(r)). Also **actour**. [a. L. *actor*, n. of agent, f. *act-* ppl. stem of *ag-ĕre* to drive, carry on, do, act. The Fr. *acteur* is later in Littré. The development of meaning took place in L.]

†**1.** A manager, overseer, agent, or factor (transl. L. *actor.*) *Obs.*

1382 WYCLIF *Gal.* iv. 2 He is vndir tutouris and actouris, til to the tyme determyned of the fadir. [**1388** under keperis and tutoris. Vulg. *sub tutoribus et actoribus.*]

†**2.** A pleader; he who conducts an action at law; **a.** the plaintiff or complainant; **b.** an advocate in civil cases; **c.** a public prosecutor. *Obs.* exc. as a term in Rom. law.

1413 LYDG. *Pylgr. Sowle* I. vi. (1859) 6 That the actour be admytted to maken his compleynt, and purpoos his askynge. **1603** GREENWEY *Tacitus, Ann.* III. xiv. (1622) 85 The publicke actor had bought Silanus bondmen, to the end they should bee examined by torture. **1625** BACON *Ess.* xxv. (Arb.) 247 Sometimes it is seene, that the Moderator is more troublesome then the Actor. **1649** SELDEN *Laws of Eng.* I. xx. (1739) 37 The king may not..determine Causes wherein himself is actor. **1768** BLACKSTONE *Comm.* III. 25 In every court there must be at least three constituent parts, the *actor, reus*, and *judex*: the *actor*, or plaintiff, who complains of an injury done. **1875** POSTE *Gaius* I. 154 The temporary representative of a Corporation for the purpose of suing and being sued, was called Actor.

3. One who acts, or performs any action, or takes part in any affair; a doer. (In later usage nearly always with fig. allusion to 4.)

1603 SHAKS. *Meas. for M.* II. ii. 37 Condemn the fault and not the actor of it. **1604** *Case is Altered* in Thynne's *Animadv.* 138 Oh wicked money, to be the Actor of such a mischiefe. **1759** ROBERTSON *Hist. Scotl.* I. I. 5 The characters of the actors are displayed. **1819** S. ROGERS *Hum. Life* 102 Now distant ages, like a day, explore, And judge the act, the actor now no more. **1875** POSTE *Gaius* Introd. 13 An actor is negligent when he is ignorant of the consequences of his act.

4. One who personates a character, or acts a part; a stage-player, or dramatic performer.

1581 SIDNEY *Def. Poesie* (Arb.) 25 There is no Arte delivered to mankinde, that hath not the workes of Nature for his principall object..on which they so depend, as they become Actors and Players as it were, of what nature will have set foorth. **1593** SHAKS. *Rich. II*, v. ii. 24 After a well grac'd actor leaues the Stage. **1646** J. HALL *Horae Vacivae* 19 God sends us not unto the Theater of this World to be mute persons, but actors. **1651** HOBBES *Leviathan* I. xvi. 80 A Person, is the same that an Actor is, both on the Stage and in common Conversation. **1748** J. MASON *Elocution* 4 The Latins by *Pronunciatio* and *Actio* meant the same thing.. hence they whose Business it is to speak publickly on the Stage, are with us called Actors. **1774** BURKE *Sp. Amer. Tax.* Wks. II. 419 Another scene was opened and other actors appeared on the stage. **1876** GREEN *Short Hist.* x. (1878) 730 Pitt was essentially an actor, dramatic in the Cabinet, in the House, in his very office.

5. *Comb.* **actor-man**, *obs.*, a (theatrical) actor; **actor-manager**, a manager of a theatre, who is also an actor; **actor-proof** *a.*, applied to a play or part in a play of which the excellence is evident apart from the standard of the actor(s). Also in other appos. uses, as ***actor-management, -playwright, -producer***. So ***actor-manage(r)*** vbs. (nonce-wds.).

1796 MISS BURNEY *Camilla* II. v. (1840), I desire to know by whose authority you present such *actormen to a young lady under my care. **1894** W. ARCHER *Theatr. 'World' for 1893* 163 As smooth, as adequate, as they could possibly have been in any *actor-managed theatre. **1895** G. B. SHAW in W. Archer *Theatr. 'World' of 1894* Pref. p. xviii, In order to bring up the list of real exceptions to the London rule of *actor-management to three. **1904** P. FITZGERALD *Garrick Club* viii. 241 What discussions, heated and other, used there to be on this topic of actor-management! **1826** F. REYNOLDS *Life & Times* II. 126, I speak of **Actor-managers* both in town, and in country. **1864** *Reader* 24 Dec. 792/1 Another mischief-working influence is that of actor-managers and manageresses. **1907** G. B. SHAW *Let. to G. Barker* 27 Feb. (1956) 75 If I am to be *actor-managered out of all my decent leading men..I shall go and be actor-managed by Alexander. **1926** FOWLER *Mod. Eng. Usage* 644/1 The *actor-playwright is invariably the better craftsman than the literary man who commences dramatist. **1927** J. P. KENNEDY *Story of Films* viii. 181 There are seventeen *actor-producers, men and women producing dramatic films and comedies. **1938** N. MARSHALL in R. D. Charques *Footnotes to Theatre* 110 Gerald du Maurier is another obvious example which can be cited against such a generalisation about actor-producers. **1895** G. B. SHAW *Our Theatres in Nineties* (1931) I. 102 Plays good enough to be comparatively '*actor-proof'. **1923** J. M. MURRY *Pencillings* 206 Molière is infinitely the better dramatist... His plays are as actor-proof as Shakespeare's. **1938** W. S. MAUGHAM *Summing Up* 151 There is no such thing as an actor-proof part.

actor, actour, obs. forms of AUTHOR *sb.*

actorish ('æktərɪʃ), *a.* [f. ACTOR + -ISH[1].] Characteristic or reminiscent of a dramatic actor; affectedly theatrical. Cf. ACTRESSY *a.*

1961 in WEBSTER. **1965** 'R. MACDONALD' *Far Side of Dollar* xxvi. 223 Hillman's personality..had romantic and actorish elements. **1976** *Times Lit. Suppl.* 13 Feb. 166/1 Usually, the trick is to produce an illusion of authenticity and neutralize the actorish qualities. **1984** *Daily Tel.* 3 Mar. 9/7 The confident, actorish voices of Alec McCowen, Norman Rodway and the rest consorted oddly with the probable condition of war criminals facing life imprisonment.

actorly ('æktəlɪ), *a.* [f. ACTOR + -LY[1].] = prec.

1959 *Times* 25 Mar. 13/4 An actorly performance, no doubt, but at the same time genuinely felt. **1969** *Daily Tel.* 7 Feb. 21/2 An ill-written, over-written actorly commentary booming forth 'stirringly' about the need to fight on. **1977** *Gay News* 24 Mar. 26/3 It is..this willingness to offer his past for scrutiny..that makes *A Postillion* a rare example in the miserable trade of actorly egoflashing. **1984** *Listener* 1 Mar. 32/1 We try to single out some quintessential actorly quality from the myriad other things that contribute to the meaning of a particular performance.

actorship ('æktəʃɪp). [f. ACTOR + -SHIP.] The quality or position of a (dramatic) actor.

1598 MARSTON *Ant. & Mell.* I. Introd. Wks. 1856 I. 3, I was never worse fitted since the nativitie of my actorshippe; I shall be hist at. **1773** in *Private Corresp. Garrick* (1831) I. 544 Worthy of your genius, (probably as equal in authorship, as it has been *proved* in actorship, to both the muses of the theatre). **1832** *Rep. Sel. Comm. Dram. Lit.* 25 If novelty were given in the shape of the regular drama, both as respects the authorship and the actorship, if I may use that word. **1840** E. B. BROWNING *Lett.* (1877) I. 17 Only you do more honour to the stage and the actorship than I could do.

actory ('æktərɪ), *a.* [f. ACTOR + -Y[1].] = ACTORISH *a.* Freq. qualifying *actor*.

1917 A. WOOLLCOTT *Let.* Oct. (1944) 38 He is a marvel of good humor, consideration and dignity—one in a thousand, and the least actory actor I have ever known—bar none. **1967** G. PLAYFAIR *Prodigy* iv. 101 George Frederick Cooke ..was a very 'actory' type of actor, as egotistical and as temperamentally unstable as he was supremely gifted. **1981** *Washington Post* 22 Dec. c9/6 Robert Prosky's narration was replete with actory details.

actress ('æktrɪs). Also 8 **actrice**. [f. ACTOR + -ESS; probably formed independently of Fr. *actrice*, which is occasionally found instead.] At first used only in the general sense, not in the dramatic; now only in the dramatic, not in the general.

†**1.** A female actor or doer. *Obs.* repl. by ACTOR.

1589 WARNER *Albion's Eng.* (1612) 335 Opportunitie, the chiefe Actresse in all attempts, gaue the Plaudite in Loue. **1596** FITZ-GEFFREY *Sir F. Drake* (1881) 25 Tasking your pens to pen a womans praise, And she the actresse of your owne disease. **1626** COCKERAM, *Actresse*, a woman doer. **1670** *Lond. Gaz.* ccccIxviii. 1 A principal Lady of the Island who was proved to be an Actress or Accomplice in the assassinate. **1712** ADDISON *Spectator* No. 273 ¶8 Vergil has, indeed, admitted Fame as an actress in the Æneid, but the part she acts is short. [*Mod.* The female prisoner appears to have been the chief actor in the tragic scene.]

2. a. A female player on the stage. (ACTOR was at first used for both sexes.)

1666 PEPYS *Diary* 27 Dec., Doll Common doing Abigail most excellently, & Knipp the widow very well, & will be an excellent actor, I think. **1700** DRYDEN *Epil. to Pilgrim* 40 To stop the trade of love behind the scene, Where actresses make bold with married men. **1711** SHAFTESBURY *Charact.* (1737) III. 368 Study'd action and artificial gesture may be allow'd to the actors and actrices of the stage. **1741** WALPOLE *Lett. to H. Mann* 6 (1834) I. 15 A bad actress, but she has life. **1790** BOSWELL *Johnson* xxiv. (Routl.) 214 This elegant and fashionable actress. **1882** *Academy* 8 July 39/2 As long as such an actress treads the boards, it is possible to take a worthy view of the functions of the theatre.

b. ***as the actress said to the bishop*** (or ***as the bishop said to the actress***): a catch-phrase mischievously implying a sexual innuendo in a preceding innocent remark.

1935 L. CHARTERIS *Saint in N. Y.* viii. 253 What's in a name?—as the actress said to the bishop when he told her that she reminded him of Aspasia. **1953** K. AMIS *Lucky Jim* xii. 123 If you don't know what to do I can't show you, as the actress said to the bishop. **1973** M. RUSSELL *Double Hit* i. 12 The player was a stereo job in moulded mahogany... 'Admiring my equipment?' Adrian re-emerged with a sandwich on a plate. 'As the actress said to the bishop. You get a terrific tone... At least, so the man assured me who installed it all: I've never managed to do exactly what he did, as the bishop said to the actress.'

3. *Comb.* **actress-manageress** (cf. *actor-manager*).

1894 G. B. SHAW in W. Archer *Theatr. 'World' for 1893* Pref. p. xxix, The time is ripe for the advent of the actress-manageress. **1937** *Times* 29 Sept. 8/3 A National Theatre that fulfilled the aspirations of actors and actreses would have to consist of plays every part of which was written for actor-managers or actress-manageresses.

actressy ('æktrɪsɪ), *a.* [f. ACTRESS + -Y[1].] Pertaining to or resembling an actress; affectedly theatrical.

1896 G. B. SHAW *Let. to E. Terry* 5 Dec. (1931) 111 You'd feel instantly with her that such a line would be actressy and that the dressing-room was the wrong *scene* for the right *line*. **1911** M. & J. FINDLATER *Penny Mony-penny* III. ii. 304 Photographs of beautiful ladies..dreadful actressy people all teeth and hair. **1958** *Observer* 9 Feb. 11/5 She talked of the theatrical digs she'd known in this part of the world. Her voice was actressy and deep.

†**actua'bility.** *Obs. rare*[−1]. [f. med.L. *actuāre* + -BILITY.] Capability of being acted upon or actuated.

1689 H. MORE *Answ. to Psych.* 115 If he acknowledge a Spiritual substance distinct from the Material, he will give Activity to the one, and Passivity or Actuability to the other.

actual ('æktju:əl), *a.* Also 4–5 actuel. [a. Fr. *actuel*, ad. late L. *actuāl-is* (in philos. and theol. writers), of or pertaining to action; f. *actu-s* acting; see ACT *sb.* and -AL[1]. Subseq. assimilated to the L. spelling.]

1. Of or pertaining to acts; exhibited in deeds; practical, active. *Obs.* exc. in ***actual grace***, ***actual sin*** (see quots.). *R.C. Ch.*

c **1315** SHOREHAM 107 Thys senne cometh nauȝt of thy ken ..Tho seggeth thys leredemen And clypyeth hyt actuel. *c* **1386** CHAUCER *Persones T.* 283 Thus is synne accomplisid ..and thanne is the synne cleped actuel. **1534** MORE *On the Passion* Wks. 1557, 1284 Original syn without actual adioyned thereto dampned the kynde of man. **1577** [see ORIGINAL A. 1 b]. **1594** HOOKER *Eccl. Politie* (1617) 47 Actuall, that holynesse, which afterwards beautifieth all the parts and actions of our life. **1605** SHAKS. *Macb.* v. i. 13 In this slumbry agitation, besides her walking, and other actuall performances, what (at any time) haue you heard her say? **1638** W. CHILLINGWORTH *Relig. of Protestants* Answ. 2, para. 163, p. 118 Not touching the Virgin Maries freedome from actuall and original sinne. **1647** H. MORE *Song of the Soul* II. ii. II. xxxviii, So when the present actuall centrall life Of sense and motion is gone. **1742** J. & C. WESLEY *Hymns & Sacred Poems* (1869) II. 338 From actual and from inbred sin Us thou hast wash'd in Thine own blood. **1855** F. W. FABER *Growth in Holiness* xxii, They [*sc.* seven supernatural gifts of the Holy Ghost] are played upon according to the needs of our spiritual life by what are called the actual impulses of the Holy Ghost, and which correspond in their subject-matter to actual grace, standing in the same relation to the habitual gifts as it does to habitual grace. **1859** *Catechism Chr. Doctr.* 18 Q. How many kinds of sin are there? A. Two; original and actual... Q. What is actual sin? A. Every sin which we ourselves commit. **1890** WILHELM & SCANNELL *Man. Cath. Theol.* I. III. II. i. 437 Around this [Habitual] Grace are grouped all other salutary Graces especially 'Actual Grace'. **1957** *Oxf. Dict. Chr. Ch.* 14/2 *Actual sin*, a sin, whether of commission or omission, which is the outcome of a free personal act of the individual will. *Ibid.* 577/1 *Actual grace*, a certain motion of the soul, bestowed by God *ad hoc* for the production of some good act. It may exist in the unbaptized.

†**2.** Abounding in action, active, energetic. *Obs.*

1470–85 MALORY *Morte d' Arth.* I. xvi. (1816) I. 30 'I wol wel,' said Arthur, 'for I see your dedes full actual.'

3. Existing in act or fact; really acted or acting; carried out; real;—opposed to *potential*, *possible*, *virtual*, *theoretical*, *ideal*. Formerly often *absol.* in *pl.* = actual qualities, actualities.

1541 COPLAND *Guydon's Quest. Cyrurg.* D iij b, Whiche cauteres are the surest, the actualles, or the potencyalles? Answere. The actualles, bycause yᵉ action of fyre is moste simple. **1587** GOLDING *De Mornay* xii. 178 And thinkest thou..that his [God's] potentials..are not stronger than thine actuals? **1651** HOBBES *Leviathan* III. xxxviii. 244 By comparison with their own actuall miseries. **1656** BRAMHALL *Replic.* iv. 160 With the Romanists themselves I distinguish between habituall and actuall Jurisdiction. Habituall Jurisdiction is derived only by Ordination. Actuall Jurisdiction is a right to exercise that habit, arising from the lawfull application of the matter or subject. **1769** *Junius Lett.* xxxv. 155 The natives of Scotland are not in actual rebellion. **1817** JAS. MILL *Brit. India* II. v. viii. 661 The nominal revenue was but a portion of the actual proceeds. **1837** CARLYLE *Fr. Revol.* I. I. II. iii. 31 Great truly is the Actual; is the Thing that has rescued itself from bottomless deeps of theory and possibility, and stands there as a definite indisputable Fact. **1853** F. W. ROBERTSON *Serm.* III. vii. 90 There is every difference between the ideal and the actual —between what a man aims to be and what he is. **1870** TYNDALL *Heat* v. §154, 131 It may be called actual energy in antithesis to possible.

4. In action or existence at the time; present, current.

1642 R. CARPENTER *Experience* II. vii. 162 If a man finde his wife in the actuall commission of Adultery, he may kill both his wife, and the Adulterer. **1790** BURKE *Fr. Revol.* 78 If this be your actual situation, compared to the situation to which you were called. **1873** BROWNING *Red Cott. N.-Cap Country* 132 Never constructed as receptacle..for him their actual lord. **1880** GEIKIE *Phys. Geog.* I. 3, 21 No telescope has yet detected any actual volcanic eruption going on in the moon. *Mod.* In the actual position of affairs in Egypt.

actual ('æktju:əl), *sb.* [f. the adj.] *pl.* Actual qualities, actualities (opposed to *ideals*).

1541, 1587 [see ACTUAL *a.* 3]. *a* **1902** S. BUTLER *Way of All Flesh* (1903) vii. 31 He may have had an ill-defined sense of ideals that were not his actuals. **1926** D. WATSON *Church at Work* x. 119 Christian ideals must be made actuals.

actualism ('æktju:əlɪz(ə)m). [f. ACTUAL *a.* + -ISM.]

c **1860** J. HINTON *Philos. & Relig.* Pref., One new word I have introduced..the word actualism..it is parallel to idealism, materialism, positivism, etc., and was adopted to express the idea that all existence is truly active or spiritual, as opposed to inert or dead. **1882** *Academy* 14 Jan. 29 It is the central doctrine of Actualism, that self-sacrifice for others is the law of life and conduct.

actualist ('æktju:əlɪst). [f. ACTUAL *a.* 3.] One who aims at actuality or realism. Hence **actua'listic** *a.*

a **1866** J. GROTE *Moral Ideals* (1876) xv. 375 To which the *actualist* ever answers, The moral world..is *given* by human constitution and circumstance. **1887** *Harper's Mag.* Jan. 324/1 In his first essay in the field of fiction he turns out an actualist, whose first wish seems to be truth to his facts and the meaning of them. **1893** *Funk's Stand. Dict.*, Actualistic. **1921** HANNAY & COLLINGWOOD tr. *Ruggiero's Mod. Philos.* 201 Over against this actualistic concept of life,..we find maintained..an absolutely intellectualistic conception. **1934** *Essays & Stud.* XIX. 145 An actualistic drawing-room play.

actuality (,æktju:'ælɪtɪ). [ad. med.L. *actuālitātem*, f. *actuāl-is*. See ACTUAL and -ITY; cf. mod.Fr. *actualité* ('a neologism.' Littré).]

†**1.** Capacity of action, activity. *Obs.*

1398 TREVISA *Barth. De P.R.* VIII. xvi. (1495) 323 The sonne hath moost actualyte and vertue of werkinge. **1647** H. MORE *Song of the Soul* II. ii. III. v, Yet falls she down at last and lowly lies..sleep doth seise her actualities. **1677** GALE *Crt. of Gentiles* III. 122 God, by reason of his infinite actualitie, permits nothing but what he wils.

2. The state of being actual or real; reality, existing objective fact.

1675 J. HOWE *Living Temple* Wks. 1834, 34/2 An infinite possibility on the part of the creature..and a proportionable infinite actuality of power on the Creator's part. **1775** J. HARRIS *Philos. Arrangem.* (1841) 365 That there are things existing in act, in reality, in actuality, (call it as you please,) we have the evidence both of our senses and of our internal consciousness. **1847** LEWES *Hist. Philos.* (1867) I. 313 Which passed from possibility into actuality. **1848** RUSKIN *Mod. Painters* I. II. I. vii. §15, 90 To sacrifice a truth of actuality to a truth of feeling. **1855** MILMAN *Lat. Chr.* XIV. iii. (1864) IX. 136 Universals are real only in God but..in potentiality rather than in actuality.

3. *pl.* Actual existing conditions or circumstances.

1665 GLANVILLE *Sceps. Sci.* 42 These distinct possibilities are founded upon distinct actualities. **1832** COLERIDGE *Table Talk* 5 Apr. 168 The public mind, which substitutes its own undefined notions or passions for real objects and historical actualities. **1852** GROTE *Greece* IX. II. lxix. 34 To look at the actualities of the present and take measure of what is best to be done for the future. **1876** M. DAVIES *Unorthod. Lond.* 250 His words would therefore be few, and directed to the actualities of the case.

4. a. Realism in description.

1850 MERIVALE *Hist. Rom. Emp.* (1865) VIII. lxiv. 83 It invests traditions and legends with the hard colouring of modern actuality. **1879** W. E. HENLEY in *Academy* 5 Apr. 298/1 Some of the characters grouped about her have a flavour of actuality.

b. *spec.* in *Cinemat.*, *Television* (see quot. 1941). Also *attrib.*

1929 H. G. WELLS *King who was King* i. §1. 10 The films began with 'actualities', the record of more or less formal current events. **1941** *B.B.C. Gloss. Broadc. Terms* 3 *Actuality*, presentation of real persons and things to give a picture of contemporary life in a particular aspect; documentary. **1944** L. MACNEICE *Columbus* 12 The radio dramatist..must select his actuality material with great discrimination. **1963** *Listener* 3 Oct. 501/2 Television is a medium far more successful at documentary or 'actuality' than at fiction.

actualization (,æktju:əlaɪ'zeɪʃən). [f. ACTUALIZE *v.* + -ATION.] A making actual; a realization in action or fact.

1824 COLERIDGE *Aids to Refl.* (1848) I. 221 The non-actualization of such power is, *a priori*, so certain. **1861** EMERSON *Cond. of Life* i. 27 The event is only the actualization of its thoughts. **1869** RAWLINSON *Anc. Hist.* 352 The constitution established..was, in part, the actualisation of the ideal of Servius.

actualize ('æktju:əlaɪz), *v.* [f. ACTUAL *a.* + -IZE.]

1. To make actual, to convert into an actual fact, to realize in action.

1810 COLERIDGE *Friend* I. xv. (1866) 65 To make our feelings, with their vital warmth, actualize our reason. **1823** DE QUINCEY *Wks.* 1860 XIV. 56 When these inert and sleeping forms are organized, when these possibilities are actualized. **1850** E. P. WHIPPLE *Ess. & Rev.* (ed. 3) I. 300 If the phrase, realizing the ideal, were translated into the phrase, actualizing the real, much ambiguity might be avoided.

2. To represent or describe realistically.

1881 *Athenæum* 9 July 39/3 Other writers..have not sufficient imaginative force to actualize a truly imaginative situation, and require the 'prop of allegory.'

actualized ('æktju:əlaɪzd), *ppl. a.* [f. prec. + -ED.] Rendered actual.

1825 COLERIDGE in *Rem.* (1836) II. 338 To distinguish being from existence—or potential being..from being actualized.

actualizing ('æktju:əlaɪzɪŋ), *ppl. a.* [f. ACTUALIZE *v.* + -ING[2].] Making actual or real; which makes real.

1824 COLERIDGE *Aids to Refl.* (1848) I. 28 Marriage contracted between Christians is a true and perfect symbol or mystery; that is, the actualizing faith being supposed to exist in the receivers, it is an outward sign co-essential with that which it signifies, or a living part of that, the whole of which it represents.

actually ('æktju:əlɪ), *adv.* [f. ACTUAL *a.* + LY[2].]

†**1.** In a way that is characterized by doing; with deeds; practically, actively. *Obs.*

1587 GOLDING *De Mornay* v. 50 Now, this vnderstanding is actualle [? *read* -alie] euerlasting, (that is..in deede) and euerlastingly actuall, (that is..doing). **1651** HOBBES *Leviathan* III. xxxv. 219 Christ shall come..to judge the world, and actually to governe his owne people. **1660** T. STANLEY *Hist. Philos.* (1701) 135/1 Those who offend actually, are most grievously punished.

†**2.** Actively, energetically. *Obs.*

1470–85 MALORY *Morte d' Arth.* (1816) I. 137 Then on foot they drew their swords, and did full actually.

3. In act or fact; as opposed to *possibly*, *potentially*, *theoretically*, *ideally*; really, in reality.

1587 GOLDING *De Mornay* xv. 232 This minde..hath being and continuance actually and of it selfe, and euen when it is seperated from the body. **1608** SIR H. WOTTON in Ellis *Orig. Lett.* I. 261 II. 99 He was heere..actually a Senator. **1775** J. HARRIS *Philos. Arrangem.* (1841) 365 Every substance that actually is, by actually being that thing, actually is not any other. A piece of brass, for example, actually is not an oak. **1782** PRIESTLEY *Matter & Spirit* I. Pref. 15, I would have every man write as he actually feels. **1868** GEO. ELIOT *F. Holt* 19 She..sat with a fixed look, seeing nothing that was actually present. **1878** JEVONS *Prim. Pol. Econ.* 52 The rates of interest actually paid in business vary very much.

4. As a present fact, at present, for the time being.

1663 GERBIER *Counsel* 60 Workmen, actually employed in every work. **1699** LUTTRELL *Brief Rel.* (1857) IV. 567 The Turks have actually evacuated Camineec. **1832** HALLAM *Const. Hist. Eng.* I. 507 The impeachment of the earl of Middlesex, actually lord treasurer of England. *Mod.* The party actually in power.

5. As a matter of fact, in truth, truly; indeed; even. Not said of the objective reality of the thing asserted, but as to the truthfulness of the assertion and its correspondence with the thing; hence added to vouch for statements which seem surprising, incredible, or exaggerated: 'He has actually sent the letter after all.'

1762 GOLDSM. *Cit. of World* cxix. (1837) 463, I had some dispositions to be a scholar and had actually learned my letters. **1849** RUSKIN *Seven Lamps* iv. §33, 124 And this principle will be actually found, I believe, to guide the old workmen. **1863** KEMBLE *Resid. Georgia* 22 This woman actually imagines that there will be no slaves in heaven. **1878** G. MACDONALD *Ann. Quiet Neighb.* vii. 121, I actually found the door standing open.

actualness ('æktju:əlnɪs). [f. ACTUAL *a.* + -NESS.] = ACTUALITY.

†**1.** Active working or operation, activity. *Obs.*

1398 TREVISA *Barth. De P.R.* VIII. xxviii. (1495) 340 One poynt of lyghte or of shynynge were suffysaunt to beshyne alle the world, for noblynesse of matere and for moast actualnesse and doynge of fourme. **1742** BAILEY, *Actuality, Actualness*, Perfection of being.

2. The quality of being actual, actuality.

1668 WILKINS *Real Char.* II. i. §3, 28, *Actualness*, existence, extant. **1755** In JOHNSON. **1876** WHITNEY *Sights & Ins.* II. xiv. 441 The real fact through whose vitality and actualness the stones were put one upon another.

actuarial (æktju:'ɛərɪəl), *a.* [f. L. *actuāri-us* ACTUARY + -AL[1].] Of or pertaining to actuaries or their profession.

1869 *Echo* 22 Nov. 1/1 Most of us are allowed to go through the span of life allotted to us in actuarial tables. **1869** *Daily News* 18 Aug., Calculated on well-known and acknowledged actuarial principles. **1879** *Ibid.* 1 Feb., The actuarial value of the annuity would be considerably more than 6,500*l.*

actuarially (æktju:'ɛərɪəlɪ), *adv.* [f. ACTUARIAL *a.* + -LY[2].] In relation to actuarial principles; on an actuarial basis.

1884 *Athenæum* 12 July 39/3 That..every society hereafter formed has its actuarially certified table. **1886** *N.*

Amer. Rev. Sept. 233 The trade-unions of England are, actuarially speaking, bankrupt. **1905** *Daily News* 12 Apr. 9/3 These schemes..were found..to be actuarially sound.

actuarian (æktjuːˈɛərɪən), *a. rare.* [f. L. *actuāri-us* + -AN.] = ACTUARIAL.

1863 A. RUMSEY *Reports, Reporting, & Reporters* 20 Pecuniary compensation, to be calculated on actuarian principles.

actuary (ˈæktjuːərɪ). [ad. L. *actuāri-us* an amanuensis, a keeper of accounts, f. *actu-s* act; see -ARY.]

1. A registrar or clerk, a notary; an officer appointed to write down the acts or proceedings of a court. Still used in the Convocation of the Province of Canterbury.

1553 FOX *A. & M.* in Cobbett's *St. Trials* I. 628 Requiring also the copies, as well of the articles as of his protestation, of the Actuaries. **1658** BRAMHALL *Consecr. Bishops* iii. 30 The same publick Notary who was Principall Actuary both at Cardinall Poles Consecration and Arch-Bishop Parkers. **1667** CHAMBERLAYNE *St. Grt. Brit.* I. II. viii. (1743) 73 To this Court [of Arches] belongeth an Actuary, a Register, and a Beadle. The office of the Actuary is to attend the court, set down the judges decrees. **1717** BLOUNT *Law Dict.*, *Actuary* (*actuarius*) is the Scribe that registers the Acts and Constitutions of the Convocation. **1879** *Whitaker's Alman.* 155, *Conv. of Prov. of Cant.* (Officérs) Vicar-General, Registrar, Actuary.

†**2. a.** The managing secretary or accountant of a public company. *Obs.*

1804 W. TAYLOR in *Ann. Rev.* II. 238 The managers and actuaries of our public companies.

b. *spec.*, one whose office it is to manage the deposits in a savings bank.

1816 E. CHRISTIAN *Plan for County Provident Bank* 19 The Actuary, in the name of the Institution, is to receive such Deposits under £20 as may be offered, which he shall enter into his Deposit Book. **1817** J. BOWLES *Provident Institutions called Savings' Banks* (ed. 3) 45 The actuary shall keep all the accounts of the institution in a regular set of books, and be responsible for the accuracy of every individual account. **1919** W. THOMSON *Dict. Banking* (ed. 2) 13/2 *Actuary*, the chief official in a savings bank.

3. An official in an insurance office, whose duty it is to compile statistical tables of mortality, and estimate therefrom the necessary rates of premium, etc.; or one whose profession it is to solve for Insurance Companies or the public, all monetary questions that involve a consideration of the separate or combined effect of Interest and Probability, in connexion with the duration of human life, the average proportion of losses due to fire or other accidents, etc.

1849 MACAULAY *Hist. Eng.* I. 283 An actuary of eminent skill, subjected the ancient parochial registers of baptisms, marriages, and burials, to all the tests which the modern improvements in statistical science enabled him to apply. **1859** *Q. Rev.* No. 211, 75 Many actuaries acknowledge the soundness of that basis for life assurance and annuity calculations.

actuate (ˈæktjuːeɪt), *v.* [f. med.L. *actuāt-* ppl. stem of *actuā-re* = *ad actum redigere* (Du Cange); f. *actu-s*, see ACT *sb.*]

†**1. a.** To reduce to action; to carry out in practice, to perform (a command, proposition, etc.). *Obs.*

1596 HUARTE *Trial of Wits* xv. 265 If there be any.. who speaketh or actuateth this in the presence of another. **1649** JER. TAYLOR *Gt. Exemp.* I. iii. §12, 88 He that neglects to actuate such discourses loses the benefit of his meditation. **1677** HALE *Contempl.* II. 68 That must..actuate such a Conviction to attain its due effect.

†**b.** To reduce into the form of an act. See ACT *sb.* 7. *Obs.*

1658 BRAMHALL *Consecr. Bps.* in *Ang. Cath. Lib.* III. 64 With their registers to actuate what is done, they do solemnly in form of law confirm the election.

†**2.** To render active, to stir into activity (a latent or inert property); to stir up, arouse, or excite. *Obs.*

1603 HOLLAND *Plutarch's Morals* 1347 And the cause which doth excite and actuate the same. **1609** —— *Amm. Marcell.* XVII. ii. 81 Who took this opportunity to actuate their boldnesse in doing mischiefe. **1655** GURNALL *Chr. in Armour* II. 506 So doth faith actuate sin in the Conscience. **1751** JOHNSON *Rambler* No. 117 ¶10 We must actuate our languor by taking a few turns round the centre in a garret.

3. a. To inspire (a thing) with active properties, to quicken, enliven, or vivify. *arch.*

1642 HOWELL *For. Trav.* (1869) 82 What kind of soule doth inform, actuat, govern, and conserve that vast empire. **1664** H. MORE *Apology* 498 The Soul is a Spirit that actuates the natural Body. **1824** COLERIDGE *Aids to Refl.* (1848) 115 Its [spirit's] property is to improve, enliven, actuate some other thing, not constitute a thing in its own name.

b. *absol.*

1664 *Knavery in all Trades* III. D 2, A Cup of Ale-berry, or Warme-Broth exhibited to his small Guts..shall actuate in all parts of his Body.

4. To move to mechanical action, to communicate motion to, to move, impel (an instrument, machine, or agent). Also *fig.*

1645 RUTHERFORD *Tryal & Triumph of Faith* (1845) 58 The devil in his element is twice a devil; he is in his own when he formeth and actuateth bloody instruments. **1750** JOHNSON *Rambler* No. 67 ¶11 Wings, which others were contriving to actuate by the perpetual motion. **1794** G. ADAMS *Nat. & Exper. Phil.* III. xxix. 191 Either of these forces is sufficient to actuate or put in motion the system of wheels and pinions. **1832** PORTER *Porcelain* 50 It has also a piston, actuated by a screw. **1879** PRESCOTT *Spkg. Telephone* 3 In 1861, Reiss discovered that a vibrating diaphragm could be actuated by the human voice.

5. To act upon, or move, the will, as motives do.

1741 RICHARDSON *Pamela* xv. (1824) I. 255 The girl has strong passions and resentments; and she that has, will be actuated, and sometimes governed by them. **1791** BOSWELL *Johnson* Ded. 1 (1816) Every liberal motive that can actuate an Authour. **1849** MACAULAY *Hist. Eng.* I. 169 The motives which governed the political conduct of Charles the Second differed widely from those by which his predecessor and his successor were actuated.

6. *intr.* To exert activity, to act.

1620 VENNER *Via Recta* 3 Consequently it not being able to actuate as it ought, putrifieth. **1629** DONNE *Serm.* cxxxvi. V. 438 The Soul that does not think, [does] not consider, cannot be said to Actuate (which is the proper operation of the Soul) but to Evaporate, not to work through the Body, but to breathe and smoke through the body. **1657** *Deuine Louer* §3. 9 Wee ought in soule with Loue to actuate towards God the intensest and continuallest..wee can. **1920** *Chambers's Jrnl.* 25 Dec. 55/1 The [human] mass..came round with an almost dismaying swiftness. 'How could such a bulk actuate with such rapidity?' Clement thought. **1924** O. LODGE *Making of Man* v. 113 He is beginning to learn.. that the portion of consciousness now actuating and made manifest in his brain is but a small part of the whole.

Hence **ˈactuator**, one who or a thing which actuates.

1889 in *Cent. Dict.* **1890** C. MERCIER *Sanity & Insanity* xii. 299 The higher nerve regions are the actuators of conduct. **1920** L. BAIRSTOW *Appl. Aerodynamics* vi. 281 W. E. Froude introduced into airscrew theory the idea of an actuator. **1931** *Electronics* Sept. 107/2 The electrostatic actuator consists of a grill or slotted plate which is slipped into the front opening of a condenser microphone. **1956** *Spaceflight* I. 24/1 Pivoting motors..to provide pitch and yaw control, movement being obtained by electro-hydraulic actuators.

†**ˈactuate,** *ppl. a. Obs.* [ad. med.L. *actuāt-us*, pa. pple. of *actuā-re*; see ACTUATE *v.*] Carried out in action; realized in fact; ACTUATED.

1662 (Nov. 24) SOUTH *12 Serm.* (1697) I. 66 And the Active informations of the Intellect, filling the Passive reception of the Will..grew actuate into a third, and distinct perfection of Practice. **1671** *True Non-Conf.* 119 By which even the gift of Miracles was actuate, made effectual.

actuated (ˈæktjuːeɪtɪd), *ppl. a.* [f. ACTUATE *v.* + -ED.] Rendered actual, or active; put into action, moved, stirred, impelled.

1652 BENLOWE *Theophila* IV. xxvii, In Sanctitie Be actuated then. **1657** T. REEVE *Plea for Nineveh* 243 It doth delight me to see a bright creature come out of the slime-heap, and to see these slime-heaps such actuated Models, that they should have the whole world wait upon them, and the Creator himselfe bow down to them. **1794** SULLIVAN *View of Nat.* I. 333 All bodies loose their parts, in proportion as they are more actuated by the power of heat. **1826** DISRAELI *Viv. Grey* IV. iv. 152 Actuated by the vilest of hatreds.

actuating (ˈæktjuːeɪtɪŋ), *vbl. sb.* [f. ACTUATE *v.* + -ING[1].] †**a.** Reducing to action, carrying out in actual practice. **b.** Moving to action, impelling, animating. (Now mostly gerundial.)

1645 BP. HALL *Content.* 132 Certain firm resolutions for the full actuating our contentment. *c* **1680** P. STERRY *Wks.* II. 226 The actuating of this in the real Performance, the making of it actual on us, in our own Persons, is then when we are New-born.

actuating (ˈæktjuːeɪtɪŋ), *ppl. a.* [f. ACTUATE *v.* + -ING[2].] Moving, inspiring, influencing.

1659 *Gentleman's Calling* (1696) 2 That actuating power, which should set them on work. *c* **1746** J. HERVEY *Medit. & Contempl.* (1818) 79 Having his will for thy rule, his glory for thy aim, and his Holy Spirit for thy ever-actuating principle. **1861** A. GEIKIE *E. Forbes* x. 288 Vanity was not the only actuating motive.

actuation (ˌæktjuːˈeɪʃən). [n. of action f. med.L. *actuāre*; see ACTUATE and -ION[1]. *Actuātio* may have been used in med.L.] A communication of motion, a bringing into action, a moving, stirring up, or urging; excitement, impulse, movement.

c **1630** JACKSON *Creed* VI. vi. Wks. V. 63 The several actuations, draughts, or replenishments, which are derived from the infinite fountain of life. **1656** H. JEANES *Fvlnesse of Christ* 390 The Actuation, the stirring up of our faith, which is our receiving and acceptance of Christs fulnesse. **1699** BURNET *39 Articles* ii. (1700) 51 By the Indwelling and Actuation of the Soul, it has another Spring within it. **1876** MAUDSLEY *Physiol. Mind* viii. 466 The whole region of motor residua [in the nervous system] might be described generically as the department of actuation. **1879** GLADSTONE *Gleanings* I. i. 55 How the best designs are spoiled by faulty actuation.

†**ˌactuˈose,** *a. Obs. rare.* [ad. L. *actuōsus* full of activity, f. *actu-s* ACTION *sb.*; see -OSE.] Full of activity, abounding in action; very active.

1677 GALE *Crt. of Gentiles* III. 22 'Ενεργεῖν, as applied to God, notes his actuose, efficacious, and predeterminate concurse in and with althings.

†**actuˈosity.** *Obs.* [f. L. *actuōs-us*, see prec., + -ITY.] Abounding activity.

1660 H. MORE *Myst. Godl.* III. iv. 66 Time present being urgent and raging like a Lion through its instant actuosity. **1677** GALE *Crt. of Gentiles* II. IV. 102 What is life but the Actuositie of the Soul informing the bodie? and what more promotes this Actuositie than Exercice?

†**ˈacture.** *Obs. rare.* [f. L. *act-* ppl. stem of *agĕre* to do + -URE; as if ad. L. **actūra*; cf. *nātūra*, *factūra*, etc.] The process of acting; action.

1593 ? SHAKS. *Lover's Compl.* 185 With acture they may be, Where neither party is nor true nor kind.

acturience (ækˈtjʊərɪəns). [f. L. *act-* ppl. stem of *ag-ĕre* to ACT *v.*, on analogy of *esurient* ad. L. *ēsurient-em* pr. pple. of *ēsurī-re* to hunger, desiderative of *ĕd-ere*, *ēs-um* to eat.] Desire to act.

a **1880** WEBSTER cites J. GROTE.

‖**actus purus** (ˌæktəs ˈpjʊərəs). *Philos.* Also **purus actus.** [med.L., 'pure act', tr. Gr. ἐνέργεια.] Actuality unmixed with potentiality; pure act (ACT *sb.* 3). Also, a mental act uncontaminated by elements of sensory awareness (see quots. 1890).

[*a* **1274** AQUINAS *Sum. Theol.* I. 14. 2 Cum igitur Deus nihil potentialitatis habeat, sed sit actus purus.] **1707–8** BERKELEY *Commonpl. Bk.* (1944) No. 701 The substance of Spirit we do not know..it being purus actus. *Ibid.* No. 828 The Will is purus actus or rather pure Spirit. **1878** S. H. HODGSON *Philos. of Reflection* II. 12 Pure energy, *actus purus*, without anything merely potential. **1890** W. JAMES *Princ. Psychol.* I. ix. 245 They are known, these relations,..by an *actus purus* of Thought, Intellect, or Reason. *Ibid.* xii. 474 The conceptualists..invent..as the vehicle of the knowledge of universals, an *actus purus intellectûs*, or an Ego, whose function is treated as quasi-miraculous...The nominalists..dislike *actus puros.*

acuate (ˈækjuːət), *ppl. a.* [ad. med. or mod.L. *acuāt-us*, pa. pple. of *acuā-re*, f. *acu-s* needle; cf. *situātus*, *fluctuātus*.] Sharpened, sharp-pointed.

1471 RIPLEY *Comp. Alch.* in Ashmole (1652) vii. 191 With a quantyte of Spyces acuate. *Ibid.* I. xiii. 132 Agaynst a brodyke of Iyron or Stele new acuate. **1880** RIDLEY in *Jrnl. Linn. Soc.* XV. No. 83. 149 Certain long acuate spicules.

†**ˈacuate,** *v. Obs.* Also 6 acuat, 7 accuate. [f. prec., or on analogy of vbs. so formed.] To make sharp or pungent, to sharpen. *lit.* and *fig.*

1542 BOORDE *Dyetary* xxii. (1870) 286 Grene gynger eaten in the moreninge, fastynge, doth acuat and quycken the remembraunce. **1657** TOMLINSON *Renou's Disp.* 219 Wine acuates the ingenuity and rouses the spirits. **1683** SALMON *Doron Med.* I. 363 Comforts the Memory, accuates the Senses. **1750** *Phil. Trans.* XLVI. 443 To be well rubb'd once in three Hours with a Mixture acuated with Spir. Sal. marin.

†**ˈacuating,** *vbl. sb. Obs.* [f. ACUATE *v.* + -ING[1].] The act of sharpening.

1753 CHAMBERS *Cycl. Supp.*, *Acuition*, in a general sense the same with acuating or sharpening.

acuation (ˌækjuːˈeɪʃən). *rare.* [n. of action f. ACUATE *v.* See -ATION.] Sharpening, rendering acute.

1837 WHEWELL *Induct. Sc.* III. xv. i. 197 Werner..had formally spoken of *truncation*, *acuation*, and *acumination*, or replacement by a plane, an edge, a point respectively, as ways in which the forms of crystals are modified.

†**acuˈition,** *Obs. rare.* [ad. med.L. *acuitiōn-em* sharpening, f. *acu-ĕre*, as if f. a ppl. stem **acuit-* for *acūt-*.] The act of sharpening.

1753 CHAMBERS *Cycl. Supp.* s.v., *Acuition*, in a general sense, the same with acuating or sharpening..The Acuition, says Gaza, is where the sound is highest in the pronunciation of a word..Acuition, in medicine and chemistry, is used for sharpening or increasing the force of any medicine.

acuity (əˈkjuːɪtɪ). [a. Fr. *acuité* (16th c. in Litt.) ad. med.L. *acuitāt-em*, f. *acu-s* needle, *acu-ĕre* to sharpen; see -ITY.] Sharpness, acuteness; as of a needle, an acid, a disease, wit.

1543 TRAHERON *Vigo's Chirurg.* II. 63 In this case suppositories and clysters having some acuity or sharpnes seme more convenient, than medicynes receyved by the mouth. *a* **1554** HOOPER *Commandm.* i. Wks. 1843–52, 272 There is no acuity nor excellency of wit..that can comprehend or compass the doctrine. **1610** HEALEY *St. Aug., City of God* 914 They excell in acuity of understanding. **1678** R. R[USSELL] *Geber* II. I. IV. xiii. 116 Water admits not the Acuity of Ignition as Ashes doth. **1872** THOMAS *Dis. Women* 145 The disease may at any time take on the characters of virulence and acuity.

aculeate (əˈkjuːlɪət), *a.* [ad. L. *acūleāt-us* furnished with a sting or prickle, f. *acūleus*, dim. of *acu-s* needle; see -ATE[2].]

1. *Zool.* Furnished with a sting.

1661 LOVELL *Anim. & Min.* 200 Flounder..They have a soft flesh, yet the Aculeate are hard. **1875** HOUGHTON *Sk. Brit. Insects* 130 The aculeate Hymenoptera are those insects furnished with a sting. **1880** *Athenæum* No. 2748, 827 Sir J. Lubbock regards the ancestral ant as having been aculeate.

2. *Bot.* Prickly, set with prickles.

1870 HOOKER *Stud. Flora* 199 *Bidens*..Fruit compressed, ribbed, ribs often aculeate.

3. *fig.* Pointed, incisive, stinging. [So in L.]

1605 BACON *Adv. Learn.* (1640) 29 The labour here is altogether, that words may be aculeate, sentences concise. **1693** BEVERLEY *Gospel Truth* 1 Any Aculeate Animadversions on..particular Expressions. **1880** R. L.

POOLE *Huguen. of Disp.* 186 Political action, hardened and aculeate by hatred.

aculeated (əˈkjuːlɪeɪtɪd), *ppl. a.* [f. prec. with the ppl. ending *-ed*, after analogy of the later pples. from vbs. in -ATE.]

1. *Nat. Hist.* Pointed, sharpened to a needle-like point; armed with prickles.

1681 WILLIS *Rem. Med. Wks., Aculeated,* Made sharp and prickly like a needles point. **1713** DERHAM *Physico-Theol.* IV. xi. 19 The mouth is.. in some [insects] aculeated; to pierce and wound Animals, and suck their Blood. **1774** BRYANT *Mythol.* I. 344 The murex is of the turbinated kind, and particularly aculeated; having strong and sharp protuberances.

2. *fig.* Pointed, incisive, keen, pungent.

1655 LESTRANGE *Charles I,* 71, A man of an acute but aculeated wit. **1813** KNOX & JEBB *Corr.* II. 170 The apothegms.. and aculeated sayings of the ancients are inestimable. **1839** DE QUINCEY *Recoll. of Lakes* Wks. 1862 II. 233, A trenchant, pungent, aculeated form of terse, glittering, stenographic sentences.

aculeation (əˌkjuːlɪˈeɪʃən). *rare.* [f. ACULEATE; see -ATION.] The state of being sharpened or pointed.

1870 SMITH *Syn. & Antonyms, Acuity..Syn.* Pointedness, Aculeation, Acumination.

aculeiform (əˈkjuːliːɪfɔːm), *a. Bot.* [f. L. *acūle-us* + -FORM.] Spine-shaped, like a prickle.

1857 BERKELEY *Cryptog. Bot.* §393, 360 Elongated aculeiform processes.

aculeolate (əˈkjuːlɪəʊlət), *a. Bot.* [f. L. *acūleol-us* a little prickle, dim. of *acūleus* + -ATE².] 'Beset with diminutive prickles.' Gray *Bot. Text-bk.*

†**aˈculeous,** *a. Obs. rare.* [f. L. *acūle-us* + -OUS.] Needle-like, sting-like; aculeate.

1658 SIR T. BROWNE *Gard. Cyrus* II. 515 The aculeous prickly plantation, upon the heads of several common thistles. **1713** DERHAM *Physico-Theol.* IV. xiv. 250 They have some aculeous Part or Instrument to terebrate, and make way for their Eggs.

‖**aculeus** (əˈkjuːlˈɪəs). Pl. aculei. [L., = a sting, dim. of *acus* a needle.]

1. *Zool.* The sting of an insect or other animal.

1828 KIRBY & SPENCE *Entomol.* IV. xlii. 162 The valves are linear, exserted, and as long as the aculeus itself.

2. *Bot.* 'A prickle; a conical elevation of the skin of a plant, becoming hard and sharp-pointed: as in the rose.' Lindley in *Treas. of Bot.*

1878 MCNAB *Bot.* 76 Prickles or aculei occurring on some brambles and roses, differ from true hairs in their originating from the epidermis, and one or more cells below it.

acumber, acumbre, earlier (and better) form of ACCUMBER *v. Obs.* to encumber.

†**acumble,** *v. Obs.* [? a. Fr. *acomble-r* to load:—L. *accumulā-re*; see ACCUMULATE.] To benumb.

a **1300** W. DE BIBLESWORTH in Wright's *Voc.* I. 161 *Jo ay la mayn si estomye* [*glossed* so acomeled (wineled)]. **1388** WYCLIF *Jer.* vi. 24 We herden the fame therof, oure hondis ben aclumsid [*v.r.* acumblid]. *c* **1440** *Prompt. Parv.* 6 Acomelyd for coulde, or aclommyde [**1499** acomyred, **1516** accombred], *Eviratus, enervatus.*

acumen (əˈkjuːmɪn, ˈækjʊmɪn). [a. L. *acūmen,* anything sharp; sharpness, point; f. *acu-ĕre* to sharpen.]

1. Sharpness of wit; quickness or penetration of perception; keenness of discrimination.

1531 ELYOT *Governor* I. xv. §4 Wherein is the chiefe sharpenes of witte, called in latin *acumen.* **1645** M. CASAUBON *Orig. Cause of Temp. Evils* 54 Neither is the jest or *acumen* of them [epigrams] any wayes improved by it. **1678** GALE *Crt. of Gentiles* III. 124 So penetrant an acumen, so profound soliditie. **1764** REID *Inq. Hum. Mind* i. §5. 102 The honour and reputation justly due to his metaphysical acumen. **1860** MOTLEY *Netherlands* (1868) I. ii. 54 Mysteries.. which no political sagacity or critical acumen could have divined.

‖**2.** *Bot.* A tapering point. Gray *Bot. Text-bk.*

1794 MARTYN *Rousseau's Bot.* xxxi. 475 *Mercurialis* has two subulate acumens or sharp points.

acumer, var. ACCUMBER *v. Obs.,* to encumber.

acuminate (əˈkjuːmɪnət), *ppl. a.* [ad. L. *acūmināt-us* pa. pple. of *acūminā-re* to point; f. *acūmen, acūmin-,* see ACUMEN.]

1. Pointed, tapered or tapering to a point. *esp.* in *Nat. Hist.*

1646 SIR T. BROWNE *Pseud. Ep.* 369 The Nightingale hath some disadvantage in the tongue; which is not acuminate and pointed as in the rest, but seemeth as if cut off. **1650** BULWER *Anthropomet.* i. 16 If the Occipitium transgresse its bounds the Head is acuminate. *a* **1661** HOLYDAY *Juv.* 210 The other [tiara] upright and acuminate, worn only by kings. **1794** MARTYN *Rousseau's Bot.* xxix. 454 You will know it by the lance-shaped, acuminate leaves. **1874** E. COUES *Birds of N.-West* 401 The tail equals, or rather exceeds, the wing in length, and consists of twenty very narrow acuminate feathers. **1875** BLAKE *Zool.* 201 The teeth are conical, acuminate, and crowded.

b. *absol.* quasi-*sb.* A pointed form.

1605 BACON *Adv. Learn.* (1640) 109 He had on his Head a pair of Hornes, riseing in a sharp acuminate to Heaven.

†**2.** Having acumen, sharp-witted. *Obs. rare.*

1654 GAYTON *Festiv. Notes* IV. v. 198 Rare, acuminate, quick and phantasticall blades of your employment, that have hundred witty Remoras for their guests.

acuminate (əˈkjuːmɪneɪt), *v.* [f. L. *acūmināt-* ppl. stem of *acūminā-re*; see prec.]

1. *trans.* To sharpen, to point; to give poignancy or keenness to.

1611 CORYAT *Crudities* 452 Where the thicknesse doth begin to be acuminated in a slender toppe. *a* **1800** COWPER in Hayley's *Life* II. 250 Tones so dismal, as to make woe itself insupportable, and to acuminate even despair. **1806** W. TAYLOR in *Ann. Rev.* IV. 613 They often supply an agreeable variation of imagery, and serve to acuminate attention. **1879** *Cornh. Mag.* Dec., 689 The work has been revised and acuminated.

†**2.** *intr.* To rise or taper to a point. *Obs. rare.*

1641 MILTON *Church Govt.* vi. (1851) 128 Their hierarchies acuminating still higher and higher in a cone of Prelaty.

acuminated (əˈkjuːmɪneɪtɪd), *ppl. a.* [f. prec. + -ED.]

1. Brought to a sharp point, pointed. *fig.* Of speech: Sharp, pointed, stinging.

1611 CORYAT *Crudities* 261 The toppe whereof on both sides above their forehead is acuminated in two peakes. **1615** CROOKE *Body of Man* 440 Pericles had an accuminated head and somewhat long. **1790** COWPER *Iliad* xv. 635, A spear Tough grain'd, acuminated, sharp with brass. **1833–48** H. COLERIDGE *North. Worthies* III. 333 So perfect a model of acuminated satire. **1866** HUXLEY *Prehist. Rem. Caithn.* 91 The palate is narrowed, and its arch somewhat acuminated in front.

2. Intellectually sharpened, made keen in discernment; acutely concentrated (in attention).

1831 G. P. R. JAMES *De L'Orme* xlvi. 313 Mounted troopers.. acuminated in every point of stratagem. **1861** H. MACMILLAN *Footn. fr. Page of Nat.* 14 We observe with speechless admiration that the Divine attention is acuminated and His skill concentrated on these vital atoms.

acuminating (əˈkjuːmɪneɪtɪŋ), *ppl. a.* [f. as prec. + -ING².] Rising or tapering to a point.

1804 JAMESON *Mineral.* I. 213 The acuminating planes form truncations on the angles. **1850** DANA *Geol.* App. I. 694 The approximated and acuminating apices of the beaks.

acumination (əˌkjuːmɪˈneɪʃən). [n. of action f. L. *acūminā-re* to sharpen; as if ad. L. **acūminātiōn-em*; see -ATION.]

1. The action of sharpening or bringing to a point; the giving point to. *lit.* and *fig.*

1837 WHEWELL *Induct. Sc.* III. xv. i. 197 Truncation, acuation and acumination, or replacement by a plane, an edge, a point respectively. **1879** *Cornh. Mag.* Dec., 689 The acumination consisting mainly in a more frequent and sarcastic repetition of the unfortunate Mr. Disraeli's titles and distinctions.

2. The product of sharpening or giving point; a tapering point.

1659 PEARSON *Creed* (1839) 270 The coronary thorns.. did also pierce his tender and sacred temples to a multiplicity of pains, by their numerous acuminations. **1804** JAMESON *Mineral.* I. 213 The extremity of the acumination is often truncated.

3. A tending towards a point.

1866 CARLYLE *Remin.* (1881) I. 183 Steadily denied acumination or definite consistency and direction to a point.

acuminose (əˌkjuːmɪˈnəʊs), *a.* [f. L. *acūmen, acumin-,* as if ad. L. **acūminōs-us,* analog. to *lūminōsus.* See -OSE.] (See quot.)

1830 LINDLEY *Introd. to Bot.* (1848) II. 357, *Acuminose,* terminating gradually in a flat narrow end.

acuminous (əˈkjuːmɪnəs), *a.* [f. L. *acūmen, acūmin-* + -OUS. See prec.]

1. Distinguished by acumen; acute.

1618 BOLTON *Florus* To Reader, Whose writings are altogether as luminous as acuminous. **1810** HIGHMORE *Jus Eccl. Anglic.* 149 The same acuminous display of talent and of science.

acuminulate (ˌækjuːˈmɪnjʊlət) *a. Bot.* [f. ACUMINATE, as if f. L. **acūminul-um,* dim. of *acūmen.*] Slightly pointed, or tapering. (In mod. Dicts.)

acunt(e, early form of ACCOUNT *v.* and *sb.*

acuntre, early form of ACOUNTER *v. Obs.*

†**acuˈpiction.** *Obs.*—⁰ [n. of action f. ACUPINGE (*pict-* ppl. stem of *ping-ĕre.*)] 'An embroydering, or as it were painting with a needle.' Bullokar 1676.

†**acupinge,** *v. Obs.*—⁰ [f. L. *acu* with a needle + *ping-ĕre* to paint, embroider.] 'To embroider.' Cockeram 1612.

acupressure (ˌækjuːˈprɛʃ(j)ʊə(r), -ʃə(r); also ˈækjuː-). [f. L. *acu* with a needle + PRESSURE *sb.*]

1. (See quot. 1865)

1859 *Proc. Roy. Soc. Edinb.* 19 Dec., Professor Simpson made a communication on acupressure as a new mode of arresting surgical haemorrhage. **1865** *Reader* 13 May 541/1 Acupressure.. consists of the artificial arrestment of the hæmorrhage from cut or wounded arteries by the pressure of a metallic needle or pin passed across their mouths or tubes.

2. = SHIATSU.

1958 F. M. HOUSTON (*title*) Healing benefits of acupressure. **1977** *Time Out* 28 Jan. 58/4 (Advt.), Acupressure therapy physiotherapist. **1978** *Science* 2 June 1029/1 A few years ago it would have been unthinkable for the federal government to lend its sponsorship to a conference on health that featured such topics as faith healing, iridology, acupressure [etc.]. **1980** *San Francisco Bay Guardian* 16–23 Oct. 14/1 Acupressure: Fingertip pressure technique that releases energy blocks in the muscular system.

acupunctuate (ˌækjuːˈpʌŋktjuːeɪt), *v.* [f. L. *acū* with a needle + PUNCTUATE.] To prick with a needle or pin; also *fig.*

1865 *Macm. Mag.* Jan., 251 That exquisite sweet malice wherewith French ladies so much delight to acu-punctuate their English sisters.

acupunctuation (ˌækjuːˌpʌŋktjuːˈeɪʃən). [n. of action f. prec.] = ACUPUNCTURATION.

1832 SOUTHEY *Lett.* (1856) IV. 305 Colchicum is often successful [in rheumatic gout], but more often fails. The same may be said of Acupunctuation.

acupuncturation (ˌækjuːˌpʌŋktjʊəˈreɪʃən). [n. of action f. ACUPUNCTURE.] The practice or process of acupuncture. *lit.* and *fig.*

1743 tr. *Heister's Surg.* 313 The famous Operation of the Chinese and Japonese, termed Acupuncturation. **1821** *Monthly Mag.* LII. 448 Acupuncturation.. consists in inserting a needle into the muscular parts of the body, to the depth, sometimes, of an inch. **1865** CARLYLE *Fredk. the Gt.* I. I. iv. 34 Her Majesty.. throws into him, as with invisible needle-points, an excellent dose of acupuncturation, on the subject of the Primitive Fathers.

acupuncture (ˈækjuːpʌŋktʃə(r) formerly ˌækjuːˈpʌŋktjʊə(r), -tʃə(r)), *sb.* [f. L. *acū* with a needle + PUNCTURE.] Pricking with a needle; a prick so made. *spec.* The insertion of needles into the living tissues for remedial purposes.

1684 tr. *Bonet's Merc. Compit.* I. 33 They have a two-fold method of Cure [in gout].. Acupuncture, and burning with their Moxa. **1801** E. DARWIN *Zoonomia* III. 254 In cases of strangulated hernia, could acupuncture.. be used with safety? **1872** THOMAS *Dis. Women* 291 Acupuncture.. may be performed by an ordinary three-sided surgical needle. **1875** M. COLLINS *Th. in my Garden* (1880) II. vi. 224 The bees this year are.. stinging with unusual sharpness of acupuncture.

Hence **ˈacupuncturist,** one who practises acupuncture.

1962 F. MANN *Acupuncture* i. 6 The acupuncturist.. has to learn to be aware of emanations so fine and subtle as to be scarcely appreciable by ordinary sense perceptions. **1972** MANAKA & URQUHART *Layman's Guide Acupuncture* I. 78 Many acupuncturists rely simply on this twenty-four-hour biorhythm. **1983** *Listener* 7 July 22/2 Our own Queen has an acupuncturist in attendance.

acupuncture, *v.* [f. the sb.] = ACUPUNCTUATE.

acurology, see ACYROLOGY.

acurse, early (and better) form of ACCURSE *v.*

acushla (əˈkʊʃlə). *Anglo-Ir.* [f. Ir. *a* O + *cuisle* vein, pulse (of the heart); cf. Ir. *cuisle mo chroidhe,* my heart's pulse, my darling.] Dear heart; darling. (Used as a term of address.)

1842 S. LOVER *Handy Andy* vi. 61 'No, *a cushla,*' whispered the aunt. **1865** DION. BOUCICAULT *Colleen Bawn* I. i. 11 Come to your own Eily, that has not seen you for two long days. Come, acushla agrah machree. **1899** SOMERVILLE & 'ROSS' *Exper. Irish R.M.* v. 112 'Come here to me, acushla,' says I to him. **1936** 'F. O'CONNOR' *Bones of Contention* 208 Cross me, acushla, and I'll shift my tent.

acustom, -ance, obs. ff. ACCUSTOM, -ANCE.

acutance (əˈkjuːtəns). [f. ACUT(E *a.* + -ANCE.]

1. The sharpness of a photographic or printed image; a numerical measure of this.

1957 T. L. J. BENTLEY *Man. Miniature Camera* (ed. 5) vi. 82 The sharpness of the edge of hard lines is now becoming known by such terms as 'acutance', 'edge sharpness', [etc.]. **1967** E. CHAMBERS *Photolitho-Offset* 268 *Acutance,* physical measure of image sharpness intended to correlate with the visual assessment of sharpness. **1979** *Mod. Photogr.* Dec. 206/1 CU's hazily described test for sharpness is more like a test for film acutance which must be measured by a microdensitometer. **1986** *Photographer* May 71/2 The resultant negs showed good tone range with even grain structure, good acutance and no loss of film speed.

2. Special Comb.: **acutance developer,** a photographic developer formulated to increase the acutance of the developed image.

[**1962** M. L. HASELGROVE *Photographer's Dict.* 77 High-acutance developers.] **1971** R. E. JACOBSEN *L. P. Clerc's Photogr.* (ed. 4) IV. xxix. 523/2 A typical *acutance developer formula is given below. **1979** *SLR Camera* June 113/1 Indeed it may be worth using an acutance developer to further increase the apparent sharpness of contre-jour pictures.

†**acutangular,** *a. Obs.* [f. ACUTE + ANGULAR.] Having acute angles; acute-angled.

1732 BERKELEY *Minute Philos.* II. 93 Whence they [triangles] are denominated æquilateral, æquicrural or scalenum, obtusangular, acutangular, or rectangular. **1752** CHAMBERS *Cycl.* s.v. *Triangle,* If all the angles be acute the triangle is said to be acutangular, or oxygonous.

acute (əˈkjuːt), *a.* (and *sb.*) [ad. L. *acūt-us* pa. pple. of *acu-ĕre* to sharpen.]

A. *adj.* 1. Sharp at the end, coming to a sharp point, pointed. ***acute angle***, one less than a right angle.

1570 Billingsley *Euclid* I. xi. 3 An acute angle is that, which is lesse then a right angle. **1599** A. M. *Gabelhouer's Phys.* 29/1 Take the extreamest acute toppes of sage. **1668** Culpepper & Cole *Bartholinus, Anat.* IV. ii. 162 Growing smaller by little and little, it terminates with an acute end. **1794** Martyn *Rousseau's Bot.* xvi. 179 The stigma which was obtuse in that, is acute in this. **1842** Gray *Struct. Bot.* iii.§4 (1880) 97 Leaves may be.. *acute*, ending in an acute angle, without special tapering. **1879** Northcott in *Cassell's Techn. Educ.* IV. 2/2 The softer the material the more acute should be the angle of the cutting tool.

2. Of diseases: Coming sharply to a point or crisis of severity; opposed to *chronic*. Also *fig.* Severe; crucial.

1667 *Phil. Trans.* II. 546 She had every year an acute disease or two. **1727** Arbuthnot *John Bull* 64 It is plainly an acute distemper, and she cannot hold out three days. **1876** tr. *Wagner's Gen. Pathol.* 13 Diseases which last but a short time are called Acute. **1877** Roberts *Handbk. Med.* (ed. 3) I. 228 Acute rheumatism is distinctly a hereditary disease. **1932** 'E. Price' *Enter—Jane* i. 11 Jane Turpin's financial position.. might well be described as acute. **1941** *Spectator* 12 Dec. 547/1 For months past a state of acute tension has existed in the Far East. **1942** *Punch* 4 Feb. 83/2 Housing Shortage Grows Acute.

b. Of a ward, bed, etc.: designated or reserved for patients with an acute disease.

1958 *Economist* 1 Nov. 402/1 St George's seems to have ousted St Thomas's from the position of being the most expensive acute hospital in the country. **1968** *Listener* 29 Aug. 258/2 Within the hospital grounds there is almost certainly a well-equipped acute-admission unit, staffed by physicians trained in psychiatry. **1977** *Lancet* 9 July 99/2 The hospital.. is planned as an integrated teaching hospital and medical school with 746 acute beds.

3. Of pain, pleasure, etc.: Acting keenly on the senses; keen, poignant, intense.

1727 Swift *Poisoning of Curll* Wks. 1755 III. I. 150 The symptoms encreased violently, with acute pains in the lower belly. **1855** Bain *Senses & Intell.* II. i. §12 (1864) 97 The pleasure is not what would be called acute, or of great intensity. **1876** Grote *Ethical Frag.* i. 10, A man may feel sympathy in the most acute degree.

†4. Of tastes or odours: Sharp, pungent. *Obs.*

1620 Venner *Via Recta* viii. 186 It.. offendeth the head with acute vapours. **1638** T. Whitaker *Bl. of Grape* 24 Let us take a taste, and principally pierce these four vessels, sweet, acute, austere, and mild.

5. Of sounds: Sharp or shrill in tone; high; opposed to *grave* or *low*. ***acute accent***: see accent 1, 2. Also applied to the mark (´) by which this is indicated, or to a letter so marked for any purpose, as *e* acute (*é*).

1609 Douland *Ornithop. Microl.* 70 An acute accent.. musically.. is the regular eleuation of the finall words or syllables according to the custome of the Church. **1656** tr. *Hobbes, Elem. Philos.* (1839) 488 Bodies when they are stricken do yield some a more grave, others a more acute sound. **1779** Johnson *L.P., Dryden* Wks. 1816 IX. 392 The English heroick [is formed of] acute and grave syllables variously disposed. **1855** Bain *Senses & Intell.* II. ii. §8 (1864) 215 The cry of a bat is so acute as to pass out of the hearing of many persons. **1875** Ouseley *Princ. Harmony* i. 3 The most acute [stave] is called the soprano.

6. Of the senses or nervous system: *actively*, Keen, sharp, quick in catching or responding to impressions. Hence *passively*, Sensitive to impressions, delicate, finely-strung.

1762 Kames *Elem. Critic.* xvi. (1833) 216 The acutest and most lively of our external senses. **1812** Miss Austen *Mansfield Pk.* (1851) 11 Her feelings were very acute, and too little understood to be properly attended to. **1817** Jas. Mill *Brit. India* II. v. v. 528 The jealousy of the Admiral was acute. **1878** G. Macdonald *Ann. Quiet Neighb.* xix. 365 His hearing is acute at all times.

7. Of the intellectual powers: Having nice or quick discernment; penetrating, keen, sharp-witted, shrewd, clever. Opposed to *dull*, *stupid*, *obtuse*. In the sense of *sharp in business*, *shrewd*, it is familiarly aphetized, esp. in U.S., to *'cute*.

1588 Shaks. *L.L.L.* III. i. 67 A most acute Iuuenal; voluble and free of grace. **1599** B. Jonson *Ev. Man Out of Hum.* III. iii. 20 The most divine, and acute lady in court. **1755** Young *Centaur* i. (1757) IV. 125 Acutest understandings in religious debates often lose their edge. **1788** Reid *Aristotle's Logic* vi. §1. 128 Chillingworth was the acutest logician as well as the best reasoner of his age. **1814** Davy *Agric. Chem.* 65 Such a circumstance could not be lost upon so acute an observer. **1863** Burton *Book Hunter* 102 Bargains may be obtained off the counters of the most acute. **1860** Bartlett *Dict. Americanisms* 112 About as cute a thing as you've seen in many a day. **1882** *Manch. Even. Mail* 31 May, American girls, in fact, appear to be as cute as the masculine Yankee.

B. quasi-*sb.* sc. accent.

1609 Douland *Ornithop. Microl.* 70 The circumflex is.. contrary to the acute, for it begins with the acute, and ends with the grave. **1824** J. Johnson *Typogr.* II. iii. 34 The five vowels marked with acutes over them.

Comb. In synthetic derivatives, in *-ed*, as **acute-angled**, having an acute angle.

†**a'cute**, *v. Obs.* [f. prec.]

1. To sharpen, quicken (a quality). *rare.*

1637 Nabbe *Microc.* in Dodsl. *O. Pl.* IX. 163 As it acutes Sloth often into diligence, despair May be hope's cause.

2. To pronounce or mark with an acute accent (perh. only in pple. acuted).

1751 Wesley in Wks. 1872 XIV. 80 Monosyllables, unless contracted, are acuted. **1775** T. Sheridan *Reading* 115 Whereas every last syllable in the Scotch is acuted.

†**a'cuted**, *ppl. a. Obs.* [f. prec. + -ed.] Made acute or sharp; marked with the acute accent (cf. *circumflexed*).

1753 Chambers *Cycl. Supp.* s.v. *Acutition*, The error of the moderns in pronouncing acuted syllables in the Greek, as long, when they are naturally short.

acutely (əˈkjuːtlɪ), *adv.* [f. acute *a.* + -ly[2].] In an acute or sharp manner; hence

1. Of things material: Sharply. (Late in this sense.)

1874 Boutell *Arms & Armour* viii. 128 Having the acutely-peaked visor or mesail lowered and closed. *Ibid.* x. 196 Acutely pointed at the toe.

2. Of senses and feelings: Keenly, delicately; sharply, poignantly.

1838 Dickens *Nich. Nick.* xii. (C.D. ed.) 89 Acutely felt by one so sensitive as Nicholas. **1842** Macaulay *Fredk. Gt.* 58 The sore places where sarcasm would be most acutely felt.

3. Of the mental faculties: With ready or quick apprehension, with keen penetration, shrewdly.

1601 Shaks. *All's Well* I. i. 221, I am so full of businesses, I cannot answere thee acutely. **1673** *Lady's Calling* I. §4. 30 Some new comer perhaps has better refined the art, and do's the same thing more acutely and ingeniously. **1756–82** J. Warton *Ess. on Pope* II. §12. 282, A line which Bentley has explained very acutely. **1864** Burton *Scot Abroad* II. ii. 158 The project was acutely conceived.

acuteness (əˈkjuːtnɪs). [f. acute *a.* + -ness.] The quality of being acute; hence

1. Of things material: Sharpness of point or edge.

1646 Sir T. Browne *Pseud. Ep.* 84 Glasse.. by reason of its acutenesse and angularity, commonly excoriates the parts through which it passeth. **1798** Greville in *Phil. Trans.* LXXXVIII. 441 The hexaedral pyramids are usually incomplete in their apex, and they vary in acuteness. **1869** *Daily News* 14 May, To appreciate for himself the poisonous odours of Barnwell Pool, the acuteness of Chesterton Corner, and the perils of the bridge.

2. Of a disease or pain: Sharpness, keenness.

1661 R. Lovell *Anim. & Min.* 438 The acutenesse of the diseases, and signes of concoction. **1732** Arbuthnot *Rules of Diet* 353 If the Patient survives three Days, the Acuteness of the Pain abates.

3. Of sounds: Shrillness, high pitch.

a **1691** Boyle (J.) This acuteness of sound will shew, that whilst, to the eye, the bell seems to be at rest, yet the minute parts of it continue in a very brisk motion. **1760** *Phil. Trans.* LI. 768 All this seems plainly to put the difference of the tones only in the acuteness or gravity of the whole.

4. Of the senses or feelings: Keenness, quickness, sensitiveness.

a **1704** Locke (J.) If eyes so framed could not view at once the hand and the hour-plate, the owner could not be benefited by that acuteness. **1764** Reid *Inq. Hum. Mind* ii. §1. 104 The acuteness of smell in some animals, shews us, that these effluvia spread far. **1823** Lamb *Elia* I. 14 (1865) 115 A constitutional acuteness to this class of sufferings. **1872** Darwin *Emotions* xiii. 342 When we direct our whole attention to any one sense, its acuteness is increased.

5. Of the mental faculties: Readiness of apprehension, keenness of penetration, shrewdness.

1627 Bp. Hall *Epistles* IV. iii. 341 To finde wit in poetry, in philosophy profoundnesse, in mathematicks acuteness. **1755** Young *Centaur* i. Wks. 1757 IV. 109 The boasted acuteness of his superior understanding. **1847** Hallam *Lit. Eur.* II. 235 It cannot be reckoned a proof of his acuteness in Zoology, that he placed the hippopotamus among aquatic animals. **1859** Geo. Eliot *Adam Bede* 166 The father and mother exchanged a significant glance of amusement at their eldest-born's acuteness.

acuti-, a combining form of L. *acūt-us* sharp, in mod.L., as *acūtifolius*; hence in Eng. words formed on them, or on the same analogy, with sense of *sharp*, *sharply*; as **acutiangle** *a. obs.*, acute-angled; **acutifoliate** *a.*, sharp-leaved; **acutilobate** *a.*, sharp-lobed.

1571 Digges *Geometrical Practise* II. iv, Mj. b, Of Acutiangle Triangles, called Oxigonia, there are three kindes.

acutish (əˈkjuːtɪʃ), *a.* [f. acute *a.* + -ish.] Somewhat acute.

1852 Dana *Crustacea* I. 510 Tooth.. acutish, not incurved.

†**acu'tition.** *Obs. rare.* [improp. f. L. *acūt-us* sharp, ppl. stem of *acu-ĕre* + -ition.] = acuition.

1753 Chambers *Cycl. Supp.*, Acutition or Acuition.

acuto- (əˈkjuːtəʊ), combining adverbial form of acute, analogous to L. *sacro-* in *sacro-sanctus*.

1. *prop.* Acutely; as in **acuto-nodose**.

1852 Dana *Crustacea* II. 929 Three abdominal segments.. sparingly acuto-nodose on the sides.

2. Acute + ; as in **acuto-grave**.

1807 J. Thelwall in *Monthly Mag.* XXIII. 30 Their distinctions of gravo-acute and acuto-grave or circumflexes.

acwell, acwench, acwick; see aquell, aquench, aquick.

-acy, *suffix* of sbs. [a branch of the wider suffix -cy, a virtual compound of -y, ME. *-ye*, *-ie*, Fr. *-ie*, L. *-ia*, with preceding *t* or *c*, though the L. was rather *-ci* + *a*, *-ti* + *a*, than *-c* + *ia*, *-t* + *ia*.] 1. ad. L. *-āci-a*, forming sbs. of quality on adjs. in *-āci-*, as *fall-* deceive, *fall-āci-* deceitful, *fallāci-a* deceitfulness, 'fallacy'; so 'contumacy, efficacy.' The corresponding Fr. words are in *-ace*; *-acy* is entirely of Eng. formation, analogous to other endings in -y, for L. *-ia*; cf. -nce and -ncy. A parallel suffix is the more frequent -aci-ty, as in *rapacity*; and an equivalent to both -acious-ness, as in *rapaciousness*, *fallaciousness*. 2. representing or imitating L. *-āt-i-a*, in med.L. often written *-ācia*, OFr. *-acie*, forming sbs. of quality, state, or condition, on nouns in *-āt-* (nom. *-ās*), being only a section of the sbs. in *-tia* from nouns in *-t-*, *-ti-*, in which the suffix was properly *-a*, and the *i* either part of the stem or connective, cf. *inerti-a*, *infant(i-a*, *mīlit-i-a*. Thus: late L. *abbāt-*, *abbāt-ia* 'abbacy', L. *prīmāt-*, med.L. *prīmātia*, Fr. *primatie*, 'primacy'; L. *optimāt-*, Fr. *optimatie*, 'optimacy'; L. *diplōmat-*, Fr. *diplomatie*, 'diplomacy'; late L. *pāpāt-* (nom. *pāpās* = *pāpa*) Anglo-L. *pāpātia* (= *pāpātus*) 'papacy.' Imitation of *primacy* has given 'supremacy,' Fr. *suprématie*. 3. repr. med.L. *-ātia*, forming sbs. of state on nouns in *-āt-us*; cf. cl. L. *-tia* from *-tus*, in *grāt-ia*, *minūt-ia*, *molest-ia*, etc. Thus, (perhaps due in part to form-association with *abbātia*, *prīmātia*, *pāpātia*,) med.L. *advocātia*, *prælātia*, *lēgātia*, 'advocacy, prelacy, legacy,' f. *advocātus*, *prælāt-us*, *legāt-us*; whence without any L. precedent, 'curacy, confederacy, magistracy,' on other words in L. *-ātus* or Eng. *-ate*. Also extended to adjs., as *accurate*, *alternate*, whence 'accuracy, alternacy' = accurate-ness, alternate-ness. So 'degeneracy, delicacy, effeminacy, intimacy, intricacy, inveteracy, legitimacy, obstinacy, privacy, profligacy, subordinacy,' etc. The cl. L. forms answering to these, when f. pples., were in *-ātiō(nem)*, as *accūrātio*, *obstinātio*, *prælātio*, *lēgātio*: hence *-ātio* has been englished as *-acy* in other words where no Eng. *-ate* exists, as *conspīrātio*, *procūrātio* 'conspiracy, procuracy.' Of others the proper L. form was *-ātus* (4th decl.) as *pāpātus*, *magistrātus*: hence in other words this has given Eng. *-acy*, as *episcopātus*, *cælibātus*, 'episcopacy, celibacy.' *Lunacy* has been formed to match *lunatic*, after the relation of *prelacy*, *diplomacy*, to *prelatic*, *diplomatic*. It thus appears that *-acy* f. *-ātus*, *-ate*, is almost entirely analogical and of Eng. formation. 4. repr. Gr. sbs. of state in -άτεια, f. nouns in -άτης, or vbs. in -ατεύειν; as πειρατής, L. *pīrāta*, pirate, πειρατεύ-ειν to pirate, πειράτεια, Anglo-L. *pīrātia*, 'piracy,' identified with L. forms like *legātia* 'legacy' above. Also in *-cracy*, Gr. sbs. in -κρατία, L. *-cratia*, Fr. *-cratie*, as 'aristocracy'; see -cracy.

acyce, obs. form of assize *sb.*

acyclic (əˈsɪklɪk), *a. Bot.* [f. Gr. ἀ not + κυκλικ-ός circular.]

1. Not arranged in circles or whorls.

1878 M'Nab *Bot.* 179 The flowers generally have the parts in whorls (cyclic). Sometimes they are wholly (acyclic) or partially spiral (hemicyclic).

2. *Dynamics*, etc. That does not move in circles.

1873 Maxwell *Electr. & Magn.* I. 137 As the negative region continues to expand till it fills all space, it loses every degree of cyclosis it has acquired, and becomes at last acyclic. **1902** *Encycl. Brit.* XXVII. 570/2 The system now behaves, as regards the co-ordinates q_1, q_2.. q_m, exactly like the acyclic type there contemplated. **1963** *New Scientist* 7 Feb. 294 A commercial-scale acyclic generator has been constructed and put to work.

3. *Chem.* Applied to an organic compound that contains no 'cycle' or ring of atoms.

1909 *Chem. Abstr.* 2145 (*title*) Cyclization of acyclic diketones. **1913** Bloxam & Lewis *Chem.* 544 There are two great divisions of organic compounds (*a*) The acyclic, open-chain, fatty or aliphatic.. series; (*b*) the cyclic or closed-chain series.

acyclovir (eɪˈsaɪkləʊvɪər). *Pharm.* [f. acycl(ic *a.* + -o + *vir*(*al DNA*) (see viral *a.*).] An antiviral drug, 9-(2-hydroxyethoxymethyl) guanine, $C_8H_{11}N_5O_3$, that is effective against some kinds of herpes.

1979 *Approved Names 1977* (Brit. Pharmacopœia Comm.) Suppl. v, Acyclovir. **1981** *Maclean's Mag.* 2 Nov. 24 The beauty of acyclovir is that it remains inactive in the body until it comes in contact with a herpes-induced enzyme. The enzyme then activates the drug. **1983** *New Scientist* 10 Mar. 642/1 One of the most publicised of the new anti-viral agents.. is acyclovir. **1987** *Sci. Amer.* Apr. 70/3 The special affinity of acyclovir for viral enzymes.. leads to potent antiviral action with minimum toxicity to the host cell.

acyde, obs. form of ASIDE.

acyl (ˈæsɪl, ˈeɪsaɪl). *Chem.* [G. *acyl* (C. Liebermann 1888, in *Ber. d. deutschen chem. Gesellschaft* XXI. 3372); cf. AC(ID, -YL.] Name used to designate an organic radical derived from an acid, as acetyl, benzoyl, etc.; an acid radical; also *attrib.* Hence **ˈacylate** *v.*, to introduce an acyl radical into (a compound); **ˌacyˈlation**.

1899 *Jrnl. Chem. Soc.* LXXVI. I. 553. **1901** *Ibid.* LXXX. I. 118 Transformation of O-Acyl Derivatives..into the Isomeric C-Acyl Derivatives. *Ibid.* 187 Wandering of Acyl Groups. **1907** *Chem. Abstr.* 1290 Indanthrene is not acylated by benzoic anhydride. **1908** *Ibid.* 2088 The reactions of phenylhydrazine and its acyl derivatives..were studied. **1910** *Ibid.* 177 Acylation of Amines and Phenols. **1910** *Encycl. Brit.* III. 756/1 With formic or acetic acids.. the para-semidines give acyl products possessing no basic character. **1949** H. W. FLOREY et al. *Antibiotics* xxi. 807 A free NH group, whose presence could be demonstrated by acylation. **1959** *Times* 6 Mar. 13/7 Various penicillins can be regarded as acyl derivatives.

acyne(n, obs. form of ASSIGN.

acyroˈlogical, *a.* ? *Obs. rare*−0. [f. Gr. ἀκυρολόγ-ος incorrect in speech (f. ἀ priv. + κῦρος authority + λόγος speech) + -ICAL.] Incorrect in use of words. Also *subst.*

1626 COCKERAM, *Acyrologicall*, An vnproper speech.

acyroˈlogically, *adv.* ? *Obs. rare*−1. [f. prec. + -LY².] Incorrectly as to use of words.

1651 BAXTER *Inf. Bapt.* 90 He saith..that the Apostle speaks acurologically and abusively.

acyˈrology. ? *Obs. rare*−1. [ad. L. *acyrologia*, a. Gr. ἀκυρολογία; see ACYROLOGICAL.] Incorrect use of language.

1656 BLOUNT *Glossogr.*, *Acyrology*, improper speech, or a speaking improperly. **1839** LADY LYTTON *Cheveley* (ed. 2) I. x. 221 His work..was meant to be..a condensation of all the 'logics' and all the 'ology's'; but, unfortunately, tautology and acyrology were the only ones thoroughly exemplified.

acyte, early form of ACCITE *v. Obs.* to summon.

†**ad**, *sb.*¹ *Obs.* 1–3. Also 3 od. [OE. *ád* cogn. w. O. and MHG. *eit*, Goth. **aids*; Gr. αἶθος fire, burning heat. The mod. repr. would be *ode.*] A fire, a blazing pile, a funeral pyre.

a **900** *Leiden Gl.*, Sweet *O.E.T.* 114, 95 *Rogus*: beel *vel* aad. *c* **1000** *Poetry of Codex Vercellensis* 1898 (1846) II. 56 And on fyrbæðe suslum beþrungen siððan wunodest ade onæled. *c* **1220** *Leg. Kath.* 1364 Bed bringen o brune a fur amidde þe burh [*v.r.* an ad]. *c* **1225** In Wright's *Vocab.* 94/2, *Rogus* od.

ad (æd), *sb.*² Colloq. abbrev. of ADVERTISEMENT and ADVERTISING. Also *attrib.* and *Comb.*, as ***ad-man***, ADMASS.

1841 W. M. THACKERAY in *Britannia* 1 May 284/1, I'll have my books properly reviewed; or else, I'll withdraw my ads. **1852** *Household Words* V. 5/2 We know that the really interesting 'ads.' are in the body of the paper. **1902** HOWELLS *Lit. & Life* 268 Ad is a loathly little word, but we must come to it. It's as legitimate as lunch. **1909** *Collier's* 22 May 15/2 So in a sense, the ad-man is a public entertainer. **1919** [see WANT *sb.*²]. **1922** JOYCE *Ulysses* 158 Best paper by long chalks for a small ad. **1933** *Scrutiny* I. 400 Like all successful ad-men he has come to believe quite uncritically in what he sells. **1942** M. MCCARTHY *Company she Keeps* (1943) v. 132 He was the Average Thinking Man..that.. ad-writers try to frighten. **1957** *Observer* 10 Nov. 15/4 That side of modern life..which bears the finger-smears of the ad. man. **1958** *Ibid.* 28 Sept. 21/7 The heroine..is straight out of the ad. pages in the shiny feminine magazines. **1959** *Spectator* 19 June 875/2, I cannot change my opinion..that 'admags' in their present form are contrary to the intentions of the framers of the TV Act.

ad-, *pref.* **1.** repr. L. *ad* prep. 'to,' cogn. w. Teut. *at*, frequent in comp. with sense of motion or direction to, reduction or change into, addition, adherence, increase, or simple intensification, as *ad-ventus*, *ad-versus*, *ad-ditus*, *ad-albātus*, *ad-ministrāre*, *ad-augēre*. Before the consonants *c*, *f*, *g*, *l*, *n*, *p*, *q*, *r*, *s*, *t*, *ad-* was in later L. assimilated, as *ac-*, *af-*, *ag-*, *al-*, *an*, *ap-*, *ac-*, *ar-*, *as-*, *at-*; and before *sc*, *sp*, *st* it was reduced to *a-* (*a-scendere*, *a-strictus*, *a-spirāre*). It remained before vowels, and the consonants *d*, *h*, *j*, *m*, *v*. It was probably assimilated before *b*, in *ab-breviāre*, for *ad-breviāre*, cf. *al-leviāre*, *attenuāre*, *accurtāre*. In OFr. *ad-* was reduced to *a-* in all cases where its character as a prefix was recognized, even before vowels, as *adōrāre*, *aörer*, *adornāre*, *aörner*, *adæstimāre*, *aesmier*. But in the 14th c. the written forms began to be artificially refashioned after L., this being in words like *alouer allouer*, *anoncer annoncer*, *atendre attendre*, only an artificial spelling, but resulting, in such as *aörer adorer*, *ajoint adjoint*, in a real change of sound. In 15th c. this fashion spread to England, where the words had originally been adopted in their OFr. forms, and was here carried out far more rigorously, attacking also words that remained unchanged in Fr., or in which the pedantic form was again rejected, as *a-dresser ad-dress*, *a-vertissement ad-vertisement*, *a-vouerie ad-vowry*. All words subsequently formed in Fr. and adopted in Eng., or formed in Eng. on L. words, or according to L. analogies, follow L. spelling. A very recent use of *ad-*, unknown to L., is to employ it in contrast to *ab-* in pairs like *ad-oral*, *ab-oral*, situated *at* the mouth, and *away from* the mouth.

2. While the refashioning of words in OFr. *a-* was going on in 16th c., mechanical imitation or pedantic assumption extended *ad-* and its variants to many words in which *a-* had quite a different origin, as L. *ab*, OFr. *en* (*an*), *es*, *re*, OE. *a* (*ar*), *on*, *æt*, etc.; as in *a*(*d*)*vance* Fr. *avancer* L. *ab-anteāre*, *a*(*d*)*debted* OFr. *endetté*, *a*(*c*)*cloy* OFr. *encloyer* L. *inclāvāre*, *admerveyl* OFr. *esmerveiller*, *a*(*f*)*fray* OFr. *esfreyer*, *a*(*f*)*force* OFr. *esforcer* L. **exfortiare*, *a*(*c*)*curse* ME. *a-curse*, *a*(*l*)*lay* OE. *a-lecȝan*, *a*(*c*)*know*(*ledge* OE. *on-cnawan*, *a*(*d*)*blast* OE. *onblæstan*, *a*(*d*)*dight* OE. *a-dihtan*, *ȝe-dihtan*, *a*(*d*)*miral* Arab. *amīr-al-*. New compounds of native words with prefix *a-* were also falsely written *ad-*, as *a*(*d*)*deem*, *a*(*d*)*doom*. In most of these words the perversion went no farther than the spelling, but in some, as *a*(*d*)*vance*, *a*(*d*)*miral*, it has distorted the spoken word.

-ad, *suffix*¹ of sbs. **1.** repr. Gr. -άδ-α (nom. -άς) forming, **a.** Collective numerals, as μονάς unity, *monad*, so *dyad*, *triad*, *tetrad*, *pentad* (especially used to class chemical elements or radicals according to the number of their combining units); *hebdomad*, *chiliad*, *myriad*, etc.; also *perissad*, *Olympiad*; *decade* retains final *e* from Fr. **b.** Feminine patronymics (in which it is a phonetic variant of *-id*), in proper names of females and districts, as *Dryad*, *Naiad*, *Troad*; often in pl. as *Pleiad-es*, *Hyad-es*, *Cyclad-es*. Hence **c.** in names of Poems, as *Iliad*, 'the lay (ᾠδή) of Ilium,' often imitated in modern times, as *Lusiad*, *Dunciad*, *Rosciad*, *Columbiad*; and **d.** used by Lindley to form family names of plants akin to a genus, as *alismad*, *liliad*, *trilliad*, *asclepiad*, etc. (on words in *-a* or after a vowel; otherwise *-id*, as in *orchid*). **2.** a. Fr. *ade-*, in *salad*, *ballad*; see -ADE the more usual form.

-ad, *suffix*² invented by J. Barclay in *A New Anatomical Nomenclature*, 1803, in the sense of 'towards' (the part denoted by the main element of the word), as CAUDAD, CEPHALAD, DEXTRAD, DORSAD, LATERAD, NEURAD.

Ada (ˈeɪdə). *Computing.* [See quot. 1979¹.] A programming language designed for use with real-time control systems. Freq. *attrib.*

1979 *SIGPLAN Notices* (Assoc. Computing Machinery) June A. p. iii, Ada has been chosen as the name for the common language, honoring Ada Augusta, Lady Lovelace, the daughter of..Lord Byron, and Babbage's programmer. *Ibid.* 1 The Ada language requires that program variables be explicitly declared. **1981** *Yearbk. Sci. & Future* 296 Ada combines many important features that were only available separately in widely different languages. **1985** *Aviation Week & Space Technol.* 1 Apr. 81/2 Ada programming support environment..has been installed at four NASA centers..to help the space agency explore the use of Ada in future projects.

†**aˈdact**, *v. Obs. rare.* [f. L. *adact-* ppl. stem of *adig-ĕre* to drive towards, f. *ad* to + *agĕre* to drive.] To drive or compel to a course.

1622 FOTHERBY *Atheomastix* I. ii. §5, 15 God himselfe once compelled the wicked Ægyptians, by flyes, and frogs.. to confesse the power of his diuine Maiestie; not vouchsafing to adact them by any other of his creatures. **1622** *Ibid.* I. vi. §4, 48 The force of Religion adacteth him.

adacted (əˈdæktɪd), *ppl. a.* ? *Obs. rare*−1. [f. prec. + -ED.] Beaten or driven in by force.

1626 COCKERAM, *Adacted*, driven in by force. **1816** JAMES *Mil. Dict.* (ed. 4) 5, *Adacted*, applies to stakes, or piles, driven into the earth with large malls shod with iron, as in securing ramparts or pontoons.

†**aˈdaction.** *Obs.*−0 [n. of action f. ADACT.] 'A driving in violently or by force.' Bullokar 1676.

adactyl(e (əˈdæktɪl), *a. Zool.* [mod. f. Gr. ἀ priv. + δάκτυλ-ος finger, toe.] = ADACTYLOUS.

1847 In CRAIG.

adactylous (əˈdæktɪləs), *a. Zool.* [f. as prec. + -OUS.] Without fingers or toes. Also applied to crustaceous animals without claws on their feet.

1858 CLARK tr. *Van der Hoeven's Zool.* II. 290, *Pseudopus Merr.*—Two rudiments of hind feet, adactylous.

†**adad** (əˈdæd), *int. Obs.* [Cf. EGAD! of which it is prob. a variation.] An expletive of asseveration or emphasis.

1663 KILLIGREW *Pars. Wedd.* in Dodsley (1780) XI. 419 You cannot, adad; adad you cannot. **1678** WYCHERLEY *Plain-Dealer* III. i. 35 Adad, I shall make thy Wife jealous of me. **1753** RICHARDSON *Grandison* li. (1781) VI. 312 Adad, adad, said he, I do not know what to make of myself. **1763** BICKERSTAFF *Love in Village* 37 Why, you look as fresh and bloomy to-day—Adad, you little slut, I believe you are painted.

adæmonist (əˈdiːmənɪst). *rare.* [f. Gr. ἀ not + δαίμον-α (evil) spirit + -IST.] (See quot.)

1837 *Pen. Cycl.* VIII. 447 Among the German adæmonists, or those who deny the personality of the devil, may also be named Wetstein, Webber, Naudæus.. Unitarians, in accordance with the scriptural adæmonists of Germany, maintain that the Bible affords no sufficient evidence of the existence of a being purely malevolent.

adæquate, obs. variant of ADEQUATE.

adage¹ (ˈædɪdʒ). [a. Fr. *adage*, ad. L. *adagium* a proverb, f. *ad* to + **agi-* root of *ajo* = *agio* I say. (Fick I. 481.) A by-form was ADAGY.] 'A maxim handed down from antiquity; a proverb.' J.

1548 HALL *Chron. Edw. IV*, an. 9, 209 He forgat the olde adage, saynge in tyme of peace prouyde for warre. **1593** SHAKS. *3 Hen. VI*, I. iv. 126 Vnlesse the Adage must be verifi'd, That Beggers mounted, runne their Horse to death. **1605** —— *Macb.* I. vii. 45 Letting, I dare not, wait vpon I would, Like the poore Cat i'th'Addage. **1642** HOWELL *For. Trav.* 25 Every Nation hath certain Proverbs and Adages peculiar to it selfe. *a* **1733** NORTH *Lives of Norths* (1826) II. 355 According to the philosophic adage, *omnes stulti insaniunt*, all fools are out of their wits. **1847** BARHAM *Ingol. Leg.* (1877) 6 That truest of adages—'Murder will out.' **1872** JENKINSON *Guide to Eng. Lakes* (1879) 189 Tourists in their anxiety to cut off a corner are sometimes induced to cross the valley, but..discover the truth of the adage 'most haste, least speed.'

‖**adage**² (ədɑːʒ). *Ballet.* [Fr., ad. It. *adagio* ADAGIO.] = ADAGIO *sb.*2 (See also quots. 1913, 1931.)

[**1913** C. D'ALBERT *Dancing*, *Adage* (l'.), when the sublimity of the subject chosen is represented by postures, attitudes, play of the arms or countenance, in any position or in pirouetting. **1931** C. W. BEAUMONT *French-Eng. Dict. Techn. Terms Classical Ballet* 1 *Adage*, Adagio. It has two meanings according to its application. (1) a dance designed particularly to enable a *danseuse*, generally assisted by a male partner, to display her grace, sense of line, and perfect balance. (2) a generic term for a series of exercises designed to develop grace, sense of line, and balance, particularly when the body is supported on one foot.] **1943** K. AMBROSE *Ballet-Lover's Pocket-Bk.* 24 Whilst tying the shoe-lace, then, imagine maintaining a pleasing serenity of expression, and grace and firmness of bearing at the same time; when some idea of the physical implications of balletic *adage* will be reached. **1957** *Times* 23 Aug. 11/1 Mr. John Gilpin shone, both in his lyrical *adages* and in the passages of *brio*. **1968** J. WINEARLS *Mod. Dance* (ed. 2) ii. 70 An Adage in dancing is a sequence of movements following one another slowly and smoothly in perfect equilibrium.

aˈdagial (əˈdeɪdʒɪəl), *a. rare.* [a. Fr. *adagial*; see ADAGE and -AL¹. Cf. *proverbial*.] Of the nature of an adage, proverbial.

a **1677** BARROW *Serm.* (1687) I. 93 That adagial verse, 'Ἀμ' ἠλέηται καὶ τέθνηκεν ἡ χάρις, No sooner the courtesie born than the resentment thereof dead. **1722** WOLLASTON *Relig. Nat.* §4, 64 Aristotle goes further than that old adagial saying (ἀρχὴ ἥμισυ παντός). **1869** *Contemp. Rev.* XII. 219 This constant resort of Theocritus to adagial expressions. **1913** BARING-GOULD & FISHER *Lives of Brit. Saints* IV. 368 The poem is of an adagial or moral character.

‖**adagietto** (əˌdɑːdʒɪːˈɛtəʊ), *adv.*, *a.*, and *sb. Mus.* [It., dim. of ADAGIO.]

A. *adv.* and *adj.* Slow(ly), but less so than adagio.

B. *sb.* A short adagio movement.

1876 STAINER & BARRETT *Dict. Mus. Terms* 17/1 *Adagietto* (*It.*), a movement diminutive of Adagio. **1909** *Monthly Musical Rec.* 1 Aug. 185/2 Adagietto for strings and harp, Gustav Mahler. **1938** P. A. SCHOLES *Oxf. Compan. Mus.* 16/1 *Adagietto* (It.), slow, but less so than adagio. **1944** W. APEL *Harvard Dict. Mus.* 15/2 *Adagietto* [It.]. (1) A tempo somewhat faster than adagio.—(2) A short adagio. **1976** *Daily Tel.* 4 Dec. 11/2 The strings surpassed themselves in the brief and intimate Adagietto—the real Mahler.

‖**adagio** (əˈdɑːdʒ(ɪ)əʊ), *adv.*, *a.*, and *sb. Mus.* [It. *ad agio* at ease, at leisure.]

A. *adv.* A direction for the musical time in which a piece is to be sung or played: Slowly; leisurely and gracefully.

c **1746** GARRICK *Musical Lady* I. Deep despair now thrums adagio. **1826** DISRAELI *Viv. Grey* VI. vi. 348 Mr. Beckendorff began an air very adagio, gradually increasing the time in a kind of variation.

B. *adj.* Of musical movement: Slow, leisurely.

1773 BARRINGTON in *Phil. Trans.* LXIII. 252, A musical bar of four crotchets in an adagio movement. **1788** A. PASQUIN *Childr. Thespis* (1792) 128 His words flow too quick to administer pleasure In adagio time, and precipitate measure. **1828** E. HOLMES *Musicians of Germ.* 70 In an adagio movement played by this gentleman..I found excellent taste.

C. *sb.* **1.** A slow movement in music; a piece of music in adagio time. Also *fig.*

1784 COWPER *Task* II. 361 [He] sells accent, tone, And emphasis in score, and gives to prayer The *adagio* and *andante* it demands. *a* **1790** T. WARTON *Wks.* I. 187 (T.) He has no ear for musick, and cannot distingish a jig from an adagio. **1867** *Cornh. Mag.* Jan. 31 The adagio is hurried till it overtakes the allegro, and the allegro apes the manners of the presto. **1876** GEO. ELIOT *D. Deronda* II. xxvii. 187 Said G. in an adagio of utter indifference.

2. A dance or ballet movement in adagio time. Also *attrib.*

1830 R. BARTON tr. *Blasis's Code of Terpsichore* II. i. 56 Can any thing be more ludicrous than to see a thick-set dancer.. gravely figure off in a slow and mournful *adagio*? **1922** BEAUCLERK & EVRENOV tr. *Svetlov's Karsavina* 16 No dancer could find a better partner in *pas de deux* or *adagio*. **1929** M. LIEF *Hangover* 179 That new adagio team I imported from Vienna. **1946** WODEHOUSE *Joy in Morning* iii. 18 He spun round with a sort of guilty bound, like an adagio dancer. **1959** *Sunday Times* 29 Mar. 11/5 This *adagio* should never be devoid of character when it is part of the full-length ballet.

†**'adagy.** *Obs.* Also 6–7 **adagie.** [ad. L. *adagium* (see ADAGE), also found unchanged, and (improperly) as *adagia*.] A by-form of ADAGE, frequent in 17th c.

1549 *Compl. Scotl.* xv. 127 Conformand til ane adagia of ane of the seuyn sapientis of rome. **1570** ASCHAM *Scholem.* II. (Arb.) 128 All adagies, all similitudes and all wittie sayinges. **1591** HORSEY *Trav.* (1857) 266 This true adagium, *Si Christum s[c]is, nihill est si cetera non s[c]is.* **1642** MILTON *Apol. for Smect.* (1851) 255 Quips and snapping adagies. **1656** JER. TAYLOR *Deus Justif.* Ep. Ded., That wise Heathen said rarely well in his little adagie. *a* **1670** HACKET *Life of Williams* I. (1693) 17 The Greek Adagy goes, *Nil sine Theseo*.

adalin ('ædəlɪn). *Chem.* Also **adaline.** [a. G. *adalin* (1910 *Medizinische Klinik* 20 Nov. 1859/1).] (See quots.)

1911 *Jrnl. Chem. Soc.* C. II. 1120 Adaline is a sedative producing light, but lasting, sleep. **1912** *Ibid.* CII. I. 244 Adaline (*a*-bromo-*a*-ethylbutyrylcarbamide).

Adam[1] ('ædəm). [Heb. *ā-dām* man.]

1. a. The name given in the Bible to the first man, the father of the human race; hence *fig.* as in the phrase ***Old Adam***, the 'old man' of St. Paul (*Rom.* vi. 6, etc.): The unregenerate condition or character.

a **1569** KYNGESMILL *Godly Adv.* (1580) 27 If you laied Adam aslepe, I meane, if you renounced all carnall affections. **1599** SHAKS. *Hen. V*, I. i. 29 Consideration like an Angell came, And whipt th' offending Adam out of him. **1846** GROTE *Greece* (1862) II. vi. 165 An impatience to shake off the old social and political Adam.

b. Phr. ***not to know*** (a person) ***from Adam***: not to recognize him; ***(as) old as Adam***: primevally old. Also, ***since Adam was a boy***, etc.

1784 *London Sessions* Feb. 400/1 Some man stopped me, I do not know him from Adam. **1795** T. WILKINSON *Wand. Patentee* IV. 129 He was so great a stranger I should not have known him from our father Adam. **1839** *Spirit of Times* 26 Oct. 397/1 As great races.. as have ever been run since Adam was a yearling. **1840** DICKENS *Old C. Shop* xxxviii, He called to see my Governor this morning,.. and beyond that I don't know him from Adam. **1867** 'COLONIST' *Life's Work Austral.* 82 Though old as Adam, love is still the theme that interests all hearts in all countries. **1900** BUCHAN *Half-Hearted* xx, I found people I didn't know from Adam drinking the old toasts. **1918** MULFORD *Man fr. Bar-20* ii. 25 You hunt up that pen you've had since Adam was a boy.

2. = ADAM'S ALE.

a **1704** T. BROWN *Wks.* 1760 IV. ii. (D.), A cup of cold Adam from the next purling spring.

Comb. ADAM'S ALE, -APPLE, -FLANNEL, -MORSEL, -NEEDLE, -WINE, q.v.

Adam[2] ('ædəm). The surname of the brothers Robert Adam (1728–92) and James Adam (1730–94) used *attrib.* or *ellipt.* (at first usu. in pl.) to designate buildings, furniture, etc., designed by them.

1872 LADY C. SCHREIBER *Jrnl.* (1911) I. 463 We got three very good 'Adam' pedestals. **1898** *Lady's Realm* July 389/1 Adams rooms. **1900** *Jrnl. Soc. Arts* XLVIII. 374/2 The 'Adams' is the most delicate and refined of all styles founded on the classic. **1903** *Connoisseur* Mar. 21 Adam, and other Furniture. **1914** H. A. VACHELL *Quinneys'* iv. §1, The sweetest table, genuine Adam. **1918** J. ALFRED GOTCH *Eng. Home* ix. 280 Robert was the most gifted, and it is his work which gave rise to the well-known 'Adam' style. **1920** GALSWORTHY *In Chancery* I. xii. 99 The fine reading-room was decorated in the Adam style. **1926** —— *Silver Spoon* I. ii, A blend between Adam and Louis Quinze. **1926** *Times* 31 Mar. 28 Beautiful Adam Residence.

adamance ('ædəməns). [f. ADAMANT *a.*: see -ANCE.] The state or quality of being adamant; firm resolve.

1954 R. HAYDN *Jrnl. Edwin Carp* 208 Mrs. Ottey's attempts to foist further tripe upon me were futile. My adamance was rewarded with.. nourishing ox-tail soup and dumplings. **1961** A. MILLER *Misfits* v. 51 She grabs his arm and her adamance astounds him. **1979** *Verbatim* Summer 12/2 Adamance, as in (from a report by a social worker in Southwark): 'He has expressed his adamance that he will become a responsible member of the community.'

Adam-and-Eve. The Biblical names of the first man and woman.

1. *dial.* A name applied locally to various plants, roots, etc. (See *E.D.D.*)

1789 B. RUSH *Let.* 8 June in T. J. Pettigrew *Mem. J. C. Lettsom* (1817) II. 439 Some of the country people call it *Adam-and-Eve*. **1808** *Monthly Mag.* 1 Dec. 421/2 *Adam and Eve*, the male and female handed orchis. **1959** *Times* 30 Dec. 8/7 A woman will carry a piece of Adam-and-Eve root in a little bag round her neck. It's really *Aplecteum hyemale*, useful in bronchial troubles.

2. As *vb.*: rhyming slang for 'believe'.

1925 FRASER & GIBBONS *Soldier & Sailor Words* 3 Could you Adam and Eve it. **1956** E. A. THORNE *Baby & Battleship* II. 89 A *baby*! Would you Adam-and-Eve it!

adamant ('ædəmənt), *sb.* and *adj.* Also 4–5 **adamaunt, -aund, ademaunt, -and; atha-, attha-, atthe-, attemant, -maunt,** 5 **admont,** 6 **adamounde.** [a. literary OFr. *adamaunt, ademaunt*, ad. L. *adamant-em* (nom. *adamas*), a. Gr. ἀδάμας, ἀδάμαντ-α, orig. adj. = invincible (f. ἀ not + δαμά-ω I tame), afterwards a name of the hardest metal, prob. *steel*; also applied by Theophrastus to the hardest crystalline gem then known, the emery-stone of Naxos, 'an amorphous form of corundum.' In L. poetically for the hardest iron or steel, or anything very hard and indestructible; also, with Pliny, the name of a transparent crystalline gem of the hexahedral system, apparently corundum or white sapphire, but extended and at length transferred to the still harder DIAMOND (q.v.) after this became known in the West. The early med.L. writers apparently explaining the word from *adamā-re* 'to take a liking to, have an attraction for,' took the *lapidem adamantem* for the *loadstone* or *magnet* (an ore of iron, and thus also associated with the ancient metallic sense); and with this confusion the word passed into the modern languages. In OE. it occurs as *aðamans*, from med.L.; and in 13th c. as *adamantines stan*, a transl. of *lapis adamantinus*, with the adj. mistaken for a sb. in apposition to *lapis*, and so englished as *stone of adamantin*. In the current form it is a 14th c. adoption of the literary Fr. *adamaunt, ademaunt*, adapted from the L. in place of the popular form *aïmant* (:—late L. **adimantem*, cf. Pr. *adiman, aziman, ayman*, Sp. *iman*) loadstone, also found in Eng.; see AYMONT. *Diamant* arose as a variant of *adamant* or *adimant*; see DIAMOND.]

Name of an alleged rock or mineral, as to which vague, contradictory, and fabulous notions long prevailed. The properties ascribed to it show a confusion of ideas between the diamond (or other hard gems) and the loadstone or magnet, though by writers affecting better information, it was distinguished from one or other, or from both. The confusion with the loadstone ceased with the 17th c., and the word was then often used by scientific writers as a synonym of DIAMOND. In modern use it is only a poetical or rhetorical name for the embodiment of surpassing hardness; that which is impregnable to any application of force.

A. *sb.* **1. a.** Without identification with any other substance.

c **885** K. ÆLFRED *Greg. Past.* (1871) 270 Se hearda stan, se þe aðamans hatte, ðone mon mid nane isene ceorfan ne mæȝ. *c* **1225** *Hali Meidenhad* 37 Ha is hardre iheorted þen adamantines stan. **1382** WYCLIF *Ezek.* iii. 9 And Y ȝaue thi face as an adamaunt, and as a flynt. *c* **1386** CHAUCER *Knt's T.* (Ellesm.) 1132 The dore was al of Adamant eterne [*v.r.* ademauntz, athamant, atthemant, athamauntz, attemant]. *Ibid.* 447 Writen in the table of atthamaunt [*v.r.* athamaunte, athamaunt]. *c* **1400** *Rom. Rose* 4181 The stoon was hard of ademaunt. **1535** COVERDALE *Zach.* vii. 12 They made their hertes as an Adamant stone. **1579** LYLY *Euphues* (1636) I. 8 The Adamant though it be so hard that nothing can bruise it, yet if the warme blood of a Goat be powred vpon it, it bursteth. **1667** MILTON *P.L.* II. 436 Gates of burning adamant Barred over us prohibit all egress. **1735** SOMERVILLE *The Chase* III. 605 On Rocks of Adamant it stands secure. **1783** COWPER *Lett.* 24 Feb. Wks. 1876, 128, I am well in body but with a mind that would wear out a frame of adamant. **1852** GLADSTONE *Gleanings* IV. xxiii. 158 Here we impinge upon a dilemma hard as adamant. **1875** FARRAR *Silence & Voices* Ser. I. 14 Around every step of our career on earth the mystery of the Infinite rises like a wall of adamant.

b. *fig.*

1642 R. CARPENTER *Exper.* II. vii. 178 For the bloud of Christ will breake the Adamant of his heart. **1828** CARLYLE *Misc.* (1857) I. 223 In collision with the sharp adamant of Fate. **1860** MOTLEY *Netherl.* I. ii. (1868) 47 The young King .. was not adamant to the temptations spread for him.

†**2. a.** Identified with the diamond. *Obs.*

1393 GOWER *Conf.* III. 112 The seconde [stone in the crown] is an adamant. *c* **1440** *Prom. Parv.*, Adamant, precyowse stone, *Adamas*. **1598** GREENE *James IV* (1861) 201 The adamant, O king, will not be fil'd But by itself. **1617** FYNES MORYSON I. III. i. 213 They say that Adamants are found here, which skilfull jewellers repute almost as precious as the Orientall. **1794** SULLIVAN *View of Nat.* I. xxix. 438 The garnet, and diamond, or adamant.

†**b.** as the natural opposite of the loadstone. *Obs.*

1398 TREVISA *Barth. De P.R.* XVI. viii. (1495) 557 This stone Adamas is dyuers and other than an Magnas, for yf an adamas be sette by yren it suffryth not the yren come to the magnas, but drawyth it by a manere of vyolence fro the magnas. **1567** MAPLET *Greene Forest* I The Adamant placed neare any yron, will not suffer it to be drawen away of the Lode Stone. **1750** *Leonardus's Mirr. Stones* 63 The Adamant.. is such an enemy to the magnet, that if it be bound to it, it will not attract iron.

†**3. a.** Identified with the loadstone or magnet. *Obs.*

1366 [under 3 b]. *c* **1400** *Rom. Rose* 1182 Right as an adamaund, iwys, Can drawen to hym sotylly The yren. **1481** CAXTON *Myrrour* II. vii. 79 In ynde groweth the Admont stone.. she by her nature draweth to her yron. **1527** WHITTINTON *Gramm.*, *Lapis ferrum attrahens*, an adamounde stone, *magnes*. **1614** J. COOKE *City Gallant* in Hazl. *Dodsl.* II. 277 As true to thee as steel to adamant. **1656** BP. HALL *Occas. Medit.* (1851) 52 The grace of God's Spirit, like the true loadstone or adamant, draws up the iron heart of man to it.

†**b.** as the natural opposite of the diamond. *Obs.*

1366 MAUNDEV. xiv. 161 Aftre that, men taken the Ademand, that is the Schipmannes Ston, that drawethe the Nedle to him, and men leyn the Dyamand upon the Ademand, and leyn the Nedle before the Ademand; and ȝif the Dyamand be gode and vertuous, the Ademand drawethe not the Nedle to him, whils the Dyamand is there present. **1579** LYLY *Euphues* K 10 The Adamant cannot draw yron, if the Diamond lye by it.

†**c.** *fig.* A magnet, centre of attraction. *Obs.*

1596 DRAYTON *Leg.* III. 67 My Lookes so powerfull Adamants to Love. **1610** *Histrio-mastix* II. 47 Your bookes are Adamants, and you the Iron That cleaves to them. **1622** HEYLIN *Cosmogr.* Introd. 4/2 (1674) The seat of Religion is not the least Adamant which draws people to it. **1625** BACON *Ess.* xviii. 523 A great Adamant of Acquaintance.

†**4.** Confusing 3 with 1 or 2. *Obs.*

1590 SHAKS. *Mids. N.D.* II. i. 195 You draw me, you hard-hearted Adamant, But yet you draw not Iron, for my heart Is true as steele.

5. *Attrib.*

1387 TREVISA *Higden* Rolls Ser. I. 221 Adamant stones [L. *lapides magnetes*]. **1535** COVERDALE *Jer.* xvii. 1 With a penne of yron & with an Adamant clawe. **1677** R. GILPIN *Dæmonol. Sacra* (1867) 38 Which might make impressions upon an iron breast or an adamant heart. **1878** B. TAYLOR *Pr. Deukalion* I. vi. 50 Solid adamant walls Seem built against the Future that should be.

B. *adj.* Unshakeable, inflexible, esp. ***to be adamant***, stubbornly to refuse compliance with requests. (The point at which the sb. use passed into adj. is not determinable.)

1936 in *Webster Collegiate Dict.* **1943** A. CHRISTIE *Moving Finger* vii. § 1. 77 Both Joanna and I tried to make her change her mind, but she was quite adamant. **1948** 'N. SHUTE' *No Highway* v. 135 C.A.T.O. were adamant that they would not carry Mr. Honey back across the Atlantic in one of their aircraft. **1960** H. E. BATES *Aspidistra in Babylon* 157 In her adamant, challenging, desperate fashion she seized my arm.

Hence **'adamantly** *adv.*

1961 *Sunday Times* 2 July 32/1 'When it's a girl her mother should be the one interviewed,' he stated adamantly.

adamantane (ædə'mænteɪn). *Chem.* [a. F. *adamantane* (Landa & Macháček 1933, in *Collection Czechoslovak Chem. Commun.* V. 4): see ADAMANT, -ANE.] A crystalline alicyclic hydrocarbon, $C_{10}H_{16}$, with a molecular structure composed of three six-sided rings of carbon atoms arranged in the manner of the crystal lattice of diamond.

1933 *Chem. Abstr.* XXVII. 2792 Adamantane, a new hydrocarbon extracted from petroleum.. has the empirical formula $C_{10}H_{16}$... The structure tricyclo[3.3.1.1^{3,7}]decane is.. assigned. **1965** *New Scientist* 8 Apr. 110/3 The new compound has certain features in common with a substance called adamantane.., which can be made by rearranging the atoms of carbon and hydrogen in tetrahydrodicyclopentadiene. **1971** *Nature* 31 Dec. 518/2 For those of our organic chemists who.. have exhausted the cubanes and adamantanes, there is a whole new world of molecular complexity in the catenanes, rataxanes, knots and loops.

†**adaman'tean,** *a.* *Obs. rare*$^{-1}$. [f. L. *adamantē-us* adj. (f. *adamant-* + -E-) + -AN.] Of adamant; of the nature or strength of adamant.

1671 MILTON *Samson* 134 Chalybean tempered steel, and frock of mail Adamantean proof.

†**ada'mantic,** *a.* *Obs. rare*$^{-1}$. [f. ADAMANT + -IC.] Having the nature of adamant (incl. loadstone).

1605 *Jeronimo* I. in Hazl. *Dodsl.* IV. 372 A silver tongue.. that, when I approach Within the presence of this demigoddess, I may possess an adamantic power.

adamantine (ædə'mæntɪn), *a.* [ad. L. *adamantin-us* a. Gr. ἀδαμάντιν-ος adj. of material, f. ἀδάμας; see ADAMANT.]

1. Made of, or having the qualities of adamant; incapable of being broken, dissolved, or penetrated; immovable, impregnable.

1382 WYCLIF *Jer.* xvii. 1 The synne of Juda writen is with an irene pointel, in an adamantyne nail. **1590** GREENE *Mourn. Garm.* (1616) 20 That set a fire with piercing flames euen hearts adamantine. **1599** MARSTON *Sco. Vill.* II. viii. 211 Vnlesse the Destin's adamantine band Should tye my teeth, I cannot chuse but bite. **1610** HOLLAND *Camden's Brit.* I. 39 To the end it might be a State Adamantine.. that is, invincible. **1662** H. MORE *Antid. agt. Ath.* Pref. Gen. 26 (1712) These are the Adamantine Laws and Tyes of Religion. **1667** MILTON *P.L.* II. 646 Three folds were brass, Three iron, three of adamantine rock. **1718** POPE *Iliad* II. 581 To count them all, demands a thousand tongues, A throat of brass, and adamantine lungs. **1727** W. MATHER *Young Man's Comp.* 68 Vertue is an Adamantine Monument, and Invincible Fortress. **1817** COLERIDGE *Biogr. Lit.* 70 The adamantine chain of the logic. **1849** MACAULAY *Hist. Eng.* II. 167, A risk which severely tried even the adamantine fortitude of Cromwell. **1865** RUSKIN *Sesame* 129 The victorious truth and adamantine purity of a woman.

adamantine spar, an old name of CORUNDUM.

1798 GREVILLE *Corundum* in *Phil. Trans.* LXXXVIII. 403 The mineral substance from the East Indies which is generally called Adamantine Spar. **1874** WESTROPP *Prec. Stones* 59 When first introduced into the European *atelier*, some ninety years ago, it [corundum] was known by the name of adamantine spar.

†**2.** Having the qualities of the loadstone; magnetic. *Obs.*

1604 DEKKER *Kings' Entert.* (1873) I. 269 All mens eyes were presently turned to the North.. like the poynts of so many geometricall needles, through a fixed and Adamantine desire. **1641** BRATHWAIT *Eng. Gentl.* 6 The eyes.. those adamantine orbes which attract affection to us. **1655** GOUGE *Comm. on Hebr.* xi. 15, III. 59 The world hath an adamantine force to draw mens hearts to it.

adamantinoma (ˌædəmæntɪˈnəʊmə). *Path.* [mod.L., f. ADAMANTIN(E *a.* + -OMA.] (See quot. 1926.) Cf. ODONTOME.

1922 W. G. CARNATHAN in *Jrnl. Tenn. Med. Assoc.* *1921–22* XIV. 408 (*title*) A study of adamantinoma, with report of a case. **1926** R. J. E. SCOTT *Gould's Med. Dict.* 31/1 *Adamantinoma*, an epithelial tumor resembling in structure the enamel organ of a developing tooth. **1931** *Nomencl. Dis.* (*Min. of Health*) (ed. 6) 84 *Adamantinoma*, fibrotic disease of the jaw. **1952** *Lancet* 1 Nov. 862/2 (*title*) The Multilocular Cystic Tumour or Adamantinoma of the Jaw.

†**adaˈmantive**, *a. Obs. rare.* [f. ADAMANT + -IVE; or perh. misprinted for *adamantine*, with 'turned n (u)' as *u* = *v*.] = ADAMANTINE.

1599 BEN JONSON *Ev. Man out of Hum.* II. iv. 166 My adamantive eyes might head-long hale This iron world to me. **1605** DANIELL *Philotas* (1717) 374 Th' Adamantive Ties Of Blood and Nature. ?**1650** *Don Bellianis of Greece* 181 It would have made any Adamantive breast to pitty them.

†**adamantize**, *v. Obs. rare*$^{-1}$. [f. ADAMANT + -IZE; but only cited in pr. pple.] To act like adamant (*i.e.* loadstone); to attract.

1605 WALKINGTON *Opt. Glass of Hum.* 3 The inveigling and adamantizing societies of some.

adamantoid (ædəˈmæntɔɪd). *Crystallog.* [mod. f. Gr. ἀδάμαντος of ADAMANT + -ειδής -form; see -OID.] 'A form of crystal occurring in the diamond, bounded by forty-eight equal triangles.' Dana.

†**ˈadamanty**, *a. Obs. rare*$^{-1}$. [f. ADAMANT + -Y[1]; cf. *rocky*, *pearly*.] Of or characterized by adamant; of the character of adamant; flinty.

1599 NASHE *Lenten Stuffe* (1871) 32 How impetrable he was in mollifying the adamantiest tyrany of mankind.

‖**ˈadamas.** [a. L. a. Gr. (also in OFr.)] = ADAMANT.

1398 [See under ADAMANT 2b.] **1684** I. MATHER *Rem.-Provid.* 73 There is a certain stone called pantarbe, which draws gold unto it; so does the adamas hairs and twigs.

†**ˈadamate**, *v. Obs.*$^{-0}$ [f. L. *adamāt-* ppl. stem of *adamā-re* to love dearly.] 'To loue dearely.' Cockeram 1612, Minsheu 1627, etc.

adambulacral (ˌædæmbjuːˈleɪkrəl), *a. Zool.* [f. L. *ad* to, at + AMBULACRA + -AL[1].] Adjacent to the ambulacra, in sea-urchins and other echinoderms.

1872 NICHOLSON *Palæont.* 113 At their outer extremities the ambulacral ossicles are articulated by the intervention of the 'adambulacral plates,' with plates belonging to the external or integumentary skeleton. **1882** SLADEN in *Jrnl. Lin. Soc.* XVI. No. 91, 204 The ambulacral spines that form the comb belonging to the first adambulacral plate have their bases arranged in a semicircular curve.

adamellite (ædəˈmɛlaɪt). *Min.* [ad. G. *adamellit* (A. Cathrein 1890, in *N. Jahrb. Mineral.* I. 74) f. Mt. *Adamello*: see -ITE[1].] A kind of granite from Mt. Adamello in North Italy.

1896 J. F. KEMP *Handbk. Rocks* 121 *Adamellite*, a name proposed by Cathrein as a substitute for tonalite. **1910** *Encycl. Brit.* VIII. 289/2 Among varietal designations given to rocks of the diorite family are.. 'adamellite' for the quartz-mica-diorite or tonalite of Monte Adamello (Alps).

Adamesque (ædəˈmɛsk), *a.* [f. the surname of the brothers *Adam* (see ADAM[2]) + -ESQUE.] Designating architecture, furniture, etc., (resembling that) designed by the Adam brothers; characteristic of their style.

1942 J. LEES-MILNE *Ancestral Voices* (1975) 10 A terrible house.., with only a vestige of the eighteenth century in the central stairwell, where there is a trace of Wyattesque or Adamesque treatment, a frieze with ram's skulls. **1951** *Archit. Rev.* CIX. 312 Davis as a last resort could always compose in the Adamesque manner. **1964** *Harper's Bazaar* Dec. 90/1 Chimney-pieces with Adamesque decorations on brand new matchwood. **1982** BARR & YORK *Official Sloane Ranger Handbk.* 135/1 An Adamesque surround in classical proportions.. should be installed if the original has gone up in smoke.

Adamhood (ˈædəmhʊd). [f. ADAM[1] + -HOOD.] *poet.* Manhood, humanity.

1857 EMERSON *Poems* 29 They discredit Adamhood.

Adamic (əˈdæmɪk), *a.* [f. ADAM[1] + -IC. Cf. Fr. *adamique*.] Of or belonging to Adam; = ADAMICAL.

1657 R. TURNER *Paracelsus* 32 The Composition of this sacred Adamick Stone, is made after the Adamick Mercury of the wise men. **1753** CHAMBERS *Cycl. Supp.*, *Adamic earth* is a name some have given to common clay. **1788** WESLEY *Wks.* 1872 VI. 412 Neither can any man, while he is in a corruptible body, attain to Adamic perfection. **1839** BAILEY *Festus* xix (1848) 210 That with man it rests to reinstate the Adamic Eden. **1868** DILKE *Greater Brit.* I. II. i. 322 The rest dressed as they pleased.. generally in Adamic style.

Adamical (əˈdæmɪkəl), *a.* [f. ADAM[1] + -ICAL.] Of or pertaining to Adam; resembling Adam, in moral freedom, nakedness, fallen condition.

1657 R. TURNER *Paracelsus* 27 The matter of the stone is understood to be Adamical. *a* **1658** CLEVELAND *Rel. of Quaker* 64 Though the Devil trapan The Adamical Man, The Saints stand uninfected. **1662** R. MATHEW *Unl. Alch.* §58, 71 To abide in their pure Adamical freedoms, pleasing themselves in all things. **1756** W. LAW *Lett. Import. Subj.* 95 All that is done from the life, the power, and natural capacity of the Adamical nature, is heathenish. **1859** R. F. BURTON *Centr. Africa* in *Jrnl. R.G.S.* XXIX. 415 Many prefer the Adamical costume, having an alacrity at twisting their solitary garment round their neck.

Adamically (əˈdæmɪkəlɪ), *adv.* [f. prec. + -LY[2].] In an Adamical manner; nakedly.

1860 H. KINGSLEY *Geoffry Hamlyn* xlvi. (D.) Standing upon the plunging-stage Adamically, without a rag upon him.

adamine, variant of ADAMITE *sb.*[2]

†**ˈAdamish**, *a. Obs. rare*$^{-1}$. [f. ADAM[1] + -ISH[1].] = ADAMIC.

1569 GOLDING tr. *Heminge's Postill.* 16 Hys newe byrth which sanctifieth the olde Adamishe and corrupt byrthe.

Adamist (ˈædəmɪst). *rare.* [f. ADAM[1] + -IST.] A follower or imitator of Adam; used for 'one who tends a garden.'

1630 J. TAYLOR (Water P.) *Wks.* II. 32/1 He calls it [his garden] Paradise, in which he playes the part of a true Adamist, continually toyling and tilling.

Adamite (ˈædəmaɪt), *sb.*[1] and *a.* [f. ADAM[1] + -ITE.]

A. *sb.*

1. A descendant or child of Adam, a human being; also, **b.** with some, a name for that section of the human race which alone they derive from Adam.

1635 HOWELL *Lett.* (1650) II. 9 Error therefore entring into the world with sin among us poor Adamites. **1821** BYRON *Heaven & Earth* I. iii, I ne'er thought till now To hear an Adamite speak riddles to me. **1865** *Reader* 28 Jan. 98/1 That the Adamites or Caucasians were created, as the Bible tells us, about 6,000 years ago.

2. An imitator of Adam in his nakedness, an unclothed man; in *Eccl. Hist.* the name of sects, ancient and modern, who affected to imitate Adam in this respect.

1628 BP. HALL *Hon. of Maried Clergie* I. §4. 743 We know well what the.. Adamites, and Apostoliques, held of matrimonie. **1657** S. COLVIL *Whig's Supplic.* (1751) 143 Some Adamits, who as the speech is, Cast off their petticoats and breeches. **1713** *Guardian* No. 134 (1756) II. 205 There was a sect of men among us, who called themselves Adamites, and appeared in publick without clothes. **1831** CARLYLE *Sart. Res.* (1858) 34 An enemy to Clothes in the abstract. A new Adamite.

B. *adj.* Descended from Adam; human. Cf. A. 1.

1860 RUSKIN *Mod. Painters* V. IX. i. §11, 203 Two states of this image.. both Adamite, both human, both the same likeness. **1870** *Athenæum* 14 May 642 The black Turanian who uniting with the white Aryan.. gave rise to a third or Adamite race.

adamite (ˈædəmaɪt), *sb.*[2] *Min.* [See quot.] A hydrous arsenate of the Olivenite group.

1837–80 DANA *Mineral.* 565 Adamite.. is a zinc olivenite. On charcoal fuses, producing a coating of oxyd of zinc. Named after Mr. Adam of Paris.

†**Adaˈmitic**, *a. Obs. rare*$^{-1}$. [f. ADAMITE + -IC.] Of, pertaining to, or resembling an ADAMITE.

1662 JER. TAYLOR *Artif. Handsom.* 164 (T.) Nor is it other than rustick or adamitick impudence to confine nature to itself, and to strip our bodies, etc.

†**Adaˈmitical**, *a. Obs. rare.* [f. prec. + -AL[1].] = ADAMITIC.

1666 G. ALSOP *Maryland* (1869) 45 Nor did I ever see.. any of those dancing Adamitical sisters. **1704** *Gent. Instruct.* 169 (D.) Nor your Adamitical garments fence virtue in London.

Adamitism (ˈædəmaɪtɪz(ə)m). [f. ADAMITE + -ISM.] The system of the Adamites.

1831 CARLYLE *Sart. Res.* (1858) 34 [Chapter on] Adamitism.

Adam's ale. Humorous name for water, as the only drink of our first parents. (See also ADAM[1] 2.)

1643 PRYNNE *Sov. Power of Parl.* II. 32 They have beene shut up in prisons and dungeons.. allowed onely a poore pittance of Adams Ale, and scarce a penny bread a day to support their lives. *a* **1845** HOOD *Drinking Song.* iv. We'll drink Adam's ale, and we get it pool measure.

Adam's apple. [In allusion to the story of the Fall.]

1. A name given to a variety of the Lime or Bergamotte (*Citrus Limetta*), and sometimes to varieties of the Orange and Shaddock.

1599 HAKLUYT *Voy.* II. 227 There came two of their Barkes neere vnto our ship laden with fruite.. which wee call Adams apples. **1615** SANDYS *Trav.* 224 The apples of Adam.. the iuyce wherof they tunne vp and send into Turky. **1725** BRADLEY *Fam. Dict.*, *Adam's Apple*.. a Fruit but little different from Lemons. **1866** LINDLEY & MOORE *Treas. Bot.* I. 292/2 Among them [limes] is one called by the Italians *Pomo d'Adamo*, because they fancy the depressions on its surface appear as if it still bore the marks of Adam's teeth.

2. The projection formed in the neck by the anterior extremity of the thyroid cartilage of the larynx.

1755 JOHNSON, *Adam's-apple*, a prominent part of the throat. **1847** CRAIG, *Adam's-apple*, so called from a superstitious notion that a piece of the forbidden fruit stuck in Adam's throat, and occasioned this prominence. **1865** *Daily Tel.* 20 July, Having the noose adjusted and secured by tightening above his 'Adam's apple.' **1872** HUXLEY *Physiol.* vii. 178 The thyroid cartilage.. constitutes what is commonly called 'Adam's apple.'

Adam's Flannel. *Herb.* The Great Mullein (*Verbascum Thapsus*). 'From the texture and appearance of the leaves.' Britten *Plant-Names.*

adamsite[1] (ˈædəmzaɪt). *Min.* A synonym of MUSCOVITE.

1837–80 DANA *Mineral.* 311 A greenish-black mica, constituting a micaceous schist or rock in Derby, Vt.—the so-called Adamsite of Shepard.

adamsite[2] (ˈædəmzaɪt). [f. the name of Roger *Adams* (b. 1889), an American chemist: see -ITE[1].] An arsenical compound for use in chemical warfare, etc.

1923 *Nature* 17 Nov. 742/2 The most remarkable results were obtained with an arsenic compound, phenarsazine, known in poison-gas warfare under the names 'D.M.' and 'Adamsite'. **1937** A. M. PRENTISS *Chemicals in War* III. xiii. 275 *Adamsite* (DM), used for cloud attack primarily against an enemy's forward elements to cause temporary casualties. **1961** *Guardian* 17 Mar. 1/7 A gas called Adamsite.. similar but superior to the German gases.. intended to make troops vomit and to tear off gas masks.

†**Adam's morsel.** *Obs.* i. q. ADAM'S APPLE.

1586 B[EARD] *La Primaudaye's Fr. Acad.* (1594) II. 94 The knot or joynt of the necke, or Adam's morsel.

Adam's Needle. [In allusion to *Gen.* iii. 7.]

1. Popular name of the Yuccas (especially *Yucca gloriosa*), plants allied to the Aloes, cultivated as garden flowers. Also ***Adam's needle-and-thread***.

1760 J. LEE *Introd. Bot.* 294/1 Adam's Needle, *Yucca.* **1861** DELAMER *Flower Gard.* 158, *Yucca*—Adam's Needle—In appearance, something between dwarf Palm-trees and Aloes. **1872** OLIVER *Elem. Bot.* II. 260 The Crown-Imperial, Asphodels, and Yucca or Adam's Needle, belong to the order [*Liliaceæ*]. **1891** *Cent. Dict.* [s.v. *Yucca*], From their sharp-pointed leaves with threads hanging from their edges, *Y. filamentosa* and *Y. aloifolia* are known as *Adam's needle and thread* and as *Eve's thread.* **1938** B. DAMON *Grandma* 73 A clump of yuccas, 'Adam's needle-and-thread'.

2. Occ. name of the plant more commonly known as Shepherd's Needle (*Scandix Pecten-Veneris*). 'From the long needle-like fruits.' Britten *Plant-Names.*

Adam's wine, Sc. phrase = Eng. ADAM'S ALE.

a-dance (əˈdɑːns, -æ-), *adv.*, prop. *phrase.* [A *prep.*[1] + DANCE.] Dancing.

1869 BLACKMORE *Lorna Doone* xxviii. (1879) 160 With hope on every beam adance to the laughter of the morning. **1870** LOWELL *Study Wind.* 238 You cannot prevent Béranger from setting all pulses a-dance.

a-dangle (əˈdæŋg(ə)l), *adv.*, prop. *phrase.* [A *prep.*[1] + DANGLE.] In a dangling state or position.

1855 BROWNING *Men & Women* I. 37 The slave that holds John Baptist's head a-dangle by the hair.

‖**Adansonia** (ædənˈsəʊnɪə). *Bot.* [mod.L. f. *Adanson*, name of a Fr. naturalist in 1794.]

1. A genus of gigantic trees (N.O. *Bombaceæ*) containing only two species, of which one is the Baobab, Monkey-bread, or Ethiopian Sour Gourd of W. and Central Africa; and the other the Cream of Tartar Tree, or Sour Gourd of N. Australia.

1797 T. HOLCROFT tr. *Stolberg's Travels* II. xciv. 485 The famous African tree, which is called Barbab, and described by.. Adanson, a French Botanist, after whom it has been named *Adansonia.* **1852** T. ROSS tr. *Humboldt's Trav.* I. ii. 62 The Adansonia or baobab of Senegal, [is] one of the oldest inhabitants of our globe. **1866** A. A. BLACK in *Treas. Bot.* 17 The *Adansonia* has, until lately, been considered the largest tree in the world, but it must now give place to the mammoth tree of California (*Wellingtonia gigantea*).

2. *Paper-making.* (See quot. 1937.)

1888 CROSS & BEVAN *Text-Bk. Paper-Making* vi. 104 Jute and Adansonia are largely used for papers where strength is of more importance than appearance. **1937** E. J. Labarre *Dict. Paper* 3/1 *Adansonia*, inner bark of *Adansonia digitata* or Baobab.. used to a limited extent for wrapping papers.

†**adapertile**, *a. Obs.*—⁰ [ad. L. *adapertilis* that may be opened, f. *ad* intensive + *aperīre* to open; see -ILE.] 'Easy to be opened.' Bailey, vol. II, 1731.

adapid ('ædəpɪd), *sb.* and *a. Palæont.* [f. mod.L. *Adap-is* rabbit, of unkn. origin (adopted as a generic name by G. Cuvier 1822, in *Ossemens Fossiles* (ed. 2) III. 265) + -ID³.] **A.** *sb.* A member of the extinct family Adapidæ of lemur-like primates, known from Eocene fossils in Europe, North America, and Asia. **B.** *adj.* Of, pertaining to, or designating this animal.

1933 A. S. Romer *Vertebr. Paleont.* xxiii. 416 The adapids are obviously proper ancestors for the typical lemurs. **1945** *Ibid.* (ed. 2) xxix. 559 To cite this list is to cite.. a number of the late Paleocene and Eocene families such as.. adapid lemurs. **1973** [see PLESIADAPOID *sb.* and *a.*]. **1977** *Univ. Michigan Contrib. Mus. Paleont.* XXIV. 246 The North American adapid subfamily Notharctinae evolved independently.

adapt (ə'dæpt), *v.* [a. Fr. *adapte-r*, ad. L. *adaptā-re*, f. *ad* to + *aptā-re* to fit; f. *apt-us* fit; see APT.]

1. To fit (a person or thing *to* another, *to* or *for* a purpose), to suit, or make suitable.

1611 Florio, *Addattare*, to fit, to adapt, to appropriate [not in ed. 1598]. *a* **1616** B. Jonson *Discov.* Wks. 1616 II. 128 He is adapted to it by nature. **1636** Healey *Epictetus' Man.* xlii. 65 Adapt the discourses of thy friends unto thine owne as neere as thou canst. **1763** Miller *Gard. Dict.*, A seminary is a seed-plot, which is adapted or set apart for the sowing of seeds. **1756** Burke *Subl. & B.* Wks. I. 182 The senses strongly affected in some one manner, cannot quickly change their tenour, or adapt themselves to other things. **1847** Yeowell *Anc. Brit. Ch.* i. 5 To have adapted poetry to the preservation of their historical memorials. **1855** Bain *Senses & Intell.* II. ii. §3 (1864) 209 The structure of the outer ear is adapted to collect and concentrate the vibrations.

2. a. To alter or modify so as to fit for a new use.

1774 Bryant *Mythol.* I. 117 It is called *Anchia*.. it signified either *fons speluncæ*, or *spelunca fontis*, according as it was adapted. **1858** Hawthorne *Fr. & It. Jrnls.* II. 199 A kind of farm-house, adapted, I suppose, out of the old ruin.

b. To construct or produce by adaptation *from*.

1805 J. Wild (*title*) Dramas Adapted (from the Original French) to the English Stage. **1849** *Athenæum* 3 Nov. 1113/3 A three-act drama adapted from the French comedy. **1852** C. Reade (*title*) The Lost Husband. A drama.. written and adapted from the French. **1911** (*title*) The Concise Oxford Dictionary of Current English adapted by H. W. Fowler and F. G. Fowler.. from The Oxford Dictionary.

3. *intr.* To undergo modification so as to fit for a new use, etc. Const. *to*. Also *absol.*

1956 M. Bryan *Intent to Kill* vi. 67 In our country, the rich have no sense of responsibility. I wonder how they will adapt to the future. **1962** *Listener* 3 May 762/1 Birds certainly adapt to the urban community, and particularly well to the suburban community. *Ibid.* 19 July 84/1 There is an absolute lack of imagination, or failure to adapt, a refusal to face the need for change.

†**a'dapt**, *ppl. a. Obs.* [f. ADAPT *v.* on analogy of ppl. adjs. like *content*, *distract*, *erect*, which were in form identical with verbs, though really adaptations of L. pples. in *-tus*; but there was no L. *adaptus*. The adj. APT may also have helped in the production of *ad-apt*.] Fitted, suited; fit.

1704 Swift *T. of a Tub* ix. Wks. 1760 I. 100 This definition of happiness.. will be acknowledged wonderfully adapt. *a* **1733** North *Lives of Norths* II. 369 Nothing could have fallen out more exquisitely adapt to Mr. North's desires.

adaptability (ədæptə'bɪlɪtɪ). [f. ADAPTABLE *a.*; see -BILITY.] The quality of being adaptable; capacity of being adapted or of adapting oneself; potential fitness. Const. *to*, *for*.

1661 R. Lovell *Anim. & Min.* 315 The manner of using, adaptability of the matter, and nature of the patient. **1796** W. Taylor in *Monthly Rev.* XIX. 513 Adaptability to define and discriminate contiguous shades of idea. **1845** Todd & Bowman *Phys. Anat.* I. 149 One of the most wonderful circumstances in the construction of the hand, is its adaptability to an infinite number of offices. **1873** Farrar *Famil. of Sp.* ii. 69 General adaptability for every purpose. **1875** Stubbs *Const. Hist.* II. xv. 293 The adaptability of his people to the execution of his design.

adaptable (ə'dæptəb(ə)l), *a.* [f. ADAPT *v.* + -ABLE, as if ad. L. **adaptābilis*.] Capable of being adapted; applicable; pliable.

1800 W. Taylor in *Monthly Mag.* X. 317 The very metre employed.. is no less adaptable to the other Gothic dialects than to the German. **1857** Toulm. Smith *Parish* 1 Principles, which are adaptable to all the changing conditions of human progress. **1865** Trafford *Geo. Geith* II. vi. 58 Before marriage men are not so adaptable as women.

adaptableness (ə'dæptəb(ə)lnɪs). [f. prec. + -NESS.] = ADAPTABILITY.

1847 In Craig.

†**a'daptate**, *v. Obs. rare.* [f. L. *adaptāt-* ppl. stem of *adaptā-re*; see ADAPT, and -ATE.] A byform of ADAPT.

1659 *Instr. Oratory* 26 Those [words] derived from the Latine.. being.. more adaptated for many discourses. **1678** Cudworth *Intell. Syst.* I. v. 690 It is your work now to Adaptate the Mortal to the Immortal.

adaptation (ædæp'teɪʃən). [a. Fr. *adaptation*, ad. late L. *adaptātiōn-em*, n. of action f. *adaptā-re*; see ADAPT. Not in Cotgr. 1632; see ADAPTING *vbl. sb.*]

1. The action or process of adapting, fitting, or suiting one thing *to* another.

1610 Healey *St. Aug., City of God* 743 They.. made a very ingenious adaptation of the one to the other. **1646** Sir T. Browne *Pseud. Ep.* III. xi. 130 A commixtion of both in the whole rather than an adaptation or cement of the one unto the other. **1782** Priestley *Nat. & Rev. Relig.* I. 29 There are.. many adaptations of one thing to another. **1881** Lubbock in *Nature* No. 618, 411 Electricity in the year 1831 may be considered to have just been ripe for its adaptation to practical purposes.

2. a. The process of modifying a thing so as to suit new conditions: as, the modification of a piece of music to suit a different instrument or different purpose; the alteration of a dramatic composition to suit a different audience; the alteration of form which a word of one language often undergoes to make it fit the etymological or phonetic system of another, as when the L. *adaptātiōnem* is taken into Fr. and E. as *adaptation*.

1790 Paley *Hor. Paul.* I. 3 His adaptation will be the result of counsel, scheme, and industry. **1846** Kingsley *Lett.* (1878) I. 140 Man has unrivalled powers of self-adaptation. **1878** C. Parry in Grove *Dict. Music* I. 89 Arrangement, or adaptation, is the musical counterpart of literary translation.

b. spec. in *Opt.* The adjustment of the eye to variations in the intensity or colour of light. Also = ACCOMMODATION 1 b.

1881 in *Syd. Soc. Lex.* **1920** *Jrnl. Gen. Phys.* II. 499 The phenomenon of retinal adaptation is one of the most familiar facts of sensory physiology. *Ibid.* 516 During the dark adaptation of the human eye, its visual threshold decreases to a small fraction of its original value in the light. **1950** L. C. Thomson in *Brit. Jrnl. Ophthalmology* Mar. 145 The sensory receptor cells in the retina.. play a part in visual adaptation. **1960** R. A. Weale *Eye & its Function* vii. 110 Chromatic adaptation experiments, in which the eye is exposed continuously to a coloured background of moderate luminance.

3. The condition or state of being adapted; adaptedness, suitableness.

1677 Hale *Prim. Orig. Man.* I. i. 2 This adaptation and congruity of these Faculties to their several proper Objects. **1751** Johnson *Rambler* No. 160 ⁋2 The benefit of this adaptation of men to things is not always perceived. **1836** J. Gilbert *Atonement* viii. (1852) 230 He perceives its adaptation to melt his mind. **1867** J. Martineau *Chr. Life* (ed. 4) 291 The adaptation of immortality to our true wants.

4. A special instance of adapting; and hence, *concr.* an adapted form or copy, a reproduction of anything modified to suit new uses.

1859 Darwin *Orig. Spec.* iii. (1873) 48 We see beautiful adaptations everywhere and in every part of the organic world. **1860** *Sat. Rev.* No. 250, 181/2 A French play is adapted by A.. B either appropriates A's adaptation or makes another. *Mod.* The word *pibroch* is our adaptation of the Gaelic *piobaireachd*, that is to say 'piper-ship.'

5. *Biol.* Organic modification by which an organism or species becomes adapted to its environment.

1859 Darwin in *Jrnl. Linn. Soc.* Zool. III. 50 The most vigorous and healthy males, implying perfect adaptation, must generally gain the victory in their contests [for the females]. **1875** *Encycl. Brit.* I. 145/2 Adaptation.. is usually restricted.. to imply such modifications as arise during the life of an individual, when an external change directly generates some change of function and structure. **1897** H. F. Osborn in *Science* 15 Oct., Ontogenetic adaptation.. enables animals and plants to survive very critical changes in their environment. **1904** H. E. Crampton in *Biometrika* III. 114 A rigid.. organization, incapable.. of structural alterations as the result of 'functional adaptation'. **1923** J. S. Huxley *Ess. of Biologist* i. 13 If the degree of adaptation has not increased during evolution, then it is clear that progress does not consist in increase in adaptation.

adaptational (ædæp'teɪʃənəl), *a.* [f. prec. + -AL¹.] Of or pertaining to adaptation.

1879 Lubbock *Scient. Lect.* ii. 42 The modifications which insect larvæ undergo may be divided into two kinds—developmental.. and adaptational or adaptive; those which tend to suit them to their own mode of life.

adaptative (ə'dæptətɪv), *a.* [f. L. *adaptāt-* ppl. stem of *adaptā-re* to ADAPT + -IVE.] Characterized by, or given to, adapting things to a purpose, or oneself to circumstances; = ADAPTIVE.

1857 Tomes *Amer. in Japan* xi. 247 The Japanese are.. a very imitative, adaptative, and compliant people. **1870** Proctor *Other Worlds* iii. 81 Adaptative power.. by which the various creatures we are acquainted with are enabled to live in comfort under all degrees of light. **1875** Stubbs *Const. Hist.* II. xv. 297 The great merit of his statesmanship is adaptative rather than originative.

adaptativeness (ə'dæptətɪvnɪs). [f. prec. + -NESS.] Ability to suit things to a purpose, or oneself to circumstances; = ADAPTIVENESS.

1881 *Harper's Mag.* Apr. 645 He possessed plenty of that Yankee adaptativeness.

adapted (ə'dæptɪd), *ppl. a.* [f. ADAPT *v.* + -ED.]

1. Fitted; fit, suitable. Const. *to*, *for*.

1610 Healey *St. Aug., City of God* 844 As spirits doe in characters and signes ad-apted to their natures. **1754** Chatham *Lett. to Nephew* v. 37 A proper behaviour, adapted to the respective relations we stand in. **1803** W. Taylor in *Ann. Rev.* I. 35 Conferring on Mr. Collins an adapted and distinguished appointment. **1875** Darwin *Insectiv. Plants* i. 3 Drosera was excellently adapted for.. catching insects.

2. Modified so as to suit new conditions.

1816 Southey *Poet's Pilgr.* iv. 52 Wks. X. 103 A race, who with the European mind, The adapted mould of Africa combined. *Mod.* Adapted comedies are being played at several theatres. *Syntax* is the adapted form in which the Greek σύνταξις is used in English.

adaptedness (ə'dæptɪdnɪs). [f. prec. + -NESS.] The quality or state of being adapted or suited; suitableness, special fitness.

1698 [R. Fergusson] *View of Eccles.* 18 Their adaptedness for their employ. **1800** W. Taylor in Robberds' *Memoir* I. 327 The adaptedness of one rhythm or form of stanza for one purpose, and of another for a different purpose, is wholly, or nearly so, the result of association. **1875** Whitney *Life of Lang.* xiv. 293 When the time for the use came, the perception of its adaptedness.. necessarily followed.

adapter, -or (ə'dæptə(r)). [f. ADAPT *v.* + -ER¹.]

1. One who adapts. **a.** One who fits or suits one thing to another. **b.** One who modifies or alters a composition to suit it to new purposes.

1801 Chalmers *Let.* in *Life* (1851) I. 48 Such adaptation speaks of a divine and intelligent adapter. **1858** De Quincey *Wks.* VI. 374 If these imaginary adapters of Homer, according to the German pretence, modernised his whole diction. **1865** *Sat. Rev.* 12 Aug. 210/1 The original author is of opinion that the adapter has not mended but marred his work. **1877** R. H. Hutton *Ess.* (ed. 2) I. 43 Intelligence is the conscious and voluntary adapter of means to ends.

2. A connecting part: in *Chem.* a tube to connect two pieces of apparatus; in *Optics*, a metal ring with screw threads to unite two lengths of a telescope; a 'sliding fitting' in an optical instrument.

1808 Sir H. Davy in *Phil. Trans.* Vol. XCIX. 454 The adaptors must have contained ·8 of a similar gas. **1867** J. Hogg *Microsc.* I. iii. 170 A flat piece of glass placed at an angle of 45° across the tube, interposed like an adapter between the objective and the microscope-body. **1875** Ure *Dict. Arts* I. 7 An adapter tube is then fitted to the lateral cylinder. This adapter enters into another tube at the same degree of inclination. **1876** Chambers *Astron.* 623 A more simple form of solar eye-piece is that which consists of an adapter in which a diaphragm plate is fitted as above.

3. *Electr. Engin.* (See quots.)

1907 T. O'C. Sloane *Stand. Electr. Dict.* (ed. 12) 11 *Adapter*, a screw coupling to engage with a different sized screw on each end; one of the uses is to connect incandescent lamps to gas-fixtures. **1913** *E. E. Becker & Co. Illustr. Catal. Sci. App.* 539 (*caption*) Plug adaptor, for tapping current off any ordinary bayonet-catch lamp-holder. **1943** *Gloss. Terms Electr. Engin.* (*B.S.I.*) 123 *Socket-outlet adaptor*, an accessory for insertion into a socket-outlet and containing metal contacts to which may be fitted one or more plugs for the purpose of connecting to the supply portable lighting fittings or other current-using appliances.

adapting (ə'dæptɪŋ), *vbl. sb.* [f. ADAPT *v.* + -ING.¹.] The action of fitting, suiting, or rendering suitable. (Now mostly gerundial.)

1632 Cotgr., *Adaptation* [Fr.] An adapting, fitting, or suiting of one thing to another. **1656** Cowley *Davideis* I. (1684) 35 An adapting of all these to the Constitution, Disposition, and Inclinations of the Patient. **1714** Swift *State of Aff.* Wks. 1755 II. I. 205, I do not know a greater mark of an able minister, than that of rightly adapting the several faculties of men. *Mod.* This clever adapting of means to ends. He is skilled in adapting French plays.

adapting (ə'dæptɪŋ), *ppl. a.* [f. ADAPT *v.* + -ING².] Rendering suitable, modifying.

1836 J. Gilbert *Atonement* iv. (1852) 91 The adapting intelligence which limited their energy to the discharge of that office.

adaption (ə'dæpʃən). [f. ADAPT *v.* as if formed on a L. ppl. stem; cf. *adopt-ion*. See -ION¹.] = ADAPTATION; the action of adapting.

1704 Swift *T. of a Tub* (1768) I. 127 For great turns are not always given by strong hands, but by lucky adaption. **1790** Blagden *Spirit. Liq.* in *Phil. Trans.* LXXX. 344 The adaption of the duties to different degrees of strength. **1860** Dickens *Lett.* (ed. 2) II. 124 There it is, needing no change or adaption.

adaptitude (ə'dæptɪtjuːd). [A mixture of ADAPT and APTITUDE.] Adaptedness; aptitude specially produced.

1842 Mrs. Browning *Grk. Chr. Poets* 129 A hedge-thorn catches sheep's wool by position and approximation rather than adaptitude. **1852** Browning *Ess. on Shelley* (1881) 16 A profound sensibility and adaptitude for act.

adaptive (ə'dæptɪv), *a.* [irreg. f. ADAPT *v.* + -IVE, as if on ppl. stem; cf. *adopt-ive*; see -IVE.] Characterized by, or given to, adaptation. ***adaptive radiation***: H. F. Osborn's term for the evolutionary process which produces divergent forms in different environments (see quots. and cf. SPECIALIZATION b).

1824 COLERIDGE *Aids to Refl.* (1848) 193 This higher species of adaptive power we call Instinct. **1854** WOODWARD *Mollusca* 56 Modifications relating only to peculiar habits are called adaptive. **1866** ARGYLL *Reign of Law* iv. (ed. 4) 185 Adaptive colouring as a means of concealment is never applied to any animal whose habits do not expose it to special danger. **1875** EMERSON *Lett. & Soc. Aims* iv. 114 Ah! what a plastic he is! so shifty, so adaptive! **1902** H. F. OSBORN in *Bull. Amer. Mus. Nat. Hist.* XVI. 92 They represent an adaptive radiation for different local habitat, different modes of feeding, fighting, locomotion, etc. **1902** —— in *Amer. Naturalist* May 353 One of the essential features of divergent evolution .. has been termed by the writer 'adaptive radiation'. This term seems to express most clearly the idea of differentiation of habit in several directions from a primitive type. **1927** HALDANE & HUXLEY *Animal Biol.* xi. 240 This adaptation to different modes of life, while .. we call it *specialization* when we are thinking only of one species of animal, is called *adaptive radiation* when we are thinking of the group as a whole.

adaptively (ə'dæptɪvlɪ), *adv.* [f. prec. + -LY^{2}.] In an adaptive manner; by way of adaptation; so as to suit special conditions.

1854 WOODWARD *Mollusca* II. 253 The form of the foot is usually characteristic of the families; but sometimes it is adaptively modified.

adaptiveness (ə'dæptɪvnɪs). [f. as prec. + -NESS.] The quality of being adaptive; the capacity or tendency to adapt one thing to another, or oneself to circumstances.

1863 J. C. JEAFFRESON *Everard's Dau.* xiii. 221 The man had .. a subtle adaptiveness as well as sincere desire to please. **1878** C. STANFORD *Symb. Christ* vi. 172 The Saviour's words have minutely particular adaptiveness to every moment of the soul's history. **1879** CARPENTER *Ment. Physiol.* I. ii. §70. 74 The adaptiveness of the movements is no proof of the existence of consciousness.

†**a'daptly**, *adv. Obs. rare*$^{-1}$. [f. ADAPT *a.* + -LY^{2}.] In a fit or adapted manner; by being adapted or fitted.

1709 PRIOR *Colin's Mist.* iii. 3 For active horsemanship adaptly fit.

†**a'daptment.** *Obs. rare*$^{-1}$. [f. ADAPT *v.* + -MENT.] Adaptation; fitting condition.

1739 H. WALPOLE *Lett.* (1861) I. 19 All the conveniences, or rather (if there was such a word), all the adaptments are assembled here that melancholy, meditation, selfish devotion, and despair would require.

†**a'daptness.** *Obs. rare*$^{-1}$. [f. ADAPT *a.* + -NESS.] The quality of being adapted, suitability; = ADAPTEDNESS.

1749 BP. NEWTON *Milton* I. Pref., The variety of the pauses, and the adaptness of the sound to the sense.

adaptometer (ædæp'tɒmɪtə(r)). [f. ADAPT(ATION + -OMETER.] (See quots.)

1917 A. DUANE *Fuchs's Textbk. Ophthalm.* (ed. 5) ii. 127 A better instrument than Förster's is the *adaptometer* of Nagel. **1928** R. J. E. SCOTT *Gould's Med. Dict.* (ed. 2) 31/2 *Adaptometer*, an instrument for measuring the time taken in retinal adaptation. **1934** H. C. WARREN *Dict. Psychol.* 6/1 *Adaptometer*, any device for measuring the course or degree of sensory adaptation, in terms of fall or rise of threshold or sensitivity. **1942** *Brit. Jrnl. Psychol.* July 4 Certain hysterical and pathological eye conditions undoubtedly affect adaptometer results.

†**adap'torial**, *a. Obs. rare.* [irreg. f. ADAPTOR, after *visitorial*, etc. There could be no *adaptor* or *adaptorius* in L.] = ADAPTIVE.

In mod. Dicts. WORCESTER cites MUDIE.

‖**Adar** ('eɪdə(r)). [Heb. *ădā̆r* of uncertain etymol.] The twelfth month of the Hebrew ecclesiastical, the sixth of the civil, year.

1382 WYCLIF 1 *Esdr.* vii. 5 The moneth of March[**1535** COVERDALE *Ibid.* The moneth Addar]. —— *Esther* iii. 7 The twelfthe moneth went out, that is clepid Adar. **1535** COVERDALE *Ibid.* The twolueth moneth, that is the moneth Adar. **1611** *Ibid.* The twelfth moneth, that is the moneth Adar. **1833** *Pen. Cycl.* I. 115/1 Adar may begin as early as the 1st of February, or as late as the 3rd of March.

[**adaration**, Souldiers pay. Cockeram 1626.]

†**adarticu'lation.** *Anat. Obs.* [mod. f. L. *ad* to + *articulātiōn-em* jointing: see ARTICULATION.] A loose jointing of two bones; one which affords room for play; specially, the jointing of a bone into a shallow socket.

1753 CHAMBERS *Cycl. Supp.*, *Adarticulation*, in some physicians, is used for Arthrodia; in others for Diarthrosis. **1853** MAYNE *Exp. Lex.*, *Adarticulation*, a term in all respects synonymous with *Arthrodia*.

ADAS ('eɪdæs). [f. the initial letters of the *A*gricultural *D*evelopment and *A*dvisory *S*ervice.] A service set up in 1971 (in place of the National Agricultural Advisory Service) under the Ministry of Agriculture, Fisheries and Food, to advise farmers and growers, to undertake research and development, and to advise and assist in Government policy measures, in matters relating to agriculture, land use, etc.

1971 (*title*) ADAS advisory papers no. 9. Soil field handbook. **1982** *ADAS Ann. Rep.* 128 ADAS provides a wide range of professional, scientific and technical services to agriculture and its ancillary industries, to Government and to many related organizations. **1984** *Oxford Times* 27 Jan. 16/10 The demonstration .. which was staged by ADAS at the Oxford University field station at Wytham, discussed some methods of reducing lamb mortality.

†**a'dased**, *ppl. a. Obs.* [f. A- *pref.* 1 intensive + *dased*; see DASE, DAZE. As *adase* is not found, it is doubtful whether *a-dased* is not merely the pa. pple. of *dase* with A *particle*, repr. earlier *i-*, *y-*, *ȝe.*] Stupefied, confused, dulled, dazzled.

a **1500** *Poem* in *Todd's Illustr.* 297 As a wytles man gretely adased, I gave no credence. **1532** MORE *Confut. Tindale* Wks. 1557, 459/1 Wold haue made euery mans eyes so adased, that no man should haue spied his falshed. **1556** ABP. PARKER *Psalt.* Ps. cxvi. 336 Myne eyes were so adasd.

‖**adat** ('adat). Also 8 **addat**. [Malay, f. Arab. *ʿāda* custom, customary law.] In the Islamic regions of S.E. Asia: custom, or customary law, particularly in contrast to Islamic religious law. Freq. *attrib.*, as ***adat law***.

1783 W. MARSDEN *Hist. Sumatra* 178 That does not affect their *addat* or customs. **1839** T. J. NEWBOLD *Straits of Malacca* II xiv. 265 Such is the adat. **1906** A. W. S. O'SULLIVAN tr. *Snouck Hurgronje's Achehnese* I. i. 77 There are .. individual cases which are controlled by an adat of native growth. **1927** *Jrnl. Compar. Legislation* IX. 149 (*heading*) Indonesian adat law. **1964** WANG GUNGWU *Malaysia* 15 The majority of people shared .. similar sets of customs and *adat* law. **1978** M. B. HOOKER *Conc. Legal Hist. S.-E. Asia* v. 149 The conflict between *adat* and Islam occurs in all the states of Malaysia and is essentially concerned with the distribution of property arising out of death or divorce.

‖**adatis, -ais, addatys** ('ædətɪs). Indian muslin.

1687 *London Gaz.* mmcclxxiii. 7 The Cargo of the last three Ships arriv'd, is as follows, viz. Atlasses 549 pieces, Addaties 1406, Bettellees 9680. **1806** *Brit. Encycl.* I. 25 *Adatais*, *Adatsi*, or *Adatys*, a muslin or cotton cloth, very fine and clear .. The finest is made at Bengal.

adatom ('ædætəm). *Physical Chem.* [f. *ad(sorbed) atom*: see ADSORB *v.*] An adsorbed atom.

1961 in WEBSTER. **1963** HIRTH & POUND *Condensation & Evaporation* 43 Nucleation .. may occur by either direct addition from the vapor or surface diffusion of an adatom. **1979** *Nature* 6 Dec. 598/1 The surface disorder may be regarded as a random distribution of surface silver vacancies or surface gold adatoms, depending on whether the alloy is gold-rich or silver-rich.

†**a'dauge**, *v. Obs. rare*$^{-1}$. [ad. L. *adaugē-re* to increase by addition, f. *ad* to + *augē-re* to increase.] To add to, augment.

1657 TOMLINSON *Renou's Dispens.* 260 Mixed with other purgatives which may adauge its imbecil purgative faculty.

†**a'daunt**, *v. Obs.* Also 6 **addaunt**. [a. OFr. *adante-r* var. of *adonter* (later *addomter*) f. *à* to + *dante-r*, *donte-r* (mod. *dompter*):—L. *domitā-re*, freq. of *domā-re* to tame.] To quell, subdue, or reduce to submission.

1297 R. GLOUC. 372 Kyng Wyllam adauntede þat folc of Walys. *c* **1300** *K. Alis* (W.) 2853 Ageyns heom thy wraththe adant. *c* **1325** *E.E. Allit. Poems* A. 157 More meruayle con my dom adaunt. **1398** TREVISA *Barth. De P.R.* xv. xii. (1495) 492 Hercules adauntyd fyrste the fiersnesse of the Amazones. *c* **1449** PECOCK *Repr.* I. vii. 37 Forto rebuke and adaunte the presumpcion of the lay persones. **1483** CAXTON *Gold. Leg.* 309/4 For to adaunte and subdue my prowde flesshe I rose at mydnyght alle the weke long. **1523** SKELTON *Garl. Laurel* 1302 With mighty corrage Adaunted the rage Of a lyon savage. **1597** DANIEL *Civ. Wares* IV. xiv. (1609) Wherewith the Rebell rather was the more Incourag'd than addaunted.

†**a'daw**, *v.*^{1} *Obs.* [f. A- *pref.* 1 + DAW, OE. *daȝian* to dawn, become day, awake; cf. MHG. *er-tagen* to dawn. Occ. found as *of-daw*, prob. by confusion with the adv. *adawe* or *of-dawe.*]

1. *intr.* To wake up, awake, from sleep, swoon, etc.

c **1300** *K. Alis.* 2265 Glitoun tho gan furst of-dawen, And his lymes to him drawen. *c* **1374** CHAUCER *Troilus* III. 1120 He gan his breeth to drawe, And of his swoun soone aftir that adawe. **1430** LYDG. *Chron. Troy* I. v. Reioyse wolde these folkes amerous .. And efte adawen of their paynes smerte. **1530** PALSGR. 417, I adawe or adawne, as the daye dothe in the mornynge whan the sonne draweth towardes his rysyng.

2. *trans.* To awaken, arouse, recall to consciousness. (The earlier instances may be intr.)

c **1386** CHAUCER *Merchts T.* 1156 Til that he be adawed verrayly. **1430** LYDG. *Chron. Troy* III. xxii. Hector .. a thousand knightes slowe That neuer were adawed of their sowe. **1447** BOKENHAM *Lyvys of Seyntys* (1835) 56 He thus ageyn was com And wel adawed of his swouwnynge. **1530** PALSGR. 417, I adawe one out of a swounde .. He fell in soche a swoune that we had moche a do to adawe hym.

†**a'daw**, *v.*^{2} *Obs.* [First used by the archaists of the 16th c.; derivation uncertain. Probably the obsolete adverb ADAWE (see next), in such a phrase as 'they did him *adawe*,' *i.e.* out of life, to death, was mistaken for a verb infinitive, *quasi* 'to quell, crush, put down,' and this in subsequent use fancied to be a compound of *awe*, after the analogy of *ad-apt*, *ad-minister*, *ad-vow*; see AD- 2.] To subdue, daunt.

1557 *Tottell's Misc.* (Arb.) 158 He adawth the force of colde. **1596** SPENSER *F.Q.* III. vii. 13 The sight whereof did greatly him adaw. *Ibid.* V. vii. 20 Like one adawed with some dreadfull spright. **1621** BP. MONTAGU *Diatribe* 85 Being overawed and adawed, as they are. **1654** USSHER *Annals* VI. (1658) 249 They .. being adawed at his constancy and resolution .. fled every man of them.

†**a'dawe**, *adv. Obs.* [For *o dawe*, a contr. form of *of dawe*, *of daȝe*, *of daȝen*, north. *of dawes*, = OE. *of daȝum* 'from days,' in sense of 'from life.' The full phrase '*of lyues dawe*' is also common. See DAW(E, DAY.] Out of life, out of existence. Usually with verbs *bring*, *do*: To put out of life, to put to death, kill.

c **1250** *Genesis & Ex.* 3545 Ðat wod folc ðor Ur of daȝe broȝten. *c* **1300** *Life of Beket* 2305 This holi man was ibroȝt of Dawe. *c* **1314** *G. Warw.* 53 He wist his folk y-slawe And thurch him brought o liue dawe. *c* **1325** *E.E. Allit. Poems* A. 282, I trawed my perle don out of daweȝ. *c* **1330** *Florice & Bl.* 634 Sithen he thoughte hem of dawe don. *c* **1370** *K. Rob. of Cysille* 133 in *E.P.P.* Hazl. I. 273, I schalle yow teche me for to knawe, And brynge yow fro yowre lyfe dawe. *c* **1420** *R. Cœur de Lion* 973 Some wolde haue hym adawe. *c* **1425** WYNTOWN *Cron.* VIII. xxvi. 29 Qwhen þat he wes dune of dawe, Ðai tuk þe Land for outyn awe. **1447** BOKENHAM *Lyvys of Seyntys* (1835) 186 He cruelly shuld be brought adawe As a transgressour of hys lawe. **1513** DOUGLAS *Æneis* VI. vii. 68 Thou with swerd was slaw, Bereft thy self the life, and brocht of daw.

adawn (ə'dɔːn), *adv.* and *pred. a.* prop. *phrase.* [A *prep.*^{1} + DAWN.] Dawning, gleaming with new light.

1881 E. H. HICKEY in *Academy* No. 459, 133 Have written ne'er a better thing than the thought a-dawn in your eye.

adaxial (æ'dæksɪəl), *a. Bot.* [f. L. *ad* to, toward + *axi-s* axle + -AL^{1}.] Toward the axis or central line. Cf. ABAXIAL *a.*

1900 B. D. JACKSON *Gloss. Bot. Terms* 5/1 *Adaxial*, the side or face next the axis, ventral. **1903** *Bot. Gaz.* XXXVI. 104 The ovaries [in Casuarina] are flattened laterally, in contrast to the adaxial flattening of the wings in Pinus.

aday, a-day (ə'deɪ), *adv.* prop. *phrase.* [A *prep.*^{1} + DAY = OE. *on dæȝe.*]

†**1.** In or on the day (in opposition to the night); by day. *Obs.*

a **1250** *Owl & Nighting.* 219 Thu singist a niȝt, and noȝt a dai. **1297** *R. Glouc.* 289 Seynt Edward þe vyfte ȝer of ys kynedom Aȝen eue aday aslawe was. *c* **1340** *Alex. & Dindimus* 425 And us bi-dewen aday · þe dewen of heuene.

2. On each day; daily. (See A *adj.*^{2} 4, and A *prep.*^{1} 8.)

c **1500** *Partenay* 4252 Full moch haue I hurd spokyn of the aday. **1526** TINDALE *Matt.* xx. 2 He agreede with the labourers for a peny a daye. **1611** *ibid.* A peny a day. **1783** ROBERTSON *Amer.* I. 163 The scanty allowance of six ounces of bread a-day for each person. **1825** *Br. Jonathan* II. 217 You would have begun with nearly three hours a-day.

adays, a-days, *adv. phr.* [A *prep.*^{1} on + *day's* gen. sing. of *day*. In OE. the gen. *dæȝes* was used adverbially = *by day, during the day*,'dæȝes and nihtes,' he is anxious 'day and night.' Subsequently, the genitive was strengthened by the prep. *a* = in, on. See A *prep.*^{1} 8 and DAY.]

†**1.** By day, during the day, in the day-time. *Obs.*

1377 LANGL. *P. Pl.* B. xv. 278 Antony a dayes · aboute none tyme, Had a bridde þat brouȝte hym bred. **1560** INGELAND *Disob. Child* (1848) 21 With broylynge & burnynge in the kytchyn adayes. **1621** BURTON *Anat. Mel.* I. ii. II. ii. (1676) 45/1 Pining a daies .. waking a nights. **1675** HOBBES *Odyssey* 59 A-days he weeping sat upon the shore. **1765** ELLWOOD *Life* (ed. 3) 149 We had also the Liberty of some other Rooms over that Hall, to walk or work in a-Days.

2. now-a-days: At the present day, during the present time.

c **1386** CHAUCER *Can. Yeom. T.* 425 Ffor any wit þat men han now a dayes [*Camb. MS.* on dayes]. *a* **1420** OCCLEVE *De Reg. Princ.* 1415 Adayes now, my sone, as men may see, O chirche to o man may nat suffise. *c* **1449** PECOCK *Repr.* II. xiii. 227 Peple now adaies ben not to be blamed. **1590** SHAKS. *Mids. N.D.* III. i. 148 Reason and loue keepe little company together, now-adayes. **1651** WITTIE *Primrose's Pop. Err.* I. ii. 4 But now adayes great is the neglect herein. **1711** GREENWOOD *Eng. Gram.* 227 One ought not promiscuously to write every Noun with a great Letter, as is the Fashion of some now adaies. **1856** E. B. DENISON *Church Bldg.* iv. 150 What would nowadays be talked of as a very fine spire.

adazzle (ə'dæz(ə)l), *adv.* and *pred. a.* [f. A *prep.*^{1} + DAZZLE.] In a dazzle; dazzling.

1832 *Blackw. Mag.* Feb. 281 Every line shall be a line of light—all a-dazzle with appropriate words. **1877** G. M. HOPKINS *Poems* (1918) 30 With swift, slow; sweet, sour; adazzle, dim. **1923** W. DEEPING *Secret Sanct.* xxix. 302 Snow .. lay on the hedges .. and all the hillsides were adazzle with it as the sun rose.

†**ad'bass**, *v. Obs. rare*$^{-1}$. [a 16th c. refashioning of ABASE after L. *ad* to + *bassus* low.] = ABASE.

1548 UDALL, etc. *Erasm. Paraphr.* Luke ii. 7 Who had for our sakes adbassed and humbled himselfe downe euen to swadling cloutes.

†adˈblast, *v. Obs. rare.* [prob. refash. of ABLAST, OE. *onblǣstan* to blow upon. See A- *pref.* 2.] To inflate, inspire.
1548 UDALL, etc. *Erasm. Paraphr.* Pref. 4 So adblasted the worlde. *Ibid. Luke* i. 44 The mother too is adblasted in suche sorte that she on her partie also beeyng replenished with the holy ghoste dyd not now kepe in the ioyes of her heorte.

‖**ad captandum (vulgus)** (æd kæpˈtændəm (ˈvʌlgəs)), *a.* and *adv. phr.* [L. *ad* for + *captandum* neuter of the gerundive of *captāre* to entice, allure.] (Calculated) to take the fancy of (the crowd).
1762 SMOLLETT *Launcelot Greaves* I. x. 201 These paltry tricks, *ad captandum vulgus*, can have no effect but on ideots. **1837** DICKENS *Pickw.* x. 95 Such an *ad captandum* argument, as the offer of half a guinea. **1882** W. JAMES *Let.* 8 Jan. in R. B. Perry *Tht. & Char. of W. J.* (1935) I. 737 Arguments which I cared little about..were used merely on account of their availability and *ad captandum* power. **1926** R. FRY *Transformations* 112 How considerable an artist lies hidden behind that *ad captandum* sentimentality. **1931** —— in W. Rose *Outl. Mod. Knowl.* 961 But vulgar and *ad captandum* as his art was, he [*sc.* Caravaggio] had a touch of genius.

adcorporate in Bailey and J.; see ACCORPORATE.

add (æd), *v.* [ad. L. *add-ĕre*; f. *ad* to + *dăre* to give, put.]
1. a. To join or unite (a thing *to* another) so as to increase the number, quantity, or importance. *spec.* in *Horse-racing* (cf. ADDED *ppl. a.* c).
c **1374** CHAUCER *Boethius* III. ix. (1868) 83 Lat vs quod she þan adden reuerence to suffisaunce and to power..Certis, quod I, lat vs adden it. **1388** WYCLIF *Hosea* xiii. 2 Thei addiden to do synne, and maden to hem a ȝotun ymage [**1382** Puttiden to. Vulg. *Addiderunt ad peccandum*]. **1570** BILLINGSLEY *Euclid* I. ii. 7 If ye adde equall thinges to equall things: the whole shalbe equall. **1593** SHAKS. *3 Hen. VI*, v. iv. 70 I need not adde more fuell to your fire. **1611** BIBLE *Matt.* vi. 27 Which of you by taking thought, can adde one cubite vnto his stature? **1756** BURKE *Nat. Soc.* Wks. I. 29 Add to the account those skirmishes which happen in all wars. **1816** *Racing Cal. 1815* XLIII. 15 The Old Stakes of 10 gs. each, with 20 gs. added. **1827** HUTTON *Mathem.* I. 8, 5 + 3 denotes that 3 is to be added to 5. **1848** *Sporting Life* 5 Aug. 277/1 By subscriptions of 20 sovs. each..with 100 added from the racing fund. **1859** TENNYSON *Guinevere* 203 Yet this grief Is added to the griefs the great must bear. **1934** *Times* 18 Oct. 5/4 The Cesarewitch Stakes, a handicap, of 25 sovs. each, with 1,000 sovs. added.
†b. To give by way of increased possession or share (*to* a person). *Obs.*
1534 TINDALE *Rev.* xxii. 18 God shall adde vnto him the plages that are wrytten in this boke. **1611** BIBLE *Matt.* vi. 33 All these things shalbe added vnto you. [*Wycl.* cast, *Tind.*, *Cranm.*, *Genev.* ministred, *Rheims* given you besides.] **1640** FULLER *Abel Rediv.* (1867) I. 18 Posterity may know who added the part of helpful Onesiphorus to this Paul in bonds. **1709** STRYPE *Ann. Ref.* liii. 532 Who seemed by the special will of God to be added to the Queen in those most difficult times.
c. †to add faith to: to give credence to, to believe. Cf. L. *addere fidem*, Fr. *ajouter foi. Obs.*
1483 CAXTON *Cato* f iiij b, Thow oughtest not euer byleue that that men sayen and reporten to the, ne to adde feythe to hit.
2. (With object unexpressed) To make an addition *to*; to increase, augment, enlarge.
1591 SHAKS. *1 Hen. VI*, I. i. 103 My gracious Lords, to adde to your laments..I must informe you of a dismall fight. **1697** DRYDEN *Virgil, Georgic* I. 420 When Autumn weighs The Year, and adds to Nights, and shortens Days. *Mod.* It adds greatly to our labour, but also to our pleasure.
3. To say or write further or in addition; to go on to say or speak.
1382 WYCLIF *Gen.* xv. 3 And Abram addide, To me forsothe thow hast not ȝouun seed. **1388** —— *Luke* xix. 11 He addide, and seide a parable [*Another MS.* He addide to. **1382** He puttinge to, seide a parable]. **1611** SHAKS. *Cymb.* v. v. 19 Further to boast, were neyther true, nor modest, Vnlesse I adde, we are honest. **1671** MILTON *P.R.* I. 497 He added not; and Satan bowing low His gray dissimulation, disappeared. **1735** POPE *Epil. Sat.* ii. 133 But let me add, Sir Robert's mighty dull. **1879** BARTLETT *Egypt to Palest.* x. 224 It may be added, in this connection, that the iron..occurs elsewhere in the Peninsula.
4. To unite (two or more things or numbers) into one sum; often with *together. absol.* To perform the arithmetical process of addition. To ***add up***, to find the sum of a column or series of numbers, to 'cast'; Also *absol;* to ***add in***, to include in a sum.
1509 HAWES *Past. of Pl.* XV. v, Who knewe arsmetryke in every degre..Bothe to detraye and to devyde and adde. **1579** DIGGES *Stratioticos* 2 To adde is to gather and knit in one many numbers or unites. *a* **1704** LOCKE (J.) As easily as he can add together the ideas of two days, or two years. **1754** D. FENNING *Brit. Youth's Instructor* (ed. 2) 12 When you have two or three rows of figures..add up the first row, [etc.]. *Ibid.* 25 To add up well..is a great Step towards Multiplication. **1796** HUTTON *Math. Dict.* 29/2 Add each column separately, and carry the overplus as before, from one column to another. **1872** HAMB. SMITH *Algebra* 2 When several numbers are added together, it is indifferent in what order the numbers are taken. **1879** COLENSO *Arithm.* 2 We then add these figures thus, 5 and 7 are 12.
5. *intr.* in phr. ***to add up***: **a.** To make the desired, expected, or correct total.
1850 DICKENS *Dav. Copp.* xli, The figures made her cry. They wouldn't add up, she said. **1864** *Good Words* 316/2 On one occasion, it struck me that a series of figures just given by the traffic-manager of a railway company, would not add up. **1885** *Sat. Rev.* 21 Feb. 243 Of the sixteen articles of diet enumerated, the percentages of five only will 'add up'. **1893** *Chambers's Jrnl.* 26 Aug. 532/1 Account books that would not add up right.
b. ***to add up to***, to amount to, to signify, to come to mean. Also *absol.*, ***to add up***, to make sense, to be significant or consistent.
1933 S. HOWARD *Alien Corn* I. 35 What is it that adds up to? A trio! **1936** *Time* 10 Feb. 23/1 The ship, plus the service, plus the passenger list, plus the Caribbean—it all adds up to the best vacation I ever had. **1938** E. S. GARDNER *Case Shoplifter's Shoe* (1939) ix. 158 All right..I wasn't home last night. So what does that add up to? **1942** *Daily Progress* (Charlottesville, Va.) 27 Apr. 8/4 How does it [*sc.* the evidence] all add up? **1945** M. ALLINGHAM *Coroner's Pidgin* xi. 88 I've tried to make it mean something else, but it doesn't add up any other way. **1945** A. J. P. TAYLOR *Course German Hist.* 8 There were and, I dare say, are many millions of well-meaning kindly Germans, but what have they added up to? **1958** *Oxf. Mag.* 6 Mar. 342/1 As a contribution to the philosophy of religion, this volume of essays does not add up to much.

addable (ˈædəb(ə)l), *a.* [f. ADD *v.* + -ABLE. A variant of ADDIBLE, formed on Fr. and Eng. analogies, without reference to a possible L. **addibilis*.] Capable of being added, or added to.
1678 COCKER *Arithm.* (J.) The first number in every addition is called the addable number, the other, the number or numbers added.

addatys, see ADATIS.

‖**addax** (ˈædæks). Also 7 addace. [L., ad. African word. '*Strepsiceroti*, quem Addacem Africa adpellat.' Plin. *H.N.* xi. 37. *post in.* §45.] A quadruped: a species of boviform or ox-like antelope, allied to the Nyl-ghau and Gnu, inhabiting Northern Africa. (*Oryx nasomaculata.*)
1693 RAY *Synop. Quadr.* 79 in Chambers *Cycl. Supp.* (1753), *Addace*, in natural history, the name by which the Africans call the common Antelope. **1847** CARPENTER *Zool.* §268 The Addax..living solitarily, or in pairs, on the borders and oases of the deserts. **1876** WOOD *Bible Animals* 141 Modern commentators have agreed that there is every probability that the Dishon of the Pentateuch was the Antelope known by the name of Addax..The ordinary height of the Addax is three feet seven or eight inches.

adde, adden, var. of *hadde, hadden*, older forms of *had.* See HAVE.

†aˈddebted, *pa. pple. Obs.* Forms 6 **adettyt, addettit, addetted, addebtit**; 7 **adebted**, 7–9 **addebted**. [f. earlier *en-detted* pa. pple. of *endet*, a. OFr. *endete-r*, *endette-r*:—late L. *indebitā-re*: see INDEBT. The Fr. prefix *en-*, like Eng. *an-*, *on-*, reduced to *a-*, afterwards refashioned as *ad-*; see A- *pref.* 10. The word seems only Scotch.] Indebted.
1513 DOUGLAS *Virgil's Æneis* x. xiv. 56 And was adettyt, for my mysdoyng Onto our cuntre, till haue sufferit pane. **1535** STEWART *Cron. Scotl.* 36060, II. 521 He wes aboue all erthlie thing, So far addettit to that nobill king. **1566** KNOX *Hist. Ref. Scotl.* Wks. 1846 I. 289, I am addetted to your Lordschip. **1639** DRUMM. OF HAWTH. *Wks.* 1711, 223 How much is Florence adebted to the noble Laurentius of Medices, for his library? **1651** CALDERWOOD *Hist. Kirk* (1843) II. 252 How muche we were addebted unto God. **1822** SCOTT *Nigel* iv. (1874) 61 His Majesty's maist gracious mother..justly addebted and owing the sum of fifteen merks.

†aˈddecimate, *v. Obs.*—⁰. [f. late L. *addecimāt-* ppl. stem of *addecimā-re*, f. *ad* to + *decimā-re* to take the tenth, f. *decem* ten.] To tithe.
1612 in COCKERAM; whence in BAILEY, JOHNSON, etc.

†aˈddecked, *pa. pple. Obs. rare*⁻¹. [f. A- *pref.* 11 + DECK. Of doubtful existence; see the quotation.] Decked, covered.
1513 DOUGLAS *Virgil's Æneis* XI. xi. 170 Than Opis lichtlie of the heuynnys glade..Persand the are with body all ouer schroude Addekkit in ane wattry sabil cloude [*Ruthv. MS.* Indekkit, *Elphinst. MS.* And dekkyt].

added (ˈædɪd), *ppl. a.* [f. ADD *v.* + -ED.] **a.** Given as an accession, increased; additional.
1606 SHAKS. *Tr. & Cr.* IV. v. 145 A thought of added honor torne from Hector. **1718** POPE *Iliad* I. 125 Perhaps, with added sacrifice and prayer, The priest may pardon. **1818** BYRON *Childe Har.* IV. cix. Till the sun's rays with added flame were fill'd. **1879** MᶜCARTHY *Hist. own Times* I. 412 An added effect was given to this well-deserved panegyric.
b. ***added sixth***: a major sixth added to a triad; the chord thus obtained.
1876 in STAINER & BARRETT *Dict. Mus. Terms.* **1931** G. JACOB *Orchestral Technique* viii. 76 *All* 'added 6ths' cannot be arranged as above. **1959** D. COOKE *Lang. Mus.* ii. 65 The Delius..reminds us that the 'lushness' of his music is often due to his use of the chord of the 'added sixth'.
c. ***added money***, esp. in *Horse-racing*, money added (by a racing association, etc.) to the stakes (cf. STAKE *sb.*² 3).
1880 *Illustr. Sporting & Dramat. News* 4 Dec. 278/3 The withdrawal of the subsidy augurs badly for the annual grant of £2,000 usually given towards the added money for the Grand Prix. **1886** *Kennel Club Calendar & Stud Book 1885* XIII. 95 Pointer Puppy Stakes..first £50 and £10 added money. **1923** *Empire Rev.* June 631 Racecourse executives are perforce more generous in the matter of added money than was the case in the pre-war days.
d. ***added value*** (Econ.) = *value added* s.v. VALUE *sb.* 2c. Also *attrib.*, esp. in ***added value tax***.
1955 C. H. MORRIS in *Proc. 48th Ann. Conf. Nat. Tax Assoc.* (1956) 19 We couldn't have had a more thorough background of the added-value theory. **1963** *Daily Tel.* 5 Apr. 14 He is considering a turnover or added-value tax. **1974** *Terminol. Managem. & Financial Accountancy* (Inst. Cost & Managem. Accountants) 24 *Added value*, the increase in market value resulting from an alteration in the form, location or availability of a product or service, excluding the cost of bought-out materials or services. Note: unlike conversion costs, added value includes profit. **1979** *Jrnl. R. Soc. Arts* May 335/2 The gap between what the customer pays and what the manufacturer or supplier has to pay for the materials and other purchases is the 'added value' or wealth created.

†aˈddeem, *v. Obs.* [f. DEEM, with pref. *ad-* in imitation of *ad-judge*: see A- *pref.* 11. There was an OE. *adéman*, but this vb. is not connected with it.] To adjudge.
1596 SPENSER *F.Q.* v. iii. 15 So unto him they did addeeme the prise. *Ibid.* VI. viii. 22 The winged god, that woundeth harts..Addeem'd me to endure this penaunce sore. **1597** DANIEL *Civ. Wares* VIII. lxxii. She scornes to be addeem'd so worthlesse base.

addend (ˈædɛnd). [ad. L. *addendus* (sc. *numerus*), gerundive of *addere* ADD *v.*: see -END.] A number which is to be added to another.
1674 S. JEAKE *Logisticelogia* (1696) 16 Place the Addends in rank and file one directly under another. [**1892** SMITH & HUDSON *Arith. for Schools* (new ed.) 6 The numbers to be added are called the *addenda*.] **1904** D. E. SMITH *Gram. School Arith.* i. 6. Numbers to be added are called *addends*. **1907** H. S. JONES *Mod. Arithm.* I. ii. 4 Addition is the process of finding *one* number..which is equivalent to two or more... The simple numbers which are to be collected into one are often called terms, or addends. **1925** D. E. SMITH *Hist. Math.* II. ii. 90 The word 'addend' was frequently used to refer only to the lower of two numbers to be added... It was also used by many writers to refer to all the numbers to be added except the top one. **1947** [see AUGEND]. **1953** *Proc. IRE* XLI. 1245/2 Addition of numbers is performed by first entering one of the numbers (the augend) in the accumulator and then giving the command to add, at the same time entering the other number (the addend). **1977** *Sci. Amer.* Sept. 85/1 We can begin with the combination in which both the addend and the augend are 0's but the carry bit from the previous column is a 1.

‖**addendum** (əˈdɛndəm). Pl. **addenda** (əˈdɛndə). [a. L. *addendum* something to be added, gerundive of *add-ĕre* to ADD. The pl. was in earlier use than the singular; cf. *miscellanea*, *minutiæ*, etc.] **a.** A thing to be added; an appendix or addition. Also *occas.* in pl. form with sing. construction: a set of addenda (esp. one appended to a book).
1794 BURNS *Wks.* IV. 179 You cannot, in my opinion, dispense with a bass to your addenda airs. **1830** MISS MITFORD *Our Village* IV. (1863) 260 The addenda of the work. **1879** O. W. HOLMES *Motley* xxi. 179 After I had gone over the instructions for the last time I wrote an addendum. **1879** *Daily News* 16 Apr. 3/6 The mover of the resolution accepted as an addendum thereto the further expression of opinion that, etc. **1840** W. BERRY *Encycl. Heraldica* IV. 1 The following Addenda has therefore been arranged in the same manner. **1936** *S.P.E. Tract* XLV. 192 A catalogue, issued in the autumn of 1935 by one of the leading American university presses, mentions, as one of the merits of a certain book, that it contains *an invaluable addenda.* **1984** *Mech. Engin.* CVI. 89/1 This addenda consists of 49 independent revisions.
b. *Mech.* A term applied to certain dimensions of toothed gearing (see quots.).
1841 R. WILLIS *Princ. Mechanism* 98 Now this addition to the radius of the pitch circle [of a gear] is called by clock-makers the *addendum*, which term I shall, for convenience, employ. **1873** RANKINE & BAMBER *Mech. Text Bk.* II. ii. 81 The radius of the pitch circle of a circular wheel is called the *geometrical radius*; that of a circle touching the crests of the teeth is called the *real radius*; and the difference between these radii, the *addendum.* **1954** *Gloss. Terms Toothed Gearing (B.S.I.)* 11 *Addendum.* 1. Of a helical or spur gear. *a. Reference addendum*, the radial distance from the reference cylinder to the tip cylinder. *b. Working addendum*, the radial distance from the pitch cylinder to the tip cylinder. 2. Of a wormwheel. Half the difference between the diameter of the pitch circle and the throat diameter. 3. Of a bevel gear. The distance from the pitch circle to the tip cone, measured on the back cone.

adder¹ (ˈædə(r)). [f. ADD *v.* + ER¹.] **1.** He who adds.
1580 HOLLYBAND *Treas. Fr. Tong.*, *Qui adjoinct*, a ioiner to, an adder to.
2. An adding-machine.
1890 *N.Y. Herald* Jan. (Advt.), The Adder is so called because really too simple to be styled a 'machine'.
3. A unit in an electronic computer (see quot. 1962).
1948 A. SVOBODA *Computing Mechanisms* ii. 37 The bar-linkage adder..consists of essentially the same parts as the linkage of Fig. 2-11. **1954** *Electronic Engin.* Sept. 376/2 The sample instruction..asks the machine to take the number.. and to add this to the contents of the accumulator... In the last 6 digits [of the instruction] is the binary code which operates the circuit to perform the required function, the adder. **1962** *Gloss. Terms Autom. Data Processing (B.S.I.)* 100 *Adder*, a unit with two or more input variables and one output variable which is equal to the sum, or a weighted sum, of the input variables.

adder[2] ('ædə(r)). Forms: 1–2 nædre, næddre, 3 nadre, 3–4 naddre, 4–5 nadder; 1–4 nedre, 2–4 neddre, 3–4 neddere, 3–7 nedder, 4–5 -ir, 5 -yr; 4 eddre, eddere, 4–5 eddyre, 5 eddyr, -ur, 5–6 -ir, 5–7 -er; 4 addre, 5– adder. *Sc.* 6 ather. *Pl.* adders; formerly 1 nædran; 2–4 nedren, neddren, naddren, addren; 3 nedres, neddres, -is; 4–5 eddres, addres. [OE. *nædre*, cogn. w. OLG. *nadra*, OHG. *natra*, *natara*, ON. *naðra*, *naðr*, Goth. *nadrs*. The initial *n* was lost in ME. 1300–1500, through the erroneous division of *a naddre*, as *an addre*. *Nedder* is still a north. dial. form. The Lindisf. Gosp. gloss has *cyn ætterna* 'brood of venomous ones,' for OE. *nædrena cynn*, but there is nowhere any form-confusion between *nædre* serpent and *ætter* venom; though, from meaning serpent generically, the word has gradually been restricted in Britain to the native viper, and its supposed foreign congeners.]

†**1. a.** A serpent; the generic name in OE. *fig.* The 'old serpent,' the devil. *Obs.*

c **950** *Lind. Gosp.* Matt. xxiii. 33 Nedra, cynn ætterna! *c* **975** *Rushw. ibid.* ȝe nedra, cynn uiperana! *c* **1000** *Ags. Gosp. ibid.* Eala ȝe næddran [*v.r.* nædran] and næddrena [*v.r.* nædryna] cynn, hu fléo ȝe fram helle dome? *c* **1160** *Hatton Gosp. ibid.* Eale ȝe næddra & næddrena kyn! —— John iii. 14 Swa swa Moises þa neddre up á-hof [*Ags. Gosp.* þa næddran *v.r.* nædran, *Lind.* ða nédræ, *Rushw.* ða nedre]. *c* **1175** *Lamb. Hom.* 53 Witeð eow þet ȝe ne beo noht þe foaȝe neddre ne þe blake tadde. *Ibid.* Nedre haueð niþ and onde. *c* **1200** *Moral Ode* 277, in *Trin. Coll. Hom.* 228 þar beð naddren and snaken, eueten and fruden. **1250** *Gen. & Ex.* 323 Eue, seide he, ðat neddre bold. *c* **1300** *Cursor Mundi* 758 þe nedder nerhand hir gun draw. **1340** *Ayenb.* 61 Hi resembleþ an eddre þet hatte serayn. **1366** Maundevile 205 Thei maken a maner of hissynge, as a neddre dothe. **1377** Langl. *P. Pl.* B xviii. 352 Lucyfer in lyknesse Of a luther addere. **1382** Wyclif *Gen.* iii. 4 Forsothe the eddre seide to the woman [**1388** serpent]. *c* **1386** Chaucer *Persones T.* 257 Dedly synne hath first suggestioun of the feend, as scheweth here by the neddir [*v.r.* naddere, adder, Hadder]. **1440** *Promp. Parv.* 135 Eddyr or neddyr, wyrme: *Serpens*. *c* **1440** *Morte Arthur* (1819) 108 An edder glode forth upon the grownde .. To kylle the adder had he thoghte. *c* **1460** *Towneley Myst.*, *Annunc.* 72 [Adam] begyled was Thrugh the edder. **1513** Douglas *Æneis* ii. iv. 8 Throw the still sey from Tenedos in feir Lo twa gret lowpit ederis with mony thraw Fast throw the fluide towart the land can draw.

†**b.** By extension, A dragon, *i.e.* a supposed serpent with wings. *Obs.*

c **1300** *K. Alis.* 5262 Grete addren comen flynge. **1366** Maundev. 27 There fleyghe out an Eddere righte hidous to see.

2. a. A small venomous serpent or snake; a viper. *spec.* The Common Viper (*Pelias Berus*): the historical and popular name, retaining the old associations, as the ideas of darting and stinging, not associated with the name *viper*.

1154 *O.E. Chron.* (Laud. MS.) an. 1137 Hi dyden heom in quarterne þar nadres & snakes & pades wæron inne. **1297** R. Glouc. 43 Nedre ny oþer wormes ne mow þer [Ireland] be noȝt. *c* **1315** Shoreham 104 So doth the naddre stinge. *c* **1386** Chaucer *Marchantes T.* 542 Lyk to the naddre in bosom sly vntrewe [*v.r.* neddre, neddere, nadder, *Petw.* adder]. **1387** Trevisa *Higden* Rolls Ser. I. 303 þe ilond Sardinia .. haþ noþer addres noþer venym, but þey haue an herbe þat hatte apium, þat makeþ men laughe hem selue to deþ. *c* **1425** Wyntown *Cron.* i. xiii. 55 Ðare [in Irland] nakyn best of wenym may lyue or lest atoure a day; As Ask, or Eddyre, Tade or Pade. **1501** Douglas *Palice of Honour* ii. xxiv. (1787) 43 A venomous ather and a serpent fell. **1535** Coverdale *Prov.* xxiii. 32 It byteth like a serpent [*Wyclif* eddere], and styngeth as an Adder [*Wyclif* kokatrice]. **1601** Shaks. *Jul. Cæs.* ii. i. 14 It is the bright day, that brings forth the Adder, And that craues warie walking. **1642** Milton *Apol. for Smect.* (1851) 291 Stung with Adders, and Scorpions. **1674** Ray *N.C. Words* 146 A Nedder. *Coluber, Anguis.* **1719** Young *Revenge* i. i. (1757) II. 107 Has the dark adder venom? So have I, When trod upon. **1810** Scott *Lady of Lake* v. xvi. Like adder darting from its coil. **1814** Carey *Dante's Inferno* xxiv. 96 Near to our side, darted an adder up. **1816** Scott *Old Mort.* 132 A pang which resembled the sting of an adder.

b. By extension, Applied in the Bible and classical translations to various poisonous snakes, as the *asp*, *basilisk*, *cockatrice*, 'deaf adder,' etc. In mod. Zoology to species of *Clotho* and other *Viperidæ*, as the Puff Adder and Horned Adder of Africa, Death Adder of N. Australia, etc.

a **1300** *E.E. Psalter* lviii. 54 Als of a neddre def als-swa þat stoppand es his eres twa. **1483** *Cathol. Ang.* A Neddyr. *Hec Aspis, hec lacerta, hic stellio, hic bisilliscus, hoc cicadrillus.* **1611** Bible *Ps.* lviii. 4 They are like the deafe adder [*marg.* or aspe] that stoppeth her eare.

3. flying adder, a widely diffused popular name of the Dragon-fly, used from Scotland to the Isle of Wight; also called *Adder-fly* and *Adder-bolt*.

4. sea adder, a species of pipe-fish *Syngnathus acus*.

5. *Comb.* as *adder-flame*, *-voice*; *adder-bitten*, *-coloured*, *-headed*, *-tongued*, adjs.; **adder-bead**, an amulet or ornament of prehistoric age, attributed to the Druids; **adder-bred** *a.*, engendered of the serpent (or devil); **adder-close**, applied by W. Morris to the enclosure in which Rognar Lodbrok was said to be stung to death; **adder-deaf** *a.* deaf as an adder, see adder 2 b; **adder-fly**, a dragon-fly; **adder-footed** *a. poet.* dragon-footed; **adder-hate** *poet.* virulent, deadly hate; **adder-like** *a.*, like an adder; also *obs.* of or pertaining to an adder, viperine; **adder-pike**, the sting-fish, or lesser weaver (*Trachinus Vipera*); **adder-stone** = adder-bead; **adders' fry**, *obs.*, brood of vipers; **adder's-meat**, pop. name of the Greater Stitchwort; **adder's-mouth**, name given in U.S. to plants of genus *Microstylis*; **adder's-spear** = adder's-tongue.

1699 E. Lhwyd in *Phil. Trans.* XXVIII. 98 The Snake-button is the same described in the Notes on Denbighshire in Camden, by the Name of Adder-Beads. **1898** Wilde *Ballad Reading Gaol* 7 The gallows-tree With its adder-bitten root. **1587** Golding *De Mornay* xvii. 271 This Diuell which hath marred .. yᵉ whole earth was a Serpent, (whom he called ὀφιογενῆ or ὀφιόνιον (?), that is to say, Snakebread or Adderbread,) which armeth men by whole troopes against God. **1870** Morris *Earthly Par.* III. iv. 85 When song arose From that Northumbrian adder-close. **1946** L. B. Lyon *Rough Walk Home* 29 Crunching the adder-coloured dung. *a* **1837** Campbell *Power of Russia* i. 7 Wks. 1837, 227 O heartless men of Europe—Goth and Gaul Cold, adder-deaf to Poland's dying shriek. **1920** E. Sitwell *Wooden Pegasus* 21 Adder-flames flare and spout From his lips. **1593** Golding *Ovid's Metam.* i. 6 When with there hundred hands a peece the Adder-footed rout Did practise for to conquer heaven. **1880** *Contemp. Rev.* March 431 Hated with the adder-hate of fear. **1874** Swinburne *Bothwell* ii. xiii. 182 What could sting you so, What adder-headed thought or venomous dream? **1611** Cotgr., *Couleuvrin* .. adderlike, of an adder. **1814** Byron *Corsair* i. xiv. Worm-like 'twas trampled—adder-like avenged. **1540** in Strype *Eccl. Mem.* vi. 232 You serpents, adders-fry, how wil ye escape the judgment of God? **1861** Pratt *Flowering Plants* I. 245 Greater Stitch-wort, Satin-flower, or Adder's Meat. **1864** T. Moore *Brit. Ferns* 17 The common Adder's-tongue is gathered by country-people for the preparation of adder's-spear ointment. **1851** D. Wilson *Preh. Annals* II. iii. iv. 126 The Adder Stone is thought by superstitious people to possess many wonderful properties. **1824** Scott *St. Ronan* III. viii. 209 What was it the old, adder-tongued madwoman dared to say of Clara Mowbray? **1946** E. Sitwell *Fanf. Eliz.* iii. 18 Adder-voices shrilling and hissing.

'adderbolt. [f. adder + bolt the arrow of a cross-bow; from the shape of its body.] A dragon-fly.

1483 Caxton *Gold. Leg.* 57/2 The eygth our lord sente to them locustes which is a maner grete flye callyd in some place an adder bolte. **1664** Power *Exp. Philos.* i. 6 In the sloe-black eye of the Dragon-fly or Adderbolt. **1703** Petiver in *Phil. Trans.* XXIII. 1414 Here is figur'd a very uncommon Libella or Adderbolt.

'adder's-grass. *Herb.* Popular name of various plants.

1. The Early Spring Orchis (*O. mascula*).

1551 Turner *Herbal* 152 Cynos orchis is called .. in Englishe adders grasse, or goukis meat. **1578** Lyte *Dodoens* 222 In English some cal it also Orchis .. Adders grasse and Bastard Satyrion.

2. Improperly for adder's-tongue.

'adder's-tongue. *Herb.* Popular name of a genus of ferns (*Ophioglossum* Linn.) which bear the fructification on a distinct simple spike springing from the base of the barren frond, which clasps it when young, so as to suggest the mouth and tongue of a serpent.

1578 Lyte *Dodoens* 135 Adders tonge is an herbe of a maruelous strange nature. **1597** Gerarde *Herball* ii. lxxxiv. §3, 327 Adders toong groweth in moist medowes throughout most parts of Englande. **1794** Martyn *Rousseau's Bot.* xxxii. 488 Adder's-Tongue has the fructification on a spike, in a jointed row along each side of it; when they are ripe, these joints gape transversely. **1820** Keats *Lamia* ii. 224 The leaves of willow and of adder's tongue. **1862** Ansted *Channel Islands* ii. viii. (ed. 2) 183 Two species of adder's-tongue are found in Guernsey.

2. Dialectally, applied loosely to various other plants, superficially more or less resembling the above, as Wake Robin, Lily of the Valley, etc. See Britten and Holland *Eng. Plant Names*.

adderwort ('ædəwɜːt). Also 1 nædderwyrt. The herb Bistort or Snakeweed (*Polygonum Bistorta*).

c **1000** *Saxon Leechd.* I. 96 Ðeos wyrt þe man .. nædderwyrt nemneð, bið cenned on wætere, & on æcerum. **1617** Minsheu *Ductor*, This hearbe hath his root crooked and winding vp, as a snake when he lieth wound vp, and therefore it is called Adderwort.

addibility (ædɪ'bɪlɪtɪ). [f. addible: see -bility.] The quality of being addible; capability of addition.

1690 Locke *Hum. Underst.* ii. xxix. (ed. 3) 204 Endless Divisibility giving us no more a clear and distinct Idea of actually infinite Parts, than endless Addibility (if I may so speak) gives us a clear and distinct Idea of an actually infinite Number.

addible ('ædɪb(ə)l), *a.* [f. add *v.* + -ible. As if ad. L. **addibilis*; and so preferred by some to addable which follows purely English and Fr. analogies.] Capable of being added.

1690 Locke *Hum. Underst.* ii. xvii. (1727) I. 88 The clearest idea it can get of infinity, is the confused, incomprehensible remainder of endless, addible numbers, which affords no prospect of stop or boundary.

addice, earlier form of adze.

addicent ('ædɪsənt). *rare.* [ad. L. *addīcent-em* pr. pple. of *addīc-ĕre*, see addict.] He who addicts or authoritatively transfers a thing to anyone. (Only as a transl. of *addicens* in *Rom. Law.*)

1880 Muirhead *Ulpian* xix. §9 Cession .. is accomplished by co-operation of three persons,—the cedent, the vindicant, and the addicent. It is the owner that cedes; he to whom the thing is ceded vindicates: the praetor addicts.

†**addict** (ə'dɪkt), *ppl. a. Obs.* [ad. L. *addīct-us* assigned by decree, made over, bound, devoted; pa. pple. of *addīcĕre*, f. *ad* to + *dīcĕre* to say, pronounce. Now replaced by addicted.]

1. Formally made over or bound (*to* another); attached by restraint or obligation; obliged, bound, devoted, consecrated.

1529 J. Frith *Antithesis* 318 Be not partially addict to the one nor to the other. **1533** —— *Agst. Rastell.* (1829) 217 As the Spirit of God is bound to no place, even so is he not addict to any age or person. **1549** L. Coxe *Erasm. Paraphr. Titus* i. 1, I Paule my selfe yᵉ addict seruaunt & obeyer, not of Moses lawe as I was once, but of God yᵉ father. *c* **1577** J. Northbrooke *Against Dicing* (1843) 6, I perceive myself something addict & tyed with the bonds of singular & great friendship. **1583** Fulke *Defence* xiii. 448 Delivering is a kind of 'dissolving,' or 'breaking from him' to whom he was before addict or bound.

2. Attached by one's own inclination, self-addicted *to* (a practice); devoted, given, inclined *to*.

1535 J. ap Rice in *Four Cent. of Eng. Lett.* (1881) 33 He seemeth to be addict to the mayntenyng of suche superstitious ceremones. **1551** R. Robinson *More's Utopia* (1869) 165, I beyng then of purpose more earnestly addict to heare. **1561** J. Daus tr. *Bullinger On Apocal.* (1573) 141 Geuen to voluptuousnes, full of surfetting, addicte to filthy lust. **1598** Marston *Met. Pigmalions Image* i. 141 Robrus .. adic't to nimble fence. **1640** *Homilies* ii. v. (1859) 301 Neither would we at this day be so addict to superstition, were it not that we so much esteemed the filling of our bellies. **1790** Cowper *Iliad* v. 1084 A foolish daughter petulant, addict To evil only.

addict (ə'dɪkt), *v.* [f. addict *a.*; or on analogy of vbs. so formed.]

1. To deliver over formally by sentence of a judge (*to* anyone). Hence *fig.* to make over, give up, surrender. *Obs.* except as a techn. term in *Rom. Law*.

1586 J. Hooker *Giraldus's Hist. Irel.* in *Holinshed* II. 61/2 With what limitation a prince may or may not addict his realme feodarie to another. **1592** tr. *Junius On Apocal.* vi. 7 That God will addict the fourth part of this world .. unto death and hell. **1670** G. H. tr. *Hist. Cardinals* ii. ii. 163 The greatest part of the day he addicts either to Study, Devotion, or other Spiritual exercises. **1774** Bp. Hallifax *Anal. Rom. Civ. Law* (ed. 4) 58 The Effects of the deceased were by the Praetor addicted, or made over, to one or more of the manumitted Slaves. **1880** [See under addicent].

†**2.** *refl.* To bind, attach, or devote oneself as a servant, disciple, or adherent (*to* any person or cause). *Obs.*

1560 J. Daus *Sleidane's Comm.* 138 a, He addicted him selfe to neyther of them: but now he semed to incline to the Emperour. **1621** *1st & 2nd Bk. of Discipline* 86 True bishops should addict themselves to a particular flocke. **1623** Bingham *Xenophon* 39 He addicted himselfe a scholar to Gorgias the Leontine. **1653** in Baxter *Chr. Concord* A 3 We do Agree and Resolve, not to addict or engage ourselves to any Party. **1655** Fuller *Ch. Hist.* iii. 208 We sincerely addict ourselves to Almighty God. **1684** *Scanderbeg Rediv.* v. 97 He would be too much addicted to the House of Austria.

†**3.** To attach (anyone) to a pursuit. *Obs.*

1660 T. Stanley *Hist. Philos.* (1701) 22 He addicted the Citizens to Arts.

4. To devote, give up, or apply habitually to a practice. **a.** *trans.* with refl. meaning. (A person addicts his mind, etc., or his tastes addict him.)

1607 Topsell *Four-footed Beasts* (1673) 247 It cannot be .. that ever he can addict his mind to grave, serious and profitable business. *c* **1630** Jackson *Creed* iv. vi. Wks. III. 68 To addict our best abilities to the service. **1662** Fuller *Worthies* (1840) III. 195 His genius addicted him to the study of antiquity. **1667** Oldenburg in *Phil. Trans.* II. 413 If these men would addict their palats to the pure fountains, and not wander after every poluted stream. **1829** Scott *Antiq.* xvi. 107 The researches to which your taste addicts you.

b. *refl.* and *pass.* (A person addicts himself, or is addicted.)

1577 Hanmer *Anc. Eccles. Hist.* (1619) 226 Addicting myself with you vnto the same busines. **1597** Shaks. *2 Hen. IV*, iv. iii. 135 To forsweare thinne Potations, and to addict themselues to Sack. **1611** Bible *1 Cor.* xvi. 15 They haue addicted themselues to the ministery of the Saints [*only occurrence*; *Wyclif*, *Rhem.* ordained, *Tindale*, *Cranmer* appointed, *Geneva* given]. **1665–9** Boyle *Occas. Refl.* (1675) Pref. 34 Addicting themselves .. to write Occasional Reflections. **1704** T. Hearne *Duct. Hist.* (ed. 3) I. 414 He addicted himself to the Discipline of Pythagoras. **1782** Priestley *Nat. & Rev. Relig.* I. 33 Persons who addict themselves to vice .. become miserable. **1846** Mill *Logic* iii. xiii. §6 (1868) 339 Such persons .. will addict themselves to history or science rather than to creative art.

Hence **a'ddicting** *ppl. a.* = addictive *a.*

1939 [see addictive *a.*]. **1965** *Listener* 23 Sept. 465/1 Lysergic acid .. is not addicting. **1970** *Nature* 22 Aug. 773/2 The use of methadone, a synthetic drug that is addicting .. is on the increase in New York. **1984** A. Hailey *Strong*

Medicine IV. xvi. 397 It was not addicting. Incredibly, adverse reports about its effect were almost nil.

addict (ˈædɪkt), *sb.* [f. ADDICT *v.*] One who is addicted to the habitual and excessive use of a drug; chiefly with qualifying sb., as ***drug, morphia addict***. Also *transf.*

1909 OSCAR JENNINGS *Morphia Habit* vi. 78 As shown by *post-mortem* examinations in morphia addicts. **1920** *Glasgow Herald* 18 Oct. 9 The Chicago Bridewell Institute for drug addicts. **1920** *Outward Bound* Oct. 38/2 The morphia addict is a doomed man. **1924** *Westm. Gaz.* 19 Dec., People who.. get into the habit of going to the chemist for drugs to induce sleep, and often end up by becoming opium, morphine, or heroin addicts. **1925** *Ibid.* 27 Jan., Even many working men are night club addicts.

addicted (əˈdɪktɪd), *ppl. a.* [f. ADDICT *v.* + -ED.]

1. Delivered over by, or as if by, judicial sentence; devoted, destined, bound. *Obs.* exc. in *Rom. Law*.

1534 MORE *On the Passion* Wks. 1557, 1280/1 The kinde of man, that was by synne addicted and adiudged to the diuel, as his perpetuall thrall. **1590** GREENE *Arcadia* (1616) 29 We be virgins, and addicted to virginitie. **1600** HOLLAND *Livy* VIII. x. 288 k, The man who is.. addicted and destined [*devotus est*] to death. **1679** PRANCE *Add. Narrative* 12 He himself was addicted to a Trade.

†**2.** Attached by one's own act; given up, devoted, inclined (*to* a person or party); naturally attached (*to* a place). *Obs.*

1560 J. DAUS *Sleidane's Comm.* 12 b, Some princes are addicted to others for stipendes. **1579** LYLY *Euphues* 105 The one was so addicted to the court, the other so wedded to the vniuersitie. **1588** in *Harl. Misc.* (Malh.) II. 62 To destroy the queen, & all her people addicted to her. **1616** SURFLET & MARKH. *Countrey Farme* 80 This bird is addicted to hot Countries. **1642** ROGERS *Naaman* 308 He was so addicted to Marius his Master. **1685** K. JAMES II. in *London Gaz.* mmxxxi/4 You are still.. addicted to the Royal Interest. **1709** STRYPE *Ann. Ref.* xxv. (1709) 246 Bishop Cheney, who was.. most addicted to Luther.

3. a. Self-addicted (*to* a practice); given, devoted or inclined; attached, prone. Const. *to*, formerly also *infinitive*; *on*, *against*; or adv. of manner, as *peevishly addicted*.

1561 T. N[ORTON] *Calvin's Inst.* II. iv. (1634) 139 His judgment and affection be so addicted unto evill. **1568** *Like Will to Like* in Hazl. *Dodsl.* III. 328 He is wholly addicted to follow me. **1580** T. LUPTON *Siquila* 75 The people are so peevishly addicted that they esteeme Wealth above Wisdome. **1597** DANIEL *Civile Wares* v. liii, Whose holy minde so much addicted is on th' world to come. **1601** SHAKS. *Twelfth N.* II. v. 222 Being addicted to a melancholy as she is. **1612** T. TAYLOR *Titus* i. 7 (1619) 140 To be addicted to the wine or strong drinke, taketh away the heart. **1618** LATHAM *New & 2nd Bk. Falconry* (1633) 36 If you doe finde her to bee tutchie or nicely addicted. **1634** T. HERBERT *Travaile* 76 They were more addicted homewards. **1660** T. STANLEY *Hist. Philos.* (1701) 149/1 He was much addicted to civil Affairs. **1661** *Grand Debate* 97 If the Magistrate would be advised by us (supposing himself addicted against you). **1703** MAUNDRELL *Jrny. Jerus.* (1732) 11 Much addicted to Merchandise. **1771** *Junius Lett.* l. 259 His majesty is much addicted to useful reading. **1850** MRS. JAMESON *Leg. Monast. Ord.* (1863) 400 Being himself addicted to his Art. **1865** LIVINGSTONE *Zambesi* xxi. 423 The blacks are more addicted to stealing where slavery exists.

b. Dependent on the continued taking of a drug as a result of taking it in the past; having a compulsion to take a drug, the stopping of which produces withdrawal symptoms.

1913 *Jrnl. Amer. Med. Assoc.* 8 Feb. 431/2 The narcotic drugs do afford pleasurable sensations to many of those not yet fully addicted to their use. **1934** *Bull. Hygiene* June 359/2 One patient became addicted in turn to morphine, dicodide and paracodine. **1958** A. KING *Mine Enemy grows Older* vi. 39 The ward physician.. told me that it was easier to get off Dolophine than regular opiates... Everybody not addicted to drugs was convinced of it. **1962** J. H. BURN *Drugs, Med. & Man* x. 110 Those who are addicted to cocaine often take it in the form of powder like snuff. **1985** *N.Y. Times* 18 Feb. C18/4 Nearly all cocaine abusers are believed to be addicted to other substances.

†**4.** *without const.* Devoted, attached. (Formerly in common use in subscribing letters.) *Obs.*

1594 BEARD *La Primaudaye's Fr. Acad.* II. Ep. Dedic., Subscr., Your Honors most addicted, T. B. **1597** T. MORLEY *Introd. Musicke* Ded., Subscr., And so I rest, In all loue and affection to you, Most addicted, Thomas Morley. **1645** MILTON *Tetrachordon* (1851) 139 With the same affections therfore, and the same addicted fidelity. **1652** GAULE *Magastrom.* 22 The superstitious and addicted profession [i.e. of magic].

addictedness (əˈdɪktɪdnɪs). [f. prec. + -NESS.] The quality or state of being addicted, or habitually given (*to* a practice); devotion, attachment.

1660 BOYLE *Seraphic Love* 47 Your past addictedness to the latter may prove serviceable to you. **1661** BAXTER *Moral Prognost.* II. §20, 49 To disable them from a total Addictedness to their proper Work. **1675** J. HOWE *View of Late Consid.* Wks. 1834, 158/1 With less.. addictedness to the interest of any party. **1788** PRIESTLEY *Lect. on Hist.* v. lxv. 523 Remarkable for their addictedness to drinking. **1865** *Reader* No. 117, 337/2 They are fanatics in their addictedness to the dance.

addiction (əˈdɪkʃən). [ad. L. *addictiōn-em*, n. of action f. *addīc-ĕre*; see ADDICT.]

1. *Rom. Law.* A formal giving over or delivery by sentence of court. Hence, A surrender, or dedication, of any one to a master.

1625 T. GODWIN *Rom. Antiq.* 170 The forme of Addiction was thus.. the party which preuailed, laid his hand on the thing or the person against which sentence was pronounced vsing this forme of words, *Hunc ego hominem siue hanc rem ex iure Quiritium meam esse dico.* **1735** BP. PATRICK *On Exodus* xx. 6 Look upon it only as a solemn Addiction of him to his Master's Service. **1751** CHAMBERS *Cycl.*, *Adjudication* is more particularly used for the addiction, or consigning a thing sold by auction, or the like, to the highest bidder. **1880** MUIRHEAD *Gaius* iii. §189 Whether this addiction made him a slave.. was a point of controversy with the old lawyers.

2. a. The state of being (self-)addicted or given *to* a habit or pursuit; devotion.

1641 *Vind. Smectym.* ii. 43 The peoples.. more willing addiction to hearing. **1675** E. PHILLIPS in *Shaks. Cent. Praise* 360 His own proper Industry and Addiction to Books. **1789** T. JEFFERSON *Writings* (1859) II. 585 Such an addiction is the last degradation of a free and moral agent. **1858** GLADSTONE *Stud. Homer* I. 237 Their addiction to agricultural pursuits. **1859** MILL *Liberty* 146 A man who causes grief to his family by addiction to bad habits.

b. The, or a, state of being addicted to a drug (see ADDICTED *ppl. a.* 3 b); a compulsion and need to continue taking a drug as a result of taking it in the past. Cf. *drug-addiction* s.v. DRUG *sb.*[1] 1 b.

[**1779** JOHNSON *L.P.*, *Philips* Wks. II. 291 His addiction to tobacco is mentioned by one of his biographers.] **1906** *Jrnl. Amer. Med. Assoc.* 3 Mar. 643/2 It matters little whether one speaks of the opium habit, the opium disease or the opium addiction. **1951** A. GROLLMAN *Pharmacol. & Therapeutics* iv. 97 Addiction refers to that condition induced by a drug which necessitates the continuation of the drug and without which physical and mental derangements result. **1960** P. GOODMAN *Growing up Absurd* ix. 180 In taking drugs for the new experience, they largely steer clear of being hooked by an addiction. **1965** *New Statesman* 3 Dec. 868/1 Addiction units tend not to be aware of the addict's tremendous need for moral support when the drug is taken from him. **1975** *Nature* 18 Sept. 188/2 Most people consider opiate addiction to comprise three major elements: tolerance, physical dependence, and compulsive craving.

†**3.** The way in which one is addicted; inclination, bent, leaning, *penchant*. Also in *pl.* *Obs.*

1604 SHAKS. *Oth.* II. ii. 6 Each man to what sport and revels his addiction leads him. **1634** PEACHAM *Compl. Gentlem.* iv. 34/2 For every man to search into the addiction of his Genius, and not to wrest nature. **1675** in *Phil. Trans.* X. 255 The genius, faculties, addictions, and humors of men of all ages.

addictive (əˈdɪktɪv), *a.* [f. ADDICT *v.* + -IVE.] Of a drug, etc.: to which one may become addicted; causing dependence, habit-forming; = ADDICTING *ppl. a.*

1939 *Harper's Mag.* Nov. 644 A chemico-pharmacological search for non-addicting drugs to replace morphine and the other addictive ones. **1969** *Daily Tel.* 27 Aug. 15/1 Cannabis is not addictive in the same way that morphine, alcohol or barbiturates are. **1982** FISHER & CHRISTIE *Dict. Drugs* (rev. ed.) 61 Amphetamine and the barbiturates are much less used now in part because they are potentially addictive.

Hence **aˈddictiveness** [-NESS], the quality of being addictive.

1977 *Sci. Amer.* Mar. 44/1 The toxicity and addictiveness of morphine were recognized only after the drug had become an established feature of clinical medicine. **1984** *N.Y. Times* 29 Aug. A23/5 If the addictiveness of smoking could be proved, the voluntary risk defense would be threatened.

addight, late f. ADIGHT *v. Obs.* to appoint, equip.

addill, obs. form of ADDLE *sb.* and *v.*

addiment (ˈædɪmənt). *Biochem.* [ad. L. **addimentum*, f. *addere* to ADD; see -MENT.] = COMPLEMENT *sb.* 5 i.

1901 *Lancet* 19 Oct. 1030/1 If an animal be.. given two M.L.D. [minimum lethal dose] and two serum equivalents it.. dies from the infection. This has been explained as due to a deficiency of addiment in the animal concerned. **1903** *Jrnl. Hygiene* Jan. 52 The supposed ferment (complement, addiment) upon which this power depends.

adding (ˈædɪŋ), *vbl. sb.* [f. ADD *v.* + -ING[1].] **a.** The act or process of putting or joining one thing to another, or of combining several quantities into one; addition. (Now mostly gerundial.)

c **1391** CHAUCER *Astrolabe* (1872) 52 Thries 20 feet ys the heyght of the Tour, with addyng of thyn owne persone to thyn eye. **1536** *Pilgr. T.* 226 in *Thynne's Animadv.* 83 It is expresse agaynst godis beading that we to his ruell shold mak any adyng. **1611** COTGR., *Adjoustement*, An adding, putting, or setting unto. **1860** TYNDALL *Glaciers* II. §1, 230 By adding sound to sound, silence may be produced.

b. *attrib.*: **adding-machine**, an instrument for the mechanical adding up of numbers.

1874 in KNIGHT *Dict. Mech.* **1911** H. S. HARRISON *Queed* viii. 102 He was as definite as an adding machine, as practical as a cash register. **1929** *Times* (weekly ed.) 7 Feb. 147/4 Clerks recording quickly on adding machines.

‖**addio** (adˈdio; ˈædɪəʊ), *int.* Also 8–9 adio. [It., f. *a* to + *dio* God: cf. ADIEU *int.*, ADIOS *int.*] A formula of civility, used in the subscription of letters, or at parting.

1789 A. SEWARD *Let.* 5 Feb. (1811) II. 236 Ask again about the quotation for Mr Croft. Adio! **1805** T. F. FREMANTLE *Let.* 1 Oct. in *Wynne Diaries* (1940) III. 211 Addio for to Night I shall leave room for a few words more. **1825** H. WILSON *Mem.* I. 48, I hate talking.. so, adio! **1866** G. MEREDITH *Let.* ? 4 June (1970) I. 338 The beauty of the walks about Shere are not to be surpassed. Addio... And all's well. Your loving George M. **1912** J. JOYCE *Let.* 22 Aug. (1966) II. 311, I am one of the writers of this generation who are perhaps creating at last a conscience in the soul of this wretched race. Addio! Jim.

addis, obs. form of ADZE.

Addison (ˈædɪsən). *Path.* The name of an English physician, Thomas *Addison* (1793–1860), used to designate the condition resulting from defective functioning of the suprarenal glands, characterized by progressive anæmia, debility, and a brown pigmentation of the skin. Also ***Addison's anæmia, Addisonian anæmia***, pernicious anæmia. Hence **ˈAddisonism**, Addison's disease. Cf. BRONZED *ppl. a.* 4.

[**1856** TROUSSEAU in *Bull. Acad. Med.* XXI. 1036 Une maladie bizarre, à laquelle M. le docteur Addison.. a donné le nom de *peau bronzée*, de *maladie bronzée*, et à laquelle je crois devoir donner désormais le nom de *maladie d'Addison*.] **1856** *Med. Times & Gaz.* 30 Aug. 230/2 Lecturing on.. the Bronze Disease, shown by Addison to be so frequently connected with disease of the supra-renal capsules, M. Trousseau suggests that it should be denominated 'Addison's Disease'. **1876** J. S. BRISTOWE *Theory & Practice Med.* IV. 582 Addison's disease occurs much more frequently in males than in females. **1906** *Lancet* 4 Aug. 288/2 Boinet has classified.. a few other diseases showing pigmentation under the title of Addisonism. **1910** *Practitioner* Jan. 126 The appearance presented by the tongue described by Dr. W. Hunter as specific for Addisonian anæmia. **1933** *Discovery* Mar. 83/1 Pernicious anaemia, or as it is more generally known, Addisonian anaemia, was first described by Addison, a physician at Guy's, in 1856. **1950** *Sci. News* XV. 132 The progress of Addison's disease can be checked by administering suitable extracts of the adrenal glands of animals.

additament (ˈædɪtəmənt). Also 6–7 **additement**, **additiment**. [ad. L. *additāment-um* f. *addit-us* pa. pple. of *add-ĕre*; see ADD.] Anything added or appended; an addition.

1460 CAPGRAVE *Chron.* 307 Thei have Seynt Austyn reule; with certeyn additamentis. **1577–87** HARRISON *England* I. II. i. (1877) 37 Whereas now prebends are but superfluous additaments unto former excesses. **1600** ABP. ABBOT *On Jonah* 593 Our great joy must be in the Lord; other things must be as appendices and additiments. **1622** MALYNES *Anc. Law-Merchant* 55 One pound [of silk] of 16 ounces was by sophistications of additements augmented to 32 ounces. **1662** FULLER *Worthies* (1840) III. 52 It is the most impure of metals, hardly meltable but with additaments. **1741** *Compl. Fam.-Piece* I. i. 32 Let the Patient take it at Bed-time in the Pap of an Apple, or some other proper Additament. **1823** LAMB *Elia* I. xvii. (1865) 134 So many pretty additaments and ornaments to that main structure.

addition (əˈdɪʃən), *sb.* Forms: 4 **addicioun**, 5 **addicion**, 5–6 **addycyon**, 6 **addycion**, 6– **addition**. [a. Fr. *addition*, ad. L. *additiōn-em* n. of action f. *add-ĕre*; see ADD.]

1. a. The action or process of adding; the putting or joining of one thing to another so as to increase it, or the joining together of several things into one amount.

c **1440** *Prom. Parv.* 6/2 Addycyon, or puttinge to for encrese, *Addicio.* *a* **1550** *Compl. Lover's Life* 201 Without addicioun Or disencrese, eyther more or lesse. **1590** SHAKS. *Com. Err.* II. ii. 130 And take vnmingled thence that drop againe Without addition or diminishing. **1635** N. CARPENTER *Geogr. Delin.* I. iv. 74 The Addition or Subtraction of some parts would make but an insensible difference. **1703** MAUNDRELL *Journ. Jerus.*, *Let. in Pref.* (1732) Accept the Whole as it was first set down, without Addition or Diminution. **1870** YEATS *Nat. Hist. Comm.* 13 The addition of a new fact to a farmer's mind often increases the amount of his harvest more than the addition of acres to his estate.

b. ***in addition***, additionally (*to*), as an additional thing or circumstance.

1902 B. T. WASHINGTON *Up from Slavery* xvii. 312 In addition to the agricultural training which we give to young men, and the training given to our girls in all the usual domestic employments, we now train a number of girls in agriculture each year. **1936** J. J. THOMSON *Recoll. & Reflections* i. 13 In addition to the lectures there were two classes a week. *Ibid.* 142 The number of research students steadily increased, and in addition many distinguished physicists came from abroad. **1979** D. MURPHY *Wheels within Wheels* xi. 150 In addition to his normal day's work in the library, he had to care for a complete invalid, shop on the way home,.. and then translate demanding tomes until one or two o'clock in the morning. **1986** *Guardian* 6 Dec. 10/4 At Chernobyl the hydrogen mixed with air and caused many secondary explosions... In addition the PWR has an exceptionally high power density.

2. The process of collecting separate numbers into one sum, which is the first rule of arithmetic.

1542 RECORDE *Grounde of Artes* (1575) 60 Addition is the gathering together and bringyng of twoo numbers or more, into one totall summe. **1827** HUTTON *Mathem.* I. 8 Addition is the collecting or putting of several numbers together, in order to find their sum, or the total amount of the whole. **1872** HAMB. SMITH *Algebra* 2 The process of addition in Arithmetic can be presented in a shorter form by the use of the sign +.

3. That which is added to anything; an appendix, augmentation, accession.

1366 MAUNDEVILE vii. 80 Thei ne know not the Addicioums, that many Popes han made. **1483** CAXTON *Cato* Pref., The said book of Cathon with some addicions and auctoritees of holy doctours. *a* **1520** *Myrroure of Our Ladye* 29 Certeyne addycions that are put therto. **1611** BIBLE *1 Kings* vii. 29 Beneath the lyons and oxen were certaine additions made of thinne worke. **1691** PETTY *Polit. Arith.* Pref. a 2 That Ireland and..other Additions to the Crown, are a Burthen to England. **1855** BREWSTER *Newton* II. xxvi. 384 Had Sir Isaac enjoyed his usual health, he would no doubt have made greater additions to the Principia.

4. Something annexed to a man's name, to show his rank, occupation, or place of residence, or otherwise to distinguish him; 'style' of address.

1494 FABYAN IV. lxix. 48 He had an addycyon put to his name, and was called for his great myght and power, Constantyne the Great. **1523** LD. BERNERS *Froissart* Pref. 2, I haue not gyuen euery lorde, knyght, or squyer his true addycion. **1604** SHAKS. *Oth.* IV. i. 105 *Iago.* How do you Lieutenant? *Cass.* The worser, that you giue me the addition. **1605** —— *Lear* I. i. 138 Onely we shall retaine The name, and all th' addition to a King. **1726** PENN *Wks.* I. 503 To set down the Names of those Justices who were present, with all their Additions and Titles. **1802** *Hull Advertiser* 13 Nov. 4/3 A List of Certificates issued..pursuant to the Acts of Parliament granting a Duty on such Certificates. Names. Addition. Places of Abode. **1936** R. W. CHAPMAN *Names* 262 The Lord President of the Council and the Financial Secretary to the Treasury are not often so named; one hardly remembers who are the owners of those additions.

†**5.** *Her.* Something added to a coat of arms, as a mark of honour; opposed to *abatement* or *diminution*. *Obs.*

1606 SHAKS. *Tr. & Cr.* IV. v. 141, I came to kill thee Cozen, and beare hence A great addition, earned in thy death. **1753** CHAMBERS *Cycl. Supp.*, The arms of a kingdom have been sometimes given, by way of *Addition*, to a private subject.

†**6.** ***point*** or ***note of addition*** in *Music*: A dot placed on the right side of a note, to signify that it is to be lengthened by one half. *Obs.*

1674 PLAYFORD *Skill of Music* I. viii. 27 This Prick of Perfection or Addition is ever placed on the right side of all Notes, for the prolonging the sound of that note it follows to half as much more as it is. **1753** CHAMBERS *Cycl. Supp.* s.v., A note of *Addition* amounts to the same, with what is by some old English authors, called *prick of perfection*. **1880** F. TAYLOR in Grove *Mus. Dict.* I. 456/2 The 'point of addition' was identical with our modern dot.

7. Chem. *attrib.*, as ***addition compound, product***, one formed by the direct addition of one substance to another without change of valency. (Cf. ADDITIVE *a.* b.) Also ***addition agent*** (see quot. 1940).

1879 *Jrnl. Chem. Soc.* XXXVI. 51 The addition-products of picramide with aniline..lost the whole of their base on exposure to the air. **1888** ROSCOE & SCHORLEMMER *Treat. Chem.* III. iv. 469 Addition Products of Phthalic Acid. **1922** T. M. LOWRY *Inorg. Chem.* II. xxiii. 275 *Addition and Substitution of Chlorine.* In general, it may be said that chlorine forms two types of derivatives, namely, (*a*) Addition-compounds..(*b*) Substitution derivatives. **1927** *Motor Cycling* 7 Dec. 104/2 This solution, the electrolyte, contains..according to numerous patents, various other materials known as 'addition agents' either to start the plate or to improve the 'throwing power' of the bath. **1940** *Chambers's Techn. Dict.* 12/2 *Addition agent,* a substance added to the electrolyte in an electro-deposition process in order to improve the character of the deposit formed.

†**a'ddition,** *v. Obs. rare.* [ADDITION *sb.* 4 used as vb.] To add something to the name of (any one); to surname or style.

1662 FULLER *Worthies* (1840) I. 266 A worthy knight, whom I forbear to name..partly because, before my pains pass the press, he will probably be honourably additioned. *Ibid* III. 228 Bale..is pleased to Addition this worthy man, Sewaldus Magnanimus.

additional (əˈdɪʃənəl), *a.* and *sb.* [f. prec. + -AL[1], as if ad. L. *dditiōnālis*. Cf. mod.Fr. *additionnel*.]

A. *adj.* Existing in addition, coming by way of addition; added; adscititious. Const. rarely *to*.

1646 SIR T. BROWNE *Pseud. Ep.* 2 There were no lesse then two mistakes, or rather additionall mendacites. **1688** *Col. Rec. Pennsylv.* I. 219 Being explanatory and additional to a former Law. **1794** SULLIVAN *View of Nat.* II. 23 A body having received an additional quantity of electric fluid, is said to be overcharged or positively electrified. **1824** DIBDIN *Libr. Comp.* 37 The last volume contains additional matter. **1870** MISS MITFORD in L'Estrange's *Life* I. vi. 198 What vile wretches these ministers are to think of putting an additional tax on dogs.

B. *sb.* An additional matter or particular; something added; an addition; an 'extra.' In the Univ. of Cambridge (Engl.) *fam.* for 'Additional Subjects of Examination in Mathematics' in the 'Previous Examination.'

1639 FULLER *Holy War* II. iv. (1840) 52 Their second master made some additionals to their profession. **1647** SPRIGG *Ang. Rediv.* IV. iv. (1854) 238 As an additional to the occurrences of these five days. **1673** W. CAVE *Prim. Chr.* II. i. 9 Having no beauty of their own [they] fly to the additionals of dresses and paintings. **1882** *Girton Rev.* July 7 The majority take the Additionals..simply because it is practically the only recognised door of admission to a Tripos.

additio'nality. [f. ADDITIONAL *a.* + -ITY.] The fact or quality of being additional; the principle of involving an additional component, esp. in financial deals; *spec.* in the E.E.C., the requirement that central funding should supplement, and not replace, national expenditure on a project.

1972 *Newsweek* 19 June 102/2 Central to their arguments is the delicate concept of 'additionality'. Under this, a developed nation would be held liable for damages caused to a developing country as a result of its antipollution measures. **1980** *Daily Tel.* 5 June 1/3 Regional fund grants have to be matched by funds from the member country... But.. there is every sign that the so-called 'additionality' requirement will become even more remote in the future. **1983** *Ibid.* 28 June 16/6 The Manpower Services Commission (MSC) decided to introduce the notion of awarding an employer a block grant of £1,850 for each of his two normal employees as long as he agrees to take on *three* additional trainees (and this 2:3 'incentive' concept is known as 'additionality').

additionally (əˈdɪʃənəlɪ), *adv.* [f. ADDITIONAL *a.* + LY[2].] In an additional manner; by way of addition; still more.

a **1665** J. GOODWIN *A being filled with the Spirit* (1867) 481 We cast in this likewise additionally, that this blessedness, etc. **1741** H. WALPOLE *Lett. to Mann* 8 (1834) I. 25 He has additionally brought over an Italian tailor—because there are none here. **1881** W. COLLINS *Black Robe* I. viii. 228 Having additionally conciliated him by means of a glass of rare liqueur.

†**a'dditionary,** *a. Obs. rare*[−1]. [f. ADDITION *sb.* + -ARY, as if ad. L. **additiōnārius*.] Additional.

1682 SIR T. BROWNE *Chr. Mor.* 105 Common gratitude must be kept alive by the additionary jewel of new courtesies.

addititious (ædɪˈtɪʃəs), *a.* [f. L. *additīci-us* (Tertull.), f. *addit-us* added + *-īci-us*, see -ITIOUS.] Characterized by having been added; due to, or of the nature of, an addition; additive. ***addititious force*** (in *Astr.*); see ABLATITIOUS.

1748 RUTHERFORD *Nat. Phil.* II. 1081 The ablatitious force upon the water at C, when the moon is in zenith, must be double the addititious force. **1833** SIR J. HERSCHEL *Astron.* xi. 351 This force is called the addititious part of the disturbing force.

additive (ˈædɪtɪv), *a.* and *sb.* [ad. L. *additīv-us*, f. *addit-* ppl. stem of *add-ĕre* to ADD; see -IVE.]

A. *adj.*

a. Characterized by, or tending to, addition; to be added.

1699 in *Phil. Trans.* XXI. 352 *Additive Ratio* is that whose Terms are dispos'd to Addition, that is, to Composition. **1751** CHAMBERS *Cycl.* s.v., Suppose the line *ac* divided in the points *b* and *x*, the ratio between *ab* and *bx* is additive; because the terms *ab* and *bx* compose the whole *ax*. **1833** SIR J. HERSCHEL *Astron.* v. 202 The quantity by which the true longitude of the earth differs from the mean longitude..is additive during all the half-year. **1840** CARLYLE *Heroes* iv. (1858) 279 The general sum of such work is great; for..all of it is additive, none of it subtractive.

b. *Chem.* Applied to a product, process, etc., characterized by addition (see ADDITION *sb.* 7).

1872 *Jrnl. Chem. Soc.* XXV. 1008 Aromatic additive compounds. **1875** BLOXAM *Chem.* (ed. 3) 84 The carbonates may be expressed either by additive formulæ, showing the bases which combine with carbonic acid to produce them, or by substitutive formulæ. **1876** *Jrnl. Chem. Soc.* XXIX. I. 338 The Laws which regulate Direct Additive Reactions. **1899** M. M. P. MUIR *Wand. Atoms* 101 Compounds..that are produced by the addition of an atom, or atoms, to the molecules of a compound..are named additive compounds. **1906** *Jrnl. Chem. Soc.* XC. I. 729 The oxidation of amines is initially an additive process.

c. Of a process of colour reproduction in which the primary colours are superimposed one upon another.

1906 E. J. WALL tr. *König's Natural-Color Photogr.* II. 71 The additive methods of three-colour photography by optical synthesis. **1932** HARDY & PERRIN *Princ. Optics* xiv. 314 Colors combined in this manner obey the laws governing the addition of stimuli. This is therefore called the *additive* method of combining colors. **1935** *Discovery* July 190/1 We can recompose colour either by adding primary coloured lights to black (by projection on to a screen in a dark room), or by *subtracting* primary coloured lights from a white light..containing all colours... Processes can thus be classified as *additive* or *subtractive*.

d. Examples of other technical uses.

1931 L. H. C. TIPPETT *Meth. Statistics* iv. 67 The Additive Nature of χ^2. A useful property of χ^2 is that several values can be added together. **1939** *Brit. Jrnl. Psychol.* July 14 If mild mental impairment were inherited by multiple Mendelian additive factors, the sibs should regress towards the norm. **1946** C. E. WEATHERBURN *First Course Math. Statist.* 177 (*heading*) Additive property of chi-square. **1959** P. B. MEDAWAR in *Listener* 17 Dec. 1068/2 The word 'additive' refers to a particular pattern of co-operation or interaction between genes. An additive pattern of interaction implies (amongst other things) that there will be no such thing as hybrid vigour in respect of intelligence.

B. *sb.* Something that is added; esp. (in various technical uses) a substance added (to a mixture, alloy, etc.) in order to impart specific qualities to the resulting product. Now esp. a substance added to food: see *food additive* s.v. FOOD *sb.* 8.

1945 *Electronic Engin.* XVII. 516/1 The use of the monomeric styrene..as an additive to the solution of the polymer in solvent. **1948** *Economist* 31 July 192/2 The supply of 'additives' for petroleum products. **1949** E. A. NIDA *Morphology* (ed. 2) iv. 103 Such bound forms are.. nonclitics—additives, replacives, subtractives. **1950** *U.S. Congr. House Delaney Rep., Select Comm. Chemicals in Food* (1951) 838 The use of additives which lead to a significant decrease in nutritive value should not be permitted. **1959** *Times* 27 Apr. (*Suppl. Rubber Ind.*) p. viii/3 In road building it is a valuable additive to road surfacing materials. **1969** *Times* 3 Mar. 5/6 The Swann committee..is considering the question of the possible dangers of additives in animal foods. **1984** M. HANSSEN *E for Additives* 8 So that foods can be moved from country to country within the Common Market, a list of additives that are generally recognised as safe has been introduced.

additively (ˈædɪtɪvlɪ), *adv.* [f. ADDITIVE *a.* + -LY[2].] In an additive manner; by way of addition.

1866 A. J. HERSCHEL in *Intell. Observer* No. 48, 444 To be applied additively for the index error. **1915** *Nation* 3 June 635/1 The series is made up additively as a combination of a double Fibonacci series. **1953** C. E. BAZELL *Linguistic Form* v. 64 The phoneme-clusters often give a clue as to which parts of the word are additively related. **1960** D. S. FALCONER *Introd. Quant. Genetics* vii. 125 Genes that show no dominance..are sometimes called 'additive genes', or are said to 'act additively'.

additivity (ædɪˈtɪvɪtɪ). [f. ADDITIVE *a.* + -ITY.] The state or condition of being additive.

1908 *Jrnl. Chem. Soc.* XCIV. II. 937 Connexion between Residual Affinity and Additivity. **1946** *Nature* 28 Sept. 452/2 Renard's assumption on the additivity of the spectra seems premature. **1964** HEISENBERG in *Cambridge Rev.* 24 Oct. 51/2 It is only on account of the long range and of the additivity of the forces from different sources that a reasonable 'classical limit' of the photon field operator exists.

'additory, *a.* [f. L. *addit-* ppl. stem of *add-ĕre* to ADD + ORY, as if ad. L. **additōrius*.] Tending to add something. (Also used *subst.*)

1659 FULLER *Appeal of Inj. Innoc.* (1840) 652 This is not contradictory, but additory, to what I have written; an additory only of suggestions and suspicions. **1727** SWIFT *Polit. Lying* Wks. 1755 III. I. 117 The additory [lie] gives to a great man a larger share of reputation than belongs to him. **1805** [see DETRACTORY *a.*]. **1897** *Amer. Jrnl. Philol.* XVIII. 27 The three distinct values of *etiam*..the temporal ('still', with negative 'yet'), the additory ('also') and the intensive ('even').

addle (ˈæd(ə)l), *sb.* and *a.* Forms: 1 **adela,** 2 **adele,** 3 **adel,** ? 5–8 **adle,** 6– **addle.** *North.* **adle** (ˈeɪd(ə)l). [OE. *adela* is cogn. w. MLG. *adele*, mod.G. *adel*, mire, puddle; O.Swed. *adel* in *ko-adel* cow-urine. (Not connected with OE. *ádl* disease.) After the OE. period found only in northern literature, except in ADDLE-EGG (where it is now treated as an adj.); but still widely diffused in the dialects.]

A. *sb.* **1.** Stinking urine, or other liquid filth; mire.

a **1000** *Enigma* in *Cod. Exon.* 110, 1 Đæt hér yfle adelan stinceþ. *c* **1000** ÆLFRIC *Homil.* II. 380 For ðære fúlnysse fenlices adelan. **1513** DOUGLAS *Virgil, Aeneis* IV. viii. 98 Scho gan behald In blak adill the hallowit watter cald Changit in the altare. **1710** RUDDIMAN *Gloss. to Douglas, Adill*, addle, rotten, stinking water. **1789** BURNS (Chambers ed.) 75 Then lug out your ladle, Deal brimstone like adle. **1847** HALLIWELL *Addle-pool*, A pool or puddle, near a dunghill for receiving the fluid from it. *South.* **1864** E. CAPERN *Devon Provinc.*, Addle-pool, stagnant water.

2. 'The dry lees of wine.' In Bailey, vol. II, 1731; whence also in Ash 1775.

B. *attrib.* and *adj.*

1. a. In **addle egg** [*addle* orig. the prec. sb. used attrib. (= med.L. *ovum ūrinæ* egg of urine or putrid liquid, a perversion of cl. L. *ovum ūrinum*, repr. Gr. οὔριον ᾠόν, wind-egg), at length, *c* 1600, treated as adj.] A rotten or putrid egg; one that produces no chicken. Applied usually to a fecundated egg in which through exposure to cold the chick dies during hatching; but also to an egg having no germ, which soon begins to decompose; and apparently sometimes to an egg no longer fit for food because partly hatched. (The idea of abortiveness led to many word-plays on *addle* and *idle*.)

a **1250** *Owl & Nightingale* 133 Ever he cuth that he com thonne, That he com of than adel-eye, Theȝ he a fro neste leie. **1563** NOWELL in Strype *Ann. Ref.* xxxvi. (1709) 377 Hatched us out such a sort of goodly decrees, worse than addle eggs. **1589** *Pappe with an Hatchet* (1844) 11 These Martins were hatcht of addle egges, els could they not haue such idle heads. **1606** SHAKS. *Tr. & Cr.* I. ii. 145 *Pan.* He esteemes her no more then I esteeme an addle egge. *Cre.* If you loue an addle egge as well as you loue an idle head, you would eate chickens i'th'shell. **1611** COTGR., *Oeuf abortif*, an addle egge, or an egge whose shell is not yet hard. **1617** MINSHEU *Ductor, An A'dle Egge* q. *idle* egge, because it is good for nothing, *oeuf qui n'a point de germe*..[Du.] *windeye* q. *ovum subuentaneum*, a windie egge. L. *Ovum urinum*, because it hath water in it like urine. **1623** —— *Span. Dict.*, *Huevo guero*, an addle egge, or rotten egge. **1632** SHERWOOD, Adle or Addle; as an Adle Egg, *Oeuf pourci, corrumpu, ou, sans germe; oeuf abortif.* **1667** DENHAM *Direct. to Painter* II. ii. 10 in *T.C.P.* (1689) 12/2 Alas, even they, though shell'd in treble Oak, Will prove an Addle Egge, with double Yolk. **1739** GRAY *Lett.* (1775) 43 We dined at Montreuil, much to our hearts' content, on stinking mutton cutlets, addle eggs, and ditch water. **1768** WILLOUGHBY in Pennant *Brit. Zool.* I. 125 Upon which lay a young one and an addle egg. **1840** GEN. THOMPSON *Exerc.* (1842) V. 191 Why must the 130 millions which are involved in railways be an addle egg? **1863** KINGSLEY *Wat. Bab.* (1878) 193 The distilled liquor of addle eggs.

b. as simple *adj.*

1592 SHAKS. *Rom. & Jul.* III. i. 25 Thy head hath bin beaten as addle as an egge for quarreling. **1643** HORN & ROBOTHAM *Gate of Lang. Unlocked* xiv. § 147 Poultry shut up in a hen-house lay eggs..and sitting on them (unlesse they be addle) they hatch young chicks. **1655** MOFFET & BENNET *Health's Improv.* (1746) 225 New Eggs are ever full, but old Eggs lose every Day somewhat of their Substance, and in the end waxing addle, stink like Urine, whereupon they were called of the Latins *Ova Urinæ*. **1781** PENNANT in *Phil. Trans.* LXXI. 70 They [Turkeys] sit on their eggs with such perseverance, that if they are not taken away when addle, the hens will almost perish with hunger before they will quit the nest.

2. a. *fig.* Empty, idle, vain; also (with reference to the decomposed or disorganized condition of an addle egg), muddled, confused, unsound.

[**1706** PHILLIPS, *Addle*, Empty or rotten; properly spoken of an Egg, and figuratively apply'd to a Hair-brain'd, Empty scull'd Fellow.]

a **1593** H. SMITH *Works* (1867) II. 480 Sudden qualm, or sullen care, Or addle-fit of idle fear. **1594** HOOKER *Eccl. Politie* III. (1617) 101 Concerning his preaching, their very by-word was Λόγος ἐξουθενημένος, Addle speech, emptie talke. **1591** LYLY *Endymion* IV. iii. 58 Till sleepe has rock'd his addle head. **1616** R. C. *Times' Whistle* v. 1835 Thus they drink round, Vntill their adle heads doe make the ground Seeme blew vnto them. **1622** M. FOTHERBY *Atheomastix* I. xi. §2, 113 The corrupt fancies of their owne addle heads. **1674** FAIRFAX *Bulk. & Selv. World* 59 Somewhat that is the fondling of our addle brains. **1693** W. ROBERTSON *Phraseol. Gener.* 1333, I wish him an ounce more wit in his addle head. *c* **1800** R. FELLOWES *Milton's 2nd Def.* (1847) 924/2 That tiresome and addle epistle which follows. *Ibid.* 923/1 The shell was no sooner broken than they loathed the addle and putrid contents.

b. as simple *adj.*

1602 T. FITZHERBERT *Apology* 15 Your owne imagination, which was no lesse Idle, then your head was addle all that day. **1621** BURTON *Anat. Mel.* III. iv. I. ii. (1651) 657 Their brains were addle, and their bellies as empty of meat as their heads of wit. **1690** DRYDEN *Don Sebastian* Prol. 24 Thus far the poet; but his brains grow addle, And all the rest is purely from his noddle. **1795** BURKE *Scarcity*, Wks. VII. 419 The brains of the people growing more and more addle with every sort of visionary speculation.

3. *dialectally.* Unsound, crazy.

1847 HALLIWELL, *Addle*, Unsound, unwell, *East.* **1876** *Surrey Prov.* (Eng. Dial. Soc.), *Adle* [ǣ·d'l] weak, shaky; said of a fence the posts of which have become loose.

C. *Comb.*

1. addle-brain, addle-head, addle-pate; one whose head is addled, a stupid bungler.

1601 *Death of Huntington* I. i. in Hazl. *Dodsl.* VIII. 219, I and my mates Like addle-pates. **1641** 'SMECTYMNUUS' *Vindic. Answ. Humb. Remonstr.* §16.205 Call them if you will, Popish fooles, and addleheads. **1849** MISS MULOCH *Ogilvies* xviii. (1875) 141 It is quite too overpowering for such addle-pates as this gentleman and myself. **1880** DISRAELI *Endymion* I. viii. 71 'Never mind Lord Waverly and such addle-brains,' said Zenobia.

2. addle-brained, addle-headed, addle-pated, *a.*; applied contemptuously to one whose intellect seems muddled.

1630 J. TAYLOR (Water Poet) *Wks.* II. 252/2 Let euery idle addle-pated gull With stinking sweet Tobacco stuffe his skull. *a* **1670** HACKET *Life of Williams* II. 166 Unstable people flock after these coachmen-preachers, watchmaking-preachers, barber-preachers and such addle-headed companions. **1848** DICKENS *Lett.* (1880) I. 202, I was quite addle-headed for the time being. **1864** *Mattie, A Stray* III. 212 Two weak addle-pated mortals, only fitted for each other. **1866** MOTLEY *Dutch Rep.* IV. v. 633 The addle-brained Oberstein had confessed..the enormous blunder which he had committed.

3. addle-headedness, fatuity.

1835 GEN. P. THOMPSON *Exerc.* (1842) III. 435 Calculate the addle-headedness of such inveterate old women, as should go about recommending to try Juno for dry nurse.

addle ('æd(ə)l), *v.*[1] [f. ADDLE *a.*; cf. to *sour*, to *wet*, to *cool*, etc.]

1. *trans.* To make addle; to muddle; to confuse (the brain); to spoil, make abortive.

c **1712** OTWAY *C. Marius* II. ii. One bottle to his Lady's health quite addles him. **1841** DICKENS *Lett.* (ed. 2) I. 43, I have addled my head with writing all day. **1849** —— *B. Rudge* (1866) I. x. 50 He addled..his brain by shaking his head. **1878** SIMPSON *Sch. Shaks.* I. 97 His cold procrastination addled the victory of Lepanto, as it had formerly addled that of St. Quentin.

2. *intr.* To grow addle (as an egg); also *fig.*

1812–21 COMBE *Dr. Syntax* XI. (Chandos) 42 Though his courage 'gan to addle, He still stuck close upon his saddle. **1829** SOUTHEY *Pilgr. Compost.* IV. Wks. VII. 266 Not one of these eggs ever addled. **1857** H. MILLER *Test Rocks* viii. 337 For in still water, however pure, the eggs in a few weeks addle and die.

†**addle** (æd(ə)l), *v.*[2] *Obs.* or *dial.* [a. ON. *ǫðla*, refl. *ǫðla-sk* to acquire (for oneself) property, f. *óðal* property. Found only in northern writers, and now exclusively dialectal, but used everywhere from Leicestershire to Northumberland; not in Scotland. (Spelt by some compilers of local glossaries *eddle*, after a false etymology in OE. *ed-léan* a reward.)]

1. *trans.* To acquire or gain as one's own; to earn.

c **1200** *Ormulum* 16102 Hemm addlenn swa þe maste wa þatt aniȝ mann maȝȝ addlenn. *Ibid.* 6235 & heore leȝhe birrþ hemm beon Rædiȝ, þann itt iss addledd. *c* **1460** *Towneley Myst., Crucif.* 218 If thou be kyng we shalle thank adylle, For we shalle sett the in thy sadylle. **1483** *Cathol. Anglic.* To Adylle: *commereri, promereri, mereri, adipisci, adquirere.* **1570** LEVINS *Manip.* To addil, *demerere*: to addle, *lucrari, mereri.* **1674** RAY *N. Countrey Wds.* 2 To *Adle* or *Addle*; to Earn. **1680** *Trial* [*at York*] in Howell *State Trials* (1816) VII. 1169 He would give me more than I could addle (that is, earn) in seven years. **1825** BROCKETT *Gloss. N. Country Wds.*, *Addle, Eddle*, v. To earn by labour. *Addlings*, labourer's wages. **1862** in *Chamber's Jrnl.* 30 Apr. 216 [West Riding of York] A good man 'll addle aboot four shillings or four and sixpence a day. **1865** HARLAND *Lanc. Lyrics* 76 He says he's addled fifty pund, An bowt a kist an' clock.

2. *absol.* Of crops: To produce, yield, ripen fruit.

1580 TUSSER *Husb.* li. 6 Where Iuie imbraceth the tree verie sore, Kill Iuie, or else tree will addle no more. **1865** *Cornh. Mag.* July 31 Crops..in Westmoreland, when they ripen well, are said to 'addle well,' as if a notion of working and earning were implied.

addled ('æd(ə)ld), *ppl. a.* [f. ADDLE *v.*[1] + -ED. But, as it seems to have existed before the verb, it was perhaps originally, like *newfangled*, etc., an assimilation of the adj. to the participial form.] Become or made addle, as an egg, or brain.

1646 SIR T. BROWNE *Pseud. Ep.* IV. vi. 194 Eggs, wherof the sound ones sink, and such as are addled swim; as do also those that are termed *hypanemiae*, or wind eggs. **1712** W. ROGERS *Voyage* (1718) 276 They found the [turtle's] eggs addled in less than twelve hours, and in about twelve more they had young ones in them completely shaped and alive. **1732** FIELDING *Cov. Gard. Trag.* II. xii. Wks. 1784 II. 330 My muddy brain is addled like an egg. **1868** GEO. ELIOT *Felix H.* 24 Things don't happen because they're bad or good, else all eggs would be addled or none at all.

addlement ('æd(ə)lmənt). [f. ADDLE *v.*[1] + -MENT.] The process of addling or being addled.

1859 HELPS *Friends in Council* Ser. II. II. xi. 286 The law of their addlement proceeds with adamantine vigour.

addleness ('æd(ə)lnɪs). [f. ADDLE *a.* + -NESS.] The quality of being addle as an egg; putrefaction.

1794 G. ADAMS *Nat. & Exper. Phil.* I. iv. 146 App., Pervious to particles of air, which..tend to produce..at length, putrefaction, or addleness in the egg.

addling ('ædlɪŋ), *vbl. sb.*[1] [f. ADDLE *v.*[1] + -ING[1].] Decomposition of an egg; muddling of the wits.

1843 E. A. POE *Purloined Let.* Wks. 1864 I. 275 An unaccountable addling of the brains.

†**addling** ('ædlɪŋ), *vbl. sb. Obs.* or *dial.* [f. ADDLE *v.*[2] + -ING[1].] Earning.

c **1200** *Ormulum* 17705 Al affterr þatt tin addlinng iss Na lasse, ne na mare. **1483** *Cathol. Anglic.* An Addyllynge; *meritum, gracia.* **1592** G. HARVEY *Pierces Supererog.* App. 3 According to Chaucer's English there can be little adling without much gabbing. **1851** *Coal-trade Terms, Northumb. & Durh.* 3 *Addlings, Adlings.*—Earnings. **1855** *Whitby Gloss.* (1864) *Addlings*, wages. 'Poor addlings,' small pay for work. 'Hard addlings,' money laboriously acquired.

'add-on, *sb.* (and *a.*) orig. *U.S.* [f. ADD *v.* + ON *adv.*] **1.** Something added to an existing object or quantity; an additional component or sum; an accessory device, esp. one designed to increase the capability of a computer, hi-fi system, etc.

1941 *Sun* (Baltimore) 27 Oct. 11 Business installment loans..are exempted from the limitations. In the case of so-called 'add-ons'..either the additional credit may be treated separately, or the combined credit may be paid in fifteen months. **1963** A. J. HALL *Textile Sci.* v. 259 Quite a large amount of the solid ingredients of the flameproofing emulsion must be deposited in the fabric to give complete protection against fire..but it is claimed that this add-on usefully increases the strength..of the fabric. **1971** *N.Y. Law Jrnl.* 23 Nov. 1/2 The ruling under the Truth in Lending Law barred such credit terms as '$6 per $100' or '6 per cent add-on'. **1974** *Petroleum Rev.* XXVIII. 558/1 After each addon is locked in place a Menck MRBS 7,000 hammer ..will drive the pile to final penetration. **1977** *Rolling Stone* 30 June 118/4 Previously most of the available automobile tape and radio units (either as factory equipment or as under-the-dash or in-dash add-ons) were nothing more than minipowered multifunction low-fi units. **1979** *Sci. Amer.* Jan. 1/2 (Advt.), New for 1979— TRS-80's numeric (calculator) keypad included on every 16K computer, and available as an add-on for present owners. **1983** *Your Computer* Nov. 18/2 OZI SOFT has released two new hardware add-ons and a large range of new Atari, VIC-20 and Commodore 64 software products from England and the United States.

2. *attrib.* or as *adj.*

1955 *N.Y. Times* 13 Feb. VIII. 7/1 Combination and add-on units now available for warm air, steam and hot-water heating are..more efficient than ever before. **1965** *Wireless World* Aug. 389/1 These can be satisfied by an add-on flywheel unit. **1974** *Times* 6 Apr. 13/5 There has been decided interest in the various 'add on' arrangements being offered in conjunction with ABC air fares. **1978** *Detroit Free Press* 16 Apr. F11/2 (Advt.), Mobile home with expanded liv rm, add-on sunroom. **1979** *Personal Computer World* Nov. 56/1 They will also be demonstrating colour add-on boards for this machine.

†**a'ddoom**, *v. Obs.* [f. A- *pref.* 11 + DOOM *v.*, probably in imitation of *adjudge*, *award*, where the pref. is etymological.] To adjudge, to award.

1599 SPENSER *F.Q.* VII. vii. 56 Now iudge then, O thou greatest goddesse trew..And unto me addoom that is my dew.

addorsed (ə'dɔːst), *ppl. a. Her.* [As if pa. pple. of vb. *addorse*, f. L. *ad* to + *dors-um* back; in imitation of Fr. *adossé*.] Turned back to back; said of two animals, or objects, on a shield.

1572 J. BOSSEWELL *Armorie* II. 45 b, The fielde is sable, two Cranes Addorsed proper. **1766** PORNY *Elem. Her.* (1777) s.v., *Addorsed, a.* The corruption of the French word *adossé*, and signifies born or set back to back. **1787** —— *Heraldry* 191 Ruby, two Keys addorsed in bend..the Arms of the Bishopric of Winchester. **1864** BOUTELL *Her. Hist. & Pop.* x. 60 Two Lions Rampant, placed back to back, are addorsed.

addoub, later f. *adoub*, ADUB *v.* to equip.

address (ə'drɛs), *v.* Also 4–5 **adress(e.** [a. (14th c.) Fr. *adresse-r*, earlier *adresce-r*, *adrece-r*, *adrecie-r* (Pr. *adreysar*, Sp. *aderezar*, It. *addirizzare*):—late pop. L. **addrictiā-re*, *addirectiā-re*; f. *ad* to + *drictiā-re*, *directiā-re* to make straight or right, f. *drictum*, *dirictum*, *directum*, straight, right: see DRESS and DIRECT. The subseq. refashioning of *a-* to *ad-* occasional in the 15th c. Fr., has been permanently adopted in Eng.; see AD-.]

Prim. sign. To straighten:—I. To make anything straight; then, to put things 'straight' or right; to put in order; to order, prepare; to array, clothe. II. To make straight the *course* of anything, to direct, to dispatch; to direct a letter, direct one's speech or oneself to, speak to. III. To direct towards an object, apply to a purpose, to apply oneself.

I. To make (a thing) straight or right.

†**1.** *trans.* To straighten up, to erect; to raise, to set up. *refl.* To raise oneself, to stand erect, *lit.* and *fig. Obs.*

c **1375** BARBOUR *Bruce* VI. 173 How he sa hardyly Addressyt hym againe thaim all. **1483** CAXTON *Gold. Leg.* 87/2 The first day that he was wasshen and bayned he addressid hym right up in the bassyn. **1620** SHELTON *Don Quixote* I. III. i. 116 He arose, remaining bended in the midst of the way, like unto a Turkish Bow, without being able to address himself.

†**2. a.** To put (things) 'straight,' or 'to rights,' to set in order; to order, arrange, draw up in line (a body of troops, etc.) *Obs.*, but cf. DRESS.

1375 BARBOUR *Bruce* XIV. 265 His men addressit he thame agane. **1523** LD. BERNERS *Froissart* I. ii. 2 [He] achyued many perilous aventures, and dyuers great batelles addressed. **1598** SYLVESTER *Du Bartas* I. iv. (1641) 33/2 The spitefull Scorpion, next the Scale addrest, With two bright Lamps covers his loathsom brest. **1598** R. BARNFEILD in *Shaks. Cent. Praise* 26 The rest Whose stately Numbers are so well addrest. **1601** HOLLAND *Pliny* I. 445 Put to their shifts, and forced for to addresse themselues, and range a nauall battell in order.

†**b.** To right what is wrong; to redress (wrongs), reform (abuses). *Obs.*

1525 LD. BERNERS *Froissart* II. lxxx. [lxxvi.] 238, I say not this to you, bycause ye sholde addresse my wrongs..by hym ye maye be addressed of all your complayntes. **1670** MILTON *Hist. Eng.* III. Wks. 1851, 95 A Parlament being call'd, to addres many things.

†**3. a.** To order or arrange for any purpose; to prepare, make ready. *refl.* To prepare oneself. Const. *to*, *unto*, *for. Obs.*, but see III.

1485 CAXTON *Paris & Vienne* 40 Eche departed fro other for tadresse suche thynges as to them shold be necessarye. **1560** Q. ELIZABETH in Ellis *Orig. Lett.* II. 158 II. 265 We will that you shall from time to time address several Schedules containing the names of all such hable Scholers. **1596** CHAPMAN *Iliad* v. 730 And Hebe, she proceeds T' address her chariot. **1633** HALL *Hard Texts* 315 Those of Media addressed their Target for a present defence. **1655** LESTRANGE *Chas. I.* 117 He..did addresse himself for the stroke of death. **1678** BUNYAN *Pilgr.* II. 201 He addressed himself to go over the River. **1818** BYRON *Childe Har.* II. lxix. When he did address Himself to quit at length this mountain-land.

†**b.** *intr.* (refl. pron. suppressed). To prepare. *Obs.*

1513 DOUGLAS *Æneis* VI. iv. 2 Sibillais commandment Enee addressis performe incontinent. **1606** SHAKS. *Tr. & Cr.* IV. iv. 148 Let vs addresse to tend on Hectors heeles.

†**4. a.** *esp.* To prepare or make ready with the *proper attire*; to accoutre, array, apparel, or attire, for any special purpose or occasion; *in later usage, simply* to clothe. (Const. to address *a person in*; also of *clothes addressing a person.*) *Obs.*; cf. DRESS.

1393 GOWER *Conf.* I. 100 As he her couthe best adresse In ragges, as she was to-tore. *c* **1425** WYNTOUN *Cron.* VI. ii. 38 Thaire ryng, thaire sceptyre, and thare crownys ar dyvcly blest Or thai in-to thaim be addrest. **1513** DOUGLAS *Æneis* IV. iv. 40 [He] wmquhile thaim gan balmyng and anoint, And into gold addres, at full gude poynt. **1567** JEWEL *Def. Apology* 349 Tecla sometime addressed her selfe in Mans apparell. **1598** YONG *Diana* 157 Kembe and addresse (louely Shepherdesse) thy silke soft haire. **1615** BP. HALL *Contemp.* XXI. 80 That soule which should be addressed, a fit Bride for thine holy and glorious majestie. **1678** QUARLES *Arg. & Parth.* 63 A Pilgrims weed her liveless limbs addrest from head to foot.

b. To put on (a garment), to don. (Also with *on.*) *Obs.* or *arch.*

1513 DOUGLAS *Æneis* XI. x. 2 Turnus hym self, als fers as ony gleid, full bissely addressyt on his weid. **1835** BROWNING *Paracelsus* iii. 81, I have addressed a frock of heavy mail.

II. To direct.

†**5.** To make straight the course or aim of (anything); to direct; to aim (a missile). *Obs.* except as a techn. phrase in *Golf*, 'to address the ball.'

c **1374** CHAUCER *Boethius* v. (1560) 224 b/1 As men seene the Carter worching in the tourning, and in the attempring or adressing of his carts or chariots. **1483** CAXTON *Gold. Leg.* 204/3 My crosse shall shewe my hede to therth and addresse my feet to heuen. **1520–41** SIR T. WYATT *Poet. Wks.* 197 Sinners I shall into thy ways address. **1598** SYLVESTER *Du Bartas* I. v. (1641) 42/2 If without wings we fly.. Through hundred sundry wayless ways addrest. **1601** SHAKS. *Twel. N.* I. iv. 15 Therefore, good youth, address thy gait unto her. **1676** HOBBES *Iliad* 159 Paris.. To him an arrow unperceiv'd addrest. **1677** MILTON *P.L.* IX. 496 So spake the enemy of mankind and towards Eve Addressed his way. **1725** POPE *Odyss.* XIII. 19 Then all their steps addrest To sep'rate mansions. **1867** *Cornh. Mag.* Apr. 494 The moment [a golfer] begins to 'address' his ball, as it is called, he expects that as a matter of course, everybody near him will become dumb and motionless.

6. a. To direct (any one) to go (*to* a person or place), to send, dispatch; to refer, introduce. Still said of a ship.

1475 CAXTON *Jason* 11, I pray yow if ye knowe any in this contre that hit may plese yow to adresse me to them. **1530** PALSGR. 417/2 I am nowe out of the waye, who shall nowe adresse me? **1570–87** HOLINSHED *Scot. Chron.* II. 19 King Edward addressed his orators into Scotland. **1660** EVELYN *Mem.* (1857) I. 355, I addressed him to Lord Mordaunt. **1715** BURNET *Hist. own Times* (1823) I. 285 He was addressed first to the Earl of Clarendon. **1882** *Charter-party*, Ship to be addressed to Charterers or their Agents at port of discharge.

†**b.** *refl.* To direct one's course, to make one's way; to betake oneself. *Obs.* (See III.)

1475 CAXTON *Jason* 30 He addressid him on that parte where he sawe the banyer royall. **1576** LAMBARDE *Peramb. Kent* (1826) 137 Into Italie whether warde he addressed himself with all speede. **1647** FULLER *Holy War* II. iii. 46 Such pilgrims as were disposed to return addressed themselves for their country. **1683** *Brit. Spec.* [He] addressed himself to the British King Arviragus.

7. a. To send as a written message *to* (some one); to write (anything) expressly that it may reach and be read by some one; to destine, inscribe, dedicate. ***to address a letter*** to one: To write and send it; in modern usage also, *techn.* to write on the outside the name and residence of the person to whom it is addressed, to 'direct' it.

1636 HEALEY *Epictetus* Ep. Ded., [He] ever wisht if these ensuing were published, they might onely bee addressed unto your Lordship. **1651** HOBBES *Leviathan* II. xxiii. 126 For the Advice is addressed to the Soveraign only. **1772** *Junius Lett.* lxviii. 355 This letter is addressed not so much to you, as to the public. **1855** PRESCOTT *Philip II* (1857) I. ii. 19 Previous to his embarkation Charles addressed a letter to his son. **1880** *P.O. Guide* 16 Letters for well-known firms and persons in London are sometimes addressed 'London' only; but this practice often causes delay.

b. *Computing.* To specify a location in (memory) or the location of (data) by means of an address, with a view to transferring data. Cf. ACCESS *v.*

1960 *Datamation* Sept.–Oct. 33/1 Three bits to address characters within the half-word. *Ibid.* 33/2 Four different character sizes may be directly addressed. **1968** N. CHAPIN *360 Programming* ii. 17 The programer identifies or names ('addresses') items of data and parts of the program. **1976** *New Scientist* 15 Jan. 120 The size of control task is limited only by the amount of memory which can be addressed. **1980** C. S. FRENCH *Computer Sci.* xiii. 72 For direct access one must be able to 'address' (locate) each record whenever one wants to process it. **1982** *Sci. Amer.* Feb. 59/2 The chips are random-access memories, or RAM's, meaning that each memory cell of the chip can be addressed independently.

8. To direct spoken words *to* any one; (implying that they are meant expressly *for* him).

a. *trans.* To address *prayers, vows, a speech, words* (*to* a person).

1490 CAXTON *How to Die* 17 The oraysons and prayers whiche [thei] adressen vnto our lorde. **1654** BAKER *Lett. Balzac* III. 134 They have addressed incense to Apes and Crocodiles. **1684** DRYDEN *Thren. August.* 2 His usual morning vows had just address'd. **1718** POPE *Iliad* v. 38 When by the blood-stain'd hand Minerva press'd The God of battles, and this speech address'd. **1849** MACAULAY *Hist. Eng.* I. 623 Her husband received her very coldly, and addressed almost all his discourse to Clarendon. **1858** O. W. HOLMES *Autocrat* xi. 109, I never addressed one word of love to the schoolmistress.

b. *refl.* To address *oneself* in speech (*to* a person).

1665 J. SPENCER *Prophecies* 53 God addrest him to men in more natural and familiar ways. **1751** FIELDING *Amelia* III. iv. Wks. 1784 VIII. 271 Some on board were addressing themselves to the Supreme Being. **1855** MAURICE *Proph. & Kings* xvii. 293 To all these different tendencies of the people's mind, Isaiah addresses himself. **1858** DE QUINCEY *Whiggism* Wks. VI. 41 To consider the Doctor as addressing himself exclusively to the lady of the house. *Mod.* He addressed himself to the reporters.

†**c.** *intr.* (by omission of obj. or refl. pron.) To address *to* a person. Also *techn.* to present a formal address, and to 'pay addresses,' to court. *Obs.*

1605 SHAKS. *Lear* I. i. 193 My Lord of Burgundie, We first addresse toward you. **1713** *Guardian* No. 45 (1756) I. 194 A man of greater fortune than she could expect would address to her upon honourable terms. **1715** BURNET *Hist. own Times* II. 32 Yet they addressed to him against it. **1754** RICHARDSON *Grandison* IV. xxxix, Miss Clements is addressed to by a Yorkshire gentleman. **1756** HUME *Hist. Eng.* vii. (1767) 524 The Commons.. addressed against the King's guards. **1765** TUCKER *Lt. of Nat.* II. 686 If either he had addressed to the studious, or I been to write for the better sort.

d. *trans.* (by omission of *to*) To speak directly to. Also with *inf. phr.* To request (the sovereign) in a formal address.

1718 POPE *Iliad* v. 518 And, calling Venus, thus address'd his child. **1782** PRIESTLEY *Matt. & Spir.* I. Pref. 12 In printed publications we, in fact, address all the world. **1827** HALLAM *Const. Hist.* xi. (1876) II. 380 The Commons.. instantly addressed the king to disband his army. **1859** DE QUINCEY *Cæsars* Wks. X. 112 The custom was that the candidate should address every voter by name. **1862** LD. BROUGHAM *Brit. Constit.* xv. 238 An obsequious assembly, which addressed him to take the title of King. *Mod.* Address the chair!

e. To deliver a prepared speech to a company or meeting (extended to any speech appealing to an audience).

1849 MACAULAY *Hist. Eng.* I. vi. 208 He now addressed the House of Peers for the first time. **1870** *Crown Hist. Eng.* 818 Mr. Hunt began to address the assembly amidst a profound silence. *Mod.* Messrs. Fawcett and Holmes will address their constituents on the work of the session.

f. *U.S.* To force (a judge) *out* (of office) by a petition to the executive. (Cf. ADDRESS *sb.* 11 b.)

1822 *Missouri Intell.* 2 July 3/2 If any of the judges have corruptly discharged their duties, impeach them. If they are incompetent, address them out. **1874** R. H. COLLINS *Kentucky* I. 27 David Ballengall, an assistant judge.. [was] 'addressed' out of office, because a Scotchman unnaturalized.

g. To speak or write to (someone) *as* (the title or name specified).

1910 A. BENNETT *Clayhanger* II. i. 153 The young man's name was Stifford, and he was addressed as 'Stiff'. **1918** A. G. GARDINER *Leaves in Wind* 113, I should like to try the experiment on Sir F. E. Smith. I should like to address him as Sir Frederic Thesiger and see how the blood of all the Smiths would take it. **1954** T. S. ELIOT *Confidential Clerk* III. 120 In order to avoid any danger of confusion You may address me as Aunt Elizabeth. **1954** J. MASTERS *Bhowani Junction* xxxix. 337 In this regiment subalterns address field officers as 'Sir', not 'Major', or 'Colonel', or even 'Chief'. **1976** *Debrett's Correct Form* (rev. ed.) VI. 353 A Senator's wife is addressed as Mrs. Doolittle.

III. (Special development of 3 influenced by 6.)

†**9.** *trans.* To apply, direct, or turn (to some object or purpose). *Obs.*

1393 GOWER *Conf.* III. 213 Where stant the verray hardiesse, There mote a king his herte adresse. **1481** CAXTON *Myrrour* I. xiv. 43 The axe doeth nothynge but cutte And he that holdeth it addressith it to what parte he wylle. **1591** GARRARD *Art of Warre* 300 To carry Ladders and such Engines, to addresse and reare them to the breach.

10. *refl.* To turn oneself with preparation, to apply oneself, to direct one's skill or energies (*to* some work or object).

1393 GOWER *Conf.* III. 259 And he, which all him hadde adressed To lust, toke thanne what him liste. *c* **1525** SKELTON *Agst. Scottes* 89 And now to begyn I will me adres, To you rehersyng the somme of my proces. **1598** *Parismus* I. (1661) 31 Parismus and the rest of the company addressed themselves to that pastime. **1633** BP. HALL *Hard Texts* 348 The captive Jewes.. shall soon addresse themselves to their returne. **1751** WATTS *Improv. Mind* I. (1801) 3 To address yourself to the work of improving your reasoning powers. **1816** J. WILSON *City of Plague* I. iv. 30 We may address ourselves to revelry. **1849** MACAULAY *Hist. Eng.* II. 67 These men addressed themselves to the task of subverting the treasurer's power.

†**11.** *intr.* (by suppression of refl. pron.) To turn the attention *to*, set about. *Obs.*

1643 MILTON *Divorce* iv. (1851) 28 Which I shall forthwith addresse to prove. **1725** POPE *Odyss.* VI. 131 But Pallas now addrest To break the bands of all-composing rest.

address (əˈdrɛs), *sb.* [partly a. Fr. *adresse*, f. *adresse-r*; partly f. Eng. vb. ADDRESS.]

I. Preparation.

†**1.** The action of making ready, the state of being ready, preparation. *Obs.*

1633 BP. HALL *Hard Texts* 408, I beheld a present representation of addresse unto a terrible judgement. **1665–9** BOYLE *Refl.* Ep. Ded., Your Importunity ingaged me (though not to the address) yet to the Publication of these Papers. **1671** MILTON *Samson* 731 But now again she makes address to speak. **1673** *Lady's Calling* Pref. 2 The Spartans notwithstanding their ready address to Empire.. could have but half a happiness. **1788** PRIESTLEY *Lect. Hist.* 20 By proper address, they are as capable of entering into any subject of speculation as they ever will be.

†**2.** That which is prepared; an appliance. *Obs.*

1598 BARRET *Theor. Warres* V. iii. 132 Bridges, barks and boats, and other Addresses and engines.. to be framed to passe riuers.

†**3.** Array, attire; dress. *Obs.*

1592 WYRLEY *Armorie* V. 100 Foorth I proceed in order clad, In weldie armes right fair addresse. **1660** BP. HALL *Rem. Wks.* 203 Secondly, here must be a light address; no Man that goes to sojourn in a strange Country will carry his lumber along with him.

4. General preparedness or readiness for an event: skill, dexterity, adroitness.

1598 SYLVESTER *Du Bartas* I. vi. (1641) 50/1 The quick, proud Courser, which the rest doth passe For apt address. **1622** BACON *Jul. Cæs.* Wks. (Bohn) 499 His ready address to extricate himself both in action and discourse: for no man ever resolved quicker, or spoke clearer. **1644** EVELYN *Mem.* I. 94 Being built exceedingly reclining, by a rare address of the architect. **1710** STEELE *Tatler* No. 3 ¶6 His Royal Highness employs all his Address in alarming the enemy. **1778** MISS BURNEY *Evelina* I. 169 The prisoner had had the address to escape. **1829** SCOTT *Antiq.* xxx. 208 Miss Griselda.. had not address enough to follow the lead. **1850** MERIVALE *Hist. Rom. Emp.* lviii. (1865) VI. 310 With the charms of beauty she combined the address of an accomplished intriguer. **1855** PRESCOTT *Philip II* (1857) I. vi. 93 The French commander had the address to obtain instructions to the same effect from his own court.

II. Direction.

5. The action of directing or dispatching (to a person or place). Still said of ships.

1882 *Charter-party*, Ship to be addressed to Charterers or their Agents at port of discharge, paying 3% address commission.

†**6.** The action of sending a written message, of inscribing or dedicating what has been written. *Obs.*

1643 MILTON *Divorce* Introd. (1847) 123/2 The address of these lines chiefly to the parliament of England might have seemed ingrateful. **1663** GERBIER *Counsel* c 8 a, The Addresse of this little Treatise to your Lordship. **1705** ADDISON *Italy* [I] can have no other Design in this Address than to declare that I am your lordship's most obliged ——.

7. a. The direction or superscription of a letter, etc.; the name of the person and place to which it is addressed or directed; the name of the place to which any one's letters are directed.

1712 BUDGELL *Spectator* No. 277 ¶6 Having learnt the Milliner's Addresse, I went directly to her house. **1848** *Vest. Creation* (ed. 3) 312 The number of letters put in without addresses is year by year the same. **1863** THACKERAY *Pendennis* lxxi. 606 His address was to his brother's house in Suffolk. *Mod.* This letter is to your address.

b. Place of residence, house.

1888 GUNTER *Mr. Potter of Texas* xix, He doesn't know where his son is to be found.., otherwise he would drive to his address at once. **1936** G. B. SHAW *Millionairess* III. 178 First I must go round to the address Tim has given me and arrange that we send them our stuff direct. **1937** *Punch* 29 Dec. 718/1 He has returned.. to the same old address in South-West London that has sheltered him so often.

fig. **1934** G. B. SHAW *Too True to be Good* II. 68 What you think is love, and interest, and all that, is not real love at all: three quarters of it is only unsatisfied curiosity. Ive lived at that address myself.

c. *Computing.* (See quot. 1956.)

1948 *Math. Tables & Other Aids Computation* III. 69 In the language of some.. more recent machine designers, they would be called 'addresses'. **1951** WILKES et al. *Prep. Programs Electronic Digital Computer* I. i. 10 The address specified in this particular order is then increased by one. **1955** ECKERT & JONES *Faster, Faster* 11 In order to tell the machine to place a word in a given storage location.. it is necessary to specify the number, or 'address', of the location. **1956** BERKELEY & WAINWRIGHT *Computers* 334/2 *Address*, digital computers. A label, name, or number identifying a register, a location, or a device where information is stored.

d. ***form of address***: the style by which a person is addressed, esp. formally.

1875 A. B. THOM *Upper Ten Thousand* p. x (*heading*) Forms of epistolary address. **1927** MRS. MASSEY LYON *Etiquette* ii. 18 Form of Address for Boys... How should a small boy be addressed formally? **1957** R. HOGGART *Uses of Literacy* ii. 34 'Our Mam', 'our Dad', 'our Alice' are normal forms of address. **1970** *Debrett's Correct Form* II. 50 Widow of a younger son of an earl. There is no difference in the form of address in widowhood. **1979** P. NORMAN *Skaters' Waltz* 110 Hers is the final authority.. wielded in such subtleties as her pre-emptive right to be known by her surname, where Miss Stella employs a familiar, somehow junior form of address.

†**8.** The act of addressing or betaking oneself to any one; recourse, application, approach for any object. *Obs.*

1611 COTGR., *Acheminement*, an addresse, introduction, entrie, ingression. **1661** BRAMHALL *Just Vind.* iii. 35 To make his first addresse for justice to a secular Magistrate. **1704** NELSON *Fest. & Fasts* x. (1739) 127 Our Addresses to Heaven are represented by Frankincense.

9. *esp.* Dutiful or courteous approach to any one, courtship to a sovereign (*obs.*) or a lady. Now always in the plural, as in ***to pay one's addresses*** to a lady.

1539 in Strype *Eccl. Mem.* I. 544 The king looked for address: and was well pleased when he had it from such as had a repute for learning. **1665–9** BOYLE *Refl.* IV. xix. 284 Procuring her to be haunted by some.. and to make an address which aims but at the Portion, not the Person. **1749** RICHARDSON *Clarissa* II. iii. 11 She did not dislike his address, only the manner of it. **1749** FIELDING *Tom Jones* (1775) III. 93 To make sham addresses to the older lady. **1854** THACKERAY *Newcomes* I. 17 The black footman persecuted her with his addresses.

10. Manner of speaking to another, bearing in conversation; accost.

1674 N. FAIRFAX *Bulk & Selv.* 17 With a goodly income of Learning, and a right handsome address of words, and well air'd periods. **1716–8** LADY M. W. MONTAGU *Lett.* 20 I. 61 A princess of great address and good breeding. **1755** JOHNSON in *Boswell* (1816) I. 240, I was overpowered.. by the enchantment of your address. **1807** CRABBE *Flattery* 11 And who that modest nymph of meek address? **1851** CARLYLE *J. Sterling* II. ii. (1872) 93 His address, I perceived, was abrupt, unceremonious.

11. a. A discourse specially directed to any one, a formal speech of congratulation, respect, thanks, petition, etc., *esp.* the formal reply of the House of Lords or Commons to the Royal Speech at the opening of Parliament; and, in modern usage, a set discourse, a speech addressed to, or appealing to an audience. (Expressing less oratorical style, than a *speech*; less systematic treatment of a theological subject than a *sermon*.)

1751 CHAMBERS *Cycl.*, *Address*, a discourse presented to the king, in the name of a considerable body of his people. **1759** ROBERTSON *Hist. Scot.* I. ii. 154 They joined with this view, in an address to the regent. **1855** PRESCOTT *Philip II* (1857) I. ii. 28 The magistrates of the cities through which he passed welcomed him with complimentary addresses. **1870** *Crown Hist. Eng.* 808 Lord Liverpool moved the Address.. the debate lasted two nights, the Address being finally carried by a majority of 163. **1872** A. J. ELLIS in *Trans. Philol. Soc.* 1873, 1 To make our Anniversary conform to those of other learned Societies, by delivering an annual address. *Mod.* The proceedings consist of prayer, singing of hymns, short and stirring addresses.

b. A formal request, directed to the executive by both branches of the legislature, requesting the removal of a judge from office. *U.S.*

1822 *Missouri Intell.* 2 July 3/2 If any of the judges.. must be removed, even without cause, still let it be done by address. **1882** H. ADAMS *J. Randolph* 132 The Constitutions of England, of Massachusetts, of Pennsylvania, authorized the removal of an obnoxious judge on a mere address of the legislature.

12. *attrib.* (in sense 7) ***address-book***, ***-card***.

1877 LADY C. SCHREIBER *Jrnl.* (1911) II. 42 Several mentioned in the address book 'n'existent pas'. **1854** *Poultry Chron.* I. 354/2 So as to have all the purchasers' address-cards quite ready by the close of the show.

addressable (əˈdrɛsəb(ə)l), *a.* *Computing.* [f. ADDRESS *v.* + -ABLE.] Allowing the assignment of an address and therefore capable of being individually accessed. Of (a) memory: in which all locations can be separately accessed.

1953 *Proc. IRE* XLI. 1267/2 An important property of the 701 is that any full word of 36 bits.. can be split into two half words of 18 bits.., each half word being separately addressable. **1961** *Communications Assoc. Computing Machinery* IV. 434/1 Addressable registers. **1967** *Technology Week* 23 Jan. 11/2 (Advt.), Memory uses 32-bit words, is addressable and alterable by 8-bit bytes, half words, words, and double words. **1973** *Sci. Amer.* July 6/2 (Advt.), The HP-45 is the first pocket calculator with *nine* addressable memory registers besides its operational stack. You can store data in each one—any number that appears on the display—and recall it to the working register whenever you want. **1983** *Listener* 20 Oct. 37/3 Special 30-minute discs allow trick playback and fast access to individually 'addressable' frames.

addressed (əˈdrɛst), *ppl. a.* Also **addrest**. [f. ADDRESS *v.* + -ED.]

†1. Erected, raised. *Obs.*

1595 SPENSER *Colin Clout* 563 She.. like a goodly beacon high addrest.

†2. Well-ordered, accomplished. *Obs.*

1475 CAXTON *Jason* 12 Jason the most adressid knight that euer was in mirmidone. **1596** SPENSER *F.Q.* I. xi. 11 Full jolly knight he seemde, and wel addrest. **1597** DANIEL *Civile Wares* (1717) II. 13 Never this Island better peopl'd stood, Never more Men of Might, and Minds address'd.

†3. Made ready, prepared, 'dressed,' as food. *Obs.*

1387 TREVISA *Higden* (1527) I. xlii. 42 b In Brytayne ben hote welles wel arayed and adressed to the use of mankynd. **1567** MAPLET *Greene Forest* 84 The Ele being killed & addressed in wine whosoeuer chaunceth to drinke of that wine so vsed, shall euer after lothe wine. **1597** SHAKS. *2 Hen. IV*, IV. iv. 5 Our Nauie is addressed, our power collected. **1633** BP. HALL *Hard Texts* 394 They were accordingly addressed for their execution upon the third part of the inhabitants.

4. Arrayed, attired, trimmed, dressed. *arch.*

1393 GOWER *Conf.* I. 134 The better addressed and arraied. **1398** TREVISA *Barth. De P.R.* (1495) XII. iii. 411 A goshawke is adressyd wyth dyuersyte of pennes and fetheres. **1513** DOUGLAS *Æneis* X. xiii. 178 His ȝallow lokkis brycht, That ayre was kemmyt and addressit rycht. **1597** DANIEL *Civile Wares* VI. xxviii. When faire Europa sate With many goodly Diadems addrest. **1820** SHELLEY *Sens. Plant.* 29 The rose like a nymph to the bath addrest, Which unveiled the depth of her glowing breast.

5. Directed, dispatched, aimed.

1598 SYLVESTER *Du Bartas* I. ii. (1641) 14/2 Anon, from North to South, from East to West, With ceasless wings, they drive a ship addrest. **1793** SMEATON *Edystone Lighth.* §15 The large copper plate print addressed to Prince George of Denmark. **1810** SOUTHEY *Kehama* X. 21 Wks. VIII. 84 The shaft, unerringly addrest, Unerring flew, and smote Ereenia's breast.

6. Directed as a letter, superscribed with the name of the person for whom it is intended.

Mod. The letter has been posted insufficiently addressed. An addressed envelope was found in his pocket.

†aˈddressedness. *Obs. rare*⁻¹. [f. prec. + -NESS.] The quality or state of being addressed or prepared; preparedness.

1633 BP. HALL *Hard Texts* 378 His ready addressednesse to the gracious works of his mediatorship.

addressee (əˌdrɛˈsiː). [f. ADDRESS *v.* + -EE.] One who is addressed; *spec.* the person to whom a letter, packet, etc., is addressed.

1810 R. PETERS *Let.* 25 Nov. in W. Jay *Life J. Jay* (1833) II. 332 Nothing must go with a pamphlet but the mere direction, under the pains and penalties of sousing the correspondent or *addressee* in all costs of enormous postage. *a* **1832** BENTHAM *Essay on Lang.* in *Wks.* (1843) viii. 328/1 By the addresser, the sign is presented to the addressee. *a* **1858** DE QUINCEY *Wks.* VI. 328 Out of five thousand addressees, if nine-tenths declined to take any notice of his letters. **1880** *P.O. Guide* 235 When the addressee resides beyond the free delivery, porterage is charged. **1884** *N. & Q.* 12 July 22/1 The strong presumption this offers in favour of this youthful nobleman as the addressee of the sonnets.

addresser (əˈdrɛsə(r)). [f. ADDRESS *v.* + -ER¹.] One who addresses; one who sets right (*obs.*); one who pays addresses (*obs.*); the signer or deliverer of an address; the person who addresses or directs a message or letter to any one.

[**1495** *Addresseress* is quoted.] **1681** LUTTRELL *Brief Rel.* (1857) I. 100 The addressers.. adjourned to the Divill tavern, and there signed the addresse. **1748** RICHARDSON *Clarissa* xvii. (1811) II. 112 It is dangerous to be laid under the sense of an obligation to an addresser's patience. **1844** LD. COCKBURN *Jrnl.* II. 86 As an addresser of the lower orders—he has no existing equal. **1881** *Echo* 7 Nov. 4/6 *Advt.*, Envelope and circular addressers.

†aˈddresseress. *Obs. rare*⁻¹. [f. prec. + -ESS.] A female addresser, who directs or sets right.

1495 CAXTON *Vitas Patr.* (W. de Worde) I. xlii. 69 bb, Our lady.. the very adresseresse of theym that ben out of the waye.

addressing (əˈdrɛsɪŋ), *vbl. sb.* [f. ADDRESS *v.* + -ING¹.] **1. a.** The action of righting, preparing; acting with address or dexterity (*obs.*); of directing or speaking directly to. (Now mostly gerundial.)

1601 BP. BARLOW *Serm. Paules Crosse* Pref. 3 The addressing my selfe to this sermon. **1603** FLORIO *Montaigne* II. xvii. (1632) 362 Of addressing, dexteritie, and disposition, I never had any. **1611** COTGR., *Adressement*, an addressing.. or setting in the nearest and readiest course. *a* **1682** in *Roxb. Ballads* IV. 256 With Abhorring and Adressing their time is spent. **1845** CARLYLE *Cromwell* (1871) I. 29 Immense sumptuosities, addressings, knight-makings, ceremonial exhibitions. *Mod.* Blamed for wrongly addressing the letter.

b. *attrib.*: **addressing-machine**, a machine for printing addresses on newspaper-wrappers, etc.

1865 *U.S. Pat.* 47,142 (*title*) Addressing-Machine.. a Machine for Printing the Directions on Newspapers or Wrappers. **1953** *Vocab. bibliothec.* (*Unesco*) 160/1 Addressing machine; addressograph.

2. *Computing.* The method or process of allocating addresses in the memory of a computer (ADDRESS *sb.* 7 c); the system for identifying or referring to locations in memory. Freq. *attrib.* Cf. *direct addressing* s.v. DIRECT *a.* 7; *indirect addressing* s.v. INDIRECT *a.* 2 a.

1957 *IBM Jrnl. Res. & Devel.* I. 131/1 The addressing system should make the average access time.. as small as possible. **1962** [see *indirect addressing* s.v. INDIRECT *a.* 2 a]. **1964** T. W. MCRAE *Impact of Computers on Accounting* i. 10 Our next job is to assign an address to each word. Our addressing system is quite arbitrary. **1971** J. H. SMITH *Digital Logic* vi. 126 Each core in the plane is threaded with additional 'read' and 'write' wires which together with the 'addressing' co-ordinates *X* and *Y* are used to put information into and out of core memories. **1982** *Sci. Amer.* Jan. 117/1 Instructions are coded patterns of bits that specify the operations to be done and carry addressing information for gaining access to memory. **1984** *Personal Software* Winter 24/2 The mode 3 addressing system is based on the use of two bits to indicate the base colour to be found at each of two adjacent points.

addressing (əˈdrɛsɪŋ), *ppl. a.* [f. ADDRESS *v.* + ING².] Forming a straight line; preparing; directing; issuing an address.

1523 LD. BERNERS *Froissart* I. ccxii. 237 All Iles addressing to the landes.. we helde in the tyme of the sayd treatye. **1705** PERRY *Hist. Coll. Am. Col. Ch.* I. 156 The addressing Clergy have the general favor of the people. **1773** BURKE *Pres. Discont.* Wks. II. 289 An addressing house of commons.

†aˈddression. *Obs. rare.* [f. ADDRESS in imitation of forms like *oppress-ion*, *confess-ion*, *aggress-ion*.] The direction of one's course.

1596 CHAPMAN *Iliad* VI. 371 (1857) I. 147 My wife with her advice inclin'd This my addression to the field. **1615** —— *Odyss.* I. 438 To Pylos first be thy addression then.

†aˈddressly, *adv.* *Obs. rare*⁻¹; 5 **adresly**. [f. ADDRESS *sb.* + -LY³.] With good address, courteously.

c **1425** WYNTOWN *Cron.* IX. xxvii. 317 Commendyt heily.. his manere As he hym hawyt adresly.

aˈddressment. *Obs.* [a. Fr. *adressement*; f. *adresser* to ADDRESS.] The act of addressing. **a.** Putting right, adjustment. **b.** Direction or dedication of a writing. **c.** Of the face or outward attention: Attitude. **d.** Of the mental attention: Devotion of attention, application.

1525 *Q. Margaret of Scotl.* I. 369 After the good addresment of that your borderers and your commissioners concludes. **1630** LORD *Persees* 29 We make addressment to the third Tract.. which layeth downe their Law. **1641** BRATHWAIT *Eng. Gentlew.* Ded., This addreessement of mine [my book] to his daughter. **1646** J. GREGORY *Notes on Script.* 81 The Great Atonement was performed towards the East, quite contrary to all other manner of addressment in their devotion.

addressograph (əˈdrɛsəʊgrɑːf, -æ-). [f. ADDRESS *sb.* + -O + -GRAPH.] An addressing-machine for printing addresses. (Proprietary term.)

1908 *Modern Business* Sept., Index to Advertisers p. iii/2. **1924** *Public Opinion* 11 July 37/1 The addresses have that dull, uninteresting look that an addressograph gives them. **1958** *Observer* 7 Dec. 3/6 Barbara, an addressograph operator. **1964** *Economist* 25 July 371/2 Many companies had already progressed by way of the addressograph plate to the punched card.

addressor (əˈdrɛsə(r), -ˌɔː(r)). [f. ADDRESS *v.* + -OR.] One who signs or joins in signing a formal address; one who addresses a formal document, as the addressor of a Letter of Credit.

1691 *New Disc. of Old Intreague* Introd. 5 With greater Gust than our Addressors sold Their Liberty for Lust. **1806** W. TAYLOR in *Ann. Rev.* IV. 64 A meeting of the addressors had nominated him as their chairman.

addressy (əˈdrɛsɪ), *a.* *nonce-wd.* [f. ADDRESS *sb.* + -Y¹.] Having the character or aspect of an address, or speech directed to an audience.

1870 *Echo* 23 Nov., Upon the unsectarian point their utterances are 'addressy.'

†addubiˈtation. *Obs. rare.* [ad. L. *addubitātiōn-em* a doubting, f. *addubitā-re* to incline to doubt, f. *ad* to, towards + *dubitā-re* to DOUBT.] The suggestion of a doubt.

1631 GOUGE *Expos. Ps.* cxvi. (1868) 78 The manner of expressing his profession is by a rhetorical addubitation. **1655** —— *Hebr.* (1866) I. 315 By way of addubitation or supposition.

adduce (əˈdjuːs), *v.* [ad. L. *addūc-ĕre* to lead to, to bring forward or allege; f. *ad* to + *dūc-ĕre* to lead.] To bring forward (verbally) for consideration, to cite, to allege.

1616 N. BRENT *Hist. Counc. Trent* (1629) 545 For better proofe many authorities of the Fathers were adduced. **1678** *Trans. at Crt. Spain* 88 Though all that I have adduced, be sufficient to convince every disinterested person. **1769** ROBERTSON *Charles V*, III. VIII. 88 In proof of this they adduced many arguments. **1806–31** A. KNOX *Rem.* (1844) I. 90 He adduces Martin Luther as an instance of clearness respecting justification. **1870** BOWEN *Logic* ix. 305 Supported by better reasons than he has been able to adduce.

adduceable (əˈdjuːsəb(ə)l), *a.* [f. ADDUCE + -ABLE.] Another form of ADDUCIBLE, on analogy of adjectives in -ABLE not adopted from L.

1869 *Pall Mall G.* 11 Oct. 1 The rapid improvement.. is confirmed by such statistical facts as are adduceable.

adduced (əˈdjuːst), *ppl. a.* [f. ADDUCE + -ED.] Brought forward in a statement, cited, alleged.

1790 PALEY *Hor. Paul.* Rom. ii. 17 The two congruities last adduced depend upon the time. **1860** FARRAR *Orig. Lang.* 205 Attempts have, indeed, been made to connect Hebrew and Sanskrit, but the adduced points of osculation are.. few and dubious.

adducent (əˈdjuːsənt), *a.* *Phys.* [ad. L. *addūcent-em*, pr. pple. of *addūc-ĕre*; see ADDUCE.] Bringing or drawing towards a given point or common centre; attribute of the muscles, called ADDUCTORS. Opposed to *abducent*.

1694 GWITHER *Physiognomy* in *Phil. Trans.* XVIII. 120 We see great Drinkers with Eyes generally set towards the Nose, the adducent Muscles being often employed to let them see their loved Liquor in the Glass. **1713** DERHAM *Physico-Theol.* IV. ii. 99 Which is the case of the Adducent and Abducent Muscles [of the eye]. **1843** WILKINSON *Swedenborg's Anim. Kingd.* I. viii. 225 The glands have four vessels, two adducent or afferent.

adducer (əˈdjuːsə(r)). [f. ADDUCE + -ER¹.] One who adduces, or brings forward in a statement.

1810 COLERIDGE *Friend* (1865) 115 Principles, from which the adducers of these arguments loudly profess their dissent. **1817** —— *Ess. on own Times* (1850) III. 952 The charge, as far as it allows even a plausible excuse for the adducer, implies a complete ignorance.

adducible (əˈdjuːsɪb(ə)l), *a.* [f. ADDUCE, as if ad. assumed L. **addūcibil-is*, vbl. adj. f. *addūc-ĕre*; cf. *condūcibilis*. See -BLE.] Capable of being adduced or produced in a statement.

1799 COLERIDGE *Ess. on own Times* (1850) II. 344 The only argument.. which.. is fairly adducible against it.

adduct (əˈdʌkt), *v.* *Phys.* [f. L. *adduct-* ppl. stem of *addūc-ĕre* to lead to: see ADDUCE.] To draw towards a common centre or median line.

1836–9 TODD *Cycl. Anat. & Phys.* II. 528/1 When the thumb is adducted the first dorsal interosseous projects considerably. **1870** W. ADAMS in *Lancet* 13 Aug. 236/2 The thigh is flexed and adducted so that the knee is drawn across the opposite thigh.

adduct (ˈædʌkt), *sb.* *Chem.* [ad. G. *addukt* (Diels and Alder 1931, in *Ann. d. Chem.* 191), f. ADD(ITION *sb.* + PROD)UCT *sb.*¹ (G. *produkt*).] An addition product (see ADDITION *sb.* 7).

1944 *Brit. Pat.* 552,644 3 Equal parts of the cyclopentadiene adduct of maleic anhydride and blown linseed oil.. were reacted together. **1952** *Chem. Abstr.* 9953 Urea and thiourea adducts, dinitrobiphenyl adducts, cyclodextrin adducts.. are treated.

adducted (əˈdʌktɪd), *ppl. a.* *Phys.* [f. ADDUCT *v.* + -ED.] Drawn towards the median line.

1836–9 TODD *Cycl. Anat. & Phys.* II. 790/2 The limb.. became so strongly adducted as to cross the median line. **1872** HUXLEY *Physiol.* vii. 174 A limb.. is adducted, when it is brought to the middle line.

adduction (əˈdʌkʃən). [a. Fr. *adduction* (16th c. in Litt.), ad. med.L. *addūctiōn-em*, n. of action,

f. *addūcĕre*: see ADDUCE.] The action of bringing to or towards.

†**1.** The action of bringing a thing to something else; *spec.* the alleged bringing of our Lord's body and blood into the elements, transubstantiation. *Obs.*

1638 FEATLEY *Transubst.* 182 Such an adduction importeth onely a translocation.

2. The action of adducting; in *Phys.* the opposite of abduction.

1656 tr. *Hobbes's Elem. Philos.* (1839) 343 The bending of a line is either the adduction of diduction of the extreme parts. **1666** J. SMITH *Solomon's Old Age* (1676) 62 If we consider how they [the muscles] can stir the limb inward, outward..can perform adduction, abduction. **1709** BLAIR *Osteogr. Eleph.* in *Phil. Trans.* XXVII. 129 The motion of the Humerus..is rather Flexion and Extension, than Adduction or Abduction. **1872** HUXLEY *Physiol.* vii. 174 The different kinds of movements which the levers thus connected are capable of performing are called..abduction and adduction.

3. The action of adducing or bringing forward facts or statements.

1764 SWINTON in *Phil. Trans.* LIV. 399 The Chaldee term being of the singular number..the adduction of it seems altogether impertinent. **1836** J. GILBERT *Chr. Atonem.* ii. (1852) 44 The adduction of such parts of Scripture as furnish an obvious ground for the conclusion. **1860** GOSSE *Rom. Nat. Hist.* 280 These attributes are so characteristic..that..their adduction gives a measure of authority to the statement.

adductive (əˈdʌktɪv), *a.* [f. L. *addūct-* ppl. stem of *addūc-ĕre* + -IVE, as if ad. L. **addūctīvus*: see ADDUCE.] Tending to lead towards, bringing to something else. Formerly applied *spec.* to the change said to be wrought in transubstantiation.

1638 FEATLEY *Transubst.* 182 Suarez drives this nayle to the head, by a meere adductive action. **1654** JER. TAYLOR *Real Pres.* (1836) 659 If we ask what conversion it is..at last it is found to be adductive. **1674** BREVINT *Saul at Endor* 411 For bringing their Imaginary Christ from Heaven; which is the English of their Adductive Motion. **1855** P. J. BAILEY *Mystic.* 90 The achate, wealth adductive, and the mind Of the immortals gladdening.

adductor (æˈdʌktə(r)). *Phys.* [a. L. *addūctor* a bringer to; also in the *Phys.* sense.] A muscle which draws any limb, or part of the body, towards the trunk or main axis, or which folds or closes extended parts of the body. Also *attrib.* with *muscle*.

1746 PARSONS *Hum. Physiogn.* i. 17 in *Phil. Trans.* XLIV. The Adductor arises tendinous and fleshy from the edge of the Hole of the optic Nerve. **1836** TODD *Cycl. Anat. & Phys.* I. 296/1 There are [in birds] most commonly three adductors of the thigh. **1859** CARPENTER *Anim. Physiol.* i. (1872) 41 The animal forcibly draws them together by its adductor muscle.

†**aˈddulce**, *v. Obs.* Forms: 5 **adoulce**, 6 **addoulce**, 7 **addoulse**, **adulce**, **addulce**. [orig. a. MFr. *adoulcir*, also written *addoulcir*; (mod. *adoucir*) to sweeten:—late L. *addulcīre*; f. *ad* to + *dulcis* sweet. Subseq. refashioned after L.] To sweeten, to render pleasant or palatable (a thing); to soothe, mollify (a person).

1475 CAXTON *Jason* 20b, Shalle not the Rigour..of my noble lady be myned and adoulced by my habondant prayers? **1552** HULOET *Abcedarium*, Addoulce or mitigate with swetnes, *Permulceo*. *c* **1592** G. HARVEY *Sonnets* xv. 69 Then would I so my melody addoulce. **1617** MINSHEU *Ductor*, To Addoulse, or mitigate with sweetenesse, Fr. *addoulcir, addoucir*; It. *addolcire*. **1622** BACON *Henry VII*, 90 With great show of their king's affection, and many sugared words, seek to addulce all matters between the two kings. **1655** DIGGES *Compl. Ambass.* 263 The answer you see..is adulced so much as may. **1655** FULLER *Ch. Hist.* IX. 203 The Queen having lately Adulced him with fair language. **1679** PRANCE *Add. Narrat.* 18 For the addulcing and ascertaining his Friends and Partizans beyond the Seas. **1696** PHILLIPS, *Addoulce* (French) to sweeten, mollifie, or asswage. [Not in ed. 1706.]

-ade, *suff.* of sbs. **1. a.** Fr. *-ade*, ad. Pr., Sp. or Pg. *-ada* or It. *-ata*:—L. *-āta*, subst. use of fem. of pa. pple., as in pop. L. *strāta* (sc. *via*) a *paved* way, a 'street.' The native Fr. form of this suff. is *-ée*, as in *entrée*, *acolée*; *-ade* appeared first in the adaptation of Provençal words in *-ada*, as *ballade*, Pr. *ballada*, and became established as the reg. form in which Pr., Sp. or Pg. words in *-ada*, or their It. cognates in *-ata*, were adapted in Fr. In some cases these supplanted the native Fr. forms as *accolade*, ad. It. *accollata*, for OFr. *acolee*; in mod.Fr. *-ade* has become a living suffix, on which new words are formed, as *gasconnade*, *cannonade*, *fusillade*. From Fr., words in *-ade* have been adopted in Eng., without change (exc. that the early *ballade*, *salade*, have become *ballad*, *salad*) as in *accolade*, *ambassade*, *ambuscade*, *arcade*, *balustrade*, *bastonnade*, *brigade*, *cannonade*, *cascade*, *cavalcade*, *comrade*, *crusade*, *enfilade*, *escalade*, *esplanade*, *fanfaronnade*, *lemonade*, *marmalade*, *masquerade*, *palisade*, *parade*, *rodomontade*, *serenade*, *tirade*. In imitation of these some have been formed in Eng. itself, as *blockade*, *gingerade*, *orangeade*. The sense is analogous to the pa. pple., and to Eng. sbs., in *-ate*, as *acetate*, *mandate*, *syndicate*; hence **a.** An action done; as in *blockade*, *cannonade*, *fusillade*, *crusade*, *parade*, *tirade*. **b.** The body concerned in an action or process; as in *ambuscade*, *ambassade*, *brigade*, *cavalcade*, *comrade*. **c.** The product of an action, and, by extension, that of any process or raw material; as in *arcade*, *colonnade*, *masquerade*, *lemonade*, *marmalade*, *pomade*.

Equivalent forms, all:—L. *-āta*, appear in *son-ata* (a. It.), *arm-ada* (a Sp.), *lev-ee*, *soir-ée* (a Fr.), *voll-ey*, *arm-y* (a. OFr. *volee*, *armee* = *armata*, *armada*, *armade*).

2. a. Fr. *-ade*, ad. (directly or through L.) Gr. -αδ-α (nom. -ας); as in *decade*, *nomade*. The ordinary Eng. form of this suffix is *-ad*: see -AD I.

3. ad. Sp. or Pg. *-ado*, or cogn. It. *-ato*, the masculine form answering to No. 1 above, and having **a.** the same meaning, as in *brocade*, embossed (stuff); or **b.** that of a person affected, as in *renegade*, one who has *re-denied* his faith. These also remain as *-ado*, cf. *desperado*.

a-dead (əˈdɛd), *adv.* and *pred. a.* [f. A- *pref.* 11 + DEAD; apparently due to form-assoc. w. *a-live*, *a-sleep*, *a-cold*, but not analogous.] Dead.

1879 E. ARNOLD *Light of Asia* 101 As ye lie asleep so must ye lie A-dead.

†**aˈdead-en**, *v. Obs.* Forms: 1 **adeadan**, **adydan**, 2–3 **adead-en**. [f. A- *pref.* 1, intensive + *deád-an* to make dead. Cf. Ger. *ertödten*.]

1. *trans.* To kill, put to death; deaden, mortify.

c **1000** ÆLFRIC *Gen.* ix. 11 Ic nelle heononforð eall flæsc adydan. *c* **1230** *Ancren Riwle* 112 No þing neuer nes þerinne þet hit muhte adeaden.

2. *intr.* To die.

c **1230** *Ancren Riwle* 150 þe bouh, hwon he adeadeð, he hwiteð wiðuten..& worpeð his rinde. Al so god dede þet wule adeaden forworpeð hire rinde, þet is, unheleð hire.

†**adeal.** *Obs.* 4–6 Also **adele**, **adell**, **adeale**. Properly two words *a deal*, a part; used in negative phrases *not a deal*, *never a deal* = not, or never a bit; not at all. See DEAL.

c **1400** *Rom. Rose* 6402 This ought thee suffice wele, Ne be not rebel never adele. *Ibid.* 7435 For he ne drede him not adele. **1430** LYDG. *Chron. Troy* I. vi. Some..lyke it neuer adell. *c* **1450** LONELICH *Grail* xxx. 220 And Salomon..there aȝens spak neuere adel. **1534** MORE *On the Passion* Wks. 1557, 1369/2, I doubte it neuer adeale.

†**aˈdeath**, *adv.*, prop. *phrase. Obs.* [A *prep.*[1] + DEATH *sb.* Cf. *a-live*.] In death.

c **1315** SHOREHAM 7 God thorwe miracles ketheth hit A-lyve and eke a-dethe.

†**aˈdeave**, *v. Obs.* [f. A- *pref.* 1 + DEAVE, OE. *deaf-ian* to make deaf.] To deafen, strike deaf.

c **940** *Sax. Leechd.* II. 38 Wið earena adeafunge. *c* **1315** SHOREHAM 103 Ac purgatorie and helle hy beth So lyte byleved, That what somevere men telleth, Ben throf al adeved.

‖**ˈadeb.** [Arab.] (See quot.)

1743 R. POCOCK *Egypt* 175 in (1753) Chambers *Cycl. Supp.*, Adeb, in commerce, the name of a large Egyptian weight..consisting of 210 okes, each of three rotolos, a weight [*i.e.* the rotolo] of about two drams less than the English pound.

†**adeˈcastic(ke**, *a. Obs.*$^{-0}$ [f. Gr. ἀδέκαστ-ος impartial (vbl. adj. f. ἀ priv. + δεκάζ-ειν to bribe) + -IC. Also used subst.] 'One that will doe iust howsoeuer.' Cockeram 1626.

adeem (əˈdiːm). [ad L. *adim-ĕre* to take to oneself from, take away, f. *ad* to + *em-ĕre* to take; assimilated to REDEEM.] To take away; *spec.* in *Rom. Law*, to revoke the bequest of (a legacy, etc.).

1845 STEPHEN *Laws of Eng.* II. 206 Where a specific legacy is so adeemed, the legatee has no longer any claim under the will. **1880** MUIRHEAD *Ulpian* xxiv.§29 A legacy that has been bequeathed may be adeemed either in the same testament or in a codicil confirmed by it.

ˈadeep (əˈdiːp), *adv.* prop. *phrase.* [A *prep.*[1] in + DEEP.] Deeply, deep.

1850 MRS. BROWNING *Poems* II. 286 We shout so adeep down creation's profound, We are deaf to God's voice.

adel, obs. f. ADDLE.

‖**adelantado** (aðelanˈtaðo). [Sp., substantive use of pa. pple. of *adelantar* to advance, promote, f. *adelante* before, forward, f. *ad* to, at + *el* the + *ante* before.] A Spanish grandee; a lord-lieutenant or governor of a province.

1599 NASHE *Lenten Stuffe* (1871) 99 As complete an Adelantado, as he that is known by wearing a cloak of tuft-taffeta eighteen years. **1610** B. JONSON *Alchemist* III. iii. (1616) 641 [He is] an Adalantado, A Grande. **1783** ROBERTSON *Amer.* I. 258 Ferdinand..appointed him Adelantado, or Lieutenant-governor of the countries upon the South Sea. **1876** BANCROFT *Hist. U.S.* I. ii. 62 Marquez, nephew to the Adelantado.

‖**adelaster** (ædiːˈlæstə(r)). *Bot.* [mod. f. Gr. ἄδηλος not manifest + ἀστήρ, -έρα star.] A provisional name for a plant of which the flowers are unknown, so that it cannot be as yet referred to its proper genus.

1866 LINDLEY & MOORE *Treas. Bot.* 18 All Adelasters are therefore provisional names, to be abandoned as soon as the true names of the plants so called can be ascertained.

Adélie (əˈdeɪliː). Also **Adelie**. The name of Adélie Land in the Antarctic, used *attrib.* or *ellipt.* of a kind of penguin (*Pygoscelis adeliæ*) found there.

1907 E. A. WILSON in *Nat. Antarctic Exped. 1901–4* Nat. Hist. II. II. 40 We had Adélie Penguins in the water all around us. *Ibid.* 39 The numbers of adult Adélies rapidly increased. **1919** SHACKLETON *South* i. 6 During the day we had seen adelie and ringed penguins. **1930** J. S. HUXLEY *Bird-Watching* iv. 68 Adelie penguins lay their eggs in a little depression bordered by stones. *Ibid.*, An Adelie rookery in the Antarctic. **1959** *New Biol.* XXIX. 107 The truly Antarctic birds are the Emperor and Adélie penguins.

adeling. See ATHELING.

adelo- (əˈdiːləʊ, ˈædɪləʊ), comb. form of Gr. ἄδηλος not manifest or evident, unseen, in **adelocoˈdonic** *a.* (see quot.); **adeloˈmorphic**, **-ˈmorphous** *adjs.*, applied to the central cells of the peptic glands.

1871 G. J. ALLMAN *Gymnobl. Hydroids* 30 The gonophore is always borne as a bud... It may be referred to one or other of two principal types, based respectively on the greater or less approach to the completely formed medusa. The peculiar condition by which one of these types is characterised may be termed phanerocodonic, while that which distinguishes the other may be designated as *adelocodonic. **1891** W. D. HALLIBURTON *Text-bk. Chem. Physiol.* xxx. 633 These cells [of the cardiac glands] were called principal cells by Heidenhain, *adelomorphic cells by Rollett, and central cells on account of their position. **1875** A. GAMGEE tr. *Hermann's Elem. Hum. Physiol.* ii. 99 'Hauptzellen' (Heidenhain), or '*adelomorphous cells' (Rollett).

adelopod(e (əˈdiːləpɒd). [f. Gr. ἄδηλος not seen + πόδα (πούς) a foot.] 'An animal whose feet are not apparent.' Craig 1847.

Adelphi (əˈdɛlfɪ). The name of a group of buildings in London between the Strand and the Thames, laid out by the four brothers, James, John, Robert, and William Adam (see ADAM[2]) and hence called *Adelphi* (Gr. ἀδελφοί brothers); the name of the theatre in the vicinity of these buildings, at which a certain type of melodrama was prevalent *c* 1882–1900, and so allusively.

1894 *Queen* 17 Mar. 432/1 Those who expected that the advent of a new Adelphi dramatist would be marked by a new development in Adelphi drama. **1902** *Encycl. Brit.* XXVII. 517/1 The 'Adelphi' as opposed to the 'Drury Lane' type of drama has recently died out in the West End. **1903** CHESTERTON *R. Browning* ii. 45 A whiff from an Adelphi melodrama. **1928** —— *Generally Speaking* 231 His trouble cannot have been as deep as hell and as shallow as an Adelphi play.

‖**-adelphia** (əˈdɛlfɪə), *suffix. Bot.* [Gr. -αδελφία (in comb.) brotherhood, f. ἀδελφός brother.] Collection of stamens into a bundle; as in the Linnæan class-names *Monadelphia*, *Diadelphia*, *Polyadelphia*.

1858 CARPENTER *Veg. Physiol.* §456 The more or less complete union of the filaments of the stamens into bundles, or brotherhoods; on account of which the termination *adelphia* is applied to the number of such bundles.

adelphic (əˈdɛlfɪk), *a. Bot.* [ad. Gr. ἀδελφικός brotherly.] 'In Botany, having the stamens into a parcel or parcels.' Craig 1847.

adelphogamy (ædɛlˈfɒgəmɪ). *Zool.* [f. Gr. ἀδελφός brother + γάμος marriage, after MONOGAMY.] The mating of brothers and sisters, as in certain ants.

1926 W. M. WHEELER tr. *R.A.F. de Réaumur's Nat. Hist. Ants* 244 'Adelphogamy', or mating between males and virgin females of the same formicary undoubtedly occurs. **1928** C. K. OGDEN tr. *Forel's Soc. World of Ants.* I III. ii. 406 Marriage takes place..between newly-matured brothers and sisters sprung from the same mother... Hence this is a clear and evident case of perpetual and constant *adelphogamy*.

adelpholite (əˈdɛlfəlaɪt). *Min.* [mod. ?f. Gr. ἀδελφός brother + λίθος stone.] A Columbate of iron and manganese, found associated with Columbite in Finland.

1868 DANA *Mineral.* 525.

adelphous (əˈdɛlfəs), *a. Bot.* [f. Gr. ἀδελφ-ός brother + -OUS.] Having the stamens grouped or united: generally in comp. as *monadelphous*, *diadelphous*.

1855 HOOKER & ARNOT *Brit. Fl.* 151 Order *Bryonia*, Filaments, 3—Adelphous. **1870** BENTLEY *Bot.* 249 The union of the filaments may take place in one or more bundles, the number being indicated by a Greek numeral prefixed to the word adelphous.

ademand, **-mant**, obs. forms of ADAMANT.

†**a'dempt**, *ppl. a. Obs.* [ad. L. *ademptus* pa. pple. of *adimĕre*; see ADEEM.] Taken away, removed.

1432–50 TREVISA *Higden* (Rolls Ser.) I. 17 Part is adempte and loste þro the slawthe of wryters. **1549** LATIMER *Seven Serm. bef. Edw. VI* (1869) 54 Without al sinister suspicion of anye thynge in the same added or adempte. **1561** *Queen Esther* (1862) Our lyfe and godes from us were adempte.

†**a'dempted**, *ppl. a. Obs. rare*⁻¹. [f. prec. + -ED. Cf. *exempted*.] Taken away, adeemed.

1590 H. SWINBURN *Testaments* 281 The will of the testator is not presumed to be altered, nor the legacie adempted.

ademption (ə'dɛmʃən). [ad. L. *ademptiōn-em* n. of action, f *adimĕre*: see ADEEM.]

A taking away; mostly in *Law*, a revocation of a grant, or bequest.

1590 H. SWINBURN *Testaments* 277 Ademption is a taking away of the legacie before bequeathed. *c* **1630** JACKSON *Creed* IV. v. Wks. III. 42 Whether ademption of equal portions from things equal leave not such equality betwixt them as it found. **1765** BURN *Eccl. Law* IV. 263 If a man gives a portion to his daughter by will, and afterwards advances her with the like sum, it shall go in ademption of the legacy. **1880** MUIRHEAD *Ulpian* xxiv. §29. 420 The words of ademption were to be a repetition of those of bequest, with the addition of a negative.

‖**'aden.** *Phys. Obs.* Pl. *aden-es.* [Gr. ἀδήν, ἀδέν-α, an acorn; a gland.] A gland.

1653 URQUHART *Rabelais* I. xliv. He cut clean thorough the jugularie veins..even unto the two Adenes, which are throat-kernels. **1706** PHILLIPS, *Aden* (in *Anat.*) a glandule or kernel in an Animal Body: some also take it for a swelling in the groin, the same as *Bubo*. **1775** ASH, *Aden* (not used) a glandule, a bubo.

aden-, adeni-, adeno-, combining forms of prec. in Gr., mod.L and Eng.

‖**adenalgia** (ædɪ'nældʒɪə). *Med.* [mod.L. f. ADEN- + -ALGIA.] 'Pain seated in a gland: a painful swelling in a gland.' Craig 1847.

adeniform (ə'dɛnɪfɔːm, 'ædɪnɪfɔːm), *a.* [ad. mod.L. *adeni-formis*, f. ADEN + -FORM.] Having the form or appearance of a gland; adenoid.

1853 MAYNE *Exp. Lex.*

adenine ('ædɪnɪn). *Chem.* Also -in. [ad. G. *adenin* (A. Kossel 1885, in *Ber. d. deutschen chem. Gesellschaft* XVIII. 79), f. G. ἀδήν gland + -INE⁵.] A crystallizable base, $C_5H_5N_5$, found in certain glands and animal and vegetable tissues.

1885 *Jrnl. Chem. Soc.* XLVIII. II. 566 The author [*sc.* A. Kossel] has isolated from the pancreatic gland of the ox, a new base, $C_5H_5N_5$, to which he gives the name *adenine*. **1887** A. M. BROWN *Anim. Alkaloids* II. i. 75 Adenine, $C^5H^5N^5 3H^2o$, is in large transparent crystals, contains three molecules of water of crystallization. **1911** [see ADENOSINE]. **1937** *Thorpe's Dict. Appl. Chem.* I. 140 *Adenine*..discovered in the pancreatic gland and spleen of the ox, occurs in all vegetable and animal tissues rich in cells. .. It has been extracted from tea leaves..from beet juice, [etc.]. **1960** *New Biol.* XXXI. 34 The base in the biologically most important nucleotide is adenine.

adenitis (ædɪ'naɪtɪs). *Path.* [mod.L., f. Gr. ἀδήν gland + -ITIS.] Inflammation of a gland.

1848 DUNGLISON *Med. Lex.* (ed. 7). **1853** ERICHSEN *Sci. & Art Surg.* xxxiii. 448 Inflammation of the lymphatic glands, or adenitis. **1879** *St. George's Hosp. Rep.* IX. 654 Erysipelas and adenitis in 6, 1 of whom died. **1949** H. W. FLOREY et al. *Antibiotics* I. i. 62 The best results were obtained in osteitis of the small joints, adenitis, [etc.].

adenocarcinoma (,ædɪnəʊkɑːsɪ'nəʊmə). *Path.* [f. ADENO- + CARCINOMA.] A malignant adenoma.

1889 in *Cent. Dict.* **1900** *Jrnl. Amer. Med. Assoc.* 31 Mar. 775/1 *Adenocarcinoma.* Nine tumors show the general plan of the gland. **1907** *Practitioner* Aug. 191 What appeared to be an adeno-carcinoma. **1962** *Lancet* 13 Jan. 85/2 The much higher proportion of adenocarcinomas in the 'spontaneous' tumours.

adenocele ('ædɪnəʊsiːl) *Path.* [mod.f. ADENO- + Gr. κήλη tumour.] An adenoid tumour; see quot. under ADENOID.

1879 *Syd. Soc. Lex.*

adenography (ædɪ'nɒgrəfɪ). [f. ADENO- + -GRAPHY.] Description of the glandular system.

1721 In BAILEY. **1753** CHAMBERS *Cycl. Supp.*, *Adenography*, that branch of anatomy which describes the glands, and glandular parts of the body.

adenohypophysis (,ædɪnəʊhaɪ'pɒfɪsɪs). [mod.L. (Berblinger, 1932), f. ADENO- + HYPOPHYSIS.] The glandular or anterior part of the hypophysis.

1935 DORLAND & MILLER *Med. Dict.* (ed. 17) 48/1 *Adenohypophysis*, the anterior or glandular portion of the hypophysis as distinguished from the neurohypophysis. **1952** [see ADRENOCORTICOTROP(H)IN]. **1962** *Lancet* 2 June 1177/2 Results of experiments on laboratory animals suggest that the long-term administration of steroid preparations containing œstrogen may have a harmful effect on the adenohypophysis.

adenoid ('ædɪnɔɪd), *a.* and *sb. pl.* [ad. Gr. ἀδενοειδής glandular; f. ἀδέν- gland + -ειδής -form; see -OID.]

A. *adj.* Gland-like; glandular.

1839 K. GRANT *Hooper's Med. Dict.* (ed. 7) 35/2 *Adenoides*, adenoid; glandiform; resembling a gland. **1863** W. TURNER *Paget's Surg. Pathol.* 548 The name adenoid sarcomata is sometimes applied to these tumours of the mammary gland. **1873** KLEIN *Handb. Physiol. Lab.* iii. 45 It remains to describe the so-called adenoid tissue. By this term is understood, a dense reticulum of branched cells, the processes of which are short but of great delicacy. **1878** BRYANT *Surgery* I. 99 Should a tumour be present in a gland ..the probability of its being an adenoid or glandular tumour cannot be overlooked.

B. *sb. pl.* Adenoid growths or vegetations.

1891 *Medical Annual* 341 Admitting that usually adenoids make their appearance during childhood. **1901** CHEYNE & BURGHARD *Man. Surg. Treatm.* v. 365 The removal of the adenoids is more easily accomplished during the earlier and deeper stage of the anæsthesia. **1912** OSLER & MCCRAE *Princ. Med.* (ed. 8) 468 'Adenoids' have become recognized as one of the most common and important affections of childhood.

adenoidal (ædɪ'nɔɪdəl), *a.* [f. prec. + -AL¹.] **a.** Having the appearance of a gland. **b.** Having the voice or appearance of one suffering from adenoids. Hence **ade'noidally** *adv.*

1919 F. HURST *Humoresque* 195 Whole rows of ladies, with the slightly open-mouthed, adenoidal expression of vicarious romance, sat forward in their chairs. **1925** 'J. SUTHERLAND' *Circle of Stars* xvii. 167 The adenoidal young daily maid had gone. **1933** ST. JOHN ERVINE *Theatre in my Time* vii. 43 A player with a distinctive and adenoidal voice. **1941** L. A. G. STRONG *Bay* 9 The father began to scold, the son to expostulate adenoidally.

adenoidectomy (,ædɪnɔɪ'dɛktəmɪ). *Surg.* [f. ADENOID(S *sb. pl.* + Gr. ἐκτομή cutting out.] Excision of the adenoids.

1906 in DORLAND *Med. Dict.* (ed. 4). **1936** *Lancet* 28 Nov. 1274/2 (*caption*) A Ring Knife for Adenoidectomy. **1955** *Sci. News Let.* 15 Jan. 39/3 Surgery..was performed on 70% of the hospitalized children, with tonsillectomies and adenoidectomies accounting for over half of the surgical cases.

adenoidy ('ædɪnɔɪdɪ), *a.* = ADENOIDAL *a.* b.

1926 F. M. FORD *A Man could Stand up* II. iii. 143 The impossible, adenoidy, Cockney subalterns. **1932** J. B. PRIESTLEY *Dangerous Corner* I, But which was the husband? Was it the one with the adenoidy voice?

adenological (,ædɪnəʊ'lɒdʒɪkəl), *a.* [f. ADENOLOGY + -ICAL.] Of or pertaining to adenology; dealing with the structure of the glands.

1753 CHAMBERS *Cycl. Supp.*, *Adenography*..or the adenological part of anatomy.

adenology (ædɪ'nɒlədʒɪ). [f. ADENO- + -LOGY.] That part of Physiology which treats of the glands.

1753 CHAMBERS *Cycl. Supp.*, *Adenography* is the same with what some others call *Adenology*. **1879** *Syd. Soc. Lex.*

adenoma (ædɪ'nəʊmə). [mod.L., f. Gr. ἀδήν gland: see -OMA.] A benign tumour with the structure or appearance of a gland or originating in a gland (cf. ADENOCARCINOMA). Hence **adenomatous** (-'əʊmətəs) *a.*, of the nature of an adenoma, glandular.

1870 W. TURNER *Paget's Surg. Path.* (ed. 3) xxviii. 558 Glandular tumour, Adenoid tumour, or Adenoma. **1870** T. HOLMES *Syst. Surg.* (ed. 2) IV. 578 Adenomatous or Glandular Growths. **1899** *Allbutt's Syst. Med.* VIII. 737 Adenoma of the coil-gland. **1907** *Practitioner* Sept. 343 The more difficult ones to deal with were those in which the adenomatous change was widely disseminated, and a whole lobe or more had to be excised, owing to the impossibility of removing the adenomata singly. **1964** L. MARTIN *Clinical Endocrinol.* (ed. 4) iii. 82 Solitary hypersecreting adenomatous nodules do rarely arise.

adenopathy (ædɪ'nɒpəθɪ). *Path.* [f. ADENO- + -PATHY, Gr. -πάθεια suffering.] Disease of the glandular system.

1879 *Syd. Soc. Lex.* **1879** BRYANT *Surgery* II. 179 Adenopathy or bubo is a common complication of the simple as well as of the infecting chancre.

adenophorous (ædɪ'nɒfərəs), *a. Bot.* [f. ADENO- + -φορος -bearing.] Bearing or producing glands.

adenophyllous (,ædɪnəʊ'fɪləs), *a. Bot.* [f. ADENO- + Gr. φύλλ-ον leaf + -OUS.] Bearing glands on the leaves; glandular-leaved.

WEBSTER cites HENSLOW.

adenose (,ædɪ'nəʊs), *a.* [ad. mod.L. *adenōsus*, see ADEN- and -OSE.] Full of glands, glandulous.

1853 MAYNE *Exp. Lex.*

adenosine (ə'dɛnəʊsɪn). *Biochem.* Also adenosin. [ad. G. *adenosin* (P. A. Levene and W. A. Jacobs 1909, in *Ber. d. deutschen chem. Ges.* XLII. 2703), blend of ADENINE and RIB)OSE.]

a. A nucleoside ($C_{10}H_{13}N_5O_4$) found chiefly in striated muscle tissue and derived from ribose nucleic acid.

1909 *Chem. Abstr.* 2563, *d*-Ribose is also produced by the hydrolysis of adenosin. **1911** *Jrnl. Biol. Chem.* IX. 171 The other nucleoside (adenosine) is composed of d-ribose and adenine, and upon acid hydrolysis gives directly precipitable adenine. **1929** *Jrnl. Physiol.* LXVII. p. xxxvi, The activity of adenosine liberated from the picrate is of the same order as the substance isolated from heart muscle. **1954** *Lancet* 22 May 1071/1 Hereditary spherocytosis (H.S.)... In some H.S. bloods both the metabolic defect and the fragility were reversible with mannose, glucose, or adenosine.

b. *Comb.*, as ***adenosine monophosphate*** (abbrev. *A.M.P.*), ***diphosphate*** (*A.D.P.*); and esp. ***adenosine triphosphate*** (*A.T.P.*), a derivative of adenosine important as a source of energy for the contraction of muscles and for other biochemical processes.

1911 *Jrnl. Biol. Chem.* IX. 180 This is a demonstration of adenosine-desamidase in the practical absence of guanosine-desamidase. **1929** *Science* LXX. 381/1 The adenosine phosphoric acid isolated about two years ago from voluntary muscle is not identical with that obtained from yeast nucleic acid. **1938** *Chem. Abstr.* 6271 Reduction of Cz by the substrate is favored by addn. of adenosine diphosphate. **1939** *Ibid.* 187 Di-adenosine tetraphosphate consists of one mol. adenylic acid and 1 mol. adenosine triphosphate. **1939** M. STEPHENSON *Bacterial Metabolism* (ed. 2) iv. 80 Under the influence of the enzymes in yeast-juice and extracts of dried yeast..A.T.P. can be dephosphorylated in two ways. **1950** *Arch. Biochem.* XXVIII. 346 Adenosine diphosphate and monophosphate were equally as effective as the triphosphate. **1954** *Sci. Amer.* May 44/2 The particles in the cytoplasm of fruit cells..take up inorganic phosphate and add it to adenosine monophosphate (AMP) to form the diphosphate (ADP) and triphosphate (ATP). **1960** *New Biol.* XXXI. 34 The nucleotide itself is called adenosine monophosphoric acid (AMP).

adenotomy (ædɪ'nɒtəmɪ). [f. ADENO- + Gr. -τομία cutting.] Dissection of or incision into a gland.

1847 In CRAIG.

adenous ('ædɪnəs), *a. Phys.* [f. ADEN- + -OUS] = ADENOSE *a.*

1864 In WEBSTER.

adenovirus (ædɪnəʊ'vaɪərəs). *Path.* [f. ADENO(ID *a.* + VIRUS.] Any of certain viruses causing respiratory diseases, first found in adenoid tissue of man. (Called 'adenoid degeneration agent' by W. P. Rowe and others in *Proc. Soc. Exp. Biol.* (1953) LXXXIV. 573.)

1956 ENDERS et al. in *Science* CXXIV. 119/2 Agreement was reached on the term *adenovirus group*, which suggests a characteristic involvement of lymphadenoid tissue, as well as the tissue of the first reported isolation. **1957** *Times* 22 Nov. 15/4 During recent years American workers have isolated an increasing number of viruses from the throats of individuals with what are generically known as upper respiratory infections—that is, infections of the nose, throat, pharynx, and larynx. At least 14 such viruses have been now isolated, and it is these which are now classified under the title of adenoviruses. **1961** *Lancet* 23 Sept. 718/1 Our results have shown that the H.A. of adenoviruses was a specific, though highly complex, phenomenon.

†**adent**, *v. Obs.*⁻⁰ [a. Fr. *adente-r* (Cotgr.) to mortice, to fasten, f. *a* to + *dent* tooth.] 'To fasten (*old word*).' Kersey 1708. Bailey 1721 and 1800.

adenyl ('ædɪnɪl). *Chem.* [f. ADEN(INE + -YL.] A radical contained in adenine. Hence **ade'nylic** *a.*, esp. ***adenylic acid***, a nucleotide found in red blood corpuscles, muscle, etc., consisting of adenine, ribose, and phosphoric acid.

1894 GOULD *Illustr. Dict. Med.*, Adenyl. **1894** *Jrnl. Chem. Soc.* LXVI. I. 156 The nucleïc acid prepared from the thyroid gland of calves yields adenine on boiling with water, and is therefore termed adenylic acid. **1936** *Ann. Reg. 1935* II. 54 Muscle study showed that the chemical changes accompanying contraction are a complicated chain of linked reactions involving creatine, adenylic, and phosphoric acid, and carbohydrates and the complexity grows. **1946** *Nature* 23 Nov. 746/2 Here also the hydrogenation would be accompanied by a hydrolysis of the coenzyme molecule followed by a transfer of the phosphate of the adenylic acid to other phosphate acceptors.

‖**Adephaga** (ə'dɛfəgə), *sb. pl.* [prop. adj. pl. neut. of Gr. ἀδηφάγ-ος voracious (sc. *animalia*) f. ἄδην enough + -φαγος eating.] A name applied to a family or group of Beetles, also called *Carnivora*, and divided into the two sections of *Geodephaga* and *Hydradephaga*. An occ. sing. is **Adephagan.**

1842 BRANDE *Dict. Sci.* 15 *Adephagans, Adephaga*, a family of carnivorous and very voracious coleopterous insects.

‖**adeps** ('ædɛps). [L., = fluid fat, grease.] Animal fat, lard.

1657 *Phys. Dict., Adeps*, fatness. **1683** SALMON *Doron Med.* I. 271 If you desire the *Adeps* rather than the Spirit. **1836–9** TODD *Cycl. Anat. & Phys.* II. 817/2 The texture of the *glutaeus minimus* resembled adeps more than healthy muscular fibre.

adept (ə'dɛpt, 'ædɛpt), *a.* and *sb.* [ad. L. *adept-us* having attained, f. pple. of *adipisci* to attain, acquire; f. *ad* to, at + *ap-* to get.]

A. *adj.* Completely versed (*in*); thoroughly proficient; well-skilled.

a **1691** BOYLE (J.) If there be really such adept philosophers as we are told of. **1755** H. CROKER *Ariosto's Orl. Furioso* XVIII. clxxiv. I. 297 Where the learned Alpheus slept..Physician, in astrology adept. **1782** COWPER *Hope* 350 Beaus adept in ev'rything profound, Die of disdain. **1861** L. L. NOBLE *After Icebergs* 325 Scarecrows—a peculiar walk of art, in which the painter..became sufficiently adept to frighten..the little creatures that pulled up the corn.

B. *sb.* [In med.L. *adeptus* was used subst. and assumed by *alchemists* that professed to *have attained* the great secret. In Eng. the L. form was at first used, with pl. *adepti.*] Hence, 'He that is completely skilled in all the secrets of his art.' J. One that has attained to proficiency in anything.

1663 BUTLER *Hudibras* I. i. 546 In Rosicrucian lore as learned, As he that *Vere adeptus* earned. **1665** in *Phil. Trans.* I. 112 The several processes of the reputed *Adepti.* **1685** *Lond. Gaz.* mmlxxii/4 Four Books..concerning the secrets of the Adepts. **1704** T. HEARNE *Duct. Hist.* (ed. 3) I. 401 Unintelligible to all but Adepti. **1785** REID *Intell. Powers* II. viii. 271 Queens became adepts in Des Cartes' philosophy. **1831** SCOTT *Kenilw.* xviii. (1853) 193 Varney heard the adept's door shut and carefully bolted. **1863** BURTON *Book Hunter* 124 The greatest adepts abandoning the effort in despair.

Hence **a'deptly** *adv.*, in an adept manner; skilfully, adroitly.

1954 *Funk & Wagnalls New Pract. Stand. Dict.* I. 17/2. **1973** *Latin Amer.* 25 Dec. VII. 52. 414/1 Caamaño's guerrilla invasion..which Balaguer used most adeptly to exploit divisions among his opponents. **1984** *N.Y. Times* 4 Nov. XXI. 27/4 These seniors still play their games vigorously and adeptly.

†**a'depted,** *ppl. a. Obs. rare*$^{-1}$. [f. prec. + -ED. Cf. *adempt-ed.*] Gained, acquired.

c **1595** NORDEN *Spec. Brit., Cornwall* (1728) 55 For a memoriall of their valor and adepted dignitye, they have caused the historye of the exployte to be registred in the window.

†**a'deptical,** *a. Obs.* [f. ADEPT-IST, after analogy of *chemist chemical, botanist botanical.*] Of or pertaining to an adeptist; alchemical.

1662 J. CHANDLER *Helmont's Oriatrike* 157 They who study in Adepticall things, do strive to promote their labour of wisdom by the objects of sight. *Ibid.* 7 Medicine Adeptical. **1801** BARRETT *Magus* 26 According to the Adeptical philosophy.

†**a'deption.** *Obs.* Also **adepcion.** [ad. L. *adeptiōn-em* an attaining, n. of action f. *adipisci*; see ADEPT.] An obtaining, gaining, or attainment.

1548 HALL *Chron., 23 Edw. IV* (1809) 339 Sith the adepcion of the Croune. **1605** BACON *Adv. Learn.* II. 12 Adeption of a crowne, by Armes and Tytle. **1655** LESTRANGE *Charles I,* 8 Before his adeption of the crown.

†**a'deptist.** [f. ADEPT *a.* + -IST.] A professed adept, a skilled alchemist.

1662 J. CHANDLER *Helmont's Oriatrike* 2 Hypocrates, a man of a most rare gift, and a partaker with the Adeptists. **1671** J. WEBSTER *Metallogr.* i. 16 Lock'd up in the breasts of a few mystical authors or Adeptists. **1715** KERSEY *Adepts* or *Adeptists,* the obtaining sons of art, who are said to have found out the grand elixir, commonly called the philosopher's stone.

adeptness (ə'dɛptnɪs). [f. ADEPT *a* + -NESS.] The quality of being adept; skill, proficiency.

1881 SAINTSBURY in *Academy* 5 Feb. 92 None the less does *Vane's Story* complete the proof of Mr. Thomson's poetical adeptness.

adeptship (ə'dɛpt-ʃɪp). [f. ADEPT *sb.* + -SHIP.] The condition or rank of an adept; special proficiency.

1882 *Church Times* 17 Feb. 104 Jesus in their system is but an Adept..who gained his adeptship by an ascetic diet.

adequacy ('ædɪkwəsɪ). [f. ADEQUATE *a.*: see -ACY.] The state or quality of being adequate or sufficient for any purpose; sufficiency.

1808 WYVILL *Intolerance,* Their immediate effect was great: the adequacy of it becomes continually more visible. **1832** LYELL *Princ. Geol.* II. 309 We do not, therefore, anticipate that the reader..will object to the adequacy of the cause proposed. **1870** BOWEN *Logic* x. 336 The test of the adequacy of a Concept is its more or less complete enumeration of the essential qualities of the real thing. **1924** ANNE D. SEDGWICK *Little French Girl* II. viii, The deliberate adequacy with which madame Vervier advanced to meet the occasion.

adequate ('ædɪkwət), *a.* Also 7 **adæquat, adæquate.** [ad. L. *adæquāt-us* equalized, pa. pple. of *adæquā-re*: see next.] Const. *to* (*with* obs.).

†**1.** Equal in magnitude or extent; commensurate; neither more nor less. *Obs.*

1628 T. SPENCER *Logick* 108 Those things are equall.. which are adæquate in magnitude. **1662** FULLER *Worthies* (1840) III. 140 He grew so tall in stature, that a hole was made for him in the ground, to stand therein up to the knees, so to make him adequate with his fellow-workmen. **1677** HALE *Prim. Orig. Man.* 311 No finite Being can be an adequate Image of an infinite Being or Perfection. **1750** JOHNSON *Rambler* No. 150 ¶3 Acquisitions of man are not always adequate to the expectations.

2. a. Commensurate in fitness; equal or amounting to what is required; fully sufficient, suitable, or fitting.

a **1617** P. BAYNE *Ephes.* (1658) 123 To justifye is not the sole adæquate or full act of it. *c* **1685** In Somers's *Tracts* II. 444 They were at a stand for want of Words adequate to it. **1738** WARBURTON *Div. Legat.* II. 148 Wit consists in using strong metaphoric Images in uncommon and adequate Allusions. **1771** *Junius Lett.* lvii. 294 People..have no adequate idea of the endless variety of your character. **1817** JAS. MILL *Brit. India* II. v. iii. 389 A remedy which was far from adequate to the disease. **1860** W. COLLINS *Wom. in White* II. 275 Is language adequate to describe it? *a* **1870** MISS MITFORD in L'Estrange *Life* I. iv. 100 Mr. Herbert does me a very great honour in thinking me adequate to the Copenhagen subject.

b. Without const.: equal to the occasion, competent to deal with the situation.

1924 ANNE D. SEDGWICK *Little French Girl* II. ix, Alix, in Maman's place, poured out their coffee, heavy-eyed, but still adequate.

c. In slightly derogatory sense: hardly sufficient or acceptable; barely reaching a minimum standard.

1900 M. BEERBOHM in *Sat. Rev.* 24 Feb. 234/1 It [the production of a play] was simply what the dramatic critics call 'adequate', meaning 'inadequate'. **1958** *Times* 12 Feb. 3/1 The standard rapidly sinks to a level which is, at best, adequate but at worst incompetent.

3. *Logic.* Fully answering to, or representing.

1690 LOCKE *Hum. Underst.* II. xxxi. (1695) 207 Those [Ideas] I call Adequate, which perfectly represent those Archetypes, which the Mind supposes them taken from; which it intends them to stand for. **1724** WATTS *Logic* I. vi. §5 (1822) 116 A definition must be universal, or as some call it, adequate; that is, it must agree to all the particular species or individuals that are included under the same idea. **1846** MILL *Logic* I. viii. §3 (1868) 152 The only adequate definition of a name is..one which declares the facts.

†**'adequate,** *v. Obs.* Also 7 **adæquate.** [f. L. *adæquāt-* ppl. stem of *adæquā-re* to make or become level or equal; f. *ad* to + *æquāre,* f. *æquus* level, equal.]

1. To equalize; to make equal or sufficient.

1622 FOTHERBY *Atheomastix* II. ii. §7. 208 A truly intellectuall obiect, exactly adequated and proportioned vnto the intellectuall appetite. **1671** *True Non-Conformist* 16 Adequating the guilt and punishment. **1691** E. TAYLOR *Behmen's Theos. Phil.* 68 What adequated and priviledged him.

2. To equal, to be equal to, or sufficient for.

1599 NASHE *Lenten Stuffe* (1871) 29 Her sumptuous porches, and garnished buildings, are such, as no port-town in our British circumference..may suitably stake with, or adequate. **1635** SHELFORD *Disc.* 227 Though it be an imposibilitie for any creature to adequate God in his eternitie. **1699** *Phil. Trans.* XXI. 291 The Husk being.. divided into Five Points, Adequating the Segments of each Flower.

adequately ('ædɪkwətlɪ), *adv.* [f. ADEQUATE *a.* + -LY^2.] In an adequate manner.

†**1.** With complete equality, with perfect correspondence; exactly. *Obs.*

1656 tr. *Hobbes' Elem. Philos.* (1839) 76 Place is that space which is possessed or filled adequately by some body. **1689** H. MORE *Answ. Psychop.* 121 You confound Substance and Matter, as if they adequately signified the same. **1692** BENTLEY *Boyle Lect.* vii. 222 Adapting itself to the figure of every Pore, may adequately fill them.

2. In a manner fitted to satisfy the requirements of the case; sufficiently, suitably.

1690 B[OYLE] *Chr. Virtuoso* I. 71 Many of which [points of Supernatural Experience] are not to be Adequately estimated by the same Rules. *a* **1763** SHENSTONE *Ess.* 186 A man of sense can be adequately esteemed by none other than a man of sense. **1821–30** LD. COCKBURN *Mem. his Time* 254 The grounds of divorce were, that I had never been adequately of his party. **1877** MRS. BRASSEY *Voy. Sunbeam* xv. (1878) 268 No words could adequately describe such a scene.

3. *Logic.* With perfect correspondence of idea to object.

1628 T. SPENCER *Logick* 191 Life and Rationalitie are attributed vnto man..adæquatly: so as, all that is in Life, and Rationalitie, is sayd to belong to man: and all that is in man, is denoted, and set out by life, and rationalitie. **1722** WOLLASTON *Relig. Nat.* iii. §3 (1738) 42 Those ideas or objects, that are immediate, will be adequately and truly known to that mind, whose ideas they are.

adequateness ('ædɪkwətnɪs). [f. as prec. + -NESS.] The quality of being adequate.

†**1.** Equality; commensurability; exact correspondence in extent or scope. *Obs.*

1664 H. MORE *Myst. Iniq.* 261 The Adequateness of these Parallelisms demonstrated by comparing the Seventeenth and Thirteenth Chapters.

2. Correspondence in fitness; sufficiency; suitableness.

1672 T. C[RANE] *Div. Provid.* 7 The wonderful adequateness of a dispensation. **1728** EARBERY tr. *Burnet's State of Dead* I. 243 The adequateness of Punishments and Rewards. **1852** F. W. ROBERTSON *Lect.* 176 Only a few..can comprehend with something like adequateness the Cosmos, or order of the Universe.

adequation (ædɪ'kweɪʃən). [ad. L. *adæquatiōnem,* n. of action, f. *adæquāre*: see ADEQUATE *v.*]

1. The action of equalizing, or making equal or commensurate; commensuration.

1651 N. BIGGS *New Dispens.* §295. 218 There is required an adæquation of the remedy to the indisposition. **1684** tr. *Bonet's Merc. Compit.* III. 87 The concoction and maturation of Defluxions, is the moderation or adequation of their substance. **1866** *Q. Rev.* CXIX. 74 The growing strength of criticism in society must be met by the continuous adequation of a like reflective strength in the individual.

†**2.** The action or fact of equalling. *Obs.*

1589 NASHE *Anat. Absurd.* 42 Let vs with Themistocles, set before our eyes one of the excellentest to imitate, in whose example insisting, our industry may be doubled, to the adequation of his praise.

3. The result of equalizing or rendering adequate; produced equivalency; *concr.* an equivalent.

1605 TIMME *Quersit.* II. iv. 116 The perfect combination, adequation, equabilitie of elements. **1626** ANDREWES *Serm.* (1856) I. 185 Then are the words uttered true, when there is a just adequation between them and the mind. **1662** FULLER *Worthies* I. 98 The arme of King Edward the first..is notoriously known to have been the adequation of a yard. **1726** PENN *Wks.* I. 452 There ought to be an Adequation and Resemblance betwixt all Ends, and the Means to them.

4. *Linguistics.* [a. G. *adäquation* (J. Stöcklein, *Bedeutungswandel der Wörter* (1898) 20 et seq.)] A semantic process whereby the meaning of a word or phrase changes under the influence of the type of context in which it typically occurs.

1931 G. STERN *Meaning & Change of Meaning* xiv. 387, I define adequation as an unintentional sense-change consisting in a shift of attention from one characteristic of the word referent to another. **1933** [see PERMUTATION 4b]. **1967** R. A. WALDRON *Sense & Sense Devel.* vi. 135 No change of meaning occurs in such cases until there is adequation, or change in the word's criteria of reference. **1974** *Semiotica* XII. 20 An anticipated sense fails to undergo unique constitution since it is predetermined in whole blocks of words. These words identify with the adequation on hand... A referential reversal has set in. **1979** *Lore & Lang.* Jan. 23 'Adequation' is the process whereby a purely iconic or symbolic image is projected onto an objective reality.

adequative ('ædɪkweɪtɪv), *a.* [ad. med.L. *adæquātīv-us,* f. *adæquāt-* ppl. stem of *adæquā-re*: see ADEQUATE *v.* and -IVE.] Of or pertaining to adequation; adequate; equivalent.

1823 SCOTT *St. Ronan* xxvi. Wks. 1830 XXXIV. 119 Without some adequative motive. **1865** *Pall Mall G.* 17 May 11 It is difficult to turn even French or German into critically adequative English.

†**a'dequitate,** *v. Obs.*$^{-0}$ [f. L. *adequitāt-* ppl. stem of *adequitā-re* to ride up to.] 'To ride by.' Cockeram 1626.

†**adequi'tation.** *Obs.*$^{-0}$ [n. of action, f. ADEQUITATE.] 'A riding towards.' Bullokar 1676.

adermin (ə'dɜːmɪn). Also **adermine.** [G. (R. Kuhn and G. Wendt 1938, in *Ber. d. deutschen chem. Ges.* LXXI. 1534), f. A- 14 + Gr. δέρμα skin + -IN *suffix*^{1}.] Pyridoxin; vitamin B_6.

1938 *Brit. Chem. & Physiol. Abstr.* 505 It is converted by acetic anhydride into acetyladermin, b.p. 85–90°/0·0001 mm., transformed by HCl into adermin hydrochloride, m.p. 204–205° (decomp.). **1939** GYÖRGY & ECKARDT in *Nature* CXLIV. 512/2 The term *adermin,* because it is misleading, should be abandoned. .. The term *pyridoxin* appears to be appropriate.

Ades, obs. variant of HADES.

ades(e, obs. form of ADZE.

†**a'desed,** *ppl. a. Obs.*$^{-0}$ [f. L. *adēs-* ppl. stem of *aded-ĕre* to eat up + -ED.] 'All eaten up.' Cockeram 1626.

adesmy (ə'dɛsmɪ) *Bot.* [mod.f. Gr. ἄδεσμος unbound (f. ἀ priv. + δεσμός a bond) + -Y.] Defective coherence or adherence between vegetable organs.

1879 *Syd. Soc. Lex.*

adespota (ə'dɛspətə), *sb. pl. Bibliography.* [neut. pl. of Gr. ἀδέσποτος without owner, f. ἀ- priv. + δεσπότης master, DESPOT.] Literary works not attributed to (or claimed by) an author.

Orig. used as a title of collections of anonymous Greek poetry.

1897 *Times* 27 Oct. 10 A bibliographical papper on Burns's *adespota*; verses fugitive, unsanctioned, or apocryphal. **1904** A. W. POLLARD in *Library* 2nd Ser. V. 20 The cards were then sorted out according to countries, towns and presses, with a large section of 'adespota'. **1913** R. B. MCKERROW *Printers' & Publ. Devices* Introd. p. 1, To lump together a large number of blocks of every date and style in a class of *Adespota.*

adespotic (ædɪ'spɒtɪk), *a. rare*$^{-0}$. [f. A- *pref.* 14 not + DESPOTIC. Gr. ἀδέσποτος = 'without master.'] 'Not absolute, not despotic.' Craig 1847.

adessenarian (æˌdɛsɪ'nɛərɪən). *Eccl. Hist.* [f. med.L. *adessenarii* (see -AN); f. *adesse* to be present; a 'name first framed by Prateolus.'] One who held the real presence of Christ's body in the Eucharist, but not by transubstantiation.

1751 CHAMBERS *Cycl., Adessenarii,* called also *Impanatores.* **1835** J. ROBINSON *Theol. Dict.* s.v., *Adessenarians* were a branch of the Sacramentarians.

adessive (æ'desɪv), *a. Gram.* [f. L. *adesse* to be present + -IVE.] Denoting the case used (in Finnish, etc.) to express position in or presence at a place.

1860 *Trans. Philol. Soc. 1857* 38 Cases are genitive, dative and the like all the world over... The extent to which they are also caritive, adessive and the like has yet to be investigated. **1890** C. N. E. ELIOT *Finnish Gram.* 131 The first member (inessive, adessive, essive) denotes originally rest in a position. **1890** GATSCHET *Klamath Indians* II. I. 486 Adessive case in -kshi. **1956** A. H. WHITNEY *Teach Yourself Finnish* (1959) 89 The Adessive Case has the ending *-lla -llä*.

†**ade'termine**, *v. Obs. rare.* [f. A- *pref.* 11 + DETERMINE.] To bring to an end, terminate.

1413 LYDG. *Pylgr. Sowle* II. xli. (1859) 46 Theyr iourney was fully adetermyned. *Ibid.* v. i. 69 Now ben ended the peynes and tormentes, and fully adetermyned.

‖**ad eundem** (æd eɪ'ʊndɛm), *adv. phr.* [L., short for *ad eundem gradum* to the same degree.] Of the admission of a member of one university to another: to the same degree or status (as that already held elsewhere). Also *transf.*, of the admission of a member of any institution or society into another.

1711 *Spectator* 30 May, You are invited to be admitted *ad eundem* at Cambridge. **1783** H. WALPOLE *Let. c* 6 Dec. (1971) XXV. 454 He shall be admitted *ad eundem*..into the Church of Rome. **1860** B. F. WESTCOTT *Let.* Dec. (1903) I. 217 The great event this morning was my admission *ad eundem*. **1885** *Athenæum* 29 Aug. 267/1 Graduates came.. and supplicated for incorporation *ad eundem*, as a matter of usage so unvarying as to be almost a right. **1952** A. M. SULLIVAN *Last Serjeant* xxxi. 280 They added an assurance that if I was to join the Inner Temple *ad eundem* the Benchers would be glad to have me as a member at the occurrence of the next vacancy. **1977** K. M. E. MURRAY *Caught in Web of Words* xiii. 248 The University Statutes [of Oxford] did not allow him to be given a doctorate *ad eundem* by virtue of his Edinburgh degree.

‖**à deux** (adø), *adv.* and *a.* [F., for two, between two.] Of, for, or pertaining to, two people.

1876 STAINER & BARRETT *Dict. Mus. Terms* 18/2 *A deux*, for two voices or instruments. **1886** R. BROUGHTON *Dr. Cupid* II. iv. 85 Some keen happiness à deux; some two happy souls together blent. **1900** H. G. WELLS *Love & Mr. Lewisham* vi. 55 A splendid isolation *à deux*. **1911** M. BEERBOHM *Zuleika D.* x. 170 The young man..at once thrifty and infatuate, had planned a luncheon *à deux*. **1928** D. H. LAWRENCE *Woman who rode Away* 14 This dictating business, this ten hours a day intercourse, *à deux*. **1963** *Listener* 24 Jan. 157/2 Strindberg regards marriage as a ghastly solitary confinement *à deux*.

adeve, var. of ADEAVE *v.* obs. to deafen.

adevism ('ædɪvɪz(ə)m). [f. Gr. ἀ priv. + Skr. *dēva* god + -ISM.] A term introduced by Prof. Max Müller, to express a disbelief in the legendary deity or deities, as distinguished from *atheism* or disbelief in a God.

1878 MAX MÜLLER *Hibbert Lect.* 303 Their atheism will more correctly be call Adevism, or a denial of the old Devas.

†**a'dew**, *v. Obs. rare.* [f. A- *pref.* 11 + DEW.] To BEDEW.

c **1430** LYDG. *Bochas* IV. ix. (1554) 105 b, By influence of heauenly fate adewed. ? *c* **1450** ? LYDG. *Life of oure Ladye* I. iv. (R.) The soyle to adewe with her swete stremes.

adew(e, obs. form of ADIEU.

adfected (æd'fɛktɪd), *ppl. a.* [A specialized variant of AFFECTED.] Compounded. Of equations in *Algebra*: Containing different powers of an unknown quantity.

1695 ALINGHAM *Geom. Epit.* 89 The Method of finding the root of an adfected equation. **1728** CAMPBELL in *Phil. Trans.* XXXV. 515 Every adfected quadratick Æquation $ax^2 - Bx + A = o$, whose Roots are real. **1870** TODHUNTER *Algebra* xx. 169 Quadratic equations which contain the first power of the unknown quantity as well as the square are called adfected quadratics.

adfiliate, -ation, obs. var. AFFILIATE, -ATION.

adfluxion (æd'flʌkʃən). [A special variant of AFFLUXION with more emphasis on the prefix.] A flowing *towards*; an attracted flow.

1829 *Edin. Rev.* L. 160 The one is termed an impulsion, and the other an adfluxion of the sap.

adfriction, adgeneration, obs. variants of AFFRICTION, AGGENERATION.

†**adgenicu'lation**, *Obs.* [n. of action, f. L. *adgeniculā-ri*, f. *ad* to + *genicul-us* a little knee: see GENICULATION.] A kneeling to or towards.

1659 LESTRANGE *Alliance Div. Off.* 487 Consequently no adgeniculation at the altars.

adglutinate (æd'gl(j)u:tɪnət), *a. Bot.* [f. L. *adglūtināt-us* (also *aggl-*) glued to; = AGGLUTINATE.]

1858 GRAY *Bot. Text-bk.* s.v., *Adglutinate*, same as accrete.

†**ad'habitate**, *v. Obs.*—⁰ [f. late L. *adhabitāt-* ppl. stem of doubtful vb. *adhabitā-re* to dwell near, f. *ad* to + *habitā-re* to dwell.] 'To dwell nigh.' Cockeram 1626.

†**adhalate**, *v. Obs.*—⁰ [f. L. *adhālāt-* ppl. stem of *adhālā-re* to breathe upon.] 'To breathe or blow on.' Cockeram 1626.

†**adhamate**, *v. Obs.*—⁰ [f. L. *adhāmāt-* ppl. stem of doubtful vb. *adhamā-re* to secure, f. *ad* to + *hāmus* hook, *hāmātus* alluring.] 'To hooke, to bind.' Cockeram 1626, Blount 1656.

†**adha'mation**. *Obs.*—⁰ [n. of action, f. prec.] 'A taking hold like a hook.' Bullokar 1676.

adhere (æd'hɪə(r)), *v.* Also 7 **adhære**. [a. Fr. *adhére-r* (15th c. in Litt.), ad. L. *adhærē-re* to stick to, f. *ad* to + *hærē-re* to stick.]

1. a. *intr.* To stick fast, to cleave, to become or remain firmly attached, *to* a substance, as by a glutinous surface, or by grasping, etc.

1651 *Rawleigh's Ghost* 96 The stalks do not adhere or cleave to the boughes by any *fibræ*. **1764** REID *Inq. Hum. Mind* v. §2. 120 When the parts of a body adhere so firmly that it cannot easily be made to change its figure, we call it hard. **1849** RUSKIN *Seven Lamps* iii. §22. 90 These mouldings nearly adhere to the stone. **1860** TYNDALL *Glaciers* I. §3. 30 The fragments of snow that adhered to the staff. *Mod.* These labels do not adhere well.

b. *fig.*

c **1620** A. HUME *Orthogr. Brit. Tong.* (1865) 32 An adverb is a word adhering mast commonlie with a verb. **1781** GIBBON *Decl. & F.* II. xli. 517 Flattery adheres to power, and envy to superior merit. **1854** J. ABBOTT *Napoleon* (1855) II. xxx. 559 A straggling village adhered to the sides of a vast ravine.

2. a. To cleave *to* a person or party; to be a close companion, partizan, or follower.

1597 BACON *Ess.* (Arb.) 76 Meane men must adheare, but great men, that haue strength in themselues, were better to maintaine themselues indifferent, and neutrall. **1602** SHAKS. *Haml.* II. ii. 21 Two men there are not liuing To whom he more adheres. **1651** HOBBES *Leviathan* I. xi. 49 It disposeth men to adhære, and subject themselves to those men. **1690** LUTTRELL *Brief Rel.* II. (1857) 124 High treason in adhering to the King's enemies. **1849** MACAULAY *Hist. Eng.* II. 129 These people..with few exceptions, adhered to the Church of Rome. **1865** GROTE *Plato* I. iv. 165 Thrasyllus adhered to Aristophanes on so many disputable points.

†**b.** *refl. Obs.*

1633 STAFFORD *Pac. Hib.* xxiv. (1821) 448 Or haue combined, or adhered themselves to any her majestie's enemies.

3. To cleave *to* an opinion, practice, or method; to continue to maintain or observe. ***to adhere to a decision***, etc.: to confirm or approve it by a subsequent decision.

1656 BRAMHALL *Replie* 42 In things not necessary a man may fluctuate safely between two opinions..without certain adherence, or adhere certainly without Faith. **1756** BURKE *Vind. Nat. Soc.* Wks. I. 64 The lawyer has his positive institutions too, and he adheres to them with veneration. **1772** *Junius Lett.* lxviii. 338 In one instance, the very form is adhered to. **1879** B. TAYLOR *Germ. Lit.* 68, I shall adhere to the plan stated in the beginning of these lectures.

†**4.** *without const.* To be coherent, to 'hang together,' as a story; to be consistent with itself or with circumstances, to agree. *Obs. rare.*

1598 SHAKS. *Merry W.* II. i. 62 They doe no more adhere and keep place together, then the hundred Psalms to the tune of Greensleeues. **1605** —— *Macb.* I. vii. 52 Nor time, nor place Did then adhere, and yet you would make both.

5. *Bot.* To be naturally united or soldered to what is normally an *unlike* part, as a distinct whorl of the inflorescence; to be adnate.

1857 HENFREY *Bot.* 94 Adhesion may exist between the inner and outer circles of the floral envelopes..or the calyx, corolla, and stamens may all adhere to the pistil.

adherence (æd'hɪərəns). Also 7 **adherance**. [a. Fr. *adhérence*, ad. L. *adhærentia*: see ADHERENCY.]

1. The action of sticking or holding fast (*to* anything, or together).

1612 T. TAYLOR *Titus* iii. 7 (1619) 670 A thing is ours two waies, 1. by infusion, inherence, or adherence; or 2. by account or reckoning. **1794** SULLIVAN *View of Nat.* I. 435 Siliceous earths are characterized by..a total want of flexibility, and adherence to each other, when minutely divided. **1875** SWINBURNE *Ess.& Stud.* 338 Another child clings to his leg..The helpless adherence of the slighted older child.

2. Attachment (*to* a person or party); adhesion.

1634-46 J. ROW (father) *Hist. Kirk Scotl.* (1842) 44 The causses of adherence and divorcements ought also to appertaine to them [ministers]. **1660** R. COKE *Just. Vind.* Ep. Ded. 8 Your constant adherence to the Church. **1754** SHERLOCK *Disc.* I. i. (1759) 2 The ground of their Constancy and Adherence to Christ. **1852** CONYBEARE & HOWSON *St. Paul* (1862) I. xi. 374 His present host and hostess had now given their formal adherence to St. Paul.

3. Persistence in a practice or tenet; steady observance or maintenance. Const. *to*.

1638 CHILLINGWORTH *Relig. Prot.* I. ii. §154. 112 God's Spirit..may work a certainty of adherence beyond a certainty of evidence. **1769** BURKE *State Nat.* Wks. II. 144 What does he mean by talking of an adherence to the old navigation laws? **1869** J. MARTINEAU *Ess.* II. 424, I profess adherence to the English psychological method. **1879** GLADSTONE *Gleanings* II. v. 219 An uncompromising adherence to what was right.

4. *Bot.* = ADHESION 4; adnation.

1857 HENFREY *Bot.* 94 Adherence of sepals and petals.

†**5.** A particular instance of adhering; adherent matter or circumstance. Cf. ADHERENCY 2. *Obs.*

1531 ELYOT *Governour* (1580) 166 Unto this noble vertue [fortitude] be attendant, or as it were continuall adherences, diuers uertues. **1650** JER. TAYLOR *Holy Living* (1727) 94 To discern his own infirmities and make discovery of his bad adherences. **1667** in *Phil. Trans.* II. 426 Every one of these small adherances is turned into a little Vermicle.

adherency (æd'hɪərənsɪ). *arch.* Also 7 **adhærency**. [ad. L. *adhærentia*, n. of action and state, f. *adhærent-em* pr. pple. of *adhærē-re*: see ADHERE and -NCY.]

1. The quality or state of being adherent; companionship; attachedness.

1647 JER. TAYLOR *Lib. Prophes.* xviii. 235 By vertue of its adherency and remanency in their flesh; it did that work. **1692** BEVERLEY *Concil. Disc.* 8 Christ..bare as deep a share of adherency in our sin, as could consist with an unspotted Purity from any inherency of sin in himself. **1820** COLERIDGE *Lett. Convers. &c.* I. viii. 51 The passions of the adherency to the former [the Stuarts], if not the adherency itself, [was] extant in our own fathers' or our grandfathers' times.

†**2.** That which is adherent; adhering matter or circumstance. Cf. L. *adhærentia*. *Obs.*

1608 TOPSELL *Serpents* 748 Not *lana*, wooll, but *lamygo* [? *lanugo*], that is, a vapoury adhærency of a thing which flyeth from the strokes of hammers upon hot burning iron. **1657** T. REEVE *God's Plea* 30 The compleatest actions of men have an adhærency of evill cleaving to them. **1681** *Whole Duty of Nations* 60 The reputation of Religion..often suffers by those unnecessary adherencies.

†**3.** An adhering party; a following. *Obs.*

1582-8 *Hist. James VI* (1804) Not againes the Lords..or onie of thair adherencis in this laitt actioun. **1633** BP. HALL *Hard Texts* 399 A great part of the Romane adherencie shall fall off from her. **1662** H. STUBBE *Indian Nectar* 4 The late changes in our Nation have disengaged me from my former adherencies.

adherent (æd'hɪərənt), *a.* and *sb.* Also 7 **adhærent**. [a. Fr. *adhérent*, ad. L. *adhærent-em* pr. pple. of *adhærē-re*: see ADHERE.]

A. *adj.*

1. Sticking fast (*to*), clinging, attached materially.

1615 SANDYS *Trav.* 215 On the South side vpon a rocke, and adherent, stood the castle. **1725** POPE *Odyssey* v. 547 Close to the cliff with both his hands he clung, And stuck adherent. **1857** J. G. WOOD *Com. Obj. Sea-sh.* 45 It is better that they [porphyra] should be adherent to some stone or shell. **1869** PHILLIPS *Vesuv.* viii. 240 Marked by two bands of adherent incrustation.

2. *fig.* Attached as an attribute or circumstance.

1588 FRAUNCE *Lawiers Logike* I. viii. 41 An adjunct is eyther inherent in the subject, or adherent to it. **1651** HOBBES *Leviathan* II. xxvii. 151 A Passion so adhærent to the Nature of man. **1725** WATTS *Logic* ii. §4. Wks. 1814 VII. 325 Modes are said to be inherent or adherent..Adherent or improper modes arise from the joining of some accidental substance to the chief subject, which yet may be separated from it; so when a bowl is wet or a boy is cloathed, these are adherent modes. **1825** COLERIDGE *Wks.* II. 213 The transitoriness adherent to all antithesis; for the identity or the absolute is alone eternal.

†**3.** Attached in sympathy, or as a companion, partizan, or follower. Const. *to*. *Obs.*

? *c* **1400** *Test. Love* I. (R.) My seruauntes shoulden..bee adherand to his spouse. **1451** in Rymer *Foedera* (1710) XI. 291 All othir that woll be to Me adherent in this Party. **1548** HALL *Chron.* Ed. IV. an. 3 All persones which were adherent to his aduersaries part. **1602** FULBECKE *First Pt. of Parallele* 86 It is treason..to be adherent to the King's enemies.

4. *Bot.* United to each other, though normally not only distinct but belonging to distinct whorls of the plant or flower; adnate.

1830 LINDLEY *Nat. Syst. Bot.* 44 The stamens slightly adherent to the base of the petals. **1872** OLIVER *Elem. Bot.* II. 157 The coat of the latter [Sweet Chestnut] is a perianth, adherent to an inferior ovary.

B. *sb.*

1. One who adheres to a person, party, or system; a partizan, follower, or supporter. Const. *of* a person, *of* (*to* obs.) a thing.

c **1460** FORTESCUE *Abs. & Lim. Mon.* (1714) 66 His said Kyng had made such End, with him, his Adherents and Fautours, as he desired. **1528** MORE *Heresyes* III. Wks. 1557 222/1 Luther and his adherentes holde this heresy, that all holy order is nothing. **1606** HOLLAND *Suetonius* 137 The dependants and adhærents of Seianus. **1758** JOHNSON *Idler* No. 10 ¶10 Jack Sneaker is a hearty adherent to the present establishment. **1849** MACAULAY *Hist. Eng.* I. 22 The adherents of Lancaster rallied round a line of bastards, and the adherents of York set up a succession of impostors. **1862** H. SPENCER *First Princ.* I. i. §1. (1875) 4 The presumption that any current opinion is not wholly false, gains in strength according to the number of its adherents.

†**2.** That which adheres to anything; an attached property or quality. *Obs.*

1636 HEALEY *Epictetus* xxxi. 37 All those goods which are peculiar adherents to the nature of man. **1645** MILTON *Tetrachordon* (1851) 162 Not a true limb..but an adherent, a sore, the gangrene of a limb.

adherently (æd'hɪərəntlɪ), *adv. rare*—⁰. [f. prec. + -LY².] In an adherent manner. Todd 1818.

adherer (æd'hɪərə(r)). ? *Obs.* [f. ADHERE + -ER¹.] One who adheres or gives his adhesion (*to* an act, proposal, etc.). More general and loose in its application than *adherent*, which implies a *professed* or *organized adherer*.

1635 F. WHITE *Sabbath-day* 192 A labyrinth, out of which he and his adherers [*printed* adheres] will not easily free themselves. **1649** DRUMM. OF HAWTH. *James V.* Wks. 1711, 106 It is an errour of state..to condemn to death the adherers to new doctrine. **1650** J. ROW (son) *Hist. Kirk Scotl.* (1842) 485 This Supplication given in to the Councill, the number of adhearers there to multiplied daylie. **1733** SWIFT *Choice of Recorder* Wks. 1745 VIII. 286 A firm adherer to the established church.

adherescent (ˌædhɪˈrɛsənt), *a. rare*⁻¹. [ad. L. *adhærēscent-em* pr. pple. of *adhærēsc-ĕre*, inceptive of *adhærē-re* to ADHERE.] Tending to adhere; adhesive.

1775 FIELDING in *Phil. Trans.* IX. 229 These subdivided parts [of a guinea] are by some observed to lose in a great degree their adherescent quality.

adhering (ædˈhɪərɪŋ), *vbl. sb.* [f. ADHERE + -ING¹.] The act or process of sticking, clinging, or remaining attached. (Now mostly gerundial.)

1611 COTGR., *Adhesion*, an adhering, cleaving, sticking fast unto. **1681** MANTON *Serm. on Ps.* cxix. 92 Wks. 1872 VII. 426 The adhering of the soul to the promises is the unquestionable way to obtain a sound peace. **1754** CHATHAM *Lett. to Nephew* iv. 23 A more serious danger is.. the adhering perhaps to false and dangerous notions. *Mod.* The limpet has the power of adhering firmly to the rock.

adhering (ædˈhɪərɪŋ), *ppl. a.* [f. ADHERE + -ING².] Sticking, clinging, abidingly attached.

1657 *Divine Loue* 197 Yet by the Grace of God will I haue noe adheringe Affection to them. **1695** WOODWARD *Nat. Hist. Earth* (1723) 19 Metallick or mineral matter, adhering firmly in Lumps to the Outsides of them. **1807** CRABBE *Par. Reg.* III. 189 Then from the adhering clasp the keys unbound.

adhesion (ædˈhiːʒən). Also 7 **adhæsion**. [a. Fr. *adhésion*, ad. L. *adhæsiōn-em*, n. of action, f. *adhæs-* ppl. stem of *adhærē-re* to ADHERE.]

1. a. The action of sticking (*to* anything) by physical attraction, viscosity of surface, or firm grasping. Also a particular instance of such clinging. In *Path.* The unnatural union of surfaces consequent upon inflammation. In *Med.*, also a benign union of tissue as in healing (now *rare*). Also *spec.* in *Physical Chem.* (see quots.).

1645 HOWELL *Lett.* v. 11 To the nutrition of the body, there are two Essentiall conditions requir'd..concoction and agglutination or adhæsion. **1661** BOYLE *Spring & Weight of Air* I. iv. (1682) 10, I could not find the Adhesion of the Finger to the Tube to be near so strong as our author related. **1794** SULLIVAN *View of Nat.* I. 120 The strong adhesion of two leaden balls which touch by polished surfaces. **1800** J. BURNS *Diss. Inflammation* II. ii. 5 We are then chiefly to search after, and extract foreign bodies, when we apprehend that their removal may permit the inflammation to be resolved, and adhesion to take place. **1804** ABERNETHY *Surg. Observ.* 224 A very slight adhesion had taken place between the sigmoid flexure of the colon and ..the peritoneum. **1813** [see INTENTION 10 b]. **1853** MAYNE *Expos. Lex.* 19/1 *Adhesion*, term for that property by which certain bodies attract others; or for the power by which their particles adhere to each other. **1860** TYNDALL *Glaciers* II. §23. 352 A new adhesion occurs which holds the pieces together. **1867** *Brit. Med. Jrnl.* 26 Oct. 356/1 The imposing circumstances of the operation have made all surgeons feel the..necessity of closing the wound at once..and endeavouring to obtain reunion of the abdominal wall..by direct adhesion, uncomplicated by suppuration. **1875** F. BUCKLAND *Log-book* 125 One of the most remarkable adhesions of oysters that ever came under my notice. **1876** *Encycl. Brit.* V. 56/1 The forces which are concerned in these phenomena are those which act between neighbouring parts of the same substance, and which are called forces of cohesion, and those which act between portions of matter of different kinds, which are called forces of adhesion. **1948** GLASSTONE *Physical Chem.* (ed. 2) vii. 483 This work is a measure of the energy required to separate the solid from the liquid and is called the *work of adhesion* between solid and liquid. **1959** P. WEISS in W. B. Patterson *Wound Healing & Tissue Repair* i. 3 These observations..reveal the existence of highly specialized ultramicroscopic devices for cellular attachment (rather than plain adhesion), which must be taken into account when considering the mobilization of the epidermis for wound healing. **1980** *Conc. Med. Dict.* 10/2 In primary adhesion there is very little granulation tissue; in secondary adhesion the two edges are joined together by granulation tissue.

b. *fig.*

a **1641** BP. MONTAGU *Acts & Mon.* (1642) 122 He was.. separated from us in inseparable adhesion to perfection. **1779** J. MOORE *View of Soc.* II. xcvi. 436 There are, however, so many repelling points in the American and French characters, that I cannot imagine the adhesion between them could be of long duration.

c. *Mech.* The grip (of a wheel on a track, etc.) produced by friction, or the friction itself. Also *attrib.*

1862 W. J. M. RANKINE *Man. Civ. Engin.* III. i. 639 The '*adhesion*', as it is called, or force which prevents the driving wheels from slipping on the rails. **1889** *Cent. Dict.*, *Adhesion-car*, a railroad-car provided with means for increasing the adhesive or tractive power beyond that due merely to the weight imposed upon the rails. **1902** *Encycl. Brit.* XXXII. 167/2 Adhesion lines..may be either of normal or of narrow gauge. *Ibid.* 168/1 A wet rail will prevent the use of the theoretical adhesion of the driving wheels. **1933** *Discovery* Feb. 57/2 A proposed adhesion railway to follow up a forest-clad Serra in South America. **1958** *Engineering* 14 Mar. 342/1 The high cost of these locomotives is apparently justified from the good adhesion characteristics.

2. The action of attaching oneself, or of remaining attached, to a person, party, or tenet, as a partizan, supporter, or follower. ***to give in one's adhesion***: to declare oneself an adherent, join as a supporter. .

1624 BP. MONTAGU *New Gagg* 164 For faith is an adhesion unto God. **1646** SIR T. BROWNE *Pseud. Ep.* I. vi. 20 The mortallest enemy unto knowledge..hath been a peremptory adhesion unto authority. **1732** LEDIARD *Sethos* II. VIII. 166 [It] carries with it the condition of a sincere adhæsion to my interest. **1846** PRESCOTT *Ferd. & Isab.* I. iv. 197 The Pimentels..now openly testified their adhesion to her [Isabella's] niece. **1851** HUSSEY *Papal Power* iii. 136 John.. and the Synod under him, sent in their adhesion to Rome. **1861** TROLLOPE *Tales of all Countries* (ser. 2) (1863) 295 His first idea had been that so close a connection..would be delightful. He had blushed as he had given in his adhesion. **1863** KINGLAKE *Crimea* (1876) I. xiii. 209 Austria had never ceased to declare her adhesion to her accustomed policy.

3. *Psych.* Intimate and involuntary association of ideas and action.

1855 BAIN *Senses & Intell.* II. i. 322 (L.) There grows up in course of time an adhesion between the tension of the rotator muscles and the several movements of walking, and at last they coalesce in one complete whole. *Ibid.* 325 It is within the cerebral hemispheres that the adhesion takes place.

4. *Bot.* Union of organs by confluence of normally *unlike* parts, such as the distinct floral whorls; in opposition to *cohesion*, the coalescence of *like* parts, such as the margins of organs in the same whorl.

1857 HENFREY *Bot.* 94 No case is known of adhesion of the three inner circles, with a free calyx. **1872** OLIVER *Elem. Bot.* I. iv. 27 Union of corolla to stamens, or ovary to calyx, or of stamens to corolla or to pistil, is due to adhesion—parts of different whorls or series being concerned.

5. a. Any substance or circumstance which adheres; an attendant, appendage, or accessory. *rare.*

1827 CARLYLE *Misc.* I. 14 Casting off all foreign, especially all noxious adhesions. **1839–47** TODD *Cycl. Anat. & Phys.* III. 748/1 The adhesions which are formed by the consolidation of coagulable lymph.

b. *Med.* A mass of fibrous connective tissue joining two surfaces that are normally separate.

1743 tr. *Heister's Surg.* 300 Having freed the disordered Artery from its Adhesions. **1793** M. BAILLIE *Morbid Anat.* i. 6 Such adhesions are to be considered as the consequence of previous inflammation. **1895** *Brit. Med. Jrnl.* 5 Jan. 1/2 The fibro-serous adhesions between the stomach and the parietes were as firm as ever. **1967** J. CYRIAX in Rob & Smith *Clin. Surg.* XIII. xii. 315 Adhesions form, especially after a sprain at the knee or ankle, when healing of a minor ligamentous rupture is allowed to take place during insufficient movement. **1974** PASSMORE & ROBSON *Compan. Med. Stud.* III. I. xix. 87/2 Adhesions are a common cause of intestinal obstruction.

adhesive (ædˈhiːsɪv), *a.* and *sb.* Also 7 **adhæsive**. [a. Fr. *adhésif*, *-ive*, as if ad. L. **adhæsīvus*. See ADHESION and -IVE.]

A. *adj.* **1.** Having the property of adhering; sticky. ***adhesive tape***, a strip of paper or film coated with adhesive, for fastening packages, etc.

1775 GOOCH in *Phil. Trans.* LXV. 374, I apply a circular plaster, moderately adhesive. **1791** E. DARWIN *Bot. Gard.* II. 36 The paste, made by boiling wheat-flour in water, ceases to be adhesive after having been frozen. **1858** H. MILLER *Cruise of Betsey* ii. 258 The Blackpots clay is..so adhesive, that I now felt..as if I had got into a bed of birdlime. **1934** in WEBSTER. **1951** *Good Housek. Home Encycl.* 28/1 Seal the tin with adhesive tape.

2. Furnished with an appliance for adhesion. ***adhesive envelope***, one having a gummed flap.

1854 MAYHEW *Lond. Lab.* I. 287 The envelopes are sold at from 6*d.* to 15*d.* the dozen: the higher-priced being adhesive.

3. *fig.* Apt or tending to adhere, cling to, or persevere in.

1670 G. H. tr. *Hist. Cardinals* III. ii. 262 To render the election of the Pope more tedious, and pernicious, that is, more adhæsive to the World. *a* **1748** THOMSON (J.) If slow, yet sure, adhesive to the track, Hot steaming up. *a* **1845** HOOD *Craniol.* iv. (1871) 333 What severs man and wife? a simple Defect of the Adhesive pimple.

B. *sb.* **a.** [The *adj.* used *absol.*] An adhesive substance.

1912 *Sci. Amer.* 17 Aug. 144/3 Gluten, gum arabic, dextrine, are also..used, though their use is mainly that of simple adhesives. **1958** *Observer* 11 May 10/3 There is no universal adhesive. If the manufacturer claims that the adhesive is good for leather, it probably is. It's no good using it for a teacup handle.

b. *Philately.* An adhesive postage stamp (opp. one impressed on a card or wrapper, etc.).

1881 *Stamp-Collector's Ann.* 9 The 5, 20, and 50 pf. adhesives have now followed the example of the 10 pf. **1893** H. EWEN (*title*) Priced Catalogue of the Used Postage Adhesives of Great Britain.

adhesively (ædˈhiːsɪvlɪ), *adv. rare*⁻⁰. [f. prec. -LY².] 'In an adhesive manner.' Todd 1818.

adhesiveness (ædˈhiːsɪvnɪs). [f. as prec. + -NESS.]

1. The quality of being adhesive; the power of adhering; stickiness, viscosity, tenacity. *lit.* and *fig.*

1839 LADY LYTTON *Cheveley* (ed. 2) II. ix. 283 Adamantine adhesiveness to a particular principle. **1868** *Morn. Star* 6 Mar., The adhesiveness and tenacity of this cement are truly extraordinary.

2. *Phren.* The faculty of forming and maintaining attachments to persons. *Psych.* The tendency to association of ideas which is the basis of memory.

1815 SPURZHEIM *Physiognom. Syst.* Pref. 9 Attachment indicates only the effect of this faculty, and I require a name to express the faculty of producing such effect..and it seems to me that the sound attachiveness would be infinitely more disagreeable than adhesiveness. **1868** BAIN *Mental & Moral Sc.* II. i. 88 Natural adhesiveness usually shows itself in special departments—aptitude for languages, for science, for music, etc. **1879** CHAMBERS *Encycl.* s.v. *Phrenology*, Adhesiveness is strongest and its organ largest in woman.

†**adˈhibit**, *ppl. a. Obs.* [ad. L. *adhibit-us*, pa. pple. of *adhibē-re* to hold towards, bring to, employ in, f. *ad* to + *habē-re* to hold.]

1. Brought or let in, admitted *to.*

1543 GRAFTON *Contn. Harding's Chron.* 492 To whiche counsel there were adhibite very fewe, and they very secrete.

2. Brought into application, employed, used.

1528 GARDINER in Pocock *Rec. Ref.* I. xl. 78 The maintenance of this town..requireth your grace's help and comfort to be adhibite in time. **1671** *True Non-Conformist* 118 Anointing..the accustomed Symbole, adhibite in the exercise of the Gift of healing.

adhibit (ædˈhɪbɪt), *v.* [f. prec., or on analogy of vbs. so formed.]

1. To take in, let in, admit (a person or thing).

1528 GARDINER in Pocock *Rec. Ref.* I. li. 121 Whose counsels the popes heretofore have most commonly adhibite and followed. **1565** JEWEL *Repl. M. Harding* (1611) 133 The conference betwixt Sylla..and Bocchus King of Numidia, had by meane of Interpreters adhibited of both parts. **1611** SPEED *Hist. Gt. Brit.* IX. xviii. 40 To which counsell..there were adhibited very few. **1742** BAILEY, *Adhibit*, to admit. **1880** MUIRHEAD *Gaius* II. §116 It avails nothing that the testator's *familia* has been sold, the witnesses adhibited.

2. To put to or upon, to affix.

1567 MAPLET *Greene Forest* 48 It joyneth togither those sinews which are cut, being adhibited and used plaister like. **1768** BOSWELL *Corsica* iii. (ed. 2) 239 We impose taxes and contributions, we adhibit our seals. **1849** ALISON *Hist. Europe* I. iv. §52. 488 Will he adhibit to subsequent decrees a sanction? **1862** *Advt. in Old Mort.*, The Subscribers to the Shilling Edition of the Waverley Novels..will receive a set of Adhesive Labels, which may be adhibited to the back of the Volumes.

3. To apply, employ, use, give, devote.

1574 T. NEWTON *Health of Magistr.* 71 So that so muche space and time in the use thereof be adhibited. **1605** CAMDEN *Rem.* 233 Wherevnto ought to be adhibited, first fervent prayers then a lowely minde. **1656** EARL MONM. *Advt. fr. Parnass.* 264 The pernitious disease of polititians.. not to adhibit faith to such actions as have a certain affected appearance of extraordinary goodness.

4. To apply as a remedy, to administer.

1654 T. WHITAKER *Blood of Grape* 33 (T.) Wine also that is dilute may safely and profitably be adhibited in an apozemicall forme in fevers. **1725** BRADLEY *Fam. Dict.* s.v. *Stinking Breath*, Let this Bolus be adhibited Morning, Noon and Night. **1864** R. F. BURTON *Dahome* I. 123 Nothing but the strongest drink, constantly adhibited, carried him through his trials.

adhibited (ædˈhɪbɪtɪd), *ppl. a.* [f. prec. + -ED.] Admitted, applied, employed, administered.

c **1555** HARPSFIELD *Divorce of Hen. VIII* (1878) 45 The wife and the man may with their mutual consent adhibited and foregoing enter into religion.

adhibiting (ædˈhɪbɪtɪŋ), *vbl. sb.* [f. as prec. + -ING¹.] The action of admitting, applying, or administering. (Now gerundial.)

1720 BLAIR in *Phil. Trans.* XXXI. 37 Next to the adhibiting of the Bitters in substance, such as Wormwood, Gentian, and Camomile Flowers, this is the most convenient way of administring them. **1859** R. F. BURTON in Jrnl. R.G.S. XXIX. 390 In common diseases..they will condescend to such profane processes as adhibiting sternutatories.

adhibition (ædhɪˈbɪʃən). [ad. L. *adhibitiōn-em* admission, application, n. of action, f. *adhibē-re*: see ADHIBIT *a.*] The action of adhibiting; **a.** of affixing; **b.** of applying, employing, administering.

1654 T. WHITAKER *Blood of Grape* 55 The adhibition of dilute wine. **1742** BAILEY, *Adhibition*, A taking or applying to. **1835** L. HUNT *Lond. Jrnl.* No. 53. 98 An apple pie was improved by the adhibition of a quince. **1848** ARNOULD *Mar. Insur.* I. iii. (1866) I. 142 The adhibition of the Seal of the body corporate. **1838** *Chambers' Jrnl.* No. 331 quoting *Edin. Rev.* on *Homœop.*, Every sickness..must by the adhibition of proper medicines be converted into a similar, but more energetic artificial sickness.

‖**ad hoc** (æd hɒk). [L., lit. 'to this'.]

a. For this purpose, to this end; for the particular purpose in hand or in view.

1659 R. BAXTER *Key for Catholics* II. iv. 451 *Ad hoc* the Magistrate is the only Judge what is sound doctrine. **1809** *Edin. Rev.* Jan. 433 The conscripts are..examined..by a special commission, created *ad hoc* by the prefect. **1875** W. R. GREG *Misc. Ess.* (1882) vi. 147 A sum not far off two millions per annum will have to be provided *ad hoc* by the Chancellor of the Exchequer.

b. *attrib.* or as *adj.* Devoted, appointed, etc., to or for some particular purpose.

[**1853** GREVILLE *Mem.* (1887) III. I. ii. 51 There are already symptoms of a possible combination *ad hoc.*] **1879** in E.

Yates *Time* I. 3 The special matter that brought about the *ad hoc* departure from the Lawrentian policy. **1900** *Daily News* 18 Apr. 7/1 The discussion of the constitution of the educational authorities was sensational, inasmuch as it led to the Conference declaring for the ad hoc principle. **1904** *Fabian News* Aug. 29/1 A report..on the total abolition of *ad hoc* bodies was read. **1928** ABP. CANTERBURY in *Daily News* 8 Feb. 10/1 A growing sense of the usefulness of Reservation of the ad hoc kind. **1955** *Times* 14 May 11/1 He was still employed by the B.B.C. on an *ad hoc* basis as a programme producer.

c. Hence (nonce-wds.): **ad hoc** *v.*, to use *ad hoc* measures or contrivances, to improvise; so **adhoc(k)ing** *vbl. sb.*; **ad hoc-ery**, the use of such measures; **ad 'hocism** (also as one word), the use of *ad hoc* measures, esp. as a deliberate means of avoiding long-term policy; **ad-hoc-ness**, the nature of, or devotion to, *ad hoc* principles or practice.

1930 A. FLEXNER *Universities* II. 71 '*Ad-hoc-ness*', if..I may be permitted to invent an indefensible word, is not confined to courses or curricula. **1936** *Mind* XLV. 249 There is a suspicion of '*ad-hoc*-ness' about the 'explanation'. **1960** C. RAY *Merry Eng.* 136 The Civil Servant who complained..about 'all this adhocking'. **1960** *20th Cent.* Dec. 588 The Children's Department, generous-hearted, chaotic, brilliantly ad-hocing. **1961** *Economist* 14 Oct. 124/1 Britain thrives on 'anomalies' and 'ad hoc-eries'. **1968** D. R. GADGIL in Bhagwati & Desai *India Planning for Industrialization* (1970) viii. 132 The first [difficulty] is the lack of a coordinated view and of a frame of considered policy... It is..related to the short-term, departmental view that Secretaries and others take... Ad hocism in policy decisions is the result. **1969** *Guardian* 2 Oct. 11/4 The first rule of non-design or Ad Hocism is to alter as little as possible. **1972** N. SILVER in Silver & Jencks *Adhocism* II. i. 105 As soon as one sees that there can be an actual policy of contingent, resourceful action, or adhocism,..this mongrel creativity..appears everywhere. **1981** *Times of India* 30 Aug. 8/5 The adhocism exhibited at all levels.

‖**ad hominem** (,æd 'hɒmɪnɛm), *phrase.* [L. *ad* to, *hominem* acc. of *homo* a man.] A phrase applied to an argument or appeal founded on the preferences or principles of a particular person rather than on abstract truth or logical cogency.

1599 R. PARSONS *Temp. Ward-Word* vi. 79 This is an argument..which logicians call, *ad hominem*. **1633** W. AMES *Fresh Suit* I. x. 105 Some arguments, and answers are *ad hominem*, that is, they respect the thing in quæstion, not simply, but as it commeth from such a man. **1748** HARTLEY *Observ. on Man* I. iii. §2. 359 The Argument here alleged is only one *ad hominem*. **1787** BENTHAM *Def. of Usury* viii. 83 This argument *ad hominem*, as it may be called.

†**ad'horn**, *v. Obs. rare*$^{-1}$. [f. L. *ad* to + HORN.] Used (jocularly, and with ref. to *adorn*), for 'to plant horns on,' to cuckold.

1605 CHAPMAN *All Fools* in Dodsl. *O.P.* (1780) IV. 146 O yes, he adores you and adhorns me. **1612** —— *Widdowes Teares* (Plays 1873) III. 9 While you adhorne their temples.

†**ad'hort**, *v. Obs.* [ad. L. *adhortā-ri* to encourage, urge on; f. *ad* to + *hortā-ri* to incite.] To urge, exhort, incite.

1539 TAVERNER *Gard. Wysdome* II. 42 b, Adhortynge offycers and rulers to punysh offendours. **1598** R. BERNARD *Terence's Eunuch* III. v, I adhort them thereto, and they make readie with speede. **1605** CAMDEN *Rem.* 231 Sadolet adhorted him vnto the studie of Philosophy. **1631** DONNE *Biathanatos* (1644) 130 The writers in the Romane Church ..obliquely adhort these inordinate Fasts and other disciplines.

†**adhor'tation**, *Obs.* [ad. L. *adhortātiōn-em*, n. of action, f. *adhortāt-* ppl. stem of *adhortā-ri*: see ADHORT.] Exhortation to or toward anything; encouragement, persuasion.

1536 CHEKE *Remedy for Sedition* E i b, The swete adhortations, the hyghe and assured promises that God maketh unto us. **1651** J. F[REAKE] *Agrippa's Occ. Philos.* To Trit. 4 Your ardent adhortation put courage and boldness into me. **1659** GELL *Amendm. Bible* 604 A forcible cohortation, adhortation, or manifold exhortation. [Also in mod. Dicts.]

adhortative (æd'hɔːtətɪv), *a.* [f. ADHORTAT(ION + -IVE.] Expressing adhortation or exhortation: applied to the verbal mood which expresses an exhortation.

1845 STODDART *Gram.* in *Encycl. Metrop.* I. 52/2 Some writers have distinguished from the imperative, the precative, the deprecative, the permissive, the adhortative, [etc.]. **1934** PRIEBSCH & COLLINSON *Germ. Lang.* vi. 316 The adhortative *gehen wir*. **1963** VISSER *Hist. Syntax Eng. Lang.* I. iii. 190 In the Pres. D. suggestive or adhortative questions in which *to be* is construed with *to do* (as in: 'Why *don't* you *be* reasonable?').

†**ad'hortatory**, *a. Obs.* [f. L. *adhortāt-* (see ADHORTATION) + -ORY, as if ad. L. **adhortātōrius*.] Of or pertaining to adhortation; hortatory; persuading or urging to a course.

1660 T. STANLEY *Hist. Philos.* III. II. 119 This 'Wear not a Ring' is likewise adhortatory. **1697** POTTER *Antiq. Greece* I. xxvi. (1715) 164 Some adhortatory Lessons..are to be privately inculcated. [Also in mod. Dicts.]

adiabat (eɪ'daɪəbæt). *Physics.* [f. ADIABAT(IC *a.*] = *adiabatic curve* s.v. ADIABATIC *a.* 2.

1945 F. A. BERRY et al. *Handbk. Meteorol.* v. 348 The lines are also called adiabatics (or adiabats). **1979** *Nature* 19 Apr. 686/1 Of the uncertainties beneath the photosphere only the value of the adiabat deep in the convection zone substantially influences the oscillation frequencies. **1983** *Physical Rev.* A. XXVIII. 1738 The shock front portion is on the Hugoniot curve whereas the rear part is closer to an adiabat.

adiabatic (,ædɪə'bætɪk, ,eɪdaɪə'bætɪk), *a.* and *sb. Physics.* [f. Gr. ἀδιάβατ-ος not to be passed through (f. ἀ not + διά through + βατός passable, vbl. adj. f. βα-ίν-ειν to go) + -IC.]

A. *adj.*

1. Impassable to heat; involving neither loss nor acquisition of heat.

1859, 1877 [Implied at sense 2.] **1882** SIEMENS in *Nature* XXV. 603 Let us suppose that the attenuated matter in space has a temperature of 160° on the absolute scale, and that it is 3000 times more rarified than when it reaches by adiabatic compression the solar photosphere. **1933** *Flight* 2 Feb. 99/2 Closed, or adiabatic, cockpits, wherein the pressure could be kept at 430 mm.

2. ***adiabatic curve, line***: a curve or line produced by plotting the changes in volume and pressure of a gas during an adiabatic process; = ADIABAT.

1859 W. J. M. RANKINE *Man. Steam Engine* III. iii. 302 A certain curve NN passing through A, which may be called a curve of no transmission, or adiabatic curve. *Ibid.*, 346 Each adiabatic line for a perfect gas is a curve of the hyperbolic kind. **1877** WORMELL *Thermodyn.* 130 If a substance can expand without gain or loss of heat, and a curve is drawn, such that the abscissa and ordinate of any point respectively represent the volume of a unit of mass, and the corresponding pressure for unit of area, this curve is termed an adiabatic line. **1922** GLAZEBROOK *Dict. Appl. Physics* I. 946/2 The calculation fixes a point in the adiabatic line of the pressure-volume diagram for expansion from the initial conditions. **1957** *Encycl. Brit.* XIV. 178/1 This equation, which gives the form of the adiabatic curves for a perfect gas, shows that these..are steeper than the isothermal curves. **1975** *Optics & Spectroscopy* XXXIX. 610/1 We calculated the upper bound of the total adiabatic potential curve of the ground state.

B. *sb. ellipt.* for *adiabatic curve*; the relationship expressed by an adiabatic curve.

1884 *Nature* 21 Aug. 403/2 Mr. W. Peddie gave a communication on the isothermals and adiabatics of water near the maximum density point. **1928** N. SHAW *Man. Meteorol.* II. p. xx, The word 'adiabatic' is also used as an abbreviation for adiabatic curve which shows the relation between the pressure and temperature of a mass of air when the adiabatic condition is rigorously maintained. **1945** [see ADIABAT]. **1967** CONDON & ODISHAW *Handbk. Physics* (ed. 2) III. ii. 24/1 This Hugoniot adiabatic is shown in Fig. 2.5 in comparison with the usual isentropic adiabatic.

adiabatically (,ædɪə'bætɪkəlɪ), *adv. Physics.* [f. prec. + -AL[1] + -LY[2].] In an adiabatic manner; so that heat neither enters nor leaves (a substance).

1882 *Eng. Mech.* No. 887. 48 In a non-conducting cylinder, the fluid expanding adiabatically.

adi'abolist (ædɪ'æbəlɪst). *rare*$^{-1}$. [f. Gr. ἀ priv. + διάβολ-ος devil + -IST.] One who does not believe in the existence of a devil.

1646 GAULE *Cases of Consc.* 2 Both for the Atheist and the Adiabolist.

adiactinic (,ædɪæk'tɪnɪk), *a. Chem.* [f. A- *pref.* 14 + DIACTINIC.] Not diactinic; not transmitting the chemical rays of light.

1880 *Nineteenth Cent.* Mar. 529 Those substances which are chemically transparent are said to be diactinic; while those which are chemically opaque are, of course, adiactinic.

‖**Adiantum** (ædɪ'æntəm). *Bot.* [L., ad. Gr. ἀδίαντον maiden-hair, prop. adj. 'unwetted,' f. ἀ not + διαίν-ειν to wet; so called from the way in which the surfaces of the fronds resist wetting.]

1. A genus of ferns, having more or less wedge-shape pinnules on slender black shining stems, and marginal sori, covered by distinct indusia, of which one species (*A. Capillus Veneris*), commonly called True Maiden-hair, is a rare native of Britain.

1706 PHILLIPS, *Adiantum*, The Herb Maiden-Hair, so call'd because its Leaves take no wet. **1866** MOORE *Treas. Bot.* 20 In *Adiantum* the spore-cases are not attached to the frond, but to the under side of the indusium.

2. *Herb.* and *pop.* The Black Maiden-hair, a species of Spleenwort (*Asplenium Adiantum-nigrum*).

1866 *Cornh. Mag.* Nov. 536 Maidenhair, black adiantum, and blue violets hanging from the brink.

adiaphanous (ædɪ'æfənəs), *a.* [f. Gr. ἀ priv. + *diaphanous*.] Not translucent, opaque.

1658 T.C. in S. Austin *Naps upon Parnassus* sig. B 3, Upon the Gurmundizing Quagmires and most Adiaphanous Bogs, of the Author's obnubilated Roundelayes. **1826** KIRBY & SPENCE *Introd. Entomol.* IV. xlvi. 285 *Adiaphanous*..which does not transmit the light at all. **1833** J. WATERWORTH tr. *Véron's Rule Cath. Faith* 77 Nor will our adversaries ever be able to prove..that actions, which are prescribed by human laws, continue..indifferent or adiaphanous. **1855** J. SCOFFERN in *Orr's Circle Sci.* IV. 103 We have transcalent and non-transcalent substances.. corresponding with the expressions *diaphanous* and *adiaphanous.*

†**adi'aphoracy, -icie**, improp. ff. ADIAPHORY.

1612 COCKERAM, *Adiaphoricie*, indifferency. **1847** CRAIG, *Adiaphoracy*, indifference, neutrality.

†**adi'aphoral**, *a. Obs.* [f. Gr. ἀδιάφορ-ος, indifferent + -AL[1].] Indifferent in the eyes of the church, or of theologians; = ADIAPHOROUS I.

1593 G. HARVEY *Pierce's Supererog.* 92 Why may not such ..condescend to a like toleration of matters adiaphorall?

adiaphorism (ædɪ'æfərɪz(ə)m). [f. Gr. ἀδιάφορ-ος indifferent + -ISM.] Religious or theological indifference; indifferentism, latitudinarianism.

1866 *Macm. Mag.* Oct. 472 Much that has of late been called Toleration has been only adiaphorism. **1881** STANLEY *Chr. Inst.* viii. 167 If this absolute adiaphorism could be made to take possession of the popular mind.

adiaphorist (ædɪ'æfərɪst), *sb.* and *a.* [f. as prec. + -IST.]

A. *sb.*

1. One indifferent about points of theological discussion; an indifferentist, or latitudinarian.

1645 *Lib. of Consc.* 30 When the Magistrate is a Nullifidian, Neutralist, and Adiaphorist. **1710** W. HUME *Sacr. Succession* 169 There is one text, which..if it confound not our adiaphorists, may make them indifferently modest.

2. *Eccl. Hist.* A member of a sect so called; moderate Lutherans, who held some things, condemned by Luther, to be indifferent or non-essential.

a **1564** BECON *Articles of Chr. Relig.* Wks. 1844, 401 In the freewill men, in the libertines, in the Adiaphorists. **1738** NEAL *Hist. Puritans* (1822) I. 56 Those who complied [to the Interim of Charles V] were for the most part Lutherans, and carried the name of Adiaphorists. **1832** MACAULAY *Burleigh* (1854) 233/1 Those German Protestants who were called Adiaphorists..considered the Popish rites as matters indifferent.

B. *adj.* Theologically indifferent.

1882 *Spectator* 11 Feb. 195/1 Fused, as Catholicism and Protestantism once seemed likely to become fused, while England for a moment became Adiaphorist.

adiaphoristic (ædɪæfə'rɪstɪk), *a.* [f. prec. + IC.] Relating to adiaphorism or the *adiaphora*.

1844 MACLAINE tr. *Mosheim's Eccl. Hist.* XVI. II. i. §28 That violent scene of contention..called the *Adiaphoristic* controversy.

adiaphorite (ædɪ'æfəraɪt). = ADIAPHORIST A. 2.

1753 CHAMBERS *Cycl. Supp.* **1847** CRAIG.

‖**adiaphoron** (ædɪ'æfərɒn), *a.* and *sb. arch.* Pl. adiaphora. [Gr. ἀδιάφορ-ον, adj. neut., indifferent; f. ἀ not + διάφορος differing; f. διά apart + φέρειν to bear.] A thing indifferent, upon which the Church has given no decision; a non-essential. (Once very common as a theological term.)

1553-87 FOXE *A. & M.* (1596) 51/1 The celebration of Easterdaie remained adiaphoron, as a thing indifferent in the church. *a* **1652** J. SMITH *Sel. Disc.* iv. 126 These we may safely reckon, I think, amongst our adiaphora in morality, as being in themselves neither good nor evil. **1865** PUSEY *Truth. & Off. Eng. Ch.* 207 Images are to be reckoned among the adiaphora, which do not belong to the substance of religion.

adiaphorous (ædɪ'æfərəs), *a.* [f. Gr. ἀδιάφορ-ος indifferent + -OUS.]

1. Indifferent, immaterial, non-essential; neutral.

1635 F. WHITE *Sabbath* 27 Divine Lawes..command or prohibite actions, which before the position of the outward Law, are adiaphorous. **1647** JER. TAYLOR *Lib. Prophes.* Ep. Ded. 7 Matters adiaphorous, as meats and drinks and holy dayes. *Ibid.* v. 93 We are taught to have no obligation in them but to be adiaphorous. **1657** TOMLINSON *Renou's Disp.* 220 Wine therefore is adiaphorous and indifferent, good or evil, as its use is good or evil. **1748** HARTLEY *Observ. on Man* I. ii. §1. 116 The Sensations [the tangible Qualities of Bodies] are for the most part, adiaphorous ones.

†**2.** *Chem.* Neutral in chemical properties; neither alkaline nor acid. *Obs.*

a **1691** BOYLE (J.) Our adiaphorous spirit may be obtained, by distilling the liquor that is afforded by wood and divers other bodies.

3. *Med.* Incapable of doing either harm or good.

WEBSTER cites DUNGLISON.

†**adi'aphory.** *Obs.* [ad. Gr. ἀδιαφορία: see quot.] Indifference, indifferentism.

1660 T. STANLEY *Hist. Philos.* (1701) 98/2 The Opinion which he taught was ἀδιαφορία, indifference. **1742** BAILEY, *Adiaphory*, indifferency.

‖**adiapneustia** (,ædɪəp'njuːstɪə). *Med.* [Gr. ἀδιαπνευστία f. ἀ not + διά through + πνευστ-, f. πνέ-ειν to breathe.] Defective or impeded perspiration.

1706 PHILLIPS, *Adiapneustia*, a breathing thro' the Pores of the Body. **1742** BAILEY, *Adiapneustia*, a Diminution or Obstruction of Natural Perspiration. **1879** *Syd. Soc. Lex.*

adiate ('ædɪeɪt), *v. Roman-Dutch Law.* [app. irreg. f. L. *adīre* to approach + -ATE[3].] *trans.* To accept (an inheritance) as heir under a will; in South Africa, to accept as beneficiary under a will. Hence **adiation** (ædɪ'eɪʃən).

1829 in J. W. KNAPP *Rep. Cases Privy Council* (1831) I. 111 Adiation (*aditio in hereditatem*) is a question more of intention than action. **1845** C. HERBERT tr. *Grotius' Introd. Dutch Jurispr.* II. xx. 143 An instituted heir, who adiates freely the inheritance, may deduct therefrom a fourth part. *Ibid.* xxi. 147 Repudiation must take place after the inheritance falls in by death and before adiation. **1896** JUTA *Selection of Leading Cases* II. 111 If the survivor has adiated and accepted benefits under the will. **1915** R. W. LEE *Roman-Dutch Law* IV. i. 286 If he [*sc.* the 'extraneus heres'] accepted or acted as heir, he was said to 'adiate' the inheritance (*adire hereditatem*), and from that moment was in the position of a universal successor.

adiathermic (ˌædɪəˈθɜːmɪk), *a. Physics.* [f. Gr. ἀ not + διάθερμ-ος warmed through + -IC.] (See quot.)
1867 W. MILLER *Elem. Chem.* I. 271 Melloni terms those bodies..which do not so allow this transmission of heat..athermanous or adiathermic.

† **ˈadible**, *a. Obs. rare*⁻¹. [ad. late L. *adibilis* accessible, f. *adī-re* to go to: see -BLE.] Accessible.
1568 C. WATSON *Polyb.* 87b, To keep themselves continually in the sides of the mountains and in adible wayes.

adicity (æˈdɪsɪtɪ). *Chem.* [f. -AD I, after *atomicity*.] Combining capacity, according as an element or non-saturated compound is a *monad*, *dyad*, etc.
1882 ODLING in *Nature* XXV. No. 642, 379 A consideration of the valency or adicity of the elements.

‖ **ad idem** (ædˈɪdɛm), *adv. phr.* [L., lit. 'to the same (thing)'.] On the same point, making direct reference to the matter in hand, à propos.
1574 WHITGIFT *Defense of Aunswere to Admonition* III. vi. 187 Hitherto you haue proued nothing in question, neyther haue you reasoned *ad idem.* **1674** J. OWEN *Discourse concerning Holy Spirit* III. v. 271 The Opposition is not *ad idem.* **1885** *Law Times* 30 May 80/2 The letters show that the parties were never *ad idem.* **1928** C. S. LEWIS *Let.* 1 Apr. (1966) 126 The discussion ended..with the infuriating statement that we were not *ad idem* on the connotation of the word control. **1983** *Financial Times* 19 Feb. 5/6 We think you have a strong case for claiming that there is no contract on the ground that there was no consensus ad idem.

adieu (əˈdjuː), *int.*, also *adv.*, *sb.*, and ellipt. *vb.* Forms: 4–7 adew(e; 5–7 adue; 5 adyeu, adieux; 6 adeu; 7 adiew(e; 4– adieu. [a. Fr. *adieu*, f. *a.* to + *dieu* God, i.e. 'I commend you to God!' originally said to the party left, as 'Farewell!' was to the party setting forth.]

A. *int.*

1. An expression of kind wishes at the parting of friends, sinking into a mere formula of civility at parting. Good-bye! farewell! *arch.*
1393 GOWER *Conf.* II. 250 He saide: Adewe my swete may. **1440** J. SHIRLEY *Dethe of James* 29 Adieux. To God I you beteche. **1509** HAWES *Past. Pl.* xx. xix, Farewell, swete herte! farewell farewell, farewell! Adieu, adieu! **1587** FLEMING *Contn. Holinshed* III. 292/1 So with this grace good queene now heere adue. **1697** DRYDEN *Virgil, Past.* iii. 123 (1721) Adieu my Dear, she said, a long Adieu. **1850** TENNYSON *In Mem.* lvii. 16 And 'Ave, Ave, Ave,' said, 'Adieu, adieu' for evermore.

2. *fig.* An expression of regret at the loss or departure of anything; or a mere exclamatory recognition of its disappearance; = Away!, no longer, no more, all is over with.
c **1400** *Test. Love* II. (1560) 292/1 Adewe and adewe blis. *c* **1430** LYDG. *Bochas* III. vii. (1554) 79a, Touching defence, adue al hardinesse. **1586** G. WHITNEY in Farr's *S.P.* (1845) I. 209 Adve, deceiptfull worlde, thy pleasures I detest. **1586** JAMES VI in Ellis *Orig. Lett.* I. 222. III. 14 Then adeu with my dealing with thaime. **1652** ASHMOLE *Theatr. Chem. Brit.* xiii. 216 Adew my song and al my notes cler. **1777** HUME *Ess. & Treat.* I. 377 Adieu to all ideas of nobility, gentry, and family.

B. *adv.*

† 1. *to go adieu*: to go away, depart finally. *Obs.*
1513 DOUGLAS *Æneis* I. vi. 174 Thus he repreuis, bot sche is went adew. **1575** CHURCHYARD *Chippes* (1817) 151 And set the world agoing once adue It is mutch like a streame that hath no stay.

2. *to bid or say adieu* (*to*): to take affectionate, regretful, or formal leave of. (Here it approaches the character of a noun.)
1413 LYDG. *Pylgr. Sowle* II. lxv. (1859) 59, I bad hym adyeu. **1624** H. SMITH *6 Serm.* 11 Bid conscience adiewe. **1771** *Junius Lett.* xlii. 221 The king..bids adieu to amicable negociation. **1818** SCOTT *Hrt. Midl.* (1873) 119 The old man arose and bid them adieu.

C. Hence *sb.* An affectionate or formal leave-taking; a parting word; a farewell; esp. *to make* or *take adieu.*
c **1374** CHAUCER *Troyl.* II. 1084 And said, he wold in trouthe alwey hym holde, And his adew made. **1592** WARNER *Albion's Eng.* VIII. xl. (1612) 196 Their eies..now looke their last adew. **1601** SHAKS. *All's Well* II. i. 53 Too cold an adieu. **1606** —— *Ant. & Cl.* IV. v. 14 Write to him, gentle adieu's, and greetings. **1653** A. WILSON *James I*, 251 The Queen spoke her own Adieu in French. **1702** POPE *Sappho* 111 Sure 'twas not much to bid one kind adieu. *c* **1815** MISS AUSTEN *Northang. Ab.* (1833) I. xv. 98 His adieus were not long. **1855** TENNYSON *Daisy* 85 What more? we took our last adieu.

D. *ellipt.* as *v.* To bid farewell to; to take leave for ever of.
1602 CAREW *Cornwall* 111a, Shepherd adiews his swymming flocke, The Hinde be whelmed haruest hope.

† **aˈdight**, *v. Obs.* Forms: *Inf.*? 1 adiht-an; 2–3 adiht-en; 3–4 adiȝt-e(n, adyȝht-e; 4 adyte; 4–6 adyght(e; 6 adight, addight. *Pa. pple.* 1–3 adiht, *later* adiȝt, adyȝt, adyht, adyght, adight. [f. A- *pref.* 1 intensive + *diht-an* to compose, set in order: see DIGHT. In 16th c. the prefix was erroneously refashioned as *ad-*, after words from Fr. in *a-*:—L. *ad-*.]

1. To prepare, dispose, order, appoint.
c **1220** *Leg. St. Kath.* 1382 Þe deore Drihtin..haueð adiht us to dei to drehe þis deað. *a* **1250** *Owl & Night.* 326 And so ich mine song adiȝte. *c* **1315** *Pol. Songs* II. 329 [He] adihteth him a gay wenche. *c* **1325** *E.E. Allit. Poems* A. 349 Deme dryȝtyn, euer hym adyte.

2. To 'appoint' with attire; to equip, attire, dress, deck.
c **1400** *Gamelyn* 634 Yonder ben tuo yonge men, wonder wel adight. *c* **1450** LONELICH *Grail* xxxvi. 125 Ryaliche sche was adyht. *c* **1460** *Lybeaus Disconus* 227 in Ritson *Met. Rom.* II. 10 An hawberk bryght, That rychely was adyght. **1581** STUDLEY *Seneca's Trag.* 191 And mee addight In shape, that may be suitable vnto my playntiffe plight.

† **aˈdighting**, *vbl. sb. Obs.* Also 6 addighting [f. prec. + -ING¹.] Preparing, preparation.
1567 MAPLET *Greene Forest* 49 Wolfbane..which the huntesman vseth..with the which after their addighting they destroy Wolues.

† **adiˈgression.** *Obs. rare.* [perh. by attraction of article *a* in phrases like 'to make a digression.'] = Digression.
1482 *Monk of Evesham* (1869) 35 And nowe after this adigression go we ageyne to the narracion.

adill, obs. form of ADDLE.

† **ˈadimate**, *v. Obs. rare*⁻¹. [improp. f. L. *adimĕre* to take away (see ADEEM) + -ATE³.]
1657 TOMLINSON *Renou's Disp.* 339 Woodbind..adimates singultion.

† **aˈdimpleate**, *v. Obs. rare*⁻¹. [improp. f. L. *adimplē-re* to fill up (f. *ad-* intensive + *implē-re* to fill) + -ATE³.] To fill up.
1657 TOMLINSON *Renou's Disp.* 328 It adimpleats ulcers with flesh and cures them.

† **adimˈpletion.** *Obs. rare*⁻¹. [ad. L. *adimplētiōn-em* completing, fulfilling, n. of action f. *adimplē-re*: see prec.] Completion, fulfilment.
1650 *Repl. Sanderson* 10 We owe time, which may suspend the adimpletion of a Promise, but not its obligation.

† **aˈdin**, *v. Obs. rare.* Forms: 3 adune, 5 adene. [f. A- *pref.* 1 intensive + DIN *v.*, OE. *dynian*, f. *dyne* sb. noise, DIN.] To din; to deafen, stun with noise.
a **1250** *Owl & Night.* 337 Mid þine pipinge þu adunest þas monnes earen þar þu wunest. **1426** AUDELAY 78, I was adenyd of that dynt, Hit stonede me, and mad me stont.

‖ **ad infinitum** (ˌæd ɪnfɪˈnaɪtəm), *adv. phr.* [L. *ad* to, *infīnītum* infinity, prop. neut. of adj. *infīnītus* endless.] Without limit, endlessly, for ever.
1678 BUNYAN *Pilgr.* Apol. 17 I'll put you by your selves, lest you at last Should prove *ad infinitum.* **1733** SWIFT *On Poetry* Wks. 1755 IV. I. 194 A flea Hath smaller fleas that on him prey, And these have smaller still to bite 'em, And so proceed *ad infinitum.* **1860** ADLER *Provenc. Poet.* iii. 48 The character of their execution varied *ad infinitum.*

adinole (ˈædɪnəʊl). *Min.* A variety of ALBITE.
1837–80 DANA *Mineral.* 351 Adinole is probably albitic; it is reddish, from Sala, Sweden.

‖ **ad interim** (ˌæd ˈɪntərɪm), *adv. phrase*, also used as *adj.* [L. *ad* to, for, *interim* adv. 'meanwhile' used subst.] *adv.* During the intervening time, meanwhile. *adj.* Temporary.
1856 *Farmer's Mag.* Nov. 377 That *ad interim* the recommendations of the Lords Committee of 1851 would be acted upon. **1880** SIR E. REED *Japan* I. 123 The story of the *ad interim* empress or regent..has already in the main been told. *Mod.* An *ad interim* injunction was granted.

† **adinˈvention.** *Obs.* [ad. L. *adinventiōn-em*, n. of action f. *adinvenī-re*, f. *ad* to, in addition + *invenī-re* to INVENT.] An invented addition.
1413 LYDG. *Pylgr. Sowle* II. xliii. (1859) 49 They peruertyn hooly Scripture. cloutynge with vycyous adinuencyons the lawe of Crystes Gospel. *c* **1630** JACKSON *Creed* XII. cxxii. Wks. XII. 165 Additions or adinventions unto the ancient or primitive canon of Catholic faith.

‖ **adios** (ædɪˈɒs), *int.* (and *sb.*) [Sp. *adiós* f. *a* to + *dios* God; cf. ADIEU, ADDIO *int.*] Goodbye! Farewell! Also as *sb.*, a parting salutation.
1664 F. WILLOUGHBY *Jrnl.* 14 Nov. in J. Ray *Observations Journey Low-Countries* (1673) 495 The common..forms of salutation are..*A Dios.* **1841** G. BORROW *Zincali* I. II. iv. 285 'Adios,' said I, for I but too well knew what was on the carpet. **1899** *Scribner's Mag.* Jan. 114/2 There being some ill here.., I gave them remedies and departed after many adioses. **1912** G. FRANKAU *One of Us* vii. 59 At length they sallied from their dimitied Staterooms and waved *adios* to the Limited. **1940** C. MCCULLERS *Heart is Lonely Hunter* I. iv. 53 '*Adios*,' Jake said. 'I'll be back sometime soon.' **1984** *N.Y. Times* 21 June B4/6 'Adios, amigo,' he said as the train arrived.

† **ˈadipal**, *a. Obs.*⁻⁰ [ad. L. *adipāl-is* greasy, f. *adip-em* fat.] 'Fat or gross.' Blount 1656.

† **ˈadipate**, *v. Obs.*⁻⁰ [f. L. *adipāt-us* fatty, greasy, f. *adip-em* fat.] 'To feed fat.' Cockeram 1626.

adipescent (ædɪˈpɛsənt), *a.* [f. L. *adip-em* fat + -ESCENT in imitation of ppl. adjs. f. inceptive vbs. as *adolescent, obsolescent.*] Becoming fatty.
1847 D. CRAIGIE *Elem. Anat.* VI. i. §2 (1848) 1032 The adipescent transformation of the organ.

adipic (əˈdɪpɪk), *a. Chem.* [f. L. *adip-em* fat + -IC.] In ***adipic acid***, $C_6H_{10}O_4$, a dibasic, diatomic acid, obtained by the oxidation of fats with nitric acid.
1877 FOWNES *Man. Chem.* II. 349.

adipocellulose (ˌædɪpəʊˈsɛljuːləʊs). [f. ADIPO(SE + CELLULOSE.] A compound of cellulose and suberin, as in cork tissue.
1888 MORLEY & MUIR *Watt's Dict. Chem.* I. 721/1 This view of its [cork's] constitution..is summed up in the group term Adipocellulose, by which it is proposed to designate them. **1895** C. F. CROSS et al. *Cellulose* II. 228 We..adopt the terms Suberose and Cutose for the compound adipo-celluloses. **1900** JACKSON *Gloss Bot. Terms* 6/1 *Adipocelluloses*, a group of bodies which constitute the cuticular tissues of leaves and fruits. **1937** E. J. LABARRE *Dict. Paper* 96/1 *Adipo-cellulose*, a compound so termed because on reduction it yields acids analogous to those obtained by the reduction of fats and cork tissue. The group embraces the cuticular tissue of such plants as straw, esparto and cotton.

adipocerate (ædɪˈpɒsəreɪt), *v. rare*⁻⁰. [f. ADIPOCERE + -ATE³ in imitation of *ulcerate.*] 'To convert into adipocere.' Craig 1847.

adipoceration (ædɪˌpɒsəˈreɪʃən). *rare*⁻⁰. [n. of action f. prec.] 'The process of changing into adipocere.' Craig 1847.

adipocere (ˈædɪpəʊˌsɪə(r)). Also **adipocire**. [a. Fr. *adipocire* (1787); f. L. *adip-em* fat + Fr. *cire*, L. *cēra* wax.] A greyish white fatty or saponaceous substance, chiefly *Margarate of Ammonia*, spontaneously generated in dead bodies buried in moist places or submerged in water; supposed to be produced by the reaction of ammonia upon the margarine and oleine of the animal fat and muscular fibre.
1803 NICHOLSON *Jrnl. Nat. Philos.* 135 This fluid [alcohol] when boiling, dissolves about its own weight of adipocire. **1836** TODD *Cycl. Anat. & Phys.* I. 56/1 Adipocere..is a soap composed of margaric acid and ammonia. **1877** ROBERTS *Handbk. Med.* (ed. 3) I. 63 The conversion of muscle into adipocere after death is a form of fatty degeneration.

adipoceriform (ˌædɪpəʊˈsɪərɪfɔːm), *a.* Having the form or appearance of adipocere.
1878 *Syd. Soc. Lex.* Adipoceriform tumours.

adipocerous (ædɪˈpɒsərəs), *a.* [f. prec. + -OUS.] Of the nature of adipocere.
c **1850** A. S. TAYLOR *Med. Jurisp.* (1873) I. vii. 129 The adipocerous state of the body could not have been brought about in less than six weeks. **1852** ROSS tr. *Humboldt's Trav.* II. xvi. 54 Sebaceous and adipocerous matter, capable of being used in the fabrication of soap.

adipose (ˌædɪˈpəʊs), *a.* and *sb.* [ad. mod.L. *adipōs-us* fatty; f. *adeps, adip-em* fat.]

A. *adj.* Of or pertaining to adeps, or animal fat; fatty. ***adipose fin***: a small, rayless, fleshy dorsal fin present in certain fishes, notably those of the salmon family. ***adipose tissue***: the vesicular structure in the animal body, which contains the fat.
1743 tr. *Heister's Surg.* 324 Encysted Tumours in the adipose Parts of the Neck. **1794** PALEY *Nat. Theol.* xi, The cellular or adipose membrane which lies immediately under the skin. **1804** G. SHAW *Gen. Zool.* V. I. 59 *Adipose fin small, pale, and tipped with brown. *c* **1854** CARPENTER *Man. Phys.* I. iii. (1856) 165 Adipose tissue is composed of isolated cells..which have the power of appropriating fatty matter from the blood. **1881** MIVART *Cat* 18 Fat, or adipose tissue, consists of round or oval vesicles containing an oily matter. **1887** F. DAY *Brit. & Irish Salmonidæ* 227 Three had a slight orange tinge on the adipose fin, and..a few red spots on the body. **1962** K. F. LAGLER et al. *Ichthyol.* vi. 183 In some fishes, such as the trouts and their relatives (Salmonidae;..), and the catfishes (Ictaluridae), one of the dorsal fins has no rays at all and is a fleshy structure termed an adipose fin. **1979** L. CACUTT *Brit. Freshwater Fishes* iv. 91 Here is another relative of the widespread salmon family, wearing that badge of fishy aristocracy, the adipose fin.

B. *sb.* [sc. substance.] The animal fat; the oil or fat which fills the vesicles of the adipose tissue; which in life is semifluid, but at death becomes solid, and is known as suet or tallow.
1865 A. L. ADAMS in *Intell. Observ.* No. 42, 435 The external adipose on the loins.

adiposeness (ˌædɪˈpəʊsnɪs). [f. prec. + -NESS.] The state of being fat; fatness.
1868 HELPS *Realmah* viii. (1876) 227 What are the component parts of adiposeness?

adiposis (ædɪˈpəʊsɪs). *Path.* [mod.L., f. L. *adip-*, *adeps* fat: see -OSIS.] Obesity or fatness of the body; fatty degeneration (of an organ).
1842 DUNGLISON *Med. Lex.* (ed. 3).

adiposity (ædɪˈpɒsɪtɪ). [f. mod.L. *adipōs-us* fat + -ITY.] Fatness; or tendency to fatness.
1859 LEWES *Phys. Com. Life* I. ii. 149 Vinegar helps to keep down an alarming adiposity. **1876** HARLEY *Mat. Med.* 320 Too free a use of sugar leads to adiposity.

adipous (ˈædɪpəs), *a.* [ad. Fr. *adipeux -euse* (16th c.).] Abounding in or characterized by fat; fat; fatty. (Less technical than ADIPOSE.)
1667 OLDENBURG in *Phil. Trans.* II. 553 Many Vessels, which may be call'd Adipous or Fatty. **1721** BAILEY, *Adipous*, Full of fat, greasy. [Also in ASH 1775, WEBSTER, etc.]

‖**aˈdipson.** *Med.* [Gr., neut. of ἄδιψος not thirsty, f. ἀ priv. + δίψα thirst.] A drink that allays thirst.
1651 N. BIGGS *New Disp.* §229, 166 A drink in the infancy of a feaver should be an *adipson.*

adipsous (əˈdɪpsəs), *a.* *Med.* [f. as prec. + -OUS.] Allaying thirst.
1879 *Syd. Soc. Lex.*

adipsy (ˈædɪpsɪ). *Med.* [f. as prec. + -Y³.] Absence of thirst.
WEBSTER cites DUNGLISON.

adistance (əˈdɪstəns), *adv.* prop. *phr.* [A *prep.*¹ + DISTANCE.] In or to a distance; afar.
1809 J. BARLOW *Columbiad* v. 275 A side-seen storm, adistance driven.

adit (ˈædɪt). Also 7 **adyt**, 7–8 **audit, addit.** [ad. L. *adit-us* approach, access; f. *ad* to + *itus* going, f. *īre* to go.]
1. An approach; *spec.* a horizontal opening by which a mine is entered, or drained.
1602 CAREW *Cornwall* 11 b, They cal it the bringing of an Addit or Audit when they begin to trench without, and carrie the same thorow the ground to the Tynworke, somewhat deeper then the water doth lie, thereby to giue it passage away. **1662** FULLER *Worthies* IV. 3 By Adyts, making their entrance..into the Mountain, at the lowest levell thereof. **1704** RAY *Creation* II. 251 It being impossible to make any Addits or Soughs to drain them. **1841** TRIMMER *Pract. Geol. & Min.* 237 Many of the beds of coal are worked by means of adits driven into the sides of the hills.
2. The action of approaching or coming to; access, entrance, approach.
1847 TENNYSON *Princess* VI. 283 Yourself and yours shall have free adit. **1859** HELPS *Friends in C.* Ser. II. II. ix. 186 Some means of adit to the imperial Executive.

†**aˈdition.** *Obs.*⁻⁰ [ad. L. *aditiōn-em* n. of action f. *adīre*, f. *ad* to + *īre* to go.] 'A going or coming nigh to.' Bailey 1731, whence in J. etc.

aditus (ˈædɪtəs). *Zool.* [L., lit. 'approach', f. *adīre*, f. *ad* to + *īre* to go.] An incurrent canal in a sponge. Hence **adital** (ˈædɪtəl) *a.*
1887 SOLLAS in *Encycl. Brit.* XXII. 415/1 The prosopyles ..may..be prolonged into..a *prosodus* or *aditus*... By the extension of the prosodal or adital canals..a still higher differentiation is reached.

Adivasi (ædɪˈvɑːsɪ), *sb.* (and *a.*) Also with small initial. [a. Hindi *ādivāsī* original inhabitant.] A member of the aboriginal tribal peoples of India. Also *attrib.* or as *adj.*
1941 A. V. THAKKAR *Probl. Aborigines in India* 2 We can ill afford to allow such a huge population as that of the Adivasis to remain any longer illiterate, ignorant and labouring under..abject poverty. **1955** [see MANCHU-TUNGUS]. **1967** *Economist* 9 Dec. 1060/1 They have to devote special attention to massive sections of the people, like Harijans (untouchables); Adivasis (tribals); [etc.]. **1979** *Times of India* 17 Aug. 5/6 The Union government has evolved a number of schemes for the development of fisheries, dairies and poultry in Adivasi areas in various parts of the country.

adj.¹, abbrev. of ADJECTIVE *a.* and *sb.*
1668 J. WILKINS *Ess. towards Real Character* II. xii. 295 *Filial* is the Adj. **1755** JOHNSON. **1836** RICHARDSON *Eng. Dict.* **1884** *N.E.D.* I. p. xxvi. **1903** 'T. COLLINS' *Such is Life* (1944) 44 When anybody calls him a Port Phillipper..he comes out straight: 'You're a (adj.) liar,' says he, 'I'm a Cornstalk, born in New South Wales.' **1953** H. C. WYLD *Hist. Mod. Colloq. Eng.* (ed. 3) ix. 325 The following additional examples of Pl. Adj. may be noted, all from Paston Letters—*certeins notables and resonables causes.* **1985** *Neuphilologische Mitteilungen* LXXXVI. 236 Transformational grammar..derives Adj + N from N—*is*—Adj but not vice versa.

Adj.² (ædʒ), colloq. abbrev. of ADJUTANT *sb.* 2.
1930 R. BLAKER *Medal without Bar* iv. 29 The Adj. [wants you]. He sent the office Corporal along in a great hurry. **1959** 'D. BUCKINGHAM' *Wind Tunnel* v. 37, I signed a 'blood chit' in the Adj.'s office, absolving everyone from blame if I broke my neck.

†**aˈdjacence.** *Obs. rare.* [f. late L. *adjacentia* (see ADJACENCY) as if through Fr.; see -NCE.] The state or condition of lying near.
1605 BACON *Adv. Learn.* II. 30 Their adiacence to forreine or vnlike bodies. **1652** URQUHART *Jewel* Wks. 1834, 270 The Latines' vicinity and neer adjacence to Rome. **1870** SMITH *Syn. & Antonyms, Contact..Ant.* Proximity, Adjacence.

adjacency (əˈdʒeɪsənsɪ). [ad. late L. *adjacentia*, n. of state f. *adjacent-em*: see ADJACENT. In med.L. the pl. *adjacentiae* was in common use for *'loca vicina'* dependencies.]
1. The quality or state of being adjacent, or of lying near; contiguity.
1805 B. MONTAGU tr. *Bacon's De Sap. Veter.* (1860) 217 Regard is justly had to contiguity, or adjacency, in private lands and possessions. **1858** DE QUINCEY *Autobiog. Sk.* Wks. II. 37 All great cities that ever were founded have sought out, as their first and elementary condition, the adjacency of some great cleansing river.
2. That which lies near. *pl.* Adjacent or contiguous places, environs, precincts, vicinity.
1646 SIR T. BROWNE *Pseud. Ep.* 64 At that point the needle conforms unto the true Meridian, and is not distract by the vicinity of Adjacencyes. **1726** DE FOE *Hist. Devil* (1822) 61 He pitches his grand army, or chief encampment, in our adjacencies, or frontiers. **1809** PINKNEY *Trav. France* 29, I returned to Calais, and was accompanied to the immediate adjacency by one of the parties. **1866** CARLYLE *E. Irving* 272 The Palais Royal and adjacencies.

adjacent (əˈdʒeɪsənt), *a.* and *sb.* [ad. L. *adjacent-em* pr. pple. of *adjacē-re* to lie near; f. *ad* to + *jacē-re* to lie. Cf. Fr. *adjacent*, 16th c. in Littré.]
A. *adj.*
1. Lying near or close (*to*); adjoining; contiguous, bordering. (Not necessarily *touching*, though this is by no means precluded.) ***adjacent angles***, the angles which one straight line makes with another upon which it stands. Also *fig.* in *Logic* of nearness in resemblance.
c **1430** LYDG. *Bochas* v. xiii. (1554) 132 a, There wer two cuntries therto adiacent. **1509** BARCLAY *Ship of Fooles* (1570) 104 [He] warred on other realmes adiacent. **1606** SHAKS. *Ant. & Cl.* II. ii. 218 A strange inuisible perfume hits the sense Of the adiacent Wharfes. **1663** GERBIER *Counsel* 6 The Houses adjacent, and those which are opposite. **1745** DE FOE *Eng. Tradesm.* XI. xxxiv. 72 Those parts of Essex, Surrey, and Kent, which lie adjacent to London. **1789–96** J. MORSE *Amer. Geog.* I. 302 The adjacent inhabitants had assembled in arms. **1827** HUTTON *Course of Math.* I. 317 The sum of the two adjacent angles DAC and DAB is equal to two right angles. **1846** MILL *Logic* III. xxi. §4 (1868) II. 108 With a reasonable degree of extension to adjacent cases. **1860** TYNDALL *Glaciers* I. §2. 20 Furnishing ourselves with provisions at the adjacent inn.
†**B.** *sb.* That which is adjacent, or lies next to anything; an adjoining part; a neighbour. *Obs.*
1610 HEALEY *St. Aug., City of God* 721 The LXX rather expressed the adjacents, then the place it selfe. **1635** SHELFORD *Disc.* 220 (T.) He hath no adjacent, no equal, no corrival. **1725** DE FOE *Voy. round World* (1840) 224 The whole place and its adjacents.

adjacently (əˈdʒeɪsəntlɪ), *adv. rare*⁻⁰. [f. prec. + -LY².] So as to lie near to, contiguously. Craig.

†**adject,** *ppl. a.* and *sb. Obs.* [ad. L. *adject-us* pa. pple. of *adjic-ĕre* to lay to; f. *ad* to + *jac-ĕre* to cause to lie, lay, throw.]
A. *ppl. a.* (æˈdʒɛkt). Annexed, joined; adjective.
1432–50 TREVISA *Higden* Rolls Ser. I. 195 By whiche chaunce that londe and see adiecte to hit toke hit name. **1612** BRINSLEY *Pos. Parts* (1669) 41 How is a Participle declined? With Number, Case, and Gender, as a Noun Adject.
B. *sb.* (ˈædʒɛkt). An addition, additament; added qualification.
1672 T. JACOMB *On Rom.* viii. (1868) 216 He is God..not a made god, a contradiction in the adject. **1677** GALE *Crt. of Gentiles* II. IV. 154 Doth it not implie a contradiction in the Adject, that man should make a right use of his natural abilities or prepare himself for the reception of supernatural grace?

adject (əˈdʒɛkt), *v.* [ad. L. *adjectā-re* to put to, add, freq. of *adjic-ĕre*, see prec.; thus having the appearance of being f. ADJECT *a.*] To annex, add, or join.
1432–50 TREVISA *Higden* Rolls Ser. I. 89 The foreseide Arsaces adiecte to his empyre the realme of Hircanes. **1538** LELAND *Itin.* III. 108 Sum Bisshop of Winchester renewed the old Fundation adjecting more Lande. **1662** FULLER *Worthies* xxiv. (1840) I. 93 They made the child's name by adjecting the syllable son to the appellation of the father. **1733** LINDSAY *Interest of Scotl.* 107 They adjected this Condition. **1832** J. AUSTIN *Lect. Jurisp.* lvi. (1879) II. 925 The law adjects to the title an element which is properly accidental.

†**aˈdjectament.** *Obs. rare*⁻¹. [ad. med.L. *adjectāment-um* that which is added; f. *adjectā-re*; see prec. and -MENT.] Anything thrown in by way of addition; an addition.
1630 NAUNTON *Fragm. Reg.* (1870) 44 Sir Christopher Hatton..besides the graces of his person and dancing, had also the adjectaments of a strong and subtill capacity.

adjected (əˈdʒɛktɪd), *ppl. a.* [f. ADJECT *v.* + -ED.] Added on, annexed, appended (*to*).
1538 LELAND *Itin.* III. 26 (R.) Removid from Cairmærdinshire, and adjected to Pembrokeshire. **1609** SKENE *Rej. Mag.* 55 Gif the donator fulfills not the condition adjected to the donation. **1727** WODROW *Corr.* (1843) III. 307 A debate about the adjected words *as to his Deity.* **1832** J. AUSTIN *Lect. Jurisp.* lvii. (1879) II. 935 Many remarks touching solemnities adjected to alienations apply *mutatis mutandis* to solemnities adjected to other titles.

adjectician (ædʒɛkˈtɪʃən), *a. Rom. Law.* [f. L. *adjectīci-us* = ADJECTITIOUS + -AN.] (See quot.)
1880 MUIRHEAD *Gaius* 448 *Adjectician actions*, The so-called *actiones adjecticiæ qualitatis*, praetorian actions against a *paterfamilias* in respect of debt contracted by a *filiusfamilias* or a slave.

†**aˈdjecting,** *vbl. sb. Obs.* [f. prec. + -ING¹.] Adding.
1639 DRUMM. OF HAWTH. *Wks.* 1711, 230 If it be asked whether adjecting or omitting be more to be tolerated? I answer, Adjecting.

adjection (əˈdʒɛkʃən). Also 4 **adieccioun.** [ad. L. *adjectiōn-em* addition, n. of action, f. *adjicĕre*; see ADJECT *ppl. a.*]
1. The action of adding, adding on, annexing or appending; addition.
c **1374** CHAUCER *Boethius* (1868) 176 þe propre nature of it ne makeþ it nauȝt. but þe adieccioun of þe condicioun makiþ it. **1598** B. JONSON *Ev. Man in Hum.* IV. viii. 5 Without adjection Of your assistance. **1664** H. MORE *Myst. Iniq.* 309 The adjection of this last part of the Interpretation is of special consequence. **1832** J. AUSTIN *Lect. Jurisp.* xxx. (1879) II. 567 Much of the positive law is custom turned into law by the adjection of the legal sanction.
†**2.** The result of adding on; that which is added; an addition. *Obs.*
1556 PONET *True Obed.* 19 (R.) This word [church] signifieth not euery congregaucion (but with an adiection, as I hate the malignant church). **1646** SIR T. BROWNE *Pseud. Ep.* 257 The fabulous adjections of succeeding ages, unto the veritable acts of this Martyr. **1691** RAY *Acc. of Errors* 163 Words formed from Verbs..by a syllabical Adjection. **1704** EARL CROMARTY in *Lond. Gaz.* mmmmxxxvii/4, I may justly fear what I can say, will prove a Diminutive Adjection.

adjectitious (ædʒɛkˈtɪʃəs), *a.* [f. L. *adjectīci-us*, f. *adjectus* (see ADJECT *a.*) + -OUS. See -ITIOUS.] Of the nature of adjection or addition; additional.
1652 URQUHART *Jewel* Wks. 1834, 200 Adjectitious syllabicals annexible to nouns and verbs. **1703** MAUNDRELL *Journ. Jerus.* (1732) 135 The adjectitious Buildings are of no mean Architecture.

adjectival (ædʒɛkˈtaɪvəl), *a.* (*sb.*) [f. L. *adjectīv-us*: see ADJECTIVE + -AL¹. (A modern formation to provide a more distinctly *adjective* or *adjectival* form to the word ADJECTIVE, this having become commonly a sb.)]
A. *adj.*
a. Of or belonging to the adjective.
1797 W. TAYLOR in *Month. Rev.* XXIV. 558 All the regular inflexions which bestow on it [a noun] a privative, an adjectival, or a verbal form. **1858** MARSH *Eng. Lang.* vi. 135 Our adjectival ending in *-ble.*
b. = ADJECTIVE *sb.* 1 b.
1910 H. G. WELLS *New Machiavelli* (1911) I. ii. 31 My mother would never learn not to attempt to break him of swearing..refusing to assist him to the adjectival towel he sought. **1932** D. L. SAYERS *Have his Carcase* viii. 92 The decease of a damned dago, hr'rm, in an adjectival four-by-three watering-place like Wilvercombe. **1959** G. MITCHELL *Man who grew Tomatoes* xiii. 167 Beresford told him to take his adjectival charity elsewhere.
c. Of writing style, etc.: abounding in adjectives, characterized by the free use of adjectives.
1928 *Sat. Rev.* 28 July 127/1 The style is too adjectival. **1965** *New Statesman* 22 Oct. 604/3 The intensely adjectival nature of her writing... Miss Murdoch is the most adjectival novelist ever.
B. as *sb.* An adjective or adjectival form; a phrase, clause, etc. having an adjectival function.
1870 J. H. TRUMBULL *Indian Geogr. Names* 39 The adjectivals employed in the composition of Algonkin names are very numerous. **1961** [see PRENOMINAL *a.* b]. **1964** S. JACOBSON *Adverbial Positions in Eng.* II. 205 No examples are given of..adverbs which are pure modifiers of adverbials, adjectivals, nominals, or functionals. **1972** HARTMANN & STORK *Dict. Lang. & Linguistics* 5/1 *Adjectival*, a name given by some grammarians to a structure which functions as an adjective or modifier,..but which cannot take the normal inflexions of an adjective.

adjectivally (ædʒɪkˈtaɪvəlɪ), *adv.* [f. ADJECTIVAL *a.* + -LY².] In an adjectival manner, as an adjective; + ADJECTIVELY *adv.*
1867 F. W. FARRAR *Greek Syntax* Introd.§38 The fact that substantives are frequently used adjectivally. **1928** E. G. R. WATERS *St. Brendan* p. cxcvi, The tonic forms of the possessive pronouns are frequently used adjectivally.

adjective (ˈædʒɛktɪv), *a.* [a. Fr. *adjectif, -ive*, ad. L. *adjectīv-us*, f. *adject-us*; see ADJECT *a.* and -IVE.]
A. *adj.* Of the nature of an addition or adjunct.
1. *Gram.* Naming or forming an adjunct to a noun substantive; added to or dependent on a substantive as an attribute. ***noun adjective***: a word standing for the name of an attribute, which being added to the name of a thing describes the thing more fully or definitely, as a *black* coat, a body *politic*; now usually called an *adjective* only, see B.
1414 DK. OF EXETER *to Henry IV* in Hall's *Chron.* (1809) 55 Scotland is like a noun adjective that cannot stand without a substantive. **1561** T. N[ORTON] *Calvin's Inst.* I.

xiii. (1634) 46 All other names of God [except Jehovah] are but adjective names of addition. **1612** BRINSLEY *Posing of Parts* (1669) 3 *Q.* How many sorts of Nouns have you? *A.* Two: a Noun Substantive, and a Noun Adjective.. A noun adjective is that cannot stand by itself, without the help of another word to be joyned with it to make it plain. **1875** WHITNEY *Life of Lang.* vi. 103 The variation of an adjective word for gender and number and case.

2. Hence, *gen.* Not standing by itself, dependent. Used *spec.* of colours that are not permanent without a basis.

1622 HEYLIN *Cosmogr.* III. (1682) 113 The People, the most Adjective of any that we have met with hitherto; able at no time to stand by themselves. *a* **1628** F. GREVILLE *Life of Sidney* (1652) 120 Our Modern Conquerors would craftily entice the Noun-adjective-natured Princes and subjects of this time to submit their necks. **1813** E. BANCROFT *Perm. Colours* I. II. i. 341 Adjective colours owe their durability, as well as their lustre, to the interposition of some earthy or metallic base. **1856** GROTE *Greece* XI. II. lxxxv. 257 The women were treated on both sides as adjective beings.

3. Of *Law*: Relating to procedure, the subsidiary part of law; opposed to *substantive*, relating to the essential justice of law.

1808 BENTHAM *Scotch. Ref.* 5 The system of procedure, or adjective branch of the law. **1870** *Daily News* 12 May, Law may be divided into Law and Procedure; Law Substantive and Law Adjective.

B. *sb.* [The adj. used *absol.*]

1. a. A 'Noun Adjective' (see A. 1.); one of the Parts of Speech.

1509 HAWES *Past. Pl.* v. x. A nowne substantyve Might stand wythout helpe of an adjectyve. **1597** BP. HALL *Satires* VI. i. In epithets to join two words in one. Forsooth, for adjectives can't stand alone. **1690** LOCKE *Hum. Underst.* III. viii. (1695) 267 Our simple Ideas have all abstract, as well as concrete Names: The one whereof is a Substantive, the other an Adjective; as Whiteness, White; Sweetness, Sweet. **1865** MARSH *Eng. Lang.* xiv. §11 The only striking peculiarity of the English adjective.. is its invariability, or want of distinct forms for different cases, genders and numbers.

b. Euphemistically substituted for an expletive adjective; usu. *attrib.*

1851 DICKENS in *Househ. Words* 14 June 270/1, I won't, says Bark, have no adjective police and adjective strangers in my adjective premises! I won't, by adjective and substantive! [**1888** KIPLING *Soldiers Three* (ed. 3, 1889) 66 They.. slept until it was cool enough to go out with their 'towny', whose vocabulary contained less than six hundred words, and the Adjective.] **1894** *Idler* Feb. 102 To know where the adjective blazes they are going. **1900** E. WELLS *Chestnuts* 29 Now.. we must have some (adjective) fun.

2. Hence, *gen.* That which cannot stand alone; a dependent; an accessory.

1639 FULLER *Holy War* v. xviii. (1840) 274 Subjects should be adjectives, not able to stand without their prince. **1658** OSBORN *King James* (1673) 516 Those Northern Adjectives, not able to subsist without England. **1801** FUSELI *Lect. on Art* ii. (1848) 394 In Parmigiano's figures action is the adjective of the posture.

3. *Comb.* or *Attrib.*, as ***adjective clause, phrase*** (*i.e.* one equivalent in function to an adj.), ***notion***, etc.

1860 ABP. THOMPSON *Laws of Thought* §26, 39 Every verb may be resolved into an adjective-notion; 'he loved' is explained by 'he was loving,' 'he hopes' by 'he is hoping.' **1881** WHITNEY *Mixt. in Lang.* 23 What is the relation of genitive-position in a given tongue to adjective-position?

adjective ('ædʒɛktɪv), *v.* [f. the adj.]

1. To make adjectival; to form or change into an adjective.

1659 *Instruct. Oratory* 27 The adjectiving of the Substantive, by adding *-s.* **1786** H. TOOKE *Purley* (1840) 650 Some languages have adjectived more; and some languages have adjectived fewer of these moods and Tenses.

2. To furnish with an adjective. Also *intr.* (*colloq.*) to use adjectives.

1804 *Med. & Physical Jrnl.* XII. 335 *Vaccine*, French, is from Latin:.. Milk is by Pliny adjectived with the word, *lac vaccinum.* **1871** EARLE *Philol. Eng. Tongue* 341 Clough took the liberty of thus adjectiving Lord Macaulay.. 'I have only detected one error myself, but it is a very Macaulayesque one'. **1920** *Sunday at Home* Apr. 423/2 In her place I think I should have 'adjectived' a good deal more.

adjectived ('ædʒɛktɪvd), *ppl. a.* [f. ADJECTIVE *v.* + -ED.] Made adjective; used as or turned into an adjective; qualified by an adjective or adjectives.

1786 H. TOOKE *Purley* (1798) 634 The sign, when thus adjectived, is not to be used by itself or to stand alone. **1892** 'H. S. MERRIMAN' *From one Generation to Another* xi, He paid for his pleasure in.. the adjectived items [i.e. 'ripping', 'topping'] of hospitality.

adjectively ('ædʒɛktɪvlɪ), *adv.* [f. ADJECTIVE *a.* + -LY².]

a. In an adjectival manner; after the manner of an adjective.

1548 W. THOMAS *Ital. Dict.* (1567) *Secondo, -a,* adiectively, sometimes do signifie the seconde in number. **1607** TOPSELL *Four-footed Beasts* (1673) 9 The Latins use them adjectively to signifie any angry, stubborn, froward, or ravening man. **1816** J. GILCHRIST *Philos. Etym.* 145 When *he* and *she* are used adjectively, as a *he-goat*, a *she-goat.* **1870** BOWEN *Logic* v. 145 Sometimes the Exclusive particles *only, one, sole*, etc., are annexed adjectively to the Predicate.

b. (Cf. ADJECTIVE *sb.* 1 b.)

1918 *Pilot* (Boston, U.S.) 9 Feb. 4/7 The effect of zero weather.. on the public.. is adjectively bad.

adjectiving ('ædʒɛktɪvɪŋ), *vbl. sb.* [f. ADJECTIVE *v.* + -ING¹.] The making or rendering adjectival.

1659 [See ADJECTIVE *v.* 1] **1786** H. TOOKE *Purley* (1840) 639 Such words.. would have been much better and more properly obtained by adjectiving our own words.

adjectivism ('ædʒɪktɪˌvɪz(ə)m). [f. ADJECTIVE *sb.* + -ISM.] The (excessive) use of adjectives.

1890 *Sat. Rev.* 5 Apr. 423/1 All our isms—Romanticism, Naturalism, Socialism, Æstheticism, Undogmaticism, Adjectivism. **1904** G. S. HALL *Adolescence* II. xvi. 467 Adjectivism, adverbism, and nounism, or marked disposition to multiply one or more of the above classes of words.

adjectivity (ædʒɪk'tɪvɪtɪ). [f. ADJECTIVE *sb.* + -ITY.] Addiction to the free use of adjectives.

1889 *Sat. Rev.* 5 Jan. 22/1 The adjectivity of his description. **1894** *Athenæum* 14 Apr. 469/1 Mrs. Ward.. has checked the reckless fluency of her 'adjectivity'.

adjectivize ('ædʒɪktɪˌvaɪz), *v.* [f. ADJECTIVE *sb.* + -IZE.] To make into an adjective. So **'adjectiˌvized** *ppl. a.*

1901 *Publ. Mod. Lang. Assoc. Amer.* XVI. 142 The completely adjectivized participle. **1949** E. A. NIDA *Morphology* (ed. 2) iv. 100 Derivational morphemes may.. adjectivize nouns, *truthful.*

adjoin (ə'dʒɔɪn), *v.* Forms: 4 **aioyne, ajoine**; 5–6 **adione, adjone**; 5–7 **adioyne, adjoyne**; 7– **adjoin.** [a. OFr. *ajoin-, ajoign-*, stem of *ajoindre*, mod. *adjoindre*:—L. *adjung-ĕre* to join to; f. *ad* to + *jung-ĕre* to join.]

†**1.** *trans. lit.* To join on; to join or unite (a person or thing *to* or *unto* another). *Obs.*

c **1325** [See ADJOINT, *pa. pple.*] *c* **1350** *Will. Palerne* 1753 The posterne of that perles erber þat was to meliors chaumber choisli a-ioyned. *c* **1400** *Destr. Troy* IV. 1135 Iason full iustly aioynet to my-seluon,.. Draw furthe in the derke. **1530** PALSGR. 417/2 If they be ones asondre, we shall have moche ado to adjoyne them. **1548** UDALL, etc. *Erasm. Paraphr. Matt.* i. 20 Adjoyne her unto the. **1602** SHAKS. *Haml.* III. iii. 20 A massie wheele.. To whose huge spoakes, ten thousand lesser things Are mortiz'd and adioyn'd. **1659** HAMMOND *On Ps.* cxviii. 27, 594 To them were adjoyned branches of trees.

2. *fig.* To join on as an adjunct or supplement; to add, annex, attach, or append; to subjoin. Const. *to, unto. arch.*

c **1400** *Destr. Troy* I. 292 A god.. þat ajoinet was Iobeter to his iuste nome. *a* **1509** in Ellis *Orig. Lett.* I. 23 I. 55 Police and wisdom is to be adjoyned to the Popes Holynesse in this behalve. **1594** J. KING *Jonah* (1864) 187 The epithet is very fitly adjoined to vanity. **1616** HAYWARD *Sanct. Troubled Soule* II. §11 (1620) 292 Thou wouldest adioyne our sins vnto thee. **1649** SELDEN *Laws of Eng.* I. xiv. (1739) 26 And so unto the Lay-power was the Ecclesiastical adjoined in this Work. **1724** WATTS *Logic* I. iv. §7 (1822) 75 I might adjoin another sort of equivocal words. **1865** *Daily Tel.* 6 Nov. 5/2 A secretary, with a handsome salary, is adjoined to the commissioners.

†**3.** *refl.* To adjoin *oneself to*: To join. *Obs.*

1533 BELLENDENE *Livy* II. (1822) 204 Cam ane huge multitude of Volschis and Equis, and adjonit thaim to the tentis of Sabinis. **1640** FULLER *Abel Rediv., Bucer* (1867) I. 179 He adjoined himself to the order of the Dominicans. **1656** JEANES *Fvlnesse of Christ* 45 Such Proselytes as adjoyned themselves thereunto.

†**4.** *intr.* (by suppression of refl. pron.) To join; to come into union or contact. Const. *to. Obs.*

c **1400** *Destr. Troy* II. 350 To this souerayne Citie þat yet was olofte Iason aioynid. *Ibid.* XXXII. 12782 This Egea ajoinet to hir iust spouse. **1484** CAXTON *Curial* 4 Hys tormentis adione to our lyf in such wyse that, etc. **1589** GREENE *Menaphon* (Arb.) 73 Maugre al the shepheards adjoining, he mounted her behind him. **1671** J. WEBSTER *Metallogr.* iv. 61 His censure upon it, and his own opinion adjoyned.

†**5.** *intr.* To be or lie close, or in contact; to be contiguous. Const. *to, on, with. Obs.*

1479 R. ROKEWOOD in *Bury Wills* (1850) 53 A mees called Pachette, and an other mees called Coles, adioynand togedyr in Euston. **1578** T. N., tr. *Conq. W. India* Pref. 3 Part of India, which adjoyneth with Brazil. **1652** C. STAPYLTON *Herodian* 61 The Roman Empire to defend and hold Against the Barb'rous people that adjoyne. **1725** POPE *Odyssey* VI. 317 Close to the bay great Neptune's fane adjoins. **1794** S. WILLIAMS *Hist. Vermont* 242 The towns in Vermont which adjoined to Connecticut river.

6. *trans.* (by omission of *to*) To be contiguous to or in contact with.

1745[See under ADJOINING 1 b.] **1817** JAS. MILL *Brit. India* II. v. iv. 430 The Mahrattas would in that case immediately adjoin Carnatic. **1870** WILSON *Churches of Lindisf.* 76 The head of the tomb adjoins the west wall.

7. *Math.* (See quot. 1903 and cf. ADJUNCTION 3 a.)

1903 L. E. DICKSON *Theory Algebraic Equations* vi. 62 In the language of Galois.. we derive the domain R¹ = (1, i) from the included domain R = (1) by *adjoining* the quantity i to the domain R. **1904** [see ADJUNCTION 3 a].

¶ Used also for ENJOIN. [See A- *pref.* 10.]

c **1400** *Destr. Troy* VI. 2197 I Aioyne thee this iorney with ioy for to take. **1590** A. MUNDAY in *Harl. Misc.* (Malh.) II. 180, I am adioyned such a penaunce.

†**a'djoinant**, *ppl. a.* and *sb. Obs.* Also **adioynaunt, adioynant.** [a. OFr. *ajoinant*, MFr. *adjoinant* (mod.Fr. *adjoignant*), pr. pple. of *adjoindre*. See ADJOIN.]

A. *ppl. adj.* Adjoining; lying next; contiguous.

1494 FABYAN v. cxviii. 94 Assautis vpon yᵉ Saxons nexte to hym adioynaunt. **1557** T. PHAER *Æneid* VII. S iij, Along dame Circes coast adioynant next their course they cut. **1602** CAREW *Cornwall* 116 a, To the town there is adjoynant in site,.. an ancient Castle.

B. *sb.* One living close by; a near neighbour.

1548 HALL *Chron.* (1809) 186 To greve and hurte his Neighbors and Adjoynauntes of the realme of Englande.

†**a'djoinate**, *ppl. a. Obs. rare*⁻¹. [f. ADJOIN *v.* after ppl. adjs. in -ATE from L.] Joined, allied.

1470 HARDING *Chron.* cxlvii. His brother Edward and he associate To Ierusalem their voiage then auowed, Two semely princes together adioynate [*v.r.* adunate].

†**a'djoinder.** *Obs. rare*⁻¹. [a. Fr. *adjoindre* vb. inf. (see ADJOIN) used subst. Cf. *rejoinder.*] Something joined to; an addition or appendix.

1604 PARSONS *Three Conversions* Contents, The third Tome.. hath for his adioinder in the end A review of Ten publike Disputations.

adjoined (ə'dʒɔɪnd), *ppl. a.* [f. ADJOIN *v.* + -ED.]

†**1.** *lit.* Joined, united. Const. *to, unto. Obs.*

1509 FISHER *Wks.* 300 The Soule of this noble prynces, whiche had the Body adioyned vnto it.. as Syster and Brother. **1622** MALYNES *Anc. Law-Merch.* 12 There was added 11 daies called *Æpactæ*, as adioyned daies. **1695** ALINGHAM *Geom. Epit.* 11 The Angle *ABD* contained under the adjoined lines *BA, BD.*

2. *fig.* Joined as an adjunct, added, annexed, attached; appended or subjoined. Const. *to. arch.*

1528 MORE *Heresyes* I. Wks. 1557, 148/1 Ther must be none errour adioyned therto. **1684** BAXTER *Cath. Comm.* 37 Davids Lies are recorded without adjoyned reproof.

†**a'djoinedly**, *adv. Obs.* [f. prec. + -LY².] Unitedly; by way of union or conjunction.

1721 STRYPE *Eccl. Mem.* I. xxiv. (R.) They have adjoinedly, naturally, corporally, and really, the true body and blood of Christ.

†**a'djoiner.** *Obs. rare*⁻¹. [f. ADJOIN *v.* + -ER¹.] He who, or that which, adjoins or lies next; a neighbour.

1627–8 FELTHAM *Resolves* (1647) 298 The giddy ayrinesse of the French, I shall rather impute to their dyet of wine, and wilde foule, than to the difference of their clyme, it being so near an adjoyner to ours.

adjoining (ə'dʒɔɪnɪŋ), *ppl. a.* [f. ADJOIN + -ING².]

1. a. Lying next, contiguous, adjacent; neighbouring.

1494 FABYAN VI. cc. 208 Other countrees adioynynge dyd the same. **1794** SULLIVAN *View of Nat.* I. 291 The seas, forests, and adjoining mountains. **1849** MACAULAY *Hist. Eng.* II. 506 To step aside into some adjoining room.

b. with const. of the vb. See ADJOIN 5, 6.

1523 FITZHERBERT *Husb.* (1534) E 4 Adioynynge to the ende of the same, make an other lyttell folde. *a* **1593** MARLOWE *Dido* I. i. 374 The land.. Adjoining on Agenor's stately town. **1606** SHAKS. *Ant. & Cl.* IV. x. 5 Our Foote Vpon the hilles adioining to the Citty, Shall stay with vs. **1667** E. CHAMBERLAYNE *St. Gt. Brit.* I. I. iii. (1743) 6 Eton, a village adjoining to Windsor. **1745** in *Col. Rec. Penn.* V. 29 Who had Lands adjoining the Road. **1864** D. MITCHELL *Wet Days* 62 Adjoining this is a tower.

2. *fig.* Pertaining, belonging; connected.

1494 FABYAN I. iv. 11 With also the Commodities therunto adioynynge. **1603** HOLLAND *Plutarch's Mor.* 28 The words and sentences either adjoyning, or intermingled with those speeches. **1869** BUCKLE *Civilis.* III. v. 417 Considerations, which are to be taken partly from the adjoining sciences.

†**adjoint**, *pa. pple.* and *sb.*¹ *Obs.* Also 4 **anioynt.** [a. OFr. *ajoint*:—L. *adjunct-um* ADJUNCT.]

A. *pple.* Adjoined, united.

c **1325** *E.E. Allit. Poems* A. 894 And to the gentyl lombe hit arn anioynt [*ed.* amoynt].

B. *sb.* [The pple. used subst.] A helper, aider; an adjunct, addition.

1597 DANIEL *Civ. Wares* IV. lxix, Here with these grave Adjoynts (Then learned Maisters) they were taught to see Themselves. **1639** H. AINSWORTH *On Pentat., Lev.* xiii. 1, 66 *Sapachath* is an adjoynt to the swelling, and an adjoynt to the Bright-spot. *c* **1700** *Gentlem. Instr.* (1732) 108 You are, Madam, I perceive, said he, a publick Minister, and this Lady is your Adjoint.

adjoint ('ædʒɔɪnt), *sb.*² and *a.* [mod.Fr. *adjoint*, pa. pple. of *adjoindre* to ADJOIN, used as an appellative. Mod.Fr. form of prec.]

‖**A.** *sb.*² (with pronunc. adʒwɛ̃). Official title of a French civil officer who assists the maire; also, an assistant professor in a French college.

1835 *Blackw. Mag.* XXXVIII. 19 The lower professors or *adjoints* cannot, in one instance out of twenty, rise above their actual position. **1864** SALA in *Daily Tel.* 16 Aug., Halting to exchange official commonplaces with.. the adjoint of the mayor. **1865** *Pall Mall G.* 6 Nov. 10, Arab adjoints are to be associated with European mayors in towns and villages.

2. *Math.* An adjoint matrix, equation, etc.

1889 T. CRAIG *Treat. Linear Differential Equations* I. xiii. 471 When Chapter I was written.. I had not seen Forsyth's memoir, and had not been able to find an adopted English term for Lagrange's '*équation adjointe*', so I used the word *adjunct*, suggested by the German '*adjungirte*', and not unlike the French '*adjointe*'. It seems better now, however, to employ the word *associate*, or, when speaking simply of Lagrange's '*équation adjointe*', the word *adjoint*. *Ibid.* 483 The adjoint of the quantic *S*. **1902** A. R. Forsyth *Theory Differential Equations* IV. vi. 253 It is clear that $wp(v)$ is a perfect differential if $P(w) = 0$, shewing that the original equation is the adjoint of the Lagrangian derived equation. **1907** M. Bôcher *Introd. Higher Algebra* vi. 77 By the adjoint A of a matrix **a** is understood another matrix of the same order in which the element in the ith row and jth column is the cofactor of the element in the jth row and ith column of **a**. **1942** R. P. Agnew *Differential Equations* xii. 254 If *L* denotes the operator $L = a_0D^2 + a_1D + a_2$, then the adjoint (or adjoint operator) is $L^* = \bar{a}_0D^2 + (2\bar{a}_0' - \bar{a}_1')D + (\bar{a}_0'' - \bar{a}_1' + \bar{a}_2)$. **1972** M. Kline *Math. Thought* xxxix. 936 The integrals are of the form $\int \frac{\phi(x, y)}{\partial f/\partial y \; dx}$ where ϕ is a polynomial (an adjoint) of .. the degree $n - 3$. **1976** M. A. Morrison et al. *Quantum States* vi. 153 These matrix elements are defined by simple matrix multiplication—for example, $\langle\chi_1 S^2 \chi'\rangle \equiv \chi^\dagger S^2 \chi'$, where the row vector χ' is the adjoint of χ, the complex conjugate of the transpose of χ. **1980** A. J. Jones *Game Theory* iii. 145 If we define the adjoint of *M* by $\text{adj}M = (A_{ji})^T$ if $r > 1$, $\text{adj}M = 1$ if $r = 1$, then for all square matrices *M* we have $M\text{adj}M = (\det M)I$, where *I* is the identity matrix.

B. *adj.* *Math.* Of a matrix: equal to the transpose of the cofactors (or in quantum mechanics, of the complex conjugate) of a given square matrix. Of a differential equation: related to a given differential equation in such a way that its solutions are integrating factors and its integrating factors solutions of the given equation. Of a transformation or operator: (see quot. 1959). Generally, pertaining to adjoint quantities or their relationships.

1889 T. Craig *Treat. Linear Differential Equations* I. xiii. 478 The typical variable of the set is the variable of the Lagrangian adjoint equation. *Ibid.* 482 Suppose the quantics .. to be adjoint. **1902** A. R. Forsyth *Theory Differential Equations* IV. vi. 253 The two equations are reciprocally adjoint to one another. **1923** J. Hadamard *Lect. Cauchy's Probl.* ii. 59 The relation between two adjoint polynomials is a reciprocal one. **1937** E. C. Kemble *Fund. Princ. Quantum Mech.* x. 350 We define the adjoint matrix to A as a matrix obtained .. by replacing each element by its conjugate complex quantity and then interchanging rows and columns. We denote the adjoint of A by $A^\dagger$. *Ibid.* 353 The matrix of the operator adjoint to α is readily seen to be the adjoint $\alpha^\dagger$ of the matrix α. **1942** R. P. Agnew *Differential Equations* xii. 254 Prove that the adjoint of the adjoint of the operator *L* .. is *L* itself. **1959** G. & R. C. James *Math. Dict.* 6/1 Two linear transformations T_1 and T_2 are said to be adjoint if $(T_1x, y) = (x, T_2y)$ for any *x* in the domain of T_1 and *y* in the domain of T_2. **1978** *Nature* 19 Oct. 643/1 According to Pontryagin's maximum principle, (1) can be minimised by maximising the hamiltonian $H(c, t) = -[\alpha s^2(t) + \beta\delta c^3(t) + \gamma c(t)p(t)]$ with unknown adjoint variable $p(t)$. **1984** S. L. Ross *Differential Equations* xi. 574 The special situation in which the adjoint equation .. of Equation (11.110) is also Equation (11.110) itself.

adjourn (ə'dʒɜːn), *v.* Forms: 4 aiorne, 4–6 aiourne, 5–6 ajourn(e, 6 adiorn(e, 6– adjourn. [a. OFr. *ajorne-r*, *ajurne-r*, *ajourne-r*:—late L. *adiurnā-re*, *adjurnā-re* 'diem dicere alicui,' Ducange, f. *ad* to + late L. *jurnus*, *jornus* (cf. It. *giorno*, Pr. *jorn*, Fr. *jour*) a day:—cl. L. *diurn-us* daily, lasting for a day: see journal. The occasional MFr. *ad-* for *a-*, rejected in mod.Fr., has been retained in Eng. since 6.]

†**1.** *trans.* To appoint (one) a day for his appearance; to cite or summon for a particular day; to remand (one) for justice to another day or occasion. *Obs.*

1330 R. Brunne *Chron.* 309 He aiorned þam to relie in þe North at Carlele. *c*1360 Chaucer *A.B.C.* 158 Ladi, vn to þat court þou me aiourne þat cleped is þi bench. **1530** Palsgr. 419/2, I adjourne, I monisshe or warne one to apere afore a judge at a daye certayne: *Je semons*. I am adjourned by the bysshops offycers. **1600** Holland *Livy* xlii. xxii. 1128 The Pretour .. adjourned [*jussit*] the defendant to make appearance in the court upon the Ides of March. **1660** Howell, To Adjourn, or Cite to Apeer, *citare*, *appellare*.

2. To defer or put off (a time, action, or state), *prop.* to another day; also indefinitely; to postpone, defer, put off.

1430 Lydg. *Chron. Troy* v. xxxvi, For they them caste the time not aiourne, For daye and nighte with her they soiourne. **1559** *Myrroure for Mag.*, *Suffolk* xxii. 4 Fro place to place to adiourne it divers times. **1589** Warner *Albion's Eng.* vi. xxxi. (1612) 152 My Deitie adiornde therefore, in humaine forme I wowe. **1600** Chapman *Iliad* xvi. 74 No more let them ajourn Our sweet home-turning. **1725** Pope *Odyssey* xii. 33 This day adjourn your cares. **1847** Bushnell *Chr. Nurt.* iv. (1861) 102 Every law of physiology must be adjourned. **1861** Emerson *Cond. Life* ii. 50, I adjourn what I have to say on this topic.

3. To adjourn (a meeting): To put off or defer its further proceedings to another day; to discontinue or dissolve it, in order to reconstitute it at another time or place.

1494 Fabyan an. 1433 (R.) Parlyament .. was aiourned onto Seynt Edwardes day. **1613** Shaks. *Hen. VIII*, ii. iv. 232 'Tis a needfull fitnesse That we adiourne this Court till further day. **1741** Middleton *Cicero* (1742) II. vi. 6 The Consul .. immediately adjourned the Senate into the Capitol. **1880** W. MacCormac *Antis. Surgery* 71 The meeting .. was adjourned for a fortnight.

†**4.** *refl.* (as in 5). *Obs.*

*a*1626 Bacon *Adv. to Villiers* (R.) By [the king] alone are they prorogued and dissolved; but each house may adjourn itself. **1641** in Rushworth's *Hist. Coll.* iii. (1692) I. 496 The Lords and Commons may Adjourn themselves to any place. **1669–70** Marvell *Corr.* 134 Wks. 1875 II. 300 The House .. then adjourned themselves till Thursday.

5. *intr.* (from *refl.*) Of persons met for business: To suspend proceedings and disperse for a time agreed upon, or *sine die*, that is, without specifying any day for reassembling. Also, to separate in order to meet at another *place*; hence *fam.* to remove the place of meeting, without the intervention of any time save that occupied by the change of place.

1641 in Rushworth's *Hist. Coll.* iii. (1692) I. 496 Touching the Houses Adjourning to any other place at their pleasure. **1718** Pope *Iliad* xix. 289 The speedy council at his word adjourn'd. **1781** Gibbon *Decl. & F.* III. xlviii. 25 From the church the people adjourned to the hippodrome. *c*1815 Miss Austen, *Northang. Ab.* (1833) I. xv. 94 They thence adjourned to eat ice at a pastry-cook's.

†**a'djournal.** *Obs.* [f. prec. + -al[2].] Adjournment, respite, or postponement (of a sentence).

1609 Skene *Reg. Maj.* 171 Ane act is made in court, quhereby he and his cautioner are oblished to assith and satisfie the partie within the space foresaid, quhilk is called ane act of Adjournall. **1620** Sanderson *35 Serm.* (1681) I. 149 The removal or adjournal of temporal punishments, which otherwise had speedily overtaken them. **1829** Scott *Hrt. Midl.* i. 16 In the State Trials, or in the Books of Adjournal.

adjourned (ə'dʒɜːnd), *ppl. a.* [f. adjourn + -ed.]

†**1.** Cited, *prop.* for a fixed day; summoned. *Obs.*

1577 Fenton *Guicciardin* xviii. (1599) 832 Such as were absent .. were adiorned, and taxed at rates to nourish the armie. **1608** Sylvester *Dubartas* 243 Wolves and panthers waxing meek and tame, .. Adjourned by Heaven, did in my presence com.

2. Deferred, postponed; held over to another time.

1699 Dryden *Palam. & Arcite* iii. 188 The day To distance driven, and joy adjourn'd with long delay. **1876** Freeman *Norm. Conq.* II. vii. 147 Let the meeting stand adjourned.

adjourner (ə'dʒɜːnə(r)). [f. adjourn *v.* + -er[1].] One who adjourns or is in favor of an adjournment.

1893 *Columbus* (Ohio) *Even Disp.* 24 Aug., The weakening among Senators .. upon which .. the confidence of the early adjourners is based. **1893** *Westm. Gaz.* 25 Nov. 7/2 There were only 44 adjourners, while 142 members preferred to proceed with the .. business.

adjourning (ə'dʒɜːnɪŋ), *vbl. sb.* [f. adjourn + -ing[1].] A putting off to another time or place, adjournment. (Now mostly gerundial.)

1641 [See under adjourn 5.] *Mod.* They talk of adjourning the meeting till tomorrow.

adjournment (ə'dʒɜːnmənt). [a. MFr. *adjournement*:—OFr. *ajornement*; see adjourn and -ment.]

1. The act of adjourning, or of putting off till another day, or indefinitely.

1641 *Termes de la Ley* 11 Adjournement, is when any Court is dissolved and determined, and assigned to be kept againe at another place or time. **1762** Hume *Hist. Eng.* (1806) IV. lxv. 789 The parliament met, according to adjournment. **1875** Stubbs *Const. Hist.* III. xx. 480 The distinction between adjournment and prorogation, in so far as the one belongs to the houses and the other to the crown, is a modern distinction.

2. The state of being adjourned; the interval during which the business of an assembly is formally deferred.

1670 in Somers's *Tracts* I. 28 During one Day's Adjournment made by the House. **1875** Stubbs *Const. Hist.* II. xiv. 126 A day's adjournment was granted.

3. Special Comb. **adjournment debate**: in the House of Commons, a debate on the motion that the House be adjourned, *spec.* one used as an opportunity for raising other matters (except those requiring legislation); also **adjournment motion**.

1944 D. C. Brown in *Hansard Commons* 28 Nov. 2403, I have been thinking about the arrangements now in operation for the half-hour *Adjournment Debate. **1984** *Financial Times* 16 May 6 The Commons debate on Hong Kong today is likely to be a low-key affair. It is to be an adjournment debate, so a vote is most unlikely. **1933** E. L. Spears in *Hansard Commons* 26 July 2598 May I give notice that I will raise the question on the *Adjournment Motion on Friday? **1984** J. Archer *First among Equals* xxx. 360 The Speaker called the Secretary of State for Wales to move the adjournment motion on the problems facing the Welsh mining industry.

†**a'djoust**, *v.* *Obs.* Also 5 aiust, 6 adjust. [a. MFr. *adjoust-er* (mod. *ajouter*), OFr. *ajouster*, *ajoster*, *ajuster* to place beside; in 14th c. to add:—late L. *adjuxtā-re* = *approximāre*, f. *ad* to + *juxtā* hard by, close to. Occ. written *adjust* either in imitation of one of the OFr. spellings, or of med.L. *adjustāre*, formed on Fr. *ajouster*, *ajuster*, under the false idea that these were f. *ad* and *jūstum*; but to be distinguished from the modern adjust, q.v.]

1. To put a thing (to one) for consideration; to bring forward, suggest.

*c*1374 Chaucer *Boethius* ii. (R.) (? ed. 1561) For whan time is I shal moue and aiust soch things, that percen hem ful depe. [*The words* and aiust *are not in ed. Morris E.E.T.S.* 43.] *a*1521 *Helyas* in Thoms' *E.E.P. Rom.* (1858) III. 90 She never proponed it, but myselfe adjusted it to her.

2. To put one thing to another, to add. *Esp.* in *adjouste feyth*, OFr. *ajouster fey* to give faith or credence.

[From the Palsgrave quot. it appears that *adjoust* was obs. in 1530. See adjute, which seems to be a readoption of the word from Fr. *adjouter*.]

1474 Caxton *Chesse* iv. viii. I6 He adjousted wyth al that he had founden thys game. **1483** —— *Cato* c viij, Man ought not to beleue no adjouste feyth to the sayeng of many one. —— *Gold. Leg.* 316/4 Adjoustyng woodenes to wodenes. **1484** —— *Chyualry* 88 They adiouste feyth to deuynours. **1484–5** —— *Curial* 1 Thou adioustest other causes that meve the therto. **1530** Palsgr. 417/2, I adjoust or joyne togyther, *Je adjouste* .. and this terme is not yet used [*i.e.* no longer] in our comen speche though Lydgate have it ofte tymes.

adjudge (ə'dʒʌdʒ), *v.* Forms: 4–5 aiuge, aiugge, 5 adiuge, 6 ajudge, 6– adjudge. [a. OFr. *ajuge-r*, earlier *ajugier* (mod. *adjuger*):—L. *adjūdicā-re*: see adjudicate. The *a-* was refashioned as *ad-* in Fr. in 14th c.; the *d* was still mute in Fr. in 16th c., but has been fixed in mod.Fr., and in Eng. since Caxton.]

1. *trans.* To settle, determine, or decide, judicially; to adjudicate upon.

*c*1374 Chaucer *Boethius* i. iv. 325 (1868) þe peyne of þe accusacioun aiuged byforn. **1628** Coke *on Littleton* i. i. §11 (1633) 18/1 And so was it adiudged in the Court of Common Pleas. **1664** Butler *Hudibr.* ii. ii. 346 Will not Fear, Favour, Bribe and Grudge The same case several ways adjudge. **1775** Burke *Sp. Conc. Amer.* Wks. III. 107 When their removal shall be adjudged by his majesty in council. **1850** Gladstone *Gleanings* V. lxxvii. 218 A right to govern, to decide, to adjudge, for spiritual purposes. **1861** Stanley *East. Ch.* ii. (1869) 78 The differences which it was called to adjudge.

2. To pronounce or decree by judicial sentence (a thing *to be*, or *that* it is so and so).

1563 Grafton *Hen. II*, an. 9 His moveables were adiudged to be confiscate to the king. **1582** N. T. (Rhem.) *Luke* xxiii. 24 And Pilate adiudging their petition to be done. **1630** Prynne *Anti-Armin.* 101 Wee may .. adiudge it to be the Doctrine of our English Church. **1660** H. Finch *Trial of Regic.* 10 This was adjudged horrid Treason by two Acts of Parliament. **1662** Fuller *Worthies* (1840) II. 468 The king's grant was adjudged void. **1846** Hawthorne *Mosses* ii. iii. (1864) 68 And almost adjudged himself a criminal. **1852** Miss Yonge *Cameos* II. xx. 216 It was adjudged that the handsome knight must abide by his own terms.

†**3.** To determine in one's own judgment; to deem, consider, reckon, regard, or judge (a thing *to be*, or *that* it is so and so). *Obs.*

*c*1400 *Destr. Troy* viii. 3718 The gentils aiuges hom two iuste goddis. *Ibid.* x. 4271 Gentils aiugget, & for iuste held, þat in þat bare yle bothe borne were þai first. **1494** Fabyan vii. ccxlvi. 289 A great comete or blasyng starre, the whiche the Frenshe men, with also the foresayde eclypce, adiudged for pronostiquykys & tokens of the Kynges deth. **1548** Geste *Priuee Masse* 72, I adjudge it a present worthy your worship. **1564** Haward *Eutrop.* ix. 99 Divers adjudged that he was a scrivener's sonne. **1644** Heylin *Laud* ii. 387 An impossible design, .. as some .. did adjudge. **1719** *Col. Rec. Penn.* III. 68 It was adjudged Convenient to Defer the Consideracon of that address. **1729** Burkitt *N.T.*, *Matt.* xxvi. 7 Nothing is adjudged too dear for Christ.

†**4.** To try judicially, judge, pass sentence on. *Obs.*

1509 Hawes *Past. Pleas.* xi. viii, That the comon wyt. Maye well a judge the perfyt veritie Of theyr sentence. **1605** Camden *Rem.* 5 The Archbishops of Canterbury .. were adiudged by the Popes. **1623** Sanderson *Serm.* Ad. Mag. iii. (1674) 122 When they had been convicted in a fair trial, .. then to have adjudged them according to the Law. **1659** Hammond *On Ps.* i. 6, 6 They shall all be severely adjudged by him.

5. To sentence or condemn (any one *to* a penalty, or *to do* or *suffer* something).

*c*1400 *Destr. Troy* xxxiii. 13031 Engest he adiuget, .. Nakid thro the noble toune onone to be drawen. **1548** Udall, etc. *Erasm. Paraphr. Luke* Prol. 14 He shal bee adjudged .. to the tormentes of the diepe pitte of hell. *c*1555 R. Lindsay *Hist. Scotl.* (1728) 189 The Cardinal and prelates .. condemned him of heresy, and adjudged him to be burnt. **1638** *Penit. Conf.* vii. (1657) 131 Quoth the Pope, I am adjudged to eternal death. **1660** H. Finch *Trial of Regic.* Here lies Thomas Scot, who adjudged to death the late King. **1756** Burke *Vind. Nat. Soc.* Wks. 1842 I. 18 Sending me from the court to a prison, and adjudging my family to beggary and famine. **1878** P. Bayne *Pur. Rev.* v. 205 By a company of Puritan soldiers, .. Charles was adjudged to die.

6. To award judicially; to grant, bestow, or impose by judicial sentence (a thing *to* or *unto* a person).

1494 Fabyan vii. 319 That he wolde be obedyent vnto the court of Rome, and stand and obey all thyng yt the same court woll adiuge hym. **1588** Shaks. *Tit. A.* v. iii. 144 Hither hale that misbelieving Moore, To be adiudg'd some direfull slaughtering death. **1649** Selden *Laws of Eng.* ii. xxvii. (1739) 119 Both parts carry themselves so cunningly, as it is hard to adjudge the Garland. **1774** Bryant *Mythol.* I. 101 The battle .. was fought at Gaugamela .. It is also adjudged to Arbela. **1789–96** J. Morse *Amer. Geog.* I. 437 Adjudging and conferring degrees. **1837** Whewell *Hist. Induct. Sc.* (1857) I. 333 The umpire who was to adjudge the prize.

1855 Prescott *Philip II*, I. i. i. 3 The great prize of the empire was adjudged to Charles.

adjudged (əˈdʒʌdʒd), *ppl. a.* [f. prec. + -ED.]

1. Determined, decided, or settled judicially.

c **1374** [See ADJUDGE 1.] **1737** Waterland *Euchar.* 3 The Reports, Precedents, and adjudged Cases are allowed to be of considerable Weight for determining Points of Law. **1742** Fielding *Jos. Andr.* II. iii. (1815) 49 It is an adjudged case and I have known it tried. **1827** Hallam *Const. Hist.* (1876) III. xv. 157 Our law is mainly built on adjudged precedent.

†**2.** Judged, deemed, regarded, held. *Obs.*

c **1440** *Morte Arthure* (Hall) 73 The gentileste jowelle ajuggede with lordes. **1608** Hieron *Wks.* I. Qqq [689] They are aiudged to be a kind of confining and limiting of God's Spirit.

3. Sentenced, doomed.

1590 Shaks. *Com. Err.* I. i. 147 Thou art adiudged to the death, And passed sentence may not be recal'd. **1671** Milton *Samson* 286 Without reprieve adjudged to death, For want of well pronouncing Shibboleth.

4. Awarded judicially. See ADJUDICATION 4.

1799 J. Robertson *Agric. Perth* 433 If..the lease be forfeited or adjudged any time before the last years of the contract.

adjudger (əˈdʒʌdʒə(r)). [f. ADJUDGE + -ER[1].] One who awards or gives judicially; an awarder.

1832-4 De Quincey *Cæsars*, Wks. 1862 IX. 99 The fabulous adjudgers of future punishments.

adjudging (əˈdʒʌdʒɪŋ), *vbl. sb.* [f. ADJUDGE + -ING[1].] The action of deciding judicially, sentencing, decreeing, or awarding. (Now mostly gerundial.)

1689 *Myst. Iniq.* 24 We had a new Court of Inquisition erected for the adjudging and punishing of them. **1734** tr. *Rollin's Anc. Hist.* (1827) I. 151 The adjudging the prize of glory to him. *Mod.* In adjudging him the victor.

adjudgment (əˈdʒʌdʒmɛnt). Also **adjudgement** in J. [f. ADJUDGE *v.* + -MENT.] The act of adjudging, adjudication; a decree, judicial sentence, or award.

1699 Sir W. Temple *Introd. Hist. Eng.* (R.) The adjudgment..came to be given by one or two, or more persons. **1723** Le Neve *Lives of Abps.* I. 242 (T.) The right of presentation was adjudged for the King..and such adjudgement was afterwards confirmed by the house of Lords. **1820** Foster *Evils of Pop. Ignor.* 62 Numbers of that community, having conspired to obtain this adjudgment.

adjudicate (əˈdʒ(j)uːdɪkeɪt), *v.* [f. L. *adjūdicāt-* ppl. stem of *adjūdicā-re*, 1. to award, 2. to give sentence; f. *ad* to + *jūdicā-re* to JUDGE.]

†**1.** *trans.* To adjudge; to award; 'to give something controverted to one of the litigants, by a sentence or decision.' J. *Obs.*

1700 [See ADJUDICATING 1.] **1731** In Bailey vol. II, whence in Johnson.

2. *trans.* To try and determine judicially; to pronounce by sentence of court.

1775 Ash, *Adjudicate, v. tr.* To determine any claim in Law. **1859** J. Lang. *Wander. India* 53 He had been called upon to adjudicate the affair in a court of justice. **1864** C. Clerk in *Morn. Star* 2 Feb., Instead of nations adjudicating their prizes in their own courts, they should be allowed to carry them for adjudication into the courts of neutrals. **1870** *Echo* 10 Nov., [He] was adjudicated a bankrupt yesterday by Mr. Spring Rice.

3. *intr.* To sit in judgment and pronounce sentence; to act as a judge, or court of judgment.

1840 Jeffrey in Ld. Cockburn's *Life* II. Let. 165 Each of the Courts..must have an equal right..to adjudicate upon it. **1848** Bright *Sp.* (1876) 161, I would establish..a special court in Ireland to adjudicate on all questions connected with the titles and transfers of landed property. **1857** M. Hopkins *Handbk. Average* 393 It is said that he ought not to adjudicate as to his own fees.

adjudicating (əˈdʒ(j)uːdɪkeɪtɪŋ), *vbl. sb.* [f. prec. + -ING[1].]

†**1.** An adjudging or awarding. *Obs.*

1700 *Paper to W. Penn* 12 He does decree also an addiudicating of them upon that Account to eternal Glory.

2. A sitting in judgment, or pronouncing sentence, upon a claim. (Mostly gerundial.)

1842 Macaulay *Fredk. Gt., Ess.* (1877) 675 Men whose lives were passed in adjudicating on questions of civil right.

adjudication (əˌdʒ(j)uːdɪˈkeɪʃən). [ad. L. *adjūdicātiōn-em*, n. of action, f. *adjūdicāre*: see ADJUDICATE. The Fr. *adjudication*, 16th c. in Littré, may be the immediate source.]

1. The act of adjudicating or adjudging; an awarding or settling by judicial decree.

1691 Blount *Law Dict., Adjudication*, A giving by Judgment, a Sentence, or Decree. **1772** Pennant *Tours in Scotl.* (1774) 353 The courts of law had made an adjudication in his favour. **1814** Wellington in Gurwood's *Desp.* XII. 87 The adjudication should take place in the Courts of Admiralty. **1857** M. Hopkins *Handbk. Average* 373 Arbitrators should not..introduce in their award questions which have not been left to their adjudication. **1871** Smiles *Character* v. (1876) 153 The adjudication of the medal.

2. A judicial sentence, or award.

1782 Burke *Sp. on Ref.* Wks. X. 96 Any adjudication in favour of natural rights. **1825** T. Jefferson *Wks.* 1859 I. 16 They would not..acknowledge the adjudications of our courts. **1880** Muirhead *Gaius* iv. §39, 42 The clauses of a formula are these,—the demonstration, the intention, the adjudication, and the condemnation... The adjudication is the clause whereby the judge is authorized to adjudicate a thing to one in particular of the litigants, as when co-heirs are suing for partition of an inheritance.

3. *Law.* A decree in bankruptcy.

1869 *Latest News* 17 Oct., The adjudication was made on the petition of Mr...a creditor for 140*l*. **1870** *Daily News* 10 Oct., The act of bankruptcy was a declaration of insolvency made by his lordship on the 29th of September, and the adjudication was now made by consent.

4. *Scotch Law.* An attachment of heritable estate as security, or in satisfaction of a debt. (See ADJUDGED 4.)

adjudicative (əˈdʒ(j)uːdɪkeɪtɪv), *a.* [f. ADJUDICATE + -IVE; as if ad. L. **adjūdicātīvus*.] Having the character or attribute of adjudicating.

1848 Arnould *Mar. Insur.* II. iii. (1866) II. 594 Although this do not appear in the adjudicative part of the sentence.

adjudicator (əˈdʒ(j)uːdɪkeɪtə(r)). [a. assumed L. **adjūdicātōr*, n. of agent, f. *adjūdicāre*: see ADJUDICATE.] One who adjudicates; who settles a controverted question, or awards the prize in a competition. .

1835 *New Monthly Mag.* XLV. 20 It is the best adjudicator we can have, for rather than condemn rashly, it acquits both parties. **1860** R. A. Vaughan *Hours w. Mystics* II. x. ii. 194 Two successive bodies of adjudicators were impanelled and dissolved, unable to arrive at a decision. **1870** *Daily News* 8 Feb., (Cambridge) Smith's (Mathematical) Prizes.—The adjudicators are the Chancellor, Vice-Chancellor, etc. **1875** Miss Braddon *Strange World* III. i. 49 Lady Cheshunt was one of the lady adjudicators.

adjudicature (əˈdʒ(j)uːdɪˌkeɪtjʊə(r), -tʃə(r)). [f. ADJUDICATE + -URE, as if ad. L. **adjūdicātūra*.] The process of adjudicating; adjudication.

1859 F. W. Robertson *Lect. on 1 Cor.* iii. 1-10, (1878) 40 The difficulty in social adjudicature is, to determine who ought to be the leaders, and who are to be the led; to abolish false aristocracies, and to establish the true.

†ˈ**adjugate**, *v. Obs.*[—0] [f. L. *adjugāt-* ppl. stem of *adjugā-re* to couple to; f. *ad* to + *jugāre* to yoke: cf. *conjugate*.] 'To yoke or couple to.' Bailey, vol. II, 1731; whence in Johnson, Ash, etc.

†ˈ**adjument.** *Obs.* [ad. L. *adjūment-um*, contr. from *adjuvāmentum*, f. *adjuvā-re* to assist: see ADJUVANT.] Help, assistance. Also of persons: A help, helper, or assistant.

1607 Walkington *Optick Glasse* 3 Such thinges as may either be obnoxious or an adjument to nature. **1641** in Rushworth's *Hist. Coll.* III. (1692) I. 287 Adjuments or Assistants to the Bishops in Cathedrals as be the Archdeacons abroad. **1663** R. Taylor *Cromwell* (1672) Pref. 3 By a mixt adjument of Tumults and Arms..did Cromwel usurp the Soveraignty.

adjunct (ˈædʒʌŋkt), *ppl. a.* and *sb.* [ad. L. *adjunct-us* pa. pple. of *adjungĕre* to join to; f. *ad* to + *jung-ĕre* to join.]

A. *adj.* Joined or added (*to* anything); connected, annexed; subordinate. Also spec. (*U.S.*) ***adjunct professor***, (in some institutions) a university or college teacher ranking immediately below a professor.

1595 Shaks. *John* III. iii. 57 Though that my death were adiunct to my Act By heauen I would doe it. *c* **1600** —— *Sonnets* xci. Euery humor hath his adiunct pleasure. **1826** *Catal. Univ. Cambridge* (*Mass.*) 6 John W. Webster, M.D., Adjunct Erving Professor of Chemistry. **1827** Southey in *Q. Rev.* XXXV. 191 Underived as it is from any parent or adjunct dialect. **1840** J. Quincy *Harvard Univ.* II. 305 In 1808, John Collins Warren, M.D., and in 1809, John Gorham, M.D., were appointed Adjunct Professors. **1870** Bowen *Logic* v. 144 Whether the adjunct word or clause is to be considered as Explicative or Limitative. **1931** W. G. McAdoo *Crowded Years* ii. 24 My father was invited to Knoxville as Adjunct Professor of History and English in the University of Tennessee.

B. *sb.* (Cf. L. *adjunctum* and Fr. *adjoint*.)

1. Something joined to or connected with another, and subordinate to it in position, function, character, or essence; either as auxiliary to it, or essentially depending upon it.

1588 Shaks. *L.L.L.* IV. iii. 314 Learning is but an adiunct to our selfe, And where we are, our Learning likewise is. *a* **1677** Barrow *Serm.* Wks. 1716 II. 103 His folly ariseth from worse causes, hath worse adjuncts, produceth worse effects. **1794** Paley *Evid.* III. viii. (1817) 387 Other articles of the Christian faith..are only the adjuncts and circumstances of this. **1846** Grote *Greece* (1862) II. iii. 61 Each with its cluster of dependent towns as adjuncts. **1875** Stubbs *Const. Hist.* II. xvi. 369 The king..confirms the charters with their adjuncts.

2. A person joined to another in some office or service; *spec.* applied to a class of Associates of the Royal Academy of Sciences at Paris, instituted in 1716. Also *spec.* (*U.S.*) = *adjunct professor*.

a **1639** Wotton (J.) He made him the associate of his heir-apparent together with the Lord Cottington (as an adjunct of singular experience and trust) in foreign travels. **1751** Chambers *Cycl.* s.v. *Academy*, Establishing a new class of twelve adjuncts to the six several kinds of sciences cultivated by the Academy. **1753** —— *Cycl. Supp.*, *Adjuncts* of the gods ..were a kind of inferior deities..To Mars was adjoined Bellona and Nemesis. **1831** Scott *Kenilw.* xxv. (1853) 254 Said his unexpected adjunct. **1876** D. C. Gilman *University Probl.* (1898) 29 Promoting them because of their merit to successive posts, as scholars, fellows, assistants, adjuncts, professors, and university professors. **1877** *Monthly Packet* XXIV. 373 This employment of Colleagues, or rather Adjuncts, in the duties of the office.

3. A personal addition or enhancement; a quality increasing a man's native worth.

1610 Healey *St. Aug., City of God* 342 The midlemost are divine, and happy adjuncts of the wise man onely. **1635** Naunton *Fragm. Reg.* in *Phenix* (1708) I. 205 A Gentleman, that..had also the Adjuncts of a strong and subtil Capacity. **1821** Byron *Mar. Fal.* IV. i. (1868) 334 There Youth, which needed not, nor thought of such Vain adjuncts, lavish'd its true bloom, and health.

4. A qualifying addition to a word or name.

1608 Norden *Surveyor's Dial.* 176 If a man should aske a Scholler..what adiunct he would giue vnto a man, dwelling in a Country village or house: hee would say hee were *Villanus* or *Villaticus*. **1622** Heylin *Cosmog.* III. (1673) 5/2 Called from hence Pontus by the Latines, the adjunct of Euxinus coming on another occasion. **1876** Freeman *Norm. Conq.* I. App. 534 Almost always coupled with one of its geographical adjuncts 'West,' 'East,' or 'South.'

5. a. *Gram.* Any word or words expanding the essential parts of the sentence; an amplification or 'enlargement' of the subject, predicate, etc.

1589 Nashe *Alm. for Parrat* 5 His auncient burlibond adiunctes, that so pester his former edition with their vnweldie phrase. **1751** Chambers *Cycl.*, *Adjuncts*, in rhetoric and grammar, are certain words or things added to others; to amplify the discourse or augment its force. **1881** Mason *Eng. Gram.* 149 The basis and type of the Adverbial Adjunct is a substantive in an oblique case, used to limit or define the signification of a verb or adjective.

b. In Jespersen's terminology, a word or group of words of the second rank of importance in a phrase or sentence. Cf. PRIMARY *sb.*, SUBJUNCT.

1914 O. Jespersen *Mod. Eng. Gram.* II. i. 2 In the combination *extremely hot weather..hot*, which defines *weather*, is a secondary word or an adjunct. **1924** —— *Philos. Gram.* vii. 97 It will be useful to have the special names *adjunct* for a secondary word in a junction, and *adnex* for a secondary word in a nexus. *Ibid.* 98 Other examples of substantives as adjuncts are *women* writers, a *queen* bee, *boy* messengers, and (why not?) *Captain* Smith. **1934** M. Callaway in *Language* X. 366 As used by Jespersen, 'adjunct' covers both 'attribute' and 'appositive' as used by Sweet. **1935** W. F. Leopold in *Jrnl. Eng. & Germ. Philol.* XXXIV. 415 The 'principals', 'adjuncts', and 'subjuncts' of his [Jespersen's] *Modern English Grammar* have now given way to the simpler and more mechanical terms 'primary', 'secondary', and 'tertiary'.

6. *Logic.* Anything added to the essence of a thing; an accompanying quality or circumstance; a non-essential attribute.

1588 Fraunce *Lawiers Logike* I. ii. 5 b, Who thinke that Judgement is not any severall part of Logike, but rather an adiunct or propertie generally incident to the whole Art. **1628** T. Spencer *Logick* 57 An adiunct is that to which something is subiected, and whatsoever doth externally belong, or happen to any subiect. **1833** I. Taylor *Fanat.* iii. 60 The one species of ardent emotion differs from the other more in adjuncts and objects, than in innate quality or character.

adjunction (əˈdʒʌŋkʃən). [ad. L. *adjunctiōn-em*, n. of action, f. *adjunct-* ppl. stem of *adjung-ĕre*: see ADJUNCT. Cf. Fr. *adjonction* (14th c. in Littré.)]

1. The joining on or adding of a thing or person (*to* another).

1618 Raleigh *Rem.* (1644) 270 That supposition, that your Majesties Subjects give nothing but with adjunction of their own interest. **1650** R. Stapylton *Strada's Lower Countrey Warres* III. 71 It never entered into his mind, by that adjunction of Bishops to impose the Spanish Inquisition upon the Low-countreys. **1817** Coleridge *Biogr. Lit.* 182 This adjunction of epithets for the purpose of additional description. **1868** *Daily News* 20 June 5/1 The adjunction of the telegraph business to the Post Office.

2. That which is joined on or added; an adjunct. ? *Obs.*

1603 Holland *Plutarch's Mor.* 1355 The second syllable θε is an adjunction idle and superfluous. **1606** —— *Sueton.* Annot. 2 By *Curia* simply without any adiunction, is ment *Curia Hostilia*.

3. *Math.* [ad. F. *adjonction* (Galois 1846).] The relation holding between sets when without overlapping one another they are so 'joined' or continuous as to form another complete set; also, the process of putting them into this relation.

1896 *Bull. Amer. Math. Soc.* Dec. 103 The formation of an algebraic 'domain' and..the nature of the process of 'adjunction' introduced by Galois. **1904** F. Cajori *Theory of Equations* xiii. 135 This process of obtaining the domain $\Omega(a)$ from Ω is called *adjunction*. We say that we *adjoin a* to Ω and obtain $\Omega(a)$. **1947** Courant & Robbins *What is Math.?* (ed. 4) iii. §2. 132 It is assumed that $\sqrt{\kappa}$ is a new number not lying in *f*, since otherwise the process of adjunction of $\sqrt{\kappa}$ would not lead to anything new.

4. *Logic.* The operation consisting in the joint assertion in a single formula of two previously asserted formulæ (see quot. 1932). Now often called *conjunction*.

1932 Lewis & Langford *Symbolic Logic.* vi. §1. 126 *Adjunction.* Any two expressions which have been separately asserted may be jointly asserted. That is, if p has been asserted, and q has been asserted, then pq may be asserted. **1962** Kneale *Devel. Logic* ix. §4. 550 In *Principia Mathematica*, which allows inference from P and $P \supset Q$ to Q, it is possible to dispense with Lewis's rule of adjunction because $p \supset [q \supset (p.q)]$ is a theorem.

adjunctive (əˈdʒʌŋktɪv), *a.* and *sb.* [ad. L. *adjunctīvus*, f. *adjunct-us*: see ADJUNCT and -IVE.]

A. *adj.* Having the character or quality of contributing (*to*) or forming an adjunct.

a **1820** N. DRAKE *Lit. Hours, Crit. 'Farmer's Boy,'* The imagery and adjunctive circumstances are original. **1855** I. TAYLOR *Restor. Belief* 189 These affirmations are all of them adjunctive to his proper subject. **1859** MRS. SCHIMMELPENNINCK *Princ. Beauty* I. vi. §18 The adjunctive phases of Beauty may be broadly classed under two heads.

B. *sb.* [The adj. used *absol.*] That which is, or may be, used as an adjunct; a thing or person of the nature of an adjunct. *rare*$^{-0}$.

1755 JOHNSON, *Adjunctive*, 1. He that joins. 2. That which is joined.

adjunctively (əˈdʒʌŋktɪvlɪ), *adv.* [f. prec. + -LY².] In an adjunctive manner; as an adjunct.

1818 In TODD. **1829** I. TAYLOR *Enthus.* ii. (1867) 52 The great facts of Christianity possess adjunctively the means of exciting in a powerful degree the emotions that belong to the imagination as well as those that affect the heart. *Mod.* A clause is a sentence adjunctively dependent on some word of a main sentence.

adjunctly (əˈdʒʌŋktlɪ), *adv. rare*$^{-0}$. [f. ADJUNCT *a.* + -LY².] In an adjunct manner; in auxiliary conjunction with.

1818 in TODD.

adjuration (ˌædʒ(ɪ)ʊˈreɪʃən). [ad. (directly or through Fr. *adjuration*, 16th c. in Litt.) L. *adjūrātiōn-em*, n. of action f. *adjūrā-re*: see ADJURE.] The action of adjuring; a solemn charging or appealing to (one) upon oath, or under penalty of a curse; an earnest appeal.

1611 COTGR., *Adjuration*, An adjuration, or conjuration; an earnest swearing unto; also, th' exaction of an oath from others. *a* **1638** MEDE *On Zach.* iv. 10, Wks. I. 42 S. Paul speaks in adjuration to Timothy, 'I charge thee (saith he) before God, and the Lord Jesus Christ, and the Elect Angels.' **1738** CLARKE *Wks.* II. cxxv. (R.) Our Saviour when the high-priest adjured him by the living God, made no scruple of replying upon that adjuration. **1803** MISS PORTER *Thadd. Warsaw* i. (1831) 5 My sobs followed this adjuration. **1858** FROUDE *Hist. Eng.* IV. xxiii. 530 An adjuration as vain as it was earnest. **1858** GLADSTONE *Homer* III. 160 The Rivers are expressly invoked, in this character, by Agamemnon in the adjuration of the Poet: and are associated with the deities that punish perjury after death.

b. *spec.* in exorcism.

c **1386** CHAUCER *Persones T.* 529 Thilke horrible sweryng of adjuracioun and conjuraciouns, as doon these false enchauntours or nigromanciens. **1621** BURTON *Anat. Mel.* II. i. I. i. (1651) 221 Our Pontificiall writers retain many of these adjurations and forms of exorcismes. **1635** PAGITT *Christianogr.* I. iii. (1636) 158 An Adiuration of the Divell and a Renuntiation or renouncing of him. **1751** CHAMBERS *Cycl.*, *Adjuration*, a part of exorcism, wherein the devil is commanded in the name of God, to depart out of the body of the possessed. **1875** B. TAYLOR *Faust* I. vi. 109 Come, draw thy circle, speak thine adjuration.

adjuratory (əˈdʒ(j)ʊərətərɪ), *a.* [ad. L. *adjūrātōri-us*, f. *adjūrātōr*, n. of agent f. *adjūrā-re*: see ADJURE.] Of or pertaining to adjuration; containing a solemn charge or appeal.

1815 *Hist. J. Decastro* II. 317 He..ought to name the impediment as soon as the parson has read the adjuratory charge. **1881** *Echo* 28 Apr. 1/5 An oath which, so far as its adjuratory terms were concerned, was to him no more than if a man uttered 'By Jove!' as an exclamation.

adjure (əˈdʒ(j)ʊə(r)), *v.* [ad. (directly or through Fr. *adjurer*) L. *adjūrā-re* to swear to (a thing), also, in late L., to put (one) to an oath; f. *ad* to + *jūrā-re* to swear, f. *jūs, jūr-* oath. Our earliest instances occur as translating L. *adjūrāre*.]

†**1.** To put (one) to his oath; 'to impose an oath upon another, prescribing the form in which he shall swear,' J.; to bind under the penalty of a curse. *Obs.*

1382 WYCLIF *1 Kings* xviii. 10 He hath adjurid (Vulg. *adjuravit*) alle rewmes and folkis, for thi that thou art not foundun. **1539** BIBLE ('great') *1 Sam.* xiv. 28 Thy father adiured the people [WYCLIF, boond the puple with an ooth], saying: Cursed be the man that eateth any sustinaunce. **1611** —— *Josh.* vi. 26 Ioshua adiured them at that time, saying, Cursed be the man before the Lord, that riseth vp and buildeth this city Iericho. **1612** MASON *Anat. Sorcerie* 75 We are constrained to make an English word of the Latine, saying (we adjure). **1643** MILTON *Doct. Divorce* II. xvii. (1847) 152/2 The woman..was adjured by the priest to swear whether she were false or no.

2. To charge or entreat (any one) solemnly or earnestly, as if under oath, or under the penalty of a curse. Const. *inf.* or *subord. cl.*

1483 CAXTON *Gold. Leg.* 78/2 Raguel desired and adjured (Vulg. *adjuravit*) Thobie that he shold abyde with hym. **1597** T. MORLEY *Introd. Musicke* Pref., The earnest intreatie of my friends daily requesting, importuning, and as it were adiuring me. **1611** BIBLE *1 Kings* xxii. 16 How many times shall I adiure thee, that thou tell me nothing but that which is true? **1718** POPE *Iliad* xv. 794 Nestor most.. exhorts, adjures, to guard these utmost shores. **1849** MACAULAY *Hist. Eng.* II. 168 His friends adjured him to take more care of a life invaluable to his country. **1850** MRS. BROWNING *Dead Pan* xxi. Poems II. 417 Gods! we vainly do adjure you. **1873** J. G. HOLLAND *Arth. Bonnic.* i. 15 Standing by the truth, as he so feelingly adjured me to stand.

adjured (əˈdʒ(j)ʊəd), *ppl. a.* [f. ADJURE + -ED.]

†**1.** Bound by oath. *Obs.*

1598 YONG *Diana* What cruell minde, what angry brest displaied, With sauage hart, to fiercenes so adiured.

2. Solemnly charged, earnestly entreated or appealed to.

1671 MILTON *Samson* 853 Solicited, commanded, threaten'd, urg'd, Adjur'd by all the bonds of civil duty. **1697** DRYDEN *Æneid* II. 209 (Lat. 155) Ye sacred altars! from whose flames I fled, Be all of you adjur'd.

aˈdjurement. ? *Obs.* [ad. L. *adjūrāmentum*, n. of action, f. *adjūrā-re*: see ADJURE.] A solemn or earnest entreaty.

1382 WYCLIF *Tob.* ix. 5 Thou seest how Raguel hath coniurid me, whos adiurement I mai not dispisen [Vulg. *cujus adjuramentum spernere non possum*].

adjurer, -or (əˈdʒ(j)ʊərə(r)). [f. ADJURE + -ER¹. The spelling in *-or* imitates the legal JUROR: see -OR.] One who adjures.

1382 WYCLIF *Prov.* xxix. 24 The adiurere he herith [Vulg. *adjurantem audit*] and not shewith. **1611** COTGR., *Adjurateur*, An adjuror or earnest swearer. **1838** LD. LYTTON *Leila* I. iv. 33 As he spoke, the adjuror himself rose, lifting his right hand.

adjuring (əˈdʒ(j)ʊərɪŋ), *ppl. a.* [f. ADJURE + -ING².] Charging upon oath; exorcising.

1637 MILTON *Comus* 858 Add the power of some adjuring verse. **1641** —— *Ch. Govt.* ii. (1851) 105 He closes up the Epistle with an adjuring charge.

adjust (əˈdʒʌst), *v.* [a. 16th c. Fr. *adjuste-r* (now *ajuster*). The OFr. *ajuster, ajoster, ajouster* = It. *aggiustare, aggiostare* (:—late L. *adjuxtāre*), gave rise to a med.L. *adjustare*, which was naturally, though erroneously, taken as a derivative of *ad* + *jūstus*, and so consciously used. After Fr. *ajouster* became *ajouter*, so that its formal relationship to *aggiustare* and *adjustare* was lost sight of, a new Fr. *adjuster* was formed after the latter, and received those senses of *ajouster*, which seemed to approach to L. *jūstus*, Fr. *juste*. In It. and Sp. also the mod. sense of *aggiustare*, *ajustar*, has been influenced by association with *jūstus*. Thus mod.Fr. *ajuster* may be viewed as a refashioning or re-forming of OFr. *ajouster*:—*adjuxtāre*, after *à* + *juste*. See also ADJOUST.]

1. a. To arrange, compose, settle, harmonize (things that are or may be contradictory, differences, discrepancies, accounts). To adjust *an average*: see ADJUSTER, ADJUSTMENT 4.

1611 COTGR., *Adjuster*, To adjust, place justly, set aptly, couch evenly, joyne handsomely, match fitly, dispose orderly, severall things together. *a* **1667** COWLEY *Shortn. Life* Wks. 1684,137 If we could but learn to number our days ..we should adjust much better our other Accounts. **1710** STEELE *Tatler* No. 24 ¶ 14 To ratify the Preliminaries of a Treaty adjusted with Monsieur Torcy. **1723** DE FOE *Col. Jack* (1840) 254 I had no difficulty left but what would soon have been adjusted. **1741** H. WALPOLE *Lett. to H. Mann* 7 (1834) I. 20 I believe the Euston embroil is adjusted. **1759** ROBERTSON *Hist. Scotl.* I. vi. 444 Four were named on each side to adjust their differences. **1762** H. WALPOLE *Vertue's Anecd. Painting* (1786) III. 52, I am desirous of adjusting the pretensions of the three Le Fevres. **1817** JAS. MILL *Brit. India* II. v. viii. 650 Balances, which appeared on adjusting the books of the Presidency. **1866** J. MARTINEAU *Ess.* I. 145 We own the difficulty of clearly adjusting their relation.

b. *Insurance.* In a case of General Average, to determine (the claims and liabilities of all parties concerned); also more widely, to assess (the amount which a claimant for compensation or indemnity is entitled to receive).

1755 N. MAGENS *Ess. on Insurances* I. 5 (*heading*) Damages which occur in foreign Parts, and are adjusted there, ought to be settled here. **1808** A. ANNESLEY *Law of Marine Insurances* II. vii. 91 When..the amount which each insurer is to pay, is settled, it is usual for the underwriter to indorse on the policy, 'Adjusted this loss at so much *per Cent.*' **1842** [see ADJUSTMENT 4]. **1904** HALSBURY in *Law Rep. Appeal Cases* 173 Where two areas are being divided and each becomes responsible for its own administration, and where previously they possessed property, it is obvious enough that they must have some mode of adjusting the division of the property which each possessed prior to such separation. **1922** V. DOVER *Handbk. Marine Insurance* v. 80 Provision is made in the Institute Clauses for general average and salvage to be adjusted according to the law and practice obtaining at the place where the adventure ends. **1952** L. M. CURRIE *Consequential Fire Loss Insurance* xxxvii. 166 We conveyed your agreement to the loss being adjusted on a departmental basis. **1966** W. H. RODDA *Property & Liability Insurance* xix. 467 The insurance agent may have the responsibility of adjusting small losses... A large loss is more likely to result in some disagreement between the adjuster and the insured. **1980** *Oxf. Compan. Law* 25/1 Under the York-Antwerp Rules, 1950, general average falls to be adjusted both as regards loss and contribution on the basis of values at the time and place where the maritime adventure ends.

†**2. a.** *ellipt. intr.* To adjust (sc. differences, or oneself): To come to terms, or to an understanding; to arrange. *Obs.*

1647 EVELYN *Mem.* (1857) III. 6 Persuading him to adjust with the holy agitators. *a* **1733** NORTH *Lives of Norths* III. 228 We had adjusted two days after to go down and agree for Besthorp.

b. To adapt oneself *to*; to get used to. Also *absol.*

1924 J. J. B. MORGAN *Psychol. of Unadjusted School Child* III. viii. 121 It may be that the child will not adjust and will later develop a more serious form of dissociation. **1938** E. BOWEN *Death of Heart* II. iv. 244 'He is not really: he's in my brother's office.' 'Well, after all,' said Evelyn, adjusting to this. **1955** *Amer. Dialect Soc.* XXIV. 14 The inability of the criminally-inclined to 'adjust' to normal society. **1962** *Listener* 9 Aug. 207/1 He may try to adjust by staying with people of the same group as his family. **1962** *Amer. N. & Q.* Sept. 4/1 He adjusted rapidly to the rough life of the open range.

3. a. To arrange or dispose (a thing) suitably in relation to something else, or to a standard or purpose. Const. *to*, rarely *by*, *with*.

1664 in *Phil. Trans.* I. 13 Having there adjusted his watches. **1690** LOCKE *Hum. Underst.* III. ix. §5 Wks. 1727 I. 219 No..settled standard..to rectify and adjust them by. **1710** STEELE *Tatler* No. 86 ¶2 There was a great point in adjusting my behaviour to the simple Squire. **1730** ADDISON *Chr. Relig.* (J.) Nothing else in view, but to adjust the event to the prediction. **1756** BURKE *Vind. Nat. Soc.* Wks. I. 64 They have adjusted the means to that end. *a* **1800** BLAIR (J.) Nothing is more difficult than to adjust the marvellous with the probable. **1860** MAURY *Phys. Geog. Sea* xii. 531 To adjust the pendulum of his clock to the right length. **1862** H. SPENCER *First Princ.* I. iv. §25 (1875) 84 The external relations to which the internal ones are adjusted.

b. *refl.* Const. *to*.

1859 GEO. ELIOT *Lifted Veil* in *Blackw. Mag.* July 39/2 Our impulses, our spiritual activities, no more adjust themselves to the idea of their future nullity. **1888** MRS. H. WARD *R. Elsmere* II. xvii. 85 Lady Charlotte's eye-glass, having adjusted itself for a moment to the distant figure of the Rector..turned back towards the squire. **1943** J. S. HUXLEY *Evol. Ethics* iii. 22 The individual..can adjust himself..to the ethical standards of his society.

4. a. To arrange or dispose (a thing) suitably in relation to its parts; to put in proper order or position; to regulate, systematize.

1667 MILTON *P.L.* VI. 514 Sulphurous and nitrous foam ..with subtle art Concocted and adjusted. **1704** SWIFT *T. of Tub* i. 23 Reducing, including, and adjusting every genus and species within that compass. **1750** JOHNSON *Rambler* No. 94 ¶4 Milton understood the force of sounds well adjusted. **1754** SHERLOCK *Disc.* i. (1759) I. 7 The motions of the stars had been observed and adjusted. **1864** BURTON *Scot Abroad* I. ii. 100 The symmetrical and scientifically adjusted court precedency of France.

b. *esp.* of clothes, armour, and the like; in which sense also *to adjust oneself*.

c **1735** POPE *Donne Sat.* IV. 242 See them..adjust their clothes. **1761** SMOLLETT *Gil Blas* X. iv. (1802) III. 151, I.. dressed myself in a hurry. Just as I had done adjusting myself, my secretary coming in. **1838** J. GRANT *Sk. in London* 187 'Sir,' said Mr. Abel Smith, adjusting his collar, 'if we don't go together, we don't go at all.' **1864** MISS BRADDON *Hen. Dunb.* iii. 25 His tremulous hands could scarcely adjust his spectacles. **1878** BOSW. SMITH *Carthage* 232 The men had hardly time to adjust their armour or to draw their swords.

c. *intr.* for *pass.* To be capable of being adjusted.

1917 *Harrods Gen. Catal.* 757/2 Canvas Adjustable chair, adjusting to six positions. **1943** *Mod. Lang. Notes* LVIII. 12 Bed-lamps *attach* and *adjust* easily. **1982** *Habitat Catal. 1982/83* 109/1 The barrel, of lacquered brushed aluminium, can adjust right up to the neck of the lamp.

adjustable (əˈdʒʌstəb(ə)l), *a.* [f. ADJUST + -ABLE.] Capable of being adjusted. ***adjustable pitch***: freq. *attrib.* (with hyphen), applied to an aeroplane propeller the blade angle of which can be adjusted when the engine is at rest (opp. *variable pitch*). Also *absol.*, a pitch setting capable of such adjustment.

1775 MASKELYNE in *Phil. Trans.* LXV. 500 Which wanted nothing to make it an excellent instrument but to have the plumb-line made adjustable. **1795** SIR W. HERSCHEL in *Phil. Trans.* LXXXV. 388 The plate on the west is fixed, but that on the east is adjustable. **1832** BABBAGE *Econ. Manuf.* 27 The opening of the valve..being adjustable at the will of the engine-man. **1851-9** SIR J. HERSCHEL in *Man. Sci. Enq.* 126 The lower level [of the mercury] in the cistern is adjustable to contact with a steel or ivory fiducial point. **1909** *Car* 5 May 451/1 Look to your propeller which..has an adjustable pitch. **1934** *Flight* 15 Feb. 156/1 The airscrews are of the three-bladed adjustable-pitch type. **1949** *Gloss. Aeronaut. Terms* (*B.S.I.*) II. 19 *Adjustable-pitch propeller*, a propeller, the blades of which can be adjusted to a desired pitch when not rotating.

†**adjustage** (əˈdʒʌstɪdʒ). *Obs. rare.* [a. Fr. *ajustage*: see ADJUST and -AGE.]

1. = ADJUSTMENT. *rare.*

1598 SYLVESTER is cited by Webster and Worcester.

2. A pipe or opening through which water is discharged so as to form a jet; = ADJUTAGE.

1725 BRADLEY *Fam. Dict.* s.v. *Reservatories*, To play a Jetteau of the thickness of four or five Lines, that is, one whose Adjustage is four or five Lines diameter..the Passage or Mouth of the Adjustages should be four times less than the Opening or Diameter of the Pipes of the Conduit.

adjustation (ˌædʒʌˈsteɪʃən). *rare.* [n. of action f. med.L. *adjustā-re*: see ADJUST.] The action of adjusting; = ADJUSTMENT.

1866 J. B. ROSE *Virgil's Ecl. & Georg.* 150 The difficulty in the Roman adjustation of the year was that they had not our hours, minutes, and seconds.

adjusted (əˈdʒʌstɪd), *ppl. a.* [f. ADJUST + -ED.]

1. Arranged, composed, harmonized, settled.

a **1674** CLARENDON *Hist. Reb.* I. I. 14 All the overtures they had made being adjusted. **1750** JOHNSON *Rambler* No. 13 ¶13 Promises of friendship are useless and vain, unless they are made in some known sense, adjusted and acknowledged by both parties. **1811** L. M. HAWKINS *Countess & Gertr.* I. 243 A species of thrift, which by an adjusted balance of caprice and parsimony, saved nothing in the event.

2. Disposed or arranged so as to fit or answer (*to* something); adapted.

1777 HUME *Ess. & Treat.* I. 109 It is rapid harmony, exactly adjusted to the sense.

3. Properly ordered or regulated.

1675 OGILBY *Brit.* Pref. 4 This, if accurately adjusted.. would conduce..to the Regulation of Latitudes. **1865** MOZLEY *Miracles* viii. 175 Who could stand firm, and maintain a moderate and adjusted ground against the strong tendencies to extravagance.

4. Adapted to one's environment (often preceded by defining word, as *well adjusted*). Cf. ADJUSTMENT I.

1924 J. J. B. MORGAN *Psychol. of Unadjusted School Child* I. i. 4 It is the function of the parent and teacher to encourage the successfully adjusted children. **1940** R. S. WOODWORTH *Psychol.* (ed. 12) xviii. 590 If an individual is participating intelligently and wholeheartedly in what is going on in his environment, we have no hesitation in calling him well adjusted. **1957** D. KARP *Leave me Alone* vi. 97 Don't talk to me about being 'adjusted'.

adjuster (əˈdʒʌstə(r)). [f. ADJUST + -ER[1].]

a. One who adjusts, settles, or regulates. Spec. in *Insurance*, a person who assesses liabilities and claims arising out of loss, damage, etc.; ***average adjuster***: see AVERAGE *sb.*[2] 4b.

1673 E. HICKERINGILL *Gregory* 252 Designed for a Confession of Faith, the Adjuster of Controversies. **1713** *London Gaz.* 16–19 May 3/2 Your Majesty..the steddy Arbiter and grand Adjuster of the Affairs of Europe. **1756** J. WARTON *Ess. on Pope* II. 298 Collectors of various readings, and adjusters of texts. **1830** *Examiner* 31 Jan. 82/2 If the adjusters have the best of the bargain, it binds; if not, the contract is void. **1862** *Standard* 24 Apr. [One] who has had large experience as a compass adjuster. **1870** *Daily News* 13 July, An association of Average Adjusters of London has recently been formed, with a view to the arbitration and examination of claims. **1934** A. WOOLLCOTT *While Rome Burns* 243 This play had been written..by a young insurance adjuster.

b. Something that adjusts (in various technical uses).

a **1884** KNIGHT *Dict. Mech.* Suppl. 6/1 *Adjuster* (*Surgical*), an instrument for bringing into coaptation the parts in case of ruptured perineum. **1909** *Westm. Gaz.* 6 Apr. 4/1 The steering-gear, too, is fitted with an adjuster at the base of the steering column.

adjusting (əˈdʒʌstɪŋ), *vbl. sb.* [f. ADJUST + -ING[1].] The process of arranging or disposing things suitably to one another or to a purpose. (Now mostly gerundial.)

1667 G. C. in *H. More's Div. Dial.* (1713) Pref. 3 The Adjusting of the Phenomena of the World to the Goodness of his Providence. **1790** BEATSON *Nav. & Mil. Mem.* I. 8 The adjusting of so many pretensions, and the reconciling so many different powers to them. **1794** HOME in *Phil. Trans.* LXXXV. 18 In the adjusting of the eye to different distances. *Mod.* In adjusting the terms of the lease.

adjustive (əˈdʒʌstɪv), *a.* [f. ADJUST *v.* + -IVE.] Tending to adjust, concerned with adjustment.

1883 ROMANES *Mental Evol. in Anim.* i. 17 Adjustive movements due to reflex action, and adjustive movements accompanied by mental perception. *Ibid.* 18 Adjustive action. **1935** *Brit. Jrnl. Psychol.* July 109 Only 'Adjustive' and 'Receptive' processes are dealt with. **1952** *New Biol.* XIII. 50 Thirdly there are the incoming stimuli which inform the pilot all the time of the discrepancy between the performance and his intention, and which also convey back to him results of his adjustive movements.

†**aˈdjustly**, *adv. Obs.* [irreg. f. ADJUST, by form-assoc. with *just, justly*.] With self-adjustment, with ready adaptation to circumstances.

1681 *Relig. Cler.* 230 He can easily and adjustly act the Scholar or the Gentleman as occasion requires.

adjustment (əˈdʒʌstmənt). [ad. Fr. *ajustement*: see ADJUST *v.* and -MENT.]

1. The process of adjusting; setting right, regulating, arranging, settling, harmonizing, or properly disposing; freq. in contexts of emotional adaptation.

1644 MILTON *Jus Pop.* 60 Fit for that adjustment of time, and other circumstances. **1678** *Trans. at Crt. Spain* II. 92 There arose new difficulties in the adjustment of our troubles. **1769–90** SIR J. REYNOLDS *Disc.* xi. (1876) 25 His principal care and attention seems to have been fixed on the adjustment of the whole. **1814** SCOTT *Waverley* xlii. (1862) 187 The rest of the apparel required little adjustment. **1869** TYNDALL *Light* §177, 26 The eye possesses a power of adjustment for different distances. **1881** ROUTLEDGE *Science* i. 12 The adjustment of the calendar was a subject which received much attention. **1881** MIVART in *Nature* No. 614, 326 Of all the races of men they are the mightiest and most noble who are, or by self-adjustment can become, most fit for all the new conditions of existence in which by various changes they may be placed. **1912** A. A. BRILL tr. *Freud's Sel. Papers on Hysteria* I. 8 Those psychic traumas which are not rectified by reaction are also prevented from adjustment by associative elaboration. **1922** R. S. WOODWORTH *Psychol.* iv. 72 Much used..are 'adjustment' and 'mental set', the idea here being to liken the individual to an adjustable machine which can be set for one or another set of work. **1957** P. HALMOS *Towards Measure of Man.* ii. 40 Modern psychologists and psychiatrists distinguish two major stages in the process of adjustment. The instinctual development of the infant.. and the treatment he receives from his environment..combine in a primary process of adjustment. .. A secondary process of adjustment..goes on from about the fifth year of life till its end. **1959** *Times Lit. Suppl.* 16 Jan. 29/2 Three of them emerge to face life again; the fourth.. refuses to make the effort of adjustment.

2. The state or condition of being adjusted, or put in proper order; arrangement, settlement.

1689 *Lond. Gaz.* mmccccclxv/3 The Business of Holstein was in a very fair way to an Adjustment. **1713** *Guardian* No. 27 (R.) Say if there be not a connexion, and adjustment, and exact and constant order discoverable in all the parts of it. **1798** WELLINGTON in *Gen. Desp.* I. 5 A regular mode of bringing to an amicable adjustment..any questions which might hereafter arise. **1840** CARLYLE *Heroes* (1858) 272 The Poet indeed, with his mildness, what is he but the product and ultimate adjustment of Reform, or Prophecy, with its fierceness? **1863** FAWCETT *Pol. Econ.* III. iii. 321 The prices obtained for the produce..cause everything to be in a state of perfect adjustment.

3. An arrangement or means whereby things are adjusted.

1736 BUTLER *Anal.* I. v. 131 Unsettle the adjustments and alter the proportions, which formed it. **1793** WOLLASTON *Transit Circle* in *Phil. Trans.* LXXXIII. 138 The adjustments of the Ys are both of them at the same end of the axis, opposite to the divided circle and the microscopes. **1871** TYNDALL *Frag. Sc.* I. vi. (ed. 6) 207 This instrument, with its wheels and verniers, and delicate adjustments.

4. *Comm.* The settlement among various parties of their several shares in respect of claims, liabilities, or payments; as the ***adjustment of the policy*** or ***adjustment of general average*** in Marine Insurance.

c **1670** in Burton's *Diary* (1828) III. 548 Yesterday the said resident signed the adjustment of the sum, with the deputies of the States General. **1842** PARK *Law Mar. Insur.* I. vi. 267 The policy had been adjusted by the defendant at 50*l.* per cent., and it was contended that he was now bound by that adjustment. **1848** ARNOULD *Mar. Insur.* I. iv. (1866) I. 182 The several underwriters, as this indorsement is submitted to them, sanction it with their initials, and this is called the adjustment of the policy. *Ibid.* III. iv. II. 772 The ascertainment of the damage done and of the sums to be paid in contribution by the parties or their underwriters, is called the adjustment of general average.

5. *attrib.* in ***adjustment award***, ***committee***, ***levy***, ***method***.

1897 C. H. JUDD tr. *Wundt's Outl. Psychol.* iii. 257 The *adjustment-methods*. Among these, we have..the 'method of minimal change', and then as a kind of modification of this for the case of adjustment until equality is reached, the 'method of average error'. **1904** KIPLING *Traffics & Discov.* 251 The Adjustment Committee—the umpires of the Military Areas. **1920** *Act 10 Geo. V*, c. 4 §2 If the profits.. exceed the sum apportioned to that undertaking,..the excess shall be payable to the Controller by the owner of the undertaking and shall be recoverable as a debt due to the Crown, and the amount so payable is in this Act referred to as adjustment levy. *Ibid.*, Any sum so payable [by the Controller] is in this Act referred to as adjustment award.

adjustor (əˈdʒʌstə(r)). *Anat.* and *Zool.* [f. ADJUST *v.*, after L. agent-nouns in *-or*, as *retractor*.] Name for certain muscles in Brachiopoda; see quot. 1895. Also *attrib.* in ***adjustor muscle***.

1895 SHIPLEY in *Cambr. Nat. Hist.* III. 477 There are three pairs of adjustor muscles..called respectively the central.., external.., and posterior..adjustors, whose action adjusts the shells when all contract together, and brings about a certain sliding movement of the shells on one another when they act independently. **1923** *Glasgow Herald* 11 Aug. 4 The more adjustors a creature has, the higher its capacity for effective behaviour.

†**adjutable**, *a. Obs.*$^{-0}$ [ad. L. *adjūtābilis*, f. *adjūtā-re* to help: see ADJUTANT and -ABLE.] 'That may help, helping.' Bailey 1721. ('*Not used.*') Ash 1775.

adjutage, ajutage (əˈdʒ(j)uːtɪdʒ, ˈædʒ(j)ʊtɪdʒ). [a. Fr. *ajutage*, variant of *ajoutage*, f. *ajouter* to add, join on: see also ADJUTAGE, another form of the word. Mod.Fr. has also *ajoutage* and *ajustage*, in accordance with the two forms *ajouter* and *ajuster*, to which the early *ajouster* has given rise: see ADJUST.] *lit.* An adjustment, adaptation, or addition: hence in *Hydraulics*, A tube adapted or adjusted to a pipe or aperture through which water passes, so as to determine the character of the jet; the efflux-tube or mouthpiece of an artificial fountain.

1707 PHILLIPS, *Ajutage*, the spout for a *Jet d'Eau*, or Pipe that throws up Water in any Fountain. **1751** CHAMBERS *Cycl.* s.v., It is chiefly the diversity in the Ajutages that makes the different kinds of fountains. **1808** J. WEBSTER *Nat. Philos.* 117 It will issue at the adjutage or aperture. **1828** HUTTON *Course of Math.* II. 251 If an adjutage be turned upward, the jet will ascend to the height of the surface of the water in the vessel. **1829** U.K.S. *Nat. Philos.* I. *Hydraulics* i. 4 The spouting or flowing of water through jets or adjutages. **1873** ATKINSON tr. *Ganot's Phys.* (ed. 3) 157 A cylindrical or conical efflux tube or adjutage is fitted to the aperture.

adjutancy (ˈædʒ(j)ʊtənsɪ). [f. ADJUTANT; as if ad. L. **adjutantia*: see -NCY.]

1. The office or rank of an adjutant.

1775 R. ALDEN in H. P. Johnston *N. Hale* (1901) 157, I would accept of a lieutenancy but should prefer an adjutancy. **1796** JANE AUSTEN *Let.* 9 Jan. (1952) 3 He has got a scheme..about getting a lieutenancy and adjutancy in the 86th. **1820** OUTRAM in Goldsmid's *Life* I. 27 An adjutancy is thought by the generality of people to be a very arduous and responsible situation. **1880** *Athenæum* 24 July 103/1 Having apparently retained the acting adjutancy up to that time.

2. *fig.* Official order.

1791 BURKE *Appeal to Old Whigs* Wks. 1842 I. 527 It was, no doubt, disposed with all the adjutancy of definition and division.

adjutant (ˈædʒ(j)ʊtənt), *a.* and *sb.* Also corruptly **agitant**. [ad. L. *adjūtant-em* pr. pple. of *adjūtā-re* to assist, freq. of *adjuvā-re* to assist; f. *ad* to + *juvā-re* to help. See -ANT.]

A. *adj.* Helping, auxiliary, assistant.

1676 BULLOKAR, *Adjutant*, helping. **1880** BURTON *Q. Anne* II. ix. 58 With adjutant vessels and small craft there were upwards of a hundred and fifty sail.

B. *sb.*

1. An assistant or helper. Now *rare* in the general sense.

1622 R. HAWKINS *Voy. to S. Sea* (1847) 84 The pilot, or his adjutants, which are the same officers which in our shippes we terme the master and his mates. **1644** BULWER *Chiron.* 17 The Hands so surpassing in dignity all the other corporall adjutants of man's wit. *a* **1733** NORTH *Examen* III. vii. §54. 542 These [petitions] were put into the Hands of Agitants and Sub-agitants in the Countries about. **1856** KANE *Arctic Explor.* II. xix. 191 Taking with me Morton, my faithful adjutant always.

2. *Mil.* An officer in the army whose business it is to assist the superior officers by receiving and communicating orders, conducting correspondence, and the like.

1600 HOLLAND *Livy* XXXVIII. xlvii. 1013 My ten adjutants [*pr.* adjacents] or suffraganes [*legatis*], whome our ancestors thought good to give unto their Generals in the war. **1622** BACON *Jul. Cæs.* Wks. 1860, 503 In great battles he would sit in his pavilion, and manage all by adjutants. **1751** CHAMBERS *Cycl.*, *Adjutant* is the same that we otherwise call *Aid-Major*. **1868** *Regul. & Ord. Army* §857 All guards are, previous to marching on duty, to be inspected and sized by the Adjutant.

3. *Ornith.* (Also **adjutant-bird, -crane, -stork.**) A gigantic species of stork (*Ciconia Argala*) native to India; so called from its stiff quasi-military gait when walking.

1798 PENNANT *Hindostan* II. 156 The Argali or Adjutant, or Gigantic Crane of Latham. **1831** TYERMAN & BENNET *Voy. & Trav.* II. xlv. 343 The adjutant-crane is a privileged carrion-eater throughout India. **1857** S. OSBORN *Quedah* ix. 110 The tall adjutant..a very king of fishing birds. **1880** *Daily Tel.* 28 Oct., The adjutant-bird and the black turkey buzzard.

ˌadjutant-ˈgeneral.

1. *Mil.* An officer who assists the general of an army.

1645 in Rushworth's *Hist. Coll.* I. IV. 34 Adjutant-General Flemming, being engaged in a single encounter, shot his enemy. **1770** *Junius Lett.* xl, Who advised the King to appoint Mr. Luttrell adjutant-general to the army in Ireland? **1844** *Regul. & Ord. Army* 54 To report to the Adjutant-General, as soon as possible after its march, the [corps'] state and condition with respect to Arms, Ammunition, and general equipment.

2. Among the Jesuits, a superintendent of a province or country, conducting its business and correspondence under the supervision of the General of the Order.

1753 CHAMBERS *Cycl. Supp.*

ˈadjutator. [n. of agent f. L. *adjūtā-re* to assist: see ADJUTANT.] *lit.* A helper, an assistant.

As first used in 1647, only a bad spelling of AGITATOR, originating with soldiers familiar with *adjutants* (often pronounced and occas. written AGITANT) and the *adjutors* of 1642. But writers unacquainted with the function of these 'agitators,' mistook *adjutator* (understood in its etymological sense) for the proper form. Hence, it has been occas. used in the general sense of 'helper.'

1647 [See AGITATOR.] **1656–7** in Burton's *Diary* (1828) I. 333 Sexby was once an adjutator. **1662** *Life of Fuller* 29 Such feeble Adjutators or Helpers (as he pleased to style them). **1670** HOBBES *Behemoth* 335 To put it into the head of these adjutators. **1876** GREEN *Hist. Eng. P.* 548 The Adjutators had taken a step which put submission out of the question.

†**aˈdjute**, *v. Obs.* [a. Fr. *ajoute-r*, in 16–17th c. *adjouter*, to add. See ADJOUST and cf. ADJUTAGE, AJUTAGE, Fr. *ajoutage*. The spelling was perh. due to false etymology connecting the word with L. *adjūtāre* (whence it is derived by Dr. Johnson, who also explains it as 'To help').] To add.

1524 PACE in Strype *Eccl. Mem.* I. II. 29 Able..to discomfit the Turque and his armie..ye, if there were therunto adjuted fifty thousand moo. **1633** B. JONSON *Love's Welc. at Welbeck*, Six bachelors as bold as he, Adjuting to his companee.

aˈdjutor[1]. [a. L. *adjūtor*, n. of agent, f. *adjuvā-re* to help: see ADJUTANT.] A helper, assistant. Also rarely used for ADJUTANT B. 2.

1531 ELYOT *Governor* II. x. (1557) 118 Adjutours and supporters. **1592** WYRLEY *Armorie* 104 Companions, bold adjutors of thy acts. **1642** *Declar. Lords & Comm., For Rais. Forces* 22 Dec. 7 That the Lord Lievtenants..appoint one experienced Souldier in every Regiment to be an Adjutor.. to exercise the severall Companies of the sayd Regiments. **1652** GAULE *Magastrom.* 321 Darius the King, with some adjutors of like dignity, entred into a pact. **1670** J.

FLAMSTEED in Rigaud *Corr. Sci. Men* (1841) II. 96 My friend, who is my sole adjutor, knows your hand. **1874** CARLYLE *Let.* 27 Apr. (1904) II. 306 Tait and some of his adjutors can set to work next day. **1893** *Nat. Observer* 15 Apr. 540/2 That gentleman, as became an adjutor of the greatest living thing in petticoats, was equal to the occasion.

† **a'djutor**[2]. *Phys. Obs.* [ad. Fr. *adjutoire* ('the upper bone of the arme toward the shoulder; so called by some anatomists.' Cotgr. 1611), ad. L. *adjūtōrium.*] Properly the *humerus*, but applied also to the *ulna*. See ADJUTORIUM, ADJUTORY.

1541 R. COPLAND *Guydon's Quest. Cyrurg.* Yᵉ fyrste parte of the great hande that is named vlna or adiutor.

† **adju'torious,** *a. Obs. rare*⁻¹. [f. L. *adjūtōri-us* ADJUTORY + -OUS.] Helpful, affording aid.

1657 TOMLINSON *Renou's Disp.* 209 To which parts their faculties are destined as adjutorious.

† **'adjutory,** *a.* and *sb. Obs.* [ad. L. *adjūtōri-us* serving to help, also subst. masc. 'a helper,' neut. *-ōrium* 'a means of help,' f. ADJUTOR; see -ORY.]

A. *adj.* Helping, contributing aid. *spec.* in *Phys.* applied to certain bones of the arm, from their assisting in raising the hand.

1612 WOODALL *Surg. Mate* Wks. 1653, 155 The arm-pit, or hollow place..under the upper round end of the adjutory bone. **1656** BLOUNT *Glossogr.*, The two bones which extend from the shoulders to the elbow are called adjutory ones. [Repeated with little or no variation in PHILLIPS, KERSEY, BAILEY.] **1706** PHILLIPS, *Adjutory*, aiding or helping.

B. *sb.*

1. A helper (L. *adjūtōrius*).

1552 LYNDESAY *Monarche* (1866) 6270 Tharfor, cal god to be thi adiutory.

2. *Phys.* A bone of the arm; prop. the *humerus*, but with some the *ulna*. (med.L. *os adjutorium.*)

1541 R. COPLAND *Guydon's Quest. Cyrurg.*, Towarde the elbowe ben receyued yᵉ roundnesses graduales of the adiutory.

3. Help, assistance. (L. *adjūtōrium.*)

c **1505** DUNBAR *To King* xvii, I haif belief, In howp, Schir, of your adjutory. **1678** GALE *Crt. of Gentiles* III. 125 The Dominicans have reached the Marrow of Divine adjutorie.

† **a'djutrice.** *Obs. rare*⁻¹. [a. Fr. *adjutrice* a female helper, ad. L. *adjūtrīc-em*, nom. *adjūtrix*: see next.] A female assistant.

1609 HOLLAND *Amm. Marcell.* XXVI. ii. 286 Fortune, the adiutrice of good purposes.

† **a'djutrix.** *Obs.*⁻⁰ [L. *adjūtrix*, fem. of ADJUTOR.] A female helper.

1721 in BAILEY, whence in JOHNSON, etc.

† **'adjuvable,** *a. Obs. rare*⁻¹. [ad. assumed L. **adjuvābil-is*, f. *adjuvā-re* to assist: see ADJUVANT and -ABLE.] Helpful.

1599 A. M. *Gabelhouer's Bk. Physic* 10/2 This corroborateth the Braynes, and is adiuvable to the Memorye.

adjuvancy ('ædʒ(j)uːvənsɪ). [f. ADJUVANT *a.*: see -ANCY.] Assistance, help.

1884 W. STANILAND *Songs after Sunset* 54 Whose designing flattery Bought my adjuvancy with foul intent. **1896** *Durham Univ. Jrnl.* XII. 14 The students.. endeavoured to secure his adjuvancy in their theological studies.

adjuvant ('ædʒ(j)uːvənt), *a.* and *sb.* [a. Fr. *adjuvant* (16th c. in Litt.), ad. L. *adjuvant-em*, pr. pple. of *adjuvā-re* to assist; f. *ad* to + *juvā-re* to help.]

A. *adj.* Assisting, aiding, helpful, auxiliary.

a **1614** P. LILIE *2 Serm.* (1619) 3, I doe not say they are principall causes, but instrumentall, adjuvant, secundary, inferiour causes. **1650** GREENHILL *On Ezek.* (1874) Ded. 4 It is my unhappinesse that I cannot be sufficiently adjuvant to such Princely beginnings. **1836** TODD *Cycl. Anat. & Phys.* I. 645/2 Used as adjuvant respiratory organs. **1874** WEBSTER *Rep. Patent Congress at Vienna* IV. 355 An examination system which should be adjuvant and advisory to the applicant.

B. *sb.* [The adj. used *absol.*] A person or thing helping or aiding; a help, helper, or assistant. *spec.* in *Med.* A substance added to a prescription to assist the action of the principal ingredient or 'base.'

1609 YELVERTON in *Archæol.* XV. 51 (T.) I have only been a careful Adjuvant, and was sorry I could not be the efficient. **1654** T. WHITAKER *Bl. of Grape* 2 (T.) These [plants] are adjuvants by reason of their cathartique quality. **1865** HUXLEY *Ethnology* in *Crit. & Addr.* 1873, vii. 138 The value of philology as an adjuvant to ethnology. **1875** WOOD *Therap.* (1879) 83 *Serpentaria*, An elegant stimulant tonic, especially useful as an adjuvant to more powerful bitters.

† **'adjuvate,** *v. Obs.* [f. L. *adjuvāt-* ppl. stem of *adjuvā-re*; see prec.] To assist or aid.

1599 A. M. *Gabelhouer's Bk. Physic* 34/2 The one might somewhat adiuvat the other. **1634** J. B[ATE] *Myst. Nat.* 112 Nature being but a little adjuvated or seconded with Art. **1657** TOMLINSON *Renou's Disp.* 335 Eyebright..doth with much efficacy adjuvate the eyes. **1708** MOTTEUX *Rabelais* V. xxiii, Your frequently experimented Industry..continually adjuvates you to perficiate all things in so expeditious a manner.

adle, obs. or dial. form of ADDLE.

† **'adle.** *Obs.* Forms: 1 ádl. *North.* 3 **adle**. [from same root as *ad* burning, hence orig. inflammation, fever. It does not seem to have survived the 12th c. in southern Eng., where it would have become *odle*. Not connected with ADDLE in *addle-egg*.] Sickness, disease.

c **1000** *Ags. Gospels* Matt. x. 1 And hældun ádle, and ælce untrumnysse. *c* **1160** *Hatt. Gosp.* ibid., And helden adle, & ælche untrumnysse. *c* **1200** *Ormulum* 4803 Onn all hiss bodiȝ her & tær þurrh an full atell adle.

adlegation (,ædlɪ'geɪʃən). [ad. L. *adlēgātiōn-em* (more commonly *allēgātiōn-em*, whence in another sense ALLEGATION), n. of action, f. *adlēgā-re* to depute to, f. *ad* to, in addition + *lēgā-re* to depute.] The right formerly claimed by the states of the German Empire of associating delegates or ambassadors of their own with those of the emperor in treaties and negotiations relating to the public concerns of the empire; hence distinguished from *legation* or the sending of envoys on the private affairs of each state.

1753 CHAMBERS *Cycl. Supp.* s.v., The bishops have the right of adlegation in treaties which concern the common interest, but no right of legation for their own private affairs .. The emperor allows the princes of Germany the privilege of *legation*, but disputes that of *adlegation*.

Adlerian (æd'lɪərɪən), *a.* [See -IAN.] Of, pertaining to, or characteristic of the psychologist Alfred *Adler* (1870–1937) or his teaching. Also *sb.*, a follower or adherent of Adler.

1924 *Brit. Jrnl. Med. Psychol.* IV. 226 Cases of Adlerian neuroses when the organic inferiority engenders..anxieties. **1933** *Times Lit. Suppl.* 2 Mar. 151/2 This latest medical pamphlet contains three papers in which Adlerian psychology is applied to various phases of child life. **1941** H. G. WELLS *You can't be too Careful* v. i. 237 A certain section of the mixture of peoples called the Jews..suffers from an Adlerian assertiveness. *Ibid.* VI. i. 269 A natural Adlerian revolt against the overbearing religious dogmatisms of the Middle Ages. **1959** *Times Lit. Suppl.* 1 May 257/4 They were thus given to..a mixed audience..of all 'schools' of dynamic psychology: Freudians, Adlerians, eclectics and a few Jungians. **1966** *Listener* 13 Jan. 71/2 The Adlerian principle of compensation for inferiority.

ad lib., abbrev. of AD LIBITUM *adv. phr.*

1811 in T. BUSBY *Dict. Mus.* (ed. 3). **1894** STEVENSON & OSBOURNE *Ebb-Tide* I. v. 66, I'll have fizz *ad lib.*, or it won't wash. **1900** in A. E. T. WATSON *Young Sportsman* 27 The catalogue may be extended *ad lib.* for those who require their spring-balance weighing-machine, vaseline,..and small bottle of odourless paraffin. **1931** *Times Lit. Suppl.* 24 Sept. 719/3 Now he could have all he wanted for his mass methods —living material *ad lib.*, hundreds of test-tubes for his cultures in place of dozens. **1962** N. DEL MAR *R. Strauss* I. vi. 183 He never gave them [saxophones] any solo work, marked them *ad lib.*, and..omitted them in his own performances.

B. *adj.* (,æd'lɪb). Extemporized, improvised, spontaneous, unrehearsed. orig. *U.S.* Also as *sb.*, something spoken or played extempore (chiefly *U.S.*).

1925 *Amer. Speech* I. 36/1 'Can the ad lib!' which means, politely, 'Will you be good enough to hush!' **1935** *Peabody Bulletin* (Baltimore) Dec. 42/2 Licks: Phrases used in solo choruses that are..catchy. They occur in 'ad lib solos' or hot choruses. **1948** *Daily Tel.* 11 June 5/4 That was an ill-considered ad lib remark. **1958** G. LASCELLES in P. Gammond *Decca Bk. of Jazz* viii. 107 With his early big band..he retained a reasonable ad-lib feeling.

ad-lib (,æd'lɪb), *v.* orig. *U.S.* [f. prec.] *trans.* and *intr.* To speak extempore; to announce without script, improvise (words, etc.) esp. in the course of a stage or broadcast performance. Hence **ad-'libbed** *ppl. a.*, improvised; **ad-'libber**, one who ad-libs; **ad-'libbing** *vbl. sb.* and *ppl. a.*

1919 F. HURST *Humoresque* 265 'Easy money, friends,' Miss Hoag would *ad lib.* to the line-up outside her railing. **1926** WHITEMAN & MCBRIDE *Jazz* iii. 73, I remember one day asking one of my English musicians, 'Can you ad lib?' ..'Certainly,' answered the man, rather nettled, 'I can ad lib anything.' **1927** *Sat. Even. Post.* 5 Mar. 54/3 The text of musical plays..is much more flexible..and considerable 'ad libbing', as impromptu speeches are called, is indulged in. **1929** *Bookman* (U.S.) Mar. 149/2 'Ad-libbing' is improvising. 'When Jones got lost back stage I had to ad-lib all over the place until he came on.' **1936** *Harper's Mag.* 2 Apr. 573/1 The preacher or orator whose message is canned beforehand never reaches the emotional heights of persuasion that his 'ad libbing' brother does on a rival rostrum. **1938** *Scrutiny* VII. 216 It seems much more likely from the extensive *ad-libbing* (to borrow a word from the Americans) Mr. Roberts allows himself that Hulme's positions were useful to him in working out problems that are preoccupying him. **1939** ADELER & WEST *Remember Fred Karno* vi. 69 In the sketch he 'ad-libbed' a bit, to use Fred Karno's phrase. **1940** *Amer. Speech* XV. 65 Fadiman is a carbolic ad libber. **1956** C. W. MILLS *Power Elite* i. 15 The easy ad-libbed gags the celebrity 'spontaneously' echoes. **1958** I. BROWN *Words in Our Time* 15 The adlibber in the theatre is one who introduces what are called 'gags'. **1958** 'N. SHUTE' *Rainbow & Rose* iii. 95 The whole squadron in the stalls chi-hiking at us and Judy ad-libbing back at them across the footlights.

‖ **ad libitum** (,æd 'lɪbɪtəm), *adv. phr.* [L. *ad* to + *libitum* pleasure, pa. pple. used subst. of *libet* it pleases.] At one's pleasure; to the full extent of one's wishes, as much as one desires. In *Music* opposed to *obbligato*.

1610 FOLKINGHAM *Art of Survey* II. vi. 58 These may be contrived in Parallelograms, Squares, Circles..compassed and tricked *ad libitum*. **1671** LOCKE *Hum. Underst.* (*Draft B*) (1931) §70 p. 139 Imperfect ideas, and consequently words, *ad libitum* by every particular man made use of for signs of those ideas. **1705** HICKERINGILL *Priest-Craft* II. i. 14 Afterwards comes another King..and quite contrary disannuls, *ad libitum*, the Acts of Uniformity and Conformity. **1724** in *Short Explic. For. Wds. Mus. Bks.* 7. **1823** *Harmonicon* Mar. I. 40/2 Air, with accompaniments, ad libitum, for the flute, by T. A. Rawlings. **1845** J. E. WARNER *Lessons in Music* 200 Sometimes the movement is expressly committed to the taste of the performer by placing the term *ad libitum*..over the passage. **1848** LYTTON *Harold* I. i. 38 To marry wives *ad libitum*. **1878** E. J. HOPKINS in Grove's *Dict. Mus.* I. 20 An accompaniment..is said to be Ad libitum when..it is not essential to the complete rendering of the music. **1922** JOYCE *Ulysses* 691 *Love's Old Sweet Song*..open at the last page with the final indications *ad libitum, forte*, [etc.]. **1944** W. APEL *Harvard Dict. Mus.* 16 *Ad libitum*, an indication which gives the performer the liberty: (1) to vary from strict tempo..(2) to include or omit the part of some voice or instrument..(3) to include a cadenza according to his own invention.

Hence as *adj.*

1769 GRAY *Jrnl.* 10 Oct. in *Corresp.* (1935) III. 1103 Many neat buildings of white stone, but a little disorderly in their position ad libitum like Kendal. **1801** T. BUSBY *Dict. Mus.* s.v., We speak of an *Ad Libitum* pause; or, an *Ad Libitum* cadenza. **1821** *Edin. Rev.* XXXV. 343 Armed with an *ad libitum* reserve of fool-hardiness. **1823** *Harmonicon* June I. 83/1 Clementi has arranged for the piano-forte, with *ad libitum* accompaniments, many of the best symphonies of Haydn and Mozart.

‖ **ad litem** (æd 'laɪtɛm). *Law.* [L.] For a lawsuit or action (applied esp. to a guardian appointed for such a purpose).

1768 W. BLACKSTONE *Commentaries on Laws of England* III. xxvii. 427 The court of exchequer can only appoint a guardian *ad litem*, to manage the defence of the infant if a suit be commenced against him. **1838** [see GUARDIAN 2 b]. **1883** LORD COLERIDGE in *Law Rep. Queen's Bench Div.* XI. 252 Guardians ad litem are relieved from the duty of answering interrogatories. **1959** JOWITT *Dict. Eng. Law* I. 884/1 A guardian *ad litem* is a person appointed to defend an action or other proceeding on behalf of an infant..or a lunatic or idiot not so found..who is defendant or respondent to a proceeding in the court. **1961** *Lancet* 12 Aug. 366/1 The husband, by the Official Solicitor as his guardian *ad litem*, denied the allegation.

adlocution, obs. form of ALLOCUTION.

† **adlu'bescence.** *Obs. rare*⁻¹. [f. L. *adlubēscent-em*, pr. pple. of *adlubēsc-ĕre* to find pleasure in; as if a. Fr. *adlubescence*, ad. L. **adlubēscentia*.] Pleasure, delight.

1673 MARVELL *Rehears. Transp.* II. (1674) 102 Such an expansion of heart, such an adlubescence of mind..that he could scarce refrain from kissing it.

ad-man: see AD.

admarginate (æd'mɑːdʒɪneɪt), *v. rare.* [f. L. *ad* to + *margin-em* edge, border + -ATE[3], as if f. L. **admarginā-re*; cf. *emarginate*.] To add or note in the margin.

a **1834** COLERIDGE in WEBSTER, Receive candidly the few hints which I have admarginated for your assistance.

admass ('ædmæs). Also **ad-mass**. [f. AD advertisement + MASS *sb.*[2]] (See quot. 1955.) That section of the community which is easily influenced by mass methods of publicity and entertainment; also applied to the advertising, etc., processes or agents themselves.

1955 J. B. PRIESTLEY & J. HAWKES *Journey down Rainbow* iii. 51 *Admass.* This is my name for the whole system of an increasing productivity, plus inflation, plus a rising standard of material living, plus high-pressure advertising and salesmanship, plus mass communications, plus cultural democracy and the creation of the mass mind, the mass man. **1957** *Times Lit. Suppl.* 4 Oct. 593/2 The broadening cultural pattern in the age of ad-mass. **1957** *Listener* 10 Oct. 583/2 Ordinary, intelligent people..who do not wish to be caught up in the Admass culture, yet whose education has not provided them with a complete means to resist it. **1959** N. MARSH *Singing in Shrouds* v. 97 The entire Commercial TV admass.

admaxillary (æd'mæksɪlərɪ), *a. Phys.* [f. L. *ad* to, at + MAXILLARY, f. L. *maxilla* jaw. Cf. *adambulacral*, and see AD-.] Connected with the jaw, or maxillary system.

1881 KLEIN in *Jrnl. Microsc. Sc.* Jan. 116, I propose to call these two glands, viz. connected with the parotid and the submaxillary, as the *admaxillary* glands, and to distinguish ..the latter as the lower or inferior admaxillary gland.

admeasure (æd'mɛʒ(j)ʊə(r), -ʒə(r)), *v.* Also 4–5 **amesure**. [a. OFr. *amesure-r*:—late L. *admensūrā-re*, f. *ad* to + *mensūrā-re* to measure, f. *mensūra* MEASURE. Occ. refashioned after L. as *admesurer* in MFr., whence the established Eng. form.]

† **1.** To assign a measure or limit to (a thing), to keep in measure; to moderate, limit, control. *Obs.*

1340 *Ayenb.* 150 He makeþ man wytvol, and wys, and amesureþ alle þing. *a* **1450** *Knt. de la Tour* 25 Here is a good ensaumple to amesure in this matere bothe herte and thought. **1627** SIR E. COOK in Rushw. *Hist. Coll.* (1659) I. 512 The Common-Law hath admeasured the Kings Prerogative.

†**2.** To apply a measure to; to measure out. *Obs.*

1481 EARL WORCESTER (Caxton) *Tulle on Friendsh.* iv. 7 Ne lete us amesure it [virtue] after the magnyfycence of wordes. **1599** SANDYS *Europæ Spec.* (1632) 5 The admeasuring of devotions by tale on beads. **1697** *View of Penal Laws* 51 All Keel-boats..that before they be admeasured..shall carry any coal, shall be forfeited.

3. To measure out to (a person); to apportion; to assign to each claimant his rightful share.

1641 *Termes de la Ley* 11 Where a woman is endowed..of more than she ought to have..the woman shall be admeasured, and the heire restored to the overplus. **1656** J. TRAPP *Expos. Matt.* xxii. 11 (1868) II. 233 [God] is in the assemblies of his saints..to admeasure unto them in blessing as they do to him in preparation. **1809** TOMLINS *Law Dict.* s.v. *Common*, It recites a complaint that the defendant hath surcharged the common; and therefore commands the sheriff to admeasure and apportion it... Upon this suit all the commoners shall be admeasured.

admeasured (æd'mɛʒ(j)ʊəd, -ʒəd), *ppl. a.* Also 4–5 amesured. [f. A(D)MEASURE *v.* + -ED.] Kept within measure or bounds; measured, apportioned.

1340 *Ayenb.* 258 Zuo ssolde he by wel ytempred and amesured ine hyperþe and ine lhestinge. **1489** CAXTON *Faytes of Armes* I. vii. 17 Not testyf, hastyf, hoot ne angry but amesured and attemporat. **1647** WARD *Simple Cobler* (1843) 51 Civill Liberties and Proprieties admeasured to every man to his true *suum*.

admeasurement (æd'mɛʒ(j)ʊəmənt, -ʒər-). [a. OFr. *amesurement*, occ. later spelling *admesurement*: see ADMEASURE and -MENT.]

1. The process of admeasuring; applying a measure in order to ascertain or compare dimensions.

*a***1626** BACON *Hist. Alienations* (J.) In some counties they are not much acquainted with admeasurement by acre. **1767** T. HUTCHINSON *Hist. Prov. Mass. Bay* iii. 326 When the terror is so great, no dependance can be placed upon the admeasurement of time in any person's mind. **1842** MRS. BROWNING *Grk. Chr. Poets* (1863) 134 Too low for admeasurement with Spenser.

2. Absolute or comparative dimensions; size, dimensions, proportions.

1790 BURKE *Fr. Revol.* Wks. V. 237 The middle term for the rest of France is about nine hundred inhabitants to the same admeasurement. **1853** MAURICE *Proph. & Kings* xxvii. 465 Accurate admeasurements in feet and cubits seem as if they must relate to a visible, not to an invisible fabric. **1870** DISRAELI *Lothair* lxxii. 380 His steam-yacht Pan, of considerable admeasurement.

3. The ascertainment and apportionment of just shares in anything, as in an inheritance or a common.

1598 KITCHIN *Courts Leet* (1675) 187 Admeasurement lies between commoners. **1650–4** USSHER *Annals* VI. (1658) 374 A further admeasurement of corn among his army. **1691** BLOUNT *Law Dict.*, *Admeasurement* is a Writ which lies, for bringing those to Reason, or a Mediocrity, that usurp more than their share. **1768** BLACKSTONE *Comm.* III. 238 By writ of admeasurement of pasture.

admeasurer (æd'mɛʒ(j)ʊərə(r), -ʒərə(r)). [f. ADMEASURE + -ER[1].] 'One who admeasures.' Craig 1847, and mod. Dicts.

admeasuring (æd'mɛʒ(j)ʊərɪŋ, -ʒərɪŋ), *vbl. sb.* [f. ADMEASURE + -ING[1].] Measuring; apportionment.

1599 [See under ADMEASURE 1].

admensuration (æd,mɛnsjʊə'reɪʃən). [ad. late L. *admensūrātiōn-em* = *reductio ad mensūram*, n. of action, f. *admensūrā-re* to assign a measure to, f. *ad* to + *mensūra* MEASURE.] = ADMEASUREMENT.

1673 MARVELL *Rehears. Transp.* II. 182 Some of 'm have more and some perhaps less than is absolutely necessary. 'Tis pity that you were not at the admensuration. **1778–80** BURROWS *Rep.* I. 263 (JOD.) He has remedy; viz. either by admensuration, or assize of novel disseisin.

admenuse, refash. f. AMENUSE, *v. Obs.*, to lessen.

admerall, obs. form of ADMIRAL.

†**admerveylle, -aylle**, *v. Obs.* [A refashioning of earlier *amerveil(le*, a. OFr. *amerveillie-r*, earlier *émerveillier*, *esmerveillier* to marvel, admire; with *a-* :—*es-* :—L. *ex-*, confused with *a-* :—L. *ad.* This pseudo-etymological spelling arose in MFr., whence introduced into Eng. by Caxton; mod.Fr. has restored *émerveiller.* See AMERVEIL; also A- *pref.* 10 and AD-.] *trans.*, *intr.*, and *pass.* To marvel; marvel at, wonder at, admire.

1474 CAXTON *The Chesse* 49 Whan Pirrus vnderstood this he was gretly admeruaylid. **1485** —— *Chas. the Gt.* 53, I am wel admeruaylled fro whens that cometh. **1495** —— *Vitas Patr.* (W. de Worde), I. i. 6ab, He admerueyled and was heuy and sory. **1506** *Ordin. Crysten Men* (W. de Worde) I. vii. 59 Such nobles..no tonge may suffycyently speke, nor understandynge byleue comprehende nor duely admeruaylle [*printed* aduerуaylle].

†**ad'metiate**, *v. Obs.* [improp. f. L. *admētī-ri* to measure to + -ATE[3].] 'To measure.' Cockeram 1612, whence in Todd.

admin., colloq. abbrev. of ADMINISTRATION, ADMINISTRATIVE *a.*, or ADMINISTRATOR. Freq. *attrib.*, as ***admin. block, building.*** Also *ellipt.*, administration building, administrative order, etc.

1942 T. RATTIGAN *Flare Path* II. ii, Probably challenge me to a duel or something. Rapiers at dawn behind the Admin Block. *Ibid.* 67, I'd have a fine time as a Squadron Leader admin. at a training school. **1951** A. C. CLARKE *Sands of Mars* viii. 98 There was nothing very exciting about Admin. It might have been any office building. *Ibid.* x. 119 She worked in the Admin. building. **1955** J. CHRISTOPHER *Year of Comet* i. 17 You are under San Diego for admin but any reports you make go direct to Graz. **1958** *Spectator* 15 Aug. 219/3 All this is in part an admin. problem. **1961** W. BUCHAN *Helen All Alone* 26 A mass of practical details—sheer 'admin'.

adminicle (æd'mɪnɪk(ə)l). Also 8 -cule. [ad. L. *adminicul-um* a prop. Cf. Fr. *adminicule*, in Cotgr.]

1. Anything that aids or supports; an auxiliary.

*a***1556** CRANMER *Wks.* I. 37 (D.) The author would have the sacraments..to be adminicles as it were. **1597** J. KING *Jonah* xxxv. (1864) 223 They adjoin fasting and sackcloth..as adminicles..to that effectual prayer of theirs. **1788** REID *Aristotle's Log.* iv. §2. 74 The invention contained in these verses is..so great an adminicle to the dexterous management of syllogisms. **1847** GROTE *Greece* III. II. x. 99 The senate of five hundred..was a permanent adjunct and adminicle of the public assembly. **1872** *Daily News* 2 Oct. 5 Floriculture and other adminicles of civilisation.

2. *Law.* Supporting or corroboratory evidence; that which, without forming complete proof in itself, contributes to prove a point. In *Sc. Law*, Any document or writing tending to prove the existence and tenor of a lost deed, which if it existed would have been full evidence.

1706 PHILLIPS, *Adminicle*..In Civil-Law, it signifies imperfect Proof. **1829** SCOTT *Hrt. Midl.* xxiii. 178 Only as adminicles of testimony, tending to corroborate what is considered as legal and proper evidence.

3. *Archæol.* In *pl.* Ornaments which surround the figure on a medal or coin.

1751 CHAMBERS *Cycl.* s.v., Among antiquaries, the term *Adminicles* is applied to the attributes or ornaments, wherewith Juno and some other figures are represented on medals.

adminicular (,ædmɪ'nɪkjʊlə(r)), *a.* [f. L. *adminicul-um* + -AR, as if ad. L. **adminiculāris.*] Helpful, auxiliary, corroboratory. (Said chiefly of evidence.)

1676 BULLOKAR, *Adminicular*, helpful. **1726** AYLIFFE *Parergon* 445 The Aid of some adminicular Proof. *c***1817** J. HOGG *Tales & Sk.* (1837) II. 201 Whatever proves adminicular to its concentration is meritorious. **1847** WHARTON *Law-Lex.* (1872) 33 *Adminicular evidence*, explanatory or completing testimony.

†**admi'niculary**, *a.* and *sb. Obs.* [An incorrect form (as if f. a L. **adminiculārius*, not analogical.)] = ADMINICULAR; also used *subst.*

1652 URQUHART Jewel *Wks.* 1834, 254 Dotations..should be most subservient to the use of those that afford literatory adminicularies of the longest continuance. *a***1818** tr. *Rabelais* III. 34 (T.) Auxiliary suffrage, or adminiculary assistance.

adminiculate (,ædmɪ'nɪkjʊleɪt), *v. Sc. Law.* [f. L. *adminiculāt-* ppl. stem of *adminiculā-re* to prop up.] To support by corroboratory evidence. (Chiefly in pa. pple.)

1829 SCOTT *Hrt. Midl.* xxiii. 187 Bolstered up or supported, or, according to the law phrase, adminiculated, by other presumptive circumstances.

adminicu'lation. ? *Obs. rare*[−1]. [n. of action, f. prec.] The process of giving help or support.

*a***1670** HACKET *Life of Williams* II. 217 (D.) Some plants grow straight, some are help't by adminiculation to be straight.

‖**adminiculum** (,ædmɪ'nɪkjʊləm). *Nat. Hist.* Pl. -a. [L.; see ADMINICLE.]

1. *Entom.* In *pl.* Kirby's name for the short spines or teeth on the abdominal segments of certain insects, pupæ or grubs, whereby they make their way through any substance in which they burrow.

1815 KIRBY & SPENCE *Entom.* III (1826) 255 The *adminicula* or short spines..with which the dorsal segments of the abdomen of some pupæ are armed.

†**2.** *Bot.* Scopuli's name for all those organs, such as tendrils, with which plants cling to any support, called by Linnæus *fulcra. Obs.*

administer (æd'mɪnɪstə(r)), *v.* Also 4 **amynistre**, 5 **ammynyster**, 5–6 **admynystre**, **-er.** [a. OFr. *aministre-r*, a semi-popular adaptation of L. *administrā-re*, 1. to minister to (any one), 2. to manage; f. *ad.* to + *ministrāre* to serve, to MINISTER. In 14th c. the Fr. began to be refashioned after L., as *administrer*, and this spelling soon became the only one in Eng.]

1. *trans.* To manage as a steward, to carry on, or execute (an office, affairs, etc.); to manage the affairs of (an institution, town, etc.)

*c***1374** CHAUCER *Boeth.* IV. (1868) 135 He [God] amynistreþ in many maneres and in dyuerse tymes by destyne, þilke same þinges þat he haþ disponed. **1413** LYDG. *Pylgr. Sowle* IV. xxxiv. (1483) 82 The gouernement of a reame shold be admynystred and executed by suche as were of grettest bounte. **1651** HOBBES *Leviathan* III. xlii. 291 They that administer the secular affairs of the Church. **1756** C. LUCAS *Ess Waters* III. 242, I could never learn how, or by whom, that charity is administered. **1865** GROTE *Plato* I. xix. 564 Pericles administered Athens. **1868** M. PATTISON *Academ. Organ.* §4, 109 Each college has one or more bursars who administer the finances.

b. *absol.*

1866 MOTLEY *Dutch Rep.* IV. i. 546 Much incapacity to govern was revealed in this inordinate passion to administer.

2. *Law.* To manage and dispose of the goods and estate of a deceased person, either under a will, or by official appointment under *Letters of Administration.*

*c***1430** *Polit. Rel. & Love Poems* 29 Peyse wisely the besynes and the purpose of them wich ammynyster thy goodes. **1809** TOMLINS *Law Dict.* s.v. *Executor*, The Ordinary shall depute the nearest and most lawful friends of the deceased to administer his goods.

b. *absol.* To act officially as an executor or administrator.

1602 FULBECKE *First Pt. Parallele* 44 Hee shall not haue an action of debt against the executour of his coexecutour, although the partie indebted did not administer in his life-time. **1714** [ARBUTHNOT & POPE] *M. Scriblerus* (J.) Neal's order was never performed, because the executors durst not administer. **1870** PINKERTON *Guide to Administr.* 9 When a stranger is about to administer, a renunciation should be obtained in writing from those who are by law entitled.

3. *trans.* To execute or dispense (justice).

1509 FISHER *Wks.* 1876, 297 And admynystre ryght and Iustyce to euery party. **1876** FREEMAN *Norm. Conq.* II. viii. 286 The citizens disliked the rule of William on account of the strict justice which he administered.

4. *trans.* To execute or perform (offices of religion); to dispense (a sacrament). A rare obs. const. is (of a person) ***to be administered***: to receive the sacrament.

1495 CAXTON *Vitas Patr.* (W. de Worde) I. xlii. 70ab, I neuer receyued hym syth I was admynystred in the chyrche of saynt Johan. **1585** ABP. SANDYS *Serm.* (1841) 252 We in our churches have both the gospel preached, and the sacraments..administered. **1611** BIBLE *2 Cor.* viii. 19 This grace which is administred by vs. **1735** WESLEY *Wks.* 1872 I. 17 I..administered the Lord's Supper to six or seven communicants. **1855** PRESCOTT *Philip II*, I. ix. (1857) 175 It was thought proper to administer extreme unction to him.

b. *absol.*

1590 GREENWOOD in *Conferences* III. 57 By the Bishops calling, you administer, and by none other. **1634** J. CANNE *Necess. Separ.* (1849) 33 A true vocation and calling by..ordination of that faithful people where he is to administer.

5. To tender (an oath *to* any one).

1593 SHAKS. *Rich. II*, I. iii. 182 Sweare by the duty that you owe to heauen..To keepe the Oath that we administer. **1751** JORTIN *Serm.* (1771) IV. i. 4 To administer an oath to a man. **1802** MAR. EDGEWORTH *Mor. Tales* (1816) I. 223 The oath, which has just been administered to you.

6. To apply or perform (any branch of the healing art). *Obs.* exc. as, To give (medicine *to*).

1541 R. COPLAND *Galyen's Terap.* 2Ci, They that by reason & Methode admynyster the arte of medycyne do cure yᵉ vlceres. **1667** *Phil. Trans.* II. 537 The Physitians administring this operation. **1743** tr. *Heister's Surg.* 277 His Attendants should stand ready to administer the Dressings. **1747** in *Col. Rec. Penn.* V. 136, I administer'd the Medicines to Shikalimy. **1804** ABERNETHY *Surg. Observ.* 109 If a surgeon..administers mercury in one of the diseases.

b. *absol.*

1845 FORD *Handbk. Spain* i. 47 The patient however must administer to himself.

7. Hence *fig.* To dispense, furnish, supply, or give (anything beneficial, or assumed to be beneficial, to the recipient; extended humorously to a *rebuke*, a *blow*, etc.) Const. *to.*

1489 CAXTON *Fayt of Armes* III. xxi. 219 Euery noble man shulde peyne him self after hys powere to administre unto him helthe of witte and aduyse. **1628** DIGBY *Voy. Medit.* 56 A place that administred meanes of such debauchednesse. **1713** STEELE *Englishm.* No. 38, 243 The Joy which this Temper of Soul administers. **1789–96** J. MORSE *Amer. Geog.* I. 296 These annual orations administered fuel to the fire of liberty. **1852** THACKERAY *Esmond* III. vii. (1876) 377 She kept him by her side to nurse the baby and administer posset to the Gossips. **1865** *Morn. Star* 31 Mar., By invading the North he might administer his old antagonists another severe blow.

b. *intr.* (obj. omitted.) To contribute beneficially, to minister *to.*

1712 *Spectator* No. 477, ¶1 A Fountain..administers to the Pleasure, as well as the Plenty of the Place. **1779** J. MOORE *View of Society* xiv. (1789) I. 99 Who are supposed to administer to the King's pleasures. **1872** R. ANDERSON *Missions Am. Board* III. xi. 164 He was soon able to administer to the comfort of his associates.

†**ad'minister**, *sb. Obs.* [a. L. *administer* an attendant, f. *ad* to + *minister* a servant.] One who administers or ministers to others; a minister or administrator.

1506 *Ordin. Crysten Men* (W. de Worde) IV. xxi. 248 To make admynysters unto the poore. **1586** T. ROGERS *39 Art.* (1607) 234 The public ministers of the word are to be the administers of the Sacraments. **1650** HOWELL *Lett.* II. 4 They serve the dead and living; they becom Attorneys and administers. **1677** GALE *Crt. of Gentiles* II. III. 172 These Apuleius cals Administers and Salvation-bringers.

administered (æd'mɪnɪstəd), *ppl. a.* [f. prec. + -ED.] **a.** Managed, carried on; dispensed, tendered.

1538 STARKEY *England* 46 Cyvyle ordur and polytyke law, admynystyrd by offycers and rularys. **1651** HOBBES *Leviathan* II. xxx. 176 The Kingdome of God, (administred by Moses,) over the Jewes. **1809** TOMLINS *Law Dict.* s.v. *Oath*, The Oath of Allegiance, as administered for upwards of six hundred years. **1865** *Pall Mall G.* 6 Nov. 10 The highly administered Arabs of the Tell or cultivated districts. *Mod.* *a* **1884** The dose administered was deadly poison.

b. ***administered price*** (Econ.), a price determined not by market forces but by administrative action (of a large company or of government).

1935 G. C. MEANS *Industr. Prices* (74th U.S. Congress 1 Sess. Senate Misc. Doc. No. 13) 1 A market price is one which is made in the market as the result of the interaction of buyers and sellers... An administered price is..a price which is set by administrative action and held constant for a period of time. **1936** J. M. KEYNES *Gen. Theory Employment* V. xix. 268 'Administered' or monopoly prices..are determined by other considerations beside marginal cost. **1965** *Observer* 10 Oct. 7/2 The once popular 'administered price' theory, in which a giant like U.S. Steel moved first, and the rest automatically played follow my leader. **1984** *Times* 4 Apr. 13/3 There is no profitable future in the production of unsalable goods at administered prices.

administerial (æd,mɪnɪ'stɪərɪəl), *a.* [f. ADMINISTER *v.* on analogy of *ministerial* (f. L. *ministerium*) and its apparent relation to *minister*.] 'Pertaining to the administration or government.' Craig 1847.

administering (æd'mɪnɪstərɪŋ), *vbl. sb.* [f. ADMINISTER *v.* + -ING[1].] The action of managing; of ministering; or of supplying, giving.

1678 BUTLER *Hudibr.* III. i. 1276 What makes rebelling against Kings A good old Cause?—Administerings. *Mod.* He thought of administering a sharp reproof.

administering (æd'mɪnɪstərɪŋ), *ppl. a.* [f. as prec. + -ING[2].] Managing; ministering; supplying.

1685 tr. *Bossuet, Doctr. Cath. Ch.* §4, 7 Angels..being established by God's order, as administring Spirits.

administrable (æd'mɪnɪstrəb(ə)l), *a.* [f. L. *administrā-re* to ADMINISTER + -BLE, as if ad. L. **administrābilis*.] Capable of administration.

1818 In TODD. **1832** J. AUSTIN *Lect. Jurisp.* li. (1879) II. 865 The Scotch law of succession in moveables (that is, administrable property).

administrant (æd'mɪnɪstrənt), *a.* and *sb.* [a. Fr. *administrant* pr. pple. of *administrer*: see ADMINISTER *v.*]

A. *adj.* Acting, managing affairs; executive.

1602 SIR W. SEGAR *Honor, Mil. & Civ.* IV. xxi. 236 The officers Administrant are to precede; next to them the Vacants. **1855** H. REED *Lect. Eng. Hist.* vii. 238 Justice is made to appear almost self-administrant.

B. *sb.* One who administers or conducts any office or affair; an acting officer.

1602 SIR W. SEGAR *Honor, Mil. & Civ.* IV. xxi. 236 To begin with Administrants and their order among themselues. **1873** BROWNING *Red Cott. N.-Cap Country* 254 The Church is sole administrant, Since sole possessor of what worldly wealth Monsieur Léonce Miranda late possessed.

†**ad'ministrate**, *ppl. a. Obs.* [ad. L. *administrāt-us* pa. pple. of *administrā-re*: see ADMINISTER *v.*] Administered.

1637 GILLESPIE *Eng. Pop. Cerem.* III. i. 5 Baptisme might not be administrat in private places. **1671** *True Non-Conformist* 226 These faithful men, by whom it [the oath] was administrate. **1715** in Wodrow's *Corr.* (1843) II. 96 To have got favourable Justices of the Peace to have administrate the Allegiance and Assurance.

administrate (æd'mɪnɪstreɪt), *v.* [f. L. *administrāt-* ppl. stem of *administrā-re*: see ADMINISTER (cf. *demonstrate*, etc.).] **1.** A by-form of ADMINISTER *v.* (a sacrament, oath, medicine).

1651 CALDERWOOD *Hist. Kirk* (1843) II. 38 That no maner of person, in time coming, administrat anie of the sacraments secreetlie. **1733** G. CHEYNE *Eng. Malady* (1735) Pref., When Lithotomy cannot be administrated. **1855** MILMAN *Lat. Chr.* III. v. (1864) II. 70 The delinquent clerk might be deprived for a time of his power of administrating sacred things.

2. To manage or direct (affairs). Now usu. *absol.* or *intr.* Cf. ADMINISTER *v.* 1.

a **1639** J. SPOTTISWOOD *Hist. Ch. Scot.* (1655) V. 241 A Lieutenant should be appointed..with full authority to administrate all affairs. **1848** *Tait's Mag.* June 397/2 The people is sovereign, its representatives administrate. **1934** G. B. SHAW *On Rocks* Pref. 150 What was formerly called'real property' is replaced by ordinary personal property and common property administrated by the State. **1965** *New Statesman* 17 Sept. 400/3 Bishops, prime ministers, official people loved it... One is simply administrating in a fantasy world. **1981** *Times* 29 Apr. 9/6 The machinery of such aid is still primed by administrators eager to go out and administrate.

3. To organize or manage the recording and application of information in (a list, register, etc.).

1977 *Wandsworth Boro' News* 16 Sept. 19/4 (Advt.), Part-time..ledger clerk required to administrate sales ledger (mechanised). **1982** *Times* 12 Oct. 12/6 A claims register, administrated by an International Sea Bed Authority, would have been a simple answer.

administrating (æd'mɪnɪstreɪtɪŋ), *vbl. sb.* [f. prec. + -ING[1].] Managing, conducting affairs; administration. (Mostly gerundial.)

1862 RUSKIN *Unto this Last* 74 Whether the stream shall be a curse or a blessing, depends upon man's labour, and administrating intelligence [= intelligence in managing or administrating]. **1873** *Brit. Q. Rev.* Jan., 93 Thanks to the system in vogue for administrating our naval affairs.

administration (æd,mɪnɪ'streɪʃən). Also 4–6 **admynystracion, -cioun, -tyon,** etc. [ad. L. *administrātiōn-em*, n. of action, f. *administrā-re*: see ADMINISTER *v.* The Fr. *administration* (13th c. in Littré) may be the immed. source.]

†**1.** The action of administering or serving in any office; service, ministry, attendance, performance of duty. *Obs.* in general sense.

1382 WYCLIF *2 Cor.* iv. 1 Therfore we hauynge this administracioun, or office [Vulg. *administrationem*]..faylen not. **1484** CAXTON *Curial* iij b, Thanguysshes that he hath suffred in admynystracion publycque. **1526** TINDALE *1 Cor.* xii. 5 Ther are differences of administracions, and yet but one lorde [WYCLIF seruycis, *Rheims* ministrations, **1611** administrations]. **1676** HALE *Contempl.* I. 356 No man's condition is desperate so long as the Physician continues his administration. **1791** BOSWELL *Johnson* (1816) I. 18 All the stores of nature and of art stand in prompt administration.

†**2.** Performance, execution *of*. *Obs.*

1598 BARKCLEY *Felicitie of Man* (1631) 309 Hee that buyeth an office, must sell the administration of it. **1611** BIBLE *2 Cor.* ix. 12 For the administration of this seruice.. is abundant also by many thanksgiuings vnto God [WYCLIF mynysterie, TINDALE ministracion].

3. Management (*of* any business).

c **1374** CHAUCER *Boethius* I. (1560) 199/2, I..desired to put foorth in execucion and in act of commen administracion thilke things that I had learned. **1494** FABYAN VII. 547 Rule and gouernaunce of the same kyngedome and lordeshyppes, with all admynystracions of the same. **1538** STARKEY *England* 4 Admynystratyon of the maters of the commyn wel. **1769** ROBERTSON *Chas. V*, VI. VI. 107 In him was vested the sovereign administration of the revenues. **1868** RUSKIN *Polit. Econ. Art* i. 18 The principles which are right in the administration of a few fields, are right also in the administration of a great country.

4. *ellipt.* The management of public affairs; the conducting or carrying on of the details of government; hence, sometimes, used for *government*.

1681 H. NEVILE *Plato Rediv.* 79 All the difficulty in our Administration, hath been to regulate our own Nobility. **1771** *Junius Lett.* xlix. 254 The real injuries they received from every measure of your grace's administration. **1825** T. JEFFERSON *Autobiog.* Wks. 1859 I. 50, I resigned the administration at the end of my second year. **1851** MARIOTTI *Italy* i. 25 Salutary reforms in every branch of administration.

5. a. The executive part of the legislature; the ministry; now often loosely called the 'Government.'

1731 *Gentlem. Mag.* (1806) I. 9 A Defence of the measures of the present Administration. **1783** COWPER *Priv. Corr.* (1824) I. 250 The deplorable condition of the country, insisted on by the friends of administration, and not denied by their adversaries. **1790** BEATSON *Nav. & Mil. Mem.* I. 17 Our Administration took alarm thereat. **1840** MACAULAY *Clive* 84 A rapid succession of weak administrations..had held the semblance of power.

b. *transf.* The period of office of a particular government, president, etc. *U.S.*

1796 G. WASHINGTON in *Deb. Congr. U.S.* (1849) 17 Sept. IV. ii. 2880 In reviewing the incidents of my administration, I am unconscious of intentional error. **1889** in *Cent. Dict.* **1927** D. S. MUZZEY *History* 484 During Harrison's administration..expenditures had mounted steadily. **1948** W. R. BENÉT *Reader's Encycl.* 550/1 The charter of the United States Bank was vetoed during [President] Jackson's administration. **1984** *Washington Post* 4 Sept. c6/3 She.. served as an ambassador to Denmark during the administration of President Franklin D. Roosevelt.

6. *Law.* The management and disposal of the estate of a deceased person by an executor or administrator. *spec.* As opposed to *probate*, The authority to administer the estate of an intestate, as conferred by ***Letters of Administration*** granted, formerly by the Ordinary, now by the Probate Division of the High Court of Justice.

1538 STARKEY *England* 127 The prerogatyfe gyven to the same Byschope of Canterbury, wherby he hath..the admynystratyon of intestate godys. **1574** tr. *Littleton's Tenures* §200 If that he make no executours when he entreth into religion, then the ordinary may commit the administration of his goods to others, as if he were dead indeed. **1708** *Bickerstaff Det.* in *Swift's Wks.* 1755 II. I. 166 Once a term she is cited into the court to take out letters of administration. **1852** McCULLOCH *Taxation* II. vi. §3 (ed. 2) 300 The court by which the probate or administration is granted. **1867** E. V. WILLIAMS *Executors & Administr.* III. I. ii. (1867) II. 885 Co-executors..are regarded in law as an individual person..the acts of any one of them, in respect of the administration of the effects, are deemed to be the acts of all.

7. The action of administering something to others: **a.** Dispensation (of a sacrament, of justice, etc.). **b.** Giving or application (of remedies). **c.** Tendering (of an oath).

c **1315** SHOREHAM 57 The signe hys of thys sacrament The bisschopes blessynge, Forth myd the admynystracioun. **1474** CAXTON *Chesse* II. i. A 8 b, He ought alwey thynk on the gouernement of the royame & who hath thadmynystracion of justyce. **1597** SHAKS. *2 Hen. IV*, v. ii. 75 In the administration of his Law. **1635** PAGITT *Christianogr.* 66 For the Administration of the Sacrament of Baptisme. **1677** HALE *Prim. Orig. Man.* 232 These severe Administrations of War could not be without great Desolations. **1768** BLACKSTONE *Comm.* III. 73 To rectify and redress any mal-administrations of justice. **1875** WOOD *Therap.* (1879) 195 In poisoning by oxalic acid, the immediate administration of an antidote is of the utmost importance.

administrational (æd,mɪnɪ'streɪʃənəl), *a.* [f. prec. + -AL[1].] Of or pertaining to administration; administrative.

1862 RAWLINSON *Five Gt. Mon.* V. vii. (1873) III. 429 The administrational merits of Darius..have obscured his military glories.

administrative (æd'mɪnɪ,streɪtɪv), *a.* [ad. L. *administrātīv-us*; f. *administrāt-* ppl. stem: see ADMINISTER and -IVE.]

1. Pertaining to, or dealing with, the conduct or management of affairs; executive.

1731 BAILEY, *Administrative*, pertaining to administration. **1794** LD. HOOD in Nicolas's *Disp. & Lett. Nelson* (1845) I. 399 Captain Young..returned to the Victory with two Officers and two of the Administrative Bodies. **1850** KINGLAKE *Crimea* VI. x. 399 The administrative troubles of the winter campaign. **1858** HAWTHORNE *Fr. & It. Jrnls.* II. 234 He was in his element as an administrative man. **1872** YEATS *Growth & Viciss. Comm.* 34 A municipal oligarchy..insured some degree of administrative skill.

†**2.** Of the nature of stewardship, or delegated authority; 'used in contradistinction to dominion or power in propriety.' *Obs.*

1753 CHAMBERS *Cycl. Supp.* s.v., 'Tis contraverted whether the power given to Augustus were only *administrative*, or proper and immediate.

3. *absol.* quasi-*sb.* An administrative body; a company of men entrusted with management.

1876 *Academy* 13 May, 455/3 Grossly unjust to the more prominent administratives and executives concerned.

administratively (æd'mɪnɪ,streɪtɪvlɪ), *adv.* [f. prec. + -LY[2].] In an administrative manner; in respect to administration.

1837 *Athenæum* 18 Nov. 846/2 To render Hungary, if not completely, at least administratively, independent of Austria. **1860** *Westm. Rev.* No. 34, 503 As fast as a government, by becoming representative, grows better fitted for maintaining the rights of citizens, it..grows administratively unfitted for other purposes. **1871** *Daily News* 2 Jan., A post which is administratively subordinate to the Treasury.

administrator (æd'mɪnɪ,streɪtə(r), ,ædmɪnɪ'streɪtɔ:(r)). [a. L. *administrātor* n. of agent, f. *administrāre*: see ADMINISTER. Cf. Fr. *administrateur* (16th c. in Litt.).]

1. One who administers; one who manages, carries on, or directs the affairs of any establishment or institution; a steward, manager, or acting governor.

1533 BELLENDENE *Livy* III. (1822) 306 Quhilk is ane richt proffittabil thing in administratoris of grete materis. **1675** BAXTER *Cath. Theol.* II. i. 177 Jesus Christ..is Gods Administrator General of the humane world. **1705** LUTTRELL *Brief Rel.* (1857) V. 627 Danish troops were marching to dislodge the forces of the administrator of Holstein. **1859** MILL *Liberty* v. (1865) 68/1 The administrators of the Poor Rate throughout the country. **1880** *Daily News* 15 Apr. 5/6 The Acting Administrator of Griqualand West.

2. *absol.* One who has the faculty of managing or organizing. Cf. *manager*.

1855 MACAULAY *Hist. Eng.* IV. 14 All the implements of war had been largely provided by Louvois, the first of living administrators. **1870** *Standard* 16 Nov., What is really wanted for the pacification of Marseilles is a new superior administrator.

3. One who executes or performs the official duties of religion, justice, etc.; one who dispenses or ministers to the public in such matters.

1563 MAN *Musculus' Com. Places* 272 b, We bee not makers of sacramentes, but administrators of them. **1651** BAXTER *Inf. Bapt.* 95 The Holiness which is the ground for the Administrator to baptize. **1865** MAULE in *Cornh. Mag.* Oct., 429 The answers to them by the judges may embarrass the administrators of justice.

b. One who applies, proffers, or gives anything.

1828 LANDOR *Imag. Conv.* Wks. 1846, I. xxxvi. 227 Bonds may hold the weak; the stronger break them, and strangle the administrator.

4. One to whom authority is given to manage estates, etc. for the legal owner during his minority, incapacity, etc.; a trustee, a steward. *esp.* in *Sc. Law.* 'A person legally empowered to act for another whom the law presumes incapable of acting for himself' (*Encyc. Brit.*), as the father of children under age.

1599 SANDYS *Europæ Spec.* (1632) 53 To be administrators of Abbeys, Bishopricks and other benefices. **1622** BACON *Hen. VII* (J.) Whether he did it in his own right, or as administrator to his daughter.

5. A person officially appointed to manage and dispose of the estate of one who dies without appointing executors, or whose appointed executors cannot or do not act; an executor dative.

1514 FITZHERBERT *Justyce of Peas* (1538) 127 Yf any person hauing shepe of his owne happen to be made executor or administratour. **1641** *Termes de la Ley* 12, *Administrator* is he to whom the Ordinary committeth the administration of goods of a dead man for default of an Executor. **1824** DIBDIN *Libr. Comp.* 455 Would not trust them to the custody of a careless heir, or mercenary administrator. **1870** PINKERTON *Guide to Administr.* 11 The administrator must bear in mind that he has nothing to do with the real estate of decedent.

administratorship (æd'mɪnɪstreɪtəʃɪp, ˌædmɪnɪ'streɪtəʃɪp). [f. prec. + -SHIP.] The position or office of an administrator.

1590 SWINBURN *Testaments* 251 Whether of them were to be admitted to the administratorship, in case the testator had died intestate. **1865** CARLYLE *Fred. Gt.* I. III. xii. 300 This first crisis, of getting into the Prussian Administratorship..our vigilant Kurfürst..has successfully managed.

administratress (æd,mɪnɪ'streɪtrɪs). *rare.* [f. ADMINISTRATOR + -ESS, on Eng. analogies; cf. *waitress, actress.*] A female administrator.

1775 MRS. BOSCAWEN in *Mrs. Delany, Lett.* Ser. II. II. 176, I will allow your word 'administratress,' and I understand it.

†**admini'stratrice.** *Obs.* [a. Fr. *administratrice*, ad. It. *administratice*:—L. *administrātrīc-em.*] A female administrator.

a **1520** *Myrroure of Our Ladye* 53 As a busy administratrice mercyful & pytuous she visited the nedy syke men.

administratrix (æd,mɪnɪ'streɪtrɪks). [a. L. *administrātr-ix*, fem. of ADMINISTRATOR: see -TRIX.]

1. *gen.* A female administrator; an administratress.

1790 BURKE *Fr. Revol.* Wks. V. 63 The princess Sophia was named..as a temporary administratrix. **1859** G. WILSON *Life of Forbes* iv. 126 A mighty change passing over Medicine as an administratrix of substances, which in one sense are food, in another medicine, in another poison.

2. *spec.* A woman appointed to administer the estate of an intestate.

1626 COCKERAM, *Administratrix*, a woman in that place [*i.e.* as administrator]. **1642** FULLER *Holy & Prof. State* xi. (1840) 27 Her daughter had little comfort to be executrix or administratrix unto her. **1751** CHAMBERS *Cycl.* s.v. *Administrator*, If a woman have goods thus committed to her charge, or administration, she is called administratrix.

¶ The special meaning is the earlier; and it is due to its technical use as a legal term that the Latin form of the word has been retained, rather than the still earlier *administress*, and the later *administratress* and *administratrice*.

†**ad'ministrer.** *Obs.* [f. ADMINISTER *v.* + -ER[1]. Cf. OFr. *amenistrere, -eor, -eur*:—L. *administrātōr, -em*, afterwards supplanted by the learned form *administrateur.*] One who administers, *esp.* who administers anything to another.

1495 CAXTON *Vitas Patr.* (W. de Worde) I. li. 105 bb, Goo hens thou wicked and peruerted admynystrer of malice. **1631** DONNE *Biathanatos* A 1 Poysons, which the nature of the disease, and the art of the Administrer made wholesome. **1654** GENTILIS *Servita's Hist. Inquis.* (1676) 843 But where the Administrer hath all his requisite qualities, it is necessary to withstand his excesses.

†**ad'ministress.** *Obs. rare.* Also admynystresse. [a. MFr. *administresse*, earlier *amenistresse, amenistreresse*, fem. of *amenestrere*: see prec. and -ESS.] A woman who administers or ministers to others; a dispenser of benefits.

1483 CAXTON *Gold. Leg.* 255/4 Marye moder of Jhesu crist admynystresse and seruaunt. **1616** CHAPMAN *Musæus* (1858) 217 A Light [Hero's torch] that was administress of sight To cloudy Venus.

†**ad'ministry.** *Obs. rare*[−1]. [f. ADMINISTER *v.*; after *minister, ministry.*] The action of administering or ministering to; administration.

1616 CHAPMAN *Sonnets* ii, Poesy is not so remov'd a thing From grave administry of public weals As these times take it.

†**ad'minutive,** *a. Obs. rare*[−1]. [f. ? med.L. *adminūt-* ppl. stem of *adminu-ĕre* (f. *ad* to + *minuĕre* to lessen; cf. ME. AMENUSE, OFr. *amenuser*) + -IVE.] Characterized by diminution, tending to grow less.

1656 TRAPP *Expos. Rev.* xiii. 3 (1868) 763/1 Cotton the Jesuit confesses..that now the Christian Church is but adminutive.

admirability (ˌædmɪrə'bɪlɪtɪ). *rare*[−0]. [ad. L. *admīrābilitas*, n. of quality f. *admīrābilis*: see ADMIRABLE and -TY.] = ADMIRABLENESS.

1731 In BAILEY, whence in JOHNSON, etc.

admirable ('ædmɪrəb(ə)l), *a.* [a. Fr. *admirable*, in OFr. *amirable*:—L. *admīrābil-em*, f. *admīrā-ri*: see ADMIRE and -ABLE.]

†**1.** To be wondered at; wonderful, surprising, marvellous. *Obs.*

1596 SPENSER *F.Q.* I. vii. 36 He..was knowne right well To have done much more admirable deedes. **1601** SHAKS. *All's Well* II. i. 26 *Lord.* Oh 'tis braue warres. *Parr.* Most admirable, I haue seene those warres. **1639** FULLER *Holy War* I. vi. (1840) 8 It may justly seem admirable how that senseless religion should gain so much ground on Christianity. **1660** MILTON *Free Commw.* 431 Not only strange and admirable, but lamentable to think on. **1718** J. CHAMBERLAYNE *Relig. Philos.* (1730) I. vi. §10 All the admirable curiosities observable in the Heart. **1794** SULLIVAN *View of Nat.* II, He has in his words something θειοντι [? θεῖόν τι], divine and admirable.

Hence, by insensible gradations,

2. Exciting gratified surprise, or wonder united with approbation, esteem or reverence. In later usage the idea of *wonder* disappears, and the word is a mere exaggerated or emphatic way of expressing *estimable, excellent, approvable, likable, pleasing.*

1598 SHAKS. *Merry W.* II. ii. 234 You are a gentleman of excellent breeding, admirable discourse. **1604** MARLOWE *Faustus* 70 Helen of Greece was the admirablest lady that ever lived. **1678** HOBBES *Decam. Phys.* i. 1 What so many do so highly praise must be very admirable. **1754** CHATHAM *Lett. to Nephew* iv. 28 The admirable dispositions you have towards all that is right and good. **1788** V. KNOX *Wint. Even.* I. II. xiv. 200 The dialogue of an admirable author. **1825** M^cCULLOCH *Pol. Econ.* II. §2, 99 The admirable machinery invented by Hargreaves. **1856** KANE *Arctic Expl.* I. xi. 29 Crimped seal-skin boots or moccasins, an admirable article of walking gear. **1867** DICKENS *Lett.* (1880) II. 288 His wife takes admirable care of him.

¶ Also used formerly as *sb.* and *adv.*, and as name of a butterfly; see ADMIRAL 5.

1598 SYLVESTER *Du Bartas* I. iii. (1641) 23/2 Sure, in the Legend of absurdest Fables I should enroll most of these admirables. **1611** SHAKS. *Cymb.* II. iii. 19 A wonderful sweet aire, with admirable rich words to it. **1725** DE FOE *Voy. round World* (1840) 291 Made them roast a piece of venison ..admirable well.

admirableness ('ædmɪrəb(ə)lnɪs). [f. prec. + -NESS.] The quality of being admirable; wonderfulness; wonderful excellence; estimableness.

1607 *Mis. Enforced Marr.* IV. in Hazl. *Dodsl.* IX. 540 The admirableness of her virtues. **1675** T. BROOKS *Golden Key* Wks. 1807 V. 593 The greatness of God's love, the vehemency of his love, and the admirableness of his love. **1677** HALE *Prim. Orig. Man.* 343 The admirableness of these Phænomena. **1851** RUSKIN *Stones of Ven.* III. ii. §44, 64 The principal church in Italy was built with little idea of any other admirableness than that which was to result from its being huge.

admirably ('ædmɪrəblɪ), *adv.* [f. ADMIRABLE + -LY[2].] In an admirable manner; marvellously, wonderfully (*obs.*); in a manner exciting wonder and pleasure; excellently.

1593 R. HARVEY *Philad.* 4 So you may deny almost euery actors Actes, that hath liued admirably in the worlde. **1615** SANDYS *Trav.* 19 Being borne by a tempest vnto this Iland, and so admirably deliuered. **1664** PEPYS in *Shaks. Cent. Praise* 318 'Macbeth,' a pretty good play, but admirably acted. **1725** DE FOE *Voy. round World* (1840) 102 Calicoes, muslins, wrought silks, some of them admirably fine. **1769** *Junius Lett.* iv. 21 He handles his weapon most admirably. **1855** MACAULAY *Fredk. Gt.* 87 The Prussian army..was also admirably trained and admirably officered. **1863** KEMBLE *Resid. Georgia* 47 The pigs thrive admirably here.

admiral ('ædmɪrəl), *sb.* Forms: 3–4 **amyrayl, amrayl,** 5 **amyrayle, amerayle;** 4 **amyral,** 4–5 **amyrall(e, amerel(le,** 5 **amyrel(le,** 5–6 **amiral, amerall(e, amrall, amrel(le;** 3 **admirail, -ale,** 4–5 **admyral,** 4–6 **admyrall(e, admiralle,** 5–6 **admerall,** 5–7 **admirall,** 5– **admiral.** Also 3 **admirald,** 5 **amireld;** 4 **ameraunt,** 7 **admirant.** [a. OFr., ad. Arab. directly, or through med.L. or some other Rom. lang. The Arabic *amīr* commander, (f. *amara*, to command, order,) commonly Englished AMEER, EMIR, occurs in many titles followed by *-al-* '(of) the,' as in *amīr-al-umarā* ruler of rulers, *amīr-al-mā* commander of the water, *amīr-al-bahr*, commander of the sea, the earliest of which is *amīr-al-mūminīn* commander of the faithful, assumed by the Caliph Omar, and Latinized in many forms by the early chroniclers (see *Amirmumnes* in Du Cange). As *amīr* is constantly followed by *-al-* in all such titles, *amīr-al-* was naturally assumed by Christian writers as a substantive word, and variously Latinized as *amīr-ālis, -allus, -ālius, -ārius*, OFr. *amiral, -ail, -aill, -ayl*, Pr. *amirau, amirar, amiralh*, Pg. *amiralh*, It. *amiraglio*. But as is usual with foreign words, popular etymology was soon at work on these original forms, assimilating them to more familiar words, (1) by treating the *am-* as = Fr. and Pr. *am-*:—L. *adm-*, and refashioning it accordingly as med.L. *admīr-ālis, -allus, -ālius, -ārius*, OFr. *admiral, -ail*; (2) by assimilating it to other Arabic words in *al-* (which prob. began in Spain) as med.L. *almirallus*, OSp. *almiralle, almirage*, It. *almiraglio*, OFr. *almiral, -ail*; (3) by assimilating the ending to familiar Teutonic or Romance suffixes, as med.L. *amir-aldus*, OFr. *amiralt, -ault, -aut* (after names like Reginald), Sp. *almirante* (? after *imperante*), OFr. *amirant, admirant*; (4) by confusing the refashioned forms in *adm-* with derivatives of L. *admīrāri* to wonder at, whence med.L. *admīrābilis* ('Rex Africæ qui dicitur vulgariter *admirabilis mundi*'), *admīrandus, admīrātus* (these again with the initial variations *am-, amm-, alm-*), whence Pr. *amiratz*, OFr. *amiret, amiré, amirauble, amirafle, amirand*, etc., etc. In Eng. the chief form represents OFr. *amiral, -ayl*, reduced in 16th c. by phonetic gradation to *amrel*, a pronunciation still common with sailors. But the refashioned *admirale, -ail* occurs as early as 1205, and became regular after 1500 as the literary form. Variants in *-ald, -aunt*, after med.L. *amiraldus*, and OFr. *amirant*, are also found in ME. As in the other languages the original meaning was 'Emir, Saracen commander, ruler under the Caliph or Sultan'; the modern maritime use is due to the office of *amīr-al-bahr* or *amīr-al-mā* 'Ameer of the sea' (Sp. *almirante de la mar*), created by the Arabs in Spain and Sicily, continued by the Christian kings of Sicily, and adopted successively by the Genoese, French, and English under Edward III as 'Amyrel of the Se,' or 'admyrall of the navy.' After the original use became obsolete about 1500, *admiral* was used in the naval sense, without any qualification, as an English title.]

†**1.** An emir or prince under the Sultan; any Saracen (or 'infidel') ruler or commander. *Obs.*

c **1205** LAYAMON 27668 Þat on admiral: of Babiloine he wes ældere. *Ibid.* 27689 Þeos admirale sone, Gecron is ihate. **1297** R. GLOUC. 407 An amrayl þere bysyde.. Ȝeld hym vp to Cristene men. *Ibid.* 409 Þe kyng of Camele made pays, & an amyrayl also, And ȝeue hem gret garyson. *a* **1300** *K. Horn* 95 Þanne spak on admira[l]d, Of wordes he was bald. *c* **1314** *Guy Warw.* 101 With that come forth an amireld, A Sarrazin. **1366** MAUNDEVILE (1839) v. 38 Be the Cytees and be the Townes ben Amyralles, that have the Governance of the Peple. *c* **1380** *Sir Ferumb.* 1920 'Y haue y-hurd .vj. of my fon,' saide þe Amyrelle. *Ibid.* 532 Ne faȝt he neuere ȝet in felde: wyþ kyng ne Ameraunt, pat he ne asloȝ ouþer madem ȝelde. **1393** GOWER *Conf.* I. 196 Where that an heathen admiralle Was lorde. *c* **1430** LYDG. *Bochas* V. v. (1554) 126 a, Old Hanniball Which of Chartage was chief Admirall. *c* **1450** *Merlin* xviii. 281 Maglaant, an amyrall saisne cruewell and felon. **1483** CAXTON *Gold. Leg.* 190/4 Sone of the admyralle of babylone which was named exerses. **1490** —— *Eneydos* xxvii. 104 Pluto the grete god of hell admyrall of the styge. [**1561** J. DAUS tr. *Bullinger on Apoc.* (1573) 124 b, After Mahomet him selfe they had in order xxv Amirals (for so they called their Kings or Princes).]

2. The commander-in-chief of the navy of a country; in England, formerly, the title of 'an officer or magistrate that has the government of the king's navy, and the hearing and determining all causes, as well civil as criminal, belonging to the sea' (Cowel), also styled more fully *Lord High Admiral*, whose administrative duties are now in commission, and discharged by five *Lords Commissioners of the Admiralty*, and his judicial functions vested in the *High Court of Admiralty*.

1460 CAPGRAVE *Chron.* 250 The Erl of Arundel, Richard, was mad amyrel of the se. **1480** CAXTON *Chron. Eng.* ccxliii. 290 Erle of kente made Admyral of Englond for to kepe the see. **1494** FABYAN VI. cxcvii. 203 Elfricus, that than was mayster or admyrall of the Kynges nauy. **1513** ARNOLD *Chron.* (1811) 47 Syr Edward Howard, the Amerall, with other, was drownyd. **1549** EDWARD VI *Death warrant* in *Facsim. of National MSS.* II. xliv, Sir Thomas Seymour knyght, Lorde Seymour of Sudeley, late Highe Admyrall of our Realme of Englande. **1556** *Chron. Grey Friars of Lond.* (1852) 37 The lorde amrelle of France came into Ynglond. *Ibid.* 54 Sir John Dudley that was amrelle of the see was made yerle of Warwyk [1547]. **1699** LUTTRELL *Brief Rel.* (1857) IV. 558 [The King of Spain] will suddenly recall to court the admirant of Castille. **1772** PENNANT *Tours in Scotl.* (1774) 161 The Earl of Bute is admiral of the county..but no way dependent on the lord high admiral of Scotland. **1868** CHAMBERS *Encycl.* I. 46 The office of Lord High Admiral was last filled by H.R.H. the Duke of Clarence, afterwards William IV.

3. A naval officer of the highest rank; the commander of a fleet or squadron; a flag-officer. In England there are four grades—***Admiral of the Fleet***, ranking with a field-marshal in the army; ***Admiral, Vice-Admiral***, and ***Rear-Admiral***, ranking with a general, lieutenant-general, and major-general respectively. Formerly they were also divided into classes denominated from the colours hoisted by them, ***Admirals of the Red, White,*** or ***Blue Squadron***.

Hence ***Admiral of the Blue***, an obs. jocose name for a *tapster* (from the colour of his apron).

c **1425** WYNTOUN *Cron.* VII. ix. 99 Slwe þe amyrale of þat flot. **1475** *Bk. of Noblesse* (1860) 16 Johan erle of Hontyndon was made cheif admyralle of a new armee to rescue Harflue.

1606 SHAKS. *Ant. & Cl.* III. x. 2 Thantoniad, the Egyptian Admirall, With all their sixty flye. **1656** MILTON *Lett. of State* Wks. 1738 II. 198 One Giles, a French-man, a petty Admiral of four Ships. **1688** *Lond. Gaz.* mmccclvi./3 Sir Roger Strickland, Rear Admiral of England, rides present Admiral in the Downs of a Squadron of Ships. **1731** *Poor Robin* (N.) As soon as customers begin to stir, The Admiral of the Blue, crys, Coming, sir! **1853** *Encycl. Brit.* II. 142 For nearly a century we had no Admiral of the Red Squadron.

4. The privileged commander of a fishing or merchant fleet.

Fishing boats in the North Sea often fish in company—in fleets. They are all under the command of one man, who gives the orders when to shoot the nets, haul them, etc. He is called the 'Admiral'.—R. G. Marsden. (Cf. ADMIRALTY 7.)

1708 *Royal Proclm.*, June 26, in *Lond. Gaz.* mmmmccccclii, It is..Enacted, That whoever should after the said Five and twentieth Day of *March*, first enter with his Fishing-Ship, any Harbour or Creek in *Newfoundland*, should be for that Season Admiral of the said Harbour or Creek, and should reserve so much Beech or Flakes as should be necessary for his Boats, and One over, as a Privilege..; and the Master of the Second Fishing-Ship Entring such Harbour.., shall be Vice-Admiral, and the Master of the Third Ship.., Rear-Admiral for that Season ..All Differences..shall be determin'd by the Fishing Admirals in the several Harbours; and an Appeal is given from such Judgment to the Commanders of the Men of War appointed Convoys for *Newfoundland*.

5. = *admiral ship* (cf. Fr. *le vaisseau amiral*. Milton's *ammiral* is in imitation of It. *ammiraglia* 'an admirall or chief ship' (Florio); cf. *ammiraglio*, later form of *almiraglio*: see above): The ship which carries the admiral; the Flagship. Also applied to the most considerable ship of a fleet of merchantmen, or of the vessels employed in the Newfoundland cod-fishery.

1588 in *Harl. Misc.* (Malh.) II. 52 The admiral and another ship of four hundred tons. **1590** WEBBE *Trav.* (1868) 19 The Harry appertayning to the company of the Marchants, was our Vice-admirall. **1622** R. HAWKINS *Voy. to S. Sea* 19 The admirall of the Spanish armada was a Flemish shippe. **1667** MILTON *P.L.* I. 294 The mast Of some great Ammiral. **1725** DE FOE *Voy. round World* (1840) 79 Under orders of the great ship as admiral. **1865** CARLYLE *Fredk. Gt.* II. VII. vi. 317 Tall branchy timbers yonder, one day to be masts of admirals.

6. Pop. name of two European species of butterfly (fam. *Vanessidæ*), distinguished as the ***Red*** and the ***White*** Admiral (*Vanessa Atalanta*, and *Limenitis Sibylla*). The name belonged at first to the former, also (perh. originally) the *Admirable*; see ADMIRAL *a.*

1720 ALBIN *Nat. Hist. Eng. Insects* Plate III, A most beautiful Fly called the Admiral Butter-fly. **1798** E. DONOVAN *Nat. Hist. Brit. Ins.* VIII. 20 The red admirable Butter-fly is certainly a very common species. **1868** BARING-GOULD *Silver Store* 116 Admirals on bark of oak Tarry till a sunny stroke O'er their scarlet stripes and rings Drinks the water from their wings.

7. *Conch.* = *admiral-shell*: A collector's name for certain beautiful shells of the genus *Conus*.

1748 SIR J. HILL *Gen. Nat. Hist.*, *Anim.* 137 The admiral-shell, the voluta with a broad yellow fascia, with a punctuated line in it. **1819** *Pantologia* I. s.v., There are four species of this shell, viz. the grand-admiral, the vice-admiral, the orange-admiral, and the extra-admiral.

8. *Attrib.* and *Comb.*, as ***admiral court, galley, ship***, etc.; also **admiral-in-chief** or **admiral-general**, the supreme naval commander.

1681 *Lond. Gaz.* mdcliv/4 An Act concerning the Jurisdiction of Admiral-Court. **1770** LANGHORNE *Plutarch's Lives* (1879) I. 138/1 Themistocles was sacrificing on the deck of the admiral-galley. **1600** HOLLAND *Livy* XXXVI. xliv. 943 c, Livius..advaunced forward with the Admirall ship [*prætoria nave*]. **1692** *Lond. Gaz.* mmdcclxi/1 The Admiral Ship, which is to carry 70 Guns. **1699** *Ibid.* mmmdxxx/2 Baron Jewell is made Admiral General. **1849** GROTE *Greece* (1862) V. II. lxi. 343 An act of direct insubordination.. towards the admiral-in-chief.

† **'admiral**, *a. Obs.* Also **admirall, admirale**. [A by-form of ADMIRABLE, caused by confusing that word with ADMIRAL *sb.*, of which one of the med.L. forms was *admirabilis*, as in Matthew Paris, ann. 1251, *Regi Marok, quem Admirabilem mundi appellare consuevimus*. As *admirabilis* was thus used for *admiral*, there was apparent authority for using *admiral* for *admirable*.] Admirable.

1611 SPEED *Hist. Gt. Brit.* VI. xxviii. (1632) 123 For his admirall height, he was admitted..into the ranke of a common souldier. ?**1650** *Don Bellianis of Greece* 77 Else could no knights in the world perform such admirale deeds.

† **'admiraless.** *Obs. rare*[−1]. [f. ADMIRAL *sb.* + -ESS.] The wife of an admiral.

1611 COTGR., *Admirale*, an Admirallesse.

Admiralissimo (ædmɪrə'lɪsɪməʊ). [f. ADMIRAL *sb.* + *-issimo* after GENERALISSIMO.] An informal title of rank applied to the supreme commander of (combined) naval forces.

1911 LD. FISHER *Let.* 22 Nov. in R. S. Churchill *Winston S. Churchill* (1969) II. Compan. II. xvii. 1341 From this time forth you must make no appointment afloat for anyone senior to Jellicoe otherwise you will be in a fix in two years time when you wish him to be Admiralissimo! **1914** PRINCE LOUIS OF BATTENBERG *Let.* 27 Aug. in M. Gilbert *Winston S. Churchill* (1971) III. Compan. I. 63 Your general dispositions and the measures taken by you from July 27th until you handed over the Command in the Mediterranean to the French Admiralissimo are fully approved by Their Lordships. **1928** G. CAMPBELL *My Mystery Ships* v. 73 Queenstown would have been an excellent place to have had a sort of Admiralissimo of all the approaches to the British Isles from the westward and southward. **1951** W. S. CHURCHILL *Second World War* IV. I. xiv. 220 Yamamoto, the Japanese Admiralissimo [in 1942].

admiralling ('ædmɪrəlɪŋ), *vbl. sb.* [f. ADMIRAL *sb.* used as vb. + -ING[1]. (Cf. *went a-colonelling*, Hudibras.)] Being or acting as an admiral.

1838 GEN. P. THOMPSON *Exerc.* (1842) IV. 332 'An admiral is to sail to a given port' (it was in the admiralling days).

admiralship ('ædmɪrəlʃɪp). [f. ADMIRAL *sb.* + -SHIP.]

1. The office or position of an admiral.

1617 MINSHEU, *Admiralship*, the estate and office of the Admirall. **1872** *Daily News* 5 Aug., The steamer was commanded by her own legal master, but the admiralship of the day was shared by Mr. Pegler.

2. Capability of performing the duties of an admiral.

1873 MASSON *Drumm. of H.* viii. 172 All faith in his generalship and admiralship for the rest of the war had been lost.

admiralty ('ædmɪrəltɪ). Forms: 5 **amyralte, amrelte, ameralte**; 6 **amraltie, amiraltye, admiraltie**; 6- **admiralty**. [a. OFr. *admiralté*, *amiraulté*; see ADMIRAL and -TY.]

1. The office or jurisdiction of an admiral, or of the Lord High Admiral; admiralship.

1327-1485 *Pol. Poems* II. 158 Cheryshe marchandyse, kepe thamyralté, That we bee maysteres of the narowe see. **1538** LELAND *Itin.* VII. 87 The Wyndowes be full of Rudders..his Badge or Token of the Amiraltye. **1600** HOLLAND *Livy* XLIII. xi. 1162 k, The admiraltie of the navy. **1668** PEPYS *Diary* (1877) V. 386 The Duke of York's regiment is ordered to be disbanded, and more, that undoubtedly his Admiralty will follow. **1846** PRESCOTT *Ferd. & Isab.* II. xvi. 117 Exclusive right of jurisdiction over all commercial transactions within his admiralty.

†**2.** The department under command of the admiral; the naval branch of the public service; the navy. *Obs.*

1465 *Manners & Househ. Exps. Eng.* 473 My master hathe receyvid of doctor Aleyn, sen he ocupyd in the Ameralte, but xxxiij.s. iiij.d. *a* **1626** BACON *Union of Eng. & Scot.* (T.) For admiralty or navy, I see no great question will arise.

3. That branch of the Executive which superintends the navy; the power or officers appointed for the administration of naval affairs; in England (until 1964) the ***Lords Commissioners of Admiralty***.

1459 BRACKLEY in *Paston Lett.* 341 I. 497 The bokys of regystre of the amrelte [were] takyn a wey from my Lord Scalys men. **1679** DK. YORK in Pepys V. 131 It is Mr. Pepys, who now, upon this change in the Admiralty, is like to suffer. **1758** in *Phil. Trans.* LI. 461 Sir Charles Wager, first lord of the admiralty. **1833** MARRYAT *Peter Simple* (1863) 435 His case was strongly recommended to the consideration of the Lords Commissioners of the Admiralty. **1855** MACAULAY *Hist. Eng.* IV. 233 Meanwhile the admiralties of the allied powers had been active.

4. a. That branch of the administration of justice which deals with maritime questions and offences. ***Court of Admiralty***: the tribunal for the trial and decision of such causes, formerly presided over by the Lord High Admiral, whose jurisdiction is now transferred to the Probate, Divorce, and Admiralty Division of the High Court of Justice; also elliptically called ***The Admiralty***.

1589 *Marprel. Tr., Hay any Work.* (1844) 46 Yea but Civilians liue by the court of Amraltie. **1666** PEPYS *Diary* IV. 131 Sir R. Ford would accept of one-third of my profit of our private man-of-war, and bear one-third of the charge, and be bound in the Admiralty. **1667** *Ibid.* IV. 281 This Judge of the Admiralty, Judge Jenkins. **1768** BLACKSTONE *Comm.* IV. xix, The high court of admiralty, held before the lord high-admiral of England, is not only a court of civil, but also of criminal jurisdiction. **1853** *Encycl. Brit.* II. 145 By the 6th and 7th Will. IV. c. 53, the admiralty jurisdiction is extended to Prince of Wales' Island, Singapore, and Malacca.

b. In full ***Admiralty coal***, a type of large steam coal supplied to the Royal Navy under contract.

1914 *Coal & Iron* 11 May 709/2 For best Admiralities up to 20s. is still being quoted. **1915** *Ibid.* 4 Jan. 337/2 Best Admiralty large steams are not dealt in to any extent, the Naval authorities still controlling supplies. **1928** *Daily Mail* 9 Aug. 12/3 The Ferndale Collieries, which are among those producing the finest Admiralty coals in the world.

5. The building where the Admiral or Lords of the Admiralty transact business.

1617 MINSHEU, *Admiraltie*..the place where the Admirals office is kept. **1661** R. BURNEY *Κέρδιστον Δῶρον* 66 He takes the Flag down from the main Top-mast head, when he pleases at the Admiralty. **1879** *Whitaker's Almanac* 302/2 Public and Private Buildings..Admiralty, Horse Guards, Treasury, War Office.

†**6.** A station for ships of war in charge of an admiral. *Obs. rare.*

1677 YARRANTON *Eng. Improvem.* 40 Ships for the Royal Navy may..be kept either in an Admiralty at Wexford, or in some Port near.

†**7.** A sailing in company (originally for mutual defence against pirates). *Obs. rare.* [PARDESSUS *Coll. Lois Maritimes* II. 548 'Toutes les lois et coutumes anciennes de la Hollande, de la Basse Saxe et de la Baltique, emploient le mot *admiralitas*, *amirauté*, pour désigner les *voyages de conserve*.]

1622 MALYNES *Anc. Law-Merch.* 180 When ships do enter into Admiraltie one with another, whosoeuer breaketh the Admiraltie is bound to answer the damage which shall happen thereby. —— *Laws of Hanse Towns* 24 When ships do enter into admiralty one with another, they shall be bound to keep together, and to stay for each other.

8. *Rhet.* Command of the seas (esp. in phr. ***the price of admiralty***).

1893 KIPLING 'Song of the English' in *Eng. Illustr. Mag.* May 535 If blood be the price of admiralty Good God, we ha' paid in full! **1923** E. K. CHATTERTON *Auxiliary Patrol* viii. 121 By the end of the following year three more mine-sweepers..and three more motor-boats had also gone, with, of course, loss of life. Such was the inevitable price of Admiralty.

† **ad'mirance.** *Obs. rare*[−1]. [a. OFr. *admirance*, f. *admirer*: see ADMIRE and -ANCE.] Admiring, admiration.

1596 SPENSER *F.Q.* V. x. 39 Who with right humble thankes him goodly greeting..With great admiraunce inwardly was moved.

admiration (,ædmɪ'reɪʃən). Also 5-6 **-cyon, -cion, -tyon.** [a. Fr. *admiration* (14th c. in Littré), ad. L. *admīrātiōn-em*, n. of action f. *admīrā-ri*: see ADMIRE.]

1. The action of wondering or marvelling; wonder, astonishment, surprise. *arch.*

1506 *Ordin. Crysten Men* (W. de Worde) I. vii. 73 Yf he haue admyracyon that one essence of deite be in thre persones. **1611** BIBLE *Rev.* xvii. 6 When I saw her, I wondred with great admiration. **1642** FULLER *Holy & Prof. St.* IV. xvi. 323 Admiration is the daughter of ignorance. **1662** EVELYN *Sylva* (1679) 9 In admiration at the universal negligence. **1719** DE FOE *Crusoe* 331 But now the Admiration was turned upon another Question, (viz.) what could be the Matter. **1826** SCOTT *Woodst.* xxv. Wks. 1830 II. 143 Phœbe stood gaping in admiration at the sudden quarrel. **1852** SIR W. HAMILTON *Discuss.* 14 How it could ever be doubted..may well be deemed a matter of the profoundest admiration.

2. a. Agreeable surprise; wonder mingled with reverence, esteem, approbation; hence, in late usage, pleased or gratified contemplation.

1589 PUTTENHAM *Eng. Poesie* II. xii. (1811) 91 To bring the world into admiration of their lawes and Religion. **1617** WITHER *Fidelia* in *Juvenil.* 1633, 480 That love which Admiration first begot, Pitty would strengthen. *c* **1680** BEVERIDGE *Serm.* (1729) I. 10 Take heed that you have not men's persons in admiration. **1860** TYNDALL *Glaciers* I. §11, 72 One large star in particular excited our admiration. **1871** RUSKIN *Fors Clav.* v. 17 Admiration—the power of discerning and taking delight in what is beautiful in visible Form, and lovely in human Character. **1876** MOZLEY *Univ. Serm.* vii. 146 The test of true admiration is pleasure.

b. Phr. ***to admiration*** [cf. F. *à merveille*], so as to elicit admiration; in an admirable or excellent manner. Slightly *arch.*

1633 W. AMES *Fresh Suit* Pref., This book..hath made all things evident to them, even to admiration. *a* **1680** EVELYN *Diary* May an. 1646 (1955) II. 501 They are curious in Straw-worke among the Nunns, even to admiration. **1681** H. MORE *Expos. Proph. Dan.* App. I. 259 You shall find this part of the Prophecy fulfilled to admiration. **1793** SMEATON *Edystone Lightho.* §152 The Buss in all the past bad weather had indeed rode it out to admiration. **1821** C. LAMB *Old Benchers* in *Lond. Mag.* Sept. 282/2 [He] moulded heads in clay or plaister of Paris to admiration, by the dint of natural genius merely. **1930** V. WOOLF *Beau Brummell* 5 He..tied his cravat to admiration.

†**3.** The faculty of exciting either wonder or agreeable surprise and approbation; admirableness. *Obs.*

1534 LD. BERNERS *Golden Bk. of M. Aurel.* (1546) E b, Theyr fewe wordes and good workes haue lefte vs exaumple of great admiracion. **1610** SHAKS. *Temp.* III. i. 38 Admir'd Miranda! Indeede the top of admiration. **1642** JER. TAYLOR *God's Judgem.* I. I. xxix. 133 [They] found him to be starke dead, not without markes upon him of wonderfull admiration.

4. An object of admiration or wonder; a marvel. In mod. usage only in the phrase ***the admiration of***, with a distinctly verbal reference.

1490 CAXTON *Eneydos* xxvii. 97 The harde and sorowfull admyracions that thenne made palmyreus that was maistre of eneas shippe ben declared. **1548** *Compl. Scotl.* (1801) 86 Ther is ane vthir admiration of the variant course of the moone. **1601** SHAKS. *Alls Well* II. i. 91 Now, good Lafew, Bring in the admiration, that we with thee May spend our wonder too. **1716-8** LADY M. W. MONTAGUE *Lett.* I. xxii. 69 The young prince..is the admiration of the whole court. **1833** HT. MARTINEAU *Brooke Farm* xii. 133 Joe's house is the admiration of all who know what comfort is.

5. ***note of admiration***: the mark (!) affixed to words, phrases, or sentences, intended to be uttered with an intonation of exclamation or surprise.

1611 SHAKS. *Wint. T.* V. ii. 12 The changes I perceiued in the King and Camillo, were very Notes of admiration. **1611** COTGR., *Admiratif*, Th' admirative point, or point of admiration (and of detestation) marked, or made thus! **1719** SWIFT *To Yng. Clerg.* Wks. 1755 II. II. 8 To skip over all sentences where he spied a note of admiration at the end. **1859** J. LANG *Wand. India* 387 You will have the Commander-in-Chief down upon you with five-and-twenty notes of admiration at the end of every sentence.

admirative ('ædmɪ,reɪtɪv, æd'maɪərətɪv), *a. rare.* [a. Fr. *admiratif*, *-ive*; f. *admirāt-* ppl. stem of *admirā-ri*: see ADMIRE and -IVE.] Pertaining to or characterized by wonder or admiration.

1611 COTGR. [see prec. 5.] **1641** BP. MONTAGU *Acts & Mon.* 160 The common people, ignorant, credulous, and admirative. **1861** C. M. INGLEBY *Compl. View* 148 Admirative comments in the Edinburgh and Saturday Reviews.

admiratively (see prec.), *adv.* [f. prec. + -LY².] In an admirative manner; with pleasurable approbation.

1882 C. M. I. in *N. & Q.* 1 Apr. 245/2 So wonderfully applicable..that it may be admiratively quoted just now.

†**admi'rator.** *Obs. rare*⁻¹. [a. L. *admīrātor*, n. of agent, f. *admīrā-ri* to ADMIRE.] An admirer; a wonderer.

1603 HARSNET *Declar. Pop. Impost.* 110 When we have instructed their Admirator in the secret causes..we shal ease him of his labour and cause his wonderment to cease.

admire (æd'maɪə(r)), *v.* [a. Fr. *admire-r*, a refashioning of OFr. *amirer*:—L. *admīrā-ri* to wonder at; f. *ad* at + *mīrā-ri* to wonder.]

1. *intr.* To feel or express surprise, or astonishment; to wonder, to marvel, to be surprised.

†**a.** *simply. Obs.*

c **1590** GREENE *Fr. Bacon* ix. 233 Lordings, admire not if your cheer be this, For we must keep our academic fare. **1626** T. H. *Caussin's Holy Crt.* 7 This would make you admire, your haire stand an end, and bloud congeale in your ueynes. **1697** MOLYNEUX in *Locke's Lett.* (1708) 238, I should have much more admired had they been otherwise.

b. with *at.*

1600 ROWLANDS *Letting of Hum. Blood* i. 48 Vttring rare lyes to be admired at. **1650** FULLER *Pisgah Sight* II. vi. 150 King Ahab stood admiring at the miracle. **1656** BAXTER *Ref. Pastor.* 348 It maketh me admire at the fearful deceitfulness of the heart of man. **1708** SWIFT *Baucis & Phil.* 148 And she admir'd as much at him. **1759** MARTIN *Nat. Hist.* I. 271 Posterity may justly admire at their being demolished. **1865** CARLYLE *Fredk. Gt.* III. VIII. iv. 17 A result, which Friedrich Wilhelm not a little admires at.

c. with *subord. cl. arch.* or *dial.*

1600 HOLLAND *Livy* I. xli. 24 A great concourse of the People, admiring what the matter was. **1642** FULLER *Holy & Prof. State* II. iii. 59 We may more admire that so beastly a drunkard lived so long. **1681** CROWNE *Hen. VI*, IV. 38, I admire my Lord of Glocester is not come. **1694** *Provid. of God* 147, I admired why I should be suspected. **1701** PENN in *Pa. Hist. Soc. Mem.* IX. 45, I admire how thou couldst stay so long. **1794** GODWIN *Caleb Williams* 176, I admire that the earth does not open and swallow you alive. **1848** DICKENS *Dombey* 316 Mrs. Chick admires that Edith should be, by nature, such a perfect Dombey.

†**d.** with *inf. Obs.* or *dial.* Also *U.S.*, to like, be desirous (*to* do something).

1645 HOWELL *England's Tears* 173 The Italian admires to see a people argue themselves thus into arms. **1676** HOBBES *Iliad* XXIV. 386 You would admire to see him look so fresh. *a* **1770** J. MECOM *Lett. to B. Franklin* (1859) 194, I should admire to come and see and hear all about every thing. **1816** PICKERING *Vocab.* s.v., *To admire*, to like very much, to be very fond of. This verb is much used in New England in expressions like the following: I should admire to go to such a place; I should admire to have such a thing, &c. **1839** MARRYAT *Diary Amer.* II. 223 'Have you ever been at Paris?' 'No; but I should admire to go.' **1869** MISS ALCOTT *Little Wom.* I. ix. 134, I admire to do it. **1876** B. HARTE *Gabriel Conroy* IV. i, 'Why didn't you come into the parlour?' she said... 'I didn't admire to to-night,' returned Gabriel. **1939** J. STEINBECK *Grapes of Wrath* xx. 348 'Well, I'd admire to git a hand,' said the young man.

2. *trans.* To view with wonder or surprise; to wonder or marvel at. *arch.*

c **1590** GREENE *Fr. Bacon* ii. 40 England and Europe shall admire thy fame. **1642** FULLER *Holy & Prof. State* II. ix. 83 He accounts their examples rather to be admired then imitated. **1682** *Lond. Gaz.* mdccxxvii/3 We cannot but admire and dread those restless Men. **1714** ADDISON *Spect.* No. 575 ¶6 How can we sufficiently admire the Stupidity or Madness of these Persons? **1738** WARBURTON *Div. Legat.* I. 68 That Disorder in the Life of Man, which Moralists so much admire. **1876** FARRAR *Marlb. Serm.* iv. 36 One hardly knows whether most to admire the stupidity of such a degradation or to detest its guilt.

Hence, by insensible gradations,

3. a. To regard with pleased surprise, or with wonder mingled with esteem, approbation, or affection; and in modern usage, To gaze on with pleasure.

1594 H. WILLOBIE in *Shaks. Cent. Praise* 10 You must admire her sober grace. **1596** SHAKS. *Tam. Shr.* I. i. 29 We do admire This virtue, and this morall discipline. **1660** T. STANLEY *Hist. Philos.* (1701) 31/2 Some Vulcan's and Minerva's arts admire. **1751** HARRIS *Hermes* (1841) 113 Admiring only the authors of our own age. **1807** CRABBE *Par. Reg.* III. 163 Thus long she reign'd, admired, if not approved. **1860** TYNDALL *Glaciers* I. §16. 118, I had occasion to admire the knowledge and promptness of my guide. **1878** G. MACDONALD *Ann. Quiet Neighb.* xxx. 526 She could admire good people.

b. To express admiration for, to praise. Also *absol.*

1833 J. ROMILLY *Diary* 16 Jan. (1967) I. 26 Harraden admired to me the beauty of his boy..—as plain as his Father. **1852** LYTTON *My Novel* x. xiii. 231 Randal had.. called twice and found her at home, and been very bland and civil, and admired the children. **1872** GEO. ELIOT *Middlem.* III. VI. liv. 196 To an aunt who does not recognise her infant nephew as Bouddha, and has nothing to do for him but to admire, his behaviour is apt to appear monotonous. **1916** G. B. SHAW *Pygmalion* v. 176 You didnt thank her, or pet her, or admire her, or tell her how splendid she'd been. **1925** F. SCOTT FITZGERALD *Great Gatsby* v. 110 With enchanting murmurs Daisy admired this aspect or that of the feudal silhouette against the sky. **1940** DYLAN THOMAS *Portrait of Artist as Young Dog* 73 We walked home together. I admired his bloody nose. He said that my eye was like a poached egg, only black. **1956** C. BUSH *Case of Extra Man* II. vi. 80 All I ever do in the matter of her clothes is dutifully admire. **1986** *Guardian* 10 Dec. 1/3 Colonel North looked suitably chastened.., but seemed pleased when conservative congressmen admired his medals and praised him as a national hero.

†**4.** *causal.* To astonish, to surprise. *Obs. rare.*

c **1650** *Don Bellianis* 204 A Tent..with so many gallant Devices, that it admired every beholder.

†**ad'mire,** *sb. Obs.* [f. the vb.] The act of admiring, admiration.

1591 G. MARKHAM *Sir R. Grinuile* clxvii, But with all kindnes, honor, and admire To bring him thence. **1602** WARNER *Albion's Eng.* x. lix. (1612) 261 Natures Mynion, eyes Admier. **1613** ROWLANDS *Knave of Hearts* (N.) He thus concludes his censure for admire

admired (æd'maɪəd), *ppl. a.* [f. ADMIRE *v.* + -ED.]

1. Regarded with admiration; wondered at; contemplated with wonder mingled with esteem, etc.; wonderful, surprising.

c **1430** *Pol. Rel. & Love Poems* 49, 453 And ther-too schee was well emyred. **1592** SHAKS. *Rom. & Jul.* I. ii. 89 All the admired Beauties of Verona. **1621** HOWELL *Lett.* (1650) II. 50 Venice..the admiredst city in the world. **1709** POPE *Ess. Criticism* 502 Then most our trouble still when most admird. **1867** INGELOW *Story of Doom* III. 77 And half-shut fans of his admirèd wings.

2. Astonished; struck with wonder.

a **1700** *Ballads on Gt. Frost* 1683–4 (1844) 4 All stand admir'd, and very well they may To see such pastimes.

admiredly (æd'maɪərɪdlɪ), *adv.* [f. prec. + -LY².] In an admired manner; surprisingly.

1637 SYDENHAM *Serm.* 218 Tho' in their own condition admiredly happy heretofore.

admirer (æd'maɪərə(r)). [f. ADMIRE *v.* + -ER¹.]

1. One who admires, wonders at, or views with surprise and pleasure, or with pleasure only.

1605 BACON *Adv. Learn.* I. vii. §5 (1873) 54 There was not a greater admirer of learning [than Trajan]. **1710** ADDISON *Whig-Exam.* No. 2 ¶1, I never yet knew an Author that had not his admirers. **1839** DICKENS *Lett.* (1880) I. 27 A little tribute from an unknown but ardent admirer of your genius.

2. 'In common speech, a lover.' J.

a **1704** T. BROWN *Comical View* Wks. 1730 I. 163 'Tis by your beauty that you make so many of your admirers hang and drown themselves every year. **1874** BLACK *Pr. Thule* 35 Vexed by the incomprehensible conduct of her reputed admirer.

admiring (æd'maɪərɪŋ), *vbl. sb.* [f. ADMIRE *v.* + -ING¹.] Viewing with wonder, reverence, esteem, pleasure. (Now mostly gerundial.)

1603 FLORIO *Montaigne* (1634) 492 That other faculty.. often causeth sport and breedeth admiring. **1633** P. FLETCHER *Piscat. Ecl.* III. xii. 17 Live in her love, and die in her admiring. **1761–2** HUME *Hist. Engl.* V. lxviii. (1806) 133 Instead of admiring that a palpable falsehood should be maintained.

admiring (æd'maɪərɪŋ), *ppl. a.* [f. ADMIRE *v.* + -ING².]

1. Wondering; regarding with loving wonder; full of admiration.

1626 D'EWES in Ellis *Orig. Lett.* I. 322 III. 217 The presence of soe deare a king drew admiring silence. **1784** TRUMBULL in Sparks' *Corr. Am. Rev.* (1853) IV. 68 The scoff of an admiring world. **1879** MCCARTHY *Hist. own Times* ii. 313 The voice of admiring friends was tumultuously raised to predict splendid things for him.

†**2.** Causing wonder or admiration. Cf. ADMIRE *v.* 4. *Obs.*

1610 GWILLIM *Heraldry* III. xxii. (1660) 235 Dolphins here are in their naturall form of swimming, wherein they use to marshale their great troopes in admiring order.

admiringly (æd'maɪərɪŋlɪ), *adv.* [f. prec. + -LY².] In an admiring manner; with admiration; with fond looks.

1601 SHAKS. *All's Well* V. iii. 44 Admiringly my Liege, at first I stucke my choice vpon her. **1823** MOORE *Loves of Angels* II. xxviii. 575 When I've seen her look above At some bright star admiringly. **1876** FREEMAN *Norm. Conq.* III. xii. 217 Two such men must have looked admiringly on each other's great deeds.

†**admirize,** *v. Obs. rare*⁻¹. [improp. f. ADMIRE or ? Fr. *admirer* + -IZE. Cf. *acclimate* and *acclimatize.*] To wonder.

1702 LOGAN in *Pa. Hist. Soc. Mem.* IX. 108 Orders to proclaim the queen have arrived in Virginia..but none here, which makes many admirize.

‖**ad misericordiam** (æd ˌmɪzɛrɪ'kɔːdɪəm). [L.] Of an appeal, argument, etc.: to mercy, to pity.

1824 *Edin. Rev.* XLI. 55 The fallacy of those arguments *ad misericordiam* on which the agriculturists now principally rest their claims to protection. **1863** THACKERAY *Round. Papers* 73 No day passes but that argument *ad misericordiam* is used. **1885** *Manchester Exam.* 27 Feb. 5/3 He now made an *ad misericordiam* appeal for an extension of that time, on the ground of his ignorance of the practice. **1929** E. MARJORIBANKS *Marshall Hall* x. 359 Later, in his final speech, he was making an appeal *ad misericordiam* for his client.

admissibility (æd,mɪsɪ'bɪlɪtɪ). [f. ADMISSIBLE; see -BILITY. Cf. mod.Fr. *admissibilité.*] The quality of being admissible; admissibleness.

1778–80 BURROWS *Reports* IV. 2058 The counsel for the defendant objected to the admissibility of the evidence. **1801** W. TAYLOR in *Monthly Mag.* XI. 290 A hybrid word, and therefore of equivocal admissibility. **1849** BEST *Evidence* (1870) 10 The admissibility of evidence is a matter of *law*, but the weight or value of the evidence is matter of *fact.*

admissible (æd'mɪsɪb(ə)l), *a.* [a. Fr. *admissible*, ad. late L. *admissibilem*, f. *admiss-* ppl. stem of *admitt-ĕre*: see ADMIT and -BLE.]

1. Worthy of being entertained as an idea or project; allowable.

1611 COTGR., *Admissible* [Fr.]. admittable, admissible, fit to be admitted, received, allowed of. **1677** HALE *Prim. Orig. Man.* I. vi. 126 Suppose that this Supposition were admissible. **1753** RICHARDSON *Grandison* (1781) V. x. 58 He used to pay his duty to me, and ask blessing the moment he came in, if *admissible* (Is that a word, Harriet?). **1859** MILL *Liberty* 171 What amount of public control is admissible for the prevention of fraud by adulteration.

b. *Law.* Allowable as judicial proof.

1849 BEST *Evidence* (1870) 116 The parol evidence of a witness [as to the contents of a lost document] is admissible, though there is a copy of the document.

2. Capable or worthy of being admitted to an office or relation, or to the use of a place. (Differs from ADMITTABLE, as *admission* from *admittance.*)

1775 ASH, *Admissible*, worthy of being admitted. **1849** MACAULAY *Hist. Eng.* II. 14 They were admissible to political and military employment. **1852** MCCULLOCH *Taxation* (ed. 2) II. v. 215 The average Gazette price of muscovado sugar, admissible to the English markets. **1868** M. PATTISON *Academ. Organ.* §5, 239 Let all who choose be admissible to our lectures.

admissibleness (æd'mɪsɪb(ə)lnɪs). [f. prec. + -NESS.] The quality of being admissible; capability of being entertained or allowed.

1861 *Press* IX. 779/3 The admissibleness of such a system.

admissibly (æd'mɪsɪblɪ), *adv. rare*⁻⁰. [f. as prec. + -LY².] In an admissible manner; so as to be entertained, or allowed.

1818 in TODD.

admission (æd'mɪʃən). [ad. L. *admissiōn-em*, n. of action f. *admiss-* ppl. stem of *admittĕre*: see ADMIT. Cf. Fr. *admission*, late, not in Cotgr. 1632.] The action of admitting to some position, standing, or privileges; distinguished from ADMITTANCE the literal action of letting in to a place.

1. a. The action of admitting to a place and its privileges, into a society or company of men, or class of things. Attributed also to the person admitted; thus = the fact of being admitted, access.

1622 BACON *Henry VII* (J.) There was also enacted that charitable law, for the admission of poor suitors without fee. **1630** NAUNTON *Fragm. Reg.* (1870) 17 Charged by her expresse command to look precisely to all admissions into the Privy-Chamber. **1651** BAXTER *Inf. Bapt.* 14 Baptizing is the Act, or Sign of their solemn admission. **1790** PALEY *Hor. Paul.* I. 6 They have never found admission into any catalogue of apostolical writings. **1828** LANDOR *Imag. Conv.* (1846) 218 Elegance in prose composition is mainly this: a just admission of topics and of words. **1851** RUSKIN *Stones of Ven.* xvii. (1874) I. 188 They have free admission of the light of Heaven.

b. *attrib.*, as ***admission fee, money, ticket.***

1667 SPRAT *Hist. Roy. Soc.* 77 (T.) Some small admission-money and weekly contributions amongst themselves. **1779** *Mirror* 12 June, I shall..present you with a dozen admission tickets. **1825** *Morning Chron.* 2 June 3/2 To give him a general passport to the Theatre, without paying any admission money. **1829** H. FOOTE *Compan. Theatres* 32 The lowering of the admission-money to the boxes. **1842** *Knickerbocker* XX. 498 Certain persons..being stationed at the gates to exact..admission fees. **1888** GUNTER *Mr. Potter of Texas* xx, No one demands an admission fee.

c. *ellipt.* for *admission fee, ticket.*

1792 *Observer* 4 Mar. 4/2 A mere admission for thirteen years sold the other day for fifty-eight guineas. **1802** G. F. COOKE in W. Dunlap *Mem. of G.F.C.* (1813) I. 216 Dispatched a note containing an admission for two on Monday evening to Covent-Garden theatre. **1833** I. F. ALDRIDGE *Let.* in *N. & Q.* (1872) 4th ser. X. 211/1, I enclose an admission for the printers, and one for yourself.

2. Reception or acceptance into an office or position; appointment, institution.

1494 FABYAN VI. cxcvi. 200 After yᵉ deth of Edgare, stryfe arose amonges the lordes for admyssion of theyr kyng. **1588** FRAUNCE *Lawiers Logic* Ded. ¶4 b, Having once knowen the price of an admission, Salting, and Matriculation, with the intertayning of Freshmenne in the Rhetorike schooles. *c* **1680** BEVERIDGE *Serm.* (1729) I. 17, This formal admission of St. Matthias into the number of the apostles. **1726** AYLIFFE *Parergon* 39, *Admission* is when the Patron presents a Clerk to a Church that is vacant, and the Bishop upon Examination admits and allows of such Clerk to be fitly qualify'd. **1818** MISS MITFORD in L'Estrange's *Life* II. xi. 45 Poor Miss Phœbe was in that state which is of all others most favourable to the admission of a new lover—she had just lost an old one.

3. a. The admitting (*of* anything) as proper, valid, or true; acknowledging, allowing, or conceding.

1538 STARKEY *England* 128 You are veray esy in the admyssyon of thes fautys in the spiritualty. **1661** BRAMHALL

Just. Vind. ii. 15 In admission of the same discipline, and subjection to the same supream Ecclesiastical authority. **1794** SULLIVAN *View of Nat.* II. The admission of supernatural truths, is much less an active consent, than a cold and passive acquiescence. **1807** MARSHALL *Constit. Opin.* (1839) 45 To the admission of this testimony great and serious objections have been made.

b. *Law* and *gen.* A concession, an acknowledgement.

1808 PEAKE *Evidence* 17 His wife's admission that she had agreed to pay 4*s.* a week was allowed to be given in evidence. **1846** MILL *Logic* II. iii. §2 (1868) 205 To press the consequences of an admission into which a person has been entrapped. **1868** HELPS *Realmah* xv. (1876) 410 I decline.. to make more admissions than I can help. **1876** J. F. STEPHENS *Law of Evid.* xv. An admission is a statement, oral or written, suggesting any inference as unfavourable to the conclusion contended for by the person by whom or on whose behalf the statement is made.

¶ Admision *c* 1450 in tr. *Higden* Rolls Ser. I. 105 is a misprint for *a diuision* (Higd. *limitem*).

admissive (æd'mɪsɪv), *a.* [ad. L. *admissīv-us*, f. *admiss-* ppl. stem of *admitt-ĕre*; see ADMIT and -IVE.] Characterized by admitting; tending to admit.

1778 HARTLEY *Swedenborg's Heaven & Hell* (1851) Pref. 48 But this.. is the sole effect of that grace which they are not admissive of. **1823** LAMB *Elia* 482 It would be a good face if it were not marked by the small-pox—a compliment which is always more admissive than excusatory.

admissory (æd'mɪsərɪ), *a.* [f. L. *admissor* n. of agent f. *admitt-ĕre* (see ADMIT) + -Y, as if ad. L. **admissōri-us.*] Of or pertaining to admission.

[Not in CRAIG 1847.] **1859** WORCESTER cites *Ecl. Rev.*

†**ad'missure.** *Obs. rare*⁻¹. [ad. L. *admissūra* putting to, admission (of male to female), f. *admiss-* ppl. stem of *admitt-ĕre*; see ADMIT and -URE.] Pairing of animals.

c **1420** *Pallad. on Husb.* IV. 875 Til yeres x she [the mare] for this admyssure Is goode.

†**ad'mistion.** *Obs.* [ad. L. *admistiōn-em* (also *admixtiōn-em*), see ADMIXT.] A by-form of ADMIXTION.

1660 T. STANLEY *Hist. Philos.* (1701) 482/1 That the admistion of some humors, in those who are unsound, excites Phantasies. **1697** WALLIS in *Misc. Curiosa* (1708) II. 317 The admistion of Charcole being chiefly to keep the Parts separate.

admit (æd'mɪt), *v.* Also 5-6 **amit, amitte, amytte.** [orig. a. OFr. *amett-re*:—L. *admitt-ĕre* to let to or into; f. *ad* to + *mittĕre* to send, let go. In 15th c. the Fr. was refashioned after L. as *admettre*, in the wake of which the Eng. also became *admit.*] To let come or go in, (1) willingly, as a person does, (2) by physical capacity as a thing. The secondary meanings are earlier in Eng. than the primary, for which native words were in use.

I. As the action of a voluntary agent.

1. To allow to enter, let in, receive (a person or thing). **a.** (*to* or *into* a place, real or ideal).

1530 PALSGR. 417/2, I admyt or retain to a rome or otherwyse, *Je admets.* **1667** MILTON *P.L.* XI. 596 The heart Of Adam, soon enclin'd to admit delight. **1713** SWIFT *Cadenus* Wks. 1755 III. II. 17 Yet some of either sex.. She condescended to admit. **1755** JOHNSON *Dict.* Pref., Obsolete words are admitted, when they are found in authours not obsolete. **1850** TENNYSON *In Mem.* xxxii. 2 No other thought her mind admits. **1860** TYNDALL *Glaciers* I. §25. 184, I had opened the little window of the cabin to admit some air.

b. into any office, position, or relation; *spec.* in *Law*, into the possession of a copyhold estate.

1473 WARKWORTH *Chron.* 13 Kynge Herry was amitted to his crowne and dignite ageyne. *c* **1480** *Childe of Bristowe* 57 in Hazl. *E.P. Poetry* 113 Any science that is trouthe y shal amytte me therto. **1494** FABYAN V. cxxviii. 110 Woldist thou not admit suche one for thy freende? **1534** LD. BERNERS *Gold. Bk. of M. Aurel.* (1546) Lvj, They amytted hym a citezen and dweller in Rome. **1660** JER. TAYLOR *Worthy Commun.* i. §2. 38 We are admitted to pardon of our sins if we repent. **1713** *Guardian* No. 2 (1756) I. 13, I was admitted a commoner of Magdalen-Hall in Oxford. **1715** BURNET *Hist. own Times* I. (R.) The triers of all those who were to be admitted to benefices. **1768** BLACKSTONE *Comm.* III. 203 If the tenant.. does not within a limited time apply to the court to be admitted a defendant. **1809** TOMLINS *Law Dict.* s.v. *Copyhold*, If the lord refuses to admit he shall be compelled in Chancery.. But that Court will not grant a *mandamus* to admit a copyholder by descent. **1876** FREEMAN *Norm. Conq.* IV. xviii. 127 With what readiness they were admitted to the royal kiss. **1878** BOSW. SMITH *Carthage* 49 Begging that we would admit his prisoners to ransom.

c. *to do* anything.

1413 LYDG. *Pylgr. Sowle* I. viii. (1859) 6 In euery ryghtwys court skyle is that the actour is admytted to maken his compleynt. **1538** STARKEY *England* 192 Only such.. schold be admyttyd to practyse in causys. **1722** DE FOE *Hist. Plague* 55 The houses and villages refusing to admit them to lodge. **1747** in *Col. Rec. Penn.* V. 113 The Ship was admitted to come up to the City.

†**d.** into the number or fellowship *of. Obs.*

1632 MILTON *L'Allegro* 38 Mirth, admit me of thy crew. **1713** *Guardian* No. 151 (1756) II. 265 Jack.. was sent up to London, to be admitted of the Temple. **1788** *New Lond. Mag.* 157 Who afterwards admitted him of his Privy-Council.

2. *fig.* To allow a matter to enter into any relation to action or thought.

a. To consent to the performance, doing, realization, or existence of; to allow, permit, grant.

a **1423** JAMES I *King's Quair* IV. ix, Gif mercy sall admitten thy servise. **1483** CAXTON *Gold. Leg.* 169/1 They wold not accorde that he shold be amytted to be worshypped. **1513** DOUGLAS *Æneis* V. xiii. 72 Amit [*v.r.* admit] my asking, gif so the fatis gydis. **1601** SHAKS. *Twel. N.* I. ii. 45 She will admit no kinde of suite, No, not the Duke's. **1682-3** *Penn. Arch.* I. 55 Desiring thee to admitt, that the people may have the Nomination. *c* **1750** SHENSTONE *Elegy* xvii. 1 Stern Monarch of the winds! admit my pray'r. **1817** JAS. MILL *Brit. Ind.* II. V. v. 534 Tippoo, in the mean time, had admitted no delay.

b. To allow or receive as valid or lawful; to acknowledge.

1538 STARKEY *England* iv. 125 Seyng you graunte the Pope.. to be hede.. you must need admit also apellatyon thereto. **1595** SHAKS. *John* II. i. 200 Let vs heare them speake, Whose title they admit, Arthurs or Iohns. **1805** WELLESLEY *Desp.* 451 We did not admit his claim to tribute. **1849** MACAULAY *Hist. Eng.* II. 208 His power to dispense with Acts of Parliament had been admitted.

c. To accept as true, or as a fact, to concede.

1532 MORE *Confut. Tindale* Wks. 1557, 668/1 That the scripture is not true, but because yᵉ churche saith so and admyt it. **1677** HALE *Prim. Orig. Man.* II. iv. 159 Though an Eternal Succession of Men were admitted. **1777** PRIESTLEY *Matt. & Spir.* xx. (1782) I. 257 Descartes'.. principle was admitting nothing but what his own consciousness obliged him to admit. **1849** MACAULAY *Hist. Eng.* I. 155 Admitting the virtues of the late king. **1876** FREEMAN *Norm. Conq.* I. v. 330 The outline of the story may, I think, be admitted.

d. With *subord. cl.* To allow, concede, grant (either from conviction, or for the sake of argument).

1538 STARKEY *England* 107 Hyt ys to be admyttyd.. that then a nother ys to be chosen. **1603** KNOLLES *Hist. Turks* (1638) 197 But admit he were able to bring an hundred thousand. **1697** POTTER *Antiq. Greece* I. xxvi. (1715) I. 173 All Genuine Citizens.. shall have permission of leaving their Estates to whom they will, admit they have no Male-children alive. **1849** MACAULAY *Hist. Eng.* I. 159 The moderate Episcopalians would admit that a bishop might lawfully be assisted by a council.

¶ In these senses *admit* is sometimes followed by *of.*

1649 SELDEN *Laws of Eng.* I. lix. (1739) 110 Had she been as willing to have admitted of the Laws. **1699** BENTLEY *Phalaris* 62 We admit of the present Calculation. **1774** CHESTERFIELD *Lett.* I. xiii. 43 Luxury and ease were not admitted of at Sparta. **1828** SCOTT *F.M. Perth* I. 4 With our equals in age only, for in dignity we admit of none.

e. *admit to* (something): to acknowledge (a weakness, etc.); to confess to (doing or being something).

1936 'M. INNES' *Death at President's Lodging* viii. 148, I felt at the time, I think, that I would rather be hanged than admit to it. **1963** 'J. LE CARRÉ' *Spy who came in from Cold* x. 95 Money like that was a *douceur* for discomforts and dangers Control would not openly admit to. **1968** S. HILL *Gentleman & Ladies* xi. 148 Now perhaps you will admit to a condition of forgetfulness? **1980** *Washington Post* 12 June D1/6 Brown.. admits to 'a weakness for blondes'.

II. As the action of an involuntary agent.

3. *trans.* To be the channel or means of admission to; to afford entrance, let in. Also *absol.*

1703 MAUNDRELL *Journ. Jerus.* (1732) App. 7 Compassed with good Walls and five Gates, which admitted into it. *Mod.* This order admits the whole party. The ticket admits to the meeting, but not to the conference. A key which admits to the garden.

4. To have the capacity to allow to enter, to have room for.

1661 DRYDEN *Coron. Chas. II*, 66 Not that our wishes do increase your store, Full of yourself, you can admit no more. **1781** J. MOORE *View of Soc.* xli. (1790) I. 451 A staircase sufficiently wide to admit a man to ascend. **1789-96** J. MORSE *Amer. Geog.* II. 24 [A] commodious harbour, which admits only one ship to enter it at a time. *Mod.* The passage admits two abreast.

5. To allow of the co-existence or presence of; to lie open to, be capable of, or compatible with.

a. *trans. Obs.* or *arch.*

1538 STARKEY *England* ii. 45 Me semyth felycyte ys the most perfayt state, wych admyttyth no degre. **1606** SHAKS. *Tr. & Cr.* IV. iv. 9 My loue admits no qualifying crosse. **1699** BENTLEY *Phalaris* 407 *Προτρέπω* in the sense of Exhortation admits a Dative Case after it. **1803** WELLESLEY *Desp.* 228 This movement admits the uninterrupted march of the combined forces. **1850** TENNYSON *In Mem.* cvii. 5 The time admits not flowers or leaves To deck the banquet.

b. with *of.*

1718 *Free-thinker* No. 65, 67 This is a character in Life, the sublimity of which admits not of Mediocrity. **1802** MAR. EDGEWORTH *Moral T.* (1866) 216 Her son's conduct admitted.. of no apology. **1873** MAX MÜLLER *Science of Rel.* 284 So firmly established as hardly to admit of the possibility of a doubt.

admittable (æd'mɪtəb(ə)l), *a.* Also 5-7 **admittible.** [f. prec. + -ABLE. The earlier *admittible* follows the analogy of *credible*, etc., repr. L. forms in *-ibilis*; but *admittibilis* is not found, and the late L. was *admissibilis.* See ADMISSIBLE and -BLE.] Formerly = ADMISSIBLE, but now limited more closely to the literal sense of ADMIT: Capable of being admitted to a place or as a fact.

a **1420** OCCLEVE *De Reg. Princ.* 3120 A man to slee by lawe it is lisible, That slaughter afore God is admyttible. *c* **1555** HARPSFIELD *Divorce Hen. VIII* (1878) 75 A dispensation is sooner admittable in affinity than in consanguinity. **1646** SIR T. BROWNE *Pseud. Ep.* 152 This appellation is not admittible in propriety of speech. *Ibid.* 274 A conceit.. not admittable in Philosophy, much lesse in Divinity. **1726** AYLIFFE *Parergon* 40 For as the Law then stood, a Deacon was admittable.

admittance (æd'mɪtəns). [f. ADMIT + -ANCE, cf. *remittance*; after Fr. and Eng. analogies in *assistance, attendance*, etc. The analogical formation on L. *admittens* would be *admittence.*] The action of admitting, now confined to the literal sense of giving entrance, the fig. ideas connected with *admit* being expressed by ADMISSION.

1. The action of admitting, letting in, or giving entrance; permission to enter. Usually attributed to the person admitted: ' our admittance (by the porter) into the grounds' rather than 'the porter's admittance of us'; thus = the fact of being admitted, entrance given or allowed.

a. *lit.* into a place.

1593 THYNNE *Let.* in *Animadv.* (1865) 97 Whene your Lordship will vouchsafe mee admyttance to your presence. **1611** SHAKS. *Cymb.* II. iii. 73 'Tis Gold Which buyes admittance. **1635** NAUNTON *Fragm. Reg.* in *Phenix* (1708) I. 208 He came up *per ardua*.. not pulled up by Chance, or by any gentle admittance of Fortune. *a* **1704** LOCKE (J.) There are some ideas which have admittance only through one sense. **1731** ARBUTHNOT *On Aliments* (J.) As to the admittance of the weighty elastic parts of the air into the blood. **1837** CARLYLE *Fr. Rev.* (1872) I. VII. ix. 238 He gets admittance through the locked and padlocked grates. *Mod.* 'No admittance except on business.'

b. *fig.* into an office, position (*arch.*), or society (*obs.*) Mostly replaced by ADMISSION.

1594 HOOKER *Eccl. Pol.* III. (1617) 124 Therefore a solemne admittance [to office in the Church] is of such necessitie, that without it there can be no Church-Politie. **1611** SPEED *Hist. Gt. Brit.* VII. xxxix. (1632) 400 Without the admittance of any Secondary or Viceroy to rule there vnder him. **1649** SELDEN *Laws of Eng.* II. xxxv. (1739) 160 The Pope had no admittance unto his ancient Claim. **1743** J. MORRIS *Serm.* viii. 230 The condition of our admittance into his favor.

c. *spec.* in *Law*, into a copyhold estate. The act by which the copyholder is put in actual and legally recognized possession.

1741 T. ROBINSON *Gavelkind* vi. 98 Who dies before Admittance. **1768** BLACKSTONE *Comm.* II. 370 *Admittance* is the last stage, or perfection, of copyhold assurances. **1809** TOMLINS *Law Dict.* s.v. *Copyhold*, The consent of the lord to the surrender shall be adjudged a good admittance. If the steward accept a fine of a copyholder, it amounts to an admittance. But delivering a copy is no admittance.

†**2.** Hence, The habit or faculty of being admitted; admissibility. *Obs. rare.*

1598 SHAKS. *Merry Wiv.* II. ii. 235 You are a gentleman of excellent breeding, admirable discourse, of great admittance.

†**3.** The action of admitting as valid or satisfactory; acceptance, sanction. *Obs.*

1598 SHAKS. *Merry Wiv.* III. iii. 61 The Tyre-valiant, or any Tire of Venetian admittance. **1622** MALYNES *Anc. Law-Merch.* 424 All other coynes inhaunced aboue the Par of Exchanges heretofore calculated amongst Merchants, and especially with the admittance of Princes.

†**4.** The action of admitting the truth (of a tenet), either from conviction or for argument's sake. *Obs.*

1589 PUTTENHAM *Eng. Poesie* (1869) 235 This figure is much vsed by our English pleaders.. which they call to confesse and auoid.. I call it the figure of admittance. **1635** J. SWAN *Spec. Mundi* v. §2 (1643) 165 We fall into other absurdities upon the admittance of this tenet.

5. *Electr.* The reciprocal of impedance, measured in mhos.

1887 O. HEAVISIDE in *Phil. Mag.* XXIV. 482 It is naturally suggested to call J the 'admittance' of the combination. But it is not to be anticipated that this will meet with so favourable a reception as impedance, which term is now considerably used. **1931** *B.B.C. Year-Bk.* 435/1 *Admittance*, the admittance of a circuit is the reciprocal of its impedance or apparent resistance. **1949** *Electronic Engin.* Apr. 145 A method is presented for finding the input admittance of an amplifier.

admitted (æd'mɪtɪd), *ppl. a.* [f. ADMIT + -ED.]

1. Allowed to enter; taken in.

1606 SHAKS. *Ant. & Cl.* V. ii. 140 'Tis exactly valewed, Not petty things admitted. **1661** DRYDEN *Coron. Chas. II*, 110 Beyond your court flows in the admitted tide. **1815** MOORE *Parad. & Peri* 334 Upon whose bank admitted souls Their first sweet draught of glory take.

2. a. Received into an office or relation, instituted.

a **1555** LATIMER in Foxe *A. & M.* III. 398 To inhibit a Preacher of the Kings admitted, is it not to disobey the King? **1881** *Daily Tel.* 25 Oct. (*Advt.*) Wanted.. an admitted solicitor as Managing Clerk.

b. *admitted clerk*, a clerk qualified by admission to the roll of solicitors kept by the Law Society.

1906 A. BENNETT *Whom God hath joined* i. 6 He was an 'admitted' clerk in a solicitor's office. That is to say, he had acquired the right to practise for himself as a solicitor, but he did not practise for himself. **1961** *Times* 9 Feb. 2/6 Wanted, Admitted or Unadmitted man.. experienced in conveyancing and trust accounts.

3. Received as true or valid; received, accepted, acknowledged.

1846 MILL *Logic* I. iii. §3 (1868) 54 But this is an admitted departure from correctness of language. **1851** H. SPENCER *Soc. Stat.* I. iii. §1 We may therefore safely consider it as an admitted truth.

admittedly (æd'mɪtɪdlɪ), *adv.* [f. prec. + -LY².] In an admitted or acknowledged manner; by general admission; confessedly, acknowledgedly.

1804 W. TAYLOR in *Ann. Rev.* II. 318 Both these classes of revenue are admittedly progressive. **1865** CARLYLE *Fredk. Gt.* IV. XI. i. 24 Many Acts of Parliament admittedly rather wise. **1879** M. ARNOLD *Falkland* in *Mixed Ess.* 228 The good which we admittedly have in the England of to-day.

admitter (æd'mɪtə(r)). [f. ADMIT + -ER¹.] One who admits, who gives official reception, or mental assent.

1581 MULCASTER *Positions* 284 The admitters to schooles haue a great charge. **1585** ABP. SANDYS *Serm.* (1841) 120 The admitters of ministers are too lavish in our days. *a* **1656** HALES *Gold. Rem.* (1688) 359 The first Admitters of all Ground of Science.

admittible, variant form of ADMITTABLE.

†**ad'mittie.** *Obs. rare*⁻¹ also **admitty.** [f. ADMIT, in imitation of *inquir-y*, *expir-y*, etc.] Admittance.

a **1616** B. JONSON *Love Restored* 58 (edd. 1616, 1640) Your . . rude good-fellowship must seeke some other spheare for your admittie [edd. 1838, 1875, admitty].

admitting (æd'mɪtɪŋ), *vbl. sb.* [f. ADMIT + -ING¹.] Willing or official reception; mental assent; acknowledgment. (Now gerundial.)

1598 FLORIO, *Matriculatione*, a matriculation, registring, or admitting. *Mod.* Afraid of admitting the whole truth.

admix (æd'mɪks), *v. rare.* [f. L. *ad* to + MIX:—OE. *misc-an*; in imitation of L. *ad-miscēre*, and perh. directly due to the ppl. adj. ADMIXT, ad. L. *admixt-us*, being taken as a regular Eng. pple. *admix-t*.] *trans.* and *intr.* To mingle with something else; to add as an ingredient.

1533 J. FRITH *Answ. to More* (1829) 382 First, you shall understand, that in the wine, which is called Christ's blood, is admixed water. **1593** BILSON *Govt. Chr. Ch.* To Reader 6 Levites being admixed with them to direct them. **1859** TODD *Cycl. Anat. & Phys.* V. 275/1 The blood of the bronchial arteries is poured directly into the pulmonary artery, with the venous blood of which it admixes.

admixt (æd'mɪkst), *ppl. a.* [ad. L. *admixt-us* pa. pple. of *admiscē-re* to mix with, f. *ad* to + *miscē-re* to mingle; afterwards taken as the pa. pple. of an assumed Eng. vb. ADMIX, and spelled *admix-ed*.] Mingled with; added as an ingredient.

c **1420** *Pallad. On Husb.* I. ix, Withouten moolde admixt, nor sandy lene. **1651** CARTWRIGHT *Roy. Slave* (NARES) Like those better spirits, that have nothing of earth admixt. **1671** J. WEBSTER *Metallogr.* xiii. 214 Having something of purple coloured raw silver admixed. **1803** in *Phil. Trans.* XCIII. 14 *Dry* . . merely implies free from mechanically admixed water.

†**ad'mixt,** *v. Obs. rare*⁻¹. [f. prec.] = ADMIX.

1570 DEE *Math. Pref.* 5 Not supposing, nor admixtyng any thyng created . . to . . represent those Numbers imagined.

admixtion (æd'mɪkstɪən). Also 7 **admixion.** [ad. L. *admixtiōn-em* (also *admistiōn-em*), n. of action, f. *admixt-* or *admist-*, ppl. stem of *admiscēre*; see ADMIXT. The form ADMISTION also occurs.] The mingling of one thing with another; the addition of an ingredient; admixture.

1432–50 TREVISA *Higden* Rolls Ser. I. 389 But now thei be amendede thro' the admixtion of Englische men. **1599** SIR J. HAYWARD *Hen IV*, I. 140 A people uncorrupt, without admixtion of forreine manners of bloud. **1615** CROOKE *Body of Man* 466 It is made of Arteries onely without any admixtion of Veines. *c* **1681** SIR T. BROWNE *Tracts* 132 Confusion, admixtion and corruption [of language] in length of time. **1822** T. TAYLOR *Apuleius* II. 33 Two cups already half-full of water, only waiting for the admixtion of wine.

admixture (æd'mɪkstjʊə(r)). [f. L. *admixt-* (see prec.) + -URE, as if ad. L. **admixtūra*; cf. *mixtūra*.]

1. The action or process of mingling one substance with another, or of adding as an ingredient; the fact of being so mingled.

1605 TIMME *Quersitanus* III. 184 Out of hearbes . . waters are extracted by simple distillation, without the admixture of any other liquor. **1704** RAY *Creation* Pref. 8 By the Admixture of that which is false, [they] render that which is true suspicious. **1791** HAMILTON *Berthollet's Art of Dyeing* II. II. §6. 306 Compound colours . . are formed by the admixture of simple ones. **1861** STANLEY *East. Ch.* ii. (1869) 72 It is important to notice this admixture of secular and lay authority.

2. That which is mixed with anything; an alloy, an alien element.

1665 GLANVILLE *Scepsis Sci.* 71 Natural Theory hath been very much hindered and corrupted by metaphysical admixtures. **1818** ACCUM *Chem. Tests* 126 Increasing the admixture of oxymuriate. **1850** MERIVALE *Hist. Rom. Emp.* (1865) I. ii. 52 Its original patrician element might in time be completely absorbed in the plebeian admixture. **1878** GREEN *Coal* i. 7 The shales contain a large admixture of sand.

admod, variant of EDMOD *a. Obs.* humble.

admonish (æd'mɒnɪʃ), *v.* Forms: 4–6 **amonest;** 4 **ammonest, amonist;** 5 **amonace, amonesshe, -esche;** 5–6 **admonest;** 6 **admonase, admonyss, -ysch, -yssh;** 6– **admonish.** [a. OFr. *amoneste-r*:—late L. *admonestā-re* an unexplained derivative form of L. *admonēre*. In Eng. the final *-t* was at length taken as the ppl. ending, leaving the stem as *amoness*, *amonase*, which soon by form-association with vbs. like *abolisse*, *abolish*, became *amonesh*. Meanwhile the prefix also was refashioned after L., giving *admonest*, *admonesse*, *admonish*. The refashioning of the termination is seen in the following:

c **1386** CHAUCER *Parsons T.* 509 Whan a man is sharpely amonested in his schrift to forleten his synne. So *Ellesmere* and *Christch. MSS.*; *Camb.* amonestid, *Petw.* amonased, = amonest, *Selden* amonesshed, *Lansd.* amonesched.]

1. *gen.* To put (a person) in mind of duties; to counsel against wrong practices; to give authoritative or warning advice; to exhort, to warn.

c **1374** CHAUCER *Boethius* (1868) 171 ȝif þou erþely man wexest yuel . . þis figure amonesteþ þe. **1382** WYCLIF *1 Cor.* iv. 14, I amoneste *or warne* [ȝou] as my moost dereworthe sones. *c* **1400** *Apol. for Lollards* 93 Feiþful prestis ammonest þe peple. **1489** CAXTON *Fayt of Armes* IV. xiii. 270 Thus oughte the sayde wysemen to exorte and admoneste them. **1534** LD. BERNERS *Gold. Bk. of M. Aurel* (1546) Kij, Admonishe her often, and reproue her but seldome. **1611** BIBLE *2 Thess.* iii. 15 Count him not as an enemy, but admonish him as a brother. **1667** MILTON *P.L.* IX. 1174, I warned thee, I admonished thee, foretold The danger. **1807** CRABBE *Libr.* 44 Fools they admonish and confirm the wise. **1824** DIBDIN *Libr. Comp.* 92 He makes our hearts reprove, admonish and comfort us.

b. *absol.*

1375 BARBOUR *Bruce* VIII. 348 Bot he mycht nocht amonist swa That ony for him vald turne agane. **1754** CHATHAM *Lett. to Nephew* v. 39 When they [servants] are bad, pity, admonish, and part with them if incorrigible.

†**2.** To call to mind, inculcate (a thing). *Obs.*

c **1386** CHAUCER *Melibeus* 328 In manye othere places he amonesteth pees and accord [*Corpus* amonysscheþ]. *c* **1400** *Apol. for Lollards* 32 To preche is in siche maner to a monest good þingis, as Crist bad His disciplis do.

3. To put (one) in mind *to do* a duty; to charge (a person) authoritatively, to exhort, urge (always with a tacit reference to the danger or penalty of failure). Const. *inf.* or *subord. cl.*; (*to* rare and obs.)

c **1325** *E.E. Allit. Poems* B. 818 Loth . . his men amonestes mete for to dyȝt. **1340** *Ayenb.* 8 þis heste ous amonesteþ þet we ous loky þet we ne wreþþi uader ne moder. **1480** CAXTON *Chron. Eng.* VII. (1520) 84 We admonest you fyrste in the popes halfe that ye make full restytucyon. **1523** LD. BERNERS *Froissart* I. ccccxix. 733 Admonyst your people to do well their deuoyre. **1557** *Kynge Arthur* v. viii, Syrs I admonest you that thys daye ye fyght . . as men. **1611** BIBLE *Transl. Pref.* 11 Doth not a margine do well to admonish the Reader to seeke further? **1709** STRYPE tr. *Beza* in *Ann. Ref.* (1824) I. xliv. 174 To send their letter . . to the queen and bishops, to admonish them to their duty. **1781** GIBBON *Decl. & F.* II. xli. 502 He admonished the usurper to repent of his treason. **1860** TYNDALL *Glaciers* I. §16. 117 Bennen admonished me to tread in his steps.

4. To put (a person) in mind of anything to be avoided; to warn or caution against danger, error, or fault. Const. usually *of*, rarely *against*, *for*, or *subord. cl.*

1541 ELYOT *Image of Gov.* (1549) 49 He would admonest or warne him of his lacke in diligence. **1718** *Free-thinker* No. 68, 87, I promised . . to admonish the Ladies against the Innovation of Masquerades. **1754** SHERLOCK *Disc.* (1759) I. x. 289 Moses was sent . . to reprove and admonish the People for their manifold Transgressions. **1785** *Rolliad.* Ded. (1799) 21 To admonish them, how they rush into future dangers. **1855** PRESCOTT *Philip II*, I. II. xii. 277 A gallows erected on an eminence admonished the offenders of the fate that awaited them.

5. To put (a person) in mind of a thing forgotten, overlooked, or unknown; to give formal or express notice; to notify, apprize, or inform. Const. *of* or *subord. cl.*

1574 tr. *Marlorats Apocalips* 3 Miracles doe teache men and admonishe them of Gods will. **1586** THYNNE *Contn. Holinshed* in *Animadv.* 70, I am to admonish thee, good reader, that . . I have neither word for word, nor sentence for sentence, set downe the writings of Lesleus. **1661** BRAMHALL *Just. Vind.* vii. 198 So soon as he shall be admonished of the Kings pleasure. **1710** BERKELEY *Princ. Hum. Knowl.* I. §44 [They] only admonish us what ideas of touch will be imprinted in our minds. **1844** LINGARD *Hist. A.-Sax. Ch.* (1858) II. i. 11 Admonished her of the obligations which it imposed. **1851** CARLYLE *Sterling* I. ii. (1872) 10 Descended, too, from the Scottish hero Wallace, as the old gentleman would sometimes admonish them. **1855** PRESCOTT *Philip II*, II. (1857) 281 The duchess of Parma admonished her brother that the lords chafed much under his long silence.

admonished (æd'mɒnɪʃt), *ppl. a.* [f. prec. + -ED.] Exhorted, urged, cautioned, warned, informed.

1489 CAXTON *Faytes of Armes* I. i. 1 Admonested of veray affeccion and good desyre. **1659** PEARSON *Creed* (1839) 279 His own wife, admonished in a dream, sent unto him. **1784** COWPER *Task* II. 593 But thus admonish'd we can walk erect.

admonisher (æd'mɒnɪʃə(r)). [f. ADMONISH + -ER¹.] One who admonishes or gives authoritative advice; a monitor.

1570 T. WILSON in *Ascham, Scholem.* (Arb.) Pref. 7 Your good admonisher, and teacher in your yonger yeares. **1617** HIERON *Wks.* II. 113 [What] a blessing to haue such a faithfull admonisher in ones bosome. **1840** BROWNING *Sordello* v. 411 Courteously He turned then, even seeming to agree With his admonisher.

admonishing (æd'mɒnɪʃɪŋ), *vbl. sb.* [f. ADMONISH + -ING¹.] The action of exhorting, cautioning or authoritatively counselling, or of notifying; admonition. (Now mostly gerundial.)

c **1374** CHAUCER *Boethius* (1868) 149 Certys ryȝtful is þin amonestyng and ful digne by auctorite. **1375** BARBOUR *Bruce* IV. 533 We haf thre thingis, That makis vs amonestyngis For to be vorthy. **1570** ASCHAM *Scholem.* (Arb.) 28 Cherefull admonishinge, and heedefull amendinge of faultes. *a* **1688** BUNYAN *Mr. Badman* (1767) I. 738, I cannot conceive since their sin was so conspicuous that my admonishing the world thereof should turn to their detriment. *Mod.* Tired of admonishing them in vain.

admonishing (æd'mɒnɪʃɪŋ), *ppl. a.* [f. as prec. + -ING².] Warning, advising.

1611 COTGR., *Monitoire*, monitory, monishing, admonishing. **1866** GEO. ELIOT *F. Holt* IV. xxxvii. 58 He would be to her as if he belonged to the solemn admonishing skies.

admonishingly (æd'mɒnɪʃɪŋlɪ), *adv.* [f. prec. + -LY².] In an admonishing manner; by way of admonition, or authoritative counsel.

1850 LYNCH *Theoph. Trinal* ii. 18 Patience and wisdom say admonishingly, Not now—not yet. **1861** GEO. ELIOT *Silas M.* 52 Nodding his head aside admonishingly.

admonishment (æd'mɒnɪʃmənt). Forms: 4–6 **amoneste-,** 5–6 **amonyste-, admoneste-,** 6 **admonishe-,** 6– **admonishment.** [a. OFr. *amonestement*, later *admonestement*; f. *amonester*; see ADMONISH and -MENT.] The action of admonishing, or fact of being admonished; also an act of admonishing, a reproof, warning; admonition.

c **1300** *K. Alis.* (W.) 6974 The kyng amonestement herde; Quykliche thennes he ferde. **1475** *Bk. of Noblesse* 79 Joachym king of Juda despraised the admonestementis . . of God. **1494** FABYAN VII. 644 The rulers of Parys, by the amonystement of the sayd John, ordeynyd good and sure watch. **1560** J. DAUS *Sleidane's Comm.* 457 b, He vnlesse he obeye admonishementes ought of his Byshop to be excommunicated. **1606** SHAKS. *Tr. & Cr.* v. iii. 2 To stop his eares against admonishment. **1691** J. NORRIS *Pract. Disc.* 189 The whole course of our Saviour's Actions tends to our instruction and admonishment. **1815** SOUTHEY *Roderick* v. 282 Disdaining all admonishment. **1850** WORDSWORTH *Prel.* IV. 90 Grateful for that admonishment, I hushed my voice.

admonition (ˌædmə'nɪʃən). Also 4–6 **amonicioun, -cion;** 6 **ammonycyon, admonicion;** 6– **admonition.** [a. OFr. *amonition*, later *admonition*; ad. L. *admonitiōn-em*, n. of action, f. *admonē-re* to ADMONISH.]

1. The action of admonishing; authoritative counsel; warning, implied reproof.

c **1374** CHAUCER *Boethius* (1868) 13 Nedeþ it ȝitte, quod I, of rehersyng or of amonicioun. **1506** *Ordin. Crysten Men* (W. de Worde) IV. xxi. 281 Take payne by ammonycyon or otherwyse that restytucyon were made. **1604** ROWLANDS *Looke to it* 20 You that liue as you please, do what you list, and admonition vtterly resist. **1611** BIBLE *1 Cor.* x. 11 These things . . are written for our admonition. **1757** JOHNSON *Rambler* No. 155 ¶6 Few are persuaded to quit it by admonition or reproof. **1861** GEO. ELIOT *Silas M.* 7 Feeling bound to accept rebuke and admonition as a brotherly office.

2. An act of admonishing; a warning, reproof; an utterance or statement of grave counsel or censure, *esp.* of ecclesiastical censure.

1526 TINDALE *Tit.* iv. 10 A man that is geuen to heresie, after the fyrst and the seconde amonicion, avoyde. **1655** FULLER *Ch. Hist.* IX. 102 Admonition is the lowest of Ecclesiasticall censures. **1753** CHAMBERS *Cycl. Supp.* s.v., By the ancient canons, nine monitories, or Admonitions, at due distance, are required before excommunication. **1843** LYTTON *Last of Barons* I. iv. 57 He now called to mind the admonitions of his host. **1870** BRYANT *Homer* I. VI. 184 The timely admonition changed The purpose of his brother.

†**admo'nitioner.** *Obs.* Also **admonishioner** in Hales. [f. ADMONITION + -ER¹.] One who gives admonitions; a monitor. *spec.* in *pl.* The Puritans who in 1571 presented an 'admonition' to Parliament, condemning the ceremonies of the Church of England.

1586 ROGERS *39 Art.* (1607) Pref. 8 Even the admonitioners themselves . . hold the substance of religion with us. **1594** HOOKER *Eccl. Pol.* v. 240 The admonitioners did seeme at the first to allow no prescript forme of prayer at all. *a* **1656** HALES *Gold. Rem.* (1688) 135 Teaching us to make our former sins and impieties admonishioners unto us. [So always.]

admonitive (æd'mɒnɪtɪv), *a.* ? *Obs. rare*⁻¹. [f. L. *admonit-* ppl. stem of *admonē-re* to ADMONISH

+ -IVE, as if ad. L. **admonitīv-us*.] Of or pertaining to admonition; admonitory.
a **1677** Barrow *Serm.* (1683) II. xxvi. 370 This kind of suffering to the devout Fathers did seem .. full of instructive and admonitive emblemes.

admonitively (æd'mɒnɪtɪvlɪ), *adv. rare*$^{-0}$. [f. prec. + -LY^2.] In an admonitive manner; by admonition.
(In mod. Dicts.)

admonitor (æd'mɒnɪtə(r)). ? *Obs.* [a. L. *admonitor* n. of agent; f. *admonit-* ppl. stem of *admonē-re* to ADMONISH; see -OR.] One who admonishes; an admonisher; a monitor. *spec.* = ADMONITIONER.
1547 Hooper *Answ. to Bp. of Winch.* Wks. 1852, 177 He [Judas] departed out of Christ's company, and with all diligence sought how to have his admonitor slain. **1655** Fuller *Ch. Hist.* IX. 102 If the Parliament complied not with this Admonitors desires. *a* **1763** Shenstone *Ess.* 222 Conscience .. at most times a very faithful and a very prudent admonitor.

admonitorial (æd,mɒnɪ'tɔərɪəl), *a. rare.* [f. L. *admonitōri-us*, f. *admonitor* (see prec.) + -AL^1.] = ADMONITORY.
1848 Dickens *Dombey* ii. (D.) Miss Tox .. in her instruction of the Toodle family had acquired an admonitorial tone.

admonitorily (æd'mɒnɪtərɪlɪ), *adv.* [f. ADMONITORY + -LY^2.] In an admonitory manner; with warning or reproof.
1845 Carlyle *Cromwell* (1871) IV. 30 [They might] reproachfully or admonitorily appeal to it.

admonitory (æd'mɒnɪtərɪ), *a.* [ad. L. *admonitōri-us*; see ADMONITOR and -Y.] Of or pertaining to an admonitor; giving or conveying admonition; warning.
1594 Hooker *Eccl. Pol.* I. §8 (J.) The sentence of reason is either mandatorie .. or else permissiue .. or thirdly, admonitorie. **1679** in Somers's *Tracts* I. 44 This little Admonitory Address. **1818** Scott *Hrt. Midl.* 279 The clergyman .. fixed upon her a glance, at once steady, compassionate, and admonitory. **1865** Dickens *Mut. Friend* xi. 254 A raised admonitory finger.

admonitrix (æd'mɒnɪtrɪks). [a. L. *admonitrix* fem. of *admonitōr*; see ADMONITOR.] A female admonitor; a monitress.
1860 L. Hunt *Autobiogr.* IV. 105 Our admonitrix, who spoke in no measured terms, was her Serene Highness herself.

admortization (ædmɔːtɪ'zeɪʃən). *rare.* [a. Fr. *admortization*, *-isation*, ad. med.L. (12th c.) *admortizātiōn-em*, n. of action f. *admortizā-re* = *admortificā-re*, *admortī-re* to reduce to mortmain; really a latinizing of OFr. *amortir*, *amortiss-ant*, assimilating it to vbs. of Gr. origin in *-īzare*: see -IZE. More commonly AMORTIZATION.] The reduction of lands or tenements to mortmain.
1753 Chambers *Cycl. Supp.*, *Admortization* denotes the acquisition of lands, by a monastery, college, church, chapel, or even lay corporation.

† **ad'motion.** *Obs. rare*$^{-1}$. [ad. L. *admōtiōn-em*, n. of action f. *admovē-re*; see ADMOVE.] A bringing into contact.
1603 Harsnet *Pop. Impost.* 86 And this was but an Admotion or touch of the Girdle. [Bailey 1731, not in *ed.* 1742.]

admotive (æd'məʊtɪv), *a.* [f. L. *admōt-* ppl. stem of *admovē-re*; see ADMOVE and -IVE.] Characterized by motion towards.
1879 *Syd. Soc. Lex.* Admotive germination: That in which the episperm containing the end of the cotyledon more or less tumefied remains fixed laterally near the base of the cotyledon.

admount, occas. 16th c. form of AMOUNT *v.*

† **ad'move**, *v. Obs.* [ad. L. *admovē-re* to move to or towards, f. *ad* to + *movēre* to move.]
1. To move to or towards, to apply (a thing *to* or *unto* another.) 'A word not in use.' J.
c **1420** *Palladius on Husb.* I. 276 And first be moolde admoved And after dounge. **1549** Coverdale *Erasmus' Paraphr. 1 Ep. John* ii. 8 Through discrete sobrenes we maye be admoued vnto the light. **1646** Sir T. Browne *Pseud. Ep.* 74 If unto the powder of Loadstone or Iron we admove the North pole of the Loadstone.
2. To promote, advance. (A Latinism.)
1839 J. Rogers *Antipopopr.* Introd. §23 That the work will serve and admove the cause of God and goodness.

† **admovent**, *ppl. a. Obs.*$^{-0}$ [ad. L. *admovent-em* pr. pple. of *admovē-re*: see ADMOVE.] 'Moving to.' Bailey, vol. II, 1731. '*Not much used.*' Ash 1775. (Perh. only in Dicts.)

† **admurmu'ration.** *Obs.*$^{-0}$ [ad. L. *admurmurātiōn-em*, n. of action f. L. *admurmurā-re* to murmur at.] 'A murmuring at.' Bailey 1731. 'The act of murmuring.' Ash 1775. (Never used.)

admyral, -all(e, -ald, -el, obs. ff. ADMIRAL.

† **'adname.** *Obs.* [f. L. *ad* to + NAME *sb.* an englishing of mod.L. *adnōmen* and Fr. *adnom*; see ADNOUN.]
1753 Chambers *Cycl. Supp.* [See under ADNOUN.]

adnascence (æd'næsəns). [f. ADNASCENT on anal. of sbs. in -NCE, a. Fr. *-nce*:—L. *-ntia*.] Adhesion of parts to each other, by the whole surface.
1879 *Syd. Soc. Lex.*

† **ad'nascent**, *a. Obs.* [ad. L. *adnāscent-em*, pr. pple. of *adnāsci* or rather *adgnāsci*, commonly *agnāsci* to grow upon; f. *ad* to + *gnāsci* to be born.] Growing or produced upon something else.
1664 Evelyn *Silva* (1776) 448 Moss, which is an Adnascent plant.

† **adna'scentia**, *sb. pl. Obs.*$^{-0}$ [L. neut. pl. of pr. pple. *adnāscens* (sc. things).] (See quot.)
1706 Phillips, *Adnascentia* .. Branches which sprout out of the main Stock as in the Veins and Arteries. **1731** Bailey, vol. II, *Adnascentia* (with Botanists) those excrescencies which grow under the earth, as in the Lily, Narcissus, Hyacinth, etc. which afterwards become true roots.

adnate ('ædneɪt), *a.* [ad. L. *adnāt-us*, more commonly *agnātus*, f. *ad* to + *(g)nātus* born. See also AGNATE.]
† **1.** Added to something naturally existing. *Obs.*
1677 Gale *Crt. of Gentiles* II. IV. 141 There is an adnate or acquired hardnesse by custome in sin.
2. *Phys.* and *Bot.* Attached congenitally by the whole surface; grown to congenitally.
1661 Lovell *Hist. Anim. & Min.* 312 The pancreas .. is adnate to the fundus of the ventricle. **1666** J. Smith *Solomon's Old Age* (1752) 155 The adnate or the enate parts, either the epiphyses or the apophyses of the bones. **1696** Phillips, *Adnate Tunicle*, the common Membrane of the Eye called *Conjunctive*. **1830** Lindley *Nat. Syst. Bot.* 11 The ovarium, to the surface of which it is adnate. **1856** Woodward *Mollusca* 130 Eye-pedicels short, adnate with the tentacles, externally. **1857** Henfrey *Elem. Bot.* §202 If the filament runs up the back of the anther as it were .. the anther is adnate.

adnation (æd'neɪʃən). [n. of action f. prec.; see -ION^1.] Attachment of surfaces; growth to. *esp.* in *Bot.* Adhesion of different whorls of the inflorescence to each other.
1842 Gray *Struct. Bot.* vi. §3 (1880) 179 Union of contiguous parts of different circles [of the inflorescence] = Adnation.

‖**ad nauseam** (æd 'nɔːsɪæm). [L., = 'to sickness'.] To a sickening extent, so as to excite disgust.
[**1616** T. Adams *Sacrifice of Thankefulnesse* 34 Wee haue heard this often enough. *Ad nauseam vsque*.] **1647** J. Trapp *Comm. upon Four Evang.* Matt. vi. 7, p. 196 Doe not iterate or inculcate the same things odiously & *ad nauseam*. [**1693** N. Mather in J. Owen *Two Discourses concerning Holy Spirit* sig. A 3, They are not filled .. with novel and uncouth Terms foreign to the Things of God, as the manner of some Writers is *ad nauseam usque*.] **1814** *Edin. Rev.* Apr. 73 He had already spoken *ad nauseam* on this very subject. **1907** W. De Morgan *Alice-for-Short* xxv, His frequent use of this expression compels repetition *ad nauseam*. **1955** *Bull. Atomic Sci.* Jan. 15/1 The cliché that fear is altogether and always uncreative is being repeated ad nauseam.

adnect, -nexion, obs. forms of ANNECT, -NEXION.

adnex ('ædnɛks). *Gram.* [f. AD- + NEX(US.] In Jespersen's terminology, a word (usu. a verb) or group of words of secondary importance in a 'nexus' or predicative relation.
1924 [see ADJUNCT B. 5b]. **1924** O. Jespersen *Philos. Gram.* vii. 100 Finite forms of verbs can only stand as secondary words (adnexes), never either as primaries or as tertiaries. **1933** —— *Syst. Gram.* 17 *The dog runs*, nexus: *runs* .. is adnex to *dog*. **1933** A. R. Radcliffe-Brown *Andaman Islanders* (rev. ed.) 504 In nexus the primary precedes the adnex, or in other words the nominative precedes the verb.

adnexa (æd'nɛksə), *sb. pl. Anat.* [a. L. *adnexa*, neut. pl. of *adnexus* joined, f. *adnectere*: see ANNEX *v.*] Structures adjoining or attached to a larger organ and having a related function.
1893 Dunglison *Dict. Med. Sci.* (ed. 21) 23/1 *Adnexa*, appendages. **1906** *Brit. Med. Jrnl.* 6 Jan. 12/1 In lepra anaesthetica the eyes may remain unaffected if the nerves supplying the adnexa of the eye remain free. **1935** [see *salpingography* s.v. SALPINGO-]. **1984** *Times* 26 Mar. 12/5 Two had blunt injuries to the eye and adnexa.
Hence **ad'nexal** *a.*
1913 in Dorland *Med. Dict.* (ed. 7) 39/1. **1965** *Gynaecologia* CLX. 322 Adnexal resistances varied in size. **1976** *Path. Ann.* XI. 64 Smallpox and vaccinia produce intraepidermal vesicles, involvement of adnexal elements, and an underlying dermal reaction.

adnexed (æd'nɛkst), *ppl. a. Bot.* [f. L. *adnex-us*, pa. pple. of *adnectĕre* (see ANNEX *v.*) + -ED^1.] Applied to the gills of certain fungi that reach but do not join the stem.
1836 Berkeley *Fungi* II. 107 Gills adnexed. **1891** W. G. Smith *Berkeley's Outl. Brit. Fungology* Suppl. 8 Gills adnexed, shining white. **1947** F. A. & F. T. Wolf *Fungi* vii. 360 (*caption*) Diagrams representing the manner in which gills of mushrooms may be attached to the stipe... Free, Adnate, Decurrent, .. Adnexed.

† **ad'nichil**, *v. Obs.*$^{-0}$ [a. Fr. (14th–15th c.) *adnichille-r*, mod *annihile-r*, ad. L. *adnihilā-re*, *annihilā-re* to ANNIHILATE.]
1706 Phillips, *Adnichiled* (old Law-word) annulled, brought to nothing, or made void.

adnichilate, adnihilate, obs. ff. ANNIHILATE.

adnize, variant of AGNIZE *v. Obs.* to recognize.

adnominal (æd'nɒmɪnəl), *a.* [f. L. *adnōmen*, var. of *agnōmen* + -AL^1.] Of or belonging to an adnoun; attached to a noun.
1845 J. W. Gibbs *Philol. Stud.* (1857) 63 This case [genitive], being in its origin the adnominal case, or case joined to a noun. **1860** J. Hadley *Grk. Gram.* §488 The adjective in the former case [attributive use] is purely adnominal, belonging exclusively to its substantive.

† **adnomination**, obs. f. AGNOMINATION, a word-play, paronomasia.
1628 Wither *Brit. Rememb.* VI. 280 Compos'd of Clinchings, and Adnominations.

† **ad'note**, *v. Obs. rare*$^{-1}$. [ad. L. *adnotā-re* (also *annotā-re*) to put a note to, remark; f. *ad.* to + *notā-re* to mark, f. *nota* a mark. More commonly ANNOTE.] To note, remark, observe.
1558 W. Forrest *Grisild the Sec.* (1875) 79 In this mateir is to bee adnoted What euyl counsell with Pryncys maye induce.

adnoun ('ædnaʊn). [mod. f. L. *ad* to + NOUN, on the model of *adverb*. Also in mod.Fr. *adnom*, and mod.L. *adnōmen*; the cl. L. *adnōmen*, var. of *agnōmen*, had a different sense.] A word added or joined to a noun substantive, an adjective; *spec.* used by some grammarians for an adjective used substantively.
1753 Chambers *Cycl. Supp.*, *Adnoun*, *Adnomen*, or *Adname*, is used by some grammarians to express what we more usually call an adjective. *a* **1834** Coleridge *Notes Theol. & Polit.* 401 The modification of the noun by the verb is the Adnoun or Adjective. **1876** Bancroft *Hist. U.S.* II. xxxvi. 415 The verb, says Elliot, is thus changed to an adnoun.

adnounce, obs. form of ANNOUNCE.

† **ad'nubilated**, *ppl. a. Obs.*$^{-0}$ [f. L. *adnūbilāt-* ppl. stem of *adnūbilā-re* to involve in clouds; f. *ad* to + *nūbilā-re* to cloud, *nubil-us* cloudy; f. *nūbes* cloud.] 'Darkened or clouded.' Bailey, 1731.

adnul, obs. form of ANNUL.

† **ad'number**, *v. Obs.* [f. L. *ad* to + NUMBER *v.*, in imitation of L. *adnumerāre* to count or reckon to.] To reckon into a number, count in; to take into account.
c **1526** J. Frith *Disput. Purgat.* (1829) 134 Howbeit I will not adnumber it for an argument. **1561** T. N[orton] *Calvin's Instit.* IV. 108 They may be adnombred among the heires of the heauenly kingdome. *Ibid.* 111 To be adnumbred among his people.

adnychellate, obs. form of ANNIHILATE.

ado (ə'duː), *sb.*, properly *v. inf.* = **at do**, which was the fuller form. [In Norse *at* is the prep. used with the inf. = Eng. *to*; see A- *pref.* 5. Hence in northern Eng., as still used in north Lanc. and Westm. 'a bit o' summat at eat.' *Ado* is thus a northern dialect form for *to do*, which has in certain phrases, and as a sb., passed into general use.]
1. *pres. inf.* To do; in northern writers in all constructions; in others only after *have*, in phrase *to have ado*. (Cf. Fr. *avoir affaire*, orig. *avoir à faire* to have a-do, or to do.)
? **1280** *Kemble's Cod. Dipl.* II. 186 Na man sal have at do. **1375** Barbour *Bruce* x. 349, I mycht nocht suffice thar-to, Sa mekill suld be thare ado. *c* **1400** *Rom. Rose* 5083 Al that thei han ado. *c* **1460** *Towneley Myst.* 181 We have othere things at do. *c* **1466** Sir J. Paston in *Lett.* 566 II. 295 Fur I woll nowt have ado ther with. *c* **1550** Cheke *Matt.* vi. 34 Eueri dai hath inough adoo with her own troble. **1637** Gillespie *Eng. Pop. Cerem.* I. viii. 25 We are dead to them, and have nothing adoe with them. *c* **1817** J. Hogg *Tales* (1837) II. 194, I wonder what he had ado in appearing to me?
2. In doing, being done; at work, astir.
1577 Fleetwood in Ellis *Orig. Lett.* II. 202 III. 56 Upon Thursday there was nothing ado but preaching of Sermondes. **1628** Earle *Microcosm.* xxvii. 58 Only an eager bustling, that rather keeps ado than does anything. **1634–46** J. Row (father) *Hist. Kirk* (1842) 291 The tryell of presbyteries is the principall thing that is ado at this tyme. **1637** Rutherford *Lett.* 97 (1862) I. 248 The remembrance .. raised a great tempest & (if I may speak so) made the devil ado in my soul. **1698** J. Newton in *Phil. Trans.* XX. 263 How now, what is here ado?
¶ Hence through such phrases as ***much ado***, ***little ado***, ***more ado***, by taking the adverbs as adjs. qualifying *ado* the latter was viewed as a sb., and so construed in ***a great ado***, ***any ado***,

etc. The transition may be seen in the following quotations, in the first of which *ado* is still the inf., in the second the sb., in the third it may be either.

1563 *Homilies* II. (1859) 191 To have any thing ado with him. *Ibid.* 178 That any true christian ought to have any ado with filthy and dead images. *Ibid.* 472 St. Paul had much ado for the staying of that matter.

3. *sb.* (pl. rare, *adoes, ados.*) Doing, action, business, fuss. ***without more ado***: without further work, ceremony.

c **1380** *Sir Ferumb.* 1495 Þe lordes buþ þan a-paste: wyþoute more a-do. **1440** *Prom. Parv.*, A-do, or grete bysynesse, *Sollicitudo.* **1489** CAXTON *Faytes of Armes* II. xxxviii. 160 They that by the see wol go, be it in armee or to som other adoo. **1535** COVERDALE *Ps.* xlv. 6 The Heithen are madd, the kyngdomes make much adoo. **1592** SHAKS. *Rom. & Jul.* III. iv. 23 Weele keepe no great adoe, a Friend or two. **1634–46** J. ROW (father) *Hist. Kirk* (1842) 162 The King's Majestie..imployed them at his pleasure in some particular adoes. **1755** B. MARTIN *Mag. Arts & Sc.* III. xi. 237 The Ancients made much more ado about this Season of the Year than we. **1876** FREEMAN *Norm. Conq.* III. xii. 85 William wanted a wife, and they were married without more ado.

4. Action or work forced upon one, labour, trouble, difficulty. ***with much ado***: with much trouble or difficulty.

1485 CAXTON *Chas. the Gt.* 221 And made no more a-doo to bere hym, than dooth a wulf to bere a lytel lambe. **1513** MORE *Hist. Edwd. V*, 6 His Mother the Dutches had much adoe in her travell. **1548** UDALL, etc. *Erasm. Paraphr. Mark* v. 27 She had with muche ado wounde her selfe out of the prease of people. **1650** FULLER *Pisgah Sight* IV. vi. 105 Their clothes were made large and loose, easie to be put on, without any adoe. **1742** WESLEY *Wks.* 1872, I. 357, I had much ado to sit my horse. **1850** CARLYLE *Latter-d. Pamphl.* I. 56 Unhewed forests, quaking bogs;—which we shall have our own ados to make arable and habitable. **1876** FREEMAN *Norm. Conq.* I. iii. 129 Tribes which the Kings had much ado to keep in even nominal subjection.

†**ado**, *pa. pple. Obs.* or *dial.* [for earlier *ido, ydo, ydon* done; see A- *particle.* Still in common use in s.w. dialects; see '*Exmoor Scolding*.'] Done. ***dead for ado***: dead for done, dead and done with, dead 'for good.' ***once for ado***: once for done, once for all.

1554 *Interlude of Youth* in Hazl. *Dodsl.* II. 16 Youth, I pray thee have ado, And to the tavern let us go. *a* **1638** MEDE *Wks.* III. ix. 599 If the Cæsarean state may revive..how shall we ever know when it is dead for adoe? **1642** ROGERS *Naaman* 849 Be persuaded to settle once for adoe upon the promise.

-ado, *suffix* of sbs. **1.** a. Sp. or Pg. *-ado* masc. of pa. pple., as *El Dorado* the gilded:—L. *deaurātus*; *desperado* one out of hope:—*desperātus*; *tornado* (Pg.) that which is turned or whirled; *renegado* one who has re-denied the faith, now *renegade.*

2. An ignorant sonorous refashioning of sbs. in *-ade*, a. Fr. *-ade* fem. (= Sp. *-ada*, It. *-ata*) probably after the assumed analogy of *renegade* = *renegado*; e.g. *ambuscado, bastinado, bravado, barricado, carbonado, camisado, crusado, grenado, gambado, palisado, panado, scalado, stoccado, strappado*, all of which in Sp. have (or would have) *-ada.* So *armado* obs. var. of *armada.*

‖**adobe** (ə'dəʊbɪ, ə'dəʊb). Also **adobi, -ie,** and (all *obs.*) **adaube, adobey, adoby,** etc. [Sp.; f. *adob-ar* to daub, to plaster:—late L. *adobāre*; see ADUB. (Dozy derives the Sp. from Arab. *aṭ-ṭōb*, = *al-ṭob*, prob. a Coptic *tōb*, Egypt. hierog. *t·b*, of same meaning; but Minsheu 1623 has '*Adobe de barro*, mortar, clay.') Adopted in U.S. from Mexico, and popularly made into *dobie.* In Eng. sometimes with *e* mute, after mod.Fr. (in Littré's Supp.).]

1. An unburnt brick dried in the sun.

1748 *Earthquake Peru* (ed. 2) iii. 268 Adobes, that is, large Bricks, about two Feet long. **1834** J. L. STEPHENS *Centr. Amer.* (1854) 224 The houses in Costa Rica are..built of adobes or undried bricks two feet long and one broad, made of clay mixed with straw to give adhesion. **1845** GREEN *Texian Exped.* viii. 91 The guard..occupied a small adoby house. **1850** G. HINES *Voyage* 188 Two or three small buildings are enclosed in an adobey wall. **1865** E. B. TYLOR *Early Hist. Man.* iv. 99 Adobe, in which form and as dobie, it is current among the English-speaking population of America. **1879** E. S. BRIDGES *Round the World* 12 He..has a nice little adobi house. **1880** EARL DUNRAVEN in *19th Cent.* Oct. 593 Small settlements..consisting only of two or three mud, or rather adobe, houses.

2. A house made of adobe. *U.S.*

1821 DEWEES *Lett. from Texas* (1852) 21 The remainder of the buildings are adobes. **1881** *Amer. Naturalist* XV. 25 The adobe at one moment seemed near, and the next very far off. **1898** F. REMINGTON *Crooked Trails* 25 A little broken adobe.

3. *Geol.* The loess-like earth or clay from which adobe bricks can be made; a deposit of this material; (see quot. 1889). Also a 'cement' made from this clay.

1856 G. H. DERBY *Phoenixiana* (1859) xix. 133 We have.. Indians employed..in mixing adobe for the type moulds. **1869** BROWNE *Adv. Apache Country* 118 This concrete, or adobe, was cast in large blocks, several feet square. **1889** I. C. RUSSELL in *Geol. Mag.* July 291 A peculiar calcareous clay which is used..for the manufacture of sun-dried bricks, known by the Spanish name 'adobe'. The earth from which these bricks are made is also designated by the same name. We have therefore adopted it..as a convenient term by which to designate the fine subaërial accumulations in general, exclusive of eolian sands. **1944** A. HOLMES *Princ. Physical Geol.* II. xiii. 269 In the semi-arid regions of the western States and in the Mississippi valley there are thick deposits of *adobe* which correspond in all essentials to the loess of Europe and Asia.

4. *attrib.* (See also examples under sense 1.)

1841 T. J. FARNHAM *Great Western Prairies* 136 We spent the 2d and 3d most agreeably with Mr. Walker in his hospitable adobie castle. **1845** J. C. FRÉMONT *Exp. to Oregon* 245 We gave a shout at the appearance on a little bluff of a neatly built *adobe* house with glass windows. **1895** *Outing* (U.S.) Aug. 355/1 The centenarian bells that hang from buckskin thongs in the adobe towers. **1897** *Ibid.* Feb. 457/1 A mile or so of broad adobe country road. **1951** R. BRADBURY *Illustr. Man* (1952) 123 Newer and better fireworks..banged against adobe café walls.

†**a'dod,** *int. Obs.* [for *Ah God!* cf. *adad, agad, egad, ecod,* etc.]

1708 MRS. CENTLIVRE *Busie Body* II. i. 30 Adod, I don't like those close Conferences. **1762** FOOTE *Orators* I. (1780) 9 Adod, away, in a hurry, Alice and I danced to Pewterers Hall.

a-doing (ə'duːɪŋ), *adv.* and *pred. a.* (prop. *phr.*) Now *arch.* [f. A *prep.*[1] + DOING *vbl. sb.*; often construed as quasi-*pr. pple.*] Being done; in the process of happening.

1526 TINDALE *New Testament Colossians* iv. 9 They shall shewe you of all thynges which are adoynge here. **1624** R. BURTON *Anat. Melancholy* (ed. 2) III. ii. mem. v. v. 456 Blessed is the wooing, That is not long a doing. **1842** BARHAM *Sir Rupert the Fearless* in *Ingol. Leg.* 2nd Ser. 40 Thrice happy's the wooing That's not long a-doing! *a* **1907** F. THOMPSON *St. Ignatius Loyola* (1909) 281 While these things were adoing in the eyes of the world. **1954** M. OLIVER *Failing Wine* II. vi. 158 Mary was perfectly aware of what was a-doing.

†'**adolent,** *ppl. a. Obs. rare*[−1]. [ad. L. *adolēntem* pr. pple. of *adolē-re*, occ. used in med.L. for the inceptive *adolēscēntem*: see Du Cange.] Growing, adolescent.

c **1420** *Pallad. on Husb.* IV. 30 Lest it adolent Be letted to encrece and wex stronge.

adolesce (ædə'lɛs), *v.* [Back-formation f. ADOLESCENT.] *intr.* To become adolescent or pass through adolescence.

1909 H. G. WELLS *Tono-Bungay* II. iv. 214 He does his silly utmost to prevent our reading and seeing the one thing, the one sort of discussion we find..supremely interesting. So we don't adolesce; we blunder up to sex. **1934** G. B. SHAW *On the Rocks* 166 The training of the scholar and the sportsman may split and diverge as they adolesce; but they must start from a common training and a common morality as children. **1938** L. MACNEICE *I Crossed the Minch* ix. 128 In September I shall be thirty. How much longer..shall [I] take over adolescing?

adolescence (ædəʊ'lɛsəns). [a. Fr. *adolescence* (14th c., Littré), ad. L. *adolēscentia*; see next.] The process or condition of growing up; the growing age of human beings; the period which extends from childhood to manhood or womanhood; youth; ordinarily considered as extending from 14 to 25 in males, and from 12 to 21 in females. Also *fig.*

c **1430** LYDG. *Bochas* IX. xxv. (1554) 207 b, Afterward in their Adolescence Vertuously to teach them. **1647** HOWELL *Lett.* (1650) I. 423 Those times which we term vulgarly the old world, was indeed the youth or adolescence of it. **1760** STERNE *Tr. Shandy* I. 439 System of education, for the government of my childhood and adolescence. **1865** CARLYLE *Fredk. Gt.* IX. xx. xiii. 242 Ballot-Box Influenza! One of the most dangerous Diseases of National Adolescence. **1876** ROGERS *Pol. Econ.* vii. 2 An infant had its price which rose as the child reached adolescence.

adolescency (ædəʊ'lɛsənsɪ). [ad. L. *adolēscentia* n. of state f. *adolēscent-em* pr. pple. of *adolēsc-ĕre* to grow up.] The quality or state of being adolescent, or in the growing age. Properly distinguished from ADOLESCENCE, as *youthfulness* is from *youth*, as in 'a protracted adolescence,' but 'evidences of adolescency.'

1398 TREVISA *Barth. De P. R.* VI. i. (1495) 186 Adolescencia duryth the thyrd vii yere..and after this adolescenciaes aege comyth the aege that is callyd juventus. **1495** CAXTON *Vitas Patr.* (W. de Worde) I. liv. 110 bb, In his adolescencie he was Paynem. **1502** ARNOLD *Chron.* (1811) 157 The iij. age is adholocencye and endurith vnto xxv. yere age. **1603** FLORIO *Montaigne* (1632) I. xxvii. 92 The first and beardlesse youth of his adolescency. **1719** *Freethinker* No. 138 in *Philol. Anglic.*, In the seasons of puerility and adolescency.

adolescent (ædəʊ'lɛsənt), *sb.* and *a.* [as sb. a. Fr. *adolescent* (15th c.) ad. L. *adolēscent-em* growing up, a youth, prop. pr. pple. of *adolēsc-ĕre* to grow up: see ADULT. The subst. use is the commoner in L., and much earlier in Fr. and Eng. than the adj.; the latter is probably taken direct from L.]

A. *sb.* A person in the age of adolescence; a youth between childhood and manhood.

1482 *Monk of Evesham* (1869) 103 A certen adolescente a yonge man. **1495** CAXTON *Vitas Patr.* (W. de Worde) I. li. 104 bb, He admonested..the adolescentes as his chyldren. **1815** W. TAYLOR in *Monthly Rev.* LXXVI. 498 Conveying, without indecency, to adolescents many facts concerning the human frame.

B. *adj.* Growing towards maturity; advancing from childhood to maturity.

1785 COWPER *Tirocin.* 219 Schools, unless discipline were doubly strong, Detain their adolescent charge too long. **1809** J. BARLOW *Columb.* VIII. 149 Unfold each day some adolescent grace. **1878** B. TAYLOR *Pr. Deukal.* III. i. 100, I see Near manhood in thy adolescent limbs.

†**a'dolorate,** *v. Obs. rare*[−1]. [irreg. f. A- *pref.* 11 + L. *dolor* grief + -ATE[3].] To vex, grieve.

1598 FLORIO, *Dogliare*, to greeue, to molest..to adolorate.

†**a'dommage,** *v. Obs. rare*[−1]. [for earlier *endommage*, ENDAMAGE; see A- *pref.* 10.] To endamage, damage or injure.

1475 CAXTON *Jason* 31 His armures were adommaged.

†**Adon.** *Obs.* [a. Fr. *Adon*, a. L. *Adon*, another form of *Adonis* (q.v.).] Adonis; a fop or exquisite.

1592 SHAKS. *Ven. & Ad.* 769 'Nay then,' quoth Adon. **1630** DRUMM. OF HAWTH. *Poems* 172 The Graces Darling, Adon of our plaines.

‖**Adonai** (ə'dəʊnaɪ, ædəʊ'neɪaɪ). Also **Adonay.** [Heb. *ădōnāi* my Lords (f. *ādōn* lord), one of the names given in O. T. to the Deity, and represented in the A.V. by 'Lord' in ordinary type; also substituted by the Jews, in reading, for the 'ineffable name' JHVH = *Jahveh* or *Jehovah*, the latter of which is said to owe its vowels to being 'pointed' by the Masoretes with those of the word *ădōnāi.*] A name of the Supreme Being.

1483 CAXTON *Gold. Leg.* 230/2 She thenne..prayed in thys maner, O adonay lord Jhesu crist. **1557** *Sarum Primer* i. O greate and marveilous Lord, Adonay.

Adonean (ædəʊ'niːən), *a.* [f. L. *Adōnē-us* + -AN.] Of or belonging to Adonis.

a **1864** FABER in WEBSTER, Fair Adonean Venus.

Adonian (ə'dəʊnɪən), *a.* [f. L. *Adōnī-us* + -AN.] = ADONIC.

1651 T. STANLEY *Poems* 56 She then her old Adonian fire retains. **1871** *P.S. Lat. Gramm.* 480 The Adonian Verse is so intimately connected with the third Sapphic line that Hiatus at the close of the latter is unusual, and words are sometimes divided between the two verses.

Adonic (ə'dɒnɪk), *a.* and *sb.* [ad. Fr. *adonique*, ad. med.L. *adōnicus*, after L. *Sapphicus, Ionicus*, etc.]

A. *adj.* Of, or relating to Adonis; in L. and Gr. *Prosody*, epithet of a metre, consisting of a dactyl and spondee (– ◡◡ | – –).

1678 PHILLIPS, *Adonick Verse*..so called from *Adonis*, for the bewailing of whose death it was first compos'd.

B. *sb.* An Adonic verse or line.

1753 CHAMBERS *Cycl. Supp.* s.v. We meet with Adonics by themselves without sapphics, as also sapphics without Adonics. **1805** *Edin. Rev.* VI. 374 The sapphics..were broken at a longer interval by the adonic.

Adonis (ə'dəʊnɪs). [Gr. prop. name; ad. Phœn. *adōn* lord; title of a Phœnician divinity; in Heb. a name of God.]

1. A beautiful or handsome young man.

1622 MABBE tr. *Aleman's Guzman d'Alf.* II. ii. 21 My Master..made me another *Adonis*, in the neatnesse and gallantry of my cloathes, and delicacie of Perfumes. **1624** MASSINGER *Parl. Love* II. ii, A leper,..in respect of thee, Appears a young Adonis. **1765** TUCKER *Lt. Nat.* I. 457 Two such Adonises talking so sweetly of our reciprocal passion! **1768** TUCKER *Lt. Nat.* II. I. xxiii. 225 How it would divert our ladies below to hear two such Adonises talking so sweetly of our reciprocal passion! *a* **1800** COWPER *On Female Inconstancy*, She who call'd thee once her pretty one, And her Adonis, now inquires thy name. **1888** GUNTER *Mr. Potter of Texas* viii, George! in a month this chap 'll be an Adonis.

†**2.** A particular kind of wig. *Obs.*

1760 H. WALPOLE quoted in *Blackw. Mag.* III. 167 He had a dark brown adonis and a cloak of black cloth. **1775** GRAVES *Spir. Quix.* III. xix. (D.) A fine flowing adonis or white periwig.

3. A genus of plants, N.O. *Ranunculaceæ*, of which the common species is called Pheasant's Eye.

1597 GERARDE *Herball* lxxiv. §2. 310 The red flower of Adonis groweth wilde in the west parts of Englande among their corne. **1741** *Compl. Fam.-Piece* II. iii. 358 Fennel-leav'd perennial Adonis. **1861** PRATT *Flower. Plants* I. 14 Adonis (Pheasants' eye)..Name from 'Adonis'..whose blood was fabled to have stained the flower.

4. A species of butterfly (*Polyommatus Adonis*), also known as the Mazarine or Clifden Blue.

†**A'donist.** *Obs.* [f. ADONAI + -IST.]

1751 CHAMBERS *Cycl.* s.v. *Adonai*, We find great disputes in authors, concerning the use and acceptation of the word Adonai; particularly, whether it is always read for the word Jehovah. This has given rise to two opposite sects among Hebraists, called Adonists and Jehovists.

adonitol (ə'dɒnɪtɒl). *Chem.* [ad. G. *adonit* (E. Merck *Bericht über das Jahr 1892* (1893) 26), f.

mod.L. *Adōnis*, generic name: see ADONIS 3, -OL.] = RIBITOL.

1893 *Jrnl. Chem. Soc.* LXIV. 291 The annual report for 1892 issued by Merck, of Darmstadt, contains a description of a crystalline pentahydric alcohol obtained from *Adonis vernalis*, and named adonitol. **1944** *Jrnl. Amer. Chem. Soc.* LXVI. 1906/1 Schulz and Tolleus condensed adonitol with aqueous formaldehyde through the action of concentrated hydrochloric acid and obtained a methylene derivative. **1948** [see RIBITOL]. **1954** [see PENTITOL].

adonize (ˈædənaɪz), *v.* [a. (16th c.) Fr. *adonise-r*; see ADONIS and -IZE.] *trans.* and *intr.* Of men: To make an Adonis of; to adorn; to dandify.

1611 COTGR., *Adoniser*, to adonize it; to resemble Adonis; to imitate, or counterfeit the graces, or beautie of Adonis. **1761** SMOLLETT *Gil Blas* XII. xiv. (1802) III. 418 Three good hours, at least, in adjusting and adonizing myself. **1865** *Pall Mall G.* 11 Aug. 9/2 They may be Adonizing at Truefit's.

†**a-doors.** *adv. Obs.* Prop. written separately **a** doors; less commonly **a** door. A phonetic reduction apparently of both *of doors, o' doors* (see A *prep.*^{2}), and *at doors* (cf. *a-do*); common 6–8 in the phrases *forth a doors, out a doors, in a doors*, for which also the full forms occur.

1526 TINDALE *John* xii. 31 Nowe shall the prynce off this worlde be cast out a dores. **1532** MORE *Conf. Barnes* viii. Wks. 1557, 804/2 Ye shall beare no part of that flesh foorth a dores. **1581** MARBECK *Bk. of Notes* 393 Charitie driueth feare out a doores. **1607** TOPSELL *Four-footed Beasts* (1673) 487 He taketh one..and draweth him in adoors. **1647** R. STAPYLTON *Juvenal* 38 Out a' doore I'm hurld. **1675** HOBBES *Odyssey* 51 She saw him coming in a door. *Ibid.* 204 And with two dogs at's heels went out a door. **1777** SHERIDAN *Trip to Scarb.* III. iii. 504 Here, run in a-doors quickly.

¶ Cf. the full phrases:

c **1325** *E.E. Allit. P.* C. 268 In at a munster dor. **1590** SHAKS. *Com. Err.* IV. iv. 36 Driuen out of doores with it when I goe from home. *a* **1593** MARLOWE *Jew of Malta* II. ii. 283 As you went in at doors. *a* **1654** GATAKER *Spirit. Watch* 79 (T.) She would not go out at doors.

†**a'doperate,** *v. Obs.* [f. med.L. *adoperāt-* ppl. stem of *adoperā-re* to use; f. *ad* to + *operāre* to work: see OPERATE.] To bring into operation, employ, use.

1632 J. HAYWARD *Eromena* 88 By the secret intelligence of the meanes already adoperated. **1681** NEVILLE *Plato Rediv.* 19 Without the Sword, which in this Case was never adoperated.

adoperation (æˌdɒpəˈreɪʃən). *rare*$^{-1}$. [n. of action f. med.L. *adoperā-re*; see prec. and -TION.] Application, employment.

1817 PEACOCK *Melincourt* II. 56 By a skilful adoperation of these means..he might himself become the lord and master of the lands.

adopt (əˈdɒpt), *v.* [a. Fr. *adopte-r* (16th c. in Litt.) ad. L. *adoptā-re* to choose for oneself, *esp.* a child; f. *ad* to + *optāre* to choose; prop. a freq. vb. f. an obs. pple. **opt-us*, f. **op-ĕre* to wish.]

1. a. *gen.* To take (any one) voluntarily into any relationship (as *heir, son, father, friend, citizen*, etc.) which he did not previously occupy. Const. *as* (*to, unto, sb. in appos.* obs.).

1548 HALL *Hen. VII*, an. 7 (R.) He did adopt to his heyre of all his realmes and dominions, Lewes the XI. **1598** R. BARCKLEY *Felicitie of Man* III. (1603) 158 Adopting mee to his sonne in law. **1593** SHAKS. *3 Hen. VI*, I. i. 135 May not a King adopt an Heire? *c* **1735** POPE *Hor. Ep.* I. vi. 108 Adopt him son or Cousin at the least. **1757** JOHNSON *Rambler* No. 142 ⁋12 Those whom he happens to adopt as favourites. **1782** COWPER *Retirement* 725 Friends, not adopted, with a schoolboy's haste, But chosen with a nice discerning taste. **1818** HALLAM *Middle Ages* (1872) II. 91 They were adopted into the Diet.

b. To choose (an applicant) as a candidate for election to the House of Commons.

1879 G. C. BRODRICK *Polit. Stud.* 270 The indifferent and wavering electors..will be less disposed to gravitate towards him than if he had been unanimously recommended and unanimously adopted. **1905** *Times* 21 Dec. 10/3 This meeting of Unionist electors..deeply regrets the precipitate action of the council of the Constitutional Union in adopting him [*sc.* Ld. Robert Cecil] as Unionist candidate for East Marylebone. **1922** *Mid Cumberland & N. Westmorland Herald* 4 Nov. 5/1 Major-General Sir Cecil Lowther, the late Member, was adopted as candidate for the ensuing election. **1969** M. RUSH *Sel. Parliamentary Candidates* ii. 53 The recommended candidate, Angus Maude, used the phrase 'If you adopt me...' no less than ten times, although at the end of the meeting members were handed printed posters urging electors to 'Vote for Maude'. **1979** J. GRIMOND *Memoirs* vi. 97 Had Lady Glen-Coats not recommended me to the Liberals there, I should never have been adopted—and probably would never have been an M.P. at all.

c. To take up the cause or campaign for the release of (a political prisoner).

1961 *Amnesty* 11 July 4/1 Anyone who writes to Amnesty to ask 'Can I adopt a prisoner?' is asked to take on the case not of one prisoner but of three. **1969** *Listener* 13 Feb. 196/2, I have no idea..what part, if any, such Amnesty devices as letters written to governments and judicial authorities by Amnesty groups which 'adopt' particular prisoners..play in securing [their] release. **1977** *Daily Mirror* 15 Mar. 23/5 Groups exist..which 'adopt' particular individuals as David Markham 'adopted' Bukovsky. It would be good to see this practice spreading.

2. a. *esp.* (Without complement, and sometimes *absol.*) To take as one's own child, conferring all the rights and privileges of childship, or such of them as the law permits to be thus conferred.

1604 SHAKS. *Oth.* I. iii. 191, I had rather to adopt a Child, then get it. **1750** CHAMBERS *Cycl.* s.v., Pope John VIII adopted Boson, king of Arles, which perhaps is the only instance in history of adoption in the order of ecclesiastics. **1873** MISS BROUGHTON *Nancy* III. 20 My child! my child!.. what possessed me to marry you? why did not I adopt you instead?

b. Of a local authority: to take over (from private ownership, etc.) responsibility for a road, etc.

1862 *Act.* 25 & 26 *Vict.* c. 61 §45 It shall and may be lawful for the Council of every such Borough in England and Wales..to adopt all or any of such Parish Roads and Highways as the Council shall in its Discretion consider advisable. **1907** *Justice of Peace* (*Reports*) LXXI. 564/3 In 1904 the widening and laying out of Stubbington Avenue as a road forty feet wide for the whole of its length was completed, but it had never been adopted by any resolution of the council of the plaintiffs. **1958** *Times* 22 Mar. 7/6 A frontager who considers that they [*sc.* roads] should have been adopted.

†**3.** To receive a graft, as a tree. [L. *fac ramum ramus adoptet* Ov. *Rem.* 195.] *Obs.*

1601 HOLLAND *Pliny* (1634) II. Fit one [vine stocke] to the other, ioyning pith to pith, and then binding them fast together so close, that no aire may enter between, vntill such time as the one hath adopted the other.

4. a. To take up (a practice, method, word, or idea) from some one else, and use it as one's own; to embrace, espouse.

1607 SHAKS. *Cor.* III. ii. 48 Which, for your best ends, You adopt your policy. **1749** CHESTERFIELD *Lett.* 205 II. 280 Adopt no systems, but study them yourself. **1850** KINGSLEY *Alt. Locke* (1876) I. 11 He might possibly not have adopted the costume of the island. **1879** FROUDE *Cæsar* xxiii. 397 These men had married Egyptian wives and had adopted Egyptian habits.

b. *Philol.* (as used in this Dict.) To take a word from a foreign language into regular use without (intentionally) changing its form.

Thus: We have adopted the modern German names of several rocks and minerals, as *gneiss, hornblende, quartz*, and *nickel*.

5. To take (a course, etc.) as one's own (without the idea of its having been another's), to choose for one's own practice.

1769 *Junius Lett.* xxxv. 160 You cannot hesitate long upon the choice which it equally concerns your interests and your honour to adopt. **1833** HT. MARTINEAU *Manch. Strike* ix. 92 He adopted one posture, from which he determined not to move. **1875** HIGGINSON *Hist. U.S.* xvii. 164 His resolutions were adopted by a small majority.

†**6.** *causal.* To make over to any one as his child, adherent, or subject; to affiliate, attach. [L. *se alicui adoptare.*] *Obs.*

1725 POPE *Odyss.* xv. 521 Sold to Laertes by divine command, And now adopted to a foreign land.

†**7.** To name after; to name anew after an adoptive parent; to christen or rechristen. [L. *aliquid* (*suo nomini*) *adoptare.*] *Obs.*

1601 HOLLAND *Pliny* (1634) I. 109 When you are past Smyrna, you come into certain plains, occasioned by the riuer Hermus, and therefore adopted in his name.

8. To approve, to confirm (accounts, reports, etc.).

1906 GALSWORTHY *Man of Property* 178, I propose then that the report and accounts be adopted. **1958** *Oxford Mail* 16 Aug. 8/7 The best balance sheet the club has ever had was unanimously adopted at the annual general meeting of the Oxford Club League.

adoptability (əˌdɒptəˈbɪlɪtɪ). [f. ADOPTABLE: see -BILITY.] Capability of being adopted or chosen. *concr.* An adoptable thing.

1843 CARLYLE *Past & Pr.* II. xvii. (D.) The Liturgy..was what we can call the Select Adoptabilities..from that wide waste imbroglio of prayers already extant.

adoptable (əˈdɒptəb(ə)l), *a.* [f. ADOPT + -ABLE.] Capable of being adopted; fit to be adopted.

1843 CARLYLE *Past & Pr.* (1858) 171 His..metaphor was found adoptable. **1862** R. H. PATTERSON *Ess. Hist. & Art* 68 An 1–18th being the smallest difference of [musical] pitch adoptable without confusion.

†**a'doptant,** *a.* and *sb. Obs.* [a. Fr. *adoptant*, ad. L. *adoptant-em* pr. pple. of *adoptā-re* to ADOPT. Cited as sb. only.] **a.** *adj.* Adopting. **b.** *sb.* One who adopts, or takes a child as his own.

1671 FLAVEL *Fount. of Life* xv. 42 Both flow from the Pleasure and Goodwill of the adoptant.

†**a'doptate,** *v. Obs. rare*$^{-1}$. [f. L. *adoptāt-* ppl. stem of *adoptā-re* to ADOPT.] = ADOPT.

1662 PETTY *Taxes & Contrib.* 12 Having calculated these numbers, to adoptate a proportion of chirurgeons, apothecaries, and nurses to them.

adoptative (əˈdɒptətɪv), *a.* [f. L. *adoptāt-* ppl. stem of *adoptā-re* to ADOPT + -IVE; as if ad. L. **adoptātīv-us.*] Of or pertaining to adoption; adoptive.

1615 BP. HALL *Contempl.* IV. xxii. (1833) 395 A spiritual and adoptative sonship. **1875** MCCLELLAN *New Test.* 623 Adoptative or other legal parentage, in opposition to the natural.

adopted (əˈdɒptɪd), *ppl. a.* [f. ADOPT + -ED.]

1. a. Taken voluntarily or admitted into any relationship not formerly occupied; *esp.* that of a child.

c **1590** GREENE *Friar Bacon* ix. 204, I accept thee here Without suspence as my adopted son. **1600** SHAKS. *A. Y. L.* I. ii. 246 To be adopted heire to Fredricke. **1741** MIDDLETON *Cicero* (1742) II. vi. 65 The only instances of Foreigners, and adopted Citizens who had ever advanced themselves to either of those honors. **1823** LAMB *Elia* II. vii. (1865) 277 An adopted denizen of the sea.

b. *spec.* of a road (cf. ADOPT *v.* 2b).

1938 *Times* 31 May (Building Soc. No.) ix/3 Roads are either adopted or unadopted. **1951** E. BARKER *Princ. Soc. & Polit. Theory* II. iii. 50 An 'adopted' road is incorporated into the road system of a town.

2. Taken up or chosen as one's own; assumed.

1660 DRYDEN *Astr. Red.* 70 These virtues Galba in a stranger sought, And Piso to adopted empire brought. **1763** J. BROWN *Poetry & Mus.* §11, 184 Their [the Romans'] Music and Poetry was always borrowed and adopted. **1876** FREEMAN *Norm. Conq.* II. x. 458 Gisa does not seem very warm in his patriotism for his adopted country. *Mod. Rose*, though an adopted word, is now as familiar as *daisy*.

adoptedly (əˈdɒptɪdlɪ), *adv.* [f. prec. + -LY^{2}.] In an adopted manner; by adoption.

1603 SHAKS. *Meas. for M.* I. iv. 47, *Luc.* Is she your cosen? *Isa.* Adoptedly; as schoole-maids change their names, By vaine, though apt affection.

adoptee (ədɒpˈtiː). [f. ADOPT *v.* + -EE^{1}.] An adopted person.

1892 *Sat. Rev.* 6 Aug. 179/1 That odd provision of French law which permits adoption—in case the adoptee has saved the life of the adopter. **1962** *Guardian* 16 Nov. 8/7 The.. psychiatric figures for adoptees.

adopter (əˈdɒptə(r)). [f. ADOPT + -ER^{1}.]

1. One who adopts into any relation, *esp.* that of sonship; an adoptive father.

1572 HULOET *Abecedarium*, Adopter, that makes the adoption, *Adoptator*. **1611** SPEED *Hist. Gt. Brit.* VI. cxviii. 99 Antoninus..did not onely equall his Adopter and Predecessours, in wisdome and other princely qualities. **1741** MIDDLETON *Cicero* II. vi. (1742) 13 The Adopter was not full twenty years old, when he adopted a Senator, who was old enough to be his father. **1870** WYNTER in *Athenæum* 6 Aug. 174 The..speculative father of six children, who sought charitable adopters for his offspring.

2. One who takes up any opinion or plan; *prop.* from another; also *gen.* as a matter of choice.

1829 SCOTT *Antiq.* xxxv. 244 The rash adopters of the more obvious etymological derivations. **1876** M. ARNOLD *Lit. & Dogma* 218 A practical rule, which, if adopted, would have the force of an intuition for its adopter also.

3. *Chem.* A tube connecting two pieces of apparatus; *esp.* one which connects the retort and receiver in apparatus for distillation. Also called ADAPTER.

1767 WOULFE in *Phil. Trans.* LVII. 411 The retort was set in a reverberatory furnace, and an adopter and quilled receiver luted to it. **1822** IMISON *Sc. & Art* II. 10 Conical tubes that fit into another, for lengthening the necks of retorts..are called adopters.

adopting (əˈdɒptɪŋ), *vbl. sb.* [f. ADOPT + -ING^{1}.] A choosing or taking as one's own, or into any relationship, *esp.* as a child; adoption.

1591 PERCYVALL *Sp. Dict.*, *Ahijamiento*, adopting, *adoptatio*. **1861** GEO. ELIOT *S. Marner* 313 That was the only adopting I ever heard of: and the child was transported when it was twenty-three.

adopting (əˈdɒptɪŋ), *ppl. a.* [f. ADOPT + -ING^{2}.] That adopts.

1717 LADY M. W. MONTAGUE *Lett.* 47 II. 44 The adopting fathers are generally very tender to these children. **1850** L. HUNT *Autobiog.* xv. (1860) 238 Torn from the arms of her adopting father.

adoption (əˈdɒpʃən). [ad. (directly or through Fr. *adoption*) L. *adoptiōn-em* n. of action, f. obs. ppl. stem *adopt-*, whence also *adoptā-re* to ADOPT. In late L. *adoptio* was used instead of *adoptātio*, the n. of action, from *adoptā-re.*]

1. The action of voluntarily taking into any relation; *esp.* of taking into sonship. **a.** *viewed actively*.

1387 TREVISA *Higden* (Rolls Ser.) V. 213 Þe sacrament of adopcioun [*sacramento adoptionis*] i.e. baptism. **1483** CAXTON *Cato* a iiij. The second [kind of cousin] is legale, the whiche cause is by adopcyon. **1581** MARBECK *Bk. of Notes* 15 The Lawiers..define Adoption to be a legitimate act imitating nature, found out for their solace and comfort, which haue no children. **1602** SHAKS. *Haml.* I. iii. 62 The friends thou hast, and their adoption tride, Grapple them to thy Soule, with hoopes of Steele. **1755** SHERLOCK *Disc.* I. viii. 230 The Spirit itself, that is the Spirit of Adoption, which Christians receive, is one Witness. **1875** H. E. MANNING *Holy Ghost* i. 18 We are made sons of God by adoption.

b. *fig.*

1644–58 CLEVELAND *Gen. Poems, &c.* (1677) 118 As Chickens are hatcht at Grand Cairo by the Adoption of an Oven.

c. *viewed passively*, The fact of being so adopted; adopted relation or condition.

1382 WYCLIF *Rom.* viii. 23 We vssilf sorwen withynne us for the adopcioun of goddis sones, *that is..the staat of Goddis sones bi grace* [TINDALE adopcion, CRANMER adopcyon, *Genevan, Rheims*, **1611** adoption]. **1494** FABYAN VII. ccxxxiii. 268 The kynge shulde take hym for his sone of adopcion, and ryghtefull heyre. **1823** LAMB *Elia* Ser. II. xxii.

(1865) 388 It could not taste of death, by reason of its adoption into immortal palaces.

2. a. The act of taking up and treating as one's own; acceptance, espousal.

1598 SHAKS. *Merry Wives* II. ii. 309, I shall.. stand vnder the adoption of abhominable termes. **1769** BURKE *Pres. State Nat.* Wks. II. 121 They may add to the publick calamity of their own measures, the adoption of his projects. **1821** CRAIG *Drawing & Paint.* vi. 347, I cannot, therefore, recommend this mode of miniature painting to your adoption. **1878** SEELEY *Stein.* III. 550 The country of his own adoption.

b. *Philol.* (as used in this Dict.) The taking of a word belonging to a foreign language into regular use in our own, without (intentional) change of form; a special instance of this process.

Thus: The English word *hotel* is an adoption of the modern French (as *hostel* was of the Old French) living descendant of Latin *hospitāle*; in *hospital* we have a French and English adaptation of the Latin word itself. These facts are thus symbolized: Eng. *hotel*, a. mod.Fr. *hôtel*:—OFr. *hostel*:—L. *hospitāle*. Eng. *hospital*, a. OFr. *hospital*, ad. L. *hospitāle*.

c. *passively*, The fact of being so taken up and accepted; the being adopted.

1755 JOHNSON *Pref. to Dict.*, Which [words].. must depend for their adoption on the suffrage of futurity. **1879** in *Cassell's Techn. Educ.* IV. 10/2 The great advantages of their adoption in all great metropolitan centres.

d. Of a road: see ADOPT *v.* 2 b.

1890 *Act 53 & 54 Vict.* c. 59 §41 Adoption of private streets... The urban authority.. may.. declare the whole of such street or part of a street to be a highway repairable by the inhabitants at large.

3. Of accounts, reports, etc.: approval, confirmation (cf. ADOPT *v.* 8).

1881 *Evening News* 26 July 3/6 The chairman in moving the adoption of the report said it was with great satisfaction that he informed the shareholders of the favourable traffic receipts of 1880.

4. *attrib.* and *Comb.*, as (sense 1) ***adoption agency, order, society.***

1944 *N.Y. Times* 26 Apr. 17/1 (*heading*) Curbs *adoption agencies. Governor Edge signs bill to end commercialization. **1975** D. LODGE *Changing Places* i. 25 Have the baby. Get it adopted—no sweat, the adoption agencies are screaming for new stock. **1926** *Law Times* 6 Mar. 194/1 If an application for an *adoption order is made by spouses they must both be parties to it. **1950** *Act* 14 *Geo. VI* c. 26 § 1(1) An adoption order may be made on the application of two spouses authorising them jointly to adopt an infant. **1972** *Times* 28 Jan. 16/3 Delay in the hearing of cases concerning children should be reduced to the minimum, Mr Justice Latey said.., granting an adoption order and dispensing with parental consent. **1939** *Act* 2 & 3 *Geo. VI.* c. 27 § 1(1) It shall not be lawful after the appointed day for any body of persons to make any arrangements for the adoption of a child unless that body is a registered *adoption society or a local authority. **1984** *Adoption Rules* (Statutory Instrument No. 265) Reg. § 2(1) In these rules ..'adoption agency' means a local authority or approved adoption society.

adoptional (ə'dɒpʃənəl), *a.* [f. prec. + -AL[1]. Cf. *nation-al*, etc.] Of or belonging to adoption.

1861 W. H. MILL *Pantheist. Princ.* (ed. 2) 212 Leaving them [the Evangelists] to describe severally the natural and the adoptional lines of this, and withholding the descent of the only true parent.

adoptionism (ə'dɒpʃənɪz(ə)m). *Eccl. Hist.* [f. ADOPTION + -ISM.] The tenets of the ADOPTIONISTS.

1874 BLUNT *Dict. of Sects* 8 By contemporaries Adoptionism was regarded as identical with.. Nestorianism.

adoptionist (ə'dɒpʃənɪst). *Eccl. Hist.* [f. ADOPTION + -IST.] One of a sect who maintained that Jesus Christ is the son of God by adoption only; commonly known under their Latin appellation of *adoptiani*. Also used *attrib.*

1847 in CRAIG. **1853** C. HARDWICK *Hist. of Chr. Ch.* iii. 66 The controversy known as the Adoptionist, but in reality a phase of Nestorianism revived. **1874** BLUNT *Dict. of Sects* 7 The Gnostics were in a certain sense Adoptionists.

†**a'doptious,** *a. Obs. rare*$^{-1}$. [f. ADOPTION, after analogy of *ambition, ambitious*, etc., as if f. L. **adoptiōsus*.] Of, or connected with, adoption.

1601 SHAKS. *All's Well* I. i. 187 With a world Of pretty fond adoptious christendomes That blinking Cupid gossips [*i.e.* christenings of adopted children for which Cupid stands godfather].

adoptive (ə'dɒptɪv), *a.* [a. Fr. *adoptif, -ive*, ad. L. *adoptīvus* characterized by adoption: see ADOPT and -IVE.]

1. Due to adoption, as an adoptive son, father, etc.

c **1430** LYDG. *Bochas* VII. viii. (1554) 170 a, Sonne adoptife ..Of sayd Galba. **1432–50** tr. *Higden* Rolls Ser. VII. 510 The holy kyng Edward.. made William Norman his sone adoptivus. **1534** LD. BERNERS *Gold. Bk. of M. Aurel.* (1546) X viij, She is thy mother adoptiue, and my natural wife. **1598** SYLVESTER *Du Bartas* I. i. (1641) 4/1 A Hen that fain would hatch a Brood, Some of her own, some of adoptive bloud. **1641** MILTON *Ch. Discip.* I. iii, The adoptive and cheerefull boldnesse which our new alliance with God requires. **1748** CHESTERFIELD *Lett.* 176 II. 155 The herd of mankind can hardly be said to think; their notions are almost all adoptive. **1876** FREEMAN *Norm. Conq.* I. 710 That the adoptive brother should be preferred to the brother by blood. **1880** W. CORY *Mod. Eng. Hist.* I. 189 To sacrifice himself to Greece as his adoptive country.

2. Fitted or inclined to adopt, having the habit of adopting.

a **1834** LAMB *Lett.* xvii. 164 There is adoptive as well as acquisitive sacrifice. **1880** G. A. SALA in *Illust. Lond. News* 18 Dec. 587 Surely the English language is the most receptive and most swiftly adoptive in the world.

adoptively (ə'dɒptɪvlɪ), *adv.* [f. prec. + -LY[2].] In an adoptive manner; by way of adoption.

1844 MAITLAND *Dark Ages* 482 For it is one thing to be so [i.e. one with God] adoptively, and another to be so substantially. **1844** B. THORPE *Ælfric's Hom.* I. 259 God, the Father Almighty, has one Son naturally, and many adoptively [A. Sax. *gewiscendlice*].

‖**ador.** [L.] The grain used in sacrifices, spelt.

c **1420** *Pallad. on Husb.* x. 41 In mene lande of ador or of whete, An acre lande to strikes IIII is mete.

adorability (ə,dɔərə'bɪlɪtɪ). [f. ADORABLE; see -BILITY.] The quality of being adorable; adorableness.

1637 GILLESPIE *Eng. Pop. Cerem.* III. iv. 64 If adorability agree to the humanity of Christ, then may his humanity help and save us. **1794** BURNS in *Wks.* IV. 173 The adorability of her charms. **1832** COLERIDGE *Table Talk* Apr. 4 Both Laelius and Faustus Socinus laid down the adorability of Jesus in strong terms.

adorable (ə'dɔərəb(ə)l), *a.* [a. Fr. *adorable*, ad. L. *adōrābil-em* worthy of worship; f. *adōrā-re*; see ADORE + -ABLE.]

1. Worthy of worship or divine honour.

1611 COTGR., *Adorable*, adorable, worthy, or fit to be adored. **1654** BAKER *Lett. Balzac* III. 105 And make me a thing adoreable and divine. **1756** BURKE *Subl. & B.* Wks. I. 228 We discover the adorable wisdom of God in his works. **1794** SULLIVAN *View of Nat.* III. 399 That adorable Being who governs all.

2. By exaggeration, said of anything to which one is passionately attached. Now also in increasingly trivial use, charming, delightful.

1710 SHAFTESBURY *Charact.* III. i. (1737) II. 349 A way to make very adorable Places of these Silvan Habitations. **1766** ANSTEY *Bath Guide* (1779) 139 I'm griev'd to the heart Without cash to depart, And quit this adorable scene. **1847** DISRAELI *Tancred* VI. ix. (1871) 469 The ever adorable had truly quitted the mountains. **1900** 'FLYNT' & 'WALTON' *Powers that Prey* ii. 37 It may be doubted whether Richard 'looked' adorable; for the most part he looked uncommonly sharp and hard. **1908** E. M. FORSTER *Room with View* ii. 25 Look at that adorable wine-cart! How the driver stares at us, dear, simple soul! **1960** C. DAY LEWIS *Buried Day* ii. 39 John McCormack, an adorable man, handsome as the top of the morning, racy and bawdy of tongue, a heroic figure with the simplicity of the heroic and a heart of gold.

adorableness (ə'dɔərəb(ə)lnɪs). [f. ADORABLE + -NESS.] The quality of being adorable; 'worthiness to be adored.' Bailey 1731, whence in J.

1806 DAWSON *Phil. Angl.* s.v., The adorableness of the divine nature is demonstrated in the works of creation and providence. **1876** GEO. ELIOT *Dan. Der.* III. xxii. 177 What suffused adorableness in a human frame where there is a mind that can flash out comprehension and hands that can execute finely!

adorably (ə'dɔərəblɪ), *adv.* [f. ADORABLE + -LY[2].] 'In a manner worthy of adoration.' J.

1806 DAWSON *Phil. Angl.* s.v., O adorably great and glorious majesty of heaven and earth!

adoral (,æ'dɔərəl), *a.* [f. L. *ad* to, at + *ōr-* mouth + -AL[1].] Situated at the mouth. Cf. ABORAL.

1882 SLADEN in *Jrnl. Linn. Soc.* XVI. 194 The first or most adoral transverse ambulacral combs of two neighbouring rays touch one another at their bases.

adorally (,æ'dɔərəlɪ), *adv.* [f. prec. + -LY[2].] In the direction of or towards the mouth.

1882 SLADEN in *Jrnl. Linn. Soc.* XVI. 196 The thickened extremity being directed adorally.

adorant (ə'dɔərənt), *a. poet.* [f. ADORE *v.* + -ANT[1].] = ADORING *ppl. a.*

1819 KEATS *Fall of Hyperion* (1905) I. 283 'Shade of Memory'—Cried I, with act adorant at her feet. **1893** *19th Cent.* Nov. 842, I.. make petition on adorant knee.

adorat. 'A chymical weight of four pounds.' Phillips 1678.

Also in Kersey, and Bailey.

adorate, obs. variant of ODORATE, scented.

adoration (,ædə'reɪʃən, ,ædɔə-). [a. Fr. *adoration*, ad. L. *adōrātiōn-em*, n. of action f. *adōrā-re*; see ADORE.]

1. The act of worshipping, or paying divine honours; worship, reverence.

1543 JOYE *Expos. Daniel* iii. (R.) Muche more execrable is it to serue or worship them [images] with any reuerent behauiour ether by adoracion, prostracion, knelyng, or kissing. **1667** MILTON *P.L.* III. 351 With solemn adoration down they cast Thir Crowns inwove with Amarant and Gold. **1774** BRYANT *Mythol.* II. 174 The Greeks in times of old.. paid their adoration to rude unwrought stones. **1855** MILMAN *Lat. Chr.* II. IV. vii. (1864) 344 The Church may draw fine and aërial distinctions between images as objects of reverence and as objects of adoration. **1860** TYNDALL *Glac.* I. §25, 187 That deep and calm beauty which suggests the thought of adoration to the human mind. **1866** LIDDON *Bampt. Lect.* vii. (1875) 362 Adoration is no mere prostration of the body, it is the prostration of the soul.

2. *fig.* The exhibition of profound regard and love.

1601 SHAKS. *Twel. N.* I. v. 274 *Ol.* How does he loue me? *Vio.* With adorations. **1859** GEO. ELIOT *Ad. Bede* 29 That adoration which a young man gives to a woman whom he feels to be greater and better than himself.

3. *techn.* A method of electing a pope.

1599 SANDYS *Eur. Spec.* (1632) 146 Two third parts of their voyces.. are requisite to him, that either by adoration or in Scrutinie shall winne that glorie. **1670** G. H. tr. *Hist. Cardinals* III. ii. 286 The third way of creating Popes, is by *Adoration*, which is perform'd in this manner; That Cardinal, who.. desires to favour any other Cardinal.. puts himself before him in the Chappel, and makes him a low Reverence; and when it falls out that two thirds of the Cardinals do the same, the Pope is then understood to be created. **1860** FROUDE *Hist. Eng.* V. 296 There was a moment when the feeling was so far in his [Pole's] favour that he might have been chosen on the spot by adoration.

†**4.** Kissing the hand as a sign of honour. *Obs.*

(Prob. never so used, but given in the following passage as the 'right sense' of the word *adore*, as if formed from Lat. *ad* to + *os, oris*, the mouth.)

1614 SELDEN *Titles* 41 Adoration, and Salutation with a kisse of the hand, is all one in the right sense of the word.

a'dorative, *a.* [f. *adōrāt-* ppl. stem of *adōrā-re* to ADORE + -IVE.] Of or pertaining to adoration. Also, adoring.

1637 S. RUTHERFORD *Lett.* 179 (1862) I. 429 Not a formal thanksgiving but an annunciation or predication of Christ's death—concional, not adorative. **1855** J. C. JEAFFRESON in *Fraser's Mag.* LI. 559/2 Such is the boy's state of mind, adorative and confident. **1861** *Temple Bar* III. 284, I always quitted the college amidst a commotion of adorative assurances. **1885** J. C. JEAFFRESON *Real Shelley* II. ix. 271 A tribute of adorative homage.

adoratory (ə'dɒrətərɪ). *rare.* [ad. med.L. *adōrātōrium*, f. *adōrātōr* a worshipper.] A place of worship: specially applied like the med.L. to those of pagans.

1800 M. KEATINGE tr. *Diaz, Conq. Mex.* 16 On the shore they found some adoratories or temples, built of lime and stone, and containing idols made of clay and wood.

adore (ə'dɔə(r)), *v.* Forms: 3–4 **aoure**, 5 **adoure**, 6– **adore.** [a. OFr. *aöre-r, aüre-r, aoure-r*:—L. *adōrā-re* to address, salute, reverence, in late L. to worship; f. *ad* to + *ōrā-re* to speak, entreat, beg, f. *ōr-* (nom. *ōs*) mouth. Refash. in 14th c. Fr. as *adourer, adorer*, whence Eng. *adore*. See AOURE.]

1. To worship as a deity, to pay divine honours to. (Now almost confined to poetry.)

c **1305** *St. Kath.* in *E.E.P.* 31 Here godes noþing nere: þat hi aourede hem to. **1340** *Ayenb.* 135 Yef þou wilt þanne lyerni god to bidde and to aouri ariȝt. **1483** CAXTON *Gold. Leg.* 268/1 He was adoured and worshyped of all the peple as a god. **1484** —— *Chyualry* 4 To preye and adoure god Almyghty. **1557** SURREY *Æneid* II. (R.) My father.. Spake to the gods, and tholy sterre adored. **1611** BIBLE *Bel* 4 The king worshipped it, and went daily to adore it. **1628** PRYNNE *Cens. of Cozens* 18 We may worship them in their Pictures —though wee may not Adore the Pictures themselues. **1732** POPE *Ess. on Man* III. 198 Be crown'd as Monarchs, or as Gods adored. **1738** C. WESLEY *Hymn*, Rejoice! the Lord is King! Your Lord and King adore! *c* **1860** J. S. B. MONSELL *Hymn* 'O worship the Lord,' Kneel and adore Him, the Lord is His name!

2. (In the usage of R.C. Ch.) To reverence with relative or representative honours.

1582 N. T. (Rhem.) *Heb.* xi. 22 By faith Iacob dying, blessed euery one of the sonnes of Ioseph; and adored the toppe of his rodde. **1762** SMOLLETT *Hist. Eng.* an. 1689 (R.) He was met by a procession of popish bishops and priests.. bearing the host, which he publickly adored. **1839** KEIGHTLEY *Hist. Eng.* II. 69 He forbade the practice of creeping to the cross and adoring it.

3. *absol.* and *intr.* To offer worship.

1582 N. T. (Rhem.) *Acts* x. 25 Cornelius came to meete him, and falling at his feete adored. **1664** H. MORE *Myst. Iniq.* 279 Pretending that a piece of bread is the very body of Christ.. and is adored towards accordingly. *a* **1826** HEBER *Hymn* 'Holy, Holy, Holy,' Gratefully adoring, our songs we raise to thee. **1843** E. JONES *Sensat. & Event* 12, I adore to it again.

4. *techn.* To kiss the hand, to a sovereign, etc. (So explained by Selden, but perh. never so used.) *Obs.* Also, To elect (a pope) by ADORATION.

1614 SELDEN *Titles* 40 Προσκυνῶ is truly interpreted in *Adosculor* (if the composition bee lawfull) or *Adoro*; both signifying to honor by kissing the hand. **1670** G. H. tr. *Hist. Cardinals* III. II. 272 The Cardinals meeting in the Gallery, to go together and adore him in his Chamber.

5. *fig.* To reverence or honour very highly; to regard with the utmost respect and affection. Now (also in trivial use), to like very much.

1594 SHAKS. *Rich. III*, I. ii. 177 Let the Soule forth that adoreth thee. **1599** MARSTON *Scourge of Vill.* III. ix. 218 My soule adores iudiciall schollership. **1718** POPE *Iliad* ix. 453 Slave as she was, my soul adored the dame. **1766** ANSTEY *Bath Guide* VIII. (1779) 61 The tender soft sex I shall ever adore. **1849** MACAULAY *Hist. Eng.* I. 575 The great mass of the population abhorred Popery and adored Monmouth. **1883** H. C. LUKENS *Jets & Flashes* 40 I'm a freshman at Yale, as was daddy before me; The girls of New Haven, egad, they adore me. **1922** JOYCE *Ulysses* 740 You will always think of the lovely teas we had together scrumptious currant scones and raspberry wafers I adore. **1938** W. B. YEATS *New Poems* 26 Sobriety is a jewel That I do much adore. **1950** D. CUSACK *Morning Sacrifice* I. in *Three*

Austral. Three-Act Plays 204 You know I simply adore cooking. **1954** O. SITWELL *Four Continents* xiv. 276 She.. spent her spare time in writing letters to her mother, whom plainly she adored, in chapel-going, and in hotel..politics. **1960** C. DAY LEWIS *Buried Day* ii. 44, I adored physical contact with my father in those days.

¶ By confusion of ME. *adore-n* and *adorn-e(n*, and contact of meanings in sense of *honour*, used for ADORN.

1596 SPENSER *F.Q.* IV. ii. 46 Like to the hore Congealed drops, who do the morn adore. *c* **1624** FLET. & MASS. *Elder Brother* IV. iii. (fol. 2, 118) Armlets for great queens to adore.

adored (ə'dɔːəd), *ppl. a.* [f. ADORE *v.* + -ED.] Worshipped, revered, highly reverenced, regarded with profound affection.

c **1325** *E.E. Allit. P.* A 368, I forloyne my dere endorde. **1653** CRASHAW *Sacr. Poems* 164 At Thy adorèd feet, thus, he lays down His gorgeous tire Of flame and fire. **1713** POPE *Winds. For.* 301 Old warriors whose ador'd remains In weeping vaults her hallow'd earth contains. **1762** HUME *Hist. Eng.* lxix. (1806) V. 198 To seek a second time, through all the horrors of civil war, for his adored republic. **1855** MACAULAY *Hist. Eng.* IV. 163 The husband of her adored friend.

† **a'dorement.** *Obs. rare.* [f. ADORE *v.* + -MENT after analogy of words in *-ment* a. from Fr., as *judgement*, *commandment*, etc.] The act of adoring; adoration. ('A word scarcely used.' J.)

1646 SIR T. BROWNE *Pseud. Ep.* I. iii. 11 The literall and downe-right adorement of Cats, Lizards, and Beetles. *Ibid.* I. xi. 46 That reasonable spirits would never firmely be lost in the adorement of things inanimate.

adorer (ə'dɔːrə(r)). [f. ADORE + -ER[1].]

1. One who adores; a worshipper; a votary.

1602 WARNER *Albion's Eng.* XIII. lxxvii. (1612) 318 Iupiter ..of whom euen his Adorers write euill Taches many an one. **1615** BEAUM. & FLET. *Cupid's Rev.* I. i. (T.) Adorers of that drowsy deity. **1667** MILTON *P.L.* IX. 143 And thinner left the throng Of his adorers. **1850** MERIVALE *Rom. Emp.* V. xlii. 12 Which had..driven his adorers from his shrine with blows and menaces.

2. *fig.* An ardent admirer, a lover.

1611 SHAKS. *Cymb.* I. iv. 74, I professe my selfe her Adorer, not her Friend. **1665** GLANVILLE *Scep. Sci.* 70 And who that adorer of Des-Cartes that professeth Scepticism? *a* **1704** T. BROWN *Wealth* Wks. 1730 I. 86 They were fain of accusers, to become the adorers of Scipio. **1853** MISS MITFORD in L'Estrange's *Life* III. xiv. 256 As to the adorers of Alfred Tennyson, they unluckily haunt one at all seasons.

adoring (ə'dɔərɪŋ), *vbl. sb.* [f. ADORE + -ING[1].] The giving of worship or reverence, or expressing ardent regard; adoration. (Now mostly gerundial.)

1633 P. FLETCHER *Purple Is.* VI. v. 66 Two shepherds most I love with just adoring. **1684** BURNET tr. *More's Utopia* 183 The contemplating God in his Works, and the adoring him for them. **1820** KEATS *S. Agnes* vi, Young virgins might have visions of delight, And soft adorings from their loves receive.

adoring (ə'dɔərɪŋ), *ppl. a.* [f. ADORE *v.* + -ING[2].] Worshipping, reverencing, showing ardent regard.

1652 CRASHAW *Sacr. Poems* 153 It comes, among The conduct of adoring spirits. **1827** KEBLE *Chr. Y.* Trin. Sund., Teach the adoring heart to fall. **1839** SIR R. GRANT *Bk. Praise* (G.T.) 71 Saviour when in dust to Thee Low we bend the adoring knee. **1866** GEO. ELIOT *F. Holt* I. viii. 205 Not one of those bland, adoring, and gently tearful women.

adoringly (ə'dɔərɪŋlɪ), *adv.* [f. ADORING *a.* + -LY[2].] In an adoring manner; with adoration, or ardent admiration.

1824-5 *Life of Dean Hook* I. 57 Your most devoted adoringly affectionate nephew. **1844** *Vest. Creat.* (ed. 3) 240 Such a degree of wisdom..as we only can attribute adoringly to the one Eternal and Unchangeable. **1859** MASSON *Milton* I. 438 They appear, dance round him adoringly.

adorn (ə'dɔːn), *v.* Forms: 4-5 **aourne**, 5 **aorne**, 5-6 **adourne**, 5-7 **adorne**, 6- **adorn**. [a. OFr. *aōrne-r*, *aūrne-r*, *aourne-r*, (later *adourne-r*, *adorne-r*):—L. *adornā-re* to fit out, to deck out; f. *ad* to + *ōrnā-re* to furnish, to deck. The *d* of pref. *ad-*, regularly dropped in OFr., began to be inserted again by the Fr. scribes in 14th c., and has regularly appeared in Eng. since the end of the 15th. See also the form ANORN.]

I. To be an ornament to.

1. To beautify as an ornament does; to be an ornament to; to add beauty or lustre to.

c **1374** CHAUCER *Troylus* III. Proem 2 O blisfull light, of which the bemes clere Adornith al the thryd hevyn faire. **1659** DRYDEN *On Death of Cromw.* vii, No borrow'd bays his temples did adorn. **1667** MILTON *P.L.* IX. 840 Of choicest Flours a Garland to adorne Her Tresses. **1775** BURKE *Sp. Conc. Amer.* Wks. III. 94 The venerable rust that rather adorns and preserves, than destroys the metal. **1851** RUSKIN *Stones of Ven.* (1874) I. Pref. 7 The circular temple of the Croydon Gas Company adorned the centre of the pastoral and sylvan scene.

2. *fig.* To add lustre to, as a quality does.

1398 TREVISA *Barth. De P.R.* XV. lxxiii. (1495) 515 Moost noble ryuers, Ganges Indus and Hispanes, that aourne the countre of ynde. **1666** DRYDEN *Ann. Mirab.* 176 Thousands were there Whose names some nobler poem shall adorn. **1742** W. COLLINS *Ecl.* I. 40 Each softer virtue that adorns the fair. **1848** L. HUNT *Jar of Honey* ix. 119 The following might have adorned the pages of Spenser. *Mod.* The piety which adorns his character.

3. Hence, Of a person: To add to the honour, splendour, or attractiveness of anything, by his presence.

1534 *Gold. Bk. M. Aurel.* (1546) E, The holie senate was adorned with olde prudente persons. **1712** STEELE *Spect.* No. 527 ¶2 The pitying Goddess easily comply'd, Follow'd in Triumph, and adorn'd her Guide. **1727** POPE *Dunc.* III. 134 And a new Cibber shall the stage adorn. **1795** SEWEL tr. *Hist. Quakers* I. II. 143 That every one, in your respective places, may adorn the truth. **1870** L'ESTRANGE *Life of Miss Mitford* I. iv. 108 Three such women as have seldom adorned one age and one country.

II. To furnish with ornaments.

4. To fit out or furnish with anything that beautifies; to deck, ornament, beautify, decorate, or embellish (*with*). Now chiefly *poetic.*

1430 LYDG. *Chron. Troy* II. xvi, I can my worke..Right as me lyst, adourne and make fayre. *a* **1450** *Knt. de la Tour* 39 To see you in suche pompe and pride to aorne suche a carion as is youre body. **1483** CAXTON *Gold. Leg.* 268/2 Our sauyour went to his passion on horsbacke aourned as a kynge. **1530** PALSGR. 417/2, I adorne, I beautyfy with fayre clothes or otherwyse. *Jadorne.* **1580** BARET *Alvearie*, To be adourned with garlandes and Roses on their heades. **1591** SHAKS. *1 Hen. VI*, V. iv. 134 Adorne his Temples with a Coronet. **1607** TOPSELL *Serpents* (1653) 805 The female.. maketh much of her young ones, licking and adorning their skins. **1611** BIBLE *Is.* lxi. 10 As a bride adorneth herselfe with her iewels. **1718** *Freethinker* No. 150 in *Philol. Anglic.*, He would take as much care to adorn his mind as his body. **1807** CRABBE *Par. Reg.* II. 318 A decent room Adorned with carpet, formed in Wilton's loom. **1853** *Arabian Nights* (Routl.) 584 Begin to adorn yourself in one of your most elegant dresses.

5. *fig.* To embellish with any property or quality.

1430 LYDG. *Chron. Troy* III. xxv, To magnifye And adourne it with his eloquence. **1530** PALSGR. 417 It is better to adorne the with vertues. **1586** T. B. tr. *La Primaudaye's Fr. Acad.* II. 195 The gifts and graces, wherewith God daily adorneth and enricheth his children. **1652** NEEDHAM tr. *Selden's Mare Cl.* 9 Most deservedly adorned with divers other honors in his own country. **1756** BURKE *Subl. & B.* Wks. I. 298 The many great vertues with which he has adorned his mind.

† **6.** To deck out speciously, dress up, 'get up,' prepare. *Obs.*

1589 NASHE *Anat. Absurd.* 6 Are they not ashamed..to adorne a pretence of profit mixt with pleasure. **1622** FOTHERBY *Atheom.* I. v. §3. 34 No man adorneth disputation against him.

¶ By confusion of *ador-en* and *adorn-(en*, helped by the sense of *honour*, in which both meet: To adore.

1470 HARDING *Chron.* lxvii, Mars, the God of Armes, they did adorne. **1480** CAXTON *Ovid's Metam.* x. v, She wolde leve this contre in [which she] was aorned and worshipped. **1581** NUCE tr. *Seneca's Octavia* 174 b, Augustus..Whom as a God in minsters we adorne. *a* **1600** *Soutar descryvit* in *Ever-Green* (1761) I. 118 Kneiland full lawly on thair Kneis, Thair Gods till adorn.

† **adorn**, *sb. Obs.* [f. the vb.] Adornment.

1592 WYRLEY *Armorie* 44 With brave Bundutia or Viragoes best..She may compare for valerous adorne. **1596** SPENSER *F.Q.* III. xii. 20 Without adorne of gold or silver.

† **adorn** (ə'dɔːn), *a. rare*[−1]. [f. It. *adorno*, short for *adornato* adorned:—L. *adōrnātus* pa. pple. of *adōrnā-re*: see ADORN *v.*] Adorned, ornate.

1667 MILTON *P.L.* VIII. 576 She will acknowledge thee her head, Made so adorn for thy delight the more.

† **adornate**, *v. Obs. rare*[−1]. [f. L. *adōrnāt-* ppl. stem of *adōrnā-re*: see ADORN. The Eng. repr. of L. *adōrnā-re*, as ADORN is of Fr. *adorner.*] To adorn.

1577 FRAMPTON in *Arber's App. Jas. I. Counterbl. Tob.* 81 To adornate Gardens with the fairnesse thereof.

† **ador'nation.** *Obs.* [n. of action f. L. *adōrnāt-* ppl. stem of *adōrnāre*: see ADORN. As if ad. L. **adōrnātiōn-em.*] The act of adorning; also that with which anything is adorned; adornment, decoration; ornament.

1597 J. KING *Fun. Serm.* in *Comm. on Jonah* (1864) 320 Making show to the world, under his glorious adornations, that he is of some better substance. **1616** T. ADAMS *Pract. Wks.* (1861) II. 439 Fair monuments of her beauty and adornation. **1631** MARKHAM *Way to Wealth* 3. II. ii. (1668) 87 They are so useful for adornation. **1676** BULLOKAR, *Adornation*, a decking or trimming. [So **1721** in BAILEY. **1775** ASH, 'Not much used.']

adorned (ə'dɔːnd), *ppl. a.*; also 5 **aourned**, 5-6 **adourned.** [f. ADORN *v.* + -ED.]

1. Furnished or decked, with things that add beauty or worth; beautified, decorated, ornamented.

1481 CAXTON *Myrrour* Prol. 1 Sette by declaracion in fair and Aourned volumes. **1490** —— *Eneydos* ii. 15, A coffre well rychely adourned wyth many precyous stones. **1548** HALL *Chron.* (1809) 52 The Monarchial prince, or adourned Kyng. **1593** SHAKS. *Rich. II*, V. i. 79 She came adorned hither like sweet May. **1667** MILTON *P.L.* x. 151 Adorned She was indeed, and lovely. **1730** THOMSON *Autumn* 206 Loveliness, Needs not the foreign aid of ornament, But is, when unadorned, adorned the most.

2. *fig.* Furnished with properties or qualities that confer distinction or give delight.

1475 CAXTON *Jason* 5 b, The herte adourned with vertue rendrith the man noble. **1667** MILTON *P.L.* II. 446 Adorn'd With splendor, arm'd with power. **1727** SWIFT *Gulliver* III. iv. 200 Adorned with integrity and honour. **1794** SULLIVAN *View of Nat.* II. 261 Adorned with eloquence, piety, and persuasion.

adorner (ə'dɔːnə(r)). [f. ADORN *v.* + -ER[1].] He who, or that which, adorns.

1818 BYRON *Ch. Harold* IV. cxxx, O Time! the beautifier of the dead, Adorner of the ruin. **1862** LYTTON *Strange Story* I. 32 Poet or painter might have seen an image equally true to either of these adorners of the earth.

adorning (ə'dɔːnɪŋ), *vbl. sb.* [f. ADORN *v.* + -ING[1].] Adornment, ornamentation, decoration.

1398 TREVISA *Barth. De P.R.* X. iii. (1495) 374 The elementes ben not bare of arayeng and aournynge. **1580** BARET *Alvearie*, The fayre greene adourning of the bankes with grasse. **1611** BIBLE *1 Pet.* iii. 3 Whose adorning, let it not bee that outward adorning, of plaiting the haire. **1635** R. N. tr. *Camden's Eliz.* I. 33 For the more plentifull adorning of their wits. **1669** H. MORE *Seven. Ch.* vi. (T.) Her prankings and adornings in the splendour of their altars.

adorning (ə'dɔːnɪŋ), *ppl. a.* [f. ADORN *v.* + -ING[2].] Adding or giving beauty or splendour; embellishing; ornamental, decorative.

1659 *Gentleman's Calling* (1696) 30 The most adorning Accomplishments of a Gentleman. **1775** ASH, *Adorning*, ornamenting, embellishing, decking-up. *Mod.* Traces of his adorning pencil.

adorningly (ə'dɔːnɪŋlɪ), *adv.* [f. prec. + -LY[2].] In an adorning manner; so as to adorn; decoratively. (In mod. Dicts.)

adornment (ə'dɔːnmənt). Forms: 5 **aournement**, **aornement**, 5-6 **adournement**, 6 **adornament**, 6-7 **adornement**, 6- **adornment.** [a. OFr. *aournement*, later *adournement*, *adornement*; f. *aourner*, *adourner*, to ADORN + -MENT, as if:—L. **adōrnāmentum*, to which the Eng. spelling was occasionally assimilated.]

1. The action of adorning, or embellishing; embellishment, ornamentation.

1480 CAXTON *Ovid's Metam.* x. vi, He..made to her many fayre aornamentis. **1614** RALEIGH *Hist. World* (J.) The heavens, before they had motion and adornment. **1641** MILTON *Ch. Govt.* II. (1851) 145 All the industry and art I could unite to the adornment of my native tongue. **1877** MRS. BRASSEY *Voy. in Sunbeam* x. (1878) 163 The finest description used for personal adornment.

2. A thing employed to adorn; an ornament, a decoration. With *pl.*

1489 CAXTON *Faytes of Armes* I. v. 11 The ladies them self brought theyr jewellis and ryche adournemens. **1543** BLOMEYR in *Richm. Wills & Invent.* (1853) 47 Decent kepyng and wesshyng of the adornaments belongyng to the altars. **1814** BYRON *Corsair* III. viii. 40 My steps will gently tread With these adornments. **1850** BLACKIE *Æschylus* I. 28 Thou hast won thee rich adornments. **1859** MRS. SCHIMMELPENNINCK *Beauty* I. ix. §29 The colouring, adornments, and furnishing of a room.

adorty, adorthy, ? obs. form of AORTA, with *a-* changed to *ad-* after A- *pref.* 7.

1541 COPLAND *Guydon's Quest. Cyrurg.* What veynes passe betwene the kydnees ouer the spondyles? *A.* There passe the veyne adorty. *Ibid.* The veynes called kyllis, and adorthy.

adosculation (æ,dɒskjuː'leɪʃən). [n. of action, f. *adōsculāt-* ppl. stem of *adōsculā-ri* to give a kiss to; f. *ad* to + *ōsculā-ri* to kiss; f. *ōscul-um* a little mouth, dim. of *ōs* mouth.]

1. Impregnation of animals or plants by mere external contact, without intromission.

1674 GREW *Anat. Plants* IV. v. §9 (1682) 173 By many Birds, where there is no Intromission, but only an Adosculation of Parts. **1753** CHAMBERS *Cycl. Supp.* s.v., Divers kinds of birds and fishes are also impregnated by adosculation.

2. The insertion of one part of a plant into another.

1731 BAILEY, vol. II, *Adosculation* (in Botany) a joining or insertion of one part of a plant into some cavity, as it were mouth to mouth. [WEBSTER cites CRABB.]

‖ **adossée** (adose, ə'dɒsɪ), *ppl. a. Her.* [Fr. pa. pple. of *adosser* to turn the back to; f. *à* to + *dos* back.] Turned back to back. (See the Eng f. ADDORSED.)

1753 CHAMBERS *Cycl. Supp.*, *Adossée* is used, in heraldry, to denote two figures or bearings, placed back to back.

† **a'dote**, *v. Obs. rare*[−1]. [f. A- *pref.* 1 + DOTE.] To become silly.

c **1350** *Will. Palerne* 2054 He wax neiȝh out of wit · for wraþ þat time & for dol a-doteþ.

† **a'doted**, *ppl. a. Obs.* [f. prec. + -ED.] Grown silly, become foolish; infatuated.

c **1230** *Ancren Riwle* 222 Ase dusie men & adotede. *Ibid.* 272 So he bringeð ofte aȝean into þe adotede soule..þeo ilke sunnen. **1393** GOWER *Conf.* III. 4 It falleth, that the most wise Ben other while of love adoted.

adoub(e, variant of ADUB *v. Obs.* to equip.

† **a'doubt**, *v. Obs. rare*[−1]. [phonetic var. of REDOU(B)T, a. Fr. *redoute-r.*] To fear, dread.

c **1400** *Destr. Troy* IV. 1097 Ye noblist of nome þat neuer man adouted.

†**adoubted**, *ppl. a. Obs.* [f. prec. + -ED.]
1. Redoubted, dreaded; formidable.
c **1314** *Guy Warw.* 111 The more adouted thou schalt be. **1340** *Alex. & Dind.* 970 To his adoutede duk · dindimus sente.
2. Frightened, afraid.
1471 SIR J. PASTON in *Lett.* 668 III. 5 Be ye not adoghtyd off the worlde, ffor I trust all schall be well.

adoutry, obs. form of ADULTERY.

adown (əˈdaʊn), *adv.* and *prep. arch.* Forms: 1 of dúne, 1–2 adún(e, 2 odune, 3 adun, 3–5 adoun(e, 4–6 adowne, 4– adown. [OE. *of dúne* off the mount, *de monte* (see DOWN *sb.*), cf. OFr. *à val*:—L. *ad vallem* to the valley, used in the same sense. As early as 2, the reduced form *a-dūn* was aphetized to *dūn, doun,* DOWN, which soon became the ordinary prose form. But *adown* never became obs., and still survives as a poetic variant of *down.*]
A. *adv.*
1. To a lower place or situation; downward, down. With vbs. of motion, and pleonastically with vbs. signifying descent; as *fall, sink, alight, sit, kneel.*
c **975** *Rushw. Gosp.* Luke iv. 9 ȝif sunu godes arð, asend ðeh hiona of-dune [*Lindisf.* aduna, *W. Sax.* nyþer]. *a* **1000** CYNEWULF *Judith* 291 Hi ðá hreowiȝ móde Wurþon hira wæpen of dúne. *c* **1000** ÆLFRIC *Man. Astron.* 16 Se ne gæð næfre adune under þyssere eorðan. *a* **1090** *O.E. Chron.* (Laud MS.) an. 1083 And þa oðre ða dura bræcon þær adune and eodon inn. *c* **1175** *Lamb. Hom.* 61 Þe engles adun follon in to þe þosternesse hellen. **1280** *Havelok* 567 And caste þe knaue adoun so harde. *c* **1380** *Sir Ferumb.* 717 Eyþer enpeynede him with al ys miȝt: to dyngen oþer adoun. *c* **1400** *Sege off Melayne* 1480 He tuke his spere owt of reste adownn. **1480** CAXTON *Chron. Eng.* clxxviii. 159 The brayne fel adoun vpon the ground. **1596** SPENSER *F.Q.* I. vii. 24 Thrise did she sinke adowne in deadly swownd. **1717** PARNELL *Poet. Wks.* (1833) 17 And drops his limbs adown. **1808** SCOTT *Marmion* v. viii, His gorgeous collar hung adown. **1870** MORRIS *Earthly Par.* I. I. 418 Till the wretch falls adown with whirling brain.
†2. In a lower place; *esp.* on earth, here below. *Obs.*
c **1000** ÆLFRIC *Man. Astron.* 16 On wintierliere tide hi beoð on niht uppe, & on dæȝe adune. *c* **1386** CHAUCER *Maunc. T.* 1 Whan Phebus duelt her in this erthe adoun. **1501** DOUGLAS *Pal. Hon.* Prol. I. viii, O May thou Mirrour of Soles.. Till eurie thing adown respirature [= refreshing].
†3. *fig.* To a lower condition or state. Hence, to *bring adown*: to bring to an end. *Obs.*
c **1175** *Lamb. Hom.* 205 Ðet blisfule bern.. ðet þuruh his holi passiun werp þene deouel adun. **1205** LAYAMON 19686 A þat Sæxisce men · setten us a-dune [**1250** a-doune]. *c* **1230** *Ancren Riwle* 266 Buh adun þine heorte. **1384** CHAUCER *Leg. G. Wom.* 250 Ester ley thou thyn meknesse al a-doun. **1393** LANGL. *P. Pl.* C. XI. 94 And with þe pyk putte adoune.. Lordes þat lyuen as hem lust. *c* **1430** *Syr Generides* 5418 To bring al this werre a doune. **1587** *Myrroure for Mag., Morgan* vii. 1, If once I might put her adowne.
†4. *fig.* In a lower condition or state. *Obs.*
1297 R. GLOUC. 376 Monye heye men of þe lond in prison he huld strong.. And ȝyf þat eny hym wraþþede, adoun he was anon.
B. *prep.* (with a defining obj.)
1. In a descending direction upon or along.
c **1374** CHAUCER *Troyl.* II. 764 Adoune the staire anon right tho she went. **1596** SPENSER *F.Q.* I. vii. 31 [His] scaly taile was stretcht adowne his back full lowe. **1710** PHILIPS *Pastorals* I. 34 To chase the lingring Sun adown the Sky. **1725** POPE *Odyss.* XVII. 365 Adown his cheek a tear unbidden stole. **1812** BYRON *Ch. Harold* I. lxxxix, Fresh legions pour adown the Pyrenees. **1868** HAWTHORNE *Amer. Note-Bks.* (1879) I. 50 There is also a beautiful view from the mansion, adown the Kennebec.
2. *fig.* Of time.
1839 LOWELL *Threnodia* Wks. 1879, 2 He did but float a little way Adown the stream of time. **1877** M. ARNOLD *New Sirens* in *Poems* I. 40 Adown life's latter days.

†**adownright**, *adv. Obs.* 2–3 adun-riht(es. [f. OE. *adún* down + *riht* straight.] Straight down, DOWNRIGHT.
c **1175** *Pater Noster* 90 in *Lamb. Hom.* 59 Alle dor and fuȝel ifliht: lete he makede adunriht. Þene Mon.. his neb upward he wrohte. *c* **1230** *Ancren Riwle* 60 Sweordes dunt is adunriht. **1250** LAYAMON 29894 And adun rihtes slowen: al þat hii neh comen.

†**a'downward**, *adv.* and *prep. Obs.* For forms see ADOWN. [f. ADOWN + -WARD.]
A. *adv.* = DOWNWARD.
a **1090** *O.E. Chron.* (Laud MS.) an. 1083 Þa Frencisce men.. scotedon á-dunweard mid arewan toweard þam haliȝ dome. **1205** LAYAMON 9298 Hamun arnde upward: & oðer while adunward. *c* **1230** *Ancren Riwle* 140 Þet heui ulessis, Þet draweð hire aduneward. *c* **1374** CHAUCER *Boethius* 7 Þus þis compagnie of muses I-blamed casten wroþely þe chere adounward to þe erþe.
B. *prep.* = ADOWN *prep.*
1205 LAYAMON 1920 Corineus.. hine fusde mid mæine, aduneward þa clude.

†'**adox(e.** *Obs. rare*⁻¹. [f. Gr. ἄδοξ-ος (occasionally = παράδοξ-ος, opposed to common sense), f. ἀ priv. + δόξα opinion.] An absurdity.
1624 HAYWARD *Suprem.* 5 Who esteemed that which I had said, not for a Paradoxe, but for an Adoxe, or flat absurditie.

†**a'doxal**, *a. Obs. rare*⁻¹. [f. Gr. ἄδοξ-ος (f. ἀ priv. + δόξα opinion) + -AL¹.] Not according to right reason; absurd.
1652 GAULE *Magastrom.* 107 But the contrary, in most, or all; not orthodoxall, but paradoxall, heterodoxall, adoxall.

†**a'doxy.** *Obs.*⁻⁰ [ad. Gr. ἀδοξία ill-repute, f. ἄδοξος, f. ἀ without + δόξα reputation.] 'Ignominy, shame; slander, infamy.' Blount 1656.

†**a'doyle**, *adv. Obs. rare*⁻¹. [A *prep.*¹ on + DOYLE squint, given by Halliwell as a Gloucestershire word.] Askew, awry.
c **1450** J. RUSSELL *Bk. Nurture* in *Babees Bk.* 139 Wrye not youre nek a doyle as hit were a dawe.

adoze (əˈdəʊz), *adv.*, prop. *phrase.* [A *prep.*¹ on, in + DOZE.] In a doze, or dozing state.
1849 *Blackw. Mag.* LXVI. 23 Lying on banks a-dose or poetising. **1868** BUCHANAN *Wallace* I. ii, I hoped to find them, Drugged with the Gallic potion, all adoze.

adp-, obs. form of APP-.

‖**ad personam** (æd pəˈsəʊnæm), *phr.* [L., to a particular individual.] **a.** Of an appointment: (assigned) personally; (allocated) on an individual basis. **b.** Of an argument, etc.: directed at a person (rather than his or her position).
1964 P. F. ANSON *Bishops at Large* vii. 243 He was allowed to retain the see of Selsey.. with the rank of Archbishop *ad personam*. **1966** *Rep. Comm. Inquiry Univ. Oxf.* II. 372 The stipends of a number of tutorial fellows are fixed *ad personam*; for example, fellows with major college offices of a permanent or semi-permanent nature.. often receive a lower college stipend. **1983** *Summary World Broadcasts: Eastern Europe* (B.B.C.) 11 July A1/3 What is also striking in revisionist reactions is the launching of clearly ad personam attacks.

adpress (ædˈprɛs), *v.* [f. L. *adpress-* ppl. stem of *adprim-ĕre*, f. *ad-* to + *prem-ĕre* to press.] *trans.* To press closely to a surface, to lay flat.
1872 DARWIN *Emotions* iv. 100 Birds when frightened, as a general rule, closely adpress all their feathers.

adpressed (ædˈprɛst), *ppl. a.* [f. prec. + -ED.] Pressed close to, lying flat against, as the hairs on the stems of some plants, etc.
1828 KIRBY & SPENCE *Entom.* II. xix. 124 The dorsal segments are covered with shining adpressed hairs. **1876** HARLEY *Mat. Med.* 412 Twigs, densely covered with minute, imbricated, adpressed leaves.

‖**adpromissor** (ˌædprəʊˈmɪsə(r), -ɔː(r)). *Rom. Law.* [a. L. *adprōmissōr* one who is security, f. *ad-* in addition + *promitt-ĕre* to PROMISE.] One who gives bail or security.
1875 POSTE *Gaius* III. 402 The adpromissor at different epochs of the law appears as sponsor, fidepromissor, fidejussor.

†**ad'pugn(e**, *v. Obs.*⁻⁰ [ad. L. *adpugnā-re* to fight against, attack, f. *ad* to, at + *pugnā-re* to fight.] 'To fight against.' Cockeram 1626.

adq-, obs. form of ACQ-.

adrad (əˈdræd), *ppl. a.*¹ *Obs.* or *arch.* Forms: 3 adræd, 3–6 adred, adrad(de, 5 adrade, adrede, 5–6 adredde, 6 adread; revived in 9 as adrad, (adread). [Probably weakened form of *of-drad*, pa. pple. of OF-DREDE to frighten, terrify. *Of-drad* and *a-drad* are used synonymously from 1200 to 1300, about which date the former disappears.] Frightened, greatly afraid, put in dread. Const. *gen.* or *of*; *dat. inf.*; *subord. cl.*; W. Morris has *at*.
c **1200** *Trin. Coll. Hom.* 31 Þe engel quað to hem ne be ȝe naht ofdredde. **1205** LAYAMON 7575 His men weoren of-dredde [**1250** a-dradde]. *Ibid.* 10952 Adræd he wes swiðe [**1250** adred]. **1377** LANGL. *P. Pl.* B. XIX. 21 For alle derke deuelles · aren adradde to heren it. *c* **1384** CHAUCER *Hous of F.* 928 Loke thou ne be Adrad of hem. *a* **1420** OCCLEVE *De Reg. Princ.* 1275, I am adredde God is not in this place. *c* **1440** *Generydes* 3867 He was full sore adrede of his comyng. *c* **1440** *Morte Arthur* (1819) 47 The quene of dethe was sore A drade. **1549** CHALONER tr. *Erasm. Moriæ Enc.* Rivb, He nothyng helde hymself adradde of drunken Marke Anthony. **1580** SIDNEY *Arcadia* (1622) 126 Thinking to make all men adread. **1600** TOURNEUR *Metamorph.* liv. 377 (1878) 208 The beast gan looke as one that were adrad. **1855** SINGLETON *Virgil* I. 390 Her sister heard it breathless, and adread. **1870** MORRIS *Earthly Par.* III. IV. 147 Thereat adrad He turned him round. *Ibid.* I. I. 19, I was the less adrad Of what might come.

†**a'drad**, *ppl. a.*², dreaded. See ADREAD *v.*¹

adradial (æˈdreɪdɪəl), *a.* and *sb. Zool.* [mod. f. L. *ad* to, at + *radius* ray + -AL¹.]
A. *adj.* Situated near or beside a ray.
1880 E. R. LANKESTER in *Nature* XXI. 414 An organ may be.. per-radial, inter-radial, or adradial in position.
B. *sb.* An adradial organ.
1888 ROLLESTON & JACKSON *Anim. Life* 717 The adradials open one into each of the eight meridional or ctenophoral vessels. **1892** J. A. THOMSON *Outl. Zool.* x. 134 Tentacles —first four corresponding to the angles of the mouth (perradials), and then other four (interradials) between these, and then eight intervening adradials.

†**adragant.** *Obs.* [a. Fr. *adragant(e* a popular corruption of *tragacanthe*] = TRAGACANTH.
1725 BRADLEY *Fam. Dict.* I. s.v. *Appetite*, Gum Adragant half an Ounce. **1775** BRUCE in *Phil. Trans.* LXV. 416 It resembles gum adragant much in quality.

†**a'draw**, *v. Obs.* Forms as in DRAW *v.* [f. A- *pref.* 1 out, away + DRAW.]
1. *trans.* To draw out; *esp.* to draw (a sword).
1205 LAYAMON 16487 Aldolf his gode sweord adroh. **1297** R. GLOUC. 361 Adraweth ȝoure suerdes. **1330** R. BRUNNE *Chron.* 400 Robert.. hys gode suerd adrou. **1340** *Ayenb.* 218 Come naȝt beuore God mid zuorde adraȝe and mid blodi honden. **1380** *Sir Ferumb.* 2281 Hure swerdes þan þay adrowe.
2. *intr.* To withdraw oneself.
c **1430** *Octouian Imp.* (W.) 357 Awey fro hem he wold adrawe. *c* **1450** *Siege of Rouen* in *Archæol.* XXI. 67 The trewys adrew and warre toke hys way.

†**a'dray.** *Obs.* [f. prec. See DRAY.] Withdrawal.
1303 R. BRUNNE *Handl. Synne* 4671 Haldyst þou forwarde, certys nay, Whan þou makyst swyche a-dray.

adraynt, pa. pple. of ADRENCH *v. Obs.* to drown.

adread (əˈdrɛd), *ppl. a.*, var. ADRAD *ppl. a.*¹ *arch.*
1580, 1855 [see ADRAD *ppl. a.*¹]. **1887** T. MARTIN tr. *Schiller's Ring of Polycrates* in *Blackw. Mag.* Nov. 684 Back drew the monarch, all a-dread.

†**a'dread**, *v.*¹ *Obs.* Forms: *Inf.* 1 andræd-an, ondræd-an; 2–4 adred-en, adrede. *Pa. t.* 1 ondreórd, ondréd, ondredde; 2 adred(e, 3 adredde, 4 adrad(de. *Pa. pple.* 1 ondræden; 3–6 adrad. [f. A- *pref.* 4 = *and-* against, towards + *drædan* to dread. Cf. OSax. *and-, ant-, an-drâdan*, OHG. *intrâten*. In OE. *and-* before initial *d* became *an-*, which, following the analogy of the prefix *an-*, became OE. *on-*, and ME. *a-*. See AND- and AN-.]
1. *trans.* To dread, to fear greatly.
a **900** *Beow.* 3353 þæt þu him on drædan ne þearft. *c* **950** *Lindisf. Gosp.* Matt. xiv. 5 He ondreard þæt folc. *c* **975** *Rushw. Gosp.*, *ibid.* Anddreord him þæt folc. *c* **1000** *Ags. Gosp.*, *ibid.* He adred him þæt folc. *c* **1160** *Hatton Gosp.*, *ibid.* He adrede him þæt folc. *c* **1175** *Lamb. Hom.* 69 Þet we þene fend noht ne adreden. *c* **1399** *Pol. Poems & Songs* (1859) II. 6 The pes is sauf, the werre is ever adrad.
2. *intr.*
a **1075** *O.E. Chron.* (Laud MS.) an. 1013 Hi ondreddon þat he hi fordon wolde. **1205** LAYAMON 8744 Nu þu scalt adreden [*l.t.* adrede] for þine ær dæden. *c* **1380** *Sir Ferumb.* 3146 Noþyng þay ne adradde.
3. With *refl. pron.* (Orig. *dat.*, with or without *acc.* of the thing.) To fear for oneself; to be afraid.
a **1000** CYNEWULF *Elene* 81 (Grein), Ne ondraed þu þé. *a* **1000** *Ags. Gosp.* Luke ii. 9 Hi him mycelum eȝe adrédon.. Nelle ȝe eow adrǽdan [*MS. A.* on-]. *c* **1160** *Hatton Gosp.*, *ibid.* Hyo heom mycel eiȝe adredden.. Nelle ȝe eow ondræden. *c* **1200** *Moral Ode* 124 in *Trin. Coll. Hom.* 223 He maiȝ him sore adrade. *c* **1300** *Rel. Songs* iv. Hwenne ich thenche of domes-dai ful sore ime adrede. *c* **1320** *Sir Tristr.* 288 Ganhardin seighe that sight, And sore him gan adrede.

†**adread**, *v.*² *Obs.*; also 5 adrede. *Pa. t.* 6 adrad. [:—earlier OF-DREAD, OE. *of-drædan.*] To make afraid, terrify. Cf. ADRAD *ppl. a.*
c **1314** *Guy Warw.* 47 No was ther non in that ferrede That of his liif him might adrede. **1603** HARSNET *Pop. Impost.* 135 With these they adrad, and gasten, sencelesse old women.

†**a'dread, adreid**, *adv.* prop. *phrase*; *Sc. Obs.* [A *prep.*¹ on, in + DREAD *sb.*] For fear, lest.
1501 DOUGLAS *Pal. Honour* III. lxv. (1787) 76 Zit studie nocht ouir mekill, adreid thow warie.

a-dream (əˈdriːm), *adv.* prop. *phr.* [A *prep.*¹ + DREAM *sb.*] In a dream, dreaming. Also *pred. a. poet.*
1830 *Blackw. Mag.* Feb. 276/2 That sets the imagination dimly a-dream of mermaids. **1854** S. DOBELL *Balder* xxiv. 141, I lie a-dream. **1909** W. J. LOCKE *Septimus* ii. 23 He stared into vacancy, his pale blue eyes adream. **1923** D. H. LAWRENCE *Birds, Beasts & Flowers* 115 And slowly, very slowly, as if thrice adream, Proceeded to draw his slow length curving round. **1933** W. DE LA MARE *Fleeting* 68 Adam and Eve lay adream.

†**a'dreamed, a'dreamt**, *pa. pple. Obs.* [f. DREAM *sb.* or *v.*; exact formation uncertain. The form is that of a pa. pple. of a vb. *adream, or *dream.* No instances of the vb. *a-dream* have been found; and the prefix is prob. A *particle*, southern form of the ppl. prefix *y-*, as in *a-been.* See DREAM *v.*] In phr. *to be adreamed*: to be visited by a dream, to dream.
1556 WITHALS *Dict.* (*ed.* 1634 in Nares) Hee is adreamd of a dry summer. **1605** *Play of Stucley* 359 in *Sch. Shaks.* (1878) I. 172, I was adreamt to night that he paid me all. **1684** BUNYAN *Pilgr.* II. 76, I was a Dreamed that I sat all alone. **1736** FIELDING *Pasquin* IV. i, I was a-dream'd I overheard a ghost.

adrectal (æˈdrɛktəl), *a. Zool.* [f. AD- + RECTAL *a.*] Situated at or near the rectum; *spec.* of or pertaining to the purpuriparous glands of certain molluscs.

1883 *Encycl. Brit.* XVI. 648/2 The presence of glandular plication of the surface of the mantle-flap..and an adrectal gland (purple-gland).

†**adree**, *v. Obs.* Forms: *Inf.* 1 **adreóȝan**, 3 **adriȝe, adrie.** *Pa. t.* 1 **adreaȝ, adreah.** *Pa. pple.* 1 **adroȝen.** [f. A- *pref.* 1 intensive + *dreóȝan* to perform, endure, DREE, cogn. w. Goth. *driugan* to perform military service.]

1. To carry on, practise, pass (life, time, etc.). Only in OE.

c **1000** ÆLFRIC *on O.T.* (Sweet 57) Men ðe heora lif adruȝon on ealre idelnisse.

2. To bear, endure, or suffer.

a **1000** *Andreas* 1488 Earfeðo þe he adréah. *a* **1300** *K. Horn* 1067 (Lumby 1035) Ne miȝte heo a-driȝe, þat heo ne weop wiþ iȝe. ? *a* **1400** in Halliwell *Dict.* s.v. *Adrye*, Ther is not soche a knyȝt..þat his strok miȝt adrie.

†**adref-e**, *v. Obs.* Forms: *Inf.* 1 **adræf-an**, 2 **adref-en.** *Pa. t.* 1 **adræf-de**, 2 **adrefde.** *Pa. pple.* 1 **adræfed**, 1–2 **adrefed.** [f. A- *pref.* 1 intensive + *dræf-an* to drive, chase.] To drive forth, or away.

c **1150** *Cott. Hom.* 223 God..adrefde hi út of paradis. *c* **1175** *Lamb. Hom.* 219 Se almihti sceappende..hi alle adrefde of heofan rices mirhðe.

‖**ad referendum** (æd rɛfəˈrɛndəm). [mod.L., = 'for reference'.] In diplomatic use, a phr. describing the acceptance of proposals by representatives subject to the assent of their principals.

1781 J. ADAMS in *Wks.* (1852) VII. 488 They will take the proposition *ad referendum* immediately. **1787** *Gentl. Mag.* 1015/2 Congress have taken this generous offer of his *ad referendum.* **1815** WELLINGTON *Dispatches* (1838) XII. 287 The agreement was read to the whole, and taken *ad referendum* by the Russian and Prussian Ministers. **1906** HARDY *Dynasts* II. v. i. 258 Prince Eugène will..make the formal offer in his name... Which I can but receive *ad referendum.*

adregh, -eich, -eigh, variants of ADRIGH *adv.*

adreint, pa. t. of ADRENCH *v. Obs.* to drown.

†**adrelwurt.** *Herb. Obs.* [Cf. OE. *adreminte*, supposed to be the same plant.] Feverfew.

HALLIWELL cites early list of plants in *MS. Harl.* 978.

‖**ad rem** (æd rɛm). [L.] (Pertaining or pertinent) to the matter or subject in hand; to the purpose.

1608 MIDDLETON *Fam. Love* v. H4, *Ad rem, ad rem*, master Poppin: leaue your allegories,..and to the point. **1621** BURTON *Anat. Mel.* To Rdr. 40 To speake *ad rem*, who is free from passion? **1680** J. HOWE *Let. to Person of Qual.* 23 What I can find in his Sermon hath any aspect or design that way is either *ad rem*, or *ad hominem.* **1865** RUSKIN in *Daily Tel.* 7 Sept. (Cent. Dict.), Your statements of practical difficulty are..more *ad rem* than my mere assertions of principle. **1905** *Spectator* 4 Feb. 180/2 It is more *ad rem* to consider whether a satisfactory answer to Newman's question is to be found in the second book on our list. **1940** *Mind* XLIX. 174 It can hardly be regarded as *ad rem* in our present discussion that is directed to *human* knowledge.

adrenal (æˈdriːnəl), *a.* and *sb.* [f. AD- 1 + L. *rēnes* kidneys: cf. RENAL *a.* and *sb.*]

A. *adj.* = SUPRARENAL *a.*; ***adrenal cortical hormone***, adrenocorticotrophic hormone.

1875 HUXLEY & MARTIN *Elem. Biol.* xiii. 173 The Adrenal glands are yellow bodies imbedded in the ventral face of the kidney. **1921** L. BERMAN *Glands regulating Personality* vii. 150 Christina may be adrenal cortex centred and so masculinoid. **1927** *Lancet* 8 Oct. 745/2 (*title*) Virilism due to an Adrenal Cortical Hypernephroma. **1934** *Ann. Reg. 1933* 60 Harris devised a chemical test for vitamin C, which is probably ascorbic acid and a specific constituent of the adrenal cortex. **1946** *Lancet* 10 Aug. 203/1 As the nitrogen output rises..so the urinary content of adrenal cortical hormone reaches relatively enormous levels. **1950** *Sci. News* XV. 132 The adrenal gland..is readily distinguishable into two parts, the rind or cortex, and the core or medulla.

B. *sb. pl.* Suprarenals.

1882 *Trans. Path. Soc.* XXXIII. 341 Adrenals. **1883** *Encycl. Brit.* XV. 365/1 The 'suprarenal bodies' or 'adrenals'. **1927** HALDANE & HUXLEY *Anim. Biol.* i. 18 The adrenals, the parathyroids, the pancreas, the reproductive organs, and probably other organs also produce internal secretions.

adrenalectomy (æˌdriːnəlˈɛktəmɪ). *Surg.* [f. prec. + Gr. ἐκτομή cutting out.] Excision of the adrenal glands. So **aˌdre-naˈlectomized** *ppl. a.*

1910 *Lippincott's New Med. Dict.* 22/2 *Adrenalectomy*, excision of suprarenal body. **1918** *Amer. Jrnl. Physiol.* 1 May 103 The following protocols are samples of our negative experiments on adrenalectomized rabbits. **1936** *Nature* 18 July 124/2 A high potassium intake is detrimental to the life of adrenalectomized animals. **1946** *Lancet* 3 Aug. 179/2 Adrenalectomy has not proved a satisfactory method of treating patients in whom prostatic cancer shows recrudescence after relief through castration.

adrenaline (æˈdrɛnəlɪn, æˈdriːn-). Also **-in.** [f. ADRENAL + -INE⁵.] A hormone secreted by the adrenal glands and affecting circulation, muscular action, etc.; also (**A-**), this substance extracted from the adrenal glands of animals or prepared synthetically and used for medicinal purposes (U.S. trade name); cf. EPINEPHRINE.

See quot. 1901 for the discovery of the substance and the invention of the name, which have, however, been claimed also for Dr. Norton L. Wilson.

1901 *Amer. Jrnl. Physiol.* V. 457 The most important contribution to our knowledge of the active principle of the suprarenal gland..is from Dr. Jokichi Takamine who has isolated the blood-pressure-raising principle of the gland in a stable and pure crystalline form... To this body..he has given the name 'Adrenalin'. **1902** *Jrnl. Chem. Soc.* LXXXII. I. 68 It is claimed that suprarenin is identical with Takamine's adrenalin. **1907** OSLER & MCCRAE *Syst. Med.* I. 758 Experimentally..adrenalin..has a powerful influence on carbohydrate metabolism. **1920** *Discovery* Mar. 88/2 Adrenaline prescribed for Addison's disease. **1922** J. C. SQUIRE in *Public Opinion* 3 Mar. 202/1 The toad secretes too much adrenalin. **1962** *Lancet* 29 Dec. 1337/1 When adrenaline is infused intravenously the vein used stands out as a white cord.

adrenalism (æˈdriːnəlɪz(ə)m). [f. ADRENAL + -ISM.] The state arising from incorrect functioning of the adrenal glands; suprarenalism.

1922 G. B. SHAW in S. & B. Webb *Eng. Prisons under Local Govt.* p. lxiii, The stigmata of adrenalism.

†**aˈdrench**, *v. Obs.* Forms: *Inf.* 1 **adrenc-an**, 2– **adrenche(n.** *Pa. t.* 1–3 **adrenc-te**, 2–3 **adrengte, adrente, adreinte**; 4 **adraynte**, 4–5 **adreynte.** *Pa. pple.* 1 **adrenc-ed**, 2–3 **adrenct, adrent, adreint**; 4–5 **adreynt, adraynt.** [f. A- *pref.* 1 intensive + DRENCH, OE. *drencan*, causal deriv. of *drink*. Cf. Ger. *ertränken.*] *lit.* and *fig.* throughout.

1. To give to drink.

1340 *Ayenb.* 92 He uoluelþ þe herte of loue..and him adrengþ of ane zuetnesse wonderuol. *Ibid.* 251 And hire adraynkþ and makeþ him dronke of holy loue.

2. *trans.* To submerge, to drown.

a **1000** *Ags. Met. Ps.* cv. 10 Heora feondas flód adrencte. *c* **1150** *Cott. Hom.* 225 Ic nelle henon forð mancyn mid watere adrenche. *c* **1175** *Lamb. Hom.* 141 Heo wende to gederes, and adreinte pharao. **1297** R. GLOUC. 437 Hys sones were þat alyue, þat adrencte were atte laste. **1387** TREVISA *Higden* Rolls Ser. I. 195 Helle was adraynt in that see [*submersa*]. **1494** FABYAN V. cxxx. 112 Yᵉ last bishop was a dreynte.

3. *refl.* To drown (oneself).

c **1230** *Ancren Riwle* 230 Te swin anonriht urnen & adreinten ham suluen iðer see. **1340** *Ayenb.* 50 An ȝuo moche drinke; þet hy ham adrencheþ. **1413** LYDG. *Pylgr. Sowle* I. xiii. (1859) 10 Adrenchyng hym self, as it were, in worldly vanyte.

4. *intr.* (by omission of refl. pron.) To be drowned, or drown; to perish in the water; to 'go down,' as a ship. (In this const. it = ADRINK, and often interchanges with it; see first quot.)

1205 LAYAMON 2206 Ferde into ane watere · þer inne he adronc [**1250** a-dreint]. *c* **1230** *Ancren Riwle* 220 þer adreinte Pharao, & hore uoan alle. *c* **1305** *Pilate* in *E.E. Poems* (1862) 118 þo com þer a gret tempest..þat schipes adreynte þere menie on. **1377** LANGL. *P. Pl.* B. x. 408 And men þat maden it · amydde þe flode adreynten.

adrenergic (ædrɪˈnɜːdʒɪk), *a.* [f. ADREN(ALINE + Gr. ἔργ-ον work + -IC.] Of the sympathetic nerve-fibres: liberating adrenalin or a substance resembling adrenalin; also, stimulated by adrenalin.

1934 H. H. DALE in *Jrnl. Physiol.* LXXX. 11 P, We seem to need words which will briefly indicate action by two kinds of chemical transmission, due in the one case to some substance like adrenaline, in the other case to a substance like acetylcholine, so that we may distinguish between chemical function and anatomical origin. I suggest the words 'adrenergic' and 'cholinergic' respectively. **1935** *Ann. Reg. 1934* II. 53 There was increased recognition of the cholinergic mechanism as having the more general application in the functions of the nervous system and of the adrenergic mechanism as being a more specialised and a more recent development. **1955** *Sci. News Let.* 19 Mar. 179/2 Adrenergic chemicals inhibit, or stop, transmission of nerve impulses across the nerve junctions called synapses. Cholinergic chemicals excite, or give the go signal, to such impulses.

adrenin (æˈdriːnɪn). Also **-ine.** [f. ADREN(AL + -IN¹.] = ADRENALINE.

1908 E. A. SCHÄFER in *Brit. Med. Jrnl.* 30 May 1281 It would..be well to substitute the term 'adrenin' for the proprietary name 'adrenalin'. **1910** *Year-Bk. Pharmacy* 177 (*heading*) Adrenine as an Emergency Treatment in Cases of Non-corrosive Poisoning. **1932** *Discovery* Oct. 339/1 Adrenin, the internal secretion of that ductless gland the suprarenal capsule.

adreno- (æˈdriːnəʊ, æˈdrɛnəʊ), comb. form of ADRENAL *a.* and *sb.*, and ADRENALINE, as in **aˈdrenochrome** [G. *adrenochrom* (*Chem. Zentralbl.* (1909) II. 1584)], a red oxidation product of adrenalin; **aˌdreno-ˈcortical** *a.*, of or pertaining to the adrenal cortex or the hormone which it secretes; **aˌdrenoˈgenital** *a.*, of or pertaining to the adrenal glands and the genitals; **aˌdrenoˈlytic** *a.*, inhibiting the effect of adrenalin or the action of adrenergic nerves; also *sb.*; **aˌdrenoˈtrop(h)ic** *a.*, = ADRENO CORTICOTROP(H)IC *a.*

1913 DORLAND *Med. Dict.* (ed. 7) 39/2 *Adrenochrome, a sulphur compound of the suprarenal gland for the internal treatment of skin diseases. **1962** *Lancet* 27 Jan. 201/1 Practically none, or none at all, of the infused adrenaline could have been metabolised via adrenochrome or its products in either schizophrenic or normal subjects. **1936** H. D. ROLLESTON *Endocrine Organs in Health & Disease* iii. 64 Corticotropic..or *Adreno-cortical Stimulating Hormone. **1941** *Lancet* 8 Mar. 313/2 A case of adreno-cortical syndrome. **1949** *Vitamins & Hormones* VII. 294 Both the sex hormones and the adrenocortical hormones are involved in the regulation of protein, carbohydrate, and electrolyte metabolism. **1931** *Brit. Med. Jrnl.* 2 May 746/1 The accentuation of the male secondary sexual characters..may be most aptly described under the heading of 'Virilism', rather than..as the '*Adreno-genital syndrome'. **1947** *Proc. Soc. Exp. Biol. & Med.* LXVI. 152/2 Dibenamine..is primarily a powerful *adrenolytic, but a weak sympathicolytic agent. **1948** *Ibid.* LXVII. 298 Several sympathicolytic substances have mainly adrenolytic properties. **1932** *Lancet* 12 Aug. 347/1 (*title*) The *adrenotropic hormone of the anterior pituitary lobe. **1938** *Encycl. Brit. Bk. of Yr.* 227/2 The adrenotrophic, thyrotrophic, and gonadotrophic hormones.

adrenocorticotrop(h)ic (æˈdriːnəʊˌkɔːtɪkəʊˈtrɒfɪk, -ˈtrɒpɪk), *a.* [f. ADRENO- + CORTICO- + TROPHIC *a.*] Stimulating or controlling the adrenal cortex; esp. ***adrenocorticotrop(h)ic hormone*** (abbrev. *A.C.T.H.*), a hormone produced by the pituitary gland which influences the action of the adrenal cortex.

1936 *Proc. Soc. Exp. Biol. & Med.* XXXV. 281 (*title*) Effect of Adrenocorticotropic Extracts on Accessory Reproductive Organs of Castrate Rats. **1937** *Ibid.* 649 Preparation and biological assay of adrenocorticotropic hormone. **1938** J. D. REESE & H. D. MOON in *Anatomical Rec.* LXX. 543 The..increase in the adrenal of normal rats following administration of the adrenocorticotrophic hormone of the anterior hypophysis is well known. **1944** *Anatomical Rec.* LXXXIX. 163 Effect of adrenocorticotropic hormone (ACTH) on the anterior pituitary of the adrenalectomized young male rat. **1950** *Lancet* 7 Jan. 11/1 A.C.T.H. seems to be the most promising tool medical investigators have today. **1962** *Lancet* 28 Apr. 888/1 Acute failure was precipitated by the adrenocorticotrophic stimulus of isoniazid.

Hence **aˌdrenocorticoˈtrop(h)in** [-IN¹] = *adrenocorticotrop(h)ic hormone.*

1952 *Proc. Soc. Exp. Biol. & Med.* LXXIX. 252 (*title*) Cytologic Changes in Rat Adenohypophysis Following Administration of Adrenocorticotrophin or Cortisone. **1959** *New Biol.* XXVIII. 131 Some tumours of the pituitary gland secrete abnormally large amounts of a hormone, adrenocorticotrophin, known as ACTH for short, which is required for the normal maintenance and function of the adrenal cortex.

adres(se, early form of ADDRESS *v.* and *sb.*

‖**adret** (adre). *Geogr.* [F. (orig. dial.), f. *à* to + OFr. *dre(i)t*: see ADROIT *a.*] A (mountain) slope which faces the sun. Cf. UBAC.

1931 *Geogr. Rev.* XXI. 424 The valley has an east-west trend and so a well defined *adret* (sunny side) and *ubac* (shady side). **1936** R. PEATTIE *Mountain Geogr.* iv. 90 An exception to the law of exposure is found in the existence of sunny slopes on an *ubac*. These slopes are the 'secondary *adrets*'. **1937** A. GARNETT *Insolation & Relief* i. 4 The familiar contrasts of land utilisation on *adret* and *ubac* slopes.

adrie, adriȝe, forms of ADREE *v. Obs.*

adrift (əˈdrɪft), *adv.* prop. *phr.* [A *prep.*¹ on, in + DRIFT. Cf. *afloat.*]

1. In a drifting condition, drifting, at the mercy of wind and tide.

1624 CAPT. SMITH *Virginia* I. 16 The ship yet went so fast a drift. **1667** MILTON *P.L.* XI. 832 With all his verdure spoiled, and trees adrift. **1748** ANSON *Voy.* II. ix. (ed. 4) 318 They had immediately turned the canoe adrift. **1853** KANE *Grinnell Exp.* xxxviii. (1856) 353 Caught and carried adrift on disengaged ice-floes.

2. *fig.* **a.**

1690 LOCKE *Hum. Underst.* II. vii. §3 And so we should..let our Thoughts (if I may so call it) run adrift, without any Direction or Design. **1728** YOUNG *Love of Fame* v. (1757) 138 The mind, when turn'd adrift, no rules to guide, Drives at the mercy of the wind and tide. **1832** HT. MARTINEAU *Hill & Valley* vii. 106 The concern must be closed and all these people turned adrift. **1878** BLACK *Green Past. & Picc.* xvii. 139 To cut myself adrift from my relatives.

b. Of a serviceman or merchant seaman: absent without leave; late returning from leave. Also of an object: unfastened, missing. *colloq.* (chiefly *Naut.*).

1919 W. H. DOWNING *Digger Dial.* 7 *Adrift*, see A.W.L. **1942** *Gen* 1 Sept. 13/1, I mustn't be adrift too late. [*Note* (1 Oct. 61/2): The words 'too late' are..superfluous.] **1946** J. IRVING *Royal Navalese* 20 *Adrift*, absent without leave; late for Divisions or a muster... In a secondary sense it also means that something has become undone or unfastened. **1960** C. MACINNES *Mr. Love & Justice* 7 A bad discharge-book, too: adrift in Yokohama and repatriated at official expense. **1962** C. EVANS *Heart of Standing* 19 Make sure you get everything checked in and signed off, because if there's anything adrift it will come off your slop chit, nobody else's. **1979** N. W. ALLINGTON *Fireman!* ii. 28 Anything not secured properly is said to have 'come adrift'.

c. Short or wide of a target, estimate, etc.; behind (the position or score of a competitor). Freq. const. *of. colloq.*

1976 *Leicester Mercury* 14 Oct. 46/1 Rose was adrift with a couple of penalties before Leicestershire opened their account. **1976** *Evening Post* (Nottingham) 15 Dec. 23/2 She finished third in 2 min. 14.2 sec.—well adrift of Katrina Colebrook who set a new UK indoor best time of 2 min. 5 sec. **1977** J. LAKER *One-Day Cricket* 66 Their score had reached a wonderful 276 for 4, only 52 runs adrift. **1978**

Guardian Weekly 15 Jan. 1/3 That will leave the United States 100 billion dollars adrift on its balance of payments. **1983** *Times* 6 June 18/2 Reed..was already £16m adrift at the pretax level at the nine-month stage.

†a-drigh, *adv. Obs.* prop. *phr.* Forms: 3–6 on dregh(e, on dryȝe, o dreghe, o dreih, a dreȝ(e, a dreigh, a drigh. [A *prep.*[1] + *dreȝe, dreghe*, extent, length, distance: see DREGH.] At or to a distance, away, off.

c **1325** *E.E. Allit. Poems* B. 71 Þus þay droȝ hem a-dreȝ. **1330** R. BRUNNE *Chron.* 194 He bad þam alle draw þam o dreih. *c* **1340** *Gaw. & Gr. Knt.* 1031 Þere he dreȝeȝ hym ondryȝe. **1393** GOWER *Conf.* II. 46 The kinges doughter.. drewe her adrigh. *c* **1400** *Destr. Troy* XXVIII. 11647 Why draghesÞou on dregh Þes dedis so ferr? **1513** DOUGLAS *Æneis* II. xi. 56 My spous on dreich efter our trais sall hy.

†a'drink, *v. Obs.* Forms as in DRINK. [f. A- *pref.* 1 intensive + DRINK, OE. *drinc-an*. Cf. Germ. *ertrinken*.] *lit.* To swallow too much water; hence,

1. To be drowned.

c **880** K. ÆLFRED *Bæda* III. xxiv. 221 Mycele má moncynnes adranc on ðam wætere. **1205** LAYAMON 2490 In ane deope watere · Þer heo adronken. *c* **1230** *Ancren Riwle* 58 Heo unwreih Þene put Þ hit adronc inne. *a* **1300** *K. Horn* 971 Þe knaue Þer gan adrinke.

So *to be adrunken*.

1205 LAYAMON 2497 Þat ilke water · Þer Abren was adrunken [*l.t.* adronke.] **1297** R. GLOUC. 430 In Þe se adronke he was.

adrip (ə'drɪp), *adv.* and *pred. a.*, prop. *phr.* [A *prep.*[1] + DRIP.] In a dripping state.

1830 *Blackw. Mag.* July 142 A head of hair all adrip like that of Neptune. **1867** D. MITCHELL *Wet Days* 84 And the pelted leaves all wincing and shining and adrip. **1881** *Atlantic Month.* XLVII. 251 Oars adrip with silver foam.

†a'drive, *v. Obs.* Forms as in DRIVE. [OE. *adrífan*, f. A- *pref.* 1 away, on + *drífan* to DRIVE.] To drive away, chase, pursue, follow up.

a **1000** *Laws of Æthelstan* v. §8. 4 (Bosw.) Adrífe ðæt spor út of his scire. *c* **1175** *Lamb. Hom.* 115 He scal..heordom for-beodan, and Þeouas addriuan, of his erde.

adrogate ('ædrəʊgeɪt), *v.* Also arrogate. [A specialized form of ARROGATE, f. L. *adrogāt-* ppl. stem of *adrogā-re* or *arrogāre*, to ask or claim to oneself, to adopt one whose consent may be legally asked, f. *ad* to + *rogāre* to ask. *Arrogate* was formerly used in all senses, but mod. writers on *Rom. Law* have appropriated this differentiated form for the special sense.] *Rom. Law.* To adopt a person who was at the time *sui juris*, or his own master, and under the *potestas* or legal power of no one else.

1649 JER. TAYLOR *Great Exemp.* III. §15. 89 He did arrogate John..into Maries kindred, Making him to be her adopted son. **1651** W. G. tr. *Cowel's Inst.* 164 There is nothing hinders, but that the English may adrogate or adopt, and be adopted..the consent of both parties is solely essentiall. **1861** MAINE *Anc. Law* vi. (1876) 180 When a Roman citizen adrogated a son, i.e. took a man, not already under *Patria Potestas*, as his adoptive child. **1875** POSTE *Gaius* I. (ed. 2) 90 Women, being incapable of exercising parental power, could not, properly speaking, adrogate.

adrogated ('ædrəʊgeɪtɪd), *ppl. a.* [f. prec. + -ED.] *Rom. Law.* Adopted, when *sui juris* or of full age and under no *potestas*.

1875 POSTE *Gaius* I. (ed. 2) 129 The children who follow an adrogated parent suffer diminution of head. **1880** MUIRHEAD *Gaius* 450 Results for the adrogated or adopted child.

adrogating ('ædrəʊgeɪtɪŋ), *ppl. a.* [f. ADROGATE + -ING[2].] That adrogates.

1880 MUIRHEAD *Gaius* 450 Results for the adrogating or adopting parent.

adrogation (,ædrəʊ'geɪʃən). Also **arrogation**. [ad. L. *adrogātiōn-em* n. of action f. *adrogā-re*: see ADROGATE.] *Rom. Law.* The technical name of adoption where the person adopted was his own master, or under no *potestas*.

1581 J. MARBECK *Bk. of Notes* 15 Arrogation they saie is, when he which is his owne man, and at libertie, is receiued in steede of a sonne. But Adoption is, when hee which is receiued, is vnder an other man's power. **1682** W. EVATS tr. *Grotius' Peace & War* 115 Arrogation or Adoption, whereby a man translates himself into the Family of another. **1705** STANHOPE *Paraphr.* I. 321 This the Lawyers call'd Adrogation, or perfect Adoption. **1833** *Penny Cycl.* s.v. *Adoption*, The Prussian law does away with all distinction between adoption and arrogation. **1880** MUIRHEAD *Gaius* I. §99 This species of adoption is called adrogation; because both he who is adopting is asked, *rogatur*, whether he will have as his lawful son him he is about to adopt, and he who is being adopted is asked whether he submits, and the people is asked whether it ordains that so it shall be.

adrogator ('ædrəʊ,geɪtə(r)). Also arrogator. [a. L. *adrogātor* n. of agent f. *adrogā-re* to ADROGATE.] *Rom. Law.* He who adrogates.

1774 HALLIFAX *Rom. Civ. Law* (1795) 58 He..by that species of adoption, called Arrogation, transferred himself and all his rights, except such as perished by the change of family, to the Arrogator. **1880** MUIRHEAD *Gaius* 40 If a man who..has children in his *potestas* give himself in adrogation, not only does he himself become subject to the *potestas* of the adrogator, but his children do so too in the character of grandchildren.

adroit (ə'drɔɪt), *a.* [a. Fr. *adroit*, orig. adv. phrase *à droit* according to right, rightly, properly, f. *à* to + *droit* right, OFr. *dreit*:—late L. *drictum, directum*:—cl. L. *directum* right: see DIRECT. Subseq. used as adj., and in this sense adopted in Eng.] Possessing address or readiness of resource, either bodily or mental; having ready skill, dexterous, active, clever.

1652 EVELYN *France* (R.) The best esteemed and most adroit cavalry in Europe. **1678** BUTLER *Hudibras* III. i. 365 He held his talent most adroit, For any mystical exploit. **1718** *Free-thinker* No. 150, 326 The Right-Hand and Arm of most Men are..more adroit than the Left. **1809** W. IRVING *Knickerb.* XI. vii. (1849) 122 The adroit bargain by which the island of Manhattan was bought for sixty guilders. **1825** *Br. Jonathan* I. 269 They played about one another now like adroit wrestlers. **1860** MOTLEY *Netherl.* (1868) II. xiii. 139 Adroit intriguers burned incense to him as to a god.

adroitly (ə'drɔɪtlɪ), *adv.* [f. prec. + -LY[2].] In an adroit manner; with ready skill; dexterously, cleverly.

1748 CHESTERFIELD *Lett.* 163 (1792) II. 92 Do you use yourself to carve adroitly and genteely? **1817** JAS. MILL *Brit. India* II. v. v. 515 Words..so adroitly ambiguous, as in fact to evade the question. **1849** W. IRVING *Mahomed & Succ.* xii. (1853) 51 He used his left as adroitly as his right hand. **1850** MERIVALE *Rom. Emp.* V. xlii. 14 Tiberius..replied adroitly, that it was not for him to choose or to reject any particular charge.

adroitness (ə'drɔɪtnɪs). [f. ADROIT + -NESS.] The quality of being adroit; ready skill, dexterity, cleverness, either bodily or mental.

1742 tr. *Klimius, Iter Subter.* vii. 87 The Person's dexterity and adroitness. **1850** MRS. STOWE *Uncle Tom's C.* xxiii. 226 Henrique..valued himself on his gentlemanly adroitness in all matters of gallantry. **1879** FROUDE *Cæsar* vi. 55 To Sylla's combined adroitness and courage Marius owed the final capture of Jugurtha.

adronc, -nken, pa. t. and pple. of ADRINK *v. Obs.*

adroop (ə'dru:p), *adv.* and *pred. a.*, prop. *phr.* [A *prep.*[1] + DROOP.] In a drooping position.

1879 J. D. LONG *Æneid* XI. 1128 Her neck adroop, she last let go her spear.

†a'drop. *Alch. Obs.* (See the quot.)

1471 RIPLEY *Comp. Alch.* II. (Ashm. 1652) 135 These two and no mo Be our Magnesia, our Adrop. **1610** B. JONSON *Alch.* II. iii. (1616) 627 Your moone, your firmament, your adrop. **1753** CHAMBERS *Cycl. Supp.*, *Adrop*, among alchemists, denotes either that precise matter, as lead, out of which the mercury is to be extracted for the philosopher's stone; or it denotes the philosopher's stone itself, inasmuch as this is also called *saturn* and *plumbum*, or lead. CASTELLUS [*Lex. Med.* Geneva 1746] *in voc.*

adrostral (æ'drɒstrəl), *a. Zool.* [mod. f. L. *ad* to, at + *rostr-um* beak, mouth + -AL[1].] Pertaining to or situated at the beak or snout.

1878 BELL tr. *Gegenbauer's Comp. Anat.* 457 The presence of special cartilages (rostral and adrostral) in front of the primordial cranium of the larvæ of Anura.

†a'drough, *adv. Obs.*

1698 *Bucaneers of Amer.* ii. 151 We set our sail adrough, and so drove to the Southward.

†adrough(e, adrowe, *v. Obs.* Forms: *Inf.* 1 **adrúȝian, adruwian**; 2–3 **adruȝien, adruwien, adruien**; 4 **adrouȝe**. *Pa. pple.* 1 **adrúȝod, adruwod**; 2–3 **adruwed**. (All southern.) [f. A- *pref.* 1 intensive + *druȝian* to (become) dry, see DROW *v.* and DROUGHT. There was also an OE. *adrýȝan* to (make) dry, which seems to have been confused in 2–3 in the south with *adruwien*, so that the latter is used in the senses of both the earlier verbs.]

1. *intr.* To dry up, to become dry, withered, etc.

c **1000** ÆLFRIC *Gen.* viii. 11 Þa wætera wǽron adruwode. *c* **1000** *O.E. Gosp.* Matt. xiii. 6 Hiȝ adruwodon and forscruncon. *c* **1160** *Hatton Gosp.* ibid., Hyo adruwedon and forscrunken. *c* **1175** *Lamb. Hom.* 133 Sum..feol an uppe Þe stane and Þer adruȝede. *c* **1230** *Ancren Riwle* 150 Auh adruieð Þe bowes, & iwurðet hwite rondes..Hwon hit is so adruwed. *c* **1315** SHOREHAM 34 Ȝef thou wylt, man, thorȝ thy schryft Lat thy senne al a-drouȝe.

2. *trans.* To dry, dry up. (In this sense it seems to take the place of OE. *adrýȝan*; see first quot.)

c **940** *Sax. Leechd.* II. 70 Adrige beana & geseoÞ butan sealte. *c* **1230** *Ancr. Riwle* 220 He adruwede Þe Reade See.

adrowse (ə'draʊz), *adv.* and *pred. a.* prop. *phr.* [A *prep.*[1] in + DROWSE.] In a drowsy state.

1866 MRS. A. WEBSTER *Circe* 41 And if my heart must always be adrowse In a hush of stagnant sunshine.

adry (ə'draɪ), *adv.* and *pred. a.* [f. DRY *a.* prob. in imitation of *acold, athirst*; see A- *pref.* 11.] In a dry or thirsty condition; thirsty.

1599 *Warn. Faire Wom.* II. 610 Nay, prethee fill my cup.. How say you now, sir? was I not a-dry? **1628** DIGBY *Voy. to Medit.* 94 Att the ebbe shee [the ship] remained all adry. **1714** GAY *Sheph. Week* Wks. 1745 I. 82 Your herds for want of water stand adry. **1830** HOOD *Haunted Ho.* I. xxvi, The Fountain was a-dry.

†a'drylle, *v. Obs. rare.* [f. A- *pref.* 1 away + DRILL, in mod. Kentish dial. to slide away.] To slide or slip away.

c **1315** SHOREHAM 90 Meche hys the mede that hym worthe By [= be it] so that he na drylle. *Ibid.* 114 The fyfte senne hys sleuthe..Wanne man leteth adrylle That he god ȝelde schel.

ads, a variant of ODS, a 'minced' form of *God's*, formerly used in various oaths; as **adsbud** (for *God's blood*), **adsheart** (*God's heart*), etc.

1693 CONGREVE *Old Bachelor* III. vi. (1866) 158 Adsbud, who's in fault, mistress of mine? **1741** RICHARDSON *Pamela* xxi. (1824) I. 271 Ads-dines, madam, said he, what of all that! *Ibid.* xxviii. I. 45 Ads-heartikins! you young gentlemen are made of iron and steel, I think. **1751** SMOLLETT *Per. Pickle* lxxxvii. (1779) IV. 35 Adsoocks! ye baggage, cried the lover. **1812** H. & J. SMITH *Rej. Addr.* (1873) 94 I'll catch at the handle, add's life!

adscititious (,ædsɪ'tɪʃəs), *a.* Also **ascititious**. [f. L. *adscīt-* (*ascīt-*) ppl. stem of *adscīsc-ĕre* to admit, accept, or receive from others (f. *ad* to + *scīsc-ĕre* to acknowledge, approve by vote, inceptive of *scī-re* to know) + -ITIOUS, as if f. L. **adscīt-īcius*.] Assumed, adopted from without; 'taken in to complete something else, though originally extrinsic; supplemental; additional.' J.

1620 BACON *Nov. Org.* II. xlviii. 542 They therefore called this [motion] perpetual and proper..and they called the others adscititious. **1697** EVELYN *Numism.* ix. 305 Such adscititious Habits as may be contracted by Institution, Discipline and custom. **1783** MARTYN *Geog. Mag.* II. 517 The adscititious inhabitants of Terra Firma. **1847** HAMILTON *Rew. & Punishm.* III. (1853) 127 Immortality being adscititious, may be withheld. **1864** MAX MÜLLER *Sc. Lang.* Ser. II. vi. (1868) 261 These initial vowels..are not radical, but merely adscititious in Greek.

adscititiously (,ædsɪ'tɪʃəslɪ), *adv. rare.* [f. prec. + -LY[2].] In an adscititious manner; supplementally. (In mod. dicts.)

adscribe, rarely used for ASCRIBE and SUBSCRIBE.

1603 B. JONSON *Sejanus* V. v. 4 Beare it [an Edict] to my fellow Consul to adscribe. **1665–6** in *Phil. Trans.* I. 252 He adscribes them to the same cause. **1864** G. M. HOPKINS *Let.* 14 Aug. (1938) 64, I am adscribed third into Alfred Erskine and Bond.

adscribed (æd'skraɪbd), *ppl. a.* [formally pa. pple. of *adscribe*, L. *adscrīb-ĕre*, f. *ad* to + *scrīb-ĕre* to write; also written *ascrībĕre*, whence in other senses ASCRIBE.] Described upon, applied to a given line or dimension of a figure.

1685 WALLIS *Secants* in *Misc. Cur.* 1708 II. 9 Which formed an Adscribed Figure made up of those Parallelograms.

adscript ('ædskrɪpt), *a.* and *sb.* [ad. L. *adscrīpt-us* pa. pple. of *adscrīb-ĕre* (more commonly *ascrībĕre, ascrīptus*); see prec.]

A. *adj.*

1. Written after, as distinguished from *subscript*.

1875 LIGHTFOOT *Col. & Philem.* (1876) 251 The iota adscript was still written.

2. For med.L. *adscriptus* (*glebæ*) attached (to the soil). Said of feudal serfs, who were transferred along with the estate to which they hereditarily pertained.

1822 *Edin. Rev.* XXXII. 291 Consider the men as being in some measure adscript to the glebe.

B. *sb.*

†1. *Math.* A natural tangent, so called because applied to the circumference of a circle. *Obs.*

1722 G. MACKENZIE *Scot. Writers* III. 520 To these Tables of Sines, Bressius added the Table of Natural Tangents, which he call'd Adscripts. **1867** SMYTH *Sailor's Word-Bk.*, *Adscripts*, sometimes used for the tangents of arcs.

2. = A. 2 used subst.

1849 CARLYLE *Nigger Quest.* 44 The Blacks in Java are already a kind of Adscripts. **1876** BANCROFT *Hist. U.S.* I. xvii. 496 Not only destitute of political franchises, but mere adscripts to the soil.

3. A comment or note added to a manuscript; esp. one which in error becomes incorporated in the text.

1889 W. G. RUTHERFORD *Thucyd. IV* p. xxxiv, In place of this word [*scholium*]..I would suggest another..if we anglicise the Latin *adscriptum* on the analogy of *postscript* and *rescript* we get exactly what we want. *Ibid.* p. xl, Adscripts combined with glosses may modify the whole structure of a sentence. **1898** F. BLASS *Philol. of Gospels* 161 The record of its original place must have been preserved.. by some adscript..*Here comes in the passage on the adulteress.* **1929** E. LOBEL in *Classical Q.* XXIII. 78 A very large number of marginal or interlinear adscripts have made their way into the text of A[c].

adscripted (æd'skrɪptɪd), *ppl. a.* [f. ADSCRIPT *a.* and *sb.* + -ED.] = ADSCRIPT A 2.

1878 F. A. WALKER *Money* I. vi. 126 The conscripted and adscripted laborers in the mines, those drawn by lot and those born to the service.

adscription (æd'skrɪpʃən). [ad. L. *adscrīptiōn-em* (also *ascrīptiōn-em*) n. of action, f. *adscrīb-ĕre* or *ascrīb-ĕre* to write to, to add in writing. Commonly ASCRIPTION, exc. in senses 2, 3.]

1. = ASCRIPTION.

1857 SIR F. PALGRAVE *Norm. & Eng.* II. 510 Good Queen Anne has no peculiar claim to that adscription of benignity. **1880** WARREN *Bk.-plates* xviii. 194 The purport, date, and adscription of each individual book-plate.

†**2.** *spec.* The describing of one geometrical figure about, or within, another; a general term including circumscribing and inscribing. *Obs.*

1660 T. STANLEY *Hist. Philos.* (1701) 9/1 The second, third, fourth, and fifth propositions of the fourth Book of Euclid..concerning the adscription of a Triangle and a Circle.

3. [From med.L. *adscriptus glebæ*; see ADSCRIPT.] Attachment as a feudal inferior.

1872 E. ROBERTSON *Hist. Ess.* 159 This personal adscription to the overlord is the real source of the feeling.. described as 'clannish.'

adscriptitious (ædskrɪp'tɪʃəs), *a.* [f. L. *a(d)-scriptīci-us* enrolled + -OUS; see ADSCRIPT and -ITIOUS.] Bound by adscription.

1831 HEIDIGER *Didoniad* I. 6 Ye simple Nine; to dream, when we began, That we were adscriptitious thralls to Quatrain.

adsignification (æd,sɪgnɪfɪ'keɪʃən). [ad. med.L. *adsignificātiōn-em* n. of action f. *adsignificā-re* to make evident, denote; f. *ad* to + *significā-re* to SIGNIFY.] (See quot.)

1753 CHAMBERS *Cycl. Supp.*, *Adsignification*, among school-men, the act of noting or signifying a thing, with the addition of the time when it happened. **1798** TOOKE *Purley* 648, I did not mean to deny the adsignification of Time to all the participles.

adsignify (æd'sɪgnɪfaɪ), *v. rare.* [ad. L. *adsignificā-re*: see prec. and -FY.] To signify an action with an addition of time, as is done by the tenses of the verb.

1798 TOOKE *Purley* (1857) 654 The other Participles.. are indeed merely those Moods and Tenses adjectived, and do truly therefore adsignify Manner and Time.

adsistency, obs. variant of ASSISTANCY.

†**adsolve**, *v. Obs. rare*^−1. Perh. a misprint; perh. for *a-solve* = *re-solve*, as in ADOUBTED.

1605 CHAPMAN *All Fooles* Plays 1873 I. 132 Durst my Sonne thus.. Adsolue to runne beyond Sea to the warres?

adsorb (æd'sɔːb), *v.* [Back-formation from ADSORPTION.] **1.** *trans.* To collect by adsorption.

1882 [implied in ADSORBING *ppl. a.*] **1906** *Bio-Chem. Jrnl.* I. 485 As to other factors which influence the adsorption v. Bemmelen points out the following:—(1) the adsorbing substance, (2) the solvent, (3) the substance to be adsorbed. **1923** *Discovery* Sept. 231/2 Impurities deposited on or adsorbed by the crystals. **1928** W. A. CASPARI *Struct. & Prop. Matter* ii. 37 Some charcoals will adsorb hundreds of times their bulk of gas. **1934** *Discovery* July 198/2 Clay behaves like an insoluble weak acid, in that it can react with, and adsorb the actions of electrolytes in the soil. **1938** R. W. LAWSON tr. *Hevesy & Paneth's Man. Radioactivity* (ed. 2) xvii. 163 A cation will be adsorbed.. when it forms with the anion of the adsorbing salt a compound, the solubility of which in the solvent is small.

2. *intr.* To undergo adsorption, become adsorbed. Const. *on (to)*, *to.*

1919 *Chem. Abstr.* XIII. 2477 A strongly adsorbable ion will supersede one possessing a lower adsorbing ability. **1958** *Yearbk. Agric.* 1957 (U.S. Dept. Agric.) 751/1 *Adsorb*, to accumulate on a surface. **1972** *Science* 5 May 516/3 Soluble viral antigens also adsorbed rapidly to the monolayers. **1973** *Sci. Amer.* May 32/1 When such a gas is cooled, it tends to adsorb as a thin film on the walls of the vessel rather than condense into droplets. **1974** *Nature* 8 Mar. 126/1 Caesium-137.. does not adsorb significantly on to sedimentary material and is easily detected at very low concentrations.

Hence **adsorba'bility**, the degree to which a substance is adsorbable; **ad'sorbable** *a.*, capable of being adsorbed; **ad'sorbed** *ppl. a.*, collected by adsorption; **ad'sorbent**, an adsorbing substance; **ad'sorbing** *ppl. a.*; **ad'sorbate** [-ATE^4], the material which is adsorbed; an adsorbed substance.

1882 *Nature* XXVI. 139 Continuing his researches on 'adsorption', or condensation of gases on surfaces of solids, Herr Kayser.. has studied the influence of the adsorbing material. **1906** *Bio-chem. Jrnl.* I. 494 In all my experiments with charcoal some trypsin has remained merely adsorbed, and therefore transferable to added casein and active. **1914** *Chem. Abstr.* VIII. 2845 The displacement of one adsorbable substance by another possessing this property to a higher degree. **1919** *Ibid.* XIII. 2477 The adsorbability of a salt is detd. by that of its component ions. **1924** *Proc. R. Soc.* A. CVI. 57 Gases known from previous experiments not to be adsorbable by tungsten. **1928** W. A. CASPARI *Struct. & Prop. Matter* ii. 38 Animal and vegetable fibres.. are tolerably good adsorbents, owing to the large surfaces presented by their internal structure. **1936** *Jrnl. Soc. Chem. Industry* 18 Sept. 724/1 Advantage is taken of marked differences in the adsorbability of the constituents.. to perform a separation into two fractions, a more and a less adsorbable. **1937** *Thorpe's Dict. Appl. Chem.* (ed. 4) I. 150/1 Enabling the adsorbed solvents to be recovered and the adsorbents to be regenerated.. for further use. **1938** *Nature* 26 Nov. 946/1 The first International Standard for Vitamin B, which consisted of an adsorbate of the antineuritic vitamin. **1952** *New Biol.* XII. 102 When only monomolecular layers of the crystal are interacting with the adsorbate, more symmetric crystals can exercise such actions, if adsorption takes place on an asymmetric crystal face. **1964** *Ann. N.Y. Acad. Sci.* CXVI. 552 Such things as volatility, water- or lipid-solubility, adsorbability, and so on may affect the *strength* of an odor. **1975** *Electroanalytical Chem.* LIX. 344 (*heading*) On the mechanism of electrode reactions in presence of foreign, neutral adsorbable organic compounds. **1978** P. W. ATKINS *Physical Chem.* xxviii. 943 We suppose that the adsorbed molecules are in dynamic equilibrium with the free molecules.

adsorption (æd'sɔːpʃən). [f. L. *ad* to, towards + *-sorption*, see ABSORPTION.] **a.** The process by which specific gases, liquids or substances in solution adhere to the exposed surfaces of materials, usually solids, with which they are in contact.

1882 in *Nature* XXVI. 139 'Adsorption,' or condensation of gases on surfaces of solids. **1904** R. A. LEHFELDT tr. *Nernst's Theor. Chem.* 129 Adsorption.—Charcoal shaken with an iodine solution or placed in an atmosphere of iodine vapour condenses appreciable amounts of iodine on its surface; this is known as 'adsorption'. **1912** E. HATSCHEK *Introd. Physics & Chem. Colloids* (1913) i. 5 One other property of colloids.. is their capacity for taking dissolved substances out of solution and retaining them... This phenomenon.. is now generally called 'Adsorption'... Specially striking is the power of 'selective adsorption'.. possessed by many substances. **1928** W. A. CASPARI *Struct. & Prop. Matter* ii. 37 Adsorption from liquids is of the highest technical importance.

b. *attrib.* and *Comb.*, as ***adsorption force***; **adsorption compound**, a compound formed between an adsorbing surface and the substance adsorbed; **adsorption isotherm**, a curve plotted to show the relative proportion of adsorption and concentration in a fluid or solution at a constant temperature.

1908 *Chem. Abstr.* 1571 (*title*) Colloids and their Adsorption Compounds. **1913** *Ibid.* 438 Negative adsorption isotherms. **1918** A. M. WILLIAMS in *Proc. R. Soc. Edin.* XXXIX. 48 (*title*) Adsorption isotherm at low concentrations. **1920** C. F. CROSS & E. J. BEVAN *Paper-Making* (ed. 5) i. 65 The lignocelluloses are adsorption compounds of lignones and cellulose. **1938** R. W. LAWSON tr. *Hevesy & Paneth's Man. Radioactivity* (ed. 2) xv. 147 Non-specific adsorption forces do not play a part in this process.

Hence **ad'sorptional** *a.*, pertaining to adsorption.

1928 W. A. CASPARI *Struct. & Prop. Matter* ii. 35 Adsorptional effects are by no means limited to the liquid state.

adsorptive (æd'sɔːptɪv), *a.* [f. ADSORPT(ION + -IVE.] Of, exhibiting, or causing adsorption. Also *fig.*

1913 *Jrnl. Agric. Res.* I. 188 The presence of other mineral substances added to the soil may or may not increase or decrease the rate at which this adsorptive phenomenon takes place. **1940** GLASSTONE *Text-bk. Physical Chem.* xiv. 1173 Under these conditions the adsorptive capacity of the charcoal is relatively so high that it is able to bring about a considerable reduction of pressure. **1957** G. E. HUTCHINSON *Treat. Limnol.* I. xi. 703 The adsorptive material in oxidized mud. **1978** J. UPDIKE *Coup* (1979) v. 193 There was in our young hero.. an adsorptive chemical will that made him adhere to just those surfaces that would have repelled him.

Hence **adsorp'tivity**, adsorptive power or capacity.

1962 *Lebende Sprachen* VII. 33/1 *Adsorptivity*, spezifische Adsorption. **1979** *Nature* 30 Aug. 765/2 The adsorptivity of various sulphur and other compounds and the physical and optical effects of adsorbed gases such as H_2S and SO_2 thereon need to be studied.

†**adspi'ration.** *Obs.* [ad. L. *adspīrātiōn-em* (commonly *aspīrātiōnem*) n. of action, f. *adspīrā-re*, *aspīrā-re* to blow or breathe upon, to favour; f. *ad* to + *spīrā-re* to breathe. Usually ASPIRATION.] Gracious or favouring breath; favour, patronage.

1532 MORE *Confut. Tindale* Wks. 1557, 357/2 Without the adspiracion and helpe of whose especiall grace no laboure of man can profite.

adstipulate (æd'stɪpjʊleɪt), *v. Rom. Law.* [f. L. *a(d)stipulāt-* ppl. stem of *a(d)stipulā-ri* to join in a bargain, f. *ad* to, in addition + *stipulā-ri* to bargain.] To act as second stipulant or receiving party to a bargain, attaining thereby an equal claim with the principal stipulant.

1880 MUIRHEAD *Gaius* III. §114 A son, however, who is in the power of his father, may effectually adstipulate.

adstipulation (æd,stɪpjuː'leɪʃən). *Rom. Law.* [ad. L. *a(d)stipulātiōn-em* n. of action f. *a(d)stipulā-ri*; see prec. and -ION^1.] The addition of, or acting as, a second receiving party in a bargain.

1880 MUIRHEAD *Gaius* III. §114 Adstipulation by a slave is of no avail.

adstipulator (æd'stɪpjʊ,leɪtə(r)). *Rom. Law.* [a. L. *a(d)stipulātor* n. of agent f. *a(d)stipulā-ri*; see ADSTIPULATE and -OR.] (See quot.)

1880 MUIRHEAD *Gaius* III. §110 It is in our power, in entering into a stipulation, to conjoin with us a third party, who stipulates in the same terms as we have done; such a person is commonly called an *adstipulator*.

adstratum (æd'strɑːtəm). *Linguistics.* [mod.L., ad. Du. *adstraat* (M. Valkhoff, *Latijn, Romaans, Roemeens* (1932), p. 17), f. L. *ad* to + *strātum* STRATUM, after SUBSTRATUM 5, SUPERSTRATUM 2.] Elements or features of a language which are identified by linguists as responsible for linguistic change in another language which is otherwise dominant over it.

1939 J. WHATMOUGH in *Rep. 5th Congrès International des Linguistes* 48 'Superstratum' (and, if I understand it aright 'adstratum') are not exposed to the same dangers as the 'substratum' theory. **1954** [see SUBSTRATUM 5 b]. **1956** [see SUBSTRATUM 5 a]. **1976** [see SUPERSTRATUM 2 a]. **1978** *Language* LIV. 424 Substrata, adstrata, superstrata, and dialect-borrowing may all have been at work, in differing degrees, in various regions and at various times.

adstrict, -ion, -ory, obs. variants of ASTRICT, -ION, -ORY.

adstringe, -ent, obs. variants of ASTRINGE, -ENT.

adstupiate, *v. Obs.*^−0 [?] 'Greatly to esteem riches.' Cockeram 1626.

adsuki, var. ADZUKI.

‖**adsum** ('ædsʌm). [L.] 'I am here', as an answer in a roll-call, etc.

1593 SHAKS. *2 Henry VI*, I. iv. 26 *Spirit.* 'Ad sum' **1854** THACKERAY *Newcomes* II. xlii. 373 He lifted up his head a little, and quickly said 'Adsum!' and fell back. It was the word we used at school, when names were called. *c* **1909** D. H. LAWRENCE *Collier's Friday Night* (1934) ii. 56 Ne'er mind; I'll say 'adsum' every time. *Recording Angel*; 'Ernest Lambert.'—'Adsum!' **1915** J. E. G. HADATH *Sheepy Wilson* i. 2 Before ever he had uttered his first *Adsum* or slipped timidly for the first time into form.

adtemper, obs. variant of ATTEMPER.

†**a'dub**, *v. Obs.* Forms: 5 adube, adubbe, 5–6 adoub(e, 6 addoub(e. [a. OFr. *adube-r*, *adoube-r*, *adubbe-r*, *adoubbe-r*, to equip a knight, to array; f. *à* to + *douber* to DUB.]

1. To invest with the insignia of knighthood; to knight; to dub.

c **1450** *Merlin* 122 Thei shull neuer be dubbed of no man till thow a-dubbe hem and yeve hem armes. *a* **1521** *Helyas* in Thoms' *E.E.P. Rom.* III. 148, I shal adube you knight.

2. To equip, array, invest, accoutre.

1475 CAXTON *Jason* 28 b, Jason and the Syriens adoubed them. **1480** —— *Ovid's Metam.* XII. xxii, Appollo adoubed hyme with a thycke clowde.

†**a'dubbed,** *ppl. a. Obs.*; also **adoubed, add-.** [f. prec. + ED.] Equipped, arrayed, accoutred.

1475 CAXTON *Jason* 117 Ye shall do her to be adoubed for to bringe her in to your countrey. **1481** —— *Myrrour* I. v. 25 Precyous bookes richely lymned storyed and wel adoubed. **1580** SIDNEY *Arcadia* III. (1654) 277 Saying hee would go to the island bravely addoubed.

†**a'dubment.** *Obs.* [a. OFr. *adoubement*, *adubement*, f. *aduber*; see ADUB and -MENT.] Adornment, decoration.

c **1325** *E.E. Allit. Poems* A. 84–5 Þe sunne beme3 bot blo & blynde, In respecte of þat adubbement. The adubbement of þo downe3 dere Garten my goste al greffe for-3ete.

†**'adulable**, *a. Obs.*^−0 [ad. L. *adūlābil-is*, f. *adūlā-ri*: see ADULATE and -BLE.] 'To be flattered.' Cockeram 1626.

‖**adularia** (ædjuː'lɛərɪə). *Min.* [f. *Adula* name of a mountain in Switzerland.] A variety of Orthoclase.

1798 GREVILLE *Corundum* in *Phil. Trans.* LXXXVIII. 412 The texture of the matrix appears sometimes like adularia, and confusedly crystallized. **1850** C. DAUBENY *Atom. Theory* xii. (ed. 2) 416 In glassy felspar.. there is more soda than in orthoclase and adularia, the minerals usually found in granite.

adulate ('ædjʊleɪt), *v.* [f. L. *adūlāt-* ppl. stem of *adūlā-ri* to fawn upon like a dog, to flatter servilely. Cf. Fr. *adul-er*, used since the 15th c.] To flatter basely or slavishly; to do servile or indiscriminating homage to.

1777 DALRYMPLE *Trav. Spain & Port.* xxxix, The way to preferment here is by.. adulating some superior, who probably is a despicable character. **1794** D'ISRAELI *Curios. Lit.* (1848) I. 154 He actually condescended.. to adulate the unworthy Christina of Sweden. **1858** *Times* 12 Nov. 7/3 Adoring and adulating absolute monarchy. **1880** W. S. GILBERT *Patience* I. 9 What is there to adulate in me! Am I particularly intelligent?

adulating ('ædjʊ,leɪtɪŋ), *ppl. a.* [f. prec. + -ING^2.] Basely flattering, fawning.

1734 tr. *Rollin's Anc. Hist.* (1827) I. Pref. 8 A set of adulating courtiers. **1796** MISS BURNEY *Camilla* VIII. ix, His adulating airs as little suited that character, as his inclination.

adulation (,ædjuː'leɪʃən). Forms: 4 adulacioun, adulacion, adulation. [a. OFr. *adulacion*, ad. L. *adūlātiōn-em*, n. of action f. *adūlā-ri*: see ADULATE.] Servile flattery or homage; exaggerated and hypocritical praise to which the bestower consciously stoops.

c **1380** CHAUCER *Bal. Good Counsail* (R.) Men woll.. call faire speache adulacion. **1429** *Pol. Poems* (1859) II. 145 Eschew flatery and adulacioun. **1538** BALE *Thre Lawes* 964 By fayned flatterye, and by coloured adulacyon. **1582** N. T.

(Rhem.) *1 Thess.* ii. 5 For neither haue we been at any time in the word of adulation, as you know. **1599** SHAKS. *Hen. V*, IV. i. 271 Thinks thou the fierie Feuer will goe out With Titles blowne from Adulation? **1766** GOLDSM. *Vic. Wakef.* iii. 18 Adulation ever follows the ambitious, for such alone receive pleasure from flattery. **1858** O. W. HOLMES *Aut. Brkf. Table* xii. 115, I have two letters on file; one is a pattern of adulation, the other of impertinence.

adulator (ˈædjʊˌleɪtə(r)). [a. L. *adūlātor* n. of agent, f. *adūlā-ri*: see ADULATE, cf. Fr. *adulateur.*] One who offers praise consciously exaggerated or unmerited; a servile or hypocritical flatterer.

[Not in COTGR. 1611, who defines *Adulateur* Fr. as A flatterer, cogger, smoother, soother, fawner, clawback. Not in SHERWOOD 1650.] **1696** PHILLIPS, *Adulator*, a Flatterer, a fawning Fellow, a Claw-back. **1779** J. SULLIVAN in Sparks' *Corr. Am. Rev.* (1853) II. 367 Could you have believed that those Adulators .. would become your bitter enemies? **1835** I. TAYLOR *Sp. Despotism* vi. 259 Constantine .. by his adulators styled Chief bishop of the Church. **1854** tr. *Lamartine's Celebr. Charact.* II. 40 Aristophanes, a vile adulator of the follies and superstitions cherished by vulgar ignorance.

†**adulaˈtorious**, *a. Obs.* [f. L. *adūlātōri-us* ADULATORY + -OUS.] A by-form of ADULATORY.

1664 R. BAILLIE *Lett.* 145 The way here of all preachers .. has been, to speake before the Parliament with so profound a reverence as .. made all applications to them toothless and adulatorious.

†**adulaˈtoriously**, *adv. Obs.* [f. prec. + -LY².] In an adulatory manner.

1602 FULBECKE *Pand. Law of Nat.* 21 Against whom rather adulatoriously then aptly Alciat replyeth, that no prescription of time wil hold place against the Empire.

adulatory (ˈædjʊlətərɪ), *a.* [ad. L. *adūlātōri-us* of or belonging to a flatterer; f. *adūlātor*. Cf. obs. Fr. *adulatoire.*] Of or belonging to an adulator; full of adulation; servilely or fulsomely flattering.

1611 COTGR., *Adulatoire* (Fr.), Adulatorie, belonging to flattery, full of cogging. **1652** URQUHART *Jewel* Wks. 1834, 276 [He] thinks no better of adulatory assentations then of a gnat[h]onic sycophantizing. *a* **1733** NORTH *Lives of Norths* I. 386 After the adulatory manner of a court. **1790** BURKE *Fr. Revol.* 40 Dr. Price, in this sermon, condemns very properly the practice of gross, adulatory addresses to kings. **1838–9** HALLAM *Hist. Lit.* I. I. iv. §52. 296 He wrote to Leo X. in a style rather too adulatory.

†**adulatress.** *Obs.* [f. ADULATOR + -ESS. Cf. L. *adūlātrix*, Fr. *adulatrice.*] A female adulator; a woman who flatters with servility.

1572 in HULOET.

adulce, earlier f. ADDULCE *v. Obs.* to sweeten.

Adullamite (əˈdʌləmaɪt). [f. *Adullam*, name of a place in the tribe of Judah, where there was a noted cave, + -ITE.]

1. *prop.* An inhabitant of Adullam.

1382 WYCLIF *Gen.* xxxviii. 12 Yras the sheepherd of the flok, Odollamyte in Tampnas. **1611** *Ibid.* He and his friend Hirah the Adullamite.

2. a. A frequenter of the cave of Adullam. *fig.* A nickname applied in 1866 to certain members of the British House of Commons, who seceded from the Liberal party then in power, from dissatisfaction with their attempt to carry a measure of Parliamentary Reform. The name originated with an expression in a speech by Mr. Bright; see quot. 1866¹. More widely, a member of a dissenting political group.

[Cf. BIBLE *1 Sam.* xxii. 1, 2. **1834** *Examiner* 14 Dec. 794/2 Perhaps, he will show how David, supported by the ragamuffins of the cave of Adullam, prevailed against the King, .. but he must admit that the Adullamites respected the person of the King, though they disregarded his opinions. **1866** BRIGHT *Sp.* (1876) 349 The right hon. gentleman is the first of the new party who has expressed his great grief, who has retired into what may be called his political Cave of Adullam, and he has called about him 'every one that was in distress and every one that was discontented.'] **1866** *Pall Mall G.* No. 440, 66/1 The other leading Adullamites. **1880** MᶜCARTHY *Hist. our Own Times* IV. l. 65 The little third party were at once christened the Adullamites, and the name still survives and is likely long to survive its old political history. **1981** *Age* (Melbourne) 24 Oct., Don Chipp is an Adullamite. And the Democrats are, in the biblical sense, 'everyone in distress, in debt, and discontented'.

b. *attrib.* or as *adj.* Of or pertaining to the seceders of 1866. Also *transf.*, esp. of other political dissenters; radical, unorthodox.

1880 J. MCCARTHY *Hist. own Times* IV. li. 77 [Lord Derby] had at once invited the leading members of the Adullamite party to accept places in his Administration. **1963** *Times Lit. Suppl.* 10 May 348/3 The statesman, the politician, the historian .. is also the youthful war correspondent .. and the prolific journalist of the Adullamite 1930s. **1982** *Guardian* 31 July 8/1 A series of opinion poll results which suggested the relegation of the Conservative Party to an Adullamite rump.

adult (əˈdʌlt, ˈædʌlt), *a.* [ad. L. *adult-us* pa. pple. of *adolesc-ĕre* to grow up; but perh. as first used a direct adoption of the Fr. *adulte*, a 16th c. adaptation of the L. Though once used by Elyot, not really naturalized till the middle of the 17th c., being unknown to Cotgrave, Florio, and Minsheu, in translating Fr. *adulte*, It. and Sp. *adulto*.]

A. *adj.*

1. a. Grown up, having reached the age of maturity. (Of men, and, in mod. use, of animals.)

1531 ELYOT *Governour* II. i. (R.) Soche persons being now adulte, that is to sei passed their childehode. [**1611** COTGR., *Hors de paye* (Fr.), Adultus, past breeching .. growne a tall man, or, a full-growne man.] **1653** BAXTER *Chr. Conc.* 10, I intend to have the Names of all the Members in a Church-Book (the Adult in one Colume and the Infants in another). **1726** AYLIFFE *Parergon* 369 An adult Age is above the age of Puberty, and under that of twenty-five years. **1836** THIRLWALL *Greece* III. xxiv. 360 They put to death all the adult citizens, and enslaved the women and children. **1871** DARWIN *Desc. Man.* I. i. 13 The orang is believed not to be adult till the age of from ten to fifteen years.

b. Of persons: characteristically mature in attitude, outlook, etc.; also, befitting or suitable for adults, as opp. to children or youngsters. Cf. GROWN-UP *ppl. a.* 2.

1929 E. BOWEN *Joining Charles* 144 In eight years or so the children will .. really matter. They'll have all sorts of ideas and feelings; they'll be what's called 'adult'. **1930** V. SACKVILLE-WEST *Edwardians* vi. 291 They played the childish games, with the adult game lying behind them. **1945** E. WAUGH *Brideshead Revisited* I. ii. 41 It seems to me that I grew younger daily with each adult habit that I acquired. **1960** *Times* 25 Apr. 4/1 Their [*sc.* a football team's] mental approach was conditioned largely by their adult effervescent captain, Blanchflower. **1976** G. GORDON *100 Scenes from Married Life* 79 Robert called Edward by his first name when confiding in him, when the boy felt that he and his father were discussing adult matters [etc.].

c. Applied *euphem.* to premises or productions ostensibly restricted to adult access, as ***adult cinema***, ***entertainment***, ***movie***, etc.; pornographic, sexually explicit. *N. Amer.*

1958 *New Musical Express* 20 June 11/2 (Advt.), Unusual adult photo sets. S.a.e. Free exciting offer. **1972** *Harper's Bazaar* July 55/3 Nude shows and the misnomered 'adult' cinema can flower. **1977** *Guardian Weekly* 10 July 17 The governor of California could be seen emerging from a restaurant in the middle of one of the gaudier blocks of strip shows, massage parlors and 'adult' entertainments in this city. **1978** *Verbatim* Sept. 5/2 As one child speaking to another in a *New Yorker* cartoon succinctly puts it, 'Adult means "dirty".' .. We have 'adult' movies, books, and magazines. **1984** *Tampa* (Florida) *Tribune* 2 Apr. 16A/3 Rentals for adult videos outstrip purchases by 12 to 1.

d. Of accommodation: designed for the use of elderly persons. Hence also, of or pertaining to the elderly. *N. Amer.*

1968 *Globe & Mail* (Toronto) 13 Jan. 4/5 (Advt.), Forest Hill, 1 bedroom, small adult building. **1984** *Tampa* (Florida) *Tribune* 2 Apr. 6B/5 According to our recently released study of adult home buying habits in Hillsborough County, The Tampa Tribune has strong readership among all types of home buyers.

2. *fig.* Of anything growing, as a plant, a language: Matured, full-grown.

1670 G. H. tr. *Hist. Cardinals* I. II. 55 Heresie (that is but Schism adult). **1752** CHAMBERS *Cycl. Supp.* s.v., Adult plants .. differ from immature ones in that they contain more oil, and less salt. **1838** SIR JAS. MACINTOSH in *Encycl. Brit.* (ed. 7) 294 He can as rarely hazard glaring innovations in diction, at least in an adult and mature language like ours.

B. *sb.*

1. a. A person adult; one who has reached maturity. ***adult baptism***: the baptism of those only who are ecclesiastically adults, or of the years of discretion; opposed to *infant baptism.*

1658 BAXTER *Saving Grace* §4. 26 Neither common nor proper Grace is ordinarily infused (at least into the Adult). **1686** BP. COMPTON *Episc. Lett.* 34 (T.) The Jews, when they admitted adults into their synagogues. **1752** CHAMBERS *Cycl. Supp.* s.v., Several conditions and preparations were required at the baptism of adults. **1797** GODWIN *Enquirer* I. x. 90 Treat the child .. as he would an adult. **1851** H. SPENCER *Soc. Stat.* xvii. §1 They must say what rights are common to children and adults, and why.

b. ***adult illiteracy***, ***illiterate***, ***literacy***; **adult education**, the further education of those over ordinary school age (as in the universities), but commonly used of that provided by local educational authorities, etc.; **adult training centre**, a training centre at which (esp. young mentally handicapped) adults learn practical and other skills.

1851 J. W. HUDSON (*title*) The history of *adult education. **1922** G. M. TREVELYAN *Brit. Hist. in 19th Cent.* 164 The case of adult education received its first stimulus from the Industrial Revolution in the desire of mechanics for general scientific knowledge, and the willingness of the more intelligent part of the middle class to help to supply their demand. **1942** *Spectator* 6 Mar. 244/3 The Cambridgeshire Technical Institute .. is the centre of adult education, both humane and vocational, in Cambridge and district. **1958** *Whitaker's Almanack* 509 Adult Education is carried on in the United Kingdom by universities and university colleges .. local education authorities .. and by a wide variety of voluntary organizations. **1973** A. LOCKE in *Times* 6 Aug. 13/4 Growing concern about the problem of *adult illiteracy in Britain. **1977** *Grimsby Even. Tel.* 14 May 5/7 Craig .. was attending a school for adult illiteracy and had the chance to go to a rehabilitation centre in Leicester. **1973** A. LOCKE in *Times* 6 Aug. 13/5 The dearth of suitable reading books for *adult illiterates. **1961** *Brit. Survey* July 22 Among other notable activities undertaken in the programme are .. mass education, especially the *adult literacy campaign, women's and children's welfare, [etc.]. **1975** *Language for Life* (Dept. Educ. & Sci.) xix. 278 Since 1950 adult literacy programmes in England have provided at least 30,700 adults with instruction for a period of 6 months or one school term. **1962** *Training of Staff of Training Centres for Mentally Subnormal* (Min. of Health) 9 The diploma course for the staff of *adult training centres is also open to both men and women. **1978** *Dumfries & Galloway Standard* 21 Oct. 1/5 Also on the council's priority list is the 39-place adult training centre in Annan.

adultage; perh. two words, *adult age*.

a **1670** HACKET *Life of Williams* I. 75 And was not this come to adultage for tryall after seventeen years vexation in it first and last.

†**aˈdulted**, *ppl. a. Obs. rare.* [ADULT + -ED.] Grown to maturity, matured.

1645 HOWELL *Lett.* 32 (1688) I. 253 Now that we are not onely Adulted, but Ancient Christians, I believe the most acceptable Sacrifice we can send up to Heaven, is Prayer and Praise. **1656** BLOUNT, *Adulted*, grown to full age, come to his full ripeness, force and bigness.

†**aˈdulter.** *Obs.* Forms: 4 **avouter**, 4–5 **avowtier**, **avowter(e**, 5 **avoutere**, 5–6 **advouter**, **advoutour**, **advoutre**, 6–7 **adulter**. Strictly speaking, *avouter* and *adulter* are *two* words, as distinct in form as *chapter* and *capital*, but as the meaning was always identical, and the one form was gradually changed into the other, it is most convenient to treat them together; and so with all their derivatives. [In its oldest form a. OFr. *avoutre* (Pr. *avoutre*, *-ro*) *aöutre*:—L. *adulterum* (etymol. uncertain, perh. f. *ad.* to + *alter* other, different); afterwards assimilated to the L. as *ad-vouter*, *ad-voulter* (MFr. *advoultre*); so as to become at length in form a direct adoption of the L. See also ADULTERER.] An adulterer.

1382 WYCLIF *Luke* xviii. 11, I am not as othere men, raueynouris, vniust, auouters, as also this pupplican [**1388** auoutreris]. *c* **1386** CHAUCER *Friar's T.* 72 Or an Auowtier or a paramour [*other MSS.* auouter, -ir, *Harl.* avouter]. *a* **1420** OCCLEVE *De Reg. Princ.* 64 Who so lithe with his neighbores wyfe Is cursed, and who is ony advoutour. **1440** *Promp. Parv.*, Avowtere (*v.r.* avowtrere, avowterere) *Adulter, Adultera.* **1502** ARNOLD *Chron.* (1811) 175 Noterye and knowen fornicatours or auouteres. **1535** COVERDALE *Luke* xviii. 11 Robbers vnrighteous aduouters or as this publican. **1537** TINDALE *Exp. 1st Ep. John* v, The covetous, the extortioners, the adulter, the backbites. **1545** COVERDALE *Def. Poore Man* Wks. II. 485 God will judge fornicators and advoutres. **1587** *Lyrics* etc. in *Eng. Garner* II. 84 When he first took shipping to Lacedæmon, That adulter I mean. **1645** MILTON *Tetrach.* (1851) 244 It would be strange that he .. should become an adulter by marrying one who is now no other mans wife.

†**adulter**, *v. Obs.* Forms: 4 **avoutre** (**vowtre**), 5 **advouter**, 6 **adulter**. [orig. a. OFr. *avoutre-r*:—*aöutrer*:—L. *adulterā-re* to debauch, to corrupt; f. *adulter*. Subseq. refashioned after L.]

1. *intr.* To commit or practise adultery.

c **1400** *Apol. for Loll.* 87 þey kepe noiþer clene lif, ne wedding, but .. vowtrand, or doing a vowtri. *c* **1550** CHEKE *Matt.* xix. 9 Whosoever loouseth himself from his wijf .. and marieth an oþer, he adultereth, and whosoever marieth yᵉ loousead awai, advoutereth. *c* **1616** B. JONSON *Epigr.* I. 26 He adulters still; his thoughts lie with a whore. **1755** JOHNSON, 'A word not classical.' **1775** ASH ('not much used').

2. *fig.* To corrupt, debase; = ADULTERATE.

1382 WYCLIF *2 Cor.* ii. 17 Auoutrynge þe worde of God. **1598** SYLVESTER *Du Bartas* (1878) 146 With vile Drugs adultering her Face. **1651** CARTWRIGHT *Cert. Relig.* I. 89 Thou, O Luther, corruptest and adulterest the Scriptures.

adulterant (əˈdʌltərənt), *a.* and *sb.* [ad. L. *adulterant-em* pr. pple. of *adulterā-re*: see ADULTER *v.* Prop. an adj., but usually subst.]

A. *sb.* That which adulterates, or is employed to adulterate anything. (J. says 'The person or thing which adulterates'; but it does not seem ever to have been used in Eng. of a person.)

1755 JOHNSON n.q. **1861** *Jrnl. Soc. Arts* IX. 488/2 Mr. John Horsley of Cheltenham has also found copper as an adulterant in the bread and flour of that place. **1881** A. GRIFFITHS *Sc. Gossip* No. 203. 248 By a careful microscopical examination these adulterants can be easily found out.

B. *adj.* Adulterating.

1881 *Philad. Rec.* No. 3470. 2 Adulterant agents and processes rest on no better principle than short measures and false weights.

adulterate (əˈdʌltərət), *ppl. a.* [ad. L. *adulterāt-us*, pa. pple. of *adulterā-re*; see ADULTER *v.*]

1. Defiled, or stained by adultery, either in origin or conduct; adulterous.

1590 SHAKS. *Com. Err.* II. ii. 142, I am possest with an adulterate blot, My bloud is mingled with the crime of lust. **1594** —— *Rich. III*, IV. iii. 69 Th' adulterate Hastings. **1607** TOPSELL *Four-footed Beasts* (1673) 129 And so enjoyed the Adulterate woman for his wife. **1651** W. G. tr. *Cowel's Instit.* 27 Adulterate Issue. **1755** SMOLLETT *Don Quix.* (1803) I. 103 Not .. held as a legitimate member, but some adulterate brood. **1857** H. REED *Lect. Brit. Poets* viii. 272 The low tastes of a worthless and adulterate generation.

2. Of things: Spurious, counterfeit; of base origin, or corrupted by base intermixture.

1592 DANIELL *Compl. Rosamond* 20 Th' adulterate Beauty of a falsed Cheek, Vile stain to Honour and to Women eke. **1599** THYNNE *Animadv.* (1875) 69 Yt wolde be good that Chaucers proper woorkes were distinguyshed from the adulterat. **1622** *Rawleigh's Ghost* 237 Many false and adulterate miracles. **1634** HABINGTON in *Shaks. Cent. Praise* 200 That adult'rate wine Which makes the zeale of Amsterdam divine. **1658** J. R. tr. *Mouffet's Theat. Insectes* 908 Not of good Honey indeed, but of base, adulterate, impure trash. *a* **1680** BUTLER *Rem.* (1759) I. 57 Not only slight what they enjoin, But pay it in adulterate Coin. **1681** HOBBES *Rhetorick* I. xvi. 40 The Judge ought to discern between true and adulterate Justice. *a* **1703** POMFRET *Poet. Wks.* (1833) 113 Adulterate Christs already rise, And dare to' assuage the angry skies. **1721** AUBREY *Misc.* 222 The rest [women] are adulterate in face, but much more in Behaviour. **1724** SWIFT *Drapier Lett.* 3 Wks. 1761 III. 57 Let England be satisfied—and keep their adulterate copper at home. ? **1833** H. COLERIDGE *Poems* II. 387 Purge the silver ore adulterate. **1867** SWINBURNE *Ess. & Stud.* 165 If he has not himself burnt a pinch or two of adulterate incense.

adulterate (əˈdʌltəreɪt), *v.* [f. L. *adulterāt-* ppl. stem of *adulterā-re*; it replaces the earlier ADULTER *v.*]

†**1.** *intr.* To commit or practise adultery (*absol.* or *with* any one). *Obs.* (Repl. by *To commit adultery.*)

1595 SHAKS. *John* III. i. 56 Sh' adulterates hourely with thine Vncle Iohn. **1615** T. Adams *White Devill* 51 'Time' adulterating with the harlot 'Fraud,' begot a brood of 'Noverints.' *a* **1675** LIGHTFOOT *Misc.* 201 Whom, from whom, and with whom we must not kill, steal, nor adulterate. **1698** VANBRUGH *Prov. Wife* III. i. (1730) 153 If I cou'd but catch her adulterating, I might be divorc'd from her. **1860** TH. MARTIN *Horace* 226 And the turtle-dove adulterate with the falcon and the kite.

†**2.** *trans.* To defile by adultery; to debauch. *Obs.*

1613 HEYWOOD *Silver Age* II. i, That durst presume to adulterate Juno's bed. **1649** MILTON *Tenure of Kings* (1847) 234/1 To murder Uriah and adulterate his Wife. **1657** TRAPP *Comm. Esther* ii. 12 II. 119 Their bodies were first adulterated and then vitiated. **1678** MARVELL *Growth of Pop.* Wks. 1875 IV. 257 That..the clergy should, by remaining unmarried, either frustrate human nature if they live chastly, or, if otherwise, adulterate it.

3. Of things: To render spurious or counterfeit; to falsify, corrupt, debase, esp. by the admixture of baser ingredients.

1531 ELYOT *Governour* (1834) 162 He that..adulterateth his coin, with a more base metal. **1532** MORE *Confut. Tindale* Wks. 1557, 636/2 The scripture [they] adulterate and viciate with false gloses. **1611** CORYAT *Crudities* 266 They adulterate their faces. **1673** *Ess. to Revive Educ. Gentlew.* 22 Not truly to adorn, but to adulterate their Bodies. **1677** GALE *Crt. Gentiles* I. Introd. 7 The minds of young Students ..adulterated and corrupted with false Principles. **1711** ADDISON *Spect.* No. 165 ¶1 The present war has.. adulterated our tongue with strange words. **1785** REID *Intell. Powers* II. iii. 249 Philosophy has been, in all ages, adulterated by hypotheses. **1822** IMISON *Sc. & Art* II. 152 They are apt to adulterate the bread sometimes with alum, and also with chalk.

adulterated (əˈdʌltəreɪtɪd), *ppl. a.* [f. prec. + -ED.]

†**1.** Defiled by, tainted with, or guilty of adultery. = ADULTERATE *a.* 1. *Obs.*

1607 TOPSELL *Four-footed Beasts* (1673) 576 An adulterated woman desiring to make away her jealous husband.

2. Corrupted, debased, spurious, counterfeit; *in modern usage*, corrupted by admixture of a baser ingredient. = ADULTERATE *a.* 2.

1610 CARLETON *Jurisd.* 73 Cælestinus..resolued with shame ynough to stand for the adulterated Canon. **1640** FULLER *Joseph's Coat* iii. (1867) 128 Jezebel..stopped up the leaks of age with adulterated complexion, and painted her face. **1675** OTWAY *Alcib.* III. ii. (1735) 36 Your Guards I'll with adulterated wine secure. **1723** BP. NICHOLSON in Ellis *Orig. Lett.* II. 446 IV. 332 Losing all our Gold and Silver in exchange for Halfpence and farthings of an adulterated metal. **1853** KANE *Grinnell Exped.* xvii. (1856) 132 The adulterated breeds of the Danish settlements. **1876** MISS BRADDON *J. Haggard's Dau.* I. 9 No adulterated coffee, no sanded sugar, came from his stores.

adulterately (əˈdʌltərətlɪ), *adv.* [f. ADULTERATE *a.* + -LY².] In an adulterate manner; with an admixture of falseness; corruptly.

a **1619** DONNE *Biathan.* 46 Every Sect will a little corruptly and adulterately call their discipline Naturall Law. **1818** in TODD, and subseq. Dicts.

adulterateness (əˈdʌltərətnɪs). [f. ADULTERATE *a.* + -NESS.] The quality of being adulterate; debased or counterfeit state; spuriousness.

1666 FULLER *Waltham Abb.* (1840) 272 Adultery in men, and adulterateness in money, both hardly reclaimed. **1731** in BAILEY; also in JOHNSON and mod. Dicts.

adulterating (əˈdʌltəreɪtɪŋ), *ppl. a.* [f. ADULTERATE *v.* + -ING².] Debasing, corrupting, making counterfeit or spurious, by base admixture.

1869 LD. ELCHO in H. of Comm. *Daily News* 2 July, Amongst the adulterating articles were the husks of rice.. and acorns.

adulterating (əˈdʌltəreɪtɪŋ), *vbl. sb.* [f. ADULTERATE *v.* + -ING¹.] The action of corrupting, debasing, or falsifying, esp. by spurious admixture.

1610–31 DONNE *Select.* (1840) 176 Almost euery means between God and man, suffers some adulteratings and disguises; but prayer least. **1753** CHAMBERS *Cycl. Supp.*, The adulterating of gems is a curious art. *Mod.* [*gerundial*], Chicory is used for adulterating coffee, beans and iron-rust for adulterating chicory.

adulteration (əˌdʌltəˈreɪʃən). [ad. L. *adulterātiōn-em*, n. of action, f. *adulterā-re*: see ADULTER *v.*]

1. The action of adulterating; corruption or debasement by spurious admixture.

1506 *Ord. Crysten Men* (W. de Worde) Prol. 4 Folowe the pathes and the wayes of theyr adulteracyon. **1603** FLORIO *Montaigne* I. xlvi. (1632) 150 The most obscure houses are most apt unto adulteration, and falsification. **1626** BACON *Sylva* VIII. §798 To make the compound pass for the rich metal simple is an adulteration or counterfeit. **1751** CHAMBERS *Cycl.*, We have laws against the Adulteration of coffee, tea, tobacco, etc. **1823** BYRON *Don Juan* XII. lxiii, Merely innocent flirtation, Not quite adultery, but adulteration. **1859** MILL *Liberty* 171 Public control is admissible for the prevention of fraud by adulteration. **1864** *Weekly Desp.* 14 Aug., Even chicory, we find, does not escape adulteration.

2. The result of adulterating; an adulterated condition, product, or substance.

1655 FULLER *Ch. Hist.* II. 154 Though there be much Adulteration therein, yet I conceive the main Bulk and Body thereof uncorrupted. **1756** BURKE *Vind. Nat. Soc.* Wks. I. 35 Free from the mixture of political adulterations. **1775** ADAIR *Amer. Ind.* 164 Indians, who are free from adulteration by their far-distance from foreigners. **1859** JEPHSON *Brittany* vii. 87 We actually adulterate our adulterations.

adulterator (əˈdʌltəreɪtə(r)). [a. L. *adulterātor* a corrupter; n. of agent f. *adulterā-re*; see ADULTER *v.*]

†**1.** One who defiles by adultery; an adulterer. *Obs.*

1632 HEYWOOD *Iron Age* II. IV. i. 411 The adulterator of his Soueraignes bed.

2. One who falsifies, corrupts, or debases anything by spurious additions or admixtures.

1678 CUDWORTH *Intell. Syst.* 17 The depravers and adulterators of the atomical philosophy. **1870** *Echo* 7 Feb., The Board of Commerce of Delft tried to combat the adulterators, and for that purpose sent real butter of good quality to England.

†**adultered,** *ppl. a. Obs.* [f. ADULTER *v.* + -ED.] Corrupted, debased; adulterate.

1624 CAPT. SMITH *Virginia* (1629) 221 Seeing what paines the Spaniards take to bring them to their adultered faith.

adulterer (əˈdʌltərə(r)). Forms: 4–5 **avou-, avow- -terer, -terere, -tereer, -trer, -trere, -treer;** 4–7 **avouterer;** 5–7 **advou-, advow- -terer, -trer,** etc.; 6 **advoterer, advoulterer, aduoulterer, adoulterer;** 6– **adulterer.** [f. *avouter*, ADULTER *v.* + -ER¹, term. of male agent. Cf. rare OFr. *avoutrier* and fem. *avoltreresse*. (For the gradual change of the word under L. influence from *avouterer* to *adulterer*, see ADULTER *sb.* and *v.*) Already in Wyclif interchanged with the earlier *avouter*, and in the middle of 17th c. *adulter-er* (in its various forms), more distinctly expressing the agent, displaced *adulter* and its forms. Cf. *cater-er, fripper-er, sorcer-er*, and see -ER¹.]

1. One who commits adultery; who violates a marriage-bed, whether his own or another's.

c **1370** WYCLIF *Agst. Begging Friers* (1608) 53 If there be anie cursed Jurour, extortioner or avowtrer. **1382** —— *Ps.* xlix. 18 With avoutereres thi porcioun thou leidist. —— *Deut.* xxii. 22 Eyther shal die, that is the auowtreer and the auowtresse [**1388** auowter and auowtresse]. *c* **1386** CHAUCER *Pars. T.* 805 (Petw. MS.) þise aduoutrers breken þe temple of god spiritually [*other MSS.* avowtiers, auoutyeris, aduoutres]. *c* **1449** PECOCK *Repr.* I. xviii. 103 Summe ben founde.. to be greet lecchouris, summe to be avoutreris. **1509** BARCLAY *Ship of Fooles* (1570) 65 Keping the dore while the auoutrer is within. **1513** DOUGLAS *Æneis* XI. vi. 106 The sle adultrare occupiis his stede. **1535** COVERDALE *Job* xxiv. 15 The aduouterer, that wayteth for the darcknesse. **1541** BARNES *Wks.* 1573, 319/1 Certayne men doe affirme those men to bee aduoulterers. **1549** *Prayer-Bk., Exhort. at Comm.*, If any here be a blasphemer, aduouterer [**1552** adulterer], or bee in malyce or envie. *c* **1585** PILKINGTON *Wks.* 1841, 642 And called him proud, advoterer, a thief and heretic. **1611** BIBLE *Heb.* xiii. 5 Whoremongers and adulterers [*Wycl.* auoutreris (auouteris), *Tind.* advoutrars, *Cranm.* aduoutrers, *Genev.*, *Rhem.* aduouterers] God will judge. **1629** COKE *1st Pt. of Instit.* 72 b, If shee goeth willingly with or to the auowtrer. **1653** BAXTER *Chr. Conc.* 70 Hereticks, Advouterers, Church-robbers. **1686** DRYDEN *Hind. & P.* III. 1216 Reeking from the stews, adulterers come. **1708** *Termes de la Ley* 68 Avowterer is an Adulterer with whom a married woman continues in Adultery. **1879** FARRAR *St. Paul* II. 306 (transl. *Sueton.*) This husband or adulterer of three queens [Felix].

b. Also of a woman = ADULTERESS.

c **1550** CHEKE *Matt.* v. 32 Whosoever divorceth his wife, except it be for fornications cause, doth mak her an adulterer. **1557** N. T. (Genev.) *Rom.* vii. 3 She shal be called an adulterer.

†**2.** One who adulterates, corrupts, or debases; an ADULTERATOR. *Obs. rare.*

1650 URQUHART *Rabelais* (1807) III. 295 Usurers, apothecaries, cheats, coiners, and adulterers of wares.

adulteress (əˈdʌltərɪs, -trɪs). Forms: 4–5 **avoutres, avoutresse, avowtresse,** 6 **advoutrice,** 6–7 **advoutresse, advouteresse,** 7 **adultresse, adulteresse,** 8– **adulteress,** *occ.* **adultress.** [The form in *-trice* imitates Fr.; but the earliest form is a. OFr. *avotresse, avoutresse* f. *avoutre*; cf. *maître, maîtresse*, and see -ESS. It is thus, formally, the feminine of ADULTER, not of the later *adulter-er.*] A woman that commits adultery.

1382 WYCLIF *Lev.* xx. 10 Thurȝ deth dye both the lecchour and the auowtres [**1388** bothe auowter and auowtresse]. **1502** ARNOLD *Chron.* (1811) 275 Yf ony weddyd woman bee aduoutrice. **1548** HALL *Chron.* (1809) 365 To pretende that his awne mother was an avoutresse. **1553** UDALL *Rois. Dois.* (1869) 81 Thou didst helpe the aduoutresse that she might be amended. **1567** JEWEL *Def. of Apol.* (1611) 176 She is twice an Aduouteresse. **1611** SHAKS. *Wint. T.* II. i. 78 But be't knowne..Shee's an Adultresse. **1611** BIBLE *James* iv. 4 Ye adulterers and adulteresses. **1625** BACON *Ess.* xix. 303 This kinde of danger, is then to be feared..that they be aduoutresses. **1626** MASSINGER *Rom. Actor* I. iii, Bringing on the stage a loose adulteress. **1697** DRYDEN *Virgil* (J.) Helen's rich attire; From Argos by the fam'd adult'ress brought. **1784** COWPER *Task* III. 64 Th' adultress! what a theme for angry verse. **1845** WHEWELL *Elem. Morality* IV. v. §728 The adulteress was to be repudiated and otherwise punished.

adulterine (əˈdʌltəraɪn), *a.* and *sb.* [ad. L. *adulterin-us* born of adultery, spurious; f. *adulter*. Used first in the fig. sense.]

A. *adj.*

1. Born of adultery.

1751 CHAMBERS *Cycl.* Adulterine children are more odious than the illegitimate offspring of single persons. **1875** MAINE *Hist. Inst.* ii. 53 Matthew O'Neill was an adulterine bastard.

2. Of or relating to adultery.

1865 *Pall Mall G.* 25 Aug. 9/1 The demand for homicidal and adulterine fiction is enormous.

3. *fig.* Spurious, counterfeit; due to adulteration.

1542 BECON *Potation for Lent* Wks. 1843, 87 To try the adulterine, feigned, and false, from the sincere, germane, and true learning. **1546** *Suppl. of Commons* 92 Forget not your owne youthe, when these adulterine trees were too stronge for you. **1621** BURTON *Anat. Mel.* II. iv. I. i. (1676) 226/2 A knave Apothecary..may doe infinite harme, by.. adulterine drugs, bad mixtures. *a* **1667** JER. TAYLOR *Serm.* (1678) 182 As adulterine Metals retain the Lustre and Colour of Gold, but not the Value. **1865** KINGSLEY *Herew.* xx. (in *Gd. Wds.* 417/2) The French look on us monk-made knights as spurious and adulterine, unworthy of the name of knight.

4. Illegal, illegitimate, unlicensed; *esp.* in *Eng. Hist.* 'adulterine' castles, guilds.

1640 BP. HALL *Episc. by Div. Right* II. §8. 130 It is enough that it is adulterine, for that it is not named by the Apostles. **1753** CHAMBERS *Cycl. Supp.*, *Adulterine* marriages, in St. Augustine's sense, denote second marriages, contracted after a divorce. **1776** ADAM SMITH *W.N.* (1869) I. I. x. 130 When any particular class of artificers or traders thought proper to act as a corporation or guild without a charter, such were called adulterine guilds. **1829** HEATH *Grocers' Comp.* (1869) 39 Upon the Pipe Roll of the 26th Henry 2nd is a return of the adulterine Gilds in the city of London. **1851** TURNER *Dom. Archit.* II. Introd. 23 The erection of numerous fortresses, adulterine castles they were termed, as built without license from the crown. **1875** STUBBS *Const. Hist.* I. x. 333 The adulterine or unlicensed castles, by whomsoever erected..are to be destroyed.

B. *sb.* An illegitimate child. *rare.*

1798 H. COLEBROOKE *Hindu Law* (1801) II. 480 'Cunda' is explained, by Amera, an adulterine begotten during the husband's life-time.

†**a'dultering,** *ppl. a. Obs.* [f. ADULTER *v.* + -ING².] Corrupting, debasing, adulterating.

1599 MARSTON *Scourge of Vill.* I. iii. 185 Shall cock-horse, fat-pauncht Milo staine whole stocks Of well-borne soules, with his adultering spots?

adulterism. *rare.* [f. ADULTERIZE; see -ISM.]

1870 POWER *Handy-book ab. Books* 91 (quoting O. HAMST *Martyr to Bibliog.*), *Adulterism*, name altered or adulterated, as d'Alton (Dalton), de Foe (Defoe).

adulterize (əˈdʌltəraɪz), *v. arch.* [f. ADULTER *sb.* + -IZE. Cf. *tyrannize*, etc.] To commit adultery.

1611 COTGR., *Adulterer* (Fr.), to commit adultery, to play the adulterer, to adulterize it. **1625** F. MARKHAM *Booke of Honour* 190 Examine the Decalogue in the old Law..that saith 'Doe not adulterize.' **1643** MILTON *Divorce* II. xvii. 152 If the wife attempted..such things as gave open suspicion of adulterizing. **1871** F. J. FURNIVALL pref. to *Laneham's Lett.* 71 Other spiritual fathers..haunt ale-houses, adulterize with women.

adulterous (əˈdʌltərəs), *a.* Also 5–6 **advoutrous,** 6 **advout-, advoulterous.** [f. ADULTER + -OUS, after anal. of words ad. Fr. or L. in *-ous.*]

1. Pertaining to, or characterized by the practice of adultery.

1470–85 MALORY *Morte Arthur* (1634) I. 197 Knights that be advoutrous or lecherous, shall not be happy nor fortunate in the wars. **1526** TINDALE *Matt.* xii. 39 The evyll and advoutrous generacion seketh a signe [*Cranm.*, *Genev.*, *Rhem.* adulterous, **1611** adulterous.] **1535** COVERDALE *Hosea* iii. 1 Go yet thy waye & wowe an aduouterous woman. **1549** OLDE tr. *Erasm. on Ephes.* Prol. II. 105 Blasphemous swearyng; advoulterous lyving. **1606** SHAKS. *Ant. & Cl.* III. vi. 94 Th' adulterous Anthony, most large in his abhominations. **1667** MILTON *P.L.* IV. 753 By thee [wedded love] adulterous lust was driven from men Among the bestial herds to range. **1814** SOUTHEY *Roderick* xx. Wks. IX. 179 Efface the shame Of their adulterous birth. **1841** EMERSON *Meth. Nat.* (1875) II. 233 It is the office..of this age to annul that adulterous divorce. *Mod.* The offspring of this adulterous union.

†**2.** Born in adultery, adulterine. *Obs.*

a **1593** MARLOWE *Dido* III. ii. 828 Lustful Jove and his adulterous child. **1607** TOPSELL *Serpents* (1653) 807 They were adulterous, and the children of strangers.

3. Pertaining to, or characterized by, adulteration; spurious, counterfeit, adulterate. *arch.*

1567 MAPLET *Greene Forest* 21 All adulterous and counterfayted Mettals it doth betray. **1586** FERNE *Blazon of Gentrie* 238, I meane not only that they be vnperfect, but also adulterous and dishonorable. **1635** F. WHITE *Treat. Sabbath* Ep. Ded. 20 We haue justly rejected all counterfeit and adulterous Traditions. **1743** *Lond. & Country Brewer* (ed. 2) II. 127 There are Thousands in the Nation..that are guilty of this adulterous Part of Brewing. **1771** SMOLLETT *Humph. Clinker* 806 An adulterous mixture, brewed up of nauseous ingredients. **1808** WILFORD *Sacr. Isles* in *Asiat. Res.* VIII. 252 He took out one or two leaves and substituted others with an adulterous legend.

adulterously (əˈdʌltərəslɪ), *adv.* [f. ADULTEROUS + -LY[2].] In an adulterous manner.

1599 SANDYS *Eur. Spec.* (1632) 41 Children adulterously begotten. **1643** MILTON *On Divorce* II. ii. (1847) 138/1 A patent to wed another adulterously. **1723** PRIDEAUX *Mahomet* 152 (T.) No man should be allowed adulterously to take to wife her that is at the same time the wife of another. **1922** JOYCE *Ulysses* 718 The matrimonial violator ..had not been outraged by the adulterous violator of the adulterously violated.

adultery (əˈdʌltərɪ). Forms: 4–5 **avowter, avowtrie, -tri, -tery, avouterye;** 4–6 **avoutrie, -try;** 5 **avutrie, avoutri, -trye, -terie, avowtrye; adultery, -trye** (only in Sc. and north. writers); 5–6 **avoutrye, -tery, -terye, advoultrye,** 5–7 **advowtry, -trie, advoutrie, -try,** 6 **advoutri, -treye, adoutry, aduoultrie, -try, adoultry,** 6–7 **adultry, -trie, -terie,** 6– **adultery.** [a. OFr. *avouterie, avoutrie*, earlier *aöuterie, aülterie*, n. of condition f. *avoutre, aöutre*:—L. *adulter*, see -Y; found alongside of *avoutire*, earlier *aöutire, aültere*:—L. *adultĕrium*, occas. also in Eng. as *avowter*. In 14th c. Fr. a learned form *adultère* was formed afresh on L. *adulterium*, and gradually superseded the popular *avoutire* and *avouterie*; under the same influence the Eng. *avoutrie* was progressively refashioned as *advoutrie* or *aduoutrie, aduoultrie, adoultry, adultry, adultery*, thus ending in a direct Eng. repr. of *adulterium*, and practically a distinct word from *avoutrie*, though connected with it by every kind of intermediate form. This latinized type had also been used by Scotch and northern writers as early as 1430. *Advowtry* survived to 1688.]

1. Violation of the marriage bed; the voluntary sexual intercourse of a married person with one of the opposite sex, whether unmarried, or married to another (the former case being technically designated ***single***, the latter ***double adultery***).

1366 MAUNDEV. 249 ȝif ony man or woman be taken in Avowtery or Fornycacyoun, anon thei sleen him. *c* **1370** WYCLIF *Agst. Begging Friers* (1608) 31 Fryars suffren mightie men, fro yeare to yeare, live in avowtrie. **1386** CHAUCER *Parson's T.* 766 Thilke stynkynge synne of lecherie that men clepe auowtrie (*v.r.* avoutrie, auouterie, advoutrie[2], aduoutre). **1400** *Apol. for Loll.* 78 If þe first woman may not proue her contract, þan þe secound schal be his wif, bi resoun of avowter. *c* **1418** *Pol. Poems* (1859) II. 247 So overset with avutrie. *c* **1425** WYNTOUN *Cron.* VI. ii. 87 Bot a wykkdy wyf had he Ðat levyd in-til Adultery. *c* **1460** *Cov. Myst.* (1841) 10 A woman.. The whiche was taken in adultrye. **1485** RICHARD III in *Paston Lett.* 883 III. 317 Doughter unto Dame Katryne Swynford and of her in double Avoutry gottyn. **1491** CAXTON *How to Die* 6 The woman that was taken in aduoultrye. **1525** LD. BERNERS *Froissart* xliii. II. 139 She was but a bastarde, and borne in aduoutrye. **1533** ELYOT *Castel of Helth* III. xii. 67 Hym, which had committed adoutry with his mayster's wyfe. **1541** BARNES *Wks.* 1573, 187/2 That you shal depose a kyng, bycause hee lyueth in adoultry. **1570** ASCHAM *Scholem.* (1863) 81 Knightes that do kill..and commit fowlest aduoulteres. **1611** BIBLE *John* viii. 4 This woman was taken in adultery, in the very act. [*Wycl.* avoutri, *Tind.* advoutry, *Cranm.* aduoutry, *Genev., Rhem.* aduoutrie, *Gen.* 1590 adulterie.] **1641** W. CARTWRIGHT *Ordinary* IV. v. (1651) 75 There shall be no Advowtry in my ward. **1648** HERRICK *To his Book* Wks. 1859, 409 She'l runne to all adulteries. **1660** R. COKE *Elem. Power & Subj.* 194 Deadly sin, of Fornication, Avowtry, and such like. **1677** BAXTER *Let.* in *Answ. Dodwell* 114, I heard, when I was young, of one, or two, that for Adultery stood in a White Sheet in the Church. **1688** *Pol. Ballads* (1860) I. 265 As long as you've pence, y' need scruple no offence, For murder, advoutery, treason. **1835** THIRLWALL *Greece* I. viii. 327 Adultery was long unknown at Sparta.

b. Extended in Scripture, to unchastity generally; and by various theologians opprobriously used of any marriages of which they disapproved, as of a widower, a nun, a Christian with a Jewess, etc. (***interpretative adultery***). Also *fig.* in Script. to giving the affections to idols, idol-worship; and in *Eccl. writers* to the enjoyment by any one of a benefice during the life-time of the legal incumbent, or to the translation of a bishop from one see to another (***spiritual adultery***). See Chambers *Cycl. Supp.* 1753, s.v.

1388 WYCLIF *Jer.* iii. 9 Bi liȝtnesse of hir fornicacioun sche defoulide the erthe, and dide auowtrie with a stoon, and with a tree. **1590** BIBLE (Genev.) *Matt.* v. 28 Whosoever looketh on a woman to lust after her, hath committed adulterie with her already in his heart. **1611** BIBLE *Jer.* iii. 9 Shee defiled the land, and committed adultery with stones and with stockes. **1753** CHAMBERS *Cycl. Supp.* s.v. A kind of second marriage, which was esteemed a degree of adultery. **1872** FREEMAN *Hist. Ess.* (ed. 2) 17 He is rebuked by Saint Dunstan who pronounces the marriage to be mere adultery.

¶ 'Used in ancient customs for the punishment or fine imposed for that offence, or the privilege of prosecuting for it.' Chambers, *Cycl. Supp.* 1753, whence in subseq. Encyclopædias and Dicts. But Spelman, who is quoted for it, gives it only (and that erroneously) as a use of the L. *adulterium*.

†**2.** Adulteration, debasement, corruption. *Obs.*

1609 B. JONSON *Epicene* I. i, Such sweet neglect more taketh me, Than all th' Adulteries of Art. **1673** *Lady's Calling* II. iii. §20. 92 Nor must she think to cure this by any the little adulteries of art: she may buy beauty, and yet can never make it her own.

adulthood (əˈdʌlthʊd). [f. ADULT *a.* + -HOOD.] = ADULTNESS.

c **1870** COWDEN CLARKE in *Two Gent. Verona* (ed. Rolfe 1882) 26 *Twelfth Night*..was written in the full vigour and adulthood of his [Shakspere's] conformation.

adultly (ˈædʌltlɪ, əˈdʌltlɪ), *adv.* [f. ADULT *a.* + -LY[2].] In a manner indicative of adultness; in adult fashion.

1957 *New Yorker* 19 Jan. 24/3 We noticed a responsible-looking man and two small, adultly dressed boys studiously proceeding from work to work. **1958** *Spectator* 22 Aug. 246/2 A few little girls seemed adultly surprised at the yaws-stricken children photographed on the UNICEF stand. **1969** R. WOLLHEIM *Family Romance* 177 If only I could think like my father, adultly. **1973** M. AMIS *Rachel Papers* 32 Rachel arrived in a group of four—what looked like a random car-load—but stayed alone by the door, arms folded adultly.

adultness (əˈdʌltnɪs). [f. ADULT *a.* + -NESS.] The state of being adult; complete development.

1754–64 SMELLIE *Midwifery* II. 58 The gums being cut the teeth appeared in the adultness of those in grown persons.

†**aˈdumber, -bre,** *v. Obs. rare*[−1]. [a. MFr. *adumbre-r, adombre-r*, refash. of OFr. *aümbrer, aombrer*:—L. *adumbrā-re* to shadow forth, to overshadow: see ADUMBRATE.] To overshadow, obscure.

1535 STEWART *Cron. Scotl.* 23663 II. 118 The cruell dartis with mony awfull ganȝe.. The dais licht adumbrit.

†**aˈdumbered,** *ppl. a. Obs.* [f. prec. + -ED.] Overshadowed.

1609 J. DAVIES *Holy Roode* (1876) 26 (D.) Serene thy woe-adumbred front, sweet Saint.

adumbral (əˈdʌmbrəl), *a.* [f. L. *ad* to + *umbra* shade + -AL[1]; with reference to *adumbrāre*, ADUMBRATE *v.* 4.]

1. Of overshadowing nature; shady.

1845 *Blackw. Mag.* LVII. 246 This circular adumbral and pluvial roofing had to be adapted to the female head.

2. *Zool.* A shortened equivalent of ADUMBRELLAR.

1881 E. R. LANKESTER in *Jrnl. Microsc. Sc.* Jan. 124 The cells of the adumbral walls are like those of the ring-canals.

adumbrant (əˈdʌmbrənt), *a. rare*[−0]. [ad. L. *adumbrant-em* pr. pple. of *adumbrā-re*; see ADUMBRATE.] Shadowing forth, representing in outline.

1731 in BAILEY, vol. II. Also in JOHNSON and mod. Dicts.

adumbrate (əˈdʌmbreɪt), *v.* [f. L. *adumbrāt-* ppl. stem of *adumbrā-re* to overshadow, to shade, to shadow out; f. *ad* to + *umbrā-re* to shade.]

†**1.** To shade (a picture), to represent with due light and shade so as to complete what has been sketched or delineated. (So in L.) *Obs.*

1599 NASHE *Lenten Stuffe* (1871) 113 Whose resplendent laud and honour, to delineate and adumbrate to the ample life, were a work that would, etc.

2. To represent the shadow of (anything), to draw or figure in outline; to outline; to sketch; to give a faint indication of.

1641 FRENCH *Distillation* Ep. Ded. A iiij b, I crave leave to adumbrate something of that art which I know you will be willing..to promote. **1692** BP. OF ELY *Answ. Touchstone* 223 Which is not expressly prepounded..but adumbrated and obscurely indicated. **1817** JAS. MILL *Brit. India* II. v. ix. 706 Its duties were very ill defined, or rather not defined at all, but only adumbrated.

3. *fig.* To represent a substance by its 'shadow' or emblem; to shadow forth, to typify; hence, to foreshadow, prefigure, as 'coming events cast their shadows before.'

1581 MARBECK *Bk. of Notes* 147 Abolished by the glorie of Christ, whose death and passion they [burnt offerings] did adumbrate. **1611** J. GUILLIM *Heraldrie* xxvi. 181 The Griffon..will neuer be taken aliue; wherein hee doth adumbrate or rather liuely set forth the propertie of a valorous Souldier. **1637** GILLESPIE *Eng. Pop. Cerem.* I. viii. 28 All Rites..our Holy-dayes among the rest, serve onely to adumbrate and shadow foorth something. **1677** GALE *Crt. of Gentiles* I. II. vi. 72 Noah..is adumbrated to us, not only in Saturne, but also in Prometheus. **1872** H. MACMILLAN *True Vine* i. 32 What qualities in Christ are adumbrated by the vine?

4. To overshadow; to shade, obscure.

1670 G. H. tr. *Hist. Cardinals* II. iii. 180 The lustre of his good qualities is in some measure adumbrated by certain defects. **1681** *Trial of S. Colledge* 41 To adumbrate our Actions, for fear we should be discovered. **1835** MARRYAT *Jac. Faithf.* v. 18 [He] was kneeling at the bedside, his nose adumbrating the coverlid of my bed. **1860** J. P. KENNEDY *Horse Shoe R.* v. 55 The building was adumbrated in the shelter of a huge willow.

adumbrated (əˈdʌmbreɪtɪd), *ppl. a.* [f. prec. + -ED.] Shadowed forth; represented faintly or in outline.

1706 PHILLIPS, *Adumbrated*, shadowed, resembled. **1877** CAIRD *Philos. Kant* iv. 64 The vaguely adumbrated idealism of the Siris.

adumbration (ædʌmˈbreɪʃən). [ad. L. *adumbrātiōn-em*, n. of action, f. *adumbrā-re*; see ADUMBRATE.]

†**1.** Shading in painting. *Obs.*

1531 ELYOT *Governor* (1580) 207 Alexander..came to the shop of Apelles..reasoned with him of lynes, adumbrations, proportions and other lyke things perteining to imagery.

2. Representation in outline, sketching; and *concr.* an outline, a sketch; a shadowy figure; a faint or slight sketch or description.

1552 HULOET, Adumbration or light description of a house side or front, where the lyue [? line] do answer to the compasse and centrye of euerye parte. *Scenographia.* **1586** *Let. to Earl Leycester* 2 Her inward vertues, whereof it is impossible for mee to make the least adumbration. **1656** JEANES *Fulnesse of Christ* 14 Painters, whose first rude or imperfect draught is termed a shadow, or adumbration, upon which they lay afterwards the lively colours. **1677** GALE *Crt. of Gentiles* II. III. 90 The Pagan Philosophers had some kind of..dark adumbration or shadowy description of the first principles of Nature. **1872** MIVART *Anat.* 290 The only faint adumbration of such organs, outside Man's Class, is to be found in Pigeons. **1876** LOWELL *Among my Bks.* II. 43 Nor capable of being told unless by far-off hints and adumbrations. **1880** H. JAMES *Benvalio* I. 346 Like the dim adumbration of the darker half of the lunar disk. **1882** *Times* 4 May, The Prime Minister's adumbration of measures.

3. Symbolic representation typifying or prefiguring the reality.

1622 FOTHERBY *Atheom.* 27 Which three Arts haue apparently an adumbration of the Trinity. **1650** GREGORY *Serm. on Resurr.* 60 Death as it is here..under the type and adumbration of sleep. **1748** HARTLEY *Observ. Man* I. iii. §1. 319 An Emblem, or Adumbration of our Passage through the Present Life. **1858** E. H. SEARS *Athanasia* vii. 58 The reality of which earth is only a dull and feeble adumbration.

4. *Her.* An outline figure.

1610 GUILLIM *Heraldrie* II. iii. 42 Adumbration, or Transparency, is a cleere exemption of the substance of the Charge, or thing borne, in such sort as that there remaineth nothing thereof to be discerned, but the naked and bare proportion of the outward lineaments thereof.

5. Overshadowing; shade, obscuration.

1653 MANTON *Expos. James* i. 17 in *Wks.* 1871 IV. 110 Stars, according to their different light and posture, have divers adumbrations. **1658** SIR T. BROWNE *Gard. Cyrus* II. 549 The sight being..circumscribed between long parallels and the ἐπισκιασμὸς and adumbration from the branches. **1863** LONGF. *Wayside Inn* Interl. III. 9 Above them..its awful adumbration passed, A luminous shadow, vague and vast.

adumbrative (əˈdʌmbrətɪv), *a.* [f. L. *adumbrāt-* ppl. stem of *adumbrā-re* (see ADUMBRATE) + -IVE.] Having the attribute of shadowing forth, faintly indicating, figuring, or typifying.

1837 CARLYLE *Fr. Rev.* (1872) II. I. x. 44 Mute monuments pathetically adumbrative of much. **1865** —— *Fredk. Gt.* V. XIV. iii. 178 'Bob Monopoly, the late Tallyman' (adumbrative for Walpole, late Prime Minister). **1858** KITTO *Bible Illustr.* Morn. Ser. III. 149 They are remarkably typical or adumbrative of that larger and greater work of God in the soul of man.

adumbratively (əˈdʌmbrətɪvlɪ), *adv.* [f. prec. + -LY[2].] In an adumbrative manner; so as to represent or indicate in a shadowy way.

1865 CARLYLE *Fredk. Gt.* V. XIV. iii. 178 England, or, as it is adumbratively called, 'the Manor of St. James's.'

adumbrellar (ˌædʌmˈbrɛlə(r)), *a. Zool.* [mod. f. L. *ad* to, at + UMBRELLA, applied to the disc of *Acalepha*, + -AR. Cf. *adactinal, adoral.*] In sea-blubbers: Pertaining to the upper surface of the *velum* or marginal ridge, which is turned towards the 'umbrella' or disc, in opposition to the *abumbrellar* or lower surface.

1881 E. R. LANKESTER in *Jrnl. Microsc. Sc.* Jan. 131 The ectoderm of the adumbrellar surface of the velum.

adun(e, early form of ADOWN.

†**adunate,** *ppl. a. Obs. rare*[−1]. [ad. L. *adūnāt-us* pa. pple. of *adūnā-re* to unite; f. *ad* to + *ūnāre* to make one, f. *ūnus* one.] United, joined in one.

1470 HARDING *Chron.* cxlvii, Two semely princes together adunate [*v.r.* adioynate].

adunation (ædjuːˈneɪʃən). [ad. L. *adūnātiōn-em* n. of action f. *adūnā-re* to unite: see prec.] Union or combination into one.

1551 CRANMER *Answ. to Gardiner* 352 (T.) Before the adunation in the Virgin's womb, the godhead and manhood were two natures. **1612** WOODALL *Surg. Mate* Wks. 1653, 90 The cure is not so safe to sew it up..because his adunation is uncertain. **1680** BOYLE *Scept. Chymist.* 94 The cold does not cause any Real Union or Adunation of these Bodies. **1881** OVERTON *Wm. Law* 275 This analogy—one might almost say this adunation—of the spiritual and the natural worlds.

adunc (əˈdʌŋk), *a.* Also 7 **adunque**. [ad. L. *adunc-us* bent in; f. *ad* to + *uncus* adj. hooked, sb. a hook.] Hooked; bent inward.

1626 BACON *Sylva* §238 Parrets have an adunque Bill. **1697** EVELYN *Numism.* ix. 297 The Nose..if Aquiline or Adunc. **1872** M. COLLINS *Pr. Clarice* I. v. 74 The astute bill-discounter, adunc of nose.

†**aˈduncate**, *ppl. a. Obs. rare*⁻¹. [ad. med.L. *aduncāt-us* pa. pple. of *aduncā-re*; f. L. *ad* to + *uncā-re* to hook: see ADUNC.] Bent inward; hooked; = ADUNCOUS.

1661 R. LOVELL *Anim. & Min.* The nailes are in..those of the rapacious aduncate.

aduncate (əˈdʌŋkeɪt), *v.* [f. med.L. *aduncāt-* ppl. stem of *aduncā-re*; see prec.] To curve inward. (Cited only in pa. pple.)

1823 LOCKHART *Reg. Dalton* v. iii. (1842) 302 You shall see the son of a London tailor strut past..with a beak as extravagantly aduncated as if, etc.

aduncity (əˈdʌnsɪtɪ). ? *Obs.* [ad. L. *aduncitas* n. of state, f. *adunc-us* ADUNC; see -ITY.] 'Crookedness; flexure inward; hookedness.' J.

1589 [HALLIWELL quotes RIDER]. **1626** COCKERAM, *Aduncity*, hookednes, crookednesse. **1714** [ARBUTHNOT & POPE] *M. Scriblerus* Pope's Wks. 1824 VII. 71 The aduncity of the pounces and beaks of the hawks, is the cause of the great and habitual immorality of those animals.

aduncous (əˈdʌŋkəs), *a.* [f. L. *adunc-us* ADUNC + -OUS.] Hooked, bent inward, incurved.

1656 BLOUNT *Gloss.*, *Aduncous*, crooked downwards, hooked. **1713** DERHAM *Physico-Theol.* IV. xv. 257 They are characteristics of Rapacious birds, to have Aduncous Bills and Talons. **1869** GROOM-NAPIER *Gloss. Bot. Terms* 521, *Aduncous*, crooked or hooked.

†**aˈdunct**, *a. Obs.* A badly formed variant of ADUNC, ADUNQUE, simulating the form of a pa. pple.

1635 HEYWOOD *Hierarchie* III. 157 Of Democritus his Atomes, some are light..some Cornered, others 'Adunct.'

adune, var. of ADIN *v. Obs.* to stun with noise.

†**aduˈnite**, *v. Obs.* [f. L. *ad* to + UNITE, f. L. *ūnī-re*. There was no L. *adūnīre*, but *adūnāre*: see ADUNATE.] To unite or join to.

1662 J. CHANDLER *Helmont's Oriatrike* 256 It might be adunited within the Cup-board.

†**aduˈniting**, *vbl. sb. Obs.* [f. prec. + -ING¹.] Uniting together.

1662 J. CHANDLER *Helmont's Oriatrike* 67 The water doth sustain as much pressing together, going to ruine, and aduniting, as great Stones or Mettalls do overpoyse the water in weight.

†**aˈdure**, *v. Obs.* [ad. L. *adūr-ĕre* to burn, scorch; f. *ad* to + *ūr-ĕre* to burn.] *trans.* or *absol.* To burn completely, to calcine; to scorch, parch.

c **1420** *Pallad. on Husb.* II. 354 And askes with, the heete apart to putte Of dounge indoon, lest it adure and lette. **1599** A. M. tr. *Gabelhouer's Bk. Physic* §3, 22/1 Flea a little Mouse, take the intestines..adure them in a piptken. **1620** VENNER *Via Recta* vi. 93 It adureth the blood. **1626** BACON *Sylva* §319 Such a degree of Heat..doth Mellow, and not Adure.

†**aˈdurent**, *ppl. a. Obs. rare*⁻¹. [ad. L. *adūrent-em* pr. pple. of *adūr-ĕre*: see prec.] Burning, hot and dry.

1626 BACON *Sylva* §460 Nitre, the spirit of which is less Adurent than salt.

adurol (ˈædjʊərɒl, ˈædjʊrɒl). [G.] A haloid substitution product of hydroquinone, used as a photographic developer.

1899 *Brit. Jrnl. Photogr.* 3 Mar. 139/1 Adurol is a new photographic developer, said to be obtained from hydroquinone by a patented process. **1912** G. MARTIN *Industr. Chem.*, *Org.* 659 'Adurol' developer consists of the stock solutions: (A) 10 g. adurol + 80 g. cryst. sod. sulphite + 500 c.c. H_2O; (B) 60 g. K_2CO_3 + 500 c.c. H_2O.

†**adush**, *v. Obs.* [f. A- *pref.* 1 + DUSH.] To cause to fall heavily, to precipitate.

c **1220** *Hali Meid.* 41 Heo þet tus aduste hire heuenliche fader adun.

a-dusk (əˈdʌsk), *adv.* and *pred. a.*, prop. *phr.* [A *prep.*¹ in + DUSK *sb.* after analogy of *alight*, *afire*.] In dusk, in gloom; gloomy, dark.

1856 MRS. BROWNING *Aurora Leigh* I. 502 You wish to die and leave the world a-dusk For others.

adust (əˈdʌst), *ppl. a.* [ad. L. *adūst-us* pa. pple. of *adūr-ĕre*: see ADURE. A favourite term of the medical writers of the middle ages; see sense 3, in which it was found in most of the mod. languages. The Fr. *aduste* (15th c.) may therefore be the immediate source of the Eng.]

1. Scorched, seared; burnt up, calcined; dried up with heat, parched. Also *fig.*

1550 BALE *Eng. Votaries* II. 41 b, Lyke an adust conscyenced hypocrite. **1623** ROWLANDSON *Bless. in Blasting* 40 Being burnt, or made adust, by some extraordinary heat of the sunne. **1637** NABBE *Microcosm.* in Dodsl. IX. 124 Provoke me no more; I am adust with rage. **1667** MILTON *P.L.* XII. 634 With torrid heat, And vapour as the Lybian air adust. **1684** tr. *Bonet's Merc. Compit.* VI. 179 The Vulgar now and then cure putrid Fevers by taking of adust Wine. **1755** HALES *Distillation* in *Phil. Trans.* XLIX. 327 Its more disagreeable adust taste. **1854** DE QUINCEY *Revolt. Tartars* Wks. IV. 152 The camels..these arid and adust creatures. **1857** *Fraser's Mag.* LVI. 69 African islands ..whose desolate and adust beauty sets the imagination all on fire.

2. Of colour: Brown, as if scorched by fire, or by the sun; sunburnt.

1596 NASHE *Saffron Walden* 110 Of an adust swarth chollericke dye. **1601** HOLLAND *Pliny* (1634) I. 28 Which stone is shewed at this day..carrying a burnt and adust colour. **1678** *Lond. Gaz.* mcccxxv/4 One Mary, a Lecestershire woman..complection somewhat adust..Run away from, etc. *c* **1760** SMOLLETT *Ode to Indep.* 67 Arabia's scorching sands he crossed..Conductor of her Tribes adust. **1845** FORD *Handbk. Spain* I. ii. 202 Here everything is adust and tawny, from man to his wife, his horse, his ox or his ass.

3. Applied to a supposed state of the body and its humours, much spoken of in the earlier days of medicine, its alleged symptoms being dryness of the body, heat, thirst, black or burnt colour of the blood, and deficiency of serum in it, atrabilious or 'melancholic' complexion, etc. *Obs.* exc. in general sense, atrabilious, sallow, gloomy in features or temperament.

c **1430** LYDG. *Min. Poems* (1840) 197 Ay ful of yre, of malys, and rancour, Drye and adust and a gret wastour. **1542** BOORDE *Dyetary* xi. (1870) 261 Burnt breade and hard crustes,—doth ingendre color aduste and melancoly humours. **1576** BAKER *Gesner's Jewell of Health* 63 a, Cares of the mynde..of adust flewme engendred. *Ibid.* 101 a, This purgeth choller adust, and melancholie. **1646** SIR T. BROWNE *Pseud. Ep.* 335 In Fevers and hot distempers from choler adust is caused a blacknesse in our tongues, teeth and excretions. **1657** *Physical Dict.* The blood is then said to be adust, when by reason of extraordinary heat the thinner parts are evaporated, and the thicker remain black and dreggy. **1728** POPE *Dunc.* II. 33 No meagre muse-rid mope adust and thin. **1820** W. IRVING *Sk. Bk.* II. 91 That plodding spirit with which men of adust temperament follow up any tract of study. **1880** *Athenæum* 27 Mar. 414 The tall, somewhat adust and worn woman standing by a table.

†**aˈdust**, *v. Obs.* [f. prec.] To burn, to scorch, to sear; to dry up with heat. Also *fig.*

1550 BALE *Eng. Votaries* I. 46 b, An hondred thousande conscyences dyd he..aduste with his Romyshe faythe. **1633** T. N[EWTON] *Lemnie's Touchst. Complex.* 64 Beards of the colour of brasse: for that the haires are neither adusted by the Sunne, nor yet by any inward heat. **1667** MILTON *P.L.* VI. 514 Sulphurous and Nitrous Foame..Concocted and adusted they reduced To blackest grain.

adust (əˈdʌst), *adv.* and *pred. a.*, prop. *phr.* [A-*prep.*¹ of state + DUST; after analogy of *a-blaze*, *a-sleep*.] In a dusty condition, affected by dust. [So explained by the author quoted.]

1863 GEO. ELIOT *Romola* in *Cornh. Mag.* VII. 297 He was tired and adust with long riding.

†**aˈdusted**, *ppl. a. Obs.* [f. ADUST *v.* + -ED.]

1. = ADUST *a.* 1.

1550 BALE *Apol.* 63 What your adusted conscyence thynketh of it I can not tell. **1642** HOWELL *For. Trav.* (1869) 74 Those rayes which scorch the adusted soyles of Calabria.

2. = ADUST *a.* 2.

1550 NICOLLS *Thucyd.* 57 (R.) Thair skynne was as redde colour adusted, full of a lyttle thynne blaynes.

3. = ADUST *a.* 3.

1607 TOPSELL *Four-footed Beasts* (1673) 19 [They] eat the flesh of Asses, which begetting in their body much melancholick and adusted humor, causeth them to fall into the *Elephantia* or spotted leprosie. **1620** VENNER *Via Recta* iv. 77 Red Herrings give a very bad and adusted nourishment.

†**aˈdustible**, *a. Obs.* [a. Fr. *adustible*; see ADUST *a.* and -BLE.] Capable of being burnt, or dried with fire.

1611 COTGR., *Adustible*, adustible, burnable, wasteable, parchable. **1650** ASHMOLE *Chymical Coll.* 102 The unctuous, adustible, phlegmatick, and evaporable parts. [In BAILEY, JOHNSON, and mod. Dicts.]

†**adustion**. *Obs.* [ad. L. *adūstiōn-em* n. of action f. *adūr-ĕre*: see ADURE. In the medical vocabulary of most modern lang. in 16th c. (see sense 3), and possibly in Eng. immed. from Fr.]

1. The action or process of burning, scorching, heating to dryness, or parching.

1594 PLAT *Jewell-ho.* 3 The more you distil at once..the oyles will be in lesse daunger of adustion. **1601** HOLLAND *Pliny* (1634) I. 424 The faults and imperfections of pitch.. are known by..the very adustion thereof. **1673** in *Phil. Trans.* VIII. 6128 The Peripateticks, who derive the Saltness of the Sea from the Adustion of the water by the sun-beams. **1725** BRADLEY *Fam. Dict.* s.v. *Gravel*, Turpentine-powder, which is made by Way of Adustion, or drying in the Sun.

2. The state of being burnt, or scorched; parched dryness.

1559 MORWYNG *Evonymus* 218 Fire in destillation dothe more procure the savoure of adustion and brentnesse. **1650** ASHMOLE *Chymical Coll.* 103 Decoct it in Dung, because by Inhumation, Adustion is taken away. **1725** BRADLEY *Fam. Dict.* s.v. *Distilling*, The least Savour of Smoke or Adustion.

3. The state of being ADUST in sense 3; hotness and dryness of the humours of the body.

1533 ELYOT *Castel of Helth* (1541) 6 The lyver in hete distempered hath moche blacke choler toward age by adustion of red choler. **1621** BURTON *Anat. Mel.* I. iii. III. (1651) 207 Adustion of humours makes men mad. **1658** CULPEPPER *Astrol. Judgem. Dis.* 90 Such diseases as come of adustion of blood, as the Pestilence.

†**aˈdustive**, *a. Obs.* [f. L. *adūst-* ppl. stem of *adūr-ĕre* (see ADURE) + -IVE, as if ad. L. **adūstīvus*.] Burning, scorching, fiery.

1633 T. ADAMS *Exp. 2 Pet.* ii. 4 (1865) 282/1 God's power shall separate the clarity of fire from the adustive virtue. **1678** R. R[USSELL] tr. *Geber* II. I. IV. ii. 86 The adustive unctuosity of Sulphur..which is easily inflamed.

†**aˈdustness**. *Obs. rare*⁻¹. [f. ADUST *a.* + -NESS.] The state of being adust; scorching heat.

1652 FRENCH *Yorksh. Spa* xiv. 106 Consider whether there be not abundance of terrene adustness in the bowels of the earth.

advail, advale, obs. forms of AVAIL and AVALE.

‖**ad valorem** (ˌæd vəˈlɔərɛm), *adv. phr.* [L. = (according) to value, (in proportion) to worth.] A phrase (properly adverbial, but more commonly attributive) meaning 'in proportion to the value,' applied to a mode of levying customs-duties upon goods, when these are taxed at rates proportioned to their estimated value.

1711 *Act 10 Anne* xix. §34 The said Books, Prints and Maps as are to pay the said Duties *ad Valorem*. **1787** PITT *Sp. on Customs Bill* 21 Mar., Particularly the case of *ad valorem* duties. **1825** *Edin. Rev.* XLIII. 76 Silk goods are to be freely admitted..on payment of an *ad valorem* duty of 30 per cent. **1866** CRUMP *Banking* iv. 88 Cheques drawn out of the United Kingdom are..required to have *ad valorem* foreign stamps.

advance (ædˈvɑːns, -æ-) *v.* Forms: 3-6 **avaunce**, 3-5 **avaunse**, (4 **avonci**), 4-7 **avance**, 5 **avanse** (**awawns** *Sc.*), 5-6 **advaunce**, 6 **avawnce** (**awance** *Sc.*), 6- **advance**. [a. OFr. *avance-r*, *avancie-r*:—pop. L. *abanteā-re*, f. late L. *abante* (Fr. *avant*) away before, f. *ab* off, away + *ante* before. The form *advance*, due to mistaking initial *a* for a representative of L. *ad*, as in *a(d)venture*, occasional in 15-16th c. French (in which, the *d* being mute, it was merely an artificial spelling) has been established in Eng. as a permanent perversion of the word. So in *advantage*. See AD- 2.]

I. To move forward *in place.*

1. a. *trans.* To move, put, or push (a thing) forward. Also *fig.*

1509 HAWES *Past. Pl.* XXXIII. xvi, His glave he did agaynst me advaunce. **1611** HEYWOOD *Gold. Age* III. i. 48 Brauely aduance your strong orbicular shields. **1667** MILTON *P.L.* II. 682 Execrable shape, That dar'st, though grim and terrible, advance Thy mis-created Front athwart my way. **1718** POPE *Iliad* XI. 721 Who spread their bucklers, and advance their spears. **1844** DISRAELI *Coningsby* VI. v. 240 The sofa which Sidonia had advanced to the middle of the room. **1875** H. ROGERS *Superh. Orig. Bible* ix. (ed. 3) 386 Man has advanced the frontier of physical science.

†**b.** *refl.* To move (oneself) forward. *Obs.*

1483 CAXTON *Gold. Leg.* 19/2, I shal avaunce me and goo to fore you into galylee. *a* **1528** SKELTON *Bowge of Courte* 88 Auaunce yourselfe to aproche. **1610** HOLLAND *Camden's Brit.* (1637) 60 He..avanced himselfe before the ensignes on foot.

2. a. *intr.* (by omission of refl. pron.) To move or go forward; to proceed.

1513 DOUGLAS *Æneis* VI. x. 116 Agane returnis he, and thay auance. **1607** SHAKS. *Cor.* I. iv. 25 Aduance, braue Titus. **1645** EVELYN *Mem.* (1857) I. 161 After we were advanced into this noble and altogether wonderful crypt. **1725** DE FOE *Voy. round World* (1840) 330 They had by swimming and wading together advanced about a mile. **1839** KEIGHTLEY *Hist. Eng.* II. 43 The duke of Norfolk, as general of the royal forces, advanced to Doncaster. **1860** TYNDALL *Glaciers* I. §10. 65 The crevasses as I advanced became more deep and frequent.

b. Of a colour: to appear to be nearer to the eye than other colours in the same plane; to stand out.

1876 S. R. KOEHLER tr. *von Bezold's Theory of Color* v. 197 Another point to which attention must be called concerns the advancing and retiring qualities of certain colors... Warm hues advance while the cold retire; if the brightness is not equal, the light colors advance while the dark retire. **1908** J. A. H. HATT *Colorist* vii. 41 Beside the distinction of luminous and sober in colors, we also have the attributes of warm and cold, also advancing and retiring. **1958** *Listener* 24 July 131/2 This is well known to artists, who call red an advancing, and blue a receding colour.

3. *intr. fig.* To go forward or make progress in life, or in any course.

a **1704** LOCKE (J.) They who would advance in knowledge ..should not take words for real entities. **1775** JOHNSON in

Boswell (Routl.) xxv. 224 As a man advances in life, he gets what is better than admiration,—judgment. **1865** RUSKIN *Sesame* 107 He only is advancing in life, whose heart is getting softer, whose blood warmer. **1866** CRUMP *Banking* i. 14 We are surprised that neither the Greeks nor the Romans advanced further than they did [commercially].

4. *trans.* To forward any process or thing that is in course; to further, promote, help on, aid the success, completion, or perfection of.

c **1230** *Ancren Riwle* 156 Ðet tet swuðest auaunceð & furðreð hit, þet is onlich stude. **1297** R. GLOUC. 503 Thine cause.. We auauncieth. **1393** GOWER *Conf.* III. 187 Wherof men ought ensample take The gode lawes to avaunce. *c* **1420** *Pallad. on Husb.* I. 1144 Thi bakhous therwith all thou maist avance. **1538** STARKEY *England* 3 To study to maynteyn and avaunce the wele of thys same your cuntrey. **1655** CULPEPPER *Riverius* To Reader, All which wil very much advance the cure. **1799** WELLESLEY *Desp.* 90 He advanced his hostile preparations. **1856** KANE *Arctic Explor.* I. 20 The officials.. vied with each other in efforts to advance our views.

5. *refl.* and *intr.* Of a process or thing in course: To go on towards completion or perfection.

1644 MILTON *Educat.* (1788) I. 140 If there were any secret excellence..[these ways would] give it fair opportunities to advance itself by. **1855** TENNYSON *To F. D. Maurice* 39 How gain in life, as life advances, Valour and charity more and more? **1875** FORTNUM *Maiolica* iv. 38 From 1520 to 1540 the art constantly advanced in this duchy. **1879** C. HIBBS in *Cassell's Techn. Educ.* IV. 117/1 Tightened up with screws as the work advances.

6. To put forward (a statement, suggestion, or claim) for notice or acceptance; to put forth, to bring forward; to offer, propose, present.

1509 HAWES *Past. Pl.* XII. v, Evermore they [poets] do to them avaunce Nurture, maner, and al gentylnes. **1665** J. SPENCER *Proph.* 29 They presently become considerable, are advanced the common Subjects of Discourse. **1699** BENTLEY *Phalaris* The very learned Mr. Dodwell has advanced some other Arguments. **1718** J. CHAMBERLAYNE *Relig. Philos.* (1730) II. xix. §45 It may be safely advanced that there falls about 20 inches of Rain yearly. **1829** SOUTHEY *All for Love* ix. Wks. VII. 207 Claim to him as thy Bondsman thou Canst never more advance. **1848** RUSKIN *Mod. Painters* I. I. I. i. §4. 5, I have accordingly advanced nothing in the following pages but with accompanying demonstration.

II. To move forward *in time*.

7. *trans.* To make earlier (an event or date); to hasten, accelerate.

1481 CAXTON *Myrrour* III. x. 153 They abregge their dayes and auaunce their deth. **1549** CHALONER tr. *Erasm. Moriae Enc.* G iii b, Elde and horenes which his own wilfull studie avaunced to him before his tyme. **1611** TOURNEUR *Ath. Trag.* v. ii. 149 All the wealthie benefits My death aduances you. **1854** J. ABBOTT *Napoleon* xxxvii. (1855) I. 569 To advance the moment when the public rights of Europe.. will be definitely established.

8. a. To make earlier the date of a payment; to pay before it is legally due. Hence, to pay or lend on security, either real or personal, of future re-imbursement.

1679-88 *Secr. Serv. Moneys* (1851) 63 For interest and gratuity for advancing the Duchess of Portsmouth's quarter ..25 daies £12 5*s.* 5*d.* **1820** CAREY *Guide to Funds* 27 The Bank advanced £400,000 more to government. **1882** *Charter-party*, One third to be advanced in cash, on account of Freight, if required on signing Bill of Lading. *Mod.* The pawnbroker declined to advance more than 3 shillings on the article. I will advance him £50 on your note-of-hand.

b. *absol.* with *on.*

1866 CRUMP *Banking* iii. 84 Dock-warrant and bills of lading are frequently advanced on.

III. To move upward.

9. *trans.* To raise or lift up. *lit.* and *fig. arch.*

1475 *Bk. of Noblesse* (1860) 22 Put forthe youre silf, avaunsing youre corageous hertis to werre. **1513** DOUGLAS *Æneis* v. iv. 134 Thare happy chance So gan the breistis of the vtheris awance [*v.r.* avance]. **1610** SHAKS. *Temp.* I. ii. 408 The fringed Curtains of thine eyes aduance. **1624** HEYWOOD *Gunaik.* III. 156 Advancing his wife from the earth. **1697** POTTER *Antiq. of Greece* III. ix. (1715) 78 The signal to be given..was a Purple Coat, which was to be advanc'd in the Air. **1712** POPE *Messiah* 25 See lofty Lebanon his head advance. **1814** WORDSWORTH *Wh. Doe of Ryl.* III. 158 At need he stood, advancing high The glittering, floating Pageantry.

10. a. *trans.* To raise or promote (a person) in rank or office, to prefer. Hence *gen.* To put in a better or more advantageous position.

1297 R. GLOUC. 77 And bihet hym, þat, ȝef þer of wel auaunsed he were To ȝelde more god to Rome. **1366** MAUNDEVILE v. (1839) 38 Whan the Soudan will avance any worthi Knyghte, he makethe him an Amyralle. **1461-83** *Lib. Nig. Dom.* in *Househ. Ord.* (1790) 50 The King's grace avaunceth these preests and clerks by prebends, churches, etc. **1538** ELYOT in Ellis *Orig. Lett.* I. 142 III. 115 My saide Lord Cardinal.. advauncid me to be Clerk of the Counsayle. **1576** THYNNE in *Animadv.* (1865) 113 Good vertue hym advanced above the reste. **1611** BIBLE *Esther* iii. 1 Ahasuerus ..aduanced him, and set his seate aboue all the princes. **1667** MILTON *P.L.* VIII. 148 Determin'd to advance into our room A Creature form'd of Earth. **1728** YOUNG *Love of Fame* iii. (1757) 106 The man that's nearest, yawning, they advance. **1876** FREEMAN *Norm. Conq.* II. ix. 314 His eagerness to advance his family may well have offended others.

†**b.** *construction transposed. Obs.*

1623 W. L'ISLE *Testim. Antiq.* Pref., Oswald avoided out of the most notable Churches the Clarkes, and advanced the same places with men of the order of Monkes.

c. *refl.* To push oneself forward in rank or station.

1340 *Ayenb.* 82 Hy ne þencheþ ne studieþ bote ham zelue to auonci. **1475** *Bk. of Noblesse* (1860) 46 They alway avaunsid hem forthe withe the formost. **1563** *Homilies* II. (1859) 480 It shall make us not to avaunce ourselves before our neighbour.

11. *Law.* To provide for children, especially in anticipation of the provisions of a settlement or will.

1411 SIR T. LANGEFORDE in *E.E. Wills* (1882) 17 And it falle þat sche deie, or scheo be a-vauncyd, þan wille y þat þe forseyd C:li. be don for my sowle. **1574** tr. *Littleton, Tenures* 55 b, Shee shall haue nothing in the remenaunt for that..she is sufficientlye advaunced. **1809** TOMLINS *Law Dict.* s.v. *Hotchpot*, If a child advanced by the father, do after his father's decease challenge a child's part with the rest.

†**12.** *fig.* To extol, to magnify (in words). *refl.* To boast. *Obs.* Cf. AVAUNT, VAUNT.

1413 LYDG. *Pylgr. Sowle* III. iii. (1483) 51 Ful wel myght the bocher auauncen hym self, and seyn that al other bochers had nought so moch flesshe hangynge in theyr howses. **1483** CAXTON *Gold. Leg.* 267/1 He had no more wylle to auaunce hym. *c* **1526** FRITH *Disput. Purgat.* (1829) 153 Bless the Lord; praise and advance him for ever. **1551** ROBINSON tr. *More's Utopia* (1869) 44 You shall in vaine aduaunce your selues of executing iustice vpon fellons. **1633** BP. HALL *Hard Texts* 477 Thou advancest thyselfe to be as that glorious Cherub which covereth the Ark of God. **1660** JER. TAYLOR *Worthy Commun.* i. §5. 97 Let no man advance the preaching of the word of God, to the disparagement..of the Sacraments.

†**13.** To raise in amount or number, increase. *Obs.*

1576 LAMBARDE *Peramb. Kent* (1826) 271 Lanfranc advaunced the number of the Monkes from 30 to 140. **1650** FULLER *Pisgah Sight* IV. iv. 66 What a mass of money might he have advanced for himselfe.

14. To raise in rate or price.

1691 PETTY *Polit. Arith.* iv. 67 The Rent of Land is advanced by reason of Multitude of People. *Mod.* The Bank of England has advanced the rate of discount to 5%.

15. *intr.* To rise in price.

1882 *Daily News* 19 Aug. 7/1 Brush Light shares advanced in a prominent manner..Indian Rupee Paper has fractionally advanced.

†**16.** *intr.* To be over in amount; to be in excess. (Cf. It. *avanzare.*) *Obs.*

1557 NORTH *Dial. of Princes* (1582) 26 To speake truely, in princes houses there is more offence in that that avaunceth then in that that wanteth. **1601** SIR A. SHERLEY *Trav. to Persia* (1613) 71 All his Goods and Lands, should be sold, for the satisfaction of those men..If anything advanced, it should be giuen to his children.

IV. To advantage.

†**17.** *trans.* To advantage, benefit, profit (any one). *Obs.*

c **1386** CHAUCER *Prol.* 246 It may not avance, As for to delen with no swiche pouraille.

†**18.** *intr.* To be advantaged; to benefit, profit. *Obs.*

c **1440** *Cokwolds Daunce* 165 in *E.P.P.* 45 Ffor any cas that may be tyde, Schall non ther of a vanse.

advance (æd'vɑːns, -æ-), *sb.* [partly a. Fr. *avance*, n. of action, f. *avancer*, partly subst. use of Eng. vb.; see prec.]

I. A going forward, onward, or upward.

1. The action of going forward or onward; forward motion; progression (in space). Also *ellipt.* The order (bugle-call) to move forward.

a **1674** CLARENDON (J.) The manner of the enemy's advance. **1815** SCOTT *Lord of Isles* v. xx, When, in retreat or in advance, The serried warriors move at once. **1858** HAWTHORNE *Fr. & Ital. Jrnls.* (1872) I. 4 This my first advance into French territory. **1868** *Queen's Regul. & Ord. Army* §1131 When the train is ready to proceed the Advance will be sounded.

2. a. *fig.* Onward movement in any process or course of action; progress.

1668 PEPYS *Diary* (1877) V. 323 Thence to Cooper's, and saw his advance on my wife's picture. **1751** JOHNSON *Rambler* No. 147 ¶3, I made very quick advances in different kinds of learning. **1855** TENNYSON *Maud* I. I. vii, These are the days of advance, the works of the men of mind. **1859** BUCKLE in *Fraser's Mag.* May 509 Who, among our living writers, had done most for the advance of knowledge.

b. A step forward, a degree of progress actually accomplished.

1860 DICKENS *Lett.* (1880) II. 110 It is a very great advance on all your former writing.

3. A personal approach; a movement towards closer acquaintance or understanding; an overture. Esp. in *pl.*, amorous overtures or approaches.

1678 DRYDEN *All for Love* IV. (R.) Th' advance of kindness which I made, was feign'd. **1692** *Lond. Gaz.* mmdccxxx/1 The Pope's Ministers think there have already been Advances enough made on their side. *a* **1706** C. SACKVILLE in Johnson *Wks. Eng. Poets* (1779) XI. 202 She never stays till we begin, But beckons us herself to sin.. Desire's asleep, and cannot wake, When women such advances make. **1802** WELLESLEY *Desp.* 218 The Resident has prudently rejected every advance of this nature. **1817** COLERIDGE *Sibylline Leaves* 137 True, I woo'd her..but she Met my advances with empassion'd pride. **1842** MACAULAY *Fredk. Gt.* in *Ess.* (1877) 690 Frederic had some time before made advances towards a reconciliation with Voltaire. **1891** G. MOORE *Impressions & Opin.* 138 The Duke would make some absent-minded advances, which in an absent-minded way would be repelled. **1898** G. B. SHAW *Philanderer* I. 108 No woman writes such a letter to a man unless he has made advances to her. **1959** M. CUMBERLAND *Murmurs in Rue Morgue* xi. 71 Men don't make 'advances' any longer. Modern man propositions a girl. **1959** D. EDEN *Sleeping Bride* ii. 10 Teaching English to..French children was one thing, but having to fight off advances from their father was another.

4. A rise in amount, value, or price.

1677 YARRANTON *Eng. Improv.* 153 There would be ten thousand pound per annum advance in the Kings Customs yearly. **1866** CRUMP *Banking* vii. 155 An advance in the Bank of England rate of discount. **1882** *Daily News* 23 Aug. 7/1 Austrian Gold Rente showing an advance of ½ per cent.

†**5.** An elevation; a rise (in space). *Obs. rare.*

1655 LESTRANGE *Chas. I*, 137 The Communion Table.. placed at the East end, upon a graduated advance of ground.

II. A putting forward.

†**6.** The action of forwarding; furtherance; ADVANCEMENT. *Obs.*

1528-1696 in *Sel. fr. Harl. Misc.* (1793) 412 The end for which they at first were chosen, viz. The advance of their protector's interest.

†**7.** The putting forward of statements; the statement put forward; assertion, allegation. *Obs.*

1699 BENTLEY *Phalaris* 235 Mr. B.'s advances upon this Topic.

8. Payment beforehand or in anticipation; payment on security of future re-imbursement. Hence, a sum of money so furnished, a loan.

1681 NEVILLE *Plato Rediv.* 81 Who may Imploy their Advance to better profit elsewhere. **1727** ARBUTHNOT *John Bull* 104 We have something by way of advance. **1727** SWIFT *Wks.* 1755 III. I. 153 A week's wages advance. **1786** BURKE *Agst. W. Hastings* Wks. 1842 II. 188 The advance to the company's use of a sum of money, amounting to fifty thousand pounds. **1866** CRUMP *Banking* iii. 84 Life assurance policies are almost invariably objected to as security for advances.

9. A briefing given (to a political figure) before an event; preparation (esp. by local publicity) for the visit of a public figure. Cf. *advance man*, sense 12a below. *U.S.*

1968 MRS. L. B. JOHNSON *White House Diary* 5 Apr. (1970) 651, I knew that I was about to go home by car for a fifteen-minute advance before the press arrived at the Ranch on the bus. **1971** *New Yorker* 12 June 30 'Good advance' means that the candidate is mobbed at the airport by fervent, unmanageable crowds. **1979** H. KISSINGER *White House Years* xix. 742 Whisked by a group of Communist Chinese to locations for which there had been no 'advance' and in which they would have no way of telling who constituted a security risk.

III. A being forward.

10. The state or position of being before, to the front, or above; precedence, anticipation. Usually in adv. phr. *in advance*: **a.** Of place, In front, ahead; **b.** Of time, Beforehand; **c.** In the position of having advanced money on account. Also prep. phr. *in advance of*: Before, in front of, ahead of, beyond.

1668 CHILD *Disc. Trade* (ed. 4) 11 Much in advance of the rates of goods. **1742** YOUNG *Night Th.* VII. 89 Men perish in advance, as if the sun Should set ere noon. **1761** SMOLLETT *Gil Blas* x. vii. (1802) III. 142, I paid the first year's annuity per advance. **1786** JEFFERSON *Writings* (1859) II. 2 Without this supply, Mr. Grand would have been in advance for the United States. **1851** RUSKIN *Mod. Painters* (1856) IV. v. v. §22. 82 Which I could not refer to in advance without anticipating all my other illustrations. **1860** TYNDALL *Glaciers* I. §1. 1 As wood opens in advance of a wedge driven into it. **1869** HUXLEY in *Sci. Opin.* 21 Apr. 464/1 Hutton was in advance of the geological speculation of his time.

IV. †**11.** One who has been advanced to office. (Prob. for Fr. *avancé.*) *Obs. rare.*

1496 *Dives & Pauper* (W. de Worde) IV. xxiv. 191/2 Patrons fynde full ofte ther auaunces full unkynde to them & full proude.

V. 12. a. *Comb.* and *attrib.*, as ***advance-account, agent, announcement, -freight, notice, publicity***; **advance copy**, a copy of a book sent out in advance of publication; **advance growth** (see quots.); **advance(d) guard**, a guard before or in front of the main body of an army; also *fig.*, = AVANT-GARDE 2; **advance man** *N. Amer.*, one sent ahead to make preparations for the visit of a politician (†formerly, of a performing company), esp. by attracting crowds; **advance-money, -payment** = ADVANCE *sb.* 8; **advance note** (see quot. 1886); **advance-proofs, -sheets**, parts of a forth-coming work supplied previously to its publication.

1882 SWEET & KNOX *Texas Siftings* 38 Do you think I am the advance agent of a variety show? **1897** *Congress. Rec.* Mar. 177/1 That grand advance agent of prosperity, William McKinley. **1885** *Art Annual* 1 (Advt.), Advance, Announcements from the Prospectus for 1885/86. **1899** *Academy* 25 Nov. 591 Mr. Donnelly conceived the request to be for an advance copy. **1903** E. ALMACK *Eikon Basilike* Pref. p. iv, The present edition has been set up from an 'advance copy' of the first edition. **1891** W. SCHLICH *Man. Forestry* II. ii. 155 In almost every mature wood groups of young growth are found, which have sprung up here and there before the regeneration cuttings have been commenced; such young growth is called 'advance growth'. **1953** *Brit. Commonw. For. Terminol.* I. 11 *Advance growth*, young trees which have established themselves in openings in the forest, or under the forest cover, before regeneration fellings are begun. **1677** *Lond Gaz.* mccxliv. 4 Troops of the two Armies, who had the Advanced-guards. **1758** in *Essex Inst. Coll.* XVIII. 113 The Advance Guard..have cleared off the Trees and built Breastworks. **1876** BANCROFT *Hist. U.S.* III. x. 435 Virginia volunteers formed the advance-guard. **1898** G. B. SHAW *Our Theatres in Nineties* (1932) III. 309 That is why Mr Pinero, as a critic of the advanced guard in modern life, is unendurable to me. **1931** C. ST. JOHN *E. Terry & B. Shaw* 297 His refusal..made him specially obnoxious to the advance guard of the drama. **1959** *Times* 20

Feb. 11/6 Poplar became the advanced guard in London Labour. **1959** *Times Lit. Suppl.* 6 Nov. p. xxix/1 Advance guard Americans are convinced..that..Abstract Expressionism radiates the world over. **1906** *Daily Colonist* (Victoria, B.C.) 1 Jan. 16/3 The Savage Opera company in which the advance man says there are 200 people will present grand opera in English at the Victoria theatre. **1970** *Time* 2 Nov. 7/1 Ron Walker, Nixon's chief advance man, told the police to let the protesters in. **1973** M. Truman *Harry S. Truman* i. 31 These days candidates send swarms of advance men into every city before they arrive. They are equipped with lavish amounts of money and every known publicity device. **1701** *Lond. Gaz.* mmmdccxi. 1 The 50000 Pistoles which the French were to pay him by way of Advance-money. **1845** *Act 8 & 9 Vict.* c. 116 §7 The Owner ..of any Merchant Ship..shall not pay or advance, nor give ..an Advance Note for any Part of the Wages of any Seaman [etc.]. **1886** *Encycl. Brit.* XXI. 606/1 Advance notes—that is, documents promising the future payment of money on account of a seaman's wages conditionally on his going to sea. **1900** T. E. Pemberton *Kendals* 281 If this much-advertised play were as original, as artistic, as great as the advance notices have painted it. **1880** *Paper & Print. Trades Jrnl.* No. 32, 27 The plates, advance-proofs of which we have seen. **1932** D. L. Sayers *Have his Carcase* iv. 56 Good advance publicity means sales. **1870** Power *Handy-bk. ab. Bks.* 91 Advance sheets..supplied elsewhere previous to publication, generally for simultaneous reproduction.

b. *attrib.* passing into *adj.* Effected (placed, given, provided, etc.) in advance; prior. Freq. as ***advance notice, warning.***

a **1910** 'Mark Twain' *What is Man?* (1917) 268 There were other advance-advertisements. One of them appeared just before Caesar Augustus was born... It was a dream ..[of] Caesar Augustus's mother, and interpreted at the usual rates. **1933** *Rep. Departmental Comm. Traffic Signs* (Ministry of Transport) v. 55 Advance warning signs should not be provided unless owing to a turn in the road, or for some other reason, signals are not visible at a distance of at least 100 yards. **1936** *Variety* 29 July 42/3 (*heading*) Not much advance sale for two suspended N.Y. hits. **1940** *Gloss. Highway Engin. Terms (B.S.I.)* 63 *Advance sign*, a sign or device placed at such a distance before a road junction is reached as to give early direction and guidance to traffic. **1962** E. Roosevelt *Autobiogr.* xviii. 147, I visited as many government projects as possible, often managing to arrive without advance notice so that they could not be polished up for my inspection. **1972** *Accountant* 25 Sept. 378/1 The three aims of avoiding transitional penalties, securing a windfall ACT (advance corporation tax) relief for dividends paid before that date and escaping an ACT forfeit for dividends paid after it. **1979** A. Hailey *Overload* I. ii. 13 Perhaps the intruder had advance information about the layout of the plant, though this would not have been essential.

advanceable (æd'vɑːnsəb(ə)l, -æ-), *a.* ? *Obs.* [f. ADVANCE *v.* + -ABLE.] Capable of being advanced, put forward, or promoted.

1656 Jeanes *Fvlnesse of Christ* 57 The greatest height of honour, and power, that the humane nature is advanceable. **1677** Hale *Prim. Orig. Man.* 311 Animals are advanceable by Industry and disciplinable Acts to a great perfection.

advanced (æd'vɑːnst, -æ-), *ppl. a.* [f. ADVANCE *v.* + -ED.]

1. Moved forward, standing or being to the front; *esp.* in military phr. ***advanced guard*** (see ADVANCE *sb.* V.), ***post, works.***

1795 Hotham in Nicolas's *Disp.* (1845) II. 11 The French ships were seen by our advanced Frigates. **1810** Scott *Lady of L.* II. xxxiv, With foot advanced, and blade half-bared. **1855** Macaulay *Hist. Eng.* IV. 98 The advanced guard of the English army. **1879** *Fortif.* in *Cassell's Techn. Educ.* IV. 138/1 'Advanced-works' are those which are occasionally added to the ordinary works of a permanent front.

2. a. *fig.* Far on in life or time, or in any course of action, or march of ideas; sometimes *spec.* of women, esp. those advocating or favouring women's rights or equality with men.

1534 Ld. Berners *Gold. Bk. M. Aurel.* (1546) P iij b, In the most highest trees the force of wyndes is most aduanced. **1628** Digby *Voy. Medit.* (1868) Pref. 19 He had attained a very advanced period of life. **1646** Sir T. Browne *Pseud. Ep.* I. vii. 25 Our advanced beliefs are not to be built upon dictates. **1776** Gibbon *Decl. & F.* I. 326 A very advanced season of life. **1846** Mill *Logic* III. xi. §2 (1868) 512 The most advanced truths of mathematics. **1863** Kemble *Resid. Georgia* 74 The season is too little advanced. **1871** *N.Y. Tribune* 2 Feb. (De Vere), The shortsightedness of the advanced female to the interest of her own cause. **1876** C. M. Yonge *Womankind* xxii. 177 The advanced school [of brides] are said to prefer a civil marriage. **1879** *Standard* 25 Apr., He is an advanced Liberal. **1895** S. Hale *Lett.* (1919) 288 She is a lion-hunter *enragée*, advanced female, views, everything. **1896** M. Corelli *Mighty Atom* ii. 24 Two or three ugly 'advanced' young women who have brought their bicycles and go tearing about the country all day.

b. Of study: on a higher level than the elementary; of a degree: (usu.) superior to a bachelor's degree; ***advanced level***, the higher of the two levels of the General Certificate of Education most commonly taken by candidates, as a university entrance qualification, etc. (a third, 'scholarship', level may be taken conjointly with the advanced level); abbrev. *A level* s.v. A III; cf. *ordinary level* s.v. ORDINARY *a.* 5 e and *GCSE* s.v. G III. f.; *spec.* in some universities: ***advanced student***, one who, because of qualifications obtained at a former place of study, is admitted to a more advanced course than would normally be available to him; so ***advanced status***, etc.

1790 *Laws of Harvard Coll.* 7 No person shall be admitted to an advanced standing, unless..he shall be found qualified. **1871** L. H. Bagg *At Yale* 689 Whether an 'advanced student' comes from a private tutor or from another college, or drops from a higher class at Yale, makes little difference. **1892** *Brigham Young Acad. Circular* 12 Requests for examination for advanced credit must be made to the faculty in writing. **1916** *Oxf. Univ. Gaz.* 22 Nov. 138/2 In a Congregation to be held on Tuesday, January 30, 1917..the form of Statute creating a new status of Advanced Student..will be promulgated. **1947**, etc. Advanced level [see ORDINARY *a.* 5 e]. **1952** M. McCarthy *Groves of Academe* (1953) vi. 113 We don't insist on the Ph.D. or even the Master's; in fact, we regard advanced degrees as a liability. **1963** *Oxf. Univ. Gaz.* 20 June 1484/2 Permitted to transfer from B.Litt. Status to Advanced Status. **1981** D. Rowntree *Dict. Educ.* 103 The examinations are organised by nine separate examining boards and are at two levels: *Ordinary level* and *Advanced level*.

c. ***advanced passenger train***, a prototype high-speed passenger train developed by British Rail, having a mechanism designed to tilt the coach bodies as the train rounds a bend (see quot. 1986); abbrev. *A.P.T.* s.v. A III.

1969 *Railway Mag.* Jan. 22/2 (*caption*) Model of British Railways proposed Advanced Passenger Train... It should be capable of speeds up to 150 m.p.h. **1971** *New Scientist* 10 June 624/1 Speed and comfort are the essence of the Advanced Passenger Train. **1976** P. R. White *Planning for Public Transport* viii. 172 The boldest attempt to make use of existing rail networks is the Advanced Passenger Train. **1982** *Railway Mag.* Jan. 53 We are desperately anxious to see the Advanced Passenger Train succeed. **1986** *Mod. Railways* Feb. 75/1 The collapse of the Advanced Passenger Train project has left InterCity services on the West Coast main line in a 1970s 'time warp'.

†**3.** Promoted. *Obs.*

1460 Fortescue *Abs. & Lim. Mon.* (1714) 137 The Clerks of his Chapell that have Wifes, or be not avaunsyd. **1681** Dryden *Abs. & Achit.* II. 48 Pamper'd Corah when advanced to court.

†**4.** Raised, elevated (physically). *Obs.*

1576 Gascoigne *Princely Pleas.* (1821) 5 Six Trumpeters hugely advanced, much exceeding the common stature of men. **1596** Spenser *F.Q.* II. i. 23 To see the Redcrosse thus advaunced hye. **1604** Edmonds *Observ. on Cæsars Comm.* 133 That all men performe their directions with their pikes aduanced. **1667** Milton *P.L.* I. 536 Th' Imperial ensign, which full high advanc't Shon like a meteor. **1673** *Vain Insolency of Rome* 35 The people could observe him advanced a Cubit above the earth.

5. Raised (in amount), increased.

1782 Cowper *Lett.* 23 Nov. Wks. 1876, 122 The advanced price of grain.

†**6.** Set off to advantage. *Obs.*

1554 Philpot *Examin. & Writ.* (1842) 389 Thou wouldst have churches well furnished with altars..avanced with lights and tapers.

advancement (æd'vɑːnsmənt, -æ-). Forms: 3–6 **avaunce-**; 4–6 **avance-**; 6 **avaunse-, advaunce-**; 6– **advancement.** [a. Fr. *avancement*, f. *avancer*: see ADVANCE and -MENT.] The action or fact of advancing.

1. The raising of any one to a higher rank or position; promotion, preferment.

1297 R. Glouc. 312 He ȝef hym such auauncement as he wolde. **1330** R. Brunne *Chron.* 103 On oþer wise he salle haf auancement. **1413** Lydg. *Pylgr. Sowle* IV. xxxiii. (1483) 82 They coueyte nought to be neyhe the kyng for no corrupte cause ne hope of auauncement. **1599** Thynne *Animadv.* (1865) 24 You seme to attribute the advancemente of the Pooles to William de la poole. **1602** Shaks. *Haml.* III. ii. 62 Nay, do not thinke I flatter: For what aduancement may I hope from thee? **1660** Milton *Free Commw.* 449 The Civil Rights and Advancements of every Person according to his Merit. **1700** Luttrell *Brief Rel.* (1857) IV. 661 Mr. Ryley's advancement to the excise. **1853** Thackeray *Eng. Hum.* 3 His hopes of advancement in England failing, Swift returned to Ireland.

2. *Law.* The promotion of children in life, especially by the application beforehand of property or money to which they are prospectively entitled under a settlement or will; also the property so applied.

1411 Sir T. Langeforde in *E. E. Wills* (1883) 17 þe Silver þere-of spendyd to þe avauncement of lucie, my dowter. **1574** tr. *Littleton, Tenures* 55 b, Shee shall have nothing in the remenaunt for that..she is sufficientlye advaunced to whiche advauncement shee agreeth. *a* **1626** Bacon (J.) The jointure or advancement of the lady, was the third part of the principality of Wales. **1768** Blackstone *Comm.* II. 517 But if the estates so given them, by way of advancement, are not quite equivalent to the other shares, the children so advanced shall now have so much as will make them equal.

†**3.** Extolment, lauding; vaunting. *Obs.*

1330 R. Brunne *Chron.* 196 What tyme or whan I mad auancement with þe alone to fight. **1564** Becon *Gen. Pref. to Wks.* (1843) 16 To seek the glory of God, the avancement of his blessed name. **1646** Sir T. Browne *Pseud. Ep.* 213 Thus is it also esteemed no small advancement unto this number [7] that the Genealogy of our Saviour is summed up by 14. that is, this number doubled.

4. The helping forward of anything in process toward completion or perfection; furtherance, promotion; improvement.

1551 Robinson tr. *More's Utopia* 13 For the auauncement and commoditie of the publique wealth. **1589** Fletewood in Ellis *Orig. Lett.* I. 229 III. 31 As touching the avaunsement of Religion. **1605** Bacon (*title*) Twoo Bookes of the Proficience and Aduancement of Learning. **1658** Bramhall *Consecr. Bps.* xi. 234 Ceremonies are advancements of Order, decency, modesty. **1810** Horsley *Sermons* I. x. (R.) The joint advancement of the virtue and the happiness of the people.

†**5.** A going forward. *lit.* and *fig.* *Obs.* See ADVANCE I, 2.

c **1730** Swift (J.) This refinement makes daily advancements, and, I hope, in time will raise our language to the utmost perfection. **1817** Jas. Mill *Brit. India* II. v. iv. 450 They retired upon the brisk advancement of the grenadiers. **1825** McCulloch *Pol. Econ.* I. 10 The advancement of nations in civilization.

6. Advancing or advanced condition.

1793 Smeaton *Edystone Lightho.* §271 [I] gave an account of the advancement of our works. **1868** Hawthorne *Amer. Note-Bks.* (1879) II. 139 We have water-melons in good advancement.

†**7.** The advancing or putting forward of a statement or assertion. *Obs.*

1532 Thynne *Ded. Chaucer* in *Animadv.* (1865) App. 25 Very remysse in the settyng forthe or avancement..of the histories therof.

†**8.** The advancing or paying beforehand of money; payment in advance. *Obs.* See ADVANCE *sb.* 8.

1649 Evelyn *Mem.* (1857) III. 47 The Common Council require double security..of this last advancement.

advancer (æd'vɑːnsə(r), -æ-). Also 6 **avauncer, avancer.** [f. ADVANCE *v.* + -ER[1].] He who or that which advances.

1. One who moves (a person or thing) forward or upward; **a.** physically (*obs.*); **b.** to higher rank or station (*obs.*); **c.** to a better or more advantageous condition; a promoter.

1538 Leland *Itin.* I. 40 This old Mounsun is in a maner the first avauncer of his Family. **1548** Hall *Chron., Hen. VII* anno 11 (R.) Suche as haue bene ayders and auauncers of Perkyns foolishe enterprice. **1610** Holland *Camden's Brit.* I. 208 Revolting from King Edward his advancer most ingratefully. **1639** Fuller *Holy War* v. xxix (1840) 295 Chiefest mover and advancer of this war. **1741** Middleton *Cicero* (1742) III. §10. 183 You will find me, not onely the favorer, but the advancer of your dignity. **1856** Emerson *Eng. Traits* 28 Navigation..is the most potent advancer of nations.

†**2.** One who extols or lauds; an extoller, supporter. *Obs.*

a **1546** Elyot *Let.* in *Governour* (1836) 286 The boasters and advancers of the pompous authority of the Bishop of Rome. **1656** Trapp *Expos. Rom.* iv. 16 (1868) 497/1 Paul was a great advancer of the grace of God. **1677** Hale *Prim. Orig. Man.* 10 The Supposition of Epicurus,..and his Advancer, Gassendus.

†**3.** *Rhet.* Amplification, auxesis, or climax. *Obs.*

1589 Puttenham *Eng. Poesie* (1869) 226 We call this figure by the Greeke originall the *Auancer* or figure of encrease because euery word that is spoken is one of more weight then another.

4. One who puts forth (a statement); an asserter.

1843 J. T. Coleridge in Stanley *Life of Arnold* II. i. 20 A confident advancer of his own opinions.

5. One who gives (money) before it is legally due, or who lends it for any purpose.

a **1733** North *Lives of Norths* III. 167 The goldsmiths, who gained by the melting trade, were advancers to the Treasury. **1748** Richardson *Clarissa* (1811) VI. 363 She mistrusted, that I was the advancer of the money.

6. A second branch of a buck's horn.

1496 *Bk. of St. Albans* d ij, Two braunches fyrste pawmyd he must have And four avauncers. **1751** Chambers *Cycl.*, *Advancer*, among hunters, is one of the starts, or branches of a buck's attire, between the back antler and the palm. **1827** Griffith *Cuvier's Anim. Kingd.* 85 Additional advancers and spillers, or snags on the anterior and posterior parts of the palm.

advancing (æd'vɑːnsɪŋ, -æ-), *vbl. sb.* [f. ADVANCE *v.* + -ING[1].] Moving forward, or forwarding; promotion, advancement. (Now mostly gerundial, in various senses of ADVANCE.)

1388 *On 25 Articles* in *Wyclif's Wks.* 1871 III. 470 Temporale avaunsyng of sum one man. **1413** Lydg. *Pylgr. Sowle* II. xlv. (1859) 51 For theyr fyers condycions of prowde auancynge they ben caste a bak in to endeles dampnacion. **1541** Barnes *Wks.* (1573) 343/1 The practysyng and aduauncing of Idolatry. **1549** *Compl. Scotl.* (1873) 2 The contenual auansing of the deffens of oure cuntre. **1655** Gouge *Hebrews* i. 5. 37 He did not usurp it by a proud advancing of himself. *Mod.* The fact of your advancing such strange opinions hinders us from advancing your cause.

advancing (æd'vɑːnsɪŋ, -æ-), *ppl. a.* [f. ADVANCE *v.* + -ING[2].] Moving forward, approaching, progressing, increasing.

1801 Southey *Thalaba* VI. xxviii. Wks. IV. 233 And unveil'd women bade the advancing youth, Come merry-make with them! **1849** Macaulay *Hist. Eng.* II. 50 Advancing age had made no essential change in his character. **1862** H. Spencer *First Princ.* I. i. §2 (1875) 6 With advancing political opinion has come still greater restriction of imperial power. *Mod.* Heedless of the advancing tide.

advancingly (æd'vɑːnsɪŋlɪ, -æ-), *adv.* [f. prec. + -LY[2].] In an advancing manner; with onward motion, progressively.

c **1875** Proctor *Expanse of Heaven* (1877) 158 The comets of short period travel advancingly. **1882** *Contemp. Rev.* Jan. 135 They are advancingly important in the order here stated.

ad'vancive, *a.* *rare*$^{-0}$. [improp. f. ADVANCE *v.* + -IVE.] 'Tending to advance or promote.' Craig 1847.

† **ad'vant**, *v.*[1] *Obs.* [an occas. refashioning of *avant*, AVAUNT *v.*[1]] To vaunt, boast.

1541 ELYOT *Image Gov.* (1556) 20 Who can advant himselfe to be well assured from this nette of hipocrisie?

† **advant**, *v.*[2] *Obs.* [a refashioning of *avant*, AVAUNT *v.*[2], *avaunt* adv. forward.] To advance.

1605 CHAPMAN *All Fooles* 1873 I. 136 Then with a Bell regard aduant mine eye With boldnes on her verie visnomie.

advantage (æd'vɑːntɪdʒ, -æ-). Forms: 4–6 **avauntage, avantage** (*Sc.* **awawntage, awantage**); 6– **advantage**. [a. Fr. *avantage*, f. *avant* forward + -AGE; the cognate Romance forms point to the word as already formed in late L. as *abantāticum*. The occasional MFr. corrupt spelling *a(d)vantage*, as if from L. *ad-*, has been permanently adopted in Eng.; see ADVANCE *v.* The original survives in the aphetic form *'vantage, vantage.*]

I. Superior position.

1. a. The position, state, or circumstance of being *in advance* or ahead of another, or having the better of him in any respect; superior or better position; precedence, superiority, *esp.* in contest or debate.

1330 R. BRUNNE *Chron.* 314 The auantage set so hie That thou may gyue with right, whan thou wille & how. **1393** GOWER *Conf.* III. 219 And whan they wiste their avauntage, They fell anone unto the chace. **1523** LD. BERNERS *Froissart* I. cxciv. 230 Ther they had a great aduantage. **1642** ROGERS *Naaman* 19 What rescue hath the dry stubble against the advantage of fire. **1692** RAY *Disc.* iii. (1732) 32 The Advantage or Height of all the dry Land. **1751** JOHNSON *Rambler* No. 177 ⁋3 When the smallest advantage was gained against me in dispute. **1781** GIBBON *Decl. & F.* III. 63 The Gauls maintained their advantage. **1810** COLERIDGE *Friend* (1865) 20 The advantage given to the opponents of Christianity. **1849** MACAULAY *Hist. Eng.* I. 115 When the war had lasted a year, the advantage was decidedly with the Royalists.

b. To have, gain, get, give ***advantage of, over*** (***on*** obs.): superiority over. Also techn. ***to have the advantage of*** (a person): to have a personal knowledge that is not reciprocal.

1561 BECON *Sick Man's Salve* (1844) 146 Let his enemy the devil have none avantage of him. *c* **1600** SHAKS. *Sonnets* lxiv. 6, I have seen the hungry ocean gain Advantage on the kingdom of the shore. **1603** GREENWEY *Tacitus* XII. viii. (1622) 164 In skilfulnesse of the countrey [Caractacus] hauing the aduantage on vs. **1611** BIBLE *2 Cor.* ii. 11 Lest Satan should get an aduantage of vs. **1700** LUTTRELL *Brief Rel.* (1857) IV. 704 The Swedes have had an advantage against the Muscovites. **1775** SHERIDAN *Rivals* V. II. (1873) 94 You have the advantage of me, I don't remember ever to have had the honour. **1813** MISS AUSTEN *Pride & Prej.* ii. 4 You may have the advantage of your friend, and introduce Mr. Bingley to her. **1869** J. MARTINEAU *Ess.* II. 115 Unbelief has no advantage over belief.

† **c.** To ***be at, upon, advantage***: in a favourable position. *Obs.*

1375 BARBOUR *Bruce* XI. 288 We sall be at awantage thar. **1513** DOUGLAS *Æneis* XII. xi. 112 Thou.. Walkys at auantage on the wod grene. **1656** in *Burton's Diary* (1828) I. 89 Some had dined and were upon an advantage.

† **d.** With poss. pron. ***at my, his, etc. advantage***: In a position where one has the advantage or superiority. *Obs.* Cf. ABOVE C 2.

1375 BARBOUR *Bruce* VI. 66 Sua that we Sall ay at our avantage be. *c* **1386** CHAUCER *Frankl. T.* 44 Loke who that is most pacient in love, He is at his avantage al above. *c* **1430** *Hymns to Virg.* (1867) 81 Whanne age haþ us at his auauntage. **1475** CAXTON *Jason* 77 b, That they sholde slee him if they founde him at their auantage.

2. In *Tennis*, when the two sides have gained the equal number of points or games known as DEUCE, the next point or game is reckoned as *advantage* or *vantage* (i.e. temporary superiority) to the side winning it. Hence *attrib.* in ***advantage game, set***. Also *fig.*

c **1641** MILTON *Reform.* I. Wks. 1847, 10 For if the Scripture be for reformation, and antiquity to boot, it is but an advantage to the dozen, it is no winning cast. **1875** H. H. GIBBS (*Note*) In matches, advantage sets are played; and then, when the players are at say '5 games all,' either must win two games running in order to win the set. **1882** *Daily Tel.* 10 July 2/7 The first was an advantage sett, and in playing off Lawford won by 4 to 2.

† **3.** A place of vantage; *esp.* a rising ground, an elevation; = VANTAGE-GROUND. *Obs.* See III.

1386 CHAUCER *Man of L.T.* 48 Such place as thought hem avauntage For here entent. *c* **1425** WYNTOWN *Cron.* VIII. xxxvi. 53 Had he noucht fowndyn in mare hy Ane Awawntage, he had bene dede. **1614** RALEIGH *Hist. World* II. 412 Shimei.. holding himselfe upon the advantage of a mountain-side. **1633** STAFFORD *Pac. Hib.* xvi. (1821) 387 A Platforme was made upon a ground of advantage (not farre from the Campe). **1639** FULLER *Holy War* III. xxvii. (1840) 166 Egypt is a low level country, except some few advantages which the Egyptians had fortified for themselves. **1663** BLAIR *Autobiog.* vii. (1848) 96 Upon this rebuke I drew my horse to an advantage.

† **4.** A time of vantage, a favourable occasion, an opportunity, a 'chance.' *Obs.*

c **1386** CHAUCER *Man of L.T.* 118 They cannot seen in that non avantage Ne in non other way, save mariage. *c* **1400** *Destr. Troy* xv. 7051 But wirdis, þat is wicked, waitis hir avauntage. **1561** T. N[ORTON] tr. *Calvin's Instit.* IV. 137 He was compelled to watch an aduauntage to take his iourney. **1592** SHAKS. *Ven. & Adon.* 129 Make use of time, let not advantage slip. **1655** FULLER *Ch. Hist.* III. 5 [They] lie at catch, and wait advantages one against another. **1667** MILTON *P.L.* IX. 258 Watches, no doubt, with greedy hope to find His wish and best advantage, us asunder.

5. a. A favouring circumstance; anything which gives one the superiority or tends to improve one's position. (The opposite is *disadvantage.*)

1483 CAXTON *Cato* C ij, Euery man kepeth and loueth better that which he acquireth wyth payn.. thenne that whych cometh of auauntage. **1593** SHAKS. *Rich. II*, III. iii. 42 Ile vse th' aduantage of my Power. **1607** TOPSELL *Four-footed Beasts* (1673) 550 [He] compareth the wrath of Perseus standing betwixt two advantages unto a Tiger betwixt two preys. **1655** FULLER *Ch. Hist.* IX. 121 This petition, though presented with all advantage, found no other entertainment than delays. *c* **1660** *Narr. late Parlt.* in *Sel. Harl. Misc.* (1793) 406 What company of foot, and other advantages, it is not certainly known. **1716–8** LADY M. W. MONTAGUE *Lett.* I. xviii. 57 He needs not the advantage of his rank to appear charming. **1874** REYNOLDS *John Bapt.* i. §1. 12 He was himself possessed of all their advantages, while he is placed on a vantage-ground above them.

b. ***to take*** (***the*** obs.) ***advantage of*** (***by, at*** obs.), ***to make one's advantage of***, a thing: To use any favourable condition which it yields; to avail oneself of. Often in a bad sense: To seize an accidental or unintended opportunity of profiting, to overreach (a person). Also ***to take advantage*** (without const.).

1393 GOWER *Conf.* III. 322 He, that by her body wolde Take avauntage. **1598** SHAKS. *Merry Wives* III. iii. 116 To take an ill aduantage of his absence. **1618** DONNE *Serm.* cxliii. V. 851 Laban.. made advantages upon him, deluded him. **1620** SANDERSON *Serm.* Ad. Pop II. v. 155 He doth *arripere ansam*, take all advantage as it were, and lay hold on every occasion to do that. **1657** *Ibid.* (1674) Pref. §10 The Papists make a great advantage of these home-differences. **1664** POWER *Exp. Philos.* I. 16 You may see them sometimes, if you happily take the advantage. **1705** ADDISON *Italy* 6 Taking the Advantage of a Side-wind. **1817** JAS. MILL *Brit. India* II. IV. iii. 95 Inclined to make their advantage of his necessities. **1859** GEO. ELIOT *Adam Bede* II. xxxii. 331 It's them as take advantage that get advantage i' this world. **1876** FREEMAN *Norm. Conq.* III. xii. 251 Here was material enough for the craft of William to take advantage of. **1922** JOYCE *Ulysses* 370 Sad about her lame of course but must be on your guard not to feel too much pity. They take advantage. **1979** B. BAINBRIDGE *Another Part of Wood* viii. 160 May sensed he was vulnerable. She couldn't help taking advantage.

c. To ***take*** any one ***at*** (***upon, on*** obs.) ***advantage***: when the circumstances favour the taker, as by surprise, stratagem, etc.; to surprise. ***to play upon advantage*** (obs.): to cheat.

1523 LD. BERNERS *Froissart* I. xviii. 24 They wold haue ben slayn, or taken at auauntage. **1592** WARNER *Albion's Eng.* VII. xxxvi. (1612) 174 Howbeit, on aduantage plai'd Gynetta all this while. **1607** HIERON *Wks.* I. 430 The griping Nimrods of the world reioyce in their taking men vpon aduantages. **1656** BP. HALL *Occas. Medit.* (1851) 17 It were woe with any of us all, if God should take us at advantages. **1668** SEDLEY *Mulb. Garden* II. ii. (1766) 63 Your only way is to turn rook and play upon advantage. **1826** SOUTHEY in *Q. Rev.* XXXIV. 330 Once it happened that the enemy took him at advantage.

II. The result of a superior or better position.

6. a. Benefit; enhancement, improvement; increased well-being or convenience; resulting benefit. ***to one's advantage***: to one's benefit, beneficial to one.

1340 HAMPOLE *Pr. Consc.* 1012 Þat world was made to our most avantage. **1393** GOWER *Conf.* I. 194 So can I see none avauntage, But all is lost, if she abide. **1477** EARL RIVERS (Caxton) *Dictes* 143 Wisemen.. semblably do auantage to other. **1596** SHAKS. *1 Hen. IV*, I. i. 27 Those blessed feet, Which, fourteen hundred years ago, were nail'd, For our aduantage, on the bitter Crosse. **1667** MILTON *P.L.* XII. 510 Who all the sacred mysteries of Heaven To their own vile advantages shall turn Of lucre and ambition. **1772** *Junius Lett.* lxviii. 337 You shall have all the advantage of his opinion. **1843** MIALL *Nonconf.* III. 209 Tahiti cannot be colonised with advantage. **1882** *Daily News* 3 Nov. 1/2 If the Gentleman who travelled from Yeovil Junction.. with a violin case, will send his address he will hear of something to his advantage.

b. ***to advantage***: So as to increase or augment the effect of anything; advantageously, favourably.

1709 POPE *Ess. Critic.* 297 True Wit is Nature to advantage dress'd. **1858** HAWTHORNE *Fr. & It. Jrnls.* I. 303 The atmosphere has a quality of showing objects to a better advantage. **1860** TYNDALL *Glac.* I. §15. 100 To see the lower portion of this glacier to advantage. *Mod.* That dress sets off her figure to advantage.

† **7.** Pecuniary profit, gain; interest on money lent. *Obs.*

1393 GOWER *Conf.* III. 46 The seale and therupon thymage Of Thebith for his avauntage He taketh. **1413** LYDG. *Pylgr. Sowle* IV. xxxiii. (1483) 81 His rentes and revenues and suche other auantages. **1535** COVERDALE *Ps.* lxxiii. 10 There out sucke they no small auauntage. **1596** SHAKS. *Merch. Ven.* I. iii. 71 You neither lend nor borrow Vpon aduantage. **1614** RALEIGH *Hist. World* II. IV. vii. §1. 280 Forcing them to restore the spoyles with advantage. **1665** MANLEY *Grotius's Low-Countrey-Warrs* 181 Another fleet.. had fallen upon the Molucca Islands, bringing away great advantage.

† **8.** Greater quantity or number, 'more-ness'; amount or quantity over, additional amount, over-plus, excess. ***to, of advantage*** (Fr. *d'avantage, de plus*): in addition, more. *Obs.*

1340 *Ayenb.* 209 Alle þise timliche þinges þou sselt habbe to auontage. *Ibid.* 210 God dep him auontage of þe timliche guodes. **1534** LD. BERNERS *Gold. Bk. M. Aurel.* (1546) Bv. b, I saie further of aduauntage, that dyuers haue written of the tyme of the saide Marke Aureleo. **1570** KANAM in *Bury Wills* (1850) 156 One blacke stered heckforde of the age of two yeres and the aduantage. **1604** SHAKS. *Oth.* IV. iii. 84 As many to' th' vantage. **1612** SHELTON *Quix.* I. 15, 4 or 5 Sheets of Advantage at the end of the Book. **1642** FULLER *Holy & Prof. St.* I. xi. 29 She being a woman that in all her actions (to be sure to do enough) made always measure with advantage.

III. *Comb.* **advantage-ground**, a position that gives advantage or superiority to a combatant; now usually written *vantage-ground.*

1628 EARLE *Microcosm.* xxxiv. 73 He stands taller on his own bottom, than others on the advantage ground of fortune. **1659** RUSHWORTH *Hist. Coll.* I. 17 The Bohemians stood upon the advantage-ground betwixt the Imperialists and Prague. *a* **1674** CLARENDON *Hist. Rebell.* III. Ded. 10 On the advantage-ground of being established by the Laws.

☛*Phrase-key.* At my, his *a* 1 d, be at *a* 1 c, gain, get, give *a* over 1 b, have *a* of 1 b, make *a* of 5 b, of *a* 8, play upon *a* 5 c, take *a* of 5 b, take at *a* 5 c, tennis *a* 2, to *a* 6 b, 8, to one's *a* 6.

advantage (æd'vɑːntɪdʒ, -æ-), *v.* Also 5–6 **avantage**, 6 **advauntage**. [a. Fr. *avantage-r, -ier*, to cause advantage. For change from *a-* to *ad-* see ADVANCE.] To do, bring, or be of, advantage to.

1. To give an advantage or superiority to, favour.

1598 BARRET *Theor. Warres* IV. i. 117 Souldiers of great experience.. should be aduantaged in their payes. **1650** FULLER *Pisgah Sight* I. xii. 38 Judea, advantaged with the friendly City of Jerusalem. **1654** E. JOHNSON *Wonder-working Prov.* 192 Although Charles Town do not advantage such o're-topping batteries as Boston doth. **1871** LOWELL *Study Windows* 96 Boston was also advantaged with the neighbourhood of the country's oldest College.

† **b.** To place advantageously. *Obs.*

1650 FULLER *Pisgah Sight* II. iv. 115 All the cities of refuge on this side Jordan were advantaged on very high foundations. **1662** —— *Worthies* (1840) III. 116 Advantaged for western voyages by its situation.

† **c.** To set off to advantage. *Obs.*

1748 RICHARDSON *Clarissa* (1811) V. 303 How dress advantages women!

2. To further, promote, advance, contribute to the progress of (anything).

1586 J. HOOKER *Giraldus's Hist. Irel.* in *Holinsh.* II. 84/2 Hereby he.. aduantaged the flight of his capteine. **1651** HOBBES *Gov. & Soc.* vi. §4. 113 It would no whit advantage the liberty of the subject. *c* **1681** SIR T. BROWNE *Tracts* 6 Variously interspersed expressions from plants, elegantly advantaging the significancy of the Text. **1692** WASHINGTON tr. *Milton's Def. Pop.* ii. (1851) 62 Nor do you much advantage your cause by telling us Moses was a king. **1858** BRIGHT *Sp.* (1876) 301 The agriculture of this country has been advantaged by the importation of reaping machines.

† **3.** To add to the amount or value of. *Obs.*

1496–7 PLUMPTON *Corr.* 129, I have done good ther and avantaged much wood and tymber. **1594** SHAKS. *Rich. III*, IV. iv. 323 Aduantaging their Loue [? loan] with interest Of ten-times double gain of happiness. **1640** FULLER *Abel Rediv., Foxe* (1867) II. 81 Friendship.. advantaged with the sympathy of their natures. **1673** RAY *Journ. Low Countries* Pref., To advantage the Catalogue I have added thereto a brief narrative.

4. To put in a better position, prove beneficial to, benefit, profit.

1530 PALSGR. 440 This can nothyng avauntage you. **1647** FULLER *Holy War* II. xxix. 81 Some think their coming advantaged King Baldwine. **1660** T. STANLEY *Hist. Philos.* (1701) 91/1 [I] have advantaged all that conversed with me. **1686** W. DE BRITAINE *Hum. Prud.* §22. 108 Winds, which if they do not throw down, do advantage Trees. *a* **1754** FIELDING *Wife at Home* III. vi. Wks. 1784 II. 40 If you are not advantaged by the stratagem, you will be disadvantaged by the discovery. **1848** RUSKIN *Mod. Painters* II. III. II. iv. §9. 191 How far it would be possible to advantage a statue by the addition of colour, I venture not to affirm.

† **b.** *impersonal.* To profit, benefit. *Obs.*

1526 TINDALE *Luke* ix. 25 What shall itt avauntage a man? **1549** COVERDALE *Erasm. Paraphr. 1 Cor.* x. 5 Nothyng aduauntaged them to escape out of Egipte, if they caried furthe Egipte with them. **1611** BIBLE *1 Cor.* xv. 32 What aduantageth it me, if the dead rise not?

† **c.** *absol. Obs.*

1610 SHAKS. *Temp.* I. i. 34 Make the rope of his destiny our cable, for our own doth little aduantage. **1668** CHILD *Disc. Trade* (1694) 57 To leave them money without skill to use it, would advantage little.

† **5.** *refl.* To benefit oneself. ***to advantage oneself of, with***: to take advantage of. *Obs.*

1598 YONG *Diana* 187 Yet will I not aduantage me with any such remedy. **1603** FLORIO *Montaigne* II. viii. (1632) 212 No man of courage vouchsafeth to advantage himselfe of that which is common unto many. **1615** T. ADAMS *Lycanthropy* 31 They will be sure to advantage themselves of the wind. **1693** *Mem. Count Teckely* II. 149 The Christians sought for nothing but advantaging themselves at the expence of the Turks.

† **6.** To gain, profit. *Obs.*

1557 N. T. (Genev.) *Luke* xix. 15 To wyt what euery man had auantaged.

† **ad'vantageable**, *a. Obs.* Also 5–6 **av-**. [f. prec. + -ABLE.] Tending to advantage; profitable; advantageous.

1548 GESTE *Priuee Masse* 72 Nedefull to hys churche and so advantageable to him selve. **1599** NASHE *Lenten Stuffe* 25 A cowe.. what an advantageable creature she is. **1657** T. REEVE *Plea for Nineveh* Ep. Ded. 1 If ye be industrious.. ye may drive a very advantageable trade.

advantaged (æd'vɑːntɪdʒd, -æ-), *ppl. a.* [f. ADVANTAGE *v.* + -ED.] Placed at advantage; furthered, promoted; benefited, profited.

1603 SHAKS. *Meas. for M.* III. i. 265 The poore Mariana aduantaged, and the corrupt Deputy scaled. **1654** FULLER *2 Serm.* 4 Armed Power, advantaged with Policie. **1796** BURKE *Regic. Peace* Wks. 1842 II. 280 Thus advantaged, if it can at all exist, it must finally prevail. **1878** SIMPSON *Sch. Shaks.* I. 134 Philip as their nearest neighbour would be the most advantaged.

advantageous (ædvən'teɪdʒəs), *a.* Also 6–7 **advantagious.** [ad. Fr. *avantageux, -euse*, f. *avantage*: see ADVANTAGE and -OUS. The common 17th c. spelling is evidently due to looking upon the word as formed from the med.L. *avantagium*, a latinized form of *avantage*. Cf. *contagious, litigious.*]

1. Of advantage; furnishing advantages; profitable, useful, opportune, beneficial, favourable.

1598 FLORIO, *Auantaggioso*, aduantageous, hauing ods or aduantage. **1606** SHAKS. *Tr. & Cr.* v. iv. 22, I doe not flye; but aduantagious care Withdrew me from the oddes of multitude. **1667** MILTON *P.L.* II. 368 Here perhaps Som advantagious act may be achiev'd By sudden onset. **1766** BURKE *Late Administ.* Wks. II. 5 Making an advantageous treaty of commerce with Russia. *c* **1860** MAURICE *Mor. & Metaph. Philos.* IV. ix. §37. 559 Condillac is an advantageous and admirable type of the school.

b. Const. *to, for* (*unto* obs.).

1610 SHAKS. *Temp.* II. i. 49 Heere is euery thing aduantageous to life. **1618** RALEIGH *Rem.* (1664) 149 Advantagious also, as well for the publick weal, as the private person. **1630** PRYNNE *Anti-Armin.* 123 What can be more aduantagious vnto Satan. **1767** *Junius Lett.* viii. 33 A wise doctrine..equally advantageous to the king and his subjects. **1868** PEARD *Water-farming* xiii. 131 Heat is agreeable, if not advantageous to most fresh-water fish.

†**2.** Apt to take advantage, overreaching, sharp. (Cotgr. *Avantageux*, advantageous, also very forward, full of forwardness.) *Obs. rare.*

1599 SANDYS *Europæ Spec.* (1632) 226 They [Jews] are a subtile and advantagious people and wonderfully eager of gaine.

advantageously (ædvən'teɪdʒəslɪ), *adv.* [f. prec. + -LY².]

1. In an advantageous manner; with advantage; beneficially, profitably; favourably.

1602 WARNER *Albion's Eng.* XII. lxx. (1612) 293 For writers advantagiously are of the liuing read. **1677** YARRANTON *Eng. Improvem.* 16 That great and desirable Rich Trade of Fishing..which so advantageously offers it self. **1734** tr. *Rollin's Anc. Hist.* I. II. §1 (1827) 230 The scripture in several places speaks advantageously of their cavalry. **1863** KINGLAKE *Crimea* (1877) IV. ix. 235 Lord Raglan was advantageously placed. **1878** GLADSTONE *Prim. Homer* 133 Hector compares..very advantageously with the worthless Paris.

†**2.** With readiness to take (improper) advantage, eagerly. *Obs.*

1602 WARNER *Albion's Eng.* XV. xcviii. (1612) 388 Too aduantagiously from out our Rubrick they vnyoke.

advantageousness (ædvən'teɪdʒəsnɪs). [f. as prec. + -NESS.] The quality or state of being advantageous; profitableness, usefulness.

1659 BOYLE *Love of God* §18. 117 The last Property which qualify's God the fittest Object for our Love..is the Advantageousness of His to us. **1750** F. COVENTRY *Pompey the Little* v. (1788) 40 The advantageousness of the match soon prevailed with her parents. **1833** HT. MARTINEAU *Loom & Lugger* II. v. 90 The advantageousness of trade.

advaunt, variant of AVAUNT *v. Obs.* to boast.

advayle, -able, obs. forms of AVAIL, -ABLE.

advect (æd'vɛkt), *v.* [Back-formation from ADVECTION.] *trans.* To convey by (esp. horizontal) mass movement of a fluid.

1957 G. E. HUTCHINSON *Treat. Limnol.* I. vii. 512 The sources of energy are the radiation from the sun..and sky.., the heat advected by influents, [etc.]. **1964** *Oceanogr. & Marine Biol.* II. 21 A rotating mass of water would tend to have its motion retarded by the action of eddies smaller than itself, while those much larger would advect the rotating mass as a whole. **1976** *Nature* 1 Apr. 457/2 Absolute vorticity..is generated at the sides, top and bottom of the vehicle... Once generated it is advected with the air stream into the vehicle's wake. *Ibid.* 24 June 679/2 If Lake Zissaga is frozen,..it will have a high albedo and a large deficit in its local energy budget, which..must be balanced using energy advected from the surroundings.

advection (æd'vɛkʃən). [ad. L. *advectiōn-em*, n. of action from *adveh-ĕre* to carry to; f. *ad* to + *veh-ĕre* to carry.]

a. *Meteorol.* The transfer of heat by the horizontal movement of the air. Similarly, heat transfer by the vertical motion of the air, esp. in a large-scale or steady atmospheric current. Also *attrib.*, as ***advection fog.*** Hence **ad'vective** *a.*, of, or caused by, advection. Cf. CONVECTION.

1910 *Rep. Brit. Assoc. Advancem. Sci. 1909* 103 Interchange of air in the upper region would be mainly by advection and the two [upper and lower] regions might be appropriately named advective and convective regions. **1941** *Jrnl. R. Aeronaut. Soc.* XLV. 82 The non-adiabatic cooling may be due to two causes, viz., the radiative cooling of the underlying surface, and the advective cooling that results when warm air streams over a colder surface. We may therefore speak of radiation fogs, advection fogs and upslope fogs. **1951** *Compendium of Meteorol.* (Amer. Meteorol. Soc.) 783/1 The greatest convective temperature changes are produced by the vertical advection of pressure, whereas only generally small convective changes in the temperature are caused by the relative local pressure change and by the horizontal advective pressure change. **1956** J. C. SWAYNE *Conc. Gloss. Geogr. Terms* 9 *Advection fog*, a fog formed when relatively warm, moist air passes over colder land or water, e.g. the sea-fogs of the Grand Banks of Newfoundland. **1956** S. PETTERSSEN *Weather Analysis & Forecasting* (ed. 2) I. xviii. 373 It has been customary to simplify by neglecting..the term representing the vertical advection of vorticity. **1967** R. W. FAIRBRIDGE *Encycl. Atmospheric Sci.* 3/1 The distinction between convection and vertical advection is commonly a matter of scale.

b. *Oceanogr.* The horizontal or vertical transfer of material, heat, etc., brought about by the mass movement of the oceans, e.g. in currents.

1942 H. U. SVERDRUP et al. *Oceans* v. 160 Surface salinity ..was shown to depend on two terms, one that represents the external processes of evaporation and precipitation, and one that represents the internal processes of diffusion and advection. **1966** R. W. FAIRBRIDGE *Encycl. Oceanogr.* 23/1 Convectional transport is..due to small-scale..thermally induced currents..which are considered at random and treated statistically. Vertical advection is that due to steady or mean vertical currents. **1979** *Nature* 23 Aug. 651/2 The shelf sea fronts..represent a set of almost fixed geographical boundaries throughout the summer season, moved significantly only by tidal advection. **1981** *Ibid.* 22 Jan. 219/1 Lonsdale proposed two possible sources of nutrition: advection of food materials from surrounding regions [of the ocean] and bacterial chemosynthesis. **1982** *Sci. Amer.* Aug. 35/1 Downward diffusion, advection or convection between the well-mixed layer and the deeper water would increase the amount of carbon dioxide taken up by the ocean.

c. *transf.*

1975 *Nature* 30 Oct. 748/1 Within the continental tectosphere the temperatures are lower, the thermal gradients are super-adiabatic, and the dominant mechanism of heat transport is conduction, not advection.

advec'titious, *a. Obs.*$^{-0}$ [f. L. *advectīci-us* (f. *advect-us*, pa. pple. of *adveh-ĕre* to carry to; f. *ad* to + *veh-ĕre* to carry) + -OUS.] 'Which is brought or carryed unto.' Blount 1656. Whence in Phillips, Bailey, Ash, and mod. Dicts.

advehent ('ædvɪhənt), *a.* [ad. L. *advehent-em* pr. pple. of *adveh-ĕre*: see prec.] Carrying towards, afferent.

1836 TODD *Cycl. Anat. & Phys.* I. 646/2 The advehent veins of the kidneys carry venous blood to these organs.

advencoun, early form of ADVENTION. *Obs.*

advene (æd'viːn), *v.* [a. MFr. *adven-ir*, common spelling of *avenir*:—L. *advenīre* to come to, f. *ad* to + *venīre* to come.]

1. *intr.* To accede or come (*to*); to be superadded, as part of something, though not essential.

1606 OWEN *Epigr.* (NARES) Venus (saith one) spontan'ous doth advene Unt' all things. **1651** N. BIGGS *New Dispens.* §229. 166 But a momentary help is that, which advenes by phlebotomy. **1726** AYLIFFE *Parerg.* 148 The accidental of any act, is said to be whatever advenes to the act itself already substantiated. **1820–30** COLERIDGE *Rem.* (1836) III. 19 Where no act of the will advenes as a co-efficient.

2. *trans.* To come to, reach.

1839 J. ROGERS *Antipopopr.* Introd. §25 The extremity whereof I have not arrived at or advened.

†**ad'venement.** *Obs. rare*$^{-1}$. [a. MFr. *advenement*, occas. spelling of *avénement* a coming, an event, f. *avenir*: see prec. and -MENT.] That which comes or happens; an event, incident.

1490 CAXTON *Eneydos* i. 12 The aduenementes and aduersitees of warre ben doubtous and vnder the honde of fortune.

advenge, -ment, obs. forms of AVENGE, -MENT.

ad'venient, *a.* [ad. L. *advenient-em* pr. pple. of *adveni-re*: see ADVENE.] Coming (to anything) from without; additional, superadded; adventitious.

1594 *Wounds of Civ. War* IV. i. in Hazl. *Dodsl.* VII. 158 Old Marius will foresee advenient harms. **1646** SIR T. BROWNE *Pseud. Ep.* VI. xii. 336 These are the advenient and artificiall wayes of denigration. **1667** BOYLE *Orig. Form & Qual.*, The advenient Humane Soul becoming now the true Forme of the Humane Body. **1870** SMITH *Syn. & Antonyms, Future..Syn.* Forthcoming, Coming, Advenient. **1923** *Times Lit. Suppl.* 13 Sept. 596/2 There is in knowledge both an advenient physical influence from the thing and a projicient psychical reference to the thing. **1936** *Nature* 28 Mar. 522/1 Colour as experienced is..an indication..of the presence of specific chemical changes in the retina and the choroid under advenient electromagnetic influence.

Advent ('ædvənt). [a. OFr. *advent*, literary form of *auvent*:—L. *adventus* arrival, f. *advenī-re* to come to: see ADVENE. Applied in Christian literature specially to the Coming of the Saviour; whence, in the ecclesiastical calendar, the name of the period preceding the festival of the Nativity, the earliest sense in Eng. (10th or 11th c.) and the only sense in French. In the middle of the 15th c. it became in Eng. also the proper title of the Incarnation; whence extended to our Lord's anticipated Second Advent as Judge (as already in Latin, in Tertullian), and to that of the Holy Spirit at Pentecost; in modern times partly as an extension of this, partly with reference to the primary sense of 'arrival' in L., it has been used of any important arrival, or even for *arrival* simply.]

1. a. In the ecclesiastical calendar, the season immediately preceding the festival of the Nativity, now including the four preceding Sundays.

1099–1121 *O.E. Chron.* (Laud MS.) anno 1099 Osmund biscop of Searbyriȝ innon Aduent forðferde. *a* **1121** *Ibid.* anno 963 On þe fyrste sunnondæȝ of Aduent. *c* **1200** *Trin. Coll. Hom.* 3 þesse þre wuken, þe ben cleped aduent, þat is seggen on englis ure louerd ihesu cristes to cume. **1297** R. GLOUC. 463 Gret frost ther com in Aduent. **1482** *Monk of Evesham* (1869) 49 Y fastyd the dayes of aduent. **1599** THYNNE *Animadv.* (1865) 40 Nowell..is that tyme whiche is properlye called the Advente. **1611** COTGR., *Advents de Noel*, the time of advent; before Christmas. **1860** TRENCH *Serm. Westm. Abb.* i. 1 All the services of this Advent season.

b. *Advent Sunday*, the first Sunday in Advent, the Sunday nearest to the thirtieth of November.

c **1450** *Mirk's Fest.* 1 Advent Sonday..þys day..ys cleped Sonenday yn þe Aduent; þat ys, þe Sonenday of Cristys comyng. **1564** *Booke of Common Prayer* sig. C iii v° (*table*) Advent Sunday. **1627** J. COSIN *Coll. Private Devotions* sig. B 9, Advent Sunday is alwayes the neerest Sunday..to the Feast of S. Andrew. **1704** NELSON *Festiv. & Fasts* ii. (1739) 27 Advent Sundays, The four Sundays that preceed the Great Festival of our Saviour's Nativity. **1875** H. BRADSHAW in Smith & Cheetham *Dict. Christian Antiquities* I. 32/2 For lessons, Isaiah was read all through, beginning on Advent Sunday. **1977** *Conc. Oxf. Dict. Christian Church* 8/1 The first day of Advent (Advent Sunday) begins the ecclesiastical year.

2. The Coming of the Lord Jesus Christ as Saviour of the world; the Incarnation. Hence his expected Second Coming as Judge, and the Coming of the Holy Spirit as at Pentecost.

c **1440** *Gesta Rom.* ii. 7 Afore þe Advente of criste. **1582** N. T. (Rheims) *1 Thess.* iv. 15 Vve vvhich liue, vvhich are remaining in the aduent [*other versions* coming] of our Lord. **1636** PRYNNE *Unbish. Tim. & Tit.* (1661) 63 Priests and Presbyters who..imprecate the Lords Advent to the Eucharist. **1664** JER. TAYLOR *Confirm.* (R.) The perfective Unction of Chrism gives to him the advent of the Holy Spirit. **1784** COWPER *Task* VI. 866 Who, could they see The dawn of thy last advent, long desir'd, Would creep into the bowels of the hills. **1879** FARRAR *St. Paul* I. 605 On the nearness of the final Messianic Advent, the Jewish and the Christian world were at one.

3. By extension, Any important or epoch-making arrival. In modern usage applied poetically or grandiloquently to any arrival. (This use is unknown to Johnson 1755 and Todd 1818.)

1742 YOUNG *Night Th.* v. 906 Death's dreadful Advent is the Mark of Man. **1801** STRUTT *Sports & Past.* Introd. §4, 5 The advent of the Normans. **1840** HOOD *Up the Rhine* 50 Too much interested..to notice the advent of another passenger. **1850** TENNYSON *In Mem.* vi. 21 Expecting still his advent home.

adventayle, var. AVENTAIL, part of a helmet.

[**adventine,** in Johnson, copied by subseq. Dicts., from Bacon's *Nat. Hist.*, is a misprint for *adventiue*: see ADVENTIVE.]

†**ad'vention.** *Obs. rare*$^{-1}$. Only form 5 **advencoun.** [ad. med.L. *adventiōn-em* addition (Du Cange), n. of action, f. L. *advenī-re* to come to: see ADVENE.] An extrinsic addition.

c **1400** *Apol. for Loll.* 55 Al kynd of syn, felony, and abhominacoun, and new aduencouns. And in þer aduencouns þey are filid [= defiled].

†**ad'ventious,** *a. Obs. rare.* [f. prec. after *contention, contentious*, etc.] = ADVENTITIOUS.

1641 FRENCH *Distillation* vi. (1651) 177 If any skilfull philosopher could..separate this adventious impurity from gold. **1652** —— *Yorksh. Spa* xiii. 104 Rather adventious, or preternatural, then natural.

Adventist ('ædvəntɪst). Also **adventist.** [f. ADVENT + -IST.] A member of any of the various religious sects holding millenarian views. Also *attrib.* Hence **'adventism,** the principles or tenets of adventists.

Second Adventist, orig. the fuller designation of the followers of William Miller (died 1849), who promoted the doctrine that the second coming of Christ and the end of the world were near at hand, a Millerite.

1843 *Signs of the Times* 15 Nov. 109 in F. D. Nichol *Midnight Cry* (1944) x. 156 The English Adventists. **1844** in Cist *Cincinnati Misc.* (1845) I. 29 As the day approaches.. the faithful adventists continue nearly the whole time, day and night at the Tabernacle. **1874** WELLCOME *Hist. Second Advent Message* 592 (D.A.E.), Judaism is being taught. If brethren do not mean to teach it let them tell us so and not teach this under the cloak of Adventism. **1876** [see SEVENTH-DAY 2 b]. **1878** in G. L. Prentiss *Life & Lett. E. Prentiss* (1882) 504 Neither Mr. Prentiss or myself have ever had any sympathy with Second Adventists. **1883** *Encycl. Brit.* XVI. 320/2 At present the number of Millerites or Adventists is estimated at from 15,000 to 20,000. **1895** J. R. HARRIS *Union* *with God* xi. 188 The existence of an adventist movement in Jerusalem. **1927** FLINT & TAIT tr. *Fülöp-Miller's Mind & Face of Bolshevism* 78 The sects with a more rationalist tinge, the 'Adventists' and the 'New Adventists'.

‖**adventitia** (ædvən'tɪʃɪə), *sb. pl. Phys.* [L. *adventīcia*, pl. neut. of adj. *adventīcius*: see ADVENTITIOUS.] Membranous structure, usually morbid, covering but not belonging to an organ.
1876 tr. *Wagner's Gen. Pathol.* 147 The adventitia of the large veins of the abdomen. **1878** HAMILTON *Nerv. Dis.* 18 Any adventitia that may be attached to the dura mater.

adven'titial, *a.* [f. L. *adventīci-us* ADVENTITIOUS + -AL[1].] A by-form of ADVENTITIOUS. Also used *subst.*
1607 TOPSELL *Four-footed Beasts* (1673) 102 Their flesh allayeth all adventitial and extraordinary heat. **1633** T. ADAMS *Exp. 2 Pet.* iii. 5 (1865) 636/2 There be three degrees of ignorance.. Secondly, adventitial, which is accompanied with actual sin. **1652** GAULE *Magastrom.* 77 Neither doth nature prefer any creature for its adventitials or accidentals. **1901** *Jrnl. Exper. Med.* VI. 69 The adventitial lymphatic sheath is in most cases distended.

†**adven'tition.** *Obs. rare*[−1]. [improp. f. ADVENTIT-IOUS + -ION[1], after *nutritious*, *nutrition*, etc.] = ADVENTION.
1671 J. WEBSTER *Metallogr.* viii. 123 The advention and mixture of extraneous matter.

adventitious (ædvən'tɪʃəs), *a.* Also **adventicious.** [f. L. *adventīci-us*, in med.L. corruptly written *adventiti-us*, coming to us from abroad + -OUS: see ADVENT, and -ITIOUS). The occas. *adventicious* is etymologically a better spelling.]

1. Of the nature of an addition from without; extrinsically added, not essentially inherent; supervenient, accidental, casual. Cf. the obs. ADVENTIVE.
1603 HOLLAND *Plutarch's Mor.* 1307 That which is extraordinarily adventitious, unholsome and diseased. **1627** HAKEWILL *Apol.* II. ix.§6 This decay in the creatures ariseth .. from an adventicious and externall cause. **1630** HOWELL *Lett.* (1650) I. 387 Greek.. was an adventitious, no mother-language to them. **1677** GALE *Crt. of Gentiles* II. IV. 36 An adventitious joy which hath no funde or bottome. **1756** C. LUCAS *Ess. on Waters* I. 35 Our Thames.. is tainted with an infinite variety of adventitious bodies from the streets. **1831** CARLYLE *Sart. Res.* (1858) 34 When a man first strips himself of adventitious wrappages; and sees indeed that he is naked. **1846** GROTE *Greece* (1862) I. xviii. 424 An adventitious population accumulated in Attica.

2. *Law.* (See quot. 1751.)
1651 W. G. tr. *Cowel's Instit.* 17 Estate whither adventitious or bequeathed. **1751** CHAMBERS *Cycl.*, *Adventitious*, in the Civil Law, is applied to such goods as fall to a man, either by mere fortune, or by the liberality of a stranger, or by collateral, not direct succession. In this sense the word stands opposed to *Profectitious*; by which are signified such goods as descend in a direct line. **1880** MUIRHEAD *Ulpian* vi. §3 A dowry is either profecticious, that is, given by the woman's father, or adventicious, given by some other person.

3. *Nat. Hist.* Appearing casually, or out of the normal or usual place, *esp.* in *Bot.* of roots, shoots, buds, etc. produced in unusual parts of the plant.
1676 GREW *Anat. Plants* IV. I. ii. (1682) 148 There are also some spots, or rather streaks, which are adventitious; as those in the Leaves of Sonchus. **1836** TODD *Cycl. Anat. & Phys.* I. 606/1 Like all adventitious organic products, cicatrices are very readily irritated. **1842** GRAY *Struct. Bot.* iii. §2 (1880) 45 Even leaves may develop adventitious buds. **1872** OLIVER *Elem. Bot.* II. 233 The celebrated Banyan tree, remarkable for the enormous extension of its crown by means of adventitious roots.

adventitiously (ædvən'tɪʃəslɪ), *adv.* [f. prec. + -LY[2].] In an adventitious manner; by way of extraneous addition; extrinsically.
1746 WATSON in *Phil. Trans.* XLIV. 82 The Phosphori.. some of which shine of themselves naturally, as the Glow-worm and Dates; or adventitiously, as the Flesh of Animals, which most probably arises from a Degree of Putrefaction. **1852** GLADSTONE *Gleanings* IV. lxxvii. 118 A political colour has been adventitiously affixed by some persons to my publication.

adventitiousness (ædvən'tɪʃəsnɪs). [f. as prec. + -NESS.] The quality or state of being adventitious; accidental presence.
1847 TODD *Cycl. Anat. & Phys.* IX. 71/1 The character of adventitiousness is conceived to arise in three different ways.

ad'ventive, *a.* and *sb.* [f. L. *advent-* (ppl. stem of *advenī-re*, see ADVENE) + -IVE, as if ad. L. **adventīvus*. Cf. *preventive*, *inventive*.]

A. *adj.* **1.** Used by Bacon for ADVENTITIOUS. *Obs.*
1605 BACON *Adv. Learn.* II. xi. §1 The considerations of the original of the soul, whether it be natiue or adventiue. **1626** —— *Sylva* §456 (1651) The Cause may be, for that Adventiue Heat doth chear up the Natiue Juyce of the Tree.

2. *Bot.* Of a plant: growing spontaneously but not native to the locality in which it appears; imperfectly naturalized.
1867 GRAY *Man. Bot.* (ed. 5) 16, I have classified our introduced plants.. into two sorts, the thoroughly *naturalized*, and the *adventive*;.. the second, those which are only locally spontaneous. **1888** F. A. LEES *Flora of W. Yorks.* 313 It is luxuriant as to size and adventive. **1919** I. HAYWARD & G. C. DRUCE (*title*) The adventive flora of Tweedside. **1936** *Nature* 11 Apr. 600/2 A survey of the weed flora of the northern part of the United States shows that a large proportion of the adventive weeds are from Europe.

B. *sb.* **1.** An immigrant, a sojourner. *Obs.*
a **1626** BACON *Adv. Villiers* (T.) That the natives be not so many, but that there may be elbow-room enough for them, and for the adventives also.

2. An adventive plant.
1888 F. A. LEES *Flora of W. Yorks.* 313 Campanula Trachelium L... by the tram-road from Manor Coal-pits, Sheffield... An adventive here, clearly.

†**ad'ventry.** *Obs. rare*[−1]. [Formed by Ben Jonson on *adventer*, a 17th c. form of ADVENTURE *v.*, after the analogy of *entry* from *enter*.] An adventure; an enterprise or undertaking.
a **1616** B. JONSON *Voyage Itself* (R.) Act a brave work, call it thy last adventry.

†**ad'ventual,** *a. Obs. rare.* [ad. med.L. *adventuālis* pertaining to Advent, f. L. *adventus*: see ADVENT and -AL[1].] Of or belonging to Advent. (Blount in *Glossogr.* (1656) gives it as a synonym of ADVENTITIOUS.)
1614–25 J. BOYS *Wks.* 1630, 78 The first Gospel in the first Dominicall, according to the Churches account is Adventuall, a Scripture describing Christ and his Kingdome. *a* **1663** SANDERSON *Serm.* (J.) I do also daily use one other collect: as, namely, the collects adventual, quadragesimal.

adventure (æd'vɛntjʊə(r), -tʃə(r)), *sb.* Forms: 3–6 **aventure, auenture, aunter;** 3–5 **auntre;** 4 **aventer, auntyre, -our;** 4–5 **aventur, -owre, awnter, auntur(e, -er(e, anter;** 4–6 **aventre, auentour;** 5 **awentuer, awntyr;** 6–7 **adventer;** 5– **adventure.** [a. OFr. *auenture*:—L. *adventūra* (sc. *res*) a thing about to happen to any one; fut. pple. of *advenī-re* to happen: see ADVENE. The early Eng. *auen'ture* soon passed in pop. speech through the forms *a'uentur*, *'auntur*, to *aunter* and *anter* (still common in Scotl.), while *aven'ture* remained a literary form. In 5–6 the Fr. was often re-spelt *adventure* in imitation of L., a fashion which (though it soon died out in France) passed into Eng., and permanently affected the word. After 1600 the last syllable was still obscure, (-ə(r)).]

†**1. a.** That which comes to us, or happens without design; chance, hap, fortune, luck. *Obs.*
c **1230** *Ancren Riwle* 340 Swuch cas, and swuch auenture bitimeð to summe monne. *c* **1314** *Guy Warw.* 187 To the Lombardes bifel iuel auentour. **1340** *Ayenb.* 18 Guodes of aventure, ase richesses, worssipe, and heȝnesse. *a* **1400** *Metr. Hom.* 30 Fel auntour that this enfermer Was sek. *c* **1450** LONELICH *Grail* xxxviii. 109 Go As Aventure wil the lede. **1587** GOLDING *De Mornay* i. 5 As for aduenture or chaunce it is nothing els but disorder and confusion. **1594** HOOKER *Eccl. Pol.* v. (1617) 52 Infants.. whom the cruelty of unnatural parents casteth out and leaveth to the adventure of uncertain pity. **1699** DRYDEN *T. fr. Chaucer, Flower and Leaf* 605 She smiled with sober cheer, And wish'd me fair adventure for the year.

†**b. per adventure, by adventure, of adventure** (Fr. *par aventure*): By chance. The two latter are obs., the first now treated as a single word, with sense *perchance*, *perhaps*. See PERADVENTURE.
1297 R. GLOUC. 375 He rod an honteþ, & per auntre hys hors spurde. **1382** WYCLIF *Matt.* v. 25 Lest peraventure thin aduersarie take thee to the domesman. *c* **1440** *Rom. Rose* 1502 For Narcisus, shortly to telle, By aventure come to that welle. *c* **1430** LYDG. *Bochas* II. xxviii. (1554) 64 b, So befell, Remus,.. Of auenture, went ouer the wall. **1483** CAXTON *Gold. Leg.* 98 Of auenture with his handes he touched his eyen. **1557** *K. Arthur* (Copland) I. i. By adventure he mette Merlyn in a beggers araye. **1675** HOBBES *Odyss.* 210 A chopping-board was near him by adventure.

†**c. an, on, in, upon, for adventure (aunter):** In case, lest, for fear. (Orig. with *if*, *lest*, *that* added.) *Obs.* (Hence by the addition of the adverbial -INGS, the northern ANAUNTERINS.)
1362 LANGL. *P. Pl.* A. III. 72 An auenture ȝe han ȝowre hire here, and ȝoure heuene als. **1387** TREVISA *Higden* Rolls Ser. II. 295 Anaunter leste þe olde man schulde be holde a lecchour. **1393** GOWER *Conf.* III. 331 In aunter if he might amende. *c* **1430** LYDG. *Min. Poems* (1840) 45 In aunter that thou tourne unto displeasaunce. *c* **1430** *Syr Generides* 9138 And so thei ride on hunting For auenture of ony spiyng. ? *a* **1450** *Visit. Sick* in Maskell's *Mon. Rit. Eccl. Angl.* III. 3 Sinne no more on aunter thow falle wors. **1480** CAXTON *Chron. Eng.* VII. (1520) 84/2 Upon aventure me sholde lyke some other bysshopryche to gyve hym. **1551** ROBINSON tr. *More's Utopia* (1869) 57 In aunters the Englishmen shoulde sturre. **1558** KENNEDY in *Misc. Wod. Soc.* (1844) 127 Nor be led with hym that is blynd, in aventure ȝe fall baith in the fowsie.

†**2.** A chance occurrence, an event or issue, an accident. Also in *Law. Obs.*
a **1300** *Cursor Mundi* 454 Qua herd euer a warr auntur. *c* **1400** *Destr. Troy* XVI. 7327 Achilles þan auerthward þis auntre beheld. **1551** ROBINSON tr. *More's Utopia* 141 Them that kepe watche and warde in harneis before the trenche for sodeine auentures. **1663** BUTLER *Hudibras* I. i. 633 For they a sad Adventure met. **1691** BLOUNT *Law Dict.*, *Aventure* is a mischance, causing the death of a Man, without Felony. **1727** SWIFT *Gulliv.* III. i. 181, I was ready to entertain an hope, that this adventure might some way or other help to deliver me.

†**3. a.** A trial of one's chance, or of an issue; a hazard, venture, or experiment. ***to give the adventure***: to make the venture, to try the experiment. ***to stand in aventure***: to remain on trial, to hang in the balance, or in doubt. *Obs.*
c **1386** CHAUCER *Knt. T.* 328 Heere in this prisoun, moote we endure And euerich of vs, take his auenture. *c* **1400** *Destr. Troy* III. 827, I wold boune me to batell and take my bare aunter, Yon worthy wethir to wyn. *c* **1460** *Towneley Myst.* 189 By nyghtertaylle dede shuld he be, And tille oure awnter stand ilkon. **1523** LD. BERNERS *Froissart* I. ccxxxvi. 334 It behoued them to abyde their aduentur. **1535** STEWART *Cron. Scotl.* (1858) I. 85 The victorie stude lang in aventour. **1595** SHAKS. *John* V. v. 22 To try the faire aduenture of to morrow. **1607** TOPSELL *Four-footed Beasts* (1673) 150 Whereupon 'Patroclus' [one of the elephants] gave the adventure, and passed over safely. **1673** *Lady's Calling* II. III. xv. 89 Marriage is so great an adventure, that once seems enough for the whole life. **1769–90** SIR J. REYNOLDS *Disc.* xiv. (1876) 90 When we adapt the character of the landscape.. This is a very difficult adventure.

†**b. at adventure, -s:** At hazard, at random, recklessly; (*with clause*) on chance. *Obs.*
In later times sometimes improperly printed *at a venture* as in *1 Kings* xxii. 34 'A certaine man drew a bow *at a venture*' (read *at aventure*), and in SHAKS. *2 Hen. IV*, I. i. 59, where the correct 'Speake at aduenture' is printed in the *Globe* ed. 'Speak *at a venture*.'
c **1420** *Cœur de Lion* 2188 The bowmen and eke the arblasters, Armed them all at aventers. **1523** LD. BERNERS *Froissart* I. cxcii. 228 Certayn of the garyson.. rode forthe at aduenture somwhat to wyn. **1561** T. N[ORTON] tr. *Calvin's Inst.* I. 11 Yet is this no small fault, at aduenture to worship an unknowen God. **1577** tr. *Bullinger Dec.* (1592) 228 Some .. marrie at aduentures, to their owne decay, and vtter destruction. **1665** EVELYN *Mem.* (1857) III. 172 Nor was what I writ a prophecy at adventure. **1777** HUME *Ess. & Treat.* I. 172 Shall this business be allowed to go altogether at adventures?

†**c. at all adventure, -s:** At random, anyhow; *hence*, At all hazards, at any risk, whatever may be the consequence, recklessly; and *later*, At all events, at any rate, in any case. *Obs.*
1485 CAXTON *Chas. the Gt.* 193 Eche took an hors of them þat were dede, which ranne at al aduenture. **1540** WHITTINTON *Tully's Off.* I. 46 We shall do nothyng folysshly and at all aduentures. **1553** T. WILSON *Rhetor.* 47 b, Plaie as young boyes or scarre crowes do, whiche showte.. at all aventures hittie missie. **1677** HALE *Contempl.* II. 195 Be contented herein.. and be Thankful to him at all adventures. **1690** LOCKE *Hum. Underst.* IV. xvii. §2 (1727) I. 316 The Effects of Chance and Hazard, of a mind floating at all adventures. **1760** JORTIN *Life of Erasm.* II. 76 At all adventures the yoke was to be shaken off. **1793** SMEATON *Edystone Lightho.* §275 At all adventures they were to fit the outside shell of the building.

4. Chance of danger or loss; risk, jeopardy, peril. ***to put in adventure***: to put in jeopardy, to imperil, to risk, to stake. Still in *Mar. Insur.*
1297 R. GLOUC. 64 And þouȝte yt was not god To do hys lyf an auntre. *c* **1325** *E.E. Allit. P.* C. 242 His seele is on anter. **1375** BARBOUR *Bruce* I. 606 He wes in full gret auentur To tyne his lyff. **1414** BRAMPTON *7 Penit. Ps.* cx. 42 Thi lyif thou potyst in aventure. **1483** CAXTON *G. de la Tour* b vij, For who soo doth, he set his honoure in grete aduenture. **1598** YONG *Diana* 141 For my sake to put thy life in aduenture. **1615** BP. HALL *Contempl.* XXI. 79 Labouring to prevent a common mischiefe, though with the adventure of their owne. **1882** *Mar. Insur. Policies* And touching the adventures and perils which the capital stock and funds of the said Company are made liable unto. *Ibid.* Beginning the adventure upon the said Goods, Freight, and Merchandizes, from the loading thereof aboard the said Ship.

5. a. A hazardous or perilous enterprise or performance; a daring feat; hence a prodigy, a marvel.
c **1314** *Guy Warw.* 35 Now Gii wendeth into fer lond More of auentours far to fond. *c* **1325** *E.E. Allit. P.* B. 1600 To open vch a hide þyng of aunteres vncowþe. **1384** CHAUCER *Leg. G. Wom.* 953 His aventourys in the se. *c* **1400** *Destr. Troy* I. 153 In a cuntre was cald Colchos by name, Was an aunter.. a wonderfull wethur weghes to be-holde. *c* **1420** *Anturs of Arther* i. 1 (1842) 1 In the tyme of Arther thys antur be-tydde. **1583** STANYHURST *Æneis* II. (1880) 69 Throgh surgye waters with mee too seek ther auenturs. **1617** SIR L. CRANFEILDE in *Fortesc. Pap.* 42 My many and dangerous adventures in his Majesties service. **1867** PEARSON *Hist. Eng.* I. 22 The romance of a brilliant adventure.

This passed insensibly into sense 6.

b. An instance of adventurism (see ADVENTURISM 2); applied disparagingly to any act or policy considered to be dangerous, e.g. as likely to involve the country concerned in war. (Russ. *avantyura* is used in a similar sense.)
1932 [see ADVENTURISM 2]. **1957** *New Statesman* 18 May 630/1 Mr. Macmillan.. argued.. that the Suez adventure in no way influenced Egypt's attitude to the negotiations. **1958** *Listener* 30 Oct. 682/2 [citing Moscow radio] The intensification of the policy of adventure and provocation of People's China, and the drawing up of plans for a new adventure in the Taiwan Straits area. *Ibid.* 27 Nov. 864/2 Outside interference, from East or West, delays such a solution, by diverting Arab attention to political problems and adventures, and thus impeding the emergence of constructive Arab statesmanship.

6. Any novel or unexpected event in which one shares; an exciting or remarkable incident befalling any one.
1570 ASCHAM *Scholem.* I. (Arb.) 29 Adventures now a days mean experiences in travel. **1608** SHAKS. *Peric.* II. iii. 83 A gentleman of Tyre.. looking for adventures in the world. **1716–8** LADY M. W. MONTAGUE *Lett.* I. xi. 40 One of the pleasantest adventures I ever met with in my life. **1853** C.

Brontë *Villette* vi. (1876) 42 To walk alone in London seemed of itself an adventure.

7. A pecuniary risk, a venture, a speculation, a commercial enterprise.

1625 Bacon *Ess.* xxxiv. 239 He that puts all vpon Aduentures, doth often times brake, and come to Pouerty. **1668** Child *Disc. of Trade* (ed. 4) 54 Whilst interest is at 6 per cent. no man will run an adventure to sea for the gain of 8 or 9 per cent. **1683** Evelyn *Mem.* (1857) II. 179, I sold my East India adventure of £250 principal for £750. **1793** Smeaton *Edystone Lighth.* §197 Puzzolana..had been imported as an adventure from Civita Vecchia. **1832** G. C. Lewis *Use & Ab. Pol. Terms* iii. 33 Employing his capital or labour in adventures only compatible with the existence of the law.

8. The encountering of risks or participation in novel and exciting events; adventurous activity, enterprise.

c **1325** *E.E. Allit. P.* A. 64 My goste is gon in godeȝ grace, In auenture þer meruayleȝ meuen. **1596** Spenser *F.Q.* i. ix. 6 But what adventure, or what high intent, Hath brought you hether. **1600** Heywood *1st Edw. IV, Auth. to Bk.* 17 Some citizens, some soldiers, borne to adventer..When we are borne, and to the world first enter. **1603** Knolles *Hist. Turkes* (1621) 1228 So the assault was begun with great furie and adventure. **1825** *Br. Jonathan* I. 382, I felt a yearning after adventure. **1863** Burton *Bk. Hunter* 87 The auction room..calls forth courage, promptness, and the spirit of adventure.

†**9.** (By analysis of the L. elements of the word.) ? A coming, arrival, advent. *Obs.*

1623 Meade in Ellis *Orig. Lett.* i. 297 III. 162 From a delight they took in so rare an adventure of a Prince of his quality. **1649** Selden *Laws of Eng.* i. lix. (1739) 109 In their first Adventure they paced the Stage.

10. *Comb.* **adventure playground**, a playground where children are provided with miscellaneous equipment, often waste material, from which they may contrive their own amusement (see quot. 1953[1]); **adventure-school**, a school started and conducted as a private speculation.

1953 Lady Allen of Hurtwood *Adventure Playgrounds* (Nat. Playing Fields Assoc.) 3 How does an *Adventure Playground differ from the usual playground? There is no asphalt, no see-saws, swings or slides, except those created by the children themselves out of waste material freely available on the site. **1953** *Playgrounds for Blocks of Flats* (Nat. Playing Fields Assoc.) 20 The employment of a supervisor, play leader or attendant is not considered necessary, except in the case of 'adventure' (creative or building) playgrounds. **1960** *Times* 25 Mar. 24/2 A steam-roller..is for the children's 'adventure playground'. **1834** H. Miller *Sc. & Leg.* xxviii. (1857) 408 Sometimes he taught an *adventure school.

adventure (æd'vɛntjʊə(r), -tʃə(r)), *v.* Forms as in adventure *sb.* [a. OFr. *aventure-r*, f. *aventure*, adventure *sb.*]

I. To commit to chance.

1. *trans.* To take the chance of; to commit to fortune; to undertake a thing of doubtful issue; to try, to chance, to venture upon.

1330 R. Brunne *Chron.* 70 Toward þis lond þei drouh, to auenture his chance. *c* **1386** Chaucer *Reves T.* 289, I wol arise and auntre it by my fay. **1587** Fleming *Contn. Holinsh.* III. 1319/2 Readie prest to aduenture anie aduentures for your gratious fauour. *a* **1618** Raleigh *Instruct. Son* iii. (1651) 11 He adventures thy mislike, and doth hazard thy hatred. **1633** Ford *Love's Sacr.* i. ii. (1839) 78, I am loth to move my lord unto offence; Yet I'll adventure chiding. **1725** De Foe *Voy. round World* (1840) 184 From east to west..it [a voyage] may be adventured with ease. **1815** Scott *Ld. of Isles* vi. xiv, I would adventure forth my lance. **1834** Ht. Martineau *Moral* iii. 89 Surely no statesman will be found to adventure it.

2. To risk the loss of, to risk, stake; to imperil, or expose (*to* danger).

c **1300** *K. Alis.* 4265 Hors and kyng..Was auntred undur the water. *c* **1440** *Gesta Rom.* (1879) 40 Thou haddist auntred thi owne body. *a* **1535** More *Rich. III*, Wks. 1557, 51/2 For what wise merchaunt aduentureth all his good in one ship. **1648** Cottrell *Davila* (1678) 709 To adventure his Army to new dangers. **1654** Goddard in Burton's *Diary* (1828) I. 84 We had adventured our lives and liberties for the cause. **1665** Evelyn *Diary* (1827) II. 250 My Wife went back to Wotton, I not as yet willing to adventure her. **1860** Motley *Netherl.* (1868) I. vi. 300 Elizabeth was taking the diadem from her head..and adventuring it upon the doubtful chance of war.

3. *refl.* To risk oneself; to venture.

c **1350** *Will. Palerne* 3268 Of þo wiþ-inne · non wold hem out aunter. **1393** Langland *P. Pl.* C. xxi. 232 And after auntrede god hym-self · and tok adams kynde. *c* **1440** *Morte Arthure* 360, I salle auntyre me anes hys egle to touche. **1475** Caxton *Jason* 65 b, To auenture myself in the conqueste of the noble moton or flees of golde. **1509** Barclay *Ship of Fooles* (1570) 178 Howe thou thee aventrest in holowe beame. **1611** Bible *Acts.* xix. 31 Desiring him that he would not adventure himselfe into the Theatre. **1697** Potter *Antiq. Greece* iii. iv. (1715) 22 Thinking it unsafe to adventure themselves abroad. **1803** Wellington in *Gen. Desp.* I. 568 You must..take care not to adventure yourself single handed against the combined forces of those chiefs.

4. *intr.* (by omission of refl. pron.) To risk oneself, to venture, to dare to come or go (*in, into, on, upon* any place). *fig.* To venture (*on, upon* a course or action), to dare to undertake. *to adventure at* (obs. rare): to dare to attack.

c **1340** *Alisaunder* (Skeat) 902 Þe armed Atenieeins auntred hym till. *c* **1400** *Destr. Troy* xii. 4985 Þen auntred Vlexes and his erund said. **1575–6** Thynne *Let.* in *Animadv.* 54 I rashely aduentured beyoynde the course of my desertes. *a* **1581** Campian *Hist. Irel.* (1633) vii. 22 When Japheth.. adventured by ship into divers West Islands. **1581** Lambarde *Eiren.* ii. iii. 117 Staying them that doe any way aduenture towardes the breach thereof. **1596** Shaks. *1 Hen. IV*, i. ii. 192 Then will they aduenture vppon the exploit. *a* **1628** F. Greville *Life of Sidney* (1652) 33 This Narration I adventure of, to show the clearness and readiness of this Gentlemans judgment. **1642** Milton *Apol. Smect.* (1851) 293 To strike high, and adventure dangerously at the most eminent vices among the greatest persons. **1704** Swift *Batt. Bks.* (1711) 235 By this time the Spider was adventur'd out. **1797–8** Wellesley *Desp.* 779 Every man who pleases may adventure thither. **1812** Byron *Childe Har.* ii. xliii, Now he adventured on a shore unknown. **1878** E. White *Life in Christ* iii. xvii. 215 The awe under which it becomes sinful men to adventure into that Holiest Place.

5. a. *intr.* (with *inf.*) To dare, to run the risk, make the experiment; to go so far as, to venture.

1387 Trevisa *Higden* Rolls Ser. I. 29 Þe secunde book auntreþ forto telle berynge and dedes. *c* **1400** *Destr. Troy* i. 314 The Emperour Alexaunder Aunterid to come. **1490** Caxton *Eneydos* xlii. 134 Noo body durste not auenture for to goo to hym. **1594** Shaks. *Rich. III*, i. iii. 116, I dare adventure to be sent to th' Towre. **1616** Sir R. Dudley in *Fortesc. Pap.* 15 My very enemies have never adventured to esteem me ungratefull. **1678** Quarles *Arg. & Parth.* 11 [He] boldly enters, and after mutual complement adventers To break the Ice of his dissembled grief. **1719** Wodrow *Corr.* (1843) II. 431, I adventured to show him the volume I brought up. **1818** Scott *Hrt. Midl.* 288 She feared she could not safely adventure to do so.

b. *trans.* To venture to say or utter.

1881 C. E. L. Riddell *Sen. Partner* II. i. 7 'I've been looking up my songs, Mr. McCullagh,' added the eldest daughter..'And we have been practising reels,' adventured Miss Vanderton. **1898** *Daily News* 19 Oct. 3/1 He adventured the opinion that 'some members opposite' were 'unaccustomed to the amenities of debate'. **1900** L. B. Walford *One of Ourselves* xiv, 'Did he tell you about us?' she adventured, cautiously.

II. To be or come as a chance.

†**6.** *intr.* To come by chance, happen, chance, befall. Usually *impers. Obs.*

c **1400** *Destr. Troy* xx. 8235 Hit auntrit, þat Ector was angrit full euill. *Ibid.* iii. 742 And oft in astronamy hit auntres to falle, þat domes men desseuis. *Ibid.* vi. 2107 Þe Authwart answares þat Auntrid hym þere Ys knowen.

adventured (æd'vɛntjʊəd), *ppl. a.* [f. prec. + -ed.] Risked, staked; which one has run a risk for, gained at a risk, or put in danger.

1570 Ascham *Scholem.* (Arb.) 57, A fit Similitude of this adventured experience. **1863** Kinglake *Crimea* (1877) V. i. 289 He will suffer an adventured portion of his force to go on to its fate.

adventureful (æd'vɛntjʊəfʊl), *a.* [f. adventure *sb.* + -ful.] Ready for adventure, enterprizing.

a **1832** Webster cites Bentham. **1847** in Craig.

†**ad'venturely**, *adv. Obs. rare*⁻¹. Also **aventurly**. [f. adventure *sb.* + -ly[2]. Cf. *mannerly*.] Adventurously, daringly.

c **1435** *Torr. Portugal* 1230 This squier that hath brought this hede, The kyng had wend he had the dede, And aventurly gan he gone.

†**ad'venturement.** *Obs. rare*⁻¹. [f. adventure *v.* + -ment.] Running of risk.

1599 Bp. Hall *Satires* iv. iii. 35 Wiser Raymundus.. laughs at such danger and adventurement.

adventurer (æd'vɛntjʊərə(r)). [a. Fr. *aventurier, adv-*, f. *aventure* adventure *sb.*; see -er[1].]

†**1.** One who plays at games of chance, or adventures his money in such games; a gamester. *Obs.*

1474 *Ord. Royal Housh.* 29 That no person..being within our sayd sonnes householde be customable swearer, brawler, backbyter, common hasorder, adventorer.

2. One who seeks adventures, or who engages in hazardous enterprises.

1667 Milton *P.L.* x. 440 Now expecting Each hour their great adventurer from the search Of foreign worlds. **1794** Sullivan *View of Nat.* II. The first voyages into the Ægean, Euxine, and Mediterranean Seas made by the various adventurers. **1855** Macaulay *Hist. Eng.* III. 506 A succession of Irish adventurers..attempted to earn the bribe.

3. *esp.* One who engages in warlike adventures, attaching himself to no party; a soldier of fortune; also, a volunteer, one who makes war at his own risk.

1548 Hall *Chron.* (1809) 646 He gave them a Pennon of St. George and bade them, Adventure (of whiche they were called Adventurers). **1555** *Fardle of Facions* ii. xi. 244 Much lyke to our aduenturers, that serue withoute wages. **1665** Manley *Grotius's Low-Countrey-Warrs* 251 One of the famous Adventurers in the taking of Breda. **1844** Thirlwall *Greece* VIII. lxi. 78 Military adventurers ready to flock to any standard.

4. One who undertakes, or shares in, commercial adventures or enterprises; a speculator; as in the ancient Society of *Merchant Adventurers*, so named by Henry VII.

1609 Thorpe in *Shaks. Cent. Praise* 86 To the onlie begetter of these insving sonnets, Mr. W. H., all Hapinesse wisheth..the well-wishing adventvror in setting forth. T.T. **1624** Capt. Smith *Virginia* iv. 166 Fewer Aduenturers here will aduenture any more. **1644** Heylin *Life of Laud* i. 220 The party so designed shall be presented to their Lordships by the Merchant Adventurers. **1653** (27 Sept.) Ordinance for the Satisfaction of the Adventurers for Lands in Ireland, and the Arrears due to the Soldiery there. **1713** *Guardian* No. 54 (1756) I. 240, I became an adventurer in one of the late lotteries. **1855** Macaulay *Hist. Eng.* IV. 135 Private adventurers had sometimes..fitted out ships for the Eastern seas. **1881** R. W. Raymond *Mining Terms*, *Adventurers* (Eng.), Shareholders or partners in a mining enterprise.

5. One who is on the look-out for chances of personal advancement; one who lives by his wits.

1663 Gerbier *Counsel* g 1 a, Since Courtaines, Bastions, and Contrescarps are to be traced for Old Eyes, as well as for young Adventurers. **1704** Swift *T. of Tub* §1. 22 To encourage all aspiring adventurers. **1762** Goldsm. *Beau Nash* 50 Wherever people of fashion came, needy adventurers were generally found in waiting. **1879** Froude *Cæsar* xv. 224 He saw adventurers pushing themselves into office.

adventures, *adv.* see aunters.

adventureship (æd'vɛntʃəʃɪp). [f. adventure *sb.* + -ship.] Adventurous practice.

1847 J. S. Mill *Lett.* (1910) I. 131 The inordinate impulse given to..the general spirit of adventureship. **1879** Morley *Burke* ii. 33 An unpleasant taint of speculation and financial adventureship hung at one time about the whole connexion.

adventuresome (æd'vɛntjʊəsəm), *a.* [f. adventure *sb.* + -some.] Given to adventures, or to running risks; adventurous, venturesome.

1731 Bailey vol. II, *Adventuresom*, bold, daring, hazardous. **1755** Johnson, *Adventuresome*, the same with *adventurous*: a low word, scarcely used in writing. **1821** Keats *Endym.* i. 6 Adventuresome, I send my herald thought into a wilderness. **1865** *Reader* No. 151. 574/1 The most adventuresome if not foolhardy feat.

adventuresomeness (æd'vɛntjʊəsəmnɪs). *rare*⁻⁰. [f. prec. + -ness.] The quality of being adventuresome; tendency to incur hazards; boldness.

1731 Bailey vol. II, *Adventuresomeness*, venturesomeness. [Also in Johnson, etc.]

adventuress (æd'vɛntjʊərɪs). [f. adventurer, after analogy of *sorcer-er, sorcer-ess; govern-or, govern-ess*, etc. See -ess.] A female adventurer; a woman on the look-out for a position.

1754 H. Walpole *Lett. to H. Mann* 257 (1834) III. 74 There is an adventuress in the world who even in the dullest times will take care not to let conversation stagnate. **1758** Chesterfield *Lett.* 331 (1792) IV. 122 She must be a kind of *aventurière*, to engage so easily in such an adventure. **1827** Scott *Surg. Dau.* Wks. 1868 XLVIII. 365 That the gentle and simple Menie Grey should be in the train of such a character as this adventuress. **1847** Thackeray *Van. F.* xlviii. 425 The odious little adventuress making her curtsey. **1863** M. A. Power *Arab. Days* 232 A good sprinkling of foreigners, adventurers, and adventuresses.

adventuring (æd'vɛntjʊərɪŋ), *vbl. sb.* [f. adventure *v.* + -ing[1].] Risking, hazarding; trial, venture. (Now mostly gerundial.)

1580 Baret *Alvearie* A 171, A prouing, or aduenturing, a jeopparding, *Periclitatio*. **1605** Verstegan *Dec. Intell.* vi. (1628) 170 Knowing the Crowne of England to be more worth then to bee let slip for the aduenturing for. **1683** *Lond. Gaz.* mdccclvi/3 Your Majesties Subjects and Soldiers shall be always ready in the adventuring of our Lives.

adventuring (æd'vɛntjʊərɪŋ), *ppl. a.* Sc. **antrin'**. [f. as prec. + -ing[2].] Making trial of one's chance, risking, daring; venturesome, forward, audacious.

1677 Hale *Contempl.* ii. 86 It is made more bold, and confident, and adventuring. **1774** Fergusson *Ode to Bee* (1845) 18 Yet they, alas! are antrin fouk That lade the scape wi winter stock. **1796** Burke *Reg. Peace* ii. Wks. VIII. 243 A body of active, adventuring, ambitious, discontented people. **1840** Gen. P. Thompson *Exerc.* (1842) V. 248 The adventuring detachment has been allowed to move out unchecked.

adventurish (æd'vɛntjʊərɪʃ), *a.* [f. adventure *sb.* + -ish.] Somewhat connected with adventure, or with adventurism.

1852 G. P. R. James *Pequinillo* I. 238 Captivated by the shrewd, trenchant, man-of-the-world, adventureish observations of his new-found friend.

adventurism (æd'vɛntjʊərɪz(ə)m). *rare.* [f. adventure *sb.* + -ism, with special reference to *adventur-er, -ess.*]

1. The principles and practice of an adventurer or adventuress; defiance of the ordinary canons of social decorum.

1843 *For. & Col. Q. Rev.* II. 343 Concubinage, Socialism, and Adventurism, and all the practical results.

2. The tendency in a government or politician to take risks in the management of national affairs, esp. in foreign policy (cf. Russ. *avantyurizm*).

1932 H. Nicolson *Public Faces* i. 17 Only three months before they had ousted the Churchill Government on a charge of adventurism. And here..was a weapon of adventure such as no British Government had ever possessed before. **1934** —— *Curzon: Last Phase* 52 The best analogy of the British imperial system is that of an old-fashioned and conservative banking house..an identical tradition, an identical caution, the same suspicion of adventurism. **1954** *Ann. Reg. 1953* 294 The two 'deviations' were 'passivity'..and 'commandism' or 'precipitate haste and adventurism'. **1957** *Observer* 3 Nov. 1/1 Of the three official accusations against Marshal Zhukov, that of 'adventurism' appears to be based on no evidence whatever.

adventurist (æd'vɛntjʊərɪst), *sb.* [f. ADVENTURE *sb.* + -IST.] One inclined to adventurism (various senses). Also *adj.*

1920 *Public Opinion* 16 Apr. 372/2 Our own military adventurists have been unable to stampede the Government. **1943** *Amer. Speech* XVIII. 310 A mid-western newspaper headline telling of the death of Ignatius Timothy Lincoln in Shanghai a few years ago read 'Ignatius Lincoln, *Adventurist*, Dies'. **1958** I. BROWN *Words in our Time* 16 Marshal Zhukov.. was formally accused of being adventurist and personalist. **1962** *Guardian* 28 Dec. 8/2 In accusing Mr. Kruschev's Cuban policy of having been both 'adventurist' and 'capitulationist' the Peking 'People's Daily' has scored a fair point. **1963** *Ann. Reg. 1962* 214 Vigorously condemning Albanian 'adventurists and dogmatists'.

adventurous (æd'vɛntjʊərəs), *a.* Forms: 4 **auenterous, -turus, aunterous, -trous, -trose, -tres, awntrouse, anterous, -trus**; 4–5 **awnterows**; 4–6 **auntrus**; 5 **auenturouse, aventrous**; 6– **adventurous.** [a. OFr. *aventuros, -eus*, mod. *aventeureux*, f. *aventure*: see ADVENTURE *sb.* and -OUS.]

†**1.** Occurring or coming by chance; casual, fortuitous, accidental. *Obs.*

c **1374** CHAUCER *Boethius* I. vi. 28 þe folie of þise happes auenterouses. *c* **1386** —— *Melib.* 701 The dedes of batailles ben aventurous.. for as lightly is on hurt with a spere as another. *c* **1400** *Ywaine & Gawin* 3399 He wald cum at the day, Als aventerous into the place. **1440** *Promp. Parv.*, Awnterows, or dowtefulle, *Fortunalis, fortuitus.*

†**2.** Full of risk or peril; hazardous, perilous. *Obs.*

c **1350** *Will. Palerne* 921 þanne seide Alisandrine, 'auntrose is þin euel.' **1375** BARBOUR *Bruce* VIII. 495 The auenturus castell off douglas That to kepe so perelous was. **1637** MILTON *Comus* 78 To pass through this adventurous glade.

3. Prone to incur risk, venturesome, rashly daring, rash.

c **1400** *Destr. Troy* VI. 2186 Ector the eldist, and heire to my selfe, Antrus in armys. **1596** SHAKS. *1 Hen. IV*, I. iii. 191 As full of perill and aduenturous Spirit, As to o're-walke a Current, roaring loude, On the vnstedfast footing of a Speare. **1614** RALEIGH *Hist. World.* I. 150 They [Griffins] grow inraged and adventurous. **1640** SANDERSON *21 Serm.* Ad Aul. xi. 13 (1673) 155 In these doubtful cases it is safer to be too scrupulous than too adventurous. **1667** MILTON *P.L.* IX. 921 Bold deed thou hast presumed, adventurous Eve. **1794** SULLIVAN *View of Nat.* IV. 447 This.. supersedes, in my opinion, every adventurous criticism.. of late thrown upon the early knowledge of the Celts. **1875** WHITNEY *Life of Lang.* ix. 169 We resort to adventurous hypotheses for its explanation.

4. Given to, or having many adventures, enterprising, daring (without the idea of *rashness*).

c **1440** *Morte Arthure* 1624 þe awntrouseste mene þat to his oste lengede. **1509** HAWES *Past. Pleas.* XIX. ix, I wyll to the toure of Chyvalry, And for your sake become adventurous. **1697** DRYDEN *Virg. Georg.* IV. 4 Embattel'd Squadrons and advent'rous Kings. **1757** BURKE *Abridgm. Eng. Hist.* Wks. X. 253 Five great bodies of that adventurous people, under different and independent commanders. **1853** DE QUINCEY *Span. Nun* (1862) III. 95 Lawless and gigantesque ideals of adventurous life. **1861** T. WRIGHT *Ess. Archæol.* II. xiii. 17 Perhaps many an adventurous monk wandered over the intervening lands.

adventurously (æd'vɛntjʊərəslɪ), *adv.* [f. prec. + -LY².]

†**1.** By chance, casually, accidentally. *Obs.*

c **1460** *Coventry Myst.* (1841) 334 Here Longeys showyth the spere.. and he avantoresly xal wype his Eyn. **1440** *Prom. Parv.*, Awnterowsly, *Forte, fortasse, forsan.* **1480** CAXTON *Chron. Eng.* lxxv, And after that shall the moldewarpe dye aventoursly and sodeynly.

2. In an adventurous or daring manner; daringly, at a risk.

c **1314** *Guy Warw.* 83 Al auntreousliche ther he comen wes. **1599** SHAKS. *Hen. V*, IV. iii. 79 If hee durst steale any thing aduenturously. *a* **1674** MILTON *Hist. Moscow*, Wks. (1738) II. 140 Shusky.. was adventrously supply'd with some Powder and Ammunition by the English. **1723** J. SHEFFIELD Dk. of Buckhm. *Wks.* 1753 I. 93 On then, my Muse, adventrously engage To give instructions that concern the Stage.

adventurousness (æd'vɛntjʊərəsnɪs). [f. as prec. + -NESS.] The quality of being adventurous; daring; exposure of oneself to risk or peril.

1530 PALSGR. 195/2 Aventurousnesse, *aventure* (Fr.) **1647** SPRIGG *Ang. Rediv.* II. iii. (1854) 93 The great adventurousness of many of the soldiers comes fitly to be remembered. **1751** JOHNSON *Rambler* No. 129 ¶9 Fixing the just limits of caution and adventurousness. **1824** SOUTHEY *Sir T. More* (1831) II. 176 In a spirit of desperate adventurousness.

†**advenue.** *Obs. rare.* [a refashioning of AVENUE (also found in MFr.).]

1. = AVENUE.

2. Income, revenue. (Cf. OFr. *les essues et les avenues des choses que nous avons en la dite chastelanie*, anno 1283 in Godefroi.)

1600 HOLLAND *Livy* XLV. xl. 1229/1 The issue and advenues [*fructus*] of his metall mines.

adverb ('ædvɜːb). *Gram.* [a. Fr. *adverbe*, ad. L. *adverbium*, f. *ad* to + *verbum* word, verb; according to Priscian 'cujus significatio verbis adjicitur;' a literal rendering of Gr. ἐπίρρημα, something additional to the predication.] Name of one of the Parts of Speech: a word used to express the attribute of an attribute; which expresses any relation of place, time, circumstance, causality, manner, or degree, or which modifies or limits an attribute, or predicate, or their modification; a word that modifies or qualifies an adjective, verb, or other adverb. Also used *attrib.*

1530 PALSGR. 800 It is harde to a lerner to discerne the difference bytwene an adverbe and the other partes of spetche. **1620** FORD *Linea Vitæ* (1843) 64 This man not only liues but liues well, remembring alwayes the old adage, that 'God is the rewarder of aduerbes not of nownes.' *c* **1620** A. HUME *Orthogr. Brit. Tong.* (1865) 32 An adverb is a word adhering mast commonlie with a verb. **1827** COLERIDGE *Table Talk* 38 Modify the verb by the noun, that is, by being, and you have the Adverb. **1873** R. MORRIS *Eng. Accid.* xiv. §310 Adverbs are mostly either abbreviations of words (or phrases) belonging to other parts of speech, or particular cases of nouns and pronouns. *Ibid.* ix. §63 Many relational adverbs are formed from demonstrative pronouns, as *he-re, hi-ther, whe-n.* **1879** WHITNEY *Sanskr. Gram.* 352 Of still more limited use, and of noun rather than adverb-value.

adverbial (æd'vɜːbɪəl), *a.* and *sb.* [ad. L. *adverbiāl-is* (cf. mod.Fr. *adverbial*), f. *adverbi-um*: see prec. and -AL¹.]

A. *adj.* **1.** Of or pertaining to, or of the nature of an adverb.

1611 COTGR., À before an Adjective, sometimes makes it admit of an Adverbiall interpretation; as *à droict, à tort*; rightfully, wrongfully. *a* **1704** T. BROWN (*title*) in Wks. (1730) I. 38 A bantering adverbial declamation, written by Mr. Brown. **1753** CHAMBERS *Cycl. Supp.*, Adverbial numbers are sometimes used to denote once, twice, thrice. **1873** R. MORRIS *Eng. Accid.* xiv. §311 In such phrases as 'He went home,' 'They wandered north and south'.. *home, north, south* are adverbial accusatives. *Ibid.* In Elizabethan writers we find the adverbial *-ly* often omitted, as '*grievous* sick,' '*miserable* poor.'

2. Given to the use of adverbs; fond of modifying, limiting, or extending one's statements. *rare.*

1710 STEELE *Tatler* No. 191 ¶1 He is also wonderfully adverbial in his Expressions, and breaks off with a 'perhaps.'

B. *sb.* [The adj. used *absol.*]

1591 PERCIVALL *Span. Dict.* Biij, The aduerbialls, *vna vez*, once, *dos vezes*, twise. **1924** H. E. PALMER *Gram. Spoken Eng.* II. 234 The term *Adverbials* is a convenient designation of adverbs and their equivalents, viz. Group-Adverbs, Adverbial Phrases and Adverbial Clauses. **1960** I. L. GORDON *Seafarer* 44 *þurh* with an abstract noun is a frequent method of expressing the adverbial of manner or state. **1962** J. SÖDERLIND in *Contrib. Eng. Syntax* (Gothenburg Stud.) 100 Thus the names of days are used as adverbials without a preposition.

adverbiality (æd,vɜːbɪ'ælɪtɪ). [f. ADVERBIAL *a.* and *sb.* + -ITY. Cf. Fr. *adverbialité.*] The state or quality of being adverbial; adverbial form or expression.

1873 EARLE *Philol. Eng. Tong.* §441 The termination *-ly* as the English sign of adverbiality. *Ibid.* §444 The requisite display of adverbiality is accomplished with another sort of instrument.

adverbialize (æd'vɜːbɪəlaɪz), *v.* [f. ADVERBIAL + -IZE; cf. Fr. *adverbialiser.* Cited only in pr. pple.] To make an adverb of, convert into an adverb.

1804 W. TAYLOR in *Ann. Rev.* II. 632 The adverbializing *s* also occurs in *backwards, forwards, upwards.*

adverbially (æd'vɜːrbɪəlɪ), *adv.* [f. ADVERBIAL + -LY².] In an adverbial manner; with adverbial meaning.

1548 W. THOMAS *Ital. Gram.*, *La*, aduerbially signifieth, there, or thyther. **1656** COWLEY *Davideis* III. (1669) 113, I wonder none have thought of interpreting Δίκην, adverbially. **1711** GREENWOOD *Eng. Gram.* 161 There are great Numbers of Adjectives that are used Adverbially, or as Adverbs. **1873** EARLE *Philol. Eng. Tong.* §434 A new and effectual way of applying a noun adverbially was by adding it to the sentence in its genitive or ablative or instrumental case.

adverbiation (æd,vɜːbɪ'eɪʃən). [f. L. *adverbium* ADVERB + -ATION.] (See quot.)

1873 EARLE *Philol. Eng. Tong.* §451, I would propose that for such extended phraseological adverbs [as *with a good will, with a green purse*, etc.] we adopt the title of Adverbiation.

†**ad'versable**, *a. Obs.*⁻⁰ [f. L. *adversā-ri* to oppose + -BLE, as if ad. L. **adversābilis.*] 'That is adverse or contrary to.' Bailey, vol. II, 1731. 'Contrary to, opposite to.' J. 1755. 'Capable of being opposed.' Ash 1775.

†**ad'versant**, *ppl. a. Obs.* [a. MFr. *adversant*, pr. pple. of *adverser, averser* to oppose:—L. *adversant-em*, pr. pple. of *adversā-ri* to oppose oneself to, f. *adversus* opposed: see ADVERSE.] Opposing oneself, opposing; adverse, hostile (*to*).

a **1420** *Pallad. on Husb.* I. 553 Let honge aboute in dyvers places rewe, And bestes adversaunt hem wol eschewe. **1432–50** tr. *Higden* Rolls Ser. I. 87 More prompte to do ylle than to speke, coverenge thynges adversaunte with silence. **1548** UDALL, etc. *Erasm. Paraphr.* John ix. 40 Even when aduersaunt misery is immynent. *c* **1630** JACKSON *Creed* V. xlv. Wks. IV. 378 Our Saviour's advice to Martha.. is no way adversant to my intended choice.

‖**adversaria** (ædvə'sɛərɪə), *sb. pl.* Also in Eng. form **adversaries.** [L. adj. pl. *adversāria* (sc. *scripta*) things written on the side fronting us (i.e. on one side of the paper), notes, a commonplace book; f. *adversus*: see ADVERSE. Prop. pl., but in Eng. usage often a collective sing.] A commonplace-book, a place in which to note things as they occur; collections of miscellaneous remarks or observations, = MISCELLANEA; also commentaries or notes on a text or writing.

1610 HOLLAND *Camden's Brit.* I. 237 As P. Pœna in his Adversaries or Commentaries of plants hath noticed. **1713** BP. BULL *Serm.* (J.) These parchments are supposed to have been St. Paul's adversaria. **1753** CHAMBERS *Cycl. Supp.* s.v., Morhof speaks much of the use and advantages of such *adversaria* to men of letters. **1842** WHITTOCK *Compl. Bk. Trades* 482 We never spent an hour more at our repose, than in silent attention to the political adversaria of this benevolent man.

adversarial (ædvə'sɛərɪəl), *a.* [f. ADVERSARY *sb.* + -IAL.] That involves adversaries, contested (freq. of legal proceedings); characterized by adversary or combative behaviour; opposed, hostile.

1970 *Jrnl. Gen. Psychol.* Jan. 12 Such bias is a demand of the adversarial system of justice. **1972** *Law Rep.* I. 185 There are no 'issues' in the sense in which that term is used in relation to adversarial litigation in courts of law. **1977** *N.Y. Times* 23 July 18 Neighbor distrusts neighbor... Social relations are becoming adversarial. **1983** *Financial Times* 25 Oct. 16/8 A radical change in the old adversarial relationship between the steel barons and the Administration.

†**'adversarily**, *adv. Obs. rare*⁻¹. [f. ADVERSARY *a.* + -LY².] In the manner of an adversary, adversely, hostilely.

1475 *Bk. Noblesse* (1860) 50 The thinges.. whiche comethe to us adversarily or on the lift side, for oure offenses.

adversarious (ædvə'sɛərɪəs), *a. rare.* [f. L. *adversāri-us* turned towards or against (f. *adversus*: see ADVERSE) + -OUS. Used instead of the earlier adj. ADVERSARY, in order to distinguish the adj. from the sb.] Adverse, opposed, hostile.

1826 SOUTHEY *Vind. Eccl. Angl.* 275, I am not sensible of any adversarious feeling.

adversary ('ædvəsərɪ), *sb.* and *a.* Forms: 3 **aduersere,** 5 **adversaire,** 6 **adversare,** 4–6 **adversarie,** 4– **adversary.** *Sc.* 4 **adversour,** 5 **adwerser,** 6–7 **adversair, -ar, -are.** [a. OFr. *aversier, adversier*, Anglo-Fr. 13th c. *adverser* (mod.Fr. *adversaire*) sb. and adj.:—L. *adversārius* opposed, opponent, f. *adversus*: see ADVERSE and -ARY. The forms with *-arie, -ary*, as in Wyclif, directly from L. Shaks. accents '*adversary*, Milton both '*adversary* and *ad'versary.*]

A. *sb.*

1. One who, or that which, takes up a position of antagonism, or acts in a hostile manner; an opponent, antagonist; an enemy, foe. *spec.* The enemy of mankind, the Devil.

1330 R. BRUNNE *Chron.* 82 þer men him teld, who was his aduersere, Of Northfolk þe Erle Roger, men said of him treson. **1340** *Ayenb.* 238 To ouercome hire aduersarie þet is þe dieuel. **1375** BARBOUR *Bruce* XVII. 736 Thair aduersouris assail3eit swa. **1382** WYCLIF *1 Pet.* v. 8 3oure aduersarie, the deuel, as a roryng lioun goith aboute. [Also in TINDALE, CRANMER, *Geneva, Rheims*, **1611**, and *Revised.*] **1413** LYDG. *Pylgr. Sowle* I. viii. (1859) 6 Let us haue place to ben herd, and thenne oure aduersarys. *c* **1420** *Pallad. on Husb.* I. 529 Gooses dounge.. is an adversarie to every seed. *a* **1541** WYATT *Poet. Wks.* 1861, 142 Mine adversare with such grievous reproof, Thus he began. **1594** SHAKS. *Rich. III*, III. i. 182 His ancient Knot of dangerous Aduersaries To morrow are let blood at Pomfret Castle. **1667** MILTON *P.L.* II. 629 The Adversary of God and Man, Satan. *Ibid.* III. 156 Or shall the Adversary thus obtain, His end? **1771** *Junius Lett.* lxiii. 324 Our adversaries would fain reduce us to the difficulty of proving too much. **1825** *Br. Jonathan* III. 154 He.. overthrew his brutal adversaries, like a giant. **1861** J. TULLOCH *Eng. Purit.* ii. 276 A hard adversary with his pen.

2. *pl.* See ADVERSARIA.

B. *adj.* Opposed, antagonistic, hostile, inimical, adverse (*to*). *arch.* In *Law*, An adversary suit: one in which an opposing party appears.

1382 WYCLIF *1 Chron.* xviii. 10 Forsothe kyng Adadezer was aduersarie to Thou. **1398** TREVISA *Barth. De P.R.* XVIII. lxxi. (1495) 827 All the kynde of wulues is contrary and aduersary to all the kynde of shepe. **1461** *Paston Lett.* 397 II. 22 On the adversaire parte Judas slepith not. **1609** SKENE *Reg. Maj.* 8 The name of him, quha is adversare partie to him, quha is summoned (that is, the name of the persewer). **1618** BOLTON *Florus* I. xiii. 42 Manlius, in a single combat, tooke from the adversary Champion a Torques. **1710** PRIDEAUX *Orig. Tithes* iii. 149 Least we become Adversary to ourselves. **1860** J. P. KENNEDY *Rob of the Bowl* xvii. 206 Your whole life has been adversary to the good will of the father.

†**adver'sation.** *Obs. rare.* [ad. (prob. through Fr.) L. *adversātiōn-em*, n. of action, f. *adversā-ri*: see ADVERSANT.] Opposition, hostility.

1470 HARDING *Chron.* lxvii, Hym and his men to kepe frome [all] aduersacyon, of Scottes & Peyghtes. *Ibid.* lxxxviii, Eche kyng warred on others lande..And Britons also did great aduersation.

adversative (æd'vɜːsətɪv), *a.* and *sb.* [ad. L. *adversātīvus*, f. *adversāt-*, ppl. stem of *adversā-ri*: see prec. and -IVE.]

A. *adj.* Characterized by opposition; hence,

1. Of words or propositions: Expressive of opposition, contrariety, or antithesis.

1533 MORE *Apol.* xvii. Wks. 1557, 877/1 *But* being a preposicion aduersatiue. *a* **1698** SOUTH *12 Serm.* III. 111 These words are ushered in with the Adversative Particle (*But*) which stands as a note of Opposition to something going before. **1752** HARRIS *Hermes* II. (1786) 257 Of these Disjunctives some are Simple, some Adversative..the Simple do no more than merely disjoin; the Adversative disjoin, with an opposition concomitant. **1879** FARRAR *St. Paul* II. 561 The adversative force of δὲ..does seem to imply that passing shade of hesitation.

†2. Of opposing tendency or adverse nature. *Obs.*

1601 HOLLAND *Pliny* xxv. viii, Pistolochia, which herb is so adversative unto serpents, that..it will chase away all kind of serpents out of the house. **1603** —— *Plutarch's Mor.* 1143 The other is adversative, and maketh us to hate that which is foule and bad.

B. *sb.* [The adj. used *absol.*] An adversative proposition or word; one which expresses opposition.

a **1556** CRANMER *Wks.* I. 57 Every indifferent reader understandeth this adversative upon our side, that we say Christ is not received in the mouth, but in the heart. **1612** BRINSLEY *Posing of Parts* (1669) 47, *Q.* How many kinds of Conjunctions have you? *A.* Twelve. Copulatives, Disjunctives..Adversatives, etc. **1778** BP. LOWTH *On Isaiah* (ed. 12) 134 Which, being rendered as an adversative, sets the opposition in a stronger light.

adversatively (æd'vɜːsətɪvlɪ), *adv.* [f. prec. + -LY².] In an adversative manner; as expressing opposition.

a **1624** SWINBURNE *Spousals* (1686) 100 [It] standeth adversatively establishing the contrary. **1814** JAMIESON *Hermes Scyth.* 186 The terms would come to be applied adversatively.

adverse ('ædvɜːs), *a.* and *sb.* [a. MFr. *advers, -e* refashioned f. OFr. *avers, auvers*:—L. *adversus* turned towards, turned against, hostile, pa. pple. of *advert-ĕre*, f. *ad* to + *vert-ĕre* to turn. Poets have accented both *'adverse* and *ad'verse.*]

A. *adj.*

1. Acting against or in opposition to, opposing, contrary, antagonistic, actively hostile. Const. *to.*

c **1440** *Partonope* 5716 That to crystes lawe ys aduerse And leeveth on machoun. **1575** CHURCHYARD *Chippes* (1817) 12 English volunteers served during those wars, in adverse armies. **1595** SHAKS. *John* IV. ii. 172 When aduerse Forreyners affright my Townes. **1628** DIGBY *Voy. to Medit.* 47 The aduerse windes had hindered my designe of going. **1667** MILTON *P.L.* I. 103 His utmost power with adverse power opposed. **1798** JEFFERSON *Writings* (1859) IV. 210 The general spirit, even of the merchants, is becoming adverse to it. **1807** CRABBE *Par. Reg.* I. 805 On life's rough sea they sail With many a prosperous, many an adverse gale. **1868** HELPS *Realmah* viii. (1876) 239 To go over to the side of their adverse critics.

b. *Law.*

1858 LD. ST. LEONARDS *Handy Bk. Prop. Law* xxiii. 177 What I may call adverse possession, which now is a possession by a person not the owner during a certain number of years without acknowledgment of the right of the real owner, and yet not necessarily in open defiance of him.

2. Opposing any one's interests (real or supposed); hence, unfavourable, hurtful, detrimental, injurious, calamitous, afflictive. Const. *to.*

c **1374** CHAUCER *Troylus* IV. 1192, O cruel Joue and thou fortune aduerse. **1490** CAXTON *Eneydos* i. 13 But the prosperous fortune of the kynge pryam torned in to aduerse. **1601** SHAKS. *All's Well* v. i. 26 Though time seeme so aduerse, and meanes vnfit. **1671** MILTON *Samson* 192 In prosperous days They swarm, but in adverse withdraw their head. **1806–31** A. KNOX *Rem.* (1844) I. 96 Strengthened instead of being shaken by adverse circumstances. **1867** BRIGHT *Sp., Amer.* (1876) 146 The presidential election of 1860 was adverse to the cause of slavery.

3. Opposite in position.

1623 BINGHAM *Xenophon* 77 The Macrons..stood imbattled on the aduerse side of the riuer. **1753** CHAMBERS *Cycl. Supp., Adversaria*..so called because the notes were written on the adverse or opposite page. **1872** BLACKIE *Lays of Highl.* 167 He looked upon the bright green slope, that skirts the adverse hills.

B. *sb.* An adverse party, an adversary. *rare.*

1850 BLACKIE *Æschylus* II. 183 If Jove hath worsted This Typhon in the fight, we too shall worst Our adverse.

†**ad'verse,** *v.* *Obs.* *rare*⁻¹. [a. MFr. *a(d)verse-r*:—L. *adversā-ri* to be opposed, f. *adversus* ADVERSE *a.*] To be opposed or adverse to, to oppose.

1393 GOWER *Conf.* I. 219 It was a presage..Of that fortune him shulde adverse.

adversely ('ædvɜːslɪ), *adv.* [f. ADVERSE *a.* + -LY².] In an adverse manner; unfavourably; contrariwise. Const. *to.*

1607 SHAKS. *Coriol.* II. i. 61 If the drinke you giue me, touch my Palate aduersly, I make a crooked face at it. **1881** SIR W. HARCOURT in *Manch. Guard.* Feb. 12 It does not act with but adversely to the agrarian party. **1882** *Daily Tel.* 21 Feb., 2 Foreign Government bonds were adversely influenced by the political news.

adverseness ('ædvɜːsnɪs). ? *Obs.* [f. ADVERSE *a.* + -NESS.] The quality or state of being adverse; opposition, hostility; aversion.

1620 DONNE *Serm.* lxxiv. 753/3 Men, who..delight in Hostility, and have an adverseness and detestation of peace. **1680** HOBBES *Consid.* 6, A new Parliament, consisting for the greatest part of such men as the People had elected only for their adverseness to the Kings Interest.

adversifoli-ate, -ous (æd,vɜːsɪ'fəʊlɪət, -əs), *a. Bot.* [f. mod.L. *adversifoli-us* (f. L. *advers-us* opposite + *foli-um* leaf), + -ATE², -OUS.] Having leaves placed opposite each other on the stem or axis.

†**ad'version.** *Obs. rare.* [ad. L. *adversiōn-em* a turning towards, f. *advers-* ppl. stem of *advertĕre*: see ADVERT and -ION¹.] Attention, perception.

1647 H. MORE *Song of Soul* II. III. II. xlv, Our listning mind by its adversion Doth notice take. —— *Poems* 141 And yet we not [be] pressed To any adversion.

adversity (æd'vɜːsɪtɪ). Forms: 4–6 **adversite(e, adversyte(e;** 4–7 **adversitie;** 7– **adversity.** [a. MFr. *adversité*, refash. f. OFr. *aversite*:—L. *adversitāt-em* opposition, contrariety, f. *adversus*: see ADVERSE and -ITY.]

†1. The state or condition of being contrary or opposed; opposition, contrariety. *Obs.*

1382 WYCLIF *Ps.* iii. 8 For thou hast smyte all doende adversite [**1388** beynge adversaries] to me with oute cause. *a* **1420** OCCLEVE *De Reg. Princ.* 390, I was agast fulle sore of the, Leste thow thurghe thoughtfulle adversitee Not hadest stonden in the feithe aright. *c* **1450** LONELICH *Grail* xviii. 174 One bone, sire kyng, þat thow graunte me Withowten lettynge owthir adversite.

2. The condition of adverse fortune; a state opposed to well-being or prosperity; misfortune, distress, trial, or affliction. (The earliest sense in Eng.)

c **1230** *Ancren Riwle* 194 Þe uttre uondunge is mislicunge in aduersite. **1340** *Ayenb.* 27 Kuead of aventure, ase povertie oþer adversitie. **1483** CAXTON *Gold. Leg.* 399/4 Thenne late us praye..that he so gouerne us bytwene welth & aduersyte in this present lyf. **1535** COVERDALE *Prov.* xvii. 17 In aduersite a man shall knowe who is his brother [**1611** A brother is borne for aduersitie]. **1570–87** HOLINSHED *Scot. Chron.* (1806) I. 81 Adversitie findeth few friends. **1592** SHAKS. *Rom.* III. iii. 55 Aduersities sweete milke, Philosophie. **1600** —— *A.Y.L.* II. i. 12 Sweet are the vses of aduersitie. **1750** JOHNSON *Rambler* No. 150 ¶5 He that never was acquainted with adversity has seen the world but on one side. **1771** *Junius Lett.* xlix. 254 A virtuous man, struggling with adversity, [is] a scene worthy of the gods. *a* **1852** D. WEBSTER *Wks.* 1877, III. 341 The discipline of our virtues in the severe school of adversity.

3. An adverse circumstance; a misfortune, calamity, trial.

1340 *Ayenb.* 84 Þe kueades and þe aduersetes of þe wordle. *c* **1386** CHAUCER *Clerkes T.* 551 Noon accident for noon aduersitee Was seyn in hire. **1483** CAXTON *Cato* b ij. b, Strengthe for to resiste ageynst all aduersytees. **1526** TINDALE *Acts* vii. 10 And God was with him, and delivered hym out off all his adversities. **1651** HOBBES *Leviathan* II. xxxi 188 The Prosperities and Adversities of this life. **1842** LONGF. *Sp. Stud.* II. i. 1 Pray, tell me more of your adversities.

†4. Contrariness of nature; perversity. (In Shak. = perverse one, quibbler.) *Obs.*

1489 CAXTON *Faytes of Armes* III. ix. 186 The felawes muste be chaunged by som aduersyte that is in them. **1606** SHAKS. *Tr. & Cr.* v. i. 14, *P.* Who keepes the Tent now? *T.* The Surgeons box, or the Patients wound. *P.* Well said adversity.

adversour, obs. var. ADVERSARY: see -OUR.

advert (æd'vɜːt), *v.* Also 4–6 **auerte, avert(e.** [a. Fr. *avert-ir*:—late L. *advertē-re* for cl. L. *advertĕre* to turn to, also (sc. *animum*) to turn the attention of oneself or another to, to remark, admonish; f. *ad* to + *vertĕre* to turn. L. *āvertere* to turn away, AVERT, also made OFr. *avertir*, which had thus all the senses 'turn to, turn away, remark, call attention.' In 14–16th c. *avertir*, when answering to L. *advertere*, was often written *advertir*; and, since Caxton, *advert* and *avert* have been distinguished in Eng. Mod.Fr. has *avertir* (Palsg. and Cotgr. *advertir*) only in the sense of 'call the attention of another, admonish' (one of the senses of L. *advertere*). The lengthened stem of this, *a(d)vertiss-*, has given Eng. ADVERTISE, orig. a synonym of *advert*, but subseq. differentiated, so that *advert* retains the sense of 'turn one's own attention,' *advertise* that of 'direct the attention of others.' *Advert, advertise, avert*, are thus all immediately from OFr. *avertir, avertiss-ant.*]

†1. *trans.* To turn towards (*lit.* or *fig.*); to turn favourably. *Obs. rare.*

a **1423** JAMES I *King's Quair* II. vi, Till Jupiter his merci list advert And send comfort. *c* **1430** LYDG. *Bochas* II. xxviii (1554) 64 a, Beastes which ben rage of theyr nature He can aduert and make them lye full styll.

2. *intr.* To turn one's attention; to take notice, take heed, attend, pay attention. (L. *animum advertere.*) Const. *to* (*absol., subord. cl., on* obs.). *arch.* = ADVERTISE 1.

1430 LYDG. *Chron. Troy* I. ii, In so slye wyse that no man myght auerte Upon no syde but that he mente well. **1509** BARCLAY *Ship of Fooles* (1570) 42 Thinking that God doth not therto aduert. **1530** PALSGR. 440 Nowe, my yonge chyldren, if you wyl avert, you shal have the frenche tonge moch more easely than men had afore your dayes. *a* **1535** W. DE WORDE *Communycacyon* B iij, Lorde whan I on thy pouerte aduerte. **1557** BARCLAY *Jugurthe* (Paynell) b ij. b, Micipsa aduertynge that Jugurth was redy of hande to strike. **1755** B. MARTIN *Mag. Arts & Sc.* 328 We shall find it our Interest to advert on the different Degrees of the Moisture and Dryness of the Air. **1790** BOSWELL *Johnson* (1816) IV. 133 They do not advert that the great body of the Christian Church..maintain also the Unity of the Godhead. **1806** WELLINGTON in *Wellesley Desp.* 92 The British government were compelled to advert to the means of strengthening the government of the Nizam. **1875** POSTE *Gaius* (ed. 2) Introd., 14 Negligence is inadvertence to consequences to which a man might have adverted.

3. *esp.* To turn one's attention in a discourse written or spoken; to refer *to.*

1777 PRIESTLEY *Phil. Necess.* 179, I shall now advert to some other matters. **1798** FERRIAR *Illustr. Sterne* vi. 172 Mauriceau adverts to the circumstance, in his attack on the Cæsarian operation. **1861** MAY *Constit. Hist. Eng.* (1863) I. iii. 169 The king's illness was adverted to in the House of Commons.

†4. *trans.* To turn the attention to, attend to, take note of; to observe, note, notice, or heed; to consider, think of (a thing). *Obs.* = ADVERTISE 2.

1430 LYDG. *Chron. Troy* I. iii, He nought advertith the menyng fraudulent. **1432–50** tr. *Higden* Rolls Ser. I. 361 Hit is to be aduertede that the extremites of the worlde schyne in newe wondres. **1470** HARDING *Chron.* civ, Egberte..was royally accepte, With all honour yᵗ [the lordes could] aduert. **1557** BARCLAY *Jugurthe* (Paynell) a iij. b, Yf we aduert the worlde as it is. **1655** SANDERSON *Serm.* II. Pref., Frailties and infirmities..not hitherto by them adverted, because never suspected. **1692** WAGSTAFFE *Vind. Carol.* Introd. 12 If he had any fault, it was his not timely adverting his Father's dear bought experience.

†5. *trans.* To turn the attention of another to, to give warning of. *Obs. rare.* See ADVERTISE 5.

1513 DOUGLAS *Æneis* III. x. 113 Quhen horrybil thingis sere he dyd aduert.

¶ Incorrectly for AVERT. [See above.]

1578 *Ps.* li. in *Sc. Poems of 16th c.* II. 115 Fra my sinnes advert thy face.

advert ('ædvɜːt), colloq. abbrev. of ADVERTISEMENT. Cf. AD.

1860 J. BLACKWOOD *Let.* 6 Jan. in *Lett. George Eliot* (1954) III. 244, I do not mean this for announcement in the advert, but that we may consider [etc.]. **1954** J. B. PRIESTLEY *Magicians* vi. 120, I don't know what you're going to put in the adverts—the usual bilge, I suppose. **1955** 'R. GORDON' *Dr. at Large* iii. 41 'Those vacancies are already filled.' 'But the advert. only came out yesterday!'

†**adver'tation.** *Obs.* *rare*⁻¹. [improp. f. L. *advert-ĕre*, as if it were a vb. of the 1st conj.; cf. the regular deriv. ADVERSION.] The action of turning the attention; observation, notice.

c **1480** *Digby Myst.* 90 Of yower good hertes I have advertacyounes, Where-thorow, In sowle holl made ȝe be.

advertence (æd'vɜːtəns). [a. MFr. *advertance, -ence*, refashioned f. OFr. *avertance, -ence*:—late L. *advertentia* attention, notice, f. *advertentem* pr. pple. of *advert-ĕre*: see ADVERT and -NCE.] The action or process of adverting or turning the attention to; observation, notice, heed, attention, consideration. Often passing into the *habit* or *quality*, which is properly expressed by ADVERTENCY.

c **1370** CHAUCER *Troylus* v. 1258 What guilte of me? what fel experience Hath fro me rafte, allas! thyn advertence? **1430** LYDG. *Chron. Troy* I. i, Their [the ants'] wisdome their prudent advertence Besy labour and wilful diligence. **1509** BARCLAY *Ship of Fooles* 258 b, If he with good aduertence looke therein. **1557** —— *Jugurthe* (Paynell) 106 The Romayns intentifely gaue aduertens to the demeanour of their enemies. **1673** *Lady's Calling* I. v. §74, 56 A serious advertence to the divine presence is the most certain curb to all disorderly appetites. **1722** WOLLASTON *Relig. Nat.* ii. 33 The finer or nicer the advertence or reflexion is, into the more parts is the time divided. **1848** MILL *Pol. Econ.* v. vii. §2 (1876) 529 To this difference it is right that advertence shall be had in regulating taxation.

advertency (æd'vɜːtənsɪ). [ad. late L. *advertentia*: see prec. and -NCY.] The quality of being advertent or attentive; the habit of turning the attention to; attentiveness, heedfulness. (See prec.)

1646 SIR T. BROWNE *Pseud. Ep.* 386 Some errors in interpunctions or poyntings the advertency of the Reader may correct. **1683** DRYDEN *Life of Plutarch* 77 Through want of advertency he has been often guilty of that errour.

1790 Paley *Hor. Paul.* I. 7 No advertency is sufficient to guard against slips and contradictions. **1800** Stuart in *Wellesley Desp.* 569 An advertency to the former periods of history..ought to caution us to keep a watchful eye on this quarter.

advertent (æd'vɜːtənt), *ppl. a.* ? *Obs.* [ad. L. *advertent-em* pr. pple. of *advert-ĕre* to ADVERT.] Attentive, heedful.
1671 *True Non-Conf.* 483 This objection showes that you are..little advertent to the conclusion you have in hand. **1677** Hale *Prim. Orig. Man.* I. ii. 62 This requires very choice Parts, great attention of Mind..and a long advertent and deliberate connexing of Consequents.

advertently (æd'vɜːtəntlı), *adv. rare*—0. [f. prec. + -LY[2].] In an advertent manner; heedfully. (Only in mod. Dicts.) Cf. *inadvertently*.

advertique (ædvə'tiːk), *sb.* (and *a.*) [Blend of ADVERTISEMENT + ANTIQUE *a.* and *sb.*] A collectors' name for a piece of early advertising material; usu. in *pl.* Also as *adj.*
1977 *Collectors Year Bk.* '77 116/1 My own collection of advertiques includes everything conceivable, from humble packets and tins, to posters, display cases, shop display cards, promotional material, match-strikers, novelties and 'give-aways', enamelled signs, tin-plate signs and original advertising mirrors. **1980** *Brit. Bottle Rev.* Dec., Flea markets, junk shops and, alas, the word 'advertique' dealers who are to be found mainly in London.

advertise (ˌædvə'taız, 'ædvəˌtaız), *v.* Also 5 **avertise**, 5–6 **aduertyse**, 6 **advertisse**, **-es(e**, 7–9 **advertize**. [f. Fr. *avertiss-*, lengthened stem of *avertir*, as seen in pr. pple. *avertiss-ant*, pres. subj. *avertisse*, and vbl. sb. *avertisse-ment*, often written in 14–16th c. *advertir*; see ADVERT. *Advertise* was thus at first simply an alternative form of *advert*, as seen by comparing the earlier senses of both, but in their development they have been differentiated, *advert* following the usual senses of L. *advertere*, and *advertise* those of mod.Fr. *avertir*. The formation of *advertise* was probably largely due to the sb. *advertisement*; for the Fr. *convertir*, *divertir*, etc. have only given *convert*, *divert*, etc. In 6–7 the pronunciation was regularly *ad'vertis*; it was subsequently conformed to Fr. as *adver'tise*; the present tendency (in commercial usage, at least) is to say '*advertise*, apparently after the vbs. in *-ize*.]

†**1.** *intr.* To take note, give heed, consider. Const. *to*, *of*, *inf.*, or *subord. cl. Obs.* = ADVERT 2.
c **1430** Lydg. *Bochas* II. xxvii. (1554) 62 b, To wil he gaue wholy the souerantie, And aduertised nothing to reason. **1475** Caxton *Jason* 12 b, He had auertised of that they shold doo. *c* **1500** *Doctr. Good Seruants* (1842) 5 Seruauntes ought to aduertyse, To say euer trouthe and veryte. *c* **1526** Frith *Disput. Purgat.* (1829) 83 Not advertising who speaketh the words, but rather what is said.

†**2.** *trans.* To take note of, attend to, notice, observe (a thing). *Obs.* = ADVERT 4.
c **1430** Lydg. *Bochas* VI. iv. (1554) 141 b, He list not aduertise theyr prayere. **1494** Fabyan IV. lxiv. 44 Liuius Gallus, aduertysynge this myschief, and the great daunger that the Romaynes were in, drewe backe into the cytie. **1533** Frith *Mirror* (1829) 291 Advertising the kindness of God, and our promise in baptism. **1606** Bryskett *Disc. Civ. Life* 252 Yet is it to be aduertised, that it is in diuers respects that they be so exercised.

†**3.** *refl.* To turn one's attention *to.* (OFr. *s'avertir*). *Obs.*
1509 Hawes *Past. Pleas.* v. i, The lady Gramer..Dyd me receyve into her goodly scoole; To whose doctrine I dyd me advertise.

4. *trans.* To call the attention of (another); to give him notice, to notify, admonish, warn, or inform, in a formal or impressive manner. (mod.Fr. *avertir.*) **a.** *simply. arch.*
1490 Caxton *Eneydos* xxiii. 86 In this place thenne wherof I telle you, as I haue be aduertised, is a right holy woman. **1597** T. Morley *Introd. Musicke*, Annot., If thou find anything which shal not be to thy liking, in friendship aduertise me, that I may either mend it, or scrape it out. **1611** Bible *Ruth* iv. 4 Naomi..selleth a parcell of land.. And I thought to aduertise thee, saying, Buy it. **1669** Marvell *Corr.* 115 Wks. 1875 II. 276 Be pleas'd to consider thereof, and advertise me timely. **1714** *French Bk. of Rates* 205 The said Merchants shall be obliged to advertise the said Judges..under the particular Fine of 500 Livres. **1859** Sir W. Hamilton *Lect. Metaph.* xvi. (1877) I. 306 The insect is advertised and put upon the watch.

†**b.** with *inf.* To warn, admonish. *Obs.*
1494 Fabyan lxxxiii. (R.) The lordes of Britayne.. aduertysed him..to expelle & put theym out of his realme. *a* **1555** Latimer *Serm. & Rem.* (1845) 108 St. Paul advertised all women to give a good ensample of sadness, soberness, and godliness. **1664** Evelyn *Kal. Hort.* (1729) 218 Till the cold being more intense advertise you to inclose them altogether. **1778** J. Glover in Sparks' *Corr. Am. Rev.* (1853) II. 73, I have to..advertise the inhabitants to come and receive their moneys.

c. with *of*, *concerning* (*against* rare and obs.).
1462 Russe in *Past. Lett.* 456 II. 107 Chapman proposyth ..to avertise the Kyng and my Lord Tresorer ageyn me to the grettest hurt he can imagyne. **1477** Earl Rivers (Caxton) *Dictes* 78 Wherof aristotill was aduertised, and hastily departed from Athens. **1559–66** *Hist. Est. Scot.* (Wodr. Misc. 81) The Lords were advertissed of their departing. **1681** Neville *Plato Rediv.* 8 Which hindred me from advertising you of my Distemper. **1748** Smollett *Rod. Rand.* vii. (1804) 34 Being advertised by me of his design. **1825** Southey in *Q. Rev.* XXXII. 383 Some prisoners..advertised the French of this terrible danger. **1860** Freer *Hist. Hen. IV*, I. i. 47 To advertise her majesty concerning his precarious position.

d. with *subord. cl.* To notify, inform.
1454 *Let. fr. Kildare* in Ellis *Orig. Lett.* II. 39 I. 118 Please youre gracious Hynes to be advertised that, etc. **1481** Caxton *Myrrour* II. xxii. 115 Whan they be not aduertysed at what tyme such tempeste shal come. **1593** Shaks. *3 Hen. VI*, v. iii. 18 We are aduertis'd by our louing friends, That they doe hold their course toward Tewksbury. **1657** Colvill *Whigs Suppl.* (1751) 99 And how he cited ends of verse..At which some laugh'd, and some were vex'd, Ye'll be advertis'd by the next. **1794** Martyn tr. *Rousseau's Bot.* ii. 32 The young botanist should be advertised that these filicles..differ much in their form. **1850** Blackie *Æschylus* II. 325 It would be unfair not to advertise the English reader that this fine sentiment is a translation.

5. Hence (by omission of the personal object), To give notice of (anything), to notify, indicate, or make generally known.
1588 A. King *Canisius' Catech.* 256 For we offend in mony things, as I haue aduertissit also befoir. **1591** Unton *Corr.* (1847) 235 Makinge hast to advertise this our good successe. **1689** *Col. Rec. Penn.* I. 268 For y[e] Reasons advertised in y[e] Returns thereof, given by y[e] Sheriff, [it] was not a good Election. **1784** Cowper *Task* IV. 500 Vain th' attempt To advertize in verse a public pest. **1801** Mar. Edgeworth *French Gov.* (1832) 125 Ladies..come to wear pearl powder, and false auburn hair, and twenty things that are not to be advertised, you know. **1872** Bagehot *Physics & Polit.* (1876) 110 Changes bring out new qualities, and advertise the effects of new habits.

6. *esp.* To give public notice of, to make publicly known, or call attention to, by a published announcement *in* a journal, *by* a circular, etc., as 'to advertise the resolutions of a meeting'; and with various elliptical constructions, as 'to advertise goods (for sale), a child or ring (as lost),' etc.
1750 H. Walpole *Corr.* 222 (ed. 3) II. 374 A citizen had advertized a reward for the discovery of a person who had stolen sixty guineas. **1775** Burke *Sp. Conc. Amer.* Wks. III. 68 The Guinea captain attempting at the same instant to publish his proclamation of liberty, and to advertise his sale of slaves. **1809** W. Irving *Knickerb.* I. 496 That he should be missing so long, and never return to pay his bill. I therefore advertised him in the newspapers.

†**7.** *intr.* To give warning or information (*of*). *Obs.* in general sense.
1612 T. Taylor *Titus* iii. 1 (1619) 550 Ministers must take heede, that they take no more vpon them, then to advise and aduertise from the Lord. **1765** H. Walpole *Otranto* iv. (1798) 63 Isabella had sent one of the domestics before to advertise of their approach.

b. *esp.* To put a public notice in a journal, or to announce by placard in any public place. ***to advertise for***: to ask for by public notice.
1772 *Junius Lett.* lxviii. 357 He advertises for patients. **1879** *Printing Trades Jrnl.* XXIX. 38 Don't advertise unless you have something worth advertising. *Mod.* He advertises largely in the daily papers.

advertised (ˌædvə'taızd, 'ædv-), *ppl. a.* [f. prec. + -ED.]
1. Informed, notified, admonished, warned.
1475 Caxton *Jason* 54 b, The king Laomedon thus aduertised of the descente of the knightes of Greece.. ymagined anon that they were espyes. *c* **1560** *Calvin's Com. Prayer Bk.* in *Phenix* 1708 II. 213 If so be that..being brotherly advertis'd, he acknowledg not his Fault. **1622** Bacon *Hen. VII*, Wks. 1860, 340 The king was neither so shallow, nor so ill advertised, as not to perceive the intention of the French. **1802** Playfair *Huttonian Theory* 317 Seymour and myself were advertised of our approach to a junction of granite and schistus.

2. Publicly announced (as being done, being for sale, etc.).
1784 Cowper *Task* III. 668 Estates are landscapes, gaz'd upon a while, Then advertis'd, and auctioneer'd away. **1882** J. M. Wilson in *Daily News* 12 Sept. 6/6 If the Tabard were a well-managed and well-advertised hotel.

advertisee (æd,vɜːtı'ziː). [f. ADVERTISE *v.* + -EE.] One advertised for, one to whom an advertisement is addressed, or who is expected to respond to it.
1861 *Sat. Rev.* 7 Dec. 580 The precise effect which it is designed to produce on the mind of the advertisee [by an advertisement].

advertisement (æd'vɜːtızmənt). Also 5–7 **avertise-**; 6 **advertyse-**, **advertise-**; 7 **advertize-**, **averti-ment**. [a. Fr. *avertissement*, in 5–6 *advertissement*; f. *avertiss-* lengthened stem of *avertir*: see ADVERTISE and -MENT. The ordinary Eng. pronunciation has been as above since Shakspere at least: (ædvə'taızmənt) is found early in 6, and is now usual in U.S.]

†**1.** The turning of the mind to anything; attention, observation, heed. *Obs.*
1523 Skelton *Garl. Laurel* 808 Behold and se in your advertysement How these ladys..For your pleasure do there endeuourment. **1594** Hooker *Eccl. Pol.* v. (1632) 451 Men should either need much advertisement or long time for the search thereof. **1651** Jer. Taylor *Holy Liv.* (1727) 140 It helps much to attention and actual advertisement in our prayers.

†**2.** The action of calling the attention of others; admonition, warning, precept, instruction. *Obs.*
1475 *Bk. of Noblesse* 79 Joachym king of Juda despraised the admonestementis, advertisementis, and the doctrines of God. **1538** Bale *God's Promises* in Dodsley (1780) I. 14 Doth what hym lust without dyscrete advysement, And wyll in no wyse take myne advertysement. **1581** Marbeck *Bk. of Notes* 258 By the aduertisement of the Emperour, he graunted it to proceede. *a* **1652** J. Smith *Sel. Disc.* ii. 31 Some secret advertisements of their consciences. **1675** T. Brooks *Gold. Key* Wks. 1867 V. 379 Christ, in his advertisement to Philadelphia, Rev. iii. 7. **1715** Burnet *Hist. own Time* (1766) II. 108 The advertisements came to him from so many hands, that he was inclined to believe there was somewhat in it. **1827** Hallam *Const. Hist.* (1876) I. iv. 180 Parker..set forth a book called Advertisements, containing orders and regulations for the discipline of the clergy.

†**3.** The action of informing or notifying; information, notification, notice. *Obs.*
1528 Gardiner in Pocock *Rec. Ref.* 50 I. 118 As other things occurreth here worthy advertisement, we shall not fail to signify the same. **1581** Savile *Tacitus, Agricola* (1622) 192 He bedeckt not with lawrell his letters of aduertisement. **1603** Knolles *Hist. Turkes* (1621) 1189 Hatwan..being so seated..it much hindered both advertisements and victuals to be brought unto Pesth. *a* **1649** Charles I *Wks.* 230 He had avertisement that the person of the said Earl of Glamorgan was arrested. **1716** in Wodrow's *Corr.* (1843) II. 136 The first advertisement they gave of it was Clanronald's orders to his men to kindle straw.

4. A (written) statement calling attention to anything; a notification, a 'notice.' *Obs.* or *arch.*
c **1460** Fortescue *Absol. & Lim. Mon.* (1714) 122 Here followen Advertisements, for the gevyng of the Kyngs Offyces. *c* **1548** Geste *Let. to Parker* 141, I have sent..your booke againe with such notes & advertisementes that..I could well gather. **1625** Burges *Pers. Tithes* To Reader, Some Aduertisements. i. Reade All, or reade nothing. **1645** Milton *Tetrach.* Wks. 1738 I. 265 The Canons and Edicts ..with the avertiments of Balsamon and Matthæus Monachus theron. **1728** Pope *Dunciad* (1736) Advertisement to the first Edition, with note, etc. **1824** Dibdin *Libr. Comp.* 278 At the end of this volume is an advertisement to the reader.

5. A public notice or announcement: *formerly* by the town-crier; *now*, usually, in writing or print, by placards, or in a journal; *spec.* a paid announcement in a newspaper or other print. Also *fig.*
1582–8 *Hist. James VI* (1804) 141 To attend thair quietlie upoun aduertisement of the drum. **1599** Shaks. *Much Ado* v. i. 32 My griefs cry lowder then aduertisement. **1692** Luttrell *Brief Rel.* (1857) II. 566 He has published an advertisement in this days Gazet of it. **1722** De Foe *Moll Fl.* (1840) 273 An advertisement of the particulars in the common newspapers. **1868** Dickens *Lett.* (1880) II. 339 A short newspaper advertisement is all we want. **1876** Freeman *Norm. Conq.* I. App. 719 A general advertisement for the heads of his enemies. **1878** *Printing Trades Jrnl.* xxv. 27 The publishers are not in the habit of inserting gratuitous advertisements. **1952** A. Wilson *Hemlock* III. i. 216 Ours has not perhaps been the ideal advertisement for such a union.

6. = ADVERTISING *vbl. sb.* 2.
1902 *Encycl. Brit.* XXV. 94/2 Advertisement, or advertising, as the process of purchasing publicity is now more commonly called, is [etc.]. **1909** H. G. Wells *Tono-Bungay* II. iii. 194 Advertisement has revolutionized trade and industry. **1922** Joyce *Ulysses* 667 The infinite possibilities hitherto unexploited of the modern art of advertisement.

7. *attrib.* and *Comb.* (in senses 5 and 6), as ***advertisement agent***, ***board***, ***curtain***, ***-manager***, ***-sticker***.
1897 G. B. Shaw *Our Theatres in Nineties* (1932) III. 27 But there *is* a clown, who acts extensively as an *advertisement agent. **1933** H. G. Wells *Bulpington* iii. 81 Mr. Parkinson was an advertisement agent. **1880** *Harper's Mag.* Dec. 72 The *advertisement boards were freshly covered with clean notices. **1951** *Oxf. Compan. Theatre* 13/1 **Advertisement curtain*, an outer curtain or act-drop used mostly in smaller theatres, covered with advertisements of local shops and manufacturers. **1902** A. Bennett *Truth abt. Author* x, in *The Academy* 21 June 634/2, I could play Blucher at the Waterloo of the *advertisement-manager. **1778** S. Foote *Capuchin* II. 114 You became *advertisement-sticker to lottery-offices, auctioneers..and mountebank-doctors.

advertisemental (æd'vɜːtız,mɛntəl), *a.* [f. prec. + -AL[1].] Of or pertaining to advertisement.
1881 *World* 11 May 14/1 The incomparable 'Nabob Pickle' and other well-known advertisemental triumphs.

advertiser (ˌædvə'taızə(r), 'ædv-). [f. ADVERTISE + -ER[1].] One who advertises.
†**1.** One who informs, notifies, or warns. *Obs.*
c **1565** Lindsay *Hist. Scot.* (1728) 55 The first advertiser of this prosperous success brought with him Archibald Douglas's head. **1611** Cotgr., *Advertisseur*, an advertiser, informer, intelligencer. **1665–6** in *Phil. Trans.* I. 15 The solution of Plains and Solids, which had been seen (as the Advertiser affirms) before Monsieur Des Cartes had publish'd anything upon this subject.

2. One who issues a public notice or announcement.
1712 Steele *Spect.* No. 521 ¶4 He has desired the Advertiser to compose himself a little, before he dictated the Description of the offender. **1784** Cowper *Task* II. Argt., The reverend advertiser of engraved sermons. **1882** *Daily News* 4 May 1/1 Advertisers are requested to make their Post-office Orders payable to, etc.

3. A journal or other print in which advertisements are published.

1769 BURKE *Pres. State* Wks. II. 13 They have drawled through columns of Gazetteers and Advertisers for a century together. **1770** *Junius Lett.* Pref. 13 This edition contains all the letters of Junius..according to the order in which they appeared in the Public Advertiser. **1841** GEN. P. THOMPSON *Exerc.* (1842) VI. 303 Just as an advertisement in the body of some of the 'monster' advertisers of the day, amounts to next to no advertisement at all. **1882** (*title*) The Morning Advertiser.

advertising (ˌædvəˈtaɪzɪŋ, ˈædv-), *vbl. sb.* [f. ADVERTISE + -ING[1].]

†**1.** Warning, notification, information. *Obs.*
1530 PALSGR., Advertysing, *advertence* (Fr.). **1549** *Compl. Scotl.* xiii. 111 The counsel of ingland gettis..haisty aduertessing of the priuitate that is amang the lordis of scotland.

2. A bringing into notice; *spec.* by paid announcement in a printed journal, by prominent display of placards, etc.
1762 GOLDSMITH *Beau Nash* 13 By self-advertizing, attract the attention of the day. **1810** CRABBE *Borough* vii. 118 Should the advertising cash be spent, Ere yet the town has due attention lent, Then bursts the bubble. **1816** JANE AUSTEN *Emma* II. xvii. 324 There are advertising offices, and..by applying to them I should have no doubt of very soon meeting with something that would do. **1832** F. TROLLOPE *Dom. Manners* I. iv. 49 We went to the office of an advertising agent. **1843** *Edin. Rev.* Feb. 2 The advertising system. **1850** *Hunt's Merch. Mag.* XXIII. 580 Mr. V. B. Palmer keeps what he terms the '*American Newspaper Advertising Agency*'. **1863** *Chicago Post* 29 Sept. (D.A.), Last night the Varieties bloomed forth a set of magnificent new scenes and a beautiful advertising curtain. **1882** *Daily News* 4 May 1/2 The vendors undertake to defray all the expenses of..printing, advertising, legal charges. *a* **1884** *Mod.* 'There is one way of obtaining business—publicity, one way of obtaining publicity—advertising.' **1913** *Maclean's Mag.* May 135/1 We live in the Advertising Age. **1936** *Discovery* Mar. 85/1 Advertising agencies are supplied with source material for advertisements of plant products. **1962** *Rep. Comm. Broadc. 1960* 82 The [Independent Television] Authority told us that they were moving towards a reform of advertising magazines rather than to their disappearance.

advertising (ˌædvəˈtaɪzɪŋ, ˈædv-), *ppl. a.* [f. as prec. + -ING[2].]

†**1.** Adverting, attending, attentive. *Obs.*
1603 SHAKS. *Meas. for M.* v. i. 387, I was then Aduertysing, and holy to your businesse.

2. Issuing advertisements; giving public notice.
1779 W. A. SMYTH (*title*) The Publican's Guide..by which every retailer will be enabled to..sell on terms equal to..the generality of advertising merchants. **1807** CRABBE *Newspaper* 320 When lo! the advertising tribe succeed. **1882** *Daily Tel.* 6 Sept. 4/6 As a convenience to the Advertising Public, it has been thought desirable, etc.

advertorial (ædvəˈtɔərɪəl). Chiefly *U.S.* [f. ADVERT(ISEMENT + EDIT)ORIAL *sb.*] An advertisement written in the form of an editorial, which purportedly provides objective information about a commercial or industrial subject.
1961 in WEBSTER. **1968** *Heidelberg News* Sept. 3/3 There has been talk lately about 'advertorials', wrapping up an advertisement to look like an editorial. **1972** *Harvard Law Rev.* Jan. 692 'Advertorials', unlike responses required by the fairness doctrine, do allow the public both control and initiative, and therefore must be accommodated by the licensees. **1981** *Jrnl. Communication* XXXI. 79 Among the most political of the ads are advertorials, in which explicit policy positions are taken. *Ibid.* (*caption*), Example of an advertorial ad for Mobil Oil Corporation.

†**adˈvesperate**, *v.* *Obs.*$^{-0}$ [f. L. *advesperāt-*, ppl. stem of *advesperā-sc-ĕre* to draw towards evening; f. *ad* to + *vesper* evening.] 'To waxe night.' Cockeram 1626. 'To grow towards night.' Bailey 1721. Johnson, etc.

†**adˈvest**, *v.* *Obs.*$^{-0}$ [a. MFr. *advest-ir*, OFr. *avestir*:—late L. *advestī-re*; f. *ad* to + *vestīre* to clothe.] To invest, put into possession.
1611 COTGR., *Adheriter*, to advest, to put into possession.

†**adˈvesture.** *Obs.*$^{-0}$ [a. MFr. *advesture*, OFr. *avesture*; f. *a(d)vestir*: see prec. and -URE.] The act of advesting, investing, or clothing.
1611 COTGR., *Advesture*, an advesture, an investure, a cloathing or possessing with; a delivering over, a making of Liverie and seisin unto. **1650** SHERWOOD, Advesture, *advest*, *advesture* (Fr.).

advice (ædˈvaɪs). Forms: 3–5 **avis, avys,** 5 **avise, avyse, avyce** (*Sc.* 4 **awyss,** 6 **awise**); 5 **advys,** 5–6 **advyse,** 4–8 **advise,** 6– **advice.** [a. OFr. *avis* (cogn. w. Pr. *avis*, Sp. *aviso*, It. *avviso*):—late pop. L. **advīsum* view, opinion, f. *ad* to + *vīsum* seen, pa. pple of *vidēre* to see. Occ. written *advis* after L. by Fr. scribes in 14th–16th c., a spelling introduced (by Caxton) into Eng., where it permanently changed the word. In 15th c. final *-e* was added to indicate the length of the *ī*; and in 16th the *s* was written *c* to preserve the breath sound; whence the stages *avīs, advīs, advise, advice.* Senses 8 and 9 represent Sp. *aviso* (= Fr. *avis*), also used unchanged, and in the adapted form ADVISO, q.v.]

†**1.** The way in which a matter is looked at or regarded; opinion, judgment. *Obs.*
1297 R. GLOUC. 144 Þe erchbischop of Walis seide ys auys. **1330** R. BRUNNE *Chron.* 32 Bot as I herd telle I say myn auys. **1366** MAUNDEV. xxviii. 284 But that myghte not ben to myn avys. **1475** CAXTON *Jason* 11 b, Me thinketh in myn aduys that the king of Esclauonye doth euyl. **1529** MORE *Supplic. Soules* Wks. 1557, 334/1 He hath geuen hys aduise therto, and said that they haue to much. **1623** BINGHAM *Xenophon* 56, I am not of that aduice, quoth Cherisophus. **1633** G. HERBERT *Temple* 113 All things.. joyn with one advise To honour thee. **1651** HOBBES *Leviathan* II. xix. 95 With power to make known their Advise, or Desires.

†**2.** Forethought, prudence, wisdom. *Obs.*
1375 BARBOUR *Bruce* x. 269 He knew..hys gret wycht, and hys awyss, Hys traist hart, and hys lele seruice. *c* **1430** LYDG. *Bochas* I. i. (1554) 1 Considre fyrst, the Lord in His auyse..He put us bothe into paradise. **1523** LD. BERNERS *Froissart* I. cclix, Howe the erle of Cambrydge and the erle of Pembroke toke by great aduyse the garyson of Bourdeile.

†**3.** Provision for, endowment, advancement. (OFr. *avis*, portion de biens qu'un père assigne à ses puinés). *Obs. rare.*
1433 MANGEARD in *E.E. Wills* (1882) Thet the seyd Bestall be salde be the vice of the paresshens ther, as for the most avice of the sayd chirche werkes.

†**4.** Weighing of opinions; consideration, deliberation, consultation, reckoning. *to take advice*: to deliberate. *Obs.*
1366 MAUNDEV. 180 The schipmen taken here Avys here and governe hem by the Lode star. *c* **1386** CHAUCER *Melibeus* 285 It semeth þat it suffiseth to han been conseilled by thise conseillours oonly, and wiþ litel Auys [*v.r.* avis(e, auys(e, avice]. **1565** JEWEL *Repl. to Harding* (1611) 161 Whom vpon verie short aduice, hæ hath condemned. **1596** SHAKS. *Merch. Ven.* IV. ii. 6 Bassanio vpon more aduice, Hath sent you heere this ring. **1611** BIBLE *Judges* xix. 30 Consider of it, take aduise, and speake your mindes. **1654** GODDARD in *Burton's Diary* (1828) I. 7 In such manner as the Commissioners of the Admiralty, by advice with the generals of the fleet, shall think fit.

5. Opinion given or offered as to action; counsel. *spec.* medical or legal counsel.
1393 GOWER *Conf.* I. 340 So that anone by his advise There was a prive counseil nome. **1413** LYDG. *Pylgr. Sowle* IV. xxx. (1483) 77 To receyuen goodly good aduys and counceyll withouten indignacion of herte. **1605** SHAKS. *Macb.* IV. ii. 68 If you will take a homely mans aduice, Be not found heere. **1667** PEPYS *Diary* (1879) IV. 398 He is very ill of his fever, and come only for advice. **1702** POPE *Jan. & May* 84 But fix'd before, and well resolv'd was he; (As men that ask advice are wont to be). **1718** —— *Iliad* I. 361 If in my youth, ev'n these esteem'd me wise; Do you, young warriours, hear my sage advise. **1761** GIBBON *Misc. Wks.* 1814 V. 211 These are so many advices which it is easy to give, but difficult to follow. **1845** *Punch*, VIII. 1 Advice to those about to marry:—'Don't.' **1860** TYNDALL *Glaciers* I. §25, 182 Acting on his advice I had a ladder constructed in two pieces.

†**6.** The result of consultation; determination, resolve, intention, plan, design. *Obs.*
c **1440** *Arthur* 104 Arthour.. toke þe castelle & þe town at hys avyse. **1455** ARDERN in *Test. Eborac.* (1855) II. 195 That thai..myne exequies done and avyce before writen, those gudis distribute. **1513** DOUGLAS *Æneis* XII. v. 51 Thay quhilkis are desyrit peace..Ar alterit halely in ane vthir auyse. **1581** SAVILE *Tacitus, Agricola* (1622) 194 Changing aduice on the sudden..they iointly assaulted by night the ninth Legion. **1704** DRYDEN *Aureng-zebe* III. i. 1035 The fatal Paper rather let me tear, You may, but 'twill not be your best Advice.

†**7.** A decision of a deliberative body; an act; a *Senatus consultum*. *Obs. rare.*
1661 BRAMHALL *Just Vind.* vii. 173 The advises of Constance conceived by the Deputies of the German Nation in that Councel, against some special abuses of the Pope.. The advises of Ments made and concluded in that City by the States of the Empire.

8. Information given, notice; intelligence, news; in *pl.* communications from a distance. *spec.* in *Comm.* Formal or official notice from a party concerned.
1490 CAXTON *Eneydos* xxii. 82 After wyth this dreme cometh to her aduyse that her cyte and landes of Cartage are all dystroied. **1578** T. N. tr. *Conq. W. India* 114 These fifteene were spies and..beganne to flie with feare, or else to give advice. **1633** STAFFORD *Pac. Hib.* xxii. (1821) 424 A Pinnace of advice that brought the Kings Letters. **1665** PEPYS *Diary* (1879) VI. 99 Where some advice from my Lady shall meet your Lordship. **1710** STEELE *Tatler* No. 129 ¶1 A mail from Holland, which brought me several Advices. **1737** WESLEY *Wks.* 1830 I. 70 Visiting a dying man, we found him full of the freshest advices. **1745** DE FOE *Eng. Tradesm.* I. xxviii. 279 He should not pay his money till he has advice that my bills are accepted. **1849** MACAULAY *Hist. Eng.* I. 590 Advices came down to him that many thousands of the citizens had been enrolled as volunteers. **1866** CRUMP *Banking* v. 133 It is more prudent in all cases to give a banker advice of bills becoming due. **1880** *P.O. Guide* 217 The Postmaster has first to see that the signature of the payee be in agreement with the advice.

9. = ADVICE-BOAT. Cf. also *pinnace of advice* in 8.
1595 DRAKE *Voy.* (1849) 18 We took a frygotte which was an advice of the kinge's [of Spain].

10. *Comb.* or *attrib.*, as ***advice-giver***; **advice note** *Comm.*, = *letter of advice* s.v. LETTER *sb.*[1] 4 c; (see quots.); **advice-yacht** = ADVICE-BOAT.
1663 GERBIER *Counsel* d 3 a, The *Advice giver to Builders. **1885** E. B. IVATTS *Railway Managem. at Stations* 537 **Advice note*, a form, partly printed and partly written, used to advise consignees of the arrival of their goods, and requesting removal of same from the station. **1901** *Business Terms, Phr. & Abbrev.* 10 *Advice note*..is a letter giving its receiver information that some particular transaction either has been or is about to be effected on his behalf. It is usual to advise the arrival of shipments, the despatch of goods, the payment of accounts, and the shipment of goods. **1930** J. B. PRIESTLEY *Angel Pavement* x. 496 He had got up as usual, bolted his breakfast and exchanged a word or two with the Pelumptons, hurried down to the Tube, climbed into the City, sent and received advice notes, telephoned to this firm and that, [etc.]. **1983** J. M. ROSENBERG *Dict. Business & Managem.* (ed. 2) 18/1 *Advice note*, a supplier's listing of items that is sent to a customer prior to an invoice, either accompanying the merchandise or preceding it, identifying the nature and quantity of the goods but not giving prices. **1666** *Lond. Gaz.* lxvi/2 A Pleasure-Boat..after ten hours chace, put on shore near this Harbor, a Dutch *Advice-Yacht.

adˈvice-boat. 'A boat employed to bring intelligence,' J.; a dispatch-boat; called also shortly an advice. See ADVICE 8, 9, and ADVISO.
1668 *Lond. Gaz.* ccxxxviii/3 All these Men of War are to be attended by a proportionable number of Galliots, Advice Boats, and Victuallers. **1790** BEATSON *Nav. & Mil. Mem.* I. 384 While on this station, he took an advice boat from Old Spain. **1798** LD. ST. VINCENT in Nicolas's *Disp.* (1845) III. 27 A good Sparonara or Felucca..will serve for an Advice-boat during the summer months.

†**adˈviceful**, *a.* *Obs.* Also 6 **avizeful,** 7 **adviseful.** [f. ADVICE + -FUL.]

1. Considerate, thoughtful, attentive, careful.
1596 SPENSER *F.Q.* IV. vi. 26 When Britomart with sharp avizefull eye Beheld the lovely face of Artegall. *c* **1607** *Beggars Ape* (N.) Which everywhere advisefull audience bred While thus th' inditement by the clerke was read.

2. Full of counsel; skilful as an adviser.
1600 CHAPMAN *Iliad* IX. 87 The first was famous Thrasymed, adviceful Nestor's son. **1624** —— *Batrachom.* (1858) Ep. Ded. 23 Th' adviceful guide of my still-trembling star.

adview, refashioned f. AVIEW *v.* *Obs.*, to view.

†**adˈvigilance.** *Obs.*$^{-0}$ [f. L. *advigilantia*, as if a. Fr. **advigilance*: see next. Cf. VIGILANCE.] 'A diligent watching.' Bailey, vol. II, 1731.

†**adˈvigilancy.** *Obs.* *rare*$^{-1}$. [ad. L. *advigilantia*, f. *advigilant-em*, pr. pple. of *advigilā-re*: see next.] Watchfulness, vigilance, care.
1577–87 HOLINSHED *Chron.* III. 1263/2 All the nobilitie of the realme may hereby receiue admonition, and cause of further circumspection and aduigilancie.

†**adˈvigilate**, *v.* *Obs.*$^{-0}$ [f. L. *advigilāt-*, ppl. stem of *advigilā-re* to be watchful over; f. *ad* to + *vigilā-re* to watch.] 'To watch diligently.' Cockeram 1626; whence in Bailey, Ash, Todd, etc.

†**advigiˈlation.** *Obs.*$^{-0}$ [n. of action f. prec.; see -ION[1].] 'A diligent watching.' Bullokar 1676.

†**adˈviron**, *v.* *Obs.* *rare.* [a. occ. MFr. *advironne-r* for *avironner*, OFr. *avironer* to surround; (cf. *environ*).] To environ, surround.
1475 CAXTON *Jason* 17 Jason felte hym self so aduironned on alle sydes by hys enemyes. **1483** —— *Gold. Leg.* 127/3 Thys lyght of heuen aduyronned hym sodeynly.

advisability (ædˌvaɪzəˈbɪlɪtɪ). [f. ADVISABLE, on analogy of L. sbs. in *-bilitas*: see -BILITY.] The quality of being advisable; advisableness.
[Not in TODD 1818, RICHARDSON 1836, CRAIG 1847, LATHAM 1872, OGILVIE 1882. In WORCESTER 1859.] **1839** DICKENS *Nich. Nick.* xxxvi. 286 Pondering upon the advisability of this step, and the sensation it was likely to create. **1857** S. OSBORN *Quedah* iv. 57 The lesson I had learnt upon the advisability of using smoke preservers.

advisable (ædˈvaɪzəb(ə)l), *a.* Also 7–9 **adviseable.** [f. ADVISE + -ABLE.]

1. Of persons: Able to be advised; open to advice.
1661 FELL *Life of Hammond* (T.) He was so strangely adviseable, that he would advert unto the judgement of the meanest person. **1775** WESLEY in *Four Cents. Eng. Lett.* (1881) 231 Pray for an advisable and teachable temper. **1866** *Pall Mall G.* 21 May 12 Seeing, however, that it pays Derby prophets to advertise, we presume that men are sometimes morbidly advisable.

2. Of things: Proper to be advised or recommended; expedient, prudent.
1647 JER. TAYLOR *Dissuas. Popery* I. II. §16 (R.) Whether to confess to a priest be an adviseable discipline..is no part of the question. **1650** CROMWELL *Lett. & Sp.* (Carl.) Let. 87 I did not think advisable to attempt upon the Enemy, lying as he doth. **1790** COWPER *Odyssey* xv. 615 It were a course Now not adviseable. **1851** MARIOTTI *Italy* iii. 150 Various reasons..seemed to render advisable the abandonment of the Tyrol.

advisableness (ædˈvaɪzəb(ə)lnɪs). [f. prec. + -NESS.]

1. Of persons: Readiness to be advised; openness to advice. *rare.*
1673 O. WALKER *Education* (1677) 94 These then promise virtue—modesty, obedience, advisableness.

2. Of things: The quality of being advisable or expedient; expediency, propriety.

1731 BAILEY, vol. II, *Advisableness*, fitness to be advised, done, etc., expediency. **1755** in JOHNSON n.q. **1853** WAYLAND *Mem. Judson* II. iii. 109 You inquire about the advisableness of setting up a school at Amherst. **1881** *Sat. Rev.* 2 Apr. 428 Lord Coleridge..gently suggested the advisableness of hostile encounters being brought off on a foreign soil.

advisably (æd'vaɪzəblɪ), *adv.* [f. ADVISABLE + -LY².] In an advisable manner; expediently, prudently, wisely.

[Not in TODD 1818, RICHARDSON 1836, CRAIG 1847. But *unadvisably* is found earlier: **1702** *Lond. Gaz.* mmmdcccxxii. 2 A Soldier..firing unadvisably upon a Centinel..those who were left behind..were alarmed.] **1865** RUSKIN *Sesame* 45 We may advisably carry out this idea a little. **1875** —— *Lect. on Art* iv. 108 To carry the pitcher you may most advisably have two handles.

advisal (æd'vaɪzəl). *rare.* [f. ADVISE + -AL², after *devisal*, *revisal*, etc.] Advising, advice, counsel.

1850 BLACKIE *Æschylus* I. 197 The sure advisal of our voiceless guide.

advise (æd'vaɪz), *v.* Forms: 3–6 avise, 4–5 avyse, 6 avize, 5–6 advyse, 6 advyce, 6–8 advice, 4– advise. [a. Fr. *avise-r*:—late L. *advīsāre*, f. late L. *advīsum* view, opinion: see ADVICE. Refash. in 5–6 after occ. MFr. spelling *adviser*.]

†**1.** *trans.* To look at, view, observe, consider, watch; also, to watch for. *Obs.*

1297 R. GLOUC. 558 He avisede þ e ost suiþe wel. *c* **1386** CHAUCER *Doctoures T.* 124 This juge his eyghen cast Upon this mayde, avysing hir ful fast. *a* **1450** *Knt. de la Tour* 55 The serpent avised her tyme whanne Eve was from her husbonde alone. **1529** RASTELL *Pastyme* (1811) 172 He rode about the castell to advyse it. **1596** SPENSER *F.Q.* II. xii. 66 Abasht that her a straunger did avise. **1603** HOLLAND *Plutarch's Mor.* 96 They advised you well and their eie was never off, wondering to see your rich purple robes.

†**b.** *absol. Obs.*

1509 BARCLAY *Shyp of Folys* (1874) II. 29 Such ar so blynde that they can not aduyse.

†**c.** To look to, provide for (cf. OFr. *avisé*, muni, doué, Godef.). *Obs. rare.*

c **1420** *Pallad. on Husb.* v. 14 Hit doungeth landes lene, and beestes lorne For lene it fedeth uppe, and seek aviseth.

†**2.** *causal.* To make (one) observe (a thing); also, To bring (a thing) into view. *Obs.* (Cf. 10, 11.)

c **1460** *Towneley Myst.* 61 My wand he bad, in thi present, I shuld lay downe, and the avyse How it shuld turne to oone serpent. **1557** SURREY *Aeneid* IV. 461 The troubled ghost doth fray me, and advise The wronged hed by me of my deare sonne, Whom I defraud of the Hisperian crown.

†**3.** To look at *mentally*; to consider, think of, think over, ponder. *Obs.*

c **1374** CHAUCER *Boethius* (1868) 174 Yif þou wolt þan þenke and avisen þe prescience by which it knoweþ al[le] þinges. *c* **1460** FORTESCUE *Absol. & Lim. Mon.* (1714) 105 Hyt may than be advysed by the Counceile, hou such a person may be rewarded. **1578** T. N. tr. *Conq. W. India* 123 Advising them to be madde and stubborne in their opinion. **1677** YARRANTON *Eng. Improv.* 18 He advises not his Creditors, but his own interest.

b. *Sc. Law.* To consider together; to reconsider a verdict, to review or revise. (Also called 'taking into *avizandum*.')

1609 SKENE *Reg. Maj.* 121 That the Judge advise the cause, and decerne, quhether that quhilk was admitted to probation, is sufficientlie proven, or not proven. **1863** *Scotsman* 16 Mar., Some time ago the case was again heard before both Divisions, and to-day it was advised.

†**4.** To devise, to purpose. *Obs.*

c **1340** *Gawayne & Green Knt.* 45 With alle þe mete & þe mirþe þat men couþe a-vyse. **1483** CAXTON *Gold. Leg.* 128/4 They that were enuyous durst not auyse on her ony euyl fame. **1586** *Let. to Earl Leycester* 2, I did therefore aduise to haue this my letter..to be ready.

†**5.** *refl.* To bethink oneself; take thought, consider, reflect. (Fr. *s'aviser.*) Const. *of*, *on*, *upon*, *subord. cl.*; also *inf. phr.* implying caution. *Obs.* See also ADVISED 1.

1297 R. GLOUC. 547 Hii wende & auisede hom somdel vp an doun, That hii miȝte bewar of hor fon. *c* **1386** CHAUCER *Melibeus* 167 Ye moste auyse yow on it ful ofte. —— *Schipm. T.* 236 Therfor have I gret necessité Upon this queynte world to avyse me. **1393** GOWER *Conf.* III. 234 Therfore a prince him shuld advise, Er that he fell in such riote. **1491** CAXTON *How to Die* 1 Fewe there be that aduyse theym of theyr ende. **1557** N. T. (Genevan) *Matt.* xxi. 29 But afterwarde [he] aduised him selfe, and went. **1563** *Homilies* II. xvii. IV. (1640) 235 Let us well advise our selves to advouch that certainly, whereof we have no good knowledge. **1601** SHAKS. *Twel. N.* IV. ii. 102 Aduise you what you say; the minister is heere. **1623** CAMDEN *Rem.* (1637) 124 When they shall better advise themselves..they will not presse mee ouer eagerly herein. [*a* **1656** HALES *Gold. Rem.* (1688) 99 When David advised with himself.]

†**6.** *intr.* (by omission of refl. pron.) To take thought, consider, reflect, ponder, deliberate. *Obs.*

c **1374** CHAUCER *Troylus* v. 1657 He gan to taken of it hede, Avysynge of the lengthe and of the brede. **1485** CAXTON *Paris & Vienne* 30 He aduysed yf he lacked ony thynge. **1513** DOUGLAS *Æneis* VIII. i. 46 Auising wele, quhou al this thing was wrocht. **1611** BIBLE *2 Sam.* xxiv. 13 Now aduise, and see what answere I shall returne. *a* **1642** QUARLES *Glor. Cœli* in Farr's *S.P.* (1848) 139 When I behold, and well advise upon The wise man's speech. **1649** EVELYN *Mem.* (1857) III. 39 Please to advise to what persons you communicate the author of this intelligence, for he desires to be concealed. **1671** MILTON *Samson* 326 Advise Forthwith how thou oughtst to receive him.

Whence, by extension to a multitude,

7. To consider in company, to hold a consultation, to take counsel. Const. *on*, *upon*, *of*. *Obs.* exc. in ***to advise with***: to consult with.

1513–75 *Diurnal of Occurr.* (1833) 88 The quenis majestie and counsell awysit thairvpone. **1623** BINGHAM *Xenophon* 121 The other Coronels said, they would aduise, and returne him answer. **1636** HEALEY *Theophrastus' Charac.* iv. 16 Who distrusting his friends and familiars, in serious affairs adviseth with his servants. **1641** in Rushworth's *Hist. Coll.* III. (1692) I. 310 To be read in full Parliament, and to be advised of by both Houses. **1722** *Col. Records Penn.* III. 158 Chiefly to advice with them on that Head. **1852** MISS YONGE *Cameos* (1877) III. xiv. 121 Edward..merely told them that he must advise with his Council.

8. *absol.* To offer counsel, as one of a consulting body; to give advice.

1375 BARBOUR *Bruce* II. 298 As he awisyt, now have thai done. **1530** PALSGR. 441, I avyse, I rede or counsayle, *Jaduise*. **1611** BIBLE *1 Kings* xii. 6 How doe you aduise, that I may answere this people? **1850** LYTTON *My Novel* I. xi. 39 Mr. Hazeldean sowed and ploughed..very much as Mr. Stirn condescended to advise.

9. *trans.* To give counsel to, to counsel, caution, warn. **a.** at first *simply*; then with *subord. cl.* or *inf.*

1375 BARBOUR *Bruce* XVI. 134 Othir lordis that war him by Avisit the king. **1485** CAXTON *Chas. the Gt.* 194 He was taken and not slayn..to thende that he shold be aduysed to byleue in Ihesu cryst. **1509** FISHER *Serm.* Wks. 1876, 292 An olde Gentylwoman..dyde aduyse her to commende herselfe to saynt Nycholas. **1593** T. WATSON *Sonnet* v. (Arb.) 181 She..Aduised the boy what scandall it would bee. **1604** MARLOWE *Faustus* vii. 80 Well use that trick no more I would advise you. **1713** DERHAM *Physico-Theol.* III. iv. 82 Should we pretend to amend his work; Or to advise infinite Wisdom. **1860** TYNDALL *Glaciers* I. §16, 104 My host advised me to avail myself of the promising weather.

†**b.** *to*, *from*, *against* an action or course. *Obs.*

1483 CAXTON *G. de la Tour* 128 To be auised and saued from velaine reproche. **1605** SHAKS. *Lear* III. vii. 9 Aduice the Duke..to a most festiuate preparation. **1699** BENTLEY *Phalaris* 480 [He] sprinkles a little dust among the Bees, advising them to milder counsels. **1734** tr. *Rollin's Rom. Hist.* (1827) II. 358 Crœsus took upon him to advise Cambyses against his conduct. **1779** JOHNSON *L.P.*, *Pope* (1787) IV. 8 Walsh advised him to correctness.

†**c.** with personal obj. understood and cl. or phr. retained, the latter becoming at length the obj. *Obs.*

1586 *Let. to Earl Leycester* 23 They durst not aduise any security to rest in any, no not in all of them. **1613** SHAKS. *Hen. VIII*, I. i. 114 Loe, where comes that Rock That I aduice your shunning. **1728** T. SHERIDAN *Persius* iii. (1739) 47 In the next Place he advises to consider the End of our Creation.

d. with objective of the thing.

1658–9 SIR H. VANE in Burton's *Diary* (1828) IV. 183, I cannot advise it to be well for you. **1693** *Mem. Count Teckely* I. 51 Having been the first to advice the War. **1735** POPE *Sat.* i. 19 Celsus will advise Hartshorn, or something that shall close your eyes. **1798** SOUTHEY *Sonnets* xi. Wks. II. 95 Wisely was it he advised distrust.

10. To give notice or intimation, to instruct, to inform, to apprise (a person). *esp.* To send (him) formal notice (of a transaction). Const. *of*, or *subord. cl.*

1591 SHAKS. *Two Gent.* III. i. 122 Aduise me, where I may haue such a Ladder. **1622** R. HAWKINS *Voy. to S. Sea* 229 My servants..advised me ordinarily of that which past. **1710** STEELE *Tatler* No. 7 ¶7 The States are advised that the Auxiliaries of Saxony were arrived. **1855** PRESCOTT *Philip II* (1857) I. 119 He advised the constable of this at once. **1879** *Globe* 17 Sept. 7/1 [He] advised the inspector that Gaydon had committed a murder.

11. To give information of, announce (an event, transaction). (*Commercial.*)

1880 *Echo* 3 Mar., The manager..advises the landing of the first Palestine party. *a* **1891** *Comm.* Have these drafts been advised?

advisé, advisee, *ppl. a. Obs.* See ADVISY.

advised (æd'vaɪzd), *ppl. a.* For forms see ADVISE. [f. ADVISE + -ED. In its adjective use, an Eng. trans. of *avisé* (see ADVISY).]

†**1.** *pple.* Of persons: Having considered or pondered. ***to be advised***: to consider, reflect, to act after consideration. Const. *of*. *Obs.*

1375 BARBOUR *Bruce* I. 620 Ic ask ȝou respyt for to se This lettir, and tharwith awysit be. *c* **1500** *Maid & Magpie* in Halliw. *Nugæ Poet.* 43 Ye wylle wedde me now, as I trowe. I wylle be advysed, Gylle, sayd he. **1598** SHAKS. *Merry Wives* I. iii. 106 Are you a-uis'd o' that? **1602** DEKKER *Satirom.* 265 Are you advized what you doe when you hisse? **1633** HANMER *Chron. Irel.* 49 Merlin came, and being advised, said as followeth.

†**2.** Hence *adj.* (in sense of the older *avisé*, *advisee*) Deliberate, cautious, wary, judicious. *Obs.*

1475 CAXTON *Jason* 91 b, Thenke ye what ye haue to do and be ye aduised. **1579** TOMSON *Calvin's Serm. on Tim.* 893/2 Man is head of the woman, hee ought to be more aduised & wise. **1611** COTGR., *Il a du plomb en teste*, He hath a sad, aduised, or discreet pate of his own. **1702** *Eng. Theophrastus* 246 In all actions a Prince ought to be slow and advised.

†**3.** *esp.* with *well* or *ill*; both *pple.* as in 1, and *adj.* as in 2. *Obs.*

a **1375** WYCLIF *Wks.* 1880, 375 þu..art wo þat euer crist was so yuel avised to say..þes wordis. *c* **1386** CHAUCER *Miller's T.* 398 Be well avised on that ilke night..That non of us ne speke not o word. *c* **1450** *Merlin* 45 Be well a-vised that ye knowe it is he. **1580** NORTH *Plutarch* (1676) 43 To another he put forth a question, who was to be well advised of his answer. **1611** BIBLE *Prov.* xiii. 10 But with the well aduised is wisedome.

4. Of things: Considered, deliberate, intentional; *hence* well considered, judicious. (Fuller contrasts these senses.) *ill-advised*: injudicious.

c **1440** *Relig. Pieces fr. Thornton MS.* (1867) 19 Kepe vs Lorde..fra sodayne and avysede dede. **1563** *Homilies* II. xv. (1640) 199 Ought we not then by the monition of the Wiseman..to take advised heed? **1642** FULLER *Holy & Prof. State* II. xix. 127 The more advised the deed is, the lesse advised it is. **1665** J. SPENCER *Prodigies* 17 His cool and advised thoughts. **1829** I. TAYLOR *Enthus.* §10, 262 The atheistical conspiracy made its long-concerted, and well-advised and consentaneous and furious attack. **1876** FREEMAN *Norm. Conq.* I. App. 722 His statement has more the air of a deliberately advised statement. *Mod.* His conduct throughout has been very ill-advised.

†**5.** Of persons: Purposed, determined. Cf. ADVISE 4. *Obs.*

c **1325** *E.E. Allit. P.* B. 1365 Such a mangerie to makeþe man watȝ auised. **1393** GOWER *Conf.* II. 10 But she is otherwise avised Than graunte such a time assised. **1483** CAXTON *Gold. Leg.* 263/3, I..am auysed neuer to leue the.

6. Counselled. See ADVISE *v.* 9 a, and d.

1596 SHAKS. *1 Hen. IV*, IV. iii. 5 Good Cousin be aduis'd, stirre not tonight. **1871** RUSKIN *Fors Clav.* ix. 11 The better minded ones really take the advised measures.

7. Informed, apprised, warned.

1599 SHAKS. *Hen. V*, II. Cho. 12 The French aduis'd by good intelligence Of this most dreadful preparation, Shake in their feare. **1860** MOTLEY *Netherl.* (1868) II. xvii. 296 He was thoroughly advised of the disputes between the Earl of Leicester and the States.

advisedly (æd'vaɪzɪdlɪ), *adv.* Forms: 4–5 **avisily**, **avissely**; 4–6 **avisely**; 5 **avysilye**; 5–6 **avysely**, **avysseley**; 6–7 **advisedlie**; 6– **advisedly**. [Two forms are here:—1 *avisi-ly*, f. *avisè* ADVISY + -LY²; 2 ADVISED + -LY². But as *avisily* was changed by various intermediate forms to *advisedly*, it is convenient to treat the whole together.] In an advised manner.

†**1.** With watchfulness or attention; warily, attentively, carefully, circumspectly. *Obs.*

1375 BARBOUR *Bruce* II. 344 Thai saw cumand Thar fayis ridand..Arayit rycht awisely. *c* **1420** *Pallad. on Husb.* III. 356 A wegge of boone or yron putte bytwene The bark and tree..Avisily, the rynde unhurte to kepe. *c* **1440** *Morte Arthure* 3166 Avissely in þat vale he vetailles his biernez. *c* **1570** THYNNE *Pride & Lowl.* (1841) 19 Beholding him advisedly. **1651** N. BIGGS *New Dispens.* §263, 192 Let the Fontanells be advisedly closed up.

†**2.** With prudence; wisely, prudently, judiciously. *Obs.*

c **1386** CHAUCER *Manc. T.* 223 But for a litil speche avisily Is no man schent. **1391** *How the goode wife, etc.* 22 in Hazl. Ȝif any man bidde the worschipe, and wille wedde the, Avysely answere hym. *c* **1500** *Partenay* 538 Thaim aid and councell ryght auysilye. *c* **1571** HENRYSON *Mor. Fables* 40 The sheepe auisely gaue answeir in the cace. **1683** CORBET *Nonconf. Plea* 8 To do all things advisedly, honestly, peaceably..is the best means of such reputation.

†**3.** With full or calm consideration; deliberately, leisurely. *Obs.*

1483 CAXTON *Gold. Leg.* 161/1 He sente for the pryour and tolde to hym aduysedly al this vysyon. **1549** COVERDALE *Erasm. Paraphr. Col.* ii. 13 We haue aduisedly sworne to be obedient to Moses lawe. **1655** MOFFET & BENNET *Health's Improv.* (1746) 396 Mince or chew your Meat finely, eat leisurely, swallow advisedly. **1656** BRAMHALL *Replic.* vii. 295 If he had advisedly read over my assertion it is this.

4. As the result of deliberation or thought; deliberately, intentionally.

1562–3 *Act 5 Eliz.* i. §17 Suche as shall openly and advisedly deprave, by Woordes or Writinges..any of the Rites and Ceremonies. **1596** SHAKS. *Merch. Ven.* v. 253 Your Lord Will neuer more breake faith aduisedlie. **1755** MAGENS *Ess. Insur.* I. 53 If the Master of a Ship has advisedly dropt Anchor in rocky ground. **1851** HT. MARTINEAU *Hist. Peace* I. v. 56 We speak advisedly and from experience when we say that this was the general feeling. **1876** FREEMAN *Norm. Conq.* I. 533, I do this advisedly.

advisedness (æd'vaɪzɪdnɪs). ? *Obs.* Also 5 avysnes, 6 avysenesse. [orig. f. *avisè* (see ADVISY) + -NESS. Etymologically *avyseness* and *advisedness* are two words; but historically *advisedness* came in as a 'rectification' of *avyseness*, when the Eng. ppl. adj. ADVISED took the place of *avisè*, *avisy*.] The quality of being advised; prudent consideration, caution, deliberation.

c **1400** *Tundale Vis.*, *Purif. Marie* 132 Mary..gan merveyly with grete avysnes Of the wordis that he can expresse. **1509** *Payne of Evyll Maryage* 9, I was in purpoce ..for to have wedded without avysenesse A fulle fayre mayde. **1633** HOWELL *Lett.* (1650) I. 349 Such a kind of cunctation, advisedness, and procrastination is allowable also in all councils of state. **1755** S. WALKER *Serm.* ix, His Recreations also, are with much Consultation and Advisedness. **1789** BENTHAM *Princ. Legisl.* ix. §10 Advisedness with respect to the circumstances..extends the intentionality from the act to the consequences.

advisee (ædvaɪ'ziː). [f. ADVISE *v.* + -EE¹.] The person advised.

1824 *New Monthly Mag.* XI. 12 The adviser reminded the advisee of those happy days. **1856** T. CARLYLE *Let.* 25 Apr. (1923) 297 'Nobody follows advice,' they say; which means withal, 'Advice never hits the case; the case is not known to any Adviser, but only to the Advisee.' **1952** M. MCCARTHY

Groves of Academe (1953) iv. 70 To have advisees in the reading courses double up in the tutorial hour.

adviseful, variant of ADVICEFUL *a. Obs.*

advisement (ædˈvaɪzmənt). For forms see ADVISE. [a. Fr. *a(d)visement*, f. *aviser*: see ADVISE and -MENT.]

†**1.** The process of looking at or viewing; observation, notice, attention, consideration. *Obs.*

1330 R. BRUNNE *Chron.* 241 Sent þei non bifore, to wite how þei mo passe, þerfore had þei lore, for non avisement wasse. *c* **1374** CHAUCER *Troylus* v. 1811 And ther he saugh, with ful avysemente, The erratyk sterres. **1447** BOKENHAM *Lyvys of Seyntys* (1835) 14 Hyr bewte so sore dede lure Hys herte, that..of hyr he took more avysement. **1600** HOLLAND *Livy* I. xviii. 14 He had with good avisement taken a prospect and view towards the cittie.

†**2. a.** The process of viewing or considering mentally; thought, thinking, consideration, reflection, deliberation. ? *Obs.* or *dial.*

1330 R. BRUNNE *Chron.* 289 Pride and ille avisement Mishapnes oftentide, and dos many be schent. *c* **1386** CHAUCER *Mercht's. T.* 287, I warn yow wel it is no childes pley To take a wyf withoute avisement. *c* **1425** WYNTOUN *Cron.* IX. xxvii. 282 To þat rycht sone assentit he And blythly ..Wyth schort Avisment maid ansuere. **1571** GRINDAL *Articles* xviii, Whether they doe every day with good aduisement conferre one Chapter of the Latine and English togither. **1603–5** SIR J. MELVIL *Mem.* (1735) 354 After fifteen days Advisement and devout Prayer. **1709** STRYPE *Ann. Ref.* xxxvii. 390 It was the work of ten years, written with good advisement. **1794** BURNS *Wks.* IV. 319 O' gude advisement comes nae ill.

†**b.** The result of thinking; a thought, opinion, resolution, plan. *Obs.*

1535 COVERDALE *Jer.* xxvi. 13 Therfore amende youre wayes, and youre advysementes and be obedient. **1590** *Span. Invas.* in *Harl. Misc.* (Malh.) II. 159 By reason of a great calm, which fell out, no part of this advisement could be accomplished.

†**3.** *to take advisement*: to take thought, to consider or deliberate; (of a multitude) to take counsel, consult; hence, to decide, resolve. *Obs.*

1375 BARBOUR *Bruce* VII. 526 He tuk avisment vith his men, On quhat maner thai suld do then. *c* **1385** CHAUCER *Leg. Good Wom.* 1413 At the laste he tooke avysemente, To send hym into some fer countre. **1462** DAUBENEY in *Past. Lett.* 452 II. 102 Take avisment of this mater tille to morowe. *a* **1569** KYNGESMILL *Godly Advise* (1580) 4 You ought to take good advisement howe you bestowe yourselfe, least you both marie and marre yourselfe in one daie. **1597** DANIEL *Civ. Wares* (1609) I. xcii, And mus'd awhile, waking advisement takes of what had past in sleepe.

4. Combined deliberation; consultation. Now *arch.* exc. *N. Amer.* (chiefly *Law*) in phr. (*to take*) *under advisement*.

1417 T. BROKE in *E.E. Wills* (1882) 24 Iff ych haue.. mystake hir good, I wyll þat it be restored to ham..be avysement of myn Executours. **1534** LD. BERNERS *Gold. Bk. of M. Aurel.* (1546) Q vij b, Doughteres..shuld not mary without lycence, nor the emperours doughters without the aduysement of the senate. **1634–46** J. ROW (father) *Hist. Kirk Scotl.* (1842) 186 Whereupon the magistrats, after advisement, withdrew themselves. **1735** *Col. Rec. Penn.* IV. 23 Till the Bill for establishing Courts of Equity comes under advisement. **1881** *Times* 19 Feb. 5/2 The application [to the Court] was made upon advisement. **1888** *Missouri Republican* 11 Feb. 1/5 Chief Justice Waite,..on being informed that the matter wanted time to look up certain records and precedents, said the matter would be taken under advisement. **1969** D. ACHESON *Present at Creation* (1970) xviii. 161 On February 12 Secretary Byrnes heard argument and received memoranda from me, Colonel McCormack, and the geographic assistant secretaries, taking the issue under advisement. **1984** *Miami Herald* 30 Mar. 2C/2 Wilson took under advisement a motion by Pizzo that another attorney, Ron Cacciatore, be appointed by the court to assist in the defense.

5. Advice, counsel. *arch.*

c **1440** *Morte Arthure* 148 Thus schalle I take avisemente of valiant beryns. **1509** BARCLAY *Ship of Fooles* (1570) 17 The reade and advisement Of wise men, discrete, and full of grauitie, Helpeth thine owne. **1658** BROME *Cov. Gard.* v. i. 77 There's hope that he may be fetch't halfe way back again, by your fatherly advicement. **1658** S. LENNARD tr. *Charron's Wisdome* I. xx. §12 (1670) 74 Particular advisements and remedies against this evil you shall find. **1850** BLACKIE *Æschylus* II. 271 My son, Xerxes, Being young hath young conceits; and takes no note Of my advisement.

†**6.** An instruction how to act, an injunction, a warning. *Obs.*

1538 in Strype *Eccl. Mem.* App. xci, I charge and enjoyn to every curate..to accomplish these few advisements and injunctions. **1598** BARRET *Theor. Warres* II. i. 17 That they may before the enemy arriue, give aduisement. **1654** GENTILIS tr. *Servita's Hist. Inquis.* (1676) 860 The punishments which the Inquisition imposeth, are spiritual, as Abjurations, Absolutions, or Advisements.

adviser (ædˈvaɪzə(r)). Also **advisor** [-OR]. [f. ADVISE + -ER[1].]

Adviser remains the usual spelling, but *advisor* is freq. used (esp. *U.S.*) in the titles of persons whose function it is to give advice.

1. a. One who advises or counsels. Also with qualifying word, as ***legal adviser, tax adviser***, etc.

1611 FLORIO, *Avisatore*, an aduiser, an advertiser. **1651** HOBBES *Gov. & Soc.* xiv. §1. 210 When obedience is yielded to the Lawes, not for the thing it self, but by reason of the advisers will, the Law is not a Counsell, but a Command. **1741** MIDDLETON *Cicero* (1742) II. vii. 266, I..who from the very first have always been the adviser of peace. **1863** COX *Inst. Eng. Govt.* I. v. 29 The advisers of the Crown have taken upon themselves the responsibility. **1899** *Advisor* Feb. 8 Such a paper as The Advisor will be a great help to any advertisor. **1919** W. J. MAILHOIT (*title*) Mailhoit's modern advisor to grocers. **1922** JOYCE *Ulysses* 302 It was explained by his legal adviser Avvocato Pagamimi that the various articles secreted in his thirty-two pockets [etc.]. **1934** *Amer. Speech* IX. 318/1 Following the advent and acceptance in this country of *advisors*, newspapers now occasionally mention *debators*. **1952** R. FINLAYSON *Schooner came to Atia* i. 8 Timi..skilfully combined the duties of secretary,.. chauffeur, advisor on inside island politics, and trusted confidant. **1954** *Amer. Speech* XXIX. 236 To call an employee..by the undemocratic 'epithet' *subordinate*..goes against the American grain. The euphemistic terms usually substituted are *advisor* (sometimes called *adviser*), *aide*, *assistant*... *Advisor* is the term employed in the higher levels of bureaucracy, especially by the President. **1964** MRS. L. B. JOHNSON *White House Diary* 22 Apr. (1970) 116 Next was a meeting with Bois Jeuilett Jones (our friend and advisor from NEW). **1971** D. BAGLEY *Freedom Trap* iii. 64 It is natural that he have an advisor to handle the investment of these funds. **1980** G. GREENE *Dr. Fischer* i. 10 Among the Toads was..a tax adviser, Monsieur Belmont.

b. Chiefly *U.S.* At some universities, a senior member assigned individually to advise students on personal, academic, or other matters. Cf. *moral tutor* s.v. MORAL *a.* 3 d.

1887 *Lippincott's Monthly Mag.* Sept. 453 One great power of appeal..playing between teachers and students [at Harvard] is exercised through the 'advisers'. Each matriculate is expected to designate one of his professors whom he will consider his adviser while at the university. The professor is to be consulted by the student as a personal friend and guide. **1914** V. L. COLLINS *Princeton* 376 Each [first-year student] has an 'adviser' among the younger members of the faculty to whom he is encouraged to go with all or any of his perplexities. **1936** MENCKEN *Amer. Lang.* (ed. 4) 242 Most English universities have deans of faculties much like our own, and some of them have lately laid in deans of women, and even advisers to women students. **1963** F. F. LAIDLER *Gloss. Terms Home Econ. Educ.* 8 *Adviser.* (1) Counsellor on subjects relating to Home Economics (Canada). (2) One who advises the student or pupil on courses or careers (New Zealand). **1965** A. LURIE *Nowhere City* (1966) i. 4 What was he supposed to do when, in April, his adviser and protector at Harvard had disappeared into Washington?

c. (with capital initial.) An agent or representative of the British government employed as a resident adviser by a Malay sultanate. *Hist.*

British Advisers to certain States (as Kelantan and Trengganu) formerly under Siamese suzerainty were officially appointed and controlled by the Siamese Government.

[**1878** J. DOUGLAS *Let.* 17 May in *Strait's Settlements Instructions Brit. Residents* 7 in *Parl. Papers 1878–9* (C. 2410) LI. 409 His Excellency desires that you should be reminded that the Residents have been placed in the Native States as advisers, not as rulers.] **1902** W. J. ARCHER *Annex to Despatch* No. 141 15 July (Publ. Rec. Office Kew FO 69/230), On June 5th..the Siamese Minister in London.. went on to say that the Siamese Government had no intention..of withdrawing from the agreement to appoint British subjects as Advisers to the Rajahs of the Malay States. **1910** W. G. MAXWELL *Ann. Rep. Adviser to Kedah Govt.* 1 in *Parl. Papers 1910.* 1 (Cd. 5389) LXVI. 831 The first printed official report upon this State appeared over the signature of Mr. G. C. Hart, the Adviser appointed by the Siamese Government. **1954** V. BARTLETT *Rep. from Malaya* ix. 97 Each of the nine States has a similar legislature on a smaller scale, with the addition of a British Adviser who is a link between the High Commissioner and the State administration. **1969** J. M. GULLICK *Malaysia* ii. 106 There was also a British Adviser (no longer a 'Resident')... The Advisers did not reassume the executive powers of the pre-war British Residents of the F.M.S.

d. Chiefly in *pl.* A soldier sent to advise or help the government or army of a foreign country (often a euphemism for a combatant soldier).

1915 *Handbk. Turkish Army* (Intelligence Dept., Cairo) (ed. 2) 24 No attempts to form reserve divisions were noted at Constantinople during the mobilization, but there is every reason to believe that it was the policy of the Turkish military authorities and their German military advisers to form a certain number. **1939** LITTLEPAGE & BESS *In Search of Soviet Gold* xxiv. 259 The Russians have kept a number of 'advisers', military and otherwise, in Sinkiang for several years. **1955** *Economist* 11 June 927/1 Nor will the presence of thirty American military advisers constitute a United States base on Cambodian soil. **1972** *Guardian* 6 Sept. 14/6 If the Australian Labour Party wins the election and the troops come home—there are only 150 'advisers' left in Vietnam—no one doubts that ANZUK would break up. **1980** *Times* 2 Jan. 9/1 Seen from Moscow the regime of Mr Amin was squandering a Soviet investment in Afghanistan that had been built up over many years... He was also allowing a lot of Soviet advisors to be killed.

2. One who sends advice or notice of anything.

1854 DE QUINCEY in Page (1877) II. xviii. 83 To you, as being (I think) my latest adviser from Tipperary, I address my answer.

†**3.** A dispatch-boat; an A(D)VISO. *Obs.*

1658–9 in Burton's *Diary* (1828) III. 383 One-hundred-and-twenty sail, whereof ten are advisers, and as many fire-ships.

adviserate (ædˈvaɪzərət). Also **advisorate**. [f. ADVISER + -ATE[1].] **1.** An advisory body; a group of political advisers.

1946 *Washington Post* 21 Sept. 8 It is painfully obvious from the second chapter in Wallace vs. Administration that the President is ill-served by his advisorate. **1956** QUIGLEY & TURNER *New Japan* iv. 46 The Privy Council, constitutional advisorate of the emperor and the cabinet.

2. (With capital initial.) The residence of an Adviser (sense 1 c).

1960 C. BELGRAVE *Personal Column* iii. 32 The Adviserate garden in 1956.

advisership (ædˈvaɪzəʃɪp). [f. ADVISER + -SHIP.] The office of an adviser.

1868 *Pall Mall G.* 2 Dec. 8 The Law Advisership to the Castle is the most important of the remaining appointments.

advising (ædˈvaɪzɪŋ), *vbl. sb.* [f. ADVISE + -ING[1].] The action expressed by the verb *advise*. Considering, consulting, counselling, warning, notifying. (Now mostly gerundial.)

c **1450** PECOCK *Repr.* 75 Bi avisingis, and bi conseil taking. **1603** SHAKS. *Meas. for M.* III. i. 203 Therefore fasten your eare on my aduisings. **1640** FULLER *Abel Rediv.* (1867) II. 234 He approved of the vice-chancellors advising. **1866** CARLYLE *Inaug. Addr.* 171, I would not..go much into advising; but there is one advice I must give you.

advising (ædˈvaɪzɪŋ), *ppl. a.* [f. ADVISE + -ING[2].] That advises; counselling.

Mod. Advising words; an advising solicitor.

†**adˈvision.** *Obs.* A rare form of AVISION, but that which the word would have regularly received, had it survived to the 16th c.

†**adˈvisive,** *a. Obs. rare*[−1]. [f. ADVISE + -IVE. Prob. a. OFr. **avisif, -ive*.]

1. Observant, prudent. See ADVISIVENESS.

2. Supplying advice, advising, counselling.

1648 HERRICK *Wks.* II. 47 A Parænetical or Advisive Verse to his friend.

†**adˈvisiveness.** *Obs. rare*[−1]. [f. prec. + -NESS.] The quality of being advisive; thoughtfulness, prudence, discretion.

1436 *Pol. Poems* II. 200 Discrecioun, subtile avisifenesse.

†**adˈviso.** *Obs.* Pl. -oes. [ad. Sp. *aviso* advice, intelligence; also, an advice-boat:—late L. *advīsum*: see ADVICE, under the influence of which, and the cognate Eng. words, *adviso* became common in Eng., though AVISO (q.v.) was also used, and is now the only form (in sense 3).]

1. Information, intelligence; an official notification, dispatch, or 'advice.' *Obs.* (Sense retained in ADVICE 8.)

1594 CAREW *Tasso's Godfr. Bulloigne* (1881) 119 William ..This fresh aduiso sendeth you by mee. **1622** F. MARKHAM *Dec. Warre* III. ix. §4. 114 By the imployment of Spies, by Traytors or by some other advisoes.

2. *pompously*, An advice, counsel, suggestion.

1591 RALEIGH *Fight of Revenge* 15 Slandrous Pamphlets, aduisoes and Letters. **1643** SIR T. BROWNE *Relig. Med.* I. §19 Who forgetting the honest advisoes of Faith, have listened unto the conspiracy of Passion and Reason. **1676** in *Phil. Trans.* XI. 573 Our modern [writers] have been free of their Adviso's to prompt the studious.

3. (Also *caraval of adviso*.) A dispatch or advice-boat; in which sense the word survives in the form AVISO.

1624 CAPT. SMITH *Virginia* v. 179 The aduenturers sent them an aduiso with thirtie Passengers. **1642** FULLER *Holy & Prof. State* II. xxi. 138 The King of Spain knew of it, and sent a Caravall of adviso to the West Indies. **1650** R. STAPYLTON *Strada's Low Countrey Warres* VI. 8 Who dispatched back his Adviso with more then ordinary speed.

advisory (ædˈvaɪzərɪ), *a.* (*sb.*) [f. ADVISE + -ORY, as if ad. late L. **advisōrius*, f. late L. *advīsor*.]

A. *adj.* orig. *U.S.* Having the attribute of advising; giving, or tending to give, advice.

1778 *Result Convention at Ipswich, Essex* (Mass.) 45 We think therefore that the members of that court ought never to be advisory to any officer in the state. **1789** MORSE *Amer. Geogr.* (1792) 170 The churches claim no jurisdiction over each other, and the power of ecclesiastical councils is only advisory. **1809** D. RAMSAY *Hist. South Carolina* II. 20 Churches, as corporations, can enforce their by-laws, but their powers as spiritual courts are merely advisory. **1847** in CRAIG. **1862** J. CHESTER in *Macm. Mag.* Nov. 62 The expression of their opinions is advisory only. **1882** *Times* 27 Mar. 4 There was some difference of opinion in the Advisory Board.

B. *sb. N. Amer.* **1.** *spec.* A bulletin issued by a meteorological office, esp. advising of adverse weather conditions; a hurricane warning.

[**1931** E. B. CALVERT *Weather Bureau* 23 There are some 4,000,000 orchard heaters in use, in the operation of which the growers largely depend on advices and warnings given by the weather bureau.] **1936** *Monthly Weather Rev.* July 239/2 The first advice was disseminated at 9·30 a.m., E.S.T., of July 27 and advisories and bulletins followed. **1948** *World Almanac* (N.Y.) 118/2 The Hurricane and Storm-Warning Service prepares its highly important advisories and warnings. **1958** *Listener* 18 Sept. 417/1 When you have a house..anywhere near the sea, you become a devoted disciple of the Weather Bureau and its bulletins, or what are now horridly called 'advisories'. **1959** 'F. RICHARDS' *Practise to Deceive* xi. 156 The radio said: 'The latest advisory on the progress of the hurricane..indicates that Eva has altered course.' **1974** *News & Reporter* (Chester, S. Carolina) 22 Apr. 6-A/7 Growers are urged to follow the daily agricultural weather advisories. **1985** *Globe & Mail* (Toronto) 9 Oct. A9/4 Weather advisories were issued for all parts of Manitoba.

2. *gen.* A document, statement, notice, etc., which gives advice; an advisory message.

1955 *Bull. Atomic Sci.* Sept. 247/1 This advisory, which had the force of a directive because of the willing, not to say anxious, compliance of newspaper editors and publishers, forbade mention of the heaviest element in the atomic table. **1976** *National Observer* (U.S.) 12 June 3/1 A 'carefully worded' security 'advisory'. **1978** *N.Y. Times* 29 Mar. B3/4 The panel.. intended to replace a controversial advisory to druggists that appeared to counsel evasion of the law.

†**advisy, advisee,** *ppl. a. Obs.* Forms: 3–5 **avysé;** 4–5 **avise(e;** 5 **avisy, aduisy, aduysee** (*Sc.* 5 **awyssé;** 6 **awysee).** [a. OFr. *aviset, avisé,* pa. pple. of *aviser* to ADVISE.] Well-advised; circumspect, heedful, wary, cautious.

c **1300** *K. Alis.* 5261 The kyng, and his meigné, Gladdest weren and aveysè. **1330** R. BRUNNE *Chron.* 188 Of werre and of bataile he was fulle auise. **1426** *Pol. Poems* (1859) II. 137 This Henry of knyghthode moste famous, Moste avisy, and moste victorious. **1443** HENRY VI in Ellis *Orig. Lett.* III. 34 I. 79 Notable and aduisy labours and diligences. **1513** DOUGLAS *Æneis* V. ix. 35 Scharp Mnestheus war and awysee.

‖**advocaat** (ædvəʊ'kɑːt). Also **advokaat.** [Du., shortened f. *advocatenborrel* egg-and-brandy liqueur, f. *advocaat* ADVOCATE *sb.* + *borrel* drink.] A Dutch liqueur made with eggs, sugar and brandy; also, a glass of this.

1935 in A. L. SIMON *Wines & Liqueurs from A to Z.* **1938** M. ALLINGHAM *Fashion in Shrouds* xxii. 420 There's some gin and French and a little Advocaat.. in the cupboard. **1951** P. BRANCH *Lion in Cellar* vi. 78 Three gins, a cherry brandy, and an Advocaat. **1962** P. HELM *Death has Thousand Entrances* ii. 41 We drank *advokaat,* sweet and thick.

advocacy ('ædvəkəsɪ). [a. (14th c.) Fr. *advocacie, -atie, avocacie,* ad. med.L. *advocātia,* n. of state, f. *advocātus*: see ADVOCATE and -ACY.]

1. The function of an advocate; the work of advocating; pleading for or supporting.

1413 LYDG. *Pylgr. Sowle* I. xv. (1859) 15 Blysful lord!.. I haue spoken of aduocacye, soo that thou sholdest myn aduocate be. **1483** CAXTON *Gold. Leg.* 427/1 He had ocupyed and exerced moche holyly and deuoutelye the fayte of aduocacye in the bysshoppes courte. **1646** SIR T. BROWNE *Pseud. Ep.* 47 Shall he want herein the applause or advocacy of Satan. **1849** COBDEN *Sp.* 21, I will never cease the advocacy of this question. **1867** CARLYLE *Remin.* (1881) II. 13 It is a strange trade, I have often thought, that of advocacy. **1872** YEATS *Growth & Viciss. Comm.* 273 Whose voice then first began to be heard in advocacy of freedom of commerce.

2. = ADVOWSON, ADVOCATION 5.

1876 FREEMAN *Norm. Conq.* III. xii. 194 Bishop Gervase .. petitioned the king to grant the royal rights over the see, the rights of advocacy or patronage.

†**advo'cacyer,** *v. Obs.* [a. Fr. *advocacier, avocacier,* f. *avocacie* advocacy, transferred with inf. ending.] To practise as an advocate.

1506 *Ord. Crysten Men* (W. de Worde) IV. xxi. 262 Suche people the whiche misbere them for to aduocacyer synneth gretly.. The Iuge may not aduocacyer in the cause that he ought to Iuge.

†**advocary.** *Obs. rare*⁻¹. [ad. med.L. *advocāria* (cited by Du Cange from charter of 1216), f. OFr. *avoërie, avouerie,* n. of state, f. *avoeor, avoueur*:—L. *advocātōrem*: see ADVOCATOR.] ? Pleading.

c **1374** CHAUCER *Troylus* ii. 1469 Be ye not ware how that false Polyfete Is now about eftsones for you to plete, And bring on yow advocacies [*v.r.* advocatis, advocacies] newe?

advocate ('ædvəkət), *sb.* Forms: 4–5 **avocat, avoket;** 5 **advoket, -ette;** 5–7 **advocat;** 5– **advocate.** Aphetic 5–6 **voket, vocate.** [a. OFr. *avocat,* ad. L. *advocātus,* one summoned or 'called to' another, esp. one called in to aid one's cause in a court of justice; prop. pa. pple. of *advocā-re,* f. *ad* to + *vocāre* to call. The OFr. living descendant of *advocātus* was *avoët, avoé, avoué* (see ADVOWEE); *avocat* was a semi-popular adaptation of the L. title. In 14–16th c. it was often still further conformed to the L. as *advocat,* an artificial spelling, afterwards abandoned in Fr., which has caused in Eng. a permanent refashioning of the word. See AD- 2.] *lit.* One called in, or liable to be called upon, to defend or speak for.

1. One whose profession it is to plead the cause of any one in a court of justice; a counsellor or counsel. (The technical title in the Roman law courts, and in those countries which retain the Roman law, as Scotland and France; also in the Admiralty Courts, and many special tribunals existing or historical; but not in ordinary English law courts.)

Faculty of Advocates: the collective body of members of the bar in Scotland. ***Lord Advocate***, formerly ***King's*** (or ***Queen's***) ***A.***, the principal law-officer of the crown in Scotland, answering to the Attorney-General in England. ***Judge-Advocate***, the officer who manages the prosecution before a court-martial, the supreme officer for the whole army being the ***Judge-Advocate-General***. ***advocate*** is also in the city of Aberdeen a local title for a solicitor. ***devil's advocate***: see DEVIL *sb.* 25 b.

1340 HAMPOLE *Pr. Consc.* 6084 For-why þai sal þan na help gett Of sergeaunt, ne auturne, ne avoket. **1382** WYCLIF *Acts* xxiv. 1 Tertulle, sum oratour, or fair speker, or avocat. **1387** TREVISA *Higden* Rolls Ser. II. 373 For þe delyueraunce of þe advoketes and ditoures. **1393** LANGL. *P. Pl.* C. III. 61 Foragers and vytailers · and vokettus of þe Arches [*v.r.* voketts, vocates, a-uoketes, B. vokates]. *c* **1400** *Rom. Rose* 5724 Phiciciens and advocates Gone right by the same yates. They selle her science for wynnyng. **1483** CAXTON *Cato* bj, b, They may selle their scyence and kunnyng for siluer.. As done these grete auocates. *c* **1538** STARKEY *Eng.* 118 Thes hungry Aduocatys and cormorantys of the law. **1635** QUARLES *Emblems* I. v. (1718) 21 There was no client then to wait The leisure of his long-tail'd advocate. **1679** *Indictment, Trial of Langhorn* 3 The Place and Office of Advocate General of the Army aforesaid. **1768** BLACKSTONE *Comm.* III. iii, Of advocates or (as we generally call them) counsel, there are two species or degrees, barristers and sergeants. **1796** MORSE *Amer. Geog.* II. 168 The college or faculty of advocates.. may be called the seminary of Scotch lawyers. **1810** BENTHAM *Packing* (1821) 48 The duty of an advocate is to take fees, and in return for those fees to display to the utmost advantage whatsoever falshoods the solicitor has put into his brief. **1825** —— *Reward* 93 At Rome, if certain travellers may be believed, it is the custom when a saint is about to be canonized, to allow an advocate, who in familiar language is called *the advocate of the devil,* to plead against his admission. **1826** DISRAELI *Viv. Grey* I. viii. 18 To succeed as an advocate, I must be a great lawyer: and, to be a great lawyer, I must give up my chance of being a great man. **1862** LD. BROUGHAM *Brit. Constitn.* xvii. 281 A Scotch Judge making a vacancy on that Bench removed the Lord Advocate. **1876** BANCROFT *Hist. U.S.* VI. l. 373 The advocate-general Segur having drawn up the most minatory indictment.

2. *fig.* and *gen.* One who pleads, intercedes, or speaks for, or in behalf of, another; a pleader, intercessor, defender.

1340 *Ayenb.* 127 Bidde we mid al oure herte þane holy gost .. þat he by oure auocat. *c* **1405** *Lay Folks Mass-Bk., B. Pr.* II. 66 Pray specialy til oure lady saynt mary that sche becum oure auoket. **1460** in *Pol. Rel. & Love Poems* 148, I loke for loue of man my broþir, I am his avoket on euery wise. *a* **1535** W. DE WORDE *Communycacyon* Biij, Mercy was thyn aduocat chefe. **1594** SHAKS. *Rich. III,* I. iii. 87 An earnest aduocate to plead for him. **1612** DRAYTON *Polyolbion* Aij, I have (but as an Advocat for the muse) argued. **1735** POPE *Eth. Ep.* II. 30 The Frail one's advocate, the Weak one's friend. **1774** MRS. CHAPONE *Improv. Mind* II. 8 He will find an advocate in every human heart. **1828** MACAULAY *Hallam's Const. Hist.* 40 The advocates of Charles have very dexterously contrived to conceal.. the real nature of this transaction.

b. Specially, applied to Christ as the Intercessor for sinners.

1382 WYCLIF *1 John* ii. 1 We han auoket anentis the fadir, Ihesu Crist just [**1388** an aduocat]. **1509** FISHER *Wks.* 282 Jesus is.. a suffycyent vocate for vs. **1611** BIBLE *1 John* ii. 1 We haue an Aduocate with the Father, Iesus Christ the righteous. **1667** MILTON *P.L.* II. 33 Let me Interpret for him, me his advocate And propitiation. *a* **1788** C. WESLEY *Hymn* 'Light of those,' Come, thou Advocate and Saviour, Manifest thy wondrous grace. **1826** BINNEY *Hymn* 'Eternal Light,' A Holy Spirit's energies, An Advocate with God.

3. One who defends, maintains, publicly recommends, or raises his voice in behalf of a proposal or tenet. Const. *of* (*for* ? obs.).

c **1735** POPE *Hor. Ep.* II. i. 34 Advocates for folly dead and gone. **1756** LUCAS *Ess. on Waters* III. 318 The advocates for brimstone will here triumph. **1792** *Anecd. W. Pitt* I. xx. 332 Truth will continue to have her worshippers; and it may be presumed that they will.. survive the advocates of Falsehood. **1810** COLERIDGE *Friend* (1865) 128 The most respectable English advocate for the theory. **1858** MAX MÜLLER *Chips* (1880) II. xxvii. 349 The priests were.. the strongest advocates of the system of caste. **1860** MAURY *Phys. Geog. Sea* ii. §92 The advocates of the trade-wind theory.

†**4.** The secular defender or 'patron' of a church or religious house; an ADVOWEE. *Obs.*

1387 TREVISA *Higden* Rolls Ser. I. 283 Þe Romayns chees hym afterwardes for to be Seynt Petres aduokett [*tr.* **1432–50** aduocate]. **1751** CHAMBERS *Cycl., Advocate* is more particularly used, in church-history, for a person appointed to defend the rights and revenues of a church, or religious house.

'advocate, *v.*¹ Pa. pple. Sc. **advocat.** [f. L. *advocāt-* ppl. stem of *advocā-re* to call to; f. *ad* to + *vocā-re* to call.]

†**1.** To call (*to* oneself), summon, invite. *Obs.*

1555 HARPSFIELD *Divorce of Hen. VIII* (1878) 271 The emperor, minding to advocate to himself another wife.

2. *Sc. Law.* To call to a higher tribunal; to ADVOKE. See also AVOCATE.

1609 SKENE *Reg. Maj.* 55 The pley sould not be advocat fra the inferiour court, except it be proven that wrang was done in it to the persewer. **1753** CHAMBERS *Cycl. Supp.* s.v. By these letters [of Advocation], the lords of session advocate, that is call that cause from the incompetent judge to themselves.

advocate ('ædvəkeɪt), *v.*² [f. ADVOCATE *sb.* on analogy of *minister,* cf. *pilot, carpenter, doctor,* etc.]

†**1.** *intr.* To act as advocate, to plead *for. arch.*

1641 MILTON *Animadv.* §1 (1847) 58/2 It had been advocated and moved for by some honourable and learned gentlemen of the house. **1659** FULLER *App. Inj. Innoc.* (1840) 339 I wonder that the Animadvertor will advocate for their actions, so detrimental to the church. **1661** HEYLIN *Ref.* I. ii. 37, I will not take upon me to Advocate for the present distempers and confusions of this wretched Church. **1872** F. HALL *False Philol.* 75, I am not going to advocate for this sense of actual [*i.e.* as = present].

†**2.** *trans.* To defend (by action). *Obs.*

1666 PEPYS *Diary* 1 Dec., Ready.. to part with all his estate in these difficult times to advocate the King's service.

3. *trans.* To plead or raise one's voice in favour of; to defend or recommend publicly.

? **1767** BURKE *Ref. Represent.* (T.) This is the only thing distinct and sensible that has been advocated. **1789** FRANKLIN *Lett. to N. Webster 26 Dec.* Wks. 1840 X. 414 During my late absence in France, I find that several new words have been introduced into our parliamentary language. For example I find a verb.. from the substantive advocate; the gentleman who advocates or has advocated that motion.. If you should happen to be of my opinion with respect to these innovations you will use your authority in reprobating them. **1821** W. TAYLOR in *Month. Rev.* XCVI. 450 The interests of justice, of liberty, and of independence are advocated. **1850** MERIVALE *Rom. Emp.* III. xxiii. 29 They advocated its publication for their own private interests. **1860** TYNDALL *Glac.* II. §28. 396 Dr. Whewell, who advocates this view, thus expounds it.

advocateship ('ædvəkət-ʃɪp). [f. ADVOCATE *sb.* + -SHIP.] The office of an advocate: i.e.

1. of an intercessor; intercession, pleading, advocacy.

a **1568** COVERDALE *Christ's Cross* ix. Wks. III. 260 Christ's mediation, intercession and advocateship. **1656** HARDY *Serm.* xx. (1865) 125/2 The advocateship of Christ consists in a four-fold presentation. *c* **1680** HALLYWELL *Sav. of Souls* 71 (T.) This redargution of the world was made a part of the advocateship of the Holy Spirit. **1748** RICHARDSON *Clarissa* (1811) I. 232 So expect not any advocateship from me.

2. of a legal pleader.

1611 COTGR., *Advocatie*, an Advocateship; the duty or place of an Advocate. **1618** tr. *Barneveld's Apol.* Gj, After the fifteenth yeare of my Aduocateships place. **1631** B. JONSON *New Inn* II. vi. (T.) Leave your advocateship Except that we shall call you Orator Fly. **1858** CARLYLE *Fredk. Gt.* II. x. ii. 580 François accordingly sat 'in chambers'.. even became an advocate; but did not in the least take to advocateship. **1867** —— *Remin.* (1881) II. 60 He was quitting his Lord Advocateship, and returning home.

†**3.** of the patron of a church; advocation, patronage. *Obs.*

1753 CHAMBERS *Cycl. Supp.*, Princes had also another title to advocate-ship, some of them pretending to be *advocati nati* of the churches within their dominions.

†**'advocatess.** *Obs. rare*⁻¹. [f. ADVOCATE *sb.* + -ESS. Cf. *poet-ess. Advocatissa* occurs in med.L. as patroness of a benefice.

Besides this the forms ADVOCATRIX, ADVOCATRICE, ADVOCATRESS, have all been used for the feminine.]

A female advocate.

1647 JER. TAYLOR *Diss. fr. Pop.* I. §8 Therefore God hath provided us of an advocatess [*some edd.* advocatress].

advocating ('ædvəkeɪtɪŋ), *vbl. sb.* [f. ADVOCATE *v.*² + -ING¹.] The action of publicly defending, maintaining, or standing up for.

1803 W. TAYLOR in *Ann. Rev.* I. 274 Some defence for the public advocating of opinions, even when obnoxious to the majority of the house.

advocation (ædvəʊ'keɪʃən). [a. Fr. *advocacion,* earlier *avocacion* (12th c. in Godef.), ad. L. *advocātiōn-em,* n. of action f. *advocā-re,* see ADVOKE. The senses are partly taken from this, partly from med.L. *advocātio,* the function of the *advocātus,* in the various mediæval senses of that word.]

I. n. of action from L. *advocāre.*

†**1.** A calling of people to council; a summoning or convocation. *Obs.*

1474 CAXTON *Chesse* IV. i. 8 Hit apperteyneth not to hem to be of counceyls ne at the aduocacions.

2. The calling of an action before itself by a superior court. Not used in Eng. law, but the technical term in Scotland, as also in the papal court. (See ADVOKE, and ADVOCATE *v.*¹)

Bill of Advocation (*Sc. Law*) The written application to the higher court asking for removal of the action. ***Letters*** or ***Note of Advocation***, the order issued by the higher court, equivalent to an Eng. writ of *certiorari* issued by a superior Court for the removal of an action to itself.

a **1528** SKELTON *Im. Hypocr.* II. 361 He robbeth all nations With his fulminations, Advocations. *c* **1555** HARPSFIELD *Divorce of Hen. VIII* (1878) 184 The Cardinall (Wolsey) most earnestly travelled to.. stay the advocation of the said cause.. to the court of Rome. **1609** SKENE *Reg. Maj.* 62 Advocation of causes, may be admitted be reason of the iniquitie of the Judge in the inferiour court: or of his doubting, or ignorance of the cause. **1753** CHAMBERS *Cycl. Supp.* s.v., If after letters of advocation are intimated to that judge, he yet proceeds, his decree will be null. **1808** BENTHAM *Scotch Ref.* 15 Instruments of usurpation, in English practice, *pone* and *certiorari*; in Scottish, bills of advocation. **1856** FROUDE *Hist. Eng.* I. 147 Wolsey, however, failed in his protest; the advocation was passed.

†**3.** The act of calling to one's aid; an appeal (for aid or defence). *Obs.*

1598 BARCKLEY *Felicit. Man* (1631) 685 True Religion doth direct us & our prayers and advocations to one God. **1753** CHAMBERS *Cycl. Supp., Advocation,* in the civil law, the act of calling another to our aid, relief, or defence.

II. n. of office from L. *advocatus.*

†**4.** The function of an ADVOCATE (1, 2) or pleader; pleading, advocacy, advocateship. *Obs.*

1604 SHAKS. *Oth.* III. iv. 123 Alas.. My Aduocation is not now in Tune. **1651** JER. TAYLOR *Serm.* I. xxvii. 349 [Christ] sits in heaven in a perpetual advocation for us. **1767** H. BROOKE *Fool of Qual.* (1859) I. 310 Rejecting your advocation in behalf of your friend.

†**5.** The function or office of a patron (see ADVOCATE 4); guardianship, protection, or patronage of a church, or benefice; right of presentation to a living; = ADVOWSON (another form of the same word). *Obs.*

1566 in Harrington *Nug. Antiq.* 151 [He] would bestowe the advocation therof uppon my son. **1621** SANDERSON

Serm. Ad. Pop. IV. 33 (1674) 205 Parents, that have the donations or Advocations of Church Livings in their hands, must needs have some of their Children..thrust into the Ministry. **1661** BRAMHALL *Just Vind.* iv. 66 To the Kings of England..the Advocation and protection of all the Churches of England.

†**advoca'tistical**, ? *a. Obs. rare*$^{-1}$.
c **1614** *England's Way to Wealth* in Arb. *Eng. Garn.* (1882) IV. 352 We do charge also the Chancellors and Provincial Council, and the Council of Admiralty, the Advocatistical, and the Procurer General, and all other officers.

advocator ('ædvəkeɪtə(r)). [As an early word, a. late L. *advocātōr*, n. of agent f. *advocāre* to call to, but used by eccl. writers as = cl. L. *advocātus*, from the active function of the *advocātus* or helper 'called in,' as a pleader or 'caller for' justice or mercy. In mod. use f. ADVOCATE *v.*]
†**1.** An intercessor, patron (saint); = ADVOCATE *sb.* 1, 2. *Obs.*
1482 *Revel. Monk of Evesham* (1869) 52 My moste meke and dere aduocatour seynt Nicholas to whome y called.
2. One who advocates, or publicly stands up for; = ADVOCATE *sb.* 3.
1845 BROWNING *Soul's Trag.* II. Wks. 1863 II. 458 The advocators of change in the present system of things.

advocatory ('ædvə,keɪtərɪ), *a.* [f. L. *advocāt-* ppl. stem of *advocā-re* + -ORY. Cf. med.L. *advocātōri-us*, f. *advocātor*; and Fr. *avocatoire.*] Of or pertaining to the advocate.
1864 *Daily Tel.* 16 Aug., Their author is by nature rather a critic than a partisan, more inclined to the judicial than the advocatory function.

†'**advocatress.** *Obs.* [f. *advocātōr* + -ESS; prob. refashioned from the earlier ADVOCATRICE.] A female advocate.
1641 WARMSTRY *Blind Guide* 47 The Scripture..speaketh nothing of..any Advocatresse or Mediatrix towards God. **1647** JER. TAYLOR *Diss. fr. Pop.* I. §8 God has provided us of an advocatress [*v.r.* advocatess], who is gentle and sweet.

†'**advocatrice.** *Obs.* [a. MFr. *advocatrice*, ad. L. *advocātrix*, *-īcem*: see next.] A female advocate.
1384 CHAUCER *M. of God* 40 Swich an advocatrice who can dyvyne..our greeves to redresse. **1485** CAXTON *St. Wenefr.* 13 Seynte Wenefryde To whome late us praye to be a specialle aduocatryce for us. **1531** ELYOT *Governour* II. vii. (R.) The emperour reioysed to him selfe that Cinna had founde such an aduocatrice.

†'**advocatrix.** *Obs. rare.* [a. L. *advocātrix*, fem. of *advocātōr.*] A female advocate. (See two prec.)
1631 *Celestina* I. 11 His successe in bringing me such an Advocatrix. **1749** WESLEY in *Wks.* 1872 X. 105 They fly unto her as the advocatrix of the faithful.

‖**advocatus diaboli** (ædvəʊ'keɪtəs daɪ'æbəlaɪ). [mod.L.; cf. ADVOCATE *sb.*] 'Devil's advocate' (DEVIL *sb.* 25 b).
1842 H. C. ROBINSON *Let.* 29 Dec. (1927) I. 473 You are aware that here I am considered as a sort of Advocatus Diaboli. **1883** *Guardian* 21 Mar. 412/1 The mere *advocatus diaboli* who is content to damage an opponent. **1929** *Music & Lett.* X. 194 It is a pleasant thing to play *advocatus diaboli* with the knowledge that one is going to allow oneself to cross over to the angels' bench later.

†**ad'vocitate**, *v. Obs.*$^{-0}$ [f. L. **advocitā-re*, frequent. of *advocāre* (of which simple *vocitāre* occurs).] 'To call often vpon.' Cockeram 1626.

advoid, -ance, obs. forms of AVOID, -ANCE.

†**ad'voke**, *v. Obs.* [a. MFr. *advoque-r*, earlier *avoque-r*, ad. L. *advocā-re* to call to, f. *ad* to + *vocāre* to call. Cf. *convoke*, *revoke*, *provoke*, etc.] To call to oneself, to summon. *esp.* To summon a cause to a higher from an inferior tribunal. The same as ADVOCATE *v.*^{1} in Sc. Law.
1533 BP. BONNER in Froude's *Hist. Eng.* II. 147 His Holiness..would not have advoked the matter at all, but been content that it should have been determined and ended in your realm. **1535** SHAXTON in Strype *Eccl. Mem.* (1832) I. II. lxi. 224 If yee advoking this matter into your hands, by that means bear the abbot in his evil dealing. **1655** FULLER *Ch. Hist.* v. 175 By this time Queen Katharine had privately prevailed with the Pope, to advoke the cause to Rome.

advoket, -ette, obs. form of ADVOCATE.

†**advo'lation.** *Obs.*$^{-0}$ [n. of action f. L. *advolā-re* to fly to.] 'A flying towards.' Bailey 1731.

†**advo'lution.** *Obs.*$^{-0}$ [n. of action f. L. *advolv-ĕre* to roll to.] 'A rolling towards.' Bailey 1731, whence in J.

†**ad'vort**, *v. Obs.* [erroneous refashioning of *avort*, a. Fr. *avorte-r*:—late L. *abortā-re*, as in ADVANCE; see AD- 2.] To miscarry.
1572 *Lament. Lady Scotland* in *Sc. P. of 16th c.* II. 242, I trauell ȝit as I had them aduortit; The malice greit that ilk to uther beires Doth ryfe my bowells with their ciuile weirs.

advoteresse, obs. form of ADULTERESS.

†**ad'votrix.** *Obs.* [L. fem. of **advōtōr*, n. of agent f. *advovē-re* to vow to; apparently here confounded with *advocātrix*; see AVOW.] A female advocate, or intercessor.
1611 CHESTER *Cantoes* L. 11 (1878) 145 Loue is my great Aduotrix, at thy shrine Loue pleads for me.

advouch, -er, obs. forms of AVOUCH *v.*, -ER *sb.*

advoulter, advouter, -er, -ess, -ous, -y, obs. early forms of ADULTER, -ER, -ESS, -OUS, -Y.

advoure, obs. form of ADVOWRY.

†**advourer.** *Obs. rare*$^{-1}$. [f. ADVOWRY + -ER^{1}.] An advocate or patron (saint).
a **1686** DUGDALE *Life of Geste* 125 That therin those sainctes bee oncalled as advourers and ayders who bi not here presently conversant emong us.

advow(e, obs. form of AVOW *sb.* and *v.*

advowee (æd,vaʊ'iː). Forms: 3–7 avowe, 6–7 avowee, 7–9 advowee. [a. OFr. *avoué*, earlier *avoé*, *avoet*:—L. *advocāt-us* in sense of *patron*; see ADVOCATE. *Avoet*, *avoué*, was the living descendant of *advocāt-us*, of which *avocat* was a later learned adaptation, as a title. In 15th c. the scribes sometimes Latinized *avoué* to *advoué*, whence the current Eng. form: cf. ADVOWSON. Though *avowè* and *advowee* are thus the same word, the former is associated with a sense which became obs. before the form *advowee* was established; and they are here treated separately: see AVOWE.]
1. An advocate, protector or patron: *esp.* a patron saint; see AVOWE, the older form used in this sense.
2. The advocate, protector, or patron of an ecclesiastical office or benefice. One who protected and defended its interests, and thus usually became privileged to nominate or present to it; the protection has long disappeared, but the right of presentation is retained as a marketable 'property.' One who holds the advowson.
1691 BLOUNT *Law Dict.* s.v., Advowee *alias* avowe (*advocatus*) is used for him that hath right to present to a Benefice. **1691** *Case of Exeter-Coll.* 44 The Custody of Voidances, Presentments, Collations, etc. as Lords and Advowees. **1744** J. LEWIS *Life of Pecock* 252 He gave & granted them as if he were the patron or advowee of them. **1751** CHAMBERS *Cycl.*, *Advowees* were the guardians, protectors, and, as it were, administrators of the temporal concerns of the churches..They are sometimes called by their primitive name *Advowee*, though more usually *patron.*

†**advower.** *Obs.* [A refashioning of *avower*, a. Fr. *avouer* inf. used subst.] A vowing, a vow.
1502 ARNOLD *Chron.* (1811) 146 The iii parte of alle his synnes releced, and all aduowers and promyse releced.

advowre, var. form of AVOWRE, patron.

†**ad'vowry.** *Obs.* Forms: 5 advourè, 6 -ie. A variant of the word more commonly spelt AVOWRY. The spelling with *ad-* was especially common in sense 3, 'The advowson or patronage of a benefice.'
1495 *Act 11 Hen. VII*, xxxiij, The Amobreshippe of the Countie of Meryonneth with the Reglorshippes and Raglorshippes of the Advoures of the same Countie. **1593** BILSON *Govt. Christ's Ch.* 363 The gift and collation of bishoprikes and other dignities of their advourie.

†**ad'vowsance, -ante**, †**ad'vowsement.** *Obs.* [corrupt formations on *advowson* or *advowsen* (probably taken as = *advows-ing*, from an imaginary verb *advowse*, whence *advows-ance*, *advowse-ment*, on analogy of such regular forms as *cognisance*, *cognisement*, etc.]
c **1536** WHITING in Ellis *Orig. Lett.* III. II. 380 Letters.. purportinge th' empetracion of th' advousante of Batcombe in Somersetshire, together with an advousante redie writen. **1590** SWINBURN *Testaments* 44 The Lord hath no title to.. the aduowsement of a church, belonging to the villeine. **1754** GARDNER *Hist. Dunwich* 135 He granted by Fine, to Richard Abbat of Sibeton, the Advowsance of the Church of Tunstall in Norfolk.

advowson (æd'vaʊzən, -z(ə)n), *sb.* Forms: 3–4 **avoweisoun, avoweson, voweson**; 6 **avoson**; 7 **aduouson, advouson, aduowsion, advousen, advowzen**; 6– **advowson.** [a. OFr. *avoëson* (in Anglo-Fr. *advoeson*, *advowëson*, *advowson*):—L. *advocātiōn-em*: see ADVOCATION (a doublet of *advowson*). *Avoweson*, beside being refashioned as *advowson* after L., was aphetized in 4 to *voweson.*] The 'patronage' of an ecclesiastical office or religious house; the right of presentation to a benefice or living. (*orig.* The obligation to defend its rights or be its '*advocate*'; see ADVOWEE.)
1297 R. GLOUC. 471 Eni striuing..betuene a lewede & a clerc, vor holi churche thing, As vor voweson of churche. *c* **1300** *Life of Beket* 575 As for an Avoweisoun of churche. **1502** ARNOLD *Chron.* (1811) 183 All such landis, tenementis, rentys, aduousons or other poscessions. *a* **1556** CRANMER *Wks.* II. 239 Mine old suit for the receipt of Mr. Benet's advowson of the Benefice of Barnabe. **1571** *Act 13 Eliz.* xxix. §3 in *Oxf. & Camb. Enactmts.* 30 Services, annuyties, advousons of Churches. **1574** tr. *Littleton's Tenures* 4/1 Such thinges that lye not in manuell occupacion as.. avowson of a churche. **1595** ERRINGTON in *Wills & Invent. N. Counties* (1860) 253 The avoson of the rectorie of Elton. **1602** FULBECKE *1st Pt. of Parallele* 10 It is *fructus aduocationis*, and not the aduouson it selfe. **1634** PEACHAM *Compl. Gent.* iv. 31 To be set off in hope of the next advouson (which perhaps was sold before the young man was borne). **1652** NEEDHAM tr. *Selden's Mare Cl.* 342 Our Lord the King was seised of the aforesaid Advousen in time of Peace. **1663** BUTLER *Hudibras* I. i. 236 As if Hypocrisie and Non-sence Had got th' Advowson of his Conscience. **1691** BLOUNT *Law Dict.* s.v., Advowzen (*advocatio*), a right to present to a Benefice; as much as *Jus Patronatus* in the Canon Law. **1713** STEELE *Englishm.* No. 6. 37 He has lately named me for a Living, of which he had the Advowson. **1836** HOR. SMITH *Tin Trum.* I. 18 Advowson, the purchaseable right (purchaseable even by a Jew, Pagan or Mahometan) of controlling the souls of a whole parish. **1865** *Reader* 9 Sept. 279/2 The traffic in advowsons has never been actually prevented in any country.
Comb. **advowson-monger.**
1660 QUARLES *Div. Fanc.* III. lxxxii. 134 [The church] sustains th' extremes of cold and hunger, To pamper up the fat Advouson-monger.

†**ad'vowson**, *v. Obs. rare*$^{-1}$. [f. the sb. Cf. to *provision.*] To invest with the advowson.
1597 BP. HALL *Sat.* II. v, Thou servile fool, why couldst thou not repair To buy a benefice at steeple fair? There moughtest thou, for but a slender price, Advowson thee with some fat benefice.

†**ad'vowsonage.** *Obs. rare.* [f. ADVOWSON + -AGE (the suffix superfluous).] Advowson.
1528 LD. CROMWELL in Ellis *Orig. Lett.* III. 160 II. 110 Advowson in grosse, that is to saye, advowsonage onely appending to no Manor, ne yet to none acre of londe. *a* **1556** CRANMER *Wks.* II. 262 Have my friend Mr. Newman in your good remembrance for Mr. Benett's advowsonage.

advowter, -er, -ess, -ous, -y, obs. 15–17th c. forms of ADULTER, -ER, -ESS, -OUS, -Y.

advoyde, obs. form of AVOID *v.*

advoyer, obs. form of AVOYER.

advt., abbrev. of ADVERTISEMENT.
1835 *Cheltenham Chron.* 16 Apr. 2/5 We refer our readers to an advt. in an adjoining column announcing a lecture. **1890** HARDY *Let.* 5 Oct. (1978) I. 218, I shall pester you with advts. **1963** J. B. MORTON *Best of Beachcomber* 23 The leopard leads a healthy life, But cannot lose his spots. He has not tried those magic pills They sell in little pots. (Advt.). **1981** *Oxf. Dict. for Writers & Editors* 7/1 *Advt*/., *-s.*, advertisement, -s.

advys, -vyse, -vysee: see ADVICE, -VISE, -VISEE.

adwait, -wate, obs. refash. of AWAIT.

adward, obs. variant of AWARD *sb.* (Spenser).

†**ad'wesch**, *v. Obs.* Forms: 1 **adwæsc-an**, 2 **adwesc-en**, 3 **adwesch-en.** [f. A- *pref.* 1 intens. + OE. *dwæsc-an* to extinguish. Cf. ADUSH.] To quench, extinguish (fire, pain, malice, enemies).
a **1000** *Ags. Gosp.* Mark ix. 46 þar hyra wyrm ne swylt ne fyr ne bið adwæsced. *c* **1160** *Hatton Gosp.* ibid., þær heora wyrm ne swelt ne fyr ne beoð adwesced. *c* **1220** *Leg. St. Kath.* 1196 Adweschde & a dun weorp þe wiðerwine of helle.

†**ad'wite**, *v. Obs.* [var. of EDWITE or ATWITE.] To reproach, accuse, twit.
c **1430** *Hymns to Virg. & Christ* 396 (1867) 70 þe synnes þat y loued, now haten me, To conscience þei adwiten me.

†**ad'wole**, *adv. Obs.* prop. *phr.*, **a dwole.** [See DWOLE, DWALE.] In error, erroneously, mistakenly.
a **1250** *Owl & Night.* 1775 Swo heore wit hi demth adwole, That ever abid maister Nichole.

adylle, obs. form of ADDLE *v.*^{2} to earn.

‖**adynamia** (ædɪ'neɪmɪə). *Med.* [mod.L. a. Gr. ἀδυναμία, f. ἀ priv. + δύναμις power.] The want of vital power, which accompanies some fevers; physical prostration.
1830 *Westm. Rev.*, *On Fever* XII. 204 The Adynamia of the Borough has not only crept over London, but is groping its way into the outskirts of the British empire. **1875** WOOD *Therap.* (1879) 659 The serious lung-affections of low fevers are, however, largely dependent upon the general adynamia, and this adynamia is, in turn, largely the result of the excessive temperature.

adynamic (ædɪ'næmɪk), *a.* [f. prec. + -IC. Cf. mod.Fr. *adynamique.*]
1. *Med.* Of or pertaining to adynamia; characterized by, or attended with, weakness or physical prostration; asthenic.
1829 W. STOKES *Path. Observ.* (quoted in *Westm. Rev.* Jan. 1830, 308) On account of this debility being an essential character of typhoid fevers, I denominated them *adynamic.* **1859** R. F. BURTON in *Jrnl. R.G.S.* XXIX. 39 Action of a poisonous miasma upon an adynamic condition of the system.
2. *Nat. Phil.* Characterized by the absence of force.
1879 THOMSON & TAIT *Nat. Phil.* I. I. §345 The first class of fundamental modes may be called adynamic because they are the same as if no forces were applied to the system, or

acted between its moving parts, except actions and reactions in the normals between mutually pressing parts (depending on the inertias of the moving parts).

adynamical (ædɪ'næmɪkəl), *a.* [f. as ADYNAMIC *a.* + -AL.] Not dynamical.
1900 *Jrnl. Inst. Electr. Engineers* Apr. 396 The properties of electric and magnetic force are explicable upon dynamical principles; so far there is no known necessity for seeking for adynamical properties in the ether.

† **a'dynamous**, *a. Obs.*—⁰ [f. as ADYNAMIC *a.* + -OUS.] 'Weak, impowerful.' Blount *Glossogr.* 1656.

adynamy (ə'dɪnəmɪ). *Med. rare.* [Eng. adaptation of ADYNAMIA.] = ADYNAMIA.
1847 in CRAIG. **1852** WEBSTER cites *Amer. Jrnl. Science.*

† **'adyt.** *Obs. rare*⁻¹. [ad. L. *adyt-um*, now commonly used in its L. form, q.v.] An adytum, a shrine or sanctuary.
1594 GREENE *Looking Gl.* (1861) 137 Amidst the adyts of our gods..The ghosts of dead men howling walk about.

† **adyte**, *v.*[1] *Obs.* [for ENDITE; see A- *pref.* 10.] To indite.
c **1420** *R. Cœur de Lion* 1174 Kyng Richard dede a lettre wryte, (A noble clerk it gan adyte).

adyte, variant of ADIGHT *v. Obs.*, to prepare.

‖ **adytum** ('ædɪtəm). Pl. **adyta**. [L. *adyt-um* a. Gr. ἄδυτον prop. adj. = not to be entered; f. ἀ not + -δυτ-ος vbl. adj. of δύ-ειν to enter. Commonly used in the L. form sing. and pl.; at first also in the Gr., though it had already been anglicised by Greene as ADYT.] The innermost part of a temple; the secret shrine whence oracles were delivered; hence *fig.* A private or inner chamber, a sanctum.
1673 HOLYDAY *Juv.* 235 The *adyta*, whence the oracles were delivered..The Romane temples..having the ἄδυτον, answerable to the quire, unto which only priests might come. **1778** BP. LOWTH *On Isaiah* (ed. 12) 339 *Adytum* means a cavern, or the hidden part of the temple. **1800** COLERIDGE *Ess. on Own Times* I. 247 [He] carries with him the habits of a disputing club into the *adyta* of the Cabinet. **1859** IS. TAYLOR *Logic in Theol.* 46 To give the foot a place in the adytum of intellectual & moral life. **1863** W. THORNBURY *True as Steel* II. 158 But the prettiest sight of all was in the adytum—the inner room of all—where the Duchess herself sat.

adz, adze (ædz). Forms: 1 **adesa (eadesa)**, 2–4 **adese**, 5 **adse**, 6 **adys**, 6–7 **addis, addice, addes, adds, ads**, (7 **atch**), 8– **adz, adze**. [Origin of OE. *adesa* unknown.] A carpenter's or cooper's tool, like an ax with the blade set at right angles to the handle and curving inwards towards it; used for cutting or slicing away the surface of wood.
c **880** K. ÆLFRED *Bæda* iv. 3 He..bær r him æcse and adesan on handa. 11th c. *Vocab.* (in Wright 84) *Ascia*, Adesa. **1388** WYCLIF *Is.* xliv. 13 A carpenter stretchide forth a reule, he fourmyde it with an adese. *c* **1420** *Pallad. on Husb.* I. 1161 Set rakes, crookes, adses, and bycornes. *a* **1500** *Debate of Carp. Tools* 53 in Hazl. *E.P.P.* I. 81 To hym then seyd the adys, And seyd; ȝe, sir, god glades. **1530** PALSGR. 193/1 Addis a coupers instrument. *Dolovere.* **1552** HULOET, *Addice*, cowpers instrumente. *Harpago.* **1578** R. SCOT *Perfite Platf. of Hoppe Gard.* 27 Prepare a toole af yron fashioned somewhat lyke to a Coopers Addes. **1580** TUSSER *Husb.* xvii. 9 An ax and a nads, to make troffe for thy hogs. [Cf. *a nother.*] **1594** NASHE *Vnfort. Trav.* 20 Some had barres of yron..some wood-kniues, some addises for their weapons. **1598** LYLY *Mother Bombie* IV. ii. 128, I had thought I had rode upon addices between this & Canterbury. **1611** COTGR., *Doloire*, a (Coopers) ax, or addis. **1665** PEPYS *Diary* (1879) III. 254 A yew tree..which upon cutting with an addes, we found to be rather harder than the living tree is. **1681** R. KNOX *Hist. Rel. Ceylon* (1817) 174 They have also..axes, bills, houghs, atches, chissels, and other tools. **1697** DAMPIER *Voy.* (1729) I. 332 They can take it out of the Helve, and by turning it make an Adds of it. **1703** MOXON *Mech. Exerc.* 119 The Adz..hath its Blade made thin, and somewhat arching. **1772–84** COOK *Voy.* (1790) I. 60 Captain Cook having produced an iron adze. **1869** LUBBOCK *Prehist. Times* xiii. 459 The stone axes, or rather adzes, were of various sizes. **1877** BRYANT *Odyss.* v. 287 A polished adze she gave him next.
Comb. **adze-like** *a.*
1859 R. F. BURTON *Centr. Afr.* in *Jrnl. R.G.S.* XXIX. 396 It is like a child's plaything, with an adze-like iron. **1865** LUBBOCK *Prehist. Times* 452 The adze-like hatchets of the South Sea Islanders.

adze (ædz), *v.* [f. the sb.] To cut, or dress with an adze.
1845 CARLYLE *Cromwell's Lett. & Sp.* (1871) IV. 79 Hammering, adzing, sawing. **1861** *Lloyd's Weekly* 26 Oct., A shipwright..adzing a piece of timber, accidentally sliced one of his heels completely off.

† **ad'zooks**, *int. Obs.* ? or *arch.* [See ADS-.]
1761 SMOLLETT *Gil Blas* III. v. (1802) I. 264 'Adzooks! my dear,' cried I, with an air of assurance. **1841** HOR. SMITH *Moneyed Man* I. iv. 115 Adzooks! one would think I was a gambler.

adzuki (əd'zu:kɪ). Also 8 **atsuki**, 8– **adsuki**; **azuki**. [Jap.] **a.** The dark red edible beans of the annual leguminous plant *Vigna angularis*, cultivated in China and Japan; the plant itself. **b.** *attrib.* in **adzuki bean**.
1727 J. G. SCHEUCHZER tr. *Kæmpfer's Hist. Japan* I. I. ix. 121 *Adsuki*, or *Sodsu*, that is Sobeans. **1795** tr. *C. P. Thunberg's Trav. Europe, Afr., & Asia* (ed. 2) IV. 88 *Atsuki* Beans likewise (*Phaseolus radiatus*) are ground to meal. **1859** A. STEINMETZ *Japan & her People* I. vi. 273 Mixed with boiled rice and *adsuki*, or red beans, coarsely powdered. **1889** J. J. REIN *Industries of Japan* I. ii. 108 A mixture of bean-meal (Adzuki) and sugar. **1914** *Bull. U.S. Dept. Agric.* No. 119. 4 The adsuki is probably native either in Japan or in Chosen [= Korea], but the plant is not definitely known in a wild state. *Ibid.*, The adsuki bean is a summer annual. **1960** B. LEACH *Potter in Japan* vi. 132 We ate it first with shoyu sauce and then with sweet adzuki beans. **1968** J. W. PURSEGLOVE *Tropical Crops: Dicotyledons* I. 290 Adzuki bean is grown mainly in Japan and China. **1976** *Hortus Third* (L. H. Bailey Hortorium) 1156/1 Azuki bean. Erect or twining ann., to 2½ ft.

æ (usually written as a digraph or ligature, but also, and in the earliest times, separately ae) was in OE. the symbol of a simple vowel, intermediate between *a* and *e*. When short, as in *glæd, fæder*, it represented orig. Teut. short *a*, and had the power of modern Eng. *a*. in *man, glad*; when long, as in *sǽ, flǽsc*, the same sound prolonged, as in a common American pronunciation of *bear, hair, there*. After 1100 the short *æ* was generally replaced by *a* (though sometimes by *e*); the long *ǽ* continued to be written *æ* in the 12th and early 13th c., the OE. *eá* passing into the same sound and symbol, but in the development of ME. this symbol died out, and was replaced by simple *e* or *ee*. Thus OE. *sǽ, flǽsc, eár, eást* are in Ormin and Layamon *sæ, flæssh, ær, æst*, but afterwards *se(e, flesh, ere, eest*. The symbol *æ*, which thus disappeared from the language in 13th c., was re-introduced in 16th c. in forms derived from Latin words with *æ*, and (this being the Latin symbolization of Greek αι) Greek words in αι; as *ædify, æther*. But this *æ* had only an etymological value, and whenever a word became thoroughly English, the *æ* or *ae* was changed into simple *e* as *edify, ether*. The *æ* or *ae* now remains, only (1) in Greek and Lat. proper names as in *Æneas, Cæsar*; even these, when familiar, often take *e* as *Judea, Etna*. (2) in words belonging to Roman or Gr. Antiquities as *ædile, ægis*. (3) in scientific or technical terms as *ætiology, æstivation, phænogamous, Athenæum*; these also when they become popularized take *e*, as *phenomenon, Lyceum, museum, era*.

Æ initial is thus to be looked upon as an earlier spelling of *E*, and will here occur only (1) in EE. words that became obsolete, before changing to *e*, as *æ* law (OE. *ǽ*), *æ* river (OE. *eá*); (2) in words directly adopted or formed from Latin and Greek which became obsolete before changing to *e* as *ædituate*; or have not changed to *e* because they indicate ancient things as *ædile, ægis*, or are technical as *ægilops, ægrotant, ætiology*. All other words will be found under their later form in E.

In many modern books the digraph *æ* is regularly resolved as *ae*; when this is done, dissyllabic *ae* ought to be printed *aë*: thus either *ægis, aereal*, or *aegis, aëreal*; but simple *ae* is often used in both.

As to pronunciation usage differs. The analogy of the language, the practice of orthoepists, and the alternate spelling with *e*, are in favour of *æ* being treated precisely like *e* in the same position. But there is a strong tendency with classical scholars (at variance with their practice as to other long L. and Gr. vowels) to make it long (i:) in all positions. This influences popular usage to some extent, so long as *æ* is written; as soon as *e* takes its place, natural English habits prevail: cf. *æstivate, æstuary, estuary*.

† **æ**, *sb.*[1] *Obs.* Forms: 1 **eá, é**; 1–3 **æ**. [OE. *eá, é, ǽ*, cogn. w. OFris. *â, ê*, ON. *â*, OS. and OHG. *aha*, Goth. *ahwa*, L. *aqua*.] A river, a running water. See also AA[1] and EA.
896 *O.E. Chron.* 92 On twa healfe þaer é. *Ibid.* 94 Up be þære eæ..On twa healfe ðære eás. *c* **1000** *Ags. Psalms* xxxv. 8 On ðære ǽ..þú hý drencst. *c* **1200** *Ormul.* 7091 Tær iss i þatt illke land An æ Sabá ȝehatenn. **1205** LAYAMON 1400 In are swiðe feire æ þer Læire falleð i þa sæ.

† **æ**, *sb.*[2] *Obs.* Forms: 1 **æw**, 1–3 **æ**, 2–3 **e**. [OE. *æ, æw*, cogn. w. OS. *êo*, OFris. *ewa, êwe, ê, â*, OHG. *êwa, êha, êa, ê*; Skr. *ewa* course.] Law, especially the law of nature, or of God; hence, legal custom, rite, marriage.
c **975** *Rushw. Gosp.* John xv. 25 In æ hiora awriten is. *c* **1000** *Ags. Gosp.* ibid., On hyra æ awriten ys. [*c* **1160** *Hatton Gosp.* ibid., On heora laga ys awritan.] *c* **1175** *Cott. Hom.* 227 þes cenne god sælde and ȝesette æ [*vel* laga]. *c* **1175** *Lamb. Hom.* 89 Ðreo tiden beoð on þissere worlde. An is þet wes buten e, and oðer is þe þet wes under þere e, þe þridde is nu ..we ne beoð na buten e, ne we ne moten holden moyses e licamliche. *c* **1200** *Ormul.* 145 þatt hemm wass sett þurrh Godess æ.
Comb. **æu-breche**, EAU-BRUCHE, adultery.

ae (e:), mod.Sc. form of northern ME. *a*, OE. *án*, one, used adjectively. See A *adj.*[1]
In ME. and early Sc., *a* was used bef. a cons., *an, ane*, bef. a vowel, and absolutely; in mid.Sc. *ane* was used in all positions and constructions; in mod.Sc. *ae* (the Sc. spelling of final *a* long) is used bef. a sb. however beginning, *ane* only absolutely: 'he has *ae* hand, only *ane*.'

æ-, *pref.* The stress form of OE. *a-* (see A- *pref.* 1) used with sbs. and adjs., the unaccented *a-* being used with verbs. Meaning: out, off, onward, away; hence, from idea of doing away, a privative = *un-, -less*. Thus *ǽ-fyrmða* washings off, ablutions, *ǽ-gilde* without payment, *ǽ-mód* out of his mind, *ǽ-scære* unshorn, without tonsure, *ǽ-rist* arising, *ǽ-cumba* what is combed off, oakum. Only a few examples survived in ME. as *e-rede* unadvised, *æ-rist, a-rist* rise. The West Germ. dialects had two forms answering to Goth. *us-* (*ur-*): viz. OHG. *ur-*, OE. *or-* with sbs. and adjs.; OHG. *ar-, er-, ir-*, mod.G. *er-*, OE. *ar-* (rarely preserved), *a-* with vbs., *ǽ-* with sbs. and adjs. This *ǽ-* represented an earlier *ā-* for *ar-* ('*ǽmód* = '*âmód* = '*armód*, like *strǽte* = WGer. *strâte*). *Ær-* reappears in Layamon in *ær-wene, ær-witte* (where it may be due to a mixture of OE. *ǽ-* and *or-*).

-æ (-i:) *pl. suffix* of L. nouns of 1st decl. in *-a*, and romanized form of Gr. *-αι* pl. of nouns in *-ē, -a, -ēs, -as*. Retained in Eng. in words not naturalized or merely in technical use, as *alæ, laminæ, larvæ, nebulæ, striæ*. Esp. in proper names of cl. antiquity, as *Heraclidæ*, and modern names of orders and families of animals and plants as *Felidæ, Falconidæ, Geometridæ, Leguminosæ, Rosaceæ, Rosidæ, Roseæ*. In other words it varies with the Eng. form in *-as*, as *actiniæ* or *actinias*; or is retained only in technical senses as mathematical *formulæ*, theological *formulas*. In all words thoroughly popularized it yields to -s, as in *arenas, areas, auroras, hyænas, fuchsias, calceolarias, Floras, Faunas, Julias, Marias, Cleopatras*, the two *Americas*.

æac, æc, obs. forms of EKE *adv.*

æcern, æcirn, obs. forms of ACORN.

æch, obs. form of EACH.

æcial, *a.*: see ÆCIUM.

æcidial (i:'sɪdɪəl), *a. Bot.* [f. ÆCIDI(UM + -AL.] Of, pertaining to, or resembling an æcidium.
1880 *Smithsonian Rep.* 324 A monograph..by Von Thümen contains an account of the aecidial forms attacking *Coniferæ*. **1891** *Athenæum* 23 May 671/1 The extraordinary abundance and wide distribution of the teleutosporic stage as compared with the comparative scarcity of the æcidial stage. **1927** GWYNNE-VAUGHAN & BARNES *Struct. & Dev. Fungi* 268 Centrally, where the pseudoperidium arches over the aecidial contents, it is derived from the cells first cut off in each row.

æcidiospore (i:'sɪdɪəʊspɔə(r)). *Bot.* [f. ÆCIDI(UM + -O + SPORE.] A spore formed in anæcidium.
1880 S. H. VINES tr. *Prantl's Elem. Textbk. Bot.* IV. 131 Some Uredineæ are known in which æcidiospores produce æcidia. **1922** *Nature* 8 Apr. 462/2 Its recurrence is explained only through fresh infection by æcidiospores produced on Barberry.

‖ **æcidium** (i:'sɪdɪəm). *Bot.* Pl. **-a**. [mod.L., dim. of Gr. αἰκία injury.] The cup-shaped fruit borne on the mycelium of certain parasitic fungi which especially attack the orders *Compositæ, Ranunculaceæ, Leguminosæ*, and *Labiatæ*.
1867 J. HOGG *Microsc.* II. i. 291 Producing chains of orange coloured fruit or in other words an *Æcidium*. **1878** M'NAB *Bot.* 56 The mycelium gives rise to small fruit-like bodies, the *Æcidia*.

æcium ('i:sɪəm). *Bot.* [mod.L., f. Gr. αἰκία injury.] U.S. term for ÆCIDIUM. Hence **'æcial** *a.* = ÆCIDIAL *a.*; **'æciospore** = ÆCIDIOSPORE.
1905 J. C. ARTHUR in *Bot. Gaz.* XXXIX. 221 For the sorus of the first spore-stage, usually..called aecidium, [etc.]..I propose *aecium*..derivatives *aecial, aeciospore*, etc. **1907** —— in *Jrnl. Mycology* XIII. 203 Cultures of Uredineae..aecial stage. **1929** —— et al. *Plant Rusts* i. 6 Aeciospores are binucleate and germinate..by producing a hypha. *Ibid.* 11 The aecia are the essential sori produced by the gametophytic mycelium in macrocyclic rusts... The cupulate form of aecium, generally known as the cluster-cup or aecidium. **1937** *Nature* 8 May 800/2 The uredial and telial stages have regularly occurred on the gramineous hosts, and the pycnial..and æcial stages on the common barberry. **1957** *Encycl. Brit.* IX. 934/1 The aeciospores are borne in fructifications (sori) known as aecia, which are frequently cup-shaped receptacles..containing chains of spores, which arise from a primordial layer of cells at the base of the aecidium.

ædi, variant of EADI *a. Obs.* blessed.

ædicula (ɪ'dɪkjʊlə). Chiefly Roman *Archit.* [L.: see ÆDICULE.] A niche (for a statue), esp. one framed by two columns supporting a pediment or an entablature; this structure forming a shrine.

[**1819** P. NICHOLSON *Archit. Dict.* I. 4/1 *Ædicula*, otherwise called *sacellum*, generally signified a small temple; but had various significations; sometimes denoting the inner part of the temple, in which the altar and statue of the deity were placed; at other times a niche in the wall, for receiving a statue.] **1901** R. STURGIS et al. *Dict. Archit.* I. 29 *Ædicula*, in Roman architecture, a small building; by extension, a shrine set up within a large edifice. Such a shrine may be a mere box or enclosure of wood, or, perhaps, only a screen with a pedestal and statue in front of it. **1968** *Medium Ævum* XXXVII. 48 Behind the wall of the city, right, a head is to be seen in a small aedicula. **1976** *Southern Even. Echo* (Southampton) 13 Nov. 2/7 The stage is composed of a low stage where the actors recited and stately background with nooks, aediculas, and three doors opening like the front of a palace, columns, tympanum and statues all helped to make the scene more attractive.

ædicular (ɪˈdɪkjʊlə(r)), *a.* [f. ÆDICULE + -AR¹.] Of, possessing, or characterized by the presence of an ædicule or ædicules; that forms or resembles an ædicule.

1953 H. BRAUN *Hist. Architecture* v. 84 It is possibly to the development of the aedicular architecture that the ultimate decadence of the Hellenistic style can be ascribed. **1970** H. BRAUN *Parish Churches* xiii. 168 The spire and the pinnacle—the latter being the aedicular offspring of the former—are both peculiar to the Gothic style. **1979** *Jrnl. R. Soc. Arts* Nov. 777/1 The aedicular entrance gates..hide garbage cans.

ædicule (ˈɛdɪkjuːl). [ad. L. *ædicula*, dim. of *ædēs* a dwelling.] A small house or room; = ÆDICULA. Also in *Archit.*, a doorway or other opening framed to resemble an ædicula; a representation of a structural feature in miniature for ornamental purposes.

1832 W. GELL *Pompeiana* I. viii. 159 In the ædicule on the left, was probably placed the statue. **1953** H. BRAUN *Hist. Architecture* v. 84 The final development was in the form of an 'ædicule', that is to say an elevational treatment in miniature. **1959** *Everyman's Conc. Encycl. Archit.* 4 *Aedicule* (Lat. *aedicula*, dim. of *aedes*, a house), originally a small structure sheltering an altar or an image of a household god: hence, a small pedimented structure over a niche. **1970** H. BRAUN *Parish Churches* xiii. 173 The niche is a Gothic example of that favourite architectural device, the aedicule, which is a miniature reproduction, for the purposes of ornament, of some larger feature actually forming part of the structure. **1971** *Country Life* 6 May 1088/1 As a stylistic exercise its [*sc.* Skerton Bridge's] combination of five elliptical arches, bold balustrade and dividing aedicules anticipates..three more famous bridges. **1981** *Times Lit. Suppl.* 27 Nov. 1380/5 The vast cliff-like façades,..and the lonely aedicules and silhouetted columns that articulate its upper peaks, are intensely moving.

ædile (ˈiːdaɪl), *sb.* and *a.* *Rom. Antiq.* [ad. L. *ædīl-is*, prop. adj. 'having to do with buildings,' f. *ædēs*, *ædis*, a building, a house. (Used at first in the full L. form.)]

A. *sb.* A magistrate in Rome, who had the superintendence of public buildings, shows, police, and other municipal functions; hence, by extension, a municipal officer.

1580 NORTH *Plutarch* (1676) 822 How cometh it to pass thou art thus rich, that thou doest sue to be Ædilis? **1607** SHAKS. *Coriol.* III. i. 214 Ædiles seize him. **1741** MIDDLETON *Cicero* I. vi. 433 The election of Ædiles..could not easily be kept off any longer. **1879** FROUDE *Cæsar* xi. 123 The ædiles had charge of the public buildings and the games and exhibitions in the capital.

B. *adj.* [Cf. *ædīles ludi* in Plautus.]

1880 BURTON *Q. Anne* III. xviii. 194 An aedile police prohibited the erection of houses.

ædileship (ˈiːdaɪlʃɪp). Also 6 edileshippe, -shyp. [f. ÆDILE + -SHIP.] The office of an ædile; also, the duration of his term of office.

1541 PAYNELL *Catiline* vii. 12 Cicero..also made thre playes in the tyme of his edileshyp. **1601** HOLLAND *Pliny* (1634) II. 563 The plaies exhibited by him in his Ædileship. **1840** ARNOLD *Rome* II. 60 The two Scipios..have their ædileships as well as their censorships and consulships recorded.

ædilitian (ˌiːdɪˈlɪʃən), *a.* [f. L. *ædīlici-us* + -AN.] Pertaining to an ædile.

1880 MUIRHEAD *Gaius* I. §6 There are no quaestors sent to the imperial provinces, where, consequently, the aedilitian edict is not propounded.

ædility (iːˈdɪlɪtɪ). Also 6 edylite. [ad. L. *ædīlitātem* the office of ædile: see ÆDILE and -TY.] The office, or term of office, of an ædile; ædileship; superintendence of public works.

1540 WHITTINTON *Tullyes Offices* II. 98 A lytle after Lucius Crassus occupyed the roume of the edylite. **1607** TOPSELL *Four-footed Beasts* (1673) 374 Lucius Sylla, in the office of his ædility, or oversight of the Temple. **1881** *Daily Tel.* 28 Jan., The singularly energetic action of the Metropolitan Board proves in one respect how miserably weak is our general system of 'ædility.'

†**æˈdituate**, *v.* *Obs. rare*⁻¹. [f. L. *ædituāt-* ppl. stem of *æditu-āre* to act as an *æditus* or sacristan, f. *ædes* a temple.] To take charge of, as a temple-keeper.

1646 J. G[REGORY] *Notes & Observ.* (1650) 49 To affect the Dignity and Title of the Νεωκόρος, to ædituate such a piece of Divine office.

aefald, -fauld, Sc. form of AFALD *a.*, simple.

æfen, obs. form of EVEN.

æfre, æferælc, æfrich, obs. ff. EVER, EVERY.

æfter, obs. form of AFTER.

æg, obs. form of EGG.

†**ˈægæde, ˈægede.** *Obs.* [ad. ON. *á-gæti* excellence, glory, f. *á* intensive + *geta* to get.] Luxury.

c **1200** *Ormul.* 2165, I skemmtinng & inn idelleȝȝc, Inn ægæde & i leȝȝkess. *Ibid.* 8060, & all forrwerrpenn illc unnitt Off ægede & off leȝȝkess.

Aegean (iːˈdʒiːən), *a.* Also **Aegaean.** [f. L. *Aegaeus*, ad. Gr. Αἰγαῖος Aegean, + -AN.] **a.** Of, pertaining to, or situated in the area between the Greek mainland and Asia Minor, esp. ***Aegean Sea***, the name of the sea that lies between Greece and Turkey.

[**1573** T. TWYNE tr. *Virgil's Æneid* xii. sig. Mm 1, When forth it bloustringe blowes, and deape *Ægæum* sea doth raise.] **1614** W. LITHGOW *Peregrinations from Scotl.* sig. G 2 These Iles *Sporades*, are scattered in the *Ægean* sea. **1667** MILTON *P.L.* I. 746 And with the setting Sun Dropt from the Zenith like a falling Star, on Lemnos, th' Ægæan isle. **1718** H. COXWELL tr. *Odes of Horace* II. xvi. 51 In the Ægean Ocean, struck with Fear. **1820** SHELLEY *Ode to Liberty* iv, in *Prometh. Unb.* 210 Yet a speechless child, Verse murmured, and Philosophy did strain Her lidless eyes for thee; when o'er the Ægean main Athens arose. **1886** J. H. WRIGHT tr. *M. Collignon's Man. Gr. Archæol.* 373/1 (Index), Aegean Islands. **1935** HUXLEY & HADDON *We Europeans* vii. 193 Further east, near Vinca, the [Danubian] culture was modified by influences from the Aegean area. **1974** *Encycl. Brit. Macropædia* I. 117/1 Vases everywhere in the Aegean area had been decorated with designs in dark rather shiny paint.

b. Of, or associated with Bronze Age Greek civilization in the Aegean area.

1890 W. M. F. PETRIE *Kahun, Gurob & Hawara* v. 44/1 The Ha-nebu, or 'lords of the north'—a name which always means the Aegean peoples, at least in later times. **1902** *Encycl. Brit.* XXXI. 55/2 In certain localities, for instance, Cyprus, Crete, and most of the Aegean islands,.. Mycenaean remains..form in fact a stratum to be expected on the site of almost every ancient Aegean settlement. **1915** H. R. HALL (*title*) Aegean archaeology. **1933** J. L. MYRES in *Jrnl. R. Anthropol. Inst.* LXIII. 279 Even earlier Aegean periods. **1941** J. S. HUXLEY *Uniqueness of Man* iii. 92 The Aegean sailors had reached the Atlantic at latest by 2200 B.C. **1952** T. K. PENNIMAN *100 Years Anthropol.* iv. 218 Flinders Petrie..had the good fortune to find Aegean pottery in a XIIth Dynasty building at Kahun. **1974** *Encycl. Brit. Macropædia* I. 119/1 Most of what has survived of Aegean Bronze Age writing is on clay tablets.

c. ***the Aegean***, the Aegean Sea.

1814 BYRON *Corsair* (1981) III. III. i. 191 Again the Ægean, heard no more afar, Lulls his chafed breast from elemental war. **1828** J. A. CRAMER *Geogr. & Hist. Descr. Anc. Greece* I. i. 7 The Mare Myrtoum was that part of the Ægean which lay between the coast of Argolis and Attica. **1846** G. GROTE *Hist. Greece* II. II. i. 287 The Peneius, which carries off all the waters of Thessaly, finding an exit into the Ægean through the narrow defile which parts Ossa from Olympus. **1888** A. H. SAYCE *Hittites* iv. 76 From Carchemish to the Ægean. **1928** C. DAWSON *Age of Gods* viii. 184 The sea route from the Ægean to the Black Sea. **1987** *Guardian* 13 Mar. 12/3 I will state bluntly that there is not a single site in the Aegean whose material would lead a modern specialist to suppose that it was occupied by Egyptians or Levantines.

ægemony, obsolete variant of HEGEMONY.

‖**æger** (ˈiːdʒə(r)), *a.* [L., = sick.] The L. word for 'sick,' used at the Eng. universities in excusing absence on account of illness; hence, a note certifying that a student is '*æger*' or sick.

1865 *Cornh. Mag.* Feb. 227 A very common method of escaping the tedium of this duty..is 'to send in an æger;' in other words, to improvise an attack of illness.

‖**ægilops** (ˈɛdʒɪlɒps). [L. *ægilops*, a. Gr. αἰγίλωψ, f. αἴξ, αἰγός, a goat, αἴγιλ-ος, a herb eaten by goats + ὤψ eye, face.]

1. *Med.* An ulcer or fistula in the inner angle of the eye.

1601 HOLLAND *Pliny* (1634) II. 234 There is a running betweene the corner of the eie and the nose, called Ægilops; for to heale which sore, there is a soueraigne herbe of that name growing among Barly. **1751** CHAMBERS *Cycl.* s.v., If the *Ægilops* be neglected, it bursts, and degenerates into a fistula which eats into the bone.

†**2.** *Herb.* The wild-oat or other grass found as a corn-weed. *Obs.*

1601 [See under 1.] **1706** PHILLIPS, *Ægilops*: a Weed that grows amidst Corn, Darnel, Wild Oats. **1753** CHAMBERS *Cycl. Supp.* s.v., The ægilops is the *avena sylvestris*, the wild oat.

3. *Bot.* A genus of grasses, native to the south of Europe.

1872 OLIVER *Elem. Bot.* II. 278 Some botanists have tried to show that Wheat may have been derived from a South European grass, called *Ægilops*.

4. A species of Oak (*Quercus ægilops*).

1706 PHILLIPS, *Ægilops*..a kind of Tree that bears Acorns or Mast. **1865** DAUBENY *Trees of Ancients* i. 16 The *Ægilops* [of Pliny and Theophrastus] is probably the species now known as *Ægilops*..the finest and tallest of the Oaks that occur in Greece.

ægirite (ˈɛdʒɪraɪt, ˈiː-). *Min.* Also called **ægirine.** [See quot.] An ore belonging to the Amphibole group of Bisilicates.

1837–80 DANA *Mineral.* 224 Ægirite..monoclinic, and isomorphous with pyroxene..Named after Ægir, the Scandinavian god of the sea. *Ibid.* Ægirine holds the same relation to pyroxene that arfvedsonite does to hornblende.

‖**ægis** (ˈiːdʒɪs). [L. *ægis*, a. Gr. αἰγίς, of uncert. etym.; see Liddell and Scott, s.v.]

1. A shield, or defensive armour; applied in ancient mythology to that of Jupiter or Minerva.

1704 ROWE *Ulysses* III. i. 1128 She [Pallas] shakes her dreadful Ægis from the Clouds. **1760** HOME *Siege of Aquileia* IV, His adamantine ægis Jove extends. **1812** BYRON *Ch. Harold* II. xiv, Where was thine Ægis, Pallas, that appalled Stern Alaric?

2. *fig.* A protection, or impregnable defence. Now freq. in senses 'auspices, control, etc.', esp. in phr. ***under the ægis*** (***of***).

1793 HOLCROFT *Lavater's Physiog.* xxix. 137 Feeling is the ægis of enthusiasts and fools. **1836** THIRLWALL *Greece* III. xviii. 83 They were sheltered by the ægis of the laws. **1865** LECKY *Rationalism* (1878) II. 323 He cast over them the ægis of his own mighty name. **1910** *Encycl. Brit.* III. 936/2 Under the aegis of the Billiard Association a tacit understanding was arrived at that the position must be broken up, should it occur. **1958** P. GAMMOND *Duke Ellington* I. 18 They make their valuable individual contributions, but under the Ellington aegis they find themselves constantly enriched musically. **1963** *B.S.I. News* May 14/2 These basic criteria and recognized methods of assessment, drawn up under the aegis of BSI.

3. *attrib.* and *Comb.*, ***ægis-bearing, ægis-orb.***

1793 WORDSWORTH *Even. Walk* 69 The broadening sun appears; A long blue bar itsægis orb divides. **1877** BRYANT *Odyss.* v. 128 The purposes Of Ægis-bearing Jove.

ægithognathous (iːdʒɪˈθɒgnəθəs), *a.* *Zool.* [f. Gr. αἴγιθος, name of an unknown bird + γνάθος jaw.] Having the formation of palate characteristic of the family *Ægithognathæ* (perching birds, woodpeckers, swifts): see quot. 1894. Hence **ægiˈthognathism**, the condition of being ægithognathous.

1875 W. K. PARKER in *Encycl. Brit.* III. 699/1 All the *Coracomorphæ* have the ægithognathous palate. **1884** COUES *N. Amer. Birds* (ed. 2) 172 Ægithognathism..is exhibited almost unexceptionally by the great group of Passerine birds. **1894** R. B. SHARPE *Handbk. Birds Gt. Brit.* I. 1 The palate is said to be 'ægithognathous', or 'Passerine', when the *vomer* is broadened and blunt, or truncated, at the anterior end, and is not connected with the *maxillo-palatines*, which, consequently, are widely separated from each other.

æglogue, obs. form of ECLOGUE.

ægophonic (ˌiːgəʊˈfɒnɪk), *a.* *Path.* [f. ÆGOPHONY + -IC.] Of or pertaining to ægophony.

1855 G. H. BARLOW *Pract. Med.* xii. 257 The more ordinary tremulous bronchophony, or, as some have termed it, œgophonic bronchophony. **1876** J. S. BRISTOWE *Theory & Pract. Med.* II. iii. 386 The ægophonic sound..is often distinctly feebler than the normal voice-resonance.

ægophony (iːˈgɒfənɪ). *Path.* [mod. f. Gr. αἴξ (αἶγα) goat + -φωνία sound.] A tremulous resonance of the voice, like the bleating of a kid, occurring in cases of pleurisy.

1834 J. FORBES tr. *Laennec's Treat. Dis. Chest* (ed. 4) I. iii. 27 Perfect pectoriloquy..is changed..into a simple resonance..such as to be with difficulty discriminated from ægophony and bronchophony. **1853** MAYNE *Exp. Lex.* **1866** [see BRONCHOPHONY]. **1876** J. S. BRISTOWE *Theory & Pract. Med.* II. iii 386 In association with pectoriloquy, bronchophony, or ægophony there can generally be detected a distinct whiff of tubular quality.

ægre, -ness, obs. forms of EAGER, -NESS.

†**ˈægritude.** *Obs.* also 7 egritude. [ad. L. *ægritūdo* sickness, f. *æger* sick: see -TUDE.] Sickness.

1532 HENRY VIII in Burnet *Hist. Ref.* II. 168 We have augmented our ægritude and distress. **1610** HEALEY *St. Aug., City of God* XIV. vii. (1620) 478 That sorrow which Tully had rather call egritude and Virgil dolour. **1647** R. BARON *Cyprian Acad.* 34 (N.) Now, now we symbolize in egritude And simpathize in Cupid's malady.

ægrotant (iːˈgrəʊtənt). *rare*⁻¹. [ad. L. *ægrōtant-em* pr. pple. of *ægrōtā-re* to be sick; f. *æger* sick.] A sick person, an invalid.

1865 *Temple Bar* Sept. 262 There is a large class of ægrotants in this country.

‖**ægrotat** (iːˈgrəʊtæt). [prop. 3rd pers. sing. of L. *ægrōtāre* (see prec.) 'he is sick.'] **a.** In the Eng. Universities, a certificate that a student is too ill to attend at a lecture or examination. Cf. ÆGER.

1864 C. BABBAGE *Philosopher* 37, I sent my servant to the apothecary for a thing called an aegrotat, which I understood..meant a certificate that I was indisposed.

b. A degree or pass awarded to a candidate prevented from sitting an examination because of illness; also *N. Amer.*, a credit (sense 13 d) awarded for similar reasons. Also *attrib.*

1900 in J. S. Farmer *Public School Word-bk.* **1904** J. T. FOWLER *Durham Univ.* ii. 42 In 1835 no ægrotat was to be received without a medical certificate. [**1912** *Oxf. Univ.*

Handbk. 168 If a candidate in a Final Honour School has been prevented by illness from completing his examinations, the Examiners may, if in their judgement his work is of sufficient merit, place his name at the foot of each copy of the Class List, distinguishing the name or names so placed by the word 'ægrotat' or 'ægrotant'.] **1943** G. G. COULTON *Fourscore Years* xiii. 124 Spratt advised me to take an *aegrotat*, promising a testimonial which would . . do more for me than the sorry place which was sure to result from papers written in my room when I ought to be in hospital. *Ibid.* 125 Tyke . . managed to get a medical certificate which legitimated his claim for an *aegrotat* degree. **1985** *Undergraduate Calendar* (Univ. of Waterloo, Kitchener, Ontario) I. 7/2 AEG, aegrotat, credit granted due to illness.

æht, variant of AGHT *a. Obs.*, noble, valiant.

æht, æhte, obs. forms of AUGHT, EIGHT.

æie, obs. form of AWE.

æihwær, æiwær, var. AYWHERE *adv. Obs.*

aeipathy (eɪˈaɪpəθɪ). *Med.* [f. Gr. ἀεὶ ever + -παθεία feeling; see -PATHY.] 'Continued passion.' Craig 1847. 'Term for an unyielding or inveterate disease.' Mayne *Exp. Lex.* 1853.

æiðer, obs. form of EITHER.

æl, an early form of ALL.

ælc, obs. form of EACH.

ælmesse, obs. form of ALMS.

ælpi, variant of ONELEPY *a. Obs.*, single.

Æluroid (iːˈl(j)ʊərɔɪd), *a.* (*sb.*) *Zool.* [f. mod.L. *Æluroidea* neut. pl., f. Gr. αἴλουρος cat: see -OID.] Belonging to, or having the characters of, the division *Æluroidea* of Carnivora, comprising the feline and allied families; as *sb.*, an animal of this division.

1869 *Proc. Zool. Soc.* 22 Cryptoprocta is a member of the Æluroid group. *Ibid.* 27 In the presence of a short cæcum . . Hyæna conforms with the Æluroids.

-æmia (-ˈiːmɪə), *suffix.* Also (chiefly *U.S.*) -emia. [f. Gr. αἷμα blood + -IA[1].] Formative element in sbs. that denote the presence in the blood of an indicated substance or organism, usu. abnormally or in abnormal amounts; as *hypercalcæmia, hypocalcæmia, leukæmia, septicæmia, viræmia.*

æmti, obs. form of EMPTY.

†**ˈæmule**, *v. Obs. rare*⁻¹. [ad. L. *æmulā-ri*, f. *æmulus* a rival.] Early by-form of EMULATE.

1595 SPENSER *Col. Clout* 72 Yet, æmuling my pipe, he tooke in hond My pipe, before that æmuled of many, And plaid theron.

†**aˈenean** *a. Obs. rare.* Also **ahenean.** [f. L. *a(h)ēne-us* brazen + -AN.] Brazen.

1664 QUARLES *Fun. Eleg.* Wks. 1717, 418 Thou dry-brain'd Portick, whose Ahenean brest (Transcending passion) never was opprest With grief.

Æneid (iːˈniːɪd, ˈiːniːɪd). Obs. forms were Eneydos, Æneidos, Æneis, Ænead. [a. Fr. *Enéide*, f. L. *Ænēid-a* adj. prop. Greek, 'of or pertaining to *Ænēas*'; see -ID.] An epic poem describing the adventures of Æneas; *esp.* that written by Virgil.

1490 CAXTON *Eneydos* **1513** DOUGLAS *Eneis.* **1548** PHAËR *Eneidos.* **1678** CUDWORTH *Intell. Syst.* 790 Virgil, in his sixth Ænead. **1711** ADDISON *Spect.* No. 60 ¶2, I have seen half the Æneid turned into Latin Rhymes.

aeneolithic (eɪˌiːniːəʊˈlɪθɪk), *a.* [f. L. *aēneus* of copper or bronze + Gr. λίθος stone + -IC.] Of or pertaining to the period of the neolithic age in which copper was used together with flint implements. See also ENEOLITHIC.

1901 SERGI *Mediterr. Race* xii. 240 In Italy this period is termed *æneolithic*, that is to say, the period of copper and polished stone together. **1928** H. C. DAWSON *Age of Gods* iii. 51 The new cultures which entered Europe in neolithic and aeneolithic times followed two main lines of diffusion. **1937** *Proc. Prehist. Soc.* III. 357 Iberian art of the aeneolithic period influenced Ireland.

aeneous (eɪˈiːniːəs), *a. rare.* [f. L. *a(h)ēne-us*, brazen + -OUS.] Brassy; brass-coloured (like some beetles).

1815–43 in KIRBY & SPENCE *Entomol.* **1847** HARDY in *Proc. Berw. Nat. Club.* II. v. 236 Head rather small . . with the thorax aeneous.

æness, obs. form of ONCE.

ængel, obs. form of ANGEL *sb.*

æni, ænig, obs. forms of ANY.

ænigma, -tic, etc.; see ENIGMA, -TIC, etc.

ænigmatite, *Min.* a variety of KŒLBINGITE.

Æolian (iːˈəʊlɪən), *a.* [f. L. *æoli-us* adj. f. *Æolis* or *Æolus* + -AN.]

1. Of Æolis or Æolia, a district of Asia Minor anciently colonized by Greeks; Æolic. ***Æolian mode*** in *Music* 'is the ninth of the church modes.' Grove *Dict. Music.*

1589 PUTTENHAM *Arte Eng. Poesie* II. x. 70 The Dorien . . the Phrigien . . the Lydien, and . . the Eolien. **1789** BURNEY *Hist. Music* (ed. 2) I. iii. 53 The Æolian is grand and pompous though sometimes soothing. **1880** HELMORE in Grove *Dict. Mus.* I. 40/2 Mozart's Requiem may be said almost to begin and end with the Æolian scale.

2. a. Of Æolus, the mythic god of the winds; hence of, produced by, or borne on the wind, or by currents of air; aerial. ***Æolian harp***: a stringed instrument adapted to produce musical sounds on exposure to a current of air.

1605 SYLVESTER tr. *Du Bartas's Deuine Weekes & Workes* [Week] II. [Day] ii. p. 399 Th' Æolian Crowd obayes his mighty call, The surly surges of the waters fall. **1693** DRYDEN *Juvenal* x. 293 And Eurus never such hard usage found In his Eolian Prisons underground. **1791** E. DARWIN *Bot. Gard.* I. 181 You melt in dulcet chords, when Zephyr rings The Eolian Harp. **1820** SHELLEY *Prom. Unb.* IV. i. 188 The music of the rolling world Kindling within the strings of the waved air, Æolian modulations. **1880** M. D. CONWAY in *Academy* 24 Jul. 56 There is a pure aeolian quality, a music as of storms telling their secret on the strings of a heart.

b. spec. *Geol.*, of formations produced or deposited by the action of wind.

1853 R. J. NELSON in *Q. Jrnl. Geol. Soc.* IX. 201 They [the Bermudas] may be placed . . as a peculiar post-tertiary formation of a composite character . . Neptunian below and 'Æolian' above. *Ibid.* 207 (*caption*) Horizontal section of 'Æolian' rock. **1879** RUTLEY *Study of Rocks* xiv. 275 Rounded by attrition, the result of their transport by water, or in the case of aeolian rocks, of their transport by wind. **1889** I. C. RUSSELL in *Geol. Mag.* July 289 The subaërial deposits now accumulating in the arid portion of the United States may be divided into four classes: 1, Eolian Sands; 2, Talus Slopes; 3, Alluvial Cones; and 4, Calcareous Clays. **1910** *Encycl. Brit.* XI. 656/1 Some [rocks] . . are accumulated by the drifting action of wind upon loose materials, and are known as 'aeolian' formations. Familiar instances of such wind-formed deposits are the sand dunes along many parts of the sea coast. **1935** *Nature* 1 June 909/1 It seems safe to conclude that the bulk of the ridge is relatively late Pleistocene in age, and that it is essentially æolian in origin.

Æolianly (iːˈəʊlɪənlɪ), *adv.* [f. ÆOLIAN *a.* + -LY[2].] With an Æolian sound; with a sound as of an Æolian harp.

1849 SYMINGTON *Harebell Chimes* 129 Plaint melody Sung by the mermaids of the wave, Æolianly. **1886** M. F. TUPPER *My Life as Author* 393 Moaning Æolianly as it went.

Æolic (iːˈɒlɪk), *a.* [ad. L. *æolic-us* a. Gr. αἰολικός.] = ÆOLIAN I. ***Æolic Digamma***: the sixth letter of the early Greek Alphabet preserved in the Æolic dialect. ***Æolic mode***; see ÆOLIAN I.

1674 PLAYFORD *Skill of Mus.* I. 59 The Æolick Mood, was that which was of a more Airy and soft pleasing sound. **1807** ROBINSON *Archæol. Græca* v. xxiii. 534 The Phrygian mode was religious . . the Æolic, simple.

æolienne, occas. var. of ÉOLIENNE.

æolina, -ine (ˌiːəʊˈlaɪnə, ˈiːəlaɪn). [f. *Æol-us* on analogy of female names like *Carolina, -line*; see -INE[3].] (See quot.)

1876 HILES *Catech. Organ* x. (1878) 73 *Æoline*, a delicate, free reed stop. **1879** A. J. HIPKINS in Grove *Dict. Music* I. 667 In 1818 Haeckel constructed a diminutive æoline as an instrument to be used with a pianoforte. **1879** E. PROUT *ibid.* I. 40/2 The æolina may be regarded as the first germ of the Accordion and Concertina.

æolipyle, -pile (ˈiːəlɪpaɪl, iːˈɒlɪpaɪl). Also eolipyle, -pile. [a. Fr. *æolipyle* (16th c.) ad. L. *Æoli pylæ* (= Gr. πύλαι) the doorway of Æolus, *Vitruv.* i. 6, the vapour bursting from the orifice like the winds from the opened door of the cave of Æolus.] A pneumatic instrument or toy, illustrating the force with which vapour generated by heat in a closed vessel rushes out by a narrow aperture. (It is said to have been invented by Hero of Alexandria, and has had many forms and applications, but is now arranged to illustrate the reaction of the air upon the issuing stream of steam producing circular motion.)

[**1611** COTGR., *Eolipyles* (Fr.), hollow brazen bowls, etc.] **1656** tr. *Hobbes's Elem. Philos.* (1839) 425 Many other phenomena . . as those of weather-glasses, æolipyles, wind-guns. **1774** GOLDSM. *Nat. Hist.* I. 205 Experimental philosophers produce an artificial wind, by an instrument called an æolipile. **1857** CHAMBERS *Inf.* I. 388 The æolipyle is formed by a globular metallic vessel, which rests on pivots where it can revolve with perfect facility. Two tubes proceed from this ball at right angles to the pivots, shut at the extremities, but with a small aperture at the side whence steam may escape.

Æolism (ˈiːəlɪz(ə)m). [f. ÆOL(IAN *a.* or ÆOL(IC *a.* + -ISM.] A style or idiom characteristic of or restricted to the Æolic dialect of Greek.

1847 GROTE *Hist. Greece* II. xxix. 117 He composed in the Laconian dialect—a variety of the Doric with some intermixture of Æolisms. **1884** *Amer. Jrnl. Philol.* V. 521 First must be eliminated from the so-called Aeolisms all phenomena which, so far from deserving the name of Aeolisms, do not so much as occur in Aeolic. **1950** H. L. LORIMER *Homer & Monum.* viii. 459 All 'Aeolisms' . . in these two categories can be equally well explained as examples of primitive Ionic preserved by the exigencies of metre.

æolist (ˈiːəlɪst). *rare*⁻¹. [f. L. *Æol-us* the god of winds + -IST.] Used by Swift for: A pretender to inspiration or spiritual regeneration.

1704 SWIFT *T. of Tub* viii. 94 The learned Æolists maintain the original cause of all things to be wind.

æolistic (ˌiːəʊˈlɪstɪk), *a.* [f. prec. + -IC.] 'Long-winded.'

1882 *Glasgow News* 26 Sept. 4/4 Men who are thought to be wise by their solemn reiteration of the most elementary platitudes. This latter class of æolistic orators.

æolo-, combining form of *Æolus*, regarded as the impersonation of wind, found in several names of tentative musical wind-instruments, as the ***æolodicon, æolodion, æolomelodicon, æolophone.***

æolotropic (ˌiːələʊˈtrɒpɪk), *a.* [f. ÆOLOTROPY + -IC.] Pertaining to, or characterized by, æolotropy; not isotropic.

1867 THOMSON & TAIT *Nat. Philos.* I. 518 An individual body . . may be isotropic in one quality or class of qualities, but æolotropic in others. **1881** *Nature* XXIII. 475 To distort the metal tube by a definite twist, thus rendering it æolotropic as regards its electric conductivity.

æolotropy (ˌiːəˈlɒtrəpɪ). [f. Gr. αἰόλος changeful + -τροπία turning.] Change of electrical, optical, or other physical qualities consequent upon change of position, as when the refractive property of a transparent body is not the same in all directions; the opposite of *isotropy*; anisotropy.

1881 SIR W. THOMSON in *Nature* No. 628. 47 One of the most curious and interesting things in the mathematics of æolotropy. *Mod.* The well-known æolotropy of Iceland spars.

æon, eon (ˈiːən, ˈiːɒn). [a. L. *æōn*, a. Gr. αἰών age.]

1. a. An age of the universe, an immeasurable period of time; the whole duration of the world, or of the universe; eternity.

1647 H. MORE *Song of Soul* Notes 136/1 For such is the nature of *Æon* or Eternity. **1765** TUCKER *Lt. of Nat.* I. 650 He shall endure, not simply to the aion, that is, 'for ever,' but to the aion of aions. **1831** CARLYLE *Sart. Res.* (1858) 157 The mysterious Course of Providence through Æons of Æons. **1857** H. MILLER *Test. Rocks* iii. 147 The protracted eons of the Carboniferous period. **1879** FARRAR *St. Paul* I. 598 The last great æon of God's dealing with mankind.

b. *attrib.* and *Comb.*

1916 O. SITWELL in E. & O. Sitwell *20th Cent. Harlequinade* 25 From far within his æon-battered brain Well up those wanton wistful images. **1923** *Blackw. Mag.* July 61/3 The aeon-long passage of water a-down the rock has worn its surface to a glassy smoothness. **1938** W. DE LA MARE *Memory* 29 A storm-cock shrilled its aeon-old refrain. **1948** E. SITWELL *Notebk. W. Shakes.* vi. 53 In one of the most terrible aeon-moments of the play.

2. The personification of an age. In *Platonic philosophy*, A power existing from eternity; an emanation, generation, or phase of the supreme deity, taking part in the creation and government of the universe.

1647 H. MORE *Song of Soul* Notes 138/1 But Intellect or *Æon* hath in himself proper Intellectuall life. **1678** CUDWORTH *Intell. Syst.* 212 The next considerable appearance of a multitude of self-existent deities seems to be in the Valentinian Thirty Gods and Æons. **1865** LECKY *Rationalism* I. iii. 228 More commonly she was deemed a personification of a Divine attribute, an individual Æon.

3. *Geol.* Usu. eon. The largest division of geological time, composed of several eras.

1933 SCHUCHERT & DUNBAR *Textbk. Geol.* (ed. 3) v. 70 It has recently been proposed to use the name *Cryptozoic* eon . . for Pre-Cambrian time, and *Phanerozoic* eon . . for all subsequent time. **1958** [see CRYPTOZOIC *a.* 2]. **1969** *Proc. Geol. Soc. Lond.* Aug. 148 *Eon*, compounded of several eras. **1980** EICHER & MCALESTER *Hist. of Earth* ii. 48 The last 15 percent of geologic history is known as the Phanerozoic . . Eon. **1982** W. B. HARLAND et al. *Geologic Time Scale* ii. 7/2 The classification has developed traditionally on a hierarchical basis with eons (e.g. Phanerozoic), eras (e.g. Mesozoic), periods (e.g. Jurassic), [etc.].

4. *Geol.* and *Astr.* One thousand million years.

1968 R. A. LYTTLETON *Mysteries Solar Syst.* i. 5 We are now fairly certain that the planets have existed for something like 4 to 5 thousand million years, four to five aeons (to use a modern unit of time, the aeon, which avoids the confusion associated with the word *billion*). **1969** G. G. SIMPSON in F. W. Preston et al. *Diversity & Stability in Ecol. Systems* v. 165 These fossils are with considerable probability somewhat but not greatly older than the long-known and classical faunas universally recognized as early Cambrian. Their age may be on the order of 0·7 eon (700 million years). **1974** *Nature* 15 Mar. 199 (*heading*) Evidence for a ~4·5 aeon age of plagioclase clasts in a lunar highland breccia.

æonial (iːˈəʊnɪəl), *a.* [f. Gr. αἰώνι-ος eternal + -AL[1].] Age-long, eternal, everlasting.

1865 *Daily Tel.* 8 July, The Millennium of eternal Stafford Northcotes, sempiternal John Pakingtons, immutable Henleys, and æonial Whitesides.

æonian (iːˈəʊnɪən), *a.* [f. Gr. αἰώνι-ος age-long, eternal + -AN.] Eternal, everlasting.

1765 TUCKER *Lt. of Nat.* I. 650, I might insist that the term translated 'everlasting' ought to be preserved untranslated, as a kind of technical term, and called *aionian.* **1850** TENNYSON *In Mem.* xxxv. 11 The sound of streams that swift or slow Draw down æonian hills. **1867** G. MACDONALD *Poems* 109 Heaven's æonian day.

æonic (iːˈɒnɪk), *a.* [f. ÆON + -IC.] Age-long, lasting an æon.

1883 *Harper's Mag.* Sept. 622/1 Such a period of æonic sleep may have been requisite for the evolution. **1924** H. E. FOSDICK *Mod. Use Bible* 251 A world where all moral living is only an accidental episode in an æonic physical process. **1932** *Discovery* Apr. 108/1 They [palæontologists] make the very dry bones live, reconstructing ancient scenes of the aeonic drama.

æonist (ˈiːənɪst). *rare.* [f. ÆON + -IST.] One who holds the eternal duration of the world.

1806 W. TAYLOR in *Ann. Rev.* IV. 723 A third sect is growing up, who, with Toulmin, maintain the eternity of the world; they might be called Æonists.

Æpyornis (iːpɪˈɔːnɪs, ɛ-). [mod.L. (I. G. St.-Hilaire 1850, in *Ann. Sci. Nat.* (*Zool.*) XIV. 209), f. Gr. αἰπύς high + ὄρνις bird.] A genus of extinct gigantic struthious birds known from remains discovered in Madagascar; a bird of this genus.

1851 *Ann. & Mag. Nat. Hist.* VII. 163 The gigantic bird of Madagascar... We shall give to this genus the name of *Æpyornis.* **1883** *Encycl. Brit.* XV. 171/1 Madagascar was the home of.. the extinct *Æpyornis*, whose eggs, found in a sub-fossil state, are the largest known. **1895** [see DROMORNIS]. **1927** HALDANE & HUXLEY *Anim. Biol.* xii. 277 Largest flightless birds (Moa, Aepyornis, large Ostrich). **1957** R. CARRINGTON *Mermaids & Mastodons* v. 92 Several species of *Aepyornis* are now recognized, the largest still being *Aepyornis maximus*. The mounted skeleton of this bird.. has a height of just under ten feet. **1959** *Chambers's Encycl.* VIII. 779/2 There are also fossil remains of large, extinct, bird-like animals not found elsewhere, such as the Aepyronis, remnants of whose eggs are strewn over the beaches of the extreme south.

æqual, æquate, æqui-, etc.; see EQU-.

æquoreal (ɪˈkwɔəriːəl), *a. Zool.* [f. L. *æquore-us*, f. *æquor* sea + -AL¹; merely a technical anglicizing of the L.] Marine, oceanic.

1838 DR. JOHNSTON in *Proc. Berw. Nat. Club* I. VI. 175 Syngnathus æquoreus, *Linn.*, The Æquoreal Pipe-fish.

æquorin (ˈiːkwərɪn). *Biochem.* [f. mod.L. *Æquorea*, generic name, fem. of L. *æquoreus* of the sea, f. *æquor* sea: see -IN¹.] A protein mixture obtained from the jellyfish *Æquorea æquorea* that luminesces with a blue light in the presence of calcium ions and is used for detecting the ions in living tissue.

1962 O. SHIMOMURA et al. in *Federation Proc.* XXI. 401/1 The activity apparently resides in a single protein, which we name 'Aequorin', whose luminescent reaction requires Ca^{++} but not molecular oxygen. **1978** *Nature* 11 May 149/2 Direct evidence of a transient increase in intracellular free Ca^{2+} at the time of fertilisation or activation of fish and sea urchin eggs has been obtained using the photoprotein aequorin.

ær, obs. form of AIR *sb.*¹, EAR, ERE, and OAR.

ær- *pref.* See Æ- *pref.*

ærarian (ɪˈrɛərɪən), *a.* and *sb.* [f. L. *ærāri-us* fiscal, *ærāri-um* the treasury, + -AN.]

A. *adj.* Connected with the public treasury; fiscal.

1850 MERIVALE *Rom. Emp.* (1865) IV. xxxii. 19 The senate, the knights, and the aerarian tribunes.

B. *sb.* [The adj. used *absol.* sc. citizen.] A Roman citizen of the lowest, unenfranchised, class, who paid only a poll-tax (*æra pendebat*).

1872 E. ROBERTSON *Hist. Ess.* 225 The Ærarian was any contributor to the Roman treasury who was not in the enjoyment of the suffrage.

aerate (ˈeɪəreɪt, ˈɛər-), *v.* [f. L. *aer* air + -ATE³, prob. after Fr. *aér-er*, a latinized spelling of OFr. *airer, ayrer*, f. *air.*]

1. To expose to the free (mechanical) action of air, to supply with air. Also *fig.*

1799 W. NICOL *Pract. Planter* iv. 121 If we admit that fallowing and aerating land is of advantage. **1851** *Fraser's Mag.* XLIII. 633/1 Mopping the dew from their brows, or aerating their persons in the breeze. **1856** *Farmer's Mag.* Jan. 20 Mineral nutriment.. could not be restored by his process of stirring and aerating without help from manure. **1879** WRIGHTSON in *Cassell's Techn. Educ.* I. 78/2 The soil between the drains must be thoroughly aërated. **1958** *Listener* 23 Oct. 665/2 Not a breath of this was allowed to aerate this particular talk.

2. To expose to the chemical action of air; to oxygenate (the blood) by respiration.

1794 E. DARWIN *Zoonomia* I. 7 The blood.. has been thus aerated in the lungs. **1860** HARTWIG *Sea* xi. 203 The crustacean possesses a heart, which propels the blood, after it has been aerated in the gills.

3. To charge (a substance) with carbonic acid gas, formerly called fixed air. (Usually in the pple. AERATED.)

1905 *Harmsworth Encycl.* I. 82/1 A more recent introduction is the sparklet. This is a bottle with a hollow removable screw top, for holding a soft steel capsule containing liquid carbon dioxide sufficient to aerate the bottle of water.

aerated (ˈeɪəreɪtɪd, ˈɛər-), *ppl. a.* [f. prec. + -ED.]

1. Exposed to the action of the air, supplied with air, charged with air. Also ***aerated concrete*** (see quot. 1956).

1800 S. MITCHILL *Let.* 3 Dec. in T. J. Pettigrew *Mem. of Lettsom* (1817) III. 218 An opinion, held by several eminent men, that aërated pus was of an acid quality. **1862** ANSTED *Channel Isl.* 10 The water is always well aërated, there is abundant vegetation. **1875** RICHARDSON *Dis. Mod. Life* 34 The body, fed with a blood that is only partially aerated, is imperfectly heated. **1947** *Brit. Standard 1364* (*title*) Aerated Concrete Building Blocks. **1956** *Gloss. Terms Concrete* (*B.S.I.*) 13 *Aerated concrete*, lightweight concrete in which the lightness is obtained by the formation of bubbles of air or gas in the plastic mix which are retained on setting and hardening.

2. Charged with carbonic acid gas (or oxygen), so as to effervesce; raised, as bread, by means of such effervescence. Also *fig.*

1794 SULLIVAN *View of Nat.* I. 454 Ponderous spar, is a terra ponderosa, combined with the aerial acid, and aerated baroselenites. **1861** WYNTER *Social Bees* 162 In the production.. of aërated bread, the hand of the workman never touches the material. **1870** LOWELL *Among my Bks.* I. (1873) 21 The best English poetry.. is understanding aerated by imagination. **1880** BEALE *Slight Ailm.* 149 Most practitioners recommend their patients to drink special aerated waters.

aerating (ˈeɪəreɪtɪŋ, ˈɛər-), *vbl. sb.* [f. as prec. + -ING¹.] **a.** Supplying with oxygen. **b.** Charging with carbonic acid.

1860 *All Y. Round* No. 45. 443 The rapidity of the new aërating process. **1870** ROLLESTON *Anim. Life* 60 The principal aerating organ, the gills.

aeration (ˌeɪəˈreɪʃən, ɛər-). [a. Fr. *aération*, f. *aérer*; or (in modern use) independent Eng. f. AERATE, after analogy of *create, creation*, etc.: see -TION.]

†**1.** Exposure to the open air; open air life. *Obs. rare.*

1578 TYMME *Calvin on Genesis* 313 The weariness of a wandering life and irksomeness of continual aeration.

2. Exposure of all the parts of anything to the mechanical influence of the air; supplying with fresh air; airing.

1835 KIRBY *Bridgew. Treat.* (1852) II. 194 To seek those stations for oviposition that are best suited to the aeration, hatching, and rearing of their spawn. **1858** T. R. JONES *Aquar. Naturalist* 27/2 Artificial aeration of the water contained in an aquarium may sometimes be beneficially adopted. **1881** T. HUGHES *Rugby Tennessee* 137 The soil.. thoroughly drained and sweetened by aeration.

3. Exposure to the chemical action of the air; oxygenation of the blood in respiration.

1836 TODD *Cycl. Anat. & Phys.* I. 142/2 That modification of the function of aeration entitled respiration. **1879** CARPENTER *Ment. Physiol.* I. i. §15. 17 If we try to 'hold our breath,' for such a period that the aëration of the blood is seriously interfered with.

4. The charging with carbonic acid, or oxygen, so as to give briskness.

1874 KNIGHT *Dict. Mech.* I. 19/1 The aëration of sparkling champagne and Catawba is produced by adding a small amount of white sugar to the wine in bottling, the slight fermentation eliminating alcohol therefrom and liberating carbonic acid gas. **1905** *Harmsworth Encycl.* I. 81/3 Various additions are made, either to the bottle before filling, or to the liquid in bulk before aeration.

aerator (ˈɛəreɪtə(r)). [f. AERATE after analogy of L. agent nouns in -OR.]

That which supplies or charges with air. *spec.* **a.** A contrivance for fumigating grain. **b.** An apparatus for forcing air or carbon dioxide into liquids. **c.** An apparatus for aerating turf.

1861 WYNTER *Social Bees* 44 What is this park but an aërator to the race, as the one [the lung] I before looked at was to the individual? **1874** in KNIGHT *Dict. Mech.* **1891** *Sci. Amer.* 4 Apr. 218/1 Aerator.. a portable device having a receiver near the top of a standard, the receiver having numerous small perforations, while lower on the standards are pans.. for the aeration of warm and fresh milk. **1892** *Jrnl. Soc. Chem. Industry* 30 Nov. 896/1 Improvements in Æreators for Treating Liquids. **1950** *N.Z. Jrnl. Agric.* Dec. 538/1 If rain has fallen on the swath, it will be advisable to lift the swath with an aerator so that it is brought up on the top of the stubble, where it dries out rapidly. **1958** *House & Garden* Feb. 90/1 Proper surface aeration is most important for good turf and when your lawn is small this aerator is the tool to do it.

ærd, var. ERD *sb.* and *v. Obs.*, dwelling, to dwell.

aereal, obs. form of AERIAL.

aerenchyma (ɛəˈrɛŋkɪmə). *Bot.* Also †aerenchym(e. [mod.L., ad. G. *aërenchym* (H. Schenck 1889, in *Jahrb. f. wissensch. Bot.* XX. 527), after *parenchym* PARENCHYMA: see AERO-.] Soft cellular plant tissue containing many intercellular air spaces and channels, found esp. in many aquatic plants.

1893 *Funk's Stand. Dict.*, Aerenchyma. **1908** DRIESCH *Sci. & Philos. Organism* I. 175 The so-called aërenchyme, especially well developed in the water-form of *Jussiaea.* **1911** *Encycl. Brit.* XXI. 743/1 A peculiar modification of periderm is formed by the phellogen in the submerged organs.. of many aquatic or marsh-loving plants... This tissue is called aerenchym, and no doubt its function is to facilitate the respiration of the organs on which it is formed. **1965** BELL & COOMBE tr. *Strasburger's Textbk. Bot.* 82 We can distinguish assimilatory parenchyma, food-storage parenchyma, transfusion parenchyma and parenchyma specialized for ventilation (aerenchyma). **1975** W. ARMSTRONG in J. R. Etherington *Environment & Plant Ecol.* vii. 209 Plants which cannot form aerenchyma appear to be intolerant of wet habitats.

ærende, ærnde, obs. forms of ERRAND.

†**aˈereosaline**, *a. Obs.* [f. L. *āere-us* of the air + SALINE.] Of the nature of a carbonate, or salt of carbonic acid ('fixed air').

1774 BROWNRIGG *Aerated Waters* in *Phil. Trans.* LXIV. 367 Exact agreement between these aëreo-saline concretes and various neutral salts.

†**aˈereous, aˈerious**, *a. Obs.* [f. L. *āere-us* or *āeri-us*, adj. f. *āer* air, + -OUS.] Of the nature of air, airy; = AERIAL, of which it may be viewed as a by-form of earlier date.

1594 PLAT *Jewell-house* III. 81 So as the lightest or most aereous, or fierie [liquor] bee placed uppermost. **1657** AUSTEN *Fruit Trees* I. 104 Whatsoever is a thin aerious light body ascends upwards. **1677** GALE *Crt. of Gentiles* II. III. 133 Affirming that our Bodies after the resurrection should be round, aereous, and not of the same substance they now are.

ærer, ærest; see ERE, ERST.

aerial (ˈɛərɪəl; orig. eɪˈɪərɪəl, eɪˈɛrɪəl), *a.* The three-syllable pronunciation is now in general use except in poetry when the metre calls for four syllables. Also 7 **aereal.** [f. L. *āeri-us* or *āere-us* airy (f. *āer* air) + -AL¹. As L. had two forms of the adj., *āerius* a. Gr. ἀέριος, and *āereus* after L. anal. as in *aureus, ferreus*, etc., so the early spelling in Eng. varied between *aereal* and *aerial*; the latter is alone used now. Cf. *aereous* and *aerious, ethereal* and *etherial.*] Airy or of air.

I. Of air as a substance.

1. Consisting or composed of air; aeriform, gaseous. ***aerial acid***: obs. name of carbonic acid gas, as being the only aeriform or gaseous acid.

1664 POWER *Exp. Philos.* II. 118 The aërial particles may be in a new motion. **1772** PRIESTLEY *Air* in *Phil. Trans.* LXII. 153 It is not improbable but that fixed air.. may be of the nature of an acid.. Mr. Bergman of Upsal.. calls it the aërial acid.

2. Thin or attenuated as air, etherial; unsubstantial, intangible, shadowy; *hence*, immaterial, ideal, imaginary. ***aerial architecture***: building castles in the air.

1610 HEALEY *St. Aug., City of God* 349 Those creatures.. being reasonable, passive, aereall and immortall. **1651** HOBBES *Leviathan* I. xii. 53 The Latines.. thought them Spirits, that is, thin aëreall bodies. **1714** MANDEVILLE *Fable of Bees* (1725) I. 40 The breath of man, the aerial coin of praise. **1829** SCOTT *Demonol.* x. 388 She was surprised to see a gleamy figure, as of some aerial being. **1838** DICKENS *Nich. Nick.* xxvii. (C.D. ed.) 213 With such triumphs of aërial architecture did Mrs. Nickleby occupy the whole of the evening. **1855** MILMAN *Lat. Chr.* IV. vii. (1864) II. 344 The Church may draw fine and aërial distinctions.

3. Light as air, airy.

1606 BRYSKETT *Civill Life* 54 For that tender age is rather sanguine and aeriall. **1756** BURKE *Subl. & B.* Wks. 1842 I. 24 This delicate and aërial faculty, which seems too volatile to endure even the chains of a definition. *a***1802** W. L. BOWLES *Poems* I. 149 Aërial Claude shall paint The gray fane peering o'er the summer woods.

II. Of the mass of air or atmosphere.

4. Of, pertaining to, or produced in the air or atmosphere; atmospheric.

1604 SHAKS. *Oth.* II. i. 39 Euen till we make the Maine, and th' Eriall blew, An indistinct regard. **1697** DRYDEN *Virgil Georgics* (J.) Aerial honey, and ambrosial dews. **1819** SHELLEY *Prom. Unb.* II. v. 13 As the aërial hue Of fountain-gazing roses. **1860** MAURY *Phys. Geog. Sea* xv. §677. 370 On the edges of this remarkable aerial current the wind is variable. **1870** TYNDALL *Heat* vi. §206. 164 We live at the bottom of an aerial ocean.

aerial perspective.

1731 BAILEY, vol. II, *Aerial Perspective* is that which represents bodies weakened and diminished in proportion to their distance from the eye. **1851** RUSKIN *Mod. Painters* I. II. II. i. §3 Aërial perspective is the expression of space by any means whatsoever, sharpness of edge, vividness of colour, etc.

5. a. Existing or moving in the atmosphere, above the earth, flying or floating in the air.

1621 BURTON *Anat. Mel.* I. ii. I. ii. (1676) 28/1 Aeriall Spirits or Devils are such as keep quarter most part in the air. **1704** POPE *Pastorals, Spring* 16 While she [the Nightingale] sings.. All th' aërial audience clap their wings. **1836-7** DICKENS *Sketches* (1850) 78/2 Then the balloons went up, and the aërial travellers stood up. **1859** DARWIN *Orig. Spec.* vi. (1873) 142 Petrels are the most aërial and oceanic of birds.

b. *esp.* with reference to locomotion in the air by means of aircraft (***aerial navigation, ship, transport***, etc.); conducted by aircraft (***aerial attack, photography, top-dressing*** (N.Z.), ***warfare***, etc.); dropped from an aircraft (***aerial bomb, mine, torpedo***, etc.); in other uses relating to aircraft or aviation, as ***aerial camera***, ***corridor***, ***screw***, etc. Some of the collocations (listed for convenience of reference in alphabetical order) are falling into disuse in favour of the corresponding expressions with *air-* as first element (see AIR *sb.*[1] B).

1915 *Readers' Guide to Periodical Lit. 1910–14* III. 19/2 *Aerial advertising company. **1919** H. G. ANDERSON *Med. & Surg. Aspects of Aviation* i. 4 The French conceived the idea of having *aerial ambulances to convey quickly the wounded. **1919** N. J. GILL *Aerial Arm* ix. 162 Fleets and armies... These ancient services [have] to be reinforced by the new *aerial arm. **1908** H. G. WELLS *War in Air* viii. §4 The drachenflieger appeared as little flecks on either wing of this *aerial Armada. **1909** A. L. ROTCH *Conquest of Air* v. 176 In view of the possibility of this method of *aërial attack on land or sea it is unfortunate that..the United States was alone among the other first-class powers to agree to prohibit ..the discharge of projectiles and explosives from balloons. **1881** W. D. HAY *300 Years Hence* x. 246 It is the first *aërial battle—may we not say it is the last, too? **1784** *Morning Herald* 18 Mar. 2/3 The *aerial boat. **1836** *New Monthly Mag.* Sept. 60 Mr. Southey's aërial boat. **1919** N. J. GILL *Aerial Arm* vii. 136 Freedom..is blighted by the curse of *aerial bombs. **1919** N. J. GILL *Aerial Arm* 135 It is.. conceded that there is no form of frightfulness so trying to the nerves as *aerial bombing. **1945** *Ann. Reg. 1944* 21 The aerial bombing of Germany reached a new pitch of intensity. **1910** *Flight* II. 96/2 An *Aerial 'Bus for Pau... The airship is to carry eight passengers besides the crew. **1919** H. SHAW *Text-bk. Aeronaut.* xxii. 249 The modern *aerial camera is a modified form of the original 'press' camera used in the early days of aerial work. **1785** in S. Stubelius *Balloon* (1960) 54 *Aerial car [*sc.* basket of a balloon]. **1957** *Everybody's Weekly* 16 Feb. 10 Whether you want an aerial car or bus.. the amazing helicopter will do the job. **1887** tr. *J. Verne's Clipper of Clouds* xxii. 231 An *aerial combat was beginning in which there were none of the chances of safety as in a sea-fight. **1921** *Flight* XIII. 293/1 The *aerial corridor for machines entering or leaving France..has now been enlarged. **1884** *Cassell's Family Mag.* 764/2 On arriving at Villebon the *aërial craft was steered gradually round. **1910** *Flight* II. 655/1 The movement of aerial craft. **1912** *Flight* IV. 471/1 On June 8th will take place, starting from London Aerodrome, Hendon, the first *aerial Derby. **1893** *Ann. Rep. Aëronaut. Soc.* 72 Mr. Horatio Phillips has, for the first time in *aërial dynamics, conveyed a weight of 400 lbs., with the aid of superposed narrow surfaces. **1784** *Universal Mag.* LXXIV. 18 A full account of the late wonderful *Aërial Excursions. **1900** *Science* XII. 798/1 What..will become of national frontiers when the *aërial fleets can cross them with impunity? **1922** *Flight* XIV. 218/2 New ones [aeroplanes] which should bring down the rate of *aerial freight to the value of those now charged in France for first-class railway passengers. **1919** N. J. GILL *Aerial Arm* v. 100 For purposes of self-defence, one or more passengers are carried as *aerial gunners in addition to the pilot. **1918** F. H. COLVIN *Aircraft Mech. Handbk.* xxi. 311 School of *Aerial Gunnery. **1918** E. S. FARROW *Dict. Mil. Terms* 9 **Aërial Lighthouses*, aerial beacons to guide aviators at night through the atmospheric ocean. **1906** *Sci. Amer.* 21 Apr. 327/2 Compared with any other means of transportation, the *aerial line seems miraculously safe. **1920** *Discovery* Mar. 80/1 It is probable that kite balloons will be used as landmarks for the main aerial lines over the world. **1909** *Flight* I. 801/1 Baron v. Roenne gives some interesting particulars regarding a proposed *aerial liner. **1843** in S. Stubelius *Balloon* (1960) 56 The Project of Aërial Locomotion refuted... The *aërial locomotive will *then* go up, and..*not till then.* **1784** *Morning Herald* 16 Feb. 3/4 The aerial navigators..mounted in the gallery of the balloon..the cords, which held the *aerial machine, were cut. **1897** BADEN-POWELL in *United Service Mag.* Apr. 46 There are two distinct schools of inventors of aërial machines, the subject of navigable balloons being very different from that of flying machines proper. **1905** *Aeronaut. Jrnl.* Oct. 57 (*title*) The Vertical Screw Aërial Machine. **1911** *Daily Mail* 23 Aug. 3/6 A contract has also been entered into..for conveyance of the *aerial mail from London to Windsor. **1921** H. E. PORTER *Aerial Observation* viii. 342 *Aërial maps of forests have been made. **1908** *Trans. Amer. Soc. Mech. Engin.* XXX. 681 If, then, a nation can submerge a mine for the destruction of ships from underneath the water, why can it not drop an *aërial mine upon a ship from above? **1938** *Jrnl. R. Aeronaut. Soc.* XLII. 618 A new type of aerial mine has been invented... These mines are suspended under captive balloons. **1903** *Aeronaut. Jrnl.* 8 When we can order round our *aerial motor to take us straight to our destination. **1804** G. CAYLEY *Note-book* (1933) 80, I am well convinced that *Aerial Navigation will form a most prominent feature in the progress of civilization. **1922** Aerial navigation [see NAVIGATION]. **1784, 1825** *Aerial navigator [see NAVIGATOR]. **1951** *Times Wkly.* 31 Jan. 18/5 New British Aerial Navigator. The Flight Log. A new British automatic system of aerial navigation which will ease the complicated task of the pilot is going into quantity production... The equipment..automatically shows the pilot his position on a map. **1783** in *W. H. Robinson's* (Newcastle-on-Tyne) *Catal. no. 14* (1926) 49 [*Aeronautical Cartoon*], The Montgolfier, A first Rate of the French *Aerial Navy. **1909** *Sci. Amer.* 12 June 443/3 London newspapers comment bitterly on the fact that Germany spends nearly eighty times as much as Great Britain for the creation of an aerial navy. **1914** HAMEL & TURNER *Flying* xvi. 280 The *aerial observation officer must be highly trained... Nothing appears yet to have been done towards making staff officers capable of taking aerial observations. **1917** 'CONTACT' *Airman's Outings* 189 The planning of bomb raids and concerted *aerial offensives. **1897** *Scribner's Mag.* XXII. 618/1 The first *aërial photograph taken in America..was on a wet plate from a balloon over the city of Boston in 1862. **1919** H. SHAW *Text-bk. Aeronaut.* xxii. 252 Only experts can be expected to read all the information that may be contained in an aerial photograph. **1897** *Scribner's Mag.* XXII. 617/2 M. Nadar, of Paris, was one of the earliest experimenters in *aërial photography. **1937** *Discovery* Oct. 306/1 In recent years aerial photography has played an important part in revealing the location of abandoned cities, for the artificial configuration of the ground appears in the air photograph and reveals the work of man. **1868** *Ann. Rep. Aëronaut. Soc.* 37 The measure of his *aërial planes. **1911** *World of Stamps* Oct. 6/1 The first *aerial post..was that instituted in besieged Paris in 1870. **1908** H. G. WELLS *War in Air* xi. §2 The second *aerial power in Europe at this time was France. **1884** *Knowledge* VI. 230/1 The accompanying engraving represents an *aërial propeller recently patented. **1910** *Flight* II. 867/1 A 'skimmer' with an aerial propeller. **1915** *Lancet* 12 June 1249/2 The dangers of an *aerial raid. **1914** *R.F.C. Training Man.* I. 22 *Aerial reconnaissance..may be considered under three heads: strategical, tactical and protective. **1908** *Sci. Amer.* 3 Oct. 218/1 The *aerial scout [i.e. an aeroplane], rising high into the air, would command a vast field of observation. **1856** *Brit. Patent* 2993 [The] first impetus..is easily sustained and increased by turning the *aërial screw. **1867** *Ann. Rep. Aëronaut. Soc.* 31 The French Aërial Screw..was now exhibited. **1892** O. CHANUTE in *Railroad & Engin. Jrnl.* Mar. 133/2 A proposed aerial screw machine. **1784** *Morning Herald* 18 Mar. 2/3 Mr. Blanchard had..given notice of an *ærial ship in which he was to take flight through the air. **1834** *Times* 15 Aug. 3/2 It was intended, or given out so in Paris, that on the 15th instant (this day) the aerial ship of Count de Lennox was to set out on the voyage to England. **1865** *Mech. Mag.* XIV. 64/1 Mr. Low, another American aëronaut, has constructed what he terms an aërial ship. **1917** 'CONTACT' *Airman's Outings* 180 Throughout the Somme Push we were able to maintain that *aerial superiority without which a great offensive cannot succeed. **1919** *Aeronautics* 2 Oct. 322 (*heading*) Antarctic *Aerial Survey. **1921** *Ibid.* 28 Apr. 304/1 The Government of India has issued a paper which deals with some experiments in *aerial surveying which have been made. **1958** *Oxf. Mail* 27 June 1/2 Two United States..*aerial tankers landed at Brize Norton today after breaking the New York-London record. **1946** *N.Z. Jrnl. Agric.* LXXIII. 193/2 The extensive areas of copper-deficient peat; land in New Zealand provided a suitable opportunity to try out *aerial topdressing under circumstances reasonably favourable to success. **1959** A. H. MCLINTOCK *Descr. Atlas N.Z.* p. xxi, Throughout this hill country aerial topdressing has made spectacular progress in improving the carrying capacity of the land. **1896** *Invention* 6 June 356/2 Mr. Rich ..has invented an *aerial torpedo capable of dealing death and destruction to..an ordinary sized county. **1938** *News Review* 25 Aug. 24/1 Three weeks ago a Japanese aerial torpedo fell within 50 feet of him at Hankow, splashing him with mud. **1908** H. G. WELLS *War in Air* viii. §2 They were declared to be *aerial torpedo-boats, and the aeronaut was supposed to swoop close to his antagonist and cast his bombs as he whirled past. **1881** W. D. HAY *300 Years Hence* ix. 202 So important was *aërial traffic become. **1910** *Times* 21 Mar. 6/6 Aerial traffic is not to circulate at the height of less than 50 mètres over buildings and enclosed property, nor are aerial vehicles to stop over enclosed property at any height below 500 mètres. **1917** 'CONTACT' *Airman's Outings* 27 When you visit the Continent after the war,..travel by the Franco-British service of *aerial transport. **1784** *Universal Mag.* LXXIV. 20/2 The sensations of the two *aërial travellers. **1784** *Universal Mag.* LXXV. 264/1 The gallery of one of these *aerial vehicles. **1809** G. CAYLEY in W. Nicholson *Jrnl. Nat. Philos.* Nov. 167 In such proportion may aerial vehicles be loaded with inactive matter. **1784** *Morning Herald* 1 Dec. 2/4 The first ascent of the *aerial vessel. **1838** T. M. MASON *Aeronautica* 325 The first of these [restrictions] regards the form of the aerial vessel. **1909** *Times* 27 Sept. 8/2 Breakage of the propeller blade is a serious danger in every form of aerial vessel. **1908** H. G. WELLS *War in Air* viii. §2 The early battles of the *aerial war were no doubt determined by attempts to realise the old naval maxim, to ascertain the position of the enemy's fleet and to destroy it. **1895** *Knowledge* XVIII. 276/1 *Aerial warfare..likely to ensue when aerial navigation becomes an accomplished fact. **1784** *Morning Herald* 1 Dec. 2/4 The Devonshire *Aerial Yacht. **1920** Aerial yacht [see AIR *sb.*[1] B. III. 5].

6. a. Placed aloft, or at an airy height, lofty, elevated; also *fig.*

1620 *Choyce Drollery* in *Shaks. Cent. Praise* 134 Cloud-grapling Chapman, whose Aerial minde Soares at Philosophy, and strikes it blinde. **1733** POPE *Ess. Man* III. 183 Here subterranean works and cities see, There towns aerial on the waving tree. **1847** LEWES *Hist. Philos.* (1867) II. 97 Rising into the aerial altitudes of imagination.

b. ***aerial cableway***, ***ropeway***: see quots.; ***aerial railway***, ***tramway***, a track consisting of overhead wires, cables, or rails supporting carriages, usually driven by electricity; ***aerial wire***, a wire or wires (by extension also a rod, etc.) supported in the air for radiating or receiving electromagnetic waves; an antenna; hence applied to things connected with this, as ***aerial array***, ***circuit***, ***switch***, ***system***, etc. Also *sb.*, short for ***aerial wire***.

1874 KNIGHT *Dict. Mech.*, *Aerial railway*, an attempt to govern the balloon or aërostat by guiding rails or wires stretched between posts. **1889** *Cent. Dict.*, *Aerial railway*, a name sometimes applied to systems of transportation by cars suspended from a rail or rope above them. **1903** *Buddhism* I. 157 A gorgeous car..ran on an aerial ropeway to the top of the scaffolding from the Pogoda platform. **1904** *Sci. Amer.* Suppl. LVII. 23438/3 (*title*) Aerial tramways as an economic means of transportation. **1910** *Encycl. Brit.* VII. 62/2 The aerial cableway is a development of the ropeway, and is a conveyor capable of hoisting and dumping at any desired point. **1957** in *Amer. Speech* (1963) XXXVIII. 204 *Aerial tramway*, usually two enclosed cabins which counter balance each other and transport a group of skiers at once. **1959** *Chambers's Encycl.* IX. 196/1 *Aerial Ropeways* are used for transporting material in bulk over long distances and over hilly ground or valley... They consist of a series of towers carrying suspension wires to which are attached carriers for the material.

1899 MARCONI in *Jrnl. Inst. Electr. Engin.* XXVIII. 274 A vertical conductor *W*, which I will call the aërial conductor. *Ibid.* 289 The aërial wire comes through the framework of a skylight. **1902** [see ANTENNA 5]. **1906** A. F. COLLINS *Man. Wireless Telegr.* 208 Aerial, a word much used instead of the longer term *aerial wire*. *Ibid.*, Aerial switch, a switch used to throw the aerial wire into connection with the spark-gap and out of connection with the detector, and vice versa. **1908** *Westm. Gaz.* 8 Dec. 9/4 The four aerials connected with the mast cover about an acre and a half. **1913** *Yr. Bk. Wireless Telegr.* 415 *Aerial Circuit*.—Starts at the free or insulated end of the aerial and ends with the connection to earth. **1930** *Times* 25 Mar. 11/3 There appears to be no reason for supposing that an effective aerial array would need masts over 180 ft. in height. **1930** *B.B.C. Yr.-Bk. 1931* 407 One 70-foot mast supports an umbrella aerial system serving the D.F. equipment. **1937** *Discovery* Feb. 43/2 A standard dipole G.E.C. receiving aerial for television.

7. Growing, or existing, in the air or above ground, instead of underground or under water.

1624 WOTTON *Elem. Archit.* I. 10 Firre Trees, Cypresses, Cedars, and such other Aereall aspiring Plants..are..fittest for Posts or Pillars or such vpright vse. **1842** GRAY *Struct. Bot.* iii. §1. (1880) 34 Aerial Roots for climbing are familiar in the Ivy.

aerialist ('ɛərɪəlɪst). [f. AERIAL *a.* + -IST.]

1. = PILLARIST I. *rare.*

1846 W. TROLLOPE *Jortin's Eccl. Hist.* II. xxxvi. 108 [St. Simeon Stylites'] example was imitated by other aerialists of great nerve and little brains.

2. A performer on the high wire or trapeze.

1905 *Barnum & Bailey's Program* 15 A cluster of most remarkable champion aerialists. **1950** *Oxf. Jun. Encycl.* IX. 2/1 An 'aerialist' is an acrobat who performs on the tight-rope or trapeze, up in the dome of the circus tent. **1961** *Guardian* 22 May 5/1 The aerialists are so high and perilous that their bland composure fools no one.

aeriality (eɪˌɪərɪ'ælɪtɪ). [f. AERIAL *a.* + -ITY.] Aerialness; airiness, unsubstantiality.

1854 DE QUINCEY *Wks.* IV. 60 Suggesting to the reader continually the mere aeriality of the entire speculation.

aerially (eɪ'ɪərɪəlɪ, 'ɛərɪəlɪ), *adv.* [f. AERIAL + -LY[2].] In an aerial manner; airily, etherially, celestially.

1821 *Examiner* 1 Oct. 618/1 A light handkerchief..floats aërially from her neck. **1827** MOORE *Epicurean* v. (1839) 33 She glided gently and aërially round the altar. **1830** TENNYSON *Margaret* 51 Your eyes Touch'd with a somewhat darker hue, And less aërially blue. **1853** DE QUINCEY *Wks.* XIV. ii. (1862) 80 The filaments connecting my heart were so aerially fine and fantastic.

aerian (eɪ'ɪərɪən), *a. rare.* [a. Fr. *aérien* 15th c., f. L. *āeri-us*: see AERIAL and -AN.] Of or belonging to the air or atmosphere; = AERIAL.

1652 BENLOWE *Theophila* VI. lxxxiii, He curbs aerian Potentates. **1865** *Morn. Star* 22 Feb., A lecture on aerian navigation.

†**a'erical**, *a. Obs. rare*[−1]. [f. L. *āer* air, after *atmospherical*.] = AERIAL.

1660 T. STANLEY *Hist. Philos.* (1701) 326/1 Qualities are Corporeal, for they are Spirits, and aerical Intentions.

aerie, aery, eyrie, eyry ('ɛərɪ, 'ɪərɪ). Forms: 6 ayerie, æiry, 6–7 airie, 7 aiery, ayrie, earie, 8 aeiry, 7–9 aerie, airy, aery; 7 eyerie, eyery, 7–9 eyrie, 8–9 eyry. [ad. med.L. *aeria*, *aerea*, (*aria*, *area*) prob. formed on Fr. *aire* with same sense. The etym. of the latter is doubtful; Littré classes it with other senses of *aire*:—L. *ārea* (also written *aria*) 'a spot of level ground, an open place, a threshing-floor'; whence 'surface plaine du rocher où l'aigle fait son nid.' Diez, comparing Pr. *aire*, takes 'family, race, stock' as the original idea, and suggests L. *ager* or *ātrium*; Wedgewood L. *āer* through the senses of 'climate, country, residence, family.' The probability rests between *ārea* and *ātrium*; the latter, as M. Paul Meyer notes, would account well for the dubiety of gender in OFr.; *aire* m.:—*ātrium*; *aire* f.:—*ātria*. The med.L. forms appear already in 12th c. The spelling EYRIE seems to have been introduced by Spelman (*Gl.* 1664) to support his notion of its derivation from *egg*, 'Dictum a Gallico *aire*: sed utrumque a Sax. *eghe*, Germanis et Anglo-Normanis [!] *eye*, i. *ovum*...unde nidus *eyerie* vocatur, quasi ovorum repositorium.' *Eyre* was an occas. spelling of AIRE, *ayre*, the earlier form in which the OFr. had itself been adopted in ME.]

1. The nest of any bird of prey; especially, in modern usage, of an eagle; also extended to that of ravens and other birds building high in the air; and *fig.* to a human residence or retreat perched high on a rock or mountain side.

[**1224** *Chart. Forest.* cap. 13 Unusquisque liber homo habeat in boscis suis aereas accipitrum, espernarum, falconum, aquilarum & hieronum.] **1581** LAMBARDE *Eirenarcha* II. vii. 277 To take yong pigeons or yong hawkes out of their nests (or airies). **1595** SHAKS. *John* v. ii. 149 And like an Eagle o're his ayerie towres. **1618** PULTON *Coll. Statutes* 6, *Chart. Forest.* (see above) xiii, Euery Freeman shall have within his own Woods ayries of Haukes, etc. **1622** MASSINGER *Maid of Hon.* (L.) One aiery with proportion, ne'er discloses The eagle and the wren. **1622** F. MARKHAM *Bk. Honour* I. iii. §1 An Object bright enough to trie the vertue of the best Eagle (bred in the Earie of Meditation). **1667** MILTON *P.L.* VII. 424 The eagle and the stork On cliffs and cedar tops thir eyries build. **1691** BLOUNT *Law Dict.* [from Spelman], Aery or Airy of Goshawks, *rectius* Eyery (from the French Eyre, i. *ova*). **1728** THOMSON *Spring* 451 Or where the hawk, High, in the beetling cliff, his aeiry builds. **1818** KEATS *Endym.* III. 94 Wherever beauty dwells, In gulf or aerie, mountains or deep dells. **1823** SCOTT *Peveril* I. i. 2 The principles on which an eagle selects her eyry. **1861**

F. W. JACOMB in *P.P. & Gl.* Ser. 2 I. 328 These men had, from their eyrie, seen us go up the glacier.

2. The brood in the nest; the young of a bird of prey, or *fig.* a noble stock of children.

1594 SHAKS. *Rich. III*, I. iii. 264 Our ayery buildeth in the Cedars top, And dallies with the winde, and scornes the Sunne. **1598** KITCHIN *Courts Leet* (1675) 114 Also if any.. take any Hauks or Æiry of Hauks. **1602** SHAKS. *Haml.* II. ii. 354 But there is Sir an ayrie of Children, little Yases, that crye out on the top of question; and are most tyrannically clap't for't. **1604** DRAYTON *The Owle* 859 The Fesant.. Seeking for safetie bred his Ayry there. **1613** W. BROWNE *Brit. Past.* II. iv. (1772) II. 140 As an eyerie from their seeges wood, Led o're the playnes and taught to get their food.

† **'aerie,** *v. Obs.* Also 7 **ayre, ayrie.** [f. prec. sb.] To build an aerie or nest.

1616 SURFLET & MARKH. *Countrey Farme* 79 [Storks] in the time of their ayring and bringing vp of their young ones .. doe ayre and neast themselues willingly also in the tops of high Towers. **1672** JOSSELYN *New Eng. Rarities* 41 She ayries in the woods upon the high hills.

aerie, variant of AERY *a.*

aerifaction (ˌɛərɪ'fækʃən). [f. AERIFY; see -FACTION.] The action of aerifying or charging with air.

1879 *Syd. Soc. Lex.*, Aerifaction of lung.

aeriferous (ˌɛə'rɪfərəs), *a.* Also 7 **airiferous.** [f. L. *āer* air + -FEROUS. Cf. mod.Fr. *aérifère*, possibly the direct model.] Bearing or conveying air.

1687 H. MORE *App. to Antidote* (1712) 232 Who have not only observ'd the succiferous but also airiferous vessels of Plants. **1868** DUNCAN *Insect World* Introd. 16 The body of the goat-moth caterpillar is traversed in all directions by 1,572 aeriferous tubes.

aerification (ˌɛərɪfɪ'keɪʃən). [mod. f. AERIFY; see -FICATION.]

1. 'The act of becoming air, or changing from a liquid or solid into an aëriform state.' Craig 1847.

2. The process of charging with air, 'the state of being filled with air' (Craig); aerifaction.

aeriform ('ɛərɪfɔːm), *a.* [f. L. *āer* air + -FORM. Cf. Fr. *aériforme.*]

1. Of the form of air or vapour, gaseous.

1782 KIRWAN in *Phil. Trans.* LXXII. 209 This intirely depends on the state of this same substance, which, when fixed and concrete, is called *phlogiston*, and, when rarified and aëriform, *inflammable* air. **1822** IMISON *Sc. & Art* I. 126 Pneumatics is the science which treats of the mechanical properties of elastic or aeriform fluids. **1860** PIESSE *Lab. Chem. Wonders* 125 Many gases which are only known to exist in an aëriform state in our climate, become first liquids, and then solid substances.

2. *fig.* Unsubstantial, intangible, unreal.

1828 CARLYLE *Misc.* (1857) I. 176 The figures light and aëriform, come unlooked for, and melt away abruptly. **1831** —— *Sart. Res.* (1858) 104 Of Man's Activity and Attainment the chief results are aeriform.

3. quasi-*sb.* An aeriform fluid; a gaseous body.

1865 MACVICAR in *Reader* No. 147. 462/3 The volumes of aëriforms.

aerify ('ɛərɪfaɪ), *v.* [f. L. *āer* air + -FY.]

1. To turn into vapour; to make aeriform.

fig. **1821** *New Monthly Mag.* II. 362 The first symptoms of that spirit of insubordination.. were probably viewed with equal contempt by the living.. and by their aerified predecessors. **1891** 'L. MALET' *Wages of Sin* II. v. iv. 224 The aerified pleasure-seeking little world of Tullingworth.

2. 'To combine with air; to infuse air into, to fill with air.' Craig 1847. = AERATE.

1858 *Jrnl. R. Agric. Soc.* XIX. 82 Lungs which aërify their blood.

aerish, variant of AIRISH *a. Obs.*, airy.

ærist, earlier form of ARIST. *Obs.*, arising.

ærn, obs. variant of EARN.

ærndrake, ærendrake. *Obs.*; see ERRAND.

aero- ('ɛərəʊ, now rarely 'eɪərəʊ), a. Gr. ἀερο-, combining form of ἀήρ, ἀέρα, air, the atmosphere, as in ἀερομετρέειν to measure the air, ἀεροσκοπία divination by observing the heavens, etc.

a. † **aero-elastic** (in form *aereo-elastic*), *a.* (see quot.); ˌ**aero-'embolism** *Path.* (see quot. 1939); **'aerogel** *Chem.*, a gel in which the liquid has been replaced by air or gas; **aˌero-'generator**, an electric generator operated by wind; **'aerograph** = AIR-*brush*; ˌ**aero-me'chanics**, the branch of mechanics which treats of the equilibrium and motion of air and other gases, and of bodies sustained in them; **a'ero-o'titis 'media** *Med.*, inflammation of the middle ear caused by a change in atmospheric pressure; cf. *aviator's ear* (AVIATOR 2 b); **aerophagia** (-'feɪdʒɪə) *Path.*, also **ae'rophagy** [ad. F. *aé rophagie* (M. L. Bouveret 1891, in *Rev. de Méd.* XI. 148): see -PHAGY], the swallowing of air; **aero'plankton** *Biol.*, a collective name for all the forms of minute organic life drifting in the air; also *attrib.*; ˌ**aerothera'peutics** (*Syd. Soc. Lex.*, 1881), **-'therapy** = PNEUMATOTHERAPEUTICS; **ae'rotropism** *Bot.* [ad. G. *aërotropismus* (H. Molisch 1885, in *Wiener Akad. Sitzungsber.* XC. I. 137), f. Gr. τροπή turning (τρέπειν to turn): see -ISM], the property, exhibited esp. by the growing roots of plants, of bending or turning towards a source of air; hence **aero'tropic** *a.*

1747 R. JAMES *Pharmacopœia Univ.* II. iii. 146 [Temperating medicines] operate by an expansive and *aereo-elastic Quality, such as that which is inherent to Nitre. **1939** H. G. ARMSTRONG *Aviation Med.* xxi. 342 *Aero-embolism may be defined as the disease produced by a rapid decrease of pressure below 1 atmosphere, such as may occur in aircraft flights to high altitude, and which is marked by the formation of nitrogen bubbles in the body tissues and fluids. **1923** W. E. GIBBS *Clouds & Smokes* vi. 112 Frequently a low specific gravity is due to the particles possessing the very open, spongy structure of an '*aerogel'. **1923** R. WHYTLAW-GRAY et al. in *Proc. R. Soc.* A. CII. 613 It seems likely that our thicker deposits of ZnO and CdO possess a conformation closely analogous to many gels, and the term 'aerogel' suggested by Prof. Donnan is not inappropriate. **1951** *Sci. News Let.* 1 Sept. 144/1 The modern napalm bomb.. contains a silica aerogel. **1946** P. H. THOMAS (*title*) The Wind Power *Aerogenerator. *Ibid.* (Foreword), This study was made to determine the character of structures suitable for aerogenerators devoted to utility power supply. **1898** *Brit. Jrnl. Photogr.* 29 Apr. 274/1 Enlargements finished with the *aerograph in water colours. **1939** *Archit. Rev.* LXXXV. 101 (*caption*) Detail of a panel by Sigmund Pollitzer, on polished black glass, using a fine aerograph-type sand-gun nozzle which enables the sandblaster to direct the blast accurately and, by reducing the pressure, obtain gradations of tone. **1909** *Cent. Dict.* Suppl., *Aero-mechanics. **1938** *Jrnl. R. Aeronaut. Soc.* XLII. 394 A very old and fundamental principle of aeromechanics. **1937** ARMSTRONG & HEIM in *Jrnl. Amer. Med. Assoc.* 7 Aug. 419/1 In the United States the term 'aviator's or aviation ear' has begun to appear in the literature, while in Germany the terms 'barotrauma' and 'tonetrauma' have been suggested. The former are obviously unsuitable and the latter may be criticized as not being descriptive of the disease. We therefore suggest '*aero-otitis media'.. as a suitable descriptive term. **1949** *Lancet* 14 May 826/1 Clinical observations on aero-otitis media in aviators, compressed-air workers, and subjects in low-pressure-chamber tests. **1901** *Lancet* 30 Mar. 953/1 In certain cases *aerophagia takes a grave form: it produces vomiting, aggravates the dyspepsia, and leads to emaciation. *Ibid.* 953/2 In horses aerophagia is a recognized disorder and is known to horse-dealers in France as 'tic à l'air'. **1901** DORLAND *Med. Dict.* (ed. 2) 26/1 *Aerophagy. **1932** FULLER & CONARD tr. *Braun-Blanquet's Plant Sociol.* iv. 76 The quantitative investigation of the edaphon and *aeroplankton is still in its infancy, and one must be content [with].. an approximate idea of the great wealth of species of air and soil floras. **1938** *Nature* 7 May 828/1 The possible importance of the aeroplankton yeasts as virus carriers is not, of course, limited to the case of foot-and-mouth disease. **1894** C. T. WILLIAMS (*title*) *Aero-Therapeutics, or the Treatment of Lung Diseases by Climate. **1876** *Sci. Amer.* 29 July 63/1 *Aerotherapy.. Air.. is forced by steam power and kept at a pressure somewhat above that of the open atmosphere. Dr. Carlo Forlanini is the discoverer and advocate of this treatment. **1918** *Lancet* 30 Nov. 757/1 His.. suggestions.. about aerotherapy, hydrotherapy, poultices. **1889** *Cent. Dict.*, *Aërotropism. **1898** H. C. PORTER tr. *Strasburger's Text-Bk. Bot.* I. II. 263 Thermotropism.. Rheotropism.. and Aerotropism, a form of chemotropism, are additional phenomena, which have been distinguished as arising from the special action of external stimuli. *Ibid.* 281 The pollen grain then grows out into a tube which is acted upon by chemotropic (including hydrotropic and aerotropic) influences. **1919** F. O. BOWER *Bot. Living Plant* viii. 128 Such plants are described as 'pot-bound'. This condition is due to the fact that the roots grow towards a source of free oxygen... Such a response is styled aerotropism, and roots curving towards the source are positively aerotropic.

b. With reference to aircraft, aviation, travel or conveyance by aircraft, or to operations conducted by aircraft; also in various names of aircraft or their parts: as † ***aero-biplane, -bus, -car, -cycle, -engine, -meteorograph,*** † ***-motion, -photography*** (hence ***-photographic*** adj.), † ***-screw,*** † ***-surface,*** † ***-taxi,*** † ***-traffic; aero-chemical, -marine, -medical, -naval*** adjs.; also **aero club**, a club for the pursuit and promotion of aviation; also † ***aero meet,*** † ***race;*** † **aero-curve**, an occasional substitute for AEROPLANE (senses 1 and 2 b); † **aerodone** (-dəʊn), **-do'netics** (see quots.); **'aerodyne** (-daɪn) [back-formation from AERODYNAMIC *a.*], a generic term for heavier-than-air aircraft; † **aeromotive** [F. *aéromotive*, after *locomotive*], a heavier-than-air aircraft; also *attrib.*; **'aero-'motor** † (*a*) a heavier-than-air aircraft; (*b*) an aircraft motor (Funk, 1928) (chiefly *U.S.*); † **aeronat** [ad. F. *aéronat* (1889 *Aéronaute* 158), f. L. *natāre* to swim]: see quot. 1908; **aero-towing**, the towing of a glider by a light aeroplane to a height suitable for launching; also **aero-tow**, an instance of aero-towing; **a'erotrain** [ad. F. *aérotrain*], a prototype high-speed train supported on an air cushion and guided by a track (never put into full service).

1874 *Ann. Rep. Aëronaut. Soc.*, The *Aero-bi-plane or First Steps to Flight. **1906** *Daily Chron.* 11 Dec. 6/6 '*Aerobus' might be preferred [to 'airvan']. **1913** *Daily Mail* 4 Oct. 6 The Grahame-White aerobus established a new passenger-carrying record by taking up nine passengers. **1960** *Aeroplane* XCIX. 850/1 To date, the transport helicopter has been most successful in airline service as a special purpose vehicle ('aerobus') transferring passengers between airports in the Chicago and New York areas. **1965** *Guardian* 10 Feb. 1/1 The Minister.. announced that discussions were in progress for 'an aerobus' to provide cheap travel for large numbers. **1910** *Flight* 13 Aug. 634/2 Airmen.. are either Aeronauts or Aviators, according as the *Aerocar that they control is an Airship or an Aeroplane. **1926** *Chambers's Jrnl.* 14 Aug. 581/2 Aero-cars may take off from here. **1937** *Daily Herald* 16 Apr. 10/3 The second stage of an *aero-chemical attack will be the passing down of fluid poisons stored, under pressure or not, in containers carried by aircraft. **1900** *Science* XII. 799/1 Through the cooperation of the *Aëro Club, balloon races were organized. **1894** J. MEANS in *Aeronaut. Ann. 1895* 157 The design here given calls for aeroplanes as being more easily made than *aerocurves modelled after the wings of birds. **1897** O. CHANUTE in *Aeronaut. Ann.* 41 The first machine which was repaired.. was the aerocurve, with three superposed fixed surfaces. **1901** *Flying* Dec. 17 The twin-screw propelled 'aerocurve machine'. **1902** F. WALKER *Aërial Navig.* 115 Aeroplanes and Aerocurves. When these are made of fabric, yacht duck may be employed. **1901** *Sci. Amer.* 2 Mar. 130/3 Mortureux; *aerocycle with four wings. **1957** *Britannica Bk. of Yr. 1956* 512/1 *Aerocycle*, a small helicopter for use by combat infantrymen. **1907** F. W. LANCHESTER *Aerodynamics* 393 *Aerodone, from the Greek ἀερο-δόνητος, lit. *tossed in mid air; soaring.* To denote a gliding or soaring model or machine; in particular, any gliding or soaring appliance destitute of propelling apparatus or auxiliary parts; in contradistinction to *aerodrome*. *Ibid.*, *Aerodonetics*, the science specially involved in problems connected with the stability or equilibrium of an aerodone or aerodrome, or of birds in flight, and with the phenomenon of soaring. **1908** *Daily Report* 21 Nov. 2/4 'Aerodone' denotes a motorless flying machine, a glider. **1906** W. TURNBULL in *Sci. Amer.* 211/1 *Aerodyne. **1907** —— in *Physical Rev.* XXIV. 285, I use the word 'aërodyne' in preference to 'flying-machines', to denote an aëroplane-supported machine, driven by mechanical power through the air. **1934** *Shell Aviation News* No. 32. 4 There are specialists in engines, heavier-than-air craft (aerodynes), [etc.]. **1913** *Aeroplane* 6 Feb. 124/2 'Aero', which Mr. O'Gorman suggested as an abbreviation for aero-plane, is useful as a prefix, for instance in aero-show, *aero-engine, and so forth. **1963** *Listener* 17 Jan. 124/1 Rolls-Royce are to put 16,000 employees in their aero-engine division on short time. **1917** H. WOODHOUSE *Textbk. Naval Aeronautics* 100 (*caption*) The 125 horse-power *Aeromarine hydro-aeroplane. **1937** *Jrnl. R. Aëronaut. Soc.* XLI. 634 *Aeromedical research (esp. the chemistry of breathing). **1962** *Flight Internat.* LXXXI. 262/2 The 'aeromedical observer', a doctor, monitors the astronaut's physical condition. **1910** *Boston Daily Globe* 4 Sept. 21/1 *Aero meet. **1945** C. P. LENT *Rocket Research* 74/1 Friez-type *aero-meteorographs. **1878** *Ann. Rep. Aeronaut. Soc.* 44 In no case in which man has succeeded in fast locomotion by machines has he rigidly copied nature, and in every case he has beaten it. In *aeromotion man will do the same. **1881** W. D. HAY *300 Yrs. Hence* ix. 214 Health.. has been marvellously improved by the universal custom of aëromotion. **1865** C. H. TURNOR *Astra Castra* vii. 256 The balloon can only therefore be.. the prologue; the true piece is the *aeromotive, which supersedes the balloon. **1868** *Aëronaut. Soc., Catal. First Exhib.* 11 Model of an Aeromotive Engine. **1902** F. WALKER *Aërial Navig.* p. viii, The construction of dirigible balloons, aërostats, aëroplanes, and aëromotors to be.. illustrated by various types already made. *Ibid.* p. ix, The aëromotor or air-ship will always be of great value. **1935** 'J. GUTHRIE' *Little Country* vi. 139, I am working on the boat.. a hundred horse-power Curtis Vth aero-motor in her. **1903** *Aeronaut. Jrnl.* 41 A steerable balloon [is called] an *aëronat. **1908** *Daily Report* 21 Nov. 2/4 'Aeronat' is a dirigible, motor-driven balloon or airship. **1959** *Economist* 21 Feb. 663/1 United States *aero-naval strength in the Formosa Strait. **1918** H. WOODHOUSE *Textbk. Mil. Aeronautics* 93/2 Detailed description of the British *aerophotographic organization will be of great assistance. **1918** E. S. FARROW *Dict. Mil. Terms* 9 **Aëro-photography*, the art of photographing from aëroplanes or airships. **1939** *Geogr. Jrnl.* XCIII. 331 If.. we ever undertake contouring of the Highlands of Scotland.. the best way to do it will be by means of aerophotography and a plotting machine. **1912** *World Alman.* (N.Y.) 432 Cross-country *Aero Races European Circuit Race. **1902** *Flying* June 135 Studying this matter of aerocurves and *aeroscrews. **1894** J. D. FULLERTON in *Proc. Internat. Conf. Aerial Navig.* 241 Sustainer, or *aerosurface, which rests on the air. **1902** *Aeronaut. World* (U.S.) 1 Oct. 65/2 Hofman's Flying Machine.. is furnished with three large square flat aero-surfaces. **1904** J. FULLERTON *Rep. Aerial Navig.* 1 Aero-surfaces, or Flying Machines proper. **1909** *Flight* 2 Jan. 14 In the aeroplane we have something new, something that is not standardised down, and commercialised so far as to have *aero-taxis and aero-buses. **1971** N. ELLISON *Brit. Gliders & Sailplanes* ii. 20 Winch launching from these long runways gave a good launch height, and aerodromes.. eased the introduction of *aero-tow launching. **1978** A. WELCH *Bk. Airsports* ii. 40/1 But, if the glider pilot thinks he would like an aerotow back home, it is no good his ending up in any small meadow. **1938** *Times* 3 May 13/3 Yet there are two gliding clubs in England which have so far been unable to persuade the local light aeroplane clubs to arrange for *aero-towing. **1978** A. WELCH *Bk. Airsports* ii. 39/1 (*caption*) Aerotowing is a satisfactory means of launching because the glider can be taken to a suitable area of sky to start soaring. **1906** *Lancet* 15 Dec. 1674/1 (*title*) *Aero-traffic. **1965** *Guardian* 12 May 12/7 France is going ahead with a study of an '*aerotrain' system that would link cities at speeds of between 125 and 240 miles an hour... The train would ride on a monorail, suspended on a cushion of air of the Hovercraft kind. **1967** *Jane's Surface Skimmer Syst. 1967–68* 52 (*caption*) The experimental Aerotrain has attained 188 mph.. over its 4.2 mile.. long test track with the aid of a booster rocket. **1971** *Daily Tel.* (Colour Suppl.) 6 Aug. 13/3 The French have.. been working on 'aerotrains' and two are in advanced experimental operation. Riding on a cushion of air as they straddle a high central 'rail', these trains reach speeds up to 200 mph. **1977** R. WHITAKER *Fodor's Railways of World* 140 The aerotrain test track can be seen from the SNCF main line near Orleans.

aerobate ('ɛərəʊbeɪt), *v. rare.* [a. Gr. ἀεροβατέ-ειν, f. ἀερο- air + βατέ-ειν to tread.] To walk (as if) on the air.

1835 *Aristophanes' Clouds* in *Blackw. Mag.* XXXVIII. 520 *Str.* Pray who's that in the basket hung up in the air?.. Do tell me, I pray, what you're doing up there. *Soc.* Aerobating—sun-musing, pacing air.

aerobatics (-'bætɪks), *sb. pl.* [After *acrobatics*.] Feats of expert aviation, performed esp. for display. Hence **aero'batic** *a.*; **'aerobat**, one who performs aerobatics; hence as *v. intr.*, to perform aerobatics; also *trans.*

1917 'CONTACT' *Airman's Outings* 128 Watching the aerobatics and sham fights of the pool pupils. **1918** H. BARBER *Aerobatics* II. 58 There are many who.. will never shine as aerobatic pilots. **1929** *N. & Q.* CLVII. 359/2 The word *aerobat*.. is now used for an airman who does 'stunts'. **1930** *Flight* XXII. 659/1 Mr. George Murray aerobated in Capt. Broad's special Moth. **1943** T. HORSLEY *Find, Fix & Strike* 43 The pupil who 'shows off'.. or who can never take an aircraft up without aerobating it. **1955** *Times* 20 Aug. 2/5 The merit of aerobatics is that everything depends on the skill of the pilot. **1961** C. B. SMITH *Testing Time* iii. 44 Gustav Hamel, the brilliant aerobat.. was summoned by the King to Windsor to demonstrate his looping of the loop.

aerobe ('eɪərəʊb, 'ɛərəʊb). *Biol.* [ad. F. *aérobie* (Pasteur, see ANAEROBE), f. Gr. ἀήρ air + βίος life.] One of a group (*Aerobia*) of micro-organisms which live on free oxygen derived from the air. So **ae'robian, ae'robious** *adjs.*, living on the oxygen of the air; of the nature of or pertaining to aerobes; **ˌaerobi'osis**, life sustained by the oxygen of the air; **ˌaerobi'otic** (-'ɒtɪk) *a.*, pertaining to or characterized by aerobiosis, aerobic.

1879 FAULKNER & ROBB tr. *Pasteur's Ferment.* 210 The first aërobian ferment. *Ibid.*, An aërobious ferment. **1885** VINES in *Encycl. Brit.* XIX. 51/2 In aerobiotic plants the normal processes of destructive metabolism.. may be replaced for a.. time by those abnormal processes of which fermentation is the outward expression. **1886** *Buck's Handbk. Med. Sci.* III. 64/1 Those [micro-organisms] which thrive only with free oxygen; these he calls *aerobes*. **1896** *Allbutt's Syst. Med.* I. 513 Obligatory aerobes, which must be supplied with oxygen. **1933** *Biol. Abstr.* 1929 III. 2332/3 Bacteriophagy and aerobiosis. **1959** *Times Lit. Suppl.* 27 Mar. 183/2 He will know.. the meaning of an aerobiosis, the action of sulphate-producing bacteria, [etc.].

aerobic (ɛə'rəʊbɪk), *a.* [f. AEROBE + -IC.]

1. Requiring or utilizing free oxygen in the air for metabolic purposes; involving the presence of air, containing air.

1884 [see ANAEROBIC *a.*]. **1900** *Jrnl. Soc. Arts* XLVIII. 387/2 A larger number of bacteria were.. facultatively aerobic. **1949** H. W. FLOREY et al. *Antibiotics* I. II. ii. 76 One incubation may be aerobic and the other anaerobic. **1951** J. P. MARBARGER *Space Medicine* 36 The most important energy source of the organisms, the biological oxidation or aerobic respiration, is a process during which the body's nutritive substances.. are slowly combusted into water and carbon dioxide by oxygen. **1958** *Times Rev. Industry* Sept. 40/3 Aerobic fermentations. **1968** A. WHITE et al. *Princ. Biochem.* (ed. 4) x. 220 There are a number of aerobic oxidases which can utilize oxygen directly. **1968** PASSMORE & ROBSON *Compan. Med. Stud.* I. xlii. 4/1 Aerobic metabolism. **1972** *McGraw-Hill Yearbk. Sci. & Technol.* 379/1 In the surface oxygenated or aerobic soil layer, microbial and chemical conditions are very much like those in drained soil. **1975** J. G. EVANS *Environment Early Man Brit. Isles* v. 92 Peaty raw humus... Its formation takes place in an aerobic situation in which bacterial activity is inhibited by the acidic state of the vegetation. **1981** D. J. & T. J. BELLAMY *Bellamy's Backyard Safari* 69 The formation of collagen, which is an important component of all muscles, is an aerobic process (that is, it requires oxygen).

2. Of or pertaining to aerobics.

1968 K. H. COOPER *Aerobics* iii. 40 Please note where the aerobic effect began. Not in tensing your muscles.. but in walking.. about 3½ miles, up and down hills. **1978** *Guardian Weekly* 30 Apr. 20/1 The aerobic capacity, reflecting the efficiency of the lungs, the power of the heart, and the state of the vascular system, is the best single index of overall physical fitness. **1978** *Detroit Free Press* 16 Apr. C1/3 He had to work at 80 percent of his aerobic power (the maximum amount or volume of oxygen he can consume in one minute). **1983** *Observer* (Colour Suppl.) 5 June 42/1 They have introduced obsessiveness into the fun of exercise by insisting that you use stopwatches and keep taking your pulse to ensure that you are getting 'good' aerobic exercise and not 'bad' anaerobic. **1986** *Here's Health* Apr. 11/3 A good overall regime would combine weight training with an aerobic exercise like running.. to improve stamina.

ae'robically, *adv.* [f. AEROBIC *a.* + -AL[1] + -LY[2].] With a metabolic use of oxygen; in an aerobic environment.

1887 A. M. BROWN *Anim. Alkaloids* 117 Four-fifths of our tissues live aerobically; and.. the remaining fifth part.. lives anaerobically, that is, after the fashion of putrid ferment. **1962** HARRIS & GRUBER in A. Pirie *Lens Metabolism Rel. Cataract* 376 Endogenous substrates, metabolized aerobically, are capable of maintaining cation transport to at least some degree. **1971** *Nature* 3 Dec. 301/1 Mammalian spermatozoa depend for their supply of energy on extracellular sources, chiefly in the form of fructose which they utilize anaerobically and aerobically. **1984** *Jrnl. Solar Energy Engin.* CVI. 351 Five experimental runs were conducted.. to account for all weather conditions utilizing aerobically digested waste activated sludge.

aerobics (ɛə'rəʊbɪks), *sb. pl.* (const. as *sing.* or *pl.*). orig. *U.S.* [f. AEROBIC *a.*: see -IC 2.] (A method of) physical exercise for producing beneficial changes in the respiratory and circulatory systems by activities which require only a modest increase in oxygen intake and so can be maintained.

1968 K. H. COOPER *Aerobics* iii. 40 After five hours of that [*sc.* golf] you've walked well past the point where anaerobics leave off and aerobics begin. **1968** *Chicago Tribune* 9 July 1. 12/3 Under the aerobics program, a person is awarded a number of points according to the amount of exercise he does each week. **1972** *Washington Post* 16 Apr. E24/4 Aerobics stresses getting the heart, lungs and circulatory system fit. **1982** *Observer* 18 July 25/1 Aerobics have become the latest fitness craze. **1983** *Daily Tel.* 9 Nov. 19/4 If a class is billed as aerobics, your teacher should have a certificate gained in America. **1986** P. BOOTH *Palm Beach* ii. 31 The air-waves of the small, stuffy gym reverberated with the insistent drum notes as thirty pairs of track shoes beat out the rhythm of the aerobics routine.

ˌaerobi'ology. [f. AERO- + BIOLOGY.] The study of airborne micro-organisms or spores and their distribution, esp. as agents of infection. Hence **ˌaerobio'logical** *a.*; **ˌaerobi'ologist.**

1937 *Biol. Abstr.* XI. 2348/2 Aerobiology. **1942** F. R. MOULTON *Aerobiology* p. iii, Although aerobiology has developed as a specialized field of investigation only within the past ten or fifteen years, it had its origin in the pioneer experiments of Spallanzani, in 1776, and in the work of Pasteur, Tyndall and others who used the methods of the aerobiologist.. in combating the theory of spontaneous generation of life. *Ibid.* 1/2 Agriculture and medicine appear to be the general fields in which there is greatest present need for aerobiological investigations. **1951** *Nature* 27 Oct. 721/2 (*caption*) Exposures on aerobiological flight IV of 1947. **1957** H. A. HYDE in *Nature* 4 May 890/1 Aerobiology may be defined as the study of the aerial transport of plants and animals or viable parts thereof, including flying animals (such as insects) in so far as passive movement is a major factor in their dispersal.

aerocyst ('ɛərəʊsɪst). *Bot.* [mod. f. AERO- + κύστ-ις bladder: see CYST.] 'The air-cells of algals.' Lindley *Treas. Bot.*

aerodrome ('ɛərədrəʊm). [In sense 1, ad. Gr. ἀεροδρόμος *a.*, running through or traversing the air; in sense 2, f. AERO- + Gr. δρόμος course, racecourse (cf. *hippodrome*).]

†1. S. P. Langley's name for an aeroplane: = AEROPLANE 2 b. Also *attrib. Obs.*

1891 S. P. LANGLEY *Exper. Aerodynamics* 49 An actual working aerodrome model with its motor. **1896** A. G. BELL in *Smithsonian Rep.* 6 Witnessing the successful flight of some of these aerodromes. **1907** [see *aerodone* s.v. AERO- b]. **1908** G. H. BRYAN in *Nature* 29 Oct. 668 Mr. Farman mounted with M. Delagrange on the latter's aërodrome, which flew a considerable distance with a heavy load.

2. **†a.** A place where a balloon or flying-machine is housed; a hangar [Fr. *aérodrome*]. *Obs. rare.*

1902 *Westm. Gaz.* 29 Jan. 6/2 He.. soared above the Prince's castle to the aerodrome. **1921** M. CORELLI *Secret Power* viii. 79 The building.. was easily recognisable as a huge aerodrome. *Ibid.* 80 The lady of many millions had commanded an air-ship to be built.. with an aerodrome for its safe keeping and anchorage.

b. (The current sense.) A large tract of open, level ground, together with the runways, hangars and other installations, for the operation of aircraft. Also *attrib.*

1909 F. LANCHESTER in *Flight* 2 Jan. 13/1, I regret to see that the misuse of the word 'aerodrome' is receiving support in your columns... I suppose because a hippodrome is a big open space for horses, you think that an aerodrome should be a big open space for flying machines. **1909** *Flight* 20 Feb. 104/1 *Aerodrome*, a field or place set apart for the practice of flight. **1911** GRAHAME-WHITE & HARPER *Aeroplane* iv. 124 A circle had been whitewashed on the aerodrome.. to act as a mark in which the aviators were to descend. **1922** *Encycl. Brit.* XXX. 48/1 The London terminal aerodrome at Croydon, Sur., may be taken as typical of a modern air-port for commercial traffic. **1934** *Jrnl. R. Aeronaut. Soc.* XXXVIII. 725 There was erected the aerodrome beacon. **1959** *Chambers's Encycl.* I. 95/2 Siting requirements for aerodromes often conflict, as when a city lying in a valley or close to a mountain range must be served.

†aero'dromic, *a. Obs.* [f. prec. + -IC.] Pertaining to flying-machines; **†aero'dromics**, the art of constructing and using flying-machines.

1891 S. P. LANGLEY *Exper. Aerodynamics* 5 The yet inchoate art of constructing suitable mechanisms for guiding heavy bodies through the air.. which art.. I will provisionally call aerodromics. **1894** CHASE & KIRCHNER (*title*) The Coming Railroad: The Chase-Kirchner Aerodromic System of Transportation. **1896** A. G. BELL in *Smithsonian Rep.* 6 Investigations connected with aerodromic problems.

aerodynamic : see next

aerodynamics (ˌɛərəʊdɪ'næmɪks, ˌɛərəʊdaɪ'næmɪks). [f. AERO- + DYNAMICS, *i.e.* the dynamics of aerial bodies. Cf. Fr. *aérodynamique*.] The branch of Pneumatics which treats of air and other gases in motion, and of their mechanical effects. Hence **ˌaerody'namic** *a.* [cf. G. *aerodynamische* (1835)], pertaining to aerodynamics [cf. DYNAMICS[1]], esp. to the effects produced on aircraft or other solid bodies by the air through which they pass, or the effects produced in air by the motion of solid bodies through it.

In quot. 1891, the art of flying through the air by some mechanism, the use of flying-machines, aviation.

1837 *Pop. Encycl.* I. 45 Aerodynamics; a branch of aerology, or the higher mechanics, which treats of the powers and motion of elastic fluids. **1868** CHAMBERS *Encycl.* I. 56 One of the most important inquiries in Aerodynamics is the resistance offered to a body moving in air, or—which is the same thing—the pressure exerted by air in motion upon a body at rest. **1891** S. P. LANGLEY (*title*) Experiments in Aerodynamics. **1908** W. H. STORY tr. *Hildebrandt's Airships* ix. 90 Aerodynamic airships. **1920** *Advis. Comm. Aeronautics, Rep. & Mem.* No. 651, p. 5 Aerodynamic balance of the aileron. **1922** *Edin. Rev.* Oct. 214 The improvements in range and aerodynamic and engine efficiency of aircraft. **1923** GLAZEBROOK *Dict. Appl. Physics* V. 199/2 *The Main Aerodynamic Balance*.. This balance was designed so that it could be used to measure forces about three axes perpendicular to one another and the moment about a vertical axis. **1935** *Jrnl. R. Aeronaut. Soc.* XXXIX. 826 With regard to the use of sponsons or stubs, he had understood Mr. Coombes to say that one could reckon on some aerodynamic lift from the stub. **1936** *Aircraft Engin.* Sept. 241/2 The idealized case is that of a monoplane in which the aerodynamic centres of the wing and tail plane lie in one straight line. **1949** *Jrnl. R. Aeronaut. Soc.* LIII. 659/2 It provided new incentives for understanding stability and control.. aerodynamic heating.. and similar general problems. **1950** *Gloss. Aeronaut. Terms (B.S.I.)* I. 28 *Aerodynamic balance*, a balance designed for measuring aerodynamic forces or moments. **1950** *Sci. News* XV. 83 Rockets are powerful research tools... Their value in aerodynamics lies in their ability to propel full-sized or model aircraft.. at supersonic speeds in order that the unknown aerodynamic forces in play at these speeds can be measured. **1962** *Gloss. Aeronaut. Terms (B.S.I.)* I *Aerodynamic centre*, the point about which the rate of change of pitching moment with incidence is zero. *Ibid.* 5 *Aerodynamic balance*, the degree to which the hinge moment of a control surface is reduced by balancing.

So **ˌaerody'namical** *a.*, **-ally** *adv.*; **ˌaerody'namicist**, one skilled in aerodynamics.

1908 *Aeronaut. Jrnl.* 84 The design and perfection of true aërodynamical flying ships of the future. **1921** *Glasgow Herald* 8 Sept. 10/2 Department for aerodynamical research. **1928** C. F. S. GAMBLE *North Sea Air Station* x. 147 The Wight seaplane.. was of similar type to the Short, but its aerodynamical qualities were inferior to its prototype. *Ibid.* xiii. 210 Aerodynamically, it was of interest in being fitted with an air-brake in the form of adjustable flaps. **1939** *Jrnl. R. Aeronaut. Soc.* XLIII. 138 It is their duty to co-ordinate the efforts of the draughtsmen,.. designers and aerodynamicists. **1960** [see next].

aeroelasticity (ˌɛərəʊiːlæ'stɪsɪtɪ). [f. AERO- + ELASTICITY, cf. *photo-elasticity*.] **a.** A branch of mechanics dealing with the effects of aerodynamic forces on elastic bodies; esp. the non-rigid structures of aircraft; **b.** the quality of being liable to distortion by aerodynamic forces. Hence **ˌaeroe'lastic** *a.*; **ˌaeroe'lastics** *sb. pl.*, aeroelasticity (sense a); **ˌaeroela'stician**, one skilled in aeroelasticity.

1935 *Aircraft Engin.* Oct. 261/2 This branch of study, which might appropriately be labelled 'aero-elasticity', is steadily increasing in importance. **1936** *Aeronaut. Res. Comm., Techn. Rep.* 1934–35 II. 748 It was found to permit of a very convenient treatment of the aerodynamics of the reversal of aileron control problem, and applications in other 'aero-elastic' problems may be possible. **1938** *Aircraft Engin.* Mar. 73/2 With increasing speeds and the consequent continued expansion of the field of aero-elasticity, stiffness and test methods are being applied.. to wings. **1946** *Jrnl. R. Aeronaut. Soc.* L. 613 The developments in aeroelastic science during the past ten years. **1946** *Nature* 21 Dec. 897/1 The problems of aero-elasticity are.. complicated by the fact that the wings are swept back. **1947** *Jrnl. R. Aeronaut. Soc.* LI. 418/2 (*caption*) The aeroelastician's viewpoint showing mechanical vibration as outlying territory of the aeroelastic domain. **1960** *Times* 24 Oct. 2/6 Aerodynamicists.. are required for the following sections:- Aeroelastics, Stability and Control, [etc.]. **1962** *New Scientist* 8 Nov. 344/1 (Advt.), *Senior Aeroelastician*. This post is suitable for a graduate.. who has acquired a number of years experience working on aeroelastic problems of aircraft or missiles.

'aerofoil. [f. AERO- b + FOIL *sb.*[1]] A wing, aileron, tailplane or other lifting surface of an aircraft; any surface designed on similar principles; also *attrib.*, and applied to a type of ship's propeller (see quot. 1948).

1907 F. W. LANCHESTER *Aerodynamics* v. 179 The author does not employ the term *aeroplane* outside its correct signification, that is to say, to denote other than a true or *plane* aeroplane; the misuse of the word being avoided by the introduction of the word aerofoil, to denote a supporting member, or organ of sustentation of undefined form. **1914** *Aeronaut. Jrnl.* XVIII. 315 *Aerofoil*, a structure, analogous to the wing or tail of a bird, designed to obtain a reaction from the air approximately at right angles to the direction of its motion. **1920** *Conquest* I. 437/1 The effects of air-flow upon various aerofoil surfaces. **1931** *Discovery* May 147/2 The general use of what is now known as 'aerofoil' blade propellers. **1948** R. DE KERCHOVE *Internat. Maritime Dict.* (1958) 5/1 *Aerofoil propeller*, a propeller designed in accord with aerodynamic principles based on the circulation theory instead of as a true screw... The margin of efficiency of the aerofoil propeller over the true screw is about 10 to 12%. **1950** *Engineering* 24 Mar. 333/3 The propellers [of a launch] are of the standard.. type in which vertical aerofoil-section blades are fitted. **1959** *Chamber's Encycl.* XIV. 612/1 In 1923 aerofoils were first fitted to the leading edges of normal windmill sails by Dekker in the Netherlands. **1961** *Spectator* 14 July 53 Part of the aerofoil lift develops as the forward speed on the cushion increases.

aerognosy (ˌɛəˈrɒgnəsɪ). [f. AERO- + Gr. -γνωσία knowledge.] That part of science that treats of the properties of the air.
1847 in CRAIG.

ˈaerogram. [f. AERO- + -GRAM.] **1.** A message sent 'through the air', i.e. by radio.
1899 *Daily News* 20 Nov. 7/1 'Wanted, a new name for wireless telegraphy', Miss Collett, Hyde-park-mansions, suggests..'Aerogram'. **1901** *Westm. Gaz.* 20 Dec. 6/2 (*heading*) Halfpenny-a-word aerograms.
2. An X-ray photograph of an organ injected with air.
1935 DORLAND & MILLER *Med. Dict.* (ed. 17) 53/1 *Aerogram*, a roentgenogram of an organ after it has been injected with air.
3. = *air letter* s.v. AIR *sb.*[1] B III. 1. (In quot. 1920, a telegram conveyed on part of its journey by aeroplane.)
1920 *Discovery* June 173/1 The rates could be..3*d.* for letters, 1*s.* for aerograms..in addition..to local telegram rates. **1967** C. DRUMMOND *Death at Furlong Post* xi. 136 If ever you get an enquiry.., just paste letters from a piper [*sc.* paper] inside an aerogram. **1973** *Whig-Standard* (Kingston, Ontario) 18 Oct. 31/5 The domestogram..is similar to aerograms now used for mail abroad. **1982** *Daily Tel.* 8 May 6/5 Aerogram letters to British troops in the Task Force are to be carried free of charge.

aerogramme (ˈɛərəʊgræm). [a. F. *aérogramme.*] = AEROGRAM 3.
[**1954** tr. *Universal Postal Convention Provisions 1952* 119 in *Parl. Papers 1953–4* (Cmd. 9190) XXXII. 573 The aérogramme consists of a sheet of paper suitably folded and gummed, the size of which, in that form, shall be that of a postcard.] **1964** H. ROBINSON *Carrying British Mails Overseas* xxiv. 302 The folded air-letter form..has..been generally adopted..throughout the world. The Congress of the Universal Postal Union held at Brussels in 1952 provided for its general use. The front of the folded form was to bear the word *Aerogramme* and a similar indication such as 'Air Letter' in the language of the country. **1970** *N.Z. News* 8 Apr. 3/4 From October 1, 1973, the universal standardising of letter envelope formats will mean a new shape for the New Zealand aerogramme. **1979** T. BENN *Arguments for Socialism* 14 My brother Michael..and I corresponded about socialism and religion by airletter and aerogramme. **1982** N. GORDIMER in *Lit. Rev.* Oct. 44/3 There his letter was, among circulars from film clubs, bills, and aerogrammes with 'And when are you coming over' scribbled on the back.

aerographer (ˌɛəˈrɒgrəfə(r)). [f. AEROGRAPHY + -ER[1].] One who undertakes the description of the atmosphere.
1889 in *Cent. Dict.* **1945** *Jane's Fighting Ships 1943–44* 432/1 (*caption*) Aerographer [in U.S. Navy].

aerographic (ˌɛərəʊˈgræfɪk), *a.* [f. AEROGRAPHY + -IC.] Pertaining to aërography.

aerographical (ˌɛərəʊˈgræfɪkəl), *a.* [f. prec. + -AL[1].] = prec.

aerography (ˌɛəˈrɒgrəfɪ). [ad. Fr. *aérographie*, f. Gr. ἀήρ, ἀέρα, the air + -γραφία description, f. γράφ-ειν to write: see -GRAPHY.] Description of the atmosphere.
1753 CHAMBERS *Cycl. Supp.*, *Aerography*, a description of the air, or atmosphere, its limits, dimensions, properties, etc. **1818** in TODD. **1918** E. S. FARROW *Dict. Mil. Terms* 9 *Aërography*, the study of the structure of the atmosphere and charting the physical conditions at all levels. The work is done principally by kites, and balloons. **1920** *Nature* 17 June 479/2 The substitution of the new name aerography for the older meteorology has not changed the leopard's spots.

aerohydrous (ˌɛərəʊˈhaɪdrəs), *a.* [mod. f. AERO- + HYDR- (= Gr. ὕδωρ water) + -OUS. Cf. Fr. *aérohydre.*] 'Applied to minerals which contain water in their cavities.' Craig 1847.

aerolite (ˈɛərəʊlaɪt). [An alteration of AEROLITH, assimilating the ending to those of minerals in -ITE.] A stone or portion of matter which has fallen to the earth from, or rather through, the atmosphere; a meteoric stone, or meteorite. In recent usage, the name *aerolite* has been confined to those meteorites which consist of stone or other substance than meteoric iron: see AEROSIDERITE.
1815 *Encycl. Brit.* Supp. I. 65 *Aerolite*, a term recently but perhaps improperly applied to those singular substances called meteoric stones. **1870** TYNDALL *Heat* i. §12. 11 The velocity of the aërolites varies from 18 to 36 miles a second. **1881** BROOKS *Candle of the Lord* 133 God does not fling His hero like an aërolite out of the sky. He bids him grow like an oak out of the earth.

aerolith (ˈɛərəʊlɪθ). [mod. f. AERO- + λίθος stone. Cf. Fr. *aérolithe.*] The more etymological form of AEROLITE.
1819 *Pantologia* I, *Aeroliths*, air-stones: a name lately given to those solid bodies composed of several mineral substances, which have been seen to fall from the atmosphere. **1864** *Daily Tel.* 8 June, This aerolith belongs to a very rare type of meteorites: it contains carbon.

aerolithology (ˌɛərəʊlɪˈθɒlədʒɪ). [mod. f. AEROLITH + Gr. -λογία discourse: see -LOGY.] That department of science which treats of aerolites.
a **1864** WEBSTER cites DANA.

aerolitic (ˌɛərəʊˈlɪtɪk), *a.* [f. AEROLITE + -IC.] Of or pertaining to aerolites; meteoric.
1868 LOCKYER *Element. Astron.* 139 Among the largest aërolitic falls of modern times we may mention the following. **1880** *Pop. Sc. Rev.* Jan. 13 Could such bodies as aerolitic stones fall from the moon?

aerological (ˌɛərəʊˈlɒdʒɪkal), *a.* [f. AEROLOGY + -ICAL.] 'Pertaining to aerology.' Craig 1847.

aerologist (ˌɛəˈrɒlədʒɪst). [f. AEROLOGY + -IST.] 'One who is versed in aërology.' Craig 1847.

aerology (ˌɛəˈrɒlədʒɪ). [mod. f. AERO- + -λογία discourse: see -LOGY.] That department of science which treats of the atmosphere. Also *spec.* [app. ad. G. *aerologie* (W. Köpper, 1906)], the branch of meteorology which treats of the phenomena of the upper air. Hence ˌaeroˈlogical *a.*
1736 BAILEY *Dict. Britannicum* (ed. 2) Pref., *Aerology*, a Treatise or Philosophical Discourse of the Air. **1753** CHAMBERS *Cycl. Supp.*, *Aerography*..amounts to much the same with aerology. **1755** in JOHNSON. **1837** *Pop. Encycl.* I. 45, *Aerodynamics*, a branch of aerology. **1912** *Aëronaut. Jrnl.* July 166 The training he had received from his distinguished father..made any facts regarding aerology which he [C. H. Ley] might contribute well worthy of..consideration. **1917** *Geogr. Rev.* III. 397 A..movement is under way..to establish aërological stations for observers. **1932** *Discovery* Aug. 271/2 Three sets of meteorological and aerological observations were made at very different stations. **1932** *Flight* XXIV. 974/1 Aerology (meteorology) seems sound, but perhaps too brief.

aeromagnetic (ˌɛərəʊmægˈnɛtɪk), *a.* [f. AERO- + MAGNETIC *a.*] Of, pertaining to, or derived from aerial measurements of the earth's magnetic field.
1946 *Petroleum Engineer* July 78 (*caption*) Map of part of Iron County, Michigan, showing part of area of aeromagnetic survey. **1946** *Geophysics* XI. 143 One of the unsolved problems was to determine whether the depths of the upper and lower limits of the Kursk ferrous quartzites could be computed from aeromagnetic data. **1969** *Courier-Mail* (Brisbane) 22 Oct. 10/8 Prospective nickel-bearing areas in the eastern goldfields district of Western Australia are covered in 16 preliminary aeromagnetic contour maps. **1978** *Nature* 2 Feb. 488/3 He supervised the complete regional aeromagnetic survey of the United Kingdom which was published..as colour-layered 'ten-mile' aeromagnetic sheets in 1965 and 1972.
Hence ˌ**aeromagneˈtometer**, an instrument for making aeromagnetic measurements.
[**1946** J. R. BALSLEY in *Petroleum Engineer* Aug. 108/1 The obvious advantages of the air-magnetometer are its speed.. and the fact that it can be used where ground methods are.. unpracticable.] **1948** *World Oil* CXXVIII. 223 (*heading*) Aeromagnetometer profile flown from Venezuela to Texas. **1969** *New Scientist* 9 Jan. 58/2 An aeromagnetometer survey to last several months will be started shortly.

†**aeromancer.** *Obs. rare*[−1]. [f. AEROMANC-Y + -ER[1].] One who practises divination by air; a weather-prophet.
c **1400** *Apol. for Lollards* 96 Ayeromauncers þat wirkun bi þe eyre.

aeromancy (ˈɛərəʊˌmænsɪ). Forms: 4 aeromaunce, 5 -mancye, 7 -mancie (heromanty), 7– aeromancy. [orig. a. OFr. **aeromance*; afterwards modified after later Fr. *aéromancye*, *aéromantie*, or med.L. *āeromantia*; f. Gr. ἀήρ atmosphere + μαντεία prophesying: see -MANCY.] Divination by air, including augury; passing in 17th c. into the idea of *weather-forecasting, meteorology.*
1393 GOWER *Conf.* III. 45 And eke also Aeromaunce in jugement To love he bringeth of his assent. **1496** *Dives & Pauper* (W. de Worde) I. xxxvi. 77/1 Aeromancye, that is wytchecrafte done in the ayer. *c* **1590** GREENE *Fryer Bacon* (1630) 6 By Æromancy, to discouer doubts. **1607** TOPSELL *Serpents* (1653) 645 Countrey people..have learned of them Aeromantie, that is, Divination of things by the air, for they have a forefeeling and understanding of rain and windes aforehand. **1630** J. TAYLOR (Water P.) *Wks.* III. 12/2 By fire he hath the Skill of Pyromanty By Ayre he hath the Art of Heromanty. **1753** CHAMBERS *Cycle Supp.* s.v., Barometers, thermometers, hygrometers, and anemometers, are of considerable use in this kind of aeromancy.

aeromantic(k (ˌɛərəʊˈmæntɪk), *a. rare*[−1]. [f. Gr. ἀήρ air + μαντικός prophetic, f. μάντις prophet, diviner.] Belonging to divination by air.
1635 HEYWOOD *Hierarchie* VIII. (1635) 512 Using their helpe, one John Teutonicus By Aeroma[n]ticke Magicke sported thus. **1742** in BAILEY.

aerometer (ˌɛəˈrɒmɪtə(r)). [mod. f. AERO- + Gr. μέτρον measure: see -METER. Cf. mod.Fr. *aéromètre.*] An instrument for ascertaining the weight or density of air and gases.
1794 G. ADAMS *Nat. & Exp. Philos.* III. xxxiv. 390 Comparing fluids with each other by means of the hydrometer or aerometer. **1839–47** TODD *Cycl. Anat. & Phys.* III. 32/2 Attached to the same mercurial trough is placed a little apparatus termed an aerometer.

aerometric (ˌɛərəʊˈmɛtrɪk), *a.* [f. prec. + -IC: see -METRIC.] Of or pertaining to the measurement of the air. (In mod. Dicts.)
Mod. Aerometric experiments and investigations.

aerometry (ˌɛəˈrɒmɪtrɪ). [mod. f. AERO- + Gr. -μετρία measuring: see -METRY.] The measuring of the air; the science of pneumatics.
1731 BAILEY, vol. II, [the Latin form] *Aerometria.* **1751** CHAMBERS *Cycl.*, *Aerometry* includes the laws of the motion, gravitation, pression, elasticity, rarefaction, condensation, etc. of the atmospherical fluid. **1777** *Phil. Trans.* LXVII. 413 The application of the laws of aërometry. **1819** *Pantologia* I, *Aerometry*, a scientific term which has now given way to the equivalent term pneumatics.

aeronaut (ˈeɪərəʊnɔːt, ˈɛərənɔːt). [a. mod.Fr. *aéronaute*; f. Gr. ἀήρ atmosphere + ναύτ-ης sailor; f. ναῦς a ship. (The first balloon ascent was made in 1783.)]
1. One who sails through the air, or who makes balloon ascents; a balloonist. Also used of any air pilot.
1784 *Europ. Mag.* VI. 331 The intrepid Aeronaut sitting in his car. **1809** G. CAYLEY in W. Nicholson *Jrnl. Nat. Philos.* XXIV. 173 Let there be a convenient seat for the aeronaut. **1831** LARDNER *Pneumatics* vii. 340 Such a valve is also necessary in order to enable the aeronaut to descend at pleasure. **1908** H. G. WELLS *War in Air* i. §3 They flew in machines heavier than air. But they smashed... The breeze upset them..a passing thought in the mind of the aeronaut upset them.
2. *fig.* A gossamer spider which floats on films.
1845 DARWIN *Voy. of Nat.* viii. (1879) 160 The little aëronaut as soon as it arrived on board was very active.. sometimes letting itself fall and then reascending the same thread.
Hence *transf.* and *fig.*
1790 BURKE *Fr. Revol.* 355 Let us be satisfied to admire, rather than attempt to follow in their desperate flights the aëronauts of France. **1840** DICKENS *Old C. Shop* xxxiii. 277 The historian takes the friendly reader by the hand, and springing with him into the air..alights with him upon the pavement of Bevis Marks. The intrepid aeronauts alight before a small dark house.

aeronautic (ˌeɪərəʊˈnɔːtɪk, ˌɛərəʊ-), *a.* [f. prec. + -IC; cf. Gr. ναυτικ-ός pertaining to sailing.] Of or pertaining to aeronauts, or to aerial navigation; sailing the air.
1784 *Hibernian Mag.* Sept. 489/2, I shall..attempt a description of his [*sc.* Richard Crosbie's] Aeronautic Chariot. **1826** MISS MITFORD *Our Village* Ser. II. (1863) 402 The announcement of the aeronautic expedition drew at least ten thousand gazers into the good town. **1876** M. COLLINS *Blacksm. & Scholar* I. viii. 197 The aeronautic art will not be perfected until the flight of birds is more carefully studied. **1878** *Daily News* 24 Oct. 6/4 The threads of the gossamer or aeronautic spider may be now seen. **1908** H. G. WELLS *War in Air* iv. §1 The Emperor forgave him and placed him in control of the new aeronautic arm of the German forces. *Ibid.* xi. §2 None of these countries had prepared for aeronautic warfare on the magnificent scale of the Germans. **1918** E. S. FARROW *Dict. Mil. Terms* 9 *Aëronautic Maps*, maps showing the contours and configuration of the land as closely as possible to the way it looks to the aviator from the air.
Hence ˌ**aeroˈnautica** *sb. pl.* [mod.L., see AERONAUTICS], matters or facts of aeronautics.
1753 [see AERONAUTICS]. **1838** T. M. MASON (*title*) Aeronautica. **1883** *Catal. Pat. Off. Libr.* II. 4 (*title*) Aëronautica Illustrata. A complete Cabinet of Aërial Ascents and Descents from the earliest period.

aeroˈnautical, *a.* [f. prec. + -AL[1].] Of or belonging to aeronautics; connected with the navigation of the air.
1802 in *Ann. Reg.* 449/2 The extraordinary display of aeronautical dexterity..was this day prepared with consummate skill, and executed with an admirable intrepidity. **1881** PETTIGREW in *Times* 30 Mar. 9/6 That aeronautical societies had of late years been established in France. **1910** in A. E. Berriman '*Flight*' *Manual* p. vi (Advt.), Aeronautical Engineers. **1916** F. W. LANCHESTER *Aircraft in Warfare* xix. 202 The question of the future of the Aeronautical Arm is not purely the concern of the Army and Navy..it is essentially an affair of the Nation. **1957** *Technology* Mar. 8/1 Early this century the design and building of flying machines was being undertaken by pioneers with no experience as aeronautical engineers. **1959** *Chambers's Encycl.* V. 191/1 *Aeronautical Engineering.* This branch is concerned with the design and construction of both heavier-than-air and lighter-than-air types of aircraft.

aeroˈnautics. [ad. mod.L. *āeronautica*, adj. pl. neut. (see AERONAUTIC), literally 'matters pertaining to sailing the atmosphere'; in Chambers 1753 in its L. form: see -ICS.] The science, art, or practice of sailing in the air; aerial navigation.
1753 CHAMBERS *Cycl. Supp.*, *Aeronautica*, the pretended art of sailing in a vessel thro' the air or atmosphere. **1824** *Encycl. Brit.* Suppl. I. 65/2 We prefer, as more correct and appropriate [than *aerostation*], the word Aeronautics, now generally adopted to express aërial navigation. **1838** DICKENS *Nich. Nick.* xvi. (C.D. ed.) 120 Balloons of a size hitherto unknown in the history of aëronautics. **1870** *Echo* 19 Oct., Aeronautics must make many a long stride before they do much practical work, either in commerce or war.

aeronautism (ˈeɪərəʊnɔːtɪz(ə)m, ˈɛərə-). *rare*[−0]. [f. AERONAUT + -ISM.] The practice of ascending and floating in the atmosphere.
1847 In CRAIG.

aeronomy (ɛəˈrɒnəmɪ). [f. AERO-, after ASTRONOMY, *geonomy* s.v. GEO-.] The science of the upper atmosphere.
1946 S. CHAPMAN in *Nature* 30 Mar. 405/2, I propose that the word [*sc. meteorology*] be abandoned in all its many

official and unofficial uses, in favour of 'aeronomy' (with the associated words 'aeronomer' and 'aeronomic'). **1953** —— in *Weather* VIII. 62/1 *Aeronomy*.. should be adopted with the restricted sense of the science of the *upper* atmosphere. **1967** *Technology Week* 23 Jan. 96/3 $372,974 GCA Corp... for experimental and theoretical studies in planetary aeronomy. **1971** WHITTEN & POPPOFF *Fund. Aeronomy* i. 5 Aeronomy is the study of chemical and physical processes of the upper atmosphere. **1976** *Physics Bull.* June 261/2 Not only has laser physics grown from this field, but also aeronomy, now the basis of environmental research.

Hence **ae'ronomer**, a specialist or expert in aeronomy; **aero'nomic, aero'nomical** *adjs.*; **ae'ronomist** = AERONOMER above.

1946 Aeronomer, aeronomic [see above]. **1958** *Meteorol. Mag.* LXXXVII. 275 The results of this work will be eagerly awaited by oceanographers, chemists and aeronomers as well as by meteorologists. **1963** *Jrnl. Geophysical Res.* LXVIII. 2360/1 The increased value of aeronomical studies when employing various techniques simultaneously. **1966** *Britannica Bk. of Year* (U.S.) 806/1 Aeronomist. **1971** *Physics Bull.* Dec. 735/2 Its excellence as a sound survey will make it worth consideration by aeronomists, amateur and professional, at all levels. **1975** *Nature* 6 Nov. 64/1 In future studies, simultaneous observations of both dynamical and aeronomical conditions, on a spatial scale adequate to establish transport effects, will be required. **1976** *Ibid.* 24 June 678/2 Interpretation of aeronomic phenomena in SAGA is difficult and often controversial. **1978** *Ibid.* 24 Aug. 731/1 The UK,.. reporting through the UK's Science Research Council, included space scientists and aeronomers; other countries may have restricted themselves to the ground-based astronomers.

aerophane (ɛərəʊ'feɪn). [a. mod.Fr. *aérophane* f. AERO- + Gr. -φανης appearing.] A semi-transparent fabric of the nature of a thin crape.

1829 *Ladies' Pocket Mag.* I. 35 Several dresses of colored satin have long sleeves of white *crepe Aerophane, a la Mameluke.* **1830** *New Monthly Mag.* XXIX. 17 Aerophane and *couleur de soupir*.. float before me. **1871** MISS BRADDON *Lovels of Arden* v. 36 A white aerophane bonnet. **1915** *Observer* 11 July 1/3 (Advt.), White Hat, in *aerophane*, small rolled brim underlined black taffeta.

aerophobia, aerophoby (ˌɛərəʊ'fəʊbɪə, ˌɛə'rɒfəbɪ). 'The dread of air, a kind of phrenzy.' Ash 1775. Also *fig.*

1785 FRANKLIN *Lett.* Wks. 1840 VI. 526, I myself had formed this prejudice, this aërophobia, as I now account it. **1847** CRAIG, *Aerophobia*, the dread of air; a symptom of hydrophobia. **1853** MAYNE, *Aerophobia*.. aërophoby.

'aerophone (-fəʊn). [f. AERO- + -PHONE.]

1. A device invented by Edison for amplifying sound. (Disused.)

1878 *Telegraphic Jrnl.* 15 May 200/2 A company of English merchants have offered Mr. Edison £60,000 if he can successfully apply his aërophone or talking fog-horn to 'the local telegraph wires' in London. **1894** W. JERROLD *Electricians & Marvels* vi. 120 The 'aerophone' a great voice of two hundred and fifty times the capacity of the human lungs, which is designed to be used between lighthouses or lightships and vessels at sea.

2. Any musical instrument in which the sound is produced by a vibrating column of air.

1937 *Times Lit. Suppl.* 17 Apr. 288/2 Those [instruments] which employ.. a column of air (aerophones). **1959** *Collins Music Encycl.* 333/2 *Aerophones*, woodwinds, brass, and instruments using a free reed. **1960** *Times* 18 Mar. 4/6 The instrument is a thin plate from the inner side of the birch bark, technically described as an aerophone with a tongue but without a soundboard.

'aerophore (-fɔə(r)). Also **aerophor.** [f. AERO- + -PHORE. Cf. Fr. *aérophore.*] A form of respirator containing a quantity of air.

1877 *Encycl. Brit.* VI. 73/2 Apparatus, originating in France, known as aerophores, which enable the miner to carry sufficient fresh air for his own respiration, and to keep a lamp alight for a short time in a totally irrespirable atmosphere. *a* **1884** KNIGHT *Dict. Mech.* Suppl. 8/2 The aërophore devised by Herr Schultz, captain of the fire brigade at Aschaffenburg, Bavaria, depends upon the regeneration of the exhaled air, the oxygen being reproduced as it is consumed. **1931** *Discovery* Apr. 128/1 The Aerophor apparatus [for use in mines] is probably the most interesting type of all on account of the fact that it makes use of liquid air.

aerophysics (ˌɛərəʊ'fɪzɪks). [f. AERO- + PHYSICS.] The physics of the atmosphere; *spec.* the branch of physics concerned with the movement of solid bodies, as guided missiles, space vehicles, etc., through the air.

1897 A. MCADIE *Equipment & Work of Aero-Physical Observatory* 3 A laboratory.. devoted to investigation and research in aero-physics. **1948** *Jrnl. Brit. Interplanetary Soc.* VII. 177 This building.. is equipped generally with facilities for all types of basic and applied research in aero-physics, electronics, [etc.]. **1962** *Times* 16 Mar. 2/2 Advanced fields of aircraft instrumentation and aerophysics.

aerophyte ('ɛərəʊfaɪt). [mod. f. AERO- + Gr. φῠτ-όν plant.] 'Plants growing wholly in the air; such as epiphytal orchids, many lichens, bromeliads.' *Treas. Bot.* 1866. In L. pl. *aerophyta* specially applied to lichens, as the division of the Thallogens which live in the air. (Henfrey.)

1840 TIMBS *Year Bk. Facts* 190 [It] appears as an aerophyte in Nees von Esenbeck's valuable appendix to R. Brown's *Botan. Schriften.* **1858** GRAY *Bot. Text-bk.* 394 *Aërophytes*, Air-plants.

aeroplane ('ɛərəpleɪn, now rarely 'eɪərəʊ-), *sb.* [In sense 1, f. AERO- + PLANE *sb.*[3]; in sense 2, ad. F. *aéroplane* (1855), f. Gr. ἀερο- (see AERO-) + F. *plan* plane (see PLANE *v.*[2]).] **1.** A plane (or slightly curved) light framework or 'surface' forming part of a flying-machine, and serving to sustain it in the air. *Obs.* (Later called simply *plane*, also *wing.*)

1866 WENHAM in *Ann. Rep. Aëronaut. Soc.* 33 In the flying mechanism of beetles.. when the .. wing-cases are opened, they are checked by a stop, which sets them at a fixed angle. It is probable that these serve as 'aeroplanes', for carrying the weight of the insect. *Ibid.* 37 A thin steel tie-band,.. served as the foundation of the superposed aeroplanes. **1869** in *Eng. Mech.* 4 June 241/3 The dynamometer and registering apparatus, to which the aeroplanes are to be attached. **1902** F. WALKER *Aërial Navig.* 117 Air-ships as combinations of aërostat, aëroplane, and propelling apparatus. **1905** G. BACON *Balloons* 111 What are called 'aeroplanes'—large flat surfaces, light but rigid inclined at a suitable angle to the horizon.

2. †**a.** An airship provided with planes. *Obs.*

1884 *Pall Mall Gaz.* 28 Aug. 4/1 As soon as the Aero-Plane has been seen floating to and fro over the city of San Francisco, steered at pleasure this way and that, and carrying a number of passengers.

b. (The current sense.) A heavier-than-air flying-machine supported by such planes or wings and mechanically driven.

The use in quot. 1873[1] appears to derive from sense 1 and to owe nothing to Fr. *aéroplane* (Stubelius *Airship* 239).

1873 D. S. BROWN in *Ann. Rep. Aëronaut. Soc.* 17, I think [impetus] will be more requisite with respect to the aëroplane than any other vehicle. *Ibid.* 20 Mr. Bennett introduced an Aëroplane invented by a Frenchman, to be worked by a screw by motive power derived from elastic springs. **1874** *Ibid.* 65 Flight has thus been accomplished on three different principles, and the practicability of a flying-machine proved. M. Penaud.. thinks the aëroplane to be the only practicable machine. **1892** H. S. MAXIM in *Century Mag.* Apr. 957/2 Ascertaining how much power was .. required to perform flight with a screw-driven aëroplane. **1897** LANGLEY *Memoir Mech. Flight* (1911) I. ii. 7 His [*sc.* A. Pénaud's] aeroplane is a toy in size, with a small propeller whose blades are usually made of two feathers.. and whose motive power is a twisted strand of rubber. **1910** R. FERRIS *How it Flies* 453 *Aeroplane*, the type of flying machine which is supported in the air by a spread of surfaces or planes formerly flat and therefore truly 'plane' but of late more or less curved. **1920** *Blackw. Mag.* July 74/1 The perfected aeroplane is the obvious instrument to suppress war. **1934** ORVILLE WRIGHT *Let.* 10 Jan. in *Papers W. & O. Wright* (1953) II. 1162 The helicopter type of aeroplane offers several seemingly insurmountable difficulties. **1943** [see AIRCRAFT]. **1951** *Oxf. Jun. Encycl.* IV. 4/1 The power propelling the aeroplane may be of a number of types—the ordinary piston-engine (internal combustion) driving a propeller (air-screw), the gas-turbine driving a propeller, or the gas-turbine 'pure jet'.

¶ In form indicating the once common *dial.* or *vulg.* but now *obs.* pronunc. (-iːəʊ).

1876 *Pop. Sci. Monthly* Feb. 454 The areoplanes have propelling surfaces which are nearly plane and slightly inclined to the horizon. **1915** S. LEWIS *Trail of Hawk* xxii. 203 It's a new areoplane (that's the way he pronounced it), and that dingus in front is a whirling motor. **1915** *Aeronautics* 13 Oct. 256/2, I have never heard anyone pronounce aeroplane in any other way than 'airoplane', with perhaps an occasional 'arioplane' or even 'hairyoplane'. **1935** 'J. GUTHRIE' *Little Country* xxix. 411 Half a dozen veterans of the forgotten Maori wars... What with these 'aereoplanes', war, like everything else, was not what it had been!

3. *attrib.* and *Comb.*

1872 *Ann. Rep. Aëronaut. Soc.* 15 At an angle of ten degrees, about one man power would be sufficient to drive an aëroplane machine twenty miles an hour. **1896** H. S. MAXIM in *Aeronaut. Ann., Nat. & Artif. Flight*, The next machine.. was on the kite or aeroplane system. **1902** *Aeronaut. World* (U.S.) 1 Oct. 58/1 This bird-like aeroplane machine. **1914** *Lancet* 4 July 55/1 A special aeroplane constructed to accommodate, besides the aviator, a medical man and also a covered litter on which the wounded man can be placed for transport... This aeroplane ambulance [etc.]. **1920** *Proc. Air Conference, London* 96 Movement by sea is a slow business unless aeroplane carriers are available. **1923** KIPLING *Irish Guards in Gt. War* I. 50 'Aeroplane duty' was another invention of those early days. A Company was told off daily to look out for aeroplanes. **1932** H. NICOLSON *Public Faces* xi. 301 She was an aeroplane carrier of His Majesty's Navy. **1958** *Spectator* 10 Jan. 47/1 HQ Tank Corps arranged with the RFC to have daily aeroplane photographs taken of the front over which tanks would advance.

Hence **'aeroplane** *v. intr.*, to fly or glide like an aeroplane; to fly or travel in an aeroplane; ***aeroplaning*** vbl. sb.; **'aeroˌplanist**, one who flies an aeroplane. Now *rare.*

1906 *Daily Mail* 26 Nov. 7/5 The first successful aeroplanist in Great Britain will win.. as much money as the Soap Trust has already lost. **1907** *Ibid.* 19 Feb. 7/7 M. Santos Dumont.. felt that for some years to come aeroplaning would remain a sport. **1907** *Jrnl. Soc. Arts* 19 Apr. 603/1 A hawk never aeroplaned; he always balanced himself on his wings. **1911** G. B. SHAW *Blanco Posnet* Pref. 367 Motoring has its risks; aeroplaning has its risks. **1912** —— *Let. to G. Barker* 1 May (1956) 182 We went to the aeroplanists' sheds again... Flying just about to begin as usual. **1914** —— *Misalliance* 46 *Lina.* I never drink tea. *Tarleton.* Bad thing to aeroplane on, I should imagine. **1927** *Observer* 7 Aug. 3/4 We cannot ignore the fact that aeroplaning is beginning to progress as a pastime, chiefly because of traffic conditions on our roads. **1934** *Times Educ. Suppl.* 17 Feb. 49/2 Model aeroplanists [wend their way] to Hampstead Heath.

aeropleustic (ˌɛərəʊ'pl(j)uːstɪk), *a.* [mod. f. AERO- + Gr. πλευστικός belonging to sailing; f. πλευστής a sailor; f. πλέ-ειν to sail.] Of or pertaining to navigation in the air; aeronautical.

1827 POCOCK (*title*) The Æropleustic Art of Navigation in the Air.

aeroscepsy ('ɛərəʊˌskɛpsɪ). *rare.* [f. AERO- + Gr. σκέψις a viewing, f. σκέπτ-εσθαι to view.] Observation of the changes of the atmosphere; aeroscopy.

1835 KIRBY *Habits & Inst. Anim.* II. xvii. 112 Snails and slugs issue forth, when the earth is rendered moist enough by showers for them to travel easily over its surface; so that they must be endued with some degree of aëroscepsy.

aeroscopy (ˌɛə'rɒskəpɪ). [ad. Gr. ἀεροσκοπία; f. ἀήρ the air + -σκοπία viewing: see -SCOPE.] The observation of the air; divination by observing the atmosphere or heavens.

1755 in JOHNSON (as Dict. word). **1815–43** KIRBY & SPENCE *Entomol.* (1826) III. 46 If insects do not hear with them in one sense they may, by communicating information and by aëroscopy.. supply the place of ears.

ærose (ɪə'rəʊs), *a.* [ad. L. *ærōsus* of copper or brass, f. *æs, æris*, copper, brass.] Of the nature of copper or brass, coppery, brassy.

(In mod. Dicts.)

aerosiderite (ˌɛərəʊ'sɪdəraɪt). [f. AERO- + Gr. σιδηρίτ-ης of iron, iron ore; f. σίδηρ-ος iron: see -ITE.] A mass of meteoric iron; a meteorite consisting of iron-ore.

1865 A. S. HERSCHEL in *Intellect. Observ.* No. 39. 219 Some meteorites called aërosiderites. **1868** LOCKYER *The Heavens* (ed. 3) 196 Professor Maskelyne has recently made a convenient classification of meteorites into 'Aerolites or Meteoric *Stones*,' 'Aerosiderites or Meteoric *Iron*,' and 'Aerosiderolites,' which includes the intervening varieties.

aerosiderolite (ˌɛərəʊsɪ'dɪərəlaɪt). [f. AERO- + Gr. σίδηρ-ος iron + λίθος stone: see AEROLITE.] A meteorite intermediate in character between stone and iron.

1882 *Academy* 7 Jan. 13/3 The entire collection of meteorites—classified as aërosiderites, aërosiderolites, and aërolites.

aerosol ('ɛərəsɒl). [f. AERO- + SOL(UTION: see SOL *sb.*[6]] **1.** A system of colloidal particles dispersed in the air or in a gas, as mist, fog, etc.

1923 R. WHYTLAW-GRAY et al. in *Proc. R. Soc.* A. CII. 600 Aerosol is a convenient term to denote a system of particles of ultra-microscopic size dispersed in a gas, suggested to us by Prof. Donnan. **1937** *Nature* 31 July 202/1 Examination of the aerosols under the ultra-microscope showed that the particles were chain-like. **1939** *Lancet* 25 Feb. 443/2 The introduction by Trillat (1938) [*Bull. Acad. Méd. Paris*, CXIX. 64] of the conception of 'aerosols' for the purpose of air-sterilisation. **1949** H. W. FLOREY et al. *Antibiotics* II. xv. 663 The inhalation of penicillin as an aerosol.

2. A substance packed under pressure in a container with a spraying device, esp. *attrib.*, as ***aerosol bomb, pack, spray***, etc. Hence, a container of this kind.

1944 *Reader's Digest* May 45/2 Today every soldier in mosquito country is armed with an 'aerosol bomb'—a specially designed container about twice the size of a hand grenade. **1957** *Times* 25 Nov. 11/4 Special foam shaving cream in aerosol container, price 12*s.* 6*d.* **1957** *Listener* 5 Dec. 963/1 *Aerosol Paint-sprays.* Most people by now are familiar with the aerosol pack. **1958** *Vogue* July 82/1 For the beach an oily preparation is best, and these packed in aerosols are likely to be more freely and frequently applied. **1958** *Woman's Own* 10 Sept. 22/1 Does your cosmetic drawer contain either a lipbrush, hair-lacquer, scent atomiser, or an aerosol spray?

Hence as *v. trans.*, (*a*) to paint or write (graffiti, etc.) with an aerosol spray; also with the surface sprayed as obj.; (*b*) = AEROSOLIZE *v.* a; **a'erosol(l)ed** *ppl. a.*, **a'erosol(l)ing** *vbl. sb.*

1966 *New Scientist* 16 June 731/1 Instead of prescribing aerosoling *before* take off, US Public Health Service regulations leave this job to be done with passengers aboard. **1978** *Church Times* 16 June 6/3 One of the more original of the aerosolled slogans is *legalise shoplifting.* **1979** S. BRETT *Comedian Dies* i. 7 The white planks.. aerosoled with lewd invitations. **1979** *Nature* 8 Nov. 186/1 An X-ray and Mössbauer study of aerosoled iron particles subjected to different extreme oxidation modes.

aerosolize ('ɛərəsɒlaɪz), *v.* [f. AEROSOL + -IZE.] **a.** *trans.* To make into an aerosol, disperse as an aerosol. **b.** *intr.* To become dispersed as an aerosol.

1944 *Science* 14 July 34/2 A simple bottle carburetor with face mask attached was devised for human use, and 50,000 units were aerosolized. *Ibid.*, Six per cent. of the total amount of penicillin aerosolized. **1949** H. W. FLOREY et al. *Antibiotics* II. xxxviii. 1246 [They] aerosolized the penicillin with propylene glycol. **1961** *Encycl. Biol. Sci.* 146/2 An aqueous suspension of the spores of *B. subtilis, var. niger*, generally known as *Bacillus globigii* was aerosolized using commercially available nozzles. **1980** *Nature* 1 May 4/1 According to the Defense Department report, released after a Freedom of Information request from the Church of Scientology, the bacteria 'aerosolised and dispersed rapidly by the movement of trains, penetrating stations and trains in the area and persisting there for one hour or longer'.

So **ˈaerosolized** *ppl. a.*; also **ˌaerosoliˈzation**, dispersal as an aerosol; conversion into an aerosol.

1944 *Science* 14 July 31/1 (*heading*) Aerosolization of penicillin solutions. *Ibid.* 35/1 The method..allows recovery of 60 per cent. of the aerosolized penicillin in the urine. **1964** W. G. Smith *Allergy & Tissue Metabolism* viii. 81 Guinea pigs were exposed to aerosolised antigen solution. **1973** *Nature* 3 Aug. 268/1 Aerosolization of FeLV through salivary and nasal secretions may play an important role in disseminating the virus. **1976** *Ann. Rev. Microbiol.* XXX. 520 Eating, drinking, and smoking in the laboratory..lead to the ingestion and/or inhalation of aerosolized materials.

ˈaerospace. orig. *U.S.* [Space *sb.*[1] 8.] **a.** The earth's atmosphere and outer space; also *attrib.*

1958 W. A. Heflin *Aero-Space Terms* p. iii, This glossary of aero-space terms is published to give guidance in a specialized vocabulary that deals with space missiles, space vehicles, and the physical laws that govern them. **1960** *John o' London's* 7 Apr. 395/1 The Air Force now is operating in an age of 'aero-space'. **1962** *Flight Internat.* LXXXII. 113 The concept of an 'aerospace plane' that takes off from and lands on conventional airfields yet is capable of orbital flight and effective manœuvres in space is one which is actively being considered at present. **1963** *Guardian* 6 June 13/1 The change from an aircraft industry to an aerospace industry is one which has not yet been made in Britain.

b. The technology of flight in the atmosphere and in space; the industrial aspects of such flight. Usu. *attrib.*

1961 (*title*) Aerospace management. **1963** *Wall St. Jrnl.* 26 Apr. 1/1 Aerospace workers at McDonnell Aircraft Corp.'s plants. **1969** *Times* 30 Apr. 27/1 In the eight years since..1960, aerospace equipment to a value of over £325m has been supplied to customers abroad. **1976** *Survey* Summer–Autumn 221 Discrimination against defence purchases from the United States might incite American discrimination against European exports..in closely-related fields such as aerospace. **1978** *N.Y. Times* 30 Mar. B23/4 (Advt.), National sales representative co needs sales engineer, exper in aerospace, & commercial markets.

aerosphere (ˈɛərəʊsfɪə(r)). [mod. f. Aero- + Gr. σφαῖρα globe; cf. Fr. *aérosphère*.] The body of air that surrounds the earth.

1912 C. M. Doughty *Clouds* 121 And signals winged, of mens sollicitudes, From the large compass of the aerosphere Continually were received.

aerostat (ˈeɪərəʊˌstæt, ˈɛərəstæt). [a. Fr. *aérostat*, f. Gr. ἀερο-, see Aero-, + στατ-ός standing, f. vbl. root στα- stand.]

1. a. A balloon or other machine capable of supporting weight in the air. (The original name.)

1784 *Europ. Mag.* VI. 384 The first aerostat filled with inflammable air ascended from the Thuilleries on the 1st of December 1783. **1785** Cavallo *Aerost.* i. v. 82 This paper aerostat rose rapidly into the atmosphere. **1895** *Knowledge* 2 Dec. 276/2 Suppose an aërostat came overhead on warlike deeds intent, carrying dynamite missiles.

b. A generic term for lighter-than-air aircraft.

1906 *Sci. Amer.* 8 Sept. 175/1 'Aerostat'..applies merely to the ordinary balloon. **1909** C. C. Turner *Aerial Navig. To-day* 309 *Aerostat*, balloons of any form, as distinct from heavier-than-air aerial machines. **1919** W. B. Faraday *Gloss. Aeronaut. Terms* 54 *Aerostat*, a generic term for any type of aircraft which derives its lift chiefly from aerostatic forces. **1950** *Gloss. Aeronaut. Terms* (*B.S.I.*) i. 7 *Lighter-than-air aircraft* (*Aerostat*: not the preferred term).

2. An aeronaut or balloonist. (In quots. 1870, 1871, repr. Fr. *aérostier*.)

1788 R. Bage *James Wallace* (1824) 392/1 Simon the magician, the first aerostat upon record. **1806** M. Edgeworth *Leonora* II. lxv. 109 To mount with a friend in a balloon, amid crowds of spectators, who..applaud the courage of the aërostats. **1870** *Daily News* 4 Oct., The aërostat who brought from Paris the second balloon despatches. **1871** *Ibid.* 3 Jan., Improvised aerostats who, with commendable courage, undertook a perilous task.

aerostatic (ˌeɪərəʊˈstætɪk, ˌɛərəʊ-), *a.* [ad. Fr. *aérostatique*, f. Gr. ἀερο-, see Aero-, + στατικ-ός causing to stand; f. vbl. root στα- stand.]

1. Of or pertaining to the balancing or weighing of air; pneumatic.

1791 E. Darwin *Bot. Gard.* i. 83 Which [air] could not be thus accumulated..by any aerostatic laws at present known. **1828** Kirby & Spence *Entomol.* III. xxxv. 591 A celebrated French writer seems to think their origin and structure aerostatic.

2. Of or connected with the navigation of the air; aeronautic.

1783 (*title*) The Air Balloon: Or a Treatise on the Ærostatic Globe lately invented by Mons. Montgolfier. **1785** Cavallo *Aerostation* Pref., Thus the aerostat, or the aerostatic machine, is the general appellation of the flying instruments. **1812** Sir H. Davy *Chem. Philos.* 255 Hydrogene gas is..well fitted for aerostatic purposes. **1849** Mrs. Somerville *Connex. Phys. Sc.* xxxv. 381 The observations of MM. Biot and Gay Lussac during their aerostatic expedition. **1865** C. H. Turnor *Astra Castra* vii. 258 The balloon..will be employed in various works of *aerostatic photography*, for which I was the first to take patents in France and abroad seven years ago. **1957** *Observer* 17 Nov. 17/3 The author has a highly developed taste for aerostatic necrology.

aerostatical (ˌɛərəʊˈstætɪkəl), *a.* [f. prec. + -al[1].] Of or pertaining to aerostatics.

1685 in *Phil. Trans.* XV. 996 Thus we have an Intelligible and Aëro Statical account of the ascent of Vapours. **1861** P. d'Amecourt *Brit. Pat. 1929*, My aerostatical apparatus (which I intend denominating aeronef or helicoptere).

aerostatics (ˌɛərəʊˈstætɪks). [Aerostatic *a.* in pl. treated as a collective sing. after analogy of *mathematics*, etc.: see -ics. Long used in the L. form *aerostatica*.] The branch of Pneumatics that treats of the equilibrium and pressure of air, and other elastic fluids, or gases, and of bodies sustained in them: hence including aeronautics.

1753 Chambers *Cycl. Supp.*, *Aerostatica* is used by some authors for the science called by others *aerometry*. **1784** *Morning Herald* 18 Mar. 1/4 The laws of Aerostatics, Pneumatics, and Hydrostatics. **1788** Howard *Encyc.* I. 56 *Aerostatica* also denotes the doctrine of the pressure and balance of the air. **1864** H. Spencer *Illust. Progress* 121 The invention of the barometer enabled men to extend the principles of mechanics to the atmosphere; and Aerostatics existed. **1881** in *Nature* XXIII. 298 The study of the applications of aërostatics to military purposes. **1887** tr. *J. Verne's Clipper of Clouds* ii. 15 They were not engineers by profession, but simply amateurs of all that appertained to aerostatics.

aerostation (ˌɛərəʊˈsteɪʃən). [a. Fr. *aérostation*, after *navigation*: see Aerostat and -ation.]

†**1.** The science of weighing air; aerostatics. *Obs.*

1788 Howard *Encycl.* I. 56 *Aerostation*, in it's primary and proper sense, denotes the science of weights suspended in the air. **1792** A. Young *Trav. in France* 171 Important works on volcanoes, aerostation, and various other branches of natural history.

2. The art of raising and guiding balloons or other machines in the air; aerial navigation. Now applied only to the operation of lighter-than-air aircraft.

1784 *Morning Herald* 16 Sept. 3/2 Aerostation. The brothers Robert have advertised another experiment with their balloon. **1785** Cavallo (*title*) History and Practice of Aerostation. **1798** W. Taylor in *Monthly Rev.* XXVI. 512 The Montgolfiers, after their splendid discoveries in aerostation. **1881** Coxwell in *Standard* 16 Dec. 3/2 To interest him in the resources of aerostation. **1950** *Gloss. Aeronaut. Terms* (*B.S.I.*) i. 6 *Aerostation*, the operation of lighter-than-air aircraft.

ˌaeroˌthermodyˈnamic, *a.* [f. Aero- + Thermodynamic *a.*] Pertaining to the thermodynamic effects of air and other gases; ***aerothermodynamic duct***, see Athodyd; and hence **ˌaeroˌthermodyˈnamics** *sb. pl.*; **ˌaeroˌthermodyˈnamicist**, one skilled in aerothermodynamics.

1945 *Westinghouse Engineer* Mar. 51/1 The..name of 'athodyd' (from Aero-THermO-DYnamic Duct). **1946** *Jrnl. R. Aeronaut. Soc.* L. 446/2 The 'engine'..is merely a duct in which aerodynamic and thermal changes occur, and it has been described as an aero-thermodynamic-duct. **1951** D. O. Dommasch et al. *Airplane Aerodynamics* ii. 26 The necessity of considering thermodynamic effects in high-speed aerodynamics has led to the use of the term *aero-thermodynamics*, which identifies work in which thermal effects are considered. **1958** *Times Rev. Industry* May 38/3 A high-speed induced-flow transonic and supersonic [wind-] tunnel..has been installed in a new 'aerothermodynamic' laboratory. **1960** *Times* 10 Feb. 3/2 Aerothermodynamicists.

Aertex (ˈɛətɛks). Also **aertex**. [f. *aer-*, as in Aery *a.*, etc., + Tex(tile).] A proprietary name for a cotton cellular fabric; chiefly designating garments made of this, esp. ***Aertex shirt***.

1896 *Trade Marks Jrnl.* 23 Sept. 846 Aertex 197,346. Articles of Clothing. The Cellular Clothing Company, Limited, 72 and 73, Fore Street, London, E.C.; Manufacturers. **1908** *Chambers's Jrnl.* Sept. 685/1 The new sheeting..is made in accordance with the aertex cellular principles. **1936** R. Lehmann *Weather in Streets* iii. ii. 287 Jane in the camp-bed, Christopher in the old cot.., sat up in Aertex sleeping suits. **1937** Hull & Whitlock *Far-Distant Oxus* ii. 44 The wind blew through their Aertex shirts. **1953** J. Trench *Docken Dead* ii. 35 His yellow Aertex shirt was clinging to his back. **1960** L. Cooper *Accomplices* i. iv. 39 If there's anything nakeder than a man in wet aertex pants I don't know what it is. **1964** C. Mackenzie *My Life & Times* III. 21, I had..Aertex shirts bought at the very shop in Oxford Street in which they are still being sold to-day. **1984** *Guardian Weekly* 19 Aug. 20 Until about 1943 my favourite garment remained a bright scarlet Aertex shirt, for reasons unconnected with revolutionary socialism.

æruginous (iːˈruːdʒɪnəs), *a.* [ad. Fr. *érugineux, -euse*; ad. L. *ærūginōs-us* rusty, f. *ærūgin-em* verdigris, f. *æs, ær-is*, brass.] Of the nature or colour of verdigris, or copper-rust.

1605 Timme *Quersit.* iii. 158 Shal it bee free and permitted to common physitians to cal choler æruginus, vitelline, and proracious? **1651** N. Biggs *New Dispens.* § 160. 120 Partake of a canckerous æruginous quality from the brazen vessel. **1721** Bailey, *Ærugineous*, rusty. **1875** Griffith & Henfrey *Microsc. Dict.* s.v. *Calothrix*, A rare freshwater species..æruginous green, growing blackish.

‖**ærugo** (iːˈruːgəʊ). [L. = verdigris; f. *æs, æris*, brass.] The rust of copper or brass, verdigris; occasionally used for the rust of metals generally.

1753 Chambers *Cycl. Supp.* s.v., The *ærugo* of antient metals adds greatly to their value. **1845** Ford *Handbk. Spain* II. 786 With pumice and emery to scrub off the respectable ærugo.

†**æˈrumnous**, *a.* *Obs.*[—0] [ad. L. *ærumnōs-us*, f. *ærumna* toil.] 'Full of trouble.' Bailey 1721.

†**ˈærwene**, *a.* *Obs.* *rare*[—1]. [f. *ær-* away, privative, -less (= OE. *or-* and *ǽ-*) + *wén* hope; OE. *or-wéne*. See Æ- *pref.*] Hopeless, desperate.

1205 Layamon 27537 For heo weoren to kene & to ærwene and to swiðe fuhten.

†**ˈærwitte**, *a.* *Obs.* [f. *ær-* see prec. + Wit.] Witless, unwise.

1205 Layamon 22069 Þat na mon on worlde swa wod no iwurðe; no swa ær-witte gume; Þat his grið bræce.

aery (ˈɛərɪ), *a.* Also **aerie**. [ad. L. *āeri-us*, f. *āer* the air.] Aerial; hence etherial, spiritual, incorporeal, unsubstantial, visionary. (In later usage only poetic; a favourite word with Milton.)

1586 T. B. tr. *La Primaudaye's Fr. Acad.* (1594) 560 Al living creatures, whether earthie, watrie, aërie, or flying. **1634** Milton *Comus* 208 Beckoning shadows dire, And aery tongues that syllable men's names. **1667** —— *P.L.* ii. 536 Before each Van Pric forth the Aerie Knights, and couch their spears. **1727** Thomson *Summer* 585 Thus up the mount, in aëry vision wrapt, I stray. **1855** M. Arnold *New Sirens* 72 Her load of streaming tresses Weigh'd, like Ossa, on the aery soul.

Comb. **aery-light**, of aerial lightness, light as air.

1667 Milton *P.L.* v. 4 His sleep Was Aerie light, from pure digestion bred.

aery, variant spelling of Aerie.

æsample, obs. form of Example.

Aeschylean (iːskɪˈliːən), *a.* [f. L. *Aeschylus*, ad. Gr. Αἰσχύλος (see def.) + -an.] Of, pertaining to, or characteristic of Aeschylus, the Athenian tragic poet (525–456 b.c.), or his works, style, etc.

1844 J. F. Boyes *Illustr. Tragedies Æschylus & Sophocles* i. p. xxxvii, His style and expressions are so bold, as often to border on the Aeschylean. **1850** Kingsley *Alton Locke* I. ix. 138 The Eschylean grandeur, the terrible rhythmic lilt. **1871** Swinburne *Songs bef. Sunrise* 178 With wind-notes as of eagles Æschylean. **1921** *Spectator* 12 Mar. 333/1 An Aeschylean trilogy, the three connected plays, lasted most of a day. **1958** *Ibid.* 22 Aug. 257/2 The last, Æschylean novel.

æschynite (ˈɛskɪnaɪt). *Min.* [f. Gr. αἰσχύνη disgrace + -ite. Named 'by Berzelius, in allusion to the inability of chemical science, at the time of its discovery, to separate the two unlike substances, titanic acid and zirconia.' Dana.] A blackish mineral of the Tantalite group found in different parts of Russia.

†**æschyˈnomenous**, *a.* *Obs.*[—0] [f. Gr. αἰσχυνόμεν-ος ashamed, bashful + -ous.] Sensitive (plants).

1706 Phillips, *Æschynomenous* Plants (among Herbalists) those Plants which as one comes near them with the Hand, shrink in their Leaves, the same with the Sensitive. **1751** Chambers *Cycl.*, *Æschynomenous* Plants, among botanists, are those popularly called sensitive plants.

Æsculapian (ɛskjuːˈleɪpɪən), *a.* Also Esc-. [f. next + -an.] Of or belonging to Æsculapius (the god of medicine), or to the healing art; medicinal.

1622 Massinger *Virg. Mart.* iv. i, Turn o'er all the volumes Of your mysterious Æsculapian science. **1792** D. Lloyd *Voy. Life* v. 107 Æsculapian art could not restore The springs and movements into harmony. **1843** A. Bethune *Scott. Peas. Fireside* 4 The time at which Roland Bridges began his Esculapian labours.

‖**Æsculapius** (ɛskjuːˈleɪpɪəs) Also Esc-. [L.] The Roman god of medicine; hence *fig.* A physician.

1714 Mandev. *Fable of Bees* (1725) I. 298 The British Esculapius was undeniably a man of sense. **1840** Hood *Up the Rhine* 4 Besides the daily visit of routine, the Esculapius is generally sent for, in haste, some twice or thrice a week extra.

æsculetin (ɛskjuːˈliːtɪn). *Chem.* [f. L. *æsculētum* a grove or wood of *æsculus*: see next.] A bitter crystalline substance ($C_9H_6O_4$) formed by the decomposition of æsculin.

1877 Watts *Fownes' Chem.* II. 604.

æsculin (ˈɛskjʊlɪn). *Chem.* [f. L. *æscul-us* a species of oak, in mod. Bot. applied to the horse-chestnut, + -in, chem. form.] A glucoside contained in the bark of the horse-chestnut and allied trees; a crystalline fluorescent substance of composition $C_{21}H_{24}O_{13}$.

1877 Watts *Fownes' Chem.* II. 604 The aqueous solution of æsculin is highly fluorescent, the reflected light being of a sky-blue colour.

Æsopian (iːˈsəʊpɪən), *a.* Also -ean. [f. late L. *Æsōpius*: see -ian.] **1.** = Æsopic *a.* 1.

1875 *Encycl. Brit.* I. 212/1 The Latin writers of Æsopean fables. **1889** *Cent. Dict.* s.v., A fable in the Æsopian style.

2. = Æsopic *a.* 2.

1950 *Amer. Speech* XXV. 190 Thus on August 17, 1949, for the *n*th time the problem of the so-called 'Aesopian' language of American Communists came up in the course of the trial of the eleven members of the United States Politburo... Government witnesses..gave handy illustrations showing how with the aid of 'Aesopian' semantics Communists can and do say one thing but mean another. **1957** K. A. WITTFOGEL *Oriental Despotism* ix. 400 Originally Lenin used an 'Aesopian' (slave) language to speak to those oppressed by the government. **1970** M. SCAMMELL *Russia's Other Writers* 6 Pasternak, hoping for publication, had 'observed the decencies' and shrouded his message in suitably Aesopian form, while Sinyavsky and Daniel were less indirect. **1977** H. B. WEBER *Mod. Encycl. Russ. & Soviet Lit.* I. 42 Censorship..had a positive, formative impact upon the Aesopian writers' style by obliging them to sharpen their thoughts.

Æsopic (iː'sɒpɪk), *a.* Also (now *U.S.*) Esopic. [ad. late L. *Æsōpicus*, f. *Æsōpus* ad. Gr. Αἴσωπος.]

1. Of, pertaining to, or characteristic of Æsop, a semi-legendary Greek fabulist of the sixth century B.C. Hence **Æsopism** ('iːsəpɪz(ə)m), an Æsopic characteristic.

1728 CHAMBERS *Cycl.* s.v. *Fable*, Esopic Fables. **1831** CARLYLE in *Foreign Q. Rev.* VIII. 381 The old prevalence of the Didactic, especially of the Æsopic, is every where manifest. **1869** TOZER *Highl. Turkey* II. 266 The Æsopic and similar fables of later date. **1905** J. M. ROBERTSON *Did Shakes. write Titus Andron.?* 146 The Æsopism about the crow figuring at court.

2. *spec.* In relation to Russian and (Soviet) Communist literature [Russ. *ezopovskiĭ*, first so used by M.E. Saltȳkov-Shchedrin, *Unfinished Conversations* (1875) iv.; cf. Lenin *Party Organization & Party Lit.* in *Novaya Zhizn'* (1905) 13 Nov.]: using a style or language that has hidden or ambiguous meaning, *esp.* as a device to disguise dissident political writing in allegorical form and so avoid official censorship. Cf. ÆSOPIAN *a.* 2.

1927 D. S. MIRSKY *Hist. Russ. Lit.* I. 360 They are written in a language which Saltykov himself called Aesopic. It is one continuous circumlocution in view of the censorship and demands a constant running commentary. **1957** W. E. HARKINS *Dict. Russ. Lit.* 2 The great master of Aesopic language in Russian literature is Saltykov. **1977** R. HINGLEY *Russ. Writers & Society in Nineteenth Cent.* IV. xvii. 165 Despite all obstacles writers still found means of communicating. One technique was indirect allusion in 'Aesopic' language.

æst, obs. form of EAST.

†'**æstable**, *a. Obs.*—⁰. 'Belonging to summer.' Bailey, vol. II, 1731.

æsthesia (iːs'θiːsɪə, -zɪə). [mod.L., ad. Gr. αἴσθησις (see ÆSTHESIS).] Capacity for feeling and sensation; = ÆSTHESIS.

1879 in R. HUNTER et al. *Encycl. Dict.* I. 87/3 *Æsthesia*, perception by the senses, feeling. **1931** *Times Lit. Suppl.* 8 Jan. 17/3 A general aesthesia akin to that of a creature in which the special sense organs are not yet differentiated.

æsthesics (ɛs'θiːsɪks, iː-). [formed (on the rare analogy of Gr. φυσικός from φύσις) on Gr. αἴσθησις perception, the regular *æsthetics* from Gr. αἰσθητικός being pre-occupied. Pronunciation: see Æ.]

1879 LEWES *Psychol.* 64 It would be an abstract science of Feeling, to stand beside the abstract science of Force—an Æsthesics parallel with Dynamics.

æsthesiogenic (ɛsˌθiːsɪəʊ'dʒɛnɪk), *a.* [f. Gr. αἰσθησι-ς perception + γενικός pertaining to what is born or produced, taken as = producing: see -GEN.] Producing or causing sensation.

1881 in *Nature* XXIV. 480 Researches on the phenomena of sense, motion, circulation, and respiration in hypnotism, and on their modification by æsthesiogenic agents.

æsthesiometer (ɛsˌθiːsɪ'ɒmɪtə(r)). [f. Gr. αἴσθησι-ς perception + -(O)METER.] (See quot.)

1871 HAMMOND *Dis. Nervous Syst.* 14 The æsthesiometer is an instrument for the purpose of determining the degree of tactile sensibility possessed by the patient.

‖**æsthesis** (ɛs'θiːsɪs). [Gr. αἴσθησις a perceiving, f. vbl. stem αἰσθε- perceive.] The perception of the external world by the senses.

1851 RUSKIN *Mod. Painters* II. III. I. ii. §1 The term 'æsthesis' properly signifies mere sensual perception of the outward qualities and necessary effects of bodies. **1879** LEWES *Psychol.* 87 The antithesis between facts and feelings, Physis and Æsthesis.

æsthesodic (ɛsθɪ'sɒdɪk), *a. Phys.* [mod. f. Gr. αἰσθησι-ς sensory perception + ὁδ-ός way, path + -IC. In mod.Fr. *esthésodique*.] Of nerves: Providing a path for sensory impulses; conveying sensations from the external organs to the brain or nerve centres.

1878 M. FOSTER *Physiol.* III. v. §3. 488 They speak of it accordingly as kinesodic and æsthesodic, as simply affording paths for motor and sensory impulses.

æsthete ('ɛsθiːt, 'iːsθiːt). [ad. Gr. αἰσθητής one who perceives; cf. *athlete*.] One who professes a special appreciation of what is beautiful, and endeavours to carry his ideas of beauty into practical manifestation. Cf. ÆSTHETIC *a.* 4 and *sb.* 3.

1881 BURNAND in *Daily News* 31 Jan. 2/3 The matter-of-fact, slily-humorous, but quiet American colonel, who descends like a bomb-shell in the midst of the æsthetes. **1881** *Spectator* 2 July 859 The sham æsthete never chooses pretty colours. **1882** W. HAMILTON *Æsthetic Movement* p. vii, The *Æsthetes* are they who pride themselves upon having found out what is the really beautiful in nature and art, their faculties and tastes being educated up to the point necessary for the full appreciation of such qualities. **1914** C. MACKENZIE *Sinister Street* II. III. i. 516 My dear chap, he was absolutely barred. M' tutor used to like him, but..I don't mind telling you, he's really an æsthete.

æsthetic (ɛs'θɛtɪk: see below), *a.* and *sb.* Also **esthetic**. [mod. ad. Gr. αἰσθητικ-ός, of or pertaining to αἰσθητά, things perceptible by the senses, things material (as opposed to νοητά things thinkable or immaterial), also 'perceptive, sharp in the senses'; f. vb. stem αἰσθε- 'feel, apprehend by the senses'. Applied in Germ. by Baumgarten (1750–58, *Æsthetica*) to 'criticism of taste' considered as a science or philosophy; against which, as a misuse of the word found in German only, protest was made by Kant (1781, *Crit. R.V.* 21), who applied the name, in accordance with the ancient distinction of αἰσθητά and νοητά, to 'the science which treats of the conditions of sensuous perception,' a sense retained in the Kantian philosophy, and found in English *c* 1800. But Baumgarten's use of *æsthetik* found popular acceptance, and appeared in Eng. after 1830, though its adoption was long opposed. (See below.) Recent extravagances in the adoption of a sentimental archaism as the ideal of beauty have still further removed *æsthetic* and its derivatives from their etymological and purely philosophical meaning. 'The pronunciations (ɛs'θɛtɪk, iːs'θɛtɪk, ɛs'θiːtɪk, iːs'θiːtɪk), are all in use; the second is at present most common in London' (*N.E.D.*, 1884).]

¶ The following quotations illustrate the history of the word:

1832 *Penny Cycl.* I. 156 Æsthetics (*Æsthetik*) is the designation given by German writers to a branch of philosophical inquiry, the object of which is a philosophical theory of the beautiful. **1832** *Philol. Museum* 369 Beautiful and ugly depend on principles of taste, which it would be very convenient to designate by an adjective..Some English writers have adopted the term *esthetical*. This has not however yet become an established English word.. Perception in general is something very different from that peculiar and complex modification of it which takes cognizance of the beauties of poetry and art. *Esthetics* would naturally designate the doctrine of perception in general, and might be wanted as a technical term for that purpose. By the Kantian school, indeed, esthetic is used to denote that branch of metaphysics which contains the laws of perception..As an additional reason for hesitating before we adopt *esthetic*, it may be noticed that even in Germany it is not yet established beyond contest. **1842** GWILT *Encycl. Architect.* 673 There has lately grown into use in the arts a silly pedantic term under the name of Æsthetics..it is however one of the metaphysical and useless additions to nomenclature in the arts in which the German writers abound. **1859** SIR W. HAMILTON *Lect. Metaph.* I. vii. 124 It is nearly a century since Baumgarten..first applied the term Æsthetic to the doctrine which we vaguely and periphrastically denominate the Philosophy of Taste, the theory of the Fine Arts, the Science of the Beautiful, etc.,—and this term is now in general acceptation, not only in Germany, but throughout the other countries of Europe. The term Apolaustic would have been a more appropriate designation.

A. *adj.* †**1.** Of or pertaining to sensuous perception, received by the senses. *Obs.*

1798 W. TAYLOR in *Monthly Rev.* XXV. 585 In the dialect peculiar to Professor Kant..his *receptivity* for *aesthetic* gratification [is] not delicate.

2. Of or pertaining to the appreciation or criticism of the beautiful.

1821 COLERIDGE in *Blackw. Mag.* X. 254, I wish I could find a more familiar word than æsthetic, for works of taste and criticism. **1831** CARLYLE *Sart. Res.* (1858) 77 In answer to a cry for solid pudding..comes, epigrammatically enough, the invitation to a wash of quite fluid Æsthetic Tea! **1855** BAIN *Senses & Intell.* III. iv. §27 (1864) 622 The first object of an artist is to gratify the feelings of taste, or the proper æsthetic emotions. **1872** H. SPENCER *Psychol.* (ed. 2) II. §533 The æsthetic sentiments originate from the play-impulse. *Ibid.* §535 The æsthetic character of a feeling is habitually associated with separateness from life-serving function.

3. Of persons, animals: Having or showing an appreciation of the beautiful or pleasing; tasteful, of refined taste. Of things: In accordance with the principles of good taste (or what is conventionally regarded as such).

1871 DARWIN *Desc. Man* II. xiii. 39 Birds appear to be the most æsthetic of all animals, excepting of course, man, and they have nearly the same taste for the beautiful as we have. **1875** FARRAR *Silence & Voices* III. 62 A corrupt Hellenism, which regards sin forsooth with æsthetic toleration. **1880** W. S. GILBERT *Patience* I. 24, I am a broken-hearted troubadour, Whose mind's æsthetic, and whose tastes are pure. *Mod. Colloq.* He must have æsthetic wall-paper and a dado.

B. *sb.* commonly pl. **æsthetics**, as collect. sing.: but also in sing., after Ger. *æsthetik*, Fr. *esthétique*.

1. The science which treats of the conditions of sensuous perception. *Hist.*

1798 WILLICH *Elem. Crit. Philos.* 139 Aesthetic commonly signifies the Critique of Taste, but with Kant, the science containing the rules of sensation. **1803** *Edin. Rev.* I. 253 (*Villiers, Philos. of Kant*) If the experimentalists of the Institute had abandoned their physics for..the study of transcendental æsthetics and all the refinements and abstractions of pure reason. **1825** CARLYLE *Schiller* III. 174 The only department [of transcendentalism] to which he attached himself with his ordinary zeal was that which relates to the principles of the imitative arts, with their moral influences, and which in the Kantean nomenclature has been designated by the term *Æsthetics*, or the doctrine of sentiments and emotions. **1875** *Encycl. Brit.* I. 212/1 Kant ..under the title Transcendental Æsthetic, treats of the *a priori* principles of all sensuous knowledge.

2. The philosophy or theory of taste, or of the perception of the beautiful in nature and art.

a. *pl.*

1833 *Penny Cycl.* I. 157/1 Most German writers, who have published systematic treatises on æsthetics, have followed the principles laid down by Baumgarten, Kant, or Schelling. **1862** SHIRLEY *Nug. Crit.* I. 82 John is a man of taste, and knows something of practical æsthetics. **1872** H. SPENCER *Psychol.* II. §536 To deal fully with the psychology of æsthetics is out of the question.

b. *sing.*

1822 *New Monthly Mag.* IV. 149 He accordingly applied himself diligently to study the spirit of classical Tragedy, and the principles of *Æsthetic*. **1857** T. E. WEBB *Intell. of Locke* v. 84 The two propositions which constitute the Æsthetic of the Essay. **1864** *Press* 21 May 481 Certes, we English are behind hand in æsthetic. **1868** M. PATTISON *Academ. Organ.* §5. 196 Two professors of the science [of art] and æsthetic, dealing with Painting, Sculpture, etc.

3. = ÆSTHETE; an adherent of the æsthetic movement (see above A. 4).

1883 L. TROUBRIDGE *Life amongst Troubridges* (1966) 164 The great Oscar Wilde..is grown enormously fat,..not at all the aesthetic he used to look. **1894** *Cosmopolitan* XVII. 122 The æsthetics..who proclaim the infinite superiority of art to nature. **1946** *English Studies* XXVII. 49 It is not unsympathetic to the Aesthetics, for it seeks to understand them.

4. *spec.* Of or pertaining to a late nineteenth-century movement in England of artists and writers who advocated a doctrine of 'art for art's sake'.

1868 W. PATER *Æsthetic Poetry* in *Appreciations* (1889) 213 The 'æsthetic' poetry is neither a mere reproduction of Greek or medieval poetry, nor only an idealisation of modern life and sentiment. *a* **1882** D. G. ROSSETTI *St. Agnes* in *Coll. Wks.* (1886) I. 410 The journal of the worthy poet-critic..was much too æsthetic to permit itself many readers. **1882** W. HAMILTON *Æsthetic Movement* 31 The leaders of the Æsthetic School in poetry have been styled fleshly poets, delighting in somewhat sensually-suggestive descriptions of the passions. **1950** E. H. GOMBRICH *Story of Art* xxv. 402 Whistler became a leading figure in the so-called 'aesthetic movement' which tried to make out that artistic sensibility is the only thing in life worth taking seriously.

æsthetical (ɛs'θɛtɪkal, iː-, see prec.), *a.* [f. ÆSTHETIC + -AL[1].] Of or relating to æsthetics; relating to the philosophy or theory of beauty.

Often interchanged in use with *æsthetic*, but properly distinct; thus my *æsthetical notions* are the notions I have on the subject of æsthetics; my *æsthetic faculties* are those which exercise æsthetics.

1798 WILLICH *Elem. Crit. Philos.* 104 Those judgments.. are called æsthetical, which relate to the Beautiful and the Sublime. **1832** (See under ÆSTHETIC ¶). **1837** LOCKHART *Scott* (1839) III. 77 His own æsthetical notions are indicated rather than expressed. **1870** DISRAELI *Lothair* xxxv. 182 Lady Beatrice was there, herself an artist, and full of æsthetical enthusiasm. **1876** M. DAVIES *Unorth. Lond.* 204 The æsthetical element in religious matters—that element which addresses the feeling of devotion through the channels of the senses.

æsthetically (ɛs'θɛtɪkəlɪ, iː-), *adv.* [f. prec. + -LY[2].] In an æsthetic or æsthetical manner; in relation to æsthetics, or to a standard of taste.

1827 DE QUINCEY *Murder* in *Blackw. Mag.* Feb. 200/2 It may also be treated æsthetically, as the Germans call it, that is, in relation to good taste. **1873** SYMONDS *Grk. Poets* vi. 171 The æsthetically ennobling enthusiasm for the old Greek deities. **1882** STUART-GLENNIE in *Macm. Mag.* XLV. 497 Archæologically interesting..as they might be, they were æsthetically tawdry..to the last degree.

æsthetician (ɛsθɪ'tɪʃən, iː-). [f. ÆSTHETICS + -IAN after *mathematics*, *mathematician*, etc.] One skilled in or devoted to æsthetics; a professor of taste.

1829 *Virginia Lit. Museum* I. 199/1 There is no question, which has given rise to more frequent disputation amongst Æstheticians..than that of the origin of beauty. **1845** *Blackw. Mag.* LVII. 613 The aesthetician has to lay aside nearly all terms of reprobation, in alluding to the habiliments of ladies of the present day. **1874** SULLY *Sensat. & Intuit.* 366 Æstheticians in their love of simplicity have persisted in forcing all forms of Art under this one Conception.

æstheticism (ɛs'θɛtɪsɪz(ə)m, iː-). [f. ÆSTHETIC + -ISM; cf. *critic*, *criticism*, etc.] The quality of being æsthetic; the pursuit of, or devotion to, what is sensuously beautiful.

1855 BRIMLEY *Ess.* 237 The *Lotos Eaters* carries Tennyson's tendency to pure æstheticism to an extreme point. It is picture and music and nothing more. **1876** MELLOR *Priesthood* viii. 392 If it [the Ritualistic movement] were nothing but a development of æstheticism, it might be left to pursue its course. **1882** W. HAMILTON *Æsthetic Movement* 32 It is at the Lyceum Theatre that æstheticism in all its beauty can best be seen. The present revival of 'Romeo and Juliet' may be pronounced to be the most exquisite rendering of that sweet poem.

æstheticist (ɛsˈθɛtɪsɪst, iː-). [f. ÆSTHETIC + -IST.] A professor of æstheticism; an æsthetician.

1868 *Chronicle* No. 44. 86/1 Those æstheticists of the future.

æstheticize (ɛsˈθɛtɪsaɪz, iː-), *v.* [f. ÆSTHETIC + -IZE, after *critic, criticize*, etc.] To render æsthetic, or agreeable to a refined taste, to refine.

1864 *Realm* 22 June 4 The sentimental theory of æstheticising the architecture of grimy manufacturing centres.

æsthetics: see ÆSTHETIC.

æsthiology (ɛsθɪˈɒlədʒɪ). [f. Gr. αἰσθ- or αἰσθε- vbl. stem, = perceive + -λογία discourse: see -LOGY. The formation is not analogical.] = next.

1831 D. CRAIGIE in *Encycl. Brit.* s.v. *Anatomy*, Comparative Æsthiology, or the comparative anatomy of the organs of sensation.

ˌæstho-physiˈology. [f. (not on Gr. analogy) Gr. αἰσθ- perceive + PHYSIOLOGY.] The scientific study of the organs of sensation.

1855 H. SPENCER *Psychol.* (1872) I. I. vi. 97, I deliberately adopt Æstho-physiology in preference to..Æsthesi-physiology.

† **æˈstiferous,** *a. Obs.*[−0] [f. L. *æstus* heat, tide + -FEROUS bearing, bringing.] 'Ebbing and flowing as the tide.' Bailey, vol. II, 1731. 'Turbulent as the tide.' Ash 1775.

æstival, estival (ˈɛstɪvəl, ɛˈstaɪvəl: see below), *a.* Forms: 4 **esty'vall,** 5–6 **esti'vall, 'estivall,** 6 **æ'stival,** 6– **estival, æstival.** [a. Fr. *estival* (16th c. in Littré), ad. L. *æstīvāl-is* a secondary adj. f. *æstīv-us* (see ÆSTIVE); said at first only of the (summer) solstice, afterwards used instead of *æstīvus*, as more analogous to *vernālis, autumnālis, hiemālis*. The spelling with *æ* after the Latin, is the more common in later times, especially in Nat. Hist. to which the word is chiefly restricted. The historical accentuation is *'estival* (cf. *'festival*); but *e'stīval* appears in 1590 and was adopted by Dr. Johnson, after anal. of *au'tumnal*; the initial vowel in this and the following words in *æst-* is by many pronounced (iː-).]

1. Of or belonging to summer, or the summer solstice.

1386 *Almanak of Year* (1812) 49 Fro þe stacyon of þe son estyval to þe stacyon of þe son hyemal. **1430** LYDG. *Chron. Troy* I. iii, Where halowed is the stondyng estiuall Of freshe Appollo, with his golden wayne. **1535** STEWART *Cron. Scotl.* I. 89 Fra the coluyre to tropic estivall. *c* **1590** GREENE *Poems* (1861) 303 When in æstival Cancers gloomy bower The greater glory of the heavens doth shine. **1698** [R. FERGUSON] *View of Eccles.* 106 The Estival or Brumal Temper of the Air. **1753** CHAMBERS *Cycl. Supp.*, *Æstival solstice*, the time when the sun enters the *æstival point*. **1880** M. COLLINS *Th. in Gard.* I. 235 You generally get true summer in August: this year it has been unusually æstival.

2. Appearing or produced in summer.

a **1682** SIR T. BROWNE *Misc.* 92 (R.) Beside vernal, estival, and autumnal, made of flowers, the ancients had also hyemal garlands. **1870** HOOKER *Stud. Flora* 365, *Leucojum æstivum*; leaves hibernal, flowers æstival.

æstivate (ˈɛstɪveɪt, ˈiːstɪveɪt), *v.* Also **estivate.** [f. L. *æstīvāt-* ppl. stem of *æstīvā-re* to reside during the summer; f. *æstīv-us*: see ÆSTIVE. Cf. Fr. *estiver* (16th c.).] To spend the summer. *esp.* in *Zool.* To pass the summer in a state of torpor or suspended animation. (Cf. *hibernate.*)

1626 COCKERAM, *Aestiuate*, to summer in a place. **1742** BAILEY, *Æstivate*, to sojourn or lodge in a Place in Summertime. **1854** WOODWARD *Mollusca* (1856) 49 The mollusca..æ stivate, or fall into a summer sleep, when the heat is great. **1882** *Pall Mall G.* 1 Feb. 5 The snails of the equatorial region, though they do not hibernate, yet æstivate (if we may coin a word).

æstivation, estivation, (ɛstɪˈveɪʃən, iːstɪˈveɪʃən). [mod. f. L. *æstīvāt-* ppl. stem of *æstīvā-re* (see ÆSTIVATE), after nouns of action in -TION, as if ad. L. **æstīvātiōn-em*. In the Bot. sense it is ad. mod.L. *æstīvātio* introduced by Linnæus. Lord Bacon spelt *estivation*, but the techn. spelling is commonly *æstivation*. As to the pronunciation of *æ-*, see ÆSTIVAL, and cf. *estimation*, L. *æstimātio.*]

† **1.** The passing or spending of the summer; summer retreat or residence. *Obs.*

1625 BACON *Ess.* xlv. 552 Let it be turned to a Grotta, or Place of Shade, or Estiuation. **1731** BAILEY vol. II. *Æstivation*, a dwelling or residence in a place for the summer time. **1755** JOHNSON, *Estivation*, the act of passing the summer.

2. *Zool.* The act of remaining dormant or torpid during the dry season, or extreme heat of summer; summer-sleep. Opposed to *hibernation*. Also *fig.*

1845 DARWIN *Voy. of Nat.* v. (1879) 99 Within the tropics, the hybernation, or more properly æstivation, of animals is determined not by the temperature, but by the times of drought. **1870** *Pall Mall G.* 12 Dec. 11 With what we are pleased to call the cold weather Calcutta rouses herself from her æstivation of seven long months.

3. *Bot.* Internal arrangement of a flower-bud; manner in which the petals are folded up therein before expansion; præfloration. Opposed to *vernation*, or the arrangement of the leaf-bud (flowers expanding in *summer*, and leaves in *spring*).

1830 LINDLEY *Nat. Syst. Bot.* 151 With Malvaceæ they agree in the twisted æstivation of the corolla. *c* **1875** HULME *Wild Flowers* 6 Meadow Crane's-Bill.—Calyx of five sepals, imbricate in æstivation.

† **ˈæstive,** *a. Obs.* Also **estive.** [ad. L. *æstīv-us* of summer, or heat; f. *æst-us* heat.] Of or belonging to summer; hot or burning.

1607 TOPSELL *Serpents* (1653) 719 Frogs..are likewise ingendered out of the dust of the earth by warm, æstive, and Summer showers. **1635** HEYWOOD *Hierarchie* III. 124 Auriga mounted in a chariot bright (Else styl'd Heniochus) receives his light In th' Estive circle.

† **ˈæstuant,** *a. Obs. rare*[−1]. [ad. L. *æstuant-em* pr. pple. of *æstuāre* to burn, be inflamed.] Boiling; heaving with heat.

1633 T. ADAMS *Exp. 2 Pet.* ii. 10 (1865) 419/1 Not that every tickling should draw us to marrying; but a burning, an æstuant flame.

† **ˈæstuary.** *Obs.* [ad. L. *æstuārium* (prop. adj. = tidal) a tidal opening, also a vent-hole for vapours. The L. form is also found unchanged.]

1. = ESTUARY.

1706 PHILLIPS, *Æstuary*, a Place overflow'd with Sea-water, such as the Washes and Fens in Lincolnshire. **1787** T. BEST *Angling* (ed. 2) 129 The Humber..is rather the mouth or *æstuarium* of divers rivers meeting together.

2. A vapour-bath.

1706 PHILLIPS, *Æstuary*, in a Medicinal Sense, a receiving of the Vapours or Steam of certain boiled Drugs into the Body, thro' a hole made in a Seat or Chair. **1775** ASH, *Æstuarium*, in pharmacy, a vapor-bath.

† **ˈæstuate,** *v. Obs.* Also 7 **estuate.** [f. L. *æstuāt-* ppl. stem of *æstuā-re* to be hot, boil up, bubble.] To boil; to heave; to surge up like the tide.

1620 VENNER *Via Recta* Introd. 11 A stomacke that estuateth with heat. **1648** JOS. BEAUMONT *Psyche* VIII. iii, Æstuating in her mighty toil The sea has wrought up to her highest shore. **1692** WAGSTAFFE *Vind. Carolinæ* iv. 41 Some humours might glow and estuate in the body.

† **ˈæstuating,** *vbl. sb. Obs.* [f. prec. + -ING[1].] Boiling; heaving with heat.

1674 R. GODFREY *Inj. & Abus. Physick* 88 The real producer of that æstuating and Feverishness, is not an inflamed mass of putryfyings.

† **æstuˈation.** *Obs.* Also 7 **estuation.** [ad. L. *æstuātiōn-em* n. of action, f. *æstuā-re* to boil up.] Feverish disturbance, boiling up, ebullition.

1605 BACON *Adv. Learn.* II. 74 Men in ambition..are in a perpetual Estuation to exalt their place. **1683** SALMON *Doron Med.* I. 147 Depress the feverish æstuation of the Blood. **1684** T. BURNET *Theo. Earth* 118 The fires and æstuations of it [Ætna] are excellently describ'd by Virgil.

æstuous (ˈɛstjuːəs), *a. rare.* [ad. L. *æstuōs-us*, f. *æstus* heat.] Agitated (as with heat or tide); heaving.

1844 R. M. MILNES *Mem. Many Scenes* 156 Why do I tremble at my æstuous soul, That would embrace the burning God?

† **ˈæsture.** *Obs. rare*[−1]. [f. L. *æstus* boiling, bubbling, tide, by false analogy (as if like *pasture* from *pastus*), *æstus* not being a pa. pple., and *æstūra* an impossible form in L.]

1615 CHAPMAN *Odyss.* XII. 111 For the seas retain Not only their outrageous æsture there.

† **æsymˈnetic,** *a. Obs.* [f. Gr. αἰσυμνήτ-ης an elective ruler (f. αἶσα a share) + -IC.] (See quot.)

1753 CHAMBERS *Cycl. Supp.*, *Æsymnetic monarchy*, among antient writers on government, denotes a limited elective monarchy.

æt, variant of ETE. *Obs.*, food.

æt, obs. form of AT *prep.*

æt. Also **aet.** [Abbrev. of L. *ætatis*, gen. sing. of *ætas* age.] Of or at the age of; aged (a particular number of years). Also **ætat** (ˈiːtæt, aɪ-).

[**1632** MASSINGER *Emperour of East* II. i. sig. E2, Cleanthe, daughter to the king of Epirus, Ætatis suæ, the fourteenth.] **1681** *Visitation of Northamptonshire* (Harleian Soc.) 4 William Adams, of Charwelton now living ætat: 34. **1857** TROLLOPE *Barchester T.* III. iii. 56 At the present moment Mr. Thorne, *ætat.* fifty, was over head and ears in love at first sight with the Signora Madeline Vesey Neroni, *nata* Stanhope. **1884** T. BRYANT *Pract. Surg.* (ed. 4) I. xiv. 688 A boy æt. 13, after a blow on the abdomen, walked a mile with but little assistance. **1918** G. FRANKAU *One of Them* vi. in *Poetical Works* (1923) II. 75 Jill as she was in times of sugared plenty: The Bond Street goddess, *aetat* three-and-twenty. **1952** G. SARTON *Hist. Sci.* I. xix. 492 He had spent twenty years of his youth (aet. 18–38) as a student. **1966** 'BRENT OF BIN BIN' *Up Country* (rev. ed.) ii. 20 Mary died *ætat* twelve, and her parents never troubled about the grant. **1972** *Lancet* 29 July 214 In 1956, aet. 19, had dull pain, right lower quadrant.

æteow, æteau, var. ATEW *v. Obs.*, to show.

ætern, -al, -ity, etc., obs. var. ETERN, -AL, -ITY.

æð, obs. form of OATH, and of EATH, easy.

æðel, variant of ATHEL *a.* and *sb. Obs.*, noble.

æðeling, obs. form of ATHELING.

aetheogam (eɪˈiːθɪəʊgæm). [f. Gr. ἀήθης unusual + γάμ-ος marriage.] An aetheogamous plant, a cryptogam.

1845 LINDLEY *Sch. Bot.* (1858) ix. 151, *Aëtheogams*, plants furnished with air vessels and stomates or air pores.

aetheogamous (eɪˌiːθɪːˈɒgəməs), *a. Bot.* [f. as prec. + -OUS.] A synonym of CRYPTOGAMOUS.

1842 GRAY *Struct. Bot.* ix. §2 (1880) 340 *Aetheogamous*, with sexual apparatus, and vascular tissue; or only cellular tissue.

æther, -ial, etc., occas. var. ETHER, -IAL, etc.

† **Æthiops mineral.** *Chem. Obs.* (See quot.)

1706 PHILLIPS, *Æthiops Mineral*, a Medicine made by Imbodying equal Parts of running Quicksilver and Flower of Brimstone, and then Deflagrating or Burning off the Mixture in a Crucible. **1755** JOHNSON, *Æthiops Mineral*, a Medicine, so-called from its dark colour, prepared from quicksilver and sulphur, ground together in a marble mortar to a black powder. [J. cites QUINCY.]

æthogen (ˈiːθədʒɛn). *Chem.* [f. Gr. αἶθος fire + -GEN taken as = 'producing.'] A name applied to boric nitride because of the brilliant phosphorescent light that it gives under the blowpipe.

(In mod. Dicts.)

æthrioscope (ˈiːθrɪəskəʊp). [f. Gr. αἰθρία the open sky + -σκοπός, -σκοπίον an observer.] An instrument invented by Sir John Leslie to indicate the variations of solar radiation.

1832 U. K. S. *Nat. Philos.* II. iv. 44 The Æthrioscope of Leslie is another modification of the differential thermometer.

ætiological (ˌiːtɪəʊˈlɒdʒɪkəl, ˌɛtɪ-), *a.* [f. Gr. αἰτιολογικ-ός inquiring into causes (see ÆTIOLOGY) + -AL[1].] Of or pertaining to ætiology; assigning or tending to assign a cause or reason.

1753 CHAMBERS *Cycl. Supp.*, *Ætiological*, something that assigns the cause of an effect or appearance. **1837** WHEWELL *Induct. Sc.* III. XVIII. 481 The sciences which treat of causes have sometimes been termed ætiological. **1869** HUXLEY in *Sci. Opin.* 28 Apr. 486/2 It will be ætiological speculation, if it attempts to deduce the history of the world, as a whole, from the known properties of the matter of the earth in the conditions in which the earth has been placed.

ætiologically (ˌiːtɪəʊˈlɒdʒɪkəlɪ, ˈɛtɪ-), *adv.* [f. prec. + -LY[2].] In an ætiological manner; so as to assign a cause or reason.

1849 W. FITZGERALD *Whitaker's Disput.* 403 Scripture is expounded ætiologically, when it is shewn why any thing was done or said.

† **ˈætiologue.** *Obs. rare*[−1]. [f. Gr. αἰτία cause, ground + λόγος speech. Cf. ÆTIOLOGY 1.] The cause assigned, or reason annexed to a statement.

1632 BP. SMYTH *Serm.* 43 In the aetiologue following, namely, in these words: Thou hast the words of euerlasting life.

ætiology (iːtɪˈɒlədʒɪ, ˈɛtɪ-). Also 7 **aiti-,** 8 **eti-.** [ad. L. *ætiologia*, a. Gr. αἰτιολογία giving a cause, f. αἰτία cause, reason + -λογία discourse: see -LOGY.]

1. The assignment of a cause, the rendering of a reason; also, the reason annexed, the wherefore of a command or utterance.

a **1555** BRADFORD *Wks.* 44 He addeth this ætiology or cause, saying, 'For the kingdom of heaven is at hand.' **1615** BP. HALL *Contempl.* IV. xi. (1853) 279 And consider with me the topography, the aitiology, the chronography of this miracle. **1716** HALLEY in *Phil. Trans.* XXIX. 406 The Etiology of a matter so uncommon, never before seen by my self. **1771** WOULFE *ibid.* LXI. 115 Ætiology of the Operation. *Mod.* Title of a lecture: 'The ætiology of the drinking customs.'

2. The science or philosophy of causation; that part of philosophy which treats of the demonstration of causes; the part of any special science which speculates on the causes of its phenomena.

1660 T. STANLEY *Hist. Philos.* (1701) 486/2 Whereby he conceives all DogmatickÆtiology may be refelled, as defective. **1753** CHAMBERS *Cycl. Supp.* s.v., The sceptics were professed opponents of all ætiology, or argumentation from causes. **1877** HUXLEY *Anat. Inv. An.* Introd. 35 Ætiology has for its object the ascertainment of the causes of these facts, and the explanation of biological phenomena, by showing that they constitute particular cases of general physical laws.

3. That branch of medical science which investigates the causes and origin of diseases; the scientific exposition of the origin of any disease.

1684 tr. *Bonet's Merc. Compit.* XVI. 562 Nor will it be easie ..to inquire the particular reasons of this Ail, nor to proceed in this Aitiology. **1737** R. BRACKEN *Farriery* I. vi. 36 The

Aetiology or Doctrine teaching (or rather pretending to teach) us the Knowledge of the Causes of Distempers. **1881** HUXLEY in *Nature* No. 615. 346 The important part played by parasitic organisms in the ætiology of disease.

‖**ae'tites.** *Obs.* [a. L. *āetītēs*, a. Gr. ἀετίτης prop. adj. 'of the eagle, aquiline,' subst. 'eagle stone.'] The eagle-stone; a hollow nodule or pebble of argillaceous oxide of iron, having a loose nucleus, which derived its name from being fabled to be found in the eagle's nest, and to which medicinal and magical properties were ascribed.

1579 LYLY *Euphues* (1636) F 9 The precious stone Ætites which is found in the filthy nests of the Eagle. **1626** BACON *Sylva* §154 The Ætites or Eagles Stone, which hath a little Stone within it. **1753** CHAMBERS *Cycl. Supp.* s.v., Dr. Woodward places the distinguishing characteristic of the *ætites*, in that it consists of several crusts, which have in them a cavity with matter in it, loose and moveable. **1862** *Reader* 8 July 33 Another stone, the Aetites, possessed the singular property..of detecting theft.

æuriche, ævriche, obs. forms of EVERY.

†**ævi'ternal,** *a. Obs. rare.* [f. L. *æviternus* (the full form, of which *ætern-us* is the contr., f. *ævum* an age + *-ternus* adj. suffix) + -AL[1].] Everlasting, endless, eternal.

1660 T. STANLEY *Hist. Philos.* III. II. 137 Gods placed in the highest regions of aether, aeviternall. *Ibid.* (1701) 817/1 The second or middle kind of Things is begun in time, but is without end (commonly termed æviternal).

†**ævi'ternity.** *Obs.* [f. as prec. + -ITY.] Eternal existence, everlasting duration; eternity.

1596 MYCHELBORNE in Grosart's *Sir F. Drake* (1881) Introd. 7 Penning forth his story In golden lines of Æviternitie. **1640** REYNOLDS *On the Passions* 1081 Our pursuits of them [knowledge and truth] seem infinite and unlimited, by reason of our own infiniteness and æviternity that way.

‖**ævum** ('i:vəm). *Obs. rare.* [L. = an age.] Formerly used as = ÆON, age, eternity.

1660 T. STANLEY *Hist. Philos.* (1701) 428/1 His soul ascends to the pure Æther, and lives in the happy Ævum with the blessed.

æx, obs. form of AXE.

aey, obs. variant of AYE, always.

af-, *pref.* **1.** Assimilated form of L. *ad-* to, bef. initial *f-*, as in *af-fectus, af-flātus, af-fluentia*. Reduced in OFr. to *a-*, and so adopted in Eng. But artificially restored in Fr. spelling in 4–5, whence extended to Eng. in 5–6; as in *affair, affiance, affront*, early Eng. *afaire, afiaunce, afront*. In all mod. words from L., *aff-* has been written from the first, though only one *f-* is pronounced.

2. While the words from OFr. were being refashioned after L. spelling, *af-* was substituted for *a-* in various words where it did not represent L. *af-*, as in *a(f)fray, a(f)fright*; see AD- 2.

af, *prep. Obs.* or *dial.* Occas. Sc. form of OF, OFF.

1535 STEWART *Cron. Scotl.* II. 321 Syne af his hors amang thame fell doun deid. *c* **1620** A. HUME *Orthogr. Brit. Tong.* (1865) 9 Af this voual ryseth tuae diphthonges. *Ibid.* 12 To put our men af their errour.

aface (ə'feɪs), *adv.* prop. *phr.* [A *prep.*[1] on + FACE.] In face, in front.

c **1860** LEIGHTON *Trad. Scot. Life* 174 Right aface of him.

afaint (ə'feɪnt), *adv.* prop. *phr.* [A *prep.*[1] of state + FAINT *sb.* or *v.*; cf. *a-float*.] In a fainting state.

1878 *The First Violin* III. ii, No sign of emotion, no quiver of the lips, no groan, though the heart might be afaint.

†**a'faite,** *v. Obs.* Forms: 3 **afeite, afyght(e,** 3–4 **afaite, afayte,** 4–5 **affayte, affaite.** [a. OFr. *afaitie-r, afaite-r, afeite-r*, to prepare, dispose, train, fashion:—L. *affectā-re*, freq. of *afficĕre* to move, touch, incline, f. *af-* = *ad-* to + *facĕre* to do, make. *Afaite* is thus an early doublet of AFFECT. In 14th c. the pref. *a-* was refashioned as *af-* in Fr. and Eng.]

1. To affect, influence, incline, dispose, in any way.

c **1230** *Ancren Riwle* 284 ȝif eni is þet naueð nout þe heorte þus afeited. **1340** *Ayenb.* 75 Þe wel louiynde of gentil herte and affayted.

2. To bring into any shape, to fashion, mould; to adapt or prepare *to* or *for* a purpose.

c **1230** *Ancren Riwle* 284 Þuruh so monie duntes..so swuðe ueire afeited. **1340** *Ayenb.* 212 Wordes afaited and y-sliked ueleuold. **1393** GOWER *Conf.* II. 113 He had affaited his lusty tales. *Ibid.* III. 22 His cokes ben for him affaited. *Ibid.* III. 234 He hath gere at home inough Affaited at his owne heste.

3. To fit out, array, dress.

1483 CAXTON *G. de la Tour* b i, They affayted and arayed the doughter the best wyse they myȝt.

4. To train (hawks, hounds, etc. to obedience); hence, to tame.

c **1300** *K. Alis.* 6583 Delfyns they nymeth, and cokedrill, And afyghteth, to heore wille. **1377** LANGL. *P. Pl.* B. VI. 32 And go affaite þe faucones · wild foules to kille. **1393** GOWER *Conf.* I. 84 The yonge whelpe, which is affaited.

5. To reduce, subject, subdue.

1297 R. GLOUC. 179 To Yrlond he gan wende, Vor to afayty þat lond, & to wynne ech ende. *c* **1315** SHOREHAM 111 The man the hym wole afayty Of prede that hys so heȝ. **1377** LANGL. *P. Pl.* B. XIV. 296 It affaiteth þe flesshe · fram folyes ful manye.

6. To affect with disease.

1475 CAXTON *Jason* 17 Arte thou he that arte affayted with the blanche feures for cause of my right redoubted lady.

†**a'faitement.** *Obs.* [a. OFr. *afaitement* preparation, address, n. of action f. *afaiter*; see prec. and -MENT.] Training, address, proper behaviour, breeding.

c **1300** *K. Alis.* 661 Theo thridde him taughte to play at bal; Theo feorthe afatement in halle.

†**'afald,** *a. Obs.* or *dial.* Forms: 1 **ánfeald,** 1–3 **anfald,** 4–6 **afald(e,** 5–6 **anefald,** 6 **afauld, efald,** 7 **effa(u)ld,** 8– **aefauld;** all north. after 2. Rare midl. form 5 **oonefold.** [f. A *adj.*[1], AN, one + FOLD; cogn. w. OS. and OFris. *énfáld*, ON. *einfalldr*, Goth. *ainfalþs*, mod. G. *einfalt-ig*. Confined after 12th c. to northern, and after 14th to Sc. writers, by whom reduced to *a-fald, effauld*, mod. Sc. *aefauld*. The *oonefold* of Townl. Myst. is only a transliteration of the north. *anfald*, the midl. and south. dialects having lost the word, which has however been used anew in modern times as ONE-FOLD. Cf. *two-fold*, etc.]

†**1.** Single, singular, sole, only. *Obs.*

c **1000** ÆLFRIC *Gramm.* xiii. 83 *Numerus* is ȝetel, *singularis et pluralis* ánfeald oððe meniȝfeald. *c* **1175** *Lamb. Hom.* 25 Erðon he hefde anfalde sunne and seodðan he haueð twafald. *c* **1200** *Ormul.* 11296 Swa þatt tu shule tweȝȝenn menn Wiþþ anfald name tellenn. *c* **1300** *Cursor Mundi* 6342 *Cotton MS.* Persons thre, And an-fald godd in vnite. *Fairfax MS.* Anfalde god in trinite. *Göttingen MS.* A-fold godd in vnite. *Trinity MS.* O godhede in vnite. **1375** BARBOUR *Bruce* xx. 618 The afald god in trinite. *c* **1460** *Townl. Myst.* 132 Hayll, oonefold God in persons þre! **1513** DOUGLAS *Æneis* Pref. 463 Afald Godhede, ay lesting but discrepance.

2. Simple, sincere, without duplicity; honest. (In *mod. Sc.* Jamieson.)

c **960** *Rushw. Gosp.* Matt. vi. 22 ȝif þin eȝe biþ anfald. *c* **1000** *Ags. Gosp.* ibid., ȝyf þin eaȝe bið an-feald. *c* **1175** *Lamb. Hom.* 151 Anfald oðer twafald is ech mon..Iob wes anfald rihtwis Mon, and swa god mon. *c* **1200** *Ormul.* 1537 To þeowwtenn an Allmahhtiȝ Godd Wiþþ anfald rihhte læfe. **1465** quoted in P. F. Tytler's *Hist. Scotl.* II. 388 To stand in afald kendnes, supplé, and defencs, ilk an til odir. **1513** DOUGLAS *Æneis* VII. Prol. 159 With ane fald diligence. *Ibid.* XIII. vii. 90 Traistis wele Enee afald and kynd. **1535** STEWART *Cron. Scotl.* (1858) I. 63 Come in that tyme with anefald mynd and hart. **1600** in Pitcairn *Crim. Trials* (1833) II. 284 To obey and serve, with efald and ever ready service. **1609** A. HUME (*title*) Ane Afold Admonitioun to the Ministerie of Scotland, by a Deing Brother. **1651** CALDERWOOD *Hist. Kirk.* (1843) II. 353 We sall tak effald, plaine, and upright part with him.

†**'afaldly,** *adv. Obs.* or *dial.* Forms: 1 **ánfealdlice,** 2 **anfaldeliche,** 6 **afaldly,** 7 **effauldly.** [f. prec. + -LY[2].]

1. Singly, simply.

c **1175** *Lamb. Hom.* 5 Ic eou habbe þet godspel iseid anfaldeliche nu scule ȝe understonden twafaldeliche.

2. With single-heartedness, sincerely, truly.

1533 BELLENDENE *Livy* II. (1822) 137 To mak thame stand the mair afaldly at thair opinioun. **1639** K. JAMES *Tumults in Scotl.* 143 And effauldly joine in defence and pursuit.

†**a'falle,** *v.*[1] *str. Obs.* Forms as in FALL. *Pa. t.* **afell.** *Pa. pple.* **afallen.** [f. A- *pref.* 1 intensive + FALL. Cf. *a-rise*.]

1. *intr.* To fall down; to fall (in battle); to fall (upon) as a destroyer.

c **1000** *Ags. Gosp.* Luke vi. 49 Hrædlice hit afeoll & wearð mycel hryre þæs huses. *c* **1160** *Hatton Gosp.* ibid., Rædlice hit afeol & warð mycel ryre þas huses. **1205** LAYAMON 15949 Þi wal is afallen. **1250** *Ibid.* 16929 Arere chirches þat beoþ a-valle. *c* **1230** *Ancren Riwle* 246 A muchel tentaciun..aualleð mid a softe rein of a lut teares. *c* **1380** *Sir Ferumb.* 1519 Charlis þe kyng of fraunce..is oppon my lond afalle. *c* **1420** *Pallad. on Husb.* IX. 172 And if it sholde affalle into the dale.

2. *fig.* To fall in amount, price, estimation, rank, moral state.

a **1121** *O.E. Chron.* (Laud MS.) an. 1100 On his dagan ælc riht afeoll · and ælc unriht..up arás. **1205** LAYAMON 31967 Þa afeol þat feoh here, fif and sixti ȝere. *a* **1250** *Owl & Night.* 1683 Ower prude schal avalle.

†**a'falle,** *v.*[2] *Obs.* Forms: *Inf.* 3 **afall-e(n, avalle(n.** *Pa. t.* 3 **avalde.** *Pa. pple.* 3 **afalled, -et, avalled.** [a variant of the causal AFELLEN, confused with the intr. *afallen* (see prec.), and perh. with *avalen* OFr. *avaler.*] *trans.* To fell, strike down, cut down, lay low.

1205 LAYAMON 26096 Whi þu mine maȝe a-ualled hafuest mid morðe [*later text* a-falled]. *c* **1230** *Ancren Riwle* 122 Þet a windes puf of a word mei auellen [*v.r.* afallen]. **1250** LAYAMON 2069 Hire names..beoð swiðe a-valled [*earlier t.* afelled].

†**a'fame,** *v. Obs. rare*[−1]. [prob. for an earlier *enfame*, a. OFr. *infame-r* or ? *enfame-r*:—late L. *infamā-re* to defame.] *trans.* To defame.

1375 *Disp. betw. Mary & Cross* 20 (1871) 131 Þe fruites Mooder · was neuere a-famed.

afamish, variant of AFFAMISH *v. Obs.*

‖**afanc** (avaŋk). Also 9 **avanc, avangc, addanc** (aðaŋk). [Welsh *afanc* beaver, f. med. Welsh *adanc, afanc*:—Celt. **abankos*, f. **ab-* water (whence, from the base **abona*, Welsh *afon*, Bret. *aven* river; Ir. *ab, abann* river), repr. by med. Breton *avancq* 'bièvre, espèce de castor', Ir. *abac* beaver, dwarf. Cf. L. *amnis* (f. **abnis*) stream, river, of Italo-Celtic origin.]

It seems likely that the original sense in Welsh and Irish was 'river animal' which by extension came also to mean 'water sprite'. For the semantic development of Ir. *abac*, an aquatic creature, beaver, dwarf, cf. the history of LEPRECHAUN (O.Ir. *lúchorpáin* small bodies, applied in the 8th c. to water-sprites).

An aquatic monster in Celtic mythology.

[**1781** T. PENNANT *Tour in Wales* II. 134 A deep, wide, and still water, called *Llyn yr Afangc*, or *The Beavers Pool*.] **1834** G. ROBERTS tr. *Theophilus Evans's View Primit. Ages* (*c* 1864) I. v. 129 As to the *Afanc*, it is the common opinion that he was a kind of large water-dog, with a broad tail called a Beaver. **1838** C. GUEST tr. *Mabinogion* I. 341 The Addanc of the Lake slays them once every day. *Ibid.* 381 In the Triads, mention is made of the Addanc, or Avanc of the Lake, as an aquatic monster. **1859** *Cambrian Jrnl.* VI. 146 It was a woman who enticed the avangc out of..the lake. **1923** OGDEN & RICHARDS *Meaning of Meaning* iii. 149 Before the appearance of an image, say, of an afanc, something can be observed to occur which is often misleadingly described as 'an intention of imagining' an afanc. **1960** *Listener* 29 Sept. 512/2, I hope no one revives the *afanc* which used to emerge from a lake near my house in Cardiganshire to devour cattle.

afand, afaynd, var. AFOND *v. Obs.*, to try, tempt.

afang, earlier f. AFONG *v. Obs.*, to seize.

afar (ə'fɑ:(r)), *adv.* Forms: 2–3 **of feor,** 4 **a ver, a feer, afer, afur, ofer;** 4–5 **a fer;** 5 **offerre;** 6–7 **a farre, a-farre;** 7– **afar.** Also 4 **on ferr, a ferr, afer, i-verre;** 6–7 **a farre, a-farre, a far, a-far;** 7– **afar.** [f. FAR *adv.*:—OE. *feor*, with *prep.* OF, or ON. The phrase *of feor* appears in 12th c., as an analytical form = *feorren, ferren*:—OE. *feorran*, 'from far.' (Cf. Fr. *de loin*, L. *a longe, de longinquo.*) *On ferr* appears *c* 1300, as = OE. *feor*, or a strengthening of it; (perhaps orig. an erroneous expansion of *a ferr* for *of feor*). In 14th c. both were *a fer*, and the force of the *of* being thus lost except in special connexion, the combination *from a far* took the place of the earlier *feorran, of feor, a fer*; and *a fer* = *on-feor* began to be strengthened with a following *off*. The result is that *afar* is now a synonym of the simple *far* in the local sense, chiefly used in poetry. See also FAR, FERREN.]

1. From far, from a distance. Now only with *see* and the like, *afar* being transferred from the seer to the thing seen.

c **1175** *Lamb. Hom.* 247 Þe warliche loki..and of feor bihalde alle þe cuminde. *c* **1230** *Ancren Riwle* 250 Derne uondunges þet he scheoteð of feor. *c* **1300** *Cursor Mundi* 8484 On-ferr þe golden letters scan. *c* **1320** R. BRUNNE *Medit.* 583 Mary, hys modyr folewed a ver. **1382** WYCLIF *Gen.* xxii. 4 He sawe a place a feer [**1388** seiȝ a place afer]. **1398** TREVISA *Barth. De P.R.* v. vi. (1495) 111 A depe syghte seeth aferre. *c* **1400** *Destr. Troy* v. 1642 Of heght so hoge.. to all þe prouyns þai apperit & pertis ofer. **1489** CAXTON *Faytes of Armes* I. xxv. 81 Other parte of the ost shal folowe offerre.

b. In this sense now usually preceded by *from*.

c **1315** SHOREHAM 122 The kynges thre that come ryde Fram be easte wel i-verre. *c* **1385** CHAUCER *Leg. G. Wom.* Prol. 212 And from a fer came walking in The God of Love. **1548** UDALL &c. *Erasm. Paraphr. Matt.* iv. 24 Manye brought from a farre theyr diseased. **1611** HEYWOOD *Gold. Age* I. i. 12 To strike and wound thy foeman from a farre. **1667** DRYDEN *Ann. Mirab.* cv, For now brave Rupert from afar appears. **1812** J. WILSON *Isle of Palms* I. 74 Some stately ship, that from afar Shone sudden. **1878** G. MACDONALD *Ann. Quiet Neighb.* x. 172 That foolish emulation which makes one class ape another from afar.

2. Far, far away, at or to a distance; *fig.* remotely. (Earlier *on feor.*)

c **1300** *Cursor Mundi* 12352 *Cotton MS.* Þai stod on ferr als best vnbald. *Fairf. MS.* On ferre. *Gött. MS.* On fer. *Trin. MS.* Stoden a fer as bestis wolde. *c* **1384** CHAUCER *Hous of Fame* 1215 A fer fro hem alle be hem selue. **1440** *Promp. Parv.* A-ferre, not nye (**1499** afer) *Procul.* **1475** CAXTON *Jason* 115 An hye roche to whom the see touched beneth a ferre lowe doun. **1597** SHAKS. *1 Hen. IV*, I. i. 4 New broils To be commenc'd in Stronds a-farre remote. *c* **1655** H. VAUGHAN *Peace* 2 My soul, there is a country, Afar beyond the stars. **1760** BEATTIE *Minstrel* (R.) The steep where fame's proud temple shines afar. **1817** CHALMERS *Astron. Disc.* i. (1852) 36 There are other worlds which roll afar. **1821** SHELLEY *Adonais* xiv, Afar the melancholy thunder moaned.

b. In this sense, now usually followed in prose by *off*.

1574 tr. *Marlorats Apocalips* 25 Lyke as starres are seene a farre off vpon the earth. **1578** TYMME tr. *Calvin on Gen.* 148 Hide himself in some Desert a farre off. **1586** T. B. tr. *La Primaudaye's Fr. Acad.* 95 It will be best for a man to keepe himselfe a far off. **1611** BIBLE *Gen.* xxii. 4 Abraham lift vp his eyes, and saw the place afarre off. **1660** T. STANLEY *Hist. Philos.* (1701) 2/1 Thales a Milesian, afar off by descent a Phœnician. **1833** I. TAYLOR *Fanat.* ix. 420 Whoever among the nations, afar off or near, would renounce his delusions.

Afar ('ɑːfɑː(r)), *sb.* and *a.* [Native name.] **A.** *sb.* **a.** (A member of) a Cushitic-speaking people of Jibuti and north-eastern Ethiopia. **b.** The language of this people. **B.** *adj.* Of or pertaining to this people or their language. Cf. DANAKIL *sb.* and *a.*

1856 R. F. BURTON *First Footsteps in E. Afr.* iii. 74 The singular is Dankali, the plural Danakil: both words are Arabic, the vernacular name being 'Afar' or 'Afer', the Somali 'Afar nimun'. **1869** *Jrnl. R. Geogr. Soc.* XXXIX. 188 (*title*) Narrative of a journey through the Afar country. *Ibid.* 191 The people of this village are Afar, like the others. *Ibid.* 209, I do not think we shall do wrong in calling them [*sc.* a number of small tribes] the Afars, after the language they speak. **1910** *Encycl. Brit.* I. 299/2 The Afar region is now partly under Abyssinian and partly under Italian authority. The Afars are also found in considerable numbers in French Somaliland. **1932** [see SAHO *sb.* and *a.*]. **1955** I. M. LEWIS *Peoples of Horn of Africa* 155 The name 'Danakil' first occurs in the 13th century writings of the Arab geographer, Ibn Said, and is currently used by the Abyssinians, Arabs, and Arabized Afar. **1969** [see DANAKIL *sb.* and *a.*]. **1977** *Trans. Philol. Soc. 1975* 206 As far as 'Afar is concerned there are only two consonant alternants, *-t-* and *-n-*. **1978** *Observer* 29 Jan. 10/7 Afar nationalism: the nomadic people of the Danakil plains and the Awash valley do not want their lands to be occupied by the Eritreans, the Somalis or the Amharas.

afara (ə'fɑːrə). [Yoruba.] A tall West African tree (*Terminalia superba* or *T. scutifera*) yielding a straight-grained wood; = LIMBA. Also, its timber.

1920 A. H. UNWIN *West Afr. Forests* ix. 371 *Terminalia scutifera.* Shingle Wood. Afara (Yoruba). It attains a height of about 200 feet and a girth of about 16 feet. **1934** A. L. HOWARD *Timbers of World* (ed. 2) 9 *Afara*, reported by the Imperial Institute as a wood very similar to oak in colour, and possessing a straight grain. **1955** *Nomencl. Commerc. Timb.* (*B.S.I.*) 87 The plain light-coloured wood is called light afara, light limba, limba clair or limba blanc; the figured heartwood dark afara, dark limba, limba noir or limba bariolé... White afara is a name used in Nigeria for the tree as distinct from the timber.

†**a'fare**, *v.* *Obs.* Forms: *Inf.* 1 afar-an. *Pa. t.* 1 afór. *Pa. pple.* 1 afaren, 2–4 afare. [f. A- *pref.* 1 away + *far-an* to go. After the OE. period found only in pa. pple., varying in Layamon with *ifaren*, *ifare*, so that the *a-* may be A *particle* = *i-*, OE. *ʒe-*.] To depart; *pa. pple.*, departed, gone.

a **1000** CÆDM. (Thorpe 217) Hie of Egyptum út afóron. *c* **1305** *St. Kath.* in *E.E.P.* (1862) 94 þemperour fram home was afare. **1250** LAYAMON 13533 Nau Vortiger his a-fare [*earlier text* Nu Vortiger is iuaren].

afe, -n, -ð, occas. var. of *have*, *-n*, *-th*, from HAVE *v.*

†**a'fear**, *v.* *Obs.* or *dial.* Forms: 1 afǽr-an, 2 afæren, 2–3 afer-en, 3–6 afer-e, affer-e, 6 affeare. [f. A- *pref.* 1 intensive + *fǽr-an* to frighten: see FEAR. For the late spelling *af-fear* see AF- 2. The vb. either in its full form, or aphetized to *'fear*, is still common in the dialects: see also AFEARD.] To frighten, terrify, or make afraid.

a **1000** *Ags. Metr. Ps.* lxxxix. 10 þæt heo [the spider] afære fleoʒan on nette. **1205** LAYAMON 25554 þ ene king hit a-uerde [*later text* a-ferde]. **1297** R. GLOUC. 22 þat folc forte a-fere. **1377** LANGL. *P. Pl.* B XVIII. 430 And it [*i.e.* the cross] a-fereth the fende. *c* **1380** *Sir Ferumb.* 742 þou ne afferest me noȝt so! **1413** LYDG. *Pylgr. Sowle* IV. xxx. (1483) 80 Hornes or grennyng teeth to aferen fooles. **1496** *Dives & Pauper* (W. de Worde) v. xix. 222 Clerkes may bere wepen .. to afere theues. **1596** SPENSER *F.Q.* II. iii. 20 And ghastly bug does greatly them affeare.

†**a'fear, afere, afeir**, *adv.* and *conj.* prop. *phr.* *Obs.* or *dial.* [A *prep.*[1] in + FEAR.] **A.** *adv.* In fear.

c **1386** CHAUCER *Monkes T.* 190 Ever he is afere To doon amys. **1460** *Pol. Rel. & Love Poems* (1866) 60, I am defied and putte a-ferre.

B. *conj.* For fear, lest. (Still used in Scotl.)

1552 LYNDESAY *Papyngo* (1866) 232 Afeir that he be nocht offendit.

afeard, -ed, (ə'fɪəd), *ppl. a.* Forms: 1–2 afǽred, 2–5 afered, 3 offearet, offered, 3–6 aferd, 4–6 affered, afferd; 5–6 aferde, afferde; 6 afearde, 6–7 afeard, afear'd; 7 affeard, -'d; 9 afear(e)d. [f. AFEAR *v.* + -ED. Used more than 30 times by Shakspere, but rare in literature after 1700, having been supplanted by AFRAID. It survives everywhere in the popular speech, either as *afeard*, or *'feard*; and has again been used in poetry by W. Morris.] Affected with fear or terror; frightened, afraid.

c **1000** *O.E. Gosp.* Mark ix. 6 He wæs afæred mid eʒe. *a* **1090** *O.E. Chron.* (Laud MS.) an. 1083 And þa wæron þa munecas swiðe áferede of heom. *c* **1230** *Ancren Riwle* 8 Hit wolde .. hurten ower heorte, & makien ou so offered. **1297** R. GLOUC. 388 Of noþing he nas aferd. *c* **1386** CHAUCER *Schipm. T.* 400 This wyf was not affered ne affrayed. **1483** CAXTON *Gold. Leg.* 209/1 He .. was aferd and adrad of the Sepulcre of our lord. *a* **1560** *Chaucer's Test. of Love* I. 276/1 He that is afearde of his clothes, let him daunce naked. **1563** *Homilies* (1859) 514 Why therefore shouldest thou be afeard of the danger. **1601** SHAKS. *All's Well* v. iii. 153, I am afeard, the life of Helen, lady, Was foully snatch'd. **1605** —— *Macb.* v. i. 41 Fye, my Lord, fie! A Souldier and affear'd? **1603** GREENWEY *Tacitus' Ann.* IV. xv. (1622) 114 Some came backe and shewed themselues againe, afeard for that they were seene to be afeard. **1664** PEPYS *Diary* (1879) III. 10, I am sometimes afeard that he do this only in policy. *a* **1689** *Popish Pol. Unmaskt* 122 in *T.C.P.* 23/2 Stand listning now concern'd, and much afear'd. **1868** W. MORRIS *Earthly Par.* I. 23, I was sore afeared At all the cries and wailing that I heard. *Ibid.* I. 373 She woke and heard A rustling noise, and grew right sore afeard.

afebrile (eɪ'fiːbraɪl, æ-, -fɛ-), *a.* [f. A- *pref.* 14 + FEBRILE *a.*] Unaccompanied by fever; not feverish.

1875 F. DELAFIELD tr. *von Ziemssen's Cycl. Med.* I. 124 The cases of febrile and afebrile abdominal catarrh. **1901** *Practitioner* Mar. 303 The afebrile cases of lobar pneumonia. **1952** M. E. FLOREY *Clin. Application Antibiotics* I. i. 14, 4 patients treated with penicillin for 7½ days became afebrile in 72 hours.

†**a'fede, a'feed**, *v.* *Obs.* Forms as in FEED. [f. A- *pref.* 1 intensive + FEED.] To feed, nourish.

c **1000** ÆLFRIC *Gen.* xxv. 27 Ða hiʒ áfédde wæron. *c* **1175** *Cott. Hom.* 227 He hi afedde .. mid hefenlice hlafe.

†**a'fefe, afief**, *v.* *Obs.* [? a. OFr. **afieffe-r*, **afiever*, Pr. *affeuar* to give as a fief; or for earlier ENFEFE a. OFr. **enfieffe-r* to establish in a fief; f. OFr. *fieffer*, *fiever*, f. *fief*, *fieu*, *fiu*, a feudal estate; see FIEF.] To give in fief, to enfeoff, to endow by feudal law.

c **1360** *Amis & Amiloun* 2486 Thei lete make a guode abbey, And well yt afefed tho. **1401** *Pol. Poems* (1859) II. 51 Reue men of her rest, and ferli hem afefe.

†**'afel.** *Obs.* *rare.* [a. ON. *afl* strength.] Strength, physical force.

c **1200** *Ormul.* 3717 And asse—þohh itt litell be, Itt hafeþþ mikell afell.

afeld, obs. form of AFIELD.

†**a'fell(e**, *v.* *Obs.* Forms: *Inf.* 1 afellan, afyllan; 2–3 afelle(n, avellen, afylle(n, afulle; 4 affulle (y). *Pa. t.* 1 afellde, afyllde; 2–3 afelde, afælde, afylde, afulde. *Pa. pple.* 1–2 afelled, afylled; 3 afulled, afeld. [f. A- *pref.* 1 intensive + *fellan*, *fyllan* to FELL, causal of FALL. The forms in *u* (y) for OE. *y* are s.w. See also AFALL *v.*[2]] To fell, strike down, cast down, lay low.

c **1000** *O.E. Gosp.* Luke xix. 44 And to eorþan afyllað þe and þine bearn. *c* **1160** *Hatton Gosp.* ibid., And to eorðan afelled þe, and þine bearn. **1205** LAYAMON 22814 Ær þa sweordes comen: seouene he afelde [*later text* afulde]. *c* **1230** *Ancren Riwle* 122 An ancre þet a windes puf of a word auelleð. *c* **1300** *K. Alis.* 5240 The kyng dude onon afelle Many thousand okes. *c* **1380** *Sir Ferumb.* 2494 Mo þan hundred of hure rout: þay affulde ded on þe clay.

afence, -fend, obs. variant of OFFENCE, -FEND.

afeorm, obs. form of AFFIRM *v.*

afer ('eɪfə(r)). [L., prop. adj. = African.] The south-west wind.

1667 MILTON *P.L.* x. 702 Notus and Afer black with thunderous clouds From Serraliona.

afer, var. AVER *sb.* *Obs.*, a horse; and obs. f. AFAR.

afere, obs. f. AFIRE, AFEAR, and AFFAIR.

†**a-'ferrom**, *adv.* *Obs.* Also 3–4 **on ferrum, o ferrom**. [*Obs.* in 5; a confusion of *ferrom*, *ferren*, OE. *feorran* from far, with the analytical *on feor*, *of feor*, *a feor*: see AFAR.] From afar; afar off.

1220 *St. Kath.* 1294 Icorene and of ferrene ifat [*i.e.* fetched]. *c* **1300** *Cursor Mundi* 5751 Als moyses on-ferrum thoght. **1366** MAUNDEV. xxvii. (1839) 271, I my self have seen o Ferrom in that See .. a gret Yle. *c* **1500** *Partenay* 629 Tho A ferrom saw to worthi men comyng.

afersche, obs. form of AFRESH.

†**a'feynted**, *pa. pple.* *Obs.* [Either from a vb. *afeynt*, *afaint*, f. FAINT, with A- *pref.* 1 intensive; or pa. pple. of *faint* itself, with A *particle*.] Rendered faint, enfeebled.

1393 LANGL. *P. Pl.* C. XXIII. 198 So elde and hue hit hadde afeynted and forbete.

aff (af), *prep.* and *adv.* *Sc.* [dial. form of OFF in mod.Sc.]

1733 A. RAMSAY *Tea-Table Misc.* (ed. 9) I. 8 He took aff his bonnet. **1826** J. WILSON *Wks.* 1855 I. 178 Whene'er I hear .. o' any man being killed aff his horse.

affability (æfə'bɪlɪtɪ). [a. Fr. *affabilité* (14th c. in Litt.) n. of quality f. AFFABLE: see -BILITY.]

The quality of being affable; readiness to converse or be addressed—especially by inferiors or equals; courteousness, civility, openness of manner.

1483 CAXTON *Cato* a iiij b, Drawe and enclyne hym to loue and affabylite. **1531** ELYOT *Governour* (1580) 95 Affability .. is also where a man speaketh courteysly with a sweet speach or countenance, wherewith the hearers (as it were with a delcate odour) be refreshed and allured to love him. **1603** T. WILSON in Ellis *Orig. Lett.* II. 246 III. 201 That gracious affabilitye which ther good old Queen did afford them. **1656** TRAPP *Expos. Luke* xv. i. (1868) 328/2 Affability easily allureth, austerity discourageth. **1774** MRS. CHAPONE *Improv. Mind* I. 168 Treat .. inferiors .. always with affability. **1855** THACKERAY *Newcomes* xxviii. 281 Greeting the other two gentlemen with his usual politeness and affability.

affable ('æfəb(ə)l), *a.* [a. Fr. *affable* (14th c. in Litt.) ad. L. *affābilis* easy to be spoken to; f. *affāri* or *adfāri* to address; f. *ad* to + *fāri* to speak.]

Easy of conversation or address; civil and courteous in receiving and responding to the conversation or address of others—especially inferiors or equals; accostable, courteous, complaisant, benign. (Const. *to* comparatively recent.)

1540 WHITTINTON *Tullyes Offyce* I. 50 Ulysses .. wolde shewe hym selfe to all persones effable and gentyll to speake vnto. **1545** JOYE *Expos. Dan.* xi. (R.) He was prudent, comely, princely, affable, ientle and amiable. **1596** SHAKS. *1 Hen. IV*, III. i. 168 Valiant as a Lyon, and wondrous affable. **1610** B. JONSON *Alchem.* II. iii. (1616) 628 [She is] the most affablest creatur, sir! so merry! **1667** MILTON *P.L.* VII. 42 Raphaël, The affable archangel. **1723** J. SHEFFIELD (Dk. Buckhm.) *Wks.* (1753) I. 53 Gentle his look, and affable his mien. **1876** FREEMAN *Norm. Conq.* II. vii. 27 When not stirred up by passion he was gentle and affable to all men.

†**b.** Formerly used more loosely. *Obs.*

1622 MALYNES *Anc. Law-Merch.* 501 The judiciall and affable judgements of this age. **1641** MILTON *Ch. Govt.* II. (1851) 148 The learned and affable meeting of frequent Academies. **1709** STEELE *Tatler* No. 101 ¶5 A Country Foxhunter .. shall in a Week's Time look with a courtly and affable Paleness.

affableness ('æfəb(ə)lnɪs). [f. AFFABLE *a.* + -NESS.] The quality of being affable; affability.

1615 BP. HALL *Contempl.* II. ii, Neither as God or man, doth he [Christ] take pleasure in a stern froward austerity, but in a mild affableness and amiable conversation.

affably ('æfəblɪ), *adv.* [f. AFFABLE *a.* + -LY[2].]

In an affable manner; in a manner indicating willingness to converse; courteously.

1608 NORDEN *Surueyors Dial.*, To giue his fellow workmen a congie early in the morning, and affably to call them. *a* **1616** BEAUM. & FL. *Martial Maid* III. iv. (R.) She'll .. answer affably and modestly. **1829** FONBLANQUE *England* (1837) I. 238 Some .. to whom the Duke has affably said 'Good morning.' **1869** MRS. WOOD *Rol. Yorke* III. 279 Making himself at home and enquiring affably the price of butter.

affabrous ('æfəbrəs), *a.* *rare.* [f. L. *affaber* (f. *af-* = *ad-* to + *faber* artificial, ingenious) + -OUS.]

'Skilfully made; complete; finished in a workmanlike manner.' J.

1731 in BAILEY. **1755** in JOHNSON, no quot. **1808** J. MACDONALD *Telegr. Comm.* 59 His anthology, affabrous in its nature, afforded him amusement.

†**a'ffabulate**, *v.* *Obs.* [f. L. *af-* = *ad-* to + *fābula* tale, fable, *fābulā-ri* to talk, tell tales + -ATE[3].]

To attribute by legend; to assign fabulously.

1622 HEYLIN *Cosmogr.* I. (1682) 264 Those feats of Chivalry, affabulated to him and his knights of the Round Table.

†**affabu'lation.** *Obs.*[−1] [a. Fr. *affabulation*, f. L. *af-* = *ad-* to + *fābula* fable + -TION formative of n. of action. Cf. L. *fābulātio* from *fābulāri*.] 'The moral of a fable.' J. (from Bailey.)

1649 ARNWAY *Tablet* (ed. 2) 97 As an Affabulation to the Apologue of the hinder parts.

†**a'ffabulatory**, *a.* *Obs. rare*[−1]. [f. as prec. as if ad. L. **affābulātōrius*.] Of the nature of the moral of a fable; having a moral.

1652 URQUHART *Jewel* Wks. 1834, 292 Allegories of all sorts, whether apologal, affabulatory, parabolary, etc.

affadyll, variant of AFFODILL. *Obs.*, a daffodil.

†**a'ffain**, *v.* *Obs. rare*[−1]. [f. L. *af-* = *ad-* to + ? FEIGN, formerly often spelt *fain*.] To feign to belong *to* (any one), to attribute fictitiously.

1640 BP. HALL *Chr. Moder.* 35/2 Those errors which are maliciously affained to him.

affair (ə'fɛə(r)). Forms: 3–4 afer(e, 4–5 affer(e, 5–7 affayre, 6–7 affaire, 7– affair. North. 6 effere, effaire. [a. OFr. *afaire*, *afeire*, *afere*, originally infinitive phrase *à faire* to do. Cf. the Eng. A-DO, the history of which is parallel to that of *à faire* in Fr. All the earlier instances of *affair* are northern; its general use in Eng. and later spelling, from 15th c. Fr., are due to Caxton.]

1. a. What one has to do, or has ado with; what has to be done; business, operation.

c **1300** *Cursor Mundi* 22116 *Cotton MS.* þe wicked gastes .. Him foluand in al his afers [*Edin. MS.* afferis, *Fairf. MS.* afers, *Gött. MS.* fers]. *c* **1300** *K. Alis.* 410 And tellith to Neptanabous, Alle theo aferis of Ammon. **1393** LANGL. *P. Pl.* C. VII. 152 þer beþ meny felle frekus myne afferes to aspye. *c* **1400** *Rom. Rose* 3455 Now goth wel thyn affere, He shalle to thee be debonaire. **1602** SHAKS. *Haml.* I. ii. 174 But what is your affaire in Elsenour? **1720** OZELL tr. *Vertot's Rom. Rep.* I. IV. 224 The Tribunes .. wou'd not suffer the Peoples Votes to be gathered upon any Affair whatsoever. **1793** BURKE *Pol. of Allies* Wks. VII. 127 The affair of the establishment of a government is a very difficult undertaking. **1842** LONGF. *Sp. Stud.* I. i. 5 It was a dull affair, one of those comedies. **1870** Miss Mitford in L'Estrange's *Life* I. iii. 79, I set about the grand affair of dressing. **1874** Blackie *Self-Culture* 47 Dinner is a more serious affair. **1878** Huxley *Physiogr.* Pref. 8 Seeing a book through the press is a laborious and time-wasting affair.

b. *More vaguely*, A thing that concerns any one; a concern, a matter.

1611 Bible *1 Chron.* xxvi. 32 Euery matter perteining to God, and affaires of the king. **1770** Langhorne *Plutarch's Lives* (1879) I. 98/1 When the trouble about Cylon's affair was over. **1859** Mill *Liberty* 188 The pretext that the affairs of another are his own affairs. *a* **1884** *Mod.* An affair of a few days; an affair of five shillings, at most.

2. *esp.* (in *pl.*) **a.** Ordinary business or pursuits of life, transactions between man and man.

1484 Caxton *Curial* 1, I am there where the places and affayres desioyne vs. **1559** *Myrroure for Mag., Cade* vi. 2 Medleth not with any worldes affaires. **1685** Morden *Geogr. Rect.* Ep. Ded. 1 Your..Affairs abroad have..given you a better knowledge and experience of Foreign Parts. **1750** Johnson *Rambler* No. 179 ¶9 As he did not suspect his unfitness for common affairs. **1798** Ferriar *Of Genius* 281 Some degree of similarity in the course of human affairs must often recur. **1869** J. Martineau *Ess.* II. 55 Practical sympathy with the..affairs of mankind.

b. Commercial or professional business.

1519 Sir T. Boleyn in Ellis *Orig. Lett.* I. 53 I. 149 Amongs all his other things and great affaires he is so moch desirous to mete visite and see your Grace. **1528** Perkins *Profit. Bk.* v. §342 (1642) 150 A woman shall be endowed of a Bayliwick..And so in like manner she shall be endowed of affaires. **1600** *Letting of Humours Bl.* i. 47 And there his tongue runs byas on affaires, No talke but of comodities and wares. **1751** Johnson *Rambler* No. 142 ¶7 He took his affairs into his own hands. **1871** Smiles *Charact.* iv. (1876) 107 Men of affairs, trained to business.

c. Public business, transactions or matters concerning men or nations collectively.

1605 Bacon *Adv. Learn.* II. ii. §2 The chronicle..read before Ahasuerus..contained matter of affairs. **1626** T. H. tr. *Caussin's Holy Crt.* 7 The good successe of affayres haue followed your desires. **1697** Dryden *Virgil, Georgic* IV. 260 That in the Field; this in Affairs of State, Employ'd at home. **1715** Burnet *Hist. own Time* (1766) I. 1, I had while I was very young a greater knowledge of affairs than is usual at that age. **1733** Pope *Prol. Satires* 267, I was not born for Courts or great affairs. **1849** Macaulay *Hist. Eng.* I. 447 The general expectation was that he would be immediately placed at the head of affairs, and that all the other great officers of state would be changed.

3. *sing.* Vaguely, and with intentional indefiniteness, of any proceeding which it is not wished to name or characterize closely; as a military 'action' or engagement of undefined character, a political job, a duel (***affair of honour***), an intrigue (***affair of love***), etc.

1702 Steele *Funeral* I. (1704) 21 To marry a Woman after an Affair with her. **1732** Berkeley *Minute Philos* (1732) I. 46 In our Dialect a vicious Man is a Man of pleasure..a Lady is said to have an affair, a Gentleman to be a gallant, a Rogue in business to be one that knows the world. **1741** Middleton *Cicero* (ed. 3) II. vii. 196 After the affair of Pindenissum, an exploit of more éclat and importance. **1753** Hanway *Trav.* (1762) II. I. i. 3 The french..calling it *an affair of honor*. **1774** Mrs. Chapone *Improv. Mind* I. 182 If your friend should..intend to carry on an affair of love. **1816** Scott *Old Mort.* xvii. (1868) 730 The enemy persevered in their attack—the affair was fiercely disputed. **1826** Disraeli *Viv. Grey* VII. viii. 434 Every affair of any character during the late war was fought over again in the tent. **1837** Dickens *Pickw.* ii. 20 'I want your assistance..in an affair of honour,' said Mr. Winkle. **1855** Macaulay *Hist. Eng.* III. 216 The strenuous opposition..offered to the government..in the affair of Wood's patent. **1922** Joyce *Ulysses* 230 The annual dinner you know. Boiled shirt affair. **1933** N. Coward *Design for Living* I. 19 We could carry on a backstairs affair for weeks without saying a word about it.

4. Loosely and familiarly of things material, in which use *affair* freq. serves merely as a peg to support an epithet, 'a *poor* affair,' etc. Cf. *concern.*

1802 Mar. Edgeworth *Moral T.* I. xx. (1816) 189 His wife was no grand affair..a merchant's daughter. **1845** Darwin *Voy. Nat.* viii, The Plata looks like a noble estuary on the map, but is in truth a poor affair. **1866** Wenham in *Ann. Rep. Aëronaut. Soc.* 37 The affair [a glider] falling over sideways, broke up the right-hand set of webs. **1879** H. Northcott in *Cassell's Techn. Educ.* IV. 344/1 In this example the cone-headstock is a very small affair. **1903** H. G. Wells *12 Stories* 11 He did not make the affair large enough to carry a man... The first flight of this first practicable flying machine took place over some fields near Burford Bridge. **1905** *Smart Set* Sept. 127/1 There were holes for the eyes and strings that tied the affair and held it in place.

†**5.** Doing, action, performance. *Obs. rare.*

c **1500** *Lancelot* 983 Wich ware to few aȝaine the gret affere Of galiot. **1596** Chapman *Iliad* v. 503 Mars..with his best affair, Obey'd the pleasure of the Sun.

†**6.** Mode of doing; bearing, deportment, appearance, conduct. [Very common in OFr. Here only in Sc. writers.] *Obs.*

1375 Barbour *Bruce* I. 361 He wes off full fayr effer, Wyss, curtaiss, and deboner. [Cf. *Vie S. Alexi* 31, *Il est home de boen afere, Douz et creable et debonere.*] *c* **1425** Wyntoun *Cron.* IX. xxvii. 315 Commendyt heily his affere His aporte and his manere. *c* **1500** *Lancelot* 3043 Yhowr manhed, yhour worschip, and affere. *Ibid.* 3059 Most knychtly of affere. *c* **1505** Dunbar *Daunce* in Warton II. 445 Frawart was their affeir. **1575** in *Pref. to Laneham's Lett.* 73 That fre answerd with fayr afeir.

†**7.** Fortune, rank, dignity. [Very common in OFr. in phr. *de haute afaire, de grant afaire, de povre afaire*, etc. In Eng. ? only in Caxton.] *Obs.*

1480 Caxton *Ovid's Metam.* XIV. xii, She was ryche and of grete affayre. **1481** —— *Myrrour* III. xxi. 180 Our lord god is moche myghty, & of a right hye affayre.

‖**affaire** (əˈfɛə(r)). [Fr.] = affair 3; *esp.* (often in form ***affaire de*** (or ***du***) ***cœur***, 'an affair of the heart', a love affair, an amour, an amatory episode.

1809 *Q. Rev.* II. 349 The connection with Egeria resolves itself, of course, into an *affaire du cœur.* **1819** T. Hope *Anastasius* I. viii. 174 The only thing he could have liked..was an *affaire de cœur* with the favourite Sultana. **1845** Geo. Eliot *Let.* 6 Apr. (1954) I. 185 My unfortunate 'affaire' did not become one 'du coeur'. **1908** 'Ian Hay' *Right Stuff* ii. 28 In either case the *affaire* terminates then and there. **1928** A. Waugh *Nor many Waters* v. 208 That life of parties and *affaires* that had seemed so infinitely desirable in the early twenties. **1940** M. Dickens *Mariana* iv. 93 The affaire Goss was only something to add a spice to school life, and did not affect in any way her love for him. **1956** A. Wilson *Anglo-Saxon Att.* II. ii. 280 But you and she had an *affaire de cœur*! **1958** —— *Middle Age of Mrs. Eliot* II. 271 It would be so awful to have one of those office affaires that they have in the women's mags.

‖**affairé** (afɛːre), *a.* [Fr.] Busy, involved.

1901 'Linesman' *Words by Eyewitness* xiii. 266 The great Public, *affairé* and astute as it is. **1927** *Blackw. Mag.* Nov. 600/1 The attractive and affairée young lady..appropriated him for her own mysterious ends. **1928** D. H. Lawrence *Let.* 7 Jan. (1962) II. 1032 Well, don't be too *affairé.* **1954** E. Jenkins *Tortoise & Hare* xvi. 214, I hear Hunter is very much *affairé* with his little typist.

affaminait, obs. form of effeminate.

†**aˈffamine.** *Obs. rare*$^{-1}$. [f. famine *sb.*, ? after Fr. *affamement.*] Famine.

c **1450** Lonelich *Graal* II. 356 A gret affamyne amonges hem was.

†**affamish**, *v. Obs.* Also 7 **afamish.** [f. Fr. *affame-r*, OFr. *afamer, afemer*, = Pr. *afamar*, It. *affamare*, pointing to a late L. or early Rom. **affamāre*, f. *ad* to, *famem* hunger. Many OFr. vbs. in *-er* had variants in *-ir*, *-iss-ant* (whence Eng. -ish); cf. affeeble, affeeblish; on this analogy other Fr. vbs. in *-er* received the ending *-ish* in Eng.]

1. *trans.* To afflict with hunger or famine; to starve.

1568 Bible ('Bishops') *Gen.* xlii. 55 All the land of Egypt was affamished. **1615** Byfield *On Coloss.* i. 21 (1869) 125/2 The deadness of his heart, which afamisheth the soul in spiritual things. **1633** Bp. Hall *Hard Texts* 249 The foolish slothful man..affamisheth himselfe with wilfull idleness.

2. *intr.* (fr. *refl.*) To suffer or perish from hunger.

1622 Bp. Hall *Serm.* 130 That men may not affamish, whom God hath fed. **1655** G. Hall *Triumphs of Rome* 123 Beggars which are ready to affamish for want.

†**aˈffamished,** *ppl. a. Obs.* Also **-ysit.** [f. prec. + -ed.] Afflicted with hunger, famished, starving.

1552 Lyndesay *Monarche* 5495 Affamysit for falt of fude. **1615** T. Adams *Pract. Wks.* (1861) I. 429 To become the food of the affamished sons of men. **1657** Trapp *Comment. Esther* iv. 11 II. 143 King Joram [heard] the affamished woman that called to him for justice.

†**aˈffamishing,** *vbl. sb. Obs.* [f. as prec. + -ing^1.] Afflicting with hunger; famishing, starving.

1649 Bp. Hall *Cases of Consc.* v. (1654) 37 To raise himself by the affamishing of others. *Ibid.* IV. i. 288 To preserve him from affamishing.

†**aˈffamishing,** *ppl. a. Obs.* [f. as prec. + -ing^2.] That afflicts with hunger or starves; starving.

1650 Bp. Hall *Balm of Gilead* (J.) I tell thee of..their affamishing meals; their nightly watchings.

affamishment (əˈfæmɪʃmənt). [f. affamish *v.* + -ment.] The act of famishing or starving with hunger; the state of being starved; starvation.

1590 J. Greenwood *Sland. Art.* Pref. A 2 To the vtter vndoing and affamishment of them. **1615** Crooke *Body of Man* 99 In time of necessity and affamishment. **1855** Singleton *Virgil* I. 327 Rueful despite and foul affamishment.

affatuate (əˈfætjuːət), *a.* [f. (on analogy of *infatuate*) L. *ad* to + *fatuus* silly. There is no corresponding L. compound.] Infatuated.

1834 Sir H. Taylor *Artevelde* II. v. ii. Wks. 1864 I. 259 By art of witchcraft so affatuate, That for his love they'd dress themselves in dowlas And fight with men of steel.

†**aˈffatuated,** *ppl. a.* [f. as prec. with ppl. ending -ed. Cf. *infatuated.*] Infatuated.

1649 Milton *Eikonokl.* Pref. Wks. 1851, 332 [They] are so much affatuated, not with his person, only, but with his palpable faults, and doat upon his deformities.

affear, affeard, variants of afear, afeard.

affear, variant of affere *v. Obs.*, to apportion.

aˈffect, *sb. Obs.* exc. in sense 1 e. [ad. L. *affectu-s*, n. of completed action, f. *affic-ĕre* to act upon, dispose, constitute.] Disposition or constitution.

I. Mental.

1. a. The way in which one is affected or disposed; mental state, mood, feeling, desire, intention.

c **1374** Chaucer *Troylus* III. 1342 And therto dronken had as hotte and stronge As Cresus did, for his affectes wronge. **1528** Roy *Rede me* (Arb.) 117 Goode christen men with pure affecte. **1531** Elyot *Gov.* (1557) II. vii. 104 Contrary to his owne affectes and determinate purposes. **1533** Tindale *Supper of the Lord* Wks. III. 266 God is searcher of heart and reins, thoughts and affects. **1580** Sidney *Arcadia* (1622) 351 She gaue a dolefull way to her bitter affects. **1626** Bacon *Sylva* §97 The affects and Passions of the Heart and Spirits, are notably disclosed by the Pulse.

esp. **b.** Inward disposition, feeling, as contrasted with external manifestation or action; intent, intention, earnest, reality. Contrasted with *chere* or outward appearance; and with *effect* or result.

c **1400** *Rom. Rose* 5489 Fully to knowen, without were, Freend of affect, and freend of chere. *c* **1449** Pecock *Repr.* V. v. 509 This man ouȝte loue in affect and in effect his owne bodi more than the bodi of his fadir. **1552** Latimer *Serm. in Linc.* vii. 127 Restitution must be made eyther in effect or affect, thou must be sorry in thy hart and aske God forgiueness. **1591** Florio *Second Frutes* 35, I accept the affect, in lieu of the effect. **1615** T. Adams *Lycanthr.* 6 Reall in his right, in his might: Royall in his affects and effects.

c. Feeling, desire, or appetite, as opposed to *reason*; passion, lust, evil-desire.

1531 Elyot *Governour* (1580) 109 Temperance..is the moderatrice..of al motions of the minde, called affects. **1545** Joye *Expos. Daniel* iv. G 4 These flaterers so nyghe them in fauour, feding their affectes. **1591** Greene *Maidens Dreame* xxv, He bridled those affects that might offend. **1619** Middleton *Temple Masque* Wks. V. 144 No doubt affects will be subdued with reason.

d. Biased feeling, partiality.

1557 Earl Surrey in *Tottell's Misc.* (Arb.) 29 An eye, whose iudgement none affect could blinde.

e. *Psychol.* [G. *affekt.*] (with pronunc. ˈæfekt). (See quots.)

1891 J. M. Baldwin *Handbk. Psychol.* II. 314 Affects..are the feeling antecedents of involuntary movements; as motives, including affects, are the inner antecedents of acts of will. **1894** W. James *Coll. Ess. & Rev.* (1920) 358 We may also feel a general seizure of excitement, which Wundt, Lehmann, and other German writers call an *Affect*, and which is what I have all along meant by an emotion. **1923** *Wkly. Westm. Gaz.* 24 Mar. 181 Their psychic lives are overfull of complexes, levels and affects. **1926** W. McDougall *Outl. Abnormal Psychol.* 26 The terms 'affect' and 'affective' denote the emotional-conative aspect of all mental activity.

attrib. and *Comb.*

1934 H. C. Warren *Dict. Psychol.* 7/1 *Affect psychoses*, psychoses which are especially characterized by disturbances in the emotional life. **1943** *Horizon* VIII. 271 The personality, rich in affect-life. **1944** *Mind* LIII. 180 The dream-process is an affect-regulative mechanism. **1949** A. Koestler *Insight & Outlook* v. 68 The affect-amplifying emergency-mechanisms of the sympathico-adrenal system became gradually superfluous. **1951** C. Kluckhorn in Parsons & Shils *Towards Gen. Theory Action* IV. ii. 390 Affect-laden customs or traditions. **1958** *Listener* 17 July 93/2 These areas of the brain..have come to be known as the 'pleasure' centres and 'pain' centres... Perhaps it would be best to call them the 'affect' systems, one which seems to be particularly related to positive affect (or pleasantness) and the other to negative affect (or unpleasantness).

2. Disposition, temper, natural tendency.

1541 Elyot *Im. Govern.* 35 To knowe the sundry wittes, maners, affectes, and studies of men. **1588** Shaks. *L.L.L.* I. i. 152 For euery man with his affects is borne. **1592** Greene *Conny catching* Pref. i, Time refineth mens affects. **1606** Bryskett *Civill Life* 50 Plato..distinguisheth these two affects, into both these faculties of the soule.

3. *esp.* Feeling towards or in favour of; kind feeling, affection.

1440 *Promp. Parv.* Affecte, or welwyllynge, *Affectus.* **1543** Becon *Policy of War* Wks. 1843, 234 Her private affect toward her children. **1586** J. Hooker *Giraldus's Hist. Irel.* in *Holinsh.* II. 55/1 Vtterlie void of that affect, which is naturallie ingraffed in man. **1593** Shaks. *Rich. II*, I. iv. 30 Wooing poore Craftesmen, with the craft of soules..As 'twere, to banish their affects with him. **1596** Southwell (*title*) Consolatorie Epistle for afflicted minds, in the affects of dying friends. **1633** Ford *Loves Sacrif.* I. ii. (1839) 78 Madam, I observe, In your affects, a thing to me most strange.

4. An affectation, a trick.

1588 Fraunce *Lawiers Logike* I. v. 31 b, This were an affect of an extemporall Rhetor to salute a man by name without premeditation.

II. Physical.

5. The way in which a thing is physically affected or disposed; especially, the actual state or disposition of the body.

1605 Bacon *Adv. Learn.* II. ix. §3 (1873) How far the humours and affects of the body do alter or work upon the mind. **1626** —— *Sylva* §835 The true passages and processes and affects and consistencies of matter and natural bodies. **1679** Brian *Pisse-proph.* 7 The symptoms and affects of the sick party.

6. *esp.* A state of body opposed to the normal; indisposition, distemper, malady, disease; 'affection'.

1533 Elyot *Castel of Helth* (1541) 54 Vomyte amendeth the affectes of the raynes. **1563** T. Gale *Antidot.* II. 9 Very precious in burnings and scaldings and lyke affectes. **1616** Surflet & Markh. *Countrey Farme* 245 It is of great vse for the affects of the lungs. **1679** tr. *Willis's Pharm. Ration.* in

Blount's *Nat. Hist.* (1693) 112 Who presently after drinking Coffee became worse as to those Affects.

†**a'ffect**, *ppl. a. Obs.* [ad. L. *affect-us* pa. pple. of *afficĕre* to do something to, to act upon, influence, dispose, incline; f. *af-* = *ad-* to + *facĕre* to do.] Disposed, inclined = AFFECTED II.

c **1400** *Apol. for Loll.* 88 þey are more affect to o ymage þan to an oþer. **1538** STARKEY *England* ii. §19, 47 Euery cuntrey, cyty, and towne lyke wyse affecte and disposyd.

affect (əˈfɛkt), *v.*[1] [a. Fr. *affecte-r* (15th c.), ad. L. *affectā-re* to aim at, aspire to, endeavour to have, pretend to have; freq. of *afficĕre* (f. *ad* to + *facere* to do) to put to, hence refl. (*se facere ad*) to put or apply oneself to, to aim at. See also AFFECT *v.*[2]]

†**1.** *trans.* To aim at, aspire to, or make for; to seek to obtain or attain. **a.** a thing. *Obs.*

1483 CAXTON *Gold. Leg.* 263/1 Roch affectyng no mortal glorye hyd his lignage. **1593** SHAKS. *2 Hen. VI*, IV. vii. 104 Have I affected wealth, or honour? **1605** BACON *Adv. Learn.* I. vii. §27 (1873) Cæsar did extremely affect the name of king. **1615** SANDYS *Trav.* 105 Elated with these beginnings, he affected the empire of the world. **1655** FULLER *Ch. Hist.* IX. 192 He with more earnestness refused a Bishoprick, then others affected it. **1675** T. BROOKS *Gold. Key* Wks. 1867 V. 21 Gracious hearts affect that which they cannot effect. **1721** STRYPE *Eccl. Mem.* (1816) II. 200 Was beheaded on Tower hill for affecting the kingdom. **1725** POPE *Odyssey* XI. 386 The Gods they challenge, and affect the skies. **1794** PALEY *Nat. Theol.* xxiii. 390 How should the blind animal affect sight, of which blind animals..have neither conception nor desire?

†**b.** *to do* a thing.

1589 BERNARD *Terence* Ded., I have affected to make knowne the good will I doe..beare to you. **1611** BIBLE *Ecclus.* xiii. 11 Affect not to be made equall vnto him in talke. **1776** T. JEFFERSON *Autobiog.* Wks. 1859 I. 22 He has affected to render the military independent of, and superior to, the civil power.

2. To be drawn to, have affection or liking for; to take to, be fond of, show preference for; to fancy, like, or love. **a.** a person. *arch.* or ? *Obs.*

?*a* **1550** *Robin Hood* in *E.E.P. Rom.* (1858) II. 91 He, whom he most affected..was called little John. **1580** NORTH *Plutarch* (1676) 43 Their favourers and lovers, which did affect and entertain them. **1601** SHAKS. *Twel. N.* II. v. 28 Maria once told me, she did affect me. **1623** BINGHAM *Xenophon* 39 Alwaies soure and cruell, so that Souldiers affected him as children doe their Schoolemaster. **1627** FELTHAM *Resolves* I. xvi. Wks. 1677, 28 It learns him in his patience, to affect his Enemies. **1633** BP. HALL *Hard Texts* 223 Those that affect me shall be sure not to lose their love. **1690** W. WALKER *Idiom. Ang-Lat.* 13, I do not affect you, *non amo te.* **1760** STERNE *Tr. Shandy* (1802) VIII. xxxiv. 192 All the world knows that Mrs. Wadman *affects* my brother Toby.

b. a thing. *arch.*

1593 DRAYTON *Eclogues* v. 45 Nor things so base doe I affect at all. **1639** FULLER *Holy War* I. xv. (1840) 25 Who never cordially affected this war. **1656** BRAMHALL *Replic.* i. 71 Persons..who doe passionately affect Episcopacie. **1720** SHADWELL *Timon* I. II. 302 No man can justly praise But what he does affect. **1735** POPE *Donne Sat.* II. 76 Takes God to witness he affects your cause. **1875** F. I. SCUDAMORE *Day Dreams* 5 Nor do I greatly affect the early thrush.

c. a thing touching one's own practice: To like to practise, use, wear, or frequent.

1589 NASHE *Alm. for Parrat* 15 a, As in garments so in gouernment continually affecting new fashions. **1642** FULLER *Holy & Prof. St.* IV. xiv. 319 She much affected rich and costly apparell. **1646** SIR T. BROWNE *Pseud. Ep.* 373 The Turkes without scruple affect the name of Mahomet. **1660** T. STANLEY *Hist. Philos.* (1701) 85/2 Socrates little affected Travel, his Life being wholly spent at home. **1665** WITHER *Lord's Pr.* Pref., They who superstitiously affect this Form of Prayer. **1704** HEARNE *Duct. Histor.* (1714) I. 416 Dionysius affected Plato's Conversation. **1718** *Free-thinker* No. 75. 142 The little Genius affects Wiles. **1854** THACKERAY *Newcomes* I. 126 That peculiar costume which he affected. **1862** *Lond. Rev.* 23 Aug. 168 He affected the back Ministerial benches.

d. *to do* a thing. ? *Obs.*

1660 T. STANLEY *Hist. Philos.* (1701) 28/2, I affect above all things to live under a Democracy. **1699** EVELYN *Acetaria* (1729) 180 Some affect to have it fry'd a little broun and crisp. **1751** JORTIN *Serm.* (1771) V. viii. 172 The greatest monarchs have affected to be called Father of their country.

†**e.** *absol.* To incline or like. *Obs.*

1606 SHAKS. *Ant. & Cl.* I. iii. 71, I go from hence Thy Souldier, Seruant, making Peace or Warre, As thou affects. **1643–5** in *Sel. fr. Harl. Misc.* (1793) 301 His malady increased or diminished as he [his man] affected.

3. Of animals and plants: To frequent naturally or habitually, to haunt, to inhabit.

1616 SURFLET & MARKH. *Countrey Farme* 285 Iuniper affecteth the tops of mountaines. **1793** G. WHITE *Nat. Hist. Selb.* xviii. (1853) 210 Here and there a bird may affect some odd peculiar place. **1849** MRS. SOMERVILLE *Connex. Phys. Sc.* §27. 305 Groups of algæ..affect particular temperatures or zones of latitude. **1873** BROWNING *Red Cott. N.-Cap* 1076 Tessellated pavement,—equally Affected by the scorpion for his nest.

4. Of things: To have or display a natural tendency toward, to tend to assume or put on.

1612 DRAYTON *Poly-olbion* v. *notes* 80 Their tongues did naturallie affect..the British Dialect. **1664** POWER *Exp. Philos.* III. 158 A contrary posture to that which it naturally affects. **1756** BURKE *Subl. & B.* Wks. 1842 I. 57 Any body ..affecting some regular shape. **1850** C. DAUBENY *Atomic Th.* viii. (ed. 2) 269 Why the same body should sometimes affect one crystalline form, and sometimes another?

5. To show ostentatiously a liking for; to make an ostentatious use or display of; to take upon oneself artificially or for effect, to assume.

1605 SHAKS. *Lear* II. ii. 102 Who hauing beene prais'd for bluntnesse, doth affect A saucy roughnes. **1663** BUTLER *Hudibr.* I. i. 94 A Babylonish Dialect, which learned Pedants much affect. **1715** BURNET *Hist. own Time* (1766) I. 17 He affected the grandeur of a regal court. **1735** POPE *Hor. Ep.* II. i. 97 Spenser himself affects the obsolete. **1781** GIBBON *Decl. & F.* II. xxxiv. 283 He at first affected a stern and haughty demeanour. **1796** MORSE *Amer. Geog.* I. 781 They affected the appellation of patriots. **1855** MACAULAY *Hist. Eng.* IV. 135 To affect the character of loyal men. **1866** ROGERS *Agric. & Prices* I. xiv. 250, I am not botanist enough to affect any judgment on the subject.

b. To assume the character of (a person).

1595 SHAKS. *John* I. i. 86 The accent of his tongue affecteth him. *a* **1616** B. JONSON *Discov.* (T.) Spenser, in affecting the ancients, writ no language. **1729** T. COOKE *Tales, etc.* 27 Her Sire, affecting now the tender Man. **1865** CARLYLE *Fredk. Gt.* II. VI. viii. 217 He affected the freethinker, and carried libertinism to excess.

c. with *inf.*: To 'profess,' take upon one.

1720 WATERLAND *Serm.* 56 Some of late have affected very much to say that all things were created through the Son. **1724** DE FOE, etc. *Tour thr. Gt. Brit.* (1769) IV. 273 The Lochs..which some affect to call the River Aber. **1853** MAURICE *Proph. & Kings* viii. 123 He affected to restore the idolatry which Aaron had sanctioned in the wilderness. **1856** KANE *Arctic Expl.* I. xxviii. 363 Every one who affects to register the story of an active life.

Hence, by imperceptible gradations,

6. a. To put on a pretence of; to assume a false appearance of, to counterfeit or pretend.

1661 BARROW *Serm.* I. i. 4 He affects commendations incompetent to him. **1723** J. SHEFFIELD (D. of Buckhm.) *Wks.* (1753) I. 290 Who..would soon have shewn A real rage, which now he but affected. **1813** SCOTT *Rokeby* v. xvi. 209 Each look and accent, framed to please, Seemed to affect a playful ease. **1837** DISRAELI *Venetia* I. viii. (1871) 40 He had ever affected a haughty indifference on the subject.

b. with *inf.* (or gerund).

1603 DANIEL *Defence Rhime* 13 (1717) 12 We smooth up a weak confused Sense, affecting Sound to be unsound. **1679** SHEFFIELD & DRYDEN *Ess. on Sat.* 70 How that affects to laugh, how this to weep. **1753** SMOLLETT *Ct. Fathom* (1784) 138/1 Although Fathom looked upon this proposal as an extravagant symptom of despair, he affected to approve of the scheme. **1816** SCOTT *Antiq.* (1879) II. xxv. 52 He tired, or affected to tire. **1848** DICKENS *Dombey* (C.D. ed.) 33 "Oh you beauties!" cried Susan Nipper, affecting to salute the door by which the two ladies had departed. **1879** M. ARNOLD *Irish Cath.* in *Mixed Ess.* 100, I have never affected to be surprised..at the antipathy of the Irish to us.

†**7.** *absol.* To assume artificial or pretended manners; to put on airs. *Obs. rare.*

1631 CORNWALLYES *Ess.* xxiii, Affectation begets Extremities: Man is allowed onely the middle way, he strayeth when he affects. **1692** LADY RUSSELL *Let.* 21 July, I take some care not to affect in these retirements.

affect (əˈfɛkt), *v.*[2] [f. (directly or through Fr. *affecter*) L. *affect-* ppl. stem of *afficĕre* to do to, act on, influence, attack with a disease; also, to put to, attach to; f. *ad* to + *facĕre* to do, make. The L. frequentative *affectāre* (see prec.) had also rarely the sense of 'attack as a disease,' whence sense 1 might be taken, merely as another branch of the preceding verb; but the others can be referred only to *afficĕre*. Though all the senses are in mod.Fr., our 1–4 are not in Cotgr. (1611–50), who has only to 'fasten or tye on; destinate (or bind for); assigne or appoint unto;' whence our sense 5, though this is also a less common use of L. *afficĕre* (*aliquid ad aliquem*). It corresponds formally, and in sense partly, to the earlier AFAITE, which was obs. long before the introduction of this.]

1. To attack, lay hold of, act upon contagiously, or attaint (as, or after the manner of, a disease). Rare in the active voice in earlier usage.

1606 SHAKS. *Tr. & Cr.* II. ii. 59 And the will dotes that is inclineable To what infectiously it selfe affects. **1722** DE FOE *Plague* 77 The inward gangrene affected their vitals. **1782** F. HOME *Clin. Exper.* 283 Affected with pain in his loins, which affects the thigh-joint. **1881** *Daily Tel.* 27 Dec., The returning pilgrims..were the means of affecting the people of the districts through which they passed.

†**2.** To attaint *with* a crime or offence: 'a phrase merely juridical.' J. *Obs.*

1726 AYLIFFE *Parergon* 59 She shall have alimony..unless you can affect them with Fraud.

3. To lay hold of, impress, or act upon (in mind or feelings); to influence, move, touch.

1662 FULLER *Worthies* (1840) III. 159 A passage that affected me with wonder. **1667** MILTON *P.L.* v. 97 The trouble of thy thoughts this night in sleep Affects me equally. **1722** DE FOE *Moll. Fl.* (1840) 238 When once we are hardened in crime no fear can affect us. **1780** BURKE in *Corr.* (1844) II. 354, I do not think I have ever on any occasion seemed to affect the House more forcibly. **1832** HT. MARTINEAU *Life in Wilds* vii. 99 The honour paid to her husband had affected her. **1876** BLACK *Madcap V.* xviii. 161 The sportsman was not affected with all these taunts and jeers.

4. To make a material impression on; to act upon, influence, move, touch, or have an effect on.

1631 SANDERSON *Serm.* II. 6 Oils and ointments..affect three distinct senses. **1667** MILTON *P.L.* x. 653 The Sun.. so to move, so shine, As might affect the Earth with cold and heat. **1667** BOYLE *Orig. Formes & Qual.* 26 External bodies being fitted to affect the Eye, others the Ear, others the Nostrils. **1764** REID *Inq. Hum. Mind* v. §2. 121 The effluvia of bodies affected our hearing. **1817** MALTHUS *Population* I. 360 Causes, which affect the number of births or deaths, may or may not affect the average population. **1840** MACAULAY *Clive* 70 This system..might affect the amount of the dividends. **1846** PRESCOTT *Ferd. & Isab.* I. Introd. 17 No person could be affected in life or property, except by a decision of this court. **1855** BAIN *Senses & Intell.* (1864) II. i. §11. 93 Bodily exercise indirectly affects all the organs of the body.

5. To apply specially; to assign, to allot; to attribute. (Only in passive voice, as in mod.Fr., though in 17th c. Fr. active, as in L.)

1611 COTGR., *Nantir*, to consigne..to tye fast; affect, appoint, or point out, one thing for th' indemnitie, or assurance, of another. **1807** W. TAYLOR in *Ann. Rev.* V. 296 Broker is become a nobler designation than formerly, and is now affected to agents of exchange. **1847** THACKERAY *Van. Fair* III. viii, One of the domestics was affected to his special service. **1868** M. PATTISON *Academ. Organ.* §4. 108 Of our total endowment fund, one, and the smallest third, is affected to the promotion of science and learning.

affectability (əˌfɛktəˈbɪlɪtɪ). [f. next + -ABILITY.] = AFFECTIBILITY.

1894 *Q. Rev.* Oct. 303 The coloured lens of 'affectability' through which they look at most things, makes them strikingly unfit to discourse in the abstract of justice. **1908** D. F. HARRIS *Functional Inertia of Living Matter* i. 1 Affectability can, then, be defined as the power, tendency, capacity, or disposition to be affected by a stimulus, i.e., to *exhibit response.* **1919** W. MCDOUGALL *Introd. Soc. Psychol.* (ed. 14) 449 The most fickle and shallow temper results from the opposite conjunction, namely, high affectability with low intensity and persistence. **1961** *Brit. Med. Dict.* 51/2 *Affectability*, the quality or state of being responsive to a stimulus.

affectable (əˈfɛktəb(ə)l), *a.* = AFFECTIBLE *a.*

1764 J. ERSKINE *Law of Scotl.* (ed. 3) 57 Neither is the right assignable by the minister, or affectable with his debts. **1766** KAMES *Decis. Crt. Sess. 1742* 39 The proper effects of the office-bearer will not be affectable by such a diligence. **1920** E. WALKER in F. S. Marvin *Rec. Dev. Europ. Thought* xi. 275 Neither honour nor artistic personality is affectable by external considerations.

†**affectate**, *ppl. a. Obs.* [ad. L. *affectāt-us* assumed, affected, feigned, pa. pple. of *affectā-re* to aim at: see AFFECT *v.*[1]] **a.** Of a thing: Assumed unnaturally, forced, strained, stilted. **b.** Of a person: Assuming artificial airs; = AFFECTED I. 4, 6.

1559 ELYOT *Dict.*, *Accercitum dictum*, an oracion to much affectate or as we saie to farre fet. **1578** N. T. (Genev.) *1 Cor.* Argt., Puffed vp with vaine glory, and affectate eloquence. **1606** HOLLAND *Suetonius* 18 Affectate forced phrases and curious ynkehorne termes. **1635** J. HAYWARD *Banish'd Virg.* 170, I like not the being an affectate follower of the common stile.

†**affectate**, *v. Obs.* [f. AFFECTATE *a.*, or L. *affectāt-* ppl. stem of *affectā-re*: see prec.] A more Latinized by-form of AFFECT *v.*[1]

1560 J. DAUS *Steidane's Comm.* 134 b, He..maye not affectate rule and gouernment, and playe the tyraunt. **1582** G. MARTIN *Discov.* in *Fulke's Def.* (1843) 202 You affectate to thrust the word 'image' into the text, when there is no such thing in the Hebrew or Greek. **1588** FRAUNCE *Lawiers Logike* I. iv. 27 The like absurditie would it bee..to affectate such woordes as were quite worne out at heeles and elbowes long before the nativitie of Geffrey Chawcer. **1595** LODGE *Def. Stage Plays* (1853) 9 What made Austin so much affectate that heavenly fury?

†**affectated**, *ppl. a. Obs.* [f. prec. + -ED.] = AFFECTATE, *ppl. a.*, and AFFECTED I. 4.

1580 BARET *Alvearie*, A 194 Much affectated: farre fette.. A stile or oration to much affectated wyth strange words. **1617** J. RIDER Much affectated, *Putidulus*..A little affectated, *Putidiusculus.*

†**affectately**, *adv. Obs.* [f. AFFECTATE *a.* + -LY[2].] = Affectedly.

1635 J. HAYWARD *Banish'd Virgin* 136 There was not any species of simplicity that I counterfeited not affectately.

affectation (æfɛkˈteɪʃən). [ad. (directly or through Fr. *affectation*, 16th c. in Litt.) L. *affectātiōn-em* a pursuit after, an aspiring to, f. *affectā-re*: see AFFECT *v.*[1] Sense 6 is a direct adoption of one sense of Fr *affectation.* See AFFECT *v.*[2] 5.]

†**1.** A striving after, aiming at; a desire to obtain, earnest pursuit. Const. *of. Obs.*

1549 SIR W. PAGET in Strype *Eccl. Mem.* (1816) II. 295 His opinion to be good to the poor, and affectation of the good word of the commons. **1608–11** BP. HALL *Medit.* (1627) III. 95 To be caried away with an affectation of fame is so vaine and absurd. **1617** J. RIDER, Affectation, a curious desire of a thing which nature has not given, *Affectatio.* **1659** PEARSON *Creed* (1839) 293 Pretended sedition and affectation of the crown. **1711** STEELE *Spect.* No. 6 ¶4 The Affectation of being Gay and in Fashion, has very nearly eaten up our Good Sense and our Religion.

†**2.** Inclination towards, affection, liking, fondness (*of*). *Obs.*

1607 TOPSELL *Four-footed Beasts* (1673) 390 No conscience of religion can avert the monstrous love of delights from the affectation of men. **1641** LD. BROOKE *Disc. Nat. Episc.* I. ii. 4 If a Minister once come to lose the heart and affectations of his people. **1795** GIBBON *Autobiogr.* in *Misc. Wks.* (1814) I. 115 Nor was I displeased at her preference and affectation of the manners, the language, and the literature of France.

3. A displayed or ostentatious fondness for; studied display *of*.

1548 UDALL, etc. *Erasm. Paraphr.* 371 Affectation of eloquence. 1600 B. JONSON *Cynthia Rev.* v. i. 6 The affectation Of an enforc'd, and form'd austeritie. 1686 DRYDEN *Hind & P.* I. 395 Affectation of an ancient line. 1716–8 LADY M. W. MONTAGUE *Lett.* I. xxv. 80 It was not an affectation of showing my reading. 1855 PRESCOTT *Philip II*, I. ii. (Routl.) 29 His dress..was rich and elegant, but without any affectation of ornament. 1861 T. WRIGHT *Ess. Archæol.* II. xiv. 60 This affectation of Latin reached its greatest height in..the reign of James I.

4. Artificial or non-natural assumption of behaviour; artificiality (of manner); putting on of airs.

1593 NASHE *Christ's Teares* 2 a, The superfluous affectation of my prophane puft vp phrase. 1598 SHAKS. *Merry Wives* I. i. 152 What phrase is this, He heares with eare? Why, it is affectations. 1642 HOWELL *For. Trav.* (1869) 63 Hee must abhorre all affectations, all forced postures and complements. 1776 GIBBON *Decl. & F.* I. xxii. 616 His simplicity was not exempt from affectation. 1827 CARLYLE *Misc.* I. 10 The essence of affectation is that it be assumed. 1872 BLACK *Adv. of Phaeton* iii. 29 Her pretty affectations of petulance.

5. As that which is artificial is often unreal, this passes imperceptibly into, Unreal assumption; hollow or false display; simulation, pretence.

1581 SIDNEY *Def. Poesie* (1622) 527 That hony-flowing matron Eloquence, apparelled, or rather disguised in a curtisan-like painted affectation. 1625 BACON *Ess.* xxxviii. (1862) 160 A Mans Nature is best perceived in Privatenesse, for there is no Affectation. 1750 JOHNSON *Rambler* No. 20 ¶1 Affectation, or a perpetual disguise of the real character by fictitious appearances. 1866 J. MARTINEAU *Ess.* I. 191 Their profession..becomes an empty affectation. 1873 BUCKLE *Civilis.* III. v. 321 Some people affect to carry on trade for the good of others; but this is mere affectation.

†6. Special application, destination, or attribution. *Obs. rare.*

1611 COTGR., *Nantissement*..a publicke, or legall affectation, fastening, appointing, or pointing out of one thing for the securitie or indemnitie of another.

affectationist (æfɛkˈteɪʃənɪst). [f. prec. + -IST.] One who indulges in affectation or artificiality.

1873 F. HALL *Mod. Eng.* 177 'Adamantiferous,' etymologically correct, would never answer; but all except pedants or affectationists would be satisfied with 'diamond-producing.'

†**affecˈtatious**, *a. Obs. rare*⁻¹. Of the nature of affectation. (In the quotation read instead of *affectations* in Shaks. *Merry Wives* I. i. 152.)

1687 M. CLIFFORD *Notes on Dryden* iii. 12 For to me, as Parson Hugh says in Shakespear, they seemed Lunacies, it is mad as a mad Dog, it is affectatious.

†**affectator**. *Obs. rare.* [a. L. *affectātor* n. of agent f. *affectāre*: see AFFECT *v.*[1]] = AFFECTER.

1610 HEALEY tr. *Vives on St. Aug. City of God* 318 Hee was an affectator of glory. 1733 BAILEY tr. *Erasm. Colloq.* (1877) 79 (D.) Those affectators of variety seem equally ridiculous.

affected (əˈfɛktɪd), *ppl. a.* [f. AFFECT + -ED. Really consists of *three* words: 1. pa. pple. of AFFECT *v.*[1] = earlier *affectate*; 2. adj. f. AFFECT *sb.* + -ED; 3. pa. pple. of AFFECT *v.*[2]. To some extent the senses are confused, through the formal identity of the words.]

I. Pa. pple. of AFFECT *v.*[1], = earlier AFFECTATE.

†1. Sought after, aimed at, desired. *Obs.*

1597 DANIEL *Civ. Wares* v. xc, Twixt Yorke, and the affected sov'raignty. 1602 CAREW *Cornw.* 14 b, With other lesse beneficiall and affected commodities. 1608 BP. HALL *Epistles* I. iii, It is at once had and affected. 1649 MILTON *Eikonokl.* Pref. (1847) 274/1 A work assigned rather than by me chosen or affected.

†2. Fondly held, cherished; entertained of choice, intentional. *Obs.*

1589 T. B. tr. *La Primaudaye's Fr. Acad.* 150 Man having by nature imprinted in his soule an affected and earnest inclination to his soveraigne good. 1623 W. LISLE tr. *Sax. Treat. on O. & N.T.* Pref. 13 Grosse, wilfull, and affected ignorance. 1640 *Prerog. Parl.* in *Sel. fr. Harl. Misc.* (1793) 241 Make the world know, that his cruelty was not affected. 1705 STANHOPE *Paraphr.* I. 171 Their Love and Preference of Darkness is more affected and obstinate.

†3. Loved, beloved. *Obs.*

1600 CHAPMAN *Iliad* VIII. 318 In all the desperate hours Of his affected Hercules. 1624 CAPT. SMITH *Virginia* (1629) 78 They should live with Powhatan as his chiefe affected. 1626 W. SANDYS *Ovid's Metam.* 216 Her speare..Kist his affected lips without a wound. 1640 FULLER *Joseph's Coat* viii. (1867) 190 Some sacrifice the reverence to this admired preacher, and others almost adore that affected pastor. 1654 GAYTON *Festiv. Notes* IV. ii. 183 His love to his affected, though some 106 years posthumus Kinsman.

4. Assumed or displayed artificially; put on for effect: non-natural, artificial, stilted, 'got up.'

1594 C[AREW] *Huarte's Exam. Wits* (1616) 136 To haue a readie tongue of his own, and not affected, choice words. 1642 MILTON *Militia* A 4, I have not used any affected style. 1678 ROCHESTER in *Shaksp. Cent. Praise* 364 But does not Dryden find..Shake-spear's stile Stiff and affected? 1723 J. SHEFFIELD (D. of Buckhm.) *Wks.* 1753 I. 51 An air affected, and a haughty mien; Something that seems to say, I would be seen. 1855 MACAULAY *Hist. Eng.* IV. 645 His diction, affected and florid, but often singularly beautiful and melodious, fascinated many young enthusiasts.

5. Assumed falsely or in outward semblance merely; pretended, simulated.

1663 GERBIER *Counsel* g i a, Those Lines must be visible, no affected ones, nor small as a haire. 1679 SHEFFIELD & DRYDEN *Ess. on Sat.* 67 Dissembling still in either place, Affected humour, or a painted face. 1751 JOHNSON *Rambler* No. 153 ¶11 Without any of the heir's affected grief or secret exultation. 1850 LYNCH *Theoph. Trinal* v. 85 This their dull sadness..is affected and heartless. 1879 MCCARTHY *Hist. own Times* I. 30 His real or affected levity gave way to a genuine and lasting desire to make her life happy.

6. Of persons: Full of affectation; non-natural or artificial in manner, pretentious, assuming airs. (An extension of 4; not directly from pa. pple.)

1588 SHAKS. *L.L.L.* v. i. 15 He is too picked, too spruce, too affected, too odde. 1689 SHADWELL *Bury Fair* I. i. 122 Conceited affected Jades. 1703 ROWE *Fair Penit.* II. i. 440 Each affected She that tells my story. 1735 POPE *Hor. Ep.* II. i. 105 Damn all Shakespear, like th' affected Fool. 1858 HAWTHORNE *Fr. & It. Journ.* I. 157 She seemed to be her actual self, and nothing affected or made up.

II. = earlier AFFECT *ppl. a.*, L. *affectus*. [were formed by distinctive ppl. ending -ED; or from AFFECT *sb.* + -ED[2], as in *mind-ed*, *will-ed*, etc.]

1. Having an affection (formerly *affect*), disposition, or inclination of any kind; disposed, inclined.

1587 FLEMING *Contn. Holinsh.* III. 372/2 That will judge to the contrarie, unless he be parciallie affected. 1598 BARRET *Theor. Warres* I. ii. 12 Let him make choise of the armes..whereunto he findeth himselfe most affected and fit. 1611 COTGR., *Addonné*, given, bent, affected, addicted, inclined. 1611 BIBLE *2 Macc.* xiv. 5 And asked how the Iewes stood affected. 1682 HEWER in *Pepys' Diary* VI. 144 Variously discoursed of as people were affected and inclined. 1684 BUNYAN *Pilgr.* II. 151 How stands the country affected towards you? *c* 1815 MISS AUSTEN *Persuas.* (1833) II. ix. 390 You might, some time or other, be differently affected towards him.

b. Usually with the direction of the affection or disposition indicated by *well*, *ill*, etc. Well- or ill-disposed, or -conditioned (mentally).

1553–87 FOXE *A. & M.* (1596) 136/1 If anie good men were well affected or minded toward religion. 1605 SHAKS. *Lear* II. i. 100 No marvaile then, though he were ill affected. 1611 BIBLE *Acts* xiv. 2 Made their mindes euill affected against the brethren. 1647 SPRIGG *Ang. Rediv.* IV. ix. (1854) 315 Many well affected citizens also went forth. *a* 1674 CLARENDON *Hist. Rebell.* II. VI. 90 The Major part..being cordially Affected to the Government. 1832 LYTTON *Eug. Aram.* ix. 60 You are an honest man, and well affected to our family.

†2. *esp.* Having a favourable affection or inclination; favourably disposed or inclined; attached, partial (*to*). *Obs.*, but cf. *dis-affected*.

1535 STEWART *Cron. Scotl.* II. 557 On to his sone affectit so wes he. 1553–87 FOXE *A. & M.* (1596) 136/2 Ethelstan..was so affected towards Odo. 1584 A. MUNDAY (*title*) A Watchwoord to Englande..Written by a faithfull affected Freend to his Country. 1618 *Shoemaker's Holiday* i. (1862) 6, I hear my cousin Lacy Is much affected to your daughter Rose. 1622 HEYLIN *Cosmogr.* IV. (1682) 93 The men are much affected to hunting. 1690 EVELYN *Mem.* (1857) II. 319 On suspicion of being affected to King James.

†3. Of bodily disposition or tendency: -conditioned; -disposed. *ill-affected* = indisposed. *Obs.*

1586 T. B. tr. *La Primaudaye's Fr. Acad.* II. (1594) 139 When the bodie is well affected. 1615 LATHAM *Falconry* (1633) 104 When you do perceive your Hawke to be ill affected in that place.

III. Pa. pple. of AFFECT *v.*[2] = L. *affectus*. Apparently first = 'laid hold of' by a disease (L. *affectus morbo*), and so apparently connected with II. 3, above; then extended to what lays hold of, touches, or moves the mind or feelings, or moves physically.

1. a. Laid hold of (by a disease), under the influence of; attacked, seized, afflicted; tainted, distempered, diseased. Const. *with*.

a 1619 DONNE *Biathan.* 63 To confesse, that those times were affected with a disease of this naturall desire of such a death. 1633 T. N[EWTON] *Lemnie's Touchst. Complex.* 120 The body is mutually affected, and alike distempered. 1751 CHAMBERS *Cycl.* s.v. *Affection*, The sick are frequently mistaken as to the place affected. 1806 T. PAINE *Yellow Fever* in *Misc. Wks.* II. 180 Of the same extent as the affected part of a city. 1857 T. WATSON *Lect. Physic* xxviii. (ed. 4) 502 To conclude that the side towards which the mouth was drawn was the affected side. 1864 *Daily Tel.* 26 May, The accused was mentally affected, her father and three of her aunts having all been insane. 1868 *Public Opin.* 2 May 460/1 On examination of the affected region with the hand.

†b. *fig.* Seized or possessed. *Obs.*

1579 LYLY *Euphues* (1636) G b, Lest being affected with barbarisme, they be also infected with their vncleane conuersation. 1656 N. BERNARD *Life of Ussher* 28 He was so affected with chronology and antiquity.

†2. Mentally influenced, moved, impressed; interested or taken up. Const. *with*. *Obs.*

1626 MASSINGER *Rom. Actor* Ded., Such as are only affected with jigs and ribaldry. 1673 *True Worship of God* 64 If Pulpit Discourses were not so frequent, people would be more affected with them. 1756 BURKE *Subl. & B.* Wks. I. 173 The imagination and passions are little or nothing affected.

3. Moved, influenced, or touched in the feelings; usually to sympathy, sorrow, or sadness. Const. *by* (*with* obs.).

1633 BP. HALL *Hard Texts* 32 Hee is more affected with the recovering of that one sheepe..than with the safety of the rest. 1751 JOHNSON *Rambler* No. 187 ¶2 Ajut was so much affected by the fondness of her lover. 1781 GIBBON *Decl. & F.* III. 53 Deeply affected by his own reproaches. 1855 PRESCOTT *Philip II*, I. i. (Routl.) 9 They were deeply affected, and not a dry eye was to be seen in the assembly.

4. Moved, influenced, acted upon, physically or materially. Const. *by* (*with* obs.).

1748 HARTLEY *Observ. Man* I. i. §1. 30 The Vibrations.. may be affected with four sorts of Differences. 1762 DUNN in *Phil. Trans.* LII. 468 Trees and bushments of equal magnitude at other times, but in their affected state as much larger. 1783 GEORGE III in Dk. of Buckingham's *Crt. Geo. III*, II. 219 Preventing the public finances from being materially affected. 1849 MURCHISON *Siluria* iv. 71 The latter strata, affected..by a slaty cleavage. 1878 HUXLEY *Physiogr.* 188 The water is affected even more than the land.

†5. *Math.* Compounded; = ADFECTED, the special form now restricted to this sense. *Obs.*

1717 B. TAYLOR *Extr. of Roots* in *Phil. Trans.* XXX. 610 Method of extracting the Roots of affected Equations. 1802 WOODHOUSE *ibid.* XCII. 115 The terms affected with x^n.

†b. *by extension*. *Obs.*

1652 URQUHART *Jewel* Wks. 1834, 276 He had his proper name affected with the agnominal addition of Parresiastes.

6. Specially applied; appointed, assigned, allotted; attributed. (Cf. Fr. *affecté* and AFFECT *v.*[2] 5.)

1611 COTGR., *Nanti*..affected unto; fastened or tied on; appointed, or pointed out for; or to whom a thing is affected; on whom it is fastened; for whom it is appointed. 1850 THACKERAY *Penden.* xxii. (1863) 181 A female servant.. affected to his private use. 1871 *Daily News* (*Let. fr. Paris*) 21 Jan., Horses..affected to military purposes.

affectedly (əˈfɛktɪdlɪ), *adv.* [f. AFFECTED *a.* I. + -LY[2].] In an affected manner; with affectation or affection.

†1. With aim or desire, with true intent; intentionally, sincerely, earnestly.

1596 CHAPMAN *Iliad* II. (355 *note*) Simple, well-meaning, standing still affectedly on telling truth. 1628 EARLE *Microcosm.* lxxviii. 161 One not hasty to pursue the new fashion, nor yet affectedly true to his old round breeches. 1690 LOCKE *Hum. Underst.* (1727) I. IV. x. §10. 293, I have affectedly made use of this measure..because I think it would be of general convenience. 1738 WARBURTON *Div. Legat.* I. Ded. 26 [He] goes affectedly out of his way to do it.

†2. With favourable affection; affectionately, lovingly. *Obs.*

1611 TOURNEUR *Ath. Trag.* IV. iv. 123 Methinkes she's very affectedly enclin'd To young Sebastian's company o' late.

3. With affectation or studied art; artifically, fancifully. (Opposed to *simply* or *naturally*.)

1617 HOLYOKE *Dict. Etym.* II. *Affectatè*..affectedly, with overmuch curiosity. 1646 SIR T. BROWNE *Pseud. Ep.* 359 Some..have beene so affectedly vaine as to counterfeit Immortality. 1673 *Ladies Calling* I. i. §14 Their gesture, their language, nay sometimes their habit too being affectedly masculine. 1787 BONNYCASTLE *Astron.* xii. 198 His philosophical notions are..affectedly mysterious and obscure. 1838 HALLAM *Hist. Lit.* I. I. vi. §16. 369 If 'Gospel light,' as Gray has rather affectedly expressed it, had not 'flashed from Boleyn's eyes.' 1876 FREEMAN *Norm. Conq.* I. App. 683 The person affectedly described as 'Lupus' is really Archbishop Wulfstan.

4. With studied simulation; with appearance rather than reality; pretendingly, hypocritically. *Obs.*

1656 DU GARD *Lat. Unlocked* §674. 207 Do nothing affectedly, dissemblingly, appearingly for fashions sake. 1795 T. HURLSTONE *Crotchet Lodge* 41, *Miss Crotchet.* O, dear Doctor [turning from him affectedly]. 1839 JAMES *Louis XIV* II. 336 Terrified at a tumult, that he had at first affectedly despised. 1861 FLOR. NIGHTINGALE *Nursing* 35 An affectedly sympathising voice, like an undertaker's at a funeral.

affectedness (əˈfɛktɪdnɪs). [f. AFFECTED *a.* I. + -NESS.] 'The quality of being affected or of making false appearances.' J.; = AFFECTATION.

1652 FRENCH *Yorksh. Spa* xvii. 23 Neither do I do it out of any affectedness to contradict D. Deane's judgement. 1873 F. HALL *Mod. Eng.* 100 There is a repulsive affectedness in this.

affecter (əˈfɛktə(r)). Also 7–8 **affector**. [f. AFFECT *v.*[1] + -ER.]

†1. One who has an affection for, a lover. *Obs.*

1568 C. WATSON *Polyb.* 16 b, I think they were deceyved (as affectoures are accustomed). 1590 MARLOWE *1st Pt. Tamburl.* v. ii, Madam, your father, and the Arabian King The first affecter of your excellence, Come now. 1622 HEYLIN *Cosmogr.* (1682) II. 178 Famous for Government, affectors of Freedom. 1638 VENNER *Tobacco* (1650) 404 These idle affectors of Tobacco.

2. A professed adherent or practiser (*of* anything); an ostentatious or pretentious user, possessor, or professor.

1580 *2nd & 3rd Blast* (1869) 100 A great affecter of that vaine Art of plaie making. 1628 EARLE *Microcosm.* xlii. 93 A great affecter of wits and such prettinesses. 1660 T. STANLEY *Hist. Philos.* (1701) 87/2 Vain affecters of Words, ignorant of those things which they professed. 1723 BLACKALL *Wks.* I. 499 Our Saviour was no Affecter of Novelty in Devotion. 1750 JOHNSON *Rambler* No. 20 ¶14 The affector of great excellencies. 1830 COLERIDGE *Ch. & St.* 168 There are few [charges], if any, that I should be more anxious to avoid than that of being an affecter of paradoxes.

†3. *absol.* An affected person. *Obs.*

1607 P. C. tr. *H. Stephen's World of Wonders* 238 Neither can these fine finicall affecters alleadge the Italian tongue.. to warrant their pronunciation. 1611 COTGR., *Affectateur*, an affector; one that (curiously) imitates a fashion, or takes on him a habit, which either becomes or befits him not.

affectibility (ə͵fɛktɪˈbɪlɪtɪ). [f. AFFECTIBLE: see -BILITY.] The quality or state of being affectible.

1847 in CRAIG.

affectible (əˈfɛktɪb(ə)l), *a. rare.* [f. L. *affect-* ppl. stem of L. *affic-ĕre* (see AFFECT *v.*^{2}) + -IBLE, as if ad. L. **affectibilis*.] Capable of being affected.

a **1834** COLERIDGE *Notes Theol.* (1853) 2 That He could not lay aside the absolute, and, by union with the creaturely, become affectible.

affecting (əˈfɛktɪŋ), *vbl. sb.* [f. AFFECT *v.* + -ING^1.] The process of the vbs. AFFECT in various senses; now mostly gerundial.

1. Aiming at, showing fondness for, ostentatiously displaying, pretending.

1564 HAWARD *Eutrop.* To Reader 7 The affectynge and desyre of the attaynynge of the Greeke, Latyne, Italian and other tounges. **1649** DRUMM. OF HAWTH. *Wks.* 1711, 162 If any part of his work distaste the reader, it will be the extreme affecting of policy. *Mod.* The folly of affecting ignorance of what had happened.

2. Assuming artificial airs.

3. Moving of the emotions.

1756 BURKE *Subl. & B.* Wks. 1842 I. 30 Pain and pleasure, in their most simple and natural manner of affecting.

affecting (əˈfɛktɪŋ), *ppl. a.* [f. AFFECT *v.* + -ING^2.]

†**1.** (From AFFECT *v.*^{1}) Loving, affectionate, solicitous. *Obs.*

1616 SURFLET & MARKH. *Countrey Farme* Ded., Darius in his deepe affecting desire, made choice of many such subiects and Captaines. **1619** HUTTON *Follie's Anat.* (1842) 48 To gratulate their kinde affecting host.

†**2.** (From AFFECT *v.*^{1} 5.) Using affectation; affected. *Obs.*

1598 SHAKS. *Merry Wives* II. i. 145, I neuer heard such a drawling-affecting, rogue. **1611** COTGR., *Pinsegreneur d'Amadis*, a Phrasemonger..affecting speaker.

†**3.** (From AFFECT *v.*^{2}) Arresting the mind; impressive. *Obs.*

1665 J. SPENCER *Proph.* 101 When we suddainly awake out of some very affecting dream. **1768** BLACKSTONE *Comm.* I. 12 How much more serious and affecting is the case of a superior judge. **1779** JOHNSON *Milton* 154 Epick poetry.. relates some great event in the most affecting manner.

4. Acting upon the emotions; moving, touching; thrilling; pathetic.

1720 ROWE *Ulysses* II. i. 46 Oh Nature, how affecting are thy Sorrows! **1756** BURKE *Subl. & B.* Wks. I. 231 Beauty in distress is much the most affecting beauty. **1790** *Cook's Voy.* III. VI. 2239 On hearing the recital of his affecting catastrophe. **1855** PRESCOTT *Philip II*, I. i. (Routl.) 9 Even the most stoical, was touched by this affecting scene.

†**5.** Having a physical influence. *Obs.*

1794 S. WILLIAMS *Hist. Vermont* 46 Nor is the cold so affecting to the human body.

affectingly (əˈfɛktɪŋlɪ), *adv.* [f. prec. + -LY^2.] In an affecting manner; touchingly, pathetically.

1788 LORD SYDNEY in Dk. of Buckingham's *Crt. Geo. III* (1853) I. 438 Attention..of the value of which he has shewn himself affectingly sensible. **1841** SPALDING *Italy* II. 27 Prefatory verses, which contain an affectingly humble self-review. **1871** *Athen.* 8 Apr. 423 It is when he has warmed to his work..that his words read the most affectingly.

affection (əˈfɛkʃən), *sb.* Forms: 3 **affectiun**, 4–5 **affectioun**, **affeccyone**, **affeccoun**, **affeccioun**, **affecsioun**, 5–6 **affectione**, 6– **affection**. [a. Fr. *affection*, an early ad. L. *affectiōn-em* disposition, inclination, fondness, f. *affic-ĕre*: see AFFECT *v.*^{2}]

I. *Generally* and *literally*.

1. a. The action of affecting, acting upon, or influencing; or (when viewed passively) the fact of being affected.

1660 T. STANLEY *Hist. Philos.* (1701) 134/2 Whether the same affection hapneth to any one, and to him that is next him from white, neither is he able to say. **1756** BURKE *Subl. & B.* Wks. 1842 I. 28 There is no difference in the manner of their being affected, nor in the causes of the affection. **1794** J. HUTTON *Philos. Light, etc.* 11 The reciprocal affection of those bodies. **1846** MILL *Logic* I. iii. §4 (1868) 57 Besides the affection of our bodily organs from without. **1879** CARPENTER *Ment. Physiol.* I. v. 186 The spots of the retina by the affection of which they are produced.

b. *Celtic Philol.* Mutation or umlaut of a vowel under the influence of a following sound.

1911 J. MORRIS JONES in *Encycl. Brit.* XXVIII. 269/1 Short vowels have been affected by vowels in succeeding syllables. These 'affections' of vowels are as follows:—(*a*) I-affection, caused by *i* in a lost termination..(*β*) A-affection ..(*γ*) Penultimate affection. **1913** —— *Welsh Gram.* 89 Affection is of two kinds in Welsh: 1. ultimate, when it takes place in the syllable which is now the last, having been brought about by a sound in a lost termination; 2. non-ultimate, when it takes place in the present penult or antepenult, the affecting sound being generally preserved in the ultima. **1937** LEWIS & PEDERSEN *Conc. Comp. Celt. Gram.* 3 Changes due to vowel affection in Ir. (> *i*),..in W. (> *y*, *ei*),..in Co. *y* is found written *e* where there is no affection. **1953** K. JACKSON *Lang. & Hist. Early Brit.* 578 It would be better..to date *ā*-affection in the first half or middle of the fifth century.

II. Of the mind.

2. a. An affecting or moving of the mind in any way; a mental state brought about by any influence; an emotion or feeling.

c **1230** *Ancren Riwle* 288 þreo degrez beoð þerinne [in carnal desire] þe uorme is cogitaciun: þe oðer is affectiun: þe þridde is kunsence. *c* **1385** CHAUCER *Leg. G. Wom.* 1518 Withouten any other affeccioun Of love, or any other ymaginacioun. **1545** ASCHAM *Toxoph.* (Arb.) 146 A man..is subiecte to inmeasurable affections. **1625** tr. *Gonsalvius's Sp. Inquis.* 1 Accompany the outward motions of the players, with some inward affection. **1723** BLACKALL *Wks.* I. 70 Mercy..is an affection of the Mind. **1764** REID *Inq. Hum. Mind* ii. §9. 112 The smell of a rose is a certain affection or feeling of the mind. **1878** HOPPS *Rel. & Mor. Lect.* xvii. 53 It is simply impossible to reveal anything to a human being except through his reason, his conscience, or his affections.

b. The representation of feeling or emotion.

1624 WOTTON *Archit.* (J.) Affection is the lively representation of any passion whatever, as if the figures stood not upon a cloth or board, but as if they were acting upon a stage.

†**3.** *esp.* Feeling as opposed to reason; passion, lust. *Obs.*

1398 TREVISA *Barth. De P.R.* III. vi. (1495) 53 Affeccions ben foure Joye Hope Drede and Sorowe. **1567** *Triall of Treas.* (1850) 4 Slaues to their lustes and affection. **1596** SPENSER *F.Q.* II. iv. 34 Most wretched man, That to Affections does the bridle lend! **1611** BIBLE *Rom.* i. 26 For this cause God gaue them vp vnto vile affections. **1643** MILTON *Soveraigne Salve* 25 A will over-ruled by enormous affections or passions. **1681** HOBBES *Rhetor.* i. 1 Anger, Envy, Fear, Pity or other Affections. **1736** BUTLER *Anal.* II. vii. 357 Over and above our reason and affections.

†**4.** State of mind generally, mental tendency; disposition. *Obs.* in general sense.

1540 WHITTINTON *Tully's Offyces* III. 125 Suche affection of mynde, that I do no man wronge bycause of my profyte. **1622** FOTHERBY *Atheom.* II. viii. §1. 279 Good Affections, which are præparatiues vnto Vertue. **1756** BURKE *Subl. & B.* Wks. 1842 I. 34 Let the affection be what it will in appearance, if it does not make us shun such objects.

5. *esp.* State of the mind towards a thing; disposition towards, bent, inclination, *penchant*. *arch.*

1330 R. BRUNNE *Chron.* 162 To þat sollempnite com lordes of renoun, þat weddyng forto se, for grete affectioun. *c* **1385** CHAUCER *Leg. G. Wom.* 793 This Tesbe hath so grete affeccioun, And so grete lykynge Piramus to see. *c* **1386** —— *Melibeus* 284 Ye have schewed to youre counseilours.. youre affeccioun to Make werre. **1481** CAXTON *Myrrour* I. v. 20 It was all their affeccion, intencion and reson to knowe god. **1549** *Compl. Scotl.* x. 83 The inglismen exponis the prophesye of merlyne to there auen affectione. **1561** T. N[ORTON] tr. *Calvin's Instit.* II. 125 Where anger or hatred is, there is an affection to hurt. **1604** ROWLANDS *Looke to it* 10 Lawyers that wrest the Law to your affection. **1625** BACON *Ess.* vii. (1862) 25 If the Affection or Aptnesse of the Children, be Extraordinary, then it is good, not to crosse it. **1642** ROGERS *Naaman* Ep. Ded. 2 A few good reaches and affections after holinesse are not enough for us. **1762** KAMES *Elem. Critic.* (1833) 483 Affection, signifying a settled bent of the mind toward a particular being or thing. **1877** MOZLEY *Univ. Serm.* iii. 69 The two desires..are in fact bound up with each other in one affection, and make but one affection between them.

6. a. Good disposition towards, goodwill, kind feeling, love, fondness, loving attachment.

1382 WYCLIF *2 Macc.* xiv. 37 Nychanore..that for affeccioun, *or loue*, was clepid fadre of Jewis. *c* **1385** CHAUCER *Leg. G. Wom.* 1421 Made he to Jason Gret chiere of love & of affecciouu. *c* **1440** *Promp. Parv.*, Affecцyon, or hertyly wellwyllynge, *Affectio*. **1488** CAXTON *Chastysing of Goddes Chyldern* xxiii. 61 Affeccion is a wylfull bowyng or enclinyng of a mannys hert with loue to a nother man. **1599** SHAKS. *Much Ado* II. i. 175, *Cl.* How know you he loues her? *Iohn.* I heard him sweare his affection. **1611** BIBLE *Transl. Pref.* 6 The Church of Rome would seeme at the length to beare a motherly affection towards her children. **1698** J. NORRIS *Pract. Disc.* IV. 289 To love one another, with the most Heroic and Divine Affection. **1749** FIELDING *Tom Jones* IX. v. (1840) 135 We are no sooner in love than it becomes our principal care to engage the affection of the object beloved. **1868** GEO. ELIOT *Felix H.* 22 Affection and satisfied pride would again warm her later years.

b. *esp.* in *pl.*

1604 SHAKS. *Oth.* I. iii. 112 Did you..Subdue, and poyson this yong Maides affections? **1768** STERNE *Sent. Journey* (1778) II. 26, I never had my affections more tenderly awakened. **1851** CHALMERS *Let.* in *Life* (1815) II. 11 Give my kindest affections to my father, mother, and family. **1855** PRESCOTT *Philip II*, I. ii. (Routl.) 19 In the society of one who was now the chief object of his affections.

†**7.** Feeling against, animosity. *Obs.*

1485 CAXTON *Chas. the Gt.* 44 And he cometh rennyng agenst me wyth affectyon mortal. **1589** BP. COOPER *Admon.* 22, I heare some crie out with earnest affection against me. **1600** HAKLUYT *Voy.* (1810) III. 164 They uttered their old spiteful affection towards vs.

†**8.** Biased feeling, partiality. *Obs.*

1547 J. HARRISON *Exhort. to Scottes* 227 Weigh the querell indifferently, and without affeccion. **1559** KENNEDY in *Misc. Wodr. Soc.* (1844) 271 The anceant fatheris..without affectioun schaws truelie thair jugement. **1577** HANMER *Anc. Eccles. Hist.* (1619) 452 Very partiall..and led very much with affection.

III. Of the body.

9. A bodily state due to any influence.

1541 R. COPLAND *Galyen's Terap.* 2 A iii, Euery vlcere is eyther symple and alone without other dysposytyon or affectyon begynnynge with it. *c* **1660** SOUTH *Serm.* Prov. iii. 17 (1715) I. 3 To place Men with the furious Affections of Hunger and Thirst in the very Bosom of Plenty. **1756** BURKE *Subl. & B.* Wks. 1842 I. 59 Why certain affections of the body produce such a distinct emotion of mind.

10. *esp.* An abnormal state of body; malady, disease.

1541 R. COPLAND *Galyen's Terap.* 2 G ij, In all suche affections behoueth purgacyons. **1633** T. N[EWTON] tr. *Lemnie's Touchst. Complex.* 4 Throwne into sundry diseases and innumerable affections. **1646** SIR T. BROWNE *Pseud. Ep.* 198 Affections both of Lungs and weazon. **1804** ABERNETHY *Surg. Observ.* 157, I mean here only to advert to those rheumatic affections. **1853** LYTTON *My Novel* VII. iii. 342 Died, sir, suddenly, last night. It was an affection of the heart.

IV. Of substances or essences.

11. A temporary or non-essential state, condition, or relation of anything; a mode of being.

1567 MAPLET *Greene Forest* 32 The coldenesse or other affection of the Aire about it. **1643** SIR T. BROWNE *Relig. Med.* I. §35 The spirits walke..freely exempt from the affection of time, place, and motion. **1674** N. FAIRFAX *Bulk & Selv.* 99 Motion, which is an all-reaching affection or belonger to each bit of the world. **1677** GALE *Ct. of Gentiles* II. IV. Proem. 7 The affections of propositions are either absolute or relate: absolute affections are quantitie and qualitie. **1751** CHAMBERS *Cycl.* s.v., The generality of Peripatetics divide Affections into internal; as motion, and finiteness: and external, as place, and time. **1802** PLAYFAIR *Huttonian Theory* 337 To be veined or not veined, is an affection of granite, that seems..accidental. **1842** W. GROVE *Correl. Phys. Forces* (1867) 106 Electricity is that affection of matter or mode of force which most distinctly and beautifully brings into relation other modes of force.

12. Hence, A property, quality, or attribute.

1588 W. KEMPE *Educ. Children* sig. G 3^r, The Rhetoricall pronounciation and gesture fit for euery word, sentence, and affection. **1625** SIR H. FINCH *Law* (1636) 225 There remaineth yet one generall and common affection scattered throughout the whole Law..which we call an Action. **1657** J. SMITH *Myst. Rhet.* 3 The affections of Tropes..are such qualities as may put ornament upon any of the forementioned Tropes. **1659** PEARSON *Creed* I. 504 Holiness and catholicism are but affections of this Church. **1751** HARRIS *Hermes* (1841) 153 It fares with tenses as with other affections of speech. **1820** MAIR *Tyro's Dict.* (ed. 10) 389 *Attributum*, an affection, an attribute. **1860** FARRAR *Orig. Lang.* i. 20 Thought is merely an affection of perishable matter.

V. From AFFECT *v.*^{1}, confused with AFFECT *v.*^{2}

†**13.** The act of affecting or assuming artificially; = AFFECTATION. *Obs.*

1553–87 FOXE *A. & M.* (1596) 171/2 He..dooth answer againe, by cauilling sophistication, & by meere affection. **1588** SHAKS. *L.L.L.* v. i. 407 Taffata phrases, silken tearmes precise, Three-pil'd Hyperboles, spruce affection. **1603** *Hist. Eng.* in *Harl. Misc.* (Malh.) II. 415, I dislike affection of foreign and new-coined words, when we have good and sufficient store of our own. **1631** SANDERSON *Serm.* II. 2/2 Affection in this, as in every other thing, is both tedious & ridiculous. **1686** in *Misc. Curiosa* (1708) III. 230 A most inconvenient affection of Monasyllabical Words. **1776** SHERIDAN *Sch. Scandal* I. i, With the very gross affection of good nature.

affection (əˈfɛkʃən), *v.* [a. Fr. *affectionne-r*, f. *affection*. Cf. *love*, to *love*; *honour*, to *honour*.] To have affection for; to like, love.

1584 *Copie of a Leter* 31 A goodlie Gentlewoman, whom the Earle affectioned much. **1598** SHAKS. *Merry Wives* I. i. 234 Can you affection the 'o-man..can you carry your good wil to ye maid? **1765** H. WALPOLE *Otranto* v. (1798) 79, I do not think my lady Isabella ever much affectioned my young lord, your son. **1863** COWDEN CLARKE *Shaks. Char.* viii. 207 Malvolio..is the only person in the play who does not affection the gay and sweet-spirited jester. **1880** *Cornh. Mag.* XLII. 659 Those underground regions he affectioned.

affectional (əˈfɛkʃənəl), *a.* [f. AFFECTION *sb.* + -AL^1. Cf. *rational*.] Of or pertaining to the affections; having affections.

1859 T. PARKER *Exper. as Minister* 112 The leading Reformers are men of large intellect, of profound morality, earnest, affectional men. **1862** F. HALL *Refut. Hindu Philos.* 228 Affectional cognition is a property of the mind. **1864** E. SARGENT *Peculiar* I. 65 The affectional part of his nature was touched.

†**aˈffectionally**, *adv. Obs.* (in quotation *effectionally*.) Affectionately; earnestly.

a **1657** BALFOUR *Ann. Scot.* (1824) II. 83 That he effectionally deall with the Frenche Kinge, that the Scotts merchants trading in France..may haue free trade.

affectionate (əˈfɛkʃənət), *a.*, formerly also *pple.* [Latinized adaptation of Fr. *affectionné* pple. and adj., on analogy of *orné*, *ornate*, *déterminé*, *determinate*, etc. See -ATE^2. Parallel forms are AFFECTION -ED with the Eng. ppl. ending, and AFFECTIONATED with that ending added, as in *nominate*, *nominated*, *separate*, *separated*.]

†**I.** = Pa. pple. of AFFECTION *v.* Cf. Fr. *affectionné*. Held in affection, beloved. *Obs. rare.*

1494 FABYAN VII. 675 (1811) Another of the affeccionat seruantes of kyng Lowys..and thus two of the derest beloued seruantes.

II. *adj.* Possessed of affection. Cf. AFFECTIONED.

†**1.** Mentally affected, disposed, inclined. *Obs.*

1533 MORE *Answ. to Poysoned Bk.* Wks. 1557, 1053/2 Heare howe Christes audience..wer affeccionate to this euerlasting liuely bred. *a* **1535** —— *Wks.* 584 (R.) The wille as it happeth..at the time to be well or euill affectionate. **1540** WHITTINTON *Tully's Offyces* III. 121 If we shall be so affectionate that euery man shall spoyle and robbe..an other man. **1657** *Penit. Conf.* ix. 282 Thus stood St. Paul affectionate unto the Corinthians.

†2. Unduly affected, biased, prejudiced, partial. *Obs.*

1530 PALSGR. 328/2 Upright, indifferent bytwene party and party, and not affectionate. **1553–87** FOXE *A. & M.* 865 b, Judges not indifferent but very much affectionate against me. **1589** BP. COOPER *Admon* 129 It is but an affectionate iudgement of some, when they impute the onelie cause to be in bishops. **1611** SPEED *Hist. Gt. Brit.* VII. xliv. 358 Subiect to the censures of euery affectionate and malignant reporter.

†3. Passionate, wilful, self-willed, headstrong, obstinate. *Obs.*

1542 UDALL tr. *Erasm. Apophth.* (1874) 35 Affeccionate appetites, perturbyng and corruptyng, the tranquilitee of the mynde. **1548** HALL *Chron.* (1809) 774 He..was not pityful, and stode affectionate in his owne opinion. **1554** KNOX *Faythfull Admon.* E iv, The vsurped gouernment of an affectionate woman is a rage without reason. **1600** HOLLAND *Livy* XXVI. ii. 583/3 The inconsiderate wils of rash affectionate souldiours. **1726** PENN *Tracts* in *Wks.* I. 478 The affectionate Passions, and voluntary Humilities, of a Sort of People, whose Judgment goes always in the rear of their Affections.

†4. Eager, ambitious, earnest. *Obs.*

1598 FLORIO, *Zelatore*, a iealous affectionate man. **1605** BACON *Adv. Learn.* II. vii. §2 (1873) I am..zealous and affectionate to recede as little from antiquity. **1654** MARVELL *Corr.* Let. 2 Wks. 1875 II. 12, I have an affectionate curiosity to know. **1705** STANHOPE *Paraphr.* III. 424 No Man is more affectionate in pressing a good Life than this Apostle. **1750** JOHNSON *Rambler* No. 87 ¶5 Their labours, however zealous or affectionate, are frequently useless.

†5. **a.** Well affected, kindly inclined, favourable (*to* a proposal or thing). *Obs.*

1543 *State Pap. Hen. VIII*, I. 754, I am thought affectionate to these parties here. **1622** BACON *Hen. VII*, 50 They being affectionate unto the quarrell of Britaine. **1647** MAY *Hist. Parl.* II. vi. 104 The Trained Bands were..so affectionate to that cause. **1761** HUME *Hist. Eng.* I. xv. 370 Tournay..containing above sixty thousand inhabitants who were affectionate to the French government.

b. quasi-*sb.* A well-affected person, a favourer. *rare.*

1628 EARLE *Microcosm.* lvi. 122 Men esteem him for this a zealous affectionate, but they mistake him many times, for he does it but to be esteemed so.

6. Of persons, animals: Having warm regard or love, loving, fond, tenderly-disposed.

1586 JAMES VI in Ellis *Orig. Lett.* I. 224 III. 22 Youre most loving and affectionat brother and Cousin James R. **1603** HOLLAND *Plutarch's Mor.* Ded. 1 This generall ioy of affectionate and loyall subjects. **1605** SHAKS. *Lear* IV. vi. 276 Your (Wife, so I would say,) affectionate Seruant. Gonerill. **1769** *Junius Lett.* xxxv. 154 Your subjects..are affectionate enough to separate your person from your government. **1814** SOUTHEY *Roderick* viii. Wks. IX. 76 A gentle heart, a soul affectionate, A joyous spirit fill'd with generous thoughts. **1879** GEO. ELIOT *Theo. Such* vi. 119 An affectionate-hearted creature.

7. Of things: Expressing or indicating love or affection; tender.

a **1586** SIDNEY (T.) Beholding this picture I know not with how affectionate countenance, but, I am sure, with a most affectionate mind. **1655** DIGGES *Compl. Ambass.* 144 To present his affectionate Commendations unto her Majestie. **1725** DE FOE *Voy. round World* (1840) 158 The affectionate carriage of this poor woman to her infant. **1756** BURKE *Subl. & B.* Wks. I. 236 The French and Italians make use of these affectionate diminutives even more than we. **1855** PRESCOTT *Philip II*, I. iv. 74 Philip, taking an affectionate farewell.. took the road to Dover. **1876** GEO. ELIOT *Dan. Der.* IV. lxii. 238 Babli, by which affectionate-sounding diminutive is meant, etc.

†**a'ffectionate**, *v. Obs.* [f. AFFECTIONATE *a.*, or latinized adaptation of Fr. *affectionn-er* on analogy of *terminer*, *terminate*, *élever*, *elevate*, etc. Cf. AFFECTION *v.*, the direct adoption of the Fr. word.]

1. To have affection for, to regard with affection.

c **1590** GREENE *Friar Bacon* (1630) 42, I will reply, which or to whom my selfe affectionates. **1593** *Tell-trothe's N. Yr's. Gift* 30 If mens love be simplie good, women cannot but affectionate them. **1615** HEYWOOD *Foure Prentises* I. 223 Whom..I do more affectionate. **1654** USSHER *Ann.* VII. (1658) 815 Honouring him that was dead, and greatly affectionating the widow Agrippina.

2. *refl.* [after Fr. *s'affectionner à* = *s'attacher.*] To attach oneself.

1603 FLORIO *Montaigne* I. iv, Those who affectionate themselves to Monkies, and little Dogges. **1620** SHELTON *Quixote* IV. xix. 153 He saw me, courted me, I gave ear to him, and..I affectionated myself to him.

†**a'ffectionated**, *ppl. a. Obs.* [f. prec. + -ED; or rather f. AFFECTIONATE *a.* after the appearance of the vb. By-form of AFFECTIONATE; cf. AFFECTIONED.]

1. Inclined or disposed; with *to*, *unto*, favourably inclined, tenderly disposed, attached.

1578 FLORIO *Firste Frutes* Ep. Ded., Your Honours..well favouring and affectionated mind, both unto me, and all other. **1620** SHELTON *Quixote* III. xviii. 119, I am somewhat affectionated to Poesy and to read good Poets. **1651** J. ROCKET *Chr. Subj.* (1658) iii. 21 Hee delights to see you..so graciously affectionated as to pray for them. **1722** WODROW *Corr.* (1843) II. 679 No sort of persons were more entirely affectionated to his Majesty's government and family.

2. Unduly inclined or biased; swayed by affection; partial.

1586 J. HOOKER *Giraldus's Hist. Irel.* in *Holinsh.* II. 134/2 In deciding of all matters he was vpright and iust, being not affectionated nor..corrupted for anie mans pleasure. **1587** FLEMING *Contn. Holinshed* III. 309/1 Without reproch of being affectionated or corrupted.

3. = AFFECTIONATE 5, 6.

1580 SIDNEY *Arcadia* (1622) 19 If he did but only repeate the lamentable, and truely affectionated speeches. **1624** CAPT. SMITH *Virginia* (1629) 142 A vigilant and faithfull counceller, as hee is an affectionated brother. **1631** in *Harl. Misc.* (Malh.) IV. 156 By her Majesty's most affectionated and bound in all humble Duty, W.H.

affectionately (ə'fɛkʃənətlɪ), *adv.* [f. AFFECTIONATE *a.* + -LY[2].] In an affectionate manner.

†1. With strong inclination; eagerly, zealously, earnestly. *Obs.*

1588 W. AVERELL *Combat of Contrar.* B, Their beholders ..while they affectionatlie gaze on their painted pride, doe lose the reason of men and become like stones. **1609** HOLLAND *Amm. Marcell.* XV. iii. 32 A man at all times affectionately given [*avidum*] to entertain the worst matters. **1723** BLACKALL *Wks.* I. 487, I can see no Reason why we may not as well use the Lord's Prayer (provided that we do it devoutly and affectionately) twice, thrice or oftener.

†2. With a biased or partizan spirit; partially, interestedly. *Obs.*

1610 CARLETON *Jurisd.* 14 Persecution began against them, that were called Albingenses: whose opinions are made hainous by some that write affectionately.

3. With favourable disposition, kindly, lovingly, fondly.

1606 SHAKS. *Tr. & Cr.* III. i. 74 My lord Pandarus: honey-sweet lord..commends himselfe most affectionately to you. **1611** BIBLE *1 Thess.* ii. 8 Being affectionately desirous of you, we were willing to haue imparted vnto you. [WYCLIF We desiryng ȝou with greet loue.] **1650** FULLER *Pisgah Sight* II. xii. 247 Strange, that strangers..should so affectionately bemoan the death of a man no whit related unto them. **1814** WORDSWORTH *Excursion* V. 101 As a king Is styled, when most affectionately praised, The father of his people. **1853** LYTTON *My Novel* IV. xvi. 199 Mrs. Riccabocca took her husband's proffered hand affectionately.

affectionateness (ə'fɛkʃənətnɪs). [f. AFFECTIONATE *a.* + -NESS.] The quality of being affectionate; passing from **a.** Earnestness, heartiness (in earlier use), to **b.** Kindness, loving disposition, fondness (in later use).

1669 HONYMAN *Surv. Naphtali* II. 244 Persons not equally allowed by Christ to be in the ministry, may be equal in the manner of their utterance, seeming affectionateness.. earnest manner of application. **1740–87** *Lett. Miss Talbot, etc.* (1808) 283 A fair-dealing kind of affectionateness, ready to encourage and acknowledge its liking of all amiable people. **1826** MISS MITFORD *Our Village* II. (1863) 453 The generosity and affectionateness of the motive. **1827** HARE *Guesses at Truth* (1859) 515 The strong affectionateness of womanhood. **1858** THACKERAY *Virginians* ii. 19 The affectionateness of the present greeting. **1877** MOZLEY *Univ. Serm.* ix. 201 The affectionateness of beseeching looks and supplicating voices.

affectioned (ə'fɛkʃənd), *ppl. a.* [f. AFFECTION *sb.* + -ED[2]; probably imitated from Fr. *affectionné*. See also AFFECTIONATE *a.*, a latinized form of the same word; and cf. the senses of both.]

1. Disposed, inclined (in any way). *arch.*

c **1555** HARPSFIELD *Divorce Hen. VIII* (1878) 29 Reasons which may seem sufficient to any indifferent affectioned man. **1561** T. N[ORTON] tr. *Calvin's Instit.* II. 109 So affectioned and minded by the direction of the spirit that they desire to obey God. *a* **1581** CAMPIAN *Hist. Irel.* XI. ix. 110 They sate upon him diversely affectioned. **1611** BIBLE *Rom.* xii. 10 Bee kindly affectioned one to another with brotherly loue. **1631** B. WEBBE *Quietnesse* (1657) 107 To be affectioned to love one another. **1881** N. T. (Revised) *Rom.* xii. 10 Be tenderly affectioned one to another.

†2. Swayed by the affections; biased, partial. *Obs.*

1589 PUTTENHAM *Eng. Poesie* (1869) 166 Such manner of forraine and coulored talke to make the iudges affectioned.

†3. Passionate, wilful, self-willed, obstinate. *Obs.*

1582 BENTLEY *Monum. Matrones* II. 177 No teares can staie him from his affectioned tyrannie. **1601** SHAKS. *Twel. N.* II. iii. 160 An affection'd Asse, that cons State without booke, and vtters it by great swarths.

†4. Eager, ambitious; zealous. *Obs.*

1534 LD. BERNERS *Gold. Bk. M. Aurel.* G vij b, Those fathers that ar so extremly affectioned, to haue theyr chyldren to begynne as olde men. **1567** in Strype's *Ann. Ref.* I. (1709) 503 To destroye all suche as be affectioned, or make claime to the same kingdome. **1623** HART *Arraign of Urines* Ded., Great Princes have beene affectioned favourers of Physicke and Physitians.

†5. Well affected, kindly disposed. *Obs.*

1539 BIBLE ('Great') *1 Thess.* ii. 8 As a norsse cheryssheth her chyldren, so were we affeccyoned towarde you. **1601** W. T. tr. *Ld. Remy's Civ. Consid.* 7 His citizens, being inclined and affectioned to the French, were much displeased. **1640** FULLER *Abel Rediv., Luther* (1867) I. 57 He was very lovingly affectioned towards his children.

†6. Loving, fond; affectionate (in mod. sense). *Obs.*

1578 N. T. (Genev.) *Matt.* Argt., To forsake the world.. and with most affectioned hearts embrace this incomparable treasure freely offred vnto vs.

affectionless (ə'fɛkʃənlɪs), *a.* [f. AFFECTION *sb.* + -LESS.] Without affection; without bias, unbiased, passionless.

1598 SYLVESTER *Dubartas* (1608) 576 Upon the Law thy Judgements alwayes ground And not on man; for that's affectionless. **1959** B. WOOTTON *Social Sci. & Social Path.* iii. 81 Bowlby's celebrated study of affectionless thieves.

†**a'ffectious**, *a. Obs.* [f. AFFECTION on analogy of *caution*, *cautious*, *action*, *actious*, etc.: see -IOUS. The etymological form is AFFECTUOUS, q.v.] = AFFECTIONATE; earnest, cordial, loving.

1581 MARBECK *Bk. of Notes* 845 True prayer is an earnest and affectious communication of the heart with God. **1607** *Trag. of Nero* (N.) A fare-well kisse, Kisse of true kindnesse and affectious love. **1775** ASH, *Affectious* (not used).

†**a'ffectiously**, *adv. Obs.* [f. prec. + -LY[2].] = AFFECTIONATELY, AFFECTUOUSLY; earnestly, cordially, kindly.

1430 LYDG., *Chron. Troy* III. xxii, Theyr gladnesse when he hath perceyued Spake vnto theim full affectiously. **1755** JOHNSON, *Affectiously*, in an affecting manner. *Dict.*

affective (ə'fɛktɪv), *a.* [a. Fr. *affectif*, *-ive*, ad. med.L. *affectivus*; f. *affect-* ppl. stem of *affic-ĕre*: see AFFECT *v.*[2] and -IVE.]

†1. Earnest, zealous. *Obs. rare.*

1549 *Compl. Scot.* 148 Throucht ane affectyue loue that there prince hes touart them.

†2. Affectionate, loving. *Obs. rare.*

1656 BP. HALL *Breathings of Devout Soul* (1851) 158 Cast me off with scorn, for casting any affective glances upon so base a rival.

†3. Existing in feeling or disposition, as distinguished from external manifestation. *Obs. rare.*

1633 T. ADAMS *Exp. 2 Pet.* ii. 1 (1865) 223 This world God loved, affective before all time, effective in time.

†4. Of affectation; artificially assumed. *Obs. rare.*

1641 BRATHWAIT *Eng. Gent.* 4 That which is most native and least affective deserves choisest acceptance.

†5. Having the quality of affecting; tending to affect or influence; influential, operative. *Obs.*

1656 TRAPP *Exp. Matt.* vii. 20 (1868) 132/1 Knowledge, not apprehensive only, but affective too. **1678** *Lively Oracles* viii. §42, 318 Other manner of impressions, more affective and more lasting then bare reading will leave.

†6. Having the quality of influencing the emotions: affecting. *Obs.*

1654 WHITLOCK *Manners of Eng.* 525 (T.) By affective meditations to view, as re-acted, the tragedy of this day [Good Friday]. **1715** BURNET *Hist. own Times* 695 He was a judicious preacher, more instructive than affective.

7. **a.** Of or pertaining to the affections or emotions; emotional.

1623 BP. HALL *Serm.* Wks. V. 138 This monosyllable (heart)..comprises all that intellective and affective world, which concerneth man;..when God says, The heart is deceitful, he means the Understanding, Will, Affections are deceitful. **1659** HARDY *Serm.* xlii. (1865) 266/2 Pride..as well in the intellectual as in the affective faculty. **1865** LECKY *Rationalism* (1878) I. 391 Act upon and develope the affective or emotional side of human nature. **1876** MAUDSLEY *Physiol. Mind* i. 36 The affective functions of the brain..are the foundations of the emotions, and impulses.

b. *Psychol.* Of, pertaining to, or characterized by feelings or affects (see AFFECT *sb.* 1 e).

1891 J. M. BALDWIN *Handbk. Psychol.* II. xiii. 313 Affective Nature of All Stimuli to Movement... Stimuli.. are all phenomena of feeling. **1897** tr. *T. Ribot's Psychol. of Emotions* 1 In all affective manifestations there are two elements: the motor states or impulses, which are primary; the agreeable or painful states, which are secondary. *Ibid.* xi. 153 Others recall the circumstances *plus* the revived condition of feeling. It is these who have the true 'affective memory'. **1912** A. A. BRILL tr. *Freud's Sel. Papers on Hysteria* (ed. 2) i. 7 Some important memories..on their return acted with the full affective force of new experiences. **1922** *Brit. Jrnl. Psychol.* (*Gen. Sect.*) Oct. 121 Love and hate ..are built of emotional stuff—they are *affective* phenomena. **1926** [see AFFECT *sb.* 1 e]. **1950** D. RIESMAN in *Psychiatry* XIII. 1/2 His [Freud's] own deep affective involvement in an idea.

Comb. **1895** *Amer. Jrnl. Psychol.* VII. 81 *Gemüthsvorgang*, affective or affective-conative process. **1921** D. H. LAWRENCE *Psychoanalysis* i. 22 The great affective-passional functions and emotions. **1925** I. A. RICHARDS *Princ. Lit. Crit.* xi. 91 The affective-volitional aspect of mental activity. **1947** M. M. LEWIS *Lang. in Soc.* i. 20 British psychologists ..have suggested the term 'orectic' as an equivalent of 'affective-conative'.

c. ***affective fallacy*** (see quots.).

1948 W. K. WIMSATT & M. C. BEARDSLEY in *Poetry* Dec. 155 Affective fallacy...a confusion between the poem and its *results* (what it *is* and what it *does*)... The affective fallacy is coupled with the intentional fallacy.., the former being a confusion between the poem and its results, the latter a confusion between the poem and its origins. Examples of the affective fallacy range from Plato's feeding and watering of the passions, Aristotle's counter-theory of catharsis, and the Longinian 'transport' of the audience. **1959** *Times Lit. Suppl.* 20 Feb. 97/1 The Affective Fallacy, for Mr. Wimsatt ..is the fallacy of the *frisson*, of the excited response to the isolated single line; or, more broadly, of the admirer of Dylan Thomas, say, who says: 'I don't understand a word of it, but how wonderful!'

affectively (ə'fɛktɪvlɪ), *adv.* [f. prec. + -LY[2].] In an affective manner.

†1. In respect to inward disposition. *Obs.*

1649 ROBERTS *Clavis Bibl.* Introd. iii. 53 In some sense God cannot repent, *viz.* Affectively, in respect of his essence.

†2. In a manner that influences conduct, etc. *Obs.*

1654 TRAPP *Exp. Phil.* iii. 10 (1863) 609/1 And may know him..not apprehensively only, but affectively.

3. As regards the affections; emotionally.

1852 A. P. Forbes *Nicene Creed* 324 The highest happiness consists intellectually in the sight of God, and affectively in the adherence of the will to the Supreme Will.

affectivity (æfɛkˈtɪvɪtɪ). *Psychol.* [f. AFFECTIV(E *a.* 7 b + -ITY.] Emotional susceptibility.

1907 *Brain* XXX. 160 The extent of this expectation curve rises in normal individuals, depending upon their varying degree of affectivity. **1917** C. R. Payne tr. *Pfister's Psychoanalytic Method* xi. 303 In it [i.e. autistic thinking] the affectivity predominates. **1924** A. A. Brill tr. *Bleuler's Textbk. Psychiatry* i. 32 Under the term affectivity we comprise the affects, the emotions, and the feelings of pleasure and displeasure. **1952** V. Gollancz *My dear Timothy* xx. 360 Nursing is, for mother and child, one long delightful and highly charged game, in which the easy warm affectivity of a lifetime is set up.

affectless (əˈfɛktlɪs), *a.* [f. AFFECT *sb.* + -LESS.] Characterized by lack of feeling, emotionless, cold.

1947, 1958 [implied at AFFECTLESSNESS]. **1964** *Listener* 23 July 133/1 Far more of the horrors of our age have been caused by affectless persons than by sadists. **1967** G. Legman *Fake Revolt* 23 Affectless persons deny..that.. anything can touch them. **1975** *New Yorker* 26 May 18/2 Malick appears to be saying that mass-culture banality is killing our souls and making everybody affectless. **1978** P. Roth *Professor of Desire* 72, I am so affectless and withdrawn that a rumor among the junior faculty members has me 'under sedation'. **1984** *Washington Post* 10 June (Bk. World) 12 Even that audience..may be dismayed by Donaldson's droning, affectless delivery.

affectlessness (əˈfɛktlɪsnɪs). [f. prec. + -NESS.] Detachment; alienation; incapacity to feel emotion.

1947 *Amer. Imago* IV. 89 (*heading*) Trends in affectlessness. **1958** C. Geertz *Modjokuto Relig. of Java* vi. 120 *Iklas*, that state of affectlessness, is the watchword, and although it is often difficult to achieve, it is always striven for. **1964** M. B. Scott in I. L. Horowitz *New Sociol.* xv. 250 All the synonyms for alienation—affectlessness, aloneness, dehumanization, etc. **1967** G. Legman *Fake Revolt* 22 *Cool* is the new venereal disease. Total affectlessness, the inability to *feel*. **1983** *Financial Times* 28 Oct. i. 12 It takes only a tiny failure of dramatic imagination to turn what should be the stare of poignant stoicism into the stare of vacant affectlessness.

† **aˈffectly,** *adv. Obs.* [f. AFFECT *a.* + -LY².] = AFFECTEDLY (? earnestly, or pretendedly).

1628 Bp. Hall *Hon. of Maried Clergie* i. ix. 750 He, being suspected of Priscillianisme, wrote affectly against that heresie,—at last, foulely fell to that which he disclaimed.

affector, variant of AFFECTER.

aˈffectual, *a.* [a. OFr. *affectuel*, f. L. *affectus*: see AFFECT *sb.* and -AL¹. Cf. *effectual*, AFFECTUOUS, AFFECTIVE, AFFECTIONATE.]

† **1.** Earnest, ardent, eager, hearty. *Obs.*

1483 Caxton *Gold. Leg.* 389/2 God hath beholden your affectuel deuocyon fro heuen. **1552** Huloet *Abcedarium*, Affectuall desyres, *Ambiciosæ preces*. **1581** Riche *Farewell to Milit. Prof.* (1846) 169 With affectuall and manifest argumentes to perswade her.

2. Of or pertaining to the affections or emotions. Now revived in *Sociol.* and *Psychol.* (see AFFECT *sb.* 1 e).

1604 T. Wright *Passions of Mind* v. §3. 175 Reasonable persuasions resemble words, affectuall passions are compared to deeds. **1946** Gerth & Mills tr. M. Weber in *From Max Weber* (1947) iii. 56 'Affectual' action, which flows purely from sentiment, is a less rational type of conduct. **1965** E. E. Evans-Pritchard *Theories Primitive Relig.* v. 117 Conservative and relatively changeless societies in which affective, or affectual, sentiments predominate. **1976** *Interdisciplinary Sci. Rev.* I. 179/2 These range from the purely purposive use..to the not-so-purposive fostering of affectual relationships between members of a sodality or other defined groups. **1982** *Contemp. Psychoanal.* Oct. 571 The *shared elements* [of paranoia and depression] are: a genesis of childhood affectual deprivation, manipulativeness, allergy to coercion,..and anger. **1983** *Ethos* Spring/Summer 76 In the absence of an affectual tie to her husband,..the young wife cultivates unusually strong reciprocal links with her children.

† **3.** = AFFECTIVE 3. *Obs.*

a **1655** T. Adams *Wks.* 1862 I. 205 (D.) Lust not only affectual, but actual is dispensed with.

aˈffectually, *adv.* [f. prec. + -LY².] = AFFECTIONATELY.

† **1.** With eager desire, earnestly. *Obs.*

1483 Caxton *G. de la Tour* f iij b, Moche affectually I praye yow as my right dere daughters. **1495** Caxton *Vitas Patr.* (W. de Worde) II. 184 b/1 Some folke..prayed hym thre dayes duryng affectually that he wolde delyuer..the poore syke. **1509** Fisher in *Wks.* 1876, 303, I pray you al nowe affectually to praye, and for her..to say one Pater-Noster.

† **2.** Lovingly, fondly; affectionately (in mod. sense). *Obs.*

1447 Bokenham *Lyvys of Seyntys* (1835) 53, I love my wyf as affectually..as any man dothe his. *c* **1530** Ld. Berners *Arthur* (1814) 91 Whan Arthur was within the tente wyth the ladyes, who affectually behelde him.

3. That arouses emotion. Cf. AFFECTUAL *a.* 2.

1951 S. F. Nadel *Found. Social Anthropol.* 31 Affectually orientated actions, in which the end-result is a psychological (emotional) state of the actor.

† **affectuˈosity.** *Obs.*—⁰ [a. Fr. *affectuosité*, ad. med.L. *affectuōsitas*, n. of quality, f. *affectuōsus*: see next.] 'Affection' Bailey. 'Passionateness' J.

† **aˈffectuous,** *a. Obs.* [a. Fr. *affectueux* (14th c.), ad. L. *affectuōs-us*, f. *affectus*: see AFFECT *sb.*] Full of affection or 'affect.'

1. Earnest in feeling or desire; eager, ardent, hearty.

1494 Fabyan vi. clxxxv. 184 He was affectuse in his desyre. **1519** Sir T. Boleyn in Ellis *Orig. Lett.* i. 53 I. 147 As harty and affectuous recommendacions from your Grace. *c* **1656** Bp. Hall (*title*) The great mystery of godlinesse laid forth by way of affectuous and feeling meditation.

2. Well disposed; loving, affectionate, tender.

1460 Capgrave *Chron.* 152 That same Gilbert was ryth affectuous vnto the Heremites of Seynt Austin. **1575** Painter *Pal. Pleas.* I. 206 Mine affectuous accentes, my sorowful words, and feruent sighes.

3. Emotional; moving the emotions.

1674 Playford *Skill of Musick* i. xi. 39 In some kind of Musick less Passionate and Affectuous..Points of Division may be used.

4. Influential, effective, successful. *rare.*

1674 Playford *Skill of Musick* i. xi. 43, I have found it to be a more affectuous way to Tune the Voice.

† **aˈffectuously,** *adv. Obs.* [f. prec. + -LY².] In an 'affectuous' manner.

1. With earnest feeling or desire (see AFFECT *sb.*); earnestly, ardently, eagerly.

1450 Q. Margaret in *Four Cent. Eng. Lett* (1881) 8 Praye you right affectuously, that, at reverence of us, ye will have oure said squire. **1494** Fabyan v. xcvii. 71 Both she and Seynt Remigeus prayed so affectuously that the childe was restoryd. **1552** Huloet *Abcedarium*, Affectuouslye, or ardentlye. *Auide.* **1569** T. Newton *Cicero de Senect.* 53 b, Neyther affectuously to be desired, nor without cause to be lefte and forsaken. **1645** in Harrington's *Nugæ Antiq.* 72 Most affectuouslye beseaching your Grace.

2. With favourable or loving feeling; affectionately (in mod. sense); kindly, lovingly, tenderly.

1447 Bokenham *Lyvys of Seyntys* (1835) 51 Lorde thou knowyst how affecteuously I hym now love and evere have do. **1481** Earl Worcester *Tully on Frendship* iv. 10 We should love our frend as affectuously as our self. *c* **1530** Ld. Berners *Arthur* (1814) 91 All other ladyes and damoyselles affectuously beheld hym. **1549** Coverdale *Erasm. Paraphr. Phil.* i. 7 My minde is so affectuously set towards you.

† **aˈffeeble,** *v. Obs.* [a. OFr. *afebli-er* (also *afebl-ir*), f. *à* to + *febli-er* to weaken, f. *fieble*, now *faible*, FEEBLE.] To weaken, enfeeble.

1480 Caxton *Ovid's Metam.* xii. xiv, Thou hast this daye overmoch grevyd and affeebled my peple. *c* **1534** tr. *Polyd. Verg., Eng. Hist.* II. 68 Which affeebled no litle the force of Englande. **1599** Hakluyt *Voy.* II. i. 88 For euer to affeeble the repaires and for to abash us..day and night they ceased not to shoot great artillery.

† **aˈffeebled,** *ppl. a. Obs.* [f. prec. + -ED.] Weakened, enfeebled.

1577–87 Harrison *Descr. Eng.* i. ii. xxiii. 348 Strengthening the affeebled members.

† **aˈffeeblish,** *v. Obs. rare.* [f. OFr. *afebliss-*, extended stem of *afeblir* (mod. *affaiblir*): see AFFEEBLE. Cf. FEEBLISH *v.*] A by-form of AFFEEBLE.

1483 Caxton *G. de la Tour* h iij b, Wyn taken ouer mesure ..affeblysshed the brayne.

affeer (əˈfɪə(r)), *v.* Also 5 affure, 6 affer, 7 affear. [a. OFr. *afeure-r, afeure-r* (Anglo-Fr. *afere-r, affere-r*), earlier *aforer* (Sp. *aforar*):—late L. *affora-re* to fix the price, or market-value, f. *ad* to + *forum* market, in late L. also 'market-price.']

1. To fix or settle the amount of an amercement, to assess; to reduce to a fair or equitable amount.

1467 *Ordin. Worc.* in *E.E. Gilds* 395 Affurers of good name and fame..to assesse and affure all such amerciaments. **1516** *Modus tenendi Cur. Baronum* (Pynson) C i, Chose ii. iii. or iiii. afferers to affer the court. **1523** Fitzherbert *Surveying* 21 [See AFFEEROR]. **1581** Lambarde *Eiren.* iv. xvi. (1602) 541 By the great Charter that Amercement and summe of money, which he is to pay.. ought to be assessed & affeered by the good and lawful men of the neighbourhood. **1641** *Termes de la Ley* 13 The amerciament of every Juror shall be affeered according to his offence. **1738** *Hist. View Crt. Excheq.* iii, They used likewise to affere, or bring in their own Assessments, just as the Freemen in a Court-Baron do affere the assessments of those who are absent. **1768** Blackstone *Comm.* IV. iv. xxix. 379 Amercements imposed by the superior courts on their own officers and ministers were affeered by the judges themselves.

2. *fig.* To settle, confirm.

c **1440** *Partonope* 3128 The bisshope he gan his tale subtilly All affere and seyde. **1605** Shaks. *Macb.* iv. iii. 34 Great Tyrrany, lay thou thy basis sure, For goodnesse dare not check thee! wear thou thy wrongs, The Title, is affear'd.

† **aˈffeerance.** *Obs.* [prob. a. Anglo-Fr. **afferance*, f. *afferer*: see AFFEER and -ANCE.] The act or process of affeering; assessment.

c **1432** *MS. Roll of York Mercers' Myst.* 10–11 *Hen. VI*, Recd.—of diverse persones that wer afferyd in ye tyme of Robert of ȝarow—& hafe noght payde thaire afferaunce. **1641** *Termes de la Ley* 13 But if a towne be amerced..the afeerance shall be generall.

affeering (əˈfɪərɪŋ), *vbl. sb.* [f. AFFEER + -ING¹.] The settling of amercements or fines.

1738 *Hist. View Crt. Excheq.* v. 81 They were not worth the Affeering.

affeerment (əˈfɪəmənt). [f. AFFEER + -MENT.] The action of affeering or assessing.

1641 *Termes de la Ley* 13 The amerciment is the act of the Court, & the affeerement the act of the Jury. **1738** *Hist. View Crt. Excheq.* iii. 39 They assessed the Escuage, which was the Nature of an Afferement of a Sum of money. **1768** Blackstone *Comm.* IV. iv. xxix. 379 By the assessment or affeerment of the coroner.

affeeror (əˈfɪəə(r)). Also 5 affurer, 6–7 afferour, 7 affearer. [a. OFr. *affeureur, aforeur* (Anglo-Fr. **affereur, -our*):—late L. *afforātōr-em*, n. of agent f. *afforā-re*: see AFFEER.] He that affeers.

1467 *Ordin. Worc.* in *E.E. Gilds* 395 Affurers of good name. **1523** Fitzherbert *Surveying* 21 The othe of afferoure: I shall truely affere this court, and highe no man for no hate, ne lowe no man for no loue, but to sette euery man truely after the quantite of his trespace. **1615** Manwood *Lawes of Forest* xxv. §1. 252/2 They shal be amerced and their amercement shall be affeared by affearers there. **1641** *Termes de la Ley* 13 Affeerors are such as be appointed in Court leets, &c. to mulct such as have committed any fault which is arbitrably punishable, & for which no expresse penalty is prescribed by Statute. **1768** Blackstone *Comm.* IV. 373 This method, of liquidating the amercement to a precise sum, is usually done in the court-leet and court-baron by affeerors, or jurors sworn to affeere, that is, tax and moderate, the general amercement according to the particular circumstances of the offence and the offender.

† **affeir, affere,** *v. north. dial.* [a. OFr. *afer-ir*, *affer-ir*, to belong, pertain; impers. *afiert* it belongs, behoves; (Pr. *afferir*):—late L. **afferīre*, f. *ad* to + *ferīre* to strike, *fig.* to reach, affect. Though common in Anglo-Fr., *aferir* seems to have been adopted only in north. Eng. and Sc., where it is retained, esp. in Sc. law, to the present day, and usually spelt EFFEIR.] *impers.* To fall by right, appertain, become, be proper or meet.

1375 Barbour *Bruce* i. 162, I sall..Hald It, as It afferis to king. *c* **1450** *Merlin* 225 And dide hym grete honour as affiered to so high a man. **1470** Harding *Chron.* xciij, As to suche a prince of nature should affere. **1513** Douglas *Eneis* v. iii. 54 To turn agane, as thaim afferis. **1552** Lyndesay *Dreme* (1866) 279 Sum swyft, sum slaw, as to thare kynde afferis. **1609** Skene *Reg. Maj.* 21 He salbe punissed conforme to the maner & quantitie of the crime, as affeires of Law.

† **affeiring** (əˈfɪərɪŋ), *ppl. a. Sc.* Also 6 affeirand, 7– effeiring. [pr. pple. of AFFEIR *v.*] Properly pertaining, appropriate, meet, proportionate. (Still used in Scotl.: see EFFEIRING.)

1535 Stewart *Cron. Scotl.* III. 374 Artalȝerie affeirand for the weir. **1683** *Act of Council* (Wodr. II. 318) Such as will not [take the Test] that these be put under caution under great sums effeiring to their condition and rank. **1800** *Mod. Sc.* (Jamieson s.v.) 'It's no sae ill, affeiring to.'

† **aˈffellowship,** *v. Obs. rare*—¹. [formed on FELLOWSHIP *sb.* apparently in imitation of *accompany*.] To be in fellowship with, to accompany.

1559 *Homilies* i. (1859) 91 Sicknesses and painful diseases ..use commonly to come to sick men before death, or at the least accompany or affellowship death, whensoever it cometh.

affend, obs. variant of OFFEND.

affenpinscher (ˈæfən,pɪnʃə(r)). [G., f. *affe* monkey, APE + *pinscher* terrier.] A small breed of dog, related to the Brussels griffon.

1903 W. D. Drury *Brit. Dogs* (ed. 3) lxii. 629 The Affenpinscher is an alert, intelligent little dog of some 7 lb. to 8 lb. in weight. It has a round skull well covered with stiff hair... The colour is different shades of red, as well as grey and yellowish: while there is often a black mask. **1922** J. Maxtee *Popular Toy-Dogs* ii. 47 In Germany there is the Affenpinscher, which unquestionably is one of the chief constituents that were used in producing the Griffon Bruxellois.

affer(e, obs. form of AFFAIR.

† **afferant,** *ppl. a.* and *sb. Obs.* [a. OFr. *afférant*, *afèrant*, falling by right, appropriate, proportionable; pr. pple. of *afèrir*: see AFFEIR.]

A. *adj.* Falling by right, pertaining, befitting, appropriate: see also AFFEIRING.

1480 Caxton *Ovid's Metam.* xv. iv, It is not afferant that man shall slee another beeste for to fede withal his body.

B. *sb.* Portion properly falling to one, share, proportion. (Cf. OFr. *a l'aferant, a son aferant*, proportionally.)

c **1400** *MS. Bodl.* 546 (Halliw.) Thei have a longere tayl than the hert, and also he hath more grece to his afferaunt than the hert. **1475** *Bk. Noblesse* 43 The habondaunce of noble men of chevalrie, passing alle othir landes, after the quantite and afferaunt of youre roiaume.

affere, obs. form of AFFEER *v.* and AFFEIR *v.*

afferent (ˈæfərənt), *a.* [ad. L. *afferent-em* pr. pple. of *affer-re* to bring to; f. *af-* = *ad-* to + *ferre* to bear.] Bringing or conducting inwards or towards. Chiefly in *Phys.* as afferent nerves, vessels.

1839–47 TODD *Cycl. Anat. & Phys.* III. 646/2 The former are called efferent, the latter afferent fibres. **1845** TODD & BOWMAN *Phys. Anat.* II. 274 These vessels being styled afferent as they enter the gland, and efferent as they leave it. **1860** H. SPENCER in *Macm. Mag.* I. 395 An impression on the end of an afferent nerve is conveyed to some ganglionic centre, and is thence usually reflected along an efferent nerve to one or more muscles which it causes to contract. **1870** ROLLESTON *Anim. Life* 52 One of the afferent pulmonary veins.

afferme, -ly, obs. form of AFFIRM, -LY.

†**a'fferre**, *v. Obs. rare*[−1]. [f. *afferr*, early form of AFAR *adv.*] *refl.* To remove, go to distance. (Fr. *s'éloigner*.)

c **1380** *Sir Ferumb.* 5565 After hem prikede duk Rolant,& Olyuer his felawe; Ac or þay afferrede hem oȝt myche þen Mo þan an .C. of þe heþemen Had hy tweyne a-slawe.

†**a'ffesed**, *ppl. a. Obs. rare*[−1]. [f. A- *pref.* 11 (written *af-*) + FEEZE, or perh. pa pple. of FEEZE with A *particle* = *y-*.] Scared, alarmed, perturbed.

1614 W. BROWNE *Sheph. Pipe* Wks. 1772, 25 She for a while was full sore affesed.

‖**affettuoso** (af,fɛttu'oso), *a. Mus.* [It. = with feeling, affecting.] With feeling; a direction placed over a single passage, or at the commencement of a movement, 'in which case a somewhat slow time is intended.' Grove. Hence *fig.* as sb.

1724 *Short Explic. For. Words in Mus. Bks.* 7 *Affetto*, or *con affetto*, or *affettuoso*, by which Words is signified, that the Musick must be performed in a very moving, tender, or affecting Manner, and therefore not too fast, but rather slow. **1766** C. ANSTEY *New Bath Guide* (ed. 2) II. ix. 70 *Song.* 'Tis this that makes my Chloe's lips Ambrosial sweets distil; *Affettuoso.* **1796** BURKE *Regic. Peace* i. Wks. VIII. 132 The tender, soothing strains, in the affettuoso of humanity. **1813** 'H. HORNEM' [= BYRON] *Waltz* 4 A..tune, that reminded me of the 'Black Joke', only more 'affettuoso'. **1962** *Times* 2 Feb. 13/3 Ornate and affettuoso composer.

affiance (ə'faɪəns). Forms: 4 **afy-**, 4–6 **affiaunce**, 5 **affyanse**, 5–6 **affyaunce**, 4– **affiance**. [a. OFr. *afiance*, n. of action f. *afier* to trust: see AFFY.]

1. The action of confiding, or fact of having faith, in a person, quality, etc.; faith, trust. Const. *in*, rarely *on* (*subord. cl.*, *upon*, *to*, *unto*, obs.)

1330 R. BRUNNE *Chron.* 87 Þat he so suld þe barons had affiance. *c* **1340** *Gaw. & Gr. Knt.* 642 Alle his afyaunce vpon folde watȝ in þe fyue woundeȝ Þat cryst kaȝt on þe croys. **1475** *Bk. Noblesse* (1860) 41 That ever we shulde put affiaunce and trust to the Frenshe partie. **1549** COVERDALE *Erasm. Paraphr. Heb.* xi. 24 Puttyng his affyaunce in God. **1633** BP. HALL *Hard Texts* 125 Repose the whole affiance of your hearts upon me. **1741** RICHARDSON *Pamela* (1824) I. 104 How well I did to put my affiance in his goodness. **1859** TENNYSON *Elaine* 1348 My Lancelot, thou in whom I have Most love and most affiance. **1862** TRENCH *Miracles* Introd. 93 A true affiance on Him who is the Giver of this faith.

†**2.** Confidence generally; assurance. *Obs.*

1483 CAXTON *Gold. Leg.* 16/4 Who is he that is not ravysshid to hope of affyaunce? **1548** UDALL, etc. *Erasm. Paraphr. John* ix. 34 The Phariseis beyng sore prouoked with the beggars great affyaunce, made no aunswere. **1591** *Troubl. Raigne of K. John* II. (1611) 92 There's no affiance after periurie. **1633** T. ADAMS *Exp. 2 Pet.* ii. 2 (1865) 243/2 Abraham in affiance of this truth ventured to forsake his country. **1753** RICHARDSON *Grandison* (1781) I. xxxix. 282 My prayers..have not that affiance with them that they used to be attended with.

3. The pledging of faith; solemn engagement; *esp.* the plighting of troth between two persons in marriage, a marriage contract.

1489 CAXTON *Faytes of Armes* IV. iv. 238 Not sayeng trouthe af hys promesse and affyaunce made. **1528** PERKINS *Profit. Bk.* v. §442 (1642) 191 Endowment ought to bee made immediately after affiance made betwixt them at the Church doore. **1557** *K. Arthur* (W. Copland) I. iii, He made affyaunce to the kynge for to nourysshe the chylde. **1628** COKE *on Littleton* I. v. §39 (1633) 34/1 After affiance and troth plight between them. **1783** MARTYN *Geog. Mag.* I. 20 The affiance is compleated by a prayer. **1809** TOMLINS *Law Dict.*, *Affiance*, the plighting of troth between a man and a woman, upon agreement of marriage.

†**4.** Hence *fig.* Intimate relationship, affinity. *Obs.*

1594 HOOKER *Eccl. Pol.* v. (1632) 350 Religion and Superstition have more affiance..then Superstition and Prophaneness. **1601** CHESTER *Love's Martyr* xliii (1878) 45 Merlin, that did alwaies loue the King, As bearing chiefe affiance to his countrey.

affiance (ə'faɪəns), *v.* Also 6 **affyaunse, affiaunce.** [a. OFr. *afiance-r*, f. *afiance*: see prec.]

1. To promise (anything) solemnly, to pledge.

1523 SKELTON *Garl. Laurel* 545 Affyaunsynge her myne hole assuraunce.

2. *esp.* To promise solemnly in marriage; to betroth, to engage. Commonly in the passive.

1555 *Fardle of Facions* II. xii. 288 Aftre that he [the Prieste] affiaunceth them both with one ringe. **1603** SHAKS. *Meas. for M.* v. i. 227, I am affianced this mans wife, as strongly As words could make vp vowes. **1627** *Lisander & Cal.* v. 87 Argire..determined to affiance her selfe unto him. **1769** ROBERTSON *Chas. V*, III. x. 210 To affiance their young Queen to his son the Dauphin. **1847** DISRAELI *Tancred* VI. vii. (1871) 452 Tancred was affianced to the daughter of Besso.

affianced (ə'faɪənst), *ppl. a.* [f. prec. + -ED.]

1. Promised in marriage; betrothed, engaged.

1580 BARET *Alvearie* A 200 Affiaunced and promysed in mariage, *Desponsatus.* **1865** CARLYLE *Fredk. Gt.* II. VIII. iii. 315 And Wilhelmina is the affianced Bride of Friedrich of Baireuth.

†**2.** Hence *fig.* Closely related; akin. *Obs. rare.*

1607 TOPSELL *Four-footed Beasts* (1673) 7 Yet is their head and tip of their tail yellow, so that the Martins before mentioned, seem to be affianced to these.

†**3.** Assured by pledge or promise. *Obs.*

1725 POPE *Odyssey* I. 162 Stranger! whoe'er thou art, securely rest, Affianc'd in my faith.

†**a'ffiancer.** *Obs.*[−0] [f. AFFIANCE *v.* + -ER[1].] One who makes a contract of marriage between two persons.

1755 in JOHNSON [as a 'Dict.' word].

affiancing (ə'faɪənsɪŋ), *vbl. sb.* [f. AFFIANCE *v.* + -ING[1].] An engaging in marriage; a betrothing.

1617 MINSHEU, An Affiancing or betroathing. **1660** HOWELL, An Affiancing, *Fiançailles.* **1755** in JOHNSON [as 'Dict.' word].

affiant (ə'faɪənt). [a. Fr. *affiant*, earlier *afiant*, pr. pple. of *afier*: see AFFY.] One who makes an affidavit; a deponent. (Only used in U.S.)

1850 BURRILL *Law Dict.* (U.S.). **1882** *An Amer. Depos.* in *Standard* 15 Apr. 2/3 Affiant also states that said —— made habitual and frightful use, in his practice, of the poisonous drug aforesaid.

†**a'ffiantly**, *adv. Obs. rare*[−1]. [f. AFFIANT (in sense of giving faith, trusting) + -LY[2].] With trust, confidently.

a **1641** BP. MONTAGU *Acts & Mon.* 543 We may chuse whether we will affiantly beleeve any thing that is not written.

a'ffich(e, *v.* Also 4 **affitch**, 5 **afficche, -yche.** [a. Fr. *affiche-r*, OFr. *afichier*, cogn. w. Pr. *afícar*, *afiquar*, Sp. *afijar*, It. *afficcare*, for the origin of which Diez assumes a late L. **affigicāre*, f. *ad* to + **figicāre*, deriv. form of *figĕre* to fix; cf. *fodĕre*, *fodicāre*, *pendĕre*, *pendicāre*, whence Fr. *pencher*.]

†**1.** To fix to, affix. *Obs.*

1382 WYCLIF *2 Kings* xviii. 16 The platis of gold, the whiche he hadde affitchide. **1393** GOWER *Conf.* II. 211 Right only for the coveitise Of that they sen a womman riche, Ther wol they alle her loue affiche. *c* **1450** *Merlin* 117 He afficched hym so in the sturopes that the horse bakke bente.

‖**2. a.** (afiʃ). Inf. **afficher**, pa. pple. **affiché**. To parade, flaunt; to advertise or give notice of. Cf. AFFICHE. Now *rare* or *Obs.*

1827 J. S. MILL *Speech* in *Archiv f. Sozialwissensch.* (1929) LXII. 460 It will become the fashion..to affiche ignorance and boast of it as if it were a merit. **1841** C'TESS BLESSINGTON *Idler in France* I. 319, I doubt whether the general mass of the upper class would *afficher* their piety as much as they do now if their regular attendance at divine worship was less likely to be known at the Tuilleries. *a* **1854** MILL *Early Draft Autobiogr.* (1961) 104, I ceased to *afficher* sectarianism. **1867** 'OUIDA' *Under Two Flags* I. vii. 129 No reception, no garden party..[was] fashionably *affiché* without being visited by him.

b. *refl.* To appear or be seen in public *with* a member of the opposite sex. Now *rare.*

1835 E. GROSVENOR *Let.* in G. Huxley *Lady Elizabeth & Grosvenors* (1965) vii. 151 He has been affiché-ing himself in the most public and disgraceful manner with a Jewess of the very worst character. **1904** H. O. STURGIS *Belchamber* x. 137 I'll drop him a hint to be more careful and not to go and *afficher* himself. **1921** W. J. LOCKE *Mountebank* xiii. 160 Any fool could see she was in love with the man. And they had *affichéd* themselves together all over the place. **1935** D. L. SAYERS *Gaudy Night* iv. 66 If one intended to break off a connection with anyone, it was perhaps not the best opening move to *afficher* one's self with him at Ferrara's.

‖**affiche** (æ'fiːʃ, Fr. afiʃ). [F., f. *afficher*:—L. type **affigicāre* (see AFFICHE *v.*).] A paper containing a notice to be affixed to a wall, etc.; a placard, poster.

[**1757** M. POSTLETHWAYT tr. *J. & P. L. Savary's Univ. Dict. Trade* (ed. 2) I. 23/2 *Affiche*, so the French call those bills, or advertisements, which are pasted up in public places.] **1818** MOORE *Fudge Fam. Paris* viii. 87 Then we stare into shops—read the evening's *affiches.* **1819** H. BUSK *Vestriad* v. 241 Soon those who spell the grand affiche peruse. **1833** T. HAMILTON *Men & Mann. Amer.* (1843) I. 11, When the sphere of my intelligence became enlarged with regard to this *affiche* [*sc.* placard on a wall]. **1884** J. SHARMAN *Cursory Hist. Swearing* i. 6 The usual notice-board..covered with a trellis-work of crimson tape for the purpose of retaining the various *affiches.* **1920** *Punch* 31 Mar. 249/1 A couple of lurid *affiches* which declared that 'Exhampton Is So Exhilarating'.

†**affic'titious**, *a. Obs.*[−0] [f. L. *affictīci-us* annexed, f. *afflict-* ppl. stem of *affing-ĕre* to add to by inventing: see -ITIOUS.] 'Feigned or counterfeit.' Blount *Glossogr.* 1656.

†**affi'dation.** *Obs. rare*[−1]. [ad. med.L. *affīdātiōn-em*, f. *affīdā-re*: see AFFIDAVIT and -TION.] A solemn promise of fidelity.

1613 DANIEL *Hist. Eng.* 62 The Empresse swore, and made affidation to the Legat..The same oath and affidation tooke likewise her brother. **1755** in JOHNSON.

†**affi'dature.** *Obs.*[−0] [ad. med.L. *affīdātūra*, f. *affīdāre*: see AFFIDAVIT and -URE.] 'Mutual contract.' Bailey, vol. II, 1731.

affidavit (æfɪ'deɪvɪt). *Law.* [late and med.L. *affīdāvit* = has stated on faith or oath, perf. t. of *affīdāre*, used for *fidem dăre*: see AFFY.] A statement made in writing, confirmed by the maker's oath, and intended to be used as judicial proof. (In legal phrase the deponent *swears* an affidavit, the judge *takes* it; but in popular usage the deponent *makes* or *takes* it.)

1622 MALYNES *Anc. Law-Merch.* 227 Which by Affidauit must be certified. *a* **1677** BARROW *Serm.* (1810) I. 9 An illustrious affidavit of God's wonderful propensity to bless and save mankind. **1755** SMOLLETT *Quix.* (1803) IV. 60, I will make affidavit, that I have really and truly returned, and repaid the sum borrowed. **1853** *Encycl. Brit.* II. 200 Justices are permitted to take affidavits in any matter by declaration. **1872** THACKERAY *Christm. Bk.* 100 Of this I am ready to take an affidavit any day. [**1860** HOTTEN *Slang Dict.* s.v. *Davy*, 'On my *davy*,' on my affidavit, of which it is a vulgar corruption.]

Comb. or *attrib.*

1678 BUTLER *Hudibr.* III. i. 485 Held up his Affidavit Hand, As if h'had been to be arraign'd. **1808** BENTHAM *Scotch Ref.* 93 The favourite sort of evidence already mentioned—affidavit evidence. *Ibid.* 23 The affidavit-maker (deponent) remaining subject to examination.

affied (ə'faɪd), *ppl. a. arch.* [f. AFFY *v.* + -ED.] Affianced, betrothed. Also *fig.*

c **1500** *Partenay* 5087 In noble Bretain gan he to mary, Affyed and sured to a gret lady. **1596** SPENSER *F.Q.* IV. viii. 53 Though affide unto a former love. **1659** J. DAY *Blind-Beggar* (1881) 8 The Lady Elizabeth, your noble Daughter, Is my affied wife. **1855** BAILEY *Mystic* 18 His [soul] Affied to God.

†**a'ffier.** *Obs. rare*[−1]. [f. AFFY *v.* + -ER[1].] One who trusts or confides.

a **1641** BP. MONTAGU *Acts & Mon.* 204 He baptizeth somewhere some, such as be his Believers and Affiers in him.

†**a'ffile**, *v. Obs.* 4–6. Also **afile, affyle.** [a. OFr. *afile-r*:—late L. *affīlā-re*, f. *af-* = *ad-* to + *fīl-um* a thread, also (in late L.) the edge of a cutting instrument.] To file down, polish, sharpen. *lit.* and *fig.* (Cf. Fr. *affiler la langue.*)

c **1386** CHAUCER *Prol.* 712 He moste preche, and wel affyle his tunge, To wynne silver [*v.r.* afile, affyle]. **1393** GOWER *Conf.* II. 113 Mercury, which was all affiled, This cow to stele he came desguised. **1485** CAXTON *Chas. Gt.* (1880) 167 A grete axe of fyn steele bended and affyled that there was noo side but it cutted. *c* **1520** *Compl. of them to late maryed* (1862) 3 All yonge lovers sholde them so affyle, That they love trewely.

affiliable (ə'fɪlɪəb(ə)l), *a.* [f. L. *affīli-* (stem of *affīliāre*: see AFFILIATE) + -ABLE; as if ad. L. **affīliābilis*.] Capable of being affiliated on, or causally traced to. Const. *on*, *upon*.

1862 H. SPENCER *First Princ.* II. viii. §69 (1875) 207 Geological processes which these marine currents effect, are affiliable upon the force which the sun radiates. *Ibid.* II. viii. §67 (1875) 202 Due to forces affiliable on the like or unlike forces previously existing.

affiliate (ə'fɪlɪeɪt), *v.* [f. L. *affīliāt-* ppl. stem of *affīliā-re* to adopt; f. *af-* = *ad-* to + *fīli-us* a son; app. in imitation of mod.Fr. *affilier* (ad. *affīliāre*).]

I. Of adopting into the position of a child.

1. To adopt as a child: but always *fig.* of a parent institution adopting or attaching others to itself as branches, or of a society adopting a member.

1797 W. TAYLOR in *Monthly Rev.* XXIII. 530 The sophists of rebellion..affiliated an antient sect, the machinations of which formed the secrets of the arrere or occult lodges of free masonry. **1860** *Times* 30 Nov. 6/5 Why does not the great firm..affiliate provincial tan-yards?

2. a. To attach a smaller institution *to*, or connect it *with*, a larger one as a branch thereof; to unite or attach a member formally to a society. Const. *to*, *with*, according as the idea of filial union, or connexion, is thought of.

1761 SMOLLETT *Gil Blas* I. i. (Routl.) 171 The very sharpers with whom I had been affiliated at Toledo. **1794** W. BURKE in *Burke's Wks.* 1842 VII. 318 The great patriarchal jacobiniere of Paris, to which they were (to use their own term) affiliated. **1880** M. L. MEASON in *Macm. Mag.* 426 Ampleforth has only been affiliated to the London University during the last four years.

b. *refl.*

1866 *Spect.* 1 Dec. 1332 That colleges..be allowed to affiliate themselves to the University of Oxford.

c. *intr.* (refl. pron. omitted.) To connect or associate oneself *with*; to rank oneself under the banners of.

1860 *Times* 28 Nov. 10/1 The party in the South that affiliates with the Republicans. **1879** TOURGEE *Fool's Errand* xxi. 125 To affiliate somewhat coolly with the party of reconstruction.

II. Of imputing or fixing as *the* child.

3. *Law.* To fix the paternity of an illegitimate child *on* the putative father (for the purpose of maintenance). In this sense apparently introduced by the Act cited below; the term in previous Acts was *filiate*. Hence *gen.* To refer or ascribe (a child) *to* its proper parent.

1834 *Act 4 & 5 Will. IV*, lxxvi. §69 To charge or affiliate any such Child or Children on any Person as the reputed or putative Father thereof. **1836** W. ROBINSON *Justice of Peace* II. vi. 539 In that year a bastard child was affiliated upon him. **1844** A. S. TAYLOR *Med. Jurisp.* lxix, There would be no medical ground for affiliating the child to one man rather than the other. **1868** GLADSTONE *Juv. Mundi* vi. (1870) 172 Sarpedon, who is directly affiliated to Zeus.

4. *fig.* To father *on* or *upon*, attribute *to*, trace origin to.

1844 H. ROGERS *Ess.* I. ii. 84 The compositions which Captain Thomson's indiscriminate admiration would fain have affiliated to his muse. **1855** H. SPENCER *Psychol.* (1872) I. III. iv. 311 How do these facts..affiliate the faculty of hearing on the primary vital processes? **1872** E. ROBERTSON *Hist. Ess.* 194 Our venerable Abbey of Westminster, when ..in search of a pedigree, sought to affiliate itself upon the Archbishop [Dunstan].

affiliate (a'fɪlɪət), *ppl. a.* and *sb.* [ad. L. *affīliātus* pa. pple. of *affīliā-re* to adopt: see prec.]

A. *adj.* Affiliated, received into intimate connexion.

1868 BROWNING *Ring & Bk.* x. 492 The much befriended man, The man almost affiliate to the church.

B. *sb.* A recognized auxiliary, as an affiliated organization, company, etc.

1879 TOURGEE *Fool's Errand* xxi. 126 Scorn for their associates and affiliates of the North. **1930** *Economist* 4 Oct. 608/1 The establishment of German bank 'affiliates' has also helped considerably the development of the Amsterdam bill market. **1931** G. T. CARTINHOUR *Branch, Group & Chain Banking* v. 74 Control of a number of banks may be exercised directly or indirectly by a particular bank through a security affiliate as well as a holding company. **1953** *Economist* 18 July 189/1 Two affiliates of the internationally owned Iraq Petroleum Company.

affiliated (ə'fɪlɪeɪtɪd), *ppl. a.* [f. AFFILIATE *v.* + -ED.] Adopted as a child or fixed in paternity. Usually *fig.* United in a dependent relation, as the branches of a society to the central organization.

1795 in *Monthly Rev.* XVI. 528 Soliciting the provincial affiliated societies to separate from the republicans. **1850** ALISON *Hist. Europe* VII. xlii. §35. 117 Surrounding France with a girdle, not of affiliated republics, but of dependent dynasties. **1863** MRS. JAMESON *Leg. Monast. Ord.* 138 And numbered, within a century after its foundation, 3000 affiliated monasteries.

affiliation (əfɪlɪ'eɪʃən). [a. mod.Fr. *affiliation* (Cotgr.), ad. med.L. *affīliātiōn-em* n. of action f. *affīliāre*: see AFFILIATE[1].]

1. 'Adoption; the act of taking a son.' Chambers. The establishment of sonship.

1751 CHAMBERS *Cycl.* s.v., Among the antient Gauls, *Affiliation* was a sort of adoption only practised among the great. **1867** J. MARTINEAU *Chr. Life* (ed. 4) 117 Let there be a conscious affiliation with God.

2. a. Adoption, by a society, of subordinate branches; union of branches to a supreme or central organization.

1799 S. TURNER *Hist. A.-Sax.* (1828) II. VI. 258 The hoary advocates of a new system..whose Affiliation and credit multiplied their power. **1868** M. PATTISON *Academ. Organ.* §5. 195 The numerous art-schools scattered over the country in affiliation to the establishment at South Kensington.

b. An affiliated part of an organization. Also *concr.*, a particular establishment (e.g. a hotel) that is an affiliated part of an organization (*U.S.*).

1818 *Ann. Reg. 1817* 22 Busily..at work, establishing branches and affiliations. **1922** *Daily Mail* 14 Nov. 4 (Advt.), The London Joint City and Midland Bank or its affiliations, the Belfast Banking Company, Ireland, and the Clydesdale Bank, Scotland. **1977** *Washington Post* 18 Apr. D12 The franchise program brought the prestigious Blackstone Hotel in Chicago into the chain last winter and more in-city affiliations are planned. **1979** *Tucson Mag.* June 16/2 In the early 1960's, Kerr found employment in two Maricopa County hotel restaurants..both five-star affiliations.

c. Association, connection, esp. in politics. *U.S.*

1852 *Congress. Globe* 15 Mar., App. 323/3 Certain merchants with whom he has affiliations in New Mexico. **1862** *Ibid.* Jan. 589/2, I am here almost without any affiliation in political sentiment. **1893** *Congress. Rec.* Feb. 2301/1 The black man..is being educated, and can see where his political affiliation can best be allied. **1904** ROOSEVELT in *N.Y. Times* 23 Mar. 2, I have not the slightest idea what your political affiliations are.

d. Relationship, esp. as perceived within a group of similar things thought to have derived from a common source; = AFFINITY 3. Chiefly *Philol.*

1936 S. ROBERTSON *Devel. Mod. Eng.* 20 Old Armenian.. is thought to have affiliations with the ancient Phrygian. *Ibid.* 36 The closest affiliations of English..are..with the Low German languages. **1962** E. J. DOBSON in Davis & Wrenn *Eng. & Medieval Stud.* 128 (*title*) The affiliations of the manuscripts of *Ancrene Wisse*. **1977** C. F. & F. M. VOEGELIN *Classification & Index World's Lang.* 171 *Affiliation.* Wider relationships of Indo-European have been most commonly claimed to be with Semitic or Egyptian in Afroasiatic.

3. The fixing of the paternity of a child. Also *fig.* The fathering of a thing upon any one; and, the assignment of anything to its origin.

1830 HOR. SMITH *Tin Trum.* (1870) 15 Man has been termed the child of affliction, an affiliation of which the writer does not recognise the truth. **1836** W. ROBINSON *Justice of Peace* II. VI. 541 The original order of affiliation was not actually destroyed, but only suspended during the lives of the husband and mother. **1859** *Edin. Rev.* No. 293. 50 The question of the originality of Greek art or of its affiliation on Egypt.

4. *Comb.*, as **affiliation order** (see quot. 1914).

[**1836**: see sense 3.] **1880** *Justice of Peace* 24 Jan. 64/3, I was concerned for the respondents in an appeal from an *affiliation order. **1909** *Rep. Sel. Comm. Bastardy Orders* 67 in *Parl. Papers* VI. 717 Special provision is required for enforcing arrears due under an Affiliation Order. **1914** *Act 4 & 5 Geo. V* c. 6 § 7 In this Act..the expression 'affiliation order' means an order made under the Bastardy Laws Amendment Act, 1872..adjudging a man to be the putative father of a bastard child and ordering him to pay a sum of money weekly or otherwise to the mother of the bastard child or to any other person who is named in the order. **1984** *Financial Times* 17 Feb. 19 What of maintenance and affiliation orders, made in favour of the child for no reason other than tax avoidance?

affiliative (ə'fɪlɪətɪv), *a.* Chiefly *Psychol.* [f. AFFILIATE *v.* + -IVE.] Seeking to associate with another or others, sociable, friendly, sympathetic; ***affiliative motivation*** (see quot. 1964).

1950 P. A. SOROKIN *Altruistic Love* 248/1 Affiliative tendencies. **1959** S. SCHACHTER *Psychol. of Affiliation* i. 2 This general class of affiliative behavior. **1964** M. ARGYLE *Psychol. & Social Probl.* ii. 25 Affiliative motivation is the drive to seek close, warm and intimate social situations, to be accepted and liked by others. **1967** —— *Psychol. Interpersonal Behaviour* ii. 40 The warm, friendly, or 'affiliative' style consists of..physical proximity, certain kinds of bodily contact, eye-contact, smiling, a friendly tone of voice, and conversation about personal topics. **1973** *Jrnl. Genetic Psychol.* June 185 Femininity involved being more ..affiliative. **1976** *Harvard Business Rev.* Mar.–Apr. 100 If a male employee asks for time off to stay at home with his sick wife to help to look after her and the kids, the affiliative manager agrees.., because he feels sorry for the man and agrees that his family needs him. **1978** S. DUCK *Study of Acquaintance* ii. 46 Affiliative behaviour will clearly..be beneficial to the species. **1984** *U.S. News & World Rep.* 12 Mar. 70/1 Individuals..displaying the 'relaxed affiliative motive'. These are people who need to have friendly relationships with others.

†**affinage.** *Obs.*$^{-0}$ [a. Fr. *affinage*, n. of process f. *affiner*: see AFFINE *v.* and -AGE.] 'A fineing or refining of metals.' Blount *Glossogr.* 1656. 'The act of refining metals by the cupel.' J.

affinal (ə'faɪnəl), *a.* [f. L. *affīnis* a relative + -AL[1], as if ad. L. **affīnālis*; cf. *fīnālis*.]

†**1.** *Music.* (See quot.) *Obs.*

1609 J. DOULAND *Ornithop. Microl.* 27 Of the Affinall Keyes of Tones. The Keyes (which we call Affinall) be the Letters which end irregular Songs..viz. *alamire* wherein ends euery song of the First and Second transposed Tone. *Ibid.*, Let euery transposition be from a Finall to a fift the proper Affinall.

2. Related by marriage; derived from the same stock or source.

1846 GROVE *Contrib. to Sc.* 327 That chemical and physical attraction are affinal, or produced by the same mode of force. **1882** A. MACFARLANE *Consanguinity* 5 As this group embraces the relationships by affinity, it may be denoted by affinal.

a'ffine, *sb.* and *a.* [a. Fr. *affin*, OFr. *afin*:—L. *affīn-em*, adj. and sb., related, or a relation, by marriage, lit. 'bordering upon,' f. *ad* to + *fīn-is* end, border.]

A. *sb.* A relation by marriage; also, less strictly, one connected or akin, a connexion.

a **1509** HENRY VII in Ellis *Orig. Lett.* I. 23 I. 55 His Cousyn and affyne the king of Spayne. **1614** RALEIGH *Hist. World* I. 164 The name of Belus, and other names affines unto it. **1641** PRYNNE *Antipathie* 98 Hee that could but onely reade..should likewise as affines and allies to the holy Orders, be saved, and committed to the Bishops prison. **1893** *Spectator* 6 May 592/1 Because they [a son and his father's goddaughter] are in some sense close spiritual affines. **1950** M. WILSON in Radcliffe-Brown & Forde *African Syst. Kinship* 124 The crux of Nyakyusa ideas of marriage: relations between *affines* (abako) are ideally permanent—a divorce should never occur; a dead husband should be replaced by his heir, a dead wife by her younger sister or brother's daughter.

B. *adj.* **1.** Closely related.

1650 W. CHARLETON tr. *J. B. van Helmont's Ternary of Paradoxes* sig. f4, Whatever soundeth but analogous or affine, that doth Reason positively judge, consonant and homogeneous to verity. **1657** TOMLINSON *Renou's Dispens.* 267 Thymelæa indeed and Chamelæa are affine both in form and nature. **1883** *Academy* 13 Oct. 240/1 [The statement is] free from that acrimonious spirit in which writers of a creed more affine to that of the Church of England frequently indulge when criticising her traditions. **1927** C. C. MARTINDALE *Relig. of World* 67 Man with one part of himself was affine to the rest of creation, and with another, was affine to God.

2. *Math.* Preserving finiteness (see quots.).

[**1748** L. EULER *Introd. in Analysin Infinitorum* II. xviii. 239 Quia Curvæ hoc modo ortæ inter se quandam Affinitatem tenent, has Curvas *affines* vocabimus.] **1918** VEBLEN & YOUNG *Projective Geom.* II. iii. 72 Any projective collineation transforming a Euclidean plane into itself is said to be affine; the group of all such collineations is called the affine group, and the corresponding geometry the affine geometry. **1923** A. S. EDDINGTON *Math. Theory of Relativity* vii. 214 If a displacement AB is equivalent to CD, then AC is equivalent to BD. This is the necessary condition for what is called affine geometry. **1923** P. FIELD *Projective Geom.* 21 An Affine Transformation..is a perspective having the centre of perspective at infinity.

†**a'ffine,** *v. Obs. rare*$^{-1}$. [a. Fr. *affine-r*, OFr. *afiner* (Pr. and Sp. *afinar*, It. *affināre*):—late L. **affīnā-re* f. *af-* = *ad-* to + *fīn-em* end.] To refine.

1601 HOLLAND *Pliny* (1634) II. 473 Very proper it [quicksilver] is therefore to affine gold.

affined (ə'faɪnd), *ppl. a.* [ad. Fr. *affiné*, f. *affin*, see AFFINE *a.*; with Eng. ppl. ending -ED. No. Fr. *affiner* or Eng. vb. *affine* existed in this sense.]

1. Joined in affinity; related, connected.

1597 J. KING *Jonah* (1864) xxxv. 275 Those that are affined unto him in the flesh. **1606** SHAKS. *Tr. & Cr.* I. iii. 25 The Wise and Foole, the Artist and vn-read..seeme all affin'd, and kin. **1866** HUXLEY *Prehist. Rem. Caithn.* 131 So far as cranial characters go..all the people whom I have enumerated are affined. **1879** MCCARTHY *Own Time* II. xxv. 224 They were thus affined by a double tie to the Russian people.

2. Bound by any tie.

1604 SHAKS. *Oth.* I. i. 39 Be judge yourself, Whether I in any iust terme am Affin'd To loue the Moore.

†**a'ffining,** *ppl. a. Obs. rare*$^{-1}$. [f. *affine*, stem of prec. + -ING[2].] Having close connexion or relation; appropriate.

1606 WARNER *Albion's Eng.* XIV. lxxxiii. 346 Iacob..That to his Births, his Burials, euen his Wels, as good or ill Did then and there betide, gaue names affining.

affinitative (ə'fɪnɪˌteɪtɪv), *a. rare*$^{-0}$. [f. L. *affīnitāt-em* AFFINITY + -IVE; cf. *quantitative*.] Of the nature of affinity, as 'an affinitative resemblance.'

affinitatively (ə'fɪnɪˌteɪtɪvlɪ), *adv. rare*$^{-1}$. [f. prec. + -LY[2].] By way of affinity.

a **1859** WORCESTER cites *Phil. Mag.*

affinition (æfɪ'nɪʃən). [f. stem of AFFINED, *affinity*, after *defined*, *definition*: see -TION. *Affinition* is in 16th c. Fr. in sense of AFFINE *v.*] Formation or recognition of affinity.

1879 HOWELLS *L. of Aroostook* xiv. 165 By some infinitely subtle and unconscious affinition she relaxed toward him.

affinitive (ə'fɪnɪtɪv), *a.* [f. AFFINITY after *infinity*, *infinitive*: see -IVE.] Characterized by affinity; closely connected or related.

1651 WILLAN *Astræa* A iij, By the Reflection of your affinitive eminence in Vertue and Beauty, It hath presumed to assume a Being more communicable. **1880** J. HATTON *Three Recruits* I. I. i. 10 The kitten playing with that ball of yellow thread somehow struck Oliver North as affinitive to his own position.

affinity (ə'fɪnɪtɪ). Forms: 4–5 **afinite**, 4–6 **affinite, affynyte, affynite**, 5–6 **affynytye, affinyte, affynitie, affinytye, affynytie**, 6–7 **affinitie**, 6– **affinity**. [a. Fr. *afinité*, *affinité*, ad. L. *affīnitāt-em*, n. of state f. *affīn-is*: see AFFINE *sb.*]

I. Affinity by position.

1. a. Relationship by marriage; opposed to *consanguinity*. Hence *collect.* Relations by marriage.

1303 R. BRUNNE *Handl. Sinne* 7379 Or ȝyf he wyþ a womman synne þat sum of hys kyn haþ endyde ynne..He calleþ hyt an affynyte. *c* **1315** SHOREHAM 70 Alle here sybbe affinitè. **1483** CAXTON *G. de la Tour* C viij b, Be he of his parente his affynyte or other. **1509** FISHER *Wks.* 1876, 293 What by lygnage what by affinite she had xxx. kinges & quenes within the iiii. degre of maryage vnto her. **1649** SELDEN *Laws Eng.* I. lv. (1739) 98 Many..that by affinity and consanguinity were become English-men. **1726** AYLIFFE *Parergon* 326 Affinity is a Civil Bond of Persons, that are ally'd unto each other by Marriage or Espousals. **1849** MACAULAY *Hist. Eng.* I. 172 He was closely related by affinity to the royal house. His daughter had become, by a secret marriage, Duchess of York.

b. In *R.C. Ch.*: The spiritual relationship between sponsors and their godchild, or between the sponsors themselves, called in older English *gossip-red* (cf. *kin-red*).

c **1440** *Relig. Pieces fr. Thornton MS.* (1867) 13 His sybb frendes or any oþer þat es of his affynyte gastely or bodyly. **1751** CHAMBERS *Cycl.* s.v., The Romanists talk of a spiritual Affinity, contracted by the sacrament of baptism and confirmation. **1872** FREEMAN *Hist. Ess.* (ed. 2) 23 When he has succeeded in placing the bar of spiritual affinity between the King and his wife.

2. Relationship or kinship generally between individuals or races. *collect.* Relations, kindred.

1382 WYCLIF *Ruth* iii. 13 If he wole take thee bi riȝt of affynyte the thing is wel doo. **1440** J. SHIRLEY *Dethe of K. James* (1818) 7 With many other of thare afinite. **1494** FABYAN IV. lxx. 49 He therfore with helpe of his affynyte and frendes, withstode the Romaynes. **1677** GALE *Crt. Gentiles* I. I. ix. 47 The great Identitie, or at least, Affinitie that was betwixt the old Britains, and Gauls. **1794** G. ADAMS *Nat. & Exp. Philos.* III. xxxii. 316 The labour of individuals.. weaves into one web the affinity and brotherhood of mankind. **1872** YEATS *Growth & Viciss. Comm.* 37 The affinities of the people which connected them..with the Semitic races of Arabia.

3. *Philol.* Structural resemblance between languages arising from and proving their origin from a common stock.

1599 Thynne *Animadv.* (1865) 66 The latyne, frenche, and spanyshe haue no doble W, as the Dutche, the Englishe, and suche as have affynytye with the Dutche. 1659 Pearson *Creed* (1839) 245 We know the affinity of the Punic tongue with the Hebrew. 1796 Morse *Amer. Geog.* I. 80 Between some of these languages, there is indeed a great affinity. 1859 Jephson *Brittany* xx. 313 To trace the affinities of words in different languages.

4. *Nat. Hist.* Structural resemblance between different animals, plants, or minerals, suggesting modifications of one primary type, or (in the case of the two former) gradual differentiation from a common stock.

1794 Sullivan *View of Nat.* I. 458 Thus we shall find that antimony has an affinity with tin. 1830 Lyell *Princ. Geol.* (1875) II. iii. xxxiv. 250 The species are arranged.. with due regard to their natural affinities. 1862 Darwin *Orchids* iii. 115 In the shape of the labellum we see the affinity of Goodyera to Epipactis. 1872 Nicholson *Palæont.* 353 The true Reptiles and the Birds.. are nevertheless related to one another by various points of affinity.

5. *fig.* Causal relationship or connexion (as flowing the one from the other, or having a common source), or such agreement or similarity of nature or character as might result from such relationship if it existed; family likeness.

1533 Elyot *Castel of Helth* (1541) 35 By reason of the affinitie whiche it hath with mylke, whay is convertible in to bloude and fleshe. 1540 Morysine tr. *Vives Introd. Wysdome* C iij, Vyces and their affynities, as foolyshnes, ignorancy, amased dulnesse. 1642 R. Carpenter *Experience* iii. v. 46 What is the reason that Grace hath such marvellous affinity with Glory? 1795 Mason *Ch. Mus.* i. 76 The sound of every individual instrument bears a perfect affinity with the rest. 1855 H. Reed *Lect. Eng. Lit.* ii. (1878) 74 Philosophy and poetry are for ever disclosing affinities with each other. 1861 Tulloch *Eng. Purit.* iv. 421 This spiritual affinity between Luther and Bunyan is very striking.

†**6.** Neighbourhood, vicinity. [OFr. *afinité.*] *Obs.*

1678 R. Russell tr. *Geber* iv. ii. 242 The third Property is Affinity (or Vicinity) between the Elixir and the Body to be transmuted. 1770 Hasted in *Phil. Trans.* LXI. 161 Some kinds of wood.. decay by the near affinity of others.

II. Affinity by inclination or attraction.

†**7.** Voluntary social relationship; companionship, alliance, association. *Obs.*

1494 Fabyan v. ciii. 78 Gonobalde.. promysed ayde to his power. Lotharius, of this affynyte beyng warned, pursued the sayde Conobalde. 1580 North *Plutarch* (1676) 4 That so many good men would have had affinity with so naughty and wicked a man. 1611 Bible *2 Chron.* xviii. 1 Now Jehosaphat.. ioyned affinitie with Ahab.

8. Hence *fig.* A natural friendliness, liking, or attractiveness; an attraction drawing to anything.

1616 Surflet & Markh. *Countrey Farme* 322 For this dung, by a certaine affinitie, is gratefull and well liked of Bees. 1652 French *Yorksh. Spa* viii. 71 With this hath the spirit of the Spaw water great affinity. 1832 Ht. Martineau *Each & All* iv. 61 Natural affinities are ever acting, even now, in opposition to circumstance. 1860 Maury *Phys. Geog. Sea* ii. §70 So sharp is the line, and such the want of affinity between those waters.

9. *esp.* Chemical attraction; the tendency which certain elementary substances or their compounds have to unite with other elements and form new compounds.

1753 Chambers *Cycl. Supp.* s.v., M. Geoffroy has given [in 1718] a table of the different degrees of affinity between most of the bodies employed in chemistry. 1782 Kirwan in *Phil. Trans.* LXXIII. 35 Chymical affinity or attraction is that power by which the invisible particles of different bodies intermix and unite with each other so intimately as to be inseparable by mere mechanical means. 1831 T. P. Jones *Convers. Chem.* i. 22 Elective affinity, or elective attraction, you will find spoken of in every work upon chemistry. *c* 1860 Faraday *Forces of Nat.* iii. 93 This new attraction we call chemical affinity, or the force of chemical action between different bodies.

10. A psychical or spiritual attraction believed by some sects to exist between persons; sometimes applied concretely to the subjects or objects of the 'affinity.'

1868 Dixon *Spir. Wives* I. 99 All these Spiritualists accept the doctrine of special affinities between man and woman; affinities which imply a spiritual relation of the sexes higher and holier than that of marriage. *Ibid.* II. 204 Such natures as, on coming near, lay hold of each other, and modify each other, we call affinities.

III. Special Comb. **affinity group** *U.S.*, a group or association of people sharing a common purpose or interest; *spec.* one allowed certain privileges when chartering an aeroplane.

1970 *Hearings Subcomm. Transportation of Comm. Interstate & Foreign Commerce* (91st. U.S. Congress 2 Sess.) 8 Legitimate *affinity groups, the American Legion, the American Bar Association, the Knights of Columbus [etc.]. 1976 *Time* 19 Jan. 62 No longer does the traveler have to belong to a so-called affinity group, such as a club or union, to qualify for the reduced rates. 1984 *Amer. Banker* 22 June 4 Insurance companies increasingly look to third-party channels for marketing their products. They include sponsored markets, such as employers and associations; affinity groups in banks and real estate enterprises; [etc.].

affirm (əˈfɜːm), *v.* Forms: 4–5 aferm(e, 4–6 afferm(e, 6–7 affirme, 6– affirm. [a. OFr. *afermer, -ier*:—L. *affirmā-re*, f. *af-* = *ad-* to + *firmā-re* to make firm, f. *firm-us* strong. In 16th c. the spelling was refashioned after the L., as Fr. *affirmer*, Eng. *affirm.*]

†**1.** *trans.* To make firm; to strengthen; to confirm, to support (an institution, purpose, proposition). *Obs.*

1330 R. Brunne *Chron.* 316 The pes þei suld afferme, for drede of hardere cas. *c* 1425 Wyntoun *Cron.* ix. v. 27 Ðan þai Welle afermyd hys cunnand. 1485 Caxton *Chas. the Gt.* 1 The cristen feyth is affermed and corrobered by the doctours of holy chyrche. 1534 Ld. Berners *Gold. Bk. of M. Aurel.* (1546) K k v, The goddis assure & affirme eueryhing.

2. *Law.* To confirm or ratify (a judgment, law).

c 1386 Chaucer *Melibeus* 84 He consented to here counseilyng, and fully affermed here sentence. 1393 Gower *Conf.* I. 257 The lawe was confermed In due form and all affermed. 1628 Coke *On Littleton* I. iii. §32 (1633) 28/1 This judgement was affirmed in a Writ of Error. 1825 J. Wilson *Wks.* 1855 I. 38 Well then—appeal to posterity.. and posterity will affirm the judgement with costs. 1855 Macaulay *Hist. Eng.* III. 388 Twenty-three peers voted for reversing the judgment; thirty-five for affirming it.

†**3.** To confirm or maintain (a statement made by another); to maintain or stand to (a statement of one's own). *Obs.*

1393 Gower *Conf.* III. 172 And alle tho Affermen that, which he hath tolde. *c* 1440 *Gesta Rom.* xx. 68 He shalle afferme my word, and sey as I seid. 1599 Shaks. *Hen. V*, v. ii. 117, I said so, deare Katherine, and I must not blush to affirme it. 1611 Bible *Acts* xii. 15 But she constantly affirmed that it was euen so. 1670 Baxter *Cure of Ch.-div.* iii. Pref. §4 When one hath said it the rest will affirm it.

4. Hence, To make a statement and stand to it; to maintain or assert strongly, to declare or state positively, to aver. Const. *subord. cl., inf., simple obj.*

c 1374 Chaucer *Boethius* ii. 34, I dar wel affermen hardyly, þat ȝif þo þinges.. hadde ben þine, þou ne haddest not lorn hem. 1382 Wyclif *Wisd.* Prol., Thys booc the Jewis afermen [1388 affermen] to ben of Filon. *c* 1400 *Apol. for Loll.* 29 It semiþ to me þat is foly to a ferme in þis case oiþer ȝie or nay. *c* 1450 Lonelich *Grail* xlvii. 501 Holy chirche afermeth also, How long King Mordreins lyvede þere. 1523 Ld. Berners *Froissart* I. ix. 8 For this that ye say and affirme me I thanke you a thousande tymes. 1599 Shaks. *Hen. V*, i. ii. 43 Yet their owne Authors faithfully affirme, That the Land Salike is in Germanie. 1616 Purchas *Pilgr.* (1864) 2 None of credit.. hath affirmed himselfe to haue seene this Vnicorne, but in picture. 1702 Pope *Jan. & May* 160 Nay, if my Lord affirm'd that black was white, My word was this, your honour's in the right. 1850 Lynch *Theoph. Trinal* ii. 19 Let us often affirm the clearness that is in God. 1877 Lytteil *Landmarks* iii. i. 104 That such a report existed in Claudian's time cannot now be affirmed.

b. *absol.*

1366 Maundev. xiv. (1839) 159 As thei beyonde the See seyn & affermen. 1382 Wyclif *1 Tim.* i. 7 Not vndirstondinge.. of what thingis thei affermen [Tindale, *Genev.*, 1611 whereof they affirme]. 1657 Trapp *Ezra* i. 3 II. 4 Many there were—who affirmed deeply of being the people of God. 1667 Milton *P.L.* viii. 107 Not that I so affirm.

c. To make a formal declaration or affirmation. Const. as in 4, and *absol.* See affirmation 5.

c 1400 *Destr. Troy* xix. 7999 He affyrmit with faithe & with fyn chere, All þo couenaundes to kepe. 1424 *Paston Lett.* 4 I. 13 The seyd William.. affermyd a pleynt of trespas. 1751 Chambers *Cycl.* s.v. *Affirmation, Anno* 1721, the following form was settled.. I, A. B. do sincerely, solemnly, and truly, declare and affirm. 1863 Cox *Inst. Eng. Govt.* i. viii. 129 Quakers and others, now permitted by law to affirm instead of swearing.

5. *Logic* and *Gram.*, *trans.* and *intr.* To make a statement in the affirmative (as opposed to the *negative*). See affirmative A. 4, B. 1.

1581 Sidney *Astrophel* Wks. 1622. 552 For Grammer sayes.. That in one speech two Negatiues affirme. 1628 T. Spencer *Logick* 172 An Axiome is Affirmed when the band of it is affirmed. 1870 Bowen *Logic* vii. 210 To affirm the Reason or the Condition is also to affirm the Consequent or the Conditioned; and to deny the Consequent is also to deny the Reason.

affirmable (əˈfɜːməb(ə)l), *a.* [f. prec. + -able, as if ad. L. *affirmābilis.]

†**1.** Affirmative, positive. *Obs.* See affirmably.

2. Capable of being affirmed or asserted. Const. *of.*

1611 Cotgr., *Affermable*, affirmable, avouchable. 1643 Prynne *Sov. Power Parl.* iii. 116 What is truely affirmable of the one, is of the other too. 1824 Coleridge *Aids to Refl.* (1848) I. 228 The grounds on which the fact of an evil inherent in the will is affirmable. 1846 Mill *Logic* vi. x. §5 (1868) II. 517 This seems to be affirmable of the conclusions arrived at.

affirmably (əˈfɜːməblɪ), *adv.* [f. prec. + -ly[2].] In an affirmable manner.

†**1.** Affirmatively, positively. *Obs.*

1470 Harding *Chron.* lxix, I cannot wryte of suche affirmably [*v.r.* affirmandlye]. 1489 Caxton *Faytes of Armes* ii. vi. 102 The Lacedemonyens had ordeyned affirmably that.. they shulde kylle and slee al the men and women.

2. 'In a way capable of affirmation.' Todd 1818.

affirmance (əˈfɜːməns). [a. OFr. *afermance, -aunce*, later *affermance*, f. *afermer*: see affirm and -ance.]

1. A confirming.

1531 Elyot *Governor* ii. xiv. (1557) 139 To the affirmaunce whereof they adde to others. 1659 Godfrey in Burton's *Diary* (1828) III. 541 Rather an affirmance than an exclusion of the old peerage. 1794 Paley *Evid.* i. ii. i. §7 (1817) 327 Which come merely in affirmance of opinions already formed. 1824 H. Campbell *Love-lett. Mary Q. of Scots* 295 An affirmance or corroboration of all that has been added by his predecessors against Mary. 1885 *Century Mag.* XXIX. 730 The affirmance of the judgment of the court below by the General Term.

2. *esp.* Of laws, verdicts, etc.: Ratification.

1528 Perkins *Profit. Bk.* v. §377 (1642) 163 That statute is but an affirmance of yᵉ common law in that point. 1657 Burton in *Diary* (1828) II. 19 The Countess's Jury brought in another and a raging verdict.. in affirmance of the private verdict they had given. 1798 Dallas *Rep.* ii. 84 Detinue and replevin are actions in affirmance of property. 1808 Bentham *Sc. Reform* 112 The affirmance or reversal of the decree appealed from. 1888 Bryce *Amer. Commw.* I. 505 A majority of the Supreme court seems to have placed upon this ground.. its affirmance of that competence of Congress to declare paper money a legal tender for debts.

3. An assertion, a strong declaration.

1494 Fabyan i. xxvi. 18 Here now endyth yᵉ lyne or ofspryng of Brute, after yᵉ affermaunce of moste wryters. 1553–87 Foxe *A. & M.* (1596) 182/2 One named *Joannes de temporibus*, which by the affirmance of most of our old histories, liued 361 yeers. 1612 Drayton *Poly-olbion* Notes ii. 34 Of whom Bale dares offer affirmance, that.. hee first taught the Britons to make Beere. 1781 Cowper *Convers.* 65 They swear it, till affirmance breeds a doubt. 1819 Scott *Ivanhoe* II. xiv. 258 His lightest affirmance would weigh down the most solemn protestations of the distressed Jewess.

affirmant (əˈfɜːmənt), *a.* and *sb.* [? a. Anglo-Fr. *afermant, affirmant*:—L. *affirmant-em* pr. pple. of *affirmā-re*: see affirm and -ant.]

A. *adj.* Affirming.

B. *sb.* One who affirms, who makes a statement or declaration.

1747 in *Col. Rec. Penn.* V. 117 A Company of Foreigners, which this Affirmant believes to be Spaniards. 1865 Grote *Plato* I. vi. 243 Socrates being opposed to him under the unusual disguise of a youthful and forward affirmant.

affirmation (æfəˈmeɪʃən). [a. Fr. *affirmation* (14th c. Godef.), ad. L. *affirmātiōn-em* n. of action f. *affirmā -re*: see affirm.] The action of affirming.

1. The action of confirming anything established; confirmation, ratification (*esp.* of laws).

a 1533 J. Frith *Answ. Bp. Rochester* k 2 (R.) For a more vehement affyrmacyon he doubleth his owne wordes. 1645 Milton *Tetrach.* Wks. 1738 I. 246 To establish by Law a thing wholly unlawful and dishonest, is an affirmation was never heard of before. 1860 Forster *Grand Remonstr.* 2 The Petition of Right.. was but the affirmation and re-enactment of the precedents of three foregoing centuries.

2. The action of asserting or declaring true; assertion. *esp.* assertion in the affirmative, as opposed to the negative.

1611 Shaks. *Cymb.* i. iv. 63 This gentleman, at that time vouching, (and vpon warrant of bloody affirmation,) his [mistress] to be more Faire. 1743 Tindal tr. *Rapin's Hist.* VII. xvii. 127 Whether more credit were to be given to her bare negation than to their affirmation. 1831 Carlyle *Sart. Res.* (1858) 11 Instead of Denial and Destruction, we were to have a science of Affirmation and Reconstruction. 1872 Darwin *Emotions* xi. 273 A single nod implies an affirmation.

3. *Logic.* 'A positive judgment, implying the union or junction of the terms of a proposition' (*Encycl. Brit.*); predication.

1656 tr. *Hobbes's Elem. Philos.* (1839) 23 Abstract names proceed from proposition, and can have no place where there is no affirmation. 1788 Reid *Aristotle's Logic* i. §4. 14 Affirmation is the enunciation of one thing concerning another. 1877 E. Conder *Basis of Faith* iv. 161 A judgment is an assertion, affirmative or negative. Affirmation and denial are as the opposite motions of the same wheel; the extensor and contractor muscles of the same limb.

4. The words in which anything is asserted; an assertion, declaration, or positive statement.

a 1593 H. Smith *Wks.* (1867) II. 63 Paul's affirmation, who saith, 'Such as the root is, such are the branches.' 1651 Hobbes *Leviathan* i. iv. 17 It be a false affirmation to say *a quadrangle is round.* 1876 J. Parker *Paraclete* ii. xviii. 324 The bold affirmation that we have no sensation of efficiency is probably best met by a bold affirmation to the exact contrary.

5. *Law.* A formal and solemn declaration, having the same weight and invested with the same responsibilities as an oath, by persons who conscientiously decline taking an oath.

1695 *Act 7 & 8 Will. III*, xxxiv, Every Quaker.. shall instead of the usual Forme be permitted to make his or her Solemne Affirmation or Declaracion. 1745 De Foe *Eng. Tradesm.* I. xvi. 138 To be examined on oath, or if a quaker on affirmation. 1878 Lecky *Eng. in 18th Cent.* II. vii. 427 Giving their affirmation the value of an oath.

affirmative (əˈfɜːmətɪv), *a.* and *sb.* [a. Fr. *affirmatif, -ive* (13th c. Littré) ad. L. *affirmātīv-us*, f. *affirmāt-* ppl. stem of *affirmā-re*: see affirm and -ive.]

A. *adj.*

†**1.** Strengthening, corroborative; confirmatory. *Obs.*

1509 Hawes *Past. Pleas.* xvi. xlix, No worldely thyng can be wythout stryfe, For unto pleasure payne is affyrmatyfe. 1580 Hollyband *Treas. Fr. Tong.*, *Da*, for *Dea*, a word affirmative, as *ouy da*, yea forsooth. *a* 1674 Clarendon *Hist.*

Reb. I. II. 106 He received the affirmative advice of all the Judges of England.

†**2.** Strong in assertion; positive, dogmatic. *Obs.*

1650 JER. TAYLOR *Holy Liv.* (1727) 102 Be not confident and affirmative in an uncertain matter. **1734** tr. *Rollin's Anc. Hist.* (1827) V. XIV. 364 He at first speaks in an affirmative tone of voice.

3. *Logic.* Expressing the agreement of the two terms of a proposition.

1570 BILLINGSLEY *Euclid* I. vii. 17 A proposition vniuersall affirmatiue is most agreable to sciences. **1628** T. SPENCER *Logick* 188 A definition must be vniversall, and affirmatiue. **1860** ABP. THOMSON *Laws of Thought* §75. 128 Where a judgment expresses that its two terms agree, it is called Affirmative.

4. a. Hence, Asserting that the fact is so; answering 'yes' to a question put or implied; opposed to *negative*.

1628 BP. HALL *Hon. of Maried Clerg.* I. §28. 759 This negatiue charge implyes an affirmatiue allowance. **1638** *Penit. Conf.* vii. (1657) 133 Therefore the Commission runnes in words affirmative, and not negative. **1651** HOBBES *Leviathan* III. xlii. 290 The ordinary way of distinguishing the Affirmative Votes from the Negatives, was by Holding up of Hands. **1751** CHAMBERS *Cycl.* s.v., In grammar, authors distinguish affirmative particles; such is, *yes.* **1849** GROTE *Greece* (1862) VI. II. lxvii. 48 The negative and the affirmative chains of argument. **1851** H. SPENCER *Soc. Stat.* xxxii. §4 This question seems to claim an affirmative answer. **1865** CARLYLE *Fredk. Gt.* X. XXI. vi. 104 Görtz Junior.. after some intense brief deliberation, becomes affirmative.

b. ***affirmative action*** (U.S.), action taken to affirm an established policy; *spec.* positive action by employers to ensure that minority groups are not discriminated against during recruitment or employment.

1935 *N.Y. Times* 2 July 15/1 If.. the Board shall be of the opinion that any person.. has engaged or is engaging in any such unfair labor practice, then the Board shall.. issue.. an order requiring such person.. to take such affirmative action, including reinstatement of employees with or without back pay, as will effect the policies of this Act. **1961** *N.Y. Times* 7 Mar. 27/3 The contractor will take affirmative action to ensure that applicants are employed, and that employees are treated, during employment, without regard to their race, creed, color or national origin. **1974** *National Observer* (U.S.) 9 Mar. 4/3 'The hospital, once life support was begun, was committed to it,' Mitchell said. 'To follow the parents' wishes would have been to violate medical precepts. It was the difference between not starting life support at all and terminating it. In other words, inaction versus affirmative action.' **1984** *Gainesville* (Florida) *Sun* 28 Mar. 1B/6 She has prosecuted affirmative action cases for eight years.

†**5.** *Math.* Of quantities: Positive, or real; opposed to *negative* or less than nothing. *Obs.*

1693 E. HALLEY *Algebra* in *Phil. Trans.* XVII. 964 Which is affirmative when $2rp$ is less than $dr - dp$, otherwise negative. **1789** WARING in *Phil. Trans.* LXXIX. 187 When n is a given quantity, and $n - \frac{1}{2}$ not a whole affirmative number.

B. *sb.* [sc. mode, proposition, statement.]

1. a. The affirmative mode in a proposition; that which affirms or asserts. ***to answer in the affirmative***; to answer 'yes,' or that it is so.

c **1400** *Beryn* 2605 Ffor then were they in the affirmatyff, and wold preve anoon. **1532** MORE *Answ. Frith.* Wks. 1557, 841/1 If he will bydde me proue the affyrmatiue. **1663** GERBIER *Counsel* 108 The one will resolve on the affirmative. **1725** DE FOE *Voy. round World* (1840) 84 They all very cheerfully answered in the affirmative. **1861** GEO. ELIOT *Silas M.* 38 'Well; yes—she might,' said the butcher, slowly, considering that he was giving a decided affirmative, 'I don't say contrary.'

b. Used quasi-*advb.* = YES *adv.* Cf. NEGATIVE *sb.* 1 d. orig. and chiefly *U.S.* in signalling and radio communication.

1876 G. M. ROBESON *Gen. Signal Bk. U.S. Navy* 37 Affirmative.. *assent, consent, permission, yes* (When this signal is made it means one of the above words, according to circumstances, or permission to do that which has been asked.) **1908** *Boat Bk.* (U.S. Navy) VIII. cxxi. 91 The affirmative-flag, when hoisted *in answer* to a signal, means assent, consent, permission granted, or 'Yes'. **1953** J. A. MICHENER *Bridges at Toko-Ri* 17 'Is his wingman still with him?' 'Affirmative.' **1962** J. GLENN in *Into Orbit* 220 'That's affirmative,' I said. 'Landing bag is on green.' **1976** T. O'BRIEN *Northern Lights* II. 186 'You awake over there?' 'Affirmative.'

2. An affirmative word or proposition; opposed to a *negative*.

1588 FRAUNCE *Lawiers Logic* I. ii. 49 b, Affirmative is that which doth affirme and lay downe something to bee or imagined to bee. **1601** SHAKS. *Twel. N.* v. i. 24 If your foure negatiues make your two affirmatiues. **1628** COKE *On Littleton* I. §1 (1633) 6 b, Witnesses cannot testifie a negatiue, but an affirmatiue. **1725** WATTS *Logic* II. ii. §2 In Latin and English two negatives joined in one sentence make an affirmative. **1870** BOWEN *Logic* vi. 169 Two judgments which are alike in Quality, either both Affirmatives or both Negatives.

†**3.** A statement affirmative of, or asserting something; an assertion, or affirmation. *Obs.*

1646 SIR T. BROWNE *Pseud. Ep.* 73 That affirmative which sayes the Loadstone is poyson. **1660** JER. TAYLOR *Worthy Commun.* i. §4. 75 That he is a priest in heaven appears in the large discourses and direct affirmatives of St. Paul.

affirmative (ə'fɜːmətɪv), *v.* [f. the sb.] *trans.* To agree to (a suggestion or remark).

1861 G. MEREDITH *E. Harrington* III. xii. 203 Andrew again affirmatived his senior's remarks. **1871** —— *H. Richmond* II. xvii. 234 He.. affirmatived her motion to ring the bell for the servants.

affirmatively (ə'fɜːmətɪvlɪ), *adv.* [f. AFFIRMATIVE *a.* and *sb.* + -LY[2].] In an affirmative manner.

1. By way of assertion or express declaration.

1533 MORE *Apol.* xlviii. Wks. 1557, 924/2 He did but speake it affirmatiuely, and wil not holde it opinatiuely. **1612** T. TAYLOR *Titus* ii. 10 (1619) 431 The Apostle extendeth the former precept, and in this forme of words affirmatiuely propoundeth it. **1860** MASSEY *Hist. Eng.* III. xxx. 362 That the right of Parliament to provide for the exigency.. should be affirmatively stated.

2. In the affirmative mood, so as to assert that a disputed or doubtful thing is; opposed to *negatively*.

1491 CAXTON *How to Die* 11 Who someuer shall mowe affyrmatyfly ansuere to these askynges. **1570** BILLINGSLEY *Euclid* I. vii. 17 Sciences vsing demonstration, conclude affirmatiuely. **1639** ROUSE *Heav. Univ.* i. (1702) 6 And they had answer'd him affirmatively. **1794** SULLIVAN *View of Nat.* I. 429 The question, I confess, is difficult, however affirmatively it may have been determined by philosophers. **1840** CARLYLE *Heroes* iv. 239 The people answered affirmatively.

†**3.** *Math.* Positively, as a positive quantity. *Obs.*

1789 WARING in *Phil. Trans.* LXXIX. 174 The co-efficients are to be taken affirmatively, or negatively, according as *s* is an even or odd number.

affirmatory (ə'fɜːmətərɪ), *a.* [f. L. *affirmāt-* ppl. stem of *affirmā-re* (see AFFIRM) + -ORY, as if ad. L. **affirmātōri-us*, f. *affirmātor* an affirmer.]

Giving or tending to give affirmation or to make an assertion; affirmative, assertive.

1651 HOBBES *Gov. & Soc.* ii. §20. 32 An Oath may as well sometimes be affirmatory, as promissory. **1860** MASSEY *Hist. Eng.* III. xxx. 361 Mr. Pitt moved three resolutions.. the second, affirmatory of the right and duty of both Houses to, etc.

affirmed (ə'fɜːmd), *ppl. a.* [f. AFFIRM + -ED.]

†**1.** Made firm, established, strengthened, confirmed. *Obs.*

c **1300** *K. Alis.* 7356 Afeormed faste is this deray; Hostage y-take, and treuth y-plight. *a* **1450** *Knt. de la Tour* 51 He had hoped to haue turned her, but she was so afermed in goodnesse, that it wolde not be. **1541** R. COPLAND *Guydon's Quest. Cyrurg.*, In the vpper roundnes therof is affyrmed the holownesse of the pyt or morteys bones.

†**2.** Confirmed, corroborated (by new statements). *Obs.*

c **1440** *Prom. Parv.*, Affermyd, or grawntyd be worde, *Affirmatus.* **1552–5** LATIMER *Serm. & Rem.* (1845) 149 A story, written by a Spaniard.. and affirmed by many godly and well learned men.

3. Maintained, positively asserted, declared.

1611 COTGR., *Affirmé*, affirmed, avouched. **1641** LD. BROOKE *Disc. Nat. Episc.* I. v. 21 To an *Affirm'd* Syllogisme, every part must be affirm'd. *Mod.* The picture affirmed to have been stolen.

affirmer (ə'fɜːmə(r)). [f. AFFIRM + -ER[1].] One who affirms: **a.** who confirms, or supports (*obs.*); **b.** who asserts or declares; **c.** who maintains what is disputed or denied, as opposed to the *denier*.

1540 COVERDALE *Confut. Standish* Wks. II. 374 Ye.. report us to be the affirmers of your wicked words. **1611** COTGR., *Affirmateur*, an affirmer, soother, avoucher. **1637** GILLESPIE *Eng. Pop. Cerem.* II. vii. 29 His Majesties Auctority, did.. exeeme the affirmers from the paines of probation. **1860** *West. Rev.* No. 36, 419 But the proof lies with the affirmer. **1865** *Reader* 30 Sept. 371/1 It is chiefly as an affirmer of positive doctrine that Plato has been influential.

affirming (ə'fɜːmɪŋ), *vbl. sb.* [f. AFFIRM + -ING[1].] (Now gerundial.)

†**1.** A strengthening, confirmation, or corroboration. *Obs.*

c **1450** LONELICH *Graal* II. 184 Thanne was this a gret afermeng To here creaunce. *a* **1520** *Myrroure of Our Ladye* 77 Amen.. ys a worde of affermynge, and ys as moche as to say, as Treuly, or Faythfully.

2. An asserting positively; affirmation.

c **1440** *Prom. Parv.*, Affermynge, *Affirmacio.* **1530** PALSGR. 193/2 Affermyng, *Affirmation* [Fr.]. **1655** FULLER *Ch. Hist.* IV. 130 If his foes affirming be a proof, why should not his friends denial thereof be a sufficient refutation? *Mod.* Do you prefer taking the oath or affirming?

affirming (ə'fɜːmɪŋ), *ppl. a.* [f. AFFIRM + -ING[2].] That affirms; asserting, maintaining the truth of anything.

1849 GROTE *Greece* VI. II. xlviii. 139 The lines just cited make him as much a contradicting as an affirming witness.

affirmingly (ə'fɜːmɪŋlɪ), *adv.* ? *Obs.* [f. prec. + -LY[2].] In an affirming manner; positively.

1470 [See AFFIRMABLY 1]. **1541** WYATT *Let.* in Wks. 1861, 19 For my part I declare affirmingly.. I never offended.

†**a'ffirmly, a'ffermely**, *adv. Obs.* [f. Fr. *affermé* made firm + -LY[2].] Firmly, strongly.

1494 FABYAN VII. ccxliv. 286 Ferrande, than Erle of Flanders, had affermely promysed to come. **1525** LD. BERNERS *Froissart* II. clxix. [clxv.] 485 We wyll holde and kepe as affermely and trewly the treuce.. as we wolde they shulde kepe with vs.

affix (ə'fɪks), *v.* [ad. med.L. *affīxā-re*, frequentative of *affīg-ĕre*, to fasten to, f. *ad* to + *fīg-ĕre* to fasten. First used by Scotch writers, and perhaps directly due to MFr. *affixer*, an occas. refash. of OFr. *afichier*, mod. *afficher* (see AFFICHE).]

1. *trans.* To fix, fasten, or make firm (a thing *to, on, upon* another). **a.** *lit.* as by a nail, a string, cement.

1533 BELLENDENE *Livy* IV. (1822) 347 The dictator affixt his tentis at Tusculum. **1535** STEWART *Cron. Scotl.* II. 482 Ane crucifix.. In quhome the image of ouir Saluiour Affixt wes. **1695** WOODWARD *Nat. Hist. Earth* IV. (1723) 218 Affixing them upon any Thing which occurs in the Way. **1734** tr. *Rollin's Anc. Hist.* (1827) I. 39 This sail was affixed to a vessel. **1827** HALLAM *Const. Hist.* (1876) I. iii. 137 Felton affixed this bull to the gates of the bishop of London's palace. **1880** *P.O. Guide* 14 Obtain postage stamps, and affix them carefully to the letters.

†**b.** To fix in occupation or possession. *Obs.*

1649 SELDEN *Laws of Eng.* I. lxviii. (1739) 178 Other Courts were rural, and affixed also to some certain place. **1654** GATAKER *Disc. Apolog.* 57 This affixed me for a longer space of time, then before, to my Bed. **1658** OSBORN *Adv. to Son* (1673) 221 A dread they have to affix the Miter in a particular Family.

†**c.** *fig.* To fix (the desires or mental faculties) *on* or *to* an object. *Obs.*

1596 SPENSER *F.Q.* III. ii. 11 She affixed had Her hart on knight so goodly-glorifyde. **1596** BELL *Surv. Pop.* III. x. 439 Ye must not affixe your mindes to these. **1640** FULLER *Abel. Rediv., Jewel* (1867) I. 365 He was so affixed to his studies.

2. *refl.* To attach oneself, cling *to*.

1796 MORSE *Amer. Geog.* I. 201 They [young opossums], from a principle of instinct, affix themselves to her teats.

†**3.** *intr.* (by omission of refl. pron.) To cling or be attached *to*. *Obs.*

1695 WOODWARD *Nat. Hist. Earth* IV. (1723) 222 Part [of these Minerals] affix to them, incrusting them over.

4. From the affixing of a *seal* (actually attached by a strip of parchment, etc.) extended to, To impress a seal, stamp, or signature, write one's 'signature,' initials, or name, add a postscript or note (*to*).

1658 BRAMHALL *Consecr. Bps.* xi. 18 And did cause his Authentick Episcopall Seale, to be there to affixed. **1771** *Junius Lett.* xlix. 254 The king.. graciously affixed his stamp. **1824** DIBDIN *Libr. Comp.* 208 But it seems to be above all price. At least, none is affixed. **1878** SIMPSON *Sch. Shaks.* I. 98 To this paper the following notes are affixed in Philip's handwriting.

b. *fig.* To attach as a stigma (*to*), to stamp or stigmatize (*with*).

1665 GLANVILLE *Scepsis Sci.* 96 Very innocent truth's are often affix't with the reproach of Heresie. **1734** tr. *Rollin's Anc. Hist.* (1827) I. 115 Affixing ridicule to them. **1805** FOSTER *Ess.* I. ii. 23 The ungracious necessity of affixing blame.

c. *fig.* To attach as an appurtenance or concomitant.

1759 HUME *Hist. Eng.* an. 1521 To bribe their indolence, by affixing stated salaries to their profession.

†**5.** *intr.* (for *refl.*) To stick as a mark or stigma; to attach. *Obs. rare.*

1802 MAR. EDGEWORTH *Moral T.* (1816) I. 224 No stain affixes to his honour from the accusation.

†**6.** *trans.* To fix upon, determine, settle. *Obs.*

1621 *1st & 2nd Bk. Discipline* 66 Another day to be affixed by your Honours. **1725** POPE *Odyss.* v. 372 The land, affix'd by Fate's eternal laws To end his toils.

affix ('æfɪks), *sb.* Also 7 **affixe**. [a. Fr. *affixe* adj. and sb., ad. L. *affix-us* fastened to, pa. pple. of *affīg-ĕre*: see prec.]

1. That which is joined or appended; an appendage, addition.

1642 JER. TAYLOR *Episcop.* (1647) 341 The ambitious seeking of a temporall principality as.. an affix of the Apostolate. *c* **1854** STANLEY *Sinai & Pal.* xi. (1858) 129 Designated like the various ranges of Maritime, Graian, Pennine and Julian Alps, by some affix or epithet. **1864** *Spectator* No. 1875, 642 Mr. Gladstone's affix to his speech on the suffrage which he calls a preface.

2. *esp.* in *Gram.* (See quot. 1865.)

1612 BREREWOOD *Lang. & Relig.* ix. 76 Framing it somewhat to their own country fashion, in notation of points, affixes, conjugations. **1753** CHAMBERS *Cycl. Supp.* s.v., The oriental languages.. differ chiefly from each other as to affixes and suffixes. **1865** HALDEMAN *Affixes to English Words* §65 *Affixes* are additions to roots, stems, and words, serving to modify their meaning and use. They are of two kinds, *prefixes*, those at the beginning, and *suffixes*, those at the end of the word-bases to which they are affixed. Several affixes occur in long words like *in-com-pre-hen-s-ib-il-it-y* which has three prefixes and five suffixes. The term *interfix* is hardly necessary for *ad* in *anim-ad-vert*, or *t* inserted as a fulcrum between two vowels as *ego-t-ism*.

†**3.** A public notice posted up. (Cf. Fr. *affiche.*) *Obs.*

1647 R. STAPYLTON *Juvenal* 48 An affix or bill of the goods being posted for the buyers to read.

4. Of a dog's name (see quots.).

1893 *Kennel Club Rules* 2 A name which has been duly registered.. cannot be again accepted for registration of a dog of the same breed, without the addition of a distinguishing number, prefix or affix. **1954** C. L. B. HUBBARD *Compl. Dog Breeders' Man.* xii. 123 Affixes consist of names attached to the names of dogs, either in front of the dogs' names (prefix) or behind (suffix) in order to identify the dogs with a particular breeder or kennel.

affixal ('æfɪksəl), *a. Gram.* [f. AFFIX *sb.* + -AL.] Pertaining to an affix.

1873 [see IMPERATIVAL *a.*]. **1953** C. E. BAZELL *Linguistic Form* 18 Basic, affixal and inflectional morphemes.

affixation (æfɪk'seɪʃən). [n. of action f. med.L. *affixāre*, freq. of *affīg-ĕre*: see AFFIX.] **1.** The action of affixing or attaching; attachment; = AFFIXION.

1851 I. TAYLOR *Wesley* (1852) 190 The affixation of a name to a Christian Institute.

2. *Morphol.* The attachment of an affix or affixes to (the root or stem of) a word.

1921 E. SAPIR *Language* iv. 75 We have reserved the very curious type of affixation known as 'infixing' for separate illustration. **1964** C. BARBER *Flux of Lang.* xv. 260 More popular words also continue to arise in large numbers, especially by affixation, conversion, and compounding. **1969** S. POTTER *Changing Eng.* iii. 70 German and Dutch, like ancient Greek, make greater use of composition (or compounding) than derivation (or affixation). **1979** *Amer. Speech 1978* LIII. 267 Ablaut does not by nature entail greater morphonemic irregularity than affixation.

affixed (ə'fɪkst), *ppl. a.* Also **affixt**. [f. AFFIX *v.* + -ED.]

1. Fixed, fastened, or appended (*to*); causally connected (*with*). Also *fig.* Devotedly attached (*obs.*).

1651 *Life of Father Sarpi* (1676) 41 His being affixt to the Divine Scripture..which he used to read from one end to the other. **1660** R. COKE *Power & Subj.* 99 His Royal capacity is affixed and inseparable with his person. **1675** OGILBY *Brit.* Pref. 4 The Distance..is signify'd by Figures affixt. **1794** ATWOOD in *Phil. Trans.* LXXXIV. 149 The balance during this motion carries with it the crank and the affixed rods. **1849** MACAULAY *Hist. Eng.* I. 378 A notice affixed in all public places. **1872** JENKINSON *Guide to Eng. Lakes* (1879) 149 The summit is reached by a ladder affixed to the stone.

†**2.** Fixed upon, appointed, settled. *Obs.*

1559 *Let.* in Tytler *Hist. Scot.* (1864) III. 396 My Lord of Huntly..will keep the affixed [time].

†**a'ffixedness.** *Obs. rare*[−1]. [f. prec. + -NESS.] The state of being affixed; devoted attachment.

1668 J. HOWE *Bless. Righteous* Wks. 1834, 267/2 A mere sordid love to the body, and affixedness of heart to the earth.

affixer (ə'fɪksə(r)). [f. AFFIX *v.* + -ER[1].] One who affixes or fastens on.

1860 W. WHITE *Round the Wrekin* xix. (ed. 2) 192 The affixers of postage stamps.

affixing (ə'fɪksɪŋ), *vbl. sb.* [f. AFFIX *v.* + -ING[1].] Attaching, fixing, fastening on, appending.

1664 H. MORE *Myst. Iniq.* 6/2 The affixing of the residence of God to a consecrated place. **1880** *P.O. Guide* 255 Best mode of affixing stamps.

†**a'ffixion.** *Obs.* [ad. L. *affixiōn-em*, n. of action f. *affix-* ppl. stem of *affīg-ĕre*: see AFFIX and -ION[1].]

The action of affixing, attaching, or fastening to; also, the state of being affixed; = AFFIXTURE.

1633 T. ADAMS *Comm. 2 Pet.* i. 4 (1865) 38 If yet the subscription of God's hand, and affixion of his seal..be not sufficient. **1653** MANTON *Smect. Rediv.* Pref. Wks. 1871 V. 502 The affixion of the name to any work being a thing indifferent. **1654** GENTILIS tr. *Servita's Hist. Inquis.* (1676) 887 To advise by Edict, Proclamation, or Affixion, are signs of superiority. **1675** T. BROOKS *Gold. Key* Wks. 1867 V. 90 It was full three hours betwixt his affixion and expiration.

†**a'ffixment.** *Obs. rare*[−1]. [f. AFFIX *v.* + -MENT.] The action of affixing, fastening to, or posting up.

1654 GENTILIS tr. *Servita's Hist. Inquis.* (1676) 832 He.. shall not be cited by Criers, nor by affixment of Schedules.

affixture (ə'fɪkstjʊə(r)). [f. AFFIX *v.*, after FIXTURE; the reg. deriv. f. L. *fixūra* would be *affixure*.]

The action of affixing or fastening to; the state of being fastened to; attachment. Cf. AFFIXION, AFFIX-ATION, -MENT.

1793 SMEATON *Edystone Lightho.* 195 The lantern having no affixture to the stone work but its own weight. **1855** MILMAN *Lat. Chr.* (1864) IV. VII. ii. 42 The perpetual affixture of the anathema to all papal, almost to all Ecclesiastical decrees.

afflate (ə'fleɪt), *v.* ? *Obs. rare*[−1]. [f. L. *afflāt-* ppl. stem of *afflā-re* to blow upon, f. *af-* = *ad-* to + *flā-re* to blow.] To blow upon or towards.

1599 A. M. *Gabelhouer's Bk. Physic* 54/1 Afflate or blowe this poulder in their Eyes.

†**a'fflate,** *sb. Obs. rare*[−1]. [ad. L. *afflātus* a blowing upon, f. *afflā-re*: see prec. Now used in the L. form.] = AFFLATUS.

1677 GALE *Crt. of Gentiles* II. III. 58 The afflate of the Holy Spirit.

afflated (ə'fleɪtɪd), *ppl. a.* [f. AFFLATE *v.* + -ED.] Breathed upon; inspired.

1850 MRS. BROWNING *Fel. Hemans* v. 4 Poems II. 210 The tripod for the afflated Woe. **1862** THACKERAY *Roundab. Pap.* (1879) II. 229 We spake anon of the inflated style of some writers. What also if there is an afflated style—when a writer is like a Pythoness?

afflation (ə'fleɪʃən). [f. *afflāt-* ppl. stem of *afflā-re*, as if ad. L. **afflātiōn-em*: see AFFLATE *v.* and -ION[1].] A blowing or breathing upon; inspiration.

1662 H. MORE *Enthus. Triumph.* (1712) 56 A sort of wild and sordid Fanaticism, such as must proceed from an afflation of an unclean complexion or habit of body. **1673** *Ladies Calling* I. §1. 32 This [piety]..is an afflation of the blessed Spirit. **1814** CARY *Dante's Parad.* IV. 36 Diversly Partaking of sweet life, as more or less Afflation of eternal bliss pervades them.

†**affla'titious,** *a. Obs. rare*[−1]. [f. L. *afflāt-*, ppl. stem of *afflā-re* (see AFFLATE *v.*) + -ITIOUS; cf. *ablatitious*.] Characterized by afflatus; inspired.

1671 *True Non-Conf.* 278 The Psalms, Doctrine, Tongue, Revelation, and Interpretation, there spoken of, appear to be inspired and afflatitious motions.

afflatus (ə'fleɪtəs). [a. L. *afflātus* a breathing upon, blast, f. *afflā-re*: see AFFLATE *v.*]

†**1.** Breathing, hissing. [L. *afflātus serpentis*.] *Obs.*

1753 CHAMBERS *Cycl. Supp.* s.v., Naturalists sometimes speak of the *afflatus* of serpents.

2. The miraculous communication of supernatural knowledge; hence also, the imparting of an over-mastering impulse, poetic or otherwise; inspiration.

1665 J. SPENCER *Prophecies* 54 Those writings being inspired by..a more gentle and easie *afflatus*. **1782** PRIESTLEY *Nat. & Rev. Relig.* I. 245 Orpheus said antient poets wrote by a divine afflatus. **1865** LIVINGSTONE *Zambesi* xxiv. 497 A migratory afflatus seems to have come over the Ajawa tribes. **1873** GOULBURN *Pers. Relig.* IV. vii. 310 When writing under the Afflatus of the Holy Ghost. **1873** SYMONDS *Grk. Poets* viii. 248 Aristophanes must have eclipsed them..by the exhibition of some diviner faculty, some higher spiritual afflatus.

3. *Med.* A species of erysipelas, so called from the suddenness of its attack. Mayne *Exp. Lex.*

†**a'fflict,** *ppl. a. Obs.* Also 5 **aflyght, aflight.** [a. MFr. *afflict* occas. refashioning of OFr. *aflit*:—L. *afflīct-um* pa. pple. of *afflīg-ĕre* to dash against, to throw down, to distress; f. *af-* = *ad-* to + *flīg-ĕre* to dash. The earlier *aflight* shows the same phonetic change as *delight* = MFr. *délit* and *délict*.]

Overwhelmed with any trouble, afflicted, distressed.

1393 GOWER *Conf.* II. 309 Her herte was so sore aflight, That she ne wiste what to thinke. *c* **1430** *Octouian Imp.* 191 Tho was the boy aflyght, And durst not speke. **1432-50** tr. *Higden* Rolls Ser. I. 193 The women of whiche cite were afflicte in ij. maneres. **1564** BECON *Christm. Banq.* Wks. 76 They [these histories] be very comfortable for poor afflict sinners. **1583** (STERNH. &) HOPK. *Ps.* lxxxviii. 16, I am afflict as dying still, From youth this many a yeare.

afflict (ə'flɪkt), *v.* Also 4 *Pa. t.* **aflight** (see prec.). [f. prec., or on analogy of vbs. so formed.]

†**1.** *trans.* To dash down, overthrow, cast down, deject, humble, in mind, body, or estate. *Obs.*

1393 GOWER *Conf.* I. 327 Cam never yet..to mannes sight Merveille, which so sore aflight A mannes herte. **1611** BIBLE *Lev.* xvi. 29 In the seuenth moneth, on the tenth day of the moneth ye shall afflict your soules. **1667** MILTON *P.L.* I. 186 And reassembling our afflicted Powers, Consult how we may henceforth most offend Our enemy.

†**2.** *intr.* To become downcast (with trouble). *Obs.*

1393 GOWER *Conf.* III. 58 Wherof the kinges herte aflight.

3. Hence, *trans.* To distress with bodily or mental suffering; to trouble grievously, torment. *refl.* To distress oneself, grieve.

a **1535** MORE *Wks.* 1080 (R.) The hope that is differred and delaied, paineth and afflicteth the soule. **1590** MARLOWE *Faustus* xiii. 80, I cannot touch his soul But what I may afflict his body with I will attempt. **1594** SHAKS. *Rich. III*, v. iii. 179 O coward Conscience! how dost thou afflict me? **1667** FAIRFAX in *Phil. Trans.* II. 546 She much afflicted her self for the Death of her Father. **1725** DE FOE *Voy. round World* (1840) 328 They had no cold to afflict them. **1771** *Junius Lett.* liv. 287 It is their virtues that afflict, it is their vices that console him. **1820** SHELLEY *Prom. Unbd.* I. i. 43 The genii of the storm..afflict me with keen hail.

†**afflict,** *sb. Obs. rare.* Also **aflight** (see AFFLICT *a.*). [f. the prec. vb.]. = AFFLICTION.

1564 BECON *Fasting* (1844) 542 The life of man upon earth is nothing else than a 'warfare' and continual afflict with her ghostly enemies. **1592** HYRDE tr. *Vives' Instr. Chr. Wom.* P ij, With the which aflight of her mind, she fell to labour of childe afore her time.

afflicted (ə'flɪktɪd), *ppl. a.* Also 6 **aflighted.** [f. AFFLICT *v.* + -ED.]

1. Cast down, depressed, oppressed, in mind, body or estate; *hence*, grievously troubled or distressed.

1534 tr. *More's On the Passion* Wks. 1557, 1389/2 Judas.. tooke a speciall pleasure to see them so aflyghted. **1558** KNOX *First Blast* (1878) 38 A deliuerer to his afflicted people Israel. **1611** BIBLE *Job* xxxiv. 28 He heareth the cry of the afflicted. **1650** JER. TAYLOR *Holy Liv.* (1727) Pref. 2 Men are apt to prefer a prosperous errour before an afflicted truth. **1781** GIBBON *Decl. & F.* III. 255 To heal the wounds of that afflicted country. **1879** MISS BRADDON *Vixen* III. 279 Here the afflicted Pamela began to sob hysterically.

2. *esp.* Grievously affected with continued disease of body or mind; suffering. Also *fig.*

1680-90 SIR W. TEMPLE *Pop. Discont.* Wks. 1731 I. 287 A Piece of Scarlet dipt in scalding Brandy, laid upon the afflicted part. **1751** JOHNSON *Rambler* No. 153 ¶19 If I propose cards, they are afflicted with the head-ach. **1864** BURTON *Scot Abroad* I. i. 15 The literary language of England became afflicted with Gallicisms. *Mod.* The afflicted child has been removed to the Asylum.

†**3.** Dejected, downcast, humble. *Obs.*

c **1593** SPENSER *Sonnet* ii, And with meek humblesse and afflicted mood. **1596** —— *F.Q.* I. Introd. 4 The argument of mine afflicted stile.

a'fflictedly, *adv.* In an afflicted manner, distressfully.

1888 DOUGHTY *Trav. Arabia Deserta* II. 169 The stranger answered him afflictedly, 'Eigh me.'

a'fflictedness. ? *Obs. rare*[−1]. [f. AFFLICTED *ppl. a.* + -NESS.] The state of being afflicted; distress.

1650 BP. HALL *Balm of Gilead* ii. §6. 54 Thou art deceived if thou thinkest God delights in the misery and afflictedness of his creatures.

afflicter (ə'flɪktə(r)). [f. AFFLICT *v.* + -ER[1].] One that afflicts or distresses; an oppressor, tormentor.

1572 HULOET in TODD. **1611** SPEED *Hist. Gt. Brit.* VIII. i. 376 These Danes..the great afflicters of the English state. **1682** *2nd Plea for Nonconf.* 77 If God hear their Prayers, then many of their Afflicters must repent. **1842** *Blackw. Mag.* LII. 451 Thine own afflictor be! And what of all thy worldly gear Thy deepest heart esteems most dear, Cast into yonder sea!

afflicting (ə'flɪktɪŋ), *vbl. sb.* [f. AFFLICT *v.* + -ING[1].] Troubling, distressing, harassment. (Now gerundial.)

1611 BIBLE *Jud.* ii. 2 So he..concluded the afflicting of the whole earth out of his owne mouth.

a'fflicting (ə'flɪktɪŋ), *ppl. a.* [f. as prec. + -ING[2].] Grievously painful, distressing.

1605 *Play of Stucley* 457 Whose afflicting pain Hath neither left him appetite nor taste. **1667** MILTON *P.L.* II. 166 We fled amain, pursu'd and strook With Heav'ns afflicting Thunder. **1705** STANHOPE *Paraphr.* II. 459 A very serious and afflicting Concern for having Offended. **1823** SCOTT *Q. Durward* II. x. 197 The farther tidings..will be afflicting to you to hear.

afflictingly (ə'flɪktɪŋlɪ), *adv.* [f. prec. + -LY[2].] In an afflicting manner; so as to distress or trouble.

1818 in TODD. **1845** *Blackw. Mag.* LVII. 371 Cato was really and afflictingly a rational drama.

affliction (ə'flɪkʃən). Also 4 **affliccioun,** 5 **-tyon,** 6 **-cion, -cyon.** [a. Fr. *affliction*, OFr. *aflicion*, early ad. L. *afflictiōn-em*, n. of action and state, f. *afflict-* ppl. stem of *afflīg-ĕre*: see AFFLICT *a.* and -ION[1].]

†**1.** The action of inflicting grievous pain or trouble. *spec.* in its earliest use, Self-infliction of religious discipline; mortification, humiliation. *Obs.*

1303 R. BRUNNE *Handlyng Synne* 309 Yn þyn afflycciouns Yn fastyng and yn orisouns. **1483** CAXTON *G. de la Tour* h vi, The sayd hooly prophete..made his prayers and his afflyctions solytaryly and secretely. **1534** MORE *Comf. agst. Tribul.* II. Wks. 1557, 1177/1 Lett hym put vppon hys bodye, and pourge the spirite by the afflyccion of the fleshe. **1611** BIBLE *2 Chron.* xviii. 26 Feede him with bread of affliction, and with water of affliction, vntill I returne in peace. **1628** tr. *Camden's Hist. Eliz.* (1688) II. 147 Affliction for Religion groweth every day heavier and heavier.

2. The state of being afflicted; sore pain of body or trouble of mind; misery, distress.

1382 WYCLIF *Ex.* iii. 7, I have seen the afflicciour of my puple in Egipte. **1485** CAXTON *Paris & Vienne* (1868) 53, I endure grete heuynes sorowe and afflyctyon. **1602** SHAKS. *Haml.* III. ii. 324 The Queene your Mother, in most great affliction of spirit, hath sent me to you. **1671** MILTON *Samson* 110 Enemies, who come to stare At my affliction. **1725** POPE *Odyss.* VIII. 32 Here affliction never pleads in vain. **1781** T. JEFFERSON *Corr.* Wks. 1859 I. 303 The affliction of the people for want of arms is great. **1816** SINGER *Hist. Playing Cards* 10 During the affliction of a famine.

3. An instance of affliction; a pain, calamity, grief, distress.

1598 SHAKS. *Merry W.* v. v. 178 To repay that money will be a biting affliction. **1652** J. BURROUGHES *Exp. Hosea* vii. 130 Afflictions are as lead to the net, the promise is as the corke. **1812** MISS AUSTEN *Mansf. Pk.* (1851) 96 So harmonised by distance, that every former affliction had its charm.

afflictionless (ə'flɪkʃənlɪs), *a.* [f. prec. + -LESS.] Free from affliction.

1874 T. HARDY *Madding Crowd* I. ix. 125 He always had a loosened tooth or a cut finger..being thereby elevated above the common herd of afflictionless humanity.

afflictive (ə'flɪktɪv), *a.* [a. Fr. *afflictif, -ive*, f. *afflict-* ppl. stem of *afflīg-ĕre* to AFFLICT, as if ad. L. **afflictīvus*: see -IVE.] Characterized by afflicting; tending to inflict continued pain or distress; distressing, painful; trying, troublesome. Const. *to.*

1611 COTGR., *Afflictif*, afflictive, grieving, molesting, tormenting. **1623** SANDERSON *Serm.* Ad. Mag. I. iii. (1674) 84 To make the afflictions of this life yet more afflictive. **1670** T. BROOKS *Wks.* (1867) VI. 176 Losses, crosses, and afflictive dispensations. **1735** SOMERVILLE *Chase* II. 191 Afflictive Birch No more the School-boy dreads. **1779** JOHNSON *L.P.*, *Ascham* Wks. IV. 635 The most afflictive symptom was want of sleep. **1833** I. TAYLOR *Fanat.* vi. 178

A military despotism .. is often less afflictive to a country in fact than in name. **1865** CARLYLE *Fredk. Gt.* VI. XVI. XV. 313 This afflictive, too aspiring King of Prussia.

afflictively (əˈflɪktɪvlɪ), *adv.* [f. prec. + -LY².] In an afflictive manner; so as to distress; painfully, grievously, troublesomely.

1677 R. GILPIN *Dæmonol. Sacra* (1867) 467 No argument .. can be more afflictively discouraging to Satan. **1682** SIR T. BROWNE *Chr. Mor.* X. ii. (T.) Who, having acted their first part in heaven .. more afflictively feel the contrary state of hell. **1865** CARLYLE *Fredk. Gt.* III. IX. xi. 191 Fleury was very pacific .. and did not crow afflictively.

† **aˈfflige,** *v. Obs.* [a. Fr. *afflige-r* (16th c. Littré) f. L. *afflig-ĕre*: see AFFLICT *a.*] An early (Scotch) form of AFFLICT *v.*

1549 *Compl. Scotl.* v. 34 Quhen ire affligis vs, ve seik nocht the vertu of patiens. *Ibid.* 1 To cure & to gar conualesse al the langorius desolat & affligit pepil.

afflight, early form of AFFLICT, AFFLICTED.

afflight, bad spelling of AFLIGHT, *Obs.*, flight.

† **aˈfflue,** *v. Obs.* [a. Fr. *afflue-r* (14th c. Littré) f. L. *afflu-ĕre* to flow towards, f. *af-* = *ad-* to + *fluĕre* to flow.] To flow towards; to flock, to congregate.

1483 CAXTON *Gold. Leg.* 431/2 So grete nombre of freres affluyng or comyng to parys oute fro alle londes. *a* **1521** *Helyas* in *E.E. Pr. Rom.* (1858) III. 29 All the people afflued from all partes.

affluence (ˈæfl(j)uːəns). [a. Fr. *affluence*, ad. L. *affluentia*, n. of state f. *affluent-em* flowing towards, pr. pple. of *afflu-ĕre*: see AFFLUE.]

1. A flowing towards a particular point; a general movement of people in any direction, a concourse, a moving crowd.

1600 HOLLAND *Livy* XLV. vii. 1205 d, The affluence of the people was so great .. that for the very prease he could not march forward. **1684** tr. *Bonet's Merc. Compit.* I. 8 Others die, when there is not a sufficient Affluence to the heart to continue the Circulation. **1759** SYMMER *Electr.* in *Phil. Trans.* LI. 380 The effluence and affluence of electrical matter. **1782** KIRWAN *ibid.* LXXII. 223 Phlogisticated air may also be formed by a rapid and copious affluence of phlogiston. **1865** CARLYLE *Fredk. Gt.* III. VIII. v. 37 There had been great affluence of company, and no lack of diversions.

2. A plentiful flow (*of* tears, words, feelings, and *fig.* fortune's gifts); profusion, exuberance.

1447 BOKENHAM *Lyvys of Seyntys* Introd. (1835) 4 Demostenes of Grece more affluence Never had in rethoryk. **1490** CAXTON *Eneydos* vi. 26 Her eyen better semed two grete sourges wellynge vp grete affluence of teerys. **1610** HEALEY tr. *St. Aug., City of God* 511 How could they either feare or grieve in that copious affluence of blisse? **1633** EARL MANCHESTER *Contempl. Mort.* (1636) 84 Man that thus lives at ease in delicacie with affluence of all things. **1849** LONGFELLOW *Kavanagh* xii. 56 Winter .. with its affluence of snows. **1867** SWINBURNE in *Fortn. Rev.* Oct. 420 The ambient ardour of noon, the fiery affluence of evening.

3. *ellipt.* Profusion or abundance of worldly possessions; wealth.

1603 HOLLAND *Plutarch's Mor.* 35 A heavenly goate whose influence Brings in riches with affluence. **1608** J. KING *Serm. 1 Chron.* xxix. 26–28, 29 The very wormes that growe out of their [Kings'] fulnes & affluence. **1713** STEELE *Guardian* No. 22 ¶3 They lived in great affluence. **1766** GOLDSM. *Vic. Wakef.* xxxii, As merry as affluence & innocence could make them. **1807** SOUTHEY *Lett.* II. 35 It was not possible to make a better use of affluence than he did. **1840** MACAULAY *Ess., Clive* II. 521 Trade revived; and the signs of affluence appeared in every English house.

† **ˈaffluency.** *Obs.* [ad. L. *affluentia*: see AFFLUENCE.] The quality or state of being affluent, profuseness, wealthiness = AFFLUENCE 2, 3.

1664 H. MORE *Myst. Iniq.* 99 Wealth and honour and affluency of all things. **1683** TRYON *Way to Health* 184 For in the midst of all their Affluencies .. they are yet most miserable.

affluent (ˈæfl(j)uːənt), *a.* and *sb.* [a. Fr. *affluent* (14th c. Godef.), ad. L. *affluent-em*, pr. pple. of *affluĕre*: see AFFLUE.]

A. *adj.*

† **1.** Flowing toward a particular place. *Obs.*

1432–50 tr. *Higden* Rolls Ser. I. 63 The stonys of whom as meltenge thro the veynes of salte mixte among theyme causethe an humor affluente. **1666** HARVEY *Anat. Consump.* (J.) These parts are .. raised to a greater bulk by the affluent blood that is transmitted out of the mother's body. **1759** SYMMER *Electr.* in *Phil. Trans.* LI. 386 The effluent current must have just as great an effect in separating them, as the affluent can have in bringing or keeping them together.

2. Flowing freely or abundantly.

1816 SOUTHEY *Lay of Laureate* Wks. X. 152 And o'er his shoulders broad the affluent mane Dishevell'd hung. **1828** MISS MITFORD *Our Village* III. (1863) 30 The beautiful Loddon, always so affluent of water, had overflowed its boundaries. **1863** BURTON *Bk. Hunter* 403 In the centre .. is an affluent fountain of the clearest water.

3. *fig.* Of the gifts of fortune, etc.: Flowing in abundance; abundant, copious, plenteous.

1413 LYDG. *Pylgr. Sowle* I. xv. (1859) 15 Thy grace alwey hath ben affluent, decrecyng nought .. though never so largely thou geue it. **1589** NASHE *Anat. Absurd.* 30 Dilating on so affluent an argument. **1725** POPE *Odyss.* XIX. 135 Their affluent joys the grateful realms confess. **1766** GOLDSM. *Vic. Wakef.* xxxii, My son was already possessed of a very affluent fortune. **1875** STUBBS *Const. Hist.* II. xvii. 625 The graceful and affluent diversity of the Decorated [style].

4. Hence, Flowing or abounding in wealth; wealthy, rich. Also *fig.* Const. *in*, rarely *of*. Freq. in phr. ***affluent society***.

1769 *Junius Lett.* i. 9 No expense should be spared to secure to him an honourable and affluent retreat. **1806** WILBERFORCE in *Life* (1838) III. xix. 246 Considering the number of affluent men connected with Pitt. **1831** W. & M. HOWITT *Seasons* 255 The orchards are affluent of pears, plums, and apples. **1837** DISRAELI *Venetia* IV. xiii. (1871) 287 Existence felt to her that moment affluent with a blissful excitement. **1846** PRESCOTT *Ferd. & Isab.* I. iv. 200 Commodities .. beyond the reach of any but the affluent. **1855** H. REED *Lect. Eng. Lit.* v. (1878) 173 The language became affluent in expressions incorporated with it from the literature of antiquity. **1958** J. K. GALBRAITH (*title*) The affluent society. **1958** *Listener* 25 Sept. 449/2 Many economists have lifted their eyes .. to the coming age of abundance; even more sociologists have inveighed vaguely against the affluent society. **1959** *Observer* 1 Nov. 1/5 Mr. James Griffiths .. attributed Labour's election defeat to its being the party of change at a time when Britain had entered the 'affluent society'.

B. *sb.* [The adj. used *absol.*; prob. after mod.Fr. *affluent* sb.] A stream flowing into a larger stream or lake; a tributary stream; a feeder.

[Not in TODD 1818, RICHARDSON 1836, CRAIG 1847.] **1833** *Penny Cycl.* I. 433 The great Missouri with its affluent the Mississippi. *Ibid.* The table-land in which the Mississippi and the affluents of Lake Superior rise. **1853** PHILLIPS *Rivers of Yorksh.* iii. 104 The only remaining affluent of importance on its northern banks, viz. the river Hull. **1878** HUXLEY *Physiogr.* 4 As the Thames rolls along, it receives a number of these feeders, or affluents.

affluently (ˈæfl(j)uːəntlɪ), *adv.* [f. prec. + -LY².] In an affluent manner; abundantly, richly.

1818 in TODD. **1873** BURTON *Hist. Scot.* VII. lxxv. 9 This deputation was not affluently adorned by rank and station.

† **ˈaffluentness.** *Obs.*$^{-0}$ [f. AFFLUENT *a.* + -NESS.] 'Great plenty.' Bailey, vol. II, 1731, whence in J. = AFFLUENCE.

afflux (ˈæflʌks). [ad. med.L. *afflux-us*, n. of action f. *afflu-ĕre*: see AFFLUE. Cf. mod.Fr. *afflux*, perh. the direct source of the Eng.].

1. A flowing towards a point; *esp.* in *Med.* of humours; also by extension, of air, a crowd of people, etc.

1611 COTGR., *Afflux*, an Afflux or Affluence, plentifull access. **1635** N. CARPENTER *Geogr. Delin.* II. vi. 82 The Affluxe and Refluxe of the Sea—is generall throughout the whole Ocean. **1661** LOVELL *Anim. & Min.* 354 Tubercles of the lungs .. are caused by the afflux or congestion of matter. **1794** SULLIVAN *View of Nat.* I. 175 There is no need of the afflux of vital air. **1872** *Pall Mall G.* 1 Aug. 10 The afflux of purchasers has much more than doubled.

2. That which flows into any place; an accession.

1661 GRAUNT *Bills of Mort.* (J.) The cause hereof .. must be by new affluxes to London out of the country. **1859** TODD *Cycl. Anat. & Phys.* V. 355/1 At this period, they [*i.e.* the villi] receive an increased afflux of blood.

† **aˈffluxed,** *ppl. a. Obs. rare*$^{-1}$. [f. AFFLUX + -ED².] That has flowed to.

1684 tr. *Bonet's Merc. Compit.* VIII. 277 In this case we have not so much regard to the humour affluent, as affluxed.

affluxion (əˈflʌkʃən). [n. of action f. *afflux-* ppl. stem of *afflu-ĕre* (see AFFLUE and -ION¹) after L. *fluxiōnem.*] A flowing towards; an afflux.

1646 SIR T. BROWNE *Pseud. Ep.* 182 An Inflammation, either simple consisting only of an hot and sanguineous affluxion. **1835** HOBLYN *Dict. Med.*, With this are associated Affluxion, or accumulation of the fluids, etc.

affly, abbrev. of AFFECTIONATELY *adv.*, used in the subscription of letters. Now *rare.*

1846 G. W. CURTIS *Let.* 30 July in *Early Lett. to J. S. Dwight* (1898) 258 Affly. yr friend, G. W. C. **1898** O. W. HOLMES *Pollock-Holmes Lett.* (1942) I. 88 Affly Yours, O. W. Holmes. **1922** JOYCE *Ulysses* 740 Be sure and write soon kind she left out regards to your father also Captain Grove with love yrs affly.

† **ˈaffodill.** *Obs.* Forms: 5 affadille, affodylle, 5–6 affadyll(e, 6 affodyl, 7 affodille, -dill, -dil. [ad. med.L. *affodillus* (*Prom. Parv.*, Turner *Lib.*, and Bailey vol. II), prob. for late L. **asfodillus*, **asphodillus*, for cl. L. *asphodilus* (Pallad.) and *asphodelus*; a. Gr. ἀσφοδελός. The form **asphodillus* (whence Ital. *asfodillo*) was prob. due, as in some other words, to the simulation of a diminutive ending. Another med.L. corruption was *affrodillus* (Turner *Lib.*), whence Fr. *afrodille.*]

1. Name of a liliaceous genus of plants, Asphodel, or King's Spear (*Asphodelus*, incl. *Anthericum*), natives of the south of Europe, and grown as garden flowers and medicinal herbs.

(In this sense *Daffodill*, and *Daffadilly*, are mentioned as variant forms of Affodil as early as 1538 and as late as 1611.)

c **1420** *Pallad. on Husb.* I. 921 With affadille upclose her hooles alle; Thai [field mice] gnawe it oute, but dede downe shal thai falle. **1440** *Prom. Parv.*, Affodylle herbe [*v.r.* affadylle], *affodillus, albucea.* [*v.r. affadilla.*] **1483** *Cathol. Angl.*, An Affodylle; *Affodillus, harba.* **1530** PALSGR. 193/2 Affadyll a yelowe floure—*affrodille.* [*Asphodelus luteus.*] **1538** TURNER *Libellus* A 3, *Asphodelus* a latinis *hasta regia* & *albucum* dicitur, a barbaris & latine lingue corruptoribus *aphrodillus* & *affodillus*, ab anglis *Affadyll* & *Daffadilly.* **1578** LYTE *Dodoens* 647 The flower .. is called in Greeke ἀνθερικός, *Anthericos*; and in Latine, as Plinie sayth, *Albucum*: in English also *Affodyl* and *Daffodyll.* [The modern *Daffodil* appears at p. 214 as *Yellow Crowbels, Yellow Narcissus, Bastarde Narcissus.*] **1611** COTGR., *Affrodille*, th' Affodille, or Asphodill flower. *Ibid.*, *Asphodele*, the Daffadill, Affodill, or Asphodill flower. *Ibid.*, *Hache royalle*, the Affodille, or Asphodill flower; especially (the small kind thereof called) the Speare for a King. **1615** MARKHAM *Eng. Housewife* 28 You must be carefull that you take not Daffodil for Affodil.

2. Applied, by confusion, to a species of Narcissus. In this sense the variant DAFFODIL (q.v.) became almost from the first the accepted form; so that eventually *Affodill* was confined to *Asphodelus*, and *Daffodil* to *Narcissus*.

1551 TURNER *Herbal* I. b iij b, I could neuer se thys herb [*asphodelos*—ryght affodill] in England but ones, for the herbe that the people calleth here *affodill* or *daffodill* is a kynd of narcissus.

† **aˈfforce,** *adv. Obs.* [for *of force*: see FORCE.] Of necessity; by compulsion or constraint; perforce.

1399 LANGL. *Rich. Redeless* IV. 21 No þing y-lafte but þe bare baggis, þan ffelle it a-fforse to ffille hem aȝeyne.

afforce (əˈfɔəs), *v.* Also 3–6 aforce, 4 aforse, afforse. [a. OFr. *aforce-r*, in one of its senses a variant of OFr. *efforce-r*, earlier *esforce-r*, *esforcie-r*:—late L. *exfortiā-re*, f. *ex* out + late L. *fortiā-re* to make strong, f. *forti-s* strong; in the other perh. a distinct formation on L. *ad* to + *fortiāre*. The med.L. *afforciāre* seems to be formed on the Fr.]

I. To apply force (= Fr. *efforcer*).

† **1.** To apply force to; to force, to compel. *Obs.*

c **1300** *K. Alis.* 789 Faste he sat, and huld the reyne .. And aforced hit [the colt] by streynthe. *c* **1330** *Arth. & Merlin* 3285 Arthour aforced him to deie.

† **b.** To force, to ravish, to violate. *Obs.*

c **1330** *Arth. & Merlin* 2360 He hath me of vilanie besought, Me to aforce is in his thought.

† **2.** *refl.* To force or strengthen oneself (*to do* a thing); to exert oneself, to do one's best, to try. (OFr. *s'aforcer*, mod. *s'efforcer.*) *Obs.*

1297 R. GLOUC. 121 And heo a forcede hom þe more, þe heþene a way to dryue. *c* **1340** HAMPOLE *Pr. Treat.* (1866) 8 Deuells þat afforces tham to reue fra vs þe hony of poure lyfe and of grace. *c* **1400** *Destr. Troy* I. 228 þat wold doutles be done .. wold þu afforce þe þerfore. *Ibid.* XXVII. 11129 Thai afforset hom felly .. The vilany to venge. *a* **1528** SKELTON *Magnificence* 257 Herein I wyll aforce me to show you my mynde.

† **3.** *trans.* To endeavour, attempt, or try. *Obs.*

1523 SKELTON *Garl. Laurel* 818 Ye must nedis afforce it by pretence of your professioun unto umanyte. *a* **1528** —— *Bowge of Crt.* 17, I was sore moued to aforce the same.

II. To add force (? properly OFr. *aforcer*).

† **4.** To add force to; to strengthen, fortify, reinforce. *Obs.*

c **1400** *Destr. Troy* XV. 6593 Then Menesteus .. afforsit hys frekys to þe fight harde. *c* **1430** LYDG. *Bochas* (1554) II. xvii. 66/1 And tafforce them, let workmen vndertake Square bastiles and bulwarkes to make.

5. *Eng. Const. Hist.* To reinforce or strengthen a deliberative body by the addition of new members; as a jury by skilled assessors, or persons acquainted with the facts. [In this sense med.L. *afforciāre* is found in contemporary records; see Blount: '*Afforcietur assisa*, let the Witnesses be encreased,' (rather, 'Let the Assise or bench be reinforced or afforced').]

1818 HALLAM *Middle Ages* (1872) II. 399 It was the practice to afforce the jury. **1870** STUBBS *Sel. Charters* Introd. 24 The jurors are at first witnesses of the fact; as business increases they are, under Edward I, afforced by the addition of persons better acquainted with the matter; a further step separates these afforcing jurors from the original twelve.

afforcement (əˈfɔəsmənt). [a. OFr. *afforcement*, f. *afforcer*: see AFFORCE and -MENT.]

1. A strengthening; a reinforcement. (See AFFORCE 5.)

1818 HALLAM *Middle Ages* (1872) II. 399 This afforcement it appears could only be made with the consent of the parties. **1874** STUBBS *Const. Hist.* I. xiii. 619 The jurors summoned were allowed to add to their number persons who possessed the requisite knowledge, under the title of afforcement.

† **2.** = AFFORCIAMENT 1. *Obs.*

1753 CHAMBERS *Cycl. Supp.*, *Afforcement*, *Afforciamentum*, in some antient charters, denotes a fortress, or work of fortification and defence.

† **aˈfforciament.** *Obs.* [ad. med.L. *afforciament-um*, f. L. *afforciā-re*: see AFFORCE and -MENT.]

1. A fortress; a fortified place.

1706 PHILLIPS, *Afforciament* (in old Records) a Fort or Strong-Hold.

2. = AFFORCEMENT 1.

1738 *Hist. View Crt. Excheq.* v. 79 There was an Afforciament of more Jurors, till they had a Verdict of twelve.

afforcing (ə'fɔəsɪŋ), *vbl. sb.* [f. AFFORCE + -ING[1].] A reinforcing or strengthening.

1875 STUBBS *Const. Hist.* III. xviii. 270 In the 'afforcing' or amending of the council.

afforcing (ə'fɔəsɪŋ), *ppl. a.* [f. AFFORCE + -ING[2].] Reinforcing; adding strength, influence, or knowledge.

1870 [See AFFORCE 5.]

afford (ə'fɔəd), *v.* Forms: 1 **ȝeforð-ian,** 2 **ȝeforð-ien, iforðian, -en,** 3 **i-forðen, i-vorðen,** 4–5 **aforth(e, avorthi,** 6 **afforthe, aforde,** 6 **afoord,** 6–7 **affoord, affoard,** 7 **affowrd,** 6– **afford.** [f. *ȝe- pref.* implying completeness + *forð-ian* to further, advance; f. *forð* forth, forward, onward. The prefix was subseq. reduced to *ă-* (see A- *pref.* 6), and this in 16th c. corrupted after L. *af-*. With the change of *ð* to *d*, cf. *burthen, burden*.] *orig.* To further, promote; *hence* achieve, manage to do, manage to give, have the power to give, give what is in one's power, supply, yield.

†**1.** To forward or advance to or towards completion: *hence,* to perform, execute, accomplish, fulfil. *Obs.*

c **1050** *O.E. Chron.* (Cott. MS.) an. 1045 He..þæt mynstre wel ȝeforðode þa hwile þe he þær wæs. **1205** LAYAMON 31561 þæt nulle he come nauere no þine heste iuorðen. *c* **1230** *Ancren Riwle* 366 (T. & C.) þi wille, þauh, & nout min, euer beon iforðet [*v.r.* ifulled].

†**2.** To carry out, accomplish, achieve, manage (something planned or desired). With *may* (= can). *Obs.*

1085 *O.E. Chron.* (Laud MS.) His feond..ne mihten na ȝeforðian heora fare. *c* **1123** *Ibid.* an. 675 Hwilc man swa haueð behaten to foren to Rome, and he ne muȝe hit forðian. *c* **1175** *Lamb. Hom.* 31 He ne mahte na mare ȝeforðian. *Ibid.* 39 Hwet ȝe sculen don ȝif ȝe hit maȝen iforðian. **1377** LANGL. *P. Pl.* B. VI. 201 And ȝaf hem mete as he myghte aforth and mesurable huyre. *a* **1420** OCCLEVE (in Halliw.), And here and there, as that my litille wit Aforthe may, eek thinke I translate hit.

3. With *inf.* or *subord. cl.* To manage (*to do* anything); with *can*: To have the means, be able or rich enough; to bear the expense.

c **1449** PECOCK *Repr.* III. v. 306 Greet lordis mowe avorthi to haue..officers undir hem forto attende. *Ibid.* 562 The comoun peple myȝten the wors avorthi in cost of money for to gete to hem thir present book. **1514** BARCLAY *Cytezen & Uplandysh.* (1847) 69, I may not aforde nowe for to spende out all. *a* **1745** SWIFT *Mod. Educ.* (J.) All families, where there is wealth enough to afford that their sons may be good for nothing. **1802** MAR. EDGEWORTH *Moral T.* (1816) I. iv. 24 She could not afford to pay. **1814** WORDSWORTH *Excurs.* I. 370 He could afford to suffer With those whom he saw suffer. **1833** HT. MARTINEAU *Brooke Farm* viii. 98 Those who could afford to try new methods. **1847** MACAULAY *Hist. Eng.* I. xii, Luxuries which few could afford to purchase.

4. With *simple obj.* **a.** To manage to give, to spare.

c **1449** PECOCK *Repr.* III. x. 336 Thei myȝten miche more avorthi into almes than thei that hadden litil. **1588** SHAKS. *L.L.L.* IV. i. 40 Praise we may afford, To any Lady that subdewes a Lord. **1667** MILTON *P.L.* IX. 912 Should God create another Eve, and I Another Rib afford. **1833** HT. MARTINEAU *Brooke Farm* vii. 89, I cannot afford them a quart a day at my own expense. **1860** TYNDALL *Glac.* I. §27. 195 The loss of a single day was more than I could afford.

†**b.** To manage to sell (at such a price). *Obs.*

1617 J. RIDER (in Halliw.), *Non possum tantulo vendere.* I cannot afford it at so little price. **1705** ADDISON *Italy* (J.) They fill their magazines in time of the greatest plenty so that they may afford cheaper. **1793** SMEATON *Edystone Lighth.* §116 The stone could be afforded at somewhat less price than Portland.

c. To manage to procure or maintain, etc.; to spare the price of, bear the expense of.

1833 HT. MARTINEAU *Brooke Farm* ii. 19, I cannot afford stockings for so many, nor shoes either. *Ibid.* vii. 87 Now they could not afford beer, except a little on Sundays. *Ibid.* viii. 93 He cannot afford a team to plough his field.

5. Without *can*: To give of what one has, to furnish, bestow, grant, yield. (Often with *to.*)

1596 J. NORDEN *Progr. Pietie* (1847) 89 To accept this church as his spouse and wife, affording himself to be her husband. **1633** G. HERBERT *Ch. Porch* iii, Gladly welcome what he doth afford. **1702** POPE *Wife of B.* 254 Kind heav'n afford him everlasting rest. **1738** WESLEY *Psalms* li. 4 Tho' I have griev'd thy Spirit, Lord, His Help and Comfort still afford. **1817** JAS. MILL *Brit. India* II. v. vii. 602 Rights which the custom of India gave, to the Prince who received over the Prince who afforded the tribute. **1853** MARSDEN *Early Purit.* Pref., Should life and leisure be afforded to the author.

6. Of things: To be capable of yielding, to have for one who asks or seeks.

1581 LAMBARDE *Eiren.* I. iv. 25 More than their owne Commission doeth afoord. **1592** SHAKS. *Rom. & Jul.* v. i. 73 The world affords no law to make thee rich. **1593** —— *Rich. II,* I. i. 177, The purest treasure mortall times afford Is spotless reputation. **1671** *True Non-Conf.* Contents, Whether the Angels of the Churches afford any ground for Bishops. **1782** PRIESTLEY *Nat. & Rev. Relig.* I. 354 Their whole history affords not a single instance. **1820** W. IRVING *Sketch Bk.* II. 8 The lives of literary men afford no striking themes for the sculptor. **1876** GLADSTONE *Hom. Synchr.* 234 The Poems afford no explanation.

7. To supply or furnish from its own resources, to yield naturally.

a **1600** Q. ELIZ. *Let.* in Beveridge *Hist. Ind.* (1858) I. I. x. 236 Commodities which our dominions may afforthe. **1589** GREENE *Menaphon* (Arb.) 50 Can a countrie cotage affoord such perfection? **1611** BIBLE *Ps.* cxliv. 13 That our garners may bee full, affoording all maner of store. **1654** BAKER *Lett. of Balzac* III. 97 As Affrick affoards Lions, and France Souldiers. **1673** RAY *Journ. Low Countries* 459 Olives..afford most oil when fully ripe. **1697** DRYDEN *Virg. Georg.* II. 716 Fruits, which, of their own accord, The willing Ground, and laden Trees afford. **1756** C. LUCAS *Ess. on Waters* III. 238 The gardens afford good supplies of the best esculent vegetables. **1879** in *Cassell's Techn. Educ.* IV. 69/2 The figure..affords a correct representation. **1878** G. MACDONALD *Ann. Quiet Neighb.* xviii. 351 The comfortable confidence afforded by the mask of namelessness.

b. In this sense rarely of persons.

1588 GREENE *Pandosto* (1843) 36 He wondred how a country maid could afoord such courtly behaviour. **1839** MURCHISON *Silur. Syst.* I. xxxviii. 530 We shall hereafter afford independent proofs of the existence of dry land.

affordable (ə'fɔədəb(ə)l), *a.* [f. prec. + ABLE.] That can be afforded, spared, or yielded.

1866 CARLYLE *Remin.* (1881) II. 169 Spasmodic writhing ..never the smallest help affordable.

affordably (ə'fɔədəblɪ), *adv.* Chiefly *U.S.* [f. AFFORDABLE *a.* + -LY[2].] So as to be affordable, cheaply, reasonably. Freq. forming attrib. collocations with pples. (often hyphened), as ***affordably-priced*** adj.

1974 *Greenville* (S. Carolina) *News* 23 Apr. c7/3 (Advt.), Affordably priced, 3 bedroom..brick and frame home. **1977** *Sci. Amer.* Apr. 95/1 (Advt.), The new HP 9896 desk-top system can fill both needs admirably and affordably. **1981** *Daily Tel.* 30 Oct. 13 (Advt.), High quality sound and vision at affordably low prices. **1984** *Real Estate Buyer* (St. Augustine, Florida) Mar. 1/3 (Advt.), Immaculately maintained and affordably priced.

afforder (ə'fɔədə(r)). [f. AFFORD + -ER[1].] One who, or that which, affords, spares, or yields.

1598 FLORIO, *Porgitore*..a bringer, an affoorder.

affording (ə'fɔədɪŋ), *vbl. sb.* [f. AFFORD + -ING[1].] A yielding, producing, sparing.

1598 FLORIO, *Porgimento*.. an affoording, a yeelding, a bringing. **1663** GERBIER *Counsel* 13 The affording of sufficient light to the rooms. **1754** SHERLOCK *Disc.* (1759) I. i. 17 The Excellency of Religion consists in affording certain Means of obtaining eternal Life.

affording (ə'fɔədɪŋ), *ppl. a.* [f. AFFORD + -ING[2].] Producing, yielding; liberal, helpful.

1873 MISS BROUGHTON *Nancy* II. 87 Perhaps she may be stupid! Certainly she is not affording.

†**a'ffordment.** *Obs.* [f. AFFORD + -MENT.] Granting, bestowal.

1633 T. ADAMS *Comm. 2 Pet.* i. 11 (1865) 126 So the Lord doth allure us by gracious affordments.

affore, afforn, obs. forms of AFORE.

afforest (ə'fɒrɪst), *v.* Also 5–6 **aforest.** [ad. med.L. *afforēstā-re* (Charter of Forests 9 Hen. III) f. *ad* to + *forēsta, forēstis,* FOREST.] To convert into forest, or hunting-ground.

1502 ARNOLD *Chron.* (1811) 208 Yf any wood other than ..his owne he aforestid..it shalbe disforestid, and yf he afforested his owne propur wood remayne it forest. **1612** DAVIES *Discov. why Irel. etc.* (1787) 124 He [Henry the Second] afforested many woods and wastes, to the grievance of the subject. **1837** W. HOWITT *Rur. Life* v. i. (1862) 352 The Conqueror's motive for afforesting so large a tract of country.

afforestable (æ'fɒrɪstəb(ə)l), *a.* [f. AFFOREST *v.* + -ABLE.] Capable of being afforested.

1928 *Britain's Industr. Future* (*Liberal Ind. Inquiry*) Index 489 Estimate of afforestable land. **1958** *Times* 24 Jan. 15/3 The planting of the total afforestable area with pines is nearing completion.

afforestation (əˌfɒrɪ'steɪʃən). [ad. med.L. *afforēstātiōn-em* n. of action f. *afforēstā-re*: see AFFOREST *v.*] The action or result of converting into forest or hunting-ground.

1615 MANWOOD *Lawes of Forest* xvi. §9. 116/2 The disafforestation of the new afforestations aforesaid. **1649** SELDEN *Laws of Eng.* I. lxiv. (1739) 130 Revoking of Charters ..Afforestations, with a train of oppressions depending there-on. **1751** CHAMBERS *Cycl.* s.v. *Purlieu*, The greatest part of the new afforestations were still remaining. **1862** *Lond. Rev.* 20 Dec. 538 Why were two churches built in the very midst of the forest immediately after the afforestation?

afforested (ə'fɒrɪstɪd), *ppl. a.* [f. AFFOREST + -ED.] Converted into forest.

1679 HOBBES *Dial. Com. Laws* (1840) 154 [They] had much land remaining in their own hands, afforrested for their recreation. **1873** *Q. Rev.* CXXXV. 154 The whole of the afforested parts of Devon.

afforesting (ə'fɒrɪstɪŋ), *vbl. sb.* [f. AFFOREST + -ING[1].] The process of converting into forest; afforestation.

1649 SELDEN *Laws of Eng.* I. lvi. (1739) 102 Unlawful Taxes, Afforrestings, and other such Oppressions. **1757** BURKE *Abridgm. Eng. Hist.* III. viii. (1812) 534 The Charter of the Forests had for its object..the prevention of future afforesting.

afforism, -ysme, obs. variants of APHORISM.

†**a'fform,** *v. Obs. rare.* [a. OFr. *aforme-r, aff-,* f. *à* to + *former* to FORM.] To form, fashion, model, according *to.*

c **1500** *Doctr. good Seruauntes* (1842) 8 To hym that is most honourable, Afforme your maners and your entent.

afformative (ə'fɔːmətɪv), *a.* (*sb.*). *Philol.* [f. AF- + FORMATIVE *a.*] Affixed as a formative element; said of a letter, syllable, etc. As *sb.,* an afformative particle; a suffix (esp. in Semitic languages). Cf. PREFORMATIVE.

1821 M. STUART *Heb. Gram.* 139 The Imperative has no Praeformatives like the Future, but only *Afformatives*, or Suffix-formatives. **1858** *Trans. Philol. Soc.* I. xii. 179 (*title*) On constant affixes and afformatives in the Hebrew language. **1864** E. B. PUSEY *Daniel* i. 47 The inflection of a passive participle by the afformatives of the preterite. **1880** B. DAVIES tr. *F. W. W. Gesenius's Heb. Gram.* 114 The characteristic *Pă'thăch* of the second syllable becomes *Shᵉwâ* before an afformative beginning with a vowel. **1942** *Antiquity* XVI. 325 The afformative of the perfect tense. **1952** *Archivum Linguisticum* IV. 61 Substantives involving both preformative *ma-* and afformative *-ān* > *-ōn* are not unknown in North-west Semitic.

afforse, obs. variant of AFFORCE.

afforst, obs. form of ATHIRST.

affrait, -ly, see AFFRAYITLY, AFRAID.

†**a'fframing,** *vbl. sb. Obs. rare*[−1]. (for aframing.) [f. A- *pref.* 1 intens. + FRAME, OE. *fram-ian, frem-ian,* to profit, avail.] Gain, profit.

1440 *Prom. Parv.,* Framynge, or afframynge, or wynnynge. *Lucrum, emolumentum.*

affranchise (ə'frɑːntʃɪz, -æ-, -tʃaɪz), *v.* 5 **afranchise,** 5–6 **affranchyse.** [f. Fr. *afranchiss-* lengthened stem of *afranch-ir* (now *affranchir*) f. *à* to + *franchir* to free; f. *franc* free: see FRANK.] To free; to set at liberty from servitude; also from an obligation.

1475 CAXTON *Jason* C b, I shall affranchyse yow of your vowe. **1477** EARL RIVERS (Caxton) *Dictes* 110 He afranchised legmon, and made him fre that afore was bonde and thralle. **1600** HOLLAND *Livy* XXXV. xxiii. 908 h, Antiochus should be sent for to affranchise Greece. **1725** COTES tr. *Dupin's Eccl. Hist.* I. III. i. 76 It cannot be said, that France..has been made Free, or affranchised, since she was free in her first original. **1863** LANDOR in *Atl. Monthly* (1866) June 702/2 Every slave, after fifteen years, should be affranchised.

affranchised (ə'frɑːntʃɪzd, -æ-), *ppl. a.* [f. prec. + -ED.] Freed, set at liberty.

1495 CAXTON *Vitas Patr.* (W. de Worde) I. cliii. 158/2 Fyrst bonde & sith afraunchised, and made free. **1611** COTGR., *Main-mis*, an affranchised person; one that is freed from seruitude. **1863** GILCHRIST *Life of W. Blake* I. 100 The affranchised tree consequently bore a luxurious crop of leaves.

affranchisement (ə'frɑːntʃɪzmənt, -æ-). [f. AFFRANCHISE + -MENT.] 'The act of making free.' Todd 1818.

1799 *Ann. Reg. 1792* (Dodsley) Hist. Eur. 81/1 The decree for the affranchisement of the mulattoes. **1887** *Harper's Mag.* Mar. 581/1 Affranchisement, independence, freedom, secured for others, had anew their echo in the hearts of the Russian people. **1931** *Times Lit. Suppl.* 8 Jan. 24/4 Mr. Woodward's reading of modern history as a gradual 'affranchisement'.

affranchising (ə'frɑːntʃɪzɪŋ, -æ-), *vbl. sb.* [f. as prec. + -ING[1].] The action of freeing. (Chiefly gerundial.)

1688 *Lond. Gaz.* mmcccxxvii/2 Since their affranchizing themselves..they have all along preserved their Liberty.

†**a'ffrap,** *v. Obs. rare.* [ad. It. *affrappare,* f. *ad* to + *frappare* to beat, knock, see FRAP; but Spenser's word is perhaps an analogical formation on *frap,* like *addoom,* etc.] To strike, strike against. (With or without object expressed.)

1596 SPENSER *F.Q.* II. i. 26 They bene ymett, both ready to affrap. *Ibid.* III. ii. 6 To tossen speare and shield, and to affrap The warlike ryder to his most mishap.

affray (ə'freɪ), *v. Obs.* or *arch.* Forms: 4 **afrai, afrey,** 4–7 **afray(e, affraye,** 4– **affray.** *Pa. t.* 4 **afrayed, affraied,** 6 **affraide, afraid.** *Pa. pple.*: see AFRAID. Also aphetic FRAY. [a. Anglo-Fr. *afraye-r, effraye-r,* early OFr. *effreer, esfreer,* 1 sing. pres. *esfrei,* (Pr. *esfredar*):—late L. *ex-fridāre*; f. *ex* out of + late L. *fridus, fridum,* ad. Teut. *friðu* (OHG. *fridu,* OSax. *friðu,* OE. *frið,* ON. *friðr*) peace. The pa. pple. AFFRAYED, 'alarmed,' acquired the meaning of 'in a state of fear,' and has since the 16th c. been treated as a distinct word: see AFRAID.]

1. To disturb, or startle, from sleep or quiet, as a sudden noise does; passing into the sense of alarm, as the effect of such startling. *arch.*

c **1325** *E.E. Allit. Poems* B. 1780 Afrayed þay no freke..& to þe palays pryncipal þay aproched ful stylle. *c* **1369** CHAUCER *Blaunche* 296 Smale foules a great hepe That had afrayed [*v.r.* affrayed, afraied] me out of my slepe. **1393** GOWER *Conf.* III. 371, I was out of my swoune affraied. *c* **1450** LONELICH *Grail* xxv. 227 And wondirly sore afrayed ȝhe was Of his noise sche herde in that plas. **1563** BARNABE

GOOGE *Eglogs* vi. (Arb.) 55 Than rest and slepe I straightway sought No Dreames dyd me afraye. **1820** KEATS *St. Agnes* xxix. The kettle-drum, and far-heard clarionet Affray his ears.

†**b.** To disturb with hostilities; to attack with an armed force. *Obs. rare.*

1467 MARG. PASTON in *Lett.* 576 II. 308 Ye wote wele that I have ben affrayd ther befor this tyme.

By imperceptible gradations the idea of *alarm* passed into that of

2. To frighten, to affect with fear; especially in the passive voice to be *affrayed* or AFRAID. *arch.*

c **1314** *Guy Warw.* 57 Now goth Gii sore desmaid, His woundes him han iuel afreyd. *c* **1315** SHOREHAM 158 For of thet he hadde her y-do He was affrayde. *c* **1386** CHAUCER *Clerkes T.* 399 Nedelees, god woot, he thoghte hire for t' affraye [*MS. Heng.* t'afraye]. **1456** *Past. Lett.* 277 I. 380, I have somwhat affrayed them, and made hem spend mony. **1523** LD. BERNERS *Froissart* I. ccxxix. 307 The whiche so affrayed them, that they had no lust to go thyder. **1637** GILLESPIE *Eng.-Pop. Cerem.* II. i. 6 If Papists..were so affrayed of Conformists. **1763-5** CHURCHILL *Duellist* I. Poems II. 7 Bid Terror, posting on the wind, Affray the spirits of mankind. **1875** B. TAYLOR *Faust* xxv. I. 212 Nay, sheathe thy sword at last! Do not affray me!

†**3.** *intr.* (*refl.*) To be afraid, to fear. (Fr. *s'effrayer.*) *Obs.*

c **1440** *Partonope* 845 She gan affray of this sodeyn caas.

4. To scare, to startle or alarm into running away, to frighten away. *arch.* Cf. FRAY.

1375 BARBOUR *Bruce* XVI. 205 [Thai] dang on thame so hardely, That all thair fayis afrayit war. *c* **1400** *Destr. Troy* VII. 3200 Þai affrayet the folke fuersly by dene, Sesit and slogh, slongen to ground. **1549** *Compl. Scotl.* vii. 70 Beand al affrayit ande fleyit for dreddour of his lyue. **1592** SHAKS. *Rom. & Jul.* III. v. 33 Since arme from arme that voyce doth vs affray. *a* **1610** BABINGTON *Wks.* 32 To prick vs to the good and to afray vs from the euill. **1855** SINGLETON *Virgil* I. 80 And with a din Affray the birds.

affray, used for DEFRAY.

1584 LODGE *Alarum agst. Vsurers* (1853) 48 Not having friends to releeve them, or money to affray their charges.

affray (əˈfreɪ), *sb.* Forms: 4-5 **afray(e**, 4-6 **affraye**, (4 **affroi**, 5 **enfray**), 4- **affray**. Also aphet. FRAY. [a. OFr. *effrei*, *esfrei*, f. *esfre-er*: see AFFRAY *v.* The form *enfray* is an erroneous expansion after the apparent analogy of *en-combre*, *a-combre*, etc.]

†**1.** The act of suddenly disturbing some one who is at rest; an attack, an assault. *Obs.*

1330 R. BRUNNE *Chron.* 176 In mirke withouten sight wille enmys mak affray. *c* **1360** *Yesterday* in *E.E.P.* (1862) 137 Þin enemy woltou · not forȝete · But ay be aferd · of his affray. *c* **1400** *Destr. Troy* XI. 4746 In diffens of þe folke þat affroi made. **1509** *Parlyament of Deuylles* xxvi, [He] strongly withstandeth myn affray. **1583** STANYHURST *Aeneis* XI. (1880) 43 Learne our fatal auentures, Thee toyls of Troians, and last infortunat affray.

†**2.** The state produced by sudden disturbance or attack; alarm; fright, terror. *Obs.*

1303 R. BRUNNE *Handlyng Synne* 1820 Betwyxe þo twey partys þe dragun lay Gresly to se wyþ grete affray. **1330** —— *Chron.* 34 Northumberland was in affray for Edred comyng. *c* **1450** LONELICH *Grail* xxv. 174 Was to hem a gret afray, Whanne they syen here Lord þere ded. **1523** LD. BERNERS *Froissart* I. ccxv. 271 Wherof the pope and cardynalles were in great affray and drede. **1596** SPENSER *F.Q.* I. iii. 12 Who full of gastly fright and cold affray Gan shut the dore.

†**3.** A disturbance, a noisy or tumultuous outburst; especially one caused by fighting, a fray. *Obs.*

1330 R. BRUNNE *Chron.* 66 Now is Edward dede þe soner for þo affrayes. *c* **1420** *Pallad. On Husb.* x. 186 And boile it so, not with to greet affray. *c* **1450** LONELICH *Graal* II. 306 Piers awook there that he lay, so astoned he was of that afray. *c* **1460** *Towneley Myst.* 179 Let no man wyt where that we war, For ferdnes of a fowlle enfray. **1513** DOUGLAS *Æneis* XII. xv. 28 Thys wourthy knycht the commen wele Romane In grete affray perturbit to rest agane And quiet sall restore. **1789** MRS. PIOZZI *France & It.* I. 216 The people are..little disposed to public affrays. **1810** SCOTT *Lady of L.* III. xiv, So swept the tumult and affray.

4. *esp.* A breach of the peace, caused by fighting or riot in a public place.

1482 CAXTON *Chron. Eng.* cclii. 323 Also this yere was a grete affraye in fleetstrete by nyȝtes tyme bitwene men of court and men of london. **1552** HULOET *Abcedarium*, Affraye betwene two men, *Monomachia*, *Pugna*. **1576** LAMBARDE *Peramb. Kent* (1826) 331, I reade not of any that was slaine in the affraye. **1691** BLOUNT *Law Dict.* s.v., An Assault is only a wrong to the party; an Affray is a common wrong. **1757** BURKE *Abridgm. Eng. Hist.* Wks. X. 352 The suppressing of riots and affrays. **1823** SCOTT *Peveril* I. vii. 127, I trust you have had no hurt in this mad affray?

affrayed (əˈfreɪd), *ppl. a. arch.* [f. AFFRAY *v.* + -ED; a recall of the old form which has become ordinarily AFRAID.] Alarmed.

1820 KEATS *S. Agnes* xxxiii, Her blue affrayed eyes wide open shone.

affrayer (əˈfreɪə(r)). Also 6 **affraier**, **affraior**, 7 **affrayor**. [f. AFFRAY *v.* + -ER[1].] One engaged in an affray; a disturber of the peace.

1553-87 FOXE *A. & M.* I. 666/2 To make these Congregations of the Lollards to be..affraiers of the people. **1581** LAMBARDE *Eiren.* II. iii. (1588) 140 Any man also may stay the Affraiors, until the storme of their heat be calmed. **1716** W. HAWKINS *Pleas of Crown* I. xxviii. (1824) I. 490 If affrayers fly to a house..[the constable]..may break open the doors to take them. **1790** DALLAS *Reports* I. 363 It is lawful to part affrayers in the house of another man.

†**aˈffraying**, *vbl. sb. Obs.* [f. AFFRAY *v.* + -ING[1].] A disturbing or alarming.

c **1450** LONELICH *Grail* xliv. 306 Whanne the deuk herde this tydyng, To hym it was a gret affrayeng.

†**aˈffrayitly, aˈffraitly**, *adv. Obs. Sc.* [f. *affrayit*, Sc. form of AFFRAYED, AFRAID + -LY[2].] In an alarmed or frightened manner; affrightedly.

1375 BARBOUR *Bruce* VI. 434 The laif fled full affrayitly. **1513** DOUGLAS *Æneis* XIII. iv. 78 Fleand thay wat not quhare, Tursing thare birdingis affraitlye here and thare. **1536** BELLENDENE *Cron. Scotl.* (1821) II. 298 The pepill, richt affrayitly, returnit to him out of all partis of the wod.

†**affrayment.** *Obs.* [f. AFFRAY *v.* + -MENT.] Given as a synonym of AFFRAY by Bailey, whence in Johnson.

1731 BAILEY, vol. II, *Affray, Affraiment* (in Common Law) is an affrightment put upon one or more persons; which may be done by an open shew of violence only, without either a blow given or a word spoken, etc. [The definition is quoted from Phillips with the addition of *Affraiment* by Bailey himself.]

†**aˈffrayne, aˈfrayne**, *v. Obs.* [f. FRAYNE, FREYNE *v.* to ask, inquire, either with A- *pref.* 1 intensive, or (as Stratmann thinks) with prep. *af*, OF, and so to *ask of* or *from*.] To question.

c **1340** HAMPOLE *Pr. Consc.* [quoted by Halliw., but not in ed. Morris] Whanne Thou schalt this werde afreyne. **1377** LANGL. *P. Pl.* B. XVI. 274, I affrayned [1393 ich fraynede] hym fyrste Fram whennes he come. *c* **1380** *Sir Ferumb.* 2146 Byfore þe Amyral þanne he goþ; & bygan him for taffrayne. *c* **1460** *Towneley Myst.* 328 My fader wakyd at the laste, And her afraynd; she told hym how she was agast.

affreight (əˈfreɪt), *v. rare*—[0]. [ad. Fr. *affréte-r*, spelt after Eng. FREIGHT.] 'To hire a ship for the transportation of goods.' Craig 1847.

affreighter (əˈfreɪtə(r)). [f. prec. + -ER[1].] 'The person who hires or charters a ship or other vessel to convey goods.' Craig 1847.

1882 *Charter-party*, Such loading berth..as the said affreighters may name.

affreightment (əˈfreɪtmənt). [ad. Fr. *affrètement* n. of action f. *affréte-r* to freight; spelt after Eng. FREIGHT.] The hiring of a vessel to convey cargo.

1755 MAGENS *Ess. Insur.* II. 101 The Agreement of Affreightment, commonly called a Charter-Party. **1848** ARNOULD *Mar. Insur.* I. vi. (1866) I. 289 Emolument derived from carrying goods on freight, or from performing certain contracts of affreightment on hire.

†**aˈffrent**, *v. Obs. rare*—[1]. [ad. Sp. *afrent-ar* to affront.] A by-form of AFFRONT.

1578 T. N. *Trans. Conquest of W. India* 229 To kill those Spaniardes who have so affrented the nation of Culhua.

†**aˈffret**, *v. Obs. rare*—[1]. [f. *af-* (= A- *pref.* 11) + FRET *v.*] To fret, annoy, trouble.

1600 ABP. ABBOT *Jonah* 247 David..was so affretted with the prosperitie of the wicked.

†**aˈffret**, *sb. Obs. rare*—[1]. [etym. doubtful; perh. f. It. *affrettare* to hasten, *affrettamento* a making speed.] 'Furious onset; immediate attack.' J.

1596 SPENSER *F.Q.* III. ix. 16 With the terrour of their fierce affret They rudely drove to ground both man and horse.

affreyd, variant of AFRAYED *ppl. a.*, rubbed.

affricate (ˈæfrɪkeɪt), *v.* [f. L. *affricāt-*, ppl. stem of *affricā-re*, to rub on or against; f. *ad* to + *fricā-re* to rub. Cf. AFFRICTION.] †**1.** 'To rub upon, or against, to grate or crumble.' Blount *Glossogr.* 1656; whence in Bailey. *Obs.*—[0]

2. To convert into an affricate (see next). Also *intr.* So **ˈaffricated** *ppl. a.*

1891 *New Eng. Dict.* s.v. CH, *Ch*..was introduced initially, in Upper German, for the affricated sound of *c* (*k*) as *chamara* (kχaˑmara). **1902** E. W. SCRIPTURE *Elem. Exper. Phonetics* xxi. 307 The 'constant diphthongs' ts tš..are affricates, that is, occlusives with fricative releases... The former seems to be an affricated t, the latter an affricated ᴛ. **1946** PRIEBSCH & COLLINSON *Germ. Lang.* (ed. 2) II. i. 118 He suspects that Ostrogoths affricated medial *t* between A.D. 553 and 580. **1964** *Language* XL. 26 The sibilant affricated in close juncture with /l/ but did not voice.

affricate (ˈæfrɪkət), *sb. Phonetics.* [ad. L. *affricātus*, pa. pple. of *affricāre*, f. *ad* to + *fricāre* to rub.] A close combination of an explosive consonant or 'stop' with an immediately following fricative or spirant of corresponding position, as in Ger. *pf*, *z* (= ts). Also called **aˈffricative.**

1880 SAYCE *Introd. Sci. Lang.* I. 270 Where a spirant or fricative is immediately preceded by an explosive, a double sound or affricative is the result (*e.g.* German *pf*, Armenian *t'š*). **1891** *New Eng. Dict.* s.v. CH (consonantal digraph), The combination CH..was introduced [into Roman spelling] to represent the Greek aspirate or affricate X. **1895** P. GILES *Man. Compar. Philol.* 70 Another series of sounds which must be..distinguished from spirants and aspirates is the affricates. **1905** L. A. MAGNUS *Respublica* 74 Here we might safely say final *c* is preserved as a sibilant or affricate. **1950** D. JONES *Phoneme* p. xii, The affricate tʃ (Eng. *ch*).

†**affriˈcated**, *ppl. a. Obs. rare.* [f. AFFRICATE *v.* + -ED.] Rubbed.

1705 HAUKSBEE in *Phil. Trans.* XXV. 2167 Nor would the Light thus produc'd, live on the Amber..but dy'd so soon as it had deserted the Affricated Woollen. **1708** —— *ibid.* XXVI. 86 The effluvia of the Affricated Tube.

affriˈcation. [ad. L. *affricātiōn-em*, n. of action f. *affricā-re*: see AFFRICTION.] †**1.** 'Rubbing upon or against.' Bailey 1721. *Obs. rare*—[1].

1706 HAUKSBEE in *Phil. Trans.* XXV. 2331 The Light..discover'd upon the Affrication of it [a glass tube] unexhausted, seem'd to be altogether on its outside.

2. The conversion (of a sound) into an affricate.

1934 *Trans. Philol. Soc.* 87 A pure tenuis passes necessarily through the stages of aspiration and affrication. **1934** PRIEBSCH & COLLINSON *Germ. Lang.* I. ii. 32 So-called assibilation or palatal affrication of *k* and *g* before front vowels. **1953** *Archivum Linguisticum* V. 69 The choice of the same diacritic mark to indicate affrication and velarization is to invite ambiguity.

†**affricke bird**, 'A coward, one in gay cloathes.' Cockeram 1626.

†**aˈffriction.** *Obs.* Also 7 **adfriction**. [ad. L. **affrictiōn-em*, n. of action, f. *affrict-* ppl. stem of *affricā-re* to rub on; f. *af-* = *ad-* to + *fricā-re* to rub. The ordinary cl. L. form was *affricātio*; the simple *fricā-re* had both *fricāt-um* and *frict-um*.] The action of rubbing one thing upon another.

1615 CROOKE *Body of Man* 234 When as in polutions or affrictions women..do loose their owne seed. **1660** H. MORE *Myst. Godl.* X. xiv. 541 The Adfriction of the pastoral medicine to a diseased Sheep. **1681** HALLYWELL *Melamp.* 115 (T.) Every pitiful vice seeks the enlargement of itself by a contagious affriction of all capable subjects.

†**aˈffriended**, *pa. pple. Obs. rare*—[1]. [f. FRIEND, by pref. *a-* or *af-*, probably intended to be factitive, after analogy of *affirm*, *afforest*; see A- *pref.* 11.] Made friends; reconciled.

1596 SPENSER *F.Q.* IV. iii. 50 She saw that cruell war so ended, And deadly foes so faithfully affrended.

†**affright, afright**, *ppl. a. Obs.* Forms: 1 **a-fyrhted**, 1-2 **a-fyrht**, 3 ? **affuruht** (Y), 4 ? **ofright**, **afriȝt**, ? **affriȝt**, **afryȝt**, 5 **affryht**, **afryht**, **afryght**, 5-6 **afright**, 6 **affright**. [pa. pple. of OE, **afyrhtan*, not found in any other part, f. A- *pref.* 1 intensive + *fyrht-an* to frighten, terrify: see FRIGHT. There appears to have been also a derivative *of-fyrhtan*, OFFRIGHT, in 12th-13th c., the pple. of which *of-fyrht* was afterwards confounded with *a-fyrht*, whence prob. the early forms marked with ? above; but the eventual doubling of the *f* is after the analogy of forms like *af-firm*, *af-fix*, from L. *ad*. A later form is AFFRIGHTED.] Struck with sudden fear; terrified, frightened.

a **1000** *Andreas* 1531 He afyrhted wearð. *a* **1000** *O.E. Gosp.* Matt. xxviii. 4 Þa weardas wæron afyrhte. *c* **1160** *Hatt. Gosp.* ibid., Þa weardes wæren afyrhte. *c* **1230** *Ancren Riwle* 362 Þe ueond is affuruht and offered of swuche. **1330** R. BRUNNE *Chron.* 158 Þe mayden Berenger scho was alle ofright. *c* **1380** *Sir Ferumb.* 1889 A-fryȝt he wax of hym sum del:so grym a was in gale. *Ibid.* 2199 Þat Þan was sore afriȝt. *c* **1450** LONELICH *Grail* xx. 10 In his herte he was wondirly afryght. **1596** SPENSER *F.Q.* II. v. 37 As one affright With hellish feends, or furies mad uprore. **1647** H. MORE *Resolution* 175 The weakned phansy sore affright With the grim shades of grisely Night.

affright (əˈfraɪt), *v. arch.* [a late formation, on FRIGHT *v.*, with A- *pref.* 11 (written *af-*); doubtless partly due to the pre-existing ppl. adj. AFFRIGHT; see prec.] To frighten, to terrify. *to **affright from***: to deter from. (Now only poetical for the prose FRIGHTEN.)

1589 NASHE in *Greene's Menaphon* (Arb.) 13 So terrible was his stile..as would have affrighted our peaceable Poets, from intermedling hereafter, with that quarrelling kinde of verse. **1593** SHAKS. *1 Hen. VI*, I. iv. 43 The Scar-Crow that affrights our children so. **1611** HEYWOOD *Gold. Age* II. i. 24 You afright me with your steele. **1675** T. BROOKS *Gold. Key* Wks. 1867 V. 129 To affright people from vicious practices. **1722** DE FOE *Moll Fl.* (1840) 102 Terrifying and affrighting me with threats. **1878** B. TAYLOR *Pr. Deukalion* IV. iv. 158 Never a wolf affrights them Here in the pasture's peace.

affright (əˈfraɪt), *sb. arch.* [f. the vb., on the analogy of the pre-existing *fright* vb. and sb.]

1. *actively*, The action of frightening or causing terror; also *concr.* A cause or source of terror.

1611 B. JONSON *Catiline* (J.) I see the gods..would humble them, By sending such affrights. **1633** BP. HALL *Hard Texts* 195 Full of troubles and dangerous affrights. **1697** DRYDEN *Æneid* (J.) The war at hand appears with more affright. **1817** COLERIDGE *Sybil. Leaves* (1862) 231 A tale of less affright, And tempered with delight.

2. *passively*, The state of sudden and great fear; terror, fright.

1596 SPENSER *F.Q.* II. iii. 19 Then dead through great affright They both nigh were. **1665** PEPYS *Diary* (1879) III. 110 This puts me into a most mighty affright. **1789** BELSHAM *Ess.* II. xl. 511 Mr. Burke, in his affright, forgets what in his calmer moments he readily concedes. **1847** BARHAM *Ingold. Leg.* (1877) 311 Thy bosom pants in wild affright.

† **aˈffrightable**, *a. Obs. rare*⁻¹. [f. AFFRIGHT *v.* + -ABLE.] Such as to frighten; deterrent.
1624 CAPT. SMITH *Virginia* VI. 214 Though the coast be rocky and thus affrightable.

affrighted (əˈfraɪtɪd), *ppl. a.* [f. AFFRIGHT *v.* + -ED. (Replaces the earlier ppl. adj. AFFRIGHT.)] Struck with sudden fear; alarmed, frightened.
1604 SHAKS. *Oth.* V. ii. 100 And that th' affrighted Globe Did yawne at Alteration. **1702** POPE *Thebais* 138 Affrighted Atlas, on the distant shore, Trembl'd. **1791** COWPER *Iliad* VI. 48 A thicket his affrighted steeds detain'd. **1876** MISS BRADDON *J. Haggard's Dau.* II. 32 Joshua looked up presently, and saw two pairs of affrighted eyes gazing at him.

affrightedly (əˈfraɪtɪdlɪ), *adv.* [f. prec. + -LY².] In an affrighted manner; with fright or alarm.
1613 DRAYTON *Poly-olbion* xxii. (T.) The day upon the host affrightedly doth look. *a* **1674** CLARENDON *Hist. Reb.* III. xv. 496 And make them affrightedly to start from Him ..whom they adored. **1860** W. COLLINS *Wom. in White* iv. 17 Looking up and down the road affrightedly.

affrighten (əˈfraɪtən), *v. arch.* [Secondary form of AFFRIGHT *v.* Cf. the relation of *fright* and *frighten*, and see -EN².] To frighten, to affright.
1630 J. TAYLOR (Water Poet) *Wks.* II. 169/1 The whilest her tongue doth thunder and affrighten. **1701** in *Lond. Gaz.* mmmdcclı/5 It is not the Terrour of the French Power.. shall affrighten us from our bounden Duty. **1794** SOUTHEY *Botany-Bay* iv. Wks. II. 88 Fit tales For garrulous beldames to affrighten babes. **1828** LANDOR *Imag. Convers.* Wks. 1868 I. 137 Wherefore, in God's name, are you affrightened?

affrightened (əˈfraɪtənd), *ppl. a. arch.* [f. prec. + -ED.] Affrighted, frightened.
1649 CLEVELAND *Elegy* 7 Wks. 1687, 198 Does his Royal Blood..Not shoot through her affrighten'd Womb? **1728** MORGAN *Hist. Algiers* I. iv. 87 The Disorder into which their affrightened Horses had put them. **1809** CRABBE *Tales* 53 Th' affrighten'd Man a due attention paid.

affrightening (əˈfraɪtənɪŋ), *ppl. a. arch.* [f. AFFRIGHTEN + -ING².] Frightful, terrifying.
1683 *Pennsylv. Arch.* I. 61 Yᵗ affrightening cruelty committed at Lewis. **1715** BURNET *Hist. own Time* (1766) II. 108 All the affrightening stories that had been brought him.

affrighter (əˈfraɪtə(r)). *arch.* [f. AFFRIGHT *v.* + -ER¹.] One who affrights or frightens; a frightener.
1612 SHELTON *Quixote* I. IV. xxv. (T.) The protector of damsels, the affrighter of giants.

affrightful (əˈfraɪtfʊl), *a. arch.* [f. AFFRIGHT *sb.* + -FUL: cf. *frightful.*]
1. Exciting fright or terror; frightening, terrifying.
1618 T. ADAMS *Pract. Wks.* (1861) II. 133 The night presents to the fantasy..many deceiving and affrightful imaginations. **1678** CUDWORTH *Intell. Syst.* 68 Spectres, Bug-bears, or Affrightful Apparitions. **1693** LUTTRELL *Brief Rel.* (1857) III. 157 That island has frequent tremblings since the great earthquake, which is very affrightfull to the inhabitants. **1800** COLERIDGE *Wallenstein* I. iii. Wks. III. 266 Here every coming hour broods into life Some new affrightful monster.
†**2.** Full of fear, timid. *Obs. rare.*
1631 MARKHAM *Way to Wealth* II. I. xiv. (1668) 71 Fishes of eager bite, most foolish, least affrightful, and soonest deceived.

affrightfully (əˈfraɪtfʊlɪ), *adv. arch.* [f. prec. + -LY².] In an affrightful manner; alarmingly.
1667 H. MORE *Div. Dial.* v. §41 (1713) 523 That I lose not my Repose this Night, or Dream affrightfully.

affrighting (əˈfraɪtɪŋ), *ppl. a. arch.* [f. AFFRIGHT *v.* + -ING².] Frightening, terrifying.
1599 A. M. *Gabelhouer's Bk. Physic* 376/1 She may also vse therof in all affrighting sicknesses. **1651** JER. TAYLOR *Serm.* I. xxvii. 344 We never heard his noises, nor have seen his affrighting shapes. **1726** PENN *Tracts* Wks. I. 558 Which needs not the extraordinary and affrighting Obligation of an Oath.

affrightment (əˈfraɪtmənt). *arch.* [f. AFFRIGHT *v.* + -MENT.]
1. † The action of frightening or terrifying, intimidation; also, a cause of fear. *Obs.*
a **1619** DONNE *Biathan.* (1648) 215 Which accompanie it with so much horror and affrightment. **1673** *Ladies Calling* II. ii. §36. 77 Invisible affrightments, the beloved methods of nurses and servants. **1721** STRYPE *Eccl. Mem.* IV. 67 Affrightments..which much terrified the mean-spirited.
2. The fact or state of being frightened; fright, sudden fear or alarm.
1604 T. WRIGHT *Passions of Mind* II. iii. 65 Choler causeth ..feares, affrightments, ill successe, and such like. **1693** LOCKE *Educ.* §167 Passionate Words or Blows from the Tutor fill the Child's Mind with Terror and Affrightment. **1748** RICHARDSON *Clarissa* vii. (1811) I. 47 [I looked] at him, when I could glance at him, with disgust little short of affrightment. *a* **1834** LAMB *Dram. Writers* 531 Their terrors want dignity, their affrightments are without decorum.

affront (əˈfrʌnt), *v.* Also 4–5 **afrount, afront.** [a. OFr. *afronte-r, afrunte-r* (cf. Pr. and Sp. *afrontar*, It. *affrontare*):—late L. *affrontā-re, adfrontā-re* f. *ad front-em* to the face. *Afronter* has in OFr. the meaning 'to strike on the forehead, to slap in the face'; hence, *fig.* to insult one to his face. The lit. meaning is not found in Eng.]
1. To insult (a person or thing personified) to his face, to treat with avowed or open indignity.
c **1315** *Pol. Songs* (1839) 337 An if a pore man speke a word, he shal be foule afrounted. **1393** LANGL. *P. Pl.* C. XXIII. 5 With neode ich mette That afrontede me foule. **1577** HELLOWES tr. *Gueuara's Gold. Ep.* 2 Not to honor vs, but to affront vs. **1665** GLANVILLE *Scepsis Sci.* i. 1 We cannot, without affronting the Divine Goodness, deny but that at first we were made wise and happy. **1757** BURKE *Abridgm. Eng. Hist.* Wks. X. 496 The Duke of Austria whom he [Richard I] had personally affronted at the siege of Acre. **1783** COWPER *Lett.* 31 May, Wks. 1876, 132 The law of our land is affronted if we say the king dies. **1824** W. IRVING *T. of Trav.* II. 34 It would have been ruin to affront them.
2. To put to the blush; to offend the modesty or self-respect of; to cause to feel ashamed. *refl.* To feel affronted, to blush (*obs.*). (Said of the feeling produced rather than of the act or purpose).
1340 *Ayenb.* 229 Vor huo þet him y[e]fþ to voule wordes, hi ham ssolle naȝt ssamie and afrounti, þet is to zigge, hi lyezeþ þe ssame. **1673** CAVE *Primit. Chr.* II. ii. 33 Without affronting their modesty. **1707** FARQUHAR *Beaux' Strat.* I. i. 9 Let me look you full in the Face, and I'll tell you whether you can affront me or no. **1741** H. WALPOLE *Lett. to H. Mann* 13 (1834) I. 38 Your friend Lord Sandwich affronted his Grace of Grafton extremely. **1809** PINKNEY *Trav. France* 22 [He] would have affronted you by his sulky reserve. *c* **1860** MAURICE *Mor. & Metaph. Philos.* IV. viii. §56. 498 [It] does not affront the family feeling.
3. To face in defiance; confront. Now chiefly *fig.*, as ***to affront death.***
1563 GRAFTON *Q. Mary* an. 6 (R.) King Philip and the French King with two most puyssaunt armies affronted eche other neere vnto the water of Some. **1596** SPENSER *F.Q.* IV. iii. 22 Who, him affronting soone, to fight was readie prest. **1661** BRAMHALL *Just. Vind.* vii. 188 How their Kings ..have all of them, in all ages, affronted and curbed the Roman Court. **1856** BRYANT *Knight's Epitaph* 37 He.. affronted death In battle-field. **1863** KINGLAKE *Crimea* (1877) III. i. 50 He was affronting great risk without due motive.
†**b.** To meet in hostile encounter, to attack. *Obs.*
1600 HOLLAND *Livy* I. xxv. 18 g, These brave brethren.. affronted [*concurrunt*] one another, and with cruell and mortall weapons gave the charge. **1642** ROGERS *Naaman* 96 A shrewd right winde, gets into the hollow of the tree, and affronts it on the rotten side. **1700** DRYDEN *Fabl. Cock & Fox* 643 [He] affronted once a cock of noble kind, And either lam'd his legs or struck him blind.
†**4.** To meet intentionally or of purpose, to throw oneself in the way of, accost, address. *Obs.*
1602 SHAKS. *Haml.* III. i. 31 That he, as 'twere by accident, may there Affront Ophelia. **1633** T. ADAMS *Exp. 2 Pet.* ii. 13 (1865) 458/1 So Jezebel painted her face, and affronted Jehu out of the window.
5. To front, to face in position; to look toward. *arch.*
1600 HOLLAND *Livy* XLIII. xviii. 1166 m, Macedonie, which regardeth and affronteth Illyricum. **1655** FULLER *Ch. Hist.* I. v. 33 But it abated the Puissance thereof [*i.e.* of Mercia], because on the West it affronted the Britans, being deadly enemies. *a* **1658** CLEVELAND *Gen. Poems, &c.* (1677) 166 We see the Sun better by looking into the Waters, than by affronting his Beams. **1873** BROWNING *Red Cott. N.-Cap Country* 654 On emergence, what affronts our gaze?
†**6.** *fig.* To face anticipatively; to prepare to meet; look out for. *Obs. rare.*
1611 SHAKS. *Cymb.* IV. iii. 29 Your preparation can affront no lesse Then what you heare off. Come more, for more you're ready.
†**7.** *causal.* To confront one thing with another; to set face to face. *Obs. rare.*
1606 SHAKS. *Tr. & Cr.* III. ii. 173 That my integritie and truth to you, Might be affronted with the match and waight Of such a winnowed puritie in loue.

affront (əˈfrʌnt), *sb.* [f. the vb. Cf. Fr. *affront* (16th c. in Littré).]
1. An insult offered to the face; a word or act expressive of intentional disrespect; a purposed indignity; an open insult or outrage; *esp.* in the phrases ***to put an affront upon, offer an affront to.***
1598 BARRET *Theor. Warres* IV. i. 102 Whereat no man ought to be offended, or take it for any affront. **1671** MILTON *P.R.* III. 160 Oft have they violated The temple, oft the law with foul affronts. **1678** BUNYAN *Pilgr.* I. 62 Though they had offered great affronts to his Person and proceedings. **1855** MACAULAY *Fredk. Gt.* 59 To resent his affronts was perilous. **1876** FREEMAN *Norm. Conq.* I. App. 630 It was certainly something to have put an open affront upon the Eastern king.
2. Offence to one's dignity or modesty, felt indignity.
1662 DRYDEN *Sat. Dutch* 27 To one well-born the affront is worse and more, When he's abused and baffled by a boor. **1716–18** LADY M. W. MONTAGUE *Lett.* II. xliv. 16 These women..look upon this..as the greatest disgrace and affront that can happen to them. **1769** *Junius Lett.* xxxv. 160 Such an object as it would be an affront to you to name. **1784** COWPER *Lett.* Mar. 29 Wks. 1876, 164 Candidates are creatures not very susceptible of affronts. **1816** SCOTT *Old Mort.* 65 The unexpected, and, as she deemed it, indelible affront, which had been brought upon her dignity. *Mod. adage.* 'Affronts are as they are taken.'
†**3.** Hostile encounter, attack, assault. *Obs.*
1599 HAKLUYT *Voy.* II. 229 [They] that were not slaine in the first affront of the entrance into the citie. **1671** MILTON *Samson* 529 And dreaded On hostile ground, none daring my affront. **1678** BUNYAN *Pilgr.* I. 103 He met with no other affront from Apollyon.
†**4.** A position of hostility or defiance; *concr.* an obstacle. *Obs.*
1642 ROGERS *Naaman* 94 Even Ministers are often great affronts in the way of poore soules. **1644** HEYLIN *Life of Laud* I. 45 His Studies in Divinity, in the exercise whereof he met with some affronts and oppositions. **1648** SYMMONS *Vind. Chas. I*, 6 To suffer it to continue in affront to their general ordinance.
†**5.** An encounter or meeting generally; accost. *Obs.*
1614 J. COOKE *Green's Tu quoq.* (Dodsl.) VII. 95 This I must caution you of, in your affront or salute, never to move your hat. **1632** HEYWOOD *Iron Age* I. II. i. 294 Whom we wil giue a braue and proud affront.

affronted (əˈfrʌntɪd), *ppl. a.* [f. AFFRONT *v.* + -ED. In sense 3 used to translate Fr. *effronté.*]
1. Insulted, offended, injured in one's dignity or modesty. (Refers to the state of feeling of the recipient of the affront.)
1706 *Col. Rec. Penn.* II. 284 He declared he was not at all affronted. **1760** G. LYTTELTON *Dialog. of Dead* xxix. (1776) II. 377, I trusted the justification of my Affronted Innocence to the opinion of my Judges. **1855** MACAULAY *Hist. Eng.* IV. 153 The affronted patrician. **1879** MISS BRADDON *Violet* III. 231 'Your mind wants balance,' said Miss Skipwith, affronted at this frivolity.
†**2.** Fronted, faced. *Obs.*
1586 FERNE *Blazon of Gentrie* 261 Shadowed with woodes and affronted with a large parke. **1708** J. CHAMBERLAYNE *St. Gt. Brit.* II. III. x. (1743) 429 Their heads upward, and affronted inward.
†**3.** [after Fr. *effronté.*] Brazen-faced, impudent; full of effrontery. *Obs.*
1656 EARL MONM. *Advt. fr. Parnassus* 66 An act of shameless and affronted impudency.

† **aˈffrontedly**, *adv. Obs.* [f. AFFRONTED *a.* 3 + -LY².] With effrontery; impudently, shamelessly.
1656 EARL MONM. *Advt. fr. Parnassus* 341 That Mahomet ..did affrontedly laugh at sacred things. **1755** CARTE *Hist. Eng.* IV. 37 The lawyers..since the beginning of his reign had most affrontedly trodden upon his prerogative.

† **aˈffrontedness.** *Obs.* [f. AFFRONTED *a.* 3 + -NESS.] Brazenfacedness, effrontery, impudence.
1656 EARL MONM. *Advt. fr. Parnassus* 228 With unheard of affrontedness, he made the whole world see, that he made use of heresie to work division amongst people, &c.

‖**affrontee** (afrɔ̃te, əˈfrʌntiː), *a. Her.* [Fr. *affronté*, pa. pple. of *affronte-r*: see AFFRONT *v.*]
1. Face to face; front to front; also called *confrontee.*
1751 CHAMBERS *Cycl.*, *Affronté*, in heraldry, is understood of animals borne in an escutcheon as facing, or with their heads turned toward each other.
2. Looking frontwise or towards the beholder.
1766 PORNY *Elem. Herald.* (1787) 151 If the Figure is set with the face looking frontways or forwards, this Position is denoted by the term *Affrontee.* **1868** CUSSANS *Handbk. Herald.* xiv. 168 The Helmet of Dukes and Marquesses also stands affronté.

affrontee (əˌfrʌnˈtiː), *sb.* [f. AFFRONT *v.* + -EE.] One who receives an affront; an insulted person.
1833 LYTTON *England* I. iv. (1840) 221 The affront once given, out at once go affronter and affrontee; they fight first and retract afterwards.

affronter (əˈfrʌntə(r)). [f. AFFRONT *v.* + -ER¹.]
†**1.** One who impudently deceives; a pretender. [Cf. mod.Fr. *affronteur.*]
1598 FLORIO, *Cantonière*, a cozener, a conycatcher, a deceiuer, an affronter. **1631** MASSINGER *Beleeve as you list* III. ii, Must I, because you say soe, Beleeve that this most miserable kinge is A false affronter?
2. One who affronts, or insults to the face.
1654 GAYTON *Festiv. Notes* IV. xxv. 283 And shee reveng'd th' affronter with a prong. **1833** [see AFFRONTEE].

† **aˈffrontery.** *Obs.* Put for EFFRONTERY.
1679 PRANCE *Addl. Narr.* 7 They have since confessed *that*..but proceed in their affrontery, to deny *this.*

† **aˈffrontfully**, *adv. Obs.* [f. AFFRONT *sb.* + -FUL + -LY².] In an affronting manner; insultingly.
1754 P. H. *Hiberniad* iv. 31 Ought then a Country..so productive of great Men, in every Walk, be affrontfully called Bœotia?

affronting (əˈfrʌntɪŋ), *vbl. sb.* [f. AFFRONT *v.* + -ING¹.] (Now mostly gerundial.)
1. The action of offering indignity or open insult; insulting defiance.
1611 COTGR., *Avillonnement*, an affronting, vexing. **1677** R. GILPIN *Dæmonol. Sacra* (1867) 388 It is no less than the open affronting of God by abusing His own favours. **1702** *Case of W. Penn* 8 By their affronting of it [the Act], and making Laws repugnant, and in opposition to it.
2. The action of facing or encountering.
1613 HAYWARD *Norm. Kings* 67 By affronting of both the Armies. **1856** RUSKIN *Mod. Painters* IV. v. xix. §15 This endurance or affronting of fearful images.

affronting (əˈfrʌntɪŋ), *ppl. a.* [f. AFFRONT *v.* + -ING².] Insulting to the face; openly offensive.
1724 WATTS *Logick* I. iv. §3 (1813) 344 Some [words] are clean and decent..others are affronting and reproachful. **1748** RICHARDSON *Clarissa* xv. (1811) II. 98 Had you not been so rudely affronting to him. **1869** R. LYTTON *Orval* 163 The blazon'd boast of his affronting flag.

affrontingly (əˈfrʌntɪŋlɪ), *adv.* [f. prec. + -LY².] In a manner which affronts; with personal indignity.
1698 *Christ Exalted* §23. 18 It looks very Boldly and Affrontingly, to teach the Holy God to speak. **1826** MISS MITFORD *Our Village* Ser. II. (1863) 271 Affrontingly gracious or astoundingly impertinent by fits and starts.

affrontingness (əˈfrʌntɪŋnɪs). [f. as prec. + -NESS.] Insulting manner or demeanour.
1853 LYNCH *Self-Improvem.* v. 124 Then there will be class pretence, hauteur, and affrontingness.

affrontive (əˈfrʌntɪv), *a.* [f. AFFRONT *v.* + -IVE, in imitation of words like *effect-ive* in which *-ive* is properly added to the L. ppl. stem.] Of affronting character or tendency.
1659 GAUDEN *Tears of Ch.* 510 Affrontive to the glory [of] God and the Honor of the Catholick Church. **1704** LOGAN in *Pa. Hist. Soc. Mem.* IX. 331 Rude and most affrontive language. **1748** RICHARDSON *Clarissa* iv. (1811) I. 23 Their behaviour..was very cold and disobliging, but as yet not directly affrontive. **1823** LAMB *Elia* Ser. II. xxiv. (1865) 410 The affrontive quality of the primitive enquiry.

aˈffrontiveness. ?*Obs.*⁻⁰ [f. prec. + -NESS.] The quality of being affrontive; personal insolence.
1721 in BAILEY; whence in ASH, TODD, etc.

†**aˈffrontment.** *Obs. rare*⁻¹. [a. Fr. *affrontement*, f. *affronte-r*: see AFFRONT *v.* and -MENT.] The action of encountering or opposing; rebuff.
1611 SPEED *Hist. Gt. Brit.* IX. xvi. (1632) 834 Vpon this affrontment he suspended the execution of that designe.

†**aˈffrontous,** *a. Obs. rare*⁻¹. [ad. Sp. *afrentoso*, f. *afrenta, afronta*, affront; cf. also Fr. *affronteur, -euse.*] Full of affront; insulting; hostile.
1598 BARRET *Theor. Warres* v. iii. 180 Those [men] are most affrontous..when being enterprised with temeritie.

†**aˈffronture.** *Obs.* [f. AFFRONT *v.* + -URE after analogy of *procedure*, etc.] The action of facing or meeting in hostility; encounter, assault.
1721 STRYPE *Eccl. Mem.* II. 240 At any approach or affronture of the enemy..they used commonly..to begin the flight.

†**ˈaffuage.** *Obs.* [a. Fr. *affouage*, f. OFr. *afouer, afoer*, to furnish with fuel:—late L. *affocā-re* to make a fire, f. *ad* to + *focus* fire.] (See quot.)
1753 CHAMBERS *Cycl. Supp., Affuiage, Affuiagium*, in antient customs, a right of cutting fuel-wood in a forest, or the like, for maintaining family-fire. **1847** CRAIG, *Affuage.*

†**aˈffulsion.** *Obs.*⁻⁰ [f. L. *affuls- ppl. stem of *affulgē-re* to shine upon + -ION¹, as if ad. L. **affulsiōn-em.*] 'A shining upon.' Bailey 1731.

†**affund,** *v. Obs. rare*⁻¹. [ad. L. *affund-ĕre*; see AFFUSE.] To pour upon.
1657 TOMLINSON *Renou's Dispens.* 664 Oyl with red or white wine affunded.

†**aˈffurnish,** *v. Obs. rare*⁻¹. [f. *af-* (= A- *pref.* 11) + FURNISH.] To furnish, provide.
a **1641** BP. MOUNTAGU *Acts & Mon.* 482 For this, therefore, it was expedient to be before affurnished.

affuse (əˈfjuːz), *v. rare.* [f. L. *affūs-* ppl. stem of *affund-ĕre* to pour upon; f. *ad-* to + *fund-ĕre* to pour. Cf. *confuse.*] To pour upon.
1683 SALMON *Doron Med.* II. 424 Affuse upon it the quintessence of Iron. **1806** BRANDE in *Phil. Trans.* XCVI. 372 I now stopped the distillation, and affused alcohol.

affused (əˈfjuːzd), *ppl. a.* [f. prec. + -ED.] Poured upon or into anything.
1676 in *Phil. Trans.* XI. 772 The affused blood does, after a sort, stagnate. **1683** SALMON *Doron Med.* I. 185 Rhenish wine affused on Salt of Tartar.

affusion (əˈfjuːʒən). [ad. (directly or through Fr. *affusion*, 16th c. in Littré.) L. **affūsiōn-em* n. of action f. *affund-ĕre*: see AFFUSE.]
1. A pouring on or into; as of water upon the body. Hence used of one method of administering baptism.
1615 CROOKE *Body of Man* 33 As it were an affusion or confluence of blood. **1652** FRENCH *Yorksh. Spa* iv. 45 Water is used outwardly..by way of aspersion or affusion (*i.e.*) sprinkling or pouring on. *a* **1677** BARROW *Serm.* (1716) II. 227 God anointed him not with an external affusion of material oil. **1780** KIRWAN in *Phil. Trans.* LXXI. 26 Growing milky on the affusion of pure distilled water. **1800** HENRY *Epit. Chem.* (1808) 238 Wash..with repeated affusions of warm water. **1872** O. SHIPLEY *Gloss. Eccl. Terms* 245 Affusion being allowed only when the child or person to be baptized is weak in health.
2. *Med.* A remedy in fevers, consisting in pouring on the patient a quantity of water, varying in temperature according to his state, but usually from 50° to 60° or 70° Fahr. Also *fig.*
1803 W. TAYLOR in *Ann. Rev.* I. 273 From the eruptive fever of democratic effervescence, countries recover by slight and temperate affusions of concession. **1844** T. GRAHAM *Dom. Med.* 752 In very acute attacks of yellow fever..we resort to the use of purgatives, and the cold affusion.
†**3.** A swelling or development of anything pulpy. *Obs. rare.*
1615 CROOKE *Body of Man* 127 A Parenchyma..or a fleshy affusion, very soft, thin, loose, and spongious.

†**aˈffy,** *v. Obs.* Forms: 4 **afye, (afyghe),** 4–6 **affye,** 4–7 **affie,** 4–8 **affy.** [a. OFr. *afie-r, afye-r*:—late L. *affīdā-re*, f. *ad.* to + *fīdāre* to trust, f. *fīdus* trusty, faithful, f. *fides* faith. Refash. in later Fr. as *affier*, whence Eng. *affy.*]
1. *trans.* To trust, confide (a thing to a person); but from the beginning *refl.* To confide oneself, trust *to, on,* or *in.*
c **1300** *K. Alis.* 4753 Joliflich he may hym in her afyghe. *c* **1325** *E.E. Allit. P.* C. 331 þose vnwyse ledes þat affyen hym in vanyté. *c* **1380** *Sir Ferumb.* 756 My godes þat y me affied on. *a* **1400** *St. Alexius* 178 To god he gan hym al Affye. *c* **1450** LONELICH *Grail* xxvi. 61 In him gan sche hire affye Aboven alle other. **1575** TURBERVILE *Bk. Venerie* 112 Let them never affie themselves in yong houndes. **1578** FENTON *Hist. Guicciardin* (1618) 232 Somewhat affying themselues in the great promises he made. **1613** *York Registry MS. Slenningford*, I much affie myself in Mr. Heughe Best' just & freindlie dealing.
2. *intr.* (by omission of refl. pron.) To confide, trust, rely, put trust. Const. *in*, rarely *on.*
1303 R. BRUNNE *Handl. Synne* 10241 þo þat þou saghe lyke maumetrye On worldly þyng þey most affye. **1330** —— *Chron.* 78 On þis Gospatrick William gan affie. **1375** BARBOUR *Bruce* x. 271 Tharfor in hym affyit he. *a* **1470** TIPTOFT *Caesar's Comm.* (1530) ii. 2 In whose great wysedome.. Cæsar much affyed. **1559** *Myrroure for Mag., Gloucester* vi, Most faulte of fayth where I most affyed. **1587** TURBERVILE *Trag. T.* (1837) 228 In whom he did affye To shew the case. **1588** SHAKS. *Tit. A.* I. i. 47 Marcus Andronicus, so I do affie In thy vprightnesse and integrity. **1622** FOTHERBY *Atheom.* 5 Affying only upon his own wit and understanding. **1642** JER. TAYLOR *God's Judgem.* I. I. xxvii. 114 Antiochus for the small trust he affied in him.. would not commit any charge..into his hand.
3. *trans.* To confide in, trust, give faith to.
1330 R. BRUNNE *Chron.* 155 To schewe counseil & skille, þat not is to affie. **1587** TURBERVILE *Epit. & Sonnets* (1837) 326 So greatly she affied him, Whilest she did beare the sway. **1633** T. ADAMS *Exp. 2 Pet.* ii. 5 (1865) 329/2 Who would not rather affy God's word with one singular Noah, than be incredulous with the whole world?
4. To assure, affirm on one's faith (a thing or fact to a person); to make affidavit.
c **1500** *Partenay* 2308 Fair nece..here I you affy That your fadir Deth auenged is well. **1530** PALSGR. 418/2, I affye, I assure or make one certayne of a thynge by my promesse. It is nat for your honour thus by your othe to affye this thyng, and nowe to go from it. **1617** MINSHEU *Ductor* 166 To Affie, Assure, Affirme on his word or credite: *vide* to Assure.
5. To secure or make fast by solemn promise; to betroth or espouse (*sc.* to oneself, or as proxy for another); to take in marriage.
c **1500** *Partenay* 6052 Neuer..wold he noght mary..No woman wold betrouth neither affy. **1587** HOLINSHED *Chron.* III. 832/2 The said duke affied the lady Marie in the name of his maister king Lewes. **1603** DRAYTON *Barons Warres* III. lxxxiv, The Prince affyes faire Philip [= Philippa] at the last. **1627**—— *Agincourt, etc.* 68 Comming to Towers, there sumptuously affide: This one, whose like no age had seene before.
6. To betroth (any one) in marriage *to* (another); to affiance.
1576 LAMBARDE *Peramb. Kent* (1826) 322 The wise Duke ..for more safetie, affied him to his daughter, to be taken in marriage. **1593** SHAKS. *2 Hen. VI*, IV. i. 80 Daring to affye a mighty Lord Vnto the daughter of a worthlesse King. **1603** DRAYTON *Barons Warres* I. xiv, To whom thy only Daughter was affy'd. **1642** BIRD *Mag. Hon.* 34 He was affied to Alice the daughter of the Earl of Moreton. **1655** DIGGES *Compl. Ambass.* 13 He was suddenly accepted by that Q. to be affied in contract of Marriage with her. **1705** ROWE *Biter* III. Wks. 1792 I. 262, I would not affy my daughter to you. [*Meant to be formal and old-fashioned.*]
7. *fig.* To engage or bind in faith (a thing *to* a person or *vice versâ*).
1566 DRANT *Medic. Mor.* A, That none contente abyde In trayned trade, that whylome choyse or chaunce to them affyed. **1625** BP. MOUNTAGU *Appeal to Cæsar* 69 (T.) Personal respects rather seem to affie me unto that Synod.

†**aˈffy,** *sb. Obs.* Also 4–5 **affye, affie.** [f. the vb.] Trust, reliance.
c **1380** *Sir Ferumb.* 2167 Wommanes wyt goþ her & þer; in hymen ys noȝt affye. *c* **1430** *Cheuelere Assigne* 10 She sette her affye in Sathanas of helle.

Afghan (ˈæfgæn), *sb.* and *a.* Also 9 **Afghaun.** [Name of the people of Afghanistan, a country lying north of West Pakistan.]
A. *sb.* **1. a.** A native or inhabitant of Afghanistan. **b.** The language of the Afghan people (= PASHTO).
1784 H. VANSITTART *Let.* 3 Mar. in *Asiatick Res.* (1790) II. 68, I venture to lay before the Society the translation of an abridged history of the Aghâns, a tribe at different times subject to, and always connected with, the kingdoms of Persia and Hindustàn. **1787** C. HAMILTON *Hist. Relation Rohilla Afgans N. Provinces Hindostan* 39 When a successor to Azmut-Oolah was appointed from Delhi, the Afgan found himself in a condition to make his own terms. **1815** M. ELPHINSTONE *Acct. Kingdom of Caubul* II. ii. 165 The Pooshtoonwulle, or usage of the Afghauns; a rude system of customary law. **1842** C. FOX *Jrnl.* 28 May (1972) 124 Carlyle ..was terribly amused. 'Poor Little Queen! She'd be glad.. if the Afghans would but submit to her conditions.' **1909** *N.E.D.*, s.v. PUSHTOO, -TU *sb.* and *a.* The native name of the language of the Afghans. **1928** W. HAIG in *Cambr. Hist. India* III. vi. 160 The subsequent rebellions in Gujarāt and the Deccan were partly due to the severity of the restrictions placed upon Afghāns in India in consequence of Shāhū's revolt. **1933** L. BLOOMFIELD *Language* iv. 62 The principal dialect areas of modern Iranian are..eastward, the Pamir dialects, Afghan (Pushto), with some 4 million speakers, and Baluchi. **1974** *Encycl. Brit. Micropædia* I. 121/3 A national awakening began among the Afghans early in the 18th century. **1980** *Daily Tel.* 12 Jan. 18/3 Presumably Kinnock and his friends do not know Afghan either.
2. a. A blanket or wrap of knitted or crocheted wool. Also *attrib.*
1833 CARLYLE *Sartor Res.* I. v, in *Fraser's Mag.* VIII. 670/1 Afghaun shawls. **1868** ELIZ. PRENTISS *Let.* 13 Dec. in G. L. Prentiss *Life & Lett. E.P.* (1882) 260 Mr. P. has come up-stairs rolled up in your afghan. **1887** STOCKTON *Hundredth Man* xxxii. 375 Miss Burns was crocheting an afghan. **1947** J. STEINBECK *Wayward Bus* xiv. 195 The bedspread, now, a giant afghan she had knitted herself in little squares.
b. A kind of sheepskin coat or jacket worn with the skin side outside, sometimes embroidered and usu. having a shaggy border. In full, ***Afghan coat.***
1973 *New Musical Express* 21 July 45/2 (Advt.), Afghan sheepskin coat. **1974** *Ibid.* 16 Nov. 60 (Advt.), Embroidered sheepskin Afghan supplied by top leading importer. Three-quarter length in various shades of brown with white shaggy hair and colourful embroidery, cleaned and washed to minimise smell. **1976** *West Lancs. Even. Gaz.* 15 Dec. I. 3/7 (Advt.), Fun furs, Afghans and oddments at silly low prices. **1980** *N.Y. Times* 11 Dec. 6A/6 Special on Afghan coats, cheap. **1983** *Ibid.* 23 Oct. x. 33/1 Young Westerners.. flaunting floor-length Afghan coats.
3. A coarse-woven rug or carpet. Also *attrib.*
1877 F. H. BURNETT *Theo* iv. 89 It was an Afghan Miss Elizabeth was making now. **1901** J. K. MUMFORD *Oriental Rugs* xii. 236 Afghan carpets. **1920** T. E. LAWRENCE *Let.* 16 Feb. (1938) 299 As for the rugs, please take any that seem worthy to you. There were two Afghans in the Arab Bureau. **1960** *News Chron.* 12 Sept. 6/4 Good quality Afghans, say 12 ft. × 9 ft., can cost anything from £110 to £250.
4. In full ***Afghan (grey)hound.*** A swift hunting dog of the Near East resembling a shaggy greyhound. Cf. BARUKHZY.
1895 [see BARUKHZY]. **1905** H. DE BYLANDT *Dogs of All Nations* I. 767 (*caption*) Ideal Afghan Greyhound. **1911** *Greyhound Stud Book* 228 The President read a letter.. admitting to the 'Appendix' of the Stud Book an imported Afghan greyhound. **1925** E. M. AITKEN *Pets* i. 28 For the purpose of classifying dogs on its registers the Kennel Club has two main divisions, sporting breeds and non-sporting breeds. These again are subdivided, the miscellaneous sporting kinds being Afghan Hounds, Basset Hounds, Beagles [etc.]. **1950** *Oxf. Jun. Encycl.* IX. 191 Carvings on the walls of the Balkh caves of Afghanistan of about 2200 B.C. show that already an Afghan Hound, almost the same as the modern Afghan, was established in that country.
B. *adj.* Of or pertaining to the Afghans or their language.
1787 C. HAMILTON *Hist. Relation Rohilla Afgans N. Provinces Hindostan* 27 The *Afgan Tartars*, whose numerous tribes (under the general denomination of PATANS) occupy all the mountainous country which forms the North-western boundary of Hindostan. **1815** [see NO *a.* 3 a]. **1833**, etc. [see senses A 2 and 4]. **1860** H. G. RAVERTY *Gulshan-i-Roh* p. v, During the last sixty years.. the cultivation of the Afghān language has, comparatively, declined. **1875** *Encycl. Brit.* I. 238 The Afghan chroniclers ..claim descent from King Saul..through a son whom they ascribe to him, called Jeremiah, who again had a son called Afghâna. **1879** GEO. ELIOT *Let.* 20 June (1956) V. 171 What a comfort that the Afghan war is concluded! *a* **1898** H. NEWBOLT 'He fell among Thieves' in *Island Race* 68 He did not see the starlight on the Laspur hills, Or the far Afghan snows. **1969** *Southerly* XXIX. 5 We..learned to..be cheeky to Chinese market-gardeners and Afghan pedlars. **1984** *Daily Tel.* 22 Sept. 8/7 (Advt.), Afghan slipper socks. .. Made in Afghanistan.

afghani (æfˈgɑːnɪ). [Pashto.] The principal monetary unit of Afghanistan, divided into 100 puls.
1927 *Statesman's Year-Bk.* 643 The following new currency was introduced in March 1926: Gold coins: the *amani*, equivalent to Rs. 20 Afghani, and the half-*amani* and the 20 *pooli*: silver coins, the Afghani rupee..and the half-Afghani. **1933** M. ALI *Progressive Afghanistan* xv. 186 Students, in addition to their monthly stipends of 50 Afghanis each, get free meals. **1934** AHMAD & AZIZ *Afghanistan* xiv. 125 The unit is an *Afghani* weighing ten grammes of silver, 900 fine, which is sub-divided into 100 *puls.* **1963** *Whitaker's Almanack* 821/1 The free rates..in June, 1960, were approximately..106 Afghanis = £1.

Afghanistanism (æfˈgænɪstəˌnɪz(ə)m). *U.S. colloq.* [f. the name of *Afghanistan* as the type of a distant land + -ISM.] Preoccupation (esp. of journalists) with events far distant, as a diversion from controversial issues at home (see quots.).
1961 H. B. JACKSON *Mass Communications Dict.* 6 *Afghanistanism*, a criticism leveled against newspaper editors for avoiding community causes and issues and for advocating causes and issues far enough away to remain unchallenged by unoriented readers. **1971** *Observer* 12 Sept. 7/4 The 'radical chic' find indignation easier about injustices in far-away America or Russia than those in our own midst: I believe this syndrome is called Afghanistanism. **1976** *Maclean's Mag.* 28 June 52 Afghanistanism..is a malady

that encourages pontification on problems far distant while conveniently ignoring the home front. **1980** *National Jrnl.* (U.S.) XII. IV. 153 In 1980,..with events in Afghanistan applying with deadly relevance to vital U.S. interests, President Carter has successfully contrived to give the practice of 'Afghanistanism' a totally opposite meaning. **1982** *Business Week* 14 June 15/1 Critics once scoffed that certain segments of the U.S. press suffered from 'Afghanistanism'... The malady..now deserves another name.

† **'afgod.** *Obs.* [OE. f. *af*, *æf* off, away + GOD; cogn. w. ON. *afguð*, OHG. *apcot*, mod.G. *abgott*; cf. Goth. *afguþs* impious, *afgudei* impiety.] The Old English word for idol or false god.

1793 *Gent. Mag.* XI. 1189 The figure on the stone was not intended to represent a griffin, but an Afgod. The Afgod was an image like a dragon placed at the feet of Woden.

afgodness. [f. prec. + -NESS.] Idolatry. (In Skinner 1671, Coles 1692, but not used since 1100.)

afibrinogenæmia (eɪˌfaɪbrɪnəʊdʒɛˈniːmɪə, æ-). *Path.* [mod.L., f. A- 14 + FIBRINOGEN + Gr. αἷμα blood: see -IA.] A condition resulting from the lack of or diminution in the amount of fibrinogen in the blood.

1943 *Biochem. Jrnl.* XXXVII. p. xvi, Studies on the Plasma Fibrinogen and other Protein Fractions in a Case of Afibrinogenaemia.

‖ **aficionado** (afiθioˈnaðo; anglicized as əfɪsɪəˈnɑːdəʊ). Pl. -os. [Sp. = amateur, f. pa. pple. of *aficionar* to become fond of, f. *afición* AFFECTION.] A devotee of bull-fighting; by extension an ardent follower of any hobby or activity.

1845 R. FORD *Handbk. Travellers in Spain* I. ii. 178 This sham fight is despised by the *torero* and *aficionado*, who aspire only to be in at the death. **1902** W. D. HOWELLS *Lit. & Life* iii. 58 The last [bull] was uncommonly fierce, and when his hindquarters came off or out, his forequarters charged joyously among the aficionados on the prisoners' side. **1957** *Times* 12 Oct. 7/6 The bull-fight is the most Spanish of spectacles... Some old *aficionados* will go so far as to say that it is dying.

1882 C. G. LELAND *Gypsies* 25 The *aficionados*, or Romany ryes, by whom I mean those scholars who are fond of studying life and language from the people themselves. **1928** F. O. LINDLEY *Diplomat off Duty* iv. 64 All amateurs, or to use a much more expressive Spanish word, *aficionados*, of bathing agree that the full flavour of the pastime is only tasted in beautiful surroundings. **1948** J. STEINBECK *Russian Jrnl.* (1949) iii. 37 A little swing band was led by Ed Gilmore, who is a swing *aficionado*. **1957** *Technology* Apr. 70/3 The *aficionados* of science fiction and golf. **1959** J. WAIN *Trav. Woman* 41, I didn't tell you I had a son who was an *aficionado* of railways, did I?

afield (əˈfiːld), *adv.* prop. *phr.* Forms: 1 on felda, 3 o felde, 4–5 a-felde, 6 afeld, 6– afield. [A *prep.*[1] in, on + FIELD.]

1. On or in the field, *esp.* of labour or battle.

a **1000** *Psalms* (Spl.) lxvii. 48 He sette foretácn his on felda Taneos. *c* **1400** *Sir Percev.* 1311 In felde for to fyght. **1591** SHAKS. *1 Hen. VI*, v. iv. 40 When thou didst keepe my Lambes a-field. **1606** —— *Tr. & Cr.* v. iii. 67 Æneas is afield. **1789** BURNS *Wks.* III. 376 My chief, amaist my only pleasure, At hame, a-fiel, at wark or leisure. **1873** DIXON *Two Queens* I. I. i. 1 Fernando was afield against the Moors in what he called a holy war. **1877** M. ARNOLD *Poems* I. 96 As afield the reapers cut a swath.

2. To or into the field; *hence*, to battle.

c **1230** *Bestiary* 398 [Ðe fox] goð o felde to a furg, And falled ðar-inne. **1377** LANGL. *P. Pl.* B. VI. 144 Helpe make morter Or bere mukke a-felde. **1566** UDALL *Royster Doyster* I. iv. (1847) 22 Oh your coustrelyng Bore the lanterne a field before the gozeling. **1676** HOBBES *Odyssey* x. 81 Then they a-field Their cattle drive. **1751** JOHNSON *Rambler* No. 138 ¶11 In harvest she rides afield in the waggon. **1870** MORRIS *Earthly Parad.* I. ii. 532 And in meantime afield he never went, Either to hunting or the frontier war.

3. Away from home, abroad; to or at a distance; *esp.* in phr. *far afield*. Also *fig.*

1413 LYDG. *Pylgr. Sowle* v. x. (1483) 101 Pacyence come pryckyng with a sobre chere and hitte Ire in the helme that it flewe a feld. **1536** BELLENDENE *Cron. Scotl.* (1821) I. 84 This Metellane..governit all materis, baith at hame and afeld, with gret felicite. **1850** KINGSLEY *Alt. Locke* xi. (1876) 124, I had..never been further afield than Fulham or Battersea Rise. **1880** SPALDING *Eliz. Demonol.* 9 It will prevent the student from straying too far afield in his reading.

‖ **afikoman, aphi-** (æfɪˈkəʊmən). Also afikomen, afikuman, etc. [Heb. *aphiqōmān*, f. Gr. ἐπικώμιον revel (G. Dalman).] Near the beginning of the Jewish Passover service, a piece broken from the second of the three cakes of unleavened bread and put aside to be eaten at the end of the meal.

1891 M. FRIEDLÄNDER *Jewish Rel.* II. 382 The part laid aside is called *afikuman*. **1892** I. ZANGWILL *Childr. Ghetto* II. I. xxv. 208 The *Afikuman* [ed. 1901, *Afikoman*], or *Motso* specially laid aside for the final morsel. **1905** *Westm. Gaz.* 20 Apr. 9/3 The Afikomen is always the centre of a little ceremony associated with..Jewish holidays, the giving of gifts. **1960** *Jewish Chron.* 8 Apr. 33/2 Grandpa split the middle matzo and hid half of it away as the *Afikoimon*.

† **a'file,** *v. Obs. rare*[−1]. Forms: 1 afýl-an. *Pa. pple.* 1 afýled, 3 afiled. [f. A- *pref.* 1 intensive + *fýl-an* to make foul; f. *fúl* foul. Cogn. w. mod.G. *erfäulen*.] To defile.

c **880** K. ÆLFRED *Gregory's Past. Care* liv. 419 Ðæt hi hi mæȝen eft afylan. *c* **1300** *K. Alis.* 1064 Men me cleputh quene afiled.

† **a'fill,** *v. Obs.* Also 2–3 afulle, 3 afeolle. [f. A- *pref.* 1 up + FILL. Cogn. w. Goth. *usfulljan*, OHG. *arfullan*, mod.G. *erfüllen*.]

1. To fill up, fill full; fulfil.

c **1000** ÆLFRIC *Gen.* IX. 1 Afyllað þa eorþan. *c* **1175** *Lamb. Hom.* 9 Ure drihten þa haued þa stronge ealde laȝe auulled mid þere newe. **1205** LAYAMON 12078 Fif scipe: of wimmonnen afulled. *Ibid.* 23554 þa burh wes wið innen: afulled mid monnien. *Ibid.* 28831 Afeolled mid blisse.

† **a'find,** *v. Obs.* Forms as in FIND. [f. A- *pref.* 1 out + FIND. Cogn. w. OHG. *arfindan*, mod.G. *erfinden*.] To find out, discover.

c **1000** *O.E. Gosp.* John viii. 4 þis wif wæs afundyn on unrihton hæmede. *c* **1200** *Trin. Coll. Hom.* 191 He auint mannes heorte emti of rihte bileue. **1205** LAYAMON 15852 þat þu scalt afinde a þisses daies ferste. *Ibid.* 30636 Al þat he auunde. *c* **1250** *Moral Ode* 56 ȝiue his for godes luue, eft heo hit scullen a-finden. *a* **1250** *Owl & Night.* 527 At than harde me mai avinde Wo geth forth, wo lith bi-hinde. *c* **1315** SHOREHAM 49 Thet thys ordre hedde Jhesus, We habbeth wel afounde. *c* **1430** *Octouian Imp.* 1659 Tho the Sarsenes afounde Her lord was slayn.

† **a'fine,** *adv. Obs.* Also 4–5 afyn(e, 5 affyn(e. [a. Fr. *à fin* at or to the end.] Finally; to the end, completely.

c **1330** *Arth. & Merl.* 50 Ac the eldest sone Constentine Was noble clerk and wise afine. *c* **1330** *Kyng of Tars* 780 Icham nou glad wel afyn. *a* **1400** CHAUCER *Rom. Rose* 3690 Til grapes be ripe and welle afyne. *c* **1420** *Liber Cure Coc.* (1865) 12 Take larde of porke..Hew hit in gobettis wele afyne. *c* **1460** *Emare* 913 When they wer well at ese afyne, Bothe of brede, ale, and wyne.

† **a'fingered,** *ppl. a. Obs.* 3–4. Also afingred, afingret. [For *af-hingered*, OE. *of-hyngred*, OFHUNGERED, f. OF + HUNGER. Cf. AHUNGERED.] Afflicted with hunger, famished, very hungry.

c **1300** *St. Brandan* 416 Hi were Afingred sore, for here mete was al i-do. *c* **1300** *Vox & Wolf* 2 A vox gon out of the wode go, Afingret so, that him wes wo. **1377** LANGL. *P. Pl.* B. VI. 269 After many manere metes his mawe is afyngred. **1547** BOORDE *Introd. Knowl.* (1870) 122 (*A Cornishman says*) Iche chaym yll afyngred.

afire (əˈfaɪə(r)), *adv.* and *pred. a.* prop. *phr.* Forms: 3 afur(e, 4 o fure, afyr, 4–5 afere, 5 afyre, 4– afire. The forms in *u* (y) are s.w., that in *e* Kentish. [A- *prep.*[1] 11 of state, in + FIRE. The full *on fyr* is not found early; Wyclif has *in fire*.]

1. On or in fire, in a state of burning or inflammation; *esp.* in phr. *to set afire*.

1205 LAYAMON 27109 þat sculden for Ardure Rome ifullen afure. **1297** R. GLOUC. 380 þe gret cyte of Medes suþþe afure he sette. *c* **1350** *Body & Soul* 347 The world shal al o fure ben. **1447** BOKENHAM *Lyvys Seyntys* 168 Wyth a brynnyng chere As alle the hous had been afere. **1480** CAXTON *Chron. Eng.* cxcii. 168 The scottes sette a fyre the stakkes of heye. **1647** FULLER *Good Thoughts* (1841) 135 If our clay cottage be not cooled with rest, the roof falls a fire. *a* **1845** HOOD *Ode to Son* i, Why, Jane! he'll set his pinafore a-fire! **1869** DICKENS *Lett.* (1880) II. 416 We have had our sitting-room chimney afire this morning.

2. *fig.* of passion, etc.

1382 WYCLIF *James* iii. 6 And it enflaumed, *or set afijre*, of helle, enflaumeth the wheel of oure birthe. [TINDALE, *Genev.*, a fyre.] **1384** CHAUCER *Leg. G. Wom.* 2493 The devyl sette here soules bothe a fere. **1604** T. WRIGHT *Passions of Mind* v. §4. 279 Lovers ire sets love afier. **1875** F. MYERS *Poems* 51 With trembling knees and heart afire.

a-first, *phr. Obs.*, at first: see FIRST.

a-five, *phr. Obs.*, in five (parts): see FIVE.

aflame (əˈfleɪm), *adv.* and *pred. a.* prop. *phr.* [A- *prep.*[1] 11 of state, in, into + FLAME.]

1. In or into flame; ablaze.

1555 BROOKES in Froude's *Hist. Eng.* VI. xxxiii. 374 But also set a-flame the fire already kindled. **1852** KINGSLEY *Androm.* 222 Lovest thou cities aflame, fierce glows, and the shrieks of the widow?

2. In a glow of light or colour, such as is caused by the reflection of flame.

1798 COLERIDGE *Anc. Mar.* III. vii, The western wave was all aflame. The day was well nigh done! **1872** DIXON *Switzers* xviii. 177 At night, the city is aflame with lamps.

3. *fig.* In a glow of excitement or intense eagerness.

1856 MRS. BROWNING *Aur. Leigh* III. 123 A tiptoe Danae, overbold and hot, Both arms a-flame to meet her wishing Jove Halfway. **1860** W. COLLINS *Wom. in White* I. 55, I am all aflame with curiosity. **1879** FARRAR *St. Paul* II. 562, I remind thee to fan aflame the gift of God which is in thee.

† **a'flaming,** *ppl. a. Obs.* [pr. pple. of vb. *aflame*, var. of ENFLAME: see A- *pref.* 10.] Inflaming, flaming, blazing up.

c **1623** *Revel. Golias* in *App. to Mapes' Poems* (1841) 291 The sting of tongues the aflaming fire doth feed.

† **a-'flank,** *adv.* prop. *phr. Obs.* [A *prep.*[1] 4 in, on + FLANK.] In flank, on the flank or side.

1601 HOLLAND *Pliny* XVII. xxiii, Afront..fortie foot: but aflanke, or on the side, twentie.

aflare (əˈflɛə(r)), *adv.* and *pred. a.* [f. A *prep.*[1] + FLARE.] Flaring; spread out, expanded; also, blazing, glowing. esp. *fig.*

1908 T. HARDY *Dynasts* III. I. vii. 40 Large pieces of canvas aflare sail away on the gale like balloons. **1924** R. CAMPBELL *Flaming Terrapin* iii. 46 Beauty ran all aflare Through nerve and bone. *Ibid.* 52 Wolfing huge coals with iron jaws aflare. **1959** *Times* 24 Mar. 15/3 When her interest was engaged the broad, strong features would be aflare with excitement.

† **a'flash,** *v. Obs. rare*[−1]. [f. A- *pref.* 1 intensive + FLASH *v.*[1]] To pour water in quantity and with force; to dash, to splash.

1387 TREVISA *Higden* Rolls Ser. I. 63 þe Rede see is nouȝt rede of kynde, but aflascheþ and wascheþ oon rede clyues and stones.

aflash (əˈflæʃ), *adv.* and *pred. a.* [f. A *prep.*[1] + FLASH.] Flashing; in a flash.

1876 G. M. HOPKINS *Poems* (1918) 85 And crush-silk poppies aflash. **1885** W. B. YEATS in *Dublin Univ. Rev.* July 136/2 Your eyes are all a-flash.

aflat (əˈflæt), *adv.* [A *prep.*[1] of position + FLAT.] In a flat position, flatly.

c **1330** *Arth. & Mer.* 9033 And Aroans with the swerd aflat. **1626** BACON *Sylva* §426 Lay all his branches a-flat upon the Ground. **1812** W. TENNANT *Anster Fair* IV. xxvii, Swop! there a jumper falls aflat upon the ground.

aflatoxin (æfləˈtɒksɪn). *Biochem.* [f. *A. fla(vus* (see def.) + TOXIN.] Any of a group of related pentacyclic lactones produced by the moulds *Aspergillus flavus* and *A. parasiticus* and highly toxic to most animals, causing cancer and liver damage; any closely related synthetic compound.

1962 *Toxicity assoc. Groundnuts* (Agric. Res. Council Interdepartmental Working Party) 2 *Aspergillus flavus*.. was shown to produce the toxic factor when grown on sterile, non-toxic nuts. In view of its origin, the toxic factor was given the name 'aflatoxin'. **1978** G. GREENE *Human Factor* III i. 102 Peanuts when they go bad produce a mould... The mould produces a group of highly toxic substances known collectively as aflatoxin. **1980** *McGraw-Hill Yearbk. Sci. & Technol.* 93/1 Foods are monitored routinely for aflatoxins.

aflaunt (əˈflɔːnt), *adv.* [f. A *prep.*[1] 11 of state + FLAUNT *v.*] In a flaunting state or position.

1568 WITHALS *Dict.* (1608) 219 (N.) Hee that of himselfe doth bragge, boast, and vaunt, Hath ill neighbours about him to set him aflaunt. **1589** PUTTENHAM *Eng. Poesie* (1869) 305 For a Courtier to know how to weare a fether, and set his cappe a flaunt. **1840** BROWNING *Sordello* IV. 363 Pennons of every blazon once a-flaunt, Men prattled.

† **'afle,** *v. Obs.* Also 3 avele. [a. ON. *afl-a*.] To gain, get, earn.

c **1200** *Trin. Coll. Hom.* 159 His mede shal ben þanne garked alse hit beoð here aueled. *Ibid.* [They] auelen · þat men hem blescen. *c* **1200** *Ormul.* 7903 Forr cnapechild iss afledd wel Affterr weppmanne kinde.

† **a'flee,** *v. Obs.* Forms as in FLEE. [f. A- *pref.* 1 away + FLEE, OE. *fleó-n*. Cogn. w. OHG. *irfliohan*, mod.G. *erfliehen*.] To flee away.

a **1000** *Guthlac* (Grein) 475 Gæst afliþ. **1205** LAYAMON 19076 þa sæiden þa cnihtes..þat þe king wes ifloȝen [**1250** afloȝe]. **1380** *Sir Ferumb.* 3132 And were afloȝen grete & smalle. **1387** TREVISA *Higden* Rolls Ser. V. 429 þe kyng.. sente for þe bisshoppes þat were aflowe. **1557** in Hazl. *E.P.P.* III. 129 He thought him well a fledde.

† **a'fleme,** *v. Obs.* Forms: 1 aflým-an, afliem-en; 2–3 aflem-en. [f. A- *pref.* 1 away + FLEME.] To drive away, expel.

1001 *O.E. Chron.*, Hy ðær aflýmede wurdon. *c* **1130** *Ibid.* (Laud MS.) an. 1124 And his sunu Willelm[he] aflemde ut of Normandi. *c* **1175** *Lamb. Hom.* 195 þene loðe deouel.. Aulem urom me ueor awei. **1205** LAYAMON 8466 He me a-flemde: sone from hirede.

† **a'fley,** *v. Obs.* or *dial.* Forms: 1 aflýȝ-an, aflíȝ-an; 2–3 aflei-en, avlei-en. *Pa. pple.* 5 aflayed, 8– *Sc.* afley'd. [f. A- *pref.* 1 away, off + *flí-ȝan* to put to flight: see FLEY.]

1. To put to flight, chase away.

c **1000** ÆLFRIC *Hom.* (Sweet 80) ȝé áflíȝdon deóflu. *c* **1000** —— *Gram.* xxviii. 166 Ic afliȝe mine fýnd. *c* **1230** *Ancren Riwle* 136 þes ston..avleieð attri þinges.

2. To discomfit: in *pa. pple.* dismayed, frightened. (Still used in Scotch.)

c **1450** *Merlin* 296 Tha[n] was the kynge loot sore aflayed. *a* **1774** R. FERGUSSON *King's Birthd.* (1845) 2 The herds would gather in their nowt..Hafflins afley'd to bide thereout To hear thy thunder.

a-flicker (əˈflɪkə(r)), *adv.* prop. *phr.* [A *prep.*[1] of state + FLICKER.] In a flickering state or condition.

1875 BROWNING *Aristoph. Apol.* 225 With age are limbs a-shake And force a-flicker!

aflight, obs. form of AFFLICT *sb.* and *ppl. a.*

† **a'flight.** *Obs. rare.* [f. A- *pref.* 1 away + FLIGHT. Not recorded in OE., but cf. *afléon* to flee away, *aflíȝan* to put to flight, *aflýȝe* flight.] Flight, flying.

c **1220** *Leg. St. Kath.* 2020 An engel..wið feorliche afluhte fleoninde aduneward. *c* **1435** *Torr. Portugal* 2043 She flew in afflight, To her birdus was she boun.

†a'flight, *v. Obs. rare*$^{-1}$. [f. A- *pref.* 11 + FLIGHT.] ? To put to flight.
1583 STANYHURST *Æneid* (Arb.) 57 Also such old enimies: policy that former aflighted And coucht in corners, with a vengeance freshly retyred.

afloat (ə'fləʊt), *adv.* and *pred. a.*, formerly *phr.* Forms: 1 **on flōte, on flōt**, 2–6 **on flote**, 6– **a flote**, 6–7 **a floate**, 6– **a-float, afloat**. [f. ON *prep.* + FLOAT *sb.*]
I. *literally.*
1. On the sea, or on any water of sufficient depth to buoy up anything; hence, in a floating condition, in opposition to being aground; at sea, in opposition to being in dock or in the dockyard. (Used also of figurative seas and streams, *e.g.* of *life.*)
993 *Battle of Maldon* (Sweet) 41 We willað..ús tó scipe gangan, on flot féran. **1023** *Charter of Canute* in *Cod. Diplom.* IV. 23 Ðæt scip bið aflote. **1070** *O.E. Chron.* (Laud MS.) an. 1037 Wæron ðá útlaȝas ealle on flote. **1587** GOLDING *De Mornay* viii. 98 The first Ship that euer was set a flote, was vpon the red Sea. **1750** JOHNSON *Rambler* No. 29 ⁋10 Whatever is afloat in the stream of time. **1756** C. LUCAS *Ess. on Waters* I. 216 In baths..a gross fat substance has been found afloat. **1851** HELPS *Friends in C.* I. 27 Send them afloat in the wide sea of humanity.
2. Of persons or goods: At sea; on board ship; *esp.* in the navy or fleet; in naval service.
1330 R. BRUNNE *Chron.* 169 Now er alle on flote, God gif þam grace to spede. **1704** ADDISON *Italy* (J.) There are generally several hundred loads of timber afloat. **1815** WELLINGTON in *Gurwood's Desp.* XII. 239 He commanded the force afloat. **1879** *Standard* 15 Apr., The quantity [of wheat] afloat is still as much as 1,421,000 qrs.
3. In a state of overflow or submersion.
1591 SPENSER *Bellay's Vis.* ix. 7 Whose out-gushing flood Ran bathing all the creakie shore aflot. **1745** GAY *Wks.* VI. 256 The meads are all afloat, the haycocks swim. **1836** MARRYAT *Midsh. Easy* xxii. 104 There was no trouble in wetting them, for the main deck was afloat.
4. In a state of suspension or floating motion in the air; buoyed up or spread out lightly like a thing floating.
1825 *Br. Jonathan* III. 316 His own hair afloat over it; like a vapour of spun gold. **1855** BROWNING *Men & Wom.* II. 5 Carelessly passing with your robes afloat.
II. From the state of a ship or other body floating on the sea, with reference to its liberty of motion, its being on the surface, its being at the mercy of the waves, its motion hither and thither, etc., are derived various figurative uses of *afloat*; as,
5. Free from embarrassments, like a ship off the ground; out of debt, paying one's way; having 'one's head above water.'
1538 LATIMER *Serm. & Rem.* (1845) 412 Shortly cometh on my half-year's rent; and then I shall be afloat again. *c* **1600** SHAKS. *Sonn.* 80 Your shallowest help will hold me up afloat. **1644** HOWELL *Lett.* (J.) My heart is still afloat; my spirits shall not sink.
6. Fully started in any career.
1559 *Myrroure for Mag.*, *Cade* xi. 1 Fortune setting us a flote. **1826** DISRAELI *Viv. Grey* VII. iii. 398 One of the most successful periodical publications ever set afloat.
7. In full swing, in full activity.
1604 T. WRIGHT *Passions of Mind* II. i. 49 While the Passion is afloate. **1728** G. CARLETON *Mem. Eng. Officer* 91 Yet all these Difficulties, instead of discouraging the Earl, set every Faculty of his more afloat. **1826** SCOTT *Woodst.* xxii. (1846) 199 Since the loss of the battle of Worcester, he had been afloat again, and more active than ever.
8. In currency in the world or in society; passing at large from one person to another; in general diffusion or circulation.
1586 T. B. tr. *La Primaudaye's Fr. Acad.* 349 The fire of sedition, which setteth a floate all kinds of impietie. **1628** DIGBY *Voy. to Medit.* Pref. (1868) 38 The many mistakes which are afloat concerning him. **1853** (3 June) BRIGHT *Sp.* 2 Various rumours were afloat. **1877** KINGLAKE *Crimea* (ed. 6) I. ii. 35 It is true that strange doctrines were afloat.
b. *Comm.* In currency as negociable documents, without coming to an actual discharge of liability.
Mod. To keep bills, 'paper,' afloat.
9. Unfixed, unsettled, adrift; moving without guide or control.
1714 ELLWOOD *Hist. of Life* (1765) 291 Applause setting his Head afloat. **1757** SYMMER in Ellis *Orig. Lett.* II. 471 IV. 403 Affairs are in a manner all afloat.

†a'flocht, *pred. a.* prop. *phr. Sc. Obs.* [A *prep.*[1] + FLOCHT; also in full *on flocht.*] In a flutter, agitated.
1513 DOUGLAS *Æneis* v. xiii. 37 Venus al on flocht, Amyd hir breist reuoluand mony a thocht. **1536** BELLENDENE *Cron. Scotl.* (1821) II. 122 My mind and body is aflocht, specially sen I herd thir innocent men sa cruelly tormentit. **1585** JAMES I. *Ess. in Poesie* (1869) 31 With spreits aflought, and sweete transported loue.

a-flore, -floor, *phr. Obs.* on the floor: see FLOOR.

aflow (ə'fləʊ), *adv.* and *pred. a.* prop. *phr.* [A *prep.*[1] 11 + FLOW.] Flowing.
1863 D. MITCHELL *My Farm* 292, I described the air as all aflow with the perfume of purple lilacs.

aflower (ə'flaʊə(r)), *adv.* and *pred. a.*, prop. *phr.* [A *prep.*[1] 11 + FLOWER.] Flowering, blooming.
1876 SWINBURNE *Erechth.* 1147 Fields aflower with winds and suns.

aflush (ə'flʌʃ), *adv.* and *pred. a.*, prop. *phr.* [A *prep.*[1] 11 + FLUSH *sb.* and *a.*]
1. (From FLUSH *sb.*) In a flushed or blushing state.
1880 E. HOPKINS *R. Turquand* II. xix. 3 A pictured lady looking down aflush with bygone love.
2. (From FLUSH *a.*) On a level.
1880 SWINBURNE *Studies in Song* 169 The bank is abreast of her bows and aflush with the sea.

aflutter (ə'flʌtə(r)), *adv.* prop. *phrase.* [A *prep.*[1] + FLUTTER.] In a flutter, agitated.
1830 GLEIG *Country Curate* I. ix. 178 All the unmarried women were a-flutter when I came among them. **1855** BROWNING *Men & Wom.* II. 147 A cornfield-side a-flutter with poppies.

afoam (ə'fəʊm), *adv.* prop. *phr.* [A *prep.*[1] + FOAM.] In a state of foam.
1849 C. BRONTË *Shirley* III. ix. 204 With steed afoam. **1864** SWINBURNE *Atalanta* 1230 At the King's word I rode afoam for thine.

afocal (eɪ'fəʊkəl), *a. Optics.* [f. A- 14 + FOCAL *a.*] Designating a lens or lens system with a focal power of zero, so that rays entering parallel emerge parallel; neither converging nor diverging.
1932 EMSLEY & SWAINE *Ophthalmic Lenses* (ed. 2) xvii. 294 The two surfaces of this central portion of the glass are practically concentric..so that the glass itself is afocal (no power). **1950** K. N. OGLE *Binocular Vision* xi. 122 The afocal type lens is a little Galilean telescope in that it consists of positive and negative surfaces, analogous to the objective and eye lenses. **1969** *Focal Encycl. Photogr.* (rev. desk ed.) 1488/1 Afocal attachments of variable magnification also exist and produce an effect similar to that of a zoom lens. **1973** *Physics Bull.* July 440/3 Afocal systems such as telescopes, binoculars and periscopic sights.

†a'fole, *v. Obs.* [a. OFr. *afole-r* to befool; f. *à* to + *fol* fool, foolish: see FOOL.] To befool.
a **1250** *Owl & Night.* 206 Ich wot he is nu suthe acoled, Nis he vor the noȝt afoled. *c* **1314** *Guy Warw.* 20 Al to michel thou art afoild, Now thi blod it is acoild.

†a'fond, *v. Obs.* Forms: 1 **afandi-an**, 2 **afandien**, 3 (south.) **afonde, avond**, 5 (north.) **afaynd.** [f. A- *pref.* 1 intensive + *fand-ian* to try, to search, causal of *find-an* to find: see FOND.]
1. *trans.* To try, make trial of, put to the test, find out by experiment.
c **1000** *O.E. Gosp.* Luke xii. 56 Lá liceteras cunne ȝe afandian heofones ansyne & eorþan: humeta na afandiȝe ȝe þas tide? *c* **1160** *Hatton Gosp.*, ibid., La liceteres cunne ȝe afandiȝen heofones ansiene & eorðan. Hu mæte na afandiȝe ȝe þas tide? *c* **1050** *Sax. Leechd.* I. 375 Þis is afandan læcecræft. *c* **1305** *Saints Lives, St. Edw.* 12 A kniȝt of Engelond As he was biȝunde see auentoures to afonde.
b. with *subord. cl.* To try, to attempt.
c **1470** HENRY *Wallace* v. 879 Sotheron wald afaynd With haill power at anys on thaim to sett.
2. To tempt (to evil).
c **1315** SHOREHAM 73 Wyth foule handlynge Other other afondeth.

‖**à fond** (afɔ̃), *adv.* [Fr., lit. 'to the bottom'.] Thoroughly, fully.
1813 WELLINGTON *Disp.* 9 May (1838) X. 366 That which ought to be done is to examine a subject of this kind *à fond.* **1928** A. CHRISTIE *Myst. Blue Train* xv. 124 The Comte de la Roche knows one subject *à fond*: Women.

†a'fong, *v. Obs.* Forms: *Inf.* 1–4 **afó-n**, 2–4 **afo**, 3–5 **afong(e**, 3–4 **avong(e**, 4 **afang(e**, **avang(e**. *Pa. t.* 1–4 **afeng**, 2–3 **aveng**, 3 **afong**. *Pa. pple.* 1 **afangen, afongen.** *Imp.* 2 **auouh**, 3 **afeoh.** [f. A- *pref.* 1 intensive + *fón* to seize, grasp: see FONG, FANG.]
1. To take by force or authority; hence, to seize, apprehend.
c **975** *Rushw. Gosp.* Matt. iv. 12 Iohannes wæs afongen. *a* **1000** *Juliana* (Grein) 320 Forht afongen, friðes orwena. **1205** LAYAMON 22628 Ȝif he [him] mihte afon, he wolde hine slæn. *c* **1314** *Guy Warw.* 74 Sir Herhaud, thou schalt afong Four hundred knightes.
2. To take (what is offered), to accept.
1205 LAYAMON 14584 Buten þu a þine daȝen afo hæðene laȝen. *a* **1250** *Owl & Night.* 841 That alle tho that hi avoth, Hi weneth that thu segge soth. *c* **1305** *St. Christoph.* in *E.E.P.* (1862) 65 He..bileouede on god anon And afeng cristendom. *c* **1314** *Guy Warw.* 94 Ac he therof nold afo.
3. To receive (a person), to welcome.
c **1000** *O.E. Gosp.* Mark xvi. 19 He wæs on heofonum afangen. *c* **1175** *Lamb. Hom.* 197 Auouh mine soule. **1205** LAYAMON 15661 Vortigerne..pa læuedi aueng: mid swiðe uæire læten. *Ibid.* 14160 Afeoh heom mid wunne. *c* **1330** *Arth. & Merl.* 2546 And him afenge with fair acord. *c* **1380** *Sir Ferumb.* 2904 Prayhede he to god Almiȝt: scholde ys soule auonge.
4. To receive, get, come into possession of.
a **1000** *Psalms* (Spelm.) xlvii. 8 We afěngon mildheortnysse ðine on midle temple. *c* **1175** *Lamb. Hom.* 131 Euric mon scal auon mede. **1205** LAYAMON 23969 He wunde afeng: feouwer unchene long. **1297** R. GLOUC. 368 As in vorste ȝer, þat he auong hys kynedom. *c* **1315** SHOREHAM 51 And at ordres avangeth hy The boke of the Godspelle. *c* **1330** *Kyng of Tars* 1016 The dethe thei scholde afonge.
b. *intr.* To be in possession.
c **1450** LONELICH *Grail* li. 220 Whethir this fyr scholde lasten longe, Oþer endelesly there stille to a-fonge.
5. To get (offspring), to conceive.
c **1305** *Judas* in *E.E.P.* (1862) 108 Ac hi no child for no þing bituene hem ne miȝte afonge. **1315** SHOREHAM 121 For so hy hyne scholde ferst avonge, Ther nys ni senne ther amonge, Ne noe flesches lykynge.
6. Of a thing: To take in, contain, to hold.
c **1300** *Beket* 2349 The contrayes wide and longe Miȝte unethe al that folc that ther com afonge.

afoot (ə'fʊt), *adv.* prop. *phr.* [A *prep.*[1] on + FOOT. The full *on fote* occurs in 13th c., and *a foot* was written as two words till the 17th. The oldest form was in the plural, *a (on) foten* = *on feet*, always in the earlier text of Layamon 1205, but altered in the later to *a fote.*]
1. On foot, *i.e.* on one's own feet, in opposition to *on horseback*, etc.
1205 LAYAMON 5908 Weoren heo of Rome: alle ridinde, þa oðere a foten [*later text* a fote]. *Ibid.* 25402 Þat folc..þat þer eoden a uoten [*later text* afote]. *c* **1325** *E.E. Allit. P.* B. 79 Þe wayferande frekez, on fote & on hors. **1366** MAUNDEV. xxii. (1839) 245, 50,000 men at horse, and 200,000 men a fote. **1489** CAXTON *Faytes of Armes* I. xxiii. 70 Folke in tho dayes faughten more on horsbacke than a-fote. **1611** BIBLE *Acts* xx. 13 Minding himselfe to goe afoote. **1681** *Lond. Gaz.* mdclxi/3 His Royal Highness walked a Foot. **1762** GOLDSM. *Cit. of World* cxxii. (1837) 474 They take coach, which costs ninepence, or they may go afoot, which costs nothing. **1849** DICKENS *Barn. Rudge* 15/1 He was mounted and I afoot.
2. On foot, in opposition to *sitting still, lying*, etc.; astir, on the move.
1530 PALSGR. 422/2 Is this woman that lay a chylde bedde a foote agayne? **1588** SHAKS. *Tit. A.* IV. ii. 29 Were our witty Empresse well a foot. **1596** —— *1 Hen. IV*, I. iii. 278 Before the game's a-foot, thou still let'st slip. **1827** COOPER *Prairie* I. vii. 100 Ishmael and his sons were all speedily afoot. **1828** SCOTT *F.M. Perth* II. 123 A party of mummers who were afoot for pleasure.
3. Hence, In active existence, in operation or employment.
1601 SHAKS. *Jul. C.* III. ii. 265 Mischeefe thou art a-foot. **1638** SANDERSON 21 *Serm.* Ad. Aul. viii. (1673) 112 Pride.. setteth contentions a foot at the first and afterwards keepeth them afoot. **1659** BIRCH in Burton's *Diary* (1828) IV. 384 The Committee of the Army is kept a-foot still, at salaries. Receivers-general and auditors are kept a-foot at the same height. **1879** ROGERS in *Cassell's Techn. Educ.* IV. 128/2 There is always a question afoot, whether the profits, etc.
4. *Comb.* **afoot-back** (after *a-horse-back*).
1592 GREENE *Groats worth of Wit* D iij b, When I was fayne to carry my playing fardle afoot-backe.

†afor(e, *prep. Obs.* [An extended form of FOR, after the analogy of *fore, a-fore. For* and *fore* were at first the same word, but *ætforan, onforan* had only the local meaning; so that *afor* is not a descendant of either of these.] For, as for.
? **1489** *Plumpton Corr.* 71 And afore the langage that Alan shold say, it is not so; he sayd none such langage. *Ibid.* 94 Sir, afor the arbage, dout yt not. **1561** J. DAUS tr. *Bullinger on Apocalipse* (1573) 9 And afore the ministers, or men, they do but onely wish.

aforce, obs. variant of AFFORCE.

afore (ə'fɔə(r)), *adv.*, *prep.*, and *conj.* Forms: 1 **onforan** (2–3 **onforen, aforen**), ? 3–4 **aforn**, 4–5 **afforn(e**, 4–6 **aforne**, 4 **affore**, 5– **afore.** [OE. *on foran* = *on*, prep. + *foran*, itself an adv. = in front, in advance, properly dative of *for*, used as adj. or sb.; cf. *æt-foran, be-foran, to-foran.* The OE. *on foran* is not of frequent occurrence, and it was only in 14th c. that *aforn, afore*, became common, taking the place of the simple FORN, FORE, OE. *foran, fore. Afore* may also in some cases represent ATFORE, OE. *ætforan* which survived to 1300. By restriction to an object *afore* became a *preposition*, and by ellipsis of a relative a prepositional *conjunction. Afore* is now mostly obsolete in literature, its place being taken by BEFORE; but it is retained in the Bible and Prayer-book, is common in the dialects generally, as well as in 'vulgar' London speech, and in nautical language. Cf. also *pinafore.*]
A. *adv.*
1. Of place: In front, in advance; in or into the fore-part. Still used in naut. lang. and in dialects.
a **1000** *Ags. Ps.* cxiii. 13 (cxv. 5) Beoð onforan eáȝan, ne maȝon feor ȝeseon. *a* **1400** *Leg. Rood* 150 And prikkede into his panne Boþe byhynde and aforn. *c* **1430** LYDG. *Minor Poems* (1840) 4 Alle clad in white, and the most principalle Afforne in reed. **1489** CAXTON *Faytes of Armes* I. ix. 23 They shuld sett theyre lifte foete a-fore. **1523** LD. BERNERS *Froissart* I. cccl. 561 Sirs, on afore to these false traytours. **1581** NUCE *Seneca's Octavia* 166 Light ashes easly puft aforne. **1655** DIGGES *Compl. Ambass.* 357 Methinks it is somewhat requisite you did send one afore. **1677** *Lond. Gaz.* mcxciv/4 Having two Guns, one afore, and the other abaft. **1769** FALCONER *Shipwreck* III. 118 While Rodmond, fearful of some neighbouring shore, Cries ever and anon, 'Loke out afore!' **1867** SMYTH *Sailor's Word-Bk.* 24 *Afore*..opposed to abaft and signifying that part of the ship which lies forward, or near the stem. *Afore*, the same as before the mast.

2. Of time: In time preceding or previous; previously, before. *arch.* but common *dial.*

1340 *Ayenb.* 271 [Hit] auore ualþ ere hit by arered. *c* **1380** *Sir Ferumb.* 2044 So þat þou ous sykerye affore. **1430** LYDG. *Chron. Troy* I. vi, He gan them sowe right as men do corne Upon the land that eared was aforne. **1526** TINDALE *1 Cor.* xi. 21 For every man begynneth a fore [*Wyclif* bifore] to eate his awne supper. **1611** BIBLE *Eph.* iii. 3 As I wrote afore [*Wyclif* aboue] in few words. **1684** BUNYAN *Pilgr.* II. (1862) 219 Had I known that afore. **1865** DICKENS *Mut. Fr.* iii. 286 Than he had done afore.

B. *prep.* [The adv. with a defining object.]

1. Of place: Before, in front of; in advance of. *arch.* in literature; still common *dial.* and in nautical language, whence the phrase ***afore the mast***, i.e. among the common seamen, who have their quarters there.

1205 LAYAMON 10413 Fulgenes him wes aforen on. *c* **1380** *Sir Ferumb.* 2282 Alle þe Sarsyns þay a-slowe: þat þay afforn hym founde. *c* **1440** *Gesta Rom.* i. 2 And fastenyd it in þe walle afore him. **1599** HAKLUYT *Voy.* II. I. 78 The Turks army was afore Rhodes. **1653** HOLCROFT *Procopius* I. 3 Ferozes..pursued without looking afore him. **1787** BURNS *Wks.* III. 216 So, took a birth afore the mast, An' owre the sea. **1827** J. WILSON *Wks.* 1855 I. 357 Plenty of life let us howp is yet afore us. **1867** SMYTH *Sailor's Word-Bk.*, *Afore the beam*, all the field of view from amidship in a right angle to the ship's keel to the horizon forward.

2. In or into the presence of. *arch.* and *dial.*

? **1250** GROSSETESTE in *Dom. Archit.* III. 75 Ete ȝe in the halle afore youre meyny. **1377** LANGL. *P. Pl.* B. v. 12 And with a crosse afor þe kynge · comsed þus to techen. **1477** EARL RIVERS (Caxton) *Dictes* 13 Be wel ware what ye speke afor your enemies. *c* **1540** WYATT *Compl. Love to Reason* 152 My froward master, Afore that Queen I caused to be acited. **1812** W. TENNANT *Anster Fair* VI. liii, Afore each half mistrusting eye. **1839** DICKENS *Ol. Twist* (1850) 60/1 'You're getting too proud to own me afore company, are you?'

b. *fig.*

1377 LANGL. *P. Pl.* B. XII. 81 Gultier as afor god. **1563** *Homilies* II. xiii. §1 (1640) 178 If we suffer to be evill spoken of for the love of Christ, this is thankfull afore God. **1642** ROGERS *Naaman* 365 Having God afore our eies.

3. Of time: Before, previously to. *arch.* & *dial.*

898 *O.E. Chron.* an. 894 [He] ȝegaderade..micelne here onforan winter. **1121** *Ibid.* (Laud MS.) an. 1116 þa ormæte reinas þe coman sona onforan August. *c* **1380** *Sir Ferumb.* 2483 If he wer now lyues man: afore þis had he come. *c* **1550** CHEKE *Matt.* xxiv. 38 As in yᵉ tijm afoor yᵉ flood. **1611** BIBLE *Is.* xviii. 5 Afore the haruest when the bud is perfect. **1660** H. FINCH *Trial of Regic.* 44 Some days afore that, there was a Committee. **1860** DICKENS *Lett.* (ed. 2) II. 109 With a certain dramatic fire in her whereof I seem to remember having seen sparks afore now.

4. Of rank or importance: In precedence of, above. *arch.* and *dial.*

1428 R. WHYTEMAN in *E.E. Wills* (1882) Y woll that Symken..haue hem [candelstekes] A-fore eny other man. **1477** EARL RIVERS (Caxton) *Dictes* 20 Loke that first affore all thingis ye loue, drede, and obeye our lord. **1662** *Bk. Comm. Prayer*, *Athanasian Creed*, In this Trinity, none is afore or after other.

C. *conj.* [elliptical use of the prep. of time, as *afore the time that* he came, *afore that* he came, *afore* he came.] Before, sooner than. Sometimes strengthened with *or*; cf. *or ere. arch.* and *dial.*

1340 *Ayenb.* 172 Auore þet he come to ssrifte. **1525** LD. BERNERS *Froissart* II. xviii. 34 In that season afore or Fraunces Atremon was putte oute of the towne. **1552** LYNDESAY *Monarche* 5326 Affore that day be done, Thare salbe signis in Sonne and Mone. **1611** BIBLE *Ezek.* xxxiii. 22 In the euening, afore hee that was escaped came. **1684** BUNYAN *Pilgr.* II. 63 That they were hanged afore we came hither. **1827** F. COOPER *Prairie* I. iii. 49 They will be here afore you can find a cover!

D. *Comb.* **1.** Of time.

a. Formerly prefixed in the sense of 'previously, beforehand' to vbs. and pples., as in **afore-bar** = preclude, ***afore-see***, ***afore-acted***, ***afore-running***.

c **1449** PECOCK *Repr.* 502 Which lettith and afore barrith.. the comaundement of God in his lawe of kinde to be doon. *a* **1564** BECON *Christ's Chron.* (1844) 552 Afore-seeing the grievous plagues. **1612** WOODALL *Surg. Mate* Wks. 1653, 185 The signs, afore-running or demonstrating of the instant disease, are these. **1700** J. MARSHALL in *Misc. Curiosa* 1708 III. 259 The afore-acted Evil that his Soul did in its other Life. **1877** J. MORLEY *Crit. Misc.* Ser. II. 35 Only as life wears on, do all its foreshapen lines come into light.

b. Still used in ppl. combinations, with the meaning, 'earlier in time or order, previously in a discourse or document,' as in **aforesaid**, **aforegoing**, and the similar **afore-cited**, **-given** *obs.*, **-mentioned**, **-named**, **-spoken** *obs.*, **-told** *obs.*

1418 CHICHELE in Ellis *Orig. Lett.* I. 2 I. 4 The avys of ȝour uncle a forseyd. **1606** SHAKS. *Tr. & Cr.* II. iii. 64 Thersites is a foole, and as aforesaid, Patroclus is a foole. **1863** KEMBLE *Resid. Georgia* 23 Our housemaid, the aforesaid Mary. **1592** tr. *Junius* on *Apocal.* i. 8 A confirmation of the afore going. **1815** WELLINGTON in Gurwood's *Desp.* X. 350 The aforegoing orders are to take effect.

1683 SALMON *Doron Med.* II. 417 The vertues you have in the aforecited place. **1741** RICHARDSON *Pamela* (1824) I. 131 For the reasons aforegiven. **1587** GOLDING *De Mornay* ix. 133 These aforementioned Philosophers also, do call the world euerlasting. **1663** GERBIER *Counsel* 92 At lower rates than the afore-mentioned. **1838** DICKENS *Nich. Nick.* xxviii. (C.D. ed.) 231 Newman wiped his eyes with the afore-mentioned duster. **1603** KNOLLES *Hist. Turkes* (1638) 183 The two valiant afore-named worthy captaines. **1845** J. H. NEWMAN *Development* 341 And converted many of the afore-named heretics. **1582-8** *Hist. Jas. VI* (1804) 38 Making his residence at Glasgow for the caus afoirtold.

2. Of place. **afore-rider** *obs.*, an avant-courier, scout; **aforeship** *obs.*, the front part of the ship.

1470 *Rebell. in Linc.* (1847) 16 Their aforeryders were com to Rotherham. **1471** *Hist. Arriv. Edw. IV* (1838) 8 Whan the Kynges aforne-ridars had thus espyed their beinge [there]. **1398** TREVISA *Barth. De P.R.* v. iii. (1495) 105 The formeste celle of the brayne highte *prora* in latyn as it were aforshyppe.

3. with *again*, *on*: see AFORNENS, AFORN-ON.

aforegoing: see AFORE D 1 b.

aforehand (əˈfɔəhænd), *adv. arch.* [f. AFORE *prep.* + HAND; cf. the much earlier BEFOREHAND. In early times generally written as two (or three) words, and even analytically *afore the hand.*] = BEFOREHAND, which is now the ordinary form.

1. With previous preparation, in anticipation, in advance. *arch.* and *dial.*

1430 LYDG. *Chron. Troy* I. v, As we were wonte aforehande for to see. *c* **1430** *Syr Generides* 378 He couth by the sterres Tel of peace and of werres. Of that he seid afor the hond My fadre alwey soth fond. **1526** TINDALE *Mark* xiv. 8 She cam a fore honde to anoynt my boddy to his buryinge warde. **1639** FULLER *Holy War* v. xxii. (1840) 280 In the nature of wages *ex pacto* contracted for aforehand. **1850** DICKENS *Lett.* (1880) I. 231 It is not possible for him to say aforehand..what it will cost.

†**2.** *adjectively.* Prepared or provided for the future. *Obs.*

1626 BACON *New Atl.* Wks. 1860, 275 The Strangers'-House is at this time rich and much aforehand, for it hath laid up revenue. **1741** RICHARDSON *Pamela* (1824) I. 216 A couple of guineas will be of use to Mrs. Mumford, who, I doubt, has not much aforehand. **1748** —— *Clarissa* (1811) III. 201 She lives reputably and is..aforehand in the world.

†**to be aforehand with**: To anticipate, to forestall, to have the first word, or make the first move. *Obs.*

1670 G. H., tr. *Hist. Cardinals* II. ii. 173 All that are in Rome do strive to be aforehand with the world. **1748** RICHARDSON *Clarissa* (1811) II. 323 A sagacity that is afore-hand with events. **1753** —— *Grandison* viii. (1781) I. 37 Let me for once be aforehand with my uncle.

†**aˈforeness.** *Obs. rare*⁻¹. [f. AFORE *adv.* + -NESS.] The state of being before; pre-existence.

1587 GOLDING *De Mornay* iv. (1617) 49 As for the euerlastingnesse, it can abide neither aforenesse nor afternesse.

aforesaid. See AFORE D 1 b.

aforethought (əˈfɔəθɔːt), *ppl. a.* and *sb.* [f. AFORE *adv.* + *thought*: see THINK. Apparently introduced as an English translation of the Old Law-Fr. *prepense* in *malice prepense.*]

A. *ppl. adj.* Thought before; entertained in the mind beforehand, premeditated.

1581 LAMBARDE *Eiren.* II. vii. (1588) 241 If two (of malice forethought) lie in await the one to kill the other. **1628** COKE *3 Inst.* 47 With malice aforethought. **1825** COBBETT *Rural Rides* 488 To make an act murder there must be malice afore thought. **1840** CARLYLE *Heroes* (1858) 204 Sheer falsehood, idle fables, allegory aforethought. **1874** L. TOLLEMACHE in *Fortn. Rev.* Feb. 231 The inveterate habit of ending stories badly, with pessimism aforethought.

B. *sb. rare.* Thinking beforehand, premeditation.

1851 SIR J. HERSCHEL *Nat. Phil.* I. iii. 55 Deliberately, of afore-thought, to devise remedies.

aforetime (əˈfɔətaɪm), *adv.* [f. AFORE *adv.* + TIME (confining *afore* to the *temporal* sense).] Before in time, in former time, formerly, previously.

1535 COVERDALE *Dan.* vi. 10 Like as his maner was to do afore tyme. **1611** *ibid.*, As hee did afore time. **1857** MISS WINKWORTH tr. *Tauler's Serm.* xxv. 391 The light in which he walked aforetime. **1880** MUIRHEAD *Gaius* I. §63 Neither can I marry her who has aforetime been my mother-in-law.

¶ Rarely *attrib.* as adj. and *absol.* as sb.

1839 BAILEY *Festus* xix. (1848) 209 Believing not the aforetime unity Of the Divine and human. **1846** GROTE *Greece* (1862) I. i. 37 Fancy, which fills up the blank of the aforetime.

†**aˈforetimes,** *adv. Obs.* [f. prec., with genitival -s¹, as in *sometime-s*, probably afterwards understood as a plural *-s.*] = AFORETIME.

1587 GOLDING *De Mornay* ix. 130 The thing which had aforetimes bene disputable among the Heathen, is now admitted as an article of faith. **1662** GLANVILLE *Lux Orient.* v. (1682) 49 Though it were granted that the soul lived aforetimes without a body.

†**aˈforeward,** *adv.* and *prep. Obs.* [f. AFORE + -WARD (defining *place* or *position*, as against *time*).]

A. *adv.* **a.** Of order: First of all, first in rank. **b.** Of place: In front.

1297 R. GLOUC. 567 So þat avoreward þe bissop hii chose of Baþe Water Giffard. *c* **1300** *Beket* 492 For ther were furst and Aforeward: the Kyng and his sone. *c* **1380** *Sir Ferumb.* 3380 Roland was þe furste of alle: þat rod afforeward.

B. *prep.* [The adv. with defining obj.] In front of.

c **1380** *Sir Ferumb.* 3923 Ac furst and afforeward alle Prykede a cosyn of þe Amyralle.

aforeye, -n, -ns, var. of AFORNENS.

†**aforˈnens,** *prep.* and *adv. Obs.* [A combination of *aforen* (see AFORE) and *aȝean*, *aȝen*, AGAIN, in which the former word appears as *aforn*, *afore*, *afor*, and the latter as *-ayen*, *-eyen*, *-yen*, *-eye*, *-ye*, or (from the adv. gen. *aȝenes*) as *-ayens*, *eyens*, *-yens*, *-ens*. Those in *-s* are mostly northern. Cf. OE. *foran-onȝeanes*: see FORNENST.]

A. *prep.* **1.** Over against, opposite. *fig.* Before, in the presence of.

1250 LAYAMON 18529 þar sat Vther þe king: in his heȝe setle. Aforneȝen him Gorlois. **1340** *Ayenb.* 18 He is wel vileyn and ontrewe auoreye his lhord. **1374** CHAUCER *Troylus* II. 1139 The yondur house, that stent aforeyens us. *c* **1425** WYNTOUN *Cron.* VII. viii. 899 Set ewyn a-for-nens Berwyke.

2. With regard to, in respect of, as concerns.

1340 *Ayenb.* 24 Auorye þet bodi: ase helþe, uayrhede.. Auorye þe ȝaule: ase clier wyt. *Ibid.* 129 Ysy hou þou art fyeble and brotel, and a-uorye þet body and a-uorye þe ȝaule.

B. *adv.* [obj. omitted.] Over against, opposite.

1388 WYCLIF *Mark* xv. 39 The centurien that stood aforn aȝens.

†**aforn-on, aforen-on,** *adv.* and *prep. Obs.* [A comb. of *aforen* (see AFORE) and ON.]

A. *adv.* In front.

1205 LAYAMON 26647 þa Bruttes to-ræsden..and smiten to a-uorenon.

B. *prep.* In front of.

1205 LAYAMON 28313 Moddred him wes auornon. *Ibid.* 10413 Fulgenes him wes aforen on [**1250** afornon].

†**aˈforrow,** *adv. Obs.* [Sc. variant of AFORE, probably formed on *aforn*, after *morn*, *morrow*.] Before.

1552 LYNDESAY *Papyngo* (1866) 227 And so befell, in tyll ane myrthfull morrow, In to my garth I past, me to repose, This bird and I, as we wer wount aforrow.

‖**a fortiori** (eɪ fɔəʃɪˈɔəraɪ, fɔətɪ-), *adv. phr.* [L. *a.* from, *fortiori* stronger (sc. *argumento*).] With stronger reason, still more conclusively.

1606 R. PARSONS *Answer to Coke* iii. 52 Yet cannot hee either *tacitè* or *à fortiore*..take vnto him, all the power.. which the said President and fellowes haue. **1712** SHAFTESBURY *Plastics* in *Second Characters* (1914) 158 From hence argument *a fortiori*: How indecent is obscenity? **1827** *Blackw. Mag.* Feb. 207/2 One might, *a fortiori*, count on *his* being murdered. **1855** H. SPENCER *Psychol.* (1872) I. II. i. 146 The expression 'substance of Mind' can have no meaning..*A fortiori*, the substance of Mind cannot be known. **1961** *New Scientist* 16 Mar. 688/1 Anyone who, being a mathematician or a scientist, loses his sight after leaving school—or, *a fortiori*, in mid-career—cannot easily escape feelings of deep dismay.

afoul (əˈfaʊl), *adv.* and *pred. a.* Orig. *Naut.* [A *prep.*¹ + FOUL: cf. *asleep.*] Entangled, in collision; fouled. Const. *of.* Phr. ***to fall, run afoul of***: to fall, run foul of (see FALL *v.* 87 and RUN *v.* 10 c). Now chiefly *U.S.*

1809 J. BARLOW *Columb.* VII. 521 With shrouds afoul. **1824** *Blackw. Mag.* Oct. 416/1 We see no reason for encouraging anybody in running afoul of other people's countries. **1840** DANA *Bef. Mast* (1854) xv. 76 After paying out chain, we swung clear, but our anchors were no doubt afoul of hers. **1841** TOTTEN *Naval Text-bk.* 328 A vessel ran a-foul of us. **1893** *Scribner's Mag.* June 793/2 He sometimes falls afoul of the night lines baited for eels. **1937** F. SCOTT FITZGERALD *Let.* July (1964) 16, I ran afoul of a bastard named de Sano. **1958** C. FERGUSON *Naked to Enemies* I. iii. 29 He stood pledged to aid them if they..fell afoul of the law on any personal matter. **1961** B. VAWTER *Consc. of Israel* ix. 244 The modern neutralist or other espouser of unpopular causes..can hardly fail to run afoul of the jingoistic society in which he lives.

†**aˈfounder,** *v. Obs.* [a. OFr. *afondre-r*, var. of *effondrer* to hollow out, undermine, swallow up. Cf. Pr. *esfondrar* and *esfondar*, L. *ex* out and *fundus* bottom: see FOUNDER.] To disable, lame.

1366 MAUNDEV. 69 His Hors shalle not ben afoundred. *c* **1400** *Beryn* Prol. 631 Ffor aftir his hete he cauȝte a cold, þurh þe nyȝtis eyre That he was nere a-found[r]it.

afraid (əˈfreɪd), *ppl. a.* Forms: 4 **afraied, affraied,** 4–6 **affrayed,** 4–7 **affraid(e,** 5 **afrayet, affrayt,** 5–6 **afrayed,** 6 **affrayd, afrayd(e,** 6– **afraid.** Also aphet. **frayed, fraid.** [Orig. pa. pple. of *afray*, AFFRAY *v.* (cf. *lay, laid*; *say, said*, etc.) which, being more used than any other part, acquired an independent standing, and has retained the spelling *afraid*, while the vb. is *affray.*]

1. As *pple.* Alarmed, frightened; hence as *adj.*, In a state of fear or apprehension, moved or actuated by fear. (As an adj. it never stands before a noun.)

1330 R. BRUNNE *Chron.* 16 þe Kyng was alle affraied. *Ibid.* 323 Alle frayed he went fro þat cite. *c* **1386** CHAUCER *Shipm. T.* 400 This wyf was nat afered ne afrayed. *c* **1420** *Anturs of Arther* xxxi. 9 (1842) 15 The freson was afrayet, and ferd of that fare. **1440** *Promp. Parv.*, Affrayed, *territus*. *c* **1500** *Lancelot* 3469 So sal thai fynd we ar no-thing affrayt. **1601** SHAKS. *Jul. Cæs.* II. ii. 101 If Cæsar hide himselfe, shall they not whisper Loe, Cæsar is afraid? **1653** HOLCROFT *Procopius* II. 54 The Roman army..were troubled and affraid. **1671** MILTON *P.R.* II. 759 Back they recoild affraid. **1864** BROWNING *Dramatis Personæ* 77, Trust God: see all, nor be afraid! **1872** J. DOOLITTLE *Chinese Vocab.* II. 684/2 Those that came were not afraid: those that were afraid did not come. **1915** T. S. ELIOT in *Poetry* VI. 132 And I have seen the eternal Footman hold my coat, and snicker, And in short, I was afraid.

2. *Const.*

a. with *of* (sometimes omitted before a clause).

1350 *Will. Palerne* 2158 He þat of þe white beres So bremli was afraied. **1483** CAXTON *G. de la Tour* f i, His wyf made semblaunt as she therof were affrayed. **1599** H. BUTTES *Diets Dry Dinner* (Arb.) 92 Such as are affrayed of roasted Pigge. **1667** MILTON *P.L.* x. 117, I..of thy voice Affraid, being naked, hid my self. *Ibid.* XII. 493 What man can do against thee, not affraid. **1678** BUNYAN *Pilgrim* I. (1862) 124, I was afraid on't at the very first. **1855** KINGSLEY *Lett.* (1878) I. 442 He first taught me not to be afraid of truth.

b. with *inf.* In fear of the consequence (to oneself) of; not having courage *to*.

1535 COVERDALE *Ex.* iii. 6 Moses couered his face, for he was afrayed to loke vpon God [WYCLIF, He darst not loke aȝens God]. **1580** SIDNEY *Arcadia* III. 317 They were affraid even to crie. **1610** SHAKS. *Temp.* I. i. 47 We are lesse afraid to be drownde then thou art. **1716–18** LADY M. W. MONTAGUE *Lett.* I. x. 37 To see me afraid to handle a gun. *c* **1735** POPE *Prol. to Sat.* 203 Willing to wound, and yet afraid to strike. **1850** MᶜCOSH *Div. Govt.* IV. ii. (1874) 498 Afraid to look upon the full purity of God.

c. with depend. cl.: *lest*, with subjunctive, introduces a deprecated contingency of which there is danger; *that*, with subjunctive, an unpleasant possibility; with indicative, an unpleasant probability or contemplated reality. The conjunctions are sometimes omitted. ***I am*** (or ***I'm***) ***afraid***: often used *colloq.* with little or no implication of fear or danger, in the sense of 'I regret to say; I regretfully or apologetically admit, report, etc.; I suspect; I am inclined to think'. Const. *that*, or simple clause.

1530 PALSG. 422/1 He was as a frayde as any man you sawe this twelve monethes that I wolde have gyven hym a blowe. **1535** COVERDALE *Tob.* vi. 14, I am afrayed lest soch thinges happen vnto me also. [**1611** BIBLE *ibid.*, I am afraid, lest, if I goe in vnto her, I die.] —— *1 Macc.* xii. 40 He was afrayed that Ionathas wolde not suffre him. **1596** SHAKS. *Merch. Ven.* I. ii. 47, I am much afraid my Ladie his mother plaid false. **1596** —— *Tam. Shrew* v. ii. 89, I am affraid sir, doe what you can Yours will not be entreated. **1635** A. STAFFORD *Fem. Glory* (1869) 98, I was affraide it would have infected my other bookes. *a* **1678** H. SCOUGAL *Importance & Difficulty of Ministerial Function* in *Wks.* (1765) 240 This.. was the humour of some in his days; and I am afraid the case is not much better in ours. **1709** ADDISON *Let.* 14 Dec. (1941) 197, I am afraid if this matter comes on it will be necessary to have Copys of the Office Books. **1740** GRAY *Let.* 16 July (1900) I. 76 Disagreeable enough (as most necessities are) but, I am afraid, unavoidable. **1813** JANE AUSTEN *Pride & Prej.* I. x. 104, I am afraid you do not like your pen. Let me mend it for you. **1816** J. WILSON *City of Plague* III. iv. 39 Perhaps thou art afraid Lest the night air may spoil its beauty. **1847** LEWES *Hist. Phil.* II. 313 He was afraid lest the poetical spirit should be swept away along with the prophetical. *Mod.* He is afraid that his dishonesty will be discovered. I am afraid that it is too true; afraid that we are not in time. We were afraid lest we should, *or* that we might hurt them. **1853** MRS. GASKELL *Cranford* iii. 47, I did many a thing she did not like, I'm afraid—and now she's gone! **1911** F. SWINNERTON *Casement* vi. 209 'I'm afraid,' said he, rather stiffly, 'that I don't know anything about his habits.' **1959** *Observer* 14 June 22/6 It would be less kind, but true, I am afraid, to find in this book a quite invincible taste for the mediocre.

d. *of* with *gerund* is found in all these senses, but chiefly = *lest* with subj., of which it is a more modern equivalent.

1727 SWIFT *Gulliver* II. viii. 174, I was afraid of trampling on every traveller that I met. **1855** BREWSTER *Newton* II. xxiv. 337 He was afraid of being known as the author of the work. *Mod.* I am afraid of bathing there = to bathe there. I was afraid of treading on somebody's toes = lest I should tread.

afraidness (əˈfreɪdnɪs). *rare.* [f. prec. + -NESS.] The quality or state of being afraid; timidity, fear.

1669 GARBUTT *Wks.* 226 The shyness and afraidness one of another. **1922** M. A. VON ARNIM *Enchanted April* xiv. 221 How deceitful her afraidness had made her. **1927** G. A. TERRILL in *Chambers's Jrnl.* 8 Jan. 94/2 He *couldn't* have held her if she had given a breath of afraidness.

A-frame (ˈeɪfreɪm). Chiefly *U.S.* [f. A + FRAME *sb.*] A frame having the shape of a capital letter A. Also *attrib.*, and *ellipt.* for something having this shape, esp. an A-frame house.

1909 *Cent. Dict.* Suppl. X. 19/2 *A-frame*, the A-shaped support for the cylinder-beam and cross-head guides of a vertical engine; the housing. **1932** *Amer. Speech* VII. 407 *A-frame*, a framework of heavy timbers in the form of a wide-spreading *A* placed at the junction of the kitchen with the main portion of the tent. It supports the proscenium of the stage. **1955** *Ibid.* XXX. 225 *A-frame*, a large upright trailer used to transport flat pieces of metal from one production operation to the next. **1967** 'T. WELLS' *Dead by Light of Moon* (1968) x. 94 There's this friend of mine whose folks own one of those crazy A-frame ski lodges. **1968** *Listener* 25 July 108/1 He was bent nearly double under a gigantic load on his A-frame and walked with a stick. **1976** P. CAVE *High Flying Birds* iii. 37, I bent down and lifted up the A-frame, getting Sweet Sue perfectly balanced.

Aframerican: see AFRO-.

†**aˈfrayed**, *pa. pple. Obs.* Also 6 **affreyd**. [Either for FRAYED with s.w. prefix *a-* for *i-*, *y-*, *ȝe-*, or with intensive *a-*.] Frayed, rubbed, worn bare.

c **1400** *Tundale Vis.* 121 And feyth with frawde is corrupt and afrayed. **1523** FITZHERBERT *Husbandry* (1534) G viij, Affreyd is an yll disease, and commethe of great labour and rydynge faste with a contynuall sweate.

afreet, afrit, afrite (ˈæfriːt). [Arab. *ʻifrīt.*] An evil demon or monster of Mohammedan mythology.

1802 SOUTHEY *Thalaba* XII. xix. Wks. IV. 431 Fit warden of the sorcery-gate, A rebel Afreet lay. **1813** BYRON *Giaour* 784 Then stalking to thy sullen grave, Go—and with Gouls and Afrits rave. **1844** DISRAELI *Coningsby* IV. ii. 115 Habitants more wondrous than Afrite or Peri.

‖**aˈfresca**, *adv. Obs.* [It. *afresco*, *aff-*.] In fresco.

a **1706** EVELYN *Diary* I. 40 The long gallery, paved with white and black marble, richly fretted and paynted afresca.

afresh (əˈfrɛʃ), *adv.* Also 6 **afresshe, afreshe**. [f. A- *pref.* 3 + FRESH, probably after analogy of *anew*, in which the *a-* is a reduction of OF. No instance of *of fresh* has been found. *On fresh* is probably a mere erroneous expansion, after such pairs as *a-sleep*, *on-sleep*, in which *a-* really = *on*.] Anew, with a fresh commencement, freshly.

1509 FISHER *Wks.* 183 Now shewe mercy vpon thy chyrche afresshe. **1594** SHAKS. *Rich. III*, I. ii. 56 Dead Henries wounds Open their congeal'd mouthes, and bleed afresh. **1603** KNOLLES *Hist. Turkes* (1638) 190 Wars began again to arise on fresh. **1751** JOHNSON *Rambler* No. 184 ¶2 The day calls afresh upon him for a new topicke. **1836** THIRLWALL *Greece* III. xxiv. 338 Existing treaties should be ratified afresh. **1853** KINGSLEY *Hypatia* iii. (1869) 35 We start afresh.

afret (əˈfrɛt), *adv.* and *pred. a.* prop. *phr.* [A *prep.*[1] + FRET.] In a fretted state.

1882 in *Gd. Wds.* 320 High are the clouds in their going, afret where the winds pursue.

†**aˈfrete**, *v. Obs.* Forms: 1 of-frét(an, 3–4 afret(e. [f. OF *prep.* from + *fret-an* to gnaw, devour: see FRET.] To devour.

c **1300** *Pol. Songs* 237 The devel huem afretye, Rau other a roste! *Ibid.* 240 The fend ou afretie, with fleis ant with felle!

afreyne, var. AFFREYNE *v. Obs.*, to question.

Afric (ˈæfrɪk), *a.* and *sb. arch.* or *poet.* Also Af(f)rick, 6 Africke. [ad. L. *Africus* African.] **A.** *adj.* Of or pertaining to Africa; African. **B.** *sb.* A native of Africa; an African Negro. *rare.*

1590 SPENSER *F.Q.* III. iii, Beyond the Africk Ismael. **1591** J. HARINGTON tr. *Ariosto's Orlando Fur.* I. i, The Moores transported all their might On Affrick seas the force of France to breake. *a* **1592** GREENE *Friar Bacon* (1594) sig. F3ʳ l. 1382 The Africke Dates *mirabiles* of Spaine. **1667** MILTON *P.L.* I. 585 Or whom Biserta sent from Afric shore. **1733** SWIFT *On Poetry* 12 So Geographers in Afric-Maps With Savage-Pictures fill their Gaps. **1876** *N. American Rev.* CXXIII. 446 Then will the Afric indeed have changed his skin and the leopard his spots. **1897** L. JOHNSON *In Ireland* 98 Make kind to him the Afric sun, The Afric stars and moon. **1956** J. MASEFIELD in *Times* 27 Jan. 9 So be the Africk visit of our Queen.

African (ˈæfrɪkən), *sb.* and *a.* Also 6–7 Af(f)rican, (6 Aph-). [OE. (only pl.) *Africanas*, ad. L. *Africānae*, f. *Africa*, sb. use of fem. (sc. *terra* land) of *Africus*, f. *Afrī* (sg. *Afer*) ancient people of N. Africa; see -AN.]

A. *sb.* **a.** A native or inhabitant of Africa; an African Negro.

In local usage applied to the particular Negro (negroid) race or races of a territory in Africa, as (*S. Afr.*) the Bantu people of South Africa.

c **888** K. ÆLFRED *Boeth.* xvi. §2 þa he feaht wið Africanas. *c* **1205** *Layamon's Brut* (1847) 25379 Mid him com moni Aufrican. *Ibid.* 27501 Of Ethipe wes þe an, þe oðer wes an Aufrican. **13..** *K. Alisaunder* (1952) 2021 And lete armen þine Affricanes. **1564** HARDING *Answ. Jewel* 61ᵛ, He being an Aphricane borne, and writing to Aphricanes. **1567** T. STAPLETON *Counterblast* Pref., I reporte me to the Africans, who falling from the vnitie of the Romaine See.. became in time Infidelles. **1671** A. WOODHEAD *Consid. Council of Trent* ii. 20 Which was the chief matter stood upon by the Affricans against Pope Bonifacius. **1687** W. D. tr. *B. Le Bovier de Fontanelle's Discourse Plurality of Worlds* iii. 50 All Faces in general are wrought according to one and the same model, but those of two great Nations, of the Europeans, for example, and Africans seem to be fram'd to two particular models. **1780** A. BUTLER *Lives Saints* IX. 172 The concurring suffrages of sixteen ancient and worthy bishops (two of whom were Africans). **1806** *Gleanings in Africa* xvi. 121 The case of the unhappy African is.. entirely different. The unoffending negro, in the forests and morasses of Africa, never so much as meditated hostility against Europe. **1849** CARLYLE in *Fraser's Mag.* XL. 672/2 Our West-Indian policy.. of keeping down the labour-market in those islands by importing new Africans. **1952** L. MARQUARD *Peoples & Pol. of S. Afr.* i. 1 Today.. 8,500,000 Africans form part of the population of South Africa.

b. *spec.* Applied to a white resident of Africa.

1815 A. PLUMPTRE tr. *Lichtenstein's Trav. S. Afr.* II. IV. xxxv. 96 Like all other settlers here, they [the French settlers] are become entirely Africans. **1923** O. SCHREINER *Thoughts on S. Afr.* ii. 77 The young English African who has never been in Europe may boast that South Africa is the finest country on earth. **1934** 'N. GILES' *Ridge of White Waters* I. xiii. 150 As an African, with Dutch blood in me, I am suspected of Republican sympathies. *Ibid.* xiv. 163 Why does the Government give the vote to Hollanders and leave good Africans out in the cold? **1953** P. H. ABRAHAMS *Return to Goli* v. 179, I am convinced that of all the whites in the plural societies of Africa only the descendants of the Trekkers have made that deeply subjective.. transition in their relations with the African earth that has made pure Africans of them.

c. A Black inhabitant of the United States, of African origin or descent; an Afro-American. Now *rare* exc. *Hist.*

1700 in *Proc. Mass. Hist. Soc.* (1864) VII. 163 It might not be unreasonable to enquire whether we are not culpable in forcing the Africans to become Slaves amongst our selves. **1721** *New-England Courant* 18–25 Dec. 1/1 On Thursday last was solemnized here the Wedding of two Africans. **1800** *Boston Selectmen* 3 Sept., All Africans and Negroes resident in this town. **1855** *Southern Lit. Messenger* Nov. 656/2 The African was not without his redeeming traits... He was not a bad specimen of the physical man. **1970** R. D. ABRAHAMS *Positively Black* vi. 149 This was the very place in which culture was stripped from the Africans. **1979** D. F. LITTLEFIELD *Africans & Creeks* i. 22 There is at present no evidence that Indians.. held Africans as slaves.

B. *adj.* **1. a.** Of or pertaining to Africa (the continent, or the ancient Roman province of that name); occurring in some specific names of plants, trees, etc. (see quots.). **b.** Belonging to or characteristic of the Negro peoples of Africa.

1564 HARDING *Answ. Jewel* f. 89ᵛ, This reconciliation.. of the Affricane churches to the catholike church. **1594** HOOKER *Eccl. Pol.* III. 128 The Africane bishopes in the Councell of Carthage. **1597, 1611**, etc. [see MARIGOLD 1 b]. **1607** TOPSELL *Foure-f. Beasts* 99 The Affrican Camels, are much more woorth then the Asian. *Ibid.* 249 A medicine made of an African Sparrow. **1624** [SCOTT] *2nd Pt. Vox Populi* 23 That (insolent and african pride) of restrayning him from that liberall.. conuerse.. with the Lady Maria Infanta. **1646** 'THOS. CARRE' *Occas. Disc.* 147 The Epist. of the Africane Bishops to Pope Celestine. **1706** PHILLIPS (ed. Kersey), *Ulpicum*.. African Garlick. **1782** LATHAM *Gen. Syn. Birds* I. II. 532 African C[uckow]. **1861** BENTLEY *Man. Bot.* 645 *Oldfieldia africana*, yields.. African Oak or African Teak. *Ibid.* 677 *Sanseviera zeylanica*.. [produces] African Hemp or Bowstring Hemp. **1869** ALLIES *Form. Christendom* II. 277 Tertullian adds the witness of the African church to that of the Asiatic and Gallic churches in Irenæus. **1913** C. PETTMAN *Africanderisms* 24 *African walnut* (*Schotia brachypetala, Sond*). A tree bearing handsome, bright scarlet flowers. The wood is said to be much like walnut, but closer in the grain, and takes a splendid polish. **1921** W. BULLOCK *Timbers for Woodwork* 24 *African Walnut*.. is a production from the west coast of Africa, being obtained from the French Congo, the Cameroons and the Nigerian territories. .. The colour of this timber is the only feature in which it compares with walnut, being quite unlike in every other respect. **1941** F. L. MULFORD *House Plants* 25 The so-called African-violet (*Saintpaulia ionantha*) is a blue-flowered, constant-blooming plant under house culture. **1958** *Economist* 13 Dec. 24/1 The idea of the 'African personality', about which African leaders talk so grandiosely.

c. Being or pertaining to a Black inhabitant of the United States.

1722 C. MATHER *Diary* 16 Jan. (1912) II. 672 My African Servant must be præpared for the Baptism, which he has been long seeking for. **1796** J. MORSE *Amer. Universal Geogr.* (ed. 3) I. 554 The African schools, into which slaves as well as free persons, of whatever age, of both sexes, are admitted gratis, and taught reading, writing, arithmetic &c. **1845** *Knickerbocker* XXVI. 334 Concert this evening, by the African Melodists. **1971** *Black World* Apr. 32 Black Theater .. should.. be utilizing.. the life-style of African peoples in America.

2. Special collocation: ***African elephant***, the species of elephant, *Loxodonda africana*, found in Africa, distinguished from the Indian by its larger ears and greater size; cf. *Indian elephant*, s.v. INDIAN *a.* 4 a.

1607 TOPSELL *Foure-f. Beasts* 192 Some Authors affirme, that the *African Elephants are much greater then the Indian. **1800** G. SHAW *Gen. Zool.* I. I. 224 The African Elephant is said to be smaller than the Asiatic: yet.. the largest tusks come from Africa. **1965** D. MORRIS *Mammals* 337 Other distinguishing characteristics of the African Elephant.. are the very large ears.. and the concave curve of the back.

Africana (æfrɪˈkɑːnə, -ˈeɪnə). [f. *Africa* + ANA *suff.*] Books, documents, or the like, relating to objects peculiar to, or connected with, Africa, in particular Southern Africa, especially those of value or interest to collectors.

1908 (*title of catalogue, Davis & Sons, Durban*) Africana: a list of work [*sic*] dealing with South Africa. **1943** *Africana Notes & News* Dec. 4 Africana is a word of many different meanings; to one it means books and other printed or manuscript material, to another it means objects other than books. For *Africana Notes and News* it is used in its widest sense, covering prints, maps,.. books, pamphlets,.. furniture, weapons, pictures and by-gones of all kinds—it is restricted only from a geographical point of view; it denotes not the whole of Africa but only Southern Africa. **1949** L. G. GREEN *Land of Afternoon* vi. 78 Greatest of all Africana collectors was Sidney Mendelssohn. **1952** E. H. BURROWS *Overberg Outspan* v. 122 A rare item of *africana* of a dozen or so pages.

Afriˈcander, Afriˈkander. Also Africaander, Afrikaander. [see AFRIKANER.]

1. = AFRIKANER 1. *obsolescent.*

1822 BURCHELL *Trav.* I. 21 All those who are born in the colony speak that language [*sc.* Dutch], and call themselves Africaanders, whether of Dutch, German, or French origin. **1834** *C. Gd. Hope Lit. Gaz.* IV. 103 (Pettman), The number of matches that have taken place between the fair

Africanders. **1882** *De Patriot* (Cape Colony) in *Encycl. Brit.* (1902) XXVI. 568/2 The Afrikander Bond has for its object the establishment of a South African Nationality by spreading a true love for what is really our fatherland. **1884** *Q. Rev.* July 150 The Africanders would hoist their own flag. *Ibid.*, An Africander republic. **1899** W. J. KNOX LITTLE *Sk. & Stud. S. Afr.* I. iv. 92 The Dutch Afrikander is wanting in this quality. The English Afrikander too suffers. **1900** A. H. KEANE *Boer States* viii. 161 Any African-born white person, whether of Dutch, English, or German origin, is an Afrikander in the social, if not in the political, sense of the term. **1905** [see *Afrikanderize* v. below]. **1939** J. S. MARAIS *Cape Coloured* v. 163 The majority of the slaves were 'Afrikaanders', that is to say Colonial-born. **1957** R. CAMPBELL *Portugal* 104 The word Afrikander is often applied by Englishmen to the human inhabitants of South Africa, who are Afrikaners without the 'd'.

2. A South African breed of cattle or sheep. Also *attrib.*

1852 *D'Urban Observer* 9 Jan. 4/1 There are..three or four recognized breeds now common in the country, viz., the *Fatherland*, the *Africanda*, and the *Zulu* and *Bastard Zulu*. *Ibid.* 4/2 Zulu cows crossed by Fatherland and Africander bulls. **1868** J. CHAPMAN *Trav. Int. S. Afr.* I. viii. 174 Rather higher than an Africander ox, with immense horns. **1874** F. OATES *Jrnl.* 6 Sept. in C. G. Oates *Matabele Land* (1881) iii. 48 Lee has just sold twelve red oxen—Africanders, with white faces. **1955** J. H. WELLINGTON *S. Afr.* II. v. 69 Non-woolled sheep..such as the Blackhead Persian, the Africander, [etc.].

3. *Bot.* = AFRIKANER 3.

1870 *Cape Monthly Mag.* Oct. 225 Yellow sorrel, pink 'Africanders', and the most lovely Magenta coloured wild 'figs'. **1915** R. MARLOTH *Flora of S. Afr.* IV. 157 *G.* [= *Gladiolus*] *grandis*..Often called the 'large brown Afrikander'. **1959** *Cape Argus* 15 Aug. 8/8 The blue afrikander (*gladiolus recurvus*..) is scenting the sandveld.

4. Afrikaans. *rare.*

1886 G. A. FARINI *Through Kalahari* xxvi. 434 A little nigger..said in Afrikander, 'That is Mr. Scott's..house.' **1902** G. M. G. HUNT (*title*) A Handy Vocabulary, English-Afrikander, Afrikander-English.

Hence **Afri'canderdom** = *Afrikanerdom*; **Afri'canderism** = *Afrikanerism*; **Afri'canderize** *v.* = *Afrikanerize* v.

1884 *Pall Mall Gaz.* 9 Oct. 2/2 Shall we throw in our lot with Afrikanderism, abjuring our nationality for evermore? **1891** *Sat. Rev.* 17 Jan. 59/2 The..apology for Afrikanderism which Sir Gordon Sprigg included in his speech on Imperial Federation. **1893** *Standard* 21 Apr. 6/2 The sympathy of Africanderdom. **1899** *Daily News* 16 Nov. 4/5 If South Africa was to be saved to the Empire, it would be by Afrikanderdom, and not by Downing-streetism. **1905** MILNER *Let.* 14 Apr. in C. Headlam *Milner Papers* (1933) II. 552 A separate Afrikander nation and State, comprising, no doubt, men of other races, who are ready to be 'afrikanderized'. **1909** *State* Dec. 701 If an English boy learns Dutch he is apt to acquire what are popularly called Dutchisms or Africanderisms.

Africanism ('æfrɪkənɪz(ə)m). [f. AFRICAN + -ISM.] An African mode of speech or idiom. Also, African qualities or characteristics in the aggregate.

1641 MILTON *Reform.* I. 38 He that cannot understand the sober..stile of the Scriptures, will be ten times more puzzl'd with the knotty Africanisms..of the Fathers. **1836** *New Monthly Mag.* XLVII. 152, I have spent some days in a town where every thing is pure Africanism. **1851** TRENCH *Exp. Serm. on Mt.* (ed. 2) Introd. ii. 27 The harsh Africanisms of Tertullian and Arnobius. **1882** B. F. WESTCOTT in Smith & Wace *Dict. Chr. Biogr.* (1887) IV. 139/2 The principles which he [*sc.* Origen] affirmed..are fitted to correct the Africanism which, since the time of Augustine, has dominated Western theology. **1884** G. W. CABLE *Creoles of Louisiana* xxxiii. 260 He [*sc.* the rich Creole] dropped..the Africanisms of his black nurse.

b. The policy which advocates that the indigenous inhabitants should have political control in Africa; African nationalism.

1957 HAILEY *African Survey* v. 251 It seems advisable on this occasion to give prominence to the use of the term 'Africanism' rather than 'nationalism'. **1959** *Cape Times* 14 Apr. 8/6 Africanism can be accepted as a solution in one sense, viz., that Africa in future must belong to the Africans, that is to those peoples who have chosen Africa as their home.

Africanist ('æfrɪkənɪst), *sb.* (and *a.*). [f. AFRICAN + -IST.] An expert or specialist in African affairs, culture, etc.

1895 *19th Cent.* XXXVIII. 455 (*heading*) Africanists in Council. **1926** E. W. SMITH *Chr. Mission in Afr.* vii. 56 A representative gathering attended by the leading Africanists of many nationalities. **1932** W. L. GRAFF *Language* xi. 433 Some Africanists make of the latter a distinct West African group.

b. An adherent of Africanism (sense b); an African nationalist.

1958 *Cape Times* 22 Dec. 12/7 What is the origin of the Africanists, the extreme Black nationalist group which recently broke away from the African National Congress? **1960** *Times* 12 Feb. 13/5 The Africanist would..like to know to what extent rule of Europeans in the West Indies ever resulted in the creation of economic privilege of the kind built up by European minorities in Africa. **1963** FENNER BROCKWAY *African Socialism* iii. 47 Touré is..the classical Africanist, unwilling to be the tool of any external Power or bloc of Powers, rejecting alike Western capitalism, European social democracy and Soviet communism.

Hence as *adj.* Also **Africa'nistic** *a.*

1958 *Spectator* 13 June 760/2 The African National Congress and other Africanist forces. **1959** *Cape Times* 28 Apr. 10/8 A Pan-Africanism, which is in a narrow and violent sense Africanistic. **1960** *Daily Tel.* 22 Aug. 8/2 Maybe Mr. Krushchev will find himself in the awkward position of being more 'Africanist' and more racialist than some of the independent African leaders themselves.

Africanity (,æfrɪ'kænɪtɪ). [f. AFRICAN *a.* + -ITY: cf. F. *Africanité.*] = AFRICANNESS.

1962 C. LEGUM *Pan-Africanism* vi. 95 Until they have 'recovered' their roots it is not possible to achieve what Senghor calls Africanity. **1969** N. HARE in A. Chapman *New Black Voices* (1972) 434 'Africanity' is the thing which 'cuts across the [O.A.U.] Festival'. **1969** *Daily Nation* (Nairobi) 7 Nov. 9/5 People of negroid stock in the Americas are generally regarded as under-dogs and perpetually foreign. We must do something to redeem their Africanity. **1972** J. R. RAYFIELD tr. *J. Maquet's Africanity* 13 Even if one.. limited the racial 'basis' of Africanity to the Black African race, one would not get a homogeneous substratum. **1973** *West Africa* 15 Oct. 1448/2 Talking to Europeans, Tagoe tends to lay on his 'Africanity' thickly.

Africanize ('æfrɪkənaɪz), *v.* [f. AFRICAN + -IZE.] To give an African character to; to make African; to subject to the influence or domination of African Negroes. Hence **,Africani'zation**; **'Africanized** *ppl. a.*; **'Africanizing** *vbl. sb.*

1853 JAS. BUCHANAN *Let.* 12 Nov. in J. F. Rhodes *Hist. U.S.* (1893) II. 26 A violent..article in the Washington *Union* charging them with an intrigue with Spain to 'Africanize' Cuba. **1856** S. CARTWRIGHT in J. F. Claiborne *Life of Quitman* (1860) II. 230 The Clayton-Bulwer Treaty, the preposterous claims..and the Africanization of tropical America. **1865** *Cincinnati Commercial* 4 July 1/2 A Yankee voice with Africanized accent. **1884** *N. Amer. Rev.* Nov. 429 When the Africanizing and ruin of the South becomes a clearly seen danger. **1905** *Tablet* 21 Oct. 649/2 They have become thoroughly Africanised, speak only the Ethiopian language. **1954** (*title*) A Statement on the Programme of the Africanisation of the Public Service (Gold Coast Govt., Accra). **1958** *Economist* 13 Dec. (African Suppl.) 7/2 The fate of Africa in the next decade, therefore, depends upon economic advance catching up with political advance in the 'Africanised' north and west. **1960** *Listener* 29 Sept. 498/2 The 'Africanization' to which so many firms have had to bow, by promoting their messengers and office boys into managing directors and retaining their Europeans merely as 'advisers'.

Africanness ('æfrɪkənnɪs). [f. AFRICAN *a.* + -NESS.] The quality or condition of being African, African character.

1961 *John o' London's* 15 June 659/1 An accent of Africanness—blackness if you will. **1961** S. HEMPSTONE *Africa* xxi. 629 Dubois..represents the first phase, in which the important feature was 'blackness', not 'Africanness'. **1971** *Black World* Oct. 10/1 Our Africanness..must operate with African 'spiritual communalism' as a philosophical base. **1973** *Ibid.* Apr. 5 Black people retain enough of their Africanness to be identifiable as such. **1980** *English World-Wide* I. 1. 90 The setting and languages leave no doubt as to its Africanness. **1981** B. B. KACHRU in Ferguson & Heath *Lang. in USA* ii. 30, I would like to discuss some typical characteristics of these other Englishes, which mark their distinctive 'Americanness', ..'Indianness', or 'Africanness'.

Africanoid ('æfrɪkənɔɪd), *a.* [f. AFRICAN + -OID.] Resembling the African types of mankind.

1899 RIPLEY *Races Eur.* 397 A long-headed member of the Africanoid races. **1921** *19th Cent.* May 884 The character-making quality did not come from Asianoid or Africanoid races, it was supplied by the Teuton.

Africanthropus (,æfrɪkən'θrəʊpəs, -'kænθrəʊpəs). *Anthropology.* [mod.L., f. *Africa* + Gr. ἄνθρωπος man.] The name given to a type of primitive hominid of the Pleistocene in Africa, known from remains found near Lake Njarasa (or Eyasi) in Tanzania. In full *Africanthropus njarasensis.*

[**1939** H. WEINERT in *Zeitschr. f. Morphologie & Anthropologie* XXXVIII. 252 Africanthropus njarasensis.] **1946** L. S. B. LEAKEY in *Jrnl. East Afr. Nat. Hist. Soc.* XIX. 43 The Eyasi Skull..has now been studied in detail by Dr. Weinert, who has created a new genus *Africanthropus* for it. **1948** A. L. KROEBER *Anthropol.* iii. 90 *Africanthropus njarasensis* is a discovery, made by Kohl-Larsen in 1935, whose definitive description is one of many delayed by World War II.

Afridi (ə'friːdɪ). Also **Afreedi.** [Pashto.] A Pathan people inhabiting the mountainous region between Pakistan and Afghanistan; a member of this people. Also *attrib.*

1815 M. ELPHINSTONE *Kingdom of Caubul* III. i. 356 The Khyberees consist of three independent tribes,..the Afreedees, Shainwaurees, and Oorookzyes. **1875** *Encycl. Brit.* I. 227/2 The Momands, Afrîdîs, Vasîrîs, &c. **1908** MRS. H. WARD *D. Mallory* I. ii. 27 In the English House of Commons, there were men..who held an Afridi life dearer than an English one. **1923** KIPLING *Land & Sea Tales* 4 The little hillsman of the North-east Indian Frontier, Afreedi, Pathan, Biluch. **1932** —— *Limits & Renewals* 209 He was a hard-bitten Afridi from the Khaiber hills.

Afrikaans (æfrɪ'kɑːns), *sb.* and *a.* Also (rarely) **Africaans.** [= Du. *Afrikaansch* (now written *Afrikaans*): see AFRICAN and -ISH.] **A.** *sb.* The modified form of Dutch spoken in South Africa. Formerly also called CAPE *Dutch*, *South African Dutch*, the TAAL.

[**1900** A. H. KEANE *Boer States* p. xix, *Taal*, Cape Dutch, called by the Netherlanders *Afrikaansch*.] **1908** *East London Dispatch* 20 Oct. 4 (Pettman), I have always regarded (high) Dutch as my mother tongue and Africaans (low Dutch) as a hodge-pot sort of a language. **1921** *Glasgow Herald* 21 July 4 The dream of the young Dutch Nationalist is of a great Dutch South African Republic, the language of which would be Afrikaans. **1925** *Times* 25 Mar. 13/2 Afrikaans, the South African form of the Dutch language,..had been introduced in schools and churches in South Africa, and there were now proposals that it should become the official language of the Union, side by side with English. **1952** [see AFRIKANER 1].

Comb. **1946** *Mind* LV. 45 In South Africa among the Afrikaans-speaking community ('the Dutch').

B. *adj.* Of, pertaining to, or designating the Afrikaans language or the Afrikaans-speaking people (cf. AFRIKANER 1).

1923 J. REYNOLDS (*title*) Maskew Miller's Afrikaans Exercises for Secondary Schools. **1927** *Off. Year Bk. of S. Afr.* 16 At present German origin seems acceptable in the case of only a few Afrikaans words. *Ibid.*, It has been calculated that the proportion of German blood in the Afrikaans colonists up to the year 1806 was about 27 per cent. *Ibid.* 22 The Afrikaans language..enjoys complete official recognition to-day. **1935** *Times* 8 Nov. 13/3 The Afrikaner Broederbond, originally a laudable society interested in Afrikaans culture..but now a secret society aiming for an independent Afrikaans form of government. **1948** *Cape Times* 25 Aug. 3 The Cape Town Afrikaanse Sakekamer (Afrikaans Chamber of Commerce).

Afrikaner (æfrɪ'kɑːnər). Also **Afrikaaner.** [Afrikaans, earlier (Cape) Du. *Afrikaander*, f. *Afrikaan* sb., African + *-d)er*, pers. suff. modelled on termination of *Hollander* Dutchman. Cf. AFRICANDER.]

1. An Afrikaans-speaking white South African, esp. one of Dutch descent; also occas. applied to any white citizen of South Africa. Also *attrib.* (Replacing AFRICANDER.)

1824 BURCHELL *Trav.* II. 619/2 (*index*) Africaánders, or Afrikaáners. **1905** R. FENTON *Peculiar People* p. vi, As General Piet Joubert said to me one day: 'We are Afrikaaners, not Dutchmen.' **1926** S. G. MILLIN *S. Africans* VI. ii. 157 The South African of Dutch descent whom one loosely and inappropriately speaks of as a Dutchman, but who prefers to define himself as an Afrikaner. **1930** *Times Lit. Suppl.* 26 June 525/2 The Afrikaaner attitude towards the British Empire. **1937** W. K. HANCOCK *Survey Brit. Commonw. Affairs* I. 269 By struggle the French Canadians and the Afrikaners won from the British respect for their individual ways of life. **1952** L. MARQUARD *Peoples & Policies S. Afr.* iii. 65 In this book Afrikaner is used to mean a South African of European extraction whose mother-tongue is Afrikaans. **1958** *Observer* 20 Apr. 4/5 In the South African general election the Nationalists..have set the Afrikaner nation upon a dominating rock.

2. = AFRICANDER 2.

1918 *Off. Year Bk. of S. Afr.* 386 There was created a distinct type [of cattle] which came to be known as the *Afrikaner*. **1939** *Nature* 11 Nov. 819/1 Zootechnical studies on Afrikaner, imported, and grade cattle.

3. *Bot.* An iridaceous South African flower belonging to any of various species of *Gladiolus* or *Homoglossum*.

1801 J. BARROW *Trav. S. Afr.* I. 25 The *Gladiolus*, which is here called *Africaner*, is uncommonly beautiful with its tall waving spike of striped flowers, and has also a fragrant smell. **1950** ADAMSON & SALTER *Flora Cape Penin.* 263 *H.* [= *Homoglossum*] *Watsonium*..Red Afrikaner. **1959** *Cape Times* 7 Sept. 2/6 Of the gladioli, the brown Afrikaners attracted most attention.

Hence **Afri'kanerdom**, the Afrikaner people or nation in South Africa; Afrikaners collectively; Afrikaner nationalism; **Afri'kanerism**, (*a*) the policy, ideals or aspirations of Afrikaners; Afrikaner nationalism; (*b*) an Afrikaans word or idiom used in South African English; **Afri'kanerize** *v.*, to bring under the influence or rule of Afrikaners; to make like an Afrikaner; so **Afri'kanerizing** *vbl. sb.* and *ppl. a.*, **Afri,kaneri'zation.**

1926 S. G. MILLIN *S. Africans* VI. i. 156 There was a spirit of Afrikanerdom abroad. **1934** A. J. BARNOUW *Lang. & Race Probl. S. Afr.* 26 This language [*sc.* Afrikaans] is to the Nationalists the hall mark of their Afrikanerism. **1935** *Cape Times* 8 Nov. 8/4 Wherever these..ministers of religion use the words 'Afrikaner' and 'Afrikanerdom' they mean 'Afrikaans-speaking Afrikaner' and 'Afrikaans-speaking Afrikanerdom'. **1942** 'B. KNIGHT' *Sun Climbs* III. xxv. 229 He is lost in his dreams of Afrikanerism. **1947** *Forum* 5 Apr. 5/2 The Afrikanerising of the cities..had gone ahead by leaps and bounds. **1952** E. H. BURROWS *Overberg Outspan* vii. 190 The afrikanerizing influence she exerted on her husband. **1952** B. DAVIDSON *Rep. S. Afr.* III. ii. 158 The 'Afrikanerization' of public life and education 'in the Christian National sense'. **1955** SARON & HOTZ *Jews in S. Afr.* xi. 207 Of those who fought on the Boer side, some were Jewish burghers who..had become thoroughly Afrikanerized. **1958** A. PATON *Hope for S. Afr.* vii. 52 As in the past Afrikaners were subject to a process of anglicization, so now English-speaking people are subject to a process of Afrikanerization. **1959** *Cape Argus* 21 Nov. 11/3 Among the words which fall in the category of Afrikanerisms, now in common use in the English language in this country, are bobotie, gousblom. **1960** *20th Cent.* July 63 The Nationalists sought to Afrikanerize the white trades unions.

Afro ('æfrəʊ), *a.* and *sb. colloq.* (orig. *U.S.*). [f. the combining form AFRO-.] **A.** *adj.* African; Afro-American. **a.** Applied to a naturally bushy, short-curled style of hair worn by some Blacks and to frizzed hairstyles in imitation of this.

1938 C. HIMES *Pork Chop Paradise* in *Black on Black* (1973) 174 Platinum blond hair puffed up atop her head in an Afro plume. **1966** T. PYNCHON in *N.Y. Times* Mag. 12 June 82 The same goes for boys who like to wear..Afro haircuts. **1969** A. YOUNG in A. Chapman *New Black Voices* (1972) 367 You need real color..nappy snaggly afro hair. **1971** *Sunday Nation* (Nairobi) 11 Apr. 6/2 Tiny transistor tape-recorders which the girls used to carry in their gigantic Afro-wigs. **1975** D. LODGE *Changing Places* v. 176 Negroes with Afro haircuts like mushroom clouds. **1984** *N.Y. Times* 3 Sept. I. 11/1 A comb used for Afro haircuts.

b. More generally, esp. with reference to styles of music, clothing, etc.

1968 *N.Y. Times* 24 May 30/1 The huts proclaim 'Love Yes, Love Now',..'Afro Ballroom', 'Leo's Casino', [etc.]. **1969** *Sunday Times* (Colour Suppl.) 9 Mar. 40/1 In clothes, Afro styling seems to be taking hold among blacks all over New York. **1970** A. D. MILLER in A. Chapman *New Black Voices* (1972) 539 Few..will doubt that the American sense of music is of Afro origin. **1971** *Community* (E. Afr. Community) Apr. 6/1 The air hostesses will be provided with aprons—an attractive afro design in two colours (beige and brown). **1984** *Washington Post* 6 Sept. B11 America's last great regional rock tradition—a jubilant party mix of the best Afro, Latin, Caribbean and Anglo spirits—faces extinction.

c. In Comb., as ***Afro-haired***, ***-wigged*** adjs.

1976 A. SCHROEDER *Shaking it Rough* xvii. 52 The *Afro-haired man steps back to the corner of the cell and sits down. **1973** *Black World* Jan. 55/1 He could see the dimples in the knees of the *Afro-wigged sales girl.

B. *sb.* **a.** An English or American person of African descent, a Black.

1942 BERREY & VAN DEN BARK *Amer. Thes. Slang* §385/14 *Negro*, Afro, black bean, [etc.]. **1970** A. D. MILLER in A. Chapman *New Black Voices* (1972) 539 The writing aimed at the heart and life of the country [*sc.* the U.S.A.] is coming increasingly from Afros. **1972** *Observer* 13 Aug. 7/2 The 'Afros' wear clenched-fist or Angela Davis badges. **1974** *Black World* June 23/1, I wouldn't be surprised if it turns out that Afros have a larger percentage of people with these *psi* abilities than other groups.

b. The name of an Afro-Cuban (esp. salsa) dance or its music. *rare.*

1956 M. W. STEARNS *Story of Jazz* xix. 248 The clavé rhythm..occurs in practically all Cuban music including the Afro, the Bolero, the Guaracha,..and so on. **1958** [see GUARACHA].

c. (Occas. afro.) An Afro hairstyle. Also *transf.* and *fig.*

1970 C. MAJOR *Dict. Afro-Amer. Slang* 19 *Afro*, 'natural' hair style..long..woolly. **1971** B. MALAMUD *Tenants* 221 A black man with a thick full beard, wearing a spiky Afro like a dangerous plant on his head. **1974** K. MILLETT *Flying* (1975) II. 194 Lila..has been to the hairdresser and got herself a Jewish afro. **1977** *New Yorker* 1 Aug. 13/2 When it's over I look out my window at the Afros of haze that the traffic has left around the street lights. **1984** *Washington Post* 19 Aug. K1/3 A young architect with..the biggest Afro this side of the Niger river.

Afro- ('æfrəʊ), used as comb. form of L. *Afer*, *Afr-* African, as in ***Afro-American*** (also *Aframerican*) adj. and sb., (a person) of African descent born in America (spec. the United States); ***Afro-Aryan*** adj., African and Aryan; ***Afro-Asian*** adj., of or pertaining to both Africa and Asia; also sb.; similarly also, ***Afro-Brazilian***, ***-Caribbean***, ***-Cuban***, ***-European***, ***-Spanish***, adjs. and sbs.

1853 *Voice of Fugitive* (Windsor, Ont.) 21 June 2/4 In our opinion, the true policy of the *Afro-American race..is to emigrate to Canada, the West Indies. **1890** *Advance* 23 Jan. 61/2 To encourage all State and local leagues..in obtaining for the Afro-American an equal chance. *Ibid.* 80/1 The Afro-American Convention in Chicago. **1898** *Westm. Gaz.* 31 May 3/1 She is a New Orleans Creole, her mother being an Afro-American, and her father a Louisiana Frenchman. **1910** H. H. JOHNSTON *Negro in New World* 390 In music the Aframerican..may achieve triumphs. **1934** C. LAMBERT *Music Ho!* III. 201 By jazz..I mean the whole movement roughly designated as such, and not merely that section of it known as Afro-American. **1939** W. HOBSON *Amer. Jazz Mus.* 29 Afro-Americans have been the chief rhythmic originators in the forty-year spread of both ragtime and jazz. **1944** H. L. MENCKEN in *Amer. Speech* XIX. 161 When the New York *Times* announced in an editorial on March 7, 1930, that it would capitalize the word *Negro* thereafter, there were loud hosannahs from the Aframerican intelligentsia. **1914** *Lancet* 4 Apr. 966/2 An *Afro-Aryan child aged 3 years, the offspring of a male African negro and a female Cingalese. **1955** *Newsweek* 17 Jan. 14/1 The critical issue at the 30-nation *Afro-Asian conference here in April ..will be a behind-scenes struggle for power between India's Nehru and Red China's Chou En-lai. **1956** *Ann. Reg. 1955* 165 The Afro-Asian conference..at Bandung.. was attended by Ministers of twenty-nine states, from Liberia to Japan, but not including Soviet Asia. **1958** *Observer* 6 July 12/6 More immediate fears tend to overshadow the long-term political value of wooing the Afro-Asians. **1946** R. BLESH *Shining Trumpets* 346 This disc is one of an *Afro-Brazilian collection. **1963** *Times* 12 June 16/6 Heitor dos Praeres..is an expert on Afro-Brazilian folklore. **1976** *Wilson Q.* Autumn 89 Afro-Brazilians represent roughly 40 percent of the total population. **1984** *Christian Science Monitor* 5 Sept. 9/4 Afro-Brazilian cults are making inroads. **1958** *Oxf. Mail* 14 Feb. 9/6 Lessons in *Afro-Caribbean dancing..for..members of the Oxford University Ballet Club. **1959** *Encounter* Dec. 53/1 In the bad old days, when..the Afro-Caribbeans had little but humiliation. **1949** L. FEATHER *Inside Be-bop* vi. 41 George Russell..penned an *Afro-Cuban drums suite. **1956** M. W. STEARNS *Story of Jazz* (1957) xix. 252 Perhaps the most stable pattern..was established by Machito and his Afro-Cubans. **1895** A. H. KEANE *Ethnology* xiv. 409 The original Aryan type..resembled that of the *Afro-European as represented by the Mauritanian Berbers. **1959** *Listener* 5 Nov. 791/2 He has the same right to talk of the land in which he has grown up as any other Afro-European. **1946** *Jazz Writings* 3/2 Spanish American rhythms in the blues (such as the rhythm of the *Afro-Spanish 'habanera', created in Havana, Cuba).

†**a'front**, *adv.* and *prep.* prop. *phr. Obs.* [A *prep.*[1] in + FRONT *sb.* Used to translate Fr. *de front* which has the same range of use.]

A. *adv.*

1. Face to face, in direct opposition; opposite.

*c*1380 *Sir Ferumb.* 1689 An hundred knyȝtes wyþ-oute faille: þer-on [*i.e.* on the bridge] affrount mowe mete. **1587** HOLINSHED *Chron.* III. 824/1 The king of England lieng afront before Tornaie. **1601** HOLLAND *Pliny* VIII. xxv, These Islanders be the only men that dare encountre him affront.

2. In front.

1587 HOLINSHED *Chron.* I. 50/1 Least his people should be assailed not onlie afront, but also vpon euerie side. **1611** SPEED *Hist. Gt. Brit.* IX. ii. 421/1 No way lay open saue onely a front. **1621** QUARLES *Hadassa*, The Bullwarks stand afront to keep thee out. **1870** SMITH *Syn. & Antonyms*, Aback, *Ant.* ahead, afront.

3. In a front; abreast.

*c*1400 *Tundale Vis.* 1001 Afrontte unneþe thei myght passe. **1596** SHAKS. *1 Hen. IV*, II. iv. 222 These foure came all a-front and mainely thrust at me. **1613** PURCHAS *Pilgr.* I. v. iii. 395 Twelve men may ride a-front through them. **1621** MOLLE *Camerarius' Liv. Lib.* V. i. 318 To containe two gallies afront with ease.

B. *prep.* [The adv. limited by a sb.] In front of.

1557 PHAËR *Æneid* VI. Q i b, Than death himself, whose neighbour next was Slepe.. and Mortal Warres afront the gate. **1610** HOLLAND *Camden's Brit.* I. 227 Two bulwarks strong afront the Foe are rais'd. **1622** CALLIS *Statute of Sewers* (1647) 25, 1600 Acres were gained from the Sea, affront the Mannor of sir Valentine Brown there.

afrormosia (æfrɔː'məʊzɪə). [G. (H. Harms in Engler and Prantl *Pflanzenfamilien* (1906) Suppl. III. 158), f. AFRO- + mod.L. *Ormosia* (1811), genus of trees.] A North and West African tree of the genus *Afrormosia* (fam. *Leguminosæ*), esp. *A. laxiflora* and *A. elata*; also, its timber.

1920 A. H. UNWIN *W. African Forests* ix. 271 Nigerian Timber Trees..*Afrormosia elata*. African Satinwood, Yellow Satinwood... The timber planes well..it is very hard and withstands the attacks of white ants. **1925** H. V. LELY *Useful Trees N. Nigeria* 11 *Afrormosia* Laxiflora..a small or medium-sized tree very common in bush or tree savannah, averaging 30 feet in height. The wood..very dark brown...is used for axe and hoe handles. **1956** *Archit. Rev.* CXX. 126/1 The furniture and joinery are of afrormosia (a wood very similar to teak in colour and quality), except for the small chairs which are black, with rush seats. **1960** *Times* 7 Mar. 3/3 A consumers' paradise of transistor radio sets, electric food mixers, and afrormosia coffee tables.

†**afrought**, *ppl. a.* [for *offruht* = *offurht*; see AFFRIGHT *a.* Cf. also OE. *anforht* timid.] Frightened, timid.

*c*1450 *Morte Arthur* 73 The bysschope spake w^{t} oute fayle, Thoughe he were nothynge afroughte.

afrown (ə'fraʊn), *adv.* and *pred. a.* prop. *phr.* [A *prep.*[1] + FROWN.] In frowning posture.

1878 JOAQUIN MILLER *Songs of Italy* 55 The lion of Venice with brows a-frown.

Afshar ('æfʃɑː(r)). A kind of Persian rug or small carpet hand-woven by nomads of the Afshar tribe in south-east Iran. Freq. *attrib.*

1913 W. A. HAWLEY *Oriental Rugs* xvi. 286 The Afshars have coarse, wiry wool for the weft, and threads of warp strung so that each half knot is distinct. **1931** [see KASHGAI b]. **1962** C. W. JACOBSEN *Oriental Rugs* 167 Not even a beginner should mistake an Afshar for a Kazak. **1975** *Oxf. Compan. Decorative Arts* 612/1 The..Niris and Afshar rugs have the cone patterns.

aft (ɑːft, æ-), *adv.* Forms: 1 æftan, (2-6 wanting), 7 afte, 7- aft. [As usual with nautical terms the early history is lost; but comparison with the derived *baft* (earlier *baftè*, *baften*, *bæftan*, *be æftan*), show it to be the OE. *æftan*, cogn. w. Goth. *aftana* from behind, f. *afta* behind; formally a superlative of *af* off, away, with primitive superlative suffix *-ta*: cf. Gr. ὕπα-τος, πρῶ-τος. The true relation of *af-ter* and *af-t* is that of Gr. πρό-τερος and πρῶ-τος; but OE. *æftan* was only an adv. of position, and it is apt to be treated in mod. Eng. as the positive of AFTER.]

†**1.** *gen.* Behind, in the rear. *Obs.*

937 *O.E. Chron., B. of Brunanburh* 63 Let him behindan ..earn æftan hwit· æses brúcan.

2. *Naut.* **a.** Of position: In or near the hinder part or stern of a ship. Also of an aircraft.

1628 DIGBY *Voy. Medit.* (1868) 3 Of aequall height fore and aft. **1706** PHILLIPS s.v., How chear ye fore and aft? *i.e.* How fares all your Ships Company? **1718** STEELE *Fish-pool* 170 Whose hold had gratings 'fore and aft'. **1863** LONGF. *Olaf* xi, Though the flying sea-spray drenches Fore and aft the rowers' benches.

b. Of motion or direction: Towards the stern, into the hinder part of the ship. Also of an aircraft.

1678 PHILLIPS, *Aft* or *Abaft*, a word us'd by Seamen to signify any Action, Motion, or Application from the Stemwards of the Ship toward the Stern; as Go *aft.* **1748** ANSON *Voyage* III. ii. (ed. 4) 425 We..began to get the guns aft. **1832** LANDER *Exped. Niger* III. xvi. 254 Call them aft, and let them stand by the arms. **1833** MARRYAT *Pet. Simple* (1863) 52 He said to us as we came on deck,—'Walk aft, young gentlemen.' **1859** W. JAMES *Nav. Hist. Gt. Brit.* IV. 73 Seized and carried aft, as the ringleader of the mutiny. **1948** 'N. SHUTE' *No Highway* ix. 242 We climbed up into the fuselage and went aft through the luggage bay.

c. *fore and aft*: from stem to stern, lengthwise. Also *attrib.*

*a*1618 RALEIGH *Inv. Shipping* 29 Needing no other addition..then a slight spar Decke, fore and afte as the Seamen call it. **1878** M. FOSTER *Physiol.* II. i. §3. 225 A certain amount of lateral and fore and aft movement.

3. Of time: Back from the present, earlier.

1674 N. FAIRFAX *Bulk & Selv.* 38 There being nothing but everlasting God..there can be no such thing as Time, or fore, or aft, at all. **1676** HOBBES *Odyssey* 299 Next him spake Alitherses, who alone Saw fore and aft.

4. *Comb.* **aft-cabin**, **aft-meal** = *after-cabin*, *after-banquet* in AFTER- *in comb.* II.

1816 *Gentl. Mag.* LXXXVI. I. 102 The aft-cabin was only wanting to make the boat complete. *a*1608 THYNNE *Debate* 49 (N) At aft-meales who shall paye for the wine? **1896** *Strand Mag.* XII. 323/1 At the fore-end and at the aft-end of the vessel. **1915** 'BARTIMEUS' *Tall Ship* i. 9 He..was precipitated through his cabin door across the aft-deck. **1948** 'N. SHUTE' *No Highway* i. 27 The aft windows of the cabin. **1961** *Engineering* 20 Jan. 123/1 The aft-engine concept pioneered..in the Caravelle..has..been adopted by Boeing for its short to medium range 727.

after ('ɑːftə(r), æ-), *adv.* and *prep.* Forms: 1-3 **æfter**, 2-3 **eafter**, 2-4 **efter**, 3-9 **after**; occas. 4-6 **aftir, -yr, -ur, -re**. North. 4-7 **efter, -ir, -yr**. [OE. *æfter* cogn. w. OS. and OHG. *aftar*, *-er*, OFris. *efter* adv. and prep., ON. *aptr* adv., *eptir* prep., Goth. *aftra* back, *aftaro* from behind, adv.; Gr. ἀπωτέρω, Skr. *apatarām*. Orig. a compar. form of *af*, L. *ab*, Gr. ἀπό, Skr. *ápa*, with compar. suffix *-ter*, -THER; = 'farther off, at a greater distance from the front, or from a point in front'; and hence in the Teutonic languages 'more to the rear, behind, later.' Used in the oldest Eng. as a separable verbal particle capable of governing a case (dat. or acc.) in composition, whence, when detached from the vb., it appeared as *adv.* or *prep.* according to the absence or presence of an object.]

¶ As adv. or prep. in separable comp.

*c*885 K. ÆLFRED *Oros.* I. x, Him æfter folȝiende wæron. *c*1230 *Juliana* (R.MS.) (1872) 32 Ant hare fan..þat ham efter sohten [*Bodl. MS.* ferden ham efter].

A. *adv.*

1. Of place or order: In the rear, behind. (With *go*, *come*, *follow*, etc.)

*c*1000 *O.E. Gosp.* Matt. xxi. 9 Ðæt folc þæt þar beforan ferde, and þæt þar æfter ferde. *c*1160 *Hatton Gosp.* ibid., Ðæt folc þe þær before ferde, & þæt þe þær æfter ferde. **1205** LAYAMON 1572 Þe king sette to fleonne and al þa ferde eafter. *c*1380 *Sir Ferumb.* 1001 & þay folȝeyeþ after wiþ rendouns. **1611** BIBLE *Luke* xxiii. 55 And the women also..followed after, and beheld the Sepulchre. *Nursery Rhyme*, Jack fell down and broke his crown, And Jill came tumbling after. *Mod.* Put your own first, and let these come after.

2. Of time: Subsequently, at a later time; afterwards. Formerly used before the vb., now only at the end of a sentence or clause, and chiefly in phr. ***before or after***, or as in 2 b.

*a*1000 *Beowulf* 24 Ðǣm eafera wæs æfter cenned. *c*1220 *Leg. St. Kath.* 1223 We mahen haue sikere bileaue to arisen alle after. **1375** BARBOUR *Bruce* I. 127 And wyst nocht quhat suld eftir tyd. *c*1400 *Destr. Troy* IV. 1439 Gyf an end hade ben now, & neuer noyet efter. **1481** CAXTON *Reynard* (Arb.) 65 Men may wel lye whan it is nede and after amende it. **1594** PLAT *Jewell-ho.* II. 40 A..substance, which you may after cleanse by ablution. **1601** SHAKS. *Jul. Cæs.* I. ii. 76 If you know, That I do fawne on men..And after scandall them. *a*1631 DONNE *Serm.* xcii. IV. 171 The very place where Solomon's Temple was after built. **1640** FULLER *Abel Rediv., Peter Martyr* (1867) I. 251 Our worthy Jewel, after bishop of Salisbury. **1756** BURKE *Subl. & B.* Wks. I. 256 All we do after it is but a faint struggle. **1768** H. WALPOLE *Hist. Doubts* 5 The king smote the young prince on the face, and after his servants slew him. *Mod.* I never spoke to him after; I was never so treated either before or after.

b. *esp.* In combination with another adv. of time or adverbial phrase, ***soon after***, ***long after***, ***an hour***, ***a year after***. The ***day***, the ***year after*** = next following.

*c*950 *Lindisf. Gosp.* Mark x. 1 Gesomnadon efter sona menigo to him. *a*1000 ? CÆDMON *Gen.* (Grein) 550 Æfter siððan. *c*1340 *Gaw. & Gr. Knt.* 1640 & efter-sones of þe same he serued hym þere. **1513** DOUGLAS *Æneis* IX. v. 40 Brocht in schort quhile eftir syne. **1536** WRIOTHESLEY *Chron.* (1875) I. 36 The morrowe after, being Satterdaie. **1611** BIBLE *John* i. 35 The next day after John stood, and two of his disciples. **1625** HART *Anat. Ur.* II. iv. 73 This flux continued..for some few dayes after. *Ibid.* II. vi. 87 She died about two months after. **1753** HANWAY *Travels* (1762) II. VIII. i. 183 Soon after the artillery..proclaimed the news to the people. *Mod.* That must have been in the week after.

B. *prep.* **I.** Of place.

1. a. With verbs of motion (expressed or implied): Following, going, or coming in the rear of, behind.

*c*1000 *Ags. Gosp.* Luke ix. 23 Ȝyf hwá wyle æfter me cuman. *c*1175 *Lamb. Hom.* 5 Al þe..folc þe eode efter him ..sungun þisne lofsong. *c*1230 *Ancren Riwle* 196 Up oðe hulles heo clumben efter us. **1297** R. GLOUC. 398 Roberd erl of Flaundres after þulke ost come. **1388** WYCLIF *Luke* xiv. 27 He that berith not his cross, and cometh aftir me. **1526** TINDALE and **1611** *ibid.*, Come after me. **1593** SHAKS. *2 Hen. VI*, v. iii. 27 Shall we after them? After them, nay, before them, if we can. **1707** *Lond. Gaz.* mmmmcccxxxiii/7 After whom rode on Horse-back a Courier of the Republick. **1816**

J. WILSON *City of Plague* I. ii. 271 That merciless ghost that walks the sea After our ship for ever. *c* **1840** J. S. KNOWLES *Virgin* I. i, The people will throng after him with shouts.

b. ***after you*** (and similar, incl. extended, expressions): a formula used in yielding precedence; ***after you with***, colloq. request for the next turn at (something).

1650 R. HEATH *Clarastella* Epigrams 33 Oh! after him is manners. *a* **1652** [see MANNER *sb.*[1] 7 a]. **1721** J. KELLY *Sc. Proverbs* 42 After you is good Manners. Spoken when our Betters offer to serve us first. **1738** SWIFT *Polite Conv.* ii. 139 Oh! Madam; after you is good Manners. **1899** R. WHITEING *No. 5 John St.* xiv. 139, I remember the fine-company style of Tildor's tea-party, 'After you's manners', whenever we passed the plate. **1927** W. E. COLLINSON *Contemp. Eng.* 31 The card-expressions now most prevalent in a figurative application are drawn in the main from bridge e.g...*after you, partner*. **1935** ISHERWOOD *Mr. Norris* ix. 136 'After you.' 'No, please.' **1955** E. POUND *Classic Anthol.* III. 152 Taught 'em to bow and stand aside, Say: after you, and: if you please.

†**2.** Of position: Behind. *Obs. rare.*

c **1380** WYCLIF *Tract.* i. 22 Crist clepide hym Sathanas and badde him go after hym. *c* **1380** *Sir Ferumb.* 2776 Spedilich in þey wente, & After hymen made þe gate faste. *c* **1400** *Apol. for Loll.* 56 Go o bak after Me, Sathanas. **1483** CAXTON *G. de la Tour* a ij, Suche ther be that lawgheth to fore yow, whiche after youre back goo mockyng. **1704** NEWTON *Opticks* (J.) Sometimes I placed a third prism after a second, and sometimes also a fourth after a third.

†**3.** Following the course of (anything extended in space); *hence*, along (a linear dimension); across or away over (an extended surface). *Obs.* or *dial.*

878 *O.E. Chron.* He [Ælfred] lytle werede .. æfter wudum for, and on mor fæstenum. *a* **1000** *Beowulf* 2854 ȝesawon þa æfter wætere Wyrm-cynnes fela. *c* **1200** *Moral Ode* 233 Þor is woninge & wop after eche strete. **1205** LAYAMON 13777 Al þat verden æfter wæi. *Ibid.* 23140 And fluȝen after þere sæ. [In Somerset a keeper says, 'You'd best go down along after that wall—after that ditch;' an apothecary says, 'the pain seems to lie after the cheek bone.' Cf. 'You had better follow the wall.']

†**b.** Along the surface of, close to. *Obs. rare.*

a **1000** *Shrine* 132 Þæt haliȝe blod orn æfter eorðan. **1523** FITZHERBERT *Husbandry* (1534) D iv, Hey commeth of a grasse called crofote, and groweth flatte, after the erthe.

4. Following with intent to overtake, pursuing, in pursuit of. **a.** Primarily, in reference to things in motion; **b.** also to things at rest, when their place is doubtful; *esp.* with *go*, *send*: in search of, in quest of, to find. ***to be after***: to be in pursuit of, trying to reach or get into the company of (a person), trying to get or do (a thing); also, to attend to, keep watch upon, 'see to'.

a. *c* **1000** ÆLFRIC *Gen.* xxxi. 36 For hwilcum gylta ferdest þu þus after me? **1154** *O.E. Chron.* (Laud. MS.) an. 1132 Þe king sende efter him. **1375** BARBOUR *Bruce* v. 511 Eftir hym in hy he sent. **1611** BIBLE *1 Sam.* xxiv. 14 After whom is the king of Israel come out? after whom dost thou pursue? After a dead dogge, after a flea. **1623** SANDERSON *35 Serm.* (1681) I. 91 He must after them, and smite them, and pluck the spoil out of their teeth. **1708** *Lond. Gaz.* mmmmccccxix/5 They stand from us, and we after them with all the Sail we can. *a* **1884** *Mod.* Run after him and catch him!

b. *c* **1000** ÆLFRIC *Deut.* vi. 14 Ne far þu æfter fremdum godum. **1061** *O.E. Chron.* (D.) Her for Ealdred biscop to Rome æfter his pallium. *c* **1175** *Lamb. Hom.* 7 God almihti sende his apostles .. efter þe assa fole. *c* **1435** *Torr. Portugal* 500 Hys squyeres bode he ther Aftyr hys armor for to far. **1611** BIBLE *Deut.* vi. 14 Yee shall not goe after other gods. **1742** RICHARDSON *Pamela* III. 201 There is nobody comes after her: she receives no Letters. **1775** SHERIDAN *Rivals* v. ii. 152 What tricks are you after now? **1856** C. M. YONGE *Daisy Chain* I. vii. 67 You are a little bit of a sloven, and .. some one must be always after you. **1876** FREEMAN *Norm. Conq.* II. x. 462 The new Metropolitan went to Rome after his pallium. *a* **1884** *Mod. fam.* There are many after this situation. She has too many followers; always some young man after her.

c. *Anglo-Ir.* With *to be* and pres. pple.: (*a*) to be in the act of; to be on the point of, desirous of, bent on (doing something); (*b*) to have just (done something).

1792 H. H. BRACKENRIDGE *Mod. Chivalry* I. IV. iii. 99 The Irishman .. utterly refused to be after fighting in any such manner. **1827** J. BARRINGTON *Personal Sk. Own Times* I. i. 208 Then it's fitter .. for you to be after putting your *sign* there in your pocket. **1848** M. KELLY tr. *Lynch's Cambrensis Eversus* I. 35 A prince who was then after renouncing the dogmas of the ancient creed. **1862** T. C. CROKER *Fairy Legends S. Ireland* 220 It is not every lady that would be after making [*sc.* would have made] such an offer. **1904** J. M. SYNGE *Shadow of Glen* (1905) 9 He's after dying on me, God forgive him. **1916** J. B. COOPER *Coo-oo-ee* viii. 93 'Gorrah!' exclaimed Mrs. O'Callaghan. 'Is he after makin' me drunk?' **1922** JOYCE *Ulysses* 295 Sure I'm after seeing him not five minutes ago. **1938** P. KAVANAGH *Green Fool* xxv. 260 If it wasn't the turnips it was the pigs were after breaking loose, or a hen they wanted me to help catch for the fowl dealer. **1958** B. BEHAN *Borstal Boy* I. 125 Well, I was after living through the winter and on the ninth I would be seventeen. **1979** *Lore & Lang.* Jan. 13, I would have enclosed the thirty-five dollars I owe you, only I'm already after sealing the envelope.

5. Hence, Denoting the aim or object of many vbs., adjs., and sbs. of action; the idea of *in pursuit of*, passing into those of *in order to overtake*, *attain to*, *come up with*, *meet with*, *find*, *discover*, *learn*; *obtain*, *get*, *have*.

†**a.** To ***stand, abide, after***; i.e. in expectation of, to catch, meet. *Obs.*

c **1200** *Ormul.* 6506 Herode king Bad affterr þeȝȝre com. **1297** R. GLOUC. 367 After betere wynd hii moste þere at stonde. *c* **1374** CHAUCER *Boethius* (1868) 13 Yif þou abidest after helpe of þi leche. **1393** LANGL. *P. Pl.* C. II. 124 Hewes in þe halyday · after hete wayten. **1515** *Festyvall* (W. de Worde) 79 b, The abbot .. stode under a pyler and abode after Thomas.

b. To ***look, see, after*** (a thing gone, going, or liable to go); hence, To look to the state of, attend to.

1375 BARBOUR *Bruce* IV. 616 Eftir the fyre he lukit fast. **1393** LANGL. *P. Pl.* C. I. 14 Esteward ich byhulde · after þe sonne. *a* **1699** LADY A. HALKETT *Autobiog.* (1875) 73 Goe to Edinburgh to looke affter my concerne. **1833** HT. MARTINEAU *Brooke Farm* i. 2 To meet the master looking after his fruit-trees. *a* **1884** *Mod.* Is there anyone to look after the cows?

c. To ***call, shout, whistle, after***. Also *fig.* (*obs.*; repl. by *for*) To seek to get by calling, whistling, etc.

1393 LANGL. *P. Pl.* C. IV. 127 The kynge fram consail cam · and callyd after mede. *c* **1500** *Cocke Lorell Bote* (1843) 12 Some stered at the helme behynde, Some whysteled after the wynde. **1709** STEELE *Tatler* No. 59 (1806) II. 87 They never call after those who run away from them. **1766** GOLDSM. *Vic. of Wakef.* iv, The very children .. will hoot after us. *Mod.* He shouted after me down the street.

d. To ***search, seek, inquire, ask, after*** (the missing, wanted, absent, or unknown).

a **1000** *Beowulf* 670 Wlonc hæleþ .. æfter hæleþum frægn. *c* **1300** *K. Alis* 1825 Uche mon soughte after socour. **1377** LANGL. *P. Pl.* B. v. 543, I seygh neuere palmere .. axen after hym. **1588** A. KING tr. *Canisius' Catech.* 22 Earnestlie seik efter thingis pleasand to the. **1591** SHAKS. *Two Gent.* I. i. 63 He after honour hunts, I after love. **1597** —— *2 Hen. IV*, I. i. 29 My Seruant Trauers, whom I sent .. to listen after Newes. **1611** BIBLE *Deut.* xii. 30 That thou enquire not after their gods. **1751** JOHNSON *Rambl.* No. 144 ¶11 This impartial and zealous enquirer after truth. **1775** SHERIDAN *Rivals* II. i, I told him you had sent me to inquire after his health. **1875** FARRAR (*title*) 'Seekers after God.' *a* **1884** *Mod.* Hearing of his illness I called to ask after him. He inquired very kindly after my parents.

e. With vbs., adjs., and sbs. of desire; as to *long*, *hanker*, *hunger*, *thirst*, *strive*; be *eager*, *greedy*; have a *hankering*, *desire*.

a **1000** *Beowulf* 3762 Him æfter deórum men dyrne langaþ. *c* **1220** *Ureisun of our Louerde* 185 Hu wilneþ after cunfort on eorþe. *c* **1400** *Gamelyn* 630 He was sore alonged after a good meel. **1535** COVERDALE *Ps.* xlii. 1 Like as the hert desyreth [**1611** panteth after] the water brokes, So longeth my soule after the, o God. **1642** ROGERS *Naaman* 479 An ardent affection after it, as one that is famished. **1709** STEELE *Tatler* No. 57 (1806) II. 64 Will Ubi, who is so thirsty after the reputation of a companion. **1796** MORSE *Amer. Geog.* I. 301 A prevailing desire after a peaceable accommodation. **1800** COLERIDGE *Wallenst.* II. iii, Because I Endeavoured after peace, therefore I fall. **1842** MACAULAY *Ess.* (1848) II. 144 He was greedy after power with a greediness all his own. **1854** THACKERAY *Newcomes* I. v. 52 This brave man thought ever of his absent child, and longed after him. **1879** C. GEIKIE *Life of Christ* lvi. 678 The priesthood had striven after kingly power and rank.

II. Of time.

6. Following in the succession of time; in succession to. Freq. in expressions of the type ***day after day***, ***man after man***.

c **1000** *Ags. Gosp.* John i. 30 Æfter me cymð wer þe me beforan ȝeworden wæs. *c* **1175** *Lamb. Hom.* 75 And ic ou wile seggen word efter word. **1297** R. GLOUC. 60 Þis Kymbel aftur hys fader kyng was of þis londe. **1599** A. M. tr. *Gabelhouer's Bk. Physic* 9/1 Doe this the continuance of 9 dayes after other, every morning. **1611** BIBLE *John* i. 30 After me cometh a man which is preferred before me. **1611**, etc. [see YEAR 7 a]. **1620** VENNER *Via Recta* vii. 115 They are not good to be taken after meat. [Cf. Grace after Meat.] **1631**, etc. [see TIME *sb.* 32]. **1674** R. STRANGE *S. Thomas Cantilupe* xxiii. 293 And soe strophe after strophe till the hymne was ended. **1798** COLERIDGE *Anc. Mar.* 115 Day after day, day after day, We stuck, nor breath nor motion. **1849** MACAULAY *Hist. Eng.* I. 262 And what was it to him who ruled after him? *Ibid.* II. 460 Turning out judge after judge, till the bench had been filled with men ready to obey implicitly the directions of the government. **1866** SALA *Barbary* 93 In front of the Grand Hotel gather group after group. **1868** DILKE *Greater Britain* I. I. iii. 34 Time after time I heard the complaint, 'The Yankees treat us shamefully, I reckon.' *a* **1884** *Mod.* Time after time I urged him to do it. **1887** [see HOUR 1 a]. **1893** BEATRICE HARRADEN *Ships that Pass* I. vii, 'It seems so little to ask,' she cried to herself time after time.

7. Subsequent to a space of time; after the interval of, at the close of. In mod. usage *after three months* varies with *three months after*, the former emphasizing the interval.

c **1000** *Ags. Gosp.* Matt. xxvii. 63 Æfter þrym daȝon ic arise. *c* **1160** *Hatton Gosp.* ibid., Æfter þreom daȝen ic arise. **1375** BARBOUR *Bruce* I. 40 The land .. Lay desolat eftyr hys day. **1382** WYCLIF *Matt.* xxvii. 63 After thre dayes I shal ryse aȝen. **1526** TINDALE *ibid.*, After thre dayes I will aryse agayne. **1582** N. T. (Rhem.) Then after fourtene yeres I vvent vp againe to Hierusalem [WYCL. fourtene ȝeer aftir; TIND. xiiii. yeares after that; CRANM. xiiii yeres thereafter; *Genev.* & **1611** fourtene yeres after]. **1625** HART *Anat. Ur.* II. v. 80 After a while she fell into a night feauer. **1641** FRENCH *Distill.* (1651) v. 109 They will after a time contract a mucilaginous slimie matter. **1753** HANWAY *Trav.* (1762) II. XIII. i. 283 After putting garrisons in these places, he marched for *Tavriz*. **1877** BROCKETT *Cross. & Cresc.* 185 After ages of submission, they became restless and rebellious. *a* **1884** *Mod.* After two years' absence Richard returned to England. After a long interval the task was resumed.

8. a. Subsequent to or later than a point of time. (Not necessarily in immediate sequence.) ***after hours***: after the regular hours of work; also, after the regular hours of opening (of a public house, etc.). Also (both senses) *attrib.* and in form ***after-hour***.

a **855** *O.E. Chron.* an. 774 Æfter sunnan setlgonge. *c* **1200** *Trin. Coll. Hom.* 47 On þe ehteðe dai efter his burþe. **1297** R. GLOUC. 407 Anon after Mydsomer þys batayle ydo was. **1384** CHAUCER *Leg. G. Wom.* 580 Afftyr the deth of Tholome .. Reynede his queen Cleopatras. *c* **1440** *Relig. Pieces fr. Thornton MS.* (1867) 25 Eftire þis sall þou wiete whilke ere þe ten comandementis. **1587** HOLINSHED *Scot. Chron.* (1806) II. 117 Adrian the .. legat came too late, as who should say, a day after the faire. **1588** A. KING tr. *Canisius' Catech.* 14 Æternal lyffe .. for yᵉ chosin eftir deathe. **1605** BACON *Adv. Learn.* II. i. §i. (1873) The narration may be before the fact as well as after. **1611** BIBLE *Jos.* x. 14 There was no day like that, before it, or after it. **1641** *Kirkcudbr. War-Comm. Minute Bk.* (1855) 98 Four dayes efter your receipt heirof. **1832** HT. MARTINEAU *Hill & Valley* viii. 124 It was long after dark. **1861** TRAFFORD *City & Suburb* (1862) 463 One night after hours he borrowed the sketch. **1879** TENNYSON *Lover's T.* 74 The eleventh moon After their marriage. *a* **1884** *Mod.* (in DICKENS) I'll work after hours and finish it. **1929** *Punch* 23 Jan. 90/2 A few austere theatricals drinking coffee and orange-juice because it was after hours. **1930** *Times Educ. Suppl.* 5 Apr. p. iv/4 These after-hour labours, done in a man's own time. **1947** in R. de Toledano *Frontiers of Jazz* xvi. 175 His unflagging interest in after-hours music. **1957** *Economist* 19 Oct. 256/2 It informed broker clients that .. after hours facilities would in future be confined to 'small routine business'.

b. Past (a certain hour). Now chiefly *dial.* and *U.S.*

1732 B. LYNDE *Diary* (1880) 24, A.M. ½ after 5 I went with son's horse. **1774** P. V. FITHIAN *Jrnl.* (1900) 271, I .. rode thence to Westmoreland Court House ten Miles by half after six. **1775** in *Essex Inst. Hist. Coll.* XLVIII. 52 We was preaded [i.e. paraded] about half after two in the morning. **1809** MAR. EDGEWORTH *Mme de Fleury* i, in *Tales Fashionable Life* II. 167 It was now half after four. **1905** *N.Y. Even. Post* 27 Jan. 3 About half after twelve the roof of the building fell in with a crash. **1961** ARTHUR MILLER *Misfits* i. 13 'Young man? You have the time?' .. 'It's twenty after nine.' '*After*!' Isabelle comes farther out on the porch and calls up to a second-floor window: 'Dear girl? It's twenty after!'

9. Of temporal and logical sequence: Subsequent to and in consequence of.

a **1000** *Beowulf* 3216 Þá þæt sweord ongan æfter heaþoswáte wanian. *c* **1280** *E.E. Poems* 20 Anoþer wol after þan · areri cuntake. **1475** CAXTON *Jason* 35 b, After that I understonde by your wordes. **1753** HANWAY *Trav.* (1762) I. VII. xcii. 426 After what has been said .. we may contemplate the superior charms of liberty. **1877** LYTTEIL *Landmarks* I. iv. 34 After what has been already said, any one will readily see that, etc. *a* **1884** *Mod.* After his behaviour to his parents, what could you expect?

10. Of temporal sequence and logical opposition: Subsequent to and notwithstanding. *esp.* in ***after all***; also (*U.S.*) as one word.

1603 SHAKS. *Meas. for M.* v. i. 347 Harke how the villaine would close now, After his treasonable abuses. **1710** PALMER *Proverbs* 69 After all our complaints of the lawyers and the law, there is no man in this kingdom too big for either. **1846** TENNYSON in *Punch* X. 106/1 Surely, after all, The noblest answer unto such Is kindly silence when they brawl. **1876** TREVELYAN *Macaulay* iii. 113 After all, as far as your verses are concerned. **1876** FREEMAN *Norm. Conq.* I. ii. 20 The Roman occupation was, after all, very superficial. *a* **1884** *Mod.* That he should continue his visits after such a rebuff is unaccountable. **1976** *Billings* (Montana) *Gaz.* 1 July (Advt. Suppl.), Afterall, the movement of people, not vehicles, is what counts. **1979** *Tucson Mag.* Feb. 29/1 Affluence, afterall, makes people mobile. **1984** *Washington Post* 2 Aug. DC12/1 Afterall, what other game accommodates so many athletes in so small a space at so slight a cost?

III. Of order.

11. Next to in point of order or importance.

c **1220** *Ureisun of Ure Lefdi* 125 To þe one is al mi trust efter þine leoue sune. *c* **1230** *St. Marh.* 13 Ich habbe efter bellzebub mest monnes bone ibeon. **1697** DRYDEN *Virgil, Pastorals* vii. 30 Codrus after Phœbus sings the best. **1777** SIR W. JONES *Arcadia* 105 And after Pan thy lips will grace it best. **1864** TENNYSON *En. Ard.* 425 'I am content,' he answer'd, 'to be loved A little after Enoch.'

IV. Of manner.

†**12.** Following as one follows a leader or guide; in obedience to, in compliance or harmony with, according to a *law*, *will*, *word*, *advice*. *Obs.*

c **975** *Rushw. Gosp.* Luke ii. 22 Gifylled werun daȝas clænsunȝe his æfter æ Moyses. *a* **1000** *Ags. Metr. Ps.* cxviii. 149 Æfter ðinum domum do me hálne. *c* **1200** *Ormul.* 119 Eȝȝþerr here ȝede swa Rihht affterr godess lare. **1340** HAMPOLE *Pr. Consc.* 6132 Hys angels þan, aftir his wille, Sal first departe þe gude fra þe ille. *c* **1380** *Sir Ferumb.* 2891 Wel sone dude þe Amyrel ⁝ after ys counseil riȝt. **1477** EARL RIVERS (Caxton) *Dictes* 21 Whether they haue obserued it [his command] after thye charge or nat. **1535** COVERDALE *John* xix. 7 After our lawe he ought to dye. **1598** SYLVESTER *Du Bartas* I. vii. (1641) 63/1 In his Name, beg boldly what we need (After his will). **1621** BURTON *Anat. Mel.* III. II. IV. i. (1651) 536 To make good musick of their own voices, and dance after it.

b. In compliance with the wishes of.

c **1386** CHAUCER *Wyf of B.* 406 And eek I pray to Jhesus schort her lyves, That wil nought be governed after her wyves [6- *text* bi]. *c* **1460** *Towneley Myst.* 209 Pylate, do after us, And dam to deth Jesus.

†**c.** In accordance with the statements of; according to (an author). *Obs.* or ? *arch.*

1483 CAXTON *Gold. Leg.* 230/4 She bad that the passyon after luke shold be redde. **1586** COGAN *Haven of Health* (1636) 30 Oates, after Galen, have like nature as Barlie. **1601** HOLLAND tr. *Pliny's Hist. World* VII. lvi. 188 Anacharsis the Scythian, or after some, Hyperbios the Corinthian, invented the cast of turning the roundell or globe.

13. In accordance with, according to a *custom, wont, fashion, manner, kind, sort, example, pattern.*

a **1000** CÆDMON *Gen.* (Grein) 396 He hæfþ mon ȝeworhtne æfter his onlicnesse. *c* **1250** *Gen. & Exod.* 1652 And kiste hire aftre kindes wune. **1483** CAXTON *G. de la Tour* K iij, To be charytable after thexemplary of our Lady. **1528** GARDINER in Pocock *Rec. Ref.* 47 I. 90 After a homely and familiar manner. **1577** *St. Aug. Manuell* 73 Looke after what sort thou showest thy self towards God. **1647** MAY *Hist. Parl.* II. ii. 34 Their.. cause lay bleeding in Ireland after so deplorable a kinde. **1668** CULPEPER & COLE tr. *Barthol. Anat.* I. viii. 17 The lower point of the Call is round after a sort. **1711** STEELE *Spect.* No. 193 ¶3 The levée of a great man is laid after the same manner. **1855** DICKENS *Dorrit* i. 1 Handsome after its kind. **1855** MACAULAY *Hist. Eng.* III. 292 The oath of office was administered after the Scotch fashion. **1866** H. LEE *Silver Age* 380 Typifying, after a fashion, the make-shift perilous way. **1871** SMILES *Character* iii. (1876) 74 Companionship after a sort. **1879** CARPENTER *Ment. Physiol.* I. ii. §82. 85 To build after one particular pattern.

b. *ellipt.* After the nature of; according to.

c **1000** *Ags. Gosp.* John viii. 15 Ȝe demað æfter flæsce. *c* **1200** *Ormul.* Ded. 2 Nu broþerr Wallterr, broþerr min Affterr þe flæshess kinde. **1382** WYCLIF *Rom.* viii. 1 Þat not aftir the fleisch wandren but after the spirit. **1534** TINDALE *ibid.*, Which walke not after the flesshe, but after the sprete. [**1588** *Rheims* according to the flesh.] **1611** *ibid.*, Who walke not after the flesh, but after the spirit. **1685** BAXTER *Paraphr. N.T.* Matt. i. 1 His reputed Legal Father after the flesh. **1882** G. SMITH in *Gd. Wds.* Mar. 212 A man after his own heart.

14. After the manner of; in imitation of; like.

c **1300** *K. Alis.* 5418 More hy than olyfaunz. Blake heueded after a palfray. *c* **1400** *Destr. Troy* v. 1613 Tilde vpon Tiber after Troy like. **1483** CAXTON *G. de la Tour* b viij, That she be arayed after the good ladyes of the countre. *c* **1570** THYNNE *Pride & Lowl.* (1841) 30 And [they] were clothed after citizens. **1710** STEELE *Tatler* No. 228 ¶4, I must.. copy after an old Almanack which I have by me. **1795** GIBBON *Autobiog.* 74 After his oracle Dr. Johnson, my friend.. denies all original genius. **1839** HALLAM *Hist. Lit.* III. iii. v. §17. 240 Some are said to dress after a lady for whom nature has done more than for themselves.

b. To *name* after.

1297 R. GLOUC. 61 Juli the emperour.. Hadde afteir hym y-clepud a moneth in the ȝer. **1480** CAXTON *Chron. Eng.* iv. 9 And Corin called it after his name cornewayle. **1849** MACAULAY *Hist. Eng.* II. 491 A succession of bands designated, as was the fashion of that age, after their leaders. **1876** FREEMAN *Norm. Conq.* III. xii. 190 Whether surnamed after the Hebrew King or not.

c. To *model, draw, compose* after.

c **1400** *Destr. Troy* XXI. 8758 A meruelous ymage.. Amyt after Ector, abill of shap. **1762** H. WALPOLE *Vertue's Anecd. Paint.* (1786) II. 52 Nicholas, the second son.. while abroad modelled after the antiques. **1845** MRS. JAMESON *Handbk. Publ. Galleries* 311 The appearance of being engraved after a drawing by Giulio Romano. *Ibid.* 313 Venus and Cupid.. a copy after Titian. **1850** —— *Sacr. & Leg. Art.* I. A portfolio of prints after the old masters. *a* **1884** *Mod.* (Titles) '*Wednesday Afternoon*' (after Longfellow). '*Jubilate*' (after the mediæval Latin hymns).

15. In a manner answering to, proportionate to, befitting, suiting. *arch.*

c **1000** ÆLFRIC *Gen.* i. 25 God ȝeworhte þære eorðan deor æfter hira híwum. *c* **1230** *Ancren Riwle* 126 Ase dude þe lefdi Iudit, efter hire efne. **1391** CHAUCER *Astrolabe* (1560) 251/2 All the Sterres of the South arisen after the degree of her longitude. *c* **1460** FORTESCUE *Absol. & Lim. Mon.* (1714) 49 The.. charge.. schal be more or less, after their long or schorte abode. **1549** LATIMER 7 *Serm. bef. Edw. VI* (1869) 51 Cut thy cloth after the mesure. **1611** BIBLE *Ps.* xxviii. 4 Giue them after the worke of their handes. [*Wyclif* aftir ther werkis.] *a* **1626** BACON (J.) According to bulk and currency and not after their intrinsick value. **1714** ELLWOOD *Hist. his Life* (1765) 234 We followed after our own Pace.

16. At the rate of (*obs.*); at (the rate of).

1530 *A proper Dyaloge* (1863) 15 Oure clargye lyue nothynge after their rate. **1587** HARRISON *England* II. i. (1877) 24 If these paie after foure shillings for land, the cleargie contribute commonlie after six shillings of the pound. **1642** *Lanc. Tracts of Civ. War* (1844) 62 To be repayed with satisfaction after eight pounds per Cent. **1643** SLINGSBY *Diary* (1836) 94 Have their pay after 6 shillings a week. **1702** *Lond. Gaz.* mmmdcccxxi/8 After the Rate of 12*s.* per Gallon. **1882** *Charter-party*, On being paid Freight at and after the rate of—shillings sterling per ton.

C. *conj.* or *conj. adv.* (elliptically from *prep.*).

1. Of time: †**a.** with antecedent and relative. *Obs.*

c **1000** *Ags. Gosp.* Matt. xxvi. 32 Æfter þam þe ic of deaþe arise. *c* **1175** *Lamb. Hom.* 51 Efter þan þet þe mon bið dead. *c* **1200** *Ormul.* 7667 Affterr þatt tatt he wass dæd.

b. with relative particle only. *arch.*

c **950** *Lindisf. Gosp.* Luke ii. 22 And æfter ðon gefylled were daȝas clænsunȝes his.. lædon hine in Hierusalem. *c* **1175** *Lamb. Hom.* 139 Efter þet ure drihten hefde þet folc adreint. *c* **1297** R. GLOUC. 230 After that Saxons and Englysse verst come thys lond to. **1382** WYCLIF *Jer.* xxxvi. 27 After that the king hadde brent the volum. **1535** COVERDALE *ibid.*, After now that the kynge had brente the boke. **1611** *ibid.*, After that the king had burnt the roule. **1880** LEWIS & SHORT *Lat. Dict.*, *Postquam*, after that, after.

c. *simply.*

c **1360** WYCLIF *De Dot. Eccl.* 22 Aftir he hadde take þe hooli Goost. **1366** MAUNDEV. 174 After thei han slayn them. **1526** TINDALE *Matt.* xxvi. 32 After I am rysen ageyne. [WYCLIF After that I schal rise aȝen.] **1611** *ibid.*, After I am risen againe. **1588** A. KING tr. *Canisius' Catech.* 31 Efter we knaw the law maker, we may rewerence him ye mair. **1753** HANWAY *Trav.* (1762) I. v. lxv. 298 After the Portuguese had settled themselves in East India. **1855** MACAULAY *Hist. Eng.* III. 10 A few days after the Revolution had been accomplished.

†**2.** Of manner: According as. *Obs.*

a. with antecedent and relative.

c **1200** *Moral Ode* 358 Sume habbed more after þan þe hi dude her.

b. with relative particle (*that* or *as*).

c **1375** *Lay-Folks Mass-Bk.* B. 8 After þat (þo boke) tellis. *c* **1394** *P.P. Crede* 732 But after þat his wynnynge is · is his well-fare. **1426** AUDELAY *Poems* 18 Uche preson schuld have his part after that he had ned. **1464–6** MARG. PASTON in *Lett.* 52. IV. 196 It is solde rythe well aftyr þat the wole was. **1506** *Ord. Crysten Men* (W. de Worde) II. ix. 112 After as saynt Gregory sayth. **1587** GOLDING *De Mornay* xiv. 201 After as any of these three powers doe reigne and beare sway.

c. *simply.*

c **1440** *Relig. Pieces fr. Thornton MS.* (1867) 7 Ilke cristene mane awe.. to take efter his elde es. **1483** CAXTON *G. de la Tour* d iiij b, Bere honoure.. to euery one after he is worthy. **1634** *Malory's Arthur* (1816) I. 22 Every knight after he was of prowess.

D. *Phr.* **at after.** (Still used in the north.)

1. *prep.* Used where we should now use *after* alone, to indicate, *time when.* (The *after* may in some cases belong to the sb. following; cf. AFTERNOON.)

1386 CHAUCER *Squires T.* 294 At after souper goth this noble king To seen this hors of bras. **1521** BRADSHAW *St. Werburge* (1848) 95 At after matyns she vsed contemplacyon. *Ibid.* 193 On saynt Katharins day at after mydnyght. **1523** FITZHERBERT *Husbandry* (1534) D ij b, Lode oute his dounge before none, and lode heye or corne at after none.

2. *adv.* Afterwards.

a **1641** STRAFFORD *Let.* in Southey's *C. Pl. Bk.* (1849) II. 172 Let shame cover me at after as a cloak.

after (ˈɑːftə(r), æ-), *a.* [OE. *þæt æfter-e*, f. *æfter* adv., = OHG. *aftar*, MHG. *after*; with superl. OE. *æftemest*, Goth. *aftuma* and *aftumists*. Senses 1, 2 are distinctly the OE. adj.; in the rest there is probably a later adjectival or quasi-adjectival use of the adv.; in expressions like *after deeds* it is especially difficult to distinguish the adj. and adv.]

I. Of time.

†**1.** The second (of two). *Obs.*

a **855** *O.E. Chron.* an. 827 Se æftera [Bretwalda] wæs Ceawlin Wesseaxna cyning. *c* **885** K. ÆLFRED *Boeth.* xix, Þam þe se æfterra deaþ ȝegripþ. **1048** *O.E. Chron.*, Neh ðære æftre Sancte Marie mæssan. *c* **1175** *Lamb. Hom.* 95 On his efter tocome [= second advent], þet is on domes deie.

2. Next, following.

c **1000** *Ags. Gosp.* Luke xiii. 33 Þy æfteran dæȝe. *c* **1160** *Hatton Gosp.* ibid., Þy æftere daiȝe. **1801** SOUTHEY *Thalaba* x. xv. Wks. IV. 361 Thou shalt not go to-morrow, Nor on the after, nor the after day, Nor ever! **1850** TENNYSON *In Mem.* cii. 158, I dream'd a vision of the dead, Which left my after morn content.

3. By extension: Later, subsequent. **a.** with *time, hours, days, years, ages*, etc. (where it may be explained as ellipt. for *after-coming*). Frequently united to its sb. by the hyphen, which has here only a syntactical value. See also AFTER- *in comb.*

1594 SHAKS. *Rich. III*, IV. iv. 293 Which after houres giues leysure to repent. **1641** *Termes de la Ley* 138 Any other after Tenant of the land. **1710** PRIDEAUX *Orig. Tithes* v. 268 The after Lawyers whose hands it passed thorough. **1731** SWIFT *Cass. & Pet.* Wks. (1755) IV. I. 164 These rhimes, A monument to after times. **1862** STANLEY *Jew. Ch.* (1877) I. iii. 54 The name was handed on to after ages. **1876** FREEMAN *Norm. Conq.* I. iv. 175 The well-known duchy of after times.

b. with n. of action or state (where it may be explained as the adv. modifying the contained vb. or adj., as *after compliance* = a complying afterwards). See AFTER- *in comb.* 7–9.

1607 SHAKS. *Cor.* II. ii. 43 The maine Point of this our after-meeting. **1758** S. HAYWARD *Serm.* 17 All his after sins were charged on himself alone. **1831** GEN. P. THOMPSON *Exerc.* (1842) I. 416 The sabrers, that produced an after compliance with their mandates. **1837** LYTTON *Athens* I. 368 These exploits were the foundation of his after-greatness. **1850** TENNYSON *In Mem.* cxvi. 4 For fuller gain of after bliss. **1853** KANE *Grinnell Exped.* viii. (1856) 59 Confirmed in our own after experience.

II. Of place.

4. Nearer the rear, hinder, posterior. Chiefly *nautical*, and probably due to *aft* (of which perh. regarded as the compar. = *more aft*): Lying nearer the stern of the ship, of or belonging to the sternward part. In numerous collocations, as *after body, cabin, end, guns, ladder, masts, part, quarter, sails, timbers, yards*, etc., which are frequently united by the hyphen. See AFTER- *in comb.* 4.

c **1200** *Trin. Coll. Hom.* 199 Ure left eare we ditteð mid ure after ende. **1440** *Promp. Parv.*, Aftyr Parte of a beste, or the hyndyr parte or the crowpe, *Clunis*. Aftyr Parte, or hynder parte of the schyppe, *Puppis*. **1795** NELSON in Nicolas's *Disp.* II. 13, I ordered the driver and after sails to be braced up. **1837** MARRYAT *Perc. Keene* xl. (1863) 281, I.. contrived to gain the after ladder and descend. **1857** LIVINGSTONE *S. Africa* iv. 80 The after part of the body has three or four yellow bars. **1879** W. H. WHITE in *Cassell's Techn. Educ.* IV. 78/2 Supposing a leak to occur in the after portion of the vessel.

III. *absol.* That which follows, subsequent time or existence; the future. Also, the rear or latter part.

1650 B. *Discolliminium* 49 He would.. turne so nimbly that he could not see which was his 'fore, which his after. **1830** TENNYSON *Poems* 98 He hath felt The vanities of after and before. **1865** *Reader* 10 June 644/3 A range of view which takes in all the before and after of Greek thought. **1903** W. S. BLUNT 7 *Golden Odes* 39 Who knows to-morrow, who the after of days, the years we see not? **1937** P. J. MCCANN *St. Benedict* 10 We can place his life and work in the sequence of a continuous development, and estimate it with reference to a before and an after.

after, colloq. abbrev. of AFTERNOON.

1890–1934 in Wentworth *Amer. Dial. Dict.* (1944) 9/1. **1906** E. DYSON *Fact'ry 'Ands* viii. 104 Iv yeh don't do yer fair share iv yacker this after, I'll punt ther slacks off yer. **1934** J. O'HARA *Appt. in Samarra* (1935) ii. 50 Tonight, or this after', when Ed showed up at the Apollo, he probably would be in a bad humour. **1939** J. MULGAN *Man Alone* xviii. 235 Boss wants us to get the hay in up top this after.

after- *in comb.* is used in various relations prepositional, adverbial, and adjectival, not always easy to separate, and in various senses. In some of these the combination is very loose, the use of the hyphen being mainly syntactical, *i.e.* to show that the grammatical relation between *after* and the following word is something else than the ordinary one of preposition and object. Cf. 'After consideration I resolved to decline' and 'After-consideration has shown me that I was wrong.' 'I should know him after years had passed' with 'I know not what after-years may bring.' Otherwise it is unnecessary, as 'the events of after years.' See AFTER *a.*

I. General senses in comb. (Words in **bold type** are treated specially under II., those in SMALL CAPITALS in their alphabetical place.)

1. As *prep.* with *sb.*, the whole forming a sb. meaning 'the time after ——': as AFTERNOON, -DINNER, -SUPPER; so ***after-church, -grave, -sales, -shave*** (also ***-shaving*** adj.); also *ellipt.*: after-shave lotion; ***-sunset, -tea.*** Also used *attrib.*, as in ***after-dinner oratory.*** See also AFTER-WAR.

1678 BUTLER *Hudibr.* III. ii. 310 The Bride to nothing but her Will, That nulls the After-Marriage still. *a* **1682** SIR T. BROWNE *Let. to Friend* (1881) 140 Leaving no earnest behind him for corruption or aftergrave. **1792** *Gentleman's Mag.* LXII. 24, I wished to accompany Miss Sophia to the after-church lecture. **1807** W. TAYLOR in Robberds' *Mem.* II. 215 This confinement of my father's takes away my after-teas. **1861** L. L. NOBLE *After Icebergs* 139 All that we anticipated of the sunset, or the after-sunset, is now present. **1895** *Daily News* 14 Sept. 5/7 The after-lunch drive was through more lovely country. **1905** E. WHARTON *House of Mirth* (1906) II. ix. 430 The noisy after-theatre supper. **1906** *Daily Chron.* 4 Jan. 6/7 A severe line is drawn by the 'after-season sale' between the masculine and feminine shop. **1914** J. COLLINGS *Colon. Rur. Brit.* I. vi. 113 The remainder of the children whose after-school career was traced went into industrial or commercial occupations. **1922** 'R. CROMPTON' *More William* iv. 69 'We di'n't ought to have set off before dinner,' said the squire with after-the-event wisdom. **1939** G. GREENE *Confid. Agent* I. ii. 72 The after-office rush was over. **1943** L. B. LYON *Evening in Stepney* 18 Be small, be mute, you after-midnight tears. **1945** *Amer. Speech* XX. 165 The after-shaving lotion may also leave your face feeling 'softer and smoother'. **1946** *Ibid.* XXI. 169 Merchandisers have emphasized terms [of lotions] used in virile, mostly expensive, sports:.. Field and Stream After Shave [etc.]. *Ibid.*, Ascot After Shave Lotion. **1955** *Times* 13 May 6/5 British manufacturers of aircraft and aero-engines are devoting special attention to 'after-sales' service. **1958** P. MORTIMER *Daddy's Gone A-Hunting* v. 27 He still managed to look suave and tidy, to emanate the bitter-sweet smell of money and after-shave. **1959** I. & P. OPIE *Lore & Lang. Schoolch.* xviii. 377 Their favourite after-dark games. **1961** *Guardian* 19 Jan. 9/7 A navy chiffon after-six dress. **1962** *Ibid.* 3 Jan. 4/1 An after-ski poncho. **1963** *Amer. Speech* XXXVIII. 203 The popularity of skiing and the after-ski atmosphere. *Ibid.* 205 After-ski boot. **1964** F. BOWERS *Bibliogr. & Textual Criticism* II. iii. 56 This bibliographical after-the-event interpretation of the Folio error.

2. As *adv.* (or *prep.*) with *vb.*, indicating succession in time, or direction in space; as **after-date, after-eye, after-go, after-send,** and other vbs. common in OE.; also in vbl. derivatives, as AFTER-COMER, -COMING; **after-beer, -liver,** etc.

1340 *Ayenb.* 58 Makeþ þe efter telleres ofte by yhyea[l]de foles and uor lyeȝeres.

3. As *adv.* with *ppl. a.*: Subsequently, later in order, as in AFTER-BORN (OE. *æfter-boren*). *esp.* later in a speech or writing: as ***after-described, -mentioned, -named, -specified, -written.***

1640 *Bk. of War Committee of Covenanters* 2 At the sight of the persones efter-specifit. **1687** *Lond. Gaz.* mmccxxi/3 Under the several Conditions, Restrictions, and Limitations after-mentioned.

4. As *adj.* with *sb.*, indicating position = hinder, posterior, **a.** as in OE. *æfter-ráp* crupper, **after-body, -brain, -breast, -nose, -wrist;** ***after-part, -truck,*** etc. (See AFTER *a.* 4.)

1824 W. IRVING *T. of Trav.* I. 41 The old gentleman had really an afterpart of his story in reserve. **1833** MARRYAT *Pet. Simple* (1863) 45 He was sharpening a long clasp knife upon the after-truck of the gun.

b. *esp.* In nautical lang.: Of or pertaining to the hinder part of the ship, nearer to the stern, as in AFTER-GUARD; **after-cabin, -leech, -oar, -sails, -yards;** ***after-ship, -part, -quarter,*** etc.

1398 TREVISA *Barth. De P.R.* v. iii. (1495) 105 Highte puppis in latyn as it were aftershyppe. **1599** HAKLUYT *Voy.* II. I. 167 Right with the maine mast or after-quarter of the shippe. **1694** MOTTEUX tr. *Rabelais* IV. xxii. 93 Hall your after-misen bowlins.—Hawl, Hawl, Hawl. **1769** FALCONER *Dict. Marine* s.v. *After,* The After-Sails usually comprehend all those which are extended on the mizen-mast, and on the stays between the mizen and main-masts. They are opposed to the head-sails. **1813** SOUTHEY *Nelson* I. i. 28 The Glasgow..was in flames, the steward having set fire to her while stealing rum out of the after-hold. *Ibid.* iii. 124 He ordered..the driver and after-sails to be brailed up and shivered. **1851** MELVILLE *Moby Dick* II. i. 1, Archy.. whose post was near the after-hatches. **1871** *Daily News* 26 Aug., She has a spacious deck saloon in the afterpart. **1883** *Man. Seamanship for Boys' Training Ships* 175 To reeve an after-guy. **1897** G. DU MAURIER *Martian* vii. 318 He made the ladies as comfortable as he could on the after-deck. **1898** KIPLING in *Morning Post* 11 Nov. 5/1 An Admiral..goes up on the after-bridge. **1933** J. MASEFIELD *Bird of Dawning* 209 An open locker against the after-bulkhead caught his eye. *Ibid.* 211 I've got to..get down into the after-hold.

5. As *adj.* with *sb.* expressing order = subordinate, inferior, remoter, as AFTER-DEAL, **after-kindred, -man, -table,** ***after-wine.*** OE. *æfter-ealo* small beer.

1398 TREVISA *Barth. De P.R.* XVII. clxxxix. (1495) 729 The after-wyne that is wrongen out of grapys.

6. As *adj.* with *sb.* expressing order in time = the latter (of two), second, secondary, following or recurring after the main occurrence: as AFTER-BIRTH, -BURDEN, -CLAP, -COURSE, -CROP, -GAME, -GLOW, -GRASS, -IMAGE, -MATH, -PIECE, -SPRING, -THOUGHT, -WORTS; **after-banquet, -baptism, -blow, -damp, -eatage, -growth, -mass, -mess, -sum, -winter;** so ***after-echo, -gust, -harvest, -meal, -paganism, -ploughing, -storm, -task.*** OE. had *æfter-gyld, -hætu, -sang.* (One main stress: *ˈaftercrop, ˈafterˌharvest.*) See AFTER *a.* 2.

a **1600** HOOKER *Serm. on Justif.* §5 The infusion of grace hath her sundrie after-meales. **1614** RALEIGH *Hist. World* II. 411 An after-harvest of many cares and discontentments. *c* **1619** HIERON *Wks.* 1620 II. 453 Wee are wise inough to put our selues to an after taske. **1624** GATAKER *Transubst.* 173 His other Arguments are drops of an after-storme. **1664** H. MORE *Myst. Iniq.* 293 Had degenerated therein into a kind of an After-Paganism. **1818** COBBETT *Year's Resid. Amer.* (1822) 57 When I have spoken of the after-culture, I shall compare the two methods of sowing. **1876** SWINBURNE *Lett.* (1960) III. 239, I cannot write of it now without feeling bitterly an aftergust or afterglow of that enthusiasm. **1885** G. SAINTSBURY *Marlborough* iv. 54 That aftergust of the plot which blew off the head of Sir John Fenwick. **1918** D. H. LAWRENCE *New Poems* 16 The after-echo of fear. **1925** O. JESPERSEN *Mankind, Nation & Individual* ix. 169 Fear of the naked word, an after-echo of the view held by savage tribes.

7. As *adv.* or *adj.* with *n. of action,* with the idea of, Following not immediately, at length, eventual, ultimate; as AFTER-PAIN, -RECKONING, -WIT; **after-cast, -proof, -roll, -taste, -treat;** so ***after-account, -chance, -consequence, -cost, -fame, -fruit, -good, -grief, -glory, -harm, -infamy, -loss, -penitence, -remedy, -rottenness, -settling, -turn.*** OE. had *æfter-yldo* later age. (One main stress: *ˈafter-aˌccount.*)

1572 BARNABE GOOGE tr. *Heresbach's Husb.* (1586) 36 b, Not sowed for present necessitie, but for other afterturnes. **1590** PAYNE *Descr. Irel.* (1841) 12 Which now dare not so for fear of after harmes. **1596** LODGE *Marg. Amer.* sig. F1, To make your after-good in deede more savourie. **1599** FENTON *Guicciardine* XIV. 641 What will be the euent and afterchaunce of things. **1612** BRINSLEY *Lud. Liter.* i. (1627) 4, I trust my after-fruits shall much increase. **1707** FREIND *Peterboro's Cond. Spain* 58 Such effects..are too often paid for by an after-reckoning. **1810** COLERIDGE *Friend* I. xiv. (1867) 62 The sense of disproportion of a certain after-harm to present gratification. **1842** H. E. MANNING *Serm.* (1848) I. 170 The shrinking anticipation of its possible after-consequences. **1860** FROUDE *Hist. Eng.* V. xxviii. 393 First the destruction of the Church as a body politic, and then an after-fruit of reaction. **1890** W. JAMES *Princ. Psychol.* I. x. 393 In the highest phase..there is no after-memory whatever until the next trance comes. **1924** S. C. CHEW (*title*) Byron in England. His fame and after-fame. **1933** *Mind* XLII. 359 The after-influence of each philosopher should be dealt with. **1937** J. M. MURRY *Necessity of Pacifism* vii. 116 The life and teaching and death and after-influence of Jesus of Nazareth.

8. As *adj.* or *adv.* with *n. of action* or *adj.,* expressing, After the event, later, and hence sometimes, late, behindhand; as AFTER-BORN, -HAND, -THOUGHT, -WIT; **after-knowledge, -view, -wise;** ***after-acceptation, -agreement, -breach, -consideration, -counsel, -deliberation, -design, -difference, -engagement, -inquiry, -fall, -meditation, -pardon, -speech, -thrift, -wrath,*** etc. (Both words have accent, but the stronger is on *after*: *ˈafter-ˌcounsel.*)

a **1600** HOOKER *Eccl. Pol.* VIII. 501 By which means of after-agreement, it cometh many times to pass. **1611** SHAKS. *Cymb.* v. iv. 189 Iump the after-enquiry on your owne perill. **1617** HIERON *Wks.* II. 91 And for the preuenting of their after-falls. **1626** BERNARD *Isle of Man* (ed. 10) 16 This fellow cannot abid after-meditation. **1634** SANDERSON *Serm.* II. 305 With God there is no after-counsel, to correct the errors of the former. **1644** QUARLES *Sheph. Oracles* ix, Give former dispensation; or at least An after Pardon. **1692** BENTLEY *Boyle Lect.* v. 158 These After-considerations are of very little moment. **1830** SIR J. HERSCHEL *Nat. Phil.* 77 It is only by after-rumination that we gather its full import.

9. As *adv.* or *adj.* with *sb.,* meaning, Coming or existing afterwards, subsequent; as in ***after-act, -action, -age, -beauty, -friend, -help, -king, -love, -state, -wisdom, -years,*** and others without limit. Not distinct from AFTER *a.* 3; the value of the hyphen, which is often omitted, is purely syntactical, and both words have a main accent: *ˈafter ˈlife, ˈafter proˈceedings.*

1591 SHAKS. *Two Gent.* III. i. 95 Scorne at first makes after-loue the more. **1594** HOOKER *Eccl. Pol.* (1617) Pref., Conference before-hand might haue eased them of much after-trouble. **1608** CHAPMAN *Byron's Trag.* I. i, And of his worth, let after ages say. **1632** MASSINGER & FIELD *Fatall Dowry* III. sig. H1, Something I must do mine owne wrath to asswage, And note my friendship to an after-age. **1640** SANDERSON *Serm.* II. 146 He meaneth to build his after-comforts upon a firm base. **1646** in J. W. Draper *Cent. Broadside Elegies* (1928) No. 17, p. 37 His fame to after-ages shall Sound out in praise. **1655** W. GOUGE *Comm. Hebr.* vi. 10 Their former diligence will be..an aggravation of their after-negligence. **1664** H. MORE *Myst. Iniq.* 474 All the importunities and necessities of after-affairs. **1680–90** SIR W. TEMPLE *Ess. Learn.* Wks. 1731 I. 297 So renowned in their own and After-ages. **1705** HICKERINGILL *Priest-Craft* II. i. 9 An After-Statute made by the said King and another Parliament. *c* **1726** GARRETSON *Pr.* 7 Unless the charitable care of some after-friend supply the defects of former education. **1736** CARTE *Life of Ormonde* II. 278 But his after-actions did not correspond to these beginnings. **1837** M. F. OSSOLI *Wom. in 19th c.* (1862) 352 Their memory is with us amid after-trials. **1842** H. E. MANNING *Serm.* (1848) I. 261 All the after-assaults of spiritual wickedness. **1862** LYTTON *Strange Story* I. 103 Though after-experience may rebuke the illusion. **1955** *Essays & Studies* VIII. 16 Compositors are far more likely than authors to allow after-ages to see their spelling idiosyncrasies.

II. Special combinations (with quotations, in alphabetical order).

ˈafter-ˌband, a subsequent band or bond after a release; †**ˈafter-ˌbanquet,** an entertainment following upon a banquet; †**ˈafter-ˌbaptism, after-baptizing,** adult baptism, anabaptism; **ˈafter-beat** *Mus.,* (*a*) a note or tone falling on an upbeat; (*b*) *spec.* the last two notes of a trill; †**ˈafter-ˌbeer,** a successor, one who lives later; †**ˈafterˌbeing,** post-existence; **ˈafter-blow** = AFTERCLAP; also *Metallurgy,* a continued period of the blow, after decarbonization is complete, in the basic Bessemer process (cf. BLOW *sb.*[2] 4); †**ˈafter-ˌbrain,** the posterior lobe of the brain, the cerebellum; **ˈafter-ˌbreast,** name proposed by Kirby and Spence for the *metathorax* of insects; **ˈafter-ˌcabin,** the cabin in the after or hinder part of the ship, having superior accommodation; **ˈaftercall, ˈafter-ˌcalling,** reclamation, a renewed demand; *also* a calling afterwards; †**ˈaftercast,** a second or later throw (at dice), an experimental result; **ˈafter-Christ,** a second Christ; **ˈafter-ˌChristian** *a.,* having ceased to be Christian; also *sb.*; hence **ˌafter-Christiˈanity; ˈafter-cure,** convalescence or further treatment taken after a period of treatment; **ˈafter-damp,** the choke-damp which rises in a mine after an explosion; **ˈafter-ˌdate,** to assign to a later date, to post-date; **ˈafter-disˈcharge,** a discharge (esp. of neural impulses) after the initial cause has been removed; **ˈafter-drops,** drops of rain which continue to fall after the cloud has passed; **ˈafter-ˌeatage,** the pasture after mowing = AFTER-GRASS; †**after-ˈeye,** to follow with the eye, to look after; **ˈafterfeed** = AFTERGRASS; †**ˈafter-frame,** superstructure; †**ˈafter-ˌgathering,** gleaning; also *fig.*; †**ˈafterˌgo,** to follow; **ˈafter-growth,** a subsequent or second growth, an after-math; also growth afterwards; **ˈafterheat** *Nucl. Sci.* (see quots. 1957, 1980); †**ˈafter-ˌkindred,** remote kindred, distant relationship; **ˈafter-ˌknowledge,** knowledge after the event, retrospective knowledge; **ˈafter-ˌleech,** the hinder edge (of a sail); **ˈafter-ˌliver,** survivor; †**ˈafter-ˌlodging,** that which lodges behind (as coarser flour in the sieve); †**ˈafter-man,** a follower, a subordinate; **aftermarket** orig. and chiefly *U.S.,* (*a*) a market for spare parts and accessories, esp. for motor vehicles; (*b*) *Stock Exchange,* a market in shares after their original issue; a secondary market; †**ˈafter-ˌmass,** the second or later mass, or feastday of a saint; †**ˈafterˌmess,** dessert, end of a feast; **ˈaftermowth** (= after-eatage); **ˈafter-nose** (see quot.); **ˈafter-ˌoar,** the hinder or rearmost oar of a boat; **ˈafter-ˌpasture** = AFTER-GRASS; †**ˈafter-proof,** outcome, realization; **ˈafter-ˌripening** (see quots.); **ˈafter-roll,** the roll of the waves after the subsidence of a storm; also *fig.*; **ˈafter-ˌsails,** 'all those on the after-masts, as well as on the stays between the main and mizen masts' Adm. Smyth; **ˈafter-ˌseason,** the latter end of the year; †**after-ˈsend,** to send after; **ˈafter-shine,** the radiance that lingers after the sun has gone down, after-glow; also *fig.*; **ˈafter-sight,** retrospective view, insight into the past; **ˈafter-sound,** a subsequent sound; an echo; cf. AFTER-IMAGE; **ˈafter-ˌsum,** the purchase money paid after the deposit, the balance; **ˈafter-swarm,** a second swarm of bees; †**ˈafter-table,** an inferior table; †**ˈafter-tale,** a subsequent reckoning, a correction; **ˈafter-taste,** a taste which remains or comes after swallowing anything; also *fig.*; **ˈafter-ˌthinker,** a reflecter; †**aftertime,** *conj.* after that; †**ˈafter-treat** = after-taste, flavour, relish; **ˈafter-view,** subsequent view, looking back; †**ˈafter-ˌwending,** following; **ˈafter-ˌwinter,** a second winter when spring is looked for, a renewal of winter; **ˈafter-ˌwise,** wise after the event, wise too late; **ˈafterwrist,** the metacarpus; †**ˈafter-ˌwriting,** postscript; **ˈafter-ˌyards,** *Naut.* the yards in the main and mizen masts.

1667 MILTON *P.L.* IX. 761 If death Bind us with *after-bands, what profits then Our inward freedom? **1577** tr. *Bullinger's Dec.* (1592) 239 Gluttonie, surfettinges, riotous *afterbanquettes, and dronkennesse. **1597** WARNER *Albion's Eng.* x. lix. 262 Which After-Banquet did their Lord for onely him prouide. **1680** W. ALLEN *Peace & Unity* 70 The Pædobaptists are as much for water-Baptism as the Anabaptists are, and hold themselves as firmly engaged by their Infant-Baptism, as they do by their *after-Baptism. *Ibid.* 64 While they remain under this perswasion, they can no more lawfully receive an *after-baptizing. **1625** W. L'ISLE *Du Bartas' Noe* 8 How long some of them lived with their forebeers and *afterbeers. **1908** R. DUNSTAN *Cycl. Dict. Mus.* 18/1 **After-beat,* last two notes of a Trill. **1927** *Melody Maker* June 597/3 The rhythmic section should support with a 'straight' but well-accented 'after-beat' rhythm. *Ibid.* Sept. 925/2 The stick taps out the second and fourth (or 'after') beats on the cymbal, thus accentuating these after-beats. **1587** GOLDING *De Mornay* vii. 92 A beginninglesse forbeing..inferreth an endlesse *afterbeing. **1663** BUTLER *Hudibr.* I. iii. 740 And they *perire,* and yet enough Be left to strike an *after-blow. **1881** *Encycl. Brit.* XIII. 346/1 The elimination of phosphorus..could be very largely effected..this action chiefly taking place during the 'after blow'. **1891** PHILLIPS & PROCHASKA tr. *Wedding's Basic Bessemer Process* iv. 104 It is useless to pour off the slag before the after-blow. **1899** H. S. BOWDEN *Relig. of Shakespeare* v. 232 He begs that his dismissal..may be at once..and not come as an after-blow to destroy his only hope. **1910** H. P. TIEMANN *Iron & Steel* 17 The period before the drop of the flame is called the fore blow, the latter one the after blow. **1615** CROOKE *Body of Man* 468 They are scituate betweene the forepart of the *After-braine and backside of the third ventricle. **1673** in *Phil. Trans.* VIII. 6153 As soon as the knife touched the cerebellum or After-brain. **1816–43** KIRBY & SPENCE *Entomol.* (1843) II. 254 You will discover in the *after-breast (*post pectus*) a rather deep cavity. **1833** MARRYAT *Pet. Simple* (1863) 196 Captain To then came out of the *after-cabin, half-dressed. **1814** WORDSWORTH *Excur.* IX. 122 Hence an *after-call For chastisement, and custody, and bonds. **1617** HIERON *Wks.* II. 92 There are no more *after-callings, when He hath once wiped out the score. **1393** GOWER *Conf.* (Halliw.) Thus ever he pleyeth an *aftircaste Of alle that he schalle say or do. **1866** CARLYLE *Reminisc.* II. 265 The aftercasts of the doctors' futile opiates were generally the worst phenomena. **1881** G. M. HOPKINS *Sermons & Dev. Writ.* (1959) 100 The Holy Ghost makes of every Christian another Christ, an *AfterChrist. **1886** C. S. DEVAS *Stud. Fam. Life* III. 274 We cannot alter the past, or be as though England..had never been a Christian country... We must of necessity be either Christian or *After-Christian. *Ibid.,* Popular writers of After-Christian France. **1911** *Month* Mar. 282 St. Paul's description of the Fore-Christians of his day applies equally to the After-Christians of ours. **1906** —— *Key to World's Progress* I. 57 Further details of *After-Christianity..are here unnecessary. **1901** W. JAMES *Let.* 6 Aug. in R. B. Perry *Tht. & Char. of W. J.* (1935) II. 199 We leave here on Saturday..and take the *after-cure in the Vosges. **1860** *Mining Gloss.* (ed. 2) 48 **After-damp,* destructive gas (carbonic acid) remaining in the workings after an explosion of fire-damp. **1869** *Echo* 29 Mar., Two others were killed by the effects of the after-damp. **1800** W. TAYLOR in *Month. Mag.* X. 223 Perhaps the ambitious fancy of Josephus has *after-dated this narrative. **1932** DORLAND & MILLER *Med. Dict.* (ed. 16) 51/2 **After-discharge,* a response to stimulation in a sensory nerve which persists after the stimulus has ceased. **1941** *Brit. Jrnl. Psychol.* July 74 After short light exposures..this after-discharge is followed by a short period of complete darkness. **1949** A. KOESTLER *Insight & Outlook* x. 148 Compare the short refractory period or afterdischarge of nerves. **1580** SIDNEY *Arcad.* III. 295 Their motions rather seemed the *after-drops of a storm, than any matter of great fury. **1760** R. BURN *Eccl. Law* (T.) The aftermowth, or *after-eatage, are undoubtedly part of the increase of that same year. **1611** SHAKS. *Cymb.* I. iii. 15 Thou should'st haue made him As little as a Crow, or lesse, ere left To *after-eye him. **1863** W. WING in *N. & Q.* III. IV. 204 The *after-feed belonging to the proprietor. **1879** *Standard* 28 Apr., Growing Crop of Grass, with afterfeed till Christmas. **1653** ASHWELL *Fides Apost.* 41 That foundation, whereon the whole *after-frame is built. **1535** COVERDALE *Jud.* viii. 2 Is not the *after-gadderynge of Ephraim better then the whole haruest of Abieser? **1548** GESTE *Priuee Masse* 78 The worshyppe *after-goeth them all. **1766** GOLDSM. *Vic. of Wakef.* vi, I called out my whole family to help at saving an *after-growth of hay. **1817** COLERIDGE *Biogr. Lit.* 106 The mind whom..he has..supplied with the germs of their after-growth. **1839** STONEHOUSE *Isle of Axholme* 62 This vert was the after-growth of that great forest. **1957** *Gloss. Terms Nuclear Sci.* (Nat. Res. Council, U.S.) 6/2 **After-heat,* heat resulting from residual activity after a reactor has been shut down. **1971** *Atlantic Monthly* June 36 The failures.. occurred in the afterheat system of the Oak Ridge Research Reactor. **1980** *Sci. Amer.* Mar. 37/2 The 'afterheat' that continues to be generated by the decay of radioactive fission products in the fuel rods..amounts to some 200 megawatts immediately after shut-down and decreases gradually over a period of seconds, minutes, days, weeks and ultimately months. **1386** CHAUCER *Melib.* 409 [Corp. & Lansd.] Yet nathelesse your kinrede is but *after-kinrede [3 *MSS.* a fer kynrede, *Harl.* and *Petw.* litel]. **1656** Hobbes *Lib. Necess. & Chance* (1841) 430 There is neither fore-knowledge nor *after-knowledge in him. **1861** Goldw. Smith *Mod. Hist.* 15 It cannot be answered by distinguishing between foreknowledge and afterknowledge. **1769** W. Falconer *Univ. Dict. Marine* Kk. 1 The foremost perpendicular or sloping edge is called the *fore* leech, and the hindmost the **after* leech. **1834** M. Scott *Cruise of Midge* (1859) 490 Look how the clear green water..pours out of the afterleech of the sail like a cascade. **1595** Sidney *Def. Poesie* (Arb.) 43 The benefit they got, was, that the *after-liuers may say, *Hæc memini.* **1641** Best *Farm. & Acc. Bks.* (1856) 104 In many places they grinde *after-logginges of wheate for theire servants pyes. **1625** Sanderson 35 *Serm.* (1681) 132 A wilful foreman that is made before-hand, and a mess of tame *after-men..that dare not think of being wiser than their leader. **1940** *Automotive Industries* 1 Jan. 33/2 The 'automotive *aftermarket', a generic term..to cover the vast market involved in servicing and maintaining America's 30,000,000 motor vehicles [etc.]. **1965** *Economist* 23 Oct. p. x/2 The independent [car] component industry is still very large. Not only does it have the lion's share of the so-called 'after market' for many items but..the vehicle manufacturers make a smaller proportion of their own requirements. **1973** *N.Y. Law Jrnl.* 23 July 3/1 [Defrauding] the public by prematurely stopping the sale of the original stock issue, opening an aftermarket, manipulating the price of the stock upward and selling to customers from the firm trading account at or above the artificially high price. **1983** *Austral. Personal Computer* Aug. 67/1 The thing that is expected to save computer makers from pricing themselves out of business is the aftermarket for products such as peripherals and software. **1984** *Observer* 28 Oct. 29/5 The only real fly in the ointment..is the future of the after-market. **1848** Petrie tr. *Ags. Chron.* 102 Nigh the *aftermass of St. Mary (8th Sept.). **1375** Barbour *Bruce* xvi. 457 Thai hade a felloun eftremess. *a* **1826** Kirby & Spence *Entomol.* (1826) III. 483 A triangular piece below the antennæ and above the nasus..this is the post-nasus or *after-nose. **1833** Marryat *Pet. Simple* (1863) 207 Who was seated upon the gunwale close to the *after-oar. **1634** Wood *New Engl. Prosp.* i. iv. (1865) There is little edish or *after-pasture, which may proceede from the late mowing. **1630** Naunton *Fragm. Reg.* (1870) 59 At the age of twenty and upwards, he was much short of his *after-proof. **1867** *Iowa Agric. Soc. Rep.* (1868) 188 To make the wine: gather the fruit with the stems on... Leave for three or four days in a cellar..thus causing *after-ripening. **1872** *Vermont Bd. Agric. Rep.* 72 Shortly after, begins after-ripening, a chemical change, whereby the starch, abundant in the unripe or green fruit, is transformed into sugar. **1935** *Forestry* IX. 30 The need of the embryo for some process of development or 'after-ripening' after the seed has been shed. **1953** *Brit. Commonw. Forest Terminol.* i. 11 *After-ripening*, biochemical or physical changes occurring in seeds ..and fruits after harvesting when ripe in the ordinary way. **1858** Froude *Hist. Eng.* III. xv. 314 Still heaving..from the *after-roll of the insurrection. **1663** Gerbier *Counsel* 28 The setting of the work in the *after-season. **1596** Spenser *F.Q.* i. v. 10 To *after-send his foe, that him may overtake. **1831** Carlyle *Sart. Res.* (1858) 102 From Suicide a certain *after-shine of Christianity withheld me. **1647** N. Bacon *Hist. Disc.* iii. 9 The honour due to great *after-sight. *a* **1878** Whyte Melville *In Lena Delta* (1885) iv. 50 Aftersight informed us of much that our foresight had overlooked. **1942** T. S. Eliot *Little Gidding* ii. 11 Speech impelled us To purify the dialect of the tribe And urge the mind to aftersight and foresight. **1909** *Cent. Dict.* Suppl., **After-sound*, a subjective sensation of sound which remains after the sound itself has ceased. **1957** L. Durrell *Bitter Lemons* 52 The beadle crashed at the church bell..and then left the silence to echo round us in wing-beats of aftersound. **1658** Reynolds *Lord's Supper* iv, Earnest useth to be paid in coyn of the same quality with the whole *aftersum. **1681** W[orlidge] *Syst. Agric.* 189 The signs of *After-swarms are more certain. **1753** Chambers *Cycl. Supp.*, The after-swarms differ from the prime, in that the latter are directed by the vulgar or the crowd of bees. **1645** Rutherford *Tryal of Faith* (1845) 266 Here is a high table and bread; and a by-board, or an *after-table. *c* **1300** *Beket* 627 On this Chartre sette here Seles: that non *Aftertale nere. **1830** Lindley *Nat. Syst. Bot.* 45 They leave a bitter unpleasant *after-taste in the mouth. **1849** C. Brontë *Shirley* II. viii. 201 It was the aftertaste of the battle. **1846** Grote *Greece* I. i. iii. 102 Promêtheus and Epimêtheus the fore-thinker and the *after-thinker. *c* **1488** *Lib. Nig. Edw. IV* in *Househ. Ord.* 1790, 34 *Aftertyme viii of these knyghtes be departed from court. **1674** N. Fairfax *Bulk & Selv.* To Reader, The *after treat will be none of the sweetest. **1693** Leighton *On 1 Pet.* iii. 11 They that know it in the sense of this *after-view..ask them what they think of it. **1800** Coleridge tr. *Schiller's Death of Wallenst.* pref., The feelings that arise from an *afterview of the original. **1951** L. MacNeice tr. *Goethe's Faust* ii. ii. 204 The afterview of that sorrowful fearful night. *c* **1300** *K. Alis.* 7280 They trussen alle in the dawenyng, And makith swithe *after-wendyng. **1601** Holland *Pliny* xviii. xxv, Putting us in good hope, that al cold weather was gone: howbeit, there ensued a most bitter *after-winter. *a* **1719** Addison (T.) These are such as we may call the *afterwise. **1615** Crooke *Body of Man* 917 Ligaments..ioyne the bones of the *After-wrest to the wrest. **1656** Du Gard *Gate of Lat. unlocked* §222. 61 The wrist [hath] eight [bones]; the after-wrist four. **1598** Florio, *Posto scritta*, a post-script, or *after-writing of a letter, a subscription. **1795** Nelson in Nicolas's *Disp.* (1845) II. 13 Braced up our *after-yards, put the helm a-port, and stood after her again.

afterbirth (ˈɑːftəbɜːθ, æ-). [after- 6; in sense 1 perh. directly from Norse; cf. Icel. *eptir-burðr*, *eftir-burðr* (*c* 1300), OSw. *efterbörd* (Ihre), Dan. *efterbyrd*.]

1. The membrane in which the fœtus is enveloped in the womb; the secundine or placenta. So called because its extrusion follows that of the infant.

1587 Golding *De Mornay* xxviii. 444 Now the world [word] *Silo* (saith Kimhi) signifieth the *Sonne of him*, and is deriued of a worde which signifieth a woman's *Afterbirth* as they terme it. **1615** Crooke *Body of Man* 81 When these vessels come vnto the secundine or after-birth they disperse through it notable braunches. **1754–64** Smellie *Midwifery* I. 241 The operator will be blamed for leaving the after-birth behind. **1855** Ramsbotham *Obstet. Mid. & Surg.* 68 It is also called the afterbirth.

2. *fig.*

1652 Benlowe *Theophila* iv. iii. 52 All New birth heart-deep groans, All after births of penitential mones, Are swallow'd up in living streams of bliss. **1879** McCarthy *Hist. own Times* I. 424 The famine had indeed many a bloody after-birth; but it gave to the world a new Ireland.

3. *Rom. Law.* (ˈafter-ˌbirth) Birth after a father's death or last will, posthumous birth.

1875 Poste *Gaius* i. 120 The institution or disinherison of a postumus born after the death of a testator..availed to save the will from rupture by afterbirth (*agnatio*) of an immediate successor.

4. Later birth, late-born children.

1871 Swinburne *Litany of Nations* 2 We thy latter sons, the men thine after-birth..O Earth.

after-born (ˈɑːftəˌbɔːn, æ-), *ppl. a.* [after- 8, 3.]

1. Born after the father's death, posthumous; in *Rom. Law*, also, Born after the father's last will.

c **1000** Ælfric *Gram.* xlvii. 275 *Posthumus*, Æfterboren, sé þe bið ʒeboren æfter bebyrʒedum fæder. *a* **1581** Campian *Hist. Irel.* ii. iii. (1633) 73 Issue two daughters, and an after-borne son called Arthur. **1880** Muirhead *Ulpian* xxii. §15 After-born descendants..such children in the womb as, were they already born, would be in our *potestas*. **1880** —— *Gaius* ii. §241 By a stranger after-born we mean a person who will not on birth be one of the *sui heredes* of the testator.

2. Younger, of later birth.

1609 Skene *Reg. Maj.* 31 Quhen the Lord..is willing to marie his eldest dochter or his after born dochter. **1768** Blackstone *Comm.* II. 251 Which daughter shall resign such inheritance to her after-born brother, or divide it with her after-born sisters, according to the usual rule of descents. **1882** Mrs. Haweis in *Belgravia* July 36 Chaucer is spoken of by his contemporaries and by the great afterborns.

ˈafter-ˌburner. Also afterburner. [f. next.] **1.** An auxiliary burner fitted to the exhaust-pipe of a turbo-jet engine to increase its thrust.

1947 *Air Reserve Gazette* Oct. 405/1 An after burner is a thrust augmentor which is, in effect, the turning of the jet pipe into an auxiliary ram-jet engine. **1948** *Sci. News Let.* 22 May 323/3 The afterburner being installed is a cylindrical device eight feet long which is attached on the exhaust nozzle of the Westinghouse turbo-jet engine which powers this plane. **1955** *Times* 30 Aug. 11/3 Afterburner, or reheat, systems provide a means of augmenting the thrust of jet engines by burning additional fuel in the jet pipe.

2. An auxiliary burner in a flue, exhaust pipe, etc., designed to burn any remaining combustible waste gases.

1956 *Proc. Amer. Soc. Civil Engineers* LXXXII. mcxvi. 2 An afterburner was designed to provide a favorable reaction zone for the completion of the oxidation of hydrocarbons in the exhaust. **1960** [see zoom *sb.* 1]. **1962** *Spectator* 28 Dec. 987/1 Perhaps afterburners will also eliminate an even more sinister product than carbon monoxide, hydrocarbons and the rest from vehicle exhausts. **1973** *Times* 12 Nov. 29/2 Stench from the Philite factory..has been eliminated by passing the waste gas through after burners. **1979** *Business Week* (Industr. ed.) 22 Oct. 80/3 In 1964 all major U.S. car manufacturers informed AMF that they would not use the afterburner.

ˈafter-ˌburning, *vbl. sb.* [cf. G. *nachbrennen*; after- 9.] **1.** In internal combustion engines, that diminishing combustion which follows the fuller force of the first ignition.

1887 J. A. Ewing in *Encycl. Brit.* XXII. 525/1 The process of combustion..is essentially gradual; when ignition takes place it begins rapidly, but it continues to go on at a diminishing rate throughout the stroke. That part which takes place after the maximum pressure is passed is the phenomenon of after-burning. **1931** A. W. Judge *Automobile & Aircraft Engines* (ed. 2) i. 59 The part of combustion which occurs after the point of maximum pressure is termed the 'after burning' portion.

2. Combustion in the after-burner of a jet-propelled aircraft.

1946 *Aeroplane Spotter* 19 Oct. 244/1 For the supersonic range of speeds, what is known as 'after-burning' was to be employed for generating even more thrust. The 'after-burning' consisted simply of fuel jets disposed annularly around the tail pipe or nozzle much in the same way as planned for the Athodyd or ram-jet. **1949** *Flight* 8 Sept. 285/1 Exhaust reheat, or 'afterburning', is the name given to the process of burning fuel in the exhaust pipe of a jet-propulsion unit.

†**ˈafter-ˌburthen, -ˌburden.** *Obs.* [after- 6.]

1. = afterbirth.

1576 Baker tr. *Gesner's Jewell of Health* 64 The water druncke in tyme of traueyle of chylde..sendeth forth the after burthen. **1688** Lady Waldegrave in *Lond. Gaz.* 22 Oct., This Deponent took the After-Burthen, and put it into a Bason of Water. **1727** Bradley *Fam. Dict.* s.v., To bring away the After-Burden, take the Leaves of fresh Smallage. **1754–64** Smellie *Midwifery* III. 398 Passing up my hand to fetch the after-burdens, there being two entirely separate.

2. *fig.*

1655 H. Vaughan *Silex Scint.* i. (1858) 116 Casting in my heart The after-burthens, and griefs yet to come.

ˈafter-care. [f. after- 9 + care *sb.*]

1. Lit. = later (i.e. after-coming) concern. Cf. after *a.* 3.

1762 Fielding *J. Wild* i. iv, in *Wks.* II. 242 An accident ..provided Mr. Wild a better tutor than any after care or expence could have furnished him with. ['after' om. in ed. 1, 1743 and in 1754 ed.] **1855** R. Browning *Men & Women* I. 229 Nor bring a moment's trouble on success With after-care to justify the same?

2. *spec.* In medical and social contexts: care or attention bestowed after the conclusion of a course of treatment, etc.; freq. *attrib.*

1854 *Poultry Chron.* I. 285/2 No after-care can then counterbalance the effects of former negligence. **1894** *Daily News* 12 Jan. 5/5 The After-Care Association facilitates the readmission of poor female convalescents from lunatic asylums into social life. **1921** *Act 11 Geo. V* c. 12 §2 Arrangements..for the after-care of persons who have suffered from tuberculosis. **1927** *Daily Tel.* 8 Feb. 13/7 Changes which are contemplated in connection with St. Dunstan's Institute..will not affect the work of after-care. *Ibid.* 3 May 14/1 Some after-care committee should protect young people from jobs which led nowhere. **1952** *Times* 21 Nov. 3/5 Problems of supervision and after-care of offenders released from prison and other institutions were being discussed. **1962** *Lancet* 27 Jan. 219/2 The delivery and aftercare should be the responsibility of the same general-practitioner/midwife team which supervised the antenatal care.

after-chrome (ˈɑːftəkrəʊm, æ-), *a.* [f. after- 9 + chrome.] Of, pertaining to, or designating a process of textile dyeing in which the material, after being dyed or printed, is treated with a chromium compound. Also as *v.*; so ***after-chroming*** vbl. sb.

1905 L. Cassella *Dyeing of Wool* 63 For shading the already afterchromed dyeings the same Anthracene Colours ..are usually applied. *Ibid.* 139 After boiling..the material is then afterchromed in the usual way. *Ibid.*, The usual quantity of bichrome need be used for afterchroming. **1922** *Encycl. Brit.* XXX. 869/2 Colouring matters of this type are known in the trade as 'after-chrome' colours. **1946** *Nature* 21 Dec. 920/2 Laboratory methods of dyeing after-chrome blacks. **1963** A. J. Hall *Textile Sci.* iv. 184 In the second (*after-chrome*) method, the wool is first dyed with the chrome mordant dye and is afterwards treated with the bichromate.

afterclap (ˈɑːftəklæp, æ-). [after- 6 + clap, blow, shock.] An unexpected stroke after the recipient has ceased to be on his guard; a subsequent surprise; 'an unexpected event happening after an affair is supposed to be at an end.' J.

a **1420** Occleve *De Reg. Princ.* 855 That after-clap in my mynde so depe Ifycched is. **1513** More *Rich. III* (1641) 404 To provide for after clappes that might happen and chance. **1535** Latimer *Serm.* I. 27 He can give us an after-clap, when we least ween. **1611** Speed *Hist. Gt. Brit.* ix. iii. 31 Who fearing afterclaps, had strongly fortified the Castle. **1663** Butler *Hudibr.* i. iii. 4 What plaguy Mischiefs and Mishaps Do dog him still with After claps. **1755** *Mem. Capt. P. Drake* II. iii. 162, I desired a Receipt to prevent any Afterclaps, which he readily granted. **1851** Melville *Whale* xviii. 101 Fear of after-claps. **1862** S. Lucas *Secul.* 12 The mitigated afterclap of this [the French] Revolution, in 1848.

ˈafterˌcomer. [after- 2, 9.] One coming after, a successor; *pl.* posterity.

1382 Wyclif *Levit.* xxii. 3 Sey to hem and to the after-comers of hem. **1563** Man *Musculus Com. Pl.* 13 a, All their after comers gat the same bleamishe and corruption. **1611** Guillim *Displ. Herald.* To Reader, I have broken the Ice, and made way to some after-commers of greter gifts and riper judgment. **1703** Maundrell *Journey* (1721) 68 They leave very little to be added by After-comers. *c* **1705** Berkeley in Fraser *Life* 448 The passage of after-comers is made more secure and easy. **1853** D. Rock *Ch. of Fathers* III. ii. xi. 55 That one church which Christ..left to be taught and governed by his apostles and their after-comers in the apostleship. **1879** G. M. Hopkins *Poems* (1918) 40 After-comers cannot guess the beauty been. **1958** E. Blunden *War Poets 1914–18* ii. 19 When after-comers walk through some well-tended war cemetery.

†**ˈafterˌcoming,** *vbl. sb. Obs.* A following state, sequel, or consequence.

1382 Wyclif *Ecclus.* iii. 32 The wis herte..in werkes of riȝtwisnesse welsum after-comyngus [1388 prosperitees] shal han. **1587** Golding *De Mornay* v. 50 The originalles, the proceedings, and the aftercommings..of men.

ˈafterˌcoming, *ppl. a.* Following, succeeding.

1594 Daniell *Cleopatra* (1717) 252 O why may not some after-coming Hand Unlock these Limits. **1598** Florio, *Futuro*, future, aftercomming. **1961** *Lancet* 22 July 189/2 Fœtal distress, the aftercoming head, and face presentation.

ˈafterˌcooler. [after- 9.] An apparatus for cooling air discharged from a compressor.

1903 W. C. Popplewell *Compressed Air* iii. 62 In some cases this intercooler is used as an 'after-cooler', through which the air is allowed to pass after leaving the high-pressure cylinder of the compressor. **1916** D. Penman *Compressed Air Practice in Mining* vi. 95 Where the capacity of the receiver is insufficient to allow the air to cool down.. after-coolers are often placed in the pipe-line somewhere between the receiver and the compressor. **1944** *Jrnl. R. Aeronaut. Soc.* XLVIII. (Abstr.) 673 Inter-coolers may be either of the air to air or liquid to air type and can be positioned either between the two stages of the supercharger (intercooler proper) or between the second stage of the engine (so-called aftercoolers). **1948** D. A. Wrangham *Heat Engines* (ed. 2) v. 94 With the object of removing moisture, coolers are sometimes fitted after the last stage, and for this reason are called *After coolers.*

after-course (ˈɑːftəkɔəs, æ-). [after- 6.]

†**1.** A later course at dinner; a dessert. *Obs.*

1580 Hollyband *Treas. Fr. Tong.*, *Desserte de table*, the banquet or after course. **1629** Parkinson *Parad.* iii. xxi. 594 The most excellent sorts of Peares, serve..to make an after-course for their masters table.

fig. **1749** J. CLELAND *Mem. Woman of Pleasure* I. 197 He gave me an after-course of pleasure, in a natural burst of tender gratitude and joy.

2. Subsequent course.

1859 MISS HENDERSON *Life of Dr. Henderson* 42 In this brief record we have a fore-shadowing of their after-course. **1922** JOYCE *Ulysses* 138 That small act..determined the whole aftercourse of both our lives.

aftercrop (ˈɑːftəkrɒp, æ-). [AFTER- 6.] A later crop after the principal one; a second crop. Also *fig.*

1562 J. WICLIF in *Richm. Wills & Invent.* (1853) 160 My lease and intrest of the aftercroppe of St. Nycolas feld. **1580** HOLLYBAND *Treas. Fr. Tong.*, *Regain, foin derriére saison*, after croppe of haye. **1616** SURFLET & MARKHAM *Countrey Farme* 112 With Autumne Hay, or the after-crop. **1740** CIBBER *Apol. Life* xiv. 268 This unexpected After-crop of Cato, largely supplied to us, those Deficiencies. **1751** SMOLLETT *Per. Pickle* (1779) IV. xciv. 142 A plenteous after-crop of delicious sprouts. **1789** COWPER *Let.* 12 Aug. (1824) II. 195 We are now gathering from our meadows, not hay, but muck..that the after-crop may have leave to grow. **1831** W. HOWITT *Bk. of Seasons* 338 Sowing wheat upon the fallows, also after crops of tares, clover, early peas.

ˈaftercrop, *v. rare.* [f. prec. after CROP *v.*] To take a second crop.

1580 TUSSER *Husb.* xviii. 20 Few after-crop much, but noddies and such.

ˈafterˌcropping, *vbl. sb.* [f. prec. + -ING¹.] The taking of a second crop.

1818 COBBETT *Year's Resid. Amer.* (1822) 82 More on this after-cropping, another time.

ˈafter-days, *sb. pl.* [AFTER- 9 and AFTER *a.* 3 a.] Later or subsequent days. Less commonly *sing.*, a subsequent day or period.

1635 QUARLES *Emblemes* II. xiii. 113 But something whispers in my dying eare, There is an After-day; which day I feare. **1700** S. WESLEY *Ep. to Friend conc. Poetry* line 451 Like old Ennius he design'd What After-days have polish'd and refin'd. **1795** SOUTHEY *Joan of Arc* I. 173 Happy those Who in the after-days shall live. **1814** WORDSWORTH *Excursion* I. 153 In the after day Of boyhood. **1828** SCOTT *F.M. Perth* xxi, That celebrated Lindsay, Earl of Crawford, who, in his afterdays, was known by the epithet of the Tiger-Earl. *a* **1878** CASWALL *Tale of Tintern* (1907) IV. v. 49 And He thine offering will repay Most fully in an after day! **1878** HOPPS *Life of Jesus* ii. 10 In after days his mother understood his meaning well. **1904** HARDY *Dynasts* I. I. iii. 43 To retrospective eyes of afterdays.

†**ˈafterdeal.** *Obs.* [AFTER- 4 *fig.* or 5 + DEAL, part, opposed to *foredeal*. Cf. Germ. *Vortheil* and *Nachtheil* with same meaning.] A disadvantage.

1481 CAXTON *Reynard* (Arb.) 107 Isegryn was wo begon, and thought he was at an afterdele. **1494** FABYAN VII. ccxl. 280 That he shuld be at so great an after deale in this warre. **1525** BP. J. CLERK *To Wolsey, MS. Cott. Vit.* VII. 7 The Frenche kyng seeth now hymself to be at suche a fordell and themperors armye at suche an afterdell, that he will no paction ne condition of treux ne peax. **1621** MOLLE *Camerarius' Liv. Lib.* v. xx. 400 Had brought themselues to such an afterdeale for the good of their countrey. **1634** *Malory's Arthur* (1816) I. 168 Oftentimes that one party was at a foredele, and anon at an afterdele.

ˈafter-death. [AFTER- 1.] An existence that follows death; a future life.

1899 W. S. BLUNT *Satan Absolved* 40 In the long after-death Ye shall be burned with fire. **1907** *Folk-Lore* June 164 That belief in an after-death or life of souls. **1929** B. JARRETT *Hist. Europe* x. 546 An after-death punishment for evil.

after-dinner (ˌɑːftəˈdɪnə(r), æ-), *sb.* [AFTER- 1.]

†**1.** As *sb.* A space of time after dinner devoted to recreation; the remainder of the day after dinner, the afternoon. *Obs.*

1576 SANDFORD (*title*) Houres of recreation or Afterdinners. **1606** SHAKS. *Tr. & Cr.* II. iii. 121 An after Dinners breath. *a* **1618** RALEIGH *Brev. Hist. Eng.* (1693) 53 Upon an After-dinner, Henry won so much at Chess of Louis..that he grew..into Choler..and threw the Chess in his face.

2. *attrib.* Taking place after, or following dinner; *esp.* before leaving the table at a festivity.

1730 SWIFT *Panegyrick on the Dean* IV. I. 142 Taking her after-dinner nap. **1790** BURKE *Fr. Revol.* 44 The sermons of the Old Jewry and the after-dinner toasts of the Revolution Society. **1826** DISRAELI *Viv. Grey* v. xiii. 238 An after-dinner anecdote, which ought to be as piquant as an anchovy toast. **1840** GEN. P. THOMPSON *Exerc.* (1842) V. 262 A drowsy after-dinner oration. **1875** HELPS *Soc. Press.* xviii. 246 The favourable after-dinner moment, when most men are most ready to promise that they will give liberally.

ˈafter-eˌffect. [AFTER- 7.] A delayed effect; an effect following after an interval.

1817 COLERIDGE *Biogr. Lit.* 226 The beneficial after-effects of verbal precision. **1927** A. H. MCNEILE *Introd. N.T.* vii. 212 Christians at the capital were still feeling the after-effects of Nero's mad outburst. **1940** 'G. ORWELL' *Inside Whale* 67 At the time this causes rebellion and vomiting, but it may have different after-effects in later life. **1949** J. F. EMBREE in M. Fortes *Social Structure* 223 The after-effects of Military Government..live on long after the period of occupation. **1956** A. H. COMPTON *Atomic Quest* v. 304 The second aftereffect is that from the..radioactive materials from the bomb itself.

after-game (ˈɑːftəgeɪm, æ-). [AFTER- 6.] *prop.* A second game played in order to reverse or improve the issues of the first; *hence* 'The scheme which may be laid or the expedients which are practised after the original game has miscarried; methods taken after the first turn of affairs.' J. ***after-game at Irish***, an old game resembling Back-gammon.

1631 SANDERSON *21 Serm.* Ad. Aul. I. (1673) 14 He had need be a good Gamester..to play an after-game of reputation. **1660** MILTON *Free Commw.* 427 Losing by a strange after-game of Folly, all the battels we have won. **1669** ETHEREDGE *Comic. Rev.* (Wright) Here's a turn with all my heart like an aftergame at Irish. **1713** ADDISON *Cato* III. vii, Still there remains an after-game to play. **1784** COWPER *Task* II. 762 What can after-games Of riper joys, and commerce with the world..Add to such erudition?

afterglow (ˈɑːftəgləʊ, æ-). [AFTER- 6.] **a.** A glow or refulgence that remains after the disappearance of any light, *esp.* that which lights the western sky after sunset; also *fig.*

1873 L. TOLLEMACHE in *Fortn. Rev.* Feb. 228 [The belief]..has left an after-glow of sentiment about the sacredness of life. **1877** MISS A. B. EDWARDS *1000 m. up Nile* xi. 296 The sun had set, the after-glow had faded, the twilight was closing in. **1881** A. J. C. HARE *Lucca* i. in *Gd. Wds.* XXII. 24 The peaks..stand out black and solemn against the infinite radiance of the afterglow.

b. *Physics.* The phosphorescent light persisting in a gas or on the screen of a cathode-ray tube after the cessation of the electric current. Also *attrib.*

1893 J. J. THOMSON *Rec. Research Electr.* ii. 185 A phosphorescent glow, which often lasts for several seconds after the discharge has ceased... All the gases I examined which do polymerize have shown the after-glow. **1934** *Nature* 28 July 140/1 At certain adjustments of pressure, velocity, and voltage, the [nitrogen] afterglow shows many of the colours of the aurora. **1943** *Electronic Engin.* XVI. 196/2 A certain amount of flicker..can be largely overcome by the use of a cathode-ray tube with a long afterglow screen. **1945** *Ibid.* XVII. 384/1 The screen of the tube has..an afterglow in total darkness of approximately 10 seconds. **1951** E. W. ANDERSON *Princ. Air Navigation* x. 176 The face of the [radar] screen is painted with a fluorescent 'afterglow' material so that the impression of the trace persists for a second or so.

after-grass (ˈɑːftəgrɑːs, æ-, -æ-). [AFTER- 6.] The grass which grows after the first crop has been mown for hay, or among the stubble after harvest. (See **after-eatage, -feed, -pasture**, under AFTER II.)

1681 J. W[ORLIDGE] *Syst. Agric.* 280 About the end of this Month you may Mow your after-grass. **1759** MARTIN *Nat. Hist.* II. 104 Their After-grass, of which they make a sort of rank Hay. **1810** WORDSWORTH *Scen. Lakes* (1823) 89 The tender green of the after-grass upon the meadows. **1813** VANCOUVER *Agric. Devon* 202 The after-grass..is usually fed off.

after-guard (ˈɑːftəgɑːd, æ-). *Naut.* [AFTER- 4 b.] 'The men who are stationed on the quarter-deck and poop, to work the after sails. Generally composed of ordinary seamen and landsmen, constituting, with waisters, the largest part of the crew, on whom the principal drudgery of the ship devolved.' Adm. Smyth.

1801 *Knight & Mason* IV. v. 60 Darby Drumconda, one of the after-guard. **1826** H. N. COLERIDGE *6 Months in W. Indies* 277 Even first lieutenants of the navy are generally sent into the after-guard. **1833** MARRYAT *Pet. Simple* (1863) 89 Now, captain of the afterguard, bring a piece of old canvass and some sand here, and clean his teeth nicely. **1927** J. SAMPSON *7 Seas Shanty Bk.* 43 If sung in proper time, it is not looked upon with favour by the afterguard.

†**ˈafterhand**, *adv.* and *prep.* *Obs.* or *dial.* [f. AFTER *prep.* + HAND; cf. *beforehand, behindhand*; formerly a phrase, *after the hand.*]

A. *adv.* Afterwards, subsequently; after the event. (Still in Sc.)

1393 GOWER *Conf.* II. 31 Then is he wise after the honde. *c* **1425** WYNTOUN *Cron.* VI. xii. 41 In-tyl hys thowcht ay wald he cast, Efterhend hys Statis all. **1634–46** J. ROW (father) *Hist. Kirk* (1842) 387 Marshall did sweare afterhend that he had not fylled him at all. **1658** S. LENNARD *Of Wisdome* II. vii. §17 (1670) 285 The wise take it before hand..and the feeble and vulgar sort, after-hand. [**1868** G. MACDONALD *Rob. Falc.* I. 65 The last time he did it, the puir auld man hostit sair efterhin'.]

†**B.** *prep.* After. *Obs. Sc.*

1552 ABP. HAMILTON *Catech.* 8 a (JAM.) Efter hend all this, thai turnit thame to the brekaris of the law, saying, etc.

after-image (ˈɑːftəˌrɪmɪdʒ, æ-). [AFTER- 6.] The impression retained by the retina of the eye, or by any other organ of sense, of a vivid sensation, after the external cause has been removed. Also *transf.*

1874 J. SULLY *Sensation & Intuition* iii. 41 Plateau sought to determine the time during which this after-image (Nachbild) continues in decreasing intensity. **1879** *Syd. Soc. Lex.* s.v., Newton suffered for many years from an after-image of the sun, caused by incautiously looking at it through a telescope. *Ibid.*, After-images may also be experienced in the case of smells, tastes, tones, and impressions of contact. **1889** G. B. SHAW in *Eng. Illustr. Mag.* Oct. 53 The after-image of the lyric drama witnessed is deeply engraved in the memory, aural and visual. **1890** W. JAMES *Princ. Psychol.* I. xv. 635 Peculiarities in an after-image, left by an object on the eye. **1962** *Listener* 12 Apr. 647/1 Though they [*sc.* abstract paintings] are concerned with *gestalt* effects, and with after-images, they are not out to batter one's eyes into submission.

afterings (ˈɑːftərɪŋz, æ-), *sb. pl.* *Obs.* or *dial.* [AFTER *adv.* + -ING¹. Cf. *innings*.]

1. The last strainings of milk from a cow. *dial.*

1796 MRS. GLASSE *Cookery* xxii. 354 Put one large spoonful of steep to five quarts of afterings. **1882** in *N. & Q.* VI. VI. 54 The first milk drawn from the cow is the poorest ..the latest drawn milk, called the 'afterings,' is the richest.

†**2.** Remaining dregs, after the main part is exhausted. *Obs.*

1609 BP. HALL *Serm.* 36 These are the ὑστερήματα, afterings of Christ's sufferings.

ˈafter-life. [AFTER- 9.] **1.** A subsequent or future life.

a **1593** MARLOWE *Hero & Leander* (1598) (Ded.) sig. A2, The impression of the man, that hath been deare unto us, living an after life in our memorie, there putteth us in minde of farther obsequies. **1615** HOBY *Curry-combe* iii. 149 Saduces..denied the Resurrection, and by consequence any after-life. **1925** F. W. NORWOOD in J. Marchant *Life after Death* 70 Concerning Jesus and the After Life. **1925** D. THOMAS *Ibid.* 104 Young children whose minds were unversed in speculations about the After Life.

2. The later period of one's life.

a **1678** H. SCOUGAL *Life of God* (1726) 204 The lessons which afflictions teach us, are then most advantageous when we learn them betimes, that we have the use of them in the conduct of our after lives. *a* **1805** WORDSWORTH *Notebook Y* in *Prelude* (1926) 556 Untutor'd minds stop here, and after-life Leads them no further. **1817** SCOTT *Harold* VI. xix, Eivir! since thou for many a day Hast follow'd Harold's wayward way, It is but meet that in the line Of after-life I follow thine. **1833** MARRYAT *Pet. Simple* (1863) 87 My history was not written in after-life. **1837** LOCKHART *Scott* I. 323 Archibald Constable, in after life one of the most eminent of British publishers. **1878** W. S. JEVONS *Pol. Econ.* Pref. 6 To instil..notions on subjects with which all must in after-life be practically conversant. **1923** J. M. MURRY *Pencillings* 77 He gives a picture of the after-life of the stockinged Fauntleroys.

ˈafter-light. [AFTER- 9.] An afterglow (also *fig.*); also, the light of what is known afterwards, hindsight.

1894 W. J. LOCKE *At Gate of Samaria* xvi. 194 She.. noticed a look upon Thornton's face,—the after-light, as it were, of a sneer, before the features had time to reset. **1923** H. E. G. ROPE *City of Grail* 47 The afterlight of sunset in those summers long gone by. **1940** W. EMPSON *Gathering Storm* 32 When this leaves the green afterlight of day. **1950** W. S. CHURCHILL *2nd World War* III. xxxiv. 585 These three documents, with which, in the afterlight..I am content.

†**ˈafterling.** *Obs.* [f. AFTER *a.* + -LING.] An inferior.

1205 LAYAMON 19117 þenne nabbeoð ure æfterlinges [*v.r.* onderlinges] nane upbreidinges.

†**ˈafterˌlithe.** *Obs.* Forms 1 Æfteraliða, 3 Efterlið. [OE. *æftera* second + *Līða* mild, serene, name of the two months June and July.] OE. name for July.

c **1200** *S. Marharete* (1862) 23 Iþe moneð þæt on ure ledene is · ald englisch efterlið inempnet.

†**ˈafterlong**, *adv.* and *prep.* *Obs.* [f. AFTER *prep.* 3 + LONG.] Lengthwise, along.

c **1320** *Castel off Loue* 724 And casteþ þat liȝt so wyde After-long þe tour and be-syde. *c* **1420** *Pallad. on Husb.* III. 139 Overward and afterlonge extende a lyne.

aftermath (ˈɑːftəmɑːθ, æ-). Also **aftermowth**; see AFTER- *in comb.* II. [AFTER- 6 + MATH mowing.] **1.** Second or later mowing; the crop of grass which springs up after the mowing in early summer. Also *attrib.* (See also AFTERGRASS, AFTERCROP.)

1523 FITZHERBERT *Surveying* 2 Yet hath the lorde the Edysshe and the aftermathe hym selfe for his owne catell. **1601** HOLLAND *Pliny* (1634) I. 506 The grasse will be so high growne, that a man may cut it down and haue a plentiful after-math for hay. **1631** G. MARKHAM *Way to Wealth* iii. II. vi. (1668) 149 Eddish, or After-math-cheese. **1673** MARVELL *Rehears. Transp.* ii. Wks. II. 251 The after-math seldom or neuer equals the first herbage. **1834** SOUTHEY *Doctor* cli. (1862) 391 No aftermath has the fragrance and the sweetness of the first crop. **1856** PATMORE *Angel in House* (1866) II. IV. iv, Among the bloomless aftermath. **1860** *Farmer's Mag.* LII. 242/1 Thus treated I would calculate on a good aftermath, to be either sold or used in the yards.

2. *fig.* Esp. a state or condition left by a (usu. unpleasant) event, or some further occurrence arising from it.

a **1658** CLEVELAND *To Mr. T. C.* 22 Rash Lover speak what Pleasure hath Thy Spring in such an Aftermath! **1851** H. COLERIDGE *Ess. & Marg.* II. 13 The aftermath of the great rebellion. **1878** *Masque of Poets* 135, I am one that hath Lived long and gathered in Life's aftermath. **1946** W. S. CHURCHILL *Victory* 5 The life and strength of Britain..will be tested to the full, not only in the war but in the aftermath of war. **1958** M. L. KING *Stride toward Freedom* vi. 102 The aftermath of nonviolence is the creation of the beloved community, while the aftermath of violence is tragic bitterness. **1960** C. DAY LEWIS *Buried Day* ii. 41, I remember, too, its aftermath—the *triste*, enervated feeling which the cold kiss of the dew spreads through one's whole body. **1979** A. STORR *Art of Psychotherapy* x. 107 Depression is sometimes an immediate aftermath of completing a piece of work. **1981** *Times* 31 July 2/5 The aftermath of the wedding seemed to mean different things to different people. Princess Anne confessed..to having 'a slight hangover from a very enjoyable wedding'.

aftermost (ˈɑːftəməst, æ-, -məʊst), *a. superl.* Forms: 1 æftemest, 2 eftemest, 4 aftermest, 8-

aftermost. [In form a treble superlative of *af-*; thus *af-te, afte-me* (Goth. *aftuma*), *afteme-st* (OE. *æftemest*, Goth. *aftumist*), with a comparative ending inserted in the later *af-te(r)-me-st*. But in OE. *afte* existed only in the adv. form *æftan* (see AFT) with positive value; **æfteme* (cf. *forme, hindeme*) is not found; and *æftemest* was treated as a superlative of *æftere* adj., and used both of time and space. Hence the corruption *aftermest* found already in 12th c.; then the word is unknown for 6 centuries, and the modern AFTERMOST may be a new formation on *aft, after*, on analogy of *foremost, hindermost*, etc.: see -MOST.]

†**1.** Hindmost, last in order. *Obs.*

c **880** ÆLFRED *Oros.* iv. 6 Đonne he sylf mid ðam fyrmestan dǽle wið ðæs æftemestan fluȝe. *c* **1000** ÆLFRIC *O.T.* 31 Đeos bóc is æftemest on ðære biblioþécan.

†**2.** Of time: Last. *Obs.*

c **1000** *O.E. Gosp.* John vii. 37 On þam æftemestan mæran freolsdæȝe. *c* **1160** *Hatton Gosp.* ibid., On þam after-mesten mæren freolsdæȝe. *c* **1200** *Trin. Coll. Hom.* 23 And elch man heren his dom bi eftemeste erdede.

3. *Naut.* Nearest the stern of the ship, most aft.

1773 HAWKESWORTH *Voy.* (T.) I ordered the two foremost and two aftermost guns to be thrown overboard. **1834** M. SCOTT *Cruise of Midge* (1863) 63 We found a cluster of people at the aftermost part of the felucca.

†**'afterness.** *Obs.* [f. AFTER *a.* + -NESS.] The quality of being after or later; posteriority.

1587 GOLDING *De Mornay* iv. (1617) 48 Time is but a measure of mouing, wherein there is both a forenesse and an afternesse. **1674** N. FAIRFAX *Bulk & Selv.* 14 To shut out formerness and afterness, which Gods everlastingness has not.

afternoon (ˌɑːftə'nuːn, æ-). [AFTER- 1 + NOON; orig. a phrase; cf. L. *post meridiem.*]

1. a. The time from mid-day to evening. Formerly preceded by *at*, now *in the, during the*; and as a date *on*.

a **1300** *K. Horn* 358 'Go nu,' quaþ heo, 'sone And send him after none.' **1450** GREGORY *Chron.* (1876) 196 That same day, the aftyr non, the Duke of Yorke roode thoroughe London. **1463** *Manners & Househ. Exp. Eng.* 228 The nyte next afore tyl the sayd day at aftyr noyn. **1527** GARDINER in Pocock *Rec. Ref.* 38 I. 73 We abide passage which we trust to have this afternoon. **1570–87** HOLINSHED *Scot. Chron.* (1806) II. 70 A terrible eclipse of the sun, at three of the clocke at afternoone. **1587** TURBERVILE *Trag. Tales* The king..To take a nappe at after noone, Into his chamber gotte. **1601** A. DENT *Path-way to Heaven* 123 These men serue God in the fore-noone, and the diuell in the after-noone. **1669** PEPYS *Diary* (1879) VI. 2 Spent the afternoon in several places. *a* **1704** T. BROWN *Com. View* Wks. 1730 I. 146 Afternoon sleepy in most churches. **1829** SCOTT *Guy M.* 217 The funeral was to proceed at one o'clock afternoon. **1842** TENNYSON *Lotos Eaters* 3 In the afternoon they came unto a land, In which it seemed always afternoon. **1877** LYTTEIL *Landmarks* II. ii. 97 She had often sat on summer afternoons admiring the majesty of the Arran Fells.

b. *pl.* as *adv.*: in the afternoon; of an afternoon. Cf. NIGHTS *adv.*

1896 *Vermont Agric. Rep.* XV. 36, I prefer to gather sap afternoons. **1911** *Rep. Lab. & Soc. Conditions in Germany* III. 31 The boys..attended school from 8 o'clock till 11 in the forenoon, and from 2 to 4 afternoons.

c. ***good afternoon***: see GOOD *a.* 10c. In informal speech often shortened to ***afternoon***. Cf. MORNING *sb.* 2b

1921 E. O'NEILL *Diff'rent* 1, in *Emperor Jones* 223 Afternoon, Harriet—and Alf. *Harriet.* Afternoon, Ma. **1954** W. FAULKNER *Fable* 141 The brigadier himself sitting at a desk..said: 'Afternoon. As you were a moment, will you?' **1966** T. FRISBY *There's Girl in my Soup* I. 5 Afternoon, Mr Hunter. Mr. Danvers's taxi is waiting.

2. *fig.* as in the ***afternoon of life***.

1594 SHAKS. *Rich. III*, III. vii. 186 Euen in the after-noone of her best dayes. **1864** TENNYSON *Aylmer's F.* 461 My lady's cousin Half-sickening of his pensioned afternoon. **1871** BURR *Ad Fidem* ix. 162 The world's latest afternoon.

3. a. *attrib.*

1577 TUSSER *Husb.* lxix. 2 Afternoone doings till suppertime come. **1633** T. ADAMS *Exp. 2 Pet.* iii. 3 (1865) 609/1 Calling for their afternoon-bevers, before they have concocted their dinners. **1711** SHAFTESBURY *Charact.* (1737) II. 258 Reading an afternoon-lecture to his pupils. **1748** RICHARDSON *Clarissa* I. xvii. 110, I will go down..and excuse your attendance at afternoon tea. **1754** FIELDING *Voy. Lisbon* (1755) 104 Our ladies..drank their afternoon tea at an alehouse. **1850** C. READE *Christie Johnst.* 155 The afternoon beams sprinkled gold on a long grassy slope. **1879** MISS BRADDON *Vixen* III. 185 How fond you gentlemen pretend to be of afternoon tea. **1882** [see TEA *sb.* 4 a]. **1903** A. BENNETT *Leonora* iii. 76 He was admiring the spacious room and herself in her beautiful afternoon dress. **1927** E. GLYN *'It'* xii. 111 She had put on her most demure garment—an afternoon frock of crimson crêpe. **1931** A. CHRISTIE *Sittaford Mystery* i. 10 Two women in afternoon frocks rose to greet the staunch old warrior.

b. *attrib.* or quasi-*adj.*, in sense 'procrastinating, slow, lazy', as ***afternoon farmer***. *dial.* (see *E.D.D.*).

1743 W. ELLIS *Mod. Husb.* June iii. 30 Others, where the Crop is thin, will not hough at all; but these are your Afternoon Farmers, as we call them. **1889** *Standard* 28 Nov. 2/1 The rain and snow..have come too soon for a few 'afternoon farmers', who have not yet put in all their wheat. **1894** *N. & Q.* V. 153/2 In West Middlesex the expression 'an afternoon farmer' is frequently used in talking of a farmer who is behind hand in his work.

4. *Comb.* **afternoon('s)-man**, a tippler.

1614 OVERBURY *A Wife, etc.* (1638) 196 Make him an afternoones man. **1621** BURTON *Anat. Mel., Democr. to Reader* (1657) 44 Beroaldus will have drunkards, afternoon men, and such as more then ordinarily delight in drink, to be mad.

Hence (*rare*) **after'noony** *a.*

1885 T. H. HUXLEY *Let.* 23 Feb. in L. Huxley *Life of T. H. H.* (1900) II. vi. 96 There is something idle and afternoony about the air which whittles away one's resolution.

after'nooner. Used in comb., as in ***Saturday-afternooner***, one who has a holiday on Saturday afternoons.

1906 *Daily Chron.* 28 July 7/6 Thus giving early-closers and Saturday-afternooners a chance. **1927** *Daily Tel.* 7 June 3/1 If the amendment which I suggest is wrong for the Saturday afternooners, it is wrong for cricket.

†**after'nooning,** *Obs.* or *dial.* The afternoon repast or *bever*.

1742 BAILEY (ed. 10) *Dondinner*, the Afternooning. *Yorksh.*

after-pain ('ɑːftəˌpeɪn, æ-). [AFTER- 7.]

1. A pain which follows later.

a **1556** CRANMER *Wks.* II. 182 Although it be pardoned, yet after-pains thereof continue so long as we live. *a* **1624** SIR N. BRETON in Farr's *S.P.* (1845) I. 196 That bitter smart That inward breeds of pleasures after-paine.

2. *esp.* (in *pl.*) The pains that follow childbirth. Also *fig.*

1667 *Decay of Chr. Piety* v. §11. 229 The throes and after-pains of conscience when sin is brought forth. **1751** CHAMBERS *Cycl.* s.v., After-pains are pains felt in the loin, the groin, etc. after the birth. **1754–64** SMELLIE *Midwifery* I. 400 Women in the first child seldom have after-pains. **1857** BULLOCK tr. *Cazeaux, Midwifery* 491 The after-pains are occasioned by the contraction of the womb.

afterpiece ('ɑːftəpiːs, æ-). [AFTER- 6.]

1. 'A farce or any smaller entertainment after the play.' J. Hence, any extra item following the main fare in a programme of entertainment; an epilogue. Also *fig.*

1779 T. HOLCROFT *Let.* in *Memoirs* (1816) III. 251 We have a new afterpiece of Mr. Sheridan's coming out this evening, 'The Critic'. **1806** *Mem. of R. Cumberland* i. 296 Eight and twenty nights it went without the buttress of an afterpiece. **1860** L. HUNT *Autobiog.* vi. 127 He could bring the tears into your eyes for some honest sufferer in an afterpiece. **1863** MRS. HOWITT tr. *Bremer's Greece* I. vi. 202 But the seven years' tragedy of Greece was still destined to have a bloody afterpiece. **1899** [see KNOCK-ABOUT, KNOCKABOUT *sb.* 1]. **1933** E. K. CHAMBERS *Eng. Folk-Play* 70 Music, dance and song, helped by patter, often turn it into an afterpiece, something like a *revue*. **1960** P. COLUM *Poet's Circuits* 115 (*heading*) After-piece. 'Wanderer's Song'. **1976** *Early Music* Oct. 394/1 An Afterpiece: a short, light work from roughly the same period as *Dido* with some connection (perhaps parodic) in subject or treatment. **1984** *Daily Tel.* 23 Nov. 18/6 'Trial by Jury' was commissioned as a mere 'after-piece' for Offenbach's 'La Perichole'.

2. *Naut.* The heel of a rudder.

after-reckoning ('ɑːftəˌrɛkənɪŋ, æ-). [AFTER- 7.] A subsequent or final account.

1623 WEBSTER *Devils Law-case* IV. ii. 566, I could never away with after reckonings. **1649** MARBURY *Obadiah* (1865) 63 We come to the after-reckoning in the day of Judgment. **1770** BURKE *Pres. Discont.* Wks. II. 291 No rules to confine, no after-reckonings to terrify. **1829** SOUTHEY *Oliver Newman* (1845) 34 Sure that no after-reckoning will arise, Of shame, or sorrow.

afters ('ɑːftəz, æ-), *sb. pl. colloq.* (formerly only *dial.* and *vulg.*). [f. AFTER *a.* or *adv.*] The course which follows the main course of a meal. Cf. SECOND *sb.*[2] 8.

1909 J. R. WARE *Passing Eng.* 3/1 Afters (Devon), sweets—pies and puddings. 'Bring in the afters' is a common satirical remark in poor Devonshire houses, especially when there are no 'afters' to follow. Also used in Scotland, *e.g.*, 'Hey mon, a dinner, an' nae afters!' **1919** *Athenæum* 29 Aug. 822/2 'Afters' is in no sense an army word..beyond the fact that the mass of the army is composed of the working classes. .. Used in its equivalent sense to sweets, pudding, entremets or dessert, it may not show much imagination. **1940** *Manchester Guardian Weekly* 11 Oct. 255 The meat course costs from fourpence to sixpence, and the 'afters', as Londoners call puddings, from twopence to threepence. **1940** 'N. SHUTE' *Landfall* x. 256 'What's he got for afters?' 'Plummy duff.' **1953** SCOTT & FISHER *1,000 Geese* x. 120 We ate our corned beef and cheese, crisp-bread and biscuits, with dates for afters.

'after-senˌsation. [AFTER- 6.] = AFTER-IMAGE (but less commonly used of visual impressions).

1867 J. MARSHALL *Outl. Physiol.* I. 431 After-sensations ..are noticed in regard to all the senses. **1874** G. H. LEWES *Problems* I. 149 We may consider the gradations of Sensation, After-sensation, Imagination, and Hallucination. **1893** DUNGLISON *Dict. Med. Sci.* (ed. 21) 28/2 *After-sensation*, continuance of impression after withdrawal of stimulating cause. **1909** E. B. TITCHENER *Text-bk. Psychol.* I. §40. 152 Followed by an after-sensation of cold. **1952** D. J. O'CONNOR *John Locke* iv. 81 It cannot be said that a red after-sensation, for example, is a property of the self who perceives it in the same sense as the red colour of a cherry is a property of the cherry.

'after-shaft. *Ornith.* [tr. mod.L. *hyporachis.*] = HYPORACHIS.

1867 W. S. DALLAS tr. *Nitzsch's Pterylography* I. i. 8 The aftershaft originates from the underside of the feather beneath the umbiliciform pit. **1871** T. H. HUXLEY *Man. Anat. Vertebr. Anim.* vi. 274 In very many birds each quill bears two vexilla; the second, called *aftershaft* (*hyporachis*), being attached on the under side of the first close to the superior umbilicus. **1884** E. COUES *Key N. Amer. Birds* (ed. 2) 84 The after-shaft, when well developed, is like a duplicate in miniature of the main feather, from the stem of which it springs, at junction of calamus with rhachis, close to the umbilicus.

'after-shock. [AFTER- 6.] A lesser shock coming after the main shock of an earthquake.

1894 *Seismolog. Jrnl. Japan* III. 72 All the after-shocks have been weaker than the respective initial earthquakes. **1903** R. D. OLDHAM in *Mem. Geol. Survey India* XXXV. II. 2 In the early months of the aftershocks, there appeared to be a distinct increase in the frequency of earthquakes. **1946** *Nature* 30 Nov. 784/2 The first, at 22 hr. 26·3 min. G.M.T., was an aftershock of the destructive Dominican Republic earthquake of August 4 off Samana Peninsula.

†**'afterspring.** *Obs.* [AFTER- 9, 6.]

1. Posterity, seed, descendants. Cf. *offspring*.

1583 GOLDING *Calvin on Deut.* viii. 43 If he should destroy the whole world and leaue no afterspring to call vpon him. **1587** —— *De Mornay* xxvii. 437 The afterspring of his children that are long hence to come.

2. ('after-ˌspring.) A second and later spring. Also *fig.*

1604 W. YONGE *Diary* 1 Never a better after-spring seen in any man's memory, at the end of June. *a* **1670** HACKET *Life of Williams* II. 30 (D.) To recreate him, and to put an after-spring into his decaying spirits.

after-supper (ˌɑːftə 'sʌpə(r), æ-). [AFTER- 1.] The time that intervened between supper (when this was at an earlier hour) and bed-time. *Obs.* or *dial.* except *attrib.*, like *after-dinner*. Also *Obs.* = RERE-SUPPER (quots. 1590 and 1637).

1590 SHAKS. *Mids. N.* v. i. 34 This long age of three houres, Between our after supper and bed-time. **1637** RUTHERFORD *Lett.* 82 (1862) I. 207 It is near after-supper. **1832** MISS MITFORD *Our Village* Ser. v. (1863) 355, I left him in the hall, just settling quietly to an after-supper nap. **1852** DICKENS *Bleak Ho.* xxxii. 312 His unpremeditated after-supper stroll. **1879** F. W. ROBINSON *Coward Conscience* I. II. vii. 254 An evening party, in the full vigour of its after-supper dances.

afterthought ('ɑːftəθɔːt, æ-). [AFTER- 6, 8.]

1. A subsequent or second thought.

a **1661** HOLYDAY *Juv.* 10 To write but on one side of the leaf, leaving the other for any after-thoughts. **1710** PALMER *Proverbs* 157 Ill nature, the afterthoughts of which strike horror and regret. **1846** GROTE *Greece* I. xxi. 551 Forced into unity..by the afterthought of a subsequent age.

2. Reflection after the act; a thought which did not occur at the time when the matter to which it refers was under consideration: hence a later expedient, explanation, or device.

1684 CHARNOCK *Attrib. God* (1834) I. 749 He cannot discover anything afterwards that may move him to take up after-thoughts. **1751** YOUNG *Night Th.* vii. 889 Annihilation is an after-thought, A monstrous wish, unborn till virtue dies. **1760** RAPER in *Phil. Trans.* LI. 799 The portico was an after-thought. **1846** MILL *Logic* II. iii. §3 (1868) 211 If any reasons were assigned, it would be necessarily an afterthought.

3. *colloq.* The youngest child in a family, esp. one born considerably later than the other children.

1914 G. B. SHAW *Misalliance* 3 Have you ever considered the fact that I was an afterthought?.. My father was 44 when I was born. My mother was 41. There was twelve years between me and the next eldest. **1965** G. MCINNES *Road to Gundagai* iii. 48 Terence was the youngest child... ('I'm a little afterthought.') **1985** *Sunday Tel.* 3 Mar. 14/8 Christopher, afterthought son of the founder member,..is allowed to sit in on the ladies' discussions.

'afterthoughted, *a.* Having afterthoughts.

1878 B. TAYLOR *Deuk.* Argt. 10 Epimetheus, the after-thoughted, who receiveth access of vigour in looking backward.

'after-time. [AFTER- 9.] A later or future time; posterity. Freq. in *pl.* (See also AFTER *a.* 3 a.)

1597 SHAKES. *2 Hen. IV* IV. ii. 52 You are too shallow (*Hastings*)..To sound the bottome of the after-Times. ? **1603** S. DANIEL *Def. Ryme* (1904) II. 380 When after-times shall make a quest of inquirie, to examine the best of this Age. **1664** S. BUTLER *Hudibras* II. iii. 170 As Withers in Immortal Rime Has registerd, to after-time. **1816** SHELLEY *Alastor* 266 To remember their strange light in many a dream Of after-times. **1842** TENNYSON *Morte d'Arthur* 35 Wheresoever I am sung or told In aftertime, this also shall be known. **1858** BAGEHOT *Coll. Wks.* (1965) II. 48 It is for the slow critic of after-times to piece together their teaching. **1902** W. JAMES *Var. Relig. Exper.* xvi. 381 As a rule they [mystical states] carry with them a curious sense of authority for after-time.

'after-ˌtreatment. [AFTER- 7.] Later or subsequent treatment.

1831 W. YOUATT *Horse* xii. 227 No after treatment will be necessary, except that the animal should be sheltered from intense heat. **1910** *Practitioner* July 29 Some of the more recently published cases of recovery in this branch of surgery have shown an advance in the after-treatment. **1925** B. BEETHAM in E. F. Norton *Fight for Everest, 1924* III. 326 The after-treatment of the [photographic] negatives is often somewhat of a nightmare. **1946** *Nature* 5 Oct. 475/1 The strength of casein fibre could be increased by after-treatment with basic zinc-chloride and formaldehyde. **1962** J. T. MARSH *Self-Smoothing Fabrics* xviii. 296 The use of sodium copper tartrate as an after-treatment. **1964** S. DUKE-ELDER *Parsons' Diseases of Eye* (ed. 14) xxvii. 427 The most important point about after-treatment is keeping the pupil well dilated.

'afterwale. [f. AFTER- 4a + WALE *sb*¹ 7.] A back wale on a horse's collar.

1889 in *Cent. Dict.* **1908** [see WALE *sb.*¹ 7]. **1946** N. WYMER *Eng. Country Crafts* v. 48 He will cut out his leather afterwales, damp them, and sew them to the body with white leather laces.

'after-war. [AFTER- 1.] The period after a war; post-war. Used esp. *attrib.* or quasi-*adj.*

1919 A. A. MILNE *First Plays* 113 The most suitable career for a young man in after-war conditions. **1931** *Times Lit. Suppl.* 17 Sept. 694/3 The numerous shady railroad flotations of the after-war period. **1939** 'G. ORWELL' *Coming up for Air* III. i. 184 It isn't the war that matters, it's the after-war. The world we're going down into.

afterward ('ɑːftəwəd, æ-), *adv.*, *prep.*, and *sb.* [OE. *æftanweard*, *æfteweard*, adj., *æftewearde* adv., f. *æftan*, AFT, + -WARD; corrupted already in OE. to *æfterweard*, *-wearde*, through influence of *æfter*, AFTER. The original is represented by AFTWARD.]

A. *adv.*

†**1.** Of place: Behind; after. *Obs.*

c **1000** ÆLFRIC *Exod.* xxxiii. 23 þu ȝesihst me æftewearde. *c* **1200** *Ormul.* 14793 Faraon wiþþ all hiss ferd Comm affterrwarrd wiþþ wraþþe. *c* **1350** *Will. & Werwolf* in *Dom. Archit.* II. 99 Bi fore went William, and after ward the quene. *c* **1400** *Destr. Troy* xx. 8198 Then Deffibus drogh furth, & to þe dede went,.. Eneas afturward with angardly mony.

†**2.** *Naut.* Backward, aftward. *Obs. rare.*

a **1618** RALEIGH *Lett.* in *Rem.* (1661) 252 To make her [a ship] swift, is to give her a large Run, or way forward, and so afterward.

3. Of time: In time following, subsequently.

1297 R. GLOUC. 6 Afturward in þis bok me schal here al þis. *c* **1380** *Sir Ferumb.* 163 Of me neuere after-wart: loue ne get he none. **1384** CHAUCER *L.G.W.* 1655 That aftyrward hat brought hire to myschef. **1440** *Promp. Parv.* Aftyrward, *Postea postmodum.* **1579** W. FULKE *Heskins's Parl.* 315 Afterwarde the mother receiued her daughter. **1605** BACON *Adv. Learn.* II. viii. §5 (1873) Afterward they come to distinguish according to truth. **1628** COKE *On Littleton* I. ii. §21 (1633) 24 b, This shall be explaned afterward. **1802** MAR. EDGEWORTH *Mor. T.* (1816) I. 207 He might afterward .. repeat some lines. **1866** NEALE *Sequences* 200 Rufus, the afterward Martyr.

†**4.** Of order: Next, then, thereafter. *Obs.*

1340 *Ayenb.* 24 [He] þengþ in his herte, uerst to þe dignete, efterward to his prosperite, efter þan to his richesses, efterward to his lustes. **1581** CAMPION in *Confer.* IV (1584) E e *b*, So being iust, he was made more iust: and so first iust, and afterward iustified.

†B. *prep. Obs. rare.*

†**1.** Of place: After, following.

c **1175** *Lamb. Hom.* 45 Ic heom wulle milcien þe weren efterward mine milce. *c* **1200** ORMIN 12727 Ta twa Leorninngcnihhtess.. ȝedenn forþ Affterrwarrd ure Laferrd.

†**2.** Of time: After.

a **1000** *Riddle* (Grein) xvi. 14 ȝif he me æfterweard ealles weorþeþ.

†**3.** Of manner: After, in quest of.

c **1230** *Hali Meid.* 37 To wearnen meidnes þat ha beon þe lasse afterward swuch þing.

†C. *conjunctively.* After (that). *Obs.*

1482 *Monk of Evesham* (1869) 24 Aftyrward that he was fully comme to hym selfe ageyne. **1607** TOPSELL *Four-footed Beasts* (1673) 400 Afterward they had sacrificed, they were delivered from the mice.

D. *sb.* A later or subsequent time; the after-life. *rare.*

1906 K. TRASK *Night & Morning* 27 Yea, all the Afterward—beyond the grave—Could have no terrors.

afterwards ('ɑːftəwədz, æ-), *adv.* [f. prec., with adverbial genitive *-es*, *-s.* At first a northern form. See -WARDS.] At a later time, subsequently. Also as sb. The future; the future life, the after-life.

c **1300** *St. Brandan* 10 And underne siththe and middai and afterwardes non. **1375** BARBOUR *Bruce* I. 588 Off hys etlyng rycht swa It fell, As I sall eftirwartis tell. **1601** SHAKS. *Jul. C.* II. i. 164 Like Wrath in death, and Enuy afterwards. **1611** BIBLE *John* xiii. 36 Thou canst not follow me now; but thou shalt follow me afterwards. **1756** BURKE *Vind. Nat. Soc.* Wks. I. 21 The war was brought home to them, first by Agesilaus, and afterwards by Alexander. **1842** J. H. NEWMAN *Ch. of Fathers* 385 In the afterwards metropolitan city of Canterbury. **1901** 'LINESMAN' *Words by an Eyewitness* (1902) 343 The little spark must keep the great cold world warm until the Afterwards. **1902** E. GLYN *Refl. Ambrosine* 285 An English girl would have a blank prospect in front of her for the afterwards. **1922** D. H. LAWRENCE *England, my England* (1924) 47 To.. mingle and commingle with the one darkness, without afterwards or forwards. *a* **1930** —— *Last Poems* (1932) 288 About the afterwards As a matter of fact, we know nothing.

after-wit ('ɑːftə,wɪt, æ-). *arch.* [f. AFTER- 7, 8.]

†**1.** Later knowledge; the knowledge of riper years or later times. *Obs.*

a **1600** HOOKER *Eccl. Politie* VI. 313 The after-wit of later days hath found out another more exquisite distinction. **1653** GAUDEN *Hieraspistes* 12 Those, that have now attained their after-wits. *a* **1680** BUTLER *Rem.* (1759) 156 Your after-wit is like to be your best.

†**2.** Second thought, reconsideration. *Obs.*

1607 A. F. in *Topsell's Four-footed Beasts* (1673) 142 Which delay hath made somewhat better, and *'deuterai phrontides,'* after wit, more meet to be perused.

3. *esp.* Wisdom after the event, that comes too late.

1579 GOSSON *Sch. Abuse* (Arb.) 18 Afterwittes are euer best, burnt Children dread the fire. **1586** G. WHITNEY in Farr's *S.P.* (1845) I. 206 After-witts are like a shower of rayne, Which moistes the soile when witherd is the graine. **1656** TRAPP *Exp. Matt.* xxv. 11 (1868) 254/1 Jehoshaphat in temporals was ever wise too late.. and paid for his after-wit. **1736** BAILEY (Fol.) *Prov.* 'After wit is everybody's wit!'

†**4.** Hence, Recognition of former folly, practical repentance, a 'coming to one's senses.' *Obs.*

1509 HAWES *Past. Pleas.* xx. v, Who that is ruled by her higher estate, Of hys after wytte shall never be shent. **1660** SWINNOCKE *Door Salv. Opened* 101 Μετάνοια signifieth.. after-wit, a change of mind, or making wise for the future.

'after,witted, *a.* Wise when too late; wanting forethought.

c **1536** TINDALE *Exp. Matt.* vi. (L), Our fashions of eating make us slothful.. afterwitted (as we call it), uncircumspect, inconsiderate, heady, rash. **1656** TRAPP *Exp. Matt.* xxv. 2 (1868) 253/1 The most imprudent, improvident, after-witted.

'afterword. [f. AFTER- 9, after *foreword.*] A passage added at the end of a book, etc., as an epilogue or the like.

1890 *Caxton's Eneydos* (E.E.T.S.) p. xx, Afterwords by F. J. Furnivall. **1900** MEAD *Fragm. Faith* 605 (*heading*) Afterword. **1911** J. GWYNN (*title*) The Present Position of Protestantism in Ireland and an Afterword. **1939** *Mind* XLVIII. 433 The after-word that he thought it essential to print.

'afterwork. [AFTER- 9.] Later work; work done afterwards.

1907 L. BINYON in *Sat. Rev.* 30 Mar. 389/2 Six leaves of a sketchbook joined together, just as they were, with no afterwork. **1958** M. L. HALL *Newnes Compl. Amat. Photogr.* 1 There is the man who considers that the picture is created the moment it is taken, to whom 'afterwork' is the work of the devil, and there is the man who spends joyful evenings printing in clouds and retouching out mistakes.

'after-world. [AFTER- 6.] **1.** A future generation; posterity.

1596 HARRINGTON *Ulysses upon Ajax*, The *afterworld shal rather pittie your lost time. **1649** DRUMM. OF HAWTH. *Cypress Grove* Wks. 1711, 122 That to after-worlds thou might'st leave some monument that once thou wast. **1913** G. MURRAY *Euripides & his Age* ii. 50 The judgement of the afterworld upon them will depend on the side we take in a never-ending battle.

2. A world after death.

1615 HOBY *Curry-combe* iv. 181 He speaks of the state of th' elect in the after-world. **1887** H. S. HOLLAND *Christ or Ecclesiastes* 128 That great after-world for which.. this age-long story of man is but a preparation. **1949** D. L. SAYERS *Dante's Divine Comedy* 17 The positions they occupy in the Three Kingdoms of the After-world.

after-wort ('ɑːftə,wɜːt, æ-). [AFTER- 6.] The second run of beer.

1725 BRADLEY *Fam. Dict.* s.v. *Brewing*, [As] for the after-worts.. what comes from the first wort will serve well enough to boil again with them. **1742** *Lond. & Country Brewer* I. (ed. 4) 48 The After-worts of small Beer come into the same Backs or Coolers where the strong Worts had just been.

'after-years, *sb. pl.* [AFTER- 9.] The years that come, came, or will come after; the later years (of a man's life, etc.). Rarely *sing.*, a later year.

1814 WORDSWORTH *Excursion* VIII. p. 378 Sottish vice.. To which in after years he may be roused. **1837** LOCKHART *Scott* I. 341 Had the subject been taken up in after years, we might have had another Marmion. **1858** W. T. MATSON *Poems* 459 Love.. sagely musing o'er Fate's riddle-book, The secret coins of many an after-year. **1869** TENNYSON *Coming of Arthur* 157 In one great annal-book, where after-years Will learn the secret of our Arthur's birth. **1902** GAIRDNER *Eng. Ch. 16th C.* iv. 45 In spite of all the frightful demoralization of his after years he retained both characters to the very end.

aftonite. *Min.* See APHTHONITE.

aftsounes, var. EFTSOONS *adv.*, soon after.

aftward ('ɑːftwəd, æ-), *adv.* [f. AFT + -WARD.] 'In the direction of the stern.' Smyth *Sailor's Wd.-bk.* Also in form aftwards, and as *adj.*

1627 JOHN SMITH *Sea Grammar* ii. 5 The.. forward or aftward beames. *Ibid.* 7 The ships quarter is from the maine mast aftward. *Ibid.* v. 19 The vse of those staies are to keepe the Masts from falling aftwards. **1887** W. MORRIS tr. *Odyss.* I. xii. 410 And the mast withal fell aftward.

aftyr, obs. form of AFTER.

afure, obs. form of AFIRE.

afurst, obs. form of ATHIRST.

afy(e, earlier form of AFFY *v.*, to give faith.

afyght(e, bad sp. of AFAITE *v. Obs.*, to subdue.

afyn, var. of AFINE *adv. Obs.*, finally.

afzelia (æf'ziːlɪə). *Bot.* [mod.L., f. the name of Adam *Afzelius* (1750–1837), Swedish botanist.] A genus of trees of tropical Africa and Asia yielding a marketable timber; a tree of this genus; also, its timber.

1797 J. E. SMITH in *Trans. Linn. Soc.* IV. 221 Twenty New Genera of Plants.. Afzelia. *Ord. Nat.* Leguminosæ.. Locus *Africa æquinoctialis*.. Nomen dedi in inventoris honorem, celeberrimi *Adami Afzelii.* **1874** LINDLEY & MOORE *Treas. Bot.* II. 1258/1 *Afzelia*,.. with.. large flowers borne in short panicled racemes at the end of the branches. **1955** *Nomencl. Commerc. Timbers* (*B.S.I.*) 10 The trade name *afzelia* is proposed for all species of this genus. In practice the West African species are usually grouped together as a single commercial timber. The East African species is usually marketed separately. **1959** *House & Garden* July 41, 3-seater settee, afzelia wood frame.

‖**ag** (ax), *int. S. Afr.* [Afrikaans, f. Du. *ach* ACH *int.*] An ejaculation expressing irritation, reproach, sympathy, etc.

1936 C. BIRKBY *Thirstland Treks* 47 Ja, we left the old village. Ag, it was a nice village and I liked it. **1958** L. VAN DER POST *Lost World Kalahari* vi. 99 'Ag! Man!' he exclaimed with a pronounced South African accent. **1964** S. MILNE *False Witness* xvi. 177 'Ag, Annie, a small boy can be in any number of places,' said Steytler reassuringly. **1969** A. PATON *Kontakion for you Departed* 105, I said to Elizabeth teasingly, *how can a Roman Catholic join in an Anglican Communion?* Elizabeth said, *Ag, there's only one God, isn't there?* **1972** [see SIS *int.*]. **1975** *Darling* (S. Afr.) 9 Apr. 95 'Ag, shame,' she babbles on, 'you should of stayed by me, Bloss!'

ag- *pref.* assimilated form of L. *ad-* to, at, before *g*, as in *ag-glūtinātus*, *ag-gravātus*, *ag-gressio*. Reduced in OFr. to *a-*, and so entered Eng. as in *a-greger*, *a-grever*, *a-grege*, *a-grieve*. Afterwards refashioned after L. in all words that survived into mod.Eng., exc. *a-gree* (*ag-grātāre*), and spelt *ag-* in all words taken from L. into mod.Fr. or Eng. As in other forms of *ad-*, erroneously substituted in 16th c. for *a-* from other sources, as *a(g)grise*, OE. *a-grísan*.

In certain words, before *g* sounded (dʒ), the original *ad-* has been preferred, as *ad-geniculate*, *ad-generate*; before *gn-* *a-* is found, as *a-gnate* (also *ad-nate*), *a-gnize*, *a-gnomen* (also *ad-nomen*).

ag (æg). Chiefly *N. Amer.* Colloq. abbrev. of AGRICULTURAL *a.*, AGRICULTURE. Cf. MIN OF AG and *War Ag* s.v. WAR *sb.*¹ 11.

1918 *Dialect Notes* V. 22 *Ag*, adj., agricultural, or pertaining to the study of agriculture. 'He is going to an *ag* school.' **1942** BERREY & VAN DEN BARK *Amer. Thes. Slang* §829/2 Ag, ag coll, aggie, cow college, an agricultural college. **1958** *Kingston* (Ont.) *Whig-Standard* 14 Jan. 6/8 Don McArthur, 'ag-rep' for Frontenac County, will be the principal speaker. **1974** *Ridge Citizen* (Johnston, S. Carolina) 18 Apr. 8/8 Feed, seed, fertilizers, farm supplies and ag chemicals are manufactured and purchased for farmer members.

‖**aga, agha** (ə'gɑː, 'ɑːgə). [Turk. *aghā* master.] **1.** A commander or chief officer in the Ottoman empire; originally a military title, but used also of civil officers and as a title of distinction.

1600 PORY *Leo's Hist. Africa* 386 Neither can they be judged by any but the Agaes. **1628** DIGBY *Voy. to Medit.* (1868) 15 The Agaw, the principall officer next to the Bass.. **1667** *Lond. Gaz.* cxxxv/2 The Aga of the Janisaries in quality of paymaster to the Army. **1865** *Daily Tel.* 6 Nov. 5/5 The different tribes.. and the aghas who are to command them.

2. Aga Khan [KHAN¹], the title successively adopted by the spiritual leader or imam of the Khoja branch of Ismaili Muslims. Also *fig.*

1842 H. C. RAWLINSON *Let.* 6 Mar. in *Parl. Papers 1843* XXXVII. 217 The Persian refugee, Agha Khan, is still a guest at Candahar. **1881** *Times* 14 Apr. 5/6 The death is announced of Aga Khan, Chief of the Khojas. **1902** *Encycl. Brit.* XXV. 163/1 The Aga Khan traced his descent from the royal house of Persia from the most remote, almost prehistoric times. **1951** W. STEVENS *Let.* 13 Apr. (1967) 716 One is either tripe or the Aga Khan of letters. **1960** H. A. R. GIBB in *Encycl. Islam* (ed. 2) I. 246 Agha Khān, properly Āḳā Khān.. was originally an honorary title at the court of the Ḳādjār Shāhs of Persia, borne by Ḥasan 'Alī Shāh, who .. fled in 1840 to Sind. **1970** [see KHOJA 2].

Aga² ('ɑːgə). [Acronym, f. the initial letters of Sw. Svenska *A*ktiebolaget *Ga*sackumulator, Swedish Gas Accumulator Company, the original manufacturers.] A proprietary name for a type of large cooking stove or range (and water-heater), burning solid fuel and (later) gas or oil. Freq. *attrib.*, esp. as *Aga cooker*, *stove*.

1931 *Trade Marks Jrnl.* 15 July 972 Aga... Bell's Heat Appliances Limited, 157 Queen Victoria Street, London, E.C.4, Manufacturers. **1937** *Ibid.* 10 Mar. 272/1 *Aga*... Cooking stoves, water heating stoves, and steam-heated hot water supply apparatus for domestic use. Aga Heat Limited,.. London, W.1; manufacturers. **1938** L. MACNEICE *I crossed Minch* vii. 98 Four Siamese cats, very large, sat on the Aga cooker. **1956** M. STEWART *Wildfire at Midnight* xvi. 129 The cook was busy over the Aga. **1962** J. CANNAN *All is Discovered* i. 10 Her daughters returned to the .. kitchen and resumed their occupation of leaning against the Aga stove and discussing their parents. **1962** I. MURDOCH *Unofficial Rose* vi. 57 The big brightly li.. stone-flagged kitchen was silent except for.. the perpetu.l purring of the Aga cooker. **1976** W. TREVOR *Children of Dynmouth* viii. 169 She said it in the kitchen,.. looki.g round from the Aga where she was frying bacon. **1986** A.

PRICE *For Good of State* II. ii. 46 A middle-aged solid fuel Aga stove.

‖**agacerie** (agasəri). [Fr.] Allurement, coquetry.

1809 *Q. Rev.* II. 182 One class of readers may perhaps be amused by the *agaçeries* of the *filles de chambre*. **1818** MRS. OPIE *New Tales* III. 95 Till her mother gave her.. a very significant frown, her *agaceries* were addressed to me. **1848** A. H. CLOUGH *Bothie* II. 13 These, I think, no less than other agaceries, cloy one. **1853** MRS. GASKELL *Ruth* I. iii. 66 He had seen others.. with many more *agaceries* calculated to set off the effect of their charms. **1883** MRS. OLIPHANT *Sheridan* v. 174 That very transparent *agacerie* by which foolish men are sometimes attracted in the lower ranks of life.

†**a'gad**, *int. Obs.* [A euphemistic alteration of *O God!* earlier *A God!*] An expletive expressive of strength of feeling, conviction, etc.; = EGAD.

1728 FIELDING *Love in Sev. Masques* I. v. Agad, and that opinion is not singular. **1752** MRS. LENNOX *Fem. Quixote* VII. xiii. II. 168 Agad! I have no great mind to a halter.

Agadic (ə'gædɪk), *a.* [f. *Agada*, a Latinized form of HAGGADA.] Of or belonging to the Haggada, legendary (Rabbinic).

1878 SCHILLER-SZINESSY in *Academy* 605/1 The beautiful, but disconnected, Agadic sayings of the ancient Rabbis. **1881** *Athenæum* 30 Apr. 592/3 He invokes also the Agadic expositions as a help for his system.

again (ə'gɛn, ə'geɪn), *adv.*, *prep.*, *conj.* Forms: 1 **ongegn, ongægn, ongeægn, ongén, onȝeán, onȝán**; later **aȝén, aȝeán, aȝán**. *South.* 2 **onȝein, oȝein, anȝen**, 2–4 **aȝein, aȝen, aȝé**, 3 **aë**, 3–4 **aȝeyn, aȝayn, ayé**, 4 **ayein, aȝeen**, 5 **ayhen, ayhé**, 5–6 **ayen(e**. *North.* 4 **ogayn(e, ogain(e**, 4–6 **agayn(e, again(e**, (*Sc.* **agane, agone**). *Midl.* 3 **onnȝænn, aȝean, aȝan, aȝeon, aȝon, agen**, 3–4 **ageyn**, 5–6 **ageyn(e, agein(e, again(e**, 5–7 **againe**, 7–9 **again**, in poets **agen**. [**1.** OE. like the cogn. langs. shows two forms: (1) *onȝeán*, earlier **onȝeaȝn*, *onȝeæȝn*, *ongægn*, **ongagn*, OHG. *in gagan*, cf. ON. *gagn* sb., *gagn-* adv. pref.; (2) *onȝén*, earlier *onȝeȝn*, *ongegn*, OS. *angegin*, OHG. *in gegin*, *in gegini* (MHG. *engegene*, *engein*, mod.G. *entgegen*), ON. *i gegn* (Sw. *igen*, Dan. *igjen*); f. *on*, in + (1) *gagn*, (2) *gegn*, best explained as:—**gag(a)na*, **gag(a)ni*, variant O- and I- stems of *gag(a)n*. Not found in Gothic. From *onȝén* came the various southern forms of which *ayen* was the type; from the earlier *ongegn*, *onȝeȝn*, the type *ayein*; from *aȝeán*, the southern and midl. types *ayan*, *ayon*; from the earlier *ongægn*, *ongæȝn* (perh. influenced later by Norse), the northern *a-gain*. The late *agen* was a mixed form between *ayen* and *again*, and showed the common literary pronunciation even when *again* was written; hence it was used by the poets down to the present century (found 1834), but this is now obs. **2.** The primary meaning of *gagn*, *gegn* seems to have been 'direct, straight' (see GAIN *a.* and *sb.*, and cf. ON. *gegn* adj.), whence *on-gegn* 'in a direct line with, opposite, facing locally,' and so extended to all ideas of meeting, opposition, reversal, recurrence, repetition. Originally a separable adverbial particle, as in *ongegn-cuman*, which, when separated from the vb., became an *adv.* or *prep.* according to the construction: *he cymeð aȝén, he him cymeð aȝén, he cymeð him aȝén, he cymeð aȝén him* or *hine*. **3.** As early as 1130 there arose in the south a variant with advb. genitive *aȝenes*, *againes*, corrupted bef. 1400 to *aȝenst*, *against* (see next word) as the prepositional form. Early in 16th c. *again* was restricted to the advb. use, and *against* alone used as *prep.* (and *conj.*). In Sc. and north Eng. where *against* was not adopted, *again* still retains all its early constructions, occasionally borrowed also by southern writers since 1525.]

A. *adv.*

1. †**a.** In the opposite direction; back. *Obs.*

993 *Batt. Maldon* 137 Ðæt spere sprengde, ðæt hit sprang onȝean. *c* **1220** *Leg. St. Kath.* 1368 & ba binden ham swa, þe fet & te honden, þat ha wrungen aȝain. **1382** WYCLIF *Ecclus.* xiii. 13 Be thou not to gredi, lest thou be put aȝeen [**1611** put back]. *c* **1400** *Apol. for Loll.* 105 þe wif of Loth, þat.. loking aȝen, was turnid in to an image of salt. *Ibid.* No man leying hand to þe plowe, and loking aȝen, is able to þe kyndam of God. **1480** CAXTON *Chron. Eng.* clxiii. 147 The walsshmen .. were so strong that they dryuen the englysshmen ageyne.

b. *esp.* with *go*, *come*, *wend*, *turn*, *throw*: back, *esp.* all the way back, back to the point of starting. *Obs.* exc. in the *arch.* and *dial.* 'turn again,' and as in d.

c **1000** ÆLFRIC *Hom.* (Sweet 77) Gecyrde se apostol onȝean mid miclum wurðmynte. **1031** *O.E. Chron.* (Parker MS.) Her com Cnut aȝan to Englalonde. **1070** *Ibid.* Swa Thomas to þam timan aȝean ferde buton bletsunga. *c* **1175** *Lamb. Hom.* 79 3if þu mare spenest of þine hwan ic aȝen cherre: al ic þe ȝelde. *c* **1200** *Trin. Coll. Hom.* 91 Elhc cristene man makeð þis dai procession fro chirche to chirche and eft agen. *c* **1250** *Gen. & Exod.* 3267 Ðo quoðen he, 'wende we a-gen, An[d] israel folc lete we ben.' *c* **1300** *Beket* 147 And was oute threo ȝer and an half, er he aȝe com. **1387** TREVISA *Higden* Rolls Ser. I. 407 Fynde and see, And þanne torne home aȝe. **1398** —— *Barth. De P.R.* IX. iii. (1495) 347 A cercle that comyth agayne into itself and is renewed. **1513** MORE *Edw. V* (1641) 17 But sith things passed cannot be called againe. **1596** SHAKS. *Tam. Shr.* II. i. 217 Nay, come againe, good Kate, I am a gentleman. **1611** —— *Cymb.* IV. iii. 1 Againe: and bring me word how 'tis with her. **1611** BIBLE *Judg.* iii. 19 Hee himselfe turned againe from the quarries. —— *Luke* x. 35 When I come again, I will repay thee [**1881** *Revised* I, when I come back again, will repay thee]. **1678** BUNYAN *Pilgrim* 9 Come then, Neighbour Pliable, let us turn again, and go home. **1742** RICHARDSON *Pamela* III. 363 Go and shut the Chamber-door and come to me again. *Arch.* 'Turn again Whittington, thrice Lord Mayor of London!' *Mod. Sc.* I have come far enough, it is time for me to turn again.

†**c.** *to and again*: to and fro, backwards and forwards. *Obs.*

1628 DIGBY *Voy. to Medit.* (1868) 7 Wee plyed to and againe the Spanish shore. **1665** PEPYS *Diary* 15 July, Staid an hour crossing the water to and again. **1697** PERRY *Hist. Coll. Am. Col. Ch.* They all sat down not at a table but to and again about the room as we are now sitting. **1702** W. J. tr. *Bruyn's Voy. to Levant* ii. 3 A white Plume of Peacocks Feathers.. which they wafted to and agen to drive off the Flies. **1719** DE FOE *Crusoe* (1858) 356 He walked along the shore, to-and-again, with his father. **1736** BAILEY (Fol.).

d. strengthened with *back*, *re*-turn; thus passing into 3. (In OE. *eft* 'again' was strengthened by *onȝeán* 'back'; in mod.Eng. *again* having taken the place of *eft* requires *back* in place of *onȝeán*.)

1052 *O.E. Chron.* (Laud MS.) And ȝewende þa Godwine eorl ut aȝean.. and ða oðra scipu ȝ ewenden heom eft onȝean to Sandwic. **1506** GUYLFORD *Pylgr.* 7 The 16th day of June we retournyd ayen to Venys. **1592** SHAKS. *Rom. & Jul.* II. iii. 8 Nurse, come backe againe. **1611** BIBLE *Prov.* ii. 19 None that goe vnto her, returne againe. **1813** SCOTT *Trierm.* II. xxii, Recall thine oath! and to her glen Poor Gyneth can return agen.

2. In reaction or reciprocal action; in return, in reply, in response, back; either of an action returned, or one done in return for it. *Obs.* or *arch.* exc. in 'Answer again,' and as in b, c.

c **1220** *Leg. St. Kath.* 1331 We nullen, ne ne duren, warpen na word aȝain. *c* **1305** *St. Edm. Conf.* 31 Hi seide aȝe þat hi ne miȝte noȝt bi so lute beo. *c* **1386** CHAUCER *Squieres T.* 124 And answere hym in his langage ageyn [*Lansd.* aȝeine, *Camb.* a-geyn]. *c* **1440** *Gesta Rom.* (1879) lx. 245 [He] wedde a ȝonge gentil damiselle to wyfe; and he loviede hir moche, and she hatide him ayene. *c* **1500** *Notborune Mayd.* (1842) 33 For neuer a dell He wyll me loue agayne. **1535** COVERDALE *Judg.* i. 7 As I haue done, so hath God rewarded me agayne. **1557** N. T. (Genev.) *Tit.* ii. 9 Not answering againe, neither pickers. **1592** SHAKS. *Ven. & Adon.* 1113 Who did not whet his teeth at him again. **1596** —— *Merch. Ven.* I. ii. 87 He would pay him againe when he was able. **1600** —— *A.Y.L.* III. v. 132, I maruell why I answer'd not againe. **1611** BIBLE *Luke* vi. 35 Doe good and lend, hoping for nothing againe. **1662** in Heath *Grocers' Comp.* (1869) 68 The which we doe faithfully promise shall be payd to you agayne. **1742** RICHARDSON *Pamela* III. 78 If he did not love me again, would he have flung his Book at my head? *c* **1840** LONGF. *Endymion* vii, Ye shall be loved again! *Mod.* (? *dial.*) Very saucy, and inclined to answer again.

b. *esp.* in *ring*, *echo*, etc. *again*, to echo back, re-echo; passing into, to sound in response or sympathy.

1561 BIBLE (Genev.) *1 Sam.* iv. 5 All Israel shouted a mightie shoute, so that the earth rang againe. [So **1611**; WYCL. thurȝ sownede. COVERD. sounded withall.] **1605** SHAKS. *Macb.* v. iii. 53, I would applaud thee to the very Eccho, That should applaud againe. **1810** SCOTT *Lady of L.* II. xix, Echo his praise agen. **1837** DICKENS *Pickw.* I. 261 He laughed till the glasses in the sideboard rang again.

c. From *echo*, extended to *creak*, *crack*, *thrill*, *shake*, *reel*, *dance*, *ache*, *shine*, *gleam*, *wink*, etc., to express sympathetic response to action, indicating the intensity of the action itself.

a **1536** TINDALE *Writings* (1849) II. 12 They make poor women howl again. **1596** SHAKS. *Merch. V.* III. ii. 205 Wooing heere, vntill I swet againe.. I gat a promise. **1623** MASSINGER *Dk. of Milan* I. i, Drink hard; and let the health run through the city, Until it reel again. **1710** PALMER *Proverbs* 53 To open upon the cry till they are hoarse again. **1837** DICKENS *Pickw.*, The wind blowing.. till every timber of the old house creaked again. *Ibid.*, Rubbing away [with the towel] till his face shone again. **1857** W. COLLINS *Dead Secret* II. 72 She gallops and gallops till the horse reeks again. *c* **1870** —— *Biter Bit.* 286 He struck his fist on the table so heavily that the wood cracked again.

3. Back into a former position or state; back.

a **1067** *Charter of Eadweard* in *Cod. Diplom.* IV. 195 Gif ani land sy owt of ðen biscopriche ȝedon, ich wille ðæt hit cume in onȝean. *c* **1250** *Gen. & Exod.* 405 And he sal bringen man a-gen In paradis to wunen and ben. **1297** R. GLOUC. 36 And a ȝeyn in his kyndom mid gret honour ydo. *c* **1350** *Will. Palerne* 4254 Til þou.. haue heled þe werwolf.. and maked to man aȝe. **1387** TREVISA *Higden* Rolls Ser. I. 119 Anon þey were i-cast vp aȝe. *a* **1400** *Covent. Myst.* 377 From dethe to lyue I am resyn ageyn. **1475** *Bk. of Noblesse* 2 For relevyng and geting ayen the said Reaume. *c* **1540** WYATT *Compl. Love to Reason* 157 'Thou gave her once,' quod I, 'but by and by Thou took her ayen from me!' **1591** SHAKS. *Two Gent.* II. i. 129 Take them againe. **1601** —— *All's Well* v. iii. 131 And would never Receive the ring again. *a* **1665** CLEVELAND *Obseq.* 40 Perhaps an *Ignis fatuus* now and then Starts up in holes, stinks and goes out agen. **1728** YOUNG *Love of Fame* v. (1757) 121 Then Like April suns, dives into clouds agen. *a* **1763** SHENSTONE *Odes* 214 'Tis yours, ye fair, to bring those days agen. **1790** WOLCOTT (Peter Pindar) *Wks.* 1812 II. 338 Go, children, to your leading-strings agen. **1818** BYRON *Childe Har.* I. vii, Monks might deem their time was come agen. **1855** H. REED *Lect. Eng. Lit.* vi. (1878) 216 Bringing.. the old books to light and life again.

b. Back in a former position or state; anew; once more as before.

c **1385** CHAUCER *Leg. G. Wom.* 72 As of the lef agayn the flour to make. *c* **1440** *Gesta Rom.* (1879) 95 He is here ayene! *a* **1447** CDL. BEAUFORT in Ellis *Orig. Lett.* I. 4 I. 8 Lette seele the Cofir aȝeyn with a signet of myn. **1624** QUARLES *Job* (1717) 215 Confess to men, I was a Leper, but am clear agen. **1712** STEELE *Spect.* No. 492. §3 These careless pretty creatures are very Innocents again. **1835** CRABBE *Par. Reg.* II. 536 And Robin never was himself again. **1849** MACAULAY *Hist. Eng.* II. 78 The principles of the treaty of Dover were again the principles of the foreign policy of England. *Mod.* Clown in the Pantomime: 'Here we are again!'

4. Repetition of an action or fact: another time; once more; any more; anew; (in quot. 1853 used as a request for repetition of what has previously been said; cf. *come again* s.v. COME *v.* 55 d).

1382 WYCLIF *Ecclus.* xxxi. 42 Bere thou not hym doun in aȝee asking. *c* **1450** LONELICH *Grail* xvi. 367 Thanne Ioseph aȝen took þat schrewe.. And bond him aȝen in alle mennes siht. **1526** TINDALE *John* viii. 21 Then sayde Iesus agayne [WYCL. eft] vnto them. *a* **1528** SKELTON *Dk. of Albaney* 153 For ye be false echone False and false agayne. **1593** SHAKS. *Rich. II*, v. iii. 133 Speake it again! Twice saying Pardon doth not pardon twaine. **1602** —— *Haml.* I. ii. 188, I shall not look upon his like again. **1611** BIBLE *Gen.* viii. 21, I will not againe [WYCL. no more] curse the ground any more for man's sake. *a* **1622** WITHER *Brit. Rememb.* 164, I saw how Cities, Commonwealths, and men, Did rise and fall, and rise and fall agen. **1736** H. BROWNE *Pipe of Tob.* (B.P.) ii. 21 Happy thrice and thrice agen, Happiest he of happy men. **1835** CRABBE *Village* I. 193 He hears and smiles, then thinks again and sighs. **1849** MACAULAY *Hist. Eng.* II. 137 He meditated the design of again confiscating and again portioning out the soil of half the island. **1853** DICKENS *Bleak Ho.* lvii. 549 'You know Mr. Skimpole!' said I. 'What do you call him again?' returned Mr. Bucket.

b. This sense is more fully expressed by ***once again***, ***over again***; and the repetition increased by ***too and again*** (obs.), ***again and again***, ***ever and again***, ***time and again***. **now and again**: occasionally, now and then.

1535 COVERDALE *1 Kings* xviii. 34 Do it yet once. And they dyd it once agayne. **1604** SHAKS. *Oth.* I. iii. 372, I haue told thee often, and I re-tell thee againe and againe. **1610** —— *Temp.* I. ii. 134, I.. Will cry it ore againe. *Ibid.* III. ii. 44 Hearken once againe to the suite I made to thee. **1659** Ross in *Burton's Diary* (1828) IV. 379 Your Committee too and again offered it as an expedient. **1703** MOXON *Mech. Exerc.* 26 You may thus work it round again and again. **1759** JOHNSON *Rasselas* xlv. (1787) 130 They came again and again, and were every time more welcome than before. **1855** MACAULAY *Hist. Eng.* IV. 91 Again and again the assailants were driven back. **1865** A. TROLLOPE *Belton Est.* ix. 96, I will come up every now and again. **1870** MORRIS *Earthly Par.* IV. 414 Time and again, he, listening to such word, Felt his heart kindle; time and again did seem As though a cold and hopeless tune he heard. **1876** FREEMAN *Norm. Conq.* III. xii. 188 The name appears over and over again. **1880** CYPLES *Hum. Exp.* iii. 63 The flesh, ever-and-again, pleasantly tingles.

5. Repetition of quantity: Once repeated; ***as much again*** = this and as much more, twice as much; ***half as much again*** = this and half as much more, one-and-a-half times as much.

1593 SHAKS. *2 Hen. VI*, IV. iii. 7 Lent shall bee as long againe as it is. **1669** BOYLE *Cont. New Exper.* I. (1682) 11 A good deal larger.. if not as large agen. *a* **1700** DRYDEN *Dufresnoy* (J.) A theatre as large and as deep again. **1709** POPE *Criticism* 81 Yet want as much again to manage it. **1774** GOLDSM. *Nat. Hist.* v. 178 The Grouse is about half as large again as a Partridge. **1878** HUXLEY *Physiogr.* 84 About half as heavy again as an equal bulk of atmospheric air.

6. Repetition locally (as on a tour): In any (or some) other place to which you may go; anywhere or somewhere besides, or further. *arch.*

1555 *Fardle of Facions* II. x. 209 Horses and mares, in suche plentie, as I beleue no parte of the earth hath againe. *a* **1626** BACON (J.) There is not, in the world again, such a spring and seminary of brave military people as in England, Scotland, and Ireland. *Mod.* You'll not meet with the like of it in London again.

7. As another point or fact. **a.** of transition or contrast: On the other hand. **b.** of simple succession: Further, moreover, in the next place, besides.

a **1533** FRITH *Answ. Rastell* §15 He saith, We have an advocate; and saith again, for our sins. **1580** BARET *Alvearie* A 222 And he againe on the other parte. **1593** SHAKS. *Rich. II*, II. ii. 113 Th' other againe Is my kinsman. *Ibid.* v. v. 15 Come, litle ones: And then, again, it is as hard to come, as for a Camell To thred the posterne of a needles eye. **1611** BIBLE *2 Sam.* xvi. 19 And againe, whom should I serue? **1694** R. LESTRANGE *Fables* (J.) Those things that we know not what to do withal, and those things, again, which another cannot part with. **1742** RICHARDSON *Pamela* IV. 87 But now again, see what succeeds to this. **1853** WALLACE *Euclid* III. v, Again, because E is the centre of the circle CDG, EC is equal to EG. **1855** MACAULAY *Hist. Eng.* III. 499 What again is the legal effect of the words?

†**B.** *prep. Obs.* or *dial.*

¶ Illustrations of the development of the prep. from separable adverbial particle.

a **1100** *O.E. Chron.* an. 1067 þá he onȝeán-cóm. *a* **1100** *Satan* 301 (Grein) [Se þe] ús onȝeán-cymeð. *a* **1100** *Hymn* iv. 59 (Grein) þonne storm cymeð mínum ȝæste onȝeȝn. *a* **1100** ÆLFRIC *Hom.* (Sweet 77) Him urnon onȝeán weras and wif. *a* **1100** *Ags. Gosp.* Luke xiv. 31 Hwæðer he mæȝe cuman aȝén þone þe hym aȝén cymð. *c* **1250** *Gen. & Ex.* 1796 Esau him cam aȝen. *Ibid.* 3912 King.. cam hem ageon. *a* **1300** *Havelok* 2024 Hwo mihte so manie stonde? *Ibid.* 3912 Hwo mouhte agey[n] so many stonde? **1340** HAMPOLE *Pr. Consc.* 7942 Nathyng þam salle ogayne-stand.

Ibid. 7964 Na thyng salle mow ogayne þam stand. *c* **1460** *Townl. Myst.* 41 My bydyng standes he not ogane.

†**1.** Of position: Opposite to, facing, in front of, in full view of. (= AGAINST 1.)

c **950** *Lind. Gosp.* Luke xix. 30 Gaas in woerc þæt onᵹeaeᵹn is [*Rushw* ongæᵹn]. *c* **1000** *Ags. Gosp.*, ibid. Farað on þæt castel þe onᵹean [*v.r.* onᵹen] inc ys. *c* **1000** ÆLFRIC *Deut.* xxxii. 49 On þam lande Moab, onᵹean Iericho. *c* **1175** *Lamb. Hom.* 3 Þane castel þet is onȝein eou. **1297** R. GLOUC. 6 Euene aȝeyn Fraunce stonde þe contre of Chichestre, Norwiche aȝeyn Denemarc, Chestre aȝeyn Yrlond. **1340** HAMPOLE *Pr. Consc.* 6366 Þe son sal þan in þe este stande.. And þe mone ogayne it in þe weste. *c* **1385** CHAUCER *Leg. G. Wom.* Prol. 48 To seen this flowre ayein the sunne sprede. *c* **1430** *Syr Generides* 8323 Right ageyn [Clarionas] he stoode. *c* **1440** *Morte Arth.* 85 The mayde knelyd the kynge a gayne. **1466** *J. Paston's Funeral* in *Lett.* 549 II. 266 To the iiii orders of fryers that rede ageyn the cors.

†**2.** *fig.* Of mental attitude or disposition: Towards, in the sight of, in regard to. = AGAINST 3.

1340 *Ayenb.* 114 Ne is hit naȝt grat þing ne grat ofservinge aye God. *c* **1430** LYDGATE *Bochas* II. xxvi. (1554) 62 a, To be piteous Ageine Cresus. *c* **1440** *Morte Arth.* 52 Ageyne the kynge trator is he. **1540** WHITTINTON *Tully's Offyce* I. 44 Howe we shulde behaue ourselfe agayn other men.

†**3.** Of motion: In a direction contrary to or facing; towards, in the direction of, forward to, to meet.

894 *O.E. Chron.*, Ða woldon ferian norð weardes.. onᵹeán ða scipu. *c* **1175** *Lamb. Hom.* 5 Ure drihten sende his ii apostles oȝein þene castel. *c* **1200** *Moral Ode* 351 Þos goð uneaðe aȝien þe cliue and aȝien þe heie hulle. *c* **1250** *Gen. & Exod.* 1438 Eliezer him cam a-gon. *c* **1300** *St. Brand.* 32 That Aȝe me..threo journeyes he wende. *c* **1380** *Sir Ferumb.* 3624 And prykeþ ys stede & forþ he nam Agayn þe hulle an heȝe. *c* **1386** CHAUCER *Man of L.T.* 293 And preyeth hir for to ride agein the queene. *c* **1440** *Morte Arth.* 24 They ran as swithe as euyr they might Oute at the gates hym agayne.

†**b.** In reception of, in welcome of. = AGAINST 5 b.

a **1300** *Havelok* 1106 Belles dede he ageyn hire ringen. **1330** R. BRUNNE *Chron.* 118 Mald þe Emperice com to lond, Þe castelle of Arondelle open ageyn hir fond.

†**4.** Advancing into forcible contact or into collision with; = AGAINST 6.

a **1300** *Havelok* 568 Hise croune he þer crakede Ageyn a gret ston. *a* **1325** *Metr. Hom.* 32 Mani pas, That than igain me casten was. *c* **1380** *Sir Ferumb.* 2850 Wiþ ys fuste harde a gerte: Gyoun agayn þe teþ. *Ibid.* 2569 Casten aȝe þe wal. *c* **1384** CHAUCER *H. of Fame* 1035 Betynge of the see.. ayen the roches holowe. *a* **1593** MARLOWE *Edward II*, II. ii. 209 Libels are cast again thee in the street.

†**5.** Towards with hostile intent; to meet in hostility. = AGAINST 11.

c **1000** *Ags. Gosp.* John xviii. 29 Hwylce wrohte bringeᵹe onᵹean þysne man? *c* **1250** *Gen. & Exod.* 3912 King.. seon, for to figten cam hem ageon. **1297** R. GLOUC. 451 Ladde ost gret ynou aȝe þe kyng & his. *a* **1305** *St. James* in *E.E. Poems* (1862) 58 Aȝen þe deuel he com adoun: & bad þe schrewe abide. **1377** LANGL. *P. Pl.* B. xix. 356 To gone agayne pryde. *c* **1400** *Destr. Troy* XVI. 7315 The Prinse hym persayuit and preset hym agayn. **1664** *Flodden Field* viii. 75 Who manfully march'd them again. [**1782** TRUMBULL *McFingal* II. (1795) 41 To each of whom, to send again ye Old Guy of Warwick were a ninny.]

†**6.** *gen.* In hostility or active opposition to (with *fight*, *strive*, *act*, *be*, *speak*, *murmur*, etc.) = AGAINST 12.

c **1000** *Ags. Gosp.* Mark ix. 40 Se þe nis aᵹen eow se is for eow [*v.r.* aᵹean; *Lind. & Rushw.* wið]. **1012** *O.E. Chron.* Wearð þa se here swiþe astyred anᵹean ðone biscop. *c* **1175** *Cott. Hom.* 219 And habbe anwealda and riche anȝen godelmichti. *c* **1200** ORMIN 1842 He shollde fihhtenn Onnȝæn ane drake. *c* **1300** *Beket* 54 Dude here beste aȝe the Prince. *Ibid.* 1456 Than contek holde in suche lond, and nameliche aë the Kinge. **1340** HAMPOLE *Pr. Consc.* 4142 Anticrist es.. Als he þat es ogayn Crist ay. **1430** *A.B.C. of Aristotle* in *Babees Bk.* 10 Argue not aȝen þat. *c* **1450** *Merlin* 55 Ye shull fight ageyn yowre enmyes. **1521** FISHER *Wks.* 311 The sermon of Iohan the bysshop of Rochester made agayn the pernicyous doctryn of Martin luuther. *c* **1550** CHEKE *Matt.* xxi. 12 Y[ei] murmured again ye good man of ye house. **1604** MIDDLETON *Five Gallants* II. iii. Wks. II. 255 Go and suborn my knave again me here. **1829** SCOTT *Antiq.* xv. 96 I'm no again your looking at the outside of a letter neither.

†**b.** In competition with, as against.

c **1385** CHAUCER *L.G.W.* 189 In preysing of the flour agayn the leefe, No more than of the corne agayn the sheefe.

†**7.** Opposed to in tendency or character, contrary to. = AGAINST 10.

c **1000** *Ags. Gosp.* Matt. v. 23 Þæt þin broðor hæfð ǽniᵹ þing aᵹen þé [*v.r.* aᵹeán; *Lind. & Rushw.* wið]. *c* **1230** *Ancren Riwle* 200 Onloðest God & most aȝean his grace. **1340** HAMPOLE *Pr. Consc.* 304 Þat men þam says ogayn þair likyng. *c* **1386** CHAUCER *Knightes T.* 1593 Al be it that it is again his kind. **1424** *Paston Lett.* 4 I. 13 Ageyn the kinges peas. **1432–50** tr. *Higden* Rolls Ser. I. 131 Hit is bareyne in pastures, ageyne the nature of other regiones. **1523** FITZHERBERT *Surveying* 4 It were agayne reason to a bridge a man of his owne right. **1596** R. H. tr. *Lavaterus's Ghostes & Spir.* 128 Licence to doo these things.. againe his owne expresse commaundement.

†**8.** In resistance to. = AGAINST 13.

1048 *O.E. Chron.*, Him láð wære ðæt hi onᵹeán heora cynehláford standan sceoldan. *c* **1230** *Ancren Riwle* 50 Þiccure aȝein þe wind. *a* **1300** *Rel. Antiq.* I. 63 Þolemod aȝean alle wowes, and in alle uveles. **1375** BARBOUR *Bruce* IV. 186 Neyll the bruce held Kyndrummy Agane his sone. **1384** CHAUCER *Mother of God* 111 We mowen make resistance Ageyn the feend. *a* **1423** JAMES I *King's Quair* II. x. Again distresse confort to seke. **1488** *Act 4 Hen. VII*, xix. §1 The defence of this land ageyn oure ennemyes outwarde.

†**9.** In return for, in exchange for; in place of, instead of. = AGAINST 14.

c **1175** *Lamb. Hom.* 15 Ne scalt þu ȝelden vuel onȝein uuel nuða. *c* **1230** *Hali Meid.* 7 Nis tis þeowdom inoh aȝain þat.

†**10.** Time: Towards, drawing near; near the beginning of. = AGAINST 18.

1096 *O.E. Chron.* (Laud MS.) Fela hungerbitene onᵹean winter ham tuᵹon. *c* **1305** *St. Edm. Conf.* 14 Aȝen eue he cudde furst his lyf. *c* **1435** *Torr. Portugal* 1940 The wynd arose ayen the nyght.

†**11.** In view of, in anticipation of, in preparation for; to meet. = AGAINST 19.

c **1230** *Hali Meid.* 31 Hwen he beoð ute, hauest aȝain his ham cume sar care & eie. *c* **1250** *Gen. & Ex.* 562 Ðat arche was a feteles good, set and limed a-gen ðe flood. **1340** HAMPOLE *Pr. Consc.* 4041 Thir takens..þat ogayn þe worldes ende shuld be. *c* **1380** *Sir Ferumb.* 1496 Þys messagers agayn þe morwe: a-rayd hem for hure message. *c* **1386** CHAUCER *Squieres T.* 134 Ageyn this lusty somerestyde. *a* **1450** *Syr Eglamore* in *Dom. Archit.* II. 202 Ageyn ye evyn ye kyng gart dyȝt A bath for ye gentyll knyȝt.

†**C.** *conj.* or *conj. adv. Obs.* or *dial.*

†**1.** In return for the adverse fact that.

a. with *relative particle*. **b.** *simply*.

c **1175** *Lamb. Hom.* 21 And he hine iblecie onȝein þe he hine acursede. *c* **1200** ORMIN 11143 [Þeȝȝ] himm sinndenn cweme, onnȝæn þatt teȝȝ Himm wærenn ær uncweme.

†**2.** Of time: Against the time that, before that.

a. with *relative particle*. **b.** *simply*.

c **1200** ORMIN 6128 All þe birrþ bitæchenn itt þe preost o Godess hallfe, Onnȝæn þatt he shall shrifenn þe. *c* **1315** *Pol. Songs* 151 Aȝeyn this cachereles cometh, thus y mot care. *a* **1400** *Sir Perceval* 192 Wolde scho noȝte with hir bere Bot a lyttille Scottes spere, Agayne hir sone ȝode. **1632** MASSINGER *City Madam* III. i, Get.. His cap and pantofles ready.. And a candle Again you rise.

†**a'gain-**, [the *adv.*], was formerly used in many verbal combinations, which are now all obsolete; of the simple GAIN- with which it varied, GAINSAY is the only surviving representative. As *again-* was originally a movable adverbial particle, as in mod.G. *entgégen-kommen*, it always had the main stress, *a'gain-ˌmeeting*. In meaning it answered to L. *re-* (compounds of which now usually replace those of *again-*) with the following varieties:

1. Against, in opposition to; *rarely* opposite: **again-behold**, to look opposite; **again-fight**, to fight against; **again-lay, -legge**, to oppose; **again-meeting**, rencounter; **again-renning**, inroad, incursion; **again-ride**, to ride against; **again-spreng(en**, to besprinkle, bespatter; **again-weight, -wiȝte**, counterweight; **again-wince**, to kick against; **again-witness**, to witness against; **again-withstand**, to resist. Also AGAIN-COME, -GO, -RISE, -SAY, -STAND, q.v.

1382 WYCLIF *Ex.* xxxvii. 9 And hemselues [*i.e.* the two cherubyn] togidere and it aȝenbiholdynge. —— *Rom.* vii. 23 An other lawe in my membris, aȝenfiȝtinge to the lawe of my soule. —— *Josh.* x. 31 And the oost.. aȝenfauȝt it. —— *Ezra* Prol., If any man forsothe aȝen legge to vs the seuenti remenoures. —— *1 Sam.* xxv. 20 Dauid and his men camen doun into aȝenmetynge of hire. —— *2 Macc.* vi. 3 The aȝein renning of yuels [Vulg. *malorum incursio*]. —— *Is.* xxix. 7 Alle þat aȝen riden and bisegeden. —— *Lev.* xiv. 44 The walles aȝen spreynt with spottis. **1340** *Ayenb.* 247 Þeruore þe ayenwyȝte of þe ulesse is zuo heuy. **1382** WYCLIF *Deut.* xxxii. 15 Ful fat maad is the loued and aȝen wynsed [**1388** kikide aȝen]. —— *Jer.* xlii. 19 Aȝenwitnessid Y haue to ȝou this day. —— *Deut.* ix. 2 To the whiche no man may aȝenwithstoond [**1388** aȝenstonde in the contrarie part].

2. Back, backward: **again-bow**, to bend back; **again-bring**, to bring back; **again-chare**, to turn back, repent; **again-clepe**, to recall; **again-drawing**, drawing back, retractation; **again-falling**, relapse; **again-fare**, to return; **again-frushe**, to start back, recoil; **again-hold**, to hold back, withhold; **again-lead**, to lead back; **again-louke**, to shut back, *recludere*; **again-put**, to push back; **again-raas**, a running back, return; **again-tell**, to report; **again-tote** *sb.*, looking back; **again-wend**, to turn back. Also AGAIN-CALL, -COME, -TURN, q.v.

1382 WYCLIF *1 Kings* vii. 26 As a leef of a lilye to be aȝen bowid. —— *Rom.* xv. 15, I wroot to ȝou of party, as aȝen bryngynge ȝou in to mynde. —— *Tob.* xii. 3 Me he hath led and aȝeen broȝt hol. *c* **1175** *Lamb. Hom.* 79 Hwan ic aᵹencherre, al ic þe ᵹelde. **1303** R. BRUNNE *Handl. Synne* 2066 Tyl sum myschaunce make hem aȝenchare. **1382** WYCLIF *Ps.* ci. 25 Ne aȝeen clepe thou me in the myddil of my daȝis. —— *Rom.* Prol., Poul aȝenclepith [reuokith] these Romayns to veri feith. —— *Ex.* iv. 7 He aȝen drewȝ [**1388** withdrew]. —— *1 Sam.* xiv. 39 With out aȝen drawynge he shal die. **1340** *Ayenb.* 116 Þet he hine loky uram ayenfallinge. **1205** LAYAMON 23158 Ȝif þu nult aȝainfaren [**1250** aȝenfare]. **1382** WYCLIF *Ex.* xv. 16 Alle the dwellers of Chanaan aȝenfrusshiden for ferde. *c* **1450** PECOCK *Repr.* 381 The same peple mowe justli withdrawe & aȝenholde the tithis. **1382** WYCLIF *Tob.* v. 15 Leden, and aȝeen lede hym to thee hol. **1315** *E.E. Psalter* (1843) xxxiv. 3 Þat filigh me, ogain-louke þam. **1382** WYCLIF *1 Sam.* xxi. 13 He aȝen put into the doris of the ȝate. **1315** *E.E. Psalter* (1843) xviii. 7 Fra heghest heven his outcome ai, And his ogaine-raas til hegh sette. **1382** WYCLIF *1 Sam.* xxii. 6 There is not that aȝen telle to me. *c* **1325** *E.E. Allit. Poems* B. 931 Ay goande on your gate, wythouten agayntote. **1205** LAYAMON 23155 Senden to þan kingen, and hahten hine aȝainwenden. **1315** *E.E. Psalter* (1843) lxxvii. 9 Sones of Effrem.. In dai of fight ere ogayne-wendand.

3. Reversal: **again-cover**, to reveal, uncover.

1382 WYCLIF *Ecclus.* xlvii. 16 His soule aȝeen couerede the erthe [**1388** vnhilide].

4. Reciprocal or reflected action; in return: **again-behest**, reciprocal or mutual promise; **again-bihote**, to be responsible or surety for; **again-bihoter**, a surety; **again-bihoting**, suretyship, responsibility; **again-bite, ayenbite**, remorse; **again-chiding**, recrimination; **again-gift**, giving in return, repayment; **again-measure**, to measure back; **again-shine**, to shine back, reflect; **again-smiting**, reaction, reverberation; **again-sound**, to resound, re-echo.

1382 WYCLIF *Heb.* xi. 17 He offride the oon bigetyn, the which hadde takyn repromyssiouns, or aȝenbiheestis. —— *Ecclus.* xxix. 23 A man aȝeenbihoteth of his neȝhebore. *Ibid.* xxix. 21 The synnere and the vnclene the aȝeenbihotere fleeth. *Ibid.* xxix. 24 Most shreude aȝenbihoting spilde manye loouende men. **1340** *Ayenb.* 5 Þis boc is ywrite Vor Englisse men þet hi wyte How hi ssolde ham zelve ssrive And maki ham klene ine þise live. Þis boc hatte huo þet writ Ayenbite of Inwyt. **1382** WYCLIF *Ecclus.* xxi. 5 Aȝeen chiding and wrongis to noȝt shul bringe substaunce. **1340** *Ayenb.* 121 Ȝefþe is ȝeuynge wyþoute aȝenȝefþe, þet is wy[þ]oute onderstondinge of aȝenȝefþe. **1382** WYCLIF *Isa.* lxv. 7, I shal aȝeen mesuren the were of hem first in the bosum of hem. —— *Ecclus.* l. 8 As the aȝenshynende bowe betweene the litle cloudis of glorie. —— *Prov.* xxvii. 19 What maner wise in watris aȝeen schinen the cheres of men. **1398** TREVISA *Barth. De P.R.* v. vi, For yf he [the eye] apprehendeþ wel and lyȝtly, with oute aȝen smytynge (*sine reverberatione*). **1382** WYCLIF *Isa.* xliv. 23 Aȝensouneth, ȝee hillis, preising.

5. Restoration to a former state; back again: **again-ask**, to ask back, require; **again-keel**, to cool again; **again-new**, to renew; **again-raise, -reyse**, to raise again; **again-seek**, to ask for, require; **again-set**, to set up again. Also AGAIN-BUY, -RISING, q.v.

1382 WYCLIF *Deut.* xxiv. 10 Whanne thow shalt aȝen aske eny thing that he owith to thee. —— *Ecclus.* xviii. 16 Whether not brennende hete the dew shal aȝeen-keelen. —— *Tit.* iii. 6 By waischynge of aȝen-bigetyng, and aȝen-newyng of the Hooly Gost. —— *John* vi. 40, I schal aȝen reyse him in the laste day. **1388** —— *Ps.* cxli. 5 Ther was not that aȝeen soȝte my soule. —— *Ezek.* xiii. 5 Nether aȝensettiden a wal for the hous of Israel [**1382** aȝen puttiden].

6. Repetition; again, over again: **again-begetting**, regeneration; **again-flower**, to bloom again; **again-know**, to know again, recognize; **again-weigh**, to reweigh; **again-writing**, a rescript or copy.

1382 WYCLIF *Tit.* iii. 5 Bi waischynge, or baptym of aȝen · bigetyng. **1382** WYCLIF *Ps.* xxvii. 7 Aȝeen flourede myn flesh. —— *1 Sam.* xxiii. 9 The which thing whanne Dauid aȝen cnewe. **1340** *Ayenb.* 57 Hit behoveþ þet he conne weȝe and ayen-weȝe þet word, huych þet hit by. **1388** WYCLIF *1 Macc.* xii. 19 This is the aȝenwriting of epistlis that the kyng sente.

†**a'gain-buy**, *v. Obs.* [AGAIN- 5.] To buy back, redeem, ransom.

1315 *E.E. Psalter* (1843) lxxiii. 2 Þou agayn-boghte yherde of þine eritage yhit. **1366** MAUNDEV. Prol. 2 How dere he aȝen boghte us, for the grete Love that he hadde to us. **1382** WYCLIF *Luke* xxiv. 21 We hopiden, for he schulde aȝen bye Israel. —— *Isa.* lxii. 12 An hoeli puple, aȝeenboȝt of the Lord. *c* **1449** PECOCK *Repr.* II. xviij. 261 Sum persoon aȝenbouȝte man bi thee, crosse, in that thou were an instrument for to aȝenbie man. *a* **1520** *Myrroure of Our Ladye* 146 He shall agenby Israel from all hys wyckednesses.

†**a'gain-buyer.** *Obs.* A redeemer.

1382 WYCLIF *Job* xix. 25, I wot, that myn aȝen-biere liueth. *c* **1449** PECOCK *Repr.* 205 Glorie, preising, and honour be to thee King, Crist! Aȝenbier! *a* **1520** *Myrroure of Our Ladye* 225 That he shulde be agenbyer of mankynde.

†**a'gain-buying**, *vbl. sb. Obs.* Redemption; ransom.

1315 *E.E. Psalter* (1843) xlviii. 9 Worth of again-biing of his saule. **1382** WYCLIF *Mark* x. 45 And ȝyue his soule, or lyf, redempcioun, or aȝen biyng, for manye. —— *Prov.* vi. 35 He shal not take for the aȝeen biȝing [**1388** raunsum] manye ȝiftis. *a* **1520** *Myrroure of Our Ladye* 213 Yet ageynebyeing myghte not come therof to mankynde.

†**a'gain-call**, *v. Obs.* [AGAIN- 2.] To call back, recall, revoke. (See also GAIN-CALL.)

1315 *E.E. Psalter* (1843) ci. 25 Ne againe-kalle me in mid of daies mine. **1609** SKENE *Reg. Maj.* 51 Gif he may repeit or againe call, that thing, before it come to the place.

†**a'gain-calling**, *vbl. sb. Obs.* Calling back, recalling.

1494 FABYAN v. lxxxvi. 64 Concernynge the agayne callyng of Childerich to his fourmer dignyte.

†**a'gain-come**, *v. Obs.* [AGAIN- 1, 2.]

1. To come against, meet with, encounter.

c **1000** *Ags. Gosp.* Luke xiv. 31 Hwæðer he mæᵹe mid tyn þusendum cuman aᵹen [*v.r.* onᵹean] þone þe him aᵹen [*v.r.* onᵹean] cymð. *c* **1160** *Hatton Gosp.* ibid., Mid teon þusenden cumen aᵹen þane þe him aᵹen kymð. **1382** WYCLIF *Gen.* xxiv. 12 Y preye, to day aᵹen-com to me [**1388** meete with me]. —— *Isa.* xxi. 14 Aᵹencomende to the thirsti berth water.

2. To come back, return: see also GAIN-COME.

c **1000** *Ags. Gosp.* Luke ix. 40 Þa se hælend aᵹén-cóm [*v.r.* onᵹeán-cóm; *Lindisf. & Rushw.* eft-com; *Hatton* aᵹen com]. **1205** LAYAMON 4436 Hit þu[h]te him seoue ȝere · ær he aȝen come [*later text* ȝein come].

†**a'gain-coming**, *vbl. sb. Obs.*

1. Coming against, encountering, meeting.

1382 WYCLIF *Isa.* vii. 3 Go out in to aȝencomyng of Achaȝ [**1388** to the meetyng of Achas].

2. Coming back, returning, return. (See also GAIN-COMING.)

1398 TREVISA *Barth. De P.R.* VI. xiii. (1495) 197 Her passynge, and ayencomynge and entrynge. *c* **1450** LONELICH *Graal* II. 343 Of ȝong age at his departyng, a knyht aforn his aȝen comeng.

†**a'gain-go**, *v. Obs.* [AGAIN- 1, 2 + GO.]

1. To go against, oppose.

1554 PHILPOT *Exam. & Writings* (1842) 340, I know that thou wilt not again go that.

2. To go back, return.

1382 WYCLIF *Gen.* viii. 3 The wateres fro the erthe ben turned aȝen, goynge and aȝen goynge.

†**a'gain-rise**, *v. Obs.* [AGAIN- 1.] To rise against, make insurrection, rebel.

1382 WYCLIF *Esther* ii. 21 And wolden aȝenrisen into the kyng and sleu him. —— *Ecclus.* xlvi. 2 To fiȝten out the enemys aȝenrisende.

†**a'gain-rising**, *vbl. sb. Obs.* [AGAIN- 5.] Rising again; resurrection. See also GAIN-RISING.

c **1380** *Prymer in English* 11, in Maskell *Mon. Rit. Eccl. Ang.* II. 177, I bileue in the hooli goost: feith of hooli chirche: comunynge of seyntis: forȝyuenesse of synnes: aȝenrisyng of fleish. **1382** WYCLIF *John* xi. 25, I am aȝen-risyng and lyf. *c* **1430** *Hymns to Virg.* (1867) 90 And how þe erþe out of þe erþe schal haue his aȝen-resynge. **1509** *Pater Noster* etc. (W. de Worde) a iij, I trowe in yᵉ holy goost, holy chirche unyversall, comunynge of sayntes, forgyuenes of synnes, agen rysynge of flesshe. [**1870** LOWELL *Among my Bks.* (1873) I. 160 Perhaps there might be a question between the old English again-rising and resurrection.]

†**a'gain-saw**, *sb. Obs.* [AGAIN- 1 + SAW a saying.] Gainsaying, contradiction.

1315 *E.E. Psalter* (1843) lxxx. 8 Þe fanded I, Ate watre of again-saw. *a* **1325** *Metr. Hom.* 29 Igain-sawe may thar nan be, Of thing that alle men may se.

†**a'gain-say**, *v. Obs.* [AGAIN- 1. *Obs.* (cf. GAINSAY.)]

1. To say nay; to refuse; to deny.

1330 R. BRUNNE *Chron.* 210 Þe Kyng William alle þis ageynsaid. *c* **1400** *Apol. for Loll.* 3 He þat may ageynsey his wombe, & despice þe goodis of þis world. **1480** CAXTON *Chron. Eng.* VI. (1520) 74/1 The kynge wolde not them agaynsaye, but asmoche as they ordeyned he graunted and confyrmed. *a* **1520** *Myrroure of our Ladye* 150 And that the reson desyreth, the sensualyte againe sayth.

2. *trans.* and *intr.* To speak against, contradict.

1382 WYCLIF *Ecclus.* iv. 30 Aȝensey thou not to the word of treuthe any maner [**1388** Agenseie thou not the]. **1395** PURVEY *Remonstr.* (1851) 76 Oo pope agenseith the sentence of a nothir. **1549** CHALONER tr. *Erasm. Mor. Enc.* E iij b, The Archestoike Seneca strongly againsaieth me. **1552-5** LATIMER *Serm. & Rem.* (1845) 40 They cannot suffer to be againsaid. **1589** PUTTENHAM *Eng. Poesie* (1869) 173 From the beginning, as to say [twixt for betwixt] [gainsay for againesay:] [ill for euill].

3. To reverse (a judgment or sentence).

1609 SKENE *Reg. Maj.* 65 Ane amerciament of ane fals dome againe said in the Justitiars court, is ten pounds.

†**a'gainsay**, *sb. Obs.* Gainsaying, objection.

1548 HALL *Chron.* (1809) 8 He tooke lande peaceably without any Againsaie or interrupcion.

†**a'gain-sayer.** *Obs.* One who speaks against or contradicts; an opponent.

1388 WYCLIF *Pref. Ep. St. Jerome* iii. (I. 63) To withstonde aȝeinseyeris. [**1382** The withseieris to withstonde.] *c* **1449** PECOCK *Repr.* 98 Proued trewe aȝens alle Aȝenseiers whiche euere thei ben. **1541** BARNES *Wks.* (1573) 227/2 Stoppe the mouthes of the agaynesayers.

†**a'gain-saying**, *vbl. sb. Obs.* Gainsaying, contradiction, opposition, contention.

1315 *E.E. Psalter* (1843) cv. 32 And gremed þai him.. At watres of againe-sainge. **1382** WYCLIF *Prov.* xviii. 18 Aȝen-seyingus lot thresteth togidere. [**1388** Lot ceesith aȝen-seiyngis.] **1413** LYDGATE *Pylgr. Sowle* IV. iv. (1483) 60 Doo hit gladly withouten ageyne seynge. **1483** ARNOLD *Chron.* (1811) 116 Without any agayn sayeng of any persone.

†**a'gain-saying**, *ppl. a. Obs.* Saying the opposite; contradictory.

c **1400** *Apol. for Loll.* Neiþer.. vnprofitable.. ne agein seying to þe wordis, ne sentence, of any seint.

against (ə'gɛnst, ə'geɪnst), *prep.* (*adv.*), *conj.* Forms: *South.* 2 **aȝænes, aȝenes**, 2-3 **aȝeines**, 3-5 **aȝeynes, aȝaines**, 4-5 **aȝeins, ayenis, ayeins, ayans**, 4-5 **aȝens, ayens**; *Midl.* 3-4 (*east*) **agenes**, 4-5 **ageynes, ageyns, agens**, 5 **ageins, agains**, (*west*) **aȝayns, -us, agaynus**; *North.* 4 **ogaynes, ogaines, agaynes**, 4-5 **agayns, agaynys**, 5 **agaynys**, *Sc.* 5-6 **agains, aganis, agans**. Also with parasitic *-t*, *South.* 4-5 **aȝenst**, 5 **aȝeynst**, 5-6 **ayenst**; *Midl.* 5-6 **ageynst(e, agenst(e, agaynst(e, againste**, 6- **against**. [Formed on *aȝen*, *ayen*, AGAIN, by genitive ending *-es*, after the kindred *tó-ȝeánes*, *to-yenes* in which a genitive, governed by *tó*, is found in the oldest English: see TOGAINS. Late in the 14th c., after the *-es* had ceased to be syllabic, the final *-ens*, *-ains* developed in the south a parasitic *-t* as in *amongs-t*, *betwix-t*, *amids-t*, probably confused with superlatives in *-st*, and *c* 1525 this became universal in literary English; *aganis*, *agains*, sinking into a dialectal northern form. The earlier forms of *againes* present all the dialectal variations found in AGAIN. The poets occasionally aphetize it to *'gainst*. Essentially a prep. (very rarely an adverb in 15th c.); but becoming by ellipsis a conj., or conjunctive adverb.]

A. I. Of position.

1. a. Directly opposite; facing, in front of, in full view of. Now generally *over against*.

c **1175** *Lamb. Hom.* 7 Þe castel þe wes aȝeines drih[t]nes twa leornikenehtes. **1366** MAUNDEV. i. 9 The tother Hond he lifteth up aȝenst the Est. *c* **1440** LONELICH *Graal* II. 199 They lokeden aȝens a mowntaygne. **1483** CAXTON *Gold. Leg.* 193/4 Saynt Marcial helde up his burdon ayenst the fyre. **1551** ROBINSON tr. *More's Utopia* 93 The men sitte upon the bench next the wall and the women againste them on the other side of the table. **1551** RECORDE *Pathw. Knowl.* II. xi, In euery triangle, the greattest side lieth against the greattest angle. **1604** DEKKER *King's Entert.* (1873) I. 299 In a direct line against them stoode the three Howres. **1611** BIBLE *Matt.* xxi. 2 Go into the village over against you. *Ibid.* xxvii. 61 Mary Magdalene, and the other Mary, sitting ouer against the sepulchre. **1695** LUTTRELL *Brief Rel.* (1857) III. 487 The Commissioners of the Admiralty satt in the new office against Scotland Yard. **1703** MOXON *Mech. Exerc.* 193 These Semi-circles must be made so exactly against each other that when.. clapt close together, the Semi-circles on both the Cheeks shall become a perfect round hole. **1741** RICHARDSON *Pamela* (1824) I. 143 And so handed me to the coach.. and sat backwards over against me.

†**b.** Exposed to (light, cold, etc.). *Obs.*

1490 CAXTON *Eneydos* xxi. 77 Theire hyghe saylles.. alle spred abrode ayenst the wyndes. **1509** HAWES *Past. Pleas.* III. ii, Turrettes fayre and hye, Which against Phebus shone so marveylously. **1595** SHAKS. *John* v. iv. 25 As a forme of waxe Resolueth from his figure 'gainst the fire. *c* **1600** —— *Sonnets* lxxiii, Those boughes which shake against the could. **1697** DRYDEN *Virg. Georg.* i. 66 While Mountain Snows dissolve against the Sun. **1752** YOUNG *Brothers* II. i. (1757) II. 228 In polish'd armour, shine against the sun.

†**2.** In the sight of, in presence of; with (L. *apud*). *Obs.*

c **1175** *Lamb. Hom.* 79 Þa þe he heuede scome aȝeines his scuppende. **1387** TREVISA *Higden* Rolls Ser. VII. 333 Pope Alisaundre aroos worschipfulliche aȝenst hym. *Ibid.* VII. 99 He schulde be to hem trewe lorde aȝenst God and þe world. **1483** CAXTON *G. de la Tour* k ij, Humble themself the one ageynst the other. *a* **1520** *Myrroure of Our Ladye* 146 Ageynste the Lorde ys mercy and plentyous redempcyon.

3. *fig.* Towards, with respect to, in regard to.

1387 TREVISA *Higden* Rolls Ser. VI. 375 Merciable aȝenst pore men. **1481** EARL WORCESTRE *Tully on Friendship* IV. 10 That our benyvolence agenst our frendes may answere evenly to the benyvolence which they bere ayenst us. **1506** *Ord. Crysten Men* (W. de Worde) I. v. 48 Charyte by some approbacyon is ayenst yᵉ fader. Fayth is ayenst the sone. Hope is ayenst the holy goost. **1557** *Apprenticeship Indenture* in *Norf. Antiq. Misc.* (1880) II. 14 He shall behave himselfe gently ageynst his seyde Master. **1871** MARKBY *Elem. Law* §155 The legal rights of subjects as against each other and the constitutional rights of subjects against the government.

4. More generally: Towards the front of, near, adjoining. Also *fig.* Still *dial.* e.g. 'I met him against the pond.'

1531 ELYOT *Governour* (1836) 156 The most damnable vice, and most against injustice.. is Ingratitude. **1669** BUNYAN *Holy Citie* 128 Against this Tophet.. was the broad wall of the City. **1725** DE FOE *Voy. round World* (1840) 66 Three of their ships lay against the walls.

II. Of motion towards.

†**5. a.** In a direction facing; towards, forward to, to meet. *Obs.*

c **1325** *E.E. Allit. Poems* B. 611 Þe good mon gos hem agayneȝ. *c* **1386** CHAUCER *Clerkes T.* 855 Agayns [*v.r.* A-geyn, a-ȝein(e, aȝeinst] his doghter hastiliche goth he. *c* **1400** *Chester Pl.* 59 Againste Abraham will I gone worshippffullye and that anon. *c* **1420** *Chron. Vilod.* 748 Þuse relekes weron comyng, with procession ageynes hem. *a* **1520** *Myrroure of Our Ladye* 258 All the people of the cyte came ageynste hym wyth ioye and wyth praysynge. **1535** COVERDALE *Gen.* xxiv. 65 What man is this that commeth agaynst us in the felde? **1566** UDALL *Royster Doyster* III. iii. (Arb.) 43 As fast as I could runne sir in poste against you. **1634** *Malory's Arthur* (1816) I. 179 Against whom came queen Guenever, and met with him, and made great joy of his coming.

†**b.** In reception of, in welcome of. *Obs.*

c **1430** *Hymns to Virg. &c.* (1867) 52 Opene þe ȝatis aȝens me!

III. Of motion into contact; pressure upon.

6. Toward and into contact with; into direct collision with. Also loosely *to run against*, to meet accidentally.

1382 WYCLIF *Acts.* ix. 5 It is hard to thee for to kyke aȝens the pricke. **1480** *Robert the Devyll* 10 Robert threw his boke ayenst the wall. **1601** SHAKS. *A.Y.L.* II. iv. 60 Till I breake my shins against it. **1610** —— *Temp.* I. i. 9 Thy cry did knock against my very heart. **1711** STEELE *Spect.* No. 96 ⁋2 Left to sob and beat my Head against the Wall at my Leisure. **1805** SCOTT *Last Minst.* I. xii, The roar of Teviot's tide, That chafes against the scaur's red side. **1820** KEATS *St. Agnes* xxxvi, Pattering the sharp sleet Against the window-panes. *a* **1884** *Mod.* The ship was dashed against the pier-head. I jostled against him in the crowd. Guess whom I ran against in London the other day?

7. Hence of force or pressure resisted, with *push*, *press*, *lean*, *hang*, *stand*, *lie*, etc.: Supported by, in contact with.

1591 SHAKS. *1 Hen. VI*, II. v. 43 Leane thine aged back against mine Arme. **1608** —— *Peric.* v. i. 51 The leafy shelter that abuts against The islands side. **1611** —— *Wint. T.* IV. iv. 818 Then.. shall he be set against a Brick-wall. **1766** GOLDSM. *Vic. Wakef.* (1806) xvi. 81 The picture.. leaned in a most mortifying manner against the kitchen wall. **1815** BYRON *Lara* I. xxi, He lean'd against the lofty pillar nigh. **1818** SCOTT *Ht. Midl.* i, He pressed his hands against his forehead. **1859** REEVE *Brittany* 236 The Chateau.. is a squat, heavy structure, much dilapidated and built against. **1871** BLACK *Dau. Heth* xxxiv. 313 Ere she knew, his arms were around her, and she was close against his bosom. *a* **1884** *Mod.* Older strata tilted against the erupted rocks. A ladder standing against a house.

8. In optical contact with something behind, projected on the visible surface of, having as background.

1805 SOUTHEY *Madoc in Azt.* xxiv. Wks. V. 360 Far visible Against the clear blue sky. **1864** D. MITCHELL *Seven Stories* 211 The trees.. darkly drawn against a bright orange sky. **1869** PHILLIPS *Vesuv.* iv. 124 The outline of the cone was plain against the illuminated vaporous atmosphere. *a* **1884** *Mod.* The pictures stand out better against the dark wall.

IV. Of motion or action in opposition to.

9. a. In the opposite direction to the course of anything, counter to. Implying adverse motion or effort.

1388 WYCLIF *Acts* xxvii. 15 Whanne the schip was rauyschid, and myȝte not enforse aȝens the wynde [**1382** into the wynde]. **1593** SHAKS. *3 Hen. VI*, I. iv. 20, I haue seene a Swan With bootlesse labour swimme against the Tyde. **1611** COTGR., *Prendre le vent*, To goe up, or against the wind. **1653** URQUHART *Rabelais* I. xxiii, He ran furiously vp against a hill. **1726** THOMSON *Winter* 180 And, often falling, climbs against the blast. **1805** FOSTER *Ess.* I. vi. 77 To swim against a torrent, to ascend against a cataract. **1879** TENNYSON *Lover's T.* 89 Slow-moving, as a wave against the wind.

b. Hence ***against the hair*** (Fr. *à contrepoil*), ***against the grain***: opposed to the natural bent.

1621 BP. MOUNTAGU *Diatribe* 168 This translation cannot passe by you, being somewhat against the haire for you. **1875** H. ROGERS *Superh. Orig. Bible* i. (ed. 3) 33 A system of ethics so much against the grain as that of the Gospel.

10. Opposed in tendency or character, contrary to; not in conformity with.

c **1250** *Gen. & Exod.* 538 Hun-wreste plaȝe.. a-ȝenes laȝe. *c* **1375** *Lay-Folks Mass-Bk.* B. 350, I haue done a-gaynes þi wille synnes mony. *c* **1386** CHAUCER *Frankl. T.* 617 It is agayns [*v.r.* a geyn, aȝein(e, aȝeinst] the proces of nature. **1387** TREVISA *Higden* Rolls Ser. I. 131 Egipte aȝenst kynde of oþer londes haþ plente of corn. *c* **1400** *Rom. Rose* 3154 Bothe ageyns resoun and right. *c* **1440** *Gesta Rom.* 4 The flesch desirith thing þat is aȝenst þe spirite, And þe spirit desirith thing aȝenst þe flesch. **1530** PALSGR. 570/1, I go against nature, or do a thynge contrarye to nature. It is a harde thyng to make a foxe do agaynst nature. **1668** CULPEPER & COLE tr. *Barthol. Anat.* I. xxiii. 57 The Opinion of.. other late Anatomists, does against all former Authority thus determine. **1676** HOBBES *Iliad* I. 329 She with them went, though much against her heart. **1708** SWIFT *Pred. for* 1708 Wks. 1755 II. I. 151 May, against common conjectures, will be no very busy month. **1763** BURKE in *Corr.* (1844) I. 48 It is against my general notions to trust to writing. **1810** COLERIDGE *Friend* (1865) 122 No power on earth can oblige me to act against my conscience. **1843** MACAULAY in Trevelyan's *Life* II. ix. 128 It goes against my feelings to censure any woman.

11. Towards with hostile intent; to meet in hostility; in hostile encounter with. *arch.*

1250 LAYAMON 22476 [He] wende aȝenest him anon [**1205** toȝeines]. *c* **1314** *Guy Warw.* 28 Ogaines Sir Gii ther com Gaier. **1388** WYCLIF *Luke* xiv. 31 If he may with ten thousynde go aȝens hym that cometh aȝens hym with twenti thousynde. *c* **1400** *Destr. Troy* XXI. 8561 But Troiell full tydely turnyt hom agaynes. *c* **1420** *Avow. Arth.* xiv. (1842) 64 A-ȝaynus the fynde for to fare. **1483** *Invent. Cross* in *Leg. Rood* 159 He wente in batayle ayenst them of perse. **1513** DOUGLAS *Æneis* VI. xv. 80 Quhidder so aganist him he went on fete, Or ȝit on horsbak. **1611** BIBLE *Luke* xiv. 31 To meete him that commeth against him with twentie thousand.

12. a. Hence, *gen.* In hostility or active opposition to, with *fight*, *speak*, *act*, *vote*, *contend*, *set*, *pit*, *be*, etc.

a **1154** *O.E. Chron.* an. 1135 Aȝenes him risen sona þa rice men þe wæron swikes. *c* **1325** *E.E. Allit. Poems* B. 1711 Bot ay hatȝ hofen þy hert agaynes þe hyȝe dryȝtyn. **1340** HAMPOLE *Pr. Consc.* 4144 Þat mykel dus ogayns Goddes lawe. **1375** BARBOUR *Bruce* I. 573 That brwyss, that presumyt swa Agayns him to brawle or ryss. **1475** *Bk. Noblesse* (1860) 8 To meove no werre ayenst no cristen man, but if he had grevously done ayenst him. **1533** MORE [*title*] A Letter impugnynge the erronyouse wrytyng of John Fryth, against the blessed Sacrament of the Aultare. **1556** LAUDER *Tractate* 236 Speking aganis godds wourd of grace. **1611** BIBLE *Gen.* xvi. 12 His hand will be against euery man, and euery mans hand against him. —— *Ps.* xxxv. 1 Fight against them that fight against me. **1663** BUTLER *Hudibr.* I. iii. 70 But what could single Valour do Against so numerous a Foe? **1679** DRYDEN, etc. *Satire* 85 First, let's behold the merriest man alive Against his careless genius vainly strive. **1849** MACAULAY *Hist. Eng.* II. 205 The whole Cavalier gentry were against him. *Ibid.* II. 37 The members who had voted against the court were dismissed. **1877** LYTTEIL *Landm.* I. i. 18 The very men who made war against the pirates.

b. Hence, expressing the adverse bearing of many verbs and nouns of action; as to *legislate*, *protest*, *argue*, *testify*; *offend*, *sin*; *cry out*, *rage*, *inveigh*, *exclaim*: a *law*, *proclamation*, *declaration*, *protest*, *argument*, *objection*, *resolution*, *action*, *proceeding*, *accusation*, *complaint*, *evidence*; *sin*, *offence*; *hostility*, *outcry*, *feeling*, *prejudice*, *rage*, *anger*, *animosity*, *bitterness*, *grudge*, etc.

c **1250** *Gen. & Exod.* 2544 King amonaphis, Agenes ðis folc hatel is. **1580** NORTH *Plutarch* (1676) 6 Then the wrath of the gods would cease against them. **1602** SHAKS. *Haml.* I. ii. 102 'Tis a fault to heaven, A fault against the dead, a fault to nature. **1621** Burton *Anat. Mel.* II. ii. I. i. (1651) 252 Laurentius excepts against them. **1630** Prynne *Anti-Armin.* 143 The Pelagians..obiect against these Conclusions. **1689** Selden *Table Talk* (1847) 225 The Law against Witches does not prove there be any. **1756** Burke *Vind. Nat. Soc.* Wks. I. 34 Arguments against artificial society. **1766** Goldsm. *Vic. W.* (1806) iv. 19 My lectures against pride. **1774** Bryant *Mythol.* II. 426 Complaint is made against the apostate Tribes. **1808** Scott *Marm.* II. vii, Charged 'gainst those who lay Prison'd in Cuthbert's islet gray. **1820** Keats *St. Agnes* x, Whose very dogs would execrations howl Against his lineage. **1849** Macaulay *Hist. Eng.* I. 218 The suffering..people raged fiercely against the government. *Ibid.* I. 265 Proceedings were instituted against the Corporation. *Ibid.* II. 82 The Commons..had protested against it. *Ibid.* II. 220 Legal evidence against him. *Ibid.* III. 13 One of the chief accusations..brought against Charles the Second. *Ibid.* III. 212 James had, in his speech.. declared against the Act of Settlement. **1854** Thackeray *Newcomes* I. xxi. 197 That common outcry against thankless children.

c. ***to be against***: to be opposed, unfavourable; the opposite of *for*, *in favour of*. Esp. in phr. ***against the government***, opposed to the established view, rulers, etc. (cf. AGIN *prep.*).

1722 Wollaston *Relig. Nat.* v. (1738) 84 There are infinite chances against the happening of it, or odds that it will not happen. **1742** Richardson *Pamela* III. 47, I am not against shewing to him all I write. **1818** Hallam *Middle Ages* (1841) I. 330 Experience..told more and more against the ordinary militia. **1850** W. Irving *Goldsm.* xiv. 174 His.. awkward manners were against him. **1860** Heavysege *Filippo* 114 Will it weigh The fors and the againsts in nicest scale? **1934** H. G. Wells *Exper. Autobiogr.* II. viii. 604 The Bastables are an anarchistic lot. Her soul was against the government all the time. **1962** *Sunday Express* 25 Feb. 6/5 Milton and Dante were usually against the Government.

d. In reference to *competition*: To ***run, compete, play a match***, etc. ***against***.

1833 Brewster *Nat. Magic* x. 243 He drew against horses, and raised enormous weights. **1854** Dickens *Hard Times* (Tauchn.) 62 A population of babies who had been walking against time towards the infinite world. **1868** —— *Mugby Junct.* (Tauchn.) 275, I always felt as if I was riding a race against time.

13. a. In resistance to, in defence or protection from.

a **1154** *O.E. Chron.* an. 1137 Æuric rice man his castles makede and aȝænes him heolden. *c* **1230** *Ancren Riwle* 14 Of fleschliche vondunges & of gostliche..& kunfort aȝeines ham. **1430** Lydg. *Chichevache* in Dodsl. *O.P.* XII. 386 Suche as can have no pacience, Ageyns yowre wyfes violence. **1477** Earl Rivers (Caxton) *Dictes* 9 Remedies ayenst sikenesse. **1561** Hollybush *Hom. Apoth.* 14a, A confection to holde in the mouth agaynste hoorsenesse. **1578** *Scot. Poems of 16th c.* II. 133 Send us support and comforting Agains our fais. **1592** Shaks. *Rom. & Jul.* II. ii. 73, I am proof against their enmitie. **1600** Hakluyt *Voy.* (1810) III. 166 Against the colde they clothe themselves in beastes skinnes. **1667** Milton *P.L.* VIII. 531 Here only weak Against the charm of Beauty's powerful glance. **1749** Fielding *Tom Jones* I. ix, The gate would have been shut against her. **1765** Tucker *Lt. of Nat.* (R.) To stop one's ears against whatever can be said in opposition to them. **1766** Goldsm. *Vic. W.* (1806) xxi. 128 Wisdom makes but a slow defence against trouble. **1849** Macaulay *Hist. Eng.* I. v. 178 It had long protected the Celts against the aggressions of the kings of Wessex.

b. Hence, Of dangers feared: To ***caution, warn***, etc. ***against***.

1682 Dryden *Medal, Ep. to Whigs*, To preserve you against Monarchy. **1710** Addison *Tatler* No. 240 ¶11 Pill which (as he told the Country People) were very good against an Earthquake. **1838** Macaulay in Trevelyan's *Life* II. vii. 9 On his guard against the sins which beset literary men. **1853** Trench *Proverbs* 113 A proverb which warns against a bad book. *a* **1884** *Mod.* Railway Notice.—'Passengers are cautioned against crossing the line.' Omnibus Notice.—'The Public are cautioned against pickpockets.'

V. Of mutual opposition or relation.

From the idea of bartering one thing *against* another, *i.e.* offering them on *opposite* sides, comes,

14. In exchange for, in return for; as an equivalent or set-off for; in lieu of, instead of. Now only *lit.*; formerly also *fig.*

1205 Layamon 8837 Aȝenes uuel ich wulle don god. *c* **1230** *Hali Meid.* 7 Aȝaines an likinge habben twa of þunchunges. *c* **1300** *K. Alis.* 6094 The kynges Losen ten ageyns on. *c* **1450** Myrc 55 Euere do gode a-ȝeynes euele. **1534** tr. *More's On the Passion* Wks. 1557, 1306/2 That agaynste his great loue we be not founde vnkynde. **1833** Ht. Martineau *Berkeley* I. iv. 74 When men used to exchange wheat against bullocks.

15. a. In the opposite scale; on the other side; as a counter-balance to.

1531 Elyot *Governor* III. xxviii. (1557) 212 Beinge exactly wayed the one agaynst the other. **1592** Shaks. *Rom. & Jul.* I. ii. 102 Let there be waid Your Ladies loue against some other Maid. **1722** Wollaston *Relig. Nat.* ii. 36 A little pain will weigh against a great deal of pleasure. **1840** Glassford Bell *Queen Mary*, Then weigh against a grain of sand the glories of a throne.

b. Hence, ***to set off against***: to place an item in an account on the *opposite* side to a previous entry, so as to cancel or diminish the latter; also *fig.*

1844 Disraeli *Coningsby* IX. vi. 337 An adequate set off against the odium that attached to their opinions. **1849** Macaulay *Hist. Eng.* xviii, Against the fall of Mons might well be set off the taking of Athlone.

†**16.** *fig.* In comparison with; in contrast to. *Obs.*

c **1300** in Wright's *Lyric P.* xxv. 68 Jesu..Al that may with eȝen se, Haveth no suetnesse aȝeynes the. *c* **1400** *Rom. Rose* 6877 Hir paroch prest nys but a beest Ayens me and my companye. **1481** Caxton *Myrrour* II. xiii. 96 We be so lytil ayenst them. **1672–3** Marvell *Rehears. Transp.* (1675) II. 137 You distinguish the elder times against these.

17. In *Betting*, against the likelihood of (a particular horse, etc., winning): denoting that the probability of losing is reckoned to exceed that of winning (by the amount specified by the odds). Also *fig.* and *ellipt.* as *advb.*

1845, **1875** [see ODDS *sb.* 5]. **1935** D. Runyon *Money from Home* 238, I long ago came to the conclusion that all life is six to five against. **1985** *Times* 20 May 12/1 As opposition to Mrs Thatcher mounts.., I hear that the Commons' unofficial bookie..offers odds of 7–4 against her still being prime minister by the end of next year.

VI. Of time.

†**18.** Drawing towards, near the beginning of, close to. *Obs.*

c **1320** *Sir Bevis* 1971 On a dai, agenes the eue. *c* **1385** Chaucer *Leg. G. Wom.* 1356 The white swan Agens his deth be-gynnyth for to synge. *c* **1440** *Morte Arth.* 103 Agaynste day he felle on slepe. **1483** Caxton *Gold. Leg.* 397/3 The Sonday ageynst euen ther came a grete multytude of fendes. **1523** Ld. Berners *Froissart* I. xviii. 20 And whan it was ageynst nyght, they came to the ryuer of Tyne. **1634** *Malory's Arthur* I. cx. 200 It happened him, against a night, to come to a fair courtlage.

19. *esp.* with some idea of preparation: In view of; in anticipation of, in preparation for, in time for.

c **1350** *St. Jerome's 15 Tokens* (1878) 92 þat God wil Aȝeins domesdai. *c* **1425** *Seven Sages* 1488 How scho myght agayens nyght Fonden a tale al newe. **1577–87** Harrison *Eng.* I. II. v. (1877) 121 This furniture is to be provided against his installation. **1642** Fuller *Holy & Prof. St.* v. xviii. 431 The moist dropping of stone walls against rainy weather. **1659** Burton *Diary* (1828) IV. 349 To shorten the business against Thursday. **1697** Locke *Lett.* (1708) 194 Some additions to my book against the next edition. **1741** Richardson *Pamela* (1824) I. 131 If I chose to order any new clothes against my marriage. **1758** Wesley in *Wks.* 1872 II. 435 Having a Sermon to write against the Assizes at Bedford. **1832** Ht. Martineau *Each & All* i. 14 Go to Covent Garden, to see the people dressing it up against sunrise. **1875** Emerson *Lett. & Soc. Aims* viii. 194 When the Queen of Sheba came to visit Solomon, he had built, against her arrival, a palace. *a* **1884** *Mod.* He has a few pounds put by against a 'rainy day.'

B. *conj.* or *conj. adv.* In reference to *time*, AGAINST *prep.* 18 is also used relatively (explainable by ellipsis as, Against (the time) at which or *that* I come, Against I come). By the time that, before. *Either of simple futurity, or futurity and contingency.* †**a.** with *relative*. *Obs.*

1393 Langl. *P. Pl.* C. xxii. 319 Aȝeynst þat þi greynes.. bygynneþ to growe, Ordeyne þe an hous, peers · to herberghen in thi cornes.

b. *simply*. *arch* or *dial.*

c **1300** in Wright's *Lyric P.* iv. 23 His hap he deth ful harde on hete, aȝeynz he howeth heune. **1577** *St. Aug. Manuell* 33 Thou preparest a table diversly furnished against I come. **1602** Shaks. *Haml.* I. i. 158 Euer 'gainst that Season comes. **1611** Bible *2 Kings* xvi. 11 Vriiah the Priest made it, against [Wyclif, Coverd. til] king Ahaz came from Damascus. **1689** Selden *Table Talk* (1847) 5 Prepare a Child against he comes to be a Man. **1749** Fielding *Tom Jones* I. iii. (1840) 3 To provide it pap..against it waked. *a* **1797** H. Walpole *George II* (1847) II. iii. 79 In getting the Bill ready against it was necessary. **1837** Dickens *Pickw.* (1847) 223/1 Throw on another log of wood against father comes home. **1848** Thackeray *Van. Fair* liv. (1866) 454 The publican shutting his shutters in the sunshine, against service commenced.

C. *adv. rare.* = AGAIN *adv.*

c **1480** *Rob. the Devyll* 8 To the chirche..and home ayenst.

D. in *comb.* rare as a variant of AGAIN: as **against-saying, against-standing**.

a **1564** Becon *Christ & Antichr.* (1844) 510 Without any resistance or against-saying. *c* **1440** *Gesta Rom.* 9 He shuld lese his life, with oute ony ayenst-stondyng.

†**a'gain-stand**, *v. Obs.* [AGAIN- 1.] *trans.* and *intr.* To stand against, withstand, resist.

c **1000** *Ags. Gosp.* Luke xi. 53 þa ongunnun ða farisei him aȝen standan [*v.r.* onȝean, *Lindisf.* wið-stonda, *Hatton* aȝén standen]. **1205** Layamon 3692 Æine..þe þe wulle aȝen-stonde [*later text* wid-stonde]. **1315** *E.E. Psalter* (1843) lxxv. 8 Wha to þe Ogaine-stand sal. **1382** Wyclif *Matt.* v. 39 Y say to ȝou, to nat aȝein-stonde yuel. *c* **1400** *Apol. for Loll.* 77 þis not aȝenstonding, þei han founden a new ordinaunce. *c* **1449** Pecock *Repr.* 479 As Jannes and Mambres aȝenstoden Moyses so these aȝenstonden treuthe. **1558** Grimalde *Tully's Office* III. 133 He semed to folow profit; but that was none where honestye againstode it. **1553–87** Foxe *A. & M.* I. 459/1 To againstond thine Enemies.

†**a'gain-stander.** *Obs.* One who withstands; a resister, an adversary.

c **1400** *Apol. for Loll.* 18 Vnriȝtwisnes in the cause, enuy of aȝen stonder.

†**a'gain-standing**, *vbl. sb. Obs.* Resisting, resistance.

1340 Hampole *Pr. Consc.* 7969 With-outen any ogayne-standyng, Or any letting of any-thyng. **1553–87** Foxe *A. & M.* I. 458/1 Thou biddest sufferen both wrongs and strokes withouten again-standing.

a'gainstness. [f. AGAINST *prep.* (*adv.*), *conj.* + -NESS.] The state or condition of being against or in opposition to an established view, etc.

1951 Paterson & Willett in *Sociological Rev.* XLIII. 90 There remains a feeling that the group is an entity, for the members have all been affected similarly by the same outside power, and there is a diffused 'againstness'. **1972** *Listener* 27 Jan. 115/2 There is only new creation out of and *against* the language taught and learned—and this 'againstness' is something the literary critic must define in evaluating a style.

†**a'gain-turn**, *v. Obs.* [AGAIN- 2.] To turn back, return.

1315 *E.E. Psalter* (1843) lxxvii. 39 Gaand and noght ogain-tornand. **1382** Wyclif *Gen.* xiv. 17 After that he was aȝen-turned fro the slawȝtir.

†**a'gainward**, *adv. Obs.* Forms: see AGAIN. [f. AGAIN *adv.* + -WARD. Cf. *outward*, *backward*. Used in most of the senses of AGAIN, of which it is to be viewed as a more distinctly adverbial form.]

1. In the opposite direction; *hence*, backward, away back, back again.

1205 Layamon 27083 Aȝeinward heo buȝen þa. *c* **1230** *Hali Meid.* 43 Ne con ha neauer ifinden na wei aȝainward. *c* **1320** R. Brunne *Medit.* 1046 Oftyn aȝenward Marye gan loke. *c* **1386** Chaucer *Man of Laws T.* 343 Sayle Out of Surrye agaynward to Ytaille. **1470** Harding *Chron.* cix, As they onto theyr shyppes agaynwarde flewe. **1634** *Malory's Arthur* (1816) II. 135 He looked still upon his horse till he saw you come in againward.

2. In return, in reply, back.

1330 R. Brunne *Chron.* 183 With slenges and magneles þei kast to Kyng Richard, Our Cristen bi parcelles kasted ageynward. *c* **1440** *Generydes* 4492 Of his loue ayenwards I am sure. *c* **1520** More in Ellis *Orig. Lett.* I. 72 I. 203 The Lettres agaynward devised and sent by my lord Admirall to her.

3. Over again; once more.

c **1380** *Sir Ferumb.* 1431 Bote ich him aȝeward gete may. *Ibid.* 3306 He hoteþ euery man: to þe assaut aȝeward come. **1413** Lydg. *Pylgr. Sowle* v. xiv. (1859) 81 Thou shalt eftsones receyue thy body, and ben to hym ayeneward conioined. **1541** R. Copland *Guydon's Quest. Cyrurg.*, Agaynwarde they ramyfye in to two partyes.

4. Conversely; *vice versâ*.

1340 *Ayenb.* 49 Of man of þe wordle to wyfman of religioun, oþer ayeanwarde of wyfman of þe wordle to man of religioun. *c* **1400** *Apol. for Loll.* 19 Ilk synning to þe deþ is an heretik; as aȝen ward a heretik is he þat synniþ to þe deþ. **1485** Caxton *Trevisa's Higden* (1527) 3 In some place I must chaunge the ordre of wordes and sette actyf for passif and agaynwarde. **1579** Spenser *Sheph. Kal.* xxxvii, When the Sun is in the signes septentrionals, their shadowes be toward the parts of the signes meridionals, and so againward.

5. Contrariwise; on the contrary; on the other hand.

1340 Hampole *Pr. Consc.* 8053 Bot þe dampned bodyse ogayn-ward Salle in helle fele payns strang and hard. *c* **1449** Pecock *Repr.* 371 When Aȝenward, if all this same receit schulde come into the hondis of grete Lordis or of Knyȝtis, it schulde not be so weel spend. **1534** More *Comf. agst. Tribul.* II. Wks. 1557, 1166/1 An occasion of meryte too, whiche the wealthye manne hath not agayneward.

‖**agal** (a'gɑːl). Also †**ageil, aggale, agghal**. [Arab. *'iqāl* bond, rope.] A fillet to keep the keffiyeh in position.

1855 J. L. Porter *Five Years in Damascus* II. xi. 87 Instead of the ample white turban, he wore the *kefîyeh* and *ageil* of the Arabs. **1920** *Blackw. Mag.* May 594/2 All three attired in costly silk robes and kefias and aggales (the band that secures the kefia or turban). **1934** *Times Lit. Suppl.* 22 Feb. 115/2 The nomadic Beduin who wear the keffiyeh and agghal. **1951** A. Christie *They came to Baghdad* v, The dignity of the Arab dress, the inevitable *Keffiyah* of black and white held in place by the black silk *agal*.

‖**agalactia** (ægə'læktɪə). *Med.* [mod.L. a. Gr. ἀγαλακτια: see AGALAXY.] = AGALAXY.

1706 Phillips, *Agalactia*, Want of milk to give suck with. **1874** Jul. Howe *Sex & Educ.* 23 Dr. Clarke sees disease chiefly in American women..In them are *ateknia*, *agalactia*, *amazia*. **1879** in *Syd. Soc. Lex.*

agalactous (ægə'læktəs), *a. Med.* [f. Gr. ἀγάλακτ-ος (f. ἀ not + γάλακτ- milk) + -OUS.] Having no milk to suckle with.

1879 in *Syd. Soc. Lex.*

agalaxy ('ægəlæksɪ). *Med.* [f. mod.L. *agalaxia* (also *agalactia*) a. Gr. ἀγαλαξία = ἀγαλακτία, f. ἀγάλακτ-ος: see prec.] A want or deficiency of milk in a mother after childbirth.

1731 Bailey, vol. II, *Agala'xy*, want of milk to give suck with. **1755** in Johnson n. q. **1864** R. F. Burton *Dahome* II. 243 Milk is not used, and animals seem to labour under a natural agalaxy.

†**a'galloch.** *Obs.* [ad. L. *agallochum*, ad. Gr. ἀγάλλοχον an adaptation of an oriental name; used also in the L. form, and in various corruptions of it, as *agalocus*, *agaloch*, etc.] 'The fragrant resinous heart-wood of *Aquilaria*; also called agila-wood, aloes-wood, and eagle-wood.' Lindley *Treas. Bot.* 1866.

1633 T. N[ewton] tr. *Lemnie's Touchst. Complex.* 202 *Agalocus* commonly called *Lignum Aloes*. **1708** Motteux *Rabelais* IV. i, Aromatic Agaloch (you call it Lignum Aloes). **1731** Bailey, *Agallachum*, Wood-aloes. **1753** Chambers *Cycl. Supp.* s.v., The *agallochum* is of a bluish purple colour.

a-gallop (əˈgæləp), *adv.* prop. *phr.* [A *prep.*[1] + GALLOP *v.* Cf. *a-float*, *a-swim*, etc.] At a gallop.
1858 MORRIS *Two Roses* 223 Rode a-gallop past the hall.

‖**a'galma.** *Obs.* [Gr. ἄγαλμα (pl. ἀγάλματα) an honour, ornament, statue, picture. Found in Dicts., but never used in Eng.]
1721 BAILEY, *Agalma*, the Image or Impression of a Seal, also a Toy. **1809** TOMLINS *Law Dict.*, *Agalma*, the impression or image of anything on a seal. *Chart Edg. Reg. pro Westmonast. Eccl.* anno 698 [That is to say it is a Greek word used in a Latin charter of the 7th c.]

agalmatolite (ægælˈmætəlaɪt). *Min.* [mod. f. Gr. ἄγαλμα, -ατος, statue, image + λίθος stone.] A name applied to various soft minerals, capable of being easily carved; properly the 'Figure-stone' or Pagodite, in which figures are cut by the Chinese.
1832 U.K.S. *Nat. Philos.* II. 28 Pyrometric pieces formed of Chinese agalmatolite. **1857** BIRCH *Anc. Pottery* (1858) I. 97 The substance chiefly employed [to glaze] was agalmatolite or steaschist. **1875** URE *Dict. Arts* s.v., The true agalmatolite is a hydrous silicate of alumina and potash, closely allied to pinite.

agama (ˈægəmə). *Zool.* [ad. native Caribbean name.] A genus of lizards, giving its name to one of the families of the Saurian Reptiles; popularly applied to one species in the British West Indies.
1817 *Blackw. Mag.* I. 187 The second order comprehends crocodiles..agamas, stellios, chameleons. **1833** *Penny Cycl.* I. 192 In the form of their heads and teeth the *agamas* resemble the common lizards, but differ in the imbricated scales which cover their tails.

‖**agamæ** (ˈægəmiː), *sb. pl. Bot.* [pl. of L. *agamus* (ad. Gr. ἄγαμ-ος unmarried) sc. *plantæ*.] A name formerly given to Cryptogams, under the idea that they were destitute of sexual organs. (In Craig 1847.)

agambo, obs. form of AKIMBO.

†**a-'game**, *adv. Obs.* prop. *phr.* [A *prep.*[1] + GAME.] In game, in sport.
*c***1374** CHAUCER *Troylus* III. 592, I seyd but agame that I wold go. —— *Compl. Mars.* 123 Take hit not a-game.

agami (ˈægəmɪ). *Ornith.* [a. Fr. *agamy* (Barrère 1741), a native name in Guiana.] The Trumpeter, a bird somewhat allied to the Crane, inhabiting tropical America.
*a***1833** BRODERIP in *Penny Cycl.* I. 194 One of these Agamis, a young bird, found its way into a farm-yard in Surrey, and associated with the poultry.

agamian (əˈgeɪmɪən), *a.* and *sb.* [f. AGAM-A + -IAN, after Fr. *agamien* Cuv.] Name given to a sub-family of the iguanians (including the genus *Agama*).
1833 *Penny Cycl.* I. 192/1 The agamians..want these additional or palatic teeth.

agamic (əˈgæmɪk), *a. Biol.* [f. Gr. ἄγαμ-ος unmarried (see AGAMOUS) + -IC.] Characterized by the absence of sexual action; in *Bot.* obs. for CRYPTOGAMIC.
1850 tr. *Humboldt, Views of Nat.* 291 Large classes of insects..subsist on agamic plants. **1859** CARPENTER *Anim. Physiol.* §747 Drones are always developed from agamic or unfertilized eggs. **1877** HUXLEY *Anat. Inv. An.* ii. 96 These present various modes of agamic multiplication by fission.

agamically (əˈgæmɪkəlɪ), *adv. Biol.* [f. prec. + -AL[1] + -LY[2]: see -ICAL.] In an agamic manner; without sexual interposition.
1877 HUXLEY *Anat. Inv. An.* iv. 206 Gyrodactylus multiplies agamically by the development of a young Trematode within the body, as a sort of internal bud.

agamid (ˈægəmɪd). *Zool.* [f. mod.L. *Agamidæ*: see AGAMA, -ID[3].] A lizard of the family Agamidæ. Also as *adj.*
1889 in *Cent. Dict.* **1934** *Geogr. Jrnl.* Nov. 393 The agamid lizard, *Phryncephalus theobaldi*. **1958** C. H. POPE *Reptiles round the World* 175 Africa has a few monitors and some agamids. **1959** *New Biol.* XXX. 79 Three related families of lizards, the iguanids, agamids, and chamaeleons.

†**'agamist.** *Obs.* [f. Gr. ἄγαμ-ος unmarried (see AGAMOUS) + -IST.] A professed celibate; one who opposes the institution of matrimony.
1553-87 FOXE *A. & M.* 1768 (R.) To exhort in like maner these agamistes and wilfull rejecters of matrimony. **1656** BLOUNT *Glossogr.*, *Agamist*, he that is unmarryed. [Not in J.]

agammaglobulinæmia (eɪˌgæməˌglɒbjʊlɪˈniːmɪə). *Path.* [mod.L., f. A- 14 + *gamma globulin* + Gr. αἷμα blood.] Lack of gamma globulin in the blood. Hence aˌgammaglobuliˈnæmic, (chiefly *U.S.*) -'emic *a.*
1952 O. C. BRUTON in *Pediatrics* IX. 722 *Agammaglobulinemia*. The complete absence of gamma globulin in human serum with a normal total protein..does not appear to have as yet been reported in the literature. **1954** *Lancet* 2 Oct. 671/2 *Agammaglobulinæmia*. A syndrome has recently been described in America in which recurrent severe infections are associated with a virtual absence of γ-globulin from the serum, the levels of the other plasma-protein fractions remaining within normal limits. **1957** *Ann. N.Y. Acad. Sci.* LXIV. 893 Antibody production in an agammaglobulinemic female. **1961** *Lancet* 29 July 246/1 In congenital agammaglobulinæmia, where the incidence of a rheumatoid-like condition is high, family studies have revealed a hereditary factor. **1966** *Lancet* 26 Nov. 1152/2 Data obtained from a normal infant born of an agammaglobulinæmic mother are the basis of this report. **1985** *Jrnl. Virol.* LV. 567/1 These piglets were agammaglobulinemic at birth.

agamogenesis (ˌægəməʊˈdʒɛnɛsɪs). *Biol.* [f. Gr. ἄγαμο-ς unmarried + γένεσις generation, birth.] The production of offspring otherwise than by the union of parents of distinct sexes (as by the simple division of a pre-existent living being, or the formation of buds, which become at length independent living beings); asexual reproduction.
1864 H. SPENCER *Illust. Progr.* 370 Species which, multiplying by agamogenesis, can people a whole shore from a single germ. **1877** HUXLEY *Anat. Inv. An.* Introd. 28 In many of the lower forms of life agamogenesis is the common and predominant mode of reproduction.

agamogenetic (ˌægəməʊdʒɪˈnɛtɪk), *a. Biol.* [f. Gr. ἄγαμο-ς unmarried + γεννητ-ός produced + -IC.] Of or belonging to agamogenesis; generating or generated without sexual union.
1870 HUXLEY *Lay Serm., Addr. & Rev.* xiii. 312 We have demonstrated, in agamogenetic phænomena, that inevitable recurrence to the original type. **1877** —— *Anat. Inv. An.* Introd. 28 There is an inverse relation between agamogenetic and gamogenetic reproduction.

agamogenetically (ˌægəməʊdʒɪˈnɛtɪkəlɪ), *adv. Biol.* [f. prec. + -AL[1] + -LY[2]: see -ICAL.] In an agamogenetic manner; by asexual reproduction.
1877 HUXLEY *Anat. Inv. An.* vii. 385 The larvae of a Dipterous insect..multiply agamogenetically in the autumn, winter, and spring.

agamoid (ˈægəmɔɪd), *a.* and *sb. Zool.* [f. AGAMA + -OID.] **A.** *adj.* Resembling, or having the form of an Agama; as 'one of the agamoid lizards.'
B. *sb.* An agamoid lizard.
1882 *Encycl. Brit.* XIV. 736/2 *Calotes* is another genus of agamoids peculiar to the East Indies. **1886** *Ibid.* XX. 469/2 The bulk of the Lacertilian fauna is composed of Skinks, Geckos, Agamoids, and *Varanidæ*.

agamont (eɪˈgæmənt). *Biol.* [a. G. *agamont* (M. Hartmann 1904, in *Biol. Centralbl.* XXIV. 25): see A- 14, GAMONT.] = SCHIZONT.
1912 [see GAMONT]. **1940** [see *merozoite* s.v. MERO- 1]. **1963** G. A. KERKUT *Borradaile & Potts's Invertebrata* (ed. 4) ii. 43 After a period of 'vegetative' existence and increase by asexual reproduction, during which the individuals [*sc.* protozoa] are known as agamonts, there appears a generation known as gamonts because they produce gametes. **1973** K. G. GRELL *Protozool.* 137 In Foraminifera ..the agamonts, after meiosis, as well as the gamonts reproduce by multiple fission.

agamous (ˈægəməs), *a.* [f. L. *agam-us* a. Gr. ἄγαμ-ος unmarried (f. ἀ priv. + γάμος marriage) + -OUS.] *lit.* Unmarried: hence *Biol.* Having no (distinguishable) sexual organs; asexual. In *Bot.* *cryptogamous* is now more commonly used.
1847 in CRAIG. **1858** GRAY *Bot. Text-bk.* 395 *Agamous*, destitute of sexes. **1876** BENEDEN *Anim. Paras.* 196 The agamous age undergoes a true moulting, the sexual age a metamorphosis.

agamy (ˈægəmɪ). [ad. Gr. ἀγαμία celibacy, f. ἄγαμος: see AGAMOUS.] Absence or non-recognition of the marriage relation.
1796 W. TAYLOR in *Month. Rev.* XXI. 492 Plato's system of agamy. **1801** —— in *Month. Mag.* XII. 578 The theory of agamy or of exempting matrimony from the notice of the magistrate.

agan, obs. f. AGONE *pa. pple.*; and of OWE *v.*

aganglionic (əˌgæŋglɪˈɒnɪk), *a. Phys.* [f. A- *pref.* 14 + GANGLIONIC.] Not characterized by ganglia.
1836-9 TODD *Cycl. Anat. & Phys.* II. 946/2 Each nerve.. is formed of one set of fibres from the gangliated part, and one from the aganglionic or motor column.

‖**aganippe.** A fountain on Mount Helicon, sacred to the Muses and giving poetic inspiration; hence *fig.* poetic power or method.
1630-95 *Life of Ant. à Wood* (1848) 36 Such towering ebullitions do not exuberate in my aganippe.

agapanthus (ægəˈpænθəs). [mod.L., f. Gr. ἀγάπη love + ἄνθος flower.] A genus of South African liliaceous plants, having large umbels of blue, violet or white flowers on a stout scape, of which the bright blue and white species are commonly cultivated for ornament; also, a plant of this genus.
1789 W. AITON *Hortus Kewensis* I. 414 Agapanthus.. African blue Lily. Nat. of the Cape of Good Hope. Cult. 1692, in the Royal Garden at Hampton-court. **1817** *Botanical Cabinet* I. 42 Agapanthus Minor..a native of the Cape of Good Hope... It differs from umbellatus both in leaves and flowers. **1874** G. M. HOPKINS *Jrnl.* 2 Oct. (1937) 214 A splendid thick-stemmed carnation-coloured lily called valotta..in the greenhouse next to an agapanthus. **1879** W. CORY *Lett. & Jrnls.* (1897) 448 He made flowering plants huddle round the trunks of trees, agapanthus under plane. **1887** RIDER HAGGARD *Jess.* i. 1 The agapanthus which is so familiar to us in English greenhouses. **1962** *New Statesman* 5 Jan. 28/2 There are one or two places in Cornwall where a much more beautiful plant than mesembryanthemum is colonising uncultivated land by seeding itself freely: agapanthus.

agape (əˈgeɪp), *adv.* prop. *phr.* [A *prep.*[1] of state + GAPE.] On the gape; with open mouth of expectation or wonder: hence *fig.* in an attitude or state of wondering expectation.
1667 MILTON *P.L.* v. 357 Their rich retinue..Dazzles the crowd, and sets them all agape. **1765** TUCKER *Lt. of Nat.* II. 73 When the moon interposes between us and the sun so as to cover his whole body, it sets every eye agape. *a***1845** HOOD *T. of Trumpet* xxxvii, At a door ajar, or a window agape. **1848** MARIOTTI *Italy* Pref. 22 Wild with excitement; agape with breathless expectation. **1855** TENNYSON *Maud* x. ii, A rabbit mouth that is ever agape.

‖**agape** (ˈægəpiː). Pl. **agapæ**, **-ai**, rarely **agapes**. [Gr. ἀγάπη brotherly love.] **1.** A 'love-feast' held by the early Christians in connexion with the Lord's Supper. Also in revived use, applied *loosely* to any Christian ritual meal. Also *transf.*
1607 R. PARKER *Scholast. Disc. agst. Antichrist* I. ii. 70 The Christians had their *Agapæ* at communions. **1696** in PHILLIPS. **1727** CHAMBERS *Cycl.* s.v., In the primitive days the Agapes were held without scandal or offence. **1837** W. & M. HOWITT *Rur. Life* (1862) VI. v. 449 The Agapai, or love-feasts of the early Christians. **1850** MRS. JAMESON *Sacr. & Leg. Art* 156 Agapæ or love-feasts. **1920** A. HUXLEY *Limbo* 77 There is a large upper chamber reserved for agapes. **1958** B. BEHAN *Borstal Boy* III. 285 He had a custom of giving a special breakfast for his Holy Communicants, which was called 'Agape', the Greek word for a love feast. **1968** *Listener* 25 July 103/1 They prayed all night in Uppsala's great Gothic cathedral,..and, towards dawn, held an agape. **1975** *Church Times* 11 Apr. 14/4 This Sunday the Parish Eucharist will be followed by an Agape in the church grounds. **1985** *Emmanuel Coll. Mag.* LXVII. 57 Subsequent events, notably agapes and informal gatherings, were also well attended.

2. Now used commonly in its simpler N.T. sense of Christian love (of God or Christ or fellow Christians: see CHARITY); freq. contrasted with Eros, earthly or sexual love.
1856 H. G. M. LASCELLES *Compensation* I. x. 88 Mr. Grant was..animated by real charity, or love, the 'Agape'—so rare to find—of which she had read and admired the true meaning in her Greek testament. **1932** A. G. HEBERT tr. *A. Nygren's Agape & Eros* I. i. 23 Christian love is essentially Agape. *Ibid.* 32 The idea of Agape is not merely a fundamental idea of Christianity, but *the* fundamental idea *par excellence*. The idea of Agape is a new creation of Christianity. **1938** J. BURNABY *Amor Dei* i. 15 From the fact that the world into which Christianity brought the Gospel of divine Agape, of God's self-giving love to men, already knew that thirst for the Divine which Platonism called Eros, it did naturally result that when Christians spoke of love they did not always mean the same thing. **1950** W. H. AUDEN *Enchafèd Flood* (1951) iii. 100 He exhibits Christian forgiveness and Christian *agape* without the slightest effort. **1953** R. NIEBUHR *Chr. Realism & Polit. Probl.* (1954) ix. 132 The *agape* form of love in the New Testament fails to be appreciated particularly in two of its facets: (*a*) the equality of the 'two loves'..(*b*)..the notion of sacrificial love. **1955** P. TILLICH *New Being* (1956) I. vi. 47 Calculating love is not love at all. Jesus did not raise the question about how much *eros* and how much *agape*, how much human passion and how much understanding was motivating the woman.

Hence **agape'istic** *a.*, (R. B. Braithwaite's term) of or characterized by Christian love.
1955 R. B. BRAITHWAITE *Empiricist's View Relig. Belief* 18 Unless a Christian's assertion that God is love (*agape*)..be taken to declare his intention to follow an agapeistic way of life, he could be asked what is the connexion between the assertion and the intention. **1966** I. T. RAMSEY *Christian Ethics* 86 When the Christian asserts, 'God is Love', he declares *primarily not* his commitment..to an agapeistic way of life, but his commitment to certain 'facts'. **1976** *Christian* III. 173 The Christian religion used language to encourage what he [*sc.* Braithwaite] called 'the agapeistic' view of life.

Agapemone (ægəˈpiːmɒniː). [irreg. f. Gr. ἀγάπη love + μονή dwelling, abode (μένειν to stay, remain).] Proper name of an association of men and women established at Spaxton in Somerset by the Rev. Henry James Prince; a similar establishment conducted by his successor, the Rev. John Hugh Smyth-Pigott, at Clapton, London. Also *gen.*, an establishment of this kind, an abode-of-love; esp. with unfavourable implication. Hence **Agapemonian** (-ˈməʊnɪən), **Aga'pemonite** *adjs.* and *sbs.*
1850 *Daily News* 22 Mar., The Agapemonites.—It is said that there is a general split amongst this deluded sect at their abode near Bridgewater. **1851** *Illustr. London News* 29 Mar. 253/3. The Agapemone, or the Abode of Love, is the residence of a religious body, which calls itself the Family of Love. **1854** *Edin. Rev.* Apr. 377 The Agapemone of Bridgwater is full of crazy fanatics. **1859** *Sat. Rev.* 30 Apr. 527/2 A carriage-full of Brothers and Sisters in Love singing the Agapemonite Psalter. *Ibid.*, Any of the subsequent Agapemonian extravagances. **1860** DICKENS *Uncommerc. Trav.* in *All Yr. Round* 29 Sept. 590/1 The happy nature of my retirement is most sweetly expressed in its being the abode of Love. It is, as it were, an inexpensive Agapemone. **1888** J. D. HOOKER *Let.* 22 Aug. in L. Huxley *Life & Lett. J.D.H.* (1918) II. 317 The moment you allow of 'promiscuous intercourse' it is all up and the thing degenerates into an agapemone. **1893** *Funk's Stand. Dict.*,

Agapemonian, *n.* **1899** *Daily News* 10 Jan. 3/3 About four years ago the deceased [Henry James Prince] assisted in the opening of..the first church of the Agapemonians. **1908** *Daily Chron.* 24 Sept. 1/1 The Agapemonites are extremely reticent about their peculiar religion. **1908** *Times* 10 Nov. 12/4 The date..on which a party of Cambridge undergraduates were going to raid the 'Agapemone' at Spaxton, and tar and feather the Rev. Smyth Pigott. **1951** M. KENNEDY *Lucy Carmichael* II. i. 86 The Staff, the Students, etc., all have to have an *agapemone* in the assembly hall, and sing carols.

† **'agapet** *Obs.* [ad. Gr. ἀγαπητ-ός, loved.] 'A lover of the fair sex; a man of pleasure,' Ash.
1736 BAILEY (Fol.) *Agapet*, a whoremaster; one that hunts after women.

agaphite ('ægəfaɪt). *Min.* [named by Fischer, 1816, after *Agaphi*, a naturalist who visited the regions of Persia where the turquoise is found. (Dana.)] A variety of turquoise.
1837-80 DANA *Min.* 581 Agaphite (or conchoidal Turquoise).

agar, obs. form of EAGER *sb.*, tidal bore.

agar ('eɪga(r)). Short for next. Also *attrib.*
1889 *Jrnl. Chem. Soc.* LVI. 817 Diffusion in Agar Jelly. **1892** *Pall Mall Gaz.* 3 Aug. 7/2 Cultures were made in broth, gelatine, and agar. **1909** *Practitioner* Nov. 596 An ordinary 2 per cent. agar medium. **1946** *Nature* 31 Aug. 293/2 A circular disk was cut from the fruit-body..and placed on a nutrient agar plate of typhoid bacillus culture.

agar-agar ('eɪgɑːr'eɪgɑː(r)). Also occas. **agal-agal.** [Malay.] Any of certain East-Indian seaweeds, esp. the Ceylon moss *Gracilaria lichenoides*, from which a gelatinous substance is extracted and used in China for soups and the manufacture of transparent silk and paper, and in bacteriology as a solidifying agent in culture media; also, this substance.
1813 W. MILBURN *Orient. Comm.* II. xxiii. 304 Agal Agal is a species of sea-weed, in which some trade is carried on by the Chinese. **1820** J. CRAWFURD *Ind. Archipelago* III. IX. ii. 181 The articles of the return cargo [to China]..embrace ..*agar-a-gar*, or sea-weed, *tripang*, or sea-slug. **1863** WATTS *Dict. Chem.* I. 61 Agar-agar or Bengal Isinglass. **1886** CROOKSHANK *Bacteriology* 65 Agar-agar has the advantage of remaining solid up to a temperature of about 45°. **1896** *Lancet* 28 Mar. 835/2 Löffler's serum agar-agar. **1929** W. DEEPING *Roper's Row* xvi. §1. 169 A culture of germs on a plate of agar-agar.

agaric ('ægərɪk, ə'gærɪk), *sb.* and *a.* [ad. L. *agaric-um* the tree fungus used for tinder, touchwood, ad. Gr. ἀγαρικ-όν (said by Dioscorides to be named from *Agaria* a place in Sarmatia). Hence mod.L. *Agaricus* given by Dillenius, and adopted by Linnæus, for a genus of *Fungi*. Shelley accents *a'garic*, Tennyson '*agaric*.]

A. *sb.*

1. *Herb.* and *Pharm.* A name given to various corky species of *Polyporus*, a genus of fungi growing upon trees; of which *P. officinalis*, chiefly found on the Larch, the 'Female Agarick' of old writers, was renowned as a cathartic, and with *P. fomentarius*, and *igniarius*, 'Male Agarick' used as a styptic, as tinder, and in dyeing. *Obs.* or *arch.*
1533 ELYOT *Castel of Helth* (1541) 79 One dramme of Agaryke and halfe a dramme of fine Reubarbe. **1551** TURNER *Herbal* II. 29 Larche tre..giueth also..ye famus medicine called Agarick..whereof some make tunder both in England and Germany for their gunnes. **1657** *Phys. Dict., Agaric*..purgeth phlegm, and opens obstructions in the Liver. **1756** *Gentlem. Mag.* XXVI. 352 The agaric sent from France, and applied as a styptic after amputations. **1836** TODD *Cycl. Anat. & Phys.* I. 229/1 Agaric and sponge entangled the blood and retained a coagulum on the spot.

2. *Bot.* A mushroom; properly one of the Linnæan genus *Agaricus*.
1777 LIGHTFOOT *Fl. Scot.* (1788) II. 1021 Little Champignion or Fairy Agaric: In dry pastures and frequently in those green circles of grass called Fairy Rings. **1820** SHELLEY *Sens. Plant* III. 62 And agarics and fungi, with mildew and mould. **1859** TENNYSON *Gareth* 728 As one That smells a foul-flesh'd agaric in the holt. **1862** COLEMAN *Woodl. Heaths, etc.* 32 The Fly Agaric..is a very handsome fungus, having a bright red upper surface.

3. = *Agaric Mineral*: see 4.
1727 CHAMBERS *Cycl., Agaric* is also a denomination given to an earthy concretion, of the colour and consistence of coagulated milk.

4. *Comb.* **agaric-gnat**, a name given by Kirby and Spence to a genus of insects (*Mycetophila*); **agaric-mineral**, a light, spongy variety of carbonate of lime, called also Rock-milk, allied to stalactites, and deposited by calcareous springs and in caverns.
1828 KIRBY & SPENCE *Entomol.* II. xvi. 7 From the antennæ in his figure, it should seem a species of agaric-gnat. **1837-80** DANA *Mineral.* 680 Agaric Mineral..Rock-milk is a very soft, white material, breaking easily in the fingers.

B. *adj.* [The sb. used *attrib.*] Of or pertaining to agarics; fungoid.
1879 *Syd. Soc. Lex., Agaric Acid*, an acid obtained from *Polyporus officinalis* by extracting with ethers. **1879** G. MACDONALD *P. Faber* I. x. 117 The efflorescent crusts and agaric tumours upon the dry bones of theology.

agariciform (ə'gærɪsɪ-, ægə'rɪsɪfɔːm), *a. Bot.* [f. L. *agaric-us* AGARIC + -FORM.] Mushroom-shaped.
1868 WRIGHT *Ocean World* 119 *Cœloptychium*..the upper part expanded, agariciform concave.

agaricoid (ə'gærɪkɔɪd), *a. Bot.* [f. AGARIC + -OID.] Of the nature of an agaric, mushroom-like.
1874 M. C. COOKE *Fungi* 8 This mycelium gives rise to the stem and cap of an agaricoid fungus.

agased, *a. Obs.* See AGAZED.

† **a'gasp**, *v. Obs. rare.* [f. A- *pref.* 11 + GASP.] To gasp (for life).
1526 SKELTON *Magnif.* 271 Galba, whom his galantys garde for agaspe.

agasp (ə'gɑːsp, -æ-), *adv.* prop. *phr.* [A *prep.*[1] 11 + GASP.] In a gasping condition; gasping, eager.
1800 COLERIDGE *Own Times* II. 395 Formerly agasp for reform, he now raves against all reformation.

Agassiz trawl ('ægəsɪz trɔːl). [f. the name of Alexander E. *Agassiz* (1835–1910), American naturalist + TRAWL *sb.*] A type of beam-trawl.
1910 *Encycl. Brit.* VIII. 573/1 (*caption*) Agassiz or Blake Trawl. From Alexander E. Agassiz's *Three Cruises of the 'Blake'*. **1936** RUSSELL & YONGE *Seas* (ed. 2) 262 A small net known as the Agassiz trawl..has the advantage that whichever way it may fall on the sea bottom it can still fish effectively. **1959** H. BARNES *Oceanogr. & Marine Biol.* i. 32 Separate problems arise in the sampling of plankton very close to the bottom... In one method, a net is mounted on an Agassiz trawl frame.

† **a'gast, a'ghast,** *v. Obs.* Forms: 2–3 **agest**, 3–6 **agast**(e, 6 (occas.) **aghast**. *Pa. t.* **agast**(e. *Pa. pple.* **agast, -ed.** [f. A- *pref.* 1 intens. + *gast-en*, OE. *gǽst-an* to frighten, alarm; see GAST, and cf. A-GAZED. The only part now in use is the pa. pple. *agast*, erroneously written AGHAST.]

1. To affright, frighten, terrify.
1205 LAYAM. 6452 þat folc hit agaste: tunes hit aweste. *c* **1230** *Ancren Riwle* 212 þe ateliche deouel schal ȝet agesten ham mid his grimme grennunge. *c* **1380** *Sir Ferumb.* 3410 þe Saraȝyns þay habbeþ sore agaste. *c* **1385** CHAUCER *Leg. G. Wom.* 1171 What may it be That me agasteth in myn slep. **1513** DOUGLAS *Æneis* IV. vi. 146 His feirfull ymage doith me agast. **1583** STANYHURST *Æneis* II. (Arb.) 66, I..was with no weapon agasted. **1596** SPENSER *F.Q.* I. ix. 21 Or other griesly thing, that him aghast.

2. *refl.*
c **1305** *E.E. Poems* (1862) 62 Cristofre him sore agaste To adrenche, so heuy þat child was.

3. *intr.* To take fright or alarm.
1300 *St. Brand.* 22 So that Brendan agaste sore, and him blescede faste.

agast, *a.* See AGHAST.

† **a'gasted,** *ppl. a. Obs.* [f. prec. + -ED.] Frightened, terrified; fuller form of AGHAST *ppl. a.*
c **1382** WYCLIF *Luke* xxiv. 37 (MS. O. a. 1420) Thei troublid and agasted gessiden hem for to se a spirit [*v.r.* agast]. **1579** TOMSON *Calvin's Serm. on Tim.* 737/1 Nothing agasted at it. *Ibid.* 699/1 The torments woulde make vs agasted [*printed* agashed]. **1583** STANYHURST *Aeneis* II. (Arb.) 59 Then shiuering moothers throgh court doo wander agasted.

† **a'gasting,** *vbl. sb. Obs.* [f. AGAST *v.* + -ING[1].] Frightening, terrifying, alarming.
1672 R. TAYLOR *Cromwell* To the agasting of Cromwell who suspected an assassinate.

† **a'gasting,** *ppl. a. Obs.* [f. AGAST *v.* + -ING[2].] That terrifies or alarms.
1593 NASHE *Christs Teares* 90/1 It woulde breede in vs such an agasting terror.

† **a'gastment.** *Obs.* [f. AGAST *v.* + -MENT. An early instance of the addition of *-ment* to a native word.] Affrightment, fright, alarm.
1594 NASHE *Terr. Night* F ij b, This terror and agastment.

agastric (ə'gæstrɪk), *a. Zool.* [f. Gr. ἀ priv. + γαστήρ, γαστρ-ός belly + -IC.] Having no distinct alimentary canal.
1836 TODD *Cycl. Anat. & Phys.* I. 43/1 Such pulmograda as..were formerly supposed to be agastric. **1867** J. HOGG *Microsc.* II. ii. 371 In..agastric Infusoria only solid alimentary particles are taken as food.

agate ('ægət), *sb.* Forms: 6–7 **agath, agget, agot,** 6–8 **agat,** 7 **agett, aggott, (nagget),** 8 **aggat, aggot,** 7– **agate.** [a. 16th c. Fr. *agathe*, ad. It. *ágatha, ágata*, f. L. *achātes* (a. Gr. ἀχάτης), whence earlier Fr. *acate, acathe*, and Eng. ACHATE, also in use.]

1. a. A precious stone; a name applied to the semi-pellucid variegated chalcedonies, with the colours disposed in parallel stripes or bands, or blended in clouds, and often with curious markings due to the infiltration of other minerals; from these variations in appearance, lapidaries distinguish many varieties, as moss agate, ribbon agate, eye agate, fortification agate, zoned or banded agate, variegated agate, brecciated agate, etc.
1570 B. GOOGE *Pop. Kingd.* IV. (1880) 39b, Jaspers, Chrysolytes and Agats doe appere. **1621** LADY A. DRURY in *Bury Wills* (1850) 166 To my sister Gawdie, my agett and pearle chaine. **1646** SIR T. BROWNE *Pseud. Ep.* 381 Many fair rooms paved with Agath. **1716-8** LADY M. W. MONTAGUE *Lett.* I. xiv. 49 A large collection of agates..of an uncommon size. **1789** BURNEY *Hist. Music* (ed. 2) IV. v. 181 Tile them with gold and pave them with aggots. **1865** LIVINGSTONE *Zambesi* xii. 261 The ground is strewn with agates for a number of miles above the falls.

b. A marble made of glass, etc., resembling agate. Also *attrib.*
1843 [see TAW *sb.*[2]]. **1921** *Glasgow Herald* 26 Nov. 6 The marbles we played with..were called 'nicks',..'agates' (black, blood and milk). **1934** *Amer. Speech* IX. 75/1 *Agates* or *Aggies*, marbles made of agate and usually used as shooters. **1952** J. STEINBECK *East of Eden* xxxvi. 365 Cal was able to develop his marble game and set about gathering in all the chalkies and immies, glassies and agates.

† **2.** *fig.* A very diminutive person, in allusion to small figures cut in agates for seals. *Obs.*
1597 SHAKS. *2 Hen. IV*, I. ii. 19, I was neuer mann'd with an Agot till now. **1599** —— *Much Ado* III. i. 65 If tall, a launce ill-headed: If low, an agot very vildlie cut.

3. An instrument used by gold-wire-drawers, having an agate fixed in it for burnishing. Cf. A glazier's *diamond*.
1751 CHAMBERS *Cycl.* s.v., The gold wire drawers burnish their gold with an *Agat*; whence the instrument, made use of on that occasion, is also called an *Agat*.

4. *Typog.* The American name of the type called in England *ruby*. Also *attrib.* (see quots.).
1838 *U.S. Mag. & Democratic Rev.* I. 61 Light faced Book and Job Printing Types..Diamond, Pearl..Agate. **1871** RINGWALT *Encycl. Print.* 24 *Agate*, the American name for a size of type between Nonpareil and Pearl, and of which there are about fourteen lines to an inch. **1884** *Chicago News Let.* 5 Apr., Commercial advertising 20 cents per line Agate measure. **1956** F. H. COLLINS *Authors' & Printers' Dict.* (ed. 10) 8/2 *Agate line* (U.S.), measure advertising space, $\frac{1}{14}$ in. deep and one column wide.

5. Sometimes erroneously confused with *gagates*, jet.
1661 LOVELL *Hist. Min.* 53 Of Sulphurs, Agath, Gagates. It's..of a black, stony earth, full of bitumen.

6. *Comb.* and *Attrib.* **agate-jasper**, a jasper veined or clouded with agate or chalcedony; **agate-onyx** (see quot.); **agate-ring**, one made of, or set with, an agate; **agate-shell**, a collector's name for the tropical genus of land-shells, *Achatina*; also called **agate-snail**; **agate-ware**, a kind of pottery coloured to resemble agate; also, enamelled iron or steel ware for household utensils; also *attrib.* Also ***agate cup, hole, mill, stone, trade, work***, etc.; ***agate eyes***; ***agate-bearing, -eyed, -forming, -handle(d)***, etc.
1875 URE *Dict. Arts* I. 32 The igneous origin of the *agate-bearing melaphyres. **1634** *Unton Inventories* 32, I give and bequeath..my *nagget cup. **1925** C. DAY LEWIS *Beechen Vigil* 30 Panic thereafter Came *agate-eyed, gibbering, past the gate. **1876** GEO. ELIOT *Dan. Der.* IV. li. 16 Deepest *agate eyes. **1710** STEELE *Tatler* No. 245 ¶2 An *Aggat-Handle Knife. **1863** TYNDALL *Heat* i. 30 The wires should be drawn through *agate holes. **1875** URE *Dict. Arts* I. 35 It is in the Idar valley, that most of the *agate-mills are situated. **1747** DINGLEY *Gems* in *Phil. Trans.* XLIV. 505 The *Agat-Onyx, of two or more Strata of white, either opaque or transparent. **1874** WESTROPP *Prec. Stones* 46 *Agate-onyx*, a variety of onyx in which the upper layer is opaque and white, the lower transparent, and either colourless or a pale yellow. This is the material most frequently employed for modern carving, and is often termed the German onyx. **1596** SHAKS. *1 Hen. IV*, II. iv. 78 This..Not-pated, *Agat ring, Puke stocking, Caddice garter, Smooth tongue, Spanish pouch. **1884** G. W. TRYON *Struct. Conch.* III. 59 Achatina, *Etym.* *Agate-shell.. Mostly African. **1889** *Cent. Dict.*, Agate-snail. **1901** E. STEP *Shell Life* xix. 379 The *Agate Snail (*Cæcilianella acicula*), though only about one-fifth of an inch in length, is interesting on several grounds. **1592** SHAKS. *Rom. & Jul.* I. iv. 55 In shape no bigger then *Agat-stone, on the fore-finger of an Alderman. **1857** J. MARRYAT *Pottery & Porcelain* (ed. 2) viii. 154 *Agate and jasper ware. **1865** JEWITT *Wedgwoods* Index, Agate-ware vases. **1879** *Cassell's Techn. Educ.* I. 367 During the reigns of Anne and George I, an improved ware was made of sand and pipe-clay, coloured with oxide of copper and manganese, forming the well-known 'agate-ware' and 'tortoiseshell-ware'.

agate (ə'geɪt), *adv.* orig. *phr.* **on gate, a gate.** [A *prep.*[1] of state + GATE *sb.*[2] way, path.] On the way, on the road; hence, a-going, in motion. (Properly a northern word.)
1554 *Interl. Youth* in Hazl. *Dodsley* II. 25 Go to it then hardily, and let us be agate. **1587** HOLINSHED *Scott. Chron.* (1806) I. 418 Some of the mills yet were now at low water set on gate, by reason the streams were so hugelie augmented. **1674** RAY *N. Countrey Wds.* s.v., *Agate*, just going, as *I am agate*. **1848** C. BRONTË *Jane Eyre* (1857) 344 I'm fear'd you have some ill plans agate. **1863** MRS. GASKELL *Sylvia's L.* I. 63 And t' cursed old pressgang's agate again.

† **'agated,** *ppl. a. Obs. rare*$^{-1}$. [f. AGATE *sb.* + -ED[2].] Marked like an agate.
1665 RAY *Flora* 47 Leaves [petals of the tulip] which, warmed by the sun..change into divers glorious colours, variously mixed, edged, striped, agoted, marbled.

agates, Sc. variant of ALGATES *adv.*, everywhere.

† **a'gateward**, *adv. Obs. north.* [f. AGATE *adv.* + -WARD.] On the road.

1647-8 A. EYRE *Diurnal* (Surt. Soc.) I rid with Robert Eyre—and agateward homewards.

† **a'gathered**, *pa. pple. Obs. rare*$^{-1}$. [? pa. pple. of *agather* vb., not otherwise found; or more probably for *i-gathered*, OE. *ʒe-gaderod*: see A *particle*.] Gathered, assembled.

1393 *Compl. Ploughm.* in *Pol. Songs* Rolls. Ser. I. 244 With the Griffon comen foules fele, Rauins, Rokes, Crowes, and Pie, Gray foules, agaðred wele.

agathism ('ægəθɪz(ə)m). *rare.* [f. Gr. ἀγαθ-ός good + -ISM; cf. *optimism.*] The doctrine that all things tend towards ultimate good, as distinguished from *optimism* which holds that all things are now for the best.

1830 *Edin. Rev.* L. 309 Wilful evil, to the degree implied in the distinction proposed between Agathism and Optimism, is inconsistent with our apprehension of his [i.e. God's] nature.

agathist ('ægəθɪst). *rare.* [f. as prec. + -IST; cf. *optimist.*] One who holds the doctrine of agathism.

1830 *Edin. Rev.* L. 294 The existence of evil compels Dr. Miller to substitute the moderate title of 'Agathist' for that of 'Optimist.' **1841** HOR. SMITH *Moneyed Man* III. x. 284 Advancing years have already made me an Agathist, a believer that every thing is for ultimate good.

agathodemon (ˌægəθəʊ'diːmən). [a. Gr. ἀγαθοδαίμων, f. ἀγαθό-ς good + δαίμων a spirit.] A good divinity or genius.

1836 LANDOR *Pericl. & Asp.* Wks. 1846 II. 376 Breaking off now and then a nose from a conqueror, and a wing from an agathodemon. **1879** M. CONWAY *Demonol.* I. III. ix. 392 The Japanese are careful to distinguish this serpent from a dragon, with them an agathodemon.

agathodemonic (ˌægəθəʊdɪ'mɒnɪk), *a.* [f. prec. + -IC.] Of or belonging to an agathodemon.

1879 M. CONWAY *Demonol.* I. III. vii. 364 The harmless serpents of Germany were universally invested with agathodemonic functions.

ˌ**agathoˌkako'logical**, *a. nonce-wd.* [f. Gr. ἀγαθό-ς good + κακό-ς bad + -LOGICAL.] Composed of good and evil.

a **1843** SOUTHEY *Doctor* I. liii. (1862) 120 For indeed upon the agathokakological globe there are opposite qualities always to be found.

'**agathopoi'etic**, *a. rare*$^{-1}$. [f. Gr. ἀγαθοποι-ός doing good, beneficent; cf. Gr. εὐποιητικός.] A proposed technical epithet for, Intended to do good, of beneficent tendency.

1838 BOWRING *Bentham's Mor. & Legisl.* xviii. §54. 133 All these trusts might be comprised under some such general name as that of agatho-poietic [*printed*-poieutic] trusts.

agatiferous (ægə'tɪfərəs), *a.* [f. AGATE *sb.* + -(I)FEROUS producing.] Producing, or rich in, agates.

1847 in CRAIG.

agatiform (ə'gætɪfɔːm, 'ægətɪfɔːm), *a.* [f. AGATE *sb.* + -(I)FORM.] Having the form or appearance of an agate.

1882 *Acad.* 10 June 420/1 When the acid solution within an agatiform deposit bursts through the bands of silica.

agatine ('ægətaɪn, -ɪn), *a.* [f. AGATE *sb.* + -INE.] 'Having the appearance of agate; of the nature of agate.' Craig 1847.

agatize ('ægətaɪz), *v.* [f. AGATE *sb.* + -IZE.] To convert into agate; to give the appearance of agate to. (Chiefly, if not exclusively, in pa. pple.)

1638 *Reliq. Wotton.* (1672) 476 Some good Flints to be Agatized by your miraculous invention. **1850** DANA *Geol.* ix. 483 Many [masses] are simply silicified or agatized.

agatized ('ægətaɪzd), *ppl. a.* [f. prec. + -ED.] Converted into or made to resemble agate.

1847 CRAIG, *Agatized*, having coloured lines and figures of agate, as *agatized* wood. **1869** PHILLIPS *Vesuv.* iv. 121 They are filled with agatized silica.

agaty ('ægətɪ), *a.* [f. AGATE *sb.* + -Y^{1}.] Of the nature of, or characterized by the presence of, agate.

1695 WOODWARD (J.) An agaty flint was above two inches in diameter.

‖**Agave** (ə'geɪviː). *Bot.* [L. *Agāve* prop. name in mythology, ad. Gr. Ἀγαυή, properly adj. fem. of ἀγαυός illustrious, highborn, adopted as a generic name by mod. botanists.] A genus of plants (N.O. *Amaryllidaceæ*), of which the chief species is the American Aloe, whose stately flower-stem (sometimes forty feet high) is produced only when the plant arrives at maturity, at the age of from ten to seventy years.

1830 LINDLEY *Nat. Syst. Bot.* 257 The wild Agave of Mexico yields a copious juice when tapped, which is fermented into a wine. **1842** TENNYSON *Daisy* xxi, The moonlight touching o'er a terrace One tall Agavè above the lake.

agaze (ə'geɪz), *adv.* prop. *phr.*; also **a gase**, and expanded, **at gaze**. [A *prep.*^{1} of state + GAZE *v.*] In a gazing attitude; on the gaze, gazing.

c **1430** *How the Good Wijf, etc.* in *Babees Bk.* (1868) 39 Go þou not into þe toun as it were a gase. **1759** ROBERTSON *Hist. Scotl.* I. III. 184 They stood confounded and at gaze. **1876** GEO. ELIOT *Dan. Der.* IV. l. 9 Fathers and sons agaze at each other's haggardness.

† **a'gazed, a'gased**, *ppl. a. Obs.* [Origin obscure. There was no vb. *agaze* (*agǽstan* taking the place of **agǽsan* in OE. = Goth. *usgaisjan*), and the sense is against its being pa. pple. of simple GAZE, with A- for *ʒe-*. Prob. a variant of *agast* (AGHAST), preserving long quantity of OE. *gǽstan* (with *agast*, *agās'd*, *agāsed*; cf. *lit*, *līghted*; *dreamt*, *drēamed*; *past*, *passed*, *pāced*), and influenced in use by to *gaze*, stand *at gaze*.] Affrighted, astounded, amazed.

c **1400** *Chester Plays* II. 85 þe were so sore agased. **1557** EARL SURREY in Tottell's *Misc.* (Arb.) 4 My spretes doe all resorte To stande agazed. **1591** SHAKS. *1 Hen. VI*, I. i. 126 The whole army stood agaz'd on him. **1600** in Farr's *S.P.* (1845) II. 438 Of vnderstanding rob'd, I stand agaz'd.

agba ('ægbə). [Yoruba.] A West African tree (*Gossweilerodendron balsamiferum*); also, its timber.

1920 A. H. UNWIN *W. Afric. Forests & Forestry* ix. 304 *Pterogopodium*, Agba, Pink Mahogany... It is a very large forest tree, with clear bole of 90 feet. **1934** A. L. HOWARD *Timbers of World* (ed. 2) 9 *Agba*, reported by the Imperial Institute as a good, useful wood of very serviceable width. **1952** *Archit. Rev.* CXII. 408/3 The desk for Unilevers, designed by Charles Kenrick, in agba, with a black bean top and reeded hardboard case.

agé, aʒé, ayé, obs. forms of AGAIN.

age (eɪdʒ), *sb.*; also 4-6 **aege**, 5 **eage**, 5-6 **aage**, 6 **aige**. [a. OFr. *aäge*, *eäge*, (11th c.) *edage* (Pr. *atge*):—late L. **ætāticum* (analogous to *umbrāticum*, *viāticum*, *volāticum*, etc.), f. *ætāt-em* age, contr. from *ævi-tātem*, n. of quality f. *ævum* an age. The OFr. word was of 3 syllables, but in the earliest recorded instances in Eng. it was already reduced to 2; Caxton's *eage*, *aage* being later attempts to restore the Fr. spelling. The mod.Fr. *âge* and Eng. *age* retain only the (lengthened) termination of the OFr. *ed-age*, *e-age*. See -AGE.]

I. A period of existence.

1. The time that any animal or vegetable has lived; the length of time that anything has existed in its present form or state; length of existence.

c **1325** *E.E. Allit. Poems* A 412, I watȝ ful ȝong & tender of age. *c* **1384** CHAUCER *Hous of Fame* 1986 In al myn age Ne saugh y suche an hous as this. **1477** EARL RIVERS (Caxton) *Dictes* 92 The said Alexander began to regne in the xviij yer of his eage. **1559** *Myrroure for Mag.*, *Dk. York* xi. 3 Prudent for their age. **1611** BIBLE *Mark* v. 42 Shee was of the age of twelue yeeres. **1665-9** BOYLE *Occas. Refl.* II. xi. (1675) 133 Those, who are of the same age with me. **1751** CHAMBERS *Cycl.* s.v., The age of a hart, etc., is chiefly judged of by the furniture of his head. **1831** *Census Quest.* in *Penny Cycl.* VI. 414/1 How many persons (including children of whatever age) are there actually found within the limits of your parish?

b. ***moon's age***: number of days since the occurrence of the new moon. So ***day's age***, ***year's age***, etc.

1636 MASSINGER *Bashf. Lov.* IV. i, Of what age is the day? **1751** CHAMBERS *Cycl.* s.v. *Moon*, To find the Moon's age:—To the day of the month add the epact of the year, and the months from March inclusive. The sum, if under 30—if over, the excess—is the moon's age.

c. ***age and area***: designating a theory that the area occupied by a culture, language, animal species, etc., is a measure of its antiquity.

1915 J. C. WILLIS in *Phil. Trans. R. Soc.* CCVI. 337 Genera will obviously tend to follow the age and area rule more closely than species. **1922** —— *Age & Area* vi. 62, I called this hypothesis, that on the average the area occupied by species in a country depended upon their age within that country, by the convenient jingle of 'Age and Area'. **1922** J. SMALL in J. C. Willis *Age & Area* xiii. 126 Inequalities more or less cancel out when the genera are taken in groups of ten or more as specified for the Age and Area hypothesis.

d. Expostulatory phr. ***be*** (less commonly ***act***) ***your age***: behave as becomes your years, *i.e.* in a responsible manner; don't be childish. orig. *U.S.*

1925 *New Yorker* 26 Sept. 18/2 (*caption*) Be Your Age. **1931** E. LINKLATER *Juan in America* II. i. 63 Aw, be your age! **1932** *Amer. Speech* June 328 *Act your age*, 'don't be childish'; 'stop the foolishness'. **1933** *Punch* 11 Jan. 29/3 *Son.* Aw shucks! Doancher know nuttin'? Cummawn, be yerr age, Paw. **1948** 'N. SHUTE' *No Highway* iii. 70 Do you think the Inspection would have let this aircraft fly if there was any danger of that sort of thing? Be your age. **1951** S. KAYE-SMITH *Mrs. Gailey* ix. 180 Rosamund..spoke irritably. 'Oh, be your age!'

e. ***of an age***: of the same age. Const. *with*.

1934 H. G. WELLS *Exper. Autobiogr.* I. iii. 105, I got more mental stimulus from some of my school-fellows who were of an age with me. *Ibid.* II. viii. 627 We were both about of an age; to be exact he was six months younger than I.

f. ***at one's age***: when one is of a particular age; ***of an age***: old enough *to* (do something).

1896 BELLOC *Bad Child's Bk. Beasts* 5 A manner rude and wild Is common at your age. **1916** G. B. SHAW *Androcles & Lion* I. 9 The men, if of an age to bear arms, will be given weapons to defend themselves..against the Imperial Gladiators. **1919** —— *Heartbreak Ho.* I. 28 Do you suppose that at my age I make distinctions between one fellow creature and another? **1961** C. G. L. DU CANN *Love-Lives Charles Dickens* x. viii. 189 It is true that the eldest boy Charles was of an age to be flying off and building a nest of his own.

2. The whole duration of the life or existence of any being or thing; the ordinary duration of life.

1535 COVERDALE *Ps.* lxxxix. 10 The dayes of oure age iij score yeares and ten. **1611** BIBLE *Gen.* xlvii. 28 The whole age of Iacob was an hundred fourtie and seuen yeeres. **1703** ROWE *Fair Penit.* v. i. 1811 Shortens her Father's Age, and cuts him off. **1853** *Encycl. Brit.* I. 233 The age of man has greatly diminished from his first creation. *Ibid.* 234 Of the ages of the lower animals little is known.

3. Such duration of life as ordinarily brings body and mind to full development; years of maturity or discretion, or what by law or custom are fixed as such. ***full age***, in Eng. Law, 21 years; hence the expressions ***of*** (***at***, ***to*** obs.) ***age***, ***under*** (***within*** obs.) ***age***, ***nonage***. ***age of discretion***, 14 years.

1382 WYCLIF *John* ix. 21 Axe ye him, he hath age, speke he of himsilf. *c* **1430** *Syr Tryamoure* 690 Of justyng canste thou ryght noght, For thou art not of age. **1509** FISHER *Wks.* 38 Till they come to aege in the ungracyous custome of synne. **1528** PERKINS *Profit. Bk.* v. §327 (1642) 144 If I dye, my heire within age. **1721** CIBBER *Rival Fools* I. i. (1754) II. 1 Sir, I'm no Boy, I have been at Age this Half-year. **1788** JOHNSON *Lett.* I. cxxviii. 278 To hinder my dear Harry from mischief when he comes to age. **1809** TOMLINS *Law Dict.* II. E 1/1 Nor can any lord of parliament sit there, until he be of the full age of twenty-one years. *Ibid.*, *Nonage*, in general understanding, is all the time of a person's being under the age of 21. **1832** HT. MARTINEAU *Demerara* i. 4 The freedom which is so precious to young people when they reach what appears to them the age of discretion. *Mod.* When did he come of age?

4. Hence, Any particular length of life which naturally or conventionally qualifies for anything. (Usually with *over* (*past* arch.), *under*.)

c **1315** SHOREHAM 63 Of ham that scholde y-wedded be Her the age thou myȝt lerne. **1382** WYCLIF *Heb.* xi. 11 Sare bareyn took vertu into conseyuing of seed, ȝhe, bi sydis, or withoute [**1388** aȝen] the tyme of age. **1526** TINDALE *ibid.*, When she was past age. [So in *Genev.*, **1611**, and *Revised*.] *a* **1884** *Mod.* This is the candidate's last chance; in another year he will be over age. There is no limitation of age for this prize.

5. A naturally distinct portion of the existence of a man or other being; a period or stage of life.

1489 CAXTON *Faytes of Armes* I. ix. 22 In tyme to come of theyre flowryng aage. **1534** LD. BERNERS *Gold. Bk. M. Aurel.* (1546) C ij b, The fearefulle dedes and enterpryses doone by Caius Jul. Cesar in his yonge age. **1600** SHAKS. *A.Y.L.* II. vii. 143 One man in his time playes many parts, His Acts being seuen ages. **1602** —— *Haml.* III. iv. 68 At your age The hey-day in the blood is tame. **1611** —— *Wint. T.* IV. iv. 108 They are giuen To men of middle age. **1736** BAILEY (Fol.) s.v. The Life of Man is divided into four different Ages, *Infancy*, *Youth*, *Manhood*, *Old Age*. **1751** CHAMBERS *Cycl.* s.v., The Age of puberty commences at 14, and ends at about 25. *c* **1815** WORDSWORTH *To Yng. Lady*, An old age serene and bright, And lovely as a Lapland night.

6. *esp.* The latter part of life, when the physical effects of protracted existence become apparent; old age.

1330 R. BRUNNE *Chron.* 114 A gode clerk wele in age. **1380** *Sir Ferumb.* 3481 Y am sumdel stryken in age. **1398** TREVISA *Barth. De P.R.* XVIII. xxvii. (1495) 788 Houndes in aege haue the Podagre. **1509** HAWES *Past. Pleas.* XI. xxxvi, Who in youth lyst nothyng to lerne, He wyl repent hym often in hys age. **1599** SHAKS. *Pass. Pilgr.* xii, Crabbed age and youth cannot live together. **1602** —— *Haml.* v. i. 79 Age with his stealing steps, Hath caught [*v.r.* claw'd] me in his clutch. *a* **1631** DONNE *Sat.* iii, Age, death's twilight. **1646** SIR T. BROWNE *Pseud. Ep.* IV. xii. 217 Many grow old before they arrive at age. **1718** POPE *Iliad* I. 96 Thus spoke the prudence and the fears of age. **1770** GOLDSM. *Des. Vill.* 100 A youth of labour with an age of ease. **1842** TENNYSON *Grandm.* xxv, Age is a time of peace, So it be free from pain. **1858** SEARS *Athan.* xiv. 122 The moroseness and peevishness of age.

b. *Cards.* The 'eldest hand' in the game of poker.

1882 C. WELSH *Poker; how to play it* 47 Before the dealer begins to deal the cards, the player next to his left, who is called the *ante-man*, or *age*, must deposit in the pool an *ante* not exceeding one-half the limit previously agreed upon. **1889** GUERNDALE *Poker Bk.* v. 33 It would be C's place to bet first, he being to the left of the Age.

7. The physical effects or qualities themselves; oldness, senility. Of things: Maturity.

c **1460** *Cov. Myst.* 139 Hese leggys here do folde for age. **1509** FISHER *Wks.* 294 For aege and febleness. **1599** SHAKS. *Much Ado* III. v. 37 When the age is in, the wit is out. **1611** BIBLE *Ecclus.* xxx. 24 Carefulnesse bringeth age before the time. **1859** J. LANG *Wander. India* 383 Bring several bottles of our Madeira, for theirs I do not like..It has not age. **1877** L. MORRIS *Hades* I. 50 The failing ear and eye, the slower limbs, Whose briefer name is Age.

II. A period of time.

8. The period of time contemporary with the lifetime of any one; the generation of men to which any one belongs. (Used in fixing a date, but not as a measure.)

1330 R. BRUNNE *Chron.* 61 Malcolm mad homage tille Edward our kyng, þat he and alle his age of Ingland sald hold þat þing. **1557** N. T. (Genev.) *Mark* xiii. 30 This age shal not passe, tyl all these thynges be done. 1611 Bible *Transl. Pref.* 5 S. Hierome..the best linguist without controuersie, of his age. *c* 1735 Pope *Donne Sat.* iv. 2 Adieu to all the follies of the age. 1849 Macaulay *Hist. Eng.* I. 183 What, in our age, would be called gross perfidy and corruption. 1876 Freeman *Norm. Conq.* III. xi. 72 A dabbler in arts and sciences beyond his age.

9. A lifetime taken as a measure of time; a generation.

1535 Coverdale *Ps.* cxliv. 13, & thy dominion endureth thorow out all ages. 1651 Hobbes *Leviathan* III. xxxiii. 203 The Writers of the New Testament lived all in lesse then an age after Christ's Ascension. 1718 *Free-thinker* No. 19. 128 A Duke is..not to be seen in a Countrey-Church above once in an Age. 1853 *Encycl. Brit.* II. 233 Nestor is said to have lived three ages when he was ninety years old.

10. A long but indefinite space of time, marked by the succession of men.

c 1400 *Destr. Troy* Prol. 6 Off aunters ben olde of aunsetris nobill, And slydyn vppon shlepe by slomeryng of Age. 1590 Marlowe *1st Pt. Tamburl.* I. i. 6 Unhappy Persia, that in former age Hast been the seat of mighty Conquerors. 1611 Bible *Eph.* iii. 5 Which in other ages was not made knowen vnto the sonnes of men. 1654 Chapman *Alphonsus* Pl. 1873 III. 212 H'as tane his leaue of me for age and age. 1816 J. Wilson *City of Plague* I. i. 39 But one dread year Hath done the work of ages. 1860 Tennyson *Locksley* 137 Yet I doubt not thro' the ages one increasing purpose runs.

b. often *loosely* in exaggeration. Also in *pl.*

1590 Shaks. *Mids. N.D.* v. i. 33 To weare away this long age of three houres. 1627 Feltham *Resolves* I. xlvii. (1677) 75 In the dead age of night. *a* 1704 T. Brown *Lett. Wks.* 1730 I. 178 This very minute seems an age. 1813 Miss Austen *Pride & Prej.* xvii. 76 The two ladies were delighted to see their dear friend again, called it an age since they had met. 1889 W. S. Gilbert *Gondoliers* II. 32 As at home we've been remaining—We've not seen you both for ages. 1922 Joyce *Ulysses* 742, I suppose he died of galloping drink ages ago.

c. occas. used for a century. (Cf. Fr. *siècle*.)

1594 Blundeville *Exerc.* III. I. xxxvi. (ed. 7) 352 The space of an hundred yeeres, called in Latine *seculum*, and in English an age. 1635 Pagitt *Christianogr.* III. (1636) 11 The end of the tenth, and beginning of the eleventh Age, after the incarnation. 1749 Wesley *Wks.* 1872 X. 43 For they [Jerome and Hilarion] did not live within the first three ages. 1848 Lowell *Fable* Poet. Wks. 1879, 149/2 Be true to yourselves and this new nineteenth age.

11. *Hist.* Any great period or portion of human history distinguished by certain characters real or mythical, as the Golden Age, the Patriarchal Age, the Bronze Age, the Age of the Reformation, the Middle Ages, the Prehistoric Age.

1297 R. Glouc. 9 Of þe world..þe firste age & tyme was from oure firste fader Adam to Noe. 1552 Lyndesay *Monarche* II. 1948 Of Weris, said he the gret outtrage Began in to the secunde aige. 1610 Shaks. *Temp.* II. i. 168, I vvould vvith such perfection gouerne Sir, T'Excel the Golden Age. 1697 Dryden *Virgil, Past.* iv. 5 The last great Age, foretold by sacred Rhymes. 1736 Bailey (Fol.), The Generality of Chronologers agree in making seven Ages [*of the World*] or Periods. 1818 Hallam (*title*) A View of the state of Europe during the Middle Ages. 1865 Tylor *Early Hist. Man.* 193 The Stone Age falls into two divisions, the Unground Stone Age, and the Ground Stone Age.

12. *Geol.* A great period or stage of the history of the Earth, distinguished by its leading physical features; an æon.

1855 Kingsley *Glaucus* (1878) 25 The Ice Age or Glacial Epoch. 1857 H. Miller *Test. Rocks* i. 53 In the Oolitic ages insects become greatly more numerous.

III. *Comb.*, as ***age-class, -determination, -distribution, -fellow, -grade*** (hence ***-grading*** vbl. sb.), ***-limit, -range, -scale, -set, -war; age-ago, -cold, -new, -proof, -weary***, adjs.; also combs. in which *age* stands in objective relation to a pr. pple., as ***age-adorning, -dispelling***; or in instrumental relation to a pa. pple., as ***age-cracked, -despoiled, -dimmed, -encamped, -enfeebled, -established, -gnarled, -honoured, -moulded, -peeled, -stricken, -worn***, etc.; or in limiting relation to a pple. or adj., as ***age-coeval, -lasting***, AGE-LONG, q.v. Also **'age-group**, a number of persons or things classed together as of similar age; hence ***age-grouping*** vbl. sb.; **'age-hardening** *Metallurgy*, (of certain alloys) the process or result of AGEING; **ageman** *obs.*, an old man; AGELESS, AGE-MATE, AGE-PRIER, q.v.

1923 Kipling *Irish Guards in Gt. War* I. 325 That *age-ago retreat from Mons. 1905 *Terms Forestry & Logging* 6 **Age class*, all trees in a stand whose ages are within given limits. 1920 R. H. Lowie *Primitive Society* xi. 302 Schurtz..is as certain of the uniform priority of age-classes when compared with clubs or secret organizations as Morgan is of the necessary priority of matrilineal descent. 1929 Age-Class [see *age-fellow*]. 1846 Hawthorne *Mosses* I. vii. 163 Lifelong and *age-coeval associations. 1950 W. de la Mare *Inward Comp.* 86 Cliffs of *age-cold stone. 1850 Mrs. Browning *Poems* II. 378 A beldame's *age-cracked voice. 1926 R. W. Lawson tr. *Hevesy & Paneth's Man. Radioactivity* xxvi. 216 *Age determination from the Helium content. 1832 W. C. Bryant *Poems* 57, I shall see the day..with an *age-dimmed eye. 1909 *Cent. Dict.* Suppl., *Age-distribution. 1934 *Planning* I. xxvii. 5 The death-rate like the birth-rate, has fallen fast in recent years, and here again the age-distribution of the population must be considered as well as the crude rate. 1913 Kipling *Songs from Books* 157 *Age-encamped Oblivion Tenteth every light that shone! 1807 J. Barlow *Columbiad* v. 531 Their maim'd, their sick, their *age-enfeebled sires. 1925 R. Graves *Welchman's Hose* 49 *Age-established brooks run dry. 1929 *N. & Q. Anthrop.* (ed. 5) II. 56 Those *Age-Fellows who have been initiated together may be looked upon as an *Age-Set* or *Age-Class*. 1954 J. G. Peristiany in *Instit. Prim. Soc.* iv. 44 To-day the council of elders, which includes..age-fellows of the wrong-doer, puts a collective curse on his head. 1933 W. de la Mare *Fleeting* 101 The *age-gnarled thorn. 1906 N. W. Thomas *Kinship Organisations* i. 2 The other kind of association, to which the name *age-grades is applied, is composed of a series of grades, through which..each man passes in succession, until he attains the highest. *a* 1942 B. Malinowski *Sci. Theory Culture* (1944) v. 50 Studying an Australian tribe, we would have to follow the small family groups..the age-grades, and totemic clans. 1948 K. Davis *Human Soc.* (1959) iv. 107 Reliance upon *age-grading is very prominent in African societies. 1950 C. F. Hockett in *Language* XXVI. 449 (*title*) Age-grading and linguistic continuity. 1904 *Gen. Rep. Census Eng. & Wales 1901* 147 The following Table, which gives the proportions of blind per million living at the earlier *age-groups, shows [etc.]. 1930 *Times Educ. Suppl.* 7 June 257/2 The public elementary school age-group 10 to 11. 1936 J. T. Jenkins *Fishes Brit. Is.* (ed. 2) 177 Probably the best method of determining the growth and age-groups..is by measuring large numbers of individuals caught together on the same ground. 1937 *Proc. Prehist. Soc.* III. 182 To divide the sites into three age-groups *merely* by observing their heights above modern sea-level. *a* 1942 B. Malinowski *Sci. Theory Culture* (1944) vi. 57 More frequently the organization according to sex is related to..*age groupings or age-grades. 1921 Hanson & Gayler in *Jrnl. Inst. Metals* XXVI. 345 The extent of the *age-hardening which takes place is roughly proportional to the amount of magnesium silicide in solution at the moment of quenching. 1932 *Discovery* May 145/1 After quenching in water from about 475°–500° C. its [duralumin's] strength increases with time. This is known as 'age-hardening' which is now recognized as an extremely important phenomenon, not confined to this type of alloy. 1839 Bailey *Festus* xxxii. (1848) 352 Between eternity and time a lapse..*age-lasting. 1898 *Strand Mag.* XV. 331/2 It is doubtful whether the inexorable *age limit will not preclude his inclusion in the next Conservative Ministry. 1917 *Aberdeen Univ. Rev.* June 259 The raising of the upper age limit [for examinees] to twenty or twenty one. 1570–1 in *Eccl. Proc. Durham* (Surt. Soc.) 225 Wm. Walker is an *aidgeman and broken in labour. 1925 D. H. Lawrence *St. Mawr* 77 The rocks.. heavy with *age-moulded roundnesses. 1938 R. Graves *Coll. Poems* 176 Time was my chronicler, my deeds *age-new. 1839 Bailey *Festus* xxvii. (1848) 325 *Age-peeled pinnacles. 1928 *Daily Express* 7 Nov. 4 Annette Kellermann..demonstrates..that she is practically *age-proof. 1929 *Nat. Soc. for Study of Educ. Yearbk.* XIV. 695 The chief concern of adults should be to make sure that.. the *age-range is kept fairly narrow. 1908 W. McDougall *Introd. Soc. Psychol.* iv. 109 The time of ripening of any instinct..is liable to be shifted forwards or backwards in the *age-scale during the course of racial evolution. 1929 *Age-set [see *age-fellow*]. 1940 E. E. Evans-Pritchard *Nuer* vi. 255 The age-set system is a further exemplification of the segmentary principle. 1954 J. G. Peristiany in *Instit. Prim. Soc.* iv. 40 The initiation rituals..provide him with an age-set; that is, with a group of age-mates who remain his social co-evals through life. 1815 Scott *Ld. of Isles* I. Introd., Some *age-struck wanderers gleans few ears of scatter'd grain. 1932 Wyndham Lewis *Doom of Youth* IV. i. 201 The '*Age-War' is really a Father-and-Children-war. 1895 W. B. Yeats *Poems* 147 And demons have lifted The *age-weary eyelids from the eyes that of old Turned gods to stone. 1836 Todd *Cycl. Anat.* I. 805/1 The infirm and *age-worn patients of Salpetrière. 1851 Hawthorne *Twice-told T.* II. xix. 267 So age-worn and woful are they. 1933 W. de la Mare *Fleeting* 135 An image of age-worn stone.

age (eɪdʒ), *v.* [f. the prec. sb.]

1. *intr.* To grow old; to become aged.

1398 Trevisa *Barth. De P.R.* xv. lxxiii. (1495) 516 Other men there ben in Inde that lyue ful longe and aegen neuer. 1440 *Promp. Parv.*, Agyn, or growyn agyd, *Seneo, senesco.* 1530 Palsgr. 418/2 Thought maketh men age a pace. 1673 Grew *Anat. Plants* II. I. ii. §2 (1682) 61 The other [skin] Postnate, succeeding in the room of the former, as the Root ageth. 1833 Praed *Poems* (1865) I. 405 Queen Mab is ageing very fast. 1861 Pearson *Early & Mid. Ages Eng.* 393 He [Henry II] stooped slightly and grew fat and gouty as he aged.

2. *trans.* To make old, to cause to grow old.

1636 Earl Manchester *Contempl. Mort.* 182 A man might age himselfe in it, and sooner grow old than weary. 1839 Bailey *Festus* (ed. 3) 12/2 Grief hallows hearts even while it ages heads. 1856 Kane *Arct. Explor.* I. xv. 173 An Arctic night and an Arctic day age a man more rapidly and harshly than a year anywhere else.

3. *Calico-printing.* To fix the mordants and printed colours in (cloth, etc.) by the process of ageing. Also *intr.*, to undergo this process. So **aged** *ppl. a.*

1849 [see AGEING *vbl. sb.* 2]. 1862 C. O'Neill *Dict. Calico Printing* 8/1 The difference of appearance will be..in favour of the aged or exposed part. 1890 W. J. Gordon *Foundry* 177 The calico..has to be dried and aged. 1910 E. Knecht et al. *Man. Dyeing* (ed. 2) II. 649 The dyeing of aged blacks. 1912 Knecht & Fothergill *Textile Printing* 138 If they [*sc.* the goods] are simply printed in aluminium mordants, one day may be quite sufficient to fully 'age' them. *Ibid.* 141 It is preferable to let them 'age' for a day or two in pile before dyeing.

4. *trans.* To mature by keeping in storage, by exposing to the air, etc.

1852 Swindells & Nicholson *Brit. Pat. 390* 1 For oxydating metallic solutions, and for ageing and raising various colouring matters. 1854 W. E. Staite *Brit. Pat. 468* 2 Madder which, technically speaking, has not been 'aged'.

5. To calculate or determine the age of (something), esp. scientifically; to assign an age to. Cf. DATE *v.* 2 e.

1887 M. H. Hayes *Soundness & Age of Horses* vi. 94 If a colonial animal in, say, September showed the condition of mouth just described, we should age him as five years old. 1954 *Vermont Life* Spring 49 The forester is able to age trees by studying the growth rings or annuli. 1970 *Nature* 23 May 692/1 These dykes have been radiogenically aged at 2,420 million years. 1971 *Country Life* 24 June 1577/1 (*caption*) Ageing a section of a tree.

6. *intr.* Of iron, the iron core of an electrical transformer: to suffer a continuously increased loss in hysteretic quality.

1896 [implied in AGEING *vbl. sb.* 4]. 1899 S. R. Roget in *Proc. R. Soc.* 23 Jan. 154 Brands of transformer steel, which are practically 'non-ageing'. 1902 *Encycl. Brit.* XXVIII. 121/1 Brands of steel are now obtainable which do not age in this manner.

-age, *suffix* of abstr. nouns, originally in words adopted from Fr., afterwards a living Eng. formative. [OFr. *-age*:—late L. *-āticum*, a favourite termination of abstr. sbs. of appurtenance, and collectives; *orig.* neuter of adjectives in *-ātic-us*. Cf. cl. L. *silv-āticus* of the wood (*silva*), It. *selv-aggio*, Pr. *salv-atge*, Fr. *sauv-age*, Eng. *sav-age*, with *viāticus* of or pertaining to a journey (*via*), *viāticum* that which pertains to a journey, provision for the way, *later* the making of a journey, Pr. *viatge*, It. *viaggio*, Fr. *viage, voyage*; *umbrāticus* of or pertaining to the shade, shady (*umbra*), late L. *umbrāticum* that which is shady, shadiness, a mass of shade, Fr. *ombrage*, Eng. *umbrage*. Afterwards a common formative in Fr. itself, as in *entour-age*; thence readopted in med.L. as *-āgium*: cf. *homāgium, cariāgium*, formed on Fr. *hommage, cariage*, which if formed in L. would have been **homināticum*, **carricāticum*.] Meaning. **1.** From names of things, indicating that which belongs to or is functionally related to, as (from Fr.) *language, potage, tonnage, umbrage, voyage*; passing into the whole functional apparatus collectively, in *baggage, foliage, plumage, village*; whence of Eng. formation *cellarage, cordage, fruitage, girderage, leafage, luggage, poundage, socage, vaultage*, etc. **2.** From names of persons, indicating function, sphere of action, condition, rank, as (from Fr.) *baronage, homage, personage, vassalage, vicinage, villeinage*, and of Eng. formation *bondage, orphanage, parsonage, porterage, umpirage*. **3.** From verbs expressing action, as (from Fr.) *advantage, damage, equipage, marriage, message, passage, pilgrimage, portage, usage*; whence of Eng. formation *breakage, brewage, cleavage, postage, prunage, steerage, wreckage*, etc.

aged (senses 1, 2, 'eɪdʒɪd; sense 3, eɪdʒd), *ppl. a.* [f. AGE *v.* + -ED, prob. orig. modelled on Fr. *âgé*.]

1. a. Having lived or existed long; of advanced age; old. ***aged parent***, applied joc. to a parent (whether elderly or not).

1440 *Promp. Parv.*, Agyd, *Antiquatus, senectus.* *c* 1460 *Cov. Myst.* 97, I am so agyd and so olde. 1535 Coverdale *Ps.* cxviii. 100 Yee I am wyser then the aged. 1607 Shaks. *Coriol.* II. iii. 176 Aged Custome, But by your Voyces, will not so permit me. 1634–46 J. Row (father) *Hist. Kirk* (1842) 290 Mr. John Malcolme being the agedest. 1718 Pope *Iliad* XXIII. 928 To Ajax I must yield the prize; He to Ulysses, still more aged and wise. 1861 Dickens *Gt. Expect.* II. vi. 92 You don't object to an aged parent, I hope? 1876 Freeman *Norm. Conq.* II. vii. 121 He was an aged man and weary of his office. 1934 A. Ransome *Coot Club* iii. 40 'Tell her we won't be late. Macaroni cheese to-night. Specially for you, A.P.' That was Starboard talking to her Aged Parent.

b. *fig.*

1611 Tourneur *Ath. Trag.* III. i. 77 Ag'd in vertue. 1874 Mahaffy *Soc. Life in Greece* ii. 28 The experience of Homeric men was aged enough to know that probity secured no man from the troubles of life.

2. Belonging to or characteristic of old age.

1588 Shaks. *Tit. A.* III. i. 7 The aged wrinkles in my cheekes. 1610 —— *Temp.* IV. i. 261 Shorten vp their sinewes With aged Cramps.

3. Of or at the age of. *spec.* of a horse.

1637 *Brass in Kendal Ch.* (Nicholson *Kend.* 68) Here vnder lyeth the body of Alice..who dyed the 25th day of March 1637, being aged 26 yeares 5 months & od dayes. 1801 *Times* 16 Apr. 4/1 The demise of a lady aged 54 years. 1869 F. Fitzwygram *Horses & Stables* lviii. 563 A moderately fresh aged horse is..more useful..than a young untried horse. 1882 *Daily News* 8 Nov. 6/5 Racing. City Cup..Hardrada, a. [*i.e.* aged more than 6] yrs., 9 st. 9 lb. *Ibid.*, Coursing. All-Aged Stakes, of 6 guineas each. 1951 E. Rickman *Come Racing with Me* ii. 17 Any horse or mare above six years is 'aged'.

Comb. †**agedlike**, *a. obs.* Having the appearance or marks of age, senile.

1530 Palsgr. 305/1 Aagedlyke, *senil.*

agedly ('eɪdʒɪdlɪ), *adv.* ? *Obs.* [f. AGED *a.* + -LY².] 'After the manner of an aged person.' J.

a 1542 Boorde *Regyment* Q ij b, For that wyll cause a man to looke agedly. 1552 Huloet, Agedlye, *Vetusté.* 1678 Gouldman, Agedly, *seniliter, vetuste.*

agedness ('eɪdʒɪdnɪs). [f. AGED *a.* + -NESS.]

1. The quality of being aged, oldness.

1530 Palsgr. 193/2 Agydnesse, *anciennete.* 1635 J. Hayward *Banish'd Virg.* 214 My wrinkles and withered agednesse. 1641 Milton *Ch. Discip.* I. (1851) 26 For Custome without Truth is but agednesse of Error. 1873

Spectator 8 Feb. 168/2 The agedness of the world, its sad want of originality.

2. The quality of having reached a stated age. *a* **1643** W. CARTWRIGHT *Poems* (N.) He still was strong and fresh, his brain was gray. Such agedness might our young ladies move To somewhat more than a Platonick love. **1881** MRS. ELLIS *Sylvestra* II. 261 That middle-agedness some men show so early.

agee (əˈdʒiː), *adv. Sc.* and *dial.* [A *prep.*[1] of state + GEE, to move to one side, from *gee!* or *jee!* a call to a horse to move to one side. Cf. *a-stray.*] Aside, on or to one side; awry; off from the straight line.

? **1800** A. CARLYLE *Autobiog.* 208, I wore my hat agee. **1837** MISS SEDGWICK *Live & let Live* (1876) 190 A looking-glass that don't make you look as if your face was all agee.

ageing, aging (ˈeɪdʒɪŋ), *vbl. sb.* [f. AGE *v.* + -ING[1].] **1. a.** Becoming old. **b.** Giving the appearance of age to.

1879 G. GLADSTONE in *Cassell's Techn. Educ.* I. 198 The hot flue leads into the ageing-room, where the cloth remains suspended. **1881** M. PATTISON in *Academy* 12 Feb. 109/3 The unfortunate effect upon us of ageing. **1882** *Daily News* 3 Jan. 2/3 A New Way to Make Old Bronzes. This 'ageing' process..is, to say the least, rather 'Gothic' than Egyptian.

2. *Calico-printing.* The action or process of fixing the colours and mordants by exposing the printed goods to the action of a warm, moist atmosphere or by running them through hot steam (see quot. 1961). Also *attrib.*

1849 J. THOM *Brit. Pat. 12,610* 4 The ageing of goods by ..passing them through a chamber containing aqueous vapour. **1850** S. PINCOFFS *Brit. Pat. 13,080* 5 Improvements in the ageing process..consist in..the mode of introducing into the ageing room..a heated and moistened atmosphere. **1859** *Ibid.*, The ageing stove. **1862** C. O'NEILL *Dict. Calico Printing* 8/2 Ageing liquor. **1881** *Instr. Census Clerks* (1885) 69 Ageing Machine Minder. **1882** *Jrnl. Soc. Chem. Industry* I. 188 To prevent condensation,..the walls of the aging [*sic*] house are double. **1961** BLACKSHAW & BRIGHTMAN *Dict. Dyeing & Textile Printing* 6 *Ageing*, originally a process in which printed fabric was exposed to a hot moist atmosphere. At the present time the term is almost exclusively applied to treatment of printed fabric in moist steam in absence of air.

3. The action or process of maturing pottery clay, wine, logwood, tobacco, etc. Also *attrib.*

1860 TOMLINSON *Arts & Manuf.* 2nd Ser. *Pottery* 31 The mixture of clay and flint..ought to be kept..in order that the materials may become more intimately united... During this ageing, as it is called, a fermentation takes place. **1874** KNIGHT *Dict. Mech.*, *Ageing* (Wine and Liquors). *Ibid.*, Wine-ageing Apparatus. **1910** E. KNECHT et al. *Man. Dyeing* (ed. 2) I. 331 Ageing or Maturing of Logwood. **1935** *Discovery* Nov. 340/2 The ageing of tobacco is dependent on the action of micro-organisms.

4. a. The continually increasing hysteresis of iron under alternating magnetization, or when subjected to great heat.

1896 D. C. & J. P. JACKSON *Alternating Currents* 539 Ageing of Transformer Cores. *Ibid.*, The ageing seems to have the greatest effect upon poor qualities of iron.

b. In various other techn. uses (see quots.).

1902 *Encycl. Brit.* XXVIII. 90/1 Ageing of lamps. **1916** *Jrnl. Soc. Chem. Industry* XXXV. 873/2 After varying periods of ageing..both [rubber] compounds are much over-vulcanised at 4½ hours. **1930** *Engineering* 19 Sept. 358/1 Artificial ageing of Duralumin. **1930** FIELD & WEILL *Electro-Plating* iv. 50 After some use a solution works better than an entirely new one. This is called 'ageing'. **1937** *Jrnl. Inst. Civil Engin.* VII. 115 There are records of the ageing of at least one pipe from which the local growth-rate [of internal roughness] can be found. **1945** *Ann. Reg. 1944* 386 The addition of small quantities of finely powdered copper ..has the added advantage of increasing the resistance [of synthetic rubber] to ageing. **1958** *Engineering* 28 Mar. 410/3 The heat-treatment furnace is designed for solution treatment and artificial ageing, as well as annealing. **1959** *B.S.I. News* Nov. 21 Tests [of copper conductors] include ..heat shock, heat ageing, [etc.].

ageing, aging (ˈeɪdʒɪŋ), *ppl. a.* [f. AGE *v.* + -ING[2].] **a.** Becoming aged, showing signs of advancing age. **b.** Giving the appearance of old age.

1862 *Com. Place Philosopher* 153 Esteemed by all, though gouty, ageing, and careworn. **1863** *Sat. Rev.* 204 Working envenomed slippers for her penurious and aging spouse. **1870** MORRIS *Earth. Parad.* I. i. 20 Many an ageing line.. Ploughed his thin cheeks.

ageism (ˈeɪdʒɪz(ə)m). Also **agism.** [f. AGE *sb.* + -ISM.] Prejudice or discrimination against people on the grounds of age; age discrimination, esp. against the elderly. Cf. RACISM b, SEXISM.

1969 *Washington Post* 7 Mar. A6/1 Dr. Robert Butler.. believes many of his Chevy Chase neighbors suffer from 'age-ism'. **1969** R. N. BUTLER in *Gerontologist* Winter 243/1 We shall soon have to consider..a form of bigotry we now tend to overlook: age discrimination or age-ism, prejudice by one age group toward other age groups. *Ibid.* 243/2 Age-ism describes the subjective experience implied in the popular notion of the generation gap. **1973** *Observer* (Colour Suppl.) 30 Sept. 61/3 In the United States, the fight against 'agism', as they describe the process of discrimination on grounds of age. **1977** *Grimsby Even. Tel.* 27 May 2/5 'Like sexism and racism, ageism has had its day,' said Dr. Alex Comfort, a world expert on ageing. Old people had to get moving and be bloody-minded to improve their lot. **1982** *Times* 2 Aug. 9/1 'Agism' is a new word in the lexicon of fashionable evils. Like..sexism and racism, it seeks to express an old evil in a new way—in this case prejudice in thought and deed against the old. **1983** *Daily Tel.* 21 Nov. 12/8 Ageism might be a joke, but it is meant only too seriously.

ageist (ˈeɪdʒɪst), *sb.* and *a.* Also **agist.** [f. prec.: see -IST.] **A.** *sb.* One who advocates or practises ageism. **B.** *adj.* Pertaining to or characterized by ageism; discriminating on the grounds of age.

1970 *Daily Tel.* 2 June 12/4 The jack-booted agists of West Sussex must be stopped before they subject the elderly to the whole terror-apparatus of the Police State. **1974** *Newsweek* 6 May 24/3 She called him 'a sexist, age-ist pig'. **1978** *Lancet* 19 Aug. 422/1 It is..extremely disheartening that you should be so ageist as to head the article 'Care of the Elderly'. 'The elderly' is a figure of speech, metonymy, in which one attribute is used to describe the whole, just as in 'the Irish', 'the blacks',..and 'the delinquents'. **1980** *Maledicta* III. 249 This was before the GAA (Gay Activists' Alliance—why not GAY? I suppose Gay American Youth would have been agist). **1983** S. DAY-LEWIS in *Daily Tel.* 21 Nov. 11/4 The proposer of the motor-cycle film said that the riders ranged from the middle-aged to the 'fresh faced and pimply' and quickly apologised in case he sounded 'ageist'.

agelast (ˈædʒɪlæst). [f. Gr. ἀγέλαστ-ος not laughing; f. ἀ not + γελαστ-ός laughable, γελαστ-ής a laugher; f. γελά-ειν to laugh.] One who never laughs.

1877 G. MEREDITH in *Times* 5 Feb. 4/5 Men whom Rabelais would have called agelasts or non-laughers.

†**age'lastic,** *a.* and *sb. Obs.* [f. Gr. ἀγέλαστ-ος (see prec.) + -IC.] 'One that never laughs.' Cockeram 1626. 'Never laughing; one who never laughs; morose, severe.' Bailey 1731.

ageless (ˈeɪdʒlɪs), *a.* [f. AGE *sb.* + -LESS.] Without old age or limits of duration; never waxing old or coming to an end.

1651 T. STANLEY *Poems* 24 Ageless ever singing. **1855** BAILEY *Mystic* 89 Fountains of ageless youth and maidenhood. **1858** NEALE *Bernard de Morlaix* 17 Peace endless, strifeless, ageless.

agelessness (ˈeɪdʒlɪsnɪs). [f. AGELESS *a.* + -NESS.] The quality of being ageless.

1905 W. WATSON *Poems* II. 137 And so the people of this land possess, Age after age, unaltering agelessness. **1906** A. C. BENSON *From a College Window* xviii, The mighty unresting Heart, to whose vastness and agelessness the whole mass of these flying and glowing suns are but as a handful of dust. **1927** *Observer* 1 May 6 He had a rare gift with boys and young men, whom he could draw out by sheer agelessness.

age-long (ˈeɪdʒˌlɒŋ), *a.* [f. AGE *sb.* + LONG.] Long with the length of an age, long as an age; lasting for an age.

1810 SOUTHEY *Kehama* XXIII. v. Wks. VIII. 189 Where the heavenly Hours Weave the vast circle of his age-long day. **1862** LYTTON *Strange Story* (1866) II. lxxxvii. 355 The age-long trees in the forest. **1878** L. MORRIS *Hades* 24 Self-inflicted death and age-long woe.

agelte, early form of AGUILT *v. Obs.*, to sin.

†**'agely,** *adv. Obs. rare*[−1]. [f. AGE *sb.* + -LY[2], after *daily, yearly.*] Coming once in each age.

1621 BP. MOUNTAGU *Diatribe* 298 Theese [first-fruits] I confesse, were not yeerely: no nor yet agely: but singularly payed, once for all.

'agemate. [f. AGE *sb.* + MATE. Cf. *playmate.*] A fellow or equal in age; a coeval.

1583 STANYHURST *Aeneis* II. (Arb.) 61 Whilst I beheld Priamus thus gasping, my syre his adgemate.

1920 *Q. Rev.* July 171 Age-mates are associated at initiation. **1951** *N. & Q. Anthrop.* (ed. 6) II. 68 Without definite age-sets there may be social and economic ties between age-mates. **1954** [see *age-set*]. **1965** *New Society* 6 May 11/1 These children saw their environment as more threatening than did their agemates.

agen, a spelling representing the southern pronunciation of AGAIN, much used by the poets from 17th to beginning of 19th c.

agen, aghen, ahen, obs. forms of OWN *a.*

agenbite, mod. rendering of AYENBITE (= remorse), used after Joyce as a conscious archaism. See note at INWIT 1, 2.

1922, etc. [see INWIT 1, 2]. **1952** DYLAN THOMAS *Let.* 6 Nov. (1966) 380 'Put it off, put it off,' 'It's too late now.'.. These agenbite-deadeners did their long-night worst, but the little voice in the dark, oh, throb, throb it went across Kansas. **1972** *Times* 17 Apr. 14 Muggeridge is haunted..by plastic grass, the possibility that dawn will be photographed as though it were dusk. What agenbite of inwit must seize the old gentleman as they lard him with make-up prior to committing him to the arms of his camera.

†**agence,** *v. Obs. rare.* [a. Fr. *agence-r* to adapt, adjust, OFr. *agencier*, f. *a* to + *gent* pretty, gentle; perh. f. L. *genitus* (well-) born. Cf. It. *agenzare*, Pr. and Cat. *agenzar.*] To fit, adapt, or adjust.

a **1631** DONNE *Aristeas* 49 There was an order of Stones in fashion of little Ovales that were Agenced and holding together and enfiled with little joncks of gold.

agency (ˈeɪdʒənsɪ). [ad. med.L. *agentia* = *facultas agendi*, n. of state f. *agent-em* pr. pple. of *ag-ĕre* to do, act.]

1. The faculty of an agent or of acting; active working or operation; action, activity.

1658 SLINGSBY *Diary* (1836) 208 Privacy..if your Hours in it are not well employed, may become as dangerous as a place of agency. **1762** EDWARDS *Freed. Will* I. v. (R.) The moral agency of the Supreme Being..differs in that respect from the moral agency of created intelligent beings. **1830** COLERIDGE *Ch. & St.* 140 The State shall leave the largest portion of personal free agency to each of its citizens, that is compatible with the free agency of all.

2. Working as a means to an end; instrumentality, intermediation.

1674 *Ch. & Crt. of Rome* 17 The Agency of the Romish Factors with the King of Spain, for the procuring a second Invasion of their Native Country. *a* **1691** FLAVEL quoted in H. Miller *Sch. & Schoolm.* ix. (1866) 87 That the moral infection came by way of physical agency. **1785** T. JEFFERSON *Corr.* Wks. 1859 I. 416 To set our treaty with the piratical States into motion, through his agency. **1815** BAKEWELL *Introd. Geol.* 439 The geologists who exclude the agency of fire from the formation of rocks. **1849** MACAULAY *Hist. Eng.* II. 175 A complete explanation and reconciliation were brought about by the agency of Gilbert Burnet. **1859** DARWIN *Orig. Spec.* Introd. 3 Requiring the agency of certain insects to bring pollen from one flower to the other.

3. Action or instrumentality embodied or personified as concrete existence.

1784 BECKFORD *Vathek* (1868) 20 An invisible agency arrested his progress. *a* **1843** SOUTHEY *To Allan Cunningham* Wks. III. 310 And still Antonides and Hooft Are living agencies. *c* **1854** STANLEY *Sinai & Pal.* i. (1858) 35 The agency by which the sea was dried up was 'a strong east wind.'

4. *Comm.* The office or function of an agent or factor.

a **1745** SWIFT (J.) Content to live cheap in a worse country, rather than be at the charge of exchange and agencies. **1800** WELLESLEY *Desp.* 715 Foreigners deal directly with the natives, or with foreign houses of agency. **1875** POSTE *Gaius* III. (ed. 2) 429 In the contract of agency..the principal is called dominus or mandator.

5. An establishment for the purpose of doing business for another, usually at a distance.

1861 *Act 19 of Legisl. Counc. India* vi, In any Circle of Issue there may be also established an Agency or Agencies of Issue in connection with a Bank or otherwise. **1882** *Daily News* 4 Sept. 6/3 General Foreign News (through Reuter's Agency). *Ibid.* 14 Oct. 8/4 (*Advt.*) Solicitor to a Debt Collecting and General Trades Protection Agency. *Ibid.* 28 Aug. 8/7 (*Advt.*) Ladies requiring English and Foreign Governesses..are invited to send particulars to the Governesses' Agency.

6. The office of an Indian agent, or the establishment forming the headquarters of one. *U.S.*

1707 *S. Carolina Statutes at Large* (1837) II. 314, I will neither directly nor indirectly trade with any Indian.. during the time of my agency. **1824** *Publ. Stat. U.S.A.* (1856) IV. 25 It shall be the duty of each Indian agent to reside and keep his agency within, or near the territory claimed by the tribe or tribes of Indians for which he may be agent. **1878** J. H. BEADLE *Western Wilds* xiii. 198 We concluded we had better see the Creeks at home, and started afoot for the Agency. **1895** C. KING *Fort Frayne* xvi. 228 Eleven o'clock came and..no further authority from the agency.

attrib. **1873** J. H. BEADLE *Undevel. West* xxv. 527 The last grain in the Agency storehouse was issued to them on the 14th. **1901** S. E. WHITE *Westerners* viii. 57 Rain-in-the-Face was at once an agency Indian and a reckless man.

7. Special Comb. **agency shop** *U.S.*, a workshop or other establishment in which employees maintain the right not to join the recognized trade union, if a sum equivalent to the union subscription is paid to the union (or to a charitable organization); an agreement or system of this kind.

1952 *Monthly Labor Rev.* (U.S. Dept. Labor) LXXIV. June p. iv, The union agreed to eliminate the union-shop provision of the previous contract and to accept the '*agency shop.' **1963** *Economist* 27 Apr. 326/1 The Douglas Aircraft Corporation..broke ranks and agreed to an 'agency shop'; this requires workers who do not join the recognised union to pay it the equivalent of union dues. **1971** *Mod. Law Rev.* XXXIV. VI. 660 Only a registered union can be a party to a valid agency-shop agreement. **1979** *N.Y. Rev. Bks.* 17 May 11/3 The constraints on the city's ability to get itself out of its destructive relationship with labor are many. The municipal unions have had an agency shop since 1977.

a'gend. Pl. **agends** (*obs.* or *arch.*), **agenda** (əˈdʒendə). [ad. L. *agendum* that which is to be done; gerundive of *agĕre* to do. The Eng. forms *agend, agends* are now apparently obs.; for the former the L. *agendum* occurs, but the only part in ordinary use is the pl. *agenda.*]

1. *gen.* in *pl.* Things to be done; matters of practice, as distinguished from matters of belief.

1753 CHAMBERS *Cycl. Supp.* s.v., Divines speak of the *agenda* of a christian, meaning the things to be practised by way of contradistinction from *credenda* or the things to be believed. **1860** MAURY *Phys. Geog. Sea* i. §67 Notwithstanding all that has been done..there still remain many *agenda.*

†**2.** Matters of ecclesiastical practice or ritual. *Obs.*

1629 ANDREWES *Answ. Cdl. Perron* 1 (L.) It is the Agend of the Church, he should have held him to. **1642** WILCOCKS *Eng. Prot. Apol.* 34 (T.) For the matter of our worship, our credends, our agends, are all according to the rule. **1775** Ash, *Agenda*, the service of the church.

3. The items of business to be considered at a meeting.

1882 *Pall Mall G.* 16 Sept. 3 The most important item in the *agenda* is to discuss the amendment of the Employers' Liability Act.

4. *coll. sing.* A memorandum book. (Cf. Fr. *agenda*.)

1753 Chambers *Cycl. Supp.*, *Agenda* is also used for a book containing notes, or memorandums of things necessary to be done. **1875** Poste *Gaius* II. (ed. 2) 300 *Codicillus* denotes..a pocket-book, an agenda.

agenda. a. Pl. of agend (sense 3), treated as a singular. Also *transf.*, a (notional) list of things to be done, of appointments, etc.; freq. in phr. ***on the agenda***. Cf. agend 1.

1907 *N.U.T. Conference Agenda (Oxford)* 30 This Conference protests against the action of the Executive in printing Supplementary Agendas for Conference. **1928** *Daily Express* 13 Jan. 1/1 Further conferences are to follow with..the Trade Union Council to tabulate agendas and settle difficulties. **1928** *Observer* 1 July 30/5 It sometimes happens that an agenda promises sensations. **1957** E. Hyams *Into Dream* II. ii. 101 It's a short agenda, by the way, only two items. **1961** in Millikan & Blackmer *Emerging Nations* x. 140 The agenda of external assistance in the economic sphere are cumulative. **1962** [see drink *sb.* 8]. **1963** *Times Rev. Industry* June 3/1 Union agendas are increasingly devoted to industrial and economic issues. **1972** T. Keneally *Chant of Jimmie Blacksmith* i. 2 The epoch-old agenda of ceremonies was kept a secret from all the women. **1975** B. Bainbridge *Sweet William* i. 7 Mrs Walton said she hadn't a spare moment. She had a busy agenda. **1982** *Sci. Amer.* Sept. 45/2 The issue is once again high on the agenda of the West German trade unions.

b. *attrib.*, *as* **agenda-paper**, the paper containing the agenda of a meeting.

1887 *Westmor. Gaz.* 10 Dec. 2/5 (Stanf.), The next business stated on the agenda paper was to sign a petition [etc.]. **1905** *Westm. Gaz.* 24 July 2/2 The Czar..and the Kaiser..are meeting to-day... We are not given the agenda-paper of their conversation.

agendum (ə'dʒɛndəm). [See agend.] = agend 3.

1898 *Westm. Gaz.* 23 Mar. 1/2 A prearranged agendum and precise rules of debate. **1920** *Daily Tel.* 25 May 12/4 To cause the closing of the session before its agendum had been fully dealt with.

agene ('eɪdʒiːn). [Trade-name in U.S.A., f. age *v.* or *sb.* + -ene.] Nitrogen trichloride used in bread-making for improving, stabilizing, and artificially ageing the flour. Hence **ageni'zation**, the addition of agene to flour; **'agenized** *ppl. a.*

1932 *Cereal Chem.* IX. 360 When nitrogen-trichloride, commercially known as 'Agene', is applied to flour..its aging effect is..to be noticed. **1937** Hackh & Grant *Chem. Dict.* (1938) 26/1 *Agene process*, the bleaching of flour with nitrogen trichloride. **1947** *Lancet* 23 Aug. 284/1 Acceptability of bread as an article of food is largely increased by the use of an 'improver'... The one in most extensive use in this country, in America, and in Western Europe is nitrogen trichloride: known commercially as 'agene'. *Ibid.*, Experiments which show that 'canine hysteria' can be produced by feeding dogs on agenised flour. **1949** *Lancet* 22 Jan. 143/2 In 1946, Sir Edward Mellanby showed conclusively that the agenisation of flour rendered it highly toxic to dogs. **1954** *Times* 22 Dec. 3/5 (*heading*) Use of Agene to be Discontinued.

agenesic (ædʒɪ'nɛzɪk), *a.* *Phys.* [f. next + -ic.] Characterized by absolute sterility.

1878 Bartley tr. *Topinard's Anthropol.* II. vii. 369 M. Broca has defined the various degrees of sexual affinity, which he calls: Abortive, Agenesic, Dysgenesic (without offspring); Paragenesic, Eugenesic (with offspring).

agenesis (a'dʒɛnɪsɪs). *Phys.* [f. Gr. ἀ priv. + γένεσις birth.] Imperfect development of the body or any part of it. Also (on Gr. analogy) **agenesia.** (Often confused with agennesis.)

1853 Mayne, *Agenesia*. **1879** *Syd. Soc. Lex.*, *Agenesis* and *Agenesia*.

agennesis (ædʒɪ'niːsɪs). *Phys.* [f. Gr. ἀ priv. + γέννησις engendering.] Male sterility, impotence. Also (on Gr. analogy) **agennesia.**

1847 Craig, *Agennesia*. **1879** *Syd. Soc. Lex.*, *Agennesis* and *Agennesia*.

agent ('eɪdʒənt), *ppl. a.* and *sb.* [ad. L. *agens*, *agentem*, acting, pr. pple. of *ag-ĕre* to act, do.]

A. *adj.* Acting, exerting power, as opposed to *patient*. *arch.*

1620 Melton *Astrolog.* 13 What a hot fellow Sol (whom all Agent Causes follow). **1678** Cudworth *Intellect. Syst.* 55 Aristotle..making it [mind] to be twofold, Agent, and Patient, concludes the former of them only to be Immortal. **1821** De Quincey *Confess.* (1862) 83 Agent or patient, singly or one of a crowd.

B. *sb.* [The adj. used *absol.*]

1. a. One who (or that which) acts or exerts power, as distinguished from the *patient*, and also from the *instrument*.

a **1600** Hooker (J.) Deliberation is..needless in regard of the agent, which seeth already what to resolve upon. **1614** Raleigh *Hist. World* I. 5 For he maketh foure originals, whereof three are agents, and the last passive and materiall. **1646** S. Bolton *Arraignm. Errour* 295 Nor are we to be meer instruments moved by the will of those in authority..but are morall Agents. **1753** Hanway *Trav.* (1762) I. III. xxviii. 118 Our first parents became accountable, because they were free agents. **1809** Tomlins *Law Dict.*, *Agent and Patient*, when the same person is the doer of a thing, and the party to whom done: as where a woman endows herself of the best part of her husband's possessions. **1870** Bowen *Logic* xii. 401 In conformity with this view, the distinction between agent and patient, between something which acts and some other thing which is acted upon, is formally abolished.

b. *Telepathy.* The person who originates the impression received by the percipient.

1882 *Proc. Soc. Psychical Research* I. 119 In Thought-transference..both parties (whom, for convenience' sake, we will call the Agent and the Percipient) are supposed to be in a normal state. **1886** [see percipient *sb.* b]. **1961** W. H. Salter *Zoar* xi. 149 Spontaneous cases [of telepathy] do occasionally occur in which no such connection between apparent agent and apparent percipient can be traced.

2. He who operates in a particular direction, who produces an effect. Of things: The efficient cause.

1656 tr. *Hobbes's Elem. Philos.* (1839) 131 The power of the agent is the same thing with the efficient cause. **1699** Bentley *Phalaris* 155 When the Samians invaded Zancle, a great Agent in that affair was Hippocrates. **1719** De Foe *Crusoe* 31, I was still to be the wilful Agent of all my own miseries. **1722** Wollaston *Relig. Nat.* (1738) v. 83 Nor can I think, that any body has such an idea of chance, as to make it an agent or really existing and acting cause of any thing. **1848** Mill *Pol. Econ.* I. vii. §3 Successful production.. depends more on the qualities of the human agents, than on the circumstances in which they work.

3. a. Hence in *mod. Science*: Any natural force acting upon matter, any substance the presence of which produces phenomena, whether *physical* as electricity, *chemical* as actinism, oxygen, *medicinal* as chloroform, etc.

1756 C. Lucas *Ess. on Waters* I. 81 Water is a most useful agent in chemistry. **1833** Brewster *Nat. Magic* xii. 298 The disintegrating and solvent powers of chemical agents. **1875** J. Dawson *Dawn of Life* vi. 134 The Rhizopods were important agents in the accumulation of beds of limestone. **1880** Geikie *Phys. Geog.* ii. xi. 100 The winds are the great agents by which the moisture of the atmosphere is distributed over the globe.

b. ***Agent Orange*** [see quot. 1970[1]], a mixture of 2,4-D and 2,4,5-T which was used as a defoliant in the Vietnam war; similarly ***Agent White***, etc.

1970 *New Yorker* 7 Feb. 34/1 These went under the names Agent Orange, Agent Purple, Agent White, and Agent Blue—designations derived from color-coded stripes girdling the shipping drums of each type of material. **1970** *Sci. Amer.* May 22/3 Agent White is a 4:1 mixture of the triisopropanolamine salts of 2,4-D and 4-amino-3,4,6-trichloropicolinic acid. *Ibid.* 23/1 Agent Blue is a water solution of sodium dimethylarsinate... It is used mainly against rice. **1972** *New Scientist* 6 Jan. 36/3 It was reported by the Washington Post that more than a million gallons of Agent Orange (the most powerful defoliant used in Vietnam and banned since April, 1970) was being shipped back to the United States... This move still leaves the less toxic Agent White and Agent Blue at the disposal of United States and South Vietnam forces. **1979** *Nature* 8 Mar. 108/3 Although it was subsequently shown that it was the dioxin contaminant..which was teratogenic and not 2,4,5,-T itself, the Bionetics study led the US Government to withdraw Agent Orange from Vietnam.

4. a. Of persons: One who does the *actual work* of anything, as distinguished from the instigator or employer; hence, one who acts for another, a deputy, steward, factor, substitute, representative, or emissary. (In this sense the word has numerous specific applications in Commerce, Politics, Law, etc., flowing directly from the general meaning.)

a **1593** Marlowe *Massacre at Paris* III. iv, Go, call the English agent hither straight. **1596** Shaks. *1 Hen. IV*, I. iii. 165 Being the Agents, or base second meanes. **1607** Topsell *Four-footed Beasts* (1673) 541 Diocletian..was Agent for the Romans in France. **1642** Howell *For. Trav.* 78 Made themselves a prey to their sollicitors and Agents. **1704** *Lond. Gaz.* mmmmxxviii/4 Mr. John Pain, Agent to the Regiment. **1745** Mrs. Delany *Lett.* 362 Agent, that is, rent-gatherer, to the dean. **1818** Miss Mitford in L'Estrange's *Life* II. xi. 22 He..employed a certain Mr. Crabtree as his agent, steward, etc. **1826** Scott *Woodst.* (1832) 189 Since the devil fell from Heaven, he never lacked agents on earth. **1847** Craig s.v., In Scots law, an agent is a solicitor for the Court of Session or other courts. **1882** *Negot. Instr. Act (India)* 40 An agent who signs his name to a promissory note, etc. without indicating thereon that he signs as agent, is liable personally on the instrument.

b. (In full ***Indian agent***.) An official appointed to represent the government in dealing with an Indian people. *U.S.*

1707 *S. Carolina Statutes at Large* (1837) II. 311 Thomas Nairne.. is..appointed the agent to reside among the Indians. **1816** *Register of Officers & Agents U.S.* 62 Indian agents have been allowed from 2 to 8 rations per day in addition to their annual compensation. **1886** Capt. Bell *Report* in *Nation* (1888) 15 Mar. 211/1 There can be but one head to an Indian agency, and the agent should be that head, if discipline is to be maintained. **1901** S. E. White *Westerners* xxxv. 317 He could not recall all the story he had told the Indian agent.

c. Ellipt. for ***road-agent*** (see road *sb.* 12). *U.S.*

1876 *Weekly Calaveras Chron.* (Mokelumne Hill, Calif.) 29 July 3/1 The driver finally succeeded in satisfying the 'agent' that no express box was carried by San Andreas. *a* **1904** S. E. White *Blazed Trail Stories* 152 Nex' time I drives stage some of these yere agents massacrees me from behind a bush.

d. A secret agent; a spy.

1932 W. H. Auden *Orators* III. 108 The agent clutching his side collapsed at our feet, 'Sorry! They got me!' **1946** *Ann. Reg. 1945* 230 Switzerland..had been full of German agents. **1956** A. H. Compton *Atomic Quest* ii. 117 Relaying secret information to Russian agents.

5. Of things: The material cause or instrumentality whereby effects are produced; but implying a rational employer or contriver.

1579 W. Fulke *Heskins's Parl.* 621 The gallowes is no agent or doer in those good thinges. **1591** Shaks. *Two Gent.* I. iii. 46 Here is her hand, the agent of her heart. **1593** Nashe *Christs Teares* 21/1 Not a nayle in it [the Crosse] but is a necessary Agent in the Worlds redemption. **1661** Bramhall *Just Vind.* 43 God doth often good works by ill agents. *a* **1842** Tennyson *Love thou thy Land* x, Nature..Thro' many agents making strong, Matures the individual form. **1878** Jevons *Prim. Pol. Econ.* 26 Whatever thus furnishes us with the first requisite of production is called a natural agent, that is, something which acts for us and assists us.

6. *Comb.* and *attrib.*, as ***agent-noun***, ***word***, etc.

1879 Whitney *Sanskr. Gram.* 374 There is hardly a suffix by which action-nouns are formed which does not also make agent-nouns or adjectives. *Ibid.* 385 Adjectives and other agent-words.

7. Special Comb. **agent-general**, the official representative of a non-sovereign country or state in the capital city of a sovereign state; *spec.* a representative of †(i) the British Crown Colonies (also, the Dominion of Canada) in London; (ii) an Australian State or Canadian (also, formerly, South African) Province in London; (iii) a Canadian Provincial or similar representative in New York and elsewhere.

1833 *Treasury Minute* 26 Mar. (Publ. Rec. Office T 29/339) 711 Altho' Lord Goderich concurs with this Board in the propriety of abolishing the several Agencies for each of these Colonies, his Lordship is of opinion that the duties to be performed..will require that the united agency should consist of two joint agents..instead of one *Agent General. **1845** *Return of Names of Agents for Colonies* 3/3 in *Parl. Papers* XXXI. 1 It is the duty of the Agents-General for the Crown Colonies to follow such directions as they may receive from the Governors of the colonies for which they respectively act, as to the conduct of its affairs in England. **1857** *Epitome of Debates Legislature S. Austral. 1857–8* 8 Sept. 512 Mr Baker asked the Commissioner of Public Works some questions relative to the appointment of an Agent-General and Immigration Agent. **1885** *List of Subscribers, Classified* (United Telephone Co.) (ed. 6) 72 Consuls, etc...Agent-General for the Cape of Good Hope, 7, Albert Mansions, Victoria Street, S.W. **1902** *Encycl. Brit.* XXXIII. 395/2 The self-governing Colonies are.. represented in London by Agents-general, whose duties are mainly of a commercial nature. **1921** *Daily Colonist* (Victoria, B.C.) 26 Mar. 4/1 When the vote for Agent-General's office comes up in the Legislature it is to be hoped that discussion will centre, not so much on the expenditure as on the duties of this London employee of the Government's at this time. **1971** *Stand. Encycl. S. Afr.* IV. 620/1 When..the Boer republics lost their independence.. like the Cape Colony and Natal, they were represented only by an agent-general in London. **1980** *Edmonton* (Alberta) *Jrnl.* 20 Mar. c3/6 He replaces Herbert Pickering, who has been assigned the new post of agent general for the Pacific Rim in Hong Kong... Mr. Pickering will also be responsible for the direction of the Alberta office in Tokyo.

'agent, *v.* [f. the sb.; cf. to *pilot*.] To act as agent in; to carry out as agent. So **'agenting** *vbl. sb.*, the work or duties of an agent.

1637–62 Baillie *Lett. & Journ.* I. 9 The Duke was carefully solicited to agent this weighty business. **1681** *Lond. Gaz.* mdcxlix/2 All Writers to the Signet..and other Persons employed in Writing or agenting. **1751** [see extractor 2 b]. **1818** Scott *Ht. Midl.* xiii. (1829) 105 I'll employ my ain man o' business, Nichil Novit, to agent Effie's plea. **1924** Galsworthy *White Monkey* II. i, A man called Smith..who's done most of the agenting for the German business. **1951** L. Z. Hobson *Celebrity* (1953) vi. 84 The deal had been 'agented' by the author's own brother.

agentess ('eɪdʒəntɪs). *rare.* [f. agent *sb.* + -ess; cf. *poetess*.] A female agent.

1757 H. Walpole *Lett.* (1820) II. 31 (D.) I shall tomorrow deliver to your agentess, Mrs. Moreland, something to send you.

agential (eɪ'dʒɛnʃəl), *a.* [f. late L. *agentia*, or L. *agenti-* stem of *agens* (see agent *a.*) + -al[1]; cf. *essential*, *prudential*.] Of or pertaining to an agent or agency.

1872 F. Hall *False Philol.* 65 Of the same class with them ['*tangential*' and '*exponential*'] is '*agential*,' a word of prime utility, as referring, indifferently, to '*agent*' and to '*agency*.' *Ibid.* 60 To obtain an *agential* substantive complementing the verb *photograph*.

agentive (eɪ'dʒɛntɪv), *a.* and *sb.* *Gram.* [f. agent *sb.* + -ive.] **A.** *adj.* Of or pertaining to a noun or suffix that indicates an agent or agency; also applied to certain verbal cases in some languages.

1903 *Amer. Anthropologist* Jan.–Mar. 26 Syntactical Cases and Appositions [in native languages of California]. Agentive, Subjunctive, Objective, Possessive. **1921** E. Sapir *Lang.* v. 87 The word *farmer* has an 'agentive' suffix *-er* that performs the function of indicating the one that carries out a given activity, in this case that of farming. **1941** E. A. Speiser *Introd. Hurrian* v. 211 Even the agentive verb is always in included position unless accompanied by the proper associative element. **1964** J. Vachek in D. Abercrombie et al. *Daniel Jones* 194 His suggestion that the morpheme /-ə/ forming the comparatives contrasts with the 'agentive' /-ə/.

B. *sb.* An agentive noun or suffix; an agentive case.

1925 E. SAPIR in *Language* I. 49 As Prof. L. Bloomfield points out to me, the agentive *-er* contrasts with the comparative *-er*, which allows the adjective to keep its radical form in -ŋg (e.g., *long* with -ŋ: *longer* with -ŋg). **1965** [see IMPERFECTIVE *sb.* 2]. **1968** C. J. FILLMORE in Bach & Harms *Universals in Linguistic Theory* 24 The cases that appear to be needed include: *Agentive* (A), the case of the typically animate perceived instigator of the action identified by the verb. **1972** L. R. PALMER *Descr. & Compar. Ling.* vii. 143 Much the same is true of the insertion of *by* before NP, for this is nothing more than an instruction on how to form the agentive. **1983** D. L. GOLD in *Comments on Etymology* XII. IX. & X. 37, *-ler* is a suffix used to form agentives from nouns, e.g., *indler* 'surfer', based on the Yiddish noun *ind*.

‖**agent provocateur** (aʒɑ̃ prɔvɔkatœːr). [Fr., = provocative agent.] An agent employed to induce or incite a suspected person or group to commit an incriminating act.

1877 W. DE HORSEY *Let.* 8 Jan. in A. Ponsonby *Henry Ponsonby* (1942) xiv. 324 You may think that I am looking through very coloured spectacles when I attribute..the Bulgarian atrocities to Russian intrigue—that Russian '*agents provocateurs*' prepared the Servian rebellion. **1896** LE QUEUX *Secret Service* viii. 169 It was hinted to an *agent provocateur* that your death would be gratifying. **1923** *Daily Mail* 1 Mar. 8 Constantinople had long been the Mecca of the professional spy and *agent provocateur*.

agentship (ˈeɪdʒənt-ʃɪp). [f. AGENT *sb.* + -SHIP.] The office or function of an agent; agency.

a **1616** ? BEAUM. & FL. *Lover's Prog.* v. i. (R.) So goodie agent! And you think there is No punishment due for your agentship? **1862** F. HALL *Refut. Hindu Philos. Syst.* 214 Hence there exists, in spirit, agentship and non-agentship.

age-old (ˈeɪdʒəʊld), *a.* [f. AGE *sb.* + OLD *a.*] Having existed for an age or ages; very old.

1910 *Sat. Westm. Gaz.* 22 Jan. 6/2 When, with self-knowledge sated, The age-old hand upon its treasure rests. **1937** C. M. ARENSBERG *Irish Countryman* v. 174 The countryman will make his last resort to age-old folk-belief. **1939** D. CECIL *Young Melbourne* viii. 239 Frederic and Emily..found all their age-old hostility towards her melting away.

†**ageoˈmetrical**, *a.* *Obs.* [f. Gr. ἀ- priv. + GEOMETRICAL.] Non-geometrical.

1668 in *Phil. Trans.* III. 686 That the Operations are not to be accounted a-geometrical, because they are not perform'd by the Sole aid of Ruler and Compass.

ageostrophic (eɪdʒiːəʊˈstrɒfɪk), *a.* *Meteorol.* [f. A- 14 + GEOSTROPHIC *a.*] Not geostrophic; *spec.* designating the wind component which when added to a geostrophic wind gives the actual wind.

[**1938** R. C. SUTCLIFFE in *Q. Jrnl. R. Meteorol. Soc.* LXIV. 502 If there is a general vertical motion in a region where the winds are quasi-geostrophic, then there is a non-geostrophic component directed along the horizontal gradient of temperature.] **1948** *Jrnl. Inst. Navigation* I. 54 Having minimised air position errors..it was possible..to make an assessment of the inherent errors of the technique i.e. those due to ageostrophic effects. **1956** *Nature* 7 Jan. 14/2 He first reduced the equations of motion to an approximate but observable form which involved the geostrophic and ageostrophic components of the wind-velocity and the radius of curvature of the isobars. **1963** *Meteorol. Gloss.* (Met. Office) (ed. 4) 9 The ageostrophic wind is of fundamental importance in that it is necessarily associated with convergence or divergence and vertical motion in the atmosphere. **1971** *Nature* 23 July 249/1 King-Hele considered the geostrophic component of the zonally averaged longitudinal wind as the prevailing wind which he observed... However,..this wind component must be rather small due to the large ageostrophic wind component which results from ion-neutral collisions. **1979** *Ibid.* 20 Sept. 190/1 This equation is invalid at fast rotation rates where motions are highly ageostrophic.

†**age-prier**. *Law.* *Obs.* [Anglo-Fr.; f. Fr. *âge* age + *prier* to pray, ask; *subst.* praying, asking; latinized *ætatem precari* or *ætatis precatio*.]

1641 *Termes de la Ley* 14, *Age prier* is when the action is brought against an infant, of lands which he hath by discent, there he shall shew the matter to the Court, and shall pray that the action may stay till his full age of 21 yeares.

ager, obs. or dial. f. EAGER *sb.*, tide, bore.

ager (ˈeɪdʒə(r)). [f. AGE *v.* + -ER[1].] **a.** An ageing apparatus or chamber. Also *attrib.*, as *ager man, minder*. **b.** = ager man. **c.** An inspector of electric lamps.

1907 *Cycl. Textile Work* VI. 126 The steam ager consists of a long chamber containing two series of rolls..over which the cloth can be passed up and down. **1912** KNECHT & FOTHERGILL *Textile Printing* 143 Mather & Platt's Rapid Steam 'Ager'..was brought out in 1879. **1921** *Dict. Occup. Terms* (1927) §308 *Ager, flash ager*; examines electric incandescent lamps, before and after cap is fitted on. *Ibid.* 398 *Ager, ager man, ager minder, age minder, ageing machine minder*..minds ageing machine.

‖**agerasia** (ædʒəˈreɪsɪə). Also **agerasy**. [Gr. ἀγηρασία eternal youth; f. ἀ priv. + γῆρας old age.] The quality of not growing old; non-appearance of the signs of age; a green old age.

1706 PHILLIPS, *Agerasia*. **1721** BAILEY, *Agerasy*. **1775** ASH, *Ageratia*. **1863** GRINDON *Life* vi. (1873) 82 Agerasia belongs only to the soul: this alone lives in perpetuity of youth.

ageratum (əˈdʒɛrətəm, *pop.* ædʒəˈreɪtəm). *Bot.* and *Herb.* [mod.L. *agĕratum*, ad. (by Linnæus) cl. L. *agĕraton*, a. Gr. ἀγήρᾰτον name of a plant in Dioscorides and Pliny, prop. neuter of ἀγήρατος not growing old, f. ἀ priv. + γῆρας, -ατος old age. Formerly also in the Gr. form.]

†**1.** *Herb.* Some kind of 'everlasting' flower, known to the ancients. *Obs.*

1567 MAPLET *Greene Forest* 31 Ageraton..is like Origan or Marigolde. **1601** HOLLAND *Pliny* (1634) II. 271 Ageraton, it is an herb of the Ferula kind..the flowers resemble buttons or brooches of gold. **1706** PHILLIPS, *Ageraton*, an Herb call'd Everlasting; Mothwort, Cotton-weed, or Maudlin. **1753** CHAMBERS *Cycl. Supp.*, *Ageratum* bears a near resemblance to the costmary. **1879** *Syd. Soc. Lex.*, *Ageraton*..was probably the *Achillea ageratum*.

2. A genus of plants (NO. *Compositæ*, Div. *Eupatoriæ*), of which one species (*A. Mexicanum*), with lavender-blue flowers in dense clustered capitules, is a favourite garden annual.

1866 W. THOMPSON in *Treas. Bot.* 30 The *Cœlestina ageratoides*, a half-hardy perennial with blue ageratum-like flowerheads, much employed in bedding, must not be confounded with the true *Ageratums*.

agerdows, Skelton's (*c* 1525) spelling of AIGREDOUX, -CE.

agerse, *phr.* *Obs.*; see AGRASS.

†**aˈgesse**, *v.* *Obs.* *rare*[−1]. [f. A- *pref.* 1 intens. + GUESS, ME. *gesse*.] To reckon on, expect.

a **1300** *K. Horn* 1181 He sede he wolde agesse To ariue in westernesse.

agest; read *a gest* 'in spirit': see GHOST.

c **1230** *Ancren Riwle* 372 Ne beo nout so ouer swuðe agest [*v.r.* igast] þet ȝe uorȝemen þe bodi.

agest(en, obs. f. AGAST(EN *v.* *Obs.*, to terrify.

agestion, obs. variant of EGESTION.

†**aˈget**, *v.* *Obs.* Forms: *Inf.* 1 **a-get-an**. *Pa. pple.* 1 **ageted**, 3 ? **aget, ageet**, 5 **agetted**. [f. A- *pref.* 1 intens. + GET.] To get hold of, seize.

937 *O.E. Chron.*, Ðær læȝ secȝ mæniȝ gárum ageted. *c* **1315** SHOREHAM 119 Tho that mayde was y-gret And wyth a present wel a-geet Fram vader oure of hevene. **1490** CAXTON *Eneydos* xv. 57 A stronge wynde..agetted theym in suche a wyse that they were lyfte vp on hyghe fro the grounde.

†**a-get**, *adv. phr.* *Obs.* [A *prep.*[1] + GET (*jet*) fashion.] According to fashion; fashionably.

a **1440** *Sir Degrevant* 1181 Greyth myn hors on hore gere And lok that thei be gay; That they be trapped a get In topteler and in mauntolet.

†**aˈgete(n, aˈȝete(n**, *v.* *Obs.* *Inf.* 1 **a-ȝéotan** *Pa. t.* 1 **aȝéat**. *Pa. pple.* 1–2 **agoten**. [f. A *prep.*[1] out + *ȝéotan* to pour, cogn. w. OS. *agiotan*, OHG. *argioȥan*, mod.G. *ergieszen*, Goth. *usgiutan*.] *trans.* and *intr.* To pour out, shed.

c **950** *Lindisf. Gosp.* Matt. xxvi. 7 Aȝeatt ofer heafud his. *c* **1160** *Hatton Gosp.* ibid., Aȝeat uppon hys heafod. *c* **1000** *Andreas* (Grein) 1443 Swá þin swát aȝét. *c* **1175** *Lamb. Hom.* 127 Ðer hit [his blood] wes agoten *in remissionem peccatorum nostrorum*.

ageusia (əˈgjuːsɪə). *Med.* [mod.L., f. Gr. ἀ- priv. + γεῦσις sense of taste.] = AGEUSTIA.

1848 in DUNGLISON *Med. Lex.* (ed. 7) 30/2. **1899** *Allbutt's Syst. Med.* VI. 797 Ageusia, therefore, implies either an extension of the neuritis into the Fallopian canal, or, according to some investigators, a concomitant lesion of the fifth nerve, which sometimes shows itself in diminished sensation over the paralysed side of the face.

‖**ageustia** (əˈgjuːstɪə). *Med.* [Gr. ἀγευστία, f. ἄγευστος not tasting; f. ἀ not + γευστός vbl. adj., f. γεύειν to taste.] Loss of the sense of taste.

1853 in MAYNE *Exp. Lex.*

agey (ˈeɪdʒɪ), *a.* *arch.*, var. AGY *a.*

1547 W. SALESBURY *Dict. in Engl. & Welshe* sig. G4[v], *Hoedloc*, agey. **1672** LOCKE *Let.* in B. Rand *Locke & Clarke* (1927) 78 Those are earthly pleasures for clodpate mortals, and we agey men contemn them. **1852** P. J. BAILEY *Festus* (ed. 5) 132 Thee, agey world, thee, universal Heaven.

ageyn, obs. form of AGAIN.

aggat, obs. form of AGATE.

†**aggeˈlation**. *Obs.* *rare*[−1]. [n. of action f. L. *aggelā-re* to stiffen with cold; f. *ag-* = *ad-* to + *gelā-re* to freeze, f. *gel-ū* frost. Cf. *congelation*.] The act of freezing to, or congealing about.

a **1681** SIR T. BROWNE *Pseud. Ep.* II. i. (ed. 1686) 41 Growing greater or lesser according unto the accretion or pluvius aggelation about the mother and fundamental atomes.

†**aˈggenerate**, *v.* *Obs.* [f. L. *aggenerāt-* ppl. stem of *aggenerā-re*, *adgenerāre* to beget in addition.] To beget or generate as an addition.

1660 T. STANLEY *Hist. Philos.* (1701) 335/1 Other things also, incommodious to those which he made, were aggenerated together with them.

†**aggeneˈration**. *Obs.* Also **adg-**. [n. of action f. prec.: see -TION.] The action of generating or producing in addition.

c **1630** JACKSON *Creed* XII. iv. Wks. XII. 29 There have been..additions unto this church without substraction; continual adgeneration without corruption. **1660** T. STANLEY *Hist. Philos.* I. VI. 60 Taking the form of a part (by aggeneration) through the digestive power of the animate body.

‖**agger** (ˈædʒə(r)). [L. *agger*, f. *agger-ĕre* (see AGGEST).] A mound; esp. the earthen mound or rampart of a camp, formed by the earth excavated from the ditch; a technical term of Roman Antiquities, extended to similar ancient works.

1398 TREVISA *Barth. De P.R.* XIX. cxxix. (1495) 938 Agger is an hepe of stones other a token in the hyghe waye. **1724** DE FOE, etc. *Tour Gt. Brit.* (1769) III. 114 Before the Gate is an Agger, said to be the Burying-place of Hengist. **1877** LL. JEWITT *Half-hrs. Eng. Antiq.* 16 A circle of somewhat irregular form..surrounded by an agger and ditch.

ˈ**aggerate** (ˈædʒəreɪt), *v.* ? *Obs.* [f. L. *aggerāt-* ppl. stem of *aggerā-re* to heap up; f. *agger* a heap: see prec.] To heap up. *lit.* and *fig.*

1553–87 FOXE *A. & M.* (1596) 359/2 Aggerating and exaggerating the fault to the uttermost. **1693** W. ROBERTSON *Phraseol. Gen.* 55 To aggerate, or heap together..To aggerate a Tree; *i.e.* to dung a Tree, or heap earth about it.. To aggerate, *i.e.* to quicken pace or going. **1775** ASH, *Aggerate* (not much used).

aggeration (ædʒəˈreɪʃən). [ad. L. *aggerātiōn-em* n. of action f. *aggerā-re*: see prec.] A heaping up; the raising of a heap. In *Archæology* the supposed raising of a mound, as an inclined plane for the elevation and erection of standing or elevated stones, such as those of Stonehenge, etc.

1692 RAY *Diss. of World* v. §1 (L.) By these various aggerations of sand and silt the sea is closely cut short and driven back. **1832** SOUTHEY *Lett.* (1856) IV. 289, I think the stones are more likely to have been raised by mechanical means than by the rude process of aggeration.

†**aggerose** (ˌædʒəˈrəʊs), *a.* *Obs.*[−0] [f. assumed L. **aggerōsus*: see AGGER and -OSE.] Full of heaps; formed in heaps.

1731 in BAILEY; whence in JOHNSON, ASH, etc.

†**aˈggest**, *v.* *Obs.* *rare*[−1]. [f. *aggest-* ppl. stem of *agger-ĕre* to carry to, heap up; f. *ag-* = *ad-* to + *ger-ĕre* to carry.] To heap up.

1655 FULLER *Ch. Hist.* IX. 47 Mountains being only the product of Noah's flood, where the violence of the waters aggested the earth. **1657** TOMLINSON *Renou's Disp.* 700 Aggesting and cohibiting the excrements.

†**aˈggestion**. *Obs.* *rare.* [ad. L. *aggestiōn-em* n. of action, f. *agger-ĕre*: see AGGEST.] A heaping up; accumulation.

1659 HAMMOND *On Ps.* lxxix. I. 397 Graves, which are made by aggestion or casting up of earth. **1684** T. BURNET in Blount's *Nat. Hist.* (1693) 443 Factitious Islands..made ..by accidental Causes, as the Aggestion of Sands and Sandbeds.

‖**aggiornamento** (adˌdʒornaˈmento; æˌdʒɔənəˈmɛntəʊ). [It., f. *aggiornare* to modernize, f. *a* to + *giorno* day.] A process of modernization or of bringing up to date; *spec.* applied to the revision of doctrines, policies, etc., in the Roman Catholic Church initiated by Pope John XXIII at the Second Vatican Council (1962–65).

[**1963** *Times* 4 June 13/1 The Italian word *aggiornamento* aptly signifies the process of adaptation that was to be undertaken [in the Church].] **1963** *New Yorker* 15 June 41 [Pope John] was eighty-one, but he was a man of today in every sense; indeed, the word 'aggiornamento', or bringing up to date, with which his reign will always be associated, itself contains an Italian form of the word 'today'. **1966** *New Statesman* 17 June 867/3 It is certainly absurd to think of a Paris-Moscow axis. The Russians are and will be extremely respectful to the General. They also know that he has been encouraging the *aggiornamento* in popular democracies, particularly in Rumania. **1969** *Daily Tel.* 9 Apr. 18/4 The splendid garb traditionally worn by Princes of the Church is the latest victim of *aggiornamento*. **1970** B. BREWSTER tr. *Althusser & Balibar's Reading Capital* (1975) II. v. 142 The ambiguous example of the Vatican II '*aggiornamento*' is a sufficiently striking proof: the effect and sign of an indisputable evolution, but at the same time a skilful adjustment to history. **1984** P. HEBBLETHWAITE *John XXIII* xiv. 313 On January 25, 1959, John announced not only the convening of the Council but also a synod for the diocese of Rome and the *aggiornamento* of canon law. **1985** *N.Y. Times* 1 Feb. 28/2 Last week another charismatic Pope, John Paul II, called for a general assembly of Roman Catholic bishops to review the results of John XXIII's *aggiornamento*.

agglate, obs. form of AGLET.

agglomerate (əˈglɒməreɪt), *v.* [f. L. *agglomerāt-* ppl. stem of *agglomerā-re*, f. *ag-* = *ad-* to + *glomerā-re* to wind or gather into a ball; f. *glomus -er-is* a clew, clue, or ball. Cf. mod.Fr. *agglomérer*, which may be immed. source of the Eng.]

†**1.** *trans.* To wind or roll into a ball. *Obs.*

1692 COLES, *Agglomerate*, to rowl together. **1721** BAILEY, *Agglomerate*, to roll or wind up into a bottom. [Whence in JOHNSON.]

2. *trans.* To gather together in a rounded mass, to combine mechanically without any adaptation of parts; to cluster or heap together.
1684 tr. *Bonet's Merc. Compit.* VI. 229 The Bloud is eventilated, and the hot particles agglomerated. **1751** JOHNSON *Ramb.* 108 ¶5 If we would know the amount of moments we must agglomerate them into days and weeks. **1873** FARRAR *Fam. Speech* ii. 44 To agglomerate a number of words without inflection or synthesis. **1878** LECKY *Eng. in 18th c.* II. ix. 636 Working men..were agglomerated by thousands in great towns. **1879** G. GLADSTONE in *Cassell's Techn. Educ.* IV. 18/1 It cannot be put into the furnace without being first agglomerated into lumps.

3. *intr.* To collect in a mass. *lit.* and *fig.*
1730 THOMSON *Autumn* 766 The hard agglomerating salts, The spoil of ages, would impervious choke Their secret channels. **1847** J. WILSON *Chr. North* I. 257 The heart and the imagination can agglomerate around them. **1869** in *Eng. Mech.* 7 May 147/3 The heated stratum of air agglomerates to an 'igneous globe.'

agglomerate (əˈglɒmərət), *ppl. a.* and *sb.* [ad. L. *agglomerāt-us*: see prec.]

A. *adj.* Gathered into a ball or cluster, or in *Bot.* into a rounded head of flowers; collected into a mass.
1828 KIRBY & SPENCE *Entomol.* IV. xlii. 155 They are divided into agglomerate ovaries and branching ovaries. **1858** GRAY *Bot. Text-bk.* 395 *Agglomerate*, heaped or crowded into a dense cluster, but not cohering. **1879** G. MACDONALD *Sir Gibbie* III. iv. 73 The sudden dispersion of its [a Scotch congregation's] agglomerate particles.

B. *sb.* [The adj. used *absol.*]

1. A collection or mass of things rudely or loosely thrown or huddled together.
1831 *Edin. Rev.* LIV. 378 A general agglomerate of all facts. **1865** CARLYLE *Fredk. Gt.* I. III. xiii. 216 This Duchy of Cleve, all this fine agglomerate of Duchies.

2. *Geol.* A mass consisting of volcanic or eruptive fragments, which have united under the action of heat; as opposed to a *conglomerate*, composed of waterworn fragments, united by some substance in aqueous solution.
1830 LYELL *Princ. Geol.* (1875) II. II. xxvii. 72 This great overlying deposit..is a white tufaceous agglomerate. **1881** GEIKIE in *Nature* No. 626. 606 The lavas and their associated agglomerates.

agglomerated (əˈglɒməreɪtɪd), *ppl. a.* [f. AGGLOMERATE *v.* + -ED.] Collected into a heap or mass.

1. Gathered into a ball or spherical mass.
1742 YOUNG *Night Th.* IX. 1911 And creations, In one agglomerated cluster, hung. **1858** LEWES *Sea-side Stud.* 259/2 One of my Daisies (*A. Bellis*) brought forth a round mass of fifteen young, agglomerated together into a ball.

2. Collected in a mass or heap; piled together; rudely or loosely united, without any mutual adaptation of parts.
1774 A. CAMPBELL *Lexiph.* (ed. 4) 6 Agglomerated asperities which may obumbrate your intellectual luminaries. **1784** COWPER *Task* III. 472 He builds Th' agglomerated pile. **1878** RAMSAY *Phys. Geogr.* xiii. 207 It is formed chiefly of the agglomerated shells of *Paludina*.

agglomeratic (ə,glɒməˈrætɪk), *a. Geol.* [f. AGGLOMERATE *sb.* 2 + -IC. Cf. *liassic, basaltic*, etc.] Of the nature of a (geological) agglomerate.
1879 RUTLEY *Study of Rocks* xii. 233 The eutaxites of the Canary Islands, and the piperno of Pianura, near Naples, are agglomeratic and banded lavas.

agglomerating (əˈglɒməreɪtɪŋ), *ppl. a.* [f. AGGLOMERATE *v.* + -ING².] Uniting into a hard mass.
1730 [See AGGLOMERATE *v.* 3.] **1869** in *Eng. Mech.* 6 Aug. 440/1 The agglomerating substance must be the 'brai sec.'

agglomeration (ə,glɒməˈreɪʃən). [ad. L. *agglomerātiōn-em*, n. of action f. *agglomerā-re*: see AGGLOMERATE *v.* Cf. mod.Fr. *agglomération*, perh. the immed. source of the Eng.]

1. The action of collecting in a mass, or of heaping together.
1774 T. WARTON *Hist. Eng. Poetry* II. 223 (T.) An excessive agglomeration of turrets..is one of the characteristick marks of the florid mode of architecture. **1850** MERIVALE *Rom. Emp.* (1865) VII. lix. 218 The Jews have grown into a nation by the agglomeration of the worst of men from all quarters. **1874** HELPS *Soc. Press.* ii. 18 The agglomeration of too many people on one spot of ground.

2. A mass formed by mere mechanical union or approximation; an unmethodical assemblage; a clustering or cluster.
1833 CARLYLE *Misc.* (1857) III. 192 Formless, blundering Agglomerations. **1859** JEPHSON *Brittany* xiii. 215 It was an agglomeration of forbidding-looking granite houses. **1866** LIDDON *Bampt. Lect.* viii. (1875) 494 Society is an agglomeration of self-loving beings. **1869** DUNKIN *Midn. Sky* 181 Orion is perhaps the finest agglomeration of stars to be found in any portion of the heavens.

agglomerative (əˈglɒmərətɪv), *a.* [f. L. *agglomerāt-* ppl. stem of *agglomerā-re* (see AGGLOMERATE *v.*) + -IVE.] Of or pertaining to agglomeration, tending to agglomerate or collect together.
1817 COLERIDGE *Poems, etc.* 139 Taylor [is] eminently discursive, accumulative, and (to use one of his own words) agglomerative. **1848** CAR. FOX *Jrnls.* (ed. 2) II. 103 His talents rather agglomerative than original.

agglutinant (əˈgl(j)uːtɪnənt), *a.* and *sb.* [ad. L. *agglūtinant-em* pr. pple. of *agglūtinā-re*: see next.]

A. *adj.*

1. Gluing, cementing; uniting closely.
1684 tr. *Bonet's Merc. Compit.* VIII. 300 A little Lint, with an agglutinant plaster..shuts the hole securely. **1758** LAYARD *Dis. Eye* in *Phil. Trans.* I. 753 Such agglutinant and contracting collyria, as may reduce the distended coats and vessels to their former size.

†**2.** *Med.* Having the property of adhering to the internal organs and making up for waste. *Obs.*
1756 GRAY *Wks.* (1825) II. 192 For which I shall beg you to prescribe me something strengthening and agglutinant, lest it turn to a confirmed phthisis. **1783** P. POTTS *Chirurg. Wks.* II. 388 This want of an agglutinant quality in the blood.

B. *sb.* [The adj. used *absol.*]

1. Any sticky or viscous substance which causes bodies to adhere together.
1752 SIR J. HILL *Hist. Anim.* 297 (JOD.) The ichthyocalla, or isingglass of the shop, famous as an agglutinant.

†**2.** *Med.* A medicine supposed to adhere to and supply the waste of tissue. *Obs.*
1718 QUINCY *Eng. Dispens.* II. 96 Of Agglutinents. **1720** GIBSON *Dispens.* I. (1734) 47 Restoratives..by their peculiar properties termed Agglutinants, or Binders. **1751** CHAMBERS *Cycl.*, *Agglutinants, agglutinantia*, in medicine a species of strengthening medicines, whose office and effect is to adhere to the solid parts of the body, and thus recruit and supply the place of what is worn off, and wasted in the animal actions.

agglutinate (əˈgl(j)uːtɪnət), *ppl. a.* [ad. L. *agglūtināt-us* pa. pple. of *agglūtinā-re* to fasten with glue; f. *ag-* = *ad-* to + *glūtinā-re* to glue; f. *glūten, -in-* glue.]

1. United as with glue; glued or cemented together.
1541 R. COPLAND *Galyen's Terap.* 2 Dj, Is it possyble.. that an vlcere caued may growe togyther and be agglutynate before that the cauyte be replete with flesshe? **1875** GRIFFITH & HENFREY *Micros. Dict.* s.v. *Calymperaceæ*, A delicate membrane agglutinate to the teeth.

2. *Philol.* Consisting of simple or root words combined into compounds, without any important change of form or loss of original meaning, as in *arrow-head-maker, castle-come-down, John-go-to-bed-at-noon.*
1850 LATHAM *Var. Man* 14 Languages, with an agglutinate, rarely an amalgamate inflexion. **1871** EARLE *Philol. Eng. Tong.* §255 These agglutinate forms, including such as *ichave, hastow, wiltu*,.. are found in great numbers.

agglutinate (əˈgl(j)uːtɪneɪt), *v.* [f. prec., or on analogy of vbs. so formed.]

1. To unite or fasten as with glue; to glue, to cement.
1586 BRIGHT *Melancholy* xiii. 69 Sundrye actions being performed, as to attract..to agglutinate, etc. **1599** A. M. tr. *Gabelhouer's Bk. Physic* 22/1 Agglutinate the same, so close that noe ayre can passe through. **1797** PEARSON in *Phil. Trans.* LXXXVIII. 33, I could just agglutinate the powder into one mass. **1863** LYELL *Antiq. Man* App. 534 Conglomerates, in which shells or casts of them are agglutinated together with sand and pebbles.

2. a. *Phys.* To cause to adhere. In an obs. sense, To add as new material repairing waste of tissue.
1620 VENNER *Via Recta* v. 83 Egges..speedily and purely nourish..because of an aptnesse that they have in their substance to be assimilated, and agglutinated to the parts of the body. **1712** tr. *Pomet's Hist. Drugs* I. 199 Moreover Sarcocol agglutinates Flesh. **1743** tr. *Heister's Surg.* 17 To agglutinate and heal wounds. **1836** TODD *Cycl. Anat. & Phys.* I. 513/2 [Lymph] by agglutinating together the fibres and layers causes the hardness which is so perceptible on pressing the diseased part.

b. *Bacteriology.* To cause agglutination or coalescence of (bacteria or red blood-corpuscles). Also *absol.* or *intr.*, to undergo agglutination. Hence **aˈgglutinating** *ppl. a.*; **aˈgglutinable**, **aˈgglutinative** *adjs.*; **agglutinaˈbility**, the quality or property of being agglutinable; **agglutiˈnation**; **aˈgglutinator**; **aˈgglutinin** (also **-inine**), an agent that causes agglutination; **aˈgglutinogen**, a substance present in bacteria or blood cells, which stimulates the formation of agglutinins; hence **aˈgglutinogenous** *a.*; **aˈgglutinoid**, an agglutinin that has lost its agglutinophoric group, but retains the haptophoric group for the cell; **aˈgglutinophore**, a molecular complex of the agglutinins to which their agglutinating property is due; hence **agglutinoˈphoric** *a.*
1896 *Lancet* 19 Sept. 806/2 The 'agglutinines' found in the serum of immunised animals. *Ibid.*, The use of the agglutinative action of human serum for the diagnosis of enteric fever. **1898** *Brit. Med. Jrnl.* 3 Sept. 589/1 Agglutinating or sedimentary properties of serums..their power of causing clumping (agglutination). *Ibid.* 592/2 A. S. F. Grünbaum..pointed out that even inanimate substances ..might be agglutinated by various serums. **1900** *Jrnl. Chem. Soc.* LXXVIII. II. 560 No satisfactory theory [to explain agglutination]..has yet been offered, although Bordet's, that an agglutinating agent (agglutinine) acting upon an agglutinable substance..is regarded as most rational. **1901** *Jrnl. Exper. Med.* V. 361 Any given race [of bacilli] does not necessarily produce the same quantities of the different constituents at different times, and hence the variations of agglutinability, virulence, etc. **1902** *Ibid.* 17 Mar. 289 Ricin, a strong agglutinator. **1903** *Jrnl. R. Microsc. Soc.* Feb. 78 The agglutinative and agglutinogenous functions are subject to the greatest variations. **1903** *Lancet* 4 Apr. 946/1 The existence of the agglutinins was one of the earliest results of modern investigations into immunity. *Ibid.* 946/2 The bacilli may lose their agglutinability,.. viz., their agglutinable substance loses its functional atom-group. *Ibid.*, A higher dilution would sometimes agglutinate when a lower one would not. *Ibid.*, Agglutinins may become converted into agglutinoids. **1904** *Jrnl. Med. Research* Oct. 314 A. JOOS..describes two other complementary agglutinable substances of the bacilli themselves, which he calls α and β agglutinogens. **1915** *Lancet* 13 Nov. 1086/2 The agglutination test..gave a positive result in practically every case of enteric fever. **1947** *Ibid.* 1 Feb. 193/1 The term 'universal donor' was introduced when it was thought there were only two corpuscular agglutinogens. **1947** *Sci. News* IV. 49 Blood grouping has become more and more complex with the discovery of new specific agglutinable (clump-forming) substances. **1948** *Ibid.* VI. 98 When blood of a wrong (incompatible) group is given in a blood transfusion, the unsuitable red cells are clotted together and broken by agglutinins in the patient's circulation. **1950** *Ibid.* XV. 106 In no case did the serum agglutinate the red cells which came from the same blood sample.

3. To combine simple words so as to express compound ideas; to compound.
1830 COLERIDGE *Table Talk* (1851) 67 The Ober-Deutsch was fuller and fonder of agglutinating words together.

4. *trans.* and *intr.* To turn into glue.
1869 in *Eng. Mech.* 30 July 412/1 Alcohol..agglutinates copal. *Ibid.*, Shellac, elemi, and mastic agglutinate [in boiling water].

agglutinated (əˈgl(j)uːtɪneɪtɪd), *ppl. a.* [f. prec. + -ED.]

†**1.** Glued or cemented up. *Obs.*
1599 A. M. tr. *Gabelhouer's Bk. Physic* 104/2 Combure a Hartshorn, in a potters oven, in an agglutinated pot.

2. United or joined as with glue or other sticky substance; cemented together.
1658 SIR T. BROWNE *Pseud. Ep.* II. i, It hath been found in the veins of minerals, sometimes agglutinated unto lead. **1835** KIRBY *Habits & Inst. Anim.* I. xii. 332 Covered with agglutinated particles of sand. **1855** GARROD *Mat. Med.* (ed. 6) 190 Smyrna opium..is made up of agglutinated tears.

agglutinating (əˈgl(j)uːtɪneɪtɪŋ), *ppl. a.* [f. as prec. + -ING².]

1. Gluing together; adhesive; closely uniting.
1664 H. MORE *Myst. Iniq.* xvii. 177 That Mystery which was..intended for the most enduring and agglutinating Cement of all those that are called by his Name. **1788** HOWARD *Encycl.*, *Albumen* is used in collyrium, on account of its cooling and agglutinating quality. **1872** DANA *Corals* ii. 153 The grains become coated by the agglutinating carbonate of lime.

†**2.** *Med.* = AGGLUTINANT A. 2. *Obs.*
1634 T. JOHNSON *Parey's Wks.* 1046 Agglutinating or agglutinative medicine is of a middle nature between the sarcoticke and the epuloticke. **1720** GIBSON *Dispens.* I. i. (1734) 25 Dragon's Blood..is very much in use by reason of its agglutinating quality.

3. *Philol.* (See quot., and cf. AGGLUTINATION 2.)
1866 FELTON *Anc. & Mod. Greece* I. ii. 20 Those [languages] which..express the grammatical relations by connecting other words loosely with the significant elements, constitute another group called the synthetic or agglutinating.

agglutination (ə,gl(j)uːtɪˈneɪʃən). [ad. L. *agglūtinātiōn-em*, n. of action f. *agglūtinā-re*: see AGGLUTINATE *a.*]

1. The action of agglutinating or gluing together; the state of adhesion or cohesion.
1541 R. COPLAND *Galyen's Terap.* 2 Ciij b, The causes that let and hyndre the agglutynacyon. *a* **1655** VINES *Lords Supper* (1677) 402 Reputed Christians and believers, by an outward profession and agglutination. **1802** SMITHSON in *Phil. Trans.* XCIII. 27 The sort of agglutination which happens between the particles of subsided..precipitates. **1878** BELL tr. *Gegenbauer's Comp. Anat.* 83 Some are distinguished by the agglutination of foreign bodies—cemented grains of sand.

2. *Philol.* The combination of simple or root words into compound terms, without material change of form or loss of meaning.
1830 COLERIDGE *Table Talk* 7 May, The Platt-Deutsch was a compact language like the English, not admitting much agglutination. **1869** FARRAR *Fam. Speech* iv. (1873) 125 Agglutination may be described as that principle of linguistic structure which consists in the mere placing of unaltered roots side by side.

†**3.** *Astron.* (See quot.) *Obs.*
1753 CHAMBERS *Cycl. Supp.*, *Agglutination* is used by some Astronomers to denote the meeting of two or more stars in the same part of the zodiac. *Agglutination* is more peculiarly understood of the seeming coalition of several stars, so as to form a nebulous star.

4. That which is agglutinated or cemented together; a mass or group formed by the adhesion of separate things.
1615 CROOKE *Body of Man* 937 Aboue the forehead as farre as to the scaly agglutinations. **1846** GROTE *Greece* II. II. ii. 344 Sparta was..but a mere agglutination of five adjacent villages. **1877** ROBERTS *Handbk. Med.* (ed. 3) I. 50 The formation of thickenings, adhesions, or agglutinations in connection with the membrane.

agglutinative (əˈgl(j)uːtɪˌneɪtɪv, -ətɪv), *a.* [f. L. *agglūtināt-* ppl. stem of *agglūtinā-re* (see AGGLUTINATE *a.*) + -IVE.]

1. Of or pertaining to agglutination; tending to produce adhesion; adhesive, cementing.

1734 R. WISEMAN *Surgery* (J.) Rowl up the member with the agglutinative rowler. **1843** HUMBLE *Dict. Geol.*, *Agglutinative*, that which has the property of causing agglutination.

†**2.** *Med.* = AGGLUTINANT A 2. *Obs.*

1634 T. JOHNSON *Parey's Wks.* 326 The Topick and particular Medicines are Agglutinative.

3. *Philol.* Characterized by agglutination; using it as the ordinary process of word-building.

1652 URQUHART *Jewel* Wks. 1834, 194 Greek hath the agglutinative faculty of incorporating words. **1861** MAX MÜLLER *Science Lang.* viii. 311 The chief distinction between an inflectional and an agglutinative language consists in the fact that agglutinative languages preserve the consciousness of their roots, and therefore do not allow them to be affected by phonetic corruption. **1875** WHITNEY *Life of Lang.* xii. 232 Such words as *un-tru-th-ful-ly* preserve an agglutinative character.

agglutinize (əˈgl(j)uːtɪnaɪz), *v. rare.* [f. L. *agglūtin-* stem of *agglūtin-āre* (see AGGLUTINATE *a.*) + -IZE.] An unnecessary by-form of AGGLUTINATE.

1872 M. B. EDWARDS *Kitty* I. xxiv. 235 'Fool that I was: fool that I am: fool that I shall be,' she said to herself again and again, conjugating the agglutinised verb in all its tenses.

aggot, obs. form of AGATE.

a'ggrace, a'grace, *v. arch. rare.* [f. A *pref.* 11 + GRACE *v.*, in imitation of It. *aggraziare, agratiare*, mod. *aggraziare* to grace; f. *ag-* = *ad-* to + *gratia, grazia*, favour.]

†**1.** *trans.* To favour. *Obs.*

1596 SPENSER *F.Q.* I. x. 18 She graunted: and that knight so much agraste That she him taught celestiall discipline.

2. To add grace to, to grace. *arch.*

1825 WIFFEN *Jerus. Deliv.* (tr. Tasso) XX. cxxiii. (1857) 493 'Unhappy arms! that from the war return With scarce a spot your mistress to aggrace.'

†**a'ggrace**, *sb. Obs.* [f. the vb.] Favour, grace.

1596 SPENSER *F.Q.* II. viii. 56 So goodly purpose they together fond Of kindness and of courteous aggrace.

aggrade (əˈgreɪd), *v. Geol.* [f. AG- + GRADE, after *degrade.*] *trans.* To fill up (a river bed, valley, etc.) with detritus. Also *intr.*, to build up by aggradation. (The opposite of DEGRADE *v.* 6.) Hence **a'ggraded, a'ggrading** *ppl. adjs.*; also **aggra'dation**, the process of raising a surface by the deposition of detritus; whence **aggra'dational** *a.*

1898 T. C. CHAMBERLIN in *Jrnl. Geol.* VI. 524 The degradation of the one furnishes the material for the aggradation of the other. **1902** *Ibid.* X. 758 The alternate depositional and aggradational work..done by the Missouri river. *Ibid.* 759 The channel at present is in a slightly aggraded and apparently still aggrading stage. *Ibid.* 760 The aggradation stage has..been inaugurated by the detour of the river... The present aggrading washes have made a little bottom in the lower twenty rods of the valley. **1904** CHAMBERLIN & SALISBURY *Geol.* (1905) I. i. 2 The deposition of material, whether on the land or in the sea, is aggradation. *Ibid.* 178 Streams carrying glacial drainage are usually aggrading streams. *Ibid.* 184 The stream in flood aggrades its plain, and degrades its channel. **1937** WOOLDRIDGE & MORGAN *Physical Basis Geogr.* xii. 173 Flood alluviation, like aggradation by gravel, is closely linked with the development of meanders. **1946** F. E. ZEUNER *Dating the Past* v. 130 In its course near the sea..a river aggrades during the mild phases and erodes during the cool phases.

aggrandizable (ˈægrænˌdaɪzəb(ə)l), *a.* [f. AGGRANDIZE *v.* + -ABLE.] Capable of being aggrandized.

1864 in WEBSTER.

†**aggrandi'zation**. *Obs.* [f. AGGRANDIZE + -ATION, after words from *-ize* = late L. *-izare*, of Gr. origin.] = AGGRANDIZEMENT.

1663 WATERHOUSE *On Fortescue* 197 (T.) No part of the body will consume by the aggrandization of the other. **1683** E. HOOKER *Pref. Pordage's Myst. Div.* 25 The Aggrandization, as I mai sai, and Exaltation, and veri Glorification of the Prince of Devils.

aggrandize (ˈægrændaɪz), *v.* [f. Fr. *agrandiss-* extended stem of *agrand-ir* (16th c. *aggr-*), prob. ad. It. *aggrandire*; f. *ag-* = *ad-* to + *grandire*, L. *grandīre* to make great; f. *grandis* large. The ending is assimilated to words of Gr. origin with -IZE.]

1. *trans.* To enlarge, increase, magnify, or intensify (a thing).

1634 T. HERBERT *Trav.* 7 (T.) The devil has infused prodigious idolatry into their hearts, enough to relish his palate and aggrandize their tortures. **1656** EARL MONM. *Advt. fr. Parnass.* 48 Making use of the calamities of others, as an instrument thereby to agrandize his authority. **1748** ANSON *Voy.* I. viii. (ed. 4) 110 That no circumstance might be wanting which could aggrandize our distress. **1855** BAIN *Senses & Intell.* III. ii. §11 The whole soul, passing into one sense, aggrandizes that sense and starves the rest. **1868** RUSKIN *Pol. Econ. Art* i. 80 The selfish and tyrannous means they commonly take to aggrandize or secure their power.

2. To increase the power, rank, or wealth of (a person or a state). Often *refl.*

1682 BURNET *Rights of Princes* Pref. 3 For the aggrandizing or maintaining his nephews and kindred. **1780** W. COXE *Russ. Discov.* 22 Every circumstance which contributes to aggrandize the Russian empire. **1800** WELLINGTON in *Gen. Desp.* I. 207 If we aggrandize ourselves at the expense of the Mahrattas. **1872** YEATS *Growth & Viciss. Comm.* 96 Venice was aggrandised by this traffic.

3. To make (a thing) appear greater; to give a character of grandeur to; to embellish, exaggerate.

1687 *Death's Vis.* (1713) Pref. 2 'Tis pleaded, that Religion aggrandizes a Poem. **1775** T. WARTON *Hist. Eng. Poetry* I. 53 Nothing could aggrandise Fingal's heroism more highly. **1779** JOHNSON *L.P., Pope* Wks. 1787 IV. 119 The ship-race, compared with the chariot-race, is neither illustrated nor aggrandised. **1848** H. MILLER *First Impr.* ix. (1857) 144 The scene, though small, is yet aggrandized with much art.

4. To make (a person) appear greater; to exalt.

1753 RICHARDSON *Grandison* (1781) III. xviii. 161 Your pretty imagination is always at work to aggrandize the man, and to lower the babies. **1823** LAMB *Elia* Ser. II. xxiv. (1865) 433 The first thing to aggrandise a man in his own conceit, is to conceive of himself as neglected.

†**5.** *intr.* To become greater; to increase. *Obs.* Cf. Fr. *s'agrandir*.

1646 HALL *Poems* 8 Follies continued till old age, do aggrandize and become horrid. **1704** *Lond. Gaz.* mmmmlxxiv/2 Could not but with Horrour see him aggrandize in Power.

aggrandized (ˈægrændaɪzd), *ppl. a.* [f. prec. + -ED.]

†**1.** Made greater, magnified, really or in appearance. *Obs.*

1722 WOLLASTON *Relig. Nat.* v. 116 Fame and reports may proceed..from small matters aggrandized.

2. Increased in rank or influence; elevated, exalted.

1790 BURKE *Fr. Revol.* 293 Who certainly would not have limited an aggrandized creature, as they have done a submitting antagonist. **1877** *Times* 16 Nov., Austria may dislike the establishment on her frontier of an aggrandized or new Court.

aggrandizement (əˈgrændɪzmənt). Also **aggrandisement**. [a. Fr. *agrandissement* (spelt by Cotgr. 1611 *aggr-*), n. of action f. *agrandir*: see AGGRANDIZE and -MENT.]

1. The action of aggrandizing or exalting in power, rank, or influence; exaltation, advancement.

1656 BLOUNT *Glossogr.*, *Aggrandisement*, a greatning, inlarging, advancement. **1670** G. H., tr. *Hist. Cardinals* II. i. 134 They..give themselves over to the aggrandizement of their Nephews. **1730** BOLINGBROKE *On Hist.* vii. (R.) He projected the aggrandizement of France. **1848** LYTTON *Harold* ix. 278 Enemies..would encounter Tostig in every scheme for his personal aggrandisement.

2. The state or condition of being aggrandized.

1734 tr. *Rollin's Anc. Hist.* (1827) I. Pref. 7 Who looked upon the fall of Jerusalem as their own aggrandisement. **1839** JAMES *Louis XIV*, III. 214 That his success and his aggrandizement were intimately united with those of France. **1871** BLACKIE *Four Phases* i. 7 Utter indifference to worldly aggrandizement.

3. *lit.* Enlargement, increase in size.

1830 LYELL *Princ. Geol.* I. 305 The aggrandizement within the estuaries far more than compensated the losses on the open coast.

aggrandizer (ˈægrændaɪzə(r)). [f. AGGRANDIZE *v.* + -ER[1].] One who aggrandizes or makes great.

1753 HANWAY *Trav.* (1762) II. xv. i. 405 The aggrandizer of religion; a title which he prefixed to his name when he mounted the throne. **1807** W. TAYLOR in *Ann. Rev.* v. 204 The nobleman who..is not the aggrandizer of his family.

aggrandizing (ˈægrændaɪzɪŋ), *vbl. sb.* [f. AGGRANDIZE *v.* + -ING[1].] The act or process of making greater, increasing, or exalting; aggrandizement.

1670 G. H. tr. *Hist. Cardinals* I. iii. 63 How much the Popes have exceeded in aggrandizing of Cardinals. **1783** WESLEY in *Wks.* (1872) IV. 245 His aggrandizing the Psalms ..even above the New Testament.

aggrandizing (ˈægrændaɪzɪŋ), *ppl. a.* [f. as prec. + -ING[2].] Increasing in power or influence.

1879 McCARTHY *Own Times* II. 351 To restrain the aggressive and aggrandizing spirit of Russia.

†**a'ggrate**, *v. Obs.* [ad. It. *aggratare* (Florio):—late L. *aggrātāre*: see AGREE].

1. To please, gratify. (= AGREE *v.* 1.)

1591 SPENSER *Teares of Muses* 406 From whom whatever thing is goodly thought, Doth borrow grace, the fancie to aggrate. **1596** —— *F.Q.* II. ix. 34 And each one sought his lady to aggrate. **1633** P. FLETCHER *Purple Isl.* VII. xxxvii, Their gleams aggrate the sight. *a* **1755** G. WEST *Abuse of Trav.* (1807) 20 But not for liberty they wagen war, But solely to aggrate their mighty lord.

2. To thank, express gratitude to.

1633 P. FLETCHER *Purple Isl.* II. ix, The Island King.. Aggrates the Knights, who thus his right defended.

¶ With these two senses cf. those of GRATEFUL, 1. pleasing, agreeable, 2. thankful.

†**'aggravable**, *a. Obs.* [f. L. *aggravā-re* (see AGGRAVATE *a.*) + -BLE.] Tending to or full of aggravation. (Cf. *peaceable, comfortable.*)

1664 H. MORE *Myst. Iniq.* 112 This horrid reproach against the Person of Christ is still the more aggravable. *a* **1733** NORTH *Exam.* II. v. 407, I have not met with any Thing of the *Genus scandalosum* so aggravable as this.

†**'aggravate**, *ppl. a. Obs.* Also 5-6 **agravate**. [ad. L. *aggravāt-us*, pa. pple. of *aggravā-re* to render heavy or troublesome; f. *ad* to + *gravā-re* to make heavy; f. *gravis* heavy.]

1. Loaded, burdened, weighed down. *lit.* and *fig.*

1471 RIPLEY *Comp. Alch.* in Ashmole (1652) v. xxxix. 157 Theyr pursys, wyth pounds so aggravate. *c* **1510** BARCLAY *Mirr. Good Manners* (1570) A ij, Faynt croked age frayle and oblivious Agrauate with yeres.

2. Loaded with the *exsecratio gravior*; under ecclesiastical censure; excommunicated.

1481 CAXTON *Reynard* (Arb.) 43 Hyt were grete repref to you, my lord the kyng..that men shold saye ye reysed and accompanyed yourself with a cursyd and person agrauate.

3. Made more serious as an offence; heightened or intensified (in a bad sense).

1548 HALL *Chron. Edward V* (R.) A small displeasure doen to you..hath been sore aggrauate. **1649** JER. TAYLOR *Gt. Exempl.* v. §20 The occasions of an aggravate crime. *a* **1733** NORTH *Exam.* I. ii. 93 Obnoxious for High Treason, or most aggravate Practices of Sedition.

aggravate (ˈægrəveɪt), *v.* Also 6 **agrauate**. [f. AGGRAVATE *ppl. a.*; used to render L. *aggravāre*, and replace the earlier AGGREGE. The appearance of the Fr. *ag(g)raver* (a Latinized refashioning of the earlier *agrever*), also adopted in Eng. as *aggrave*, probably helped the prevalence of *aggravate*. See AGGRAVE, AGGRIEVE, AGGREGE.] To make heavy or heavier; hence, to put weight on; to add weight to; to add *apparent* weight or importance, to exaggerate.

I. To put weight upon.

†**1.** *trans.* To make heavy; to load, burden, weigh down; *hence*, to cumber, impede, retard. *Obs.*

1530 PALSGR. 418/2 A folysshe answere may agravate [Fr. *agreger* ou *agrauer*] a mannes mater more than one wolde wene of. **1578** T. N. tr. *Conq. W. India* 252 That they doe not agravate or molest your subjectes. **1598** YONG tr. *Diana* 176 A great greefe aggrauateth the hart that suffers it. **1603** FLORIO *Montaigne* (1634) 147 He was so exceedingly aggravated with travell, and over-tired with wearinesse.

†**b.** To load (any one) *with*. *Obs.*

1573 TWYNE *Cont. Phayer's Æneidos* XI. H h iij b, Drances ..Standes up, and him in wordes doth blame, and aggrauates with ire. [Cf. **1513** DOUGLAS *Æneis* XI. vii. 112 Aggregeing on him wraith. L. *aggerat iras.*]

†**2.** To load or heap anything heavy *upon*. *Obs.*

1583 STUBBES *Anat. Abuses* (1877) 98 If the punishment.. were aggrauated and executed upon the offenders. **1586** T. B. tr. *La Primaudaye's Fr. Acad.* II. (1594) 62 To aggrauate so much the more his iust and fearefull iudgement vpon our heades. **1790** BURKE *Fr. Revol.* 39 In order to lighten the crown still further, they aggravated responsibility on ministers of state.

†**3.** *trans.* To lay to the charge of any one; to bring as a charge or 'gravamen' (*against*). *Obs.*

1626 MEADE in Ellis *Orig. Lett.* I. 329 III. 233 Aggravating it as an act of Rebellion. **1641** BAKER *Chron.* (1679) 80/2 Their spokesman to the King to aggravate his breach of promise. **1678** MARVELL *Corr.* 321 Wks. 1872-5 II. 580 His having appeared at the King's Bench barre, being aggravated as a new crime against him.

†**4.** *absol.* To bring charges (*upon*). *Obs.*

1672 MARVELL *Rehears. Transp.* I. 120 While he aggravates upon Religion..he doth so far alleviate and encourage Debauchery. **1679** JENISON *Narr. Pop. Plot* 39, I love to tread softly on the Graves of the deceased, and therefore shall no further aggravate.

II. To add weight to.

†**5.** *trans.* To add weight or intensity to; to strengthen, increase, or magnify. *Obs.* in gen. sense.

1549 COVERDALE *Paraphr. Erasm. Heb.* vi. 16 Men to aggrauate theyr othe do swere by hym that is greater. **1635** W. AUSTIN *Medit.* 46 All these aggravate the greatnesse of his Humility: and that, aggravates the greatnesse of his Love. **1698** in *Coll. Rec. Penn.* I. 544 Becaus Coll. Quarry, the Judge of the admiralty, aggravats it as an action of y[e] governments.

6. *esp.* **a.** Of things evil: To increase the gravity of, to make more grievous or burdensome; to make worse, intensify, exacerbate.

1597 DANIEL *Civ. Wares* II. xvi, To aggravate thine owne afflictions store. **1610** HEALEY *St. Aug., City of God* 460 Why doe we aggravate our misery? **1756** BURKE *Vind. Nat. Soc.* Wks. I. 10 To introduce new mischiefs or to aggravate and inflame the old. **1788** JOHNSON *Lett.* 143 I. 312 If grief either caused or aggravated poor Queeney's illness. **1824** DIBDIN *Libr. Comp.* 93 To aggravate the terror of his invective. **1875** BRYCE *Holy Rom. Emp.* vi. (ed. 5) 86 Its dangers from foreign enemies were aggravated by the plots of the court. **1880** GLADSTONE in *Daily News* 16 Mar. 2/8 Instead of relieving all estates up to 2,000*l.* he aggravates the duty at 500*l.*

b. Of offences: To make more heinous, or offensive; to increase in offensiveness.

1596 *Edward III*, II. i. 24 That sin doth ten times aggravate itself That is committed in a holy place. **1616** R. C. *Times' Whistle* iv. 1448 Th' offenders greatnesse aggravates th' offence. **1749** FIELDING *Tom Jones* XVIII. vii.

(1840) 262/2 Falsehood will only aggravate your guilt. **1878** GLADSTONE *Prim. Homer* 111 Gross wrong to his mother, aggravated by what follows with himself.

7. To exasperate, incense, embitter (a person); *fam.* to provoke, arouse the evil feelings of.

1611 COTGR., *Aggravanter*, to aggravate, exasperate. **1634** T. HERBERT *Trav.* 93 This aggra[va]ted the Persian king exceedingly to be so bearded. **1748** RICHARDSON *Clarissa* (1811) I. 345 If both were to aggravate her parents, as my brother and sister do mine. **1858** THACKERAY *Virg.* xvii. 134 Threats only served to aggravate people in such cases.

b. To irritate, inflame (physically).

1880 MISS BIRD *Japan* I. 366 With stinging wood smoke aggravating the eyes.

III. To add weight unduly.

8. To make the most of; to represent (a thing) as graver, more serious, or more important; to exaggerate. *Obs.* exc. in extension of 6.

c **1555** HARPSFIELD *Divorce Hen. VIII* (1878) 179 Setting forth and aggravating the great spoil late made in Rome. **1580** BARET *Alvearie* A 231 To Aggrauate and make more then it is, *Exaggerare rem.* **1674** MARVELL *Rehears. Transp.* II. 220, I have not in the least aggravated your sense or words. **1740** in *Col. Rec. Penn.* IV. 441 You have greatly aggravated the number of Servants inlisted by calling them several hundreds. **1876** FREEMAN *Norm. Conq.* III. xii. 251 It was not hard, whenever it was convenient, to insist on and to aggravate the offence.

aggravated (ˈægrəveɪtɪd), *ppl. a.* [f. prec. + -ED.]

†**1.** Heaped up, charged. *Obs.*

1603 GREENWEY *Tacitus, Ann.* IV. vi. (1622) 96 For other things aggrauated against him, he was arraigned.

†**2.** Increased, magnified. *Obs.* in gen. sense.

1548 HALL *Chron. Edw. V* (R.) Small matters aggrauated with heinous names. **1727** THOMSON *Summer* 1121 Follows the loosen'd aggravated roar, Enlarging, deepening, mingling.

3. Increased in gravity or seriousness: made worse, or more grievous; intensified in evil character.

a **1638** MEDE *Wks.* I. xxvii. 117 This Sacriledge or Sacrilegious act committed by Ananias is..partly aggravated by the inexcusableness thereof. **1712** STEELE *Spect.* No. 472 ¶1 A poor Man in the Agony of Pain, aggravated by Want and Poverty. **1810** SOUTHEY *Kehama* I. vii. Wks. VIII. 5 For who could know What aggravated wrong Provoked the desperate blow! **1862** STANLEY *Jewish Ch.* (1877) I. v. 101 Calamities..exhibited here in aggravated forms.

4. *fam.* Exasperated, incensed, irritated, provoked.

1611 COTGR., *Aggravanté*, aggravated, exasperated. **1848** DICKENS *Dombey* 516 'I'm very much obliged to you, Misses Brown,' said the unfortunate youth, greatly aggravated.

aggravating (ˈægrəveɪtɪŋ), *vbl. sb.* [f. as prec. + -ING¹.] The process expressed by the verb AGGRAVATE. (Now mostly gerundial.)

1659 MILTON *Civ. Power* Wks. 1851, 332 To the multiplying and the aggravating of sin to them both. *Mod.* Relieving the pain instead of aggravating it.

aggravating (ˈægrəveɪtɪŋ), *ppl. a.* [f. as prec. + -ING².]

†**1.** Bringing a charge against; accusatory. *Obs.*

1640-4 in Rushworth's *Hist. Coll.* (1692) IV. 250 The Articles of Impeachment..were carried up to the Lords, and a smart aggravating Speech made at the delivery of them.

2. Adding weight, effect, intensity. Usually in an evil sense, Making worse, or more heinous.

1790 BEATSON *Nav. & Mil. Mem.* I. 27 Dragged from their master's house, with very aggravating circumstances.

3. *fam.* Exasperating, irritating, provoking.

1775 ASH, *Aggravating*, exaggerating, provoking. **1825** *Br. Jonathan* III. 383 Say no more, that's enough, rather aggravatin' though, at first. **1865** DICKENS *Mut. Fr.* xv. 381 You're an..aggravating, bad old creature!

aggravatingly (ˈægrəˌveɪtɪŋlɪ), *adv.* [f. prec. + -LY².] In an aggravating manner; in a manner that makes worse, embitters, irritates, etc.

a **1680** R. ALLESTREE 40 *Serm.* (L.) If I had worded this more aggravatingly. **1748** RICHARDSON *Clarissa* (1811) I. vii. 43 My sister aggravatingly held up her hands. **1861** *All Yr. Round* 3 Aug. 447 The aggravatingly wakeful condition of the inhabitants.

aggravation (ægrəˈveɪʃən). Also 5 agrauacion. [Prob. a. Fr. *aggravation* (Cotgr. 1611) ad. L. *aggravātiōn-em*, n. of action f. *aggravā-re*: see AGGRAVATE *a.*]

†**1.** The laying on of burdens, oppression. *Obs.*

1481 CAXTON *Myrrour* III. x. 153 Nature may not suffre.. the sodeyn agrauacions ne griefs, of whiche by their folyes they trauaylle nature.

†**2.** The charging as an offence; accusation. *Obs.*

1647 MAY *Hist. Parl.* I. ix. 112 Severall Members were appointed to present those particular charges..which they all did, making large speeches in aggravation of their crimes. **1675** BAXTER *Cath. Theol.* II. i. 212, I only answer your aggravation of uncomfortableness of their Doctrine.

3. *Eccles.* (See quot.)

1611 COTGR., *Aggravation*..a curse, excommunication, or execration denounced against an obstinate offender. **1751** CHAMBERS *Cycl.*, *Aggravation*, in the Romish canon-law, is particularly used for an ecclesiastical censure, threatening an excommunication, after three admonitions used in vain. *Ibid.* From *Aggravation* they proceed to *re-aggravation*; which is the last excommunication. **1864** KIRK *Chas. the Bold* I. II. iv. 583 The Church was invited..to hurl its interdicts, excommunications, 'aggravations' and 're-aggravations.'

4. A making heavier, graver, or more heinous; the fact of being increased in gravity or seriousness.

1615 T. ADAMS *White Devill* 4 Thus the aggregation of circumstances is the aggravation of offences. **1678** CUDWORTH *Intell. Syst.* 473 Though in way of Aggravation of their crime, it be said, that they also worshipped the Creature more than the Creator. **1801** WELLESLEY *Desp.* 203 None of these evils have been diminished..their daily increase and aggravation are notorious. **1833** I. TAYLOR *Fanat.* §6. 206 Circumstances so unfavourable to virtue.. could hardly admit aggravation. **1851** MARIOTTI *Italy* 11 The consequent aggravation of hard, senseless, suspicious despotism. **1855** *Ess. Intuitive Mor.* 38 Then eternal punishment would be too great for any multiplication or aggravation of sins.

†**5.** Making the most of (in a bad sense); exaggeration. *Obs.*

1628 WITHER *Brit. Rememb.* II. 2173 But, I from aggravations will forbeare. **1699** BENTLEY *Phalaris* Pref. 33 Rhetorical aggravations above the naked and strict Truth. **1743** TINDAL tr. *Rapin's Hist.* II. XVII. 73 It might be thought, Buchanan, who hated the queen, has used aggravation, if what happened afterwards did not too evidently confirm what he said.

6. a. *fam.* The action of exasperating, or irritating. Also, an exasperating or irritating occurrence, situation, etc.; annoyance, difficulty.

1875 L. TROUBRIDGE *Life amongst Troubridges* (1966) 138 Amy and I are both hot-tempered, and I believe I have a talent for aggravation at times. **1880** 'MARK TWAIN' *Tramp Abroad* 614 A..sorely tried American student..used to fly to a certain German word for relief when he could bear up under his aggravations no longer... This was the word *Damit*.

b. (Trouble or disturbance caused by) aggressive behaviour, harassment; cf. AGGRO.

1939 L. GOLDING *Mr. Emmanuel* i. 11 If I should have a son, I should not give him such aggravation. **1969** B. RUBENS *Elected Member* (1980) xiii. 134 Throughout our childhood, it seems the only thing we gave our mothers was aggravation. And not just aggravation, but *such* aggravation. I used to think aggravation was a yiddish word. **1970** C. KERSH *Aggravations of Minnie Ashe* xiv. 196 With my aggravations you'd also use language. **1970** P. LAURIE *Scotland Yard* 287 *Aggravation*, harassment imposed either by the police or criminals on each other. **1971** J. MANDELKAU *Buttons* viii. 112 We'd been getting heavy aggravation from things in our area. **1978** *Times* 21 Jan. 2/3 Members of the public are quite able to make their own claims assisted and guided by department officials without having these people coming in and causing aggravation. **1982** R. FRIEDMAN *Proofs of Affection* vii. 84 She'd had enough aggravation with her over the *Yom Kippur* business. **1984** *Police Rev.* 16 Mar. 531/1 Aggravation emerged into the criminal vocabulary during the Fifties gang wars between Jack Spot and Billy Hill. Meaning to annoy, harass or provoke, it is a misuse of the conventional sense of the word, which, shortened to 'aggro', has travelled far beyond the boundaries of underworld conversation.

†**7. a.** A circumstance that renders more weighty or important. *Obs.* in the general sense.

1653 BAXTER *Saints' Rest* IV. ix. (1662) 745 Consider of the several aggravations of the mercy of the Spirit enabling thee thereto.

b. *esp.* 'An extrinsic circumstance or accident, which increases the guilt of a crime, or the misery of a calamity.' J.

1552-5 LATIMER *Serm. & Rem.* (1845) 351 Not any new indisposition, but one of old standing, though lately increased by fresh aggravations. **1651** BAXTER *Inf. Bapt.* 174 What a hainous aggravation of their sin it is, that they commit it after Baptism. **1791** T. PAINE *Rights of Man* (ed. 4) 135 It is no relief, but an aggravation to a person in slavery, to reflect that he was sold by his parent. **1855** BAIN *Senses & Intell.* II. ii. §11 (1864) 134 Confinement is the chief aggravation of all those impurities.

aggravative (ˈægrəˌveɪtɪv), *a.* and *sb. rare.* [f. L. *aggravāt-* ppl. stem of *aggravā-re* (see AGGRAVATE *a.*) + -IVE.] *adj.* Of or pertaining to aggravation; tending to aggravate. *sb.* That which aggravates or tends to aggravate.

a **1733** NORTH *Exam.* II. v. 319 We rose up to Oates's Plot by a Climax of Aggravatives. **1863** SALA *Capt. Dang.* II. viii. 278 By the endearing aggravative of Jemmy he is..known.

aggravator (ˈægrəveɪtə(r)). [f. AGGRAVATE *v.* + -OR, as if a. L. **aggravātor* agent-noun f. *aggravāre*: see AGGRAVATE *a.*]

1. One who, or that which, aggravates.

1598 FLORIO, *Grauatore*, an aggrauator, a grieuer, a molester.

†**2.** *slang* (also in corrupt form (*h*)*aggerawator*). A greased lock of hair. *Obs.*

1835 DICKENS in *Bell's Life in London* 4 Oct. 1/1 His hair carefully twisted into the outer corner of each eye, till it formed a variety of that description of semi-curls, usually known as 'haggerawators'. **1859** F. FOWLER *Southern Lights* 38 The ladies..are addicted to..strained hair, embellished with two or three C's—aggravators they call 'em—running over the temple. **1860** HOTTEN *Slang Dict.*, *Aggerawators* (corruption of Aggravators), the greasy locks of hair in vogue among costermongers and other street folk, worn twisted from the temple back towards the ear. **1861** *Temple Bar* I. 226 The broad bull neck, and the 'aggerawator' curl.

†**aˈggrave**, *v. Obs. rare.* Also agrave. [a. Fr. *aggrave-r* (earlier *agraver*): see AGGRIEVE.] A by-form connecting AGGRIEVE and AGGRAVATE.

1530 PALSGR. 419/1, I agrudge, I am agraved, *Je suis greuè.* **1612** T. TAYLOR *Titus* i. 12 (1619) 256 When the heart is so aggraved, the whole man is vnfit either for heauenly or earthly exercise.

‖**aˈggrave**, *sb. Obs.* [Fr.] = AGGRAVATION 3.

1725 tr. *Dupin, Eccl. Hist. 17th c.* I. v. 190 An Error, common enough, that Excommunication is not denounc'd till after the Fulmination of the Aggrave.

†**aggravidiˈzation.** *Obs. rare*⁻¹. [n. of action (see -ATION) from assumed vb. *aggravidize*, f. L. *ad* to + *gravid-us* 'heavy, weighted' + -IZE. In loc. cit., perh. an error for *aggrandisation*, though as likely to be an actual formation by the author.] Increase of weight or gravity, aggravation.

a **1641** BP. MOUNTAGU *Acts & Mon.* 404 They..opposed, accused, traduced, persecuted him many wayes, unto death ..no great evidences of any pitifull, mercifull, compassionate disposition, which received an aggravidisation in continuing the same to his name, memory, and succession.

aggregable (ˈægrɪgəb(ə)l), *a.* [f. L. *aggregā-re*: see -BLE.] Capable of being collected into one mass; that may be aggregated *with* (other property).

1570 DEE *Math. Pref.* 2 Their particular Images, by Art, are aggregable and diuisible. **1910** LD. HALSBURY *Laws Eng.* XIII. §253. 204 Property accruing to a deceased person's estate after his death..is aggregated with the other aggregable property passing on the death of such person. **1924** *Westm. Gaz.* 12 Feb., The Parliamentary estates were aggregable with the marriage settlement funds. **1927** *Daily Tel.* 12 Apr. 9/1 Property which is [so] settled..is not aggregable when passing on the death of the life tenant with the other property passing on that death.

aggregate (ˈægrɪgət, -eɪt), *ppl. a.* and *sb.* Also 4-5 aggregat. [ad. L. *aggregāt-us* united in a flock, associated, pa. pple. of *aggregā-re*, f. *ag-* = *ad-* to + *gregā-re* to collect; f. *grex, greg-em* a flock.]

A. *ppl. adj.*

1. *pple.* Collected into one body.

c **1400** *Apol. for Loll.* 16 Aggregat, or gedred to gidre in on. **1471** RIPLEY *Comp. Alch.* in Ashmole (1652) IV. viii. 146 In our Conjunccion four Elements must be aggregat. **1509** HAWES *Past. Pleas.* (1845) 181 Whan in my minde I had well agregate Every thinge that I in hym had sene. **1672** BAXTER *Bagshaw's Scandals* iv. 23 Scarce now to be numbred, any more than drops that are aggregate in a Pond. **1866** ROGERS *Agric. & Prices* I. x. 165 After the Reformation estates became more aggregate and insulated.

2. *adj.* **a.** Constituted by the collection of many particles or units into one body, mass, or amount; collected, collective, whole, total.

1659 EVELYN *Mem.* (1857) III. 116 Were I not an aggregate person, and so obliged..to provide for my dependents. **1685** MORDEN *Geogr. Rect.* 68 Polonia..is an aggregate Body consisting of many distinct Provinces. **1824** DIBDIN *Libr. Comp.* 15 Publications..of which the aggregate total is scarcely to be credited. **1859** *Edin. Rev.* No. 223, 49 Or were they but the representatives of the aggregate Hellenic races? **1876** ROGERS *Pol. Econ.* ii. 2 The aggregate amount of labour expended..is called the cost of production.

b. ***aggregate demand*** (Econ.), the total demand for, or spending on, goods, services, etc., within a particular market; conversely, ***aggregate supply***.

1894 J. N. KEYNES in R. H. I. Palgrave *Dict. Pol. Econ.* I. 541/1 The *aggregate* demand for a commodity in general use. **1899** W. E. JOHNSON in *Ibid.* III. 488/2 The aggregate supply price may be in excess of the aggregate expenses of production. **1936** J. M. KEYNES *Gen. Theory Employment* II. iii. 25 The volume of employment is given by the point of intersection between the aggregate demand function and the aggregate supply function. *Ibid.* iv. 40 A raising of the aggregate demand function, will lead to an increase in aggregate output. **1952** R. A. GORDON *Business Fluctuations* ii. 10 We may..speak of 'aggregate demand' and 'aggregate supply' in describing the forces which lead to changes in the total output of goods and services. **1958** J. K. GALBRAITH *Affluent Society* viii. 92 The immediate..cause of depression is a fall in the aggregate demand..for buying the output of the economy. **1970** C. FURTADO in I. L. Horowitz *Masses in Lat. Amer.* ii. 49 The action of these factors [etc.] ..are bound to...make the pattern of aggregate demand and the structure of aggregate supply compatible.

3. *Law.* Composed of many individuals united into one association.

1625 SIR H. FINCH *Law* (1636) 91 Corporations..whereof some are aggregate of many persons, that is to say, of a head and body: other consist in one singular person. **1771** *Act 11 Geo. III*, xix. in *Oxf. & Camb. Enactmts.* 78 Whether of University or City, aggregate or sole. **1862** LD. BROUGHAM *Brit. Constitn.* xvii. 272 Each chapter is a corporation aggregate, and each person is a corporation sole.

4. *Zool.* Consisting of distinct animals united into a common organism.

1835 KIRBY *Habits & Inst. Anim.* I. v. 164 All the polypes are aggregate animals. **1848** DANA *Zoophytes* iv. 82 Aggregate, when the polyps of a compound zoophyte are united to one another by their sides.

5. *Bot.* Consisting of florets united within a common calyx or involucre, as in scabious, honeysuckle, and valerian. Sometimes of flowers, fruits: Collected into one mass.

1693 in *Phil. Trans.* XVII. 928 Such Trees and Shrubs, whose Flower and Fruit are Aggregate, as the *Ficus.* **1794** MARTYN tr. *Rousseau's Bot.* vi. 67 An aggregate or capitate flower; or a head of flowers. **1845** LINDLEY *Sch. Bot.* (1858) iv. 42 *Lobel's Catchfly*, Flowers aggregate, tufted. **1858** GRAY *Bot. Text-bk.* 395 *Aggregate Fruits*, those formed of aggregate carpels of the same flower.

6. *Geol.* Composed of distinct minerals, combined into one rock, as granite. Cf. B *sb.* 4.

1795 MILLS in *Phil. Trans.* LXXXVI. 40 A compact aggregate substance, apparently compounded of quartz, ochraceous earth, chert, etc.

†**7.** *Gram.* Collective. *Obs.*

1683 DRYDEN *Plutarch* 34 One in the aggregate sense as we say one army, or one body of men, constituted of many individuals. **1756** BURKE *Subl. & B.* Wks. 1842 I. 69 Such as represent many simple ideas united by nature to form some one determinate composition, as man, horse, tree, castle, etc. These I call aggregate words.

8. *absol.* quasi-*sb.* (sc. state, etc.) *esp.* in phr. ***in (the) aggregate.***

1777 RICHARDSON *Dissert. Lang.* 31 Man in the aggregate, is too irregular to be reduced to invariable laws. **1852** MCCULLOCH *Taxation* II. xi. 377 These payments must amount, in the aggregate, to a vast sum. **1973** O. SACKS *Awakenings* (1976) 16 These 'footnotes' sometimes have the form and length of miniature essays, and in aggregate now constitute about one third of the book's length.

9. ***aggregate recoil***: the ejection, from the surface of a radioactive sample, of atoms additional to those which recoil on disintegrating (*B.S.I. Gloss. Terms Nucl. Sci.* 1962).

1919 R. W. LAWSON in *Nature* 13 Feb. 464/2 To the recoil of a compact cluster of atoms of the active matter when one of the atoms contained in it disintegrates with an ejection of an α-particle.. I recently gave the name of 'aggregate recoil'. **1926** —— tr. *Hevesy & Paneth's Man. Radioactivity* vi. 61 Aggregate recoil phenomena can also be observed with preparations in which the polonium was not deposited electrolytically.

B. *sb.*

1. Collected sum, sum total.

1656 tr. *Hobbes's Elem. Philos.* (1839) 77 A cause is the sum or aggregate of all such accidents.. as concur to the producing of the effect propounded. **1846** MILL *Logic* II. vii. §2 (1868) 296 Every such belief represents the aggregate of all past experience. **1877** MOZLEY *Univ. Serm.* v. 120 The general only regards his men as masses, so much aggregate of force.

2. A mass formed by the union of individual particles; an assemblage, a collection.

1650 HOBBES *De Corp. Polit.* 78 A Multitude considered as One Aggregate. **1667** BOYLE *Orig. Formes & Qual.* 30 Agitating water into froth.. that aggregate of small Bubbles. **1758** JOHNSON *Idler* No. 36 ¶9 Four is a certain aggregate of units. **1855** H. SPENCER *Psychol.* (1872) I. II. i. 159 Mind.. is a circumscribed aggregate of activities. **1869** GLADSTONE *Juv. Mundi* v. 134 That marvellous aggregate which we know as the Greek nation. **1878** P. BAYNE *Pur. Rev.* ii. 28 He was an aggregate of confusions and incongruities.

3. *esp. Physics.* A mass formed by the union of homogeneous particles (in distinction from a compound).

1692 BENTLEY *Boyle Lect.* vii. 231 The whole Aggregate of Matter would retain well-nigh an uniform tenuity of Texture. **1704** RAY *Creation* I. 114 Those vast Aggregates of Air, Water, and Earth. **1814** SIR H. DAVY *Agric. Chem.* 9 The chemical elements acted upon by attractive powers combine in different aggregates. **1870** TYNDALL *Heat* vi. §225 Snow.. is not an irregular aggregate of ice particles.

4. *Geol.* A mass of minerals formed into one rock.

1795 KIRWAN *Elem. Min.* (ed. 2) I. 338 Masses of different aggregates inhering or adhering to each other. *Ibid.* 370 Derivatives.. differ from aggregates in this, that the associated ingredients are not visibly distinct. **1830** LYELL *Princ. Geol.* I. 169 To render fit for soils, even the hardest aggregates belonging to our globe. **1869** PHILLIPS *Vesuvius* ii. 36 Pompeii was built on a mass of volcanic aggregates.

5. *Build.* Gravel, sand, slag or the like added to a binding agent to form concrete, tarmacadam, etc.

1881 *Mechanic* §1111. 522 Any waste material of a hard nature may be used as aggregate in making concrete. **1930** *Engineering* 19 Dec. 764/3 The importance of mineral aggregates for concrete. **1933** *Archit. Rev.* LXXIII. 217/1 The solid concrete balustrade has had the aggregate exposed. **1949** P. C. CARMAN *Chem. Const. of Engin. Mat.* xvi. 464 By mixing cement with sand or 'fine aggregate' and broken rock or 'coarse aggregate'.. the resulting concrete is.. stronger than cement itself. **1958** *Daily Mail* 16 July 7/2 Coated roadstone—known as 'tarmac'—which is a mixture of tar or bitumen with aggregates of natural stone or.. slags.

6. *Metallurgy.* (See quots.)

1935 A. SAUVEUR *Metallogr. of Iron & Steel* (ed. 4) i. 8 When an alloy contains more than one of these phases, it is generally referred to as an aggregate. **1958** A. D. MERRIMAN *Dict. Metall.* 3/1 *Aggregate*.. In reference to metals and alloys, the term is applied to mechanical mixtures of two or more phases. Quenched steel, for example, is an aggregate of three phases: solid solution of carbon in gamma-iron, alpha-iron and iron carbide.

aggregate (ˈægrɪgeɪt), *v.* Also 6 **agregate**. Pa. pple. at first **aggregate**, afterwards **aggregated**. [f. AGGREGATE *a.* Cf. mod.Fr. *agréger.*]

1. *trans.* To gather into one whole or mass; to collect together, assemble; to mass.

1509 HAWES *Past. Pleas.* VIII. viii, The retentyfe memory ..must ever agregate All maters thought to retayne inwardly. **1633** T. ADAMS *Comm. 2 Pet.* ii. 1 (1865) 210 The light which lay diffused abroad.. was afterwards aggregated into the body of the sun. **1794** SULLIVAN *View of Nat.* I. 71 The flux, reflux, and currents indisputably aggregated large quantities of matter. **1864** *Spect.* 1406 Population is aggregated in small villages. **1865** GROTE *Plato* I. i. 6 This peripheral fire was broken up and aggregated into separate masses.

2. *refl.* and *intr.* in sense 1.

1855 H. SPENCER *Psychol.* (1872) I. II. vii. 255 The taste of honey aggregates with sweet tastes in general. **1870** PROCTOR *Other Worlds* iv. 107 We see the polar snows aggregating. **1875** DARWIN *Insectiv. Plants* iii. 42, I distinctly saw minute spheres of protoplasm aggregating themselves.

3. *trans.* To unite (an individual) *to* (rarely *with*) an association or company; to add as a constituent member.

1651 *Life of Father Sarpi* (1676) 15 Being a year before that, aggregated to that most famous College of Padua. **1722** WOLLASTON *Relig. Nat.* v. 112 Hard to discern, to which of the two sorts, the good or the bad, a man ought to be aggregated. **1801** T. JEFFERSON *Writings* (1830) III. 456 These people are now aggregated with us. **1860** TRENCH *Serm. Westm.* iii. 22 That great thirteenth apostle, who after the Resurrection was aggregated to the other twelve.

4. *ellipt.* [from sb.] To amount in the aggregate to; to form an aggregate of. (Colloq. Cf. *to average.*)

1865 *Morn. Star* 17 Apr., The guns captured.. will aggregate in all probability five or six hundred. **1879** W. WEBSTER in *Cassell's Techn. Educ.* IV. 132/1 British vessels, aggregating 520,019 tons burden.

aggregate, erroneous for older AGGREGE q.v.

aggregated (ˈægrɪgeɪtɪd), *ppl. a.* [f. prec. + -ED. Preceded by AGGREGATE *ppl. a.*]

1. Gathered into one whole; assembled, collected; collective.

1576 LAMBARDE *Peramb. Kent* (1826) 16 These peoples, being aggregated of so many sundrie Nations. **1646** SIR T. BROWNE *Pseud. Ep.* I. vii. (1686) 20 The aggregated testimony of many hundreds. **1775** JOHNSON *Tax. no Tyr.* 61 Part of the aggregated guilt of rebellion. **1875** DARWIN *Insectiv. Plants* iii. 47 The aggregated masses in many of the cells were re-dissolved.

2. *Zool.* = AGGREGATE *a.* 4.

1846 PATTERSON *Zool.* 27 These Polypes are not separated, but aggregated.

†**3.** *Bot.* = AGGREGATE *a.* 5. *Obs.*

1706 PHILLIPS, *Aggregated Flower.*

aggregately (ˈægrɪgətlɪ), *adv.* [f. AGGREGATE *a.* + -LY².] Collectively, taken together, in the aggregate.

1750 CHESTERFIELD *Lett.* 220 (1792) II. 347 Many little things, though separately they seem too insignificant to mention, yet aggregately are too material for me to omit. **1823** T. TAYLOR (*title*) The Elements of a new Arithmetical Notation.. in which the Series discovered.. for the Quadrature of the Circle and Hyperbola, are demonstrated to be aggregately Incommensurable Quantities.

aggregateness (ˈægrɪgətnɪs). ? *Obs.* [f. AGGREGATE *a.* + -NESS.] The quality of being aggregate; collectiveness, compositeness.

1668 WILKINS *Real Charact.* 34 *Aggregateness*, Train, Troop, Company, Party.

aggregating (ˈægrɪgeɪtɪŋ), *vbl. sb.* [f. AGGREGATE *v.* + -ING¹.] Collection into a mass; gathering, grouping.

1875 DARWIN *Insectiv. Plants* xv. 354 The aggregating process spreads from the glands down the pedicels of the hairs.

aggregating (ˈægrɪgeɪtɪŋ), *ppl. a.* [f. AGGREGATE *v.* + -ING².] Collecting into a mass; forming an aggregate.

1875 WHITNEY *Life of Lang.* v. 83 An aggregating crystal.

aggregation (ægrɪˈgeɪʃən). [n. of action f. AGGREGATE *v.*, as if ad. L. **aggregātiōn-em* f. *aggregā-re*. Cf. L. *congregātio*, and late Fr. *agrégation.*]

1. a. The action or process of collecting particles into a mass, or particulars into a whole; or of adding one particle *to* an amount; collection, assemblage, union.

1564 BAULDWIN *Mor. Philos.* (ed. Palfr.) v. iv, Learning is no other thing but the aggregation of many mens sentences and acts. **1671** J. WEBSTER *Metallogr.* iii. 45 By aggregation and apposition of atoms. **1817** JAS. MILL *Brit. India* I. III. v. 638 By the continual aggregation of one individual case to another. **1875** DARWIN *Insectiv. Plants* vi. 113 The glands were blackened from the aggregation of their protoplasmic contents.

b. *Ecology.* The act or process of organisms coming together to form a group; a group so formed; = ASSOCIATION 12. (See also quot. 1927.)

1905 F. E. CLEMENTS *Research Methods in Ecology* 314. **1912** J. S. HUXLEY *Indiv. in Anim. Kingdom* iv. 110 In the making of Volvox, community-life—mere aggregation—came first, division of labour last. **1927** HALDANE & HUXLEY *Animal Biol.* xi. 235 Aggregation is the joining together of a number of separate units to form a super-unit, as when coral polyps unite to form a colony. **1929** WEAVER & CLEMENTS *Plant Ecol.* i. 3 The individuals come to be grouped, as a result of propagation, a process termed aggregation.

2. The adding of any one to an association as a member thereof; admission, affiliation.

a **1710** BP. BULL *Wks.* II. 555 (T.) The aggregation, or joyning of one's self to the worship and service of the only true God. **1796** W. TAYLOR in *Month. Rev.* XX. 537 The second [book] recounts his aggregation to the society of free-masons.

3. The state of being aggregated, assembled, or united into a whole; aggregate condition.

1646 SIR T. BROWNE *Pseud. Ep.* 10 Their individuall imperfections being great, they are moreover enlarged by their aggregation. **1794** SULLIVAN *View of Nat.* I. 297 The first state of a body, at least chymically considered, is that in which it is in the greatest possible aggregation. **1870** TYNDALL *Heat* v. §176. 143 The phenomena which accompany changes of the state of aggregation.

4. *concr.* A whole composed of many particulars; a mass formed by the union of distinct particles; a gathering, assemblage, collection.

1547 BOORDE *Breuiary* ii. 2 A fatte matter in the browes the whiche be granuluse aggregacions. **1638** CHILLINGWORTH *Relig. Prot.* I. ii. §142. 107 The Church being nothing else but an aggregation of Believers. **1833** BREWSTER *Nat. Magic* v. 106 Small spherical aggregations of siliceous matter. **1863** FAWCETT *Pol. Econ.* I. v. 71 Victoria has.. advanced from an aggregation of isolated settlements to the position of a prosperous country.

aggregative (ˈægrɪˌgeɪtɪv), *a.* [f. L. *aggregāt-* ppl. stem of *aggregā-re* (see AGGREGATE *a.*) + -IVE. Cf. late Fr. *agrégatif, -ive.*]

1. Of or pertaining to aggregation; collective.

1644 JESSOP *Angel of Ephesus* 8 Seven singular starres may signifie seven unites, whether singular or aggregative. **1661** BRAMHALL *Just Vind.* iii. 44 We have heard of late of an aggregative treason.. But never untill now of an aggregative schism. **1833** LYELL *Princ. Geol.* III. 126 An aggregative process like that which takes place in the setting of mortar.

2. Having the tendency to collect particulars into wholes; or particles into masses.

1713 *Notes to H. More's Death's Vis.* 36 That Substance.. shou'd cleave together, or have an aggregative Power. **1800** HENRY *Epit. Chem.* (1808) 227 The aggregative affinity of bodies in promoting chemical union. **1817** COLERIDGE *Biog. Lit.* I. 285 Fancy, or the aggregative and associative power.

3. Having the tendency to unite (oneself) or combine; associative, social.

1837 CARLYLE *Fr. Revol.* I. IV. iv. (1871) 122 Crabbed old friend of men! it is his sociality, his aggregative nature.

4. quasi-*sb.* = AGGREGATE A 8.

? **1792** SPELMAN *Feuds* (R.) Such customs as were in use either before the Conquest, or at the Conquest, or at any time since, in the disjunctive, not in the aggregative.

aggregato- (ægrɪˌgeɪtəʊ), combining form of AGGREGATE *a.*, in which it is used adverbially with another adjective; = AGGREGATELY-, in an aggregate manner; as in *aggregato-glomerate, -gemmate.*

1848 DANA *Zoophytes* vii. 115 Simple or aggregato-gemmate. *Ibid.* 361 Quite simple, ramose or aggregato-glomerate.

aggregator (ˈægrɪgeɪtə(r)). ? *Obs.* [agent-noun f. AGGREGATE *v.*, as if a. L. **aggregātor*, f. *aggregāre.*]

1. One who joins himself to; an adherent.

1533 ELYOT *Castel of Helth* (1541) A iiij, Yᵉ practisis of Isake, Halyabbas, Rasys, Mesue, and also of the more part of them which were their aggregatours and folowers.

2. A collector of particulars; a compiler.

1621 BURTON *Anat. Mel.* II. IV. I. iii. (1676) 230/2 Jacobus de Dondis the Aggregator repeats Ambergreese Nutmegs and all Spice amongst the rest.

†**aggregatory.** *Obs. rare*⁻¹. [f. L. *aggregāt-* ppl. stem of *aggregā-re* (see AGGREGATE *a.*) + -ORY, as if ad. L. **aggregātōrium.*] That which contains collected particulars; a compilation.

a **1500** *Bibell of Geomancye* in Hist. MSS. 1872, 112/2 Here endeth the aggregatorye other the compilatory of Geomancye.

†**a'ggrege, -'edge**, *v. Obs.* Forms: 4–5 **agrege**, **-egge**, 5 **agredge**, **-eage**, **aggregge**, 5–7 **aggrege**, 6–7 **aggredge**, 7 **aggrage**. Also aphet. **grege**. [a. OFr. *agrege-r, -ier* (Pr. *agreujar*):—late L. **aggreviā-re*, f. late L. **grevis* (cf. It. *greve*, Pr. *greu*, OFr. *grief*) for *gravis*, perh. by assimilation to *levis* (Diez). With *aggreviāre, agregier, aggrege*, cf. *abbreviare, abrégier, abridge*; *alleviāre, alegier, allege.* A MFr. form, influenced by *aggravāre*, was *agragier, aggragier*, whence Sc. *aggrage*. See AGGRIEVE and AGGRAVATE, from same L. elements].

1. *trans.* To make heavy; to make dull (the eyes or ears).

1382 WYCLIF *Lam.* iii. 7 He agreggede myn gyues. —— *Is.* vi. 10 Blynde out the herte of this puple, and his eres agregge [**1388** aggrege thou the eeris therof]. —— *Is.* lix. 1 Lo! there is not abreggid the hond of the Lord.. ne agreggid is his ere.

2. *intr.* To be heavy, to be weighed down.

1393 GOWER *Conf.* II. 389 Sacrilegge Which maketh the conscience agregge.

3. *trans.* To make graver, to aggravate.

1382 WYCLIF *Gen.* xviii. 20 The synne of hem is myche agredgyd. *c* **1386** CHAUCER *Parson's T.* 886 The circumstaunces that aggreggen mochel every synne. **1496** *Dives & Pauper* (W. de Worde) II. iv. 113/2 Wycked custome excuseth not synne but it accuseth and aggregeth synne. **1536** BELLENDENE *Cron. Scotl.* (1821) I. 42 To aggrege this importabil cruelte in mair dammaige of our commoun weill. **1663** MACKENZIE *Relig. Stoic* xiii. (1685) 137 [Which] will doubtless aggrage their punishment. **1696**

A. WEDDERBURN *David's Test., Serm.* xvi. 182 That agregges their Torment and their Misery.

4. *intr.* To grow grave, to increase in aggravation.

c **1400** *Apol. for Loll.* 4 In swelk þe synne aggregith bi resoun of þe degre.

5. *trans.* To cause to appear graver or worse, to exaggerate.

c **1386** CHAUCER *Melibœus* 53 His flaterers..empeirèd and agregged muchel of this matere. **1513** DOUGLAS *Æneis* XI. viii. 74 Than with his drede and sle contruwit fere My cryme aggregeis he on this manere. **1566** KNOX *Hist. Ref. Scotl.* Wks. 1846 I. 372 Sche..exponed hir grevous complaint, aggredging the same with many lyes. **1651** CALDERWOOD *Hist. Kirk* (1843) II. 474 These calumneis were published..and aggredged, to stirre up the subjects against the regent. **1668** HONYMAN *Surv. Naphtali* II. (1669) 15 All which this Libeller labours to aggrege. **1676** W. ROW *Suppl. Blair's Autobiog.* xi. (1848) 363 He did [as he could] aggrage Mr. James Sharp's great pains and travels for the good of the Kirk.

6. To allege as a grievance; to charge.

a **1600** *Egerton Pap.* 226 (Halliw.) Neither dyd I euer put in question yf I shoulde do you right, as you appeare to agreage.

7. To load, heap. (Perh. confused with later Fr. *agréger* = L. *aggregāre*. The Latin is *aggerat iras*.)

1513 DOUGLAS *Æneis* XI. vii. 112 Aggregeing on him wraith and malice large.

¶ **Aggrege** seems to have been obs. in Eng. *a* 1500, though retained in Scotland. In 1554 it was so unknown that Tottel changed Lydgate's *agrege* in the following passage to *agregate*, quite a different word. So in mod. Fr. *agréger* is treated as the equivalent of L. *aggregare*.

c **1430** LYDG. *Bochas* III. xx, Some tonges..Whan they perceyue that a prince is meved To agreg hys yre do their busy cure [*ed.* **1554** Tagregate his yre do their busy cure].

aggregometer (ægrɪ'gɒmɪtə(r)). [f. AGGREG(ATION + -OMETER.] An instrument for measuring the rate or degree of aggregation of platelets in a sample of blood, usu. after the removal of red and white cells.

1972 J. R. O'BRIEN in Mannucci & Gorini *Platelet Function* 48 In many ways it is a remarkable test situation in the aggregometer. **1975** DACIE & LEWIS *Pract. Haematol.* (ed. 5) xiii. 385 The aggregometer incorporates a heating block which maintains a temperature of 37°C. **1977** *Lancet* 8 Jan. 101/1 Platelet aggregation was measured in platelet-rich plasma at 37°C by the turbidometric method of Born using a Born-Michal mark-IV aggregometer connected to a pen recorder.

† **a'ggress**, *sb. Obs.* [ad. L. *aggress-us* an attack, f. *aggredi* to approach, attack: see AGGRESS *v.*] Attack, aggression.

1678 HALE *Pleas of Crown* xv. (T.) Not only to mutual defence, but also to be assisting to each other in their military aggresses upon others. **1698** J. NORRIS *Pract. Disc.* IV. 383 Upon the very first Aggress.

aggress (in *Her.*) obs. variant of OGRESS.

a'ggress (ə'grɛs), *v.* [a. Fr. *aggresse-r* (Cotgr.) earlier *agresser*, ad. med. and ? late L. *aggressāre*, freq. of *aggred-i* to approach, attack, f. *ad* to, at + *grad-i* to march, step.]

† **1.** *intr.* To approach, march forward. *Obs.* Hence **a'ggressed** *ppl. a.*; also as *sb.*

c **1575** *Cambyses* in Hazl. *Dodsl.* IV. 172 Behold, I see him now aggress, And enter into place. **1801** *Ann. Reg. 1799* II. 285/2 The aggressed party shall have been properly indemnified for the damages suffered. **1890** J. MIDDLEMASS *Two False Moves* III. iii. 37 Are you the aggressor or the aggressed? **1930** *Observer* 7 Sept. 8/7 The aggressed State would raise loans..but the service of the loans would be guaranteed by the signatory States.

2. *intr.* To make an attack; to set upon; 'to commit the first act of violence; to begin the quarrel.' J. Const. *on.* Also *transf.* (esp. in Psychol. contexts) and const. *against*. Cf. AGGRESSION 3.

a **1714** PRIOR *Ode to Q. Anne* (J.) Tell aggressing France How Britain's sons, and Britain's friends can fight. **1837** J. HARRIS *Gt. Teacher* 290 The only domains on which his empire aggresses. **1851** H. SPENCER *Soc. Stat.* xxi. §8 The moral law says—Do not aggress. **1972** *Jrnl. Social Psychol.* LXXXVII. 94 Subjects who were aggressed against 90% of the time reciprocated less harm than they received. **1973** *Guardian* 31 Jan. 14/1 To show affection to a child who is self-destructive is to aggress to him. **1976** *National Observer* (U.S.) 14 Aug. 12/2 The ultimate negative situation occurs when a parent walks out without telling the child... He feels abandoned, aggressed against, hated.

3. *trans.* To set upon, attack, assault.

1775 ASH, *Aggress, v.t.* to set upon, to attack, to begin a quarrel. **1882** *Sat. Rev.* 25 Feb. 225 Roaring lions to be going about seeking whom they may aggress (the verb, though little used, is strictly in accordance with analogy).

aggressed, bad spelling of AGREST *a.*

aggressin (ə'grɛsɪn). *Med.* Also -ine. [G.; cf. AGGRESS *v.* and -IN[1].] Bail's term (*Archiv f. Hygiene* (1905) LII. 340) for a hypothetical substance which increases the toxic effect of bacteria in the body.

1906 *Johns Hopkins Hospital Bull.* Dec. 406/2 The sterile fluid seeming..to produce conditions favorable for the growth and reproduction of the bacteria..Prof. Bail called it aggressine at the suggestion of Prof. Kruse. **1907** *Chem. Abstr.* 2804 The aggressin exudates of Bail can be separated in two parts by means of dialysis. **1913** DORLAND *Med. Dict.* (ed. 7) 42/2 *Aggressin*, a substance supposed to exist in the body of an infected animal and to hasten or make aggressive the action of the bacilli.

aggressing (ə'grɛsɪŋ), *vbl. sb.* [f. AGGRESS *v.* + -ING[1].] The action of attacking; commencing an attack.

1879 H. SPENCER *Data of Ethics* viii. §52. 139 Whether men live together in quite independent ways, careful only to avoid aggressing.

aggressing (ə'grɛsɪŋ), *ppl. a.* [f. as prec. + -ING[2].] Commencing the attack, assailing.

a **1714** [See AGGRESS *v.* 2]. **1775** ADAIR *Amer. Indians* 380 The aggressing party usually send..a friendly embassy to the other, praying them to accept of equal retribution.

aggression (ə'grɛʃən). [a. Fr. *agression*, formerly *aggr-* (16th c. in Littré); ad. L. *aggression-em* n. of action f. *aggred-i*: see AGGRESS *v.*]

1. An unprovoked attack; the first attack in a quarrel; an assault, an inroad.

1611 COTGR., *Aggression*, an aggression, assault, incounter, or first setting on. **1693** J. OWEN *Holy Spirit* 227 An extraordinary Aggression was to be made upon the Kingdom of Sathan. **1793** T. JEFFERSON *Writings* (1859) IV. 12 We have borne with their aggressions. **1818** SCOTT *Hrt. Midl.* 31 An unjust aggression upon their ancient liberties. **1830** LYELL *Princ. Geol.* (1875) II. III. xliv, The sand drift is making aggressions at certain points.

2. The practice of setting upon any one; the making of an attack or assault.

a **1704** LESTRANGE (J.) There may be also..a conspiracy of common enmity and aggression. **1721** BAILEY, *Aggression*, setting upon. **1776** ADAM SMITH *W.N.* I. Pref. 11 The business of government is to check aggression only. **1799** WELLINGTON in *Gen. Desp.* I. 17 A war of agression against the Company. **1851** MᶜCULLOCH *Taxation* III. i. 410 Hostile aggression and insult must be opposed and avenged. **1868** PEARD *Water-farming* xv. 158 The stock..will be safe from aggression. **1955** *Bull. Atomic Sci.* Mar. 97/1 This is clearly the future reserved for all those who are unable or unwilling to resist Communist aggression or infiltration. **1957** R. N. CAREW HUNT *Guide Communist Jargon* 1 Aggression can be predicated only of imperialist Powers, which is in line with the distinction made in communist theory between 'just' and 'unjust' wars. **1959** *Observer* 19 Apr. 1/4 A 21-nation United Nation General Assembly Committee has voted to delay for three years an attempt to define aggression.

3. *Psychol.* Hostile or destructive tendency or behaviour, held to arise from repressed feelings of inferiority, frustration or guilt. (Except in textbooks not clearly distinguishable from senses 1 or 2.) Also, feeling or energy displayed in asserting oneself, in showing drive or initiative; aggressiveness, assertiveness, forcefulness. (Usu. as a positive quality.)

1912 A. A. BRILL tr. *Freud's Sel. Papers on Hysteria* vii. 160 We no longer deal here with sexual passivity but with pleasurably accomplished aggressions. **1917** GLUECK & LIND tr. *Adler's Neurotic Constitution* (1921) v. 156 The neurotic succeeds in..this new line so skillfully as to manage to set up an aggression which enables him to dominate and torture others. **1918** A. A. BRILL tr. *Freud's 3 Contribs. to Theory of Sex* 22 The sexuality of most men shows a taint of aggression. **1932** S. HERBERT *Unconscious in Life & Art* 153 For the repression rouses the innate tendency to aggression against those who interfere with the original libidinous impulses. **1943** J. S. HUXLEY *Evol. Ethics* iii. 22 Victims of a distorted and hyperactive conscience, charged with aggression which seeks an outlet in attacking in others all those tendencies of which itself bears the unconscious guilty burden. **1960** A. S. NEILL *Summerhill* (1962) I. 20 Well, every child has to have some aggression in order to force his way through life. The exaggerated aggression we see in unfree children is an overprotest against hate that has been shown toward them. **1968** *Listener* 11 Jan. 59/1 So I would say that *Newsroom* is strategically well placed to be a success. It is also being presented with aggression and self-confidence. **1968** A. STORR *Human Aggression* ii. 19 Once we can bring ourselves to abandon the pleasure principle, it is easy to accept the idea that the achievement of dominance, the overcoming of obstacles, and the mastery of the external world, for all of which aggression is necessary, are as much innate human needs as sexuality or hunger. **1984** *Guardian Weekly* 9 Dec. 24/3 They'll need more aggression than they showed in allowing superiority over Coventry City at the weekend to slip away.

aggressive (ə'grɛsɪv), *a.* [f. L. *aggress-* ppl. stem of *aggred-i* (see AGGRESS *v.*) + -IVE. Cf. mod.Fr. *agressif, -ive.*]

1. Of or pertaining to aggression; of attack; offensive.

[Not in TODD 1818, RICHARDSON 1836–55. In CRAIG 1847.] **1824** SYD. SMITH *Wks.* 1869, 468 Jealous of the aggressive pleasantry of more favoured people. **1837** PALMERSTON *Opin. & Pol.* (1852) 362 The only Country in which financial difficulties constitute an obstacle to aggressive warfare. **1876** FREEMAN *Norm. Conq.* I. ii. 36 An aggressive war, as distinguished from mere plundering inroads.

absol., quasi-*sb.* The aggressive (sc. course).

1845 FORD *Handbk. Spain* I. ii. 311 Soult..at once assumed the aggressive.

2. a. Tending or disposed to attack others.

1840 MILMAN *Hist. Chr.* (1875) II. 208 To follow any rigorous impulse from a determined and incessantly aggressive few. **1868** PEARD *Water-farming* xvi. 163 Pike, and perch, the most quarrelsome, and aggressive fish. **1869** SEELEY *Ess. & Lect.* ii. 43 It included warlike and aggressive nations.

b. *Psychol.* Of, pertaining to, or characterized by, aggression (sense 3 above).

1913 A. A. BRILL tr. *Freud's Interpr. of Dreams* iv. 134 In the sexual make-up of many people there is a masochistic component, which has arisen through the conversion of the aggressive, sadistic component into its opposite. **1917** GLUECK & LIND tr. *Adler's Neurotic Constitution* (1921) v. 157 Forms of the aggressive impulse become accentuated through the feeling of inferiority. **1949** KOESTLER *Insight & Outlook* v. 56 A component..of aggressive-defensive self-assertion, has been recognized in laughter. **1950** B. WOOTTON *Test. Soc. Sci.* ii. 8 Aggressive behaviour means physical actions like letting off bombs, or, on a milder scale, giving vent to cross words or looks.

c. Self-assertive, pushful; energetic, enterprising. Chiefly *U.S.* and *Canadian colloq.*

1930 *Vancouver newspaper* (Advt.), Aggressive clothing salesman with ambition, to manage a large..store. Good salary..for the right man. **1956** *Winnipeg Free Press* 19 Jan. 34/1 We require 2 salesmen!..Only aggressive men need apply. **1959** H. E. SALISBURY *Shook-up Generation* xi. 154 'Aggressive group work'..means that instead of sitting in offices..the Youth Board goes out on to the street, finds the youngsters who are in trouble..and begins to work with them right in the neighbourhood. **1966** *Which?* Aug. 268/1 Co-operative Societies are giving private industry an example of aggressive retailing.

3. Of a substance: that attacks another substance; corrosive.

1957 G. E. HUTCHINSON *Treat. Limnol.* I. x. 665 If the pressure of CO_2 in the atmosphere is now raised, more CO_2 will enter the liquid phase and will start attacking any solid $CaCO_3$ still present. Such CO_2 is therefore said to be aggressive. **1978** *Environmental Conservation: Chemicals* (Shell Internat. Petroleum Co.) 6 Where especially aggressive materials are involved it is common practice for the pipes to be protected internally. **1980** *Nature* 1 May p. xxii/3 The Zippette can be used with acids and other aggressive liquids, as well as with organic solvents.

aggressively (ə'grɛsɪvlɪ), *adv.* [f. prec. + -LY[2].] In an aggressive manner; offensively.

1800 *Ann. Reg. 1795* (Dodsley) Hist. 145/1 Unwillingly to act aggressively, in so dubious a case, he proposed a negotiation for peace. **1847** DE QUINCEY in *Tait's Edin. Mag.* XIV. 680/2 Johnson..relied sturdily upon his natural powers for carrying him aggressively through all conversational occasions. **1849** PALMERSTON *Opin. & Pol.* (1852) 479 The impression—that England..never will be found acting aggressively against any other power. **1865** MILL *Represent. Gov.* 35/1 What then prevents the same powers from being exerted aggressively? **1882** STURGIS *Dick's Wandering* I. I. ix. 116 Two gentlemen of an aggressively artistic appearance. **1963** *Publishers' Weekly* 23 Sept. 34/1 An aggressively modern bookstore has been opened in Oxford.

aggressiveness (ə'grɛsɪvnɪs). [f. AGGRESSIVE + -NESS.] The quality of being aggressive; the disposition to attack others.

[Not in CRAIG 1847.] **1859** *Bentley's Q. Rev.* No. 3. 24 To secure Europe from the insatiable aggressiveness of France. **1881** MASSON *Carlyle* in *Macm. Mag.* XLV. 154 His fearlessness and aggressiveness in speech. **1943** J. S. HUXLEY *Evol. Ethics* viii. 68 It appears more than probable that, for instance, certain psycho-physical types are predisposed to callous and tireless aggressiveness.

aggressor (ə'grɛsə(r)). [a. L. *aggressor* n. of agent, f. *aggredi*: see AGGRESS *v.*; cf. Fr. *agresseur*, 16th c. in Littré.] He who sets upon, attacks, or assails another; he who makes the first attack, or takes the first step in provoking a quarrel. Also *attrib.*, as ***aggressor nation, state***.

[Not in COTGR. 1611–50, who renders Fr. *aggresseur*, an assailer or assaulter, hee that gives the onset, or first layes hands on his weapon, to do another violence.] **1678** PHILLIPS, *Aggressour*, an assailer of another, a beginner of a business. **1684** BURNET tr. *More's Utopia* 155 To defend themselves, or their Friends, from any unjust Aggressors. **1701** *Lond. Gaz.* mmmdccxiii/2 The French were the first Aggressors, by seizing all the Boats. **1768** BLACKSTONE *Comm.* I. 259 He may attack and seise the property of the aggressor nation. **1851** MARIOTTI *Italy* i. 44 The Austrian was the aggressor. **1930** S. O. LEVINSON in E.R.A. Seligman *Encycl. Soc. Sci.* (1935) I. 485/2 In both the American Revision and the Protocol an attempt was made to base the definition of an 'aggressor nation' on refusal of arbitration. **1940** KING GEORGE VI in *Times Weekly* 27 Nov. 11/1 My peoples and My Allies are united in their resolve to continue the fight against the aggressor nations until freedom is made secure. **1941** *Spectator* 5 Sept. 225/1 Great Britain, left to face the aggressor States alone..was keeping the enemy at bay.

† **aggresteyne.** *Obs.* A disease of the tail feathers of hawks.

1496 *Bk. St. Albans* iv, Whan ye se your hawke hurte hir fete wyth hir beke: and pullyth her tayle thenne she hath the aggresteyne. [In PHILLIPS, BAILEY, and ASH, with mere reference to the foregoing passage.]

‖ **aggri**: see AGGRY.

† **a'ggrievance** (ə'griːvəns). Also 5–6 **agreuaunce, aggr-,** 6 **agreeuance.** [a. OFr. *agrevance*, n. of action f. *agrever*: see AGGRIEVE and -ANCE.]

† **1.** That which burdens or oppresses; a burden, trouble, or hardship; a grievance. *Obs.*

1440 *Promp. Parv.*, Aggreuauns, *Gravamen, nocumentum, tedium.* **1599** FENTON *Guicciardin* XVII. 781 For remedie of which aggreeuances..the people..determined to resist with their weapons. **1649** BALL *Power of Kings* 2 That..our Kings should Redresse such Agrievances as they should complaine of. **1664** H. MORE *Myst. Iniq.* xvi. 38 Those great agonies and aggrievances of spirit that the true members of Christ are cast into by beholding such abominable practices.

2. The action of aggrieving, troubling or annoying; oppression.

1587 J. HOOKER *Hist. Irel.* in *Holinsh.* II. 172 To the aggreeuance of good subiects, & to the incouragement of the wicked. **1596** B. GRIFFIN *Fidessa* (1876) 28 Vntoward subiect of the least aggrieuance. **1819** FOSTER *Pop. Ignor.* (1834) 4 The aggrievance of things which inevitably continue in our presence.

†**3.** Aggravation. (See AGGRIEVE 3.) *Obs.*

1506 *Ord. Crysten Men* (W. de Worde) IV. xxv. 311 It is also agreuaunce of synne more or lesse of as moche that a man eteth many tymes.

aggrieve (əˈgriːv), *v.* Forms: 4–5 **agreue, agreve,** 5–6 **aggreue,** 6 **agreeue, aggreeue, agrieve,** 6– **aggrieve.** [a. OFr. *agreve-r* to render more heavy or severe:—L. *aggravā-re*: f. *ag-* = *ad-* to + *gravā-re* to load. In 14th c. the Fr. and in 15th c. the Eng. began, after L., to be written *agg-* and finally the Fr. was changed to *aggraver*. See also AGGRAVATE, AGGRAVE, and AGGREGE.]

1. *trans.* To bear heavily upon; to bring grief or trouble to; to grieve, distress, afflict, oppress. Now rarely used exc. in the passive ***to be aggrieved***: to be injuriously affected, to have a grievance or cause of grief.

1330 R. BRUNNE *Chron.* 323 Of þat ilk outrage þe fest þam sore agreued. *c* **1425** WYNTOUN *Cron.* IX. Pref. 38 Elde me masteris wyth hir Brevis Ilke day me sare aggrevis. *c* **1450** LONELICH *Grail* lii. 343 Agreved was he sore Of tydynges that him comen thore. **1514** PACE in Ellis *Orig. Lett.* I. 37 I. 110 Oon thynge doethe aggreve me ryght sore. *c* **1540** tr. *Pol. Verg., Eng. Hist.* (1846) I. 199 They aggreeved the inhabitantes with infinite mischeves. **1670** G. H. tr. *Hist. Cardinals* III. II. 289 They shall not permit the Cardinals to be aggrieved by any body. *a* **1716** SOUTH *Serm.* viii. 11 (T.) Those pains..are afflictive just so long as they actually possess the part which they aggrieve. **1849** MACAULAY *Hist. Eng.* I. 16 Both were alike aggrieved by the tyranny of a bad king.

†**2.** *intr.* To afflict oneself, to grieve, to feel grief. *Obs.*

1559 *Mirrour for Mag.* 442 (T.) My heart aggriev'd that such a wretch should reign.

†**3.** *trans.* To make more grave or serious; to aggravate, exaggerate. (= AGGREGE 3, 5.) *Obs.*

1524 *State Pap. Hen. VIII*, IV. 154 Agrieving somewhat the daungier whiche might ensue. **1541** ELYOT *Im. Gov.* 44 But yet the treason dooen also to me, aggreeueth the trespasse. **1562** ATKINSON in Strype's *Ann. Ref.* xxvi. (1709) 265 Let us therefore never go about to aggrieve the matter, or make it worse than it is. **1590** SOUTHWELL *Marie Magd. Funeral Teares* 195 Want of faith was agrieved with want of all goodnesse.

aggrieved (əˈgriːvd), *ppl. a.* [f. prec. + -ED.]

†**1.** Oppressed or hurt in spirit; distressed, troubled, annoyed, vexed (*with, at*). *Obs.* replaced by *grieved*.

c **1350** *Will. Palerne* 266 Goþ til him swiþe · lest he agreved wex. *c* **1385** CHAUCER *Leg. G. Wom.* 345 A God ne sholde nat be thus agreved, But of hys deitee he shal be stable. **1477** EARL RIVERS (Caxton) *Dictes* 77 He was gretely agreued with suche as helde the same opynyon. **1513** DOUGLAS *Æneis* II. xi. 111 Grete Goddis semand with Troy aggreuit. **1557** SURREY *Æneid* II. (R.) And great gods eke aggreued with our town. **1577** tr. *Bullinger's Decades* (1592) 561 Agreeued at, or ashamed of the thing that they haue done.

2. Injured or wronged in one's rights, relations, or position; injuriously affected by the action of any one; having cause of grief or offence, having a grievance (*at, by*).

1590 MARLOWE *1st Pt. Tambur.* I. i. 1 Brother Cosroe, I find myself agrieved. **1643** MILTON *Divorce* (1851) ii. 25 The agrieved person shall doe more manly, to be extraordinary and singular in clayming the due right whereof he is frustrated. **1790** COWPER *Iliad* I. 757 My mother, be advised, and though aggrieved Yet patient. **1859** T. LEWIN *Invas. Brit.* 61 The Britons were as much the aggrieved as the aggressive party. **1870** BOWEN *Logic* ix. 293 The Catholics had a right to feel aggrieved that these laws should be permitted to remain in the statute book.

†**3.** Injured physically; hurt, afflicted. *Obs.*

1725 BRADLEY *Fam. Dict.* s.v. *Sprain*, Rub and chafe it upon the aggrieved place. **1783** P. POTT *Chirurg. Wks.* II. 278 What disorders the aggrieved part is naturally liable to.

†**4.** Aggravated, exaggerated. *Obs.*

1513 MORE *Richd. III*, Wks. 1557, 62/1 Smal matters agreuid with heinouse names. **1559** *Myrroure for Mag., Gloc.* xxi. 1 Aggreued was also this latter offence, With former matter.

aggrievedly (əˈgriːvɪdlɪ), *adv.* [f. AGGRIEVED *ppl. a.* + -LY[2].] In an aggrieved manner.

1883 R. BROUGHTON *Belinda* xiii, 'I offered to teach it to Sarah,' he says aggrievedly. **1886** R. A. KING *Shadowed Life* vi, He growled as aggrievedly as though it was his wife. **1906** *Daily Chron.* 3 Feb. 4/4 Mr. Manktelow expressed frank incredulity and they went aggrievedly.

†**aˈggrievedness.** *Obs. rare.* [f. AGGRIEVED *ppl. a.* + -NESS.] The quality or state of being aggrieved; the feeling of injury causing grief.

1596 CAREW tr. *Huarte's Trial of Wits* xiii. 234 Through this aggreeuednes, the naturall heat encreaseth.

aggrievement (əˈgriːvmənt). *rare.* [f. AGGRIEVE *v.* + -MENT after *amendment*, etc.] The action of aggrieving; aggrievance.

1847 MRS. GORE *Castles in Air* II. i. 5 Whether Sir Robert went to the grave aware or unaware of the bitterness of his aggrievements.

aggrieving (əˈgriːvɪŋ), *vbl. sb.* [f. AGGRIEVE + -ING[1].] The bringing of grief or trouble upon; giving cause of trouble to; annoying.

1440 *Promp. Parv.*, Aggruggynge, or a-greuynge. *Aggravacio, aggravamen.*

aggrieving (əˈgriːvɪŋ), *ppl. a.* [f. as prec. + -ING[2].] Annoying, vexing; vexatious.

1841 GEN. P. THOMPSON *Exerc.* (1842) VI. 1 Sending spies..with directions to make every aggrieving and wounding report which rancour could devise.

aggro (ˈægrəʊ). *slang.* Also **agro.** [Abbrev. of AGGR(AVATION or AGGR(ESSION + -O[2].] Aggravation, aggression; deliberate trouble-making or harassment (esp. formerly by skinhead gangs: see BOVVER), violence, trouble; annoyance, inconvenience.

1969 BYRNE & FABIAN *Groupie* ix. 70 Grant launched into ..some kind of explanation about the aggressive side of his personality. After speaking about his aggro, as he called it, he shot me an accusing look. **1969**, etc. [see -O[2] a]. **1969** 'TROG' in *Daily Mail* 15 Oct. 18/6 [*Moses Maggot, a racketeer*] 'Legality is all that's necessary in this case [an eviction], Bodger. I have his lease here and it's as full of holes as a crochet tea-towel.'.. [*Bodger, a hoodlum*] 'I 'ate all that legal agro. Makes me feel redundant!' **1970** *Guardian* 14 May 22/4 A leaflet is circulating in London urging skinheads to 'work out your aggro by demonstrating against apartheid and racist sport'. **1971** J. WAINWRIGHT *Dig Grave* 122 That is not our scene, friend... Our thing does not include aggro. **1972** DANIEL & MCGUIRE *Paint House* viii. 83 This didn't stop the gang from searching out provocative situations, looking for 'aggro'. **1975** *Punch* 11 Mar. 478/1, I mean have you ever in your life seen as much aggro around as you see today? Nowadays you can't go in to buy a package of fish fingers without someone snarling at you. **1981** M. GEE *Dying, in Other Words* 103 He had to stop the titters with a bit of aggro, over the next few weeks, a bit of knuckles and a bit of razor. **1984** *Times* 13 Jan. 11/1 A certain amount of agricultural aggro is a regular part of the French way of public life. **1987** *Radio & Electronics World* Feb. 46/1 The last thing we want is aggro on the air; this is supposed to be a hobby and contests ought to be stimulating and enjoyable, not a slanging match!

aggroup (əˈgruːp), *v.* [a. Fr. *agroupe-r* (17th c.) to put into a group; f. *à* to + *grouper* to group, prob. due to phr. *à groupe*. Would be better spelt *agroup*.] *trans.* To form or arrange in a group or groups; to GROUP. Also *intr.* (for *refl.*) (Orig. a term of art.)

1695 DRYDEN *Art of Painting* §132 (R.) They aggrouppe, and contrast each other in the same manner as figures do. *a* **1700** —— (J.) Bodies of divers natures, which are aggrouped (or combined) together. *a* **1760** J. BROWNE *Design & Beauty* (1768) 103 Aggroupe the figures here, and there oppose.

aggrouped (əˈgruːpt), *ppl. a.* [f. prec. + -ED.] Arranged in a group; grouped.

1864 R. F. BURTON *Dahome* I. 219 The King and Fanti cortège then stood aggrouped to the west of the square.

aggroupment (əˈgruːpmənt). Also **agr-.** [f. AGGROUP *v.* + -MENT.] Arrangement in a group or groups.

1862 *Art Jrnl.* June 130 The time is sunset, and the mass of the broadcast aggroupment is in shade. **1864** WEBSTER, *Agroupment.* **1874** BOUTELL *Arms & Armour* iii. 42 The remarkable and celebrated aggroupment or formation known under this term 'phalanx.'

†**aˈggrudge,** *v. Obs. rare*; also 6 **agrudge,** [f. *ag-* (= A- *pref.* 11) + GRUDGE.] To grumble, express dissatisfaction or annoyance.

1470 DK. OF CLARENCE in Ellis *Orig. Lett.* II. 42 I. 136 We ..aggrudgynge of the greate enormyties and inordinate ympositions..newly layd upon you. **1530** PALSGR. 419/1, I agrudge, I am a graved, *je suis greué*, or *je suis couroucé*.

†**aˈggrudged,** *ppl. a. Obs.* Also 5 **aggroggyd.** [f. prec. + -ED.] Dissatisfied, annoyed.

1440 *Promp. Parv.*, Aggroggyd, or aggreuyd, *Aggravatus.*

†**aˈggrudging,** *vbl. sb. Obs.* Also 5 **aggruggynge.** [f. AGGRUDGE *v.* + -ING[1].] Grumbling, dissatisfaction, annoyance.

1440 *Promp. Parv.* 8 Aggruggynge, or a-greuynge. *Aggravacio, aggravamen.*

‖**aggry, aggri.** A word of unknown origin and meaning, applied to coloured and variegated glass beads of ancient manufacture, found buried in the ground in Africa; they closely resemble the *glain neidyr* or adder stone of the Britons.

1819 BOWDICH *Mission to Ashantee* 267 The variegated strata of the aggry beads are so firmly united and so imperceptibly blended, that the perfection seems superior to art. **1876** *Fam. Herald* 9 Dec. 95 Aggry beads..are supposed to be of ancient Egyptian manufacture. **1882** J. E. PRICE in *Athenæum* 11 Mar. 321/1 When the Romans occupied the country [Britain], they brought with them many African slaves who wore necklaces with aggri beads attached.

agh, aghe, obs. forms of AWE, and of OWE.

agha, variant of AGA.

aghast (əˈgɑːst, -æ-), *ppl. a.* Forms: 3–6 **agast,** 6– **aghast.** [Pa. pple. of AGAST *v.* to frighten, affright. The fuller AGASTED is also found. Cf. *roast* (beef), *roasted*. The unetymological spelling with *gh* appears first in Scotch *c* 1425 (probably influenced by *ghast, ghaist, ghost*); it became general after 1700.]

1. Affrighted, frightened, terrified. *esp.* in mod. usage, Seized with the visible or physical signs of terror or horror; struck with amazement. This change of meaning is due to misunderstanding the nature of the word, as if it were *a-ghast*, like *a-sleep, a-float*. Const. *at* (*of* obs.) the object, *with* (*for* obs.) the emotion. Rare and obs. with *inf.* and *lest*.

c **1260** *A Sarmun* in *E.E. Poems* (1862) 1 Wel mow we drede and be agast. **1382** WYCLIF *Luke* xxiv. 37 Thei, troublid and agast (*v.r.* agastid). *c* **1385** CHAUCER *Leg. G. Wom.* 1534 He was agast To love. *c* **1425** WYNTOWN *Cron.* VIII. xvi. 138 Þe scottis men..Ware gretly in þare Hart aghast. *c* **1450** LONELICH *Grail* xii. 404 For of here lyves they were Agaste. **1480** CAXTON *Chron. Eng.* ccxxxii. 251 He was agast lest it shold be ony preiudyce ayenst the pope. **1587** HOLINS. *Chron.* III. 916/2 Be not agast of your enemies. **1667** MILTON *P.L.* II. 616 With shuddring horror pale, and eyes agast. **1711** GREENWOOD *Eng. Gram.* 276 A-gast, affrighted, as it were at the sight of a Ghost. **1783** WATSON *Philip III*, (1793) I. I. 17 The garrison stood aghast at this unforeseen disaster. **1846** PRESCOTT *Ferd. & Isab.* I. x. 427 Their countenances aghast with terror. **1866** MOTLEY *Dutch Rep.* III. ii. 385 The Bishop fell on his knees, aghast at the terrible decree.

¶ *catachrestic.* Ghastly. *rare.*

1850 MRS. BROWNING *Poems* II. 161 Dead things that look aghast By the daylight.

aghastness (əˈgɑːstnɪs, -æ-). *rare.* [f. prec. + -NESS.] The state of being aghast; horror.

1881 *Punch* 14 May 221 Mrs. Vamp..threw the needful expression of hollow aghastness into her eyes.

aghe(n, aȝe(n, obs. forms of OWE *v.*, OWN.

aghen, aȝen, obs. forms of AGAIN.

agher, aȝer, obs. forms of OWNER.

aghful, -li, -nesse, obs. ff. AWFUL, -LY, -NESS.

aghill, aȝel, occ. erroneous form of ATHEL, noble.

aghlich, -ly, obs. forms of AWLY.

aght, obs. f. AUGHT *a.* something worth, worthy; also of AUGHT *sb.*, and EIGHT.

aght(e, aȝte, pa. t. of *agan*: see OWE, OUGHT.

aghtand, obs. form of EIGHTH.

aghtel, variant of ETTLE *v. Obs.*, to intend.

†**ˈagible,** *a. Obs.* [ad. med.L. *agibilis*, f. *ag-ĕre* to do: see -BLE.] Proper or possible to be done; practicable, practical. Also used *subst.*

1613 SIR A. SHERLEY *Trav. Persia* 1, Fit for agible things. **1667** WATERHOUSE *Fire of Lond.* 93 Disarming them of all agible judgment and prudent succour. **1677** GALE *Crt. Gentiles* II. IV. 2 The intermediate objects of moral Prudence are in general al agibles or practicables.

†**aˈgig,** *adv.* prop. *phr. Obs. rare.* [A *prep.*[1] + GIG; cf. *agog*, and *top, tip*.] ? In a tiff, excited.

1797 BRYDGES *Homer Travestie* II. 186 But something set her so agig She sent a monstrous great he-pig That swallow'd ev'ry thing he found.

agila (ˈægɪlə). Also 6 **aguila,** 7 **aguala,** 8 **agala,** 9 **agilla.** [ad. Sp., Pg. *aguila* in *palo de aguila, pao d'aguila* (= wood of a.): see EAGLE-WOOD and AGALLOCH.] A resin or resinous wood: = AGALLOCH, CALAMBAC. Also ***agila-wood.***

1588 Aguila [see CAYOLAC]. **1699** DAMPIER *Voy.* II. I. 8 Pepper, Lignum Aloes, and Aguala Wood. **1727** A. HAMILTON *E. Indies* II. 193 It [*sc.* the Siam Coast] produces much Agala and Sapan-woods. **1846** LINDLEY *Veg. Kingd.* 579 Aloes-wood, Agila-wood, or Eagle-wood. **1871** Agilla [see CALAMBAC]. **1881** *Spons' Encycl. Industrial Arts* 1523 Agar, Agila, Akyaw, Calambak, Eagle-wood, Kayugaru, or Lignum-aloes.

agild, OE. *ǽgilde* without compensation, without exaction of the *wer-gild*; f. Æ- *pref.* + GILD. Quoted by Spelman from the Latin text of the Laws of Ælfred, whence in some later Dicts.

agile (ˈædʒɪl, -aɪl), *a.* Also 6–7 **agill,** 7 **agil.** [a. Fr. *agile* (14th c.) ad. L. *agil-is*, f. *ag-ĕre* to do. A by-form was AGILIOUS.] Having the faculty of quick motion; nimble, active, ready.

c **1577** NORTHBROOKE *Dicing* (1843) 52 To make one more freshe and agilite [? agile], to prosecute his good and godly affaires. **1581** W. STAFFORD *Exam. Compl.* I. (1876) 23 Wee be not so agill and light as fowles & Byrdes. **1592** SHAKS. *Rom. & Jul.* III. i. 171 His agile arme, beats downe their fatall points. **1677** HALE *Prim. Orig. Man.* 3 The exercise of the Intellective Faculty makes it agil, quick, and lively. **1766** H. BROOKE *Fool of Qual.* (1859) I. 5 He cast it from him with a sudden agile jerk. **1844** THIRLWALL *Greece* VIII. lxi. 96 The advantages of a robust and agile frame. **1872** BLACKIE *Lays of Highl.* 156 Whose agile tongue doth flit From theme to theme with change of wordy war.

†**2.** Easily moved. *Obs.*

1694 WESTMACOTT *Script. Herb.* 80 All agree that it [Gophir] was a solid, light, agile wood.

agilely ('ædʒɪllɪ, -aɪllɪ), *adv.* [f. AGILE *a.* + -LY^{2}.] In an agile manner; with agility; nimbly.

1866 *Cornh. Mag.* Mar. 311 Striding grandly from tuft to tuft, splashing into soft places, lighting agilely on boulders.

†'**agileness.** *Obs.*$^{-0}$ [f. AGILE *a.* + -NESS.] 'Nimbleness, activity.' Bailey 1731; whence in J.

agiler, variant of AGUILER. *Obs.*, a deceiver.

†**a'gilious**, *a. Obs. rare*$^{-1}$. [f. L. *agili-s* (see AGILE) + -OUS. *-ous* is not now added as a formative to L. adjs. in *-lis*, though appended to other *i*-stems, as *capaci-ous*, *feroci-ous*, *alacri-ous*.] = AGILE.

1599 SILVER *Parad. Def.* in *N. & Q.* Ser. v. IV. 42 Apt bodies, both strong and agilious.

agility (ə'dʒɪlɪtɪ). Forms: 5 **agilite**, 5–6 **agylyte, -ie**, 6 **agilitie**, 6– **agility**. [a. Fr. *agilité* (14th c.) ad. L. *agilitāt-em*, f. *agilis*: see AGILE.] The quality of being agile; readiness for motion; nimbleness, activity, dexterity in motion.

1413 LYDG. *Pylgr. Sowle* v. iii. (1483) 94 Subtilite Clerte Inpassibilite and agylyte ben cleped the dowerys of the body. **1483** CAXTON *G.L.* i. 3 Agilite and lightnes of theyr bodyes. **1533** MORE *Apol.* ix. Wks. 1557, 863/2 Gyftes of nature..as wytte, bewtye, strengthe, agylytie. **1597** MORLEY *Introd. Music* 150 With a quicke hand playing vpon an instrument, shewing in voluntarie the agilitie of his fingers. **1605** BACON *Adv. Learn.* I. vii. §3 They..trust to the agilitie of their wit. **1646** SIR T. BROWNE *Pseud. Ep.* II. iv. (1686) 60 Which motion is performed by the breath of the effluvium issuing with agility. **1791** COWPER *Iliad* XI. 806 In my limbs No longer lives the agility of youth. **1801** STRUTT *Sports & Past.* Introd. 2. Exertions requiring strength and agility of body.

agilte, variant of AGUILT *v. Obs.*, to sin, wrong

†**agin(ne**, *v. Obs.* For forms see BE-GIN. [for earlier *an-ginnan*, *on-ginnan*, also found in same sense: see ONGIN, and A- *pref.* 2. Afterwards aphetized to GIN of which the pa. t. *gan* became a frequent auxiliary.] To begin.

c **1000** *O.E. Gosp.* Mark vi. 7, & agan hí sendan twám & twám. *c* **1160** *Hatton Gosp.* ibid., & angan hyo sænden twam & twam. **1205** LAYAM. 18761 Oðere weies þu most agunnen [**1250** agynne]: ȝef þu hire wult awinnen. *c* **1230** *Ancren Riwle* 74 Ne aginne hit neuer so wel. *c* **1302** *Pol. Songs* 189 The Flemmysshe..Agynneth to clynken huere basyns of bras. **1340** *Ayenb.* 197 Huo þet wile riȝtuolliche do elmesse, he ssel beuore aginne at himzelue.

agin (ə'gɪn), *prep.* Widespread dialectal var. AGAIN *prep.* (= against) and AGAINST *prep.*, often used jocularly and esp. in phr. ***agin the government***, taken to represent the typical Irishman's or countryman's attitude in politics.

1823 E. MOOR *Suffolk Words* 5 'A struv agin um as long as 'a could. **1841** LEVER *C. O'Malley* iii, 'Have ye a great spite agin him?' 'I have,' said I fiercely. **1847** *Sporting Life* 23 Oct. 114/1 A pound to a hay-seed agin' the bay. **1878** W. S. GILBERT *H.M.S. Pinafore* II. 26 I'm unpleasant to look at, and my name's agin me. **1888** *Nation* (N.Y.) 2 Aug. 81/3 It was as natural for them to support the party in power..as it was for the 'Pat' of the anecdote to reply, when asked on landing which party he belonged to: 'I'm ag'in the gover'mint.' **1904** *Athenæum* 5 Nov. 615 He was by nature 'agin' the Government'. **1920** GALSWORTHY *In Chancery* II. xii, Possession, vested rights; and anyone 'agin' 'em—outcast. 'Thank Heaven!' he thought, 'I always felt "agin" 'em, anyway!' **1920** *Punch* 21 July 53/1 To compel the poor thing [*sc.* the motor car] to crawl is 'agin natur". **1960** *Guardian* 4 Nov. 14/3 The Kennedy crowds..are noticeably..people who are agin the Government. **1961** *New Statesman* 28 Apr. 656/3 Ashington has one other grievance agin the government. 'Why don't they encourage light industry to come yere?' **1963** *Listener* 17 Jan. 120/2 The real breeder, the chap with green fingers for dealing with living things, knows that artificial insemination is 'agin nature'.

agin (ə'gɪn), *adv.* Dial. var. of AGAIN *adv.* (= once more). Cf. AGIN *prep.*

1815 D. HUMPHREYS *Yankey in Eng.* III. 58 They were done over agin, no longer than half an hour ago. **1892** 'MARK TWAIN' *Amer. Claimant* viii. 67 Blame my skin if I hain't gone en forgit dat name agin! **1906** E. DYSON *Fact'ry 'Ands* viii. 92 D'yeh mean t' tell me how Hoggy's let you loose agin after you gettin' glorious in his dry-goods, 'n' makin' his name mud all up 'n' down ther town? **1935** Z. N. HURSTON *Mules & Men* I. ix. 197 De Devil broke a anchor cable. Jack took it and broke it agin.

†'**aginate**, *v. Obs.*$^{-0}$ [f. late L. *agīnāt-* ppl. stem of *agīnā-re* to trade; f. *agīna* the tongue of a balance.] 'To retaile small wares.' Cockeram.

†'**aginator.** *Obs.*$^{-0}$ [a. late L. *agīnātōr* i.e. qui parvo lucro movetur: n. of agent f. *agīnā-re*: see prec.] 'He which retaileth.' Cockeram 1626.

†**a'ginning**, *vbl. sb. Obs.* [f. AGIN + -ING^{1}.] Beginning.

1340 *Ayenb.* 16 Prede..wes þe verste ȝenne, and þe aginninge of alle kueade. *Ibid.* 32 Ne may þe sleawolle habbe guod aginnynge oþer amendement.

agio ('ædʒɪəʊ, 'eɪdʒɪəʊ). [a. It. *agio*, *aggio* ease, convenience.]

1. The percentage of charge made for the exchange of paper-money into cash, or for the exchange of a less valuable metallic currency into one more valuable; hence, the excess value of one currency over another.

1682 SCARLETT *Stile of Exch.* 3 One party allows the other a certain profit upon the certain species he desireth; and that profit is called by the Italians Aggio. **1776** ADAM SMITH *W.N.* I. II. ii. 330 Bank money..bears an agio of four or five per cent. **1860** ELLICOTT *Life of our Lord* vii. 293 The agio exacted in changing common money into sacred, or the shekel into two half-shekels was great. **1875** JEVONS *Money* viii. 72 Yet an agio, or allowance, being made for the average depreciation, the old standard of value and money of account may be retained.

2. *loosely*, Money-changing, exchange-business.

1817 SCOTT *Rob Roy* (1855) 11 The mysteries of agio, tariffs, tare and tret. **1837** CARLYLE *Fr. Revol.* II. v. ii. 285 Chabot, disfrocked Capuchin, skilful in agio. [Cf. 'Cet homme entend l'agio.' Littré.]

3. *Comb.* ***agio-jobber***.

1837 CARLYLE *Fr. Revol.* (1871) III. IV. iv. 154 Lest Girondin Monsieurs, Agio-jobbers..corrupt their morals.

agiograph, incorrectly for HAGIOGRAPH.

agiotage ('ædʒɪəʊtɪdʒ). [a. Fr. *agiotage*, n. of action, f. *agioter* to speculate, f. *agio*: see AGIO and -AGE. The *t* is purely connective in Fr., doubtless in imitation of the mute *t* in words like *ballot*, which is sounded in *ballotage*. For the same reason *agio* was written in the 2nd ed. of the Dictionary of the Academy *agiot*.] Exchange business; hence, *loosely*, speculation in buying and selling public stocks and shares; stock-jobbing.

1829 LANDOR *Imag. Conv.* xlvii. Wks. 1846 I. 279 Vanity and agiotage are to a Parisian the oxygen and hydrogen of life. **1865** *Pall Mall G.* 22 Dec. 10 The Minister of Commerce and Public Works has issued an order against agiotage. It is forbidden to impose any agio in changing the pontifical currency. **1880** DISRAELI *Endym.* III. 61 What they mean by peace is agiotage, shares at a premium, and bubble companies.

[**agipe** (Coles 1692), error for a GIPE or GYPE.]

agist (ə'dʒɪst), *v.* [a. OFr. *agister* (*agîter*, *agitter*), f. *à* to + *gister*, *gîter* to lodge:—L. **jacitā-re*, freq. of *jacēre* to lie (perh. due to phrase *à giste*). A med.L. formation on the OFr. was *adgistāre*; cf. also *gista*, *gistum* lodging, formed on Fr. *giste*, sb. f. *gister*.]

1. To take in live stock to remain and feed, at a certain rate; *orig.* to admit cattle for a defined time into a forest, whence the constructions, to ***agist cattle***, to ***agist the forest***.

[**1224** *Chart. Forests* (see 1618). **1304** *Yearbooks Edw. I*, 23 E il agista nos bestis..nos bestis furent agistes par celuy qe l'engistement ad.] **1598** MANWOOD *Lawes Forest* xi. §1 If a man have common by a specialitie..he may not Agist other mens cattell, there to use his common. **1611** COTGR., *Glandager les porceaux*..to agist, or lay, swine in mastie woods. **1618** PULTON *Coll. Stat.* 7, tr. *Chart. Forests* ix, Euery Freeman may agest his owne Wood within our Forest [*agistet boscum suum in foresta*] at his pleasure, and shall take his pawnage. Also we doe grant that euery Freeman may driue his swine freely without impediment through our demesne Woods, for to agest them in their owne Woods [*ad agistandum eos in boscis suis propriis*]. **1691** BLOUNT *Law Dict.* s.v., This word *Agist* is also used for the taking in of other Mens Cattle into any Man's Ground at a certain Rate per week. **1839** T. STAPLETON *Plumpton Corr.* 18 Sir Robert & his heirs were also to have the pannage of the swine agisted in their own woods.

2. *intr.* Of cattle: To remain and feed for a specified time.

1598 MANWOOD *Lawes of Forest* xi. §1. (1615) 80/2 He..did put his said cattell..into the same close to Agist. **1753** CHAMBERS *Cycl. Supp.* s.v., When the lord..takes in other cattle to agist, or feed on it.

3. By extension, To rate or charge (lands or their owner) with any public burden.

1691 BLOUNT *Law Dict.* s.v., The word *Agist* is also metaphorically taken for a Charge or Burthen on a thing; e.g. *Terrae ad custodiam maris agistatae* (Selden *Mare clausum* 191) [Lands agisted or] charged with a Tribute to keep out the Sea. **1875** STUBBS *Const. Hist.* II. xv. 289 The king [Edward I] instituted the system of coastguard..and agisted or rated the land-owners of the maritime counties for its support.

†**a'gistage.** *Obs.* [f. AGIST *v.* + -AGE.] The action or function of agisting; agistment.

1691 BLOUNT *Law Dict.* s.v. *Agist*, Their [Agistors'] function is termed Agistment and Agistage. **1751** [See next].

†**agi'station.** *Obs.* [ad. med.L. *agistātiōn-em* (see Cowel), n. of action f. *agistāre*: see AGIST.] Agistment.

1751 CHAMBERS *Cycl.*, *Agistment*, *Agistage*, or *Agistation*, in law, the taking in, and feeding the cattle of strangers in the king's forest, and gathering the money due for the same.

‖**agi'stator.** *Obs.* [L. n. of agent f. *agistā-re* to AGIST.] = AGISTOR.

1809 TOMLINS *Law Dict.* s.v. *Agist*, They are also called Agistators, to take account of the cattle agisted.

agisted (ə'dʒɪstɪd), *ppl. a.* [f. AGIST *v.* + -ED.] Of animals: Taken in to feed. Of pasture, etc.: Depastured or eaten by cattle taken in at a certain rate of payment.

1779 *Chron.* in *Ann. Reg.* 221/2 Grass agisted or eaten by improfitable cattle. **1882** *Daily News* 8 Mar. 4/6 Exempting agisted stock and hired machinery from seizure.

agisting (ə'dʒɪstɪŋ), *vbl. sb.* [f. AGIST *v.* + -ING^{1}.] The taking in to pasture.

1598 MANWOOD *Lawes of Forest* xi. §1 This manner of taking in of cattell, to pasture or feede by the weeke, or by the moneth or otherwise, is called Agisting of beasts or cattell. **1695** KENNETT *Par. Antiq.* ix. 219 The Bishop..and Ralph de Warewill had liberty of agisting their hogs.

agisting (ə'dʒɪstɪŋ), *ppl. a.* [f. AGIST *v.* + -ING^{2}.] **a.** That takes in the cattle of another to pasture. **b.** Feeding on hired pasture.

1768 BLACKSTONE *Comm.* II. II. xxx. 453 The agisting farmer. **1882** *Echo* 2 Dec., We should much like to have a pulpit defence of the right to seize agisting stock.

agistment (ə'dʒɪstmənt). [a. OFr. *agistement*, f. *agiste*: see AGIST and -MENT.]

1. The action or process of agisting; the taking in of cattle or live stock to feed at a rate of so much per head; the opening of a forest for a specified time to live stock.

[**1304** *Year books of Edw. I*, 23 Q'il ad agistement a deus cents bestis.] **1611** COTGR., *Glandage*..th' Agistment, or laying of swine into Mastie woods. **1695** KENNETT *Par. Antiq.* ix. 219 To take pannage which was one farthing for the agistment of each hog. **1768** BLACKSTONE *Comm.* II. 452 If a man takes in a horse, or other cattle, to graze and depasture in his grounds, which the law calls agistment. **1813** VANCOUVER *Agric. Devon* 82 Depending upon casual and agistment stock for the consumption of his herbage. **1885** *Sheffield Tel.* 30 June (Advt.), Agistment. Good pasture for cattle and horses. **1955** *Times* 16 July 11/5 A number of cattle had to be sent away on agistment.

2. The herbage of a forest, or the right to it.

1598 [See under 3]. **1611** COTGR., *Paisson*, th' Agistment, or Herbage of woods, or forests; feeding for cattell therein. **1641** *Termes de la Ley* 15 The feed or herbage of the cattell is called Agistment.

3. The rate levied or profit made upon the pasturing of another's cattle.

1577 HOLINSHED *Chron.* an. 1198 (R.) Aduantages and profits..as in pannage and agistements. **1598** MANWOOD *Lawes of Forest* ix. §1 Agistment is most properly, the common of Herbage, of any kind of ground..or the money that is received or due for the same. **1809** TOMLINS *Law Dict.* s.v. *Agistment* is likewise the profit of such feeding in a ground or field; and extends to the depasturing of barren cattle of the owner, for which tithes shall be paid to the parson.

4. ***agistment tithe***: 'The tithe of cattle or other produce of grass lands...paid to the vicar or rector by the occupier of the land, and not by the person who may put his cattle there to graze at a certain rate per head.' *Encycl. Brit.*

1527 quoted in Hutchins' *Hist. Dorset* (1774) I. 280 The rector..shall have all the tithes of hay and agistments in the mead called Shetewel in Bradepole. **1779** in *Ann. Reg.* 221/2 A claim made by the former [the rector] of agistment tithe in kind. **1808** SYD. SMITH *Plymley's Lett.* Wks. 1859 II. 174/2 The abolition of agistment tithe in Ireland by a vote of the Irish House of Commons.

5. By extension, Any rate or charge levied upon the owner or occupier of (pasture) lands.

1618 PULTON *Coll. Stat.* tr. *Act 6 Hen. VI*, v, So that no tenants of lands or tenements..shal in any wise be spared in this and for agistments vpon the sea banks for preseruation of the said parts. **1809** TOMLINS *Law Dict.* s.v., There is agistment of sea-banks, where lands are charged with a tribute to keep out the sea.

agistor, agister (ə'dʒɪstə(r)). [a. Anglo Fr. *agistour*, f. *agister*: see AGIST and -OR.] One who agists. *spec.* An officer of the royal forests, who takes charge of cattle agisted, and accounts for the money paid for their agistment.

[**1327** *Stat.* 1 *Edw.* 3. viii, Foresters, verdours, regardours, agistours, et autres ministres de mesme le forest.] **1483** *Cath. Anglic.*, A gister: *Agistator*. **1598** MANWOOD *Lawes of For.* xi. §1. (1615) 80/1 The kings Agistors of his Forest..doe receiue and take in the beasts and cattell of euery person. **1812** W. TAYLOR in *Month. Mag.* XXXIV. 210 A forest has laws and officers of its own as foresters, verdours, rangers, and agisters. **1837** W. & M. HOWITT *Rur. Life* v. i. (1862) 357 Agistors also, to look after the agistment of cattle.

†'**agitable**, *a. Obs.* [a. Fr. *agitable*, ad. L. *agitābilis*, f. *agitā-re*: see AGITATE and -ABLE.] Capable of being agitated, easily moved, or disturbed.

1548 HALL Edw. IV, 23 A rede wyth euery wind is agitable and flexible. **1603** FLORIO *Montaigne* III. xii. (1632) 593 The mind [of the vulgar]..is lesse penetrable and agitable. **1661** *Origen* in *Phenix* (1721) I. 53 The finer and more agitable Particles. [Also in JOHNSON and mod. Dicts.]

†'**agitant**, *a.* and *sb. Obs.* [a. Fr. *agitant* pr. pple. of *agiter*, ad. L. *agitā-re*: see AGITATE *a.*]

A. *adj.* Moving, stirring, disturbing. *rare*$^{-0}$.

B. *sb.* One who stirs in, or plans, a course of action. (Cf. also ADJUTANT.)

a **1670** HACKET *Life of Williams* II. 90 (D.) The chief agitant saw that this tryal upon so firm a courage was uneffectual and ridiculous. *a* **1698** R. HOWARD *Committee* III. i. (D.) Now am I ready for any plot; I'll go find some of these agitants.

† **'agitat(e**, *pa. pple. Obs. Sc.* [ad. L. *agitāt-us* pa. pple. of *agitā-re* to move to and fro, freq. of *ag-ĕre* to drive.] Equivalent to the later AGITATED.

1. Tossed about, disturbed (mentally).

1567 *Test. K. Hen. Stewart* in *Sc. Poems of 16th c.* II. 258 Sumtyme in mynde with anger agitat.

2. Debated, discussed.

1634-46 J. Row (father) *Hist. Kirk* (1842) 183 The Kirk desyres the King..to heare everie weightie thing concerning the estate agitat.

agitate ('ædʒɪteɪt), *v.* [f. L. *agitāt-* ppl. stem of *agitā-re* (see prec.), also representing Fr. *agiter* (14th c., Littré).]

I. To move, excite.

†**1.** *trans.* To communicate action or motion to; to move, actuate. = ACT *v.* I. *Obs.*

1620 SHELTON *Quixote* III. xxxiv. 244 In the chace.. Sleep and Idleness are banished, the Pores are corroborated, the Members agitated. **1748** THOMSON *Castle Ind.* ii. 47 By whom each atom stirs, the planets roll: Who, fills, surrounds, informs, and agitates the whole.

2. To move to and fro, shake (things material).

1599 A. M. tr. *Gabelhouer's Bk. Physic* 44/1 Take fresh butter..impose the same in a little dishe, and agitate or amalgamize the same. **1667** BOYLE *Orig. Formes & Qual.* 30 In agitating water into froth. **1794** SULLIVAN *View of Nat.* I. 76 Incessant earthquakes..during which the earth was constantly agitated. **1825** SCOTT *Talism.* (1854) 141 The other refreshed his reverend master by agitating a fan of peacock-feathers. **1849** MRS. SOMERVILLE *Connex. Phys. Sc.* §30. 347 The aurora powerfully agitates the magnet.

3. *fig.* To disturb, perturb, or excite (the thoughts and feelings).

1586 JAMES VI in Ellis *Orig. Lett.* I. 224 III. 18 Knouin quhat divers thochtes have agitat my mynde. **1719** DE FOE *Crusoe* I. 233 This had agitated my Thoughts for two Hours. **1836** HOR. SMITH *Tin Trumpet* I. 13 An actor..is never so sure to agitate the souls of his hearers, as when his own is perfectly at ease.

4. Hence, To perturb or excite (*a person*) in mind or feelings; to stir up, excite, or move (a multitude) by appeals, etc.

a **1822** SHELLEY *Œdip. Tyr.* I. i, The gadfly was the same which Juno sent To agitate Io. **1824** DIBDIN *Libr. Comp.* 89 Frequently agitated with passion and prejudice. **1855** LEWIS *Early Rom. Hist.* xii. §25 Each consul forms a party, and agitates the people in favour of his own views. **1878** SEELEY *Stein.* III. 320 You are alarmed and agitated by the lamentations of those ladies.

II. To be active or busy about.

†**5.** *trans.* To do the actual work of (the affairs of another); to manage or act as an agent. Also *absol. Obs.*

1634 WOOD *New Engl. Prosp.* II. x, A King of large Dominions hath his Viceroyes..to agitate his State-affaires. **1654** FULLER *2 Serm.* 76 Let painefull Solicitours so honestly Agitate..as knowing they must give an Account to God.

6. To be busy with (mentally), consider on all sides, revolve in the mind (as a plan to be executed); to contrive busily. *arch.*

1648 COTTRELL tr. *Davila's Hist. France* (1678) 9 Whilst these things were agitated at the court. *a* **1649** CHARLES I (J.) When politicians most agitate desperate designs. **1671** MRS. BEHN *Forc'd Marriage* II. iii. 174 As if your soul were agitating something Contrary to the pleasure of this night.

7. To discuss, debate, or push forward as a question to be settled. Also *absol.*

1643 MILTON *Sov. Salve* 33 Parliament preparing, discussing, agitating, concluding what is to be done. **1756** BURKE *Sp. Amer. Tax.* Wks. II. 410 Before a repeal was so much as agitated in this house. **1785** COWPER *Tirocin.* 130 Points, which unless the Scripture made them plain, The wisest heads might agitate in vain. **1863** COX *Inst. Eng. Govt.* I. ii. 285 The question of the revival of licensed printing was repeatedly agitated in Parliament.

8. *absol.* To keep up an agitation; to keep a political or other object perpetually under discussion, so as to impress on the public mind. Const. *for*.

c **1828** MARQ. ANGLESEY (to Irish Deputation), If you really expect success, *agitate, agitate, agitate.* **1860** KINGSLEY *Misc.* II. 180 If he wants protection for them, let him agitate for the true protection. *Mod.* To agitate for a repeal of the malt tax.

agitated ('ædʒɪteɪtɪd), *ppl. a.* [f. prec. + -ED.]

†**1.** Moved, set in motion. *Obs.*

1620 [See under AGITATE *v.* 1]. **1659** HAMMOND *On Psalm* civ. 3. 516 Those agitated clouds, whereby, as with wings, the Angels fly down to us.

2. Moved to and fro; shaken, disturbed.

1660 DRYDEN *Astr. Red.* 273 As those lees, that trouble it, refine The agitated soul of generous wine. **1826** DISRAELI *Viv. Grey* II. xiii. 66 The solitary clerk no longer found time to answer the often agitated bell. **1878** HUXLEY *Physiogr.* 172 However agitated the surface of the sea may be.

3. Excited, disturbed in mind, having the feelings greatly moved.

1756 BURKE *Subl. & B.* Wks. 1842 I. 73 An impassioned countenance, an agitated gesture. **1849** MACAULAY *Hist. Eng.* I. 623 He was greatly agitated. The blood left his cheeks.

4. Debated, discussed, kept before the public by discussion.

1640-4 *Order of Commons* in Rushw. *Hist. Coll.* III. (1692) I. 355 Notes of things brought into the House, Propounded or Agitated in the House. **1675** BAXTER *Cath. Theol.* I. I. 17 It is also an agitated Controversie with them, Whether, etc. **1868** G. DUFF *Polit. Surv.* 104 The long agitated scheme for running a railway down the Euphrates valley.

agitatedly ('ædʒɪ,teɪtɪdlɪ), *adv.* [f. prec. + -LY².] In an agitated manner; with agitation.

1827 MOORE *Epicurean* xii. (1839) 156 Laying her hand agitatedly upon mine. **1862** MRS. WOOD *Mrs. Hallib.* (1864) I. viii. 48 He saw how agitatedly anxious she was.

agitating ('ædʒɪteɪtɪŋ), *vbl. sb.* [f. AGITATE *v.* + -ING¹.] The action of moving, disturbing, discussing. (Mostly gerundial.)

1667 [See under AGITATE *v.* 2]. **1732** ARBUTHNOT *Diet* 398 Violent Purging..by agitating the Humours often hurts. **1769** BURKE *St. of Nat.* Wks. 1842 I. 110 Without agitating those vexatious questions.

agitating ('ædʒɪteɪtɪŋ), *ppl. a.* [f. AGITATE *v.* + -ING².] **a.** *Eng. Hist.* Acting as AGITATORS. **b.** Disturbing, exciting.

a **1671** FAIRFAX *Short Mem.* (1699) 119 To prepare a way to this Work, this Agitating Council did first intend to remove all out of the Parliament who were like to oppose them. **1814** SOUTHEY *Roderick* xviii. IX. 162 The active agitating joy that fill'd The vale. **1868** GEO. ELIOT *F. Holt* 47 He trembled under the pressure of some agitating thought.

agitatingly ('ædʒɪteɪtɪŋlɪ), *adv.* [f. AGITATING *ppl. a.* + -LY².] In such a manner as to cause agitation.

1819 *Blackw. Mag.* VI. 160 That such a mind should have known miserable thoughts so well as to be enabled thus agitatingly to paint them. **1887** *Pictorial World* 28 Apr. 410 He had been deeply, not to say agitatingly, impressed.

agitation (ædʒɪ'teɪʃən). [a. (16th c.) Fr. *agitation*, ad. L. *agitātiōn-em* n. of action, f. *agitā-re*: see AGITATE *a.*] The action of agitating.

†**1.** The action of moving, stirring; motion, action, exercise of activity. *Obs.*

1573 BP. COOPER *Thesaur., Agitatio*, moouing, stirring, agitation, exercise. **1610** GWILLIM *Heraldry* III. xx. (1660) 217 Albeit they..have their feeding upon the earth, yet is their agitation above in the Ayre. **1633** T. N[EWTON] tr. *Lemnie's Touchst. Compl.* 167 Likewise doth the body of man become putrified..if it accustome not it selfe to exercise and agitation. **1711** F. FULLER *Med. Gymn.* 4 By Exercise then, I understand all..Motion or Agitation of the Body.

2. *esp.* The moving of (anything) to and fro; shaking.

1583 PLAT *Jewel-ho.* (1594) 47 Or use anie other devise by agitation or shaking, untill you have broken the yolke. **1659** BAXTER *Saving Faith* §12. 88 Even Agitation with pressure sometimes sets the Turners wood on fire. **1750** JOHNSON *Rambler* No. 133 ¶2 Enabled me to bear the agitation of a coach. **1860** MAURY *Phys. Geog. Sea* x. §484 Brought to the surface by the agitation of the sea.

3. A state or condition of being moved to and fro; commotion, disturbance, perturbation.

1605 BACON *Adv. Learn.* I. vii. §1 (1873) The true character of Divine Presence, coming in..without noise or agitation. **1664** POWER *Exp. Philos.* I. 21 A tremulous Motion and Agitation of rowling fumes. **1775** BURKE *Concil. Amer.* Wks. III. 27 Under them the state of America has been kept in continual agitation. **1880** CYPLES *Hum. Exp.* i. 5 A nervo-cerebral system, with specific agitations set up.. in it.

4. Mental disturbance or perturbation (showing itself usually by physical excitement).

[**1573** BP. COOPER *Thesaur., Agitatio mentis*, the agitation and exercise of mind.] **1722** DE FOE *Plague* (1756) 221, I have seen them in strange Agitations and Surprises on this Account. **1788** JOHNSON *Lett.* 207 II. 55 Think on such things as may please without too much agitation. **1816** SCOTT *Antiq.* vii, 'We thought,' replied Sir Arthur in great agitation, 'we thought we could get round Halket-head.' **1834** HT. MARTINEAU *Demerara* iv. 52 A long, deep sob broke from him, and the child, terrified at his agitation, ran away.

5. The mental tossing of a matter to and fro; consideration, debate, discussion.

1569 SHAKS. *Merch. Ven.* III. v. 5 [*Clown* says] So now I speake my agitation of the matter. **1625** BACON *Ess.* (1862) xx. 82 Things will have their first, or second Agitation; If they be not tossed upon the Arguments of Counsell, they will be tossed upon the Waves of Fortune. **1640** FULLER *Abel Rediv., Sandys* (1867) II. 192 The business in agitation very weighty. **1769** *Junius Lett.* xxiii. 112 The latest moments of your life were dedicated to the same..busy agitations. **1865** F. PARKMAN *Huguenots* (1875) i. 9 While this design was in agitation.

†**6.** Busy devising, scheming, contrivance. *Obs.*

1607 TOPSELL *Four-footed Beasts* (1673) 176 The hunter must..in hunting of a fox..drive him against the winde, and then he preventeth all his crafty and subtill agitations and devises. **1626** HOWELL *Lett.* (1650) I. 206 You heard how I was in agitation for an employment in Italy.

†**7.** *Eng. Hist.* The action of the 'Agitators' of 1647. *Obs.*

a **1671** FAIRFAX *Short Mem.* (1699) 116 The Army was almost wholly infected with this Humour of Agitation. *Ibid.* 105, I shall now descend to some particulars of their Agitations.

8. The keeping of a political or other object constantly before public attention, by appeals, discussion, etc.; public excitement. See AGITATE 8. Also, *spec.* of agitation on behalf of Communism.

1828 *Ann. Reg., Hist.* 122/2 Its[Catholic Association's] orators publicly proclaimed that 'Agitation,' as they termed it, was the object which they had in view, and that agitation they would have so long as they found it necessary. **1863** W. PHILLIPS *Speeches* iii. 53 The antislavery agitation. **1879** MCCARTHY *Own Times* I. 337 With the Manchester school began a new kind of popular agitation. Up to that time agitation meant appeal to passion..The Manchester school introduced the agitation which appealed to reason and argument only; which stirred men's hearts with figures of arithmetic, rather than figures of speech. **1923** E. RICE *Adding Machine* iii. 46 Too damn much agitation, that's at the bottom of it... Foreign agitators, that's what it is. **1946** L. HARRY GOULD *Marxist Glossary* 11 *Agitation*, the act of rousing the masses to political action around some particular social injustice. **1948** J. TOWSTER *Pol. Power in U.S.S.R.* x. 195 For the duration of the campaign, agitation points (*Agitpunkty*) are set up in the election precincts. **1957** R. N. CAREW HUNT *Guide to Communist Jargon* 3 Ozhegov's *Dictionary of the Russian Language* defines agitation as 'Oral and written activity among the broad masses which aims at inculcating certain ideas and slogans for their political education and for attracting them to the solution of the more important social and political tasks'. **1958** *Economist* 1 Nov. 427/1 But in the Soviet Union, the Department of Propaganda and Agitation is one of the seven sections of the central committee of the Communist party.

agitational (ædʒɪ'teɪʃənəl), *a. rare.* [f. prec. + -AL¹.] Of or pertaining to agitation; connected with the promotion of discussion on public questions.

1866 *Morn. Star* 14 Feb., The denunciations..which have been published are all of them so purely political, so purely agitational—if we may coin a word.

agitative ('ædʒɪ,teɪtɪv), *a.* ? *Obs.* [f. L. *agitāt-* (see AGITATE *a.*) + -IVE, as if ad. L. **agitātīvus.*] Tending to agitate, stir, or move; motive, excitative.

1687 H. MORE *App. to Antid.* (1712) 221 If a Spirit use his Agitative power moderately. **1753** CHAMBERS *Cycl. Supp.* s.v., The agitative force of the pendulum arises from three things.

‖**agitato** (ædʒɪ'tɑːtəʊ), *a. Mus.* [It.:—L. *agitātus*: see AGITATE *a.*] 'Agitated'; used in music to describe the mode or character of a movement; hence, adverbially, 'in an agitated manner, with agitation, restlessly.' Also *transf.* and as *sb.*

1801 BUSBY *Dict. Mus., Agitato*... This term signifies a broken, interrupted style of performance, calculated to shake and surprise the hearer. **1822** *Blackw. Mag.* XII. 446 Ambrogetti..sung an *agitato*. **1876** STAINER & BARRETT *Dict. Mus. Terms* 19/2 *Agitato*.., an agitated or restless style of playing or singing, in which the time and expression is broken and hurried. **1938** *Oxf. Compan. Mus.* 18/2 *Agitato, agitatamente*.., 'agitated', 'agitatedly'. **1963** J. D. SALINGER *Seymour* 177 It was my custom..to try out my new short stories on Seymour. That is, read them aloud to him. Which I did *molto agitato*, with a clearly indicated required Rest Period for everybody at the finish. **1977** *Gramophone* Aug. 306/3 Some collectors initially may prefer bolder surges and a more marked *agitato* character in the first movement. **1978** *Ibid.* June 86/1 The central *agitato* of Op. 9 No. 3 is particularly convincing. **1983** *Observer* 9 Jan. 41/3 She was terribly agitato, and can you blame her?

agitator ('ædʒɪteɪtə(r)). [a. L. *agitātor*, n. of agent, f. *agitā-re*: see AGITATE *a.* and -OR.] One who agitates. Specially:—

†**1.** *Eng. Hist.* An agent, one who acts for others (see AGITATE *v.* 5); a name given to the agents or delegates of the private soldiers in the Parliamentary Army 1647-9; in which use it varied with ADJUTATOR. *Obs.*

(Careful investigation satisfies me that *Agitator* was the actual title, and *Adjutator* originally only a bad spelling of soldiers familiar with *Adjutants* and the *Adjutors* of 1642. *Adjutator* has naturally seemed more plausible to recent writers unfamiliar with this old sense of 'agitate,' and the functions of the Agitators of 1647. J.A.H.M.)

1647 (June 4) *Two Lett. of Sir T. Fairfax to both Houses of Parlt.*, with the Advice of the Council of Warre..also the Petition of the private Souldierie of the Army..presented.. by their severall Adjutators. [*Signed*] Edward Saxby, Edward Taylor, Adjutators of the Generals Regime[nt] of Horse, etc., etc. **1647** (June 5) *Solemn Engagement of the Army* [Official paper printed under auth. of Gen. Fairfax] Upon a late Petition to the General from the Agitators in behalf of the soldiery. **1647** (June 11) in Rushw. *Coll.* (1721) VI. xv. 556 The Agitators on the behalf of the Soldiers press'd to have the Question put. [So always in Rushw.] **1647** EVELYN *Mem.* (1857) III. 6 The agitators are for certain reconciled with the army. **1650** FULLER *Pisgah Sight* II. xii. 250 Devills then dancing for joy, where once Angels (those holy Agitators) went up and down betwixt heaven and earth. *c* **1650** SIR T. HERBERT *Mem.* (T.) Active and malevolent persons of the army, disguised under the specious name of agitators, being two selected out of every regiment, to meet and debate the concerns of the army. *a* **1671** FAIRFAX *Short Mem.* (1699) 207 Now the Officers of the Army were plac'd and displac'd at the will of the new Agitators. [So always in F.] *a* **1674** CLARENDON *Hist. Reb.* III. x. 33 The common soldiers made choice of three or four of each Regiment, most Corporals or Serjeants, few or none above the degree of an Ensign, who were called Agitators, and were to be as a House of Commons to the Council of Officers. [So always in Cl.] **1827** HALLAM *Const. Hist.* (1876) II. x. 210 Those elective tribunes called Agitators, who had been established in every regiment to superintend the interests of the army (*Note* to *Agitator*: Some have supposed it to be a corruption of *adjutator*, as if the modern *adjutant* meant the same thing. But I find it always so spelled in the pamphlets of the time.)

2. One who keeps up a political agitation. After the Bolshevik Revolution freq. applied *spec.* to Communist agitators.

a **1734** R. North *Examen* (1740) I. iii. 195 The visible Agitators of all the Seditions and Troubles of King Charles the Second's Reign. **1780** Burke *Durat. Parl.* (T.) Some leading man, some agitator. **1791** Newte *Tour in Eng. & Scot.* 4 Talked of by certain political reformers and other agitators. **1828** *Ann. Reg.* 123/1 Starting against him [Fitzgerald] their own great popish leader and agitator, Daniel O'Connell. **1852** Emily Tennyson in *Rev. Eng. Stud.* (1964) XV. 402 Do not speak of him as an 'agitator'. .. The word has come to have so evil a meaning, a sort of hysterical lady meaning if nothing worse. **1853** *Encycl. Brit.* II. 240 The great agitator, Daniel O'Connell, was able to stir up the mass of the Irish nation. **1876** Bancroft *Hist. U.S.* III. xvii. 261 He was by nature an agitator, and carried into the cabinet restless activity and the arts of cabal. **1920** *Independent* 31 Jan. 161/1 Bolshevik Representative Klishke —'Soviet Russia will not allow itself to be used as a dumping ground for agitators from America.' **1931** *New Statesman* 4 July 4/1 Mr. Winston Churchill, the notorious British agitator (we adopt the phraseology of the *Morning Post* when describing M. Bukharin and other distinguished Russians now in this country) has now decided that disarmament is impossible, because of the menace of Russia. **1934** T. S. Eliot *Rock* i. 31 On the fore-stage, an *agitator* is addressing a tattered crowd. **1938** Auden & Isherwood *On the Frontier* I. ii. p. 46 *Col. Hussek.* Tcha! Another lightning strike at the Docks! .. *Mrs. Vrodny.* I'm sure it's only due to Westland agitators. **1959** *Observer* 29 Mar. 11/4 Mrs. Nora Jefferey said at the British Communist Party congress .. that the Communist aim should be: Every member a propagandist and agitator.

3. An apparatus for shaking or mixing. In various techn. uses.

1809 J. Dickinson *Brit. Pat. 3191*, Machinery for Making and Cutting Paper. *Ibid.* 7, B is an agitator consisting of a number of arms .. and this being turned .. keeps the stuff in motion. **1839** Ure *Dict. Arts* 72 The agitator is then suspended to a spring R, and .. the operator gives an alternating rapid movement, which agitates the solution. **1871** Balf. Stewart *Heat* 51 By means of an agitator every part of this tube .. may be brought to the same temperature throughout. **1937** *Times* 13 Apr. xiii/4 The paint on arrival from the manufacturers is subjected to what is termed 'agitating' or mixing. When it enters the containers it meets two more agitators, one at the top and one at the bottom of the container. **1958** *Ibid.* 2 June ix/5 Gas is used to boil the clothes and an electric agitator helps with the washing. **1958** *Listener* 19 June 1006/2 Mechanical equipment such as valves, pumps, centrifuges and agitators in the radioactive section.

agitatorial (ˌædʒɪteɪˈtɔərɪəl), *a.* [f. prec. after analogy of *dictator-ial*, etc.: see -ORIAL.] Of or pertaining to an agitator.

1863 *Sat. Rev.* 7 Feb. 185/1 Manin's whole personal and political working during those years was neither revolutionary nor agitatorial.

agitatrix (ædʒɪˈteɪtrɪks). [a. L. *agitātrix* fem. of *agitātor*: see -TRIX.] A female agitator.

1881 *Sat. Rev.* 19 Mar. 361 So the cat and the agitatrix exchanged courtesies and the agitatrix gave food to the hungry cat.

Agit-prop, agit-prop (ˈædʒɪtˌprɒp, ˈæg-). [f. Russ. *agitprop*, f. *agit(átsiya* agitation + *prop(agánda* propaganda.] A department of the Central Committee of the Russian Communist Party responsible, with its local branches, for 'agitation and propaganda' on behalf of Communism; its activities. Also, a person engaged in agitprop. Also *transf.*

1934 *N. & Q.* CLXVI. 73/1 The *A[g]itprop*, the central organ for propaganda and agitation, has sent word round to writers, newspapers and publishers, that there is to be an organisation for mass-laughter. **1935** *Time* 17 June 38/1 Far more serious, far more earnest is the Depression-born movement of workers' theatres which are currently putting on 'agit-prop' (agitational propaganda) plays in 300 U.S. cities. **1936** *Times Lit. Suppl.* 22 Feb. 146/3 Primitive 'agitprop' and mass-chant plays. **1949** 'G. Orwell' *Nineteen Eighty-Four* 307 The tendency to use abbreviations of this kind was most marked in totalitarian countries and totalitarian organizations. Examples were such words as *Nazi*, *Gestapo*, *Comintern*, *Inprecorr*, *Agitprop*. **1950** A. Koestler in *God that Failed* 51 The job of Agit.-Prop. fell to me soon after I had joined the cell. **1952** G. A. Duncan in R. S. Sayers *Banking in Brit. Commonw.* viii. 314 They [*sc.* the banks] have made no effort to counter the flood of often malicious .. but sometimes pointed *agitprop*. **1952** *Economist* 1 Mar. 508/2 Any businessman who goes to Moscow in the belief that he will be able to strike an effective blow for anything he believes in and the Communists do not is simply inviting the 'Agitprop' experts to make a monkey of him. **1959** *Spectator* 6 Nov. 629/2 The whole tone [of the play] is ten times heavier and cornier than any of the agitprop from the old Unity Theatre.

† **a'give**, *v. Obs.* For forms see GIVE. [f. A- *pref.* 1 out, away, up + GIVE. OE. *agifan* is cogn. w. OHG. *ar-*, *ur-*, *ir-*, *er-geban* (mod.G. *ergeben*), Goth. *us-giban*.]

1. *trans.* To give up, give back; render, surrender.

c **1000** *O.E. Gosp.* Matt. xxvii. 17 Hwæðer wille ȝe þæt ich eow agyfe, þe Barraban, þe þanne Hælend. *c* **1175** *Lamb. Hom.* 29 Ah soðliche al he hit mot aȝefen ȝif he hit haueð. and ȝif he hit naueð aȝefe swa muchel swa he mei. **1205** Layam. 22165 Aȝif us ure icunde lond. *a* **1250** *Owl & Night.* 139 Thos word aȝaf the niȝtingale.

2. *intr.* To give way or yield; to abandon a state of rigidity; cf. to *give*.

1681 J. W[orlidge] *Syst. Agric.* 155 As soon as your Hops are off the Kiln, .. lay them in some room or place .. that they may cool, agive, and toughen.

aglance (əˈglɑːns, -æ-), *adv.*, prop. *phr.* [A *prep.*[1] of state + GLANCE.] Glancing, gleaming.

1880 Webb tr. *Goethe's Faust* I. ii. 60 With wreath and ribbon all aglance.

aglare (əˈglɛə(r)), *adv.*, prop. *phr.* [A *prep.*[1] of state + GLARE.] In a glare, glaring.

1872 M. Collins *Pr. Clarice* II. xix. 223 His sole remaining eye aglare with furious light. **1881** *Art Jrnl.* Jan. 119 The landscape lying all aglare beneath the 'blue unclouded.'

agleam (əˈgliːm), *adv.*, prop. *phr.* [A *prep.*[1] of state + GLEAM.] In a gleaming state; gleaming.

1870 Lowell *Study Windows* 380 Those faces .. agleam with pale intellectual light.

aglet, aiglet (ˈæglət, ˈeɪglət). Forms: 5–6 aglett(e, aglott(e, agglot, 5–9 **aglet**, 6 agglet(te, aiguelet, aguelette, ayguelet, 8 aigullet, 9 (egellet) aigulet, aiglet, aiguillette. [a. Fr. *aiguillette* dim. of *aiguille* needle:—late L. *acūcula*, var. of *acicula*, dim. of *acus* needle. The phonetic changes must have been *aiguïllette*, *aigue'lette*, *aï'glette*, *a'glette*, *'aglĕt* (-ət), but early instances are wanting: in modern times it has been again made *aiglet* and AIGUILLETTE.]

1. The metal tag of a lace (formerly called *point*), intended primarily to make it easier to thread through the eyelet-holes, but afterwards also as an ornament to the pendent ends.

1440 *Promp. Parv.*, Agglot or an aglet to lace wyth alle, *Acus, aculus.* **1468** *Cov. Myst.* (1841) 241 Two dozeyn poyntys of cheverelle, the aglottes of sylver feyn. *a* **1500** in Wright's *Vocab.* 238 *Hoc mominlum*, a naglott. **1545** Ascham *Toxoph.* (Arb.) 108 Take hede .. that it be fast on with laces wythout agglettes. **1549** Latimer *7 Serm. bef. Edw. VI* (1869) 117 He made hys pen of the aglet of a poynte that he plucked from hys hose. **1603** Holland *Plutarch Mor.* 13 You put your aglet, sir, thorow the oilet that is not made for it. **1708** Kersey, *Aglet*, the Tag of a Point. **1775** Ash, *Aigullet*, a point with tags. **1834** Planche *Hist. Brit. Cost.* 236 These splendid hose .. were attached by points or laces, with tags called aguletes or aiglets (*i.e.* aiguillettes) to the doublet. **1852** Miss Yonge *Cameos* (1877) IV. xiii. 148 The message related to two letters written with an aglet plucked from his hose.

2. Hence, An ornament consisting **a.** properly, of a gold or silver tag or pendent attached to a fringe; whence **b.** extended to any metallic stud, plate, or spangle worn on the dress.

1514 Fitzherbert *Justyce of Peas* 120 We shall weare any agglettes, botons, or broches of golde or sylver, gylt, or counterfayt gylt. **1530** Palsgr. 193/2 Aiguelet to fasten a claspe in, *porte.* **1531** Elyot *Governour* (1580) 91 A millayne or French bonnet on his head full of agglets. **1551** Edward VI *Jrnl. Lit. Rem.* (1858) 325 His goune dressed with aglettes, worth 25 li. **1587** Holinshed *Chron.* III. 1207/1 On the sleeues eight and thirtie paire of aglets of gold. **1580** Baret *Alvearie* A 227 An aglet or iewell in one's cap. **1596** Spenser *F.Q.* II. iii. 26 A silken Camus .. Which all above besprinckled was throughout With golden aygulets, that glistred bright, Like twinckling starres. **1598** Florio, *Tremolante* .. aglets or spangles. **1656** Blount *Glossogr.*, *Aglet*, a little plate of any mettal, the tag of a point. **1764** R. Burn *Poor Laws* 21 No man, under the degree of a gentleman, shall wear any aglets of gold or silver.

c. *esp.* A tagged point, braid, or cord, hanging from the shoulder upon the breast in some military and naval uniforms. In this sense now officially treated as Fr., and written *aiguillette*.

1843 Lytton *Last of Bar.* II. ii. 126 No flaunting tawdriness of fringe & aiglet characterised the appearance of the baron. **1845** J. Saunders *Cabinet Pict.* 33 Little aiglets, tipped with gold, (hang) from his shoulders. **1879** *Cornh. Mag.* June 685 A handsome officer, bearing the epaulets and aiglets of a staff captain. **1882** *Navy List* July 495/2 Aides-de-Camp to the Queen are to wear a gold aiguillette on the right shoulder.

3. 'Still used in haberdashery, and denotes round white stay-laces.' *Drapers' Dictionary* 1882.

[So in mod.Fr. *aiguillette* has passed from the tag to the lace or cord, as *point* did in Eng.]

4. *Herb.* Any pendent part of a flower resembling the prec., *esp.* **a.** A catkin of hazel, birch, etc. **b.** An anther (only in Dicts., and perh. erroneous).

1578 Lyte *Dodoens* 635 The knoppes or agglettes that hang in the Birche or Hasell trees. **1598** Gerarde *Herball* I. xxxix. §2. 56 A certain long aglet or bunch, such as the Aller tree bringeth foorth. **1657** Purchas *Theatre of Insects* xiii. 72 When they gather off the Aglets, or Catkins, of the Hazel. **1708** Kersey, *Aglets* or *Aglects* (among Florists) are the Pendants that hang on the Tip-ends of Chivets and Threads; as in Tulips, Roses, etc. **1809** Parkins *Culpepper's Eng. Phys. Enl.* 127 A long bush of small and more yellow, green, scaly aglets, set in the same manner on the stalks as the leaves are. *c* **1860** Lowell *Wks.* 1879, 373/2 And [the willow] glints his steely aglets in the sun.

† **5.** A fragment of flesh hanging by the skin. Hence, a scrap, a shred. (Cf. Fr. *découper un canard par aiguillettes*, Littré.) *Obs.*

1555 *Fardle of Facions* II. x. 217 No, the begger .. getteth not an aguelette of hym. *Ibid.* App. 352 That thei should vtterly destroy him .. not leauing an agguelet of a poincte for the memorial of such hopeloste persones.

6. *Comb.* **aglet-babie**, ? A doll or (grown-up) 'baby' decked with aglets. (Explained by some as an aglet shaped like a human figure. Johnson defines *aglet* as 'A tag of a point curved into some representation of an animal, generally of a man,' but no quotations have been found bearing out this statement, which was perhaps merely hazarded as an explanation of *aglet-babie*); **aglet-headed**, having a head resembling an aglet; **aglet-hole**, a hole for passing a lace through, an eyelet-hole.

1596 Shaks. *Tam. Shr.* I. ii. 80 Giue him Gold enough, and marrie him to a Puppet or an Aglet babie, or an old trot with ne're a tooth in her head. **1789** Pilkington *Derby.* I. 330 (Jod.) Aglet-headed rush. **1600** Darrell *Demon. Possess.* 6 The boy .. burst the buttons of his Doublet & the aglet holes before both of his Doublet and Hose. —— *Detect. Harsnet* 181 The buttons of his Doublett did brust off and his aglet holees breake. **1623** Minsheu *Sp. Dict.*, Aglet-hole, *Ojéte.*

'aglet, *v. Obs. rare.* [f. the sb.] To put a tag on a point.

1530 Palsgr. 418/2, I agglet, I set on an agglet upon a poynte or a lace. *Je fene.* These poyntes be yvell bought, for some be aggletted and some nat.

† **'agleted**, *ppl. a. Obs.* Also 6 **agglated**. [f. prec. + -ED.] Furnished with aglets.

1548 Hall *Chron.* (1809) 729 A Cote of black velvet upon White Satin and tied with laces agglated with golde.

a'gley, *adv. Sc.* Also **aglee, agly.** [f. A *prep.*[1] + GLEE, GLEY *v.*] Asquint, askew, awry.

1785 Burns *To a Mouse* in *Poems* (1786) 140 The best laid schemes o' Mice an' Men, Gang aft agley. **1813** E. Picken *Misc. Poems* I. 67 We haena mense like cruel man; Yet tho' he's paukier far than we, Whatreck, he gangs as aft aglee. **1880** [see GO *v.* 4 d]. **1887** R. L. Stevenson *Underwoods* xv, Or lads that tak a keek a-glee At sonsie lasses. **1929** C. Day Lewis *Transit. Poem* II. 23 These are they who built My house and never a stone of it laid agley.

† **a'glide**, *v. Obs. rare*[−1]. [f. A- *pref.* 1 up, away + GLIDE.] To glide up or away.

c **1430** Lydg. *Minor Poems* (1840) 116 When the body ded ryse, a grymly gost a-gleed [? aglood], Then was tyme me for to stere, many a foyle I be-strood.

† **a'gliff**, *v. Obs.* Pa. pple. 3 **aglyfte, oglyft.** [f. A- *pref.* 1 + GLIFF to alarm.] To frighten. Only in pa. pple. Frightened, terrified.

1303 R. Brunne *Handl. Synne* 3587 As he stode so sore aglyfte. **1330** —— *Chron.* 70 William was oglyft .. þat falle mad him ofright. *Ibid.* 72 For William þei were oglift, & said, þat we ne dar.

a-glimmer (əˈglɪmə(r)), *adv.*, prop. *phr.* [A *prep.*[1] + GLIMMER.] In or into a glimmering state.

1860 Hawthorne *Marble Farm* (1879) II. xii. 117 To set the tarnished gilding of the picture-frames .. all a-glimmer.

aglint (əˈglɪnt), *adv.*, prop. *phr.* [A *prep.*[1] + GLINT.] Glinting, peeping through.

1879 J. D. Long *Æneid* IX. 315 Oft in the hunt have we caught sight, Aglint through valley copses, of the town.

aglist (əˈglɪst), *adv.* Also **a'glisten.** [f. A *prep.*[1] + GLIST *v.*] Glistening.

1858 Mrs. Oliphant *Laird of Norlaw* lxvi, All aglist with early morning dews and sunshine. **1891** *Murray's Mag.* Aug. 291 The garden all aglisten 'twixt two showers. **1916** E. Blunden *Harbingers* 32 Carriage-roofs aglisten with rain.

aglitter (əˈglɪtə(r)), *adv.*, prop. *phr.* [A *prep.*[1] of state + GLITTER.] In a glitter, glittering.

1865 Dickens *Mut. Fr.* II. xvi. (1872) I. 293 Mr. Lamb, all a-glitter. **1881** Miss Braddon *Asphodel* I. 66 A room all a-glitter with gilding.

aglomerular (eɪglɒˈmɛrələ(r)), *a. Ichthyol.* [f. A- 14 + GLOMERULAR *a.*] Of a kidney: lacking glomeruli, as in some fish. Of a fish: having such kidneys.

1928 *Amer. Jrnl. Anat.* XLII. 76 Three families said to include genera possessing aglomerular mesonephroi were reinvestigated. **1942** *Lancet* 3 Oct. 396/1 Renin can be obtained from the glomerular kidney of the carp and dogfish but not from the aglomerular kidney of the midshipman fish. **1959** W. Andrew *Textbk. Compar. Histol.* xi. 439 The aglomerular condition of the kidney reduces greatly the loss of water but in itself does not wholly solve the problem of osmotic regulation for bony fishes in a marine environment. **1966** *McGraw-Hill Encycl. Sci. & Technol.* V. 140/2 The aglomerular fishes represent a successful group of animals, being numerous and widely distributed. **1974** *Nature* 9 Aug. 461/1 In the absence of a glomerulus the flow of water is sustained by secretion in the upper region of the tubule, as in the aglomerular kidneys of some fishes, and not by pressure of the blood.

† **a'glopened**, *ppl. a. Obs.* [pa. pple. either of *glopen*, *gloppen*, with A *particle* for *y-*, or of a compound *a-glopen* with A- *pref.* 1 intensive.] Frightened.

a **1400** *Alexander* 874 Bees not aglopened, madame.

aglossal (əˈglɒsəl), *a. Zool.* [f. Gr. ἄγλωσσ-ος without tongue + -AL[1].] Tongueless.

1870 Rolleston *Anim. Life* 65 The aglossal Anura.

aglow (əˈgləʊ), *adv.*, prop. *phr.* [A *prep.*[1] of state + GLOW.]

1. In a glow of warmth, or of some warm colour.

1817 COLERIDGE *Biogr. Lit.* 118 Now all a-glow with colours not their own. **1871** TYNDALL *Fragm. Sc.* (ed. 6) I. iv. 125 The great mass of the Fletshorn was all a-glow. *Mod.* I was all aglow with the exercise.

2. *fig.* In a glow of (pleasurable) excitement; flushed.

a **1834** COLERIDGE *Poems* 257 Amid the tremor of a realm aglow, Amid a mighty nation jubilant. **1872** BLACK *Adv. Phaeton* xxii. 308 All her face was aglow with delight.

aglu (ˈæglu:). *Canad.* Also **agloo.** [Eskimo.] A breathing-hole in the ice, made by a seal. Cf. BLOW-HOLE 4.

1835 R. HUISH *Last Voy. Sir J. Ross Arctic Regions* 701/1 *Ag-loo*, seal-hole. **1836** *Ibid.* (rev. ed.) 303 While hunting he had found a polar bear with his head jammed into an aglu. **1882** W. H. GILDER *Schwatka's Search* 142 No work of any kind .. can be done upon new skins until the ice has formed sufficiently thickly upon the salt water to permit the hunter to seek the seal at his agloo or blow-hole. **1959** W. A. LEISING *Arctic Wings* 301 He does this by going from one hole, or aglu, to another, to keep the holes open as the ice freezes.

aglucone: see AGLYCONE.

†**aˈglut,** *v. Obs.* Also 4 **aglotye.** [f. A- *pref.* 1 intens. + GLUT.] To feed to satisfaction, to glut.

1393 LANGL. *P. Pl.* C. x. 76 Boþe in mylk and in mele, to make with papelotes, To a-glotye with here gurles, þat greden after fode. **1496** *Bk. of St. Albans* C ii, It is agluttyd and kelyd wyth the glette that she hath engendred.

aglutition (æglˌ(j)u:ˈtɪʃən). *Path.* [f. A- *pref.* 14 + L. **glūtītiōn-em* n. of action, f. *glūtī-re* to swallow: see DEGLUTITION.] Inability to swallow.

1847 in CRAIG.

†**aˈgly,** *v. Obs. rare*⁻¹. [f. A- *pref.* 1 away + GLY to glance.] To vanish, disappear.

c **1325** *E.E. Allit. Poems* A. 245 Syþen in to gresse þou me a-glyȝte.

agly, var. of AGLEY *adv.*

aglycone (əˈglaɪkəʊn). *Chem.* [ad. G. *aglykon* (A. Windaus et al. 1925, in *Zeitschr. f. Physiol. Chemie* CXLV. 38), f. A- 14 + GLYCO- + -O)NE.] The portion of a glycoside which remains when the sugar component is removed; called an **aˈglucone** when the sugar involved is glucose.

1925 JACOBS & HOFFMANN in *Proc. Soc. Exp. Biol. & Med.* XXIII. 214 The digitalis glucosides, digitoxin, and gitoxin .. contain different although possibly related aglucones, respectively digitoxigenin and gitoxigenin. **1938** A. T. CAMERON *Textbk. Biochem.* (ed. 5) iv. 94 The 'aglycone' (non-carbohydrate portion) of the glucoside. *Ibid.* v. 122 These aglycones .. possess chemnical structures which relate them to the sterols. **1941** *Ann. Reg. 1940* 344 The aglucone fraction of the cardiac glucosides .. [has] the same skeleton as cholesterol. **1964** GUTHRIE & HONEYMAN *Chem. Carbohydrates* (ed. 2) viii. 58 The non-sugar portion [of a glycoside], known as the aglycone (aglucone when the substance is a glucoside), is an alcohol or a phenol.

aglyphous (ˈæglɪfəs), *a. Zool.* [f. A- 14 + Gr. γλυφή carving + -OUS; cf. F. *Aglyphodontes* sb. pl. (A. H. A. Duméril, 1853).] Of a snake's tooth: solid, without a groove for venom. Of a snake: (belonging to a group Aglypha) having such teeth.

1893 G. A. BOULENGER *Catal. Snakes Brit. Mus.* (*Nat. Hist.*) I. 170 Beyond these three subfamilies I am unable to divide the Aglyphous *Colubridæ* into groups .. that may be regarded as natural and capable of definition. **1902** *Proc. R. Soc.* LXX. 447 *Tropidonotus*, a genus of Aglyphous or 'harmless' Colubrines. **1943** M. A. SMITH in R. B. S. Sewell *Fauna of Brit. India: Reptilia & Amphibia* III. 2 Solid teeth (aglyphous) occur in all the primitive snakes. **1956** A. S. ROMER *Osteol. Reptiles* II. 574 For these four types of dentition were coined the terms *aglyphous, opisthoglyphous, proteroglyphous,* and *solenoglyphous.* Aglyphous types lacking other specializations are customarily considered as forming a subfamily Colubrinae. **1965** R. & D. MORRIS *Men & Snakes* viii. 177 Snakes with non-poisonous saliva are referred to as Aglyphous. These have simple, small teeth all along the upper (and lower) jaws. **1969** A. BELLAIRS *Life of Reptiles* I. v. 199 Mice have died within less than an hour after subcutaneous injection of gland extract from 'harmless', aglyphous snakes such as the Indian rat snake.

Hence [as back-formation] **ˈaglyph,** an aglyphous snake.

1913 G. A. BOULENGER *Snakes of Europe* v. 57 The Aglyphs, in which the teeth are all solid. **1965** [see OPISTHOGLYPH *sb.* (*a*)].

agma (ˈægmə, ‖ˈæŋmə). *Phonol.* [a. late Gr., f. Gr. ἄγμα fragment.] A name for the sound [ŋ], orig. as it occurred in Ancient Greek when the letter γ preceded another γ, κ, χ, or a nasal consonant; a symbol standing for this sound in phonetic transcription.

1890 W. J. PURTON tr. *F. W. Blass's Pronunc. Anc. Greek* xxii. 88 Some would assume the guttural nasal, written γ, before μ and ν, on account of the traditional name *agma*; for in this name, a transposition of γάμμα, the sound itself ought according to them to occur. For this very reason however others emend ἄγγμα. **1957** [see *murmur vowel* s.v. MURMUR *sb.* 5]. **1967** DILLON & CHADWICK *Celtic Realms* ix. 207 The earliest Irish documents we have are inscriptions in a curious alphabet called *Ogam*... [*Note*] O'Rahilly appears to think that Ogam was brought into Ireland from Gaul. Richardson stresses the importance of the special sign for *ng* (agma). **1980–81** *Verbatim* Winter 14/2 Some, who do not believe that dictionary users will make the effort to interpret unfamiliar symbols like the long *s* (ʃ), IPA for the *sh* in *shoot* and other spelled forms, .. the agma (ŋ), for the *ng* in *thing*, and others, continue to use Moo Goo Gai Pan transcription.

†**ˈagminal,** *a. Obs.*⁻⁰ [ad. L. *agminālis*, f. *agmen* (*agmin-*) a troop, army.] 'Belonging to a troop.' Bailey 1731.

agminate (ˈægmɪneɪt), *a.* [f. L. *agmen* (*agmin-*) a troop + -ATE².] Arranged in a group or cluster.

1859 TODD *Cycl. Anat. & Phys.* V. 356/2 There are generally about twenty clusters of these agminate follicles.

agminated (ˈægmɪneɪtɛd), *ppl. a.* [f. prec. + -ED.] = prec.

1847–9 TODD *Cycl. Anat. & Phys.* IV. x. 103/2 The patches of agminated glands. **1874** JONES & SIEV. *Pathol. Anat.* 153 The solitary and agminated follicles of the intestines.

agnail (ˈægneɪl). Forms: 1 **angnæȝl,** 5 **agnayl, -lle,** 6 **angnaylle, angnale, agnale,** 6–7 **agnayle, agnell,** 7 **agnel, agnaile,** 7– **agnail.** [A word of which the application (and perhaps the form) has been much perverted by pseudo-etymology. The OE. *angnæȝl* is cogn. w. OHG. *ungnagel*, mod.G. dial. *anneglen, einnegeln* (E. Müller), Fris. *ongneil, ogneil*; f. *ang-* (Goth. *aggwus*, cf. *angsum*), compressed, tight, painful + *næȝl*, Goth. *nagls* nail. The latter had here the sense, not of 'finger-nail,' *unguis*, but of a nail (of iron, etc.) *clāvus*, hence, a hard round-headed excrescence fixed in the flesh; cf. *wer-næȝl*, WARNEL, a wart, lit. 'man-nail' (as opposed to 'door-nail,' 'wall-nail,' etc.). So, L. *clāvus* was both a nail (of iron, etc.) and a corn in the foot. Subsequently *-nail* was referred to a *finger-* or *toe-nail* (*unguis*), and the meaning gradually perverted to various (imaginary or real) affections of the nails: see senses 2, 3.]

†**1.** A corn on the toe or foot. *Obs.*

c **950** *Saxon Leechdoms* II. 80 Wiþ angnægle argesweorf & ealde sapan. *a* **1440** *MS. Med. Linc.* lf. 300 (in Halliw.) For agnayls one mans fete or womans. **1483** *Cath. Angl.*, Agnaylle. **1530** PALSGR., Agnayle upon ones too, *corret.* **1547** BOORDE *Breuiary* II. (1552) 3 Clauus is the latin .. In englyshe it is named cornes or agnelles in a mannes fete or toes. **1551** TURNER *Herbal* II. 2 Figges .. purge away angnaylles and suche harde swellinges. *Ibid.* (1568) 17 [Aloe] heleth also agnales when they are cut of. **1575** TURBERVILLE *Venerie* 137 They skinne a kybed heele, they fret an angnale off, So thus I skippe from toppe to toe. **1601** HOLLAND *Pliny* XX. iii, Passing good for to be applyed to the agnels or corns of the feet. **1611** FLORIO, *Fignoli*, agnels, cornes, pushes, felons or swellings in the flesh. **1611** COTGR., *Corret*, an agnaile, or little corne, vpon a toe. **1611** —— *Frouelle*, an agnell, pinne, or warnell in the toe. **1783** AINSWORTH *Lat. Dict.*, *Morticini* .. agnails, or rather corns, especially on the feet and toes.

2. Any 'painful swelling,' 'ulcer,' or 'sore,' under, about, around the toe- or finger-nail; in J. and subseq. Dicts. identified with *whitlow.* [This change of explanation seems due to pseudo-etymology; whether confusion with Fr. '*angonailles*, botches, (pocky) bumps, or sores,' Cotgr., or med.L. *anghiones, anguinalia*, carbuncles, contributed the 'ulcers' or 'sores' is uncertain; but *-nail*, misinterpreted, fixed the locality. The further identification with whitlow (in the Dicts.) seems due to collating the Gr. name of the latter παρωνυχία (f. παρ' beside + ὄνυχ- nail) with *ag-nail* (quasi *ag-* at + *nail*). Ash explains *agnail* as 'a whitlow, paronychia,' and *paronychia* as 'a perpetual sore under the root of the nail, a whitlow.']

1578 LYTE *Dodoens* 258 Good to be layde unto .. ulcered nayles, or agnayles, whiche is a paynefull swelling aboute the ioyntes and nayles. **1633** W. LANGHAM *Gard. Health* (ed. 2) 95 It draweth out splents and broken bones, and openeth noughty vlcers and agnayles, that grow about the roots of the nayles. **1656** BLOUNT *Glossogr.*, *Agnail*, a sore between the finger and the nail. **1721** BAILEY, *Agnail*, a sore at the root of the nail on the fingers or toes. **1755** JOHNSON, *Agnail*, a disease of the nails, a whitlow. **1847** CRAIG [as J.].

3. A 'hang-nail'; see quot. [*Hang-nail*, given by Halliwell as a dialect word, is evidently like the Sc. equivalent *anger-nail* (ANGER = irritation, inflammation), a corruption of *ang-nail*, putting a plausible meaning into it. That is, *ang-nail*, dialectally pronounced *hang-nail*, was explained as 'hanging' or detached nail. This explanation of *agnail* appears first in Bailey 1737 (ed. 1736 having only sense 2); the form *hang-nail* is in Craig 1847, and is now commoner in London than *agnail.*]

1742 BAILEY, *Agnail*: a sore slip of skin at the root of a nail. **1758** DYCHE & PARDON, *Agnail*; the soreness that arises from the stripping up the flesh into thin slices at the bottom and corners of the nails. **1847** HALLIWELL, *Agnail*, a hang-nail, either on the finger or toe. *Hangnails*, small pieces of partially separated skin about the roots of the finger-nails. *Various dialects.* **1879** *Syd. Soc. Lex.*, *Agnail*, a term applied to the shreds of epidermis which separate from the skin covering the root of the nail, and which, on being torn, give rise to a painful state of the fingers. **1882** *Weldon's Illustr. Dressmaker* Oct., Suppl. 6 This method practised daily will keep the nails in perfect preservation, also preventing agnails.

agname (ˈægneɪm). [f. L. *ag-* = *ad-* in addition + NAME, after L. *agnomen.*] An appellation over and above the ordinary name and surname; a 'to-name,' a sobriquet.

1834 H. MILLER *Scenes & Leg.* iv. (1857) 52 The title, or agname, of Paterhemon.

agnamed (ˈægneɪmd), *ppl. a.* [f. prec. + -ED².] Styled or called, apart from christian and surname.

1652 URQUHART *Jewel* Wks. 1834, 214 Colonel Alexander Hamilton, agnamed dear Sandy. **1834** H. MILLER *Scenes & Leg.* iv. (1857) 47 He was agnamed *Gulielmus de monte alto.*

agnate (ˈægneɪt), *sb.* and *a.* Also 6–7 **agnat,** 7 **agnet.** [a. Fr. *agnat*, ad. L. *agnāt-us* (*adgnāt-us, adnātus*) a relation by the father's side; prop. born to, added by birth, pa. pple. of *adgnā-sc-i*, f. *ad* to + *gnā-sc-i* to be born, f. stem *gen-* to beget. Another form of the word differently used is ADNATE.]

A. *sb.*

1. A kinsman by the father's side; a collateral descendant by male links from the same male ancestor.

1534 in Balfour's *Practicks* (1754) 117 Thay cannot have ony agnat or kinnisman of the father's side. **1607–40** *Roxb. Bal.* (1871) I. 449 It never shall make me looke otherwise than an agnet. **1671** *True Non-Conf.* 455 The King of Navarre, to whom, as nearest agnat, the Regencie belonged. **1840** *Blackw. Mag.* XLVIII. 143 Cognates or agnates—affinity or consanguinity—all varieties came alike to them. **1880** MUIRHEAD *Gaius* I. 156 By agnates are to be understood persons who are of kin through males.

2. A relation by descent from a common male ancestor, even though female links have intervened.

1868 CHAMBERS *Encycl.* I. 76 Agnates, in the law both of England and Scotland, are persons related through the father, as cognates are persons related through the mother. .. The intervention of females is immaterial, provided the connection be on the male or paternal side of the house.

B. *adj.* [After the use of L. *agnāt-us*, which was properly adj.]

1. Related by the father's side; also, sprung from the same forefather, of the same clan or nation.

1860 FARRAR *Orig. Lang.* ix. 199 The Agnate descendants of Shem.

2. *fig.* Allied in kind, akin; partaking of the same nature.

1782 POWNALL *Study Antiq.* (T.) By a fair reciprocal analysis of the agnate words. **1828** LANDOR *Imag. Conv.* (1846) 342 Persons who are elevated to high rank .. assume more or less of a fictitious character, but congenial and agnate, if I may say it, with the former.

agnathan (ægˈneɪθən), *sb.* and *a. Ichthyol.* Also **Agnathan.** [f. mod.L. *Agnatha* (E. D. Cope 1889, in *Amer. Naturalist* XXIII. 852), f. Gr. ἀ- A- 14 + γνάθ-ος jaw + -A 2: see -AN.] **A.** *sb.* A member of the class or superclass Agnatha of jawless fishes, which comprises hagfish, lampreys, and many extinct forms, including the earliest vertebrates.

1939 J. A. MOY-THOMAS *Palaeozoic Fishes* i. 2 The head of a hypothetical primitive Agnathan must have had a terminal mouth and been segmented in a manner similar to the rest of the body. **1978** *Sci. Amer.* Sept. 111/1 The early jawless fishes, the agnathans, are first known from late Cambrian fossils. **1984** J. S. NELSON *Fishes of World* (ed. 2) 29 The interrelationships of the agnathans have been subject to many differences of opinion.

B. *adj.* Of, pertaining to, or being an agnathan.

1974 D. & M. WEBSTER *Compar. Vertebr. Morphol.* iv. 64 Since the agnathan head skeleton lacks jaws, only the cartilages of the tongue and the lamprey's annular cartilage are involved in food gathering. **1979** *Nature* 20 Dec. 831/2 We have united the galeaspids and polybranchiaspids .. and grouped them within the same major agnathan division as the anaspids and lampreys—the Cephalaspidomorphi. **1985** A. WHEELER *World Encycl. Fishes* (ed. 2) p. vii/2 The 32 known species of lamprey and the related hagfishes are the sole survivors of the agnathan fishes, a group of great diversity in the fossil record.

agnathous (ˈægnəθəs), *a. Phys.* [f. Gr. ἀ priv. + γνάθ-ος jaw + -OUS.] Having no jaws.

1879 in *Syd. Soc. Lex.*

agnatic (ægˈnætɪk), *a.* [ad. Fr. *agnatique*: see AGNATE and -IC.] Of or pertaining to agnates; related on the father's side.

1747 CARTE *Hist. Eng.* I. 365 A lineal agnatic succession. **1880** MUIRHEAD *Gaius* II. 64 The agnatic [L. *agnatus*] curator of a lunatic is empowered .. to alienate his ward's property.

†**agˈnatical,** *a. Obs. rare*⁻¹. [f. prec. or Fr. *agnatique* + -AL¹.] = AGNATIC.

1660 R. COKE *Power & Subj.* 99 Lineal, agnatical, cognatical or collateral [descent].

agnatically (æg'nætɪkəlɪ), *adv.* [f. AGNATICAL + -LY².] In an agnatic manner; by agnation.

1861 MAINE *Anc. Law* v. 149 All persons are Agnatically connected together who are under the same Paternal Power.

agnation (æg'neɪʃən). [a. Fr. *agnation*, ad. L. *agnātiōn-em*, n. of action f. *agnāsci*: see AGNATE.]

1. Relationship through the male line; descent from a common male ancestor through male links alone, as recognized in the Salic law.

1611 GUILLIM *Heraldry* 255/1 The Agnation (which is of the Fathers side) must be preserued entire. **1861** MAINE *Anc. Law* v. 149 The foundation of Agnation is not the Marriage of Father and Mother, but the authority of the Father. **1880** MUIRHEAD *Gaius* I. §156 There is no agnation between a mother's brother and her son,—only cognation.

2. Descent from a common male ancestor, even though female links have intervened; distinguished from *cognation* or descent from the same mother, which may or may not include agnation.

1751 CHAMBERS *Cycl.* s.v., This difference was abolished by Justinian (*Inst.* 3. 10) and the females were reinstated in the right of Agnation.. hence cognation came to take in all the relations of the mother as well as father; and Agnation to be restrained to those of the father alone.

3. *fig.* Kinship by descent.

1782 POWNALL *Study Antiq.* 168 (T.) A much greater agnation may be found amongst all the languages in the northern hemisphere.

agnesite ('ægnɪsaɪt). *Min.* [See quot.]

1837–80 DANA *Mineral.* (ed. 5) 793 Agnesite.. an earthy steatite-like mineral from St. Agnes in Cornwall.. may be an impure bismuth ochre.

agnet, obs. form of AGNATE.

agnification (ˌægnɪfɪ'keɪʃən). *rare.* [f. L. *agn-us* lamb + -FICATION.] The making or representing (of persons) as lambs or sheep.

1863 NEALE *Liturgiol.*, Early frescoes which represent all kinds of Scriptural characters under the form of sheep.. The agnification of such artists, etc.

†**'agnit**, *v. Obs. rare*⁻¹. [f. L. *agnit-* ppl. stem of *agnōsc-ĕre*: see AGNITION.] = AGNIZE.

1708 MOTTEUX *Rabelais* v. xx, The silence of the Egyptians was agnited as an expressive manner of Divine Adoration.

†**ag'nition**. *Obs.* [ad. L. *agnitiōn-em* n. of action, f. *agnit-* ppl. stem of *agnōsc-ĕre, adgnōsc-ĕre*, to recognize, acknowledge; f. *ad.* to + *gnōscĕre*, f. stem *gno-* to know.] Recognition, acknowledgement.

1569 GRAFTON *Chron.* 75 The agnition of the shepeherdes. **1668** HOWE *Bless. Righteous* Wks. 1834, 247/1 Our glorifying him [God] is but the agnition of his glory. **1678** CUDWORTH *Intellect. Syst.* 471 They liked not to retain God in the Agnition, or Practical Knowledge of him. **1775** ASH, *Agnition*, an acknowledgement, an owning.

agnize (æg'naɪz), *v. arch.* Also 6–7 **agnise**, 7 **adnize**. [formed after L. *a(d)gnōsc-ĕre* to acknowledge, recognize, apprehend (f. *ad* to + *gnōscĕre* to get to know), on the analogy of *cognize* and *cognōscĕre*, *recognize* and *recognōscĕre*, derived through Fr., while *agnize* had no Fr. antecedent.]

1. To recognize, remember. *arch.*

1611 SPEED *Hist. Gt. Brit.* VI. xiv. 91 The Britaines wil agnize their owne cause, the Gaules will remember their wonted liberty. **1790** COWPER *Odyssey* XIII. 226 That ere yet agnized By others, he might wisdom learn from her. **1814** CARY *Dante's Inf.* xv. 22, I was agnized of one, who by the skirt Caught me.

†**2.** To recognize or acknowledge in any capacity; to own. Const. *for, as, inf., sb. in appos. Obs.*

1535 LEGH in Strype *Eccl. Mem.* (1822) I. II. 216 They should be driven by this means to agnize their author, spring, and fountain. **1542** UDALL *Erasm. Apophth.* (1877) 271 To agnise and knowledge Julius Cæsar for his conquerour. **1593** BILSON *Govt. Chr. Ch.* 46 Let him agnise the things that I write to be the commandements of the Lord. **1635** PAGITT *Christianogr.* App. 18 They had submitted to the Pope of Rome, and agnized him their Head. **1737** WATERLAND *Eucharist* 496 Offered up to God, for the agnizing Him as Creator of the World.

†**3.** To own the authority or claims of. *Obs.*

1581 SAVILE *Tacitus, Hist.* 7 Not accustomed to obey any lawe, to agnize any magistrate. **1593** BILSON *Govt. Chr. Ch.* To Reader, To agnise or admit the ancient and approued maner of the primitive church. **1659** LUDLOW *Mem.* (1771) 264 It was desired, That since it.. would be most safe for the protector [Richard Cromwell] to derive his authority from a right source, the words in the declaration of 'recognizing' him might be altered for 'agnizing' him; that so his right might appear to be founded upon the consent of the people represented in this assembly. **1748** T. EDWARDS *Canons Crit.* 291 (R.) Such He will crown with praise, And glad agnize before his Father's throne.

4. To recognize the existence of, to acknowledge, confess. *arch.*

1543 BECON *Policy of War* Wks. 1843, 245 Unthankful is he, that doth not agnise and knowledge the unmeasurable kindness of this most excellent prince. **1576** WOOLTON *Chr. Manual* (1851) 12 Happy is that man.. that humbly and heartily agniseth his faults. **1604** SHAKS. *Oth.* I. iii. 232, I do agnize A Naturall and prompt Alacartie, I finde in hardnesse. **1648** D. JENKINS *Wks.* 23 We doe upon the knees of our heart adnize constant Faith, Loyalty, and Obedience to the King. **1823** LAMB *Elia* Ser. I. ii. (1865) 11 Well, I do agnize something of the sort. **1855** BAILEY *Mystic* 56 None but they Who extasie divine enjoy, agnize The universal impulse.

b. *absol.*

1602 WARNER *Albion's Eng.* XI. lxiii. (1612) 275 Loue is a Lordly Feast: Agnize (so should you) so, and so despayre is part releast.

†**5.** To gain knowledge of, learn. *Obs. rare.*

c **1575** *Cambyses* in Hazl. *Dodsl.* IV. 173 The tenor of your princely will From you for to agnise.

agnized (æg'naɪzd), *ppl. a. arch.* [f. prec. + -ED.] Recognized, acknowledged.

1535 LEGH in Strype *Eccl. Mem.* (1822) I. I. 216 The king.. of late agnized & declared Supreme Head of the Church. **1735–8** LD. BOLINGBROKE *Diss. on Parties* 99 A Title.. agnized, or recognized, by his Parliament. **1790** [See AGNIZE *v.* 1.]

agnizing (æg'naɪzɪŋ), *vbl. sb.* [f. AGNIZE *v.* + -ING¹.] A recognizing; acknowledgement.

a **1557** UDALL *Luke* i. 79 (R.) With yᵉ agnisyng & knowlageyng of theyr owne synfulnesse. **1737** [See AGNIZE *v.* 2.]

'agnoetism. *Eccl. Hist.* [f. AGNOETE, -ITE + -ISM.] The doctrine or system of the Agnoites.

1753 CHAMBERS *Cycl. Supp.*, There seems to have been two kinds of *agnoetism* and *agnoetæ*.

agnoiology (ægnɔɪ'ɒlədʒɪ). *Philos.* [f. Gr. *ἄγνοια* ignorance + -(O)LOGY.] The doctrine of those things of which we are necessarily ignorant; that department of philosophy which inquires into the character and conditions of ignorance.

1856 FERRIER *Inst. Metaph.* 51 We must examine and fix what ignorance is—what we are, and can be, ignorant of. And thus we are thrown upon an entirely new research, constituting an intermediate section of philosophy, which we term the agnoiology.. the theory of true ignorance.

agnoites, agnoetes ('ægnəʊaɪts, -iːts). *Eccl. Hist.* [ad. med.L. *agnoītæ*, ad. Gr. *ἀγνοηταί*, heretics so named; f. *ἀγνοέ-ειν* to be ignorant.] An ancient theological sect who held that Christ was ignorant of some things.

1586 T. ROGERS *39 Art.* (1607) 48 The Agnoites, who held that the divine nature of Christ was ignorant of some things. **1775** ASH, *Agnoetes*, a sect who denied that Christ knew the day of judgment.

‖**agnomen** (æg'nəʊmɛn). [L. *agnōmen*, *adnōmen*, f. *ad.* to + *(g)nōmen* name; cf. *adgnō-sc-ĕre* to recognize.] In *Rom. Antiq.* A second cognomen or fourth name, occasionally assumed by Romans. Hence *loosely*, A 'to-name' or additional name subsequently acquired.

1753 CHAMBERS *Cycl. Supp.* s.v., The generality of grammarians speak of the *agnomen* as a fourth name superadded to the *cognomen* or third name, on account of some extraordinary action, virtue, or the like: as *Africanus* in Publius Cornelius Scipio Africanus. **1802** MAR. EDGEWORTH *Ennui* ix. (1832) VI. 101 She was wonderfully happy in the invention of agnomens. **1814** SCOTT *Wav.* xvii. 74 Small pale features, from which he derived his agnomen of Bean, or white.

agnomical (æg'nɒmɪkəl), *a.* [f. Gr. *ἀ* priv. + *γνώμη* thought, purpose + -ICAL; after Gr. *γνωμικός*; the Gr. form would be *ἄγνωμος*.] Of or belonging to the absence of set purpose or intention.

1881 FAIRBAIRN in *Scotsman* 24 Feb. 3 The struggle.. of the agnomical and evolutional with the statical and stationary element.

agnominal (æg'nɒmɪnəl), *a.* ? *Obs. rare*⁻¹. [f. L. AGNOMEN (*-min-*) + -AL¹.] Of or belonging to an agnomen.

1652 URQUHART *Jewel* Wks. 1834, 276 He had his proper name affected with the agnominal addition of Parresiastes.

agnominate (æg'nɒmɪneɪt), *v.* ? *Obs. rare.* [f. L. *agnōmināt-* ppl. stem of *agnōminā-re*, f. AGNOMEN; more commonly ANNOMINATE.] To bestow an agnomen on, style, nickname.

1595 *Locrine* III. ii. 161 Silver streams Which in memorial of our victory Shall be agnominated by our name. **1656** BLOUNT *Glossogr.*, *Agnominate*, to allude to ones name, to nickname. [Not in JOHNSON 1775, but in TODD 1818, and mod. Dicts.]

agnomination (æg,nɒmɪ'neɪʃən). [ad. L. *agnōminātiōn-em* (also *adn-* and in med.L. *ann-*), n. of action, f. *agnōminā-re*: see AGNOMINATE. Also written ADNOMINATION and ANNOMINATION.]

1. The giving of an agnomen or surname; the name so given. *rare*⁻⁰.

1692 COLES, *Agnomination*, a sir-name. [Not in JOHNSON 1755.] **1775** ASH, *Agnomination*, the giving of a new name.

2. *Rhet.* A kind of word-play, paronomasia; allusion of one word to another.

1588 FRAUNCE *Lawiers Logike* I. xii. 50 As for the pretty and conceipted chaunge of the woord, *argumentum ab arguendo*, it seemeth also a Rhetoricall agnomination. **1601** B. JONSON *Poetaster* III. i. 104 A kind of paranomasie, or agnomination. **1657** J. SMITH *Myst. Rhet.* 105 Agnomination is a pleasant sound of words, or a small change of names; or it is a present touch of the same letter, syllable, or word with a different meaning. **1682** KEACH & DELAUNE *Philologica Sacra* II. ii. 3 in *τροποσχημαλογια* II, Agnomination, or Likeness of Words.. is when by the Change of one Letter or Word, the Signification thereof is also changed. **1962** G. K. HUNTER *John Lyly* iv. 244 The highly patterned prose.. is not there simply because Lyly was suffering from a bad dose of agnomination or isocolon.

3. Alliteration.

1595–6 R. CAREW in *Shaks. Cent. Praise* 20 In Ecchoes and Agnominations. **1605** CAMDEN *Rem.* 27 The English and Welsh delighted much in licking the letter and clapping together Agnominations. **1789** MRS. PIOZZI *France & Italy* I. 239 They held agnominations... to be elegant.

agnosia (æg'nəʊsɪə). *Path.* [mod.L., a Gr. *ἀγνωσία* ignorance (*ἀ-* priv., *γνῶ σις* knowledge: see GNOSIS).] Freud's term (*Zur Auffassung der Aphasien*, 1891) for loss of perception (sense 7). Hence **ag'nosic** *a.*

1900 DORLAND *Med. Dict.* 27/2 *Agnosia*, loss of the perceptive power; loss of the power to recognize persons or things seen. **1940** HINSIE & SHATZKY *Psychiatric Dict.* 16/1 In psychiatry the term agnosia is employed to indicate the loss or disuse of knowledge of objects, when the knowledge appears to have been altered by emotional circumstances. **1953** E. STENGEL tr. *Freud's On Aphasia* 78 For disturbances in the recognition of objects, which Finkelnburg called asymbolia, I should like to propose the term 'agnosia'. **1953** M. CRITCHLEY *Parietal Lobes* vi. 191 The various types of visual agnosic defects. **1961** *Brit. Med. Dict.* 57/1 Agnosia is found in relation with the senses: auditory agnosia, gustatory agnosia, olfactory agnosia, optic agnosia, and tactile agnosia. **1964** M. CRITCHLEY *Developmental Dyslexia* i. 2 Another kind of dichotomy also came about, which looked upon cases of alexia without agraphia as instances of 'agnosic alexia'. **1974** E. LAUSCH *Manipulation* v. 72 People whose association areas have been damaged can still see and can describe exactly the shape and colour of what they see, but they have difficulties in recognizing what they have seen. It is hard to transpose oneself into the world of such a 'visually agnosic' person, as the doctors call it. **1976** S. S. GUBBAY (*title*) A study of developmental apraxia and agnosic ataxia.

agnostic (æg'nɒstɪk), *sb.* and *a.* [f. Gr. *ἄγνωστ-ος* unknowing, unknown, unknowable (f. *ἀ* not + *γνο-* know) + -IC. Cf. GNOSTIC; in Gr. the termination *-ικός* never coëxists with the privative *ἀ-*.]

A. *sb.* One who holds that the existence of anything beyond and behind material phenomena is unknown and (so far as can be judged) unknowable, and especially that a First Cause and an unseen world are subjects of which we know nothing.

[Suggested by Prof. Huxley at a party held previous to the formation of the now defunct Metaphysical Society, at Mr. James Knowles's house on Clapham Common, one evening in 1869, in my hearing. He took it from St. Paul's mention of the altar to 'the Unknown God.' R. H. HUTTON in letter 13 Mar. 1881.]

1870 *Spect.* 29 Jan. 135 In theory he [Prof. Huxley] is a great and even severe Agnostic, who goes about exhorting all men to know how little they know. **1874** MIVART *Ess. Relig. etc.* 205 Our modern Sophists—the Agnostics,—those who deny we have any knowledge, save of phenomena. **1876** *Spect.* 11 June, Nicknames are given by opponents, but Agnostic was the name demanded by Professor Huxley for those who disclaimed atheism, and believed with him in an 'unknown and unknowable' God; or in other words that the ultimate origin of all things must be some cause unknown and unknowable. **1880** BP. FRASER in *Manch. Guardn.* 25 Nov., The Agnostic neither denied nor affirmed God. He simply put Him on one side.

B. *adj.* Of or pertaining to agnostics or their theory.

1873 *Q. Rev.* CXXXV. 192 The pseudo-scientific teachers of what has.. been termed.. the Agnostic Philosophy. **1876** Principal TULLOCH *Agnosticism* in *Weekly Scotsm.* 18 Nov., The same agnostic principle which prevailed in our schools of philosophy had extended itself to religion and theology. Beyond what man can know by his senses or feel by his higher affections, nothing, as was alleged, could be truly known. **1880** BIRDWOOD *Ind. Arts* I. 4 The agnostic teaching of the Sankhya school is the common basis of all systems of Indian philosophy. **1882** FROUDE *Carlyle* II. 216 The agnostic doctrines, he (Carlyle) once said to me, were to appearance like the finest flour, from which you might expect the most excellent bread; but when you came to feed on it, you found it was powdered glass, and you had been eating the deadliest poison.

agnostical (æg'nɒstɪkəl), *a.* [f. AGNOSTIC + -AL.] = AGNOSTIC *a.*

1884 *Punch* 20 Sept. 135 The Agnostical or Nothingarian creed. **1886** *Sat. Rev.* 25 Dec. 849 Our Agnostical friend passed to the paradise of Mahomet. **1907** *Daily Chron.* 23 Mar. 6/4 Anthropomorphism is the most agnostical and atheistical habit of thought.

agnostically (æg'nɒstɪkəlɪ), *adv.* [f. AGNOSTIC *sb.* and *a.* + -AL¹ + -LY².] In an agnostic manner; with a leaning towards agnosticism.

1882 *Daily News* 7 Dec. 5/3 In one of his latest books he brought an agnostically-minded hero on the scene.

agnosticism (æg'nɒstɪsɪz(ə)m). [f. AGNOSTIC + -ISM.] The doctrine or tenets of Agnostics.

1870 *Spect.* 29 Jan. 135 The lecture was.. perhaps not quite so full as it should have been of his Agnosticism. **1871** R. H. HUTTON *Ess.* I. 27 They themselves vehemently dispute the term [atheism] and usually prefer to describe their state of mind as a sort of know-nothingism or Agnosticism, or belief in an unknown and unknowable God. **1877** E. CONDER *Basis of Faith* i. 25 But there is nothing *per se* irrational in contending that the evidences of Theism are inconclusive, that its doctrines are unintelligible, or that it fails to account for the facts of the universe, or is irreconcilable with them. To express this kind of polemic against religious faith the term 'agnosticism' has been adopted. **1879** HUXLEY *Hume* i. 60 Called agnosticism, from its profession of an incapacity to discover the indispensable conditions of either positive or negative knowledge. **1880** *Sat. Rev.* 26 June 819/2 In nine cases out of ten Agnosticism is but old atheism 'writ large.'

‖**'Agnus.** [L. *agnus* a lamb.] = AGNUS DEI.
1494 FABYAN VII. 472 After the thirde agnus was sayd. **1674** BREVINT *Saul & Sam.* 331 (T.) They will..carry most devoutly a scapulary, an agnus, or a set of beads about them. *Ibid.* 322 Scapularies, beads, ropes, agnusses. **1888** in E. S. Roscoe *Bishop of Lincoln's Case* (1889) 48 The words or hymn or prayer commonly known as the Agnus that is to say Oh Lamb of God that takest away the Sins of the World—Have mercy upon us. **1921** *Outward Bound* Apr. 72/1 It was a little Agnus of gold and enamel. **1936** E. UNDERHILL *Worship* xiii. 285 The *Agnus* is now sung, and the Lord's Prayer is said. **1961** *Proc. R. Mus. Assoc.* LXXXVII. 51 Another..composer..survives in only two works,..and of those two Masses one lacks the Agnus.

Comb. **agnus-bell** (in *R.C. Ch.*) the bell rung while the *Agnus Dei* is being said or sung in the Mass.
1566 in *Eng. Ch. Furniture* (1866) 103 One sanctus bell one agnus bell gone owtt of the fore sayd churche.

‖**agnus castus** ('ægnəs 'kæstəs). [L. *agnus*, a. Gr. ἄγνος name of the tree, confused with ἁγνός chaste, whence the second word L. *castus* chaste.] A tree, species of Vitex (*V. Agnus Castus*), once believed to be a preservative of chastity; called also Chaste-tree and Abraham's Balm (? Baum).
1398 TREVISA *Barth. De P.R.* XVII. xv. (1495) 612 The herbe Agnus castus is alwaye grene, and the flowre therof is namly callyd Agnus castus, for wyth smelle and vse it makyth men chaste as a lombe. *c* **1400** *Floure & Leafe* 173 A braunch of Agnus castus eke bearing In her hand. **1741** *Compl. Fam. Piece* II. iii. 386 Agnus Castus or the Chaste Tree. **1881** STANLEY *Chr. Instit.* i. 2 The sacred river rushes through its thicket of tamarisk, poplar, willow and agnus-castus.

‖**Agnus Dei** ('ægnəs 'diːaɪ, 'agnus 'deiː). [L. = lamb of God.] In *R.C. Ch.* **a.** A part of the Mass beginning with the words *Agnus Dei*; also the music set to it. Now also used in the service of the Church of England. **b.** A figure of a lamb bearing a cross or flag. **c.** A cake of wax stamped with such a figure and blessed by the Pope.
c **1400** *Apol. for Loll.* 8 Bi-twex þe consecracioun & *Agnus Dei.* **1480** CAXTON *Chron. Eng.* CCXXX. 245 After the iii *agnus dei* y seid. **1583** *Exec. for Treason* (1675) 45 Their Cakes of Wax which they call *Agnus Dei.* **1629** OWEN *Spec. Jesuit.* 44 Such little Cristall glasses, as Papists do vse to weare about their necks, with an *Agnus Dei* inclosed betweene them. **1673** MILTON *True Relig.* Wks. 1851, 418 Masses for him both quick and dead, *Agnus Dei's*, Reliques, and the like. **1845** HOLMES *Mozart* 100 The service lasted till a quarter to eleven, and an *Agnus Dei* of Haydn's was again performed. **1867** in C. Walker *Ritual Reason Why* x. 160 *What is the Agnus Dei?* It is an anthem sung by the choir during the Communion of the priest... The Choir sing thrice: 'O Lamb of God, that takest away the sins of the world', adding twice: 'have mercy upon us', and the third time: 'Grant us Thy peace'. **1887** *Church Times* 30 Dec. 1082/3 The music throughout was of the simplest character, the *Kyrie*, *Benedictus* and *Agnus Dei* being sung to Merbecke. **1974** *Oxf. Dict. Chr. Church* (ed. 2) 41/2 The Offertory leads directly to the Thanksgiving... The Fraction, which follows, may be accompanied by the Agnus Dei.

†**a'go,** *v. Obs.* Forms as in GO. [f. A- *pref.* 1 forth, away, out + GO. Cogn. w. OS. *âgangan*, OHG. *irgangan, irgân* (mod.G. *ergehen*), Goth. *us-gaggan*. Only the pa. pple. *agan, agon, agone, ago* is common after 1300, and of this the *verbal* use ceased before 1700, leaving it only as *adj.* of time: see next.]
1. To go forth, go on, proceed.
a **1000** *Ags. Ps.* lxviii. 32 Cealf..þeah þe him úpp-agá horn on heafde. **1297** R. GLOUC. 561 Ich mai honge vp min ax, febliche ic abbe agonne.
2. Of time: To depart, pass away, pass.
c **1000** *O.E. Gosp.* Mark xvi. 1 Ða sæternes dæȝ wæs agán. **1205** LAYAM. 24196 Þa æstre wes aȝonge. *Ibid.* 31889 Þa elleue ȝer weoren onfast aȝeongen. *c* **1380** *Sir Ferumb.* 2305 Þe day hym was ful neȝ agan. *c* **1435** *Torr. Portugal* 65 Ore vij. yere be ago, More schalle we here. *c* **1550** *Every man* in Hazl. *Dodsl.* I. 107 The day passeth, and is almost ago.
3. To go away, depart (from a place).
c **1175** *Lamb. Hom.* 33 Nis nawiht þeos weorld, al heo aȝeð. *c* **1230** *Ancren Riwle* 288 Hit kumeð lihtliche, ageð awei lihtliche. *c* **1260** *E.E. Poems* (1862) 14 Al hir ioi was ago. *c* **1384** CHAUCER *H. of Fame* 365 He Was forthe vnto his shippes agoon. *c* **1420** *Pallad. on Husb.* II. 379 And when thaire huske agooth hem thai beth ripe. **1482** *Monk of Evesham* (1869) 112 The wownde so clene agonne, that no tokyn of hyt..remaynyd. **1586** FERNE *Blazon of Gentrie* 21 Our sheepe shearing feastes..been all agone. **1674** MARVELL *Rehears. Transp.* II. 76 The Author therefore..took a great fright lest all were ago.

ago, agone (ə'gəʊ, ə'gɒn), *ppl. a.* and *adv.* Forms: 4-5 **agoon**, 5-6 **agon**, 6- **agone**; also 4-6 **agoo**, 6-7 **agoe**, 4- **ago**. [pa. pple. of the preceding vb., used as adj. qualifying some noun of time, expressed or understood; in the latter case always preceded by *long = long time.* The full form *agone* had been contracted to *ago* in some dialects long before this usage began, in end of 14th c.; *ago* became the ordinary prose form from Caxton, but *agone* has remained dialectally, and as an archaic and poetic variant to the present day.]
A. *ppl. adj.* Gone by; by-gone; past. (Now always *follows* its noun.)
c **1314** *Guy Warw.* 58 For it was ago fif yer That he was last ther. *c* **1386** CHAUCER *Wife's T.* 7 (Lansd.) I speke of mony a hundred ȝere a-go. **1388** WYCLIF *Gen.* xxi. 2 As ȝistirdai, and the thridde dai agoon. *c* **1450** *Knt. de la Tour* 158 It is not yet longe tyme agoo that suche custume was vsed. **1528** MORE *Heresyes* II. Wks. 1557, 179/2 Nowe quite gone manye yeares a goo. **1601** SHAKS. *Twel. N.* V. i. 204 O he's drunke, sir Toby, an houre agone. **1611** BIBLE *1 Sam.* xxx. 13 Three dayes agone I fell sicke. **1718** *Free-thinker* No. 61, 42 Some Years agoe they were remarkable for the narrowest Hats in the Kingdom. *a* **1849** HOR. SMITH *Addr. Mummy* i, In Thebes's streets three thousand years ago. **1846** HAWTHORNE *Mosses* I. iv. 70 And that's full fifteen minutes agone. **1869** 'MARK TWAIN' *Innoc. Abr.* xxi. 212 Some two and forty years agone the good count rode hence to fight for Holy Cross. **1914** W. OWEN *Let.* 19 July (1967) 267 So you are at last getting the Curtains, about which we fidaddled so long a year & more agone! **1933** H. ALLEN *Anthony Adverse* I. II. xiii. 170 It's over ten years agone, you know, since... **1980** *Amer. Speech 1976* LI. 245 Among recent coinages I miss *admanity*, a worthy successor to Thomas Carlyle's *gigmanity* a century agone.
B. *adv.* in *Long ago*: a long while ago, in time long gone, long since. Chaucer has also *yore ago.*
c **1366** CHAUCER *Compl. Pity* 1 Pite that I haue sought so yore agoo. **1377** LANGL. *P. Pl.* B. XVIII. 271, I þis lord knowe, it is longe ago I knewe him. **1417** CLIFFORD in Ellis *Orig. Lett.* II. 29 I. 90 It liked to youre seyd Hyghnesse not longe agon to wryte to me. **1548** UDALL, etc. *Erasm. Paraphr. Matt.* xvi. 2 Ye would haue beleued me long agon. **1633** FORD *Broken Heart* III. v. (1839) 63 'Tis long agone since first I lost my heart. **1833** HT. MARTINEAU *Loom & Lug.* I. v. 89 Dead and gone long ago.
¶ Corrupt form. See A *prep.*[2]
c **1538** STARKEY *England* 88 Not many yerys of-goo.

agog (ə'gɒg), *adv.* Also 6 **on gogge**. [perh. ad. OFr. *en gogues* (15th c. in Littré '*il estoit en gogues*'; Cotgr. '*estre en ses gogues* to be frolicke, lustie, lively, wanton, gamesome, all-a-hoit, in a pleasant humour; in a veine of mirth, or in a merrie mood'), f. *gogue* 'fun, diversion,' of unknown origin. (See conjectures in Diez and Skeat. Prof. Rhys finds no etymon in Celtic.) Cf. also Fr. *vivre à gogo* to live like a lord, in abundance; see Littré.] In eager readiness, expectation, or desire; on the move, astir. Const. *inf.*, *on*, *upon*, *for*, *with*, *about*. In some instances now regarded as pred. adj.: eager, keen.
1542 UDALL *Erasm. Apophth.* (1877) 329 Beeying set agog to thinke all the worlde otemele. **1559** *Myrroure for Mag.*, *Glendour* xxiii. 1 And for to set us hereon more agog. **1575** TURBERVILLE *Booke of Venerie* 92 To sette mens myndes on gogge. **1600** HOLLAND *Livy* XLV. xxxv. 1225 c, These words set them agog [*His verbis incitatis*]. **1656** TRAPP *Exp. John* xi. 53 (1868) 385/2 To set men agog upon mischief. **1663** COWLEY *Cutter of Colem. St.* v. xiii. (1710) II. 892, I ha' set her agog to Day for a Husband. **1782** COWPER *Gilpin* x, Six precious souls and all agog To dash through thick and thin. **1792** GOUV. MORRIS in Sparks' *Life* (1832) II. 230 They are now agog with their republic. **1865** CARLYLE *Fredk. Gt.* V. XIII. ix. 100 The Eldest, age fourteen, had gone quite agog about my little Girl, age only nine. **1887** M. ARNOLD in *Fortnightly Rev.* July 2 Still, still I see the figure smart—Trophy in mouth agog to start, Then, home return'd, once more depart. **1903** H. JAMES *Ambassadors* III. vii. 67 He was now so interested, quite so privately agog, about it, that he had already an eye to the fun it would be to open up to her afterwards. **1922** JOYCE *Ulysses* 440 *Mrs Breen* (*All agog*): O, not for worlds. **1951** R. CAMPBELL *Light on Dark Horse* vi. 97 When we had got the spectators agog we would dive in. **1979** B. MOORE *Mangan Inheritance* I. 27 Everyone agog, everyone loves gossip.

agoggled (ə'gɒg(ə)ld), *ppl. a. rare*[−1]. [f. A- *pref.* 11 + GOGGLED.] = GOGGLED.
1862 A. LEIGHTON *Trad. Scott. Life* 8 A man a little agoggled in his eyes.

agogic (ə'gɒdʒɪk), *a.* [f. Gr. ἀγωγός leading, guiding, f. ἄγειν to lead + -IC.]
†**1.** Of or pertaining to modelling in wax.
1662 EVELYN *Sculptura* I. i. 7 Neither the Paradigmatic, Agogic, or any of the Plastic [Arts], can Genuinely..be call'd Sculpture.
2. *Mus.* [G. *agogik* (Riemann 1884).] Applied to a kind of accent consisting in a lengthening of the time-value of the note. Also **a'gogical** *a.* So **a'gogics**, the use of agogic accents.
1893 J. S. SHEDLOCK tr. *Riemann's Dict. Mus.* (1899) 13/1 Agogic accent is the name given by H. Riemann..to the slight prolongation of the note-value, in rhythms, which are in conflict with the species of time. *Ibid.*, Agogics..relates to the small modifications of *tempo*..which are necessary to genuine expression. **1921** *Mus. Assoc. Proc. 1919–20* 23 Treatises..on Aesthetics, Expression, Agogics, Phrasing. **1922** S. GREW *Art of Player-Piano* 62 'Agogic restraint' is the term found by German pedagogues to describe this detail of *rubato*. *Ibid.* 63 Clashings of discordant notes may be..intensified by an 'agogical' pressure. **1962** *Times* 15 Jan. 14/4 There are subtleties of agogic accent.

‖**à gogo** (a gogo) *phr.* Also **à go-go**. [Fr.] In abundance, galore, no end of.
1965 *Economist* 25 Dec. 1416/2 A lot more has been added, even before *après ski* life *à gogo* begins. **1966** *New Yorker* 24 Sept. 52 This is really nothing but Leninism à go-go! **1967** *Listener* 6 Apr. 468/3 (*heading*) Franglais à gogo. **1967** *Observer* 7 May 21/4 At Expo every nation is petrochemical a-go-go.

agoing; see A *prep.*[1] 13 b and GO *v.*

a'gomphious (ə'gɒmfɪəs), *a.* [f. Gr. ἀγόμφι-ος toothless + -OUS.] Toothless.
1879 in *Syd. Soc. Lex.*

‖**agon** ('ægəʊn). [Gr. ἀγών, orig. 'a gathering or assembly' (f. ἄγ-ειν to lead, bring with one), *esp.* for the public games; hence 'the contest for the prize at the games,' and by extension, 'any contest or struggle.' The pl. is usually in the Gr. form ἀγῶνες *agones* (ə'gəʊniːz).] **1.** *Gr. Antiq.* A public celebration of games, a contest for the prize at those games; also *fig.*
a **1660** HAMMOND *Serm.* (T.) Fit for combats and wrestlings and so came out to practise in these agones. *c* **1660** SANCROFT *Serm.* (1694) 106 (T.) They must do their exercises too—be anointed to the agon and to the combat. **1846** GROTE *Greece* II. II. iv. 422 Those religious games or agônes instituted by Herakles.
2. A verbal contest or dispute between two characters in a Greek play. Also *transf.*
1887 *Amer. Jrnl. Philol.* VIII. 197 The participants in an Agon are the Choros.., the two antagonists, the judge, and the clown. **1914** F. M. CORNFORD *Origin Attic Comedy* i. 2 What is now generally called the *Agon*, a fierce 'contest' between the representatives of two parties or principles, which are in effect the hero and villain of the whole piece. **1918** R. C. FLICKINGER *Greek Theater & its Drama* 41 The *agon*, a 'dramatized debate' or verbal duel between two actors, each supported by a semi-chorus. **1932** T. S. ELIOT *Sweeney Agonistes* 23 Fragment of an Agon.

†**'agonal, -el,** *sb. Obs. rare*[−1]. [? subst. use of Fr. *agonal*, ? *agonel*, quasi *liber agonalis* 'book of agonies': cf. *manual*, Fr. *manuel.*] A martyrology.
1610 HOLLAND tr. *Camden's Brit.* (1637) 220 An old Agonel. **1695** GIBSON tr. *ibid.*, We find it in an ancient Agonal.

agonal ('ægənəl), *a.* [f. Gr. ἀγών (see AGON) + -AL.] **1.** Of or pertaining to an AGON.
1770 tr. *Mme. Fiquet du Boccage's Lett.* II. 38 Sea-fights are now exhibited in the agonal circus called the square of Navonne. **1838** *Fraser's Mag.* Nov. 516 Come to us Our saviour, and the patron of our games: And with thee come our Agonal deities all.
2. [f. AGONY.] Of, pertaining to, or occurring during agony, esp. the death agony.
1901 *Jrnl. Exper. Med.* Jan. 344 A condition which, if not due solely to agonal contraction, might at least favor the production of diverticula in the upper part. **1961** *Lancet* 29 July 266/1 Antemortem autolysis may occur when the agonal period is drawn out.

agonarch ('ægənɑːk). *rare*[−0]. [ad. Gr. ἀγωνάρχ-ης a judge of a contest, f. ἀγών (see AGON) + -αρχης ruler.] 'A judge or overseer in feats of activity, a master of revels.' Blount *Glossogr.* 1656; whence in mod. Dicts.

agone (ə'gɒn), *ppl. a., arch.* and *poet.* = AGO, q.v.

agoniadin (ə'gəʊnɪədɪn). *Chem.* [f. *Agoniada* + -IN.] A glycoside, $C_{10}H_{14}O_6$, contained in Agoniada or Agonia bark (obtained fr. *Plumieria lancifolia*).
1872 WATTS *Dict. Chem. 2nd Supp.* 30.

agonic (ə'gɒnɪk), *a.* [mod. f. Gr. ἄγων-ος, ἀγώνι-ος, without angle (f. ἀ priv. + γωνία angle), + -IC.] Having or making no angle, having no inclination; as in ***agonic line***, the irregular line passing through the two magnetic poles of the earth along which the magnetic needle points directly north or south; the line of no magnetic variation.
1863 ATKINSON tr. *Ganot's Physics* VIII. §674 In certain parts of the earth the magnet coincides with the geographical meridian. These points are connected by an irregularly curved imaginary line, called a line of no variation or agonic line.

†**a'gonious,** *a. Obs.* [a. Fr. *agonieux* (cf. It. *agonioso*): see AGONY and -OUS.] Full of agony.
1494 FABYAN VI. clxi. 154 Lewys had long lyen in this agonyous sykenes. **1683** TRYON *Way to Health* 575 The harsh astringent fierce original Poysons do..put Nature into an agonious Condition.

agonism ('ægənɪz(ə)m). ? *Obs.*[−0] [ad. Gr. ἀγώνισμα a contest, or its prize, f. ἀγωνίζ-εσθαι: see AGONIZE.]
1. A combat, an athletic match.
1742 BAILEY, *Agonism*, a Combat or Trial of Skill. **1755** JOHNSON and **1775** ASH, *Agonism*, contention for a prize.
2. The prize of a contest.
1656 BLOUNT *Glossogr.*, *Agonism*, the reward or prize won by activities; the reward of victory.

agonist (ˈæɡənɪst). [ad. Gr. ἀγωνιστ-ής a combatant in the games.] **1.** 'A contender for prizes.' J. *rare*

1626 COCKERAM, *Agonist*, a Champion. **1859** I. TAYLOR *Nilus* in *Ess. etc.* 1859, 161 Happiest of mothers am I, who have borne so noble an agonist.

2. A person engaged in a contest or struggle; a protagonist. (For the *spec.* sense in quot. 1914 cf. AGON 2.)

1914 F. M. CORNFORD *Origin Attic Comedy* v. 71 Three, or sometimes four, rôles are involved in the *Agon*... First there are the two Adversaries (as we shall call them). For the sake of convenience, we shall distinguish them as the 'Agonist' and the 'Antagonist'. The Agonist is the hero, who is attacked, is put on his defence, and comes off victorious. **1921** *Glasgow Herald* 4 Aug. 5/3 He knows too well the respective roles of agonist and spectator of life. **1933** E. K. CHAMBERS *Eng. Folk-Play* 23 The culminating point of the Drama is of course the Combat. It will be convenient to call the champion who falls the Agonist and his vanquisher the Antagonist. **1934** *Punch* 14 Feb. 195/1 Since this is a novel and not an economic treatise, the high lights are naturally focussed on particular agonists.

3. One who advertises in an 'agony column' (see AGONY 1 a).

1915 *Chambers's Jrnl.* 6 Feb. 149/1 Yet somebody must respond, or a number of the 'agonists' would require to retire..from the business. **1934** I. BROWN in *Essays of Year 1933–4* p. xx, He even scours the advertisements, for the Agonists of *The Times* are often helpful.

4. *Physiol.* A muscle whose contraction is directly responsible for the movement of a part of the body. Also ***agonist muscle***. Cf. ANTAGONIST 4.

1925 *Arch. Neurol. & Psychiatry* XIII. 291 The splendid researches of Duchenne of Boulogne, which restate Winslow's idea in even more categorical terms by claiming a simultaneous contraction of agonist and antagonist muscles during the production of movement. **1932** *Jrnl. Bone & Joint Surg.* XIV. 2 The increasing elastic tension of the antagonist and the decreasing elastic tension of the contracting agonist determine the neutral point of equilibrium. **1949** *New Gould Med. Dict.* 33/1 When flexing the elbow, the biceps is the agonist and the triceps is the antagonist. **1980** *Conc. Med. Dict.* 33/1 Antagonists relax to allow the agonists to effect movement.

5. *Pharm.* A chemical which can not only combine with a receptor (RECEPTOR 3 c), like an antagonist, but when it does so stimulates it, resulting in an observable effect.

1955 *Pharmacol. Reviews* VII. 211 The term 'reversible competitive antagonism' is used in this review to designate that type of antagonism in which the antagonist competes with the agonist by reacting reversibly with the same receptors with which the agonist reacts. **1970** *Nature* 10 Oct. 135/1 Trigonelline was found to have little pharmacological activity, being about 10^5 times less active as an agonist than acetylcholine, and with no detectable antagonist activity. **1972** BURGEN & MITCHELL *Gaddum's Pharmacol.* (ed. 7) 6/2 One of the dilemmas of pharmacology is to explain just what it is that makes some members of a drug series agonists and some antagonists. **1977** *Sci. Amer.* Mar. 44/2 All opiate agonists, or analgesically active substances, show basic similarities in their molecular architecture. **1983** *Fortune* 24 Jan. 88/2 An agonist not only fits a receptor molecule but also activates it to initiate some operation in a cell.

agonistarch (æɡəˈnɪstɑːk). [f. ἀγωνιστ-ής a combatant + ἀρχ-ός ruler.] One who trained combatants for the games.

1824 in CRABB.

agonistes (æɡɒˈnɪstiːz). [a. Gr. ἀγωνιστής (see AGONIST).] Used postpositively as epithet of a person who is an agonist (sense 2), in allusion to Milton's *Samson Agonistes*.

1932 T. S. ELIOT (*title*) Sweeney Agonistes. **1946** B. H. BRONSON (*title*) Johnson agonistes: and other essays. **1969** G. WILLS (*title*) Nixon Agonistes.

agonistic (æɡəˈnɪstɪk), *a.* [ad. Gr. ἀγωνιστικ-ός of or pertaining to an ἀγωνιστ-ής or AGONIST.]

1. a. Of or pertaining to the athletic contests of ancient Greece; *hence*, pertaining to athletic feats generally, athletic.

1648 JOS. BEAUMONT *Psyche* XI. ccvi, Smeared in 's bloody Agonistik Gore. **1753** CHAMBERS *Cycl. Supp.*, *Agonistic* amounts to much the same with *athletic*. **1857** BIRCH *Anc. Pottery* (1858) II. 32 An Agonistic inscription..reading, 'Damocleidas (was victor) in the horse race.' **1879** FARRAR *St. Paul* I. 447 The many military and agonistic metaphors in his Epistles.

b. *Zool.* Pertaining to or designating animal behaviour associated with hostility between individuals.

1951 SCOTT & FREDERICSON in *Physiol. Zool.* XXIV. 273/1 When fighting behavior is analyzed, it is found to be one of several patterns of behavior... Other common and closely related patterns are escape behavior, defensive behavior, and passivity... It is with this general group of behavioral adjustments, which may be given the name 'agonistic behavior', that this paper is concerned. **1970** *Nature* 5 Dec. 960/1 After the capture of meat there were often agonistic encounters over its possession. **1980** *S. Afr. Jrnl. Sci.* LXXVI. 415/1 The facial resultants of conflict between.. tendencies..for attack and those for flight..are sometimes referred to as the 'agonistic faces'. **1981** *Oxf. Compan. Animal Behaviour* 13/2 Agonistic behaviour may also include activities that are not aroused in direct response to an opponent, but are more a matter of routine. The early morning song of many birds, and the scent marking of territory boundaries in mammals are examples of this.

2. *Rhet.* Polemic, combative, striving to overcome in argument.

a **1660** HAMMOND *Serm.* 589 (T.) The prophetick writings were not, saith St. Peter, ἰδίας ἐπιλύσεως (I conceive in an agonistick sense) of their own starting or incitation. **1677** GALE *Crt. of Gentiles* III. Pref., A thetic and dogmatic method, rather than agonistic and polemic. **1836** H. TAYLOR *Statesman* xxx. 225 If knowledge be argumentative and wit agonistic, the society becomes an arena. *a* **1857** DE QUINCEY *Dr. Parr* (Beeton) 241 As a scholar he was brilliant; but he consumed his power in agonistic displays.

3. Strained, aiming at effect; simulating strong feeling, tending to exaggeration of feeling.

1843 CARLYLE *Past & Pres.* (1858) 250 Agonistic posture-makings. **1864** I. TAYLOR in *Gd. Wds.* 943 Long before the coming on of the modern agonistic paroxysm in literature.

agonistical (æɡəˈnɪstɪkəl), *a.* [f. prec. + -AL[1].]

1. = AGONISTIC 1. ? *Obs.*

1653 HAMMOND *N. Test.* (T.) Τελειοῦσθαι, in the agonistical notion, we have formerly explained. **1725** BLACKWALL *Sacr. Cl.* I. 335 (T.) To say nothing of the beautiful metaphors and noble agonistical terms. **1755** JOHNSON and **1775** ASH, *Agonistical*, belonging to prize-fighting.

2. *Rhet.* = AGONISTIC 2.

a **1652** J. SMITH *Sel. Disc.* i. 20 With a struggling, agonistical, and contentious reason. **1840** H. ROGERS *Ess.* II. v. 240 Aristotle has happily and aptly called the 'agonistical' or 'wrestling' style, that style by which a speaker *earnestly strives* to make a *present* audience see and feel what he wishes them to see and feel.

agonistically (æɡəˈnɪstɪkəlɪ), *adv.* [f. prec. + -LY[2].] In an agonistic manner, argumentatively.

1836 ARNOLD in *Life* (1844) II. viii. 33 Having written once agonistically, I wish next to write in another manner.

agonistics (æɡəˈnɪstɪks). [pl. of AGONISTIC *a.* used *subst.* Cf. Fr. *agonistique*, and Gr. ἡ ἀγωνιστική the agonistic (art).] That part of gymnastics which has reference to athletic combats, such as those practised in the ancient games.

1753 CHAMBERS *Cycl. Supp.* s.v., A learned work on the subject of agonistics. *a* **1859** WORCESTER cites *Q. Rev.*

† **agoˈnizant.** *Obs.* 'Certain Friers in Italy, who assisted those who were in Agonies.' Bailey.

agonize (ˈæɡənaɪz), *v.* [prob. a. Fr. *agonise-r* or its original, the med.L. *agonizā-re*, ad. Gr. ἀγωνίζ-εσθαι, to contend in the AGON, to struggle. The trans. use is however confined to Eng. and seems an independent application of the word, after the analogy of verbs in -IZE from the Gr. active -ίζειν.]

1. *trans.* To subject to agony, to torture. Also *absol.*

1583 STUBBES *Anat. Abus.* (1877) 72 And seyng her thus agonized..he demaunded of her the cause thereof. **1598** SYLVESTER *Du Bartas* 823 Or whom some serpent's sting doth agonize. **1799** SHERIDAN *Pizarro* IV. ii, The sharpest tortures that ever agonized the human frame. **1853** ROBERTSON *Serm.* Ser. IV. xvii. (1876) 220 This power of sin to agonize is traced to the law. **1856** MRS. BROWNING *Aur. Leigh* vii. 173, I will not let thy hideous secret out To agonise the man I love.

2. *intr.* To suffer agony, to writhe in pain or anguish, to be in the throes of death. (From Fr.)

1664 EVELYN *Sylva* (1776) 484 The Olive under which our blessed Saviour Agonized. **1732** POPE *Ess. on Man* I. 198 To smart and agonize at ev'ry pore. **1762** FALCONER *Shipwreck* I. 74 Where dying victims agonize in pain. **1810** T. MAURICE *Hist. Hindostan* (1820) I. I. xiii. 519 The dreadful catastrophe in which nature agonized, and a world was destroyed.

3. *intr.* To contend in the arena; to struggle or strive in physical exercise; to wrestle. (In reference to orig. Gr. sense; also in med.L. and It.) Usually *fig.*

1711 SHAFTESBURY *Charact.* (1737) III. 351 He agonizes, and with all his strength of reason endeavours to overcome himself. **1863** W. PHILLIPS *Speeches* xvi. 347 The nation agonizes this hour to recognize man as man. **1879** FARRAR *St. Paul* II. 123 [Paul] most earnestly entreats the Romans to agonise with him in their prayers to God.

4. *fig.* To make desperate or convulsive efforts for effect. Now freq. (*colloq.*), to worry intensely (*over* or *about* something); to struggle to reach a decision.

1865 *Athenæum* No. 1966. 26/2 Every one who has no real fancy seems agonizing after originality. **1872** G. MACDONALD *Wilf. Cumb.* I. xv. 246, I might agonize in words for a day and I should not express the delight. **1946** R. GRAVES *Poems 1938–1945* 25 When the pines agonized with flaws of wind And flowers glared up at her with frantic eyes. **1961** *Manas* 5 Apr. 1/1 He is a Craig's wife who agonizes about tobacco ash on the living room rug. **1961** *Texas Studies Lit. & Lang.* III. 281 Pip agonizes over the theft that his own hands have committed. **1969** *Word Study* Oct. 7/2 My purpose here is not to agonize over a sorry past. **1973** *Times* 24 May 8/6 Mr Hoover had troubles of his own while the White House was agonizing over the Pentagon Papers. **1983** *Listener* 10 Feb. 9/3 We agonised for two seconds about whether to cast McGee, the Roman Catholic husband with 'a little infection', as a Martian.

agonized (ˈæɡənaɪzd), *ppl. a.* [f. prec. + -ED.]

1. Subjected to agony, tortured, in anguish.

1583 [See AGONIZE 1]. **1828** SCOTT *F.M. Perth* III. 329 'He is dead!' screamed the agonized parent. **1876** GREEN *Short Hist.* viii. §8. 553 The agonized loyalty, which strove to save Charles.

2. Expressing agony, full of distress.

1853 KANE *Grinnell Exped.* xxxii. (1856) 279 One wild, booming, agonized note. **1882** *Daily News* 7 Mar. 5/4 His reading being interrupted by..agonised yawns, and other signs of impatience.

agonizedly (ˈæɡəˌnaɪzɪdlɪ), *adv.* [f. prec. + -LY[2].] In an agonized manner; in tones of agony or anguish.

1840 THACKERAY *Paris Sk. Bk.* (1872) 166 'Niece Matilda,' cried Sir Roger, agonizedly. **1870** *Stand.* 26 Nov., France is crying agonisedly to every one of her sons to up and help her.

agonizer (ˈæɡənaɪzə(r)). [f. AGONIZE *v.* + -ER[1].] One who agonizes; in *Society slang*, One who makes convulsive efforts for effect.

1879 *Daily Tel.* 11 Dec., The agonisers of the pianoforte.

agonizing (ˈæɡənaɪzɪŋ), *vbl. sb.* [f. AGONIZE *v.* + -ING[1].] The action of putting forth excessive exertion, struggling, suffering anguish.

1813 MRS. SCHIMMELPENNINCK tr. *Lancelot's Tour* (1816) I. 71 This agonizing must as much relate to that vile body, which even St. Paul kept under. **1882** *Pall Mall G.* 14 Nov. 5 [His] continual agonizings with his hopeless passion.

agonizing (ˈæɡənaɪzɪŋ), *ppl. a.* [f. AGONIZE *v.* + -ING[2].]

1. a. Causing agony or extreme anguish, torturing.

1686 DRYDEN *Hind. & P.* III. 287 O sharp convulsive pangs of agonizing pride! **1764** GOLDSM. *Trav.* 435 The lifted ax, the agonizing wheel. **1826** DISRAELI *Viv. Grey* II. xiii. 64 With a smile of agonising courtesy. **1861** MACAULAY *Hist. Eng.* V. 45 What Fenwick must have suffered, the agonizing struggle between the fear of shame and the fear of death.

b. ***agonizing reappraisal***, a reassessment of a policy, position, etc., painfully forced on one by a radical change of circumstances, or by a realization of what the existing circumstances really are. (Chiefly a political and journalistic catch-phrase.)

1953 J. F. DULLES in *N.Y. Times* 15 Dec. 14/3 If..the European Defence Community should not be effective; if France and Germany remain apart... That would compel an agonizing reappraisal of basic United States policy. **1958** *Economist* 18 Oct. 222/2 New Zealand..is being forced into an agonizing reappraisal of its domestic policies. **1958** *Star* 9 Dec., As if in response to new directions from an agonising reappraisal in MCC's room at lunch, the scoring spurted as Cowdrey twice swung Benaud to the leg fence.

2. Suffering agony; writhing in pain or anguish; in the throes of death.

1666 in *Phil. Trans.* I. 249 An extraordinary Restorative and Cordiall, recovering frequently with it agonizing persons. **1728** THOMSON *Spring* 586 Convulsive twist in agonizing folds. **1812–21** COMBE *Dr. Synt.*, *Consolation* I. (Chandos) 129 His agonising bosom burns.

agonizingly (ˈæɡəˌnaɪzɪŋlɪ), *adv.* [f. prec. + -LY[2].] In an agonizing manner; with painful or desperate struggles.

c **1841** KINGSLEY *Lett. & Mem.* I. 52 Struggles..which made him feel more agonizingly weak than ever. **1860** RUSKIN *Mod. Painters* V. VI. vii. §7 They..fail egregiously; —ridiculously;—it may be, agonizingly.

agonothet(e (əˈɡəʊnəθiːt, -θɛt). *Gr. Antiq.* [ad. Gr. ἀγωνοθέτης f. ἀγών contest + θέτης a disposer; f. vbl. stem θε- to place. Also used in the Gr. forms.] A superintendent or director of the great public games of Greece.

1626 COCKERAM, *Agonotheth*, a Judge in masteries of actiuity. **1734** tr. *Rollin's Anc. Hist.* IV. x. 405 Of which games the Amphictyons were judges and agonothetæ. **1865** *Athenæum* No. 1964, 818/1 The agonothet for each year. **1878** *N. Amer. Rev.* CXXVII. 505 He gravely assumed the titles of archon and agonothetes.

agonothetic (əˌɡəʊnəʊˈθɛtɪk), *a.* [ad. Gr. ἀγωνοθετικ-ός: see prec. and -IC.] Of or pertaining to an agonothete.

1731 in BAILEY; whence in JOHNSON, etc.

† **ˈagonous,** *a.* *Obs. rare*$^{-1}$. [f. med.L. *agōn* death struggle (a. Gr. ἀγών contest) + -OUS.] Struggling, engaged in mortal combat.

1683 TRYON *Way to Health* 274 This agonous condition and strugling strife of the Properties of Nature.

agony (ˈæɡənɪ). Also 4 **agonye**, 5–7 **agonie**. [prob. formed by Wyclif on the L. *agōnia* of the Vulgate; though also found in 14th c. Fr., *agonie*. The L. is a. Gr. ἀγωνία contest, hence, mental struggle, anguish; f. ἀγών, AGON q.v.] The development of the senses in Gr. was:—1. A struggle for victory in the games; 2. Any struggle; 3. Mental struggle, anguish, *e.g.* Christ's anguish in Gethsemane. But the historical appearance of the meanings in Eng. was as follows:

1. a. Anguish of mind, sore trouble or distress, a paroxysm of grief. ***agony column***, (*a*) the column of a newspaper that contains special advertisements, particularly those for missing relatives or friends, and thus often gives evidence of great distress; (*b*) a regular newspaper or magazine feature containing readers' questions about personal difficulties, with replies from the columnist; cf. *problem page* s.v. PROBLEM 7(b); ***agony aunt(ie)***, a familiar name for the (female) editor of an agony column (sense b); in extended use, an adviser on personal, psychological, etc., problems.

c **1386** CHAUCER *Miller's T.* 266 This man is falle.. In som woodnesse, or in som agonye. **1494** FABYAN v. cxvii. 91 Fredegunda..sore was abasshed, and in great fere and agony. **1611** BIBLE *2 Mac.* iii. 14 There was no small agonie throughout the whole citie. **1769** *Junius Lett.* xix. 83 He sunk under the charge in an agony of confusion and despair. **1863** BURTON *Bk. Hunter* 40 It was agony to him to hear the beggar's cry of distress. **1863** *Fun* 3 Oct. 23/2 Our own agony column. **1880** *Times* 28 Dec. 10/1 A cryptogram in the agony column. **1930** WYNDHAM LEWIS *Let.* 30 July (1963) 190 The agony-column of the Times has echoed the rage of people who considered themselves attacked in the Apes. **1975** P. MAKINS *Evelyn Home Story* 9 Perhaps the biggest obstacle the 'agony aunties' faced in the 'thirties was that neither the queries they dealt with nor the publications which printed them were taken seriously. *Ibid.* xiv. 158 The actual writing style of agony columns has changed quite noticeably over the years. **1979** *Observer* 11 Mar. 9 Marriage is something I've never wanted and writing an agony column has confirmed that.—Irma Kurtz. **1979** R. KENT *Aunt Agony Advises* xii. 265 Perhaps a university should start an agony auntie course. **1983** *Daily Tel.* 7 Nov. 3/4 Confidential counselling 'agony aunts'—to help police officers under stress is recommended in a report presented to chief constables. **1984** S. TOWNSEND *Growing Pains A. Mole* 19, I can't go on like this. I have written to Auntie Clara, the Agony Aunt.

b. Hence, Intensity or paroxysm of pleasure.

a **1725** POPE *Odyssey* x. 492 With cries and agonies of wild delight. **1877** MRS. OLIPHANT *Mak. Flor.* v. 138 He struck the marble in an agony of pleasure and content, bidding it 'Speak'!

2. *spec.* The mental struggle or anguish of Christ in the garden of Gethsemane.

1382 WYCLIF *Luke* xxii. 43 And he maad in agonye [*ether angwische or stryf*] preiede lengere. [Vulg. *Et factus in agonia, prolixius orabat.*] **1526** TINDALE *ibid.*, He was in an agonye. **1557** *Genev.*, **1611**, and *Revised, ibid.*, And being in an agonie, he prayed more earnestly. **1864** TENNYSON *Aylmer's F.* 793 As cried Christ ere His agony.

3. The convulsive throes, or pangs of death; the death struggle. (med.L. *agon mortis.*) Seldom now used in this sense without qualification, as agony *of death, mortal* agony.

1549 *Compl. Scotl.* xiv. 121 Quhen darius vas in the agonya and deith thrau. **1588** SHAKS. *L.L.L.* v. ii. 867 To moue wilde laughter in the throate of death? It cannot be, it is impossible: Mirth cannot moue a soule in agonie. **1715** BURNET *Own Time* (1766) I. 432 On a sudden she fell into the agony of death. **1836** TODD *Cycl. Anat. & Phys.* I. 800/1 The death-struggle, or agony.

4. a. Extreme bodily suffering, such as to produce writhing or throes of the body.

1607 DEKKER *Westward Hoe* (1873) II. 347 O quickly, quickly, shees sicke and taken with an Agony. **1667** MILTON *P.L.* II. 861 Here in perpetual agonie and pain. **1725** DE FOE *Voy. round World* (1840) 157 The agony the poor woman was in. **1859** TENNYSON *Elaine* 850 Brain-feverous in his heat and agony. **1864** —— *Boadicea* 84 Ran the land with Roman slaughter, multitudinous agonies.

b. *transf.* and *fig.*

1835–40 etc. [see PILE *v.*² 2b]. **1863** GEO. ELIOT *Let.* 23 Oct. (1956) IV. 111 We shall soon be in the agonies of moving. **1924** R. CAMPBELL *Flaming Terrapin* ii. 25 The mountains frown, Locked in their tetanous agonies of stone. **1932** W. B. YEATS *Words for Music* 2 Dying into a dance, An agony of trance, An agony of flame that cannot singe a sleeve.

5. A struggle or contest. (Rarely without some shade of the preceding senses.)

1677 *Decay Chr. Piety* 408 (T.) Till he have thus denudated himself of all these encumbrances he is utterly unqualified for these agonies. **1859** DE QUINCEY *Cæsars* Wks. X. 89 He was most truly in an agony, according to the original meaning of that word; for the conflict was great between two master principles of his nature. **1865** CARLYLE *Fredk. Gt.* VII. XVIII. ii. 117 Which lasted..above three hours; and was the crisis, or essential agony, of the Battle.

† **a'gonyclite.** *Obs.* [ad. L. *agonyclita*, a Gr. ἀγονυκλίτης, f. ἀ not + γόνυ knee + -κλιτ-ος bending, f. vbl. stem κλιν- bend.] 'Hereticks, in the seventh century, whose distinguishing tenet was, never to kneel, but to deliver their prayers standing.' Bailey.

1710 T. WARD *Eng. Ref.* 361 (D.) To God he will not bow his knee Like an old Agonyclitee [? for *Agonyclitæ*, L. *pl.*]

† **a-'good,** *adv.*, prop. *phr.* [A *prep.*¹ + GOOD; cf. *afresh.*] In good earnest; thoroughly, heartily.

a **1536** TINDALE *Prol. Jonah* Wks. I. 456 The nature of all wicked is, when they have sinned a good, to seek..to drive the remembrance of sin out of their thoughts. **1591** SHAKS. *Two Gent.* IV. iv. 170 And at that time I made her weepe a good. **1606** HOLLAND *Sueton.* 188 Ran in a good to helpe him. **1671** *Welch Trav.* 258 in Hazl. *E.P.P.* IV. 339 The company that stood about did laugh at him a-good. [Cf. mod. dial., To laugh a good one, run a good one, etc.]

agoon, obs. form of AGO, AGONE.

‖**agora** ('ægɒrə). *Gr. Antiq.* Pl. **agoræ**. [Gr. ἀγορά.] An assembly; hence, the place of assembly, *esp.* the market-place. Also *transf.*

1598 HAKLUYT *Voyages* I. 489 The Emperor himselfe, who hath no other seat of Empire but an *Agora*, or towne of wood, that moueth with him whithersoeuer hee goeth. **1820** T. MITCHELL *Com. Aristoph.* I. 176 The agora or forum was the resort of all the idle and profligate in Athens. **1846** GROTE *Greece* I. I. i. 2 The custom of occasionally convoking and consulting the divine Agora. **1862** E. FALKENER *Ephesus* I. iv. 63 The Greeks, in these hot climates, loved to have water in some form in the centre of their agoræ. **1886** W. T. STEAD in *Contemp. Rev.* May 654 The telegraph and the printing-press have converted Great Britain into a vast agora, or assembly of the whole community. **1941** AUDEN *New Year Let.* III. 53 The agora of work and news Where each one has the right to choose His trade, his corner and his way.

Comb. **1948** L. MACNEICE *Holes in Sky* 66 Ancient Athens Was a sparrow-chatter of agora-gibes.

agoraphobe ('ægərəfəʊb), *sb.* and *a.* [Back-formation f. AGORAPHOBIA.] **A.** *sb.* A person who suffers from agoraphobia. **B.** *adj.* Causing or conducive to agoraphobia.

1955 *New Yorker* 13 Aug. 49/1 The inmates include suicidal types, agoraphobes, and plain nervous people. **1958** *Listener* 13 Nov. 776/1 This entirely synthetic agoraphobe arcadia. **1970** *Daily Tel.* (Colour Suppl.) 4 Sept. 12/3 The agoraphobe, for example, is taken on to a large common or moor and simply left there to suffer for several hours at a time until he learns to bear it. **1984** *Forbes* (N.Y.) 18 June 82/2 Schwartz, now 60, is an agoraphobe..who rarely leaves his studio.

agoraphobia (ˌægɒrə'fəʊbɪə). *Med.* [f. Gr. ἀγορά (see AGORA) + -φοβία fear.] (See quot.)

1873 *Jrnl. Mental Sc.* XIX. 456 Dr. C. Westphal has an article on Agoraphobia; by this he means the fear of squares or open places.

agoraphobic (ˌægɒrə'fəʊbɪk), *a.* (*sb.*) [f. AGORAPHOBI(A + -IC.] Of or pertaining to agoraphobia; (one who is) suffering from or affected with agoraphobia. Also *transf.*

1884 *Lancet* 27 Dec. 1141/1 The giddiness which accompanies his agoraphobic attacks. **1898** *Lancet* 19 Nov. 1322/2 All the time that I was an 'agoraphobic' I attended church regularly with my family, but we always sat close to the door. There I was safe. **1936** A. STRACHEY tr. *Freud's Inhib., Sympt. & Anx.* VII. 89 An agoraphobic patient may be able to walk in the street provided he is accompanied.. by someone he knows and trusts. **1958** *Times* 4 Feb. 6/4 Chardin comes at once to mind as an agoraphobic figure quite unconcerned with anything outside his own four walls.

† **a-'gore-blood,** *phr. Obs.* [A *prep.*¹ in, and *gore-blood*; see GORE.] In or with clotted blood or gore.

1580 NORTH *Plutarch* (1676) 163 The Flouds and Rivers [were] running all agore-blood, by reason of the great slaughter. **1609** HOLLAND *Amm. Marcell.* XIV. vii. 14 To see ..champions wounding and killing one another, and to behold them all agore bloud [*perfusorumque sanguine*].

agot, obs. form of AGATE.

agoten, pa. pple. of AGET-EN *v. Obs.*, to pour.

agouti, agouty (ə'guːtɪ). Also **aguti.** [a. Fr. *agouti*, Sp. *aguti*, a. *aguti*, *acuti*, native Indian name.] **1.** A genus of rodents, belonging to the Cavy or Guinea-pig family; the common species (*Dasyprocta agouti*) is an animal of the size and appearance of a hare, common in the W. Indies and adjacent parts of S. America.

1731 BAILEY, *Agouty* (in America) a little Beast of the shape and size of a rabbit. **1830** E. BENNETT *Zool. Gard. Del.* I. 295 The Long-nosed Agouti..is now almost confined to St. Lucia. **1855** KINGSLEY *Westw. Ho* (1861) 281 Smoking agoutis out of the hollow trees.

2. The brindled appearance exhibited by the agouti as a result of individual hairs of its fur being banded in their pigmentation; such a banded condition of a hair or fur; any animal with such fur. Also *attrib.* or as *adj.*

1903 *Proc. Zool. Soc.* II. 73 The pigments in wild *M[us] musculus* or *sylvaticus* are..of three kinds..black..brown.. yellow... The different colour-types of fancy mice... 1. Ordinary Cinnamon (or Agouti)... This is doubtless the 'grey' of most writers... 2. Golden Agouti. Like (1) but yellower. Contains brown and yellow, without black. **1905** *Proc. Amer. Acad. Arts & Sci.* XL. 62 Its color [*sc.* that of the house mouse] is usually spoken of as gray, the 'agouti' of fanciers. **1911** R. C. PUNNETT *Mendelism* (ed. 3) v. 46 The F_2 generation from such a cross consists of agoutis and albinos in the ratio 3:1. **1912** C. J. DAVIES *Fancy Mice* (ed. 5) v. 39 Fancy mice may be roughly classified as follows:.. 1. Agouti (wild colour), carries three pigments, black, chocolate, and yellow. **1977** *Sci. Amer.* Nov. 104 (*caption*) Agouti, named for the South American rodent that exemplifies the condition, is a salt-and-pepper appearance caused by the fact that each hair of the fur has a band of reduced pigmentation below the tip. *Ibid.* 106/3 Most mammals are agouti, but most domesticated mammals are nonagouti. **1985** J. AUEL *Mammoth Hunters* xxiii. 369 Only later would the hair develop the dark and light bars of the typical agouti colouration of an adult wolf.

agrace, variant of AGGRACE *v. Obs.*

agrade, used by Florio in 1611 (not in ed. 1598) to translate It. *gradire* to be pleased with. Cf. It. *aggradare*.

agraffe (ə'græf). [a. Fr. *agrafe*, formerly *agraffe*, *agraphe*, *agrappe* (see AGRAPPES), f. *à* + *grappe*:—late L. *grappa* 7th c., ad. OHG. *chrapfo* hook, mod.G. *krappen*. Cf. Cymric *crap* hook.] **1.** A kind of hook, which fastens to a ring, used as a clasp.

a **1666** EVELYN *Diary c.* 16 Nov., an. 1643 (1955) II. 88 The agraffe of his royal mantle. **1707** *Lond. Gaz.* mmmmccclxii/2 The Present..is an Agraffe of Diamonds, and a Diamond Buckle for an Hat. **1820** SCOTT *Ivanhoe* (1830) 33 The feather of an ostrich, fastened in her turban by an agraffe set with brilliants. **1872** O. SHIPLEY *Eccl. Terms* 388 Foreign ritualists mention a sort of agrafe of pearls, worn by the pope and cardinals under this name [*rationale*].

2. Various technical uses: see quots.

1883 *Lond. & Prov. Music Trades Rev.* Mar. 13/2 Erard [in 1808]..substituting for a long, pinned wooden bridge as many little brass bridges as there were notes. The strings passing through holes bored through the little bridges, called agraffes, or studs, turned upwards towards the wrest-pin. **1900** DORLAND *Med. Dict.* 27/2 *Agraffe*, an instrument for keeping together the edges of the wound in operation for harelip. **1918** E. S. FARROW *Dict. Mil. Terms* 11 *Agraffe*,.. the coupling pin in artillery.

† **a'graith,** *v. Obs.* Also 4 **agrayth, agreith, agredy.** [f. A- *pref.* 1 intensive + GRAITH, ad. Norse *greið-a* to make ready, prepare; cogn. w. Goth. *ga-raidjan* and OE. *ȝe-rǣdan*, from which perhaps the Kentish form *agredy* below.]

1. To prepare; make ready.

c **1315** SHOREHAM 126 And yet ne were hyt noȝt inoȝ One to agredy hyre looȝ And heȝ ine hevene blysse. **1340** *Ayenb.* 14 þe pine wyþoute ende þet God heþ agrayþed to þe uorlorene. *Ibid.* 140 Alneway agrayþed, ase byeþ þe ssipmen in ssipe. *c* **1350** *Will. Palerne* 1597 Purueaunce þat prest was, to pepul agreiþed.

2. To accoutre, dress, deck.

1340 *Ayenb.* 140 Hy hise agrayþeþ and aȝet mid alle hire ournemens. *c* **1350** *Will. Palerne* 52 In gode cloþes of gold agreþed ful riche. *c* **1460** *Launfal* 904 Thyn halle agrayde and hele the walles.

3. To dress (a wound).

1340 *Ayenb.* 148 Me ssel zueteliche þe wonden agrayþi.

4. *refl.* and hence *intr.* To make oneself ready, to prepare (to do any thing).

c **1315** SHOREHAM 126 Into the blysse of hevene sty, To agredy worthy scholde hy be At hyre assumpcion. **1340** *Ayenb.* 173 He hine wolde agrayþi ase zone ase he miȝte.

† **a'graithing,** *vbl. sb. Obs.* [f. prec. + -ING¹.] Attiring; dress, decoration.

1340 *Ayenb.* 216 Hire coustouse robes, and hire oþre agrayþinges. *Ibid.* 176 Agrayþeþ hire heaueden mid precieuse agrayþinges.

agral ('ægrəl), *a. rare*⁻¹. [ad. L. *agrāl-is* = *agrār-is*, f. *ager* field, country.] Of or belonging to the fields; = AGRARIAN 4.

1866 *Intell. Observ.* No. 52. 288 Wayside and agral plants.

† **a'gramed, agremed, agromed,** *pa. pple. Obs.* [The only part found of vb. *agrame*, *agreme*, *agrome*, coinciding in form and sense with OFr. *agramir*, *agremir* (also *engr-*) chiefly used in pa. pple. *agrami*, etc.; f. *à* to (or *en* in) + *gram* adj. (Pr. *gram*, It. *gramo*) a. OHG. *gram*, angry. But OE. had also *gram* adj. and *gremian*, *gremman* vb., to enrage, ME. *gremien*, *greme*, whence *a-gremed* might have been formed with A- *pref.* 1, independently of Fr. (cf. OHG. *ergremen*). The special influence of OFr. *agrami* seems clear in the form *agramed*, but see GRAME, GREME.] Angered, vexed, enraged.

c **1300** *K. Alis.* 3310 Y am aschamed, And sore anoyed, and agramed. *c* **1314** *Guy Warw.* 84 As he that was agremed in hert. *c* **1430** *Generides* 6044 In his hert right yuel agramed. *a* **1500** *Chron. Eng.* 863 in Ritson *M.R.* II. 306 The kyng wes ful sore agromed. **1692** COLES, *Agramed*, aggrieved (*obs.*). **1775** ASH, *Agramed*, grieved (*obs.*).

agrammatism (ə'græmətɪz(ə)m). *Path.* [f. Gr. ἀγράμμᾰτ-ος illiterate (see AGRAMMATIST) + -ISM.] A form of aphasia marked by an inability to form sentences grammatically.

[**1881** *Syd. Soc. Lex.* I, *Agrammatismus*, inability to form a grammatical sentence.] **1888** F. P. FOSTER *Illustr. Encycl. Med. Dict.* I. 117/1 Agrammatism. **1909** A. PICK in *Rev. Neurol. & Psychiatry* VII. 757 When the question came under consideration, more than ten years ago, it took the form of inquiring whether we could assume for agrammatism as one of the higher mental functions a circumscribed localisation. **1956** JAKOBSON & HALLE *Fundamentals of Lang.* II. iv. 72 A typical feature of agrammatism is the abolition of inflection.

a'grammatist (ə'græmətɪst). *rare*⁻⁰. [f. Gr. ἀγράμμᾰτ-ος illiterate (f. ἀ priv. + γράμματ-α letters) + -IST; after Gr. γραμματιστής.] 'An unlearned, illiterate man.' Bailey 1731; whence in Johnson, etc.

agranulocyte (ə'grænjʊləʊsaɪt). [f. A- *pref.* 14 + GRANULOCYTE.] A leucocyte without cytoplasmic granules (see also quot. 1928). So **aˌgranulo'cytic** *a.*, of or pertaining to such a leucocyte; **aˌgranulocy'tosis** [mod.L., f. G. *agranulozytosen* (W. Schultz 1922, in *Deutsche Med. Wochenschr.* XLVIII. 1496)], an agranulocytic condition.

1927 D'A. PRENDERGAST in *Canad. Med. Assoc. Jrnl.* XVII. 446 (*title*) A Case of Agranulocytic Angina. **1928** R. J. SCOTT *Gould's Med. Dict.* (ed. 2) 43/2 *Agranulocytosis*, absence, or great decrease in the number of granulocytes. **1928** *Jrnl. Amer. Med. Assoc.* XCI. 1718/2 This case resembles..the case of agranulocytic angina first reported by Dr. Werner Schultz in 1922. **1932** DORLAND & MILLER *Med. Dict.* (ed. 16) 55/2 Agranulocyte. **1946** *Nature* 24 Aug.

270/1 Despite the severe leucopenia and agranulocytosis which developed in the rats on the purified diet, the rate of growth of the nymphs was not affected. **1954** *Sci. News Let.* 16 Jan. 36/3 The granulocyte cell is most commonly involved in myeloid leukemia and in the fighting of infections. The agranulocyte cell originates in the lymph glands and carries off waste materials.

agrapha ('ægrəfə), *sb. pl.* The sing. form **agraphon** is rare. [Gr., neut. pl. of ἄγραφος unwritten.] The collective name given to sayings attributed to Jesus but not recorded in the canonical Gospels.

[**1889** A. RESCH (*title of book written in German*) Agrapha.] **1890** *Church Q. Rev.* XXXI. 6 Resch has been successful in calling attention to some 'agrapha' which his predecessors had not noticed. **1900** B. JACKSON *25 Agrapha* 8 J. G. Körner (†1785) of Leipzig, *De sermonibus Christi ἀγράφοις*, [was] the first..to use the term Agrapha of the extra-canonical Sayings of the Lord. **1910** *Encycl. Brit.* I. 382 Agrapha (i.e. 'unwritten'), the name given to certain utterances ascribed, with some degree of certainty, to Jesus, which have been preserved in documents other than the Gospels. **1920** H. G. E. WHITE *Sayings of Jesus from Oxyrhynchus* p. xxx, Harris pointed out that *agrapha* are quoted by St. Paul, Clement of Rome and Polycarp. **1950** *Sc. Jrnl. Theol.* III. 300 In particular he lays the axe to the word *mysterion* as not being a genuine word of Jesus, in spite of the fact that an *agraphon* survives through Clement of Alexandria.

‖**agraphia** (ə'græfɪə). *Med.* [mod.L. f. Gr. ἀ priv. + -γραφία writing.] Inability to write (as a manifestation of brain-disease).

1871 *Academy* 15 Mar. 183/2 Agraphia, in which the patient speaks, but blunders sadly in writing. **1880** BASTIAN *Brain* xxix. 658 Agraphia may be appropriately enough allowed to include 'incoordinate' as well as 'paralytic' defects in the power of mental expression by Writing.

agraphic (ə'græfɪk), *a. Med.* [f. Gr. ἀ not + γραφικ-ός of writing, able to write: see -IC. The Gr. form was ἄγραφος or ἄγραπτος.] Characterized by inability to write.

1878 HAMILTON *Nerv. Dis.* 166 Whether the inability to write is due to this cause, or is really the 'agraphic' condition. **1880** MACCORMAC *Antis. Surg.* 226 At first he was quite aphasic and of course agraphic.

agraphy ('ægrəfɪ). Anglicization of AGRAPHIA.

*a***1901** MYERS *Hum. Pers.* (1903) I. 65 Elements of agraphy, of word-blindness, of word-deafness appear.

†**a'grappes**, *sb. pl. Obs.* [a. OFr. *agrappe* (mod.Fr. *agrafe*); see AGRAFFE.] 'Hooks and eyes used on armour or on ordinary dress.' Fairholt.

agrarian (ə'grɛərɪən), *a.* and *sb.* [f. L. *agrāri-us* pertaining to land (f. *agr-* field + *-āri-us*: see -ARY) + -AN. The L. was first adapted as *agrarie* (cf. *contrary*), or untranslated.]

A. *adj.*

1. *Rom. Hist.* Relating to the land: epithet of a law (*Lex agraria*) for the division of conquered lands.

[**1533** BELLENDENE *Livy* IV. (1822) 379 The law Agrarie.. put the Faderis fra the public landis, quhilkis was wranguislie possedit. **1580** NORTH *Plutarch* (1676) 647 Cæsar preferred the Law Agraria.] **1618** BOLTON *Florus* I. xxvi. 71 Spurius Cassius, suspected of affecting Soveraignty, because hee had published the Agrarian Law. **1838** ARNOLD *Hist. Rome* I. ix. 161 An agrarian law for the division of a certain proportion of the public land.

2. *gen.* Relating to, or connected with, landed property. ***agrarian outrage***, an act of violence originating in discord between landlords and tenants.

17.. in Somers's *Tracts* II. 453 Whatever Reflections may be rais'd from the Agrarian Principles. **1833** GEN. P. THOMPSON *Exerc.* (1842) II. 422 Have not your landlords brought you to the very eve of an agrarian war? **1876** ROGERS *Pol. Econ.* xiii. 23 The Irish land system familiarised the peasantry with agrarian outrages.

3. Of, relating to, or connected with, cultivated land, or its cultivation.

1792 A. YOUNG *Trav. France* 197 Signore Giobert, academician, and of the agrarian society. **1864** BURTON *Scot Abroad* II. ii. 163 The heartless agrarian devastation accompanying the movements of the Russian troops. **1867** J. DRAPER *Amer. Civ. War* I. xxvi. 445 The only bulwark.. against the clamoring rule of agrarian majorities.

4. *Bot.* Growing wild in the fields. Also, name proposed by H. C. Watson for the lowest of the altitudinal zones of vegetation, within the limits of the cultivation of corn.

1843 H. C. WATSON *Distrib. Brit. Pl.* 34 Agrarian region. **1861** BUCKMAN *Rep. Brit. Assoc.* (L.) We believe that the charlock is only an agrarian form of brassica.

B. *sb.*

1. An agrarian law.

1656 HARRINGTON *Oceana* 54 (R.) An equal agrarian is a perpetual law establishing and preserving the balance of dominion. **1823** LAMB *Elia* Ser. I. xvi. (1865) 125 The estate has passed into more prudent hands, and nothing but an agrarian can restore it.

2. One in favour of a redistribution of landed property.

1818 SOUTHEY in *Q. Rev.* XIX. 97 An Agrarian of three hours standing. **1882** GOLDW. SMITH in *Pall Mall G.* 24 May 2 The agrarians will be satisfied with nothing short of the total spoliation of the landowners.

agrarianism (ə'grɛərɪənɪz(ə)m). [f. prec. + -ISM.]

1. The principle of a uniform division of lands.

1808 W. TAYLOR in *Month. Mag.* XXVI. 109 A poor's rate ..is an assurance-premium against agrarianism: it is a quit-rent paid to the sovereign people for a recognition of individual titles of possession.

2. Political agitation or civil dissension arising from dissatisfaction with the existing tenure of the land.

1861 GOLDW. SMITH *Irish Hist.* 21 Irish agrarianism is.. the offspring of a barbarism prolonged by unhappy circumstances. **1869** *Times* 15 Oct., Condemn agrarianism by all means, pursue with whatever rigour you can those who commit or abet its crimes.

agrarianize (ə'grɛərɪənaɪz), *v.* [f. as prec. + -IZE.]

1. To apportion land by an agrarian law.

1846 in WORCESTER.

2. To imbue with the ideas of agrarianism.

1883 J. COWEN in *Pall Mall G.* 9 Jan. 1/1 Emigration has democratized the peasants; evictions have agrarianized the artisans.

agrarie, -ary, obs. by-form of AGRARIAN.

†**a'grass, agerse**, *adv.*, prop. *phr. Obs. rare*$^{-1}$. [A *prep.*[1] in + GRASS.] In the grass or blade.

1340 *Ayenb.* 36 Corn agerse, þe vines in flouringe.

agraste, pa. pple. of AGGRACE *v. Obs.*

†**a'graunte**, *v. Obs. rare.* [a. OFr. *agraunte-r*, f. *à* to + *graunter* to GRANT.] To promise, to grant.

1303 R. BRUNNE *Handl. Synne* 4163 þoghe euery day a man hyt haunte ȝyt wyl no man be hyt agraunte [pa. pple.].

agrayde, variant of AGRAITH *v. Obs.*

†**'agre**, *v. Obs. rare*$^{-1}$. [a. OFr. *agrier, aigrier* (cf. mod.Fr. *aigrir*) to torment, f. *aigre*; see EAGER *a.*] To torment, vex.

1495 CAXTON *Vitas Patr.* (W. de Worde) I. xxxvi. 33 b/2 See ye not how this folysshe hermyte agryth & scornyth us, by cause he hathe not be ouercome?

agreable, -bleté, obs. var. AGREEABLE, -BILITY.

agreage, variant of AGGREGE *v. Obs.*

†**a'great**, *adv.*, prop. *phr. Obs.* [A *prep.*[1] in + GREAT *a.* Cf. Fr. *en gros.* The expanded forms *of great, in great*, often occur.] In gross, in the gross, *en masse*; by the whole piece, lump, or lot.

1502 ARNOLD *Chron.* (1811) 72 A dwelling hous is hired of gret and aftir leten..to sondry folkis..the hirer in gret.. shall offir to God..for the rent of all. **1580** BARET *Alvearie* A 234 Agreat or altogither, *Vniuerse*. To take a worke agreat or vpon a price. **1632** BP. M. SMITH *Serm.* 9 Certaine young men..beholding fishermen making of a draught, agreed with them a-great for their draft. **1692** COLES, *Agrat*, by the great or lump. **1775** ASH, *Agreat*, by the great, by the job.

†**agre'ation.** *Obs. rare*$^{-1}$. [a. Fr. *agréation* (Cotgr.) n. of action f. *agréer*: see AGREE and -ATION.] Agreeing, agreement.

1643 PRYNNE *Sov. Power of Parl.* 201 Underneath were the signatures of the Deputies..and underneath them, was written the agreation of the Councell of State.

†**a'gree**, *adv. Obs.* [a. Fr. *à gré*, f. *à* to, at + *gré*, earlier *gred, gret*, that which pleases, gree, liking or pleasure:—L. *grāt-um* that which is pleasant or gratifying.] According to one's liking; pleasantly, kindly, in good part. *to take a-gree*, to take kindly, or in good part, to receive with satisfaction.

*c***1400** *Rom. Rose* 4349 Whom I ne fonde froward ne felle, But toke agree alle hool my play.

Also anglicized as *in, at, to gree*: see GREE *sb.*

1366 MAUNDEV. xxix. 295 That God take hire Servyse to gree. *c***1400** *Rom. Rose* 42 God graunte me in gre that she it take. *c***1430** LYDG. *Bochas* (1554) I. xviii. 33 b, Rightful iudges his sentence toke atgree.

agree (ə'griː), *v.* Also 4–6 **agre, aggre.** [a. OFr. *agré-er*, cogn. w. Pr., Sp. Pg. *agradar*, It. *aggradare*:—late L. **adgrātā-re, aggr-*, f. *ad* to + *grātāre*, to make agreeable, f. *grāt-us* agreeable. (Cf. *adæquāre, aggravāre, alleviāre.*) Also aphetized as GREE.]

I. To please or be pleased.

†1. *trans.* To be to the liking of (any one), to suit the humour of, to please. (Obj. orig. indirect, *dat.* in Fr.) *Obs.* **a.** Of a thing.

*c***1374** CHAUCER *Troylus* I. 409 If harme agre me, ye, wherto than I pleyne? [S'a mal mio grado, il lamentar che vale?] *c***1450** *Merlin* 82 Yef the kynges profer myght not agre the lady, and..hir frendes.

†**b.** Of a person: To please, to satisfy. *Obs.*

*c***1430** LYDG. *Bochas* IX. xxxviii b (1554) 217 a, Great comfort Of trust I should agreen your noblesse. *c***1450** LONELICH *Graal* II. 105 ȝow, sire, agreen I wolde ful pleyn. **1475** *Bk. Noblesse* (1860) 30 Finding bothe horsmete and mannysmete to youre soudeours..without contenting or agreing hem.

†2. To be pleased with (*prendre à gré*); to receive or take in good part; to accept favourably; to favour. (Cf. Fr. *agréez mes respects.*) Also *absol. Obs.*

*a***1500** *MS. Harl.* 7526, 35 Be mercyfulle, agre, take parte and sumwhat pardoone. **1605** BACON *Adv. Learn.* II. xiv. §3 (1873) The principles to be agreed by all. **1642** *Vind. of the King* 1 Those who will not agree the Ceremonies.

II. To make agreeable or harmonious.

†3. *trans.* To make (persons) pleased *with*, or well-disposed towards each other; to reconcile, make friends. *Obs.*

1489 *Plumpton Corr.* 82 The dayes men cannot agre us. **1530** PALSGR. 619/2, I make at one, I agre folkes that were fallen out. **1587** HOLINSHED *Chron.* II. 54 To agree the king and the pope. *Ibid.* I. 188/1 His coosen..the which trauelled to agree him with the king. **1655** J. JENNINGS *Elise* 86 The governour, desirous to agree them, had straitly forbid them fighting.

4. To bring into harmony (things that differ); to conciliate or arrange (a difference). Now only of discrepant *accounts* and the like.

1572 *Lament. Lady Scotl.* in *Sc. Poems of 16th c.* II. 247 To aggre this ciuile difference. **1596** SPENSER *F.Q.* II. iv. 3 Some troublous uprore, Whereto he drew in haste it to agree. **1638** CHILLINGWORTH *Relig. Prot.* I. iii. §7. 130 Meanes of agreeing differences are either Rationall..or voluntary. **1653** HOLCROFT *Procopius* I. 16 Having agreed the War with the Franks. **1706** ESTCOURT *Fair Example* V. I. 69 Do but agree the matter between you. **1785** T. JEFFERSON *Corr.* Wks. 1859 I. 381 His difference with the Dutch is certainly agreed. *a***1884** *Mod.* (*Book-keeping*) Have you agreed the balance? No, we have not yet agreed the items of the accounts. **1928** *Times* 15 Aug. 7/5 The actual figures of profits were agreed between the accountants.

5. To arrange, concert, or settle (a thing in which various interests are concerned).

1523 LD. BERNERS *Froissart* I. 86 Whan that this sayde trewse was agreed. **1658–9** NEVILLE in Burton's *Diary* (1828) III. 194 If you leave it without agreeing the security. **1679** BURNET *Hist. Ref.* I. 586 The king sent Sir Ralph Sadler to him, to agree the marriage. **1715** —— *Own Time* II. 380 He had agreed a match for him with his brother the duke of Zell for his daughter. **1718** POPE *Iliad* IV. 186 Did I for this agree The solemn truce? **1928** *Britain's Industr. Future* (*Liberal Ind. Inquiry*) 140 These councils should have the power to agree factory rules. **1959** *Bookseller* 13 June 1982/1 The Russians have agreed a wide list of categories. **1963** *Listener* 23 May 877/3 Miss Laski's letter.. shows once more the difficulty of agreeing a definition of mysticism.

III. To become well-disposed, to accede.

†6. *refl.* (from 3.) To make oneself well-disposed, to become favourable, to accede, consent *to*. *Obs.*

*c***1450** *Merlin* 84 The kynge hadde a-greed hym-self all to theire ordenaunce. **1523** LD. BERNERS *Froissart* I. cccvi. 461 Dame, I agre me well to your desyre. **1574** tr. *Littleton, Tenures* 110 a, I agree me to the graunte made to you.

7. *intr.* (from *refl.*) To become favourable; to give consent, to accede. **a.** with *inf.*, or *subord. cl.*

*c***1374** CHAUCER *Troylus* III. 81 Ye wolde..agreen that I may ben he. **1597** DANIEL *Civ. Wares* II. xli, The Realme.. will never gree To have a right succession overthrowne. **1658–9** BAYNES in Burton's *Diary* (1828) IV. 123 The Act of Union agrees, that they shall have thirty members. **1849** MACAULAY *Hist. Eng.* II. 119 He reluctantly agreed..that some indulgence should be granted to the Presbyterians. **1860** TYNDALL *Glac.* I. §16. 104 He then agreed to make the trial.

b. with *to* (a proposal, conditions, etc.)

*c***1400** *Destr. Troy* VIII. 3649 All agreit to þe gate with a gode wille. *c***1450** *Merlin* 85 Will ye..agreen to the acorde and ordenaunce of these worthy lordes? **1475** CAXTON *Jason* 35 They that at the firste requeste of their louers agree to them ought to be ashamed. **1535** COVERDALE *1 Macc.* i. 42 All the Heithen agreed to the commaundement of kynge Antiochus. **1591** SHAKS. *1 Hen. VI*, V. v. 88 Post..to France, Agree to any couenants. **1759** ROBERTSON *Hist. Scotl.* I. II. 105 It was not possible to agree to a proposal so extraordinary and unexpected. **1876** FREEMAN *Norm. Conq.* III. xii. 193 Till he agreed to the hard conditions.

c. *absol.* and *passive.*

1461 *Paston Lett.* 398 II. 23 If ye wol have her hom to you for a seacon..my mastre is agreed. **1476** *Plumpton Corr.* 37 You must desier the sheriffe to serve it, yf so be that ye agre not. **1534** LD. BERNERS *Gold. Bk. M. Aurel.* (1546) Nv, Thoughe fortune denie hym at one howre, yet at an other time, she agreeth. **1590** SHAKS. *Com. Err.* I. i. 61 Unwilling I agreed. **1851** MRS. BROWNING *Casa Guidi* 46 Austrian Metternich Can fix no yoke unless the neck agree.

d. with *clause*: To concede, grant, accede to the opinion, *that* a thing is so; *formerly*, a thing *to be* so.

1606 G. W[ODCOCKE] *Hist. Justine* 86 Which grace though the Godds had not agreed to be due vnto her, yet, etc. **1658–9** MORRICE in Burton's *Diary* (1828) IV. 190, I can never agree that to be law which is dissonant to reason. **1765** HARRIS *Three Treat.* I. 14 We have agreed it, replied he, to be necessary. *Mod.* I agree that he is the ablest of the candidates.

†8. To accede *to* the opinion of (a person); to assent; passing into sense of ***agree with*** (12). *Obs.*

1526 TINDALE *Acts* V. 40 To him agreed [so CRANM., *Genev.*, **1611**; WYCLIF, *Rhem.*, consented]. *a***1556** CRANMER *Wks.* I. 25 Cyril..agreed to Nestorius in the substance of the thing that was eaten. **1561** T. N[ORTON] tr. *Calvin's Instit.* I. 17 They were by no other meane brought to agree vnto him. **1580** BARET *Alvearie* A 239 To Agree to one or to be of his opinion. **1641** W. CARTWRIGHT *Lady Errant* III. i. (1651) 31, I must not agree t'you, to pass by What you have said.

IV. To come into harmony.

9. *intr.* (? for *refl.*) To come into accord or harmony, to become of one mind, make up differences, become friends. Const. *with.* Still *dialectal* 'Kiss and 'gree again.'

1489 Caxton *Faytes of Armes* I. xix. 60 He agreed and made peas wyth mayencyens. **1535** Coverdale *2 Macc.* xi. 26 Yf thou sende vnto them & agre with them. **1548** Hall *Chron.* (1809) 3 If you of yourselfes will not agre, I will not study how to agre you. **1597** Daniel *Civ. Wares* III. (R.) Till all inflamed they all at once agree. **1723** Blackall *Wks.* I. 260 To agree with our Adversary while we are in the way to Judgement. (See Bible *Matt.* v. 25.)

10. To come into accord as to something. **a.** *spec.* To come to terms about the price of anything, to bargain, contract. ? *Obs.*

1526 Tindale *Matt.* xx. 2 And he agreed with the labourers for a peny a daye[so **1611**; Wyclif, *Rhem.*, made covenant]. **1580** Baret *Alvearie* A 239 To agree or consent as concerning the act or deede, price, etc. **1669** Pepys *Diary* (1877) V. 431 To the cabinet-shops, to look out, and did agree, for a cabinet to give my wife.

b. Const. *on, as to*, (*of* obs.) a matter or point.

1523 Ld. Berners *Froissart* I. lxiii. 86 And so contynued a xv. dayes, and agreed of no poynt of effect. **1603** Greenwey *Tacitus Ann.* VI. vii. (1622) 131 To lay downe such things as they agree of. **1607** Shaks. *Timon* III. vi. 76 To let the meat coole, ere we can agree vpon the first place. **1651** Hobbes *Leviathan* II. xxiii. 125 Judges he himself agrees on. **1657** Sir C. Pack in Burton's *Diary* (1828) II. 160 It will be hard for the Committee to agree of names. **1804** W. Taylor in *Ann. Rev.* II. 273 A convention has been agreed on relative to this subject. **1876** Freeman *Norm. Conq.* III. xii. 104 Terms of reconciliation were readily agreed on.

c. with *inf.*, or *subord. cl.* Also *spec.* in phr. ***to agree to differ*** (or ***disagree***), to agree to cease trying to convince one another .

1572 *Lament. Lady Scot.* in *Sc. Poems of 16th c.* II. 248 ȝe did aggre To crowne and place him in authoritie. **1781** Gibbon *Decl. & F.* xl, They agreed to censure the corrupt management of justice and the finances. **1785** J. Wedgwood *Let.* 3 Oct. (1965) 285 The principal difficulty.. is to *agree to differ*, to agree in impartial investigation and candid argument. **1810** Coleridge *Friend* VII. vi. (1867) 379 His lordship and Sir Alexander Ball 'agreed to differ.' **1852** Dickens *Bleak Ho.* II. 43 We.. had little in common even before we agreed to differ. *a* **1884** *Mod.* They agreed that the matter should stand over for the present. **1925** A. Huxley *Those Barren Leaves* V. iv. 369 There we must agree to differ. But even if it is impossible to get at reality, the fact that reality exists and is manifestly very different from what we ordinarily suppose it to be, surely shows some light on this horrible death business. **1942** Berrey & Van den Bark *Amer. Thes. Slang* §347/2 *Disagree*, agree to disagree, beg to differ. **1977** *Guardian Weekly* 27 Feb. 9/3 'We shall agree to disagree,' a press-weary Israeli official said last week.

V. To be in harmony.

11. To be in harmony or unison in opinions, feelings, conduct, etc.; to be in sympathy; to live or act together harmoniously; to have no causes of variance. (Simply, or with *together*; or const. *with*.)

1548 Udall, etc. *Matt.* xxviii. (R.) My spirite agreeth not with the spirite of this worlde. **1596** Shaks. *Merch. Ven.* II. ii. 107 How doost thou and thy Master agree? I haue brought him a present; how gree you now? **1639** Fuller *Holy War* II. xi. (1840) 63 These cities.. agreed so well together, that they were called sisters. **1642** —— *Holy & Prof. St.* V. xix. 438 It is probable that in Noahs Ark the wolf agreed with the lambe. **1720** Watts *Divine Songs* xvii, Birds in their little nests agree. **1726** Gay *Fables* I. xxi. 43 In ev'ry age and clime we see, Two of a trade can ne'er agree. **1807** Crabbe *Par. Reg.* I. 88 And where they once agreed, to cavil now. *Adage*, 'Friends agree best separate.'

12. a. To be of the same mind as to particular points; to concur *with* a person *in* an opinion, *as to* a matter, *that* such is the fact, or (*obs.*) such *to be* the fact. (See also 7, 8.) ***I couldn't agree (with you) more***: I am in complete agreement (with you).

1494 Fabyan I. vii. 12 The more partie of wryters agreen, that he ruled this Ile of Brytayne by the terme of xl. yeres. **1580** Baret *Alvearie* A 239 The doctours discent, or the authours doe not agree in this poynt. **1652** Needham tr. *Selden's Mare Cl.* 267 As to.. its beginning, they agree with Ingulphus and Hoveden. **1663** Butler *Hudibr.* I. i. 426, I would say Eye, for h' had but one, As most agree, though some say none. **1706** De Foe *Jure Div.* I. 3 All Histories agree him to be a Tyrant. **1769** *Junius Lett.* xxxv. 162 There is one point in which they all agree. **1877** Mozley *Univ. Serm.* V. 102 Nobody supposes that the suitors in our courts agree with the judge when he decides against them. **1942** J. B. Priestley *Black-out in Gretley* viii. 185 'I couldn't agree with you more,' he said, grinning. **1953** —— *Try it Again* in *Best One-Act Plays 1952–3* 109 *Kramer*. Whatever I do can hardly make things worse. *Helen*. I couldn't agree more. **1960** L. Cooper *Accomplices* II. i. 77 You think it's a nasty cold-blooded business..? I couldn't agree more.

b. Hence, To agree *with* an opinion or statement.

1530 Palsgr. 418/2, I agree with his opynion touchyng this mater. **1781** Burke *Corr.* (1844) II. 412 To know any man's story that you cannot agree with. *Mod.* I do not agree with what has been said by the last speaker.

13. Of things: To be in harmony, to accord, to coincide in any respect. **a.** *simply*.

1570 Billingsley *Euclid* I. viii. 7 Thinges which agree together: are equall the one to the other. **1580** Baret *Alvearie* A 239 To agree or accorde: to serue to the purpose, *Congruo*. **1596** Shaks. *Tam. Shr.* V. ii. 1 At last.. our iarring notes agree. **1611** Bible *Mark* xiv. 56 Their witnesse agreed not together. **1782** Priestley *Corr. Chr.* I. III. 305 All the accounts sufficiently agree. **1871** Balf. Stewart *Heat* §70 The two scales agree almost exactly at 62° while they differ sensibly at 72°.

b. with *with*.

1494 Fabyan 3 And cause it to agre with other olde storyes. **1608** Shaks. *Peric.* II. v. 18 Mistress.. your choice agrees with mine. **1651** Hobbes *Leviathan* II. xxv. 131 It best agreeth with the conclusions they would inferre. **1674** Playford *Skill of Mus.* II. 94 Till it agree in sound with your Treble open. **1734** tr. *Rollin's Anc. Hist.* (1827) I. II. 363 The expedition.. cannot agree in time with the siege of Tyre. **1860** Tyndall *Glac.* II. §14. 301 This quite agrees with the views now generally entertained.

14. To be consistent, to answer *to*, correspond *with*.

†**a.** with *to*. *Obs.*

1526 Tindale *Mark* xiv. 70 Thou arte of Galile, and thy speache agreth therto [so Cranm., *Genev.*, **1611**]. **1625** Burges *Pers. Tithes* 50 This Statute agreeth to the best English Canon Law. **1659** Hammond *On Ps.* xvii. 13. 92 This perfectly agrees to the context. **1708** Swift *Wks.* (1755) II. 72 The constitution of the English government.. to which the present establishment of the church doth so happily agree. **1788** Reid *Aristotle's Logic* iv. §3. 77 It agrees to the rules of the figure.. it is also agreeable to all the general rules.

b. with *with*.

1580 Baret *Alvearie* A 239 The beginning agreeth with the ende, *Congruunt extrema primis*. **1588** Shaks. *Tit. A.* I. i. 306 Full well.. Agree these Deeds with that proud bragge of thine. **1661** Bramhall *Just. Vind.* iii. 40, I do not see why Monasteries might not agree well enough with reformed deuotion. **1661** Boyle *Spring & Weight of Air* III. (1682) 69 I find nothing that agrees not with my Hypothesis. **1838** Macaulay in Trevelyan's *Life* II. i. 29 He looked about to see how my Horatius agreed with the topography.

15. *Gramm.* To be in 'concord'; to take the same gender, number, case, or person; as happens in inflected languages to words in apposition, and to substantives and their attributive words, whether adjective, verb, or relative.

1530 Palsgr. Introd. 38 Adjectyves agre onely in gendre and nombre, but theyr verbes agre with theyr nominatyve cases in nombre and parsone. **1669** Milton *Gram.* II, *Concords* Wks. 1847, 468 An adjectiue with his substantiue .. agree[th] in gender and case. **1881** Mason *Eng. Gram.* §465 Pronouns must agree in gender, number, and person with the nouns for which they stand.

16. To be agreeable *to*, or in harmony *with* the nature or character of.

†**a.** To be suitable, appropriate, consonant *to*. *Obs.*

1541 R. Copland *Guydon's Quest. Cyrurg.*, Other maner of byndynge.. proprely agreeth to depe woundes. **1551** Turner *Herbal* I. (1568) 114 We have no herbe in Englande .. to whome all thes hole descriptions do agre. **1586** J. Hooker *Giraldus's Hist. Irel.* in *Holinsh.* II. 153/2 Interred in all honorable maner, as to his estate did agree. **1586** T. B. tr. *La Primaudaye's Fr. Acad.* II. (1594) 17 The worke of the creation can agree to none but to God only. **1637** Gillespie *Eng.-Pop. Cerem.* III. viii. 196 The power of Ecclesiasticall jurisdiction doth no more agree to the King, then the power of Ecclesiasticall order. **1662** More *Antid. agst. Ath.* II. ii. (1712) 45 That Hypothesis.. which will agree universally to the Air. **1671** J. Webster *Metallogr.* i. 15 Reason agreeth thereto.

†**b.** To do well *with*: formerly said of a person agreeing or doing well with food, climate, etc. *Obs.*

1525 Ld. Berners *Froissart* II. ciii. 301 To agree with the ayre not accustomed before. **1530** Palsgr. 419/1, I agre with meate or drinke, I can away wit it. **1599** Shaks. *Hen. V*, V. i. 28 Because your appetites and your disgestions doo's not agree with it [the leek], I would desire you to eat it. **1681** Burnet *Hist. Ref.* II. 162 Fagius, not agreeing with this air, died soon after. **1697** Dryden *Virg. Georg.* II. 361 Lest the Tree Translated, shou'd not with the Soil agree.

c. now only of food, climate, work agreeing or doing well with a person, etc.

1661 Lovell *Hist. Anim. & Min.*, Others are more grosse, tough and hard, agreeing chiefely with country persons and such as labour. **1669** in *Phil. Trans.* IV. 981 The Baths agree (as the vulgar speaks) with Brass, but not with Iron. **1796** Mrs. Glasse *Cookery* xv. 270 Some boil it with milk, and it is very good where it will agree. **1855** Bain *Senses & Intell.* II. ii. §5 (1864) 157 Whether a substance will agree or disagree with the stomach. **1858** Thackeray *Virginians* xvi. 126 She wondered whether the climate would agree with her. *Mod.* Sea-bathing does not agree with everybody.

†**a'gree**, *sb.* *Obs.* [f. the vb.] Agreeing, agreement.

c **1400** *Apol. for Loll.* 91 We.. may after agre worschip such þingis writun. **1590** Greene *Orl. Fur.* (1599) 8 Shame you not, Princes, at this bad agree, To wrong a stranger with discourtesie?

agreeability (əˌgriːəˈbɪlɪtɪ). Also 4 **agreablete**. [In 14th c. a. OFr. *agréableté* n. of state, f. *agréable*: see agreeable and -ty. Obsolete for 400 years, and then freshly formed on *agreeable*: see -bility. In Fr. *agréableté* was still in Cotgr. 1611; obs. in the Academy's Dict. and in Littré; revived in 1860 by Ste.-Beuve as *agréabilité*.] The quality of being agreeable; agreeableness, especially of disposition.

c **1374** Chaucer *Boethius* 1099 Al fortune is blisful to a man by þe agreablete or by þe egalite of hym þat suffreþ it [*ed.* 1560 aggreeability]. [Not in any Dict. of 16th, 17th, 18th c. In Todd 1818 only from Chaucer as above.] **1778** Miss Burney *Diary & Lett.* (1854) I. 53 She was all good humour.. and agreeability. (Surely I may make words when at a loss, if Dr. Johnson does.) **1839** Lady Lytton *Cheveley* (ed. 2) I. v. 105 His house was the focus of agreeability. **1854** Thackeray *Newc.* II. 4 Remarkable for rank, fashion and agreeability.

agreeable (əˈgriːəb(ə)l), *a.* Also **agreable, aggreable, aggreeable.** [a. Fr. *agréable* capable of pleasing, f. *agréer* to please: see agree and -able.] At a very early date aphetized to greeable.

1. a. To one's liking or taste; affording pleasure; pleasing, pleasant.

c **1384** Chaucer *H. of Fame* 1097 But for the ryme is lyght and lewed Yit make hyt sumwhat agreable. **1413** Lydg. *Pylgr. Sowle* IV. xx. (1483) 68 Fyercer than the fyre he fyndeth the and nothyng agreable. *c* **1500** *Doctr. Good Serv.* (1842) 4 Speke lytell and be agreable. **1587** Fleming *Contn. Holinsh.* III. 969/2 This man.. had doone to the king and realme right agreeable services. **1716** Lady M. W. Montague *Lett.* 2. I. 10 Nothing can be more agreeable than travelling in Holland. **1742** H. Baker *Microsc.* II. xxv. 201 The minute Spiders appear very agreeable in the Microscope. **1779** J. Moore *View of Soc.* II. 176 Two very agreeable French gentlemen. **1813** Marshall *Gardening* xix. (ed. 5) 363 Christmas rose is very hardy, a plant or two potted is agreeable enough at such a season. **1859** Lewes *Physiol. Com. Life* I. i. §6. 27 The sensation of Hunger is at first rather agreeable, but it quickly becomes unpleasant if prolonged. **1874** *Daily News* 2 June 5/5 Mr. Disraeli's definition of an agreeable man—he who agrees with us.

b. with *to*.

c **1386** Chaucer *Man of Lawes T.* 767 An heir moore agreable than this to my likynge. **1481** Caxton *Myrrour* III. xvi. 170 That he myght conduyte hym that it myght be to god agreable. **1732** Law *Serious Call* (ed. 2) 77 Neither of which can be any longer agreeable to God. **1863** *Sat. Rev.* 273 That painful manufacture of common-places which is called 'making yourself agreeable to a lady.' **1876** Freeman *Norm. Conq.* I. 650 They made themselves too agreeable to the English women.

2. Of a person: Having a liking (*to* anything); favourable, propitious; kindly-disposed, pleased, contented (*to do* anything). Now *colloquial*.

1467 Sir J. Paston in *Lett.* 570 II. 300, I kannot in no wyse fynde hyr a greable that ye scholde have her dowter. **1494** Fabyan V. lxxxiii. 61 To whose request the kynge was aggreable. **1509** Barclay *Ship of Fooles* (1570) 87 God is not sone agreable To heare their cry. **1524** Henry VIII in Strype *Eccl. Mem.* (1822) I. II. 43 The kings highnes is agreable to be a mediator. **1623** J. Bingham *Xenophon* 113 The sacrifice [*personified*] was not agreeable that day. **1850** Thackeray *Pend.* (1863) 329 'Well, sir, if Ann's agreeable, I say ditto.'

†**3.** Agreeing together; of one mind. *Obs.*

1552 Huloet, *Agreable*, of one consente, mynde, or wyll. *Concors*. **1567** Jewel *Def. Apol.* (1611) 105 The agreeable multitude of many Bishops. **1601** Holland *Pliny* (1634) I. 270 The same fishes in certaine set moneths, are good friends and agreeable enough.

†**4.** Of things (rarely of persons): Corresponding, conformable, suitable, fitting. **a.** Mutually corresponding, answering to each other. *Obs.*

1551 Recorde *Pathw. Knowl.* II. xx, You see the agreable sentence of these iij. theoremes to tende to this purpose. **1661** *Hist. Parismus* II. 80 To see whether his valour and his boastings were Agreable. **1692** Molyneux in *Locke's Lett.* (1708) 14 These two places have been stumbled at by some as not consistent. To me they appear, and are, very agreeable.

†**b.** Answering to the circumstances, or to the general order of things; suitable, fitting. *Obs.*

1601 Dolman *Fr. Acad.* (1618) 691 Which consideration is every whit agreeable in each part of the zodiacke. **1674** N. Fairfax *Bulk & Selv.* 70 'Tis agreeable, that we cannot otherwise have the heaven, in the world, than as to sence above us. **1682** Grew *Anat. Plants* III. II. iii. §14 And so make a vessel of a wider, as a more agreeable bore.

†**c.** with *with*: In accordance, in harmony; harmonious, congruous, consistent. *Obs.*

1557 Recorde *Whetst.* T iij, Their lengthe is agreable with their bredthe, and so thei make square figures. **1594** Carew tr. *Huarte's Trial of Wits* (1616) 102 That which is agreeable with his naturall abilitie. **1655** Culpepper *Riverius* I. i. 5 Blood-letting is not agreeable with Flegmatick Diseases. **1783** Boswell *Johnson* (1816) IV. 249 Your anxiety about my health is.. very agreeable with your general kindness.

d. with *unto, to*: Conformable (to a standard or design), corresponding, answering; suitable; in accordance with. Now only of things immaterial.

c **1385** Chaucer *Leg. G. Wom.* 668 Most agreable unto myn entent. **1547** Bale *Sel. Wks.* (1849) 232 Though in faith she were not agreeable to the world's wild opinion. **1548** Udall, etc. *Erasm. Paraphr. Matt.* iii. 4 His dyet was agreable unto his apparell. **1625** Burges *Pers. Tithes* 22 This is neither agreeable to Religion nor conscience. **1699** Bentley *Phalaris* §2. 28 About LXXX Years later: Which is agreeable to Suidas, who places him 'about the LII Olympiad.' **1776** Adam Smith *W.N.* I. I. v. 48 It rarely happens that these are exactly agreeable to their standard. **1855** Bain *Senses & Intell.* II. ii. §11 (1864) 195 It is agreeable to all experience.

5. In this sense it is often used *adverbially* for agreeably: In a manner answering to, in accordance with, in conformity with; according to.

1549 Latimer *7 Serm. bef. Edw. VI* (1869) 25 To accomodate hymselfe and hys matter a greable vnto the comforte, and amendemente of the audience. **1614** Selden *Titles of Honor* 285 They haue also, agreeable with the identitie of Thane and Steward, certain Stewarties at this day. **1710** Palmer *Proverbs* 249 Rakes and clowns.. will.. treat you agreeable to their own humour. **1828** Scott *F.M. Perth* III. 173 The Earl entered, agreeable to the Prince's summons.

6. *subst.* (as in mod.Fr.) †**a.** An agreeable person. Cf. *an incapable*. *Obs.*

1712 Addison *Spect.* No. 511 ¶1 There were as many ugly Women as Beauties or Agreeables.

b. *pl.* Agreeable things. Cf. *eatables*, *valuables*, etc.

1812 HENRY *Camp. agst. Quebec* 94 Accompanied by all those agreeables which render the cultivator of the earth the most happy of human beings. **1822** COLERIDGE *Lett., Convers.* II. 99 Superficial Advantages and outside Agreeables.

c. *to do* (or †*make*) *the agreeable*, to make oneself pleasant, show courteous attentions. (Cf. Fr. *faire l'agréable*.)

1825 H. WILSON *Memoirs* I. 52 It fatigues me to death to be eternally making the agreeable to a set of men who might be all buried, and nobody would miss them. **1834** J. K. TOWNSEND *Narrative* 31 Mar. in R. G. Thwaites *Early Western Travels* (1905) XXI. i. 127, I endeavored to do the agreeable to the fair ones. **1851** J. J. HOOPER *Widow Rugby's Husb.* 168 The Colonel does the agreeable to strangers.

agreeableness (əˈgriːəb(ə)lnɪs). [f. prec. + -NESS.]

1. The quality of being agreeable, or of giving pleasure; pleasingness, pleasantness.

1611 COTGR., *Agreeableté*, agreeablenesse, acceptablenesse. **1610–31** DONNE *Selections* (1840) 160 Loveliness of person, agreeableness of conversation. **1667** BOYLE *Orig. Formes & Qual.*, Beauty..is made up of Symmetry of parts, and agreeablenesse of colours. **1709** LADY M. W. MONTAGUE *Lett.* lxiv. 106 Leave me my..agreeableness and genius, but leave me also my sincerity. **1725** DE FOE *Voy. round World* (1840) 159 The agreeableness of the climate. *a* **1763** SHENSTONE *Ess.* 213 Virtue and agreeableness are, I fear, too often separated. *c* **1813** MISS AUSTEN *Northang. Ab.* (1833) I. x. 58 We have entered into a contract of mutual agreeableness. **1870** HAWTHORNE *Eng. Note-Bks.* (1879) I. 128 You might enjoy its agreeableness without suspecting it.

†**2.** The quality of being conformable *to*, or consistent *with*; conformity, consistency. *Obs.*

1557 RECORDE *Whetst.* G ij, There appeareth a greate agreablenes, between like flattes, and square numbers. **1667** H. MORE *Div. Dial.* v. xli. (1713) 523 Sing no Tragical strain in agreeableness to the last Thunder. **1690** J. NORRIS *Beatitudes* (1694) I. 166 Some Likeness or Agreeableness between the Faculty and the Good to be enjoy'd. **1710** PRIDEAUX *Orig. Tithes* ii. 43 The strength of every Precedent lyeth in its agreeableness with the Law. *a* **1797** BURKE *Ess. Drama* Wks. X. 159 The incompatibility or agreeableness of incidents..with the probable in fact, but with propriety in design.

agreeably (əˈgriːəblɪ), *adv.* In 4 agreablely. [f. AGREEABLE + -LY².] In an agreeable manner.

1. In a way which pleases, or suits the inclination; pleasantly.

c **1374** CHAUCER *Boethius* 43 With hem þat euery fortune receyuen agreablely or egally. **1597–8** BACON *Ess.* (Arb.) 20/1 To speake agreeably to him with whome we deale. **1740–61** MRS. DELANY *Life & Corr.* (1861) III. 300, I spent an hour and a half very agreeably. **1842** MACAULAY *Lays* (1864) Pref. 25 He..tells very agreeably the stories of Elfleda and Elfrida.

2. In a manner suiting, corresponding, or answering *to*; in conformity or accordance *with*.

1461 *Paston Lett.* 407 II. 34 A signement sufficient to hem aggreabili for the seid payment. **1611** BIBLE *1 Esdr.* viii. 12 Agreeably to that which is in the Law of the Lord. *a* **1745** SWIFT *Wks.* II. 28 Men should act agreeably to the motive of that respect. **1769** ROBERTSON *Chas. V*, III. x. 252 Agreeably to the manifesto which he had published. **1837** J. H. NEWMAN *Proph. Off. Church* 108 Agreeably with this anticipation, the Church of Rome..is led to profess to know not only infallibly but completely.

†**b.** without *to*: (*a*) In a way that corresponds to something else; correspondingly, conformably. (*b*) In ways that correspond to each other, in the same way, uniformly, similarly. *Obs.*

1561 J. DAUS tr. *Bullinger on Apocal.* (1573) 91/b, The Scripture euery where agreeably witnesseth, that the Saintes in heauen are free from grefes. **1563** *Homilies* II. (1859) 421 And St. Peter most agreeably writing in this behalf saith. **1596** SPENSER *F.Q.* VI. vii. 3 Two Knights..The which were armed both agreeably. **1659** HAMMOND *On Ps.* 2 And agreeably the fiftieth Psalm inscribed to Asaph. **1718** J. CHAMBERLAYNE *Relig. Philos.* II. xxii. §28 Another experiment proved the same no less agreeably.

†**c.** In a way that answers to circumstances or the nature of things; suitably, fittingly. *Obs.*

1754 RICHARDSON *Grandison* II. xxix. 269, I was shy of forcing an opportunity, as none agreeably offered.

†**a'greeance.** *Obs.* [a. OFr. *agréance*, n. of action f. *agréer*: see AGREE and -ANCE.] The act of agreeing; = AGREEMENT in several of its meanings.

1536 BELLENDENE *Cron. Scotl.* (1821) II. 333 King Johne ..to eschew the present dangeir, maid aggreance with his prelatis. **1549** COVERDALE *Erasm. Paraphr. Hebr.* iii. 6 If we dooe styll abyde in the concorde and agreaunce of the house. **1559** in Strype's *Ann.* I. I. App. xvi, The diversity of our fasting setteth forth the more the agreeance of our faith. **1599** JAS. I *Basil. Dor.* (1682) To Reader, What aggreance and conformitie he ought to keep betwixt his outward behaviour..and the vertuous qualities of his minde. **1714** MILBOURNE *Traitor's Reward* 19 In agreeance with God's laws.

agreeand, northern form of AGREEING *ppl. a.*

agreed (əˈgriːd), *ppl. a.* [f. AGREE *v.* + -ED.]

†**1.** Pleased, satisfied, contented. *Obs.*

1418 HEN. V in Ellis *Orig. Lett.* III. 27 I. 64 That he be contented and agreed in the best wyse as longeth vnto hym. *c* **1450** LONELICH *Graal* II. 233 Thanne the kyng agreed he was Of the veniawnce in that plas.

†**2.** Made pleasing or satisfactory. *Obs.*

c **1400** *Epiph.* (Turnb. 1843) 113 Unto God I say in sothenes Aboue all this agreed is hur mekenes.

3. Brought into harmony; united in feeling or sentiment.

a **1440** *Sir Degrev.* 1770 Giff ȝe holde us a-gret, Shall I never ete mete. **1535** COVERDALE *Amos* iii. 3 Maye twaine walk together excepte they be agreed amonge them selues? **1611** *Ibid.*, Can two walke together, except they be agreed? **1851** MRS. BROWNING *Casa Guidi* 100 Our Tuscans..rising up agreed And bold.

4. Come to one and the same opinion; at one as to a matter in question.

1613 SHAKS. *Hen. VIII*, v. iii. 87 Are you all agreed, Lords? **1659** STARKEY in Burton's *Diary* (1828) IV. 353 We are agreed of the substance. **1769** *Junius Lett.* iii. 18 In the two next articles, I think, we are agreed. **1833** HT. MARTINEAU *Brooke Farm* iv. 47 He and I were never agreed about matters of that kind. **1842** J. H. NEWMAN *Par. Serm.* (ed. 2) V. xvi. 261 He professes to be agreed with me.

5. a. Arranged or settled by common consent. (In this sense ***agreed on*** is now more usual.)

1613 SHAKS. *Hen. VIII*, v. i. 87 It stands agreed..by all voices. **1640** BP. HALL *Chr. Mod.* 8/2 Retired to an agreed solitariness. **1732** POPE *Ess. on Man* IV. 219 Heroes are much the same, the point's agreed. **1806** W. TAYLOR in *Ann. Rev.* IV. 256 The best standard is not yet agreed.

1596 SHAKS. *Tam. Shr.* II. i. 272 Your dowry 'greed on. **1651** HOBBES *Leviathan* II. xxv. 125 To be judged by men agreed on by Consent. **1741** RICHARDSON *Pamela* (1824) I. 221 To take leave of them and receive her agreed-on portion. *Mod.* They met at the place agreed on.

b. ***agreed syllabus*** (see quots.).

1944 *Act 7 & 8 Geo. VI*, c. 31 §114 (1) 'Agreed syllabus' means..an agreed syllabus of religious instruction. **1945** *Guide Educ. Syst. Eng. & Wales* (Min. Educ.) 57 *Agreed syllabus*, syllabus governing undenominational religious instruction in county and controlled schools, and drawn up or adopted for each area by a conference representing the religious denominations, the teachers and the L.E.A.

6. As a rejoinder: Consented to; granted, admitted, or accepted. = 'I agree to the proposal.'

1794 SOUTHEY *Bot. Bay Ecl.* ii. Wks. II. 75 Suppose we leave awhile this stubborn soil, To eat our dinner and to rest from toil. Agreed. Yon tree..Forms with its shadowy boughs a cool retreat.

agreef, agrefe, agreve, *adv. phr.* See AGRIEF.

agreeing (əˈgriːɪŋ), *vbl. sb.* [f. AGREE *v.* + -ING¹.] A coming to or being in harmony.

1548 UDALL, etc. *Mark* xiv. 14 (R.) This house presenteth vnto vs the agreyng and frendely felowshyp of the church. **1580** HOLLYBAND *Treas. Fr. Tong.*, *Accord de sons & choses differentes*, agreeing of disagreeing thinges. **1591** PERCIVALL *Sp. Dict.*, *Concorde*, agreeing. **1611** COTGR., *Agreation*, an agreement, concord, assent, consent; also, an agreeing. **1865** CARLYLE *Fredk. Gt.* I. II. iv. 65 Inextricable coil of claimings, quarrellings and agreeings.

agreeing (əˈgriːɪŋ), *ppl. a.* North. **agreeand.** [f. AGREE *v.* + -ING².]

†**1.** In conformity with, conformable, corresponding, or answering *to*. *Obs.*

1540 WHITTINTON *Tully's Offyce* I. 2 That thynge..to my dignite mooste agreynge. *a* **1555** BRADFORD *Wks.* 189 What is more necessary than meat and drink, or more agreeing to nature? **1687** SETTLE *Refl. Dryden's Plays* 4 How agreeing Images are to the Mahumetan Worship..I leave to the judicious to censure.

2. Of the same mind or nature; concurring, accordant, harmonious, unanimous.

1557 EARL SURREY *Aeneid* II. 292 The people cried with sondry greeing shoutes. **1581** LAMBARDE *Eiren.* I. ix. (1602) 38 The agreeing opinion of all the judges. **1677** GALE *Crt. Gentiles* I. III. ii. 33 In the ancient fables, there is no uniforme, and..agreeing historie to be exspected. **1703** ROWE *Fair Penit.* III. i. 1097 The kind consent of our agreeing minds. **1880** CYPLES *Hum. Exp.* iii. 51 The largest number of agreeing units.

†**3.** Suiting, doing well *with*. *Obs.*

1620 VENNER *Via Recta* v. 86 The milke will be much the more agreeing with the stomacke. **1642** ROGERS *Naaman* 110 A marveilous agreeing nature..with the corrupt sensuall appetite of man.

†**4.** *adverbially*. According *to*; = AGREEINGLY. *Obs.*

1526 TINDALE *1 Cor.* xv. 3 Christ dyed for our synnes agreynge to the scriptures [so COVERD., CRANMER, *Geneva*; *Rhem.* and **1611** according to]. **1614–25** BOYS *Wks.* 1630, 138 A Preacher then must teach agreeing to the faith.

†**a'greeingly,** *adv. Obs.* [f. prec. + -LY².] In an agreeing manner; correspondingly, consistently, agreeably, suitably. ***agreeingly to***, according to.

1562 *Burnynge of Paules Ch.* If they..ministred after one sorte, and agreinglye through the whole church it were good. **1591** PERCIVALL *Sp. Dict.*, *Concordemente*, agreeingly. **1616** SHELDON *Surv. Rom. Miracles* 32 (T.) Agreeingly to which St. Austin contendeth. **1642** ROGERS *Naaman* 41 He will order all meanes most sweetly and agreeingly, to that purpose.

agreeingness (əˈgriːɪŋnɪs). *rare*⁻⁰. [f. as prec. + -NESS.] The quality of agreeing; 'consistence, suitableness.' J.

agreement (əˈgriːmənt). Also 5–6 ag(g)rement. [a. OFr. *agreement*, *agrément*, n. of action, f. *agréer*: see AGREE and -MENT.] The action or fact of agreeing.

†**1.** The action of pleasing or contenting; satisfaction. *Obs.*

1494 FABYAN VI. ccxii. 227 After he had taryed here a certayne of tyme, to his agrement and pleasure.

†**2.** The action of consenting; consent. *Obs.*

1479 ROKEWOODE in *Bury Wills* (1850) 52 As welle by my wylle as by the aggrement of the seid Alice and Robert. **1483** CAXTON *Gold. Leg.* 85/1 He receyuyd with hys agrement the gybet of the crosse.

†**3.** A setting at one; atonement (both in its earlier sense of reconciliation, and its later sense of propitiation, satisfaction). *Obs.*

1526 TINDALE *1 John* iv. 10 Not that we loued God, but that he loued vs, and sent his sonne to make agrement for oure sinnes. **1535** COVERDALE *Ps.* xlviii. 7 No man may delyuer his brother, ner make agrement for him vnto God. ——*Hebr.* ii. 17 A faithfull hye prest in things concernynge God to make agrement for the synnes of yᵉ people. **1557** N. T. (Genev.) *1 John* iv. 10 And sent his sonne to make agreement for our sinnes [*Rhem.* and **1611** propitiation].

4. A coming into accord; an arrangement between two or more persons as to a course of action; a mutual understanding; a covenant, or treaty.

c **1400** *Destr. Troy* XIX. 7827 þe grekys by agrement of þe grete all, Sent to þe Cite soueran men two. **1523** LD. BERNERS *Froissart* I. cxv. 136 Were not of the agrement with the kyng. **1596** SHAKS. *1 Hen. IV*, I. iii. 103 Three times did they drink Vpon agreement, of swift Severnes flood. **1611** BIBLE *Dan.* xi. 6 The Kings daughter of the South shall come to the King of the North to make an agreement. **1725** DE FOE *Voy. round World* (1840) 296 We came to a good agreement with him for his reward. **1860** TYNDALL *Glac.* I. §10. 67 We accordingly entered into an agreement with our guide.

5. *Law.* A contract duly executed and legally binding on the parties making it.

1536 in *Thynne's Animadv.* (1865) App. 28 In wittyness herof the saide John Wilkinson, to this agreement hath putte his merke. **1751** CHAMBERS *Cycl.* s.v., An Agreement executory is when both parties at one time are agreed, that such a thing shall be done in time to come. **1881** F. POLLOCK *Princ. Contract* (ed. 3) 1 An agreement is, 'An act in the law whereby two or more persons declare their consent as to any act or thing to be done or forborne by some or one of those persons for the use of the others or other of them.'

6. Accordance in sentiment, opinion, action, or purpose; harmony, concord; absence of dissension.

1528 MORE *Heresyes* I. Wks. 1557, 170/1 The consent and comen agrement of the olde holy fathers. **1548** LD. SOMERSET *Epist. to Scots* 241 You loued better dissencion then vnitie, discorde then agremente. **1652** BURROUGHES *Exp. Hosea* vi. 105 Agreement in errour is farre worse than division for the sake of truth. **1654** GODDARD in Burton's *Diary* (1828) I. 155 He hath espoused Charles Stuart, with whom he is fully at agreement. **1692** [WAGSTAFFE] *Vind. Carol.* i. 24 It is not the Crowd, but agreement makes the Company. **1771** *Junius Lett.* lix. 307 Neither are we to look for perfection in any one man, nor for agreement among many.

7. Mutual conformity of things, whether due to likeness or to mutual adaptation; concord, harmony, affinity.

1398 TREVISA *Barth. De P.R.* XVI. xliv. (1495) 567 Yren hath agrement with the stone Adamas, and so the stone Adamas draweth yren to itself. **1586** T. B. tr. *La Primaudaye's Fr. Acad.* II. (1594) 531 When the image hath some agreement in forme with the thing represented. **1611** BIBLE *2 Cor.* vi. 16 What agreement hath the Temple of God with idoles? **1790** PALEY *Hor. Paul.* i. Wks. 1825 III. 6 Agreement or conformity between letters bearing the name of an ancient author, and a received history of that author's life. **1855** BREWSTER *Newton* II. xviii. 170 The agreement between his observations and the theory.

8. *Gramm.* Concord: see AGREE *v.* 15.

1669 MILTON *Gram.* II. *Concords* (1847) 468/1 The agreement of words together in number, gender, case, and person, which is called concord. **1879** J. A. H. MURRAY *Trans. Philol. Soc.* 619 In the English 'the men push the stone,' we have neither formal expression of the destination [of the action] nor formal agreement of verb and subject.

9. Mostly *pl.* Agreeable qualities, circumstances, or accessories. Now treated as Fr., *les agréments*.

1692 DRYDEN tr. *St. Euremont's Ess.* 376 The Charms and Agreements natural to Women. **1732** MRS. DELANY *Autobiog.* (1861) I. 399 She has..all the agreement of embellishments that can be desired. **1737** WARBURTON in *Boswell's Johnson* I. Introd. 50 The art of adding the agreements to the most agreeable subject in the world, which is literary history.

†**agreemony.** *Obs.* Agreeableness. A nonce-word, probably intended to suggest *acrimony*.

1678 MRS. BEHN *Sir P. Fancy* II. i. 254 Upon my reputation, Madam, you're a civil well bred person, you have all the agreemony of your sex.

agreer (əˈgriːə(r)). [f. AGREE *v.* + -ER¹.] One who agrees; an adherent.

1548 GESTE *Priuee Masse* 75 As well of thee agreers and favourers therof, as of the authors and doers of the same. *a* **1603** Q. ELIZ. in Froude *Hist. Eng.* VII. 485 The agreers ..gave more credit thereunto than unto their own wits. **1611** FLORIO, *Componitore*, a framer, an agreer, a maker.

agreeve, agreif, agreive, obs. ff. AGGRIEVE.

agregge, earlier f. AGGREGE *v. Obs.*, to aggravate.

agreith, var. of AGRAITH *v. Obs.*, to prepare, deck.

‖**agrément** (agremɑ̃). Also (*pl.*) **agrémens.** [F.: see AGREEMENT.] **1.** *pl.* = AGREEMENT 9.

1711 *Spectator* No. 28, 2 Apr., I had ghessed by the little Agréemens upon his Sign, that he was a Frenchman. **1749** CHESTERFIELD *Let.* 14 Nov. (1774) I. 489 You must.. captivate them by the *agrémens*, and charms of conversation. **1841** GEO. ELIOT *Lett.* (1954) I. 96 All the agrémens it [*sc.* honeysuckle] brings us. **1848** THACKERAY *Van. Fair* lxii. 566 We.. talked.. about the *agrémens* of the place. It was very agreeable for the English. **1863** 'OUIDA' *Held in Bondage* I. vii. 153 Lansquenet, racing, Coralies, champagne, and all one's other habitual agréments. **1904** W. JAMES *Let.* 1 Jan. in R. B. Perry *Tht. & Char. of W. J.* (1935) II. 201 America does not offer the *agréments* to a tourist which almost any part of Europe offers.

2. *Mus. pl.* Grace-notes; embellishments.

1789 BURNEY *Hist. Mus.* III. i. 87/1 Extraneous episodes, or fashionable divisions, which being the *agrémens*, or trimmings, of the times, become antiquated. **1871** J. HILES *Dict. Mus. Terms* 9 *Agréments*, graces, embellishments, ornaments. **1879** GROVE *Dict. Mus.* I. 44/1 The agrémens used in modern music.. are the acciacatura, appoggiatura, arpeggio, mordent, nachschlag, shake or trill, slide, and turn.

3. The approval given by the government of a country to a diplomatic representative of another country.

1917 E. SATOW *Guide to Diplomatic Practice* I. xiv. 193 The generally existing diplomatic practice to ask, previously to any nomination of a foreign minister, the consent (*agrément*) of the Government to which he is to be accredited. **1939** H. NICOLSON *Diplomacy* x. 236 It is customary.. to sound a foreign government privately before making a formal application for an agrément. **1955** *Times* 2 May 10/3 The present Burmese Ambassador to India has been accorded an *agrément* by the Queen as Ambassador to the United Kingdom.

agrese, variant of AGRISE *v. Obs.*, to shudder.

†**a'grest**, *a.* and *sb. Obs.* [a. Fr. *agreste*, 14th c. a. It. (and Sp.) *agreste*:—L. *agrest-is* belonging to the field, f. *ager, agr-um* field.]

A. *adj.* Belonging to the open country, wild; hence, Rustic, rude.

c **1420** *Pallad. on Husb.* XI. 324 The bay of myrte agrest. **1549** *Compl. Scotl.* (1873) 16 To support & til excuse my barbir agrest termis. **1553–87** FOXE *A. & M.* III. 637 By whose unmerciful Nature and agrest Disposition, very many were put to death. **1668** HOWE *Bless. Righteous* (1825) 227 His more uncomely and aggressed manners. **1775** ASH, *Agrest* (*not much used*) belonging to the fields.

B. *sb.* A rustic, a countryman.

1480 CAXTON *Ovid's Metam.* xv. iv, Th' agrestes that see thenne th' erbes & grasse enjoyen them.

agrestal (ə'grɛstəl), *a.* [f. L. *agrest-is* (see AGREST) + -AL[1].] = AGRESTIAL *a.* Also as *sb.*

1858 H. C. WATSON *Cyb. Brit.* III. 183 A well-established agrestal weed. **1863** J. G. BAKER *N. Yorkshire* xiv. 183 To designate the different kinds of locality we may employ a series of adjectives such as sylvestral, pratal, pascual, ericetal, uliginal, agrestal. **1926** G. C. DRUCE in J. J. Walker *Nat. Hist. Oxf. Distr.* 116 Naturally these Agrestals are not the same from one century to another. *Ibid.* 117 Closely allied to the Agrestal are the Ruderal species.

†**a'grested**, *ppl. a. Obs.* [irreg. f. AGREST *a.* and *sb.* + -ED, as if pa. pple.; cf. *adust-ed.*] Rustic, 'countrified.'

1620 VENNER *Via Recta* (1650) 70 Of unprofitable nourishment, except for agrested bodies. *Ibid.* 97 Agrested bodies that commonly digest anything that filleth the belly.

agrestial (ə'grɛstɪəl), *a.* [f. L. *agresti-s* (see AGREST) + -AL[1]. Cf. *celesti-al.*] Inhabiting the fields or open country; wild; *spec.* (Bot.) growing wild in cultivated land.

1607 TOPSELL *Serpents* (1653) 638 Other [bees] again are altogether wilde, uplandish, and agrestial. **1842** *Fraser's Mag.* Sept. 298/1 A vast accession of richly productive agrestial territory. **1855** *Jrnl. R. Agric. Soc.* XVI. 584 A large farmer.. seems to have been afflicted by.. a sense of agrestial invasion.

agrestian (ə'grɛstɪən), *a.* and *sb.* [f. as prec. + -AN. Cf. *equestri-an.*] **A.** *adj.* Belonging to the country, rustic, rude. **B.** *sb.* A rustic, a countryman.

1845 HAMILTON *Pop. Educ.* viii. (ed. 2) 184 We may now survey the agrestian population. *Ibid.* iii. 43 The figure of.. the agrestian early learns to stoop.

agrestic (ə'grɛstɪk), *a.* Also 7 **agrestick(e, -ique.** [f. L. *agrest-is* (see AGREST) + -IC. Cf. *domestic*, and for formation *forens-ic.*] Of or pertaining to the country, rural, rustic; hence, uncouth.

1620 VENNER *Via Recta* viii. 175 The strong and healthy bodies of agresticke men. *a* **1646** J. G[REGORY] *Assyr. Mon.* (1650) 222 Continual conversation with bruit beasts changed his humane disposition into a barbarous and agrestick behaviour. **1660** WATERHOUSE *Arms & Armory* 123 The residences of Princes were in tents and agrestique Pavilions. **1703** EVELYN in *Pepys' Diary* 419 He has his time for his agrestic flute. **1880** DISRAELI *Endym.* I. xxx. 279 A delightful ramble to some spot of agrestic charm.

†**a'grestical**, *a. Obs.*—[0] [f. prec. + -AL[1]. Cf. *comic, comical.*] = AGRESTIC.

1626 in COCKERAM; whence in BAILEY, ASH, TODD.

†**'agresty.** *Obs.*—[0] [f. L. *agrest-is* or Eng. AGREST + -Y[3]. Cf. *modest-y.*] Rusticity, 'clownishness.' Bailey, and Ash.

agreve, obs. form of AGGRIEVE.

agribusiness ('ægrɪbɪznɪs). orig. *U.S.* [f. AGRI(CULTURE + BUSINESS.] **1. a.** The group of industries concerned with the processing and distribution of agricultural produce or with farm machinery and services. **b.** Agriculture conducted as a modern business, esp. making use of advanced technology; a farm run in this way.

1955 *Harvard Business School Bull.* Autumn 41 'Agribusiness'—a term coined to define the many diverse enterprises which produce, process, and distribute farm products or which provide supporting services. **1960** *Farmer & Stockbreeder* 29 Mar. 78/2 The broiler industry.. had to go in for 'vertical integration'... It is not farming, it is agri-business. **1961** *Economist* 30 Dec. 1269/2 If, in the next decade, agriculture in Europe is to become 'agribusiness', employing the scale and methods of industry. **1962** *Times* 3 Dec. Agric. Suppl. i/5 So long as agriculture is carried on by farmers and not by so-called 'agribusiness'. **1968** M. PYKE *Food & Society* ix. 122 Science will inevitably bring agriculture, as it has so far been understood, to an end, and cause 'agribusiness' to take its place. **1973** *Times* 8 Aug. 7/2 Farmers under economic policies are squeezed into agribusinesses. **1976** *Sci. Amer.* Sept. 118/3 The development of American agriculture has fostered the growth of an entire agricultural industry—'agribusiness'—of which farming is only a small part. **1977** *Time* 28 Feb. 34/2 Small farms, located near cities,.. could provide food more cheaply than agribusiness can in the face of the enduring, expensive energy shortage. **1978** S. BRILL *Teamsters* x. 387 Gibbons was sent to California as a representative of the major force—other than the farm owners and agribusinesses themselves—that was holding Chavez back. **1983** *Sci. Amer.* May 78/2 In modern agribusiness the pig is attractive because of its efficiency in converting feed into food.

2. *attrib.*

1969 *Times* 14 Apr. 7/1 Pastures of the agribusiness Midlands. **1971** *Nature* 23 July 217/3 The interests of the consumer are no match for the powerful agribusiness lobby on Capitol Hill. **1977** *Time* 21 Feb. 19/2 Mexico is shipping tomatoes in quantity to the U.S. from vast agribusiness farms below the border.

Hence **'agri(-),businessman**, a man who engages in agribusiness.

1961 *New Statesman* 22 Dec. 956/3 If I were a real agri-businessman I would no doubt know the answer. **1963** G. SYKES *Poultry* p. xxiii, We must watch closely how the American agribusinessmen work in the West European and the South American countries. **1966** *Economist* 26 Feb. 819/2 The farmer who has the ability to become an 'agri-businessman' may not be able to command the capital to finance the growth of his business. **1984** *Nat. Geographic* Feb. 233/2 Agribusinessman Bill Ramsey oversees fields of cotton and barley.

agrichemical (ægrɪ'kɛmɪkəl), *a.* and *sb.* [f. AGRI(CULTURAL *a.* + CHEMICAL *a.*] **A.** *adj.* Agricultural and chemical; of or pertaining to agrichemicals. **B.** *sb.* A chemical used or produced in agriculture; also, = AGROCHEMICAL *sb.*

1958 (*periodical title*) Agrichemical west. **1962** *Sci. News Let.* 3 Nov. 291/2 Synthetic foods may become the largest of all the agri-chemical industries. **1964** *Agrichem. West* Dec. 30/1 Agrichemicals themselves are already subject to very special investigations. **1965** *Ibid.* Sept. 30/2 A couple of journalists at Wisconsin shook up the agrichemical fraternity.. when they discovered that.. farmers do not understand the terms commonly used on pesticide labels. **1967** N. SHREVE *Chem. Process Industries* (ed. 3) xxvi. 473 Farm products would be impossible.. without farm equipment and supplies, of which agrichemicals[2] are an important part. [*Note*] [2]Term adopted by the author to encompass the chemicals used in agriculture, and its related supplying, processing, and distributing industries. **1973** D. I. B. VANDER HOOVER in Y. Pomeranz *Industr. Uses of Cereals* 259 (*heading*) Industrial and agrichemical utilization of corncobs. **1985** *Marketing Mag.* (N.Z.) July 28/2 The campaign.. involves a variety of products—animal health remedies and agri-chemical products.

†**agrico'lation.** *Obs.*—[0] [ad. L. *agricolātiōn-em*, n. of action, f. *agricolā-ri* to act as husbandman, f. *agricola* a husbandman; f. *ager, agr-* field + *cola* a tenant: stem *col-* also in vb. *col-ĕre* to take care of, till, occupy, dwell.] Tillage of the ground; husbandry; the practice of agriculture.

1626 in COCKERAM; whence in BAILEY, JOHNSON, ASH, etc.

agricole ('ægrɪkəʊl). [a. Fr. *agricole*, ad. L. *agricola* (see prec.).] A husbandman; a rustic.

1656 BLOUNT *Glossogr.*, *Agricole*, a Husbandman, Farmer or Plowman. **1882** H. MERIVALE *Faucit of Bal.* III. II. xix. 159 The agricoles of Mould-on-the-Moss. *Ibid.* II. I. xxiv. 105 In nine cases out of ten, the agricole sees it not.

†**a'gricolist.** *Obs. rare.* [f. prec. + -IST.] An agriculturist.

1754 DODSLEY *Agric.* II. (R.) The pasture and the food of plants First let the young agricolist be taught. **1794** MRS. PIOZZI *Brit. Synon.* II. 271 Those who are speaking with agricolists will observe that *soil* is the word in use.

agricolous (ə'grɪkələs), *a. rare.* [f. Fr. *agricole* agricultural (ad. L. *agricola*) + -OUS. (Hardly a serious word.)] Agricultural.

1825 SYD. SMITH in *Edin. Rev.* XLII. 36 Upon sacks of wool, and on benches forensic, sit grave men, and agricolous persons in the Commons. **1880** *Contemp. Rev.* Mar. 413 The ordinary member, agricolous, or otherwise.

agricultor ('ægrɪ,kʌltə(r)). ? *Obs.* [a. L. *agricultor*, i.e. *agri cultor* a tiller of the field. Cf. mod. Fr. *agriculteur.*] 'A husbandman. The word in our language is modern, but is getting into common use.' Todd 1818. Now very rare.

1787 MARSHALL *Rur. Econ. Norf.* II. (To Reader) 6 For an agricultor cannot register an incident. **1839** J. ROGERS *Antipopopr.* vi. §2. 228 A man that keeps a vineyard, a vinedresser, or an agricultor.

agricultural (ægrɪ'kʌltjʊərəl), *a.* [f. L. *agricultūra* (see AGRICULTURE) + -AL[1]. Cf. *natural*, L. *nātūrālis.*] **a.** Of or pertaining to agriculture; connected with husbandry or tillage of the ground.

1776 ADAM SMITH *W.N.* (1869) II. IV. ix. 246 The agricultural systems of political economy will not require so long an explanation. **1814** SIR H. DAVY (*title*) Agricultural Chemistry. **1849** MACAULAY *Hist. Eng.* I. 413 Four shillings a week therefore were.. fair agricultural wages. **1849** ALISON *Hist. Europe* I. ii. §4. 121 The agricultural population, at both periods, was double the manufacturing.

b. *slang.* Applied to a clumsy stroke in cricket.

1937 PARTRIDGE *Dict. Slang* 186/1 (s.v. *cow-shot*), A more clumsy shot, made by a standing batsman, is termed an agricultural one. **1955** *Times* 25 July 3/4 Keith.. took an agricultural swing at Wardle and was bowled.

c. ***agricultural ant***: a species of ant, such as the *Pogonomyrmex barbatus* of Texas, that clears the vicinity of its nest of verdure or herbage except for that on which it feeds.

1868 *Amer. Naturalist* II. 157 Such structures are remarkable.. reminding us of the intelligence shown by the Agricultural Ant of Texas. **1882** [see HARVESTING *ppl. a.*].

agriculturalist (ægrɪ'kʌltjʊərəlɪst). [f. prec. + -IST. Cf. *natural-ist, constitutional-ist*; but the shorter AGRICULTURIST is preferred.] One engaged in agricultural pursuits; a husbandman.

1802 *Ann. Reg. 1801* Chron. 21/1 The company exceeded five hundred agriculturalists. **1812** HENRY *Camp. agst. Quebec* 93 He was an agriculturalist, which in the vagueness and uncertainty of our language is called a farmer. **1854** *Illustr. Lond. News* 14 Jan. 38 Well known as a scientific and practical agriculturalist.

agriculturally (ægrɪ'kʌltjʊrəlɪ), *adv.* [f. AGRICULTURAL *a.* + -LY[2].] With regard or reference to agriculture.

1821 *Examiner* 50/1 Why say a word about it—why not pass it agriculturally, in prudent silence? **1883** HOLME LEE *Loving & Serving* I. xi. 211 His land is poor agriculturally. **1885** *Standard* 2 Sept. 2/4 The Board have not lost sight of the dealing with the sewage agriculturally.

agriculture ('ægrɪ,kʌltjʊər, -tʃə(r)). [ad. (prob. through Fr. *agriculture*, 17th c. in Littré), L. *agricultūra*, i.e. *agri cultūra* tillage of the land: see CULTURE.] The science and art of cultivating the soil; including the allied pursuits of gathering in the crops and rearing live stock; tillage, husbandry, farming (in the widest sense).

1603 HOLLAND *Plutarch's Mor.* 9 Such tooles as pertaine to Agriculture and husbandrie. **1650** J. JONES *Judges Judged* 35 Their sweet Farmhouses, large fields, and industrious Agricultures. **1658** SIR T. BROWNE *Gard. Cyrus* II. 504 Future discovery in Botanical Agriculture. **1751** JOHNSON *Rambl.* No. 145 ¶3 If we estimate dignity by immediate usefulness, agriculture is undoubtedly the first and noblest science. **1831** SCOTT *A. Geierst.* iii. 45 A glance round the walls showed the implements of agriculture.

b. restricted to, Tillage. *rare.*

1862 STANLEY *Jew. Ch.* (1877) I. xii. 228 The lands.. were not fields for agriculture, but pastures for cattle.

agriculturer (ægrɪ'kʌltjʊərə(r)). ? *Obs.* [f. prec. + -ER[1].] One practically engaged in agriculture, a husbandman. (Prob. intended as less scientific in meaning than AGRICULTURIST.)

1812 COLERIDGE *Own Times* III. 751 The interests of agriculturers, whose products feed and clothe this large body. *a* **1864** LANDOR *Wks.* (1876) IV. 506 'Ploughman' may be accepted for any agriculturer.

agriculturism (ægrɪ'kʌltjʊərɪz(ə)m). ? *Obs. rare* —[0]. [Analogous formation on AGRICULTURIST.] 'The science of agriculture. *Modern.*' Todd 1818.

agriculturist (ægrɪ'kʌltjʊərɪst). [f. AGRICULTURE + -IST.] (At first) A student of the science of agriculture, (but soon extended to) A professed cultivator of the land, a farmer (for which AGRICULTURALIST is also used).

1760 J. SCOTT *Eclogue* ii. (Chalmers 1810) XVII. 469 Rural Business; or, the Agriculturists. **1795** J. BILLINGSLEY *Agric. Surv. Somerset* (1798) 275 That enlightened agriculturist Jethro Tull. **1814** SIR H. DAVY *Agric. Chem.* 4 Both to the theoretical agriculturist, and the practical farmer. **1849** COBDEN *Sp.* 2 We have been accused of having subjected the agriculturists of this country to a competition with foreigners. **1861** *Times* 1 June, *Re* Agriculturist Cattle Insurance Company.

†**a'grief**, *adv.* (prop *phr.*) *Obs.*; also 4–5 **agref(e, ogrefe, agreff, agreve.** [A *prep.*[1] in + GRIEF.] In

grief, as a grievance. Usually *to take agrief*: to take it ill or unkindly; the opposite of *to take a-gree* or *in gree*.

c **1300** *K. Alis.* 3785 He tok hit in heorte agref. **1330** R. BRUNNE *Chron.* 155 Þan spak Philip ogrefe. c **1386** CHAUCER *Wyf of B.* Prol. 191, I pray to al this companye.. As taketh nought agreef [*v.r.* agrief, agreff, a greue] of that I say. c **1420** *Sir Amadace* xxx. (1842) 39 Gode Sirs, take noȝte on greue, For ȝe most noue take ȝour leue. a **1440** *Sir Degrev.* 467 Madame, takes not agreve A thyng that y yow say.

agrieve, -ance, obs. forms of AGGRIEVE, -ANCE.

†**a'grill(e, agrulle** (-Y-), *v. Obs. rare.* [f. A- *pref.* 1 intensive + GRILL.] To provoke, annoy, grieve.

a **1250** *Owl & Night.* 1108 Ne dar me never eft mon a-grulle. c **1380** *Sir Ferumb.* 2195 For þat torn or þat a gon: ful sore him schal a-grille.

agrim(e, early pop. form of ALGORISM.

agrimensorial (,ægrɪmɛn'sɔːrɪəl), *a.* [f. L. *agrīmensor* land-surveyor + -IAL.] Of or pertaining to land surveying.

1878 H. C. COOTE *Romans of Brit.* 67 The incision was made in the form of a cross. This was the agrimensorial '*antica et postica*'. *Ibid.* 83 An inscribed agrimensorial stone found at Drumburgh. **1892** C. MCLEAN ANDREWS *Old Eng. Manor* 33 Mr. Coote.. believed that all Britain was laid out on the exact lines of the Roman agrimensorial system. **1958** *Antiquity* XXXII. 26 Studies agrimensorial and tenurial.

agrimony ('ægrɪmənɪ). Forms: 1 **agrimonia,** 4 **egremounde,** 4-5 **egrimoigne, egremoyne,** 4-6 **egrymoyn(e,** 5-7 **egrimonie, -y,** 6 **egremonie, agremony, agrymonye,** 5-6 **agrimonie,** 5- **agrimony.** [ad. L. *agrimōnia* (Cels.), said to be a transformation of Gr. ἀργεμώνη (Dioscor.), of unkn. etym. The Middle Eng. forms were adopted from Fr. *aigremoine.*]

1. A genus of plants (N.O. *Rosaceae*), of which one species (*A. Eupatoria*), to which the Eng. name is usually attached, is common in Britain.

1040-50 *Sax. Leechd.* I. 130 þas wyrte þe man agrimoniam, & oðrum naman garclife nemneð. c **1328** *Chester Pl.* 119 Raydishe and egremounde which be my erbes. c **1386** CHAUCER *Chan. Yeman Pr. & T.* 247 And herbes couthe I telle eek many oon, As egrimoigne, valirian [*v.r.* egremoyne, egrymoyn(e]. **1440** *Promp. Parv.*, Agrimony, or egrimony, herbe. *Agrimonia.* **1551** TURNER *Herbal* I. 177 Agrimony groweth among bushes and hedges and in myddowes and woddes. **1604** MIDDLETON *Courtly Masque* V. 196, I grant there's bitter egrimony in 'em. **1671** SALMON *Syn. Medic.* III. xxii. 389 Agrimony nobly opens the Liver and Spleen. **1866** JOHNS in *Treas. Bot.* I. 31/1 Agrimony.. contains tannin, and will dye wool of a nankeen colour.

2. Through confusion as to the application of *Eupatoria* and *Liverwort*, old names of Agrimony, the name has been, with or without qualification, extended to other plants. **a.** Bastard, Dutch, Hemp, or Water Agrimony, *Eupatoria cannabina.* **b.** Noble, Three-leaved Agrimony, *Hepatica* (Lyte). **c.** Water Agrimony, *Bidens* (Gerard). **d.** Wild Agrimony, *Potentilla anserina* (Lyte).

1578 LYTE *Dodoens* 57 There be sundry kindes of herbes called in Latine *Hepatica* or *Jecoraria*, that is to say Lyuerwortes.. The two first kindes are Bastarde Agrimonie. The third is Three leaued Agrimonie, or noble Lyuerwurte. *Ibid.* 57 In English wilde Tansie, Siluer weede, and of some wilde Agrimonie. **1597** GERARD *Herball* II. ccxl. 710 Water Hempe or Water Agrimony is seldomer found in hot regions.

agrimotor ('ægrɪməʊtə(r)). [f. L. *agri-*, *ager* land + MOTOR *sb.*] A motor tractor for agricultural work.

1917 *Town Topics* 10 Feb., The immediate future of agrimotors in this country. **1920** *Country Life* 10 Jan. p. lxi (Advt.), The Crawley Agrimotor Equal to 8 men and 16 horses.

agrin (ə'grɪn), *adv.*, prop. *phr.* [A *prep.*[1] of state, in, on + GRIN.] On the grin; in a grinning attitude.

1847 TENNYSON *Princess* V. 510 His visage all a-grin. **1849** C. BRONTË *Shirley* I. iii. 47 His hard features were revealed all agrin and ashine with glee.

agriologist (ægrɪ'ɒlədʒɪst). [f. Gr. ἄγριο-ς wild, savage + λόγ-ος discourse + -IST.] One who is versed in the history and customs of savages.

1882 *19th Cent.* Jan. 115 The mythology of the savage races, which as agriologists confidently maintained, would .. upset the whole system of comparative mythology.

agriology (ægrɪ'ɒlədʒɪ). [f. Gr. ἄγριος wild, savage: see -OLOGY.] The comparative study of the history and customs of savage or uncivilized peoples. Hence **agrio'logical** *a.*

1878 *Fraser's Mag.* XVII. 730 Trying the law.. of euphony and prosody in face of the agriology of the day. *Ibid.* 733 Mr. Sayce.. threatens to make agriological scalps the only wear in glottology. **1886** *Jrnl. Educ.* 1 Apr. 152/1 The new lights thrown on the early stages of society by.. what may be called Agriology.

†**'agriot.** *Obs.* Also 7 **egriot.** [f. 16th c. Fr. *agriote*, now *griotte.*] A sort of cherry.

1611 COTGR., *Agriotte*, the ordinary sharp, or tar[t] cherrie, which we also call, the Agriot-cherrie. **1626** BACON *Sylva* §509 The Cœur-Cherry, which inclineth more to White, is sweeter than the Red: but the Egriot is more sowre. **1725** BRADLEY *Fam. Dict.* s.v. *Waters*, Morel and Agriots, of each an Handful. **1775** ASH, *Agriot*, a kind of sour cherry.

agriproduct ('ægrɪprɒdʌkt). [f. PRODUCT *sb.*[1], after AGRIBUSINESS.] An agricultural product produced or distributed on an industrial scale; a product of agribusiness.

1977 *Business Week* (Industr. ed.) 24 Oct. 28E/1 The Farm Progress Show, a microcosm of American agriculture that brings farmers and agriproduct manufacturers together for three days each year. **1977** *Daily Tel.* 2 Nov. 9 (Advt.), Basic, staple industries such as building materials and agriproducts. **1981** *Economist* 12 Sept. 86/2 Its newly acquired agriproducts subsidiaries generated 18% of group turnover.

†**a'grise,** *v. Obs.* Forms: *Inf.* 1 **agrís-an,** 2-4 **agris-en,** 2-7 **agrise,** 3-7 **agryse,** 4-5 **agrese,** 6 **agryce, agryze, aggrise, aggryese,** 6-7 **agrize,** 7 **aggrize.** *Pa. t.* 1-3 **agrás,** 3-5 **agros,** 4 **agroos,** 5 **agrose.** *Pa. pple.* 1-4 **agrisen,** 3-4 **agrise,** 4-5 **agrised,** 5 **agresyd,** 6 **agryz'd.** [f. A- *pref.* 1 intensive + GRISE, same root as *grís* horror. Cf. *grisly.*]

1. *intr.* To shudder with terror, be full of horror; to tremble, quake, be greatly afraid or moved.

a **1000** *Laws of Cnut* (Thorpe I. 374, Bosw.) Ðæt he for helle agrise. c **1230** *Ancren Riwle* 306 Swuch ȝeor þet heouene & eorðe muwen beoðe grisliche agrisen. c **1320** *Seuyn Sages* (W.) 886 To gon therinne [*i.e.* in the forest] ech man agros. c **1380** *Sir Ferumb.* 3370 Of þe siȝte agrise he gan. c **1385** CHAUCER *Leg. G. Wom.* 830 And in his herte he sodeynly agroos, And pale he wex. c **1461** *Play of Sacr.* 902 For that presumcon gretly I agryse. **1534** MORE *Comf. agst. Tribul.* III. Wks. 1557, 1215/2 Their heartes agryce & shrynke in the remembraunce of the payne. **1598** SYLVESTER *Du Bartas* II. iv. III. (1641) 223/1 Already in each nook agrising, Fell, wall-break Famine ill-advising Howls hideously.

2. *trans.* To shudder at (with terror or abhorrence); to dread, abhor, loathe.

c **1374** CHAUCER *Boethius* (1868) 31 If þou agrisest hir fals[e] trecherie. **1382** WYCLIF *Job* xix. 17 My wif agriside my breth. **1393** GOWER *Conf.* I. 351 She hadde.. after wrought in suche a wise, All the worlde it ought agrise. **1468** *Cov. Myst.* (1841) 41 Ony worke of synful dede Oure Lord God that xulde agryse.

3. *refl.* (obj. orig. indirect—*he shuddered to himself.*)

1205 LAYAM. 11977 Haȝel and ræin þer aræs: þe hit i-seh him agras [**1250** agros]. a **1300** *K. Horn* 867 Horn him gan to agrise, And his blod arise.

4. *impers.* (cf. 'it abhors me, it repented him.')

1205 LAYAM. 13329 Þer uore me a-griseð. c **1300** *Beket* 688 Sumdel him agros. c **1460** *Lybeaus Disconus* 1884 Therfore hym grym agros. **1596** SPENSER *F.Q.* V. x. 28 And powring forth their bloud in brutishe wize, That any yron eyes, to see, it would agrize.

5. *trans.* (from impers., by defining the subject.) **a.** *active*, To horrify, terrify, affright.

c **1314** *Guy Warw.* 49 Nas ther non that him agros. **1447** BOKENHAM *Lyvys of Seyntys* 75 These wordis urban so sore dyde agryse. **1513** DOUGLAS *Æneis* IV. vii. 47 My goist sall be present the to aggrise. **1596** SPENSER *F.Q.* II. vi. 46 Engrost with mud which did them fowle agrise. **1611** FLORIO, *Legare*, to agrise or set ones teeth on edge. **1647** H. MORE *Song of Soul* I. I. xxx, Their course the best Astronomer might well aggrize.

b. *passive*, To be horrified, terrified, or afraid.

1297 R. GLOUC. 539 Tho were the porters agrise sore of thulke siȝte. **1387** TREVISA *Higden* Rolls Ser. IV. 353 Þe fader and þe moder were agrised [*abhorrerent*] for to slee þe childe. c **1430** LYDG. *Minor Poems* (1840) 141 Hooly Awstyn ..was of the caas agrised. **1613** W. BROWNE *Sheph. Pipe* I. 501 Of whose sight he full sore was agrysed.

†**a'grised,** *pa. pple. Obs.* Earlier **agrise)n.** [f. prec.] Horrified, terrified, frightened.

c **1250** *Gen. & Ex.* 667 Ðo wurðen he frigti and a-grisen. **1330** R. BRUNNE *Chron.* 237 Sone he hasted him, to mak þam alle ogrisen. c **1450** LONELICH *Grail* xiii. 870 His meyne so wownded were, That sore agresyd was he there. **1596** SPENSER *F.Q.* IV. viii. 12 Whom when she saw.. Like ghost late risen from his grave agryz'd, She knew him not.

agro- ('ægrəʊ), comb. form of Gr. ἀγρός field, used chiefly to represent AGRICULTURE or AGRICULTURAL *a.* **a.** More or less nonce-wds., as ***agro-based, -defensive, -despotic, -literate*** adjs.

1969 *National Herald* (New Delhi) 29 July 5/2 *Agro-based industries can operate during off-peak hours. **1949** *Ann. Reg. 1948* 208 The planting.. of a large-scale system of so-called '*agro-defensive' forest strips to conserve moisture, overcome the effect of dust storms, and prevent soil erosion. **1957** K. A. WITTFOGEL *Oriental Despotism* 4 Under *agrodespotic conditions the managerial bureaucracy was the ruling class. **1983** E. GELLNER *Nations & Nationalism* ii. 9 In the characteristic *agro-literate polity, the ruling class forms a small minority of the population, rigidly separate from the great majority of direct agricultural producers, or peasants.

b. Special Combs. **agrobi'ology,** the study of the breeding, nutrition, and growth of crops, esp. in relation to soil management; hence **,agrobio'logical** *a.*; **agrobi'ologist,** an expert or specialist in agrobiology; **'agrobusiness** = AGRIBUSINESS; also **'agro,businessman; agro-city:** see AGROGOROD; **agro-cli'matic** *a.*, of or pertaining to the relationship between climate and agriculture; **agro-eco'logical** *a.*, of or pertaining to the relationship between ecology and agriculture; **agro-eco'nomic** *a.*, of or pertaining to agriculture as it relates to economics; so **agro-e'conomist; agro'forestry,** agriculture in which there is integrated management of trees or shrubs along with conventional crops or livestock; **agro-mechani'zation,** the action or process of making greater use of mechanization in agriculture, esp. in developing countries; **,agrometeo'rology** (see quot. 1957); hence **,agrometeoro'logical** *a.*, **,agrometeo'rologist,** an expert or specialist in agrometeorology; **agro-'politics** *sb. pl.*, the politics of agriculture or agricultural produce; **agrotech'nology,** the application of technology to agriculture; hence **agrotech'nologist,** an expert or specialist in agrotechnology; **agro-town:** see AGROGOROD; also, a similar rural grouping in Italy.

1935 O. W. WILLCOX *Nations can live at Home* p. ix, Details of *agrobiological calculations. **1937** A. HUXLEY *Ends & Means* v. 45 No government has hitherto made any serious effort to apply modern agro-biological methods on a large scale. **1984** *Current Digest Soviet Press* 20 June 1/1 Such generalizing indices of the state of the environment and natural resources as integral indexes of the quality (purity) of air and water and the agrobiological potential of soils. **1934** O. W. WILLCOX *Reshaping Agric.* i. 13 Agricultural technology may never reach.. the full condition of perfection foreseen for it by the *agrobiologists. **1937** A. HUXLEY *Ends & Means* v. 44 A systematic exposition of the agro-biologist's case. **1984** *Fortune* 23 Jan. 32/1 Lysenko, for those who have forgotten about the once eminent Ukrainian agrobiologist, was a crackpot and intellectual crook. **1934** O. W. WILLCOX *Reshaping Agric.* ii. 31 So far as the purely mathematical principles of *agrobiology are concerned the soil can never be filled to a point beyond which some additional yield, however small, might not be obtained. **1937** A. HUXLEY *Ends & Means* v. 44 According to experts trained in the techniques of modern agro-biology, imperialism has now lost one of its principal justifications. **1976** *Survey* Summer–Autumn 71 The miracle in agrobiology promised in the very near future by the magician Lysenko. **1960** *Observer* 13 Nov. 3/1 *Agrobusiness means the application to farming of the sort of radical, unsentimental thinking that goes into business. **1983** *Engin. News-Rec.* 21 Apr. 24/2 Its thrust during the remaining years of the 1980s will continue to be on agrobusiness and energy development. **1961** *Britannica Bk. of Year* 537/1 The closer association between agriculture and commerce gave.. *agrobusinessman, chiefly represented by the poultry-farmer turned technologist, using all the aids of mechanization and big business. **1984** *Daily Tel.* 2 Nov. 16/8 He observes with horror the activities of the 'agrobusinessmen', water authorities, power stations and litter louts, who are doing their best.. to vandalise the countryside. **1937** G. T. SELIANINOV *World's Agro-Climatic Handbk.* 52 The *agro-climatic belts are divided in thermal zones by the sufficiency of warmth during the growing season. **1960** H. J. CRITCHFIELD *Gen. Climatol.* xiii. 340 Nuttonson has developed a series of agro-climatic analogues for North America by comparing climatic factors in different parts of the world. **1967** J. OLIVER in J. A. Taylor *Weather & Agric.* 187 (*heading*) Problems of agro-climatic relationships in Wales in the eighteenth century. **1981** *McGraw-Hill Yearbk. Sci. & Technol.* 80/2 Most research centers concentrate on a few major food crops adapted to a given agroclimatic zone. **1965** THRAN & BROEKHUIZEN (*title*) *Agro-ecological atlas of cereal growing in Europe. **1978** *Nature* 6 Apr. 486/3 The programme is designed to develop new quinoa varieties adapted to different agro-ecological production zones in Bolivia and elsewhere. **1958** J. P. BHATTACHARJEE *Sahajapur* p. iii, The *Agro-Economic Research Centre for East India was started at the Visva-Bharati University, Santiniketan in July, 1954. **1973** *Nature* 13 July p. vii/2 (Advt.), Collection, processing and analysis of agro-economic data relating to the structure and operation of the rural economy. **1974** *Daily Tel.* 5 Nov. 9/1 M. Rene Dumont, a French *agro-economist, said that last year one-third of all grains was consumed by cattle of rich countries. **1985** *Financial Times* 13 May 2/4 Several newspapers and agro-economists have attacked Herr Ignaz Kiechele, the Farm Minister, for his refusal to offer a compromise on the European Commission's call for a 3.6 per cent price cut for grains. **1977** J. G. BENE et al. *Trees, Food & People* 41 One of the objectives of *agroforestry is to 'domesticate' and upgrade shifting agriculture to maximize sustained production on less well-endowed land. **1979** *Canada Weekly* 3 Jan. 4/2 Agroforestry can be practised on soils that are inherently infertile.. or where climatic conditions are too extreme for 'normal' plant growth. **1984** *Forestry Abstr.* XLV. 558/1 In agroforestry systems there are both ecological and economical interactions between the different components. **1974** *Daily News* (Tanzania) 27 Sept. 1/2 Tanzania's march towards mechanised farming has been set in motion with the establishment of an *agro-mechanisation centre in Rufiji District. **1977** *Business Week* (Industr. ed.) 29 Aug. 34F/2 Tractor rehabilitation centers will be built throughout the country [*sc.* Tanzania] to provide convenient repair facilities. 'These agro-mechanization centers, which we hope to expand elsewhere, also provide the companies with long-term potential for developing their business.' **1962** WANG & BARGER *Bibliogr. Agric. Meteorol.* i. 19 (*heading*) *Agrometeorological organization and problems. **1980** (*title*) Agrometeorological crop monitoring and forecasting (UN: *FAO Plant Production & Protection Paper* No. 17). **1963** J.-Y. WANG *Agric. Meteorol.* i. 11 The *agrometeorologist must first formulate an accurate description of the physical environment and biological responses. **1974** E. C. STACEY *Peace Country Heritage* ii. 71 Stock questions to any modern agrometeorologist. **1957** J.-Y. WANG *Evaluation Techniques*

Agrometeorol. (Ph.D. Thesis, Univ. of Wisconsin) 152 **Agrometeorology*, a branch of applied meteorology which deals with weather and climate in their relation to agriculture. **1983** R. A. GOMMES (*title*) Pocket computers in agrometeorology. **1973** *Bulletin* (Sydney) 25 Aug. 68/3 The prime requisites for leadership have been .. some rustic ability as an emotional orator, and enough money to permit a virtual full-time role in *agro-politics. **1975** *Sunday Times* 16 Mar. 72 The flavour makers bring world agro-politics right into the ordinary kitchen. **1980** *Summary World Broadcasts: Eastern Europe* (B.B.C.) 12 Feb. A1/7 A total of 455 young Vietnamese have completed their training as agricultural machinery and motor mechanics, *agrotechnologists or skilled forestry workers. **1984** *Daily Tel.* 19 Oct. 14/4 Agrotechnologists are planning to produce the perfect dairy cow by the year 2000. **1937** J. D. BERNAL in C. Day Lewis *Mind in Chains* 200 There is being built up in the Soviet Union an organised science unlike anything the world has seen before... Already in several fields its results are impressive, notably in aero-dynamics, in the study of the solid state and in *agrotechnology. **1981** *McGraw-Hill Yearbk. Sci. & Technol.* 80/1 An immense quantity of agrotechnology is currently being developed by a large number of national and international agricultural research centers for the resource- and technology-poor farmers of the tropics and subtropics. **1969** *Compar. Stud. Society & Hist.* Apr. 121 Peasant agglomerations, the so-called '*agro-towns' that may number several thousand inhabitants, are fairly common in southern Italy. **1971** P. A. ALLUM *Politics & Society Post-War Naples* (1973) i. 28 Certain large peasant agro-towns (like Casoria, Marano and Marchianise, etc.) in which the population of the plain is concentrated.

agrobacterium (ˌægrɒbæk'tɪərɪəm). Also Agro-. Pl. -ia. [mod.L. (H. J. Conn 1942, in *Jrnl. Bacteriol.* XLIV. 359), f. AGRO- + BACTERIUM.] A bacterium of the genus *Agrobacterium*, which includes Gram-negative aerobic rods found in soil, several of which cause plant galls.

1966 *Jrnl. Gen. Microbiol.* XLIII. 8 We applied the same approach with a group of 45 agrobacteria. **1975** *Nature* 26 June 742/1 The acquisition of virulence by non-pathogenic agrobacteria from pathogenic agrobacteria has been demonstrated by Kerr. **1980** *Ibid.* 21 Feb. 796/1 Effective binding of agrobacteria to plant cells is a prerequisite to tumour formation. **1983** *Economist* 19 Nov. 101/3 Agrobacterium is a microbe that invades wounds in plants.

agrochemical (ægrəʊ'kɛmɪkəl), *sb.* (and *a.*) [f. AGRO- + CHEMICAL *sb.*] A chemical used in agriculture, esp. a biologically active one such as a weedkiller or a fungicide. Also *attrib.* or as *adj.* Cf. AGRICHEMICAL *a.* and *sb.*

1960 *Biol. Abstr.* 1 Jan. 215/2 Years of work by the Dolgoprudnaya Agrochemical Testing Station have proven the highly beneficial consequences of systematic application of manure in crop rotation. **1963** *Economist* 30 Mar. 1222/3, 29 per cent of its sales were accounted for by defence contracts .. and 21 per cent by agrochemical and industrial products. **1964** *Ibid.* 11 Apr. 167/1 Recent Russian purchases of chemical plant have been directed by the need for 'agro-chemicals', urgently required to improve agricultural output. **1970** *Daily Tel.* 28 Apr. 22/1 While a rapid turn-round can be expected in agrochemicals, the position in the main fertiliser market remains uncertain. **1978** *Dumfries Courier* 20 Oct. 13/3 West Cumberland Farmers are one of four co-operatives involved in the formation of a new agro-chemical marketing company. **1984** 'D. ARCHER' *Ambridge Years* 119 In my lifetime, four things have happened to revolutionize farming: mechanization, plant breeding, livestock breeding and the development of agro-chemicals.

‖**agrodolce** (ˌagro'doltʃe), *a.* [It. *agro* sour, *dolce* sweet. Cf. *piano-forte, chiar-oscuro.*] Sour and sweet blended together; = AIGRE-DOUX.

1845 FORD *Handbk. Spain* I. i. 46 In Spain, as Sappho says, Love is .. an alternation of the agro-dolce. **1854** BADHAM *Halieutics* 62 Agrodolce, as its name imports, is a blending of sweets and sours, and is made by stewing in a rich gravy, prunes, Corinth currants, almonds, pine-kernels, raisins, vinegar and wine.

‖**agrogorod** (ægrəʊ'gɔərəd). Pl. -a. [Russ., f. *agro-* as in AGRONOMIC *a.* + *górod* town.] A group of amalgamated collective farms (kolkhozes) forming an administrative unit; a 'rural city'. Also, by partial translation, **agro-city, -town**.

1951 *Soviet Stud.* Oct. III. 158 Under the leadership of the Politburo member Nikita Khrushchev, a campaign was begun for a great enlargement of the individual kolkhozy by 'voluntary' mergers, by corresponding consolidation of villages into what were proudly called 'agro-cities'. **1951** *Sun* (Baltimore) 20 Mar. 12/2 What Stalin has now launched is a program of combining Russia's 250,000-odd collective farms into not more than 100,000 giant farm enterprises, to be called agro-towns or agricultural towns. **1952** *Ann. Reg. 1951* 198 Khrushchev himself had dismissed contemptuously the earlier grandiose dreams of '*agrogoroda*', or rural cities, and had substituted the idea of '*kolkhoz* settlements'. **1959** E. CRANKSHAW *Khrushchev's Russia* 83 He [*sc.* Khrushchev] had had his wild ideas, like the premature scheme for *agrogoroda*; but he had had his good schemes too.

agro-industry ('ægrəʊɪndʌstrɪ). [f. AGRO- + INDUSTRY.] Industry which is connected with agriculture; agriculture developed along industrial lines.

[**1965** T. J. WEYGAND *Introd. Agric. Business & Industry* i. 12 Agindustry—This is a relatively new term. It refers .. to: (1) the industries producing agricultural commodities, (2) the industries and businesses supplying and servicing those engaged in agricultural commodity production, and (3) the industries and businesses performing all the necessary functions in making agricultural commodities available to the consumer.] **1969** *New Scientist* 24 Apr. 180/2 In this way [*sc.* by composting] he can create a permanent fertility and does not mine and exploit nature like so many techniques of agro-industry. **1977** *Food Policy* Feb. 44/1 The authors describe the experience, needs, and attitudes of UN agencies and a representative sample of the agroindustry firms. **1982** *Pakistan Agric.* Apr. 17/3 The present policy of the Government is to encourage entrepreneurs to set up agro-industries for this purpose.

Hence ˌ**agro-in'dustrial** *a.*, of or pertaining to agro-industry; serving both agricultural and industrial purposes.

1968 *Economist* 21 Sept. 45/3 Such nuclear desalting facilities might be the centre of agro-industrial complexes, with fresh water and fertilisers produced by atomic power, which could revolutionise life in poor, dry regions. **1971** *Daily Tel.* 5 Jan. 10/7 In Dobrudja [in Bulgaria] .. 41 co-operatives and five State farms are to be merged into nine agro-industrial complexes. **1975** A. B. SHAH in H. M. Patel et al. *Say not Struggle Nought Availeth* 111 Within each state, a programme of agro-industrial development should be taken up. **1979** *Nature* 14 June 574/3 Chemotherapy is no match for the powerful social and economic forces which have made schistosomiasis a major problem in Brazil's agro-industrial age. **1983** *Indian Jrnl. Animal Sci.* LIII. 652 (*heading*) Amino-acid composition of some agroindustrial byproducts.

agrology (ə'grɒlədʒɪ). [f. Gr. ἀγρό-ς field, land + -LOGY; cf. F. *agrologie.*] **a.** The science of soils. **b.** *spec.* In Canada, 'professional agriculture' (see quot. 1946). So **a'grologist**, an expert or specialist in agrology; a 'professional agriculturist'.

1916 B. D. JACKSON *Gloss. Bot. Terms* (ed. 3) 415/1 *Agrology*, the science of soils, and their support of special vegetation. **1946** *Statutes Prov. Saskatchewan* LXVIII. 652 'Agrologist' means any person registered as an agrologist under the provisions of this Act... 'Practising agrology' and similar forms of expression mean .. experimenting with, or advising on the application of scientific principles and practices relating to the cultivation, production, improvement .. of agricultural plants. **1962** *Careers in Prof. Agric.* (*Canadian Imp. Bank of Commerce*) 1 The need for more professional agriculturists (agrologists) in Canada.

‖**'agrom.** [app. a. Gujaráti *agrūn*, 'ulceration of the tongue from chronic disease of the alimentary canal'; Molesworth, *Marathi Dict.*] (See quot.)

1753 CHAMBERS *Cycl. Supp.*, *Agrom*, a disease frequent in Bengal, and other parts of the Indies, wherein the tongue chaps and cleaves in several places. **1879** *Syd. Soc. Lex.*, An Indian term for a rough and cracked condition of the tongue.

agromed, variant of AGRAMED *pple. Obs.*, vexed.

agronome ('ægrəʊnəʊm). *rare.* [a. Fr. *agronome*, ad. Gr. ἀγρονόμος an overseer of lands, f. ἀγρός field, land + -νόμος dispensing, f. νέμ-ειν to dispense. Cf. Fr. *astronome.*] = AGRONOMIST.

1838 *Monthly Chron.* II. 212 The rule adopted by the South American agronomes. **1881** tr. *Nordenskiöld's Voy. Vega* II. xi. 60 According to a communication from the agronome. **1945** H. G. WELLS *Happy Turning* vi. 22 The agronomes—there are no farmers in Dreamland—come along and tell us, 'We can produce all the food.'

agronomial (ægrəʊ'nəʊmɪəl), *a. rare*—[1]. [f. AGRONOMY + -AL[1].] = Agronomic (which is more analogical).

1853 LYTTON *My Novel* v. ii. (Routl.) 226 His rural eye detected the signs of a master in the art agronomial.

agronomic (ægrəʊ'nɒmɪk), *a.* [f. Gr. ἀγρονόμος: see AGRONOME + -IC. Cf. *economic* and mod.Fr. *agronomique.*] Of or pertaining to agronomy or the management of land.

1817 SOUTHEY *Life & Corr.* IV. 274 The agronomic part [of the institution] afforded funds, from the farm and the manufacture of agricultural implements. *Mod.* Agronomic science. **1891** *Times* 28 Sept. 13/5 Agronomic stations have been created for the purpose of enlightening agriculturalists. **1957** *Times* 2 July Agric. Suppl. i/2 The improved agronomic techniques .. have .. been taken up and tested by Norfolk farmers.

agronomical (ægrəʊ'nɒmɪkəl), *a.* [f. prec. + -AL[1]. Cf. *economical.*] = AGRONOMIC. Hence **agro'nomically** *adv.*, as regards agronomy, from an agronomic point of view.

1856 *Edinb. Rev.* Jan. 94 The French agronomical division of the soil is infinitely less profitable. **1877** WALLACE *Russia* vii. 114 The peasant knows of course nothing about agronomical chemistry. **1879** *Nature* 2 Oct. 542/2 An agronomical station will be placed in the same locality. **1946** K. S. CHESTER *Nature & Prevention Cereal Rusts* xiv. 199 The use of early-maturing varieties .. should not be advised until it has been determined that their culture is agronomically a sound practice in any locality concerned. **1976** *Nature* 27 May 279/2 Exploitation of this potential requires considerable work to identify the limiting environmental factors and develop agronomically feasible practices to overcome them. **1983** *Sci. Amer.* Nov. 138/2 Such agronomically important crops as alfalfa and numerous trefoils.

agronomics (ægrəʊ'nɒmɪks). [AGRONOMIC *a.* used as sb. pl. (or coll. sing.); cf. *economics.*] Agronomic science; the science of the distribution and management of the land as the original basis of national wealth.

1863 F. HALL in *Reader* 24 Jan. 95 Ancient Parsee books treated of botany, agronomics, metaphysics, and handicrafts.

agronomist (ə'grɒnəmɪst). [f. AGRONOM-Y + -IST. Cf. *econom-ist.*] One engaged in the study of agronomy; a rural economist.

1818 W. TAYLOR in *Month. Rev.* LXXXVII. 480 No Romman agronomist .. ever mentions a harvest so husbanded. **1868** *Daily News* 4 Sept., Certain agronomists are of opinion that there is a great advantage in reaping corn before its complete maturity.

agronomy (ə'grɒnəmɪ). [mod. f. assumed Gr. *ἀγρονομία n. of state, f. ἀγρονόμος: see AGRONOME, and cf. οἰκονομία. The Fr. *agronomie* may be earlier.] The management of land, rural economy, husbandry.

1814 *Sch. Good Living* 196 Equally skilled in agronomy and gastronomy, in the cultivation of the field or in the adaptation of its produce. **1881** RODWELL in *Nature* XXIV. 32 The .. papers communicated to the section of Agronomy related .. to the .. agriculture of Algiers.

agroof, see AGRUFE.

†**a'grope**, *v. Obs.* [f. A- *pref.* 1 out + GROPE.] To grope out, search, discover.

1393 GOWER *Conf.* I. 254 And after that they couthe agrope, Hath eche of hem said his entent. *Ibid.* II. 379 For who so woll it wel agrope, To hem belongeth all Europe.

agros(e, pa. t. of AGRISE *v. Obs.*

†**a'grose**, *sb. Obs.*—[0] [ad. L. *agrōsus*, f. *ager* field, land: see -OSE.] 'One which hath much lands.' Cockeram 1612.

‖**agrostis** (ə'grɒstɪs). *Bot.* [L. *agrōstis*, ad. Gr. ἄγρωστις some kind of grass; f. ἀγρός field.] A genus of grasses known commonly as *Bent*.

1753 CHAMBERS *Cycl. Supp.*, *Agrostis* is commonly used for the species of grass called *quick-grass* or *couch-grass*. **1866** MOORE in *Treas. Bot.* I. 31/2 The Falkland Islands, Nootka Sound, and Tasmania, may be quoted as some of the outlying stations for the species of *Agrostis*.

agrostographic (əˌgrɒstəʊ'græfɪk), *a.* [f. AGROSTOGRAPH-Y + -IC.] Of or belonging to agrostography. (In mod. Dicts. and Gloss. of Terms.)

agrostographical (əˌgrɒstəʊ'græfɪkəl), *a.* [f. prec. + -AL[1].] = prec.

agrostography (ægrə'stɒgrəfɪ). [f. AGROST-IS + -(O)GRAPHY description.] Description of grasses.

1753 CHAMBERS *Cycl. Supp.*, *Agrostographia*, in physiology, the history, or description of gramens, or plants of the grassy kind. **1847** CRAIG, *Agrostography*.

agrostologic (əˌgrɒstəʊ'lɒdʒɪk), *a.* [f. AGROSTOLOG-Y + -IC.] Of or belonging to agrostology.

agrostological (əˌgrɒstəʊ'lɒdʒɪkal), *a.* [f. prec. + -AL[1].] = prec.

agrostologist (ægrə'stɒlədʒɪst). [f. next + -IST.] One who is skilled in agrostology.

1882 *Amer. Jrnl. Sc.* Mar. 244 Representations which may horrify old-fashioned Agrostologists.

agrostology (ægrə'stɒlədʒɪ). [f. AGROST-IS + -(O)LOGY discourse.] 'That part of botany which treats of the grasses.' Craig 1847.

†**a'grote**, *v. Obs.* 4–5. Only in pa. pple. **agroted, -yed, -eied.** [Origin obscure; perhaps f. A- *pref.* 1 + *grot* a particle, or Norse *grautr* porridge. (Cf. also GROUT, to fill interstices with mortar.)] To cram, surfeit, cloy.

c **1385** CHAUCER *L.G.W.* 2454, I am agrotyed here byforn To wryte of hem that ben on love for-sworn. *c* **1430** LYDG. *Bochas* V. xx. (1554) 136 a, Gorges agroteyed, enbossed their entrayle Disposeth men rather to rest and slepe.

†**a'groten**, *v. Obs. rare*—[1]. Only form 5 **agrotone.** [f. prec. + -EN[2]. Cf. *fat, fatten.*] To surfeit.

1440 *Promp. Parv.*, Agrotone wyth mete or drynke [*v.r.* agrotonyn], *Ingurgito.* Agrotonyd or sorporryd wyth mete or drynke, *Ingurgitatus.*

†**a'grotening**, *vbl. sb. Obs.* [f. prec. + -ING[1].] Surfeiting, a surfeit.

1440 *Promp. Parv.*, Agrotonynge. *Ingurgitacio.*

aground (ə'graʊnd), *adv.*, orig. *phr.* [A *prep.*[1] on + GROUND.]

†**1.** On or upon the ground, either of *position* or *direction*; on the earth, to the earth. *Obs.*

1297 R. GLOUC. 378 Manne orf deyde alaground [*i.e.* all aground], so gret qualm þer was þo. **1340** *Ayenb.* 91 þe drope of þe deawe .. ualþ agrund. **1377** LANGL. *P. Pl.* B. I. 90 He is a god bi þe gospel Agrounde and aloft [**1362** on grounde]. **1490** CAXTON *Eneydos* li. 145 Eneas that sawe Mezencyus agrounde came towarde hym. **1562** *Romeus & Juliet* (in Wr.) She fel flat downe before his feete aground.

2. On or to the strand or shallow bottom of any water, where a boat or ship lodges, and is no longer 'afloat.' ***to be aground***: to be stranded; ***to run aground***: to run into a place where the ship lodges on the bottom.

c **1500** *Cocke Lorelles Bote* (1843) 6 Some at saynt Kateryns stroke a grounde. **1579** Gosson *Sch. Abuse* (Arb.) 55 A little fishe swimmeth continually before the great Whale to shewe him the shelues that he run not a ground. **1610** Shaks. *Temp.* I. i. 4 Speake to th' mariners: fall too't yarely, or we run ourselves a ground. **1719** De Foe *Crusoe* (1858) 264 The water was ebbed considerably away leaving their boat aground. **1813** Southey *Nelson* v. 149 Before the lead could be hove again he was fast aground. **1856** Kane *Arctic Expl.* I. v. 60 The bergs were aground well out to seaward.

b. *fig.*

1665 Glanville *Sceps. Sc.* xiii. 76 And run aground on that more desperate absurdity, Atheism. *a* **1687** J. M. in *Cleveland's Wks.* 1687, 282 For in Discourse his Wit did never rest, When others were aground with one dry jest. **1832** Gen. P. Thompson *Exerc.* (1842) II. 57 The arguments against competition .. all finally come aground on this rock.

‖**agroville** (agro'vil; 'ægrəʊvɪl). *temporary.* [Fr., = agrogorod.] In the Vietnam war: a South Vietnamese agricultural community established according to a policy of concentrating formerly dispersed farms, for safety against the Viet Cong; a village stronghold.

1960 *Economist* 7 May 542/1 Mr Diem's pet project, of establishing 'agrovilles'— communities of scattered farmers regrouped around modern facilities. **1961** *Ann. Reg. 1960* 358 The official policy of concentrating rural population in *agrovilles* .. met little enthusiasm from the cultivators who were thus uprooted. **1962** E. Snow *Other Side of River* (1963) lxxxv. 705 Ngo Dinh Can's answer is more 'agrovilles', which are set up like Chiang Kai-Shek's erstwhile models of 'New Life' in Kiangsi. **1966** *Economist* 18 June 1304/2 There has been scrupulous avoidance of the breakneck speed and swollen costs of Diem's ill-fated 'agroville' programme.

agrudge, -gge, var. aggrudge *v. Obs.*, to grudge.

†**a'grufe, a'gruif, a'groof,** *adv. Obs.* or *dial.* [ad. Norse *á grúfu* on the belly, face down; more commonly expanded in ME. to *on grufe*: see grufe and groveling.] With face downward, prone. (In common use in Sc. and North Eng. dial.)

1638 Adamson *Muses Thren.* 112 (Jam.) Agruif lay some, others with eyes to skyes.

agrull, variant of agrill *v. Obs.*, to annoy.

agrum, agrym(e, obs. pop. ff. algorism.

†**agrum.** *Obs. rare*⁻¹. (See quot.)

1496 *Bk. St. Albans* C ij, Whan thou seest thy hawke upon her mouth and her chekes blobbed, then she hath this sycknes called Agrum.

†**a'gruw,** *v. Obs. rare*⁻¹. [f. a- *pref.* 1 intens. + *gruw*, grue to shudder. Cf. Ger. *ergrauen*.] To cause to shudder, horrify; *impers.* to abhor.

c **1230** *Ancr. R.* 92 Ʒe schulen biholden sumetime touward te pine of helle, þet ou agruwie [*printed* agrupie] aʒean ham.

‖**agrypnia** (ə'grɪpnɪə). *Med.* [mod.L. ad. Gr. ἀγρυπνία sleeplessness.] Wakefulness, sleeplessness.

1684 tr. *Bonet's Merc. Compit.* III. 67 In curing an Agrypnia (or Want of Sleep). **1753** Chambers *Cycl. Supp.*, *Agrypnia* in the Greek church, is used for the vigil of any of the greater feast-days. **1853** in Mayne *Exp. Lex.*

agrypnode (ə'grɪpnəʊd), *a. Med.* [ad. Gr. ἀγρυπνώδης making sleepless; f. ἄγρυπνος sleepless.] Sleep-preventing.

1879 *Syd. Soc. Lex.*, *Agrypnode fever*, a fever that prevents sleep.

agrypnotic (ægrɪp'nɒtɪk), (*a.*) *sb. Med.* [a. Fr. *agrypnotique*, f. Gr. ἄγρυπνος wakeful. In imitation of *hypnotic*, Gr. ὑπνωτικός, f. ὑπνώσσ-ειν; but ἀγρυπνητικός wakeful, gives *agrypnetic*.] Anything administered to produce wakefulness.

1879 *Syd. Soc. Lex.* s.v., Coffee, tea .. and the electric bath, are reckoned among the most effectual agrypnotics.

agt, agte, obs. forms of aught *sb.* and *v.*

agterskot ('axtəskɒt). *S. Afr.* [Afrikaans, f. *agter* after + *voor)skot* advance payment, f. *voorskiet* to advance (money).] The final payment for a crop by a farmers' co-operative society or similar body to members, consisting of the difference between the total amount due for the season and the advance-payment (voorskot). Also *transf.*

1944 *Cape Argus* 18 May 7/6 More than 1,000 persons went to Rustenburg .. from many parts of the Transvaal to receive back pay (agterskot) for tobacco sold to the Magaliesberg Co-operative Tobacco Planters Association. **1950** *Ibid.* 8 Sept. 8/6 The country is reaping an 'agterskot' in reverse from devaluation. **1958** *Cape Times* 12 Dec. 2/8 An *agterskot* amounting to £31,000 is being paid to lucern seed farmers in Oudtshoorn district.

aguacate (agwa'kate). [Sp.: see avocado.] The alligator pear or avocado. Also *attrib.*

1897 *Blackw. Mag.* Nov. 686/1 Tall mangoes and aguacates. **1926** *Chambers's Jrnl.* 23 Jan. 126/2 Banana peelings, aguacate skins.

aguardiente (agwarði'ente). [Sp., = brandy, f. *agua* water + *ardiente* ardent.] A coarse kind of brandy made in Spain and Portugal. Also applied to any distilled spirituous liquor; in south-western U.S., native whisky.

[**1818** *New-Eng. Palladium* (Boston, Mass.) 28 Sept. 3/2 Isaac McLellan & Co. .. have for sale .. 100 pipes Spanish Rum or Auquedent.] **1824** W. Bullock *6 Months' Res. in Mex.* xvii. 212 Shops for the sale of native and Spanish brandy, (aguardiente). **1828, 1854** [see mescal 1]. **1899** St. Barbe *Mod. Spain* 67 Much of the fun of the fair consists in sipping *aguardiente*, a strong liqueur. **1926** D. H. Lawrence *Plumed Serp.* iv. 80 The hateful sugar-cane brandy, *aguardiente*.

ague ('eɪgjuː). Forms: 4 aguwe, 4–6 agew, 4–7 agu, 5 agwe, 6 agewe, 4– ague. [a. OFr. *ague*:—L. *acūta* sharp, used subst. in med.L. for an 'acute fever,' *fièvre ague*: see acute *a.* 2.]

†**1.** An acute or violent fever. *Obs.*

1377 Langl. *P. Pl.* B. xiii. 336, I cacche þe crompe .. Or an ague in such an angre. **1393** *Ibid.* C. xxiii. 84 Bules and bocches · and brennyng Aguwes. **1494** Fabyan vii. 377 Yᵉ kynge was taken with suche a flixe, and therwith an agu, that he kept his bedde. **1541** Barnes *Wks.* (1573) 325/1 Peters wyues mother had a gret agew. **1611** Bible *Lev.* xxvi. 16 And the burning ague, that shall consume the eyes [Vulg. *ardore*, Wyclif brennyng.]

2. *esp.* A malarial fever, marked by successive fits or paroxysms, consisting of a cold, hot, and sweating stage. The name *ague* was apparently at first given to the burning or feverish stage, but afterwards more usually to the cold or shivering stage, as being the most striking external character of the disease.

c **1386** Chaucer *Nonne Pr. T.* 140 Ye schul have a fever terciane, Or an agu, that may be youre bane. **1440** *Promp. Parv.*, Agwe, sekenes, *Acuta, querquera*. **1579** Gosson *Sch. Abuse* (Arb.) 16 Hee that hath bin shooke with a fierce ague. **1601** Shaks. *Jul. Cæs.* II. ii. 113 That same Ague which hath made you leane. **1678** Butler *Hudibr.* III. i. 653 'Tis but an ague that's reverst, Whose hot fit takes the patient first. **1719** De Foe *Crusoe* I. 101 An Ague very violent; the Fit held me seven Hours, cold Fit, and hot, with faint Sweats after it. **1859** Masson *Milton* I. 142 Confined to College by an attack of ague (then the prevalent disease of the fenny Cambridge district).

3. *loosely* or *fig.* Any fit of shaking or shivering, like the cold stage of ague; quaking.

1589 *Pappe with Hatchet* (1844) 14 And saies he will ergo Martin into an ague. **1596** Shaks. *Merch. Ven.* I. i. 23 My winde cooling my broth, Would blow me to an Ague. **1608** Bp. Hall *Epistles* I. ii, All these earthly delights! If they were sound, they are but a good day between tuo agues. **1750** Gray *Let.* in *Poems* (1775) 217 But soon his rhetorick forsook him .. A sudden fit of ague shook him, He stood as mute as poor Macleane. **1813** Scott *Rokeby* II. xi, For not to rank nor sex confined Is this vain ague of the mind.

4. *Attrib.* and *Comb.*, as in ***ague-fen, -fit, -sore***, etc.; *instrumental*, as in ***ague-struck, -shaken***, etc.: ***ague-like***; **ague-drop**, a solution of potassic arseniate, used as a remedy for ague; **ague-grass**, a name of the *Aletris farinosa*; **ague-proof** *a.*, proof against ague; **ague-shake** *v.*, to shake as with ague; **ague-shell** (see quot.); **ague-spell**, charm against ague; ague-cake, ague-tree, q.v.

1866 Kingsley *Herew.* xv. 194 One who has just come from the ague-fens. **1587** Golding *De Mornay* xii. 175 What feare, and what Agewfits they susteine in following their wicked lusts. **1858** Froude *Hist. Eng.* III. xv. 350 Cromwell .. had an ague-fit from anxiety. **1748** Richardson *Clarissa* (1811) I. 13 An ague-like lover. **1687** Clayton in *Phil. Trans.* XLI. 158 Some call it Ague-grass, others Ague-root, others Star-grass. **1605** Shaks. *Lear* IV. vi. 107, I am not agu-proofe. **1653** Shirley *Cupid & Death* 350 How will she ague-shake him with a frown! **1708** in *Phil. Trans.* XXVI. 78 Gryphites, the Hawk's-Bill, or Ague-shell. **1745** Gay *Wks.* I. 120 His Pills, his Balsams, and his Ague-spells.

ague ('eɪgjuː), *v. rare.* [f. the sb.] To affect with, or as with, ague; to seize with a quaking.

1636 Heywood *Chall. for Beauty* (T.) Whose aspect Would ague such as should but hear it told. **1796** Miss Burney *Camilla* v. vi, I am agued with trepidation. **1864** Sir F. Palgrave *Hist. Norm.* III. 379 The victor of Hastings was agued with terror when receiving his prize.

'ague-ˌcake. An enlargement of the spleen or liver caused by ague.

1641 Milton *Ch. Discip.* II. (1851) 42 A mere ague-cake coagulated of a certaine Fever they have, presaging their time to be but short. **1801** E. Darwin *Zoon.* II. 47 The liver, spleen, or pancreas; one or more of which are frequently so enlarged in the autumnal intermittents as to be perceptible to the touch externally, and are called by the vulgar ague-cakes.

agued ('eɪgjuːd), *ppl. a.* [f. ague *v.* + -ed.] Affected as with ague; ague-shaken.

1607 Shaks. *Coriol.* I. iv. 38 Faces pale With flight and agued feare. **1787** T. Jefferson *Writings* (1859) II. 304 They calculate on the spirit of the nation, and not on the agued hand which guides its movements. **1819** Crabbe *T. of Hall* xii. 680 The flame, That warm'd his agued limbs.

†**a'guerried,** *ppl. a. Obs. rare.* [f. 17th c. Fr. *aguerri* pa. pple. of *aguerrir* to accustom to war; f. *à* to + *guerre* war.] Inured or trained to war.

1767 Geo. Ld. Lyttelton ? *Hist. Hen. II* (T.) An army the best aguerried of any troops in Europe.

†**'ague-tree.** Obsolete name of the Sassafras.

1597 Gerard *Herbal* 1341 For want of an English name we are contented to call it the Ague tree, of his vertue in healing the Ague. **1712** tr. *Pomet's Hist. Drugs* I. 65 Sassafras, call'd the Ague-Tree, is rather a Root than a Wood. **1753** Chambers *Cycl. Supp.*, *Ague-Tree* is a name given to sassafras, on account of its febrifuge virtue.

aguey ('eɪgjuːɪ), *a.* [f. ague *sb.* + -y¹.] = aguish.

Mod. Our cold and aguey age.

†**a'guiled, agyled,** *pa. pple. Obs. rare*⁻¹. [f. a- *pref.* 1 or 6 + guile *v.*] Beguiled.

c **1305** *St. James* in *E.E. Poems* (1862) 59 þe deuel ʒeode awey · & huld him a-gyled sore; Nadde þe schrewe neuere so moche schame.

[**aguiler.** Ash has '*agiler* a deceiver.']

†**a'guiler.** *Obs. rare*⁻¹. [a. OFr. *aguiller*, mod. *aiguillier*, f. OFr. *aguille* needle: see aiguille.] A needle-case.

c **1400** *Rom. Rose* 98 A sylvre nedle forth I droughe, Out of an aguler [*v.r.* aguiler] queynt ynoughe.

†**a'guilt,** *v. Obs.* Forms: *Inf.* 1 agylt-an, agilt-an, 2–4 agult-en, 2–5 agilt-en, 3–4 agelt-en, agelt-e, agult-e, 4–5 agilt(e, 4–6 agylt(e, 5 aguylt(e. *Pa. t.* 1–5 agylte, agilte, 2–4 agulte, 3–4 agelte. *Pa. pple.* 1–5 agylt, agilt, 2–4 agult, 3–4 agelt, 4–5 aguylt, agulted, agilted. [f. A *pref.* 1 intens. + *gylt-an*: see guilt. The forms in *u* (*ü*) are s.w., in *e* s.e., in *i*, *y*, midl. and north.]

1. *intr.* To be guilty, transgress, offend, sin (*with*, *against*, *to*, *towards*).

c **1000** Ælfric *Gen.* xl. 1 Tweȝen afyryde men agylton wið heora hláford. *c* **1175** *Lamb. Hom.* 17 ʒif þu agultest, oðer suneȝest toward drihten. *c* **1200** *Trin. Coll. Hom.* 211 He agilt wið gode. *c* **1230** *Ancren Riwle* 346 'Mea culpa:' Ich agulte: Louerd, merci! *Ibid.* 186 Ne warien hwon me agulteð to ou. *c* **1386** Chaucer *Melib.* 860 Dampnably we have agilt ageinst youre highe lordschipe. *c* **1450** *Merlin* 19 My moder ought to be quyte, for she hath no thynge aguylte.

2. *trans.* To be guilty towards, to sin against, to offend, wrong. (The obj., orig. *dat.*, becomes *acc.*)

c **1175** *Lamb. Hom.* 195 þauh he ðe habbe swuðe agult. *c* **1200** *Trin. Coll. Hom.* 79 And naðemore haten him, þe him agilteð. *c* **1340** *Ayenb.* 65 Huanne man agelt his treuþe. *c* **1386** Chaucer *Parson's T.* 910 He hath agultid his God and defoulid his soule. *a* **1420** Occleve *De Reg. Prin.* 1399 Cast thou thyne eye abak, What thou god hast agilt in tyme past.

3. *trans.* To be guilty to the peril of, to sin away.

c **1320** *Seuyn Sages* (W.) 686 Yit had he nowt agelt his lif.

4. *causal.* To make or declare guilty.

1530 Palsgr. 418/2, I agylte of trespas. *Je fays coulpable.* Thou shalte neuer agylt me of this mater.

†**a'guise,** *sb. Obs.* Also 7 agg-. [f. guise; the prefix either for *on*, or in opposition to *dis-* in *dis-guise*. Cf. *a(c)-cord*, *dis-cord*; Spenser's *ag-grace* and *dis-grace*. There was no Fr. *aguise* or *aguiser*.] Dress, attire, array.

1483 *Cath. Angl.*, Anguice *Indula*. **1647** H. More *Song of Soul* I. I. xxiii, The glory of the Court, their fashions, And brave agguize. *Ibid.* I. III. lvi, Yclad in snowy stoles of fair agguize.

†**a'guise,** *v. Obs.* [formed on, or as, the prec. sb.] To dress, attire, array.

1591 Spenser *M. Hubberds T.* 656 Then gan this craftie couple to devize, How for the Court themselves they might aguize. **1596** —— *F.Q.* II. vi. 7 Sometimes her head she fondly would aguize With gaudy girlonds. **1598** Sylvester *Du Bartas, Adam* 12 Reave him the skill his un-skill to aguize.

†**a'guised,** *ppl. a. Obs.* [f. prec. + -ed.] Arrayed, dressed.

1596 Spenser *F.Q.* II. i. 21 Had craftily devisd To be her squire, and do her service well aguisd.

aguish ('eɪgjuːɪʃ), *a.* [f. ague *sb.* + -ish.]

1. Of the nature or character of an ague.

1665–9 Boyle *Occas. Refl.* Contents, The immoderate Heat and Cold of the Aguish Fit. **1753** Hanway *Trav.* (1762) I. III. xxvi. 110 The dews here fall heavy; and the heat of the sun .. is productive of colds and aguish pains. **1856** Miss Muloch *John Halifax* 170 It was a low agueish fever.

2. Having a tendency to produce ague.

1627 Speed *Eng. etc. Abridged* xv. §4 The ayre is temperate and pleasant, onely towards the waters somewhat aguish. **1771** Smollett *Humph. Cl.* (1815) 106 The nocturnal rheums of an aguish climate. **1850** Lyell *2nd Visit to U.S.* II. 54 A rich aguish flat, bordering the Missouri.

3. Subject to ague.

1616 Surfl. & Markh. *Countrey Farme* 191 There is nothing better .. for leane agueish persons, than the vse of the pulpe of Gourds. **1672** Davenant *Love & Hon.* (1673) 241 Which left me feeble as an aguish Girl. **1824** Byron *Juan* XVI. lxxxiii, But both were thrown away amongst the fens; For wit hath no great friend in aguish folks.

4. *fig.* Resembling an ague, in shakiness or intermittency; **a.** quaking, shivering, shaky; **b.** coming by fits and starts.

1633 FLETCHER *Purple Isl.* VIII. xxxi, A weak distrustfull heart is vertues aguish spell. **1638** COWLEY *Love's Riddle* IV. (1711) III. 119 The aguish Head of every Tree by Æolus Was rock'd asleep, and shook as if it nodded. *a* **1674** CLARENDON *Hist. Reb.* III. XI. 202 So aguish and fantastical a thing is the Conscience of Men who have once departed from the Rule of Conscience. **1865** *Pall Mall G.* 24 Apr. 4 Their panics are of the aguish or intermittent type.

aguishly (ˈeɪgjuːɪʃlɪ), *adv.* [f. prec. + -LY².] In an aguish manner; with the symptoms of an ague.

1741 RICHARDSON *Pamela* (1824) I. 89, I was very feverish, and aguishly inclined. **1748** —— *Clarissa* (1811) II. xl. 295 Shivering with cold, as if aguishly affected.

aguishness (ˈeɪgjuːɪʃnɪs). *rare*⁻⁰. [f. AGUISH *a.* + -NESS.] The quality or state of being aguish; resemblance or tendency to ague.

1731 in BAILEY; whence in JOHNSON, ASH, etc.

agult(e, variant of AGUILT *v. Obs.*, to sin.

agur, obs. form of AUGUR.

agush (əˈgʌʃ), *adv.*, prop. *phr.* [A *prep.*[1] of state, in + GUSH.] In a gushing state; gushing.

1858 HAWTHORNE *Fr. & It. Jrnls.* II. 149 The cider mill ..all agush with sweet juice.

agy (ˈeɪdʒɪ), *a. arch.* [f. AGE *sb.* + -Y¹.] Characterized by age; aged.

1664 *Floddan Field* v. 43 Lord Scroop of Upsall the agie Knight. **1839** BAILEY *Festus* ix. (1848) 103 Thee, agy world, thee, Universal Heaven.

†**aˈgye**, *v. Obs. rare.* [a. OFr. *aguie-r* to guide, f. *à* to + *guier*: see GUIDE and GUY.] To conduct, manage.

c **1460** *Launfal* 623 Sir Launfal schud be stward of halle, For to agye hys gestes alle. *Ibid.* 627 His feste for to agye. *c* **1460** *Lybeaus Disconus* 2052 Lybeauus Lambard tolde, And othre Knyghtes bolde, How hym ther gan agye.

agyled, *pa. pple.*: see AGUILED.

agylte, variant of AGUILT *v. Obs.*, to sin.

agynarious (ædʒɪˈnɛərɪəs), *a. Bot.* [f. Fr. *agynaire* (see next) + -OUS.] = AGYNARY.

1847 in CRAIG.

agynary (ˈædʒɪnərɪ), *a. Bot.* [ad. Fr. *agynaire* (De Candolle), f. Gr. ἀ priv. + γυνή woman: see -ARY.] Applied to double flowers, in which the stamens have become petals, and the pistil is wanting.

1879 in *Syd. Soc. Lex.*

agynic (əˈdʒɪnɪk), *a. Bot.* [ad. Fr. *agynique*, f. as prec.: see -IC.] Applied to the insertion of the stamens when not adherent to the ovary.

1879 in *Syd. Soc. Lex.*

†**agynous.** *a. Bot. Obs.* [f. Gr. ἀ priv. + γυνή woman + -OUS.] Without female organs.

1847 CRAIG, *Agynous* flower is the synonyme of *male* flower.

agyrate (əˈdʒaɪəreɪt), *a. Bot.* [f. A- *pref.* 14 + GYRATE.] Not disposed in whorls or circles.

1847 in CRAIG.

ah, obs. f. OWE *v.*; and var. of AC *conj. Obs.*, but.

ah (ɑː), *int.*; formerly 2–6 **a**! [perh. a. OFr. *a*, *ah*, since not found in OE. Cf. MHG. *â*, ON. *æ*. In northern dial. pronounced (eː), sometimes written *ay! eh!* the regular phonetic descendant of ME. *a*.] An exclamation expressing, according to the intonation, various emotions, as

1. Sorrow, lamentation, regret, passing into the regretful expression of a vain wish. (Actual pain or suffering is now more commonly expressed by *O! Oh!* North. dial. have *a* (eː) in both senses.)

c **1440** *Gesta Rom.* I. i. 2 A! Sir, I knowe welle that my wife is an hore. **1523** LD. BERNERS *Froissart* I. xliv. 61 A fayre uncle, your absence hath sette the frenchmen in a pride. **1611** BIBLE *Jer.* xxii. 18 They shall not lament for him, saying, Ah my brother, or ah sister. **1718** POPE *Iliad* x. 632 Yet much I fear (ah! may that fear be vain!) *a* **1842** TENNYSON *Gold. Year* 47 Ah! when shall all men's good Be each man's rule.

2. Surprise, wonder, admiration.

1826 DISRAELI *Viv. Grey* v. vi. 191 A-a-h! what a box! a Louis-Quatorze, I think?

¶ In the two prec. senses often followed by *me* (north. EH ME!). Cf. It. *ahime!*

1592 SHAKS. *Rom. & Jul.* v. i. 10 Ah me, how sweet is loue. *c* **1720** PRIOR (J.) Ah me! the blooming pride of May, and that of beauty, are but one.

3. Entreaty, appeal, remonstrance; passing in former times into simple exclamation to excite attention, where *O!* would now be used. (North. dial. still have *ā man!*)

c **1280** *A Sarmun* in E.E. Poems (1862) 1 Þer for he seiith. a! man hab munde þat of þis lif þer commiþ ende. **1382** WYCLIF *2 Cor.* vi. 11 A! ȝe Corynthis, oure mouth is opyn to ȝou. *c* **1450** *Merlin* 353 A here, Arthur, ride faste. **1593** SHAKS. *3 Hen. VI*, I. iii. 8 Ah, Clifford, murther not this innocent Child. **1711** ADDISON *Spect.* No. 130 ¶2 Ah Master, says the Gipsy, that roguish Leer of yours makes a pretty Woman's Heart ake. *a* **1843** SOUTHEY *Devil's Walk* Wks. III. 91 With throbs and throes, and ahs and ohs, Far famed his flock for frightening. **1855** TENNYSON *Maud* II. iv. 13 Ah Christ, that it were possible For one short hour to see The souls we loved.

4. Dislike, aversion; passing into contempt, mockery, exultation over or satisfaction at misfortune.

c **1435** *Torr. Portugal* 184 A! fellow! wylt thow so? **1580** BARET *Alvearie* A 253 Ah, ah, I dye poore wench in laughing thee to scorne. **1593** SHAKS. *2 Hen. VI*, IV. x. 28 A villaine, thou wilt betray me. **1611** BIBLE *Mark* xv. 29 Ah thou that destroyest the Temple, and buildest it in three dayes.

5. Opposition, objection (to what has been said). Often followed by *but*.

Mod. Ah! but I know something better than that.

6. Realization, discovery, inspiration.

c **1785** W. BLAKE *Island in Moon* iii, in *Compl. Writings* (1972) 47 'It was Phebus,' said the Epicurean. 'Ah, that was the Gentleman,' said Aradobo. **1915** CONRAD *Victory* III. vii. 245 Suddenly he moved, and murmured: 'Ah, here's the trolley.' **1934** W. B. YEATS *Words upon Window Pane* 58 Where did I put that tea-caddy? Ah! there it is. **1955** J. P. DONLEAVY *Ginger Man* xvii. 201 Ah, you want money, Miss Frost. Money is what you're after. **1972** T. STOPPARD *Jumpers* II. 62 Ah!—I knew there was something.

ah (ɑː), *v.* [f. AH *int.*] *intr.* To say 'ah' (as an expression of surprise, wonder, etc.); also, = ER *v.*

1897 'MARK TWAIN' *Foll. Equator* in *Writ.* (1900) V. 111 We..went oh-ing and ah-ing in admiration. **1924** D. H. LAWRENCE *Indians & Entertainment* in *Adelphi* Nov. 500 The men sing in unison..for hours..it goes on..gurgling, aah-h-h-ing! of the male voices. **1931** [see ER]. **1934** 'REBECCA WEST' *Mod. Rake's Progr.* 113 These visitors from the next civilisation..will walk about oh-ing and ah-ing. **1960** C. RAY *Merry Eng.* 128 The spectators ooh! and ah! and roar their delight.

ah, repr. dial. and U.S. Black pronunc. of I *pers. pron.* See A *pron.* ¶.

1869 *Good Words* 1 Mar. 171/2 Ah couldn't groind wi'out un. **1898** [see AIN'T *v.*]. **1904** *Dialect Notes* II. 423 The pronoun *I* when unemphatic is often pronounced ah, as *ah be, ah hai*ⁿ *gu*ⁿ*ty* (I'm not going to), [etc.]. **1911** D. H. LAWRENCE in *Eng. Rev.* June 424 Ah've said many a time as Ah'd fill up them ruts in this entry. **1935** Z. N. HURSTON *Mules & Men* 19 It's de strongest thing Ah ever made. **1942** W. FAULKNER *Go down, Moses* 136 'Whar you gwine?' she said. 'Ah'm goan home,' he said. **1961** S. CHAPLIN *Day of Sardine* vii. 145 Cut me throat if Ah'm lyin'..Ah never knew Ah'd so much talkin' in me; that kid draws me out. **1973** [see ME *pers. pron.* 10].

aha (ɑːˈhɑː, əˈhɑː), *int.* and *sb.* [a combination of the two interjections AH! and HA! formerly written separately, *a ha*. Cf. mod. Germ. *aha!* Fr. *ah! ah!*] **A.** *int.* An exclamation expressing, with different intonations, surprise (*arch.* or *obs.*), triumph or satisfaction, and mockery or irony.

c **1386** CHAUCER *Nonne Pr. T.* 561 They crieden, out!.. A ha the fox! and after him thay ran. **1509** *Parlyament of Deuylles* xc, 'A ha' sayd Adam, 'my God I se.' **1611** BIBLE *Is.* xliv. 16 He warmeth himself, and saith, Aha, I am warm. —— *Ps.* xxxv. 21 Yea they opened their mouth wide against me, and saide, Aha, Aha, our eye hath seene it. **1861** C. READE *Cloister & Hearth* I. 344 Next will come—Cramps of the Stomach. Aha! Then—Bilious Vomit. Aha!

B. *sb.* Used *attrib.*, as **aha experience** [tr. G. *aha-erlebnis* (K. Bühler (1908) in *Arch. Ges. Psychol.* XII. 18)], (the experience of) a moment of sudden insight or discovery; the sudden finding of a solution to a problem; also ***aha moment***, ***reaction***, etc.

1939 L. E. COLE *Gen. Psychol.* 666 '*Aha-moment*', the moment of insight. **1947** P. L. HARRIMAN *Dict. Psychol.* 18 '*Ah-ah' experience*, the sudden achievement of insight... The catch-phrase..comes, of course, from the tale about Archimedes. **1951** D. RAPAPORT tr. K. Bühler in *Organiz. & Pathol. Thought* ii. 49 Then comprehension came suddenly with an affect like 'Aha!' (not spoken)... [*Note*] To my knowledge, this is the first mention of the often-quoted aha-phenomenon. **1962** *Listener* 20 Sept. 436/2 They [*sc.* computers] sometimes reach solutions suddenly, and they do this under circumstances in which human subjects are likely to have an 'aha!' experience. **1970** A. TOFFLER *Future Shock* xv. 300 At the level of ideas or cognition, this is the 'a-hah!' reaction we experience at a moment of revelation, when we finally understand something that has been puzzling us. **1980** *Dædalus* Spring 131 Those famous moments of inspiration, one-liners, and 'Aha!' experiences that creativity studies cite.

aha, variant of HA-HA *sb.*, a sunk fence.

†**a hall**, *phr. Obs.* [see HALL; the *a* is doubtful, whether 'indef. article,' prep., or interj.] An exclamation, implying 'Make room (for a dance).'

1612 CHAPMAN *Widows Tears* Dodsl. *O.P.* (1780) VI. 185 A hall, a hall, who's without there? **1808** SCOTT *Marmion* v. xvii, And to his nobles loud did call,—Lords to the dance,—a hall! a hall!

†**a hand**, *phr. Obs.* [see A *prep.*[1] and HAND.] At hand.

1637 GILLESPIE *Eng.-Pop. Cerem.* IV. viii. 38 Taking the *Gibeonites* to dwell a farre off, when they dwelt a hand.

†**aˈhang**, *v. Obs.* Forms: *Inf.* 1–3 **ahón**, 2 **ahonge.** *Pa. t.* 1 **aheng, ahong**, 3 **ahon.** *Pa. pple.* 1 **ahongen, ahangen.** *Imp.* 1 **ahóh.** [f. A- *pref.* 1 up + HANG; confused in ME. with AN-HANG.] *trans.* and *intr.* To hang up.

c **950** *Lindisf. Gosp.* Mark xv. 14 Ahoh hine [so *Rushw.* & *Hatton*]. *Ibid.* xv. 20 Ða gilæddun hine þætte hia ahengun hine. *c* **1160** *Hatton Gosp.* ibid., þæt hyo hine ahengen. *c* **1175** *Lamb. Hom.* 41 Uppon þan treon he him sceawede þe wrecche saulen ahonge. **1205** LAYAM. 20878 Whæðer swa ich wulle don: oðer slæn oðer ahon [**1250** an-hon]. **1230** *Marharete* 3 As fisch ahon on hoke.

ahead (əˈhɛd), *adv.* (and *prep.*) [A *prep.*[1] in, at + HEAD.] Originally a nautical term. Now used *fig.* in all its senses.

1. At the head, in advance, in front (of a moving company).

1628 DIGBY *Voy. Medit.* (1868) 2 That the Admirall.. shall each seuerall night goe ahead. **1666** *Lond. Gaz.* lx/3 Our Fregats then which went on head, made sail. **1697** DRYDEN *Æneid* (J.) And now the mighty Centaur seems to lead, And now the speedy Dolphin gets ahead. **1844** DISRAELI *Coningsby* v. iv. 208 We have polled all our dead men, and Millbank is seven a-head.

2. In a position to the front, in the direct line of one's motion.

1725 DE FOE *Voy. round World* (1840) 330 They saw it just before them, or, as the seaman call it, right ahead. **1793** SMEATON *Edystone L.* §92 When it blows right a-head from Plymouth Sound. **1867** SMYTH *Sailor's Word-bk.*, *Breakers ahead!* the common password to warn the officer of broken water in the direction of the course.

3. In a position or direction pointing forward.

1596 SIR F. VERE *Comm.* 32 Their ships lay thwart with their broadsides towards us, and most of us right a-head, that we could use but our chasing pieces. **1823** F. COOPER *Pioneer* iii. (1869) 14/1 One who looked on a-head to the wants of posterity. **1873** *Brit. Q. Rev.* Jan., To enable the four guns carried in it to be fired directly ahead or astern.

4. Of motion: Forward, onward.

1762 FALCONER *Shipwr.* I. 205 The boats with rowers mann'd are sent ahead.

5. Hence, Forward or onward at a rapid pace; headforemost, headlong; also *fig.* with headlong or unchecked course, unrestrainedly. *esp.* in the phrase ***to go a-head.***

1643 MILTON *Divorce* Ded. Wks. 1847, 123/1 Such whose capacity, since their youth run ahead into the easy creak of a system, sails there at will under the blown physiognomy of their unlaboured rudiments. **1694** R. LESTRANGE *Fables* (J.) They suffer them [children] to run ahead, and, when perverse inclinations are advanced into habits, there is no dealing with them. **1741** *Compl. Family-Piece* II. i. 288 'Tis the nature of the Hart, when he is close pursued, and almost spent, to make forth on Head. **1840** GEN. P. THOMPSON *Exerc.* (1842) V. 24 We 'go ahead' quite as fast, as either the transporters or transported. **1879** BROWNING *Ivàn* 111 He understood the case galloping straight a-head.

¶ Hence the adj. phr. **go-a-head** and its compounds.

1846 KINGSLEY *Life* (1877) I. 143 It is the scientific go-a-head-ism of the day which must save us. **1865** MILL *Repres. Govt.* 26/1 The striving go-ahead character of England and the United States.

6. a. ***ahead of***: away in front of, in advance of.

1748 ANSON *Voyage* III. vi. (ed. 4) 465 A boat ahead of us waved a red flag. **1825** *Br. Jonathan* I. 385, I was working, all the time, to get ahead of Edith. **1835** SIR J. ROSS *N.-W. Pass.* xlvi. 588 The large iceberg ahead of us. **1876** GREEN *Short Hist.* Epil., The rapid development of English industry for a time ran ahead of the world's demands.

b. With reference to time: in advance of, before; esp. in pred. phr. ***ahead of one's*** (or ***it's***) ***time***, having ideas too original to be immediately accepted; also, new, original, incorporating advanced technological devices.

1901 G. B. SHAW *Devil's Disciple* III. 78 We are some minutes ahead of you already. **1920** *National Rev.* Apr. 141 Men who had sympathized with the Allied cause some years ahead of President Wilson. **1934** G. B. SHAW *On Rocks* I. 219 Women and men who are ahead of their time. They alone can lead the present into the future. They are ghosts from the future. **1947** *Redbook* Sept. 112/3 Henry's ahead of his time. **1965** A. J. P. TAYLOR *Eng. Hist. 1914–45* viii. 272 Henderson..secured the withdrawal of Allied troops from the Rhineland five years ahead of time. **1972** T. STOPPARD *Jumpers* II. 80 That astronaut..[is] going to find he was only twenty years ahead of his time. **1977** *Time* 21 Nov. 15 (Advt.), Seiko has maintained its position as world leader in Digital Quartz by consistently introducing new, ahead-of-their-time watches. **1982** *Times* 27 Feb. 13/2 Ahead of results on Monday Barclays Bank shed 5p to 351p.

7. quasi-*prep.* Short for *ahead of*.

1596 SIR F. VERE *Comm.* 32 Sir Walter Raleigh came upon my left side with his ship; and very little a head me cast his anchor.

8. Used temporally: in or for the future; in advance.

1900 W. F. DRANNAN *31 Years on Plains* 132 Johnnie West and I having enough meat ahead to last several days, we pulled out for Taos. **1907** G. B. SHAW *Major Barbara* I. 191 Charles Lomax will be a millionaire at 35. But that is ten years ahead. *a* **1918** W. OWEN *Coll. Poems* (1963) 64 Your fifty years ahead seem none too many? **1922** JOYCE *Ulysses* 602 They're full up for the next three weeks, man. God, you've to book ahead, man. **1945** E. WAUGH *Brideshead Revisited* I. v. 123 Men..in all the full flood of academic and athletic success, of popularity and the promise of great rewards ahead. **1954** TOLKIEN *Two Towers* III. iv. 90 We have a long way to go, and there is time ahead for thought. **1969** AUDEN *City without Walls* 75 When courage fails, when hopes are fading, Think on the victory ahead. **1981** R. HAYMAN *K* iv. 34 It was a relief that the dreaded examination no longer lay ahead.

a-head, *phr.* (= for each): see A *adj.*[2] 4 and HEAD.

aheap (əˈhiːp), *adv.*, prop. *phr.* [A *prep.*[1] of state, in + HEAP.] In a heap, 'all of a heap.'
1827 HOOD *Mids. Fairies* xvi, Some fresh bruit, Startled me all aheap. **1879** J. D. LONG *Æneid* II. 662 He falls aheap, and in a gush of blood Pours out his life.

†**aˈheat**, *phr. Obs.* [A *prep.*[1] of state + HEAT *sb.*] In or into heat.
1587 GOLDING *De Mornay* (1617) Pref., To chafe them a heate, that are waxed colde.

†**aˈheave**, *v. Obs.* Forms: 1 ahebb-an, 2 ahebben, ahefen, 3 aheue. *Pa. t.* 1–3 ahóf, 3 ahef. *Pa. pple.* ahafen. [f. A *pref.* 1 up + HEAVE, OE. *hebban.* Cogn. w. OS. *âhebbian*, OHG. *arhefan* (mod.G. *erheben*), Goth. *ushafjan.*] To heave, lift up.
c **1000** *Ags. Gosp.* Luke xviii. 13 Nolde furðun his eaȝan ahebban úp to þam heofone. *c* **1160** *Hatton Gosp.* ibid., Nolde for-ðan his eaȝen ahebben. *c* **1175** *Lamb. Hom.* 113 God ahef[ð] of mexe þene mon þe he wule. **1205** LAYAM. 21626 Cador his sweord ahof. **1230** *Marharete* 5 þe edle meiden ahef hire heorte [and] heaued uppward to þe heouene.

a-height (əˈhaɪt) *phr. arch.* [A *prep.*[1] + HEIGHT. The full *on height* is equally common.] On high, aloft. (Of position and direction.)
1605 SHAKS. *Lear* IV. vi. 58 From the dread Somnet of this Chalkie Bourne Looke vp a height. **1622** *Rawleigh's Ghost* 109 The brasen serpent being hanged a height. **1813** HOGG *Queen's Wake* 160 Lord Darcie's sword he forced ahight.

ahem (əˈhɛm), *int.* (and *sb.*)[a lengthened form of *hem!* an inarticulate sound made in clearing the throat.] An exclamation to attract attention to the speaker, or to give him time to consider what he is to say; also, to express disapproval by a factitious clearing of the throat. Hence as *sb.*
1763 C. JOHNSTONE *Reverie* II. 151 Hem! ahem! In the first place, said he, clearing his voice. **1814** J. BOSWELL *Justiciary Opera* 65 Gal-lery—si-lence—Ahem! **1848** G. E. JEWSBURY *Let.* 12 Aug. (1892) 252 George Sand corresponds with Miss——, and calls her the 'sister of her soul'. Ahem! **1928** R. CAMPBELL *Wayzgoose* ii. 58 Then having seen his error, [he] paled with fear And coughed—Ahem, we'll leave the matter here! **1929** D. H. LAWRENCE *Pansies* 147 They were just a bloody collective fraud, That was what their *Ahem!* meant.

ahem (əˈhɛm), *v.* [f. AHEM *int.*] *intr.* To exclaim 'ahem!'; also *trans.*, to pass off with the exclamation 'ahem!'.
1839 *Fraser's Mag.* XIX. 125 He immediately 'a-hems' away his jocularity. **1876** MEREDITH *Beauch. Career* III. ix. 166 Tuckham brushed his hand over his mouth and ahemed. **1891** —— *One of our Conq.* I. xiii. 240 He..pulled the waistcoat, and swelled it, ahemming.

ahenean, variant of AENEAN.

†**aˈhere**, *v. Obs. rare*[−1]. [prob. for ȝe-, *i-here(n*, OE. *ȝehieran*; there was no OE. *a-hieran.*] To hear.
a **1400** *Octouian* 23 Of oon the best ye mowne a-here That hyght Ottouyan.

a-hey (əˈheɪ), *int.* [a lengthened form of HEY; an exclamation to arouse the person addressed.] = Hey! ho!
1705 VANBRUGH *Confederacy* III. i, Where's this old woman?—A-hey!..nobody at home? **1751** SMOLLETT *Per. Pic.* II. lxvi. 225 Ahey!..you herring-fac'd son of a sea-calf. **1815** *Hist. J. Decastro, etc.* iii. 50 Ahey! how is all this? a blank page!

†**a-high** (əˈhaɪ), *adv.*, prop. *phr. Obs.* Forms: 4–5 a-hy, a hyȝe, 4–6 a-hygh(e, ahighe, 6–9 a-high. [A *prep.*[1] of general position, on + HIGH. The full form *on high* is now alone used.]
1. On high, aloft.
a **1300** *K. Alis.* 6236 Roches two So ahygh so any mon myghte seone. **1490** CAXTON *Eneydos* xvi. 64 He drewe sowles out of helle and made hem to come vp ahighe. **1594** SHAKS. *Rich. III*, IV. iv. 86 One heaued a-high, to be hurl'd downe below. **1676** HOBBES *Homer* 351 Their chars sometimes are in the air a high And sometimes on the ground. **1823** HONE *Anc. Myst.* 235 At the Cross in the 'Crosschepyng' were divers angels censing ahigh on the cross.
2. In high or loud tones; aloud. Cf. Fr. *en haut*, *hautement.*
1303 R. BRUNNE *Handl. Synne* 1549 She spake euer vyleyny Among here felaws al ahy. **1489** CAXTON *Faytes of Armes* II. vi. 102 He sayd thus al ahighe in audyence.

†**a-high-lone**, *adv. phr. Obs.* Prob. a mere emphasizing of *alone*, i.e. *all-one*, improperly divided as *a-lone*, whence emphatically *a-high-lone*, *an-high-lone*. Cf. *high noon*, *high carnival*, Shakspere's *high gravel blind*: see HIGH.
1597 SHAKS. *Rom. & Jul.* I. iii. 37 [*Q^o* 1597 *has*] For then she could stand high lone [*1st Fol.* 1623 alone]. **1604** MIDDLETON *Blurt* II. ii. Wks. I. 262 When I could not stand a-high-lone without I held by a thing. **1664** COTTON *Scarron.* (1692) 16 (D.) But e'er this colt..Was foal'd, and first 'gan stand an-high-lone.

‖**ahimsa** (əˈhɪmsɑː). *Hindu Philos.* [Skr., f. *a* without + *himsa* injury.] The doctrine of non-violence or non-killing.
1875 MONIER WILLIAMS *Indian Wisdom* x. 249, I am told ..that, notwithstanding the strict rules of *a-hiṃsā*, the 'Society for Prevention of Cruelty to Animals' might find work to do in some parts of India. **1884** H. JACOBI *Gaina Sutrâs* in *Sacred Bks. East* XXII. p. xxi, The stress which is laid on the ahiṃsâ or not killing of living beings. **1913** J. N. FARQUHAR *Crown of Hinduism* vii. 263 The idea at the basis of ahimsa is that all life is sacred, and that no holy man can take life. **1915** M. K. GANDHI *Speeches & Writings* (ed. 3, 1922) 236 Our religion is based upon *ahimsa*, which in its active form is nothing but Love. **1936** A. HUXLEY *Eyeless in Gaza* xi. 150 How foolish of Satan to tempt a, by definition, *ahimsa*-practising Messiah with fame, dominion, ambition. **1962** *Economist* 27 Oct. 330/2 *Ahimsa* is not the only thread in Indian political tradition.

aˈhind, aˈhint, *adv.* and *prep. dial.* [f. A- *pref.* 2 + HIND; cf. *a-fore* = *be-fore.* Early ME. had *at-hind* (OE. *æt-hindan*) as well as *be-hind.*] Behind.
1768 A. ROSS *Helenore* 68 (JAM.) And ye are following on wi' what's ahind. **1816** SCOTT *Black Dw.* iv. 26, I ance heard ane whistle ahint me in the moss. **1881** EVANS *Leicester Gloss.*, *Ahind*, behind.

a-hiˈstoric (æ-, eɪ-). [A- 14 + HISTORIC *a.*] Not historic; lacking an historical background.
1937 WYNDHAM LEWIS *Let.* 21 Nov. (1963) 246 My mind is *ahistoric*, I would welcome the clean sweep. **1941** L. B. NAMIER in *19th Cent.* Nov. 276 The Jews who, by reducing themselves to the level of a nondescript, a-historic group, cast away the dignity of a nation. **1952** AUDEN *Nones* 58 Their a-historic Antipathy forever gripes All ages and somatic types.

a-hiˈstorical, *a.* [f. A- 14 + HISTORICAL *a.*] Regardless of, or indifferent to, the historical aspect; not historical.
1957 J. C. MCKINNEY in Becker & Boskoff *Mod. Sociol. Theory* vii. 228 American sociology has been generally ahistorical in its approach to the study of society. It has instead concerned itself with the realm of 'contemporary' events. **1960** H. READ *Forms of Things Unknown* ix. 146 It will be one of my purposes..to maintain that the negation of the historical present is not to be confused with an apathetic nihilism..that on the contrary, this a-historical art..is the only positive evidence of renewal..in the visual arts of our time. **1962** EVANS-PRITCHARD *Essays Soc. Anthrop.* iii. 46 Durkheim, though perhaps not anti-historical, had been ahistorical, at any rate in the sense that his developmental studies were in the field of evolutionary typology rather than of history proper.

ahlas, obs. (Chapman's) form of ALAS.

†**a-ˈhoight, a-ˈhoit**, *adv.* (prop. *phr.*) *Obs.* [A *prep.*[1] + HOIT *v.* Cf. *hoity-toity.*] In reckless jollity; wantonly, without restraint.
1598 FLORIO, *Intresca*, iesting, iugling, dauncing, iumbling, all a hoit. **1611** COTGR., *Estre au dessus du vent*, To flourish, liue in prosperitie, be all a flaunt or a hoight. **1611** —— *Letabonde, jocund, frolicke, buxome, all-ahoight.*

a-ˈhold, *adv. phr.* [A *prep.*[1] + HOLD.] †**1.** *Obs.* 'A term of our early navigators, for bringing a ship close to the wind, so as to hold or keep to it.' Adm. Smyth.
1610 SHAKS. *Temp.* I. i. 52 Lay her a hold, a hold, set her two courses; off to Sea againe, lay her off.
2. ***a-hold of***: holding (something). Also in ***to catch, lay, take***, etc., ***a-hold of, on, upon***: see HOLD *sb.*[1] 2. Also **a-holt** (see HOLT[2]). *colloq.* or *dial.*
1872 E. EGGLESTON *End of World* xi. 77 You gripped a-holt of the truth. **1879** *Scribner's Monthly* May 17/1 With one bee a-hold of your collar..and another a-hold of each arm. *a* **1881** LANIER *Poems* (1892) 17, I will heartily lay me a-hold on the greatness of God. **1887** MORRIS *Odyss.* x. 264 He caught ahold upon me. **1925** E. HEMINGWAY *In our Time* (1926) v. 79 Nick dropped his wrist. 'Listen,' Ad Francis said. 'Take ahold again.' **1959** C. MACINNES *Absolute Beginners* 107 Some of the birds tried to get aholt of me.

-aholic (əˈhɒlɪk). *colloq.* (orig. *U.S.*). Also **-(o)holic.** The final element of WORKAHOLIC (after ALCOHOLIC *sb.* 2) used as a suffix forming sbs., as ***computerholic***, ***newsaholic***, ***spendaholic***, etc., (chiefly humorous nonce-words) denoting one who appears to be addicted to the object, activity, etc., specified; a person subject to an inordinate craving for or obsession with (something).
1965 P. WYDEN *Overweight Society* vi. 106, I was a sugaraholic...Mom kept saying, 'You eat your spinach and I'll give you a piece of candy.' **1971** *Southern Living* May 29/1 Donald Goldstein..probably knows more manufacturers personally than Porter and other club manufacturers. Goldstein, you see, is a 'golfaholic'. **1972** *Time* 24 July 53/1 Thousands of men were on it consistently enough to be dubbed 'hashaholics' by their buddies. **1973** *Times* 19 Mar. 7/1 The organization called Weightwatchers describes..its members as carboholics. **1974** *Washington Post* 2 Dec. A25/1 Until Thanksgiving Day, I had considered myself just another enthusiastic fan of pro football, not an abuser, a footballaholic. **1977** *New Scientist* 19 May 405 There are clearly more 'computerholics' in Britain than many in the business ever imagined. **1979** *Daily Tel.* 27 Oct. 15/8 All journalists, in some degree, are newsaholics. **1982** *Chicago Sun-Times* 31 Aug. 37 The guy is a womanizer, a spend-a-holic, uses dope and is strictly no good. **1985** *N.Y. Times* 13 Jan. 14/5 Barbara Shepherd, owner and manager of Book Tree,..said she was a 'bookaholic'.

A-horizon: see HORIZON *sb.*

ahorse (əˈhɔːs), *adv.* [f. A *prep.*[1] + HORSE *sb.*; cf. ME. *on hors* (HORSE *sb.* 16).] = A-HORSEBACK.
1808 R. ANDERSON *Ballads in Cumberland Dialect* 74 Frae east and west, beath rich and peer, A-horse, a-fit, caw in. **1860** W. H. RUSSELL *Diary India* II. 126 Young ladies and gentlemen..a-horse and a-foot. **1925** *Chambers's Jrnl.* Xmas No. 854/2 When he and I encountered, ahorse on a road, we pulled up our horses and conversed.

a-ˈhorseback, *adv. phr. arch.* [A *prep.*[1] of state, on + HORSEBACK.] On horseback.
1490 CAXTON *Eneydos* li. 145 Whan he was sette ahorsbacke. **1665–9** BOYLE *Occas. Refl.* II. ix. (1675) 126 The careless Wanderer..may be said to have been long a Horse-back. **1771** SMOLLETT *Humph. Cl.* (1815) 189 There were two suspicious fellows a-horseback at the end of a lane. **1852** THACKERAY *Esmond* I. v. (1876) 35 And he never was known to wear his silk, only his stuff one, a-horseback.

ahoy (əˈhɔɪ), *int. Naut.* [A *int.* + HOY.]
A. *int.* A nautical call used in hailing.
1751 SMOLLETT *Per. Pic.* (1779) I. ii. 12 Ho! the house a hoy. **1828** MOORE *Meeting of Ships* ii. 8 Ship ahoy! ship ahoy! what cheer? what cheer? **1873** SYMONDS *Grk. Poets* viii. 268 The good times when the sailor only knew enough to sing out 'Ahoy' and call for biscuit.
B. as *vb.* To call ahoy. (Cf. *to hurrah*, *halloo.*)
1881 *Century Mag.* XXIII. 54 'Schooner ahoy!' says a voice from the shore, and she ahoys.

aht, obs. f. AUGHT *sb.* and *a.*

ahtande, ahte, ahtene, obs. ff. EIGHTH, EIGHT, EIGHTEEN.

ahte, obs pa. t. of OWE, OUGHT.

ahtliche, var. AUGHTLY, *adv. Obs.*, worthily.

†**a-ˈhuff**, *adv. phr. Obs.* [A *prep.*[1] + HUFF.] In a huff.
1598 GREENE *James IV* (1861) 210 Set cap a-huff and challenge him the field.

a-hull (əˈhʌl), *adv. phr. Naut.* [A *prep.*[1] of state + HULL.] (See quot.)
1582 N. LICHEFIELD *East Ind.* 73 All this time the shippes laye a hull. **1628** DIGBY *Voy. Medit.* (1868) 78 Then wee lay a hull till wee gott a new maine course to the yard. *a* **1733** NORTH *Lives of Norths* II. 316 All this while the ship ploughed her mizen shrouds under water, and then we were fain to lie a-hull at the mercy of the sea and waves. **1867** SMYTH *Sailor's Word-bk.* s.v. *Hull*, *To strike hull* in a storm, is to take in her sails and lash the helm on the lee side of the ship, which is termed *to lie a-hull.*

a-hum (əˈhʌm), *adv. phr.* [A *prep.*[1] in + HUM.] In a hum, humming.
1859 COLEMAN *Woodl. Heaths* (1866) 120 The bright air is ..a-hum with the song of the bee.

aˈhunger, *adv.* or *pred. a.* [f. A- *pref.* + HUNGER; cf. ANHUNGERED.] Hungry; hungering.
c **1450** *Mirk's Festial* 127/10 þe pore..aboden.., sor ahongyr. **1830** *Blackw. Mag.* Mar. 511/1 The maw of the public, ahunger and athirst for stories of peril. **1922** JOYCE *Ulysses* 261 Lenehan, small eyes ahunger on her humming.

a-hungered (əˈhʌŋgəd), *ppl. a. arch.* [perh. representing a lost OE. *a-hyngred* (cf. Germ. *erhungert*), or a later formation with A- *pref.* 1 intensive; but more probably a later form of OF-HUNGERED, OE. *of-hyngred*, pa. pple. of vb. *of-hyngran* to suffer hunger, be weak with hunger, be very hungry. Cf. AFINGERED. By confusion of A- *2* and A- *3*, the prefix was sometimes expanded to *an-*, *on-*; cf. A-HIGH, AN-HUNGERED.] Oppressed with hunger; very hungry.
1377 LANGL. *P. Pl.* B. x. 59 Bothe afyngred [*v.r.* a-hungred, an-hungred] and a-thurst [*v.r.* a-thrust, a-thrist, a-furst], and for chele quake. **1398** TREVISA *Barth. De P.R.* XII. xxv. (1495) 429 Alwaye he is a hungryd whyle he liuyth. **1567** JEWEL *Def. Apol.* (R.) When their eies were ful they put vp theire kniues and rose ahungred. **1820** KEATS *Hyperion* II. 163 Saturn's ear Is all a-hunger'd. **1868** GEO. ELIOT *Sp. Gypsy* II. 194 Soothe the frightened bird And feed the child a-hungered.

a-ˈhungry, *a.* [f. HUNGRY; the prefix is due to form-assoc. with A-HUNGERED, and, perhaps, A-COLD; it was probably taken as emphatic. Also expanded to AN-HUNGRY.] Hungry, in a hungry condition.
c **1460** *Towneley Myst.* iii. 499 The ravyn is a hungrye All way. **1601** SHAKS. *Twel. N.* II. iii. 137 'Twere as good a deede as to drink when a man's a hungrie. **1832** *Fraser's Mag.* Nov. 527 The baby in the cradle is for ever a-hungry, or a-thirsty. **1852** *Tait's Mag.* XIX. 228 The Whigs..were a-thirst and a-hungry for office. **1933** C. MILLER *Lamb in Bosom* (1934) viii. 91 Jasper found that he was not a-hungry.

a-hunt (əˈhʌnt), *adv. phr.* [A *prep.*[1] + HUNT.] On the hunt.
1875 BROWNING *Aristoph. Apol.* 272 Follow you quick, with a whizz, as the hounds a-hunt with the huntsman. **1880** J. B. BROWN in *Gd. Wds.* Dec. 821 A priest of the Inquisition ahunt for blood.

a-hush (ə'hʌʃ), *adv.* (prop. *phr.*). [A *prep.*[1] in + HUSH.] In a hushed condition, hushed.
Mod. Nature seems to keep herself a-hush.

ahwene, variant of AWHENE *v. Obs.*, to vex.

ai, aie, obs. forms of AY, AYE, and of EGG.

ai ('ɑːɪ). *Zool.* [a. Braz. *aï, haï* (Fr. *aï, hay*) repr. the animal's cry.] A kind of Sloth (*Bradypus tridactylus*, family *Tardigrada*, order *Edentata*) found in South America.
1693 in *Phil. Trans.* XVII. 851 The American Creature called Ai or Sloth. **1833** *Penny Cycl.* I. 233 They emit a feeble, plaintive cry, resembling the word *Ai*, which is the origin of the name they bear among the Europeans settled in America. **1847** CARPENTER *Zool.* §241 The Ais or three-toed Sloths.. are inhabitants of the dense forests of the tropical portion of South America.

ai- in late north. and Sc. is used for long *ā*, as *aiblings, aill, ain, ait, air, tairge*, for *ablings, ale, aan* (own), *ate* (oat), *are* (oar), *targe*; mod.Sc. *airch, airm*, for *arch, arm*. Now pronounced (eː).

Aich('s) metal. [Named after the patentee Johann *Aich* (3 Feb. 1860).] An alloy of copper, zinc, and iron, used in gun-making.
1867 BLOXAM *Chem.* 342 Aich (or Gedge's) metal. **1875** HUNT & RUDLER *Ure's Dict. Arts* (ed. 7), *Aich metal.* **1958** MERRIMAN *Dict. Metallurgy* 3/1 *Aich's Metal*, a brass of the 60/40 type that has good casting properties.

aid (eɪd), *v.* Forms: 5 eyde, 5–6 ayde, 6–7 ayd, aide, 7– aid. [a. OFr. *aide-r, -ier* (Pr. *ajuda-r*):—L. *adjūtā-re*, freq. of *adjuvā-re* to give help to; f. *ad* to + *juvā-re* to help. (In the OFr. *aidier, ai-* = L. *adju-*, *d* disappearing as usual, and *u* as following secondary accent in ˌ*adju'tāre*; *i* was semi-vowel (j) = L. *j*.)]

1. *trans.* To give help, support, or assistance to; to help, assist, succour.
[*Aiding* quoted from CHAUCER *Persones T.* by Richardson is not genuine.]
1483 CAXTON *Cato* a iij b, To ayde helpe and Susteyne them in theyr necessytees. **1488** W. PASTON in *Lett.* 904 III. 344 My Lord Woddevyle and other schulde have gone over in to Breten to have eyded the Duke of Breten. **1591** SHAKS. *1 Hen. VI*, v. iii. 7 Ye choise spirits.. Appeare, and ayde me in this enterprize! **1611** BIBLE *1 Macc.* viii. 26 Neither shal they.. aide them with victuals, weapons, money, or ships. **1795** SEWEL tr. *Hist. Quakers* I. iv. 239, I would have aided him out of the country but he would not go. **1876** FREEMAN *Norm. Conq.* I. v. 286 The invasion was aided and abetted by Richard's subjects. **1878** G. MACDONALD *Ann. Quiet Neighb.* xxviii. 478 Every appliance that could alleviate suffering or aid recovery.

2. *absol.* and with *inf.*
1601 SHAKS. *Alls Well* IV. iv. 12 Where, heaven ayding.. Wee'l be before our welcome. **1611** —— *Wint. T.* v. ii. 77 All the Instruments which ayded to expose the Child. **1806** COLERIDGE *Christabel* I. 130 But this she knows.. That saints will aid if men will call.

aid (eɪd), *sb.* Forms: 5 eide, 5–7 aide, ayde, 6–7 ayd, 7– aid. [a. OFr. *aïde, ayde*, earlier *aiude*, Strasb. oaths *aiudha, adiudha* (cf. Pr. *ajudha, ajuda*, Sp. *ayuda*):—late L. *adjūta*, sb. f. pa. pple. fem. of *adiuvāre* (see prec.) analogous to sbs. in *-ée, -āta*; see -ADE.]

1. a. Help, assistance, support, succour, relief.
1475 *Bk. Noblesse* 4 Be the eide of tho thre noble prynces. **1475** CAXTON *Jason* 18 b, If the goddes be in myn ayde. **1559** *Myrroure for Mag., Rich II*, vi. 1 Neyther lakt I ayde in any wicked dede. **1607** SHAKS. *Coriol.* I. vii. 3 If I do send, dispatch Those Centuries to our ayd. **1667** MILTON *P.L.* VI. 119 His puissance, trusting in the Almighty's aid, I mean to try. **1771** BURKE in *Corr.* (1844) I. 262 You have not called in the aid of fancy. **1807** CRABBE *Par. Reg.* II. 130 Friend of distress! the mourner feels thy aid. **1868** GEO. ELIOT *F. Holt* 22 She had never dressed herself without aid.

b. *in aid of*, in support of (a cause or charity). Hence, *fig.* and *colloq.* (presumably having its origin in the freq. use of the phr. in appealing for the public support of a cause), about, concerned with; esp. in phr., often disparaging, *what's this* (or *that*) *in aid of?*, what is the meaning or purpose of this?, what is this all about?
1837 *Playbill* in M. Morley *Old Marylebone Theatre* (1960) 20 A Benefit will take place in Aid of the Funds of the New Alms Houses. **1860** S. S. HENNELL (*title*) Thoughts in aid of faith. **1881** W. S. GILBERT *Patience* I. 19 In aid—in aid of a deserving charity, I've put myself up to be raffled for! **1915** *Times* 22 Oct. 11/3 Queen Alexandra.. was present at the Empire Theatre *matinée* in Aid of the British Red Cross Society. **1918** *Punch* 20 Nov. 332 (*caption*) Oh Mother,.. they've given us a whole holiday to-day in aid of the war. *a* **1935** T. E. LAWRENCE *Mint* (1936) 127 The hut lights were on and he had brought me a tin of tea and a hot sausage roll. 'Scram up!' he called... 'What's all this in aid of?' I asked, stupidly. **1935** MARSH & JELLETT *Nursing-Home Murder* xv. 231 'That's your disillusioned expression, Fox,' said Alleyn. 'What's it in aid of?' **1942** 'BLAKE' *We Rendezvous at Ten* ii. 41 The Group Captain called down the table to Roger: 'Find out what that's in aid of, Roger, will you?' **1949** E. BOWEN *Heat of Day* xvii. 315 What you *were* in aid of.. often was a mystery to me. **1956** 'M. INNES' *Old Hall, New Hall* viii. 70 He couldn't quite make out what Olivia's questions and speculations were in aid of.

2. a. *Eng. Law.* Help or assistance in defending an action, legally claimed by the defendant from some one who has a joint-interest in the defence. *to pray in aid*: to claim such assistance. *aid-prayer*, the appeal therefor.
1625 SIR H. FINCH *Law* (1636) 367 Ayd Prayer is for Tenant for life, to request him that hath the Inheritance, to helpe him plead.. and this Ayd Prayer is for the feeblenesse of his estate. **1751** CHAMBERS *Cycl.* s.v., A city or corporation, holding a fee-farm of the king, may pray in Aid of him, if anything be demanded of them relating thereto. **1809** TOMLINS *Law Dict.* s.v., There is a prayer in aid of patrons, by parsons, vicars, etc... And also servants having done anything lawfully in right of their masters, shall have aid of them.

b. *to call* or *crave in aid*, properly a legal phrase, also in a loose transf. use.
1927 *Observer* 8 May 16/2 Imagination craves the wireless in aid. **1928** *Ibid.* 1 July 13/4 Many [bishops].. would call in aid, as justifying their action, the use of the *Jus Liturgicum* inherent in their office.

3. a. *concr.* Anything by which assistance is given in performing an operation; anything helpful, a means or material source of help. *esp.* in *pl.* aids and appliances. *spec.* in *Horsemanship* (see quot. 1751).
1597 SHAKS. *2 Hen. IV*, I. iii. 24 Surmise Of Aydes incertaine should not be admitted. **1697** DRYDEN *Virg. Georg.* IV. 465 Whom, scarce my Sheep, and scarce my painful Plough, The needful Aids of Human Life allow. **1711** F. FULLER *Med. Gymn.* 58 Exercise may deserve to be taken as a common Aid to Physick. **1751** CHAMBERS *Cycl.*, *Aids*, in the manage, are helps, or assistances, by which the horseman contributes towards the motion or action required of the horse; by a discreet use of the bridle, caveson, spur, etc... Such a horse knows his *Aids*, answers his *Aids*, etc. **1824** COLERIDGE (*title*) Aids to Reflection. **1858** GLADSTONE *Homer* I. 23 He has furnished us with some aids towards the consideration of this question. **1953** G. BROOKE *Introd. Riding* i. 16 During the period that the novice is riding his first mount, he should learn the aids (correct and combined applications of his hands and legs).

b. Freq. with defining word, as *approach, artificial, hearing, homing, legal, radio-navigational, visual aid*: see these words.
1924 *Lancet* 31 May 1140/2 A new acoustic aid for the deaf. **1955** *Oxf. Jun. Encycl.* XI. 128/2 Hearing may be greatly improved by the use of.. electrical aids which amplify sounds.

c. *spec.* Material help given by one country to another, esp. economic assistance or material help given by a rich to a poor or underdeveloped country. Also *attrib.* and *Comb.* Cf. MARSHALL.
1940 *Economist* 5 Oct. 421/1 The United States' aid to Britain would be rendered ineffective. **1946** *Ann. Reg. 1945* 100 The difficulties of procuring American aid for Britain on acceptable terms. **1951** *Ann. Reg. 1950* 337 The U.S. aid conventions with the Associated States [of Indo-China]. **1958** *Spectator* 17 Jan. 65/3 Congress would like to buy missiles with foreign-aid money. **1964** *Listener* 16 Apr. 614/1 Since the Soviet Union and.. China have joined in the game of competitive aid-giving the Western Powers, it is argued, cannot afford to drop out. **1968** M. PYKE *Food & Society* xi. 165 Considerable thought has been given to the effectiveness of aid as a means of achieving the economic development and hence, presumably, the improved nutritional status, of poor countries. **1970** *Theol. Stud.* XXXI. 261 Such aid can also salve the conscience of Christians in the countries that control the world economy. **1974** M. B. BROWN *Econ. of Imperialism* iv. 95 The underdeveloped countries complain also of the overpricing of goods and shipping in their manufactured imports from developed lands, particularly in the case of aid-supported supplies. **1981** *Nat. Westminster Bank Q. Rev.* Aug. 36 Aid, or official development assistance (ODA).

d. As the second element in the names of events, etc., organized to raise money for particular charitable causes (see quots.), as *Band Aid, Live Aid*, etc.
Based on *Band Aid*, the name of the rock music group formed by Bob Geldof in Oct. 1984 to raise money for famine-relief in Ethiopia.
1984 *Times* 12 Dec. 3/2 *Do They Know It's Christmas*, [a record] on which Boy George, Sting, George Michael, members of Duran Duran, Status Quo, and U2 appear under the joint name of Band Aid. **1985** *Music Week* 2 Feb. 2/3 Britain has been the source of musically-based political commentary—from the mostly British composition of Band Aid to Frankie Goes to Hollywood. **1985** *Times* 11 July 32/1 The failure of Live Aid to penetrate the poorer countries is unlikely to affect adversely the amount of money it makes. *Ibid.* 5 Nov. 13/1 The fashion world is smouldering with gossip about Fashion Aid, which takes off like a rocket at the Albert Hall tonight. **1985** *Sunday Tel.* (Colour Suppl.) 29 Dec. 5/2 Other events such as Visual Aid, the sale of limited edition prints at auction, and School Aid, in which.. schoolchildren are to be asked to contribute pocket money for famine relief. **1986** *Daily Tel.* 24 Sept. 5/2 Top performers due to appear in 'Classic Aid' to raise money for refugee relief will include Vladimir Ashkenazy, [etc.].

4. *Eng. Hist.* A pecuniary grant in aid; a grant of a subsidy or tax to the king for an extraordinary purpose. *Later*, an exchequer loan.
c **1460** FORTESCUE *Abs. & Lim Mon.* (1714) 52 For the expensis wherof, he schal not so sodenly have Ayde of his People. **1523** LD. BERNERS *Froissart* I. ccclxxxvii. 663 The kyng and his counsayle wolde generally reyse vp throughe all Fraunce ayedes, fowages, tayles and subsydes. **1669** MARVELL *Corr.* 130 Wks. 1875 II. 294 The House did.. vote an aid to his Majesty not exceeding the summe of 400,000*l.* **1702** *Lond. Gaz.* mmmdcccix/8 Dropt.. a Talley on the Fourth 4*s.* Aid of 100o*l.* No. 2058. **1862** LD. BROUGHAM *Brit. Const.* xii. 166 For the granting of an aid or supply to the crown.

5. *Feudal System.* A pecuniary contribution by a feudal vassal to his lord; limited by *Magna Carta* to three special occasions.
1590 SWINBURN *Testaments* 72 The lordes lost their.. aids, 'Pur faire fitz chiualer & pur file marier.' **1649** SELDEN *Laws of Eng.* I. lxii. (1739) 125 The aids were of three kinds, one to make the Lord's eldest Son Knight, the other to marry his eldest Daughter; the third to help him to pay a relief to his Lord Paramount. **1753** CHAMBERS *Cycl. Supp.* s.v., The bishops also received aids, *auxilia episcopi.* **1768** BLACKSTONE *Comm.* II. 63 Aids were originally mere benevolences granted by the tenant to his lord, in times of difficulty and distress. **1868** CHAMBERS *Encycl.* I. 92 These Aids were abolished by 12 Car. II. c. 24.

6. *French Hist.* (*pl.*) Customs-dues. *Court of Aids*, the Court that supervised the customs-dues.
1714 *Fr. Bk. Rates* 29 Mr. John Rouvelin, Farmer-General of our Aids. **1753** CHAMBERS *Cycl. Supp.*, *Aids*, in French laws, denote a duty paid on all goods sold and transported either out of, or into the kingdom. **1792** A. YOUNG *Trav. France* 20 The house of the first president of the court of aids.

7. a. A person who renders help or assistance; a helper, an assistant; *pl.* auxiliaries. (Cf. Fr. *aide*, L. *auxilium*, and Eng. *help*, all applied to persons.)
1569 *Epitaph on Bonner* in *Harl. Misc.* I. 615 His ayds took always pain To keep their god, their hope, their trust. **1587** HOLINSHED *Chron.* I. 37/2 He had no legionarie souldiers, but certeine bands of aids. **1611** BIBLE *Tobit* viii. 6 It is not good that man should bee alone, let vs make vnto him an aide like to himselfe [cf. WYCLIF *Gen.* ii. 18 An help lijk to him self]. **1738** WESLEY *Ps.* cxxi. 1 The Lord that built the Earth and Skies Is my perpetual Aid. **1838** ARNOLD *Rome* I. 397 He was at the head of a mighty army; for the Latins and the Hernicans had brought their aids.

b. *U.S.* = AIDE. See also AID-DE-CAMP.
1780 S. HOLTEN in *Essex Inst. Coll.* (1920) LVI. 94 One of General Lincoln's aids is arrived with the accounts of the surrender of Charlestown. **1832** J. P. KENNEDY *Swallow Barn* I. xix. 190 Ned and myself formed part of his retinue, like a pair of aids somewhat behind the commander-in-chief. **1907** *Chicago Tribune* 8 May 2 Gen. A. W. Greely.. arrived with his.. aids.

8. *Comb.* and *attrib.*, chiefly in sense 7, as **aid-band, -cohort, -force, -soldier**; or in sense 5, as **aid-money**: (all *obs.*). Also **aid-major** *obs.* an adjutant; **aid-post**, a post at which wounded soldiers receive first medical attention; **aid-prayer** in *Law*: see 2.
1600 HOLLAND *Livy* XXX. xxxiii. 763 c, Then he embattailed the aid souldiers [*auxilia*] of the Ligurians. **1603** GREENWEY *Tacitus Ann.* XII. viii. (1622) 166 They intercepted two ayde-bandes. **1610** HOLLAND *Camden's Brit.* II. 65 A small powre of Aid-forces. **1635** BACON *Use of Com. Law* 32 Ayde money to make the Kings eldest son a knight, or to marry his eldest daughter. **1670** COTTON *Espernon* III. XII. 632 The Office of Aide Major to the Regiment of Guards. **1691** *Lond. Gaz.* mmdcc/2 *L'Assurance* Aid-Major killed. **1916** 'BOYD CABLE' *Action Front* 49 To walk.. to the nearest aid-post and hospital. *a* **1917** E. A. MACKINTOSH *War, the Liberator* (1918) 149 The Aid Post was like a shambles with blood and wounded men.

aidable ('eɪdəb(ə)l), *a.* [f. AID *v.* + -ABLE; cf. MFr. *aidable*, refash. on OFr. *ayable*:—L. *adjūtābilis* serviceable, f. *adjūtā-re*: see AID *v.*]
†**1.** Capable of aiding; helpful. *Obs. rare.*
1594 CAREW tr. *Huarte's Trial of Wits* vii. (1596) 94 Such bodily qualities as are aidable to that effect.
2. Capable of being helped. *rare*$^{-0}$.

aidance ('eɪdəns). [a. MFr. *aidance*, f. *aider*: see AID *v.* and -NCE.] Assistance, aid; means of help.
1593 SHAKS. *2 Hen. VI*, III. ii. 165 Aydance 'gainst the enemy. **1633** P. FLETCHER *Purple Isl.* VI. I, Who when for ought the aged Grandsire sends, With swift yet backward steps his helping aidance lends. **1810** COLERIDGE *Friend* (1865) 61 All the aidances given by religion. **1860** TH. MARTIN *Horace* 111 Apollo's self his aidance lent.

aidant ('eɪdənt), *a.* and *sb.* Also 5 **ayante, aydaunt**, 6 **aydant**. [a. OFr. *aiant, aidant* pr. pple. of *aider* (also *aier*): see AID *v.*]
A. *adj.* Helping, assisting; helpful.
1483 CAXTON *Gold. Leg.* 420/1 Saynt Thomas whos merytes be unto us aydaunte and helpyng. **1605** SHAKS. *Lear* IV. iv. 17 Be aydant and remediate In the good man's distress! **1830** COLERIDGE *Ch. & St.* 179, I would gladly be aidant, as far as my poor mite of judgment will enable me. **1855** BAILEY *Mystic* 91 The topaz, aidant in all holy rites.
B. *sb.* A helper, assistant. *rare.*
1475 CAXTON *Jason* 11 The ayantes and helpers of the quene. **1611** COTGR., *Aide*, an aidant, helper. **1879** SIR R. PHILLIMORE in *Law Rep. Prob. Div.* V. 33 The Court is now called upon to be an aidant to the enforcement of a judgment given by a Portuguese Court.

aid-de-camp, occas. (chiefly *U.S.*) var. AIDE-DE-CAMP.
1690 R. DAVIES *Jrnl.* 4 Aug. (1857) 134 Scravenmore's aid-de-camp came to us again. **1732** [see AIDE-DE-CAMP]. **1762** C. BRIETZCKE *Diary* 9 Feb. in *N. & Q.* (1959) CCIV. 136/2 Jack spoke to Mr. Percival in the Boxes who was aid de camp to Hodgson. **1776** *Jrnl. Cont. Congress* V. 418 Resolved, That the aids de camp of the commander in chief rank as lieutenant colonels. **1878** J. H. BEADLE *Western Wilds* xxxiii. 532 He.. was made full captain and aid-de-camp of General McClellan.

aide, short for AIDE-DE-CAMP. Also more widely (chiefly *N. Amer.*), (one employed as) an assistant, an ancillary worker; freq. with qualifying word indicating the sphere of work. Cf. AID 7.

1777 J. M. LINCOLN *Papers R. Lincoln* (1904) 11 They.. fired on the flag and killed an ade. **1826** COOPER *Mohicans* xxxiii, Attended by the aide of Montcalm with his guard. **1837** J. F. COOPER *Recoll. Europe* I. v. 177 The prefects are no more than so many political *aides*, whose duty it is to carry into effect the orders that emanate from the great head. **1864** SALA in *Daily Tel.* 23 Nov., If he made a gesture.. an attentive aide bustled forward. **1876** LODGE in *N. Amer. Rev.* CXXIII. 117 Picked out by Washington to serve as his confidential aide. **1881** H. W. NICHOLSON *From Sword to Share* xvii. 114 The Bishop and his *aides* are making strenuous efforts to build a permanent stone edifice. **1930** *Amer. Speech* VI. 112 S.F. Inspector made aide to postmaster. **1952** *Manch. Guard. Weekly* 12 June 3/2 General MacArthur.. is on inactive status, but he receives .. the services of three military aides. **1956** R. MACAULAY *Towers of Trebizond* ii. 18 She often took me with her on such expeditions, as illustrator, courier and general aide. **1962** K. KESEY *One flew over Cuckoo's Nest* I. 95 You may need a month of bedpans and slab baths to refresh your appreciation of just how little work you aides have to do on this ward. **1972** *New Society* 12 Oct. 115/1 (Advt.), London Borough of Hammersmith. Social Services Department. Family Aide... This new post has been created to supplement the activities of social workers in intensive efforts to support families and individuals at risk. **1984** *Daily Tel.* 26 Nov. 15/5 There is domiciliary care.. offered by 200 home helps, 18 aides and their organisers.

aided ('eɪdɪd), *ppl. a.* [f. AID *v.* + -ED.] **a.** Assisted.

1549 COVERDALE *Erasm. Paraphr. Hebr.* xi. 32 Who beyng ayded with the helpe of God achiued manye wonderful enterprises. **1611** COTGR., *Aidé*, aided, helped. **1816** CHALMERS *Let.* in *Life* (1851) II. 71 All that minuteness which the aided eye of man has been able to explore.

b. *spec.* Receiving financial aid; esp. (of a school) assisted by monetary grants from the government. So *grant-aided*, *state-aided*, adjs. (see at first element).

1882 [see STATE *sb.* 40b]. **1943** *Educ. Bill, Explan. Memorandum* (Cmd. 6492) 5 Aided schools: The managers of these schools will continue to appoint their own teachers and have the teachers' salaries and other maintenance charges paid by the local education authority.

‖**aide-de-camp** (ˌɛddəˈkɑ̃, ˈeɪddəˌkɒŋ). *Mil.* Pl. aides-de-camp. [Fr., lit. *camp-assistant*: see AID *sb.* 7.] An officer who assists a general in his military duties, conveying his orders, and procuring him intelligence.

1670 COTTON *Espernon* III. XI. 578 The Duke.. writ to St. Torse Aide de Camp, who commanded them. **1732** LEDIARD *Sethos* II. IX. 304 He declar'd him, from that instant, his aid-de-camp. **1808** WELLINGTON in Gurwood's *Desp.* IV. 14 That spare room may be kept for my horses and those of my Aides-de-Camp. **1844** *Queen's Regul. & Ord. Army* 61 A Subaltern Officer is not eligible to hold the appointment of Aide-de-Camp, until he has been present with his Regiment at least two years.

aide-de-campship (ˌeɪddəˈkɑ̃ʃɪp). [f. prec. + -SHIP.] The office or position of aide-de-camp.

1882 *Standard* 9 May 5/2 An aide de campship to the Queen is placed at the disposal of the First Lord of the Admiralty.

‖**aide-mémoire** (ˈeɪdmɛmwɑː(r), ɛdmemwar). [F., f. *aider* to help + *mémoire* MEMORY.] An aid to the memory; esp. in diplomatic use, a memorandum (cf. MEMOIR 2).

1846 G. G. LEWIS et al. (*title*) Aide-Mémoire to the Military Sciences. **1855** H. LAXTON (*title*) Examples of Building Construction, intended as an Aide-Memoire for the Professional Man. **1885** *Athenæum* 1 Aug. 151/1 *Catalogue Illustré du Salon*.. is more than a very useful *aide mémoire* of the great collection. **1923** *Westm. Gaz.* 3 July, No written document on the subject of the British questionnaires, even in the way of an aide memoire, will be handed to the Foreign Secretary. **1941** AUDEN *New Year Let.* I. 312 This aide-mémoire on what they say. **1955** *Times* 1 Aug. 5/6 The United States has sent to Bulgaria a strongly worded aide-mémoire, transmitted through the Swiss Government, protesting against the 'brutal attack'. **1957** *BBC Handbk.* 23 An agreement reached in 1947 between the BBC, the Government, and the Opposition, and embodied in an *Aide-Mémoire*.

aider ('eɪdə(r)). [f. AID *v.* + -ER[1]. Cf. OFr. *aidere*:—L. *adjūtātōr*.] One who, or that which, aids; a helper, assister, or supporter; a help, assistance.

1514 PACE in Ellis *Orig. Lett.* I. 37 I. 111 Th[ose that] were ayders and supporters here off suche. **1602** FULBECKE *1st Pt. Parall.* 9ix, This is felony in them, their aydors, and counsellors. **1660** R. COKE *Pow. & Subj.* 224 Every such offender, his ayders and abettors, shall be apprehended. **1677** HALE *Prim. Orig. Man.* IV. viii. 380 The Tenders and Ayders of his Grace and Guidance. **1841** LANE *Arab. Nights* III. 496 She found for herself no aider save weeping.

†**'aideress.** *Obs.* [f. prec. + -ESS.] A female helper; an adjutrix.

1491 CAXTON *How to Die* 21 Ayderesse and helper of all anguysshe.

aidful ('eɪdfʊl), *a.* [f. AID *sb.* + -FUL.] Full of, or abounding in, aid; helpful.

1598 ROWLANDS *Betr. of Christ* 53 Christs night-disciple aidfull did agree, To take his bodie from that guiltie tree. **1603** DANIEL *Epistles* (1717) 342 Thy Worthiness, and England's Hap beside Set thee in th' aidfull'st Room of Dignity. **1649** HALL *Cases of Consc.* IV. i. (1654) 290 When hee might be likely by his coming forth to bee aidfull to his said Parents. **1850** LYNCH *Theoph. Trinal* ix. 168 The fathers.. are yet amongst us as beneficent and aidful spirits.

aiding ('eɪdɪŋ), *vbl. sb.* [f. AID *v.* + -ING[1].] Helping, assistance. (Mostly gerundial.)

1839 KEIGHTLEY *Hist. Eng* II. 66 On condition of their aiding him to effect it.

aiding ('eɪdɪŋ), *ppl. a.* [f. AID *v.* + -ING[2].] Assisting, helping; helpful.

1552 HULOET, Aydynge or succourynge, *Auxiliaris.* **1594** SHAKS. *Rich. III*, I. iii. 96 She may helpe you to many faire preferments, And then deny her ayding hand therein. **1656** EARL MONM. *Advt. fr. Parnass.* 112 That he should be ayding to them upon all occasions. **17..** *Col. Rec. Penn.*, They shall in all cases be aiding to all its officers.

aidless ('eɪdlɪs), *a. poet.* [f. AID *sb.* + -LESS.]

†**1.** Affording no help, of no service, unserviceable, useless. *Obs.*

1674 GODFREY *Inj. & Abus. Phys.* 88 When the Apothecaries Drugs have proved aidless.

2. Bereft or void of help, unassisted, helpless.

1607 SHAKS. *Coriol.* II. ii. 116 Alone he entred The mortall Gate of th 'Citie.. aydelesse came off. **1637** MILTON *Comus* 574 The aidless innocent Lady, his wished prey. **1832** TENNYSON *Morte d' Arthur* 41 It is not meet, Sir King, to leave thee thus, Aidless, alone.

AIDS (eɪdz). Also **Aids.** [Acronym: see def.] **1.** Acquired immune deficiency syndrome: an illness (often if not always fatal) in which opportunistic infections or malignant tumours develop as a result of a severe loss of cellular immunity, which is itself caused by earlier infection with a retrovirus, HIV, transmitted in sexual fluids and blood. Freq. *attrib.* Cf. *acquired immune deficiency syndrome* s.v. ACQUIRED *ppl. a.* (a).

1982 *Morbidity & Mortality Weekly Rep.* 24 Sept. 508 CDC defines a case of AIDS as a disease, at least moderately predictive of a defect in cell-mediated immunity, occurring in a person with no known cause for diminished resistance to that disease. *Ibid.* 10 Dec. 653 The infant had no known contact with an AIDS patient. **1983** *New Scientist* 3 Feb. 289/1 In just one year the list of people at risk from AIDS has lengthened from male homosexuals, drug-abusers and Haitians, to include the entire population [of the U.S.A.]. **1983** *Observer* 26 June 10/9 Across the country, AIDS hysteria is being encouraged. **1984** *McGraw-Hill Yearbk. Sci. & Technol. 1985* 68/1 Many AIDS patients experience malaise, fevers, anorexia, and weight loss for weeks, months, or years prior to the documentation of their initial opportunistic infection. **1985** *Daily Tel.* 22 July 15/8 A cancer clinic in the Bahamas has been ordered to close.. after two patients.. were given serum infected with HTLV-III, the deadly virus which causes Aids. **1987** *Sunday Times* (Colour Suppl.) 21 June 35/3 One of the mysteries of HIV is why the virus can lie dormant in some people for long periods, possibly for life, while in others Aids develops more quickly.

2. Special Comb. **AIDS-related** *a.*, related to or associated with AIDS; *spec.* in ***AIDS-related complex***, a set of symptoms that often precedes the full development of AIDS, including lymphadenopathy, fever, weight loss, and malaise.

1983 *N.Y. Times* 1 May I. 26/5 St. Jude Children's Research Hospital in Memphis.. will look at potential drug treatments in animals for an AIDS-related form of pneumonia, pneumocystis carinii. **1984** *European Jrnl. Cancer & Clin. Oncol.* XX. 169/1 This syndrome has occasionally been described as 'pre-AIDS' or 'AIDS-related complex'. **1986** *Daily Tel.* 3 Feb. 5/5 Of 34 mothers who gave birth to children with Aids at his hospital, only four had any symptoms of the disease or Aids-related complex, a milder form. **1987** *Economist* 28 Feb. 93/2 After a female prostitute.. died.. from AIDS, the government launched big campaigns aimed at preventing the spread of the virus, so spreading interest in AIDS-related stocks.

†**'aiel.** *Obs.* 4–5. Also 4–5 ayel(e, ayell(e, (eile), 5 aiell(e, ayle, ayeull, 6 ayal, 9 ael. [a. OFr. *aïel*, *ael*, *aïeul*, *aïol* (Pr. *aviol*):—late L. **aviol-us*, dim. of *avus* grandfather.] A grandfather, forefather.

1377 LANGL. *P. Pl.* B. xv. 317 To ȝiue fram ȝowre eyres · þat ȝowre ayeles ȝow lefte. *c* **1386** CHAUCER *Knt's. T.* 1619, I am thyn Aiel [*v.r.* eile, ayell] redy at thy wille. **1460** CAPGRAVE *Chron.* 97 The same heresi of Crist in whech his fader and his ayle was infecte. **1480** CAXTON *Chron. Eng.* VI. (1520) 75 b/1 Richarde duke of Normandye, that was ayeull to Duke Wyllyam. **1502** ARNOLD *Chron.* (1811) 18 In time of Kynge Herry ayal unto Kynge Herry our Ayal.

b. *Law.* ***Writ of Aile, Ayle, Ayel, Ael.***

1625 SIR H. FINCH *Law* (1636) 267 A writ of Ayell after the death of his grandfather or grandmother. **1768** BLACKSTONE *Comm.* III. 186 A writ of *ayle*, or *de avo*. **1809** TOMLINS *Law Dict.*, *Aile*.. A writ which lies where a man's grandfather being seised of lands and tenements in fee simple the day that he died, and a stranger abateth or entereth the same day, and dispossesses the heir of his inheritance. **1865** NICHOLS *Britton* II. 59 Writs of Cosinage of Ael.

aiery, variant of AERIE, an eagle's nest.

aiger, obs. or dial. f. EAGER *sb.*, tidal bore.

aight, obs. form of AIT.

aighted, aighteth, obs. forms of EIGHTH.

aiglent wine, 'Mustie wine.' Cockeram 1626.

aiglet, obs. form of AGLET.

aiglette, obs. form of EAGLET.

aigre, obs. f. EAGER *a.* esp. in sense of sour.

‖**aigre-doux, -ce,** *a.* In 6 agerdows. [Fr. *aigre* sour, *doux, -ce* sweet.] Compounded of sweet and sour. Cf. AGRO-DOLCE.

1523 SKELTON *Garl. Laurel* 1250 He wrate an Epitaph for his grave stone With wordes devoute & sentence agerdows. For he was ever agaynst Goddis hows.

aigrette ('eɪgrɪt). Also 8 **egrette, aigret.** [a. mod.Fr. *aigrette*, the EGRET or Lesser White Heron, whose head is 'adorned with a beautiful crest composed of some short and two long feathers, hanging backward.' The name was in Fr. transferred to the crest itself, extended to similar plumes borne by other birds, or worn by ladies in a head-dress, as the tuft of a helmet, etc. Thence it has received in modern times further extension in the language of Science. As the word was already in use in the form *egret(te* for the bird, this spelling was also at first used in the present sense.]

1. The Lesser White Heron: see EGRET.

1845 *Blackw. Mag.* LVII. 42 The white aigrette; superior in size to the common heron.

2. A tuft of feathers such as that borne by the Egret and some other birds; a spray of gems, or similar ornament, worn on the head.

a **1645** W. BROWNE *Temple Masque* 147 Egrettes with a greene fall. **1759** in *Phil. Trans.* LI. 37 They contain an infinite number of prickles, which are.. brilliant, like an aigrette of glass. **1784** BECKFORD *Vathek* (1868) 27 To the third my aigret of rubies. **1843** PRESCOTT *Mexico* I. ii. (1864) 11 A human skull.. surmounted by an aigrette of brilliant plumes and precious stones. **1878** LADY HERBERT tr. *Hübner's Round the World* II. iv. 326 He wore a colossal aigrette, made of bamboo and horse-hair.

3. Hence applied in *Science* to tufts of similar appearance, as the feathery pappus of composite plants like the Dandelion; the feathery tufts on the heads of certain insects, etc.; luminous rays seen shooting out from behind the moon in solar eclipses, or at the ends of electrified bodies.

1816 KEITH *Physiol. Bot.* II. 404 Furnished with an aigrette or down, as in the case of the Dandelion. **1828** KIRBY & SPENCE *Entomol.* III. xxix. 176 Some have the anterior aigrettes disposed like the arms of a cross. **1879** LOCKYER *Elem. Astron.* iii. xviii. 103 Rays of light, called aigrettes, diverge from the Moon's edge, and appear to be shining through the light of the corona.

4. *Comb.* as ***aigrette-like.***

1873 HERSCHEL *Pop. Lect.* iii. §43. 128 Till it assumed at length that superb aigrette-like form.

‖**aigue-marine.** *Obs.* [Fr., = OFr. *aigue*:—L. *aqua* water + *marin, -e* of the sea.] French name of the beryl; also called AQUAMARINE.

1765 DELAVAL in *Phil. Trans.* LV. 21 The colour will be blueish, and bordering on the colour of the aigue marine. **1837–80** DANA *Mineral.* 245 Beryl or 'Aigue-marine.'

aiguille ('eɪgwiːl, 'eɪgwɪl). [a. Fr. *aiguille* (cogn. w. It. *aguglia*, Pr. Pg. *agulha*, Sp. *aguja*):—late L. **acūcula* for *acicula*, dim. of *acus* needle. For the sense cf. the similar Eng. use of *needle*.] A slender, sharply-pointed peak (of rock); *esp.* the numerous peaks of the Alps so named.

1816 BYRON in Moore's *Life* (1866) 311 Mont Blanc and the Aiguille of Argentières both very distinct. **1835** *Penny Cycl.* IV. 501 s.v. *Blanc, Mt.*, The upper surface is extremely irregular, and a considerable number of rocks rise from it, which, from their resemblance to pyramids or steeples, are called aiguilles, or needles. **1862** DANA *Man. Geol.* 680 Granite is well known to run up into lofty needles (or aiguilles).

aiguillesque (ˌeɪgwɪˈlɛsk), *a.* [f. prec. + -ESQUE. Cf. *picturesque*.] Shaped like an aiguille.

1856 RUSKIN *Mod. Painters* IV. v. xv. §31 He gives more of the curved aiguillesque fracture to these upper crests.

aiguillette (ˌeɪgwɪˈlɛt). [a. mod.Fr. *aiguillette*; for the historical forms see AGLET.] = AGLET; specially applied to the ornamental tags on military and naval uniforms, and some liveries.

1816 'QUIZ' *Grand Master* I. 14 A figure, in the garb of war, Dress'd in an Egellet and Star. **1854** DE QUINCEY *Sp. Mil. Nun* Wks. III. 60 Some bright ornament, clasp, or aiguillette, on Kate's dress. **1882** *Adm. Uniform Reg.* in *Navy List* July 495 The aiguillete is always to be worn with full dress and on state occasions.

aiguilletted (ˌeɪgwɪˈlɛtɪd), *ppl. a.* [f. prec. + -ED.] Ornamented with aiguillettes or aglets.

1853 H. D. WOLFF *Spanish Life* 52 The riders wear.. a jacket, aiguilletted and embroidered.

aik, aiken, obs. north. form of OAK, OAKEN.

aikido (aɪˈkiːdəʊ). [a. Jap., lit. 'a way of adapting the spirit', f. *ai* together + *ki* spirit + *do*: see JUDO.] A Japanese art of self-defence, also practised as a sport, which takes advantage of the opponent's strength to subdue him.

1956 K. TOMIKI *Judo* 102 Mr. Moritaka Ueshiba.. made many additions to the art [of jujutsu], and it is now known as *aikido*. **1966** [see KENDO]. **1975** *New Yorker* 23 June 33/2 The best aikido master in the United States—aikido being a martial-art form that involves spinning the body a great deal. **1976** *Milton Keynes Express* 2 July 3/1 Demonstrations of aikido, country dancing, and brass band playing followed the opening ceremony. **1984** *New Yorker* 7 May 44/3 Fifty students of aikido..are swirling, turning, twisting, depositing their partners on the shiny floor.

aikinite (ˈeɪkɪnaɪt). *Min.* [named after Dr. A. Aikin.] A Sulpharsenite ore, containing bismuth, lead, and copper, crystallizing in needle-shaped crystals, belonging to the prismatic or ortho-rhombic system.

1837–80 DANA *Mineral.* 100 Aikinite..color blackish lead-gray, with a pale copper-red tarnish.

†**ail**, *a. Obs.* Only found in the forms: 1 **eᵹle**, 2–3 **eille**, **eil**, 4 **eyle**. [OE. *eᵹle*:–**agljo*- cogn. w. Goth. *aglus*.] Loathsome, troublesome.

a **1000** *Riddles* (Grein) lxxi. 16 ȝif me ordstápe eᵹle wæron. **1205** LAYAMON 3282 Heore þuhte swiþe eille of æðelene hire fædere [*later text* eil]. *c* **1225** *Hali Meid.* 25 To don hit þat te þuncheð uuel of & eil for ta heren. *c* **1320** *Cast. Loue* 223 Eyle and hard and muche.

ail (eɪl), *v.* Forms: 1 **eᵹl-an**, 2 **eȝl-en** (Orm. **eȝȝl-enn**), 2–3 **eil-en**, **eil-e**, 4–5 (**eale**), **eyl(en**, **eil(en**, **eil(e**, 4–6 **eyl(e**, 5–7 **ayle**, **aile**, 4– **ail**. [OE. *eᵹl-an* cogn. w. Goth. *aglj-an*; f. *eᵹle*, **agljo*-: see prec.]

†**1.** *trans.* To trouble, afflict. *Obs. rare.*

c **940** *Sax. Leechd.* II. 122 Wið wyrmum þe innan eglað. *a* **1000** *Judith* xi. 64 Ðæt he mid láððum ús eᵹlan móste. **1352** MINOT *Poems* viii. 41 Schent war tho schrewes And ailed unsele.

2. *impers.* To trouble, afflict, affect unusually. (Now restricted to *interrog.*, *rel.*, and *indef.* sentences, as *what ails you? if anything ailed me.*)

a. physically.

1086 *O.E. Chron.* (Laud MS.) an. 1086 (Earle 220) Him ȝeyfelade, and þ him stranglíce eᵹlade. *c* **1230** *Ancr. R.* 276 Nu a uleih mei eilen þe, & makien þe to blenchen. **1362** LANGL. *P. Pl.* A. VII. 121 Such seknes vs eileþ. *c* **1440** *Gesta Rom.* 68 Maister, what eileth the, thou art lepre? *c* **1450** *Merlin* 52 He myght wele a-rise, for hym eyleth noon evell. **1535** COVERDALE *Ps.* cxiv. 5 What ayled the (o thou see) that thou fleddest? [**1611** ailed; WYCLIF, What was to thee.] **1722** DE FOE *Plague* 184 Some have sent for physicians to know what ailed them. **1850** MRS. STOWE *Uncle Tom's C.* xxiv. 231 'I don't see as anything ails the child,' she would say.

b. mentally. (mod. Sc. *what ails you at me?* = What cause of dissatisfaction have you with me?)

c **1090** *L. St. Edm.* Procœm., Me e[ᵹ]leþ swyðe. *c* **1200** ORMIN 4766 Bilammp himm oþerr wa þatt mare mihht himm eȝȝlenn. *a* **1300** *Cursor M.* 20301 Leuedi quat ails te. **1483** CAXTON *Gold. Leg.* 386/1 And demaunded hym what hym eyled and why he sorowed. **1535** COVERDALE *1 Sam.* xi. 5 What ayleth the people that they wepe? [**1611** aileth; WYCLIF, What hath the puple.] **1690** W. WALKER *Idiom. Ang.-Lat.* 18 What ails you to be sad? *a* **1842** TENNYSON *Miller's Dau.* xii, My mother thought, What ails the boy? For I was alter'd, and began To move about the house with joy.

†**3.** *impers.* To interfere with, obstruct, prevent.

c **1380** *Sir Ferumb.* 1560 'Sir duk,' quaþ Rolond, 'what eyleþ þe? þer ne buþ noȝt xxx[ti] þare.' **1440** *Promp. Parv.*, Eylyn, *Obsto.* *c* **1440** *Generydes* 3411 What aylith the to fight? **1563** MAN *Musculus Com. Pl.* 286b, What eyleth it [*quid impedit*] but by the same reason he should be baptised.

4. *intr.* (By mistaking the personal obj., which in early times usually preceded the impersonal vb. for the subj.) To have something the matter with one.

a. physically: To be ill, to be indisposed.

c **1425** WYNTOUN *Cron.* VIII. xxxv. 131 And wyth a gud will and a stowte He sayd, þat he wald ayl na-thyng. *c* **1450** *Merlin* 3 Know ye ought what thise bestes eiled thus for to dye? **1601** SHAKS. *All's Well* II. iv. 6 If she be very well, what does she ail, that she's not very well? **1702** PRYME in *Phil. Trans.* XXIII. 1076, I know not what I ail, says he, I cannot swallow any Beer. **1742** RICHARDSON *Pamela* III. 78 And when he ails ever so little..he is so peevish. **1869** *Pall Mall G.* 18 Aug. 4 No wonder, the *Lancet* says, that diarrhœa has prevailed, and that the children ail.

†**b.** mentally: To be in trouble; to be affected by. *Obs.* or *dial.* (mod. Sc. *to ail at*, as in 2b.)

c **1250** *Gen. & Ex.* 3809 ȝet he aȝlen on here red. *c* **1450** *Merlin* xxix. (1877) 586 Whan Merlin..herde hem make soche doell he asked hem what thei eiled. *a* **1528** SKELTON *Magnyfyc.* 2393 For who loueth God can ayle nothynge but good. **1635** QUARLES *Embl.* II. v. (1718) 82 Thou ask'st the Conscience what she ails. **1714** ELLWOOD *Autobiog.* 20, I knew not what I ayled, but I knew I ayled something more than ordinary: and my Heart was very heavy. *c* **1817** HOGG *Tales & Sk.* III. 191 'What can the fool mean?' said old Richard, 'What can he ail at the dogs?'

ail (eɪl), *sb.*[1] Forms: 3 **eil**, **eile**; 7 **ayle**, **aile**, 7– **ail**. [subst. use of AIL *v.*; but the 13th c. instances are probably subst. use of AIL *a.* The sb. is wanting in OE. though found in Goth. *aglo*.] Trouble, affliction; affection, illness, ailment.

c **1230** *Ancren Riwle* 50 þe blake cloð also.. deð lesse eile to þen eien. *Ibid.* 62 Heo habbeð idon muchel eil to moni on ancre. **1642** ROGERS *Naaman* 143 Long custome hath stupified their hearts, and made them senselesse of their ayle. **1734** WATTS *Reliq. Juv.* (1789) 218 Buzzing all my ails into the ears of my friends. **1812** COMBE (Dr. Syntax) *Picturesque* IV, And ointments, too, to cure the ail Of her cropp'd ears and mangled tail. **1852** MOIR *Scot. Sab.* iii. Poet. Wks. II. 39 Soother of life, physician of all ail.

†**ail**, *sb.*[2] *Obs.* or *dial.* Forms: 1 **eᵹl**, 2 **eiȝle**, 3–7 **eile**, 4 **eyle**, **yle**, 6 **ayle**, 6–8 **aile**, 8 **ail**. [OE. *eᵹl* cogn. w. Germ. *egel*, *agele*, orig. Teut. **agli*.] The awn of barley, or other corn.

[Still used in the Eastern Counties.]

c **1000** *O.E. Gosp.* Luke vi. 41 Hwi ᵹesihst þu þa eᵹle on þines broþor eaᵹan? *c* **1160** *Hatton Gosp.* ibid., Hwi ȝesyhst þu þa eiȝle on þines broðer eaȝen? *c* **1230** *Ancren Riwle* 270 Forto winden hweate & scheaden þe eilen & tet chef urom þe clene cornes. **1398** TREVISA *Barth. De P.R.* XVII. cx, The beste [nard] is smoþe..with small yles [*ed.* 1535 eiles]. **1578** LYTE *Dodoens* 461 The eares (of barley) be..set ful of long bearded sharpe ayles. **1620** VENNER *Via Recta* (1650) 23 Wheat..whose eares are bare and naked without eiles. **1787** WINTER *Syst. Husb.* 310 Barley should likewise be..well shook in a sack by two men, to be cleared from ailes.

ailantery (eɪˈlæntərɪ). Improp. **ailanthery**. [a. mod.Fr. *ailanterie*, cf. *shrubb-ery*. See -ERY.] A grove of Ailanto trees.

1867 *Chambers's Jrnl.* XXXVIII. 128 Have formed what they call an 'ailanthery' so as to afford the [silk] worms the best possible chance of thriving.

ailantho, **ailantus**: see AILANTHUS.

‖**ailanthus** (eɪˈlænθəs). *Bot.* Also **ailante**, **ailanto**, **ailantus**. [f. *Aylanto*, the native Amboyna name, said to mean 'Tree of the gods,' or 'of heaven,' whence mod.L. *Ailantus* (in English often corrupted to *Ailanthus*, as if the termination contained Gr. ἄνθος flower), Fr. *ailante*.] A large East Indian tree (N.O. *Simarubaceae* or *Xanthoxylaceæ*), grown in S. Europe for ornament and shade, the pinnated leaves of which are the favourite food of a species of silk-worm. 'The name "Japan Varnish" seems to have been applied to it through some mistake.' Also ***ailanthus-tree***.

1807 T. MARTYN *Miller's Gardener's & Botanist's Dict.* I. I. sig. Pi/1, The Ailanthus grows very fast in our climate, and ..is proper for ornamental plantations. **1845** HIRST *Poems* 158 O'er me let a green Ailanthus grow..the Tree of Heaven. **1853** *Harper's Mag.* VI. 848/2 The poor Ailanthus-tree has..been outlawed by Congress. **1861** *Times* 23 July, This silkworm lives in the open air on a very hardy plant called the 'ailante,' or Japan varnish tree. **1866** C. A. JOHNS in *Treas. Bot.* 32 *Ailantus*, the *Vernis du Japon* of the French ..is in its native countries, China and India, called Ailanto. Its German name *Götterbaum* is said to be a translation of *Ailanto.* **1878** BLACK *Green Past. & Picc.* xxx. 240 The acacia-looking ailanthus along the pavements. **1936** J. DOS PASSOS *Big Money* 259 An unwashed window that looked out on cindery backyards and a couple of ailanthustrees. **1941** T. S. ELIOT *Dry Salvages* i. 7 The rank ailanthus of the April dooryard. **1974** K. MILLETT *Flying* (1975) II. 197 An ailanthus, the only ratlike tree that can grow in our soil. **1975** *New Yorker* 31 Mar. 35/3 It faces south and is at eye level with chimney pots and the tops of ailanthus trees.

ailantic (eɪˈlæntɪk), *a. Chem.* Improp. **ailanthic**. [f. AILANT(H)-US + -IC.] Of or pertaining to the ailanthus; as ***ailantic acid***.

1879 *Syd. Soc. Lex.*, *Ailanthic Acid*, an acid prepared from the bark of the *Ailanthus excelsa*.

ailantine (eɪˈlæntɪn), *a.* and *sb.* Improp. **ailanthine**. [f. AILANT(H)-US + -INE[1].] **A.** *adj.* Of or belonging to the ailanthhus, or the silk-worm that feeds on it. **B.** *sb.* Silk from the *Bombyx Cynthia* or ailanthus silk-worm.

1861 *All Y. Round* 9 Feb. 423 Ailanthine, or the silk of the bombyx which feeds on the leaves of the *Ailantus glandulosus.* **1863** *Ibid.* 11 July 467/1 Ailanthine sericulture would remain in great measure unproductive.

aile, obs. form of AISLE; and var. AIEL, *Obs.*

aileron (ˈeɪlərən). [a. F. *aileron*, dim. of *aile* wing.] One of the hinged flaps on the trailing edge of a wing of an aeroplane for maintaining or restoring its balance when flying.

1909 *Aero* 25 May 1 The ailerons or small planes between the main surfaces are used instead of wing-flexing for balancing. **1916** *Air* I. 11 Elevator surface and aileron surfaces which are constructed of steel frames covered with linen. **1937** *Jrnl. R. Aeronaut. Soc.* XLI. 191 Partial flap (slotted or split type) combined with drooping ailerons. **1953** *Sci. News* XXIX. 99 The ailerons on an aircraft are usually situated on the trailing edges of the wings and extend approximately halfway along the wing from the tips.

ailette (eɪˈlɛt). Formerly **alet**. [a. Fr. *ailette*, OFr. *alete*; dim. of *aile* wing:—L. *āla*.] A steel plate worn by men-at-arms on their shoulders, the prototype of the modern epaulette.

c **1440** *Morte Arthure* 2565 An alet enamelde he oches in sondire. **1834** PLANCHÉ *Brit. Costume* 108 Towards the close of this [Edward I's] reign those curious ornaments called ailettes, or little wings, from their situation and appearance, are seen on the shoulders of knights.

ailing (ˈeɪlɪŋ), *vbl. sb.* [f. AIL *v.* + -ING[1].] = AILMENT.

1862 T. TROLLOPE *Marietta* II. ix. 149 Seeing in it the signs of ailing. **1867** LADY HERBERT *Cradle Lands* ii. 60 Whose hard-won experience in Eastern ailings renders them invaluable in suggesting the proper remedies.

ailing (ˈeɪlɪŋ), *ppl. a.* [f. AIL *v.* + -ING[2].] **a.** Afflicted, affected with illness, suffering.

1598 FLORIO, *Manco*..failing, ayling, wanting. **1759** DILWORTH *Pope* 15 So far in justice to his prudence as a great poet, and an ailing man. **1810** CRABBE *Borough* vii. 248 A potent thing, 'twas said, to cure the ills Of ailing lungs —the oxymel of squills. **1880** MISS BRADDON *Barbara* xviii. 128 He kept a hospital..for his friends' ailing dogs.

b. *fig.* Of business or financial concerns.

1962 *Daily Tel.* 28 Mar. 24/6 The decision will then be whether to cut off the ailing limbs [of the railway services] without mercy or keep them alive with regular injections of the taxpayers' money. **1976** *Ann. Reg. 1975* 21 The Government's 'Santa Claus policy of bailing out the ailing giants of industry'. **1981** *Times* 16 June 17/4 Evidence of an improvement in the ailing United States economy. **1986** *Marketing* 11 Sept. 2/3 Zanussi has undergone a major restructuring programme as Electrolux has tried to make the ailing Italian giant profitable.

[**ailingness** (Richardson, from Tytler) Error for ALANGE-, ELENGENESS.]

ailment (ˈeɪlmənt). [f. AIL *v.* + -MENT added to an Eng. vb.] The fact of ailing; bodily or mental indisposition; disorder, sickness.

1706 PHILLIPS, *Ailment*, a light disorder or indisposition of the body. **1710** PHILIPS *Pastorals* ii. 24 For much it may relieve thy Woe To let a Friend thy inward Ailment know. **1741** RICHARDSON *Pamela* (1824) I. xxvi. 279 Taken with slight stomach ailments. **1834** HT. MARTINEAU *Farrers* iii. 37, I know his ailments to be from an uneasy mind.

ailurophil(e) (aɪˈl(j)ʊərəʊfaɪl, -fɪl). Also **aeluro-**, **ailouro-**. [ad. Gr. αἴλουρος cat + -PHIL, -PHILE.] A lover of cats. Cf. AILUROPHOBE.

1931 J. C. SMOCK *Greek Element in Eng. Words* I. 7/1 Ailuro-..phile/phobia/pus. **1948** J. S. G. SIMMONS in *Times* 4 Dec. 1/3 (Advt.), Oxford—Lecturer and wife, aelurophiles ..seek flat. **1952** *Britannica Bk. of Year* 666/1 *Ailurophile* .., a lover of cats. **1957** *Observer* 22 Dec. 9/6 A creature of moods and temperament that they [*sc.* the children] seem to enjoy as much as any adult ailourophile. **1976** *Publishers Weekly* 13 Sept. 97/2 Ailurophiles can indulge their favorite pastime: celebrating the wonder of the feline. **1982** *Times Lit. Suppl.* 23 July 803/4 Shackleton Bailey is a confessed aelurophil.

ailurophobia (aɪl(j)ʊərəʊˈfəʊbɪə). [mod.L., f. Gr. αἴλουρος cat + -PHOBIA.] Morbid fear of cats. Hence **aiˈlurophobe**, one affected with ailurophobia; **ailuroˈphobic** *a.*

1905 S. W. MITCHELL in *Amer. Med.* IX. 851 (*title*) Of ailurophobia and the power to be conscious of the cat as near, when unseen and unheard. **1905** A. LANG in *Morning Post* 16 June 4/3 Female ailurophobes are just as capable of not knowing that a cat is in the room..as of saying that it is there when it is not. *Ibid.*, Finding a lady, rather ailurophobic, in a low dress at dinner Tippoo suddenly leaped up and alighted on her neck. He was never so friendly with non-ailurophobes. **1920** C. VAN VECHTEN *Tiger in House* (1921) ii. 30 Cats only give affection where it is deserved, except..when they annoy an ailurophobe with their attentions.

aim (eɪm), *v.* Forms: 3–7 **ame**, 4 **eyme**, 4–7 **ayme**, 6–7 **aime**, 7– **aim**. [In this word probably two vbs. are confounded, 1. Picard. *amer*, OFr. and Pr. *esmer*:—L. *æstimā-re*; 2. OFr. (*aasmer*, *aemer*, *eesmer*, *eamer*,) *aesmer*:—late L. *ad-æstimā-re*.]

†**1.** *trans.* To esteem, consider, take account of. *Obs.*

1382 WYCLIF *Ps.* cxliii. 3 Or the sone of man, for thou eymest hym [**1388** Thou arettist him of sum valu]. *c* **1400** *Destr. Troy* III. 762 Iff þe any thing have amyt abill me to, þat þe me faithfully informe.

†**2.** To estimate, calculate, reckon (a number or value). *Obs.*

1330 R. BRUNNE *Chron.* 240 An arme of þe se men kennes þe depnes may non ame. *c* **1350** *Will. Palerne* 1596 No mon vpon mold · miȝt ayme þe noumber. *c* **1440** *Morte Arthure* 4069 And alle Arthurs oste was amede with knyghtes Bot awghtene hundrethe of alle.

†**3.** To guess, to conjecture. (With *simple obj.* or *subord. cl.*) *Obs.*

1382 WYCLIF *Prov.* xxiii. 7 For in licnesse of a deuynour ..he eymeth [**1388** gessith] that he knowith not. —— *1 Sam.* i. 13 Heli therfor eymyde hir dronken. *a* **1593** H. SMITH *Wks.* (1866) I. 268 No marvel if he did aim that his death was near at hand. **1602** WARNER *Albion's Eng.* X. lix. 258 Supposing, by her Blushings, all would ayme her altred plight.

†**4.** To calculate, devise, arrange, plan. *Obs.*

c **1400** *Destr. Troy* V. 1679 Oppon þe auter was amyt to stond An ymage full noble. *Ibid.* V. 1562 Ymagry ouer all amyt þere was, Of beste and babery. **1604** SHAKS. *Oth.* III. iii. 223 My speech should fall into such vilde successe Which my Thoughts aym'd not.

5. To calculate one's course with a view to arriving (at a point); to direct one's course, to make it one's object to attain. Hence *fig.* To have it as an object, to endeavour earnestly. Const. (*to* obs.) *at*; *dat inf.*; sometimes *for*, perhaps by confusion with *make for*. †**a.** *refl. Obs.*

c **1400** *Destr. Troy* XVI. 7229 Ector to Achilles amyt him sone.

b. *intr.* Also with infinitive: to intend; to attempt (formerly chiefly *dial.* and *U.S.*, now *colloq.*)

1330 R. BRUNNE *Chron.* 98 Whan Henry was ryued þer, þer he wild ame. *c* **1400** *Destr. Troy* V. 2023 Antenor Amyt after anone To the palis. **1598** J. DICKENSON *Greene in Conceipt* 24 Which aym'd wholly at singularitie, glorying to bee peerelesse in hir pompe. **1602** MARSTON *Antonios Revenge* V. i. sig. I 2[r], Alberto drawes out his dagger, Maria her knife, ayming to menace the Duke. **1613** Shaks. *Hen. VIII*, III. i. 138 Madam, you wander from the good We ayme at. **1649** Selden *Laws of Eng.* II. xxvi. (1739) 116 That ease and rest that the King aimed to enjoy. **1665** in *Rhode Isl. Col. Rec.* II. 120 And this the Court hath done, aimeing alsoe therein to save the towne. **1758** S. Hayward *Serm.* xvi. 471 Perfection is what the Christian is aiming at. **1785** Hutton *Bran New Wark* (1879) 24 Aaiming to hev a good conscience. **1872** Jenkinson *Guide Eng. Lakes* (1879) 293 Aim for the Steeple. **1878-** in *Eng. Dial. Dict.* **1879** Froude *Cæsar* ix. 91 In politics they aimed at being on the successful side. **1891** Hardy *Tess* (1892) xxv. 204 Aiming to arrive about the breakfast hour. **1909** J. Bigelow *Retrosp.* I. iii. 57 A[n]..article in which I aimed to compare and contrast the duties of Roman lawyers with those of our own time and country. **1940** F. van Wyck Mason *Stars on Sea* II. viii. 283 A seaman called through tattooed hands, 'We ain't Spanishers. We don't aim to harm you.'

6. a. *intr.* To calculate or estimate the direction of anything about to be launched (at an object); to deliver a blow, or discharge a missile (at anything) with design or endeavour to strike. Hence *fig.* To try to hit, gain, or bring into one's power; to have designs upon, to seek to obtain. Const. *at*.

c **1380** *Sir Ferumb.* 735 And eymede ful euene to ȝyue þe strok. **1573** Twyne *Æneid* XI. (R.) This goddesse faire.. from this hillocke farre at Aruns aimes within her sight. **1659** Pearson *Creed* (1839) 230 Our translation, aiming at the sense, rendereth it, etc. **1718** Pope *Iliad* IV. 130 Aim at his breast, and may that aim succeed. **1769** *Junius Lett.* Pref. 18 Those who persuade you to aim at power without right. **1821** W. Russel *Mod. Europe* I. xxxvii, Edward..aimed at the absolute sovereignty and dominion of that kingdom.

b. ***to aim off*** (in *Rifle-Shooting*), to alter the aim to allow for the wind. So ***aiming-off*** vbl. sb., ***aim-off*** sb. Also *transf.*

1918 E. S. Farrow *Dict. Mil. Terms* 12 *Aiming-off*, altering the point of aim laterally, so as to give deflection to the rifle-barrel without using the wind gauge. **1931** *Small Arms Training* (*War Off.*) V. v. 70 Aiming off for wind.., using wind-gauge to give effect of wind. **1932** J. A. Barlow *Elements Rifle Shooting* iv. 44 We have to learn to aim at some spot other than the one which we want to hit... We will leave for the moment the business of judging the amount of aim-off required and concentrate on the problem of how to aim off. **1957** *Spaceflight* I. 64/2 One of the most difficult problems in the launching of a guided missile, that of aim-off, is entirely eliminated, as the rocket flies continuously within the guiding beam, always endeavouring to intercept its target.

7. *trans.* To direct (a missile, or blow); especially, to direct it with the eye before its discharge; to point or level a gun, etc. (*at*). Hence *fig.* to direct any act or proceeding against. Also *transf.*

1573 Phaër *Æneid* x. (R.) Then Turnus, aiming long in hand a dart of sturdy oke..at Pallas forth it flung. **1603** Drayton *Odes* xvii. 67 Which didst the Signall ayme, To our hid forces. **1702** Logan *Pa. Hist. Soc. Mem.* IX. 99 Hee aimed a blow home at the charter. **1727** Arbuthnot *John Bull* (1755) 11 Mrs. Bull aimed a knife at John. **1776** M. Angelo *Juv. Sports* (ed. 2) ix. 81 If you stand too far from it [the wicket], you may be knocked out by the bowler, before you can recover your bat after aiming a stroke. **1849** Macaulay *Hist. Eng.* II. 210 The laws enacted..against the Roman Catholics had really been aimed at himself. **1927** *Punch* 4 May 480/2 The maid appeared again, aimed me at the consulting-room and loosed me off. **1962** *Which?* Oct. (Car Suppl.) 139/2 Offside headlamp [was] aimed high.

8. *absol.* In both the preceding senses: To take aim; to form designs.

1588 Shaks. *Tit. A.* IV. iii. 65 My Lord, I aime a Mile beyond the Moone. **1608** —— *Peric.* II. v. 47 That never aim'd so high, to love your daughter. **1651** Hobbes *Leviathan* II. xxv. 136 They look about with two eyes, yet they never ayme but with one. **1779** Cowper *Olney Hymns* 'Jehovah Nissi,' Who gave him strength to sling And skill to aim aright. *Mod. dial.* [To a boy throwing stones] 'Now then, Charlie, you mustn't aim.'

aim (eɪm), *sb.* [the vb. used *subst.*]

†**1.** Estimation of probability; conjecture, guess.

c **1400** *Destr. Troy* xv. 7088 Ector, be ame of his speche, Knew hym for his cousyn. *c* **1420** *Siege of Rouen* in *Archæol.* XXI. 62 Theroff had oure Kynge an awme. **1565** Jewel *Repl. Harding* (1611) 59 Wee lead not the people by aimes and ghesses. **1601** Shaks. *Jul. C.* I. ii. 163 What you would worke me to, I haue some ayme. **1625** Bacon *Essays* xvii. 347 The taking an Aime at diuine Matters by Human.

†**2.** The action of making one's way towards a point; course, direction. *Obs.*

1549 Olde tr. *Erasm. Paraphr. 1 Tim.* i. 19 Lest he shuld chaunce to goe quyte out of his ame altogether. **1679** Coles, I am quite out of my aim, *Non ubi terrarum sim scio.*

3. The act of aiming, or pointing the course of anything; the direction or pointing of a missile at that which it is intended to strike; *esp.* in phr. ***to take*** (***make*** obs.) ***aim***.

c **1430** *Syr Generides* 5959 To cleue his heid the king made ame. **1590** Shaks. *Mids. N.* II. i. 157 A certaine aime he tooke At a faire Vestall. **1667** Milton *P.L.* II. 712 Each at the head Level'd his deadly aime. **1818** Scott *Hrt. Midl.* 40 The rearmost soldiers turned, and again fired with fatal aim and execution. **1868** Q. Victoria *Life in Highl.* 72 Macdonald whispered that he saw stags, and that Albert should wait and take a steady aim.

†**b. to give aim**: To guide one in his aim, by informing him of the result of a preceding shot. *Obs.*

1545 Ascham *Toxoph.* 161 Yet, there is one thing whiche many archers vse, yat shall cause a man haue lesse nede to marke the wether, and that is Ame gyuing. *Ibid.* Gyuing Ame..hindreth the knowledge of shotyng, and maketh men more negligente. **1653** Middleton & Rowley *Sp. Gypsey* II. (N.), I myself give aim thus: *wide*, four bows; *short*, three and a half.

†**c. to cry aim**: 'To encourage the archers by crying out "*Aim!*" when they were about to shoot.' Nares. Hence, To encourage, applaud, abet. *Obs.*

1589 R. Harvey *Pl. Perc.* 21 Shake handes & be friendes, meet halfe way, and I standing iump in the middle will crie aime to you both. **1595** Shaks. *John* II. i. 196 It ill beseemes this presence to cry ayme To these ill-tuned repetitions. **1625** [Beaum. & Fl.] *Maid of Inn* v. iii, Must I cry aim To this unheard of insolence?

†**4.** Direction or guidance given. *Obs.*

a **1625** Fletcher *Hum. Lieut.* (1st fol.) 127 We know without your aime, good woman. **1627** Speed *Eng. etc. Abridged* xxxiv. §8 [Houses of religion broken up] vnder the ayme of King Henry the eight. **1643** Milton *Sov. Salve* 39 Posts of direction for Travellers..to give you ayme. **1705** Stanhope *Paraphr.* III. 54 A Passage which seems to give us some Aim for judging.

5. *fig.* The act of directing the efforts towards an object; design, intention, purpose.

1632 Sanderson 12 *Serm.* 553 We cannot attain to the full of our first aymes. **1667** Milton *P.L.* I. 41 With ambitious aim Against the Throne and Monarchy of God. **1738** Wesley *Ps.* xxxii. 2 Free from Design, or selfish Aim. **1870** Bryant *Homer* I. I. 4 'Twere well, Since now our aim is baffled, to return.

†**6.** A thing aimed at; a mark, or butt. *Obs.* in lit. sense.

c **1325** *E.E. Allit. Poems* C. 128 Schomely to schort he schote of his ame. **1594** Shaks. *Rich. III*, IV. iv. 90 A garish Flagge To be the ayme of euery dangerous Shot. **1598** Florio, *Segno*..a white or ayme or blanke to shoote at. **1632** Sanderson 12 *Serm.* 50 But because my ayme lyeth another way; I can but poynt at them, and passe.

7. *fig.* A thing intended or desired to be effected; an object, purpose.

1625 Burges *Pers. Tithes* 3 My chiefe ayme in this discourse is..to pull sundry honest Christians out of a damnable sinne. **1651** Hobbes *Leviathan* II. xxviii. 162 The aym of Punishment is not a revenge, but terrour. **1734** Pope *Ess. on Man* iv. 1 O Happiness! our being's end and aim! **1860** Tyndall *Glac.* I. §2. 9 Our first aim was to cross the Wengern Alp. **1876** Green *Short Hist. of Eng. People* Pref. 5 The aim of the following work is defined by its title.

8. *colloq.* The person who aims. Cf. *a good shot.*

1881 Miss Laffan *Weeds* in *Macm. Mag.* XLIV. 392 He was a good aim too.

9. *Comb.* and *Attrib.* as **aim-certain** *a.*, sure of one's aim; **aim-frontlet**, a frontlet or front-piece to assist in taking aim. Also aim-crier.

1878 *Masque of Poets* 11 Plunge aim-certain in the living stream. **1849** *Mem. Kirkaldy of Grange* xxviii. 335 All the cannon of those days were levelled, raised or depressed by means of a wedge called the aim-frontlet, hollowed to receive the muzzle under which it was placed.

†**'aim-crier.** *Obs.* [see aim *sb.* 3 b, c.] An encourager, applauder; one whose help is confined to words alone. Also, one who 'gives aim.'

1622 F. Markham *Bk. Hon.* v. ix. 196 Like Ayme-cryers, they stand and direct him a neerer way to his owne marke. **1638** G. Markham *Eng. Arcadia* (N.) Thou smiling aim-crier at princes' fall. *Ibid.* Her own creatures, like aim-criers, beheld her mischance with nothing but lip-pity.

aimed (eɪmd), *ppl. a.* [f. aim. *v.* + -ed.]

†**1.** Estimated. *Obs.*

1382 Wyclif *Lev.* xxvii. 19 He shal adde the fifthe part of the eymed money.

2. Directed or pointed at a mark, or in a particular direction; also *fig.*

1635 A. Stafford *Fem. Glory* (1869) 179 Temptations aym'd at her, broke like Haile against a Rocke. **1795** Southey *Joan of Arc* viii. 176 Wks. I. 134 An archer's hand, Palsied with fear, shot wide his ill-aim'd shaft.

3. ***aimed at***: Taken as a point of destination, or as a mark or butt; sought to be reached or struck.

a **1674** Clarendon *Hist. Reb.* I. I. 24 Which was the discovery principally aimed at.

aimel, variant of amel *v. Obs.*, to enamel.

aimer ('eɪmə(r)). [f. aim *v.* + -er[1].] One who aims.

1590 Greene *Neuer too late* (1600) 116 Gentlemen, all riuals in loue & aymer[s] at one fortune. **1611** Cotgr., *Guigneur*..a winker; an aimer with one eye, as a Gunner taking his leuell. **1679** Coles, An aimer at, *Petitor*. **1869** Mozley *Ess.* (1878) II. 398 Natural selection designs perfectly..it always hits, because the aimer is, in truth, the mark.

aimful ('eɪmfʊl), *a. rare*$^{-0}$. [f. aim *sb.* + -ful.] Full of aim or purpose, as 'an aimful effort.'

aimfully ('eɪmfʊlɪ), *adv. rare*$^{-1}$. [f. prec. + -ly[2].] In an aimful manner; with settled purpose.

1882 T. Davidson in *Fortn. Rev.* July 16 To work aimfully, and to use her strength to the best advantage.

aiming ('eɪmɪŋ), *vbl. sb.* [f. aim *v.* + -ing[1].] The action of the verb aim: direction, pointing, levelling a gun, etc. (Now mostly gerundial.) ***aiming point***, in *Gunnery* (see quots.).

1587 Golding *De Mornay* xviii. 282 The true welfare of man consisteth in his true end or..aming point. *a* **1716** South *Serm.* I. xii. (R.) This is always done with forecast and design; with a steady aiming, and a long projecting malice. **1842** J. H. Newman *Par. Serm.* (ed. 2) V. iii. 50 Aim at things, and your words will be right without aiming. **1910** *Encycl. Brit.* I. 692/1 In war, the target, even if visible, is often indistinct, and in this case..an 'aiming point'..a conspicuous point quite apart and distinct from the target, has to be employed. **1918** E. S. Farrow *Dict. Mil. Terms* 12 *Aiming Point*, in gunnery, a stationary object..upon which the panoramic sight is directed after the proper deflection is set off.

aiming ('eɪmɪŋ), *ppl. a.* [f. aim *v.* + -ing[2].] Directing oneself, or a missile, towards an object; designing, intending, tending towards, with, or as the result of, calculation or design.

1643 Milton *Divorce* I. vi. (1847) 129/1 Love..having but one eye, being born an archer aiming. *c* **1746** Hervey *Medit. & Contempl.* (1818) 24 The blow came from an aiming, though invisible hand.

aimless ('eɪmlɪs), *a.* [f. aim *sb.* + -less.] Void of aim or object; purposeless. Also, void of the means of taking aim.

1627 May *Lucan's Phars.* (1631) III. 23 In his blind aymelesse hand a Pile he shooke. **1690** Dryden *Don Sebast.* (T.) The Turks, half asleep, ran about in aimless confusion. **1827** Hood *Hero & Leander* lxxxv, Thine arrows miss me in the aimless dark! **1870** Morris *Earth. Par.* II. III. 236 A life of aimless ease and luxury.

aimlessly ('eɪmlɪslɪ), *adv.* [f. prec. + -ly[2].] In aimless manner; without object or purpose.

1851 Robertson *Serm.* Ser. IV. vi. (1872) 55 'We are consumed'—perish aimlessly like the grass. **1860** *Q. Rev.* No. 215. 297 Intrigues begin aimlessly and close fruitlessly.

aimlessness ('eɪmlɪsnɪs). [f. aimless *a.* + -ness.] The quality of being aimless; want of aim, or definite purpose.

1859 *Bentley's Q. Rev.* No. 3. 26 In spite of this aimlessness the wealth and empire of England are constantly increasing. **1882** *Cornh. Mag.* Feb. 168 The aimlessness of Nature.

aimont, variant of aymont; see also adamant.

aimworthiness ('eɪm,wɜːðɪnɪs). *rare*$^{-1}$. [f. aim *sb.* Cf. *trustworthiness.*] Excellence of aim.

1869 Blackmore *Lorna Doone* liv. (D.) These worthy fellows waited not to take good aim with their cannon.. trusting in God for aimworthiness.

ain, north. f. one and own *a.*; and obs. pl. of eye.

ainalite ('eɪnəlaɪt). *Min.* 'A cassiterite (from Finland) containing nearly 9 p.c. of tantalic acid.' Dana.

aince, ainis, ains, north. dial. forms of once.

aind, north. variant of ande, *Obs.*, breath.

aine, variant of ayne, eigne, elder.

‖**aîné** (ene), *a.* [Fr.: cf. ayne *a.*, eigne *a.*] Senior; (the) elder, eldest: usu. appended to a name to distinguish between members of a family. Cf. fils, père 2, 3.

1792 A. Young *Trav. France* I. 133, I had letters for Mons. Cadot L'ainé, a considerable manufacturer. **1883** *Academy* 20 Jan. 43 MM. Got, Delaunay, Maubant, Coquelin *aîné*, Febvre. **1900** G. Meredith *Let.* ? 12 Dec. (1970) III. 1386 Nothing doing there at present; Sarah [Bernhardt] and Coquelin *aîné* away. **1911** T. E. Lawrence *Let.* 16 Dec. (1938) 129 Touma ainé wants rent for the store room. **1930** E. Pound *XXX Cantos* xxix. 135 Expecting the heir ainé be killed in battle..And the page repented and told this To Nicolo (ainé) Pitigliano. **1985** *Financial Times* 16 Mar. I. 15/3 Loeb's has held a trade tasting of Paul Jaboulet Ainé's '83 Rhônes.

ain't (eɪnt), *v.*[1] *dial.* and *colloq.* [A contracted form of *are not* (see an't), used also for *am not*, *is not*, in the pop. dialect of London and elsewhere; hence in representations of Cockney speech in Dickens, etc.,and subsequently in general informal use. The contraction is also found as a (somewhat outmoded) upper-class colloquialism. Cf. *wŏn't, dŏn't, cân't, shân't.*]

1778 Miss Burney *Evelina* (1873) I. xxi. 87 Those you are engaged to ain't half so near related to you as we are. **1829** Lamb *Life & Lett.* (1860) I. 348 An't you glad about Burk's case? **1865** Dickens *Mut. Fr.* iii. 12 'You seem to have a good sister,' 'She ain't half bad.' **1873** C. H. Smith *Bill Arp's Peace Papers* 201, I thought I was but I aint. **1875** Trollope *Prime Minister* I. xiii. 203, I ain't thinking of her marrying. I don't want her to marry. **1898** *Eng. Dial. Dict.* I. 198/2 Aint ah *or* am ah nūt? **1919** Mencken *Amer. Lang.* 146 *Ain't* is already tolerably respectable in the first person ..'*ain't* I in this?' **1938** V. Woolf *Let.* 3 Oct. (1980) VI. 278, I believe politics will bring L..to London. And I've not the spirit to pack up and go without him. Ain't I a craven? **1959** W. Miller *Cool World* 8, I aint paying that kind of bread.

ain't (eɪnt), *v.*[2] *dial.* and *vulg.* var. *hain't*, have not, has not.

1845 Simms *Wigwam & Cabin* Ser. I. 7 But you ain't said, ..who was your Carolina gineral. **1875** in *Eng. Dial. Dict.* s.v. *Have* v. I. ii. **1880** Tourgée *Fool's Err.* II. x. 473, I ain't done nothing. **1884** 'Mark Twain' *Huck. Finn.* xxxv. 360 He ain't had no experience. **1887** Mary E. Wilkins *Humble Romance* 3 You've been crying, ain't you? **1910** W. M. Raine *B. O'Connor* iii. 37 We ain't got one chance in a hundred, Jim. **1914** *Dialect Notes* IV. 70 He ain't got sense enough to carry guts to a bear. **1917** Mathewson *Sec. Base Sloan* xiv. 195 More than that I ain't got the right to say.

1940 W. FAULKNER *Hamlet* I. i. 15 He is going to charge Ab twenty bushels of corn for it against his crop that Ab ain't even planted yet. **1959** W. MILLER *Cool World* 8 That piece aint been worth no fifteen dollas since you was a little boy Priest.

Ainu ('aɪnuː). Also 9 Aino. [Ainu, lit. 'man'.] The name of a Caucasoid people in Japan and the U.S.S.R. and of the language spoken by them. Also *attrib.*

1819 tr. *Golovnin's Recoll. Japan* v. 242 Their manners shew that the Ainu and Kuriles are one people. **1843** J. C. PRICHARD *Nat. Hist. Man* xxi. 226 (*heading*) The Ainos, or Kurilians. **1864** J. HUNT tr. *Carl Vogt's Lect. Man* v. 127 We find a small, nearly extinct tribe of the Kuril islands,—the Ainos,—whose body is so completely covered with shaggy hair, that it gave rise to the Japanese tradition, that the Aino mothers suckled young bears, which gradually became men. **1880** I. L. BIRD *Unbeaten Tracks in Japan* II. 37 He spoke both Aino and Japanese in the low musical tone which I find is characteristic of Aino speech. **1880** D. P. PENHALLOW in *Sci. Amer.* Suppl. 4 Sept. 3884/2 As an article of clothing, for which use alone it appears to be utilized, the Aino cloth has several good qualities. *a* **1884** KNIGHT *Dict. Mech.* Suppl. 12/2 *Aino cloth*, a cloth made by the Ainos..from the divided fibers of the elm, beaten so as to obtain bast layers, which are split and woven. **1893** A. H. S. LANDOR (*title*) Alone with the Hairy Ainu. **1931** H. G. WELLS *Work, Wealth & Happiness of Mankind* (1932) xiii. 666 The existence of really primitive and undeveloped peoples in small numbers, like the white hairy Ainu or the pygmies. **1932** W. L. GRAFF *Language & Languages* xi. 411 Ainu, spoken by some 20,000 people in the southern part of the island of Sakhalin.

‖**aïoli** (ajoli). [Fr. *aïoli* (Trésor, 1744), f. mod.Pr. *aioli*, f. *ai* (F. *ail*) garlic + *oli* (F. *huile*) oil.] Garlic mayonnaise, orig. a speciality of Provence.

1914 A. E. HOUSMAN *Let.* 2 May (1971) 134 Aioli at Pascal's was rather nasty, perhaps because lukewarm. **1923** W. J. LOCKE *Moordius & Co.* vi. 75 Aioli. It's the national sauce of Provence—mayonnaise made with pounded garlic. **1931** F. M. FORD *Return to Yesterday* I. ii. 23 A meridional French with as strong a Southern accent as that of garlic in *aïoli*. **1951** E. DAVID *French Country Cookery* 69 Prepare an aïoli, that is to say, a mayonnaise with garlic. **1966** *Daily Tel.* 9 Nov. 13/4 Delicious fried *moules* with *aioli* sauce. **1976** [see PESTO].

air (ɛə(r)), *sb.*[1] Forms: 3–5 eir, 4–5 eyr, 4–6 eyre, aier, 4–7 ayre, 5 eyir, eire, 5–6 eyer, ayer, 5–7 aire, 6 eyere, 6–7 ayr, 7 aër, 7– air. [Br. I. II. a. OFr. *air* (Pr. *air, aire*, Sp. *aire*, Pg. *ar*, It. *aire, aere*):—L. *āer-em*, a. Gr. ἀήρ, ἀέρ-α, f. ἄ-ειν, ἀ-ῆναι (ἀε-) to blow, breathe. (Mod.It. has largely substituted *aria*:—L. *āerea* adj. for *aere*. Cf. Florio 1598 '*Aere* (*aire, aira*) the aire. Also, an aspect, countenance, cheere, a look or apparance in the face of man or woman. Also, a tune or aire of a song or ditty.' '*Aria*, as *aere*, the aire.') Br. III. IV. did not arise from I. in Eng. but were adopted *c*1600 from Fr. *air* = *apparence, extérieure, manière d'être*, also *suite de tons et de notes qui composent un chant*, the connexion of which with atmospheric *air* is disputed.

1. Littré makes them two words, identifying *air*, manner, with OFr. *aire* 'area, open place, AERIE' q.v. (which was occasionally masc.) through the chain of ideas 'nest, stock, family, family character, derived manner,' comparing phrases like *faucon de bon aire*, hawk of a good sort (stock, aerie); but no *formal* connexion can be traced between OFr. *aire* and mod. Fr. *air*, while OFr. *aire* never had the sense of 'external appearance,' which is moreover quite a late sense of mod.Fr. *air* (end of 16th c.). Diez, after Burguy, inclines to identify the two senses, through the ideas of 'air, breath, spirit, character, manner,' comparing the range of L. *spiritus*, originally 'breath, air.' 2. It seems probable that the sense of 'manner' was adopted in Fr. from It. in which it is of old standing (see Florio above). Diez says that the Pr. *di bon aire* (Fr. *de bon aire*) was adopted in It., and *aire* treated as the native *aere, aire, aria*, whence *di buon' aria*; hence it is not impossible that the development of senses supposed by Littré, may have taken place in It. and thence been transferred in 16th c. to Fr. *air*. 3. But it is more probable that there was no confusion with *aire* = aerie, and that the idea of *manner*—'*external* manner, appearance, mien,' rather than 'innate character'—is a simple extension of the idea of the 'enveloping or affecting atmosphere special to a place, or situation' as when one is said to carry with him the 'air of the office' (Fr. *air du bureau*), or to catch 'the air of the court,' Shaks. (see below; cf. La Bruyere 'L'air de cour est contagieux, il se prend à Versailles, comme l'accent normand à Rouen') which Littré himself refers to 'atmosphere,' and which is not separable from 'an air of gentility, of truth,' etc. This would also best accord with Br. IV. undoubtedly of It. origination, *aere, aria*, (see Florio above), here translating L. *modus* 'manner,' also 'musical mode, metre, measure, melody.']

A. I. Atmospheric air.

1. a. The transparent, invisible, inodorous, and tasteless gaseous substance which envelopes the earth, and is breathed by all land animals; one of the four 'elements' of the ancients, but now known to be a mechanical mixture of oxygen and nitrogen, with the constant presence of a small quantity of carbonic acid gas, and traces of many other substances as contaminations.

c **1300** in Wright's *Pop. Sc.* 120 þe four elementz, of wham we beoþ iwroȝt: the fur..th-eir..siþþe þe water and siþþe þe urþe. **1384** CHAUCER *H. Fame* III. 260 In his substance is but aire. **1393** GOWER *Conf.* III. 33 As the plover doth of aire, I live, and am in good espeire. *c* **1440** in *Household Ordin.* (1790) 433 Stop hit well that no eyre goo oute. **1565** GOLDING *Ovid's Met.* IX. (1593) 227 Scarce her toong the aier hits. **1604** SHAKS. *Oth.* III. iii. 322 Trifles, light as ayre. **1610** —— *Temp.* IV. i. 150 These our actors..Are melted into ayre, into thin ayre. **1651** HOBBES *Leviathan* III. xxxiv. 207 Aire, and aeriall substances, use not to be taken for Bodies, but..are called Wind, or Breath. **1660** JER. TAYLOR *Worthy Commun.* i. §2. 43 Truth is the aire they breath. **1674** PETTY *Disc. bef. Royal Soc.* 117 The Vnder-water-Air within the Vessels of Water-Divers, who the lower they go, do find their stock of Air more and more to shrink. **1751** CHAMBERS *Cycl.* s.v., We can actually weigh Air. **1878** HUXLEY *Physiogr.* 39 As transparent, as colourless, as invisible as the air we breathe.

b. *fig.* With reference to its unsubstantial or impalpable nature.

1692 SOUTH *12 Serm.* (1697) I, Entertain'd only with the Air of Words and Metaphors.

c. The air considered as a medium for the transmission of radio waves; colloq. = RADIO *sb.* 2, esp. in phr. ***on the air***, (being) broadcast by radio transmission; so ***off the air***.

1927 *Observer* 11 Dec. 16 The only New York church which is 'on the air'. **1928** *Daily Express* 13 Apr. 11/1 They will speak into the microphone as usual, but before being put 'on the air' their voice modulations will be turned upside down. **1940** *N. & Q.* CLXXIX. 66/1 On and off the air. **1955** *Times* 9 May 10/5 Radio and, particularly, television will play a large part in the election, and the campaign of the air has already begun. **1956** A. H. COMPTON *Atomic Quest* 255 The Hiroshima radio went off the air. **1964** *Evening Standard* 4 Feb. 16/2 Every policeman on the beat may be 'on the air' in a few years. Experiments with pocket radios ..have established that they..can be of immense value to the constable on patrol.

attrib. **1928** *Sunday Dispatch* 16 Dec. 12/2 Air Hogs.. Certain people..have been interrupting wireless transmission by crude signals from a private station. **1944** *Amer. Speech* XIX. 49 The New York agencies..spread *fifth column* over the pages of every subscribing newspaper in the country and onto the air waves as well. **1955** T. H. PEAR *Eng. Soc. Differences* xi. 246 The listening public's approval or disapproval of the 'air-time' given to each.

†**2.** Any aeriform body 'permanent' as a *gas*; 'transient' as a *vapour*. *Obs.*

'*Factitious* or *artificial air*, a name given by Boyle to all those elastic fluids which he found produced in chemical experiments, and to be different from the air of the atmosphere.' *Pantologia* 1819.

The following are the chief of these obsolete uses:

Acid or ***Marine Air***, Muriatic Acid Gas; ***Alkaline Air***, Ammoniacal Gas, ***Fixed Air***, Carbonic Acid Gas; ***Dephlogisticated***, or ***Vital Air***, Oxygen; ***Sparry Acid Air***, Fluoric Acid Gas; ***Inflammable Air***, Hydrogen; ***Hepatic Air***, Sulphuretted Hydrogen; ***Phlogisticated Air***, Nitrogen; ***Mephitic Air***, Carbonic Acid Gas, and Nitrogen.

1641 FRENCH *Distill.* vi. 177 This..gold nature would have perfected into an elixir but was hindred by the crude aire, which crude aire is..nothing else but..sulphur. **1692** BOYLE *Hist. Air* in Chambers *Cycl.* s.v., Various solid and mineral bodies..being plunged in corrosive unelastic menstrua..afford a considerable quantity of permanently elastic air. *c* **1700** NEWTON in Chambers *Cycl.* s.v., Gunpowder generates air by explosion. **1751** CHAMBERS *Cycl.* s.v., The difference between permanent and transient *Air* amounts to the same as that between vapour and exhalation. **1774** PRIESTLEY (*title*) 'Experiments and Observations on different kinds of Air.' **1789** HOWARD *Royal Encycl.* 74 Impregnation of water with fixed air. **1789** AUSTIN in *Phil. Trans.* LXXX. 55 A jar perforated with brass rods, such as is used for inflaming airs. **1819** *Pantol.* I. s.v., The different kinds of air, now comprehended under the general term gas.

3. The whole body of air *surrounding*, or in popular language *above*, the earth; the atmosphere; *hence*, **a.** the (apparently) free space above our heads, in which birds fly and clouds float. Also, considered as a medium for the operation of aircraft; a collective term for aircraft or aerial power; esp. in *Comb.*, as ***air arm, cover, offensive, warfare*** (see below B. III. 2). So ***by air***, by aeroplane.

c **1300** in Wright's *Pop. Sc.* 128 Th-eir is swiþe heȝ. *c* **1340** HAMPOLE *Pr. Consc.* 7642 Ane other heven es called þe ayre .. þar þe foghles has flyght. *c* **1386** CHAUCER *Squieres T.* 114 To fleen as hye in the Air [*v.r.* ayr, eir, eyre] as dooth an Egle. **1393** LANGL. *P. Pl.* C. II. 127 Somme in erþe, somme in aier · somme in helle dupe. **1413** LYDG. *Pylgr. Sowle* v. i. (1859) 68 By see and land, and in the eyer abouen. **1488** CAXTON *Chast. Goddes Chyld.* 8 The sonne draweth the humours up in to the ayre. **1556** *Chron. Grey Friars* (1852) 69 Abowte Ester was sene in Sussex three sonnes shenynge at one tyme in the eyer, that thei cowde not dysserne wych shulde be the very sonne. **1611** BIBLE *Eccl.* x. 20 A bird of the aire shall carry the voyce. **1652** NEEDHAM tr. *Selden's Mare Cl.* Pref., The Romanes had shut up the Rivers and Lands, and in a manner the very Aër. **1652** BROME *Jov. Crew* II. 388 While their sublimed spirits daunce i' th' Ayr. **1712** ADDISON *Spect.* No. 553 ¶3 To suspend our coffee in mid-air, between our lips and right-ear. **1808** SCOTT *Marm.* VI. xxv, As if men fought upon the earth, And fiends in upper air. *c* **1840** LONGF. *Not always May*, The sun is bright—the air is clear, The darting swallows soar and sing. **1917** LD. FISHER *Let.* 11 July in R. H. S. Bacon *Life Ld. F.* (1929) II. xxi. 303 The air is going to win the war. **1919** *Daily Tel.* 17 Feb. 6/4 (*headline*) Egypt to the Cape by Air. *Ibid.* 19 Feb. 12/6 (*headline*) Heroes of the Air. *Ibid.* 13/4 (*headline*) Who Owns the Air? **1944** *Picture Post* 9 Sept. 8 We'd got the air, we'd got the guns. **1945** *Hutchinson's Pict. Hist. War* 27 Sept.–13 Mar. 54 Our land-based air was very thin indeed. *fig.* **1855** H. REED *Eng. Lit.* x. (1878) 311 The upper air of poetry is the atmosphere of sorrow.

b. The ***open air***: the unconfined space outside buildings, exposed to the weather. Often *attrib.*

1653 HOLCROFT *Procopius* I. 20 The brazen Statue of Minerva in the open ayre. **1683** TRYON *Way to Health* 287 Moderate Exercises in open Airs, which is profitable for all People. **1756** BURKE *Subl. & B.* Wks. I. 193 A greater light than you had in the open air. *Mod.* An open air meeting; a great open air demonstration.

c. in the air. *fig.* 1. *a.* In the moral or intellectual atmosphere of the time, in men's minds everywhere abroad; *b.* in an unfixed or uncertain state, in doubt; colloq. phr. (***up***) ***in the air***, of persons: in doubt, uncertain; of ideas or theories: speculative, hypothetical; *c.* (slang) ***up in the air***: excited, as in anger (orig. *U.S.*). 2. *Milit.* (see quot. 1882). 3. ***to build in the air, form castles in the air***: to form unsubstantial or visionary projects; see also CASTLE.

1875 A. W. WARD *Hist. Eng. Dram. Lit.* I. iv. 325 The appreciation of Shakspere and the dramatic art perceptible in both these great writers was, as the phrase is, in the air, —in the air, *i.e.*, breathed by those who stood on the height of European culture. **1879** FARRAR *St. Paul* I. 642 These expressions and points of view were not peculiar to Philo. They were, so to speak, in the air. *a* **1884** *Mod.* The spirit of doubt is in the air.

1752 H. WALPOLE *Let.* 28 Oct. (1903) III. 124 Don't look upon this paragraph as a thing in the air. **1797** T. JEFFERSON *Writ.* 1859 IV. 186, I consider the future character of our republic as in the air; indeed its future fortune will be in the air, if war is made on us by France. **1910** GALSWORTHY *Justice* IV, Keep him in the air; I don't want to see him yet. .. Keep him hankering. **1933** D. L. SAYERS *Murder must Advertise* viii. 140 You might have let somebody know. I was left rather up in the air this morning. **1940** in Harrisson & Madge *War begins at Home* v. 107, I didn't hear anything for a long time. They sort of leave you in the air. **1943** W. TEMPLE *Let.* 8 June (1963) 80 The faith he professes in that book is very much up in the air and devoid both of practical and philosophical attachments. **1956** C. WILSON *Outsider* ii. 44 The reader is left feeling oddly 'up in the air' about it all. No happy finale, no dramatic tying up of loose ends. **1956** *Essays in Criticism* VI. 193 By modern standards the article is a bit up in the air.

1906 *N.Y. Even. Post* 13 Jan. 4 Representatives..have ..'gone up in the air' because they could not 'land' their men. **1928** E. WALLACE *Again Sanders* ii. 49 Abiboo, who is a strict Mussulman, got up in the air because Bones suggested he might have been once a guinea-pig. **1930** *Punch* 21 May 577/3 Why the Prime Minister should have 'gone up in the air', as they say, because it appeared in print that Gandhi was about to be arrested..was not revealed.

1865 M. ARNOLD *Ess. Crit.* 261 No intelligent man can read the *Tractatus Theologico-Politicus*..without feeling that, as a speculative work, it is, to use a French military expression, *in the air*; that, in a certain sense, it is in want of a base and in want of supports. **1882** D. GARDNER *Quatre Bras, etc.* 200 The extreme left of the Allied front..was, in military dialect, 'in the air'—that is, protruded into the open country, without natural or artificial protection to its outer flank. **1923** KIPLING *Irish Guards in Gt. War* I. p. x, There was hardly an operation in which platoons..brigades, or divisions were not left with one or both flanks in the air.

1594 SHAKS. *Rich. III*, III. iv. 100 Who builds his hope in ayre of your good Lookes. **1601** *Imp. Consid.* (1675) 60 Mr. Saunders (building Castles in the Air amongst his Books). **1757** WESLEY *Wks.* 1872 IX. 304 A mere castle in the air.

d. ***to give*** (a person) ***the air***: to dismiss (him); to reject. Also with *get*. *U.S. slang.*

1900 G. ADE *More Fables in Slang* 85 (*title*) The Fable of why Essie's Tall Friend got the Fresh Air. **1924** P. MARKS *Plastic Age* 202 'How about my studies?' Hugh retorted. 'I suppose you want me to give them the air.' **1934** WODEHOUSE *Thank You, Jeeves* x. 135 Surely you don't intend to give the poor blighter the permanent air on account of a trifling lovers' tiff? **1949** R. GRAVES *Seven Days in New Crete* xvii. 207, I couldn't change her views..nor could she convert me to hers, even when she threatened to give me the air.

e. ***to give*** (a ball) ***air***: in *Cricket*, to deliver (a ball) with a high trajectory. In *Football*, etc., to keep the ball constantly in movement.

1920 E. R. WILSON in P. F. Warner *Cricket* 88 Slow bowlers are right to 'give the ball air' to a nervous or slow-footed batsman. **1929** *Daily Express* 7 Nov. 18/7 The ball was given plenty of 'air', the pace of the passing and the accuracy of handling a greasy ball reflecting the greatest credit on every one concerned. **1932** *Ibid.* 20 Sept. 10/2 He is doing what every good footballer seeks to do when the play becomes too close. He is opening up the game by 'giving the ball fresh air'.

4. A special state or condition of the atmosphere, as affected by temperature, moisture or other invisible agencies, or as modified by time or place, as the ***night air***, one's ***native air***; approaching the senses of *weather* and *climate*.

1479 J. PASTON in *Lett.* 849 III. 265 Ye wyllyd me..to hast me ought of the heyer that I am in..her must I be for a season. **1529** WOLSEY in *Four Cent. Eng. Lett.* 10, I must be removyd to some other dryer ayer. **1583** B. RICH *Phyl. & Em.* (1835) 13 It was very good for ill Ayres in a mornyng. **1649** JER. TAYLOR *Great Exemp.* II. §12. 57 The spirits of the body have been bound up by the cold winter ayre. **1656** HAMMOND *Leah& Rachel* (1844) 10 Change of ayre does much alter the state of our bodies. **1703** *Lond. Gaz.* mmmdccccxxi/1 To remove from the *Vatican* to his Palace at *Monte Cavallo*, as being a better Air. **1708** POPE *Solit.* 3 Content to breathe his native air In his own ground. **1765** CHURCHILL *Gotham* II. 20 Nor waste their sweetness in the desert air. **1860** W. COLLINS *Wom. in White* (1861) 292 As soon as [they]..can travel, they must both have change of air. *Mod.* Are you afraid of the night air?

5. The fresh unexhausted air of the outer atmosphere, as distinguished from that exhausted of its oxygen in confined spaces.

c **1440** *Generydes* 1984 The Sowdon toke the waye, Owt of the Cite to take the ayre. **1588** Greene *Pandosto* (1843) 45 The king would go abroad to take the ayre. **1623** Massinger *Duke of Milan* III. ii, Say I am rid Abroad to take the air. **1727** Swift *Gulliver* II. viii. 163 To give me air in hot weather as I slept. **1745** De Foe *Eng. Tradesm.* I. x. 83 He goes to take the air for the afternoon. **1813** Miss Austen *Pride & Prej.* ii. 171 She resolved soon after breakfast to indulge herself in air and exercise. *a* **1838** L. E. L[andon] *May day* 200 Clear sky, fresh air, sweet birds, and trees. *Mod.* The bones crumbled to dust on exposure to the air.

6. Air contaminated by gaseous exhalations or emanations; *hence*, the contaminating exhalations themselves; miasma. (Cf. It. *mal' aria.*)

c **1230** *Ancr. R.* 104 þicke eir in hire huse stunch . . and strong breð ine neose. **1366** Maundev. xxvii. 276 To voyden away alle wykkede Eyres and corrupciouns. *c* **1430** Lydg. in *Dom. Archit.* III. 39 From endengeryngе of all corrupcion, From wycked ayre, & from inffexion. *c* **1538** Starkey *England* II. ii. 179 Some corrupt and pestylent Ayre. **1601** Holland *Pliny* (1634) I. 72 The aire arising out of it so noisom and pestiferous for birds. **1712** Pope *Rape Lock* II. 83 Suck the mists in grosser air below. **1861** Flor. Nightingale *Nursing* 12 His goods are spoiled by foul air and gas fumes.

†**7.** Exhalation affecting the sense of smell; effluvium, odour, redolence; the 'atmosphere' sensibly diffused by anything. *Obs.*

c **1430** Lydg. *Bochas* II. xiv. (1554) 53 The ayre of meates and of baudy cookes Which all day rost and sede. **1509** Hawes *Past. Pleas.* VII. i, Wyth flowres of all goodly ayre. **1523** Ld. Berners *Froissart* I. ccccxxiii. 741 The kyng disloged fro Rosbeque, bycause of the eyre of the dead bodyes. **1607** Topsell *Four-footed Beasts* (1673) 133 The Theevish Dog . . hunting Conies by the air.

8. Air in motion; a breeze, or light wind; current, or draught.

1535 Coverdale *Ezek.* xxxvii. 9 Come (o thou ayre) from the foure wyndes, & blowe vpon these slayne. **1602** Shaks. *Ham.* I. iv. 41 Bring with thee ayres from Heauen or blasts from Hell. **1633** P. Fletcher *Purple Isl.* 107 When cooler ayers gently gan to blow. **1704** Pope *Spring* 5 Let vernal airs thro' trembling osiers play. **1836** Marryat *Midsh. Easy* xxx. 116 Calms and light airs detained them for a few days. **1853** Kane *Grinnell Exped.* xiv. (1856) 106 To crowd on the canvas, and sail with gentle airs for about two miles. **1879** Froude *Cæsar* xvi. 267 On a fine summer evening, with a light air from the south. *Mod.* 'Sitting right in the air of the door.'

†**9.** Breath; also *fig.*; 'popular air' (Horace, *popularis aura*), the breath of popular applause. *Obs.*

1590 Marlowe *Edw. II*, v. iii. 270 But can my air of life continue long. **1611** Shaks. *Wint. T.* v. iii. 77 Still me thinkes There is an ayre comes from her. What fine chizzell could euer yet cut breath . . I will kisse her. **1665** J. Spencer *Prophecies* 114 There being not the least air of any promise of Prophecy made. **1710** Palmer *Proverbs* 123 A man of a weak judgment is soonest over-set by popular air. **1821** Byron *Mar. Fal.* I. i. (1868) 315 A whisper, or a murmur, or an air.

†**10.** Hence, Inspiration: confidential or secret information. *Obs.*

1622 Bacon *Hen. VII* (J.) The airs, which the princes and states abroad received from their ambassadors. **1660** R. Coke *Just. Vind.* 14 A kind of divine ayre informing men of their truth.

11. *fig.* (partly from 3, partly from 8.) Public exposure, publicity, public currency. *to take air*: to spread about among people, to 'get wind.'

1601 Shaks. *Twel. N.* II. iv. 144 Pursue him now; least the deuice take ayre. **1662** Marvell *Corr.* 35 Wks. 1872–5 II. 80 The businesse has got a litle too much aire. **1692** R. Lestrange *Josephus* I. xi. (1733) 571 For fear the Plot should take Air and be disappointed. **1734** tr. *Rollin's Anc. Hist.* (1827) IX. xx. i. 9 Nothing that passed in the senate . . was known abroad or suffered to take air. **1843** Prescott *Mexico* VI. iv. (1864) 361 Had he suffered his detection . . of the guilty parties to take air. **1878** G. Macdonald *Ann. Quiet Neighb.* vii. 113 He would not make any fuss that might bring the thing out into the air.

II. [Common in OFr. e.g. '*si se cumbat de grant air*,' '*brocha le chevau par grand hair*'; cf. L. *spiritus, animus.*]

†**12.** Impetuosity, violence, force, anger. *Obs.*

1297 R. Glouc. 51 As þis schippes with gret eir come toward londe. *Ibid.* 397 He turnde hys stede wyþ god eyr. *c* **1300** *St. Brand.* 161 The Yle quakede anon, And with gret Eir hupte al up. *c* **1305** *St. Edm.* 210 in *E.E.P.* (1862) 76 And his pamerie drouȝ So heȝe & wiþ so gret eir, as he him wolde altodryue; Seint Edmund lay & quakede.

III. Manner, appearance.

13. Outward appearance, apparent character, manner, look, style. *Esp.* in phrases like 'an air of absurdity'; less commonly of a thing tangible, as 'the air of a mansion.'

1596 Shaks. *1 Hen. IV*, IV. i. 61 The Qualitie and Heire of our attempt Brookes no diuision. **1607** —— *Timon* V. i. 25 Promising, is the verie Ayre o' th' Time; It opens the eyes of expectation. **1611** —— *Wint. T.* IV. iv. 755 Seest thou not the ayre of the Court in these enfoldings? . . Receiues not thy nose court-odour from me. **1630** Wadsworth *Pilgr.* i. 4 For feare the Heretiques of England should . . say, he changed his ayre for profit, not conscience. **1647** Jer. Taylor *Lib. Proph.* §4. 77 Unlesse other mens understandings were of the same ayre—the same constitution and ability. **1692** Dryden *St. Euremont* 30 Nothing that had the least Air of Acknowledgment. **1710** Steele *Tatler* No. 5 ¶7 Writing in an Air of common Speech. **1711** Pope *Rape Lock* Ded., It was communicated with the air of a secret. **1739** Hume *Hum. Nat.* (1874) I. II. §1. 334/2 Whatever has the air of a paradox. *c* **1815** Miss Austen *Northang. Ab.* (1833) II. vi. 133 The air of the room was far from uncheerful. **1827** Hallam *Const. Hist.* (1876) II. x. 230 The Icon has . . all the air of a fictitious composition. **1845** Ford *Handbk. Spain* i. 25 Some have at a distance quite the air of a gentleman's mansion. **1864** D. Mitchell *7 Stories* 201 The postillion gives his hat a jaunty air. **1876** Freeman *Norm. Conq.* IV. xviii. 232 The story too has in itself a mythical air.

14. a. Of a person: Mien, demeanour, attitude, gesture, manner, look. *arch.*

1599 H. Porter *Two Angry Women* (1841) 36 His ayre is pleasant and doth please me well. **1611** Shaks. *Wint. T.* v. i. 129 Your Fathers Image is so hit in you (His very ayre) that I should call you Brother. **1709** Steele *Tatler* No. 1 ¶5 He is of a noble Family, has naturally a very good air. **1711** Pope *Rape Lock* II. 98 Assist their blushes, and inspire their airs. **1714** Budgell *Spect.* No. 605 ¶8 Married Persons . . catch the Air and way of Talk from one another. **1729** Burkitt *On N. T.* Ded., Unless he sees upon us the Air and Features . . of Christ our elder Brother. **1822** Byron *Heaven & E.* I. ii, But her air, If not her words, tells me she loves another.

†**b.** Disposition, mood. *Obs. rare.*

1655 H. Vaughan *Silex Scint.* III. 233 The short-lived bliss Of air and humour. **1728** Morgan *Algiers* II. v. 320, I am well acquainted with the very Airs, the innate Disposition of the People.

†**c.** Attitude or expression (*of* any part of the body). *Obs.*

1640 T. Carew *Poems* (1824) 104 No colour, feature, lovely ayre, or grace, That ever yet adorn'd a beauteous face. **1711** Addison *Spect.* No. 98 ¶5 Nature has . . given it [the Face] Airs and Graces that cannot be described. **1729** Franklin *Ess.* Wks. 1840 II. 20 There was something in the air of his face that manifested the true greatness of his mind. **1762** H. Walpole *Vertue's Anecd. Paint.* (1786) II. 151 Admirable is the variety of attitudes and airs of heads. **1768** Sterne *Sent. Journ.* (1778) II. 4 It . . gives a better air to your face.

d. Mien or gesture (expressive *of* a personal quality or emotion).

1711 Steele *Spect.* No. 118 ¶2 Her confident shall treat you with an Air of Distance. **1736** Butler *Anal.* II. vii. 355 Determine at once with a decisive air. **1751** Johnson *Rambl.* No. 144 ¶9 He . . excites curiosity by an air of importance. **1802** Mar. Edgeworth *Moral T.* (1816) I. x. 81 He turned from the lady . . with an air of disgust. **1826** Disraeli *Viv. Grey* III. vii. 118 [He] addressed the Marchioness with an air of great interest. **1853** H. Rogers *Eclipse of Faith* 195 He tossed off the brandy and water with a triumphant air.

15. a. An assumed manner, affected appearance, show.

1660 T. Stanley *Hist. Philos.* (1701) 9 With what an Air did Zeno teach his Wise Men the Contempt of Death. **1796** *Campaigns* 1793–4 II. xi. 82 The Stadtholder's hat was pulled off with an air. **1850** Mrs. Stowe *Uncle Tom's C.* iv. 21 Said Aunt Chloe, drawing herself up with an air. **1858** J. Martineau *Stud. Chr.* 217 That he had given himself the air of a great Apostle. **1876** Geo. Eliot *Dan. Der.* I. ii. 12 Taking the air of a supercilious mentor. **1878** Bosw. Smith *Carthage* 78 The Senate thought fit to assume the air of those who were conferring a favour and managed to drive a hard bargain with the Syracusan king.

b. *esp.* in *pl.*

1704 Addison *Italy* (1733) 37 Which easily discovers the Airs they give themselves. **1717** Savage *Love in a Veil*, In France the coquet is rather admir'd for her airs. *a* **1732** Gay *Barley-Mow* 1, How many saucy airs we meet From Temple Bar to Aldgate Street. **1734** Fielding *Old Man* Wks. 1784 III. 132, I must always give myself airs to a man I like. **1742** Richardson *Pamela* III. 66 What had I to do, to take upon me Lady-airs, and resent? **1853** C. Brontë *Villette* I. (1876) 6, I hope you mean to behave prettily to her, and not show your airs. **1863** Kingsley *Wat. Babies* 6 A stuck-up fellow, who gave himself airs. **1876** Black *Madcap V.* v. 41 You will get cured of all these whims and airs of yours some day.

c. *to put on airs*: to assume an unjustified air of superiority.

1781 [see put *v.*[1] 47 d]. **1832** *Deb. Congress* 30 Jan. 203, I am aware that, at times, States have attempted to put on airs, and set up their own against federal opinions. **1860** O. W. Holmes *Prof. Breakf.-t.* v. 93 None of them like too well to be told of it, but it must be sounded in their ears whenever they put on airs. **1952** T. Williams *Summer & Smoke* II. i, It is understandable that she might be accused of 'putting on airs' and of being 'affected'.

†**16.** *spec.* Grand air; stylishness, 'style.' *Obs.*

1710 Steele *Tatler* No. 23 ¶1 She complained a Lady's Chariot . . hung with twice the Air that her's did. **1816** Miss Austen *Emma* I. iv. 25, I had no idea he could be so very clownish, so totally without air.

17. *Horsemanship.* 'The artificial or practised motions of a managed horse.' Chambers *Cycl.* 1751.

1641 Brooke *Eng. Episc.* I. ii. 5 Those Horses which are designed to a lofty Ayre, and generous manage, must be of a Noble race. *a* **1720** Gibson *Diet of Horses* ii. (ed. 3) 35 He never saw Horses go so well as they, all sorts of Aires, as well for the Manage de Guerre, as in the Leaps.

IV. In Music [= musical *mode* or modulation].

18. Connected succession of musical sounds; expressive rhythmical sequence of musical tones; song-like music, melody.

1590 Shaks. *Mids. N.* I. i. 183 Your tongue's sweet ayre More tuneable then Larke to Shepheard's eare. **1596** —— *Merch. V.* v. i. 76 If they but heare perchance a trumpet sound, Or any ayre of musicke touch their eares. **1749** *Numbers in Poet. Comp.* 32 How is it possible to accommodate the Quantity of the Notes to that of the Syllables, without spoiling the Air and Time of the Tune? **1795** Mason *Ch. Mus.* ii. 131 By the addition of too much Air by which these Masters deprived Harmony of its absolute supremacy, they robbed Church Music of its ancient solemnity. **1880** Hullah in Grove's *Dict. Mus.* I. 46 In common parlance air is rhythmical melody—any kind of melody of which the *feet* are of the same duration, and the *phrases* bear some recognisable proportion one to another.

19. a. *concr.* A connected succession of musical sounds in expressive rhythmical arrangement; a piece of music of this nature to be sung or played as a 'solo,' with or without a distinct harmonized accompaniment; a melody.

1604 tr. *Acosta's Hist. Indies* VI. xxviii. 493 With these instruments they made many kinds of Aires and Songs. **1656** Cowley *Misc.* i. (1669) 29 Whilst Angels sing to thee their ayres divine. **1678** Butler *Hudibr.* III. i. 919 For discords make the sweetest airs, And curses are a kind of pray'rs. **1684** *Lond. Gaz.* mdcccclxvii/4 Beginning with an Overture and some Aires for Violins. **1763** J. Brown *Poetry & Mus.* §12. 200 The Scotch Airs are perhaps the truest Model of artless and pathetic musical Expression, that can be found in the whole Compass of the Art. **1828** Scott *F. M. Perth* II. 219 The very airs which I have the trick of whistling. **1871** Black *Dau. Heth* xii. 115 'That "Flowers of the Forest" is a beautiful air, but you want it harmonised.' **1880** Hullah in Grove's *Dict. Mus.* I. 47 Technically, an air is a composition for a single voice or any monophonous instrument, accompanied by other voices or by instruments.

†**b.** *spec.* A light or sprightly tune or song. *Obs.* (Perhaps due to popular confusion with *airy*, or with other sense of *aria* in Ital.)

1597 Morley *Introd. Mus.* 180 These and all other kinds of light musick sauing the Madrigal are by a generall name called ayres. **1789** Burney *Hist. Mus.* (ed. 2) I. vi. 65 The word air, or as the Italians call it Aria, includes a certain piece of music of a peculiar rhythm or cadence. **1880** Hullah in Grove's *Dict. Mus.* I. 47 In the 16th and 17th centuries air represented popularly a cheerful strain.

20. That part of a harmonized composition for voices, instrument, or instruments, which manifestly predominates and gives character to it (supplying what, if sung or played alone, would be an 'air' in sense 19), as distinct from the other parts which form an accompaniment. In part-music this is usually the highest or soprano part.

1819 *Pantologia* I. s.v., Frequently, the principal vocal part is called the air. *Mod.* The air, which was at first allotted to the violins, was afterwards taken up by the clarionet. If you will sing the air, I will take the tenor.

†**21.** A harmonized melody, a part-song. *Obs.*

1597 Douland (*title*) The Firste Booke of Songes or Ayres of foure parts with Tableture for the Lute.

V. In Eastern Church. (See quot.)

c **1620** Bp. Andrewes *Minor Wks.* (1854) 99 A cloth to lay over the chalice, wrought with coloured silk, called the aire. **1850** Neale *Eastern Ch.* III. ii. 350 *note*, The second veil has no distinctive name, but the third is called ἀήρ or νεφέλη.

B. air- in *Comb.*

I. General relations, in which the hyphen has mostly a syntactical value, and also indicates a main stress on *air-*, as *'air-ˌbreathing*, *'air-ˌspun*, *'air-ˌproof*, *'air-ˌbubble*.

1. *objective*: with active pple., as ***air-breathing***, ***-crisping***, ***air-defiling***, ***-entraining*** etc., or *obj. genitive* with n. of agent or action, as ***air-breather***, ***-cleaner***, ***-cleanser***; **air-condenser**.

1559 *Mirr. Mag.* 563 (T.) Air-threat'ning tops of cedars tall. **1647** H. More *Song of Soul* III. xxxvi, Air-trampling ghosts. **1839–47** Todd *Cycl. Anat. & Phys.* III. 910/1 The air-breathers or pulmonary Mollusca. **1847** Carpenter *Zool.* §619 Air-conveying tubes, known under the name of *tracheæ*. **1855** Owen *Skel. & Teeth* 8 Air-breathing vertebrates. **1865** G. M. Hopkins *Poems* (1948) 37 Let me be to Thee as the circling bird, Or bat with tender and air-crisping wings. **1882** *Macm. Mag.* XLV. 500 Powerful air-pumping engines. **1926** *Lancet* 26 June 1292/1 The 'Deodos' Air Cleanser. The purpose of this apparatus is to purify and medicate the air of rooms and buildings by means of a vapour. **1929** *Times* 2 Nov. 4/7 The carburettor is to hand, and there is a useful air-cleaner. **1956** *Gloss. Terms Concrete* (*B.S.I.*) 7 *Air-entraining agent*, an admixture to Portland cement or to concrete which causes a small quantity of air to be incorporated . . in the concrete during mixing. **1962** *Which?* Oct. (Car Suppl.) 139/1 Stones [were] found in air cleaner.

2. *instrumental*: with passive pple., as ***air-bred***, ***air-freighted***, ***air-spun***, ***-swept***, etc.

1597 Drayton *Mortim.* 29 Ayre-bred moystie vapors. **1599** *Solim. & Pers.* III. in Hazl. *Dods.* V. 319 Air-bred eagles. **1725** Pope *Odyss.* IX. 330 Those air-bred people, and thin goat-nursed Jove. **1783** Sir J. Moore *Absence* ix. 33 Each air-form'd spectre. **1819** Shelley *Prom. Unb.* (1878) II. 89 How fair these air-born shapes. **1827** Hood *Hero & L.* xxxii, An air-blown bubble. **1839** Bailey *Festus* x. (1848) 110 This air-filled bowl. **1851** H. Melville *Moby Dick* III. xxiv. 159 Rolled in the sea like an air-freighted demi-john. **1853** M. Arnold *Scholar-Gipsy* in *Poems* 202 And air-swept lindens yield Their scent. **1901** *Guide to Felixstowe* (*Ward, Lock*) 2 It is an air-swept place, this sunny Felixstowe.

3. *similative*: as ***air-clear*** (clear as air), ***air-pale***, ***-sweet***, ***-thin***, ***-white***, etc., and *limitative*, as air-tight, ***air-proof***.

1600 Tourneur *Ovid's Met.*, *Prol.* 40 Ayre-cleare brightnes. *Ibid.* xxi. 145 Sacred lights in ayre-cleare azurie. **1879** Spon *Worksh. Rects.* 369 Waterproof but not air-proof . . the great drawback of ordinary mackintoshes. **1918** E. Sitwell *Clowns' Houses* 11 Each in an air-white crinoline. **1920** —— *Wooden Pegasus* 73 In air-pale waves. **1938** W. de la Mare *Memory* 67 A quiet, air-sweet October day. **1942** E. Sitwell *Street Songs* 31 The air-pale petals of the foam seem flowers. **1948** —— *Notebk. W. Shakes.* xii. 141 There are echoes . . some more air-thin than the sound of which they are a memory.

4. *locative*: with vbl. adj. or sb., as ***air-built***, ***air-dance***, ***air-fowling***, etc.

1605 Shaks. *Macb.* III. iv. 62 This is the Ayre-drawne-Dagger. **1658** tr. *Mouffet's Theat. Ins.* 994 The boyes . .

exercise their air-fowling not without profit and pleasure. **1727** POPE *Dunc.* III. 10 The air-built Castle, and the Golden Dream. **1784** H. WALPOLE in *Bk. of Days* I. 326, I expect that they [aeronauts] will soon have an air-fight on the clouds. **1843** MIALL *Nonconf.* III. 537 An air-built castle, which dissolves away before the gaze of reason. **1853** KINGSLEY *Hyp.* xi. 128 Swallows.. began their air-dance for the day. **1882** J. HAWTHORNE *Fortune's Fool* I. xii, The air-drawn picture of all the wondrous scenes that were in her memory. **1888** G. M. HOPKINS *Poems* (1918) 68 Cloud-puffball, torn tufts, tossed pillows flaunt forth, then chevy on an air-Built thoroughfare.

5. *attrib.* (Composed or formed) of air, as ***air-breath, -bubble, -current, -eddy, -particle, -plume, -supply, -wave.***

1600 TOURNEUR *Ovid's Met.* (1878) 175 My fearelesse ayre-plume-pen. **1756** F. HOME *Exper. Bleaching* II. iv. 76 A few hours after it has been there, air-bubbles arise, the liquor swells, and a thick scum is formed. **1765** BROWNRIGG in *Phil. Trans.* LV. 220 Air-bubbles adhering to the insides of the bottles. **1774** GOLDSM. *Hist. Earth* I. 34 (JOD.) To break these air-currents into smaller ones. **1827** CARLYLE *Misc.* (1857) I. 11 A distorted incoherent series of air-landscapes. **1851** H. MELVILLE *Moby Dick* III. i. 21 The air-eddy made by the sudden tossing of a pair of broad flukes. **1860** TYNDALL *Glac.* I. §6. 45 The minute air-bubbles which incessantly escape from the glacier. **1877** F. SCHUMANN *Man. Heating & Ventilation* 18 *Air Supply.* The following formulæ will demonstrate the necessity of a greater supply of pure air. **1881** BROADHOUSE *Mus. Acoust.* 75 Applying the visible motion of water-waves to illustrate the invisible motion of air-waves. **1885** W. B. YEATS in *Dublin Univ. Rev.* July 136/1 For there came an air-breath cool. **1909** H. G. WELLS *Tono-Bungay* III. iv. 407 That cold side that gives you the air-eddy I was beginning to know passing well. **1959** E. F. LINSSEN *Beetles* I. 112 The larvae of *Haliplus*.. must renew their air-supply at the surface of the water since they breathe through spiracles.

6. *attrib.* Of or pertaining to the air, as AIR-PLANT; **air-castle, -root, -stone**; ***air-sylph, -world.***

1817 COLERIDGE *Biogr. Lit.* 119 The wings of the air-sylph forming within the skin of the caterpillar. **1888** G. M. HOPKINS *Poems* (1918) 89 How the boys.. Are earthworld, airworld, waterworld thorough hurled. **1906** *Westm. Gaz.* 8 Sept. 13/1 We imagine ourselves stopping in just that way to chat with a friend in the highways of the air-world.

7. *attrib.* For the use, reception, passage, of air; as ***air-bag, -bottle, -furnace, -gland, -receptacle, -space, -syringe, -valve.*** Also AIR-BALLOON, -BLADDER, -BOX, -CELL, -CHAMBER, -GUN, -HOLE, -PIPE, -PUMP, -SHAFT, -VESSEL; and nearly all those in II. as **air-ball, -bath,** etc.

1732 in *Cal. State Pap., Amer. & W. Indies* 22 Feb. (1939) 230 To lett us know whether air furnaces are allow'd of, because at one of the works there is one built. **1784** WEDGWOOD in *Phil. Trans.* LXXIV. 370 Greatest heat of my small air-furnace. **1787** DARWIN in *Phil. Trans.* LXXVIII. 50 A small cell, which is kept free from air by an air-syringe adapted to it. **1836** TODD *Cycl. Anat. & Phys.* I. 99 The air-bags, for they scarcely deserve the name of lungs. *Ibid* I. 344/2 Continuous air-receptacles.. subservient to the function of respiration. **1859** TODD *Cycl. Anat. & Phys.* V. 281/2 The so-called air-gland. **1869** *Eng. Mech.* 22 Oct. 138/2 The pressure of steam.. at once closes the air-valve. **1918** *Jane's Pocket Aeronaut.* Dict. 8 *Air-bottle,* container for compressed air used for starting big engines. **1941** W. S. CHURCHILL *Speech* 25 June in *Secret Session Speeches* (1946) 28 By.. somewhat increasing the compressed air-bottle which drives them, they [*sc.* U-boats] were able to fire volleys of torpedoes.

II. Special combinations (with quotations in alphabetical order).

air-bag, a bag inflated with air, esp. one in a motor vehicle, designed to inflate upon impact so as to cushion the vehicle's occupants in a collision, or (*U.S.*) one built into a vehicle to improve the suspension; see also quot. 1836; **air-ball**, a ball inflated with air, a toy so called; **air-bath**, an arrangement for drying chemical substances; the protracted exposure of the body to the free action of the air as a form of medical treatment (cf. SUN-*bath*); **air-bed**, one with a mattress inflated with air; **air-bell** [BELL *sb.*[3]], a small bubble of air; *spec.* one formed in a photographic developer, etc., and appearing as a spot on a plate, film, or paper; **air-blast**, a blast of air; *spec.* in various technical uses (see quots.); **air-bloomery** (see quot.); **air-bone**, a hollow bone for the reception of air, as in birds; **air-brake**, one worked by the pressure of condensed air; **airbrasive** *a.* and *sb.* [A)BRASIVE *a.*] *Dentistry* (see quots.); **air-break**, (*a*) [BREAK *sb.*[1] 5] *Cricket*, a 'twist' or deviation in the air, of the ball when bowled; (*b*) [BREAK *sb.*[1] 17 b] *Electr. Engin.*, *attrib.* (see quot. 1910); **air-breathing** *a.*, applied to a jet-engine requiring the intake of air for the combustion of its fuel; **air-brick**, one perforated for ventilation; **air-brush**, a device for spraying colour over a surface by means of compressed air; also as *v. trans.*, to apply colour, paint, etc., to or (esp. in *Photogr.*) to retouch or (with *out*) to obliterate by means of an air-brush; also *fig.*; hence **airbrushed** *ppl. a.*; **airbrushing** *vbl. sb.*; **air-burst**, the bursting of a shell or bomb in the air; hence as *v. intr.*; **air-canal** (Bot.; see quot.); **air-casing**, the sheet-iron casing enclosing the base of a steamer chimney, to prevent conduction of heat to the deck; **air-castle**, a castle-in-the-air, a visionary or baseless project; **air-cavity**, one of the intercellular spaces in water-plants; **air-channel**, a channel for the passage of air, in various structures; **air-cock**, a stop-cock for letting air out or in; **air-compressor**, a machine for compressing air; **air-condenser**, an instrument for condensing air in a vessel; **air-cooled** *a.*, cooled by means of a current of air; so **air-cool** *v. trans.*, **air-cooling** *sb.* and *a.*; **air-cooler**, an apparatus or appliance for reducing the temperature; **air-core**, esp. *attrib.* (so *-cored* adj.) *Electr.*, applied to a type of transformer or coil in which the central core consists of an air-filled space instead of a magnetic material; **air-course** = AIRWAY 1; **air-crossing**, a passage or arched way to carry one air-passage over another in a mine; **air-cure**, a cure by the use of air, cf. *water-cure*; **air-cushion**, (*a*) one inflated with air instead of being stuffed; (*b*) a cushion (CUSHION *sb.* 2 a) of air; used esp. *attrib.* of a type of craft or vehicle buoyed up by a cushion of air; **air dam**, a streamlining device below the front bumper of a vehicle, a front spoiler (SPOILER 3 b); hence **air-dammed** *a.*, furnished with an air dam; **air-drain**, a covered channel round the external walls of a building to prevent damp, a 'dry area'; hence ***air-drained*** adj.; **air-drainage** (see quots.); **air-dried** *a.*, dried by the action of the air; so ***air-dry*** v. trans.; **air-driven** *a.*, actuated by means of compressed air; **air-dry** *a.*, dry to such a degree that on exposure to the air no further moisture is given off; **air-duct**, a passage for air, esp. to the air-bladder of fishes; **air embolism** *Path.*, an embolism caused by an air-bubble in the blood-stream; **air-engine**, one actuated by the elastic force of heated air; **air-escape**, a valve for allowing the escape of air from water-pipes; **air-extractor** (see quot.); **air-filter**, an apparatus for extracting extraneous particles, germs, etc., from air; **air-flow**, the flow of air, *spec.* that encountered by the surface of an aircraft in flight or by a motor-car in motion; **air-fountain**, one of which the jet is raised by condensed air; **air-freshener**, a substance or device for freshening the air (of a room); **air-gap**, a gap or hole through which air passes; *Electr.*, the air-filled space in a magnetic or electric circuit, as between the poles of a magnet or the terminals of an electrostatic machine; **air-gas**, a mixture of air and a vaporous hydrocarbon mixture (e.g. petroleum), used esp. as an illuminant; **air-gauge**, an instrument for measuring and indicating the pressure of air or gases; **air-glow** [GLOW *sb.* 2]: see quots.; **air-grating**, a grating or perforated plate for the entrance of air under floors, etc.; **air-hammer**, a large hammer moved by compressed air; **air-hardening** *a.* *Metallurgy*, applied to a metal that can be cooled in air; so ***air-harden*** v. trans., **air-hardened** *ppl. a.*; **air-head, -ing** (see quot.); **air-heater** (see quots.); **air-holder**, an air-tight vessel or receiver; **air-intake**, an inlet or duct for air; **air-jacket**, (*a*) one with air-tight lining, which, when inflated, supports the wearer in water; (*b*) a jacket (JACKET *sb.* 2) in which air or gas is circulated to diminish loss of heat from the enclosed vessel; so ***air-jacketed*** adj.; **air-layering** [cf. LAYER *v.* 1] *Hort.* (see quot. 1934); cf. CIRCUMPOSITION; **air-loop** (see quot.); **air-machine**, in a mine, a contrivance by which pure air is forced into ill-ventilated parts; **air-mass** *Meteorol.*, a body of air of uniform temperature and humidity; **air-mattress**, one inflated with air; **air-monger**, one who occupies himself with visionary projects; **air-pad**, a pad inflated with air; **air-passage**, (*a*) a passage through which air travels, e.g. the nasal passages, bronchial tubes, etc.; (*b*) *Bot.* the large intercellular space in the stems and leaves of some plants; **air-pillow** (see *air-cushion*); **air-pistol**, †(*a*) one in which the propelling power is the explosive force of inflammable gases; (*b*) one in which the propelling power is compressed air (esp. in sport and recreational use); **air-pit**, a ventilating shaft in a mine; **airplay**, the playing of recorded music (esp. a 'pop' record) over the radio; cf. PLAY *sb.* IV. 16 b; **air-poise**, an instrument for weighing air; **air-port**, [PORT *sb.*[3]] a port-hole in a ship for ventilation; also, an aperture for admitting air in a gas-burner; **air-pressure**, atmospheric pressure; pressure of air; **air-quake**, cf. *earthquake*; **air-receiver** [RECEIVER[1] 5], *spec.* a vessel for the storage of compressed air (*Funk's Stand. Dict.* 1928); **air-resistance**, the resistance of air to a moving body; **air rifle**, one actuated by the force of compressed air; **air-road** (= air-way); **air-root**, the root of an epiphyte, which hangs free in the air; **air-sac** = AIR-CELL; **air scoop**, a scoop for diverting the wind (see quots.); **air-scuttle** (= air-port); **air-seasoned** *a.*, of timber = *air-dried*; also **air-season** *v. trans.* and *intr.*, **air-seasoning** *vbl. sb.*; **air-ship**, one propelled by an air-engine; **air-shot**, (*a*) a shot in which a batsman, etc., misses the ball and inadvertently strikes only air, a miss; (*b*) a recording made from broadcast music; **air-space**, a space for the use or passage of air, e.g. for respiration, insulation, etc. (see quots.); **air speed**, the velocity of moving air or wind; †**air-spring**, elasticity of the air; **air-stone**, aerolite; **air-stove**, one which heats a stream of air passing between its surface and an outer casing; **air-stream**, (*a*) a current of air, *spec.* in *Meteorol.*; (*b*) = *air-flow*; **air suspension**, suspension which incorporates air for springing a motor vehicle; cf. *air-bag* above; **air-thermometer**, one which measures temperature by the expansion of a column of air; **air-threads**, the slender threads of the gossamer spider seen floating in the air; **air time**, time allotted for broadcasting (something) on radio or television; **air-trap**, a contrivance for preventing the escape of foul air from sewers, etc.; **air-tube**, (*a*) a tube designed for the passage of air, *spec.* SPIRACLE; (*b*) the inner tube of a pneumatic tyre; **air-tunnel** = *wind-tunnel*; **air-twist**, a spiral used for decorative effect in the stem of a wine-glass; so ***air-twisted*** adj.; **air-volcano**, an eruptive orifice from which volumes of gas are discharged with mud and stones; **air-washer** (see quot. 1949); **air-wave**, an atmospheric wave as of compression, rarefaction, or progression; **air wheel**, a balloon-tyre (see quots.); **air-whistle**, cf. *steam-whistle*. Also in various names of instruments or apparatus actuated by the elastic force of compressed or heated air (often = 'pneumatic'), as ***air-cylinder, -drill, -locomotive.*** Also AIR-LIFT 1.

1836 *Air-bag [see AIR- I. 7]. *a* **1877** KNIGHT *Dict. Mech.* I. 769/1 An india-rubber air-bag. *a* **1884** *Ibid.* Suppl. 12/2 Air bags for raising sunken ships. **1948** 'N. SHUTE' *No Highway* vii. 175 There's no equipment here to lift an aircraft of this size. We've got no air bags. **1970** *Guardian Weekly* 5 Sept. 16/3 Volvo engineers are a little worried that the airbag.. will be imposed on them before their own very detailed examination of its value and feasibility has been completed. **1971** M. TAK *Truck Talk* 1 *Air bag,* a device on tag axles that utilizes air pressure in the suspension system. **1983** *Truckin' Life* July 64/2 The truck came fitted with steel leaf springs on the steering axle and full airbags on the tandem. **1984** *Guardian* 22 Oct. 22/8 The clearly defined degree of protection universally provided by a lap-and-diagonal seat belt is complemented by a mini airbag in the steering wheel boss. **1869** *Eng. Mech.* 24 Sep. 29/2 The India-rubber coloured *air-balls, which are sold at fairs. **1881** MISS BRADDON *Asph.* I. 17 Children.. flying gaudy-coloured air-balls. **1791** BOSWELL *Johnson* (1887) III. 168 He.. walked in his room naked, with the window open, which he called taking an *air bath. **1885** *Buck's Handbk. Med. Sci.* I. 467 It is often desirable not to employ too much water, but to expose the body freely, giving an air bath. **1959** *Encounter* Oct. 48/2 Seven minutes air-bath in the shade; four minutes in the sun; then a shower. **1859** W. GREGORY *Egypt & Tunis* II. 204 We were lent two *air-beds by friends. **1815** *Air-bell [see BELL *sb.*[3]]. **1889** *Anthony's Photogr. Bull.* II. 143 Carbon Printing in Winter... The difficulty I experienced in avoiding air bells. **1945** T. H. SAVORY *Spiders Brit. Isles* (ed. 2) 53 As winter approaches the spider hibernates. Either it closes the mouth of its air-bell or it finds an empty shell.. and fills it with air. **1962** *Gloss. Terms Glass Industry* (*B.S.I.*) 38 *Air bell,* a bubble of irregular shape formed.. in the manufacture of optical glass. **1889** *Cent. Dict.*, *Air-blast. **1902** *Encycl. Brit.* XXXIII. 422/1 In.. air-blast transformers, apertures are left in the core by means of which the cooling air can reach the interior portions. **1946** H. P. YOUNG *Electr. Power Syst. Control* (ed. 2) vii. 194 Air-blast breakers can be classified into three main types depending upon the manner in which the compressed air is directed at the arc. **1845** *North Brit. Rev.* IV. 128 An *air-bloomery.. was dependent, for its blast, upon the varying currents of air that played around the hill on which it was placed. **1860** W. FORDYCE *Hist. Coal* 110 The first smelting furnace.. was undoubtedly the Air-Bloomery, a low conical structure, with small openings at the bottom for the admission of air, and a larger orifice at the top for carrying off the gaseous products of combustion. **1855** OWEN *Skel. & Teeth* 7 The extremities of such *air-bones present a light, open net-work. **1872** *Rep. Comm. Patents 1871* I. 253 Westinghouse, George, Jr.,.. Valve device for steam-power *air-brake couplings. **1945** R. B. BLACK in *Jrnl. Amer. Dental Assoc.* XXXII. 956/2 The *airbrasive process employs for its action a very fine—almost pinpoint—stream of compressed air into which a suitable finely divided abrasive agent has been introduced. **1953** I. GLICKMAN *Clin. Periodontology* xxxix. 665 *Airbrasive* which consists of fine abrasive powder (Dolemite in a stream of carbon dioxide) is used for removing surface deposits from the teeth. **1900** *Cricket* 29 Mar. 41/3 There is no necessity to mention Noble's *air-breaks any more. **1910** *Hawkins's*

Electr. Dict. 6/2 *Air Break Switch*, a type of switch designed to break the circuit in the open air or in an enclosed air space, as distinguished from an oil break switch. **1958** *B.S.I. News* Aug. 16 Heavy-duty composite units of air-break switches and fuses for voltages not exceeding 660V. **1956** in G. Merrill *Guided Missile Design, Operations Res.* III. i. 374 Pulsejet engines will initiate pressure waves of considerable energy, and the relatively long time it takes to warm-up an *air breathing engine forces consideration of the effect of heat in the exhaust gases. **1964** *Economist* 7 Mar. 891/2 Manned aircraft powered by air-breathing jets. **1889** *Cent. Dict.*, *Air-brush. **1901** *Brit. Jrnl. Photogr.* 1 Nov. 696 The ærograph [*read* aero-] is probably better known to the majority of photographers as the air-brush. **1916** 'B. Cable' *Doing their Bit* iv. 58 The quick and even painting of the shells by air-brush spray. **1934** H. Hiler *Notes Technique Painting* iii. 241 It may then be varnished..preferably with an air brush. **1941** J. C. Tobias *Man. Airbrush Technique* xxii. 116 Having transferred the design to illustration board, proceed to airbrush it. *Ibid.* xvii. 89 Airbrushed borders are often effective in giving a card distinction. **1953** O. R. Croy *Retouching* 165 Air brushing allows the photographer to concentrate on..the subject..without worrying over.. unfavourable surroundings. *Ibid.* 169 (*caption*) Photographs are air brushed with the help of masks. **1967** *Life* (Atlantic ed.) 30 Oct. 76/3 They..seldom miss an opportunity to show the expanses of both sexes once discreetly turned away from the camera or airbrushed out of view. **1983** *Times* 28 Sept. 6/6 Argentina had attempted to airbrush out the fact that it had broken off from the negotiating process. **1984** *Science* 6 Apr. 44 While viewing the material on the video monitor, the operator..can 'electronically airbrush' it to remove blemishes or add artifacts. **1917** 'Dixhuit' *Artillery Experience* v. 62 *Air-bursts of shrapnel are conspicuous. **1946** *Jrnl. R. Aeronaut. Soc.* L. 486/1 This particular rocket ..air burst over Sweden. **1950** in *Effects of Atomic Weapons* (*Los Alamos Scient. Lab.*) ii. 30 The brownish or peachlike tint of the cloud which has been reported, particularly in the Bikini 'Able' airburst, is apparently due to nitrogen dioxide. **1857** Henfrey *Elem. Bot.* §734 *Air-canals are long tubular channels, in petioles, or stems, bounded by a cellular wall. **1795** T. Wilkinson *Wand. Patentee* I. 22 By attempting a visionary comparison, which has just now struck my *air-castle imagination. **1831** Carlyle *Sart. Res.* (1858) 32 High Air-castles cunningly built of Words. **1839** W. Irving *Wolf. Roost* (1855) 217 Golden fancies, and splendid air-castles. **1840** C. Howard *Farming at Ridgemont* 140 A tunnel is formed by placing a wooden pipe..exactly over the centre of the *air-channel. **1927** Haldane & Huxley *Animal Biol.* iv. 96 These contain air-channels..which run within the bodies of elongated cells. **1800** Henry *Epit. Chem.* (1808) 56 Glass jars..provided with *air-cocks. **1874** *Air-compressor [see compressor 1 g]. **1892** P. Benjamin *Mod. Mechanism* 17 The Norfolk Compound Air-Compressor. **1908** *Westm. Gaz.* 21 July 4/2 An..ingenious air-compressor, specially designed for use on motor-vehicles. **1899** *Motor-Car World* I. 59/1 An *air-cooled Aster motor of $2\frac{1}{4}$ h.p. **1909** *Westm. Gaz.* 1 Apr. 4/1 The seven cylinders of the Gnome..when they are revolving at a high speed.. will be very efficiently air-cooled. **1914** E. A. Powell *Fighting in Flanders* iii. 73 The Lewis gun..is air-cooled. **1935** *Economist* 18 May 1141/1 A number of these aircraft are fitted with Rolls Royce engines, but the Gloster 'Gauntlet'..is equipped with an air-cooled engine. **1962** *Which?* Jan. (Car Suppl.) 4/1 Air-cooled: relies on fan-driven air, not water-filled radiator. *a* **1875** Knight *Dict. Mech.* I. 34/2 Shaler's *air-cooler. **1865** N. S. Shaler *U.S. Pat. 47,991* (*title*) *Air Cooling Apparatus. **1909** *Westm. Gaz.* 25 Mar. 2/2 The designer has adopted the expedient of revolving the cylinders en bloc around fixed cranks, whereby he is enabled to successfully adopt air-cooling. **1909** *Ibid.* 9 Sept. 4/3 The sparking plugs, which are provided with air-cooling ribs. **1894** *Phil. Mag.* XXXVII. 405 The *air-core transformer used for the experiment consisted of two coils wound one inside the other. **1906** A. Russell *Alternating Curr.* II. viii. 231 The ideal air core transformer, that is, the air core transformer the resistance of the primary coil of which is zero. **1953** Amos & Birkinshaw *Television Engin.* I. x. 265 (*caption*) Air-cored coils.., iron-cored.., Ferrite-cored. **1882** *Imp. Dict.*, *Air-course. **1937** *Times* 6 Feb. 8/5 Work on 14's face should have been stopped at least until a return air-course, far removed from the intake and leading directly to the main return, had been made. *a* **1884** Knight *Dict. Mech.* Suppl. 15/1 **Air-crossing* (Mining), an arch built over a horse-way or other road, with a passage or airway above it. **1911** *Act 1 & 2 Geo. V*, c. 50 §42 (3) All air-crossings shall..be so constructed as not to be liable to be destroyed in the event of an explosion. **1876** L. Tollemache in *Fortn. Rev.* Mar., Whether the fault lies both with the *air-cure and with the iron-cure. **1836–7** Dickens *Sketch.* (1850) 182/1 An easy chair with an *air-cushion. **1960** *Aeroplane* XCIX. 770/1 This new craft has, in fact, been designed to enable operators to obtain practical experience with air-cushion craft 'in the field'. **1962** *New Scientist* 19 Apr. 79/2 The air cushion of the VA-3 is derived from peripheral and intersecting slots. **1965** *Guardian* 5 Jan. 3/3 Air cushion vehicles—or hovercraft, if you prefer the term. **1974** *Daily Tel.* 3 July 12/3 The large *air dam at the front and the spoiler on the boot lid presumably serve some aerodynamic purpose. **1984** *Ibid.* 7 Mar. 14/5 Ventilated disc brakes are now fitted to all four wheels with the air dam being re-designed to allow a cooling flow to front brakes. **1976** *Scotsman* 24 Dec. 11/1 Inside the *air-dammed, aerofoiled saloon car challenger, there's a BMW trying to get out. **1843** *Jrnl. R. Agric. Soc.* IV. 357 An *air drain round the building is, in damp situations, highly useful. **1848** *Ibid.* IX. 341 No indications of wetness appeared on the two air-drained pieces. **1944** *Geogr. Jrnl.* June 252 Valleys and basins are more frosty, depending again on the degree to which the relief and other factors permit *air drainage from extensive uplands inland. **1948** White & Renner *Human Geogr.* IV. xx. 340/2 At night the air, which is cold and therefore heavy, drains down the slopes settling in the lower elevations. Hence danger of frost is least at the head of the piedmont plain and greatest at its foot. This.. is known as air drainage. **1889** *Cent. Dict.*, *Air-dried. **1891** W. Schlich *Man. Forestry* II. iv. 248 The Ash yields an excellent timber, hard and heavy, specific gravity when air-dried = ·75. **1908** *Chambers's Jrnl.* July 543/1 Peat which can be air-dried to such an extent that only some 25 per cent of moisture is retained. *a* **1912** *Paper Terminol.* (*Spalding & Hodge*) II. 1 *Airdried*..is applied to hand-made and exceptionally good machine-made writings and brown papers, when dried slowly by exposure to a uniform temperature. **1897** *Daily News* 1 Nov. 7/1 The *air-driven hydraulic pump. **1856** *Jrnl. R. Agric. Soc.* XVII. I. 194, I.. then allowed it to become *air-dry, by keeping it for some days in a safe place, in a heated room. **1949** *Gloss. Terms Timber* (*B.S.I.*) 13 In Great Britain the moisture content of air-dry timber may range between 14..and 23 per cent according to the season of the year and the species of timber concerned. **1870** Rolleston *Anim. Life* 75 The presence or absence of an *air-duct to the air-bladder. **1873** Dawson *Earth & Man* v. 100 In the bony pike..there is an extremely large air-bladder..communicating with the mouth by an air-duct. **1890** Billings *Med. Dict.* I. 32/2 **Air embolism*, the presence of free atmospheric air within the vascular system during life in sufficient quantity to give rise to symptoms of obstruction. **1905** *Lancet* 9 Dec. 1738/1 (*title*) Death of a Diver from Air Embolism. **1873** B. Stewart *Conserv. Force* iv. 105 The steam-engine, the *air-engine, and all varieties of heat engines. **1936** *Archit. Rev.* LXXX. p. lviii/1 The removal of smells from kitchens, of steam from bathrooms and of smoke from smokerooms is well worth while and there are a number of *air-extractor devices on the market that deserve the consideration of the architect. **1861** J. Stenhouse (*title*) The successful application of Charcoal *Air-Filters to the ventilation and disinfection of Sewers. *a* **1884** Knight *Dict. Mech.* Suppl. 15/2 *Air Filter*, a protective ventilator consisting of a cloth interwoven with thin brass wire to act as a filter for the air. **1927** *Daily Tel.* 10 Feb., Motor manufacturers are urged to provide air-filters on all motor vehicles. **1911** R. M. Pierce *Dict. Aviation* 16 **Air-flow*, the flow or movement of the air. **1915** *Aeronautics* 17 Nov. 327 Let us first see wherein mainly the behaviour of the air flow and its resistance differ from that prevailing in the case of a flat plane. **1935** *Discovery* Oct. 309/1 The occasional opening of doors is quite inadequate for regulating the air flow [in a film studio]. **1940** E. C. Shepherd *Britain's Air Power* 18 The bomber began to take on a load of ice it had not expected—ice on the edge of the wing to spoil its shape and interfere with the air-flow. **1961** P. Strevens in *Papers in Lang. & Lang. Teaching* (1965) xi. 134 If the breath-stream is forced to pass through a narrow constriction, the air-flow becomes turbulent. **1962** D. Slayton in *Into Orbit* 22 When you are re-entering the atmosphere..you must get the capsule into a position where its blunt end is pointed straight down into the airflow. **1949** *Good Housekeeping* (N.Y.) Nov. 135/1 Have you ever used an *air freshener—a special product that camouflages unpleasant odors with clean countrylike scents? **1960** *Guardian* 22 Feb. 6/7 An air-freshener in aerosol form. **1962** *Which?* Mar. 90/1 There are a great many air fresheners on the market, which claim to 'dispel', 'kill', 'neutralise' or 'suppress' unwanted smells. **1848** Mrs. Gaskell *Mary Barton* xvi, *Air-gaps were to be seen in their garments. **1899** R. Routledge *Discov. & Inv. 19th C.* (ed. 13) 541 A stout wire interrupted by an air gap in its centre provided with small brass balls. **1902** *How to make Things* 3/2 A miniature flash of lightning breaks through the insulating air-gap between the balls or oscillators. **1942** C. A. Cotton *Geomorphology* (ed. 3) vi. 73 The former gorge, or water gap, through this stratum is now no longer traversed by a stream, and becomes an 'air gap'. **1873** *Pract. Mag.* II. 399/1 *Air Gas Machine..an improved apparatus for forcing air in uniform quantities into a carbureter. **1879** *Encycl. Brit.* X. 101/2 This air-gas is now largely used both in America and Europe for lighting mansions, churches, factories, and small rural districts. **1909** *Chambers's Jrnl.* June 411/1 The application of what is generically termed 'air-gas' to domestic uses is one of far-reaching possibilities. **1841** *Civil Engin. & Arch. Jrnl.* IV. 13/1 The..instruments employed ..to determine the pressure of the steam,..namely, the barometer-gauge, the *air-gauge, etc. **1951** J. G. Vaeth *200 Miles Up* ii. 26 **Air glow*, which is a term applied to the light of the night sky (excluding starlight and moonlight), lends itself to spectroscopic examination and has been found to contain light emissions characteristic of nitrogen, oxygen, and sodium. **1958** *Sci. News* XLVIII. 12 One effect of the normal Sun on the atmosphere..is the production of the faint emission from the atmosphere at night which is called the night airglow. **1914** H. Brearley *Case-Hardening of Steel* vi. 72 The surface of the *air-hardened steel is less hard than that of water or oil quenched steel. **1930** *Engineering* 23 May 680/3 Steel A was air-hardened from 950 deg. C after soaking for 20 minutes. **1906** E. R. Markham *Amer. Steel Worker* (ed. 2) 278 The steel hardens when..exposed to the air. It is styled '*Air Hardening Steel', more generally known, however, as Self-Hardening Steel. **1839** Murchison *Silur. Syst.* I. xxxvi. 490 Ventilation is effected by means of *air-heads driven through the fault. **1881** R. Raymond in *Trans. Amer. Inst. Mining* IX. 99 Air-head, or Air-heading, *S. Staf.* A smaller passage, driven parallel with the gate-road, and near its roof, to carry the ventilating current. It is connected with the gate-road at intervals by openings called spouts. *a* **1875** Knight *Dict. Mech.* I. 49/1 **Air-heater*, a stove or furnace so arranged as to heat a current of passing air, for warmth or ventilating purposes. **1944** *Gloss. Terms Gas Ind.* (*B.S.I.*) 34 *Air heater*, an appliance designed to heat spaces by the forced circulation of large volumes of warmed air. **1806** Davy in *Phil. Trans.* XCVII. 12, I filled it with hydrogene gas from a convenient *airholder. **1918** *Jane's Pocket Aeronaut. Dict.* 8 **Air intake pipe*, a pipe fitted to the carburetter or induction system through which only air is drawn. **1922** *Encycl. Brit.* XXX. 26/2 (*caption*) Air Intake [in a wind tunnel]. **1931** T. E. Lawrence *Let.* 14 July (1938) 729 Scoop-tubes like air intakes thrust through the floor amidships. **1958** *Times* 19 June 6/3 He had been sucked into the air intake of a jet engine. **1909** *Westm. Gaz.* 4 May 4/2 An engine having specially designed *air-jackets. **1936** *Techn. Rep. Aeronaut. Res. Comm. 1934–35* I. 19 A wind tunnel investigation has been made of an air-jacketed engine. **1900** L. H. Bailey *Cycl. Amer. Hort.* II. 894/2 In a conservatory, merely a ball of sphagnum bound around the branch with twine will serve an equally good purpose... This kind of propagation is known as *air-layering. **1934** Webster, *Air layering*, a form of propagation, employed with certain plants whose branches cannot be brought to the ground for layering, in which a portion of a branch or stem, sometimes girdled, is kept covered, as by wrapping with moist soil, moss, or the like, until it forms roots and may be detached from the parent and planted... The process is specified as *pot layering* when the rooting medium is enclosed, as in a pot or box, and as *marcottage*, or *Chinese layering*, when the ball of earth or moss is merely tied about the stem. **1957** M. Free *Plant Propag.* vi. 183 In air-layering a suitable shoot is selected, the stem is wounded by removal of a cylinder of bark..where it is desired that roots should form. **1757** Smeaton in *Phil. Trans.* L. 202 On the north and south side, are two narrow windows or *air-loops. **1855** Leifchild *Cornwall Mines* 282 The underground boys work the *air-machines. **1893** F. Waldo *Mod. Meteorol.* iv. 318 If a swiftly moving *air mass moves into a quiet mass of air, then the resistance is considerable. **1942** W. G. Kendrew *Weather* xii. 65 *Air mass* is the term applied to a part of the atmosphere large enough to play an appreciable part for a period of at least some hours in the meteorology of any region. **1949** M. Mead *Male & Female* xi. 240 A hunting-trip with an *air-mattress. **1627** Feltham *Resolves* I. xv. Wks. 1677, 25 Thou *Airmonger, that with a madding thought, thus chaseth fleeting shadows. **1876** *Trans. Clinical Soc.* IX. 23 An *air-pad was applied to the tumour. **1836** Todd *Cycl. Anat. & Phys.* I. 345/1 The air-passages in birds. **1878** Rankine *Steam Engine* (ed. 9) 459 Air Passages —Blowing Apparatus—Chimney. **1911** *Encycl. Brit.* XXIII. 199/2 A foreign body in the air-passages may be impacted above the vocal cords. **1779** Ingenhousz in *Phil. Trans.* LXIX. 398 The compound of the two airs in the *air pistol takes fire. **1855** *Brit. Pat. 2,422* 1 This invention relates to certain improvements on the ordinary air pistols used as toys for children. **1872** *Ann. Rep. U.S. Patent Office Comm. Patents 1870* II. 107/1 Air-Pistol. Reuben Brooks, Jr., Rockport, Mass. **1936** H. Nicolson *Let.* 5 May (1966) 260, I do not quite like the idea of Ben being such an old cautious cissie as to refrain from shooting policemen with air-pistols. **1975** *Oxf. Compan. Sports & Games* 922/1 For air pistol shooting, the aiming mark contains scoring rings for points valued 10 to 7, surrounded by six more rings with score values from 6 down to 1 point. **1986** *Target Gun* Aug. 27/1 It is said that Richard Wang put in 5,000 shots in training with air pistol [*sic*] the week before he broke the British record. **1709** T. Robinson *Nat. Hist. Westmld.* v. 30 If the Miners should not open their *Air-Pits and keep their Thurling-Ways clear. **1839** Ure *Dict. Arts* 969 These air-pits do not in general exceed 7 feet in diameter. **1966** *Guardian* 7 June 9/3 We cannot conscientiously recommend such records for *airplay. **1976** *Sounds* 11 Dec. 31/1 If this fine song doesn't get the airplay it deserves I shall be very cross indeed. **1983** *Listener* 10 Feb. 11/2 The chart rounds .., ironically, are created by continual airplay. ? **1667** Sprat *Hist. Roy. Soc.* III. 363 (T.) Small mutations of the air.. insensible by the more common *airpoises. **1788** A. Falconbridge *Acct. Slave Trade* 24 Most of the ships..are provided, between the decks, with five or six *air-ports on each side of the ship. **1867** Smyth *Sailor's Word-bk.* 28 *Air-ports*, large scuttles in ships' bows for the admission of air, when the other ports are down. **1944** *Gloss. Terms Gas Ind.* (*B.S.I.*) 33 *Air port*, the aperture in an aerated burner adjacent to the injector through which primary air is admitted to the mixing tube. *a* **1875** Knight *Dict. Mech.* I. 50/2 Gruber's *air-pressure filter. **1946** *Nature* 9 Nov. 674/2 Using air-flow through a capillary to regulate the air-pressure difference. **1965** W. S. Allen *Vox Latina* 7 *Ceteris paribus*, stressed sounds produce greater intensity of air-pressure. **1746** Berkeley in Fraser's *Life* viii. (1871) 318 We are not to think the late shocks merely an *air-quake (as they call it). **1750** *Phil. Trans.* XLVI. 700 A certain ingenious gentleman would not allow the last shock of an Earthquake in London to be an Earthquake..but rather calls it an Airquake, because it was lateral. **1891** *Daily News* 13 Oct. 5/4 General Dyrenforth's experiments in rain-making by means of explosions, or what he calls 'terrific airquakes', have not convinced his scientific opponent. **1950** D. Gascoyne *Vagrant* 28 Till all night's spark-sprayed dome is stunned with quick air-quakes of gold. **1951** *Gloss. Terms Plastics Ind.* (*B.S.I.*) 34 **Air receiver*, (*a*) an accumulator or storage vessel charged with compressed air or inert gas used in a high pressure hydraulic system as an alternative to a weight-loaded accumulator; (*b*) an accumulator or storage vessel used as a reservoir in pneumatic systems. **1959** *B.S.I. News* Apr. 3 The welding of air receivers is likely to be separately discussed by a group of experts on welding and may become the basis for welding of pressure vessels as a whole. **1901** *Sci. Amer.* 9 Feb. 82/2 Light has recently been thrown upon the question of *air resistance of railway trains. **1908** *Aeronautics* Mar. p. xviii, Trials of a cellular aeroplane ..have demonstrated that weight is a less important factor than air-resistance. **1936** *Discovery* Feb. 40/1 To diminish air-resistance by the streamlining of both engine and train. **1902** *Sears, Roebuck Catal.* (ed. 112) 298/2 Quackenbush Improved Nickel Plated *Air Rifle..$4.35. **1958** *Daily Tel.* 30 June 15/8 A girl was injured by an air rifle. **1866** *Morn. Star* 18 Dec. 6/2 We went down the *air road, thinking that we might be able to get to the shaft that way. **1863** H. Bates *Riv. Amazons* ii. (1864) 29 The *air-roots of epiphytous plants, which sit on the boughs of the trees above. **1836** Todd *Cycl. Anat. & Phys.* I. 37/2 The *air-sac [of the Physalus]. **1879** Wright *Anim. Life* 4 The air-tubes of the lungs do not end in air-sacs. **1919** W. B. Faraday *Gloss. Aeronaut. Terms* 55 **Air Scoop*, a projecting cowl, which, by using the dynamic pressure of the relative wind or slip stream, serves to maintain air pressure in the interior of the envelope. **1920** *Flight* XII. 663/2 In Italy the British method of supplying air to the ballonets through airscoops fitted in the slipstream of the propellers is never used. **1929** *Daily Express* 1 Jan. 6/3 The air-scoops projecting from every porthole in a vain attempt to manufacture a breeze with the ship's motion, fail to fulfil their functions. **1748** Anson *Voy.* I. iv. (ed. 4) 50 The Commodore ordered six *air-scuttles to be cut in each ship. **1917** J. B. Wagner *Seasoning of Wood* x. 151 The wood is allowed to *air-season for several months to a year. *Ibid.* 154 The present methods of air-seasoning in use have been determined by long experience. **1919** H. S. Betts *Timber* v. 150 A kiln is used also when partially air-seasoned or even fully air-seasoned material is to be dried further. **1930** *Forestry* IV. 36 In air-seasoning both the temperature and humidity of the available air are dependent on local climatic conditions. **1855** W. Boyd *New York Pred.*, It ploughed gently the sea ..the *air-ship of Eric. **1956** R. Alston *Test Commentary* xix. 176 Surridge set the tone with a number of *air-shots against Davidson. **1956** M. Stearns *Story of Jazz* xix. 254 The combination of..Cuban and jazz drummers was electric and air shots of the session are now collector's items. **1963** *Times* 19 Jan. 3/3 He reached the first drop shot only at its second bounce. But having got over this and an air shot which followed soon afterwards he settled down to give a demonstration which was too much for the South African.

1976 *Gramophone* Dec. 952/3 The sound quality..leaves a lot to be desired—the tracks are all air-shots from between 1937 and 1940. **1986** *Golf World* July 157/3 Would it have been a different story if Hale Irwin had not had an air shot in the third round as he went to tap in a one-inch putt to lose by just one shot? **1889** *Cent. Dict.*, *Air-space. **1893** DUNGLISON *Dict. Med. Sci.* (ed. 21) 32/1 *Air space*, space filled with air from rupture or other injury to air-cells. **1900** *Lancet* 11 Aug. 458/1 That this conference approves that the standard of air space for dwellers in cities and large towns be raised to 500 cubic feet for every adult and to 250 cubic feet for each child under 10 years of age. **1936** *Discovery* June 197/2 It appears that the dielectric constant is lower in the case of those organs having much fatty tissue and air-spaces such as the bones and lungs. **1957** *Archit. Rev.* CXXI. 213 Rust-proof rails swing out, cabinets are double cased (airspace insulation) in zinc coated steel. **1922** *Encycl. Brit.* XXX. 27/1 The larger Eiffel tunnel gives an *air speed of 40 metres per second. **1660** BOYLE *Exp. Phys.-Mech.* i. 27 An account plausible enough of the *Air-spring. **1608** *Let.* in Wright's *Dict.*, They talk of divers prodigies..but specially *air-stones. **1879** WARREN *Astron.* vi. 123 These are called aerolites or air-stones. **1869** HARTWIG *Polar W.* 308 Soon the Polar air-streams regain their supremacy. **1913** J. C. HUNSAKER tr. *Eiffel's Resistance of Air & Aviation* 239 Stability was verified by suspending the model [aeroplane] in the air stream upon a horizontal axis. **1922** *Encycl. Brit.* XXX. 27/1 The experimental section of an Eiffel type wind tunnel consists of an air stream as it crosses an open room from wall to wall. **1958** *Times* 23 Sept. 11/4 His pilgrimage coincides with the fair example of a wet, westerly airstream. **1961** *New Scientist* 16 Mar. 672/1 Such a cooling mechanism [for rockets] is superior..because a liquid is simply swept away in the air-stream. **1961** L. F. BROSNAHAN *Sounds of Language* i. 2 The conversion of some of the kinetic energy of this airstream into acoustic energy. **1960** *Buses Illustr.* June 197/1 Following the prototype *air-suspension vehicles, four such models are now in production. **1980** *Truck & Bus Transportation* Feb. 62 One of the good things about air suspension is its ability to provide a constant vehicle riding height under any conditions of static loading. **1806** DAVY in *Phil. Trans.* XCVII. 47 A small *air-thermometer capable of being immersed in the gold cones. **1871** TYNDALL *Fragm. Sc.* (ed. 6) II. xvi. 451 Incompetent to..affect the most delicate air-thermometer. **1753** CHAMBERS *Cycl. Supp.*, *Air-threads are not only found in autumn, but even in the depth of winter. **1955** *Air-time [see sense 1 c]. **1968** *Melody Maker* 30 Nov. 7 On radio there are only two programmes giving air time to the music. **1984** *Listener* 16 Feb. 28/3 Breakfast television could still be selling the sort of airtime appeal that means good business. **1826** KIRBY & SPENCE *Entomol.* III. xxx. 154 The two prolegs, which M. Latreille thinks are *air-tubes. **1847** CARPENTER *Zool.* §619 The air-tubes of insects. **1877** *Engineering* 16 Nov. 381/3 The air-tube of a diver's dress. **1894** *Work* 315/2 Repairing Air-tube of 1892 Dunlop. **1953** J. S. HUXLEY *Evolution in Action* iii. 75 [The insects] breathe by means of air-tubes, which convey oxygen direct to the tissues. **1933** *Jane's Fighting Ships* 26 A ¼ inch scale model was prepared for testing in the *air-tunnel at the National Physical Laboratory. **1897** A. HARTSHORNE *Old Eng. Glasses* 58 The beaded stems, out of which the *air twists were derived, continued to be made in Holland. *Ibid.*, Air-twisted stems of various kinds. **1903** *Burlington Mag.* III. 63/1 The secret of the construction of two of the classes—namely, the brilliant, and the combined opaque and air-twist—seems to have been lost. **1916** J. S. LEWIS *Old Glass* 62 The air-twist probably began with a 'tear'. **1879** GEIKIE in *Encycl. Brit.* X. 250 Certain remarkable orifices of eruption..to which the names of mud-volcanoes, salses, *air-volcanoes, and macalubas have been applied. **1905** *Lancet* 25 Feb. 507/2 The Stellite Air Deodoriser..is an effectual *air-washer and as such it may obviously have numerous hygienic applications. **1949** *Gloss. Terms Refrig.* (*B.S.I.*) 4 *Air washer*, a water-spray system or other device for cleaning air, capable of serving also as a cooler, humidifier, or dehumidifier. **1879** W. JAMES in *Jrnl. Speculative Philos.* XIII. 85 Notwithstanding the brilliant conjectures of the last few years which assign different acoustic end-organs to different rates of *air-wave, we are still greatly in the dark about the subject. **1881** Air-wave [see AIR- I. 5]. **1895** H. LAMB *Hydrodynamics* Index, Air-waves, effect of viscosity on. **1930** *Flight* XXII. 404/1 The *Air Wheel..is revolutionary in design, and, as its name implies, the cover has the dual function of a tyre and wheel, being a full balloon cover mounted directly on a hub attached to the 'plane undercarriage. **1932** *Times* 29 Feb. 17/5 A new tire for small cars has been introduced... It is known as the air wheel and is based on aeronautical experience. **1870** W. BOYD *Morse Alph.*, Telegraphy by steam-whistle, *air-whistle, musical instrument, or light.

III. Of or pertaining to aircraft.

1. In numerous combinations (tending to supersede AERIAL) relating to locomotion in the air by means of aircraft, as ***air drill***, ***navigation***, ***pageant***, ***service*** [SERVICE *sb.* 32], ***traffic***; carried or conducted by aircraft, as ***air parcel***, ***photography*** (also ***-photo(graph)***), ***post***, ***survey***, ***tour*** (so ***-tourist***); ***air-flying***, ***-launched***, ***-portable*** (so ***-portability***), ***-sailing*** adjs.; also, **air-bridge**, (*a*) a link between points provided by air transport; (*b*) at an airport, a portable covered bridge to enable passengers to cross directly between the terminal and an aircraft; **air carrier** = AIRCRAFT *carrier*; **air circus** [cf. CIRCUS 2 d], a squadron of aeroplanes; an air display, an air pageant; **air Derby**, see DERBY 1 d; **air edition**, see AIRMAIL b; **air ferry**, an aircraft or system of aircraft for the conveyance of passengers and goods; **airfoil** *U.S.* = AEROFOIL; **air freight**, freight conveyed by air; also as *v. trans.*; hence ***air-freighting*** vbl. sb.; **air fuelling**, the refuelling of one aircraft by another in flight; **airgraph** (also **Airgraph**), a form of airmail registered by Kodak Ltd., in which the correspondent's letter is photographed on a reduced scale; a letter so transmitted; **air hog**, cf. *road hog* (ROAD *sb.* 12 and ROAD HOG); **air letter**, a letter conveyed by air, esp. one written on a folding form of special design; **air-mark** *v. trans.* (see quot. 1929); hence ***air marker***, ***-marking***; **air-mast**, a mast to which airships are moored; **air mile**, a nautical mile used as a measure of distance flown by aircraft; hence ***air mileage***; **air-minded** [MINDED *ppl. a.*] *a.*, interested in or enthusiastic for the use and development of aircraft; so ***air-mindedness***; **air miss** (see quots.); **air plot** (see quot. 1951); **air-pocket**, a local condition of atmosphere, as a down current or sudden change of wind velocity, which causes an aircraft to lose height suddenly; also *fig.*; **air position**, position in the air, (*a*) for tactical purposes [see POSITION *sb.* 7 c]; (*b*) that an aircraft would have reached if the flight had been in motionless air; also *attrib.*; **airscape**, a view taken from the air (cf. SCAPE *sb.*[3]); **air-sea rescue**, applied to a branch of the Royal Air Force, whose task is to rescue airmen and passengers from the sea, and to such operations; **air sense**, cf. *road sense* (ROAD *sb.*); **air-sick** *a.* [after SEA-SICK *a.*], sick from the motion of an aircraft; hence **air-sickness**; **air space, airspace**, the air considered as a medium for the operation of aircraft; **air speed**, the velocity of an aircraft (or of anything flying, e.g. a bird) in relation to the air through which it is moving; also *attrib.* and as *v. trans.*, to convey (mail, etc.) by air; hence ***air-speeded*** ppl. adj.; **air terminal**, (*a*) the terminal point of an air-line, also called *air terminus*; (*b*) the town office of an air-line, equipped for the reception of passengers; **air-to-air** *a.*, from one aircraft to another; so ***air-to-ground***, ***air-to-surface*** adjs.; **air traffic controller**, one who is responsible for regulating the movement of aircraft, esp. into and out of an airport.

1939 *Baltimore Sun* 17 Apr. 9/1 The New Zealand service will constitute the air line's second 'air bridge' of the Pacific. **1948** *Newsweek* 9 Aug. 27/1 The Berlin 'air bridge'—as the Germans call it—claimed its first American victims on July 9. **1976** *Times* 17 May 12 Access to the aircraft from the beehive [*sc.* a passenger terminal] was through canvas tunnels, the forerunners of today's movable air bridges. **1981** *Telegraph* (Brisbane) 17 Feb. 13/1 The airbridge..gives direct access from the aircraft to the terminal. **1920** *Proc. Air Conf., London* 99 Air carriers were designed and commissioned towards the end of the war. **1932** *Flight* XXIV. 1227/1 His 'Air Circus' carried 250,000 passengers. **1933** *Aeroplane* 18 Oct. 690/1 The accident arose from a collision..during an air circus. **1940** D. WHEATLEY *Faked Passports* viii. 94 After the Armistice he [Goering] was ordered to surrender the planes of his famous air-circus to the Americans. **1932** *Flight* XXIV. 584/2 A squadron of 'Furies' was given just 15 minutes in which to show off their air drill. **1916** *Aerial Age Weekly* 11 Sept. 793 (*heading*) Air Ferry over Great South Bay. **1932** *Flight* XXIV. 933/1 The daily air ferry services between Shoreham, Portsmouth and Ryde. **1912** C. M. DOUGHTY *Clouds* 119 Their air-flying enemies. **1922** *N.A.C.A.* (*U.S.*) *Rep. Nomencl. Aeronaut.* 621 Airfoil. **1930** *Flight* 29 Aug. 972/2 The addition of an airfoil fuselage. **1929** *Aerial A.B.C.* Feb.–Apr. 19 The conditions for air freight services apply to all goods which are accepted by an air traffic company. *Ibid.* May–July 41 Luggage can also be forwarded as air freight. **1959** W. D. PEREIRA *North Flight* ix. 143 Make sure that box is air-freighted to-night. **1947** *Aircraft Engin.* Jan. 27/1 Now..that civil air freighting is upon us..the problems involved in the efficient handling of freight must be tackled. **1937** *Jrnl. R. Aeronaut. Soc.* XLI. 285 Air fuelling offers another alternative, but the large aerodrome..seems the simplest of all methods of increasing the economy of air transport operation. **1941** *Engineer* 2 May 296 To meet the need for cheapening and expediting homeward postal communication from the British Forces in the Middle East, the Post Office is introducing an airgraph service. **1941** *Sphere* 6 Dec. p. i, Airgraph letters should be written in black ink. **1945** *Comment from Italy* (*Three Arts Club*) 41 For weeks now there had been little for him,—just an occasional Airgraph,—nothing more. **1955** H. & A. GERNSHEIM *Hist. Photogr.* 254 The airgraph service which operated between 1941 and 1945, in which by modern microfilm methods myriads of messages were flown between families in England and the fighting services in the four corners of the world. **1909** *Westm. Gaz.* 9 Feb. 4/1 Pointing out how the flying-machine is likely to violate every international law and rudely trespass on every private right and privilege, characterising the intrepid navigators as air-hogs and human vultures. **1949** A. R. WEYL *Guided Missiles* 108 The most powerful air-launched missile of its kind. **1951** *Jrnl. Brit. Interplanetary Soc.* X. 217 The 'Skyrocket'..adopted the technique of air-launching from a B.29. **1920** *Flight* XII. 781/2 Threepenny air-letter postage between London and Amsterdam, with the prospect of a similar charge to Paris, is getting a little nearer sanity. **1951** *Oxf. Jun. Encycl.* IV. 17/1 An air letter is written on a special form supplied by the Post Office. This is made of thin paper and impressed with a sixpenny stamp. **1929** *Times* 12 Mar. 12/2 Thousands of cities and towns throughout the States have been 'air-marked' by civic and trade associations. During last year one oil company alone painted names on 4,200 stations... These markings, together with a standardized system of indicating obstructions, such as high tension cables..have proved a very valuable aid to air pilotage. **1948** *Shell Aviation News* No. 117, 5/1 An extensive air-marking programme along Skyway One is now under way. *Ibid.* No. 122, 4/2 The Civil Aeronautics Administration is sponsoring a programme for air marking cities, towns and villages throughout the country. An air marker is a sign on rooftop or ground, visible from the air, which enables a pilot to orient himself when lost. **1927** *Daily Tel.* 1 Nov. 10/6 The selection of a site on the south side of the St. Lawrence for the erection of an Imperial airmast. **1919** *Sphere* 6 Dec. p. viii/1 Fifteen hundred air miles at 107 m.p.h. **1945** *Yorks. Post* 19 Apr. 1/1 Nulde, 20 air miles east of Amsterdam. **1948** *Jrnl. Inst. Navig.* I. 63 The aircraft's fuel consumption ..must be balanced against savings in air mileage. **1951** *Gloss. Aeronaut. Terms* (*B.S.I.*) III. 10 *Air-mileage unit*, an instrument which derives continuously and automatically the air distance flown, and feeds this function into other automatic instruments. **1928** *Daily Express* 20 June 8/3 At last, I believe, people are becoming 'air-minded'. **1927** *Glasgow Herald* 2 Nov. 13 The expansion of aviation systems and the spread of a sense of 'airmindedness'. **1930** *Flight* 3 Jan. 4 That great wave of airmindedness that followed Lindbergh's transatlantic flight. **1960** *Guardian* 10 Nov. 1/5 The new Minister did not explain..the exact technical significance of an 'air-miss'... (The Air Ministry says it is 'rather like a near miss on the ground'). **1962** *UK 'Air Pilot'* p. RAC 35 Whenever a pilot considers that his aircraft may have been endangered by the proximity of another aircraft during flight..he should make an airmiss report. **1871** *Ann. Rep. Aëronaut. Soc.* 62 The minds of many thinking men have been, during the present century, turned to this interesting subject of air navigation. **1927** *Air* Dec. 55/2 The first Birmingham Air Pageant. **1928** *Aerial A.B.C.* Apr. 20 Air parcels may be posted at any District or Branch Post Office. **1919** *Geogr. Jrnl.* LIII. 330 (*heading*) Air Photography in Archaeology. *Ibid.*, Had I not been in possession of these air-photographs the city would probably have been merely shown by meaningless low mounds. **1920** *Flight* XII. 233/1 The achievements of air photography during the War were very remarkable. **1923** *Geogr. Jrnl.* LVII. 359 Here two air-photos will certainly reveal the course of undiscovered Roman roads. *Ibid.* 363 The field archæologist has much to gain in future from an alliance with the air-photographer, particularly in England. **1959** *N. & Q.* CCIV. 1/1 From air photographs Dr. St. Joseph was able to show the size and shape of Roman fields in the Fenlands. **1942** D. C. T. BENNETT *Compl. Air Navig.* (ed. 4) v. 172 The Air Plot Method is similar in principle..but instead of flying on one constant course only, a number of courses may be followed. **1951** *Gloss. Aeronaut. Terms* (*B.S.I.*) III. 6 *Air plot*, a continuous plot of true heading steered and air distances flown. **1913** C. GRAHAME-WHITE *Aviation* v. iv. 155 A lessening of pressure—or what is more familiarly known as an 'air pocket'. **1933** *Boys' Mag.* XLVII. 24/2 We shall probably bump a bit, owing to air-pockets. **1967** *Economist* 18 Mar. 1033/1 Restoration of the tax credit of 7 per cent of the cost of new investment..had been all but inevitable in order to avoid the problem of the 'air pocket'— a drying up of orders during the months before restoration was due. **1977** *Time* 14 Nov. 32/1 Almost all of them fear that the economy will run into an air pocket during the second half of next year. **1959** *Times* 16 Jan. 10/5 The British idea was to develop an air-portable gun for both roles. **1959** *Star* 19 Feb. 9/5 Mr. Christopher Soames, Secretary for War, coined a new watchword today for Britain's all-regular Army of the future—air portability. **1917** F. A. COLLINS *Air Man* vi. 140 The English had not chosen their battlefield, or rather air-position, and thus fought at a disadvantage. **1937** D. C. T. BENNETT *Compl. Air Navig.* v. 154 The difference of the air position so obtained in relation to the ground position (i.e. the departure point) is the wind effect for the total time. **1945** *Sci. Amer.* June 349/1 One of the recently revealed secrets.. is the 'air position indicator', an instrument that..gives continuous readings of latitude and longitude plus a continuous record of nautical air miles flown. **1911** *Daily Mail* 11 Sept. 3/4 (*heading*) First Air-Post. *Ibid.*, An air post cannot be expected as yet to behave with the same clockwork regularity as an earth post. **1919** *Liverpool Jrnl. Commerce* 20 Nov. 6/4 Within the past few months regular air post services have sprung into being. **1897** *Aeronaut. Ann.* 92 The..care needed in making changes in an air-sailing machine. **1921** *Flight* XIII. 193 (*caption*) Winter in Switzerland: An airscape of the popular resort, Davos. **1941** *Flight* XXXIX. 361/1 The various rescue services..have been co-ordinated under one central control known as the Directorate of Air/Sea Rescue Services. **1941** J. A. HAMMERTON *ABC of RAF* (ed. 2) 74 Abbreviations of Titles and Terms employed by the R.A.F... A/SRS. Air Sea Rescue Service. **1942** *Aeroplane* 13 Nov. 562/3 A Supermarine Walrus of the Air-Sea Rescue Service alighted on the sea in the middle of a German minefield. **1958** *Times* 10 July 15/2 The manufacture..of..inflatable liferafts and other air-sea rescue aids. **1919** *Conquest* Dec. 65/1 The successful execution of aerial acrobatics involves the possession..of that indefinable quality which, for want of a better word, we will call 'air-sense'. **1919** *Sphere* 1 Nov. p. x/3 Outside the R.A.F. there were no records of a daily air service to guide the Avro company in organising such an undertaking. **1922** *Daily Mail* 8 Dec. 12 An 1,800 miles air service from Copenhagen to Brindisi is being planned. **1785** F. FARLEY *Bristol Jrnl.* 14 May in *N. & Q.* (1938) CLXXV. 79/1 Air sick. **1873** Air-sick [see AIRMAN]. **1908** H. G. WELLS *War in Air* vii. §1 Even the air-sick men flushed and spoke. **1958** G. GREENE *Our Man in Havana* III. ii. 123, I suppose he's feeling air-sick again. **1784** H. WALPOLE in *Bk. of Days* (1863) I. 325 If there is no *air-sickness..I would prefer a balloon to the packet boat. **1908** H. G. WELLS *War in Air* vii. §2 For a time he was not a human being, he was a case of air-sickness. **1911** R. WALLACE in Grahame-White & Harper *Aeroplane* xiii. 289 A State should have full dominion in the air space above its territory. **1959** *Listener* 19 Mar. 512/1 Persia protests to U.S.S.R. that Russian aircraft have violated her air space eighty-one times in past three months. **1961** *New Scientist* 20 Apr. 103/2 It is generally agreed that national sovereignty in the so-called 'airspace' is limited to some level above the Earth's surface. **1910** R. FERRIS *How it Flies* 453 Air-speed—the speed of aircraft as related to the air in which they are moving; as distinguished from land-speed. **1912** *Aeronautics* Dec. 391/1 It is possible with an air-speed indicator to read..how far one is above this danger point. **1937** D. C. T. BENNETT *Compl. Air Navig.* v. 165 The following abbreviations are acceptable for use in Navigation Logs..A/S = Air Speed. **1941** E. C. SHEPHERD *Military Aeroplane* 17 Height and forward speed..are shown on a sensitive altimeter and on an airspeed indicator. **1942** *Gen* 15 July 50/1 Watch that airspeed! Eleven hundred and you're levelling out. **1959** *Time* 9 Mar. 9/2 The magazines are air-speeded each week to every corner of the globe. **1976** *Early Music* Oct. 522/2 (Advt.), All prices include dispatch; USA copies by air-speeded post. **1981** *Nature* 19 Mar. p. x (Advt.), Order Form... Please send me The Lancet each week for one year... £40.00 overseas (Airspeeded). **1918** *Times* 6 Dec. 12/2 (*headline*) An Air Survey..Surveying the country by means of aerial photographs. **1924** O. G. S. Crawford (*title*) Air Survey and Archæology. **1925** *Flight* XVII. 735 (*title*) Air surveying. **1933** *Discovery* Feb. 57/1 Air surveying is used extensively by the United States Geological Survey for the preparation of topographic maps. **1921** *Aircraft Yr. Bk.* 79 The principal communities which are situated along this air route should create thoroughly modern air terminals. **1935** C. G. Grey in N. Tangye *Air is Our Concern* i. 10 Though Hounslow Heath was actually the first London Air Terminal, it was given up because it was on the wrong side of London. **1956** *Times* 2 Feb. 5/1 A temporary air terminal will be erected on the platform to take those services now being handled at B.E.A.'s Waterloo air terminal. **1919** *Sphere* 10 May 108/1 The air terminus for London is Hounslow. **1941** *Flight* XL. 48 f/2 Drogue targets for air-to-air gunnery training. **1955** *Sci. News Let.* 26 Mar. 197/3 The Air Force has unveiled its newest guided missile..described as the 'only air-to-air missile with a "brain" of its own'. **1957** *Times* 22 Aug. 6/6 Air-to-air guided missiles on wing-tip launchers. **1942** *Hutchinson's Pict. Hist. War* 10 June–1 Sept. 135 (*caption*) A..high-wing monoplane..has proved useful for reconnaissance and air-to-ground co-operation by the British. **1958** C. C. Adams et al. *Space Flight* 51 Next to nothing is known about air-to-air or air-to-surface rockets, though a few surface-to-air missiles are known. **1923** *Daily Mail* 29 Jan. 13 (*heading*) Air tours at a penny a mile. **1929** *Punch* 20 Mar. 326/3 The Minister is satisfied that before many months we air-tourists will be taking our twelve-day flips to Kenya. **1912** H. E. Richards *Sovereignty over Air* 4 We must consider the principle on which the relations of States are to be conducted with regard to air traffic. **1933** *Flight* XXV. 524/2 (*heading*) Air Traffic Control. **1951** *Oxf. Jun. Encycl.* IV. 381/2 The advent of the fast, all-weather aircraft, and the demand for frequent and regular services, have made it essential to establish strict rules for air-traffic control. **1956** *USAF Dict.* 39/1 *Air traffic controller*, an aircraft controller..responsible for providing air traffic control. Often shortened 'controller'. **1973** [see *traffic controller* s.v. traffic *sb.* 6]. **1979** *Arizona Daily Star* 5 Aug. A10/3 He told air-traffic controllers he would try to land at Hays. **1929** *Lancet* 12 Jan. 105/2 The facilities offered by air transport to patients travelling abroad. **1946** in *Amer. Speech* (1948) XXIII. 76 Air transportability. **1879** P. Brannon (*title*) The air-boat for arcustatic air-travel. **1923** G. Collins *Valley of Eyes Unseen* 326 The great strides recently made in the art of air-travel. **1963** *New Yorker* 8 June 96 Showcase is air-travel light. **1951** L. MacNeice tr. *Goethe's Faust* II. Act II. p. 205 She departs. Enter, above, the air-travellers. **1908** *Westm. Gaz.* 1 July 12/1 Thirteen persons who made a successful air-trip from the Champ de Mars. **1959** *Elizabethan* Apr. 5/3 The chance of an air-trip overseas.

2. Pertaining to the air as a sphere of offensive or defensive operations, as ***air alert, attack, -bombing*** (also ***-bomber***), ***defence, observation, offensive, reconnaissance, strike, support, supremacy, warfare***; used of a bomb, missile, etc., discharged from an aeroplane, as ***air bomb, torpedo***; also, **air control**, control of an area by means of air power (in quot. 1915 *spec.* to give the correct range for artillery fire); **air cover**, protection by aircraft during a military operation; **air-drop** (chiefly *U.S.*), the landing of troops or supplies by parachute; also as *v. trans.* & *intr.*; **air-head**, cf. *beach-head*; **air mine** (see quots.); **air power**, power of defensive and offensive action dependent upon a supply of aircraft, missiles, etc. (cf. sea-power 2); **air umbrella**, a force of aircraft used to give air protection to a military operation; **air warden** (see air-raid).

1941 *Times Weekly* 5 Feb. 2/3 In spite of air alerts and privations, the population have not lost their courage. **1959** *Times* 18 May 7/2 The reason why Strategic Air Command does not maintain an air alert, with aircraft carrying nuclear weapons in the air twenty-four hours a day. **1914** *Sphere* 26 Dec. 318/1 The possible air attack over London. **1915** Grahame-White & Harper *Aircraft in Gt. War* v. ii. 172 Air attacks on cities have appeared despicable largely because they are so new. **1941** N. Macmillan *Air Strategy* xiv. 109 A true conception of the object of the air blockade. **1914** *Sci. Amer.* 15 Aug. 113/2 (*heading*) The Air Bomb. **1915** Grahame-White & Harper *Aircraft in Gt. War* v. ii. 172 The Germans..were prepared to use every instrument ..drifting mines, air bombs. *a* **1930** D. H. Lawrence *Last Poems* (1932) 54 And most murderous of all devices Are poison gases and air-bombs Refinements of evil. **1929** F. P. Gibbons *Red Napoleon* (1930) viii. 198 American field guns ..became the target of air bombers and low flying combat 'planes. **1934** *Flight* XXVI. 141/2 The idea of air bombing, which General Groves and..his supporters are trying to popularise. **1915** Grahame-White & Harper *Aircraft in Gt. War* vi. ii. 271 It was certainly unfortunate for the Germans that, as their air control for artillery grew less effective, that of the Allies should have begun to reach its full efficiency. **1930** *Flight* 3 Jan. 1 These are the air control of Iraq and the Air Defences of Great Britain. **1942** *Hutchinson's Pict. Hist. War* 10 June–1 Sept. 245 Our bombers and fighters thrust fiercely into the attack, affording continuous and effective air cover to our attacking forces. **1916** *Sphere* 26 Feb. 207/1 (*heading*) The Problem of Air Defence. **1922** *Encycl. Brit.* XXX. 87/1 Air defence.. deals with the arrangements which deny to enemy aircraft access to vulnerable points. **1949** *Britannica Bk. of Year* 687/1 *Airdrop*, that which is dropped from an airplane, such as supplies. **1950** *Baltimore Sun* 29 Apr. (edition B*) 1/7 D-day of the exercise was marked by the biggest of peacetime airdrops. **1958** *N.Z. News* 1 July 4/1 An airdrop of prefabricated sections for ten bivouacs..was made by the New Zealand Forest Service. **1951** A. M. Ball *Compounding & Hyphenation* 23/2 Air-drop, *v.* **1955** *Time* 3 Oct. 29/2 The U.S. International Cooperation Administration this month began air-dropping 1,000 tons of rice to the 100,000 peasants who inhabit the region. **1966** H. Harrison *Plague fr. Space* iii. 33 We had airdropped in during the night. **1941** N. Macmillan *Air Strategy* xv. 128 Long range air escorts..to protect the fleets of bombers. **1784** Air-fight [see air- I. 4]. **1908** H. G. Wells *War in Air* ix. §3 The devastation and ruins of the greatest air fight in the world. **1944** *Amer. N. & Q.* Sept. 84/2 *Airhead*, the counterpart, in air action, of *beachhead*; used by Major Eliot F. Noyes..speaking before the Soaring Society of America, Aug. 5, 1944, in referring to the behind-German-lines base established by Allied gliders during the Normandy invasion. **1945** *Times* 1 Mar. 5/6 Two large 'air-heads' each with two transport strips and one light plane strip were built between Kalemyo and the river. **1944** *Times* 18 Mar. 4/7 A big-scale exercise with paratroops, air-landing units, [etc.] ..was in progress. **1914** *Sci. Amer.* 15 Aug. 114/1 The aerial mine is inferior to the sea-mine not only in its vulnerability to currents, but also in its visibility...Against..these handicaps the air-mine can oppose only its cheapness and lightness. **1939** *War Weekly* 202/3 A German sketch visualising the use of air mines against aeroplanes. The sketch shows a swarm of hydrogen-filled balloons released during an air-raid. Each balloon has hanging from it a chain with a mine attached. **1943–4** *Hutchinson's Pict. Hist. War* 27 Oct.–11 Apr. 26 Among the vast armada that was sent up against the invading force of bombers was a special squadron which towed air mines... The effect..was to catch the American aircraft in the tow ropes or destroy them by the blast from the mines. **1923** Kipling *Irish Guards in Gt. War* I. 30 Artillery fire, directed by air observation. **1944** *Times* 5 Jan. 3/1 Some of the credit for the flexibility and accuracy with which our superior weight of guns is used must go to our 'air o.p.' (observation post) squadrons... I have seen the little ' air o.p.' circling over the enemy lines. **1915** Grahame-White & Harper *Aircraft in Gt. War* vii. i. 295 (*heading*) Strategy of an Air Offensive. **1944** *Ann. Reg. 1943* 29 The British air offensive against Germany..set up a new record. **1923** Kipling *Irish Guards in Gt. War* I. 57 The days of the merciless air-patrols had yet to come. **1908** H. G. Wells *War in Air* iii. §5 The immense aeronautic park that had been established..to give Germany..the air power and the Empire of the world. **1909** in F. T. Jane *All World's Air-Ships* 327/3 'Air power' can hardly be more than one of many factors in deciding the issue of future wars. **1940** *Economist* 11 May 851/2 The superiority of air power over sea power. **1915** Grahame-White & Harper *Aircraft in Gt. War* I. ii. 25 An air reconnaissance would have told him that Blücher..was actually marching north. *Ibid.* ii. iv. 47 (*heading*) Air-Scouting and Tactics. **1945** *Times* 3 May 3/3 Destroyers of the East Indies Fleet bombarded airfields ..and followed this up with an air strike. **1944** T. H. Wisdom *Triumph over Tunisia* xvii. 143 The function of what [Air Marshal] Coningham now called the Air Striking Force. **1935** Burge *Compl. Bk. Aviation* 553/2 A deliberate attempt was made by both sides to gain air superiority. **1941** *Aeronautics* Oct. 49/2 Fortunately the Royal Navy has never completely neglected the importance of air support to naval forces. **1916** *Sphere* 29 Jan. 109 (*heading*) The latest German attempt to challenge British air supremacy. **1940** E. C. Shepherd *Britain's Air Power* 7 On an Army front air supremacy is essential to success in these days. **1874** 'Mark Twain' & C. D. Warner *Gilded Age* I. xviii. 233 Colonel Sellers..was the inventor of the famous air-torpedo. **1916** *Illustr. War News* 8 Mar. 6/1 (*caption*) A French air-torpedo caught in a tree over a German trench. **1941** *Hutchinson's Pict. Hist. War* 14 May–8 July 138 They slink along from port to port under the protection of their air umbrella. **1915** Grahame-White & Harper *Aircraft in Gt. War* v. xiv. 252 The axiom that 'might is right' may apply very forcibly to the air wars of the future. **1916** *Fortnightly Rev.* XCIX. 1062 Air warfare on the scale indicated..opens up possibilities in the way of air raids for landing considerable bodies of men.

3. Of that branch of a country's armed forces which fights in the air, as ***air arm*** [cf. fleet *sb.*[1] 1 d], ***armada, cavalry, fleet, service***; also, **air force**, a military or naval force organized for conducting operations in the air; that part of the military forces of a country (in Great Britain, the Royal Air Force) which consists of officers and men with aircraft and other necessary equipment; so in titles of officers, as ***air commodore, (vice-)marshal*** [see marshal *sb.*], ***officer***; of non-commissioned ranks, as ***air-gunner*** (hence ***-gunnery***), ***mechanic***; also ***air council, ministry*** (see quot. 1959), ***-scout, staff***; **air-bomber**, a bomb-aimer; **Air Training Corps** (abbrev. A.T.C.), an organization for the training of cadets for the Royal Air Force; **Air Transport Auxiliary** (see quot.). For *air crew, pilot* see 4; see also airman.

1917 *Flying* 19 Sept. 129/2 Why not remove the 'air arm' at once from 'the naval and military control'? **1940** E. C. Shepherd *Britain's Air Power* 7 The Navy has its own air arm designed to work with the ships of the Fleet. **1917** *Flying* 31 Oct. 225/2 The disaster which befell the German air armada. **1911** *Times* 25 Feb. 7/3 The Balloon School is being reorganized and will be transformed into an Air Battalion. **1943** *Hutchinson's Pict. Hist. War* 17 Feb.–11 May 101 We now group pilots, navigators and air bombers together on entry into the Service. **1944** *Times* 8 July 2/2 As the air-bomber takes his aim he [etc.]. **1917** 'Contact' *Airman's Outings* 203 We shall see a great extension of ground attacks by air cavalry. **1965** *Observer* 11 July 2/5 The United States is about to reinforce its troops in Vietnam with a new high-powered 'air-cavalry' division. **1919** *Flight* XI. 1044 His Majesty..has approved of new titles for the commissioned ranks of the Royal Air Force..Air Commodore. **1920** *Ibid.* XII. 113/1 The chair will be taken at 8 p.m. by Air Commodore E. M. Maitland. **1917** *Act 7 & 8 Geo. V* c. 51 An Act to make provision for the establishment, administration, and discipline of an Air Force, the establishment of an Air Council, and for purposes connected therewith. **1908** H. G. Wells *War in Air* iv. §3 The German airfleet. **1946** A. Lee *German Air Force* ii. 19 The Luftwaffe was organized territorially into Air Fleets (Luft-flotten). There were four immediately before the war. **1917** Air force [see *air council*]. **1918** *Flight* 6 June 605/1 'The Air Force Cross', to be awarded to officers and warrant officers for acts of courage. *Ibid.*, 'The Air Force Medal', to be awarded to non-commissioned officers and men for acts of courage. **1920** *Act 10 & 11 Geo. V* c. 76 §11 (2) Where possession is reasonably required for naval, military, or air force purposes. **1959** *Chambers's Encycl.* I. 185/2 The view that an air force should be free to operate independently or that it should have equal status to the land and sea forces is predominantly an Anglo-American conception. **1928** *R.A.F. Regulations Amendm. List* July 3 Airmen selected for employment as air gunners will be required initially to qualify at a short course of air gunnery. **1944** *Times* 11 Apr. 4/4 Air gunners reported they shot down 43 enemy fighters. **1917** *Flying* 18 July 480/3 Second-Lieutenant Fletcher warmly commended the gallant conduct of First Air Mechanic Merritt. **1928** C. F. S. Gamble *North Sea Air Station* i. 39 The term 'air mechanic' is in use, though no such naval rating really exists. By air mechanic is meant a man who has been through a course of training either at the Central Flying School or at Eastchurch. **1916** *Flight* VIII. 112/1 (*heading*) An Air Ministry at last. **1959** *Chambers's Encycl.* I. 197/2 *Air Ministry* is the department responsible in the United Kingdom for the organization and direction, under the minister of defence, of the Royal Air Force. **1920** *Act 10 Geo. V* c. 7 §11 (3) The expression 'air officer' means any officer above the rank of group captain. **1963** *Times* 16 Apr. 12/3 Air Vice-Marshal T. N. Coslett has been appointed Air Officer Commanding-in-Chief, R.A.F. Maintenance Command. **1939** *War Illustr.* 11 Nov. 282/3 Officers of Air Rank. **1914** *Times* 24 June 4/1 The Royal Naval Air Service..will form part of the Military Branch of the Royal Navy... A certain number [of officers] will..be selected to fill the higher posts in the Air Service. **1911** R. M. Pierce *Dict. Aviation* 19 *Air-scout*, a scout who operates in the air; an aerial observer. **1914** *Illustr. War News* 19 Aug. 43 (*caption*) The value of the air-scout: military entrenching viewed by an airman from a height of about 1000 feet. **1922** *Times* 17 Jan. 11/5 He thought him an officer very likely to become one day Chief of the Air Staff. **1940** Air Staff [see fleet *sb.*[1] 1 d]. **1941** *Times* 10 Jan. 2/3 It is proposed to establish an Air Training Corps to provide pre-entry training for candidates for air crew and technical duties. **1941** *Flight* XXXIX. 57/2 The birth of the A.T.C. **1939** *Ibid.* XXXVI. 373/2 The units have been strengthened by.. groups of pilots from..Air Transport Auxiliary. A.T.A. was originally formed by British Airways for..assisting the regular airline people to maintain communications during and after the expected full-scale bombing attacks on this country. **1919** Air Vice-Marshal [see marshal *sb.*].

4. Of persons engaged in the flying, operation, or maintenance of aircraft, as †***air-boy, -girl, navigator*** (in quot. 1834 transf.), ***pilot***, †***-sailer (-or), stewardess***; also, **aircrew**, (*a*) the crew of an aircraft (pl. *-crews*); (*b*) used *collect.* in *pl.* (*-crew*): the members of such a crew; **air hostess**, a stewardess in a passenger aircraft; airman; **airwoman** (see airman). See also 3.

1873 *Cassell's Mag.* VIII. 134/1 We saw two air-boys leaning over the side of the car. **1921** *Flight* XIII. 477/1 The two University air crews are staying there. **1939** *Aeronautics* Aug. 5/1 A source of trained men from which the Volunteer Reserve could draw for air-crew training purposes. **1940** *Times Weekly* 27 Nov. 6 It is one of the great merits of the R.A.F. curriculum..that it turns out air crews of which every member can at a pinch take over the work of any other. **1948** *Daily Tel.* 29 May 2/4 The job of the Training Wing is to train 'Air Crews', a new form of R.A.F. entry, introduced, I gather, in 1946. **1955** *Times* 25 May 11/7 It has been quite impossible for many young married pilots and aircrew to make proper provision for their dependents. **1955** *Times* 21 July 4/6 While finding that there was nothing in the aircrew's tour of duty to cause undue fatigue, the report urges that B.O.A.C. should consider some limitation of hours of duty of an aircrew at an airport. **1957** J. Braine *Room at Top* vi. 54 I'd learned to drive in the RAF: I'd shared an Austin Chummy with three of the aircrew. **1977** *R.A.F. News* 5–18 Jan. 2/1 The OCU..has trained about 7,000 aircrew of 13 air forces throughout the world. **1984** *Aviation Week & Space Technol.* 24 Sept. 93/2 The software provides connected-word recognition, which allows aircrews to control a number of cockpit functions by spoken command. **1928** *Daily Express* 20 June 1/3 All first impressions vanished... The boyish airgirl [*sc.* Miss Earheart] became a feminine woman. **1945** P. A. Larkin *North Ship* 14 The Polish air-girl in the corner seat. **1934** *Baltimore Sun* 6 Feb. 22/1 The air hostess was the overnight guest of Captain and Mrs. W. O. Schrum. **1936** *N.Z. Herald* 24 Mar., A knowledge of nursing is essential for an air hostess..for the experience of handling people. **1939** *Flight* 14 Dec. 490/1 The K.L.M. has found it wiser to employ stewards rather than Air Hostesses on the London line. **1958** *Times Lit. Suppl.* 17 Oct. 598/4 The unanimity with which air hostesses give as their reason for choosing this profession the desire to meet people and see distant places. **1834** Carlyle *Sart. Res.* ii. v. in *Fraser's Mag.* IX. 306/1 A hapless Air-navigator, plunging, amid torn parachutes, sand-bags, and confused wreck, fast enough, into the jaws of the Devil! **1915** *Sphere* 20 Feb. 198/1 A well developed system of meteorological reports can be of such help to the air navigator. **1913** *Stamp Collecting* 27 Sept. 27/2 The provisional air pilot was arguing with the Republican officials. **1918** E. Wallace *Tam o' the Scouts* 211 (*title*) Aircraft by 'An Air Pilot'. **1923** J. W. Simpson *Ess. & Mem.* 169 The confident courage that inspires air-pilots. **1834** Carlyle *Sart. Res.* ii. v. in *Fraser's Mag.* IX. 306/1 The thunderstruck Air-sailor is not wanting to himself in this dread hour. **1897** *Aeronaut. Ann., Scientific value of flying models*, The air-sailer who..adds the thrust of a screw to the forces he is accustomed to deal with. **1908** H. G. Wells *War in Air* vii. §5 Then Bert..had his first experience of the work of an air-sailor. **1936** *Punch* 9 Dec. 646/1 To Chloe, an 'Air Stewardess'. My Chloe rides the heavens in a roaring silver hull, She serves up morning coffee over Basle and Istanbul.

5. In names of various types of aircraft, as ***air ambulance*** (cf. AMBULANCE *aeroplane*), ***-bomber*** [see 2], ***-bus***, ***-car***, ***freighter***, ***liner***, †***-machine***, †***-sailer (-or)***, ***scout***, ***taxi***, ***vehicle***, ***yacht***; **air-boat**, (*a*) a lighter-than-air aircraft; (*b*) = FLYING *boat*. Also, AIRCRAFT, AIRPLANE 2, AIRSHIP, AIR-VESSEL 3.

1921 *Aeronautics* 2 June 394/1 The first air ambulance.. is painted aluminium with a large Red Cross painted on the fuselage and beneath the wings. **1933** *Lancet* 16 Dec. 1381/2 Air ambulance detachments under the British Red Cross. *Ibid.* 15 July 160/2 An air-ambulance service for the conveyance of urgent.. cases to the hospitals and infirmaries in Glasgow. **1870** tr. *F. Marion's Wonderful Balloon Ascents* III. iv. 218 The air-boat of M. Pline seems to us one of the best ideas; but the working of it presents many difficulties. **1876** C. B. MANSFIELD *Aerial Navig.* II. xiii. 436 The action of rowing an air-boat must be much simpler than the same exercise on water. **1913** *Britannica Year-bk.* 343 The second class [of seaplane], variously termed 'flying-boat' and 'air-boat', consists essentially of a long boat-shaped hull, wherein the passengers' seats are contained, and on which the planes are built up. **1926** *Glasgow Herald* 18 Aug. 9 New British all-metal air-boats. **1910** *Times* 4 May 11/6 Probably when there are air-buses we shall call their drivers airmen. **1960** *Aeroplane* XCVIII. 468/1 A subsonic short- to medium-stage high passenger-density aircraft, for operation at low fares. This we call the Air-Bus. **1829** Air-car [see AIRWORTHY *a.*]. **1911** GRAHAME-WHITE & HARPER *Aeroplane* ii. 41 Further developments, in passenger-carrying, are expected during 1911, when 'air-cars', carrying four and six occupants as their regular equipment, will be introduced. **1962** *Flight Internat.* LXXXII. Suppl. 6/3 The air car [i.e. a hovercraft] is capable of operating over land, water, sand, swamps, snow, or thin ice, with equal ease. **1930** *Pop. Sci. Monthly* Dec. 55/2 (*caption*) One of the air freighters put in service on a recently opened Pacific coast line. **1908** *Daily Mail* 25 May 7/6 The cost of working the air-liner was represented as small. **1955** *Times* 11 July 9/3 Twenty people died in the airliner, which crashed on.. a scheduled flight. **1783** *Morning Herald* 17 Sept. 3/1 In a few days I shall have finished an air-machine, which will ascend, descend, or describe at pleasure a horizontal line. **1881** W. D. HAY *300 Years Hence* xii. 326 Tenders on the opposite side of the great air-machine begin to load. **1910** *Times* 23 Aug. 7/5 People look for the coming of the day when air machines are to become a practical means of regular locomotion. **1897** *Aeronaut. Ann.* No. 3, p. 2 The development of the motorless air-sailer. **1923** *Daily Mail* 17 Apr. 8 The engineless air-sailor. **1913** GRAHAME-WHITE & HARPER *With Airmen* xi. 276 The air scouts whirl over the enemy's troops at the rate of sixty miles an hour. **1914** *Sphere* 3 Oct. p. ii, One of these dismantled air scouts. **1920** *Flight* XII. 459/2 The chief concern of the many Americans who attended Mr. Handley Page's recent lectures on aviation in the United States appeared to be to discover when air taxis would be possible. **1927** *Observer* 7 Aug. 11/3 It was an ordinary air-taxi flight from Brooklands to Ascot. **1963** *Economist* 14 Dec. 1125/3 Charter and air-taxi flights in the area. **1902** *Aeronaut. Jrnl.* July 51/1 Some accomplishment on the part of an air vehicle. **1898** *Ibid.* July 54/2 The millionaire who indulges in an air yacht. **1920** *Flight* XII. 865/1 A converted.. flying boat, fitted up as an 'aerial yacht'. .. This air yacht—elegantly furnished with two cabins seating 10 passengers.. was officially launched.. on June 22.

6. In names of parts of aircraft, or of apparatus used in aircraft or for the navigation of aircraft, as ***air chart***, ***frame*** [FRAME *sb.* 11 h], ***log***, ***map***, ***propeller*** (so ***prop*** colloq.), ***sextant***; also, **air-brake**, a movable plane or flap on the wing of an aeroplane, that can be lowered to decrease its speed; **airscrew**, a power-driven screw for producing pull or thrust by rotation in the air; a propeller.

1914 *Aeronaut. Jrnl.* July 228 Air brakes.. must not tend to produce any upsetting effect on the machine. **1928** C. F. S. GAMBLE *North Sea Air Station* xiii. 210 Fitted with an air-brake in the form of adjustable flaps in the trailing edge of the lower plane adjacent to the fuselage. **1920** *Flight* XII. 854/2 These air charts, which are constructed on Mercator's projection, measure approximately 20 ins. by 18 ins. **1951** *Oxf. Jun. Encycl.* IV. 290/1 An air map presents an accurate picture of the ground below, illustrating.. all conspicuous geographical features... An air chart, drawn to a much smaller scale and without the elaborate detail of the map, is designed simply to enable the navigator to plot his position during the journey. **1931** *Aircraft Engin.* Jan. 9/2 Enclose both engines.. in a high speed air frame. **1957** *Technology* July 187/1 A turbo-jet engine which rose straight into the air by itself with no airframe at all [the 'flying bedstead']. **1928** V. E. CLARK *Elements Aviation* 138 *Air log*, an instrument for measuring the linear travel of an aircraft relative to the air. **1943** 'T. DUDLEY-GORDON' *Coastal Command at War* xii. 115 One navigator.. always takes a portable typewriter with him on a raid... So I thought that I should do my air logs on the typewriter. **1913** GRAHAME-WHITE & HARPER *With Airmen* viii. 204 It has been decided that.. certain districts should be marked out on air-maps, and that aeroplanes should not be allowed to fly over them. **1951** Air map [see *air chart*]. **1935** T. E. LAWRENCE *Let.* 5 Apr. (1938) 867 You can push an air-prop pitch up to great steepness, so long as the revs are not extravagant. **1910** R. FERRIS *How it Flies* x. 208 The form of the air-propeller has passed through a long and varied development. [**1784** tr. *J. P. Blanchard's Jrnl.* 6 The fly, acting on the air as a screw, appeared to me the most suitable and efficacious mode which an aeronaute can adopt to advance in a calm.] **1894** *Proc. Internat. Conf. Aerial Navig., Chicago* 265 For aeroplanes driven by screw propellers.. there must always be two air screws.. rotating in opposite directions. **1914** *Aeronaut. Jrnl.* XVIII. 315 *Airscrew*, used as a generic term to include both a propellor and a tractor screw. **1916** M. A. S. RIACH *Air-Screws* ii. 14 (*heading*) The forces acting on an air-screw blade. **1951** *Oxf. Jun. Encycl.* IV. 8/2 The gas-turbine is widely used in aircraft to turn an ordinary propeller or airscrew... For long, fast journeys the airscrew-turbine is much used. **1922** *Flight* XIV. 754/3 They can now supply.. revolution indicators.. air sextants, [etc.].

7. Of land or buildings used for the operation or maintenance of aircraft, as ***air base***, ***park*** (chiefly *U.S.*), ***shed***, ***station***; also, **'airdrome** *U.S.* = AERODROME 2 b; **'air-strip**, a strip of land prepared for the taking off and landing of aircraft, often for temporary use. Also AIRFIELD, AIRPORT.

1919 *Athenæum* 23 May 360/2 'Air-base', 'aircraft',.. 'air mechanic', [etc.].. are now everyday terms. **1938** *Flight* XXXIV. 424 e/2 The cost of the Shannon air base.. will be close on half a million pounds. **1917** E. N. FALES *Learning to Fly* v. 97 The airdrome.. is used exclusively for flying, and may be as large as a mile square. **1943** Airdrome [see AIRFIELD]. **1929** *Daily Tel.* 22 Apr. 2/5 Ten air parks.. and sixty landing grounds will be provided. **1944** *Amer. Speech* XIX. 304 'Airparks', the ATS said, would be small landing fields in or near communities for the use of private flyers. **1915** *Whitaker's Almanack 1916* 464/2 French airmen raided the German air-sheds at Freiburg. **1911** *Aeronautics* Apr. 13/2 Starting and Landing Stations.. A cumbersome expression... 'Air Stations' have been suggested as alternatives. **1914** *Whitaker's Almanack 1915* 774 *Fort George* (Cromarty Firth).—British Naval Air Station. **1923** *Daily Mail* 17 July 10 Ocean Air-stations. **1942** *Newsweek* 7 Dec. 27/3 Then.. further airstrips for landing the transport planes were built by the troops as they went along the jungle trails. **1944** *Times* 18 Mar. 3/2 The American forces.. immediately began a drive for the air-strip. **1956** W. SLIM *Defeat into Victory* xii. 251 An airstrip which served as an emergency landing ground on the Hump route.

8. Of routes or courses taken through the air by anything flying, esp. by aircraft, as ***air lane***, ***road***, ***route***; also, **air corridor**, a route to which aircraft are restricted, esp. one over a foreign country. Also AIRWAY 2.

1922 *Flight* XIV. 34/1 (*heading*) Abolition of Air 'Corridors'. The regulations which have hitherto been in force relating to the 'corridors' by which aircraft might enter and leave the U.K. have now been abolished. **1948** *Daily Mail* 22 Apr. 1/3 The R.A.F. have introduced air corridors from which Russian and Eastern European planes must not stray as they fly over the British zone of Germany. **1911** R. M. PIERCE *Dict. Aviation* 16 *Air-lane*, a lane or road thru the air. **1958** *Listener* 13 Feb. 269/1 Do not think.. that the airlines fly as the crow flies... They fly along prescribed air lanes.. they meander and zig-zag. **1909** *Westm. Gaz.* 30 Aug. 2/3 Already we hear of rules of the air-road. **1926** KIPLING *Debits & Credits* 359 He Who bids the wild-swans' host still maintain their flight on Air-roads over islands lost. **1911** *Technical World Mag.* Sept. 117/2 (*title*) Marking out air routes. **1935** *Economist* 26 Oct. 816/1 The Company will continue to be the Government's chosen instrument for the operation and development of Empire air routes.

air (ɛə(r)), *sb.*[2] *Sc.* Also **aer, aire, ayr(e, er.** [ON. *eyrr*; cf. Norw. *ør*, *øyr* sandbank, gravel-bank.] A gravelly beach. (See *Sc. Nat. Dict.* s.v. AIR *n.*[4])

a **1795** G. LOW *Tour thro' Ork. & Schet.* (1879) 11 A house on the Aire.. bears the empty name of the Fish-house. **1809** A. EDMONDSTON *State Zetl. Is.* I. iii. 140 Most of the extensive beaches on the coast are called *airs*; as *Stour-air, Whale-air, Bou-air.* **1868** D. GORRIE *Summers & Winters in Orkneys* ix. 365 This aith, ayre, or spit of land. **1933** *Geogr. Jrnl.* LXXXI. 505 These 'green fish' were bought by the merchants and dried on stony ayres. **1936** *Nature* 19 Sept. 512/2 The most interesting find.. was at Braewick.. where storm water had breached an 'ayr' or storm beach.

air (ɛə(r)), *v.* [f. the sb.; cf. to *water, fire, dust.*]

1. *trans.* To expose to the open or fresh air, so as to remove foul or damp air; to ventilate.

1530 PALSGR. 419/2, I ayre or wether, as men do thynges whan they lay them in the open ayre, or as any lynen thyng is after it is newe wasshed or it be worne.. Ayre these clothes for feare of mothes. **1697** DRYDEN *Virg. Georg.* I. 359 Let him.. wicker Baskets weave, or aire the Corn. **1816** SCOTT *Old Mort.* 317 To brush and air them [doublet and cloak] from time to time. **1861** FLOR. NIGHTINGALE *Nursing* ii. 13 Always air your room from the outside air, if possible.

2. Hence, from the idea of expelling damp: To expose to heat, to dry or warm at the fire.

1610 *Ordin. R. Househ.* 338 To make fires to ayer the chamber. **1679** CROWNE *Ambit. Statesm.* II. 19 To carry charcoal in to air his shirt. **1689** LADY R. RUSSELL *Lett.* 96 II. 30, I shall come and air your beds for a night. **1722** DE FOE *Plague* 87 While the bed was airing. **1759** SYMMER in *Phil. Trans.* LI. 350 After being a little air'd at the fire. **1813** MAR. EDGEWORTH *Patron.* (1833) II. xxxi. 311 Nothing airs a house so well as a warm friend.

†**3.** To leave pasture unstocked. *Obs.*

1641 BEST *Farming* (1856) 82 Those closes.. have beene ayred ['and kept fresh,' p. 83] from St. Andrewe-day till the time that the ewes come in.

4. To expose oneself to the fresh air; to take the air. **a.** *refl.*

1611 SHAKS. *Cymb.* I. ii. 110 Were you but riding forth to ayre yourselfe. **1711** ADDISON *Spect.* No. 159 ¶2 As I was here airing myself on the tops of the mountains. **1823** LAMB *Elia* Ser. II. xi. (1865) 302 To go and air myself in my native fields. **1864** TENNYSON *Aylmer's F.* 468 And fain had haled him out into the world And air'd him there.

b. *intr.* (by omission of refl. pron.) *arch.*

1633 MASSINGER *New Way, etc.* I. ii, I'll take the air alone. You air, and air: But will you never taste but spoon-meat more? **1733** POPE *Eth. Ep.* III. 388 The well-bred cuckolds in S. James's air. **1826** MISS MITFORD *Village* Ser. II. (1863) 317 She went airing every day. **1830** T. HAMILTON *Cyr. Thornton* (1845) 121 Lady Amersham has gone out airing.. in her pony phaeton.

5. *fig.* **a.** *trans.* To wear openly, expose to public view. In modern times the meaning has been influenced by *airs*, 'affected gestures,' so as to mean, To show off, to parade ostentatiously.

1611 SHAKS. *Cymb.* II. iv. 98, I begge but leaue to ayre this jewel. **1631** CORNWALLYES *Ess.* xxiii, I have been afraid to weare fashions untill they have beene ayred by a generall use. **1847** TENNYSON *Princ.* I. 120 Airing a snowy hand and signet ring. **1878** BOSW. SMITH *Carthage* 364 To air their importance and their imbecility.

b. *refl.* and *intr.* To expose oneself publicly, to show oneself off.

1670 EACHARD *Contempt Clergy* 17 To have his name only stand airing upon the college tables. **1823** LAMB *Elia* Ser. II. xxii. (1865) 386 A poor human fancy may have leave to sport and air itself. **1874** GREEN *Short Hist.* x. §2. 742 The young sovereign who aired himself in the character.. of a Patriot King.

c. *trans.* To give expression to, to make public (an opinion, grievance, etc.).

1879 R. ELLIOT *Writ. on Foreheads* I. 13 A chance of airing some of his pet theories. *a* **1902** S. BUTLER *Way of All Flesh* (1903) lv. 251 He did not air any of his schemes to me until I had drawn him out concerning them. **1922** JOYCE *Ulysses* 624 Skin-the-Goat.. was airing his grievances. **1956** A. WILSON *Anglo-Saxon Attitudes* I. i. 17, I don't relish.. the prospect of hearing Rose Lorimer air her crazy theories. **1984** *Church Times* 9 Nov. 11/1 Whilst recognising the impact made by Billy Graham's visit, it is important to air a number of issues—particularly in view of his mission in Sheffield next year.

†**6.** *intr.* (with *away*) To pass into air, evaporate.

1627 FELTHAM *Resolves* II. lv. (1677) 272 It airs away to nothing by only standing still.

†**7.** To set to music. *Obs.* (See AIRABLE.)

1653 J. COBB *Pref. to H. Lawes' Ayres & Dial.* (D.) For not a drop that flows from Helicon But ayred by thee grows streight into a song.

8. To broadcast. Also (*U.S.*) *intr.* for *pass.*, to be broadcast. Cf. AIR *sb.*[1] A 1 c. Chiefly *U.S.*

1952 W. GRANVILLE *Dict. Theatr. Terms* 15 *Air*, to broadcast a play, or excerpts of one, on the radio. **1960** *Guardian* 12 Oct. 9/2 The independent network that aired the programme. **1973** *Publishers Weekly* 12 Mar. 9 (Advt.), After the tape was aired.. we received hundreds of calls from listeners. **1974** *Greenville* (S. Carolina) *News* 20 Apr. 10/4 'Planet Earth', which airs on ABC Tuesday, is in a way the flip side of 'Star Trek'. **1981** *Economist* 24 Jan. 28/3 The obligation to keep records of all programmes aired. **1981** *TV Picture Life* (U.S.) Mar. 32/1 *Those Amazing Animals*, which aired last August, should be a big smash.

air (ɛə(r), *Sc.* eːr), *adv. Sc.* Forms: 1 **ær**, 2–3 **ar, aar**, 4– **air(e.** [The later Sc. form of ME. northern *ar(e*, OE. *ǽr* adj., adv., prep., and conj., 'former, formerly, before'; see mod. Eng. ERE, which is only a prep. (and conj.), while Sc. *air* is only an adv. (cf. EAR-LY).]

†**1.** Before, formerly, previously.

a **822** *O.E. Chron.* an. 797 And eft wæs papa swa he ær wæs. **1205** LAYAM. 28687 þa oðere cnihtes þa at þan fehte ar weoren. *c* **1300** *K. Alis.* 5033 Hy ben broun of hare, as hy weren aar. **1375** BARBOUR *Bruce* XVIII. 211 Eduard the bruce, as I said air, Wes descumfit. **1535** STEWART *Cron. Scotl.* I. 536 The sone.. of Fyndocus as I haif said ȝow air.

2. Early, soon; opposed to *late.*

c **1200** ORMIN 6242 Beon ær & läte o ȝunnkerr weorrc. *c* **1425** WYNTOUN *Cron.* VIII. xxxiii. 145 Come I are, come I late. **1501** DOUGLAS *Pal. Hon.* II. xxix, Quha is content, rejoycit air or lait. **1651** CALDERWOOD *Hist. Kirk* (1843) II. 211 Skairse could anie of the nobilitie have accesse to her aire or late. **1725** RAMSAY *Gent. Sheph.* I. i, She jeers me air and late. **1818** SCOTT *Rob Roy* xxvii, [Baillie Nicol Jarvie *loq.*] 'Air day or late day, the fox's hide finds aye the flaying knife.'

air, dial. form of ARE: see BE.

air, north. and Sc. form of OAR, HEIR.

air(e, Sc. form of EYRE, a circuit court.

†**'airable**, *a. Obs.* [f. AIR *v.* 7 + -ABLE. Cf. *tuneable.*] Capable of being set to music.

1633 HOWELL *Lett.* (1650) II. 36 The following numbers —'Could I but catch those beamy rayes [etc.]'.. are of the same cadence as yours, and aireable.

'air-balloon. [AIR- 7.] †**1.** = BALLOON *sb.*[1] 3. *Obs.*

1753 *Publ. Advertiser* 25 May, A cascade, and shower of fire, and grand air-balloons, were most magnificently displayed.

2. A globose bag filled with gas so as to ascend in the air. Cf. BALLOON *sb.*[1] 6.

1783 [see BALLOON *sb.*[1] 6]. **1783** *Morning Chron.* 8 Sept. 3/4 The first air-balloon he made was filled with fumous particles. **1784** JOHNSON in *Boswell* III. 626 On one day I had three letters about the air balloon. **1789** MRS. PIOZZI *France & It.* I. 22 The new-invented flying chariot fastened to an air-balloon. **1829** U.K.S. *Nat. Phil.* I. vi. §51. 28 Aërostats, or air-balloons, are machines, constructed so as to be able to rise in the atmosphere. **1907** *Daily Mail* 9 July 7/4 In July 1901 M. Santos Dumont flew from St. Cloud round the Eiffel Tower and back in his steerable air balloon.

3. An inflatable toy balloon.

1895 CROKER *Village Tales* 155 The child was jumping for joy, and had a green air-balloon in his hand. **1908** H. G. WELLS *War in Air* vi. §2 Small children's air-balloons of the latest model attached to string became a serious check to the pedestrian in Central Park. **1944** O. SITWELL *Autobiogr.* (1945) I. II. vi. 227 Fashionable beauties, with psyches that resembled air-balloons, inflated, light and highly coloured.

'air-ba,lloonist. [f. prec. + -IST.] An aeronaut.

1817 KIRBY & SPENCE *Entomol.* II. xxiii. 346 The aërial excursions of our insect air-balloonist.

'air-ˌbladder. [AIR- 7.]

1. A bladder or sac filled with air in an animal or plant, as those in the fronds of sea-weeds and other floating plants; also, an 'air-hole' or vesicle in glass or cast-metal.

1731 ARBUTHNOT *Aliments* (J.) The pulmonary artery and vein pass along the surfaces of these airbladders. **1769** STRANGE in *Phil. Trans.* LIX. 55 Globular appearances, like air-bladders. **1789** LIGHTFOOT *Fl. Scot.* II. 904 Bladder Fucus.. In the disc or surface are immersed hollow sphærical or oval air-bladders. **1869** *Eng. Mech.* 15 Oct. 106/3 If too hot, it is liable to have air-bladders.

2. The swimming-bladder of fishes.

1678 CUDWORTH (J.) The airbladder in fishes seems necessary for swimming. **1772** WATSON *Isinglass* in *Phil. Trans.* LXIII. 7 The sounds, or air-bladders of fresh-water fish. **1855** OWEN *Vertebr.* I. xi. (L.) The air-bladder is lined by a delicate mucous membrane.

'air-borne, *a.* Carried through the air (see AIR- I. 2); (of aircraft) having left the ground; in flight; (of troops) carried by aircraft.

1641 MILTON *Ch. Govt.* II. iii. (1851) 173 Like aire-born Helena in the fable. **1880** *Nature* No. 532. 232 The theory ..that cholera is air-borne. **1909** C. M. DOUGHTY *Cliffs* 57 We've seaborne, airborne and now subsea fleets. **1920** *Flight* XII. 48/1 An air-borne letter delivered by hand in Paris for 2s. 6d. **1937** B. H. L. HART *Europe in Arms* iii. 30 The most striking features of the Army are its development of tank and air-borne units. **1941** *War Fortnightly* 20 June 1876/1 It [Crete] was the first occasion on which a major operation had been undertaken by air-borne troops, without the aid of sea-borne or any other troops. **1943** *Aeronautics* Feb. 48/1 An Airborne Division of the British Army.

'air-box. [AIR- 7.]

1. The AIR-CHAMBER of a fire-engine or life-boat.

1838 POE *Pym* Wks. 1864 IV. 20 Fitted.. with air-boxes in the manner of some life-boats. **1857** TOMES *Amer. in Japan* xiv. 316 These engines.. are deficient in the important part of the machine called the air-box.

2. *Mining*: 'A square wooden tube used to convey air into the face of a single drift, or shaft, in sinking.' *Northumb. & Durh. Coal-trade Terms*, 1851.

'air-ˌcell. [AIR- 7.]

Any cell or small cavity filled with air; *esp.* in *pl.* **a.** Small cells in the lungs of animals, forming the extremities of the ultimate ramifications of the bronchial tubes. **b.** Intercellular spaces or *lacunæ* in the stems, etc. of plants; air-cavities.

1787 SIR J. HAWKINS *Johnson* 590 (JOD.) The aircells of the lungs unusually distended. **1855** OWEN *Skel. & Teeth* 7 An air-cell, or prolongation of the lung,.. lines the cavity of the bone. **1860** TYNDALL *Glac.* I. §7. 56 Compact ice, filled with innumerable air-cells.

'air-ˌchamber. [AIR- 7.]

1. a. Any chamber or cavity filled with air in an animal or plant, *esp.* those in a 'chambered-shell.'

1847 ANSTED *Anc. World* iii. 43 In the Nautilus.. we find a large, powerful, and complicated shell, composed of a number of separate compartments or air-chambers. **1855** OWEN *Vertebr.* I. ii. (L.) These air-chambers between the outer table and the immediate covering of the brain.

b. A chamber filled with air in a boat, airship, etc., to provide or assist buoyancy.

1881 W. D. HAY *300 Years Hence* vii. 133 In the upper part [of the boat] was the entrance and air-chamber. **1882** *Encycl. Brit.* XIV. 570/2 The buoyancy of the institution's lifeboat.. is secured chiefly by means of a watertight deck.. and two large air-chambers, one in the bow, the other in the stern. **1908** H. G. WELLS *War in Air* viii. §1 The airship was remarkably simple to construct: given the air-chamber material, the engines, [etc.].. it was really not more complicated.. than an ordinary wooden boat had been.. before.

2. In a pump or other hydraulic machine, a receptacle containing air, the elasticity of which, when condensed, maintains a constant pressure upon the water; an air-vessel.

1873 ATKINSON tr. *Ganot's Physics* §206 The fire engine is a force pump in which a steady jet is obtained by the aid of an air-chamber.

'air-ˌchambered, *a.* [f. prec. + -ED.] Furnished with air-chambers.

1856 KANE *Arct. Explor.* I. v. 49 It [boat] was air-chambered and buoyant.

'air-conˌditioning, *vbl. sb.* [cf. CONDITION *v.* 9.] The process of cleaning air and controlling its temperature and humidity before it enters a room, building, etc., and in certain manufacturing processes. Hence **'air-conˌdition** *v. trans.*; **'air-conˌditioned** *ppl. a.*; **'air-conˌditioner**, an apparatus for conditioning the air (of a room or building).

1909 S. W. CRAMER *Useful Information for Cotton Mfrs.* (ed. 2) IV. 1395, I finally hit upon the compound word 'Air Conditioning'.. suggested by the use of the term 'conditioning' in the treatment of yarn and cloth. *Ibid.* 1411 Well-known 'Air Conditioners' of both individual and central station types. **1930** *Engineering* 11 July 34/2 Air-conditioning is dealt with fully, with the methods for washing, cleaning, humidifying, cooling and drying the air. **1930** *Discovery* Sept. 317/2 Tobacco leaf.. is extraordinarily sensitive to changes of atmospheric humidity, and this has led in recent years to much development in the matter of air-conditioning. **1933** *Archit. Rev.* LXXIII. 101 Its thirty-five stories of air-conditioned, sound-insulated.. offices. **1935** BURGE *Complete Bk. Aviation* 111/2 Air conditioners have been designed to supply fresh air, and to maintain a comfortable cabin temperature while a machine is on the ground. **1937** *Times* 22 Sept. 10/1 The trustees of the National Gallery will discuss a scheme to air-condition the gallery. **1938** *Encycl. Brit. Bk. of Year* 28/2 The built-in central plant system provides the best performance at the lowest cost wherever a number of rooms, or where one large room is to be air-conditioned... Quite recently unit air-conditioners of improved design and of relatively low cost have been produced. **1939** *Nature* 6 May 769/2 The large-scale air-conditioning and refrigeration installed in many South African gold mines enable gold companies to explore much greater depths. **1958** *Engineering* 14 Mar. 352/1 Originally, air conditioning was not introduced for reasons of comfort but was developed for the controlled processing of materials. **1958** *Times Lit. Suppl.* 28 Mar. 176/1 An admirably equipped strong room for manuscripts with its own air-conditioning and humidifying plant.

aircraft ('ɛəkrɑːft, -æ-). [f. AIR- III. + CRAFT *sb.* 9.] Flying-machines collectively; a flying-machine.

Since the 1930s commonly restricted to denote an aeroplane (as distinct from a balloon or airship) or aeroplanes collectively. The nineteenth-century examples refer to balloons and airships.

1850 J. WISE *System of Aeronautics* xvi. 102 The aircraft has but one medium, the water-craft has two. **1876** C. B. MANSFIELD *Aerial Navig.* 2 Air-craft seems an appropriate term for the whole apparatus, including boat and gas vessel, or car and balloon. *Ibid.* II. viii. 323 The inventors of air-crafts. **1903** *Aeronaut. Jrnl.* VII. 81/1 His world-famed aircrafts. **1909** *Daily Chron.* 26 Feb. 1/2 The vast commercial possibilities that the manufacture and world-wide use of air craft offer. **1910** ROTCH in *Epitome Aeronaut. Ann.*, [Suppose] an aircraft to possess the very moderate speed of 9 metres per second. **1910** *Daily Mail* 27 May 6/1 The three types of aircraft—the balloon, the airship, and the aeroplane. **1912** F. T. JANE *All the World's Air-craft* III. 7/1 It has.. been deemed advisable gradually to change the title of this annual to *All the World's Air-craft*, in order to avoid all risk of misunderstanding as to its scope—'air-craft' being apparently the only generic which cannot be associated with a single type. **1915** *Whitaker's Almanack 1916* 465/1 Sixteen German aircraft attempted to fly over the English Channel. **1933** *Aeroplane* 19 July 124/2 The Air Council will do well to make a note of the fact that the word 'aircraft', which they allow their subordinates to use in the limited sense of the word 'aeroplane', covers 23 classes of air vehicles. **1936** *Discovery* Aug. 238/1 Like all mapping cameras it is installed in the aircraft on a mount. **1942** R. HILLARY *Last Enemy* ii. 34 The proper handling of an aircraft. **1943** W. S. CHURCHILL *Second World War* (1952) V. 566 Will you please make the following terminology effective in all British official correspondence: For 'aeroplane' the word 'aircraft' should be used... It is a good thing to have a rule and stick to it. **1944** H. St. G. SAUNDERS *Per Ardua* ix. 122 The constant coast-wise patrols carried out by three kinds of aircraft, land planes, seaplanes, and airships. **1945** *Yorks. Post* 19 Apr. 1/2 Nearly 1,000 aircraft of R.A.F. Bomber Command. **1955** *Times* 9 May 10/5 An aircraft of the Queen's Flight. **1960** C. H. GIBBS-SMITH *Aeroplane* I. xv. 119 The helicopter.. soon became an indispensable type of aircraft.

b. *attrib.*, as ***aircraft hand*** [HAND *sb.* 8], abbrev. A.C.H.; **aircraft carrier**, a ship that carries and serves as a base for aircraft; so ***aircraft-carrying*** adj.

1912 *Aeronautics* Nov. 365/1, 4 machines are under construction at the Royal Aircraft Factory. **1919** *Times* 30 Dec. 4/6 The aircraft carrier Hermes.. is to be towed from the Tyne to Devonport. **1921** *Airman* Nov. 113/1 [In the] aircraft of the future.. we shall find such people as cooks, fire-fighters.. and aircrafthands; these latter, of course, to be employed as guards, and to do odd jobs which will be numerous no doubt on this type of aircraft. **1922** T. E. LAWRENCE *Let.* 1 Oct. (1938) 363, I can't ask the corporal how an aircraft hand addresses an air-vice-marshall. **1925** —— *Let.* 7 Oct. (1938) 484 Five are fitters, five are riggers, five are A.C.H.'s. **1925** *Jane's All World's Aircraft* A. 10a/1 The following are the aircraft-carrying ships owned by the British Navy. **1940** E. C. SHEPHERD *Britain's Air Power* 12 The latest aircraft carriers can carry many aeroplanes. A total of 60 would not be an over-estimate, though the exact complement of any such floating aerodrome must not be given. **1942** O. J. LISSITZYN *Internat. Air Transport* 430 (*heading*) Route miles and aircraft miles flown. **1957** *Technology* Mar. 8/1 In the short space of fifty years the aircraft industry has come a long way.

Hence **'aircraftman** (abbrev. A.C., A/C), the lowest non-commissioned rank in the Royal Air Force. Also (in non-official use) **'aircraftsman.**

1920 *Glasgow Herald* 2 Aug. 6 The demand for experienced pilots and aircraftsmen. **1921** *King's Regs. R.A.F.* 8 The ranks of Warrant Officers, Non-Commissioned Officers, and men of the Royal Air Force.. are as follows.. *Non-Commissioned Officers.* Flight Sergeant. Sergeant. Corporal. *Men in the Ranks.* Leading Aircraftman. Aircraftman. **1922** T. E. LAWRENCE *Let.* 6 Nov. (1938) 376 Address now No. 352087, A.C. 2 Ross. **1924** *Lancet* 19 Jan. 164/2 Examined the olfactory condition of 100 air craftsmen, and found only one who could not distinguish petrol, orange, or peppermint among the test solutions offered to him. **1943** C. H. WARD-JACKSON *It's a Piece of Cake* 10 *A/C Plonk*, Aircraftman 2nd Class.

So **'aircraftwoman** (abbrev. A.C.W.), the lowest rank in the women's air service.

1939 *Times* 11 Sept. 5/6 Airwomen.. will receive 2s. 2d. a day on entering, 2s. 8d. a day when mustered as aircraftwomen first class. **1941** J. HAMMERTON *ABC of RAF* 53/1 Aircraftwomen 2nd class. **1942** *Ibid.* (ed. 2) 58 *A.C.W.*, Aircraftwoman. **1943** K. B. BEAUMAN *Wings on her Shoulders* v. 57 A plotter, A.C.W. Cooper, told me about the attack on North Weald.

† **aire,** *sb.*[1] *Obs.*; also 6 aare. [a. OFr. *aire*:—L. *āra* altar.] An altar.

1581 STUDLEY *Seneca's Trag.* 57b, Nor yet deuoutly praying, at the Aares with godly guise To Pallas, president in earth, to offer sacrifice. **1652** C. STAPLYTON *Herodian* xx. 166 Distracted like men ran upon these Aires, Maximiens Honor'd Statues were defaced.

† **aire,** *sb.*[2] *Obs.* Forms: 4 air, 5 eyre, 7 ayre, 4–7 aire. [a. OFr. *aire*: see AERIE.] The earlier equivalent of AERIE.

c **1325** *Sir Tristr.* I. xxix, Aȝain an hauke of nobl air. [Cf. OFr. *faucon de gentil aire.*] *a* **1440** *Sir Degrev.* 46 Ffelle ffaukons and ffayre Haukes of nobulle eyre. **1616** SURFLET & MARKH. *Countrey Farme* 79 Some [storks] do euerie years repayre to their wonted ayres, and doe ayre and neast themselves willingly also in the tops of high Towers. **1706** PHILLIPS, *Aire* or *Airy* (among Falconers) a nest of Hawks, or other Birds of Prey; especially the Nest, which Falcons make choice of to hatch their Young in.

† **aire,** *v. Obs.* Forms: 5 eyer, 7 eyre, ayre. [f. prec. sb. Cf. to *nest.*] *trans.* and *intr.* To build an aerie, to breed as a falcon.

1472 J. PASTON in *Lett.* 708 III. 68 To cast hyr in to some wood, wher as I wyll have hyr to eyer. **1616** [See prec.] **1652** ASHMOLE *Theatr. Chem. Brit.* xxxvi. 220, I was eyred and bred in swete Paradyce.

aired (ɛəd), *pple.* and *a.* [f. AIR + -ED.]

1. Exposed to the open air, ventilated; heated so as to remove damp incurred by being in a damp air.

a **1540** T. CROMWELL *Care of Pr. Edward* in *Athen.* 3 Dec. (1842) Purely brushed, made clean, aired at the fire, and perfumed thoroughly. **1616** SURFLET *Countrey Farme* 429 The more that oyle is ayred and stirred, so much the more clear it is. **1722** DE FOE *Plague* 189 They caused the bales of goods to be opened and aired. **1756** NUGENT *Grand Tour* IV. 22 Take particular care to see the sheets aired. **1802** MAR. EDGEWORTH *Mor. T.* (1816) I. xvii. 141 To keep the room aired and swept. *Mod.* 'Well-aired beds.'

2. *fig.*

1611 SHAKS. *Wint. T.* IV. ii. 6 Though I haue (for the most part) bin ayred abroad, I desire to lay my bones there.

3. -aired, in *comb.*: having an air (breath, manner, mien, tune) of a defined kind, as in *well-aired.*

1505 in *National MSS.* I. lxvi, The said quyne ys lyke for to be of a sewit savour, and well eyred. **1674** N. FAIRFAX *Bulk & Selv.* 17 A right handsome address of words and well air'd periods. **1879** *Daily News* 16 Apr. 3/1 A string of shaggy, supercilious-aired camels. **1881** *Academy* 5 Mar. 167/3 A severe aunt and a grand-aired cousin. **1882** *Exch. & Mart* 8 Jan. 91/3 Splendid eight-aired musical box.

Airedale ('ɛədeɪl). The name of a district in the West Riding of Yorkshire; hence short for ***Airedale terrier***, one of a breed of large rough-haired dogs.

1880 DALZIEL *Brit. Dogs* 377 The Airedale or Bingley Terrier. **1889** *Ibid.* (ed. 2) II. 385 The name Terrier, applied to the Airedale, is admittedly a stretching of the term beyond its original meaning. **1916** F. M. JOWETT *Airedale Terrier* 26 A dog brimful of true Airedale character and type.

† **'aireous, -ious,** *a. Obs.* [var. of AEREOUS, modified in spelling after *air.*] = AEREOUS; aeriform.

1597 GERARDE *Herbal* II. lxxxiii. (1633) 395 Thin, airious, hot, and purging. **1665** J. SPENCER *Prodigies* 34 The vapour is more subtil and aireous.

airer ('ɛərə(r)). [f. AIR *v.* + -ER[1].] One who or that which airs; *spec.* a frame on which clothes are aired.

1775 ASH, *Airer*, One that exposes to the air. *a* **1884** *Mod.* He is an airer of most absurd opinions. **1884** *Manchester Examiner* 10 Dec. 3/6 Mrs. Jackson is no rabid airer of grievances. **1920** *Cornhill Mag.* Sept. 3/3 The 'airers' of wounded soldiers were dreaming of jaunts without hospital blue. **1959** *Which?* Aug. 94/1 Airer Driers.. all work on the same basic principle. Washing is spread out on horizontal rods and is dried by warm air from an electric heater.

airfield ('ɛəfiːld). [f. AIR- III + FIELD *sb.*] An area of land where aircraft are accommodated and maintained and may take off or land.

1935 *Aero Digest* May 13/3 Officials.. have a fundamentally clear conception of how airfield projects ought to be handled. **1936** *Baltimore Sun* 18 May 7/8 All airfields in Virginia, with one or two exceptions, are below the standard sizes recommended by the Department of Commerce. **1940** B. WARD *Russian Foreign Policy* 30 The Baltic States.. 'acquiesced' in the cession of islands, the leasing of harbours and airfields. **1943** W. S. CHURCHILL *Second World War* (1952) V. 566 For 'aerodrome' either 'airfield' or 'airport' [should be used]. The expression 'airdrome' should not be used by us.

airgonaut, airgonation, jocular forms of *aeronaut* and '*aeronautation*,' f. AIR *sb.*[1], GO, in allusion to *argonaut.*

1784 H. WALPOLE *Corr.* (1837) III. 354 You know how little I have attended to these airgonauts. *Ibid.* A sort of meditation on future airgonation, supposing that it will not only be perfected but will depose navigation.

'air-gun. [AIR- 7.] (See quot.)

1753 CHAMBERS *Cycl. Supp.*, *Air-gun*, See the article *Wind-gun* [No such article]. **1787** DARWIN in *Phil. Trans.* LXXVIII. 44 The blast from an air-gun was repeatedly thrown on the bulb of a thermometer. **1812** SCOTT in Lockhart's *Life* (1839) III. 356 To shoot one of them with an air-gun. **1829** U.K.S. *Nat. Philos.* I. vi. §52 The air-gun is an instrument for projecting balls, or other missiles, by the elastic force of condensed air.

'air-hole. [AIR- 7.]

1. A hole or passage to admit air; *spec.* A hole that forms in the ice in rapid rivers over the main current, for which it is a breathing-place.

1766 SMOLLETT *Trav.* I. xvi. 264 He said that there were air-holes at certain distances (and indeed I saw one of these). **1876** W. BOYD in Bartlett's *Dict. Amer.*, The ice on the St. Lawrence at Montreal never becomes stationary for the winter until one or more air-holes have formed in it in that neighbourhood. **1883** C. HOLDER in *Harper's Mag.* Jan. 190/1 The air-holes open and shut at the will of the insect.

2. 'The cavities in a metal casting—produced by the escape of air through the liquid metal.' Ure *Dict. Arts.*

1813 SOUTHEY *Nelson* vii. 249 [The guns] were probably originally faulty, for the fragments were full of little air-holes.

airiferous, variant of AERIFEROUS.

airified ('ɛərɪfaɪd), *ppl. a.* [f. AIR -(I)FY + -ED. Cf. *frenchified*, etc.] Made into air; fashioned in an airy manner; given to assuming airs. (*Slightingly.*)

1864 MISS YONGE *Trial* I. 61 She.. began one of her most renowned instrumental pieces.. 'Not that jingling airified thing!' cried Leonard. **1882** *Graphic* 4 Feb. 98 There is a column written in this airified optimist style in Wednesday's *Times.*

airily ('ɛərɪlɪ), *adv.* [f. AIRY *a.* + -LY[2].] In an airy manner; see AIRY.

1. In a manner exposed to the air; thinly, lightly.

1797 MRS. RADCLIFFE *Italian* vii. (1824) 566 If he had been as airily dressed as yourself. **1851** HAWTHORNE *Snow Image* (1879) 23 Airily as she was clad. **1856** KANE *Arct. Explor.* II. xi. 113 They were airily clad.. and they soon crowded back into their ant-hill.

2. Lightly, delicately, etherially.

1869 *Daily News* 15 Dec., Their details are more picturesque.. more quaintly, strangely, and airily wrought.

3. After the manner of the upper air; loftily.

1879 TENNYSON *Lover's T.* 53 There be some hearts so airily built, that they.. ride highly Above the perilous seas of Change and Chance.

4. With light hearts, gaily.

1833 TENNYSON *Poems* 102 Singing airily, Standing about the charmèd root.

5. With ostentatious air; jauntily.

1766 CHALKLEY *Wks.* 264 A young Baronet.. who at first behaved airily. **1856** MISS MULOCH *John Halifax* (ed. 17) 401 She rose to her feet, smiling airily. **1859** DICKENS *Two Cities* 121 'It is all the same,' said the spy, airily, but discomfited too; 'good day!'

airiness ('ɛərɪnɪs). [f. AIRY *a.* + -NESS.] The quality of being airy (in various senses).

1. Unsubstantiality like that of the air.

1674 N. FAIRFAX *Bulk & Selv.* 40 The same is altogether nothing but the airiness of thinking.

2. Openness to the air; breeziness.

1742 BAILEY, *Airiness*, lying open to the Air.

3. Lightness or sprightliness of motion.

1731 BAILEY, *Airiness*, briskness, liveliness. **1779** JOHNSON *L.P.* Wks. 1816 X. 164 His numbers.. commonly want airiness, lightness, and facility. **1826** H. COLERIDGE *West Indies* 78 The bird has the advantage.. in airiness and motion. **1846** T. WRIGHT *Mid. Ages* I. vii. 249 The elves and fairies in all their frolicsome airiness.

4. Sprightliness of personal manner.

1711 ADDISON *Spect.* No. 45 ⁋5 Gaiety and Airiness of Temper. **1857** DICKENS *Lett.* (1880) II. 16 Airiness and good spirits are always delightful.

5. Graceful delicacy or lightness of style.

1794 MATHIAS *Pursuits of Lit.* (1798) 336 More fancy and airiness of design. **1842** MRS. BROWNING *Grk. Chr. Poets* (1863) 181 His peculiar grace and airiness of diction.

airing ('ɛərɪŋ), *vbl. sb.* [f. AIR *v.* + -ING[1].]

1. a. The action or process of exposing to fresh or dry air, or (anything slightly damp) to heat.

1610 B. JONSON *Alch.* I. i. (1616) 610 Hee'll send word, for ayring o' the house. **1611** COTGR., *Ventilation*, a winnowing, or airing in the wind. **1626** BACON *Sylva* §343 To discharge some of the superfluous moisture.. they require Airing. **1685** in Ellis *Orig. Lett.* II. 330 IV. 89 Fire.. at Montague House.. occasioned by the Steward's airing some hangings.

b. *airing cupboard*, a cupboard for airing linen and clothing.

1917 A. WAUGH *Loom of Youth* I. vii. 82 The School House changing-room... In the far corner there was an airing cupboard. **1958** *Times* 2 June ix/3 An immersion heater... Small and compact, it is particularly suitable for fitting in an airing cupboard.

2. A walk, ride, or drive to take the air. (Now rarely of a walk.)

1629 MASSINGER *Picture* v. i, How do you like Your airing? **1704** ADDISON *Italy* (1733) 22 To give their Ladies an Airing in the Summer-season. **1791** BOSWELL *Johnson* (1831) V. 88 He frequently attended him in airings. *c* **1815** MISS AUSTEN *Northang. Ab.* (1833) I. ix. 50, I hope you have had a pleasant airing. **1836** MARRYAT *Japhet* lxxvi. 142/1 You would have no objection to take an airing in the carriage.

3. Exercising of horses in the open air.

1631 MARKHAM *Way to Wealth* I. I. i. (1668) 6 Let him [the horse] have much moderate exercise, as Morning and Evening ayrings. **1753** CHAMBERS *Cycl. Supp.* s.v., It is from long airings that we are to expect to bring a horse to a perfect wind.

4. [AIR *v.* 5.] Display, exposure to public notice.

1870 G. MEREDITH *H. Richmond* (1871) I. x. 166, I really felt that I was justified in giving my irritability an airing. **1884** *Eng. Illustr. Mag.* I. 440 It was little more than scientific gossip, and the occasional airing of certain theories. **1965** *Listener* 25 Nov. 874/3 An informative and lively series which could certainly stand another airing.

'airish, *a.* [f. AIR *sb.* + -ISH. Cf. *Spanish.*]

†**1.** Of or belonging to the air; aerial, aereous. *Obs.*

c **1384** CHAUCER *H. Fame* 964 And behelde the ayerissh bestes [*v.r.* ayryssh, ayrisshe, eyrysshe]. **1551** TURNER *Herbal* II. 165 Viscum is made of an aerishe, waterishe hote nature. **1612** T. JAMES *Iesuits Downefall* 61 He was not a meere man; but some Fairies brat, or begotten by an Incubus, or aerish spirit, vpon the bodie of a base woman.

2. Cool, fresh.

1641 BEST *Farming* (1856) 18 Betwixt 8 and 9 of the clocke; and not afore, because the morninges are airish. **1882** J. H. BEADLE *Western Wilds* xxxviii. 613 Going westward on any line one will find the winters growing dryer, also more 'airish'. **1885** 'C. E. CRADDOCK' *Prophet Gt. Smoky Mts.* 267 It air toler'ble airish in the fog.

airless ('ɛəlɪs), *a.* [AIR *sb.* + -LESS.]

1. a. *strictly*, Void of air; Hence **b.** Not open to the air, stuffy; **c.** Breezeless, still.

1601 SHAKS. *Jul. Cæs.* I. iii. 94 Nor Stonie Tower, nor Walls of beaten brasse, Nor ayrelesse Dungeon. **1847** LEWES *Hist. Philos.* (1867) I. 232 In airless space her movements would be more rapid. **1847** J. WILSON *Chr. North* I. 244 Asleep in the airless sunshine. **1861** DICKENS *Gt. Expect.* I. xi. 176 It had an airless smell that was oppressive. **1876** BUCKLEY *Hist. Nat. Sc.* xxi 176 It has to come across a great airless space before it reaches the atmosphere. **1879** W. COLLINS *Rogue's Life* vii. 95 The night was so quiet and airless. **1881** *Daily News* 7 Dec. 5/3 The inside of the coach is a mere airless box.

2. *airless injection* [INJECTION]: see quot. 1940.

1930 *Engineering* 11 July 39 (*heading*) Airless-injection oil engine at the Royal Agricultural Show. **1940** *Chambers's Techn. Dict.* 19/2 *Airless injection*, the injection of liquid fuel into the cylinder of an oil engine by a high-pressure fuel pump, so dispensing with the compressed air necessary in the early Diesel engines.

airlessness ('ɛəlɪsnɪs). [f. AIRLESS *a.* + -NESS.] The condition of being airless.

1831 J. WILSON *Unimore* in *Blackw. Mag.* XXX. 144 Idle all at once her sails Hang in the airlessness. **1857** DICKENS *Dorrit* II. xxiii, The airlessness and closeness of the house. **1885** 'LUCAS MALET' *Col. Enderby's Wife* II. iv, The shut and darkened windows produced an effect of airlessness. **1913** E. F. BENSON *Thorley Weir* i. 5 The baking airlessness of town.

airlie, obs. and dial. form of EARLY.

'air-lift. [LIFT *sb.*[2]]. **1.** [AIR- II.] A pumping device operated by compressed air.

1893 *Patent Specif.* No. 22372 My process.. I term the 'air lift' process. **1902** *Encycl. Brit.* XXXIII. 776/1 The object attained by the air-lift is precisely the same as that attained by putting a pump some distance down a bore-hole. **1917** *Proc. Inst. Mech. Engin.* 628 In an air-lift pump in operation the air-bubbles are rising through a mixture of variable density.

2. [AIR- III.] Transportation of supplies or troops by air, esp. during a state of emergency. Also as *v. trans.*, hence **'airlifted** *ppl. a.*, **'airlifting** *vbl. sb.*

1945 *Life* 17 Dec. 112/2 General Ho Ying-chin used the American air lift to pass four crack American-equipped.. armies over the heads of the Communists into Shanghai. **1948** *News Chron.* 20 Sept. 1/1 This is the first British plane to crash on the air lift, which began in June. **1949** *Baltimore Sun* 5 Jan. 7/1 The Soviet-licensed newspaper *National Zeitung* today accused British and American officers of shunting more than 8,000 tons of airlifted coal into the black market of fuel-short Berlin. *Ibid.* 2 July 1/1 It may lead to the airlifting of other highly perishable fruits and vegetables. **1952** in *Amer. Speech* (1953) XXVIII. 50 Thus whirlybirds airlifted almost 11,000 troops to safety. **1957** *Ann. Reg. 1956* 77 The infantry battalion which had been air-lifted from Calgary to Halifax in readiness for transfer to Egypt. **1958** *Oxf. Mail* 19 July 1/2 The United States today began a massive oil airlift to save Jordan from oil starvation. **1960** *Guardian* 20 July 1/4 The United States had sent support in the airlifting of United Nations troops.

airlike ('ɛəlaɪk), *a.* [f. AIR *sb.* + -LIKE.] Resembling air.

1567 MAPLET *Greene Forest* 23 The Turches or Turcois is in colour airelike, or like to the Heauens. **1821** SHELLEY *Epipsych.* 195 On the air-like waves Of wonder-level dream.

'air-line. 1. [AIR- II.] **a.** A direct line through the air, a bee-line. Chiefly *U.S.*

1813 J. QUINCY in *Deb. Congress* 1 Jan. 544 They will not rigidly observe any air-lines or water-lines in enforcing their necessary levies. **1829** J. F. COOPER *Wish-ton-wish* ii. 27 This clearing, which by an air line might have been half a mile from the place where his horse had stopped. **1852** GROTE *Greece* IX. II. lxx. 160 If we measure on Kiepert's map the rectilineal distance, the air-line is 170 English miles. **1904** *Chicago Tribune* 1 Aug. 4 The judge held that distance was to be measured by air line or 'as the crow flies', not as the main traveled road leads. **1919** *Sphere* 22 Mar. 254/2 Flying routes will soon show a tendency to become fixed, just as birds fly along 'air lines' from point to point.

attrib. **1863** *Congress. Globe* Feb. 813/1 This is a proposition to construct an air-line railroad between Washington and New York. **1895** *Outing* Dec. 214/2 Pursuing an even air-line route across the roughest country.

b. In *nonce attrib.* use: Sent through the air.

The reference is to letters dropping through the air as a theosophical manifestation in India.

1888 KIPLING *In Black & White* 66 The Religion never seemed to get much beyond its first manifestations; though it added an air-line postal *dak*, and orchestral effects.

2. [AIR- III.] A line of aircraft for public service.

1914 *Argus* (Melbourne) 16 July 13 The Defence flying school at Point Cook has been inaccessible.. except by air line. **1937** *Discovery* May 163/2 Few people realise how vast is the network of air lines which now links up the United States with Central and South America. **1956** *Times* 2 Feb. 5/1 Work will begin this month on the.. platform above District Line railway tracks close to Cromwell Road, Earls Court, for future use as London's main air line terminal. **1958** [see AIR- III. 8].

3. A pipe or tube containing or (esp.) conducting air under pressure.

1910 *Compressed Air Mag.* Apr. 5622/2 At the end of the stroke the piston trips the tappet in the auxiliary air-line, causing the main valve to close. **1930** R. PEELE *Compressed Air Plant* (ed. 5) xv. 273 Air lines are tested from time to time by allowing the air at full pressure to remain in the closed transmission circuit long enough to observe the gage pressure. **1954** *Compressed Air Handbk.* (Compressed Air & Gas Inst.) (ed. 2) iv. 15 If an aftercooler is not employed, [when hot air is being emitted from a compressor] some of the trouble experienced with water in air lines can be overcome if small air receivers are put in the lines at frequent intervals to act as collecting tanks. **1971** *Daily Tel.* (Colour Suppl.) 12 Nov. 22/4 Any big truck lives and dies, steers and brakes, on its air-lines. **1977** *Drive* Jan.-Feb. 113/1 When motorists can be prosecuted for having incorrect tyre pressures, they have a right to expect airlines to be in as good working order as petrol pumps.

†**'airling.** *Obs.* [? f. AIR *sb.* + -LING diminutive.] A young, thoughtless person.

1611 B. JONSON *Catiline* I. i. (1692) 240 Some more there be, slight airlings, will be won With dogs and horses. **1775** ASH, *Airling* (an incorrect spelling) an earling, a young thoughtless person.

'air-lock. [AIR- I. 7.] **a.** = LOCK *sb.*[2] 10; also, a similar chamber in a space-craft, etc.

1857 *Brit. Almanac* 99 Each cylinder.. is filled with compressed air, by which it is kept free from water, and by means of chambers at the top furnished with doors or valves, on the principle of the canal lock, and called 'air-locks'. **1877** *Encycl. Brit.* VI. 63/1 A cylinder of wrought iron, within which a tubular chamber, provided with doors above and below, known as an air-lock. **1926** *Blackw. Mag.* Sept. 322/1 A diver could lie inside a great steel cylinder undergoing compression and have tea passed in to him through an airlock. **1951** A. C. CLARKE *Sands of Mars* ii. 12 Help him through the airlock when the tender couples up.

b. [AIR- I. 5.] A stoppage of the flow of liquid in a pump or pipe by a bubble of air. So **air-locking.**

1909 in WEBSTER. **1920** *Flight* XII. 219/1 The avoidance of air-locks in pipe systems. **1927** D. L. SAYERS *Unnatural Death* xi. 132 'Blew through the filler-cap,' said his lordship with a grin. 'Air-lock in the feed, old son, that's all.' **1936** *Aircraft Engin.* Nov. 321/1 Airlocking was studied in the laboratory by observing the behaviour of a fuel-air system in glass pipes.

†**'airly,** *a. Obs.* [f. AIR *sb.* + -LY[1]. Cf. *earth-ly*, *heaven-ly.*] Of air; of the nature of air; aerial.

1398 TREVISA *Barth. De P.R.* II. xix. (1495) 46 Fendes ben callyd ayrly beestes · for they lyue in kynde of bodies that ben ayrly. **1477** NORTON *Ord. Alch.* in Ashm. (1652) v. 76 Ayre.. which bare up Erth with his Aierly might. **1582** BATMAN *Barth. De P.R.* IV. i. 24 It turneth what is earthly into watrye, and watrye into airely, and airely into firie.

'airmail. [MAIL *sb.*[3]] Mail conveyed by air; a service for conveying letters, parcels, etc., by air; also *attrib.* Hence as *v. trans.*, to send by air.

1913 *Stamp Collecting* 13 Dec. 210/1 There have been many other German air mail flights. **1920** *Lancet* 11 Sept. 581/2 A Royal air mail service from London to Holland was started on July 6th. **1922** *Glasgow Herald* 4 Apr. 9 The despatch of air-mail letters.. between London and Paris. **1928** *Post Office Guide* July 55 A special Blue Air Mail label should be affixed to the top left hand corner of every Air Mail packet. **1932** S. GIBBONS *Cold Comfort Farm* xx. 272 The papers arrived by air-mail at noon. **1942** WYNDHAM LEWIS *Let.* 8 July (1963) 327 This is going to be air-mailed, and a carbon of it will go by ship. **1950** *Lancet* 8 July 70/1 Air-mail envelopes with coloured borders.

b. Applied to a type of thin paper intended for dispatch by airmail; also applied to an edition of a newspaper specially printed for conveyance by air (also called *air edition*).

1935 *Brit. Paper* Summer 13/1 A new air mail paper.. a tub-sized air-dried paper for air mail purposes. **1944** *Times Weekly* 9 Aug. 7/2 *The Times* now publishes an Air Edition daily. This consists of.. copies of full size printed on India paper. **1948** *Hansard Commons* CDXLVI. 994 Only two of our newspapers have airmail editions. **1958** *Times* 14 June 8/7 Among the exhibits here is a copy of the Air Mail edition of *The Times*, printed on paper made from Sunn Hemp.. and rag. **1959** *Engineering* 27 Feb. 262/3 [The machine] can handle a wide range of stock, from air-mail to board.

airman ('ɛəmən). [f. AIR- III. + MAN *sb.*[1], after *seaman.*] One who is engaged in the flying or operation of aircraft, esp. as a pilot or a member of an air crew; *spec.* an enlisted person in the Royal Air Force.

1873 *Cassell's Mag.* VIII. 135/2 The airmen were running.. and the balloon was pitching so much as almost to make Bob feel a little air-sick. **1910** *Daily Mail* 4 June 4/2 A flight of over forty miles above the sea, during which the airman is in continual danger. **1918** *Times* 26 Aug. 3/4 A light blue uniform has been approved for Warrant Officers, N.C.O.'s, and Airmen of the Royal Air Force. **1920** *Act 10 & 11 Geo. V* c. 30 §41 (5) The expression 'airman' means a man of the regular air force. **1924** *King's Regs. R.A.F.* p. vii, Airman, or Airmen. These words, wherever they occur, will be held to include a warrant officer, a N.C.O., an aircraftman, and a boy. **1927** T. E. LAWRENCE *Let.* 2 Dec. (1938) 553 Airmen mustn't fly machines:—that is a privilege of officers; and R.A.F. officers are very unlike R.A.F. airmen. **1934** *Lancet* 30 June 1377/1 The term 'airman' in the R.A.F. is used to designate 'other ranks' as distinguished from officers. It does not, per se, imply flying capacity.

So ˈ**airwoman**.

1911 *Chambers's Jrnl.* 6 May 364/1 Crowds were collecting..to see the first English airwoman make her widely advertised attempt on the height-record. **1941** *Hutchinson's Pict. Hist. War* 22 Jan.–18 Mar. 229 Airwomen had made an unqualified success of every trade in which they had taken the place of airmen.

airmanship (ˈɛəmənʃɪp). [f. AIR *sb.*[1], in imitation of *seamanship, horsemanship.*] Skill in managing a balloon or other aircraft; aeronautism.

1864 *Daily Tel.* 21 July, To a degree which would have paralysed his predecessors in airmanship. **1865** *Ibid.* 8 July, With what has been called 'magnificent airmanship,' he chooses his destined harbour of refuge under the lee of some shady wood. **1908** *Daily Chron.* 15 Aug. 4/6 'Airmanship' is the newest addition to the language. **1910** *Daily Mail* 4 June 4/2 When airmanship was in the elementary stage. **1955** *Times* 12 July 8/7 The emphasis in training will be on developing officers rather than airmen, though the course will include airmanship.

airmobile (ˌɛəˈməʊbɪl, -baɪl), *a. Mil.* (orig. *U.S.*). [f. AIR- III + -MOBILE.] That can be transported by air, esp. applied to ground troops organized to be moved about within a war zone by helicopter. Also *transf.*

1965 *Economist* 24 July 334/1 The [U.S.] Army has begun to create a pioneering unit, the First Cavalry Division (Airmobile)..designed primarily for very rapid surprise movements against enemy guerrillas and light infantry. **1967** *Compton Yearbk.* 124 The army was making greater use of airmobile tactics in Vietnam. **1975** *Courier-Mail* (Brisbane) 25 Jan. 1/4 There are three American divisions being sent to the Middle East... One is airmobile, one is airborne and one is armoured. **1979** *Daily Tel.* 9 July 6/5 If the security situation continues to deteriorate the Russians might then bring in their airborne and airmobile troops as well. **1983** *Times* 10 Nov. 4/8 The army has been pressing for 6 Brigade to be made air-mobile for several years.

So **air mobility**, the facility for moving (troops) about by air.

1941 N. MACMILLAN *Air Strategy* v. 43 The situation in Poland demanded air mobility.

†ˈ**airous**, *a. Obs. rare*[−1]. [f. AIR *sb.* + -OUS, after Fr. *aëreux.*] Of the nature of air, airy.

1683 TRYON *Way to Health* 651 It easily penetrates..the well-tempered Air, and so into the airous Spirits of the Hearers.

ˈ**air-pipe.** [AIR- 7.] A pipe for the passage of air; as **a.** One of the bronchial tubes in the lungs; **b.** A ventilating pipe or tube.

*c*1675 RAY (JOD.) The lungs are made up of such airpipes and vesicles. **1748** BOSCAWEN in R. Mead's *Wks.* (1762) 430 The airpipes fixed in the men of war have been of great service in this particular. **1889** F. R. STOCKTON *Gt. War Syndicate* vi. 84 If the air-pipes..could be rendered useless the crew [of the submarine vessel] must inevitably be smothered. **1899** W. S. CHURCHILL *River War* I. i. 2 The Soudan is joined to Egypt by the Nile, as a diver is connected with the surface by his air-pipe.

air-plane (ˈɛəpleɪn). [f. AIR- + PLANE *sb.*[3]]

1. The air regarded as a horizontal plane. *nonce-use.*

1874 *Belgravia* IV. 168 Not all the rudders and flappers.. can ever enable the aeronaut to navigate his machine *horizontally*—to one hand or the other of the air-plane on which he is sailing.

2. [Alteration of AEROPLANE, after AIR- III.] Also **airplane.** †**a.** = AEROPLANE 1; **b.** = AEROPLANE 2 b (esp. *U.S.*). Also *attrib.*

a. 1896 J. CHALLIS in *Invention* 13 June 380/2 The combined use of the screw and aeroplane (why not call it air plane) principles.

b. 1907 *Westm. Gaz.* 19 July 4/2 It is this ease of going against the current, with no motive force in evidence, that is ..the despair of the aeronauts with their air-planes. **1916** BUCHAN *Nelson's Hist. War* XIV. 48 Airplane reconnaissance. **1917** *N.A.C.A. (U.S.) Rep. Nomencl. Aeronaut.* 31 *Airplane*..This term is commonly used in a more restricted sense to refer to airplanes fitted with landing gear suited to operation from the land. If the landing gear is suited to operation from the water, the term 'Seaplane' is used. **1918** *King's Regs. R.A.F.* §1024A, The supply of patent fire-extinguishers is to be limited to the following services:—Motor boats. Motor vehicles. Airplanes. Seaplanes. **1928** A. LLOYD JAMES *Broadc. English* I. 21 *Aeroplane*..the [B.B.C. Advisory] Committee [on Spoken English] advises the use of the word *airplane.* **1930** H. G. WELLS *Autocr. Mr. Parham* IV. i. 279 The airplane carrier *Courageous.* **1937** *Daily Express* 2 Feb. 3/4 The islanders clamber into the airplane as though they were boarding a bus. **1956** W. A. HEFLIN *U.S. Air Force Dict.* 33/1 'Airplane' is preferred to 'aeroplane' in American usage, having received official sanction in Army publications as early as 1918.

ˈ**air-ˌplant.** [AIR- 6.] A plant which grows on a tree or other elevated object, and derives its nourishment from atmospheric moisture, as is the case with many tropical orchids.

1842 GRAY *Struct. Bot.* iii. §1 (1880) 35 Epiphytes or Air-Plants have roots which are..unconnected with the ground. **1879** B. TAYLOR *Germ. Lit.* 64 Like the air-plants of Brazil, their gorgeous blossoms and exquisite fragrance seem to spring from nothing.

airport (ˈɛəpɔət). [PORT *sb.*[1], in transf. use of sense 2.] An aerodrome, esp. one with a customs-house, to which aeroplanes resort to load and unload, and at which passengers embark or disembark. (For *air-port* in an unconnected use see AIR- II.)

In quot. 1921 [after SEAPORT], a landing-place for a seaplane.

1919 *Aerial Age Weekly* 14 Apr. 235/1 There is being established at Atlantic City the first 'air port' ever established, the purposes of which are..to provide a municipal aviation field,..to supply an air port for trans-Atlantic liners, whether of the seaplane, land aeroplane or dirigible balloon type. **1921** *Aeronautics* 19 May 351/2 The flight..was made in..two hours, the machine landing above Westminster Bridge... It was the first occasion on which the Thames had been used as an air port for a machine from abroad. **1924** *Lancet* 9 Feb. 309/2 The vigilance practised by sanitary authorities at our seaports will require to be exercised in even greater degree at the great airports of the future. **1926** *Glasgow Herald* 13 Nov. 4 The scene [at Croydon] is characteristic of the airports of all the big cities. **1933** *Jrnl. R. Aeronaut. Soc.* XXXVII. 22 Another important feature of night lighting is the airport beacon, usually of the rotating or flashing type, and mounted upon the terminal building. **1943** [see AIRFIELD]. **1946** *Daily Tel.* 26 July 6/3 The course began at the helicopter airport at Bridgeport.

ˈ**air-pump.** [AIR- 7.] A machine for exhausting the air out of a vessel by means of the strokes of a piston. (Formerly called *Pneumatic Engine* and *Wind Pump*; subsequently used in steam engines.)

1660 BOYLE *New Exper.* i. (1682) 4, I put Mr. G. and R. Hook to contrive some Air-pump that might not like the other need to be kept under water. **1664** POWER *Exp. Philos.* II. 121 That excellent Tractate of Experiments of Esq. Boyle's, with his Pneumatical Engin or Ayr-pump. **1692** BENTLEY *Boyle Lect.* viii. 284 Exhausted Receivers of Air-pumps. **1711** ADDISON *Spect.* No. 21 ¶7 For want of other Patients [they] amuse themselves with the stifling of Cats in an Air-Pump. **1728** YOUNG *Love of Fame* v. (1757) 126 Like cats in air-pumps, to subsist we strive On joys too thin to keep the soul alive. **1802** TREVITHICK & VIVIAN *Brit. Pat. 2599* In the steam engines constructed and applied according to our said Invention..we use a new method of condensing by an injection above the bucket of the air pump. **1812** SIR H. DAVY *Chem. Philos.* 26 Otto de Guericke of Magdeburgh invented the air-pump. **1875** *Encycl. Brit.* I. 429/2 *Air-pump*, in steam-engines, is the pump which draws the condensed steam, along with the air which is always mixed with it, and also the condensing water..away from the condenser, and discharges it into the hot well.

ˈ**air-raid.** [RAID *sb.*] A raiding attack by aircraft upon an enemy. Also *attrib.*, as ***air-raid alarm, precautions*** (abbrev. A.R.P.), ***shelter, warden*** (also ***air warden***), ***warning.***

1914 *Whitaker's Almanack 1915* 823/1 British air raids on Cologne and Dusseldorf. **1916** [see *air warfare*, AIR- III. 2]. **1916** LANCHESTER *Aircraft in Warfare* 190 Air-raids on Great Britain by Zeppelin do not pay. **1917** *Flying* 1 Aug. 18/2 The Home Secretary stated..that air-raid warnings would be given by signal rockets. **1919** 'I. HAY' *Last Million* p. xi, Above all, we hope to see the air-raid shelters gone. **1935** N. HAMMER (*title*) A Catechism of Air Raid Precautions. **1935** *Lancet* 27 Apr. 1018/1 Mr. Mander asked the Home Secretary the precise nature of the work to be carried out by the Home Office Air-raids Precautions Department at 5, Princes-street, Westminster. **1936** *Ibid.* 19 Dec. 1465/2 Each subdivision being required to make its own plans for police and fire brigade services, rescue, [etc.] ..and air-raid wardens. **1937** *Ibid.* 2 Oct. 812/2 A.R.P. These sinister initials are being made more and more familiar by a spate of books on air-raid precautions. **1938** *Times Weekly* 27 Jan. 8/2 The appointment by local authorities in Great Britain of voluntary air wardens and fire-fighters. **1938** *Lancet* 9 July 90/2 The current theory is that there will be an air-raid warning, after which the population will go to shelters..and stay there till the all-clear signal. **1940** *Times Weekly* 7 Aug. 18 This was the first time that his Majesty had had the experience of an air-raid alarm sounding while carrying out a tour of inspection.

ˈ**air-ˌshaft.** [AIR- 7.] A straight passage (usually vertical) for the admission of air into a mine or tunnel.

1692 RAY *Creation* I. 69 By the sinking of an Air-shaft, the Air hath liberty to circulate. **1753** CHAMBERS *Cycl. Supp.* s.v., The damps..make it necessary to let down air-shafts. **1789** MRS. PIOZZI *France & It.* I. 196 One of the natives.. made a sort of mine, or airshaft.

airship (ˈɛəʃɪp). Formerly **air-ship.** [f. AIR- III. + SHIP *sb.*[1]; cf. G. *luftschiff.*] A dirigible motor-driven balloon, *spec.* one of an elongated cigar-shaped form having the gas-bags enclosed inside a rigid structure; also, esp. in the U.S., applied generally to other types of aircraft.

1819 in J. Milbank *First Cent. Flight in Amer.* (1943) v. 71 To ascend first in a balloon of the common construction, and afterwards to carry into operation his principles for navigating airships. **1838** T. M. MASON *Aeronautica* 327 Count Lennox's air-ship [*sc.* a balloon]. **1891** O. CHANUTE *Aerial Navig.* 7 It was not until 1852 that Henri Giffard.. laid down the foundation for eventual success by ascending with a spindle-shaped air ship driven by a steam-engine. **1894** —— *Progr. Flying Machines* 66 In 1885 Mr. Foster patented an air ship consisting of two screws. **1900** [see ZEPPELIN]. **1910** C. C. TURNER in *Jrnl. R. Soc. Arts* LVIII. 156/1 The common word airship can be applied to all vessels that travel in the air, but it is gradually becoming restricted to the dirigible balloon. **1927** —— *Old Flying Days* xxv. 344 To this day the Americans call aeroplanes 'airships'. **1950** *Gloss. Aeronaut. Terms (B.S.I.)* I. 46 *Airship*, a power-driven lighter-than-air aircraft.

b. *fig.*

1829 CARLYLE in *Foreign Rev.* III. 449 Over all which Chamouni-needles and Staubbach-Falls, the great *Persifleur* skims along in this his little poetical air-ship. **1833** —— *Sart. Res.* I. xi. in *Fraser's Mag.* VIII. 682/1 What vacant, high-sailing air-ships are these, and whither will they sail with us?

Hence †ˈ**airshipman.**

1904 *Pall Mall Mag.* Jan. 12/1 We air-shipmen are steamboat captains and not sailing yachtsmen.

†ˈ**airsome,** *a. Obs.* [f. AIR *sb.* + -SOME.] Airy, aereous.

1602 WARNER *Alb. Eng.* XI. lxvi. (1612) 283 On airesome Mountaines helde hee then his Court. **1674** N. FAIRFAX *Bulk & Selv.* 86 So as the surface might not be some airsom body, but all such thick or fast body.

airt (ˈɛət, *Sc.* eːrt), *sb. Sc.* Forms: 5–6 **art, arth,** 6– **airth, airt.** [app. a. Gael. *aird, àrd,* Irish *ard,* a height, top, point, also quarter of the compass. (Found only in Scottish writers from 15th c. to 18th c., but also used in some north. Eng. dialects, and recently by some Eng. writers.] A quarter of the heaven or point of the compass; a direction.

1470 HARDING *Chron.* lxxviii, And yf any met another at any arte [*v.r.* arcte]..he shuld his felowe tell His auentures. *c*1470 HENRY *Wallace* I. 308 Our kyne are slayne..And othir worthi mony in that art. *a*1500 *Wisd. Solomon* (R.R. 11) The sonne..cerclis the erd about all artis anis euery day [*Eccles.* i. 5]. **1535** STEWART *Cron. Scot.* (1858) I. 298 In sindrie airthis baith be south and north. **1552** LYNDESAY *Monarche* 5600 Angellis sall passe in the four airtis. **1637** RUTHERFORD *Lett.* No. 94 (1862) I. 244 Oh, if I c[d] turn my sails to Christ's right airth! **1730** T. BOSTON *Mem.* App. 30 They can have little hope from that airth. **1788** BURNS *Wks.* IV. 293 Of a' the airts the wind can blaw, I dearly like the west. **1839** DE QUINCEY *Recoll. Lakes* Wks. 1862 II. 36 Suppose..a pole, 15 feet high..with two cross-spars to denote the airts (or points of the compass). **1863** ATKINSON *Whitby Gloss.*, *Airt* or *Airth*, quarter or direction. 'The wind blows from a cold easterly airt.' **1866** KINGSLEY *Herew.* xxxiv. (1877) 425 He sent out spies to the four airts of heaven. **1876** MORRIS *Sigurd* III. 170 The airts whence the wind shall blow.

airt (ɛət, *Sc.* eːrt), *v. Sc.* [f. the sb.] To shew the direction or point out the way to any place; to direct, guide.

1787 BURNS *Wks.* 74 Her kind stars hae airted till her A good chiel wi' a pickle siller. *c*1810 TANNAHILL *Poems* (1846) 111 Ah! gentle lady, airt my way Across this langsome lonely moor. **1818** SCOTT *Hrt. Midl.* xix (1829) 159 To keep sight of my ain duty, or to airt you to yours.

air-tight (ˈɛətaɪt), *a.* [AIR- 3.] **a.** So tight as to be impermeable to air.

[Not in TODD 1818.] **1760** J. FERGUSON *Lect.* vi. II. 194 Push the open end of the glass tube through the collar of leathers..which it fits so as to be air-tight. **1833** BREWSTER *Nat. Magic.* xiii. 345 Shut up in an air-tight breathing-box. **1857** EMERSON *Poems* 86 You captives of your air-tight halls, Wear out in-doors your sickly days.

b. *fig.* (As one word.) That cannot be faulted, incontrovertible. Cf. WATERTIGHT *a.* 1 fig. *U.S.*

1929 W. FAULKNER *Sound & Fury* 236, I never found a nigger yet that didn't have an airtight alibi for whatever he did. **1955** D. W. MAURER in *Publ. Amer. Dial. Soc.* XXIV. 145 Sometimes..there is an *airtight* arrangement under which the pickpockets who pay off are protected, while..those who do not may be arrested and framed. **1969** J. A. MCPHERSON in A. Chapman *New Black Voices* (1972) 163 They took the seniority clause apart word by word, trying to figure a way to get at Doc. But they had it written airtight. **1978** *Sci. Amer.* Aug. 15/1 He..eventually found a lengthy, complex proof for 294 and 1,028 that he believes is airtight. **1986** R. FORD *Sportswriter* ix. 238 He hated everything I had ever liked and had airtight arguments for why they were laughable.

air-tight (ˈɛətaɪt), *sb. U.S.* [f. the adj.]

1. An air-tight stove.

1844 'JONATHAN SLICK' *High Life N.Y.* II. xxxi. 227 Speakin' of stoves, Par, I got..what they call an air-tight. **1909** J. C. LINCOLN *Keziah Coffin* i. 12 The stovepipe was attached to the 'air-tight' in the dining room.

2. An article of food put up in an air-tight vessel.

1897 A. H. LEWIS *Wolfville* 330 What's air-tights?.. Air-tights is can peaches, can tomatters, an' sim'lar bluffs. **1907** S. E. WHITE *Arizona Nights* I. xvi. 219 On top of a few incidental pounds of *chile con*, baked beans, soda biscuits, 'air tights', and other delicacies.

Hence ˈ**air-ˌtightness.**

1852 D. BOOTH *Art of Brewing* (ed. 2) 65 Pay the strictest attention to the air-tightness of the vats.

air-tightly (ˈɛːəˌtaɪtlɪ), *adv.* [f. AIR-TIGHT *a.* + -LY[2].] In an air-tight manner.

1800 HOWARD in *Phil. Trans.* XC. 238 By means of a leather collar, the neck can be air-tightly closed.

ˈ**air-vessel.** [AIR- 7.]

1. *Nat. Hist.* Any vessel whose function is to contain air; especially, the tracheæ or respiratory tubes of insects, and the spiral vessels in plants. Also *fig.*

1676 Grew *Anat. Plants* II. iii. (1682) 70 The Lignous Part is also Compounded of Two kinds of Bodies *scil.* succiferous or Lignous and Aer-Vessels. **1692** Ray *Creation* I. (1704) 82 Insects.. having more Air-vessels for their Bulk. **1753** Chambers *Cycl. Supp.*, *Air-vessels* are found in the leaves of all plants. **1819** *Pantologia*, s.v., Air-vessels are distinguished from sap-vessels. **1857** Geo. Eliot *Amos Barton* ii in *Blackw. Mag.* LXXXI. 7/1 We are poor plants buoyed up by the air-vessels of our own conceit.

2. *Hydraulics*; = air-chamber.

1744 J. T. Desaguliers *Course Exper. Philos.* II. xii. 510 A large Copper Air-Vessel, which receives the Water forced into it by the Action of 2 pumps. **1819** *Pantologia*, s.v., *Air-vessels*.. metalline cylinders placed between the two forcing-pumps in the improved fire-engine. *c* **1850** *Nat. Phil.* (S.S.B.A.) 90 The fire-engine consists of two forcing-pumps, both communicating with an air-vessel.

†**3.** [air- III.] A flying-machine. *Obs.*

1821–2 Byron in Medwin *Conversat. Ld. B.* (1824) I. 199, I suppose we shall soon travel by air-vessels; make air instead of sea-voyages. **1916** *Sphere* 9 Dec. 183 The strafing of Germany's zeppelin fleet: a pictorial presentation of the air vessels brought down and wrecked.

†**4.** The gas-bag of a balloon. *Obs.*

1870 *Sci. Amer.* 8 Jan. 33/2 An air vessel of 100 feet diameter, two thirds filled with coal gas.. would be all sufficient for a practicing machine.

airward ('ɛəwəd), *adv.* [f. air *sb.* + -ward.] Toward the air, upward.

1820 Keats *Hyperion* II. 82 When the muse's wings are airward spread. **1880** G. Macdonald *Book of Strife* 247 All winged things came from the waters first; Airward still many a one from the water springs. **1937** W. de la Mare *This Year, Next Year*, With whirr of wing Will airward spring.

airwards ('ɛəwədz), *adv.* [f. air *sb.* + -wards.] = prec.

1855 Thackeray *Shabby Story* iv. (D.) Eagles.. sail down from the clouds.. and soar airwards again.

'airway. Also **air-way.**

1. a. A passage for air, esp. one for ventilation in a mine.

1851 [see intake *sb.* 4]. **1880** *Colliery Guard.* 5 Nov., [It] drives the gas, in a diluted state, into the airways, and so carries it away to the upcast. **1908** *Daily Chron.* 7 Mar. 5/5 Free the return air-way from noxious gases.

b. A passage for air into the lungs; also, *spec.* a device to keep this passage open.

1908 *Lancet* 15 Feb. 491/1 Should there be much jaw spasm at the moment when it is desired to introduce the 'air-way' it may be necessary to separate the teeth by means of a Mason's gag. **1911** *Ibid.* 11 Nov. 1335/2 Insisting on the routine use in every administration of an anaesthetic of establishing an oral airway by means of a mouth-prop and tongue-clip. **1962** *Ibid.* 28 Apr. 879/2 To protect the patient against obstruction of the airway, endotracheal intubation with a cuffed tube is highly desirable during abdominal surgery.

2. a. A route through the air, esp. one regularly followed by aircraft from airport to airport. Also (freq. *pl.*) = air-line 2.

1873 *Punch* 1 Feb. 44 [This book] professes to give.. account of the.. customs of.. one of the planets... Are their railways, or airways, or whatever their means of locomotion may be called, as well managed as our own? **1908** *Westm. Gaz.* 3 Oct. 3/2 An impression of 1920... Extract from Passenger Handbook of the Great Eastern Airway Company for June. **1911** L. Blériot in Grahame-White & Harper *Aeroplane* 218 The Atlantic will, also, beyond doubt have its regular 'airway'. **1920** *19th Cent.* Aug. 333 It is the business of an airway to sell speed at a price. **1937** *Discovery* May 163/2 A message was sent to an airways agent. **1946** G. B. Shaw *Geneva* Pref. 7 The houses and factories, the railways and airways, the orchards and furrowed fields. **1958** *Economist* 1 Nov. 434/2 Outside the airways.. the need is for international agreement on a standard form of navigation. **1958** *Economist* 1 Nov. 434/2 When the airways control is completed, they will not be allowed to fly 'see and be seen' in British air lanes. **1971** D. Potter *Brit. Eliz. Stamps* xii. 130 Cambrian Airways, when they took over the operation of some internal routes previously operated only by BEA, inherited the airway service. **1985** *N.Y. Times* 18 Mar. A4/4 We warn all international airways that all Iranian airspace is considered a prohibited zone.

b. airway beacon (see quot. 1940).

1937 *Aeronaut. Res. Comm. Rep. & Mem.* No. 1793 p. 1 Light signals used in aviation.. on or near the airway, airway beacons. **1940** *Chambers's Techn. Dict.* 19/2 *Airway beacon*, a powerful light (often flashing a morse sign), for the guidance of aircraft.

3. A radio channel (cf. air *sb.*¹ 1 c). *U.S.*

1934 in M. Weseen *Dict. Amer. Slang* xii. 165. **1946** *Baltimore Sun* 10 Oct. 18/8 By that time a radio broadcaster had appeared with a portable microphone but Ted had nothing for the airways, even after most of the other players had taken their turns at the 'mike'.

airworthy ('ɛəˌwɜːðɪ), *a.* Also **air-worthy.** [f. air- III + -worthy, after seaworthy *a.*] Of aircraft: in a fit condition for travelling through the air. Hence **'airˌworthiness.**

1829 *Mech. Mag.* XI. 181 The airiner has time, in all cases (assuming that the air-car is air-worthy) to concert proper measures for his safe descent. **1864** M. Reid *Cliff-Climbers* lii. 342 Whether their aërial ship would prove herself air-worthy. **1909** *Westm. Gaz.* 11 May 5/2 That their vessel would be airworthy when completed. **1909** H. G. Wells *Tono-Bungay* IV. i, I had satisfied myself.. of the real air-worthiness of Lord Roberts *β* [*sc.* a dirigible balloon]. **1920** *Flight* XII. 1182/2 Ensuring that machines are maintained in an airworthy condition after the issue of the airworthiness certificate. **1955** *Times* 23 May 6/2 The results.. will be reviewed by the Air Registration Board, and their bearing on airworthiness certification will be considered.

airy ('ɛərɪ), *a.* Forms: 4–7 **ayery**, 6–7 **ayry(e, -ie, airie,** 7 **aiery,** 6– **airy.** [f. air *sb.* + -y¹. See also aery, a parallel form after L. *āeri-us.*]

I. Of the atmosphere.

†**1.** Of or belonging to the air. **a.** Naturally produced or performed through the air, pneumatic, atmospheric. **b.** Living in the air; aerial. *Obs.*

1398 Trevisa *Barth. De P.R.* III. xviii, þe herynge is ayery, for al wey it is gendrid by ayer. **1551** Recorde *Pathw. Know.* Pref., Nether motion, nor time, nor ayrye impressions coulde hee aptely declare, but by the helpe of Geometrye. **1623** Favine *Theat. Hon.* III. xi. 348 His pace equalled the flight of the ayrie Birdes. *a* **1656** Hales *Gold. Rem.* (1688) 9 Meteors and airy speculations. **1677** Hale *Prim. Orig. Man.* II. ix. 208 Insects, whether aiery, terrestrial, or watry.

2. Performed or taking place in the air as an action; aerial.

1624 Quarles *Sion's Eleg.* (1717) 380 And to the Air breathes forth her Airy moans. **1790** Wolcott (P. Pindar) *Wks.* 1812 II. 260 And wings o'er Trees and Towers its airy way. **1874** J. Sully *Sensat. & Intuit.* 104 Pleasant visions of airy castles. **1878** E. White *Life in Christ* I. ii. 18 If that has been the object of the airy voyage.

3. Placed high in the air: aerial; lofty. Hence, ethereal, heavenly. (Now only *poetical.*)

c **1590** Marlowe *Faustus* i. 126 Like women or unwedded maids Shadowing more beauty in their airy brows. **1635** Swan *Spec. Mundi* iv. §2 (1643) 68 Not onely the Aiery heaven.. but under the whole Heaven. **1643** Denham *Cooper's Hill* 217 His proud head the aery Mountain hides Among the Clouds. **1725** Pope *Odyss.* IV. 700 Him thus exulting.. A Spy distinguish'd from his airy stand. **1808** Scott *Marm.* VI. xix, Beneath the castle's airy wall. **1879** Tennyson *Lover's T.* 11 From his mid-dome in Heaven's airy halls.

4. Exposed to the open air, abounding in or open to free currents of air; *hence*, breezy.

a **1596** Spenser (J.) To range abroad.. Through the wide compass of the airy coast. **1683** Tryon *Way to Health* 287 Airy Houses & Rooms. **1713** Pope *Windsor For.* 167 O'er airy wastes to rove. **1779** Johnson *L.P.*, *West* Wks. 1787 IV. 199 He was seduced to a more airy mode of life. **1821** J. Clare *Vill. Minstrel* I. 195 The morning breeze, healthy and airy. **1863** Miss Braddon *Eleanor's Vict.* I. ii. 22 She had been accustomed to large airy rooms.

II. Of the substance air.

5. Composed of air, of the nature of air; hence, in modern use, Having the consistency or appearance of air merely, air-like, immaterial.

1398 Trevisa *Barth. De P.R.* IV. vii, The pure and ayery matter. **1533** Elyot *Cast. Helth* (1541) 1 Rather erthy, watry, airy, and fyry, than absolutely erth, water, ayre, & fyre. **1563** W. Fulke (*title*) A goodly Gallerye.. to behold the naturall Causes of all Kynde of Meteors, as wel fyery and ayery, as watry and earthly. **1612** Woodall *Surg. Mate* Wks. 1653, 20 A volatile uncertain ayrie substance. **1651** Hobbes *Leviathan* IV. xlv. 352 They can put on Aiery bodies .. to make them Visible. **1704** Addison *Italy* 3 Thin airy Shapes that o'er the Furrows rise. **1849** Mrs. Somerville *Connex. Phys. Sc.* xxxvii. 445 These thin and airy phantoms vanish in the distance.

6. Like air in its lightness and buoyancy. (Used appreciatively.) **a.** Light in appearance; thin in texture, as if capable of floating in the air.

1598 Florio, *Fungoso*, spungie, airie, light, as a mushrome. **1633** Donne *Poems* (1650) 41 Like gold to ayery thinnesse beat. **1831** Scott in Lockhart's *Life* (1839) X. 47 The French chain-bridge looked lighter and airier than the prototype. **1849** Miss Muloch *Ogilv.* i. 3 The airy evening dress she wore. **1865** *Cornh. Mag.* 302 The airiest of chintz muslins.

b. Light in movement, elastic as air.

1642 Howell *For. Trav.* 30 The one Quick and Ayry, the other Slow and Heavy. **1810** Scott *Lady of L.* I. xviii, Elastic from her airy tread. **1878** C. Stanford *Symb. Christ* ix. 237 To still the airy foot and to quench the brightness of that radiant eye.

c. Lively, sprightly, merry, gay, vivacious.

1644 Milton *Educ.* (1738) 136 Others.. of a more delicious and airy spirit. **1630–95** *Life Ant. à Wood* (1848) 70 Violins.. being more airie and brisk than viols. **1673** Dryden *Marr.-a-la-Mode* v. i. Wks. III. 270 To be very Aiery, with abundance of Noise, and no Sense: Fa, la, la, la, &c. **1674** Playford *Skill of Mus.* I. x. 33 This Mood is much used in Airy Songs and Galiards. **1714** Ellwood *Life* (1765) 95 An airy Piece she was; and very merry she made herself at me. **1826** Disraeli *Viv. Grey* v. vii. 206 Miss Fane combated all the objections with airy merriment.

d. Light, delicate, graceful in fancy or conception. (Fr. *spirituel.*)

1779 Johnson *L.P.*, *Pope* Wks. 1787 IV. 16 The Rape of the Lock, the most airy.. of all his compositions. **1818** Hazlitt *Eng. Poets* xi. (1870) 54 The fancy of Spenser; and .. the airy dream that hovers over it. **1864** Neale *Seaton. Poems* 86 And flutes make airier music float. **1879** *Standard* 27 May, The airiest of wits, he was one of the gayest squib writers that ever lived.

7. Like air in its (apparently) intangible or empty character. (Used depreciatively.)

a. Unsubstantial, vain, empty; unreal, imaginary.

1590 Shaks. *Mids. N.* v. i. 16 The Poets pen.. giues to air[i]e nothings a locall habitation And a name. **1615** Sandys *Trav.* 145 The aiery title our Richard the first did purchase. **1644** Milton *Areop.* (Arb.) 49 Plato.. making many edicts to his ayrie Burgomasters. **1649** Selden *Laws Eng.* II. ii. (1739) 8 A General without an Army, the Title big, but airy. *a* **1704** T. Brown *Epigr.* Wks. 1730 I. 123 Airy visions of imagin'd food. **1749** Smollett *Regic.* I. iii. (1777) 20 The vain resource of Fancy's airy dreams. **1847** Lewes *Hist. Philos.* (1867) I. 115 And peoples an airy void with airy nothings. **1876** Mozley *Univ. Serm.* iv. 94 Goodness was to them but an airy ideal.

b. Flimsy, superficial, flippant.

1598 B. Jonson *Ev. Man in Hum.* I. i. 81 Your gentilitie.. an ayrie, and meere borrow'd thing. **1627** Feltham *Resolves* I. xxix. (1677) 51, I will never deny my self an honest solace, for fear of an airy censure. **1710** Shaftesbury *Charact.* (1737) III. i. 8 These.. may easily be oppressive to the airy Reader. **1712** Hughes *Spect.* No. 525 ¶3 It was determined among those airy Criticks. **1750** Johnson *Rambler* No. 175 ¶15 Him whose airy negligence puts his friend's affairs.. in continual hazard. **1865** Dickens *Mut. Fr.* xv. 259 Said Eugene with airy contempt.

c. Speculative, imaginative, visionary.

1667 *Pref. to H. More's Div. Dial.* (1713) 14 Not simply a Platonist, but an aiery-minded one. **1790** Burke *Fr. Rev.* Wks. V. 331 Subliming himself into an airy metaphysician.

8. (Derived from or influenced by air *sb.*¹ III.)

†**a.** Assuming airs, making lofty pretensions. *Obs.*

1606 Warner *Albion's Eng.* xv. xcviii. (1612) 390 Ayrie Saints, our Hypocrits we meane.

†**b.** Of a good air, manner, bearing, presence. *Obs.*

1689 *Gazophyl. Angl.*, An ayry man, from the Fr. *Aire*, comliness, or a good presence. **1699** Garth *Dispens.* iv. (1760) 60 The Slothful, negligent; the Foppish, neat; The Lewd are airy; and the Sly, discreet.

9. *Comb.*

1879 G. M. Hopkins *Poems* (1918) 46 The gold-wisp, airy-grey Eye, all in fellowship.

airy, obs. and dial. form of area.

airy-fairy ('ɛərɪ'fɛərɪ), *a. colloq.* [After Tennyson's 'airy, fairy Lilian' (*Lilian*, 1830).]

1. Delicate or light as a fairy. Also as *sb.*

1869 W. S. Gilbert *Bab Ballads, Only a Dancing Girl* iii, No airy fairy she, As she hangs in arsenic green, From a highly impossible tree, In a highly impossible scene. **1898** *Westm. Gaz.* 1 Oct. 8/1 The low-necked airy-fairy ladies' ball gown. **1907** *Ibid.* 30 Mar. 16/1 To find partners for the airy-fairy creatures.

2. Fanciful (in disparaging sense).

1920 D. H. Lawrence *Lost Girl* iv. 55 He had already an airy-fairy kind of knowledge of the whole affair. **1957** F. Hoyle *Black Cloud* iv. 85, I am concerned with facts not with motives, suspicions, and airy-fairy nothingness. **1966** *Listener* 8 Sept. 336/2 Favoured by.. some men of the market place, whose ideas I believe to be airy-fairy.

aisch, aissh, obs. forms of ash and ask.

aisel, -ell(e, -il, early var. eisell. *Obs.*, vinegar.

aisle (aɪl). Forms: *α.* 4–5 **ele, hele,** 5 **ille, eill(e, eyle,** 5–6 **yle, ylle,** 5–8 **ile,** (5 **ilde**). *β.* (6 **yland**) 6–8 **isle.** *γ.* 8 **aile, ayle,** 8– **aisle.** [Orig. a. OFr. *ele*, *eele*:—L. *āla* wing (contr. from *axilla*). Refashioned in Fr. after L. as *aelle* 15th c., *æle*, *aile* 16th c.; in 15th–16th c. Fr. also occas. written *aisle* in imitation of med.L. *ascella*, the common term for the wing of a building, for L. *axilla*. In Eng. confused in 15th. c. with *ile*, *yle* island (perh. with the idea of a detached or distinct portion of a church), and refashioned with this, *a*1700, as *isle*; recently modified after Fr. *aile* to *aisle*. The latter spelling is thus a cross between *isle* and *aile*, and has no connexion with earlier Fr. *aisle*. It was hesitatingly admitted by Johnson 1755; see quot. 4b. Lat. *āla* besides being confounded in mediæval use with *aula*, was confused with OFr. *alee*, Fr. *allée*, Eng. *alley*, which led to a mixture of the senses of *aisle* and alley; while the confusion with *ile*, *isle*, made *yland* an occasional Eng. equivalent, and *insula* the ordinary Lat. rendering in 15–16th c.]

1. A wing or lateral division of a church; the part on either side of the nave, usually divided from the latter by a row of pillars.

α. *c* **1370** *Inscr. in Cawston Ch.*, 'Orate pro animâ Roberti Oxburgh.. qui istud ele fieri fecit.' **1398** in *Reg. Test. Ebor.* I. 219 Ecclesiæ de Schirefhoton ad ponendum plumbum super le south hele xxs. **1410** *Ibid.* IV. 42 The foresaid Richard hase undirtaken for to make the south eill. **1418** in *E.E. Wills* (1883) 38 þat it go to þe Lee Cherche, to þe Eyle. **1428** *Ibid.*, The Ille of the toon Side of the Cloistere. **1428** in *R. Test. Eb.* II. 665 In portica qui vulgariter yᵉ yle S.M. dicitur. **1463** in *Bury Wills* (1850) 38 If ther be maad an ele ther the vestry is. **1471** Sir J. Paston in *Lett.* 676 III. 16 The grounde off the qwyr is hyer than the grownde off the ilde. **1490** in *R. Test. Eb.* IV. 60 To be beried in the Trinite church, in the north ile. **1533** *Ibid.* XI. 61 In the ylle affore our Lady. **1577** Hanmer *Anc. Eccles. Hist.* (1619) 189 He builded seats and goodly yles on either side. **1596** Nashe *Saffron Walden* 121 Then he comes vpon thee with I'le, I'le, I'le. Hee might as well write against *Poules* for hauing three Iles in it. **1681** Wyndham *King's Concealm.* 85 He sate in an Ile distinct from the body of the Congregation. **1711** Pope *Temp. Fame* 265 And arches widen, and long iles extend. **1756** J. Warton *Ess. on Pope* (1782) I. §6. 339 The long ile of a great Gothic church.

β. **1590** *Wills & Invent. N. Counties* (1860) II. 183 In the portch in the south yland of the church. **1673** Ray *Journ. Low Countries* 261 A double isle on each side the nave. **1711** Steele *Spect.* No. 20 ¶2 One whole isle has been disturbed with one of these monstrous starers. **1772** Pennant *Tours in Scotl.* (1774) 58 On the isles on each side are some strange legendary painting. **1796** Pegge *Anonym.* (1809) 251 One cannot approve of the mode of writing *isles* of a church..

The absurdity appears from the will of Richard Smith, Vicar of Wirksworth, made in 1504, wherein he makes a bequest for the reparation '*Imaginis S'ti Marie* in insulâ *predicti eccles. de Wyrkysworth*.'

γ. **1742** RICHARDSON *Pamela* III. 397 As up the Ayle, with Mind disturb'd, I walk. **1755** [See 4 b]. **1782** V. KNOX *Ess.* (1819) II. lxviii. 54 As he treads the solemn aile. **1789** [see 4 a]. **1821** W. CRAIG *Drawing &c.* vii. 368 Grave-stones occasionally found in the ailes. **1848** LYTTON *Harold* IV. ii. 85 As the swell of an anthem in an aisle.

[δ. **1358** in *Reg. Thoresby* (York), In posteriori parte porticus sive aulæ.. in loco eminenciore dicti porticus sive alæ.]

2. *fig.*

1789 E. DARWIN *Loves of Plants* iv. 9 Long ailes of Oaks. **1818** KEATS *Endymion* IV. 977 Through the dark pillars of those sylvan aisles. **1854** J. ABBOTT *Napoleon* (1855) II. xxi. 385 Through the deep aisles of the forest. **1878** B. TAYLOR *Deukal.* II. v. 93 Arching aisles of the pine, receive us.

†**3.** ***cross aisle***: a transept. *Obs.*

1451 in *R. Test. Eb.* II. 157 Ad facturam—de lez crosse yles. *a* **1500** W. WORCESTRE 290 (in Parker's *Gloss. Arch.* s.v.) Longitudo de la crosse eele.. In medio de la crosse eele scituatur. **1662** FULLER *Worthies* III. 144 The Cross Isle of this Church is the most beautifull and lightsome of any I have yet beheld. **1772** *Hist. Rochester* 58 At the entrance of the choir is a great cross isle.

4. By extension of the strict architectural meaning, used also for: **a.** Any division of a church.

1762 H. WALPOLE *Vertue's Anecd. Painting* (1786) III. 106 A pillar in the middle isle of the church. **1789** MRS. PIOZZI *France & It.* II. 100 Warwick Castle would be contained in its middle aisle. **1835** WHEWELL *Germ. Churches* (ed. 2) 26 Among the liberties taken with language .. I should mention the employment of the word 'aisle' for the central space, nave or choir, as well as for the lateral spaces of a building. **1836** PARKER *Gloss. Arch.* s.v., Many writers of authority apply the word *Isle* to the central as well as the lateral compartments. Thus Brown Willis [*a* 1760] has 'middle Isle' repeatedly, and even describes the Cathedral Church of Man as consisting of two single Isles crossing each other. **1861** NICHOLSON *Annals of Kendal* 42 The church.. consists of the nave, chancel, and four side aisles, so that it consists of five open aisles.

b. (By confusion with ALLEY) A passage in a church between the rows of pews or seats. ***broad aisle*** (U.S.): see BROAD *a.* D. 2.

1731–42 BAILEY, *Isles*, Certain straight Passages between Pews within a Church. **1755** JOHNSON, '*Aisle* [Thus written by Addison, but perhaps improperly, since it seems deducible only from either *aile* a wing, or *allée* a path, and is therefore to be written *aile*.] The walks in a church or wings of a quire.' **1766** *Goody Two-Shoes* (1881) 55, I then walked up and down all the Isles of the Church. **1856** E. B. DENISON *Ch. Build.* iii. 113 An aisle is.. a wing, not a passage, as people seem to imagine who talk of the 'middle aisle' of a church. **1871** *Congreg. Year-bk.* 410 The aisles and lobbies of the church are laid in tiles.

5. a. A passage-way in a building (esp. a theatre, cinema, etc.), a train, etc. orig. *north. dial.* and *U.S.*

1755 in J. N. SCOTT *Bailey's Dict.*, *Isle*.. a long passage in a church or public building. **1827** *Western Monthly Rev.* I. 73 The long aisles of all the stories [of a factory] to the fourth loft. **1842** FANNY BUTLER in *Bentley's Misc.* XII. 2 The seats .. are placed down the whole length of the vehicle, one behind the other, leaving a species of aisle in the middle for the uneasy.. to fidget up and down. **1851** J. J. HOOPER *Widow Rugby's Husb.* 103, I have seen him.. charge.. into one door of the court-house, dash furiously along the aisle [etc.]. **1873** *Sat. Rev.* 22 Nov. 662/2 The Deputy-Sheriff placed his prisoners in the smoking-car of the train... The aisle was packed. **1880** L. WALLACE *Ben-Hur* v. xiii, As the four stout servants carried the merchant in his chair up the aisle [in the circus], curiosity was much excited. **1890** *N. & Q.* 19 July 53/1, I have heard the space between the counters of a shop called 'the aisle' in Liverpool. **1903** A. I. BACHELLER *Darrel of Blessed Isles* xiv. 148 Small boys would be chasing each other up and down aisles [of the school]. **1909** *Daily Chron.* 16 Feb. 4/7 [In America] all gangways and narrow paths whether in theatres, shops, or omnibuses, are 'aisles'. **1921** WODEHOUSE *Jill the Reckless* xviii. 260 The audience began to move up the aisles. **1961** R. GRAVES *More Poems* 33 Bring the charge-nurse scuttling down the aisle With morphia-needle levelled. **1965** G. MELLY *Owning Up* vi. 61 Pat would.. scurry down the coach aisle.

b. Colloq. phr. ***to have, lay, send*** (people) (***rolling***) ***in the aisles***: to make (an audience) laugh uncontrollably; to be a great theatrical success. Also *transf.*

1940 WODEHOUSE *Quick Service* xii. 136, I made the speech of a lifetime. I had them tearing up the seats and rolling in the aisles. **1943** D. W. BROGAN *Eng. People* vii. 202 This trick had the population, white and coloured, rolling in the aisles. **1954** N. COWARD *Future Indef.* I. 17 This, to use a theatrical phrase, had them in the aisles! In fact, two of my inquisitors laughed until they cried. **1959** *Sunday Express* 11 Oct. 6/5 A book that sends my English friends rolling in the aisles. **1959** *Times* 14 Dec. 13/4 We looked forward to a school play which would really lay them in the aisles.

6. A double row of wheat-sheaves set up to dry. *local.*

1794 T. DAVIS *Agric. Wilts.* 76 The general custom of Wiltshire, is, to set up the sheafs in double rows,.. and the sheaves so set up are called an aile. **1839** 'M. GRAY' *Last Sentence* II. III. i. 206 Paler gold of piled sheaves 'in aisle' on upland slopes. **1904** *Daily Mail* 10 Sept. 3/7 In the Isle of Wight, what is locally described as an 'aisle' of corn standing in a field.. was struck by lightning.

aisled (aɪld), *ppl. a.* Also 6 ilid, islid. [f. prec. + -ED².]

1. *adj.* Furnished with an aisle or aisles.

1538 LELAND *Itin.* I. 51 The Chirch of Stratflere is larg, side ilid and crosse ilid. *Ibid.* V. 82 Ther ly 4 notable Chapelles on the South syde of this Chirche crosse islid. **1820** KEATS *Lamia* II. 130 All down the aisled place. **1879** SCOTT *Lect. Archit.* II. 32 A Roman basilica, with an aisled nave and an unaisled choir.

2. *pple.* Located in an aisle. Cf. *housed, stabled.*

1818 BYRON *Childe Har.* IV. cliv, Majesty, Power, Glory, Strength and Beauty, all are aisled In this eternal ark of worship undefiled.

aisleless (ˈaɪllɪs), *a.* [f. AISLE + -LESS.] Unfurnished with aisles.

1849 FREEMAN *Archit.* 374 The tall narrow faces of an aisleless apse. **1865** STREET in *Englishm. Mag.* Feb. 121 There is hardly any obstruction to the view and the effect is almost that of an aisleless Church.

aisliche, -ment, obs. ff. EASILY, EASEMENT.

aisur, obs. north. form of AZURE.

ait¹ (eɪt). Forms: (1 *íʒʒað, íʒeoð*), 2 eyt, 3 æit, eit, 7–8 eyt, eyet, eyght, 8 aight, ayte, 7– ait, 9 eyot. [OE. *íʒʒað, íʒeoð* was perh. a dim. of *ieʒ, íʒ*, island (though the ordinary power of *-að* was to make abstr. nouns, as in *huntað* hunting). The subsequent phonetic history is obscure: the normal descendant of *íʒʒað* would be *ieth* (cf. *flieth*); the vowel of ME. *eyt* might arise from an OE. variant *éʒað*, as in *éʒ* isle for *íʒ* (cf. also ON. *eið* 'peninsula,' in Shetland *eid* 'a tongue of land'); but the *t* is unexplained; the later *-et*, and mod. *-ot*, are artificial spellings after *islet* (MFr. *islette*) and mod.Fr. *îlot*.] An islet or small isle; especially one in a river, as the aits or eyots of the Thames.

894 *O.E. Chron.*, Hie fluʒon ofer Temese buton ælcum forda þa up be Colne on anne iʒʒað. *c* **1000** ÆLFRIC *Hom.* (Sweet 77) þa asende hé hine.. to ánum iʒeoðe þe is Paðmas ʒeciʒed. **1052–67** *Charter of Eadweard* in *Cod. Dipl.* IV. 211 On máden and on eyten, on waterin and on weren. **1205** LAYAMON 23872 Ferde to þan æite mid aðele his wepnen [**1250** He wende to þan yllond]. **1649** R. HODGES *Plainest Direc.* 2 The Ait where the Osiers grew. **1677** COLES, An Eyet, Eyght. *Insula minima in fluento.* **1725** DE FOE, etc. *Tour Gt. Brit.* II. 70 Not far from Maidenhead Bridge, is a small Aight or Islet in the River. **1772** BARRINGTON in *Phil. Trans.* LXII. 289 A man near Brentford says, that he hath caught them [swallows] in this state in the eyt opposite to that town. **1835** T. HOOK *G. Gurney* (1850) I. iv. 61 The ayte opposite Mrs. Forty's excellent inn. **1851** SIR. F. PALGRAVE *Norm. & Eng.* I. 321 Not presqu'isles, but completely eyots and islands. **1864** R. F. BURTON *Dahome* 33 A semi-stagnant stream, dotted with little green aits. **1880** *Times, Thames Conservancy*: All Steam tugs are to be placed outside Chiswick Ait.

Comb. **ait-land**, *obs.*, an island.

1205 LAYAMON 1117 Logice hatte þat eitlond [**1250** yllond] *Ibid.* 21750 Sixti æit-londes· beoð i þan watere longe.

ait², **aitt**, *Sc.* and *north. dial.* = OAT.

1513–75 *Diurn. Occurrents* (1833) 181 Aittis and peis growand thair about. **1570** *Wills & Inv. N. Counties* (1835) I. 344 Fywe bollis quheit & fywe bollis beir & aitts. **1786** BURNS *Wks.* III. 13 An' Aits set up their awnie horn.

aitch (the letter); see ACHE *sb.*³ and H.

aitch (eɪtʃ). Name of the letter H; cf. ACHE *sb.*³ Also *Comb.*, as ***aitch-dropping, -free*** adjs. Hence **ˈaitchless** *a.*, that does not aspirate his *h*'s.

1887 H. BAUMANN *Londinismen* p. xvi, Avowing himself 'An Aitch Dropper'. **1892, 1894** [see H 1 a, 2]. **1900** G. SWIFT 75 The aitch-less 'Arry. *Ibid.* 115 A bounder of the aitch-dropping type. **1903** SHAW *Man & Superman* II. 50 This man takes more trouble to drop his aitches than ever his father did to pick them up. **1907** *Daily Chron.* 9 July 3/3 Humanity, with a capital aitch. **1925** *Contemp. Rev.* June 746 The aitch-free accent. **1937** 'G. ORWELL' *Road to Wigan Pier* xiii. 257 Even the aitchless millionaire, though sometimes he.. learns a B.B.C. accent, seldom succeeds in disguising himself as completely as he would like to.

aitch-bone (ˈeɪtʃˌbəʊn). Forms: 3 nage-, 6–9 nache-, 5 hach-, 9 aitch-, H-, each-bone. And corruptly 6 ise-, 7 ice-, 8 ize-, 9 ische-, ash-, edge-bone. [As shown by Mr. H. Nicol (Phil. Soc. 3 May 1878) orig. *nache-* or *nage-*bone, bone of the buttock, a. OFr. *nache, nage*:—late L. **natica*, prop. adj. f. *nati-s* buttock; see NACHE. The initial *n* being lost by coalescence with *a* (as in *a nadder, an adder*) *a nache, an ache* has been phonetically narrowed to *aitch, each*, corrupted as *ash, ische*, and falsely refashioned as *H-, ice-, edge-*bone.] The bone of the buttock or rump; the cut of beef lying over this bone.

[*c* **1300** *Langtoft's Chron.* in *Pol. Songs* 295 The fote-folke Puth the Scotes in the polke, and nakned their nages. **1523** FITZHERBERT *Husb.* §57 Upon the hucbone and the nache by the tayle. **1784–1815** A. YOUNG *Ann. Agric.* (in Britten 97) The catch or point of the rump.. The nache in some writers; also the tail-points by others.] **1486** *Bk. St. Albans* f 3 b, Kerue vp the flesh ther vp to the hach-boon. **1576** *Exp. Queens table* in Nichols's *Progr.* II. 8 Ise-bones.. 2 st... 2d. **1691** RAY *S. & E. Country Wds.*, *Ice-bone*, a rump of beef [*Norf.*]. **1703** THORESBY *Lett. to Ray*, *Ize-bone*, the huckle-bone, the coxa [*Yorksh.*]. *c* **1818** *Yng. Woman's Compan.*, The hind quarter contains the sirloin.. and the isch, each, or ash-bone. **1822** KITCHINER *Cook's Oracle* 151 H-Bone of Beef. (*Note.* In Mrs. Mason's *Ladies Assistant* [1773] this joint is called 'Haunch-bone'; in Henderson's *Cookery*, 'Edge-bone'; in *Domestic Management* [1810] 'Aitch-bone'; in Reynold's *Cookery*, 'Ische-bone'; in Mrs. Lydia Fisher's *Prudent Housewife*, 'Ach-bone'; in Mrs. M'Iver's *Cookery*, 'Hook-bone.' We have also seen it spelt 'Each-bone,' and 'Ridge-bone,' and we have also heard it called 'Natch-bone.') **1828** CARR *Craven Gloss.*, *Nache-bone*. **1873** E. SMITH *Foods* 48 The proportion of bone.. is the greatest in the head, shins, and legs and the aitch bone. **1876** *Echo* 6 Dec. 1/3 *Present Prices*:—Beef.. Aitch-bone 7½d. per lb.

aith, obs. or dial. form of OATH.

aither, obs. and dial form of EITHER.

aitiology, obs. variant of ÆTIOLOGY.

aiver, aix, obs. or dial. forms of AVER, AXE.

ajar (əˈdʒɑː(r)), *adv.*¹ Forms: 6 on char, ? a char. [f. A *prep.*¹ + CHAR, OE. *cyrr, cerr* a turn. The 18th c. *at jar* was on false analogy; see next.] Of a door or window: On the turn, slightly opened.

[*c* **1400** *Beryn* 355 The doer shall stond char vp; put it from yew sofft.] *a* **1513** DOUGLAS *King Hart* (1874) I. 98 The dure on char it stude. **1513** —— *Æneis* VII. Prol. 129 Ane schot wyndo vnschet a lytill on char. **1708** SWIFT *Abol. Chr. Wks.* 1755 II. I. 90 Opening a few wickets, and leaving them at jar. **1786** BECKFORD *Vathek* (1868) 92 With a large door in it standing ajar. **1815** SCOTT *Ld. of Isles* V. iii, But the dim lattice is ajar.

ajar (əˈdʒɑː(r)), *adv.*² prop. *phr.* [A *prep.*¹ of state + JAR *sb.* discord, quarrel; or for earlier *at jar*.] In a jarring state, out of harmony, at odds.

1553–87 FOXE *A. & M.* (1843) VIII. 170 You are at jar amongst yourselves. **1860** HAWTHORNE *Marble Farm* (1879) I. xiii. 129 Any accident.. that puts an individual ajar with the world. **1877** HT. MARTINEAU *Autobiog.* I. 83 My temper was so thoroughly ajar.

†**a'jax.** *Obs.* Jocularly for *a jakes*; see JAKES.

1588 SHAKS. *L.L.L.* v. ii. 581 Your Lion that holds his Pollax sitting on a close stoole, will be giuen to Aiax. **1596** HARINGTON (*title*) The Metamorphosis of Ajax. **1611** COTGR., *Retraict*, an Aiax, Priuie, house of Office.

ajee (əˈdʒiː), *adv. Sc.* and *dial.* [A *prep.*¹ of state + JEE: see AGEE.] Aside, off the straight line; *hence* (of a gate) ajar. Also *fig.*

1733 RAMSAY *Tea-Table Misc.* (ed. 9) I. 35 Let ne'er a new whim ding thy fancy a-jee. **1793** BURNS *Wks.* IV. 98 Comena unless the back-yett be a-jee. **1816** SCOTT *O. Mort.* 257 His brain was a wee ajee, but he was a braw preacher for a' that.

ajog (əˈdʒɒg), *adv.*, prop. *phr.* [A *prep.*¹ + JOG.] On the jog, jogging.

1879 MEREDITH *Egoist* II. v. 100 Riding slack.. ajog homeward from the miry hunt.

ajoin, ajourn, obs. ff. ADJOIN, ADJOURN.

ajoint (əˈdʒɔɪnt), *adv.* prop. *phr.* [A *prep.*¹ on + JOINT.] **a.** On a joint or pivot. **b.** Jointed, supple, in motion.

1840 BROWNING *Sordello* II. 304 Like some huge throbbing-stone, that, poised a-joint, Sounds. **1856** MEREDITH *Shaving of Shagpat* 324 A monkey all ajoint with tricks.

ajostle (əˈdʒɒs(ə)l), *adv.* or *pred. a.* [f. A *prep.*¹ + JOSTLE.] Jostling; in a jostle.

1893 *Nat. Observer* 22 July 246/2 The quiet distance is all a-jostle and a-quake. **1908** A. S. M. HUTCHINSON *Once aboard Lugger* VI. v. 323 George put a hand to his head. This young man's senses were ajostle and awhirl.

ajoupa (əˈdʒuːpə). [Fr., repr. the Creole name.] In the West Indies, a hut or wigwam built on piles and covered with leaves or branches.

1871 KINGSLEY *At Last* I. viii. 298 A tribe of Chaymas built their palm-leaf ajoupas upon the very spot where the lake now lies.

ajutage, variant of ADJUTAGE.

ajutment (əˈdʒʌtmənt). *rare*⁻¹. [A purely imitative formation on JUT *v.* after *abutment*.] A jutting out, or projection.

1833 MARRYAT *Pet. Simple* (1846) III. iii. 323 Each hill, at its ajutment towards the sea, crowned with a fort.

ak(e, variant of AC *conj. Obs.*, but.

ak(e, obs. or dial. form of OAK.

akalat (əˈkælət). [Native (Bulu) word.] A native name of babblers of the genus *Illadopsis* in West Africa, and of chats of the genus *Sheppardia* in East Africa.

1930 G. L. BATES *Handbk. Birds W. Afr.* 379 Malacocincla fulvescens fulvescens. Brown Akálat *Bulu* Akalat. *Ibid.* 381 Malacocincla cleaveri batesi. Blackcap Akalat... The Blackcap Akalat is similar in habits to the others. **1953** D. A. BANNERMAN *Birds of West & Equat. Afr.* II. 847 In the White-breasted Akalat (*I. rufipennis*) the throat and middle line of the belly are white; in the Blackcap Akalat the under parts are even whiter.

akale, variant of ACALE *ppl. a. Obs.*, cold, frozen.

Akan (ˈɑːkən), *a.* and *sb.* Forms: 7 Arcanys, 8 Acanni, Acanny, -s, 9- Akan. [Native name.] The name of a group of Negro peoples inhabiting Ghana and neighbouring regions of West Africa, and of their group of languages.

1694 T. PHILLIPS in *Coll. of Voyages & Travels* (1732) VI. 224/2 The Arcanys, who are the best traders to our ships and castles, and have the purest gold, are an inland people. **1705** tr. *W. Bosman's New Descr. Guinea* vi. 77 Next.. we come..

to the description of Acanny, whose Inhabitants.. were famed for great Traders... And that which they vended was always so pure and fine, that to this day the best Gold is called by the Negroes, Acanni Sica, or Acanny Gold. **1897** J. M. SARBAH *Fanti Customary Laws* I. 2 The Akan language is nevertheless the parent language—the language of diplomacy and courtiers. *Ibid.* 3 The words 'Akan' (Akanfu) arose probably from the way the Mfantsifu referred to those who remained at Takieman. The word Akan to our mind means a remnant. **1923** R. S. RATTRAY *Ashanti* ix. 113 The Brong are, in my opinion, undoubtedly a branch of the Akan stock, to which the Ashanti and the Fanti belong.

akasa, akasha (ɑː'kɑːʃə). *Hindu Philos.* [Skr. *ākāśá-* ether, atmosphere.] One of the five elements: ether (see quot. 1858[1]). Hence **a'kasic, a'kashic** *adjs.*, of, pertaining to, or existing in the akasa.

1858 H. T. COLEBROOKE *Relig. & Philos. Hindus* vi. 154 Five elements, produced from the five elementary particles or rudiments... A diffused, etherial fluid (*ácáśa*), occupying space: it has the property of audibleness, being the vehicle of sound, derived from the sonorous rudiment or etherial atom. *Ibid.* x. 253 The Bauddhas do not recognise a fifth element, *ácáśa*, nor any substance so designated. **1885** *1st Rep. Comm. Soc. Psychical Res.* 30 The akâsic substratum of ponderable things. **1917** 'RAMACHARAKA' *14 Lessons in Yogi Philos.* vi. 105 These akasic records contain the 'memory' of all that has passed. **1938** M. FIRTH tr. *F. Werfel's Hearken unto Voice* i. 17 In some incomprehensible way.. *akâsha* contains in each of its particles, simultaneously and pervading the whole of space, all the phenomena and happenings of the cosmos. **1962** F. BANKS *Frontiers of Revel.* v. 66 An 'akashic record', that showed me.. the truth of the assertion that 'the universal ether is the recording angel of the Christian terminology'.

akathisia, acathisia (ækə'θɪsɪə). *Path.* [mod.L., ad. Czech. *akathisie* (L. Haškovec in *Sborn. Klin. v Praze* (1901–2) III. 193), Fr. *akathisie*, f. Gr. ἀ- priv. (A- *pref.* 14) + κάθισις sitting: see -IA.] Inability to sit; morbid fear of sitting. Also used *joc.* (quot. 1938).

1904 *Jrnl. Nerv. & Ment. Dis.* XXXI. 195 *Akasthesia* [sic]. The symptom which the author has called by this name consists in the development of peculiar involuntary movements whenever the patients attempt to seat themselves. **1938** S. BECKETT *Murphy* vii. 119 It was true that Cooper never sat, his acathisia was deep-seated and of long standing. **1953** E. PODOLSKY *Encycl. Aberrations* 3/2 The inability to sit down or the dread to sit down is known as acathisia. **1961** *Lancet* 29 July 267/2 Akathisia.

akatown, obs. variant of ACTON, HAQUETON.

ake, earlier and better spelling of ACHE *v.*

ake ('ækɪ, Maori 'ake). Also **ake-ake** ('akeake, anglicized 'ækɪækɪ); 9 **aki, aki-aki, haki.** [Maori.] The native name in New Zealand for the small hardwood tree *Dodonæa viscosa* and trees of the genus *Olearia*, as *O. traversii.*

1835 W. YATE *Account of N.Z.* (ed. 2) ii. 47 Aki, called the *Lignum vitæ* of New Zealand. **1840** J. S. POLACK *Manners N. Zealanders* II. 261 The *Akki* a species of *lignum vitæ*, when young is much used for boat-timbers. **1844** *Barnicoat's Jrnl.* (MS.) 188 New Zealand woods, totara, haki, mairi. **1847** *Annals of Diocese of N.Z.* (*S.P.C.K.*) 239 Akeake (Metrosideros buxifolia), very hard and heavy, fit for cabinet work. **1851** MRS. R. WILSON *New Zealand* 43 The ake (Dodonæa spatulata) and towai.. are almost equal, in point of colour, to rosewood. **1851** E. WARD *Jrnl.* 3 June (1951) 189 The largest of the akiaki trees. **1851** H. R. RICHMOND *Let.* 15 June in *Richmond-Atkinson Papers* (1960) I. ii. 97 The hakihaki for the handles of axes. **1879** J. HECTOR *Handbk. N.Z.* 94 Ake.—A small tree, 6–12 feet high. Wood very hard, variegated black and white; used for Native clubs. **1882** W. D. HAY *Brighter Britain!* II. 195 The Ake-ake.. gives a handsome wood for cabinet work. **1917** *Chambers's Jrnl.* 6 Jan. 90/2 The dense scrub, consisting of silver-pine, ake-ake, and alpine vegetation. **1928** W. BAUCKE *Where White Man Treads* (ed. 2) 246 The Chathams grew only one durable timber, the ake-ake, which, because of its insufficient bulk, was seldom without heart-rot, shakes, and other blemishes.

akee, var. ACKEE.

†**a'keep**, *v. Obs. rare*[−1]. [f. A- *pref.* 1 intens. + KEEP *v.*] *intr.* To keep, remain.

1250 LAYAMON 26937 Hii comen in one wode.. and seide ȝam bitwine, þat þar hii wolde akepe [**1205** kepen].

akehorne, obs. erron. form of ACORN.

akela (ɑː'keɪlə). [The name of 'the great gray Lone Wolf, who led all the Pack by strength and cunning' in Kipling's Jungle Books, a. Hindi *akelā* single, solitary.] The adult leader of a pack of Cub Scouts (formerly Wolf Cubs); a cub-master or cub-mistress.

1924 *Boy Scouts Imperial Jamboree* 62/2 The 7,000.. raised one great voice in the Grand Howl: 'Akela, we'll do our best'. **1950** *Pack Holidays & Cub Camping* (Boy Scouts Assoc.) 6 Throughout this book the term 'Akela' denotes the Cub Scouter.. whilst the expression 'Old Wolves' includes Akela and all the grown ups helping her. **1966** *Courier-Mail* (Brisbane) 6 July 4/5, I was surprised and shocked. So were other akelas (Scout mistresses). **1977** *S. Wales Guardian* 27 Oct. 4/5 Akela Mr. Emyr Rees invested new members into the cub pack and gave awards to boys who had gained badges during the past months. **1983** J. DEFT *Beaver Leader's Handbk.* 6 Even today a Cub Scout Leader is often known as 'Akela'.

†**a'kele**, *v. Obs.* Forms: 1 **acél-an**, 3–5 **akelen.** [f. A- *pref.* 1 intens. + *célan*:—*cœ́lan* to cool, f. *cól* cool; properly *trans.* while *acólian*, ACOOL, was *intr.*, but the constructions were confused, and after *akele* became obs., *acool* was used for both.]

1. *trans.* To make cold, to cool.

c **880** K. ÆLFRED *Metr.* vii. 17 (Grein) Ne bið his þurst acéled. **1297** R. GLOUC. 442 And þe anguysse of hys doȝter.. akelde hym wel þe more, so þat feble he was. *c* **1400** *Court of Love* 1076 For love may thy freill desire ackele.

2. *intr.* To become cold, to cool.

c **1380** *Sir Ferumb.* 4492 Ys blod scholde sone a-kele. **1393** GOWER *Conf.* II. 91 If love be to hote, In what maner it shulde akele.

†**a'ken(ne**, *v.*[1] *Obs.* [f. A- *pref.* 1 intens. + KEN *v.*[1] Probably in OE.; cf. OHG. *arkennan*, mod.Germ. *erkennen.*] To recognize, to reconnoitre.

1250 LAYAMON 7243 He þis lond a-kende [**1205** he þis lon ikende]. *Ibid.* 25430 Hit were þe kenlokeste men þat eni man akende [**1205** þa æi mon ikende]. *c* **1300** *K. Alis.* 3468 At the othir side akennynge, They sygh Darie the kyng. **1599** *Soliman & Pers.* v. in Hazl. *Dodsl.* V. 354 His ships were past a kenning from the shore.

†**a'ken(ne**, *v.*[2] *Obs.* Forms: 1–2 **acenn-an**, 2–3 **akenn-en.** *Pa. t.* 1–2 **ac-**, 2–3 **akende.** *Pa. pple.* 1–2 **acenned**, 2–3 **akenned, -et.** [f. A- *pref.* 1 forth, out + *cenn-an* to give birth to: see KEN *v.*[2]] To bring forth, to bear. (Most common in pa. pple.)

c **880** K. ÆLFRED *Boeth.* xxxi. § 1 Swa swa wif acenþ bearn. *c* **1000** ÆLFRIC *Gen.* iii. 16 On sarnysse ðu acenst cild. *c* **1175** *Lamb. Hom.* 227 þa ðer hire time com hi acennede. *c* **1220** *Leg. Kath.* 332 He was akennet of Marie, a meiden.

akene, occas. var. (Gray *Struct. Bot.*) of ACHENE.

†**a'kenned**, *ppl. a. Obs.* [pa. pple. of prec.] Born.

c **975** *Rushw. Gosp.* Matt. ii. 1 þa soþlice akenned wæs hælend. *c* **1175** *Cott. Hom.* 219 And his wisdom, of him selfe efre acenned. *c* **1200** ORMIN 7141 þatt he to manne cumenn iss, Soþ Godd off Godd ankennedd. *c* **1230** *Juliana* 5 Al of heaðene cun icumen & akennet.

†**a'kennedness.** *Obs.* 1–2. Also **accen-, akynnednysse.** [f. prec. + -NESS.] Birth; generation.

c **1000** *Ags. Gosp.* Luke i. 14 Maneȝa on his acennednysse ȝefaȝniað. *c* **1160** *Hatton Gosp.*, Akynnednysse. *c* **1175** *Lamb. Hom.* 209 þurh þin akennednesse in a meidenes licame.

†**a'kenness.** *Obs.* 1–3. Also **acennisse, accennisse.** [f. AKEN *v.*[2] + -NESS, prob. contr. for prec.] Birth, generation.

c **950** *Lindisf. Gosp.* Luke i. 14 Moniȝo in accennisse his biðon glæde. *c* **975** *Rushw. Gosp.* John ix. 1 Monno blindne from acennisse. *c* **1230** *Hali Meid.* 45 Gabriel.. brohte hire þe tidinge of godes akenesse.

†**a'kenning**, *vbl. sb. Obs.* [f. AKEN *v.*[2] + -ING[1]. Already in 12th c. we find this written *acennende*, an instance of the early confusion of the sb. in *-ing* and pple. in *-end.*] Bearing, generation, birth.

c **1175** *Lamb. Hom.* 237 Ure acenneng wes ful.. His clene acennende clénséde ure fule acennende.

akephalisis, obs. variant of ACEPHALISIS.

†**aker.** *Obs. rare*[−1]. (See quot.)

1601 TATE *Househ. Ord. Edw. II* (1876) §49. 33 Two valletes of office, which are called akers which shal receve the vessel of the meisnies kitchen by indenture from the Esquiller: thei shall scoure it & keepe it, both in travel & sojorne.

aker, obs. f. ACRE; and var. ACKER, tidal bore.

akeratophorous (əˌkɛrə'tɒfərəs), *a. Zool.* [f. Gr. ἀ priv. + κέρατ-(κέρας) horn + -PHOROUS bearing.] Not bearing horns; unhorned.

1859 TODD *Cycl. Anat. & Phys.* V. 537/2 In the akeratophorous Ruminantia the reed is relatively smaller.

aker-spire, -d, obs. or dial. f. ACROSPIRE, -D.

1631 MARKHAM *Way to Wealth* III. II. vii. (1668) 174 For want of turning when the Malt is spread on the floor, it comes or sprouts at both ends, which Husbands call Aker-spired.

akest, pa. pple. of ACAST *v. Obs.*, to throw down.

aketon, -toun, obs. var. ACTON, HAQUETON.

akimbo (ə'kɪmbəʊ), *adv.* (and *a.*) Forms: 5 **in kenebowe**, 7 **on kenbow, a kenbow, a kenbol, a kenbold, on kimbow, (a-gambo)**, 7–8 **a-kemboll**, 8–9 **a kembo, a kimbo**, 8– **a-kimbo, akimbo.** [Deriv. unknown. Prof. Skeat (Append.) gives a suggestion of Magnussen, comparing the earliest known forms with Icel. *keng-boginn, -it*, 'crooked' (Vigfusson), lit. 'bent staple-wise, or in a horse-shoe curve'; other suggestions are *a cambok* in the manner of a crooked stick (ME. *cambok*, med.L. *cambūca*, see CAMMOCK); *a cam bow* in a crooked bow. None of these satisfies all conditions.

The difficulty as to *a-cambok, a cam bow*, is that no forms of the word show *cam-*, from which the earliest are the most remote. The Icel. *keng-boginn* comes nearer the form, but there is no evidence that it had the special sense of *a-kimbo*, and none that the latter ever had the general sense of 'crooked.' It also postulates an early Eng. series of forms like **keng-bown* or **keng-bowed, *keng-bow, *akengbow*, quite unknown and unaccounted for.]

Of the arms: In a position in which the hands rest on the hips and the elbows are turned outwards. Now usu. hyphenless. Also *transf.* and *fig.* (see quots.), and as *adj.*

c **1400** *Beryn* 1837 The hoost.. set his hond in kenebowe. **1611** COTGR. s.v. *Arcade.* To set his hands a kenbow. **1627** PEACHAM *Compl. Gent.* (1634) V. xx. 247 The armes of two side-men on kenbow. **1629** GAULE *Holy Madnesse* 92 With his armes a kemboll. *a* **1642** SIR T. URQUHART *Tracts* (1782) 71 With gingling spurrs, and his armes a kenbol. **1644** BULWER *Chiron.* 104 (L.) To set the arms a-gambo and a-prank. **1678** WYCHERLEY *Plain-Dealer* II. i. 23 He has no use of his Arms, but to set 'em on kimbow. **1681** HOBBES *Rhet.* III. xv. 126 Setting his arms a-kenbold. **1711** STEELE *Spect.* No. 187 ¶3 She would clap her arms a kimbow. **1727** ARBUTHNOT *John Bull* 72 John was forced to sit with his arm a-kimbo. **1748** RICHARDSON *Clarissa* (1811) V. 317 She set her huge arms akembo. **1782** MISS BURNEY *Cecil.* II. iii. 170 Putting his arms akembo with an air of defiance. **1879** BROWNING *Ned Bratts* 143 Both arms a-kimbo. **1922** JOYCE *Ulysses* 516 The Fan (folded akimbo against her waist). **1943** I. BROWN *Just Another Word* 24 'She got terribly akimbo' became a species of Mayfair slang for what was earlier called 'high horse'. I have also heard it used by stage people for over-acting. 'So and so was a bit akimbo to-night.' **1959** *New Yorker* 5 Dec. 146 He tended to match all of Coleman's near-atonal plunges with akimbo melodic lines of his own.

†**a'kimed**, *ppl. a. Obs. rare.* [Der. uncert. Cf. KIME, a simpleton, silly fellow. Stratmann compares MHG. *erkümen* to become sick and wretched.] Confounded, struck speechless or silly.

1205 LAYAMON 26354 Aset þe kaisere: swulc he akimet [**1250** dombe] weore, And ansdware nauer nan: no aȝæf þissen eorle. *c* **1220** *Leg. Kath.* 1297 Al ȝe beon blodles, ikimet, of ow seluen, Hwider is ower wit & ower wisdom iwent?

akin (ə'kɪn), *adv.* and *a.* orig. *phr.* Also aphetic **kin.** [contr. from *of kin*, which is also found: see A *prep.*[2] = of, and KIN.]

A. *adv.* (The phrase *of kin* added to adjectives.)

1. Of kin, by way of family or blood relationship.

1558 GRIMALDE *Tully's Offices* I. 21 They be injurious to their next akinne. **1699** PEPYS in *Diary* VI. 217 To forfeit their whole inheritance to the next a-kin. **1859** OWEN *Lect. on Mamm.* App. B. 80 He might think that the orangs were nearer akin to man than the chimpanzees.

2. Of things: Of nature or character; in character. ***near a kin***: near in nature or character.

1633 P. FLETCHER *Pisc. Eclogs* v. xiii, To Love, Fear's neare akinne. **1713** *Guardian* No. 170 (1756) II. 348 The manufacture of paper is very near a-kin to that of linen. **1878** R. W. DALE *Lect. Preach.* iii. 63 Desultoriness and indolence are very near akin.

B. *adj.* (Only as predicate or complement.)

1. Of the same kin or family; related by blood.

1586 T. B. *La Primaudaye's Fr. Acad.* 2 These fower gentlemen being of kin, and neere neighbors. **1673** CAVE *Prim. Chr.* III. ii. 297 We should reckon ourselves akin and obliged to love all Mankind. **1754** FOOTE *Knights* I, The gentleman says as how mother and he are akin. **1839** KEIGHTLEY *Hist. Eng.* I. 40 Dunstan was of noble birth, and even akin to the royal family.

2. Of things: Of the same kind; allied, related, in character or properties.

1603 SHAKS. *Meas. for M.* II. iv. 113 Lawful mercy Is nothing kin to fowle redemption. **1665** GLANVILLE *Sceps. Sci.* Addr. 19 An Imaginary World of our own Making, that is but little a kin to the real one that God made. **1723** WODROW *Corr.* (1843) III. 25 Divisions somewhat of akin to yours have been for some time in the University of Glasgow. **1853** MAURICE *Proph. & Kings* vi. 98 The two doctrines seem closely akin. **1860** TYNDALL *Glac.* I. §22. 155 The sensation was akin to giddiness.

†**a'kind**, *a. Obs.*, variant of AKIN due to confusion of KIN and KIND. (? quasi *akinned.*)

1600 LANE *Tom Tel-Troth* 127 Patience, a cosin hath calde Sufferance Neerely akind. **1657** FULLER *Comm. Jonah* (1868) 198 They are.. a-kin'd unto the unjust Judge.

‖**akinesia** (ækɪ'niːsɪa). *Phys.* [a. Gr. ἀκινησία quiescence, f. ἀ priv. + κίνησις motion, f. κῑνέ-ειν to move.] Loss of the power of voluntary movement; paralysis of the motor nerves. (Also called **akinesis**, not according to Gr. analogy.)

1878 M. FOSTER *Physiol.* III. vi. §4. 511 Anæsthesia (a loss of sensation) and akinesia (a loss of movement). **1878** HAMILTON *Nerv. Dis.* 306 A condition of akinesis and prostration takes the place of the irritable nervous state.

akinesic (ækɪ'niːsɪk), *a. Phys.* [f. prec. + -IC.] Opposed to movement, not producing movement.

1879 in *Syd. Soc. Lex.*

akinetic (eɪkɪ'nɛtɪk), *a.* [f. A- 14 + KINETIC *a.*; in medical use, after AKINESIA.] Lacking movement, stationary, static; now *spec.* in *Med.*, characterized or affected by akinesia.

1889 *Sat. Rev.* 30 Nov. 605/1 The Toryism which, without being merely 'akinetic', takes the true Tory attitude and asks whether rationally making the best of things as they are is not better than never-ending experiments. **1927** I. S. Wechsler *Textbk. Clin. Neurol.* iv. 319 Sometimes [in cases of apraxia] spontaneous movements alone are lost: this is known as akinetic apraxia. **1934** R. R. Grinker *Neurol.* xxv. 831 The toneless fits or akinetic attacks comprise a not infrequent type of [epileptic] attack. **1941** *Brain* LXIV. 273 In a case of cystic tumour of the 3rd ventricle we have observed a peculiar mental state which may be described as akinetic or trance-like mutism. **1977** *Brain's Dis. Nervous Syst.* (ed. 8) xxii. 1104 Attacks in which falling occurs but in which there are no convulsive movements are often called akinetic epilepsy. **1983** *Oxf. Textbk. Med.* II. xi. 109/1 Any child or young adult presenting with any form of dyskinesia or akinetic-rigid syndrome..should be investigated to exclude Wilson's disease.

Akita (əˈkiːtə). [Name of a district in northern Japan.] A medium-sized dog of Japanese breed.

1928 F. T. Barton *Kennel Encycl.* 8/1 *Akita.* The title of this breed came from the name of the district, in the northern part of Japan. **1945** C. L. B. Hubbard *Observer Bk. Dogs* 17 *Akita*..is a typical Spitz, with broad-pointed skull, stiff 'fur' on the back but softer hair elsewhere, and a curled ..and bushy tail. **1948** —— *Dogs in Britain* xvii. 170 The Shika Inu is popularly called the Akita and is the only member of the breed to have been imported into Britain.

akka, var. ACKER.

Akkadian (əˈkeɪdɪən), *a.* and *sb.* Also Accadian.[f. *Akkad*, *Accad*, name of a city (prob. to be identified with *Agade*) founded by Sargon I, and of the northern part of ancient Babylonia: see -IAN. Cf. F. *accadien*, G. *akkadisch.*] **A.** *adj.* **1.** Formerly, of a dialect related to Sumerian (see note s.v. SUMERIAN *a.*). **2.** Of or belonging to an eastern Semitic language of northern Babylonia, known from cuneiform inscriptions, or to the people of this region or their culture. **B.** *sb.* **1.** The Akkadian language. **2.** An inhabitant of Akkad or northern Babylonia.

c **1855** E. Hincks (*title*) On the Relation between the newly-discovered Accadian Language and the Indo-European, Semitic, and Egyptian Languages. **1874** Sayce in *Trans. Soc. Biblical Archæol.* III. 468 Elamu..is but a translation of the old Accadian name Susiana. *Ibid.* 484 In both Elamite and Susian, as well as in Accadian, the genitive relation may be expressed by simple position. **1875**, **1878** [see SUMERIAN *a.* and *sb.*]. **1884** Sayce *Fresh Light fr. Anc. Mon.* ii. 24 The Accadians had been the inventors of the pictorial hieroglyphics..afterwards developed into the cuneiform..system of writing. **1921** G. A. F. Knight *Nile & Jordan* iii. 31 The still earlier non-Semitic Akkadian civilization which the dynastic Babylonians dethroned. *Ibid.*, Eridu..means in Akkadian 'the city of the good (god)'. **1948** D. Diringer *Alphabet* i. i. 49 In the long development of the cuneiform writing of the Mesopotamian Semites, we can distinguish in particular six periods: (1) The Early Accadian period and Ur III, roughly from the middle of the twenty-fifth century B.C. to the middle of the twenty-second century B.C. **1958** A. Toynbee *East to West* liii. 160 The Akkadians themselves had acquired the vast irrigated oasis in the waist of Mesopotamia where the two rivers all but meet.

akker, var. ACKER.

akmite, var. ACMITE

aknee (əˈniː), *adv.* prop. *phr.* Forms: 1–3 on cneowe, 3 a cneowe, a cnouwe, 4 a knowe, a cneo, akneo, a cne. Also in *pl.* 3 a cneon, a kneon, 4 aknen; *north.* 3 o cnewwess, 4 a knewes. [f. ON *prep.* + KNEE. Obs. *a*1500, but used in sing. by Southey. In plural we now say *on my* (*his*, etc.) *knees.*] On one's knee or knees.

c **1200** *St. Marherete* lxvii, Malchus herde thes wordes, he sette him acne. **1205** Lay. 29573 He lai on cneowe ibede. *Ibid.* 14305 Reowen sæt a cneowe [**1250** a cnouwe]. *c* **1300** *Beket* 1696 And to his fet ful akneo. *c* **1300** *K. Alis.* 3540 And made mony knyght aknawe, On medewe. **1805** Southey *Madoc in Azt.* vii. Wks. V. 250 Aknee they fell before the Prince.

†**b.** with *pl. Obs.*

c **1200** Ormin 6467 Fellenn dun o cnewwess. *c* **1230** *Ancr. R.* 44 Ualleð akneon to ðer eorðe. *Ibid.* 16 Efter þis ualleð acneon to ower crucifix. *a* **1300** *K. Horn* 340 (Halliw.) Tho Athelbius astounde Fel aknen [334 in *ed.* 1866, anon] to grounde. *c* **1330** *Arth. & Merl.* 2353 To forn him aknewes sche fel.

aknow, earlier and better form of ACKNOW *v.*

akoint, -ed, obs. forms of ACQUAINT, -ED.

akoluthic (ækəˈluːθɪk), *a.* Also acoˈluthic [f. Gr. ἀκόλουθος following + -IC.] Following, subsequent; *spec.* R. Semon's term (G. *akoluthe* in *Die Mneme* (ed. 2) 1908, p. 18) designating the phase following the initial excitation of a sensation.

1921 B. Russell *Analysis of Mind* ix. 175 At the beginning of a stimulus we have a sensation; then a gradual transition; and at the end an image. Sensations while they are fading are called 'akoluthic' sensations. **1923** B. Duffy tr. *Semon's Mnemic Psychol.* vi. 136 To describe these after-effects which are immediately connected with synchronous ones I have chosen the term 'acoluthic'. *Ibid.* 137 In the acoluthic phase excitation, of which the intensity begins to diminish rapidly when the stimulus ceases,..results nevertheless in sensations which we describe as acoluthic.

akre, obs. f. ACORN, perhaps due to taking the final *-n* in the form *akern*, as a sign of plural.

1572 Bossewell *Armorie* ii. 74 b, An Akre, or maste of the Oke tree. [**1882** 'Still the common form in Sussex.'—A. Smith.]

akrochordite (ækrəʊˈkɔːdaɪt). *Min.* Also acro-. [ad. Sw. *akrochordit* (G. Flink 1922), f. Gr. ἀκροχορδών wart: see -ITE[1].] Hydrated basic arsenate of manganese and magnesium found in small spherical aggregates.

1922 G. Flink in *Geol. Fören. Förh.* XLIV. 776 Summary. *Akrochordite*,..the individual grouped in wartlike aggregations. Found in..Långban mines. **1932** W. E. Ford *E. S. Dana's Textbk. Min.* (ed. 4) V. 720 *Akrochordite*..Mono-clinic. In spherical aggregates of minute, nearly parallel crystals. **1955** M. H. Hey *Index Min. Species* (ed. 2) 255 *Akrochordite.* $Mn_4Mg(AsO_4)_2(OH)_4 \cdot 5H_2O$... Syn. Acrochordite.

aksis, obs. form of ACCESS, 'fit, fever, ague.'

akvavit, var. AQUAVIT.

akyr, obs. ACRE; and obs. var. ACKER *sb.*

al, obs. form of ALL, retained in comp. in *albeit*, *almighty*, *almost*, *alone*, *already*, *although*, *always*.

al- *pref.*[1] The assimilated form of L. *ad-* to, before *l*. In OFr. reduced to *a-*, as in *alier*, for which however *al-* was often restored as an 'etymological' spelling in 14–15th c. in Fr. and Eng. In modern words adopted or formed from Latin the *al-* is always retained, as *allegation*, *alliterate*. Sometimes erroneously for *a-* in other words as *a(l)lay*.

al- *pref.*[2] The Arabic article *the*, retained as an essential part of the word in various words of Arabic origin, adopted in Eng. as *alcohol*, *alcove*, *alcoran*, *algebra*, *alkali*, *almagest*, *almanac*, etc.

-al *suffix*[1], of adjs. and sbs. **I.** *adj.* **1.** repr. L. *-āl-em* (*-ālis*, *-āle*, stem *-āli-*) adj. suff. = 'of the kind of, pertaining to,' varying in some words with *-ār-em*, the form always used when *l* preceded; thus *tāl-*, *quāl-*, *nātāl-*, *ōrāl-*; *ālār-*, *stellār-*, *regulār-*; *līneāl-* and *lineār-*. In words that survived, *-ālem* became in OFr. and hence in early Eng. *-el*, as *mortālem*, *mortel*. But, to some extent in Fr. and entirely in Eng. this was afterwards refashioned after L., as *-al*, on the analogy of which L. adjs. in *-ālis* and Fr. in *-el* have since been englished without limit. **2.** The number of these adjs. in *-ālis* has been immensely increased in med. and mod. L.; and in the mod. Rom. langs. and E. this has become a suffix addable to any L. sb., as seen in *agmin-al*, *bas-al*, *cordi-al*, *document-al*, *margin-al*, *nation-al*, *pred-al*, *circumstanti-al*, *constitution-al*, *denomination-al*, *longitudin-al*, *proportion-al*, *providenti-al*, *prudenti-al*, *antipestilenti-al*, none of which are found in ancient L. Following L. precedent (as in *boreāl-em*, *hebdomadāl-em*, *theātrāl-em*) *-al* is also suffixed to Gr. sbs., as in *baptism-al*, *cathedr-al*, *coloss-al*, *chor-al*, *octagon-al*, *patriarch-al*. **3.** In L., secondary adjs. in *-ālem* were formed on other adjs., esp. when these were used substantively, as in *æqu-um æquāl-em*, *annu-um annuāl-em*, *diurn-um diurnāl-em*, *infern-um infernāl-em*, *vern-um vernāl-em*. This process has been greatly extended in the mod. langs., esp. in E. where *-al* (like *-ous*) is a living formative, freely applied to L. adjs. in *-eus*, *-ius*, *-uus*, *-rnus*, *-is*, and other endings, to give them a more distinctively adj. form; thus, *aere-al*, *corpore-al*, *funere-al*, *senatori-al*, *continu-al*, *individu-al*, *perpetu-al*, *etern-al*, *patern-al*, *celesti-al*, *terrestri-al*, *magnific-al*. This is extended to Gr. adjs. in *-κός*, *-οειδής*, which also frequently gave substantives (*music*, *tactics*, *rhomboid*), so that, as adj. suffixes, *-acal*, *-ical*, *-oidal* occur earlier in E. than the simple *-ac*, *-ic*, *-oid*; when the two co-exist, as in *comic-al*, *tragic-al*, *historic-al*, that in *-ic*, etc. means 'of or belonging to' the thing, that in *-ical* 'relating to, dealing with, indirectly or remotely connected with' the thing, as a *historic* answer, a *historical* treatise, a *comic* paper, a *comical* idea. See -AC, -IC, -OID. Other suffixes are also added, as in *central-ly*, *-ize*, *-ization*, *formal-ity*.

II. *sb.* **4.** Adjs. in *-al-* in various genders and numbers were used substantively in L., thus *rivāl-is*, *annāl-es*, *animal*, *tribūnal*, *sponsāli-a*, *Baccānāli-a*. Many of these have been adopted in E., directly or through Fr., as *rival*, *annals*, *animal*, *Bacchanals*, *penetralia*, *Saturnalia*; and the number has been increased by the mod. sb. use of many which were only adj., or did not exist in L., as *cardinal*, *principal*, *moral*, *oval*, *signal*, *regimentals*, *canonicals*. **5.** Nouns in *-ālia* (neut. pl.) which survived into OFr. became *-aille* (fem. sing.) with pl. *-ailles*, adopted in ME., as *-aylle*, *-aille*, later *-aile*, *-al*, as L. *sponsāli-a*, OFr. *espousaille-s*, E. *spousaille*, *spousaile-s*; L. **battālia*, OFr. *bataille*, Eng. *bataille*, *-aile*, *-ail*, now *battle*. On this analogy, *-aille*, *-ail*, *-al* became an Anglo-Fr. and E. formative of nouns of action on vbs. of Fr. or L. origin, as in AFr. *arrivaille* arrival; so of later formation (some quite modern) 'revival, survival, approval, removal, avowal, renewal; acquittal, committal, transmittal, refutal, recital, requital; dismissal, perusal, refusal, carousal, rehearsal, reversal, revisal, reprisal, surprisal; dis-, inter-, pro-, re-, sup-, trans-posal; trial, denial, decrial'; occas. also on native final-accented vbs. as 'bestowal, betrothal, beheadal.' *Bridal* and *burial* simulate this ending, but have a different origin; yet they have probably aided the prevalence of these nouns of action in *-al* in mod. Eng.

-al, *suff.*[2] *Chem.* The first syllable of ALDEHYDE and ALCOHOL, used to form the names of substances which are aldehydes or derived from alcohol; e.g. *bromal*, *butyral*, *chloral*, *ethal*. Also as a general termination for pharmaceutical products, as *barbital*, *hormonal* (sb.).

‖**ala** (ˈeɪlə). Pl. **alæ** (ˈeɪliː). [L. *āla* a wing, an arm-pit, a side apartment.]

1. *Phys.* Any wing-like process; *esp.* one of the lateral cartilages of the nose.

1755 *Phil. Trans.* XLIX. 193, I laid the intire bone bare.. even down to the ala of the nose. **1856** Todd & Bowman *Phys. Anat.* II. 111 The great ala of the sphenoid. **1864** Spencer *Illust. Progr.* 11 The flatness of the alae of the nose.

2. *Bot.* †**a.** An axil, or junction of branch and trunk (*obs.*). **b.** One of the side petals of a papilionaceous corolla. Gray *Struct. Bot.*

1794 Martyn tr. *Rousseau's Bot.* v. 50 Branches which grow from their alæ, or axils.

3. *Arch.* A side apartment or recess of a Roman house. (Hence AISLE of a church.)

1832 Gell *Pompeiana* I. i. 9 The atrium has two alæ in one of which is an altar.

‖**à la** (ˈɑ ˌlɑ), *phr.* [Fr. *à la* (sc. *mode*) in the manner.] **a.** After the manner, method, or style of; in such phr. as ***à la Française***, and hence ***à la Reine*** (= *à la mode de la Reine*), ***à la Roi***, etc. Also ***à la débandade***: in confusion or disorder; ***à la fourchette***: see *fork-breakfast* (FORK *sb.* 16); also, eaten informally; ***à la Russe***: in Russian fashion; *spec.* designating a meal for which the table is dressed with flowers and dessert, while the courses are served from other tables or from another room. See also À LA CARTE, À LA PAGE.

1589 Puttenham *Eng. Poes.* iii. xxv. 250 The breech a la *Françoise.* **1646** Suckling *Fragm. Aurea* 61 As ill a Mine [= mien] as this Act has, 'twas *a-la-Romansci*, as you may see by a Line of Mr. Shakespears [cf. *Jul. C.* v. iii. 90]. *a* **1666** Evelyn *Diary* 19 Nov. an. 1644 (1955) II. 259 A deepe basso-relievo a l'antique. **1739** R. West *Let.* 21 June in Walpole *Lett.* (1857) I. 22 We supped à l'Angloise. Imprimis, we had buttock of beef. **1812** [see FORK *sb.* 16]. *a* **1823** D. Wordsworth *Second Tour Scot.* in *Jrnls.* (1941) II. viii. 353 Sheltered in the Cabin, and took a breakfast *à la fourchette*—not at the gentry end. *a* **1828** —— *Tour Continent* in *Ibid.* II. 20 An elegant gauze mob-cap with flowers, and robe *à la française.* **1828** Scott *Jrnl.* 3 Mar. (1890) II. 135, I do better *à la débandade* than I could with rules of regular study. **1828** *Souvenir* II. 95 (Stanford), The collar..is of fancy spotted silk, tied à-la-Russe, and fastened at the back of the neck. **1851** *London at Table* ii. 41 Serving a dinner *à la Russe.* **1863** *Blackw. Mag.* Mar. 305/2 The modern service *à la Russe*, adopted in all good houses, has struck a decisive blow at the old English heavy dinners. **1874** J. H. Walsh *Dom. Econ.* ix. ii. 701/1 A table set out *à la Russe* for a party of eighteen. **1919** G. B. Shaw *Heartbreak Ho.* p. xx, Police raid *à la Russe.* **1926** D. H. Lawrence *Plumed Serp.* vii. 123 Some of the organdie frocks had green legs and green feet, some had legs *à la nature.* **1939** A. Toynbee *Stud. Hist.* IV. 440 A pair of mounted men-at-arms..were eventually to drive the legionary off the field *à la débandade.* **1957** V. Nabokov *Pnin* 157 A supper *à la fourchette.*

b. *Cookery.* In the names of particular dishes, denoting the manner in which they are prepared; as ***à la broche***, ***brochette***: (cooked) on a spit or skewer; ***à la meunière***: see MEUNIÈRE.

1653 I. D. G. tr. *De la Varenne's French Cook* 58 Joint of Mutton after the Kingly manner (a la royale). **1723** J. Nott *Cook's & Confectioner's Dict.* No. 49B Beef a la Braise. *Ibid.* No. 59C To dress a Carp a la daube..take the Carp, fill the body..with this Farce, set it a stewing..pour on it your Ragoo and serve it up. **1747** H. Glasse *Art of Cookery* ii. 20 Beef *à la Daub. Ibid.* 24 Leg of Mutton *à la Royale. Ibid.* 44 *To à la Daube* Pigeons. **1853** E. K. Kane *U.S. Grinn. Exped.* xxxiv. 309 He made me this morning an idea of white bear's liver, *à la brochette.* **1882** *Englishman* 2 Dec. 3/5 *Entrees*, Chicken à la Stanley. Lamb Cutlets à la Reform. **1906** Mrs. Beeton *Househ. Managem.* lxii. 1652 *À la Broche*, roasted in front of the fire on a spit or skewer. **1959** R. Postgate *Good Food Guide* 31 What it can claim real distinction for is its cooking à la broche; chicken, duck or game roasted on the spit should be chosen.

c. With English sbs. and names.

1808 JANE AUSTEN *Let.* 15 June (1932) 189 Yesterday passed quite *à la* Godmersham. **1814** —— *Mansf. Park* II. x. 218 Her happiness on this occasion was very much a-la-mortal, finely chequered. **1881** W. S. GILBERT *Patience* I, An attachment *à la* Plato for a bashful young potato. **1926** GALSWORTHY *Silver Spoon* II. x. 191 As for Foggartism, they didn't—*à la* 'Evening Sun'—pooh-pooh it.

alabamine (ælə'bæmɪn). (*Disused.*) [f. *Alabama*, name of a State in U.S.A. + -INE[5].] The name originally proposed for ASTATINE. Cf. also ANGLO-HELVETIUM.

1932 F. ALLISON et al. in *Jrnl. Amer. Chem. Soc.* LIV. 616 We suggest the name Alabamine and symbol Am for element 85. **1936** *Nature* 13 June 969/2 The problems of illinium, masurium, virginium, and alabamine.

†**ala'bandic.** *Obs.*$^{-0}$ [f. L. *Rosa alabandica*, 'of Alabanda,' in Pliny. Misprinted in Coles 1692, *Alabandie*, and so copied by Bailey and Ash.]

1678 PHILLIPS, *Alabandic*, a kind of Rose with whitish leaves; some will have it to be the Provence Rose, which is respected more for its doubleness, than for its sweetness or use. **1775** ASH, *Alabandy*, the damask rose.

†**ala'bandical,** *a. Obs.*$^{-0}$ [? f. L. *alabandic-us* of Alabanda, app. confused in med.L. (see Ducange) with *alalandic-us* ? latinized form of OE. *æl-lendisc*, OTeut. *alilandisc* foreign.] (See quot.)

1656 BLOUNT *Glossogr.*, *Alabandical*, barbarous or sottish. **1775** ASH, *Alabandical*, belonging to the damask rose.

†**ala'bandine.** *Obs.* Also 4 **alabaunderryne, alabraundyne.** [a. L. *alabandina* (sc. *gemma*), f. *Alabanda* a city of Caria.]

1. A precious stone known to the ancients; now called ALMANDINE.

*c***1325** *E.E. Allit. Poems* B. 1471 Alabaunderrynes, & amaraunȝ. **1366** MAUNDEV. xx. 219 The rede [gems] ben of Rubies & of Grenaȝ & of Alabraundynes. **1398** TREVISA *Barth. De P.R.* XVI. xiii. (1495) 558 Alabandina is a precious stone clere and somdeale red. **1567** MAPLET *Greene Forest* 2 b, The Gem Alabandine.. is somewhat more rare, and in colour cleare. **1658** PHILLIPS, *Alabandine*, a kind of stone, that provokes to bleed [*ed.* 1678 Alabandine or Amandine; *ed.* 1706 Almandine only].

2. A synonym of ALABANDITE.

alabandite (ælə'bændaɪt). *Min.* [f. *Alabanda* (see prec.) + -ITE, as being perhaps the *Alabandina* of the ancients, whence the synonym ALABANDINE.] A native sulphate of manganese, called also *Manganblende* of iron-black colour, and sub-metallic lustre, occurring, massive, or crystallized in cubes and octohedrons, in Mexico, Transylvania, etc. Dana.

alabarch ('æləbɑːk). [ad. L. *alabarch-es*, a. Gr. ἀλαβάρχ-ης of unkn. origin.] Title of the chief magistrate of the Jews at Alexandria under the Ptolemies, and Roman emperors.

1727 LARDNER *Wks.* (1838) I. 87 Philo's brother Alexander was alabarch of the Jews in Egypt. **1879** FARRAR *St. Paul* I. 227 Ethnarch, as well as Alabarch, was a title of Jewish governors in heathen cities.

alabaster, obs. var. ARBLASTER, a crossbowman.

alabaster ('ælə,bɑːstə(r), -æ-, ,ælə'bɑːstə(r), -æ-). Forms: 4 **alabaustre, alabast,** 4–6 **alabastre,** 6 **aliblaster,** 6–7 **alablaster,** 4– **alabaster.** [a. OFr. *alabastre* (mod.Fr. *albâtre*), ad. L. *alabaster, -trum*, a. Gr. ἀλάβαστρος, prop. ἀλάβαστος; said to be from name of a town in Egypt. The spelling in 16–17th c. is almost always *alablaster*; app. due to a confusion with *arblaster* a cross-bowman, also written *alablaster*.]

A term applied to fine translucent varieties of carbonate or sulphate of lime, especially to the pure white variety of the latter used for vases, ornaments, and busts. In *Mineralogy*, massive fine-grained *sulphate* of lime or gypsum, occurring white, yellow, red, or delicately shaded (*Modern* or *Gypseous* Alabaster); as distinguished from the translucent or variegated varieties of stalagmitic *carbonate* of lime, included under the name by the ancients, and used by them for holding unguents (*Oriental* or *Calcareous* alabaster).

1375 BARBOUR *Bruce* XX. 588 Schir archibald his sone gert syne Of alabast [*v.r.* alabastre] bath fair and fyne, Ordane a towme full richly. *c***1386** CHAUCER *Knts. T.* 1052 Of alabaster whit and reed coralle [*v.r.* alabastre]. **1440** *Promp. Parv.*, Alabaster, a stone, *Alabastrum, Parium.* **1596** SHAKS. *Merch. Ven.* I. i. 84 Why should a man whose bloud is warme within Sit like his Grandsire cut in Alablaster? **1600** DEKKER *Fortun.* Wks. I. 124 It were better to let the memory of him shine in his owne vertues..than in Alablaster. **1771** SMOLLETT *Humph. Cl.* (1815) 96 He had a skin as fair as alabaster. **1870** YEATS *Nat. Hist. Comm.* 374 Statuary Alabaster is obtained from the Miocene and Pliocene strata in Tuscany and in Egypt. **1875** URE *Dict. Arts* I. 41 The Oriental alabaster, or alabaster of the ancients, is to be carefully distinguished from the mineral now commonly known as alabaster; the former is a *carbonate*, the latter a *sulphate* of lime.

2. A box made of alabaster in which the ancients sealed up unguents; often with L. pl. *alabastra*.

1398 TREVISA *Barth. De P.R.* XIX. cxxviii. (1495) 933 Alabastrum is a vessell for oyntment. **1753** CHAMBERS *Cycl. Supp.* s.v., Others define *alabaster* by a box without a handle, deriving the word from the privative α and λαβη handle. **1861** KING *Antique Gems* (1866) 88 Little jars for holding perfumes, which were called alabastra.

†**3.** An ancient liquid measure. *Obs.*

1753 CHAMBERS *Cycl. Supp.*, *Alabaster* is also said to have been used for an ancient liquid measure, containing 10 ounces of wine or 9 of oil.. In this sense the *alabaster* was equal to half the sextary.

B. *adj.* (orig. *attrib.* use of *sb.*)

a. Of alabaster, as a material.

1526 TINDALE *Matt.* xxvi. 7 A woman, which had an alablaster boxe of precious oyntment. [*Genev.*, *Rhem.*, **1611**, alabaster box; WYCLIF, boxe of alabastre.] **1605** *Delightes for Ladies* 29 Take your beries and grinde them in a Alablaster morter. **1815** SCOTT *Ld. of Isles* III. xxviii, Mermaid's Alabaster-grot. **1864** BOUTELL *Heraldry* xx. 338 The very perfect alabaster effigy of a knight.

b. Like alabaster, in whiteness, smoothness, etc.

1580 SIDNEY *Arc.* (1622) 427 [He] set his dagger to her Alablaster throate. **1594** SHAKS. *Rich. III*, IV. iii. 11 Gentle babes..girdling one another Within their alabaster innocent arms. **1616** SURFLET & MARKH. *Countrey Farme* 417 Tender or delicate pear, such as alabaster pear. **1649** LOVELACE *Poems* (1659) 63 Thy Alablaster Lady will come home. **1851** RUSKIN *Stones Ven.* (1874) I. xxi. 239 Look at the clouds, and watch the delicate sculpture of their alabaster sides.

alabastrian (ælə'bɑːstrɪən, -æ-), *a. rare*$^{-0}$. [f. prec. + -IAN.] 'Pertaining to, or like alabaster.' Craig.

alabastrine (ælə'bɑːstrɪn, -æ-, -aɪn), *a.* [ad. med.L. *alabastrinus*: see ALABASTER and -INE.] Of or resembling alabaster.

1598 SYLVESTER *Du Bartas* II. iv. I. (1641) 202/1 Her Alabastrine well-shapt Limbs. **1757** MILLES in *Phil. Trans.* L. 28 They seem to be an alabastrine spar. **1829** SIR T. LAUDER *Moray Floods* (ed. 2) 234 Perpendicular streaks of a beautiful alabastrine whiteness.

‖**alaba'strites.** [L., a. Gr. ἀλαβαστρίτης, more correctly ἀλαβαστίτης, prop. adj. (sc. λίθος stone).] The ancient or calcareous alabaster, of which ointment pots were made.

1601 HOLLAND *Pliny* (1634) II. 624 The stone Alabastrites is found about Alabastrum a city in Egypt.. white of colour it is, and intermedled with sundry colours. **1848** WEBSTER, *Alabastrite.* **1874** WESTROPP *Prec. Stones* 132 The name alabastrites was applied to the marble from its being chiefly employed for Alabastra or unguent jars.

alabastron (,ælə'bɑːstrən, -æ-). [a. Gr. ἀλάβαστρον globular perfume jar.] = ALABASTER 2.

1848 G. DENNIS *Cities & Cemeteries of Etruria* I. p. c, An *alabastron* of stone from Chiusi.. having a hole in the crown for pouring out the ointment or perfume. **1928** D. H. LAWRENCE *Etruscan Places* (1932) iii. 79 A servant.. presumably offering the *alabastron*, or ointment-jar. **1940** *Antiquity* XIV. 245 Among other shapes (of pots) the alabastron is prominent.

‖**alabastrum** (ælə'bɑːstrəm, -æ-). *Bot.* [Cf. *virides alabastros*, used of rose-buds in Pliny.] (See quot.)

1706 PHILLIPS, *Alabastrum* or *Alabastrus*.. Among Herbalists, the Bud or green Leaves of Plants, which enclose the bottom of the Flowers, before they are spread. **1858** GRAY *Bot. Text-bk.* 395 *Alabastrum*, a flower-bud.

alablaster, obs. f. ALABASTER and ARBLASTER.

‖**à la bonne heure** (a la bɔn œːr), *phr.* [Fr., lit. 'at the right time'.] 'Well done!', 'fine!': freq. used ironically.

1750 CHESTERFIELD *Let.* 26 Apr. (1932) IV. 1528 If you can amuse yourself with that low play till supper, *à la bonne heure.* **1878** H. JAMES *Europeans* II. v. 211 'Surely, marriage was what you proposed.' 'Yes; but we didn't wish to force her.' 'A la bonne heure! That's very unsafe, you know.' *a***1930** D. H. LAWRENCE *Etruscan Places* (1932) 12 To my detractors I am a very effigy of vice. *A la bonne heure!*

†**alabre.** *Obs.* [?] (*Wright expl.* A kind of fur.)

*a***1500** *MS. Rawlinson* 137, 25 (Halliw.) And eke his cloke with alabre, And the knottes of golde.

‖**à la carte** (ælæ'kɑːt). [See A LA and CARTE[1] 5.] 'By the card (or menu)': said of meals which are ordered at a hotel or restaurant in separate items, each having its specified price. (Distinguished from a TABLE D'HÔTE meal, which is served at a fixed inclusive price.) Also *transf.*

1826 SHERER *Ramble in Germany* 252 He will find comfortable apartments, civil attendance, excellent fare, *à la carte*, at any hour. **1914** 'I. HAY' *Lighter Side School Life* vii. 189 If you want to have your son educated *à la carte*, you must get a private tutor for him. **1933** MRS. C. S. PEEL *Life's Enchanted Cup* xvi. 211 A restaurant for the staff, where meals were served *à la carte.* **1944** RUNYON (*title*) Runyon à la carte. **1966** *Automobile Assoc. Members Handbk.* 1966/67 30 A minimum charge for the à la carte menu.

†**a'lacche,** *v. Obs.* Pa. t. alehte. [f. A- *pref.* I intens. + LACCHE.] To get hold of, catch.

1154 *O.E. Chron.* (Laud MS.) an. 1123 Se kyng alihte dune of his hors and alehte hine betwux his earmes. *c***1380** *Sir Ferumb.* 3098 And laiden a-doun hur fon, Alle þat þai þan alacche miȝt: þer na ascapedem non.

alace, obs. form of ALAS.

alack (ə'læk), *int.* Also **alac, alacke,** and *north.* **alaik, alake.** [(As suggested by Prof. Skeat) f. A *int.* Ah! O! + *lak* (north. *laik*) LACK, failure, fault, reproach, disgrace, shame; hence, used in 'crying out upon' a thing in depreciation or reprobation. Also aphetized *lack!*] An exclamation originally of dissatisfaction, reprobation, or deprecation = *pity or shame that it should be so*; and hence of regret or surprise. Occ. with a dative obj. Now *arch., poet.* or *dial.*

*c***1480** *Robt. Devyll* 25 Alacke, sayd the Duke, yet am I gladde. **1513** DOUGLAS *Æneis* IV. x. 20 Thus fynaly scho out bradis, alaik! **1544** BALE in *Harl. Misc.* (Malh.) I. 269 Alac, Sir, why do ye say so? **1599** H. PORTER *Angry Women* (1841) 54 Where I shall be adiudged, alack the ruthe, To penance for the follies of my youth! **1610** SHAKS. *Temp.* I. ii. 152 Alack, what trouble Was I then to you? **1773** GOLDSM. *She Stoops* v. ii. (1854) 68 Alack, mamma, it was all your own fault. *a***1842** TENNYSON *Old Year* 47 Alack! our friend is gone.

b. *esp.* in phr. **alack the day! alack-a-day!** originally 'Shame or reproach to the day! Woe worth the day!' but in later usage of mere surprise, and aphetized ***lack-a-day!***

1592 SHAKS. *Rom. & Jul.* IV. v. 23 Shee's dead, deceast, shee's dead: alacke the day! **1703** STEELE *Tender Husb.* II. i, Alack-a-day, Cousin Biddy, these idle romances have quite turn'd your head. **1834** M. SCOTT *Cruise Midge* 177 Alas and alackaday both the pig and the wig were drowned.

†**a'lack.** *adv.* (*pred. a.*) *Obs. rare.* [A *prep.*[1] + LACK, after *asleep.*] Lacking, wanting, missing.

*a***1528** SKELTON *Magnyf.* 2558 Sodenly promotyd and sodenly put back, Soddenly commendyd, and suddenly fynde a lacke. **1587** TURBERVILLE *Epit. & Sonn.* (1837) 317 But now (Alas) she is alacke.

†**a'lacrative,** *a. Obs. rare*$^{-1}$. [irreg. f. L. *alacr-is* + -ATIVE; or perhaps f. ALACRITY, on apparent analogy of *infinity, infinitive*, etc.] Of or pertaining to alacrity; lively, sprightly.

1657 T. MAY *Satyr. Puppy* 37 A Comick Fancy wrinst in sparkling Claret..could not wander in alacrative Sence, more then I do now.

†**a'lacriate,** *v. Obs. rare*$^{-1}$. In 7 all-. [f. L. *alacri-s* + -ATE[3]. Cf. *humili-ate.*] = ALACRIFY.

1657 TOMLINSON *Renou's Disp.* Pref., All to allacriate the spirit of Man.

alacrify (ə'lækrɪfaɪ), *v. rare*$^{-0}$. [f. L. *alacri-s* (see ALACRIOUS) + -FY.] To fill with alacrity.

1864 in WEBSTER.

†**a'lacrious,** *a. Obs.* [f. L. *alacri-s* brisk, lively + -OUS. Cf. *hilari-ous.*] Brisk, lively, active.

1602 WARNER *Albion's Engl.* Epit. (1612) 376 His alacrious Intertainments, and vpright Gouernment. **1640** JACKSON *Wks.* I. Pref., Alacrious endeavours to redeem time. *a***1660** HAMMOND *Wks.* IV. 550 (R.) 'Twere well if we were a little more alacrious. [Not in JOHNSON, but in mod. Dicts.]

†**a'lacriously,** *adv. Obs.* [f. prec. + -LY[2].] In an alacrious or brisk manner; briskly; with alacrity.

1611 SPEED *Hist. Gt. Brit.* IX. viii. (1632) 568 The next morning alacriously they addressed to the fight. **1667** *Decay Chr. Piety* i. §9. 207 He cannot but run alacriously, who has the prize in his eye. **1674** *Govt. Tongue* iv. §8. 118 Thus Epaminondas alacriously expired. **1755** in JOHNSON; and in mod. Dicts.

†**a'lacriousness.** *Obs. rare*$^{-1}$. [f. ALACRIOUS + -NESS.] The quality of being alacrious; alacrity.

*a***1660** HAMMOND *Serm.* 553 (T.) To infuse some life, some alacriousness into you for the purpose.

alacritous (ə'lækrɪtəs), *a. rare*$^{-1}$. [f. ALACRIT-Y + -OUS; cf. *felicitous.*] = ALACRIOUS.

1870 HAWTHORNE *Eng. Note-Bks.* (1879) I. 90 A brisk, alacritous, civil, cheerful young man.

alacrity (ə'lækrɪtɪ). [ad. L. *alacritāt-em*, n. of quality f. *alacer* brisk (also in It. *alacrità*): see -TY.] Briskness, cheerful readiness, liveliness, promptitude, sprightliness.

*c***1510** MORE *Picus* Wks. 1557, 8/1 That meruelouse alacritee languished. **1594** SHAKS. *Rich. III*, V. iii. 73, I haue not that alacrity of spirit, Nor cheere of Minde that I was wont to haue. **1687** T. BROWN *Saints in Uproar* Wks. 1730 I. 79 With what wonderful alacrity you scamper'd over the Alps. **1710** STEELE *Tatler* No. 34 ¶2 It immediately gives an Alaçrity to the Visage and new Grace to the whole Person. **1791** COWPER *Il.* v. 145 She wing'd him with alacrity divine. **1820** SCOTT *Monast.* xv. 98 He accepted with grateful alacrity.

Aladdin (ə'lædɪn). [The name of the hero of *Aladdin, or the Wonderful Lamp*, a story from the Arabian Nights, subsequently popular as a pantomime, ad. Arab. *'Alā 'al Dīn*, lit. 'nobility of faith': cf. ALADDINIZE *v.*] **1. a.** ***Aladdin's lamp***, a magic lamp whose genie could grant any wish of the holder; usu. in fig. contexts. Cf. GENIE 1 b and *Slave of the Lamp* s.v. SLAVE *sb.*[1] 1 d.

1804 M. EDGEWORTH *Pop. Tales* II. 118 Good will is almost as expeditious and effectual as Aladin's lamp. **1823** BYRON *Don Juan* XII. xii. 11 Yes! ready money *is* Aladdin's lamp. **1853** J. R. LOWELL in *Putnam's Monthly* June 688 When I was a beggarly boy, And lived in a cellar damp, I had not a friend nor a toy, But I had Aladdin's lamp. **1963** N. STREATFEILD *Vicarage Family* xvii. 193 You have never begun to work..yet you expect, as if you had Aladdin's lamp, just to give it a rub—and hey presto, there you are at the top of the form.

b. ***Aladdin lamp***, a proprietary name for a type of oil- or paraffin-lamp; also *absol.*

1920 *Trade Marks Jrnl.* 19 May 956, 24 hours Daylight Aladdin... Kerosene Lamps and Parts thereof... *Jack Imber*, 134–135, Bank Chambers, Holborn, London... 24th October 1919. **1926–7** *Army & Navy Stores Catal.* 200 The Aladdin paraffin mantle lamp. **1938** L. MACNEICE *Earth Compels* 25 The Aladdin lamp mutters in the boarded room. **1943** R. GODDEN *Rungli-Rungliot* 29 The lamps are Victorian... To me they are far preferable to Aladdins. **1957** J. BRAINE *Room at Top* xxvi. 211 Roy began to snore, his snortings and rumblings competing with the steady hiss of the Aladdin lamp. **1962** *Times* 1 Jan. 13/4 We use paraffin in Aladdin lamps.

2. ***Aladdin's cave***, a place where great wealth is stored; a treasure-house of jewels or other valuables. Usu. *transf.* and *fig.*

1884 R. KIPLING in *Civil & Mil. Gaz.* 22 Mar. 3/3 With the vivid sunlight streaming in upon thousands of rainbow-coloured glass drops,..it seemed as unreal as Alladin's Cave. **1922** A. M. HYAMSON *Dict. Eng. Phr.* 9/1 *Aladdin's cave of wealth, an*, vast stores of wealth. **1957** J. BRAINE *Room at Top* xvi. 150, I was taking Susan not as Susan, but as a Grade A. lovely, as the daughter of a factory-owner, as the means of obtaining the key to the Aladdin's cave of my ambitions. **1963** A. LUBBOCK *Austral. Roundabout* 170 That rough little room was an Aladdin's Cave! Glass cases lined the walls in which glittered great nuggets of gold and shimmering silver, [etc.]. **1968** J. M. WHITE *Nightclimber* xxii. 171 What Aladdin's cave was on the other side of the door? Spoils from Venice, Cyprus, Byzantium, the Crusades? **1986** *Good Housekeeping* May 51/1 Down in London's Soho is..an Aladdin's cave of cotton jerseys, silks, velvets and unusual cloths.

Aladdinize (ə'lædɪnaɪz), *v. nonce-wd.* [f. *Aladdin* of the magic lamp in the Arabian Nights + -IZE.] To transform as if by magic.

1861 C. HODGSON *Resid. Japan* 235 The whole house may be Aladdinized into one room.

alagarto, obs. form of ALLIGATOR.

alaik, alak(e, obs. or dial. forms of ALACK.

alairy (ə'lɛərɪ), *adv. dial.* [Cf. ALIRY *adv.*] (See quots.)

The expression is doubtless much older but printed evidence is lacking.

1916 'N. DOUGLAS' *London Street Games* 5 There are other ball-games, such as..One-Two-Three-And-A-Lairy (I wish I knew what a-lairy meant). **1958** *Medium Ævum* XXVII. 113 The game often played by little girls, in Northern England at least, where the player bounces a ball on the ground, catching it with one hand, keeping the score by chanting 'One, two, three, alairy..', and accompanying each 'alairy' with a circular swing of the leg so as to describe a loop around but not obstruct the rising ball. **1959** I. & P. OPIE *Lore & Lang. Schoolchildren* vii. 108 One, two, three a-lairy, My ball's down the airie.

‖**ala'la.** [Dor. Gr. ἀλαλά a loud shout, hence a war-cry.] A shout used by the ancient Greeks in joining battle; a (Greek) battle-cry.

1675 HOBBES *Odyss.* 299 More than half with alalaes up start. —— *Iliad* 214 With alalaes the mighty armies close.

alalia (ə'lælɪə). *Med.* [f. Gr. ἀ priv. + λαλία talking.] Loss of the power of speech.

1878 HAMILTON *Nerv. Dis.* 162 In 1840, Lordat..who became aphasic himself, described the disease under the name of alalia. **1879** *Syd. Soc. Lex.* s.v., When all the letters are gone, the alalia is said to be complete.

alalite ('æləlaɪt). *Min.* [f. *Ala*, name of place in Tyrol + -LITE.] A variety of Malacolite or Diopside, one of the many forms of Pyroxene.

1837–80 DANA *Mineral.* 214 Alalite..occurs in broad right-angled prisms, colorless to faint greenish or clear green.

alalonga (ælə'lɒŋgə). Also -lunga. [mod.L., a. local It. *alalonga*, f. *ala* fin + *longa* (It. *lunga*) long.] An albacore, *Thunnus* (*germo*) *alalonga.*

1854 C. D. BADHAM *Prose Halieut.* xi. 201 The trembling thunnies, pelamyds, and alalongas, which covered the bottom of the net. *Ibid.* 203 Alalongas, whose long pectorals had been draggled in the mire.

alamanda, alamander, erron. varr. ALLAMANDA.

alamandine (ælə'mændɪn). [ad. med.L. *alamandina*, altered f. L. *alabandina* (*gemma*), f. *Alabanda* a city of Caria.] A kind of garnet. Cf. ALMANDINE *sb.*

1895 J. W. ANDERSON *Prospector's Handbk.* (ed. 6) 96 Garnet (including carbuncle, alamandine, pyrope, &c.). **1921** W. W. WATTS in *Trans. Scott. Ecclesiol. Soc.* 152 A ring with an alamandine (a garnet-coloured stone).

alambic, obs. form of ALEMBIC.

†**a'lamed**, *ppl. a. Obs.* [f. A *pref.* 1 or 6 + *lamed*: see LAME: cf. Ger. *erlahmt*.] Lamed.

a **1250** *Owl & Night.* 1602 Ah thu me havest sore i-gramed, That min heorte is wel neh a-lamed.

‖**alameda** (ala'meda). [Sp.] A public walk or promenade with a row of trees on each side.

1797 *Encycl. Brit.* IV. 10/1 The public walk, or Alameda, is pleasant in the evening. **1807** R. SOUTHEY *Lett. fr. England* iii. 26 Every town has not its Norney [as in Exeter] as with us its *alameda*. **1843** BORROW *Bible in Spain* li. (1872) 290 There is a public walk or alameda on the northern ramparts. **1845** DARWIN *Voy. Nat.* xv. (1873) 331 The boasted alameda.

†**ala'mire.** *Obs.* Also 6 **alamyre**. [f. *a, la, mi, re*, names of musical notes.] The note A which in other hexachords is *la, mi*, and *re.*

a **1528** SKELTON *Col. Clout* 107 And solfa so alamyre. **1654** GAYTON *Festiv. Notes* 83 (T.) She ran through all the keys from a-la-mi-re to double gammut. **1760** STILES in *Phil. Trans.* LI. 699 Our natural scale, beginning with Are, and ending with Alamire.

alamite. *Obs.*

1458 CHAWORTH in *Test. Ebor.* (1855) 227 Hengyng for ye halle and parlor of tapisserwork, and alle the kuchyns of tappisserwerk with alamitez.

alamodality (æləməʊ'dælɪtɪ). [a. mod.L. *alamodalitas*, f. *alamodal-is*, f. *à-la-mode*: see next. *Alamodal* seems not to occur.] The quality of being *à la mode*, or of following the fashion of the time; fashionableness.

1753 CHAMBERS *Cycl. Supp.*, *Alamodality*, a study or endeavour to accommodate a man's self in point of behaviour, dress, conversation, and other actions of life, to the reigning taste of custom, from a motive of complaisance, and to avoid the imputation of ill-breeding. *Ibid.*, A German writer..has a dissertation express on *alamodality* in writing (Geamœnius *de Alamodalitate Scribendi*). **1834** SOUTHEY *Doctor* xx. (D.) Doubtless it hath been selected for me because of its *alamodality*—a good and pregnant word.

‖**à la mode** (‖a la mɔd, 'æləməʊd), *phr.* Also 7–9 **alamode**.[Fr., in the manner or fashion (15th c. in Littré), adopted in Eng. in 17th c. as an *adv.*, and used also as *adj.* and *sb.* In the advb. sense now again treated as Fr. Formerly often written *all-a-mode*, as if containing *all*. Cf. *all alive, all-agog.*]

1. a. *phr.* In the fashion, according to the fashion.

1649 SELDEN *Laws of Eng.* I. lxxi. (1739) 198 Commanders that are never a-la-mode but when all in Iron and Steel. **1655** FULLER *Ch. Hist.* I. 14 With Bands, Cuffs, Hats and Caps, 'al a mode' to the Times. **1657** SANDERSON *Serm.* (ed. 4) Pref. 1, I confess they are not Alamode. **1680–1** *Roxb. Bal.* (1883) IV. 631 And All-a-mode of the brisk Monsieur, In the midst of the Pit, like ourselves we do sit. **1751** CHESTERFIELD *Lett.* 241 (1792) III. 108 If you can get that name generally at Paris, it will put you à la mode.

b. *Cookery.* Of a dessert: served with ice-cream. *U.S.*

1903 *Everybody's Mag.* VIII. 6/2 Tea and buns,..apple pie à la mode and chocolate were the most serious menus. **1928** *Delineator Cook Bk.* 734 'Pie a la mode' is pie served with ice-cream. **1949** L. DE GOUY *Pie Book* 65 Apple Pie... Serve warm or cold, with cheese, a la mode or with whipped cream. **1971** 'D. HALLIDAY' *Dolly & Doctor Bird* v. 67 We had..apple pie *à la mode*. *À la mode* in the United States means ice-cream. **1985** *N.Y. Times* XXI. 29/3 Highlights are the chocolate mousse cake, with its intense, creamy filling, and the nearly black chocolate cake, served à la mode in a pool of surprisingly insipid butterscotch sauce.

2. *adjectively*, Fashionable; according to some particular fashion.

1650 LOVELACE *Poems* (1817) II. 53 Where now each alamode inhabitant, Himself and's manners both do pay you rent. **1693** LOCKE *Educ.* 67 That plainness of Nature, which the Alamode People call Clownishness. **1713** STEELE *Englishm.* No. 40. 260 All sorts of Perukes the most Alamode. **1761** SMOLLETT *Gil Blas* III. v. (1802) I. 266, I began by five or six à-la-mode bows.

b. *esp.* in ***alamode silk*** (see 4); ***alamode beef***: Scraps and remainders of beef boiled down into a thick soup or stew.

1686 *Lond. Gaz.* mmcxxvi/4 Very good black narrow Lute-Strings, and Alamode-Silks. **1753** CHAMBERS *Cycl. Supp.*, Writers on cookery give the preparation of *alamode* or larded beef. *Collins*, Salt and Fish, p. 132. **1831** MACAULAY *Johnson* (1860) 88 His taste in cookery formed in..Alamode beef-shops, was far from delicate. **1843** HOOD *Turtles* i, Alamode-beef and greens.

†**3.** *subst.* A fashion or temporary mood. *Obs.*

1654 WHITLOCK *Mann. Engl.* 354 (T.) Her alamodes are suitable shapings of her mind to all changes of occurrences. **1683** KENNET tr. *Erasm. Moriæ Enc.* 44 For an old man to marry a young wife..is become the A la mode of the times.

4. A thin, light, glossy black silk.

1676 *Lond. Gaz.* mxcix/4 Several Pieces of wrought Silk, as Taffaties, Sarcenets, Alamodes, and Lutes. *Ibid.* mxciii/4 Sarcenet and Alamode Hoods. **1702** *Ord. in Counc.* 8 Mch. in *Lond. Gaz.* mmmdccxci/4 To wear Hatbands of Black English Alamode covered with Black Crape. **1861** MACAULAY *Hist. Eng.* V. 53 Regular exchange of the fleeces of Cotswold for the alamodes of Lyons.

†**ala'modeness.** *Obs. rare*$^{-1}$. [f. À LA MODE *a.* + -NESS.] Fashionableness.

1669 PENN *No Cross* xv. §8 Wks. 1726 I. 357 And Men become Acceptable by their Trims and the Alamodeness of their Dress and Apparel.

†**ala'modic**, *a. Obs. rare*$^{-1}$. [ad. mod.L. *alamodicus*; f. *à la mode*: see À LA MODE and -IC.] Fashionable; in accordance with prevailing taste.

1753 CHAMBERS *Cycl. Supp.* s.v. *Alamode*, Grapius has a dissertation on alamodic, or artificial sermons.

alamort, ‖**à la mort** (ælə'mɔːt, Fr. alamɔːr), *adv.* (*pred. a.*). [Fr. *à la mort* to the death: as *elle estoit chargée à la mort* Palissy (16th c.). Formerly quite naturalized; now often treated as Fr. Sometimes corrupted to *all amort* (cf. *al a mode, all agog*); and at length AMORT was occasionally used without *al* or *all*, being taken as = Fr. *à mort* 'to death.']

1. *adv.* To the death, mortally.

1592 WYRLEY *Armorie* 155, I drooping passe as one stroke alemort. **1725** in *Biblioth. Biblica* III. 142 The Raven ominous (as Gentiles holde), What time she croaketh hoarsely a la morte. **1833** GEN. P. THOMPSON *Exerc.* (1842) II. 479 The combat à la mort was of their own beginning.

2. *adj.* Sick to death, mortally sick; dispirited.

1592 LILLY *Midas* v. ii. 60 How now, Motto, all a-mort? **1596** SHAKS. *Tam. Shr.* IV. iii. 36 What sweeting all-amort? *a* **1658** CLEVELAND *Gen. Eclipse* vii, The whole World is al-a-mort. —— *Content* 24 Drink the A la mort Sun down and up agen. **1700** DRYDEN *Wife of Bath's T.* 340 Mirth there was none, the man was 'a-la-mort.' **1753** RICHARDSON *Grandison* (1781) I. xvi. 107 Ah my poor boy! Thus alamort! **1820** KEATS *St. Agnes* viii, She sighs..all amort.

†**ala'mort**, *v. Obs. rare*$^{-1}$. [f. prec.] To become mortally sick, to pine.

1705 HICKERINGILL *Priest-cr.* IV. (1721) 215 One Bishop would not, of old, be pleased with a fat Bishoprick, but Chagrin and Alamort, because not Archbishop.

†**alan**[1]. *Obs.* Also **alaun(t, alant, allan, allaund, aland.** [a. OFr. *alan, alant, allant*; cf. It. and Sp. *alano*, Pg. *alão*, med.L. *alanus*.] A large species of dog used to hunt or bait wild animals; a wolf-hound.

c **1386** CHAUCER *Knt's. T.* 1290 Aboute his Chaar ther wenten white Alauntz [*v.r.* alantz, alauntis]. **1525** LD. BERNERS *Froissart* II. xxiv. 65 Foure coursers and two Allans of Spaygne. **1572** BOSSEWELL *Armorie* II. 86 Three Allaundes, whiche be a certaine kinde of dogges of great stature. **1742** BAILEY, *Alandes*, wolf dogs. *Chauc.* **1801** STRUTT *Sports & Past.* I. i. 17 Alauntes, or bull-dogs. **1825** SCOTT *Talism.* (1863) 47 Three alans..wolf-greyhounds, that is. **1845** *Blackw. Mag.* LVII. 776 The snowy alauns. **1864** BOUTELL *Heraldry* ix. 63 Another heraldic Dog, a mastiff with short ears, is distinguished as an Alant.

Alan[2] ('ælən). Pl. **Alani** (ə'lɑːnɪ, ə'leɪnɪ), **Alans.** [ad. L. *Alānus, -i.*] A member of an ancient Scythian people, first encountered near the Caspian Sea. Also *attrib.* or as *adj.* Hence **A'lanic** *a.*, of or pertaining to the Alani.

a **1450** tr. (prose) *Vegetius' De Re Militari* 19 b For þow among gothus and alanus & hunus horsmen vsen to ben armed. **1598** HAKLUYT tr. *J. de Plano Carpini's Tartars* in *Princ. Navigations, Voiages* I. 66 On the South side it hath the Alani. **1601** P. HOLLAND tr. *Pliny's Nat. Hist.* IV. xii. p. 83 The bastard and degenerate Scythians..and anon the Alani. **1614** A. GORGES tr. *Lucan* x. p. 443 He whom the fierce Alanis might, Nor Scythians rage could ought affright. **1776** GIBBON *Decl. & F.* I. xii. 329 He had negotiated with the Alani, a Scythian people, who pitched their tents in the neighbourhood of the lake Mœotis. **1875** *Encycl. Brit.* I. 442/1 The Alani were frequently in conflict with the Roman power. **1913** E. H. MINNS *Scythians & Greeks* iv. 37 Klaproth first proved in 1822 that the Ossetes are the same as the Caucasian Alans. *Ibid.* xviii. 555 The Alan or Tauric tongue. *Ibid.* [The name] is almost certainly Iranian, but we cannot take this as throwing light on the Tauri for it is more probably Alan. **1930** C. A. MACARTNEY *Magyars* 2 They [*sc.* the Magyars] moved southward, and were in contact with Alanic and other Caucasian elements. **1932** C. H. DAWSON *Making of Europe* v. 87 Reinforced by ..Sarmatian Alans from across the Danube. *Ibid.*, Gothic and Alan contingents, serving under their own leaders, became the mainstay of the Roman armies.

aland (ə'lænd), *adv.* prop. *phr. arch.* [A *prep.*[1] on, in + LAND. The full *on lande, on þam lande*, and the intermed. *o þe lande, o lande* also occur.]

†**1.** Position: In the land, in the country. *Obs.*

c **1150** *O.E. Chron.* (Laud MS.) an. 1137 þa was corn dære ..for nan ne wæs o þe land. **1297** R. GLOUC. 389 And destrude al þat lond, þat no gode alonde nas. *a* **1400** *Octouian* 1628 The Kyng of Masydonye com ryde With hys ost alond. **1568** in *Bannat. MS.* in Gilchrist's *Scot. Bal.* II. 104 Iok tuk Jynny be the hand..And made a brydell up alland. **1879** JAMIESON *Scot. Dict.*, *Up-a-land*, at a distance from the sea; in the country.

2. On the dry land (in opposition to the water or sea); ashore. ? *Obs.*

c **1175** *Lamb. Hom.* 165 He deð al þat his wil is, a wettre and alonde. **1377** LANGL. *P. Pl.* B. XVI. 189 Alle þat lyf hath A-londe & a-watre. **1582** LICHEFIELD *Disc. E. Ind.* 159 Two shippes..in the water were likewise burnt, besides other three that were a land. **1608** SHAKS. *Peric.* II. i. 31, I marvel how the fishes live in the sea..Why, as men do a-land. **1697** DRYDEN *Virgil* (1806) II. 213 And in mid ocean left them moor'd a-land. **1809** J. BARLOW *Columb.* v. 815 Howe leads aland the interminable train, While his bold brother still bestorms the main.

3. Motion: To the land or shore, ashore.

c **1300** *St. Brand.* 114 A lute havene he fonde tho, Alond hi wende there. **1475** CAXTON *Jason* 57 They hadde not sette foot a lande. **1580** NORTH *Plutarch* (1676) 8 Ariadne..[was] so sore sea-sick..he was forced to put her aland. **1675** HOBBES *Odyss.* 91 Vulcan is now at Lemnos gone a land.

1805 SOUTHEY *Madoc in Azt.* xxv. Wks. V. 368 Could they but aland Set foot. **1870** MORRIS *Earthly Par.* I. I. 50 A well-hooped cask our shipmen brought aland.

†**a'land**, *v. Obs. rare.* [f. prec. phr.] To come ashore, land.

1570–87 HOLINSHED *Scot. Chron.* (1806) II. 295 Forthwith alanded at Leith Octavian a Frenchman. **1586** THYNNE in *Animadv.* App. 86 On which [shore]..the Saxons were woont to alland, and then to spoile the Countrie.

†**a'landward**, *adv. Sc. Obs.* [A *prep.*[1] on + LAND + -WARD; cf. *to us-ward*; now LANDWARD.] In the country, in opposition to town or burgh.

1609 SKENE *Reg. Maj.* 69 Ane burges dwelland allandward. *Ibid.* 141 Na burges dwelland a landwart, sould haue lot, nor cavill with burgesses dwelland within burgh.

†**alange**, *a. Obs.* Also **alenge, -inge**. [A variant of ELENGE, OE. *ǽlenge*, lengthy, tedious, f. æ- intensive + *lenge*, secondary form of *lang*, long:—OTeut. **langjo-*.] Protracted, tedious, wearisome, dreary, lonely. Also, [by confusion with *elelende, ellende*, ELEND; cf. the confusion of *-ende* and *-ing* in pples.] strange, foreign.

c **1330** *Arth. & Merl.* 4269 In time of winter alange it is. *c* **1386** CHAUCER *Wife's T.* 343 Pouerte is this, al-though it seme alenge [*v.r.* elenge, alenge⁻³, alinge] Possession that no wight wol chalenge. *a* **1420** OCCLEVE *De Reg. Princ.* 121 Her spirites..Thought that craft unlusty & alenge. **1440** *Promp. Parv.*, Alange, or straunge (**1499** alyande) *Extraneus, exoticus.* *c* **1515** *Compl. too late Maryed* (Halliw.), Now am I out of this daunger so alenge.

†**a'lange**, *v. Obs. rare*⁻¹. [f. prec. adj.] To make tedious, dreary, or lonely.

c **1330** *Arth. & Merl.* 4212 The leves fallen of the tre, Rein alangeth the cuntre.

†**alangely**, *adv. Obs. rare*⁻¹. [f. ALANGE *a.* + -LY[2].] Tediously, drearily; *also* strangely.

1440 *Promp. Parv.*, Alangely, or straungely (**1508** alyaundly) *Extranee.*

†**alangeness**. *Obs. rare.* [f. ALANGE *a.* + -NESS.] Tediousness, weariness, loneliness; *also* strangeness.

c **1320** *Seuyn Sages* (W.) 1736 His serjaunts ofte to him come, And of alangenes him undernome, And bade him take a wif jolif. **1440** *Promp. Parv.*, A-langeness, or strawngenesse (**1508** alyaundnesse) *Extraneitas.*

alanine ('ælənaın). *Chem.* [f. AL(DEHYDE), whence obtained by Strecker in 1849, + -INE; the *-an-* is a 'euphonic' insertion. (H. Roscoe.)]

1. The 'acid' monamide $C_3H_7NO_2 = CH_3-CH(NH_2)-CO(OH)$, derived from lactic acid by replacement of the alcoholic hydroxyl by NH_2, called also lactamic and α-amidopropionic acid; an organic base isomeric with lactamide, acting also in certain combinations as an acid.

1863–79 WATTS *Dict. Chem.* I. 63 Alanine crystallises..in colourless needles having the form of oblique rhombic prisms united in tufts. The aqueous solution has a sweet taste.

2. Extended (in pl.) to the group of acid amides (amic or amidic acids), of which the preceding substance is taken as the type, derived as above from the diatomic monobasic acids, or 'lactic series.'

1877 WATTS *Fownes' Chem.* 381 These amic acids..form saline compounds both with acids and with bases, the basic character, however, predominating. Hence, they are often designated by names ending in *-ine*, the ordinary termination for organic bases, glycollamic acid being designated as glycocine, lactamic acid as alanine, leucamic acid as leucine, etc. They are also designated, as a group, by the name *Alanines.*

alanna (ə'lænə). *Anglo-Ir.* Also **alan(n)ah**. [Ir. *a leanbh* my child!] My child! Used as a form of address or as a term of endearment.

1839 C. J. LEVER *Confessions H. Lorrequer* iii. 29 Shutting one eye knowingly, with an air of great secrecy, [he] whispered out, 'Miss Betty—Miss Betty, alanah!' **1841** 'H. LORREQUER' [C. J. LEVER] *Ch. O'Malley* I. iii. 16 'Do you want to break your neck entirely?' 'No Brackely, not mine.' 'Whose then, alannah?' **1847** A. TROLLOPE *Macdermots* I. viii. 176 Who else, should I main, alanna; sure isn't he your own beau? *Ibid.* xii. 307 Every one that entered, said, 'Well, Mary,' or, 'Well, alanna, how's yourself?' **1907** G. B. SHAW *John Bull's Other Island* III. 56 Come on, alanna, an make the paste for the pie. **1922** JOYCE *Ulysses* 580 Ireland's sweetheart, the king of Spain's daughter, alanna. **1948** T. H. WHITE *Elephant & Kangaroo* xxiii. 183 Jump in, alannah.

alant, variant of ALAN, a wolf-hound.

alantin (ə'læntın). *Chem.* [mod. f. Germ. *alant*, the Elecampane, *Inula Helenium* + -IN.] A synonym of INULIN, a starchy substance, obtained from the roots of elecampane, angelica, potato, etc.

1847 in CRAIG.

†**a'lantom**, *adv.* prop. *phr. Sc. Obs.* [? corruption of Fr. *à lointain.*] At a distance.

1686 G. STUART *Joco-ser. Disc.* 72 Some of our Lads being very kind Alantom followed me behind. **1721** BAILEY *Alantom*, at a distance. *N*[*orth*] *C*[*ountry*].

alap (a'lɑːp). Also **alaap, alapa**. [a. Hindi *ālāp*, late Skr. *ālāpa*, prob. f. Skr. *ālāpya*, lit. 'that which is to be spoken or sung'.] In Indian music, the improvised introductory section of a raga.

1891 C. R. DAY *Mus. & Mus. Instruments of S. India* iv. 41 To convey in writing an adequate idea of what an alâpa consists is..difficult; it is not exactly a song..; neither is it an air, for it is not confined in its rhythm. An alâpa may be said to be rather a kind of rhapsody, which abounds with grace and embellishments of all kinds, and is formed by an extension, according to the murchana, of the notes of the râga, in such a way that all the characteristics of that râga are prominently shown. **1898** [see DHRUPAD]. **1957** *New Oxf. Hist. Mus.* I. iv. 213 It is customary to preface the performance of a *râga*..with a prelude, called *âlâpa*, in which, against the note chosen for the function of *sa*, the salient points are pointed. **1959** *Listener* 23 Apr. 736/1 There is the breathless tone..when the alap quickens. **1972** P. HOLROYDE *Indian Mus.* 266 In Hindustani music the elaboration of the alaap is an indication of depth..of musicianship, whereas in the Carnatic it is often curtailed for the main body—the gat—of the raga. **1980** *Early Music Gaz.* Jan. 16/3 Particularly in the protracted alap of his [*sc.* Ravi Shankar's] opening solo raga, it was clear that the process of tuning..is of vital concern.

‖**à la page** (alapaʒ). [Fr., lit. 'at the page'; *être à la page*, to be up to date.] Up to date, up to the minute.

1936 A. HUXLEY *Eyeless in Gaza* ii. 12 His awful suspicions that people are beginning to find him a bore, no longer *à la page.* **1948** *Mind* LVII. 522 These vagaries were in a sense useful, because they put Campanella more *à la page* than ever. **1961** *Times* 14 Feb. 6/7 In medieval times.. ladies 'thought it indispensable' to carry small pocket mirrors kept in shallow circular lidded boxes (which sounds à-la-page today). **1963** *Sunday Express* 6 Oct. 19/2 To be really *à la page*, which is how the girls in Paris are at the moment, invest also in a small chunky handbag.

†**'alapat**, *v. Obs. rare*⁻¹. [f. med.L. *alapāt-* ppl. stem of *alapā-re* to slap, f. *alapa* a slap.] To slap or strike.

1609 J. MELTON *Sixe-fold Polit.* 185 [125] Not with a wand to alapat and strike them.

alar ('eılə(r)), *a.* [ad. L. *ālār-is*, f. *āla* a wing: see -AR.]

1. Of or pertaining to a wing or wings.

1847 in CRAIG. **1860** EMERSON *Cond. Life* 171 The bone or the quill of the bird gives the most alar strength, with the least weight. **1874** COUES *Birds of N.-W.* 544 Audubon mentions one nearly ten feet in alar expanse.

2. Winglike or wing-shaped.

1839–47 TODD *Cycl. Anat. & Phys.* III. 829/2 The alar bones..are in reality distinct elements of the cranium. **1845** TODD & BOWMAN *Phys. Anat.* I. 127 The knee affords some remarkable examples of these folds, in what are known as the alar ligaments.

3. *Bot.* and *Phys.* Belonging to the axil or axilla, axillary.

1858 GRAY *Bot. Text-bk.* 395 *Alar.* From *ala* in the sense of axilla, therefore axillary or in the forks. **1879** *Syd. Soc. Lex.*, *Alar vein*, a vein which, after collecting blood from the axilla, joins the axillary vein.

†**a'lard**, *v. Obs. rare*⁻¹. [f. A- *pref.* 1 or ? 6 + LARD *v.*, a. Fr. *larde-r*; or ad. Fr. *enlarder*: see A- *pref.* 10.] To fatten.

c **1380** WYCLIF *Serm.* (1879) I. xx. 52 Man fattid and alardid wendiþ awey fro God.

†**a'large**, *v. Obs.* [a. OFr. *alargir* to enlarge, f. *à* to + *large* LARGE.]

1. *trans.* To make larger, increase; give largely.

c **1380** WYCLIF *Serm.* (1879) I. xxxv. 93 Herfore preyden disciplis to alarge hem bileve. —— *Gen.* xxxii. 12 Alarge my seed as the grauel of the see. **1395** ? PURVEY *Remonst.* (1851) 51 To alarge othir mayntene his seculer lordshipe. *a* **1560** *Chaucer's Dream* 156 Such part in their nativity Was them alarged of beauty.

2. *intr.* (OFr. *s'alargir.*) To extend oneself.

1382 WYCLIF *Ps.* v. 1 In tribulacioun thou hast alargid to me. [**1388** Thou spraddest out to me. *Cf. OFr.* (in Godef.) En ma tribulatiun il s'est alargi a mi. Vulg. *In tribulatione dilatasti mihi.*]

†**a'larger**. *Obs. rare*⁻¹. [f. ALARGE + -ER[1].] One who extends. *perh.* One who gives largely.

c **1380** *Prymer* in Maskell's *Mon. Rit. Eccl. Ang.* II. 122/2 God, the alarger of forȝyuenesse and autour of mannys heelthe.

†**a'larging**, *vbl. sb. Obs.* [f. ALARGE + -ING[1].] Enlargement, increase.

1388 WYCLIF *Ezek.* xxxi. 7 Ful fair in his greetnesse, and in alargyng of hise trees.

alarm (ə'lɑːm), *sb.* Forms: 4–7 **alarme**, 6–7 **all arme**, 7 **all-arm, all' army**, 6– **alarm**. Also: 4 **alarom**, 6 **alarome**, 7 **allarum**, 6– **alarum**. [a. OFr. *alarme*, a. It. *allarme* = *all' arme!* 'To (the) arms!' orig. the call summoning to arms, and thus, in languages that adopted it, a mere interjection; but soon used in all as the *name* of the call or summons. Erroneously taken in the 17th c. for an English combination *all arm!* and so written; cf. similar treatment of *alamode* and *alamort*. From the earliest period there was a variant *alarum* due to rolling the *r* in prolonging the final syllable of the call, now restricted to an alarm-signal, as the peal or chime of a warning bell or clock, or the mechanism producing it. (The earlier pronunciation, following *alarm*, was (ə'lɑːrəm); but this has given way to (ə'lɛərəm) and (ə'lærəm).) Hence also, by aphesis, LARUM.]

I. As a phrase.

†**1.** *int.* An exclamation meaning 'To arms!' *Obs.*

1393 LANGL. *P. Pl.* C. XXIII. 92 'Alarme! Alarme!' quaþ þat Lorde. **1523** LD. BERNERS *Froissart* I. lxxxviii. 111 He began to cry a larum, treason, treason. **1535** COVERDALE *Jer.* li. 14 Which with a corage shall crie Alarum Alarum agaynst the. **1600** HOLLAND *Livy* 331 (R.) Showting as he could, crying al'arme, help help citizens.

†**2.** *adverbially*, with *ring*, etc. *Obs.*

1523 LD. BERNERS *Froissart* I. lxxx. 101 It was commaunded to sounde the watche bell alarm, and euery man to be armed. *Ibid.* I. ccccxi. 717 The townes all about range their belles alarum.

†**3.** quasi-*sb.* The call to arms, whether by using the exclamation *alarme!* or by any equivalent means. With ***cry, lilt, sound, blow, strike***, etc. *Obs.*

c **1325** *E.E. Allit. Poems* B. 1207 Loude alarom vpon launde lulted was þenne. **1523** LD. BERNERS *Froissart* I. xviii. 20 Often tymes in the day there was cryed alarum. **1580** BARET *Alv.* A 284 To blowe alarme, *Bellicum canere.* **1593** SHAKS. *2 Hen. VI*, V. ii. 3 When the angrie Trumpet sounds alarum. **1594** —— *Rich. III*, IV. iv. 148 Strike alarum, drummes!

II. As *sb.* with *pl.*

4. a. A call to arms; a signal calling upon men to arm. ***alarums*** (or ***alarms***) ***and excursions***, a stage-direction occurring in slightly varying forms in Shakes. *Hen. VI* and *Rich III* (e.g. *3 Hen. VI*, V. ii. *init.*); hence used playfully by recent writers for: skirmishing, confused fighting or onsets, sudden divagations, etc. (see sense 11 below).

1548 HALL *Chron.* (1809) 680 When the alarme came to Calice, euery man made to horse and harnes. **1600** HOLLAND *Livy* III. (1659) 81 The al'army was given on all hands: and no cry heard but 'Arme,' 'Arme.' **1609** C. BUTLER *Fem. Mon.* (1634) 130 As if the Drum did sound an all-arm. **1705** J. ROBINS *Hero of Age* II. ii. 3 Now first is beat the General Alarm, Now sounds to Horse. **1711** POPE *Rape Lock* v. 48 And all Olympus rings with loud alarms. **1864** SKEAT *Uhland* 21 And when th' alarum thrills the air, And beacons on the mountains flare. **1891** [see CRASH *sb.*[1] 5]. **1895** K. GRAHAME *Golden Age* 29 Alarums and Excursions. **1907** W. RALEIGH *Shakesp.* iv. 102 The whole First Act of *Coriolanus* is..full of alarums and excursions and hand-to-hand fighting. [**1910** G. K. CHESTERTON (*title*) Alarms and Discursions.] **1922** BARRIE *Courage* 9, I want you to hold.. That to gain courage is what you come to St. Andrews for. With some alarums and excursions into college life.

b. A message or news of approaching hostility.

1812 BYRON *Childe Har.* II. lxxii, Tambourgi! thy larum gives promise of war. **1815** SOUTHEY *Roder.* xx. 3 From east and west..the breathless scouts Bring swift alarums in.

5. A warning sound of any kind to give notice of danger, or to arouse or attract attention; *esp.* a loud and hurried peal rung out by a tocsin or alarm bell; or a chime rung out by a clock to awaken sleepers.

1592 *No-body & Some-b.* (1878) 328 Sound out a sodaine and a shrill Alarum. **1611** SPEED *Hist. Gt. Brit.* VII. xxxviii. (1632) 397 Awaked with the suddaine Allarum. **1642** JER. TAYLOR *God's Judg.* I. I. vii. 14 The frogges..filling every corner of his land sounded him an alarme. **1846** LYTTON *Lucr.* (1853) 185 A larum loud enough to startle the whole court from its stillness. **1842** MACAULAY *Lays, Armada*, At once the loud alarum clashed from all her reeling spires.

6. *fig.* **a.** A warning. **b.** An incitement (*obs.*).

1584 LODGE (*title*) An Alarum against Usurers. **1620** SHELTON *Don Quix.* IV. xiii. 103 A kind of black Meat, called Caviary..a great Alarum to the Bottle. *a* **1670** HACKET in Walcott's *Life* (1865) 169 Curious music upon costly instruments is an admirable alarm for devotion. **1686** W. DE BRITAINE *Hum. Prud.* §16. 75 Your Wisdom will be but an Alarm to them never to come unprovided. **1850** MERIVALE *Rom. Emp.* (1865) VIII. lxiv. 91 It is an alarum rung in the ears of a careless generation.

7. The apparatus or mechanism which sounds the alarm; also *fig.* Also *ellipt.* = *alarm-clock*.

1586 BRIGHT *Melanc.* xiii. 66 Automaticall instruments as clockes, watches and larums. **1655** MRQ. WORC. *Cent. Inv.* lxxii. §2 If a stranger open it, it setteth an Alarm a-going, which the stranger cannot stop from running out. **1682** SIR T. BROWNE *Chr. Mor.* 38 Thou hast an alarum in thy breast. **1788** WESLEY *Wks.* 1872 VII. 69, I procured an alarum, which waked me the next morning at seven. **1832** BABBAGE *Econ. Manuf.* viii. (ed. 3) 59 The various kinds of alarums connected with clocks and watches. **1910** A. BENNETT *Clayhanger* III. vi. 366 The ticking parcel drew the discreet attention of the doctor...'It's only an alarm,' said Edwin.

8. A warning of danger of any kind; especially one given in such a way as to startle or arouse the unwary; *esp.* in the phr. ***to give*** or ***take the alarm.***

1591 GARRARD *Art of Warre* 76 In giving Alarome to the enimie. **1594** NASHE *Vnfort. Trav.* 15 What did I now but one day made a false alarum in the quarter where they lay. **1624** CAPT. SMITH *Virgin.* I. 8 The towne took the Alarum before I ment it. *a* **1674** CLARENDON *Hist. Reb.* I. I. 29 [Words] which gave the first alarum to the Duke to apprehend his own Ruin. **1772** *Junius Lett.* lxviii. 355 Your natural benevolence took the alarm. **1867** LADY HERBERT *Cradle L.* viii. 215 The alarm was given that the Bedouins were upon them. *Mod.* It proved to be a false alarm.

9. *Fencing.* 'A step or stamp made on the ground with the advancing foot.' Chambers *Cycl. Supp.*

1579 GOSSON *Apol.* (Arb.) 75 Players haue chosen such a Champion as when I giue the Allarm winnowes his weapon. **1707** SIR W. HOPE *Fencing* iv. 102 in Chambers *Cycl. Supp.*, The motion of the sword-hand may in this case be attended with the appel or alarm of the advanced foot.

10. A loud noise or disturbance, of such a kind as to startle or perturb; din. *arch.*

1523 EARL SURREY in Ellis's *Orig. Lett.* I. 77 I. 217 The horses of his company brake lowse.. in suche nombre that it caused a marvelous alarome. **1596** SHAKS. *Tam. Shr.* I. i. 131 Though it passe your patience & mine to endure her lowd alarums. **1684** T. BURNET *Theor. Earth* II. 61 You see what disorders in nature, and what an alarum, the eruption of one fiery mountain is capable to make. **1820** KEATS *Hyperion* III. 105 What divinity Makes this alarum in the elements?

†**11.** A sudden or unexpected attack; necessitating a rush to arms; a surprise; an assault. *Obs.* exc. as in sense 4.

1587 FLEMING *Contn. Holinshed* III. 1021/2 Their men readie at all times to serue in euerie alarum and skirmish. **1605** SHAKS. *Macb.* v. ii. 4 Their deere causes Would to the bleeding, and the grim Alarme Excite the mortified man. **1660** HEXHAM *Dutch Dict.*, *Een Storm*, an assaulting, or an Al-arme. **1681** DRYDEN *Abs. & Achit.* II. 567 The doubtful nations watch his arms, With terror each expecting his alarms.

12. a. A state of surprise with fear or terror, suddenly excited by apprehension of danger; excitement caused by danger apprehended. Esp. in phr. ***alarm and*** (orig. ***or***) ***despondency***.

1587 D. FENNER *Def. Ministers* C 4 If Maist. D. Bridg. had not hitte on this cause of allarum. **1602** SHAKS. *Haml.* II. ii. 532 A blanket in th' Alarum of feare caught vp. **1711** STEELE *Spect.* No. 11 ¶5 Such Fears and Alarms as they were there tormented with. **1807** CRABBE *Par. Reg.* III. 599 Awe in each eye, alarm in every face. **1821** SCOTT *Kenilw.* xxiii. (1853) 235 The alarms of her guide made more impression on the Countess's mind. **1879** *Act 42 & 43 Vict.* c. 33 §5 Every person subject to military law who.. by word of mouth or in writing spreads reports calculated to create unnecessary alarm or despondency.. shall.. be liable to suffer penal servitude. **1950** V. PENIAKOFF *Private Army* II. v. 128 A message came on the wireless for me. It said: '*Spread alarm and despondency*'... The date was, I think, May 18th, 1942. **1957** 'N. SHUTE' *On the Beach* viii. 249 They don't want to create alarm and despondency until they've got to.

b. In modified sense: apprehension; uneasiness as to consequences.

1833 *Reg. Deb. Congress* 26 Feb. 1781 This General Assembly views with alarm.. the proposition.. for abandoning.. the principle of protection. **1834** *Ibid.* 18 Feb. 604 They regard with alarm the late measures of the President. **1937** I. GERSHWIN *Foggy Day*, I viewed the morning with alarm, The British Museum had lost its charm.

13. *Comb.* and *Attrib.* as ***alarm shock, alarm signal.*** Also **alarm-bird**, a name applied to various birds, as the kookaburra, the wattled peewit (*Lobivanellus lobatus*) of Australia, the African touracou (*Schizorhis concolor*), etc.; **alarm call, cry** = ALARM-*note*; **alar(u)m-clock, -watch**, one with an apparatus which can be set to ring loudly at any particular hour, so as to awaken sleepers, or excite attention; **alarm-cord**, the cord of an alarm-bell, *esp.* (*U.S.*) the communication-cord on a railway train; **alar(u)m-gauge**, an appliance attached to a steam-engine to give warning of a dangerous pressure of steam or deficiency of water in the boiler; **alarm-gun, -cannon**, a gun fired to give notice of danger, or to call to vigilance; **alarm-note**, the note of a bird when startled; **alarm-word**, a watchword. Also ALARM-BELL, -POST, q.v.

1848 J. GOULD *Birds of Austral.* VI. pl. 9 *Lobivanellus lobatus*.. has obtained the name of the Alarm Bird from its rising in the air, flying round and screaming at the approach of an intruder. **1940** V. POHL *Bushveld Adv.* vii. 155 The popular belief that the 'Go-away' or 'Alarm birds' scare off game. **1938** *Brit. Birds* XXXII. 93 The alarm call was a single note repeated several times before the bird took to wing. **1876** BANCROFT *Hist. U.S.*, V. xxiii. 592 A man-of-war in New York Bay fired alarm-cannon. **1697** A Larum Clock [see LARUM *sb.* 3]. **1751** *Boston News-Let.* 10 Oct., Eight day and small alarm clocks. **1835** J. TODD *Student's Manual* 69 The students in Yale.. have generally the alarm-clock. **1961** C. MCCULLERS *Clock without Hands* iv. 90 He.. would not let himself day-dream in the morning after the alarm clock went off. **1872** E. EGGLESTON *End of World* v. 40 In behind the donjon chimney he pulled an alarm cord. **1920** H. ELIOT HOWARD *Territory in Bird Life* iv. 139 The wary Redshank, poised on flickering wings, forgets its mournful alarm cry. **1928** D. H. LAWRENCE *Lady Chatt.* x. 134 The mother hen's wild alarm-cries. [**1757** *General Orders* 53 (D.A.E.), After the larem gun is fired.] **1760** S. NILES *Indian Wars* in *Mass. Hist. Soc. Coll.* (1861) ser. IV. V. 433 Alarm-guns were fired at St. George's Fort. **1826** G. R. GLEIG *Campaigns Brit. Army at Washington* (ed. 2) xii. 165 Wherever a light-house or signal station was erected, alarm guns were fired. **1879** *Wild Life in S.C.* 163 If you should disturb the blackbird.. he makes the meadow ring with his alarm-note. **1801** SOUTHEY *Thal.* XII. xxiv. Wks. IV. 433 Over the surface of the reeling Earth, The alarum shock was felt. **1665** PEPYS *Diary* 14 July (1876) III. 193 Up betimes by the helpe of a larum watch. **1678** T. HERBERT *Mem.* (T.) You shall have a gold alarmwatch, which, as there may be cause, shall awake you. *a* **1875** E. H. KNIGHT *Dict. Mech.* I. 57/2 *Alarm-watch*, an instrument not necessarily a time-piece, with going works, and adapted to.. sound an alarm after a specific interval of time. **1828** SCOTT *F.M. Perth* I. 102 Crying the alarm-word of the town.

alarm (ə'lɑːm), *v.* Also 6–7 **allarum, alarum.** [f. the sb. Cf. Fr. *alarmer*, of which Littré has no instance bef. 17th c.; not in Cotgr. 1611, either as Eng. or Fr.]

†**1.** To call to arms. **a.** *intr. Obs.*

c **1590** MARLOWE *2nd Pt. Tambur.* III. iii, Trumpets and drums, alarum presently. **1718** POPE *Iliad* II. 93 Now, valiant chiefs! since heaven itself alarms, Unite.

†**b.** *trans. Obs.*

1645 PAGITT *Heresiogr.* (1662) 287 They alarumed the trained-band that was to watch all that day. **1671** CROWNE *Juliana* I. 4 The troops are all alarum'd.

†**2.** To rouse to action, urge on, incite. *Obs.*

1605 SHAKS. *Macb.* II. i. 53 Wither'd Murther, Alarum'd by his Centinell, the Wolfe, Whose howl's his Watch.. towards his designe Moves like a Ghost. **1662** FULLER *Worthies* I. 237 This allarumed the Londoners to rescue poor Pateshul. **1710** STEELE *Tatler* No. 47 ¶2 At Epsom, there is at present a young Lady.. who has alarmed all the Vain and the Impertinent to infest that Quarter. **1768** BEATTIE *Minst.* I. iv, Nor him whose sordid soul the love of gold alarms.

3. To arouse to a sense of danger, to excite the attention or suspicion of, to put on the alert.

1651 JER. TAYLOR *Serm.* (1850) i. 18 Alarumed into caution and sobriety. **1684** OTWAY *Atheist* v. (1735) 113 If you squeak, and think to alarum the house. **1727** DE FOE *Apparitions* vi. 94 To alarm us at the approach of impending mischief. **1783** COWPER *Task* III. 185 Great crimes alarm the conscience. **1849** MACAULAY *Hist. Eng.* II. 250 For the purpose of alarming the guards.

†**b.** To inform or notify of anything dangerous, to warn. *Obs. rare.*

1711 STEELE *Spect.* No. 80 ¶3 Before Brunetta could be alarmed of their Arrival.

4. To keep in excitement; to disturb, perturb.

1661 C. LYTTELTON in *Hatton Corr.* (1878) 22 We have beene mightily alarumd here with reports of plotts. **1697** DRYDEN *Virg. Georg.* IV. 86 Intestine Broils allarm the Hive. **1872** BLACK *Adv. Phaeton* xvi. 222 Sellers of fruit and of fish.. alarming the air with their invitations.

5. To strike with fear or apprehension of danger; to agitate or excite with sudden fear.

1653 A. WILSON *James I*, 189 The King was again Alarum'd by this Protestation. **1711** ADDISON *Spect.* No. 7 ¶2 A Screech-Owl at Midnight has alarmed a Family more than a Band of Robbers. **1817** JAS. MILL *Brit. India* II. IV. iv. 128 These events alarmed (him) into submission. **1877** in *Fam. Herald* 27 Oct. 406/1 You alarm me with that long prologue. *Mod.* I am alarmed at the aspect of affairs.

6. *intr.* To sound like an alarm or alarum.

1839 POE *Ho. of Usher* Wks. 1864 I. 306 The noise of the dry and hollow-sounding wood alarummed and reverberated throughout the forest.

alarmable (ə'lɑːməb(ə)l), *a.* [f. ALARM *v.* + -ABLE.] Liable to be alarmed or excited; excitable.

1813 W. TAYLOR *Month. Mag.* XXXV. 139 A more delicate and alarmable sensibility. **1841** *Chambers's Journ.* 4 Sept. X. 260 A suspicious and very alarmable individual.

a'larm-,bell, a'larum-,bell. A bell rung as a signal of danger or on a sudden emergency; as the tocsin of burghs in olden times. Also *fig.*

1597 SHAKS. *2 Hen. IV*, III. i. 17 A common Larum-Bell. **1641** HINDE *J. Bruen* lviii. 175, I feare.. that the Alarum Bell of your conscience is silenced. **1781** GIBBON *Decl. & F.* III. xlix. 108 The alarum-bell rung to arms in every quarter of the city. **1834** CARLYLE *Fr. Rev.* I. III. viii. 128 The alarm-bell bursts forth, ominous; and peals and booms all day. *a* **1849** POE *Bells* Wks. 1859, 75 Hear the loud alarum bells —Brazen bells!

alarmed (ə'lɑːmd), *ppl. a.* Also 7–8 **allarum'd, alarum'd.** [f. ALARM *v.* + -ED.]

1. Called to arms, aroused, on the watch.

1605 SHAKS. *Lear* II. i. 55 He saw my best alarum'd spirits, Bold in the quarrel's right. **1667** MILTON *P.L.* IV. 986 On th' other side Satan allarm'd Collecting all his might dilated stood. **1871** *Daily News* 23 Jan., The French are taking to these attacks seemingly.. The front line is standing 'alarmed.'

2. Disturbed, excited by the prospect of danger.

1650 FULLER *Pisgah Sight* IV. vi. 100 The young man, late at night allarum'd out of his bed, with the noise. **1722** DE FOE *Plague* 30 Deceivers fed their fears and kept them alarmed. **1827** HOOD *Mids. Fairies* cx, And prompt fresh shifts in his alarum'd ears. **1828** SCOTT *F.M. Perth* v. (1874) 55 Her efforts implied alarmed modesty rather than maidenly coyness.

alarmed (ə'lɑːmd), *a.* [f. ALARM *sb.* + -ED².] Fitted or protected with a (burglar, fire, etc.) alarm or alarms. Chiefly *pred.*

1969 V. CANNING *Queen's Pawn* vi. 83 Windows in the far wall overlooking a small yard and garden, each window alarmed and burglar proof. **1976** *Liverpool Daily Post* 11 Dec. (Advt.), Warehouse to let, suitable for wholesale or light industrial use, alarmed. **1982** *Amer. Speech* LVII. 197 This door is locked and alarmed between 11 p.m. and 6 a.m. **1985** *Oxford Times* 13 Sept. 4 They even ripped off the front of the club bar, believing it to be alarmed, to gain access to cash, spirits and cigarettes.

alarmedly (ə'lɑːmɪdlɪ), *adv.* [f. ALARMED *ppl. a.* + -LY².] In an alarmed manner; frightenedly.

1880 MISS BROUGHTON *Sec. Thoughts* I. I. xi. 199 Looking alarmedly round at the breakfast-table for restoratives.

alarming (ə'lɑːmɪŋ), *ppl. a.* [f. ALARM *v.* + -ING².] Disturbing or exciting with the apprehension of danger.

1680 BURNET *Rochester* (1692) 86 With such allarming Evidences. **1769** *Junius Lett.* ii. 14 The last charge.. is of a most serious and alarming nature. **1855** MACAULAY *Hist. Eng.* IV. 278 But one alarming report followed another fast.

alarmingly (ə'lɑːmɪŋlɪ), *adv.* [f. prec. + -LY².] In an alarming manner; so as to excite alarm or apprehension.

1787 BURNS *Lett.* 60 Wks. 1875, 349 Alarmingly ill of a sore throat. **1856** FROUDE *Hist. Eng.* I. 8 So far from increasing, manufactures had alarmingly declined.

alarmism (ə'lɑːmɪz(ə)m). [f. ALARM *sb.* + -ISM.] The profession or practice of the alarmist; persistent tendency to raise alarm needlessly.

1867 *Spect.* 20 July 793 [A] speech.. powerful and logical, yet extravagant in its alarmism. **1881** *St. James's Gaz.* 12 Feb., 'Panic' and 'alarmism.'

alarmist (ə'lɑːmɪst). [f. ALARM *sb.* + -IST.]

a. One addicted to raising alarms; *hence*, who raises alarm on very slight grounds, or needlessly; a panic-monger.

1793 BURKE *Corr.* 23 Aug. (1844) IV. 135 We must continue to be vigorous *alarmists.* **1802** SYD. SMITH *Wks.* 1859 I. 11/1 The panic of this alarmist is so very great. **1849** COBDEN *Sp.* 8 Those wicked alarmists and panic-mongers whom I will never forgive.

b. *attrib.*

1800 *Aurora* (Philadelphia) 28 Nov. (Thornton), The little alarmist Jacobin doctor found he had mistaken his man. **1802** SYD. SMITH *Wks.* 1867 I. 13 This was another gentleman of the alarmist tribe. *c* **1842** LD. CAMPBELL *Autobiog.* (1881) II. 153 Alarmist or disappointed Whigs. **1870** *Daily Tel.* 18 July, Rumours of an alarmist character, some of them wildly improbable, were circulated.

alarm-post (ə'lɑːm,pəʊst). 'The ground appointed to each Regiment, by the Quarter-Master-General for them to march to in case of an Alarm from the enemy.' Bailey 1721.

1694 *Regulation for Garrison Duty* in J. Muller *Syst. Camp-Discipline* (1757) 1 Each Regiment to have an Alarm-post to repair to, in case of Fire, or any other extraordinary Alarm. **1794** NELSON in Nicolas's *Disp.* (1845) I. 386 Our troops.. in ten minutes at farthest would be at the bridge from the alarm-posts. **1844** *Regul. & Ord. Army* 180 Although a Regiment or a Division may remain for a single night only in a quarter, yet an Alarm-Post is invariably to be established.

alarum. A variant of ALARM, formerly used in all the senses of the word, but now restricted, exc. in poetical use, to the peal or chime of a warning bell or clock, or the mechanism which produces it: see ALARM *sb.* 5, 7.

alary ('eɪlərɪ), *a.* [ad. L. *ālāri-us*, f. ALA wing: see -ARY.] Of or pertaining to wings or *alæ.*

1658 SIR T. BROWNE *Gard. Cyrus* iv. 181 The lower leaf [of leguminous plants] closely involving.. the alary or wingy divisions. **1836–9** TODD *Cycl. Anat. & Phys* II. 945/2 It is the first alary nerve, and is given to the future anterior pair of wings. **1837** *Blackw. Mag.* XLII. 821 Can't I use part of the fortune in advancing my great project of alary aerostation? **1877** HUXLEY *Anat. Inv. An.* vii. 434 The alary muscles.

alas (ə'lɑːs, -æ-), *int.* Also 4– **allas**, 4 **alaas, allaas.** *Sc.* 4–7 **allace, alace.** *Aphet.* 6–7 **'las, lass.** [a. OFr. *ha las, a las* (mod.Fr. *hé -las*), f. *ha!* = AH! + *las, lasse* wretched, orig. 'weary':—L. *lassum* weary. Cf. Pr. *ai las*; It. *ahi lasso.* In these languages the adj. took the gender of the speaker, *las, lasso*; *lasse, lassa.* The later Fr. form *helas!* is occas. found in Eng.; also in 16th c. an aphetic '*las!*] An exclamation expressive of unhappiness, grief, sorrow, pity, or concern. Occ. with dat. obj., or with *for.*

c **1260** *Signs bef. Judg.* in *E.E. Poems* (1862) 10 Alas louerd wat sul we tak we þat abbiþ sin i-wroȝt. *c* **1386** CHAUCER *Sqrs. T.* 491 That I was bred, allas that harde day. *c* **1394** *P. Pl. Crede* 754 Alaas! þat lordes of þe londe · leueþ swiche wrechen. *c* **1400** *Destr. Troy* XXIV. 9716 Hit happis vs suche harmes to haue now, alace. *c* **1525** SKELTON *Col. Cloute* 1022 Helas! I say, helas! How may this come to passe? *a* **1593** MARLOWE *Jew of M.* IV. iii. 314 'Las, I could weep at your calamity! **1604** SHAKS. *Oth.* IV. ii. 42 Alas the heauy day: why do you weepe? **1667** MILTON *P.L.* x. 461 Alas, both for the deed and for the cause! **1842** J. H. NEWMAN *Par. Serm.* VI. iii. 32 Alas for our easy sensual life. **1870** MORRIS *Earthly Par.* I. I. 36 Alas, the happy day! the foolish day! Alas! the sweet time, too soon passed away!

Alaska (ə'læskə). The name of a State in the north-west of the United States, used *attrib.* to designate things connected with it in origin: as ***Alaska cedar, pine***, trees indigenous to western N. America; ***Alaska sable, seal***, used in the fur trade as spurious names for skunk and other pelts.

1884 SARGENT *Rep. Forests* 7 The most valuable species of the northern Coast Forest [is].. the Alaska cedar (*Chamaecyparis* [*nootkatensis*]). **1897** *Boston Even. Transcript* 11 Sept. 24/3 Skunk skins are one of the biggest items in the fur market. They go under the attractive name of 'Alaska sable'. **1897** SUDWORTH *Arborescent Flora* 45 *Tsuga mertensiana*.. Alaska Pine [of] Northwestern lumbermen. **1910** *Encycl. Brit.* I. 475/1 The yellow or Alaska cedar, a very hard and durable wood of fine grain and pleasant odour. **1921** A. C. LAUT *Fur Trade of America* iv. 43 Skunk as skunk simply wouldn't sell; so skunk became 'Alaska sable'. *Ibid.* iii. 33 Plucked otter is sold dyed for Alaska seal.

b. baked Alaska, a dessert consisting of a centre of sponge cake and ice cream with a light covering of rapidly cooked meringue.

1909 FARMER *Boston Cook Book* 448 Baked Alaska... Make meringue of eggs and sugar.., cover a board with white paper, lay on sponge cake, turn ice cream on cake.., cover with meringue, and spread smoothly. Place on oven grate and brown quickly in hot oven. **1954** *Menu (M/S Stella Polaris)* 13 Dec., Tenderloin Steak with Vegetables—Baked Alaska.

Alaskan (əˈlæskən), *a.* and *sb.* [f. prec. + -AN.] **A.** *adj.* Of or pertaining to Alaska (see prec.) and its inhabitants.

1868 F. WHYMPER *Travel in Alaska* xxii. 255 The 'medicine man' of the Tchuktchis (and also of the North Alaskan peoples, who use the same term) was.. represented in Greenland. **1890** FRAZER *Golden Bough* II. 116 Alaskan hunters preserve the bones of sables and beavers out of reach of the dogs for a year. **1921** *Contemp. Rev.* Feb. 286 It seems certain that the Alaskan races.. are of the same ultimate stock as ourselves. **1936** *Discovery* July 200/2 Archaeological evidence is conclusively in favour of an Alaskan origin [for the Eskimo].

B. *sb.* A native or inhabitant of Alaska.

1871 *Lakeside Monthly* July 16 (*title*) The Alaskans at home. **1881** C. M. WILLARD *Life in Alaska* (1884) 16 It is the custom of the Alaskans to compel the murderer to stay beside the corpse until it is finally disposed of. **1924** *Chambers's Jrnl.* 19 Apr. 325/1 The largest of all.. as the Alaskans call it, the 'tyee' salmon, sometimes weighs over one hundred pounds.

†**aˈlask-i**, *v.* *Obs.* *rare*$^{-1}$. [a. ONFr. *alaskie-r* (and *alaski-r*) to let loose, f. *à* to (or *es* out) + *laskier*, *laskir*, mod.Fr. *lâcher*:—late L. *las-cāre*, cl. L. *laxāre*, f. *lax-us* loose.] To let loose, release.

1250 LAYAM. 8838 Ich wole.. alaski him of care [**1205** lutlien ich wulle his kare].

†**aˈlast**, *adv.* prop. *phr.* *Obs.* [A *prep.*[1] of order in a series, at + LAST. Layamon has a fuller *a þan laste*, beside *at þan laste*, and Ormin *att lattste.*] In the last place; at last.

c **1230** *Ancr. R.* 42 Alast þet uerset, 'Ecce ancilla Domini.' *c* **1320** *Cast. Loue* 457 So þat Pees a-last vp-breek. **1340** *Ayenb.* 139 Alast hit is wone of þe poure manne þet.. he ne heþ none ssame to acsi.

‖**alastor** (əˈlɑːstə(r), -æ-). *rare.* [a. Gr. ἀλάστωρ the avenging deity, f. ἀ priv. + λαστ-, f. λαθεῖν to forget.] A relentless or avenging spirit, a Nemesis.

1810 W. TAYLOR *Month. Mag.* XXIX. 350 Imps, alastors, and every other class of cacodemons. **1812** *Ibid.* XXXIV. 234 The midnight mass will soon be read, Which even the alastors dread.

alastrim (əˈlæstrɪm). [Pg., f. *alastrar* to spread.] A contagious eruptive disease resembling smallpox.

1913 DORLAND *Med. Dict.* (ed. 7), *Alastrim*, same as *amaas*. **1922** *Times* 19 May 10/4 Last week no fewer than 38 cases of smallpox were notified in England and Wales... One of these cases was notified as 'alastrim'. [**1926** *Encycl. Brit.* Suppl. III. 559/2 An outbreak [of mild smallpox] in South Africa was described by de Korté in 1904, under the name of Amaas or Kaffir-pox, another by Ribas in Brazil in 1910, under the name of Alastrim.]

alate (əˈleɪt), *adv.* prop. *phr.* *arch.* [A *prep.*[2] of + LATE.] Of late, lately.

c **1400** *Destr. Troy* x. 4176 Of shame and of shenship shapyn vs alate. **1509** HAWES *Past. Pleas.* (1845) 16 The goodly portres.. axed me from whence I came alate? *c* **1590** GREENE *Poems* 119 Where chilling frost alate did nip, There flasheth now a fire. **1670** WALTON *Lives* III. 151 How art thou chang'd from what thou wert a late. **1842** MRS. BROWNING *Poems* (1878) 219 But the Harpies alate In the storm came, and swept off the maidens.

†**aˈlate**, *v.* *Obs.* *rare*$^{-1}$. [a. OFr. *alaite-r*, *-ier*:—L. *adlactā-re* to give milk to; f. *ad* to + *lac*, *lact-* milk.] To give milk to, suckle.

a **1521** *Helyas* in *E.E. Pr. Rom.* (1858) III. 56 The vii children were nourished and alated [*printed* alaced] of the saide white goate.

alate (ˈeɪleɪt), *a.* [ad. L. *ālāt-us*, f. *āla* a wing; cf. *caudate* and L. *togātus*: see -ATE.] Winged; having wings or side appendages resembling wings in shape or general appearance.

1668 WILKINS *Real Char.* 118 Alate seed-vessels; or Keys. **1763** STUKELEY *Palæogr. Sacra* 73 Nainby—Lincolnshire—from an alate temple there. **1857** HENFREY *Elem. Bot.* 76 Sometimes the stalk-like petiole is winged (alate), a narrow plate of the blade structure running down its margins. **1876** G. BUCKTON *Brit. Aphid.* (Ray Soc.) I. 86 The alate females are never so plentiful as the apterous.

alated (ˈeɪleɪtɪd), *a.* [f. L. *ālāt-us* ALATE + -ED, according to the ordinary Eng. representation of L. *-ātus*: cf. *elate* and *elated* from *ēlā tus.*] Winged, having wings.

1653 WATERHOUSE *Apol. Learn.* 56 (L.) Power, like all things alated, seldom rests long in any continued line. **1697** in *Phil. Trans.* XIX. 679 This hath alated or winged Leaves. **1753** CHAMBERS *Cycl. Supp.*, The bat is the only alated or winged quadruped, properly speaking. **1879** H. PHILLIPS *Coins* 17 On the obverse Pallos Nikephora with alated helmet.

‖**alaternus** (ælәˈtɜːnəs). *Bot.* Also **alatern.** [f. L. *āla* wing + *ternus* three.] An evergreen shrub (*Rhamnus Alaternus*) belonging to the genus *Rhamnaceæ* or Buckthorns.

1607 TOPSELL *Four-footed Beasts* (1673) 189 They love Tamerisk.. and a tree called Alaternus, which never beareth fruit but only leaves. **1711** PETIVER in *Phil. Trans.* XXVII. 393 Great broad Alatern. **1794** MARTYN *Rousseau's Bot.* xvi. 207 The Alaternus, formerly so shorn and beclipped in hedges.

alation (eɪˈleɪʃən). [a. Fr. *alation*, f. L. *ālāt-us* winged: see ALATE and -ION[1]. Cf. *foliation.*] A winged condition; 'the mode in which the wings of insects are formed and disposed upon the body.' Craig 1847.

Mod. Bot. The alation of the stem is more conspicuous in other species of the pea.

alaunt, variant of ALAN, a wolf-hound.

†**alaˈventure**, *Obs.* *rare*$^{-1}$. In phr. *at alaventure*. [A mixture of Eng. *at aventure* and corresp. Fr. *à l'aventure.*] Used by Caxton for *at aventure*: see ADVENTURE *sb.* 3 b.

1489 CAXTON *Faytes of Armes* I. xxiv. 75 Al dedes of bataylle ben doon at alaventure.

†**aˈlay**, *v.* *Obs.* *rare.* [?] The specific term for 'to carve' a pheasant.

1508 *Termes of a Keruer* in *Babees Bk.* 265 Vntache that curlewe. Alaye that fesande. Wynge that partryche. **1838** P. PARLEY *Tales ab. Christm.* xxxiii. 302 The good people of those days would not say *cut up*, but *alay* a pheasant.

alay, earlier and better spelling of ALLAY.

alay, variant of ALLY, a kind of marble.

†**aˈlayne**, *v.* *Obs.* *rare*$^{-1}$. [f. A- *pref.* 1 intens. + LAYNE to hide.] To hide, conceal.

c **1400** *Sowdane* 1497 The sowdan sore them affrayned What that ther names wer; Rouland saide, and noght alayned.

†**alazony.** *Obs.*$^{-0}$ [ad. Gr. ἀλαζονεία, -νία bragging, imposture.] 'Arrogancy or pride.' Blount *Glossogr.* 1656.

alb (ælb). Forms: 1–9 **albe**, 4–7 **aube**, 5 **awbe**, **awlbe**, 5–6 **aulbe**, 6– **alb.** [OE. *albe*, ad. late L. *alba*, for *tunica* or *vestis alba* a white tunic or garment, a shirt. The form *aube* is a later adoption of the Fr. *aube*:—*alba*, and was the usual one in Eng. in the 14th and early 15th c.; in the 16th the two were mixed in *aulbe*, *awlbe.*] A tunic or vestment of white cloth reaching to the feet, and enveloping the entire person; a variety of the surplice, but with close sleeves; worn by clerics in religious ceremonies, and by some consecrated kings.

a **1100** *Canons of K. Edgar* in *Anc. Laws* II. 250 þæt ælc preost hæbbe subuculam under his alban [*dat. or acc. of* albe]. *c* **1200** *Trin. Coll. Hom.* 163 Te albe sol, and hire smoc hwit. **1340** *Ayenb.* 236 Ine þe aube and ine þe gerdle above. **1440** *Promp. Parv.*, Awbe (**1499** Awlbe). *Alba, poderis.* **1483** CAXTON *Gold. Leg.* 359/2 Saynt Martyn appiered to hym cladde in an aulbe. **1566** *Engl. Ch. Furn.* (1866) 30 Item an alb—whearof wee have made a surples. **1606** G. W[OODCOCKE] *Hist. Justine* Ll iij, Hee [Sigismund].. was buryed in his regall Albe in Vngaria. **1649** JER. TAYLOR *Gt. Exemp.* II. viii. 68 Whose albes of baptisme served them also for a winding sheet. **1820** SCOTT *Monast.* xxxvii, Array yourselves also in alb and cope. **1846** KEBLE *Lyra Innoc.* (1873) 171 Who daily in the Holy Place wears the bright albe.

alba (ˈælbə). [Pr., f. Rom. **alba* (cf. Sp. *alba* dawn), f. L. *albus* white.] A dawn-song of the Provençal poets. Cf. AUBADE.

1821 *New Monthly Mag.* I. 284 The *Albas* and the *Serenas* of the Provençal poets were the stanzas, which were sung by them at the break or close of day, in honour of their mistresses. [**1934** A. JEANROY *La Poésie des Troubadours* II. vii. 292 Réveillés, à l'aurore, par le cri du guetteur, deux amants qui viennent de passer la nuit ensemble se séparent en maudissant le jour qui vient trop tôt; tel est le thème, non moins invariable que celui de la pastourelle, d'un genre dont le nom est emprunté au mot *alba*, qui figure parfois au début de la pièce, et régulièrement à la fin de chaque couplet, où il forme refrain.] **1936** C. S. LEWIS *Alleg. Love* iv. 196 Before them lies the morning and the beautiful antiphonal *alba*.

albacore (ˈælbəkɔə(r)). Also 6 **albo-**, 6– **albi-**, 8 **albe-**, 9 **alber-**. [a. Pg. *albacor*, *-bacora*, *-becora* (Sp. *albacora*, Fr. *albicore*); f. Arab. *al* the + *bukr*, pl. *bakārat*, a young camel, a heifer, whence also Pg. *bacoro* a young pig. The Fr. form *albicore* is also in use.] A fish; prop. a large species of Tunny (*Thynnus*), found in the Atlantic, near W. Indies. Applied also to a kindred species in the Pacific; and loosely to others of the genus.

1579 T. STEVENS *Lett. fr. Goa* in Hakluyt II. 583 In the sea, the fish which is called Albocore, as big as a salmon. **1696** OVINGTON *Voy. Surat* 48 We likewise met with shoals of Albicores (so call'd from a piece of white Flesh that sticks to their Heart). **1766** GROSE *Voy. East Ind.* I. 5 The Albacore is another fish of much the same kind as the Bonito. **1782** P. BRUCE *Mem.* XII. 424 Baracuda, ship-jacks. albecores. **1845** DARWIN *Voy. Nat.* viii. (1873) 162 The flying-fish and their devourers the bonitos and albicores. **1860** MAURY *Phys. Geog. Sea* iii. § 158 A few years ago, great numbers of Albercore.. entered the English Channel. **1868** *Daily News* 14 Sept., Capture of an Albacore at Dawlish.

alban (ˈælbən). [f. L. *alb-us* white + -AN.] A white crystalline resinous substance extracted from gutta-percha on treatment with alcohol or ether.

1863 WATTS *Chem. Dict.* (1872) I. 64. **1879** *Syd. Soc. Lex.*, *Alban* forms from 14 to 16 per cent. of gutta percha.

Albanian (ælˈbeɪnɪən), *a.*[1] and *sb.*[1] *Hist.* [f. med.L. *Albania* Scotland (Ir. *Alba*, gen. *Alban*) + -AN.] **A.** *adj.* Of or pertaining to Scotland. **B.** *sb.* A Scot. So **Albanic** (ælˈbænɪk) *a.* [cf. Ir. *Albanach*, Gael. *Albannech*], Scottish.

1561 NORTON & SACKV. *Gorboduc* v. ii. 137 The proude attemptes of this Albanian prince. **1779** A. BUTLER *Lives of Saints* (ed. 2) I. 446 St. Gildas the Albanian, or the Scot. **1865** T. MᶜLAUCHLAN *Early Scott. Ch.* xvi. 208 The great convention at Drumceat in Ulster, where the question of Albanic independence was fully discussed.

Albanian (ælˈbeɪnɪən), *a.*[2] and *sb.*[2] [f. *Albania* (see below) + -AN.

Albania is the med.L. and general mod. name of the country, which is called *Shqipnija* by the inhabitants, who call themselves *Shqipetars*; in med.Gr. Ἀλβανία, with variants Ἀλβανητία, Ἀρβανητία, the inhabitants being called Ἀλβάνοι, Ἀλ-, Ἀρβανῆτες (in Turkish ARNAUT).]

A. *adj.* Of or pertaining to Albania, a country in the western part of the Balkan peninsula, its inhabitants or their language.

1596 Z. I. tr. *J. de Lavardin's Hist. Scanderbeg, King of Albanie* ix. 381 The Albanian souldiers enclining to the peace which had bene so longe demanded. **1788** GIBBON *Decl. & F.* VII. lxviii. 466 In the Albanian war, he [*sc.* Mahomet II] studied the lessons.. of his father. **1813** *Q. Rev.* Oct. 283 The Hungarian and the Albanian languages have some traits of resemblance to each other. **1869** TOZER *Highl. Turkey* I. 186 The Mahometans are mostly Albanian. **1905** M. E. DURHAM *Burden of Balkans* x. 227 A young Albanian officer. **1920** —— in *Contemp. Rev.* Aug. 210 The long-forbidden Albanian language was printed.

B. *sb.* **1.** A native or inhabitant of this country.

1596 Z. I. tr. *J. de Lavardin's Hist. Scanderbeg, King of Albanie* x. 387 Mahomet.. might at this time haue bene beaten downe.. if Italy & the other Prouinces of Christendom would haue.. harkened to the.. admonitions of the Hungarians, the Greekes, and the Albanians. **1788** GIBBON *Decl. & F.* VI. lxvii. 457 Under his [*sc.* Scanderbeg's] conduct, the Albanians were invincible. **1813** *Q. Rev.* Oct. 284 The Albanians speak a language of which a considerable portion is Greek, Latin, German, Sclavonian or Turkish. **1920** *Contemp. Rev.* Aug. 210 Freed from Turkish prohibition,.. the cult of the national language became almost a religion to the Albanians.

2. The language of this people (the descendant of Ancient Illyrian).

1813 *Q. Rev.* Oct. 283 The Finnish is said to have some coincidence with the Greek, the Hungarian with the Finnish, and the Albanian with all its neighbours. **1905** M. E. DURHAM *Burden of Balkans* xii. 298 Books printed in Albanian by the Church press at Skodra. **1920** —— in *Contemp. Rev.* Aug. 210 Up till 1908 the foreign schools, where alone Albanian could be taught as a written language, had for political purposes frequently changed the spelling of their school books. *Ibid.* 212 He [*sc.* Essad Pasha] could only understand Turkish and Albanian.

Albanian (ælˈbeɪnɪən), *a.*[3] and *sb.*[3] *Hist.* [L. *Albānia.*] **A.** *adj.* Of or pertaining to the ancient province of Albania on the Caspian Sea.

1607 TOPSELL *Four-f. Beasts* 146 These Dogges growe to an exceeding greate stature, and the next vnto them are the Albanian Dogs. **1788** GIBBON *Decl. & F.* IV. xl. 110 The name of Caspian or Albanian gates, is properly applied to Derbend. **1853** *Encycl. Brit.* II. 444/1 The whole country, formerly called Albania, now goes under the names of Daghistan, Schirwan, and Leghistan... The ancient historians take notice of the Albanian men as tall, strong-bodied, and.. of a very graceful appearance. **1948** D. DIRINGER *Alphabet* II. v. 327 A potsherd from Old Ganja may contain an Albanian inscription.

B. *sb.* **1.** A native or inhabitant of this province.

1579 NORTH *Plutarch* 695 The Albanians lye towards the East, and Mare Caspium. **1781** GIBBON *Decl. & F.* II. xix. 153 The king of the Albanians, who led his independent tribes from the shores of the Caspian. **1948** D. DIRINGER *Alphabet* II. v. 327 Many ancient and modern savants dare to connect the Albanians of the Balkans with the Caucasian Albanians.

2. The language of this people.

1948 D. DIRINGER *Alphabet* II. v. 327 According to some scholars, Caucasian Albanian still survives in the Udi language.

albarello (ælbəˈrɛləʊ). Also **alberello.** [It. *alberello* pot, phial, app. dim. of *albero*, *albaro* (silver)-poplar, f. late L. *albarus* white poplar, f. L. *albus* white.] A Majolica jar used esp. as a container for drugs.

1873 C. D. E. FORTNUM *Maiolica* p. lxxv, The *albarello*.., or drug pot, universally known under that name, is made of different sizes and always of one piece. **1893** *Funk's Stand. Dict.*, Alberello. **1904** H. WALLIS (*title*) Italian Ceramic Art: The Albarello, a Study in early Renaissance Maiolica. **1925** B. RACKHAM in R. Fry et al. *Chinese Art* 17 The jar is no less pleasing. In shape it approaches the *albarello* of the Near East and Italy. **1950** *Ashmolean Mus. Dutch & Flemish Still-life Pictures* 173 A blue pottery *albarello* with foliage. **1959**

G. SAVAGE *Antique Coll. Handbk.* 71 It was also fashionable for pharmacies to be gaily decorated with painted drug-jars, the most popular being the tall, waisted jar known as the *albarello*, which was originally derived from Persia, by way of Moorish Spain.

albata (æl'beɪtə). [a. L. *albāt-a* fem. of *albāt-us* whitened, clothed in white.] A metallic composition imitating silver; white metal, German silver.

1848 *Bachel. Albany* 111 The argentine and the albata did their best to look silvery. **1861** SALA *Baddington Peer.* II. 232 He was not the genuine article, but a substitute, a kind of albata, or Sheffield plate.

†**al'bation.** *Obs.* [ad. med.L. *albātiōn-em*, n. of action f. *albāre* to whiten.]

1. A term used by the alchemists for the alleged process of whitening metals, especially of transmuting copper into silver; = ALBIFICATION.

1879 in *Syd. Soc. Lex.*

2. Dusting; ? *orig.* dusting with a white powder.

1612 WOODALL *Surg. Mate* Wks. 1653, 268 Albation is the abstraction of dust, moths, gret, adhering to a thing with an Hares foot, feather, spather, knife, or the like. **1658** PHILLIPS, *Albation* (chem.) a dusting with a hare's foot [not in ed. 1678].

albatross ('ælbətrɒs). Forms: 7 **algatross**, 7–8 **albi-**, 8 **albe-**, 8– **albatross**. [Apparently a modification of ALCATRAS, applied to the Frigate-bird, but extended through inaccurate knowledge to a still larger sea-fowl, and in this sense altered to *albi-*, *albe-*, *albatross* (perhaps with etymological reference to *albus* white, the albatross being white, while the *alcatras* was black). *Algatross* in 17th c. may be an intermediate form; *albatross* has not been found bef. 1769. The word has now passed into most of the mod. langs. (Du. *albatross*, G. *-tross*, *-tros*, Fr. *-tros*, It. *-tro*, Pg. *-troz*, Sp. *-troste*), but seems to have originated in Eng. (or ? Du.)]

†**1.** The Frigate-bird, = ALCATRAS 2. *Obs.*

1732 MORTIMER in *Phil. Trans.* XXXVII. 448 While the Albitrosse are setting and hatching their Young, their Heads change from Brown to Scarlet, and become Brown again afterwards. **1748** ANSON *Voy.* I. vi. (ed. 4) 76 Their bills are narrow, like that of an Albitross. **1753** CHAMBERS *Cycl. Supp.*, *Albitrosse*, the name of a large sea-bird, common about Jamaica, and in many other places. This is a thievish creature and principally feeds on the prey which another sea-bird, called the booby, provides for itself.

2. a. The English name of a family of birds allied to the Petrels (Order *Tubinares*), which inhabit the Pacific and Southern Oceans. The great Albatross, *Diomedea exulans*, to which the name is usually applied, is the largest of sea-fowls.

1681 GREW *Mus. Reg. Soc.* 73 The Head of the *Man of War*; called also *Albitrosse*. [Figured; clearly *Diomedea*.] **1697** DAMPIER *Voy.* an. 1691 (1703) I. 531 They [sailors] have several other signes, whereby to know when they are near it, by the sea-fowl they meet at sea, especially the Algatrosses, a very large long-winged fowl. **1698** FRYER *E. India & Persia* 12 Those feathered Harbingers of the Cape ..Albetrosses. **1719** SHELVOCKE *Voy.* in Harris I. 202 These were accompanied with Albitrosses, the largest sort of sea-fowls. **1768** (Dec. 24) COOK *Voy.* (1790) I. 30 We shot an albetross, which measured between the tips of its wings nine feet and an inch. **1769** (Jan. 26) *Ibid.*, The Albatrosses proved very good eating. **1798** COLERIDGE *Anc. Mar.* II. xiv, Instead of the cross, the albatross About my neck was hung. **1845** DARWIN *Voy. Nat.* viii. (1879) 162 It has always been a mystery to me on what the albatross..can subsist. **1865** LUBBOCK *Preh. Times* 367 Ear-rings made of albatross-down.

b. *fig.* [In allusion to Coleridge's *Ancient Mariner*: see sense 2a quot. 1798.] A source or mark of misfortune, guilt, etc., from which one cannot (easily) be free; a burden or encumbrance. Cf. MILLSTONE 3a.

1936 DYLAN THOMAS in *First Comment Treasury* (1937) 77 The old forget the grief, Hack of the cough, the hanging albatross. **1955** O. NASH in *McCall's* July 6/2 For when you're cross, Amanda, I feel an albatross Around my neck. **1963** *Times* 16 Feb. 9/7 The Director of Recruiting, with the albatross of '165,000' removed from about his neck, has already started to attack the problem of balance. **1973** M. AMIS *Rachel Papers* 11, I am a member of that sad, ever-dwindling minority..the child of an unbroken home. I have carried this albatross since the age of eleven. **1985** *Toronto Life* Sept. 41/2 He got rid of that albatross, the accumulated deficit.

3. *Golf.* A score of three under par on a hole; a hole played in three under par. Cf. EAGLE *sb.* 1d.

1937 *Evening News* 13 Aug. 14/5 Philip H. Savory, of Old Souls Manor Golf Club, Barnet, playing in a four-ball match for his club at Barnet, secured an albatross on the 13th, which is a 545-yards hole. **1965** *Times* 14 July 4/1, I may be excused for dwelling at length on one stroke, but it is seldom that one has the chance to write about an albatross which became the key to an historic round. **1975** H. COTTON *Golf* iv. 109 That 235-yard spoon shot had put him down in two—a double eagle (or albatross). **1983** *Times* 15 July 23 (*heading*) Rogers sets scene for runaway start at Royal Birkdale with an albatross.

albe, variant of ALB.

albe. [Anglicized form of ALBUM, in sense 1.] *Rom. Antiq.* A tablet on which anything is inscribed; a register.

1697 POTTER *Antiq. Greece* (1715) I. xxvi. 165 If any Debtor shall be blotted out of the Albe, or Register. **1807** ROBINSON *Archæol. Gr.* I. xxx. 114 If any debtor should be blotted out of the albe, or register, before he had discharged his debt.

†**al'be,** *conj. Obs.* or *arch.* Also **al be, allbe, all be.** [prop. a phrase *all be*, contr. for *all be it*, = *although it be* (*that*): see ALL *adv.* and ALBEIT.] Although it be that; although.

1. = ALBEIT 1.

c **1386** CHAUCER *Sqrs. T.* 97 Al be that I kan nat sowne his stile [*v.r.* al be it]. **1493** *Petronylla* (Pynson) 79 Albe that he excellyd in richesse He besy was to haue hir in mariage.

2. = ALBEIT 2.

c **1400** *Purific.* (Turnb. 1843) 128 Thou mekely com thyn offurryng in thyn hond All be the law sett on the no bond. *a* **1586** SIDNEY in Farr's *S.P.* I. 68 Allbe thousands here, Ten thousands there decay. **1603** B. JONSON *Sejanus* IV. v, Ay, but his fear Would ne'er be mask'd, allbe his vices were. **1825** SOUTHEY *Paraguay* IV. xix. Wks. VII. 83 And in their hearts, albe the work was rude, It raised the thought of all-commanding might.

3. = ALBEIT 3.

1596 SPENSER *To Beautie* 149 Oft it falles..That goodly Beautie, albe heavenly borne, Is foule abused.

albecore, obs. variant of ALBACORE.

†**albe'dene,** *adv. Obs.* 3–5. Also **al bidene, alle bidene, al bydene, albydene, all bedene.** [Really two words ALL BEDENE, i.e. 'all soon,' but so much used together that *all* preserved little of its force. Cf. *although*.] Forthwith, immediately.

a **1300** *Havelok* 730 And thrie, he gat it al bidene. *c* **1320** *Syr Bevis* 3685 And men told hem albedene How the geaunt Ascopard In a castel hire hadde to ward. **1330** R. BRUNNE *Chron.* 45 Lyndeseie he destroied quite alle bidene. *c* **1400** *Syr Percyv.* 2278 Grete lordes and the qwene Welcomed hym al-bydene. *c* **1450** *Erle of Tolous* 1211 Betwene them had they chyldyr fyftene Doghty Knyghtys all bedene.

†**albedi'neity.** *Obs.* [f. L. *albēdin-em* whiteness, as if on an adj. **albēdine-us*, + -ITY.]

1652 URQUHART *Jewel* Wks. 1834, 195 Hexeity, and albedineity..are words exploded by such as affect the purity of the Latine diction.

‖**albedo** (æl'biːdəʊ). [L. *albēdo* whiteness; f. *alb-um* white.] **1.** Whiteness; *spec.* in *Astr.* The proportion of the solar light incident upon an element of the surface of a planet, which is again diffusedly reflected from it. Hence in extended use, applied to the proportion of light reflected from various surfaces. Also *attrib.*

1859 *Monthly Not. R.A.S.* XX. 103. **1878** NEWCOMB *Pop. Astron.* 549 When the albedo of a body is said to be 0·6. **1879** *Syd. Soc. Lex.* s.v., Urinary conditions..were called the crystalline, the snowy, the limy, and the limpid albedo. **1936** *Brit. Jrnl. Psychol.* Jan. 313 Experiments on albedo perception. **1936** *Nature* 11 July 70/1 The albedo of different types of soil and vegetation. **1937** *Jrnl. R. Aeronaut. Soc.* XLI. 410 The albedo of clouds and the earth's surface.

2. A white structure, tissue, or material (Webster 1934); *spec.* the white pith of the inner peel of citrus fruits.

1949 J. B. S. BRAVERMAN *Citrus Products* iii. 77 Penetrating further into the peel of citrus fruit, one comes to the white, spongy, parenchymatous layer (mesocarp), generally known as the albedo.

3. *Nuclear Physics.* (See quots.)

1949 W. E. SIRI *Isotopic Tracers* v. 134 The effect of a reflector..is expressed in terms of its albedo γ, defined as the ratio of the number of neutrons that flow back in across the boundary to the number that flow out. **1962** *Gloss. Terms Nucl. Sci.* (*B.S.I.*) 8 *Albedo*, of a given object, the fraction of radiation (e.g. slow neutrons) reflected from it (Symbol: β).

albedony. 'Whiteness.' Cockeram 1626.

albeit (ɔːl'biːɪt), *conj.* [prop. a phrase *all be it* (*that*); in full, *all though it be that*. This is only a particular instance of *all* with a verb in subjunctive (see ALL *adv.* 10), in which the conjunctive phrase becomes a *quasi*-word. The nom. pron. *it* was also often dropped, whence the shorter *all be*, ALBE. Before the synthesis was complete, *all be it* had, in past tense, *all were it*.]

1. Even though it be (*that*); admitting (*that*).

c **1460** FORTESCUE *Abs. & Lim. Mon.* (1714) 30 Albeit that the Frenche Kyng's Revenuz be..miche gretter. **1603** KNOLLES *Hist. Turkes* (1621) 1150 Albeit that a great number of them were slain, yet fell they out againe. **1862** C. STRETTON *Chequered Life* I. 125 From that day to this we have never met—albeit that he has had my best wishes.

†**b.** *Pa. t.* Even though it were. *Obs.*

c **1374** CHAUCER *Boethius* (1868) 5 Al were it so þat sche was ful of so greet age.

2. *That* omitted: Even though it be that; even though, although, though.

c **1385** CHAUCER *Leg. G. Wom.* 1359, I may well leese a worde on yow, or letter, Albeit I shal be never the better. *c* **1420** *Chron. Vilod.* 530 He had gret fere, Albut þaw hit ner no nede. **1532** MORE *Confut. Tindale* Wks. 1557, 688/2 All bee it he coulde not saye naye. **1611** SHAKS. *Cymb.* II. iii. 61 A worthy Fellow, Albeit he comes on angry purpose now. **1805** SOUTHEY *Madoc in W.* I. Wks. V. 8, I shall live to see the day, Albeit the number of my years well nigh Be full. **1878** LEVER *Jack Hinton* xxvi. 184 Their voices, too, albeit the accent was provincial, were soft and musical.

3. In *contr. clause*: Even though, even if, although.

1795 SOUTHEY *Joan of Arc* I. 365 And I am well content to dwell in peace, Albeit inglorious. **1847** THACKERAY *Van. Fair* xix. (1879) I. 198 When a certain (albeit uncertain) morrow is in view. **1853** KANE *Grinnel Exp.* xxvii. (1856) 225 The sun, albeit from a lowly altitude, shone out in full brightness.

albercore, variant of ALBACORE.

alberge, obs. Fr. and Eng. form of AUBERGE.

albergo (æl'bɜːgəʊ). Pl. **alberghi.** Occas. anglicized **alberg.** [It.: cf. AUBERGE.] An inn (in Italy).

1617 MORYSON *Itin.* I. 154 Three houses like Colledges, called *Albergi*, for those that make long stay in the Citie. **1673** RAY *Journ. Low C.* 303 The *Alberghi* or Halls of the eight several Nations..of the Order. **1808** 'HELEN ST. VICTOR' *Ruins of Rigonda* I. 137 By your naming payment, I should suppose that you had mistaken my poor Cottage for an Albergo, some distance from this. **1889** 'F. PIGOT' *Strangest Journ.* 149, I was thus able..to rest at the country albergs. **1926** *Spectator* 20 Feb. 318/2 Ostia..consisted of a few forlorn houses, a modest *albergo*, and a wilderness of sand.

Albert ('ælbət). Also in full **Albert chain.** [named after Prince Albert, the Consort of Queen Victoria.] **1.** A kind of watch-chain.

1861 *Daily Rev.* (Edinburgh) 16 Dec. 4/5 (Advt.), Rings, Eardrops, Albert and Guard Chains. **1865** DICKENS *Let.* 22 Apr. (1880) II. 228 What's an Albert chain? **1883** *Daily News* 5 Feb. 3/4 Stealing..a silver watch and Albert chain. *Mod. Advt.* Lost, a gold albert with two seals. **1922** JOYCE *Ulysses* 431 Wearing gent's sterling silver waterbury keyless watch and double curb Albert with seal attached.

2. Albert Medal, a medal awarded since 1866 for 'gallantry in saving life at sea or on land'. Abbrev. A.M. (see A III).

1866 *Times* 16 June 7/4 The Queen has conferred the decoration of the Albert Medal on Samuel Popplestone. **1902** *Encycl. Brit.* XXXI. 340/1 The Albert Medal..consisting of two classes.

3. A size of writing paper.

1859 *Stationers' Hand-bk. & Guide Paper Trade* (ed. 2) II. 71 *Albert*, a fancy note paper, of any sort, $3\frac{7}{8}$ by 6 inches, produced from foolscap 8vo. **1876** *Stationer's Price & Cost Book* 3 *Albert Note*..is the 8vo of Fcap., $3\frac{7}{8}$ by 6 inches, and it may be had at any price, according to the quality of paper from which it is cut. *c* **1912** *Paper Terminol.* (*Spalding & Hodge*) II. 1 *Albert*, a standard size of note paper. *Ibid.* 18 Albert, about $3\frac{7}{8}\times 6$. **1954** *Ibid.* 11 *Albert*, a standard size of ..notepaper 6×4 in.

Alberti bass (æl'bɜːtɪ beɪs). *Mus.* [f. the name of Domenico *Alberti* (*c* 1710–1740), an Italian musician + BASS *sb.*[5]] A style of bass accompaniment consisting of broken chords or arpeggios.

1876 STAINER & BARRETT *Dict. Mus. Terms* 20/1. **1954** *Grove's Dict. Mus.* (ed. 5) 93/2 It is not very probable that he [Domenico Alberti] actually invented the 'Alberti Bass',.. but he certainly brought it into undue prominence in his sonatas. **1957** *Encycl. Brit.* I. 527/1 An extremely familiar, but nowadays little-esteemed, formula of arpeggio accompaniment..known as the Alberti bass.

albertite ('ælbətaɪt). *Min.* [f. *Albert* (county), New Brunswick + -ITE.] A jet-black bituminous mineral found in 1849 in New Brunswick, supposed to be the residue left on the drying up of a great body of petroleum.

1875 URE *Dict. Arts* I. 41 Albertite has been largely used in the United States for the distillation of oil and coke. **1881** *Echo* 23 July 1/6 The coal..resembles the Albertite found in New Brunswick.

'albert-type. [after name of the inventor.] A method of printing in ink from photographic plates; also, the picture thus produced.

1875 VOGEL *Light & Photog.* xv. 245 These Albert-types ..approach, but do not equal, the silver copies in beauty.

albescent (æl'bɛsənt), *a.* [ad. L. *albēscent-em* pr. pple of *albēsc-ĕre* to grow white; f. *alb-us* white.] Growing or becoming white; shading or passing into white.

1831 W. & M. HOWITT *Seasons* 306 The galaxy stretches its albescent glow athwart the northern sky. **1868** DARWIN *Var. An. & Plants* I. vi. 184 The croup being blue instead of snow-white; but the tint varies, being sometimes albescent.

albespyne, -ine ('ælbɪspaɪn). *arch.* [a. OFr. *albespine*, *aubespine* (mod. *aubépine*), Pr. *albespin*:—L. *alba spīna* white thorn.] Whitethorn, hawthorn.

1366 MAUNDEV. ii. (1839) 13 Braunches of Albespyne, that is White Thorn. **1881** F. T. PALGRAVE *Vis. Eng.* 79 A bower Of reedmace and rushes fine, Fenced with sharp albespyne.

†**albeston(e.** *Obs.* [a. OFr. *albeston*, variant of *abeston*, *asbeston*, a. L. *asbeston*, acc. of ASBESTOS, q.v. (OFr. has also *abestos*). *Albeston* is perhaps due to fanciful association with *alb-us* white; in

Eng. the termination was assimilated to *stone*, quasi 'white-stone.'] = ASBESTOS.

1398 TREVISA *Barth. De P.R.* XVI. xi. (1495) 558 Of albestone.. was made a candyll sticke, on whyche was a lantern so brennynge that it myght not be quenched wyth tempeste nother with reyne. **1567** MAPLET *Greene Forest* 2 Albeston.. being once set on fire, can neuer after be quenched.

† **albe'times**, *adv. phr. Obs.* = ALL BETIMES; see ALL *adv.*, and cf. *albedene*.

1634 *Malory's Arthur* (1816) II. 218 He that is my father shall be known openly, and albetimes.

Albian ('ælbɪən), *a.* and *sb. Geol.* [ad. Fr. *Albien* (1842, A. D'Orbigny, *Paléont. franç. terrains crétacés*), f. *Alba* (now *Aube*), a department of France + -IAN.] Epithet of a division of the Cretaceous formation in Europe (see quot. 1910); belonging to or found in this, as a fossil.

1847 in R. Chambers *Vestiges* (ed. 6) xii. 163 [citing translated statement of F. J. Pictet] Is it probable that the albian fauna had been completely annihilated, and then.. replaced by a fauna altogether new, and so similar to it? **1910** *Encycl. Brit.* I. 505/1 In England it is usual to regard the Albian stage as equivalent to the Upper Greensand *plus* Gault, that is, to the 'Selbornian' of Jukes-Browne.

albicant ('ælbɪkənt), *ppl. a.* [ad. L. *albicantem* pr. pple. of *albicā-re*: see ALBICATION.] Becoming or growing white.

1879 in *Syd. Soc. Lex.*

albication (ælbɪ'keɪʃən). [n. of action f. L. *albicāt-* ppl. stem of *albicā-re* to whiten, f. *alb-us* white.] The process of growing white; *esp.* The development of white or light patches, spots, streaks, bands, etc., in the foliage of plants, as in variegated hollies, sycamines, geraniums, grasses, etc.

1879 *Syd. Soc. Lex.* s.v., This anomaly is hereditary; a good example of it is afforded by the *Phalaris arundinacea*, which presents bands alternately of white and green. It is not yet certainly known whether albication is a pathological change or not.

albicore, variant of ALBACORE.

† **'albid**, *a. Obs. rare*[−1]. [ad. L. *albid-us* whitish, f. *alb-us* white; see -ID.] Whitish.

1657 TOMLINSON *Renou's Disp.* 264 Its flowers are albid.

† **albifi'cation**. *Obs.* [a. Fr. *albification*, ad. med.L. *albificātiōn-em*, n. of action f. *albificā-re*: see ALBIFY.] The process or art of making white. (Chiefly as a term in Alchemy.)

c **1386** CHAUCER *Chan. Yem. Prol. & T.* 252 Oure fourneys eek of calcinacioun, And of watres albificacioun. **1592** LILLY *Galathea* II. iii. 233 It is a very secret science, for none almost can understand the language of it [e.g.] .. *albification*. [Also in BAILEY (not in JOHNSON), TODD, and mod. Dicts.]

† **'albifi,cative**, *a. Obs.* [f. med.L. *albificāt-* ppl. stem of *albificā-re* (see ALBIFY) + -IVE.] Having the power or tendency to make white.

1471 RIPLEY *Comp. Alch.* (in Ashm. 1652) Pref. 128 Albyfycative shall be the Syxt [Gate of Alchemy].

albiflorous (ælbɪ'flɔːrəs), *a. Bot.* [f. mod.L. *albiflōr-us* (f. L. *alb-us* white + *flōr-* flower) + -OUS.] Having white flowers.

1879 in *Syd. Soc. Lex.*

† **'albify**, *v. Obs.* [ad. med.L. *albificāre*, f. *albus* white; see -FY.] To make white, to whiten.

1599 A. M. tr. *Gabelhouer's Bk. Physic* 73/2 It.. exemptteth all impuritye, and albifyeth the teeth. **1606** N. BRETON *Sidney's Ourania*, As a Red Bricke by water's Albified.

Albigenses (,ælbɪ'dʒensiːz), *sb. pl.* [med.L. (12th c.), f. *Albīga*, L. name of Albi, a city in south-west France.] The name of a sect of Catharist heretics of the south of France in the 12th and 13th centuries.

1625 PURCHAS *Pilgrims* II. VIII. vi. 1254 By exciting Princes and People to roote them out.. thus Innocent the third oppressed the Albigenses. **1646** [see TABORITE]. **1692** P. ALLIX (*title*) Remarks upon The Ecclesiastical History of the Antient Churches of the Albigenses. **1757** A. BUTLER *Lives of Saints* III. 397 The abominations of the heresy of the Albigenses. **1832** [in title below]. **1910** *Encycl. Brit.* I. 505/2.

Hence **Albi'gensian** *a.* and *sb.*, **Albi'gensic** *a.*

1604 R. PARSONS *Treat. Three Convers. Engl.* II. Ep. ded., Manie different sectaryes of opposite opinions,.. as Waldensians, Albigensians,.. Thaborits.. & Lutherans. **1828** G. S. FABER *Sacr. Cal. Prophecy* III. 28 The Albigensic church of the south of France. **1832** S. R. MAITLAND *Albigenses & Waldenses* 14 Fugitive Waldensians (not Albigensians) driven out of Lyons. *Ibid.* 17 Either the Albigensian, or Waldensian, sect. **1922** H. J. WARNER (*title*) The Albigensian Heresy.

albin(e ('ælbɪn). *Min.* [mod. f. L. *alb-us* white + -INE, min. form.] Name given by Werner (1817) to an opaque white variety of the mineral apophyllite found in Bohemia. Dana.

albines ('ælbɪnz), *sb. pl. Veg. Phys.* [mod. f. L. *alb-us* white + -INE.] Small colourless bodies found associated with aleuron grains.

1879 in *Syd. Soc. Lex.*

albiness ('ælbɪnɪs). [f. ALBIN-O + -ESS; cf. *negro*, *negress*.] A female albino.

1808 T. S. TRAILL *On Albinoes* in *Phil. Trans.* XIX. 85 Her mother's first child, a girl, is also an albiness.. the fifth, a boy, is an albino. **1852** *Cassell's Pop. Educ.* II. 76/2 If an Albino marry an Albiness, etc. **1858** HOLMES *Aut. Breakf. T.* (1865) 72 *Negative* or *washed* blondes, arrested by nature on the way to become albinesses.

albinism ('ælbɪnɪz(ə)m). [? a. mod.Fr. *albinisme*: see ALBINOISM.] The state or condition of being an albino.

1836 TODD *Cycl. Anat. & Phys.* I. 86/2 St. Hilaire.. supposes that there are two species of Albinism, one the effect of disease, the other a true anomaly. **1839** TIMBS *Year-Bk. of Facts* 174 Albinism in a Swallow. **1859** DARWIN *Orig. Spec.* i. (1873) 10 Every one must have heard of cases of albinism.. appearing in several members of the same family.

albinistic (ælbɪ'nɪstɪk), *a.* [f. ALBINISM: see -ISTIC.] Of, pertaining to, or affected with albinism.

1880 in WEBSTER *Suppl.* **1912** *Brit. Mus. Return* 115 Skull of an albinistic Pekinese Spaniel.

albino (æl'biːnəʊ, æl'baɪnəʊ). Pl. -os. [a. Sp. or Pg. *albino* (originally applied by the Portuguese to white negroes on the coast of Africa) an appellative f. *albo* white.] Used *attrib.* in all senses.

1. A human being distinguished by the congenital absence (partial or total) of colouring pigment in the skin, hair, and eyes, so that the former are abnormally white, and the latter of a pink colour, and unable to bear the ordinary light.

1777 ROBERTSON *Amer.* II. 69 The former are called Albinos by the Portuguese. **1808** (See under ALBINESS). **1819** *Pantologia* s.v., *Albinos*.. first noticed by the Portuguese as existing among African negroes. **1834** U.K.S. *Nat. Philos.* III. 62/1 The albino varieties in mankind. **1879** G. HARLAN *Eyesight* ii. 15 The eyes of albinos are pink.. from the red blood in the vessels of the choroid in which also pigment is absent.

2. By extension, Any animal having the same peculiarity, as white mice, rabbits, cats, elephants, etc.

1859 DARWIN *Orig. Spec.* v. 163 A white ass, but not an albino. **1865** TYLOR *E. Hist. Man.* x. 274 In Africa, the albino buffalo shares the sanctity of the elephant. **1874** COUES *Birds of N.-W.* 47 A curious partial albino, which had the plumage irregularly blotched with pure white.

3. Sometimes also said of plants in which no chlorophyll is developed in the leaves.

1879 *Syd. Soc. Lex.*, *Albino plants* may be obtained by causing them to germinate and grow in a damp place. No chlorophyll is formed and they are said to be etiolated.

albinoid ('ælbɪnɔɪd), *a.* [f. ALBINO + -OID.] Resembling an albino; having the appearance of an albino.

1965 P. WYLIE *They both were Naked* I. v. 232 A short, dumpy, and albinoid person. **1971** 'A. BURGESS' *MF* iv. 46 He was fair and pale, almost albinoid.

albinoism (æl'biːnəʊɪz(ə)m, -'baɪn-). [f. ALBINO + -ISM. Cf. *heroism*.] The state or condition of being an albino; = ALBINISM.

1868 CHAMBERS *Encycl.* I. 110 Albinoism is always born with the individual. **1881** J. G. WOOD in *Sund. Mag.* Feb. 126 Birds are very subject to albinoism.

albinotic (ælbɪ'nɒtɪk), *a.* [f. ALBINO + -OTIC.] Of, pertaining to, or affected with albinism: = ALBINISTIC *a.*

1872 COUES *N. Amer. Birds* 237 Albinotic or melanotic, and other abnormally colored specimens.

Albion ('ælbɪən). *poet.* or *rhet.* [OE. *Albion*, f. L. *Albion*, *-ōnis* (Pliny), Gr. Ἀλουίων (Ptolemy):—Celtic **Albio*, gen. **Albionis*, whence Ir.-Gael. *Alba*, gen. *Alban* Scotland (cf. med.L. *Albania*: see ALBANIAN *a.*[1]); usu. referred to **albho-* (L. *albus*) white, the allusion being to the white cliffs of Britain.] Great Britain. Phr. ***perfidious Albion***, rendering F. *la perfide Albion*, a rhetorical expression for 'England', with reference to her alleged treacherous policy towards foreigners.

The phr. 'la perfide Albion' is said to have been first used by the Marquis de Ximenès (1726–1817) (*N. & Q.* (1932) CLXII. 107/2).

c **900** tr. *Bæda's Hist.* (1890) I. i. 24 Breoton is garsecges ealond, ðæt wæs iu geara Albion haten. *c* **1205** *Layamon's Brut* (1847) 1243 Albion hatte þat lond. **1387** TREVISA *Higden* (Rolls) II. 5 Firste þis ilond hiȝte Albion, as it were þe white lond. *c* **1399** CHAUCER *Purse* l. 22 in *Wks.* (1894) I. 406 O conquerour of Brutes Albioun. *a* **1592** GREENE *Fr. Bacon* (1594) sig. E2ᵛ, As if that Edward gaue me Englands right, And richt me with the Albion diadem. **1593** SHAKES. *2 Hen. VI* I. iii. 48 Is this the Gouernment of Britaines Ile? And this the Royaltie of Albions King? **1605** —— *Lear* III. ii. 91 Then shal the Realme of Albion, come to great confusion. [**1653** J. BOSSUET *Œuvres* (1816) XI. 469 L'Angleterre, ah! la perfide Angleterre, que le rempart de ses mers rendoit inaccessible aux Romains.] **1713** POPE *Windsor-For.* 5 When Albion sends her eager Sons to War. **1757** GRAY *Progr. Poesy* II. st. iii in *Odes* 9 When Latium had her lofty spirit lost, They sought, oh Albion! next thy sea-encircled coast. **1841** W. M. THACKERAY in *Fraser's Mag.* June 711/2 Ferocious yells of hatred against perfidious Albion were uttered by the liberal French press. [**1846** R. FORD *Gatherings fr. Spain* iv. 37 If there be a thing which '*La perfide Albion*', 'a nation of shopkeepers', dislikes,.. it is a bankrupt.] **1850** WORDSW. *Prel.* (1926) x. 239 Since I had seen the surge Beat against Albion's shore. **1903** A. MCNEILL *Egregious English* 11 The French dislike of perfidious Albion may be reckoned to a great extent an intermittent matter. **1941** H. G. WELLS *You can't be too Careful* III. viii. 146 There I was—a lovely crossing—saying Adieu to the white cliffs of Albion. **1958** *Observer* 18 May 9/4 He [*sc.* General de Gaulle] felt it to be essential.. that he should maintain a proud and haughty demeanour towards 'perfidious Albion'.

albite ('ælbaɪt). *Min.* [mod. f. (by Gahn and Berzelius 1814) L. *alb-us* white + -ITE, min. form.]

1. a. A feldspathic mineral, usually white, differing from common feldspar in containing soda instead of potash; white or soda feldspar.

1843 HUMBLE *Dict. Geol.*, *Albite*.. forms a constituent part of the greenstone rocks in the neighbourhood of Edinburgh. **1879** RUTLEY *Rocks* x. 88 The species albite and anorthite are isomorphous.

b. *Comb.* **albite-felsite**, a variety of albite; **albite porphyry**, a porphyry containing crystals of albite. Hence **albiti'zation** (see quot. 1940).

1909 *Geol. Mag.* VI. 250 (*title*) Albitization of Basic Plagioclase Felspars. **1940** *Chambers's Techn. Dict.* 20/2 *Albitisation*, in igneous rocks, the process by which a soda-lime feldspar (plagioclase) is replaced by albite (soda-feldspar). **1959** J. J. REED in G. J. Williams *Econ. Geol. N.Z.* (1965) x. 156/2 The hardness of the argillites is due largely to albitization.

albitic (æl'bɪtɪk), *a. Min.* [f. prec. + -IC.] Of the nature of, or containing, albite.

1837–80 DANA *Min.* 352 Veins of albitic granite are often repositories of the rarer granite minerals.

albitite ('ælbɪtaɪt). *Min.* [f. ALBIT(E + -ITE.[1]] A form of albite (see quot. 1940). Hence **albi'titic** *a.*

1896 H. W. TURNER in *Amer. Geologist* XVII. 380 Some of these dikes are composed of coarsely granular albite only. Such a rock may be called an albitite. **1940** *Chambers's Techn. Dict.* 20/2 *Albitite*, a rare type of soda-syenite consisting almost entirely of albite, with a small content of coloured silicates. **1955** BROWN & DEY *India's Min. Wealth* (ed. 3) xvii. 636 Intermediate in composition are the albititic jadeitites which grade into the albitites—granulitic rocks composed almost exclusively of untwinned albite.

alblast, -er, obs. forms of ARBALEST, -ER.

albocore, obs. variant of ALBACORE.

albocracy (æl'bɒkrəsɪ). *rare*[−1]. [f. L. *alb-us* white + -*(o)cracy*, ad. Gr. -(ο)κρατία government.] Government by 'white' men or Europeans.

1880 CUST *Ling. Ess.* 303 The same albocracy, so striking in British India, flourished famously under the Ptolemies.

albolith ('ælbəlɪθ). [f. L. *alb-us* white + Gr. λίθος stone.] A name given to a white cement prepared from magnesia and silica.

1875 in URE *Dict. Arts.*

† **albonie**. *Obs.* [= *All-bony*.] = ALL-BONE.

1597 GERARD *Herbal* 43.

‖ **albo'rak**. *Obs.* [Arab. *al-burāq* the splendid, lightning-flashing, f. *baraqa* to flash, lighten.] The white steed on which Mohammed was said to have been carried up to heaven; a white mule.

1635 SWAN *Spec. Mund.* (1670) 410 The Alborach is a fair white beast like an ass, frequent in the Turkish Territories. **1847** CRAIG, *Al Borak*.

alborne, obs. form of AUBURN.

albuginean (ælbjuː'dʒɪniːən), *a.* [f. mod.L. *albūgine-us* (see next) + -AN.] Of or resembling the white fibrous tissue of the eye and of the testicle.

1836 TODD *Cycl. Anat. & Phys.* I. 354/1 Invested with a strong and dense albuginean tunic.

albugineous (ælbjuː'dʒɪniːəs), *a.* [f. mod.L. *albūgine-us* (f. *albūgin-em*, see *albūgo*) + -OUS.] **a.** = ALBUGINEAN. **b.** Of the nature of the white of an egg, albuminous.

1543 TRAHERON tr. *Vigo's Chirurg.* (1586) 430 Albugineus is that, yᵗ pertaineth to the white of the eye. **1664** POWER *Exp. Philos.* I. 60 You shall observe in perfect Sanguineous Animals a circulation of an albugineous chylic-matter before the bloud have a being. **1836–39** TODD *Cycl. Anat. & Phys.* II. 263/2 An elementary organic solid, called by him the albugineous fibre.

† **al'buginous**, *a. Obs. rare*[−1]. [ad. Fr. *albugineux* (f. as if:—L. **albūginōs-us*): see ALBUGO and -OUS.] Of the white of an egg; albuminous.

1646 SIR T. BROWNE *Pseud. Epid.* 50 Egges I observe will freeze, in the generative and albuginous part thereof.

†**al'buginousness.** *Obs.* [f. prec. + -NESS.] Albuminousness, albumen, white of an egg.
1599 A. M. tr. *Gabelhouer's Bk. Physic* 48/1 Take..the albuginousnes of a nue layed Egge.

‖**albugo** (æl'bju:gəʊ). [L. *albūgo, -gin-*, whiteness, also a disease of the eye (*oculorum albūgines* Pliny), f. *albus* white.]
1. A disease of the eye, in which a white opaque spot forms upon the transparent cornea.
1398 TREVISA *Barth. De P.R.* VII. xvi. (1495) 234 Another euyll of the eyen we calle a webbe and Constantin calleth it Albugo. **1633** T. ADAMS *Exp. 2 Pet.* iii. 18 [Pride] is like the albugo, or white spot in the eye, which dimmeth our understanding. **1704** *Lond. Gaz.* mmmmix/4 Ungula's, Albugo's..and all other Distempers relating to the Eyes. **1853** MAYNE *Exp. Lex.*, *Albugo*, a white opacity of the cornea.
†**2.** The white of an egg; albumen. *Obs.*
1706 PHILLIPS, *Albugo*..Also the white of an Egg.

album[1] ('ælbəm). Pl. **albums.** [a. L. *album* a blank tablet for entries, subst. use of neut. sing. of adj. *alb-us* white. At first used in Eng. professedly as a Latin word, and so inflected: see *in albo* below, as we say *in toto*.]
1. *Rom. Antiq.* A tablet on which the prætor's edicts and other public notices were recorded for public information; afterwards extended to other lists.
1753 CHAMBERS *Cycl. Supp.* s.v., The high-priest entered the chief transactions of each year into an *album*, or table, which was hung up in his house for the public use. **1868** SMITH *Dict. Antiq.* s.v., The album was so called because it was either a white material, or a material whitened.
2. A blank book in which to insert autographs, memorial verses, original drawings, or other souvenirs. According to Johnson 'a book in which foreigners have long been accustomed to insert the autographs of celebrated people.'
1651 *Reliq. Wotton* (1672) 30 Was requested by Christopher Flecamore to write some sentence in his *Albo*. *Ibid.* 69 In his Album of Friends after the German custome. **1652** BENLOWE *Theoph.*, Who in Loves *Albo* are enrol'd Unutterable Joyes behold. **1757** CHESTERF. *Lett.* 319. IV. 87, I do not mean a German album, stuffed with people's names and Latin sentences. **1848** THACKERAY *Van. F.* lxiii. (1853) 533 Grignac..made caricatures of Tapeworm in all the Albums of the place.
3. 'A book at public places in which visitors enter their names.' Webster. (This in England is called a *Visitors' Book*.)
1775 W. MASON *Gray* (JOD.) I remember..to have seen at the convent of the Grande Chartreuse an album of this fashion; and was invited to insert my name in it, as a foreigner. **1822** J. FLINT *Lett. fr. Amer.* 294 In the album kept at one of these [taverns]..a hundred folio pages had been written with names within five months.
4. A book for reception of photographic cartes and views, or of postage-stamps, crests, or other things which are collected and preserved; a scrap-book. Also *attrib.*
1859 *All Y. Round* No. 30. 79 An album full of photographs. **1878** *Paper & Print. Jrnl.* xxv. 11 A still greater novelty is an album containing twenty-four Welsh costumes. **1936** C. J. WEST *Bibliog. Pulp & Paper Making* 612 Changes in the composition of thick album paper and oiled paper. **1937** E. J. LABARRE *Dict. Paper* 97/1 Album papers and boards are cover papers, or double thick pasted board..intended for photographic albums.
5. *attrib.*, passing into *adj.* Applied to verses of a sort or quality suitable for inclusion in an album (often with disparaging implication).
1918 V. WOOLF *Writer's Diary* 7 Aug. (1953) 3 I'm much impressed by the extreme badness of B's [Byron's] poetry. .. Why did they think this album stuff the finest fire of poetry? **1953** C. DAY LEWIS in *Proc. Brit. Acad.* XXXVII. 163 Album verse that ranges between the inept and the perfunctory.
6. A long-playing gramophone record or a set of such records.
1957 *Gramophone* Apr. 427/2 That he was too little appreciated in his lifetime makes this memorial album (another record is to follow) even more..important. **1963** *Oxford Mail* 28 Jan. 6/6 Many jazz album covers have little connection with the contents. **1967** *Times* 16 Dec. (Advt.), A four record album with illustrated colour brochure.

‖**'album**[2]. *Obs.* [L. *album* white.]
1. *Path.* Leucorrhea.
1527 L. ANDREW tr. *Brunswyke's Distyll. Waters* G v, Good agaynst that Album or whyte in women.
2. Rent paid in white money or silver.
1691 BLOUNT *Law Dict.*, *Album*, used for white Rent, or Rent paid in Silver. **1775** ASH, *Album* (in old records) Rent paid in silver.

albumean, *a.* Of or relating to albums.
1829 LAMB *Lett.* xvii. 156, I have fled hither to escape the albumean persecution.

albumen (æl'bju:mɪn). [a. L. *albūmen* (*albumin-*) white of an egg, f. *albus* white.]
1. The white of an egg.
1599 A. M. tr. *Gabelhouer's Bk. Physic* 52/1 Take..the Albumen of 4 Egges. **1753** CHAMBERS *Cycl. Supp.* s.v., There is most albumen in the obtuse end of an egg. **1869** HUXLEY in *Fortn. Rev.* Feb. 135 The white or albumen of an egg.
2. The substance which exists nearly pure in the white of an egg, and forms a constituent of animal solids and fluids, and of the tuberous or fleshy roots, and seeds of plants. See ALBUMIN.
1800 HENRY *Epit. Chem.* (1808) 304 The white of an egg affords a good example of animal albumen. **1822** IMISON *Sci. & Art* II. 138 Albumen is the principle constituent of the serum of blood. **1858** CARPENTER *Veg. Phys.* §32 These compounds,..gluten, fibrin, albumen, caseine, etc., form the basis of all vegetable and animal tissues.
3. *Bot.* The substance interposed between the skin and embryo of many seeds, of which it usually constitutes the eatable part. It varies greatly in consistency and amount, and is sometimes entirely wanting.
1677 GREW *Anat. Plants* IV. iii. §9 The *Albumen* or clear Liquor out of which they are bred. **1830** LINDLEY *Nat. Syst. Bot.* Introd. 32 The substance which surrounds the embryo is called the Albumen. **1857** HENFREY *Elem. Bot.* §298 The body of the seed is composed either of the embryo alone, or of the embryo imbedded in a mass of tissue, called the endosperm, perisperm, or albumen.
4. *attrib.* Designating a photographic paper or plate coated with albumen; also denoting a process using such a paper or plate.
1856 R. HOWLETT *Methods Printing Photogr. Pict.* 7 The Albumen Process. The most simple process for obtaining positive prints is that upon albumenized paper. **1867** SUTTON & DAWSON *Dict. Photogr.* 126 This consists in subjecting sensitised albumen-paper to the fumes of ammonia. **1889** *Internat. Ann. Anthony's Photogr. Bull.* II. 403 The albumen paper asserts its old place in the photographic galleries. *Ibid.*, The clearness..of the albumen pictures.

albumenize (æl'bju:mɪnaɪz), *v.* Also **-min-**. [f. ALBUMEN + -IZE.] To cover or impregnate with albumen; in photography, to coat paper with an albuminous solution. (Usually in pa. pple.)

albumenized (æl'bju:mɪnaɪzd), *ppl. a.* [f. prec. + -ED.] Coated with albumen.
1853 R. HUNT *Man. Photog.* 278 A sheet of positive albuminized paper. **1868** *Q. Rev.* No. 248, 354 The production of albumenized paper for the purposes of the photographer consumes a large number of the whites of fresh eggs.

albumenizer (æl'bju:mɪnaɪzə(r)). [f. as prec. + -ER[1].] One who albumenizes.
1879 *Daily Tel.* 25 Oct. (*Advt.*) Albumenizers.—The Imperial Company have vacancies for several first-class hands.

albumenizing (æl'bju:mɪnaɪzɪŋ), *vbl. sb.* [f. as prec. + -ING[1].] Coating with albumen.
1853 *N. & Q.* Ser. I. VIII. 396 That is coated again with the albumenizing mixture. **1869** *Eng. Mech.* 15 Oct. 102/2 I give the recipes for albumenising.

albumess. A female keeper of an album.
1829 LAMB *Lett.* II. (1841) 65 My albumess will be catechised on this subject.

albumin (æl'bju:mɪn). *Chem.* [a. mod.Fr. *albumine*, f. L. *albūmin-* stem form of ALBUMEN.]
One of the classes of ALBUMINOIDS, containing such as are soluble in water (= ALBUMEN 2), or in dilute acids or alkalis (*acid* or *alkali albumins*.)
1869 ROSCOE *Chem.* 434 Albumin is seen in one of its purest forms in the white of egg. **1879** *Syd. Soc. Lex.* s.v., By some it is believed that ovum-albumin is a compound of several forms of albumin. **1881** *Nature* No. 615. 352 The derived albumins noted as acid-albumins.

albuminate (ælbju:mɪneɪt). [f. L. *albūmin-* (see ALBUMEN) + -ATE[4].] The combination of albumin with certain bases, in which the albumin acts as a very feeble acid.
1859 LEWES *Phys. Com. Life* I. ii. 90 Schmidt's researches prove fat to be less easily combustible in the organism than the carbo-hydrates, and even than albuminates. **1863** WATTS *Chem. Dict.* (1879) I. 69 Albuminate of Soda is contained in blood-serum.

albuminated (ælbju:mɪneɪtɪd), *ppl. a.* [f. as prec. + -ATE[3] + -ED.] = ALBUMENIZED.
1879 in *Syd. Soc. Lex.*

albuminiferous (æl,bju:mɪ'nɪfərəs), *a.* [f. as prec. + -(I)FEROUS.] Producing or supplying albumen.
1859 TODD *Cycl. Anat. & Phys.* V. 66/1 The albuminiferous part of the oviduct.

albuminimeter (æl,bju:mɪ'nɪmɪtə(r)). [f. as prec. + -(I)METER.] A polarizing apparatus for measuring the amount of albumen in a liquid.
1879 in *Syd. Soc. Lex.*

albuminin (æl'bju:mɪnɪn). [a. Fr. *albuminine*; see ALBUMIN and -IN.] Couerbe's name for the substance of the cells which enclose the white of birds' eggs.
1863 in WATTS *Chem. Dict.*

albuminiparous (æl,bju:mɪ'nɪpərəs), *a.* [f. L. *albūmin-* (see ALBUMEN) + *-par-us* bearing + -OUS: see -(I)PAROUS.] Producing albumen.
1855 OWEN *Invert. An.* 561 Both invaginated tubes enter the albuminiparous sac.

albuminization (æl,bju:mɪnaɪ'zeɪʃən). *Biol.* [f. next + -ATION.] (See quot.)
1843 T. ADDISON in *Guy's Hosp. Rep.* Ser. II. I. ii. 370 This re-conversion of a tissue into albumen I would express by the term albuminization.

albuminize (æl'bju:mɪnaɪz), *v. Biol. rare*[−0]. [f. L. *albūmin-* (see ALBUMEN) + -IZE.] To convert into albumin.

albumino- (æl'bju:mɪnəʊ), combining adverbial and adjectival form of ALBUMEN; cf. *acuto-*.
1. *adv.* Albuminously, as in **albumino-fibrous.**
1836 TODD *Cycl. Anat. & Phys.* I. 60/2 Albumino-gelatinous tissues. **1878** BRYANT *Pract. Surg.* I. 83 An albumino-fibrous material.
2. *adj.* Albuminous, as in **albumino-chloride.**
1849-52 TODD *Cycl. Anat. & Phys.* IV. 1155/2 The white aphthous mass..albumino-fibrin. **1869** *Eng. Mech.* 28 May 229/3 The albumino-choride of silver.

albuminoid (æl'bju:mɪnɔɪd), *a.* and *sb.* [f. L. *albūmin-* (see ALBUMEN) + -OID.] Not in Craig 1847.
A. *adj.* Like or resembling albumen; of the same character as albumen.
1859 LEWES *Phys. Com. Life* I. ii. 128 These four albuminoid substances, namely albumen, fibrine, caseine, and gluten. **1869** HUXLEY in *Fortn. Rev.* Feb. 135 All living matter is more or less albuminoid.
B. *sb.* in *pl.* = *Albuminoid Principles*: A class of organic compounds (also called *Proteids*), which form the chief part of the organs and tissues of animals and plants; they are composed of carbon, oxygen, nitrogen, hydrogen, and a little sulphur, and are divided into *Albumins, Globulins, Fibrins, Derived Albumins, Coagulated Proteids, Peptones*, and *Amyloids*.
1873 BALF. STEWART *Conserv. Force* vii. 177 The plastic matters of which vegetable structure is built are of two kinds, amyloids and albuminoids. **1876** M. FOSTER *Phys.* (1879) 647 Proteids..are frequently spoken of as albuminoids.

albuminoidal (æl,bju:mɪ'nɔɪdəl), *a.* [f. prec. + -AL[1].] Of the nature of an albuminoid.
1864 *Reader* No. 86. 239/2 A new albuminoidal substance.

albuminone (æl'bju:mɪnəʊn). *Chem.* [f. ALBUMIN + -ONE.] (See quot.)
1878 KINGZETT *Anim. Chem.* 71 Albuminoids being converted into albuminones, or substances soluble in alcohol and not coagulable by heat.

albuminose (æl,bju:mɪ'nəʊs), *a.* and *sb.* [ad. mod.L. *albūminōs-us*: see ALBUMEN and -OSE.]
A. *adj.* = ALBUMINOUS.
a **1859** WORCESTER cites SMITH. **1880** GRAY *Bot. Text-bk.* 395 *Albuminose*, said of seeds provided with albumen.
B. *sb.* A crystalloid substance derived from albumen by the action of pepsin in weak acid solutions.
1847-9 TODD *Cycl. Anat. & Phys.* IV. 163-2 Bonchardat obtained a substance by digesting moist fibrin in water.. which he called albuminose.

‖**albuminosis** (æl,bju:mɪ'nəʊsɪs). *Path.* [f. L. *albumin-* (see ALBUMEN) + -OSIS, formative of names of diseases.] A condition of the blood in which the proportion of albumen is increased.
1879 in *Syd. Soc. Lex.*

albuminous (æl'bju:mɪnəs), *a.* [f. as prec. + -OUS; cf. Fr. *albumineux*.]
1. Of the nature or character of albumen or albumin; having the same composition as the white of an egg.
1791 NICHOLSON *Chem.* 514 The albuminous part, or serum, coagulates. **1879** C. CAMERON in *Cassell's Techn. Educ.* IV. 368/1 In the case of young animals, a diet rich in albuminous substances is necessary.
2. *Bot.* Containing a store of albumen in the seed: see ALBUMEN 3.
1830 LINDLEY *Nat. Syst. Bot.* 57 Albuminous solitary pendulous seeds. **1842** GRAY *Struct. Bot.* ii. (1880) 14 Seeds are distinguished into albuminous and exalbuminous, those supplied with and those destitute of albumen.
3. *fig.* Insipid.
1865 CARLYLE *Fredk. Gt.* III. IX. i. 65 Nothing but a kind of albuminous simplicity noticeable in them; no wit, originality, brightness in the way of uttered intellect.

albuminousness (æl'bju:mɪnəsnɪs). [f. prec. + -NESS.] The state of being albuminous.
1864 in WEBSTER.

‖**albuminuria** (æl,bju:mɪ'njʊərɪə). *Path.* [f. L. *albūmin-* + Gr. οὖρ-ον urine.] The presence of albumen in the urine. Hence **albumi'nuric** *a.*
1842 DUNGLISON *Dict. Med. Sci.* (ed. 3) 30/1 *Albuminuria*, the condition of the urine in which it contains albumen. **1854** JONES & SIEV. *Path. Anat.* 607 We regard albuminuria ..only as an indication that the kidney is the seat of a passive hyperæmia. **1876** tr. *Wagner's Gen. Path.* 538 Albuminuria, the escape of albumen through the kidney. **1879** *St. George's Hosp. Rep.* IX. 500 One male, aged 40, was the subject of long-standing albuminuric disease. **1908** *Practitioner* Jan. 15 Examination of the fundus, revealing albuminuric retinitis.

albumose (ˈælbjuːməʊs). *Chem.* [f. ALBUM(IN + -OSE[2].] An intermediate digestion-product of albuminous matter, passing into peptone; a species of proteose.

1884 *Jrnl. Chem. Soc.* XLVI. 1389 A new method of preparation..whereby four different forms of albumose are separated. **1889** G. M'GOWAN tr. *Bernthsen's Org. Chem.* 516 Albuminous matters undergo change when acted upon by the juices of the stomach at a temperature of 30–40°, pepsin converting them in the first instance into Anti- and Hemi-albumoses, both of which then go into peptone; trypsin likewise gives rise to the two above albumoses. **1891** [see PTOMAÏNE]. **1946** *Nature* 20 July 87/1 The albumoses and allied compounds, constituting about 14 per cent of the material [*sc.* meat extract], although supplying first-class protein, are of small quantitative significance in the diet.

alburn, obs. form of AUBURN.

alburn (ˈælbɜːn).

1. = ALBURNUM [of which it is an Eng. ad.].

2. A fish; the Bleak [in L. *alburnus* on account of its silvery white appearance].

1753 CHAMBERS *Cycl. Supp.*, *Alburnus.* [*Alburn* in mod. Dicts.]

alburnous (ælˈbɜːnəs), *a.* [f. ALBURN-UM + -OUS.] Of, or of the nature of, alburnum.

1803 KNIGHT in *Phil. Trans.* XCIII. 289 Between the cortical and alburnous substances. **1814** SIR H. DAVY *Agric. Chem.* 72 In bulbous roots, the alburnous substance forms the largest part of the vegetable.

alburnum (ælˈbɜːnəm). [a. L. *alburnum*, f. *albus* white.] The whiter, softer, and more recently formed wood in exogenous trees, between the bark and heart-wood; the sap-wood.

1664 EVELYN *Silva* (1776) 524 That whiter, softer, fatty part called by the antients *Alburnum.* **1791** E. DARWIN *Bot. Gard.* I. 96 Sap-wood or alburnum. **1809** *Nat. Hist.* in *Ann. Reg.* 793/1 The buds of trees invariably spring from their Alburnum. **1872** MACMILLAN *True Vine* iii. 121 The branch, in its most vital part, must come into closest contact with the vine in its most vital part,..the two alburnums and the two libers.

†**alˈbysi, alˈbyssi**, *adv.* *Obs.* [f. ALL in a concessive sense, although, even though (cf. ALBEIT) + BUSY, earlier *bysi.* Lit. *even though busy, even though with trouble or pains*, hence *with difficulty, hardly.* Cf. Fr. *à peine.*] Hardly, scarcely, barely.

1297 R. GLOUC. 81 Ac albysi were yt ten ȝer, ar heo here aȝeyn were. *c* **1425** *Seven Sag.* (P.) 1559 'Sire,' quod the stiwarde anoon, 'Al byssi schal I fynde oon.'

alcade, var. ALCALDE; and erron. f. ALCAYDE.

alcahest, variant of ALKAHEST.

alcaic (ælˈkeɪɪk), *a.* and *sb.* Also 7 alch-. [ad. L. *alcaic-us*, a. Gr. ἀλκαικ-ός; f. Ἀλκαῖ-ος prop. name of a lyric poet of Mytilene about 600 B.C.]

A. *adj.* Of or pertaining to Alcæus, or pertaining to the kind of verse invented by him.

a **1637** B. JONSON *To Himself* (J.) Leave things so prostitute And take th' Alcaick lute. **1753** CHAMBERS *Cycl. Supp.* s.v., The Alcaic Ode consists of four strophes, each of which contains four verses. **1878** *N. Amer. Rev.* CXXVII. 379 The Alcaic and Sapphic metres.

B. *sb.* in *pl.* Alcaic strophes.

1630 J. TAYLOR (Water P.) *Wks.* II. 161/1 If a Poet should examine thee Of Numbers, Figures, Trimeters, Alchaicks. **1793** SOUTHEY *Nondescr.* i. Wks. III. 57 In sapphics sweetly incensed; glorified In proud alcaics. **1863** KINGLAKE *Crimea* (1876) I. viii. 118 Smooth Eton Alcaics.

alcaid, variant of ALCAYDE.

‖**alcalde** (alˈkalde). Also **alcade.** [Sp., ad. Arab. *al-qāḍī* the judge, f. *qaḍa(y* to judge. The same word as a Turkish title is englished CADI. Sometimes in Fr. form *alcade.*] A magistrate of a town, a sheriff or justice, in Spain and Portugal.

1615 BEDWELL *Arab. Trudg.*, *Kadi* or *Alkadi*..signifieth also a Iudge. **1666** *Lond. Gaz.* lxi/2 The Alcalde sent an Alguazil..to the Admiral. **1842** LONGF. *Sp. St.* iii. 2 Why that was Pedro Crespo, the alcalde! **1861** MOTLEY *Dutch Rep.* II. 263 A requisitory letter to the alcades, corregidors, and other judges of Castille.

alcali, etc., obs. variant of ALKALI, etc.

alcamist, -my(e, obs. ff. ALCHEMIST, -MY.

†**ˈalcamyn(e.** *Obs.* 5–6. Also **alkmuyne, alcumyn(e.** [f. *alcamy*, early form of ALCHEMY + -INE[2].] = ALCHEMY 3.

1432–50 tr. *Higden* Rolls Ser. VI. 41 An ydole of auricalke or alkmuyne. **1440** *Promp. Parv.* Alkamye metalle (**1499** alcamyn) *Alkamia.* *a* **1529** SKELTON *Why come ye nat* 904 To copper, to tyn, To lede, or alcumyn. **1557** N. T. (Genev.) *Rev.* i. 15 His fete lyke vnto fyne brasse [*marg.* or alcumyne].

alcanamy, obs. form of ALCHEMY.

alcanet, obs. variant of ALKANET.

‖**alˈcanna, alˈcana.** *Bot.* [a. Sp. *alcana, alcaña*, a. Arab. *al-hennā*, name of the shrub. See also HENNA and ALKANET.] The oriental shrub, Egyptian Privet (*Lawsonia inermis*, N.O. *Lythraceæ*), or its leaves and young shoots, used by eastern nations to dye parts of the body reddish orange; henna.

1625 HART *Anat. Ur.* II. v. 81 If any annoint his bodie with the iuyce of the berries of the hearbe *Halcana.* **1646** SIR T. BROWNE *Pseud. Epid.* 383 Alcanna being greene, will suddenly infect the nailes and other parts with a durable red. **1753** CHAMBERS *Cycl. Supp.* s.v., From the berries of alcana an oil is extracted of a very agreeable smell.

¶ *Alkanna* is in mod. Botany the generic name of the Alkanet (formerly *Anchusa tinctoria*).

alcapton, alcaptonuria: see ALKAPTON.

alcargen, alcarsin: see ALK-.

‖**alcarraza** (ælkəˈrɑːzə, Sp. alkəˈrɑːθə). [Sp., ad. Arab. *al-kurrāz* = *al* the + *kurrāz* pitcher.] A porous earthenware vessel used for cooling water by evaporation.

1818 *Encycl. Brit. Suppl.* III. 257 The Moors introduced into Spain a sort of unglazed earthen jugs named.. *alcarrazas.* **1871** BALF. STEWART *Heat* §118 In hot climates porous vessels called Alcarazas are used for cooling water.

†**ˈalcatote.** *Obs. rare.* [Orig. unkn. Occurs as *alkitotle* in the *Exmoor Courtship*, Devonsh. dial., in the glossary to which it is suggested to be connected with *elk*, older Eng. *alce*, said to be 'subject to fits of epilepsy'; the L. *alca* an auk, a stupid bird, may also be suggested; the second part perhaps = *toti* giddy; as if giddy elk or giddy auk.] 'A silly elf or foolish oaf.' *Gloss. Ex. Scolding.*

1638 FORD *Fancies* IV. i. (1811) 186, I am..an oaf, a simple alcatote, an innocent. **1746** *Exmoor Courtsh.* (Elw.) 577 Go, ya Alkitotle, why dedst tell zo?

†**ˈalcatras, -ace, -ash.** *Obs.* [a. Sp., Pg. *alcatraz*, probably (as shown by Devic) a variant of Pg. *alcatruz* the bucket of a 'noria,' or water-raising wheel for irrigation, in Sp. *arcaduz, alcaduz*, a. Arab. *al-qādūs.* This name seems to have been applied (perhaps already by the Arabs in Spain) to the Pelican, in accordance with the idea that this bird draws up water in its great beak, in order to carry it to its young in the desert, whence also the Arabs now call it *saqqā* 'water-carrier' (Lane). By mistaken identification it was transferred to other large oceanic birds, and by English voyagers to the Frigate-bird, whence eventually, in a modified form, to the ALBATROSS, q.v.]

‖**1.** Spanish and Portuguese name of the pelican; applied loosely to sea-mews and allied birds.

[**1564** SIR J. HAWKINS *Voyage* (1878) 15 We ankered by a small Island, called Alcatrarsa, wherein..we found nothing but sea-birds, as we call them Ganets, but by the Portingals called Alcatrarses, who for that cause gaue the said Island the same name. **1598** FLORIO, *Alcatrazzi*, a birde as bigge as a goose, and liues on fishes, a sea gull. **1623** MINSHEU *Sp. Dict.*, *Alcatráz*, a kinde of fowle like a seamow, a great eater of fish.] *a* **1700** *Addit. MS.* 5008 (Halliw.) Ned Gylman took an alcatrash on the mayn topmast yerd, which ys a foolysh byrd, but good lean rank meat. **1852** T. ROSS tr. *Humboldt's Trav.* I. iv. 147 The shores..were peopled with alcatras, egrets, and flamingoes. **1853** *Ibid.* III. xxix. 188 A dreadful slaughter of the young alcatras, grouped in pairs in their nests. This name is given, in Spanish America, to the brown swan-tailed pelican of Buffon.

†**2.** Given by English voyagers to another sea-fowl of the same order, the Frigate Bird, *Tachypetes aquilus. Obs.*

1593–1620 R. HAWKINS *Voy.* (in 1593) *S. Sea* (1847) 71 The alcatrace is a sea-fowle..His head like unto the head of a gull, but his bill like unto a snytes bill,..He is almost like to a heronshaw... He is all blacke, of the colour of a crow, and of little flesh; for he is almost all skinne and bones. He soareth the highest of any fowle that I have seene, and I have not heard of any, that have seene them rest in the sea. **1604** DRAYTON *Owle* 549 Most like to that sharpe-sighted Alcatras, That beates the Aire above the liquid Glasse. **1692** COLES, *Alcatrace*, a fowl like a Heron.

†**3.** ? A species of albatross ('prob. the sooty albatross, *Diomedea fuliginosa*'; Prof. Newton). *Obs.*

1775 DALRYMPLE in *Phil. Trans.* LXVIII. 403 Two black alcatrasses. Many pintado birds, sheerwaters, etc., one alcatrass.

‖**alcavala** (alkəˈvɑːlə). [Sp. *alcabala, alcavala*, ad. Arab. *al-qabālah* the tax, duty, impost (Fr. *gabelle*), f. *qabala* to receive.] (See quot.)

1776 ADAM SMITH *W.N.* (1869) II. v. ii. 498 The famous *Alcavala* of Spain..was at first a tax of ten per cent..upon the sale of every sort of property. **1846** PRESCOTT *Ferd. & Isab.* III. xvi. 167 The alcavalas of the grandmasterships of the military orders.

‖**alcayde** (ælˈkeɪd, Sp. alˈkaɪde). Also 6 **alcaydy,** 8 **alcaid.** [Sp. *alcaide*, formerly *alcayde*, the captain of a castle, ad. Arab. *al-qāʼid* the leader, f. *qāda* to lead.] The governor or commander of a fortress; the warden of a prison; (in Spain, Portugal, Barbary, etc.)

1502 ARNOLD *Chron.* (1811) 232 The honorable Peter Gracia Carnayl, alcaydy ordinary of this said towne. **1698** *Lond. Gaz.* mmmcccxxii/1 The Alcayde, who Commands the Moors. **1707** *Ibid.* mmmmcccli/2 Into the Custody of the Alcaid of Tangier. **1846** PRESCOTT *Ferd. & Isab.* II. xiii. 30 The sufferings of the citizens softened the stern heart of the alcayde.

¶ Sometimes confounded with ALCALDE.

1753 CHAMBERS *Cycl. Supp.*, *Alcaid* is also written *Alcade, Alcalde*, and *Alcayd.* The Spanish alcaid answers in good measure to the French prevost, and English justice of peace.

‖**alcazar** (alˈkɑːθar). [Sp., a fortress, a castle, ad. Arab. *al-qaçr* = *al* the + *qaçr* in pl. a castle.] A palace, fortress.

1615 BEDWELL *Arab. Trudg.*, *Alcasar, Alkazar*, The palace, the kings house. **1846** PRESCOTT *Ferd. & Isab.* II. ix. 454 Their permanent residence was assigned in the old alcazar of Seville.

†**alce.** *Obs.* [a. L. *alce* (also *alces*).] An elk.

1541 ELYOT *Image Gov.* (1556) 81 Alces, brought for the nonce out of the great wooddes of Germany. **1617** HORN & ROB. *Gate Lang. Unl.* xvii. §193 The alces hide cannot be pierced with cutting. **1678** PHILLIPS, *Alce*, a wild Beast.. hath no joynts in his legs, and therefore doth never lye down but lean to Trees..This beast in English we answerably call an *Elk.* **1753** CHAMBERS *Cycl. Supp.*, The *Alce* or *Elk.*

alchahest, obs. form of ALKAHEST.

alchemic (ælˈkɛmɪk), *a.* Also **alchym-.** [ad. med.L. *alchimic-us* or Fr. *alchimique.* See ALCHEMY and -IC.] Of or pertaining to alchemy. Also *fig.*

1815 F. BARRETT *Alchem. Philos.* Pref., The same alchemic knowledge is ascribed to Saint John the Divine. **1835** *Blackw. Mag.* XXXVII. 440 Sweet as ottar of roses distilled by the alchymic sun. **1856** R. VAUGHAN *Ho. w. Mystics* II. VIII. viii. 290 Theosophists who mingled in hopeless confusion, religious doctrine, and alchemic process.

alchemical (ælˈkɛmɪkəl), *a.* Also 6–7 **alchimicall,** 7–9 **alchymical.** [f. med.L. *alchimicus* or Fr. *alchimique* + -AL[1].] Of or relating to alchemy.

1585 THYNNE in *Holinshed* III. 1168/2 Alchimicall art. **1605** CAMDEN *Rem.* (1657) 187 Made by projection or multiplication alchymicall. **1788** PRIESTLEY *Lect. Hist.* v. xxxvi. 264 The later Greeks had likewise many alchemical writers. **1853** FARADAY *Lect.* Introd. 9 The early days of chemical, or more properly speaking, alchemical philosophy.

alchemically (ælˈkɛmɪkəlɪ), *adv.* [f. prec. + -LY[2].] In an alchemical manner; according to alchemy. Also *fig.*

1657 CAMDEN *Rem.* (ed. 6) 187 Raymond Lully would prove it as Alchymically. **1801** W. TAYLOR in *Month. Mag.* XI. 132 Earth which has been alchemically exposed to the sun's rays.

alchemico- (ælˈkɛmɪkəʊ), combining adverbial form of ALCHEMIC (cf. ACUTO-); = prec.

1856 R. VAUGHAN *Ho. w. Mystics* II. VIII. vii. 74 The alchemico-astrotheologico jargon of the day.

alchemist (ˈælkɪmɪst). Forms: 6 **alkemyste, alckmist,** 6–7 **alchimist(e, alcumist,** 6–9 **alchymist,** 7– **alchemist.** [a. OFr. *alquemiste, alkemiste*; cf. It. *alchimista*, a. med.L. *alchymista*: see ALCHEMY and -IST. Earlier forms were ALCHEMISTER, ALKANAMYER.] One who studies or practises alchemy. Also *fig.*

1514 BARCLAY *Cyt. & Uplandyshm.* (1847) 23 As Alkemystys, wenynge by polecy Nature to alter. **1546** *Supplic. Comm.* 77 An alckmist, or a goldsmith. **1578** LYTE *Dodoens* I. xciv. 136 Alchimistes also do make great accompt of this herbe. **1607** SHAKS. *Timon* v. i. 117 You are an Alcumist, make Gold of that. **1635** QUARLES *Embl.* IV. iv. (1718) 203 Lord, what an alchymist art thou, whose skill Transmutes to perfect good from perfect ill! **1790** BURKE *Fr. Revol.* 250 Delivered over blindly to every projector and adventurer, to every alchymist and empiric. **1831** CARLYLE *Sart. Res.* (1858) 146 Brightening London-smoke itself into gold vapour, as from the crucible of an alchemist.

†**ˈalchemister.** *Obs.* Forms 4–5 **alcamister, -ystre, alkamyster(e, -istre,** 5–6 **alchymister,** 6 **alcumister.** [f. OFr. *alquemiste, alkemiste* + -ER[1], the native termination of the agent being added, as in *barrist-er, chorist-er, astronom-er*, etc.] The earlier form of ALCHEMIST.

c **1386** CHAUCER *Chan. Yem. Prol. & T.* 651 Whan this alcamister saugh his tyme [*v.r.* alcamystre, alkamystre, -mistre, -mystere, -mistrie]. **1477** NORTON *Ord. Alch.* in Ashm. (1652) 10 An Alchimister wise. **1576** BAKER tr. *Gesner's Jewell of Health* 173 b, A certaine Alchymister in Padua. **1586** FERNE *Blaz. Gentrie* Of the nature of Alcumisters.

alchemistic (ælkɪˈmɪstɪk), *a.* Also 7–9 **alchym-.** [f. ALCHEMIST + -IC.] Of or pertaining to alchemy or alchemists.

1689 PACKE tr. *Glauber* I. 240 The Alchymistick Virtues absconded in Vitriol. **1846** SABINE tr. *Humboldt's Cosm.* (1849) II. 342 What was accidentally remarked in alchemistic laboratories. **1854** LADY LYTTON *Behind Scenes* II. II. xiii. 310 The true alchymistic secret of accumulation —that of saving farthings.

alchemistical (ælkɪˈmɪstɪkəl), *a.* Also 6 **alcum-,** 7 **alchim-,** 7–9 **alchymistical.** [f. ALCHEMIST +

-ICAL. In earlier use than ALCHEMISTIC.] Of or relating to alchemists, or to their pursuits.

1560 J. DAUS tr. *Sleidane's Comm.* 119 b, Chaungeth leade into golde, farre exceadinge all the Alcumisticall multipliers that euer were. **1653** A. WILSON *James I*, 155 A new Alchimistical way to make Gold and Silver Lace with Copper. **1754** HUXHAM in *Phil. Trans.* XLVIII. 835 Whatever may have been boasted by the alchymistical visionaries. **1829** *Edin. Rev.* L. 257 The style is alchymistical, and therefore obscure. **1858** *Cassell's Art Treas.* 294 Vandyck..impoverished himself in his alchemistical researches.

† **'alchemisting**, *vbl. sb. Obs.* [f. ALCHEMIST used as a vb. + -ING[1].] Alchemical treatment; transmutation; counterfeiting.

1648-9 C. WALKER *Hist. Indep.* III. 50 It is a Mocking, a Counterfeiting, an Adulterating and Alchimisting of Justice.

† **alchemistry** ('ælkɪmɪstrɪ). ? Obs. Forms: 6-7 **alcum-, alchumistrie,** 7 **alcum-, alchym-,** 8- **alchemistry.** [f. ALCHEMIST + -RY. Cf. *chemistry, sophist-ry, rogue-ry*, etc.] The art or practice of the alchemists; alchemic art, alchemy.

1570 FOXE *A. & M.* (ed. 2) 1549/1 And farther you dyd meddle with the selling of the kinges landes. Also, you commaunded multiplication and Alcumistry to be practised, to abuse the kinges coyne. **1609** N. BRETON *Poste w. Pack.*, Touching Alchymistry I heare much but believe little. **1611** COTGR., *Alquemie*, Alchumie, Alchumistrie. **1791** BERGMAN *Chem. Ess.* III. 134 A person who has no faith in the changes of alchemistry. **1817** DRAKE *Shaks. & Times* II. 154 Alchemistry was one of the foolish pursuits of the day.

alchemize ('ælkɪmaɪz), *v.* Forms: 7 **alcumise, -ize,** 7-9 **alchymize,** 7- **alchemise, -ize.** [f. ALCHEM-IST, which on analogy of words in -IST, implied a vb. in *-ize*. Cf. *baptist* and *baptize*.] To change, as by alchemy; to transmute.

1603 H. CROSSE *Vertue's Commonw.* (1878) 43 The Artificer [would] Alcumize his Instruments into gold. **1683** tr. *Erasmus Mor. Encom.* 94 These subtleties are Alchymized to a more refined Sublimate. **1850** MRS. BROWNING *Poems* II. 231 Darkly brown thy body is, Till the sunshine, striking this [*i.e.* the hair], Alchemise its dulness.

alchemized ('ælkɪmaɪzd), *ppl. a.* [f. prec. + -ED.] Changed, as by alchemy; transmuted; *hence*, counterfeit.

1647 WARD *Simple Cob.* (1843) 5 Alchymized coines. **1818** KEATS *Endym.* I. 781 Till we shine Full alchemiz'd and free of space.

alchemizing ('ælkɪmaɪzɪŋ), *ppl. a.* [f. as prec. + -ING[2].] Transmuting, transforming as if by alchemy.

1873 SYMONDS *Grk. Poets* i. 29 The alchemizing touch of the Greek genius had transformed languages, cities.

alchemy ('ælkɪmɪ). Forms: 4-5 **alkamy(e, alknamy(e, alkenamye, -emye, alconomy(e,** 5 **alcanamy,** 6 **alkemy, alcomye, alchumie,** 6-7 **alchimie, -ymie,** 7 **alkimy, -camy, -cumy,** 7-8 **alchimy,** 6- **alchymy,** 7- **alchemy.** [a. OFr. *alquimie, -emie, -kemie, -camie* (also *ar-*), ad. med.L. *alchimia* (Pr. *alkimia*, Sp. *alquimia*, It. *alchimia*), a. Arab. *al-kīmīā*, i.e. *al* the + *kīmīā*, apparently a. Gr. *χημία, χημεία*, found (c. 300) in the Decree of Diocletian against 'the old writings of the Egyptians, which treat of the *χημία* (transmutation) of gold and silver'; hence the word is explained by most as 'Egyptian art,' and identified with *χημία*, Gr. form (in Plutarch) of the native name of Egypt (land of *Khem* or *Khamè*, hieroglyphic *Khmi*, 'black earth,' in contrast to the desert sand). If so, it was afterwards etymologically confused with the like-sounding Gr. *χῡμεία*, pouring, infusion, f. *χυ-* pf. stem of *χέ-ειν* to pour, cf. *χῡμός* juice, sap, which seemed to explain its meaning; hence the Renascence spelling *alchymia* and *chymistry*. Mahn (*Etym. Unt.* 69) however concludes, after an elaborate investigation, that Gr. *χῡμεία* was probably the original, being first applied to pharmaceutical chemistry, which was chiefly concerned with juices or infusions of plants; that the pursuits of the Alexandrian alchemists were a subsequent development of chemical study, and that the notoriety of these may have caused the name of the art to be popularly associated with the ancient name of Egypt, and spelt *χημεία, χημία*, as in Diocletian's decree. From the Alexandrians the art and name were adopted by the Arabs, whence they returned to Europe by way of Spain. Of the 14-15th c. forms, *Alconomy* was evidently assimilated to Astronomy, the two sciences going together.]

1. The chemistry of the Middle Ages and 16th c.; now applied distinctively to the pursuit of the transmutation of baser metals into gold, which (with the search for the alkahest or universal solvent, and the panacea or universal remedy) constituted the chief practical object of early chemistry.

1362 LANGL. *P. Pl.* A. XI. [152 Astronomye is hard þing] 157 Experimentis of Alconomye [*v.r.* alkenemye, alknamye]. **1377** *Ibid.* B. x. 212 Experimentz of alkamye [*v.r.* alkenemye, alconomie, alle kyn amye] þe poeple to deceyue. **1393** GOWER *Conf.* II. 84 They founde thilke experience Which cleped is alconomy. **1398** TREVISA *Barth. De P.R.* XVIII. xvi. (1495) 776 The asshes of a cokatrice be acountyd good and proffytable in werkyng of Alkamye: and namely in tornynge and chaungynge of metalle. **1509** BARCLAY *Ship of Fooles* (1570) 211 The vayne and disceatfull craft of alkemy. **1601** SHAKS. *Jul. C.* I. iii. 159 That which would appeare Offence in vs, His Countenance, like richest Alchymie, Will change to Vertue. **1621** BURTON *Anat. Mel.* I. ii. IV. vii. (1651) 167 What is.. Alcumy, but a bundle of errors? **1683** PETTUS *Fleta Min.* II. 1 Alchimie..an Art of Distilling or Drawing Quintessences out of Metals by Fire. **1776** GIBBON *Decl. & F.* I. 371 Philosophy, with the aid of experience, has at length banished the study of alchymy. **1837** WHEWELL *Induct. Sc.* (1857) I. 232 It has been usual to say that Alchemy was the mother of Chemistry.

2. *fig.* Magic or miraculous power of transmutation or extraction.

c **1600** SHAKS. *Sonn.* xxxiii, A glorious morning.. Guilding pale streames with heauenly alcumy. **1640** QUARLES *Enchir.* lxiii, It is a Princely Alchymie, out of a necessary Warre to extract an honourable Peace. **1824** BYRON *Don. J.* II. cciii, Wisdom, ever on the watch to rob Joy of its alchemy. **1872** BLACKIE *Lays of Highl.* 35 Toilsome Nature's patient alchemy.

†**3.** A metallic composition imitating gold; 'alchemy gold.' Hence applied to a trumpet of such metal, or of brass as its chief constituent. *Obs.*

1440 *Promp. Parv.*, Alkamye, metalle (**1499** alcamyn) *Alkamia.* **1483** *Cath. Angl.* Alcanamy, *corinthium.* **1513** DOUGLAS *Æneis* XII. iv. 130 In byrnist gold and finest alcomye. **1611** SPEED *Hist. Gt. Brit.* Concl., Coines of gold, siluer, alcumy and copper. **1667** MILTON *P.L.* II. 516 Four speedy cherubim Put to their mouths the sounding alchymie. **1677** *Lond. Gaz.* mcclxiv/4 One Livery Coat.. with Alcomie Buttons. **1691** *Ibid.* mmdclxxxvi/4 A Hair Camlet Wastecoat with Alkimy Buttons. **1695** *Ibid.* mmmlxxi/4 A strip'd Wastcoat with plain Alcomy Cuffs. **1812** W. TENNANT *Anster Fair* v. ii, King James's trumpeter aloud should cry Through his long alchemy the famous name.

†**4.** *fig.* Glittering dross. ('All is not gold that glitters.') *Obs.*

1591 HARRINGTON *Orl. Fur.* (Trench *Sel. Gl.* 4) Though the show of it were glorious, the substance of it was dross, and nothing but alchymy and cozenage.

5. *attrib.* (See 3.)

1657 J. TRAPP *Comm. Ps.* xiii. 6 II. 600 Alchimie-gold.. will not passe the seuenth fire.

† **'alchemy**, *v. Obs.* Also **alchyme, alkime.** [f. ALCHEMY *sb.* 3. Cf. to *silver, tin, lacquer*, etc.] To plate or wash with another metal; to alloy.

1615 T. ADAMS *Blacke Devill* 42 So true Gold is alchymed over with a false sophistication. **1622** MALYNES *Anc. Law-Merch.* 277 They cause them to be Alkimed like silver. **1627** FELTHAM *Resolves* I. xviii. (1677) 32 It will Alchymy the gold of vertue.

alcheringa, (æltʃə'rɪŋgə). Also **'alchera, 'altjira, A-.** [Austral. Aboriginal, lit. = 'dream-time'.] In the mythology of some Australian Aboriginal peoples, the 'golden age' when the first ancestors were created.

1899 SPENCER & GILLEN *Nat. Tribes Central Australia* ix. 324 'It was so in the Alcheringa,' was considered as perfectly satisfactory by way of explanation. **1910** *Encycl. Brit.* X. 162/2 The Arunta believe that the souls of the primal semi-bestial ancestors of the Alcheringa or 'dream time' are perpetually reincarnated. **1939** S. DELL tr. *Jung's Integr. Personality* (1941) iii. 92 The palæolithic Australians.. identify themselves..with their ancestors of the so-called alcheringa period. **1959** S. H. COURTIER *Death in Dream Time* iv. 43 Alchera..is the name given by Central Australian tribes to the time when the world was being made. *Ibid.*, The natives..who had learned the white man's tongue found the word *dream* to come nearest to what they meant by *Alchera*. **1965** W. E. H. STANNER in R. & C. Berndt *Aborig. Man in Austral.* 214 A full understanding of the Aboriginal view of life and the world requires a careful study of the whole body of doctrine about the Dream Time (*altjira, bugari*).

alchermes, obs. form of ALKERMES.

alchim-: see ALCHEM-.

† **'alchimistie**, = ALCHEMISTRY (?misprint.)

1578 FLORIO *1st Frutes* 14 There are others that practise a newe kynde of Alchimistie.

† **alchitran, alkitran.** *Obs.* Forms: 4 **alkatran,** 7 **alkitrum,** 8 **alchitran, -am, -kytran.** [a. OFr. *alketran, alquitran*, a. Sp. *alquitran*, Pg. *alcatrão* (med.L. *alquitranum, alchitrum*, It. *catrame*, mod.Fr. *goudran, -on*), ad. Arab. *al-qaṭrān* or *al-qiṭrān*, the resin of fir-trees, pitch, tar; f. *qaṭara* to drop.] The liquid resin or pitch which flows from fir-trees; extended by the early chemists to: **a.** oil of cedar and juniper; **b.** mineral pitch, tar, bitumen; and, vaguely, to other substances.

c **1325** *E.E. Allit. P.* B. 1035 Alum & alka[t]ran, that angré arn boþe. **1366** MAUNDEV. ix. 99 About that [Dead] See growethe moche Alom and of Alkatran. **1658** J. R. *Mouffet's Theat. Ins.* 1123 Abenzoar prescribes, to anoynt the hair with the lesser Centaury, and Alkitrum. **1753** CHAMBERS *Cycl. Supp.*, *Alchitram*, among the alchemists, denotes sometimes the oil of juniper, sometimes liquid pitch, and sometimes arsenic prepared by ablution. This is otherwise written *alchitram* and *alchitran*; sometimes *alchytran* and *alkytran*. **1879** *Syd. Soc. Lex.*, *Alchitrum, Alchytran, Alketran, Alkitram, Alkitran*, [variously expl. as] the impure liquid resin of *Pinus sylvestris*; a resin obtained from the cedar tree; oil of cedar; oil of juniper; *pix liquida* or tar; arsenic prepared by washing; a term for the residuum after distillation.

† **al'chitrean**, *a. Obs. rare*[−1]. [f. med.L. *alchitre-us* adj. f. *alchitrum* (see prec.) + -AN.] Of or pertaining to the resin of the Pine.

1560 P. WHITEHORNE *Ord. Sould.* (1588) 46 For to make them [fireworks], there must be taken Rosen Alchitrean, quicke Brimstone, etc.

alchym-: see ALCHEM-.

† **alchy'mistrical**, = ALCHEMISTICAL (?mispr.).

1682 SCARLETT *Exchanges* A 4 Pref., As if there were some Alchymistrical cunning used by them.

† **alchymusie.** *Obs.*

1587 GOLDING *De Mornay* xxv. (1617) 429 Afterward he (who would prophecy) must gather together the beames of the Skie into a mirror, which they call Alchymusie, made according to the Rules of Catoptrick.

alcion, obs. form of HALCYON.

Alcmanian (ælk'meɪnɪən), *a.* Also **Alc'manic.** [f. L. *Alcmānius*, f. *Alcmān*, Gr. *'Αλκμάν*, the name of a Greek lyric poet of the 7th c. B.C.] Used to designate a dactylic tetrameter, or a distich consisting of a dactylic hexameter followed by this verse. Also *sb.*, an Alcmanian verse or distich. (See also quot. 1853.)

1850 P. SMITH in W. Smith *Dict. Gr. & Rom. Biogr.* I. 107/1 The shorter dactylic lines into which Alcman broke up the Homeric hexameter... The Cretic hexameter was named Alcmanic, from his [Alcman] being its inventor. **1853** *Encycl. Brit.* II. 453/1 *Alcmanian*, an ancient lyric kind of verse, consisting of two dactyles and two trochees: as *Virgini|bus pue|risque| canto.* **1879** J. W. WHITE tr. *J. H. H. Schmidt's Rhythmic & Metric* 95 The Alcmanian group, consisting of a dactylic hexameter followed by a dactylic tetrameter. **1962** D. S. RAVEN *Greek Metre* 84 *Alcmanic*, a name given to the dactylic tetrameter -∪∪-∪∪-∪∪-(-)..., and, in Latin, to its combination by Horace with the hexameter.

alcoate, alcohate ('ælkəʊ(h)eɪt). A shortened form of ALCOHOLATE.

1828 *Pen. Cycl.* (1833) I. 281/2 Dr. Graham has shown that, like water, it [alcohol] combines with bodies in definite proportions: these compounds he calls alcoates. **1833** FYFE *Chem.* (ed. 3) 649 The chlorids of common metals were found to be acted on in the same way, alcoates being formed. **1875** URE *Dict. Arts.* I. 58 Alcoholates or Alcoates.

alcogel ('ælkədʒel). *Chem.* [f. ALCO(HOL + GEL(ATIN: see GEL.] A gelatinous precipitate from a colloidal solution in alcohol.

1864 [see ALCOSOL].

alcogene ('ælkədʒiːn). [mod. f. ALCO(HOL) + -GEN(E taken as = producer.] The vapour-cooler in distilling apparatus.

1828 S. GRAY *Operat. Chem.* 767 The dephlegmator, or alcogene, contained in the tub.

alcohol ('ælkəhɒl). Also 6-8 **alcool, alcho(h)ol, alcohole.** [a. med.L. *alcohol*, ad. Arab. *al-koḥ'l* 'collyrium,' the fine powder used to stain the eyelids, f. *kaḥala*, Heb. *kākhal* to stain, paint: see *Ezekiel* xxiii. 40. It appeared in Eng., as in most of the mod. langs. in 16th c. Cf. Fr. *alcohol*, now *alcool*.]

†**1.** *orig.* The fine metallic powder used in the East to stain the eyelids, etc.: powdered ore of antimony, stibnite, or antimony trisulphide (known to the Greeks in this use as *πλατυόφθαλμον στίμμι*); also, sometimes, powdered galena or lead ore. *Obs.*

[MINSHEU *Sp. Dict.* (1623) *Alcohól*: a drug called Antimonium; it is a kinde of white stone found in siluer mynes. JOHNSON *Lex. Chym.* (1657) 12 *Alcohol* est antimonium sive stibium.]

1615 SANDYS *Trav.* 67 They put betweene the eye-lids and the eye a certaine black powder..made of a minerall brought from the kingdome of Fez, and called Alcohole. **1626** BACON *Sylva* §739 The Turkes have a Black Powder, made of a Mineral called Alcohole; which with a fine long Pencil they lay under their Eye-lids. **1650** BULWER *Anthropomet.* iv. 69 A Mineral called Alcohol, with which they colour the hair of their Eye-brows. **1819** *Pantol.* s.v., The ladies of Barbary tinge their hair, and the edges of their eyelids, with *al-ka-hol*, the powder of lead ore..That which is employed for ornament and is principally antimony, is called *al-cohol* or *isphahany*.

†**2.** Hence, by extension (in early *Chem.*): Any fine impalpable powder produced by trituration, or especially by sublimation; as ***alcohol martis*** reduced iron, ***alcohol of sulphur*** flower of brimstone, etc. *Obs.*

1543 TRAHERON tr. *Vigo's Chirurg.*, The barbarous auctours use *alchohol*, or (as I fynde it sometymes wryten) *alcofoll*, for moost fine poudre.[*Alcofoll* is Catalan.] **1605** TIMME *Quersit.* I. xvi. 83 If this glasse be made most thinne in alchool. **1657** *Phys. Dict.*, *Alcolismus*, is an operation.. which reduceth a matter into allcool, the finest pouder that is. **1661** LOVELL *Anim. & Min.* 3 The alcohol of an Asses spleen. **1751** CHAMBERS *Cycl.*, *Alcohol* is sometimes also used for a very fine impalpable powder. **1812** SIR H. DAVY

Chem. Philos. 310, I have already referred to the alcohol of sulphur.

†**3. a.** By extension to fluids of the idea of sublimation: An essence, quintessence, or 'spirit,' obtained by distillation or 'rectification'; as ***alcohol of wine***, essence or spirit of wine. *Obs.*

[LIBAVIUS *Alchymia* (1594) has *vini alcohol* vel *vinum alcalisatum* a mispr. or perhaps misconception for *alcolizatum*, see ALCOHOLIZATED; JOHNSON *Lex. Chym.* (1657) 13, *Alcohol vini*, quando omnis superfluitas vini a vino separatur, ita ut accensum ardeat donec totum consumatur, nihilque fæcum aut phlegmatis in fundo remaneat.]

1672 *Phil. Trans.* VII. 5059 Assisted by the *Alcool* of Wine. **1706** PHILLIPS, *Alcahol* or *Alcool*, the pure Substance of anything separated from the more Gross. It is more especially taken for a most subtil and highly refined Powder, and sometimes for a very pure Spirit: Thus the highest rectified Spirit of Wine is called *Alcohol Vini.* **1731** ARBUTHNOT *Aliments* (J.) *Sal volatile oleosum*..on account of the alcohol or rectified spirit which it contains. **1753** CHAMBERS *Cycl. Supp.*, *Alcohol* is used by modern chemists for any fine highly rectified spirit. *Ibid.* Method of preparing *Alcohol of Wine.* **1794** PEARSON in *Phil. Trans.* LXXXIV. 395 Alcohol of gall nut (tincture of gall nut).

b. *fig.* Quintessence, condensed spirit.

1830 COLERIDGE *Lect. Shaks.* II. 117 Intense selfishness, the alcohol of egotism.

4. (Short for *alcohol of wine*, this being the most familiar of 'rectified spirits.') The pure or rectified spirit of wine, the spirituous or intoxicating element in fermented liquors. Also, *popularly*, any liquor containing this spirit. ***absolute*** or ***anhydrous alcohol***: alcohol entirely free from water.

1753 CHAMBERS *Cycl. Supp.* s.v. *Spirit*, Water is a solvent to alcohol or spirit of wine. **1760** *Phil. Trans.* LI. 824 Alcohol, or spirit of wine, has been more generally used. **1806** VINCE *Hydrost.* ii. 25 Pure spirits, called alcohol. **1814** SIR H. DAVY *Agric. Chem.* 134 The intoxicating powers of fermented liquors depend on the alchohol that they contain. **1873** COOKE *Chem.* 14 Alcohol has never been frozen. **1875** URE *Dict. Arts* I. 43 The separation of absolute alcohol would appear to have been first effected about 1300 by Arnauld de Villeneuve. *Ibid.* 65 If wood-spirit be contained in alcohol, it may be detected..by the test of caustic potash. **1879** RIDGE *Temper. Primer* 129 Life assurance offices have found that the average length of life of total abstainers is greater than that of drinkers of alcohol.

5. a. *Organ. Chem.* An extensive class of compounds, of the same type as spirit of wine, composed of carbon, hydrogen, and oxygen, some of which are liquid and others solid.

They may be regarded as water (HOH) with one of its hydrogen atoms replaced by a hydro-carbon radical as Methyl (CH_3), Ethyl (C_2H_5), Propyl (C_3H_7), Butyl (C_4H_9), Amyl (C_5H_{11}) etc., according to the character of which, the alcohol is *monocarbon* or *methyl*, *dicarbon* or *ethyl*, *tricarbon* or *propyl*, etc.; or as paraffins (Methane CH_4, Ethane C_2H_6, Propane C_3H_8, etc.) with one or more of their hydrogen atoms replaced by equivalent atoms of hydroxyl (HO), according to the number of which atoms replaced, the alcohol is *monatomic*, *diatomic*, *triatomic*, etc. Tricarbon alcohols are *primary* or *secondary*, tetracarbon and higher alcohols are *primary*, *secondary*, or *tertiary*, according as the carbon atom united to the hydroxyl atom is also directly in contact with *one, two, three* other carbon atoms of the molecule. *Isomeric* alcohols are such as have the same percentage composition but a different arrangement of atoms in the complex molecule, and are physically different substances. The number of possible alcohols is apparently unlimited. [This extension of the name to a genus was made by Dumas and Péligot in 1834–5, in pointing out the analogy between wood-spirit (Methyl alcohol) and spirit of wine; in 1836, they identified another member of the series in ethal (Cetyl alcohol); in 1844, Cahours found another (Amyl alcohol) in Fusel oil; after which the recognition of 'alcohols' went on rapidly.]

common (vinous or vinic) ***alcohol*** (see prec. sense) is a *primary, monatomic, dicarbon* or *ethyl* alcohol, C_2H_6O, and may be considered as water, in which one atom of hydrogen is replaced by an atom of *ethyl*, or C_2H_5; thus $C_2H_5.OH$ instead of H.OH.

1850 DAUBENY *Atom. Theory* vii. (ed. 2) 222 The term ..*alcohol* indicates a class, some members of which, far from being volatile, are not even liquid. **1863** WATTS *Dict. Chem.* (1872) I. 99 The first eight alcohols are liquid. Cetyl alcohol is a solid fat: cerylic and myricylic alcohols are waxy. **1875** URE *Dict. Arts* I. 42 We speak of the various alcohols. Of these, common or vinous alcohol is the best known. **1879** G. GLADSTONE in *Cassell's Techn. Educ.* IV. 106/1 Resistance to the action of Alcohols, Acids, and Alkalies.

b. In full ***alcohol fuel***, a fuel used in internal combustion engines, guided missiles, etc.

1901 *Sci. Amer.* LXXXIV. 344/3 (*title*) Alcohol as fuel for motor carriages. *Ibid.*, The champions of the alcohol motor scored another triumph in the Paris-Roubaix races. **1904** GOODCHILD & TWENEY *Technol. & Sci. Dict.* 11/1 *Alcohol fuel*..In France and Germany cheap alcohol, made from potatoes or beetroot, is utilised to a considerable extent in place of petrol. **1935** *Jrnl. R. Aeronaut. Soc.* XXXIX. 470 These engines are fitted with positive super-chargers and run on exceptionally high compression ratios on alcohol fuel. **1940** *Chambers's Techn. Dict.* 20/2 *Alcohol fuel*, volatile liquid-fuel consisting wholly, or partly, of alcohol, able to withstand high-compression ratios without detonation. **1958** *Aero-Space Terms* 3/1 *Alcohol*, ethyl alcohol (C_2H_5OH) or methyl alcohol (CH_3OH), used with liquid oxygen as a bipropellant. *Ibid.*, Ethyl alcohol and liquid oxygen were used in the German V-2.

alcoholate ('ælkəhɒ,leɪt). *Chem.* [f. ALCOHOL + -ATE. Contr. forms ALCOATE, ALCOHATE, are also found.] A crystalline compound in which alcohol acts as water of crystallization.

1863 in WATTS *Dict. Chem.* **1875** URE *Dict. Arts.* I. 58 Alcoholates are in general rather unstable combinations, and are almost always decomposed by water.

alcoholature (ælkəʊ'hɒlətjʊə(r)). *Med.* [f. mod.L. *alcoholāt-us* alcoholized + -URE] An alcoholic tincture prepared with fresh plants.

a **1864** PARRISH *Pharmacy* (1874) 603 The class of tinctures called by the French alcoolatures. **1879** *Syd. Soc. Lex.*, In the same manner are prepared..alcoolatures of leaves of pulsatilla.

alcoholic (ælkəʊ'hɒlɪk), *a.* and *sb.* [f. ALCOHOL + -IC.]

A. *adj.* **1.** Of or belonging to alcohol.

1790 KERR tr. *Lavoisier's Chem.* 51 The combination of alkohol with caloric, becomes alkoholic gas. **1800** HOWARD in *Phil. Trans.* XC. 217 The alcoholic liquor was likewise evaporated to a dry salt. **1809** NICHOLSON in *Brit. Encycl.* V. II. xvi, In making alcoholic tinctures. **1836** C. REDDING *Mod. Wines* xv. (ed. 2) 326 Some ingenious observations.. upon the alcoholic principle in wine. *Ibid.* App. xxviii. 411 The mean alcoholic strength of wines. **1845** *Pen. Cycl.* Supp. I. 73/1 A moderate use of alcoholic drinks. **1871** TYNDALL *Fragm. Sc.* (ed. 6) II. xii. 260 The true alcoholic fermentation. **1882** *Med. Temp. Jrnl.* No. 50. 77 Symptoms of chronic alcoholic poisoning.

2. Preserved in alcohol.

1852 DANA *Crustacea* I. 185 The specimen, an alcoholic one, has a pale brown colour.

3. Using or employing alcohol.

1856 KANE *Arct. Explor.* II. 405 The differences which alcoholic thermometers exhibit.

4. Addicted to alcohol (cf. sense B. 2 below).

1957 *Times Lit. Suppl.* 8 Nov. 670/5 The girl is virtually imprisoned by the neurotic, psychotic and (it is apparent by this time) alcoholic novelist.

B. *sb. pl.* **1.** Alcoholics = alcoholic liquors.

1870 *Food Jrnl.* 1 Apr. 141 Any restriction on the sale of alcoholics.

2. a. One who is addicted to excessive consumption of alcoholic drinks, a drink addict.

1891 G. T. KEMP in *Q. Jrnl. Inebriety* Jan. (Funk), Chronic alcoholics. **1907** *Daily Chron.* 4 Sept. 3/1 There is ..a time coming when the alcoholic will be a rarity. **1909** *Westm. Gaz.* 25 Feb. 8/1 Warning him that deceased was a 'chronic alcoholic', and must have a bottle of port a day.

b. ***Alcoholics Anonymous*** (orig. *U.S.*), an association for the mutual support and rehabilitation of alcoholics, founded at Akron, Ohio, in 1935. Abbrev. *A.A.* (see A III. 1).

1939 'BILL W.' *Alcoholics Anonymous* ii. 27 We, of *Alcoholics Anonymous*, know one hundred men who were just as hopeless as Bill. All have recovered. They have solved the drink problem. **1941** *Sat. Even. Post* 1 Mar. 9/1 They were members of Alcoholics Anonymous, a band of ex-problem drinkers who make an avocation of helping other alcoholics to beat the liquor habit. **1951** I. SHAW *Troubled Air* ii. 28 You're jittery... Maybe you ought to join Alcoholics Anonymous. **1962** *Lancet* 2 June 1193/2, 7 men attended meetings of Alcoholics Anonymous regularly. The impression was that those that helped most by A.A. are the more stable and more intelligent. **1974** M. C. GERALD *Pharmacol.* xii. 232 The most successful organization has been Alcoholics Anonymous (AA), an informal fellowship of former alcoholics whose goal is the rehabilitation of alcoholics. **1984** *N.Y. Times* 2 Jan. 21/2 The Roman Catholic rectory serves twice a week as the meeting place for the local chapter of Alcoholics Anonymous.

alcoholically (ælkəʊ'hɒlɪkəlɪ), *adv.* [f. prec. + -AL[1] + -LY[2].] In an alcoholic manner; after the manner of alcohol.

1876 tr. *Schutzenberger's Ferment.* 187 Dextrin, inulin, and sugar of milk do not ferment, alcoholically, in the presence of Mucor racemosus.

alcoholicity (,ælkəhɒ'lɪsɪtɪ). [f. ALCOHOLIC + -ITY. Cf. *catholicity*.] Alcoholic quality.

1874 H. VIZETELLY *Rep. Vienna Exhib.* IV. 8 A wine distinguished..by greater alcoholicity.

alcoholimetric (ælkəʊ,hɒlɪ'mɛtrɪk), *a. Chem.* = ALCOHOLOMETRIC.

1869 *Eng. Mech.* 7 May 148/2 The alcoholimetric degree of the solution rises.

alcoholism ('ælkəhɒ,lɪz(ə)m). [ad. mod.L. *alcoholismus*; see under ALCOHOL 2, and -ISM.] The action of alcohol upon the human system; diseased condition produced by alcohol.

1852 M. HUSS *Chron. Alkohols-Krank.* Pref., Ich habe dieser Krankheit einen neuen Namen, nämlich *Alcoholismus chronicus* beigelegt. **1860** W. MARCET *Chron. Alc. Intox.* Introd., The valuable publication on chronic alcoholism by Magnus Huss of Stockholm. **1869** *Daily News* 8 Dec., The deaths of 2 persons from alcoholism. **1879** tr. *Busch's Bismarck* II. 189 The doctors complain of the bad effects of alcoholism, which makes slight wounds serious. **1882** *Med. Temp. Jrnl.* No. 52. 160 The term alcoholism..denotes merely cases which come directly from the toxic action of alcohol.

alcoholist ('ælkəhɒlɪst). [See -IST. Cf. ALCOHOLISM.] One who is addicted to, or advocates, drinking alcoholic drinks.

1888 *Forum* (N.Y.) Sept. 103 Of 250 chronic alcoholists nearly 90% had fatty degeneration of the liver. **1894** *Pop. Sci. Monthly* Nov. 99 A moderate alcoholist. **1920** W. J. LOCKE *House of Baltazar* iii, Old Jack Bonnithorne, the champion alcoholist of the moorland.

†**alcoholizated**, *ppl. a. Obs.* Also **alcolizated**. [f. mod.L. *alco(ho)lizāt-us*; see ALCOHOL 3 + -ED.] = ALCOHOLIZED 2.

1641 FRENCH *Distill.* iv. (1651) 99 Of the best alcolizated Wine. *Ibid.* vi. 192 The best alcholizated Spirit of Wine.

alcoholization (,ælkəhɒlaɪ'zeɪʃən). [ad. mod.L. *alcoholīzātiōnem* n. of action f. *alcoholīzāre*: see ALCOHOLIZE. Cf. Fr. *alcoolisation*.]

†**1.** Reduction to a fine powder; pulverization sublimation. *Obs.*

1678 PHILLIPS, *Alcoholization*, a reducing of any solid matter into an extream fine and subtle powder. **1753** CHAMBERS *Cycl. Supp.*, *Alcoholization* is also used for pulverization.

†**2.** Refinement to an essence or essential spirit; rectification of a spirit. *Obs.*

1678 PHILLIPS, *Alcoholization*, in Liquids, is the depriving of Alcohols or Spirits of their flegm or waterish part; so that they consume and fume away with the matter wherein they were dipt. **1721** BAILEY, *Alcoholization*, a reducing Bodies to a fine and impalpable Powder; also a freeing of Spirits from Phlegm and waterish Parts. **1753** CHAMBERS *Cycl. Supp.*, *Alcoholization* is one way of volatilizing alkali's.

3. Saturation with spirit of wine.

1879 *Syd. Soc. Lex.*, *Alcoholisation*, the saturation or mixture of a substance with alcohol.

4. Subjection of the human or animal system to the influence of alcoholic stimulants.

1852 *Illustr. Lond. N.* 23 Sept. 327 Fifteen pigs were treated daily upon various descriptions of alcohol, and then killed after the process of alcoholisation had gone on for some time. **1871** *Sat. Rev.* 1 Apr. 398/2 Misery, discord, perhaps disgrace follows neglect of incipient alcoholization.

alcoholize ('ælkəhɒ,laɪz), *v.* [ad. mod.L. *alcŏholīzā-re*: see ALCOHOL 3 and -IZE. Cf. Fr. *alcoholiser*.]

†**1.** To reduce to an impalpable powder; to sublime. *Obs.*

1686 W. HARRIS tr. *Lemery's Chym.* (ed. 2) 40 To Alcoholize, or reduce into Alcohol, signifies to Subtilize as when a mixt is beaten into an impalpable powder.

†**2.** To concentrate to an essential spirit, rectify.

1686 W. HARRIS tr. *Lemery's Chym.* I. xxii. (ed. 3) 464 Spirit of Wine well Alcoholized. **1799** W. TAYLOR in Robberds' *Mem.* I. 296 Let those [literary compositions] of uncertain value be afterwards concentrated..alcoholized, and have their aroma distilled into a quintessential drop of otr.

3. To saturate with alcohol; to subject to the influence of alcohol.

alcoholized ('ælkəhɒ,laɪzd), *ppl. a.* Also 8 **alcol-**, **alcool-**. [f. prec. + -ED.]

†**1.** Reduced to an impalpable powder or sublimate; sublimed. *Obs.*

†**2.** Refined to an essential spirit, rectified. *Obs.*

1686 [see prec.] **1753** CHAMBERS *Cycl. Suppl.*, *Alcoholized* is understood of things which are reduced to an alcohol. In this sense, we meet with alcolized spirits, alcolized powders, etc. This is otherwise written alcoolized, and amounts to much the same as subtilized, rectified, etc.

3. Saturated with alcohol; subjected to the influence of alcohol.

1862 *Cornh. Mag.* VI. 320 The blood of alcoholized animals. **1879** CARPENTER *Ment. Phys.* II. xvii. 651 As the alcoholized blood takes more and more hold of the brain.

alcoholizer ('ælkəhɒ,laɪzə(r)). [f. ALCOHOL + -IZE + -ER[1].] = ALCOHOLIST

1890 'R. BOLDREWOOD' *Miner's Right* xxiv, I pity those alcoholisers... And they are often such Bayards in their sane periods.

alcoholizing ('ælkəhɒ,laɪzɪŋ), *vbl. sb.* [f. as ALCOHOLIZED *ppl. a.* + -ING[1].] The process of converting into or saturating with alcohol.

1706 PHILLIPS, *Alcoholization*, the Act of Alcoholizing or reducing any solid Substance into a fine Powder; But in Liquids, it is the depriving Alcohols or rectified Spirits of their Phlegm or waterish Parts.

alcoholmeter (ælkəʊ'hɒlmɪtə(r)) = next.

1859 in WORCESTER. **1864** WEBSTER cites URE. **1882** *Times* 14 Mar. 5/1 Spanish wines being admitted at a shilling per gallon up to 36 degrees of Syke's alcoholmeter.

alcoholometer (,ælkəhɒ'lɒmɪtə(r)). [f. ALCOHOL + -(O)METER. Cf. Fr. *alcoolomètre*.] An instrument for measuring the proportion of absolute alcohol in a liquor.

1859 in WORCESTER. **1875** URE *Dict. Arts* I. 59 Sykes's hydrometer, or alcoholometer, is the one employed by the Board of Excise.

alcoholometric (,ælkəʊhɒləʊ'mɛtrɪk), *a.* [f. ALCOHOLOMETER + -IC.] Of or pertaining to alcoholometry.

alcoholo'metrical, *a.* [f. prec. + -AL[1].] Relating to alcoholometry. (More common in the shortened form ALCOOMETRICAL.)

alcoholometry (,ælkəhɒ'lɒmɪtrɪ). [f. ALCOHOL + Gr. -μετρία: see -METRY.] The process of testing the proportion of absolute alcohol in liquors.

1863 WATTS *Chem. Dict.* (1872) I. 81 (*Article*) Alcoholometry. **1875** URE *Dict. Arts.* I. 61 [On the] Alcoholometry of liquids containing besides alcohol, Saccharine Matters, etc.

alcohometer (ælkəʊ'hɒmɪtə(r)) = ALCOHOLOMETER. Craig 1847.

alcolizated, obs. form of ALCOHOLIZATED.

alcomy(e, obs. form of ALCHEMY.

‖**al'conde**, *Obs.* [Sp. *alconde*, comb. of Arabic *al* the + Sp. *conde* count, earl:—L. *comitem*: see COUNT.] A (Spanish) count or grandee.

c **1486** *Bk. St. Albans Heraldry* (Dallaway App. 71) Prouves of Knighthode done before alcondis in honour of renowne.

alconomy(e, obs. form of ALCHEMY.

alcool, obs. form of ALCOHOL.

alco'ometer, -try, shortened forms of ALCOHOLOMETER, -TRY.

1864 in WEBSTER. **1875** URE *Dict. Arts* I. 58 Alcoholometry or Alcoometry.

alcoometrical (,ælkəʊəʊ'mɛtrɪkəl), *a.* [f. ALCOOMETRY + -ICAL.] Of or pertaining to alcoometry; as ascertained by an alcoholometer.

1875 URE *Dict. Arts* I. 51 Alcoometrical Table of real Strength.

alcoothionic (,ælkəʊəʊθaɪ'ɒnɪk), *a.* [f. ALCOHO(L) + Gr. θεῖον sulphur + -IC.] = Œnothionic.

1879 in *Syd. Soc. Lex.*

Alcoran (ælkɒ'rɑːn, 'ælkɒrɑːn, -æn). *arch.* Forms: 4–5 **alkaron, -oun,** 6 **alcharon,** 6–7 **alchoran(e, alcorane, alcaron,** 7 **alcheron,** 7– **alcoran** 8 **alkoran.** [a. (immed. from Fr. *alcoran*) Arab. *al-qorān*, the recitation, reading, f. *qaraɂa* to recite, read.] The sacred book of Mohammedans; the Koran (which is now the usual form).

1366 MAUNDEV. xii. 139 The holy book Alkaron that God sente hem be his messager Machomete. *c* **1386** CHAUCER *Man of Lawes T.* 199 The holy lawes of our Alkaroun [*v.r.* alkaron], Geven by Goddes messangere Makamete. **1532** MORE *Confut. Tindale* Wks. 1557, 340/1 As the Turkes doe, bidde men belieue in Machometes alchoran. *Ibid.* 651/1 Mahomettes alcharon. **1642** HOWELL *For. Trav.* (Arb.) 85 They so adore the *Alcoran* that they never put it under their girdles. **1651** CALDERWOOD *Hist. Kirk* (1843) II. 297 The Turkes for the maintenance of their Alcaron. **1655** GOUGE *Comm. Hebr.* iii. 7, 320 The Turks Alcheron, the Jews Cabala..are..to be detested. **1728** MORGAN *Algiers* II. iv. 293 The first chapter of the Al-Coran. **1777** HUME *Ess. & Treat.* II. 443 A sacred book, such as the Alcoran. **1796** MORSE *Amer. Geog.* II. 586 Called the Koran, or Alkoran, by way of eminence, as we say *the* Bible.

b. *fig.*

a **1659** CLEVELAND *Obseq.* 26 A Text on which we find no Gloss at all, But in the *Alcoran* of Gold-smiths Hall!

alcoran, *v. Obs.* [f. the sb.] To make into a Koran or inspired book.

a **1678** MARVELL *Poems, First Anniv.*, Prophecies fit to be alcoran'd.

†**alco'ranal**, *a. Obs. rare*⁻¹. [f. ALCORAN + -AL¹.] Belonging to the Koran.

1652 URQUHART *Jewel* Wks. 1834, 234 In an alcoranal paradise.

Alcoranic (ælkɒ'rænɪk), *a.* Also **alk-.** [f. ALCORAN + -IC.] Of or pertaining to the Koran, or to Mohammedan theology.

1857 *Nat. Mag.* II. 403 Being removed from the Alkoranic school. **1859** WORCESTER, *Alcoranic.*

†**Alco'ranish**, *a. Obs.* [f. ALCORAN + -ISH.] = ALCORANIC.

1634 T. HERBERT *Trav.* (1677) 129 The Carcasses of some Alchoranish Doctors. **1762** PARKHURST *Heb. Lex.* Pref. (T.), I have called the Alcoranish Arabic a hotch-potch of several corrupt dialects of the Hebrews.

Alco'ranist. [f. ALCORAN + -IST.] One who adheres to the letter of the Koran, rejecting all subsequent additions.

1753 CHAMBERS *Cycl. Supp.*, The Persians are generally alkoranists, as admitting the alcoran only for their rule of faith.

‖**alcor'noco, alcor'noque.** [Sp. *alcornoque*, f. Arab. *al* the + *quern oco* spongy oak (Diez).]

Spanish name of the cork-oak, the young bark of which is employed in tanning under the name of *European* or *Spanish Alcornoque bark.* Extended in Spanish America to various trees yielding a similar product (*American Alcornoque*), esp. *Bowdichia virgilioides*, and species of *Byrsonima*; formerly also used in medicine.

[**1823** HUMBOLDT *Nova Genera* VI. 376 *Bowdichia virgilioides, Alcornoco* incolarum.] **1832** G. DON *Gen. Syst.* II. 464, *Bowdichia*: At the mouth of the Orinoco where it is commonly called *Alcornoque.* **1866** *Treas. Bot.* 35, *Alcornoco* or *Alcornoque* Bark, the bark of several species of *Byrsonima*; the Alcornoque of Spain is the bark of the cork-tree. *Ibid.* 161, *Bowdichia*: The bark is of a reddish brown colour, and is known as Alcornoco bark. **1873** BENTLEY *Man. Bot.* 459 The bark [of *Bowdichia*] with that of one or more species of *Byrsonima* is said to form the American Alcornoco or Alcornoque Bark of commerce.

alcosol ('ælkəsɒl). *Chem.* [f. ALCO(HOL + SOL(UTION: see SOL *sb.*⁶] A colloidal solution in alcohol.

1864 T. GRAHAM in *Proc. R. Soc.* XIII. 337 If I may be allowed to distinguish the liquid and gelatinous hydrates of silicic acid by the irregularly formed terms of hydrosol and hydrogel of silicic acid, the two corresponding alcoholic bodies now introduced may be named the alcosol and alcogel of silicic acid. **1922** A. W. STEWART *Physico-Chem. Themes* ix. 160.

alcove (æl'kəʊv, 'ælkəʊv). [a. Fr. *alcôve*, ad. Sp. Pg. *alcova, alcoba*, ad. Arab. *al-qobbah*, i.e. *al* the + *qobbah* a vault, a vaulted chamber; f. *qubba* to vault.]

1. A vaulted recess; especially, **a.** 'A recess, or part of a chamber, separated by an estrade or partition, and other correspondent ornaments; in which is placed a bed of state, and sometimes seats to entertain company.' J. In Spain applied also to the recess for the bed in an ordinary chamber.

[**1623** MINSHEU *Sp. Dict., Alcoba*, a closet, a close roome for a bed.] **1676** D'URFEY *Mad. Fickle* IV. ii. (1677) 43 D'ee hear 'em Sir— they're yonder in th' Alcove. **1678** PHILLIPS, *Alcove*, a recess within a chamber for the setting of a Bed out of the way; where for state many times the Bed is advanced upon two or three ascents with a rail at the feet. **1688** in BURNET *Own Time* (T.) Of these eighteen were let into the bed-chamber; but they stood at the furthest end of the room. The ladies stood within the alcove. **1725** POPE *Odyss.* III. 510 Deep in a rich alcove the prince was laid, And slept beneath the pompous colonnade. *a* **1733** NORTH *Lives of Norths* I. 272 A large hall was built with a sort of alcove at one end for distinction. **1753** HANWAY *Travels* (1762) I. VII. xcii. 422 His bed..was in a small alcove or niche. **1878** G. MACDONALD *Ann. Quiet Neighb.* vi. 74 She emerged from a recess in the room, a kind of dark alcove.

b. An arched recess or niche in the wall of any building or apartment, of a cave, etc.

1786 COWPER *Gratitude* 33 This china that decks the alcove Which here people call a buffet. **1830** MILMAN *Hist. Jews* I. I. (ed. 2) 21 The common cemetery..is usually hewn out of the rock..with alcoves in the sides, where the coffins are deposited. **1856** MISS MULOCH *John Halif.* 159 John and I were in the alcove of the window. **1872** O. SHIPLEY *Gloss. Eccl. Terms* 175 In England these [Easter] sepulchres are often permanent alcoves.

2. A recess in a garden or pleasure ground, originally in the surrounding wall or hedge; but in later usage, Any covered retreat, a bower or summerhouse.

1706 ADDISON *Rosamond* I. vi, Amaranths, and Eglantines, With intermingling sweets have wove The particolour'd gay Alcove. **1766** C. ANSTEY *Bath Guide* ix. 58 Some to *Lincomb's* shady groves, Or to *Simpson's* proud Alcoves. **1817** COLERIDGE *Biogr. Lit.* 249 The women and children feasting in the alcoves of box and yew. **1863** MRS. HOWITT tr. *Bremer's Greece* II. xvi. 146 A lofty rugged rock, formed by nature into a rude alcove. **1870** D. ROSSETTI *Poems, Jenny* (1871) 123 And in the alcove coolly spread Glimmers with dawn your empty bed.

alcoved (æl'kəʊvd), *ppl. a.* [f. prec. + -ED.] Made as an alcove, vaulted, arched.

1865 J. CAMERON *Malayan Ind.* 76 The ceilings of the principal rooms are alcoved.

alcum-: see ALCHEM-.

alcumyn, variant of ALCAMYNE, *Obs.*

alcyon, variant of HALCYON.

alcyon ('ælsɪən). *Zool.* = ALCYONIUM.

1868 WRIGHT *Ocean W.* vi. 121 The Alcyonaria are so designated from their principal type, that of the Alcyons.

alcyonarian (,ælsɪə'nɛərɪən), *a.* and *sb.* [f. mod.L. *Alcyonaria* + -AN.] **A.** *adj.* Belonging to the *Alcyonaria*, a sub-order of Actinoid Zoophytes; see ALCYONIUM. **B.** *sb.* A zoophyte of that group.

1878 SPRY *Cruise Challenger* i. 13 Twelve gigantic alcyonarian polyps. **1880** MOSELEY in *19th Cent.* No. 38, 617 The deep sea must be lighted here and there by greater or smaller patches of luminous alcyonarians.

alcyonic (ælsɪ'ɒnɪk), *a. Zool.* [f. ALCYON-IUM + -IC.] Of or pertaining to Alcyonium.

1847 in CRAIG.

alcyonite ('ælsɪənaɪt). [f. ALCYON-IUM + -ITE a formative of names of minerals and fossils.] A fossil zoophyte related to *Alcyonium.*

1822 J. FLINT *Lett. fr. Amer.* 261 The rocks contain.. millepores, favocites, alcyonites, corals. **1865** W. WHITE *East Eng.* II. 174 Agates, carnelians, Alcyonites..may be picked up by those who know how to look for them.

‖**Alcyonium** (ælsɪ'əʊnɪəm). [L., ad. Gr. ἀλκυόνιον Bastard-sponge, so called according to Dioscorides from its resemblance to the nest of the ἀλκυών or Halcyon.] A genus of zoophytes, giving its name to the sub-order *Alcyonaria*, forming firm fleshy masses, a species of which is popularly called Dead Man's Fingers, and Cow's Paps.

1752 *Phil. Trans.* XLVII. 460 Call'd madrepora, lithophyton or alcyonium. **1786** *Ibid.* LXXVI. 444 Infinite variety of corals, madrepores, alcyoniums. **1857** WOOD *Com. Obj. Sea.* vi. 116 When placed in clear sea-water, the alcyonium soon begins to put forth a few crystalline columnar polyps.

alcyonoid ('ælsɪənɔɪd), *a. Zool.* [f. ALCYON-IUM + -OID.] Resembling or allied to Alcyonium. Also used *subst.*

1862 DANA *Man. Geol.* 163 Alcyonoid Polyps. **1872** —— *Corals* i. 80 The Alcyonoids include some of the gayest and most delicate of coral shrubs.

†**ald**, *a. Obs.* or *dial.* [OE. *ald* became in WS. *eald*, whence the later *æld, eeld, yeald,* ELD; in midl. it became in due course OLD, but remained in the north as *ald, auld*, mod. dial. *aald, aad, aud*, in use from Scotland to Shropshire in the W., and Lincolnshire in the E.] The following quotations illustrate the form; for sense see OLD.

c **950** *Lindisf. Gosp.* Luke i. 18 Ic am ald. *c* **1175** *Lamb. Hom.* 43 An ald mon. *c* **1340** HAMPOLE *Pr. Consc.* 749 Alde men. **1375** BARBOUR *Bruce* I. 17 Aulde storys that men redys. **1513–75** *Diurn. Occurrents* (1833) 33 The ald enemies of Ingland. *c* **1620** A. HUME *Brit. Tong.* (1865) 28 An ald man sould be wyse. **1790** BURNS *Tam o' Shanter* 15 Auld Ayr wham ne'er a town surpasses.

†**ald**, *sb. Obs.* 3–6. [variant of ELD:—OE. *eldu*, influenced by the adj. *ald*, old. Also found in midl. dial. as OLD.]

1. Age, duration of life or existence.

c **1200** ORMIN 14426 Þis middellærdes ald iss all o sexe daless dæledd.

2. An age, or secular period of the world.

c **1200** ORMIN 2373 Swa summ i þatt ald Wass laȝhe to ben fesstnedd.

3. Old age, the advanced state or period of life.

1205 LAYAM. 19411 Bruttes hafden muchil mode..for þas kinges alde. *c* **1430** *Seven Sages* (P.) 641 He wille brynge the adown in olde. **1535** STEWART *Cron. Scotl.* I. 444 Vnsaturabill bayth in ald and youth. **1551** ABP. HAMILTON *Catech.* 69 a, Fra the tyme of thair youthede to the tyme of thair auld.

†**ald(e, ald-en**, *v. Obs.* [OE. *aldi-an*, f. *ald* old; still retained in 2–3 as *ald-ien, ald-en*; whence in 3–4 the midl. *old-en*; see OLD *v. Eld-en* (see ELDE *v.*) is a parallel form from WS. *eald-ian.*] To grow old.

c **825** *Vesp. Ps.* vi. 9 Ic aldade betwih alle feond mine. *c* **1175** *Lamb Hom.* 109 þeo hearte ne aldeð naut.

†**alday**, *adv. phr. Obs.* [= ALL DAY; cf. *alway.*]

1. Every day (see ALL A 3); *hence*, Continually, always. (Cf. Fr. *tous les jours, toujours.*) *Obs.*

1297 R. GLOUC. 92 Þe grete tresour þat he alday nom. **1387** TREVISA *Higden* VI. xvii. Rolls Ser. VII. 103 We dye alday [*Quotidie morimur*], but none overcomeþ. **1393** GOWER *Conf.* Prol. 15 To hem that shall it alday rede. **1477** PYMPE in *Paston Lett.* 794 III. 185 That wrytith, sendith, and wisshith alday your wele More than his owne. **1483** CAXTON *Gold. Leg.* 73/3 What shal I aldaye wryte.

2. The whole day, all day (which is the usual form; see ALL A 1. Cf. Fr. *tout le jour, toute la journée*).

1297 R. GLOUC. 197 Þey ech of vs sete alday, þe beste red to rede, Betere ansuere ne ssolde we fynde.

‖**al'dea, aldee.** *Obs.* [Pg. *aldea* (Fr. *aldée*), ad. Arab. *al-dayɂa* the farm, village.] A village or villa (in Portugal or its colonies).

1698 J. FRYER *East Ind. & Persia* 71 Pleasant Aldeas or country seats of the Gentry. **1780** DUNN *New Direct.* (ed. 5) 110 The coast is filled with Aldees or villages of the Indians.

aldehydate ('ældɪhaɪdeɪt). *Chem.* [f. next + -ATE.] A salt in which aldehyde acts as a monobasic acid.

1863 WATTS *Dict. Chem.* (1879) I. 111 Aldehydate of silver ..Aldehydate of Ammonium, Aldehyde-ammonia, or Acetyl Ammonium $C_2H_3O.NH_4$.

aldehyde ('ældɪhaɪd). [= *Al. dehyd.* abbreviation for *Alcohol dehydrogenatum*, i.e. Alcohol dehydrogenated, or deprived of hydrogen.]

1. A colourless, very volatile fluid of suffocating smell, obtained by the oxidation of alcohol, which by further oxidation is converted into Acetic Acid.

1850 DAUBENY *Atom. Theory* vii. (ed. 2) 193 By the action of oxidizing agents on alcohol..we produce aldehyde. **1862** *Cornh. Mag.* VI. 320 That during the earlier stages of the sojourn of alcohol in the body, it was converted only to aldehyde, or acetic acid, which are lower degrees of oxidation than that represented by carbonic acid and water.

2. An extensive class of compounds of the same type as the above; and bearing the same relation to the alcohols, from each of which a corresponding *aldehyde* is derived by the removal of two atoms of hydrogen. (Called by Gmelin *Aldides.*)

Thus Methyl Alcohol CH_4O, Methyl Aldehyde CH_2O; common or Ethyl Alcohol C_2H_6O, common or Acetyl Aldehyde, or Acetaldehyde, C_2H_4O, which has two

polymeric modifications called *Metaldehyde* and *Paraldehyde*.
1863 WATTS *Dict. Chem.* (1879) I. 111 Many aldehydes are obtained directly from plants, either existing ready formed in the plants, or being given off as volatile oils on distilling the plants with water. **1873** —— *Fownes' Chem.* 538 Aldehydes are compounds intermediate between alcohols and acids. **1881** ABNEY in *Nature* XXV. 191 Par-aldehyde has three molecules of aldehyde in its one molecule.

Comb. **aldehyde-ammonia**: see ALDEHYDATE. **aldehyde green**, a dye, also called aniline green or emeraldine, prepared by the action of aldehyde on magenta. **aldehyde-resin**, a resinous substance obtained by heating aldehyde with potash in aqueous or alcoholic solution. (Watts.)

aldehydic (ældɪˈhaɪdɪk), *a.* [f. prec. + -IC.]
1882 *Nature* 16 Mar. 457 The formation of albumin by condensation of aldehydic groups with amido groups.

al dente (æl ˈdɛnteɪ, ‖al ˈdente), *adv.* (and *adj.*) *phr.* [a. It., lit. 'to the tooth'.] Of pasta, etc.: (cooked) so as to be tender but still firm when bitten.
1935 M. MORPHY *Recipes of All Nations* 133 In Italy it [*sc.* pasta] is cooked 'al dente', as they call it—sufficiently firm to be felt 'under the tooth'. **1958** W. BICKEL tr. *Hering's Dict. Cookery* 600 Macaroni must be cooked in plenty of boiling salt water 'al dente', i.e. done but not soft. **1960** *Harper's Bazaar* Oct. 153/1 Spaghetti cooked *al dente*. **1978** *Chicago* June 210/2 For dessert, we ordered apple strudel. Served hot, the strudel had a generous supply of *al dente* apples, and the leaves, though not especially crisp, were enjoyable. **1984** *Listener* 5 Apr. 10/2 Our vegetables are cooked *al dente*. Should you require your vegetables well done, please advise on placing your order.

alder (ˈɔːldə(r)), *sb.*[1] Forms: 1 alor, -aer, -er, 1–2 alr, 3 olr, 4–8 aller, 7–8 allar; 4–5 aldir, aldyr, 4– alder. By-forms: 5 ellyr, 7– eller, owler, ouller. [With OE. *alor*, *aler*, cf. ON. *ölr*, *elrir*, OHG. *elira*, *erila*, mod.G. *erle*, *eller*. The *d* was a phonetic development, as in *alder-best* (see ALL D 3), and the dialectal *celder* = *cellar*, etc. The historical form *aller* survived till 18th c. in literature, and is still general in the dialects. *Owler* (= *aüler*, or *olr*) used by Cotton, etc., survives in Lancashire, etc.]

1. A tree (*Alnus glutinosa*) related to the Birch, common in wet places over the northern hemisphere, from Europe to N.W. America and Japan, the wood of which resists decay for an indefinite time under water.
c **700** *Epinal Gloss* (Sweet 38) *Alnus*: alaer *Erf.* aler. **882** *Chart. Ælfred* in *Cod. Dipl.* V. 124 Norð úpp of ðǽre ie úpp on ðone ibihtan alr; of ðám ibihtan alre on scortan dic. *c* **940** *Sax. Leechd.* II. 32 Oxan slyppan . . & alor rinde. *a* **1300** in Wright *Voc.* 91 *Alnus*, olr. *c* **1386** CHAUCER *Knts. T.* 2063 The names how the trees highte, As ook, fir, birch, asp, aldir [*v.r.* alder -yr]. **1483** *Cath. Angl.*, An ellyrtre: *alnus*. **1502** ARNOLD *Chron.* (1811) 164 Graf it in a stoke of elme or aller. **1567** MAPLET *Greene Forest* 30 The Alder tree (which by corrupt and accustomed kinde of speaking they commonly call the Elder). **1578** LYTE *Dodoens* 756 The blowinges of Alder are long tagglets. **1601** HOLLAND *Pliny* (1634) I. 493 Pines, Pitch trees, and Allar, are very good for to make . . pipes to conuey water. **1616** SURFLET *Country Farme* 504 The Aller or Alder-tree . . doth serue . . to lay the foundations of buildings vpon, which are laid in the riuers, fens, or other standing waters, because it neuer rotteth in the vvater, but lasteth as it vvere for euer. **1635** BRERETON *Trav.* (1844) 149 Cleared of the oullers and under-wood. **1676** COTTON *Angler* II. (1863) 240 Plant willows or owlers about it. **1727** POPE, etc. *Art of Sinking* 109 And to the sighing alders, alders sigh. **1791** NEWTE *Tour Eng. & Sc.* 240 The oak, aller, birch, and ash, shoot up from the old stock. **1794** MARTYN *Rousseau's Bot.* xxviii. 434 Alder is of the same genus with the Birch. **1799** J. ROBERTSON *Agric. Perth* 206 Willows, allers, and other brush-wood are grubbed up. **1870** MORRIS *Earthly Par.* I. I. 172 Amid rushes tall Down in the bottom alders grew.

2. black alder, berry-bearing alder, or, with modern botanists, **alder buckthorn** (*Rhamnus Frangula*), a European shrub, formerly thought to be allied to the preceding tree.
1579 LANGHAM *Gard. Health* (1633) 10 The iuice of blacke Allder . . is yellow. **1597** GERARD, *Alnus nigra, Blacke Aller*. **1794** MARTYN *Rousseau's Bot.* xvi. 206 Berry-bearing Alder . . grows in woods, is a black looking shrub. **1861** PRATT *Flower. Plants* II, Alder Buckthorn . . Plant perennial . . its bark affords a good dye.

3. Pop. extended to various other shrubs or trees, as Black Alder (N. Amer.), *Prinos verticillatus*; White Alder (N. Amer.), *Clethra alnifolia*; (S. Afr.) *Platylophus trifoliatus*; Red Alder (S. Afr.), *Cunonia capensis*.

4. *Comb.*:
a. *instrumental*, as *alder-fringed*, *-skirted*, etc.
1845 HIRST *Poems* 48 Adown the alder-margined lane The throstle sings. **1858** H. MILLER *Sch. & Schm.* (1858) 164 The dark hills and alder-skirted river of Strathcarron.

b. *attrib.*, as *alder-branch*, *-brake*, *-pile*, *-tree*, *-wood*; **alder-buckthorn** (see 2); **alder-carr**, a piece of wet ground where alders grow; **alder-fly** (also ellipt. **alder**) = ORL-*fly*.
1850 MRS. BROWNING *Poems* I. 344 Near the alder-brake We sigh. **1440** *Promp. Parv.* Aldyr-kyr (alder-kerre, alderkar). *Alnetum, locus ubi alni et tales arbores crescunt*. **1828** H. DAVY *Salmonia* 24 The fly you see is called by fishermen the alder fly, and is generally in large quantities before the May fly. **1859** C. KINGSLEY *Glaucus* (ed. 4) 195 The water-crickets . . change into . . the dark chocolate 'Alder' (Sialis lutaria). **1875** [see ORL-*fly*]. **1902** *Encycl. Brit.* XXV. 447/2 Among the flies which are general favourites with dry-fly fishers are the . . alder . . and the May-fly. **1928** *Daily Express* 11 Aug. 4/2 On Dartmoor streams . . I found a small alder and a black gnat as effective as anything. **1862** COLEMAN *Woodl. Heaths* 62 Alder-wood, if kept constantly under water, is almost imperishable . . It is said that on Alder-piles the beautiful arch of the famous Rialto of Venice is supported.

† **ˈalder**, *sb.*[2] *Obs.* Forms: 1 aldor, -ur, 1–2 (late WS. ealdor), 2–4 alder, ælder, (ældere, eldere). [f. *ald* old + *-or* suffix forming sbs.; cf. OFris. *alder* parent. The pl. *aldras*, WS. *ealdras*, 'ancestors,' is to be distinguished from *ęldran* (WS. *ieldran*, *yldran*) 'elders,' compar. of *ald* old, used in same sense. In Layamon the two words are confused.]

1. Parent, ancestor, elder (chiefly in *pl.*). [In this sense only in OE.; superseded by the compar. of the adj. *ald* (*eald*), *ęldran*: see ELDER.]
? *a* **800** CÆDMON *Gen.* (Grein) 1578 Ða com ærest Cam . . þær his aldor læᵹ. *c* **885** K. ÆLFRED *Bæda* I. xxvii, Ure eldras þa ǽrestan menn. [—— *Oros.* I. i. 1 Ure yldran.]

2. The head of a family or clan; a patriarch, chief, prince, or ruler. (Used to translate L. titles, as *senior*, *princeps*, *dominus*, *dux*.)
c **600** *Beowulf* 697 Beowulf is min nama: wille ic asecgan . . min ǽrende aldre þinum. *c* **950** *Lindisf. Gosp.* Matt. xxvii. 1 [Vulg. *Omnes principes sacerdotum et seniores populi*] . . Alle aldor sacerda & ældro ðæs folces. *c* **975** *Rushw. G.* Ealle aldur sacerdæs & ældre þæs folces. *c* **1000** *Ags. G.* Ealle þæra sacerda ealdras . . and þæs folces ealdras. *c* **1160** *Hatton G.*, Ealle þare sacerda ealdres . . and þas folkes ealdres. *c* **1175** *Cotton Hom.* 219 Hare alder þat he mihte beon. **1205** LAYAM. 16562 þu scalt beon alder [**1250** louerd]. *Ibid.* 23436 Frolle, þe ælder wes of France [**1250** king]. *Ibid.* 3122 Aganippes wes ihaten: hæleðen he wes ældere [**1250** eldere]. *c* **1340** *Gaw. & Gr. Knt.* 95 A vncouþe tale . . Of alderes, of armes, of oþer auenturus.

† **ˈalder**, *a. compar. Obs.* or *dial.* [f. ALD old. In OE. the compar. properly took umlaut *ęldra* for *aldira*, whence mod. ELDER; but a north. and midl. form *alder*, without umlaut, appears in 12th c., whence by usual change of long or lengthened *a* to *o* the mod. OLDER. *Alder*, *aulder* continues to be the form in Sc. and north. dialects; and occurs as an affected archaism in other writers *c* 1600.]
1205 LAYAM. 3750 Of þan aldre sustren. *Ibid.* 8199 þe king nom þreo aldere men [**1250** holde men]. *c* **1325** *E.E. Allit. P.* A. 620 And ay the ofter, þe alder þay were. **1581** STUDLEY tr. *Seneca's Medea* 134 b, The wood in alder-time . . Did spread his shade on gladsome soyle; no shade remayneth now. **1610** HOLLAND tr. *Camden's Brit.* I. 806 Those that liv'd in alder time [*Mod. Sc.* aulder, *Northumb.* auder].

alder-, variant of ALLER- gen. pl. of ALL, used in comb. as *alder-best*, *alder-liefest*: see ALL D 3.

† **ˈalderdom.** *Obs.* Also 1 aldordom (WS. ealdordom). [f. ALDER *sb.*[2] + -DOM; cf. *kingdom*.] Lordship, chief authority.
c **950** *Lindisf. Gosp.* Luke xix. 20 þætte saldon hine ðæm aldordóm. *a* **1000** *Metr. Ps.* cxiii. (cxiv.) 2 Hæfdan ealdurdóm ofer Israhélas. *c* **1200** ORMIN 18278 Ræfeþþ þe þin allderrdom.

† **ˈalderelde.** *Obs.* [f. *alder* older (perh. confused with *alder-* in *alder-most*) + ELD.] Extreme old age.
a **1300** *E.E. Psalter* lxx. 18 Til in un-elde and alder-elde.

† **ˈalderling.** *Obs.* or *dial.* [perh. f. ALDER *sb.*[1] + -LING.] A term applied to some fresh-water fish, called also dialectally *aller-trout*.
1655 MOUFFET & BENN. *Health's Improv.* (1746) 283 Gray Trouts . . lurk . . like the Alderlings under the Roots of great Alders. *Ibid.* 268 Alderlings are a kind of Fish betwixt a Trout and a Grayling. **1661** LOVELL *Anim. & Min.* 232 Alderling . . lie ever in deep water under some old and great Alder.

alderman (ˈɔːldəmən). Forms: 1–2 aldormann (late WS. ealdor-), 3 allderrmann, aldurmon, 4 elder-, heldar-, aldur-, aldreman, 5 aldir-, aldyr-, 4– alderman. (8–9 Historical ealderman, ealdorman.) [f. OE. *aldor* (*ealdor*): see ALDER *sb.*[2] + MAN, i.e. the *man* who occupied the position held in an earlier stage of society by the *aldor*, patriarch or chief of the clan.]

The *aldor* (or *ealdor*) was thus a natural rank, the *aldorman* its political equivalent. But the distinction necessarily faded away; the Northumbrian and Mercian Gospel glosses constantly have *aldorman* for the WSax. *ealdor*, and in WSax. itself *ealdorman* differed from *ealdor* solely in its more restricted and technical use.

1. A senior, signor, superior, ruler; a noble or person of high rank.

In OE. the special title of one exercising authority under the king, over a former kingdom, as Mercia, a district, or county; a viceroy or lord-lieutenant. Used also to translate Lat. *princeps*, *subregulus*, *optimas*, *satrapa*, *dux*, *comes*, *præpositus*; and, in a more general sense, many other words, as *pontifex*, *architriclinus*, *presbyter*, *senator*, etc. The special title was mostly supplanted by *earl* under the Danish dynasty; the more general sense continued for several centuries, and gave rise to 2 and 3. For the OE. title, recent historical writers have used the late West-Saxon and Kentish *ealdorman*; but the general OE. form was *aldormann*.

a. As O.E. title.
750 *O.E. Chron.* (Parker MS.) Her Cuþred cyning ᵹefeaht uuiþ Æþelhun þone ofermedan aldorman. *c* **855** *Ibid.* an. 495 Her cuomon tweᵹen aldor-men on Bretene, Cerdic and Cynric his sunu. **894** *Ibid.* Æþered ealdormon, and Æþelm ealdorman, and Æþelnoþ ealdorman, and þa cinges þegnas. **1205** LAYAM. 1420 Numbert hehte þe alder mon, þe sculde þas ernde don. **1591** LAMBARDE *Arch.* (1635) 249 Before the divisions of the Realms into Shires, every large territorie had an Alderman, or Governour. **1599** THYNNE *Animadv.* (1865) 33 Brightnothus, aldermanne, erle, or duke, of northumberlande. **1761** HUME *Hist. Eng.* I. App. i. 93 The Aldermen, or governors of counties, who after the Danish times, were often called Earls. **1839** KEIGHTLEY *Hist. Eng.* I. 76 After the Danish conquest, the title of Ealdorman was changed for that of Earl. **1862** LD. BROUGHAM *Brit. Const.* x. 136 The Earl, Eorlderman, or Governor of the county. **1876** FREEMAN *Norm. Conq.* I. iii. 75 The chieftains of the first settlers in our island bore no higher title than Ealdorman or Heretoga.

b. As translation of foreign titles = ALDER *sb.*[2]
c **950** *Lindisf. Gosp.* John ii. 8 Brengeð ðæm aldormen [*Ags. & Hatton G.* ealdre; Vulg. *architriclino*]. *c* **1000** *Ags. Gosp.* Matt. xx. 21 Ealdormenn wealdað hyra þeoda [*L. & R.* aldormenn; Vulg. *principes*]. *c* **1200** ORMIN 14061 And son se þatt bridgume comm, þatt allderrmann himm seᵹᵹde. **1387** TREVISA *Higden* Rolls Ser. IV. 313 Tiberius exilede many of þe aldermen [i.e. of the senators]. *c* **1394** *P. Pl. Crede* 691 Aungells & Arcangells . . And alle Aldermen, þat bene *ante tronum*. *c* **1550** CHEKE *Matt.* xxvii. 1 Al ye hedpriestes and ye aldermen of yᵉ people, took councel again Jesus. **1618** BOLTON *Florus* I. i. (1636) 6 Called . . for their antiquitie, 'Senators,' or Aldermen.

† **2.** The headman, ruler, governor, or warden of a guild. *Obs.*
1130 *Pipe Roll 31 Hen. I*, Ut sit aldermannus in Gilda Mercatorum [at York]. **1180** *Admerciamenta de Gildis adulterinis* (Madox *Hist. Excheq.* 490) Gilda unde Goscelinus est Aldermannus. **1316** *E. Eng. Gilds* xxviii. 73 Be þe ordinaunce of þe Alderman and of þe gilde breþeren. **1368** *Ibid.* xx. 55 If ani broþer be ded wit-owten þe toun, þe aldirman xal do þe belleman gon for þe soule. **1494** *Ibid.* 188 The Alderman of the seid Gilde shalbe at Seynt Katerynis Chapell aforeseid, with all his Bredern. **1649** SELDEN *Laws of Eng.* I. xxxiii. (1739) 50 By custom they grew to be Fraternities, or Corporations under one Magistrate or Head, whom they called Alderman.

3. Since the guilds became identified with the corporation or ruling municipal body: A magistrate in English and Irish cities and boroughs, next in dignity to the mayor; properly, as in London, the chief officer of a ward.
c **1200** *Trin. Coll. Hom.* 55 On him rixleð lichamliche wil, alse eldrene man on his burh. **1229** *Lib. de Ant. Leg.* 6 Omnes aldermanni et magnates civitatis per assensum universorum civium. *c* **1330** *Arth. & Merl.* 5105 The alder man Ich with his ward cam. *c* **1386** CHAUCER *Prol.* 372 Euerich for the wisdom þat he kan Was shaply for to been an Alderman [*v.r.* aldirman, aldurman]. **1428** in Heath *Grocers' Comp.* (1869) 7 For the fyrste dynner imade in the parlore to oure Aldermen . . £5 6*s*. 8*d*. **1594** SHAKS. *Rich. III*, III. vii. 66 The Maior and Aldermen . . Are come to haue some conference with his Grace. **1611** COTGR. s.v. *Abbé*, Alderman's pace, a leasurely walking, slow gate. **1629** GAULE *Holy Madn.* 94 What an Alderman's pace he comes. **1667** E. CHAMBERLAYNE *Gt. Brit.* I. 201 The 26 Aldermen preside over the 26 Wards of the City [of London]. All the Aldermen that have been Lord-Mayors, and the three eldest Aldermen that have not yet arrived to that honourable Estate, are by their Charter Justices of the Peace. **1784** COWPER *Sofa* 61 Elbows still were wanting; these some say, An alderman of Cripplegate contrived. **1878** STUBBS *Const. Hist.* III. 565 The title of alderman, which had once belonged to the heads of the several guilds, was transferred to the magistrates of the several wards into which the town was divided, or to the sworn assistants of the mayor, in the cases in which no such division was made.

† **4.** 'Formerly, there were also Aldermen of Hundreds.' Chambers *Cycl.* 1751.
1596 SPENSER *State of Irel.* 107 When I come to appoint the Alderman, that is the head of the Hundreth.

5. *slang.* **a.** (See quots.)
1782 G. PARKER *Hum. Sketches* 31 Nick often eat a roast fowl and sausage with me, which in cant, is called an Alderman double slang'd. **1859** LORD W. LENNOX *Pict. Sporting Life* I. vi. 169 A turkey, garnished with sausages—technically termed, an alderman hung in chains.

† **b.** = JEMMY *sb.* 6. *Obs.*
1872 DIPROSE *London & London Life* xxi. 159 The 'alderman' . . is a 'head bar', which would open any safe. The smaller bars were called 'citizens'. **1883** *Standard* 14 May 5/8 A complete set of safebreaking tools had been . . left behind, including wedges, an 'alderman', a jemmy.

aldermanate (ˈɔːldəmənəɪt). [ad. med.L. *aldermannātus*, f. *aldermannus* after *senatus*, *consulatus*, etc. See -ATE.] The office or dignity of alderman; the aldermen collectively.
1875 STUBBS *Const. Hist.* III. xxi. 581 We must trace the existence of the aldermanate . . to the ancient guild system.

aldermancy (ˈɔːldəmənsɪ). *rare.* [f. ALDERMAN + -CY (cf. *captain-cy*), after *magistracy*, *lieutenancy*, in which the suffix, really *-y*, is apparently *-cy*.] The office of an alderman. (In mod. Dicts.)

ˈaldermaˌness. An alderman's wife.
1840 BARHAM *Ingol. Leg.* 16 With the swate Peeresses . . And Aldermanesses and the Boord of Works.

aldermanic (ɔːldəˈmænɪk), *a.* [f. ALDERMAN + -IC; in imitation of words of Fr., L., or Gr. origin in *-ic*, as *German-ic*. The native adj. is ALDERMANLY.] Of, pertaining to, or like an alderman: **a.** (municipal.)

1770 WILKES *Corr.* (1805) IV. 32 For fear of growing more dull than usual in this thick aldermanic air. **1799** SOUTHEY *Nondescr.* vi. Wks. III. 72 Aldermanic bliss. **1819** SHELLEY *Pet. Bell* Wks. 1839, 240 Lunches and snacks so aldermanic. **1837** LOCKHART *Scott* IV. xli. 166 The feast was.. gorgeous; an aldermanic display of turtle and venison. **1870** HAWTHORNE *Eng. Note-Bks.* (1879) II. 19 Quite as dull in their aldermanic way. **1878** M. HAY *Under the Will* I. 47 The aldermanic luxury of turtle soup. **1882** F. BUCKLAND *Jottings Anim. Life* 255 A good plump seal or an aldermanic walrus.

b. (Old English.) Also *ealdormanic*.

1861 PEARSON *E. & Mid. Ages Eng.* 173 Probably in most shires there were several families of ealdormanic rank, from whom the holder of office was selected by the king, with advice and consent of his witan.

†**alderˈmanical**, *a. Obs. rare*$^{-1}$. [f. ALDERMAN + -ICAL] = prec.

1653 BROME *Damois.* II. i. 403 See my Aldermanicall Father-in-Law!

†**alderˈmanikin.** *nonce-wd. Obs.* [f. ALDERMAN; see MANIKIN.] A little or young alderman.

1640 BROME *Antip.* III. ii. 277 *Item*, a love Epistle for the Aldermanikin his sonne.

aldermanity (ɔːldəˈmænɪtɪ). [f. ALDERMAN + -ITY in humorous imitation of *human, humanity*, etc.: see -ITY.]

1. The quality or office of an alderman.

1625 B. JONSON *Staple of News* III. ii, I would fain see.. a treatise of aldermanity truly written! **1823** LAMB *Elia* Ser. II. xxiv. (1865) 408 How would certain topics, as aldermanity.. have sounded to a Terentian auditory?

2. The body of aldermen. (Cf. *admiralty*.)

1632 B. JONSON *Magn. Lady* v. vii, 'Twill purchase the whole Bench of Aldermanity.

aldermanlike (ˈɔːldəmənlaɪk), *a.* and *adv.* [f. as prec. + -LIKE.]

A. *adj.* Like, or becoming to, an alderman.

1612 SHELTON *Don Quix.* I. iv. 20 (T.) All in a grave posture and with an aldermanlike pace. **1779** MISS WILKES in *Wilkes' Corr.* (1805) IV. 285 On Friday morning; I shall arrive, alderman-like, with some Dorking fowls for your acceptance. **1831** BLAKEY *Free Will* 68 What Swift says about its being an alderman-like virtue.

†**B.** *adv.* After the manner of an alderman. *Obs.*

1617 J. RIDER *Dict.*, Aldermanlike, *Senatorie, patricie*, adv.

aldermanly (ˈɔːldəmənlɪ), *a.* [f. ALDERMAN + -LY[1].] Like, or becoming to, an alderman.

1720 SWIFT *Wks.* 1755 II. II. 23 Exigencies wanting a reasonable infusion of this aldermanly discretion.

aldermanry (ˈɔːldəmənrɪ). Also 5–6 aldyrmanry. [f. ALDERMAN + -RY, med.L. 13th c. *aldermaneria*. Cf. for the form *yeomanry*, for the sense *deanery, archdeaconry*.] A district of a borough having its own alderman, a ward; *also*, the dignity or rank of an alderman.

c **1229** [STUBBS *Const. Hist.* III. 561 'Early in the reign of Henry III.. the name *Aldermaneria* seems to be used exchangeably with *Warda*.'] **1502** ARNOLD *Chron.* 37 an. 1384 From yᵉ office of aldyrmanry vtterly and percysly to cessen. **1608** DEKKER *Dead Terme* F iv b, Those Diuisions or Partages [of London], are called Wardes or Aldermanries, being 26 in number. **1698** STOW *London* (ed. Strype 1754) I. II. i. 347/1 The ancient division of this City was into Wards or Aldermanries. **1841** HOR. SMITH *Moneyed Man* I. viii. 250 The city assembly, the vulgar, untitled balls of the Aldermanry.

aldermanship (ˈɔːldəmənʃɪp). [f. ALDERMAN + -SHIP; this is the most legitimate term for the office.] The office, position, or quality of an alderman; **a.** municipal.

1494 FABYAN VII. 331 He was dyschargyd of his aldermanshyp. **1502** ARNOLD *Chron.* 37 an. 1384 They owe not to be remeued fro the office of aldyrmanshyp wythout certayn cause. **1714** FORTESCUE-ALAND in *Fortescue's Abs. & Lim. Mon.* 37 Our English termination, ship, as in Stewardship, Aldermanship, Worship. **1772** WILKES *Corr.* (1805) IV. 139 Mr. Martin does not accept the aldermanship. **1871** *Daily News* 6 Nov., The Vacant Aldermanship.

2. Old Eng. (Recent writers have used the late West Saxon *ealdorman*.)

1861 PEARSON *E. & Mid. Ages Eng.* 251 Ealdormanships of counties and towns. **1875** STUBBS *Const. Hist.* I. vi. 160 The original idea of the ealdormanship is, magistracy or jurisdiction, as implied in the attribute of age. **1876** FREEMAN *Norm. Conq.* I. iii. 80 Their progress from the ealdormanship of a corner of Hampshire to the Imperial crown.

Aldermaston (ˈɔːldəmɑːstən). The name of a village in Berkshire, site of the Atomic Weapons Research Establishment, used *attrib.* and *ellipt.* of demonstrations and protest marches by 'anti-bomb' demonstrators, as ***Aldermaston march, marcher***.

1958 *Observer* 2 Nov. 6/1 There are plenty of Aldermaston badges, with their semaphore symbol of ND—nuclear disarmament. **1958** *Times Lit. Suppl.* 28 Nov. 689/4, I am not a Communist, a pacifist or an Aldermaston marcher. **1960** *New Left Rev.* Nov.–Dec. 5/2 Next year's Aldermaston will really be a *fighting* Aldermaston. **1962** *Guardian* 19 Oct. 3/2 Neutralist and pacifist movements abroad.. call their marches 'Aldermastons'.

aldern (ˈɔːldən), *a.* and *sb.* Also 1 ælren, 3 allerne, 5 alloren. [f. ALDER *sb.*[1] + -EN. Its subst. use is prob. due to comb. like *aldern-tree*; but there may have been a confusion with ELDER, ELDERN.]

A. *adj.* Of alder.

1001 *Cod. Dipl.* III. 316 To þam ælrenan stobbe. **1398** TREVISA *Barth. De P.R.* XVII. 684 The pine tre, and alloren tree.. deep under þe grounde dureþ and lesteþ longe tyme. **1622** MAY *Virgil* (J.) Then aldern boats first plow'd the ocean.

B. *sb.* = ALDER *sb.*[1]

c **1250** W. DE BIBLESWORTH in Wright *Voc.* 171 *Coupet de aunne* (of allerne). **1607** TOPSELL *Four-footed Beasts* (1673) 220 If the right eye of a Hedge-hog be fryed with the oil of Alderne or Linseed, and put in a vessel of red brasse, and afterward anoint his eyes therewith, as with an eye-salve, he shall see as well in the dark as in the light.

Alderney (ˈɔːldənɪ). [The name of one of the Channel Islands.] Properly, the designation of the cattle bred in Alderney; popularly used *attrib.* or *ellipt.* as a general name for the cattle (mostly light or dark fawn-coloured) of the Channel Islands, including those of Jersey and Guernsey; also, an animal of this breed.

1771 SMOLLETT *H. Clinker* I. 2 Let Morgan's widow have the Alderney cow. **1772** F. BOSCAWEN *Let.* 11 July in C. F. Aspinall-Oglander *Admiral's Widow* (1942) v. 34 We.. have a great deal of garden, two fields and an Alderney cow. **1816** JANE AUSTEN *Emma* I. iv. 50 Eight cows, two of them Alderneys. **1834** YOUATT *Cattle* 267 The Alderney, considering its voracious appetite.. yields very little milk. **1853** MRS. GASKELL *Cranford* i. 7 An old lady had an Alderney cow, which she looked upon as a daughter. **1854** DICKENS *Hard Times* II. x, She didn't give any milk, ma'am; she gave bruises. She was a regular Alderney at that. **1875** in J. Coleman *Cattle Gt. Brit.* 139 The Channel Island breed of cattle, popularly known in this country as 'Alderneys', consists of two classes... The Guernsey is the larger of the two, usually of a light fawn colour... The Jersey class is smaller. **1910** *Encycl. Brit.* V. 539/2 (*Cattle*) The term Alderney is obsolete, the cattle of Alderney being mainly a type of the Guernsey breed. **1918** GALSWORTHY *Five Tales* v. 292 Listening to the starlings and skylarks, and the Alderney cows chewing the cud.

†**ˈaldership.** *Obs.* Only form 2 **alderscipe.** [f. ALDER *sb.*[2] + -SHIP.] Chiefship, lordship.

c **1175** *Cotton Hom.* 219, *Dominationes* hlafordscipe, *principatus* alderscipen.

ˈalderˌwoman. [f. ALDERMAN, after pairs like *gentleman, -woman*.] †**1.** An alderman's wife; cf. ALDRESS, ALDERMANESS. *Obs.*

1557 in W. H. Turner *Sel. Rec. Oxford* (1880) 264 Mʳᵉˢ. Brydgman shall go nexte unto the Alderwomen. **1640** BROME *Antip.* III. ii. 276 *Item*, an Elegy for Mistris Alderwoman.

2. A woman holding the position of an alderman.

1768 MORANT *Hist. Essex* II. 400/2 A Gild of women of our Lady's Lights, to which belonged an Alderwoman, and two wardens. **1895** [see MAYORESS 2]. **1900** *Daily News* 24 May 3/1 The London Government Act of last year.. prohibited women serving as alderwomen or councillors on borough Councils.

†**ˈaldest**, *a. superl. Obs.* or *dial.* [f. ALD old; see ALDER *a.* to which it belongs.]

1205 LAYAM. 6947 þe aldeste hæhte Fulgenius [**1250** þe eldest]. *Ibid.* 2105 þe ældeste broðer. **1297** R. GLOUC. 233 þe aldest hous al so. *c* **1325** *E.E. Allit. P.* B. 1333 Bolde Baltaȝar, watȝ his barn aldest. (*Mod. Sc.* auldest.)

aldfader, -father, obs. dial. var. ELDFATHER.

aldide (ˈældaɪd). *Chem.* [f. ALD(EHYDE) + -IDE.] Gmelin's name for the aldehydes as a class; see ALDEHYDE 2.

Aldine (ˈældaɪn, ˈɔːldaɪn), *a.* and *sb.* [ad. mod.L. *Aldinus, -a* (sc. *editio*), f. *Aldus*, latinized form of *Aldo* (see below.)] The designation of the editions of Greek and Latin classics (including many *principes*) printed or published at Venice by Aldo Manuzio (the more familiar name of Teobaldo Manucci, 1450–1515), and his family (*c* 1490–1597); also applied to certain styles of display types. As *sb.*, an Aldine book or edition.

The device characteristic of Aldine books is a figure of a dolphin on an anchor.

1802 DIBDIN *Classics* Introd. 27 A most beautiful copy of this Aldine edition. **1827** *Ibid.* (ed. 4) II. 342 The Aldine Demosthenes of 1504. *Ibid.* 343 This edition.. departs from the Aldine in some places. **1837** HALLAM *Hist. Lit.* I. I. iii. 257 (Aldus).. introduced (in 1501) a new Italian character, called Aldine. **1862** BURTON *Bk. Hunter* 101 Old editions of the classics in vellum bindings—Stephenses or Aldines. **1880** A. LANG *XXII Ballades in Blue China* 24 In rich men's shelves they take their ease—Aldines, Bodonis, Elzevirs! **1883** *Pall Mall Gaz.* 18 Sept. 3/2 An Aldine dolphin. **1895** [see DOLPHIN 4].

Aldis[1] (ˈɔːldɪs). *Aldis lens*: see quot. 1911.

1904 J. T. TAYLOR *Optics Photogr.* xxx. 204 This optician [*sc.* Hugh Lancelot Aldis] applied for another patent, which was granted in February, 1902. The construction is known as the Aldis lens. **1911** *Encycl. Brit.* XXI. 511/1 In 1902 H. L. Aldis issued the 'Aldis lens', *f*/6, a doublet composed of a cemented meniscus in front and single double-convex back lens.

Aldis[2] (ˈɔːldɪs). The name of Arthur Cyril Webb *Aldis*, used *attrib.* or *ellipt.* in the proprietary names of certain of his inventions, as ***Aldis lamp*** (for signalling in Morse code), ***Aldis (unit) sight*** (for artillery, aircraft, etc.).

1917 *R.N.A.S. Anti-Submarine Rep. No. 3* 4 The Aldis lamp used in surface craft, trawlers, etc., for communication with aircraft has given satisfactory results. **1918** J. M. GRIDER *War Birds: Diary* 11 July (1927) 231 His altimeter and Aldis sight were both hit. **1928** C. F. S. GAMBLE *North Sea Air Station* xv. 280, I at once reported the incident by means of Aldis lamp to H.M.S. *Dryad*. *Ibid.* xvi. 295 In some instances the ring was mounted in a telescope of unit magnification, one of the best examples of which was the Aldis sight. **1944** 'N. SHUTE' *Pastoral* viii. 190 Would you like me to make him a signal on the Aldis, sir, and tell him to bale out? **1962** *Oxf. Illustr. Dict.* 18/2 *Aldis lamp*, signalling lamp, used esp. in navy and air force, in which Morse signs are transmitted by rotating a mirror at whose focus the light is located.

aldo- (ældəʊ), before a vowel **ald-**, used as combining form of ALDEHYDE in the names of chemical compounds as ***aldo-hexose, -keten, -pentose***; **aldoxim(e**, the oxime of an aldehyde.

1883 *Jrnl. Chem. Soc.* XLIV. 1104 Lactones are not converted into aldoximes by the action of hydroxylamine. **1906** SUDBOROUGH *Bernthsen's Org. Chem.* 308 The relationship of the aldohexoses to the aldopentoses. **1907** J. B. COHEN *Org. Chem. Adv. Stud.* I. 295 An aldehyde sugar containing six atoms of carbon would be termed an aldo-hexose. *Ibid.* 310 Aldo-Pentose. **1912** F. G. POPE *Mod. Research Org. Chem.* 276 Two classes of ketens have been recognized, namely, the keto-ketens.. and the aldo-ketens.

aldol (ˈældɒl). *Chem.* [f. ALD(EHYDE) + (ALCOH)OL; see -OL.] A clear viscid neutral liquid of composition $CH_3.CH(OH).CH_2.CHO$, polymerous with acetyl aldehyde; so called because regarded by Wurz as intermediate in constitution and properties between aldehyde and alcohol; previously called *acraldehyde*.

1874 WATTS *Dict. Chem.* 2nd Supp. 38 *Aldol* possesses the reducing powers of the aldehydes. **1878** —— 3rd Supp. 54 *Aldol*.. is the aldehyde of butene-glycol.

aldolase (ˈældəleɪz). *Biochem.* [a. G. *aldolase* (O. Meyerhof et al. 1936, in *Biochem. Zeitschr.* CCLXXXVI. 301): see ALDOL and -ASE.] An enzyme present in muscle extract.

1940 *Chem. Abstr.* 7947 The zymohexase of Meyerhof and Lohmann.. and aldolase are identical. **1941** DORLAND & MILLER *Med. Dict.* 69/1 *Aldolase*, an enzyme in muscle extract which causes aldol condensations between phosphodihydroxyacetone and aldehydes to produce ketophosphoric acid. **1964** G. H. HAGGIS *Introd. Molecular Biol.* ii. 34 Samples of aldolase and glyceraldehyde-3-phosphate dehydrogenase (enzymes involved in glycolysis) were obtained and crystallized.

aldor, -ur, OE. forms of ALDER *sb.*[2], chief.

aldormann, OE. form of ALDERMAN.

aldose (ˈældəʊs). *Chem.* [f. ALD(EHYDE + -OSE[2].] An aldehyde sugar.

1894 *Jrnl. Chem. Soc.* LXVI. II. 489 (*title*) Reaction for aldehydes: differentiation of aldoses and ketoses. **1900** W. H. HOWELL *Amer. Text-Bk. Physiol.* (ed. 2) I. 561 Bodies.. possessing either the constitution of an aldehyde-alcohol,—CH(OH)CHO, called aldoses, or of a ketone-alcohol. **1902** J. J. R. MACLEOD in A. P. Beddard et al. *Pract. Physiol.* II. i. 161 Chemically, monosaccharides are either aldehydes or ketones, the former are called aldoses, the latter ketoses.

aldosterone (ˌældəʊˈstɛrəʊn, -ˈstɪərəʊn). *Biochem.* [f. ALDO- + STER(OL + -ONE.] A steroid hormone isolated from the adrenal gland. Hence ˌ**aldoˈsteronism**, a disease characterized by excessive amounts of aldosterone in the blood and urine.

1954 *Lancet* 12 June 1226/2 Because of the presence of an aldehyde group at the 18 position on the steroid ring the name 'aldosterone' has been proposed (in place of 'electro-cortin'). **1955** *Ibid.* 4 June 1167/1 Many cases of potassium-losing nephritis.. were really cases of primary aldosteronism. **1962** *Ibid.* 1 Dec. 1125/2 When aldosterone antagonists became readily available patients were included only when diuresis was complete.

†**ˈaldress.** *Obs.* [f. ALDER *sb.*[2] + -ESS; ? short for *alder*maness.] The wife of an alderman or mayor.

1608 *York Reg. MS.* 7 [John Bramhall, alderman of Pontefract, desires to be buried] at the end of the maiors and aldresses stall. **1692** R. THORESBY *Dairy* I. 220 After with relations.. to the funeral of Aldress Hick. **1713** *Ibid.* II. 180 Madam Nevile was this day buried—also was another aldress interred.

aldrin (ˈældrɪn). [f. the name of Kurt *Alder* (1902–1958), a German chemist + -IN[1].] A white crystalline insecticide.

1949 *U.S. Dept. Agric. Release Interdepart. Comm. on Pest Control*, (*title*) Aldrin, a coined name for an insecticidal product. **1953** *Ann. Reg. 1952* 412 A new American insecticide, aldrin, was used.. to supplement other methods of [locust] control. **1955** D. E. H. FREAR *Chem. of Pesticides* (ed. 3) 62 *Aldrin*, the first published tests on the material were made by Kearns, Weinman, and Decker early in 1949. This compound . . was later assigned the coined name *aldrin*, chosen because it was made by the Diels-Alder reaction.

aldur-, OE. form of ALDER *sb.*[2]

† ˈ**aldur-ˌfather.** *Obs.* [App. a confusion betw. *ald-father* ancestor and *aller-father* father of all, first parent.] Ancestor, progenitor.
1340 *Alex. & Dind.* 1050 þin aldur-faþur, alixandre · al þat haþ used.

aldyr, -man, obs. ff. ALDER *sb.*[1], ALDERMAN.

ale (eɪl). Forms: 1 alu (WS. ealu, ealo), 2– ale (5 aale, aylle, 5–6 alle, Sc. 6–7 ail, aill; in mod. dial. yale, yall, yaäle, yell, yill). [OE. *alu*, cogn. w. OS. *alo*, ON. *öl* (:—*alu*), has been shown by Mr. J. Platt to be a *-t* stem:—**alut*, hence gen. and dat. *aloð*, *ealoð*, 12th c. *aleð*:—**alutaz*, *aluti*: see first quot.]

1. An intoxicating liquor made from an infusion of malt by fermentation. Various ingredients have at various times been added to impart flavour; at present hops or other bitters are in use.

Ale and *beer* seem originally to have been synonymous. The Alvismál says 'öl heitir með mönnum, en með Ásum bjórr,' it is called 'ale' among men, and among the gods 'beer.' After the introduction into England of 'the wicked weed called hops' (*Retn. to Edw. VI's Parlt.*) c 1524, 'beer' was commonly hopped; at present 'beer' is in the trade the generic name for all malt liquors, 'ale' being specifically applied to the paler coloured kinds, the malt for which has not been roasted or burnt; but the popular application of the two words varies in different localities.

c **940** *Sax. Leechd.* II. 268 Do healfne bollan ealoð to, and ȝehæte þæt ealu. *c* **1000** *Hept. Judg.* xiii. 4 Ne he ealu ne drince næfre oððe win. *c* **1200** *Trin. Coll. Hom.* 13 þe man þe hit meðeð riht . þe suneð aleð gestninge. **1205** LAYAM. 24440 Ne mai hit na mon suggen on his tale: of þan win and of þan ale. *a* **1300** *Havelok* 14 Fil me a cuppe of ful god ale. **1377** LANGL. *P. Pl.* B. v. 219, I bouȝte hir barly malte · she brewe it to selle, Peny ale and podyng ale. **1466** *Paston's Funer.* in *Lett.* 549 II. 268 For vii barels of bere, xviijs. vid.—For iiii barels of alle, xiiis. iiiid. **1485** MALORY *Arthur* (1816) II. 445 Wyn & aale. ? **1531** *Plumpton Corr.* 230, I am faine to eate browne bread & drink small alle. **1535** STEWART *Cron. Scotl.* II. 660 Of wyne and aill takand thame sic ane fill. **1542** BOORDE *Dietary* x. 256 Ale is made of malte and water; and they the whiche do put any other thynge to ale than is rehersed, except yest, barme, or godes-good, doth sofysticat theyr ale. **1594** PLAT *Jewel-ho.* III. 16 It is the Hoppe onelie which maketh the essential difference betweene Beere and Ale. **1591** SHAKS. *Two Gent.* III. i. 304 Item, she brewes good Ale. **1613** —— *Hen. VIII*, v. iv. 11 Do you looke for Ale and Cakes heere, you rude raskalls? **1725** BRADLEY *Fam. Dict.* s.v. *Malt Liquor*, Ale is more diuretick than Beer; that is, unhopp'd Liquor more than that which has Hops in it. **1770** J. MASSIE *Tax on Malt* 8 A Pint of Ale or strong Beer, costs the Ale-seller, only Five Farthings. **1853** THACKERAY *Engl. Hum.* 240 Then they sallied forth for Rochester on foot, and drank by the way three pots of ale. [**1864** TENNYSON *North. Farmer*, I've 'ed my point o' yaäle ivry noight sin' I beän 'ere.]

†**2. a.** In the phrases **at the ale (at þen ale, at þe nale, atten ale, atte nale, at nale)**, and **to the ale**, 'the ale' is put for, (*a*) The ale which is being drunk, hence ale-drinking; (*b*) The stock or supply of ale at the disposal of the public, and hence the place where the ale is, the ale-house. *Obs.*

1362 LANGL. *P. Pl.* A. Prol. 42 Feyneden hem for heore foode, fouȝten atte alle [*v.r.* at þe ale, at þe nale, at nale]. *c* **1386** CHAUCER *Freres T.* 49 And make hym grete feestes atte nale [*v.r.* at þe nale, att nale]. **1480** CAXTON *Descr. Brit.* 40 When they drynke atte ale They telle many a lewd tale. *c* **1500** *Carp. Tools* in Halliw. *Nug. Poet.* 19 When thei have wroght an oure ore two, Anone to the ale thei wylle go. **1591** SHAKS. *Two Gent.* II. v. 61 Thou hast not so much charity in thee as to goe to the Ale with a Christian. **1617** ASSHETON *Jrnl.* (1848) 1 Besse, John, wyffe, self, at ale.

†**b. in (his) ale**: in the midst of drinking, under the influence of ale. *Obs.*
c **1460** *Towneley Myst.* 86 What, art thou in aylle? **1599** SHAKS. *Hen. V*, IV. vii. 47 As Alexander kild his friend Clytus, being in his Ales and his Cuppes.

3. A festival or merry-meeting at which much ale was drunk; an ale-drinking. (Cf. *a tea.*) See also BRIDAL.
1076 *O.E. Chron.*, Ðær wæs þæt bryd ealo . . Ealle þa Bryttas þe wæron at þam bryd ealoð. **1544** *Supplic. Hen. VIII*, 41 Keapinge of church ales, in the whiche with leappynge, daunsynge and kyssying they maynteyne the profett of their churche. **1583** BABINGTON *Wks.* 166 Gadding to this ale or that. **1587** HARRISON *England* I. II. i. (1877) 32 The superfluous numbers of idle waks . . *church-ales, helpe-ales* and *soule-ales* called also *dirge-ales* with the heathenish rioting at *bride-ales* are well diminished. **1635** J. TAYLOR (Water P.) *Life of T. Parr* C ij b, T'a Whitson Ale, Wake, Wedding, or a Faire. **1857** TOULM. SMITH *Parish* 504 There was also an Ale called the Mary-Ale, held, it must be presumed, on one of the days consecrated to the Virgin Mary. **1879** *Wild Life in S.C.* 140 In this locality, Clerk's Ale, which used to be rather an event, is quite extinct. **1882** SKEAT *Etym. Dict.* s.v., *Bridal*, lit. a bride-ale. (There were leet-ales, scot-ales, church-ales, clerk-ales, bed-ales, and bride-ales.)

†**4. buttered ale**: a beverage composed of sugar, cinnamon, butter, and beer brewed without hops. *Obs.*

1662 PEPYS *Diary* 5 Dec., And give him a morning draught of buttered ale. **1667** *Ibid.* 28 Sept., It will cost him . . £300. in ale, and £52. in buttered ale.

B. ale- in *comb.*

I. General syntactic relations.

1. *objective*: with active pple., as ***ale-brewing, -drinking, -swilling***, etc.; or *obj. genitive* with n. of agent or action, as ***ale-brewer, -dealer, -drinker, -monger, -seller, -selling***, etc.; ALE-CONNER, -TASTER.
c **1510** *Cocke Lorelles Bote* 8 Potycaryes, ale brewers, and bakers. **1765** TUCKER *Lt. Nat.* I. 475 The speciallest species of ale-drinking . . rhetoricians. **1769** BUCHAN *Dom. Med.* vii. (1826) 36 There are few great ale-drinkers who are not phthisical. **1786** COWPER *Corr.* (1824) II. 91 A shoemaker and an alemonger have proposed themselves as joint candidates to succeed us. **1833** GEN. P. THOMPSON *Exerc.* (1842) II. 490 If the ale-dealers keep any of the razors for their own use.

2. *instrumental*: with passive pple., as ***ale-blown, -born, -crummed, -fed, -washed.***
1592 CHETTLE *Kind-Harts Dr.* (1841) 15 Where the one in a sweaking treble, the other in an ale-blowen base, carowle out such adultrous ribaudry. **1599** SHAKS. *Hen. V*, III. vi. 82 Ale-washt Wits. **1599** NASHE *P. Peniless* E ij, Elderton consumed his ale-crummed nose to nothing. **1836** GEN. P. THOMPSON *Exerc.* (1842) IV. 152 That ale-born business the Restoration.

3. *attrib.* Of, made of or with, ale, as ***ale-sop, -stain***; ALE-BERRY.
c **1450** in Wright *Voc.* 242 Hec offa, a ale-sope.

4. *attrib.* Of, for, or connected with (the manufacture, sale, or use of) ale, as ***ale-brewhouse, -cup, -duty, -feast, -glass, -pot, -tun***, etc. Also ALE-BENCH, -BUSH, -COST, -DRAPER, -HOOF, -HOUSE, -KNIGHT, -POLE, -STAKE, -WIFE; and most of those in II.
a **1000** *Beowulf* 995 Se þe on handa bær hroden ealo-wæge. *c* **1500** *Col. Blowbol* in Halliw. *Nug. Poet.* 1 He rensyd had many an ale picher. **1583** BABINGTON *Wks.* 165 Idle, or tossing the alepot with their neighbours. **1620** VENNER *Via Recta* ii. 39 Our common Ale-pot drunkards. **1699** *Lond. Gaz.* mmmdxiii/4 A small Ale-brewhouse. **1777** WATSON in *Phil. Trans.* LXVIII. 876 A narrow-bottomed ale glass.

II. Special combinations with quotations (in alphabetical order).

ale-barrel, a barrel for ale, a measure of 36 (formerly 32) gallons; †**ale-boly**, ? = *ale-bouilli*, ALE-BERRY; †**ale-brue**, = ALE-BERRY; †**ale-dagger**, one worn for use in ale-house brawls; †**ale-dame**, = ALE-WIFE[1]; †**ale-fat** (= **ale-vat**); **ale-firkin**, a small barrel of ale, a measure of 9 (formerly 8) gallons; **ale-gallon** (see quot.); **ale-grains**, refuse malt left after brewing; **ale-grounds** (? = prec.); **ale-kilderkin**, a half-barrel of ale; †**ale-man** (see quot.); †**ale-meat**, = ALE-BERRY; †**ale-passion**, headache after drinking ale; †**ale-pock**, an ulcer caused by drinking ale; **ale-score**, a reckoning for ale consumed; †**ale-shot** (= prec.); †**ale-silver** (see quot.); †**ale-stand**, the bar of an ale-house; †**ale-taker**, purveyor of ale; **ale-tap**, strictly the tap whence ale is drawn, *hence* the room or place where it is kept; †**ale-toast**, a toast in ale, *fig.* a roisterer or tippler; †**ale-tunning**, brewing of ale; **ale-vat**, a vat in which ale is brewed; **ale-wort**, the fermenting infusion of malt; **ale-yeast**, yeast produced in the brewing of ale.

1743 *Lond. & Country Brewer* II. (ed. 2) 157 The *Ale-Barrel of 32 Gallons. **1828** CARLYLE *Misc.* (1857) I. 201 Computing excise-dues upon tallow, and gauging *alebarrels! *c* **1500** *Col. Blowbol* in Halliw. *Nug. Poet.* 1 And afterward their toke hym many a throw Of good *ale boly that he had i-blowe. **1542** BOORDE *Dyetary* xii. (1870) 264 *Ale-brues, caudelles and colesses for weke men and feble stomackes . . is suffered. **1589** *Pappe w. Hatchet* (1844) 8 He that drinkes with cutters, must not be without his *ale dagger. **1694** WESTMACOTT *Scrip. Herb.* 230 These things are not so much as thought on by our *Ale-dames. *a* **1000** *Sax. Leechd.* II. 142 Under þæt *ealo-fæt. **1596** *Unton Invent.* 13 One *yelfate, one cooler. **1608** ARMIN *Nest Ninn.* (1842) 36 Jack Miller sang his song . . and lookt like the poter of the *ale-fat. **1743** *Lond. & Country Brewer* II. (ed. 2) 157 The *Ale-firkin of 8 Gallons. **1800** COLERIDGE *Sib. Leaves* II. 223 They snatch'd him from the sickle and the plough To gauge *ale-firkins. **1827** HUTTON *Course Math.* I. 28 The *Ale Gallon contained 282 cubic or solid inches. **1630** J. TAYLOR (Water P.) *Wks.* I. 147/2 A messe of warme *Ale-graines from a Brewhouse. **1572** B. GOOGE tr. *Heresbach's Husb.* (1586) 133 Take a quart of *allegroundes, and seeth them. **1743** *Lond. & Country Brewer* II. (ed. 2) 157 The *Ale-Kilderkin of 16 Gallons. **1693** W. ROBERTSON *Phraseol. Gen.* 504 An *Aleman, or ale-house-keeper. **1699** *Phil. Trans.* XXI. 403 The Diet . . was of Mutton-Broth, *Ale-Meat, Poacht-Eggs. **1593** *Bacchus Bountie* in *Harl. Misc.* (1809) II. 271 A passing preseruatiue against the *ale-passion, or paine in the pate. **1601** HOLLAND *Pliny* (1634) II. 128 Sauce-fleame, *ale-pocks, and such like vlcers in the face. **1816** *Q. Rev.* XV. 454 The *ale-scores of a village landlady. **1626** SPELMAN *Gloss. Arch.* 506 *Quasi dictum à* scot, i. *pecunia, et* ale, i. *cervisia: quod inverso vocabulo alii* an *aleshot *nuncupant.* **1691** BLOUNT *Law Dict., Ale-silver*, a Rent or Tribute yearly paid to the Lord Maior of London, by those that sell Ale within the City. **1588** *Marprel. Ep.* (1843) 54 Whereby he might . . visit the *alestond. **1455** in *Househ. Ord.* (1790) 20 The *Aletakers—Richard Joskyn, etc. **1828** SCOTT *F.M. Perth* II. Pref. 3 And when I die, as needs must hap, Then bury me under the good *ale-tap. **1691** SHADWELL *Scowrers* I. i. Wks. IV. 313 Every night thou clearest the streets of . . idle rascals, and of all *Ale-toasts and Sops in brandy. *a* **1529** SKELTON in *Harl. Misc.* (Malh.) III. 476 Elynoor Rummin, with her good *ale-tunning. *a* **1000** 'Ealaþ-wyrt, *cervisia mustea*' Somner. **1737** BRACKEN *Farriery* (1756) I. xxvi. 225 Give the Horse . . two quarts of warm *Ale-wort. **1741** *Compl. Fam.-Piece* I. ii. 194 Take . . a Pint of good *Ale-yeast.

aleak (əˈliːk), *adv.*, prop. *phr.* [A *prep.*[1] of state + LEAK.] In a leaking state or condition.
1859 in WORCESTER. *Mod.* The vessel is aleak.

†**alear(e**, *a. Obs. rare*$^{-1}$. [? ad. L. *āleār-is* belonging to dice.] ? Fated, ? chance-directed.
1581 STUDLEY tr. *Seneca, Herc.* 203 Why dastard dost thou feare? I spoylde thy father Hercules; this hand, this hand aleare Hath murdred him.

aleatico (æliːˈætɪkəʊ). [It.] A sweet Italian red wine.
1821 SHELLEY *Let.* 5 Aug. (1964) II. 313 If you take any wine let it be Aleatico. **1824** ALEX. HENDERSON *Hist. Wines* vi. 237 The *Aleatico*, or red muscadine . . is produced in the highest perfection at Montepulciano. **1921** A. HUXLEY *Crome Yellow* xx. 221 The carminative virtues . . of Marsala, of Aleatico, of stout, of gin.

aleatoric (eɪliːəˈtɔərɪk), *a.* [f. L. *āleātōr-ius* (see ALEATORY *a.*) + -IC.] Dependent on uncertain contingencies; done at random.
1961 *Times* 28 July 13/5 Indeterminate, or aleatoric music. **1962** *Publishers' Weekly* 12 Mar. 19 A new art form, known as 'aleatoric', meaning subject to elements of chance, is making headway among the younger generation of poets in Europe. Its leading exponent . . Maxwell Volker . . creates poetry by cutting out single words or long strips from newspapers and magazines which he haphazardly pastes together to create aleatoric verse.

aleatory (ˈeɪliːətərɪ), *a.* [ad. L. *āleātōri-us*, f. *āleātor* a dice-player, f. *ālea* a die, the dice.] Dependent on the throw of a die; *hence*, dependent on uncertain contingencies.
1693 URQUHART *Rabelais* III. xlii, So continually fortunate in that aleatory way of deciding Law Debates. **1818** H. COLEBROOKE *Oblig. & Contr.* I. 17 If the equivalent consist in the risk of loss, or the chance of gain, dependent on an uncertain event, the contract is contingent and aleatory or hazardous. **1879** MOTLEY in Holmes *Life* xxi. 168 Such an aleatory process seemed an unworthy method in arbitrations.

aleavement, var. ALLEVEMENT. *Obs.*, relief.

aleaven, obs. form of ELEVEN.

ˈ**ale-ˌbench.** Also 1 ealo-benc, 6 alle benche. [ALE- 4.] A bench in or before an ale-house.
a **1000** *Beowulf* 2062 Gum-manna fela, in ealo-bence. **1547** *Homilies* I. xii. I. (1640) 89 Which upon the Ale-benches or other places, delight to set forth certaine questions. **1556** ROBINSON tr. *More's Utopia* (1869) 26 An other sorte sytteth vpon their allebencheis . . amonge their cuppes. **1644** QUARLES *Whipper Whipt* in *Chertsey Libr.* I. 171 A pack of Alebench Whistlers. **1678** BUNYAN *Pilgr.* I. 134 So will he talk when he is on the Ale-bench. **1849** MACAULAY *Hist. Eng.* II. 429 Wild rumours . . flew without ceasing from coffeehouse to coffeehouse and from alebench to alebench.

† ˈ**aleberry.** *Obs.* Forms: 5 ale-bre, -brey, albery, 5–7 alebery. [f. ALE- 3 + OE. *briw* pottage, brewis: changed by its unaccented position to *bre*, *brey*, varying phonetically with *-bery*, of which *-berry* is a corruption due to erroneous etymology. Cf. *bread-berry.*] Ale boiled with spice and sugar and sops of bread; also called *alebrue*, and *alemeat* (see ALE- in *comb.* II).
c **1420** *Lib. Cure Coc.* (1862) 53 Alebre þus make þou schalle With grotes and safroune and good ale. **1440** *Promp. Parv.*, Albery, *vel* alebrey [**1499** albry] *Alebrodium, fictum est.* **1543** BECON *Agst. Swear.* Wks. 1843, 373 They would taste nothing, no, not so much as a poor aleberry . . until they had slain Paul. **1630** J. TAYLOR (Water P.) *Gt. Eater* 12 His appetite . . needed the assistance of cawdle, iulep, alebery.

alebromancy (Blount and Cocker after *alebromantie* in Cotgr.), a mistake for ALEUROMANCY.

† ˈ**ale-bush.** *Obs.* [ALE- 4; see BUSH.] A tavern sign.
1599 H. PORTER *Angry Wom.* (1841) 102, I might haue had a pumpe set vp with as good Marche beere as this was and nere set up an ale-bush for the matter.

‖ ˈ**alec.** [L.] A herring; a pickle or sauce of small herrings or anchovies.
c **1520** ANDREWE in *Babees Bk.* (1868) 230 Alec, the heringe, is a Fisshe of the see . . when he is fresshe taken he is a very delicious to be eten. **1854** BADHAM *Halieut.* 71 Alec, like garum, was at once the name of a fish and of a sauce made from it.

alecithal (əˈlɛsɪθəl), *a. Embryol.* [f. A- 14 + Gr. λέκιθος yolk: see -AL.] Of an ovum: with little or no food-yolk.
1880 BALFOUR *Comp. Embryol.* I. iii. 90 It is convenient to distinguish the ova which segment uniformly by some term; and I should propose for this the term alecithal, as implying that they are without food-yolk, or that what little food-yolk there is, is distributed uniformly. [*Note*] For this term as well as for the terms telolecithal and centrolecithal I am indebted to Mr. Lankester.

alecize ('ælɪsaɪz), *v. rare.* [f. L. *ālec* + -IZE. Cf. L. *ālēcātus.*] To dress with alec sauce.
1854 BADHAM *Halieut.* 145 The modes of dressing so approved a fish were endless. One way was to alecize or halecize it.

Aleck (in *smart Aleck*): see SMART *a.*

aleconner ('eɪl,kɒnə(r)). Also 4-6 **alekonner,** 6-7 **alecunner.** [f. ALE- 1 + CONNER, OE. *cunnere* a trier.] An examiner or inspector of ale: 'An officer appointed in every court-leet, and sworn to look to the assize and goodness of bread, ale, and beer, sold within the jurisdiction of the leet.' Phillips 1706. 'Four of them are chosen annually by the common-hall of the city; and whatever might be their use formerly, their places are now regarded only as sinecures for decayed citizens.' Johnson 1755. Still a titular office in some burghs.
c **1350** *Chart. Edw. III* in *Liber Albus* 316 Serement de Alekonners. **1566** DRANT *Horace, Sat.* iv. C b, Not Tygille nor such alecunners my workes do overprye. **1630** *Tincker of Turvey* Ep. Ded. 4 The autenticall drinke of England, the whole barmy-tribe of ale-cunners never layd their lips to the like. **1683** LUTTRELL *Brief Rel.* (1857) I. 278 Some of the liveries of the companies mett, and..chose..Mr. Welling to be aleconner. **1859** H. RILEY *Liber Albus* Introd. 61 Immediately a brewing was finished, it was the duty of the brewer..to send for the Ale-conner of the Ward, in order to taste the ale. **1876** *Encycl. Brit.* (ed. 9) I. 476 In London four aleconners are still chosen annually by the liverymen in common hall assembled on Midsummer Day.

alecost ('eɪlkɒst). Also 6-7 **ale-coast.** [f. ALE- 4 + COST. ad. L. *costum, -us, -os,* a. Gr. *κόστος* an unidentified plant used as spice.] A Composite plant (*Balsamita vulgaris* or *Chrysanthemum balsamita*) allied to Tansy, so called because formerly much used for giving to ale an agreeable aromatic and bitter flavour.
1589 COGAN (in Prior *Plant-names*). **1597** GERARD *Herbal* II. cxcviii. 524 Called in English Costmarie and Ale-coast. **1676** BEAL in *Phil. Trans.* XI. 587 Ale-cost..famous for dispatching the maturation of Ale and Beer. **1866** W. BOOTH in *Treas. Bot.* 119 The common Costmary or Alecost is a native of Italy, whence it was introduced in 1568.

† **alec'torian.** *Obs.* [f. Gr. *ἀλέκτωρ* cock + -IAN.] (See quot.)
1398 TREVISA *Barth. De P.R.* XVI. xvi. (1495) 558 Alectoria is a stone that is founde in the mawes of capons and is lyke to dymme cristall. **1586** BRIGHT *Melanch.* xxxix. 257 The Alectorian or Cockes stone..wherewith (as it is reported) the famous Milo Crotonien alway stoode invincible. **1678** PHILLIPS, *Alectorius*..a precious stone of a waterish colour.

alectoromachy (ə,lɛktə'rɒməkɪ). [See following words.] A variant of ALECTRYOMACHY.
1847 in CRAIG.

alectoromancy (ə'lɛktərəʊ,mænsɪ). Also 7-8 **alectromancy.** [f. Gr. *ἀλέκτωρ* cock + *μαντεία* divination.] A variant of ALECTRYOMANCY.
1652 GAULE *Magastrom.* 165 Alectromancy [divining] by cocks or pullen. **1731** BAILEY, *Alectoromancy*, an ancient divination, in which they made use of a cock in discovering secret and unknown transactions of future events. **1758** *Ann. Reg.* 275/2 The mysteries of chyromancy, alectromanchy and catoptromanchy. **1847** in CRAIG.

alectryomachy (ə,lɛktrɪ'ɒməkɪ). *rare*⁻⁰. [f. Gr. *ἀλεκτρυών* cock + *-μαχία* fighting.] Cock-fighting.
1656 BLOUNT *Glossogr.* **1731** BAILEY. **1775** ASH, etc.

alectryomancy (ə,lɛktrɪəʊ,mænsɪ). [f. Gr. *ἀλεκτρυών* cock + *μαντεία* divination. Cf. Fr. *alectryomancie.*] Divination by means of a cock with grains of corn.
1684 *Phil. Trans.* XIV. 706 The author singles Alectryomancy for the subject of this book. **1819** *Pantol., Alectoromantia*, an ancient kind of divination by means of a cock, called also *Alectryomancy*.

‖ **alectryon** (ə'lɛktrɪən). [Gr.] A cock.
1873 LONGF. *Emma & Eginh.* 110 The crowing cock, The Alectryon of the farmyard and the flock.

† **'alecy.** *nonce-wd. Obs.* [f. ALE after *lunacy.*] Mental aberration, due to ale-drinking; intoxication.
1598 LILLY *Moth. Bombie* IV. ii. 127 To arrest a man that hath no likenesse of a horse, is flat lunasie or alecie.

aledge, obs. form of ALLEGE.

† **'ale-,draper.** *Obs.* or *dial.* [f. ALE- 4 + DRAPER, perhaps originally jocular, in allusion to *linen-draper*, etc.] An alehouse-keeper.
1655 R. YOUNGE *Charge agst. Drunk.* 13 These godlesse Ale-drapers, and other sellers of drink. **1743** *Lond. & Country Brewer* IV. (ed. 2) 300 Most of our Brewers and Ale-Drapers care not what horrid Stuff they prepare and vend. **1747** in *Parish Reg. of Scotter, Linc.*, [Buried] July 8th Thomas Broughton, Farmer and Ale Draper. **1855** ATKINSON *Whitby Gloss., Ale-draper*, an alehouse keeper, or publican; a term now obsolete.

† **'ale-,drapery.** *Obs.* [f. prec. + -Y³.] Ale-selling.
1592 CHETTLE *Kind-Harts Dr.* (1841) 20 Two milch maydens that had set vp a shoppe of Ale-drapery.

alee (ə'liː), *adv.* [a. ON. *á hlé*, a sea phrase as in Eng., f. *á* on, in the direction of + *hlé* shelter: see LEE.] On or toward the lee or sheltered side of the ship; away from the wind; to leeward. Also as an order = *put alee.*
1399 LANGL. *Rich. Redeless* IV. 74 þan lay the lordis a-lee with laste and with charge, And bare aboute þe barge. *c* **1575** *Hickscorner* in Hazl. *Dodsl.* I. 161 Ale the helm, Ale, veer. *c* **1648** DAVENANT *Wint. Storms*, Alee, or we sink! *a* **1826** HOOD *Wee Man* xi, Good sir, the boat has lost her trim, You must not sit a-lee. **1859** W. JAMES *Nav. Hist. Eng.* II. 223 The helm of the George was instantly put a-lee. **1865** CARLYLE *Fred. Gt.* II. VI. ix. 229 Such a sea as never was; and breakers now close alee.

† **a-leeward,** *phr. Obs.* [A *prep.*¹ + LEEWARD.] Toward the sheltered side, to one side.
1623 MINSHEU *Sp. Gram.* 81 *Traér de tema la gorra*..To set his hat to the good aleward, on one side the head.

aleft (ə'lɛft), *adv.*, prop. *phr.* [A *prep.*¹ of direction + LEFT.] On or to the left hand.
c **1330** *Arth. & Merl.* 8149 Aleft he smot and Aright. **1821** SOUTHEY *Vis. Judgm.* Wks. X. 225 Lightning and thunder Volleying aright and aleft amid the accumulate blackness.

alegar ('ælɪgə(r), 'eɪlɪgə(r)). Forms: 6 **aleger, alligar,** 6-7 **all-, aliger,** 7 **alegre,** 8 **aleager,** 6- **alegar.** [f. (after *vinegar*) ALE + *egre, eger,* EAGER, = Fr. *aigre* sharp, sour.] Sour ale; vinegar formed by the acetous fermentation of ale; malt-vinegar.
1542 BOORDE *Dyetary* xxxiv. (1870) 296 Soure and tarte thynges, as venegre and aleger [*v.r.* alceger, alegar]. **1586** COGAN *Haven Health* (1636) 189 Some make it of Ale onely ..but that is rather Aliger than Vinegar. **1598** FLORIO, *Agresto*..vertiuice, alligar. **1598** STOW *Surv.* (ed. Strype 1754) II. v. xv. 324/2 Corrupt Vinegar, Beeregre, and Alegre. **1741** *Compl. Fam.-Piece* I. iii. 218 Boil Alegar, scum it, and pour it over them. **1837** CARLYLE *Fr. Rev.* I. IV. iv. 200 Whose small soul, transparent wholesome-looking as small ale, could by no chance ferment into virulent alegar?.. We shall see. **1881** EVANS *Leicestersh. Gloss.* s.v., *Alegar* is to ale what vinegar is to wine. The old home-made article is now seldom procurable.

alegarto, obs. form of ALLIGATOR.

† **a'leger,** *a. Obs. rare*⁻¹. [ad. OFr. *alègre*:—late L. *alăcr-em.* Cf. It. *allegro.*] Lively, cheerful.
1626 BACON *Sylva* §738 The Root, and Leafe Betell; The Leafe Tobacco; And the Teare of Poppy,..doe all Condense the Spirits, and make them Strong, and Aleger.

alegge, obs. form of ALLAY and ALLEGE.

ale-hoof ('eɪlhuːf). Forms: 3-4 **heyhoue,** 4 **haihay-, hale-houe,** 6-7 **ale-hove, ale-hoofe,** 7-9 **ale-hoof.** [Formerly *ale hove*, from OE. '*hófe*, *viola*' (Ælfric) in allusion to its alleged use in brewing instead of hops; perhaps a corruption of the earlier *hay-hove*, 'hedge-hove,' influenced by misunderstanding of another early name, *tun-hove*, f. *tún* enclosure. Among the various kinds of *hófe* mentioned in OE. there is no *ale-hófe.* See HOVE.]
The herb ground-ivy (*Nepeta Glechoma*); also formerly called *hay-* or *hey hove*, *horse-hove*, and HOVE.
a **1300** W. DE BIBLESWORTH in Wright *Voc.* 162, *Eyre terestre*, heyhowe. *c* **1350** ARDERNE *Practica* in *Promp. Parv.* 250 Haihoue, *vel* halehoue, *vel* folfyt, *vel* horshoue. **1579** LANGHAM *Gard. Health* (1633) 8 Alehoofe, ground iuie, gilrunbith ground, or Tudnoore. **1597** GERARD *Herball* II. ccc. 705 Commonly called..ground Iuie, Alehoof, Gill creepe by ground, tunehoofe, and Cats foote. *Ibid.* 707 The women of our northren parts..do tun the herbe Alehooue into their ale, but the reason thereof I know not. **1656** RIDGLEY *Pract. Physic* 284 Let him take often with a spoon Water of Ale-hove. **1676** BEAL in *Phil. Trans.* XI. 587 Alehoof, or Ground-Ivy, famous for dispatching the maturation of Ale and Beer. **1859** E. CAPERN *Bal. & Songs* 128 Where ale-hoof and the borage, too, Held forth their gems of blue.

'ale-house. [ALE- 4.] A house where ale is retailed; *hence*, a tippling house.
a **1000** *Laws of Ethelb.* Thorpe I. 292 On eala-huse. *c* **1200** *Trin. Coll. Hom.* 11 Untimeliche eten alehuse. **1303** R. BRUNNE *Handl. Synne* 5978 At þe alehous make þey marchaundye. *c* **1450** *Knt. de la Tour* 44 His parisshenes gone forthe to the ale hous or to a taverne. **1599** SHAKS. *Hen. V*, III. ii. 12 Would I were in an Ale-house in London. **1670** EACHARD *Contempt Clergy* 122 If upon Sunday the church doors be shut, the ale-houses will be open. **1787** BENTHAM *Def. Usury* xiii. 159 The stuff fit to make a prodigal of is to be found in every alehouse. **1849** MACAULAY *Hist. Eng.* I. 295 The redcoats filled all the alehouses of Westminster.
b. *attrib.* (Cf. also ALE-KNIGHT.)
1553 T. WILSON *Rhet.* 2 b, Scurrilitie or alehouse jestyng would bee thought odious. **1583** GOLDING *Calvin on Deut.* li. 305 These Tauernhaunters or Alehouseknightes which counterfeit the preachers. **1601** DENT *Pathw. to Heaven* 248 You are..a drinker, a common ale-house-haunter. **1765** TUCKER *Lt. Nat.* II. 528 Exercising the trade of a butcher, or an ale-house keeper. **1855** TENNYSON *Maud* I. iv. ii, And Jack on his ale-house bench has as many lies as a Czar.

alehte, pa. t. of ALACCHE *v. Obs.*, to catch.

aleing, aling ('eɪlɪŋ), *vbl. sb.*, *nonce-wd.* [f. ALE taken as a vb. (cf. *to wine*) + -ING¹.] Drinking of ale or treating to ale.
1870 *Daily News* 28 Sept., There was a wining and dining, or better, a beering or aleing and dining of the 'Southern brethren.'

aleiptic (ə'laɪptɪk), *a.* ? *Obs. rare.* [ad. Gr. *ἀλειπτικ-ός*, f. *ἀλείπτης* a gymnastic trainer, orig. an anointer, f. *ἀλείφ-ειν* to anoint.] Of or belonging to gymnastic 'training.'
1660 T. STANLEY *Hist. Philos.* (1701) 423/1 The Aleiptick art, and, its nearest ally, Medicine, are design'd for the cure of Bodies.

aleive, var. ALLEVE *v. Obs.*, to relieve.

† **'ale-'knight.** *Obs.* [f. ALE 4 + KNIGHT, used derisively; cf. *carpet-knight*, *knight of the ellwand*, etc.] A votary of the ale-house, a tippler.
1575 *Eccl. Proc. Chester* [The Vicar of Whalley, Lanc., is charged with being] a common dronker and ale knight. **1598** E. GILPIN *Skial.* (1878) 55 There brauls an Ale-knight for his fat-grown score. **1664** H. MORE *Myst. Iniq.* 325 S. Urban for Ale-Knights or Pot-Companions. **1864** CHAMBERS *Bk. Days* II. 597 This man was a regularly dubbed ale-knight, loved barley wine to the full.

alem, obs. form of ALUM.

Alemannic (ælə'mænɪk), *a.* and *sb.* Also formerly **All-, -anic.** [ad. late L. *Alemannicus*, f. *Alemannī* pl., Gr. *'Αλαμανοί*, ad. Germ. **Alamanniz*, prob. f. ALL + MAN *sb.*¹ and so denoting a wide alliance of peoples.] The name of a confederation of Germanic tribes occupying the territory between the Rhine, the Main, and the Danube; also, of the dialects of Old High German spoken by them or the modern representatives of these in Alsace, Switzerland, and S.W. Germany. Also **Ale'mannian** *a.* and *sb.*; **Ale'mannish** [after G. *Alemannisch(e)*, *a.* and *sb.*
1776 GIBBON *Decl. & F.* I. xi. 310 Aurelian had chosen these veteran troops..whose valour had been severely tried in the Alemannic war. **1797** *Encycl. Brit.* I. 469/2 Allemannic language. **1813** *Q. Rev.* 258 German, Himina. Alemannish, Himil. Classical German, Himmel. **1814** J. JAMIESON *(title)* Hermes Scythicus: or, the radical affinities of the Greek and Latin languages to the Gothic: illustrated from the Moeso-Gothic, Anglo-Saxon, Francic, Alemannic. **1842** *Penny Cycl.* XXIV. 268/1 Suabian branch [of modern High German]... *Allemannic*, commonly so called in the south-west corner of the Black Forest. **1879** *Encycl. Brit.* X. 517/2 For Bavarian we may quote some old glossaries, for Alemannian the interlineary versions of the Benedictine Rule. *Ibid.* 519/2 Alemannian is best characterized by its rigidly keeping its original vowel qualities. **1888** WRIGHT *O.H.G. Primer* 1 Upper German, spoken in the highlands of South Germany, and consisting of the Alemanic and Bavarian dialects. **1934** PRIEBSCH & COLLINSON *German Lang.* II. vii. 326 The Alemannic Group includes Swabian. **1951** E. S. DUCKETT *Alcuin* iii. 98 The new Queen, Liutgard, was of Alemannian origin.

alembic (ə'lɛmbɪk). Forms: 4 **alambic, -ik, alembyk,** 4-5 **-ike, -yke,** 4-7 **-eke,** 7 **alimbeck, alembicke,** 7-8 **-eck,** 7-9 **-ick,** 7- **-ic.** [a. Fr. *alambic*, ad. (ultimately) Arab. *al-anbīq*, i.e. *al* the + *anbīq* a still; ad. Gr. *ἄμβῑκ-*, *ἄμβιξ* a cup, beaker, the cap of a still. Aphetized as early as 15th c. to *lembick*, LIMBECK, and the full form scarcely appears till the 17th.]
1. An apparatus formerly used in distilling, consisting of a *cucurbit* or gourd-shaped vessel containing the substance to be distilled, surmounted by the *head* or *cap*, or *alembic* proper, the beak of which conveyed the vaporous products to a *receiver*, in which they were condensed. It is now superseded by the *retort* and *worm still.*
c **1374** CHAUCER *Troylus* IV. 520 This Troylus in teres gan distille, As licour out of alambic, fulle fast. *c* **1386** —— *Chan. Yem. Prol. & T.* 241 Concurbites, and alembikes eeke [*v.r.* Alambike, alembyke, alembeke.] **1563** T. GALE *Antidot.* II. 33 Destill them in a glasse alembike accordyng to arte. **1612** WOODALL *Surgeon's M.* Wks. 1653, 212 Fill your Alimbeck but two third parts of Copperas. **1678** R. R[USSELL] *Geber* II. I. IV. xiii. 118 The Alembeck and its Cucurbit must be both of Glass. **1725** BRADLEY *Fam. Dict.* s.v. *Earth*, Chymists by their Alembick shew us plainly what this Salt is. **1800** HENRY *Epit. Chem.* (1808) 91 An alembic of pure silver, furnished with a glass head. **1851** LONGF. *Gold. Leg.* I. 28 In alembics finely wrought, Distilling herbs and flowers.
2. *fig.*
a **1613** OVERBURY *A Wife, &c.* (1638) 111 Making a brokers Shop his Alembicke, [he] can turn your silkes into gold. **1790** BURKE *Fr. Rev.* 135 The hot spirit drawn out of the alembick of hell, which in France is now so furiously boiling. **1789** G. WHITE *Selborne* (1853) II. xxix. 243 In heavy fogs..trees are perfect alembics. **1814** SCOTT *Wav.* I. ii. 17 The cool and procrastinating alembic of Dyer's Weekly Letter. **1856** BRIMLEY *Ess.* 229 Passed through the alembic of a great poet's imagination.

† **a'lembic,** *v. Obs.* [f. sb.; cf. Fr. *alambiquer.*] To distill as in an alembic; = ALEMBICATE.
1635 PERSON *Var.* I. i. 8 The heavens are of a fift substance, not alembecked out of the foure elements. *a* **1666** J. SHIRLEY *Closet of Rar.* (ed. 5) 9 To distill, or rather

alembick, spirit of wine. **1749** H. WALPOLE *Corr.* (1837) I. 138 The important mysteries that have been alembicked out of a trifle.

alembicated (əˈlɛmbɪkeɪtɪd), *ppl. a.* [f. L. type **alembicatus* + -ED[1]. Cf. F. *alambiqué.*] Of ideas, expression, etc.: over-refined, over-subtilized (as if by passing through an alembic).

1786 MRS. PIOZZI *Anecd. Johnson* 197 His mind was like a warm climate, which brings every thing to perfection suddenly and vigorously, not like the alembicated productions of artificial fire, which always betray the difficulty of bringing them forth when their size is disproportionate to their flavour. **1818** LADY MORGAN *Fl. Macarthy* I. i. 8 Theories of alembicated refinement. **1823** *New Monthly Mag.* VII. 194 Alembicated systems for explaining conduct, and reconciling contradictions of character, are rarely satisfactory. **1836** CROKER *Johnson.* I. 63 The alembicated productions of artificial fire. **1913** W. RALEIGH in *Eng. Rev.* May 228 The prose style of Boccaccio . . is not a simple style—rather it is curious and alembicated.

alembication (əˌlɛmbɪˈkeɪʃən). [f. as prec. + -ATION.]

1. Over-subtlety or over-refinement of expression.

1893 STEVENSON *Vailima Lett.* 2 June (1895) 271 This sort of trouble . . produces nothing when done but alembication and the far-fetched.

2. Refinement; concentration; = DISTILLATION 3 b, 4 c.

1936 *Proc. Brit. Acad.* XXI. 195 The masterpieces of this process of alembication are the views of Petworth Park, painted in about 1830. **1951** O. DOWNES in *N.Y. Times* 24 Mar. 9/3 The reading [of Verdi's 'Requiem'] was the alembication of a lifetime's thought and experience.

alembroth (əˈlɛmbrɒθ). [A word of the Alchemists, of unknown origin.] An old name for the double chloride of mercury and ammonium, $2(NH_4Cl.HgCl) + H_2O$, formerly believed to be a universal solvent.

1471 RIPLEY *Compl. Alch.* in Ashm. 1652, 190 Sal Alkaly, sal Alembroke, sal Attinckarr. **1726** BAILEY *Alembroth, Alembor,* the philosophers salt, the key of art. **1753** CHAMBERS *Cycl. Supp., Alembroth* is represented as partaking of the nature of halonitrum and alum. The word is said to be of Chaldee origin, and its natural meaning to be the *key of art.* **1879** *Syd. Soc. Lex.* s.v., The preparation *Sal alembroth,* also called salt of wisdom.

† **a'leme,** *v. Obs.* Forms: 2–3 **aleome, aleme, alime, alume** (-y-). [f. A- *pref.* 1 intens. + LEME, OE. *léom-an* to shine.] To illumine.

c **1200** *Trin. Coll. Hom.* 107 Godes giue is betere, þe alimeð þe man of fiffolde mihte. *Ibid.* 109 Ure drihten [*i.e.* God] . . ure ihesu christi alemeð þe selue sunne, þe alle oðre þing aleomeð. *Ibid.* 141 Hur eiðer alumð þe se. *c* **1230** *Serm.* in *Reliq. Ant.* I. 128 þe lihted alle men þe . . aleomed ben.

alemesse, obs. form of ALMS.

Alençon (alɑ̃sɔ̃). [The name of a town in the department of Orne, north-western France.] Applied *attrib.* and *absol.* to a lace made originally at Lonray near Alençon, a hand-made print lace of point de France. Cf. *point d'Alençon* s.v. POINT *sb.*[3] b.

1853 *Morning Post* 31 Jan. 5/2 Mlle Palmyre is making 20 full dresses:—one is in white brocade . . one of blue velvet, ornamented with Alençon lace. **1865** F. B. PALLISER *Hist. Lace* xiii. 171 A few observations remain to be made respecting the dates of Alençon point. *Ibid.* 172 France . . has no rival in her points of Alençon and her white blondes, or her black silk laces. To begin with Alençon, the only French lace not made on the pillow. **1872** *Young Englishwoman* Oct. 541/2 Under sleeves of grey satin, with white satin creves, are finished off with deep upturned Alençon lace cuffs. **1953** M. POWYS *Lace & Lace-Making* ix. 143 The Empress Eugenie was married to Napoleon III in the finest Point d'Alencon lace... It is said that 'Her Alencons dazzled the eye!' **1977** H. FAST *Immigrants* I. 68 She changed into a dressing gown of pale blue velvet and Alençon ruffled lace.

a'lene, *v. Obs.* [f. A- *pref.* 1 intens. + OE. *lǽnan* to grant, LEND.] To lend, grant, give.

c **1000** ÆLFRIC *Gloss.* in Wright 21, *Pignus,* alæned feoh. **1250** LAYAM. 24000 Ech man brouke his hom: þat god him aleneþ. *Ibid.* 31603 Waþer ich þe aleane wolle: þat þing þat þou ȝeornest.

† **a'length,** *adv.* and *prep.,* prop. *phr.* [A *prep.*[1] + LENGTH. Cf. *across.*]

A. *adv.* In the direction of the length, lengthwise, longitudinally.

c **1400** *Destr. Troy* XI. 4751 The grekes . . Layn ladders alenght & oloft wonnen. **1534** FITZHERB. *Husb.* xlii, Laye a lyttell terre ther vpon, and stroke it alengthe in the bottom of the woll. **1601** HOLLAND *Pliny* IX. xxx, He would stretch the same [his feet] alength and make them serve in stead of an helme to steere withall. **1775** ASH, *Alength,* at full length.

B. *prep.* [the adv. restricted to a definite obj.] In the direction of the length of, lengthwise to.

c **1540** *Practyse of Cyrurg.,* In all other places rome must be made a length the membres.

aleph (ˈɑːləf, ˈæləf, -ɛf). Also 4 **Allef,** 5–7 **Alephe,** and with capital initial. [a. Heb. and Phoenician *āleph,* lit. 'ox'; the character may have developed from the hieroglyph of an ox's head: see ALPHA.]

1. The name of the first letter of the Phoenician and Hebrew alphabets, whence it came to be used in a number of Semitic languages to represent the glottal stop; in post-biblical Hebrew, the numeral 1.

a **1300** *S. Eng. Legendary* (Laud) (1878) ȝwi was Allef furst bi founde? Of alle lettres he is þe furste. *c* **1400** MANDEVILLE *Trav.* (1725) 132 The Lettres, that the Jewes usen . . and the names . . in manere of here *A.B.C.* . . Alephe. **1677** T. HERBERT *Trav.* (ed. 4) 124 The first verse of the first chapter of Genesis where the letter Alephe is six times found. **1875** *Encycl. Brit.* I. 608/2 The Phoenician alphabet consisted of twenty-eight letters, which for convenience we may call by the names of their Hebrew equivalents. These were (1) Aleph (2) Beth, (3) Gimel, [etc.]. **1944** AUDEN *For Time Being* (1945) 67 O where is the garden of Being that is only known in Existence As the command to be never there, the sentence by which Alephs of throbbing fact have been banished into position. **1976** J. F. A. SAWYER *Mod. Introd. Biblical Hebrew* 8 The Alphabet... Aleph not pronounced, except between vowels where it stands for a glottal stop.

2. *Math.* A transfinite cardinal number; ***aleph-null, -zero,*** the smallest such number, the cardinal of the set of integers. [Adopted in this sense, as G. *alef,* by G. Cantor 1895, in *Math. Ann.* XLVI. 492.]

[**1903** B. RUSSELL *Princ. of Math.* xxxvii. 309 The number of finite numbers . . is transfinite. This number Cantor denotes by the Hebrew Aleph with the suffix o; for us it will be more convenient to denote it by a_0]. **1913** *Athenæum* 3 May 497/1 The authors deal with . . the construction of Cantor's aleph-numbers. **1915** P. E. B. JOURDAIN tr. *Cantor's Contrib. Theory Transfinite Numbers* 103 (*heading*) The smallest transfinite cardinal number aleph-zero. **1920** A. S. EDDINGTON *Space, Time & Gravitation* iii. 59 It reminds us of the mathematicians' transfinite number Aleph; you can subtract any number you like from it and it still remains the same. **1963** B. S. JOHNSON *Travelling People* i. 19 It would be a noble achievement to find the square root of aleph one... He began looking now: square roots he knew about, a little, but aleph one meant very little to him. **1969** H. HORWOOD *Newfoundland* iii. 11 A poetic equation with black and white as its limits . . the aleph-null of a transfinite reality. **1979** *Sci. Amer.* Nov. 29/2 The continuum hypothesis . . states that there is no infinite number between aleph-null (the number of positive integers) and aleph-one (the number of real numbers).

† **alepine, alapeen.** *Obs.* A mixed stuff either of wool and silk or mohair and cotton.

1739 in *Observ. Wool. Manuf.* (in *Drapers' Dict.*), *Alapeen.* **1757** DYER *Fleece* III. 480 Cheyney, and baize, and serge, and alepine . . and the long countless list Of woollen webs.

† **'ale-pole.** *Obs.* [ALE- 4.] A pole or post set up as the sign of an ale-house; an ale-stake.

1533 FRITH *Answ. More* (1829) 331 The alepole is not the ale itself which it doth signify or represent. **1587** HOLINSHED *Chron.* II. 22/2 Booths, and alepoles are pitched at Saint James his gate. **1616** J. DEACON *Tobacco Tort.* 57 The hungry Hostesses ale-pole.

‖ **alerce** (əˈlɛrθeɪ). [Sp. *alerce,* f. L. *laricem* LARCH.] An American tree allied to the larch.

1845 DARWIN *Voy. Nat.* xiv. (1879) 298 Mules bringing alerce-planks and corn from the southern plains. *Ibid.* xiii, A red cedar or an alerce pine.

alerion (əˈlɪərɪən). *Her.* [Fr. *alérion* (12th c.), med.L. *alariōn-em* some large bird of prey of the eagle kind. Of unkn. origin. Borel makes it an augmentative of OFr. *aillier,* which Diez considered might be Germ. *adler* or *adelar* an eagle.] An eagle without beak or feet.

1605 CAMDEN *Rem.* (1614) 180 Geffray of Boullion . . at one draught of his bowe . . broched three feetlesse birds called Allerions vpon his arrow. **1731** BAILEY, *Allerions* (in Heraldry) are small birds painted without beak or feet, like the martlet or martinet. Others say they are like eagles without beak or feet. **1862** H. WHEATLEY *Anagrams* 92 The House of Lorraine took for their arms, an *alerion* (a small eagle, with neither beak nor claws), from the word *alerion* being a transposition of *Loraine.*

alert (əˈlɜːt), *adv., a.,* and *sb.* [a. Fr. *alerte,* formerly *allerte, à l'airte,* 16th c. ad. It. milit. phr. *all' erta* on the watch, on the look-out = *alla* to the, at the, *erta* a look-out, 'a high watch tower' (Florio), literally something *erected* or raised aloft, fem. of *erto,* pa. pple. of *ergere*:—L. *ērigĕre* to ERECT. From being used as an adv. phr., *stare all' erta, se tenir à l'erte* 'to stand on the watch,' it became a predicative and complemental, and at length an attributive adj. and a sb. When *alert* was established as a real adj. in Eng., the adv. phr. became 'on the alert,' etymologically pleonastic = on the *à l'erte.* Cf. the similar histories of *alarm, alamort, alamode,* in which adv. phrases have become more or less adj. or sb.]

A. *adv.* On the watch, on the look-out: hence *adj.* (in the compl. or pred.) Watchful, vigilant, wide-awake. **a.** as a military term.

1598 BARRET *Theor. Warres,* Gloss. 249 *Alerta,* an Italian word, vsed vnto the souldiers, when there is any suspition of the enemy, and signifieth to be watchfull, carefull, and ready. **1618** R. WILLIAMS *Act. Low Countr.* 27 (T.) The prince finding his rutters alert (as the Italians say). **1707** FREIND *Peterboro's Cond. Spain* 213 Dear Jones, prove a true Dragoon, be diligent and alert. **1780** *Ann. Reg.* 64/1 Their situations were often so alert that no persons slept out of their clothes. **1879** FROUDE *Cæsar* xxiv. 417 The Pompeys were alert on the water to seize stray transports or provision ships.

b. generally.

1735 GEO. LD. LYTTELTON *Pers. Lett.* (1776) I. 186 The people were kept Alert and upon their guard. **1799** S. TURNER *Anglo-Sax.* (1828) I. vii. 169 Caledonian wanderers would be alert to profit by the opportunity. **1866** MACGREGOR *1000 M. in Rob Roy* 1 An interest ever varied . . keeps fully alert the energies of the mind. **1880** CYPLES *Hum. Exp.* vi. 152 Every sense is stirring; he is wholly alert.

B. *adj.* **a.** Quick in attention and motion, lively, brisk, active, nimble. *Comb.,* as ***alert-looking*** adj.

1712 ADDISON *Spect.* No. 403 ¶5, I saw an alerte young Fellow that cocked his Hat upon a Friend of his. **1818** SCOTT *Rob Roy* 115 He is an alert, joyous, and lively old soul. **1859** THOREAU *Lett.* (1865) 180 You can . . carry any fortress with an army of alert thoughts. **1926** F. W. CROFTS *Insp. French & Cheyne Myst.* xix. 270 A tall, alert-looking young man entered the room.

b. Compared *-er, -est,* or *more, most.*

1754 RICHARDSON *Grandison* (1766) V. 73 Miss Byron . . is one of the alertest in [these amusements]. **1767** BURKE *Corr.* (1844) I. 134, I never knew him talk in a more alert, firm, and decided tone. **1793** SMEATON *Edystone L.* §298 One of the most alert of the masons. **1843** CARLYLE *Past & Pres.* (1858) 272 None of the alertest.

C. *sb.* [mod.Fr. *alerte,* subst. use of the original phrase, used as a military call. Cf. *alarm.*]

1. a. The call to 'look out' for an attack; an alarm; *hence,* that which amounts to such a call, a 'waking up,' a sudden attack or surprise.

1803 WELLINGTON in Gurwood *Desp.* II. 286, I am glad to find that you have given the Enemy an Alert. **1826** SCOTT *Woodst.* vii. (1846) 79 No man ever saw me drink when an alert was expected. **1870** *Ev. Standard* 17 Sept., In case of an alert, every battalion, every company, and every man know their stations.

b. *spec.* A signal given by means of a siren or hooter to indicate that an air attack is imminent; an air-raid alarm or warning; also, the state of preparedness so produced or the period during which this alarm is in effect. (Used esp. in the war of 1939–45.)

1940 W. S. CHURCHILL in *Hansard Commons* 5 Sept. ser. v. CCCLXV. 46 It was felt that the red warning should be taken merely as an alert. *Ibid.,* We immediately resumed our work under the conditions of alert. **1940** *Flight* 26 Sept. 243/2 London had three 'Alert' warnings in the morning of Monday, September 16, each lasting about half an hour. **1941** [see AIR- III. 2]. **1949** E. BOWEN *Heat of Day* viii. 151 There were no alerts just at present, not so much as a yellow.

2. on the alert: on the look-out, on the watch. (Takes the place of the earlier *alert* adv. = *all' erta.*)

1796 *Campaigns* 1793–4 II. vi. 31 The troops were . . kept constantly on the Alerte. **1827** HARE *Guess. Truth* Ser. I. (1873) 181 Open evil at all events does this good: it keeps good on the alert. **1835** MARRYAT *Jac. Faithf.* xxxviii. 132 But those who were stationed at the look-out were equally on the alert. **1882** *19th Cent.* No. 69, 736 The men are for ever on the alert to find out something wrong.

alert (əˈlɜːt), *v.* Formerly *rare.* [f. ALERT *a.* Cf. *content.*] To make alert, to rouse to vigilance. Also **a'lerted** *ppl. a.*; **a'lerting** *vbl. sb.* and *ppl. a.* (Cf. ALERT *sb.* 1 b.)

a **1868** W. WHITMAN *Chants Dem.* Poems 155 When the fire-flashing guns have fully alerted me. **1941** *Baltimore Sun* 19 Dec. 14/7 Directors of civilian defense air-raid control centers will alone be responsible for . . alerting their . . districts. **1943** *Ibid.* 12 Jan. 5/3 An alerted zone. **1948** *Cape Times Week-end Mag.* 17 Jan. 2/3 All bank tellers and others handling large sums have now been alerted. **1950** *Evening News* 11 Feb. 1/1 The Shrewsbury Flood Warden Service was alerted to-day. **1954** A. W. FIELDING *Hide & Seek* ix. 114 We spent the whole night with our senses more alerted than the situation . . demanded. **1955** *Financ. Times* 10 Sept. 4/2 The advantages of alerting the public to economic realities. **1958** *Times Lit. Suppl.* 9 May 256/4 Something of such a writer's concentrated quality gives even his most expansive verse an alerting brevity.

alertly (əˈlɜːtlɪ), *adv.* [f. ALERT *a.* + -LY[2].] In an alert manner; on the watch to act; *hence,* briskly, actively, nimbly.

1787 MRS. DELANY *Corr.* Ser. 2 III. 454 She is as upright, and walks as alertly, as when you saw her. **1865** CARLYLE *Fredk. Gt.* IX. xx. ix. 168 Henri had to . . stand alertly on his guard.

alertness (əˈlɜːtnɪs). [f. ALERT *a.* + -NESS.] The quality of being alert; quickness in observing and acting; briskness, activity, nimbleness.

1714 *Spectator* No. 566 ¶4 That Alertness . . which is usually so visible among Gentlemen of the Army. **1748** ANSON *Voy.* II. vi. (ed. 4) 271 His alertness rendered it impossible to seize him. **1816** MISS AUSTEN *Emma* III. ix. 333 The alertness of a mind which could neither be undecided nor dilatory. **1873** BUCKLE *Civilis.* III. v. 281 A certain alertness and vigour of understanding.

† **a'lese,** *v. Obs.* Forms: 1 **alés-an** (WS. **alýsan**), 2–3 **ales-en,** s.w. **alus-en** (-y-). [f. A- *pref.* 1 out,

away + *lés-an*: see LESE. Cf. Germ. *er-lösen*.] To release, deliver.

a **1000** *Ags. Gosp.* Matt. vi. 13 Ac alys us of yfele. *c* **1160** *Hatton G.* ibid., Ac ales us of yfele. *c* **1175** *Lamb. Hom.* 87 He us alesde from deofles þewdome. *c* **1230** *Ancr. R.* 124 Uorte..alesen him ut of pine. *c* **1250** *Moral Ode* 136 Ne bidde ic no bet beo a-lused [*c* **1200** alesed] a domesdai of bende. *a* **1400** *Leg. Rood* (1871) 180 þat bonde me alese of bondes, Of unkind dede.

† **a'lesedness, a'lesendness.** *Obs.* [f. OE. *alésend* pr. pple. and *alésed* pa. pple. of ALESE + -NESS.] Deliverance, redemption.

c **1000** *Ags. Gosp.* Matt. xx. 28 Mannes Sunu..sealde his sawle lif to alysednesse for maneȝum. *c* **1160** *Hatton G.* ibid., To alesendnysse for maneȝen. *c* **1175** *Lamb. Hom.* 129 Of þissere alesednesse.. Dauid þe prophete seide. *c* **1175** *Cotton Hom.*, Heo wolde man beon..for ure alysendnisse. *c* **1230** *Hali Meid.* 11 Meidenhad is..worldes alesendnesse.

† **a'leseness, a'lesness.** *Obs.* [f. ALESE *v.* + -NESS.] Redemption, ransom.

c **950** *Lindisf. Gosp.* Matt. xx. 28 Sella sawel his alesenis fore moniȝum. *c* **975** *Rushw. G.* ibid., For monȝum to alesnisse. *a* **1000** *Crist* (Grein) 1474 þinre alýsnesse. *c* **1175** *Cotton Hom.* 263 He sende ihesu crist..to ure alesnesse. *c* **1230** *Hali Meid.* 11 Meidenhad is heuene cwen & worldes alesnesse [*printed* alefnesse].

† **a'lesing,** *vbl. sb. Obs.* [f. ALESE *v.* + -ING[1].] Release.

c **1175** *Lamb. Hom.* I. 143 I warpen ine eche pine wiþ-uten alesinge. *c* **1220** *Leg. St. Kath.* 1153 Sum walde hopen & habbe bileaue to his alesunge.

† **a'less,** *v. Obs. rare*$^{-1}$. [f. LESS *a.*, by form-association with vbs. from Fr. apparently formed on adjs., as *a-base*: cf. *amenuse*.] To make less, lessen, diminish.

1496 *Dives & Paup.* (W. de Worde) VIII. ix. 289/1 He must alesse the hyre that the fermer sholde paye.

† **'ale,stake.** *Obs.* [f. ALE- 4.]

1. A stake or post set up before an alehouse, to bear a garland, bush, or other sign, or as a sign itself; an alepole. Also *fig.*

c **1386** CHAUCER *Prol.* 667 A garland had he set upon his heed, As gret as it were for an ale-stake. **1509** BARCLAY *Ship of Fooles* (1570) 32 To the wine and ale stakes to renne. **1532** MORE *Confut. Tindale* Wks. 1557, 642/1 Set vp for a bare signe, as a tauerners bush or tapsters ale stake. **1553-87** FOXE *A. & M.* (1684) II. 50/1 This Popish Decree and Indulgense, as a new Merchandise or Ale-stake to get Money. **1693** W. ROBERTSON *Phraseol. Gen.* 64 An Ale-stake ..*vide* May-pole.

2. A frequenter of the alehouse; a tippler or sot.

1583 BABINGTON *Wks.* 104 If he be a drunken alestake, a ticktack tauerner. **1656** TRAPP *Exp. 1 Tim.* iii. 3 (1868) III. 641/1 No Ale-stake, tavern-haunter, that sits close at it.

alet, obs. form of AILETTE.

† **a'let,** *v. Obs.* [f. A- *pref.* 1 out, away + LET, OE. *alǽtan*, cogn. w. OS. *âlâtan*, OHG. *arlâzan*, Goth. *uslêtan*.] *trans.* To let go; also *intr.* to 'give.'

c **1000** *Ags. Gosp.* John x. 18 Ic hæbbe anweald mine sawle to alætan. *c* **1160** *Hatton G.* ibid., To alætene. **1205** LAYAM. 15932 Let alæten þis wæter & wei weorpen. *c* **1420** *Pallad. on Husb.* IX. 103 A potters potte uneled wol alete.

'ale-,taster. [ALE- 1.] An officer appointed to examine or try the ale sold within his jurisdiction, an ALE-CONNER.

1523 FITZHERB. *Surv.* 20 b, I shall true constable be..true ale taster, trewe wodewarde. **1641** *Termes de la Ley* 18 Ale-taster is an officer appointed and sworne in every Leet to looke that the due assise be kept of all the Bread, Ale, and Beere sold within the Jurisdiction of the Leet. **1876** ROGERS *Pol. Econ.* xx. 12 The keeper of an ale-house was fined, if he broached a cask, without giving notice to..[the] ale-tasters.

† **a'lethe,** *v. Obs. rare.* [f. A- *pref.* 1 intens. + LETHE, to soften.] To soften, mitigate.

c **1420** *Pallad. on Husb.* XI. 434 Yit leve a litel hool oute atte to brethe Mane heetes estuant for to alethe.

alethiology (ə,liːθɪ'ɒlədʒɪ). *rare.* [f. Gr. ἀλήθεια truth + -(O)LOGY.] The doctrine of truth, that part of logic which treats of truth.

1837-8 SIR W. HAMILTON *Logic* iv. 69 (L.) The first part [of logic] treats of the nature of truth and error, and of the highest laws for their discrimination, Alethiology.

alette (ə'lɛt). *arch.* [a mod.Fr. *alette*, OFr. *alete*, cogn. with It. *aletta*, dim. of *ala* wing; in form a doublet of AILETTE.] (See quot.)

1816 JAMES *Mil. Dict.* (1816) 10 *Alette* (Fr.) in architecture, the sides of a pier between the arcades: alettes also signify jaumbs, or piedroits. **1838** BUTTON *Dict. Arch.* 7 *Alette*, a small wing; also applied to a pilaster, or buttress.

† **'aletude.** *Obs.*$^{-0}$ [ad. L. *aletūdo*.] 'Fatness of the body, grossness.' Blount *Glossogr.* 1656.

aleukæmic (æl(j)uː'kiːmɪk, eɪ-), *a. Path.* Also -emic. [f. A- 14 + LEUKÆMIC *a.*] Not characterized by a high white-cell count; esp. in *aleukæmic leukæmia*.

1904 A. STENGEL in *Amer. Jrnl. Med. Sci.* CXXVIII. 524 Some authorities regarded the latter [*sc.* splenic anæmia] as an aleukæmic variety of splenic leukæmia. **1949** *Blakiston's New Gould Med. Dict.* 562 *Aleukemic leukemia*, a form of leukemia in which the total leukocyte count is normal, despite leukemic changes in the tissues and qualitative changes in the blood. **1962** *Lancet* 13 Jan. 64/2 When splenomegaly occurred alone the initial diagnosis was often obscure, and 3 cases had been diagnosed as aleukæmic leukæmia.

aleuromancy (ə'ljʊərəʊ,mænsɪ). *rare.* [a. Fr. *aleuromancie*, ult. f. Gr. ἄλευρον flour + μαντεία divination; the compound ἀλευρομαντεῖον already existed in Gr.] An ancient kind of divination performed by means of meal or flour.

1656 BLOUNT *Glossogr.*, *Aleuromancy*, divination by barley meal mixed with wheat. **1693** URQUHART *Rabelais* III. xxv. Disclosed unto you..by aleuromancy, mixing the flour of wheat with oatmeal. **1775** in ASH; and in mod. Dicts.

aleurometer (æljʊ'rɒmɪtə(r)). [f. Gr. ἄλευρ-ον flour + -(O)METER.] An instrument for measuring the quantity of gluten in flour.

1844 *Athen.* No. 1112 The Aleurometer, the purpose of which is to indicate the panifiable properties of wheat flour.

aleuron(e (ə'ljʊərən, -əʊn). [ad. Gr. ἄλευρον flour.] An albuminoid or proteinous substance found in amorphous granules in the seeds of plants, etc.

1869 S. W. JOHNSON *How Crops Grow* 92 Hartig.. distinguished them by the name *Aleurone*, a term which we may conveniently employ. By *Aleurone* is..meant..those organised granules found in the plant, of which the albuminoids are chief ingredients. **1875** BENNETT & DYER *Sachs' Bot.* 55 The aleurone grains of oily seeds contain no oil. **1879** *Syd. Soc. Lex.*, *Aleuron* masses or crystals are found in the vitellus of the ova of fishes and other vertebrata.

aleuronic (æljʊ'rɒnɪk), *a.* [f. prec. + -IC.] Of or pertaining to aleuron.

1879 *Syd. Soc. Lex.* s.v. *Albines*, The aleuronic mass is composed of two concentric vesicles.

Aleut ('əl(j)uːt, (U.S.) 'ælıuːt). [Origin unknown, perh. from a native word.] **a.** A native of the Aleutian Islands. Also *attrib.* **b.** The language of this people, distantly related to Eskimo.

1780 W. COXE *Acc. Russ. Disc. betw. Asia & Amer.* 263 The inhabitants of Unalashka..now begin to call themselves by the general name of Aleyut, given them by the Russians. **1881** *Encycl. Brit.* XII. 826/1 Of the Aleuts, whose collective name is 'Ungungun', or 'People', there are two divisions. *Ibid.* 826/2 The Thlinkeet language seems to be completely isolated, showing nothing beyond the faintest verbal resemblance to the Aleut. **1890** *Independent* (N.Y.) 9 Oct. 1/2 The word *Aleut*, pronounced *al-lee-yoot*, is of uncertain origin. *Ibid.*, The Aleuts themselves do not recognize the word, their own name for their tribe being Oonangan. **1936** *Discovery* Nov. 351/2 It is not certain that the skull found..is that of an Aleut. **1956** J. WHATMOUGH *Lang.* iii. 41 Aleut was reduced to picture writing even in the last century. **1962** *Listener* 25 Oct. 690/1 The anatomical knowledge of the Aleut Eskimo.

Aleutian (ə'l(j)uːʃən), *a.* and *sb.* [f. prec. + -IAN.] **A.** *adj.* Of or pertaining to the Aleutian Islands off the western coast of Alaska. **B.** *sb.* A native of the Aleutian Islands.

1780 W. COXE *Acc. Russ. Disc. betw. Asia & Amer.* (*map facing title-p.*), Aleütian Islands. **1814** tr. *G. H. von Langsdorff's Voy. & Trav.* II. ii. 48 The Aleutians are not addicted to smoking, but are passionately fond of snuff. **1870** *Alaska Times* (Sitka) 7 May 2/3 On last Monday afternoon war was declared between the Sitka Si-washes and the native Aleutians. **1902** *Encycl. Brit.* XXV. 242/2 The Aleutian district derives its name from traditions of islands beyond the Oliutorsk Cape of Kamchatka. **1911** FRAZER *Golden Bough* (ed. 3) I. i. iii. 123 An Aleutian hunter of sea-otters. **1937** *Times Lit. Suppl.* 4 Dec. 923/1 A fair crossing of the Aleutian ledge.

alevin ('æləvɪn). [a. Fr. *alevin*, according to Littré for **alevain*, f. OFr. *alever* to rear:—L. *adlevāre*, f. *ad* to + *levāre* to raise; like *nourrain* from *nourrir*.] Young fish, fry.

1868 PEARD *Water-farm.* vii. 75 The havoc committed on the eggs, and alevins. **1882** F. FRANCIS in *Gd. Wds.* Sept. 603 Into your hatching-boxes, amongst your trout and salmon eggs, or alevins.

† **a'lew.** *Obs. rare*$^{-1}$ (in Spenser). = HALLOO.

1596 SPENSER *F.Q.* v. vi. 13 Yet did she not lament with loude alew, As women wont.

'ale-wife[1]. [ALE- 4 + WIFE in sense of *woman*.] A woman that keeps an ale-house.

1393 LANGL. *P. Pl.* C. IX. 330 þe best and brounest · þat brewesters [*v.r.* *c* 1400 ale-wiuys] sellen. *a* **1500** *Carp. Tools* 43 in Hazl. *E.P.P.* I. 81 He wones to nyȝe the ale-wyffe. **1587** HARRISON *Engl.* I. II. vi. 161 Such slights also have the alewives for the utterance of this drinke. **1596** SHAKS. *Tam. Shr.* Ind. ii. 23 Aske Marrian Hacket the fat Ale-wife of Wincot, if shee know me not. **1663** *Flagel.*, *O. Cromwell* (1672) 17 The Ale-wives of Huntingdon..when they saw him coming would use to cry out to one another, shut up your Dores. **1789** MRS. PIOZZI *France & It.* I. 17 A flat silver ring on her finger, like our ale-wives. **1865** T. WRIGHT *Caricature & Grot.* viii. 139 The ale-wife is pouring her liquor from her jug.

ale-wife[2] ('eɪlwaɪf). Pl. **ale-wives.** [Prob. a transf. use of prec., with reference to the large belly of the fish.] An American fish (*Clupea serrata*) closely allied to the herring.

1633 in *New Plymouth Col. Rec.* (1855) I. 17 Whereas God, by his providence, hath cast the fish called alewiues or herrings in the middest of the place. **1634** in *Mass. Col. Rec.* (1853) I. 114 [He] is to sell the Alewyves hee takes there at 5 s. the thousand. **1652** J. ELIOT *Let.* 28 Feb. in *Strength out of Weakness* 5 Where the Fish we call Alewives come, there we built a Bridge. **1670** S. CLARKE *Acc. Plantations* 37 Big-bellied Alewives, Mackrils richly clad With Rainbow colours. **1847** in CRAIG. **1852** M. PERLEY *Rep. Fish. N. Brunsw.* (ed. 2) 208 The ale-wive appears in great quantities in the Chesapeake, in March. **1870** LOWELL *Study Wind.* 15 The refuse of the gasworks..supplied him [the crow] with dead alewives in abundance.

† **ale'xander,** *sb.*[1] *Obs.* Alexandrine or Alexandrian work; a species of striped silk.

1500 in *Ann. Reg.* 1768, 134 A compleat hanging of broad Alexander. **1882** BECK *Draper's Dict.*, *Alexander*, Bourde de Alisaundre, Burdalisaunder..In 1327 Exeter has a chasuble of Bourde de Elisandre of divers colours.

Alexander (ælɪg'zɑːndə(r), -æ-), *sb.*[2] A kind of cocktail.

1930 H. CRADDOCK *Savoy Cocktail Book* I. 18 Alexander Cocktail, ½ Dry Gin, ¼ Crème de Cacao, ¼ Sweet Cream. **1951** N. BALCHIN *Way through the Wood* vii. 98 The sort of places where one always drinks Alexanders. **1958** A. L. SIMON *Dict. Wines* 55/1 *Alexander*, (1) ⅓ gin; ⅓ Crème de Cacao; ⅓ cream. Frappé. (2) ¾ jigger Rye Whisky; ¼ jigger Bénédictine; twist orange peel on top.

Alexander (ælɪg'zɑːndə(r), -æ-), *sb.*[3] The name of Frederick Matthias *Alexander* (1869–1955), Australian-born physiotherapist, used *attrib.* and in the possessive to designate a technique developed by him for controlling postural behaviour as an aid to improved living.

1932 J. DEWEY in F. M. Alexander *Use of Self* p. xv, Mr. Alexander's technique gave a direct and intimate confirmation in personal experience of the fact of central control. **1941** A. HUXLEY in *Sat. Rev. Lit.* 25 Oct. 18/2 Alexander's technique for the conscious mastery of the primary control is now available, and..it can be combined ..with the technique of the mystics for transcending personality. **1942** —— *Let.* (1969) 473 Given mysticism and such psycho-physical techniques as the Bates method and the Alexander method, it is possible to conceive of a totally new kind of education. **1973** W. BARLOW *Alexander Principle* i. 9 Men and women who are pre-eminent in their various spheres..have gladly accepted the help that the Alexander principle has to offer them. **1980** *Times* 8 Apr. 12/6, I have no doubt that the wide range of therapeutic techniques practised there (..Massage, Reflexology, Alexander Technique,..) are of the greatest value for the growth towards wholeness. **1981** *Washington Post* 9 Mar. C5/2 Carol Boggs..formerly on the dance faculty at American University, uses the Alexander Technique to help people 'retrain postural and movement habits so they don't have pain'.

† **Ale'xander,** *v. Obs. nonce-wd.* [f. prop. name *Alexander*, in reference to the renown of Alexander the Great.] To praise as an Alexander; to extol.

1700 DRYDEN *Cock & Fox* 660 Ye princes..Alexander'd up in lying odes.

alexanders (ælɪg'zɑːndəz, -æ-). Forms: 1 **alexandre,** 3–4 **alisaundre,** 5–6 **alysaunder,** 7 **allis-, alys-,** 8 **ales-,** 7–9 **alis-,** 6– **alexander(s.** [Cf. Fr. *alexandre* (Lyte's *Dodoens*), *alisandre* Palsg., *alisaundre, alissandere* Godef., med.L. name *Petroselinum Alexandrinum*, a synonym of *P. Macedonicum*. The note in Holland's *Pliny* (1634) II. 30 that *alisanders* is 'a corrupt word from *olus atrum*, as if one would say *olusatres*,' seems disproved by the 10th c. *alexandre*.]

An umbelliferous plant (*Smyrnium Olusatrum*), called also Horse-parsley, formerly cultivated and eaten like celery.

c **940** *Sax. Leechd.* II. 120 Wyrc to drence alexandre. *c* **1300** in Wright *Lyric P.* v. 26 With alisaundre thare-to, ache ant anys. **1440** *Promp. Parv.*, Alysaunder, herbe, or stanmarche, *Macedonia*. **1578** LYTE *Dodoens* 608 In Frenche *Grand Ache* or *Alexandre*..in English, *Alexanders*. **1579** LANGHAM *Gard. Health* (1633) 11, Alysander, the seeds drunke alone..dissolueth winde and griping in the body. **1580** TUSSER *Husb.* xl, Herbes and rootes for sallets and sauce, Alexanders, at all times. **1669** J. W[ORLIDGE] *Syst. Agric.* (1681) 270 Now sow..Sellery, Smallage, Allisanders. **1813** MARSHALL *Gard.* xv. (ed. 5) 214 Alexander is a culinary plant, formerly much used, but has given way to celery. **1861** PRATT *Flower. Pl.* III. 9 Smyrnium (Alexanders).

Alexander's Foot. A composite plant (*Anacyclus Pyrethrum*), also called Pellitory of Spain, closely allied to camomile.

1597 GERARD *Herball* 619 In French *Pied d Alexandre*, that is to saie, *Pes Alexandrinus*, or Alexanders foote. **1678** PHILLIPS, *Alexander's Foot*, a Plant, whose Root resembles a foot. [Also in BAILEY and ASH.]

Alexandra (ælɪg'zɑːndrə, -æ-). **1.** The name of *Alexandra* (1844–1925), wife of King Edward VII, used *attrib.* to designate a manner of walking affected by fashionable society in imitation of her limp when she was Princess of Wales. So **Ale'xandrian** *a.*[3] (*temporary.*)

1870 G. M. HOPKINS *Further Lett.* 1 Mar. (1956) 110 He is going to make use of the 'Alexandrian step' when he can walk, that is the step wh. suddenly became the thing at court when the Princess of Wales got lame with a sore knee. **1876** *Chambers's Jrnl.* 15 Jan. 35/1 The Grecian bend and the Alexandra limp—both positive and practical imitations of physical affliction. **1880** C. M. YONGE *Autobiogr. P. Applecheeks* in *Bye-words* 304 Her Alexandra limp, and all her most unnatural airs.

2. In full *Alexandra fly*: an artificial fly used by anglers.

1880 F. FRANCIS *Bk. Angling* (ed. 5) viii. 286 A fly with a silver twist body and a bunch of peacock herl for the wing, which they [*sc.* trout] have a great fancy for, the fly minnow, known as the Alexandra in fact. **1882** D. FOSTER *Scientific Angler* xii. 199 Gaudily-dressed lake flies.. are good. But the combination more suitable.. is the dressing known as the 'Alexandra fly'. This is as large as a full-sized Sewin fly .. the shank carefully wrapped with broad silver tinsel, to represent the body. **1926** *Chambers's Jrnl.* XVI. 601/1, I have an Alexandra, a confection of peacock feather and tinsel.

Alexandrian (ælɪg'zɑːndrɪən, -æ-), *a.*[1] and *sb.*[1] [f. L. *Alexandri-us* + -AN.] = ALEXANDRINE.

1751 CHAMBERS *Cycl.* s.v., Chapman's translation of Homer consists wholly of *Alexandrians.* **1753** —— *Supp.* s.v., He had been deceived in supposing the alexandrian verses to have corresponded to the ancient heroics.

Alexandrian (ælɪg'zɑːndrɪən, -æ-), *a.*[2] and *sb.*[2] [f. L. *Alexandrīa*, Gr. Ἀλεξάνδρεια, the capital of ancient Egypt in classical times: see -AN.]

1. Of, pertaining to, or characteristic of, Alexandria. As *sb.*, an inhabitant of Alexandria.

1584 GREENE *Gwydonius* 63 But if yᵉ Alexandrians obtained yᵉ conquest, yᵉ Duke of Metelyne should peacably depart the countrie. **1606** SHAKES. *Ant. & Cl.* II. vii. 102 This is not yet an Alexandrian Feast. **1607** TOPSELL *Four-f. Beasts* 627 The Babilonians and the Alexandrians loued diuersity of colours in their garments. **1611** BIBLE *Acts* vi. 9 Certaine of the Synagogue.. of the Libertines, and Cyrenians, and Alexandrians, and of them of Cilicia, and of Asia, disputing with Steuen. **1671** A. WOODHEAD *Consid. Council Trent* vii. 104 Arius, an Alexandrian Presbyter. **1775** ASH *Dict., Alexandrian*, a native of Alexandria. **1875** *Encycl. Brit.* I. 494/1 The famous lighthouse.. cost 800 talents, which, if Alexandrian, is equivalent to £248,000. **1949** *Oxf. Classical Dict.* 35/2 The Alexandrian citizenship was allowed to continue and carried with it certain privileges.

2. Belonging or akin to the schools of philosophy in Alexandria, esp. those which produced Philo Judaeus, the Neo-Platonists Ammonius, Plotinus, Iamblichus, and the Christian fathers Clement of Alexandria and Origen. As *sb.*, a member or follower of one or other of these schools.

1753 E. CHAMBERS *Cycl.* Suppl. s.v., The chief Alexandrian philosophers, were Ammonius, Plotinus, Origen, Porphyry, [etc.]. **1809** E. JERNINGHAM (*title*) The Alexandrian School; or, A Narrative of the First Christian Professors in Alexandria. —— *Ibid.* 18 The Alexandrians at length silenced the adverse party. **1840** *Q. Rev.* June 67 What in Plato was a religious philosophy, became, in the hands of the Alexandrians, a philosophical religion. *Ibid.*, John Smith, Cudworth, Norris, and More, were Alexandrian, not Athenian Platonists. **1858** DONALDSON *Contin. C. O. Müller's Lit. Anc. Greece* III. liii. 172 Gnosticism originated in the Orientalized Platonism of the Alexandrians. **1883** FARRAR *Ep. Hebrews* Introd. 35 The most marked feature of the Epistle to the Hebrews is its Alexandrian character. *Ibid.* 36 It is Alexandrian in its method of dealing with Scripture.

3. Belonging or akin to the school of Greek literature, esp. poetry, which flourished at Alexandria under the Ptolemies, and is regarded as a 'silver age'; derivative, imitative, artificial, addicted to recondite learning. As *sb.*, a member or imitator of this school, or a writer who shows himself to be a kindred spirit.

1840 *Q. Rev.* June 110 The great mass of Alexandrian literature has perished by its own acknowledged worthlessness. **1858** DONALDSON *Contin. C. O. Müller's Lit. Anc. Greece* II. xlv. 449 Of all the writers of the Alexandrian school, the bucolic poets have enjoyed the most universal and permanent popularity. **1877** SELLAR *Virgil* 42 Virgil.. has used the Alexandrians more freely than any other Greek writers, with the exception of Homer. **1887** MAHAFFY *Gr. Life & Thought* xi. 235 Antimachus of Colophon.. certainly was great enough to set up a model which had fatal effects on the Alexandrians. **1904** T. R. GLOVER *Stud. Virgil* 68 Ovid adds to his Alexandrian learning an air of humour which gives it quite a new complexion. **1958** *Times Lit. Suppl.* 7 Feb. 76/1 An Alexandrian style that abounds in hidden allusions, a version.. of the academic rococo.

Hence **Ale'xandrianism**, the method and doctrine of the philosophical and Christian schools, or the style and characteristics of the literary school, mentioned above.

1860 WESTCOTT *Introd. Study Gosp.* i. 75 The society of the Therapeutæ was indeed the practical corollary of Alexandrianism. **1878** J. C. COLLINS *Tourneur's Plays* II. 223 Lycophosed... This is a good instance of Tourneur's Alexandrianism. **1883** FARRAR *Ep. Hebrews* Introd. 38 The Alexandrianism of the Epistle appears most clearly in the constant parallels which it furnishes to the writings of Philo. **1960** H. READ *Forms of Things Unknown* II. vi. 97 Alexandrianism, which is another name for cultural decadence.

Alexandrine (ælɪg'zɑːndrɪn, -æ-), *a.*[1] and *sb.*[1] [a. Fr. *alexandrin*, the exact origin of which is disputed, some deriving it, according to Ménage, from the name of *Alexandre Paris*, an old French poet who used this verse, others from the fact that several poems on Alexander the Great were written in it by early poets (one by the said Alexandre Paris): see Littré.]

A. *adj.* Applied to a line of six feet or twelve syllables, which is the French heroic verse, and in English is used to vary the heroic verse of five feet.

1589 PUTTENHAM *Eng. Poesie* (1869) 86 This meeter of twelue sillables the French man calleth a verse Alexandrine. **1756-82** J. WARTON *Ess. Pope* I. 199 (T.) The harmony of his numbers, as far as Alexandrine lines will admit.

B. *sb.* An Alexandrine line or verse.

1667 DRYDEN *Ann. Mirab.* Pref., They write in Alexandrins or verses of six feet. **1709** POPE *Crit.* 359 A needless Alexandrine ends the song That like a wounded snake, drags its slow length along. **1860** *All Y. Round* No. 67, 392 Says Spenser, in one of his fine, drowsy, murmuring alexandrines.

Alexandrine (ælɪg'zɑːndrɪn, -æ-, -aɪn), *a.*[2] and *sb.*[2] [a. Fr. *alexandrin*, ad. L. *alexandrīnus*, f. *Alexandrīa* prop. name.]

A. *adj.* **a.** Of or belonging to Alexandria; Also *spec.* = ALEXANDRIAN *a.*[2] 2, 3.

B. *sb.* **a.** A kind of embroidery named from that town. **b.** = ALEXANDRIAN *sb.*[2] 2, 3.

? *a* **1500** *MS. Rawlinson* C. 86, 121 (Halliw.) A mauntelle of hermyn Coverid.. with Alexandryn. **1605** TIMME *Quersit.* III. 178 Take.. of the treacle Alexandrine 2 ounces. **1876** BANCROFT *Hist. U.S.* II. xli. 535 Plato and the Alexandrine philosophers. **1877** SELLAR *Virgil* 42 Yet even in him [*sc.* Horace] the influence of the Alexandrine tone is apparent, especially in his treatment of the subjects taken from the Greek mythology. **1893** C. T. CRUTTWELL *Lit. Hist. Early Christ.* II. 442 The Alexandrine Fathers. **1904** T. R. GLOVER *Stud. Virgil* 165 From Euripides and the Alexandrines the love motive found its way into Latin poetry. **1923** J. B. BURY *Hellen. Age* i. 3 The Latin poets.. owed more to.. the Alexandrines.

Hence **Ale'xandrinism** = ALEXANDRIANISM.

1880 CHEYNE *Proph. Isaiah* I. 238 Hence the Greek writer of Wisdom need not be credited with Alexandrinism. **1901** J. C. COLLINS *Ephem. Crit.* 336 He [*sc.* Catullus] has not, indeed, escaped the taint of Alexandrinism.

alexandrite (ælɪg'zɑːndraɪt, -æ-). *Min.* [Named from Alexander I, Czar of Russia; see -ITE.] A variety of chrysoberyl found in the Ural Mountains.

1837-80 DANA *Min.* 155 Alexandrite of emerald-green color.

alexia (ə'lɛksɪə). *Path.* [mod.L., badly f. A- 14 + Gr. λέξις speech (λέγειν to speak, confused with L. *legere* to read), after AGRAPHIA.] Inability to see words or to read; word-blindness.

1878 G. B. SHATTUCK tr. *von Ziemssen's Cycl. Med.* XIV. 774 It is.. by no means easy to say how much of the alexia and paralexia is to be ascribed to the hemiopia. **1904** TITCHENER tr. *Wundt's Physiol. Psychol.* I. 305. **1964** in de Reuck & O'Connor *Disorders of Language* 215 Alexia occurs significantly more often in left-handed people with left-sided lesions than in right-handed people with similar lesions.

† **ale'xicacon, -kakon.** *Obs.* [a. Gr. ἀλεξίκᾰκ-ος, -ον keeping off evil, f. ἀλέξ-ειν to keep off + κακόν evil.] A preservative against evil; a safeguard.

1635 HEYWOOD *Hierarch.* VIII. 552 That their great Alexikakon was a meere figment and Imposture. **1721** BAILEY, *Alexicacon*, a remedy against all evils. **1731** BAILEY and **1775** ASH, *Alexicacon*, A medicine to expell any ill humours from the body.

alexin (ə'lɛksɪn). *Biochem.* Also **alexine.** [a. G. *alexin* (H. Buchner 1891, in *Münchener Med. Wochenschr.* XXXVIII. 437/1, in form *alexine*), f. Gr. ἀλέξειν to ward off + -IN[1].] A name for a class of substances found in blood-serum, having the capacity of destroying bacteria, etc., and thus guarding against infection; *spec.* = ADDIMENT, COMPLEMENT *sb.* 5 i.

1892 *Brit. Med. Jrnl.* II. 728/2 Proteid substances capable of killing bacteria, and now known as alexins, can be obtained from the bodies of various animals. **1896** *Allbutt's Syst. Med.* I. 568 Buchner.. suggested that the destructive power of serum is due to certain proteid substances, to which, unfortunately, he gave the name of alexins. **1901** *Jrnl. Chem. Soc.* LXXX. II. 256 Alexin is found in larger quantity in the polynuclear leucocytes than in normal blood serum of dogs and rabbits. **1904** [see THERMOLABILE *a.*]. **1949** H. W. FLOREY et al. *Antibiotics* I. i. 62 The bacilli so treated formed an excellent antigen for the fixation of alexine.

† **a,lexi'pharmac,** *sb.* and *a.* *Obs.* [a. Fr. *alexipharmaque* (16th c.), ad. mod.L. *alexipharmacum*, ad. Gr. ἀλεξιφάρμακον a remedy against poison; prop. adj. neut. 'keeping off poison'; f. ἀλέξ-ειν to ward off + φάρμακον poison. At first used only in the Gr. or L. form; after adaptation as *alexipharmac* it was also used adjectively, and finally by form-assoc. made ALEXIPHARMIC.]

A. *sb.* An antidote against poison.

1671 SALMON *Syn. Med.* III. xvi. 366 Alexipharmaks, called also Alexiteria, are such as resist poison. **1776** BRYANT *Mythol.* III. 107 The people.. made use of it by way of an alexipharmack and amulet. **1797** *Edin. New Disp.* II. 242/1 This root has been much celebrated as an alexipharmac.

B. *adj.* = ALEXIPHARMIC.

1699 *Phil. Trans.* XXI. 55 This is endowed with Alexipharmac Vertues. **1725** BRADLEY *Fam. Dict.* s.v. *Lemon*, The Rind is Alexipharmac and Cordial.

† **a,lexi'pharmacal,** *a.* and *sb.* [f. prec. + -AL[1]. Prop. the adj. form of ALEXIPHARMAC *sb.*]

A. *adj.* = ALEXIPHARMIC.

1643 E. GREAVES *Morbus Epid.* 11 Some Alexipharmacall Medicine. **1646** SIR T. BROWNE *Pseud. Ep.* III. xxiii. 168 The Horn of a deer is Alexipharmacal. **1692** in COLES.

B. *sb.* = ALEXIPHARMIC.

1607 TOPSELL *Serpents* 775 So effectuall a remedy, or so notable an alexipharmacall.

‖ **a,lexi'pharmacon, -um.** [the orig. Gr. ἀλεξιφάρμακον, and its L. ad. *alexipharmacum*, used as Eng.] = ALEXIPHARMIC.

1605 TIMME *Quersit.* II. vii. 134 This is the summe of all alexipharmacons. **1657** *Phys. Dict., Alexipharmaca*, medicines to resist the plague, and poyson. **1744** BERKELEY *Tar Water in Plague*, Tar water.. is a great alexipharmacum and cordial.

alexiphar'matical, *a.* Erroneous form for ALEXIPHARMACAL, imitating *grammatical*, etc.

1607 TOPSELL *Serpents* (1653) 623 Preserved safe and sound by this alexipharmatical medicine.

alexipharmic (ə,lɛksɪ'fɑːmɪk), *a.* and *sb.* [Modified from ALEXIPHARMAC by form-association with the ending -IC, as in *tonic*, *diuretic*, etc.]

A. *adj.* Preserving from the effects of poison; counteracting or driving away poison; having the quality or nature of an antidote.

1671 SALMON *Syn. Med.* III. xxii. 393 Marigold, the flowers are Alexipharmick. **1761** *Brit. Mag.* II. 117 Alexipharmic boluses and neutral draughts. **1830** LINDLEY *Syst. Bot.* 233 Supposed by the Indian doctors.. to be alexipharmic.

B. *sb.* An alexipharmic medicine or application; a remedy or preservative against poison; an antidote or 'counterpoison.'

1683 SALMON *Doron Med.* II. 394 A mighty great Cordial, alexipharmick, and counter-poyson. **1751** JOHNSON *Rambler* No. 120 ¶2 They filled his apartments with alexipharmics, restoratives, and essential virtues. **1768** PENNANT *Brit. Zool.* 20 The horns were employed as alexipharmics. **1836** M. CHAPMAN *Prom. Bd.* in *Blackw. Mag.* XL. 730 Alexipharmic was there none or drug.

† **a,lexi'pharmical,** *a.* *Obs.* [f. prec. + -AL[1].] Of the nature of an alexipharmic or antidote.

1650 BAXTER *Saints' Rest* IV. iii. (1662) 640 As Alexipharmical Medicines preserve the heart. **1670** *Phil. Trans.* V. 1177 Alexipharmical Plants, as Scordium, Rue and the like.

alexipyretic (ə,lɛksɪpaɪ'rɛtɪk), *a.* and *sb.* [f. Gr. ἀλεξι- warding off + πυρετ-ός fever + -IC.]

A. *adj.* Helpful against fever. **B.** *sb.* A febrifuge.

1753 CHAMBERS *Cycl. Supp.*, Confounding alexiterics with alexipyretics. **1847** in CRAIG. **1879** in *Syd. Soc. Lex.*

alexir, erroneous form of ELIXIR.

† **a,lexi'terial,** *a.* *Obs.* [f. med.L. *alexiterium* (see ALEXITERY) + -AL[1].] = ALEXITERIC.

A. *adj.*

1607 TOPSELL *Serpents* (1653) 657 Sufficient store of alexiterial medicines for the expulsing of this grief. **1712** tr. *Pomet's Hist. Drugs* I. 24 Several People will have it that this Root is Alexiterial. **1751** CHAMBERS *Cycl., Been* or *behen*.. its aromatic, cardiac, and alexiterial virtues.

B. *sb.*

1673 *Phil. Trans.* VIII. 6170 Divers Receipts of Cordials and Alexiterials. **1753** in CHAMBERS *Cycl. Supp.*

alexiterian = ALEXITERIC; a superfluous variant.

1879 in *Syd. Soc. Lex.*

alexiteric (ə,lɛksɪ'tɛrɪk), *a.* and *sb.* [f. med.L. *alexiter-ium* (see ALEXITERY) + -IC.]

A. *adj. properly*, Having the power to ward off contagion; but *used as* Having the properties of an antidote, alexipharmic.

1706 PHILLIPS, *Alexiterical* or *Alexiterick*, that preserves from or drives out Poison, and hinders its mischievous effects in a Humane Body. **1879** *Syd. Soc. Lex., Alexiteric*, having the properties of an *Alexeterium*: antidotal.

B. *sb.* A preservative against contagion or poison.

1694 WESTMACOTT *Scrip. Herb.* 92 The berries [of juniper].. are a great Diuretick, Sudorifick, and Alexiterick. **1712** tr. *Pomet's Hist. Drugs* I. 26 One of the greatest Alexitericks in the World. **1753** in CHAMBERS *Cycl. Supp.*

† **alexi'terical,** *a.* *Obs.* [f. prec. + -AL[1].] = prec.

1742 BAILEY, *Alexiterical, Alexiterick*, that which preserves from or drives out Poison; also that is good against Fevers of a malignant kind, by promoting sweat. **1775** in ASH.

† **a'lexitery,** *sb.* and *a.* *Obs.* [ad. med.L. *alexiterium* (also used unchanged) remedy, alleviation, a. Gr. ἀλεξητήριον a safeguard, a protection; prop. neut. of adj. ἀλεξητήριος

keeping off, defending; f. ἀλέξ-ειν to ward off.] = ALEXITERIC.

A. *sb.*

1657 Tomlinson *Renou's Disp.* 189 Having drunk of the Decoction..or some other Alexitery. **1684** tr. *Bonet's Merc. Compit.* VI. 211 No Alexiterium for a pestilential poison. **1671** *Phil. Trans.* VI. 3015 The heart or liver of a viper is one of the greatest Alexitery's in the world.

B. *adj.*

1727 Bradley *Fam. Dict.* s.v. *Fraxinel,* The Root of the Fraxinel is cordial, opening and alexitary.

alexithymia (eɪlɛksɪˈθaɪmɪə). *Psychol.* [Back-formation from next: see -IA[1].] An affective disorder characterized by inability to recognize or express emotions.

1976 J. C. Nemiah et al. in O. Hill *Mod. Trends Psychosomatic Med.* III. xx. 434 Some patients with severe, life-threatening or debilitating bodily conditions may develop an alexithymic picture... This..has been termed ..'secondary alexithymia'. **1979** *Amer. Jrnl. Psychotherapy* XXXIII. 17 There has been an accumulation of studies..of an affective and cognitive disturbance which Sifneos has called 'alexithymia'. **1983** *Amer. Jrnl. Psychiatry* CXL. 1307/2 Alexithymia may serve as a nidus around which various disciplines can interface.

alexithymic (eɪlɛksɪˈθaɪmɪk), *a.* and *sb. Psychol.* [f. A- 14 + Gr. λέξις speech + θῡμ-ός soul + -IC.]

A. *adj.* Displaying or characterized by an inability to recognize and express emotions. **B.** *sb.* An alexithymic person.

1972 P. E. Sifneos *Short-Term Psychotherapy* vi. 81 Schizophrenic patients who are notorious for having 'a lack of affect' can at times have violent emotional explosions... The ability, then, not only to recognize and express emotions but also to verbalize them is significant... I would like to introduce the term alexithymic..to describe patients who present these difficulties. **1976** [see ALEXITHYMIA]. **1979** *Amer. Jrnl. Psychotherapy* XXXIII. 18 Alexithymic individuals generally are unable to put their emotions into words. **1982** *London Rev. Bks.* 15 July–4 Aug. 21/4 Alexithymics are, quite simply, bores. **1983** *Amer. Jrnl. Psychiatry* CXL. 1308/1 Once someone can be called alexithymic a more comprehensive understanding of that individual follows.

†**aˈley.** *Obs. rare*[−1]. [a. OFr. *alie, alye* (also *alis*), mod.Fr. *alise, alize,* ad. OHG. *eliza,* mod.G. *else(beere)*; the suppression of the *s* in the OFr. is anomalous.] The fruit of the Wild Service tree.

c **1400** *Rom. Rose* 1377 Cherys, of which many oon fayne is, Notes, aleys [*v.r.* aleis], & bolas.

‖**alezan** (aləˈzɑ̃). [Fr., ad. Sp. *alazan,* of doubtful origin; accord. to Devic, f. Arab. *al* the + *hals-ā* fem. of *aḥlas* a bay horse.] A sorrel horse.

1848 Lytton *Harold* II. iii. 43 The snow-white steed of Odo; the alezan of Fitzosborne.

alfa (ˈælfə), var. HALFA.

1857 [see HALFA]. **1883** *Nature* XXVII. 299/2 English journals, many of which are printed on paper made from alfa, a plant cultivated in those remote regions [*sc.* Algeria], and manufactured in England. **1935** S. Beckett *Echo's Bones* (note *ad fin.*), 250[*sc.* copies] on Alfa paper numbered 1 to 250. **1937** E. J. Labarre *Dict. Paper* 141/2 Esparto.. also termed Alfa.

‖**alˈfalfa** (ælˈfælfə). [Sp. *alfalfa* 'three-leaved grasse, clovers grasse' (Minsheu), formerly *alfalfez,* identified by Pedro de Alcalá with Arab. *alfaçfaçah* 'the best sort of fodder,' Freytag.] Spanish name for a variety of Lucerne, in use also in parts of the United States.

1845 Darwin *Voy. Nat.* xvi. (1873) 339 The beds of alfarfa, a kind of clover. **1881** W. White *Cameos fr. Silverl.* I. One species took possession of an alfalfa field. **1882** *Harper's Mag.* Apr. 690 Hay and its substitutes alfalfa and lucern.

‖**alfaqui** (alfəˈkiː). [Sp. *alfaquí,* ad. Arab. *al-faqīh,* i.e. *al* the + *faqīh* one skilled in divine things, f. *faqiha* to be wise.] (See quot.)

1615 Bedwell *Arab. Trudg., Alfakih, Alfaqui, Fakih, Faqui* or *Faquinus*..is in the Mosquits or temples of the Mohametanes, one, that in the manner of a Priest, doth their diuine Seruice, readeth the Law, and doth interpret and expound the same. **1630** Wadsworth *Pilgr.* v. 39 The Priest called their *Alfaqui,* conjured the fish. **1846** Prescott *Ferd. & Is.* I. ix. 382 'Woe is me?' exclaimed an ancient Alfaki. *Ibid.* II. vi. 387 The counsels and authority of some of the chief alfaquis.

alfast = all fast: see AL- and ALL- E 6.

alfe, obs. form of ELF and of HALF.

†**alˈferes.** *Obs.* Also alfierez, -feeres, -ferez, -faras; alfere, -a, -o. [a. OSp. and Pg. *alféres* (mod.Sp. *alférez*) ensign, ad. Arab. *al-fāris* cavalier or knight, f. *faras* horse. Often made pl., with sing. *alfere -a -o*; cf. Fr. *alfier,* It. *alfiere.* (In later Sp. and It. also confused with *alfir,* see ALFIN, as name of the bishop in chess.)] An ensign, a standard-bearer.

1591 Gerrard *Art Warre* 166 The Alfieres of everie Regiment. **1595** T. Maynard *Drake's Voy.* (1849) 10 Losinge my Alfierez Davis Pursell. **1598** Barret *Theor. Warres* II. i. 21, I have seene..the Alferes themselves to passe into other ranks to fight, leauing the Ensigne with the Abanderado. **1631** B. Jonson *New Inn* III. i (N.) Jug here, his alfarez; An able officer. **1633** T. Stafford *Pac. Hib.* xxiii. (1821) 431 With a sealed Letter to the Lord Deputie, by an Alfeeres. *Ibid.* xxi. 420 Two Captaines, 7 Alferoes. ?*c* **1640** *Embl. Parthen. Sodal.* 49 (N.) The heliotropium, or sunflower, 'is the true alferes, bearing up the standard of Flora.' **1679** in Howell's *State Trials* (1816) VII. 347 There are no lieutenants in all the Flanders companies, only Captains and Alfara's. **1708** Kersey, *Alferes,* an Ensign-bearer.

†**alfet.** [Anglicized form of med.L. *alfetum,* latinized form of OE. *ál-fæt,* f. *ál* burning + *fæt* vat, vessel (cf. *ál-ȝeweorc* tinder), in Laws of Æthelstán.] The cauldron used in the ordeal of scalding water. (Not Eng. since 1100; mod. form would be *ole-vat.*)

a **1000** *Anct. Laws* I. 226 Sí þæt álfæt ísen oþþen æren, léaden oþþe lǽmen. [**1678** Du Cange, *Alfetum.*] **1678** Phillips, *Alfet,* a kind of Ordeal anciently used, which was by a great Caldron of scalding water, into which the accused person was to put his arm up to the elbow, and if hurt he was held guilty, if not acquitted. [In Bailey, Ash, Tomlins, etc., but only from Du Cange.]

alfilaria (ælfɪˈlɛərɪə). Also -eria. [Mexican Sp., f. Sp. *alfiler* pin, from the shape of the carpels.] (See quots.)

1868 *Overland Monthly* Aug. 180/1 Burr clover,..alfalfa, bunch grass and alfilaria represent the general pasture of the mountains. **1888** Farmer *Americanisms,* Alfilaria (*Erodium cicutarium*). Also known as Storksbill, Pin-grass, Filaree, &c. A valuable forage plant of the dry regions from Colorado and New Mexico to Southern California. **1897** B. Harraden *Hilda Strafford* 115 Carpets of the little pink blossom of the alfilaria, the first spring flower.

Also **alfileˈrilla.**

1889 in *Cent. Dict.* **1897** *Outing* (U.S.) XXIX. 551/2 The sleek Herefords lifted their white faces from the ferny circlets of alfilerilla.

†**ˈalfin, ˈalphin.** *Obs.* Forms: 5 **alphyn(e, aufyn, awfyn, 6 alfyn.** [a. OFr. *alfin, aufin* (med.L. *alphinus,* It. *alfino, alfido*), f. Sp. *alfil* (*arfil*), Pg. *alfil* (*alfir*), a. Arab. *al-fīl* the elephant, Skr. *pīlu*; the piece in chess called the *alphin,* and now the *bishop,* having had originally with the Indians, Chinese, and Persians the figure and name of an *elephant.*]

1. Former name of the *bishop* in chess.

c **1440** *Gesta Rom.* 70 Som tyme hy and som tyme lowe, among aufyns and pownys. *Ibid.* 62 The secunde, *scil.* alphyne, renneth iij. poyntes, both vpwarde and dounewarde. **1474** Caxton *Chesse* II. iii. B 8, The alphyns ought to be made and formed in manere of Juges syttyng in a chayer. *Ibid.* IV. iv. K 8, The alphyn goeth alwey corner-wyse. **1530** Palsgr. 194/1 Alfyn, a man of the chesse borde. **1562** Rowbotham in *Archæol.* XXIV. 203 The Bishoppes some name Alphins, some fooles, and some name them Princes; other some call them Archers. **1801** Strutt *Sports & Past.* IV. ii. 275 The alfin was also denominated by the French fol, and with us an archer, and at last a bishop.

2. *fig.* with reference either to the Fr. name *fol* fool, or to the awkward and formerly limited moves of the alfin. (Cf. 'Alanus in Parabolis,' quoted in Du Cange, 'Sic inter schachos *Alphinus inutilis* extat, Inter aves bubo.')

c **1440** *Morte Arth.* 1343 Myche wondyre have I, þat syche an alfyne as thow dare speke syche wordez!

Alfisol (ˈælfɪsɒl). *Soil Sci.* [f. *alfi-,* arbitrary prefix + -SOL.] A type of leached basic or slightly acid soil with a clay-enriched B horizon, found chiefly in humid temperate and subtropical regions.

1960 *Soil Classification: 7th Approximation* (U.S. Dept. Agric.) xiv. 202/1 The Alfisols include most soils that have been called Noncalcic Brown soils, Gray-Brown Podzolic soils, and Gray-Wooded soils, [and] many that have been called Planosols. **1972** [see ULTISOL]. **1976** *McGraw-Hill Yearbk. Sci. & Technol.* 367/1 Alfisols on glaciated land surfaces 20,000 years old..are commonly associated with Entisols a few hundred years old on floodplains.

†**alˈforge, alˈforja.** *Obs.* [Pg. *alforge,* Sp. *alforja,* according to Diez, ad. Arab. *al-khorj* the store, supply, provision, f. *kharaja* to proceed.]

1. A wallet, a leather bag, a saddle-bag.

1611 Timberlake 2 *Eng. Pilg.* in *Harl. Misc.* (1753) I. 341 A few Raisins and Bisket, such as we carried in our Alforges. **1779** Johnson *Wks.* 1787 IV. 417 Came down to the sea-side with their aliforges, or leather-bottles, to traffic for water.

2. The cheek-pouch of a baboon.

a **1704** T. Brown *Highlander* Wks. 1730 I. 117 As monkeys their alforges stuff with nuts. **1748** Smollett *Rod. Rand.* xviii. (1804) 112 A great bag of loose skin hanging down in wrinkles like the alforjas of a baboon.

†**al-fort,** *conj. Obs.* [f. ALL *adv.* + FORT, until.] Even till, even to, = Fr. *jusqu'à, jusqu'à ce que.*

c **1300** *Vox & Wolf* 17 To erne, Alfort he come to one walle.

Alfredian (ælˈfriːdɪən), *a.* Also Ælfredian. [f. *Alfred* + -IAN.] Characteristic of Alfred, King of the West Saxons (871–899), or of his writings.

1826 J. J. Conybeare *Illustr. Anglo-Saxon Poetry* 258 The style of these Ælfredian versions is distinguished from that of the Cædmonian school by its great simplicity of diction. **1871** H. Sweet *Alfred's Past. Care* p. vi, I have given..a short sketch of the characteristics of Alfredian English as distinguished from those of the later period. **1899** C. Plummer *Two Saxon Chrons. Parallel* II. p. cxiv, The Alfredian Chronicle up to 892, itself compiled from earlier materials under Alfred's supervision. **1930** *Times Lit. Suppl.* 2 Jan. 14/3 The preverb *ge-* in Alfredian English. **1933** C. L. Wrenn in *Trans. Philol. Soc.* 74 We may then consider how far our material will enable us to deduce Alfred's norm, and then inquire more fully into Sweet's own 'normalized Early West Saxon'—or *Alfredian,* as we have seen that it should strictly be termed. **1935** A. H. Smith *Parker Chron. 832–900* 8 The 'Ælfredian' Chronicle was circulated throughout the kingdom.

‖**alfresco** (ælˈfrɛskəʊ), *adv.* [It. phr. *al fresco* on the fresh, in the fresh or cool air; to paint *al fresco* on the fresh plaster, to dine *al fresco* in the open air.]

1. = FRESCO; *painted* on a plaster surface while still fresh or moist.

1764 Harmer *Observ.* vii. §40. 304 It is superior to the al-fresco, and the Mosaic work. **1886** *Athenæum* 6 Mar. 333/1 The prehistoric artist worked *al fresco,* executing patterns or figures. **1939** *Burlington Mag.* Sept. 108/1 The painting of the flesh—which is consistently *al fresco.*

2. In the open air; also *attrib.* open-air-.

1753 Mrs. Heywood *J. & J. Jessamy* I. v. 53 It was good for her ladyship's health to be thus alfresco. **1761** Smollett *Gil Blas* IV. i. 113 To ventilate my passion here al fresco. **1811** L. M. Hawkins *Countess* I. ii. 32 A little lad who had reported an *alfresco* orchestra as consisting of two horns and a hautboy. **1816** Jane Austen *Emma* III. vi. 92 Mr. Woodhouse was safely conveyed in his carriage..to partake of this al-fresco party. **1881** *Daily Tel.* 23 Feb., The pillared archway of Clement's Inn..a once favourite 'al fresco' emporium of hot eel soup.

3. Used as vb. with obj. *it.*

1822 L. Hunt *Recoll. Writers* 214 Of putting on his shirt as he returns, or even of alfrescoing it without one.

ˈalfridary. *Astrol.* [Of obsc. orig.; cf. Arab. *faraḍa, 'cernere,'* to cut into, define, decree, also to define beforehand a time, to fix on an hour; whence *fariyḍah,* sb. a fixed and defined part. The *-aria* must be Romance ending.] (See quot.)

1614 *Albumazar* II. v. (N.) I'll finde the cuspe, and alfridaria. **1647** Lilly *Chr. Astrol.* clxxi. 733 Lords of the Septenniall yeers, vulgarly called Lords of the Alfridary, are thus: If the Native be borne by day, the ☉ governes the first seven yeers after the Birth, ♀ the next seven, ☿ the next seven, and so in order. **1708** Kersey, *Alfridary,* a temporary Power which the Planets have over the Life of a Person. **1775** in Ash.

Alfur, -o (ˈælfʊə(r), ælˈfʊərəʊ). [ad. Pg. *alfuori* 'the outsider,' f. Arab. *al* the + *fuori* outside:—L. *foribus* out of door, *fores* doors. (R.N. Cust.)] A member of a race or group of races in Celebes and the surrounding islands, distinct from the Malay and Negrito, but perhaps intermediate between them. Hence **Alfurese** *a.*

1878 Cust *Mod. Langs. E. Ind.* 147 The seven Alfurese languages of which we have vocabularies. **1879** *Syd. Soc. Lex.* Alfurian Race: the Alfurs. **1881** A. Keane in *Nature* XXIII. 251 The fusion of yellow, white, and black produces the so-called 'Alfuros' in the East.

Alfvén (ˈælfveɪn, -ən). *Physics.* The name of Hannes *Alfvén* (b. 1908), Swedish physicist, used with reference to his work in magnetohydrodynamics, as **Alfvén speed** (or **velocity**), the speed of an Alfvén wave; **Alfvén wave,** a transverse magnetohydrodynamic wave travelling in the direction of the magnetic field in a magnetized plasma (described by Alfvén in 1943).

1956 *Proc. R. Soc.* A. CCXXXIII. 359 The first *p*-mode is an Alfvén wave propagating with Alfvén's phase velocity. **1960** J. M. Wilcox et al. in *Physics of Fluids* III. 15/1 The generation and propagation of Alfvén waves in a gaseous discharge plasma have been reported recently at Berkeley and Harwell. Such hydromagnetic waves were first postulated by Alfvén to account for certain properties of sun spots. **1962** W. B. Thompson *Introd. Plasma Physics* iv. 50 V_A is the Alfvén speed, an important speed in magnetohydrodynamics. *Ibid.* 51 The Alfvén velocity is large. *Ibid.* vii. 142 This motion, which is common to both ions and electrons, is exactly that experienced by a fluid transmitting Alfvén waves. **1971** I. G. Gass et al. *Understanding Earth* xviii. 259/1 The solar wind is supersonic, in the sense that its speed is ten times the Alfvén wave speed. **1978** *Nature* 26 Oct. 725/2 Accreting matter can pile up at the magnetopause (which in the case of a pulsar would be made up of very low frequency electromagnetic Alfvén waves).

alfyn, variant of ALFIN, *Obs.*

alg (ælg). *rare.* [Anglicized form of L. *alga* or Fr. *algue.*] = ALGA.

1882 F. v. Mueller (*title*) Mosses, Lichens, Algs, and Fungs..indigenous to Australia.

‖**alga** (ˈælgə). Pl. **algæ** (ˈældʒiː). [L. *alga* sea-weed.] A sea-weed; in *pl.* One of the great divisions of Cryptogamic plants, including sea-weeds and kindred fresh-water plants, and a few aerial species.

1551 Turner *Herbal* (1568) 110 Alga whiche is a common name vnto a great parte of see herbes..is commonly called in englyshe see wrak. *a* **1637** B. Jonson *Masques at Crt.* (T.) Oceanus was garlanded with alga, or sea-grass. **1660** Dryden *Astr. Red.* 119 With alga who the sacred altar strews. **1753** CHAMBERS *Cycl. Supp.*, The alga's are some marine..others fluviatile. **1794** MARTYN *Rousseau's Bot.* x. 114 Algæ, having..the seeds either like a meal on the leaves or inclosed in bladders. **1832** LYELL *Princ. Geol.* II. 78 These banks of algæ in the Northern Atlantic. **1849** MRS. SOMERVILLE *Connex. Phys. Sc.* xxvii. 301 The snow itself..produces a red alga.

algæology, -ist, bad forms of ALGOLOGY, -IST.
1854 H. MILLER *Sch. & Schm.* xviii. (1866) 193 Now that algæology has become a science. **1857** —— *Test. Rocks* i. 18 Families familiar to the modern algæologist. **1882** tr. *Nordenskiöld's Voy.* xiv. 242 Whose speciality is Algæology.

algal ('ælgəl), *a.* and *sb.* [f. L. ALGA + -AL[1].]
A. *adj.* Of the nature of an alga or sea-weed. ***Algal alliance***: Lindley's lowest division of the Thallogens, containing the sea-weeds and their allies.
1846 LINDLEY *Veg. Kingd.* 8 The near approach of the two realms being through the Algal alliance. **1862** H. MACMILLAN in *Macm. Mag.* Oct. 465 Merely an algal condition of the common mould. **1866** R. TATE *Brit. Mollusks* iv. 185 By clearing off the algal growth.
B. *sb.* A plant of the algal alliance; an ally of the *algæ*.
1848 LINDLEY *Introd. Bot.* II. 122 The mode of propagation in Algals is extremely variable. **1854** BALFOUR in *Encycl. Brit.* V. 69 In many Algals the cellular spores are surrounded by cilia.

‖ **'algalie.** *Surg. Obs.* [a. Fr. *algalie*, *algarie*, ad. med.L. *algalia*, *argalia*, identified by Ménage with med.Gr. ἀργαλεῖον (used in same sense) for ancient Gr. ἐργαλεῖον 'instrument,' f. ἔργον work. (Littré.)] (See quot.)
1746 ZOLLMAN in *Phil. Trans.* XLIV. 177 In this manner I thrusted an Algalie (or hollow Catheter) into the Bladder.

† **alga'rad.** *Obs.* [a. Fr. *algarade*, ad. Sp. *algarada* 'a sudden assault with a great crie' (Minsheu); f. med.L., Pg. and ? Sp. *algara* a raid (a. Arab. *al-ghārah*, i.e. *al* the, *ghārah* raid) + *-ada*, see -ADE.] A hostile incursion, a raid upon an enemy's territory.
1649 DRUMM. OF HAWTH. *James II*, Wks. 1711, 35 As the French made an algarad by sea upon Kent. —— *James IV*, 63 To suppress their incursions and algarads.

† **algarde.** *Obs.* [f. name of a place.] A Spanish wine formerly celebrated.
a **1400** *Sqr. Low Deg.* 756 (in *Dom. Arch.* II. 134) Mount rose, & wyne of Greke, Both algrade, & respice eke. *c* **1440** *Morte Arth.* 202 Osay and algarde, and oþer ynewe, Rynisch wyne and Rochelle, richere was never.

† **algarot, -oth.** *Chem. Obs.* [a. Fr. *algaroth*, f. name of the inventor Victor Algarotti, a physician of Verona.] An emetic powder, consisting of a compound of trichloride and trioxide of antimony, not now used.
1706 PHILLIPS, *Algarot*, a Chymical Preparation made of Butter of Antimony. **1798** M. & R. EDGEWORTH *Pract. Educ.* I. 96 Butter of antimony, powder of algaroth, and salt of alembroth, may yet long retain their ancient titles amongst apothecaries. **1801** *Phil. Trans.* XCI. 378 White oxide of antimony, formerly called Algaroth Powder.

‖ **alga'rroba.** [Sp. *algarroba*, ad. Arab. *al-kharrūbah*, applied to the same.] **a.** The CAROB tree and bean (also called Locust-pod). **b.** A South American mimosa with pods of similar flavour.
1845 DARWIN *Voy. Nat.* xvi. (1873) 359 A few algarroba trees, a kind of mimosa. **1866** *Treas. Bot.*, *Algaroba bean*, the fruit of *Ceratonia Siliqua*. **1873** BENTLEY *Bot.* (ed. 3) 504 The legumes of *Prosopis dulcis*..are used as a food for cattle, under the name of *Algorobo*.

† **algate, -s,** *adv. Obs.* or *dial.* Also 3-4 **allegate**, 4- **algates**. [lit. *alle gate* = every way: see GATE *sb.*[2] Cf. ON. *alla götu*, and Ormin's *whatt gate* what way? how? The extended form *algates* began in the n.e. *c* 1300; the *-s* was probably analogical, after *always*, etc. (originally genitive). As no difference of meaning appears between *algate* and *algates*, they are not here separated.]
1. Of circumstance and time: Always, continually.
c **1200** *Trin. Coll. Hom.* 23 Wunede mid his apostles for to þe fowertuðe dai, noht alegate, ac stund-mele. *c* **1320** R. BRUNNE *Medit.* 358 He bad hem algates wake and pray. **1388** WYCLIF *2 Cor.* v. 6 We ben hardi algatis [**1611** alwayes confident]. *c* **1449** PECOCK *Repr.* II. viii. 188 We ouȝten algatis abstene and forbere. **1583** STANYHURST *Aeneis* I. (1880) 20 Through thy freendlye trauaile mee dooth King Iuppiter algats Tender. **1587** HOLINSHED *Chron.* II. i. 59 These strangers in Ireland would algate now be also called and accompted Normans.
2. In every way, any way, any how; by all or any means.
c **1230** *Ancr. R.* 398 ȝif þi luue nis nout forto ȝiuen, auh wult allegate þet me bugge hire. *a* **1330** *Sir Otuel* 69 And seide, algate he wolde preue, That Ich am in misbeleue. **1430** LYDG. *Chron. Troy* I. vi, That ye algates desyre to haue a do. **1450** MYRC 1560 Algate make hym telle the. **1565** JEWEL *Repl. Harding* (1611) 36 The Host once Consecrated of the Priest, is algates to bee receiued, whether of many together, or one alone. **1580** G. HARVEY *Three Witie Lett.*, Seeing you gentlewomen will allgates have it so.
3. At all events, at any rate, in any case; whatever may happen.
c **1386** CHAUCER *Sompn. T.* 329, I deme the, thou most algate be deed. *c* **1430** LYDG. *Bochas*, That we algate shall dye bothe two. **1496** *Dives & Paup.* (W. de Worde) I. l. 90 Algates he wolde haue the freres on the lefte honde. **1513** DOUGLAS *Æneis* II. (1710) iii. 80 Now haist my pane, sen al gatis I mon de. **1600** FAIRFAX *Tasso* II. xlii. 47 For a space there must he algates dwell.
4. All the way, altogether.
1330 R. BRUNNE *Chron.* 185 Philip now wille me faile, & alle gate wend me fro. *c* **1386** CHAUCER *Sqrs. T.* 238 Which is vnknowe algates vnto me [*v.r.* algat, -e]. *c* **1449** PECOCK *Repr.* 395 This IX[e] trouthe is Algatis to be holde. **1596** SPENSER *F.Q.* II. i. 2 Una now he algates must forgoe. **1625** L'ISLE *Du Bartas* 60 When algate the top of this Tower had raught unto the clouds.
5. Of sequence: However that may be; yet, nevertheless, notwithstanding, after all.
a **1300** *Cursor M.* 16392 Him haf algat we will. *c* **1386** CHAUCER *Pers. T.* 291 Although ther be difference betuen these tuo causes of drenching, algates the schip is dreynt. *c* **1450** J. RUSSELL *Bk. Nurture* in *Babees Bk.* (1868) 142 Mynse hem smalle in þe siruppe: of fumosite algate be ye feerynge. **1570** THYNNE *Pride & Lowl.* (1841) 36 Alas, quoth I, this is great crueltye: All gate, I bad them all be of good cheere. **1614** W. BROWNE *Sheph. Pipe* Wks. 1772, 22, I have a fear and dread algate.
6. Of place: Everywhere. (This is now the common meaning of the word in the northern dialects, in which alone it survives, along with the cognate ***any gate, na-gate, sumgate***.)

algatross, obs. form of ALBATROSS.

algazel, early form of GAZELLE.

algebra ('ældʒɪbrə). Also 6 **algeber**, **algiebar**. [a. It. *algèbra* (also Sp. and med.L.), ad. Arab. *al-jebr* the redintegration or reunion of broken parts, f. *jabara* to reunite, redintegrate, consolidate, restore; *hence*, the surgical treatment of fractures, bone-setting. Also in phr. *ʿilm al-jebr wa'l-muqābalah*, i.e. 'the science of redintegration and equation (opposition, comparison, collation),' the Arabic name for algebraic computation. In this sense the first part of the Arabic title was taken into It. in 1202, as *algèbra*; the second part, *almucābala*, was used by some med.L. writers in the same sense. The 16th c. Eng. *algeber* (fancifully identified by early writers with the name of the Arabic chemist *Geber*) was either taken directly from Arab. or from Fr. *algèbre*; but the It. *algèbra* became the accepted form (accented '*algebra* by 1663).]
† **1.** The surgical treatment of fractures; bonesetting. (A popular sense which probably survived from the Arabs in Spain; still in Sp.) *Obs.*
1541 R. COPLAND *Guydon's Formul.* X iij, The helpes of Algebra & of dislocations. **1565** J. HALLE *Hist. Expost.* 19 This Araby worde Algebra sygnifyeth as well fractures of bones, etc. as sometyme the restauration of the same. [**1598** FLORIO, *Algèbra* [It.] the arte of bone-setting. **1623** MINSHEU, *Algèbra* [Sp.] bone-setting. *Algebrísta*, a bone-setter.]
2. The department of mathematics which investigates the relations and properties of numbers by means of general symbols; and, in a more abstract sense, a calculus of symbols combining according to certain defined laws.
'Hence various *algebras*: as ***commutative algebra***, in which the symbols obey the law of commutation; ***linear algebra***, in which the symbols are linearly connected; ***quadruple algebra***, or quaternions; and the ***algebra of logic***, in which the symbols represent not numbers or quantities, but other objects of thought, as classes or qualities of things, or statements concerning things.' R. Harley, F.R.S.
1551 RECORDE *Pathw. Know.* II. Pref., Also the rule of false position, with dyuers examples not onely vulgar, but some appertaynyng to the rule of Algeber. **1557** —— *Whetst.* E iv, This Rule is called the Rule of Algeber, after the name of the inuentoure, as some men think..But of his vse it is rightly called the rule of equation. **1570** BILLINGSLEY *Eucl.* x. Introd. 229 That more secret and subtill part of Arithmetike, commonly called Algebra. **1570** DEE *Math. Præf.* 6 The very name is *Algiebar*, and not *Algebra*: as by the Arabien Auicen, may be proued. **1579** DIGGES *Stratiot.* 70 Farther to wade in the large sea of Algebra and numbers cossical. *Ibid.* 55 This Art of Algebra or Rule of Cosse as the Italians terme it. **1610** B. JONSON *Alchem.* I. i. (1616) 607 Your alchemy, and your algebra. **1621** BURTON *Anat. Mel.* Democr. (1657) 45 Geber, that first inventer of Algebra. **1658** PHILLIPS, *Algebra*, or the Analytical Art. **1663** BUTLER *Hud.* I. i. 126 And wisely tell what hour o' th' day The clock does strike, by Algebra. **1775** BURKE *Sp. Conc. Amer.* Wks. III. 33 A proportion beyond all the powers of algebra to equalise and settle. **1781** COWPER *Convers.* 22 And if it weigh the importance of a fly, The scales are false, or algebra a lie. **1837** HALLAM *Hist. Lit.* (1847) I. 238 [In Italian] *co* or *cosa* stands for the unknown quantity; whence algebra was sometimes called the *cossic* art. **1849** DE MORGAN *Double Algebra* II. i. 98 Algebra..got its Arabic name, I have no doubt, from the *restoration* of the term which completes the square, and *reduction* of the equation by extracting the square root. The solution of a quadratic equation was the most prominent part of the Arabic algebra. **1860** MOTLEY *Hist. Netherl.* III. 102 Passionless as algebra.

algebraic (ældʒɪ'breɪɪk), *a.* [f. prec. + -IC. Cf. the more regularly formed Fr. *algébrique*.] Of or pertaining to algebra, occurring *in* algebra.
1662 HOBBES *Seven Prob.* Wks. 1845 VII. 60, I have to prove..the algebraic calculation. **1673** KERSEY *Algebra* (1725) 31 Two or more Algebraic quantities. **1681** SIR G. WHARTON *Wks.* 1683, 44 The so long sought for Equation of three discontinued Numbers in Algebriaque proportion. **1684** *Lond. Gaz.* mdcccclxxxv/4 Algebraick Arithmetick, made easie for the commonest capacity. **1827** HUTTON *Course Math.* I. 182 Algebraic Fractions have the same names and rules of operation, as numeral fractions in common arithmetic. **1858** HOLMES *Aut. of Breakf. T.* xi. 101 These expressions come to be the algebraic symbols of minds which have grown too weak to discriminate.

algebraical (ældʒɪ'breɪɪkəl), *a.* [f. ALGEBRA + -ICAL.] Of or relating to algebra, in which algebra occurs; involving or using, dealing with or treating algebra. (Formerly used = ALGEBRAIC, but prop. disting. as an objective from possessive genitive: an ***algebraic*** symbol, an ***algebraical*** treatise.)
1571 DIGGES *Geom. Pract.* IV. Pref. T b, I intend..geometrically by Algebraycall Calculations to search out the sides. **1579** —— *Stratiot.* 32 The working of supputations Algebraicall. **1679** MOXON *Math. Dict.* 172 Signs, or Symbols now commonly used by some Algebraical Writers. **1736** HERVEY *Mem.* I. 52 Lord Bolingbroke in the algebraical phrase less than nothing. **1837** WHEWELL *Induct. Sc.* (1857) II. 348 The affectation of algebraical formality. **1868** G. AIRY *Pop. Astron.* v. 173 The process is algebraical.

algebraically (ældʒɪ'breɪɪkəlɪ), *adv.* [f. prec. + -LY[2].] In an algebraic or algebraical manner; in algebraic terms, by algebraic processes.
1666 COLLINS in Rigaud *Corr. Sci. Men* (1841) I. 118 A treatise of conics..algebraically performed. **1673** KERSEY *Algebra* (1725) 63 Various Arithmetical Questions Algebraically resolved. **1695** *Lond. Gaz.* mmmlxxxv/4 Euclids second Book..Algebraically Demonstrated. **1837** HALLAM *Hist. Lit.* III. iii. §82 The great discovery that geometrical curves may be expressed algebraically.

† **'algebraism, -rism.** *Obs.* [f. ALGEBRA + -ISM; see next.] Properly an operation or expression in algebra; algebraic symbolism.
1753 CHAMBERS *Cycl. Supp.*, *Algebraism*, or *Algebrism*, is affectedly used, in some writers, for algebra itself. In which sense, we read of the application of algebraism.

algebraist, -rist ('ældʒɪ,breɪɪst, -rɪst). [f. ALGEBRA + -IST. As the final *a* of *algebra* is no part of the stem, *algebrism*, *algebrist*, *algebrize*, are more correct, as well as easier forms of these three words. Cf. Fr. *algébriste*, It. and Sp. *algebrista*.] One versed in algebra.
1673 *Phil. Trans.* VIII. 6073 A Body of Algebra prepared for the Press by that eminent Algebraist Mr. John Kersey. **1691** WOOD *Ath. Oxon* I. col. 871 He had the Character among the *Vertuosi* of a very good Algebrest. **1748** HARTLEY *Observ. Man* I. iii. §1 ¶80 Letters..used by Algebraists to denote Sums and Differences. **1831** GEN. P. THOMPSON *Exerc.* (1842) I. 468 When the algebraist speaks of multiplying by a negative quantity.

algebraize, -rize ('ældʒɪbraɪz), *v.* [f. ALGEBRA + -IZE; see prec.] To reduce to algebraic form, to perform or solve by algebra.
1841 *Blackw. Mag.* L. 633 When a child throws out his five fingers..he has algebraized before he can speak.

† **alge'brician.** *Obs.* [f. ALGEBRA or It. *algebrico* (Fr. *algébrique*) by form-assoc. with *arithmetician*, *geometr-ician*, etc.] = ALGEBRAIST.
1579 DIGGES *Stratiot.* 48 One Prime, or one Roote as commonlye Algebricians tearme it. **1680** HOBBES *Consid.* 51 You Algebricians and Non-conformists, do but fain it, to comfort one another.

algefacient (,ældʒɪː'feɪʃ(ɪ)ənt), *a. Med.* [f. L. *algē-re* to be cold + *facient-em* pr. pple. of *facĕre* to make; cf. L. *calefacere* to make warm.] 'Cooling, having the power to make cold.' *Syd. Soc. Lex.* 1879.

† **algere.** *Obs.* [? f. OE. *ǣl* eel + *gár* spear. Cf. Fl. *aalgeer*, *elger*, instrumentum dentibus mucronatum, quo anguillæ figuntur. H. Hettema in *Trans. Phil. Soc.* 1858, p. 145.] An eel-spear: see ELGER.
a **1500** *MS.* in *Promp. Parv.* 186 *Contus*, an algere, a shaft, a dartt, a polloure. *Fuscina*, a hoke for fysshe, an algere.

Algerian (æl'dʒɪərɪən), *a.* and *sb.* [f. *Algeria* + -AN.]
A. *adj.* Of or pertaining to Algeria or Algiers, in northern Africa. Also *ellipt.*, Algerian wine. ***Algerian onyx***: see quot. 1904.
1874 [R. L. PLAYFAIR] *Handbk. Trav. Algeria* 4 Algerian hotels are similar to the French country hotels. *Ibid.* 212/2 The mosque..owes its chief interest to its 8 columns of Algerian onyx. **1904** GOODCHILD & TWENEY *Technol. & Sci. Dict.* 10/1 *Oriental alabaster*, a stalagmitic variety of calcite; of white or brownish concentric laminæ. Used as an ornamental stone under the name Algerian onyx. **1912** 'R. DEVEREUX' *Asp. Algeria* ix. 165 In 1906 Algerian wine was introduced into the English market. **1953** R. FULLER *2nd Curtain* i. 10 The waiter came with a bottle of Algerian wine. *Ibid.* 11 Garner shielded his face with his glass of Algerian.

1958 *Times* 26 May 6/1 The Algerian insurrection has now spread to..Corsica.

B. *sb.* An inhabitant or native of Algeria or Algiers.

1625 PURCHAS *Pilgrimes* II. IX. xii. 1564 Opinions foolish and Deuilish in Algier. These Algierians haue the foolish conceits of other Mahumetans..that Fooles and Dwarfes are Saints. **1914** M. D. STOTT *Real Algeria* iii. 41 The Algerian regards his own intelligence and aptitude in every respect superior to that of the Frenchman.

Algerine (ældʒəˈriːn), *sb.* and *a.* [f. *Alger-ia* + -INE[1].] **A.** *sb.* **1.** An inhabitant or native of Algiers or Algeria; esp. a pirate from Algiers.

1657 J. SOMER 12 May in *Cal. Clarendon State Papers* (1876) III. 287 Their whole fleet under Blake was destroyed by the Algerines. **1669** PEPYS *Diary* 26 Jan. (1896) VIII. 211 The Algerines have broke the peace with us. **1728** J. MORGAN *Hist. Algiers* II. 433 Hassan Basha, with his Algerines, determined to attack that small Peninsula. **1785** JEFFERSON *Writ.* (1894) IV. 25 The Algerines..have taken two of our vessels. **1819** SALAMÉ *Narr. Exped. Algiers* 39 At a few minutes before three, the Algerines, from the Eastern battery, fired the first shot at the Impregnable. **1870** THORNBURY *Old Stories* 249 The Algerines stood astonished at the English audacity. **1890** S. LANE-POOLE *Barbary Corsairs* 302 The French..beating back the Algerines as they advanced.

†**2.** *transf.* One who acts like a pirate. Hence **Alge'rineism**. *U.S. Obs.*

1841 FOOTE *Texas & Texans* 83 A transaction which will ..call down retributive vengeance upon these American Algerines. **1844** *Congress. Globe* 11 Mar. 360/1 The gentleman from Rhode Island had talked of 'ruffianism' in that State, and of 'Algerines'; but if the proposition he made to this House was not a specimen of 'Algerineism', he apprehended it was not to be found in Rhode Island. *a* **1861** WINTHROP *John Brent* (1883) vii. 57 He's one er them Algerines what don't know a dark hint, till it begins to make motions.

3. A popular name for one of the cetaceans; a dolphin or porpoise. Also as *adj.*

1849 H. MELVILLE *Mardi* I. xiii. 63 Of a somewhat similar species [to the Black Fish]..were the Algerines; so called, probably, from their corsair propensities; waylaying peaceful fish on the high seas. **1851** —— *Moby Dick* I. xxxi. 228 *Algerine Porpoise.* A pirate. Very savage. He is only found, I think, in the Pacific. **1911** *Cent. Dict.*, *Algerine*, a grampus: because common off the coast of Algiers.

B. *adj.* Of or belonging to Algiers or Algeria; characteristic of Algiers pirates.

1657 R. CLEMENT 31 Mar. in *Cal. Clarendon State Papers* (1876) III. 265 The money sent by the Turks to hire the Algerine fleet has been lost at sea. **1682** in L. Hertslet *Treaties* (1820) I. 63 In like manner no Algerine passenger being on board any ship or vessel in enmity with the said King of Great Britain shall be in any way molested. **1728** J. MORGAN *Hist. Algiers* I. 348 The Algerine Turks. **1772** H. WALPOLE *Let. to W. Cole* 15 Dec. (1818) 84 The plunder of your prints by that Algerine hog. **1818** FEARON *Sketches* 150 He [*sc.* the captain] is an American, tall, determined, and with an eye that flashes with Algerine cruelty. **1819** SALAMÉ *Narr. Exped. Algiers* 175 It is well known that the Algerine government are very rich, by their plundering at sea. **1864** MRS. GASKELL *French Life* i, in *Fraser's Mag.* Apr. 438/2 The window-curtains and portières are made of handsome dark Algerine stripe. **1870** THORNBURY *Old Stories* 250 An Algerine frigate. **1873** *Handbk. Trav. Algeria* (John Murray) 22 The audacity of the Algerine pirates at this time was unparalleled. **1925** E., O. & S. SITWELL *Poor Young People* 3 Wears an Algerine turbane.

algerite (ˈældʒəraɪt). *Min.* [named (1849) after Mr. F. Alger + -ITE.] A variety of Wernerite; 'an altered scapolite, related to pinite.' Dana.

algesimeter (ældʒɪˈsɪmɪtə(r)). [f. Gr. ἄλγησις sense of pain + -METER.] = ALGOMETER. Hence **al,gesi'metric** *a.*

1896 *Index-Catal. Libr. Surg.-Gen. U.S.* I. 252/1 Algesimeter. **1925** C. FOX *Educ. Psychol.* xii. 343 An algesimeter, an instrument for exerting a pressure of known intensity on the surface of the skin. **1953** *Brit. Jrnl. Psychol.* Nov. 284 Rey..found a very much wider threshold scatter for his algesimetric results.

algetic (ælˈdʒɛtɪk), *a.* [f. Gr. ἀλγέ-ειν to feel pain (of which the vbl. adj. would analogically be *ἀλγητ-ός) + -IC.] (See quot.)

1879 *Syd. Soc. Lex.*, *Algetic*, producing, or having relation to, pain.

alȝen for *halȝen* = saints: see HALLOW.

algicide (ˈældʒɪsaɪd). Also (*rare*) **'algacide**. [f. ALGA + -CIDE 1.] That which kills algæ; *spec.* a preparation used for destroying algæ.

1904 *Science* 9 Dec. 805/1 (*title*) The use of Copper Sulphate as an Algacide in the Treatment of Water Supplies. **1909** *Cent. Dict.* Suppl., Algicide. **1950** *Endeavour* IX. 143/1 Algae may cause serious trouble in waterworks, in small fish-ponds, and even on the soil of commercial gardens and on house walls, so that the need for algicides is obvious.

algid (ˈældʒɪd), *a.* Also **'algide**. [a. Fr. *algide*, ad. L. *algid-us* cold; f. *algē-re* to be cold: see -ID.] Cold, chill, chilly; especially pertaining to or designating the cold stage of an ague. *Spec.* in ***algid cholera***, Asian cholera, which is marked by copious watery alvine discharges, etc.

1626 COCKERAM, *Algide*, chill with cold. **1661** LOVELL *Anim.& Min.* 202 The [frog's] heart applied to the back bone helps algid agues. **1847** E. A. PARKES *Res. Path. & Treatm. Asiatic or Algide Cholera* i. 4, I have ventured to employ the term 'Algide Cholera' as a synonym for the 'Cholera gravior' of Orton and others. **1859** R. BURTON in *Jrnl. R.G.S.* XXIX. 142 The hot fit is unusually long and rigorous, compared with the algid stage. **1864** —— *Dahome* II. 249 The algid breath of the desert wind. **1873** F. T. ROBERTS *Theor. Pract. Med.* 685 Epidemic, Asiatic, Algide, or Malignant Cholera. *Ibid.* 690 Stage of Collapse. Algide Stage. **1889** *Buck's Handbk. Med. Sci.* VIII. 610 Algid dysentery. **1901** DORLAND *Med. Dict.* (ed. 2) 162/2.

algidity (ælˈdʒɪdɪtɪ). [f. prec. + -ITY, as if f. L. **algiditas*. Cf. *rigidity*.] Coldness, chilliness; esp. that caused by collapse of the vital functions.

1656 BLOUNT *Glossogr.*, *Algidity*, Algor, great cold or chilness. **1674** COLES *Lat. Dict.*, Algidity, *algor*. **1879** *Syd. Soc. Lex.*, *Algidity*, a state of coldness and collapse.

†**'algidness.** *Obs.*$^{-0}$ [f. ALGID + -NESS.] The state of being algid; chillness; algidity.

1731 in BAILEY; whence in JOHNSON.

algif(e = all if: see AL-, ALL *adv.* C 13.

algific (ælˈdʒɪfɪk), *a. rare.* [ad. L. *algific-us* causing cold; f. *algē-re* to be cold + *-ficus* making: see -FIC.] Causing cold, chilling.

1692 in COLES; **1731** in BAILEY; whence in JOHNSON (Algifick), ASH, etc.

†**al'gifical,** *a. Obs.* [f. L. *algific-us* + -AL[1].] = prec.

1656 BLOUNT *Gloss.*, *Algifical*, which makes chill or cold.

algin (ˈældʒɪn). *Chem.* Also **'algine**. [f. ALGA + -IN[1].] A nitrogenous substance, resembling gelatin, obtainable from certain algæ. So **'algic** or **al'ginic acid; 'alginate**, a salt of alginic acid.

1883 E. C. C. STANFORD in *Chem. News* XLVII. 255/2 This fluid contains a unique substance..to which, from its source [*sc.* sea-weed], I have given the name algin. **1885** *Jrnl. Soc. Chem. Ind.* IV. 520/1 Insoluble algin, or alginic acid, has a sp. gr. of 1·5, and closely resembles horn. **1888** *Chambers's Encycl.* I. 160 The cell-walls of our common brown seaweeds..all contain algin. **1897** C. T. DAVIS *Manuf. Leather* xxxvii. 505 Algine dissolved in water in the proportion of 12 to 100. **1915** *Jrnl. Chem. Soc.* CVIII. I. 932 Constituents of the cell walls of the *Fucoideae* are..algin, the calcium salt of algic acid. **1937** *Thorpe's Dict. Appl. Chem.* I. 201 Commercial algin or sodium alginate. **1940** J. B. SPEAKMAN in *Textile Manufacturer* LXVI. 464/2 Since sodium alginate dissolves in water to give solutions of high viscosity, whereas calcium alginate is insoluble, filaments are readily obtained. **1946** *Lancet* 24 Aug. 279/1 Calcium alginate filaments can be prepared as an absorbable hæmostatic gauze for application to oozing surfaces... Alginates..are relatively cheap, and can be sterilised by heat. **1955** *Times* 14 July 9/3 The establishment in Scotland, during the Second World War by the Ministry of Supply, of factories to produce alginates—the salts of alginic acid extracted from the brown seaweeds.

algist (ˈældʒɪst). [f. ALGA + -IST. Cf. *Flora, florist.*] One who studies algæ.

1869 *Pall Mall G.* 29 Sept. 10, Scientific algists are botanizing among the sea-weeds.

algodonite (ælˈgɒdənaɪt). *Min.* [named (1857) from *Algodones*, near Coquimbo + -ITE.] A native arsenide of copper, Cu_3As, of whitish colour and metallic lustre.

1837–80 DANA *Min.* 37 A transported mass of mixed whitneyite and algodonite, weighing 95–100 lbs., was found on St. Louis R.

algoid (ˈælgɔɪd), *a.* [f. ALGA + -OID.] Of the nature of an alga.

1874 M. COOKE *Fungi* 12 The supposed algoid nature of gonidia.

Algol[1] (ˈælgɒl). *Astr.* [ad. Arab. *al ghūl* (see GHOUL).] The β star of the constellation Perseus, of variable brightness.

1390 GOWER *Conf.* VII. 1329 The thridde [star]..Is hote Algol the clere rede. **1706** [see MEDUSA'S HEAD[1]]. **1855** *Astron. Jrnl.* IV. 57/1 Algol, or β *Persei*, unquestionably belongs to the most remarkable of all the variable stars. **1880** E. C. PICKERING in *Proc. Amer. Acad. Arts & Sciences* XVI. 1 (*title*) Dimensions of the Fixed Stars, with special reference to Binaries and Variables of the Algol Type. **1909** [see DEMON 3]. **1935** AUDEN & ISHERWOOD *Dog beneath Skin* II. v. p. 111 Alan lifting his eyes sees The Bear, the Waggoner, the Scales And Algol waxing and waning as his hope. **1965** *Listener* 20 May 740/2 Algol..seems to shine steadily for two and a half days..and then exhibits a ..'wink' lasting for several hours.

Algol[2] (ˈælgɒl). [f. ALGO(RITHMIC *a.* + L(ANGUAGE *sb.*[1]] An international algebraic language for use in programming computers.

1959 PERLIS & SAMELSON in *Numerische Mathematik* I. 41 (*title*) Report on the Algorithmic Language Algol. **1959** *Oxf. Univ. Gaz.* 3 Dec. 361/2 Dialgol, a dialect of Algol. **1961** *Times* 3 Oct. (Computer Suppl.) p. x/7 Algol..is used widely as a communication language.

algolagnia (ælgəʊˈlægnɪə). *Path.* [mod.L., f. G. *algolagnie* (A. von Schrenck-Notzing, *Sugg.-Therap.* (1892) III vii. 125), f. Gr. ἄλγος pain + λαγνεία lust.] A form of sexual perversion (see quots.). Hence **algolag'nistic** *a.*

1900 DORLAND *Med. Dict.* 31/1 *Algolagnia*, abnormal and distorted activity of sexual impulse toward persons of opposite sex, including sadism, masochism, etc. **1908** M. E. PAUL tr. *I. Bloch's Sexual Life of our Time* xxi. 558 De Sade ..collected almost all the facts..regarding the algolagnistic phenomena in ethnology. **1924** E. & C. PAUL tr. *L. C. Baudouin's Psycho-Analysis & Aesthetics* 101 The word 'algolagnia' was coined to denote the inner unity of a tendency embracing two instincts, the instinct of suffering and that of making others suffer, the pathological forms of these instincts being known as 'masochism' and 'sadism' respectively. **1940** HINSIE & SHATZKY *Psychiatric Dict.* 20/1 Sadism thus came to be known as active algolagnia, while masochism was called passive algolagnia. **1949** H. HARE *Swinburne* vi. 126 This active sadism is expressed over and over again throughout *Poems and Ballads*... The algolagnia is carried to the last extreme.

algological (ælgəˈlɒdʒɪkəl), *a.* [f. ALGOLOGY + -ICAL.] Of or pertaining to algology.

1830 R. GREVILLE *Algæ Brit.* Pref. 1 Engaged in Algological researches on the Continent. **1863** *Athenæum* 18 July 82 The finest algological specimens. **1881** *Nature* No. 590, 359 Remarks on the most recent algological publications.

algologist (ælˈgɒlədʒɪst). [f. ALGOLOGY + -IST.] One who prosecutes the scientific study of algæ or seaweeds; a student of algology.

1830 R. GREVILLE *Algæ Brit.* Pref. 3 The more systematic Algologists. **1881** HERVEY *Sea Mosses* 444 One of the most celebrated algologists of Europe.

algology (ælˈgɒlədʒɪ). [f. L. *alga* sea-weed + -(O)LOGY.] That part of botanical science which relates to algæ or seaweeds.

1849 LANDSBOROUGH *Brit. Seaweeds* Pref. 7 British algology is making..rapid progress. **1881** HERVEY *Sea Mosses* 42 The earliest American worker in the field of algology.

algometer (ælˈgɒmɪtə(r)). [f. Gr. ἄλγος pain: see -METER.] An instrument for measuring degrees of sensitiveness to pain. So **algometric** (ælgəʊˈmɛtrɪk) *a.*, pertaining to such measurement; **algometry** (-ˈɒmɪtrɪ), the use of the algometer.

1880 *Index-Catal. Libr. Surg.-Gen. U.S.* I. 190/1 (*heading*) Algometry. **1890** in BILLINGS *Med. Dict.* **1892** *Fortn. Rev.* Mar. 355 By experiments made with the electric algometer it is clearly shown that woman is inferior to man [in general sensibility, including sensitiveness to pain]. **1897** E. W. SCRIPTURE *New Psychol.* 303 The pressure algometer consists..of a strong spring by means of which a rubber disc or point is pressed against the surface to be tested. **1904** G. S. HALL *Adolescence* II. 4 Other algometric tests..have led to somewhat different results.

Al'gonkian, *a.* and *sb.* [Var. of next.]

1. See next.

2. *Geol.* An epithet designating a period between the Archæan and the Palæozoic; proterozoic. As *sb.*, this period or system of rocks (in the U.S.A.).

These rocks are a feature of the region of Lake Superior, a territory of the Algonquian Indians.

1890 J. W. POWELL in *10th Ann. Rep. U.S. Geol. Survey* I. 20 At a recent conference of geologists..it was decided to make but one period of the Agnotozoic, and the name 'Algonkian' was chosen to designate that period. **1893** —— in *14th Ann. Rep. U.S. Geol. Survey* I. 100 The chronologic series from the Algonkian up to the Cretaceous. **1893** GEIKIE *Text-bk. Geol.* VI. I. §ii. 715 Another enormous succession of rocks comprised under the general name of 'Algonkian', but consisting of several distinct formations, separated from each other by unconformabilities. **1925** J. JOLY *Surface-Hist.* v. 80 These are probably of Algonkian age; that is, they are some of the earliest rocks in which life has been recognized.

Algonquian, -kian (ælˈgɒŋkɪən, -ŋkw-), *a.* and *sb.* [f. ALGONQUIN, by alteration of ending: see -IAN.] **A.** *adj.* Of or belonging to a large group of N. American Indians which includes the Algonquin tribe proper. **B.** *sb.* **1.** A member of this group. **2.** Any one of the languages or dialects spoken by the people of this group.

1885 J. W. POWELL in *Bur. Amer. Ethnol. Rep.* VII. 47 The area formerly occupied by the Algonquian family was more extensive than that of any other linguistic stock in North America. **1891** J. C. PILLING (*title*) Bibliography of the Algonquian Languages. *Ibid.*, Pref. p. iii, The Algonquian speaking peoples. **1900** tr. *Deniker's Races of Man* 526 The original home of the Algonquians was the region around Hudson's Bay. **1907** F. W. HODGE *Handbk. N. Amer. Ind.* I. 40/1 The Central Algonquians are tall. **1938** R. H. LOWIE *Hist. Ethnol. Theory* vi. 63 He recognized the criteria of..the 'Omaha' system and indicated its occurrence among the Algonkian..family. *Ibid.* vii. 84 He [*sc.* Tylor] definitely ascribes the latter view only to Algonkians, Fijians, and Karens.

Algonquin, -kin (ælˈgɒŋkɪn), *sb.* and *a.* [a. F. *Algonquin*, perh. contracted f. *Algoumequin* (17th c.). In Micmac *algoomeaking* or *-making* means 'at the place of spearing fish and eels'.] **A.** *sb.* **1.** An Indian of a people encountered in the districts of Ottawa and Quebec; also used as collect. sing., this people. **2.** More widely = ALGONQUIAN *sb.* **3.** The language of this people. **B.** *adj.* Pertaining to any of the above.

1625 PURCHAS *Pilgrims* IV. 1607 The Estechemins, Algoumequins, and Mountainers. **1667** TRACY in Fernow *N.Y. Documents* (1853) III. 151 By our authority wee haue hindred the Algonquins from making warre upon them [*sc.* the Dutch]. **1698** L. HENNEPIN *New Discov. Contin.* xxiv. 95 The Algoncains; *orig.* les Algonkains. **1705** BEVERLEY *Virginia* III. 24 A sort of general Language, like what Lahontan calls the Algonkine. **1705** J. HARRIS *Navigantium* II. 909/2 [We] made towards them, crying out in the

Iroquese and Algonquin Languages. **1765** *Exped. Henry Bouquet* (1868) 153 Nipissins, Algonquins, living towards the heads of the Ottawa river. **1778** T. Hutchins *Topogr. Descr. Virginia* etc. 67 Alagonkins. **1845** H. R. Schoolcraft *Onéota* 171 The Algonquin tribes. **1851** —— *Ind. Tribes U.S.* I. 306 Their language is pure Algonquin. **1865** Parkman *Pioneers of France* in *Wks.* (1899) I. xii. 383 This neighborhood was the seat of the principal Indian population of the river [Ottawa], ancestors of the modern Ottawas.. Usually called Algoumequins, or Algonquins, by Champlain and other early writers,—a name now always used in a generic sense to designate a large family of cognate tribes. **1867** —— *Jesuits N. Amer.* in *Ibid.* II. 4 Tribes speaking various Algonquin languages and dialects. **1884** C. G. Leland *(title)* The Algonquin Legends of New England, or Myths and Folk Lore of the Micmac, Passamaquoddy, and Penobscot Tribes. **1949** J. Brodrick *Proc. Saints* 199 She composed.. a prayer book in Algonquin.

algophobia (ælgəʊˈfəʊbɪə). *Path.* [mod.L., f. Gr. ἄλγος pain + -phobia.] Morbid fear of pain.
1897 in R. W. Greene et al. *Lippincott's Med. Dict.* 33/2.

algor (ˈælgə(r)). [a. L. *algor* cold, cognate with *algē-re* to be cold. Cf. *humor, vigor, terror,* etc.] Cold, chilliness; especially that experienced in the onset of fever.
c **1420** *Pallad. on Husb.* xi. 55 For over colde doo douves dounge at eve Aboute her roote, algour away to dryve. **1656** in Blount *Glossogr.* **1753** Chambers *Cycl. Supp.*, *Algor* is used to denote a preternatural coldness or chilness in a part. **1879** *Syd. Soc. Lex.*, *Algor*, the sense of coldness experienced in the onset of fever; chilliness, rigor.

algorism (ˈælgərɪz(ə)m). Forms: α. 3–6 **augrim,** 4 **-ym,** 5 **-ime, -yme, awgrym, algram,** 6 **agrym(e, -ime,** 7 **agrum, algrim.** β. 4–6 **algorisme,** 5 **-ysme, algarism,** 6 **algarosme, aulgorism(e, augrisme,** 7–9 **algorism, algorithm.** [a. OFr. *augorisme, algorisme, augorime*; ad. med.L. *algorism-us* (cf. Sp. *guarismo* cipher), f. Arab. *al-Khowārazmī*, the *native of Khwārazm (Khiva)*, surname of the Arab mathematician Abu Ja'far Mohammed Ben Musa, who flourished early in the 9th c., and through the translation of whose work on Algebra, the Arabic numerals became generally known in Europe. (Cf. '*Euclid*' = plane geometry.) *Algorisme* being popularly reduced in OFr. to *augorime*, English also shows two forms, the popular *augrime*, ending in *agrim, agrum*, and the learned *algorism* which passed through many pseudo-etymological perversions, including a recent *algorithm* in which it is learnedly confused with Gr. ἀριθμός 'number.']

1. a. The Arabic, or decimal system of numeration; *hence*, arithmetic. ***numbers of algorism***, the Arabic or Indian numerals. ***cypher in algorism***, the figure 0; a 'mere cipher,' a dummy.
c **1230** *Ancr. R.* 214 [He] makeð þerinne figures of augrim, ase þeos rikenares doð þ habbeð muchel uorto rikenen. **1340** *Ayenb.* 1 þe capiteles of þe boc.. byeþ ywryte.. by þe tellynge of algorisme. *c* **1391** Chaucer *Astrol.* (1872) 5 Ouer the wiche degrees ther ben nowmbres of augrym. **1393** Gower *Conf.* III. 89 Of arsmetique the matere Is.. What algorisme in nombre amounteth. **1399** Langl. *Rich. Redeless* iv. 53 As siphre.. in awgrym, That noteth a place, and no thing availith. **1483** *Cath. Ang.*, Algarism (*v.r.* Algram); *algarismus, abacus.* **1530** Palsgr. 476/2, I caste an accomptes with counters after the aulgorisme maner. *Ibid.* 684/2, I reken, I counte by cyfers of agrym. **1532** More *Conf. Barnes* viii. Wks. 1557, 772/1 Mysse-pryntynge those fygures of Algorisme, because the figure of .9. and the figure of .6. be all in maner one, if thei be contrary turned. **1542** Recorde *Gr. Artes* (1575) 40 Corruptyle written.. Augrim for algorisme, as the Arabians sounde it. **1549** Chaloner *Erasm. Moriæ Enc.* L iij b, Other men stande for no more than Ciphres in Algorisme. **1561** T. N[orton] *Calvin's Inst.* (1634) Pref. 3, I have.. quoted the Sections also by their due number with the usuall figure of Algorisme. **1553–87** Foxe *A. & M.* III. 265 As a Cypher in Agrime. **1566** Drant *Hor. Sat.* ii. B 2 As well by augrisme tell the gravell of the sea. **1591** Garrard *Art Warre* 129 Good knowledge in the Mathematikes specially in Algarosme, Algebra, and Geometrie. **1593** Peele *Edw. I*, 84 Neither one, two, nor three, but a poor cypher in agrum. **1625** L'Isle *Du Bartas* 140 The treasures hoard of Algrim mysteries. **1699** *Phil. Trans.* XXI. 262 The Indian Algorism (or Calculation by the Numeral Figures now in use). **1837** Hallam *Hist. Lit.* I. i. ii. §30. 114 Matthew Paris observes that in Greek.. any number may be represented by a single figure, which is not the case.. in Algorism. **1861** T. Wright *Ess. Archæol.* II. xv. 70 The figures of the algorismus are identical in every respect with the characters of the abacus.

b. *Attrib.* **algorism-stones,** counters.
c **1386** Chaucer *Millere's T.* 24 His augrym stoones, leyen faire apart. *a* **1535** More *Let.* (J.), I send now to my good daughter Clement her algorisme stone.

2. = algorithm 2.
1960 [see algorithm 2].

algorismic (ælgɒˈrɪzmɪk), *a. rare.* [f. prec. + -ic.] Pertaining to algorism, arithmetical.
1861 T. Wright *Ess. Archæol.* II. xv. 73 In the fourteenth century.. these algorismic numerals became generally used.

† **ˈalgorist.** *Obs.*⁻⁰ [ad. med.L. *algorista*, f. *algorismus*, by confounding this with Gr. words in -ισμος, as *agonismus, agonista.*]
1656 Blount *Glossogr.*, *Algorist*, one skilful in reckonings or figuring.

algorithm (ˈælgərɪð(ə)m). [f. algorism, influenced by Gr. ἀριθμός 'number.']

1. = algorism 1 a.
1699 *Phil. Trans.* XXI. 263 The Algorithm or Numeral Figures now in use. **1774** T. Warton *Hist. Eng. Poetry* III. 46 The first who brought the algorithm from the Saracens. **1852** R. Grant *Hist. Phys. Astron.* Introd. 9 The ingenious algorithm of the Indians.

2. *Math.* A process, or set of rules, usually one expressed in algebraic notation, now used esp. in computing, machine translation and linguistics.
1938 Hardy & Wright *Introd. Theory of Numbers* x. 135 The system of equations.. is known as Euclid's algorithm. **1960** E. Delavenay *Introd. Machine Transl.* 129 *Algorithm* or *algorism*.., used by computer programmers to designate the numerical or algebraic notations which express a given sequence of computer operations, define a programme or routine conceived to solve a given type of problem. **1964** F. L. Westwater *Electronic Computers* ix. 146 An Algorithm is a set of rules for performing a calculation. **1966** Owen & Ross tr. *Revzin's Models of Lang.* ii. 22 A.. more convenient way of arranging the phonemes is suggested. It is given by an instruction (an 'algorithm') consisting of six points.

3. *Med.* A step-by-step procedure for reaching a clinical decision or diagnosis, often set out in the form of a flow chart, in which the answer to each question determines the next question to be asked.
[**1968** L. B. Lusted *Introd. Med. Decision Making* iii. 70 Two.. [studies] show that an algorithm in terms of a computer program can be developed for a computer based medical history system.] **1970** *Scottish Med. Jrnl.* XV. 378 (*heading*) Flow charts, diagnostic keys and algorithms in the diagnosis of dysphagia. **1985** *Brit. Med. Jrnl.* 23 Mar. 916/1 The algorithm illustrates the steps towards establishing a functional and aetiological diagnosis.

algorithmic (ælgəˈrɪðmɪk), *a.* [f. algorithm + -ic.] Expressed as or using an algorithm or algorithms. Cf. Algol² and prec. 2.
1881 J. Venn *Symbolic Logic* iv. 98 'Symbolic', as I understand it, being almost exactly the equivalent of 'algorithmic'. **1940** *Mind* XLIX. 249 He thinks of the subject [*sc.* the calculus] not merely as an algorithmic method. **1959** [see Algol²]. **1960** *Communic. Assoc. Comput. Mach.* III. 300 The algorithmic language has three different kinds of representation—reference, hardware, and publication. **1964** *Language* XL. 167 Further syllabic studies for algorithmic prediction of English parts of speech.

algory. 'Chilnesse.' Cockeram 1626.

† **algose** (ˌælˈgəʊs), *a. Obs.* [ad. L. *algōs-us*, f. *alga* sea-weed: see -ose.]
1731 Bailey, *Algose*, full of weeds or reets called alga. [Ash 1775 has '*Algose*, cold, chilly,' an evident error.]

algous (ˈælgəs), *a.* [f. L. *algōs-us*: see prec. and -ous.] Of, pertaining to, or full of sea-weeds.
1742 Bailey, *Algous* [of Alga, a Sea-weed], full of weeds. **1851** Wells & Bliss *Sci. Ann.* 324 The atmospheric dissemination of algous plants.

algraphy (ˈælgrəfɪ). [ad. G. *algraphie* (J. Scholz 1896, in *Papier Zeitschr.* XXVIII. i. 1450), f. al(uminium: see -graphy; cf. lithography.] The art or process of printing from aluminium plates. Hence **alˈgraphic** *a.*
Scholz did not use the term in the orig. patent of 1893 (Germ. Patent D.R.P. 72470).
1897 *Studio* Sept. 244/2 An alternative device which would give equal facilities to the artist, and would preserve the technical character of lithography, while it would remove the necessity for depending upon the use of lithographic stone itself,.. a process.. discovered by Mr. Scholz of Mayence, who has patented his invention under the name of 'Algraphy'. **1898** *Daily Chron.* 14 Oct. 3/1 The algraphic plate is a substitute for the ordinary lithographic stone. **1914** E. H. Richter *Prints* 10 Plates of metal are often substituted for stone (zincography, algraphy).

‖ **alguacil** (algwaˈθiːl). Pl. **alguaciles,** (Anglicized) **-s.** [Sp.: see alguazil.] Either of two mounted constables in 17th-century costume who lead the team of bullfighters into the ring, keep order during the fight, and award trophies (ears, etc.) to the matadors under his direction.
1910 *Encycl. Brit.* IV. 789/2 The bull-fight begins with a grand entry of all the bull-fighters with *alguaciles*, municipal officers in ancient costume, at the head. **1932** E. Hemingway *Death in Afternoon* vi. 63 The alguacils ride up to under the president's box to ask for the key to the red door of the toril where the bull is waiting. **1967** McCormick & Mascareñas *Compl. Aficionado* iii. 72 In toreo, the entrance into the plaza by the *alguaciles* (mounted deputies of the president of the corrida), the matadors, their cuadrillas, and the muleteers.

‖ **alguazil** (ælgwəˈzɪl, Sp. algwaˈθil). [Sp. *alguazil* (now *alguacil*), earlier forms of which in Pg. are *al-vazil, al-vazir*, ad. Arab. *al-wazīr*, i.e. *al* the, *wazīr* vizier, minister, officer, f. *wazara* to carry, carry on, = L. *gerere.*] Originally the same word as *vizier*, the meaning of which descended in Spain through that of *justiciary* or *justice*, to *warrant-officer* or *serjeant.*
1598 Barret *Theor. Warres* Gloss. 249 *Alguazil*, a Spanish word, is an officer attendant on the Campe-maister Generall, to apprehend offenders, and to see execution done. **1651** A. Weldon *Crt. K. James* 43 An Allagozy, which is a great officer or judge in Spain. **1670** *Lond. Gaz.* ccccxcvii/3 The Alguasils having got together about 150 persons, set upon 20 Souldiers. **1706** Phillips, *Alguazil*, a Sergeant or Officer that arrests People in Spain. **1712** W. Rogers *Voy.* (1718) 200 Algozils or Serjeants. **1841** Macaulay *Ess.*, *Hastings* 623 Died of rage and shame in the gripe of the vile alguazils of Impey. **1843** Prescott *Mexico* ii. ii. (1864) 78 An alguasil suddenly sprang on him from behind and pinioned his arms. **1880** *Daily Tel.* 22 Sept., The powers of the School Board and their alguazils cease with the lighting of the street lamps.

algum (ˈælgʌm). [Heb. *algūm*, a foreign word; see quot.] A tree mentioned in the Bible (*2 Chron.* ii. 8), also called erroneously (*1 Kings* x. 11) almug, said to have been brought from Ophir; variously surmised to be a species of acacia, cedar, or cypress, but probably a kind of sandalwood.
1578 Bible (Genev.) *2 Chron.* ii. 8 Send mee also cedar trees, firre trees, and Algummim trees. **1611** *ibid.*, Algume trees. **1721** Bailey, *Algum* or *Almug.* **1873** Max Müller *Sc. Lang.* I. 232 *The algum-tree*.. is supposed to be the sandal-wood-tree.. One of the numerous names for this tree in Sanscrit is *valguka.* This *valguka*, which points back to a more original form *valgu*, might easily have been corrupted by Phœnician and Jewish sailors into *algum*, a form, as we know, still further corrupted, at least in one passage of the O.T., to *almug.* Sandal-wood is found indigenous in India only, and there chiefly on the coast of Malabar.

Alha, obs. form of Allah.

‖ **Alˈhagi** (ælˈhɑːdʒɪ). *Bot.* [mod.L. (Rauwolf 1537), ad. Arab. *al-ḥāj*, used by Avicenna.] A genus of leguminous plants, some of which produce a kind of manna.
1769 Sir J. Hill *Fam. Herb.* (1812) 17 There is a kind more rare, called Persian manna; this is produced by the shrub called alhagi. **1847** Craig s.v., The manna of this country.. has nothing to do with Moor's Alhagi or Hebrew manna.

Alhaji (ælhædʒɪ). Also **Alhajji;** fem. **Alhaja.** [a. Hausa, ad. Arab.: see prec.] In Nigeria: = hadji, hajji; a Nigerian who has made the hadj.
1945 J. Patterson in *Ann. Rep. N. Prov. Nigeria 1944* 1 The account of the year's events from Katsina records the death of the Emir Alhajji Muhammadu Dikko, C.B.E., a man with a high idea of service to this Government and to his people. **1953** *Nigeria Handbk.* 298 Emir of Katsina, Alhaji the Hon. Usuman Nagogo, C.B.E., M.H.R. **1966** C. Achebe *Man of People* xiii. 158, I remember the first time I woke up in the hospital and felt my head turbanned like an Alhaji. **1977** *Sunday Times* (Lagos) 2 Jan. 12 (*caption*) The 1976 Hajj is now behind us, but its memories linger in many Nigerian homes as new alhajis and alhajas swell the ranks of Nigerians who have performed the pilgrimage. **1981** *Glaxo Group News* Mar. 9/4 Viewers saw and heard Glaxo Nigeria chairman Alhaji Chief Edu perform the ceremony.

Al-Haj(j) (ælˈhædʒ). Also **Al-Hadjdj.** [a. Arab. *al-ḥājj*: see al-² and hadji.] = hadji, hajji
1836 E. W. Lane *Acct. Mod. Egyptians* I. iii. 110 It is not by the visit to Mek'keh.. that the Moos'lim acquires the title of *el-hha'gg* (or the pilgrim). **1927** *Encycl. Islam* II. 201/2 *Al-Ḥādjdj 'Omar*, a.. conqueror in the Sūdān, founder of the Tuculor Kingdom (1797–1864). **1949** J. S. Trimingham *Islam in Sudan* iv. 124 The pilgrimage (*ḥajj*) to the Holy Places is a great ambition, but.. not very many go. He who does returns.. to be feasted and honoured, for his *ḥajj* brings to his family the *baraka* of the Holy Places. Henceforth he is called *al-Ḥājj* and his achievement is commemorated on his house which has its façade whitewashed and designs.. painted on it. **1956** J. V. Morais *Leaders of Malaya* 8/2 The Sultan of Selangor Sir Hisamuddin Alam Shah Alhaj ibni Almarhum Sultan Ala-iddin Sulaiman Shah... In August, 1952, made a pilgrimage to Mecca and is the first Malay Ruler to have done so. **1969** *Whitaker's Almanack 1970* 758/1 The words 'Al Haj' or 'Haji' indicate that the person so named has made the pilgrimage to Mecca.

Alhambra (ælˈhæmbrə). [ult. ad. Arab. *alḥamrāʼ* i.e. the red (house).] The palace of the Moorish kings at Granada.

Alhambresque (ælhæmˈbrɛsk), *a.* [f. prec. after *picturesque*: see -esque.] After the fanciful style of the ornamentation of the Alhambra.
1862 Timbs *Year Bk. Facts* 123 The ceiling is Alhambresque in style.. and of the most delicate colours.

‖ **alˈhandal.** *Pharm. Obs.* [a. Arab. *al-ḥanḍal.*] Arabic name of the Colocynth or Bitter Cucumber (*Citrullus Colocynthis*) formerly applied to its purgative extract.
1683 Salmon *Doron Med.* ii. 463 Rhubarb, Sena, Troches alhandal.

alheal, obs. form of all-heal.

alhenna: see alcanna, henna.

alhidad, -a, -e, obs. forms of alidad.

alhuet, i.e. all what: see al-, all.

ali- (ælɪ), in *Anat.* combining form of L. *āla* wing (as in *aliform, aliped, alisphenoid,* etc.) denoting 'pertaining to the "wings" or lateral expansions' of certain parts, as **aliˈethmoid** *a.*, pertaining to the lateral expansions of the ethmoid bone of certain birds; also **aliethˈmoidal** *a.*; **aliˈnasal** *a.*, pertaining to the lateral parts of the nostrils; **aliˈseptal** *a.*,

pertaining to a cartilaginous partition in the nasal passage of the embryo of a bird; also as *sbs.*
1869 W. K. PARKER in *Philos. Trans. R. Soc.* CLIX. 759 The rudiments of the 'aliethmoidal' and 'aliseptal' cartilages of the nasal labyrinth. *Ibid.* 800 The roots of the cartilaginous aliethmoid. *Ibid.* 780 The alinasal fold. *Ibid.* 798 The alinasals give rise to the nasal turbinal.

aliage, var. ALLIAGE. *Obs.*, alliance.

aliant, aliaunt, obs. forms of ALIEN.

alias (ˈeɪlɪəs, ˈælɪəs), *adv.* and *sb.* [a. L. *alias* 'at another time, otherwise'; adopted in Eng. chiefly in the latter sense.]
‖**A.** *adv.* Otherwise (called or named). Now written in *italics*.
1535 STEWART *Cron. Scotl.* II. 354 Callit Gillelmus alias Gilmoure. **1607** SHAKS. *Coriol.* II. i. 48 Violent testie Magistrates (alias Fooles). **1709** *Lond. Gaz.* mmmmdlxi/4 The Parish of Stepney, alias Stebonheath. **1840** HOOD *Up Rhine* 202 Louisa Brachman, *alias* Sappho..threw herself from a gallery, two stories high.
B. *sb.* (with *pl.* **aliases.**)
1. Another name, an assumed name.
1605 CAMDEN *Rem.* (1614) 147 An *Aliàs* or double name cannot preiudice the honest. **1831** *Edin. Rev.* LIII. 364 He has been assuming various aliases. **1861** MACAULAY *Hist. Eng.* V. 92 The monk who was sometimes called Harrison and sometimes went by the alias of Johnson.
†**2.** *Law.* A second or further writ issued after a first had failed of its effect, so called from the words *Sicut alias præcipimus* (as we on another occasion command) which occurred in it. *Obs.*
1672 MANLEY *Interpr.*, *Alias* Vide *Capias alias.* **1714** SIR W. SCROGGS *Pract. Courts* (ed. 3) 173 Then the Plaintiff may have an Alias. **1768** BLACKST. *Comm.* III. 135 To delay his obedience to the first writ, and..wait till a second and a third, called an *alias* and a *pluries*, were issued. **1809** TOMLINS *Law Dict.* s.v. *Capias*, An *alias* writ..to the same effect as the former.

†**ali'ation.** *Obs.*$^{-1}$. [f. L. *ali-us* another + -ATION after *alter-ation*, *vari-ation*.] Change in quality.
1780 HARRIS *Philol. Enq.* 361 A man from hot becomes cold, from ruddy becomes pale. Motion of this species has respect to the genus of quality, and may be called *aliation.*

Ali Baba (ˈælɪ ˈbɑːbɑː). The name of the principal character in *Ali Baba and the Forty Thieves*, from the Arabian Nights, used *attrib.* (and *absol.*), as **Ali Baba basket**, a tall laundry basket resembling in shape the oil-jars in which the thieves hid to attack Ali Baba.
1968 R. JEFFRIES *Traitor's Crime* iii. 33 He took off his shirt and put it in the Ali Baba basket for washing. **1971** H. C. RAE *Marksman* II. vii. 158 Soiled linen [was] stripped from the beds and stuffed into the Ali Baba basket. **1976** *Newmarket Jrnl.* 16 Dec. 5 (Advt.), 'Ali Baba' linen baskets ..from £8.60. **1978** *Jrnl. R. Soc. Arts* CXXVI. 367/2, I recall..being confronted with stall after stall displaying wine baskets, Ali Babas and place mats, all culturally foreign articles, all woven in the traditional palm techniques of the area.

alibi (ˈælɪbaɪ), *sb.* formerly *adv.* [a. L. *alibi* elsewhere, in another place, old locative case of *alius* another.]
‖**A.** *adv.* **a.** Elsewhere.
1727 ARBUTHNOT *John Bull* 70 The prisoner had little to say in his defence; he endeavoured to prove himself Alibi. **1777** ERSKINE *Institutes* (ed. 5) IV. 499 The defender will be allowed to proue, that..he was alibi.
b. *attrib.* quasi-*adj.*
1858 THACKERAY *Virginians* xxxv. (1878) 275 Women are not so easily cured by the alibi treatment.
B. *sb.* **a.** The plea of having been *elsewhere* at the time when any alleged act took place.
1743 FIELDING *J. Wild* in *Miscellanies* III. IV. iii. 303 A single *Alibi* would have saved them. **1774** *Ann. Reg.* (1778) XVII. 135/2 Clearer proofs of an alibi than can frequently be produced. **1855** MACAULAY *Hist. Eng.* IV. 523 For some of the prisoners an alibi was set up. **1862** *Sat. Rev.* 15 Mar. 291 They have got to establish alibis for her. **1939** T. S. ELIOT *Old Possum's Pract. Cats* 34 He always has an alibi, and one or two to spare: At whatever time the deed took place—Macavity wasn't there!
b. *colloq.* In weakened sense: an excuse, a pretext; a plea of innocence; a person providing an excuse, etc. orig. *U.S.*
1912 *Collier's* 20 Apr. 15/2 'Getting your alibi ready?' asked Zeider. **1922** W. T. TILDEN *Lawn Tennis* i. 1 Don't offer alibis for losing. **1936** W. HOLTBY *South Riding* v.§3. 297 Pip's devotion gave her, she considered, a complete alibi in all charges of frustration and virginity. **1949** 'C. HARE' *When Wind Blows* xiv. 181 Tom and Maureen are my alibis. **1951** L. P. HARTLEY *Fellow Devils* xxi. 216 Low spirits make you seem complaining..I have an alibi because I'm going to have a baby.
Hence ˈ**alibi** *v. trans.*, to clear by an excuse; to provide an alibi. orig. *U.S.* Also (in *U.S.*) *intr.* Both *colloq.*
1909 P. ARMSTRONG *Alias Jimmy Valentine* (MS.) 111, I'm going to alibi Doyle until he'll think he's lost his eye sight. *Ibid.*, You cant get away from the scar on your left wrist if you alibied yourself into hell. **1917** *Collier's* 13 Oct. 16/1, I ain't trying to alibi, it was a solid bone play. **1926** J. BLACK *You can't Win* i. 3, I am not lugging in the fact..to alibi myself away from anything. *Ibid.* xx. 318, I could say I was looking for his room and he would alibi for me. **1930** 'E. QUEEN' *French Powder Myst.* xxxi. 257 There's a sagacious chauffeur to alibi one. **1958** J. CANNAN *And be a Villain* iv. 111 Aunt Primrose..hadn't opportunity. She's alibi-ed by Mrs. Fitch.

alibility (ælɪˈbɪlɪtɪ). [ad. Fr. *alibilité*, f. L. *alibilis*: see ALIBLE and -TY.] The capacity of a nutritive substance for absorption; assimilativeness.
1879 in *Syd. Soc. Lex.*

alible (ˈælɪb(ə)l), *a.* [f. L. *alibil-is*, f. *al-ĕre* to nourish: see -BLE.]
1. Nutritive, nourishing.
1656 BLOUNT *Glossogr.*, *Alible*, nourishable, comfortable. **1684** tr. *Bonet's Merc. Compit.* VI. 167 The bloud..could scarce assimilate the alible Juice. **1775** ASH, *Alible*, nourishing. **1879** *Syd. Soc. Lex.*, *Alible Substance*, the nutritive portion of the chyme, as distinct from the excrementitious.
2. 'Which may be nourished.' J. *rare*$^{-0}$.
1755 in JOHNSON. **1775** in ASH.

alicant (ælɪˈkænt, in 17th c. ˈælɪkənt). Forms: 6 **alycaunt, alle-, aligaunte,** 6–7 **alle-,** 7 **ale-, alligant,** 7– **alicant(e.** A kind of wine made at Alicante in Spain.
c **1500** *Col. Blowbol* in Halliw. *Nug. Poet.* 10 Rede wyn.. and Alycaunt, in whom I delite. **1547** RECORDE *Judic. Ur.* 36 b, Darke red wyne, and Allegaunte. **1604** DEKKER *Honest Wh.* I. i, You'll blood three pottles of Aligant. **1625** [BEAUM. & FL.] *Maid of Inn* IV. ii, Butter'd beer, coloured with Alligant [cf. SHAKS. *Merry Wives* II. ii. 69]. **1626** BACON *Sylva* §56 Bedew it with a little Sack or Alegant. **1656** BLOUNT *Glossogr.*, Alicante, where great store of Mulberries grow, the juyce whereof makes the true *Alicant* wine. **1693** W. ROBERTSON *Phraseol. Gen.* 68 Aligant or Alicant, wine.

Alice (ˈælɪs). **1.** The name of the heroine of two books by 'Lewis Carroll' (C. L. Dodgson, 1832–98), 'Alice's Adventures in Wonderland' (1865) and 'Through the Looking-Glass' (1871), used allusively with reference to these books, their heroine or her fantastic adventures. So ***Alice-in-Wonderland*** used *attrib.*; ***Alice band***: a type of hair-band, as worn by Alice in Tenniel's illustrations to 'Through the Looking-Glass'.
1925 D. H. LAWRENCE *Let.* 6 Oct. (1962) II. 857 England is the most fantastic Alice-in-Wonderland country. **1931** *Observer* 19 Apr. 22/2 They [*sc.* trout] flourish and increase in size..at an Alice-in-Wonderland rate. **1935** E. BOWEN *House in Paris* I. ii. 34 'Oh, don't be such a baby!' said Henrietta..with her most Alice-ish air. **1940** *N. & Q.* CLXXIX. 395/1 Tweedledee in the first of the Alice books. **1945** E. BOWEN *Demon Lover* 170 Weeks of exile from any hairdresser had driven Miss Bates to the Alice-in-Wonderland style. **1955** 'C. BROWN' *Lost Girls* xiii. 141 Holding it [*sc.* her hair] in place with an Alice band. **1959** *Sunday Express* 14 June 1/4 Princess Anne, wearing a dress of flowered silk and an Alice band over her fair hair. **1961** *Guardian* 21 Mar. 2/4 A £1,500 council house is costing my city over £6,000. This is an Alice in Wonderland situation.
2. The name of *Alice* Roosevelt Longworth, daughter of the American President Theodore Roosevelt, used *attrib.* to designate a light greenish-blue colour. orig. *U.S.*
1921 *Collier's* 19 Feb., Mood change carefree to gay record-creation causing such change Alice blue gown. **1946** T. JONES *Skinny Angel* 149 She sat straight-spined on the edge of her chair as she said this, a lovely figure in Alice blue. **1959** *Woman's Own* 16 May 12/3 An Alice blue dress.

ˈ**alichons.** [cf. mod.Fr. *alluchons*, in Cotgr. *allochons*, the teeth of a toothed wheel.] 'The wings or ladles of a wheel.' Ash 1775.

alicyclic (ælɪˈsɪklɪk, -ˈsaɪk-), *a. Chem.* [ad. G. *alicyclisch* (E. Bamberger 1889, in *Ber. d. Deut. Chem. Ges.* XXII. 767), f. ALI(PHATIC *a.* + CYCLIC *a.* 7.] Combining the properties of aliphatic and cyclic compounds (see CYCLIC *a.* 7).
1891 *Jrnl. Chem. Soc.* LX. II. 1097 Alicyclic Homology. **1900** E. F. SMITH tr. *von Richter's Org. Chem.* II. 18 Aliphatic-cyclic or alicyclic saturated and unsaturated compounds. **1907** J. B. COHEN *Org. Chem. Adv. Stud.* I. 553.

alidad(e (ælɪˈdæd, ˈælɪdeɪd). Also 4 **allidatha,** 6–7 **alhidada,** 7–9 **alhidad(e,** 8– **alidad(e.** [In mod. form, a. Fr. *alidade*, in earlier, a. med.L. *alhidada* (cf. Sp. *alhidada, alidada*), ad. Arab. *al-ʿiḍādah*, the revolving radius of a graduated circle; f. *ʿaḍd*, *ʿaḍid*, *ʿaḍud*, the *humerus* or upper arm (which revolves in its socket).]
The index of an astrolabe, quadrant, or other graduated instrument, carrying the sights or telescope, and showing the degrees cut off on the arc of the instrument. In the astrolabe it revolved at the back, and was called by Chaucer the *Rule*.
c **1450** Insertion in MS. L of Chaucer's *Astrolabe* (Skeat 81), ed. 1561, 164/1 Ley thy rewle of thy astrolabye, that is to sey, the allydatha [*ed.* 1561 Allidatha], vpon þe day in the Kalendre off the Astrolabye, & he schall shewe the thy degree of the sonne. **1571** DIGGES *Geom. Pract.* I. xxix, Note bothe what degrees the Alhidada cutteth of the circle, and the perpendiculare of the semicircle. **1611** COTGR., *Alidade*, Th' Alhidada of an Astrolabe; the rule which turneth on the back thereof. **1679** MOXON *Math. Dict.* 5 Alhadida..a word seldom used by English authors..signifies only the Label or Index that moves upon the centre-pin of an Astrolabe. **1762** PARSONS in *Phil. Trans.* LIV. 162 Moved in the limb by a vertical motion in either direction by the alidad alone. **1834** U. K. S. *Nat. Philos.* III. xiii. 66/1 Morin went so far as.. to attach a telescope to the alhidade of what he calls a planisphere. **1837** WHEWELL *Induct. Sc.* (1857) I. 178 The alidad of an instrument is its index, which possesses an angular motion. **1878** NEWCOMB *Pop. Astron.* 579 *Alidade*, a movable frame carrying the microscopes or verniers of a graduated circle.

†**a'lie,** *v.*^{1} *Obs.* Forms as in LIE *v.* [f. A- *pref.* 1 + LIE.]
1. To lie down, subside, become extinct. (The intr. vb. of which ALLAY *v.*^{1} = *a-lay* is the causative.)
a **1000** *Beowulf* 5764 Nú sceal..eall eðelwyn ·eowrum cynne leófum alicȝean. **1200** *St. Marhar.* 12 Ant þat liht alei lutlen ant lutlen. **1205** LAYAM. 26298 Nu is hit muchel leod-scome! ȝif hit scal þus a-ligge. *c* **1230** *Ancr. R.* 246 A muchel wind alið mid a lutel rein.
2. To lie towards or lean.
1583 STANYHURST *Æneid* IV. 101 His rackt wit he tosseth, Now to this od stratagem, now too that counseyl alying.

†**a'lie,** *v.*^{2} *Obs. rare.* [var. of ELIE.] To anoint.
c **1360** *Amis & Amil.* 2194 Yif he wald..slen his children tvay, Alien his brother with the blode. *Ibid.* 2330 He tok that blood that was so bright And alied that gentil knight.

alien (ˈeɪlɪən), *a.* and *sb.* Forms: 4–6 **alyen(e,** 5 **aliaunte,** 5–6 **aliente, alyaunte,** 6 **aleyn, alyon, aleaunt,** 6–7 **aliant, -aunt, -ent,** 7 **alliant,** 4–8 **aliene,** 4– **alien.** [a. OFr. *alien, allien*:—L. *aliēn-us* of or belonging to another person or place; f. *ali-us* other, another + *-ēn-us*: see -EN, -ENE. The *-t* so commonly added, esp. to the sb., was due to form-assoc. with ppl. words in *-nt*, *-nd*, in which there was an organic tendency to drop the final mute (cf. *gyane* for *giant*, etc.), in the literary struggle against which, *t* was added where it had not been dropped; cf. *tyrant*, *pageant*, *ancient*.]
A. *adj.*
1. *gen.* Belonging to another person, place, or family; strange, foreign, not of one's own.
1340 HAMPOLE *Prose Tr.* 45 Ffra þe soueranye joy and gastely swetnes in þe blysse of Heuene he sall be aliene. **1382** WYCLIF *Gen.* xxxv. 2 Doth awey alyen goddis, that ben in the mydil of ȝow. *c* **1600** SHAKS. *Sonn.* lxxviii, Euery Alien pen hath got my vse. **1697** DRYDEN *Virg. Eclog.* VIII. 62 In Desarts thou wert bred..Alien of Birth. **1791** COWPER *Iliad* XVI. 75 As I had been Some alien wretch. **1820** KEATS *Ode to Night.* 67 Ruth..stood in tears amid the alien corn. **1880** MORRIS *Ode of Life* 86 To watch by alien sick-beds.
2. a. *esp.* Of a foreign nation and allegiance.
c **1450** J. RUSSELL *Bk. Nurture* in *Babees Bk.* 191 Take hede he must to aliene commers straungeres, and to straungers of þis land. **1503** *Act 19 Hen. VII*, xxiii. 11 That no spirituell person ne straunger Aleyn be chargeable. **1809** TOMLINS *Law Dict.* s.v., Obsolete statutes..prohibiting alien artificers to work for themselves in this kingdom. **1849** MACAULAY *Hist. Eng.* I. 185 Disastrous war and alien domination. **1862** STANLEY *Jew. Ch.* (1877) I. x. 202 The Gibeonites..were an alien race.
b. alien priory, priory alien: a monastic establishment dependent upon and owing obedience to a mother-abbey in a foreign country.
1502 ARNOLD *Chron.* (1811) 184 The priory alyen of Lynton. **1598** R. HAKLUYT *Voy.* I. 18 To conceale from the Priors Aliens..the secret affaires of his Realme. **1611** SPEED *Hist. Gt. Brit.* IX. xv. (1632) 786 One hundred and tenne Priories aliant were suppressed. **1753** CHAMBERS *Cycl. Supp.* s.v., Upon breaking out of wars, the king usually seized on the *alien priories*, took their lands into his own hands. **1845** STEPHEN *Laws of Eng.* II. 679 The alien priories, that is, such as were filled by foreigners only.
3. a. Foreign in nature or character; belonging to something else; of foreign or other origin.
1673 O. WALKER *Educ.* (1677) 185 Chusing fit and convenient from improper and aliene. **1756** BURKE *Subl. & B.* Wks. I. 101 Habit alone has reconciled his palate to these alien pleasures. **1841** MYERS *Cath. Th.* IV. §32. 329 To introduce an alien and confusing element into our judgments. **1874** SAYCE *Compar. Philol.* viii. 321 It may sometimes be difficult to detect the presence of an alien myth.
b. *Science Fiction.* Of or pertaining to an (intelligent) being or beings from another planet; that derives from another world. See sense 1 b of the sb. below.
1944 *Astounding Sci. Fiction* June 72/1 An alien ship, all right. *Ibid.* 76/2 He looked at the thing. It was alien.., horribly different from anything on Earth. **1967** *Guardian* 5 Sept. 1 Six mysterious flying saucer-shaped objects were found in..Southern England yesterday... Was this an alien attempt to establish life on this planet? **1986** *Los Angeles Times* 15 Nov. VI. 12/3 As for Tomlin, *does* she believe in alien beings and UFOs?
c. Of a plant: brought from another country or district and subsequently naturalized. Cf. sense 5 of the sb.
1903 S. T. DUNN (*title*) A preliminary history of the alien flora of Britain. **1919** HAYWARD & DRUCE *Adventive Flora of Tweedside* p. ix, In former times at Galashiels the effluents from the woollen mills carrying seeds washed out in the course of scouring found their way in to the river... In the near future, therefore [as a result of a new system of drainage], instead of a large alien flora appearing along the rivers only a few sporadic species can be expected to occur. **1960** N. POLUNIN *Introd. Plant Geogr.* iv. 119 It is said that the majority of alien plants in Australia and New Zealand come from Europe. **1983** *Jrnl. Adelaide Bot. Garden* VI. 124

By 1855..there were 114 alien species recorded as naturalised in South Australia.

4. Of a nature or character differing *from* (*of* obs.), far removed from, inconsistent with.

1382 WYCLIF *John* Prol., He is founde alien fro corupcioun of fleisch. 1398 TREVISA *Barth. De P.R.* II. iv. (1495) 30 Aungels ben alyene and clene of all erthely cogytacyon. 1528 GARDINER in Pocock *Rec. Ref.* I. li. 121 Somewhat alien and discrepant from the expectation of the king's highness. 1667 MILTON *P.L.* IV. 572 His looks Alien from Heaven, with passions foul obscured. 1709 SWIFT *T. Tub* Wks. 1768, 140 Neither do I think such an employment alien from the office of a wit. 1855 H. REED *Eng. Lit.* ix. (1878) 294 This uncouth style, so alien from genuine English. 1874 HELPS *Soc. Press.* iv. 61 To seize upon this wise bequest, and to devote it to alien purposes.

This passes imperceptibly into

5. Of a nature repugnant, adverse or opposed *to*.

1720 WATERLAND *8 Serm.* 146 All Things, or Persons whatsoever, that are seperate from, or aliene to; that are not necessarily included in..God the Father. 1780 BURKE *Econ. Ref.* Wks. 1842 I. 238 A system of confusion remains, which is not only alien, but adverse to all economy. 1833 I. TAYLOR *Fanat.* vi. 177 Popery is alien to the climate and to the races of the Western world. 1875 MCLAREN *Sermons* Ser. II. vii. 125 Good, alas! is but too alien and unwelcome.

6. *fig.* Unkindly, unsympathetic, with the 'cold stare' of the stranger. *rare.*

1849 C. BRONTË *Shirley* xxvii. 399 The stars shone alien and remote.

7. *Comb.* **alien-looking**: of foreign or strange appearance.

1861 GEO. ELIOT *Silas M.* I The shepherd's dog barked fiercely when one of these alien-looking men appeared.

B. *sb.* [the adj. used absol.]

1. a. A person belonging to another family, race, or nation; a stranger, a foreigner.

1330 R. BRUNNE *Chron.* 37 þe reame salle men se Gouerned þorgh aliens kynde, & euermore fro þe. *c*1340 HAMPOLE *Pr. Consc.* 1377 For we dwell here als aliens. 1382 WYCLIF *Matt.* xvii. 24 Of her owne sonys, ether of alyenys, *or other mennys sones?* 1387 TREVISA *Higden* Rolls Ser. VII. 33 A new aliaunte [*advena*] scholde expelle olde inhabitators. 1535 COVERDALE *Job* xix. 15, I am become as an aleaunt in their sight. 1563 *Homilies* II. (1859) 358 He that speaketh in a tongue unknown shall be unto the hearer an alient. 1611 BIBLE *Ps.* lxiv. 8 An aliant vnto my mothers children. —— *Ex.* xviii. 3, I haue bene an alien in a strange land. 1796 SOUTHEY *Penates* Wks. II. 281 Mourning his age left childless, and his wealth Heapt for an alien. 1861 GEO. ELIOT *Silas M.* 2 Those scattered linen-weavers, emigrants from the town into the country, were to the last regarded as aliens by their rustic neighbours.

b. *Science Fiction.* An (intelligent) being from another planet, esp. one far distant from the Earth; a strange (usu. threatening) alien visitor.

1953 'W. TENN' *Of all Possible Worlds* (1958) 57 The first of the aliens stepped out in the complex tripodal gait that all humans were shortly to know..so well. 1960 K. AMIS *New Maps of Hell* (1961) i. 20 Some excellent stories have been written about non-communicating aliens, from *The War of the Worlds* onwards. 1984 *Times* 30 Nov. 15/4 A gentle, speechless alien of black human form lands in Harlem, whither he is pursued by a pair of white bounty-hunters from outer space.

2. *fig.*

1596 SHAKS. *1 Hen. IV*, III. ii. 34 Almost an alien to the hearts Of all the Court. 1675 TRAHERNE *Chr. Ethics* v. 65 An alien to felicity, and a foreiner to himself. 1755 YOUNG *Centaur* iv. Wks. 1757 IV. 203 Vengeance is an alien to thy most amiable nature. 1865 DICKENS *Christm. Bks.* (C.D. ed.) 212 An alien from my mother's heart.

3. a. *esp.* One who is a subject of another country than that in which he resides. A resident foreign in origin and not naturalized, whose allegiance is thus due to a foreign state.

1330 R. BRUNNE *Chron.* 96 þat aliens suld non hent hauen of Normant. *c*1425 WYNTOUN *Cron.* II. viii. 40 All Alienys þai banyst hale. 1480 CAXTON *Chron. Eng.* v. (1520) 47 b/2 In his tyme shall his lande be multeplyed with alyauntes. 1547 BOORDE *Introd. Knowl.* vii. 144 In Englande howe many alyons hath and doth dwell of all maner of nacyons. 1628 COKE *On Litt.* 8 a, An Alien that is borne out of the Kings ligeance. 1850 MAURICE *Mor. & Met. Philos.* (ed. 2) 8 The Jewish people..in Egypt, are regarded as a dangerous body of aliens. 1871 MARKBY *Elem. Law* §122 An alien is a person who belongs to a different political society from that in which he resides.

b. *transf.* A word from one language used but not naturalized in another language.

1884 *New Eng. Dict.* p. ix, *Aliens* are names of foreign objects, titles, etc., which we require often to use, and for which we have no native equivalents. 1926 FOWLER *Mod. Eng. Usage* 193/2 Only faddists will engage in alien-hunting and insist on finding native substitutes for *tête-à-tête*, *agent provocateur*, [etc.]. 1933 *Shorter Oxf. Eng. Dict.* p. vii, *Natives* are words of Old English origin, *denizens* are borrowings from foreign languages which have acquired full English citizenship, *aliens* are words that retain their foreign appearance and to some extent their foreign sound.

4. One separated, or excluded *from* (the citizenship and privileges of a nation).

1549 COVERDALE *Erasm. Paraphr. Hebr.* vii. 6 Melchisedech..was an alyaunt from the Jewishe nacion. 1557 N. T. (Genev.) *Eph.* ii. 12 Reputed aliantes from the commen welth of Israel. 1738 WESLEY *Ps.* xiii. I An Alien from the Life of Grace. 1837 J. H. NEWMAN *Par. Serm.* I. 13 Not as if aliens from God's mercies.

5. *Bot.* (See quot.)

1847 H. WATSON *Cybele* 63, *Alien*, [a plant] now more or less established, but either presumed or certainly known to have been originally introduced from other countries. *Ibid.* 153 An imperfectly established alien. 1903 S. T. DUNN *Prelim. List Alien Flora Britain* 4 There are..many species here classed as aliens which are old and well-established weeds in cultivated land, roadsides, and field borders. 1960 N. POLUNIN *Introd. Plant Geogr.* viii. 221 The discontinuation of a road or railway-line is apt to have a similar effect, and even those aliens which have managed to spread from the immediate vicinity of the travelled track usually disappear when Man's influence is removed. 1961 E. SALISBURY *Weeds & Aliens* i. 18 Blackberry and Sweet Briar, deliberately introduced into New Zealand in the early days of colonisation, furnish examples of aliens that have become noxious weeds. 1987 *New Scientist* 12 Feb. 38/2 Most aliens have escaped from gardens and cannot reproduce as well as common species that are native to Britain.

6. *Comb.* **alien-friend**, **(alien-amy)**, **alien-enemy**, law-terms designating an alien owing allegiance to a country which is for the time being in alliance, or at war, as the case may be, with the country in or to which he is an alien; **aliens duty**, the special duty formerly paid by aliens on imports and other mercantile transactions; ***alien-born***, etc.

1522 *Act 14 Hen. VIII*, ii, No Stranger, being Alien borne ..shall take, retaine or keep into his or their seruices any maner of Journyman. 1625 SIR. H. FINCH *Law* (1636) 28 Any body may seise the goods of an alien enemy, to his owne vse. 1641 *Termes de la Ley* 18 Every alien friend may by the Common Law have and get within this Realme. 1706 *Lond. Gaz.* mmmmcclxxxviii/3 Exposed to publick Sale, 26 Bags of Spanish Wooll..paid Aliens Duties. 1753 CHAMBERS *Cycl. Supp.*, *Aliens duty* is otherwise called petty customs, and navigation duty. 1853 WHARTON *Pa. Digest* §20. 94 An alien enemy cannot maintain an action during the war in his own name.

alien ('eɪlɪən), *v.* Also 4–6 alyen(e, 4–9 aliene. [a. OFr. *aliéne-r*:—L. *aliēnā-re* to estrange or make another's; f. *aliē n-us*: see ALIEN *a.*] = ALIENATE, of which it is the earlier equivalent.

1. *trans.* To convert into an alien or stranger. Usually *fig.* To estrange, turn away in feelings or affection, to make averse or hostile, or unwelcome.

*c*1374 CHAUCER *Boethius* 27 þei may not al arace hym ne alyene hym in al. 1382 WYCLIF *Ecclus.* xi. 36 She shal.. alienen thee fro thi propre weies. *c*1555 HARPSFIELD *Divorce Hen. VIII* (1878) 189 To aliene the fast and entire mind, which his highness beareth to your holiness. 1633 STAFFORD *Pac. Hib.* i. (1821) 227 The fame..would alien me to loath this kind of life. *a*1674 CLARENDON *Hist. Reb.* I. II. III The hearts of his Subjects were not then alien'd from their duty to the King. 1864 LD. DERBY *Iliad* I. 661 Yet shalt thou.. rather thus Be alien'd from my heart. 1870 LOWELL *Among Bks.* Ser. I. (1873) 157 Poetry had not been aliened from the people.

2. To transfer the property or ownership of anything; to make over to another owner. (In this sense often written *aliene*, and pronounced ('eɪljiːn).)

1413 LYDG. *Pylgr. Sowle* I. xxx. 34 A servaunt may make no testament..to alyene ony goodes out of his lordes hond. *c*1595 J. NORDEN *Spec. Brit.*, *Cornw.* (1728) 14 None may alien or dispose of his tynn, till it be coyned. 1614 RALEIGH *Hist. World* II. 451 He might alien the Crowne from his naturall Heires. 1658 BRAMHALL *Consecr. Bish.* viii. 189 If he alien any Lands belonging to his See. 1768 BLACKSTONE *Comm.* II. 289 He was not empowered to aliene. 1876 K. DIGBY *Real Prop.* v. §2. 216 If tenant in tail aliened the land with warranty.

†**3.** *refl.* and *intr.* To turn away, go off. *Obs.*

1382 WYCLIF *1 Macc.* vi. 24 The sonys of oure peple for this thing alieneden hem fro vs. 1541 R. COPLAND *Guydon's Quest. Cyrurg.*, Whan it is seen that it [the pulse] alyeneth to vnequalyte, and that it minissheth, the veyne ought to be stopped.

alienability (ˌeɪlɪənəˈbɪlɪtɪ). [f. ALIENABLE: see -BILITY.] The quality of being alienable; capability of being transferred to other ownership.

[1707 *Lond. Gaz.* mmmmccclv/1 With Orders to maintain the Inalienability of the Fief.] 1780 BURKE *Econ. Ref.* Wks. III. 316 His principal grounds of doctrine for the alienability of the domain. 1874 LD. SELBORNE *Rep. Comm. Ch. Patron.* Q. 103. 13 Altering the law as to the alienability of property.

alienable ('eɪlɪənəb(ə)l), *a.* [f. ALIEN *v.* + -ABLE. Cf. Fr. *aliénable*, perh. the direct source.] Capable of being alienated, or transferred to the ownership of another.

1611 COTGR., *Vendible*, vendible, sellable, alienable. 1643 D. DIGGES *Unlawf. Taking Arms* i. (1647) 4 Their nerves and sinewes are not alienable, as their money and goods. 1751 CHAMBERS *Cycl.* s.v. *Alienation*, Crown lands are only alienable under a faculty of perpetual redemption. 1832 I. TAYLOR *Sat. Even.* 465 Looking to things exterior and alienable, as his wealth. 1876 BANCROFT *Hist. U.S.* I. x. 334 All lands and heritages were declared free and alienable.

alienage ('eɪlɪənɪdʒ). [a. Fr. *aliénage* (1398 in Godef.), f. *alien*: see -AGE.] The state or condition of an alien; the legal standing of an alien.

1809 TOMLINS *Law Dict.* s.v. *Abatement*, Alienage is a plea in abatement, now discouraged, and seldom used. 1863 LINCOLN *Message to Congr.* 8 Dec., Exemption from military service..on the ground of alienage.

†**'alienar(e.** *Obs.* [f. ALIEN *a.* + *-ar* north. form of -ER[1] ending of the agent.] An alien, a stranger.

1513 DOUGLAS *Æneis* VII. ii. 165 To be thy mach sall cum ane alienare.

†**'alienate**, *ppl. a.* and *sb. Obs.* Also 5 **alyenate**, 6 **alyenat**, 6–7 **alienat**. [ad. L. *aliēnāt-us* pa. pple. of *aliēnā-re*: see ALIEN *v.*]

A. *ppl. adj.*

1. Estranged, withdrawn or turned away in feeling or affection.

1430 LYDG. *Chron. Troy* II. xii, Fer from hym selfe, he was so alyenate. 1582–8 *Hist. James VI* (1804) 17 The heartis of people are alienate from the lawfull prince. 1614 RALEIGH *Hist. World* II. 431 And as all alienate resolved hearts doe, they served themselves..with impudent excuses. *a*1745 SWIFT *Misc.* (J.) The Whigs are..wholly alienate from truth. 1814 CARY *Dante*, *Purg.* XIX. 113, I was a soul in misery, alienate From God.

2. Foreign in nature or character, alien.

1599 A. M. tr. *Gabelhouer's Bk. Physic* 21/1 When as the woman is gravid with any alienat excrescence. 1620 VENNER *Via Recta* iii. 57 They are..vnwholsome, and alienate from the taste of wholsome meates. 1660 T. STANLEY *Hist. Philos.* (1701) 296/1 Nothing was more alienate from the comprehension of Sciences, than Poetry.

3. Used as pple. of ALIEN *v.*

1513 BRADSHAW *St. Werburge* 204 Some other..diuers libertes haue alienate. 1538 STARKEY *England* 151 Prouysyon made that nothyng schold be alyenat to the fraud of the law.

4. *Bot.* = ALIENATED 4.

1839 HOOPER *Med. Dict.*

B. *sb.* An alien, stranger.

1552 LATIMER *Lord's Prayer* v. II. 68 And keep us from invasions of alienates and strangers. 1566 STAPLETON *Ret. Untr. Jewel* iv. 157 Whosoeuer eateth the lambe without this house, he is an alienat.

alienate ('eɪlɪəneɪt), *v.* [f. ALIENATE *ppl. a.* : see -ATE.]

1. To make estranged; to estrange, or turn away the feelings or affections of any one; = ALIEN *v.* I.

1548 UDALL etc. *Erasm. Paraphr. Matt.* vi. 12 And alienat not thy mynde awaye from us. 1614 RALEIGH *Hist. World* II. 366 Jotham..sought by his best perswasions to alienate the Sechemites. 1740 CIBBER *Apol.* (1756) I. 285 Who had so visibly alienated the hearts of his theatrical subjects. 1769 BURKE *State Nation* Wks. II. 113 Such projects have alienated our colonies from the mother country. 1855 MILMAN *Lat. Chr.* (1864) V. VIII. viii. 19 If Matilda's pride had not alienated Henry of Winchester.

2. To transfer to the ownership of another. Also *absol.* = the earlier ALIEN *v.* 2.

1513 BRADSHAW *St. Werburge* 203 Other have been glad to alienat the patronage of certayne churches. 1651 HOBBES *Govt. & Soc.* viii. §6. 130 The Lord may sell his Servant, or alienate him by Testament. 1681 DRYDEN *Abs. & Achit.* 434 What means he then, to Alienate the Crown? 1776 ADAM SMITH *W.N.* (1869) II. v. ii. 455 The vassal could not alienate without the consent of his superior. 1855 MACAULAY *Hist. Eng.* IV. 647 The King was not at perfect liberty to alienate any part of the estates of the Crown.

3. *fig.* (combining I and 2) To turn away, transfer.

1621 BURTON *Anat. Mel.* II. ii. IV (1676) 179/2 If such voluntary tasks..will not..alienate their imaginations. 1712 ADDISON *Spect.* No. 414 ¶4 To alienate so much ground from Pasturage. 1750 JOHNSON *Rambl.* No. 148 ¶11 Who alienates from him the assistance of his children. 1832 HT. MARTINEAU *Homes Abr.* ix. 127 This is done by alienating capital from its natural channels.

†**4.** [One of the senses of L. *aliēnāre.*] To alter, change, or make a thing other than it is. *Obs.*

1553–87 FOXE *A. & M.* III. 538 Neither favour of his Prince..nor any other worldly respect could alienate or change his purpose.

alienated ('eɪlɪəneɪtɪd), *ppl. a.* [f. prec. + -ED.]

1. Estranged, withdrawn in feeling or affection.

1561 J. DAUS tr. *Bullinger on Apocal.* (1573) Pref. II Sequestred and alienated from the true religion of Christ. 1667 MILTON *P.L.* I. 452 His eye surveyed the dark idolatries Of alienated Judah. 1719 YOUNG *Revenge* I. i. Wks. 1757 II. 110 With absent eyes, and alienated mien. 1856 FROUDE *Hist. Eng.* II. vii. 210 Tokens..of alienated feeling, if not of alienated act. 1881 N. T. (Revised) *Eph.* ii. 12 Alienated from the commonwealth of Israel, and strangers from the covenant of the promise.

2. Transferred to other ownership.

1611 COTGR., *Aliené*, aliened, alienated..sold, or made away. 1759 ROBERTSON *Hist. Scotl.* (1802) I. I. 234 He found his revenues wasted or alienated. 1876 FREEMAN *Norm. Conq.* IV. xvii. 59 Some parts of the alienated lands were in course of William's reign restored.

†**3.** Made other or different; altered. *Obs.*

1605 VERSTEGAN *Dec. Intell.* viii. (1628) 262 Also written Heughe, and alienated among strangers vnto Hugo.

†**4.** *Bot.* (See quot.) *Obs.*

1853 MAYNE *Exp. Lex.*, *Alienatus*, Applied to first leaves, which give way to others different from them.

alienating ('eɪlɪəneɪtɪŋ), *vbl. sb.* [f. as prec. + -ING[1].] The act of estranging, or transferring to another owner. (Mostly gerundial.)

1591 PERCIVALL *Sp. Dict.*, *Agenamiento*, casting off a sonne, alienating. 1645 MILTON *Tetrach.* (1851) 230 Law more justly did permitt the alienating of that evil which mistake made proper. 1704 ADDISON *Italy* 15 Never entertain'd a Thought..of alienating any Part of these Revenues. 1849 ALISON *Hist. Eur.* I. iii. §151. 423 It was intended to conciliate—it had the effect of alienating.

alienating ('eɪlɪəneɪtɪŋ), *ppl. a.* [f. as prec. + -ING².] Estranging, or transferring to other ownership.

1661 *Pet. Peace* 1 Exasperating and alienating differences.

alienation (ˌeɪlɪə'neɪʃən). Also 5–6 **alyenacion, -cyon.** [a. MFr. *alienacion*, ad. L. *aliēnātiōn-em*, n. of action f. *aliēnā-re*: see ALIEN *v.*]

1. a. The action of estranging, or state of estrangement in feeling or affection. Const. (*of* obs.) *from*.

1388 WYCLIF *Job* xxxi. 3 Alienacioun of God is to men worchynge wickidnesse. **1621** BURTON *Anat. Mel.* III. iii. I. i, Alexander..saw now an alienation in his subiects hearts. **1670** G. H. *Hist. Cardinals* II. iii. 298 The alienation shew'd by the Pope from the French. **1770** BURKE *Pres. Discont.* Wks. II. 275 They grow every day into alienation from this country. **1862** STANLEY *Jew. Ch.* (1877) I. xvii. 323 The alienation of the people from the worship of the sanctuary.

b. spec. ***alienation of affection(s)***: see quot. 1961. *U.S.*

[**1861** *Rep. Cases Wisconsin Supr. Court 1860* XI. 430 The evidence offered by the defendant, for the purpose of showing that the affections of the wife had been previously alienated..should have been admitted.] **1867** in N. Howard *Practice Rep. Supreme Court N.Y.* XXXII. 145 Does such alienation of affection—such refusal to recognize and receive the plaintiff as her husband, and to live with him as his wife —..constitute a cause of action, when caused as charged in the complaint? **1922** *Dominion Law Rep.* LXVI. 144 An affection that was merely flickering faintly with life might be finally killed by the act of adultery. Would even this not be an alienation of affection? **1933** in S. N. Grant-Bailey *Lush on the Law of Husband & Wife* (ed. 4) i. 36 It would seem that the English temperament is sufficiently sagacious to make the importation into the English law of the alienation of affection as a ground for action so remote as to be a negligible danger. **1949** M. MEAD *Male & Female* xv. 299 Alienation-of-affection cases between two men, which assume that the woman is a gently pliant lily, ring just as false. **1961** WEBSTER, *Alienation of affection*, the transfer of a person's affection from someone who has certain rights or claims to such affection to a third person who is held to be the instigator or cause of the transfer.

c. *Marxism.* (See quot. 1962.) (Marx's term *Entäusserung*, which he used in 'Zur Judenfrage', *Deutsch-Französische Jahrbücher*, 1844, has been rendered by 'self-alienation' and 'dehumanization' as well as by 'alienation'.)

1926 H. J. STENNING tr. *Marx's Sel. Essays* 95 After Christianity had completed the alienation of man from himself..Judaism [could] attain to general domination and turn the alienated individual..into alienable and saleable objects. **1958** *Listener* 7 Aug. 194/1 Marx, or at any rate the early Marx, has used a concept, Hegelian in origin, which Berdyaev found immensely fruitful for his own discussion of the idea of objectivity: the concept of 'alienation'. Men turn or are turned into impoverished things, dependent on power outside themselves. **1962** E. KAMENKA *Ethical Foundations Marxism* 12 The philosophico-ethical conceptions that underlie the younger Marx. Chief among these conceptions is that of 'alienation': the notion that in modern capitalistic society man is estranged or alienated from what are properly his functions and creations and that instead of controlling them he is controlled by them.

d. *Theatr.* In full ***alienation effect.*** [tr. G. *verfremdungseffekt* (Brecht, 'Verfremdungs effekte in der chinesischen Schauspielkunst', 1937, in *Schriften z. Theater*, 1957).] An effect sought by the German playwright Brecht and followers, aimed at the destruction of many of the conventions of theatrical illusion.

[**1948** E. R. BENTLEY *Brecht's Private Life of Master Race* 91 The meaning of the device is, in a word, *Verfremdung*. The audience is put at a distance from the events related, is prevented from identifying itself with any character because each actor is all the time shifting roles.] **1949** —— in *Theatre Arts* Jan. 38/2 It is Brecht's contention that..we need a kind of acting..that will set the action before us rather than involve us in the action... The German word which Brecht has made up to describe the distancing or estranging of the action is Verfremdung, here translated as 'alienation'. Any device which promotes such alienation is called an A-effect. **1956** K. TYNAN in *Observer* 2 Sept. 10/2 The famous 'alienation-effect' was originally intended to counter balance the extravagant rhetoric of German classical acting. **1956** S. WANAMAKER in *Internat. Theatre Ann.* 125 His [Brecht's] principal theory: objectivity of the spectator, distancing, alienation of the audience's feeling and involvement. **1962** *Listener* 29 Nov. 932/2 This method of description seems almost like a parallel to Brecht's 'alienation effect'. We watch, we judge, but we do not participate.

2. a. The action of transferring the ownership of anything to another.

1430 LYDG. *Chron. Troy* v. xxxvi, Kinges in theyr bedde are slawe; Whiche bringeth in alyenacyon By extorte tytle false successyon. **1463** in *Bury Wills* (1850) 26 Wich obligacion must be maad at euery alyenacion in a notable summe. **1587** HARRISON *Engl.* I. II. ii. 48 Hereford..paid to Rome at everie alienation 1800 ducats at the least. **1661** BRAMHALL *Just Vind.* iii. 39 Prohibiting..the alienation of Lands to the Church. **1699** LUTTRELL *Brief Rel.* (1857) IV. 580 Mr. Charles Boyl..succeeds..as receiver of the alienation office. **1788** PRIESTLEY *Lect. Hist.* v. lii. 405 Price, however, supposes alienation; and a common standard of value supposes a frequent and familiar alienation. **1876** K. DIGBY *Real Prop.* x. §1. 368 By alienation is meant the intentional and voluntary transfer of a right.

b. The taking of anything from its owner.

1583 BABINGTON *Wks.* 319 The forbidding of stealth which is an alienation of an other mans goodes to our selves.

c. Diversion of anything to a different purpose.

1828 LD. GRENVILLE *Sinking Fund* 59 That of 1786 was ..'fortified as much as possible against alienation.'

3. The state of being alienated, or held by other than the proper owner.

1818 TODD *Dict.* s.v., The estate was wasted during its alienation.

4. Mental alienation: Withdrawal, loss, or derangement of mental faculties; insanity. (So in L.)

1482 *Monk of Evesham* (1869) 20 That he had seyd hyt of grete febulnesse of his hedde, or by alyenacion of hys mynde. **1607** TOPSELL *Four-footed Beasts* (1673) 272 It infecteth as well the heart as the brain, and causeth alienation of minde. **1748** HARTLEY *Observ. Man* I. iii. §6 Temporary alienations of the Mind during violent Passions. **1862** LD. BROUGHAM *Brit. Const.* xiii. 194 He had fallen into a state of mental alienation.

†**5.** Alteration, change. *Obs.*

1615 CROOKE *Body of Man* 503 A Hecticke Feuer in which there is an vtter alienation of the Temperament.

6. ***alienation coefficient*** or ***coefficient of alienation*** in *Statistics*: a ratio expressing the degree of lack of correlation of two variables.

1919 T. L. KELLEY in *Jrnl. Appl. Psychol.* III. 61 Just as ·484 is the coefficient of correlation between intelligence and vocational choice, so may ·875 be called the coefficient of alienation between the same two things. **1923** —— *Statist. Method* xi. 289 We have called $k_{0\cdot 12}$ the multiple alienation coefficient... We will define $k_{01\cdot 2}$ as the partial alienation coefficient. **1936** J. P. GUILFORD *Psychometric Methods* III. xi. 362 The expression $\sqrt{(1-r^2)}$ is known as the *coefficient of alienation*, and it measures the absence of relationship just as *r* measures its presence.

alienator ('eɪlɪəneɪtə(r)). [a. L. *aliēnātor* n. of agent f. *aliēnā-re*.] One who alienates.

1670 WALTON *Lives, Hooker* III. 191 With these Immunities and Lands they have entail'd a curse upon the Alienators of them. **1772** T. WARTON *Sir T. Pope* 40 (T.) Many popish bishops were no less alienators of their episcopal endowments. **1823** LAMB *Elia* Ser. I. iv. (1865) 39 There is a class of alienators more formidable..I mean your borrowers of books. **1860** FORSTER *Grand Remonstr.* 82 Mary was able to burn at her pleasure, the alienators of the abbey lands.

[**alienatory** in Webster is misprint for prec.]

aliene, a frequent variant of ALIEN *v.*; also obs. f. of ALIEN *sb.* and *a.*

aliened ('eɪlɪənd), *ppl. a.* [f. ALIEN *v.* + -ED.] = ALIENATED, of which it is the earlier form.

1. Converted into an alien, or foreigner; estranged; turned away in feeling or affection, rendered hostile.

1382 WYCLIF *Eph.* ii. 12 That weren in that tyme withouten Crist, alyened, *or maad straunge.* **1583** GOLDING *Calvin on Deut.* clxix. 1051 Wee were dispersed and aliened from our Lorde Jesus Christ. **1656** BP. HALL *Occas. Med.* (1851) 40 He, that is not ashamed of my bonds..not aliened with my disgrace. *a* **1733** NORTH *Exam.* I. iii. §134. 210 A Nation so aliened as England was, could not be regained impetuously. **1844** LD. HOUGHTON *Mem. Many Scenes* 202 Let the sound Of native and of neighbour speech No more his aliened senses reach.

2. Transferred to another owner; diverted to other uses.

1531 *Dial. Laws Eng.* II. xxxv. (1638) 123 A covenant made upon a gift to the Church, that it shall not be aliened. **1655** FULLER *Ch. Hist.* III. 78 It shall be lawful to us.. immediately to enter in the land so aliened.

alienee (ˌeɪlɪə'niː). [f. ALIEN *v.* + -EE.] One to whom the ownership of property is transferred.

1531 *Dial. Laws Eng.* II. xiii. (1638) 82 After whose death his wife asketh her dower, and the alienee refuseth to assigne it unto her. **1768** BLACKSTONE *Comm.* II. 192 If one of two joint-tenants in fee alienes his estate for the life of the alienee, the alienee and the other joint-tenant are tenants in common. **1859** BENTLEY *Q. Rev.* No. 3. 28 That an alienation should be null if the alienee should turn out a bad landlord.

alienigenate (ˌeɪlɪə'nɪdʒɪneɪt), *a.* [ad. L. *aliēnigenāt-us* pa. pple. of *aliēnigenā-re*, f. *aliēnigen-us* of foreign race, f. *aliēn-us* foreign + *-gen-us* born.] Alien-born.

1855 WINTHROP *Braddock's Exped.* 17 The throng of Hanoverian favorites around their alienigenate king.

†ˌ**alie'niloquy.** *Obs.*$^{-0}$ [ad. med.L. *aliēniloquium*, f. *aliēn-us* foreign + *loqui* to speak.] 'A talking wide from the purpose, or not to the matter in hand.' Bailey 1731; whence in Ash.

aliening ('eɪlɪənɪŋ), *vbl. sb.* [f. ALIEN *v.* + -ING¹.] = ALIENATING; the action of estranging, estrangement; or of transferring to another owner.

1382 WYCLIF *Job* xxxi. 3 And alienyng to men werkende wickednesse. **1494** FABYAN VII. 577 Yᵉ olde mayre and shryues contynued theyr offyces to the termys accustomed of theyr alienynge. **1642** ROGERS *Naaman* 409 For the aliening of his heart from the Protestant Religion. **1768** BLACKSTONE *Comm.* I. 303 In order to prevent such idiots from aliening their lands. **1875** POSTE *Gaius* II. (ed. 2) 164 A power of aliening from all who..might succeed by descent.

alienism ('eɪlɪənɪz(ə)m). [f. ALIEN *sb.* + -ISM.]

1. The position or profession of being an alien, or foreigner in a country.

a **1816** JOHNSON *N.Y. Rep.* 381 in Pickering 31 The prisoner..suggested his alienism, which was admitted. **1854** RAIKES *Eng. Const.* II. 370 (L.) They were generally justified on some plea of war or alienism. **1879** GEO. ELIOT *Theo. Such* 342 Their monetary hold on governments is tending to perpetuate in leading Jews a spirit of universal alienism (euphemistically called cosmopolitanism).

2. The study and treatment of mental diseases.

1881 *The Nation* 1 Dec. 433/1 As surgery is the very best department in medical science in this country [U.S.], alienism is the very worst.

alienisparsison (ælɪˌiːnɪ'spɑːsɪsɒn). [f. L. *aliēn-us* foreign + *spars-us* rare + *son-us* sound. The L. *alienisparsisonus* was used by Dr. J. D. Rhys in his Welsh Gram. 1592; the Eng. first as under.] In Welsh prosody, a diphthong found only in foreign words, followed by such a consonant group as *-rs* (gravisparsison) or *-dr*, *-gr* (fortisparsison); as in the word *siars* = Eng. *charge*.

1856 J. WILLIAMS *Gram. Edeyrn* §207 A syllable which has its beginning strange, and ends with a fortisparsison or gravisparsison..is called alienisparsison.

alienist ('eɪlɪənɪst). [a. mod.Fr. *aliéniste*: see ALIENATION 4 and -IST.] One who treats mental diseases; a mental pathologist; a 'mad-doctor.'

1864 *Soc. Sc. Rev.* I. 447 A distinguished alienist, and Member of the Belgian Lunacy Commission. **1881** ROMANES in *Nature* XXV. 193 All alienists are agreed as to the greater frequency of mental alienation in the summer season.

alienize ('eɪlɪənaɪz), *v.* [See -IZE.] *trans.* To make alien, reduce to the status of an alien (in quot. 1841 rendering W. *alltudio*). Hence '**alienized** *ppl. a.*, made foreign.

1841 *Anc. Laws & Inst. Wales* II. 333 Her brothers alienized her children when they gave her to an alltud. **1860** MEREDITH *Evan Harrington* iv, This extremely alienised idea of the nature of a member of the Parliament of Great Britain.

alienness ('eɪlɪənnɪs). [f. ALIEN *a.* + -NESS.] The fact or quality of being alien.

1929 A. HUXLEY *Do what you Will* 33 Absolute alienness which no amount of Esperanto and international government..will ever..completely abolish. **1939** A. J. TOYNBEE *Study Hist.* V. 363 If alienness were really a hindrance and not a help to the spread of a 'higher religion'.

alienor ('eɪlɪənə(r), -ˌɔə(r)). Also 6 -our. [late Anglo-Fr., for earlier *alienour* = Fr. *aliéneur*, f. *aliéner*: see ALIEN *v.* and -OR. Correl. with *alienee*.] One who transfers property to another.

1552 HULOET, Alienour, *alienator.* **1649** SELDEN *Laws of Eng.* I. lxvi. (1739) 152 Lands or Tenements aliened to a Religious House shall escheat to the Lord, if the Alienor take the same back to hold of that Lord. **1768** BLACKSTONE *Comm.* II. 291 For the alienor himself to recover lands aliened by him. **1876** K. DIGBY *Real Prop.* ii. §8. 93 Conveying lands by means of a fictitious or collusive suit, commenced by arrangement by the intended alienee against the alienor.

alienship ('eɪlɪənʃɪp). [f. ALIEN *sb.* + -SHIP.] The condition of an alien or foreigner.

1875 *Daily News* 12 Oct. 3/1 French sailors do not somehow attach any idea of alienship to these peoples.

†'**aliet.** *Obs.* [ad. med.L. *alietus*, or *aliaetus*, a. Gr. ἁλι-άετος sea-eagle; applied in Middle Ages in somewhat random fashion to other *Falconidæ*.] A bird of prey; in Wyclif put for the osprey or sea-eagle; in *Her.* a merlin or a sparrow-hawk.

1388 WYCLIF *Lev.* xi. 13 An egle, and a grippe, aliete and a kyte. **1398** TREVISA *Barth. De P.R.* XII. iv. (1495) 412 Alietous and a fawcon is all one byrde. **1610** GWILLIM *Displ. Her.* III. xx. (1660) 223 The Aliet is a bird of little power; And little birds are all he eats and doth devour. **1783** BAILEY, *Alet*, the true falcon of Peru, that never lets her prey escape.

†**a'liety.** *Obs.*$^{-0}$ [ad. med.L. *aliētāt-em*, f. *alius* other: cf. *varius*, *variētas*, *variety*, and see -TY.] The condition of being other or different.

1656 BLOUNT *Glossogr.*, *Aliety*, otherness; a term in Philosophy. **1753** CHAMBERS *Cycl. Supp.*, *Alterity* amounts to the same with what others call *aliety*, *alietas*.

†**a'life**, *adv.*¹ *Obs.* [Prob. formed on *lief* dear, but confused in form with *life* ?quasi 'as one's life.'] In phr. ***to love alife***: to love dearly.

1601 HOLLAND *Pliny* (1634) II. 86 Saffron loueth a-life to be trampled and trod vpon. **1603** —— *Plutarch's Mor.* 136 A busie fellow loveth a-life to step secretly into a house. **1611** COTGR. s.v. *Paresseux*, The sluggard loues alife things done to his hand. **1693** W. ROBERTSON *Phraseol. Gen.* 1325 I love that a-life; I am willing unto this.

alife (ə'laɪf), *adv.*² prop. *phr.* ?*dial.* [A *prep.*¹ in + LIFE; a modern formation on the same elements as ALIVE.] In life.

1864 MRS. LLOYD *Ladies of Polcar.* 40 Unless God keep her alife.

aliferous (ə'lɪfərəs), *a. rare*$^{-0}$. [f. late L. *ālifer* wing-bearing + -OUS.] Bearing or having wings.

1731 in BAILEY; whence in JOHNSON, &c.

aliform (ˈeɪlɪfɔːm), *a.* [ad. mod.L. *āliform-is*, f. *āla* wing + *-formis*: see -FORM. Cf. Fr. *aliforme.*] Wing-shaped.

1836 TODD *Cycl. Anat. & Phys.* I. 546/2 A very thin dilated, aliform margin. **1882** SLADEN in *Jrn. Linn. Soc.* XVI. 228 Lateral aliform extensions.

†**aˈlift**, *v. Obs.* [f. A- *pref.* 11 + LIFT.] To lift.

1590 in *Right Religion* A iij b, Kneele downe, shead teares, alift heart, and pray. **1606** *Choice, Chance, & Change* (1881) 75, I saw her come to life againe, when her eies alifted vp, she sighed out, oh friend art thou aliue?

aligerous (əˈlɪdʒərəs), *a. rare*⁻⁰. [f. L. *āliger* wing-bearing + -OUS.] Bearing wings, winged.

1731 BAILEY; whence in ASH, etc.

alight (əˈlaɪt), *v.*¹ Forms: 1 **alíht-an**, 2–4 **aliȝten**, 4 **alyȝt-en**, 4–5 **alight-e(n**, 5 **alyght(e**, 7 **alite**, 5– **alight**. *Pa. t.* 1–3 **alíhte**, 3–4 **aliȝte**, 5–6 **alight**, **alyght**, 6– **alighted**, (9 **alit**). *Pa. pple.* 1–3 **aliht**, 3–4 **aliȝt**, **alyȝt**, 4–5 **alight**, 5 **alyght**, 6– **alighted**, (9 **alit**). [OE. *alíhtan*, f. A- *pref.* 1 + *líhtan*: see LIGHT *v.*¹]

I. Referring chiefly to the action: To spring.

1. To spring or jump lightly down *from* (*of* obs.) a horse; *hence*, To dismount *from* a horse or descend *out of* a conveyance.

c **1000** ÆLFRIC *Gram.* xxx. §3. 191 *Dissilio*, ic of alíhte. **1250** LAYAM. 26337 Adun hii gonne alihte of hire gode stedes. *c* **1300** *Beket* 1854 Of his palefrai he aliȝte adoun. *c* **1450** LONELICH *Grail* lii. 585 Down he alyhte of his rownsy. *Ibid.* xxv. 151 He ne dorste..owt of his sadil alyhte. **1475** CAXTON *Jason* 10 b, Peleus and Jason were alighted from their hors. **1530** PALSGR. 420/2, I alight downe of a horse. **1578** T. N. tr. *Conq. W. India* 321 And he alyghting from his horse. *a* **1674** CLARENDON *Hist. Reb.* III. XIV. 404 His Majesty alighted out of his Coach. **1699** DRYDEN *Flower & Leaf* 304 The victors from their lofty steeds alight. **1857** DICKENS *Lett.* (1880) II. 31 Station-masters assist him to alight from carriages. **1863** MRS. JAMESON *Leg. Monast. Ord.* 36 The emperor has just alighted from his charger.

†**2.** To spring lightly, to vault *on* or *upon*, to mount. *Obs.*

c **1380** *Sir Ferumb.* 2938 And wan Ro[land] was on his [stede] alyȝt: to is felawes þanne a sede. **1509** HAWES *Past. Pleas.* XXXIII. vi, I alyght anone upon my gentyll stede.

†**3.** To spring forth. *Obs.*

c **1450** LONELICH *Grail* II. 156 From that there cam a roser ful stronge..As on tre owt of anothir scholde alyht.

II. Referring chiefly to the result: To land.

4. a. To get down from a horse or conveyance; to dismount or descend for the time; to finish one's ride, stop.

1205 LAYAM. 26618 Heo letten alle þa horsmen i þan wude alihten. *a* **1300** *Floriz & Bl.* 21 At þe selue huse hi buþ aliȝt þat blauncheflur was þat oþer niȝt. *c* **1386** CHAUCER *Clerkes T.* 925 Abouten undern gan this erl alight. **1480** CAXTON *Chron. Eng.* ccxliv. 300 They come rydyng thurgh the Cyte of london vnto seynt poules and ther they alyght. **1598** BARRET *Theor. Warres* IV i. 101 That if occasion be offered, euery mounted souldier may alight. **1596** SHAKS. *Merch. V.* II. ix. 87 Madam, there is a-lighted at your gate, A yong Venetian. **1659** in Rushw. *Hist. Coll.* I. 77 Being alighted at the Palace-gate. **1678** *Yng. Mans Call.* 364 She was fain to alite under a hedge, and there to trim her self as well as she could. **1742** RICHARDSON *Pamela* III. 351 We alighted, and walked a little way. **1824** DIBDIN *Libr. Comp.* 224 He happens to alight at an inn. **1872** JENKINSON *Eng. Lakes* (1879) 200 On alighting at the Threlkeld station cross the line.

†**b.** To stop in a course or journey, to arrive. *Obs. rare.*

1596 SPENSER *F.Q.* I. xii. 25 Fast before the king he did alight.

†**5.** *gen.* To go or come down, to descend. *Obs.*

c **1175** *Lamb. Hom.* 79 þes Mon þhet a lihte from ierusalem in to ierico. *c* **1230** *Ancr. R.* 248 God Almihti..alihte adun to helle. *c* **1260** *Signs bef. Judgem.* in *E.E.P.* (1862) 7 þe grace of ihsu..mote a mang vs nuþe aliȝte. *c* **1320** *Cast. Love* 653 He..That from hevyn to erthe alyȝht. *a* **1420** OCCLEVE *De Reg. Princ.* 1141 Right as she made me clymbe on hight..so she may make me alight. **1483** CAXTON *G. de la Tour* g viij b, As soone as she was a lyght out of her child bedde.

6. To descend and settle, to land on one's feet anywhere (and so contrasted with *falling*); hence, to land on a spot by floating, flying, or falling lightly, as a bird from the wing, a snow-flake, etc. Also of an aircraft: to land.

1297 R. GLOUC. 433 After þat our Lorde was in hys moder alyȝt. *c* **1314** *Guy Warw.* 270 Opon Sir Gy, that gentil knight, Ywis, mi love is alle alight. *c* **1320** *Cast. Love* 1291 þulke God alle þing dihte þat in þe swete Mayden alihte. *c* **1450** LONELICH *Grail* xli. 208 Goddis sone of hevene, That into þe maide alyhte. **1596** SPENSER *F.Q.* I. iii. 20 The heavie hap, which on them is alight. **1786** J. JEFFRIES *Narr. 2 Aerial Voyages* 16 After alighting for a moment..M. Blanchard threw out the remaining part of our sand ballast. **1816** J. WILSON *City of Plague* II. ii. 192 A wondrous bird That ne'er alights to fold her wings. **1818** BYRON *Mazeppa* xviii, I saw his wing through twilight flit, And once so near me he alit. *a* **1849** POE *Angel of Odd* Wks. 1864 IV. 308, I alit upon my feet. **1860** TYNDALL *Glac.* I. §18. 124 A grey cloud alighted on the shoulder of the Lyskamm. **1958** *Times* 17 Oct. 3/4 To see and feel the aircraft obeying the dictates of unseen devices..as we were about to alight along the centre-line of the runway.

7. To fall (*on* or *upon*) as a blow, or projectile, to descend and strike. *arch.*

c **1300** in Wright *Pop. Sc.* 136 No wonder þeȝ hit smite harde þer hit doþ aliȝte. *a* **1700** DRYDEN (J.), Storms of stones..Pour down and on our batter'd helms alight. **1824** WIFFEN *Tasso's Jerus. Deliv.* XI. xxxv, A huge round rock..upon his crown Alit, and rudely beat the' heroic soldier down.

8. To land, fall, or come upon anything without design; to light upon. Chiefly const. *on.*

1858 FROUDE *Hist. Eng.* IV. 549 By good fortune..I alighted on a collection of MSS. in the State Paper Office. **1925** F. SCOTT FITZGERALD *Great Gatsby* vii. 148, I realized that so far his suspicions hadn't alighted on Tom. **1961** S. GILLESPIE *Neighbour* vi. 93 Her flat was pretty much what he had expected; the apartment of a rich woman of taste, and his eye immediately alighted on a Degas. **1984** *Financial Times* 1. 19/4, I believe you may already have *alighted upon* the reason for some of the scepticism shown towards business graduates mentioned in 'Business Schools under Siege'.

†**aˈlight**, *v.*² *Obs.* [? f. A- *pref.* 1 + LIGHT *v.*², OE. *líhtan*; or LIGHT *a.* But cf. OE. *ȝelíhtan*, which may be the actual source; see A- *pref.* 6.] To make light, or less heavy; to lighten, alleviate (a burden); to relieve (the bearer).

[*c* **885** K. ÆLFRED *Past. Care* 159 Ðonne hie willað him selfum ðæt yfel..ȝelihtan. *a* **1000** *Laws Penit.* 19 (Thorpe II. 286) Mid xxx mæssan man mæȝ ȝelíhtan xii monða festen. *c* **1230** *Ancr. R.* 356 þet ich beo ilihted of hore heuinesse.] **1388** WYCLIF *Is.* ix. 1 The lond of Zabulon..was aliȝted *ether releessid.* **1393** GOWER *Conf.* II. 278, I might Some of my grete peine alight. *c* **1449** PECOCK *Repr.* v. xiii. 550 For this..cause of aliȝting poor men. **1483** CAXTON *G. de la Tour* d vij b, She wende to alyght her euylle and her synne.

†**aˈlight**, *v.*³ *Obs.* Forms: 1 **aléoht-an**, **alýht-an**, **alíhtan**, 2–3 **aliht-en**, **alyht-en**, 4 **aliȝt-en**, **alyȝt-en**, 4–7 **alight(e**, (7 **adlight**). *Pa. t.* 1–3 **alíhte**, etc., 3–4 **aliȝte**, 4–5 **alight**, 6–7 **alighted**. *Pa. pple.* 1 **alihted**, 2 **aliht**, 4–6 **alight**, 6–7 **alighted**. [Probably the two OE. verbs *a-líhtan* (? with A- *pref.* 1; cf. OHG. *arliuhtan*, mod.G. *erleuchten*) and *on-líhtan* (see A- *pref.* 2), both 'to shine upon, light up,' are here represented, if indeed the solitary OE. instance of *alíhtan* be not merely a later form of *onlíhtan.*]

1. To light, light up, illumine.

c **1000** *Ags. Metr. Ps.* cxxxviii. (-ix.) 10 þu þá onlíhtest niht, þæt heó byð dæȝe ȝelíc. *c* **1000** ÆLFRIC *Gen.* i. 15 And hiȝ..alihton þa eorþan. *c* **1175** *Lamb. Hom.* 185 þu..hauest aliht mi þester heorte. **1340** *Ayenb.* 109 þet þe holy gost ous wille alyȝte þe herte. **1393** GOWER *Conf.* II. 183 A fiery piller hem alight. **1577** tr. *Bullinger's Decades* (1592) 550 To goe about with a tallow candle to helpe or adlight the sunne at his rising. **1634** *Malory's Arthur* (1816) II. 216 They were alighted of the grace of the Holy Ghost.

2. To set light to, to light (a fire, etc.).

1340 *Ayenb.* 66 Huanne me alyȝt þet uer. *c* **1400** *Lay le Freine* 199 Anon fer sche alight, And warmed it wele aplight. **1590** *Eng. Rom. Life* in *Harl. Misc.* (Malh.) II. 183 When the schollers come they alight their lamps. **1620** SHELTON *Don Quix.* (R.) Having..alighted his lamp.

alight (əˈlaɪt), *a.* [app. orig. pa. pple. of ALIGHT *v.*³ (under which see quot. dated 1175); but placed by form-assoc. in the same series with *a-fire*, *a-blaze*, *a-sleep*, *a-live*, i.e. *on fire*, *in a blaze*, etc. and so now used only predicatively, whereas it was formerly attrib. also.]

1. Lighted, kindled, in a flame; on fire. Also *fig.*

c **1420** *Pallad. on Husb.* v. 208 A brason vessel..Alight atte nyght. **1675** T. BROOKS *Gold. Key* Wks. 1867 V. 242 To see all the world on a-light fire about them. **1743** BOLINGBROKE *Rem. Hist. Eng.* Pref., A Beacon to be kept continually alight. **1860** HAWTHORNE *Marble Farm* (1879) I. xx. 202 To set alight the devotion of the worshippers. **1863** SALA *Capt. Dang.* III. v. 156 She was alight, and ran about the scene, screaming piteously. **1876** MRS. WHITNEY *Sights & Ins.* iii. 18 The girls, of course, were all alight about it. **1878** HUXLEY *Physiogr.* 82 The number of gas-burners, lamps, or candles alight. **1882** R. STEVENSON *New Arab. N.* II. 90 The whole pavilion..had gone alight like a box of matches.

2. Lighted up, illumined. Also *fig.*

1842 MRS. BROWNING *Grk. Chr. Poets* 62 Some marbles are like new dropt snow, and some Alight with blackness. **1861** THACKERAY *Four Georges* iii. (1862) 169 The chapel was scarcely alight. **1881** SHORTHOUSE *J. Inglesant* II. i. 6 All alight with the morning sun.

†**aˈlight**, *ppl. a. Obs.* [pa. pple. of ALIGHT *v.*¹] Alighted, dismounted, arrived.

c **1386** CHAUCER *Prol.* 722 Whan we were in that hostelrie alyght. ? **1469** GREGORY *Hist. Coll.* (1876) 188 Anon as he was a lyght of hys hors, he was arestyde. **1626** SHIRLEY *Maid's Rev.* II. i, A pretty, handsome stripling new alight.

†**aˈlighten**, *v.*¹ *Obs. rare*⁻¹. [Secondary form of ALIGHT *v.*¹ Cf. the following, and see -EN².] To alight, dismount.

1697 *Lond. Gaz.* mmmcccxli/1 The Recorder also alightning,..the Proceeding from thence to Whitehall, was in manner following.

†**aˈlighten**, *v.*² *Obs.* [Secondary form of ALIGHT *v.*²; cf. LIGHT *v.*², LIGHTEN, and see -EN².] To lighten, relieve.

1530 PALSGR. 420/2, I alyghten of a burden or conforte in distresse. **1662** FULLER *Worthies* I. 282 On the fifth day Mr. Hedly died, whereby their Boat was somewhat allightned. **1781** BURNS *Corr.* (1846) 284 When for an hour or two my spirits are alightened.

†**aˈlighten**, *v.*³ *Obs.* [Secondary form of ALIGHT *v.*³ Cf. LIGHT *v.*³ *lighten*, *enlighten*; and see -EN².] To light up, illumine, enlighten.

1382 WYCLIF *1 Cor.* iv. 5 Schal aliȝtne the hid thingis of derknessis. *a* **1547** EARL SURREY *Aeneid* IV. 9 The next morow, with Phebus laump the earth Alightned clere. *c* **1630** JACKSON *Creed* IV. II. iv. Wks. III. 257 Beseeching him to alighten their hearts.

alighting (əˈlaɪtɪŋ), *vbl. sb.*¹ [f. ALIGHT *v.*¹ + -ING¹.] **a.** The action of descending or dismounting; descent, landing.

1297 R. GLOUC. 430 In þe..enleue hondered ȝer & seuene of our Lorde aly3tyn. **1548** W. THOMAS *Ital. Dict.*, *Scesa*, the alightyng or commyng downe. **1631** SALTONSTALL *Pict. Loq.* E iij b, At your first alighting hee straight offers you to see a Chamber. **1704** *Lond. Gaz.* mmmmlii/1 At Her alighting out of the Coach. **1727** SWIFT *Gulliver* III. ii. 182, I..was drawn up by pulleys. At my alighting I was surrounded by a crowd of people.

b. *Aeronaut.* = LANDING *vbl. sb.* 1 d. Also *attrib.*

1909 V. LOUGHEED *Vehicles of Air* 466 *Alighting gear*, the under mechanism of an aeroplane, used to cushion its descent and to bring it to a stop as it reaches the ground. **1914** *Aeronaut. Jrnl.* XVIII. 315 *Carriage*, that part of the aircraft..intended..to absorb the shock of alighting. **1927** *Flight* 3 Feb. 54/1 Compulsory alightings must be made at the end of each seven laps.

c. alighting-board: a board placed in or near a hen-house, bee-hive, or the like upon which hens, bees, etc., can alight.

1855 *Poultry Chron.* III. 61/2 It [*sc.* a bee] has measured every inch of the alighting-board, and now it flies off. **1926** *Chambers's Jrnl.* 12 June 435/1 Distraught bees run about on the alighting-board. **1950** *New Zealand Jrnl. Agric.* Nov. 446 The hinged alighting board [of the hen house] can be raised at night.

†**aˈlighting**, *vbl. sb.*² *Obs.* [f. ALIGHT *v.*³ + -ING¹.] The action of setting a light to, or kindling; *fig.* an incentive.

1340 *Ayenb.* 221 To moche drinke and to moche ethe is grat aliȝtinge to þe uere of lecherie.

align (əˈlaɪn), *v.* Also 7 **aline** [ad. mod.Fr. *aligne-r*, f. *à* to + *ligner*, ad. L. *līneā-re* to line, f. *līnea* a LINE; prob. due to phrase *à ligne*, 'into line.' As *line* is the Eng. spelling of Fr. *ligne* and *ligner*, there is no good reason for retaining the unetymological *g* in the derivative: see ALINER.]

1. To range, place, or lay in a line; to bring into line.

1693 EVELYN *De la Quint. Compl. Gard. Dict.*, To *Aline*, is to range, level, or lay even in, and to a strait and direct Line. Said of Walls, Rows of Trees, and sides of Banks, Allies, or Beds, which is performed with Lines fastened to Spikes fixed in the Ground or Wall. **1863** R. BURTON *Abeokuta* II. 135 Trees, so aligned that they presented a sharp edge to the gales. **1879** RUTLEY *Study Rocks* vii. 53 The cobweb is aligned on one of the faces of the crystal. **1881** *Daily News* 15 Sept. 3/4 The route will be in parts aligned and widened.

2. *intr.* (for *refl.*) To fall into line.

1877 KINGLAKE *Crimea* (ed. 6) IV. xiii. 415 The array in which Dundas consented to align with the French.

3. To bring two or more points into a straight line; spec. said of bringing the 'sights' of a rifle into line with the mark, so as to aim straight.

1860 *Hunt. Grounds O. World* Ser. I. xxvi. (ed. 2) 506 'Aiming drill'..teaching him how to 'align' his rifle, or 'aim' correctly at a mark. **1861** J. MACGREGOR in *Jrnl. Soc. Arts* IX. 477/2 A slight stoop of the head enables the eye to align the sights and the bull's-eye.

b. To get or take in a line with something else, as *e.g.* to hit with the same shot.

1853 KANE *Grinnell Exp.* xxxvii. (1856) 338 Regretting that my one ball could not align his mate.

4. *Politics.* To bring into line with a particular tradition, policy, group, or power. Also *refl.*

1934 WEBSTER s.v., To align nations against warfare. **1942** *Ann. Reg. 1941* 279 President Vargas..now showed himself..anxious to align his country with the democracies. **1955** *Treatm. Brit. P.O.W.'s in Korea (H.M.S.O.)* 2 If a prisoner refused to be educated..he was voluntarily aligning himself with the forces of reactionary capitalism.

‖**aligˈnation.** *rare.* [? Fr., f. *aligner* to ALIGN + -ATION.] = ALLINEATION, ALIGNMENT.

1866 SALA *Barbary* 331 Alignation is doing its best to spoil Oran structurally.

alignment (əˈlaɪnmənt). Also **aligne-**, **alline-**, **alinement.** [a. Fr. *alignement*, f. *aligner*: see ALINE and -MENT. The Eng. form *alinement* is preferable to *alignment*, a bad spelling of the Fr.]

1. a. Arrangement in a straight or other determined line; mode of arrangement in lines. *concr.* A line of things arranged.

1790 ROY in *Phil. Trans.* LXXX. 133 The deviation from the *allignement* horizontally or vertically. **1809** J. BARLOW *Columb.* v. 93 The crossing streets in just allinement run. **1839** MURCHISON *Silur. Syst.* I. xxx. 401 Which range from N.E. to S.W. in allinement with the other ridges. **1853** KANE *Grinnell Exp.* xli. (1856) 375 The alignment of the hills shows a northward drift. **1875** MERIVALE *Gen. Hist. Rome* lxxviii. (1877) 661 It was for this and other sacred ceremonies that its width and straight alignment were maintained. **1881** *Nature* XXV. 99 Archæological researches in the alignments or stone avenues of Kermario.

b. In various techn. uses (see quots.).

1892 *Perry & Co. Typewriter Prospectus* 2 Alignment is the first quality to be considered in purchasing a typewriter. **1904** Goodchild & Tweney *Technol. & Sci. Dict.* 11/1 *Alignment*, the correct placing in line of the parts of a machine or apparatus—*e.g.* the mandrel and loose centre of a lathe, or the front and back wheels of a bicycle. **1940** *Gloss. Highway Engin. Terms (B.S.I.)* 8 *Alignment*, the precise direction given to the centre line of a highway in plan. **1955** *Gloss. Acoust. Terms* (*B.S.I.*) 29 *Magnetic head alignment*, the adjustment of the magnetic gap in relation to the magnetic medium.

2. *spec.* Arrangement of soldiers in a line or lines; *concr.* a military 'line.'

1808 *Trial Gen. Whitelocke* I. 28 We were obliged to re-occupy our original alinement and position for pickets. **1816** James *Mil. Dict.* (ed. 4) 10 The *alignement* of a battalion means the situation of a body of men when drawn up in line: The *alignement* of a camp signifies the relative position of the tents, &c. so as to form a straight line from given points. **1829** G. Gleig *Chelsea Pensioners* (1840) 80 We had not assumed our alignement many minutes. **1860** Sir R. Wilson *Invas. Russia* 35 Its alignment had been pierced, and its communications obstructed. **1882** *Standard* 20 Nov. 5/6 Getting the Guards into their places in the general *alignement* on the Mall.

3. The drawing of a straight line in such a position that it shall pass through a particular point.

1869 *Eng. Mech.* 24 Sept. 6/1 What is known as allinement—drawing imaginary lines through two stars, and producing such lines until they pass close to, or through, others which we are seeking to identify. **1869** Dunkin *Midn. Sky* 146 The stars..are very easily found by alignment.

b. *concr.* A line (of section) through fixed points.

1879 C. King in *Cassell's Techn. Educ.* IV. 116/1 It adds much to the value of the plan if a section of the survey on any given alignment be given.

4. The action of bringing into line; straightening.

1879 C. King in *Cassell's Techn. Educ.* IV. 149/1 The straight edge of the ruler being used to guide the alignment. **1881** *Daily News* 15 Sept. 3/4 Between St. Mary-at-Hill and the Ship Tavern extensive alignments must take place.

5. *Politics.* The process or result of aligning (see align *v.* 4); the grouping or agreement of parties or powers. Also *transf.*

1933 *Planning* 25 Apr. 2 Its approach is not partisan, but cuts across existing political alignments. **1940** G. F. Hudson *Turkey, Greece & E. Medit.* 31 With Britain and France arrayed against Germany, and Italy neutral, the alinements in Western Europe are in the main those of the autumn of 1914. **1955** D. Davie *Articulate Energy* xiii. 154 The alignment of forces, for and against authentic syntax in poetry, is particularly clear. **1957** *Times* 11 May 6/3 The preservation of Jordan last month has bought time, and may have shifted the formal power of alignments of the Middle East.

6. *Comb.* **alignment chart** = nomogram; hence ***alignment diagram***.

1910 J. B. Peddle *Constr. Graphical Charts* ii. 15 A type of chart which has received considerable attention of late.. is that known as the alinement chart. *Ibid.* iii. 31 So far the alinement charts as described have only taken account of three variables. This is not a necessary limitation and we will next consider a case in which the number of variables is four. **1915** *Trans. Amer. Soc. Civil Engin.* LXXVIII. 1382 Nomographic solutions for formulas... The alignment diagram has all the advantages over diagrams plotted by rectangular co-ordinates. **1918** J. Lipka *Graphical & Mech. Computation* iii. 44 The fundamental principle involved in the construction of nomographic or alignment charts consists in the representation of an equation connecting three variables, f (*u*, *v*, *w*) = 0, by means of three scales along three curves (or straight lines) in such a manner that a straight line cuts the three scales in values of *u*, *v*, and *w* satisfying the equation.

‖**aligoté** (aligɔte). [F.] A white grape used for wine-making in Burgundy; the wine made from this grape.

1912 P. Allen *Burgundy* xvii. 247 The best wines of all are called Aligote, and the second-best—still very good—are called Pinot. **1924** H. W. Allen *Wines of France* iii. 167 The best ordinary white wines are made in Burgundy from the *aligoté* grape. *Ibid.*, The *aligoté* wine..keeps well. **1958** *Spectator* 13 June 782/3 The travelling qualities of aligote—cheapest and least fragile of white burgundies.

'aligreek. *rare*⁻¹. [A corrupt form of It. *alla Greca*, or of Fr. transl. *à la Grecque*; the moulding is in Fr. called simply *Grecque*.] A mæander, fret, or 'key' pattern; 'Greek fret' or 'Greek border.'

[*a* **1884** *Archit. Publ. Soc. Dict.* s.v. *Mæander*, As *guillochis* or *méandres* are known in Italy as *alla Greca*, so the word *grecque* is likely to remain in France the technical name of the *méandre*.] **1873** Burton *Hist. Scot.* I. iv. 156 A moulding ..called technically the single meander and the aligreek.

aliicide ('eɪlɪaɪˌsaɪd). *nonce-wd.* [f. L. *alius* another + *-cide*; in allusion to suicide.] Murder.

1868 *Punch* 19 Dec. 263/1 To take a mad freak..and commit suicide or aliicide.

alike (ə'laɪk), *a.* Forms: α. 1–2 **ȝelíc**, 2–4 **ilich(e**, 5 **yleche**. β. 4–5 **alyche** (5 **aleche**, 6 **aleeche**). γ. 2–5 **ilik(e**, 5 **illike**, **ilyke**, **ylyke**, **ylike**. δ. 5–6 **alyke**, 6– **alike**. [Here, as in alike *adv.*, two, if not three, earlier words seem blended: 1. OE. *ȝelíc* (OS. *gelîc*, *gilîc*, OFris. *gelîk*, OHG. *ge-*, *gi-*, *ga-lîh*, mod.G. *gleich*, Goth. *galeiks*, ON. *glîkr*), f. *ge-*:—*ga-* together + *líc* like; 2. ON. *álíkr* (cogn. w. OE. *anlíc*, *onlíc*, Goth. *analeiks*, OHG. *ana(ga)lîh*, MHG. *anelîch*), f. *á* prep. on, unto, to + *lik* like; 3. The OE. *anlíc* itself survived to 14th c., and would naturally also give *alike*, *alich*, as its later form; see anlike. The mod. *alike* seems mainly due to the ON., the 15th c. repr. of OE. *ȝelíc* being *ilich*; but the example of afford, and the *a-* for *ȝe-* in s.w. dial., show that *ȝelíc* might have given *alike* independently.]

Like one another, similar, of identical form or character. (Now almost always predicatively; and of, or referring to, things in the plural.)

α. *c* **950** *Lindisf. G.* Matt. xxii. 39 Ðe æftera ȝelic is ðisum. *c* **1000** *Ags. G.* ibid., Oðyr ys þysum ȝelic. *c* **1160** *Hatton G.* ibid., Oðer is þan ȝelic. *c* **1175** *Pater N.* 38 in *Lamb. Hom.* 57 And þis oðer..þis is ilich. *c* **1260** *Signs bef. Judgm.* in *E.E.P.* 10 Al we sul ben ilich. **1340** *Ayenb.* 196 Þe poure þet is ilich þe. *c* **1400** *Beryn* 736 Noon to hym I-lich of worship, ne of wele. *c* **1420** *Chron. Vilod.* 100 Thre wax candels..Every candel y leche of weyȝt.

β. *c* **1385** Chaucer *Leg. G. Wom.* 389 Al be that here stat be nat a-lyche [*v.r.* yliche⁻⁵].

γ. *c* **1175** *Lamb. Hom.* 151 Under houene ne nan is ilike. *a* **1300** *K. Horn* 502 Þer was no kniȝt hym ilik. **1391** Chaucer *Astrol.* I. xvii. 9 Than ben the daies & the nyhtes illike of lengthe. **1413** Lydg. *Pylgr. Sowle* IV. xxvi. (1483) 71 Tho two that ben y lyke.

δ. **1440** *Promp. Parv.*, Alyke or euynlyke, *Equalis*. Alyke or lyke yn lykenes, *Similis*. **1590** Shaks. *Com. Err.* I. i. 56 Male, twins, both alike. **1756** Burke *Vind. Nat. Soc.* Wks. I. 43 High, low, men, women, clergy, and laity, are all alike. **1768** Sterne *Sent. Journ.* (1778) II. 87 They are become so much alike, you can scarce distinguish one shilling from another. **1812** Combe (Dr. Syntax) *Picturesque* viii. 29 Alike the laurel to the truly brave; That binds the brow or consecrates the grave. **1837** J. H. Newman *Par. Serm.* (ed. 3) I. xvii. 255 They begin to think all religions alike.

In various other const. Now *rare.*

1535 Coverdale *Wisd.* xi. 11 Whether they were absent or present, their punyshment was alyke. **1615** T. Adams *Spirit. Nav.* 20 You see the alike distastefulness of the world and sea. **1634** Canne *Necess. Sep.* (1849) 46 It is a like to have no minister at all, as to have an idol in the place of a true minister. **1637** Earl Monm. *Romulus & Tarq.* 12 Children, for the most part, side with the belly; and their change is easie, where are alike qualities. **1640** Fuller *Joseph's Coat* vii. (1867) 181 Moses..made it in all things alike to the pattern he saw in the mount. **1653** Ashwell *Fides Apost.* 102 The Romane-Catholik, who with alike loudnes and lying proclaimes to the world, etc. **1658** J. R. *Mouffet's Theat. Ins.* 944 This of the male kinde. The female is almost alike, but somewhat more black. **1680** W. Allen *Persw. Peace* 83 To consist of somewhat alike mixture as that of the Jews of old did. **1748** Hartley *Observ. Man* I. iii. §2. ¶87 Where the Instances are alike..to that under Consideration. **1867** Morris *Jason* IX. 170 A golden glittering sun That seemed well-nigh alike the heavenly one. **1920** D. H. Lawrence *Lost Girl* vi. 112 Oh, but he was always alike. **1938** E. Bowen *Death of Heart* III. i. 339 Thomas and Portia turned their alike profiles in the direction from which the breeze came.

alike (ə'laɪk), *adv.* Forms: α. 1–2 **ȝelíce**, 2–5 **iliche**, 4–5 **ilyche**, 5 **yliche**, **ylyche**, **ylich**. β. 4–5 **aliche**, 5 **eliche**, **alych(e**, **aleche**. γ. 3–5 **olike**, **olyke**. δ. 4–5 **ilike**, **ilyke**, **ylyke**, 4–6 **ylike**. ε. 5–6 **elyke**, **elike**. ζ. 6 **alyke**, 6– **alike**. [Like the prec. represents two (or three) orig. words: 1. OE. *ȝelíce* adv., f. *ȝelíc* adj. 2. ON. *álíka* adv., f. *álíkr* adj., cogn. w. OE. *anlíce*, which may also itself be one of the sources of ME. *aliche*. Since 1500 *alike* has taken the place of all the ME. forms.] In like manner, in the same manner, in the same way, at the same rate, equally, similarly.

α. *a* **1000** *Blickl. Hom.* 119 Ne wæron ðas ealle ȝelice lange. *c* **1175** *Cotton Hom.* 219 He geð of þe fader and of þe sune ȝelice. *c* **1175** *Pater N.* 60 in *Lamb. Hom.* 57 His name is hali and efre wes iliche swiðe. *c* **1300** *St. Brand.* 714 This frut is evere iliche ripe, and this lond iliche liȝt. **1369** Chaucer *Dethe of Bl.* 9 Al is ylyche goode to me Joy or sorrowe wherso hyt be. **1485** Caxton *Trevisa's Higden* I. xliv. (1527) 44 All these iii Ilondes, Wyght, Mon and Man ben almoost yliche moche and of lyke quantyte.

β. *c* **1325** *E.E. Allit. P.* B. 1477 Al aliche dresset. **1393** Gower *Conf.* I. 297 Ever in one aliche hot. **1399** Langl. *Rich. Redeless* I. 66 All eliche grette. *c* **1440** *Morte Arth.* 194 Seyne come þer sewes sere..Ownd of aȝure alle over and ardant þem semyde, Of ilke aleche þe lowe launschide fulle hye. **1480** Caxton *Chron. Eng.* lxxvii. 63 Al shold be alych hygh.

γ. *c* **1250** *Gen. & Ex.* 2024 Al it was him olike loð. *c* **1340** Hampole *Pr. Consc.* 7560 Alle er þa noght olyke clere. *c* **1430** *St. Katherine* (Gibbs MS.) 47 Olyke endeles wyth his maker.

δ. **1377** Langl. *P. Pl.* B. xix. 436 Alle tymes y-like. *c* **1385** Chaucer *Leg. G. Wom.* 57 And evene I-like fayr & fresch of hewe. *Ibid.* 731 And bothe in love I-lyke sore they brente. **1486** *Bk. St. Alban's*, *Fysshynge* 13 Fasten theym in thee clyftes ylyke streyghte. **1579** Spenser *Sheph. Cal.* Mar., My selfe will have a double eye, Ylike to my flocke and thine.

ε. *a* **1400** *Relig. Pieces fr. Thornton MS.* 51 The gud lady Meknes þat aye elyke makis hir selfe lowly. *c* **1460** *Towneley Myst.* 57 A bush I se burnand fulle bryght, And ever elyke the leyfes ar greyn. **1513** Douglas *Æ neis* x. viii. 34 My fader ..Reputis all elike.

ζ. **1535** Coverdale *Eccles.* ix. 3 It happeneth vnto all alyke. **1611** Shaks. *Cymb.* I. vi. 148 A lady, that disdains Thee, and the devil alike. **1667** Milton *P.L.* IV. 640 All seasons and thir change, all please alike. **1712** Steele *Spect.* No. 509 ¶9 To treat his customers all alike. **1764** Goldsm. *Trav.* 81 Nature, a mother kind alike to all. **1824** Dibdin *Libr. Comp.* 87 He would sacrifice alike logic and candour. **1849** Macaulay *Hist. Eng.* I. 194 The minister's virtues and vices alike contributed to his ruin. **1879** Froude *Cæsar* ii. 18 By means which demoralised alike the givers and receivers.

Comb. †**alike-minded** *a.*, of a like mind, like-minded.

1638 Sanderson *21 Serm.* Ad Aul. viii. (1673) 118 The strong agreed well enough among themselves, and were all alike-minded, and so the weak among themselves, all alike-minded too. *a* **1656** Bp. Hall *Rem.* 82 (T.) I would to God ..all our brethren of this land, were alike-minded.

a'likeness. In 5 alyckeness. [f. alike *a.* + -ness.] Likeness, similarity, similitude.

c **1400** *Circumc.* (Turnb. 1843) 87 Lyke of alyckenes as hit is devysed That Cryst Jesus..was truly cyrcumsysed. **1920** *Times* 25 Sept. 11/6 This alikeness is not confined to the features and clothing of Americans, but it is noticeable in their thought and conversation. The whole tendency is towards levelling. **1924** *Public Opinion* 6 Dec. 572/1 The fundamental alikeness of God and man. **1960** E. Bowen *Time in Rome* ii. 65 There is an alikeness between all and any nights in the same place.

†**a'likewise.** *Obs.* Forms: 5 alyke-wise, 6 Sc. elikewise, elykewyse. [f. alike *a.* + wise *sb.*, way, manner.] Perh. in *Promp. Parv.* three words, *a like wise*, 'in like manner.'

1440 *Promp. Parv.*, Allelykely, or euynly (*v.r.* a lykewyse or euynly) *Equaliter*. **1513** G. Douglas *Æneis* I. Pref. 241 Elikewise eik this Caxtoun all in vane Crispina clippis Sibilla Cwmane. **1556** Lauder *Tract.* (1864) 34 Rycht as the sande hour in the glasse, Elykewyse dois thare tyme heir passe.

aliment ('ælɪmənt). [a. Fr. *aliment* (16th c. in Littré), or ad. its original, L. *aliment-um*, f. *al-ĕre* to nourish: see -ment.]

1. The material or means of nourishing; that which nourishes or feeds; nutriment, food.

1477 Norton *Ord. Alch.* (in Ashmole 1652) v. 76 Liquors conveieth all Aliment and Food To every part of Mans Body. **1605** Bacon *Adv. Learn.* II. (1873) xxv. §15 In the body there are three degrees of that we receive into it, aliment, medicine and poison. **1646** Sir T. Browne *Pseud. Ep.* 378 Poysons may meet with tempers whereto they may become Aliments. **1682** Grew *Anat. Plants* Introd. 3 The Aliment by which a Plant is fed. **1743** tr. *Heister's Surg.* 110 Fluid Aliments, such as Broths or Soups. **1877** Huxley *Anat. Inv. An.* iv. 204 A mouth and gullet..admit aliment to the digestive sac.

2. *fig.* That which supports or sustains the mind, a quality, state, etc.; sustenance, support.

a **1631** Donne *Serm.* lxxxi. Wks. IV. 8 The world is one body and Marriage the Aliment. **1665–9** Boyle *Occas. Refl.* IV. ix. (1675) 224 The means of grace..are piety's true and improving Aliments. **1741** Richardson *Pamela* (1824) I. 92 Mischief, love, and contradiction, are the natural aliments of a woman. **1872** Liddon *Elem. Relig.* iv. 143 Vice is not a necessary aliment, it is not even a necessary foil to virtue.

3. *Sc. Law* and *gen.* Provision for the maintenance of any one, called in Eng. Law alimony; an allowance, annuity or pension.

1640–1 *Kirkcudbr. War-Comm. Min. Bk.* (1855) 167 Allowing to the said Margaret, for hir and hir childrene thair aliment and mantenance..aught hundred merks. **1780** Howard *Prisons in Eng. & Wales* 6 The expense of sueing for the aliment. **1865** Carlyle *Fredk. Gt.* IX. xx. ix. 166 He had some pension or aliment from the Austrian Court. **1881** *Fifeshire Jrnl.* 15 Jan. 5/5 Inspector of Poor sued James Baxter for the board of his father in the Poorhouse..Decree was given for aliment at the rate of 2s. 6d. a week.

aliment ('ælɪmənt), *v.* [a. Fr. *alimente-r* (14th c. in Littré). Cf. med.L. *alimentā-re*, f. *aliment-um*: see prec.]

†**1.** To nourish, supply with food, feed. *Obs.*

1490 Caxton *Eneydos* xxix. 113 She hathe alymented and noryshed her from the owre of hyr birthe.

2. *fig.* To maintain, sustain, support.

1663 G. Mackenzie *Relig. Stoica* (1685) Addr., There is Heavenly Mannah enough to aliment us all. **1789** T. Jefferson *Writ.* (1859) III. 95 They will furnish him money liberally to aliment a civil war. **1842** Chalmers *Lect. Rom.* I. 42 Not fitted to aliment the faith and the holiness.

3. *Sc. Law* and *gen.* To make provision for the maintenance of; to pension.

1629 *Marriage Contract* in *Rep. Hist. MSS.* (1871) 168/2 To educate and aliment them according to their rank. **1837** Lockhart *Scott* (1839) V. 320 They would have alimented the honest man decently among them for a lay figure. **1861** Sir R. Phillimore *Intern. Law* (1874) IV. 239 To compel an English mother to aliment a child born in Scotland.

alimental (ælɪ'mɛntəl), *a.* ? *Obs.* [f. aliment *sb.* + -al[1], as if ad. L. **alimentāl-is*.] Of or pertaining to aliment; of the nature of food; furnishing food or nourishment, nutritious, feeding.

1586 Bright *Melanch.* iv. 20 Everie parte of that we take for nourishment is not alimentall. **1646** Sir. T. Browne *Pseud. Ep.* Pref., These weeds must lose their alimentall sappe and wither. **1706** J. Philips *Cyder* I. 132 At the Foot of ev'ry Plant To sink a circling Trench, and daily pour A just Supply of alimental Streams. **1751** Chambers *Cycl.*, *Alimentary, alimental*, something that relates to aliment, or food. [Also in mod. Dicts.]

alimentally (ælɪ'mɛntəlɪ), *adv.* ? *Obs.* [f. prec. + -ly[2].] In an alimental manner; in the way of affording aliment or nourishment; nutritiously.

1633 T. Adams *Comm. 2 Pet.* i. 6 (1865) 73 It [drink] servith alimentally for the body's strength. **1646** Sir T. Browne *Pseud. Ep.* 85 The substance of gold is invincible.. not only alimentally in a substantiall mutation, but also medicamentally in any corporeall conversion. [Also in mod. Dicts.]

ali'mentariness. ? *Obs.*—[0] [f. ALIMENTARY + -NESS.] The quality of being alimentary.

1731 BAILEY, *Alimentariness*, nourishing quality. [Also in mod. Dicts.]

alimen'tarious, *a.* *Obs.* *rare*—[1]. [f. L. *alimentāri-us* (see next) + -OUS.] = ALIMENTARY.

1684 tr. *Bonet's Merc. Compit.* x. 358 The root has something spirituous and alimentarious in it.

alimentary (ælɪ'mɛntərɪ), *a.* (and *sb.*) [ad. L. *alimentāri-us*; f. *aliment-um*: see ALIMENT and -ARY.]

1. Of the nature of aliment; alimental; nutritious.

1615 CROOKE *Body of Man* 30 To restraine the word Humors to the Alimentarie, and not to include the Excrementitious. **1667** *Phil. Trans.* II. 513 The alimentary Juyce passes through the Umbilical vessels. **1746** R. JAMES *Introd. Mouffet & B's Health's Impr.* (1746) 25 Milk loses.. a great deal of its alimentary Virtues, if once boiled. **1870** ROLLESTON *Anim. Life* 27 Dependent therefore upon ciliary action for the injection of alimentary matter.

2. Concerned with the function of nutrition. ***alimentary canal***: the whole channel or passage through the body for receiving and digesting food and ejecting excrementitious matter.

1620 VENNER *Via Recta* Introd. 8 There are some.. waters, not to be allowed for alimentary vses. **1733** G. CHEYNE *Eng. Mal.* II. viii. §5 (1734) 196 The Alimentary tubes being the first sensible Sufferers in all Bodily Maladies. **1842** WILSON *Anat. Vade Mec.* 508 The Alimentary canal is a musculo-membranous tube, extending from the mouth to the anus. **1865** L. SIMPSON *Dining* ii. (ed. 3) 27 Physics and chemistry have been called in to the aid of the alimentary art.

3. Connected with sustenance or maintenance; providing maintenance.

1751 CHAMBERS *Cycl.*, *Alimentary Law* was an old law among the Romans, whereby children were obliged to find sustenance for their parents. **1831** SOUTHEY in *Q. Rev.* XLV. 423 An alimentary pension from his family. **1875** MERIVALE *Gen. Hist. Rome* lxv. (1877) 524 Supplying the necessities of the Italians by alimentary endowments.

†**4.** Depending on the maintenance of others; supported by charity or public provision. *Obs.*

1751 CHAMBERS *Cycl.* s.v., Trajan was the first that brought up any of these alimentary boys.

†**B.** *sb.* An almsman. *Obs.*

? **1617** MINSHEU (in Wright), An *Alimentarie*, he to whom a man giveth his meat and drinke by his last will.

alimentation (ˌælɪmən'teɪʃən). [ad. med.L. *alimentātiōn-em*, n. of action f. *alimentā-re*: see ALIMENT *v.*]

1. The action or process of affording aliment; nourishment, nutrition.

1656 BLOUNT *Glossogr.*, *Alimentation*, nourishment, or that causeth or breeds nourishment. **1753** CHAMBERS *Cycl. Supp.*, *Alimentation* is used, by some naturalists, for what we more ordinarily call nutrition. **1849–52** TODD *Cycl. Anat. & Phys.* IV. 1203/2 The tentacula of the Bryozoa..are subservient to the purposes of alimentation. **1872** HUXLEY *Physiol.* i. 15 The organs which convert food into nutriment are the organs of alimentation.

2. The process of being nourished, the mode in which any one is nourished.

1605 BACON *Adv. Learn.* (1640) 170 A man that..hath thoroughly observed the nature of Assimilation and of Alimentation. **1626** —— *Sylva* §602 Plants do nourish: inanimate bodies do not; they have an Accretion, but no Alimentation. **1830** LYELL *Princ. Geol.* (1875) II. III. xliii. 477 That climate..social condition, alimentation, and mode of life may have determined originally the diversity of races.

3. The supplying with the necessaries of life; maintenance, support.

1590 SWINBURN *Testaments* 201 As if he did bequeath it vnto hir for hir alimentation. **1850** MERIVALE *Rom. Emp.* (1865) VIII. lxvi. 193 The alimentation of poor children.. was extended or increased by fresh endowments.

alimentative (ælɪ'mɛntətɪv), *a.* *rare.* [f. L. *alimentāt* ppl. stem of *alimentā-re* (see ALIMENT *v.*) + -IVE.] Connected with the supply of aliment.

1881 HUXLEY in *Nature* No. 615. 346 Abnormal states of the physiological units..[or] of their co-ordinating and alimentative machinery.

ali'mentativeness. [f. prec. + -NESS.] A more analogical equivalent of ALIMENTIVENESS.

1850 *Pop. Encycl.* s.v. *Phrenology*, Alimentativeness..is a propensity to eat and drink.

alimenter ('ælɪməntə(r)). [f. ALIMENT *v.* + -ER[1].] One who, or that which, affords aliment, or feeds.

1869 *Eng. Mech.* 24 Sept. 16/1 The automaton alimenter [for supplying water to a boiler].

alimenting ('ælɪməntɪŋ), *vbl. sb.* [f. as prec. + -ING[1].] The supplying of aliment; maintenance.

1696 *Lond. Gaz.* mmmccxxviii/2 Act anent the Alimenting of poor Prisoners.

alimentiveness (ælɪ'mɛntɪvnɪs). [f. adj. *alimentive* (not cited) + -NESS. Cf. the more analogical ALIMENTATIVE, and mod.Fr. *alimentivité*.]

The instinct which impels an animal to seek food, to which some have assigned a special 'organ' in the brain.

1825 COMBE *Syst. Phrenol.* (ed. 5) I. 280 Dr. Hoppe considers that the organ of Alimentiveness is likewise the organ of the sense of taste. **1845** *Vestig. Creat.* (ed. 3) 327 The alimentiveness of such animals as the dog..can be pampered or educated up to a kind of epicurism.

†**ali'mentous,** *a.* *Obs.* [f. Fr. *alimenteux*, f. *aliment*, as if f. L. **alimentōsus*: see -OUS.] = ALIMENTARY.

1662 H. STUBBE *Ind. Nectar* v. 78 This was refrigerating, and very alimentous. **1727** BRADLEY *Fam. Dict.* s.v. *Distilling*, Several [waters] are medicinal and alimentous.

†**'alimon,** *sb.* *Herb.* *Obs.* [Apparently a. Gr. ἅλιμον, 'a shrubby plant growing on the shore, perh. salt-wort,' Liddell & Scott; prop. neut. (sc. φυτόν) of ἅλιμος maritime. Confused by early herbalists with Gr. ἄλῑμον, 'banishing hunger,' whence this attribute ascribed to the plant.]

A plant fabled to dispel hunger; perh. *Atriplex halimus* of the Levant, identified by modern botanists with the ἅλιμον of the Greeks.

1572 BOSSEWELL *Armorie* III. 17b, Gesante an Alimon proper..The Herbe aforesaide, which he beareth, is of that nature, that it will not suffer them that taste it, to be hungrye. **1601** HOLLAND *Pliny* (1634) II. 128 Ther is an herb..called Alimon: about which writers haue erred not a little.

†**ali'monious,** *a.* *Obs.* *rare.* [f. ALIMONY + -OUS: cf. *ceremonious*.] Supplying nourishment or sustenance.

1659 *Lady Alimony* v. vi. in Hazl. *Dods.* XIV. 366 Alimonious wages To feed their boundless riot! **1666** G. HARVEY *Morbus Angl.* (J.) They are incapacitated of digesting the alimonious humours into flesh.

alimony ('ælɪmənɪ). [ad. L. *alimōnia* nutriment; f. *al-ēre* to nourish: see -MONY.]

1. Nourishment; supply of the means of living, maintenance.

1656 COWLEY *Avarice* (1710) II. 755 To see, that he should not want Alimony befitting his Condition. **1684** tr. *Bonet's Merc. Compit.* VI. 193 That she may have strength against both her enemies, she has need of more ample Alimony. **1726** AYLIFFE *Parerg.* 58 These words Alimony and Victuals are used in a larger Acceptation, and denote all kind of maintenance whatever..as Meat, Drink, Cloathes. **1827** GEN. P. THOMPSON *Exerc.* (1842) IV. 543 Paying each of the members of the aristocracy an alimony from the public purse. **1876** E. MELLOR *Priesth.* ii. 50 The age and character they [widows] must bear before they are entitled to such benevolent alimony.

b. *fig.*

1660 JER. TAYLOR *Worthy Commun.* i. §1. 18 These men will allow the Sacraments to be..spiritual alimony. *a* **1670** HACKET *Cent. Serm.* 287 His benediction is alimony enough though there were no meat in the world.

2. *esp.* The allowance which a wife is entitled to from her husband's estate, for her maintenance, on separation from him for certain causes.

1655 FULLER *Ch. Hist.* III. 58 He should appoint the said Emme Pinkney reasonable Alimony. **1721** MRS. CENTLIVRE *Marplot* II. i. 143 A wound in the reputation of an English woman, they say, only lets in Alimony. **1858** LD. ST. LEONARDS *Handy Bk. Prop. Law* XII. 73 The Court can direct the husband to pay alimony.

†**a'limp,** *v.* *Obs.* *rare.* [f. A- *pref.* 1 intens. + LIMP.] To befall, happen (to any one).

a **1000** *Beowulf* 1249 Oþþæt sæl alamp. **1205** LAYAM. 18053 þa while him a-lomp [**1250** bi-fulle] wurs.

†**a'line,** *adv.*, prop. *phr.*, *Obs.* [A *prep.*[1] in + LINE.] In a line

1391 CHAUCER *Astrol.* II. xxxviii, Draw a strike, euene alyne fro the pyn vn-to Middel prikke.

aline: see ALIGN *v.*

A-line ('eɪlaɪn), *sb.* and *a.* [f. A + LINE *sb.*[2] (see below).] **A.** *sb.* An A-line garment. **B.** *adj.* Of a garment (esp. a dress or skirt): flared from the shoulder or waist to the hem in the shape of the letter A.

1955 *Punch* 16 Mar. 348/1 Christian Dior's A-line—the most significant cipher since the S-curve of the Edwardian Gibson Girl. **1969** *Sears Catal.* Spring/Summer 20/2 A-line with smart contrast stitching. *Ibid.* 275/2 A-line skirt. Jute belt; contour top. **1976** *New Yorker* 21 June 70/1 (Advt.), In scaled-down but generous A-line with sleeves to roll or not. **1980** L. BIRNBACH et al. *Official Preppy Handbk.* 132/1 Because it is an A-line, it is never really in style or out.

alineation, variant of ALLINEATION.

alinement: see ALIGNMENT.

aliner (ə'laɪnə(r)). [f. *aline*, ALIGN *v.* + -ER[1].] One who lays out things in lines, or brings them to a straight line.

1693 EVELYN *De la Quint. Compl. Gard. Dict.*, *Aliners* are ..Men imployed in the abovesaid work of Ranging, or Levelling Rows of Trees, Walls, &c. It were well our English Gard'ners would naturalize those two Words, not being otherwise able to express their signification without a Circumlocution, and having with less necessity naturalized many other forreign terms, without so much as altering their Termination, which in these I have made perfectly English.

alio-relative (ˌælɪəʊ'rɛlətɪv), *sb.* *Philos.* [f. L. *ali-us* other + -O + RELATIVE *a.* and *sb.*] Peirce's term for 'a relation which no term can have to itself' (see quot. 1873). Hence as *adj.* = IRREFLEXIVE *a.*

1873 C. S. PEIRCE in *Mem. Amer. Acad. Arts & Sci.* IX. II. 369 Simple relatives are divisible into those which contain elements of the form (A:A) and those which do not. The former express relations such as a thing may have to itself, the latter (as cousin of ——, hater of ——) relations which nothing can have to itself. The former may be termed *self-relatives*, the latter *alio-relatives*. **1920** B. RUSSELL *Introd. Math. Philos.* (ed. 2) iv. 33 It often happens that a relation is an aliorelative without being asymmetrical. **1934** *Mind* XLIII. 224 This is also guaranteed by my definition ..provided R [*sc.* a relation] is assumed alio-relative.

aliped ('ælɪpɛd), *a.* and *sb.* [ad. L. *ālipĕd-em*, f. *āla* wing + *ped-em* foot.]

A. *adj.*

1. Wing-footed, having wings on the feet, like the figures of Mercury; *hence*, swift-footed.

1731 BAILEY and **1775** ASH, *Alipede*, nimble, swift of foot.

2. *Zool.* Having the toes connected by a membrane which serves as a wing, as in the bat.

1847 in CRAIG.

B. *sb.* An animal having the structure described in A 2; a cheiropterous animal.

1847 in CRAIG.

aliphatic (ælɪ'fætɪk), *a.* *Chem.* [f. Gr. ἀλειφατ-, ἄλειφαρ unguent, fat + -IC]. Fatty; epithet of organic compounds having an open-chain structure.

1889 M'GOWAN tr. *Bernthsen's Org. Chem.* vi. 146 The saturated alcohols yielding the saturated monobasic fatty acids, or 'acids of the aliphatic series' as they are termed. **1895** F. P. MÖLLER *Cod-liver Oil & Chem.* 7 The aliphatic series. *Ibid.* 83 The aliphatic hydrocarbons. **1958** *Sci. News* XLIX. 44 In general, dimethyl silicone fluids are readily soluble in aliphatic and aromatic hydrocarbons.

alipite ('ælɪpaɪt). *Min.* [mod. f. Gr. ἀλιπ-ής without fat, not greasy + -ITE.] An apple-green, non-unctuous, earthy mineral, containing about 33 per cent. of Oxide of Nickel; placed by Dana in his Dioptase group of Hydrous Bisilicates.

aliquant ('ælɪkwənt), *a.* *Math.* [a. Fr. *aliquante*, ad. L. *aliquant-um* somewhat, a certain amount of; f. *ali-us* some or other + *quant-us* how great, how much.] In the phrase ***aliquant part***: Contained in another, but not dividing it evenly, and so opposed to *aliquot*.

1695 W. ALINGHAM *Geom. Epit.* 17 An Aliquant part is a lesser Number in respect of a greater, when it doth not measure it exactly, as 3 is an aliquant part of 7, because it is not contained precisely any Number of times in 7. [Similarly in JOHNSON, ASH, CRAIG, etc.]

aliquot ('ælɪkwɒt), *a.* and *sb.* *Math.* [a. Fr. *aliquote*, a. L. *aliquot* some, so many, f. *ali-us* some or other + *quot* how many.]

A. *adj.* In phrase ***aliquot part***: Contained in another a certain number of times without leaving any remainder; forming an exact measure of.

1570 BILLINGSLEY *Euclid* v. def. i. 126 This..is called..a measuring part..and of the barbarous it is called..an aliquote part. **1672** *Phil. Trans.* VII. 5153 The Aliquot parts or Just Divisors. **1695** W. ALINGHAM *Geom. Epit.* 16 An aliquot part is a lesser Number in respect of a greater, when it measures it exactly, as 2 is an aliquot part of 6, because it is contained just 3 times in it. **1757** JOS. HARRIS *Money & Coins* 9 None of our coins are aliquot or even parts of our weights. **1849** MRS. SOMERVILLE *Connex. Phys. Sc.* xvii. 157 On the string at the half, third, fourth or other aliquot points.

B. *sb.* An aliquot part. (See also quot. 1955.)

1610 HEALEY *St. Aug., City of God* 434 This kinde of part we call an aliquote. **1777** SIR W. JONES *Ess.* ii. 196 Accessory sounds..caused by the aliquots of a sonorous body vibrating at once. **1866** SIR J. HERSCHEL *Fam. Lect. Sc.* 423 The length of any object stated to contain a given number of such units or its aliquots. **1955** *Gloss. Terms Radiology (B.S.I.)* 65 *Aliquot*, a small sample of radioactive material assayed in order to determine the radioactivity of the whole. **1962** *Lancet* 6 Jan. 53/2 Deep-frozen aliquots were sent to the departments where the methods were evolved.

†**a'liry,** *adv.* *Obs.* *rare*—[1]. [Cf. LIRYLONG. Perh. f. OE. *lima lyre* loss of (the use of) limbs (E. J. Dobson in *Eng. & Germ. Stud.* (1948) I. 60): then quot. 1362 would mean 'made their legs lame, acted as if paralysed'. Connection with mod. dial. ALAIRY *adv.* is also possible.] Of the legs: ? Across each other.

1362 LANGL. *P. Pl.* A. VII. 115 Summe leiden þe legges aliri [*v.r.* a lery, a lyry] as suche losels cunne.

alisaunder, obs. form of ALEXANDER(S.

†**a'lise,** *v.* *Obs.* *rare.* [f. A- *pref.* 1 (or 6) + OE. *hlīs-ian* to fame.] To report, name by report, allege by rumour or report.

c **1305** *E.E. Poems* (1862) 67 So þat me nute maide non-alised ȝe þe.

alish ('eılıʃ), *a.* [f. ALE + -ISH. Cf. *waterish.*] Having somewhat of the qualities of ale.
1707 J. MORTIMER *Husb.* (J.) Beating down the yeast gives it the sweet alish taste.

‖**alisma** (ə'lızmə). *Bot.* [a. L., a. Gr. ἄλισμα a water-plant mentioned by Dioscor.] A genus of aquatic endogenous plants, the type of N.O. *Alismaceæ*; applied esp. to the species *A. Plantago*, a plant common in ponds and ditches.
1736 BAILEY *Househ. Dict.*, *Alisma*..is sudorifick, and dissolves coagulated blood. **1863** O. MEREDITH *King of Amasis* I. II. ii. 112 Upshoots, with graceful pyramid of white thick-clustered flowers, the delicate alisma.

alismaceous (ælız'meıʃəs), *a. Bot.* [f. prec. + -ACEOUS.] Of or belonging to the N.O. *Alismaceæ* or Alismads.

alismad (ə'lızməd). *Bot.* [f. ALISMA + -AD.] A plant of the order *Alismaceæ*: see ALISMA.
1847 CRAIG s.v. *Alismaceæ*, Such plants as the *Ranunculus parnassifolius* are hardly distinguishable from Alismads.

alismal (ə'lızməl), *a. Bot.* [f. ALISMA + -AL^{1}.] Of or pertaining to alisma; epithet of Lindley's alliance of plants containing the alismads and kindred orders.

alismoid (ə'lızmɔıd), *a. Bot.* [f. ALISMA + -OID.] Alisma-like.

alisonite ('ælısənaıt). *Min.* [Named after Mr. R. E. Alison of Chili; see -ITE.] A variety of the Sulphid ore COVELLITE found in Chili.
1837-80 DANA *Min.* 84 Alisonite is an indigo-copper, containing a much larger proportion of lead than the cantonite.

alispheno- (ælıs'fi:nəʊ), combining form of ALISPHENOID *a.*, as in **alispheno-parietal**.
1866 HUXLEY *Preh. Rem. Caithn.* 153 No observer..says a word about either the alispheno-frontal, or the alispheno-parietal, sutures.

alisphenoid (ælıs'fi:nɔıd), *a.* and *sb. Phys.* [mod. f. L. *āla* wing + SPHENOID, f. Gr. σφηνοειδής wedge-shaped.]
A. *adj.* Forming the wing of the sphenoid bone at the base of the skull, or pertaining to this part.
1846 OWEN in *Rep. Brit. Assoc.* 179 'Alisphenoid' seemed to retain most of the old anthropotomical term of 'alæ majores,' or wings 'par excellence' of the os sphenoideum. **1864** HUXLEY in *Reader* 19 Mar. 365/1 The constant union of the alisphenoid with the parietal bones. **1881** MIVART *Cal.* 477 The passage thus enclosed called the alisphenoid canal.
B. *sb.* An alisphenoid bone.
1849-52 TODD *Cycl. Anat. & Phys.* IV. 1297/2 The longer basisphenoid, and shorter alisphenoids. **1866** HUXLEY *Preh. Rem. Caithn.* 150 The sutures surrounding the alisphenoid..have been prematurely ossified in the Neanderthal skull.

alisphenoidal (ˌælısfi:'nɔıdəl), *a. Phys.* [f. prec. + -AL^{1}.] Pertaining to the wings of the sphenoid bone.
1849-52 TODD *Cycl. Anat. & Phys.* IV. 1298/1 Alisphenoidal..air-cells. **1866** HUXLEY *Preh. Rem. Caithn.* 153 If alisphenoidal synostosis is the cause of the frontal depression of the Neanderthal skull.

alit, poet. pa. t. and pa. pple. of ALIGHT *v.*^{1}

†**a'lite**, *phr. Obs.* A merely graphic combination for *a lite* = a little, used in 14th–15th c. See LITE.
c **1374** CHAUCER *Troylus* III. 1568 O, ho so seeth you, knoweth you but alite! **1494** FABYAN VII. 431 Fortune, whiche sharpe was with stormys not alyte.

‖**aliter** ('ælıtə(r)), *adv. Law.* [L.] (The case is) otherwise.
1848 in WHARTON *Law Lex.* **1902** S. L. PHIPSON *Law of Evidence* (ed. 3) xxxvi. 339 Even such testimony without the production and proof of the marriage contract itself..is insufficient; though *aliter* to prove a former marriage by the *prosecutor*. **1907** J. W. SALMOND *Law of Torts* v. 162 Consequently only one action will lie, and in it full damages are recoverable for both the past and the future. *Aliter* if I have brought a heap of soil and left it on the plaintiff's land. **1946** *Law Rep.* II. 63 *Aliter* when the King's Proctor intervenes to show cause. **1971** *Mod. Law Rev.* XXXIV. VI. 687 In cases where the accused is not..provoked, he cannot kill simply in order to avoid an unlawful arrest... *Aliter*, no doubt, where the accused honestly fears that he will be beaten.

†**a'lithe**, *v.*^{1} *Obs.* [f. A- *pref.* 1 away + LITHE, OE. *líðan* to go, pass.] To pass away, go away.
1205 LAYAM. 3970 þa seoue ȝer weoren aliðene. *Ibid.* 12041 þe wind gon(d) aliðen [**1250** alegge], & þat weder leoðede.

†**alithe**, *v.*^{2} *Obs.* In 1 **a-leoði-an.** [f. A- *pref.* 1 away + *lið*, LITHE, limb. Cf. *to-lithien.*] To tear limb from limb, dismember.
a **1000** CÆDMON *Gen.* (Grein) 177 He ðæt andweorc of Adames lice aleoðede. **1250** LAYAM. 25929 Nou haueþ he.. mine leomes aliþede [**1205** al to-leðed].

†**a'lition.** *Obs. rare*$^{-1}$. [f. L. *alit-* ppl. stem of *al-ĕre* to nourish + -ION^{1}, as if ad. L. **alitiōn-em.*] The action of supplying nourishment; alimentation.
1650 BULWER *Anthropomet.* xvii. 171 Hunger..is the work of nature..admonishing us of alition.

alitrunk ('ælıtrʌŋk). [f. L. *āla* wing + *trunc-us* trunk.] The segment of an insect's body to which the wings are attached; the thorax.
1816-43 KIRBY & SPENCE *Entomol.* III. 531 The wing trunk, a happy term, which I have adopted and latinized calling it the alitrunk.

†'**aliture.** *Obs.*$^{-0}$ [ad. L. *alitūra*, f. *alit-* ppl. stem of *al-ĕre* to nourish: see -URE.] The process of nourishing; nourishment.
1721 in BAILEY; whence in JOHNSON.

†**ali'turgesy.** *Obs.*$^{-0}$ [ad. Gr. ἀλειτουργησία, f. ἀ priv. + λειτουργέ-ειν to fill a public charge: see LITURGY.] 'A franchisement, or exemption from any publick office or charge.' Bailey 1731; Ash 1775.

aliturgic (ælı'tɜ:dʒık), *a. Eccl.* [f. A- 14 + LITURGIC *a.* Cf. F. *aliturgique* and Gr. ἀλειτούργητος.] Of a day: on which the liturgy is not celebrated. So **ali'turgical** *a.*
1872 O. SHIPLEY *Gloss. Eccl. Terms*, *Aliturgical Days*, those days when the holy sacrifice is not offered. **1898** *Church Times* 7 Apr., Those who desired to communicate on that [*sc.* Good Friday] and other aliturgic days. **1912** A. FORTESCUE *Mass* 186 In the Milanese rite all Fridays in Lent are still strictly aliturgical days.

-ality, *comp. suffix* of sbs. = -AL^{1} + -ITY, after Fr. *-alité*, ad. L. *-ālitāt-em*; as L. *liberālitāt-em*, Fr. *libéralité*, *liberality*, the quality of being liberal.

‖**aliunde** (ælı'ʌndı), *adv.* Chiefly *Law.* [L.] From another person or place; from elsewhere.
1659 J. OWEN *Divine Orig. Authority Scriptures* ii. 36 That it may reach us, that we may know, and understand, and submit to its Authority, it must be testified unto *aliunde*, from some other person, or thing appointed thereunto. **1843** MILL *Logic* I. III. i. 245 Every shadow of doubt..is dispelled by evidence *aliundè*. **1884** *Law Rep., 28 Chanc. Div.* (1885) 308 The reference to the purchaser is not conclusive, for it might have been shown *aliunde* that *J. Studds* was not the purchaser. **1909** A. D. GODLEY in *Reliquiae* (1926) II. 163 What we know *aliunde* does not amount to very much. **1976** *Phipson on Evidence* (ed. 12) xxi. 378 Where the Civil Evidence Act 1968 does not apply, the special conditions of admissibility must be proved *aliunde* to the satisfaction of the judge.

†**a'live**, *v. Obs.* Forms as in LIVE. [f. A- *pref.* 1 intens. + LIVE, OE. *libban*. Cf. Ger. *erleben*.] To live. (prop. *trans.*)
c **885** K. ÆLFRED *Oros.* I. ii. §2 Hý..on bilwitnesse hyra lif alyfdon. *c* **1175** *Lamb. Hom.* 109 ȝunge monnan mei tweonian hweðer hi moten alibban.

alive (ə'laıv), *adv.* or (*pred.*) *a.*, orig. *phr.* Forms: α. 1–2 **on life**, 2–7 **on liue**, 4–6 **on lyue, on lyve**, 6 **on lyfe**. β. *Contr.*: 3 **oliue**, 3–7 **aliue**, 4 **olyve, olyfe**, 4–6 **alyve, alyue**, 5 **a lyff**, 6 **alyfe**, 6– **alive**. [A *prep.*^{1} = on, in + ME. *live*, OE. *life*, dat. sing. of *líf* LIFE. Here, as in the pl. *lives* and the vb. *live*, the *f* between two vowels took the voice-sound *v*, while *f* final remained in the nom. sing. This disguises the fact that *a-live* is only a shortened form of *on life* = *in life*. The fuller form *on live* was still current in the 17th cent.]

1. a. In life; in the living state; living.
α. *a* **1000** CÆDMON *Gen.* (Grein) 2610 Seó on life wæs wintrum yldre. **1205** LAYAM. 1378 Wel wes him on liue [**1250** aliue]. **1387** TREVISA *Higden* Rolls Ser. V. 259 þey þat were lefte no lyve. *c* **1440** *Gesta Rom.* (1879) 285 He went and bete him, and lefte hym halfe on lyve. *c* **1500** *Partenay* 4204 Fair sir, saue my life, lete me on-lif go. **1576** LAMBARDE *Peramb. Kent* (1826) 68 About which time Geffrey of Monmouth was on live also. **1602** [See 3].
β. *c* **1200** *Moral Ode* 23 Hwile he beð aliue. [*Another MS.* Hwile ȝe buð a life.] *c* **1300** *Beket* 67 Whar he scholde alyve this Gilbert fynde. *c* **1400** *Destr. Troy* XXIII. 9549 Achilles.. Might socour his Soudiours, & saue hom alyue. *c* **1440** *Morte Arth.* 802 Thus he brittenyd the bere, and broghte hyme olyfe. **1538** STARKEY *Eng.* II. ii. 136 Theyr parentys being Alyfe. **1596** SHAKS. *Merch. Ven.* II. ii. 75 God reste his soule aliue or dead. **1611** BIBLE *Josh.* ii. 13 Saue aliue my father. **1711** STEELE *Spect.* No. 254 ¶2 To be married I find is to be buried alive. **1796** MRS. GLASSE *Cookery* x. 154 Take your cod whilst alive and cut it in slices. *a* **1842** TENNYSON *May Queen* III. I., I thought to pass away before, and yet alive I am.

b. Occas. as *adj.* in *attrib.* position (senses 1 and 5).
1938 E. BOWEN *Death of Heart* III. i. 329 Portia said, in a hardly alive voice: 'I thought you said you had finished everything.' **1959** D. EDEN *Sleeping Bride* xix. 150 Her intensely alive face..her eager response. **1961** K. NORWAY *Waterfront Hosp.* iv. 67 Group Captain Hurst is the most alive man I know.

c. Colloq. phr. ***alive and well*** (***and living in*** ..), etc.: alive and active, flourishing (at the place named), esp. despite suggestions to the contrary.
1966 *New Statesman* 26 Aug. 286/3 Much of today's wittiest and most significant writing can be found scrawled on walls... How would the Englishman react to *God is alive and living in Argentina*, or *God is Dead: Nietzsche*, countered by *Nietzsche is dead: God*? **1968** *Listener* 3 Oct. 449/3 The *Daily Mail* recently began a column-length tribute to Radio Leeds with the conceivably exaggerated remark: 'The *Goon Show* is not dead. It is alive and well, living in Yorkshire and operating under the name of BBC Radio Leeds.' **1970** *New York* 16 Nov. 66/1 Entertainments..reminding us that laughter is alive and well (and not a nervous reaction to some blackness of comedy). **1974** [see MOTEL]. **1977** *Time* 5 Sept. 52/3 The last English eccentric is alive and well and living comfortably in Oakland. **1978** G. BORDMAN *Amer. Musical Theatre* xi. 656/1 A small-scale 'cabaret revue'..opened January 22 [1968] at the Village Gate... The Belgian Jacques Brel had gathered about him so loyal, persuasive a cult that by the time *Jacques Brel Is Alive and Well and living in Paris* closed it had run up..1,847 performances... At the time, when some theologians were asking 'Is God dead?' others were replying that God was alive and well in various locations. **1986** *More* (N. Z.) Feb. 19/2, I was stunned when this happened. I thought bigotry is alive and well in my community.

2. a. Often used for emphasis: 'any man alive,' any living man whatever, any man in the world.
a **1230** *Hali Meid.* 19 þeo beon to alle men oliue iliche meane. *c* **1400** *Destr. Troy* XXXII. 12814 Hir brother ho best louet of buernes olyue. *c* **1420** *Chron. Vilod.* 793 Glad and blythe was everyche a lyff. *c* **1449** PECOCK *Repr.* 535 Ouer hard to eny man on lyue. **1552** LYNDESAY *Monarche* 5062 To peirs the hartis Off euerilk Creature on lyue. **1711** STEELE *Spect.* No. 167 ¶3, I should be the most contented happy man alive. **1858** GEN. P. THOMPSON *Audi Alt. Part.* I. xxii. 81 There is no assignable cause; man alive cannot tell a reason why.

b. Hence, as intensive or expletive. *colloq.*
a **1845** HOOD *Agric. Distress* vi, Says he,'no matter man alive!' **1857** DICKENS *Christm. Carol.* 43 Why, bless my heart alive, my dear, how late you are! *a* **1860** in Bartlett *Dict. Amer.* s.v. *Sakes*, Why, sakes alive! do tell me if Enos is as mean as all that comes to.

3. *fig.* in reference, *e.g.* to *fire*, *courage*, *discontent*, *fame*, *memory*, or anything which is liable to subside, fail, or decay: In full force or vigour, unextinguished, unabated, unforgotten.
1602 CAREW *Cornwall* 38 b, Cornish gentlemen use all possible remedies..to keep it on live. **1603** SHAKS. *Meas. for M.* III. ii. 240 There is scarce truth enough aliue to make Societies secure. **1756** BURKE *Vind. Nat. Soc.* Wks. I. 61 Our boasted liberty..has only been kept alive by the blasts of continual feuds. **1849** MACAULAY *Hist. Eng.* I. 74 He kept discontent constantly alive. **1876** FREEMAN *Norm. Conq.* III. xiii. 277 The political constitution once common to every Teutonic people was still alive in England.

4. In the sentient or susceptible condition which distinguishes life from death; fully susceptible (*to* any sensation or idea); sensitive, awake, fully conscious.
1732 POPE *Ess. Man* I. 191 The touch, if tremblingly alive all o'er, To smart. **1762** FALCONER *Shipwr.* (R.) Tremblingly alive to nature's laws. **1778** BENTHAM *Penal Law* Wks. 1843 I. 456 Women..are more alive to, and susceptible of, the impression of shame than men. **1820** W. IRVING *Sketch Bk.* I. 31 My feelings were yet alive on the subject. **1878** BOSW. SMITH *Carthage* 139 Both sides were fully alive to the vital importance of the crisis.

5. a. In the active condition which distinguishes life from death; full of alacrity, lively, vivacious, brisk, quick in action. ***to look alive*** (colloq.): to make haste. (***all***) ***alive***, (***alive***), ***oh!*** (from the cry of fish sellers): very much alive and active. ***alive and kicking***: see KICKING *ppl. a.*
c **1709** *Squire Bickerstaff Detected* 7 Can any Man of common Sense think it..not much beneath the Dignity of a Philosopher, to stand bawling before his own Dore—Alive! Alive! Hoa! **1748** RICHARDSON *Clarissa* (J.) She was not so much alive the whole day, if she slept more than six hours. **1824** MISS MITFORD *Village* Ser. III. (1863) 108 The most entertaining person, the most *alive* of any one I met there. **1825** T. CREEVEY *Let.* 16 Mar. in *Creevey Papers* (1963) xii. 205 Our *York* is all alive O! He dined at Sefton's this day week as gay as a lark. **1835** MARRYAT *Jac. Faithf.* i. 5 We must be at the wharf early tomorrow morning, so keep alive. **1854** J. R. PLANCHÉ *Once upon a Time* I. iv. 16 *Sub.* Girls, where's your mother? *Chloe.* Coming at a wish. *Sub.* She is — and all alive O! like your fish. **1858** T. HUGHES *Scouring W. Horse* 29 The Squire..told the men to look alive and get their job done. **1859** [see O *int.* 3]. **1884** J. YORKSTON *Cockles & Mussels*, As she wheel'd her wheel barrow Through streets broad and narrow, Crying 'cockles and mussels alive, alive o!' **1941** 'N. BLAKE' *Abom. Snowman* xix. 215 He and Andrew have skipped together, both alive-oh. **1956** 'M. INNES' *Old Hall, New Hall* I. x. 91 Joscelyn..was suddenly struck all of a heap by Edward's all alive-oh Grecian girl.

b. *transf.* Of things, in specific uses. (See quots.)
1845 S. JUDD *Margaret* II. i. 186 Her Mother 'stirs it off' and a due quantity of the 'quick' and 'alive' crystal sweet is the result. **1892** GUNTER *Miss Dividends* xvi. 234 The locomotives..are moving about slowly, with a view to keeping themselves what is technically called 'alive'—that is their steam up, sufficient to give them power of motion. **1937** *Times* 13 Apr. p. xxv/2 The spare parts department.. carries approximately 40,000 different components, all of which are kept 'alive' for a period of no less than five years. **1943** 'T. DUDLEY-GORDON' *Coastal Command* ii. 20 It [*sc.* a torpedo] becomes 'alive' only after running through the water for a certain distance, so that the arming vane rotates a certain number of times.

c. *Electr.* Charged with electric current; connected to a source of electricity. Cf. LIVE *a.* 4.
1898 E. J. HOUSTON *Dict. Electr. Words* (ed. 4) 674/2 '*Alive*', (1) a name sometimes given to a live wire or circuit. (2) an active wire or circuit. **1958** *Which?* I. II. 6/1 If the casing becomes alive and you touch it while in contact with the bath, you may get electrocuted.

6. In a state of commotion, stirring, or swarming with things in motion.

1789 MORSE *Amer. Geogr.* 205 The markets are alive with them [*sc.* fish]. **1808** SCOTT *Marmion* v. vi, All was alive with martial show. **1849** MACAULAY *Hist. Eng.* II. 361 The whole river was alive with wherries. **1872** BLACK *Adv. Phaeton* xxvi. 362 The hotel was all alive with elderly ladies.

7. *Comb.* **alive-like** *a.*, with all the appearance of being alive.

1639 J. CLARKE *Parœmiol.* 275 He's alive, and alive-like, *Crotone salubrius.*

aliveness (ə'laɪvnɪs). [f. ALIVE *a.* + -NESS.] The quality of being alive or full of vigour. Also, sensitiveness *to* (one's surroundings, etc.).

a **1866** J. GROTE *Moral Ideals* (1876) 322 This would be the real fountain of youth, supposing.. there were energy to maintain the perpetual aliveness. **1866** MRS. CARLYLE in T. W. Reid *Life Ld. Houghton* (1891) II. xv. 146 A woman.. going about in society alive and well. To be sure, both the aliveness and the wellness 'may be strongly doubted', as they say in Edinburgh. **1892** *Independent* (U.S.) 7 Oct. 35/1 Aliveness, if we may use such a phrase, to the spirit of the age. **1921** J. WOOD in L. S. Hunter *John Hunter* ii. 18 He had all Dawson's aliveness to the world in which he lived.

†**a'lives,** *adv. phr. Obs.* Also o lives, etc. [= ALIVE *adv.*, with gen. *lives* instead of dat. *live.* The gen. was also used alone: see LIFE.] In life, alive.

a **1300** *Body & Soul* in *Mapes' Poems* (1841) 338 Alle the men that ben o lyves. *a* **1300** *Cursor M.* 22849 þe childir þat es abortiues, þaa þat er not born o-liues.

Comb. **alives-like** *a.*, living-like, lively.

1624 BP. MOUNTAGU *Gagg.* 100 Epaphroditus was then alive; and upon recovery, alives-like.

alizarate (ə'lɪzəreɪt). *Chem.* [f. ALIZARI + -ATE[4].] A salt of alizaric acid.

1875 URE *Dict. Arts* I. 70 Alizarate of potash, from which the alizarine may be thrown down as a bright yellow precipitate.

‖**Alizari** (ælɪ'zɑːrɪ). [Fr. and Sp., according to Devic, prob. ad. Arab. *al* the + *ʿaçārah* juice pressed out, extract, f. *ʿaçara* to press, extract. This is confirmed by the variant form *azala* 'la graine de garance qu'on apporte de la Turquie asiatique est appelée *azala* ou *izari*' (Bose *Dict. d'hist. nat.*, in Littré Supplt.] A commercial name of the Madder of the Levant.

1850 *Bot. Gaz.* 84 The madder, called by the ancient Greeks Erythrodanon, now bears the name of Alizari. **1875** URE *Dict. Arts* I. 158 The root of the *Rubia peregrina*, called in the Levant *Alizari*, was the material to which dyers had recourse, and large quantities of it are at the present day imported into Europe from Smyrna, under the name of *Turkey roots.*

alizaric (ælɪ'zærɪk), *a. Chem.* [f. prec. + -IC.] Of alizari or madder. *alizaric acid*: a colourless crystallized substance produced by the action of nitric acid on alizarine or rubian; = phthalic acid.

1863 WATTS *Dict. Chem.* (1879) I. 113.

alizarin (ə'lɪzərɪn). *Chem.* Also **alizarine.** [a. Fr. *alizarine*, f. ALIZARI: see -IN.] The red colouring matter of the madder root ($C_{14}H_8O_4$) discovered and named by Robiquet; now prepared from anthracene. Also *attrib.*, designating dyestuffs derived from, or similar in action to, alizarin; the colours of these dyes.

1835 HOBLYN *Med. Dict.*, *Alizarine*, the red colouring matter of madder. **1863** WATTS *Dict. Chem.* (1879) I. 114 Alizarin in the anhydrous state forms red prisms inclining more or less to yellow. **1875** URE *Dict. Arts* I. 70 In 1869 Messrs. Graebe and Liebermann made the important discovery that alizarine might be produced artificially from anthracene, one of the products of coal-tar distillation. **1876** *Jrnl. Chem. Soc.* II. 234 The contamination of the printed cotton with iron is thus prevented, and only the pure alumina lake, that is to say, the pure alizarin-red, remains upon the cotton. **1885** C. T. DAVIS *Manuf. Leather* xliii. 735 Alizarine red (a pale flesh color) is produced by rubbing the cleansed and trodden skins with a solution of alizarine or extract of madder in weak soda lye and rinsing in water. **1901** *Kynoch Jrnl.* II. 36/2 The use of picric acid as a dye has been superseded by the use of alizarine and naphtol yellows. **1954** *Archit. Rev.* CXV. 286/2 It makes a particularly good textured background for pictures, and is manufactured in six colours: natural, light corn, tobacco, strawberry, alizarin green and egyptian green. **1962** *Listener* 11 Jan. 76/1 A fortress of almost vertical rocks.. burnt umber and alizarin red.

alk, obs. form of AUK.

alkahest ('ælkəhɛst). Also alc-, alch-. [first used in med.L. by Paracelsus, and believed to have been arbitrarily invented by him with a form simulating Arabic. Used in the same forms in most of the European languages.] The 'universal solvent' of the alchemists.

1641 FRENCH *Distill.* v. 109 With his Alkahest [*printed* Altahest] all stones.. may be turned into water. **1657** G. STARKEY *Helmont's Vind.* 294 There are noble Arcana's in Nature preparable by the great Dissolvent, the liquor Alchahest. **1705** W. WORTH *Compl. Distiller* 243 The great Hilech.. of Paracelsus, called by his great Interpreter Van Helmont, *Alkahest*, from the German word *Al-gehest*, which signifies All Spirit. **1812** SIR H. DAVY *Chem. Philos.* 323 The alkahest, or universal solvent imagined by the alchemists.

b. *fig.*

1832 CARLYLE *Misc.* (1857) III. 167 Quite another alcahest is needed. **1866** ALGER *Solit. Nat. & Man* IV. 351 An intellectual alkahest, melting the universe into an idea.

alkahestic (ælkə'hɛstɪk), *a.* [f. prec. + -IC.] Of or pertaining to the alkahest; all-dissolving.

1753 CHAMBERS *Cycl. Supp.* s.v., De Bernitz has given forms and processes of alkahestic liquors. **1775** in ASH; and in mod. Dicts.

alka'hestical, *a. Obs. rare*[−1]. In 7 alch-. [f. as prec. + -ICAL.] = prec.

1657 G. STARKEY *Helmont's Vind.* 295, I shall therefore here not speak of any Alchahesticall preparations.

alkakengi, variant of ALKEKENGI.

alkalæmia (ˌælkə'liːmɪə). *Path.* [mod.L., f. ALKALI + Gr. αἷμα blood: see -IA[1].] A condition of increased alkalinity resulting from a disturbance of the acid-base equilibrium of the blood.

1922 *Lancet* 9 Sept. 560/2 (*title*) Periodic Alkalæmia with Alkalosis in the Adult. *Ibid.* 561/2 When the value of the ratio is decreased the blood reaction becomes more alkaline than normal—that is, a condition of *alkalæmia* results. **1924** *Q. Jrnl. Med.* 405 (*title*) Disturbance of the Acid-Base Equilibrium of the Blood to the Alkaline Side: Alkalæmia. *Ibid.*, In this paper only examples of alkalæmia due to alkali excess are presented, but the alkalæmia due to carbon dioxide deficit also has clinical importance. **1961** *Brit. Med. Dict.* 65/2 *Alkalæmia* a state in which there is an increase in the hydrogen-ion concentration in the blood without changes in the bicarbonate content of the blood. **1965** G. H. BELL et al. *Textbk. Physiol. & Biochem.* (ed. 6) xxxiii. 667 Raised pH, that is alkalæmia, or lowered pH, acidæmia.

alkalamide ('ælkələˌmaɪd). *Chem.* [f. ALKALI + AMIDE.] A compound uniting the characters of an amine and an amide, containing both acid and alcohol radicals, as *Ethyl-acetamide* $N{\cdot}C_2H_5{\cdot}C_2H_3O{\cdot}H$.

According to the molecules of ammonia which they represent, they are *mon-*, *di-*, or *tri-alkalamides*, which are *secondary* or *tertiary* according to the hydrogen atoms replaced. As there must be at least 2 of these, there are of course no *primary* alkalamides.

1863 WATTS *Dict. Chem.* (1879) I. 169 [Classification of compound ammonias] 3. Ammonias in which 2 or more atoms of hydrogen are replaced by *acid-* and *base-* radicles. This division we call *alkalamides*. *Ibid.* 180 There exists a class of compounds occupying an intermediate place between primary and secondary dialkalamides.

alkalescence (ælkə'lɛsəns). [f. ALKALESCENT, on the regular analogy of sbs. in -ENCE from adjs. in -ENT. Cf. mod.Fr. *alcalescence.*] The process of becoming alkaline; also = ALKALESCENCY.

1746 R. JAMES *Introd. Mouffet's Health's Impr.* 35 The Alcalescence of animal Aliments. **1807** DAVY in *Phil. Trans.* XCVIII. 41 Oxygen.. the principle of acidity of the French nomenclature, might now likewise be called the principle of alkalescence.

alkalescency (ælkə'lɛsənsɪ). [f. as prec., on regular analogy of sbs. in -NCY.] The tendency to become alkaline; slight alkaline character.

1756 C. LUCAS *Ess. Waters* III. 333 Disorders spring from an alcalescency of the humours. **1809** PEARSON in *Phil. Trans.* XCIX. 338 Affording no signs of alkalescency. **1826** PARIS *Diet* §126 (1828) 146 Writers on dietetics have descanted very learnedly upon what they please to term the .. alkalescency of certain aliments.

alkalescent (ælkə'lɛsənt), *a.* and *sb.* [f. ALKALI, as if ad. L. **alkalēscent-em*, pr. pple. of an inceptive **alkalēscĕre*, analogous to *acēscĕre* to become sour, etc. Cf. mod.Fr. *alcalescent.*]

A. *adj.* Becoming or tending to become alkaline; of a character incipiently or slightly alkaline.

1732 ARBUTHNOT *Rules Diet* 255 All Animal Diet is Anti-acid or Alkalescent. **1756** C. LUCAS *Ess. Waters* I. 186 Medicines which are chiefly alcaline or alcalescent. **1821** SHELLEY *Lett.* (1852) II. 259 Nothing but alcalescent water.

B. *sb.* An alkalescent substance.

1750 PRINGLE in *Phil. Trans.* XLVI. 555 Carrots, Turneps, Garlick.. and Colewort, were tried (as Alcalescents).

alkali ('ælkəlɪ). Forms: 4–7 alcaly, -ie, alkaly, 8 alcali, 8–9 alkali. Pl. **alkalis,** sometimes **-ies.** [a. Fr. *alcali*, ad. (ultimately) Arab. *al-qalīy*, the 'calcined ashes' of the plants *Salsola* and *Salicornia*, f. *qalay* to fry, roast in a pan; hence transferred to the plants themselves so employed.]

1. *orig.* A saline substance obtained by lixiviating the calcined ashes of marine plants; soda-ash.

c **1386** CHAUCER *Chan. Yem. Prol. & T.* 257 Salt tartre, alcaly [*v.r.* alkaly, alcaly, alcalie], and salt preparat, And combust matieres, and coagulat. **1471** RIPLEY *Comp. Alch.* in Ashm. 1652 v. 190 Sal Alkaly, sal Alembroke, sal Attinckarr. **1578** LYTE *Dodoens* 116 The axsen or asshes whiche are made of burnt Kali, is called in Latin of the Alcumistes and Glassemakers *Alumen Catinum*, but the Salte which is made of the same Axsen, is called *Sal Alkali.* **1610** B. JONSON *Alchem.* I. iii. (1616) 616 You shall deale much, with mineralls.. I know, you have Arsnike, Vitriol, Sal-tartre, Argaile, Alkaly. **1712** tr. *Pomet's Hist. Drugs* I. 102 They make of this Salt—a white Salt call'd Salt of Kali or Alkali.

2. *Bot.* The plant Saltwort (*Salsola Kali*); from the ashes of which (or of the allied *Salsola Soda*) the original *Alkali* was derived.

1578 LYTE *Dodoens* 115 It [Salsola Kali] is the right Kali or Alkali of the Arabians: some call it in English Salte-worte; we may also call it Kali or prickled Kali. **1753** HANWAY *Trav.* (1762) I. IV. xiv. 250 We found it to be.. the small sort of *kali* (or *alkali*, glass-wort: the ash of this is used in making glass and soap). **1861** MISS BEAUFORT *Egypt. Sepul.* I. xv. 337 The 'hashish el kali' which covered the ground.. the plant from the ashes of which they make potash for soap.

3. a. Any substance possessing the characteristics of soda, *i.e.* a caustic or acrid taste, the power of forming a soap with oil, and of effervescing with or neutralizing acids.

In early chemistry *alkali* was supposed to be a specific substance, which existed, *fixed* (in soda, potash), *volatile* (in ammonia). Duhamel (1736) showed that there were distinct alkalis, and these were distinguished as ***mineral alkali*** (soda), ***vegetable alkali*** (potash), ***animal alkali*** (ammonia).

1612 WOODALL *Surg. Mate* Wks. 1653, 259 Paracelsus termeth every vegetable Salt *Alkaly.* **1669** *Phil. Trans.* IV. 1055 Acids and Alcaly's mutually operate upon one another to a satiety. **1657** G. STARKEY *Helmont's Vind.* 298 Alcalyes are the fixt Salts of combustible Concretes, fixed by the activity of the fire, which were (before burning) volatile. **1682** GREW *Anat. Pl. Lect.* ii. i. §8. 240 The predominant Salt in most Minerals, and parts of Animals, is an Alkaly: in the former, usually a fixed; in the latter, a volatile Alkaly. **1685** BOYLE *Min. Waters* 85 Strong Spirit of Urine, and other volatile Alcaly's. **1732** ARBUTHNOT *Rules Diet* i. 246 Mulberries pectoral, corrective of the bilious Alkali. **1748** HARTLEY *Observ. Man* I. i. §1. ¶5 The effervescence which attends the Mixture of Acids and Alcali's. **1756** C. LUCAS *Ess. Waters* I. 9 Native or Mineral alcali is the basis of common salt. **1788** AUSTIN in *Phil. Trans.* LXXVIII. 381 A very pungent smell of volatile alkali is immediately perceived. **1822** IMISON *Sc. & Art* II. 4 If some oil and some alkali be put together they will unite and form soap. **1825** MACAULAY *Ess.*, *Milton* I. 7 The conflicting ingredients, like an acid and an alkali mixed.

b. Native alkali (i.e. various salts) existing in excess in the soil of certain areas in the Western States; hence, a region abounding in alkali. *U.S.*

1848 E. BRYANT *California* viii. 124, I found the liquid bitter with salt and alkali. **1869** S. BOWLES *Our New West* xiv. 278 In looking out.. on the starry heavens,.. one almost forgets alkali. **1872** 'MARK TWAIN' *Sketches* 119 That awful five days' journey, through alkali, sagebrush, peril of body. **1904** S. E. WHITE *Blazed Trail Stories* x. 181 They had ridden solitary over the limitless alkali of the Arizona plains.

attrib. **1848** W. CLAYTON *Latter-Day Saints' Emigr. Guide* i, Emigrants have lost many of their teams in the neighbourhood of the *Alkali lakes.* **1869** S. BOWLES *Our New West* xiv. 275 The alkali dust, dry with a season's sun, .. was thick and constant. *Ibid.* 276 Bare alkali plains stretch out.. for miles. **1871** SCHELE DE VERE *Americanisms* 177 The Alkali Flats are now crossed by the Pacific Railroad. **1878** J. H. BEADLE *Western Wilds* xxiv. 388, I am convinced there is little to see but.. alkali flats and sand-hills. **1886** *Boston* (Mass.) *Herald* 16 July, It is only an 'alkali sink'—a natural well, filled with a paste as yielding as water.

4. *fig.*

1702 *Eng. Theophr.* 141 The church of England generally preaches alcali's, the Presbyterians acids.

5. *Comm.* Any form in which the substances above mentioned are used in commerce or the arts, or manufactured from other substances; once given specially to an impure soda, now applied both to caustic soda and caustic potash, and other alkaline products.

1822 IMISON *Sc. & Art* II. 168 The alcali is one of the chief articles of expense used in bleaching. **1876** URE *Dict. Arts* I. 71 Of alkali manufactured in the United Kingdom the following quantities were exported. *Ibid.* III. 861 Before the passing of the Alkali Act, or at least before the introduction of the Alkali Bill into Parliament.

6. *Mod. Chem.* A series of the compounds called BASES, with well-marked characters, analogous to, and including soda, potash, and ammonia; they are highly soluble in water, producing caustic or corrosive solutions, which neutralize strong acids, turn vegetable yellows to brown, reds to blue, and purples to green; in the decomposition of a compound they are relatively electro-positive.

'In its most restricted, but most usual sense, it is applied to four substances only: hydrate of potassium (potash), hydrate of sodium (soda), hydrate of lithium (lithia), and hydrate of ammonium (which may be supposed to exist in the aqueous solution of ammonia). In a more general sense it is applied to the hydrates of the so-called *alkaline earths* (baryta, strontia, and lime), and to a large number of organic substances both natural and artificial, [called] *alkaloids* and *ammonium-bases.* The first four bodies are sometimes spoken of as *alkalis proper*, when it is wished specially to distinguish them from the other bases.' WATTS *Dict. Chem.* Hence, ***fixed*** or ***mineral alkalis***, the hydrates of the metals above-named; ***vegetable alkalis***, the alkaloids; ***organic alkalis***, all the organic bases containing nitrogen, whether of vegetable or animal origin.

1813 SIR H. DAVY *Agric. Chem.* 20 The fixed alkalies which were formerly regarded as elementary bodies, it has been my good fortune to decompose. **1863** WATTS *Dict. Chem.* (1879) 117 The relations of the alkalis to other substances lead to the representation of them as hydrates, or as water in which half the hydrogen is replaced by a metal or compound radicle. The earliest addition made.. to the old list of alkalis was morphia.. This was the first organic alkali, or alkaloid, which became known. **1875** URE *Dict. Arts* I. 71 Modern chemists regard all organic alkalis as derived from the type ammonia or oxide of ammonium.

7. *Comb.* **alkali act** (see quot.); **alkali-albumen, -inate**, a precipitate thrown down from an albuminous fluid treated with dilute alkali, and neutralized by dilute acid; **alkali-cellulose**, a compound of cellulose and an alkali; **alkali-metal** = ALKALINE metal; **alkali-waste**, a by-product obtained in the manufacture of soda ash, consisting of sulphide of calcium; **alkali-work**, a manufactory where the alkali of commerce is prepared, or where carbonate of soda is prepared from common salt.

1875 URE *Dict. Arts* III. 861 The Alkali Act of July 28, 1863, is 'An Act for the more effectual condensation of Muriatic Acid in Alkali works.' An alkali-work is defined as 'every work for the manufacture of alkali, sulphate of soda, or sulphate of potash, in which muriatic acid is evolved.' **1879** *Syd. Soc. Lex.* s.v., *Alkali-albumen* is not distinguishable from Casein, which is also termed the natural alkali-albumen. **1878** KINGZETT *Anim. Chem.* 69 The organic matter of pancreatic juice contains soluble albumin and alkali-albuminate. **1901** CROSS & BEVAN *Res. on Cellulose* 31 Hydrolytic changes should occur in the cellulose molecule when kept for prolonged periods as alkali-cellulose.

al'kalic, *a.* [f. ALKALI + -IC.] †**1.** = Alkaline. *Chem. Obs.*

1733 *Phil. Trans.* XXXVIII. 67 Neither..Acid, nor Alcalick, but insipid like Talck. *Ibid.* 68 Neither is it any ways Alcalick.

2. *Petrol.* Of a rock: containing more alkali metals than the average for the group it belongs to; having sufficient alkali metals to determine the mineral content; *spec.* containing more sodium and potassium than is required to form feldspar with the available aluminium and silica. †Of a mineral: rich in alkali metals.

1902 *Jrnl. Geol.* X. 569 The two rocks having almost identical chemical compositions are composed in the first case of somewhat alkalic, aluminous hornblende. **1931** *Ibid.* XXXIX. 54 Some rock series cannot be properly classified either as alkalic or as sub-alkalic. **1973** *Nature* 9 Feb. 375/2 Thus the alkalic provinces may be related to a greater depth of fusion for these rocks, by contrast with the tholeiitic composition of the ridge volcanics.

alkalifiable ('ælkəlɪˌfaɪəb(ə)l), *a. Chem.* [f. next + -ABLE.] Capable of being alkalified.

1833 FYFE *Chem.* (ed. 3) 334 The alkalifiable bodies, or those forming salifiable bases. **1853** CHAMBERS *Introd. Sc.* 80 These thirty-one are said to possess an alkaline property and to be Alkalifiable Bases.

alkalify ('ælkəlɪfaɪ), *v. Chem.* [f. ALKALI + -FY to make. Cf. mod.Fr. ppl. adj. *alcalifiant*.]

1. *trans.* To convert into an alkali, to make alkaline.

1831 URE *Dict. Chem.* 135 The alkalifying property of the metal. **1839** HOOPER *Med. Dict.* 65 Morveau conjectured hydrogen to be the alkalifying principle.

2. *intr.* To become an alkali or alkaline.

†**alkaligen**. *Chem. Obs.* [a. Fr. *alcaligène*, f. ALKALI + -GEN(E, taken to signify 'producer.'] A name proposed for nitrogen.

1790 KERR tr. *Lavoisier's Chem.* 52 It was at first proposed to call it alkaligen gas, as..it appears to enter into the composition of ammoniac or volatile alkali. **1879** *Syd. Soc. Lex.*, *Alkaligene*, nitrogen, because it is a chief constituent of ammonia.

alkaligenous (ælkə'lɪdʒɪnəs), *a. Chem.* [f. ALKALI + -GEN (see prec.) + -OUS.] Generating or producing an alkali, or alkaline qualities; as the ***alkaligenous metals***.

1846 in SMART, CRAIG. *c* **1865** J. WYLDE in *Circ. Sc.* I. 311/1 We shall divide these into three classes; namely, Alkaligeneous, Calcigeneous, and Metals proper.

†**alkalimeter** (ælkə'lɪmɪtə(r)). *Obs.* [f. ALKALI + -METER. Cf. Fr. *alcalimètre*.] An instrument for ascertaining the amount of alkali in a solution.

1828 S. GRAY *Operat. Chem.* 473 An alkalimeter of M. Descroizilles, for the purpose of ascertaining the strength of alkalies. **1873** WATTS *Fownes' Chem.* I. 335 The alkalimeters commonly used contain 50 cubic centimeters.

alkali'metric, *a.* = ALKALIMETRICAL *a.*

1844 *Mech. Mag.* XL. 335/2 Instead of using beads for preparing the alkalimetric and acidimetric test liquors.. hydrometers may..be employed. **1856** W. A. MILLER *Elem. Chem.* II. xi. 739 The 35 divisions of alkalimetric acid used in the experiment.

alkalimetrical (ˌælkəlɪ'mɛtrɪkəl), *a.* [f. ALKALI + Gr. μετρικ-ός of measuring + -AL[1].] Of or pertaining to alkalimetry.

1842 GRAHAM *Chem.* I. 552 The object of an alkalimetrical process. **1853** THUDICHUM *Urine* 66 One of the ordinary alkalimetrical methods. **1865** *Reader* 11 Mar. 290/2 When performing alkalimetrical analyses by gaslight.

alkalimetry (ælkə'lɪmɪtrɪ). [mod. f. ALKALI + Gr. -μετρία measuring. Cf. mod.Fr. *alcalimétrie*.] The measurement of the strength of alkalis; the ascertainment of the amount of free alkali contained in any solution or compound.

1821 BRANDE *Chem.* II. 354–6 (*Article*) Alcalimetry. **1827** FARADAY *Chem. Manip.* xii. 275 Alkalimetry at present consists in an estimative process dependant upon neutralization, and the use of test papers. **1860** MUSPRATT *Chem.* I. 735 The valuation of potashes, or alkalimetry.

alkaline ('ælkəlaɪn), *a.* Also 7 alkalin, 8 alcaline. [? a. Fr. *alcalin* or mod.L. *alcalīn-us*: see ALKALI and -INE.] **1. a.** Of or pertaining to alkalis; of the nature of an alkali.

1677 W. HARRIS tr. *Lemery's Chym.* I. ii. (1686) 322 Quicklime..being a substance very Alkalin, the acid points ..enter into it with force. **1718** J. CHAMBERLAYNE *Relig. Philos.* II. xviii. 6 Volatile and Alcaline Salts. **1732** ARBUTHNOT *Rules Diet* 289 Acidity..is to be cured by an alkaline Diet. **1743** *Lond. & Country Brewer* III. (ed. 2) 218 The alcaline Salt in the Ashes. **1794** J. HUTTON *Philos. Light, etc.* 210 An alkaline salt saturated with fixed air. **1849** MRS. SOMERVILLE *Connex. Phys. Sc.* xxix. 340 By reversing the poles the taste becomes alkaline. **1876** PAGE *Advd. Text-bk. Geol.* iii. 70 The alkalis and alkaline carbonates attack many rocks with great facility.

b. *fig.*

1818 SCOTT *Hrt. Midl.* 402 A mediating spirit, who endeavoured, by the alkaline smoothness of her own disposition, to neutralize the acidity of theological controversy.

†**c.** *substantively. Obs.*

1773 *Gentlem. Mag.* XLIII. 126 Alkalines cannot be attracted in waters where acids do not abound.

2. alkaline metals: the metals whose hydroxides are alkalis, *viz.* potassium, sodium, cæsium, lithium, rubidium, to which is sometimes added the hypothetical ammonium. **alkaline earths**: the oxides of calcium, strontium, and barium, which are intermediate in properties between the alkalis and 'earths' proper. Hence **alkaline-earthy** *a.*

1806 DAVY in *Phil. Trans.* XCVII. 21 Alkaline or alkaline-earthy bases. **1816** —— in Faraday's *Res.* 4 A new point of analogy between the alkalies and the alkaline earths. **1849** MURCHISON *Siluria* xii. 307 The terrestrial mass contains free alkaline metals.

3. Of soils or areas: charged or permeated with alkali. *U.S.*

1850 L. SAWYER *Way Sketches* (1926) 109 Great care should be taken to avoid the alkaline waters found along the route and the animals should never be picketed out upon the low alkaline bottoms. **1869** S. BOWLES *Our New West* xiv. 277 It would seem as if these alkaline valleys of the Great Interior Basin were too cold. **1870** *Amer. Naturalist* IV. 29 A desert section proper and one more particularly pertaining to the alkaline flats.

alkalinity (ælkə'lɪnɪtɪ). *Chem.* [f. prec. + -ITY. Cf. mod.Fr. *alcalinité*.] The quality of being alkaline; alkaline character or property.

1788 PRIESTLEY in *Phil. Trans.* LXXVIII. 157, I am still inclined to think..that phlogiston is the principle of alkalinity, if such a term may be used. **1788** CAVENDISH *ibid.*, To discover how nice a test of alcalinity the paper tinged with blue flowers was. **1863** WATTS *Dict. Chem.* (1879) I. 120 Some of these [alkaloids] rival potash and soda in the degree of their alkalinity, while in others the existence of alkaline properties is barely perceptible.

alkalinization (ˌælkəlɪnaɪ'zeɪʃən). [f. ALKALINIZE *v.* + -ATION.] The process of making or becoming (more) alkaline; reduction of acidity.

1930 *Chem. Abstr.* XXIV. 2198 (*heading*) The reciprocal action of chlorination and alkalinization of the organism in acute diseases. **1946** *Nature* 9 Nov. 673/2 It is significant that commercial hypochlorite is stabilized by alkalinization to *p*H 10, whereby free hypochlorous acid is neutralized. **1976** *Sci. Amer.* June 46/1 In the case of the vesicles the light produced not a decrease in the *p*H of the medium (acidification) but an increase in *p*H (alkalinization). **1979** *Nature* 24 May 281/2 Alkalinisation of the soil. **1983** *Brit. Med. Jrnl.* 23 July 275/1 The renal clearance of salicylate depends much more on urine pH than flow rate, and alkalinisation of the urine is therefore more important than attempts to force a diuresis.

alkalinize ('ælkəlɪnaɪz), *v.* [f. ALKALINE + -IZE. Cf. *latinize*.] To render alkaline.

1800 W. TAYLOR in Robberds' *Mem.* I. 344 By alkalinizing a hyperoxygenated mass of blood. **1876** BARTHOLOW *Mater. Med.* (1879) 161 An attempt to alkalinize the urine.

†**alkalinous**, *a. Chem. Obs. rare*⁻¹. [f. med.L. *alcalinus* + -OUS.] Of alkaline character.

1770 MCBRIDE in *Phil. Trans.* LXI. 342 They..act as acids, by saturating anything of the alcalinous kind, that they meet with.

†**al'kalious**, *a. Chem. Obs.* Also alc-. [f. ALKALI + -OUS.] = ALKALINE.

1703 MORLAND in *Phil. Trans.* XXIII. 1321 Those that.. affirm, that it is Alkalious. **1754** HUXHAM *ibid.* XLVIII. 854 The alcalious salts fix on the sulphur, and unite with it.

†**al'kalizate**, *ppl. a.* and *sb. Chem. Obs.* Also -izat, -isat(e. [ad. mod.L. *alcalizāt-um* pa. pple. of *alcalizā-re*: see ALKALIZE. Cf. Fr. *alcalisé*.]

A. *adj.* Alkalized, alkaline.

1622 BACON *Hen. VII*, 47 All sorts of Acid and Alcalizate Salts mixed with Snow are capable of freezing other Bodies. **1669** *Phil. Trans.* IV. 1055 Of a Volatile and Alcalisate property. **1673** *Ibid.* VIII. 5187 No Fixt Alcalisat Salt. **1713** SLARE *ibid.* XXVIII. 249 Sweetning and Alkalisate Remedies. **1753** CHAMBERS *Cycl. Supp.*, *Alkaline* is otherwise written, *alcaline*, *alkaleous*, *alcalious*, *alkalizate*, and *alcalizate*, which all amount to the same thing.

B. *sb. rare*⁻¹. 'That which has the qualities of alkali.' Sheridan 1797.

1681 tr. *Willis's Rem. Med. Wks.*, *Alchalisat*, a salt made of the herb kali. Also taken and applyed to salts made of herbs and shells of fishes.

†**al'kalizate**, *v. Obs.* [? f. mod.L. *alcalizāt-um*: see prec. Prob. only in pa. pple.] 'To make bodies alkaline by changing their nature, or by mixing alkalies with them.' J.

1801 *Phil. Trans.* XCI. 379 Distilled water, previously alkalizated by a sufficient quantity of ammonia.

†**al'kalizateness.** *Obs.* [f. prec. + -NESS.] The quality of being alkalizate, = ALKALINITY.

1667 BOYLE *Orig. Formes & Qual.*, This new Alkalizatenesse might proceed from the Ashes of injected coals.

alkalization (ælkəlaɪ'zeɪʃən). [n. of action, f. ALKALIZATE *v.* Cf. Fr. *alcalisation*.] The action of alkalizing, or of conferring alkaline qualities.

1719 QUINCY *Lex. Phys. Med.* 11 *Alcalization* is when any Liquor is impregnated with an alkaline Salt. **1754** HUXHAM in *Phil. Trans.* XLVIII. 850 This chiefly depends on the alcalization of the nitre. **1807** DAVY *ibid.* XCVIII. 12 Its alkalization and combustion in oxygene gas.

'**alkalize** ('ælkəlaɪz), *v. Chem.* [a. Fr. *alcalise-r*, ? ad. mod.L. *alcalizā-re*: see ALKALI and -IZE.] To render alkaline.

1749 STACK in *Phil. Trans.* XLVI. 186 What can the repeated Action of the Fire produce on Salts, in order to alkalise them? **1808** *Edin. Rev.* XII. 398 An imperfect oxyde ..which, by degrees, is fully alkalized.

alkalized ('ælkəlaɪzd), *ppl. a.* [f. prec. + -ED.] Rendered alkaline; charged with alkaline properties; impregnated with alkali.

1725 BRADLEY *Fam. Dict.* s.v. *Restor. Beer*, Tortoise-shells, Crabs-eyes, alcaliz'd Coral..imbibe and attract the Sharpness, and turn it into Sweetness. **1754** HUXHAM in *Phil. Trans.* XLVIII. 854 A strong lixivium of fixed or alkaliz'd nitre. **1847** TODD *Cycl. Anat.* III. 818/1 The alkalized lime.

alkalizing ('ælkəlaɪzɪŋ), *ppl. a.* [f. ALKALIZE + -ING[2].] That makes alkaline.

1833 *Penny Cycl.* I. 341 The alkalis..do not result from the action of any specific or alkalizing principle, being very variously constituted.

alkaloid ('ælkəlɔɪd). *Chem.* [mod. f. ALKALI + -OID. Cf. mod.Fr. *alcaloïde*.] A body resembling an alkali in properties. Applied *gen.* to all nitrogenous basic substances, natural or artificial, with alkaline reaction (*Nitrogen alkaloids*), or to all nitrogenous organic bases, whether animal or vegetable (*Organic alkaloids*); *spec.* to the *Vegeto-alkaloids* or *Vegetable alkalis*, a series of highly complex organic bases found in many plants, having mostly a very bitter taste, and powerful action on the animal system, the first of which to be discovered was *morphine* in 1817. Chemically they may be regarded as substitution compounds of ammonia. (The names of organic alkaloids are regularly formed in *-ine*, as *nicotine*, *strychnine*, *quinine*, *aconitine*, *theine*.)

1831 URE *Dict. Chem.* 135 They are called by the German chemists *alkaloids*. **1833** *Penny Cycl.* I. 158 The detection of the alkaloids in cases of poisoning by them. **1863** WATTS *Dict. Chem.* (1879) I. 120 The number of natural alkaloids now known is very great, and includes many substances which cannot in any strict sense be called alkalis. **1874** ROSCOE *Elem. Chem.* 427 The alkaloids act most powerfully on the animal economy; some, such as strychnine, nicotine, &c., form the most violent poisons with which we are acquainted, whilst others, such as quinine and morphine, act as most valuable medicines.

2. *attrib.* or *adj.*

1859 in WORCESTER. **1882** T. STEVENSON in *Echo* 11 Mar. 3/2 An alkaloid extract which contained a trace of morphia.

alkaloidal (ælkə'lɔɪdəl), *a.* [f. prec. + -AL[1].] Of the nature of an alkaloid; pertaining to alkaloids.

1879 in *Syd. Soc. Lex.* **1880** B. DYER in *Daily News* 7 Oct. 6/7 The fact..would rather point to the alkaloidal theory. **1882** T. STEVENSON in *Echo* 11 Mar. 3/2 The first alkaloidal extract contained more alkaloid than was accounted for by the morphia.

alkalosis (ælkə'ləʊsɪs). *Path.* [mod.L., f. ALKAL(I + -OSIS.] A condition of excessive alkalinity in the body-tissues and blood. Cf. ACIDOSIS.

1912 *Chem. Abstr.* 642 The meat intoxication is due to a condition of alkalosis, the alkalosis probably being brought about by 'NH_3 salts'. **1930** *Q. Jrnl. Med.* XXIII. 393 'Acidosis' is herein defined as a reduction in the bicarbonate content of the blood plasma..and 'alkalosis' as an increase above normal in this substance. **1965** J. R. ROBINSON *Acid-Base Regulation* (ed. 2) xiii. 31 It therefore seems preferable to restrict the terms 'acidosis' and 'alkalosis' to conditions in which the total concentration of buffer base is less than or greater than the normal.

†'**alkalous**, *a. Obs.* 7–8 alc-. [f. ALKALI + -OUS: cf. ALKALI-OUS.] = ALKALINE.

1683 PETTUS *Fleta Min.* II. 5 Salts of that Quality are called alcalous. **1742** *Lond. & Country Brewer* I. (ed. 4) 11 An alcalous and balsamic Quality.

alkamy(e, -anamye, obs. forms of ALCHEMY.

†**alkanamyer.** *Obs.* [f. *alkanamy* (see prec.) + -ER[1].] An alchemist; or perhaps one who prepared or used the metal ALCHEMY.
1483 *Cath. Anglic.*, Alkanamyer [*no Lat.*].

alkane ('ælkeɪn). *Chem.* [f. ALK(YL + -ANE 2 b.] Any member of the paraffin series of hydrocarbons (see PARAFFIN *sb.* 3).
1899 E. F. SMITH tr. *von Richter's Org. Chem.* (ed. 3) I. i. 79 Saturated or limit hydrocarbons, paraffins, alkanes. **1949** F. S. & F. B. KIPPING *Perkin & Kipping's Org. Chem.* I. iv. 63 The names of all the hydrocarbons of this series (also called the *alkanes*) end in *ane*.

alkanet ('ælkənɛt). [? ad. Sp. *alcaneta* (also *arcaneta*), dim. of *alcana, alcaña*: see ALCANNA. The diminutive form was applied to a European plant yielding red dye, the *Anchusa* or *Alkanna tinctoria*, (formerly sometimes called *Alkanna spuria*) to distinguish it from the oriental *Alkanna = henna*. Hence it has been extended to other species of *Anchusa* and allied genera. A variant is ORCANET, a. Fr. *orcanète*, ad. Sp. *arcaneta* above.]
1. A dye-material obtained from the roots of a boraginaceous plant, which yields a fine red colour.
1326 etc. *Prices of Foreign Prod.* in Rogers *Agric. & Prices* II. 545 Anno 1326 'Alkanet ½lb. @ 1/8,' anno 1334 and 1376 'Alkanet 1lb. @ /8.' *c* **1440** in *Househ. Ord.* (1790) 256 Take alkenet ii penyworth, and frie hit in faire grese. **1601** HOLLAND *Pliny* II. (1634) 96 With an addition of Orchanet it will be red. **1725** BRADLEY *Fam. Dict.* s.v. *Lip*, Add a little Orcanet to give it a Colour. **1791** HAMILTON tr. *Berthollet's Dyeing* I. Introd. 11 Others again prepared their cloth with alkanet. **1876** URE *Dict. Arts* I. 89 Oil coloured by alkanet is used for staining wood in imitation of rosewood.
2. The plant whose root yields the dye, *Anchusa* or *Alkanna tinctoria*, N.O. *Boraginaceæ*, also called Orchanet, Dyer's Bugloss, Spanish Bugloss, and Bugloss of Languedoc.
1567 MAPLET *Greene Forest* 55 Orchanet, of the Romaines and Greekes is called Anchusa. **1578** LYTE *Dodoens* 9 The first [of the smal Buglosses] is called in French *Orchanette*, in English Alkanet, or Orchanet. **1616** SURFLET *Countr. Farme* 332 Red [Waxe is made] by putting the root of Alkanet vnto common Wax. **1725** BRADLEY *Fam. Dict.* s.v. *Orkanet*, The Orkanet grows in the Southern Parts of France. **1796** WITHERING *Bot. Arrangem.* II. 226 The root of the foreign Alkanet that is kept in the shops. **1828** S. GRAY *Operat. Chem.* 541 Alkanet root gives a fine colour.
3. Applied to kindred plants: **a.** Common (English) Alkanet (*Anchusa officinalis*); **b.** Evergreen Alkanet (*A. sempervirens*); **c.** Bastard Alkanet (*Lithospermum arvense*); **d.** Alkanet (of America), (*L. canescens*).
1597 GERARD *Herbal* II. cclxxi. 657 The Alkanets flower and flourish in the sommer moneths. **1861** PRATT *Flower. Pl.* IV. 50 The roots of most of the Alkanets furnish some slight degree of red colouring matter.

alkanna: see ALCANNA.

alkany, obs. or dial. form of ALKANET.
1741 *Compl. Fam.-Piece* I. i. 82 Colour it with Alkany Roots.

alkapton (æl'kæptɒn). *Med.* Also **alcapton.** [a. G. (C. Boedeker 1861, in *Ann. d. Chemie u. Pharm.* CXVII. 101), f. AL(KALI + Gr. *κάπτον*, neut. pres. pple. of *κάπτειν* to swallow greedily.] A reducing substance which causes urine, left standing, to turn dark through oxidation. Also *attrib.* Hence **alkapto'nuria** [-URIA], the disease in which this substance is present; **alkapto'nuric** *a.* and *sb.*
1888 *Jrnl. Chem. Soc.* LIV. 1121 Alcaptonuria... A certain kind of human urine darkens on the addition of alkalis. Bödeker..isolated from such urine a substance to which he gave the name 'alcapton'. **1899** GARROD in *Jrnl. Physiol.* XXIII. 512 The urine of an alkaptonuric individual. *Ibid.*, Alkapton urines. *Ibid.*, Some cases of alkaptonuria. **1905** —— & HELE *Ibid.* XXXIII. 198 An adult male alkaptonuric.

alkargen (æl'kɑːdʒɪn). *Chem.* [f. ALKAR(SIN) + (OXY)GEN.] (See quot. 1877)
1843 J. S. MILL *Logic* III. ix. §1. 482 The substance called alkargen, discovered by Bunsen,..has not the slightest injurious action upon the organism. **1877** WATTS *Fownes' Chem.* 232 Cacodylic or Dimethyl-arsenic Acid, also called Alkargen.

alkarsin (æl'kɑːsɪn). *Chem.* [f. ALK(ALI) + ARS(ENIC) + -IN, in reference to its preparation.] A heavy poisonous liquid, spontaneously inflammable, with disgusting odour of garlic, formed by distillation of arsenious oxide and dry acetate of potash, supposed to be a variable mixture of cacodyl and its oxidation products.
1850 DAUBENY *Atom. Theory* vii. (ed. 2) 219 Cadet's fuming liquor also called alkarsine. **1875** BLOXHAM *Chem.* 524 Alcarsin has the properties of a base; it is capable of combining with the oxygen acids to form crystalline salts.

alkatran, early form of ALCHITRAN, *Obs.*, pitch.

alke, obs. form of ELK.

‖**alke'davy.** *Obs.* [ad. (perh. indirectly) Arab. *al-qāḏawī*, i.e. *al* the + *qāḏawī* of the CADI or ALCALDE (sc. *alqaçr* the palace).] The palace of a cadi or alcalde.
1631 HEYWOOD *Maid of West* IV. (1874) 313 Fill our Alkedavy, the great Pallace. *Ibid.* V. 329 Beare him hence Alcade Into our Alkedavy.

‖**alkekengi** (ælkɪ'kɛndʒɪ). *Bot.* Forms: 5 **alkenkengy,** 6 **alkakinge,** 6–7 **alkakengie,** 7 **alkakeng(e, alcakengie,** 8 **alkakengi.** [med.L. *alkekengi* f. Arab. *al-kākanj, al-kākenj*, i.e. *al* the + Pers. *kākanj* a 'kind of medicinal resin from a tree growing in the mountains of Herat.' Freytag. 'Nightshade,' Hopkins *Pers. Dict.* Cf. It. *alcachengi*, Sp. *alquequenje*, Fr. *alkékenge*, which also appears as an earlier Eng. form.]
1. A plant (*Physalis Alkekengi* Linn.) N.O. *Solanaceæ*, also called Winter-Cherry from its ornamental scarlet fruit.
1440 *Promp. Parv.*, Alkenkengy, herbe morub. *Morella rubea.* **1551** TURNER *Herbal* II. 142 Alkakinge..hath the same vertue that gardin nyghtshad hath. **1597** GERARD *Herbal* II. lii. 271 The red winter Cherrie is called..in English red Nightshade..and Alkakengie. **1605** TIMME *Quersit.* III. 181 Take of alkakeng berries, twenty in number. **1676** BULLOKAR, *Alkakangi.* **1742** BAILEY, *Alkakengi*, winter cherry, the Fruit of one sort of the Plant Night-shade. **1783** AINSWORTH *Thesaur.*, *Halicacabus*, a red winter cherry, red nightshade, alkakengy.

alkemy, -enamy(e, obs. forms of ALCHEMY.

alkene ('ælkiːn). *Chem.* [f. ALK(YL + -ENE.] Any member of the olefine series of hydrocarbons.
1899 [see OLEFINE]. **1944** L. F. & M. FIESER *Org. Chem.* iii. 53 The Geneva system provides the convenient generic term alkene, which designates the hydrocarbons of the series comprising ethylene and its homologues. **1964** N. G. CLARK *Mod. Org. Chem.* vi. 87 Thus the olefins are systematically known as the 'alkenes'.

†'**alker.** *Obs.* A sort of custard.
1381 *Forme of Cury* 120 (in Wright) For to make rys alker. Tak figys and raysons, and do away the kernelis.

†**alkermes** (æl'kɜːmɪz). *Obs.* [a. Fr. *alkermès* ad. (ult.) Arab. *al-qirmiz*, i.e. *al* the + *qirmiz* KERMES.]
1. The Kermes, or Scarlet Grain insect (the female of *Coccus Ilicis*), formerly supposed to be a berry, and sometimes described erroneously as a 'gall.'
1621 BURTON *Anat. Mel.* II. v. I. v, Alkermes comforts the inner parts. **1624** CAPT. SMITH *Virginia* VI. 216 The..Fruits are of many sorts and kinds, as Alkermes, Currans, Mulberies, etc. **1718** QUINCY *Compl. Dispens.* 83 Of Alkermes, The Juice of the Berries is wonderfully grateful to the Palate, and a fine Cordial.
2. A once famous confection or cordial of which the kermes 'berry' was originally an ingredient.
1605 BACON *Adv. Learn.* IV. ii. 164 Venice treacle, mithridate, diascordium, the confection of alkermes. **1626** —— *Sylva* §965 Kermes, which is the principal ingredient in their cordial confection Alkermes. **1692** TRYON *Good House-w.* (ed. 2) i. 6 A rich Cordial of Alchermes that I'll send you. **1704** COCKER *Dict.*, *Alkermes*, an Excellent Confection against swoonings, it is made of Gold, Amber, Pearl and the like. **1753** CHAMBERS *Cycl. Supp.* s.v., The confection alkermes has undergone divers changes and censures.

alkimy, obs. form of ALCHEMY.

†'**alkin,** *a. Obs.* Forms: (1 **alra cynna,** ? **alles cynnes**), 2–3 **alles cunnes (-y-),** 3–4 **alle kunnes, alle kinne,** 4–5 **alkyns, alkyn(e,** 5–6 **alkin, alken.** [orig. genitive phrase, sing. or pl., *alles cynnes* of every kind, '*omnis generis*,' *alra cynna* of all kinds, '*omnium generum*,' which being placed before the noun on which they depended, as *alra cynna fúᵹlas* fowls of all sorts, *alles cunnes deor* beasts of every kind, became treated more or less as adjs., and finally reduced to *alkins, alkin.* It is doubtful whether they occur before 1100, though OE. has phrases parallel to *alra cynna* in *maneᵹra cynna wítu* 'afflictions of many kinds.' *Ps.* x. 7. Modern usage reverses the syntactic relation in *all kind of, all kinds of.* See KIN and KIND.] Of every kind or sort; every kind of, all kinds of.
c **1175** *Lamb. Hom.* 79 Alles cunnes wilde dor. *c* **1200** ORMIN 850 Onn alle kinne wise. *c* **1230** *St. Juliana* 35 Ha greiðið þe..Alles cunnes pinen. *a* **1330** *Florice & Bl.* 793 þer was alle kunnes gleo. **1340** HAMPOLE *Pr. Consc.* 613 Alkyn filthe. **1377** LANGL. *P. Pl.* B. x. 177 Of alkinnes craftes · I contreued toles. **1460** in *Pol. Rel. & L. Poems* (1866) 105 Alken synnes wer wroȝt in me. **1552** LYNDESAY *Complaynt* 300 Wors than thay in alkin thyng.

alkine ('ælkaɪn). *Chem.* [ad. G. *alkin* (A. Ladenburg 1881, in *Ber. d. Deut. Chem. Ges.* XIV. 2126) f. ALC(OHOL + -INE[5].] †**1.** Ladenburg's name for a tertiary base containing an alcoholic group; also called *alkamine. Obs.*
1882 *Jrnl. Chem. Soc.* XLII. 165 *Alkines*... *Piperpropylalkine*..dissolves in water with evolution of heat. **1886** E. F. SMITH tr. *von Richter's Org. Chem.* 264 Oxy-alkyl bases may be obtained from the allyl amines... The bases obtained from the secondary amines are *alkamines* or *alkines*. **1904** *Jrnl. Chem. Soc.* LXXXVI. I. 685 Alkines combine with the haloids of organic alkyloxy- or acetooxy-acids... The products closely resemble the difficultly prepared, unsubstituted alkine esters in their physiological action.
2. Also '**alkyne** (now the usual form). Any member of the acetylene or ethyne series of hydrocarbons, with the general formula C_nH_{2n-2}, containing a triple bond.
1909 in *Cent. Dict.* Suppl. **1938** *Jrnl. Org. Chem.* II. 1 In 1913 Lebeau and Picon reported that 1-alkynes were produced in good yield by the action of certain alkyl iodides on sodium acetylide in liquid ammonia. **1944** L. F. & M. FIESER *Org. Chem.* iv. 75 The properties of some of the members of the alkyne series.

alkitran, variant of ALCHITRAN, *Obs.*, pitch.

alkmuyne, variant of ALCAMYNE.

alknamy(e, obs. form of ALCHEMY.

alky ('ælkɪ). *slang* (orig. and chiefly *U.S.*). Also **alchy, alki(e).** [Abbrev. of ALCOHOL and (sense 2) ALCOHOLIC *sb.*: see -Y[6], -IE.] **1.** Alcohol; *spec.* (illicit) alcoholic liquor. Freq. personified in early use.
1844 *Akron* (Ohio) *Buzzard* 25 June 3/1 After strong devotional homage before the throne of old King Alchy, [he] is in the habit of manifesting his affection for his family by severely beating them. **1858** J. A. STONE *Put's Golden Songster* 15 'Old Alky' makes their bowels yearn, They stagger round and fall. **1921** P. & T. CASEY *Gay-Cat* xx. 187 There ain't nothin' stronger in th' booze line than pure alky mixed with jamocha. **1927** *Amer. Speech* II. 389/1 Drinking has supplied its quota of words to the vag's lexicon. Alki and hall come from alcohol and explain themselves. **1929** D. RUNYON in *Cosmopolitan* Nov. 73/1 Ripping and tearing at each other..as to who shall have what in the way of business privileges of one kind and another, including alky, and liquor, and gambling. **1930** *Amer. Mercury* Dec. 454/1 *Alky*, alcohol. 'He's in the alky racket.' **1962** *Parade* (Austral.) Oct. 20/3 Soon Pretty Louie had his first batch of 'alky' cooking on crude apparatus in a broken-down Brooklyn warehouse. **1970** R. & J. PATERSON *Cranberry Portage* iv. 22 All they [*sc.* bootleggers] need is a shack and a can of alky.
2. A drunkard or alcoholic.
1960 WENTWORTH & FLEXNER *Dict. Amer. Slang* 3/2 *Alky, alki, alchy*... 5 A drunkard, esp. a jobless, homeless alcoholic. **1962** A. FRY *Ranch on Cariboo* xx. 209 What it's like to be an alky, I guess. **1964** B. BEAVER *Hot Sands* 16 Ben Tickell, the regular night porter, was an alkie if ever she had seen one. **1970** *N.Z. Listener* 21 Dec. 8/4 You might draw an alky who stops at every pub. **1983** M. GEE *Sole Survivor* xii. 124, I had done an article on alkies, winos, meths drinkers, sleepers-out. **1986** *City Limits* 9 Oct. 63 Nazi sympathizers, alkies, junkies and the unemployed.

alkyd ('ælkɪd). [f. ALKY(L + ACI)D.] In full ***alkyd resin.*** Any of a group of synthetic resins (see quot. 1929). Also *attrib.* and *Comb.*
1929 *Chem. Abstr.* 2308 Alkyd resins include all complexes resulting primarily from the interaction of a polyhydric alc[ohol] and polybasic acid. **1943** E. A. BEVAN in R. S. Morrell et al. *Synthetic Resins & Allied Plastics* (ed. 2) xi. 281 The alkyd resins, sometimes known as 'glyptals', are formed by the condensation of polybasic acids with polyhydric alcohols. **1943** *Jrnl. R. Aeronaut. Soc.* XIV. Abstr. 480 Alkyd type finishes are relatively new. **1958** *Woman* 22 Feb. 14/2 Choose an alkyd-based enamel.

alkyl ('ælkɪl). *Chem.* [f. G. *alk(ohol* ALCOHOL + -YL.] In full ***alkyl radical.*** Any of the series of radicals derived from paraffin hydrocarbons by the removal of a hydrogen atom, as methyl (CH_3), ethyl (C_2H_5), etc. So *attrib.* or as *adj.*, derived from, or related to, the paraffin series of hydrocarbons. Formerly also called *alphyl.* Cf. ARYL.
1879 *Jrnl. Chem. Soc.* XXXVI. 522 (*title*) Boiling points of the ethereal salts of hydroxy- and alkyloxy-acids. **1882** *Ibid.* XLII. 831 (*title*) Synthesis of so-called alkyl disulphoxides. **1883** *Ibid.* XLIV. 919 Action of the Alkyl-derivatives of the Halogen-substituted Fatty Acids on Aniline. *Ibid.* 276 The alkyl salts of the $C_nH_{2n}O_2$ series. **1889** M'GOWAN tr. *Bernthsen's Org. Chem.* 37 The halogen alkyls, $C_nH_{2n+1}X$. **1906** M'GOWAN & SUDBOROUGH *Bernthsen's Org. Chem.* 22 The monovalent residues, C_nH_{2n+1} (methyl, ethyl, etc.), which form the radicals of the monovalent alcohols, $C_nH_{2n+1}OH$, are frequently termed *alkyls*, or *alphyls*, while the divalent residues, C_nH_{2n}, are known as *alkylenes*. **1953** *Sci. News* XXX. 91 One of the detergents..is an alkyl sulphate, with an average chain-length of about eight to ten carbon atoms. **1957** *Technology* July 168/4 Detergents usually contain a surface active agent, alkylbenzenesulphonate, which influences surface adsorption and, incidentally, causes the familiar foaming (of doubtful utility). **1964** N. G. CLARK *Mod. Org. Chem.* viii. 125 These compounds may also be regarded as alkyl-substituted water molecules.
Hence '**alkylate** *v. trans.*, to introduce an alkyl radical into (a compound); so '**alkylated** *ppl. a.*, '**alkylating** *ppl. a.* and *vbl. sb.*, **alky'lation**; '**alkylate** *sb.*, a product of alkylation; '**alkylene**, an olefine of the ethylene series.
1889 M'GOWAN tr. *Bernthsen's Org. Chem.* 46 Olefines or Hydrocarbons of the Ethylene Series (Alkylenes): C_nH_{2n}. *Ibid.* 272 Alkylated ureas. **1900** *Jrnl. Chem. Soc.* LXXVIII.

I. 619 Dimethyl Sulphate as an Alkylating Agent. *Ibid.* LXXVII. I. 729 Alkylation by means of Dry Silver Oxide and Alkyl Halides. **1903** *Amer. Chem. Jrnl.* Apr. 293 The acylhalogenalkyl(alphyl)amines, by treatment with zinc ethyl, are simply reduced and not alkylated. **1904** F. P. Foster *Appleton's Med. Dict.* 86/1 *Alkylate*, a compound derived from a monatomic alcohol by the substitution of a metal for the hydroxylic hydrogen. **1958** *New Scientist* 8 May 23/1 There are alkylation processes at Stanley in Cheshire, and at Shellhaven, the latter for making those alkylates used in detergents. **1961** *Lancet* 29 July 250/1 Chemotherapy with various alkylating agents. **1964** N. G. Clark *Mod. Org. Chem.* vi. 98 In the presence of strong acids (concentrated sulphuric acid or hydrofluoric acid) or aluminium chloride, $AlCl_3$, olefins react with tertiary paraffins, whereby the alkyl group corresponding to the olefin is attached to the paraffin; the paraffin is said to undergo 'alkylation'.

alkyne, see ALKINE 2.

all (ɔːl), *a.*, *sb.*, and *adv.* Forms: *Sing.* 1– all (late WS. 1–3 eall, eal), 1–7 al (*north.* 4–5 alle). *Pl.* 1–5 alle (WS. 1–3 ealle, *north.* 2–7 al), 5– all. For early inflected forms, see below, D. [Common to all the Teutonic stock, but not found beyond: cf. OS. *all*, *al*, OFris. *al*, *ol*, OHG. *al* (*all-er*), ON. *all-r*, Goth. *all-s*. Properly adj. but passing on one side into a sb., on the other into an adv. As an adj. it usually precedes, but sometimes follows its sb.]

A. *adj.* I. with *sb.*

1. With *sb. sing.* The entire or unabated amount or quantity of; the whole extent, substance, or compass of; the whole.

a. with proper names, names of substances, and abstracts, *all England*, *all flesh*, *all wisdom*, *all speaking*; also with *day*, *night*, *spring*, *summer*, *Lent*, *August*, and other definite portions of time.

886 *O.E. Chron.*, And him all Angel cyn to cirde. *a* **1000** *Metr. Ps.* lv. 9 Ic ealne dæȝ, ecne Drihten wordum weorðiȝe. *c* **1175** *Lamb. Hom.* 17 Þrouwede deð for al moncun. *c* **1175** *Cott. Hom.* 225 Of þan wearð eft ȝestaþeled eall middenard. *c* **1325** *E.E. Allit. P.* B. 779 In longyng al nyȝt he lengeȝ. **1340** *Ayenb.* 17 To huam alle triacle went in to venym. **1382** Wyclif *Matt.* xxviii. 18 Al power is ȝouun to me, in heuene and in erthe. **1473** Warkw. *Chron.* 3 And so Kynge Edward was possessed of alle Englonde. **1535** Coverdale *Judg.* xix. 13 Tarye at Gibea or at Ramah allnight. **1611** Bible *1 Pet.* i. 24 All flesh is as grasse. **1665** Marvell *Corr.* 50 (1872–5) II. 186, I..beseech God to continue you in all health and well-fare. **1763** J. Brown *Poetry & Mus.* v. 79 Horace.. hath set him above the old Philosophers, as a Teacher of all Virtue. **1849** Macaulay *Hist. Eng.* I. 576 At Exeter all Devonshire had been gathered together to welcome him. **1862** Trench *Miracles* Introd. 12 This speaking is diffused over all time.

(*b*) All that is possible, the greatest possible. **1594** Shaks. *Rich. III*, iv. i. 57 *St.* I in all haste was sent. *A.* And I with all vnwillingnesse will goe. **1879** *Wild Life in S.C.* 258 A weasel..makes all speed into the fern.

b. with a defining word (dem. or poss. adj., genitive case, etc.) *all* precedes def. word, or, less usually, follows the sb.

855 *O.E. Chron.*, Ofer al his rice. **860** *Ibid.*, To allum þam rice. **870** *Ibid.*, Þa Deniscan..þæt lond all ȝe eodon. *c* **1280** *A Sarmun* in *E.E.P.* (1862) 7 Of al þis ioi þer nis non end. **1297** R. Glouc. 122 And schewede hem al þe wey wyder he schulde wende. *c* **1386** Chaucer *Knts. T.* 660 And songen al the roundel lustily. **1593** Shaks. *Rich. II*, iii. ii. 174 You haue but mistooke me all this while. **1667–8** Marvell *Corr.* 84 (1872–5) II. 231 We are, as for all other your kindnesse, obliged to you. **1682** Dryden *Medal* 304 Frogs and Toads and all the Tadpole Train. **1830** Tennyson *May Queen* ii. 24 And all the world is still. **1847** —— *Princess* i. 193 With all my heart, With my full heart.

c. So when the sb. is understood, as *all this*, *all that*, *all mine*, *all your friend's*. *All* now follows *it*; as *take it all* (or *all of it*).

a **700** on *Ruthwell Cross*, Ic þæt al biheald. *c* **1175** *Lamb. Hom.* 49 God þe al þis heom haueð isend. *c* **1220** *Hali Meid.* 31 Þat heo hit al weldeð. *c* **1300** *Leg. Rood* 18 Al hit com of one more. *Mod.* All this is distasteful to me. I see it all now.

†**d.** Following *the*. *Obs. rare.*

1297 R. Glouc. 367 Þer nas prince in þe al worlde of so noble fame. *c* **1449** Pecock *Repr.* 313 Ech preest which schulde folewe thilk ensaumpling thoruȝ the al fulnes and likenes of it.

†**e.** Followed by *a*. *Obs.* repl. by *a whole*.

c **1300** *St. Brand.* 60 Her ȝe habbeth al a ȝer meteles i-beo. **1340** Hampole *Pr. Consc.* 3010 A malady..lastand alle a yhere. *c* **1350** *Will. Palerne* 2215 Þei trauailed al a niȝt. *c* **1386** Chaucer *Frankl. T.* 620 She wepeth, wailleth, al a day or two. **1523** Ld. Berners *Froissart* I. liv. 75 Ther was one [assault] endured al a day.

2. With *sb. pl.* The entire number of; the individual components of, without exception. (*All* precedes the sb. or defining adj.; rarely, in poetry, follows the sb.).

a. without defining word. Also in phr. (*to be*) *all things to all men*.

878 *O.E. Chron.*, Him to comon onȝen Sumor sæte alle and Wilsætan. *c* **1000** *Sax. Leechd.* I. 296 Wið ealle wundela, genim þas wyrte. **1154** *O.E. Chron.* (Laud MS.) an. 1135 Þa þestrede þe dæi ouer al landes. *c* **1220** *Hali Meid.* 5 Freo ouer alle fram alle worldliche weanen. **1366** Maundev. ii. 10 Alle Men knowen not that. **1382** Bible (Wycliff) *1 Cor.* ix. 22 To alle men I am maad alle thingis. **1570** Ascham *Scholem.* ii. (Arb.) 118 Marke all aiges. **1606** Shaks. *Ant. & Cl.* i. iv. 9 A man who is th' abstracts of all faults That all men follow. **1611** Bible (A. V.) *1 Cor.* ix. 22 To the weake became I as weake, That I might gain the weake. I am made all things to all men, that I might by all meanes save some. **1742** Young *Nt. Th.* i. 424 All men think all men mortal, but themselves. **1763** Churchill *Prophecy of Famine* 11 If they, directed by Paul's holy pen, Become discreetly all things to all men, That all men may become all things to them, Envy may hate, but justice can't condemn. **1807** Crabbe *Par. Reg.* iii. 52 All men have done, and I like all, amiss. **1860** Abp. Thomson *Laws of Th.* §77. 131 The word All in its proper logical sense means 'each and every;' but it stands sometimes for 'all taken together.' **1873** Symonds *Grk. Poets* iii. 89 Theognis bids his friend (Cyrnus) be as much as possible all things to all men. **1940** Wodehouse *Quick Service* ix. 86, I pointed out to him that it is of the essence of a barmaid's duties that she be all things to all men. **1973** *Times* 25 Apr. 25/4 The agency's charter tries to gloss over..these fundamental differences by instructing..its president and his staff to be all things to all men.

b. with defining word. (Also with sb. understood, as *all those*, *all mine*, *all Henry's*.)

885 *O.E. Chron.*, And þa scipo alle ȝeræhton. *c* **1000** *Ags. Gosp.* Matt. xxvi. 35 Ealle þa oþre leorning-cnihtas. *c* **1175** *Cott. Hom.* 219 He and halle his iféren. *c* **1175** *Lamb. Hom.* 97 Ealle þas þing and moniȝe oðre. **1362** Langl. *P. Pl.* A. i. 55, I fonde þere Freris, alle þe foure ordres. **1660** T. Stanley *Hist. Phil.* (1701) 113/1 He form'd a Law, which all the old Men follow'd. **1782** Cowper *J. Gilpin* 114 The dogs did bark, the children screamed, Up flew the windows all. **1849** Macaulay *Hist. Eng.* I. 171 They had watched all his motions, and lectured him on all his youthful follies.

c. with a pers. or rel. pron. (In the nom. *all* was formerly often prefixed; e.g. *all we*, for which the mod. usage is *we all*, or *all of us*.)

c **1000** Ælfric *Saints' L.* i. 140 Ealle hí sind on Godes ȝesihðe. *c* **1175** *Lamb. Hom.* 125 Ure drihten and ure alesend i-unne us allen. *c* **1200** *Moral Ode* 176 Ealle he scullè þuder come. **1382** Wyclif *Isa.* liii. 6 Alle wee as shep erreden. [**1611** Alle we like sheepe haue gone astray.] **1557** More *Edward V* (1641) 15 The place that they al preach of. **1562** J. Heywood *Prov. & Ep.* (1867) 79 Euery man for him selfe, and god for us all. **1593** Shaks. *Rich. II*, iii. ii. 142 Yea, all of them at Bristow lost their heads. **1665** Ld. Dorset, To all you Ladies now on Land. **1711** Addison *Spect.* No. 93 ¶1 We all of us complain of the Shortness of Time. **1798** Coleridge *Anc. Mar.* iv. iv, And they all dead did lie. **1820** Keats *St. Agnes* xi, They are all here to-night. *Mod.* We all know him; all of us have said so at times; I saw you all; I have heard it from all of you. He took down all our names, *or* the names of all of us. 'And so say all of us.'

d. *all very well*, fine or acceptable as far as it goes (implying that it may be unsatisfactory in other ways); similarly *all very fine* (*and large*) (now *arch.*).

c **1853** C. Brontë *Villette* II. xix. 67 This would have been all very well, if he had not added to such kindly and unobtrusive evidence a certain wilfulness in discharging what he called debts. **1887** *Referee* 7 Aug. 2/4 How many people passed the turnstiles at the Alexandra Palace I am not in a position to say, but that the attendance was all very fine and large is beyond dispute. **1953** C. Day Lewis *Italian Visit* iii. 34 Terribly apt to ask what Our all-very-fine sensations were in aid of. **1961** *Essays & Stud.* 21 It is all very well to scoff at H. G. Wells because much of his writing betrays a perky mediocrity, if you have a vision of life not indeed identical with his but somewhat comparable in scope. **1985** *New Yorker* 19 Aug. 27/2 One has heard of holiday romances, which are all very well, but really, in one's own home!

†**3.** = Every. L. *omnis*, Fr. *tout* (*tout homme*). *Obs.* exc. as in b.

This use, unknown to OE., seems to have begun with *thing*, in which the sing. and pl. being alike, *alle thing* passed from pl. into coll., and then simple sing. In later times often combined, *althing* (cf. *anything*, *something*, *nothing*), and used advb.: see below C 2b. *All day* seems to be after Fr. *toujours*. The extension to *all-kin*, *all-gate*, *all man*, *all body*, etc., seems northern; *aa'thing*, *aa'bodie*, *aa'gate*, are still common Sc. for *everything*, *everybody*, *every way*. (See also infra C 2b.)

c **1000** Ælfric *Saints' L.* i. 136 God ælmihtiȝ wát ealle þing togædere..ealle þing þe æfre wæron. *c* **1175** *Lamb. Hom.* 7 Wurðian alre erest þin feder and þin moder ouer alle eordliche þing. **1297** R. Glouc. 371 Edgar Aþelyng And kyng Macolom were þo glade þoru alle þyng. **1398** Trevisa *Barth. De P.R.* iv. xi, And þis we seeþ al day [*quotidie*], with oure yen [*ed.* 1582 this we see each day]. **1526** Tindale *Phil.* ii. 14 Do all thynge [**1611** all things] without murmuryngе. **1549** *Bk. Com. Prayer, Pref. on Ceremonies*, Some bee so newe fangle that they woulde innovate all thyng [**1604** all things]. **1556** Lauder *Tract.* 144 Ȝour..dewtie..That ȝe aucht tyll all Creature. **1558** Kennedy in *Wod. Soc. Misc.* I. 174 Lat all Christiane man haue refuge to the juge. **1570** Ascham *Scholem.* 62 Good order in all thyng.

b. *esp.* with *kin* (obs.: see ALKIN), *kind*, and *manner*.

1366 Maundev. xx. 215 Spices and alle manere of marchaundises. **1535** Coverdale *Josh.* iii. 15 All maner watris of the londe. **1548** Udall etc. *Erasm. Paraphr.* Pref. 14 Void of almaner parcialitie of affection. **1607** Shaks. *Timon* i. i. 67 All kinde of natures that labour on the bosome of this Sphere. *a* **1609** ? Shaks. *Lover's Compl.* 121 All kind of arguments. *c* **1680** Beveridge *Serm.* (1729) II. 21 Avoid all manner of evil. **1711** Steele *Spect.* No. 32 ¶2, I shall be quite out of all manner of Shape. **1817** Jas. Mill *Brit. Ind.* II. v. iv. 437 Orders which might be construed all manner of ways. *Mod.* All kind of drollery.

4. = Any whatever. In universally exclusive sentences or clauses; as *without all* (cf. L. *sine omni*). Now only in such phr. as *beyond all question*, *doubt*, *controversy*, etc., or where the exclusion is expressed by a verb, as *to deny*, *disclaim*, *renounce*, *all connexion*.

c **1400** *Apol. for Loll.* 72 If þe kirk, wiþ out oole autorite, solempnize matrimoyn forbidun of þe general kirk. *c* **1449** Pecock *Repr.* iv. ix. 472 Nile ȝe swere alwise. **1587** Holinshed *Scot. Chron.* (1806) I. 315 Such of the people as ..fell into their hands, were slaine without all mercie. **1605** Shaks. *Macb.* iii. ii. 11 Things without all remedie, Should be without regard. **1652** Needham tr. *Selden's Mare Cl.* 75 The Carthaginians enjoyed the command of the Sea without all Controversie. **1847** Longf. *Ev.* i. iii. 10 Without all guile or Suspicion..was he. **1855** Macaulay *Hist. Eng.* III. 382 He disclaimed all intention of attacking the memory of Lord Russell.

II. *absol.*

5. As antecedent to relative: All *that*, all *those*, the accompanying demonstrative having been dropped from the earliest times before the relative *that* (*what* obs., cf. Ger. *alles was*), which latter is now often dropped also: 'all we have' = all *that that* we have.

827 *O.E. Chron.*, Al þæt be suþan Humbre wæs. **874** *Ibid.*, On allum þam þe him læstan woldon. *c* **1320** *Cast. Loue* 535 Ichulle al don þat þi wille is. **1587** Golding *De Mornay* i. 8 Yee Rivers, and all that euer is. **1607** Shaks. *Tim.* iv. ii. 35 To haue his pompe, and all what state compounds. **1667** Milton *P.L.* ix. 569 To tell thee all What thou commandst. **1690** Locke *Hum. Underst.* Wks. 1727 I. i. iv. §11. 25 This is all could be infer'd from the Notion of a God. **1790** Burke *Fr. Rev.* 43 To derive all we possess as an inheritance from our forefathers. **1850** Tennyson *In Mem.* xxiii. 17 And all we met was fair and good, And all was good that Time could bring.

6. Followed by *of*: in *sing.* The entire amount, every part, the whole; in *pl.* Every individual, all the members or examples. (This const. is comparatively modern, and is probably due to form-assoc. with *none of*, *some of*, *little of*, *much of*, *few of*, *many of*.) *Rare*, exc. with pronouns, as *all of it*, *of whom*, *of which*, *of them*. Also, as much as, altogether, quite; *for all of* (cf. FOR *prep.* 26b) *U.S.*, as far as concerns (a person or thing).

[See pronominal examples under 2c.]

c **1800** Montgomery *Hymn*, 'Tis not the whole of life to live, Nor all of death to die. **1858** Sears *Athan.* x. 81 The Sadducees held that all of human existence was bounded between birth and death. **1903** T. B. Aldrich *Ponkapog Papers* (1904) 169 All of Herrick's geese were swans. **1932** J. H. Frederick *Devel. Amer. Commerce* vii. 77 There were insufficient American vessels to handle all of the traffic.

1829 R. C. Sands *Writings* (1834) II. 57 Miss Cross, who was all of six feet high. **1854** M. J. Holmes *Tempest & Sunshine* xix. 124 No;—he may have her and go to the old boy for all of Josh. **1883** 'Mark Twain' *Life on Miss.* xviii. 220 It must have been all of fifteen minutes..of dull, homesick silence. **1911** H. S. Harrison *Queed* xvii. 209 Thus they parted, almost precipitately, and, for all of him, might never have met again in this world. **1944** 'G. Graham' *Earth & High Heaven* i. iii. 65 He was all of thirty-three, solitary and unsure of himself.

7. a. as *pl.* = All men, all people.

c **1000** *Ags. Gosp.* Mark xiii. 37 Soðlice þæt ic eow secȝe, eallum [*Lindisf.*, *Rushw.* allum, *Hatt.* eallen] ic hit secȝe. **1382** Wyclif *Eph.* iv. 6 O God, and fadir of alle, the which is aboue alle men, and by alle thingis, and in vs alle. **1593** Shaks. *Rich. II*, iii. ii. 160 Some poyson'd by their Wiues, some sleeping kill'd, All murther'd. **1611** Bible *1 Tim.* iv. 15 That thy profiting may appeare to all. **1711** Addison *Spect.* No. 122 ¶2 Beloved and esteemed by all about him. **1878** *Birm. Weekly Post* 2 Feb., An inn in Marlborough has the sign 'The Five Alls.' They are—a king, with the motto, 'I govern all;' a bishop, with 'I pray for all;' a lawyer, 'I plead for all;' a soldier, 'I fight for all;' a labourer, 'I pay for all.'

b. In scoring at games, denoting that both sides have made the stated score; e.g. *love all* = neither side has scored.

1742 Hoyle *Short Treatise Whist* xi. 25 Suppose the Game to be Nine all. **1837** T. Bacon *First Impr. fr. Nat. in Hindostan* I. 252 In the fourth 20, they were even; 67 all. **1878** *Laws of Lawn-Tennis* 12 If both players win five games, the score is called games-all. **1883** *Nat. Hist. Jrnl. & School Reporter* VII. 155 Up to within ten minutes when time was called the score was one goal all. **1898** Love all [see LOVE *sb.* 10b]. **1965** *Listener* 17 June 915/2 Game all. Dealer West.

8. a. as *sing.* = Everything.

c **1000** Ælfric *Saints' L.* i. 139 God is æȝhwær eall. **1470** Malory *Arthur* (1816) I. 303 But in God is all. **1589** *Pap w. Hatch.* (1844) 21 Alls as it is taken; marie the diuell take al. **1667** Milton *P.L.* i. 105 What though the field be lost? All is not lost. **1785** Crabbe *Newsp.* 235 Something to all men, and to some men all. **1870** Lowell *Study Wind.* 211 Browning..draws nearer to the all-for-point fashion of the *concettisti*, with every poem he writes. **1866** G. Macdonald *Ann. Q. Neighb.* i. 10, 'I wanted to see yer face, sir, that was all.'

b. all but: Everything short of. *Hence* (*adverbially*) Almost, very nearly, well nigh, (also with hyphen) used *adject.*, almost complete or entire; in ellipt. use: almost; also as *sb.*

1598 J. Bastard in Farr's *S.P.* II. 306 Man..All but resembleth God, all but his glasse, All but the picture of his maiestie. *a* **1678** Marvell *Poems* Wks. III. 412 Society is all but rude To this delicious solitude. **1810** M. L. Weems *Let.* in *Wks.* (1929) III. 14 Doctor Fendall..sold 60 doll[ar]s all but. **1816** Tuckey *Narr. Exped. R. Zaire* (1818) i. 18 Negro washerwomen, whose state of *all but* nudity. **1831** Carlyle *Sart. Res.* ii. ii. 111 The all-but omnipotence of early culture. **1862** Stanley *Jew. Ch.* (1877) I. v. 87 These were all but unknown to Greeks and Romans. **1866** Pusey *Mirac. Prayer* 12 An all-but-infinite variety of phænomena. **1878** Bosw. Smith *Carthage* 203 The best and all-but-sufficing answer. **1881** Gilbert *Patience* 11 *Col.* (apologetically). I'm afraid we're not quite right. *Ang.* Not supremely, perhaps, but, oh, so all-but! Oh, Saphir, are they not quite too all-but? **1914** 'I. Hay' *Knight on Wheels* xix. 192 Most of them are Impossibles, but there are a good many All-Buts. **1920** 'W. S. Palmer' *Christianity & Christ* 43 Until the great all-but-men brought forth true men. **1935** W. Empson *Poems* 3 Our all-but freedom.

c. and all: And everything *else*, and everything connected therewith, *et cetera*; *hence*, Too, also, as well (especially in dial. speech; Sc. 'Woo'd an' married an' a''). **and all that**: and all the rest of it, *et cetera*.

c **1535** TINDALE *Wks.* 1849 II. 11 He will save Devils and all. **1538** BALE *Thre Lawes* 1007 The wolle, skynne, flesh and all. c **1540** CROKE *Ps.* li, The walles, and all, shalbe made newe. **1662** MORE *Antid. Ath.* III. x. (1712) 120 Down came John, Pipe and all. **1681** *Trial S. Colledge* 29 *Jeff.* Who were the All? *Dugdale.* King and Clergy-men and all. **1702** DE FOE *New Test.* in Somers *Tracts* (1751) III. 14 They did it to Purpose, carried all before them, subdued Monarchy, cut of their King's Head, and *all that.* **1828** SCOTT *F.M. Perth* I. 37 With smithy, bellows, tongs, anvil, and all. **1857** HELPS *Friends in C.* Ser. I. I. 122 'Region of subtle sympathies,' and all that.

d. all in all: All things in all respects, all things altogether in one. Also *adverbially* and *subst.* (See **in all** below, 9 d.)

1539 ('great') and **1611** BIBLE *1 Cor.* xv. 28 That God maye be all in all [WYCLIF, alle thingis in alle thingis, TINDALE, all in all thinges]. **1596** R. CAREW in *Shaks. Cent. Praise* 20 Will you have all in all for Prose and verse? **1767** FORDYCE *Serm. Yng. Wom.* I. i. 27 Mirth and diversion are all in all. a **1824** CAMPBELL *On receiv. Seal* xii, The all-in-all of life—Content! **1824** BYRON *Don J.* II. clxxxix, They were All in all to each other. **1859** TENNYSON *Vivien* 248 And trust me not at all or all in all. **1878** —— *Q. Mary* III. vi. 136 Their Flemish go-between And all-in-all.

e. *phr.* **when all comes (goes) to all**: when everything is summed up, wound up, cleared up, explained; when one gets to the bottom of everything. *arch.*

1519 HORMAN *Vulg.* 123 Whan it cometh all to all. **1526** SKELTON *Magnyf.* 1732 For your sake, what so ever befall; I set not a flye, and all go to all. **1580** NORTH *Plutarch* (1676) 141 When all came to all nothing was done. **1668** PEPYS *Diary* 19 Aug., When all come to all, a fit of jealousy about Tom.

f. In phr. after an oath or obscenity, as *damn all*, nothing at all. Cf. BUGGER *sb.* 2 e.

1922 JOYCE *Ulysses* 417 Proud possessor of damnall. **1926** D. L. SAYERS *Clouds of Witness* x. 187, I'll tell you my story as shortly as I can, and you'll see I know damn all about it. **1930** BROPHY & PARTRIDGE *Songs & Slang* 114 *Damn all*, nothing. Used to give emphasis... A bowdlerization of a foul expression. **1939** J. MULGAN *Man Alone* iii. 31 There's —— all grows up here.

9. Hence, in many prepositional phrases.

a. Preceded by *above, after, before, beyond, for*, = Everything, (or often) everything else, everything to the contrary. Hence, ***after all***: after considering everything to the contrary, nevertheless; ***once for all***: once only; ***for good and all***: finally (see GOOD).

1611 BIBLE *Hebr.* x. 10 By the which will we are sanctified ..once for all. **1712** STEELE *Spect.* No. 462 ¶1 But after all he is very pleasant Company. **1763** BOSWELL *Johnson* (1826) I. 356 Here it is proper, once for all, to give a true and fair statement. **1768** STERNE *Sent. Journ.* (1778) II. 11, I stopp'd to bid her adieu for good and all. **1809** W. IRVING *Knickerb.* VII. xi. (1849) 440 Yet after all he was a mere mortal. **1849** MACAULAY *Hist. Eng.* I. 172 Above all, he had been long an exile.

b. at all: In every way, in any way. Formerly only *affirmatively* = altogether, wholly (now only *Irish*, dial., and *U.S. local*); now often in negative or interrogative sentences, or conditional clauses: e.g. *I did not speak at all*; *did you speak at all? if you spoke at all.*

c **1350** *Will. Palerne* 283, I þe coniure · & comande att alle. c **1400** *Epiph.* (Turnb. 1843) 110 Myrre betokneth to us at all Of hys monhode that is mortall. **1513** DOUGLAS *Eneis* Prol. 34 My waverand wyt, my cunnyng febill at all. **1535** COVERDALE *Jer.* vi. 14 Sayenge: peace, peace, when there is no peace at all. **1552–5** LATIMER *Serm. & Rem.* (1845) 52 They were careless at all, they thought all things were cock-sure. **1611** BIBLE *1 Sam.* xx. 6 If thy father at all misse me. **1849** MACAULAY *Hist. Eng.* II. 557 If he refuses to govern us at all, we are not bound to remain..without a government. **1876** FREEMAN *Norm. Conq.* III. xii. 185 Without any form of trial at all. *Ibid.* IV. xvii. 55 For that very cause, it soon ceased to be a garrison at all. **1894** CAINE *Manxman* II. 56 Is the woman mad at all? **1895** J. BARLOW *Strangers at Lisconnel* 262 And what at all have you got there? **1916, 1932** in H. WENTWORTH *Amer. Dial. Dict.* (1944) 34/2. **1945** *Amer. Speech* XX. 15 This affirmative use, although it has disappeared from speech at the formal level, lives on in Irish dialect and in colloquial speech in certain parts of America, especially after a superlative, as in the sentence 'We had the best time at all'.

†(*b*) *substantively. Obs.*

1672 MARVELL *Reh. Transp.* II. 3 He is so self-sufficient, and an At-all of so many capacities.

c. for all, *adv.* and *prep.*, Notwithstanding: see FOR.

a **1400** *Kyng of Tars* 1134 [He] smot him so fer al his scheld. **1526** TINDALE *Acts* xvi. 39 They have beaten us openley..for all that we are Romans. **1611** BIBLE *John* xxi. 11 For all there were so many, yet was not the net broken. **1741** RICHARDSON *Pamela* I. 28 Sit still, Pamela, and mind your Work, for all me. *Ibid.* IV. 178 A sad Situation I am in ..for all that. **1795** BURNS, 'A man's a man for a' that.'

d. in all: In the whole number, all together; *also*, in whole.

c **1380** *Sir Ferumb.* 4387, V. hundred knyȝtis in al þay wore. **1387** TREVISA *Higden* Rolls Ser. III. 363 He lived in alle þre and sixti ȝere. **1611** BIBLE *1 Chron.* ii. 6 Fiue of them in all. **1654** GENTILIS tr. *Servita's Hist. Inquis.* (1676) 870 It is received either in part or in all, or in part or in all laid aside. **1856** *Farmer's Mag.* Jan. 33 'Work, work, work!' are the in-all and the end-all of existence to him. **1882** *Mar. Ins. Policy*, All and every other Person or Persons to whom the same doth, may, or shall appertain, in Part, or in All.

†**e. mid all** (*obs.*), **with all**: †(*a*) Altogether, quite (*obs.*); (*b*) see WITHAL.

c **885** K. ÆLFRED *Gregory* xix. 144 Ða hie swiðe stiðliche arasiað, & mid ealle ofðrysceað. c **1175** *Lamb. Hom.*, Mid alle fordon. c **1230** *Ancr. R.* 100 A grim word mid alle. a **1300** *E.E. Psalter* xxi. 27 Loove Laverd þai sal with al. **1297** R. GLOUC. 28 He lette close fyur in metal quoynteliche withalle.

f. of all, from its use after a superlative, as in *first of all* (see D. II) was formerly used elliptically = Most of all, beyond all.

1590 MARLOWE *Edw. II*, IV. v, Vild wretch, and why hast thou, of all unkind, Borne arms against thy brother. **1605** ANDREWES *Serm.* (1841) II. 158 From each part;—but of all, from the last part. **1649** LOVELACE *Poems* 30 She Whom thou of all ador'st. **1711** ADDISON *Spect.* No. 135 ¶4 First of all by its abounding in monosyllables.

†**g. over all**: Everywhere (Ger. *überall*, Fr. *partout*). *Obs.*

1297 R. GLOUC. 375 Tresour aboute & oþer god oueral apertelyche. c **1386** CHAUCER *Prol.* 549 Over al there he cam.

h. with all: see e (above) and WITHAL.

III. Combined with other adjectives.

†**10.** Emphasized by *whole*: **all whole, whole all** (see ALLWHOLE), **all and whole**, entire; *advb.* entirely. *Obs.*

c **1449** PECOCK *Repr.* I. viii. 39 These ij officis maken the hool al werk. *Ibid.* I. ii. 11 It upon which the al hool substaunce of the wal..stondith. *Ibid.* II. vii. 177 It is open ynouȝ to alle hem whiche wolen biholde al the hool proces ..But according to the hool al processe. **1579** W. FULKE *Heskins's Parl.* 154 All the whole vpper house is manifestly contrarie vnto it. **1601** HOLLAND *Pliny* (1634) I. 402 The lower sort of these trees the floud coucreth all and whole.

†**11. all both, all two.** *Obs.* (Fr. *tous les deux*.)

c **1420** *Chron. Vilod.* 892 þey weron as bleynd all bothe, y wys, as ever was ony stok or stoune.

12. Distributed to each member or part of the whole, by the forms *all and some* (arch.), *one and all, each and all, all and each, all and sundry*, etc.

a. Of these **all and some** (see SOME) has the longest history.

c **1325** *Cœur de L.* 5846 They that wolde nought Crystene become, Richard leet sleen hem alle and some. c **1386** CHAUCER *Knts T.* 1329 These lordes alle and some Been in the Sonday to the citė come. **1460** *Play Sacr.* 402 Whyle they were alle together & sum..Comedite corpus meum. **1600** HOLLAND *Livy* XXVII. xiii. 637 e, To endeavour and strain themselves, both all and some [*singulis universisque*]. **1681** DRYDEN *Abs. & Achit.* II. 457 Now stop your noses, readers all and some. **1870** MORRIS *Earthly Par.* II. III. 478 Two hours after midnight all and some Into the hall to wait his word should come.

¶ It has been suggested that in this phrase *some* was a corruption of *isame* (*isome*) 'together,' but the phonology shows that it is not so; with the first quot. above cf. this from the same poem:

c **1325** *Cœur de L.* 4385 Among the toun folk was no game; To counsayl they gaderyd hem insame.

†**b.** *al and som* (*some*) was also used in sing., as if confused with *sum*; = The whole sum, the sum total; *advb.* entirely. *Obs.*

1303 R. BRUNNE *Handl. Synne* 169 þe tale ys wrytyn al and sum In a boke of *Vitas Patrum.* c **1380** *Sir Ferumb.* 3014 He shridde him þer-with..& cloþed him al & some. c **1386** CHAUCER *Wife's T.* Prol. 91 This is all and som [*v.r.* sum, some, somme]. c **1480** *Childe of Bristowe* 338 in Hazl. *E.P.P.* 123 By that the fourtenyht was come, his gold was gon, al and some. **1520–41** WYATT *Wks.* (1861) 173 Henceforth, my Poins, this shall be all and sum. **1625** tr. *Gonsalvio's Sp. Inquis.* Pref., Herein resteth all and some concerning these matters.

c. *one and all, all and each, each and all, all and sundry, all and every.*

1513 DOUGLAS *Æneis* IX. viii. 16 With huge clamoure followand ane and all. **1782** COWPER *J. Gilpin* 239 And all and each that passed that way Did join in the pursuit. **1816** SCOTT *Old Mort.* xxxvi, All and sundry his moveable goods and gear..inbrought to his Majesty's use. **1837** J. LANG *New S. Wales* I. 185 Rendering it virtually imperative on all and sundry to follow his example.

B. *sb.* (through the absolute use in A 8.)

1. Usually with *poss. pron.*, as ***our all***: Everything that we have, or that concerns or pertains to us; whole interest, concern, possession, property.

1627 FELTHAM *Resolves* Wks. 1677, I. xxxi. 55 He shall not command the All of an honest man. **1681** NEVILE *Plato Rediv.* 235 Those matters..which concern our All. **1707** ADDISON *State of War* 242 Our All is at stake. **1722** WOLLASTON *Relig. Nat.* viii. 157 When two persons throw their all into one stock as joint-traders for life. **1794** BURKE *Corr.* (1844) IV. 221 We are, as I think, fighting for our all. **1862** TRENCH *Mirac.* iii. 143 Whatever it was, it was their all.

b. In this sense it has been used with a *pl.*

1721 MRS. CENTLIVRE *Perpl. Lovers* I. 267 I'd pluck up a courage, pack up my Awls and match with him. **1752** FIELDING *Amelia* VII. iii. (1775) 296 [My father] bid me pack up my alls and immediately prepare to quit his house. **1763** BICKERSTAFF *Love in Vill.* 44 So pack up your alls, and be trudging away. [Still a common phrase in Scotland.]

c. Antithetically, with *little.*

1631 QUARLES *Sampson* (1717) 280 That little All Was left, was all corrupt. **1738** JOHNSON *London* 189 [You] leave your little all to flames a prey. **1738** WESLEY *Hymn*, '*Long have I viewed*,' My little All I give to Thee. **1755** JOHNSON *Boswell* (1826) I. 226 No man is well pleased to have his all neglected, be it ever so little. *Mod.* Many a struggling tradesman lost his little all in the fire.

2. Whole being, entirety, totality.

1674 FAIRFAX *Bulk & Selv.* 145 The laws of motion, in the round All of bodies. **1761** LAW *Comf. Weary Pilgr.* (1809) 86 This pure love introduces the creature into the all of God. **1843** CARLYLE *Past. & Pr.* 169 An All of rotten Formulas.

3. Whole system of things, τὸ πᾶν, the Universe.

1598 J. BASTARD in Farr *S.P.* II. 316 Man is the little world (so we him call), The world the little god, God the Great All. **1612** WITHER *Prince Henry's Obs.* in *Juven.* (1633) 298 Living in any corner of this All. **1649** DRUMMOND Wks. 1711, 25 Come see that King, which all this all commands. **1714** MANDEVILLE *Fab. Bees* (1733) II. 21 The beautiful all, must be the workmanship of one great architect of power and wisdom stupendious. **1839** BAILEY *Festus* xxviii. (1848) 329 The atom and the all Commune and know each other. **1850** CARLYLE *Latt.-day Pamph.* vi. (1872) 200 No pin's point can you mark within the wide circle of the All where God's Laws are not.

C. *adv.* **I.** General construction.

1. *All* adj. is often separated from the sb. which it defines, by an auxiliary vb. or clause, and so appears to refer to the predicate; as 'Zion our mother is all wofull,' where *all*, originally an attribute or complement of *Zion*, comes to be viewed as qualifying *woful* = *altogether* woful.

a **1000** CÆDMON *Gen.* (Grein) 756 Hit is Adame nu eall forgolden. c **1200** ORMIN 9579 Issraæle þeod tatt wass All wesste & all forrworrpenn. c **1220** *Hali Meid.* 21 Ah al is meidenes song unlich þeose. **1382** WYCLIF *Prov.* xii. 3 The roote of riȝtwis men shal not ben al moued. **1483** CAXTON *G. de la Tour* C vij, The lady wente oute of her wytte and was al demonyak. **1533** MORE *Answ. Poysoned Bk.* Wks. 1557, 1056/1 His exposicion flitteth all fro the poynte. **1611** BIBLE *Nah.* iii. 1 Woe to the bloody City, it is all full of lyes and robberie. **1814** BYRON *Corsair* III. xv. 18, I am not all deserted on the main. **1826** DISRAELI *Viv. Grey* VII. v. 405 His Royal Highness all smiles, and his Consort all diamonds. **1850** LYNCH *Theoph. Trinal* xi. 224 Another is all frivolity. **1879** TENNYSON *Lover's T.* 59 Six stately virgins, all in white.

2. Whence, as true *adv.* modifying adj. or adv.: Wholly, completely, altogether, quite (cf. ALL- E. 6, 7).

a **1000** *Crist* (Grein) 1221 Eall æfter rihte. c **1200** *Trin. Coll. Hom.* 191 þurch onde com deað in to þe worelde al umbegonge. **1340** *Ayenb.* 89 Nou ich þe habbe al uolliche ysseaued þet ich leue. **1375** BARBOUR *Bruce* I. 392 All othir contenance had he. c **1425** WYNTOUN *Cron.* VI. vi. 29 Hyr chyld-ill al suddanly Travalyd hyr sa angrily. **1541** ELYOT *Image Govt.* 33 But it succeeded all other wise. **1693** *Mem. Count Teckely* I. 57 They endeavour all anew to put those.. in a state uncapable. **1793** SOUTHEY *Triumph of Wom.* 63 Wks. II. 7 All hopelessly our years of sorrow flow. **1849** MACAULAY *Hist. Eng.* II. 480 All at once..the whole fleet tacked. **1880** BROWNING *Clive* 28 All-agog to have me trespass.

†**b.** In this sense **all thing** was also used. (Cf. '*nothing* loath.') *Obs.*

1534 MORE *Comf. agst. Trib.* III. Wks. 1557, 1217/1, I am not all thinge afearde in this case. **1605** SHAKS. *Macb.* III. i. 14 It had bene as a gap in our great Feast, And all-thing vnbecomming. **1665** RAY *Flora* 189 The flowers are not all-thing so broad.

c. In idiomatic hyperbolic use, esp. in phr. *to go all* ——.

1932 S. GIBBONS *Cold Comf. Farm* v. 71 She will..go all arty-and-crafty. **1934** A. HUXLEY *Beyond Mexique Bay* 254 We will assume that the Indians have gone all hygienic. What are the results? **1935** *Punch* 16 Oct. 448/2 If Mr. Morley does go all Rider Haggard for a few pages towards the end of the book the circumstance is scarcely to be deplored. **1947** M. GILBERT *Close Quarters* iii. 50, 'I have questioned Canon Beech-Thompson,' replied Pollock shortly. 'And got an imperial raspberry?' said Halliday... 'I suppose he went all Crockford at once.'

3. Even, just; passing into a mere intensive or emphasizing adjunct. (Cf. ALSO.) *arch.*

1579 W. FULKE *Heskins's Parl.* 195 Al bicause he would not acknowledge the presence of Christ. **1633** P. FLETCHER *Purple Isl.* v. lxviii, All so, who strives..To bring his dead soul to the joyfull skie. **1720** GAY *Blackeyed Susan*, All in the Downs the fleet was moored. **1808** SCOTT *Marm.* I. xi, He.. Gave them a chain of twelve marks' weight All as he lighted down.

4. All through, wholly, entirely, without admixture.

1705 *Lond. Gaz.* mmmmclix/4 Stolen..a black Gelding.. trots all, except forced, and then paces a little. *Ibid.* mmmmclv/4 Trots and gallops all. *Ibid.* mmmmclxxviii/4 Paces all.

II. Special constructions.

5. all one. †**a.** All together. *Obs.* **b.** (also **all a.**) One and the same, quite the same. **all of a**: see A *adj.*[2] 3. (See also ALONE.)

1205 LAYAM. 29080 þa weoren heo al an. c **1380** WYCLIF *Wicket* 5 It is..all one to denye Christes wordes for heresye and Christe for an heretyke. **1581** MARBECK *Bk. Notes* 935 It is all one water whether Symon Peter, or Symon Magus be christened in it. **1691** RAY *Acc. Errors* in *Coll. E.W.* 154 As for the vulgar and illiterate it is all one to them. **1702** *Eng. Theophr.* 138 That which a man causes to be done, he does himself, and 'tis all a case. **1719** DE FOE *Crusoe* (1858) 373 It was all one, he could not sleep. **1768** BLACKSTONE *Comm.* IV. 20 What persons are, or are not, capable of committing crimes; or, which is all one, who are exempted from the censures of the law. **1829** SCOTT *Guy M.* xxxvi, 'It's a' ane to Dandie.' a **1884** *Mod.* It's all one to me whether I go or stay. **1930** C. WILLIAMS *War in Heaven* iii. 35, I gather it's all one to you whether we take it or leave it?

c. all for [FOR *prep.* 7 a], entirely in favour of, on the side of. *colloq.*

1864 A. TROLLOPE *Can you forgive Her?* xix. 150, I am all for Mr. Cheesacre..I can't abide anything that's poor. **1934** D. L. SAYERS *Nine Tailors* II. ii. 105, I'm all for a treasure-hunt. **1945** J. B. PRIESTLEY *Three Men in New Suits* iii. 38 'You've got to..see that the country's run properly.' 'I'm all for that,' said Herbert.

6. Pleonastically in the combinations ALL-WHOLE, ALL-WHOLLY, ALL-UTTERLY, q.v. (See also A 10.)

7. With adverbs of degree, *all* gives emphasis, = Quite, altogether, as *all so*, *all too*. (*All so* is now obs., exc. in the combined form ALSO q.v.)

a **1000** *Ælfred's Death* (Grein) 13 Eal swá ȝebundenne. *c* **1200** *Moral Ode* 328 Of þesse riche we þencheð to ofte, of þare alto selde. *c* **1384** CHAUCER *H. of Fame* 288 Dido.. That loued alto sone a gest. **1587** HOLINSHED *Scot. Chron.* (1806) II. 175 The King.. did send forth, but all too late, Andrew Wood. **1597** SHAKS. *2 Hen. IV*, v. ii. 24 Our argument Is all too heavy to admit much talke. **1805** SOUTHEY *Madoc in Az.* xvii. Wks. V. 322 Give me the boy.. he travels all too slow. **1831** CARLYLE *Sart. Res.* (1858) 182 Thy all-too Irish mirth and madness. **1840** GEN. P. THOMPSON *Exerc.* (1842) V. 191 War is all soon enough when it cannot be helped. **1921** JOYCE *Lett.* (1957) 160 The last word (human, all-too-human) is left to Penelope. **1932** D. GASCOYNE *Roman Balcony* 75 On farms, on all-too-barren fields. **1952** AUDEN *Nones* 23 Far from tall Restituta's all-too-watchful eye.

8. With adv. *the*: By that amount, to that extent, just so much.

1600 SHAKS. *A. Y. L.* I. ii. 102 All the better: we shalbe the more Marketable. **1879** TENNYSON *Lover's T.* 82 He was all the more resolv'd to go.

9. With adverbs of place: In all directions, in every part; as *all about*, *all round*. Special idioms are ***all along*** (see ALONG), ALL OUT, ALL OVER, ALL ROUND, ***all together*** or ALTOGETHER, ***all one*** or ALONE q.v.

c **1300** *Beket* 2253 And crope ek as emeten alaboute. *Ibid.* 820 Seint Thomas was albenethe. **1480** CAXTON *Descr. Brit.* 4 Britayne is all aboute xlviii sithe lxx thousand paas. **1699** BENTLEY *Phalaris* 130 He is all-over mistaken. **1879** TENNYSON *Lover's T.* 75 Beheld All round about him.

10. With conjunctions. †**a.** With *if* and *though* in **if all, though all,** *all* emphasized the supposition or concession, = Even if, even though. Thus: *if all they keep* = if wholly or really they keep, even if they do keep. *Obs.*

c **1330** R. BRUNNE *Chron.* 37 Þof alle Edgar þe gate, Estrild þi moder ware. **1366** MAUNDEV. ii. 13 3if alle it be so, that Men seyn. *c* **1375** WYCLIF *Antecrist* 145 If al þei kepen neiþer.

†**b.** The more common order was **all if, all though**; the former is now obs., the latter written as one word ALTHOUGH q.v.

1340 HAMPOLE *Pr. Consc.* 3045 Þe saul, al-if it haf na body. *c* **1380** WYCLIF *3 Treat.* 17 Al 3if thei shulen aftir be dampnyd. **1514** BARCLAY *Cyt. & Uplandyshm.* 41 All if I would, it were but shame. **1557** —— *Jugurtha* (Paynell) A ij, All if he haue power so to do.

†**c.** With the subj. mood, *though* or *if*, being expressed by the reversed position of vb. and subject (as in *be they* = *if they be*), were omitted, leaving *all* apparently = *although*. Thus: *al be I* = *all though I be*. *Obs.* exc. in synthetic phrases ALBEIT, ALBE q.v.

c **1365** CHAUCER *ABC* 46 Al have I ben a beste in witte and dede, Yet, Lady! thou me close in with thyn grace. *c* **1384** —— *H. Fame* 1820 Al be ther in me no Iustice Me lyst not doo hyt nowe. *c* **1386** —— *Prol.* 736 Al speke he never so rudely, ne large. **1532** MORE *Conf. Tindale* Wks. 1557, 385/2 All were he neuer so olde eare he were baptysed. **1560** H. COLE *Lett. to Jewel*, We brought more than ye were able to answer, all were it no Scriptures, nor Councels, nor Doctours. **1599** BP. HALL *Satires* III. i. 50 All could he further then earths center go. **1659** FULLER *App. Inj. Innoc.* (1840) 532 From whence came Smith, albe he knight or squire, But from the smith that forgeth at the fire.

11. With prep. of extension in space or time, *all* gives completeness, as *all round*, *down*, *over*, *through*, etc.

1622 MIDDLETON etc. *Old Laws* v. i, That's equal change all the world over. **1795** NELSON in Nicolas's *Disp.* II. 11 The wind all round the compass. **1849** MACAULAY *Hist. Eng.* II. 455 All down the Rhine, from Carlsruhe to Cologne. **1875** HIGGINSON *Hist. U.S.* xxvi. 264 This made a great excitement all over the country.

†**12.** With prep. referring to a point of space: Quite, entirely. ***all to naught***, to absolute nothingness, 'away to nothing.' ***to call all to naught***: to vilify. Cf. 15 below. *Obs.*

c **1175** *Lamb. Hom.* 35 Þu forwurðest eca.. al to nohte. *c* **1230** *Ancr. R.* 380 [He] tukeð ham alto wundre. *c* **1300** *Beket* 22 The Princes Douȝter.. that hire hurte al upe him caste. **1559** *Homilies* I. (1859) 134 David, when Semei did call him all to naught, did not chide again. **1592** SHAKS. *Ven. & Ad.* 993 It was not she that call'd him all to naught. *a* **1617** P. BAYNE *Ephes.* (1658) 102 Hee.. doth give his son all to death. **1626** BACON *Sylva* §540 The sap is not so frank as to rise all to the boughs.

13. With *to* of the *dative inf.*: Expressly, just.

c **1300** *Beket* 99 Red alto afonge. **1607** HIERON *Wks.* II. 249 The Spirit of God came.. all to shew how these men were inabled of God.

†**14.** *all* emphasized the particle combined with a vb.:

c **1386** CHAUCER *Prol.* 76 Al bismotered with his habergeon.

b. Especially with the prefix *to-* = 'asunder' (LG. *ter-*, HG. *zer-*, L. *dis*), as in *to-break*, *to-burst*, *to-cut*, *to-gnaw*, *to-hew*, *to-rend*, *to-rive*, *to-shake*, *to-shiver*, *to-tear*, *to-tread*, *to-wend*. Thus *all to-broken*, (G. *all zerbrochen*) 'quite broken in pieces.' As these derivative vbs. were at length rarely used without *all*, the fact that the *to-* belonged to the vb. was lost sight of, and it was written separate, or even joined to *all*, as *al to-torn*, *al to torn*, *alto torn*. *Obs.*

a **1000** *Gregory's Dial.* III. xvi. (Cott. MS. 77 *b*) Þæt he sceolde beon eal to sliten from ðam clifstanum. *c* **1200** *Trin. Coll. Hom.* 113 Ure helende.. alto shiurede þe ȝiaten. *c* **1330** *Arth. & Merl.* 4853 That he tak he alto rof. *c* **1400** *Sege off Melayne* 262 Riche hawberkes were all to-rent. *c* **1449** PECOCK *Repr.* v. i. 484 That her ordre schulde be alto broke. **1483** CAXTON *Gold. Leg.* 236/1 They.. were alle to cutte with the stones. **1493** W. DE WORDE *Communyc.* (1535) B iij, With thy tongue thou me all to terest. **1587** FLEMING *Contn. Holinshed* III. 1991/1 Which the Scots in times past haue all to broken. **1611** BIBLE *Judg.* ix. 53 And a certaine woman cast a piece of a milstone vpon Abimelechs head, and all to brake his scull. **1637** MILTON *Comus* 380 Her wings.. Were altoruffled, and sometimes impaired.

†**15.** Hence, by form-assoc., *all to*, *allto*, *alto* was extended to other verbs as = 'wholly, completely, utterly, soundly'; in later times esp. with vbs. in *be-*; as *all-to-befool*, *all-to-begod*, *all-to-beblubber*, *all-to-benight*. *Obs.*

1534 MORE *Comf. agst. Trib.* III. Wks. 1557, 1224/1 She fel in hand with hym and all to rated him. **1538** LATIMER *Serm. & Rem.* (1845) 398 We be fallen into the dirt, and be all-to dirtied, even up to the ears. **1549** CHALONER tr. *Erasm. Moriæ Enc.* D iij b, Beyng all to laught to scorne. **1551–76** GRINDAL *Fruitf. Dial.* Wks. 1843, 48 To kneel and crouch down and all-to be-god him. **1589** GREENE *Menaphon* (Arb.) 69 Her cheekes all to be blubbered with her jealous teares. **1591** G. FLETCHER *Russe Commonw.* 141 And so al to be-sprinkleth.. the image gods. **1611** COTGR., *Papilloteux*, All-to-bespangled.. set thicke with spangles. **1647** I. C. *Char. Lond.-Diurn.* 3, I wonder my Lord.. is not once more all-to-be-traytor'd. **1674** FAIRFAX *Bulk & Selv.* 53 The wide, thick, all-to-be deckt heap of visible beings. **1682** N. O. *Boileau's Le Lutrin* I. 314 Him too the bounteous Dean All-to-be-Blesses. **1684** BUNYAN *Pilg.* II. 48 She all-to-be-fooled me.

D. Obsolete uses of early inflected forms.

(The inflexions were: *Sing. acc. masc.* 1–2 **alne,** 2–3 **alle,** *dat. m. & n.* 1 **allum,** 2–3 **-en,** 2–4 **-e;** *dat.* & *gen. f.* 1–3 **alre,** 2–4 **alle;** *gen. m. & n.* 1–3 **alles.** *Pl. nom.* & *acc.* 1–5 **alle;** *dat.* 1 **allum,** 2–4 **-en,** 2–5 **-e;** *gen.* 1–2 **alra,** 2–4 **-re,** 3–4 **aldre,** 3–6 **aller, alder, alþer, alther,** also *passim*, **alir, aldir, -yr, althir; alleris, altheris,** etc. These survived longest in the south, none being retained by northern dial. after 13th c. exc. gen. pl. In midl. dial. *all* sing. and *alle* pl. were still distinguished by Wyclif and Chaucer.)

†**I.** The gen. sing. **alles** was used adverbially: Altogether, at all, wholly, entirely. (Fr. *du tout*.)

a **1100** *O.E. Chron.* an. 1018 Þæt gafol.. wæs ealles lxxii þusend punda. **1205** LAYAM. 3077 Þa hit alles up brac. *c* **1230** *Ancr. R.* 88 Hwon hit alles cumeð forð. **1297** R. GLOUC. 17 Corineus was alles wroþ. *c* **1320** *Cast. Loue* 659 Whon he wolde alles bicome man.

II. The gen. plur. **alra, alre, aller, alder, alther,** 'of all' was used down to 1600.

†**2.** With *sb.* **a.** governed by sb. (To 1200.)

a **1000** CYNEWULF *Elene* (Grein) 816 Allra cyninga þrym. *c* **1175** *Lamb. Hom.* 33 He is alra kinge king. *Ibid.* 217 Heo is ælra þinga angin.

b. governed by superlative. (To 1300.)

a **1000** *Scópes Widsið* 15 Ealra ricost monna cynnes. *c* **1200** *Moral Ode* 351 Þer is alre meruþe mest. **1297** R. GLOUC. 135 Þat ys aller mon worst, þat me euer sey with ye.

†**3.** *absol.* with a superlative, *orig.* either before or after; *subseq.* always prefixed, and becoming at length a mere intensifying prefix. Prefixed to any superlative, as *aller-best* 'best of all,' *aller-blivest*, *-erst*, *-farthest*, *-fairest*, *-feeblest*, *-first*, *-foulest*, *-highest*, *-last*, *-least*, *-liefest*, *-longest*, *-most*, *-next*, *-truest*, *-worst*, etc.; of which ***alderliefest*** 'dearest of all, very dear,' was a common epithet in 16th c.

a **1000** *Metr. Ps.* cviii. 28 Him si abrogden hiora sylfra sceamu swyðust ealra. *a* **1000** CÆDMON *Gen.* (Grein) 337 Ofermetto ealra swiðost. **1154** *O.E. Chron.* (Laud MS.) an. 1135 Alre fyrst Balduin de Reduers. **1297** R. GLOUC. 44 Grete townes in Engelond.. And London aller most. *a* **1300** *Cursor M.* 7391 Quar es þin alþer-yongest son? *c* **1374** CHAUCER *Troylus* v. 576 Myn alderlevest lady deere, So wommanly. *Ibid.* III. 240 My altherlevest lord, and brothir dere. **1382** WYCLIF *1 Sam.* ix. 10 Altherbest is thi word; com, go we. *a* **1400** *Relig. Pieces fr. Thornton MS.* (1867) 31 He es alþir-myghtyeste, althirwyseste, and alswa althire-beste. **1481** CAXTON *Myrrour* I. xiii. 42 God created nature alther-first. **1502** ARNOLD *Chron.* (1811) 43 Our alther lieuest uncles. **1587** GASCOIGNE *Wks.* 163 To mine Alderlieuest Lord I must indite a wofull case. **1590** T. WATSON *Egl., Walsingham* 386 Thou, Spencer, art the alderliefest swaine. **1593** SHAKS. *2 Hen. VI*, I. i. 28 Mine Alder liefest Soueraigne.

†**b.** In later times when the nature of *alther* was forgotten, it was erroneously written *all there*.

a **1450** *Syr Gowghter* 172 Huntyng he loved al there best. *c* **1500** *Partenay* 2490 Ywon all ther first ther he edified. **1513** DOUGLAS *Æneis* v. ix. 21 All thare last The antiant kyng Acestes. **1537** LYNDESAY *Q. Magd.* 150 The greit Maister of houshold all thare last.

†**c.** Ignorance of the true meaning, with consciousness of its intensifying force, produced many remarkable constructions.

c **1250** *Gen. & Ex.* 3997 On ilc alter fier alðerneðer. *c* **1320** *Seuyn Sag.* (W.) 2298 On alder twenti devel wai. *c* **1330** *Florice & Bl.* 27 In the althrest fairest sete. *c* **1430** LYDG. *Chron. Troy* I. v, For there was one thyng closed in her hert An alderother in her chere declared. **1630** *Tinck. Turvey* 56 An alder leefer swaine, I weene, In the barge there was not seene.

†**4.** In concord with a pron. pl. possessive: *our*, *your*, *their aller*; where modern language has *of us all*, *belonging to them all*, etc. (Cf. L. *omnium nostrum parens*.) Later northern writers, to whom the *-er* had no longer a genitive force, added a second possessive ending, making *alleris*, *alders*, *althers*. (Cf. *our-s*, *their-s*, *both-er(s)*.)

c **1230** *Ancr. R.* 52 Eue vre alre moder. *Ibid.* 94 Hore alre crune. *a* **1300** *Cursor M.* 469 For þare aller right. **1330** R. BRUNNE *Chron.* 162 Þat I be ȝour aller broþer. **1377** LANGL. *P. Pl.* B. XVI. 205 Adam was oure aller fader. *c* **1380** *Sir Ferumb.* 2884 By-for hure alre siȝt. *c* **1386** CHAUCER *Prol.* 823 Vp roos oure hoost and was oure aller cok [*v.r.* alþer, alder]. **1401** *Pol. Poems* II. 65 Crist, our aller duke. *a* **1423** JAMES I *King's Q.* III. xl, I will that Gud-hope.. be, ȝoure alleris frende. *c* **1430** *Syr Gener.* 5244 The gates thei shet bi here althers consent. *c* **1460** FORTESCUE *Abs. & Lim. Mon.* 144 The Harmes.. ben now by hym turnyd into our aller Good. **1513** DOUGLAS *Æneis* XII. i. 40, I sall reuenge and end our alleris offence.

E. all- in *comb.*

Combinations with *all-* as first element have existed from the earliest times, and have become, since *c* 1600, unlimited in number. In some groups the combination is merely syntactic, though even there individual instances of long standing have become true compounds; cf. the gradation in *all alive*, *all-important*, *all-powerful*, *almighty*. The stress is not on *all* except in a few real compounds as *'always*, *'also*. On these combinations as well as on simple phrases, *derivatives* are freely formed in which the loose union or non-union of the original elements is cemented by the formative process, so that *all* is no longer merely in syntactic combination with the rest of the word; thus *all-pervadingness*, *all-eyed*, cannot be analysed as *all* + *pervadingness*, *all* + *eyed*, but only as (*all-pervading*) + *-ness*, (*all eyes*) + *-ed*. The following general classification contains I. Simple combinations; II. Derivatives formed on these, and on phrases. Words in SMALL CAPITALS are treated in their alphabetical place in the sequel.

I. Simple combinations.

1. *adject.* with sb., as ALL-FOUR(S, -HAIL, -HALLOWS, -MIGHT, -NIGHT, -SAINTS, -SOULS, -SPICE (and their derivatives); **all-power,** omnipotence; ***all-wisdom***.

c **1680** J. PORDAGE *Myst. Divin.* 55 The Power of all Powers, yea All-power it self. **1827** *Edin. Rev.* XLVI. 320 Here it has assumed.. a sort of all-wisdom.

2. *adject.* with adv. (formerly an oblique case of sb. or pron.), as ALGATE, ALWAYS, ALLWHERE, -WHITHER.

3. *substant.* (*genit.*) with sb. = 'of all, universal,' as ALL-FATHER; ***all-monarch***, ***-parent***, ***-soul***; esp. as *obj. gen.* with verbal agents, when there is an accompanying ppl. form in *-ing* (see 7), as ***all-commander*** (cf. *all-commanding*), ***-creator***, ***-destroyer***, ***-encompasser***, ***-giver***, ***-knower***, ***-maker***, ***-seer***, ***-sustainer***, etc.

1594 SHAKS. *Rich. III*, v. i. 20 That high All-seer, which I dallied with. **1598** SYLVESTER *Du Bartas* I. iii. (1641) 21/2 The All-Monarch's bounteous Majesty. *Ibid.* 24/2 Th' eternall All-Creator. **1613** ZOUCHE *Dove* in Farr's *S.P.* 320 To this All-maker's prayses sing. **1621** BURTON *Anat. Mel.* III. ii. I. i, That mischievous all-commander of the Earth. **1795** T. TAYLOR *Met. Apul.* (1822) 184 The all-powerful and all-parent Syrian goddess. **1850** MRS. BROWNING *Prom. Bnd.* I. 163 Zeus, the all-giver. **1870** BRYANT *Homer* II. XIII. 13 Saturn's son, The all-disposer. **1870** H. MACMILLAN *Bible Teach.* i. 26 The invisible shrine of the All-encompasser,—the All-sustainer. **1879** WHITNEY *Sanskr. Gram.* Introd. 20 The emancipation of the soul, and its unification with the All-soul. **1890** W. JAMES *Princ. Psychol.* I. x. 362 These declarations on Kant's part of the utter barrenness of the consciousness of the pure self, and of the consequent impossibility of any deductive or 'rational' psychology, are what, more than anything else, earned for him the title of the 'all-destroyer'. **1902** —— *Var. Relig. Exper.* vi. 138 Only by an All-knower can we finally be judged. **1909** —— *Pluralistic Universe* iii. 126 Again, the absolute is always represented idealistically, as the all-knower.

4. *substant.* (*obj.*) with vb. inf., as ALL-HEAL; **all-hold,** that which holds all.

1496 *Dives & Paup.* (W. de Worde) I. xxxiv. 73/1 Settynge of mete or of drynke by nyght on the benche, for to fede All holde, or gobelyn.

5. *advb.* with sb., as ALL-BONE; ***all-heart*** (i.e. wholly heart), a name of the elm tree; ***all-sayer***. And in attrib. phrases such as **all-rail,** wholly by rail, **all-slavery, all-talk** , wholly, altogether (given to) talk. In *attrib.* phrases: made wholly of (a substance), as ***all-aluminium***, ***-metal***, ***-steel***, ***-wool*** (also *fig.*) ; containing or consisting of something exclusively, as ***all-fire***, ***-freight*** (hence *all-freighter*), ***-grass***, ***-male***, ***-star*** [STAR *sb.*[1] 5]; ***all-sea***, cf. *all-rail*. (Cf. also IV below.)

1567 MAPLET *Greene Forest* 41 b, The Elme.. is called of some All heart. **1624** BARGRAVE *Serm.* 21 Our Saviour.. found some all-sayers and no-doers, so others that would outdoe all faith. **1833** GEN. P. THOMPSON *Exerc.* (1842) II. 479 The 'all slavery' party in England,—who wherever two or three were gathered together to oppress, were there in the midst of them. **1863** W. PHILLIPS *Speeches* iii. 50 The all-talk party. **1879** *Lumberman's Gaz.* 3 Dec., The first all-rail shipment of lumber. **1882** *Daily News* 4 Mar., The demand is most apparent in all-wool dress goods. **1868** *Chambers's Encycl.* X. 268/1 Many of the names used in the all-wool class are retained in this, with the addition of the word 'union', as union merino. **1876** G. M. HOPKINS *Wr. Deutschland* (1918) st. 23 To bathe in his fall-gold mercies, to breathe in his all-fire glances. **1889** *Daily Even. Bulletin* (San Francisco) 13 July 1/6 Manager Harris' team is not now so much of an 'all star aggregation' now as it was. **1908** A. W. TILBY *Eng. People Overseas* I. i. 32 It now became evident that the all-sea route was really the safest. **1912** MRS. P. CAMPBELL *Let. to G. B. Shaw* (1952) 25 An 'all star' show is fit only for Kings and Queens! **1912** W. RALEIGH *Let.* 12 Jun. (1926) II. 379 He.. uses only all-wool five-star Romany when he orders a drink. **1927** W. E. COLLINSON *Contemp. Engl.* 89 All-steel houses. **1927** *Melody Maker* Aug. 785 (Advt.), One of the greatest 'all-star' records ever issued. **1930** *Engineering* 7 Feb. 159/3 A new ambulance aeroplane has recently been delivered... It is an all-metal machine. **1933** *Ann. Reg. 1932* II. 47 One of the most expensive of the year's [cinema] productions was 'Grand Hotel', which had a showy all-star cast. **1933** *Discovery* Oct. 325/2 An all-aluminium train was exhibited for the first time at the Chicago World's Fair this year. **1941** G. STAPLEDON in H. J. Massingham *Engl. & Farmer* vii. 148 To the holders of these all-grass farms I would address myself. **1960** *Times* 14 Nov. 13/6 British companies that fly regular long haul all-freight flights. **1961** *Ann. Reg. 1960* 429 This play had an all-male cast. **1961** *Guardian* 24 Jan. 14/1 As an all-freighter in airline use it is unique.

6. *advb.* with adj., = 'wholly, altogether, infinitely.' About twenty of these combinations are found in OE. including *eall-beorht, -ȝearo, -ȝeleáflic, -gréne, -gylden, -hálig, -hwít, -íren, -isiȝ, -mihtiȝ, -nacod, -niwe, -riht, -seolcen, -teaw, -weald, -wérlic.* Of these ALL-HOLY, and ALMIGHTY, survived into ME. and were reinforced from time to time by -WITTY, *-worthy, -wise,* -GOOD, *-merciful, -just.* Since 1600, the number of these has been enormously extended, *all-*having become a possible prefix, in poetry at least, to almost any adj. of quality. Thus, ***all-able, -beauteous, -bitter, -black, -bountiful, -brilliant, -complete, -constant, -content, -divine, -dreadful, -earnest, -eloquent, -essential, -evil, -fair, -glorious, -golden, -gracious, -holy, -important, -just, -lavish, -lovely, -merciful, -peaceful, -perfect, -potential, -powerful, -praiseworthy, -prolific, -puissant, -pure, -rapacious, -righteous, -sacred, -substantial, -surfy, -true, -various, -vast, -wondrous.*** Hence as *sb., all-fair, -wise.* Also with the implication 'entirely, exclusively', as ***all-coloured, -red*** (sense 13 below), ***-white.***

a **1000** ? CÆDMON *Sat.* 522 (Gr.) Englas eall-beorhte. CYNEWULF *Andreas* 799 Eorþan eall-gréne. ÆLFRIC *Judg.* xvi. 16 ȝebunden mid eallniwum rápum. *c* **1340** [See ALL-WITTY]. *c* **1375** WYCLIF *Antecrist* 137 Chef bischop& kynges son alworþiest. **1585** ABP. SANDYS *Serm.* (1841) 292 Three Persons and one almighty and all-merciful God. **1586** T. B. tr. *La Primaudaye's Fr. Acad.* II. 574 He must bee all-good, al-just, and almightie. **1600** TOURNEUR *Transf. Metamorph.* xii. 78 (1878) 194 Where shall I find a safe all-peacefull seat. **1611** SHAKS. *Cymb.* III. v. 95 *Pis.* Oh my all-worthy lord. *Clo.* All-worthy villaine, Discouer where thy Mistris is at once. **1626** G. SANDYS *Ovid's Met.* VIII. 166 One who did despise All-able Gods. **1613-30** DRUMM. OF HAWTH. *Poems* Wks. 1711, 46/2 Earth's all-thorny soyl. *Ibid.* 47 Of the first world an all-substantial man. *c* **1656** BP. HALL *Invis. World* II. ii, The bliss-making presence of the All-glorious God. **1670** EACHARD *Contempt Clergy* 41 The all-wise patron, or all-understanding justice of the peace. **1692** E. SCARISBRICK *Life Lady Warner* (ed. 2) v. i. 294 Hereby to encrease her confidence in his All-Powerful assistance. **1725** POPE *Odyss.* XXIII. 303 Such future scenes the all-righteous powers display. **1765** TUCKER *Lt. Nat.* I. 503 We judge of the All perfect by ourselves. **1781** GIBBON *Decl. & F.* II. 139 His all-powerful virtue, and celestial fortune. **1785** T. DWIGHT *Conq. Canäan* II. 29 Flowers all-beauteous. **1794** T. TAYLOR *Pausanias* I. 304 He employed all-various purifications. **1839** HALLAM *Hist. Lit.* IV. IV. iii. §54. 95 The soul is united to an all-perfect Being. **1839** W. IRVING *Wolfert's Roost* (1855) 63 They [the modern languages] are all-important. **1842** H. E. MANNING *Serm.* (1848) I. xx. 303 Christ.. was all-pure. **1847** EMERSON *Poems* 15 This monument of my despair Build I to the All-Good, All-Fair. **1849** HARE *Par. Serm.* (1849) II. 112 The one living, eternal, all-worthy Sacrifice. **1851** BUCKLEY tr. *Homer's Il.* 60 She beheld the all-beauteous neck of the goddess. *Ibid.* 91 His step-mother, all-fair Eëribæa. **1855** MACAULAY *Hist. Eng.* IV. 379 Bowed down by fear of the allpowerful Campbells. **1861** W. GRESLEY *Sophr. & Neol.* 140 It is of that all-essential and vital character. **1862** LYTTON *Strange Story* II. 258 Is not the Creator omniscient? if all-wise, all-foreseeing? If all-foreseeing, all pre-ordaining? *a* **1889** G. M. HOPKINS *Poems* (1918) 71 Thundering all-surfy seas. **1899** *Daily News* 28 Oct. 7/6 An all-white framework of symmetrical petals. **1929** D. H. LAWRENCE *Pansies* 30 The All-wise has tired us of wisdom. **1937** *Burlington Mag.* Nov. 211/2 The meaning of certain all-important words. **1939** *Ibid.* Sept. 124/1 Rogier's all-powerful personality. **1940** 'G. ORWELL' *Inside Whale* 47 Something resembling the colonial attitude.. exists.. in all-white communities. **1958** *Times* 13 Aug. 5/4 Whose last musical, also with an all-coloured cast, was *Carmen Jones.* **1960** *Guardian* 21 Mar. 1/4 Negroes arrested after refusing to leave two all-white public libraries, were each released on bail.

¶ These are connected with the next by forms in *-ent,* and *-ive,* from L. pr. pples. and vbl. adjs., as ***all-efficient, -perficient, -potent, -prepotent, -prevalent, -sufficient; all-comprehensive, -inclusive, -miscreative, -perceptive, -persuasive, -pervasive.***

1594 HOOKER *Eccl. Pol.* II. (1617) 79 The Testimonies of God are al-sufficient vnto that end for which they were giuen. **1623** DRUMM. OF HAWTH. *Cypress Gr.* Wks. 1711, 121 The wise and all-provident Creator. **1660** R. COKE *Power & Subj.* 75 The good will and pleasure of the All-prepotent God. **1675** BAXTER *Cath. Theol.* II. I. 233 He himself who is God Allsufficient. **1684** T. BURNET *Th. Earth* I. 320 That great all-comprehensive thought. **1711** SHAFTESBURY *Charact.* (1737) II. 365 That all-prevalent wisdom which you have establish'd. **1790** BURKE *Fr. Rev.* 287 Your all-sufficient legislators have forgot one thing that seems essential. **1821** SHELLEY *Prom. Unb.* I, The all-miscreative brain of Jove. **1879** FROUDE *Cæsar* ii. 17 Moral habits are all-sufficient while they last. **1885** W. JAMES *Coll. Ess. & Rev.* (1920) 282 Dr. Royce's novel reason for believing that all that is has the foundations of its being laid in an infinite all-inclusive Mind. **1910** —— in *Hibbert Jrnl.* VIII. 758 There is no complete generalisation,.. no all-pervasive unity. **1944** H. A. HODGES *W. Dilthey* iv. 54 There is no all-inclusive purpose which could constitute the meaning of life. **1965** *Engl. Studies* Feb. 2 His suspicion is all-inclusive.

b. (Cf. IV below.) Representative of the whole, as distinguished from part, of an area or country, as ***all-American*** (hence as *sb.*), ***-Russian.***

1888 *Outing* (U.S.) Nov. 166/2 The All-American team.. is composed of men picked from the ranks of the representative ball teams of America. **1920** *Ibid.* Nov. 84/3 The little cripple, sometime All-American. **1920** B. RUSSELL *Pract. & Theory Bolshevism* v. 76 The All-Russian Soviet, which is constitutionally the supreme body. **1959** *Times Lit. Suppl.* 14 Aug. 469/4 All-American footballer.

7. *advb.* with pr. pple. as in prec., but often as the object of the verbal action. With exc. of ALL-WIELDING q.v. found already in OE., no examples of this combination occur much before 1600; in modern times their number is unlimited, though many are used only in poetry. Examples: ***all-absorbing, -accepting, -acting, -affecting, -afflicting, -appointing, -arranging, -attempting, -availing, -bearing, -beholding, -bestowing, -binding, -blessing, -canning, -cheering, -commanding, -composing, -comprehending, -conceiving, -concerning, -confounding, -conquering, -consuming, -containing, -convincing, -covering, -creating, -daring, -deciding, -defying, -despising, -destroying, -devouring, -dimming, -disposing, -embracing, -encompassing, -ending, -enduring, -energizing, -enlightening, -enveloping, -filling, -forgetting, -governing, -grasping, -healing, -hearing, -heeding, -including, -involving, -judging, -justifying, -knowing, -loving, -maintaining, -ordering, -pervading, -pitying, -pondering, -prevailing, -preventing, -protecting, -providing, -quickening, -reaching, -relieving, -ruling, -satiating, -satisfying, -saving, -seeing, -shaking, -soothing, -space-filling , -subduing, -sufficing, -surpassing, -surrounding, -sustaining, -swallowing, -swaying, -telling, -tolerating, -transcending, -triumphing, -turning, -understanding, -upholding, -working.***

a **1000** *Cod. Exon.* (Th.) 474 Alwaldend God. **1588** SHAKS. *L.L.L.* II. i. 21 All-telling fame Doth noyse abroad. **1592** —— *Rom. & Jul.* I. i. 141 The all-cheering sunne. **1594** —— *Rich. III,* III. i. 78 To all posteritie, Euen to the generall all ending day. **1599** MARSTON *Sc. Villanie* III. ii. 232 Close his eyes with thy all-dimming hand. *Ibid.* II. v. 195 O brawny strength is an all-canning charme. **1603** *Patient Grissil* 16 When all-commanding love your hearts subdue. **1605** SHAKS. *Lear* III. ii. 6 All-shaking Thunder. **1607** HIERON *Wks.* I. 427 It hath pleased the all-disposing God to remooue you. **1610** G. FLETCHER *Christs Victorie* xxiv, He heau'ns al-seeing eye, He earths great Prophet. **1612** DRAYTON *Poly-olb.* ix. *note* 152 The Druids inuocation was to one All-healing or All-sauing power. *Ibid.* vii. *note* 109 That All-knowing Isaac Casaubon. *Ibid.* v. *note* 76 What all-appointing Heauen will. **1623** DRUMM. OF HAWTH. *Cypress Gr.* Wks. 1711, 124 That all-sufficient and all-sufficing happiness. *c* **1630** —— *Wks.* 1711, 31/1 All-acting vertues of those flaming tow'rs. *Ibid.* 32/2 See, all-beholding King. *Ibid.* 29/2 Uncreate Beauty, all-creating Love. *Ibid.* 43/1 The greatest gift, that.. The all-governing pow'rs to man can give. *Ibid.* 30/1 Thy all-upholding might her malice reins. **1655** H. VAUGHAN *Silex Scint.* I. (1858) 15 Some drops of thy all-quickning blood. **1667** MILTON *P.L.* x. 591 Second of Satan sprung, all conquering Death. **1674** N. FAIRFAX *Bulk & Selv.* 99 Motion, which is an all-reaching affection or belonger to each bit of the world. **1710** PALMER *Proverbs* 376 Our conduct is in view of an all-seeing eye. **1741** RICHARDSON *Pamela* (1824) I. xx. 268 The all-surpassing pleasure that fills the worthy breast. **1742** YOUNG *Nt. Th.* VIII. 1150 All-bearing, all-attempting, till he falls. **1765** TUCKER *Lt. Nat.* I. 596 Offspring of all-protecting Jove. *Ibid.* 666 The all-space-filling mundane soul. **1768** BOSWELL *Corsica* iii. (ed. 2) 164 Looking up to an all-ruling Providence. **1807** J. BARLOW *Columbiad* x. 483 Her cloudless ken, her all pervading soul Illume, sublime and harmonize the whole. **1827** KEBLE *Chr. Year* Tues. bef. Easter, Thine all-pervading look. *Ibid.* Purific., An all-defying, dauntless look. **1834** J. S. MILL in *Monthly Repos.* VIII. 387 The universal and all-absorbing struggle to be or to appear rich. **1847** J. D. MORELL *Hist. View Speculative Philos.* (ed. 2) I. 15 Researches.. so wide and all-embracing in their extent. **1848** A. BRONTË *Tenant Wildf. Hall* II. xviii. 365, I cannot live here, and be for ever silent on the all-absorbing subject of my thoughts and wishes. **1848** L. HUNT *Jar of Honey* vii. 92 The all-including genius of Shakspeare. **1848** J. R. LOWELL *Oak* 42 in *Poet. Wks.* (1873) 76/2 Lord! all thy works are lessons,—each contains Some emblem of man's all-containing soul. **1857** EMERSON *Poems* 25 The all-loving Nature Will smile in a factory. **1863** (26 Mar.) BRIGHT *Sp.* (1878) 125 Christian morality ever widening and all-blessing in its influence. **1866** G. M. HOPKINS *Poems* (1948) 147 My all-accepting fixèd eye. **1870** BRYANT *Homer* I. III. 94 O all-beholding and all-hearing Sun! **1880** W. JAMES *Will to Believe* (1897) 237 The vague Asiatic profession of belief in an all-enveloping fate. **1882** SHORTHOUSE *J. Inglesant* II. 131, I see traces of this all-pervading truth. **1892** W. B. YEATS *C'tess Kathleen* Pref. 8 No dramatic method elastic and all-containing enough. **1902** W. JAMES *Var. Relig. Exper.* vi. 142 The jealousy of the gods, the nemesis that follows too much happiness, the all-encompassing death. **1907** —— *Meaning of Truth* (1909) vi. 157 We get nearer and nearer to realities, we approximate more and more to the all-satisfying limit. **1912** W. DE LA MARE *Listeners* 82 This all-encompassing hush. **1930** 'R. CROMPTON' *William's Happy Days* vi. 129 Lounging at his ease—the gracious, generous all-providing male. **1932** W. B. YEATS *Words for Music* 14 All-destroying sword-blade, still Carried by the wandering fool. **1935** *Burlington Mag.* Nov. 235/1 Art, which, like human nature, should be all-embracing in its scope. **1939** R. CAMPBELL *Flowering Rifle* II. 66 The former all-accepting soar above To triumph over death and die for love. **1940** L. MACNEICE *Last Ditch* 9 Night came down upon the bogland With all-enveloping wings.

8. *advb.* with pa. pple. = 'wholly, completely'; sometimes assuming an instrumental relation = 'by all.' Rare bef. Shakspere. Examples: ***all-accomplished, -admired, -appalled, -armed, -dreaded, -enlightened, -enraged, -honoured, -licensed, -praised, -seen, -shunned, -starred, -watched.*** (These pass by ambiguous combinations, as *all-watched,* 'wholly watched through,' or 'being all watch,' into group 12.)

1596 SHAKS. *1 Hen. IV,* III. ii. 140 This gallant Hotspur, this all-praysed Knight. **1599** —— *Hen. V,* IV. Cho. 38 The wearie, and all-watched night. **1605** —— *Lear* I. iv. 220 This, your all-lycenc'd Foole. **1606** —— *Ant. & Cl.* II. vi. 16 All-honor'd, honest Romaine Brutus. **1607** —— *Timon* IV. ii. 14 His disease of all shunn'd pouerty. **1611** —— *Cymb.* IV. ii. 271 Th' all-dreaded Thunderstone. *c* **1612** SYLVESTER *Lachr. Lachrim.* Poems (1633) 1149 O, All-admired, Benign and Bountious! O All-desired (right) Panaretos! *a* **1631** DRAYTON *Triumph of David, ibid.* 114 How this vnarmed youth himselfe would beare Against th' all-armed giant (which they feare). *c* **1630** DRUMM. OF HAWTH. *Wks.* 1711, 10/1 False delights.. my all-appalled mind so do affray. **1725** POPE *Odyss.* XIII. 483 Oh all-enlightened Mind! Inform him. **1756** TOLDERVY *Hist. Two Orphans* IV. xxxiii. 184 Where the modest, and all-accomplished landlady, Mrs. Rogers, was.. invited to sit down. **1842** TENNYSON *Sir Galahad* in *Poems* II. 178 All-arm'd I ride, whate'er betide Until I find the holy Grail. **1865** G. M. HOPKINS *Poems* (1948) 142 And I must have the centre in my heart To spread the compass on the all-starr'd sky. **1917** D. H. LAWRENCE *Look! We have come Through!* 101 There, sure in sinless being, All-seen, and then all-seeing.. We might have lain.

9. *advb.* with vb. = 'wholly, completely.' *rare.*

1839 BAILEY *Festus* ix. (1848) 104 Whether the sun all-light thee or the moon.

II. Synthetic derivatives of comb. and phrases.

10. *sb.* **a.** from 6, as ***all-alikeness, aloneness, -fullness, -powerfulness, -whiteness, -wiseness;*** **b.** from 6 ¶, as ***all-defiance, -inclusiveness, -sufficience, -potency, -prevalency, -sufficiency;*** **c.** from 7, as ***all-absorbingness, -knowingness, -meaningness, -pervadingness, -prevailingness.***

a. **1614** RALEIGH *Hist. World* II. 259 The loue and kindnesse of his all-powerfulnesse. **1656** JEANES *Fvlnesse of Christ* 382 That all-fulnesse which dwelleth in Christ. **1670** EACHARD *Contempt Clergy* 56 The all-powerfulness of aqua-fortis. **1824** SOUTHEY *Sir T. More* (1831) I. 52 It would be disparaging his own all-wiseness. **1860** RUSKIN *Mod. Paint.* V. VIII. iv. §19 He must be able to bear the all-wrongness. *a* **1897** W. JAMES in R. B. Perry *Thought & Char. W. James* (1935) I. 482 Evolution is a change from a nohowish untalkaboutable all-alikeness to a somehowish.. not-all-alikeness. **1921** D. H. LAWRENCE *Sea & Sardinia* v. 164 Save us from proletarian homogeneity and khaki all-alikeness. **1924** *Glasgow Herald* 17 July 9 London's vastness.. [is] yet capable of baffling him and impressing him with a feeling of strangeness and 'all-alone-ness'. **1927** E. GRUNDY *Happy Pianist* vi. 32 C major [scale] is technically the most difficult, on account of its 'all-whiteness'. **1956** D. GASCOYNE *Night Thoughts* 18 Cave-night which every night His all-aloneness drives him back into. **1957** *New Biol.* XXII. 57 These disturbing cases, which test to the limit our faith in the all-powerfulness of Natural Selection.

b. **1619** J. SEMPILL *Sacrilege Sacredly Handled* vii. 79 Hee vseth Tithing, as a chiefe argument to confirme them in the Al-sufficiencie and Eternitie of Christs Priest-hood. **1641** *Prel. Episcop.* A b, All-sufficiency.. to furnish us.. with spiritual knowledge. **1642** H. MORE *Song of Soul* I. I. II. liv, What thing not done by his all-potencie? *a* **1797** WALPOLE *George II* (1847) III. i. 16 The Duke of Bedford.. reflected on Pitt's all-sufficience. **1826** E. IRVING *Babylon* II. VII. 235 The doctrine of Christ, and the all-prevalency of his kingdom. **1845** CARLYLE *Cromwell* (1871) V. 136 With pious all-defiance front the World. **1865** PUSEY *Truth & Off. Eng. Ch.* 108 The all-sufficiency of the Intercession of our Divine Redeemer. **1870** SMITH *Syn. & Antonyms, Ubiquity, Syn.* Omnipresence. All-pervasiveness. **1882** W. JAMES *Let.* 8 Jan. in R. B. Perry *Thought & Char. W. James* (1935) I. 738

What are they but limitations to the all-inclusiveness of any single being? **1938** R. H. LOWIE *Hist. Ethnol. Theory* ix. 131 We are struck by the all-inclusiveness of his interests.

c. 1654 E. JOHNSON *Wonder-wrkg. Prov.* 56 The honour of his All-seeingness. **1674** N. FAIRFAX *Bulk & Selv.* 23 The naked essence of God is as much his all-knowingness, his all-fillingness, or his onefoldness, as his everlastingness. *c* **1830** COLERIDGE in *Blackw. Mag.* (1882) 119 The abominable no-meaningness..The all-meaningness..of the lectures. **1849** J. S. MILL *Lett.* (1910) I. 146 The limitation may be in our faculties, and in the allpervadingness, to us, of a contrary experience. **1862** F. HALL *Hindu Philos. Syst.* 64 In the matter of omnipresence,—or, rather, all-pervadingness. **1945** *Scrutiny* XIII. 131 The all-absorbingness of the purpose.

11. *adv.* from the same, as ***all-powerfully***; ***all-sufficiently***; ***all-convincingly***.

1649 ROBERTS *Clavis Bibl.* 308 How..all-sufficiently able God is, in performing of his Promises. *Mod.* An all-convincingly genuine inscription.

12. *adj.* in *-ed*, formed on phrases (chiefly since 1600), as ***all-aged*** of all ages, ***all-coloured***, ***all-shaped***, ***all-sized***, ***all-eyed***, being 'all eyes,' ***all-sided*** (hence ***all-sidedness***), ready or skilful on all sides, versatile. These have the stress on *all*: 'all-ˌsided.

1621 G. SANDYS *Ovid's Met.* I. (1626) 7 All-colour'd Iris, Iuno's messenger. **1630** J. TAYLOR (Water P.) *Wks.* II. 61/2 Al-shaped Proteus. **1658** J. R. tr. *Mouffet's Theat. Ins.* 899 Let that all-eyed Argus tell. **1765** TUCKER *Lt. Nat.* II. 478 Persons of all sized apprehensions. **1862** M. HOPKINS *Hawaii* 275 One of those rapid, intelligent, all-sided men. **1876** *Coursing Calendar* 51 The Craven Cup, for all-aged bitches, contained some already known to fame. **1880** RUSKIN *Bible of Amiens* i. 3 All-coloured velvets, pearl-iridescent colombettes. **1881** W. JAMES in *Unitarian Rev.* XVI. 407 May you still be the champions of mental completeness and all-sidedness. **1882** *Daily News* 8 Nov. 6/5 Coursing. All-Aged Stakes, of 6 guineas each. **1905** *Terms used in Forestry* 15 *Many-aged*, a forest through all parts of which many different classes of trees tend to distribute themselves. When all age classes are thus distributed, the forest is all-aged. **1933** *Times* 2 June 15/6 We are sick of the weak-kneed, allsidedness of people who see everything and do nothing.

III. 13. Special Combs.: **all-ages**, horses of all ages entered for a race; **all-along** *adv. Bookbinding* (see quot. 1960); **all-court** [COURT *sb.*[1] 4] *a.*, in *Lawn Tennis* applied to a game played both from the base-line and from near the net; **all-electric** *a.*, using only electrical power; **all-in-one** *a.* = *one piece* adj. s.v. ONE *numeral a.* 33; also *ellipt.* as *sb.*, a one-piece foundation garment (see quot. 1939); **all-or-none**, (*a*) used esp. *attrib.* of the nature of a response of a muscle or nerve fibre, etc., to a stimulus (see quots.); (*b*) = ALL-OR-NOTHING 2; **all-points bulletin** *N. Amer.*, a radio alert broadcast throughout a police radio network, giving details of a crime, suspect, etc.; also *fig.* and *ellipt.* as ***all-points*** (colloq.); abbrev. *APB* (see A III. 1); **all-red** *a.*, used to indicate a telegraph-line, a trading route, etc., lying throughout in British territory (from the practice of colouring British and Imperial territory red in our maps); **all risks**, applied *attrib.* to a type of comprehensive insurance; **all-sliming** *vbl. sb.* and *ppl. a.* (*Mining*), applied to the process of reducing all the ore to slime (see SLIME *sb.* 4) in the extraction of gold; so ***all-slimed*** adj.; **all-sorts** (cf. SORT *sb.*[2] 12 b), as *sb.* (see quots.) and *attrib.*; *spec.* of confectionery (in full ***liquorice all-sorts***), a mixture of black-and-white or brightly coloured sweets containing liquorice; **all-terrain vehicle** *N. Amer.*, a light-weight motor vehicle suitable for use in rough country; abbrev. *ATV* (see A III. 1); **all-through** *a.*, of a journey: performed without a change of conveyance; **all-time** *a.*, (*a*) taking one's full time; (*b*) of a record level or figure, etc., for all time up to the present (orig. *U.S.*); **all-up** *a.*, of a postal service, mail, etc.: (with all items) sent by air at surface-mail rates, when this results in earlier delivery (see quot. 1980); **all-up (weight)**, the total (weight) of the machine, crew, passengers and cargo of an aircraft when in the air; **all-welded** *a.*, having all the joins welded (opp. *riveted*, etc.); **all-wing** *a.*, of aircraft (see quot. 1956).

1876 *Coursing Calendar* 323 The *all-ages were not a good lot, but they contained one or two who had already distinguished themselves this season. **1880** J. W. ZAEHNSDORF *Art Bookbinding* 167 When a volume is sewed, and the thread passes from kettle-stitch to kettle-stitch, or from end to end in each sheet, it is said to be sewed '*all-along'. **1960** G. A. GLAISTER *Gloss. of Book* 5/2 *All along*, the method of hand sewing the sections of a book on cords or tapes when the thread goes from kettle-stitch to kettle-stitch inside the fold of each section. Also used to describe a machine-sewn book in which each section has the full number of stitches. **1927** *Observer* 5 June 21 His main weakness is a preference for the base-line rather than the *all-court game. **1920** *Electr. Rev.* 27 Feb. 274/2 On Friday, last week..a Press visit to the '*All-Electric House' exhibited..at the Ideal Home Exhibition, took place. **1924** S. R. ROGET *Dict. Electr. Terms* 4/2 *All-electric Signalling*, automatic or other railway signalling in which the signals are actuated as well as controlled electrically. **1960** AUDEN *Homage to Clio* 25 This all-electric room Where ghosts would feel uneasy. **1939** M. B. PICKEN *Lang. Fashion* 2/1 **All-in-one.* Foundation garment or corselet consisting of girdle and brassière, made with or without a pantie. **1956** *Vogue* 1 Mar. 212/1 An all-in-one made of nylon satin and Darleen elastic. **1961** *Seventeen* Oct. 169 Shape up to your feminine potential in this all-in-one sweep that molds and holds you...the world's first bra to follow nature's curves uninterrupted by seams. **1967** S. BECKETT *Stories & Texts for Nothing* 86, I deduced it all from nature, with the help of an all-in-one. **1977** *Wandsworth Boro' News* 7 Oct. 8/3 The platforms on which the teachers' desk used to be had been removed many years ago, as had the all-in-one wooden and iron desks and seats of the pupils. **1985** *Evergreen* Spring 55/1 His wife..would be plump, creating the greatest demand in the country for 'roll-ons' and all-in-one foundation garments. **1900** J. BURDON-SANDERSON in Sharpey-Schafer *Text-bk. Physiol.* II. 449 The characteristic relation of response to stimulus known as the '*all or none' principle, according to which the vigour of the response evoked by a stimulus adequate to produce an effect, is independent of the strength of the stimulus. **1912** E. H. STARLING *Princ. Human Physiol.* v. 230 The rule of 'all or none'..was first enunciated for heart muscle. **1920** W. H. R. RIVERS *Instinct & Unconscious* vi. 45 There is [in these reactions] an absence of graduation... They tend to occur in their full strength. This form of reaction is known in physiology as the 'all-or-none' reaction. **1928** J. T. MACCURDY *Comm. Princ. Psychol. & Physiol.* 168 Adrian.. found that, in the isolated fibre, the strength of the impulse, once it was set up, remained constant and could not be increased by augmenting the strength of the stimulus. This is known as the all-or-none law of the nerve impulse. **1932** J. S. HUXLEY *Probl. Rel. Growth* vi. iv. 178 The 'all-or-none' law of the action of the sex-hormones on comb-growth. **1934** *Discovery* June 165/1 The mechanism of repression is an all-or-none mechanism. **1940** AUDEN *Another Time* 70 Are her fond responses All-or-none reactions? **1976** *CB Mag.* June 77/3 Pick it off a milepost on the roadside and turn on the lights in your car—they have an *all points out on you. **1960** *All-points bulletin [see A III. 1]. **1969** *Daily Colonist* (Victoria, B.C.) 13 July 6/3 An all-points bulletin then was put out for the arrest of the former mental patient. **1977** *Amer. Speech* 1975 L. 55 *All-points-bulletin* n, earnest plea for help, as in a course. 'I'm sending out an all-points-bulletin for my English class.' **1984** *Tampa* (Florida) *Tribune* 28 Mar. 1B/2 The police issued an all-points bulletin for the truck as the museum employee drove innocently toward Delray. **1895** G. HUTCHISON in *N.Z. Hansard* XCI. 854 Arguments..in favour of the '*All Red' line. **1923** *Daily Mail* 12 Mar. 9 A huge 'All-Red' aeroplane, spanning the Empire in such a series of great, long-distance night-and-day flights as shall obviate any necessity for alighting on foreign soil. **1911** *Law Times Rep.* CV. 413/2 The insurance is to be a complete insurance against all risks..an insurance which would be known as an *all risks insurance. *Ibid.* 412/2 Lloyd's 'all risks' policy was inadequate. **1962** D. TENCH *Law for Consumers* vi. 74 It is a mistake to imagine that a comprehensive policy covers the consumer against every conceivable happening... Even an 'All Risks' policy does not cover you against all risks. **1934** *Brit. S. Afr. Ann.* *1934–35* 103/2 Two or three-stage grinding..reduces all the ore to an *all-slimed product. **1920** A. H. FAY *Gloss. Mining & Mineral Industry* 26/2 **All-sliming*, crushing all the ore in a mill to so fine a state of subdivision that only a small percentage will fail to pass through a 200-mesh screen. **1933** *Brit. S. Afr. Ann.* *1933–34* 97/2 The extended 'all-sliming' process plant came into full commission in November, 1929. **1955** *Times* 20 May 19/1 The reduction plant has been converted to operate on an all-sliming basis, and it is expected that this modification will result in small improvements in reduction costs and gold residue values. **1823** 'JON BEE' *Slang* 3 **All sorts*, or All Nations, spirits compounded of all the drippers in a cellar, and the pewter save-all on a gin-shop counter. **1931** W. HOLTBY *Poor Caroline* iii. 76 Pink sugared hazel nuts, and Liquorice All Sorts. **1937** W. DE LA MARE *This Year, Next Year*, An all-sorts shop. **1961** *20th Cent.* Feb. 99 The architectural all-sorts of the actor's metropolitan Mecca. **1970** *Time* 23 Nov. 41 Proliferating from Maine to California, they [*sc.* off-road vehicles] now include 200,000 dune buggies,..1,100,000 snowmobiles and, newest of all, 25,000 *all-terrain vehicles (ATV's). **1973** *Globe & Mail* (Toronto) 5 July 1/7 The select committee studying motorized snow vehicles and all terrain vehicles spent the better part of a day's sitting listening to an expert about noise. **1912** MRS. HUGH FRASER *Further Remin.* i. 10 After an *all-through journey from Rome, our train crawled into the Gare de Lyons. **1930** H. G. WELLS *Autocr. Mr. Parham* I. i. 4 An *all-time job with a garrulous advertisement contractor. **1933** *Sat. Even. Post* 10 June 61 Brings cost of power to new all-time low. **1939** 'N. BLAKE' *Smiler with Knife* ii. 29 An all-time high in adenoidal growth. **1959** N. MARSH *Singing in Shrouds* vi. 110 An all-time-low in inhibitions and an all-time-high in what it takes. **1959** *Observer* 29 Mar. 3/3 The market in industrial equities had soared by the end of 1958 to an all-time peak. **1937** *Rep. Proc. 14th Conf. ASLIB* 76 The ceremonial send-off from Southampton of the first '*all-up' Empire Air Mail. **1964** H. ROBINSON *Carrying British Mails Overseas* xxiii. 291 Sir Philip Sassoon..informed the Commons in December 1934 of..the decision to carry *all* of the first-class mail by air ...Up to this time the Imperial surface rate had been..1½d for an ounce. The new 'all-up' rate was set at 1½d but for a half ounce only, with no special fee for conveyance by air. **1968** *Economist* 13 July 41/3 A major diversion of first-class mail from the railways to the airlines, reflecting the determination of the postal authorities to shift to 'all-up' handling of inter-city first-class mail. **1980** *Postal Rates Overseas* (Post Office) 4 Feb. All-up to Europe... Letters and postcards are sent by air whenever this will result in earlier delivery. **1933** *Jrnl. R. Aeronaut. Soc.* XXXVII. 774 We have been able to build a flying boat with an *all-up weight of 56 tons. **1958** *Economist* 25 Oct. 349/3 New York airport, for one, has too short a runway to permit it to take off at full all-up weight. **1936** *Ibid.* 18 Jan. 150/2 The first *all-welded spiral guide-frames gasholder to be built in this country is now in course of erection at Newhaven. **1931** *Flight* 25 Sept. 970a/1 The ideal *all-wing type of airplane would incorporate only wing formation, utilising all power output for lifting purposes. **1956** W. A. HEFLIN *U.S. Air Force Dict.* 42 *All-wing*, of an airplane: Designed and built as a single wing, without conventional fuselage or empennage.

IV. In modern (esp. 20th-century) use, *all* with a sb. forms an attrib. phr.: **a.** with names of countries, states, etc., denoting that the whole is concerned; **b.** with words denoting a period of time: lasting or functioning throughout that period, as ***all-day***, ***-night*** (hence ***all-nighter***: see NIGHTER, also (chiefly *U.S.*) a task, etc., that takes all night.); **c.** (with the sb. either in sing. or pl.) denoting that all the persons or things expressed by the sb. are concerned or included. (Cf. also senses E. 5, 6 b above.)

a. 1853 'C. BEDE' *Verdant Green* I. xi. 102 Verdant's score was always on the *lucus a non lucendo* principle of derivation ..and he felt that he should never rival a Mynn or be a Parr with any one of the 'All England' players. **1878** (*title*) Laws of Lawn-Tennis, as adopted by The Marylebone Cricket Club, and The All England Croquet and Lawn-Tennis Club. **1904** *Independent* (U.S.) 27 Oct. 951/1 The selection of 'All-America' teams seems to have become a mania. **1906** *Dublin Rev.* Oct. 332 We are forced onwards to the necessity of an all-world State if we would escape an all-world anarchy. **1928** *Manch. Guardian Weekly* 28 Sept. 242/3 The all-India leaders. **1937** *Ann. Reg.* *1936* II. 133 The All-Africa Convention. **1952** C. P. BLACKER *Eugenics* viii. 160 In 1926..there took place..the first All-Union [i.e. in U.S.S.R.] census of population.

b. 1861 [see ALL-NIGHT-MAN]. *a* **1870** in *Dict. Amer. Eng.*, An all-day horse. **1888** A. C. GUNTER *Mr. Potter of Texas* xx, The..Press Club..just beginning to assume its usual all-night gayety and brilliancy. **1895** [see NIGHTER]. **1901** *Dialect Notes* II. 134 *All-day sucker*, a piece of candy on small stick to be disposed of by sucking for some time. **1906** 'O. HENRY' *Four Million* 215 An all-night lunch Counter. **1930** B. MAINE *Rondo* I. ii. 38 There are some who profess to find excitement in encountering..all-nighters on the Embankment. **1939** J. STEINBECK *Grapes of Wrath* xxvi. 330 Ever' place you look is restaurants... Lookit that all-nighter there. **1955** A. HUXLEY *Genius & Goddess* 32 You know those enormous lollipops on sticks that children lick at all day long? Well, that's what her fear was—an all-day sucker. **1959** E. K. WENLOCK *Kitchin's Road Transport Law* 8/2 A cheap 'all-day' ticket. **1967** *Melody Maker* 28 Jan. 11 'It's an all-nighter,' he revealed. 'And I want you to play three 45 minute spots.' **1968–70** *Current Slang* (Univ. S. Dakota) III–IV. 2 *All-nighter*, a long, difficult job; a cram session. **1978** J. WAMBAUGH *Black Marble* xi. 247 She felt like telling him it would be the last all-nighter until he accepted impending middle age. **1984** *Nutshell* (Gainesville, Fla.) Spring 88/3 Don't let schoolwork pile up into an interminable string of all-nighters.

c. 1909 *Westm. Gaz.* 8 Nov. 7/1 The National All-Grades Movement of the Amalgamated Society of Railway Servants. **1928** *Times* 3 July 16/6 The new all-purpose Fairey Napier aeroplane. **1928** *Manch. Guardian Weekly* 23 Nov. 401/3 The all-parties Constitution. *Ibid.* 26 Oct. 328/2 Six-cylinder Thornycroft all-weather body cars. **1929** *Punch's Almanack 1930* 4 Nov. p. xxxv, The All-Mains set draws its power from the house electrical supply. **1930** *Times Educ. Suppl.* 8 Mar. 107/4 With the present system of parochial 'all-age' schools it had not been possible to provide for the..needs of the pupils. **1933** *Jrnl. R. Aeronaut. Soc.* XXXVII. 2 In Europe our aerodromes, being surfaced with excellent turf, are available for landing in every direction. In other words, they are 'all way' fields and the envy of the Americans. **1937** *Discovery* Feb. 44/2 An alternative [television] set incorporating an 8-valve all-wave sound receiver. **1939** D. CECIL *Young Melbourne* v. 114 A petition was brought forward in the House of Lords asking for an all-party Government. **1955** W. W. DENLINGER *Complete Boston* I. 159 The dog..was many times Best Dog in Show at all-breed shows. **1955** *Times* 8 July 5/1 The Gloster Javelin delta winged all-weather fighter, which is soon to go into service with the R.A.F. **1960** *Farmer & Stockbreeder* 1 Mar. 142/1 An all-purpose mounted implement capable of drastically reducing the time and labour spent in preparing seed beds.

†a'llaborate, *v. Obs.*[—0] [f. L. *allabōrāt-* ppl. stem of *allabōrā-re* to toil at, f. *al-* = *ad-* to, at + *labōrā-re* to labour.] 'To labour vehemently.' Blount *Glossogr.* 1656; whence in Bailey.

†a'llaborateness. *Obs.*[—0] [f. assumed *allaborate* ppl. adj., ad. L. *allabōrāt-* (see prec.) + NESS.] 'A being well wrought.' Bailey 1731.

†allabo'ration. *Obs.*[—0] [n. of action f. ALLABORATE *v.* + -TION.] 'A labouring strenuously.' Bailey 1731.

‖alla breve (ˌalla 'brɛve), *adv. phr. Mus.* [It., = according to the BREVE.] (See quot.)

1806 CALLCOTT *Mus. Gram.* iii. 30 The barred Semicircle is used to denote a quicker Movement, and is called Alla Breve. **1879** E. PROUT in Grove *Dict. Mus.*, *Alla Breve*, originally a species of time in which every bar contained a breve or four minims; hence its name..Modern alla breve time simply differs from ordinary common time by being always beaten or counted with two minims in the bar, and therefore is really quick common time.

‖alla capella (ˌalla ka'pɛlla), *adv. phr. Mus.* [It., = according to (the manner of) the chapel.] = prec.

1847 in CRAIG. **1879** E. PROUT in Grove *Mus. Dict.* I. 53/2 *Alla Breve*..This time, chiefly used in the older church music..was also called *Alla Capella*.

allactite (æ'læktaɪt). *Min.* [ad. Sw. *allaktit* (A. Sjögren 1884, in *Geol. Fören. Förhandl.* VII.

109), f. Gr. stem ἀλλακτ-, ἀλλάσσειν to change: see -ITE[1].] A native arsenate of manganese.

1892 DANA *Syst. Min.* (ed. 6) 800 *Allactite*... Monoclinic... Numerous vicinal planes in the prismatic zone. **1920** *Brit. Museum Return* 145 Allactite from Sweden.

allagite ('ælədʒaɪt). *Min.* [mod. f. Gr. ἀλλαγή change, alteration + -ITE min. form.] An altered variety of the mineral RHODONITE, classed by Dana as a carbonated variation, of a dull-green or reddish-brown colour.

allagostemonous (ˌæləgəʊ'stiːmənəs), *a. Bot.* [f. (by Gleditsch and Mönch) Gr. ἀλλαγή change + στήμων thread.] (See quot.)

1880 GRAY *Bot. Text-bk.* 395. *Allagostemonous*, with stamens alternatively inserted on the torus and on the petals.

Allah ('ælə). [a. Arab. *allāh* the (true) God, contr. of *al-ilāh*, i.e. *al* the + *ilāh* god = Aram. *ĕlāh*, Heb. *ĕlōah*.] The name of the Deity among Mohammedans.

1702 ROWE *Tamerl.* I. i. 14 Well has our holy Alha mark'd him out The Scourge of lawless Pride. **1753** HANWAY *Trav.* (1762) II. XV. i. 403 The Tartars when they believe themselves to be dying, repeat this word, *allah, allah,* continually. **1840** CARLYLE *Heroes* (1858) 235, I make but little of his [Mahomet's] praises of Allah.

Allahism ('ælɪz(ə)m). [f. prec. + -ISM.] The Mohammedan conception of the attributes of God.

1881 SEELEY in *Macm. Mag.* July 170/1 [Bonaparte] had imagined.. some fusion apparently of Rousseau's Deism with the Allah-ism of Mohammed.

allamanda, Alla- (ælə'mændə). Also erron. **alamanda, alamander.** [mod.L. (Linnæus 1771), f. the name of the Swiss scientist J. N. S. *Allamand*.] A plant of the genus so named of apocynaceous trees of tropical America, cultivated for their large funnel-shaped yellow flowers.

1796 CURTIS in *Bot. Mag.* X. pl. 338 Willow-leaved Allamanda. **1879** W. CORY *Lett. & Jrnls.* 7 Oct. (1897) 449 An alamanda with big petals of a very lovely yellow. **1918** C. W. BEEBE *Jungle Peace* iv. 83 The sheets of bougainvillea blossoms, of yellow allamandas.. brought joy to the eye and the nostril. **1957** P. MANSFIELD *Final Exposure* xiv. 213 The wind had been.. beating the branches of the alamander against the wall and plucking the pale flowers from the stems.

Comb. **1918** W. H. HUDSON *Far Away* xxii. 294 The large alamanda-like flower of a purest divine yellow.

‖**alla marcia** (ˌala 'martʃia), *adv.* (*adj.* and *sb.*) *phr. Mus.* As a musical direction: in the style of a march. Also as *adj.* and *sb.*

1876 STAINER & BARRETT *Dict. Mus. Terms* 20/2 *Alla marcia*, in the style of a March. **1888** L. A. SMITH *Music of Waters* 14 Solo. *Alla marcia.* Haul on the bow-lin', the fore and main-top bow-line. **1947** A. EINSTEIN *Mus. Romantic Era* xi. 131 A trio entitled *Phantasiestück* (Op. 88, 1842), consisting of Romance, Duet, and Alla Marcia. **1964** *Listener* 19 Mar. 498/3 A source from which Prokofiev drew inspiration for his piquant *alla marcia* type of movement. **1982** *N.Y. Times* 8 Sept. c2/1 Largo (five minutes' rest). *Conductor*: 'Some congestion ahead of us. We'll be moving shortly.'.. Alla marcia, assai vivace.

allamotti, -monti, -moth, dial. names for the Stormy Petrel. Montague *Ornith. Dict.* 1802.

allan, var. of ALAN.

allane, obs. form of ALONE.

allanerly, variant of ALLENNARLY.

allanite ('ælənaɪt). *Min.* [named after T. Allan, a mineralogist + -ITE, min. form.] A brownish-black mineral, akin to Epidote, consisting mainly of the oxides of cerium and iron, with silica.

1843 HUMBLE *Dict. Geol.*, *Allanite*, an orthitic melane-ore .. brought from Greenland. **1880** DANA *Min.* 287 Allanite is a cerium-epidote.

allantoic (ælæn'təʊɪk), *a. Phys.* [f. ALLANTOIS + -IC: cf. mod.Fr. *allantoïque*.] Of or belonging to the allantois.

1836 TODD *Cycl. Anat. & Phys.* I. 47/1 Certain acids almost peculiar to individual animals such as the.. allantoic. **1850** DAUBENY *Atom. Theory* xi. (ed. 2) 365 The allantoic fluid of the cow. **1880** HUXLEY in *Nature* No. 583. 203 The existing horse has a diffuse allantoic placentation.

allantoid (ə'læntɔɪd), *a.* and *sb. Phys.* [mod. ad. Gr. ἀλλαντο-ειδής; f. ἀλλάντ- sausage + -ειδ ής shaped: see -OID, and cf. mod.Fr. *allantoïde*.]

A. *adj.* Of or pertaining to the allantois.

1633 P. FLETCHER *Purple Isl.* II. xxiii, The last, from Urine-lake with waters base, In the allantoid sea empties his flowing race. **1836** TODD *Cycl. Anat. & Phys.* I. 646/2 In which [the Batrachia] during fœtal life no allantoid membrane is ever formed.

B. *sb.* The allantoid membrane or ALLANTOIS.

1667 *Phil. Trans.* II. 512 Then he proceeds to the description of the *Allantoides*. **1847-9** TODD *Cycl. Anat. & Phys.* IV. 744/1 The allantoid in the mare does not form a closed bag.

allantoidian (ælæn'tɔɪdɪən), *a.* and *sb. Zool.* [ad. Fr. *allantoïdien*: see prec. and -IAN.] **A.** *adj.* Having the fœtus furnished with an allantois. **B.** *sb.* An animal whose fœtus is so furnished.

1861 HULME *Moquin-Tandon's Med. Zool.* II. II. 62 Allantoidians = Mammalia, Aves, Reptilia.

allantoin (ə'læntəʊɪn). *Chem.* [mod. f. ALLANTO-IS + -IN chem. form. Cf. Fr. *allantoïne*.] A crystalline substance, $C_4N_4H_6O_3$, the nitrogenous constituent of the allantoic fluid.

1845 TODD & BOWMAN *Phys. Anat.* I. 9 Allantoin, an analogous compound to urea. **1863** WATTS *Fownes' Chem.* (1877) II. 412 Allantoïn.. is found in the allantoïc liquid of the fœtal calf.. It is produced artificially.. by boiling uric acid with lead dioxide and water.

allantois (ə'læntəʊɪs). *Phys.* [mod.L. in form, a factitious sing. f. the earlier form *allantoïdes*, ad. Gr. ἀλλαντο-ειδής: see ALLANTOID.] The fœtal membrane (so named by ancient anatomists from its form in a calf) found only in mammals, birds, and reptiles, which lies between the amnion and chorion, and forms a means of communication between the fœtal and maternal blood.

1646 SIR T. BROWNE *Pseud. Ep.* 270 The Allantois is a thin coat seated under the Corion, wherein are received the watery separations conveyed by the Urachus. **1691** RAY *Creation* (1701) 82 Abundance of urine in the Allantoides. **1879** *Syd. Soc. Lex.* s.v., [In birds] by its proximity to the shell, the allantois is an important respiratory organ.

allanturic (ælæn'tjʊərɪk), *a. Chem.* [f. ALLANT-OIS + URIC.] Epithet of an organic acid obtained from allantoin or from uric acid.

1863 WATTS *Chem. Dict.*, *Allanturic Acid* $C_3H_4N_2O_3$.. is a white solid body, slightly acid, deliquescent, nearly insoluble in alcohol. **1879** *Syd. Soc. Lex.*, *Allanturic acid*, an acid obtained by Pelouze by treating allantoin with nitric acid.

‖**alla prima** (ˌalla 'priːma, ˌælə 'praɪ-), *advb. phr.* passing into *sb.* [It., lit. 'at once'.] The direct method of painting without underpainting.

1849 M. P. MERRIFIELD *Orig. Treatises Arts of Painting* I. vi. p. cxxxiv, Paolo Veronese painted generally *alla prima* with more body than Titian.. so that the finished picture was little more than the abbozzo; that is, he painted up his picture at once. **1961** M. LEVY *Studio Dict. Art Terms* 12 *Alla prima*, direct painting. The completion of a painting by a single application of pigments, in contrast to a painting which is completed in stages by the application of successive layers of pigments.

†**a'llaqueate,** *ppl. a. Obs. rare*$^{-1}$. [f. L. *ad* to + *laqueāt-us* entangled, snared, f. *laque-us* a noose.] Ensnared, captivated.

1535 STEWART *Cron. Scotl.* III. 503 And quhen he saw the fairnes and the fame Of this virgin.. Allaqueat wes with hir speciositie.

allar, obs. and dial. form of ALDER (tree).

‖**allargando** (alar'gando). *Mus.* Pl. **allargandi.** [It., pres. pple. of *allargare* to broaden.] A musical direction indicating that the time is to be made slower and slower and the tone fuller; also a passage of music in this style.

1893 J. S. SHEDLOCK tr. *Riemann's Dict. Mus.* 19/1 *Allargando*, becoming broader (slower); specially used in place of *ritardando* (*rallentando*), where the tone is to be increased. **1959** D. COOKE *Lang. Mus.* v. 256 The first three notes.. are accented and held back (*allargando*): there is the maximum of rhetorical emphasis here. **1961** *Times* 28 Jan. 3/7 A tendency to break the flow of the music by introducing *ritardandi, allargandi.*

all-around, *a. U.S.* = ALL-ROUND *a.*

1883 [see AROUND *adv.* 4]. **1886** *Harper's Mag.* June 18/2 This arrangement gives a clear sweep.. enabling the forward gun to cover an all-around fire. **1904** *Brooklyn Daily Standard Union* 7 July 6 Our army in the Philippines seems to be composed of 'all-around' men. **1904** *Forum* Oct. 257 The most comprehensive and in many ways the best all-around American city school exhibit. **1920** *Harvey's Weekly* 5 June 4/1 Senator Knox is the best-equipped all-around international statesman.

Hence **all-a'roundness.** *U.S.*

1888 *Voice* (N.Y.) 6 Sept., The all-aroundness of our chieftain's character. **1929** D. H. LAWRENCE *Paintings* sig. E 1ᵛ, But intuition needs all-aroundness, and instinct needs insideness.

allas, obs. variant of ALAS.

†**a'llation.** *Obs. rare*$^{-1}$. [f. L. *allāt-* ppl. stem of *afferre* to bring to or into + -ION[1].] The action of bringing to; importation, introduction.

1657 TOMLINSON *Renou's Disp.* 158 Sassafras.. which at its first allation was sold dear.

allative ('ælətɪv), *a. Gram.* [f. L. *allāt-* ppl. stem of *afferre* to bring to + -IVE.] Denoting the case used in some languages, e.g. Finnish, to express motion to or toward.

1860 *Trans. Philol. Soc. 1857* 34 The declension of the personal pronouns [in the Tushi Language] is as follows.. Singular.. Affective.. Allative. **1924** O. JESPERSEN *Philos. Gram.* xiii. 182 Finnish has no dative proper, but the 'allative' which expresses motion to or into the neighbourhood of, often corresponds to the Aryan dative. **1928** *Mod. Lang. Rev.* Apr. 137 Thus, he might say, in Finnish the indirect object is in the allative case. **1939** L. H. GRAY *Found. Lang.* vii. 194 The Eskimo *allative*, denoting that toward which an action tends. **1951** *Archivum Linguisticum* III. 57 An allative-dative type of case suffix.

†**a'llatrate,** *v. Obs. rare*$^{-1}$. [f. L. *allatrāt-* ppl. stem of *allatrā-re*, f. *ad* to + *latrāre* to bark.] To bark out.

1583 STUBBES *Anat. Abus.* I. (1880) 158 Let Cerberus, the dog of hel, alatrate what he list to the contrary.

†**a'llaud,** *v. Obs. rare*$^{-1}$. [ad. L. *allaudā-re*, f. *ad* intensive + *laudā-re* to praise.] To bepraise.

1657 TOMLINSON *Renou's Disp.* 132 He is more commended and allauded.

†**a'llaudable,** *a. Obs.*$^{-0}$ [ad. L. *allaudābilis*: see prec. and -ABLE.] 'Praiseworthy.' Bailey 1731.

allay (ə'leɪ), *v.*[1] Forms: 1 alecȝ-an, 2-4 alegg-e(n, 4 aley-e, alai-e, 4-6 alay-e, 5-7 alay, allaye, 6- allay. *Pa. t.* 1 aleȝde, aléde, 2 aleiȝde, 2-4 aleide, 3-4 aleyde, 4 alede, 4-5 alaide, 5-6 alayd(e, 5-7 alayed, alaid, 6-7 alaied, allayd, 6- allayed. *Pa. pple.* 1 aleȝd, aléd (etc. as in pa. t.), 6-9 allayed. [f. A- *pref.* 1 + LAY, OE. *lęcȝan*, causal of *licȝan* to lie. OE. *alęcȝan* (cogn. w. Goth. *uslagjan*, OHG. *irleccan*, mod.G. *erlegen*) was inflected : Imper. *aleȝe, alecȝað*; Ind. pres. *ic alecȝe, þú aleȝest, he aleȝ(e)þ, we alecȝað*; Pa. t. *aleȝde, aléde*; Pa. pple. *aleȝd, aléd*; whence ME. *aleggen* (ə'lɛdʒən); *aleye, alaye* (ə'lɛɪə, ə'leɪə, ə'leɪ), *alleggeþ*; *I alegge, þou aleyest, he aleyeþ, we aleggeþ* or *aleggen* ; *aleyde* ; *aleyd, -eid, -ayd, -aid*; levelled *c* 1400, by substitution of *aleye* for *alegge* all through ; as inf. *to aleyen, alaye(n, alay(e*; subsequently mis-spelt ALLAY, after words from L. in *all-* (see AD- 2). In its two forms, *alegge* and *aleye*, this vb. was formally identical with 4 other vbs. of Romance origin; viz. 1. *alegge*, ALLEGE *v.*[1]:—L. *alleviāre*; 2 *alaye*, ALLAY *v.*[2]:—L. *alligāre*; 3. *aleye*, ALLAY *v.*[3]:—L. *allēgāre*; 4. *alegge*, ALLEGE *v.*[2] = OFr. *alléguer*, L. *allēgāre*, a learned form of ALLAY *v.*[3]. Amid the overlapping of meanings that thus arose, there was developed a perplexing network of uses of *allay* and *allege*, that belong entirely to no one of the original vbs., but combine the senses of two or more of them. Those in *allay* are placed at the end of this word.]

I. Unmixed senses: To lay from one, lay aside or down; put down; put down the proud, pride, tumult, violence; to quell, abate.

†**1.** To lay, lay down, lay aside. *Obs.*

c **970** *Canons of K. Edgar* in *Anc. Laws* II. 286 Alecȝe þonne his wæpna. *c* **1000** *Ags. G.* Luke ii. 16 Hiȝ ȝemetton .. ðæt cild on binne aléd. *c* **1160** *Hatton G.* ibid., Gemetton þæt chyld on binne aleiȝd.

†**2.** To lay aside (a law, custom, practice); *hence*, to set aside, annul, abolish, destroy the legal force of (anything). *Obs.*

c **1175** *Lamb. Hom.* 91 Þenne beoð eowre sunnen aleide. *Ibid.* 115 He scal wicche creft aleggan. **1205** LAYAM. 7714 Þurh þa luue of þan feo feond-scipe aleggen. **1297** R. GLOUC. 144 Gode lawes, þat were aleyd, newe he lette make. *c* **1350** *Will. Palerne* 5240 Þan william wiȝtli.. a-leide alle luþer lawes. **1413** LYDG. *Pylgr. Sowle* IV. xxxvi. (1483) 84 Worshyp is aleyde and neuer shal retourne.

†**3.** To abandon, give up (a course of action). *Obs.*

a **1330** *Sir Otuel* 38 Bi me he sente the to segge, Thou sscoldest Christendom alegge. *c* **1380** *Sir Ferumb.* 3300 Hot þat þyn assaut be noȝt aled : and let by-gynne hit newe.

†**4.** To put down, bring low, quell (a person). *Obs.*

c **1000** ÆLFRIC *Josh.* x. 13 Hiȝ aledon heora fynd. *c* **1175** *Lamb. Hom.* 91 Ic alegge þine feond under þine fot-sceomele. *c* **1300** in Wright *Lyric P.* xxxvii. 105 Alle thre shule ben aleyd, with huere foule crokes. **1387** TREVISA *Higden* Rolls Ser. III. 237 [The Greeks] schulle be aleyde [*obruentur*] wiþ the multitude of Perses.

†**5.** To put down or overthrow (a principle or attribute of men). *Obs.*

a **1000** *Sec. Laws of Cnut* (Thorpe I. 380) Unriht alecȝan. *c* **1200** *Trin. Coll. Hom.* 11 Unbileue is aiware aleid, and rihte leue arered. *c* **1300** *Beket* 1928 Forto awreke ous wel of him and alegge his prute. *c* **1440** *Arthur* 219 Thy pryde we wolle alaye. **1593** SHAKS. *2 Hen. VI*, IV. i. 60, I, and alay this thy abortiue Pride. **1642** ROGERS *Naaman* 205 Wherby carnall reason is somewhat alaied and abated. **1659** PEARSON *Creed* (1839) 88 Sufficiently refuting an eternity, and allaying all conceits of any great antiquity.

†**6.** To put down by argument, confute, overthrow. *Obs. rare.*

a **1250** *Owl & Night.* 394 Heo ne miȝte noȝt alegge That the hule hadde hire i-sed.

†**7.** To cause to lie, to lay (dust, etc.). *Obs. rare.*

1642 FULLER *Holy & Prof. St.* v. xiv. 413 That in Noahs floud the dust was but sufficiently allayed.

8. To put down or repress (any violence of the elements, as heat, wind, tempest); to calm, assuage, 'lay' a storm. (This and the next sense are perhaps influenced by ALLEGE *v.*[1]: see 11 below.)

1488 CAXTON *Chastys. Goddes Chyld.* 12 Hete is thenne ful colde and alayed. **1580** BARET *Alv.* A 282 The tempest is alaied. **1610** SHAKS. *Temp.* I. ii. 2 If by your Art (my deerest father) you haue Put the wild waters in this Rore; alay them. **1781** J. MOORE *Italy* (1790) I. ii. 23 One of the virtues of the holy water [is] that of allaying storms. **1847** DISRAELI *Tancred* III. iv. (1871) 183 The fervour of the air was allayed. **1862** TRENCH *Mirac.* iv. 147 Having allayed the tumult of the outward elements.

9. To quell or put down (any disturbance in action or any tumult of the passions); to appease.

c **1380** *Sir Ferumb.* 1373 Y-blessed mot þou be, For aled þow hast muche debate. **1387** TREVISA *Higden* Rolls Ser. IV. 293 Forto alegge þe outrage of þe kyngdom of Jewes. **1600** FAIRFAX *Tasso* XIX. xx. 340 Tancred..Asswag'd his anger and his wrath alaid. **1623** BINGHAM *Xenophon* 35 To allay, if he could, these distrusts, before they broke out into open hostilitie. **1697** DRYDEN *Virg. Georg.* IV. 131 This deadly Fray, A Cast of scatter'd Dust will soon allay. **1711** ADDISON *Spect.* No. 16 ¶4 If I can any way asswage private Inflammations, or allay publick Ferments. **1855** PRESCOTT *Philip II*, I. II. xi. 265 The best means of allaying the popular excitement. **1863** KINGLAKE *Crimea* (1876) I. xiv. 236 Words tending to allay suspicion. **1880** MCCARTHY *Own Time* III. xxxii. 48 Various efforts were made to allay the panic.

†**10.** *intr.* (for *refl.*) To subside, sink, abate, cease; to become mild. *Obs.*

1526 TINDALE and **1557** (Genev.) *Mark* iv. 39 And the wynde alayed. **1561** HOLLYBUSH *Hom. Apoth.* 33 a, For assone as the stomake perceyveth the savoure of the bread, then doth the wambling alaye. **1593** SHAKS. *3 Hen. VI*, I. iv. 146 And, when the Rage allayes, the Raine begins. **1723** WODROW *Corr.* (1843) III. 78 If there were any room to hope that your hearts were allaying.

II. Confused with ALLEGE *v.*[1] to *lighten* or *alleviate*, both verbs being in 14th c. *alegge*, and both used of *pains*, etc., so that *alegge peine* was in the one sense = *quell* pain, in the other = *alleviate* pain. Both senses might be expressed by *abate*, and they came to be regarded as the same word, so that from *c* 1400 *alaye* was used for *alegge* in both (cf. Caxton's 't' *alegge* thurste,' see ALLEGE *v.*[1] 2, Gower's 'to *allay* thurst'); and finally *alegge* became obs., and *allay* remained with the combined meaning.

11. To subdue, quell (any trouble, as care, pain, thirst); to abate, assuage, relieve, alleviate.

[*c* **1220** *Ureisun Ure Lefdi* 133 þu miht lihtliche..al mi sor aleggen. **1250** LAY. 25684 Al þis lond he wole for-fare: bote þou alegge oure care.] **1393** GOWER *Conf.* III. 11 Which may his sory thurst allay. *Ibid.* III. 273 If I thy paines mighte alaie. **1578** LYTE *Dodoens* 341 The roote Rhodia..alayeth head ache. **1667** MILTON *P.L.* x. 566 Fondly thinking to allay Thir appetite. **1681** WYNDHAM *King's Concealm.* 76 The pleasantness of the Host..allayed and mitigated the weariness of the Guests. **1768** BEATTIE *Minstrel* II. xxxii, I would allay that grief. **1836** MACGILLIVRAY tr. *Humboldt's Trav.* xix. 283 These Indians swallow quantities of earth for the purpose of allaying hunger.

III. Confused with ALLAY *v.*[2], to alloy, mix, temper, qualify. The two verbs were from the 15th c. completely identical in form, and thus in appearance only different uses of the same word. (The earlier of the following senses are more closely related to the next vb. than to this; but it is, on the whole, more convenient to place them here, than under a word which is obs. or arch. in its own proper sense.)

†**12.** To temper (iron, steel, etc.) *Obs.*

1409 *Roll for Building Durham Cloisters*, Pro alayng secur', chyselle, wegges. **1486** *Bk. St. Albans* (1810) h iij, Ye shall put the quarell in a redde charkcole fyre tyll that it be of the same colour that the fyre is. Thenne take hym oute and lete hym kele, and ye shall find him well alayd for to fyle.

13. To temper or abate (a pleasure or advantage) by the association of something unpleasant.

1514 BARCLAY *Cyt. & Uplondyshm.* 48 Because one service of them continuall Allayeth pleasure. *a* **1670** HACKET in Wolcott's *Life* (1865) 175 If the comfort of our joy be not allayed with some fear. **1759** JOHNSON *Rasselas* xxvi. (1787) 71 Benefits are allayed by reproaches. **1796** MORSE *Amer. Geog.* I. 310 The principal circumstance that allayed the joys of victory. **1839** HALLAM *Hist. Lit.* III. III. iii. §131. 115 But this privilege is allayed by another, *i.e.* by the privilege of absurdity.

†**14.** To dilute, qualify (wine with water, etc.). *Obs.*

c **1450** J. RUSSELL *Bk. Nurt.* in *Babees Bk.* (1868) 132 Watur hoot & cold, eche oþer to alay. **1470** HARDING *Chron.* lxxii, He vsed the water ofte to alaye His drynkes. **1533** ELYOT *Cast. Helth* (1541) 32 White wyne alayd with moche water. **1655** CULPEPER *Riverius* XV. v. 419 Clysters..made of Vinegar allaied with Water. **1676** HOBBES *Odyss.* IX. 212 Which when he drank, he usually allaid With water pure.

†**15.** *fig. Obs.*

1586 T. B. tr. *La Primaudaye's Fr. Acad.* Ded., To alay the strength of the word of Christ with the waterish sayings and fables of men. **1650** FULLER *Pisgah Sight* IV. vii. 125 God..allaying the purity of his nature, with humane Phrases.

16. To abate, diminish, weaken, mitigate.

1603 FLORIO *Montaigne* (1634) 624 To allay or dim the whitenesse of paper. **1628** PRYNNE *Cens. Cozens* 96 This pretence..will not mittigate nor allay his Crime. **1748** CHESTERF. *Lett.* 166 II. 111 Neither envy, indignation, nor ridicule, will obstruct or allay the applause which you may really deserve. **1805** FOSTER *Ess.* II. iv. 169 They must allay their fire of enterprise. **1842** H. ROGERS *Introd. Burke's Wks.* 59 To allay and temper its splendour down to that sober light which may enable his audience to see his argument.

†**allay** (əˈleɪ), *v.*[2] *Obs.* or *arch.* Forms: 4–5 **alay(e**, 5–8 **allay(e**, (8–9 ALLOY). [a. ONFr. *aleyer*, *alayer* (mod.Fr. *aloyer*), a variant of *alier*, *allier*, ALLY:—L. *alligā-re* to combine, f. *al-*, *ad-* to + *ligāre* to bind. (*Ligāre* gave in OFr., according to accent, inf. *lier*, pres. t. *leie*, *leies*, *leiet*, *lions*, *liez*, *leient*, whence, by levelling of forms, two verbs *lier*, *je lie*, etc., and *leier*, *je leie*, etc. So *ad-ligāre* gave *alie-r*, and *aleie-r* (*alai-er*), now *allier* and *aloyer* (Cotgr. *allayer*), with differentiation of meaning. Cf. Fr. *plier* and *ployer*:—L. *plicāre*; OFr. *desplier*, *despleier*, *desploier*, mod.Fr. *déployer*, Eng. *display*:—L. *displicāre*.) At a later period the Fr. *aloyer* and sb. *aloi*, in reference to metals, were explained by false etymology from *à loi* (reduced) to law, or to legal standard. In Eng. this vb. has been confused with the prec., from identity of form and contact of meaning. In the original sense it is now changed to ALLOY, after mod.Fr.]

1. To mix (metals); *esp.* to mix with a baser metal, so as to lower the standard or quality.

1377 LANGL. *P. Pl.* B. xv. 346 þe metal, þat is mannes soule With synne is foule alayed. **1530** PALSGR. 420/1, I allaye, as mettals be alayde or as sylver or golde is with their mixture. **1587** HARRISON *Engl.* I. II. xxv. 363 The finesse of the metall began to be verie much alaied. **1649** LOVELACE *Poems* (1659) 93 The Gold allayd almost halfe brasse. **1687** SETTLE *Dryden's Plays* 51 That to convert gold Ore into silver, he allays it with common Sand. **1796** PEARSON in *Phil. Trans.* LXXXVI. 439 Hardening copper..by allaying it with iron.

2. *fig.* To mix with something inferior, to contaminate, debase; to deteriorate or detract from.

1447 BOKENHAM *Lyvys of Seyntys* 282 For both of men and wummen also The molde these dayis ys so sore alayde Wyth froward wyl. **1639** FULLER *Holy War* v. ix. (1840) 257 Debased and allayed with superstitious intents. **1642** —— *Holy & Prof. St.* I. vii. 17 He doth not so allay his servants bread..to make that servants meat which is not mans meat. **1769** ROBERTSON *Charles V*, III. VIII. 66 His extraordinary qualities were allayed with no inconsiderable mixture of human frailty.

¶See at the end of the prec. word, a number of senses combining the ideas of ALLAY, to alloy, or deteriorate, and ALLAY, to put down, abate, reduce, which might equally follow here. When these arose, the two verbs, originally distinct, had come to be viewed as one.

†**a'llay**, *v.*[3] *Obs.* Forms: 4–5 **aleye, alleie, alay.** [a. OFr. *aleie-r*, *alaier*, *alleyer* to declare on oath:—L. *allēgā-re*, *adlēgā-re*, to send to or for, cite, adduce, produce in evidence, f. *ad* to + *lēgāre* to depute, send. The popular OFr. *aleyer* was superseded at an early date by *a(l)léguer*, a forensic adaptation of the L. original, and in Eng. *allege* has similarly replaced *allay*.] To cite, adduce, allege.

1356 WYCLIF *Last Age of Ch.* 32 He aleyeþ Gregor seiynge þus. *c* **1380** —— *Prelates* vii. (1879) 70 Sathanas..aleid holy writt to crist. **1387** TREVISA *Higden* Rolls Ser. VI. 371 Rollo ..alleyeþ þe manere and usage of his contray. **1393** GOWER *Conf.* II. 66 She him preide, And many another cause alleide, That he with her at home abide. **1470** HARDING *Chron.* cxvii, Kyng Knowt to him alayde These wordes there, & thus to hym he sayde.

†**a'llay**, *sb.*[1] *Obs.* Forms: 4–6 **alaye, alaie,** 5–6 **aley,** 6 **alay,** 6–7 **alley, allaye,** 7–8 **allay.** [a. ONFr. *aley*, *alay* (mod.Fr. *aloi*; med.L. *alleium*, *alaium*), f. *aleier*, *alayer*, *aloyer*: see ALLAY *v.*[2] Confused in late OFr. with the phr. *à loi* 'to law, to legal standard,' which probably influenced senses 3, 6. See also ALLOY. Further confused in Eng. with ALLAY *v.*[1]]

I. Original sense; = ALLOY. *lit.* and *fig.*

1. Admixture of metals; *esp.* admixture with a baser metal. *concr.* A mixture of metals, a metallic compound.

c **1386** CHAUCER *Clerkes T.* 1111 The gold of hem hath now so bad alayes [*v.r.* alayis, alaies, layes, laies] With bras. **1480** *Pol. Rel. & L. Poems* 45 Trewe metalle requireth non alay. *a* **1626** BACON *Physiol. Rem.* (R.) Gold incorporates with copper in any proportion, the common allay: gold incorporates with tin, the ancient allay. **1641** *Termes de la Ley* 19 Allay is the temper or mixture of gold and silver with baser mettall. **1675** *Phil. Trans.* X. 346 As many mixtures or degrees of allay as you think fit. **1719** D'URFEY *Pills* (1872) II. 306 Those that know finest metal say, No Gold will coin without Allay. **1796** PEARSON in *Phil. Trans.* LXXXVI. 421 This allay of ten parts of copper with one part of steel. **1809** TOMLINS *Law Dict.*, *Allay*, the mixture of other metals with silver or gold.

2. Inferior metal mixed with one of greater value.

1377 LANGL. *P. Pl.* B. xv. 342 As in lussheborwes is a lyther alay, and3et loketh he lyke a sterlynge; þe merke of þat moneie is good, ac þe metal is fieble. **1473** WARKW. *Chron.* 4 To the same ryolle was put viij d. of aley. **1605** CAMDEN *Rem.* (1657) 185 A pound of money containeth twelve ounces, two easterlings and one ferling, and the other allay. **1625** BACON *Ess.* i. (Arb.) 501 Mixture of Falshood, is like Allay in Coyne of Gold and Siluer; which may make the Metall worke the better, but it embaseth it. **1678** BUTLER *Hudibr.* III. ii. 482 For Fools are stubborn in their way As Coins are hard'ned by th' Allay. **1743** TINDAL *Rapin's Hist.* II. XVII. 62 Queen Elizabeth reduced the Silver coin to eleven Ounces, two Pennyweight fine, and eighteen Pennyweight allay. **1852** A. RYLAND *Assay of Gold* 2 The added metal is called the 'allay' or 'alloy.'

3. Degree of purity or mixture of gold or silver; standard; intrinsic quality.

? **1424** in Arnold *Chron.* 31 This yere was ordeyned yᵉ alay of golde. **1523** LD. BERNERS *Froissart* I. ccciv. 454 Money, bothe whyte and blacke, of the same forme and alay as is in Parys. **1586** FERNE *Blaz. Gentry* 126 A large reuennue..if you will consider the computation and alley of money then currant. **1676** *Phil. Trans.* XI. 814 To know adulterated Wares from those that be of the true standard-Allay. **1676** *Man. Goldsm.* 4 Which degree of allay..is commonly called the Sterling Allay.

4. *fig.* Admixture of something that detracts from or diminishes the value, the intrusion or presence of any impairing element.

1599 FENTON *Guicciard.* III. 133 There is no earthly blisse so perfect, which hath not his aley with some bitternesse or bale. **1649** JER. TAYLOR *Gt. Exemp.* §12 The best and most excellent..had an allay of viciousness. **1660** WATERHOUSE *Arms & Armory* 112 That were..a baston of allay [*i.e.* of bastardy] to that Gentleman. **1710** M. HENRY *Comm. Gen.* xxviii. 1–5 While there is such an allay as there is of sin in our duties, we must expect an allay of trouble in our comforts. **1796** MISS BURNEY *Camilla* v. i, Good-nature gives pleasure without any allay.

5. *fig.* Alien element, especially such as lowers the character of anything.

a **1619** DONNE *Biathanatos* (1644) 71 The Authors..have somewhat remitted the intensnesse of Martyrdome, and mingled more allayes..and not made it of so great value. **1675** *Art of Contentm.* I. §15. 180 If we compare our blessings with our allaies, our good things with our evil. **1774** BRYANT *Mythology* II. 276 He borrows many exalted notions from Christianity; and blends them with the basest allay.

6. *fig.* Intrinsic character, quality, temper, vein, composition, complexion. Cf. Fr. *de bon aloi*, *de mauvais aloi*.

1630 NAUNTON *Fragm. Reg.* (1870) 15 Participating in this more of her Father than Mother, who was of inferiour allay. *a* **1674** CLARENDON *Hist. Reb.* I. IV. 287 The Committee.. prepared other Votes of a brighter allay. **1680–90** TEMPLE *Pop. Discont.* Wks. 1731 I. 268 Noble Families would not be exhausted by Competition with those of meaner Allay.

II. Senses affected by, or wholly derived from, ALLAY *v.*[1]

7. Dilution (of wine, etc.).

1531 ELYOT *Governour* (1580) 36 Galen will not permit, that pure wine without alaye of water, should..be given to children. **1632** B. JONSON *Magn. Lady* III. i. 496 He only takes it in French wine, With an allay of water.

8. Abatement, tempering of the force of anything.

1614 RALEIGH *Hist. World* II. v. iii. §16. 454 Whose temper needed the allay of a more staied wit. *c* **1618** FLETCHER *Double Marr.* v. i, You are of a high and cholericke complexion And you must have allayes. **1654** GODDARD in Burton's *Diary* (1828) I. 84 Standing armies, at best, were dangerous..let us temper them with what allays we can. **1738** WESLEY *Hymn 'Come Holy Spirit,'* ii, Come, Thou our Passion's cool Allay. **1758** S. HAYWARD *Serm.* Introd. 19 A considerable allay to our grief.

9. Repression, check, stoppage, retardment.

1630 NAUNTON *Fragm. Reg.* (1870) 37 He was one of the great allayes of the Austerian embracements. **1655** FULLER *Ch. Hist.* II. 80 All these his excellent Practices Bede dasheth with this Allay. **1672** MARVELL *Reh. Transp.* I. 123 Thereby to give more temper and allay to the common and notorious Debauchery. **1726** BUTLER *Serm. Rolls Chap.* xii. 235 The Principles in our Mind may be contradictory, or checks and Allays only..to each other.

†**a'llay**, *sb.*[2] *Obs.* Also 7–8 **alay.** [a. Norm. Fr. *alais* = OFr. *eslais*, '*élan, saut*,' f. *eslaissier* to let out, let off. Cf. RELAY = Fr. *relais* (with which this is confounded by Phillips and Ash.] The act of laying on the hounds.

1486 *Bk. St. Alban's* F j, Than let thyn houndes all togeder goo That called is an Allay. **1575** TURBERVILLE *Bk. Venerie* 243 When they tarrie till the rest of the kennell come in, and then cast off, it is called an Allay. ? **1594** PERCY *Faery Past.* 150 (Halliw.) With greyhounds..I made the alay to the deere. **1630** J. TAYLOR (Water P.) *Wks.* I. 93 Avauntlaye, Allaye, Relaye. [See ABATURE.] **1658** PHILLIPS, *Alay*, a Term us'd in Hunting, when fresh Dogs are sent into the Cry. **1775** ASH, *Alay*, an addition of fresh dogs to the cry.

allayed (əˈleɪd), *ppl. a.*; also 5–6 **alayed.** [f. ALLAY *v.*[1] and *v.*[2] + -ED.] The senses are combined as in the vbs.

†**1.** Mixed with an inferior metal, debased; = ALLOYED. *Obs.*

c **1400** *Epiph.* (Turnb. 1843) 121 For gold of trowth ys falsly now alayed. **1671** FLAVEL *Fount Life* ii. 4 The best creature-delights one in another are mixed, debased and allayed. **1738** WARBURTON *Div. Legat.* I. 453 The Good.. was allayed with Evil.

2. Mingled with water, etc.; tempered, qualified.

1528 PAYNELL *Salernes Regim.* L ij b, The wyne..shulde be alayde with moche water. **1552** HULOET, Alayde wyne, *Aquaticum Vinum.* **1684** tr. *Bonet's Merc. Compit.* III. 108 Acids allayed with a lixivious Salt. *a* **1704** T. BROWN *Quakers Grace* Wks. 1730 I. 107 Thy judgements are tart unless allay'd with the sugar of thy mercy.

3. *gen.* Mixed, mingled, modified.

1683 BURNET tr. *More's Utopia* 125 An entire healthiness ..not allayed with any Disease. **1819** R. CHAPMAN *James V*, 131 In human life our gladness is still allayed with sorrow. **1857** EMERSON *Poems* 146 Of the same stuff, and so allayed, As that whereof the sun is made.

4. [f. ALLAY *v.*[1], or from LAY with A- *pref.* ? 6, 10, or 11.] Laid, set (cf. *inlaid*).

1509 Barclay *Ship of Fooles* (1570) 245 Resplendaunt is all thy apparayle Alayed gayly with pearles. *Ibid.* (1874) II. 289 My stremynge standardes alayd with sundry hewe.

allayer (əˈleɪə(r)). [f. ALLAY *v.*[1] (*v.*[2]) + -ER[1].] He who or that which allays, modifies, or restrains.
1615 A. Niccholes *Marr. & Wiv.* xi. in *Harl. Misc.* (1744) II. 158 Indigence and Want, two great Allayers of Affection. 1631 *Celestina* I. 20 O head, the allayer of my passion! O reliever of my torment! 1666 Harvey *Morb. Anglic.* ? (J.) Phlegm and pure blood are reputed allayers of acrimony.

allaying (əˈleɪɪŋ), *vbl. sb.* [f. as prec. + -ING[1].] †1. Abatement of violence; moderation; cessation.
1635 Swan *Spec. Mundi* v. §2 (1643) 168 The storms and showers which often happen upon the allaying of a wind.
2. Dilution with water, etc.; mitigation, modification.
1528 Paynell *Salernes Regim.* L ij b, To moche alayenge with water wolde distroye naturall heate. 1648 Sanderson *Serm.* II. 237 Advice towards the allaying of those heats and distempers. 1802 Lamb *J. Woodvil* III. 616 These high and gusty relishes of life, sure Have no allayings of mortality in them.
†3. Admixture of an inferior metal; = ALLOYING.
1796 [See ALLAY *v.*[2] I.]

allaying (əˈleɪɪŋ), *ppl. a.* [f. as prec. + -ING[2].] Diluting, tempering.
1607 Shaks. *Coriol.* II. i. 52 A cup of hot Wine, with not a drop of alaying Tiber in't. *a*1658 Lovelace *To Althea* (R.) Flowing cups run swiftly round With no allaying Thames.

†**aˈllayment.** *Obs. rare.* Also 6 alai-. [f. as prec. + -MENT. Cf. OFr. *alaie-, aloie-ment.*] Admixture of a modifying element or agent; mitigation.
1606 Shaks. *Tr. & Cr.* IV. iv. 8 If I could temporise with my affection Or brew it to a weake and colder pallat, The like alaiment could I giue my griefe. 1611 —— *Cymb.* I. v. 22 To try the vigour of them [thy Compounds], and apply Allayments to their Act.

†**allbone** (ˈɔːlbəʊn). *Bot. Obs.* Also all-bonie, all-bones. [ALL- E 5 + BONE: transl. Gr. name ὁλόστεον from the 'jointed skeleton-like stalks,' Prior, p. 4, though Pliny, and others after him, thought the name ironical, on principle of *lucus a non lucendo.*] A name given in the herbals to the Greater Stitchwort (*Stellaria Holostea* L.).
1597 Gerard *Herbal* 43 The Grecians call this plant ὁλόστεον: in Latine *Tota ossea*: in English All-bonie. 1601 Holland *Pliny* (1634) II. 283 Holosteon; which the Greeks so call by the contrary, for the word signifieth All-bone.

all clear, *phr.*, also used as *sb.* A signal giving information that there is no danger; *spec.* the signal that hostile aircraft have left the neighbourhood ('raiders passed'). Also *attrib.* and *transf.*
1902 J. Conrad *Youth* 9 There was a moment of confusion, yelling, and running about. Steam roared. Then somebody was heard saying, 'All clear, sir.' 1917 *Times* 18 Oct. 6/3 It has been decided that the 'All clear' signal after air raids shall in future be given by bugle calls. 1922 Wodehouse *Girl on Boat* xvii. 282 Webster had promised to come and knock an all-clear signal on the door. 1923 —— *Inimit. Jeeves* v. 55 The effect she had on me whenever she appeared was to make me want to slide into a cellar and lie low till they blew the All-Clear. 1936 *Economist* 15 Feb. 347/2 The 'all-clear' for armament expansion on a great scale is being given. 1939 T. S. Eliot *Old Possum's Practical Cats* 40 The [railway] signal goes 'All Clear!' 1939 *War Weekly* 3 Nov. 41/2 The alarm was at 2.30 and the 'all clear' half an hour later. 1942 *Hutchinson's Pict. Hist. War,* 18 Mar.–9 June 9 (*caption*) After the 'All Clear'... Malta after a 'raiders passed' signal had been given, showing the people about to resume their daily occupations. 1945 E. Waugh *Brideshead Rev.* I. iii. 70, I felt a sense of liberation and peace such as I was to know years later when after a night of unrest, the syrens sounded the 'All Clear'.

alle, obs. form of AWL.

alleage, variant of ALLIAGE. *Obs.*, alliance.

allecret: see HALECRET.

†**aˈllect**, *v. Obs.* Also alect. [ad. L. *allectā-re* to allure, freq. of *allicĕre* to allure, f. *al-* = *ad-* to + *lic-ĕre*, in comp. = *lac-ĕre* to entice. By-forms were ALLICIT and ALLICIATE.] To entice, allure.
1528 More *Heresyes* IV. Wks. 1557, 275/1 To allect ye people by preaching. 1534 —— *On the Passion* 1274/1 The other lesse euils, that he alewred and alected her with. 1552 Huloet, Allect, or styre with some pleasaunte meane. *Allicio, Duco.*

†**allecˈtation.** *Obs.*$^{-0}$ [ad. L. *allectātiōn-em*, n. of action f. *allectā-re*: see ALLECT.] An alluring.
1656 in Blount; 1692 in Coles; 1721–1800 in Bailey.

†**aˈllected**, *ppl. a. Obs.* [f. ALLECT + -ED.] Enticed, drawn forth.
1691 E. Taylor *Behmen's Theosoph.* iii. 4 Restrains or confines their allected virtues.

†**aˈllection.** *Obs. rare*$^{-1}$. [ad. L. *allectiōn-em*, n. of action f. *allic-ĕre* (see ALLECT), not used in this sense, for which *allectātio* was substituted.] An alluring or enticing; enticement.
1640 Bp. Reynolds *Passions* xlii, The allection, enticing, and insinuation of the sensitive appetite.

†**aˈllective**, *a.* and *sb. Obs.*; also 6–7 **alective**. [ad. med.L. *allectīvus*, f. *allect-* ppl. stem of *allicĕre*: see ALLECT and -IVE.]
A. *adj.* Having the power or tendency to allure; alluring, enticing.
*a*1560 *Remed. Love* 14 (T.) Most allective bait. 1592 G. Harvey *Pierce's Supererog.* in *Archaica* II. 211 Her bewtifull and allective stile as ingenious as elegant. 1610 Holland *Camden's Brit.* I. 811 What mindes th' allective shade of gold stirres not. 1775 Ash, *Allective* (not used), alluring.
B. *sb.* That which has power to allure.
1531 Elyot *Governor* I. v. (1557) 16 There is no better alectiue to noble wittes. *c*1577 Northbrooke *Dicing* (1843) 117 What better alectiue coulde Satan deuise. 1675 *Art of Contentm.* I. §5. 177 Generous contemt of sensual allectives.

allectuary, obs. form of ELECTUARY.

allegate, obs. variant of ALGATE.

†**ˈallegate**, *v. Obs.* Also 6 **allygate**. [f. L. *allēgāt-* ppl. stem of *adl-, allēgā-re* to send a message, to cite; to adduce, bring forward; f. *ad* to + *legāre* to commission.] A by-form of ALLEGE *v.*[2]
*a*1529 Skelton *Col. Cloute* 1164 How darest thou, losell, Allygate the Gospel Agaynst us? 1599 Peele *Sir Clyomon* (1829) III. 68 Ah, why should I this allegate? 1639 Rouse *Heav. Univ.* viii. (1702) 107 Ambrose.. allegates for Interpretation and Confirmation of this place, the words of Christ to St. Peter.

†**ˈallegate**, *ppl. a. Obs.* [ad. L. *allēgāt-us* pa. pple. of *allēgā-re* to commission, delegate. Cf. *adlegation.*] Deputed, delegated.
1649 Ball *Power of Kings* 6 These things they may doe as Judges Allegate, or Umpeeres for the People.

allegation (ælɪˈgeɪʃən). Also 5–6 **allegacioun, alegacion, adlegacyon.** [a. Fr. *allégation*, ad. L. *adl-, allēgātiōn-em*, n. of action f. *allēgā-re*: see ALLEGATE *v.* Sometimes spelt *adl-* in 5–6.] The action of alleging; the matter alleged.
1. The action of making a charge before a legal tribunal; the charge or matter undertaken to be proved.
1483 Caxton *Cato* A vij, After alle allegacions and compleyntes made of bothe partes. 1490 —— *Eneydos* xxix. 113 An aunswere to the adlegacyons of Proserpyne. 1494 Fabyan VII. ccxxi. 243 Whan Thomas had harde all the alegacions, he denyed all. 1593 Shaks. *2 Hen. VI*, III. i. 181 To sweare False allegations to o'rethrow his state. 1772 *Hist. Rochester* 128 Their allegations against their Spiritual governor were groundless. 1823 Lingard *Hist. Eng.* VI. 202 The king's counsel laboured to prove three allegations. 1862 Ld. Brougham *Brit. Const.* xix. §6. 356 An officer of the court takes the allegation, the libel, or the interrogatories.
†2. A statement made in excuse; a plea; the alleging of a reason. *Obs.*
*c*1510 More *Picus* Wks. 1557, 27 Saye not thou lackest myght, Suche allegacions foly it is to vse. 1589 Bp. Cooper *Admon.* 115 That the people.. did euer use such allegations for their owne excuse. 1614 Raleigh *Hist. World* II. 431 This allegation of 'raggione del stato' did serue as well to uphold, as.. to bring in this vile Idolatry. 1622 R. Hawkins *Voy. S. Sea* (1847) 206 In case he excuse himselfe with this allegation.
3. The action of asserting or affirming what one is prepared to prove; an assertion, affirmation, averment.
1532 More *Confut. Tindale* Wks. 1557, 507/1 To proue you the foly of that allegacion. 1594 Plat *Jewell-ho.* I. 19 My former allegation, that those oysters are nourished with salt. 1630 Levett *Bees* (1634) 63 This allegation is true: for I have often seene a hive cast a swarme, and within foure dayes cast another. 1658 Bramhall *Consecr. Bish.* xi. 10 The proofe of both these allegations. 1712 Steele *Spect.* No. 498 ¶3, I thought their allegations but reasonable. 1830 Lyell *Princ. Geol.* (1875) I. II. xxv. 644 Nor ought we to call the allegation in question. 1869 Gladstone *Juv. Mundi* iii. 105 Without any allegation of a rigid uniformity.
4. *esp.* An assertion without proof, a mere assertion.
1635 R. Bolton *Affl. Consc.* ii. 162 With unprofitable mixtures of human allegations. 1775 Boswell *Johnson* xxiv. 221 He also persevered in his wild allegation that he questioned if there was a tree between Edinburgh and the English border older than himself. 1856 E. Bond *Russia in 16th c.* (Hakl. Soc.) Introd. 79 The specious allegation that 'the whole country of Russia was not able to receave so much of English commodities as wear now brought.' 1870 *Daily News* 25 July 5 The allegation of an excited orator.
†5. The action of citing or quoting (a document or author); the matter cited or quoted; citation, quotation. ? *Obs.*
1561 T. N[orton] tr. *Calvin's Inst.* IV. xvi. (1634) 663 Baptisme of infants [is] proved by allegations brought to disprove it. 1628 T. Spencer *Logick* 120 The bare allegation of Aristotles words. 1671 Flavel *Fount. Life* ix. 23 Which words are an allegation out of Moses. 1673 Penn *Chr. Quaker* xv. 569 The Allegation of that Scripture against us.
¶ Also by confusion for ALLIGATION, q.v.

allegator, obs. form of ALLIGATOR.

†**ˈallegator.** *Obs.* [n. of agent f. L. *allēgāt-* ppl. stem of *allēgā-re*: see ALLEGE *v.*[2] and -OR.] He who alleges or affirms.
1681 *Relig. Cler.* 81 'Tis not the first time that Holy Scripture hath been the Argument when the destruction of the Allegatour hath proved the consequence.

†**aˈllege**, *v.*[1] *Obs.* Also 4–5 **alegge, allege,** 4–6 **allegge,** 5 **alledge,** 6 **alege.** [a. OFr. *alege-r, alegier* (14th c. *alléger*):—L. *alleviā-re* to lighten, f. *al-* = *ad-* to + *levis* light. Cf. Pr. *aleujar*, It. *alleggiare*, and L. *abbreviare*, Fr. *abréger*: see ABRIDGE.]
1. To lighten (one) *of* any burden.
*c*1340 Hampole *Pr. Consc.* 3894 Pardon.. sal þam avail, To allege þair saules of payne. *c*1450 Lydg. *Mass Bk.* (1879) 394 Ffor to alleggen the wery lemys of her grete berthene. 1483 Caxton *Gold. Leg.* 266/3 He felte hym a lytell alledged and eased of his payne.
2. To lighten, alleviate, diminish (a burden, grief, pain); or to abridge the duration of a trouble.
1382 Wyclif *Is.* ix. 1. The firste tyme is aleggid, *or maad liȝt*, the lond of Zabulon. 1387 Trevisa *Higden* Rolls Ser. VII. 195, I pray ȝow now þat ȝe allegge [*allevietis*] my tourmentes. *c*1400 *Rom. Rose* 2588, I wolde this thought wolde come ageyne, For it alleggith welle my peyne. 1481 Caxton *Myrr.* I. v. 18 They setted not of mete and drynke, but for talegge their hungre and thurste. 1530 Palsgr. 420/2, I alege, I lyghten or comforte. *Je alege*; I allevyate, I make lyght the mynde or body. *Je allege.*
¶ In this sense now represented by ALLAY *v.*[1] The infinitive and certain other parts of these two vbs. were formally identical in ME., and when *aleggen*, :—OE. *alecȝan*, was levelled to *aleye, allay* (as explained under that vb.), this was also substituted for *aleggen* = OFr. *alegier*, giving the modern 'to *allay* hunger, pain, grief, fear': see ALLAY *v.*[1] II. Spenser has *alegge* as an archaism for *allay*:
1579 Spenser *Sheph. Cal.* Mar., The joyous time now nigheth fast, That shall alegge this bitter blast.

allege (əˈlɛdʒ), *v.*[2] Forms: 3–5 **alegg-e, aleg-e,** 4–6 **allegge,** 5–9 **alledge,** 5–6 **adledge,** 6–7 **alledg, aleage, alleage, alleadg, alleadge,** 4– **allege.** [Though *allege* answers exactly in *sense* to L. *allēgāre* and its Fr. adaptation *alléguer*, its soft *g* (dʒ) shows that it is not an adoption of this, which would have given *alleague*. But there was an OFr. *esligier*:—late L. **exlītigāre* to clear at law, of which the Norm. form was *aligier, alegier*. This was latinized in England, as *adlēgiāre*, a word in regular use in the laws of the Norman kings (see Du Cange); and this *adlēgiāre* (as if f. *ad lēgem*) was evidently treated also as the equivalent of *aleier* (as if f. *a lei*), the true OFr. descendant of L. *allēgāre* (see ALLAY *v.*[3]). Hence, in later AFr., *alegier* (*aleger, alegger*), and its Eng. adoption *alege, allege*, though formally descended from *exlītigare*, were used as = L. *allēgāre*. (Cf. the technical use of the latter in Roman Law, in 'adlēgāre sē ex servitūte in ingenuitātem,' to release oneself .. by adducing reasons.) As in Fr. the forensic *alléguer* supplanted the popular *aleier*, so in Eng. *allege* took the place of ALLAY *v.*[3].
Connexion of *alegier* (:—**exlītigare*), *aleier* (:—*allēgāre*), *adlegiāre*, and *alegge, allege*:
Tristan I. 3217 (Michel), Se devant lui sui *alegie*, Qui me voudroit ares sordire? *Laws of Wm. I*, xxxix. §1 (Schmid) Seit en la forfaiture le rei de XL sols, s'il ne pot *aleier* [*Lat.* nisi purgare se possit] que plus dreit faire nel sout. *Ibid.* II. i, Francigena compellatus *adlegiet* se in jure jurando [*OE.* lādiȝe hine mid āðe] contra eum. *13 Rich. II*, II. i, Si la chartre de mort de homme soit *alegge* devant qiconques Justices. *Early transl.* If a charter of the death of a man be *alleadged* before any justices.]
1. To declare upon oath before a tribunal, to give testimony for or against; hence, to bring forward as a legal ground or plea, to plead. *Obs.* exc. *fig.*
*c*1325 *E.E. Allit. P.* A. 702 For-þy to corte quen þou schal com.. þer alle oure causeȝ schal be tryed, Alegge þe ryȝt. *c*1330 *Florice & Bl.* 689 Ȝif thai ought aȝein wil allegge Hit uer nowt right jugement Withouten answere to acoupement. 1413 Lydg. *Pylgr. Sowle* I. ii. (1483) 3 Yf thou canst ought alledgen · that may be ageynst hym · come byfore the Juge. 1540 T. Cromwell in Ellis *Orig. Lett.* II. II. 170, I haue no merits or good works which I may alledge before thee. 1605 Thynne in *Animadv.* App. 112 The arguments alledged agaynst Him by the Advocate. 1711 Addison *Spect.* No. 293 ¶1 It was alledged against him that he had never any Success in his Undertakings. 1773 Burke *Corr.* (1844) I. 421 All the arguments he alleges for his safety.
b. with *clause*.
*c*1300 *Beket* 1396 And bad him answere for hir stat: and aleggi for him hou hit were. *c*1400 *Destr. Troy* XXXIII. 13072 þan alleggit the lede to the leue prinses, All þe dere þat he did.. Was barly by biddyng of his bright goddes. 1660 R. Coke *Power & Subj.* 201 The Clerk holdeth him to his Clergy, alleadging that he ought not before them thereupon to answer. 1710 Steele *Tatler* No. 256 ¶1 The Prosecutor alledged, That he was the Cadet of a very ancient Family. 1779 Johnson *K. Prussia* Wks. 1787 IV. 542 Alledges that his predecessors had enjoyed this grant above a century.
†c. *absol. Obs.*

c **1440** *Gesta Rom.* (1879) 165 And yf we wolle thus alegge ayenste þe devil. **1628** HOBBES *Thucydides* (1822) 67 They alleged much to haue him, yet he deliuerd him not.

2. To cite, quote (an author or his authority) *for* or *against. arch.*

1366 MAUNDEV. x. 119 Thei knowen alle the Bible, and the Psautere: and therfore Allegge thei so the Lettre. *c* **1384** CHAUCER *H. Fame* 314 Non other auttour a-legge I. *c* **1386** —— *Merch. T.* 414 And for he wolde his longe tale abregge He wolde noon auctoritee allegge [*v.r.* alegge]. *c* **1440** *Gesta Rom.* 33 And allege holy scripturis aȝenst synnerys. **1541** BARNES *Wks.* (1573) 209/2 To whom I aunswered . . aleaging Saint Augustine for mee. **1616** R. C. *Times' Whistle* iii. 885, I can alleadge mine author for it. **1653** MILTON *Consid. Hirelings* 59 With what face or conscience can they alleage Moses . . for tithes? **1724** A. COLLINS *Gr. Chr. Relig.*, To alledge the passages of the Old Testament. **1878** R. W. DALE *Lect. Preaching* v. 118 The greatest names can sometimes be alleged for opinions which are incredible.

3. Hence *gen.* To plead as an excuse; to adduce or urge as reason.

c **1440** *Gesta Rom.* (1879) 56 Whenne þe wise man saw þat, he gan to alegge resons. **1519** R. PACE in Ellis *Orig. Lett.* I. 56 I. 157 The Electors speke agaynst hym and allege reasons whye he schulde nott be electidde. **1560** J. DAUS tr. *Sleidane's Comm.* 107 b, He adledged certen causes, why it ought so to be. **1598** YONG *Diana* 209, I alleaged some excuses to the contrary. **1660** T. STANLEY *Hist. Philos.* II. III. 16 Tertullian alleadgeth another reason. **1762** GOLDSM. *Beau Nash* 213 Refused to lend a farthing, alledging a former resolution against lending. **1835** THIRLWALL *Greece* I. ix. 344 Sparta did not draw the sword till she had injuries and insults to alledge.

b. with *clause.*

1600 HAKLUYT *Voy.* III, Alleadging how much it would be for our credite and profite. **1622** WITHER *Philarete* (1633) 688 Were she Vaine, she might alledge, 'Twere her Sexes priviledge. **1741** BETTERTON in Oldys *Eng. Stage* ii. 27 Alledging the greater the Temptation, the greater the Glory to resist. **1878** SEELEY *Stein* II. 450 England would give nothing beyond arms and ammunition, alleging that her Spanish enterprise occupied her wholly.

4. To advance (a statement) as being able to prove it; *hence*, to assert without proof; to affirm, predicate.

1377 LANGL. *P. Pl.* B. XI. 88 Þei wol allegen also, quod I, and by þe gospel preuen [it]. **1494** FABYAN V. xcv. 69 But Policronica alledgyth yᵗ honour vnto Vter Pendragon his brother. **1586** T. B. tr. *La Primaudaye's Fr. Acad.* II. (1594) 27 Wee must not therefore alledge anie imperfection in the creation of the woman. **1676** CLARENDON *Surv. Leviathan* 145 Who . . will ever venture to alledg any matter of fact that he is not sure of? **1690** LOCKE *Hum. Underst.* II. i. (ed. 3) 44 But Men in love with their Opinions, may not only suppose what is in question, but alledge wrong matter of fact. **1781** GIBBON *Decl. & F.* III. xlviii. 29 Where much is alleged, something must be true. **1879** H. SPENCER *Data of Eth.* ii. §5. 15 In neither case can conduct be alleged.

b. with *clause.*

1330 R. BRUNNE 247 The kyng algid thei were of his tresour. *c* **1425** WYNTOUN *Cron.* VI. viii. 673 Þe mwnkys . . Allegyd þat þat electyoun Fell to þame. **1551** TURNER *Herbal* II. 37 Some . . alledge . . that Cypros is the tre which is called in Italy Ligustrum. **1711** ADDISON *Spect.* No. 267 ¶1 Those who alledge it is not an Heroick Poem. **1794** SULLIVAN *View Nat.* I. 27 He alleges that there are several elementary bodies. **1860** TYNDALL *Glac.* II. §27. 379 It has since been alleged that ours was unnecessary labour.

† **a'llege**, *v.*³ *Obs.* Form: 4 alegge. [ad. L. *allēgā-re* to dispatch to, f. *ad-* = *al-* to + *lēgāre* to dispatch, send.] In the phr. *to allege prayer* (= L. *allēgāre preces*): to address prayer.

1382 WYCLIF *Wisd.* xviii. 21 A man . . bi encens preȝing aleggyng, withstod to the wrathe [**1388** He aleggide preier].

allegeable (əˈlɛdʒəb(ə)l), *a.* [f. ALLEGE *v.*² + -ABLE.] Capable of being alleged or adduced as evidence, authority, excuse, etc.

1542 HENRY VIII *Declar.* 206 The passing ouer of tyme . . is not allegable in prescription for the losse of any right. *a* **1656** HALES *Gold. Rem.* (1688) 464 Notwithstanding any reason allegable against it. *a* **1716** SOUTH *12 Serm.* Wks. 1717 V. 36 Is there so much as the least Shadow of excuse alledgeable. [In JOHNSON and mod. Dicts.]

† **a'llegeance**¹. *Obs.* Forms: 4–5 alegeance, -aunce, -eaunce, all-, allegg-, erron. allegiance. [a. OFr. *alegeance, alejance*, mod. *allégeance*, f. *aléger* to relieve: see ALLEGE *v.*¹, and -ANCE.] Alleviation, lightening, relief.

1297 R. GLOUC. 85 Mo and mo þer come for enlegeance to habbe of heore wo. *c* **1315** SHOREHAM 42 Alleggaunce of his sennes. *a* **1400** *Relig. Pieces fr. Thornt. MS.* 8 In lyghtenes and alegeance of þaire sekenes. *c* **1400** *Rom. Rose* 4570 Sende me socour or allegeaunce. *c* **1430** LYDG. *Bochas* II. vii. (1554) 49 b, And of his peyne feleth alegeaunce. **1483** CAXTON *Cato* h vij, Alegeaunce of a ryght grete and heuy fardel.

† **allegeance**². *Obs.* or *Sc.* Forms: 4 allegiaunce, 5 allegyaunce, 6 allegeaunce, 6–7 alledgance, -eance, allegeance. [f. ALLEGE *v.*² + -ANCE. Cf. OFr. *alégance, allégance*, med.L. *allegantia* = *allegātio.* Chiefly Sc. after 1500.] The action of producing in court, of citing in evidence, or asserting as capable of proof; allegation.

c **1400** *Apol. for Loll.* 60 A juge, ȝeuing a sentens aȝen a innocent man after allegiaunce & prouid, sinniþ deadly. *c* **1410** N. LOVE *Bonaventura's Mirr.* (Gibbs MS.) xxxix. 83 Here lawgheþ þe lollarde and scorneþ holy chyrche in allegeaunce of suche myracules. **1502** ARNOLD *Chron.* (1811) 119 Callyng before vs the same partyes . . herd their complayntis contrauersies allegeauncis and greuauncis. **1548** *Compl. Scotl.* 31 Sic opinions ande allegeance suld nocht haue audiens amang cristin pepil. *c* **1630** DRUMM. OF HAWTH. *Vind. Hamiltons* Wks. 1711, 239 Alledgeances, of which they can give no reason. **1671** *True Non-Conf.* Pref., How foolishly doth he second his allegeances? **1711** *Countrey-Man's Let.* 94 The alledgeance of the said approbation . . is not only groundless but utterly false.

allegeance, obs. variant of ALLEGIANCE.

alleged (əˈlɛdʒd), *ppl. a.* [f. ALLEGE *v.*² + -ED.]

1. Produced in court, brought forward or adduced as legal ground, or as a reason.

1613 SHAKS. *Hen. VIII*, II. iv. 225 The sharp thorny points Of my alleadged reasons. **1689** *Tryal of Bish.* 26 The Fact alleadged in the Commitment. **1790** PALEY *Hor. Paul* i. 4 The coincidences alleged. **1840** HOOD *Up Rhine* 326 The alleged reason for my recall. **1844** LEVER *Tom Burke* xxxiv. (1857) 324 The charges alleged against me.

2. Cited, quoted (properly as an authority).

c **1449** PECOCK *Repr.* III. xvii. 391 Poul also in his alleggid text. **1559** MORWYNG *Evonymus* Pref., The authors alledged in this Boke. **1656** BRAMHALL *Replic.* iii. 149 The Author alledged, doth testifie. **1836–7** SIR W. HAMILTON *Metaph.* xxxvii. II. 334 Which Aristotle has so well illustrated in the passage alleged to you.

3. Asserted as capable of proof; *hence*, asserted but not yet proved; *or*, asserted but not admitted.

a **1674** CLARENDON *Hist. Reb.* I. III. 139 All the particulars alleadged. **1828** SCOTT *F.M. Perth* III. 241 During his alleged illness. **1855** H. SPENCER *Psychol.* (1872) I. IV. iii. 420 This alleged explanation . . is simply a disguised mode of shelving them as inexplicable. **1876** FREEMAN *Norm. Conq.* I. 734 The alleged parentage of her son was generally doubted.

allegedly (əˈlɛdʒɪdlɪ), *adv.* [f. prec. + -LY².] In an alleged manner, by way of assertion.

1874 *Rep. Vienna Exhib.* IV. 649 The creation of fresh marks allegedly superior, to the disadvantage of the existing ones.

† **a'llegement**¹, **alegement.** *Obs.* [a. OFr. *al-, allégement*, f. *aléger* to lighten: see ALLEGE *v.*¹ and -MENT.] Lightening, alleviation, relief.

c **1400** *Rom. Rose* 1890 A precious oynement . . to yeve alegement Upon the woundes. **1413** LYDG. *Pylgr. Sowle* (Wright) To don allegementis To ffolkes whiche be not glade. **1483** CAXTON *Gold. Leg.* 235/4 It dyd hym none alegement. **1485** —— *Chas. Gt.* 97 Grete alegement of tormente.

allegement² (əˈlɛdʒmənt). [f. ALLEGE *v.*² + -MENT.] The act of alleging, allegation, affirmation.

1516 *Plumpton Corr.* 217 The Counsell derecteth proses against them. Howbeyt, I made aledgment for your mastership. **1634** SANDERSON *21 Serm.* Ad. Mag. iii. (1673) 284 They come to Samuel with many complaints and alledgments in their mouths. **1660** H. MORE *Myst. Godl.* VII. iii. 280 The second Alledgement . . is still more frivolous. **1831** HEIDIGER *Didoniad* II. 49 'Woman loves power,' is a well-known allegement.

alleger (əˈlɛdʒə(r)). Also 6 alledger, 7 -eadger. [f. ALLEGE *v.*² + -ER¹.] One who alleges, or cites.

1579 W. FULKE *Heskins's Parl.* 64 A long speache . . against M. Heskins the alledger of it. **1624** GATAKER *Transubstant.* 67 This alleadger of him fareth as ill as in the former allegation. *a* **1691** BOYLE (J.) The narrative, if we believe it as confidently as the famous alleger of it appears to do.

allegiance (əˈliːdʒəns, əˈliːdʒ(ɪ)əns). Forms: 4–5 al- allegeaunce, alie- alligiaunce, 5 alegeawns, 6 allegians, -gance, -giauns, -gyaunce, 6–7 alleagiance, allegeance, 7 aleige-, alleageance, 6– allegiance. [A derivative of LIEGE, q.v., OFr. *lige, liege*, late L. *ligius*: whence OFr. *ligance, ligeance, ligence* (Cotgr.); med.L. *ligiantia, ligeantia, ligentia, ligantia* (erroneously associated with *ligāre* to bind); ME. *ligeaunce*, ? *legeance*. Of the latter, *allegiance*, 14th c. *alegeaunce*, was orig. merely a variation, the *a-* being prefixed perh. through confusing the word with another legal term, ALLEGEANCE², with which it was, at first, *formally* identical. The word was of Eng. formation, med.L. *allegiantia* being formed on it, and mod.Fr. *allégeance* according to Littré and Diez adopted from Eng.]

† 1. The relation of a liege lord; lordship. *Obs.*

c **1400** *Destr. Troy* VI. 2326 Yff it like your Aliegiaunce, þat I, your lefe son, Be sent . . it shall vs wele like. *Ibid.* XXI. 8909 And his alligiaunce lelly I will loute to. *c* **1425** WYNTOUN *Cron.* VII. viii. 14 Hys Lord be detful allegeawns.

2. The relation or duties of a liege-man to his liege-lord; the tie or obligation of a subject to his sovereign, or government.

1399 LANGL. *Rich. Redeless* I. 9 Of alegeaunce now lerneth a lesson oþer tweyne Wherby it standith and stablithe moste. **1494** FABYAN VII. 324 He had, contrary his allegeaunce, made homage vnto Lewys. **1588** GREENE *Pandosto* (1607) 7 To diswade his subiects from their allegance. **1593** SHAKS. *2 Hen. VI*, v. i. 179 Hast thou not sworne Allegeance unto me? **1651** HOBBES *Leviath.* I. xii. 60 Subjects may be freed from their Alleageance. **1768** BLACKSTONE *Comm.* I. I. x. 284 Natural allegiance is therefore perpetual. **1824** DIBDIN *Libr. Comp.* 115 To take the oaths of allegiance and supremacy. **1845** STEPHEN *Laws of Eng.* II. 399 We shall now pass from the duties of the sovereign to those which are owing to him from his people, and which are comprehended in the single word allegiance.

3. *fig.* The recognition of the claims which anything has to our respect and duty.

1732 POPE *Ess. Man* III. 235 Love all the faith, and all th' allegiance then. **1808** SCOTT *Marm.* V. 10 Nor to that lady free alone Did the gay king allegiance own. **1830** SIR J. HERSCHEL *Stud. Nat. Phil.* 27 Their allegiance (so to speak) to natural science. **1851** HELPS *Friends in C.* I. 22 There is something to which a man owes a larger allegiance than to any human affection.

allegiance, variant of ALLEGEANCE¹, ². *Obs.*

allegiancy (əˈliːdʒ(ɪ)ənsɪ). [var. of prec.: see -NCY. Cf. *abundancy*.] = ALLEGIANCE.

1643 PRYNNE *Rome's Master-Piece* (ed. 2) 28 To seduce him from his Allegiancy. **1881** W. ALLINGHAM in *Athenæum* 6 Aug. 175/1 He Be shot who wavers in allegiancy.

allegiant (əˈliːdʒ(ɪ)ənt), *a.* (and *sb.*) [f. ALLEGIANCE, on analogy of adjs. in -ANT accompanying sbs. in -ANCE.] Giving allegiance, loyal. Also as *sb.*, one who owes or renders allegiance; a subject.

1613 SHAKS. *Hen. VIII*, III. ii. 176, I can nothing render but Allegiant thankes. **1848** *Blackwood's Mag.* LXIV. 227 He proved anything but allegiant to Shakspeare. **1854** PATMORE *Angel in House* I. I. xii, The wretch, whom . . His own allegiant thoughts despise. **1886** *N. Amer. Rev.* CXLII. 125 Strangers shall have the same personal rights as the allegiants. **1888** TOURGÉE *Lett. to King* v. 67 In the one sense it [*sc.* the word 'citizen'] is used to distinguish the American people from the allegiants of a foreign power.

† **a'lleging**, *vbl. sb.*¹ *Obs.* [f. ALLEGE *v.*¹ + -ING¹.] The action of making lighter; alleviation.

c **1450** LONELICH *Grail* liii. 245 In aleggeng of my peyne.

alleging (əˈlɛdʒɪŋ), *vbl. sb.*² [f. ALLEGE *v.*² + -ING¹.] The action of adducing as evidence; citing, quoting; the making of an assertion.

1531 *Dial. Laws of Eng.* II. l. (1638) 155 If such alleagings should be accepted in the law. **1533** FRITH *Agst. Rastell* (1829) 231 This alleging of Paul for the establishing of the law. *Mod.* After alleging his experience.

allegoric (ælɪˈgɒrɪk), *a.* Also 4 -ik, 7 -ick. [a. Fr. *allégorique*, ad. L. *allēgoric-us*, a. Gr. ἀλληγορικ-ός: see ALLEGORY and -IC.] Of or pertaining to allegory; of the nature of an allegory; constituting or containing an allegory.

1388 WYCLIF *Is.* Prol., 'Literal' ether historial vndurstondyng techith what thing is don; allegorik techith what we owen for to bileue. **1549** *Compl. Scotl.* iv. (1873) 29 That passage of the text nedis nocht ane alligoric expositione. **1671** MILTON *P.R.* IV. 389 A kingdom they portend thee, but what kingdom, Real or allegorick, I discern not. **1762** H. WALPOLE *Vertue's Anecd. Paint.* (1786) I. 234 Having painted an allegoric piece of Strength vanquished by Wisdom. **1827** DE QUINCEY in *Blackw. Mag.* XXI. 14 Allegoric personages; that is, impersonated abstractions expounded by emblems.

allegorical (ælɪˈgɒrɪkəl), *a.* [f. prec. + -AL¹.] Of or belonging to allegory; consisting of, formed by, or occurring in allegory.

1528 TYNDALE *Obed. Chr. Man* Wks. I. 303 They divide the scripture into four senses, the literal, tropological, allegorical, and anagogical. **1577** VAUTROULLIER tr. *Luther's Ep. Gal.* 217 Sina the allegorical Agar. **1657** J. SMITH *Myst. Rhet.* 5 An Allegorical signification: as, when Peter by the Arke of Noah, signifies Baptism. **1756** BURKE *Subl. & B.* Wks. I. 167 Its chimeras, its harpies, its allegorical figures are grand. **1829** CARLYLE *Misc.* (1857) I. 272 Quitting this idle allegorical vein. **1841** SPALDING *Italy* II. 24 Heathen deities and allegorical personages appear in a kind of drama.

allegorically (ælɪˈgɒrɪkəlɪ), *adv.* [f. prec. + -LY².] In an allegoric or allegorical manner; by way of, or by means of, allegory; figuratively.

1577 tr. *Bullinger's Decades* (1592) 330 Some . . thinke it very profitable and an excellent thing to construe Homer and Virgil allegorically. **1641** BRATHWAIT *Engl. Gentl.* 102 In many places are wee allegorically and not literally to cleave to the Text. **1774** T. WARTON *Hist. Eng. Poetry* Dissert. III. (1840) I. 200 Writers who affect to interpret allegorically. **1859** MASSON *Milton* I. 542 An acted pageant, with speeches, etc. by persons allegorically dressed.

allegoricalness (ælɪˈgɒrɪkəlnɪs). ? *Obs.*—⁰ [f. as prec. + -NESS.] The quality of being allegorical.

1731 in BAILEY; whence in JOHNSON.

'**allegorism** (ˈælɪgərɪz(ə)m). *rare.* [f. ALLEGORIZE. Cf. *baptize, baptism.* See -IZE.] The use of allegory; the allegorical method of interpreting Scripture. (Cf. ALLEGORIST.)

1889 *Sat. Rev.* 18 May 613/1 [His views] rest upon what the early Fathers called Allegorism—that is, on the spiritual, not the literal, interpretation of our Lord's words. Nor is Allegorism 'Gnostic'. **1901** *Jewish Encycl.* I. *Allegorical interpretation* [of Scripture]. Expositors of this system may be called allegorists; the system itself, allegorism. **1919** P. H. OSMOND *Myst. Poets Engl. Ch.* 350 No doubt there is a rather slippery descent from this type of mysticism, through symbolism, to mere allegorism.

allegorist (ˈælɪgərɪst). [f. ALLEGORIZE: cf. *baptize, baptist.* See -IST.] One who constructs allegories, or writes allegorically; *rarely*, one who expounds allegorically.

1684 T. BURNET *Theor. Earth* iii. 49 It cannot be understood . . as these allegorists pretend. **1756** J. WARTON *Ess. Pope* (1782) II. §8. 34 The pencil of Spenser is as powerful as that of Rubens, his brother allegorist. **1841**

D'ISRAELI *Amen. Lit.* (1859) II. 123 Every tale is accompanied by the gloss of a pious allegorist. **1849** MACAULAY *Hist. Eng.* II. 228 Bunyan is.. decidedly the first of allegorists.

†**allegorister**, *rare*$^{-1}$. [f. prec. + -ER[1], an unnecessary agential termination. Cf. *chorist-er*, *barrist-er*.] = ALLEGORIST.

1841 D'ISRAELI *Amen. Lit.* (1859) II. 125 In a lengthened allegory.. the allegorister tires of his allegory.

allegorization (ˌælɪgɒraɪˈzeɪʃən). [f. ALLEGORIZE, as if ad. L. **allēgorizātiōn-em*, n. of action f. *allēgorizā-re*: see -ATION.] Allegorical representation or interpretation.

1827 DE QUINCEY in *Blackw. Mag.* XXI. 14 Temperance and Constancy, are simply impersonated abstractions and not allegorizations. **1846** GROTE *Greece* I. I. xvi. 563 Proclus is full of similar allegorisation both of Homer and Hesiod.

allegorize (ˈælɪgəraɪz), *v.* [a. Fr. *allégorise-r*; ad. L. *allēgorizāre*, f. Gr. ἀλληγορία (see ALLEGORY), an analogous form to *prophētizāre*, *evangelizāre*, etc., f. assumed Gr. *ἀλληγορίζειν: see -IZE.]

1. *trans.* To make or treat (a thing) as allegorical; to turn it into, or explain it as, an allegory.

1596 HARINGTON *Metam. Ajax* 6, I will not spend time to allegorize this story. **1678** CUDWORTH *Intell. Syst.* 316 Plutarch and Synesius Allegorized those Egyptian Fables of Isis and Osiris, the one to a Philosophical, the other to a Political sence. **1724** A. COLLINS *Gr. Chr. Relig.* 81 The Jews began to allegorize their sacred books. **1882** FARRAR *Early Chr.* I. 104 His attempt to allegorise the distinction between clean and unclean animals.

2. *intr.* **a.** To give allegoric explanations, to expound allegorically. **b.** To construct, or utter, allegories.

1581 FULKE *Agst. Allen* 223 (T.) After his manner he allegorizeth upon the sacrifices of the law. **1603** HOLLAND *Plutarch's Mor.* 1300 The Greeks allegorize that Saturne is time, Juno the aire. **1782** PRIESTLEY *Corr. Chr.* I. I. 24 One method of allegorizing.. took its rise in the East. **1875** MASSON *Wordsw., Shelley, etc.* 239 Some writers are not moved to allegorize so easily as others.

3. To allegorize (a person) *out of* (anything): to take away from by the use of allegory. To allegorize (a thing) *away*: to get rid of by means of allegory. ? *Obs.*

1667 E. CHAMBERLAYNE *State Gt. Brit.* I. III. i. (1743) 150 Charged with allegorising away the whole History of the Crucifixion. **1678** CUDWORTH *Intell. Syst.* 795 Our High-flown Enthusiasts.. quite Allegorize away.. the Outward Resurrection of the Body. **1726** PENN *Tracts* Wks. I. 583 To Allegorize Christ out of His Divinity.

allegorizer (ˈælɪgəˌraɪzə(r)). [f. prec. + -ER[1].] One who allegorizes: **a.** who expounds allegorically; **b.** who speaks in allegories.

1677 R. GILPIN *Dæmon. Sac.* (1867) 165 The allegorizers and inventors of mysteries.. are ravished with the discovery of a new nothing. **1736** COVENTRY *Phil. Conv.* v. (T.) The Stoick philosophers.. were great allegorizers in their theology. **1824** COLERIDGE *Aids to Refl.* (1848) I. 254 The fond humour of the mystic divines, and allegorizers of Holy Writ.

allegorizing (ˈælɪgəˌraɪzɪŋ), *vbl. sb.* [f. as prec. + -ING[1].] The treatment or expounding of anything as an allegory; the using of allegories.

1579 W. FULKE *Heskins's Parl.* 11 His wicked allegorizing vpon the scriptures. **1677** R. GILPIN *Dæmon. Sac.* (1867) 164 Upon the occasion of Origen's allegorizing. **1751** JORTIN *Serm.* (1771) I. i. 2 The Pagan Philosophers fell into the Allegorizing way. **1880** SAINTSBURY in *Academy* 3 Jan. 6/1 The open allegorising which simply makes use of the unfamiliar appliances to tell a familiar story.

allegorizing (ˈælɪgəˌraɪzɪŋ), *ppl. a.* [f. as prec. + -ING[2].] Converting into or treating as an allegory.

1860 ELLICOTT *Life of our Lord* viii. 405 The interesting, but too minutely allegorizing comments of Augustine.

allegory (ˈælɪgərɪ). Forms: 4–7 **allegorie**, 5–6 **allegorye**, 6– **allegory**. [ad. L. *allēgoria*, a. Gr. ἀλληγορία, *lit.* speaking otherwise than one seems to speak, f. ἄλλος other + -ἀγορία speaking; cf. ἀγορεύω to speak, orig. to harangue, f. ἀγορά the public assembly. Cf. Fr. *allégorie*, perh. the direct source of the Eng. The L. *allegoria* was occas. used unchanged in 16th c.]

1. Description of a subject under the guise of some other subject of aptly suggestive resemblance.

1382 WYCLIF *Gal.* iv. 24 The whiche thingis ben seid by allegorie, or *goostly vndirstondinge* [Vulg. *per allegoriam*]. **1477** EARL RIVERS (Caxton) *Dictes* 66 The sayd Platon dide teche his sapyence by allegorye. **1589** PUTTENHAM *Eng. Poesie* (1869) 196 Properly and in his principall vertue Allegoria is when we do speake in sence translatiue and wrested from the owne signification, neuerthelesse applied to another not altogether contrary, but hauing much conueniencie with it. **1712** PARNELL *Spect.* No. 501 ¶1 Some of the finest compositions among the ancients are in allegory. **1840** CARLYLE *Heroes* (1858) 207 Allegory and Poetic Delineation, as I said above, cannot be religious Faith.

b. *attrib.*

1532 MORE *Confut. Tindale* Wks. 1557, 415/1 These heretikes nowe not onely rob the churche in an allegorye sense. —— *Answ. Frith* 835/1 The wordes of Chryste might beside the lyttarall sence bee vnderstanden in an allegorye.

2. An instance of such description; a figurative sentence, discourse, or narrative, in which properties and circumstances attributed to the apparent subject really refer to the subject they are meant to suggest; an extended or continued metaphor.

1534 MORE *On the Passion* Wks. 1557, 1340/1 It might be taken for an allegory or some other trope or figure. **1577** VAUTROULLIER tr. *Luther's Ep. Gal.* 149 The allegorie of the two sonnes of Abraham, Isaacke and Ismael. **1611** BIBLE *Gal.* iv. 24 Which things are an Allegorie. **1751** JOHNSON *Rambl.* No. 176 ¶11 They discover in every passage.. some artful allegory. **1846** T. WRIGHT *Mid. Ages* II. xix. 257 The spirited and extremely popular political allegory of the 'Vision of Piers Ploughman.'

3. An allegorical representation; an emblem.

a **1639** W. WHATELEY *Protot.* I. xi. (1640) 154 These two mothers and the children borne of them were allegories, that is, figures of some other thing mystically signified by them. **1769** BURKE *State Nat.* Wks. II. 134 Procrustes.. with his iron bed, the allegory of his government. **1882** MRS. PITMAN *Mission Life in Greece* 30 That Hercules is only an allegory of the sun.

†**'allegory**, *v. Obs.* [f. the sb. Perh. misprint for *allegorize*.] To ALLEGORIZE.

1554 WHITGIFT *Defense* 571 (R.) Some do allegorie vpon this place, saying that Christ is lifted vp by the preaching of the gospell.

‖**a'llegrement**, *adv.* [Fr. *allégrement*, f. *allègre*: see next.] In a lively manner, briskly, gaily.

1604–9 DONNE *Let.* in *Wks.* 1839 VI. 322 Make therefore to yourself some Mark and go towards it Allegrement.

‖**allegresse** (aleˈgrɛs, æliːˈgrɛs). [Fr. *allégresse*, n. of state f. *allègre*:—L. *alácrem* for *álacrem*, acc. of *alacer* brisk, sprightly: see ALACRITY and -ESSE.] Gaiety, gladsomeness.

1652 URQUHART *Jewel* Wks. 1834, 223 They raised their shouts of allegress up to the very heavens. **1853** *Ch. Auchester* III. 170 He.. glanced into the room with an air of allegresse to bid me adieu. **1878** J. PAYNE *Lautrec*, Hymning the golden allegresse Of wedded love.

‖**allegretto** (alleˈgrɛtto), *a. Mus.* [It., dim. of ALLEGRO.] Somewhat brisk; less brisk than '*allegro*.' (Used also as *adv.* and *sb.*; cf. next.)

1740 in J. GRASSINEAU *Mus. Dict.* 3. *a* **1817** JANE AUSTEN *Lesley Castle* in *Love & Freindship* (1922) 70, I had.. constantly hollowed whenever she played, *Bravo, Bravissimo,.. allegretto,..* and *Poco presto* with many other such outlandish words, all of them.. expressive of my admiration. **1833** [see ANDANTINO *adj.*]. **1877** G. B. SHAW *How to become Mus. Critic* (1960) 13 The symphony.. was very fairly played, especially the *allegretto.* **1879** [See ALLEMANDE *sb.* 2]. **1966** *Listener* 3 Mar. 329/2 A supremely concentrated account of the allegretto.

‖**allegro** (It. alˈlegro, æˈlɛgrəʊ), *a.*, *adv.*, and *sb.* [It. *allegro*, irreg. repr. of L. *alácrem* for *álacrem*, acc. of *álacer* brisk.]

A. *adj.* In orig. It. sense: Lively, gay, merry.

1632 MILTON (*title*) L'Allegro.

B. *adv.* and *adj.* **1.** *Music.* Brisk, lively, quick; one of the five grades of musical pace and character, being the quickest except *presto*. Used advb. in directions as 'to be taken *allegro*,' and adject. as 'allegro time.'

1721 BAILEY, *Allegro*, a Term in Musick when the Movement is quick. **1752** [see PRESTO *a.*[1]]. **1963** AUDEN *Dyer's Hand* 487 The tempo indication is *allegro assai*... The duet.. is sung *allegro assai*.

2. *Philol.* Applied to a word or phrase conventionally shortened in actual speech.

1939 L. H. GRAY *Found. Lang.* iii. 65 Only words of very common use have these double forms (*lento-* and *allegro-*forms). **1964** R. H. ROBINS *Gen. Linguistics* viii. 347 The reduction or abbreviation of the forms of frequently used words ('allegro forms' like *howd'yedo*, and *yes'm* for *yes madam*).

C. *sb. Mus.* A movement in allegro time.

1683 PURCELL *Sonnata's III Parts* Pref., *Allegro*, and *vivace*, a very brisk, swift, or fast movement. **1754** LD. CHESTERFIELD in *World* 14 Nov. 588 His adagio's, his allegro's.. and his jiggs. ?**1777** J. SKINNER *Tullochg.*, Their allegros and a' the rest, They canna please a Scottish taste, Compared wi' Tullochgorum. **1875** OUSELEY *Mus. Form* xi. 52 The first movement of a symphony is usually an allegro, a tolerably brisk piece. **1876** G. B. SHAW *How to become Mus. Critic* (1960) 10 The first portion is an *allegro agitato*. **1947** A. EINSTEIN *Mus. Romantic Era* xi. 125 With no other composer than Mendelssohn does there appear so frequently in the Allegro movements the indication *con fuoco* or *appassionato*.

allele (ˈæliːl). *Biol.* Also **allel**. [ad. G. *allel*, abbrev. of ALLELOMORPH] = ALLELOMORPH. Hence **a'llelic** *a.*; **a'llelism** = ALLELOMORPHISM.

1931 J. A. JENKINS in *Univ. Calif. Publ. Agric. Sci.* VI. 390 The most probable assumption is that.. there are many different combinations of alleles. **1934** *Genetics* July 310 (*title*) Alleles of the Mallard Plumage Pattern. **1935** *Science* 12 July 37/2 Allelic.. allelism. **1939** *Nature* 11 Nov. (Suppl.) 822/1 D. Ferriman found that oxycephaly and acrocephalosyndactyly are dominant conditions, probably allelomorphic, and that a third allele may be acholuric jaundice. **1940** HINSIE & SHATZKY *Psychiatric Dict.* 21/1 Each gene is an allele of, or is allelic to, the other.. Brown and blue eyes in man are alleles of each other, as is red and white color in snapdragons. **1953** J. S. HUXLEY *Evol. in Action* i. 26 Each particular kind of gene can exist in a number of slightly different forms or 'allels', each allel exerting a slightly different effect in development. **1956** C. H. WADDINGTON in A. Pryce-Jones *New Outl. Mod. Knowl.* 232 Geneticists speak of the whole family of genes.. as occupying a 'locus'. The different members of the family are the 'alleles' of the locus.

alleleu (ælɪˈljuː). *nonce-wd.* An outcry.

1865 CARLYLE *Fredk. Gt.* I. I. v. 40 The universal alleleu of female hysterics.

allelomorph (æˈliːləʊmɔːf). *Biol.* [f. Gr. ἀλλήλ- one another + -O + μορφή form.] One of several alternative forms of the same gene, occupying the same relative positions in homologous chromosomes. Hence **aˌllelo'morphic** *a.*, pertaining to or of the nature of allelomorphs; **aˌllelo'morphism**, the existence, transmission, or inheritance of allelomorphs.

1902 BATESON & SAUNDERS in *Rep. Evol. Com. R. Soc.* I. 159 [If] two similar gametes meet, their offspring will be no more likely to show the other allelomorph than if no cross had ever taken place. *Ibid.* 127 The strictly allelomorphic or Mendelian distribution of characters among the gametes. *Ibid.* 142 It does not appear as yet that simple allelomorphism occurs between any two colours, of which neither is xanthic or albino. **1906** R. H. LOCK *Variation, Hered. & Evol.* vii. 184 The dominant and recessive allelomorph seem to represent respectively the presence and absence of something. *Ibid.* x. 265 Allelomorphic characters. **1914** T. H. MORGAN in *Amer. Naturalist* XLVIII. 502 (*title*) The theoretical distinction between multiple allelomorphs and close linkage. *Ibid.*, Dexter pointed out that the mode of treatment that Nabours followed.. is the procedure of multiple allelomorphism. **1949** DARLINGTON & MATHER *Elements Genetics* v. 114 In addition to such simple allelomorphs, however, particular loci in scores of species show whole series of alternatives, multiple allelomorphs as they are called. **1957** E. B. FORD *Butterflies* ix. 188 Three, four, or more forms of the same gene have on occasion been encountered, so giving rise to 'multiple allelomorphs'.

alleluia (ælɪˈl(j)uːɪə), *int.* and *sb.*[1] [a. L. *Allēlūia*, a. Gr. ἀλληλούϊα, the Septuagint representation of Heb. *hallēlū-yāh*, *i.e.* praise ye Jah or Jehovah, now more commonly written as in the A.V. of the O.T., HALLELUJAH.] An exclamation meaning 'Praise the Lord,' which occurs in many psalms and anthems. *Hence*, A song of praise to God.

1382 WYCLIF *Rev.* xix. 6 A vois of a greet trumpe.. seiynge alleluya [TINDALE Alleluya, *Rhem.* Allelu-ia, **1611** Alleluia]. **1398** TREVISA tr. *Barth. De P.R.* IX. xxviii. (1495) 364 At Ester Alleluya is songe. *c* **1400** *Epiph.* (Turnb. 1843) 1880 They song all ther with myld chere Aleluya with vocys soo clere. **1691** J. NORRIS *Pract. Disc.* 121 The Burthen of whose Devotion lay in Anthems and Alleluiahs. **1864** ENGEL *Mus. Anc. Nat.* 99 Trilling the tongue against the roof of the mouth.. is all that constitutes the Alleluia of the ancients.

alleluia (ælɪˈl(j)uːɪə), *sb.*[2] *Obs.* or *dial.* ['Bears the same name in Ger., Fr., It., Sp.' Prior. Etymon uncertain; see the quotations.] The wood sorrel (*Oxalis Acetosella*).

1543 TRAHERON *Vigo* (1586) 430 Alleyluya.. a kind of three leaved grasse, which is sowre in tast. **1551** TURNER *Herbal* II. 74 Oxys.. is called alleluya, because it appereth about Easter, when Alleluya is song agayn, or wodsore: but it shuld be called wodsour or sorell. **1662** MORE *Antid. agst. Ath.* II. vi. (1712) 57 The Leaf of Balm, and of Alleluia or Wood-Sorrel.. are Cardiacal. **1725** BRADLEY *Fam. Dict.*, *Cuckow-Bread*, or *Alleluia*. **1830** WITHERING in Britten *Plant-n.* s.v., *Alleluia*, probably from its being called in the South of Italy *Juliola*, whence also its officinal name *Luzula*.

alleluiatic (ælɪˌl(j)uːɪˈætɪk), *a.* [ad. L. *allēlūiatic-us* f. *allēlūiā*, after *drama*, *dramatic-us*, etc.] Of or pertaining to the Alleluia or Hallelujah.

[**1639** USSHER *Brit. Eccl.* xi. Wks. 1847 V. 381 Celebratissimam victoriam Alleluiaticam.] **1844** *St. German* in *Eng. Saints* xiv. 158 Which goes in history by the name of the Alleluiatic Victory [when the Britons under Germanus by shouting Hallelujah gained a bloodless victory over the Pagan Saxons and Picts]. **18..** W. STAUNTON *Eccl. Dict.* (ed. 4) App. 3, *Alleluiatic Sequence*, the hymn beginning with the words 'The strain upraise.'

†**alle'lykely**, *adv. Obs.* [comb. of ALL *adv.* + LIKELY or perh. for *alike-ly*.] Equally.

1440 *Promp. Parv.*, Allelykely, or euynly (*v.r.* a lyke wyse, or euynly), *Equaliter*.

‖**allemande** (aləˈmɑ̃ːd, -ˈmand, ˈæləmænd, ˈælmænd), *sb.* [a. mod.Fr. *allemande* German (sc. *dance*). For the various historical forms under which the word was formerly englished, see ALMAIN.]

1. a. A name given to various German dances.

1775 SHERIDAN *Rivals* III. iv. 130 These outlandish heathen allemandes and cotillons are quite beyond me! *a* **1790** in *Scots Songs* II. 56 The Spaniards dance fandangos well, Mynheer an all'mand prances.

b. A figure in which the gentleman turns his partner, in square or country dancing.

1808 T. WILSON *Analysis Country Dancing* 7 *Allemande*, the lady at A, and Gentleman at B, pass round each other, the Lady in the circle C, and the Gentleman in the circle D, returning to their situations at AB. **1949** A. CHUJOY *Dance Encycl.* 6/1 A characteristic figure is that in which the gentleman turns the lady under his arm and vice versa. There is a hint of this in the 'allemand' of American square dancing. **1952** HUNT & UNDERWOOD *Eight Yards of Calico* 28 An allemande may be done with either hand, with the partner or the corner. Its commonest use is in the 'left hand around with your corner' figure. **1979** I. HALL in *Notes on teaching Scottish Country Dancing* 51 The next two figures which in dancing terms flow naturally into each other (the Double reel of 4 into the circular Allemande) have a change of tune at their interface.

2. A piece of music forming one of the movements of the Suite.

1685 *Lond. Gaz.* mmlxxxi/4 Airs for the Violin, To wit, Preludes, Fuges, Allmands, Sarabands. **1833** *Penny Cycl.* I. 346 Handel, and other composers of his period..never intended their allemandes to be so fast as they are performed by modern players. **1879** E. PROUT in Grove *Mus. Dict.* I. 55/2 The allemande is a piece of moderate rapidity—about an allegretto—in common time.

3. *Cookery.* **allemande sauce** [F. *sauce allemande*, also used], a rich velouté sauce thickened with egg yolks. Also *ellipt.*

[**1827** 'M. DODS' *Cook & Housewife's Man.* (ed. 2) 329 *Sauce à l'Allemand, or German Sauce*..is extensively used for dressed meat-dishes.] **1863** MRS. BEETON *Bk. Househ. Managem.* x. 244 Sauce Allemande, or German Sauce. **1868** M. JEWRY *Warne's Model Cookery & Housek. Bk.* 54/1 *Allemande*, reduced white velouté sauce, thickened with cream and yolks of eggs, seasoned with nutmeg and lemon-juice. **1951** *Good Housek. Home Encycl.* 332/1 *Allemande Sauce*, a rich version of velouté sauce.

allemande, *v.* [f. the sb.] **1.** *trans.* To move (a person) as in an allemande.

1821 GALT *Annals of Parish* xxxviii. 308 He..allemanded her along in a manner that should not have been seen..out of a king's court.

2. *intr.* To dance an allemande. Also *fig.*

1830 *Fraser's Mag.* I. 298/1 With what grace might he *allemand* in a quadrille. **1835** *Nautical Mag.* July 416 A girl in the same set, who was tying her shoe-string when she ought to have been allemanding. **1890** BARING-GOULD *Arminell* xlviii, The love-making below stairs is..full of restraints and shynesses, of setting to partners, and allemanding about them.

3. *imp.* (A call to) execute the figure of an allemande. Freq. as ***allemande left, right***, etc.

1808 T. WILSON *Analysis Country Dancing* 128 The following short figures are generally performed in half a strain of eight bars, or a whole strain of four bars, as, Turn Your Partner, Right and Left, Allemande, Half Figure, [etc.]. **1883** C. PHELPS in *Harper's Mag.* Jan. 284/1 What pressure of hands was exchanged when Sandy authorized 'alamande left'! **1937** TOLMAN & PAGE *Country Dance Bk.* ii. 33 Allemande Left..Couples turn back to back and walk 4 steps to meet their corner. **1953** T. H. NEOH *Square Dance Calling Simplified* 13 The 'Allemande Right' is done with your own partners and right hands are used instead of left. **1966** C. R. & M. B. JENSEN *Beginning Square Dancing* 22 Allemande left and allemande thar; right and left and make a star. **1977** *Express* (Brisbane S.W. Suburbs ed.) 16 Nov. 19/3, I have even danced to a Japanese caller who used the same 'allemande left' and 'do-sa-do' as callers use everywhere. **1983** *Amer. Square Dance* Jan. 59/2 Allemande thar (all with partners) Shoot the star and go *red hot*.

allemontite (æləˈmɒntaɪt). *Min.* [f. *Allemont*, in Dauphiné, where found + -ITE.] A native alloy of antimony and arsenic; *Arsenical antimony*.

1837–80 DANA *Min.* 18, *Allemontite*..Color tin-white, or reddish-gray.

Allen (ˈælɪn). A proprietary name used *attrib.* in the names of various tools, etc., produced by the Allen Manufacturing Co., of Hartford, Conn., esp. **Allen key**, a kind of spanner designed to fit into and turn an Allen screw; **Allen screw**, a screw with a hexagonal socket in the head.

1930 *Buck & Hickman Catal.* 1055 Allen Safety Set Screws. **1961** *Which?* Nov. 282/2 Users felt that it was a nuisance to have to use an Allen-key (a small spanner) to tighten the Helvetia's needle. **1967** KARCH & BUBER *Offset Processes* viii. 295 Loosen the Allen screws..and turn the eccentric collars..at each side of the duplicator. **1972** *Pract. Motorist* Oct. 165/1 We took a plug out at the top. Under it ..was the top of the hinge pin which has a recess in the head to take an Allen key. **1972** *Trade Marks Jrnl.* 3 May 838/1 Allen..Set screws, cap screws, shoulder screws; plugs for pipes and oil plugs..all made of common metal and incorporating hexagonal shaped sockets. The Allen Manufacturing Company..Hartford, Connecticut, United States of America; Manufacturers and Merchants. **1976** A. HILL *Summer's End* ii. 35 When you'r not using the gun, yo' threads these plugs into the barrel ends like this, sithee. This allen-key teks 'em out when yo' wants to shoot it. **1978** *Official Gaz.* (U.S. Patent Office) 9 May 174/1 The Allen Wrench People. The Allen Manufacturing Company. Multiple class.

allenarly (əˈlɛnəlɪ), *adv. north. dial.* and *Sc.* Forms: 4–7 **allanerly(e**, 6 **alanerly**, 6–7 **allanerlie**, 6–8 **allenerly**, 6– **allenarly.** [f. ALL *adv.* + ANERLY singly.]

1. Solitarily, alone; only, solely, merely. (Still in Sc. law.)

1340 HAMPOLE *Prose Tr.* 4 Allanerly þay may ioye in Ihesu þat lufes hym in þis lyfe. **1375** BARBOUR *Bruce* v. 281 That he wald cum all-anerly For to spek with him priuely. **1535** STEWART *Cron. Scotl.* (1858) I. 216 Thus am I left allanerlie allone. **1549** *Compl. Scotl.* 3 ȝour grace deseruis nocht to be callit ane nobil, alanerly throcht ȝour verteouse verkis. *c* **1565** R. LINDSAY *Hist. Scotl.* (1728) 37 Ambitiousness cometh never of God, but allenarly of the devil. **1687** *Royal Procl.* in *Lond. Gaz.* mmccxxi/3 To accept of Our Indulgence allenarly, and none other. **1711** *C. M. Lett. to Curat*, 'Tis all the Child of his own Fancy allenerly. **1818** SCOTT *Hrt. Midl.* xxxix. 308 On whilk..the gospel shineth allenarly, and leaveth the rest of the world in utter darkness.

2. *adj.*, Only, sole.

1533 BELLENDENE *Livy* (1822) I. 86 His empire..was under the governance of ane allenerly persoun. **1587** HOLINSHED *Scot. Chron.* (1806) II. 51 James our second and allanerlie son.

allene, synonym of ALLYLENE.

†**aˈlleniate**, *v. Obs. rare*$^{-1}$. [f. L. *al-* = *ad-* to + *lēnis* soft, gentle. Formed on the analogy of *abbreviate*, *alleviate*, etc., against Latin usage which made the vb. *lēnīre*.] To soften, render gentle.

1620 VENNER *Via Recta* ii. 34 Drunkennesse..doth (as they say)..alleniate and make quiet the animall powers. **1642** ROGERS *Naaman* 45 How doth the Lord turne the eies of Crocodiles, to Doves eies, alleniate, and draw the hearts of fathers to the children.

aller, obs. gen. pl. of ALL (see ALL D.), and obs. form of ALDER *sb.*^{1}

allergic (æˈlɜːdʒɪk), *a.* [f. next + -IC.] Pertaining to or characterized by allergy.

1911 C. E. VON PIRQUET in *Arch. Internal Med.* VII. 265 The allergic condition does not occur immediately after the first injection. *Ibid.* 428 The practical method of diagnosis by the allergic reactions will be extended to other diseases. **1919** *Jrnl. Amer. Med. Assoc.* LXXIII. 759/2 Allergic action of drugs. **1925** W. W. DUKE *Allergy, Asthma* 246 A large proportion of patients with asthma, 'allergic coryza', erythema,..and even allergic shock, are actually sensitive specifically and solely to the action of a physical agent, such as light, heat, cold, or mechanical irritation. **1926** SOLLMANN *Pharmacol.* (ed. 3) 86 Allergic hypersusceptibility is a special type of idiosyncrasy in which the patient reacts to special substances. **1958** *Immunology* I. 22 Allergic reactions have occurred in human patients after treatment with ACTH.

b. *fig.* Sensitive (esp. antipathetic) *to. colloq.*

1937 *New Yorker* 23 Jan. 20 (*caption*) He's allergic to Philadelphia scrapple. **1942** *Punch* 26 Aug. 169/3 Colonels have a curious effect on me. Quite frankly, I am allergic to them. **1958** *Observer* 5 Oct. 19/4 Allergic as I am to opera on television..I cannot be relied on for an objective opinion of the B.B.C.'s two-hour presentation.

allergy (ˈælədʒɪ). *Path.* [ad. G. *allergie* (von Pirquet 1906, in *Münchener Mediz. Wochenschr.* LIII. 1457/2), f. Gr. ἄλλος other, different + ἔργεια (known only in comp. ἐνέργεια: see ENERGY), used for 'reactivity': see -Y^{3}.] The altered degree of susceptibility of a body produced by a sensitizing dosage of or exposure to some foreign material; more widely, hypersensitivity to the action of some particular foreign material, as certain foods, pollens, micro-organisms, etc.

1911 C. E. VON PIRQUET in *Arch. Internal Med.* VII. 260 We might rightly use the word 'allergy'..as a clinical conception. **1919** *Jrnl. Amer. Med. Assoc.* LXXIII. 759/2 Coca's classification of hypersensitiveness into 'anaphylaxis' and 'allergy' will serve to clarify this whole field... Anaphylaxis is an antigen antibody reaction, artificially induced by immunologic processes. Allergy is used to express the natural hypersensitiveness of the individual not produced by immunologic processes. **1925** W. W. DUKE (*title*) Allergy, Asthma, Hay Fever, Urticaria and Allied Manifestations of Reaction. *Ibid.* 20 Wells and others contend that 'allergy' is a broad useful term, for under its heading can be described a group of peculiar phenomena of altered reactivity the underlying cause of which is as yet unproved. **1959** *Which?* Sept. 116/2 The person who is specifically sensitive to some article of food—for instance, shellfish—may make himself very ill after only a mouthful. This is *true* allergy... True allergy or specific sensitivity to synthetic detergents is rare.

b. *fig.* A feeling of antipathy to some thing or person.

1944 AUDEN *For Time Being* (1945) 118 Before the Diet of Sugar he was using razor blades And excited soon after with an allergy to maidenheads. **1951** KOESTLER *Age of Longing* 186 The European public..had developed a violent allergy to all kinds of rationing, saving and public-spirited exhortation.

Hence **ˈallergen** [after ANTIGEN], a substance producing allergy; **allergenic** (æləˈdʒɛnɪk) *a.* Also **ˈallergist**, one who specializes in allergic phenomena.

1912 *Jrnl. Pharm. & Exp. Therap.* III. 232 The same amount of allergen given in lesser concentration elicits a more intense reaction. **1913** DORLAND *Med. Dict.* (ed. 7), Allergen..allergenic. **1923** *Westm. Gaz.* 16 Feb. 8/6 The majority of cases of spasmodic asthma were due to some allergen. **1934** WEBSTER, Allergist. **1942** in F. R. Moulton *Aerobiology* 7 Relatively little is known about air-borne bacteria as possible allergens. **1945** *Lancet* 22 Dec. 822/1 (*heading*) Alarums of an Allergist. **1957** *New Scientist* 7 Nov. 39/1 These agents [*sc.* antibodies] are called allergens when they produce allergic reactions like hay fever.

allerion, variant of ALERION.

Allerød (ˈalərød). Also **Alleröd**. The name of the type site near Copenhagen, Denmark, used *attrib.* and *absol.* to designate a Late Glacial interstadial in Europe between the Older and the Younger Dryas, *c* 9500 BC, marked by the spread of birch, willow, and pine.

1920 *Danmarks Geol. Undersøgelse* II. *Raekke* XXXIV. 260 The warm period of the Late Glacial Age: the Allerød Period. **1928** K. JESSEN in V. Madsen et al. *Geol. Denmark* 133 On Bornholm, Sjælland, Møen, Fyn and in East Jylland evidence has been found of a considerable climatic oscillation, the Allerød Oscillation, in lateglacial times... We find at the bottom Dryas Clay, above that mud with macrophyllous birch,..which bears witness to a higher summer temperature; at the top is Dryas Clay again. **1946** F. E. ZEUNER *Dating Past* iii. 62 The Alleröd oscillation..was a time with climatic conditions more genial than before *and after*. **1957** G. E. HUTCHINSON *Treat. Limnol.* I. i. 26 Organic deposits of Alleröd age. **1973** P. A. COLINVAUX *Introd. Ecol.* vii. 100 The [climatic] episode was also tied in to a glacial retreat, during the Allerød, and a readvance in younger Dryas time. **1974** *Encycl. Brit. Micropædia* I. 255/1 During the Allerød in Britain, glaciated regions were restricted to the highlands of Scotland.

allers (ˈæləz), repr. dial. and colloq. pronunc. of ALWAYS *adv.* Cf. ALLUS *adv.*

1866 R. B. MARCY *Thirty Yrs. Army Life* xii. 359 Me an him..allers 'llowed that them there Massys was considdible on bar and other varmints. **1886** F. H. BURNETT *Little Lord Fauntleroy* xiii. 247 She was allers up to her tricks. **1913** D. H. LAWRENCE *Sons & Lovers* i. 14 'They're working very late now, aren't they?'..'No later than they allers do.' **1931** *Amer. Speech* VII. 90 The chillern allers kept their mouths shet in the presence o' their elders.

†**ˈallevate**, *v. Obs. rare*$^{-1}$. [f. L. *allevāt-* ppl. stem of *allevāre*: see ALLEVE.] To raise up, lift. Used also for ALLEVIATE.

1613 R. C. *Table Alph.*, *Allevate*, asswage, or make more easie and light. **1696** *Money masters all Things* (1698) 39 He scarce can allevate his Feet off Ground.

†**alleˈvation.** *Obs. rare.* [ad. L. *allevātiōn-em* a raising up, an alleviating, f. *allevāre*: see ALLEVE.] = ALLEVIATION (for which, in the second instance, it may be a mispr.).

1502 *Ord. Cryst. Men* (W. de Worde) IV. iii. (1506) 170 And this alleuacyon they fynde by certayne operacyons. **1689** *Myst. Iniq.* 40 That an explanation of these Impositions, and such Allevations, be allowed to the tenderly Considerate.

†**aˈlleve**, *v. Obs.* In 6 **aleive**. [prop. *aleve*, a. OFr. *aleve-r*:—L. *adl-*, *allevāre*, to lift up, raise, relieve, lighten, f. *ad* to + *levāre* to raise (cf. *levis* light).] To relieve, alleviate.

a **1546** EARL SURREY *Lett.* xxvi. (R.) To th' intent his majesty's charges might be aleived.

alleve(n, -the, obs. forms of ELEVEN, -TH^{1}.

†**aˈllevement.** *Obs.* Also 6 **aleave-**. [a. OFr. *alevement*, f. *alever*: see ALLEVE *v.* and -MENT.] Relief, alleviation.

1599 *Soliman & Pers.* II. in Hazl. *Dodsl.*, Yet this is some allevement [*v.r.* aleavement] to my sorrow.

†**aˈlleviate**, *ppl. a. Obs.* [ad. L. *alleviāt-us*, pa. pple. of *alleviā-re* to lighten, f. *al-* = *ad-* to + *levis* light. Used for some time as pa. pple.]

1. Lightened in weight.

1471 RIPLEY *Comp. Alch.* in Ashm. 1652, v. xxxix. 157 Pursys, wyth pounds so aggravate, Whych by Phylosophy be now allevyat.

2. Extenuated, palliated.

1671 *True Non-Conf.* 34 That which you call cruelty.. will quickly be alleviat to moderation.

alleviate (əˈliːvɪeɪt), *v.* [f. prec. 'Reckoned by Heylin, in 1656, among uncouth and unusual words.' Todd.]

†**1.** To make lighter, diminish the weight of. *Obs.*

1665–6 *Phil. Trans.* I. 157 Such as have exact Wheel-Barometers may try whether Odors or Fumes do alleviate the Air.

2. To lighten, or render more tolerable, or endurable; to relieve, mitigate. Also *absol.*

1528 PAYNELL tr. *Salernes Regiment* 22 Milk..alleviateth the griefes of the breast. *a* **1656** BP. HALL *Balm of Gil.* i. §ii. (1863) 6 To alleviate the sorrows of their heavy partners. **1712** STEELE *Spect.* No. 450 ¶3, I..found means to alleviate, and at last conquer my Affliction. **1871** NAPHEYS *Prevent. Dis.* III. ii. 619 To alleviate the sufferings of the invalid. **1876** MOZLEY *Univ. Serm.* v. 120 Hope alleviates the sorrow of that home. **1888** MRS. H. WARD *R. Elsmere* xli, The constant effort to serve and to alleviate.

†**3.** To lighten the gravity of (an offence); to extenuate, palliate. *Obs.*

1768 BLACKSTONE *Comm.* IV. 15 The violence of passion, or temptation, may sometimes alleviate a crime. **1777** R. WATSON *Philip II* (1793) II. xiv. 181 They began to alleviate the outrages of the soldiers.

alleviated (əˈliːvɪeɪtɪd), *ppl. a.* [f. prec. + -ED.] Lightened, mitigated.

1792 COWPER *Lett.* 25 Nov. Wks. 1876, 405 My melancholy seemed a little alleviated for a few days. **1882** BEECHER *Chr. World Pulpit* 13 Nov. 6 My father's public teaching may be called alleviated Calvinism.

alleviating (əˈliːvɪeɪtɪŋ), *vbl. sb.* [f. as prec. + -ING^{1}.] The action of making lighter, less grave, or less severe. (Mostly gerundial.)

1691 RAY *Creation* (1714) 149 [These] conduce much to the alleviating the body and facilitating the flight (of birds). **1757** JOHNSON *Rambl.* No. 183 ¶2 The hope of alleviating the sense of our disparity. **1758** —— *Idler* No. 31 ¶11 The misery..he has many means of alleviating.

alleviating (əˈliːvɪeɪtɪŋ), *ppl. a.* [f. as prec. + -ING^{2}.] Lightening, mitigating, extenuating.

1789 BENTHAM *Princ. Legisl.* xi. §42 The alleviating circumstance is only a matter of presumption.

alleviation (əˌliːvɪˈeɪʃən). [n. of action f. ALLEVIATE, as if ad. L. **alleviātiōn-em*.] The action of lightening weight, gravity, severity, or pain; relief, mitigation.

1625 J. HART *Anat. Ur.* I. ii. 31 The disease gave her some reasonable time of intermission, with some alleuiation of the accidents. **1646** SIR T. BROWNE *Pseud. Ep.* 270 Alleviation of spirits.. may also ensue. **1750** JOHNSON *Rambl.* No. 76 ¶5 It has always been considered as an alleviation of misery not to suffer alone. **1771** *Antiq. Sarisb.* 4 Small Alleviation of the yoke of Servitude. **1833** I. TAYLOR *Fanat.* vi. 195 Some grateful alleviation of the inward torment. **1876** FREEMAN *Norm. Conq.* I. App. 662 An alleviation of the heavy imposts under which the people groaned.

alleviative (əˈliːvɪətɪv), *a.* and *sb. rare.* [f. *alleviāt-* ppl. stem of *alleviāre* (see ALLEVIATE) + -IVE.]

A. *adj.* Of an alleviating nature or tendency.

1823 *Examiner* 24 Aug. 552/3 Any measure alleviative of distress. **1931** *Birmingham Post* 13 May 7/5 He was admitted to hospital for an alleviative operation.

B. *sb.* That which tends to alleviate; a palliative.

1672 *Corah's Doom* 126 (T.) Some cheering alleviatiue to lads kept in pure slavery to a few Greek and Latin words.

alleviator (əˈliːvɪeɪtə(r)). [f. ALLEVIATE + -OR, as if a. L. **alleviātōr* n. of agent f. *alleviāre*.] He who, or that which, alleviates; a lightener, or reliever.

1811 LAMB *On being Hanged* Wks. 560 That kindest alleviator of human miseries. *a* **1823** COMBE in *Half-hrs. Authors* II. 128 A powerful alleviator of the fatigue of walking. **1882** *Cornh. Mag.* Feb. 157 An alleviator of the evils of his individual life.

alleviatory (əˈliːvɪətərɪ), *a.* [f. ALLEVIATE + -ORY; after L. adjs. in *-ōrius*, f. agent-nouns in -OR.] Having the attribute of relieving.

1865 CARLYLE *Fredk. Gt.* X. XXI. ix. 183 The chief Berlin Doctor.. began some alleviatory treatment.

allevin, obs. form of ELEVEN.

†**a'llevy**, *v. Obs. rare*⁻¹. [a. Fr. (15–16th c.) *a(l)lévie-r*:—L. *alleviā-re*.] A by-form of ALLEVIATE.

1566 DRANT *Hor. Sat.* iii. B vj, Let discipline allevied be, in measure, to the vyce.

alley (ˈælɪ). Forms: 4–6 **aley, aleye,** 5 **aly, alaye,** 6 **ally,** 6– **alley.** *Pl.* **alleys,** formerly often **allies.** [a. OFr. *alee*, mod.Fr. *allée*, 1. the act of walking, passage, 2. a walk or passage.]

I. A walk, a passage.

†**1. a.** A passage in or into a house; a covered way. *Obs.*

1388 WYCLIF *1 Kings* vii. 2 He bildide foure aleis [**1382** aluris] bitwixe the pilers of cedre. *c* **1400** *Destr. Troy* XII. 4978 Mony long chaumburs, Goand vp by degrees þurgh mony gay alys. **1475** CAXTON *Jason* 86 b, For ther was no more.. but a litil aleye from her chambre to his. **1480** —— *Chron. Eng.* VII. (1520) 115 b/2 An aleye that stretcheth out of the warde under the erth into the forsayd castell. **1525** LD. BERNERS *Froissart* II. cxvi. [cxii.] 334 The aley vnder couert endured fro their garyson a seuen or eight leages.

b. *fig.*

1602 SHAKS. *Ham.* I. v. 67 The natural Gates and Allies of the Body.

II. *esp.* A bordered walk or passage.

2. a. A walk in a garden, park, shrubbery, maze, or wood, generally bordered with trees, or bushes; an avenue; also the spaces between beds of flowers or plants, or between the rows of hops in a hop-garden.

1382 WYCLIF *Song of Sol.* xi. 1, I am the flour of the feeld, and the lilie of aleyes. *c* **1386** CHAUCER *Frankl. T.* 285 And in the Aleyes [*v.r.* aleyes, -eis, -ies] romeden vp and doun. **1440** *Promp. Parv.*, Aley yn gardyne. *Peribolus.* **1578** LYTE *Dodoens* XX. 575 Wild [purslowe] groweth of his owne accorde in wayes and alies of gardens. **1594** PLAT *Jewell-ho.* I. 48 Throughout all the allies of his hop garden. **1599** SHAKS. *Much Ado* I. ii. 10 Walking in a thick pleached alley in my orchard. **1601** HOLLAND *Pliny* (1634) I. 527 The allies that lie between the beds. **1625** BACON *Ess.* (Arb.) 563 These closer alleys must be ever finely gravelled. **1637** MILTON *Comus* 311 Each lane, and every alley green Dingle or bushy dell of this wild wood. **1716–8** LADY M. MONTAGUE *Lett.* I. x. 36 At the end of the fine alley in the garden. **1809** BRYDONE *Sicily* xxi. 217 The approach to Palermo is fine. The alleys are planted with fruit-trees. **1848** L. HUNT *Jar of Honey* ix. 125 A walk down an alley of roses. **1849** RUSKIN *7 Lamps* ii. §xv. 43 Pictured landscapes at the extremities of alleys and arcades. **1861** DELAMER *Kitchen Gard.* 41 Beds four feet in width, with a foot-wide alley between each bed. **1863** LONGF. *Wayside Inn, Theolog. T.* 93 He walked all night the alleys of his park. **1867** MISS BRADDON *Rup. Godwin* I. i. 4 Under the shelter of a long alley of hazel and filbert trees. **1878** R. STEVENSON *Inland Voy.*, With alleys of trees along the embankment.

b. *fig.*

1765 TUCKER *Lt. Nat.* I. 554 We are now striking into another alley, and starting a different question.

3. a. A passage between buildings; hence, a narrow street, a lane; usually only wide enough for foot-passengers. ***blind alley***: one that is closed at the end, so as to be no thoroughfare; a *cul de sac*. ***the Alley***, particularly applied to Change Alley, London, scene of the gambling in South Sea and other stocks. (In U.S. applied to what in London is called a *Mews*.)

c **1510** *Cocke Lorelles Bote* 6 Also in ave maria aly, and at westmenster, And some in shordyche. **1583** STANYHURST *Aeneis* ii. (1880) 66 Through crosse blynd allye we iumble. **1615** SANDYS *Trav.* 12 The buildings meane, the streets no larger than allies. **1687** *Lond. Gaz.* mmccxcviii/4 In a paved Alley near St. Sepulchres Church in London. **1711** ADDISON *Spect.* No. 8 ¶3 The Lanes and Allies that are inhabited by Common Swearers. *c* **1713** H. CAREY (*title*) Sally in our Alley. **1720** *The Bubblers Medley* (*title*) Stock Jobbing Cards, or the Humours of Change Alley. **1720** SWIFT in *Bk. of Days* I. 146 There is a gulf where thousands fell.. A narrow sound though deep as hell, 'Change Alley' is the dreadful name. **1722** DE FOE *Plague* 167 The mortality was great in the yard or alley. **1728** NEWTON *Chronol. Amend.* v. 340 Buildings.. with a walk or alley between them. **1775** ASH, *Alley*.. the place in the city of London where the public funds are bought and sold. **1861** STANLEY *East Ch.* ii. (1869) 62 The dark corners of London alleys. **1863** R. CHAMBERS *Bk. of Days* I. 146 Exchange Alley was the seat of the gambling fever. **1876** *World* No. 107, 12 Some who write of Courts, are more familiar with alleys.

b. A back-lane running parallel with a main street. *U.S.*

1729 in *Baltimore Town Rec.* (1905) 10 The commissioners.. shall cause the same Sixty Acres to be.. divided into convenient Streets, Lanes, and Allies, as near as may be into Sixty equal lots. **1747** *Ibid.* 22 To Survey the Same and lay it out into Lotts with convenient Streets and Alleys. **1817** S. R. BROWN *Western Gaz.* 90 There are three streets,.. besides lanes and alleys. *Ibid.* 101 Each block of lots has the advantage of two 16 feet alleys. **1835** J. MARTIN *Gazetteer Virginia* 139 Fire plugs are connected with the distributing pipes at every intersection of the alleys with 2nd and 3rd streets. **1890** J. A. RIIS *How other Half Lives* (1891) 21 A notorious Fourth Ward alley.

c. ***to be up a person's alley***: to be up a person's street (see STREET *sb.*). *slang.*

1931 M. E. GILMAN *Sob Sister* v. 65 It's about time a good murder broke, and this one is right up your alley. **1936** D. CARNEGIE *How to win Friends* (1938) IV. viii. 247 Bridge will be in a cinch for you. It is right up your alley. **1941** AUDEN *New Year Let.* II. p. 37 All vague idealistic art That coddles the uneasy heart, Is up his alley. **1954** R. BISSELL *High Water* (1955) iii. 32 Right up your alley with Donald Duck and Mickey Mouse and all them other uplifting characters you are always studying up on. **1965** *New Statesman* 9 Apr. 583/2 Its slogans and chirpy recommendations are right up her spiritual alley.

4. a. A long narrow enclosure for playing at bowls, skittles, etc.

a **1400** *Squyr of lowe Degre* 804 An hundreth knightes, truly tolde, Shall play with bowles in alayes colde. **1615** *Country Contentm.* in Strutt *Sports & Past.* (1876) 363 Flat bowles being best for allies, your round byazed bowles for open grounds. **1661** PEPYS *Diary* 5 June, Sir W. Pen and I went home with Sir R. Slingsby to bowles in his ally. **1801** STRUTT *Sports & Past.* (1810) 237 The little room required for making these bowling alleys was no small cause of their multiplication. **1844** *Ord. & Regul. Army* §438 Skittle Alleys are repaired by the Royal Engineer Department.

b. *fig.*

1594 PLAT *Jewell-ho.* III. 2 The aire will be a player, vnlesse you can keepe it out of the Alley perforce. **1612** BACON *Ess.*, *Cunning* (Arb.) 434 Such Men are fitter for Practise, then for Counsell; And they are good but in their own Alley: Turne them to New Men, and they have lost their Ayme.

5. A passage between the rows of pews or seats in a church. Still used in the north. In the south corruptly replaced by AISLE.

[**1464** in *Test. Ebor.* II. 268 In medio ambulatorii coram crucifixo.] **1508** *Ibid.* VII. 28 [To be buried] afore yᵉ rode in yᵉ ally. **1558** in *Richmond Wills* 180 To be buried in the mydde allie before the quere dore. **1603** HOLLAND *Plutarch's Mor.* 1295 Temples, which in some places have faire open Isles and pleasant allies. **1686** OLDHAM *Satyrs* 193 At Church.. you in the Alley stand, and sneak. **1697** BP. OF LINCOLN in Southey *Comm.-Pl. Bk.* Ser. II. 68 So strait a place as an ally of the Church. **1776** WESLEY *Wks.* 1872 IV. 71 The church was crowded, pews, alleys, and galleries.

¶ As *aisle* was erroneously put for *alley*, so *alley* has been used for *aisle* (*ala*).

1731 DERBY in *Phil. Trans.* XLI. 229 The Leads and Timber of great Part of the North Alley of the Church was broke in.

6. In a printing-office, the space between two compositors' stands, or between two printing-presses.

1871 RINGWALT *Encycl. Pr.* 27. **1875** SOUTHWARD *Dict. Pr.* 4.

7. A passage or free space between two lines of any kind.

1756 WARTON *Ess. Pope* II. §8. (1782) 30 It is a description of an alley of fish-women. **1856** KANE *Arct. Expl.* I. xxv. 329 We were in an alley of pounded ice-masses.

8. The AMBULACRUM in the shell of an echinoderm.

1835 KIRBY *Hab. & Inst. Anim.* I. vi. 208 Those parts (of the shell of sea urchins) void of spines called the alleys.

†**9.** = ALURE: a gallery round the roof. *Obs.*

c **1380** WYCLIF *Sel. Wks.* (1869) I. 110 Aboue þe pynacle of þe temple þat sum men seyen weren þe aleis.

10. *Comb.* or *Attrib.* as ***alley maker, making,*** etc. **alley cat** (chiefly *U.S.*), a cat that frequents alleys, a stray cat, also (*U.S. slang*) *transf.* (see esp. quot. 1942).

1552 HULOET, Aley maker, *Topiarius.* Aley makynge, *Topiaria.* **1904** *Atlantic Monthly* Mar. 369/1 If you were just an alley-cat you wouldn't even get the chloroform. **1914** E. POUND in *Blast* I. 50 For her laughter frightens even the street hawker And the alley cat dies of a migraine. **1916** DON MARQUIS in *Evening Sun* (N.Y.) 1 Sept. 10/4 Ours is the zest of the alley cat. **1926** S. LEWIS *Mantrap* iv. 44 Thinking up a way of insulting that mangy alley cat! **1941** *Time* 16 June 85/1 [list of words not to be used in film scripts] Alley cat (applied to a woman). **1942** BERREY & VAN DEN BARK *Amer. Thes. Slang* §418. 2 *Ragamuffin*.. alley cat. *Ibid.* §439. 2 *Slut*, alley cat. *Ibid.* §507. 2 *Prostitute*, alley cat. **1946** M. DICKENS *Happy Prisoner* viii. 149 They're as quarrelsome as a couple of alley cats.

alley, var. ALLY, a kind of marble.

alleyed (ˈælɪd), *ppl. a.* [f. ALLEY + -ED².] Laid out as an alley, or with alleys.

1475 *Bk. Noblesse* 70 The gardins so welle aleyed to walke upon. **1808** SCOTT *Marm.* II. x, The arcades of an alley'd walk. **1813** —— *Rokeby* IV. xxi, Through the alleyed walk we spied With hurried step my Edith glide.

alley-way (ˈælɪweɪ). orig. *U.S.* Also **alloway** (ˈæləweɪ). [f. ALLEY + WAY *sb.*¹] A narrow passage or avenue, e.g. between houses or between rows of cabins in a ship.

1788 P. M. FRENEAU *Misc. Wks.* 223 The article stipulated .. that the alley-way should be sufficient for the passing and repassing of the plaintiff. **1854** *Harper's Mag.* IX. 849/2, I was taken to the Auburn state-prison. And as I walked along the concealed alley-ways,.. I bethought me of my theft of fruit. **1888** *Murray's Mag.* III. 238 The covered way, or 'alloway', on the port side, which led from the quarter-deck to the fore part of the ship. **1891** C. ROBERTS *Adrift Amer.* 231 Alley-way between the after-deck house and the bulwarks. **1894** *Outing* (U.S.) XXIV. 286/2 The main street of this town was as dirty as the filthiest alley-way found in any large city of America. **1920** *Blackw. Mag.* Jan. 108/2 A local marshman as a guide, or you will soon find yourself lost in the maze of alleyways through the giant reeds. **1924** WODEHOUSE *Bill the Conqueror* xi. 193 Her decks and alleyways were crowded with voyagers and those who had come to see those voyagers off.

'all-ˌfather. [ALL- E 3 + FATHER, after ON. *Al-fadir.*] The father of all, the universal father.

1. a. *orig.* A title of Odin, the *Al-fadir* of the Edda.

1810 W. TAYLOR in *Month. Mag.* XXIX. 321 Nor, by Al-father, shall it be conniv'd at. **1864** KINGSLEY *Rom. & Teut.* iii. (1875) 69 Woden, the All-father, was superior to one of his sons.

b. Transferred to Jupiter.

1870 BRYANT *Homer* I. VIII. 239 The All-Father took his golden scales.

c. Applied to God.

1826 KIRBY & SPENCE *Entomol.* III. xxxv. 694 The wisdom and skill of the Allfather. **1850** C. KINGSLEY *Alton Locke* II. xv. 225 Had we not an All-Father?.. Did He not love us, too, even as we loved each other? **1874** M. COLLINS *Th. in Garden* (1880) II. i. 11 Doing that which is right, you grasp the hand of the Allfather, and that grasp gives safety. **1945** AUDEN *Coll. Poetry* 69 Only the All-Father Can change the cast or give them Easier lines to say.

ˌall-'fatherly, *a. rare.* [f. prec. + -LY¹.] Of, or like, the universal father.

1839 BAILEY *Festus* viii. (1848) 98 One all-Fatherly source of light and life.

all-fired (ˈɔːl-ˌfaɪəd), *a.* and *adv. slang.* [said to be euphemism for *hell-fired*.] Infernal; hence an intensive. (Chiefly in U.S.) Hence as *adv.*

1837 HALIBURTON *Clockm.* (1862) 115 What an all fired scrape he got into. **1837** *Yale Lit. Mag.* II. 149 Star's an all-fired good ox. **1861** HUGHES *Tom Brown at Oxford* III. vii. 130, I knows I be so all-fired jealous, I can't abear to hear o' her talkin', let alone writin' to ——. **1862** —— in *Macm. Mag.* V. 244/1 [*Berksh. peasant says*] A went off wi' th' most all-fired noise. **1935** M. M. ATWATER *Murder in Midsummer* x. 96 Tell him to get all-fired busy on it.

all-firedly (ˈɔːl-ˌfaɪədlɪ), *adv. slang.* [f. prec. + -LY².] Unusually; excessively.

1833 A. GREENE *Life & Adv. Dr. Duckworth* II. 176 He was seldom downright drunk; but was often all-firedly sprung. *a* **1860** MILNE *Farm Fence* 8 (in Bartlett) Wonder if it is rum that makes potatoes rot so all-firedly. **1924** H. DE SÉLINCOURT *Cricket Match* vi. 192 I'm most all-firedly sorry about it.

all-flower-water. (? Euphem.) Cow's urine; as a remedy.

1839 OTWAY *Tour in Connaught* 142 Salt, the blood of a black hen, and allflower-water. **1876** *N. & Q.* Ser. v. VI. 358 In this nineteenth century I know a poor woman who took all-flower-water. **1879** in *Syd. Soc. Lex.*

All Fools' Day. [prob. orig. with jocular reference to *All Saints, All Souls*.] A humorous name for the 1st of April; the day popularly appropriated to practising upon one's neighbour's credulity. (Only of modern use.)

1712 SWIFT quoted in Hone *Ev. Day Bk.* (1826) I. 205 'A due donation for All Fool's Day.' **1760** *Poor Robin's Alm.* in BRAND *Pop. Ant.*, The first of April some do say Is set apart for All-Fools Day. **1777** BRAND *Pop. Ant.* 398 *All-Fools'* Day, a corruption it should seem of *Auld* i.e. *Old* Fools' Day. **1823** LAMB *Elia* (1868) 65 All Fools' Day. The compliments of the season to my worthy masters.

all fours (ˌɔːl ˈfɔəz), *sb. phr.* [i.e. *all four* card*s*.] **1.** A game at cards, played by two; 'so named from the four particulars by which it is reckoned, and which, joined in the hand of either of the parties, are said to make all-fours. The ***all four*** are ***high, low, Jack,*** and ***the game***.' Johnson.

1707 FARQUHAR *Beaux' Strat.* v. i. 57 Can you play at Whiste, Sir? No, truly, Sir. Nor at all-fours? Neither. **1775** SHERIDAN *St. Patrick's Day* I. ii. 293 To drink bohea tea, and play at allfours on a drum head. **1851** MAYHEW *Lond. Lab.* (1854) I. 13 The usual games are all-fours, all-fives, and cribbage.

2. A game at dominoes, in which points are scored only when the sum of the pips at the two extremes are four or a multiple thereof.

all fours (ˌɔːl ˈfɔəz), *phr.* [formerly *all four*, sc. *extremities*. The *-s* was added prob. during the 19th century; not in Johnson 1808.] All four legs of a quadruped, or the legs and arms of a man. In the phrase *to go* (*crawl*, etc.) *on all fours*.

1563 *Homilies* II. xiii. II. (1640) 184 A bruit beast, creeping upon all foure. **1611** BIBLE *Lev.* xi. 42 Whatsoeuer goeth vpon all foure. [**1535** COVERDALE *ibid.*, All that goeth vpon foure or mo fete.] **1777** ROBERTSON *Amer.* (1783) II. 436 These spies..will creep on all-four, like cats. **1814** SCOTT *Wav.* xxxviii, Edward..could perceive him crawling on all-fours.

2. *fig.* **to run on all fours**, *i.e.* fairly, evenly, not to limp like a lame dog. **to be**, or **stand, on all fours**: to be even or on a level, to present an exact analogy or comparison (*with*).

1710 SIR J. ST. LEGER in Somers' *Tracts* (1751) III. 248 Tho' the Comparison should not exactly run upon all four when examined. **1877** *Daily Tel.* 15 Mar., It must stand on all fours with that stipulation. **1883** *Daily News* 8 Feb. 3/7 The decision I have quoted is on all fours with this case.

ˌall-ˈgood, *a.* [ALL- E 6.] Wholly or infinitely good.

1586 tr. *La Primaudaye's Fr. Acad.* II. 565 God, who is aljust, almightie, and algood. **1857** EMERSON *Poems* 23 This monument of my despair Build I to the All-Good, All-Fair.

allgood (ˈɔːlgʊd), *sb.* [ALL- E 6.] A popular name of the herb (*Chenopodium Bonus-Henricus*), also called English Mercury, and Good King Henry.

1578 LYTE *Dodoens* 560 Algood groweth..about wayes and pathes and by hedges. **1616** SURFLET & MARKH. *Country Farm* I. 58 Take the leaues of Plantaine..Mallowes, Allgood. **1853** *N. & Q.* Ser. I. VIII. 36/1 Mercury Goose-foot..It is also called All-good.

ˌall ˈhail, *int. phr.*, *sb.*, *v.* [ALL- E 1 + HAIL health.] A salutation: *lit.* (I wish you) all health! Hence, **A.** *int.* expressing affectionate recognition or welcome.

c **1400** *Rom. Rose* 3219 She seide: 'Alhayle, my swete freende!' **1526** TINDALE *Matt.* xxviii. 9 Iesus met them sayinge: All hayle! [WYCLIF Heil ȝe!]. **1821** BYRON *Cain* I. 1 Jehovah, with returning light, All-hail.

B. *sb.* A bidding All-hail! a salutation of respect and welcome.

1605 SHAKS. *Macb.* I. v. 57 Great Glamys! worthy Cawdor! Greater then both, by the all-haile hereafter! **1826** SCOTT *Woodst.* x, Frequently repeated his welcomes and all-hails.

C. *v.* To salute with All-hail! to salute a new king, a long-absent friend, etc.

1605 SHAKS. *Macb.* I. v. 8 Missiues from the King, who all-hail'd me, 'Thane of Cawdor.' **1615** A. STAFFORD *Heauenly Dogge* 90 The Sun..shines freely, and is of all-hailed. **1805** SOUTHEY *Madoc in W.* i. Wks. V. 5 The happy mariners all-hail Their native shore.

all-hail, -hal, -hale, north. ff. ALL-WHOLE.

all-haillie, -halelie, north. ff. ALL-WHOLLY.

All-Hallow, -s (ˌɔːlˈhæləʊz). [ALL- E 1 + *hallows* pl. of *hallow*, OE. *hálȝa*, a holy (man), a saint. The nom. pl. *hálȝan* passed through the forms *halwen, halowen, halowe, halowes*. The gen. pl. *hálȝena* with *-tide*, *-day*, became *halwene, halwen, halowen, hallowen, hallown, hallon, hollan, holland*.]

1. All saints, the saints (in heaven) collectively. (Often as dedication of a church.)

c **1000** ÆLFRIC *Gram.* ix. §18. 43 *November*: se mónað ongynð on ealra hálȝena mæssedæȝ. *c* **1375** *Layfolk's Mass Bk.* 8 To God full of myght, And to his modir mayden bryght, And to alle halouse here. **1413** LYDG. *Pylgr. Sowle* v. vi. (1859) 78 In the feste of al halowen, euery saynt..taketh his owne place. *c* **1450** *Knt. de la Tour* 106 The pistelle upon the feest of alhalwynne. **1494** FABYAN VII. ccxx. 242 Vsed to swere by Alhalowes, that he had nat one peny. **1528** MORE *Heresyes* II. Wks. 1557, 196/1 Ye conclude yᵉ thinge displeasant to god and to all hallowes. **1552** LYNDESAY *Complaynt* 190, I hald thareto, man, be allhallow. **1565** CALFHILL *Answ. Treat. Crosse* (1846) 67 The devout fathers..did consecrate a church in the same place unto All-Hallous. **1646** *Ordin. Lords & Comm.* 9 Alhallowes in Bread Street.

2. = All Hallows' Day, or All-hallowmas. *arch.*

1503 *Plumpton Corr.* 183 If he come againe afor alhallowes. **1647** CRASHAW *Poems* 21 How fit our well-rank'd Feasts do follow, All mischief comes after All-Hallow.

3. ***All Hallows' Day***: All Saints' Day; the first of November. *arch.*

1483 CAXTON *G. de la Tour* G vij, Thepystle of al hallowen day. **1493** *Festivall* (W. de Worde 1515) 147 b, Good frendes suche a daye ye shall haue all halowen daye. **1552** *Chron. Grey Friars* 76 On alhallon day began the boke of the new servis of bred and wyne in Powlles. Item after allhollan day was no more communyon but on the sondayes.

4. ***All Hallow Eve***: the eve of All Saints. (See also HALLOW-E'EN.) *arch.*

1556 *Chron. Grey Friars* 17 Thys yere the towne of Depe was tane..on Halhalon evyn. **1603** SHAKS. *Meas. for M.* II. i. 130 *Clo.* Was't not at Hallowmas, master Froth? *Fro.* Allhallond-Eue. **1698** STOW *Surv.* (ed. Strype 1754) I. I. xxix. 304/1 These Lords (of misrule) beginning their rule at Alholland Eve.

5. ***Allhallowmass***: the feast of All Saints. *arch.*

1083 *O.E. Chron.* (Laud MS.) Æfter ealra halȝena mæsse dæȝ. *c* **1325** *Cœur de Lion* 5878 And wente home at Alhalewemeise. **1330** R. BRUNNE *Chron.* 145 Þe moneth of Nouembre, after Alhalwemesse. *c* **1425** WYNTOUN *Cron.* VIII. xiii. 177 Fra þe Alhalowmes..til yhule he bydand wes. **1598** SHAKS. *Merry W.* I. i. 211 Upon Allhallowmas last, a fortnight afore Michaelmas. **1725** H. BOURNE *Antiq. Vulg.* xix, Lighted tapers..were then wont to cease till the next All-hallow-mass.

6. ***Allhallowtide***: the season of All Saints. *arch.*

1548 *Chron. Grey Friars* 57 This yere before Alhallontyd was sett up the howse for the markyt folke in Newgate market for to waye melle in. **1549** DK. SOMERSET in Strype *Eccl. Mem.* VI. 409 Parliament cannot be assembled before Allhallowntide. **1578** R. SCOT *Hoppe Garden* 17 Cut your Poales betweene All hallowentyde and Christmas. **1592** MASCALL *Plant. & Graff.* 16 Betwixt Alhallowtide & Christmas. **1653** WALTON *Angler* 222 About All-hollantide, when you see men ploughing up heath-ground. **1679** BURNET *Hist. Ref.* 290 The final payment being to be at allhallontide. **1743** *Lond. & Count. Brewer* III. (ed. 2) 171 From Michaelmas to Alhollantide, their Well-Water has such an earthy ill Quality.

7. ***All-Hallown Summer***: a season of fine weather in the late autumn; also *fig.* brightness or beauty lingering or reappearing in old age. Apparently *Obs.*, but worthy of revival, as much superior to its equivalents, *St. Martin's Summer* (from French), and the *Indian Summer* of America.

1596 SHAKS. *1 Hen. IV*, I. ii. 178 Farwell the latter Spring! Farwell, Alhollown Summer!

ˈall-ˌheal. [ALL- E 4.]

†**1.** A balsam or medicine that heals all wounds; a heal-all or panacea. *Obs.*

1630 DRAYTON *Muses Elys.*, *Nymphal* v. Wks. 1793, 621/2 This all-heal..New wounds so quickly healing. **1633** G. HERBERT *Offering* iv. in *Temple* 141 There is a balsome..which doth both cleanse and close all sorts of wounds..Seek out this All-heal.

2. A name applied to various plants, in consequence of virtues ascribed to them, as—

†**a.** The Mistletoe. †**b.** An umbelliferous plant, *Opoponax Chironium*, native to the S. of Europe. **c.** The Great Valerian (*V. officinalis*). †**d.** The Milfoil or Yarrow. **e.** A local name ('in Cheshire and Yorkshire' Britten and Holl.) of the plant also called Self-heal (*Prunella vulgaris*). **f. Clown's Allheal**: A name given by Gerard to the Woundwort (*Stachys palustris*).

1597 GERARD *Herbal* 850 Hercules Alheale or Woundwoort. *Ibid.* 851 Clownes Woundwoort or Alheale. **1598** FLORIO, *Achilea*, the hearb Yarrow, All-heale, Nose-bleed, or Milfoile. **1601** HOLLAND *Pliny* (1634) I. 497 They call it [Mistletoe] in their language All-Heale, (for they haue an opinion of it, that it cureth all maladies whatsoeuer). **1725** BRADLEY *Fam. Dict.* s.v. *Cancer*, Take the Flowers and Stems of the Herb All-Heal (the Flowers are white and very small).

all-ˈhid. [From the words called out by the hiding party.] The game of 'Hide-and-Seek.'

1608 TOURNEUR *Rev. Trag.* III. v. 82 A lady can At such al-hid beguile a wiser man.

ˌall-ˈholy, *a.* [ALL- E 6.] Altogether or infinitely holy.

a **1000** *Metr. Ps.* cxxxi. 8 Đú earce eart eall háliȝra. *c* **1360** WYCLIF *De Dot Eccl.* 10 He was clepid þe pope & hed of alhooli chirche. **1586** T. ROGERS *39 Art.* (1607) 35 The all-holy and sacred scripture. **1865** PUSEY *Truth Eng. Ch.* 273 In the Name of the All-Holy Trinity.

†**ˈall-hood.** *Obs. rare*$^{-1}$. [f. ALL + -HOOD. (app. formed in loc. cit. as an explanation of *allodium*.)] Entire estate, entirety.

1722 WOLLASTON *Relig. Nat.* vi. 136, *P* has therefore the all or all-hood of it.

allia, variant of ALLYA, *Obs. Sc.*, an ally.

alliable (əˈlaɪəb(ə)l), *a. rare.* [a. Fr. *alliable*, f. *allier* to ally, combine: see ALLY and -ABLE.] Able to enter into alliance or union.

1795 BURKE *Scarcity* Wks. VII. 415 Poor meagre diet, not easily alliable to the human constitution. **1796** —— *Regic. Peace* Wks. 1842 II. 310 How far it is in its nature alliable with the rest. **1852** JAMES *Pequin.* I. 265 Fancy is alliable to all things but dulness.

alliably (əˈlaɪəblɪ), *adv. rare*$^{-1}$. In 6 **aliably**. [f. prec. + -LY².] In an alliable manner; by way of alliance or affinity.

1592 G. HARVEY *Pierce's Supererog.* in *Archaica* II. 86 Honour aliably belongeth to redoubted Seniours.

alliaceous (ælɪˈeɪʃəs), *a.* [f. L. *alli-um* garlic + -ACEOUS.] **a.** Of or pertaining to the botanical genus *Allium*, including garlic, onions, leeks, etc. **b.** Having the smell or taste of garlic and onions.

1792 *Phil. Trans.* LXXXII. 303 It had, like the rest of the powder in the tube, an alliaceous smell. **1818** ACCUM *Chem. Tests* 162 The alliaceous odour peculiar to arsenic. **1828** KIRBY & SPENCE *Entomol.* II. xxi. 240 Many wild bees are distinguished by their pungent alliaceous smell. **1861** E. LANKESTER *Food* 267 All belong to the same genus allium, hence we call them alliaceous plants.

†**ˈalliage.** *Obs.* In 5 **aliage**, 6 **alleage**. [a. Fr. *al-, alliage*, f. *allier*: see ALLY and -AGE.] Alliance.

c **1450** *Roll* in *3rd Rep. Comm. Hist. MSS.* (1872) 279/2 The Frenshemen alied them selfe and enlarge their amite, and their aliage to suche as were beste oute of the kynge's amite. **1546** BALE *Eng. Votaries* I. (1550) 41 b, The late ouerthrowe of the monasteries, couentes, colleges, and chaunteries, alleages of uncleane spretes.

alliance (əˈlaɪəns), *sb.* Forms: 3–7 **aliˈance**, 3–6 **alyˈance**, 4–5 **alyˈaunse, allyˈaunce**, 4–6 **ali-, aly-, alliˈaunce, 5 alyans, alyˈawns**, 6–8 **allyance**, 4– **aˈlliance**. By-form 3 **enlyance**. [a. OFr. *aliance*, 14th c. *alliance*: see ALLY and -ANCE; repr. L. *alligantia* (found in med.L.) n. of state, f. *alligant-em* pr. pple. of *alligāre*. Accented *alliˈance* in 16th c.] The state of union or combination; the action of uniting or combining.

1. Union by marriage, affinity; union through marriage or common parentage, relationship, kinship, consanguinity.

1297 R. GLOUC. 12 He bygan to loue Brut so muche..þat he wyllede..to hym enlyance. *Ibid.* 295 To spouse hyre ..þat he myȝte, þoru alyance, eny help vndergo. *c* **1365** CHAUCER *A.B.C.* 60 He vouchedsafe..Become a man as for our alliaunce [*v.r.* allyaunce, aliaunce, aliance]. **1393** GOWER *Conf.* III. 280 Which of sibred in aliaunce For ever kepten thilke usaunce. **1469** J. PASTON *Lett.* 612 II. 357 Consyderyng the alyans betwyx yow. **1481** CAXTON *Myrr.* II. viii. 85 Mariages and Alyaunces that they doo and make wyth the sarasyns. **1548** COVERDALE *Erasm. Paraphr. Hebr.* ii. 17 Ioyned vnto hym with so streighte a bonde of alyaunce or consanguinitie. *a* **1674** CLARENDON *Hist. Reb.* I. Pref. 18 The Allyance was undeniable; there were Children born of it. **1729** BURKITT *On N.T.*, *Mark* iii. 3 Alliance by faith is more valued by our Saviour, than alliance by blood. **1877** LYTTEIL *Landm.* IV. viii. 225 The descendants of Scottish and Celtic alliances may have acquired the Gaelic tongue.

2. a. Combination for a common object, confederation, union offensive and defensive; especially between sovereign states.

1366 MAUNDEV. xviii. 195 To breke the Alliance and the Acord. *c* **1374** CHAUCER *Boethius* (1868) 141 Þer nis none alyaunce bytwixe good[e] folke and shrewes. *c* **1425** WYNTOUN *Cron.* VII. viii. 170 In fermly festnyd alyawns To þe Kyng. **1477** EARL RIVERS (Caxton) *Dictes* 106 Him that hath made any aliaunce or promesse with his ennemyes. **1519** SIR T. BOLEYN in Ellis *Orig. Lett.* I. 53 I. 148 The unfeyned amytie and aliance that is established betwixt you. **1682** *Lond. Gaz.* mdcclxvii/1 An Offensive and Defensive Alliance is concluded between the French King and the Duke of Savoy. **1781** GIBBON *Decl. & F.* II. xlv. 707 The peace and alliance of the two empires were faithfully maintained. **1815** WELLINGTON in Gurwood's *Desp.* XII. 282 A treaty of alliance which I have signed with the Ministers of the Emperors of Austria and Russia. **1878** SEELEY *Stein* III. 430 That Alliance of the European Sovereigns which is somewhat inaccurately spoken of as the Holy Alliance.

b. ***Alliance Party***, the name given to any of various political parties, *esp.* one formed of Roman Catholic and Protestant moderates in Northern Ireland in 1970; freq. with ellipsis of *Party*. Also (as *Alliance*), the name applied to the political collaboration of the Liberal and Social Democratic Parties in Britain from 1981.

1970 *Economist* 25 Apr. 17/2 This revolt of the moderates was salutary. Their showing encouraged them to announce the formation of the new Alliance party, for Protestants and Roman Catholics alike, on Tuesday. **1975** *Times* 22 Apr. 2/8 The leaders of the three power-sharing parties, Alliance, SDLP and UPNI. **1977** *Belfast Tel.* 14 Feb. 11/6 Alliance councillor Mrs. Muriel Pritchard has appealed to candidates in the May local government elections not to stick posters on public property. **1977** *Financial Times* 6 Apr. 7/2 It was the 20,000 Fijian voters who deserted their traditional Alliance Party to vote for other Nationalist candidates. **1981** *Times* 1 Oct. 5/8 An amendment..stating that, as the Social Democratic Alliance had decided to support an organization opposing Labour MPs, the Alliance was now ineligible for affiliation to the party. **1983** *Whitaker's Almanack 1984* 687 Members of the Northern Ireland Assembly...Alliance Party...Democratic Unionist Party [etc.]. **1985** *Church Times* 14 June 12/5 It is..because these Christian values are apparently being cast off by the present leadership of the Conservative Party..that many Christians are turning to the Alliance.

3. Community or relationship in nature or qualities; affinity; inclusion in the same class.

1677 R. GILPIN *Dæmon. Sac.* (1867) 28 This word is ranked with others, as being of the same alliance. **1754** SHERLOCK *Disc.* (1759) I. iv. 153 Corrupt Principles..have no Alliance with Reason. **1833** I. TAYLOR *Fanat.* x. 451 The ordinary alliance of the moral sentiments with the imagination. **1860** MANSEL *Prolegom. Log.* (ed. 2) Pref. 6 The alliance established of old between Logic and Metaphysics.

†**4.** *collect.* People united by kinship or friendship; kindred, friends, allies. *Obs.* [Perh. confused with *Alliants*, OFr. *alians*; cf. ACCIDENCE.]

1366 MAUNDEV. xviii. 195 Accorded be here Frendes or be sum of here Alliance. **1393** GOWER *Conf.* I. 199 Thilke alliaunce, By whom the treson was compassed. *c* **1400** *Destr. Troy* XXVIII. 11390 Antenor also was abill of fryndes, Large of aliaunce. **1548** UDALL etc. *Erasm. Paraphr. Mark* vi. 4 His alyance, kinnesmen, and famyliares. **1601** SHAKS. *Jul. C.* IV. i. 43 Therefore let our Alliance be combin'd. **1655** GOUGE

Comm. Hebr. xi. 15 III. 58 This Country..where their kindred, alliance, and other friends were.

†**5.** *individual*, A kinsman, relation, or ally. *Obs.*

1536-7 in *Reg. Abp. Lee, York MS.*, To Thomas Hugaite, my allyaunce, my best doublet. **1586** FERNE *Blaz. Gentrie* Ded., A worshipful friend and allyance of mine. **1654** USSHER *Annals* VII. (1658) 801 He requested that..he would give him leave to see again his alliances.

6. *Bot.* A name given by Lindley to groups of Natural Orders of plants, considered to be allied to each other in general structure; thus the *Glumal Alliance* of Endogens contains the *Grasses*, *Cyperaceæ*, and three other allied orders.

1836 LINDLEY *Nat. Syst.* (ed. 2) xiv, Classes, sub-classes, groups, alliances, and orders. **1838** —— in *Penny Cycl.* X. 126 The terminations of the names express their value; the groups end in *-osæ*; the alliances in *-ales*; the orders in *-aceæ*; the suborders in *-eæ*. **1848** —— *Veg. Kingd.* 8 The near approach of the two realms being through the Algal alliance. **1866** J. BALFOUR in *Treas. Bot.* 267 A natural order of dicotyledons, characterizing Lindley's chenopodal alliance.

¶ By confusion, for ALLEGIANCE.

a **1581** CAMPIAN *Hist. Irel.* II. i. 58 The subjects whom they had schooled, to breake allyance towards the King of Leinster. **1714** BURNET *Hist. Ref.*, The bishops did all renew their alliance to the king.

alliance (əˈlaɪəns), *v. rare.* [f. prec. sb. Cf. OFr. *aliancier*, and Eng. *affiance*.]

1. *trans.* To join in alliance, to ally.

a **1688** CUDWORTH *Serm.* 62 (L.) It is allianced to none but wretched, forlorn, and apostate spirits.

2. *intr.* To form alliances, ally oneself.

1782 T. PAINE *To Abbé Raynel* (1791) 50 Courts..are relatively republics with each other. It is the first and true principle of alliancing.

alliancer (əˈlaɪənsə(r)). *rare.* [f. prec. + -ER[1].] One who enters into or belongs to an alliance.

1653 URQUHART *Rabelais* (1807) III. 265 We sailed right before the wind..leaving those odd alliancers.

†**aˈlliant**, *a.* and *sb. Obs. rare.* [a. Fr. *alliant*, OFr. *aliant*, pr. pple. of *allier* to ALLY.]

A. *adj.* In alliance, in league; related, akin.

1551 ROBINSON tr. *More's Utop.* (1869) 118 This kynde of learninge..is sumwhat allyaunte to them.

B. *sb.* One in league; an ally.

1620 *Reliq. Wotton.* (1672) 532 Princes, Catholick Estates and Alliants, have excluded from this present Treaty the Kingdom of Bohemia. **1656** BLOUNT *Glossogr.*, *Alliant* or *Ally*, one that is in league, or of kindred with another.

alliant, -aunt, obs. forms of ALIEN.

alliarious (ælɪˈɛərɪəs), *a. rare*[—0]. [f. med.L. *alliāri-us* of the nature of *allium* + -OUS.]

1879 in *Syd. Soc. Lex.*

†**ˈalliate**, *a. Obs. rare.* [ad. L. *alliāt-us* composed of ALLIUM: see -ATE.] Composed of garlic, having garlic as an ingredient.

1661 LOVELL *Anim. & Min.* 235 Eaten with alliate sauce.

allice, allis (ˈælɪs). *Zool.* Also 7 **allowes**. [a. Fr. *alose*:—L. *alōsa, alausa*, the shad.] A fish of the Herring family, more commonly called the **allice-shad** (*Alosa communis*) found in the Severn.

1620 VENNER *Via Recta* iv. 75 The Allowes is taken in the same places that Sammon is. **1777** PENNANT *Brit. Zool.* (1812) III. 463 The Severn Shad is sometimes caught in the Thames, though rarely, and called *Allis* (no doubt *Alose*, the French name) by the fishermen. **1882** *Standard* 2 Mar. 2/8 The Allice shad is an excellent fish, and attains to a weight of four or five pounds.

allicholly, jocosely in Shaks. for MELANCHOLY.

1591 SHAKS. *Two Gent.* IV. ii. 27 Now my yong guest; me thinks your' allycholly. **1598** —— *Merry W.* I. iv. 163 Shee is giuen too much to Allicholy and musing. **1736** H. WALPOLE *Lett.* (1861) I. 8 A disconsolate wood-pigeon in our grove..is so allicholly as any thing.

†**aˈlliciate**, *v. Obs.* [f. Fr. *alicier, allicier*, to attract, entice, irreg. f. L. *allic-ĕre*. See also ALLICIT, ALLECT.] To allure, entice, attract.

1568 C. WATSON *Polyb.* To Reader, The matter is of importance inough to alliciate al men to the reading hereof. **1620** VENNER *Via Recta* viii. 166 My counsell is..that the stomacke be by no meanes vntimely alliciated vnto meate. **1657** TOMLINSON *Renou's Disp.* 404 They may alliciate watry and serous humours to those parts.

†**aˈlliciency.** *Obs.* [f. ALLICIENT *a.* (see -NCY) as if ad. L. **allicient-ia*, n. of quality f. *allicient-em*.]

The quality of being attractive; attractiveness; attractive power or influence.

1646 SIR T. BROWNE *Pseud. Ep.* 66 If the Loadstone attract, the steele hath also its attraction; for in this action the Alliciency is reciprocall. **1665** GLANVILLE *Sceps. Sci.* xx. 126 The feigned Central alliciency is but a word. **1755** in JOHNSON; and in mod. Dicts.

allicient (əˈlɪʃənt), *ppl. a.* and *sb. rare.* [ad. L. *allicient-em* pr. pple. of *allic-ĕre* to entice to; f. *al-* = *ad-* to + *-licĕre* = *lacĕre* to catch with a noose or gin (*laqueus*), to entrap.]

A. *adj.* Attracting.

1831 P. HEIDIGER *Didon.* I. 20 All rosy smiles..Allicient, blooming like immortal Hebe.

B. *sb.* Anything attracting; that which attracts.

1658 J. ROBINSON *Eudoxa* 121 (T.) The awakened needle, with joy, leapeth towards its allicient.

†**aˈllicit**, *v. Obs.* [f. L. *allicĕre*, after *elicit* f. *ēlicĕre, ēlicit-um*; but the pple. of *allicĕre* was *allect-um*, from which the etymological derivative is ALLECT. See also ALLICIATE.] To entice, attract.

1725 CHEYNE *Health & Long Life* 79 (L.) To allicite blood and spirits to the parts most distant.

†**aˈllide**, *v. Obs.*[—0] [ad. L. *allīd-ĕre* to dash against, f. *al-* = *ad-* to + *līdĕre* = *læd-ĕre* to dash or strike violently.] 'To dash or hit against.' Bailey 1721; whence in Ash 1775, etc.

allied (əˈlaɪd), *ppl. a.* Forms: 3 **alied**, 5 **alyed**, 6 **allyde, alide**, 7 **allyed**, (8 **allay'd**), 4- **allied**. [f. ALLY *v.* + -ED.]

1. United, joined: **a.** by kindred or affinity.

1297 R. GLOUC. 65 To be in such mariage alied to þe emperour. *c* **1400** *Destr. Troy* IV. 1284 A knight noble, Aliet vnto Lamydon by his lefe suster. **1587** TURBERVILLE *Trag. T.* (1837) 33, I to thee am verie neere allyde. **1591** SHAKS. *Two Gent.* IV. i. 49 A Lady..alide vnto the Duke. **1725** POPE *Odyss.* VI. 186 Bless'd are the brethren who thy blood divide, To such a miracle of charms allied. **1861** MACAULAY *Hist. Eng.* V. 103 A German Princess nearly allied to the Imperial House.

b. by league or formal treaty.

1393 GOWER *Conf.* III. 275 The route apostazied Of hem that ben to him allied. **1490** CAXTON *Eneydos* xii. 46 Wher is he that shalle..make warre ayenste the thus alyed? **1611** SHAKS. *Wint. T.* I. ii. 339 Courts and kingdomes Knowne, and ally'd to yours. **1860** MAURY *Phys. Geog. Sea* xix. 803 The celebrated Black Sea storm which did so much damage to the allied fleet. **1870** KNIGHT *Crown Hist. Eng.* lix. 800 The Treaty of Vienna..had bound the Allied Powers to make war together upon Napoleon.

c. generally. ? *Obs.*

1483 CAXTON *Cato* d vij b, When two good frendes ben wel alyed to gyder they ben stronger. **1611** BIBLE *Wisd.* viii. 17 To be allyed vnto wisedome, is immortalitie. **1667** MARVELL *Corr.* 36 Wks. 1875 II. 82 A friend..sincerely devoted and allyed to your interests.

2. *fig.* Related, connected by nature, properties, or similitude, akin.

1603 SHAKS. *Meas. for M.* III. ii. 108 The vice is of a great kindred: it is vvell allied. **1681** DRYDEN *Abs. & Achit.* 163 Great wits are sure to madness near allied. **1709** CODRINGTON in *Garth's Dispens.* (1709) Pref., So near allay'd in Learning, Wit, and Skill. **1854** HOOKER *Himal. Jrnls.* II. xviii. 50 Various allied insects. **1856** KANE *Arct. Expl.* II. xvii. 180 An anomalous spasmodic disorder, allied to tetanus.

alligant, obs. f. ALICANTE; catachr. for ELEGANT.

alligar, obs. form of ALEGAR.

alligarta, obs. form of ALLIGATOR[2].

†**ˈalligate**, *ppl. a. Obs. rare*[—1]. [ad. L. *alligāt-us* pa. pple. of *alligāre* to bind to, f. *al-* = *ad-* to + *ligāre* to bind, tie.] Bound together, connected.

1542 RECORDE *Gr. Artes* (1575) 419 Dyuers parcels of sundry pryces..alligate, bounde, or mixed togither.

alligate (ˈælɪgeɪt), *v.* ? *Obs.* [f. prec., or on analogy of vbs. so formed.]

†**1.** To tie or unite (one thing to another). *Obs.*

1626 COCKERAM, *Alligate*, to binde, or tie vp. **1677** HALE *Prim. Orig. Man.* IV. ii. 305 By the same Divine Ordination ..the Faculties specifically belonging to every Individual were annexed and alligated to it.

2. To perform the arithmetical process of alligation.

1671 SALMON *Syn. Med.* III. 501 Alligate alternately the quality of the Medicine proposed, with the degree of the Simple with which you desire to raise or depress it.

†**ˈalligated**, *ppl. a. Obs.* [f. prec. + -ED.] Bound, connected, united.

1677 HALE *Prim. Orig. Man.* IV. viii. 375 Connatural Instincts alligated to their nature.

alligation (ælɪˈgeɪʃən). [ad. L. *alligātiōn-em*, n. of action f. *alligāre*: see ALLIGATE.]

1. The action of attaching by some bond; the state of being attached, physical conjunction. *rare.*

a **1555** RIDLEY *Wks.* 266 Christ's church is universally spread throughout the world, not contained in the alligation of places. **1651** J. F. *Agrippa's Occult. Phil.* 92 Vitall vertue is sent..from the trunk to the twig graffed into it, by way of contact and alligation. **1868** SEYD *Bullion* 238 Iridium is found..in alligation with the latter metal.

2. The 'Rule of Mixtures'; the arithmetical method of solving questions concerning the mixing of articles of different qualities or values.

1542 RECORDE *Gr. Artes* (1575) 419 Alligation..hath his name, for that by it there are dyuers parcels of sundry pryces, and sundrie quantities, alligate, bounde or mixed togither. **1695** ALINGHAM *Geom. Epit.* 73 The Rules of Fellowship, Alligation, with others. **1827** HUTTON *Course Math.* I. 133 *Alligation* teaches how to compound or mix together several simples of different qualities, so that the composition may be of some intermediate quality, or rate. It is commonly distinguished into two cases, Alligation Medial, and Alligation Alternate. **1833** *Pen. Cycle.* I. 348/2 *Alligation*..by which the price of a mixture is found when the price of the ingredients is known.

†**alliˈgator**[1]. *Obs.*[—0] [a. L. *alligātōr*, agent-noun f. *alligā-re* to bind: see ALLIGATE *a.*] One who binds or ties.

1706 PHILLIPS, *Alligator*, a Binder or Tyer of the Vines to their Stakes. **1731** BAILEY, *Alligator*, a binder.

alligator[2] (ˈælɪgeɪtə(r)). *Zool.* Forms: 6 **lagarto, alagarto, aligarto**, 7 **alegarto, alligarta, allegater, aligator**, 7-8 **allegator**, 7- **alligator**. [orig. ad. Sp. *el* or *al lagarto* the lizard, (pointing to a dial. L. *lacarta* for *lacerta*,) applied *par excellence* to the gigantic saurians of the New World. In Eng. the word soon became *allagarto, alagarto*, reduced to *alegarto, alligarta*, whence by pop. corruption *alligarter, allegater, alligator*, the medial (ɑː(r)) becoming (ɑː) now (eɪ), and the final *o* taking *r*, as in *'tatur* (potato), *buffaler, feller*, etc. As the spelling *alligator* had a literary and etymological appearance, it was established in the lang., and has since been adopted in Fr.

('Some of our older writers on..America affirm that it is merely a modification of the Indian word *legateer* or *allegater*.' *Penny Cycl.* I. 349.)]

1. a. A genus of saurian reptiles of the crocodile family, also called Caymans, of which the various species are found in America; popularly the name is extended to all large American Saurians, some of which are true crocodiles.

1568 J. HORTOP (Hakl. Soc.) III. 580 In this river we killed a monstrous Lagarto or Crocodile. **1577** FRAMPTON *Joyfull Newes* II. (1596) 73 b, Caimanes, that are called Lagartos. **1591** A. KNIVET in Purchas *Pilgr.* IV. 1228 Aligartos (which we call in English crocodiles). **1593** R. HAWKINS *Voy. S. Sea* (1847) 178 In this river, and all the rivers of this coast, are great abundance of alagartoes. **1614** RALEIGH *Hist. World* I. 96 The Crocodiles (now called Alegartos). **1614** B. JONSON *Barth. Fair* II. vi. (1631) 28 Who can tell, if..the Alligarta hath not piss'd thereon? **1623** SHAKS. *Rom. & Jul.* V. i. 43 (*1st Fol.*) In his needie shop a tortoyrs hung, An Allegater stuft [**1597** *1st Qo.* Aligarta]. **1663** COWLEY *Vis. Cromwell* in *Verses, &c.* (1669) 71 He must have his prey of the whole Indies both by Sea and Land, this great Aligator. **1692** COLES, *Alegator*, a Jamaica Crocodile. **1697** DAMPIER *Voy.* (1729) I. 256 We found no Allegators here, tho' there are several. **1699** GARTH *Dispens.* II. 19 And near, a scaly Alligator hung. **1738** MORTIMER in *Phil. Trans.* XL. 345 The Spaniards first gave them the Name of Allagarto..and from the Words Al Lagarto, our English Sailors have formed the Word Alligator. **1756** *Ibid.* XLIX. 640 A young allegator..here laid before you. **1824** W. IRVING *T. Trav.* II. 254 Like alligators sleeping in the mire. **1880** HAUGHTON *Phys. Geogr.* iii. 82 The alligator thrives in the neighbourhood of New Orleans. **1882** *Daily News* 8 June 5/3 The profession of alligator farming has been developed in California.

b. [absol. use of sense 4 c below.] Alligator skin or material resembling this; also *pl.*, shoes of alligator or mock-alligator skin (orig. *U.S.*).

1905-6 *T. Eaton & Co. Catal.* Fall & Winter 180/1 Buff alligator, inside frame, moire silk lined,..colors tan, brown, blue and green. **1951** *Vogue* 1 Mar. 194 Take it for granted —the red shoe..for city, country: alligator. **1952** *Creative Footwear* Mar. 24/1 Easter footwear for women is already being sold, and the shell pump in alligator. **1978** J. WAMBAUGH *Black Marble* xv. 341 There was no way he could..clean the blood and feces from his imitation alligators.

2. *Mining.* **a.** A rock-breaker operating by jaws. **b.** A 'Squeezer' or machine for reducing the puddle-ball to a compact mass. Raymond's *Gloss.*

3. a. *U.S. slang.* A non-playing devotee of swing music, a hep-cat. (No longer in use.)

1936 *Delineator* Nov. 10/2 You are there as an alligator, so don't applaud. **1939** *Collier's* 8 Apr. 9/2 It's this jive, hep-cat, alligator, jitterbug craze—this swing mania! **1943** *N.Y. Times* 9 May II. 5/5 The alligators started to fall in at the crack of dawn. **1952** C. R. COOPER *Teen-Age Vice* (1959) iv. 58 Alligators and hep-cats, or non-performing swing fans.

b. In rhyming catch-phrase ***see you later, alligator (in a while, crocodile)***, etc., used at parting. Cf. ABYSSINIA and SEE *v.* 12 e. *slang.*

1957 R. C. GUIDRY *See you later, Alligator* (song) 3 See you lat-er, al-li-ga-tor, Aft-er 'while, croc-o-dile,—Can't you see you're in my way, now, Don't you know you cramp my style? **1959** I. & P. OPIE *Lore & Lang. Schoolch.* ii. 17 Rhyme seems to appeal to a child as something funny and remarkable in itself, there being neither wit nor reason to support it... Hence the way lines of current dance songs become catch phrases..'See you later, alligator'—'In a while, crocodile', repeated *ad nauseam* in 1956. **1960** P. MORTIMER *Saturday Lunch with Brownings* 38 'See you later, Alligator.' 'See you in a little while, Crocodile.' **1960** J. MACLAREN-ROSS *Until Day she Dies* ii. 32 'Alligator,' she seemed to say, before the crowd closed round and hid her from sight. **1978** J. WAMBAUGH *Black Marble* v. 67 Giving Tyrone McGee a chance to grin malevolently..and say, 'Catch you later, alligator'.

4. a. *Comb.* **alligator apple**, the fruit of a West Indian tree, *Anona palustris*; **alligator gar**: see GAR *sb.* b (also *alligator snapper, terrapin, turtle*: see at second element); **alligator pear**, the fruit of a West Indian tree, *Persea gratissima* (also called *Laurus persea*), allied to the laurels; **alligator tortoise**, a large species of marsh tortoise (*Chelydra serpentina*, fam. *Emydidæ*), found in the waters of Carolina, also called the

Snapping Turtle; **alligator wood**, the timber of a West Indian tree, *Guarea Swartzii*.

1866 M. T. MASTERS in *Treas. Bot.* 70 The fruit is called the Alligator Apple, but is not eaten as it contains a narcotic principle. **1821** in *Texas Hist. Q.* VII. 300 Found another Karanqua encamp at which was..Alligator heads and the skins of Alligator Gars. **1843** [see GAR *sb.*]. **1944** *Reader's Digest* July 110 A huge alligator gar rips their nets to pieces, destroying the labor of weeks. **1763** GRAINGER *Sug. Cane* I. *note* 9 The avocato, avocado, avigato, or, as the English corruptly call it, alligator-pear. **1861** TYLOR *Anahuac* ix. 227 There is a well-known West Indian fruit which we call an avocado or alligator-pear, and which the French call 'avocat' and the Spaniards 'aguacate.' All these names are corruptions of the Aztec name of the fruit, 'ahuacatl.' **1884** GOODE *Nat. Hist. Aquat. Anim.* 153 An Alligator Snapper of perhaps forty pounds weight. **1835** W. G. SIMMS *Partisan* 317 Three enormous terrapins of that doubtful brood which the vulgar in the southern country describe as the alligator terrapin. **1888** Alligator terrapin [see SNAPPER *sb.*[1] 7 c]. **1842** J. E. DE KAY *Zool. N.Y.* III. 8 The Snapping Turtle..is one of our largest turtles... In other sections, it is known under the names of Logger-head, Alligator Turtle and Couta. **1885** J. S. KINGSLEY *Stand. Nat. Hist.* III. 452 The elongated tail of this animal..has..given rise to the popular name, 'alligator-turtle'. **1725** SLOANE *Jamaica* ii. 24 Alleygator or Musk-Wood..The Smell [of the trunk] is sweet like Musk, or that of an Alleygator, whence the name. **1837** MACFADYEN *Fl. Jamaica* 173 The Alligator Wood.

b. Used *attrib.* of a device or apparatus, as clips, forceps, etc., resembling in form or action the jaws of an alligator (cf. sense 2).

a **1884** KNIGHT *Dict. Mech.* Suppl. 22/1 Alligator Forceps. **1940** *Chambers's Techn. Dict.* 23/1 *Alligator wrench*, a tool with fixed serrated jaws, used for twisting and screwing pipes into position. **1952** *Brit. Jrnl. Psychol.* XLIII. 86 Alligator clips with platinum electrodes soldered to the jaws were attached to the rat's ears.

c. *attrib.* Of shoes, handbags, etc.: made of alligator skin or material resembling this. orig. *U.S.*

[**1869** W. H. H. MURRAY *Adventures in Wilderness* 26 A pair of huge alligator-leather boots.] **1892** *Harper's Mag.* Feb. 486/2 'Are you the man who invented paper soles for shoes?'.. 'Yes, sir; also..paper alligator bags.' **1895** *Montgomery Ward Catal.* Spring & Summer 519/2 Men's genuine alligator slippers. **1897** *Sears, Roebuck Catal.* 252/2 Fine alligator club bag, made of selected goat skin. **1950** 'N. SHUTE' *Town like Alice* vii. 202 The only work she really knew about was fancy leather goods, alligator shoes and handbags and attaché cases. **1984** *Washington Post* 27 Aug. (Business Suppl.) 15/1 Cedar Post..was one of the first stores in that area that sold alligator boots.

ˈalligatoring, *vbl. sb.* orig. *U.S.* The cracking and retraction of paint, varnish, etc., caused by contraction.

1911 *Engin. News* (N.Y.) 27 July 121 Many of the paints which lack any evidence of cracking, checking, or alligatoring. **1953** *Glossary Paint Terms (B.S.I.)* 11 *Crocodiling or alligatoring*, a drastic type of crazing producing a pattern resembling the hide of a crocodile.

† **aˈlligature.** *Obs.*[—0] [ad. L. *alligātūra*, f. *alligāre*: see ALLIGATE *a.* and -URE.]

1. 'A tying or binding to.' Bailey 1726.

2. 'The link or ligature by which two things are joined together. *Dict.*' J.

† **aˈllige**, *v. Obs. rare*[−1]. In 7 adl-. [f. L. *adl-*, *alligāre* (see ALLIGATE *a.*); cf. *oblige.*] = the more usual ALLIGATE *v.*

1650 W. CHARLETON *Paradoxes* 60 The mind after once it is alligated to the body, alwaies flowes downward.

all-in. Also **all in.** **1.** As predicative adj.

a. Exhausted. *colloq.*

1903 A. D. MCFAUL *Ike Glidden* xxii. 201 The horse was holding steady up to his clip, but it could be easily seen that he was 'all in'. **1904** ADE *Breaking into Society* 53 'I'm all in,' said the Wreck. **1916** 'B. M. BOWER' *Phantom Herd* xiv. 244 You better find him right there in the blizzard—hurt maybe—anyway just about all in. **1952** M. LASKI *Village* iii. 56 You look all in... Been doing too much, that's what it is.

b. Completely or wholeheartedly involved.

a **1910** 'O. HENRY' *Strictly Business* (1917) xx. 221 'On the dead level,' said Cork, holding her close with one arm, 'when it comes to you, I'm all in.' **1925** W. DEEPING *Sorrell & Son* viii. 76, I am all in on this adventure. Either we touch port—or we founder. **1933** H. G. WELLS *Shape of Things to Come* III §1. 263 It was becoming impossible to retain self-respect, to be happy within oneself, unless one was 'all in' upon that one sound objective.

2. As attrib. phr.: Inclusive of all; in *Wrestling*, without restrictions. Also *absol.*

1890 *Daily News* 17 Feb. 3/6 The all-in [Billiards] tournament at the Westminster Aquarium. **1900** N. GOULD *Settling Day* xvi. 135, 'I'll take that wager.' 'All in, run or not?' **1908** *Westm. Gaz.* 6 June 9/3 The 'all-in' system—that is to say, railway and hotel accommodation combined. **1913** J. E. G. HADATH *Schoolboy Grit* viii. 88 A fight is just a fight: Catch-as-catch-can, All-in, and Best-your-enemy-anyhow! **1924** F. W. THOMAS *Rain & Shine* 125 Our Double-Decked Combination Endowment and All-in Policy. **1927** *Daily Tel.* 7 Mar. 2 The exceptionally high all-in cost of 1*s.* 1½*d.* per lb. **1927** *Manch. Guardian Weekly* Oct. 329/2 A notable appeal for disarmament and all-in arbitration. **1929** *Times* 8 Jan. 14/1 The two-part tariffs comprise a domestic 'all-in' rate and a business 'all-in' rate. The charge per unit for electricity for..lighting, heating, cooking, and domestic and business appliances is 1*d.* per unit. **1934** E. J. HARRISON *Wrestling* ii. 16 Alike, therefore, in the Cumberland and Westmorland, Græco-Roman, Catch-as-Catch-Can, All-in, or even the Japanese *sumo* styles of the art, lightweights do not usually contend against heavyweights. *Ibid.* v. 68 Any aspirant for mat honours..will not seek to explore and master the mysteries of All-in until he has gained a good working knowledge of orthodox Catch-as-Catch-Can. **1944** 'G. ORWELL' in *Horizon* X. 242 To the extent that all-in wrestling is worse than boxing.

allineate (əˈlɪniːeɪt), *v. rare*[−1]. [f. L. *ad* to + *līneāt-* ppl. stem of *līneā-re* to draw a line. Cf. *delineate.*] = ALIGN.

1864 SIR J. HERSCHEL *Pop. Lect.* (1871) v. 184 The intended base line [must be] allineated by placing a telescope a little beyond one of its proposed extremities.

allineation, alin- (əlɪniːˈeɪʃən). [n. of action f. prec.; cf. *delineation.*]

1. = ALIGNMENT 1.

1860 *Builder* XVIII. 333/2 Even the cross streets..will claim some attention, not only to their width, but their allineation. **1881** *Daily Tel.* 31 Jan., The magnificent alineation of the New Law Courts.

2. = ALIGNMENT 3.

1837 WHEWELL *Induct. Sc.* I. iv. §1 (L.) The positions are described by means of alineations. **1863** J. DRAPER *Devel. Europe* vi. (1865) 150 Hipparchus also undertook to make a register of the stars by the method of alineations. **1866** PROCTOR *Handbk. Stars* Pref. 6 The great advantage..that the allineations of the stars are preserved.

3. The position of two or more bodies in a straight line with a given point, as of two planets in a line with the sun.

1882 YOUNG *Sun* v. 150 In some cases, sun-spot minima have coincided with the allineation of the two planets.

allinement, var. of ALIGNMENT.

† **alling(e**, *adv. Obs.* Forms: 1 allunga (WS. eallunga), 2–3 allunge, 3 allinge, 3–4 allynge, 4–5 allyng. [f. ALL, prob. instrumental case of an abst. sb. *allung* totality.] Wholly, entirely, altogether, quite, indeed.

c **880** K. ÆLFRED *Boeth.* xxx. 2 Ðe allunga underþeóded biþ unþeawum. *a* **1000** ? CÆDMON *Gen.* 477 (Grein) Eallenga sweart. *c* **1000** ÆLFRIC *Deut.* iv. 31 He eallinga ne adiligaþ eow. *c* **1000** *Ags. Gosp.* Matt. xxvi. 45 Slapað eallunga, and restað eow. *c* **1160** *Hatton G.* ibid., Slæpeð eallunge, & resteð eow. *c* **1175** *Lamb. Hom.* 185 Turn me allunge to þe. *c* **1230** *Ancr. R.* 228 Ne suffre þu nout þet te uoend allunge lede us into uondunge. **1297** R. GLOUC. 48 Þat heo shoulde allyng faile. *a* **1375** *Joseph of Arim.* 440 Hit is not allynge to carpe. *c* **1420** *Pallad. on Husb.* XII. 42 Kitte hem shortte..not v Feet longe allyng.

† **allings**, *adv. Obs.* Forms: 2 allunges, 4 -ynges, 5 -inges. [f. prec. with genitival *-s*, as in *always*, *backwards*, etc.: see -LINGS.] = prec.

c **1175** *Lamb. Hom.* 31 And þa ȝet hit were wel god moste ic alunges festen. **1366** MAUNDEV. 189 It is not allynges of suche savour. *c* **1430** *St. Katherine* (1884) 1 [Hit] was not allinges so plener in þat quayere as hit was drawe by me tofore.

alliotical: see ALLŒOTICAL.

allis, obs. variant of ALLICE.

allisanders, obs. form of ALEXANDERS.

allision (əˈlɪʒən). ? *Obs.* [ad. L. *allīsiōn-em*, n. of action f. *allīd-ĕre*: see ALLIDE.] The action of dashing against or striking with violence upon.

a **1631** DONNE *Serm.* lxxvi. 774 a, That the Allision of those clouds have brought forth a thunder. **1633** T. BROWN *Exp. 2 Pet.* ii. 3 (1865) 268/1 Breaking out with an Allision. **1683** SALMON *Doron Med.* I. 159 For their mutual 'Allision.' *a* **1728** WOODWARD (J.) By the boisterous allision of the sea. **1755** in JOHNSON; and in mod. Dicts.

alliteral (əˈlɪtərəl), *a. rare.* [f. ALLITER(ATE) after *literal*: see -AL[1].] Characterized by alliteration; an attribute applied by Appleyard (1850) to the Caffre group of languages.

1850 APPLEYARD *Kafir Lang.* 26 The alliteral class forms the second and principal division of South African languages. **1864** MAX MÜLLER *Sc. Lang.* II. 12 The Kafir, or, as Appleyard calls them, alliteral languages.

alliterate (əˈlɪtəreɪt), *v.* [f. L. *al-*, *ad-* to + *littera* letter + -ATE[3], on the analogy of *obliterate*, f. L. *oblitterāt-um*, *oblitterā-re*, already formed in L.]

1. *intr.* Of words: To begin with the same letter or group of letters, to constitute alliteration.

1816 SOUTHEY *Lett.* (1856) III. 27 Moreover, the two L's alliterate well.

2. Of persons: To compose alliteratively.

1826 *Q. Rev.* XXXIV. 13 The letters with which we alliterate.

alliterate (əˈlɪtərət), *ppl. a.* [f. as prec., on analogy of *literate*, *illiterate*, and L. *litterātus.*] Alliterated; formed or placed so as to alliterate.

1871 R. F. WEYMOUTH *Euph.* 4 The alliterate words often have more than one letter the same: 'Thou hast tried me, therefore trust me: I never yet failed, and now I will not faint.'

alliterated (əˈlɪtəreɪtɪd), *ppl. a.* [f. ALLITERATE *v.* + -ED.] Composed with or characterized by alliteration.

1776 JOHNSON *Lett.* (1788) I. 331 Smollett's heroes, who in every alliterated novel, Roderick Random or Peregrine Pickle, are always employed by their author to kill a dog. **1859** *Sat. Rev.* 20 Aug. 229/2 Imitation of the old epic alliterated long lines of the Northern poetry.

alliterating (əˈlɪtəreɪtɪŋ), *ppl. a.* [f. as prec. + -ING[2].] Producing alliteration; beginning with the same letter as another word.

1846 T. WRIGHT *Ess. Mid. Ages* I. i. 14 In the Saxon poetry..the first line often contains but one alliterating word.

alliteration (əˌlɪtəˈreɪʃən). [n. of action f. ALLITERATE *v.*: see -ATION.]

1. *gen.* The commencing of two or more words in close connexion, with the same letter, or rather the same sound.

1656 BLOUNT *Glossogr.*, *Alliteration*, a figure in Rhetorick, repeating and playing on the same letter. **1749** *Power Pros. Numbers* 71 That which some call Alliteration, *i.e.* beginning several Words with the same Letter, if it be natural, is a real Beauty. **1763** CHURCHILL *Proph. Famine* Poems I. 101 Apt Alliteration's artful aid. **1831** MACAULAY *Johnson* 126 Taxation no Tyranny..was..nothing but a jingling alliteration which he ought to have despised. **1871** R. F. WEYMOUTH *Euph.* 4 'Delightful to be read, and nothing hurtfull to be regarded; wherein there is small offence by lightnes given to the wise, and lesse occasion of loosenesse profferred to the wanton.' Lilie's favourite form of alliteration is well marked in this sentence.

2. The commencement of certain accented syllables in a verse with the same consonant or consonantal group, or with different vowel sounds, which constituted the structure of versification in OE. and the Teutonic languages generally. Thus from the beginning of Langland's *Piers Ploughman*, text C.:

In a *s*omere *s*eyson · whan *s*ofte was þe sonne,
Y *sh*op me into *sh*robbis · as y a *sh*epherde were;
In *a*bit as an *e*rmite· vn*h*oly of werkes,
Ich *w*ente forth in þe *w*orlde · *w*onders to hure,
And *s*awe meny *c*ellis · and *s*elcouthe þynges.

1774 T. WARTON *Eng. Poetry* (1840) I. Diss. I. 38 The Islandic poets are said to have carried alliteration to the highest pitch of exactness. **1846** T. WRIGHT *Ess. Mid. Ages* I. i. 14 The form of Saxon poetry is alliteration—not rhyme. **1871** EARLE *Philol. Eng. Tong.* §626 Alliteration did not necessarily act on the initial letter of the word.

alliterational (əˌlɪtəˈreɪʃənəl), *a. rare.* [f. prec. + -AL[1]: cf. *conversational.*] Characterized by, or abounding in, alliteration. Cf. ALLITERAL.

1858 *Penny Cycl.* Supp. II. 377/2 The language of the Kaffir supplies a broad distinction between them and other African races. They are prefixional and alliterational.

alliterative (əˈlɪtərətɪv), *a.* [f. ALLITERATE *v.* + -IVE, as if ad. L. **allitterātīv-us.*] Pertaining to or characterized by alliteration.

1764 GOLDSM. *Trav.* Introd. (JOD.) Criticisms in favour of alliterative care and happy negligence. **1774** T. WARTON *Eng. Poetry* (1840) II. x. 108 Alliterative measure, unaccompanied with rhyme. **1855** MILMAN *Lat. Chr.* (1864) IX. XIV. vii. 232 The alliterative verse of the Old Anglo-Saxon. **1865** *Sat. Rev.* 15 July 76/2 The old alliterative cry ['Measures not Men'] is reversed.

aˈlliteratively, *adv.* [f. prec. + -LY.] In an alliterative manner; with alliteration.

1823 HONES *Anc. Myst.* 25 Mary is greatly astonished, and she is thus alliteratively addressed by the Angel, 'Mayde, most mercyfull, and mekest in mende.' **1881** *Punch* 19 Mar. 124 Alliteratively..described as 'beastly bellowing.'

aˈlliterativeness. [f. as prec. + -NESS.] The quality of being alliterative.

1818 COLERIDGE *Lit. Rem.* (1836) I. 92 You cannot read a page of the Faery Queene..without perceiving the intentional alliterativeness of the words.

alliterator (əˈlɪtəˌreɪtə(r)). [f. ALLITERATE *v.* + -OR, on analogy of L. agent-nouns f. ppl. stems. Cf. L. *litterātōr* a teacher of letters.] One who makes use of alliteration.

1755 COLMAN & THORNTON in *Connoiss.* No. 83 The alliterator must be as busily employed to introduce his favourite vowel or consonant, as the Greek poet to shut out the letter he had proscribed.

allituric (ælɪˈtjʊərɪk), *a. Chem.* [f. ALL(OXAN) whence obtained by Schlieper in 1848 (+ *-it-* meaningless) + URIC.] In *Allituric acid*, a product of the disintegration of alloxantin.

1863–79 WATTS *Chem. Dict.*

‖ **Allium** (ˈælɪəm). *Bot.* [L. *allium* garlic, of unkn. origin.] A large genus of Liliaceous plants, of which garlic, the onion, leek, chive, shallot, and the British wild flower Ramsons are species.

1807 CRABBE *Par. Reg.* I. 602 High-sounding words our worthy gardener gets..He *Allium* calls his onions and his leeks. **1866** *Cornh. Mag.* Nov. 538 In the shade, grey periwinkles wind among the snowy drift of allium.

allmand, obs. form of ALLEMANDE.

allmesse, obs. form of ALMS.

ˌall-ˈmight, *sb.* [ALL- E 1.] All power, omnipotence. (See also ALMIGHT.)

c **1440** *Arthur* 452 Suche alle myght comeþ of god. **1589** PUTTENHAM *Eng. Poesie* (1869) 209 By his allmight, that first created man. **1862** TRENCH *Mirac.* vi. 187 Trust in the all-might of Him, to whose help he had appealed.

allness ('ɔ:lnɪs). [f. ALL + -NESS.] Universality.
a **1652** J. SMITH *Sel. Disc.* ix. (1821) 419 Triumphing.. in his own nothingness, and in the allness of the Divinity. **1816** COLERIDGE *Lay Serm.* 339 The science of the universal, having the ideas of oneness and allness as its two elements. **1839** BAILEY *Festus* xxviii. (1848) 335 With God All oneness and sole allness lives alone.

†ˌ**all-'night.** *Obs.* [ALL- E I.] A service of food, fuel, or light for the whole night.
1526 *Househ. Ord. Hen. VIII*, 152 That there be no playing of disse or cards used in the same chamber, after the King be served for All-night. **1626** BACON *Sylva* §372 In the Court of England, there is a Service which they call All-night; which is a great Cake of wax, with the Wicke in the middest. *a* **1685** *Househ. Ord. Chas. II* (1790) 369 From eight of the morning untill All-night is served, in the Presence Chamber.

†ˌ**all-'night-man.** *Obs.* [= *Man* astir *all night.*] A former name for body-snatchers, or men who disinterred corpses by night in order to sell them to medical students for dissection.
1861 RAMSAY *Remin.* Ser. II. 133, The body-lifters, or 'all-night-men,' as they were wont to be called.

allo- ('æləʊ), combining form of Gr. ἄλλος other, different, as in ALLOTHEISM, ALLOCHIRIA, etc. Also in various technical and scientific subjects: **1.** *Chem.* Used to distinguish one of two organic isomers, as ***allocinnamic***, ***-maleic***, ***-mucic*** (acids).
1893 *Jrnl. Chem. Soc.* LXIV. I. 513 Allocinnamic acid. **1894** *Ibid.* LXVI. I. 173 Allofurfuracrylic Acid and the Formation of Allo-Acids. *Ibid.*, The allo-form of cinnamyl-acrylic acid. **1949** S. & L. M. MIALL *New Dict. Chem.* (ed. 2) 21/1 With sterols and related substances the prefix allo- should indicate that rings A and B are in the trans position to each other, but allocholesterol is an exception.
2. *Biol.* In comp. with *-ploid*, as ALLOPOLYPLOID, ALLOTETRAPLOID: having sets of chromosomes derived from different species by hybridization (opp. AUTO- c).
3. In *Philology*: see ALLOGRAPH[2], ALLOMORPH[2], ALLOPHONE.
4. *Biol.* and *Med.* Used to refer to genetically dissimilar individuals of the same species.

alloantigen (æləʊ'æntɪdʒən). *Immunol.* [f. ALLO- + ANTIGEN.] = *isoantigen* s.v. ISO- a.
1964 G. D. SNELL in *Transplantation* II. 657/2 The substitution of alloantigen and alloantibody would create a wholly convenient, consistent, euphonious and etymologically appropriate vocabulary. **1971** [see *isoantigen* s.v. ISO-]. **1973** *Nature* 12 Oct. 286/1 The mother can, and often does, make antibodies to some of the alloantigens of her foetus even though maternal and foetal circulations are entirely separate. **1980** R. C. BURTON in R. B. Herberman *Natural Cell-Mediated Immunity against Tumors* 28 Ly-5 is an alloantigen which is expressed on most cells of the lymphohemapoietic system.
Hence ˌ**alloanti'genic** *a.*
1969 *Transplantation* VIII. 435 Twenty-five different alloantigenic specificities determined by the *H-2* locus have been described.. by workers in a number of laboratories. **1978** *Nature* 26 Oct. 711/1 A new Thy-1 alloantigenic specificity is defined in the mouse. **1985** *Brit. Med. Jrnl.* 14 Sept. 696/1 It has become increasingly likely that immunological disturbances in haemophilia are caused by the aetiological agent for AIDS rather than by any alloantigenic response to denatured protein.

allobarbitone (ˌæləʊ'bɑ:bɪtəʊn). [f. ALLO- + BARBITONE.] A white crystalline compound, diallylbarbituric acid ($C_{10}H_{12}N_2O_3$), used as a sedative and hypnotic.
1934 *Lancet* 22 Dec. 1404/2 The claim is made.. for allobarbitone B.P.C... that it alleviates pain. **1953** *Faber Med. Dict.* 18/2 *Allobarbitone*, a hypnotic similar to barbitone, more rapidly excreted and of less prolonged action.

†**allo'brogical**, *a.* *Obs.* [f. L. *Allobrogic-us* of the Allobroges + -AL[1].] An epithet applied in 17th c. to Presbyterians or Calvinists, in allusion to the fact that Geneva was anciently a town of the Allobroges.
1640 BP. HALL *Episc.* III. §5. 245 See on what shelves of land this late Allobrogicall device is erected. **1646** *Burden of Issach.* in *Phenix* (1708) II. 265 Altho this allobrogical Brood maintain Parity, there be notwithstanding some few Patriarchs who rule and over-rule all.

allocable ('æləkəb(ə)l), *a.* [f. ALLOCATE *v.*, with omission of *-at-* by analogy with *imitable*, etc.: see -ABLE.] Of revenue, resources, etc.: that may be allocated or assigned.
1929 *Rep. Brit. Economic Mission Austral.* (Dominions Office) II. 10 Only a fraction of the interest allocable.. is being received. **1942** *Rep. Tax Cases 1938–1941* XXIII. 709 £642 is allocable on a time basis to the short period ending the 5th April, 1935. **1965** *Federal Suppl.* CCXL. 921/1 The accounts of the constituent banks are allocable to the local and national markets, as follows: [etc.]. **1973** *N.Y. Law Jrnl.* 2 Aug. 14/8 The Partnership shall pay.. 47.368% of all distributions allocable to the Limited Partners. **1980** *Nat. Westminster Bank Q. Rev.* Aug. 24 For the unallocable benefits such as defence and law this is unavoidable but the same obviously does not apply to allocable benefits such as health and education.

allocate ('æləkeɪt), *v.* [f. med.L. *allocāt-* ppl. stem of *allocāre*; f. *al-*, *ad-* to + *locāre* to place.] Formerly only in Scottish writers; not in J. or T.
1. To set or lay apart for a special purpose, to apportion, assign, to give one as his special portion or share.
1640–1 *Kirkcudbr. War-Comm. Min. Bk.* (1855) 157 To allot and allocate to thame and ilk ane of thame.. ane competent localitie. **1733** P. LINDSAY *Int. Scotl.* 23 This Meeting may then appoint and allocate such a Proportion of the Poors Money. **1821** DE QUINCEY *Confess.* (1862) 68 That very sum which the Manchester Grammar School allocated to every student. **1872** E. ROBERTSON *Hist. Ess.* 251 A system of allocating the public revenues amongst wealthy capitalists.
2. To attach locally.
1842 DE QUINCEY in Page *Life* I. xv. 332 Lasswade, to which nominally we allocate ourselves.
3. To fix the locality of, localize.
1881 LOCKYER in *Nature* 28 July 298 We can allocate the absorption of the hydrogen, magnesium, and so on; we can see where they are absorbing. *Ibid.* 317 Kirchhoff allocated the region where the absorption.. took place at a considerable height in the atmosphere of the sun.

†'**allocate,** *ppl. a.* *Sc.* *Obs.* [ad. med.L. *allocāt-us*; used as pa. pple. of prec. vb.: see -ATE.] Allotted, assigned.
1717 WODROW *Corr.* (1843) II. 336 The stipend.. mortified or legally allocate for this.

†'**allocate,** *sb.* *Obs.* [ad. med.L. *allocātum* an allowance, pa. pple. of *allocāre*, used absol.] An allowance or grant.
1709 STRYPE *Eccl. Mem.* II. II. xxx. an. 1552 An allocate for the D. of Suffolk for 40*l.* ayear given him by the king.

'**allocated** ('æləkeɪtɪd), *ppl. a.* [f. ALLOCATE *v.* + -ED.] Allotted, assigned.
1864 SALA in *Daily Tel.* 27 Sept., Somebody has stolen the money allocated for municipal improvements.

allocation (æləʊ'keɪʃən). [a. Fr. *allocation*, ad. med.L. *allocātiōn-em*, n. of action f. *allocāre* (see ALLOCATE *v.*), or perh. direct ad. med.L.]
1. a. The action of apportioning or assigning to a special person or purpose; apportionment, assignment, allotment.
1833 CHALMERS *Constit. Man* (1835) I. vi. 275 At the first allocations of property. **1850** MERIVALE *Rom. Emp.* (1865) VIII. lxiii. 55 Domitian.. had respected this allocation of the imperial treasures. *c* **1854** STANLEY *Sinai & Pal.* ii. (1858) 133 The allocation of the particular portions of Palestine to its successive inhabitants. **1876** *N. Amer. Rev.* CXXIII. 456 The whole subtle question of the allocation of powers under the Constitution.
†**b.** *concr.* A portion of revenue, etc. assigned to a distinct purpose, constituting a fixed charge upon it. *Obs.*
1535 GARDINER in Strype *Eccl. Mem.* (1822) I. I. xxx. 328 In the deductions and allocations.. we have followed in our judgment.. the words of our instructions. *c* **1630** JACKSON *Creed* IV. III. iii. Wks. III. 393 Revenues without such allocations or deductions. *Ibid.* XI. xliii. Wks. XI. 291 We shall be able to make the deductions or allocations somewhat equal.
†**c.** A portion of revenue settled on a particular person; an allowance. *Obs.*
1658 PHILLIPS, *Allocations* are also the Allowances of Officers under a Prince or Nobleman.
d. *spec.* The allotment of available materials, provisions, etc., by the government or other authority.
1940 *Economist* 24 Aug. 237/1 The Select Committee recommends that allocation—that is, the rationing of materials—should be centralised and applied to every material that is scarce enough to form a bottleneck in the process of production. **1951** E. A. G. ROBINSON in D. N. Chester *Lessons Brit. War Econ.* iii. 57 As the war developed the need for critical allocation of resources increased progressively. **1951** R. PARES *Ibid.* x. 154 The allocation and use of scarce resources.
e. A portion allocated in this way.
1940 *Times* 6 Feb. 5/3 Allocations will be based on the actual sales made by the butchers. **1947** J. HAYWARD *Prose Lit. since 1939* 19 Commercial publishers.. had some cause to resent the intrusion of a rival with an unlimited allocation of paper. **1947** *Ann. Reg. 1946* 30 [The Minister of Food] has been successful in getting an allocation of 1,550,000 tons [of rice] for India.
2. The action of allowing or admitting an item in an account; also, the item so allowed. (A common sense in med.L.)
1658 PHILLIPS, *Allocation*, properly a Placing or Adding to. In a Law sense, an Allowance made upon an Account in the Exchequer. **1681** BLOUNT *Glossogr.*, *Allocation*.. also allowance made upon an account. **1751** CHAMBERS *Cycl.*, *Allocation, Allocatio*, the admitting or allowing of an article in an account.. Allocation is also an allowance made upon an account; used in the exchequer.
3. The placing or adding of one thing to another; disposition, arrangement.
1656 BLOUNT *Glossogr.*, *Allocation*, a placing or adding unto. **1755** in JOHNSON. **1838** HALLAM *Hist. Lit.* II. III. ii. §58. 447 That inconsequent allocation of his proofs which frequently occurs in his writings.
4. Placing; fixing in a place; localization.
1855 OWEN *Vertebr.* Introd. 5 (L.) The allocation of the.. albuminous electric pulp in a special cylindrical cavity.

allocator ('æləkeɪtə(r)). [f. ALLOCATE *v.* + -OR.] One who or that which allocates (something).
1934 *N.Y. Times* 6 Apr. 35/6 The district allocator.. shall make every effort to avoid inequities that may exist in the availability of supplies of crude oil to refiners. **1953** P. C. BERG *Dict. New Words* 28/2 *Allocator*, a person who is responsible for, or engaged in, allocation. **1972** *Computer Jrnl.* XV. 198/1 The function must therefore claim a new vector from the storage allocator. **1980** *N.Y. Times Mag.* 10 Aug. 32/2 In Japan, the Government is a major allocator of investment funds.

‖**allocatur** (æləʊ'keɪtə(r)). [med.L. *allocātur* 'It is allowed.'] A certificate given by the proper authority at the termination of an action, allowing costs.

allocentric (ˌæləʊ'sɛntrɪk), *a.* *Psychol.* [f. ALLO- + -CENTRIC.] Centred in the object; concentrating on or interested in an object in itself rather than in its relation or relevance to oneself. Opp. AUTOCENTRIC *a.*
1927 T. BURROW *Social Basis of Consciousness* II. vii. 188 The type of personality whose course is the exact opposite [of that of the autocentric individual].. is the *allocentric* type. **1959** E. G. SCHACHTEL *Metamorphosis* ix. 220 The *allocentric attitude*.. is one of profound interest in the object, and complete openness and receptivity toward it. **1970** *Jrnl. Gen. Psychol.* Oct. 235 The allocentric or creative personality is interested in objects for their own sake. **1982** *Jrnl. Genetic Psychol.* Dec. 203 (*heading*) Facilitation of children's allocentric placement by reducing task complexity and providing a verbal rule.

allochiria (æləʊ'kaɪərɪə). *Path.* Also **allocheiria**. [mod.L., f. ALLO- + Gr. χείρ hand: see -IA[1].] A condition in which a sensation is referred to a point other than the true one (esp. the corresponding point on the other side of the body).
1881 H. OBERSTEINER in *Brain* IV. 153 The patient is not clear.. as to which side of the body has been touched. I would term the phenomenon 'Sensory Allochiria', or shortly 'Allochiria' or confusion of sides. **1907** E. JONES in *Brain* XXX. 525 Under the name allochiria two fundamentally different conditions have hitherto been confused. A patient's mistake in determining the side of the stimulus may be (i) part of a general defect in localisation.. or (ii) a specific defect independent of any error in localisation. **1910** *Lancet* 1 Jan. 44/2 The difficult subject of allochiria. By this term neurologists have commonly understood the false reference of a point stimulated to a corresponding spot on the opposite side of the body. **1943** I. S. WECHSLER *Textbk. Clinical Neurol.* (ed. 5) 44 In certain cerebral lesions.. a patient sometimes refers the sensation to a corresponding spot on the opposite limb (*allocheiria*).
So **allo'chiral, -'cheiral** *adj.* (*a*) relating to the other hand; *spec.* = HETEROCHIRAL *a.* (Funk 1893); so ***allo'chirally*** adv.; (*b*) pertaining to or exhibiting allochiria.
1889 W. THOMSON *Math. & Physical Papers* (1890) III. 410 Two men of exactly equal and similar external figures would be allochirally similar if one holds out his right hand and the other his left. **1900** DORLAND *Med. Dict.* 32/1 *Allochiral*, exhibiting reversed symmetry; having the relation of the right hand to the left. **1911** T. L. STEDMAN *Med. Dict.* 28/2 *Allochiral*, relating to or suffering from allochiria.

allochroic (æləʊ'krəʊɪk), *a.* [f. Gr. ἀλλόχρο-ος changed in colour (see ALLOCHROOUS).] 'Changeable in colour, shot-colour.' *Syd. Soc. Lex.* 1879.

allochroite (æ'lɒkrəʊaɪt). *Min.* [mod. f. Gr. ἀλλόχρο-ος (see prec.) + -ITE, min. form.] An iron-garnet, made by Dana a sub-variety of Andradite, found in Norway and elsewhere.
1837–80 DANA *Min.* 269 Named *Andradite* by the author after the Portuguese mineralogist, d'Andrada, who described and named [1800] the first of the included sub-varieties Allochroite.. The original *allochroite* was a manganesian iron-garnet of brown or reddish-brown color, and of fine-grained massive structure.

allochromatic (ˌæləʊkrəʊ'mætɪk), *a.* [f. Gr. ἄλλος other, different + χρῶμα, -ατ-ος colour + -IC.]
Of or pertaining to change of colour; exhibiting or seeing colours different from what they really are.
1879 in *Syd. Soc. Lex.*

allochroous (æ'lɒkrəʊəs), *a.* [f. Gr. ἀλλόχρο-ος changed in colour (f. ἄλλος other + χροιά colour) + -OUS.] Changing colour; *spec.* as a symptom of disease.
1811 in HOOPER *Med. Dict.* **1847** in CRAIG (Allochrous).

allochthon (æ'lɒkθən). *Geol.* [G., or back-formation f. next.] An allochthonous rock formation; opp. AUTOCHTHON 4.
1942 M. P. BILLINGS *Struct. Geol.* x. 181 Rocks.. have traveled many miles from their original place of deposition and are said to be *allochthonous*.. these rocks are sometimes called the *allochthon*. **1957** *Amer. Geol. Inst., Gloss. Geol.* 7/2 *Allochthon*, rocks that have been moved a long distance from their original place of deposition by some tectonic process, generally related to overthrusting or recumbent folding, or perhaps gravity sliding. Used in contrast to autochthon. **1961** J. CHALLINOR *Dict. Geol.* 15/2 The 'allochthon' (allochthonous folds and thrust masses) is the far-travelled ground.

allochthonous (æ'lɒkθənəs), *a. Geol.* [f. G. *allochthon* (K. W. von Gümbel 1888, in *Grundzüge d. Geologie* I. II. v. 615), f. ALLO- + χθών, χθονός earth, soil: see -OUS.] Applied to organic deposits and rock formations: consisting of or formed from transported material; not formed *in situ* (opp. AUTOCHTHONOUS *a.* c).

1911 E. A. N. ARBER *Nat. Hist. Coal* v. 110 We now turn to the alternative hypothesis of the Drift theory or Allochthonous formation of coal as Gümbel termed it... The material, which formed the mother substance of coal seams, was, on this view, always drifted..and transported from a distance. **1916** C. C. FORSAITH in *Bot. Gaz.* LXII. 33 Allochthonous peat (that type of peat which has been deposited by a gradual accumulation of floated, drifted, and windblown vegetable material in permanent and more or less quiet bodies of open water). **1932** J. A. STEERS *Unstable Earth* iii. 114 Nappes characteristic of the true geosyncline which have often been moved far from their place of origin, and to which the term allochthonous is applied. **1939** W. H. TWENHOFEL *Princ. Sedimentation* v. 162 Before fossil plants may be used to reconstruct a physical environment it must first be determined whether the plant material is autochthonous, that is, whether it grew where it is found; or allochthonous, that is, whether it was transported to where it is found. **1942**, **1961** [see prec.].

alloclase ('æləʊkleɪs). *Min.* [mod. f. (Ger. *alloklas* 1866) Gr. ἄλλος other, different + κλάσις fracture; so called because it shows a different cleavage from other minerals with which it has been confounded.] = next.

1875 URE *Dict. Arts.*

alloclasite (æ'lɒkləsaɪt). *Min.* [Dana's systematic name for prec., with -ITE, min. form.] A mineral containing sulphur, arsenic, bismuth, and cobalt, with traces of iron, zinc, and other metals, found in the Banat; placed by Dana in the pyrite division of Sulphids.

1868 DANA *Min.* 80 The supposed glaucodot of Orawicza is alloclasite.

allocute ('æləkju:t), *v. rare*$^{-1}$. [f. L. *allocūt-* ppl. stem of *alloqu-i* to address, speak to; f. *al-*, *ad-* to + *loqui* to speak: cf. *attribute*, *comminute*.] *intr.* To deliver an allocution; to address formally.

1860 *Times* 11 Oct. 6/2 The Pope can allocute and Francis II can protest.

allocution (æləʊ'kju:ʃən). Also 7 adl-. [ad. L. *adl-*, *allocūtiōn-em*, n. of action f. *alloqui*: see prec.]

1. *Rom. Antiq.* A formal address or exhortation by a general to his soldiers; hence in *R.C. Ch.* A public address by the Pope to his clergy, or to the Church generally.

1689 SIR G. WHELER *Anc. Ch.* 91 (T.) In adlocutions to the army. **1697** EVELYN *Numism.* v. 182 To these add their Discipline, Adlocutions, Oaths of Fidelity. **1702** ADDISON *Medals* i. (1727) 19 Many ancient Customs as sacrifices.. Allocutions..preserved on Coins. **1753** CHAMBERS *Cycl. Supp.* s.v., The usual form in *Adlocutions* was *fortis esset ac fidus*. **1842** *Blackw. Mag.* LI. 729 They..represent the popes in that act which, in Roman antiquity, is called allocution. **1858** WISEMAN *Four Last Popes* 336 The text of the allocution is not accessible.

2. *gen.* The action of addressing or exhorting; hortatory or authoritative address.

1615 T. ADAMS *Leaven* 109 That comfortable allocution —'Good and faithfull servant, enter thou into thy masters joy.' **1848** THACKERAY *Van. F.* xlix, After this vigorous allocution, to..his 'Hareem.'

†**3.** A speaking to, addressing or accosting. *Obs.*

1754 LAVINGTON *Enthus. Methodists* III. 86 St. Teresa, who had so many Rapts, Visions, and Allocutions with our Lord.

allod, alod ('æləd). [ad. L. *a(l)lōdium*, *alōdis*, *alōdus*, the first more commonly used unchanged. Cf. Fr. *alode* (Cotgr. 1611).] = ALLODIUM.

1689 BURNET *Tracts* I. 62 There are some Lands that are Frank-alod. **1848** HALLAM *Mid. Ages* Suppl. Notes (1868) I. 146 The former derivation of *alod*. **1872** E. ROBERTSON *Hist. Ess.* 131 Small freeholders in allod. **1875** STUBBS *Const. Hist.* I. iii. 53 The alod is the hereditary estate derived from primitive occupation.

†**a'llodge**, *v. Obs.* Also 4–5 aloge, alogge. [a. OFr. *aloge-r*, *-ier*, f. *à* to + *loger* to lodge, after phr. *à loge*; cogn. w. It. *alloggiare*: see LODGE.]

1. *trans.* To place, pitch, lodge.

c **1330** *Arth. & Merl.* 2096 On that ich fair roume To aloge her paviloun. **1598** BARRET *Theor. Warres* v. ii. 150 To alodge a camp commodiously, is a point of great skill.

2. *intr.* To lodge, sojourn.

1604 T. WRIGHT *Pass. Mind* I. ix. 32 The heart is the peculiar place where that Passions allodge..They will allodge longer with you than you would haue them.

†**a'llodgement.** *Obs.* Also 6 al-, 7 allogia-. [f. ALLODGE + -MENT, after It. *allogiamento* lodging, 'also, a place where a campe or soldiers bee quartered.' Florio; f. *allogiare*.] Lodging; in *pl.* soldiers' quarters.

1598 BARRET *Theor. Warres* I. ii. 13 The plot of the alodgement according to the disposition of the ground. **1622** F. MARKHAM *Bk. Warre* IV. vi. §6. 144 The Serieant-Maior ..shall proportion out all Allodgements and Encampings. **1644** EVELYN *Diary* (1827) I. 90 The allogiaments of the garrison are uniforme. **1755** T. CROKER *Ariosto's Orl. Fur.* XIV. 62 I. 200 In this place pastoral allodgements were.

allodial, alodial (ə'ləʊdɪəl), *a.* and *sb.* [ad. med.L. *al(l)ōdiāl-is*, f. ALLODI-UM + -AL^1. Cf. Fr. *al-*, *allodial* (Cotgr.).] As to spelling see *allodium*.

A. *adj.* **1.** Of or pertaining to an allodium; held in absolute ownership.

1656 BLOUNT *Glossogr.*, *Allodial Lands*, free Lands, for which no Rents, Fines, nor Services are due. **1677** HOBBES *Dial. Comm. Laws* 199 When a Man holds his Land from the gift of God only, which Lands Civilians call Allodial. **1795** BURKE *Abridgm. Eng. Hist.* Wks. 1842 II. 549 These estates ..were not fiefs; they were to all purposes allodial. **1876** FREEMAN *Norm. Conq.* I. iii. 95 The King..might have his ancient allodial property.

2. Of or pertaining to the holding of land in absolute ownership; e.g. ***the allodial system*** as opposed to the *feudal system*.

1747 CARTE *Hist. Eng.* I. 364 The same privileges and allodial rights as had been enjoyed by the original proprietors. **1761** HUME *Hist. Eng.* I. App. II. 246 Territory ..possessed by an allodial or free title. **1875** STUBBS *Const. Hist.* I. ii. 34 We dare not say that we have a perfect alodial system.

3. Owning an allodium; holding in absolute ownership.

1857 SIR F. PALGRAVE *Norm. & Eng.* II. 264 A patch of arable tilled by the remaining allodial rustics. **1872** FREEMAN *Eng. Const.* 77 The feudal tenant holding his land of a lord by military service, gradually supplanted..the allodial holder who held his land of no other man.

B. *sb.* **1.** Allodial lands.

1769 *Ann. Reg.* 163/1 The King of Naples as possessor of the allodials of the family of Farnese. **1807** COXE *House of Austria* xxii. (L.) The allodials were adjudged to the sons of Robert and Elizabeth.

2. An allodial holder; an allodiary.

1778 LD. MALMESBURY *Priv. Lett.* I. 371 Room ought to have been left for the claims of the Allodiels.

allodialism (ə'ləʊdɪə,lɪz(ə)m). Also alod-. [f. prec. + -ISM.] The allodial system.

1864 KIRK *Chas. the Bold* II. IV. iii. 413 Feudalism supervening on allodialism. **1875** STUBBS *Const. Hist.* I. vii. 207 A progress..from alodialism to feudalism.

allodialist (ə'ləʊdɪəlɪst). Also alod-. [f. ALLODIAL + -IST.] An allodial proprietor.

1805 *Edin. Rev.* VI. 223 That allodialists 'held in contempt beneficiary and feudal tenures' we have never read. **1845** STEPHEN *Laws of Eng.* I. 174 The allodialist held of no one, but enjoyed his land as free and independent property.

allodiality (ə,ləʊdɪ'ælɪtɪ). *rare.* [ad. Fr. *allodialité*, n. of quality f. *allodial*: see -TY.] The quality of being allodial, of holding or being held in free ownership.

1848 HALLAM *Mid. Ages* Suppl. Notes (1868) I. 163 The party claiming alodiality.

allodially (ə'ləʊdɪəlɪ), *adv.*; also alod-. [f. ALLODIAL + -LY^2.] In an allodial manner; by allodial tenure.

1776 ADAM SMITH *W.N.* I. III. iv. 413 Rights possessed allodially by the great proprietors of land. **1874** STUBBS *Const. Hist.* I. ii. 34 The land..is held alodially.

†**a'llodian**, *a. Obs.* [f. L. *allōdi-um* + -AN.] = ALLODIAL.

1672 MANLEY *Interpr.*, *Allodian Lands* are free Lands, which pay no Fines or Services.

allodiary (ə'ləʊdɪərɪ). Also alod-. [ad. L. *al(l)ōdiāri-us* (common in Domesday Book): f. ALLODIUM; see -ARY.] The holder of an allodium.

[**1628** COKE *On Litt.* 1 b, The Booke of Domesday: and tenants in Fee simple are there called *Alodarii* or *Aloarii*.] **1875** STUBBS *Const. Hist.* I. v. 89 The alodiaries of Domesday.

allodification (ə,lɒdɪfɪ'keɪʃən). [f. L. *allōdi-um* + -FICATION, as if on a vb. *allodify, of which no instance is cited.] The conversion of land into allodium; the making of it absolutely freehold.

1875 *Blackie's Pop. Encycl.* I. 119/1 In such *allodification*, a part of the value must be paid as a compensation to the former lord. **1879** BARING-GOULD *Germany* I. 52 The result of the allodification has therefore been to sever the gentry from the soil.

allodium, alodium (ə'ləʊdɪəm). [a. med.L. *al-*, *allōdium* (frequent in Domesday Book,) f. Ger. **alôd*, *allôd*, 'entire property,' found in the Salic Law in latinized form *alod-is*, 'in W.Goth. documents *alaudes*' (Diez), f. ALL + OLG. *ôd* (OHG. *ôt*, OE. *eád*, ON. *auðr*), 'estate, property, wealth' (Goth. **auds* in *audags*, OE. *eádiᵹ* wealthy, fortunate, happy). With *allōdium* cf. med.L. *clenōdium* a trinket, f. Ger. *kleinod*, lit. a 'little piece of property.' Occasionally englished as AL(L)OD, AL(L)ODY. Usage varies, in this word and its derivatives, between *al-* and *all-*. In med.L., forms in *al-* are more usual.] An estate held in absolute ownership without service or acknowledgement of any superior, as among the early Teutonic peoples; opposed to *feudum* or *feud*.

1628 COKE *On Litt.* 1 b, For in the law of England we have not properly *Allodium*, that is any subject's land that is not holden, unlesse you will take *Allodium* for *Ex solido*, as it is often taken in the Booke of Domesday. *Ibid.* 5 a, In Domesday, *Alodium* (in a large sense) signifieth a free mannor. *a* **1660** HAMMOND *Serm.* (T.) Allodium, not from any ἀλλ' ἐκ Διὸς *but from God*, as the lawyers have derived that word. **1751** CHAMBERS *Cycl.*, *Allodium* and *patrimonium* are frequently used indiscriminately. **1839** KEIGHTLEY *Hist. Eng.* I. 77 *Allodium*, land held in full propriety.

†**allody, alody.** *Obs. rare*$^{-1}$. = prec.

1650 ELDERFIELD *Civ. Right of Tythes* 54 No alodyes left amongst us.

alloe, obs. form of ALOE.

allœopathist (æli:'ɒpəθɪst). *Med.* [f. Gr. ἀλλοῖο-ς of a different kind + πάθ-ος affection + -IST.] = ALLOPATHIST (which is the more usual form).

1849 *Hahnemann's Organon* Introd. 28 However..he may affect to be a homœopathist, [he] is and will always remain a generalizing allœopathist.

‖**allœ'ostropha**, *a.* or *sb. pl.* [Gr. ἀλλοιόστροφα adj. pl. neut. 'consisting of irregular strophes'; f. ἀλλοῖος different in kind + στροφή strophe. A modern writer would have adapted the word as *allœostrophous*.] (See quot.)

1671 MILTON *Samson* Pref., The measure of verse used in the chorus is of all sorts..being divided into stanzas or pauses, they may be called Allœostropha.

allœotic (æli:'ɒtɪk), *a. Med.* [ad. Gr. ἀλλοιωτικ-ός fit for changing; f. ἀλλοι-οῦν to change; f. ἀλλοῖ-ος of different kind; f. ἄλλος other, different.] Capable of bringing about a change in the constitution (technically *allœōsis*); alterative.

1853 in MAYNE *Exp. Lex.* **1879** in *Syd. Soc. Lex.*

†**allœ'otical**, *a. Med. Obs. rare*$^{-1}$. In 7 alliot-. [f. as prec. + -AL^1.] = prec.

1657 TOMLINSON *Renou's Disp.* 507 The Syrupe of Succory..is alliotical..and purgative.

allo-erotism (,æləʊ'ɛrətɪz(ə)m). *Psychol.* Also -e'roticism. [ad. G. *alloerotismus* (Freud 1899, *Let.* to W. Fliess 9 Dec. in *Aus d. Anfängen d. Psychoanalyse* (1950) 324), f. ALLO- + EROTISM, EROTICISM.] Erotism aroused by another person (opp. AUTO-EROTISM). So **allo-e'rotic** *a.* [cf. G. *alloerotisch* (Freud 1899).]

1921 J. C. FLÜGEL *Psycho-anal. Stud. of Family* ii. 14 (To use a convenient term of Ferenczi's) allo-erotic aspects of the mind. **1934** H. C. WARREN *Dict. Psychol.* 10/1 Allo-eroticism, allo-erotism. **1936** *Brit. Jrnl. Psychol.* XXVI. 284 The contrast between object-love, or allo-erotic libido, and self-love, narcissistic libido. **1954** MOSBACHER & STRACHEY tr. *Freud's Let. 9 Dec. 1899 to W. Fliess* in *Origins of Psycho-Analysis* 304 The lowest of the sexual strata is auto-erotism. .. This is superseded by allo-erotism (homo- and hetero-). *Ibid.*, Hysteria..is allo-erotic; the main highway it follows is identification with the beloved person.

allogamy (æ'lɒgəmɪ). *Bot.* [mod. f. Gr. ἄλλος other, different + -γαμία marrying, f. γάμος marriage.] Cross-fertilization.

1879 in *Syd. Soc. Lex.* **1880** GRAY *Struct. Bot.* vi. §4. 216 Cross fertilization, or Allogamy, the action of the pollen of one flower on the pistil of some other flower of the same species.

allogeneic (æləʊdʒɪ'ni:ɪk, -'eɪɪk), *a. Immunol.* [f. ALLO- + Gr. γένος, γέν-ε race, kind + -IC; cf. ALLOGENEITY.] Derived from a genetically dissimilar individual of the same species; occurring between two such individuals.

1961 P. A. GORER et al. in *Nature* 25 Mar. 1025/1 We therefore propose 'allogeneic'; this should be pronounced 'allogeneeic', but even if pronounced 'allojeenic' it should not sound like 'allergenic'. **1973** *Ibid.* 12 Oct. 329/1 The placenta, which is foetal in origin and therefore allogeneic in the mother, is not rejected during pregnancy. **1982** *Brit. Med. Jrnl.* 13 Nov. 1394/1 The increasing use of highly immunosuppressive regimens for allogeneic and autologous marrow transplantation.

Hence **alloge'neically** *adv.*

1971 *Nature* 12 Mar. 114/2 The first group [of mice] was immunized allogeneically to CBA male mice. **1984** *Internat. Jrnl. Cell Cloning* II. 263 Rodents transplanted with allogeneically mismatched marrow or spleen cells.

allogeneity (,æləʊdʒɪ'ni:ɪtɪ). *rare.* [f. Gr. ἀλλογενή-ς of another race, (f. ἄλλο-ς other + γέν-ος, γένε-, kind) + -ITY.] Difference of nature.

1825 COLERIDGE *Rem.* (1836) II. 336 Its hetero- or rather its allo-geneity, that is, its diversity, its difference in kind.

allogeneous (æləʊ'dʒi:nɪəs), *a. rare.* Incorr. -genous [f. as prec. + -OUS.] Of different nature, diverse in kind.

1842 *Blackw. Mag.* LI. 726 Stone, brick, and stucco.. unite their allogenous surfaces. **1920** *Glasgow Herald* 6 May 6 The Russia of the Soviets is still the old Muscovite tyranny which denies to allogenous races the right to live. **1950** *Jrnl. Theol. Stud.* I. 102 The body from Mary, with its *centrum vitae*, afforded to God the Word an allogenous manward *prosopon*.

allogenic (ælǝʊˈdʒɛnɪk), *a.* [f. Gr. ἀλλογενή-ς (see ALLOGENEITY) + -IC.]
 1. *Geol.* (See quot. 1888.)
 1888 F. H. HATCH in J. J. H. Teall *Brit. Petrogr.* 423 *Allogenic* (*Allothigenic*), applied to such minerals as are of more ancient origin than the rocks which they compose. **1893** [see AUTHIGENIC *a*]. **1937** WOOLDRIDGE & MORGAN *Physical Basis Geogr.* xix. 277 Many..of these streams are 'allogenic', deriving much of their water from terrains beyond the Chalk outcrops.
 2. *Ecology.* Caused by external factors, opp. AUTOGENIC *a.* (see also quot. 1962).
 1931 W. B. MCDOUGALL *Plant Ecol.* (ed. 2) xix. 259 Successions that are brought about by the reactions of the plants themselves are sometimes called autogenic successions while those caused by climatic or physiographic factors are called allogenic successions. **1934** *Geogr. Jrnl.* LXXXIII. 499 The further stages in the succession may be brought about by the operation of external factors alone, and when this is so the succession is termed an allogenic succession. **1962** H. HANSON *Dict. Ecol.* 14 *Allogenic succession*, the kind of succession in which one kind of community replaces another because of a change in the environment which was not produced by the plants themselves, e.g., decrease in soil moisture by improved drainage.

allogenous, *a.*: see ALLOGENEOUS *a.*

allogiament, obs. form of ALLODGEMENT.

allogonite (æˈlɒgǝnaɪt). *Min.* [mod. f. Gr. ἄλλος other, different + γωνία angle + -ITE, min. form.] A synonym of HERDERITE.
 1878 LAWRENCE tr. *Cotta's Rocks Class.* 134 Allogonite is the name given by Winkler to certain dark grey or reddish rocks..an intimately blended compound of labradorite with the basalts.

allograft (ˈælǝʊgrɑft), *sb. Med.* and *Biol.* [f. ALLO- + GRAFT *sb.*[1]] A graft between genetically dissimilar individuals of the same species.
 1961 P. A. GORER et al. in *Nature* 25 Mar. 1025/1 'Allogeneic graft' could, and probably will, be abbreviated to 'allograft'. **1974** R. M. KIRK et al. *Surgery* ii. 34 Homograft..also known as an allo-graft..is a graft transferred to a member of the same species. **1983** *Nature* 14 July 121/1 The way in which the maternal immune system is regulated during pregnancy to allow the survival of the fetal allograft remains unsolved.
 Also as *v. trans.*, to graft or transplant between genetically dissimilar individuals of the same species; **ˈallografted** *ppl. a.*
 1968 *Transplantation* VI. 65 The blood flow increase induced by acetylcholine in the allografted kidneys is shown. **1972** *Brit. Jrnl. Surg.* LIX. 541/1 The results obtained when both kidneys were allografted in the pig are described. **1972** *Nature* 7 Apr. 314/2 Techniques have been developed at the Institute of Orthopaedics for allografting articular cartilage with varying amounts of underlying bone. **1975** *Ibid.* 1 May 2/2 Allografted skin does not behave like vascularised organs.

allograph[1] (ˈælǝgrɑːf, -æ-). [mod. f. Gr. ἄλλος other + γραφή writing. Cf. *autograph.*] A writing or signature made by one person on behalf of another.

allograph[2] (ˈælǝʊgrɑːf, -æ-). *Philol.* [f. ALLO- 3 + GRAPH(EME.] **a.** A particular form of a letter of an alphabet. **b.** One of a number of letters or letter-combinations representing a phoneme; thus *f* (in *friend*) and *gh* (in *cough*) are two of the allographs representing the phoneme /f/. Hence **alloˈgraphic** *a.*
 1951 R. A. HALL JUN. in *Archivum Linguisticum* III. 117 We now have *allomorph* and *morpheme*, *alloseme* and *sememe*, *allograph* and *grapheme*. **1956** A. MCINTOSH in *Trans. Philol. Soc.* 43 At other times it [*sc.* the word 'letter'] is used of the particular allographic form a grapheme may have in a given context, e.g. when we speak of 'the *s* used in final position in Greek'; again it may be used of a single instance of an allograph, as when we say 'that's a badly formed letter'. **1962** *Amer. Speech* XXXVII. 229 A proposal to describe graphemes in terms of phonemic model, i.e., grapheme: phoneme::graph: phone::allograph: allophone. **1963** *Language* XXXIX. 234 We might imagine that an Arcadian, struck by the fact that the Laconians sometimes spelled with ⟨wo⟩ what was to him simply /oː/, introduced ⟨wo⟩ here, considering it merely an initial allograph of ⟨o⟩.

allom, obs. form of ALUM.

allomerism (æˈlɒmǝrɪz(ǝ)m). *Chem.* [mod. f. Gr. ἄλλος other, different + μέρ-ος part + -ISM.] A term applied by Cooke to the variation in chemical constitution without change of form, incident to those minerals that contain isomorphous constituents which may wholly or partially replace one other.
 Allomerism is well shown in *Amphibole*; its typical composition is RO . SiO_2 in which RO represents any two or more of the bases magnesia (MgO), lime (CaO), oxide of iron (FeO), oxide of manganese (MnO), soda (N_2O), potash (K_2O) or water (H_2O); while the silica (SiO_2) is usually partly replaced by alumina (Al_2O_3) and often by the isomorphous sesquioxide of iron (Fe_2O_3).

allomerous (æˈlɒmǝrǝs), *a.* [f. as prec. + -OUS.] Liable to variation in constituent elements or as to the proportion in which these are present, without change in crystalline form.
 Allomerous is (to some extent) the correlative of *isomorphous*; hornblende, tremolite, and edenite are isomorphous minerals, being varieties of the allomerous amphibole (see prec.); but distinct minerals are also isomorphous, as gold, platinum, and zinc; phosphate of lime (apatite) and phosphate of lead (pyromorphite); sesquioxide of iron and sesquioxide of manganese; which are not varieties of a single allomerous substance, though, as in the case of the two last mentioned, they may appear as isomorphous constituents of an allomerous compound mineral like amphibole or pyroxene.

allometry (æˈlɒmɪtrɪ). *Biol.* [f. ALLO- + -METRY.] (See quot. 1936.) Hence **alloˈmetric** *a.*, pertaining to or exhibiting allometry.
 1936 HUXLEY & TEISSIER in *Nature* 9 May 780/2 To denote growth of a part at a different rate from that of a body as a whole or of a standard, we propose the term *allometry*. *Ibid.*, *Positive* and *negative allometry* denote respectively growth-rates of the part above and below that of the standard. **1938** *Nature* 3 Sept. 437/2 Limbs must exhibit positive heterogony, or allometry..during fœtal development. **1940** G. R. DE BEER *Embryos & Ancestors* iv. 25 The relative growth-rates of the allometric organ and of the body remain constant during long periods. **1941**, **1942**, **1949** [see ALLOMORPHOSIS 2]. **1959** *Chambers's Encycl.* I. 276/1 The huge claws of the adult lobster and the armament of the stag are thus evidently the outcome of a strongly positive allometric growth.

allomorph[1] (ˈælǝʊmɔːf). *Min.* [f. ALLO- + Gr. μορφή form.] A distinct crystalline form without change of chemical composition. Hence **alloˈmorphic** *a.*[1], **alloˈmorphism**.
 1866 KING & ROWNEY in *Q. Jrnl. Geol. Soc.* XXII. I. 187 All these varieties are considered to belong to one axial system—the monoclinate; but being obviously of other forms than one, and as they are all chemically alike, we propose to call them *allomorphs*. Like aragonite, calcite is also subject to allomorphism. *Ibid.* 193 It is our present impression that flocculite is merely an allomorph of serpentine. *Ibid.*, There is an allomorphic variety of serpentine known as chrysolite.

allomorph[2] (ˈælǝʊmɔːf). *Philol.* [f. ALLO- 3 + MORPH(EME.] A morphemic alternant; one of two or more morphs making up a morpheme. Hence **alloˈmorphic** *a.*[2]
 1948 E. A. NIDA in *Language* XXIV. 420 Morphemic alternants can conveniently be called allomorphs. Accordingly, allomorphs are related to morphemes as allophones are related to phonemes. **1949** —— *Morphology* (ed. 2) ii. 21 Allomorphic differences of tone may be described in terms of different tonal surroundings. **1951** TRAGER & SMITH *Outl. Eng. Struct.* II. 60 Suffixes, especially inflectional ones, usually have many allomorphs. **1953** C. E. BAZELL *Ling. Form* i. 8 Allomorphs are not to be regarded as segments, since this way of treating them gives rise to the impression that they are not minimal units. **1962** E. F. HADEN et al. *Resonance-Theory Linguistics* iii. 30 The forms..*showed*,..*handed*,..are..analyzable into stem + suffix:../ʃow/ + /d/, /hænd/ + /id/... Each of these endings signals the same grammatical meaning, namely, 'past', and they can all be classed together in the morpheme {-D} (or {past})... The several allomorphs of this morpheme ({M_1}) are statable as sets of phonemes, but more accurately as sets of allophones.

allomorphite (ælǝʊˈmɔːfaɪt). *Min.* [mod. f. Gr. ἀλλόμορφος of strange shape (f. ἄλλος other, different + μορφή form) + -ITE, min. form.] A mineral, allied to barytes or barite, of which Dana makes it a variety, having the form and cleavage of ANHYDRITE.
 1837–80 DANA *Min.* 617 *Allomorphite*..probably pseudomorphous; Breithaupt regards it as a case of dimorphism.

allomorphosis (ælǝʊˈmɔːfǝsɪs, -mɔːˈfǝʊsɪs). *Biol.* [f. ALLO- + MORPHOSIS.] **1.** = METAMORPHOSIS (Mayne *Expos. Lex.* Add. 1860).
 2. Evolutionary allometry: a term used for comparison of different phylogenetic groups (see quots.).
 1941 J. S. HUXLEY et al. in *Nature* 23 Aug. 225/1 We wish to suggest that *allometry* be the covering term, and *allomorphosis* the term for phylogenetic comparison. This indicates that all these differences..concern differing rates of growth in the individual, and..different (morphological or chemical) patterns brought about..in the completed individual of different groups. *Ibid.*, *Allomorphosis*, the relation of parts of organisms at some definite age to wholes or parts also at some definite age, but of different groups (races, varieties, species, genera). **1942** J. S. HUXLEY *Evolution* ix. 529 For comparison of relative proportions in different types it will..be best to use *allomorphosis*.. keeping allometry as a general and inclusive term. **1949** *Blakiston's New Gould Med. Dict.* 42/1 *Allomorphosis*, a type of allometry which deals with the relation of a part to the whole, or to another part, in a series of organisms..as the relation of jaw length to skull length of the adult in a series of breeds of dogs.

† **allonˈgation.** *Obs. rare*[−1]. [f. *allongāt-* ppl. stem of late L. *allongā-re* + -ION[1]. Cf. *elongation.*] A lengthening out; extension, continuation.
 1665–6 *Phil. Trans.* I. 309 The Nerves, holding at one end to the Brain, whereof they are but Allongations.

† **aˈllonge**, *v. Obs. rare*[−1]. [a. Fr. *allonge-r* to lengthen, draw out, lunge; f. *à* to + *long* long; or ? f. late L. *allongāre.*] To lunge.
 1668 R. LESTRANGE *Vis. Guevedo* (1708) 80 He..leapt a step backward, and with great agility, alonging withal.

† **aˈllonge**, *sb.*[1] *Obs.* [a. Fr. *allonge* lengthening, drawing out, etc.; f. *allonger*: see prec.]
 1. A lunge, thrust.
 1731 BAILEY, *Allonge*, a thrust or pass at the enemy. **1755** in JOHNSON; and in mod. Dicts.
 2. A long rein, when the horse is trotted in the hand. J.

‖ **allonge** (aˈlɔ̃ʒ), *sb.*[2] [a re-adoption of the Fr. word.] A slip of paper gummed to the end of a bill of exchange or promissory note, to give room for further endorsements when the back of the document itself will hold no more.
 1862 BYLES *Bills of Exch.* (ed. 8) 138 The supernumerary indorsements may be written on a slip of paper annexed to the bill, called, in French, an *allonge*.

‖ **allons** (alɔ̃). [Fr., 1st pers. pl. imp. of *aller* to go.] 'Let us go.' Also as *int.*, = 'Well!'
 1669 DRYDEN *Wild Gallant* v. 70 Allons Isabelle! courage! **1694** CONGREVE *Double-Dealer* I. i. 9 Come, Gentlemen, *allons*. **1765** STERNE *Tr. Shandy* VII. i. 6 *Allons*! said I; the post boy gave a crack with his whip—off I went. **1826** M. R. MITFORD *Our Village* II. 58 *Allons, messieurs*, over this gate, across this meadow. **1864** TROLLOPE *Can You forgive Her?* I. xxvii. 211 'Allons donc,' said Lady Glencora... Alice now followed her out of the room. **1925** D. H. LAWRENCE *Refl. Death Porcupine* 131 This is the philosophic problem: to find the way ahead. *Allons*!—there is no road before us. **1954** W. STEVENS *Let.* 15 Mar. (1967) 825 If in ten years I seem to be fifty, allons!

allonym (ˈælǝnɪm). [a. mod.Fr. *allonyme*, f. Gr. ἄλλος other + -ώνυμ-ος -named, f. ὄνομα, Æol. ὄνυμα name. Cf. *synonym.*] **a.** The name of some one else assumed by the author of a work. **b.** A book bearing the name of some one other than its author.
 1867 O. HAMST *Martyr to Bibliogr.* 21 Allonym (Allonymous). False proper name. Work published in order to deceive, under the name of some author or person of reputation, but not by him, as Peter Parley (Annual).

allonymous (æˈlɒnɪmǝs), *a.* [f. prec. + -OUS. Cf. *anonymous*, *synonymous*, etc.] Published or appearing under the name of some one other than the real author; falsely attributed to an author.

† **aˈlloo**, *v. Obs.* [for HALLOO.] To urge on with cries.
 1708 J. PHILLIPS *Cyder* I. 26 Alloo thy furious Mastiff, bid him vex the noxious herd.

allopalladium (ˌælǝʊpǝˈleɪdɪǝm). *Min.* [mod. f. Gr. ἄλλος other + PALLADIUM.] Native palladium crystallizing under the hexagonal system.
 1837–80 DANA *Min.* 12 *Allopalladium*..from Tilkerode, in the Harz, in small hexagonal tables with gold.

allopath (ˈælǝpæθ). [a. mod.Fr. *allopathe*, f. *allopathie* ALLOPATHY, by form-assoc. with such pairs as *philosophie*, *philosophe*, *astronomie*, *astronome*; the analogy being merely apparent and opposed to the etymology, a. Gr. ἀλλοπάθος in the sense of *allopath* being quite impossible.] A practitioner of allopathy.
 1830 *Edin. Rev.* L. 519 The common large-dose-dispensing Allopath. **1842** BLACK *Homœop.* i. 10 The few specifics employed by allopaths.

allopathetic (ˌælǝʊpǝˈθɛtɪk), *a. rare*[−0]. [f. ALLOPATHY, after *apathy*, *apathetic.*] = ALLOPATHIC.

allopathetically (ˌælǝʊpǝˈθɛtɪkǝlɪ), *adv. rare*[−0]. [f. prec. + -AL[1] + -LY.] = ALLOPATHICALLY.

allopathic (ælǝʊˈpæθɪk), *a.* [ad. mod.Fr. *allopathique*: see ALLOPATHY and -IC. Due to form-assoc. with words like *botanie*, *botanique*, etc., and not derivable from Gr. παθικός passive.] Of or pertaining to allopathy.
 1830 *Edin. Rev.* L. 513 The allopathic..method..hopes to cure disease by exciting some dissimilar affection. **1844** T. GRAHAM *Dom. Med.* 330 Some of the allopathic school, who order poisons every day, and almost wholesale. **1870** *Daily News* 29 Sept., Various medical journals of the allopathic profession.

allopathically (ælǝʊˈpæθɪkǝlɪ), *adv.* [f. prec. + -AL[1] + -LY.] In an allopathic manner; according to the methods of allopathy.
 1842 BLACK *Homœop.* i. 2 Medicines may be applied.. Allopathically and Homœopathically. **1865** *Pall Mall G.* 15 June 9 Homœopathically or allopathically..with globules or with Glauber salts.

allopathist (æˈlɒpǝθɪst). [f. ALLOPATHY + -IST.] One who professes or practises allopathy.
 1844 LAURIE *Homœop.* Pref. 6 The Allopathist, willing by fair experience to put the system to the test. **1881** *Scribn. Mag.* XXII. 305 The allopathist calls the homeopathist a 'quack,' and the latter regards the former as a 'butcher.'

allopathy (æˈlɒpǝθɪ). [mod. f. (first used in Ger. (*allopathie*) by Hahnemann) Gr. ἄλλος other, different + -πάθεια, f. πάθος suffering.] 'The curing of a diseased action by the inducing of another of a different kind, yet not necessarily diseased.' *Syd. Soc. Lex.* A term applied by homœopathists to the ordinary or traditional medical practice, and to a certain extent in common use to distinguish it from HOMŒOPATHY.

1842 BLACK *Homœop.* i. 2 The term Allopathy, as a general term, is applied to the present prevailing system of medicine. **1863** J. HOLLAND *Lett. Joneses* xx. 291 No man of sense believes that allopathy is all wrong and homœopathy all right.

allopatric (æləʊ'pætrɪk), *a. Biol.* [f. ALLO- + Gr. πάτρᾱ fatherland: see -IC.] Applied to organisms that occupy different geographical areas. Opp. SYMPATRIC *a.* Hence **allo'patry**, the occurrence of allopatric forms.

1942 E. MAYR *Systematics & Origin of Species* vii. 149 Two forms (or species) are *allopatric*, if they do not occur together, that is if they exclude each other geographically. **1953** —— et al. *Methods & Princ. Syst. Zool.* ii. 29 Closely related allopatric forms are usually subspecies of a polytypic species. *Ibid.* v. 101 The word *allopatric* is essentially an antonym of *sympatric* and means therefore geographical distribution without geographical overlap. There are five kinds of allopatry that may be encountered by the taxonomist. **1958** *Canadian Jrnl. Zool.* XXXVI. 148 Reproductive isolation is more likely to be present between closely related sympatric species than between closely related allopatric species. **1960** *Evolution* XIV. 82/1 The best estimate of the course of geographic speciation comes from analysis of disjunct, allopatric populations.

allophanate (æ'lɒfəneɪt). *Chem.* [mod. f. Gr. ἀλλοφανής (see next) + -ATE[4].] A salt of allophanic acid.

1863 WATTS *Chem. Dict.* I. 133 Allophanate of amyl forms nacreous scales, unctuous to the touch, and without taste.

allophane ('æləʊfeɪn). *Min.* [mod. ad. Gr. ἀλλοφανής appearing otherwise, f. ἄλλος other + φαίνειν to show, appear.] A mineral classed by Dana as the first of his Sub-silicates; a hydrated silicate of alumina, with colour sky-blue, green, brown, or yellow, which it loses under the blowpipe; whence the name.

1843 HUMBLE *Dict. Geol.*, *Allophane*.. gelatinizes in acids. **1875** URE *Dict. Arts* I. 90 Allophanes have been found containing from 14 to 19 per cent. of oxide of copper, which gives them a green colour.

allophanic (æləʊ'fænɪk), *a.* [mod. f. Gr. ἀλλοφανής (see prec.) + -IC.] Of or pertaining to anything which changes colour or appearance; as ***allophanic acid*** $C_2H_4N_2O_3$, a monureide of carbonic acid only known in the form of salts or ethers.

1863 WATTS *Chem. Dict.* I. 132 By passing the vapour of cyanic acid into absolute alcohol, Liebig and Wöhler obtained in 1820 a peculiar ether.. the ether of a peculiar acid which they called allophanic acid. *Ibid.* I. 133 Allophanate of Ethyl or Allophanic Ether, $C_4H_8N_2O_3$.

allophite ('æləʊfaɪt). *Min.* [mod. f. (Ger. in 1873) Gr. ἄλλ-ος other, different + ὀφίτης serpentine, f. ὄφις serpent.] A hydrous silicate of the Margarophyllite section, consisting chiefly of silica, alumina, and magnesia.

1880 DANA *Min.* App. II. 2 *Allophite*.. distinguished from serpentine by its inferior hardness.

allophone ('æləʊfəʊn). *Philol.* [f. ALLO- 3 + PHONE(ME.] Any of the variants making up a single phoneme.

1938 B. L. WHORF *Lang., Thought, & Reality* (1956) 126 Allophones or positional variants. **1941** TRAGER & BLOCH in *Language* XVII. 223 Sound-types as members of a phonemic class are called allophones. **1949** C. E. BAZELL in *Archivum Linguisticum* I. 4 Two comparisons are familiar, the one between the allophones of a phoneme and the alternants of a morpheme, the other between the allophones and the semantic variants of the morphemic *Gesamtbedeutung*. **1957** S. POTTER *Mod. Linguistics* ii. 39 A phoneme is a closely coherent group or bundle of sounds consisting of one more frequent phone, or chief member, together with other related phones or allophones which take its place in particular contexts. **1964** R. H. ROBINS *Gen. Linguistics* iv. 131 Members of phonemes are often called *phones* or *allophones*, and it is common practice to write phone symbols between square brackets and phoneme symbols.. between oblique brackets. Thus [t] and [tʰ] are allophones of the /t/ phoneme.

Hence **allo'phonic** *a.*, of or pertaining to an allophone; **allo'phonically** *adv.*

1938 B. L. WHORF *Lang., Thought, & Reality* (1956) 126 Allophonic constellation. **1953** L. F. BROSNAHAN *Some O.E. Sound Changes* 82 By themselves these inducing phones are unable to induce anything more than those allophonic modifications of the affected vowels which are present in normal speech. **1956** D. JONES *Outl. Eng. Phonetics* (ed. 8) x. 49 The words [*sc.* F. *loup, boucle*] may be transcribed allophonically.. as *lu, bukl̥*, *l̥* representing a voiceless *l*.

allophyle ('æləʊfɪl), *sb.* and *a. rare.* [ad. L. *allophȳl-us*, a. Gr. ἀλλόφῡλ-ος of another tribe, alien, f. ἄλλος other, different + φυλή tribe.]

1. An alien; a Philistine.

1577 *Test. 12 Patriarchs* 48 The kindred of the allophyles or of the gentiles.

2. = ALLOPHYLIAN. (Cf. mod.Fr. *allophyle*, introduced by Quatrefages after Prichard.)

1879 in *Syd. Soc. Lex.*

Allophylian (æləʊ'fɪlɪən), *a.* and *sb.* [f. L. *allophȳl-us* (see prec.) + -IAN.] A term introduced by Prichard to designate the languages of Asia and Europe, which are neither Aryan nor Semitic; sometimes extended to all the languages of the world outside these families, sometimes made equivalent to 'Turanian.' **A.** *adj.*

1844 J. PRICHARD in *Blackw. Mag.* LVI. 328 Among the Allophylian nations, on the other hand, a rude and sensual superstition prevailed. **1865** *Athenæum* No. 1960, 688/1 This so called Turanian or Allophyllian family of languages. **1866** LAING *Preh. Rem. Caithn.* 4 Stonehenge.. has been assigned.. to the remote antiquity of some unknown Allophylian race.

B. *sb.*

1881 *Q. Rev.* Jan. 41 The Californian Indian is no allophylian.

allophytoid (æ'lɒfɪtɔɪd). *Bot.* [f. Gr. ἄλλος other, different + PHYTOID, f. Gr. φυτόν plant + -OID.] A separated vegetable bud differing from the plant from which it originates.

1858 CARPENTER *Veg. Phys.* §397 When the phytoids are of the usual form they are called isophytoids, whilst the differing form is called an allophytoid.

allopolyploidy (ˌæləʊ'pɒlɪplɔɪdɪ). *Biol.* [ad. G. *allopolyploidie* (Kihara and Ono 1927, in *Zeitschr. für Zell. und Mikr. Anat.* IV. 480), f. ALLO- 2 + POLYPLOIDY.] The state or occurrence of a polyploid having its sets of chromosomes derived from different species by means of hybridization.

1928 DARLINGTON in *Jrnl. Genetics* XIX. 243 A useful distinction has been made amongst polyploids.. according as their gametic complements are constituted by the reduplication of similar series (auto-polyploidy), that is, by the doubling of the chromosome number in a theoretically pure line, or by the combination of dissimilar series (allopolyploidy), that is, by doubling in a hybrid. **1930** E. MÜNTZING in *Hereditas* XIII. 293 As to the nature of the chromosome increase the case may be one of auto-polyploidy (doubling of the same genome) or allo-polyploidy (addition of different genomes). **1952** *New Biol.* XIII. 46 Among the newer crops which have arisen by allopolyploidy in recent years, the most notable are the various berries related to blackberry and raspberry of the genus *Rubus*.

Hence ˌ**allo'polyploid**, a polyploid of this type. Also as *adj.*

1928 DARLINGTON in *Jrnl. Genetics* XIX. 243 It is impossible to draw any but an arbitrary line across the innumerable gradations between a pure type, as pure as inbreeding can produce, and a hybrid;.. it is thus impossible to distinguish in absolute terms between an allo-polyploid and an auto-polyploid. **1938** E. B. FORD *Study Heredity* iv. 95 The polyploids.. belong to the group called autopolyploids, in which all the sets of chromosomes are derived from the same species. More striking.. are the allopolyploids, which result from chromosome doubling after hybridization. **1953** *Rep. 13th Internat. Hort. Congress 1952* 66 Allopolyploid or amphidiploid groups [of plants].. should be treated as species.

allopurinol (æləʊ'pjʊərɪnɒl). *Pharm.* [f. ALLO- + PURIN(E + -OL.] A bicyclic pyrimidine derivative which inhibits the enzyme xanthine oxidase and hence uric acid production, and is used in the treatment of gout and other conditions involving excess uric acid; 1*H*-pyrazolo[3,4-*d*]pyrimidin-4-ol, $C_5H_4N_4O$.

1964 YÜ & GUTMAN in *Amer. Jrnl. Med.* XXXVII. 885/2 Our chief interest in testing the new drug, now designated allopurinol, was to determine its efficacy in cases of primary and secondary gout. **1966** *New Scientist* 16 June 692/3 Allopurinol is an example of the still comparatively small group of therapeutic substances which have been developed by chemists and pharmacologists in an attempt to regulate some specific chemical reaction within the cell. **1974** M. C. GERALD *Pharmacol.* iv. 75 Allopurinol's development was based upon adequate biochemical knowledge of gout. **1983** *Oxf. Textbk. Med.* II. XIX. 106 In the early stages of treatment [of chronic granulocytic leukaemia], and particularly if the white cell count is very high, allopurinol, 400–600 mg daily, should be given.

alloquial (ə'ləʊkwɪəl), *a. rare*⁻¹. [f. L. *alloqui-um* address (f. *al-* = *ad-* to + *loqui* to speak) + -AL[1]; cf. ALLOCUTION.] Of, or pertaining to, the action of addressing others; contrasted with *colloquial* or conversational.

1840 DE QUINCEY *Style* in *Blackw. Mag.* XLVIII. 11 There are no such people endured or ever heard of in France as *al*-loquial wits; people who talk *to* but not *with* a circle.

alloquialism (ə'ləʊkwɪəˌlɪz(ə)m). *rare.* [f. prec. + -ISM: cf. *colloquialism*.] A phrase or manner of speech used in addressing.

1872 R. BURTON *Unexpl. Syria* I. App. 264 The alloquialisms of a people new to me.

† **'alloquy.** *Obs.*⁻⁰. [ad. L. *alloquium* an address or speech.] 'The act of speaking to another; address, conversation.' J.

1626 COCKERAM, *Alloquie*, communication or speech. **1731** BAILEY, *Alloquy*, talking with another.

alloren, obs. form of ALDERN.

all-or-nothing, all or nothing. 1. Applied *attrib.* to a piece of mechanism in a repeating watch (see quot. 1940); also used *absol.*

1765 *Ann. Reg. 1764* 79/1 The all or nothing piece [in a watch]. **1843** *Penny Cycl.* XXVII. 108/1 (*Watch, Repeating*) The whole.. carried by the all-or-nothing piece *TR*. *Ibid.* 108/2 When the quarter-rack is brought back to its original position.. the part *m* will have passed between the end *R* of the all-or-nothing, which in its passage *m* will have pressed outwards. **1940** *Chambers's Techn. Dict.* 22/2 *All-or-nothing piece*, a piece of the mechanism of a repeating watch which either allows the striking of the hours and quarters or entirely prevents it.

2. As phr., indicating that a principle, policy, etc., must be accepted without qualification or not at all; also *attrib.*

1862 EMERSON *Jrnl.* Jan. (1914) IX. 361 My estimate of my own mental means and resources is all or nothing; in happy hours, life.. infinitely rich, and sterile at others. **1882** W. JAMES *Will to Believe* (1897) 292 The silly hegelian all-or-nothing insatiateness. **1891** W. WILSON tr. *Ibsen's Brand* v. 290 *The Figure.* All these fell and pallid spectres can be laid with *three words*. *Brand.* Speak them! *The Figure.* All or nothing! **1936** J. C. POWYS *Maiden Castle* (1937) vi. 222 They don't need your damned all-or-nothing truths! **1950** B. WOOTTON *Test. Social Sci.* iii. 49 Questions which (like nearly all the significant issues in life) cannot but be matters of more or less are constantly answered in terms of yes or no, all or nothing. *Ibid.* vi. 132 The peculiarity of religious systems is that this threat to security has a peculiar all-or-nothing character. **1957** R. N. CAREW HUNT *Guide to Communist Jargon* p. xiv, The 'all-or-nothing' nature of communist thinking, which leads to the rejection as 'opportunism' of whatever stops short of the absolute goal of revolution. **1960** in L. Pincus *Marriage* i. 21 An all-or-nothing response in which the infant feels itself and its world to be entirely good, or entirely bad.

3. = *all-or-none (a)*: see ALL III. 13.

1922 *Encycl. Brit.* XXXII. 104/2 In the case of the heart muscle, this fact has long been known and was given the name of the 'law of all-or-nothing'... This law has now been shown to hold for voluntary muscle and for nerve. **1932** *Times Lit. Suppl.* 11 Feb. 93/2 The 'all-or-nothing' law of nervous conduction. **1964** J. Z. YOUNG *Model of Brain* ii. 23 We now know that nerve fibres are able to propagate all-or-nothing signals with a high safety factor and without decrement.

allosteric (æləʊ'stɛrɪk, -'stɪərɪk), *a. Biochem.* [f. ALLO- + STERIC *a.*] Pertaining to or involving a change in an enzyme's affinity for a substrate as a result of a change in its conformation by the attachment of a molecule not analogous to the substrate molecule at a site other than the substrate binding site; pertaining to any change in conformation caused by the attachment of a ligand.

1962 MONOD & JACOB in *Cold Spring Harbor Symp. Quantitative Biol.* XXVI. 391/1 In 1954, Novick and Szilard discovered that the synthesis of a tryptophan precursor.. was inhibited by tryptophan... The work of Umbarger.. demonstrated that, in many pathways, an early enzyme is so constructed as to be strongly and specifically inhibited by the.. endproduct... The most remarkable feature of the Novick-Szilard-Umbarger effect is that the inhibitor *is not a steric analogue* of the substrate. We propose therefore to designate this mechanism as 'allosteric inhibition'. **1962** H. A. KREBS in A. Pirie *Lens Metabolism Rel. Cataract* 351 In competition inhibitions, substrate and inhibitor react with the same site of the enzyme molecule. Allosteric inhibitions involve different sites. **1970** R. W. MCGILVERY *Biochem.* xiii. 247 There evidently is a second site on the protein, allosteric rather than catalytic, at which ATP also binds and causes a modification of the protein structure to an inactive form. **1971** J. Z. YOUNG *Introd. Study Man* iii. 64 Such 'allosteric' proteins may.. be the basis of regulation of gene action. **1982** J. L. YORK in T. M. Devlin *Textbk. Biochem.* iv. 171 The modulating ligands that bind at the allosteric site are known as the allosteric effectors or modulators.

Hence **allo'sterically** *adv.*; **allo'sterism** = ALLOSTERY.

1967 *Proc. Nat. Acad. Sci.* LVIII. 1955 If the ion affinity center of an ionophore could be altered allosterically by energy-linked reversible configurational changes, it would acquire the requisites for promoting active transport. **1976** *Ann. Rev. Microbiol.* XXX. 288 Both the *S. faecalis* and *L. casei* malic enzymes were shown to be allosterically regulated proteins. **1977** *Jrnl. Protozool.* XXIV. 3/2 With the concepts 'cooperativity' and 'allosterism' plainly before us, let us begin to look at some cell patterns. *Ibid.* 6/2 It is allosterically controlled by binding at other sites of the dimer. **1982** J. L. YORK in T. M. Devlin *Textbk. Biochem.* iv. 175 The relationship between allosterism and cooperativity has been confused in many recent texts.

allostery ('æləʊstɪərɪ). *Biochem.* [f. ALLOSTER(IC *a.* + -Y[3].] (The theory of) allosteric phenomena.

1966 *New Scientist* 4 Aug. 271/2 (*heading*) Allostery: a starting point. **1975** *Nature* 4 Sept. 76/2 He.. provided evidence for a low molecular weight compound such as a steroid hormone, specifically changing the conformation of a protein molecule. This concept, subsequently termed allostery by others, is an important one not only in endocrinology but for most of molecular biology and biochemistry. **1982** J. L. YORK in T. M. Devlin *Textbk. Biochem.* iv. 171 (*heading*) Allostery and cooperativity.

allot (ə'lɒt), *v.* Also 6–7 **alot, allott.** [a. OFr. *alote-r* (mod. *allotir*), f. *à* to + *loter, lotir* to divide by lot, or into lots, f. *lot* lot, a Teut. word (Goth. *hlauts*, OHG. *hlôz*, OE. *hlot*) of early adoption in the Rom. langs.; It. *lotto*, Pg. *lote*,

OFr. *lot*, whence the vbs. It. *lottare*, Pg. *lotar*, Fr. *loter*, *lotir*.]

1. To distribute by lot, or in such way that the recipients have no choice; to assign shares authoritatively; to apportion.

1574 tr. *Littleton's Tenures* 52 b, The landes in fee-simple bee alotted to yᵉ younger daughter in allowance of the tenementes tayled allotted to the elder daughter. **1618** BOLTON *Florus* (1636) 167 To allot them out some proportions of Land, instead of pay. **1660** PEPYS *Diary* 22 May, I spent an hour at allotting to every ship their service. **1766** GOLDSM. *Vic. Wakef.* xxvi. (1857) 184, I allotted to each of my family what they were to do. **1858** BRIGHT *Sp.* 285 How your Members shall be allotted to the various constituent bodies.

†**b.** *intr.* To fall by lot, to be apportioned. *Obs.*

1574 tr. *Littleton's Tenures* 53 b, That other ploughe lande that allotteth to yᵉ purparty of that other.

2. Of any absolute authority, the Deity, fate, etc.: To assign as a lot or portion *to*; to appoint (without the idea of distribution).

a **1547** EARL SURREY *Æneid* II. (R.) The wofull end that was allotted him. **1587** TURBERVILLE *Trag. T.* (1837) 21 For thus the Goddis alotted had her paine. **1681** DRYDEN *Abs. & Achit.* I. 252 Heaven has to all allotted, soon or late, Some lucky revolution of their fate. *a* **1842** TENNYSON *Will Waterpr.* 218 The sphere thy fate allots. **1860** MAURY *Phys. Geog. Sea* xvii. §728 The climate which the Creator has.. allotted to this portion of the earth.

3. Hence *gen.* To assign to a special person as his portion; to appropriate to a special purpose.

1574 tr. *Marlorat's Apocalips* 11 Those then that be chosen vnto Bishoprikes, haue allotted to them, not a soueraintie, but a seruice. **1596** B. GRIFFIN *Fidessa* (1876) 30 This hap her crueltie hath her alotten. **1624** CAPT. SMITH *Virginia* v. 190 The house and land he had allotted for himselfe. **1718** *Free-thinker* No. 2. 10 He has a seat allotted him in each theatre. **1758** JOHNSON *Idler* No. 101 ¶4 Ten years I will allot to the attainment of knowledge. **1809** WELLINGTON in *Gen. Disp.* V. 33 Obliged to allot the Portuguese carts.. to the purpose of removing the wounded soldiers.

†**4.** To make it the lot of, to appoint, destine (a person *to do* something). *Obs.*

1588 GREENE *Pandosto* (1607) 24 Vulcan was allotted to shake the tree. **1589** *Hay any Work* 45 Why was John of London alotted.. to pay him 40 pounds? **1591** SHAKS. *1 Hen. VI*, v. iii. 55 Thou art alotted to be tane by me. **1677** HALE *Prim. Orig. Man.* II. viii. 204 We will allott only two of these six to attain to the state of Men and Women.

†**5.** *fig.* To attribute as due or proper. *Obs.*

1598 BACON *Sacred Med.* x. 125 Nothing can be more iustly allotted to be the saying of fooles then this—'There is no God.' **1750** JOHNSON *Rambl.* No. 172 ¶6 Scarce any man is willing to allot to accident, friendship, etc... the part which they may justly claim in his advancement.

6. *Amer. colloq.* ***to allot upon*** (occas. without prep.): to count or reckon *upon*.

1816 PICKERING *Vocab. U.S.* 31, *I allot upon* going to such a place. **1840** HALIBURTON *Clockm.* (1862) 93 And I allot we must economise or we will be ruined.

allotetraploid (ˌæləʊˈtɛtrəplɔɪd), *a.* and *sb. Biol.* [f. ALLO- 2 + TETRAPLOID.] = AMPHIDIPLOID *a.* and *sb.*

1930 W. J. C. LAWRENCE in *Genetica* XII. 272 Hybrid tetraploid (allo-tetraploid). *Ibid.* 277 The most probable origin of an allotetraploid would seem to be hybridisation of two self-incompatible diploid species. **1938** E. B. FORD *Study Heredity* x. 225 The allotetraploids.. may be quite fertile forms, though sterile with the two species from which they are derived. *Ibid.* 239 An allotetraploid plant is as completely isolated from its parent species as if it had been transported to a desert island. **1957** M. ABERCROMBIE et al. *Dict. Biol.* 14 *Allotetraploid* (*amphidiploid*), allopolyploid which arises when an ordinary hybrid between two different species, containing a set of chromosomes from each parent, doubles its chromosome number. An ordinary hybrid is usually sterile because its chromosomes cannot pair during meiosis. But if it becomes an allotetraploid it solves this difficulty because each chromosome then has a homologue with which it can pair... Artificial preparation of allotetraploids has great scope in the production of new agricultural and horticultural varieties.

Hence **alloˈtetraploidy**, the state or occurrence of such a tetraploid.

1942 J. S. HUXLEY *Evolution* iii. 87 Allotetraploidy is almost confined to plants, because of the favourable conditions provided by their vegetative growth for the rare chromosome-doubling.

allotheism (ˈæləʊˌθiːɪz(ə)m). [f. Gr. ἄλλος other + θεός god + -ISM. Cf. *atheism*, *polytheism*.] The worship of other or strange gods.

1660 JER. TAYLOR *Duct. Dubit.* II. ii. vi. §29 In the first commandment.. polytheism and allotheism are forbidden. **1863** J. MURPHY *Comm. Gen.* xli. 37 Sharply-defined systems of polytheism and allotheism.

allothigenic (æˌlɒθɪˈdʒɛnɪk), *a. Geol.* [ad. G. *allothigene* (E. Kalkowsky 1880, in *Neues Jahrb. f. Min.* 4), f. Gr. ἀλλοθι elsewhere: see -GENIC.] See quot.; opp. AUTHIGENIC *a.*

1888 [see ALLOGENIC *a.* 1].

allotment (əˈlɒtmənt). [a. Fr. *allotement*, formerly *al-*, f. *aloter*: see ALLOT and -MENT.]

1. a. The action of allotting or assigning as a share; apportionment; appointment.

1574 in Heath *Grocers' Comp.* (1869) 11 That this and the other Companies should, after the rateable and proportionable allotment, provide their shares thereof. **1774** BRYANT *Mythol.* I. Pref. 6 Colonies went abroad without any regard to their original place of allotment. **1790** COWPER *Odyss.* III. 10 To each they made Allotment equal of nine sable bulls. **1882** *Globe* 24 July 8/3, 10*s.* per share payable on Application; 10*s.* per share on Allotment.

b. A deed of allotment; an assigning document.

1772 *Hist. Rochester* 95 The only allotment to be met with is to the dean and one prebendary.

c. *spec.* The payment of part of a seaman's wages to a nominated person; also, the amount so paid; esp. *attrib.* in ***allotment note***, a note authorizing such an allotment.

1867 SMYTH *Sailor's Word-Bk.* 32 *Allotment*, a part of the pay apportioned monthly to the wives, children, mothers, or destitute fathers of the warrant and petty officers, seamen, and marines. **1894** *Act 57 & 58 Vict.* c. 60 §141 (2), The seaman may require that a stipulation be inserted in the agreement for the allotment by means of an allotment note, of any part (not exceeding one half) of his wages in favour either of a near relative or of a savings bank. **1953** 'R. GORDON' *Doctor at Sea* vi. 82 Long voyages and young wives don't mix. You leave the allotment of your pay and if you don't get a letter at every port you wonder what's up.

2. The destiny allotted to any one; lot in life, fate.

1674 *Govt. Tongue* x. §6 (1684) 157 Our behavior towards God, whose allotments we dispute. **1754** FIELDING *Jon. Wild* II. xii. Wks. 1784 IV. 195 No man is born into the world without his particular allotment. **1828** CARLYLE *Misc.* (1857) I. 122 The stinted allotments of earthly life are as a mockery to him.

3. A share or portion allotted to one.

1629 COKE *1st Pt. Inst.* 167 a, In this case euery one of them ought to stand to their chance and allotment. **1768** BLACKSTONE *Comm.* II. 83 The elder sons.. migrate from their father with a certain allotment of cattle. **1850** BLACKIE *Æschyl.* II. 27 He called his gods together, and assigned To each his fair allotment.

4. *esp.* A portion of land assigned to a special person, or appropriated to a particular purpose. *spec.* A small portion of land let out for cultivation (see quot. 1959).

1674 SCHEFFER *Lapland* vi. 15 The Finlanders.. have a certain division or allotment called Lappio. *a* **1745** BROOME (J.) A vineyard, and an allotment for olives and herbs. **1768** BLACKSTONE *Comm.* II. 45 Large districts or parcels of land were.. dealt out again in smaller parcels or allotments to the inferior officers. **1845** *Penny Cycl. Supp.* I. 88 The most convenient mode of giving [country labourers] gardens is to divide a field near the village into small allotments.. The bishop of Bath and Wells commenced the letting of allotments in 1807, but it is only since 1830 that its adoption has become common. **1917** *Times* 14 Aug. 3/3 Holders of municipal allotments.. claim for loss by malicious damage, the hearts of 700 cabbages having been cut out. **1922** *Encycl. Brit.* XXX. 81/2 The powers conferred upon the [Food Production] Department by D.O.R.A., which were delegated to town and urban district councils, enabled them to take possession of any unoccupied land for the purpose of letting it as allotments. **1944** *Amer. Speech* XIX. 294 In Britain the playing of tennis and golf has been succeeded by the weekend pastime of working in one's 'allotment', which is a kind of 'Victory Garden'. **1959** *Chambers's Encycl.* I. 276/2 *Allotment*, a small plot of land let for cultivation, sometimes by private landowners but usually by local authorities for individuals or allotment associations. They were originally provided for country labourers by their overlords, but now are found in and near towns.

†**5.** *Comm.* The division of a ship's cargo into equal portions, the particular portion falling to each purchaser being decided by lot; *also* in *pl.* Descriptions of the divided portions. *Obs.*

1703 *Lond. Gaz.* mmmdccclxxxii/4 Inventories of the Ships, and Allotments of the Goods may be seen at the said Hall. **1705** *Ibid.* mmmmcxxxv/3 Printed Copies of the Allotments of the said Goods. **1751** CHAMBERS *Cycl.*, *Allotment* of goods, is when a ship's cargo is divided into several parts, bought by divers persons, etc.

6. *Comb.* or *Attrib.*, chiefly in sense 4: **allotment letter**, also ***letter of allotment*** (see quot. 1882 and cf. sense 1 a, quot. 1882). **allotment system**, the division of land into small plots to be held for cultivation by the poorer classes at a small rent; hence ***allotment-garden***, ***-gardening***, ***-holder***, etc.

1863 DICKENS *Uncommercial Traveller* in *All the Year Round* 1 Aug. 542/1 Certain allotment-gardens by the road-side. **1876** FAWCETT *Pol. Econ.* II. viii. 238 The granting of allotment-gardens would do much for the labourers. **1959** *Chambers's Encycl.* I. 276/2 There is in Britain a legal distinction between allotments and allotment gardens (Allotments Act, 1922) important as regards determination of tenancy and compensation. **1944** AUDEN *For Time Being* (1945) 113 Allotment gardening has become popular. **1848** J. S. MILL *Pol. Econ.* I. ix. §4. 1. 180 The labour which the peasant, or even the allotment holder, gladly undergoes. **1920** Allotment holder[see next]. **1882** R. BITHELL *Counting-House Dict.* 169 *Letter of Allotment*, a letter issued in answer to a letter of application for a portion of a public loan, or for shares in a commercial undertaking. **1909** A. E. DAVIES *Money, Stock & Share Markets* xii. 98 Once the allotment letter has been posted it is impossible for the applicant to withdraw his application. **1955** *Times* 15 July 13/1 The allotment letters were being posted by the Bank of England last evening. **1845** *Penny Cycl. Supp.* I. 90 The allotment system, when limited to the giving a labourer a small plot of garden-ground, presents many advantages. **1868** PEARD *Water-farm.* ii. 13 A piece of ground parcelled out under the allotment system.

allotmenteer (əˌlɒtmənˈtɪə(r)). [f. ALLOTMENT + -EER.] One who holds or rents an allotment (of land).

1920 *Evening Times* (Glasgow) 1 Oct. 4 Allotment holders .. have had fine weather for the ingathering of their crop, and the average of quality—as shown at the recent exhibition arranged by allotmenteers..—is very high. **1959** *Times* 21 Apr. 15/5 As an 'allotmenteer' of over 30 years' standing, I must challenge the suggestion.. that an allotment cannot be a thing of beauty.

allotriomorphic (æˌlɒtrɪəʊˈmɔːfɪk), *a. Min.* [ad. G. *allotriomorph* (H. Rosenbusch *Mikrosk. Physiog. d. Massigen Gest.* (1886) i. 11), f. Gr. ἀλλότριος belonging to another (ἄλλος other) + μορφή form: see -IC.] = XENOMORPHIC *a.* (opp. *idiomorphic*). Hence **aˌllotrioˈmorphically** *adv.* Cf. ANHEDRAL *a.*

1887 *Geol. Mag.* Mar. 123 The form of an individual mineral in a rock may.. be.. dependent on causes other than the molecular forces proper to the mineral (*allotriomorphic*). **1888** [see XENOMORPHIC *a.*]. **1888** W. S. BAYLEY in *Amer. Naturalist* Mar. 209 When none of the constituents are ..[idiomorphically] developed the structure is *allotriomorphically granular*. **1922** C. H. DESCH *Metallography* (ed. 3) ix. 179 Each grain [of metal] is, to use the mineralogical term, an 'allotriomorphic' crystal, the outline of which is determined by the presence of neighbouring grains. **1958** A. D. MERRIMAN *Dict. Metallurgy* 5/1 *Allotriomorphic*, a term applied to crystals which have taken their shape from their surroundings and have not been allowed to develop the contours prescribed by their crystalline form.

allotrope (ˈæləʊtrəʊp). [Back-formation f. ALLOTROPY.] An allotropic form of a substance. Also *fig.*

1889 *Cent. Dict.*, *Allotrope*, one of the forms in which an element having the property of allotropy exists: thus, the diamond is an allotrope of carbon. **1942** J. N. GREENWOOD *Gloss. Metallographic Terms* (ed. 2) 6 The importance of allotropes in connection with metals and alloys is that they constitute different phases, and increase the possibilities of changing the mechanical properties by heat treatment. **1968** *Listener* 6 June 750/2 Walton evokes various allotropes of Old England that are.. gently sauced with the Mediterranean. **1978** *Times Lit. Suppl.* 24 Nov. 1357/3 Among the various allotropes of Jonathan Miller cited above, we must number also the entertainer and wit.

allotrophic (æləʊˈtrɒfɪk), *a. Med.* [mod. f. Gr. ἄλλος other, different + -τροφ-ος nourishing (f. τρέφειν to nourish) + -IC.] Susceptible of a change as to nutritive or physiological properties, without any change in physical or chemical characters.

1879 in *Syd. Soc. Lex.*

allotropic (æləʊˈtrɒpɪk), *a.* [f. Gr. ἀλλότροπ-ος (see ALLOTROPY) + -IC.] Of or pertaining to allotropy; having different physical properties, though unchanged in substance.

[Not in CRAIG 1847.] **1849** SCHROETTER in *Rep. Brit. Assoc.* 42 The allotropic red phosphorus was not ignited by friction. **1869** MRS. SOMERVILLE *Molec. Sc.* I. i. 16 Sulphur becomes allotropic by the continued application of heat. **1873** H. SPENCER *Sociol.* ix. 225 The constitution of ozone as an allotropic form of oxygen.

alloˈtropical, *a.* [f. prec. + -AL[1].] = prec.

1853 FARADAY *Lect.* Introd. 40 We can only demonstrate the allotropical substance to be phosphorus by reducing it to its original state.

allotropically (æləʊˈtrɒpɪkəlɪ), *adv.* [f. prec. + -LY[2].] In an allotropic manner.

1870 W. GROVE *Correl. Phys. Forces* (ed. 6) 169 Elementary gases are changed allotropically.

allotropicity (æˌlɒtrəˈpɪsɪtɪ). *rare.* [f. ALLOTROPIC + -ITY. Cf. *electricity*.] Capacity for assuming allotropic forms; allotropic nature.

1853 FARADAY *Lect.* v. 231 Sulphur is a simple body; and this circumstance greatly increases our astonishment at its allotropicity.

allotropism (æˈlɒtrəpɪz(ə)m). [mod. f. Gr. ἀλλότροπ-ος (see ALLOTROPY) + -ISM.] Allotropy viewed as a principle or process.

1851 *Art Jrnl. Catal. Exhib.* II. v*/2 The allotropism, as this peculiar state has been called by Berzelius, of charcoal, plumbago and the diamond. **1858** LEWES *Sea-side Stud.* 211 Chemical changes, both of decomposition and allotropism. **1881** LOCKYER in *Nature* No. 617. 397 The substances in which allotropism is most marked are all metalloids which have not been found in the sun.

allotropize (æˈlɒtrəpaɪz), *v. rare.* [mod. f. Gr. ἀλλότροπ-ος (see ALLOTROPY) + -IZE.] To change the physical properties of a body without change of its substance.

allotropized (æˈlɒtrəpaɪzd), *ppl. a.* [f. prec. + -ED.] Changed in physical properties by, or in accordance with, allotropy.

allotropy (æˈlɒtrəpɪ). [mod. ad. Gr. ἀλλοτροπία variation, changeableness, f. ἀλλότροπος of other manner; f. ἄλλος other, different + τρόπος turn (of mind), manner, f. τρέπ-ειν to turn.] The variation of physical properties without change of substance to which certain elementary bodies are liable, first noticed by Berzelius in the case of charcoal and the diamond.

1850 ANSTED *Elem. Geol.* 151 Isomorphism, a converse phenomenon to that of allotropy. **1863** WATTS *Chem. Dict.* II. 423 Instances of inorganic isomerism are usually called instances of allotropy.. Sulphur, phosphorus, carbon, and many other elements present.. examples of allotropy.

allottable (əˈlɒtəb(ə)l), *a.* [f. ALLOT + -ABLE.] Capable of being allotted or apportioned.
1869 *Echo* 10 Feb., They [game] are virtually fed within confines, at a cost ascertainable and allottable.

allotted (əˈlɒtɪd), *ppl. a.* [f. ALLOT + -ED.] Assigned by lot, or as the lot or portion of any one; apportioned, appointed.
1587 *Myrr. Mag., Rudacke* iv. 2 Each had a kingdome aloted his part. **1670** MILTON *Hist. Brit.* Wks. 1738 II. 48 In Kent, their own allotted dwelling. **1725** POPE *Odyss.* IV. 906 Must my servant-train The allotted labors of the day refrain? **1863** KEMBLE *Resid. Georgia* 124 Her allotted task was not done.

allottee (əˌlɒˈtiː). [f. ALLOT + -EE.] One to whom an allotment is made.
1846 *Blackw. Mag.* LX. 62 The national gaming-table was open to men of every class. Peer and peasant..were alike entitled to figure as allottees. **1880** *Fortn. Rev.* May 746 The allottee found it to pay him better to sell those plots. **1882** *Daily News* 16 Dec. 2/3 [He] never agreed to become an allottee of shares from the company.

allotter (əˈlɒtə(r)). [f. ALLOT + -ER[1].] One who allots or apportions.
1862 TRENCH *Mirac.* xxxiii. 473 He claims to be the allotter of the several portions of his servants.

†**a'llottery.** *Obs. rare*⁻¹. [perh. a. Fr. *alloterie, f. *allotir* (cf. *lottery*, a. Fr. *loterie* f. *lotir*); perh. an Eng. formation on *allot*: see -ERY.] The action or result of allotting; assignment of a share.
1600 SHAKS. *A.Y.L.* I. i. 77 Giue mee the poore allottery my father left me by testament.

allotting (əˈlɒtɪŋ), *vbl. sb.* [f. ALLOT + -ING[1].] A giving by lot, or as the lot or share of any one; apportionment, assignment. (Mostly gerundial.)
1598 FLORIO, *Sortimento*..an allotting by lot. **1611** COTGR., *Allotement*..an allotting, or laying out vnto euery one his part. **1618** BOLTON *Florus* III. iii. 168 Lawes touching the allotting out of Grounds. **1711** *Tatler* (J.) A man cannot be too scrupulous in allotting them their due portion.

allotype (ˈæləʊtaɪp). [f. ALLO- + TYPE *sb.*[1]] **1.** *Taxonomy.* A paratype of the opposite sex to the holotype.
1910 R. A. MUTTKOWSKI in *Bull. Public Museum Milwaukee* I. 10 The following suggestions to designate the types properly are made: *allotype*..for the sex not designated by the holotype... It can be contained in the original as well as in any subsequent description by other authors. **1962** GORDON & LAVOIPIERRE *Entomol. for Students of Med.* liii. 325 Sometimes one of these 'paratypes' (always of the opposite sex to the holotype) is singled out and designated as the 'allotype'. **1984** *Internat. Jrnl. Acarol.* X. III. 145 The male of *Limnesia cooki* Conroy and the male of *Piona triangularis* (Wolcott) are described from different locations in Wisconsin. The specimens are designated as Allotypes for the respective species.
2. *Immunol.* [a. F. *allotype* (J. Oudin 1956, in *Compt. Rend.* CCXLII. 2607).] An allotypic form of a protein or antigen.
1962 *Nature* 25 Aug. 786/1 An allotype the molecules of which are known to carry one or more allotypic specificities will be designated..as follows: A3 or A1, 6. **1975** *Immunogenetics* II. 288 That allotype markers exist should provide a convenient criterion for the survival of the B-cell graft. **1981** T. TADA et al. in N. Fabris et al. *Immunoregulation* 3 Many other investigators looked for idiotypes which are linked to immunoglobulin allotype genes on suppressor T cells and their hybridomas. **1983** *Ann. N.Y. Acad. Sci.* CDXVIII. 109 (*heading*) The role of rabbit immunoglobulin allotypes in an immune network. **1984** W. H. HILDEMANN *Essent. Immunol.* v. 37 Allotypes are useful in forensic medicine, anthropology, and in genetic analysis of immune responses.

allotypy (ˈæləʊtɪpɪ). *Immunol.* [ad. F. *allotypie* (J. Oudin 1956, in *Compt. Rend.* CCXLII. 2606), f. Gr. ἄλλος ALLO- + τύπος TYPE *sb.*[1]: see -Y[3].] The occurrence of a protein in antigenically distinct forms in different individuals of a species.
1962 *Nature* 19 May 658/2 It would be of interest to determine if antigenic polymorphisms of β-lipoproteins (allotypy) occur in species other than man; for example, in rabbits, where allotypy for the α- and β-globulin has already been reported. **1969** [see ALLOTYPICALLY *adv.*]. **1972** *Sci. Amer.* June 35/1 The immunoglobulin molecule consists of a 'constant' region whose amino acid composition varies among different individuals of the same species. This variation, known as allotypy, is not related to the molecule's recognition function in its role as an antibody. **1984** *Jrnl. Immunol. Methods* LXXI. 9 An allotypy in the rat species is located on the constant part of the kappa light chain.
Hence **allo'typic** *a.*, pertaining to or exhibiting allotypy; **allo'typically** *adv.*
1962 *Nature* 25 Aug. 785 The allotypic specificity is that which is not the same for all normal individuals of the same species. **1967** *New Scientist* 4 May 277/2 One position in the 'invariable' half of the [protein] chain is known in which the amino-acid may vary, being either valine or leucine. It turns out that these two alternatives (known as ' allotypic' alternatives) behave as genetic alleles. **1968** *WHO Technical Rep. Ser.* No. 402. 10 Recombination of allotypic markers identified on different IgG-cistrons have [*sic*], however, been detected. **1969** S. SELL in Smith & Good *Cellular Recognition* 208/1 If the control of expression of allotypy is similar for lymphocytes and for plasma cells, then each lymphocyte from an allotypically heterozygous donor should express only one of the two allotypic specificities supplied genetically. **1975** *Immunogenetics* II. 288 Allotypically defined sublines of the B14 strain. **1984** W. H. HILDEMANN *Essent. Immunol.* v. 37 Only one of two alternative allotypic markers is expressed in each mature B cell.

ˌall 'out, *adv. phr.* Also written 4 **alout**, 5–6 al-out(e, all-out. [See ALL C 9.]
1. *adv.* Entirely, completely, quite.
c **1300** *Beket* 1940 The lawes of his lond alout riȝt withsede. *c* **1400** *Rom. Rose* 2935 Now have I declared thee alle oute. *c* **1500** *Partenay* 866 Thay approched Columbere toun al-oute. **1513** DOUGLAS *Æneis* XI. xvi. 19 To mekil all out sa cruel punyssing. **1601** HOLLAND *Pliny* (1634) I. 10 Not all out foure moneths. *Ibid.* I. 365 Not all out so good. **1638** SANDERSON 35 *Serm.* (1681) II. 115 Our conversation ..cannot be all out so free and familiar. **1835** M. DOYLE *Common Sense for Common People* 18 *Bench*..Were you drunk? *Tom.* Not all out, I could keep my feet on the floor. **1852** W. R. WILDE *Irish Pop. Superstitions* iv. 121 In the islands of the extreme west, except from sheer old age, or some very ostensible cause, no-one is ever believed to 'die all out'.
†**2.** *esp.* **to drink all out**: to empty a bumper. *Obs.*
1530 PALSGR. 676/2, I quaught, I drinke all out. *Je boys dautant.* **1542** BOORDE *Introd. Knowl.* 151 There be many good felowes, the whyche wyll drynke all out. **1605** VERSTEGAN *Dec. Intell.* (1634) 13 To say *drink a Garaus*.. which is to say *All-out*.
†**3.** Hence *subst.* A bumper. [Cf. CAROUSE.] *Obs.*
1611 COTGR., *Alluz* (Fr.), all-out; or a carouse fully drunk up.
4. a. Using or involving all one's (or its) strength or resources; 'fully extended'; at top speed.
1895 *Windsor Mag.* I. 120/1 There is no fun in going all-out. **1919** *Punch* 19 Mar. 216/2 The car..bolted down-hill all out. **1925** E. F. NORTON *Fight for Everest 1924* 143 Irvine ..was willing.. to 'go all out', as he put it, in an utmost effort to reach the top. **1928** GALSWORTHY *Swan Song* II. vi. 149 He..made up his mind to go 'all out' for his Uncle Hilary's slum-conversion scheme. **1938** E. WAUGH *Scoop* iii. 60 One screw [*sc.* of an aeroplane] swinging slow, one spinning faster, one totally invisible, roaring all-out. **1940** *War Illustr.* 16 Feb. 110/1 Germany wants oil..but if she is to go all out for victory she must have at least 10,000,000 tons a year.
b. As *adj. phr.*
1908 *Westm. Gaz.* 29 Sept. 4/2 To put a vehicle to an all-out test. **1955** A. L. ROWSE *Expansion Eliz. England* vii. 261 Not committing herself to an all-out war in Europe. **1959** M. M. KAYE *House of Shade* iii. 39 An all-out bid for control.

ˌall 'over, *adv. phr.* [See ALL C 9.]
1. a. Over the whole extent, in every part; over the whole body, in every limb.
1577 tr. *Bullinger's Decades* (1592) 115 The properties of God..to bee all ouer, and euerie where. **1633** MASSINGER *New Way* IV. iii, I am so full of joy,—nay, joy all over. **1710** *Lond. Gaz.* mmmmdccix/4 Stray'd..a Mare..black all over. **1720** WATERLAND 8 *Serm.* 101 It was confounding the Ideas of Creator and Creature, and was all over Contradictory, and Repugnant. **1815** H. BROUGHAM *Let.* 14 July in T. Creevey *Corr.* (1903) I. xi. 243 Such an exertion ..I already *ache all over* with it. **1852** E. TWISLETON *Let.* 1 July (1928) i. 10 Both were thoroughly well-bred and polite —lady and gentleman all over. **1855** THACKERAY *Let.* 28 Apr. (1946) III. 443 His house was all over pictures, drawings, casts, statues, and medals. *a* **1884** *Mod.* I ache all over. **1903** E. BUTLER *Lett. fr. Holy Land* 42 He and Isaac are all over pistols and weapons of various sorts. **1906** *Harper's Mag.* Oct. 764 They'd been hunting all over for her. **1922** JOYCE *Ulysses* 761, I often felt I wanted to kiss him all over.
b. As *sb.* Everywhere. Chiefly *U.S.*
1904 *Post Express* (Rochester, N.Y.) 12 Sept. 3 News Flashes from All Over. **1911** *N.Y. Even. Post* 12 Jan. 16 They came from all over, and showed it. They were..from every section of the country. **1956** D. JACOBSON *Dance in Sun* I. i. 7 There were cars, we saw from the registration plates, from all over.
c. transf., *to be all over* (a person): to display great warmth or affection towards (one); *to be all over oneself* (see quot. 1925). *colloq.*
1912 E. PUGH *Harry the Cockney* x. 102 The worst of women is..they never leave you alone... They're all over you. **1923** S. KAYE-SMITH *End House Alard* I. 23, I wouldn't come yesterday. I thought your family would be all over you, and I didn't like ——. **1925** FRASER & GIBBONS *Soldier & Sailor Words* 5 *All over oneself*, extremely pleased. Over confident; e.g. 'He's all over himself because he's got leave.' 'He used to be all right, but now he's promoted he's all over himself.' **1931** A. CHRISTIE *Sittaford Mystery* v. 43 'Were they friendly?' 'The lady was..All over him, as you might say.'
d. (See OVER *adv.* 2 b.)
2. Finished, brought to a close; done for. (Cf. Ger. *vorüber.*) *it is all over with* = L. *actum est de.*
1765 C. BRIETZCKE *Diary* 16 June in *N. & Q.* (1963) CCVIII. 307/1 Walkd in the Park with Mr. Stanhope who seems to think it is all over with Us. **1805** NELSON in Southey *Life* (1813) II. ix. 260, I am a dead man, Hardy.. I am going fast:—it will be all over with me soon. **1845** CARLYLE *Cromwell's Lett. & Speeches* I. I. i. 134 Sir Thomas [Steward] makes his will in this same month of January, leaving Oliver [Cromwell] his principal heir; and on the 30th it was all over. **1857** RUSKIN *Elem. Drawing* iii. 216 If you once begin to..try this way and that with your colour, it is all over with it and with you. **1863** 'OUIDA' *Held in Bondage* I. x. 223 We were profoundly thankful when it was all over and done with. **1963** 'J. LE CARRÉ' *Spy who came in fr. Cold* xi. 101 And then I asked him, 'Is this goodbye?'—whether it was all over.

all-over, *adj. phr.* [f. prec.]
1. *colloq.* Indisposed all over or all through the body, generally ill.
1851 MAYHEW *Lond. Lab.* III. 146 It gives you an all-over sort of feeling.
2. a. Covering every part, esp. of ornamental patterns or designs (see quot. 1893).
1859 C. TOMLINSON *Illustr. Useful Arts* 39/2 The patterns of floor-cloths should not be elaborate... What are called *all-over* patterns..have the best effect. **1893** *Jrnl. Soc. Arts* XLI. 372/2 A common cry now is, that what is termed an 'all-over' treatment is best; that is, the areas of the details of the design should be nearly all equal, so that no feature should obtrude itself in the design. **1916** HAMLIN *Hist. Ornament* i. 5 In 'all-over' patterns the units are arranged along two or more intersecting systems of lines so as to cover a broad surface. **1932** *Times Lit. Suppl.* 7 July 493/1 Hazlitt's 'Conversations of Northcote'..may be met with in at least six 'original' bindings, ranging from all-over boards with label, through half-cloth and full-cloth. **1960** B. ROBERTSON *Jackson Pollock* 45 The significance of Pollock's late, all-over style, is not only aesthetic.
b. As *sb.* (See quots.)
1838 *Penny Cycl.* XI. 220/1 The amalgam for this description of work [i.e. the gilding of buttons] is brought to a much stiffer consistence than that which is used for 'all-overs'. **1916** HAMLIN *Hist. Ornament* i. 5 Continuous 'all-overs' forming a mesh of two sets of intersecting lines are called quarries. **1957** M. B. PICKEN *Fashion Dict.* 6/1 *All-over*,..fabric completely covered with a design, such as lace.
3. = OVER-ALL *adj. phr.*
1933 *Irish Press* 27 Jan. 6/2 The Irish people have answered...They have given Fianna Fáil its all-over majority. **1959** *N. & Q.* CCIV. 45/2 His all-over conclusion is that [etc.].

all-over, *sb.* [f. the adj. phr.] **1.** See ALL-OVER *adj. phr.* 2.
2. *the all-overs* (colloq., chiefly *U.S.*), a feeling of nervousness or unease (occas. of annoyance), as if affecting the subject from head to foot. Cf. sense 1 of the adj. phr.
1870 DICKENS *E. Drood* xxiii. 180 But we're out of sorts for want of a smoke. We've got the all-overs, haven't us, deary? But this is the place to cure 'em in; this is the place where the all-overs is smoked off! **1888** 'O. THANET' in *St. Nicholas* Nov. 50/1, I jes' take the all-overs every time I see paw getherin' his gun ter go out. **1893** H. A. SHANDS *Some Peculiarities of Speech in Mississippi* 70 *All-overs*, a term employed by all classes to mean *a feeling of extreme annoyance* or *vexation*; as, 'That man is so trifling it gives me the *all-overs* to look at him.' **1942** M. K. RAWLINGS *Cross Creek* ix. 167, I came to Cross Creek with such a phobia against snakes that a picture of one in the dictionary gave me what Martha calls 'the all-overs'. **1951** L. CRAIG *Singing Hills* xxiii. 218 It gives me the all-overs to have a gun pointed in my ribs.

ˌall-'overish, *a. colloq.* [f. ALL OVER *adv. phr.* + -ISH.] **1.** Having a general and indefinite sense of illness pervading the body; generally seized or indisposed.
1832 *Blackw. Mag.* XXXII. 647 He said he was all-overish, and at last he began to strain and bock. **1833** *Sk. & Eccentr. D. Crockett* 52, I wish I may be shot if I know how I felt; but I tell you what, it made me feel quite all-overish. **1851** JANE WELSH CARLYLE *Let.* 5 Mar. (1924) 347, I still feel sick and sore and miserably *all-overish*. **1929** *Daily News* 17 July 11/2 He said he had a sore throat and felt 'All-overish'.
2. Ubiquitous; over the whole extent.
1853 MARCUS DODS *Let.* 18 July (1910) 37 There was an all-overish sort of freshness about your last [*sc.* letter]. **1920** D. H. LAWRENCE *Let.* 15 Mar. (1932) 501 There are a good many English people, but fewer than [in] Capri, and not so all-overish.
3. (Cf. ALL-OVER *adj. phr.* 2.)
1885 LEWIS F. DAY in *Art Jrnl.* 45/1 The besetting danger of mere ornament is that it is so apt to be monotonous and all-over-ish.

ˌall-'overishness. *colloq.* [f. prec. + -NESS.] A general sense of illness or indisposition all through the body.
1820 M. WILMOT *Let.* 3 Mar. (1935) 53 Then poor nurse had her share [of influenza]—Mlle hers and Nanny hers—and I had an alloverishness. **1832** *Blackw. Mag.* XXXII. 647 So great was my all-overishness. **1864** C. CLARKE *Box for Season* II. 195 That indescribable all-overishness resulting from too much drink. **1882** *Society* 11 Jan. 11/1 'What's the trouble?' asked the doctor. 'I feel a sort of dislocated all-overishness.'

ˌall-'overness. [f. ALL-OVER *adj. phr.* + -NESS.] **1.** = ALL-OVERISHNESS.
1820 in *Amer. Speech* (1965) XL. 127 I'm seized with an alloverness, I faint! I die! **1828** *Blackw. Mag.* XXIV. 191, I could almost fain be sick—not *very* sick, but have a gentle all-overness—a tranquil debility. **1840** *Fraser's Mag.* XXI. 474/1, I felt attacked by the malady best designated by the term all-overness.
2. The quality of being 'all-over' (see ALL-OVER *adj. phr.* 2).
1953 *Archit. Rev.* CXIV. 194/1 There is continual interplay..between the flat, tawny-coloured all-overness and the coming out of the objects. **1955** P. HERON *Changing Forms of Art* 122 His form is very powerful; but it is distinct from the form of Renoir in that it is developed entirely in terms of this 'alloverness'.

allow (əˈlaʊ), *v.* Forms: 4–6 **alowe**, **alow**, (4 **aloow**), 5 **aloue**, 5–7 **allowe**, 6– **allow**. [a. OFr. *aloue-r* (15th c. *all-*), 1. to praise, commend:—L. *allaudā-re* (f. *al-* = *ad-* to + *laudāre* to praise); 2. to bestow, assign:—L. *allocā-re* (f. *al-* = *ad-* + *locāre* to place, stow. The two were apparently completely identified in OFr. and viewed as senses of one word, which was adopted with both senses in Eng. *a*1300. Between the two primary significations there naturally arose a variety of uses blending them in the general idea of *assign with approval*, grant, concede a thing claimed or urged, admit a thing offered, permit, etc., etc.] I. To praise, commend, approve of. II. To admit as probable. III. To permit. IV. To bestow, grant. V. To take into account, give credit for.

I. To praise, commend, sanction, view or receive with approbation. (Fr. *alouer*:—L. *allaudāre*.)

†1. *trans.* To laud, praise, commend. *Obs.* or *dial.*

c **1315** SHOREHAM 149 He wolde..be God ylyche, To be alowed. **1330** R. BRUNNE *Chron.* 281 þe gode bisshop Antoyn þer he bare þe pris, His dedes ere to alowe, for his hardynesse. **1377** LANGL. *P. Pl.* B. xv. 4 Somme lakkede my lyf · allowed it fewe. *c* **1450** *Merlin* xx. 355 Gretly were thei to a-lowe and to preise. **1532** MORE *Confut. Tindale* Wks. 1557, 672/2 Saint Mary Magdaleyn was more alowed of Christ for bestowing that costly oyntemente vpon hys heade ..then if she had solde it. **1551** TURNER *Herbal* (1568) 77, I can alowe them for theyr labores in sekyng out of symples. **1600** HOLLAND *Livy* XXVI. xiv. 594 To put that in execution which they so well allowed and approved. **1656** BP. HALL *Occas. Med.* (1857) 201 Should I be censured by a world of men, when I am secretly allowed by thee, I could contemn it. **1783** CRABBE *Village* I. Wks. 1834 II. 81 Proud To find the triumphs of his youth allow'd.

2. a. To approve of, sanction (ranging from a sense hardly differing from the prec., to that of barely passing as acceptable or defensible). *arch.*

c **1315** SHOREHAM 137 That everech man hyt moȝt alowe. **1399** LANGL. *Rich. Redeles* II. 69 'No, redely,' quod reson, 'that reule I alowe.' **1413** LYDG. *Pylgr. Sowle* I. xiii. (1859) 9 Euery wigt loueth, and maynteneth the thyng that he alowith. **1535** COVERDALE *Ps.* i. 6 For the Lorde aloweth yᵉ waye of the rightuous, but the waye of the vngodly shal perishe. *a* **1555** RIDLEY *Wks.* 390, I refused to allow the mass with my presence. **1611** BIBLE *Luke* xi. 48 Truely ye beare witnesse that ye allowe the deeds of your fathers. **1768** BLACKSTONE *Comm.* I. 425 Upon reasonable cause to be allowed by a justice of the peace.

b. *intr.* with *upon*, *of*: To approve of. (Still in some dialects as 'allow on.')

c **1534** tr. *Polyd. Verg., Eng. Hist.* II. 120 He cowld never be movyd..to alow uppon any practyse agaynst Kinge Edward. **1583** *Let.* in Fuller *Ch. Hist.* x. 159 [A thing] which I allow well of. **1660** *Trial Regic.* 142 If you countenance and allow of their authority. **1724** WODROW *Corr.* (1843) III. 141, I use still the very same freedom with him..because I know you allow of this.

3. a. To receive with approval or approbation; accept. *arch.*

a **1300** *Cursor M.* 20034 þou nu will mi wil a-lou. **1382** WYCLIF *Wisd.* iii. 14 Ther shal be ȝiue to hym..lot in the temple of God most aloowid [**1388** a moost acceptable eritage]. **1465** *Paston Lett.* 498 II. 174, I vele but littille that my gode wille ys allowed. **1611** COTGR., To Allow: *allouer, greer, approuver, accepter.* **1669** BOYLE *Occas. Refl.* I. i. (1675) 78 God mercifully allows the Will for the Effect.. favourably accepting what we can do.

†b. *intr.* with *of.* (Cf. *accept of.*) *Obs.*

1579 TOMSON *Calvin's Serm. Tim.* 1/2 The Churches, whiche did alreadie verie well allowe of him. **1748** RICHARDSON *Clarissa* (1811) I. i. 4 When I love you as never woman loved another, and when you have allowed of that concern and of that love—.

II. To accept as reasonable or valid; to admit (intellectually).

4. a. To accept as true or valid; to acknowledge, admit, grant.

1548 COVERDALE tr. *Erasm. Paraphr.* 1 *Pet.* 1 If any man allowe not the vnderstanding of Rome by Babylon. **1611** BIBLE *Acts* xxiv. 15 Hope towards God, which they themselues also allow. **1628** COKE *On Litt.* 29 b, Upon hearing the proofes either allowed or disallowed the same. **1770** LANGHORNE *Plutarch's Lives* (1879) I. 169/2 The citizens..were compelled..to allow his great abilities. **1876** FREEMAN *Norm. Conq.* II. App. 586 Her innocence shall be allowed.

b. *intr.* with *of.* (Cf. *accept*, *admit of.*)

1528 PERKINS *Profit. Bk.* ii. §158 (1642) 71 They allow of that which the principall speaketh. **1587** HOLINSHED *Chron.* I. 5/1 Manie doo not allow of this historie of Albion the giant. **1699** BENTLEY *Phal.* 362 If we allow of Their reckoning. **1724** A. COLLINS *Gr. Chr. Relig.* 133 As to what texts I have..alledg'd to you, you allow of them all. **1849** LOWELL *Biglow P.* Wks. 1879, 199 Jortin is willing to allow of other miracles.

5. with *subord. cl.* To admit something claimed; to acknowledge, grant, concede; to accede to an opinion.

1643 MILTON *Divorce* I. xiii. (1847) 135/1, I suppose it will be allowed us that marriage is a human society. **1711** STEELE *Spect.* No. 4 ⁋5 She has, I will allow, a very pleasing Aspect. **1768** FRANKLIN *Ess.* Wks. 1840 II. 370, I allow also that part of the expense of the rich is in foreign produce. **1858** HAWTHORNE *Fr. & It. Jrnls.* I. 131 He allowed that the old Pre-Raphaelites had..exquisite merits.

6. with *compl.* (*inf.* formerly omitted or expressed by *for*) To acknowledge or admit a thing *to be* something.

1593 R. HARVEY *Philad.* 36 Martia was generally allowed for ruler and king of the realme. **1624** HEYWOOD *Gunaik.* III. 144 Not allowing Porsenna a lawful judge in regard of their late league. **1712** STEELE *Spect.* No. 512 *note*, The Self-Tormentor of Terence's, which is allowed a most excellent Comedy. **1777** SHERIDAN *Sch. Scandal* II. ii. 249 They'll not allow our friend..to be handsome. **1798** BAY *Amer. Law Rep.* (1809) 43 It had been allowed for law. **1877** MOZLEY *Univ. Serm.* 129 Poetry is allowed to border upon the horizon of mysticism.

7. To come to the conclusion, to form the opinion, or state as an opinion formed. (*In Eng. and Amer. dialects.*)

Also used in aphetic form *'low*.

1580 BARET *Alv.* A 297 To Alowe, to make good or allowable, to declare to be true, *Approbo.* **1825** NEAL *Bro. Jonathan* I. ii. 28 Her large eyes would sparkle—so the men 'allowed'—like the mischief. *a* **1861** WINTHROP *John Brent* (1883) iii. 26, I allowed from seeing you handle that thar hoss, that you had got your hand in on women. **1871** G. A. TOWNSEND *Mormon Trials* 13 Well, in the first place, he allowed he was doing his religious duties, and he allowed that he had got to live with some one else. **1872** C. KING *Sierra Nev.* v. 98, I allow you have killed your coon in your day? **1875** PARISH *Dict. Sussex Dial.* 13 'Master Nappet, he allowed that it was almost too bad.' **1880** *Scribn. Mag.* June 293, 'I 'lowed I'd make him sorry fur it, an' I reckon I hev.'

III. To admit the realization of, permit.

8. a. *trans.* To concede, permit (an action or event).

1558 in Strype *Ann. Ref.* I. II. App. i. 391 The queen's proclamation..allowing only the reading of the epistles. **1651** HOBBES *Leviathan* II. xxi. 192 Where many sorts of Worship be allowed. *Mod.* Such practices are no longer allowed.

b. with *inf.*

1637 *Decree of Star Chamb.* in Milton *Areop.* xvi. (Arb.) 16 Euery person or persons, now allowed or admitted to have the vse of a Presse. *a* **1754** FIELDING *Mod. Husb.* III. vi. Wks. 1784 II. 201 Mr. Gaywit does not allow me to play at Quadrille. **1849** MACAULAY *Hist. Eng.* II. 99 He was not allowed to take advantage of the general rule.

c. Also with ellipse of inf.: to permit to go or come *in*, *out*, etc.

1864 TROLLOPE *Small House at Allington* II. xxv. 260 He could not have been allowed again into my drawing-room. **1882** BESANT *All Sorts* xiv, Then he allows the Conservatives..back again, and gives them another show. **1911** *Rep. Labour & Social Conditions Germany* III. 76 The miners who were in the company were allowed to some parts. **1915** RUPERT BROOKE *Let.* 12 Mar. in *Coll. Poems* (1918) p. cxlii, We were allowed ashore from 5 to midnight. **1924** D. GARNETT *Man in Zoo* 19 He was allowed out every evening after closing-time.

9. *refl.* To surrender oneself *to*, lend oneself *to* (*obs.*); to permit oneself to indulge *in*.

1605 SHAKS. *Lear* III. vii. 107 His roguish madness Allows itself to anything. *a* **1716** BLACKALL *Wks.* 1723 I. 149 If the Man..allows himself in that Wickedness which he thinks his Religion allows of. **1815** PALEY *Serm.* (ed. 7) vii. 126 The true child of God allows himself in no sin whatever. **1860** RUSKIN *Mod. Paint.* V. IX. v. 247 It refuses to allow itself in any violent or spasmodic passion.

10. *intr.* with *of.* To permit the occurrence or existence *of*, to admit *of*.

1732 LEDIARD *Sethos* II. IX. 290 His condition would not allow of his talking longer. **1750** JOHNSON *Rambler* No. 97 ⁋19 She tacitly allows of his future visits. **1860** TYNDALL *Glac.* I. §27. 209 The snow..sufficiently compact to allow of a stake being firmly fixed in it.

IV. To allot, assign, bestow (Fr. *allouer*:—L. *allocāre*).

†11. To assign to any one as his right or due; to accord. (With *direct* and *indir. obj.*) *Obs.*

1330 R. BRUNNE *Chron.* 77 On þe same asise serued & alowed Of alle þe franchise, þat it are was dowed. **1463** *Mann. & Househ. Exps.* 152 My mastyre alowyd hys fermour off Freffeld ffor otys..vs. xd. **1530** PALSGR. 421/1, I alowe him xiid. a day for his costes: *je luy aloue douze deniers par jour pour ses despens.* **1580** BARET *Alv.* A 302 To alow or finde ones costes or expences, *Sumptus alicui rei suggerere.* **1596** SHAKS. *Merch. V.* IV. i. 303 And you must cut this flesh from off his breast; The Law allowes it, and the court awards it.

12. a. To give, or let any one have, as his share, or as appropriate to his needs. (Const. as in 11.)

c **1370** WYCLIF *Wks.* 1880, 387 He alowid þe comonte her liflode. **1555** *Fardle of Facions* II. viii. 173 A certaine of graine allowed them at the kinges allowaunce. **1696** WHISTON *Th. Earth* IV. (1722) 320 In this Six Days' Creation one entire Day is allow'd to the Formation of the Air. **1735** POPE *Hor. Ep.* II. i. 193 Allow him but his plaything of a Pen. **1856** BREWSTER *Mart. Sc.* II. iii. (ed. 3) 143 It was arranged that the Emperor should allow him 100 florins.

b. *refl.*

1751 JOHNSON *Rambler* 13 Apr., He, therefore, that allows himself to be dissatisfied while he can perceive any error or defect, must refer his hopes of ease to some other period of existence. **1874** HARDY *Far fr. Madding Crowd* II. ii. 27 She contemplated it firmly, allowing herself, nevertheless,..to dwell upon the happy life she would have enjoyed had Troy been Boldwood. **1888** MRS. H. WARD *R. Elsmere* xvii, Robert, meanwhile..had been allowing himself a little deliberate study of Mr. Wendover. *Ibid.* xlii, Madame de Netteville allowed herself plenty of jests with her intimates. **1896** 'H. S. MERRIMAN' *Sowers* vii, He would not allow himself the luxury of being the first arrival.

†13. To give an allowance to (a person); to portion, endow. *Obs.*

a **1677** BARROW *Serm., Rew. honouring God*, Those whom he..maintains in a handsome garb, allows largely. **1712** STEELE *Spect.* No. 496 §2 The Father who allows his Son to his utmost ability.

V. To admit or take into account.

†14. To place to one's credit in an account; to reckon, count to one. *Obs.*

c **1340** HAMPOLE *Pr. Consc.* 2467 Alle the gud dedys that we haf done Onence our syns sal than sem fone; And yhit we er unsyker..Wether thai sal be alowed or noght. **1382** WYCLIF *Gen.* xv. 6 Abram leuede to God, and it was alowid to hym to ryȝtwisnes. **1440** *Promp. Parv.*, Allowyn yn rekenynge, *Alloco.* **1667** E. CHAMBERLAYNE *St. Gr. Brit.* I. II. xiii. 121 They deliver the same attested for a lawful Tally to the Clerk of the Pipe to be allowed in the Great Roll.

†15. Hence, To remit or deduct from the debit or the amount due or charged; to abate. *Obs.*

1501 in *Bury Wills* (1850) 91, I will that John Etoon haue alowyd iij *li.* to hym of the laste payment of mony that he owyth on to me. **1530** PALSGR. 420/2, I alowe or abate upon a reckenyng or accompte made.

16. *gen.* To make an addition or deduction, as the case may be, of (so much), on account of something requiring to be taken into consideration, though not formally appearing in the reckoning.

1663 GERBIER *Counsel* 87 In exchange of old lead for sheets new run, is allowed three shillings in every hundred weight for waste. **1756** BURKE *Vind. Nat. Soc.* Wks. I. 18 It will therefore be very reasonable to allow on their account as much as added to the losses of the conqueror, may amount to a million of deaths. *Mod.* You must allow an hour at least for time lost in changing trains, and waiting at stations.

17. *to allow for*: To allow what is right or fair, to make due allowance for; also *fig.* To bear in mind as a modifying or extenuating circumstance.

c **1711** ADDISON (J.) Allowing..for the different ways of making it. **1742** RICHARDSON *Pamela* III. 48 If your Ladyship will not allow for me..what will become of me? *a* **1762** LADY M. MONTAGUE *Lett.* lxxix. 131, I allow a great deal for the inconstancy of mankind. *Mod.* To allow for expansion or shrinkage, for friction or the resistance of the air, for the increase of population since the census, for the place and circumstances of a speech, etc.

allowable (əˈlaʊəb(ə)l), *a.* and *sb.* Also aphet. lowable. [a. Fr. *allouable*, f. *allouer*: see ALLOW and -ABLE.]

†1. Worthy of praise; praiseworthy, laudable. *Obs.*

1393 LANGL. *P. Pl.* C. XVIII. 130 Lowable [*v.r.* al-, allowable] was it neuere. **1413** LYDG. *Pylgr. Sowle* IV. xxix. (1859) 62 A statu, or an ymage his allowable and sadde condicions. **1580** HOLLYBAND *Treas. Fr. Tong.*, *Louable*, praise worthy, allowable, laudable. **1670** EACHARD *Contempt Clergy* 44 True and allowable rhetorick, that is, of what is decorous and convenient to be spoken. **1702** *Eng. Theophr.* 176 There is a sweeter, more noble and allowable sort of vengeance.

2. Worthy of sanction, approval, or acceptance (without rising to *praise*); satisfactory, acceptable.

1552 HULOET, Allowable, *Acceptabilis.* **1561** T. N[ORTON] tr. *Calvin's Inst.* III. xxiii. (1634) 469 If he goe about to make himselfe allowable to him [God] with innocency and honesty of life. **1580** BARET A 299 Pleasant, alowable, acceptable, *Acceptus.* **1611** BIBLE *Transl. Pref.* 9 If the olde vulgar had bene at all points allowable. **1623** SANDERSON *Serm.* Ad. Mag. ii. §8 (1674) 104 Custom had made it not only excusable but allowable.

3. a. To be intellectually admitted or conceded.

1712 STEELE *Spect.* No. 546 ⁋2 The advantages of action, show and dress on these occasions are allowable.

b. Worthy of provisional acceptance; probable.

a **1682** SIR T. BROWNE *Tracts* 3 Therein an allowable allusion unto the tropical conversion of the Sun. *Ibid.* 8 What Tremelius rendreth Spina is allowable in the sense.

4. a. Worthy of toleration, fit to be borne, permitted, endured; tolerable, permissible, admissible, excusable, legitimate. (At first in negative sentences.)

a **1568** COVERDALE *Christs Cross* viii. Wks. II. 258 Prayer for the dead is not..allowable or to be excused. **1561** T. N[ORTON] tr. *Calvin's Inst.* I. 5 There is no lawfully allowable religion, but that which is ioyned with truthe. **1625** MEADE in Ellis *Orig. Lett.* I. 310 III. 193 Devise some allowable and parliamentary way..to supply the present necessities. **1712** STEELE *Spect.* No. 555 ⁋2 The licence allowable to a feigned character. *a* **1732** ATTERBURY *Serm.* (J.) Their pursuit of it is not only allowable but laudable. **1790** JOHNSON in *Boswell* (1831) I. 454 It may be defended as a very allowable practice. **1824** MISS MITFORD *Village* Ser. I. (1863) 140 A little touch of very allowable finery in the gay window-curtains. **1868** M. PATTISON *Acad. Organ.* §5. 143 The payment of the teacher by endowment is not only allowable, it is necessary.

b. *spec.* of the restricted production of oil (see quots.). Hence as *sb. U.S.* and *Canada.*

1940 M. ALBERTSON in E. DeGolyer *Elem. Petroleum Ind.* xii. 287 Many methods of allocation of allowable oil to producers are in use. *Ibid.*, When oil-producing capacity became sufficient..restriction of production was enforced. Allowables were established for wells, leases, pools, and states. **1949** M. MUSKAT *Physical Princ. Oil Production* x. 454 Total production from the state is fixed..and this total is subdivided or prorated among the fields in the state. These prorated field 'allowables' have generally been far below..production capacities. **1960** *Guardian* 9 Sept. 10/1 Their owners..keep up the price of oil by a quota system which restricts production to so many days' output (called 'allowables') in each month.

allowableness (əˈlaʊəb(ə)lnɪs). [f. prec. + -NESS.] The quality of being allowable; permissibleness, legitimacy.

1692 SOUTH *12 Serm.* (1697) I. 329 To discourse of Lots, as to their Nature, Use, and Allowableness. **1765** TUCKER *Lt. Nat.* II. 184 To stand approved in the eyes of others for the allowableness of my attempt. **1799** W. TAYLOR in *Month. Rev.* XXIX. 147 He doubts the allowableness of his delay.

allowably (ə'laʊəblɪ), *adv.* [f. as prec. + -LY².] In an allowable manner; laudably, commendably, admissibly, permissibly, excusably, legitimately.

1588 LAMBARDE *Eiren.* II. iii. 138 More allowablie therfore writeth Marrow. **1589** PUTTENHAM *Eng. Poesie* (1869) 40 This last sort..may allowably beare matter not alwayes of the grauest. **1663** BOYLE *Exper. Phil.* (R.) I should allowably enough discharge my part. **1748** RICHARDSON *Clarissa* (1811) II. ix. 52 Your sister..may allowably be angry at you. **1850** McCOSH *Div. Govt.* II. ii. (1874) 190 There are senses in which we may allowably use the word chance.

allowance (ə'laʊəns), *sb.* Also 4 alouance, 5 alowans, 5–6 alowance. [a. OFr. *alouance*, f. *alouer*: see ALLOW and -ANCE.] The action of allowing; a thing allowed.

I. Of praising, approving, admitting, permitting.

†**1.** Praise, applause. *Obs.*

1377 LANGL. *P. Pl.* B. XI. 215 Of logyke ne of lawe In legenda sanctorum Is litel allowaunce made. *a* **1541** WYATT *Poet. Wks.* (1861) 203 Vain allowance of his own desert. **1633** BP. HALL *Hard Texts* 259 It is not the allowance or applause of men that I seek.

2. Approbation, approval; sanction; voluntary acceptance. *arch.*

1552 HULOET, Allowaunce, accepcion or estimation, *Acceptio.* **1561** T. N[ORTON] tr. *Calvin's Inst.* I. To Reader, If I did not, holding myselfe contented with the allowance of God alone, despise the iugementes of men. **1604** EDMONDS *Observ. Cæsar's Comm.* 107 They all with one consent made allowance of Vercingetorix for their Generall. **1707** *Lond. Gaz.* mmmmcccxxxvi/8 Her Creditors are required to.. assent to or dissent from the Allowance of her Certificate. **1736** BUTLER *Anal.* I. v. 130 They cannot be gratified at all ..with the allowance of the moral principle. **1807** CRABBE *Par. Reg.* III. 426 He look'd smiling on And gave allowance where he needed none.

†**3.** Admission of something claimed or charged, acknowledgement. *Obs.*

1587 GOLDING *De Mornay* xxxii. (1617) 564 This is a good proof and allowance of their innocency. **1602** SHAKS. *Ham.* III. ii. 30 The censure of the which One, must in your allowance o'reway a whole Theater of Others. **1756** BURKE *Subl. & B.* Wks. I. 232 Modesty which is a tacit allowance of imperfection.

4. Permission, tolerance, sufferance.

1628 WITHER *Brit. Rememb.* Premon. 6 Because I could not get allowance to doe it publikely. **1689** *Col. Rec. Pennsylv.* I. 261 Nor had he given Tho. Lloyd any allowance to sett his hand to any thing. **1709** STRYPE *Ann. Ref.* I. xiii. 184 Some murmur at the allowance of reading the Scriptures. **1753** RICHARDSON *Grandison* (1781) IV. iii. 22 By the Doctor's allowance, I enclose it to you. **1872** FREEMAN *Gen. Sketch* xvii. §19. 364 There were many causes of difference between them, the chief being the allowance of slavery in the South.

II. Of taking into account, allotting, granting.

5. The action of placing to one's credit, admitting as an item in an account, or allotting a sum on account of the expenses of a person or thing.

1574 tr. *Littleton's Tenures* 27 a, Such a wardeine..shall have allowance of al hys reasonable costes. **1611** BIBLE *Transl. Pref.* 1 Against Church-maintenance and allowance it is not vnknowen what a fiction was deuised. **1625** BACON *Ess.* (1874) 24 Illiberalitie of Parents in allowance towards their Children. **1845** STEPHEN *Laws of Eng.* II. 315 Allowance shall be made to him for all his reasonable costs and expenses.

†**6.** A sum allowed in account; an amount placed on the other side of the account as an equivalent; a consideration. *Obs.*

1393 LANGL. *P. Pl.* C. x. 271 Þy lord lokeþ to haue a-louance for hus [*i.e.* his] bestes, And of þe monye þow haddist þer-myd. **1574** tr. *Littleton's Tenures* 52 b, The landes in fee simple bee alotted to yᵉ younger daughter in allowance of the tenementes tayled, allotted to the elder daughter.

7. A definite portion, sum, or amount, allotted or granted to meet any expenses or requirements.

a. Of money, to meet one's expenses. In military use, esp. in *pl.* the sums of money (distinct from the *pay*) paid for various purposes or services. ***family allowance***, see FAMILY *sb.* 11.

1440 *Promp. Parv.*, Alowans, *Allocacio.* **1539** *Househ. Ord.* in *Thynne's Animadv.* Pref. 35 Then he [*i.e.* the Clerk-Comptroller] to controule the same [expenditure], giving noe larger allowance than there ought to be. **1662** J. WARD *Diary* (1839) 183 Mr. Shakspeare..had an allowance so large, that hee spent att the rate of 1,000*l.* a-year. **1711** ADDISON *Spect.* No. 295 ¶6 They consider this Allowance [Pin-money] as a kind of Alimoney. **1794** *Certain Rules & Orders to be Observed by the Corps of Fencible Infantry* (*War Office*) 15 Allowances to Officers. We are graciously pleased to grant the following allowances, *viz.* To every Captain of a Company..Fifty-six Pounds Ten Shillings *per Annum. Ibid.* 19 Every..Non-Commissioned Officer, and Private Man shall receive, in Aid of the Expence of his Necessaries, an Annual Allowance of 13s. 2½d. **1795** (*title*) Copy of Warrant for establishing a consolidated Allowance at a daily rate, for soldiers of cavalry and infantry. *Ibid.* 18 The several Allowances called Bread Money..the annual Allowance to each Man in the Infantry for Alteration of Clothing. **1802** MAR. EDGEWORTH *Moral T.* (1816) I. ix. 71 Five ten-guinea notes for your last quarterly allowance. **1837** T. BACON *First Impr. fr. Nat. in Hindostan* I. 252 Upon pay and allowances not exceeding £20 a month. **1849** MACAULAY *Hist. Eng.* II. 464 An excellent order..increasing the allowances of Captains. **1853** [see CLOTHING *vbl. sb.* 5 b]. **1888** KIPLING *Plain Tales fr. Hills, False Dawn* 40 Pay and allowances of nearly fourteen hundred rupees a month. **1949** F. MACLEAN *Eastern Approaches* II. ii. 190 They had drawn special equipment..and special pay and allowances.

b. A limited portion of food. Hence the phr. ***at no allowance***, without stint, at pleasure.

1580 BARET *Alv.* A 302 That schollers call their commons or alowance, *Demensum.* **1607** TOPSELL *Four-footed Beasts* (1673) 237 That so every beast may eat his own allowance. **1611** BIBLE *2 Kings* xxv. 30 His allowance was a continuall allowance giuen him of the king, a dayly rate for euery day. **1711** F. FULLER *Med. Gymn.* 56 The short Allowance, the Bread and Water of a Prison. **1836** MARRYAT *Midship. Easy* xiii. 44 They had but their allowance of bread and grog for one day. **1865** CARLYLE *Fredk. Gt.* III. VIII. v. 42 His people pluck him at no allowance.

c. A restricted portion of anything granted.

1637 MILTON *Comus* 308 In such a scant allowance of star-light. **1711** STEELE *Spect.* No. 14 ¶12 We had also but a very short Allowance of Thunder and Lightning. **1837** CARLYLE *Fr. Rev.* I. IV. i. 166 A popularity of twenty-four hours was, in those times [1788], no uncommon allowance.

8. a. A sum or item put to one's credit in an account; *hence*, rebate, deduction, discount. ***to make allowance***: to add to or deduct from a reckoning, in order to provide for some incidental circumstance.

1530 PALSGR. 194/1 Alowaunce for money, *alouuance.* **1552** HULOET, Allowaunce in rekenynge, *Subductio.* **1663** GERBIER *Counsel* 77 There must be an allowance for the waste of the Timber. **1740** *Act of Parl.* in Hanway *Trav.* (1762) I. I. ix. 44 With such allowances, abatements, discounts, and drawbacks..as are by law prescribed. **1794** SULLIVAN *View Nat.* I. 326 He made no allowance for what the portion of the earth in question perspired at the same time. **1860** TYNDALL *Glac.* II. §25. 363 Making allowance for the time required by the sound to ascend from the bottom. **1870** PINKERTON *Guide to Administr.* 43 The usual allowance for Administrators' commissions in Pennsylvania is five per cent. upon the personal property.

b. A deduction from the weight a race-horse is required to carry.

1823 'JON BEE' *Slang* 3 *Allowances* (turf) Mares and geldings running against horses are allowed weight (usually 3 lbs. each); also, if coming of untried parents..fillies *always* carry less than colts. **1881** *Encycl. Brit.* XIII. 202/2 The competitors carried the same weights, with the exception of a slight allowance [to fillies] for sex. **1955** *Times* 10 Sept. 3/1 By this success Robinson lost the right to claim an apprentice's allowance.

c. *Mech.* (See quots. 1940, 1958.)

1903 *Trans. Amer. Soc. Mech. Engin.* XXIV. 1173 Before making any changes in our present allowances I wrote to a number of engine builders. **1940** *Chamber's Techn. Dict.* 23/2 *Allowance*, a difference in dimensions prescribed in order to allow of various qualities of fit between mating pieces. **1958** *Van Nostrand's Sci. Encycl.* (ed. 3) 887/1 Allowance is an intentional difference in the size of mating parts. Tolerance is the permissible variation in the size of a part.

9. *fig.* The taking into account, or consideration, of mitigating, extenuating, or excusing circumstances. Usually in phr. ***to make allowance for***.

1676 DRYDEN *Dram. Wks.* IV. 75 This Honesty of theirs ought to have many Grains for its Allowance. **1711** STEELE *Spect.* No. 274 ¶1 To have proper Allowances made for their Conduct. **1748** CHESTERF. *Lett.* 173 II. 140 The spectators are always candid enough to give great allowances ..to a new actor. *c* **1812** MISS AUSTEN *Sense & Sensib.* (1849) 29 To make every allowance for the colonel's advanced state of life. **1846** MILL *Logic* VI. viii. §3 Apply their principles with innumerable allowances. **1862** TROLLOPE *Orley Farm* v. (ed. 4) 31 He made allowances for her weakness. **1876** FREEMAN *Norm. Conq.* II. vii. 4 Allowance must be made for his constant flattery of his own master.

†**10.** A balance, remainder. *Obs.*

1528 PERKINS *Profit. Bk.* v. §326 (1642) 144 If a man seised of three acres..enfeoffeth a stranger..of two of the three acres..and the wife is endowed of the third acre which remaineth as allowance of the other acres. **1552** HULOET, Allowaunce, or that whiche fulfilleth, maketh good, or vp, or supplieth that which wanteth in measure, numbre or quantity, *Supplementum.*

11. *Comb.* or *Attrib.* as ***allowance-money***, ***system***.

1700 LUTTRELL *Brief Rel.* (1857) IV. 697 One quarter of his majesties allowance money. **1746** W. THOMPSON *R.N. Advoc.* (1757) 48 Who receives the Benefit of Short Allowance-Money? **1831** *Edin. Rev.* LIII. 48 The factitious increase of population caused by the allowance-system.

allowance (ə'laʊəns), *v.* [f. the sb. Cf. to *distance*, *dower*, *portion*, etc.]

1. To put (any one) upon an allowance; to limit (him) in the amount allowed.

1839 DICKENS *Nich. Nick.* xxxiv, I have made up my mind ..to allowance him..to put him upon a fixed allowance. **1840** —— *O.C. Shop* xxxvi, Don't you ever go and say you were allowanced, mind that. **1859** MEREDITH *R. Feverel* II. i. 10, I am allowanced two glasses three hours before dinner.

2. To supply (a thing) in fixed and limited quantities; esp. in ppl. adj. **allowanced**.

1840 DICKENS *O.C. Shop* (1867) 276 I'd advise you not to waste time like this. It's allowanced here you know. **1859** *Cornh. Mag.* I. 116 The evening pannikin of tea and the allowanced pound of pemmican.

alloway: see ALLEY-WAY.

†**a'llowe, a'lowys.** [a. OFr. *al(l)ouy*, prop. *alouys*:—L. **allocātīci-um*, *-ītī-um*, one whose attribute it is to be *allocāt-us*, hired: see ALLOCATE and -ITIOUS. The final *-s* was in 14 c. Fr. occ. treated as a pl. inflexion, and so with *allowes* in Eng.] A hired servant, a hireling.

c **1483** *Chron. Lond.* (1827) 156 As wele allowes and servaunts as the maisters. **1494** FABYAN VI. cxcviii. 205 He shuld scantly haue of his owne, as alowys or seruaunt had.

allowed (ə'laʊd), *ppl. a.* [f. ALLOW + -ED.]

†**1.** Praised, approved, sanctioned, accepted as satisfactory. *Obs.*

1382 WYCLIF *Wisd.* ix. 12 My werkys shul ben aloowid [**1388** acceptable]. **1580** BARET *Alv.* A 297 No man better esteemed or alowed of his countrie men, *Nemo probatior suis.* **1728** MORGAN *Algiers* I. vi. 184 The Names of the twelve.. allowed and accepted by the majority.

2. Permitted by authority, licensed.

1589 *Hay any Work* 39 He solde it to an allowed printer. **1593** HOLLYBAND *Treas. Fr. Tong.*, An allowed cart or chariot. **1601** SHAKS. *Twel. N.* I. v. 101 There is no slander in an allow'd foole, though he do nothing but rayle. **1690** J. NORRIS *On Beatitudes* Wks. IV. 352 Moderate even in the most allow'd Enjoyments. **1829** I. TAYLOR *Enthus.* viii. 206 The allowed enjoyments of domestic life.

3. Acknowledged, admitted.

1749 CHESTERF. *Lett.* 180 II. 169 The allowed and established models of good breeding. **1872** C. HAMMOND *Text. Crit.* (1880) Introd. 8 We have the following allowed facts to start with.

4. Assigned as a portion or due share; allotted.

1440 *Promp. Parv.*, Alowede, *Allocatus.* **1578** *Cecil Papers* in *Monthly Mag.* XXXVI. 43 Havinge only duringe that tyme allowed unto him breade and water.

5. Remitted, deducted in reckoning.

1674 COLES, Allowed in Reckoning, *Substractus.*

allowedly (ə'laʊɪdlɪ), *adv.* [f. prec. (formerly pronounced *allow-ed*) + -LY².] In a manner that is allowed, admitted, or acknowledged; by general allowance or admission; admittedly.

1602 T. FITZHERB. *Apol.* 47 a, Alowdly improba[b]le in it self. **1678** MANTON 20 *Serm.* v. Wks. 1871 II. 230 Living willingly and allowedly in his sins. **1742** SHENSTONE *Ess.* (1806) 5 Allowedly more genteel. **1859** DE QUINCEY *Style* Wks. XI. 243 It may allowedly be used in all cases. **1879** *Academy* 29 The English is allowedly one of the most complete of the European languages.

allower (ə'laʊə(r)). [f. ALLOW + -ER¹.] One who allows.

†**1.** One who praises, approves, abets, countenances; a patron, or abettor. *Obs.*

c **1565** R. LINDSAY *Hist. Scot.* (1728) 45 The fortifiers and allowers of him in such wickedness. **1580** BARET *Alv.* A 303 A prouuer, an alower, a prayser, *Probator.* **1606** *King's Declar.* 13 (L.) This pretended assembly, together with their associates and allowers. **1647** N. WARD *Simple Cobbler* 14 Not onely an Allower, but an humble Petitioner, that.. Anabaptists may have due time and means of conviction.

2. One who admits, or permits.

1859 in WORCESTER.

allowing (ə'laʊɪŋ), *vbl. sb.* [f. ALLOW + -ING¹.]

†**1.** Praise, commendation, approval, applause.

1490 CAXTON *How to Die* 1 The allowynge or praysynge of the deth. **1551** TURNER *Herbal* Ded. 1 This commendacyon and alowyng of Physicions and Phisick in this playn and expressed wordes. **1580** BARET *Alv.* A 305 The approouing or alowing, *Approbatio.* **1632** SHERWOOD, An Allowing, *Approuvement.*

2. Permitting, permission.

3. The giving of a portion or allowance.

1674 COLES, Allowing (giving), *Exhibitio.*

4. Rebate, deduction.

1674 COLES, An Allowing in Reckoning, *deductio.*

¶ Capable also of being used in various other meanings of vb. ALLOW, especially gerundially, as After allowing that this might be so, etc.

allowing (ə'laʊɪŋ), *ppl. a.* [f. ALLOW + -ING².]

1. Approving, applauding.

1580 SIDNEY *Arcadia* (1622) 454 With many allowing tokens was Euarchus speech heard.

2. 'Admitting, permitting, granting, abating.' Ash 1775.

allowment (ə'laʊmənt). ? *Obs.* [f. ALLOW + -MENT; or perh. a. Fr. **allouement.*] The action of allowing or sanctioning; sanction, approval.

1579 TOMSON *Calvin's Serm. Tim.* 96/2 Bicause God would vse this man in great matters, he gaue a greater allowment of him, then he did of others. *Ibid.* 483/1 The kynde of allowement which all they must haue, that are set in any publique office.

alloxan (æ'lɒksən). *Chem.* [f. ALL(ANTOIN) + OXA(LIC) + -AN, 'so named by Liebig and Wöhler in 1838, because it contains the elements of allantoin and oxalic acid.' H. E. Roscoe.] An organic compound $C_4H_2N_2O_4$ crystallizing in large efflorescent rectangular prisms; one of the oxidation products of uric acid, being a monureide of mesoxalic acid constituted by the radical mesoxalyl CO.2(CO)″ and the urea-residue CO.(2NH)″.

1853 THUDICHUM *Urine* 81 The reaction consists in the formation of alloxan, urea, and nitrous acid. **1873** WILLIAMSON *Chem.* §317 Alloxan is formed by the action of various oxidizing agents.

alloxanate (æ'lɒksəneɪt). *Chem.* [f. prec. + -ATE[4].] A salt of alloxanic acid.

1863 WATTS *Dict. Chem.* (1879) I. 138 [Alloxanic] is a di-basic acid, forming acid as well as normal salts: the formula of normal alloxanates is $C_4H_2M_2N_2O_5$, of acid alloxanates $C_4H_3MN_2O_5$. **1865** *Intell. Observ.* No. 38, 109 Alloxanate of ammonia.

alloxanic (æləkˈsænɪk), *a. Chem.* [f. as prec. + -IC.] Of alloxan, as in *alloxanic acid*, a bi-basic acid, $C_4H_4N_2O_5$ = alloxan + H_2O.

1863 WATTS *Dict. Chem.* I. 137 Alloxanic acid forms hard white needles arranged in radiated groups or warty masses.

alloxantin (æləkˈsæntɪn). *Chem.* An organic compound, $C_8H_4N_4O_7$, crystallizing in small, 4-sided, oblique rhombic prisms; consisting of two molecules of alloxan minus 1 atom of oxygen, OC.2(NH) = 2 (OC).COC.2(OC) = 2(NH).CO.

1853 THUDICHUM *Urine* 81 On dissolving uric acid in dilute nitric acid, alloxantine is obtained. **1873** WILLIAMSON *Chem.* §319 An aqueous solution of alloxan decomposes on boiling into alloxantin.

alloy (ˈælɔɪ, əˈlɔɪ), *sb.* Also 6 **aloye**. [a. mod.Fr. *aloi*:—OFr. *alei*, retained in Norman as *alai*, *allai*, whence our earlier word ALLAY *sb.*[1], which this Parisian form has since 1600 gradually displaced. Through the erroneous fancy that Fr. *aloi* was = *à loi* 'to law,' the word, meaning originally simple 'combination, union,' came to be used specially of the mixing of baser metal with gold or silver in coinage, so as to bring it to the recognized standard, and hence of the standard itself.]

I. *literal.*

1. The comparative purity or mixedness of gold or silver; fineness, quality, standard. = ALLAY *sb.* 3.

1604 E. G. tr. *D'Acosta's Hist. Ind.* IV. xii. 245 Silver drawne with Mercurie, is so fine, that it never abates of two thousand three hundred and fourescore of alloy. **1685** MORDEN *Geogr. Rect.* 396 The Mony of this Kingdom is of a good Alloy. **1871** DAVIES *Metr. Syst.* III. 65 The civil authority stamps its image, to authenticate its weight and alloy.

†**2.** Agio of exchange (? originally an allowance for difference of standard). *Obs.*

1598 FLORIO, *L'aggio*, the aloye or losse of money by exchange, coyning, or banke. **1672** MARVELL *Reh. Transp.* I. 271 Much after the same current Rate and Standard: only there hath been some little difference in the alloy.

3. An inferior metal mixed with one of greater value; *esp.* that which is added to gold and silver coinage. = ALLAY *sb.* 2.

1719 W. WOOD *Surv. Trade* 345 Half the Silver is taken out, and Copper or other Alloy put into the place. **1860** FROUDE *Hist. Eng.* V. xxv. 109 Bad shillings, in which 4 ounces of pure metal were mixed with 8 of alloy. **1876** ROGERS *Pol. Econ.* xi. 4 Only a practised eye can detect the amount of alloy in an ornament professedly manufactured of gold.

4. The condition of combination between different metals melted together. (Without reference to their relative values.)

1827 FARADAY *Chem. Manip.* xx. 508 Making the alloy of the metal and the platina more complete. **1883** *Nature* XXVII. 351 That peculiar..form of association which metallurgists term an alloy.

5. a. A mixture of metals; a metallic compound, an amalgam. *Formerly*, A compound containing a baser metal. = ALLAY *sb.* 1. Also *attrib.*, as ***alloy steel***.

1656 H. MORE *Ant. agst. Ath.* (1712) Pref. 20 Whether this be that ancient golden Key..or one made of baser alloy. **1869** ROSCOE *Chem.* 185 In the alloys the metallic appearance and properties are preserved. **1902** *Encycl. Brit.* XXIX. 572/1 Alloy Steels and Cast Irons are those which owe their properties chiefly to the presence of one or more elements other than carbon. **1922** *Ibid.* XXXI. 927/2 Certain alloy steels..can be rendered (or kept) completely 'austenitic'..by quenching.

b. native alloy: an alloy of osmium and iridium occurring with native platinum, called also *Iridosmine*.

1875 URE *Dict. Arts* II. 918 The native alloy on account of its hardness is used to point metallic pens.

II. *figurative.*

†**6.** Intrinsic standard or character, quality, temper, vein. = ALLAY *sb.* 6. (Cf. Fr. *de bon aloi.*) *Obs.*

1596 CAREW tr. *Huarte's Trial of Wits* 2nd Proeme, If thy wit be of the common and vulgar alloy. **1643** SIR T. BROWNE *Relig. Med.* II. 13 A Soull of the same alloy as our owne. **1647** N. BACON *Hist. Disc.* ix. 27 To inhaunce the price of a Presbyter somewhat within the aloye of a Bishop. **1674** N. FAIRFAX *Bulk & Selv.* 136 Workings of so lofty and refined an alloy.

7. Admixture of that which lowers the character or takes from the value. Hence *concr.* Alien element, anything that detracts from, impairs, or sullies. = ALLAY *sb.* 4, 5.

1625 BACON *Eleg. Sent.* Wks. 1860, 193 There's no fortune so good, but it has its alloy. **1712** *Spect.* No. 548 ¶4 Every one has in him a natural alloy, tho' one may be fuller of dross than another. **1816** MISS AUSTEN *Emma* I. i. 2 Disadvantages which threatened alloy to her many enjoyments. **1849** C. BRONTË *Shirley* II. iii. 83 A base alloy of moral cowardice. **1863** MRS. JAMESON *Leg. Monast. Ord.* 166 A face..so spiritualised, so refined from all earthly alloy.

alloy (əˈlɔɪ), *v.* [a. mod.Fr. *aloyer*:—OFr. *aleier*, *alier*:—L. *alligāre*. The north. Fr. form *allayer* (= *alleyer*, *aleier*), whence our earlier ALLAY, long continued to be the standard Fr. form, and is alone found in Cotgr. 1611. Since the 17th c. it has been displaced by *aloyer* (probably by assimilation to the sb., which has been *aloi* in standard Fr. from an early period: see prec.). In the wake of the Fr., Eng. also has substituted *alloy* for the Norman *allay*, first in the sb. and then *c*1690 in the vb.]

1. To mix with a baser metal so as to reduce to a desired standard or quality. = ALLAY *v.*[2] 1.

1691 LOCKE *Money* Wks. 1727 II. 40 Most of the Silver of the World, both in Money and Vessels, being alloy'd (*i.e.* mixed with some baser metals). **1719** W. WOOD *Surv. Trade* 361 Melting of Coin for Bullion, and bringing in Bullion for Coin *alloy'd*..will be avoided. **1875** URE *Dict. Arts* I. 93 Gold and silver..when alloyed with a little copper. *Ibid.* I. 96 The alloy for silver coinage is always copper, and a very pure quality of this metal is used for alloying.

2. To mix metals (without reference to their relative value); to form compounds of two or more metals.

1822 [See ALLOYED 3]. **1839** URE *Dict. Arts* 30 When we wish to alloy three or more metals, we often experience difficulties.

3. *intr.* (*refl.*) To enter into combination with another metal.

1839 URE *Dict. Arts* 29 One metal does not alloy indifferently with every other metal. **1875** *Ibid.* I. 99 Gold and iron alloy with ease.

4. *fig.* To mix with something inferior; to lower in degree, debase, contaminate by admixture. = ALLAY *v.*[2] 2.

1703 MAUNDRELL *Journ. Jerus.* (1732) App. 9 Some [heaps of Salt] being exquisitely White, others alloy'd with Dirt. **1832** HT. MARTINEAU *Ella of Gar.* x. 117 Their external prosperity was not alloyed by troubles from within.

5. *fig.* To temper, moderate, modify. Cf. ALLAY *v.*[1]

1661 HICKERINGILL *Jamaica* 10 The heat in the day time being alwaies alloy'd with the Sea Breezes. **1875** RUSKIN *Lect. Art* ii. 42 Gentle and submissive persons, who might by their true patience have alloyed the hardness of the common crowd.

alloyage (əˈlɔɪdʒ). [a. Fr. *aloyage*, f. *aloyer*: see ALLOY and -AGE.] The art or process of alloying metals.

1790 KERR tr. *Lavoisier's Chem.* 109 To this difference in fusibility, part of the phenomena attendant upon alloyage are owing.

alloyed (əˈlɔɪd), *ppl. a.* [f. ALLOY *v.* + -ED.]

1. Mixed with a baser metal, so as to be reduced in quality.

1691 LOCKE *Money* Wks. 1727 II. 40 Fine Silver is usually dearer than so much Silver alloy'd. **1831** LARDNER *Hydrost.* viii. 164 Alloyed metals, or adulterated liquids.

2. Hence *fig.* Debased, deteriorated, through the admixture of something injurious.

1827 CARLYLE *Richter, Misc.* I. 15 This man, alloyed with imperfections as he may be, is consistent. **1869** LECKY *Europ. Mor.* I. xi. 227 Pleasures so fleeting and so alloyed.

3. Combined so as to form a metallic compound.

1822 IMISON *Sc. & Art* II. 118 They always contain native iron alloyed with nickel. **1860** URE *Dict. Arts* I. 93 Copper alloyed with zinc forms brass.

alloying (əˈlɔɪɪŋ), *vbl. sb.* [f. ALLOY *v.* + -ING[1].]

1. The action of reducing or modifying a metal by mixing a portion of an inferior ingredient.

1875 [See ALLOY *v.* 1].

2. The combining of metals.

1839 URE *Dict. Arts* 32 The alloying of given quantities of two metals of known densities. **1858** GLADSTONE *Homer* III. 499 The fusion or alloying of metals.

alloying (əˈlɔɪɪŋ), *ppl. a.* [f. ALLOY *v.* + -ING[2].] Modifying, or combining with, another metal.

1822 FARADAY *Exp. Res.* xvi. 69 To him the steel together with the alloying metals..was forwarded.

allozooid (ˌæləʊˈzəʊɔɪd). *Biol.* [f. Gr. ἄλλο-ς other, different + ZOOID, f. Gr. ζῷ-ον living being + -OID.] A separated animal bud differing in nature from the animal from which it originates.

1858 CARPENTER *Veg. Phys.* §397 The same terms are applied to animals, whence we have isozooids and allozooids.

all-ˈpurpose, *adj. phr.* Also (*rarely*) **all-purposes**. [See ALL E 1.] For all or many purposes; suitable for every occasion or use, or for use by all; = *omnipurpose* adj. s.v. OMNI-. Cf. MULTI-PURPOSE *a.*

1953 K. JACKSON *Lang. & Hist. Early Brit.* v. 188 As with the names in **catōs*, the engravers were too lazy or ignorant to use anything but the convenient all-purposes Latin *-i*. **1961** *Lebende Sprachen* VI. 39/3 All-purpose cabinet, der Allzweckschrank. **1967** *Gloss. Highway Engin. Terms* (*B.S.I.*) *All-purpose road*, a road for the use of all classes of traffic. **1979** *Dædalus* Summer 6 It is..his all-purpose, serviceable humility, that Dickens wants us to understand. **1985** *Times* 9 Apr. 14/7 He was an enviably all-purpose artist.

all right. (See RIGHT *a.* 15, *adv.* 13 c) Hence **1.** sb. use of phr., esp. in ***bit of all right***: see BIT *sb.*[2] 4 h.

2. *adj. phr.* Used to indicate approval. *colloq.*

1953 'S. RANSOME' *Hear No Evil* (1954) vii. 71 Was it an all-right evening? **1962** M. PROCTER *Body to Spare* xxv. 186 He seemed an all-right bloke to me.

†**allron.** *Obs.* ? A fabric originally made at Oleron in France.

1603 in *Verney Papers* (1853) 91 That he shall delyuer.. not only so many allrons and sale clothes for shipps as shall amount to the full somme of 100*l*. but also all such allrons and saile clothes for shippes as the said Frauncis shall or can make during the said term of 5 yeares.

ˌall ˈround, all-round, *phr.* used as *adv.*, *prep.*, and *a.* [See ALL C 9.]

A. *adv.* Everywhere around; affecting equally every one in a circle or company. In a complete circuit; so as to include all the parts of anything, or every member of a circle or company.

1728 E. CHAMBERS *Cycl.* s.v. *Foundry*, They first loosen them a little all round, with a small cutting Instrument. **1861** *Baily's Monthly Mag.* July 140 A stronger Eleven 'all round' never came from Cambridge. **1871** R. H. HUTTON *Ess.* (ed. 2) I. Pref. 15 Revelation is a light on God's character, taken all round. **1882** TENNYSON, Hands all round! God the traitor's hope confound! *a***1884** *Mod.* To make things pleasant all round. **1959** H. P. TRITTON *Time means Tucker* 7 Work was scarce and wages low, and conditions all-round were tough.

B. *prep.* Around all the parts of, round in every direction.

1805 in Nicolas's *Disp.* (1845) VII. 209 *note*, Cutter's head all round the compass during the night.

C. *adj.* Including everything in a given circle, affecting everyone or everything alike; equally developed all round. ***an all-round man***: one who is 'good all around,' or has ability in all departments.

1867 *Routledge's Every Boy's Ann.* Aug. 15 A particularly good all round cricketer. **1869** *Notes on N.W. Prov. Ind.* 98 We find an all-round rent of so much per acre charged on the cultivation. *a* **1883** *Angler's Souvenir* 270 Very few anglers are 'all round' men—*i.e.* devote themselves to the pursuit of all branches of angling alike. **1895** W. JAMES *Coll. Ess. & Rev.* (1920) 403 We find the all-round men like Washington, Cavour, and Gladstone. **1958** *New Statesman* 6 Dec. 802/3 An excellent all-round performance by the Guildford Repertory Company.

Hence **ˌall-ˈroundness**, the quality of being all-round; all-round nature or quality (cf. ALL-AROUNDNESS).

1914 W. E. BEET *Mediaeval Papacy* ii. 43 The most striking feature of Gregory's character and work was its all-roundness. **1950** A. HUXLEY *Themes & Variations* 47 Doubting the inevitability and all-roundness of progress, Biran began to feel very dubious about that Future to which the Liberals looked forward with such sanguine hope.

ˌall-ˈrounder. *fam.* [f. prec. + -ER.] He who, or that which, is all round; hence applied to a man who is able 'all round'; to a collar which fits all round, etc.

1857 J. E. RITCHIE *Night Side of London* 146 One or two awful young swells with excruciating all-rounders were present. **1860** *All Y. Round* No. 42. 369 That particularly demonstrative type of the [collar] species known as 'the all-rounder!' **1865** LD. STRANGFORD *Selection* (1869) II. 163 Dressed in full uniform, with high stand-up collar; the modern all-rounder not having got so far into Asia. **1875** *Contemp. Rev.* XXV. 741 An all-rounder in attainments ..'who had run through the circle of the sciences, and understood them all equally well'. **1938** *Times* 7 Jan. 13/6 Nor, even if the organization were bigger, would it be easy to clap the staff into their pigeon-holes, when so many jobs call for the all-rounder. **1955** *Times* 12 May 14/4 Mr. Gilbert Jessop. A Great Cricketing All-Rounder. **1959** *Listener* 5 Mar. 402/1 The academically successful student is an all-rounder. He plays games and he takes a good part in general college life.

All Saints. The saints in heaven collectively, = ALL-HALLOWS. Hence a frequent dedication of churches. *Also*, the festival on which there is a general celebration of the saints, more fully called **All Saints' Day** (first of November), instituted early in the 7th century, when the Pantheon was transformed into a Christian church; *also*, the season adjoining this festival, ALLHALLOWTIDE.

1580 TUSSER *Husb.* xii. 5 All Saintes [*marg. note* 'Hallomas'] doe laie for porke and souse, for sprats and spurlings for their house.

allseed (ˈɔːlsiːd). *Bot.* [ALL- E 1 + SEED.] A name given to various plants producing a great quantity of seed. (Often a book translation of the botanical name of the genus or species.)

a. The genus *Polycarpon*, consisting of small annual weeds, one of which is found in Engl. **b.** A species of Goosefoot (*Chenopodium polyspermum*). **c.** *Radiola Millegrana*. Prior. **d.** The Knot-grass (*Polygonum aviculare*). Pratt.

All Souls. The souls of all the pious dead; as in All Souls' College, at Oxford, founded to offer prayers for the souls of all the faithful departed. *Also*, the festival on which the church of Rome makes supplications for the souls of all the faithful deceased, more fully called

All Souls' Day. [OE. *ealra sawlena dæȝ*; the old gen. pl. came down to the 16th c. in the form *solne*.] The second of November.

1556 *Chron. Grey Friars* 33 On Alsolne day doctor Allyn beganne in the Gray freeres at afternone. **1594** SHAKS. *Rich. III*, v. i. 10 *Buck.* This is All-soules day (Fellow) is it not? *Sher.* It is. *Buck.* Why then Al-soules day, is my bodies doomsday.

All Souls' Eve. The evening of November 1st.

1805 SCOTT *Last Minstr.* VI. xvi, 'Twas All-souls' eve, and Surrey's heart beat high.

allspice ('ɔːlspaɪs). [ALL- E 1 + SPICE, so called because it has been 'supposed to combine the flavour of cinnamon, nutmeg, and cloves.']

1. An aromatic spice, also called Jamaica Pepper or Pimento, the dried berry of *Eugenia Pimenta* or Allspice Tree (N.O. *Myrtaceæ*) of the West Indies.

1621 BURTON *Anat. Mel.* II. iv. I. iv, Ambergrease, nutmegs and allspice. **1866** *Morn. Star* 17 Mar., Reduction in value of the pimento or all-spice.

2. With various epithets, applied to other aromatic shrubs: **Allspice Tree** or **Carolina Allspice**, *Calycanthus floridus*, a flowering shrub, native to U.S., and cultivated in Engl.; **Japan Allspice**, *Chimonanthus fragrans*, an early-flowering shrub introduced from China in 1766; **Wild Allspice**, *Lindera Benzoin*, a lauraceous shrub native to N.Amer., bearing an aromatic berry, said to have been used as a substitute for allspice.

1768 MILLER *Gard. Dict.* (ed. 8) Ii 3 The bark..has a very strong aromatic scent; from whence the inhabitants of Carolina gave it the title of Allspice. **1789** AITON *Hort. Kew.* II. 220 Japan Allspice. **1830** RAFINESQUE *Med. Flora* II. 236 *Lindera benzoin* has many vulgar names, Spicewood, Allspice. **1866** J. BALFOUR in *Treas. Bot.* 203 The bark of Carolina Allspice is used as a substitute for cinnamon. **1866** A. BLACK *ibid.* 270 The Japan Allspice is a much-branched shrub, and generally treated as a wall-plant in gardens.

allspicy ('ɔːlˌspaɪsɪ), *a. nonce-wd.* [f. prec. + -Y[1]; cf. *peppery*.] Of all-spice; hot, warm.

1840 HOOD *Up Rhine* 217 Poor Martha's allspicy temper.

allthing. *Obs.* or *dial.* Everything. See ALL A 3.

allto, all-to: see ALL C 14, 15.

†**allu'bescency.** *Obs.*$^{-0}$ [f. L. *adl-*, *allubēscent-em*, pr. pple. of *allubēscĕre* to be pleasing to, to find pleasure in, as if ad. L. **allubēscentia*. Cf. ADLUBESCENCE.] 'A willingness; also content.' Bailey 1731; whence in J.

allude (əˈl(j)uːd), *v.* [ad. L. *allūd-ĕre* to play with, joke or jest at, dally with, touch lightly upon a subject; f. *al-* = *ad-* to + *lūdĕre* to play.]

†**1.** *trans.* To play with, make game of, mock. *Obs.*

1535 HENRY VIII in Strype *Eccl. Mem.* I. II. App. liii, Making him [the Pope] a God, to the great deceit, alluding, and seducing of our subjects. **1577** DEE *Relat. ab. Spirits* I. (1659) 418, E. K. then came to me and said, I think there is some wicked spirit that would allude me.

†**2.** To play upon words, to refer by play of words: **a.** *intr.* To play upon, or make a play with (words); to pun. **b.** *trans.* To refer by word-play, to apply punningly. **c.** *intr.* To have a punning reference. *Obs.*

1553-87 FOXE *A. & M.* (1596) 1/1 Christ..alluding to his [St. Peter's] name, called him a rock. **1556** RECORDE *Cast. Knowl.* 4 There canne be no such allusion of woordes in the englyshe..except a man wold rather allude at the woordes, than expresse the sentence. **1605** VERSTEGAN *Dec. Intell.* v. (1628) 148 In respect of Pope Gregory his alluding the name of Engelisce vnto Angellike. *Ibid.* v. 141 The reuerent Father perceiuing this name to alude vnto the name of Angeli. **1607** TOPSELL *Four-footed Beasts* 117 Gray-hounds ..called *Windspill*, alluding to compare their swiftness with the winde.

†**3.** To refer by the play of fancy. **a.** *trans.* To refer (a thing) fancifully or figuratively, to compare symbolically, *to* (something else). **b.** *intr.* To have a fanciful or figurative reference, to correspond in a figure, *to* (something else). *Obs.*

1596 HARINGTON *Ulysses upon Ajax* (1814) 70 Now, to allude this, Philaretes, in this sort conceit me. **1613** T. ADAMS *Pract. Wks.* (1861) II. 10 (D.) Some have alluded these three, gold, myrrh, and frankincense, to..faith, hope, and charity. **1630** TAYLOR (Water P.) *Wks.* (N.) Ile at last allude her to a water-man. **1647** CRASHAW *Poems* 209 Hills and relentless rocks, or if there be Things that in hardness more allude to thee. **1655** [See ALLUDING *a.*] **1665** WITHER *Lord's Prayer* 133 The holy Ghost alludes not our most wise Creator to a foolish Potter.

4. *intr.* To have an oblique, covert, or indirect reference, to point as it were in passing.

1533 MORE *Apol.* viii. Wks. 1557, 860/1 These wordes.. allude vnto certaine woordes of Tyndall. **1711** STEELE *Spect.* No. 11 ¶1 Quotations which allude to the Perjuries of the Fair. **1713** —— *Englishm.* No. 50. 319 The following Letter alludes to an Edition of a Discourse printed in Ireland. *Mod.* This expression evidently alludes to some circumstance then well known but now forgotten.

5. *intr.* To make an indirect or passing reference, to glance at, refer indirectly *to*. (Often used ignorantly as = *refer* in its general sense.)

1574 WHITGIFT *Def. Answ.* i. (1851) I. 162 In a family the master is above the servant..whereunto Christ himself alludeth. **1651** BAXTER *Inf. Bapt.* 251 The Apostle expoundeth, and not only alludeth to these words. **1712** STEELE *Spect.* No. 510 ¶3 He alludes to enterprises which he cannot reveal but with the hazard of his life. **1787** GILPIN *Tour Lakes* (R.) The people of the country, alluding to the whiteness of its foam, call it sour-milk force. **1837** J. HARRIS *Gt. Teacher* 307 He often alluded to his poverty. **1865** DICKENS *Mut. Fr.* iv. 291, I allude to my parents.

†**6.** *trans.* To refer (a thing) as applicable, appropriate, or belonging, *to* (as a saying to that to which it refers, a name to its owner, a thing to its author). *Obs.*

1607 TOPSELL *Four-footed Beasts* 187 Men for honour of Bacchus, did dance upon certain Bottles made of Goats skins..whereunto Virgil alluded this saying; *Mollibus in pratis unctos saliere per utres*. **1634** T. HERBERT *Trav.* 137 Ninus..built Ninive, though some allude it to Assur.

†**7.** *trans.* (with *obj.*, *inf.*, or *subord. cl.*) To throw out by the way, to hint, suggest. *Obs.*

1547 J. HEYWOOD *Wit & Folly* 12, I glanset at payne of mynd, allewdyng That payne to be most payne. **1587** HOLINSHED *Chron.* III. 851/1 The king of Spaine alluded with good right, that the empire apperteined to him. **1677** HALE *Prim. Orig. Man.* III. vii. 285 To excuse this unexperienced Notion..they allude these ensuing Apologies.

alluded (əˈl(j)uːdɪd), *ppl. a.* [f. prec. + -ED.] In *alluded to*: Indirectly referred to, hinted at, meant.

1684 T. BURNET *Th. Earth* (J.) That artificial structure here alluded to. **1872** YEATS *Techn. Hist. Comm.* 22 The agency of fire alluded to above.

alluding (əˈl(j)uːdɪŋ), *vbl. sb.* [f. as prec. + -ING[1].] The making of indirect reference or allusion.

1580 HOLLYBAND *Treas. Fr. Tong.*, *Allusion*, an alluding or applying to an other thing. **1861** J. HOLLAND *Lessons in Life* vii. 99 Fond of alluding to the fact.

alluding (əˈl(j)uːdɪŋ), *ppl. a.* [f. as prec. + -ING[2].] In *alluding to*: †**a.** Suggesting a likeness to (*obs.*). **b.** Referring indirectly to, hinting at.

1655 FULLER *Ch. Hist.* VIII. 29 Sable wings somewhat alluding to those of Bats. **1672** MARVELL *Reh. Transp.* I. 197 Another expression of our Authors alluding too this way.

allume, -inous, obs. var. ALUM, -INOUS.

‖**allumette** (alymɛt). [Fr., f. *allumer* to set light to (:—late L. *adlūmināre*, f. *ad* to + *lūmen* light) + *-ette* dim. formative.] A match for lighting.

1848 LOWELL *Poet. Wks.* (1879) 127/2 Twisting an allumette out of one of you..and relighting my calumet. **1878** LADY HERBERT tr. *Hübner's Round the World* I. xii. 193 If any allumettes are discovered they are pitilessly confiscated. **1882** FROUDE *Carlyle* viii. 121 A faggot or two of cedar allumettes.

†**a'lluminate**, *v.* *Obs.*$^{-0}$ [A refashioning of earlier ALLUMINE after *illumin-ate*: see -ATE[3].] To illuminate (manuscripts).

1742 BAILEY, *Alluminate*, to enlighten, to give Grace, Light, and Ornament to the Letter painted.

†**a'lluminated,** *ppl. a. Obs.*$^{-0}$ [f. prec. + -ED.] Illuminated.

1775 ASH, *Alluminated*, Painted, coloured, embellished.

†**a'lluminating,** *vbl. sb. Obs.*$^{-0}$ [f. as prec. + -ING[1].] Illuminating.

1775 ASH, *Alluminating*, painting, colouring, embellishing.

†**a'llumine,** *v. Obs.* [a. Fr. *a(l)lumine-r*, a refashioning of OFr. *alumer* (Pr. *alumnar*, *alumenar*, It. *allumar*, *-inar*, Sp. *alumbrar*, Pg. *alumear*, *allumiar*, OCat. *alumar*):—late L. *adlūminā-re* to set light to, light up, f. *ad* to + *lūminā-re* to light, f. *lūmen* light. In some senses *aluminer* represents earlier *enluminer*, repr. L. *inlūmināre*.] To enlighten, brighten, illuminate.

1581 MARBECK *Bk. Notes* 947 They wold haue him to be worshipped of vs, who alluminating them doe reioyce.

†**a'lluminor.** *Obs.* [a. Anglo-Fr. *alluminour*:—OFr. *alumineor*, later *allumineur*, f. *alluminer* (here = *enluminer*): see prec. and -OR. Aphetized to LUMINOR and LIMNER.] An illuminator of manuscripts, a limner.

1483 *Act 1 Rich. III*, ix, Any writer, lympner, bynder, or imprynter of such bokes [*French version*: Ascun escrivener, alluminour, liour, ou enpressour, autrement dit imprintour. *16th c. transl.* Any scrivener, allumynour, reader, or printer of such bookes]. **1607** COWEL *Interpr.* (1672) Alluminor denotes one, that by his Trade coloureth or painteth upon Paper or Parchment. At this day we call such a one a *Limner*. [**1754** STOW *London* (Strype) II. v. xiv. 311 quotes Act of Rich. III with 'Alluminer.']

a'llurance. [f. ALLURE v. + -ANCE, as if a. Fr. **allurance*.] The action of alluring; allurement, enticement.

1580 BARET *Alv.* A 315 To draw by allurance: to flatter.. *Blandior.* **1587** GOLDING *De Mornay* xxvi. 396 The Scriptures haue in their lowlinesse more statelines..in their homelinesse more allurance. **1845** 'BON GAULTIER' *Bk. Ballads* 118 That the liquor hath allurance, Well I understand. **1949** O. NASH *Versus* 4 He use no lotions For allurance.

†**a'llurant,** *ppl. a. Obs.* [f. ALLURE *v.* + -ANT, as if a. Fr. **allurant*; cf. OFr. *alurant*.] Alluring, enticing, seductive.

1614 B. JONSON *Barth. Fair* Ind., A sweete Singer of new Ballads allurant.

allure (əˈl(j)ʊə(r)), *v.* Also 5–7 alure. [a. OFr. *alure-r*, *aleurrer*, *alerrer* to attract, captivate, f. *à* to + *lurer*, *leurrer* to LURE, orig. a term of Falconry.]

1. To attract by the offer of some advantage or pleasure; to tempt by something flattering or acceptable; to entice; to win over. **a.** to (or from) a person or party.

1401 *Pol. Poems* (1859) II. 54 Alle these ben alured to ȝoure sory secte. **1574** tr. *Marlorat's Apocalips* 116 He executeth the office of our mediator, gently alluring vs vnto him. **1614** RALEIGH *Hist. World* III. 58 To allure the principall of them to his partie. **1796** MORSE *Amer. Geog.* I. 67 The foreigners, whom the fame of the discoveries of the Portuguese had allured into their service. **1841** MACAULAY *Ess.*, *Hastings* 607 The military adventurers who were allured to the Mogul standards. **1847** DICKENS *Haunted Man* 210 Alluring her towards him.

b. to (or from) a place.

1531 ELYOT *Governor* (1875) 12 Excepte with some pleasaunt noyse, thei be alured and conueied vnto an other hyue. **1611** BIBLE *Hos.* ii. 14, I will allure her, and bring her into the wildernesse. **1769** GOLDSM. *Des. Vill.* 170 He.. Allur'd to brighter worlds, and led the way. **1781** COWPER *Lett.* Wks. 1876, 73 The fine weather..allures the ladies into the garden. **1845** HAMILTON *Pop. Educ.* viii. (ed. 2) 187 Many workmen are allured from the country. **1846** PRESCOTT *Ferd. & Is.* I. ii. 126 He accordingly sought..to allure him back to Spain.

c. to (or from) a course of action.

1513 MORE *Edw. V*, Ded. 2 [It] doth allure all well-disposed persons to the imitation of those things. **1534** —— *On the Passion* Wks. 1557, 1274/1 The other lesse euils, that he alewred and alected her with. **1577** NORTHBROOKE *Dicing* (1843) 104 Him that did teach and practise..vaine pastimes and playes, and did allure children vp therein. **1684** BUNYAN *Pilgr.* II. Introd. 134 Things that seem to be hid in words obscure, Do but the Godly mind the more alure, To study. **1750** JOHNSON *Rambl.* No. 170 ¶12 Had she not been allured by hopes of relief. **1870** EDGAR *Runnymede* 211 Nothing could allure him from his fidelity to the crown. **1880** MCCARTHY *Own Times* III. xlv. 381 Perhaps he had purposely allured his opponents on.

†**2.** *refl. Obs. rare.*

1603 FLORIO *Montaigne* I. xlii. (1632) 145 Such as allure themselves unto it, and that affect to honour..themselves by such service.

3. *simply*, To exercise an attractive power upon; to appeal temptingly to; to fascinate, charm.

1612 DRAYTON *Poly-olb.* v. 78 A hundred Nymphs.. Whose features might allure the Sea-gods more then thee. **1667** MILTON *P.L.* III. 573 The golden Sun in splendor likest Heaven Allur'd his eye. **1725** POPE *Odyss.* I. 185 Viands of various kinds allure the taste. **1756** BURKE *Vind. Nat. Soc.* Wks. I. 63 Some were allured by the modern, others reverenced the ancient. **1878** B. TAYLOR *Deukalion* I. ii. 17 Sad is the message, yet its sense allures.

†**4.** *gen.* To draw to or towards oneself, draw forth, attract, elicit (a thing). *Obs.*

1616 SANDYS in Farr's *S.P.* (1848) 80 O thankful then God's love alure. **1622** SPARROW *Rationale* (1661) 174 The Priests..inviting and alluring the mercy of God. **1670** COTTON *Espernon* III. x. 526 He made use of all the odious terms he could invent, to allure his Majesties Indignation. **1794** PALEY *Nat. Theol.* xx. (1819) 327 A sweet liquor allures the approach of flies.

a'llure, *sb.*[1] [f. the vb.] = ALLUREMENT.

1548 GESTE *Pr. Masse* 132 Not onlye to ryot is synne but the doctryne also therof and the allure to the same. **1590** T. WATSON *Poems* (1870) 169 Inticd from griefs by some allure diuine. **1758** WARBURTON *Div. Legat.* (ed. 10) III. 87 His images and ideas are by an insensible allure, taken throughout from crowded cities. **1901** *Westm. Gaz.* 2 Jan. 1/3 Biskra..Doré like are its allures. **1924** J. FARNOL *Loring Mystery* (1925) xix. 126 He seemed to find a strange allure in this forbidding prospect.

‖**allure** (alyr), *sb.*[2] [Fr., f. *aller* to go: see -URE.] Gait; mien, air. (See also ALURE.)

1882 SALA in *Illustr. Lond. News* 23 Sept. 323 She has all the *allures* of a duchess. **1882** MYERS *Renew. Youth* 192 O Spanish eyebrows, Spanish eyes, Voice and allures of Spain!

a'llured, *ppl. a.* [f. ALLURE *v.* + -ED.] Attracted as to a lure; drawn or enticed to a place or to a course of action.

1552 HULOET, Allured, *Allectus*. **1611** SHAKS. *Cymb.* I. vi. 46 Not so allur'd to feed. **1702** POPE *Thebais* 737 Ravenous dogs, allur'd by scented blood. **1807** CRABBE *Par. Reg.* II. 127 Not led by profit, nor allured by praise.

allurement (əˈl(j)ʊəmənt). Also 6 al-. [f. ALLURE *v.* + -MENT.]

1. The action or process of alluring, or attracting by some proffered good; temptation, enticement.

1561 T. N[ORTON] tr. *Calvin's Inst.* II. iii. (1634) 129 Will, for as much as it is drawne by allurement, cannot exclude necessity. **1601** SHAKS. *All's Well* IV. iii. 241 Take heede of the allurement of one Count Rossillion. **1671** MILTON *P.R.* II. 131 Though Adam by his wife's allurement fell. **1751** JOHNSON *Rambl.* No. 155 ¶8 When some craving passion shall be fully gratified, or some powerful allurement cease its importunity. **1796** MORSE *Amer. Geog.* I. 276 The snares of the enemy are detected, his allurements avoided. **1866** KINGSLEY *Herew.* viii. 135 She found him proof against her allurements.

2. Alluring faculty or quality; attractiveness, fascination, charm.

1579 GOSSON *Sch. Abuse* (Arb.) 22 The allurement of the other drawes the mind from vertue. **1605** BACON *Adv. Learn.* I. vii.§27 (1873) 65 A speech of great allurement toward his own purpose. **1756** BURKE *Subl. & B.* Wks. I. 228 To disentangle our minds from the allurements of the object. **1794** SULLIVAN *View Nat.* V. 398 Is it the right way to teach morality, to trick vice out with allurements? **1838** DICKENS *Nich. Nick.* xxx. (C. D. ed.) 245 The young lady.. displaying her choicest allurements.

3. The means of alluring; that which is offered or operates as a source of attraction; a lure, bait.

1548 UDALL etc. *Erasm. Paraphr. Mark* i. 13 Deceiued with the pleasaunt alurement of an apple. **1626** R. BERNARD *Isle of Man* (1627) 53 Foolish niceries, perfumings, and other allurements to dalliance. **1725** DE FOE *Voy. round World* (1840) 251 Gold..appeared to be the great allurement of the Spaniards. **1825** MCCULLOCH *Pol. Econ.* III. §3. 234 The allurements to enlist in the army.

allurer (əˈl(j)ʊərə(r)). [f. ALLURE *v.* + -ER[1].] One who, or that which, allures, attracts, or fascinates.

1580 HOLLYBAND *Treas. Fr. Tong.*, *Blandisseur*, an allurer or intiser. **1583** BABINGTON *Wks.* 272 Too much showe in apparrell..is a dangerous allurer of lust. **1690** DRYDEN *Prophetess* Prol. 11 Money, the sweet allurer of our hopes.

alluring (əˈl(j)ʊərɪŋ), *vbl. sb.* [f. ALLURE *v.* + -ING[1].]

1. The action of attracting or enticing with the prospect of advantage. (Now mostly gerundial.)

1531 ELYOT *Governor* (1834) 22 It behoueth with most pleasaunt allurynges to instill in them swete maners. **1602** FULBECKE *Pandects* 72 For the alluring of straunge Merchants into a Realme, their priuiledges must be inuiolablie obserued. **1842** J. H. NEWMAN *Par. Serm.* VI. xiv. 224 Let us be far more set upon alluring souls into the right way.

†**2.** Attractiveness, fascination, charm. *Obs.*

1586 T. B. *La Primaudaye's Fr. Acad.* 482 Nature having honoured woman with a gracious alluring of the eyes. *c* **1622** FLETCHER *Wom. Prize* I. iii. (R.) Thus despising Thee and thy best allurings.

aˈlluring, *ppl. a.* [f. ALLURE *v.* + -ING[2].]

1. Attracting or enticing to a course of action; appealing to the desires; tempting, seductive.

1577 tr. *Bullinger's Decades* (1592) 450 By alluring inticements of many faire promises. **1667** MILTON *P.L.* IX. 588 Quick'nd at the scent Of that alluring fruit. **1713** YOUNG *Last Day* II. 380 Teach me with equal firmness, to sustain Alluring pleasure, and assaulting pain. **1776** GIBBON *Decl. & F.* I. 250 The prospect of the Roman territories was far more alluring. **1855** MACAULAY *Hist. Eng.* IV. 712 The terms offered were alluring; three hundred guineas down.

2. Attractive, fascinating, charming. †**a.** of persons. *Obs.*

1587 TURBERVILLE *Trag. T.* (1837) 80 Much given to the love of light alluring dames. **1684** BUNYAN *Pilgr.* II. 82 Mercy was of a fair Countenance, and therefore the more alluring. **1732** POPE *Mor. Ess.* III. 70 Fair Coursers, Vases and alluring Dames.

b. of things.

1590 SHAKS. *Com. Err.* II. i. 89 Hath homelie age th' alluring beauty tooke From my poore cheeke? **1655** H. VAUGHAN *Silex Scint.* II. 169 Each gay, alluring ware. **1755** HERVEY *Theron & Asp.* I. 34 The loveliest Colours and most alluring Forms. **1852** MRS. JAMESON *Leg. Madon.* (1857) Introd. 31 An alluring and even meretricious beauty.

alluringly (əˈl(j)ʊərɪŋlɪ), *adv.* [f. prec. + -LY[2].] In an alluring manner; so as to attract or fascinate; temptingly, charmingly.

1611 COTGR., *Faire les doux yeux à*..to frame or set th' eyes to looke alluringly, flatteringly, or pitifully at one. **1862** LYTTON *Strange Story* II. 176 On sale at a price which seemed to me alluringly trivial. **1868** BROWNING *Ring & Bk.* VIII. 1657 And to love, Not simply did alluringly incite.

alluringness (əˈl(j)ʊərɪŋnɪs). *rare*[−0]. [f. as prec. + -NESS.] The quality of being alluring; attractiveness, charm.

1731 in BAILEY; whence in JOHNSON, etc.

allus (ˈæləs), repr. dial. and colloq. pronunc. of ALWAYS *adv.* Cf. ALLERS *adv.*

1852 DICKENS *Bleak Ho.* xlvi. 447 He wos allus willin fur to give me somethink, he wos. **1876** *Punch* 15 July 15 Do it [*sc.* the sea] allus keep a muddlin' abeaout like that? **1890** KIPLING *Barrack-Room Ballads* (1892) 15, I bring a lock of 'air that 'e allus used to wear, An' you'd best go look for a new love. **1921** H. WILLIAMSON *Beautiful Years* 94 When we be a-shootin' on um [*sc.* pheasants] in t'season, Molly allus lighter in colour than t'others, woan't rise and fly. **1937** D. L. SAYERS *Busman's Honeymoon* ii. 68 You will find Bert an' me allus ready to oblige. **1955** F. O'CONNOR *Wise Blood* v. 86, I allus have admired swimming. **1984** 'D. ARCHER' *Ambridge Years* 21 Heads too close together, Walter, you allus needs to see a'tween your horses, lad.

allusion (əˈl(j)uːʒən). [ad. L. *allūsiōn-em*, n. of action f. *allūdĕre* to ALLUDE. Cf. mod.Fr. *allusion*.]

†**1.** Illusion. *Obs.*

1618 *Hist. P. Warbeck* in *Harl. Misc.* (1793) 59 Resolved in the error of his allusion, he strongly conjectured that, etc.

†**2.** A play upon words, a word-play, a pun. *Obs.*

1556 RECORDE *Cast. Knowl.* 4 So dooth that sentence leese his beautye by the translation, for there canne be no suche allusion of woordes in the englyshe. **1576** LAMBARDE *Peramb. Kent* (1826) 426 The battail (in memorie that they threw away their coates) was called by allusion Losecoatefield. **1605** VERSTEGAN *Dec. Intell.*, Some refer *Adolescens* to Αδολεσχῶν, 'fond of chit-chat.' This is not a derivation, but an Allusion. **1677** GALE *Crt. Gentiles* II. III. 25 'As they did not like,' etc. Here is an elegant Paronomasia or allusion on the words ἐδοκιμασαν and ἀδοκιμον. **1731** BAILEY, *Allusion*, a dalliance or playing with words alike in sound but unlike in sense.

†**3.** A symbolical reference or likening; a metaphor, parable, allegory. *Obs.*

1548 UDALL etc. *Erasm. Par. Luke* Pref. (R.) By reason of sundry allusions, diuers prouerbes, many figures. **1611** COTGR., *Allusion*, an allusion, or likening; an alluding, or applying of one thing unto another. **1635** QUARLES *Embl.* Introd. (1718) 2 To see the Allusion to our blessed Saviour figured in these Types. **1641** FRENCH *Distill.* v. (1651) 117 By a sutable allusion the nutriment is taken for the life of man. **1736** BUTLER *Anal.* I. iii. 87 Virtue, to borrow the Christian allusion, is militant here. **1781** GIBBON *Decl. & F.* II. 67 If he had pursued the allusion, he must have painted many of the Gallic nobles with the hundred heads of the deadly Hydra.

4. A covert, implied, or indirect reference; a passing or incidental reference (cf. ALLUDE *v.* 5). Also *attrib.* in ***allusion book***, a collection of references to a writer or his works.

1612 DRAYTON *Poly-olb.* A 2 The verse oft, with allusion, as supposing a full knowing reader, lets slip. **1624** GATAKER *Transubst.* 95 With more special allusion and application to the water of Baptism. **1703** MAUNDRELL *Journ. Jerus.* (1732) 142 Those frequent allusions made to them in the Word of God. **1766** SIR A. MITCHELL in Ellis *Orig. Lett.* II. 515 IV. 499 His..Majesty smiling, said, I understand your allusion. **1790** PALEY *Hor. Paul.* I. I. 5 The frequent allusions to the incidents of his private life. **1824** DIBDIN *Libr. Comp.* 214 To which some allusion has been made in a preceding page. **1855** MACAULAY *Hist. Eng.* IV. 730 A very intelligible allusion to the compromise proposed by France. **1874** C. M. INGLEBY *Shaksp. Allusion-Books* I. p. i, A Section of our Reprints appears under the title of *Allusion-Books*. By this term we intend to cover not only those books which afford some *allusion*, or indirect reference, to Shakspere or to a work of his, but also those which directly deal with either: i.e. which mention him by name as the author of such and such a play, or as a poet worthy of praise or of blame. **1939** H. MACDONALD *Dryden Bibliogr.* Pref. p. viii, This book is therefore an allusion book as well as a bibliography.

allusive (əˈl(j)uːsɪv), *a.* [f. L. *allūs-* ppl. stem of *allūd-ĕre* to ALLUDE + -IVE, as if ad. L. **allūsīvus*.]

†**1.** Playing upon a word, punning. *Obs.*

1656 FULLER *Hist. Camb.* (1840) 174 Dr. Thomas Nevyle ..practising his own allusive motto, *Ne vile velis.*

b. *Her.* ***Allusive Arms***, called also *canting* or *punning* arms: those in which the charges suggest or play upon the bearer's name or title, as the martlets (OFr. *arondel* young swallow) borne by the Duke of Arundel.

2. Symbolical, metaphorical, figurative. *arch.*

1605 BACON *Adv. Learn.* II. 18 The diuision of Poesie..is into Poesie Narrative, Representative, and Allusive. **1635** BRATHWAIT *Arcad. Princ.* II. 149 The allusive meaning of these emblemes. **1672** JACOMB *Comm. Rom.* viii. (1868) 205 No better than an..allusive, metaphorical son of God. **1780** BOSWELL *Johnson* (1847) 663/1 Johnson..professed that he could bring him out into conversation, and used this allusive expression, 'Sir, I can make him rear.' **1850** LEITCH tr. *Müller's Anc. Art* §128. 102 It represents [it]..in the allusive manner of antiquity.

3. Containing an allusion; having or abounding in indirect references.

1607 TOPSELL *Four-footed Beasts* (1673) 341 According to the allusive saying of the Mantuan. *c* **1630** JACKSON *Creed* VI. xv. Wks. VII. 109 No concludent proof, but allusive only. **1662** EVELYN *Chalcogr.* (1769) 18 More allusive yet to our plate. **1864** *Spect.* No. 1875. 6 Modern ephemeral writing, being essentially allusive from the necessity of condensation, is crowded with allusions to historical facts. **1875** FORTNUM *Majolica* xv. 172 The inscription..allusive, in all probability, to the reconciliation of the rival houses.

allusively (əˈl(j)uːsɪvlɪ), *adv.* [f. prec. + -LY[2].]

1. Symbolically, metaphorically, figuratively. *arch.*

a **1660** HAMMOND *Wks.* I. 6 (J.) By which allusively are noted the Roman armies, whose ensign was the eagle. **1671** EACHARD *Observ.* 63 To take the words not litterally, but allusively. **1870** H. MACMILLAN *Bible Teach.* ii. 39 They are only used allusively, as a kind of pictorial language.

2. By way of allusion, or indirect reference.

1656 TRAPP *Exp. Matt.* v. 12 (1868) 55/1 Allusively to the walks and galleries that were about the temple. **1755** YOUNG *Centaur* vi. *Wks.* 1757 IV. 259 To speak allusively to the patriarchal vision. **1779** JOHNSON *L. P.*, *Dryden* Wks. II. 339 An incident..allusively mentioned by Dryden. **1868** HELPS *Realmah* x. (1876) 284 To write always allusively, but so that the allusions should be understood by any intelligent person. **1881** STRACHEY in *Academy* 5 Mar. 163 Trafalgar is dismissed allusively and unintelligibly in two lines.

allusiveness (əˈl(j)uːsɪvnɪs). [f. as prec. + -NESS.]

1. Symbolical or figurative quality or manner. *arch.*

1669 H. MORE *Seven Churches* ix. (T.) The multifarious allusiveness of the prophetical style. **1875** M. LOWER *Engl. Surn.* (1875) II. App. 128 The allusiveness so much objected to by the lovers of simple and non-emblematical heraldry.

2. The quality of containing or making covert or indirect reference.

1791 WHITAKER *Rev. Gibbon* (R.) The quick and short allusiveness of it [Gibbon's language]. **1863** *Sat. Rev.* 415 Half-jocular allusiveness, which is incomparably more suggestive and more full of temptation than anything else. **1871** R. H. HUTTON *Ess.* II. 299 The indirectness, the allusiveness, the educated reticence of the artists.

†**aˈllusory,** *a. Obs.* [f. L. *allūs-* ppl. stem of *allūd-ĕre* to ALLUDE + -ORY, as if ad. L. **allūsōrius*.] Of or pertaining to allusion; allusive; symbolical, figurative.

1631 DONNE *Def. Self-Murd.* (1644) 112 In the same Oration he hath another allusorie argument. **1660** H. MORE *Myst. Godl.* VII. vii. 308 It is not merely an allusorie Prefiguration of the Messiah, but a down-right Description of him. **1663** *Flagellum, O. Cromwell* (1672) 13 An unhappy allusory Omen of his after Actions.

†**all-utterly,** *adv. Obs.* Forms: 4–5 **al vtterly, alouterly,** 5–6 **aluterlie,** 5–7 **alluterlie, -ly.** [See ALL C 6, and UTTERLY. After Wyclif and Chaucer, apparently retained only by Scottish writers.] Wholly, entirely, completely; wholly and utterly, absolutely.

c **1374** CHAUCER *Boethius* (1868) 109 þei ne were nat alouterly vnknowen to me. *c* **1400** *Apol. Loll.* 54, I a cord in no þing wiþ him, but al vtterly we are contrari. *a* **1423** JAMES I *King's Q.* IV. vi, Gif thy lufe be set allutterly Of nyce lust. **1513** DOUGLAS *Æneis* IV. vi. 99 Aluterlie dissauit or dissolate. **1582–8** *Hist. James VI* (1804) 204 This was alluterly refuisit be the capitane. **1651** CALDERWOOD *Hist. Kirk* (1843) II. 387 To root out, destroy, alluterlie subvert all monuments of idolatrie.

alluvial (əˈl(j)uːvɪəl), *a.* and *sb.* [f. L. *alluvi-um* + -AL[1]. Cf. mod.Fr. *alluvial*.] **A.** *adj.* Of, pertaining to, or consisting of alluvium; deposited from flowing water; or pertaining to such a deposit. Applied to various formations, as ***alluvial cone, fan***, etc.: see the sbs.

1802 PLAYFAIR *Illustr. Hutton. Th.* 463 Contained in the soil or alluvial earth. **1850** LAYARD *Nineveh* xiii. 342 The soil, an alluvial deposit, was rich and tenacious. **1858** GEIKIE *Hist. Boulder* x. 194 Alluvial matter still darkened the water. **1878** HUXLEY *Physiogr.* 142 The rich alluvial mud of Egypt.

B. *sb.* An alluvial deposit; alluvium; *spec.* 'the common term in Australia and New Zealand for gold-bearing alluvial soil' (Morris).

1866 *Harper's Mag.* Sept. 544/1 Nearly two thousand acres of the rich alluvial at the junction of the Ohio and Great Miami rivers. **1888** 'R. BOLDREWOOD' *Robbery under Arms* III. xviii. 270 The whole of the alluvial will be taken up, and the Terrible Hollow..will re-echo with the sound of pick and shovel. **1890** *Pall Mall Gaz.* 16 Dec. 2/1 There is ..every indication of mineral wealth, but it has not been sufficiently proved yet for one to say whether there is good alluvial or not. **1944** J. A. LEE *Shining with Shiner* (1963) 60 Men were out shovelling at and turning over the alluvials.

alluvian (əˈl(j)uːvɪən), *a. rare.* [f. L. *alluvi-um* + -AN. Cf. mod.Fr. *alluvien*.] = ALLUVIAL.

1794 SULLIVAN *View Nat.* I. 493 Alluvian mountains, as they are denominated, are evidently of posterior formation. **1866** J. ROSE *Virgil Ecl. & Georg.* 81 Such the alluvian mud by mountain rills Deposited o'er valleys from the hills.

alluviated (əˈl(j)uːvɪeɪtɪd), *ppl. a.* [Back-formation from ALLUVIATION: see -ATE[3], -ED[1].] Covered or overlain with alluvium; formed of alluvium.

1928 *Proc. Indiana Acad. Sci.* XXXVII. 129 It is probably because of these obstructions in the valley that wide stretches between them possess alluviated levels attained temporarily. **1947** *N.Z. Jrnl. Sci. & Technol.* B. XXIX. 85 This mineral is deposited as layers of varying thickness on the floors of the alluviated flats bordering the hot mineral streams. **1978** *Nature* 23 Feb. 740/1 Sediment storage, transport and redeposition are also characteristic of the alluviated valley floor.

Hence **aˈlluviate** *v. trans.*, to cover or fill with alluvium.

1968 *Proc. Indiana Acad. Sci.* LXXVII. 250 Material eroded from the Mitchell Plain during middle to late Pleistocene time alluviated the subterranean systems.

alluviation (əˌl(j)uːvɪˈeɪʃən). [f. ALLUVI(UM + -ATION.] The process of depositing alluvium.

1847 C. LANMAN *Summer in Wilderness* xxii. 132 They have been striped with various colors by mineral alluviations. **1877** G. K. GILBERT *Rep. Geol. Henry Mts.* 139 The changes by planation and alluviation. **1937** WOOLDRIDGE & MORGAN *Physical Basis Geogr.* xii. 173 Flood alluviation, like aggradation by gravel, is closely linked with the development of meanders.

alluvion (əˈl(j)uːvɪən). [a. Fr. *alluvion*, ad. L. *alluviōn-em* a washing against, inundation; f. *al-* = *ad-* to + *-luvio* washing, f. *lu-ĕre* to wash.]

1. The wash or flow of the sea against the shore, or of a river on its banks.

1536 BELLENDENE *Cron. Scot.* (1821) I. Pref. 48 Ane gret tre was brocht, be alluvion and flux of the see, to land. **1665**

MARVELL *Poems* Wks. 1776 III. 288 Holland..the off-scouring of the British sand, Or what by the ocean's slow alluvion fell, Of ship-wreck'd cockle and the muscle-shell. **1753** CHAMBERS *Cycl. Supp.* s.v., Great alterations are made ..by alluvions of the sea. **1851** SIR F. PALGRAVE *Norm. & Eng.* I. 321 The isle..has not been obliterated by alluvion.

2. An inundation or overflow; a flood, especially when the water is charged with much matter in suspension.

1550 NICOLLS *Thucydides* 92 (R.) Of the whyche alluuyons and overflowynges the earthquakes (as I thynke) were the cause. **1644** HOWELL *Lett.* (1753) 456 Slow rivers, by insensible alluvions, take in and let out the waters that feed them. **1830** LYELL *Princ. Geol.* I. 349 A current of mud is produced..So late as the 27th of October, 1822, one of these alluvions descended the cone of Vesuvius.

3. The matter deposited by a flood or inundation.

1731 BAILEY, *Alluvion*, an accession or accretion along the sea-shore, or the banks of large rivers by tempests or inundations. **1833** LYELL *Princ. Geol.* III. 60 Detached alluvions covering the emerged land. **1849** F. SHOBERL tr. *Hugo's Hunchb.* 104 Every wave of time superinduces its alluvion.

4. *esp.* The matter gradually deposited by a river. = ALLUVIUM.

1779 MANN in *Phil. Trans.* LXIX. 602 The matters, so carried off, will be thrown against the opposite bank of the river..and produce a new ground, called an alluvion. **1834** BANCROFT *Hist. U.S.* I. xiii. 423 A hardy race multiplied along the alluvion of the streams. **1841** CATLIN *North Amer. Ind.* (1844) I. iii. 19 Spreading the deepest and richest alluvion over the surface of its meadows.

5. *Law.* The formation of new land by the slow and imperceptible action of flowing water.

1751 HUME *Ess., Justice* (1817) II. 483 The accessions which are made to land bordering upon rivers, follow the land, say the civilians, provided it be made by what they call alluvion, that is insensibly and imperceptibly. **1880** MUIRHEAD *Gaius* II. §70 That becomes ours which is brought to us by alluvion.

alluvious (ə'l(j)u:vɪəs), *a.* [f. L. *alluvi-us* (see next) + -OUS.] Of alluvial character, washed up.

1731 BAILEY, *Alluvious*, overflowing. **1755** JOHNSON, *Alluvious*, that which is carried by water to another place, and lodged upon something else. **1837** LOCKHART *Scott* IV. 286 The aforesaid alluvious substances which formed its shores.

alluvium (ə'l(j)u:vɪəm). Pl. alluvia, alluviums. [a. L. *alluvium* neut. of adj. *alluvius* washed against, f. *al-* = *ad-* to + *luĕre* to wash.] A deposit of earth, sand, and other transported matter left by water flowing over land not permanently submerged; chiefly applied to the deposits formed in river valleys and deltas.

1655-6 *Phil. Trans.* I. 121 Our Earth, where Alluviums are made in some places, and the Sea gains upon the Land in others. **1731** BAILEY, *Alluvia*, little islets thrown up by the violence of the stream. **1803** SYD. SMITH *Wks.* 1859 I. 53/1 An *alluvium* gained and preserved from the sea. **1830** LYELL *Princ. Geol.* I. 187 The Mississippi, by the continual shifting of its course, sweeps away..considerable tracts of alluvium. **1878** RAMSAY *Phys. Geog.* xxviii. 458 The bones of which are found in the old alluvia of rivers.

b. *fig.*

1850 KINGSLEY *Alt. Locke* vi. (1876) 66 Out of this book alluvium a hole seemed to have been dug near the fireplace. **1862** LUDLOW *Hist. U.S.* 281 The tide of emigration..left behind it a sort of alluvium of free-soil principles.

† **'allwhat,** *conj. adv.*, and *prep. Obs.* [ALL- E 1 + WHAT, occas. used in south. dial. = *what time, while, when.*]

A. *conj. adv.* (with or without *that*) All the while, while, till.

1314 *Guy W.* 81 Al what that cite y-nomen be. *c* **1315** SHOREHAM 127 Al fram Crystes ascensioun, Al wat comth hyre assumpcioun. **1340** *Ayenb.* 132 Hy clifþ an heȝ alhuet þet hi come to perfeccion.

B. *prep.* Till, until.

1340 *Ayenb.* 26 Þet no man ne may his knawe alhuet þanne þet hi byþ uol wexe. *Ibid.* 52 He uesteþ..alhuet niȝt.

all-where ('ɔ:l-hwɛə(r)), *adv. arch.* [ALL- E 2 + WHERE. At first *over all-where*.] Everywhere.

c **1430** *Hymns to Virg.* (1867) 102 But ouer al-where isþi godhede. **1526** SKELTON *Magnyf.* 1347 Foly and Fansy all where, every man doth face and brace. **1585** JAMES I *Ess. Poesie* (Arb.) 17 The pelmell chok with larum loude alwhair. *c* **1630** DRUMM. OF HAWTH. *To Fairest Fair* Wks. 31/2 All-where diffused. **1865** LOWELL *Poet. Wks.* (1879) 437, I follow all-where for thy sake.

b. In form **allwheres.** (Cf. *alway-s, sometime-s.*)

1879 J. LONG *Æneid* XI. 826 Allwheres at once their missiles stream.

allwhither (,ɔ:l'hwɪðə(r)), *adv. rare.* [ALL- E 2 + WHITHER; after *all-where.*] In every direction.

1878 B. TAYLOR *Deukalion* IV. iii. 153 Thou warrest with pure intelligence That rays allwhither from its central flame.

†**,all-'whole,** *a.* and *adv. Obs.* Forms: 4-5 al-hool, 5-6 al-hole, 6-7 all whole. *North.* 5 al hale, 5-6 all hale, al haill, 6 alhayl. [ALL- E 6 + WHOLE; cf. ALL A 10. Cf. Fr. *tout entier.*]

A. *adj.* Entire.

c **1449** PECOCK *Repr.* I. iv. 20 The seid ful al hool moral lawe of kinde..the al hool lawe with which Cristen men ben chargid. **1513** DOUGLAS *Æneis* VI. xiii. Argt., Anchyses schawis Eneas to the end Alhayl the lynage that suld fra hym discend. **1588** A. KING *Canisius' Catech.* 2 in *Cath. Tractates* (S.T.S.) 209 That Christ is alhaill contenit in the holie sacrament off the alter.

B. *adv.* Entirely.

1535 STEWART *Cron. Scot.* (1858) I. 39 Fra Clyde alhaill on to Brigantia. **1541** R. COPLAND *Galyen's Terapeut.* 2 B iv b, It is a straunge thynge, & all hole agaynst reason. **1601** HOLLAND *Pliny* (1634) I. 67 The region..all whole in the midland part of Italy.

†**,all-'wholly,** *adv. Obs.* Also 5 alholly, 6 north. al haillelie. [f. prec. + -LY[2].] Entirely.

c **1440** *Partonope* 5163 To yow alholly I do me schryfe. **1535** STEWART *Cron. Scot.* (1858) I. 277 Thair purpois wes al haillelie to fle. **1597** DANIEL *Civ. Wares* IV. lxviii, Bent All-wholly unto active worthynesse.

all-wielding (,ɔ:l'wi:ldɪŋ), *ppl. a.* Forms: 1 al-waldend, 2 al-weldinde, 3 al-wealdent, al-waldand, 4-5 alweldand(e, 5 alweldynge. [ALL- E 7 + *wielding* pr. pple. of WIELD. Cf. OE. adj. *eal-weald*, and sb. *eal-wealda.*] All-ruling, almighty.

a **1000** *Botschaft* (Grein) Alwaldend God. *c* **1175** *Lamb. Hom.* 215 Al weldinde Godd. *a* **1300** *Cursor M.* 3117 Herkens o godd þat all weldand. *a* **1300** *Credo* in *Reliq. Ant.* I. 22 Sitis on his fadir richt hand, fadir al-waldand. **1352** *Pol. Poems* (1859) I. 75 Alweldand God, of mightes maste. *a* **1400** *Chev. Assigne* 1 All-weldynge god.

†**,all-'witty,** *a. Obs.* [ALL- E 6.] Knowing all things, omniscient. (A special attribute of the Second Person of the Trinity, the 'Eternal Wisdom.')

c **1340** HAMPOLE *Pr. Consc.* 2 Þe witte of þe Son alwytty. *c* **1375** WYCLIF *De Apost. Cleri.* 86 Siþ Crist is al witty as our feiþ techiþ us. **1496** *Dives & Paup.* (W. de Worde) III. xix. 157/2 The seconde commaundement is applyed to the sone alwytty..for he knoweth all.

'all,work. Work, especially domestic work, of all kinds. ***maid of all-work***: a general servant.

1838 DICKENS *Ol. Twist* (1850) 139/2 Brittles was a lad of allwork. **1880** W. S. GILBERT *Pir. Penz.* I, A piratical maid of all work.

ally (ə'laɪ), *v.* Forms: 3-4 alie, 4-6 alye, allie, allye, 5- ally. [a. OFr. *alie-r*:—L. *alligā-re*, f. *al-* = *ad-* to + *ligāre* to bind, fasten. For change of *a-* to *al-* see AL- *pref.*[1]. Differentiated variants are ALLAY *v.*[2], ALLOY; a by-form ultimately of same origin is ALLIGATE.]

1. *trans.* To combine, unite, or join in affinity, companionship, amity, or association for a special object; now chiefly of marriage, friendly association of sovereign states, and union of nature or spirit. Const. *to, with.*

1297 R. GLOUC. 65 To be in such mariage alied to the emperour. *c* **1386** CHAUCER *Pard. T.* 288 Me were lever dye, Than I yow scholde to hasardours allye [*v.r.* alye, alleye, allie]. *c* **1425** WYNTOUN *Cron.* IV. xix. 27 Swa wythe þame til alyid be, þai and þare posteryti. **1558** Q. ELIZ. in Strype *Ann. Ref.* I. II. App. i. 389 We do by this our proclamation streightly charge and allye them to us. **1605** STOW *Ann.* 670 She allied unto her all the Knights. **1732** POPE *Ess. Man* II. 243 Wants, frailties, passions, closer still ally The common int'rest. **1837** J. HARRIS *Gt. Teacher* 17 Virtue..allies us to supreme greatness. **1847** TENNYSON *Princess* II. 51 You may with those self-styled our lords ally Your fortunes. **1862** R. PATTERSON *Ess. Hist. & Art* 33 We can never ally mahogany to vivid reds.

2. *refl.* (with same meaning and const.)

1330 R. BRUNNE *Chron.* 24 Alfride vnto Rollo sone gan him alie. **1591** PERCIVALL *Sp. Dict.*, *Aliar*, to confederate, to allie himselfe. **1635** A. STAFFORD *Fem. Glory* (1869) 59 He might have allied Himselfe to the greatest Princes. **1781** J. MOORE *Italy* (1790) I. ii. 20 This young gentleman has lately allied himself to the family..by marrying. **1849** MACAULAY *Hist. Eng.* II. 51 He allied himself closely with Castlemaine.

3. *intr.* To unite, enter into alliance. *arch.*

1330 R. BRUNNE *Chron.* 67 To Malcolme, þe Scottis kyng, Tostus alied to. *c* **1386** CHAUCER *Merch. T.* 170 Wher me lust beste to allien [*v.r.* allyen, alien]. *c* **1400** *Destr. Troy* VII. 3190 Yche lede by the last aliet þerto. **1825** T. JEFFERSON *Autobiog.* Wks. 1859 I. 31 No foreign power will ally with us. **1837** LYTTON *Athens* II. 195 If they [the Athenians] will ally with me.

†**4.** *intr.* To belong naturally. *Obs. rare.*

1330 R. BRUNNE *Chron.* 248 Now is non of age of his ancestrie May haf his heritage, to whom it salle alie.

†**5.** *trans.* To combine or mix (ingredients). *Obs.* (Cf. *allay, alloy.*)

1392 in Warner's *Antiq. Culin.*, Alye it with ȝolkes of eyren. *c* **1420** *Liber Cocorum* (1862) 34 Þere-with alye mony metes. *c* **1500** *Anc. Cookery* in *Househ. Ord.* (1790) 427 Take grene pesen..wyth gode brothe of beeff..and let hom boyle tyl hit aly hitself.

ally (ə'laɪ, 'ælaɪ), *sb.*[1] Forms: 4-6 alie, alye, 4-8 allye, (4 aleye), 5 aly, 5-7 allie, (6-7 alley), 5- ally. Occas. accented '*ally* in 7. [f. the vb.]

I. *abstract.*

†**1.** Connexion by marriage or descent; relationship, kinship, kindred. *Obs.*

c **1400** *Epiph.* (Turnb. 1843) 102 His son..Or ellis won that wer her next of alye. **1494** FABYAN IV. lxxi. 49 A noble yonge man of thaly of Helayne. **1592** WARNER *Alb. Eng.* VII. xxxv. 170 He wiu'd a Lady passing faire and of the King's Allie.

†**2.** Confederation, alliance. *Obs.*

1513 DOUGLAS *Æneis* X. ix. 22 His band of freyndschip and ally. **1553-87** FOXE *A. & M.* II. 370 A perpetual league amity and allie should be nourished between this realm and the princes of Germany.

II. *collect.* (Cf. 'to have acquaintance with'; 'to meet all his acquaintance.')

†**3.** People of one's relationship; kindred, relatives. *Obs.*

a **1400** *Cov. Myst.* (1841) 145 If I myght of myn alye ony ther ffynde. *c* **1400** *St. Alexius* (Cott. MS.) 64 With alle the beste of here Aleye. **1460** CAPGRAVE *Chron.* 286 The erl of Northumbirland cam..with alle his alye.

†**4.** People of an alliance; confederates. *Obs. rare.*

1375 BARBOUR *Bruce* XVII. 319 Or ellis thai war his allye.

III. *individual.* (Cf. 'an acquaintance.')

†**5.** A relative, a kinsman or kinswoman. *Obs.*

c **1380** *Sir Ferumb.* 4077 Othre þat ware ys cosyns oþer alyes. *c* **1386** CHAUCER *Sec. Nonnes T.* 292 'This day I take the for myn allye,' Sayde this blisful faire mayde. **1388** WYCLIF *Ex.* xviii. 5 Jetro, alie of Moises. **1482** *Monk of Evesham* (1869) 71 Cosyn and alye to the same bysshoppe. **1592** SHAKS. *Rom. & Jul.* III. i. 114 This Gentleman the Princes neere Alie. **1654** LESTRANGE *K. Charles I* (1655) 118 Upon an ally worse still, as superinducting Incest with Rape.

6. *fig.* Anything akin to another by community of structure or properties, or placed near it in classification. In *Bot.* Natural orders placed in the same ALLIANCE, q.v.

1697 DRYDEN *Virg. Georg.* III. 549 All the Weste Allies of stormy Boreas blow. **1713** DERHAM *Physico-Theol.* VII. ii. 384 From the Head and Mouth, pass we to its near Allie the Stomach. **1857** H. MILLER *Test. Rocks* xi. 496 Consisting mainly of ferns and their allies. *Mod.* The alkaline metals and their allies.

7. a. One united or associated with another by treaty or league; now usually of sovereigns or states.

1598 GREENWEY *Tacitus Ann.* XIII. ii. 180 The like number of citizens and allies should bee vnder Corbuloes charge. **1640** QUARLES *Enchirid.* ix. 1 Assayle some Alley of his rather than himselfe. **1677** SEDLEY *Ant. & Cl.* IV. i. (1766) 166 One King or ally still forsakes his side. **1769** ROBERTSON *Charles V*, VI. VI. 77 His new ally the Sultan. **1862** STANLEY *Jew. Ch.* (1877) I. xvi. 303 Ammon, the ancient ally of Israel..is the assailant. **1870** KNIGHT *Crown Hist. Eng.* 791 There were two columns of the Allies marching on Paris.

b. *spec.* (pl.) ***the Allies***, the allied forces or States (including Britain) which fought against the Central Powers in the war of 1914-18, or against the Axis in that of 1939-45.

1914 *Times* 2 Nov. 9/6 A Note was to have been presented to the Porte on Friday asking for..the withdrawal of the German officers and men from the Turkish ships [etc.]... Failing satisfaction in these respects, diplomatic relations with the Allies would cease. **1926** T. E. LAWRENCE *Seven Pillars* (1935) 7 The rebellion of the Sherif of Mecca came to most as a surprise, and found the Allies unready. **1939** *Times* 13 Nov. 7/6 (*heading*) World events in Allies' favour. **1945** A. HUXLEY *Let.* 27 May (1969) 528 It is obvious that now, even if the Allies desired to treat Germany non-punitively and in a reformatory spirit, it will be impossible for anything but the *lex talionis* to function. **1968** W. K. HANCOCK *Smuts* II. xxi. 373 At the very worst..victory in Africa would give the allies a firm base from which to counter the German thrust. **1977** V. GLENDINNING *Elizabeth Bowen* ix. 154 The days before the Allies invaded occupied France.

c. An individual who helps or co-operates with another; a supporter or associate; a friend.

1916 JOYCE *Portrait of Artist* (1969) xi. 63 He became the ally of a boy named Aubrey Mills and founded with him a gang of adventurers in the avenue. **1950** R. MACAULAY *World my Wilderness* iv. 49 She went off; each had a warm sense of having found an ally against Others. **1963** D. LESSING in *Winter's Tales* IX. 146 His sister..far from being his friend and ally..seemed positively to hate him.

8. *fig.* Anything auxiliary to another.

1853 H. ROGERS *Ecl. Faith* 6 Tractarianism is..the strict ally of Rome. **1869** BUCKLE *Civilis.* III. v. 477 Science, instead of being the enemy of religion, becomes its ally.

ally, alley, alay ('ælɪ), *sb.*[2] [Supposed to be a diminutive abbreviation of *alabaster*: cf. *Willy, Tommy*, etc.] A choice marble or taw, used by boys in playing; one of real marble or alabaster in contrast with those of terra cotta, etc.

1720 DE FOE *Duncan Campb.* iv. Wks. 1871, 401 A large bag of marbles and alleys. **1748** *Phil. Trans.* XLV. 456 Pellets, vulgarly called Alleys, which boys play withal. **1807** COLERIDGE *Own Times* III. 953 While he was playing at marbles, would quarrel with the taws and alays in his mouth, because had understood it was the way Demosthenes learnt to splutter. **1833** J. PARIS *Philos. in Sport* x. 171 Why, your taw is a brown marble, and your ally, if I rightly remember, a very white one, is it not so? **1837** DICKENS *Pickw.* (1847) 281/1 Inquiring whether he had won any alley tors or commoneys lately. **1865** MISS MULOCH *Christian's Mist.* 37 An 'ally taw,' that is, a real alabaster marble.

ally, obs. form of ALLEY.

'allya, allia. *Obs. Sc.* [The same as ALLY; the final *a* perhaps represents Fr. *é* in *allié* allied.] = ALLY *sb.*[1] in senses 2, 3, 4, 7 a.

1513-75 *Diurn. Occurr.* (1833) 166 For mantenance of the allia betwix the said king and thame. **1548** *Compl. Scotl.* 79 The atheniens and ther allya..assailȝet the persans. **1568** in Tytler *Hist. Scotl.* (1864) III. 418 All of the surname of the Hamiltons and their allya. **1651** CALDERWOOD *Hist. Kirk* (1843) II. 295 The King of France, the ancient allya of this realme.

allying (ə'laɪɪŋ), *vbl. sb.* [f. ALLY *v.* + -ING[1].] Joining, uniting; formation of alliance.

1598 FLORIO, *Parentado*, a mariage, or matching, or allying together of houses.

allyl ('ælɪl). *Chem.* [f. L. *all(ium)* garlic, onion + -YL = Gr. ὕλη substance.]

1. A monovalent hydro-carbon radical, C_3H_5, $= CH_3-CH=CH'$, obtained in the free state as a very volatile liquid, with a pungent odour resembling that of horse-radish.

1854 PEREIRA, *Mat. Med.* I. 225 Oils obtained from alliaceous and cruciferous plants..whose hypothetical radical is allyle. 1863 WATTS *Dict. Chem.* I. 140 Berthelot and De Luca in the same year [1857] isolated the radical allyl. 1870 TYNDALL *Heat* xv. §763. 528 The liquid here employed is the iodide of allyl.

2. *attrib.* as in ***allyl series, allyl compounds, allyl alcohol*** C_3H_5OH, ***di-allyl ether*** $(C_3H_5)_2O$, ***allyl isothiocyanate*** (C_3H_5NCS), ***allyl oxalate, allyl sulphide*** $(C_3H_5)_2S$, ***allyl sulphocyanide*** $C_3H_5.S.CN$, ***allyl-thio-urea*** (see THIOSINAMINE), etc.; **allyl plastic, resin**, a plastic or synthetic resin made by polymerization of an allyl compound.

1863 WATTS *Dict. Chem.* (1879) I. 56 Acrolein..the aldehyde of the allyl series. 1869 ROSCOE *Elem. Chem.* 389 The allyl sulphide is remarkable as occurring in nature as the essential oil of garlic. In like manner allyl sulphocyanide is found as the essential oil of black mustard seed. 1884 ROSCOE & SCHORLEMMER *Treat. Chem.* III. 394 *Allyl-thio-urea*, $CS.N_2H_3$ (C_3H_5), was obtained in 1834... Will.. proposed for it the name of *thio-sinamine* in place of that which had been hitherto used, namely mustard-oil ammonia. 1891 THORPE *Dict. Appl. Chem.* II. 626/2 The *volatile oil*, consisting of allyl isothiocyanate is formed from the brown mustard on addition of water. 1895 *Proc. Chem. Soc.* 216 Iodine..acts similarly to bromine on allyl-thiourea. 1907 WALKER & MOTT tr. *Holleman's Text-bk. Org. Chem.* (ed. 2) I. 323 The *iso*thiocyanic esters are also called *mustard-oils* after allyl *iso*thiocyanate, to which the odour and taste of mustard-seeds are due. 1911 *Encycl. Brit.* XXVII e 794/2 The most important derivative [of thiourea] pharmacologically is allyl-thiourea. 1943 *Mod. Plastics* Nov. 96/2 The capacity for forming or drawing the new allyl plastics into curved windows is restricted..because of the absence of plastic flow. *Ibid.* June 102 (*caption*) Physical Properties of Cast Allyl Resins and Laminated Allyl Resins. *Ibid.* Nov. 96/1 The manner in which the Columbia allyl resins differ from..commercial plastics can be clarified..by indicating why the development of the new materials has appeared desirable. 1959 *Chambers's Encycl.* X. 776/2 *The Allyl Plastics.* The allyl resins are among the newest plastic materials, and are based on allyl alcohol produced in the cracking of oil.

allylamine ('ælɪlə,maɪn). *Chem.* [f. ALLYL + AMINE.] The ammonia of the allyl series $C_3H_5NH_2$, also called Acrylamine.

1863 WATTS *Dict. Chem.* I. 146 Allylamine is obtained by the action of ammonia on iodide of allyl.

allylate ('ælɪleɪt). *Chem.* [f. ALLYL + -ATE[4].] A salt of allyl, as ***sodium allylate*** C_3H_5ONa.

1863 WATTS *Dict. Chem.* (1879) I. 141 A gelatinous mass of allylate of potassium. 1869 ROSCOE *Elem. Chem.* 389 Sodium dissolves in allyl alcohol, forming sodium allylate, one atom of typical hydrogen in the alcohol being replaced by sodium.

allylene ('ælɪliːn). *Chem.* [f. ALLYL + -ENE.] A divalent hydro-carbon radical, C_3H_4, isomeric with acetylene; consisting of allyl minus one atom of hydrogen. Also called *propine*.

1863 WATTS *Dict. Chem.* I. 112 Pure allylene, a colourless gas, having an unpleasant odour, burning with a smoky flame. 1869 ROSCOE *Elem. Chem.* 391 Allylene is formed by the action of potash upon propylene dichloride.

allylic (ə'lɪlɪk), *a. Chem.* [f. ALLYL + -IC.] Of or belonging to allyl.

1857 W. A. MILLER *Elem. Chem.* III. vi. §2. 386 Hofmann and Cahours have succeeded in discovering the allylic.. alcohol.., a compound which stands in the same relation to acrolein that ethylic alcohol does to ordinary aldehyd. 1863 WATTS *Dict. Chem.* I. 141 Allylic aldehyde (acrolein). 1873 WILLIAMSON *Chem.* §290 Allylic sulphide $(C_3H_5)_2S$,.. found to be identical with the essential oil of garlic.

allylin ('ælɪlɪn). *Chem.* [f. ALLYL + -IN.] A viscid liquid, a by-product in the preparation of allyl alcohol by distilling glycerin with oxalic acid.

1874 WATTS *Dict. Chem.* (1879) VII. 51.

Ally Sloper ('ælɪ 'sləʊpə(r)). The name of a character in a series of humorous publications, having a prominent nose and receding forehead and noted for his dishonest or bungling practices; hence used allusively.

1873 (*title*) Some Playful Episodes in the Career of Ally Sloper..pictorially portrayed by Marie Duval, and explained..by Judy's Office Boy [*i.e.* C. H. Ross]. 1877 C. H. Ross (*title*) Ally Sloper's Book of Beauty. 1884 (*title*) Ally Sloper's Half Holiday. 1901 *Ann. Brit. Sch. Athens* VI. 126 The young man[in the carnival] contents himself with..a roughly-made domino, or, thanks to the steadily increasing influx of Western culture..an 'Ally Sloper' mask. 1922 JOYCE *Ulysses* 495 Prognathic with receding forehead and Ally Sloper nose. 1925 FRASER & GIBBONS *Soldier & Sailor Words* 170 *Ally Sloper's Cavalry*, the Royal Army Service Corps. A humorous perversion of the initials of the Army Service Corps.

alma, almah ('ælmə). Also **alme, almeh.** [a. Arab. *ʿalmah*, adj. fem. 'learned, knowing'; f. *ʿalama* 'to know' (because they have been instructed in music and dancing). Cf. Fr. *almée*.] An Egyptian dancing-girl.

1814 BYRON *Corsair* II. ii. 8 While dance the Almas to wild minstrelsy. *a*1877 OUIDA *Tricotrin* I. 394 Dance like an almàh among the scarlet beans of the cottage garden.

almacantar, -er, obs. ff. ALMUCANTAR.

†**alma'chabel.** *Obs.* = ALGEBRA; being the second half of the Arabic name of the science. (Also in med.L. *almacabala*: see ALGEBRA.)

1570 DEE *Math. Præf.* 6 The Science of workyng Algiebar and Almachabel, that is, the Science of findyng an vnknowen number, by Addyng of a Number, and Diuision and æquation.

†**almacie.** *Obs.* (See quot.)

1551 TURNER *Herbal* II. 67 b, Oliues..that for rypenes fall of the tre..ar called almacles and colymbades.

†**almaçour, -ur.** *Obs. rare*[−1]. [a. OFr. *almaçor, -ur, aumaçor*, also *aumansour*, ad. (perh. indirectly) Arab. *al-manṣūr*, the (heaven-) defended, the august, f. *naṣara* to defend.] A (Saracen) grandee, a magnifico. (A common title in OFr. romances, but not so used in Arabic.)

*c*1300 *K. Alis.* 3042, After him spak Dalmadas, A riche almaçour he was [*Weber, following Linc. Inn, MS. has* almatour; *Laud MS.* 622 lf. 41 almacur].

almadia (ælmə'diːə). Also **almadie, almade.** [ad. Arab. *al-maʿdīyah* a ferry-boat, f. *ʿaday* to cross; cf. It. *almadia*, Fr. *almadie* (also used in Eng.).] A river-boat in India and Africa; in the latter applied to a canoe of bark or of a hollowed trunk; in the former also to a boat, 80 ft. in length, and of great swiftness.

[1611 COTGR. & FLORIO have it in Fr. and It. but not Eng.] 1681 BLOUNT *Glossogr.*, *Almades*, little Boats in the East-Indies, made all of one piece of wood. 1753 CHAMBERS *Cycl. Supp.*, *Almadie*, in ship-building, a small vessel used by the negroes of Africa, about four fathom long: and made usually of the bark of a tree. 1858 BEVERIDGE *Hist. Ind.* I. I. vii. 162 Four lads arrived in an almadia.

almagest ('ælmədʒɛst). Also 4 **almagesti, almageste.** [a. OFr. *almageste*, ad. (ult.) Arab. *al-majistī*, ad. (with article *al* the) Gr. μεγίστη greatest (sc. σύνταξις composition); applied by the Arabs (and previously, it is inferred, in the Greek schools of Alexandria) to the great treatise of Ptolemy, Μαθηματική σύνταξις, in contradistinction to the elementary works studied before it.] The great astronomical treatise of Ptolemy; extended in middle ages to other great text-books of astrology and alchemy.

*c*1386 CHAUCER *Miller's T.* 22 His almageste and bokes gret and smale, His astrelabre longing for his art. 1393 GOWER *Conf.* III. 134 Danz Tholome is nought the lest Which maketh the boke of almagest. 1614 SELDEN *Titles of Hon.* 74 The starres placed in his almagest are of that time. *c*1680 SIR T. BROWNE *Tracts* 179 Welcome might be a true Almagest. 1714 DERHAM *Astroth.* 6 (JOD.) The particulars.. he may find them in Riccioli's Almagest. 1805 SCOTT *Last Minstr.* VI. xvii, On cross, and character, and talisman, And almagest, and altar, nothing bright. 1878 NEWCOMB *Pop. Astron.* I. i. 32 The 'Almagest' of Ptolemy, composed about the middle of the second century of our era.

al'magra. Also **almagre.** [a. Sp. *almagra, almagre*, a. Arab. *al-maghrah* red ochre.] An ochre of a fine deep red; the *sil atticum* of the ancients; found in great quantities in Spain.

1703 MOXON *Mech. Exerc.* 286 If you would have it of the Colour of the Brick, put into it either some very fine Brick-Dust, or Almegram. 1753 CHAMBERS *Cycl. Supp.*, *Almagra*, in the cant of chemists, denotes red bole, or ruddle. 1775 ASH, *Almagra*, a fine deep red ochre.

†**'Almain,** *a.* and *sb. Obs.* Forms: 4 **almaun,** 5 **-ayn,** 6–7 **-an(e,** 4–8 **-ain,** (7–8 **almond).** [a. OFr. *aleman* (mod. *allemand*), a. Ger. *alaman*.]

A. *adj.* German.

1549 *Compl. Scotl.* 66 Thai dancit al cristyn mennis dance, ..the alman haye. 1586 T. B. *La Primaudaye's Fr. Acad.* I. 84 The emperor Frederike the II spake the Morisco, Almaigne, Italian, and French toong. 1587 HOLINSHED *Scot. Chron.* I. 3 Towards the Almaine Sea..Scotland hath the Mers. *c*1590 MARLOWE *Faustus* I. 123 Almain rutters with their horsemen's staves. 1665 MANLEY tr. *Grotius's L. Country Wars* 907 The Netherlanders belonged no more to the Almain Empire than the French did.

B. *sb.* **1.** A German.

*c*1314 *Guy Warw.* 70 The Almains ben ouer come. *c*1350 *Will. Palerne* 1165 þe almauns seweden sadly. 1398 TREVISA *Barth. De P.R.* XIX. ix. (1495) 869 Whitysshe colour in Almayns, Duchemen. 1594 BLUNDEVIL *Exerc.* III. II. vi. (ed. 7) 382 The Spanish and the high Almaines. 1635 PAGITT *Christianogr.* I. iii. (1636) 141 The Armenians did gladly receive the Almans. 1698 *Life Bl. Prince* in *Harl. Misc.* (1793) 51 Not only French, but Almains, Dutch.

2. A kind of dance. Hence ***Almain-leap.***

1549 [See *Alman haye* under A]. 1584 PEELE *Arraignm. Paris* II. ii. 28 Knights in armour, treading a warlike almain. 1611 COTGR. s.v. *Saut, Trois pas, & vn saut*, The Almond leape. 1616 B. JONSON *Devil is an Ass* I. i. (N.) And take his almain-leap into a custard. *a*1634 CHAPMAN *Alphonsus* Plays (1873) III. 238 An Almain and an upspring, that is all. *a*1701 SEDLEY *Bellamira* V. i. Wks. 1766, 179, I will leap the half almond with you.

3. A species of dance-music in slow time, afterwards included as one of the movements of the Suite.

1597 T. MORLEY *Introd. Mus.* 181 The Alman is a more heauie [measure] then this. 1651 PLAYFORD (*title*) A Musicall Banquet. The second [Part] a Collection of New and Choyce Allmans, Corants, and Sarabands, for one Treble and Basse Viol. 1676 SHADWELL *Virtuoso* III. (1720) I. 362 To play, first a grave pavin or almain. 1882 SHORTHOUSE *J. Inglesant* II. liii. 14 Sweet dance music, such as Pavins, Almains.

¶ In senses 2 and 3 now written ALLEMANDE

†**'Almaine, -any.** *Obs.* Forms: 4–5 **almeyne, -egne,** 6– **-en,** 6–7 **-ain(e, -aigne, -anie, -any.** [a. OFr. *alemaigne*:—L. *allemania* the country of the *Allemanni*.] Germany.

*c*1314 *Guy Warw.* 35 Forth he went into Speyne And after into Almeyne. 1480 CAXTON *Chron. Eng.* ccxli. 266 Hir fadre was emperour of almayne. 1556 *Chron. Grey Friars* 14 The emperar of Almen. 1562 TURNER *Baths* Ded., I was compelled..to fly into hygh Almany. 1585 JAMES I *Ess. Poesie* (Arb.) 77 *Mein*, a riuer in *Almanie*. 1586 T. B. *La Primaudaye's Fr. Acad.* I. 150 According to the custome of Almaigne. 1622 BACON *Henry VII*, 10 Fredericke the Third Emperour of Almaine. 1682 MILTON *Hist. Moscow* iv. Wks. 1847, 575/1 Ambassadors from Almany.

,almain-'rivets. A kind of light armour, first used in Germany, in which great flexibility was obtained by overlapping plates sliding on rivets.

1530 PALSGR. 516 He hath dygged hym in nat withstandyng his almayne ryvettes, *nonobstant ses cuirasses*. 1565 in *Richmondsh. Wills* (1853) 179, j almon revet..j shafe of arrowes, and other hustlements xxvjs. viijd. 1591 GARRARD *Art of Warre* 10 The forepart of a Corslet and a Headpeece, as is the Almaine Rivet. 1742 BAILEY, *Almain Rivets*, a certain light kind of Armour with Plates of Iron for the Defence of the Arms; used by Germans. 1834 PLANCHÉ *Brit. Costume* 253 Black bill-men or halberdiers, who wore the armour called almain rivet.

‖**,Alma 'Mater.** [L. *alma māter* bounteous mother.] A title given by the Romans to several goddesses, especially to Ceres and Cybele, and transferred in Eng. to Universities and schools regarded as 'fostering mothers' to their *alumni*.

1398 TREVISA *Barth. De P.R.* XIV. ii. (1495) 466 In signe and token of grete plente, a grete female ymage was made, and callyd *Alma mater*. 1718 POPE *Dunc.* III. 338 Till Isis' elders reel..And *Alma Mater* lye dissolv'd in port. 1803 SCOTT in Lockhart *Life* (1839) II. 126 The literary men of his *Alma Mater*. 1866 CARLYLE *Inaug. Addr.* 170 My dear old *Alma Mater*.

alman(e, variant form of ALMAIN.

almanac ('ɔːlmənæk). Forms: 4 **almenak,** 6–7 **almanach(e,** (6 **amminick),** 7 **almanacke,** 6–9 **-ack,** 8– **-ac.** [Appears in med.L. as *almanac(h* in end of 13th c., and soon after (though it may have been earlier) in most of the Rom. langs., It. *almanacco*, Sp. *almanaque*, Fr. *almanach*, the immediate source of which was app. a Spanish Arabic *al-manākh*; Pedro de Alcala, in his Arabic-Castilian Vocabulista (1505), has '*manākh*, almanaque, calendario'; also '*manah* (probably meant for same word), relox del sol' [sundial]. But the word occurs nowhere else as Arabic, has no etymon in the language, and its origin is uncertain. See note at end of this article.]

An annual table, or (more usually) a book of tables, containing a calendar of months and days, with astronomical data and calculations, ecclesiastical and other anniversaries, besides other useful information, and, in former days, astrological and astrometeorological forecasts.

(The 'almanacs' known to Roger Bacon and Chaucer were permanent tables of the apparent motions and positions of sun, moon, and (?) planets, whence the astronomical data for any year could be calculated. 'The calculations [of Regiomontanus, 1475] of the places of the sun and moon were the best that had been made in Europe..He speaks of them himself as "quas vulgo vocant *almanach*"' (Hallam *Lit. Eur.* 1855 I. 190). In 15th c. almanacs or *ephemerides* began to be prepared for definite periods, as 30 or 10 years, and in 16th c. for the year, with which was combined the ecclesiastical *calendar*; astrological and weather predictions appear in 16–17th c.; the 'useful statistics' are a modern feature.)

*c*1391 CHAUCER *Astrol.* Prol. 3 A table of the verray Moeuyng of the Mone from howre to howre, every day and in every signe, after thin Almenak. 1508 (W. de Worde) *Almanacke for xii. yere*, ¶This almanacke and table shall endure .xii. yere and is called after the latytude of Oxenforde (& it is taken out of the grete ephymerides or almanacke of .xxx. yere). 1543 (*title*) ¶*An Almanacke* moste exactly sette foorth for the terme of xiiii. yeres, shewing in what date, houre, minute, signe, and degre, the Moone shall bee at the tyme of her chaunge and full, with the Eclipse of the sunne and Moone, from the date of our Lorde MD xliii, vnto the date of our Lorde MD lvii. ¶Imprinted by Richarde Grafton. 1587 H. BAKER (*title*) Rules and Documentes touching the vse and practise of the common Almanaches, which are called Ephemerides. 1590 SHAKS. *Mids. N.* III. i. 54 Doth the Moone shine that night wee play our play? A Calender, a Calender! looke in the Almanack, finde out the Mooneshine. 1598 B. JONSON *Ev. Man in Hum.* III. iv. (1616) 38 These filthie Almanacks, an't were not for them, these dayes of persecution would ne're be knowne. 1599

Warn. Faire Wom. II. 556 Did ye looke in the Amminicke? **1606** DEKKER *Seven Sins* II. (Arb.) 23 Falshood and Lying thus haue had their day, and like Almanackes of the last yeare, are now gon out. **1653** WALTON *Angler* To Reader 5 They that make Hay by the fair dayes in Almanacks. *Ibid.* As useful as an Almanack out of date. **1662** FULLER *Worthies* II. 289 It was in plain truth a perpetual Almanack. **1663** COWLEY *Verses & Ess.* (1669) 126 He does not look in Almanacks to see, Whether he Fortunate shall be. **1687** T. BROWN *Saints in Upr.* Wks. 1730 I. 73 St. Longinus and St. Amphibolus, upon my infallibility, have not their fellow in the almanack. **1751** ADDISON *Freeholder* No. 22, 128 My Friend perceiving by his Almanack that the Moon was up.. left me. **1775** BOSWELL *Johnson* I. (1848) 452/2 You would reduce all history to no better than an almanac. **1802** SOUTHEY *S. Antidius* Wks. VI. 161 There was an eclipse that night, Which was not in the Almanack. **1863** KINGLAKE *Crimea* (1876) I. vii. 102 A Prince of the sort which Court almanacs describe as 'Serene.'

Comb. **almanac-maker, -man, -making.**

1611 COTGR., *Prognostiqueur*, Almanack-maker, fortune-teller, foreteller. *a* **1613** OVERBURY *A Wife, etc.* (1638) 131 An Almanack-maker Is the worst part of an Astronomer. **1650** B. *Discolliminium* 30 My skill in Almanack-making. **1654** GAYTON *Festiv. Notes* 268 (T.) Almanac-makers are forced to eat their own prognosticks. *a* **1697** EACHARD *Hobbes' State Nat.* (1705) 53 A meer Human Institution of the Almanack-men. **1708** SWIFT *Predict. for* 1708 Wks. 1755 II. I. 147 The almanack-maker has the liberty of chusing the sickliest season of the year.

[*Note.* As to the origin and history of the word *almanac*:—

1. The earliest notices are: **1267** Roger Bacon *Op. maj.* xv. (1733) 120 Antiqui astronomi ponunt principium anni circiter principium Octobris, sicut patet in expositione tabularum, quae Almanac vocantur; *Op. Tert.* xi. (1859) 36 'Hæ tabulæ vocantur *Almanach* vel Tallignum, in quibus.. homo posset inspicere omnia ea quæ in cælo sunt omni die, sicut nos in calendario inspicimus omnia festa sanctorum; *c* **1345** Giovanni Villani *Cronica* XI. xli, 'Secondo l'almanacco di Profazio Giudeo, e delle tavole Toletane dovea essere la detta congiunzione di Saturno e di Giove a di 20 del detto mese di Marzo' [where the 'Tables of Toledo' (constructed *c* 1080 by Arzachel) again point to the Arabs in Spain]. Explanations have been offered of *manākh* from Semitic sources, as Arab. *manay* to define, determine, *manā* measure, time, fate; Heb. *manāh* to allot, assign, count; Arab. *manaḥa* to present, *minḥat* a gift, all of which fail in form or sense or both.

2. Eusebius, *De Præp. Evangel.* iii. 4, quotes Porphyrius as to the Egyptian belief in astrology, in horoscopes, and so-called lords of the ascendant, 'whose names are given in the *almenichiaká* (ἐν τοῖς ἀλμενιχιακοῖς), with their various powers to cure diseases, their risings and settings, and their presages of things future.' Notwithstanding the suggestive sound and use of this word (of which however the real form is very uncertain), the difficulties of connecting it historically either with the Spanish Arabic *manākh*, or with med.L. *almanach* without Arabic intermediation, seem insurmountable. Nor does the sense really point to such tables as those described by Roger Bacon, Chaucer, and Regiomontanus.

3. *Manākh* has been identified with a L. *manacus* or *manachus*, applied in Vitruv. ix. 8 (Dialling) to a circle in a sun-dial showing the months or signs of the zodiac, an origin which would well explain Pedro's word in both senses; but the true reading of Vitruvius's word is now generally agreed to be *mēnæus* (Gr. μηναῖος monthly); and it has not yet been shown that the reading *manacus* was ever so generally known or accepted, as to make its adoption probable at the hands of any Arab astronomer in Spain. Nor has it been shown to be impossible. Of many other conjectures none are worthy of notice.]

almand(e, obs. form of ALMOND.

† **al'mander, -aunder.** *Obs.* [a. OFr. *almandier*, mod. *amandier*, repr. a L. **amygdalārius*: see ALMOND.] An almond tree.

1382 WYCLIF *Gen.* xxx. 37 Takynge green popil ȝerdis and of almanders. —— *Eccles.* xii. 5 The almaunder [**1388** an alemaunde tre] shal flouren. *c* **1400** *Rom. Rose* 1363 And almandres grete plentee, Figgis, and many a date tre.

† **al'mandin(e**, *a.* *Obs. rare.* [f. *almande*, ALMOND + *-in*, prob. northern for -EN, as in *beechen*, etc.] Of the almond tree, of almond wood.

a **1300** *Cursor M.* 6893 (Cotton) And it was an almandin wand, þat ilk frut þar-on þai fand (*Fairf.* almandine).

almandine ('ælməndɪn, 'ælmən,daɪn), *sb.* Also 7 **amandine.** [a corruption of the earlier ALABANDINE. See the change in Phillips below. Sometimes by false form-assoc. written *almondine.*]

'An alumina iron garnet of a beautiful violet or amethystine tint; the word is said to be a corruption of Pliny's alabandine, a term applied to the garnet from its being cut and polished at Alabanda.' Westropp *Prec. Stones* 1874.

1658 PHILLIPS, *Alabandine*, a kind of stone, that provokes to bleed. [*Almandine* not mentioned.] **1678** *Ibid.*, *Alabandine* or *Amandine*, a kind of blew and red Stone, which very much excites to bleeding. [Also a cross-ref.] *Almandine*, see *Alabandine.* **1696** *Ibid.*, *Almandine*, or *Alabandine*, a sort of Ruby softer and lighter than the oriental. [*Alabandine* not separately entered.] **1706** *Ibid.*, *Almandine*, a coarse sort of Ruby, etc. [*Alabandine* not entered at all.] **1804** *Edin. Rev.* III. 304 Karsten constituted some varieties of the noble garnets into almandines. *c* **1825** BEDDOES *Crocod.* in *Poems* 108 With sanguine almandines and rainy pearl. **1830** TENNYSON *Merman* 32 But I would throw to them back in mine Turkis and agate and almondine. **1872** BROWNING *Fifine* 13 That string of mock turquoise, those almandines of glass.

almandite ('ælməndaɪt). *Min.* [f. prec. with min. formative -ITE.] Dana's name for almandine as a mineral, a variety of Garnet.

1837–68 DANA *Min.* 271 Almandite or precious garnet comes in fine crystals from Ceylon, etc.

† **'al,manner.** *Obs.*, comb. form of *all manner* used *attrib.* Cf. ALKIN. [Orig. a genitive = 'of every sort': see MANNER and ALL A 3 b.]

a **1400** *Cursor M.* (Trin. MS.) Al maner þing of him bigan [*Cotton MS.* alkyn]. **1526** TINDALE *Rev.* xviii. 12 Almanner vessels of yvery and almanner vessels off most precious wodde.

almar, obs. by-form of ALMONER.

almarie, almary, obs. forms of AMBRY.

† **al'mariol(e.** *Obs. rare.* [ad. med.L. *almāriolum* (for L. *armāriolum*), dim. of *alm-*, *armārium*: see AMBRY.] A little closet or cabinet.

1807 J. T. SMITH *Antiq. Westm.* 204, 12 March [26 Edw. III].. a certain almariole in the vestry for keeping the vestments in. *Ibid.* A certain armoriol within the king's chapel.

almatour: see ALMAÇOUR.

almaund, obs. form of ALMOND.

alme, obs. form of ALUM, AAM, and ELM.

alme(h, an Egyptian dancing-girl: see ALMA.

‖ **almen'dron.** [Sp., augm. of *almendra*, *quasi* 'the great almond.'] The Brazil-nut tree (*Bertholettia excelsa*), which forms large forests on the banks of the Amazon and Rio Negro.

1852 T. ROSS tr. *Humboldt's Trav.* II. xxiv. 449 The *almendron*, or *juvia*, one of the most majestic trees of the forests of the New World. **1862** SMILES *Engineers* III. 248 And towering over all, the great Almendrons.

almener, obs. form of ALMONER.

† **'almer**, obs. by-form of ALMONER [really an independent formation on ALM(S + -ER[1]. See also ALMOWR.]

† **almere.** *Obs.* [a. OFr. *almaire*, also *armaire*, now *armoire.*] An ambry.

1547 *Lanc. Wills* I. 108 One water tubbe and one almere.

almery, obs. form of AMBRY.

almes(se, obs. form of ALMS.

almicanter, -a, -ath, obs. ff. ALMUCANTAR.

† **'almid**, *adv.* *Obs.* [f. ALL + MID with.] Withal, altogether.

c **1300** *Beket* 2312 And seide 'Almid wille her Mi bodi ich bitake.'

† **al'mifluent**, *a.* *Obs. rare*[—1]. [irreg. f. L. *almus* kindly, bounteous + *fluent-em* flowing.] Bounteous, beneficent.

1477 *Let. to Dk. Glouc.* in *York Records* 90 We.. shal evermore pray to the almyfluent God for your prosperous estate.

almi'gation. *Obs.* ? for AMALGAMATION.

1592 LILLY *Galathea* II. iii. 233 A very secret science, for none almost can understand the language of it; [*e.g.*] sublimation, almigation.

† **al'might**, *a.* *Obs.* Forms: 1 **ælmiht**, 4 **alle myght**, 4–5 **almyȝt, al-, allmyght, almicht**, (5 **almyth**), 6 **almycht**, 4–6 **almight.** [f. ALL + MIGHT, which is here probably the pa. pple. of MAY in original sense to 'have power.'] = ALMIGHTY. (Long the commoner form in poetry.)

a **1000** CÆDMON 182 Wiston drihten ælmihtne. *c* **1314** *Guy Warw.* 152 'O Lord,' he seyd, 'God Almight.' *c* **1325** *E.E. Allit. P.* A. 497 In sothful gospel of god al-myȝt. *c* **1330** R. BRUNNE *Chron.* 172, & þi messe songen, & serued God alle myght. *c* **1440** *Morte Arth.* 23 They thankid God all myght. **1546** *Primer Hen. VIII*, Blessed be God, Father almight.

† **al'mightend**, *a.* *Obs.* Forms: 3 **almichttende, almightende, almightand.** [a variant of ALMIGHTY, with pr. pple. ending, perh. corrupted from ALMIGHTIN.] = ALMIGHTY.

c **1250** *Creed* in *Rel. Ant.* I. 22 Hi true in God, fader halmichttende. *a* **1300** *Creed*, *ibid.* I. 282 Ich ileve in God, fader almightinde.

† **al'mightful**, *a.* *Obs.* [f. ALL *adv.* + MIGHTFUL.] All-powerful.

c **1250** *Gen. & Ex.* 2694 He wurð al-miȝt-ful in ðat lond. *c* **1375** *Assumpcioun* A. 219 He þat is almiȝtful kyng.

† **al'mightiful**, *a.* *Obs.* [perh. due to confusion of ALMIGHTY and ALMIGHTFUL.] = prec.

a **1400** *Cov. Myst.* 178 Allemyghtyfful fadyr, merciful kynge. **1548** UDALL etc. *Erasm. Paraphr.* Pref. 6 His almightifull power. *Ibid.* Pref. Luke 9 The almightiful word of the omnipotent father.

† **al'mightihede.** *Obs.* [f. ALMIGHTY + -HEAD.] Omnipotence.

1440 *Promp. Parv.*, Allmyghtyhede, *Omnipotencia.*

almightily (ɔːl'maɪtɪlɪ), *adv.* [f. ALMIGHTY *a.* + -LY[2].] In an almighty manner.

a **1650** P. FLETCHER *Father's Test.* (1670) 99 It is a working beauty, mightily, almightily working on every object that looks upon it.

1676 EACHARD *Contempt Clergy* 81 That the clergy are almightily furnished with learning. **1839** BAILEY *Festus* (1848) 52/1 Elements of immortality, As mind on earth almightily beseems.

† **al'mightin**, *sb.* and *a.* *Obs.* Also 2 **almihtin**, 3 **almihten, -miȝtin, -mightin, -mightten.** [variant of ALMIGHTY, with a termination imitating that of *Drihtin*, *drihten*, Lord.] An ancient form of ALMIGHTY, used *subst.* as a title of the Deity, in apposition to *God*; also alone.

c **1175** *Lamb. Hom.* 23 God almihtines milce. *Ibid.* 137 Ure lauerd God almihten. *Ibid.* 99 þe almihtin feder and þe sune. **1205** LAY. 16783 For luue of god almihten [**1250** al mihti]. *c* **1250** *Gen. & Ex.* 9 Ðan sal him almightin luuen.

almightiness (ɔːl'maɪtɪnɪs). [f. ALMIGHTY + -NESS.] The quality of being almighty, omnipotence.

a **1520** *Myrr. Our Ladye* 229 Whyche byleue not that the almyghtynesse of God myghte do suche thynges. **1535** COVERDALE *Is.* xlii. 11 Ascribinge almightynes vnto the Lorde. **1651** JER. TAYLOR *Serm.* I. xxiii. 292 To provoke God.. to defie his Almightinesse. **1810** SOUTHEY *Kehama* XXIV. xx. Wks. VIII. 206 Vain his almightiness, for mightier pain Subdued all power. **1877** J. M. CHARLTON *In Mem.* 10 To unite our puny powers with his Almightiness.

almighty (ɔːl'maɪtɪ), *a.* Forms: 1 **ælmeahtiʒ, ealmihtiʒ**, 2 **ælmihti, almihtiȝ**, 2–3 **almihti(e**, (3 **allmahhtiȝ**), 3–4 **almiȝti, -myȝti, myhti**, 4 **almihty, allmyghty**, 4–5 **almyghty, -myȝty**, 6 **allmighty**, 7 **-ie**, 6–7 **almightie**, 4– **almighty.** [f. ALL *adv.* + MIGHTY. OE. *ælmeahtiʒ* = OS. *alomahtig*, OHG. *alamahtic*: see the by-forms ALMIGHT, -IN, -END.] All-powerful, omnipotent.

1. a. Orig. and in the strict sense used as an attribute of the Deity, and joined to *God* or other title.

c **890** *Cod. Dipl.* 138 On Godes ealmihtiʒes naman. *a* **1000** *Psalm* l. (Cotton) 85 Ælmeahtiʒ god. *c* **1175** *Lamb. Hom.* 7 þenne wunet god almihti in us. *Ibid.* 97 þe almihtiȝa godes sune. *c* **1200** ORMIN 95 Biforenn Crist Allmahhtiȝ Godd. *c* **1300** *Beket* 1042 ȝe honuryeth more an urthlich King than ȝe God almiȝti do. **1366** MAUNDEV. i. 6 In the Name of God Glorious and Allemyghty. **1418** ABP. CHICHELE in Ellis *Orig. Lett.* I. 2 I. 4 Blessud be Almyȝty God. **1535** COVERDALE *Ecclus.* l. 20 To geue thankes to Allmightie God. **1611** BIBLE *Gen.* xvii. 1, I am the almightie God, walke before me. **1732** POPE *Ess. Man* I. 145 The first Almighty Cause Acts not by partial, but by gen'ral Laws. **1864** TENNYSON *En. Ard.* 783 O God Almighty, Blessed Saviour.

b. *absol. The Almighty*; a title of God.

a **1000** *Beowulf* 184 Cwæþ þæt se Ælmihtiʒa eorþan worhte. **1382** WYCLIF *Ruth* i. 20 With bitternes mych the Almyȝti hath fulfillid me. **1535** COVERDALE *Job* vi. 4 The allmighty hath shott at me with his arowes. **1611** BIBLE *Job* viii. 3 Doth the Almightie peruert iustice? **1667** MILTON *P.L.* IV. 566 To know More of th' Almighties works. **1718** POPE *Iliad* VII. 215 Grant, thou Almighty! in whose hand is fate, A worthy champion. **1878** E. WHITE *Life in Christ* 108 The same words are used by the Almighty in threatening Abimelech. *Mod.* If it should please the Almighty to spare him for a few years longer.

c. rarely in *superlative.*

1598 SYLVESTER *Du Bartas* I. vii. (1641) 60/2 Man (but Image of th' Almightiest) Without these gifts is not a Man, but Beast.

2. All-powerful (in a general sense). *spec.* (chiefly *U.S.*) ***almighty dollar*** and similar phrases.

c **1386** CHAUCER *Monkes T.* 62 O noble almighty Sampson. **1588** SHAKS. *L.L.L.* v. ii. 650 The Armipotent Mars, of Launces the almighty. **1606** —— *Tr. & Cr.* v. ii. 174 Constring'd in masse by the almighty Fenne [*v.r.* sunne]. **1782** COWPER *Hope* 655 Insensible of Truth's almighty charms. **1836** W. IRVING in *New Yorker* 12 Nov. 115 The almighty dollar, that great object of universal devotion throughout our land. **1842** DICKENS *Amer. Notes* I. iii. 63 The almighty dollar sinks into something comparatively insignificant. **1863** W. PHILLIPS *Speeches* iii. 45, I hail the almighty power of the tongue. **1891** F. W. BAIN *Antichrist* ii. 104 A mere conglomeration of fortune hunters, worshipping the Almighty Dollar. **1947** *Time* 16 June 33/1 There is a limit to the sacrifices some Britons would make for the sake of the almighty greenback.

¶ *slang.* Mighty, great; exceedingly.

1824 DE QUINCEY *Wks.* (1871) XVI. 261 Such rubbish, such 'almighty' nonsense (to speak *transatlanticè*), no eye has ever beheld. **1833** MARRYAT *Pet. Simple* (1863) 328 An almighty pretty French privateer lying in St. Pierre's.

† **al'mightyship.** *Obs. rare*[—1]. [f. ALMIGHTY + -SHIP.] = ALMIGHTINESS.

1663 COWLEY *Verses & Ess.* (1669) 130 Which arm'd him stronger, and which helped him more, Than all his Thunder did, and his Almighty-ship before.

almirah, -myra (æl'maɪrə). [ad. Urdu *almārī*, ad. Pg. *almario*:—L. *armārium*; see AMBRY.] Anglo-Indian name for a cupboard, cabinet, press, wardrobe, or chest of drawers.

1878 *Life in the Mofussil* I. 34 Sahib, have you looked in Mr. Morrison's almirah?

almis(se, obs. form of ALMS.

†**'almistry.** [? In jest for *all-mystery*.]
1621 B. JONSON *Masques* (1692) 616 Of faces and Palmestry, And this is Almistry.

almner, variant of ALMONER.

almoign, almoin (æl'mɔɪn). Also 4 **almoyn**, 6 **almoyne, -on(e**, 7 **allmone**. [In the form *almon(e*, a. OFr. *almône, almosne* (mod.Fr. *aumône*): see ALMS. *Almoign (-oin, -oyne)* is late AFr., perh. due to confusion with *alimonium*, the senses of the two words partially overlapping. But **alimosina* could of itself give *almoine*, as in *præpositum, preboide*; cf. OFr. *almoisnier, almosgner, almogner*, variants of *almosnier, aumoner*, to give in alms; also Pr. *almoynier*, beside *almonier*, almoner.]

†**1.** Alms; alms-chest; the church chest or treasury, ecclesiastical possession. (A common med.L. sense of *eleēmosyna*.) *Obs.*
c **1330** R. BRUNNE *Chron.* 239 For freres of þe croice, and monk and chanoun, Haf drawen in o voice his feez to þer almoyn.

2. Tenure by divine service, or by the performance of some religious duty. **frank almoin** or *free alms* (L. *libera eleēmosyna*): the 'tenure of lands, etc. bestowed upon God, that is, given to such people as bestow themselves in the service of God, for pure and perpetual alms; whence the feoffors or givers cannot demand any terrestrial service, so long as the lands remain in the hands of the feoffee.' Cowel. Perpetual tenure by free gift of charity.
1513 BRADSHAW *St. Werburge* (1848) 200 Many helde their landes .. by tenur' franke almoigne. **1523** FITZHERBERT *Surveying* ix. 16 Franke almoyne, homage auncetrell. **1596** BARLOW *Three Sermons* iii. 116 They hold what ever they have in Frankalmoin from God. **1641** *Termes de la Ley* 33 Allmone or Tenure in aumone, is tenure by divine service. **1672** MANLEY *Interpr.* s.v., It cannot be Frank-almoine if any certain service be expressed. **1726** AYLIFFE *Parergon* 11 (note) *Frank-Almoigne* is the same which we in Latin call *Libera Eleemosyna* or *Free Alms* in English: whence that Tenure is commonly known by the name of a Tenure in Aumone or Frank-Almoigne. **1844** WILLIAMS *Real Property Law* (ed. 12) 39 The grantees in frankalmoign .. were for ever free from every kind of earthly or temporal service.

β. Scotch form: **fre almons.**
c **1550** SIR J. BALFOUR *Pract.* 28 (JAM.) Gif the defender hald the land in name of fre almons. *Ibid.* 241 Landis gevin to thame in name of fre almonis.

almoigner, -moiner, -moisner, literary forms of ALMONER in 6-7, due to attempts to recast the current *amner* after late AFr. *almoignier* and MFr. *aulmosnier*; their influence remains in part in the mod. spelling ALMONER.

almoise, -moyse, var. ALMOSE, *Obs.*, alms.

almon, obs. form of ALMOIGN and ALMOND.

†**'almonage.** *Obs.* [a. OFr. *almosnaige, aumonnaige*, almsgiving, gift; f. *almosnier* to give alms, f. *almosne*: see ALMS and -AGE.] In phr. **frank almonage** = *frank almoin*: see ALMOIGN.
1655 FULLER *Ch. Hist.* VI. 292 None of these held of mean Lords by *franke almonage*, but all of the King *in capite per Baroniam.* **1656** —— *Serm., Best Employm.* 13 He himselfe held all that he had in Frank-Almonage, and lived on the poore mans box. **1667** WATERHOUSE *Fire of Lond.* 154 Worthy objects of your Almonage.

almond ('ɑːmənd). Forms: 3-4 **almand(e**, 3-5 **almaund(e**, 4-5 **almound(e, alemaund**, 4-6 **almonde**, (5 **almund**, 5-7 **almon**, 6 **alomond, aulmond**), 5- **almond.** [a. OFr. *almande, alemande*, earlier *alemandre, alemandle* (also *amande, amandre*); cf. Sp. *almendra*, Pg. *amendoa*, It. *mandorla, mandola*, Pr. and med.L. *amandola*; pointing to early Romanic **amendla, -ola, -ala*, from L. *amygdala*, a. Gr. ἀμυγδάλη. Cf. the change of *smaragdum* to *smeraldo*. The initial *al-* in Fr. and Sp. prob. arose in the latter, by confusing the initial *a-* (dropped in It., as if no real part of the word) with Arab. article *al-*, as in *almidon* (Fr. *amidon*), *almirante* (*amirand*), *almáraco* (*amáracum*).

The genealogy of *almond* is therefore: Gr. ἀμυγδάλη, L. *amygdala* = *ă'migdălă, ă'mingdălă*; early Rom. *ă'mendǝlă* (thence Pg. *ă'mendŏă*); splitting up into "*mendǝlă* (thence It. '*mandŏla*), *al-"mend(ǝ)lă* (thence Sp. *al'mendră*), and *al-ă'mendǝlă, al-ă'mandǝla*, whence OFr. *alĕ'mandlĕ, alĕ'mandrĕ*; OFr. and E. *alĕ'mandĕ, al'mandĕ*; E. *al'maund, 'almaund, 'almŏnd, 'āmǝnd*.]

1. The kernel of a drupe or stone-fruit, the produce of the almond tree, of which there are two kinds, the sweet and the bitter.
a **1300** *Cursor M.* 6895 Almandes [*v.r.* almondes, -maundes, -mound] was groun þar-on. **1388** WYCLIF *Numb.* xvii. 8 The blossoms .. weren fourmed in to alemaundis [**1382** almaundes]. **1398** TREVISA *Barth. De P.R.* XVII. iii, Yf a foxe eteþ almoundes he schal dye. **1463** *Mann. & Househ. Exps.* 217 *Item*, vjl. almundys, xviijd. **1542** BOORDE *Dyetary* xii. (1870) 263 Almons be hote & moyste; it doth comforte the brest. **1586** BRIGHT *Melanch.* xl. 267 Oile of bitter alomonds. **1611** BIBLE *Gen.* xliii. 11 Myrrhe, nuts, and almonds. **1769** SIR J. HILL *Fam. Herb.* (1812) 5 Sweet almonds are excellent in emulsions. **1814** SIR H. DAVY *Agric. Chem.* 83 The principal part of the almond .. [is] a substance analogous to coagulated albumen.

2. The tree which bears almonds, *Amygdalus communis* (N.O. *Rosaceæ*), closely allied to the genus *Prunus*, which contains the plum, peach, nectarine, etc. Often in comb. as ***almond-tree***.
1697 DRYDEN *Virg. Georg.* I. 272 Mark well the flowring Almonds in the Wood. **1735** MILLER *Gard. Dict.* s.v. *Amygdalus*, The common Almond .. is cultivated more for the beauty of its flowers, than for its fruit. **1870** YEATS *Nat. Hist. Comm.* 78 The almond and the palm flourish together.

3. A comfit enclosing an almond kernel.
1855, 1892 [see SUGARED *ppl. a.* 1 d].

4. A kernel similar to the almond.
1712 tr. *Pomet's Hist. Drugs* I. 85 Two or three Nuts or Berries, which contain in each a little luscious Almond.

5. Anything shaped like an almond, whether solid or superficial, as: **a.** An ornament of that shape; **b.** A name given by lapidaries to pieces of rock crystal used in adorning branch candlesticks; **c.** An oval with pointed ends.
1853 RUSKIN *Stones of Ven.* II. ii. §12. 22 Six balls, or rather almonds, of purple marble.

d. Applied *attrib.* to eyes shaped like an almond, esp. of certain Asian peoples. So ***almond-eyed*** adj.
1870 'MARK TWAIN' *Wks.* (1900) XIX. 145 An 'unsuspecting, almond-eyed son of Confucius'. **1891** WILDE *Critic as Artist* in *Intentions* 179 The almond-eyed sage of the Yellow River. **1915** W. S. MAUGHAM *Of Human Bondage* xxii. 94 He [a Chinaman] laughed .. and his almond eyes almost closed as he did so. **1935** *Discovery* Aug. 244/1 Mongol is but a generic term, associated with almond eyes and high cheek bones.

e. *attrib.*, of a face.
1878 WILDE *Ravenna* 8 The almond-face which Giotto drew so well.

6. The tonsils: also called ***almonds of the throat, jaws***, or ***ears***. The latter name is also given to 'a small lymphatic gland over the mastoid process or below the external ear,' *Syd. Soc. Lex. arch.*
1578 LYTE *Dodoens* I. lxxxi. 120 Ulcers of the aulmondes or kernels of the throte. **1607** TOPSELL *Four-footed Beasts* (1673) 500 Goats milk .. gargarized in the mouth, is very effectual against the pains and swellings of the almonds. **1641** BAKER *Chron.* (1679) 401/1 The Almonds of her Jaws began to swell. **1709** *Phil. Trans.* XXVI. 318 A pain on the left side about the Almonds of the Ear. **1835** HOBLYN *Dict. Med.*, *Almonds of the Ears*, a popular name for the exterior glands of the neck.

†**7.** Other almond-shaped animal organs: *esp.* **a.** The operculum of a whelk; **b.** Some part of a rabbit's leg. *Obs.*
c **1450** J. RUSSELL *Bk. Nurture* in *Babees Bk.* (1868) 60 His [the whelk's] pyntill & gutt almond & mantille awey þer fro ye pitt. **1627** PEACHAM *Compl. Gent.* xxi. (1634) 253 To make Paste to last long, you may use .. those parts of a Connies legges which are called the Almonds. **1631** MARKHAM *Way to Wealth* II. I. xiii. (1668) 70 Those parts of the Conies leg which is called the Almond of the Coney.

8. The delicate pink colour of the almond blossom. Also, a light shade of yellow or yellowish brown. ***almond black***, a pigment similar to peach-black (PEACH *sb.*[1] 6). ***almond green***, a shade of greyish green.
1835, 1869 [see *peach-black* s.v. PEACH *sb.*[1] 6]. **1879** *Daily News* 13 June 2/2 Cream colour, relieved with cardinal, and almond adorned with the same fashionable hue. **1920** *Textile Color Card Assoc. Amer.* Fall 2/1 Almond O. 3831. **1923** *Index to Color Names* (Textile Color Card Assoc. of U.S. Inc.) 1 Almond green 5864 Sp. '23. **1934** *Dict. Colour Standards* (Brit. Colour Council) 17 *Almond green, Russian Green*, B.C.C. 10. General representation of samples submitted by Textile and other Colour Using Industries. **1977** *Western Morning News* 30 Aug. 4/1 (Advt.), 1974 (N) Rover 2200 TC. Almond. One owner. 29,000 miles.

9. From its colour: A kind of pigeon, more fully called the ***Almond Tumbler***.
1735 J. MOORE *Columbarium* 39 But amongst all [the colours of Tumblers], there is a Mixture of three Colours, vulgarly call'd an Almond, perhaps from the Quantity of Almond colour'd Feathers that are found in the Hackle: Others call it an Ermine. **1765** (*title*) A treatise on domestic pigeons .. to which is added, a most ample description of that celebrated and beautiful pigeon called the Almond Tumbler. **1854** *Poultry Chron.* I. 359/2 Marks in the Almond Tumbler... Should it be an almond, it will most likely have a great deal of black about it. **1867** TEGETMEIER *Pigeons* ii. 113 The feathers of the Almond should be covered with a metallic lustre or gloss. **1883** *Stand.* 11 Jan. 3/6 The almond tumbler, a round plump bird.

10. *Comb.* and *Attrib.*, in which *almond* stands in simple attributive relation, as ***almond blossom, colour, flower, fruit, shape, wood***; in attributive relation of material, as ***almond cake, custard, paste***, etc.; or in similative or instrumental relation to a pa. pple., as ***almond-leaved, -scented, -shaped***; ***almond-shaded***. Also **almond-comfit** = ALMOND 3; **almond-kernel** (= ALMOND 1, 6); **almond oil**, the expressed oil of bitter almonds, or benzoic aldehyde; **almond-peach**, a hybrid between the almond and peach, cultivated in France; **almond rock, snow**, confections made with almonds; **almond tree**, the tree that bears almonds, also *fig.* (from the colour of its flowers) grey hair; **almond tumbler** (see ALMOND 9); **almond willow**, or almond-leaved willow, *Salix amygdalina*; **almond-worts**, Lindley's name for the plants of his N.O. *Drupaceæ* or stone-fruits. Also ALMOND-BUTTER, -MILK, q.v.
a **1842** TENNYSON *To the Queen* 16 The sun-lit almond-blossom shakes. **1751** CHAMBERS *Cycl.*, *Almonds* give the denomination to a great number of preparations in confectionery, cookery, etc. whereof they are the basis; as *Almond* cakes, *Almond* cream .. *Almond* paste, *Almond* snow. **1853** MRS. GASKELL *Cranford* xv. 299 If a little child came in to ask for an ounce of almond-comfits .. she always added one more. **1440** *Promp. Parv.*, Almaunde frute (**1499** almon) *Amigdalum.* **1601** HOLLAND *Pliny* (1634) II. 146 Tonsils or Almond-kernels on either side of the throat. *a* **1845** HOOD *T. of Trumpet* xiii, The almond-oil she had tried. **1629** J. PARKINSON *Parad.* III. xv. 582 The Almond Peach, so called, because the kernell of the stone is sweete, like the Almond, and the fruit also somewhat pointed like the Almond in the huske. **1880** MISS BRADDON *Asph.* II. 95 The golden tinge of the almond pound-cake. **1859** SALA *Tw. round Clock* 56 The relative merits of almond-rock and candied horehound. **1880** *Daily News* 6 May 5/5 Almond rock and peppermint drops. **1881** WILDE *By Arno* in *Poems* 162 The almond-scented vale. *a* **1790** T. WARTON *Poems* 60 (JOD.) Carmel's almond-shaded steep. **1830** *Edin. Rev.* LII. 71 Amydaloid is a rock containing almond-shaped cavities. **1388** WYCLIF *Eccles.* xii. 5 An alemaunde tre schal floure. **1590** *Pasquil's Apol.* I. E b, Vpon whose siluer heads the Almond-tree hath blossomde. **1611** BIBLE *Jer.* i. 11, I see a rodde of an almond tree. *a* **1763** SHENSTONE (T.) Trees more and more fady, till they end in an almond-willow. **1867** LADY HERBERT *Cradle L.* i. 3 Floors .. made of ebony and almond-wood.

ˌalmond-'butter. (See quot. 1753.)
1586 COGAN *Haven Health* (1636) 182 An other kinde of butter made of Almonds with Sugar and Rose water, called Almond Butter. **1606** *Wily Beguiled* in Hazl. *Dodsl.* IX. 285 He speaks nothing but almond-butter and sugar candy. **1753** CHAMBERS *Cycl. Supp.*, *Almond-butter* is a preparation made of cream and whites of eggs boiled; to which is afterwards added, blanched almonds.

ˌalmond-'furnace. [Corruption of *Allemand* or *Almain*, i.e. German, *furnace*.] Name of a furnace used in the refining process to separate metals from cinders and other dross, and for the reduction of slag of litharge to lead.
1674 RAY *Smelting Silver* in *Collect.* 116 Another Furnace they have which they call an Almond Furnace. **1751** CHAMBERS *Cycl.* s.v., The Almond-furnace, called also the sweep, is usually six feet high, four wide, and two thick; it is built of brick.

ˌalmond-'milk. (See quot. 1753.)
c **1430** *Recipes* in *Babees Bk.* (1868) 61 Take Almaunde Milke & 3olkys of Eyroun. **1598** HAKLUYT *Voy.* I. 97 It leaueth behind it a taste like the taste of almon milke. *a* **1678** MARVELL *To Dr. Witty* Poems 74 The doctor doth Stint them to cordials, almond-milk, and broth. **1753** CHAMBERS *Cycl. Supp.*, *Almond-milk* is a preparation made of sweet blanched almonds and water, of some use in medicine, as an emollient.

almondy ('ɑːməndɪ), *a.* [f. ALMOND + -Y[1]. Cf. *sugary*.] Having almonds, or the characteristics or properties of almonds.
1847 LYELL in *Life* II. 132 The almondy scent of the flowers is very strong and delicious. **1853** *Mem. Stomach* 11 The sweet almondy taste of the delicious food my poor mother gave me.

almoner[1] ('ælmənə(r), 'ɑːm-). Forms: *α.* 3-4 **aumoner(e, amoner**, 3-5 **aumener(e**, 4-5 **-eer**, 5 **awmener, -eer, (ambynowre), amener**, 5-7 **amner**, 6-7 **almner, almener, almonar**, 6- **almoner.** *β.* 5-7 **almosner**, 6 **-osiner**, 7 **-oisner, ausmoner.** *γ.* 6 **almoigner, almoygner, -or, almoiner.** *δ.* 5 **aumere, almer, -ar**, 6 **-owr**; 5 **awmerer**; 6 **amonerer.** [a. OFr. *aumoner, aumonier* (12th c. *almosnier*, 13th *aumosnier*, 15th *aulmosnier*, mod. *aumônier*):—late L. **almosinārius* for *eleēmosynārius*, prop. adj. 'connected with alms,' sc. *homo*, f. *eleēmosyna* ALMS. But perh. partly due, esp. in sense 3, to OFr. *almosnère, -eor*, later *-eur*:—L. *eleēmosynātor -ātorem* an alms-giver.

The native development was *aumoner, aumener, aumner, amner* (ā) the regular form in 16th c. But the Renascence brought up a number of artificial spellings, after later Fr. *aulmosnier, ausmonier*, AFr. *almoignier*, and their med.L. adaptations, under the influence of which and the native *alms, amner* has been artificially refashioned as *almner, almener, almoner*, and the pronunciation has followed the spelling. The 15th c. *aumere, almer*, and Sc. *almowr*, are direct formations on *aumes, almes*; *aumer-er, amoner-er* seem to be f. *awmere, awmener*, a purse; see ALMONER[2].]

1. An official distributor of the alms of another; the name of a functionary in a religious house, in the household of a bishop, prince, or other person of rank. Sometimes applied to the chaplain of a hospital, or other institution.

In the royal household of Great Britain there is a titular ***Hereditary Grand Almoner*** besides the ***Lord High Almoner***, and ***Sub-almoner***, who are clergymen.
α. *c* **1300** *Cursor M.* 15219 Judas .. Was iesu crist aumoner [*v.r.* aumener(e]. **1366** MAUNDEV. XIX. 210 Whan the covent of this abbeye hath eaten, the awmener let bere the releef to the gardyn. **1444** *Polit. Poems* II. 220 The awmeneer seyth he cam to late. **1494** FABYAN VII. 586 The lord of Awdeley amner, in stede of the erle of Cambrydge. **1548** HALL *Chron.* 790 Dr. Fox the Kynges Amner made an eloquent oracion in Latin. **1591** PERCIVALL *Sp. Dict.*, *Limosnero*, an almener. **1630** BRATHWAIT *Eng. Gent.* (1641) 242 These deferre giving, till they cannot give, making their executors their

almoners. **1647** HAWARD *Crown Rev.* 31 Gentleman Amner: Fee, 11*l.* 8*s.* 1*d. ob.*; Subamner: Fee, 6*l.* 16*s.* 10*d. ob.* **1654** LESTRANGE *K. Charles I*, 176 There came to London from Cardinal Richelieu.. his Chaplain and Almner. **1667** E. CHAMBERLAYNE *St. Gt. Brit.* I. II. xii. (1743) 97 The Lord Almoner disposes of the king's alms. **1748** RICHARDSON *Clarissa* (1811) III. xxxvi. 209 He is now and then my almoner. **1867** J. MARTINEAU *Chr. Life* (ed. 4) 178 The almoner of God to the poor and sad. **1870** *Daily News* 10 Nov., The almoners of the Berliner Hülfsverein.

β. **1483** CAXTON *Gold. Leg.* 124/3 He [saynt Johan] was called almosner or amener. **1553–87** FOXE *A. & M.* (1596) 1693/1 The almosiner, a phisition, and a surgeon to attend upon them. **1586** *Wills & Inv. N.C.* (1860) 134 To the almosiners of this towne of Middlesburghe. **1601** TATE tr. *Househ. Ord. Ed. II*, §19. 55 For the ausmoner & al under him. **1617** JAMES I *Patent* in *Lib. Mun. Hib.* I. ii. 81 To erect and establish an office of Almosner in this our realm of Ireland.

γ. **1528** MORE *Heresyes* I. Wks. 1557, 164/2 Doctor Mayo, sometyme almoygner to king Henry the seuenth. **1564** GRINDAL *Fun. Serm.* Wks. 1843, 32 The Bishop of Rochester, chiefe Almoygnor. **1598** STOW *Surv.* (ed. Strype 1754) II. ix. 718/1 All Almoisners and houses of Almoise.

δ. ? *c*1400 in *Dom. Arch.* III. 133 The aumere a rod schall haue in honde. *c*1430 LYDG. *ibid.* III. 133 Humble compassion was his awmerer. **1450** *Old Will* in *Academy* 27 Sept. (1882) 231/2 The thonne of þame the þo almer and the tother of yame the tother almar. *c*1510 *Bonaventura's Myrrour* (Pynson) viii. Dj, Theyr amonerers or tresourers myght lightly have had it in hande. *a*1600 *Mem. of Spottiswood* 3 (JAM.) To stay with the queene and attend her Maiestie as her Almowr.

2. *fig.*

1822 B. CORNWALL *Lys. & Ione* I Iris.. Is the Spring's almoner.. and scatters Upon the subject world, dyed flowers and sweets. **1873** SIR J. HERSCHEL *Pop. Lect.* ii. §20. 62 The sun is the almoner of the Almighty.

†**3.** One who gives alms largely; an alms-giver. *Obs.* or *arch.*

1303 R. BRUNNE *Handl. Synne* 5575 Seynt Joan þe aumonere. **1340** *Ayenb.* 190 Ine þe lyue of Ion þe amoner. *a*1400 *Relig. Pieces fr. Thornton MS.* 53. Mercy hir syster salle be ambynowre þat gyffes to alle. **1483** [See in 1 β]. **1580** BARET *Alv.* A 365 An *Amner*, or giuer of almes, seemeth to be deriued of this French worde *Aumosnier*, and therefore ought rather to be written *almonar*. **1585** ABP. SANDYS *Serm.* (1841) 193 Who for his liberal relieving of the needy was surnamed the Almner. **1591** H. LOCKE in Farr's *S.P.* I. 138 An amner to the poore that helpless cry. **1607** HIERON *Wks.* I. 389 [Dorcas] was a discreet, iust, compassionate, cheerefull, simple-hearted almoner. **1874** J. HOLLAND *Mist. Manse* ix. 156 Who found the largess in her palms And him the friendly almoner.

4. A hospital official who has duties concerning patients' welfare (also formerly concerning patients' payments).

1896 M. STEWART in *Mag. Lond. School Med. for Women* May 146 The appointment of an almoner is an experimental measure which has been adopted conjointly by the [Royal Free] Hospital and the Charity Organisation Society. **1922** *Encycl. Brit.* XXXI. 384/2 Many hospitals had adopted the almoner system, that is, specially appointed hospital employees who approach the individual patient who comes to hospital, explain the needs of the hospital, and invite the patient to contribute according to his ability. **1964** *Times* 10 Oct., The almoner has died, at least in name,.. giving way to a new title, Medical Social Worker.

†**'almoner²**. *Obs.* Forms: 4–5 au-, awmener, awmer, alner. [a. OFr. *aumosnière*, *aumonière* (med.L. *almonaria*):—L. **eleēmosynāria*, prop. adj., sc. *bursa*, *arca*, etc., a place for alms.] An alms-purse; a bag, a purse.

*c*1330 *Sir Degarré* 5, I tok hit out and haue hit er, Redi in min aumener. **1375** BARBOUR *Bruce* VIII. 490 Quhen he ded wes.. Thai fand in-till his awmener A letter. *c*1400 *Rom. Rose* 2087 Thanne of his awmener he drough A litell keye. *Ibid.* 2270 Weare streit gloves, with awmere Of silk. *c*1460 *Launfal* 319, I wyll the yeve an alner, Imad of sylk. **1834** PLANCHÉ *Brit. Costume* 89 Berengaria.. is represented with a small pouch called an *aulmonière*.

almonerer, amonerer, *Obs.*: see ALMONER 1 δ.

almonership ('ælmənəʃɪp). [f. ALMONER¹ + -SHIP.] The office or position of an almoner.

1847 *Blackw. Mag.* LXI. 2 To this almonership no salary was attached.

almonry ('ælmənrɪ). Also 5 almosnerye. [a. OFr. *au(l)mosnerie* (mod. *aumônerie*); f. *au(l)mosnier* (mod. *aumônier*) ALMONER: see -RY.]

1. A place where alms were distributed; the residence of an almoner.

*a*1480 CAXTON *Advt.* in Douce *E.T. Fragm.* 1 Late hym come to Westmonester in to the almonesrye at the reed pale. [? *mispr. for* almosnerye]. **1598** STOW *Survey* (ed. Strype 1754) II. VI. iii. 634/2 The place wherein this Chapel and Alms-house stand was called the Elemosinary or Almo[n]ry, now corruptly the Ambrey; for that the alms of the Abbey are there distributed to the poor. **1770** THORPE in *Phil. Trans.* LXI. 154 Given in very ancient times to the use of the almonary or almonry of that abbey. **1859** TENNENT *Ceylon* I. III. xi. 407 The king erected almonries at the four gates of the capital.

†**2.** = ALMONER², or perh. = AMBRY 3. *Obs. rare.*

*a*1536 TINDALE *Exp. Matt.* Wks. II. 88 Love will make me put my hand into my purse, or almonry.

almorie, obs. form of AMBRY.

†**almose.** *Obs.* 5–6. Also 6 almoys(e, almoise, almos. [A literary variant of ALMS, affected by many writers, chiefly ecclesiastical, in 16th c.; apparently a partial refashioning of 'almesse, 'almes, after med.L. *elimosina*, perhaps owing something to the contemporary northern ALMOUS, and (especially Sir T. More's *almoise*, *almoyse*) to the late Anglo-Fr. *almosne*, *almoisne* of the lawbooks.]

1. = ALMS I.

1528 MORE *Heresyes* IV. Wks. 1557, 263/2 Good workes, almoyse, fastyng. **1535** JOYE *Apol. Tindale* 43 Releifed by their dayly almose. *c*1550 CHEKE *Matt.* vi. 2 When yow givest ẏin almos. **1559** *Bk. Comm. Prayer, Pr. for Ch. Mil.*, We humbly beseche the most mercifully to accepte our almose [1604 alms]. **1562** TURNER *Baths* 14 b, Clenge thyne herte from al synne and deal almoys. **1578** FLORIO *1st Frutes* 73 b, To doo almose unto the poore.

b. *sing.* with pl. *almoses* = ALMS 1 b.

1483 CAXTON *Gold. Leg.* 431/1, He.. gafe for god largelye almoses to yᵉ blynde. **1553–87** FOXE *A. & M.* (1596) 1075/2 All the praiers, suffragies, almoses, fastinges.

2. *fig.* = ALMS 2.

1513 MORE *Rich. III*, Wks. 1557, 44/2 It wer almoise to hange them. **1532** —— *Confut. Tindale* Wks. 1557, 446/1 [They] be burned vp & fal as flatte to ashen as it were almoyse all obstinate heretiques dyd.

3. *Comb.*: see ALMS 4.

†**'almoseir, almousser, almaser.** *Sc. Obs.* [f. ALMOUS, *almos* + -ER¹.] = ALMONER¹ 1.

1501 DOUGLAS *Pal. Hon.* iii. 542 (1874) I. 68 Pietie is the kingis almoseir. *c*1501 DUNBAR *Dance* 15 (1860) 165 Then cam in the maister almaser. **1581** *Acts Jas. VI* (1814) 236 His hienes preceptor and maister almousser.

almosiner, -osner, -oisner, literary variants of ALMONER, refashioned in 16th c. after Fr. *aulmosnier* and L. *eleēmosynārius*.

almost ('ɔːlməʊst, -məst; when emphatic or used in reply to a question, 'ɔːlməst), *adv.* Forms: 1 almæst, ealmæst, ælmæst, 2 ælmest, 2–4 almest, 3 all-masst, almaste, 4–5 almeste, -moost, 4–6 -moste, 5 allemost, 7 allmost, 4– almost. Also 8– a'most, still used dial., and aphet. 'most; mod. Sc. amaist, 'maist. [f. ALL + MOST *adv.* = *mostly*.]

†**1.** *adj.* or *adv.* Mostly all, nearly all; for the most part. *Obs.*

*a*1000 BÆDA in Thorpe *Hom.* II. 466 (Bosw.) Hit is eal mǽst mid háligra manna naman geset. **1036** *O.E. Chron.* Mæst ealle þa þegenas be norðan Temese. **1091** *Ibid.*, Seo scipfyrde.. ælmæst earmlice forfór. **1130** *Ibid.*, Se burch for-bernde æl-mæst. *c*1200 ORMIN 9617 þatt Issraæle þeod allmasst þa shollde beon forrworrpen. **1417** in *E.E. Wills* (1882) 24 Thys twey Lynis I wrete almeste with myn owne Hond. **1570** ASCHAM *Scholem.* II. (Arb.) 133 Thies giuers were almost Northmen. **1658** tr. *Mouffet's Theat. Ins.* 1093 The women.. do that work almost.

2. *adv.* Very nearly, wellnigh, all but: **a.** qualifying a verb or attribute.

*c*1200 in *Cod. Dipl.* V. 18 Fram ðe heðe forðriȝte to herdeies ouerende almest. **1250** LAY. 19328 H' is almest dead. *a*1300 *E.E. Psalter* cxviii. 87 Almaste in erthe þai me forname. *c*1386 CHAUCER *Frankl. T.* 443 They were come almoost [*v.r.* almost(e)] to that Citee. **1432–50** tr. *Higden* I., The heete of hit is ioynede allemoste with heuyn. **1531** ELYOT *Governour* (1834) 31, I had almost forgotten where I was. **1580** BARET *Alv.* A 323 It is almost twelue a clocke, *Duodecima instat.* **1611** BIBLE *Acts* xxvi. 28 Almost thou perswadest mee to bee a Christian. **1639** J. CLARKE *Paræmiol.* 3 Almost was never hang'd. *a*1674 CLARENDON *Hist. Reb.* II. VI. 134 The flame of this Common Combustion hath almost devour'd Ireland. **1710** PALMER *Proverbs* 232 They had a'most as live be call'd anything, as to be thought too old for an agreeable conversation. **1756** BURKE *Vind. Nat. Soc.* Wks. I. 11 Diet.. confined almost wholly to the vegetable kind. **1816** SCOTT *Black Dw.* iv. 26 As sair vexed amaist for you as for me. **1849** MACAULAY *Hist. Eng.* I. 597 He was almost within sight of their city. **1869** J. MARTINEAU *Ess.* II. 190 Mistakes.. on almost every page. **1879** MᶜCARTHY *Hist. Own Times* I. 199 Passionate and almost hysterical declamation.

b. qualifying a sb. with implied attribute.

1552 HULOET, Almost nyght, *serum lumen.* **1599** SHAKS. *Much Ado* v. i. 113 You are almost come to part almost a fray. **1709** J. COLLIER *Ess. Mor. Subj.* II. (ed. 6) 193 The almost Omnipresence of an Advantage is a Circumstance of Value. **1808** SOUTHEY *Lett.* (1856) II. 108, I am a heretic requiring toleration, an almost Quaker. *c*1875 WHITNEY *Essen. Eng. Gram.* 382 His almost impudence of manner.

3. With a negative: ***almost no*** = scarcely any; ***almost never*** = scarcely ever, etc.

1523 LD. BERNERS *Froissart* I. ccxv. 270 Bycause they were so great a company, almoost nothynge helde agaynst theym. **1548** UDALL etc., *Erasm. Paraphr. John* iii. 32 But no man almoste recieueth his witnes. **1652** NEEDHAM tr. *Selden's Mare Cl.* 335 So that the French King had neither any shore almost, nor any considerable use of Sea-affairs. **1777** R. WATSON *Philip II* (1793) III. XXIV. 314 His affairs almost never prospered where he was not present. **1857** H. REED *Brit. Poets* vi. 200 Of Shakspeare we know almost nothing. **1875** HIGGINSON *Hist. U.S.* xxv. 252 There were almost no roads.

†**4.** Used to intensify a rhetorical interrogative. (L. *quis fere.*) *Obs.*

1595 SHAKS. *John* IV. iii. 42 Or do you almost thinke, although you see, That you do see? **1615** BEDWELL *Moham. Imp.* K iiij, In what page almost shal you not meet with some exoticke and strange terme? **1670** SOUTH *Serm.* (1737) III. 123 Whom almost can we see who opens his arms to his enemies? **1748** G. WHITE *MS. Serm.*, Who almost are there who do not know these things?

†**almous.** *Obs.* or *dial.* Forms: 3–5 almus, 5 -ws, -ows, 5–6 -ouse, 5–7 -ous, 8–9 mod.Sc. awmous. [a. ON. *almusa*, cogn. w. OE. *ælmysse*: see ALMS. *Almous* is thus, so far as Eng. is concerned, a word of independent origin.]

1. = ALMS I.

*a*1300 *Cursor M.* 19813 þin orisuns and þin almus Es knauin hei in goddes hus. *c*1340 HAMPOLE *Pr. Consc.* 3722 þan availles almus, messe, and bedes. *c*1425 WYNTOUN *Cron.* VI. ii. 67 He wes a man of almous grete. **1564** BECON *Pref. to Wks.* (1843) 20 Niggardly, grudging, and unwilling almous. **1566** KNOX *Hist. Ref.* Wks. 1846 I. 150 A poore man.. asking of his almouse. **1609** SKENE *Reg. Maj.* 64 The wife may give almous moderatly, without consent of hir husband. **1816** SCOTT *Antiq.* xx. 139 'I thank you for your awmous,' said Ochiltree.

b. *sing.* = ALMS 1 b.

1826 J. WILSON *Noct. Ambr.* Wks. 1855 I. 185 White slaves, about the doorcheek, haudin out their hauns for an awmous.

2. = ALMS 2.

*c*1450 HENRYSON *Mor. Fab.* 85 It were almous thee for to draw and hing.

3. *Comb.*: see ALMS 4.

†**almowr.** *Sc. Obs.* By-form of ALMONER¹. [really an independent formation on ALM(S + -OUR, and cogn. w. *almer* and *aumere*. See ALMONER¹ δ.]

alms (ɑːmz). Forms: 1 ælmysse, 1–3 ælmesse (2–3 ælmisse, elmisse, 2–4 elmesse), 2–6 almesse (2–4 almisse, 4 alemesse, allmesse, 5 almese), 2–7 almes (2 elmes, 3 almys, 4 almis, 5 elmys, 6 allmes), 7–9 alms. Pl. wanting; formerly 4–6 almessis, almesses; since 7 the sing. *alms* has also been used as pl. [OE. *ælmysse*, obl. cases *ælmyssan*, cogn. w. ON. *almusa* (Dan. *almisse*, Sw. *almosa*), OFris. *ielmisse*, OS. *alamósna*, OHG. *alamuosan* (MHG. *almuosen*, mod.G. *almosen*), pointing to a com. OTeut. **alemosna* or **alemosina*, a. pop. L. **alimosina* (whence Pr. and OSp. *almosna*, OFr. *almosne*, It. *limosina*), a perversion (due perhaps to sense-association with *alimōnia*) of *elimosina*, *elemosina*, orig. *eleēmosyna* (Tertull., 3rd c.) ad. Gr. ἐλεημοσύνη compassionateness (n. of qual. f. ἐλεήμων compassionate, f. ἔλεος compassion, mercy).

The final -*n* in OE. was early treated as inflexional, and disappeared from the nom.; in recent times the final -*s* of the reduced form *almes*, *alms*, has also been treated as a plural inflexion. For the *y* in OE. *ælmyssan* from **alimosina*, cf. *mynet*, *mylen*, repres. Lat. *moneta*, *molina*. In ME. the s.e. dialects long retained forms with initial *e*, *elmesse*, *elmes*. Distinct by-forms are the northern ALMOUS, *awmous*, an independent adoption of Norse *almusa*; the 16th century literary ALMOSE, *almoyse*; and the legal ALMOIGN, *almone*, from AFr.]

1. Charitable relief of the poor; charity; originally and especially as a religious duty, or good work; const. with *do*, *make*, *work*. Afterwards applied especially to the material substance of the relief, and const. with *give*, *bestow*, etc.

a. *abstract.* or *collect.* without plural.

*a*1000 ? CÆDM. *Dan.* 587 (Gr.), Syle ælmyssan. *c*1000 *Ags. Gosp.* Matt. vi. 2 þonne þu þine ælmessan dó. *c*1160 *Hatton G.* ibid., þanne þu þine ælmesse do. *c*1175 *Lamb. Hom.* 23 Hu miht þu don þine elmesse. *Ibid.* 137 Al ðe almisse þe mon deð. *c*1200 *Trin. Coll. Hom.* 29 þenne þu almesse makest. *Ibid.* 131 Ure gode dedes, on elmes, and on oðre þinge. *Ibid.* 157 On oðer wise man silleð his almes. **1250** GROSTESTE in *Dom. Arch.* III. 82 That youre almys be kepyd ..to poure men. **1297** R. GLOUC. 330 He was.. of hys almesse large & fre. **1340** *Ayenb.* 17 Prede makeþ of elmesse zenne. **1366** MAUNDEV. xviii. 199 To gadre hem precyous Stones and Perles, be weye of Alemesse. *c*1386 CHAUCER *Man of Lawes T.* 70 Hir hond ministre of fredom and almesse. *c*1400 *Apol. for Loll.* 111 Wil þu not do almis of oker & vsur; þat is, do not swilk defautis to do almis þerof. *c*1440 *Gesta Rom.* (1879) 17 Tythes and oblacions, and othere almese. *c*1469 EBESHAM in *Past. Lett.* 596 II. 333 Sende me for almes oon of your olde gownes. **1581** MARBECK *Bk. Notes* 27 This word Almes, importeth as much as mercie. **1587** FLEMING *Contn. Holinshed* III. 1312/2 The distributors of this almesse to the poore. **1666** PEPYS *Diary* (1879) IV. 189 To be buried at the Almes of the parish. **1790** COWPER *Odyss.* XVIII. 2, A public mendicant.. seeking alms. **1816** J. WILSON *City of Plague* I. i. 202 Do you pity me? Then give me alms.

b. As *sing.* (with *pl.* obs. since 16th c.) A charitable donation, a gift of charity, a benefaction.

*c*1375 WYCLIF *Anticrist* 131 Crist's almes.. was encresed to twelve lepful. **1377** LANGL. *P. Pl.* B. xv. 306 þat Freres wolde forsake hir almesses. **1382** WYCLIF *Acts* x. 2 Doynge manye almessis to the peple. *c*1449 PECOCK *Repr.* 550 *bis*, If religiose persoones.. receyve myche and grete Almessis. **1535** COVERDALE *Acts* iii. 3 He desyred to receaue an almesse [1611 asked an almes]. **1541** BARNES *Wks.* 1573, 274/1 Our eatyng, our drynkyng, our almesses, our prayers. **1711** ADDISON *Spect.* No. 269 ¶4 A Beggar Man that had asked an Alms of him. **1848** KINGSLEY *Saint's Trag.* II. viii. 59 Every alms is a fresh badge of slavery.

c. as *pl.* [from the collective sense, assisted by treating the final -*s* as a pl. inflection, as in *riches*.] Things given in charity.

1557 N. T. (Geneva) *Acts* x. 4 Thy prayers and thy almes are come vp into remembrance [Gr. ἐλεημοσύναι, *Wycl.* almes-dedis, *Tind.* almeses, *Coverd.* allmesses, *Cranm.* almeses, *Rhem.* almes-deedes, **1611** almes. But cf. *v.* 2 ἐλεημοσύνας πολλάς, *Wycl.* many almessis, *Tind.* moche almes, *Coverd.* moch almesse, *Cranm.* moch almes, *Gen.* much almes, *Rhem.* many almes-deedes, **1611** much almes; so that in v. 4 it may likewise be sing. notwithstanding the Gr.] **1647** BP. CORBET *Poems* (1807) 122 His alms were such as Paul defines. **1686** DRYDEN *Hind & P.* III. 106 For alms are but the vehicles of prayer. **1865** *Pall Mall G.* 2 May 3 The Alms are thus given by himself to himself.

†**2.** *fig.* A meritorious action, a good deed, a service to God, a charity. Often *ironically*. *Obs.*

c **1430** LYDG. *Bochas* (1544) Prol. 30 It is almes to correcten and amend The vicious folke. **1523** LD. BERNERS *Froissart* I. ccxcv. 437 It is a great almesse to confort maydens in their distresse. **1528** MORE *Heresyes* I. Wks. 1557, 137/1 It had ben great almes the priour, & shee had ben burned togyther. **1577** *Test. 12 Patriarchs* 143 It were more alms to let him go, and to beat you. **1623** SANDERSON *35 Serm.* Wks. 1681 I. 87 If he be hungry, it is alms to feed him; but if he be idle and untoward, it is alms to whip him.

3. *Law.* **a.** Tenure by alms, see ALMOIGN; **free alms** = *frank almoign*. **b. reasonable alms**: a portion of the estate of an intestate allotted to the poor.

1530 *Proper Dyaloge* (1863) 25 And over thys that saye more suttelly that they occupye not this by tytle of secular lordshyppe but by tytle of perpetuall allmes. **1726** AYLIFFE *Parergon* 11 *Frank-Almoigne* is the same which we call.. Free Alms in English.

4. *Comb.*, **a.** *general*: with *alms* in objective relation to a pr. pple. or as obj. gen. to n. of action or agent, as *alms-giving* (pple.), *alms-giver*, *-giving* (sb.); in instrumental relation to a pa. pple., as *alms-clothed*, *-fed*; and in attributive relations, of material, as ***alms-bread***, ***-money***; of purpose (for giving or receiving), as ***alms-basin***, ***-bowl***, ***-box***, ***-chest***, ***-gate***, ***-purse***; of causal connexion (giving or receiving), as ***alms-body***, ***-folk***, ***-man***, ***-people***, ***-priest***, ***-woman***.

1879 O'CONNOR *Beaconsfield* 220 An almsgiving Church. *a* **1631** DONNE *Serm.* xxxvii. 365 A liberall Almsgiver sends to persons that never know who sends. **1690** J. NORRIS *Pract. Disc.* IV. 302 To prove to them that Almes-giving is a Duty. **1764** BURN *Hist. Poor Laws* 205 Almsgiving, among the vulgar, hath engrossed the name of charity. **1670** G. H. *Hist. Cardinals* II. I. 111 Twenty thousand Crowns out of the Alms-money. *Ibid.* 107 They break open the Alms-box. **1753** CHAMBERS *Cycl. Supp.*, The erecting of such alms-chest in every church, is enjoined by the book of canons. **1611** *Tarleton's Jests* (N.), Tarlton called Burley-house gate ..the lord treasurers almes-gate, because it was seldom or never opened. **1530** PALSGR. 194/1 Almes purse, *bovrse avlmosnieres*. **1659** BURROUGHS *Beatit.* (1867) 12, A poor godly alms-body. **1587** HOLINSHED *Chron.* III. 830/1 He founded a faire large almes-house for an almose priest or schoolemaister, and thirteene poore almes folke. *c* **1490** *Reg. Civ. Ebor.* 366 a, The said almus women be fully content & paid. **1865** H. STAUNTON *Gt. Sch., Eton* ii. 10 Alms-women who occupy the place once held by the Bedesmen.

b. *esp.* †**alms-deal, -dealing**, distribution of alms; †**alms-drink**, the remains of liquor reserved for alms-people; **alms-gift**, alms-giving, also = ALMOIGN; **alms-land**, land held in frank almoign; †**alms-penny**, a penny given in charity or as a gratuity; †**alms-room**, an apartment in an alms-house; †**alms-tub**, a large vessel in which the remains of food were preserved for distribution in alms; †**alms-wine**, wine given in alms; †**alms-work** (= ALMS-DEED).

Also ALMS-BASKET, -DEED, -DISH, -FEE, -FOLK, -HOUSE, -MAN, q.v.

c **1175** *Lamb. Hom.* 135 þe apostel us muneȝeð here to.. elmasdele. **1563** *Homilies* II. xi. II. (1859) 389 Merciful almose-dealing is profitable to purge the soul. **1606** SHAKS. *Ant. & Cl.* II. vii. 5 They haue made him drinke Almes drinke. *c* **1250** *Gen. & Ex.* 2464 Chirche-gong, elmesse-gifte, and messe-song. **1882** J. HARDY in *Proc. Ber. Nat. Club* IX. 474 The Abbot..held one carrucate of land..in pure alms-gift. **1809** BAWDWEN *Domesday Bk.* 135 The Almsland of the poor is contained within this limit. **1595** PEELE *Old Wive's T.* (N.), Father, here is an alms-penny for me. *a* **1589** *Petition in Robinson's Gold. Mirr.* (1850) Introd. 12 One of the twelve Allmose Rowmes at Westminster. **1680** SHADWELL *Wom.-Capt.* I. Wks. 1726 III. 347 Whose beards stunk of beef and brewis, and his breath like the fume of an alm's-tub. **1461-83** *Ord. R. Househ.* 73 Wynes, almeswynes to houses of relygyouse & for wynes of yeftes. *c* **1200** ORMIN 10118 To wirrkenn allmesswerrkess.

'alms-ˌbasket. The basket containing the public alms, or those of any charitable society.

1565 J. CALFHILL *Answ. Treat. Crosse* (1846) 4 Your exhibition belike failed you, and therefore ye thought to pick a quarrel to the alms-basket. **1634** *Churchw. Acc. St. Marg. Westm.* in Nicholls (1797) 42 To carry the Almes baskete for the poore of our parish. *a* **1640** J. DAY *Parl. Bees* (1881) 29 We must not come neare But stand Amongst almsbasket men! *a* **1670** HACKET in Walcott *Life* (1865) 156 Take the plenty of the earth to your own table..and feed Him with your Alms-basket.

to live on the alms-basket: to live upon public charity, or on what others voluntarily give.

1588 SHAKS. *L.L.L.* v. i. 41 O they haue liu'd long on the almes-basket of words. **1628** tr. *Camden's Eliz.* IV. (1688) 603 That he should be forced to live upon the Alms-basket.

'alms-deed. [f. ALMS + DEED, from the early phrase to *do alms*.]

1. An act of almsgiving; a deed of charity to the poor, especially as a religious good work.

c **1175** *Lamb. Hom.* 107 ȝif þe ȝunge bið butan hersumnesse, and þe richen butan elmesdedan. *c* **1340** HAMPOLE *Prose Tr.* (1866) 11 To helpe þaire sawles with almous dedes and prayers. *c* **1450** *Merlin* 94 And dide many faire almesse dedes. *a* **1564** BECON *Art. Chr. Rel.* (1844) 468 Thy almose-deeds and thy prayers are come up into heaven. **1611** BIBLE *Acts* ix. 36 This woman was full of good works and almes deeds. **1875** STUBBS *Const. Hist.* III. xxi. 600 Almsdeeds were always regarded as a religious duty.

†**2.** The practice of almsgiving, charity. *Obs.*

c **1200** *Trin. Coll. Hom.* 207 He haueð ofte forlete almes-dede. *c* **1315** SHOREHAM 37 Almesdede senne quenketh, Ase water that fer aquencheth. *c* **1386** CHAUCER *Man of Lawes T.* 1058 In vertu and in holy almes-dede They lyven alle. *c* **1450** LONELICH *Grail* lvi. 50 Mochel almesdede ded he trewly. **1593** SHAKS. *3 Hen. VI*, v. v. 79 Murther is thy Almes-deed; Petitioners for Blood thou ne're put'st back.

†**3.** A meritorious action, a good work = ALMS 2.

c **1430** LYDG. *Bochas* IV. v. (1554) 103/b, They dempte it was an almesse dede To set theyr londe in quiet. **1519** HORMAN *Vulgaria*, It is an almesdede to help the chevalry of Rhodes agaynst the Turkes. **1828** SCOTT *F.M. Perth* III. 10 It were an alms deed to leave him there.

'alms-dish. A dish or plate for the reception of alms, used in churches, in the houses of the charitable, or carried by beggars.

1381 in *Test. Ebor.* I. 114 Je devise al priour du dit Couent ..les mazers et le grant almesdych d'argent. *c* **1460** *Bk. Curtasye* in *Babees Bk.* 325 In þe lordys cupp þat leuys vndrynken, Into þe almesdisshe hit schalle be sonken. **1469** *Ord. R. Househ.* 89 The almes-disshe, to be gyven to the moste needy man or woman. **1785** BURNS *Jolly Beggars* 24 While she held up her greedy gab Just like an aumos dish. **1859** *Autobiog. Beggar-boy* 9 Many of the farmers' wives kept what was then called an aumous dish; this was a small turned wooden dish, and was filled according to the deserts of the claimants or the feeling of the donor.

'alms-fee. The payment also called Peter's pence, and Rome-scot, anciently made to the pope.

a **1000** in Thorpe *Anc. Laws* I. 432 Eac of maneȝum landum mare land-riht arist to cyniȝes ȝebanne..ælmes-feoh & cyric-sceat. **1691** BLOUNT *Law Dict.*, *Almsfeoh*, or *Aelmesfeoh*, that is, Peter-Pence, anciently paid in England on the first of August, and given by King Ina. **1848** KEMBLE *Saxons in Eng.* II. x. (L.), He strictly commands payment of tithe, cyricsceat and almsfee.

'alms-folk.

1. Persons supported by alms; almsmen and almswomen.

1587 HOLINSHED *Chron.* III. 830/1 Thirteene poore almes folke. *a* **1704** T. BROWN *Lett.* Wks. 1730 I. 184 Railing..like almsfolks at the churchwardens. **1811** COLERIDGE *Notes Theol. & Pol.* 366, I alone am lord of fire and light; other creatures are but their alms-folk.

†**2.** Almsgivers. (Cf. ALMSMAN 2.) *Obs.*

1709 STRYPE *Ann. Ref.* I. 233 (T.), This knight and his lady had the character of very good alms-folks.

†**'almsful,** *a.* *Obs.* [f. ALMS + -FUL.] Abounding in alms, beneficent to the poor; charitable.

c **1175** *Lamb. Hom.* 143 þe herbe[r]gers, þe polemode, þe elmesfulle. *c* **1200** ORMIN 9931 Mec and milde and allmessfull. *c* **1300** *Beket* 1676 Gode men beoth and almesful. **1393** LANGL. *P. Pl.* C. VII. 48 þat ich were · wel holy and wel almesful. *c* **1449** PECOCK *Repr.* 335 Goostlie almysful preestis.

'alms-house. A house founded by private charity, for the reception and support of the (usually aged) poor. *Formerly*, The house where the alms of a monastery were distributed, and the hospitality of the convent dispensed.

1440 *Promp. Parv.*, Almesshowse, *Xenodochium*. **1509** *Bury Wills* (1850) 111 The seyd poor dwellyng in yᵉ seyd almeshowsyn. **1576** GRINDAL *Articles of Inquiry* Wks. 1843, 172 Whether your hospitals, spitals, and almose-houses, be well and godly used. **1712** ADDISON *Spect.* No. 549 ⁋3, I may build an alms-house..for a dozen superannuated husbandmen. **1858** WISEMAN *Four Last Popes* 238 Humble alms-houses founded by an eminent merchant.

†**'almsless,** *a.* *Obs.* [ALMS + -LESS.] Without alms, giving no alms.

c **1311** *Pol. Songs* 255 For pride hath sleve, the lond is almusles.

almsman.

1. One supported by alms, or by funds bequeathed for the support of the poor; a bedesman. Also *fig.*

a **1000** *Sax. Leechd.* I. 400 Đonne nime man uncuþ sæd æt ælmesmannum. **1205** LAYAM. 19662 Nu wenden forð þa cnihtes..On ælmes-monnes claðes. **1440** *Promp. Parv.*, Almesmann, Elimosinarius. **1593** SHAKS. *Rich. II*, III. iii. 149 My gay Apparrell, for an Almes-mans Gowne. **1649** BP. HALL *Cases of Consc.* III. vii. (1654) 229 Ye proud ignorants, that call your ministers your almes-men. **1820** KEATS *Isabella* xiii, Bees, the little almsmen of spring bowers. **1866** ROGERS *Agric. & Prices* I. v. 120 The garb of the fourteenth century is still seen in the almsman's gaberdine.

2. An almsgiver. *arch.*

1483 CAXTON *G. de la Tour* c iij b, [He] was a grete almes-man to the poure. **1587** HOLINSHED *Chron.* III. 835/1 He was a good almes-man, and greatly releeued the needie. **1876** FREEMAN *Norm. Conq.* I. vi. 511 King John also was a great almsman.

almucantar (ælmə'kæntə(r)). Forms: 4 **almykantera, almicantera,** 6 **-ath,** 7 **almucanturie, almicantarath,** 6-8 **almicanter,** 8 **almicanther,** 7-8 **almucantar,** 7-9 **almacanter, -ar.** [a. Fr. *almicantarat* or *almucantarat*, also med.L. *almi-*, *almucantarath*; ad. Arab. *almuqanṭarāt*, pl. (with article) of *muqanṭarah* (cited by Golius in sense of 'sundial'), deriv. of *qanṭarah*, a bridge, an arch.] **1.** *pl.* Small circles of the sphere parallel to the horizon, cutting the meridian at equal distances; parallels of altitude. (The horizon itself was reckoned the first almucantar.) Also used in *sing.*

c **1391** CHAUCER *Astrol.* II. §5 The almykanteras in thin astrelabie ben compownet by two & two, where-as some Almykanteras in sondri Astrelabies ben compownet by on and on. **1594** DAVIS *Seamans Secr.* II. (1607) 8 Almicanters are circles of altitude..and are described upon the Zenith. **1594** BLUNDEVIL *Exerc.* III. I. xix. (ed. 7) 320 The first Almicanterath is the very oblique Horizon it selfe. *a* **1625** FLETCHER *Bloody Bro.* IV. ii, Look upon the Astrolabe; you'll find it Four almucanturies at least. **1672** STRODE in Rigaud *Corr. Sci. Men* (1841) II. 441 The sun's almacanters delineated on an horizontal dial are hyperbolas, except when the sun is in the equator. **1768** SMEATON in *Phil. Trans.* LVIII. 170 To describe an almicanther and azimuth circle. **1783** MARTYN *Geog. Mag.* I. Introd. 37 Almicanters are parallels of altitude. **1837** WHEWELL *Induct. Sci.* (1857) I. 178 The circles of the spheres termed almacantars and azimuth circles. **1863** W. CHAUVENET *Man. Spherical & Pract. Astron.* I. i. 19 Small circles parallel to the horizon are called *almucantars*. **1923** D. CLARK *Plane & Geodetic Surv.* II. ii. 83 The almucantar, or small circle of equal altitudes.

2. A telescope fitted with horizontal wires and mounted on a float resting on mercury, used for observing the rising and setting of stars.

1880 S. CHANDLER in *Sci. Observ.* III. No. 5. 36, I propose to call the instrument [for the determination of time and latitude] the 'Almacantar,' from an Arabic astronomical term, now obsolete in its general use. **1901** *Proc. Durham Philos. Soc.* II. 6 In the Almucantar we claim that the telescope turns with faultless truth about its theoretical axis of rotation. **1920** *Nature* CV. 329/1 The almucantar, in which horizontality is secured by the device of floating the whole in a mercury bath.

3. *Comb.* **almucantar-staff.** (See quots.)

1706 PHILLIPS *Almacantar-staff*, a Mathematical Instrument usually made of Box or Pear-tree, with an Arch of 15 Degrees, to take Observations of the Sun at the times of its Rising and Setting; in order to find the Amplitude, and consequently the Variation of the Compass. **1876** CHAMBERS *Astron.* 91 Almacantar Staff, an instrument formerly used for determining the amplitude of an object.

almuce, early form of AMICE.

almug ('ælmʌg). [Heb. *almūg*, for *algūm*: see ALGUM.] A variant of ALGUM (probably only an erroneous spelling of the word in Heb., but more used by Eng. writers).

1611 BIBLE *1 Kings* x. 11 The nauie also of Hiram.. brought in from Ophir, great plentie of Almug trees. **1614** RALEIGH *Hist. World* II. 423 The Almaggin trees brought from Ophir. **1671** *Phil. Trans.* VI. 3074 He shews out of Josephus..what is meant by the Almyggim Wood.. namely, the Indian Pine. **1753** CHAMBERS *Cycl. Supp.* s.v., Critics have long disputed about the nature and kind of the almug-tree. **1867** J. INGELOW *Stor. Doom* II. 94 He sat below an almug tree.

†**almury.** *Obs. rare.* [a. (ult.) Arab. *al-muṛī*, i.e. *al* the + *muṛī* indicator, agent-noun f. 4th form of *raṛay* to see.] 'The "denticle" or tooth-like point or pointer situate on the Rete of the astrolabe near the "head" of Capricorn.' Skeat.

c **1391** CHAUCER *Astrol.* I. xxiii, Thin almury is cleped the denticle of capricorne or else the kalkuler.

†**al'muten.** *Astrol. Obs.* [Corrupt for *almutaz* (so in OFr.) a. Arab. *al-muṛtaz*, i.e. *al* the + *muṛtaz* prevailing, f. 8th form of *ṛazz* to be powerful.] The prevailing or ruling planet in the horoscope.

a **1625** FLETCHER *Rollo* v. ii, All these shew him to be th' almuten..Yes; he's Lord of the Geniture. **1632** MASSINGER *City Madam* II. ii, And Mars Almuthen, or lord of the horoscope. **1651** N. BIGGS *New Dispens.* §165 The Ascendant and Almuten in its own Horizon. **1721** BAILEY, *Almuten*, the Lord of Figure, or strongest Planet in a Nativity.

almyghty, obs. variant of ALMIGHTY.

almykantera, obs. form of ALMUCANTAR.

almyra, variant of ALMIRAH.

almys, obs. form of ALMS.

†**aln.** *Obs.* [ad. L. *alnus*.] An alder(-tree).

1589 FLEMING *Virg. Ecl.* VI. 31 Turned into alntrees tall.

alnage ('ɔːlnɪdʒ). Forms: 5-7 **aulnage,** 7 **aulneage,** 7- **alnage.** [a. OFr. *aulnage* (mod. *aunage*), f. *aulner*, *auner* to measure by the ell; f. *alne*, *aulne*, *aune* ell (cogn. w. Pr. *alna*, *auna*, It. *auna*):—late L. *alena*, a. OTeut. **alina* (Goth. *aleina*, ON. *alin*, OHG. *elina*, OE. *eln*, Eng. *ell*) cogn. w. L. *ulna*, Gr. ὠλένη the fore-arm.]

1. Measurement by the ell. *spec.* Official inspection and measurement of woollen cloth, and attestation of its value by the affixing of a leaden seal.

[**1477** *Act 17 Ed. IV*, v. in Pulton *Coll.* (1632) 379 To let to ferme the subsidie and aulnage of Clothes which ought to be sealed.] **1668** CHILD *Disc. Trade* (1694) 3 The business of the Aulnage, which doubtless our predecessors intended for a scrutiny into the goodness of the commodity. **1736** CARTE *Ormonde* I. 141 Alnage was to remain as already settled by law.

2. The fee paid for the above measurement.

1622 *Rep. Hist. MSS.* (1874) 311/2 The pettie farm (various items, viz... Alnage, £820). 1689 Atkins *Parl. & Pol. Tracts* (1734) 231 A Case that concerns meerly his Revenue, as this of the Aulneage was.

alnager ('ɔːlnɪdʒə(r)). Forms: 5–7 **aulneger**, 6 **-geour**, 7 **-geor**, **alnageor**, **-eager**, **allnager**, 7–8 **alneger**, 7–9 **aulnager**, 7– **alnager**. [a. OFr. *aulnegeor*, n. of action f. *aulnage*: see prec.] A sworn officer appointed to examine and attest the measurement and quality of woollen goods. The office was abolished by 11 & 12 Will. III. c. 20.

[1350 *Act 25 Edw. III*, i. Totes maneres des draps vendables..soient aunez par le Auneour de Roi (16th c. transl. All manner of cloths vendible..shall be measured by the kings Aulnegeour).] 1581 Lambarde *Eiren.* iv. iv. (1602) 416 Sundry other fees of Officers there be, as of Alnageours, Gaugeours. 1666 *Lond. Gaz.* lxvi/2 A Bill for Regulating old and new Draperies, and appointing an Alneagers Office for sealing them. 1755 Carte *Hist. Eng.* IV. 149 Some abuses of the aulnager. 1838 J. Holt in *Mem.* II. 32, I was deputy alnager..which produced me from £80 to £100 a year.

Alnaschar (æl'næʃə(r)). The name of a beggar in the 'Arabian Nights' who destroys his means of livelihood because he indulges in visions of riches and grandeur; applied allusively to a person given to such illusions. Also *attrib.* Hence **Al'naschar̃ism**; **Al'nascharize** *v. intr.*

1712 Addison *Spect.* No. 535 13 Nov., Alnaschar was entirely swallowed up in this chimerical Vision. 1812 M. Edgeworth *Tales Fash. Life* IV. i. 13 With maternal *Alnascharism*, she had, in her reveries, thrown back her head with disdain, as she repulsed the family advances of some wealthy, but low-born heiress. 1840 *New Monthly Mag.* LIX. 349 Higgins had been Almascharizing [*sic*]—building *chateaux en Espagne*. 1840 Thackeray *Shabby Genteel Story* vi. in *Fraser's Mag.* Aug. 236/2 'I'll..make designs hallusive of my passion for her.' And so our pictorial Alnaschar dreamed and dreamed. 1849 —— *Pendennis* I. xxxiii. 329 What an Alnaschar I am because I have made five pounds by my poems. 1853 Mrs. Gaskell *Ruth* I. ii. 55 She..was busy with Alnaschar visions of wide expenditure. 1896 G. B. Shaw in *Contemp. Rev.* Feb. 205 Those delicious Alnaschar dreams.

†**al'nath.** *Astrol. Obs.* [Arab. *al-naṯh* from *naṭaḥa* to butt, aim at with the horns.] The first star in the horns of Aries; hence, the 'first mansion of the moon.'

*c*1386 Chaucer *Frankl. T.* 553 He knew ful wel how fer Alnath was shoue ffro the heed of thilke fixe Aries aboue.

alner, variant of almoner². *Obs.*, a purse.

*c*1460 *Launfal* 319, I wyll the yeve an alner I-mad of sylk and of gold cler.

†**'alner, aulner.** *Obs. rare.* [a. OFr. *aulnère*, *aulneor*, mod.Fr. *auneur* (:—L. *alenātor*) n. of agent f. *aulner* to measure by the ell: see alnage and -er.] = alnager.

1483 *Act 1 Rich. III*, viii. §4 Nor make eny persone or persones to be Aulner..but such as be experte in Cloth makyng. [in Pulton 1632: No person..to be Aulneger.]

alneway, obs. form of alway.

alnight: see allnight.

aload (ə'ləʊd), *adv.*, prop. *phr.* [A *prep.*¹ in, on + load.] In load.

1601 Holland *Pliny* (1634) II. 176 Labouring beasts which haue Apples and such like fruit aload, wil quickly shrinke and complaine vnder their burden.

†**a'loathe,** *v. Obs.* [f. a- *pref.* 1 intens. + OE. *láðian* to loathe.] *trans.* To loathe, detest. *intr.* To become loathesome, to cause disgust.

1205 Layam. 25930 Mi lif me is a-laðed. 1250 *Ibid.* 2258 His leofe dowter was Locrin a-loþed. *a*1250 *Owl & Night.* 1277 Nis noht so hot þat hit nacoleþ..Ne noht so leof þat hit naloþeþ.

†**a'loathing,** *ppl. a. Obs. rare*⁻¹. [f. prec. + -ing².] Loathing, disliking, unwilling.

1382 Wyclif *Luke* Prol., To schewe God as wel to men willinge, as to profite to men aloothinge [*v.r.* lothende].

alocasia (æləʊ'keɪzɪə, -'keɪʒ(ɪ)ə). *Bot.* [Said to be an alteration of colocasia.] A plant of a genus from tropical Asia cultivated for its foliage, closely allied to colocasia.

1860 *Bot. Mag.* LXXXVI. t. 5190 Alocasia Metallica. Bronze-leaved Alocasia. 1882 *Garden* 4 Feb. 86/3 Alocasias ..should be potted before growth begins. 1884 *De Candolle's Orig. Cultivated Pl.* 75 Apé, or Large-rooted Alocasia—*Alocasia macrorrhiza.*

alod, -ial, -iality, etc. variants of allod, etc.

aloe ('æləʊ). Forms: *pl.* 1 **aluwan, alewan, alwan,** 2–6 **aloen,** 4–6 **alowes,** 6 **allowes,** 4– **aloes;** *sing.* 5– **aloe.** [OE. *aluwan*, pl. of *aluwe*, *alue*, ad. L. *aloē*, a. Gr. ἀλόη, properly the drug and plant described in senses 2–5; but used also in the Septuagint and N.T. to translate Heb. *akhālīm*, *akhālōth* (cf. Skr. *aguru*, Hind. *aghil*) the Agalloch, probably from the similarity of the words. In consequence of this confusion, the word came to be applied in the modern languages, both to the fragrant resin or *aloes* of the Bible, and the bitter drug or *aloes* proper. The former is indeed the earliest use in Eng., where also the word was orig. always plural.]

†**1.** *pl.* The fragrant resin or wood of the agalloch (q.v.), derived from species of two East Indian genera, *Aloexylon* and *Aquilaria*. See lign-aloes.

*c*950 *Sax. Leechd.* II. 174 Alwan wiþ untrymnessum. *c*1000 *Ags. Gosp.* John xix. 39 Brohte wyrt-ȝemang and alewan. *c*1160 *Hatton G.* ibid., Wyrt-ȝemang and aloen. 1382 Wyclif *ibid.*, A medlynge of myrre and aloes. 1398 Trevisa *Barth. De P.R.* xvii. v. (1495) 606 Alowes is a tree wyth moste swete smelle. 1535 Coverdale *Ps.* xliv. 8 All thy garmentes are like myrre, Aloes and Cassia. 1541 R. Copland *Guydon's Formul.* Tij, Decoction of thure, mastice, aloen. 1599 Hakluyt *Voy.* II. 229 He sendeth another small ship euery yeere to Cauchin China to lade there wood of Aloes. 1741 *Compl. Fam.-Piece* I. i. 93 Take ..Aloes Cicatrina, purest Frankincense..of each half an Ounce. 1865 *Public Opin.* 7 Jan. 19 The Canticles record in one verse..frankincense, myrrh, and aloes—the last meaning the wood of the aloexylum agallochum.

2. A genus of plants (N.O. *Liliaceæ*, sect. *Aloinæ*) containing several species, succulent herbs, shrubs, or trees, with erect spikes of flowers, and bitter juice.

1398 Trevisa *Barth. De P.R.* xvii. vi. (1495) 606 Aloe is the frute of a certen herbe that hyght Aloe..The juys thereof is wronge and sod on the fyre and afterwarde dryed in the sonne. 1477 Earl Rivers (Caxton) *Dictes* 68 The bittrenesse of the aloe tre distroyeth the swittenesse of the hony. 1551 Turner *Herb.* (1568) 17 The nature of the herbe Aloe is to hele woundes. 1578 Lyte *Dodoens* 353 We may call it in English Aloë, herbe Aloë, or Sea Aygreene. 1769 Sir J. Hill *Fam. Herb.* (1812) 6 The socotrine aloe is a very beautiful plant, the leaves are like those of the pine-apple. 1830 Lindley *Nat. Syst. Bot.* 274 Aloes are mostly found in the southern parts of Africa. 1877 Thomson *Voy. Challenger* I. ii. 113 Clumps of aloes with their rich crimson spikes.

3. (Usually *pl.*) A drug of nauseous odour, bitter taste, and purgative qualities, procured from the inspissated juice of plants of the genus *Aloe*.

1398 [See 2]. 1477 Norton *Ord. Alch.* in Ashm. 1652 v. 70 Odours misliking, as Aloes and Sulphure. 1543 Traheron *Vigo's Chirurg.* (1586) 430 Aloe is the liquor of an herbe, brought unto us out of India. 1618 Latham *2nd Bk. Falc.* (1633) 140 Aloes, the iuyce which is vsed in physicke is moderately hot..extreame bitter. 1756 Burke *Subl. & B.* Wks. I. 100 All men are agreed to call..aloes bitter. 1875 Wood *Therap.* (1879) 462 Aloes is a stomachic, stimulant cathartic.

4. *fig.* Bitter experiences, trials, etc.

1526 Skelton *Magnyf.* 2383 Bytter alowes of herde adversyte. 1617 Hieron *Wks.* II. 203 He purgeth and bringeth low by the bitter aloes of the law. 1630 Brathwait *Eng. Gent.* (1641) 256 Hee attempers his actractivest pastimes with a little alloes.

†**5.** Some mineral resembling the drug. *Obs.*

1601 Holland *Pliny* (1634) II. 271 Aboue Ierusalem.. there is a certain minerall Aloe to be found, growing in manner of a mettal within the ground.

6. Applied popularly to other plants having some supposed resemblance to the genus *Aloe*, chiefly the Agave or 'American Aloe' (famed for its rare flowering).

1682 Wheler *Journ. Greece* i. 27 Here I saw Aloes in flower. 1752 Miller *Gard. Dict.* (ed. 6) H 2 A vulgar Error ..relating to the large American Aloe; which is, that it never flowers till it is an hundred Years old. 1843 Prescott *Conq. Mexico* (1854) 3 Plantations of the aloe or maguey (*Agave americana*). 1866 Moore in *Treas. Bot.* 29 The American Aloe appears to have been first introduced to Europe in 1561.

7. *Comb.* **aloes-wood** (= aloe 1); *aloe-like*.

1807 Martyn *Miller's Gard. Dict.* 3 B b, The aroma of Aloes wood is a disease. 1830 Lindley *Nat. Syst. Bot.* 77 Aloes wood, a fragrant resinous substance of a dark colour, is the inside of the trunk of the *Aquilaria ovata* and *A. Agallochum*. 1866 *Treas. Bot.*, *Aloes-Wood*, the wood of *Aloexylon Agallochum*. 1839 Bailey *Festus* xxx. (1848) 345 There are some hearts, aloe-like, flower once, and die [see 6].

aloed ('æləʊd), *ppl. a.* [f. aloe + -ed².]

1. Mixed or flavoured with, or as with, aloes; bitter. Cf. *honied*, etc.

1627 Feltham *Resolves* i. xxiv. Wks. 1677, 43 Conceit of a surviving name, sweetens Deaths Aloed portion.

2. Planted or shaded with aloes. Cf. *willowed*.

1855 Browning *Old Pict. Flor.* in *Men & Wom.* II. 30 As I leaned and looked over the aloed porch.

†**alo'edary.** *Obs.* [ad. L. *aloēdārium*, a. Gr. ἀλοηδάριον, f. ἀλόη aloe.]

1. *Med.* A purgative medicine, having aloes as a chief ingredient. (In mod. medical Dicts. **aloedarium.**)

1753 Chambers *Cycl. Supp.*, *Aloedary*..denotes a purgative medicine, wherein aloes is an ingredient.

2. *Bot.* A treatise on the genus Aloe.

1753 Chambers *Cycl. Supp.* s.v., Munting has published an aloedary at the end of his history of the *Herba Britannica*.

aloetic (æləʊ'ɛtɪk), *a.* and *sb.* [f. Gr. ἀλόη aloe; by form-assoc. with *diuretic*, etc. but not analogous.]

A. *adj.*

1. *Med.* Of the nature of aloes; having aloes as an ingredient.

1706 Phillips, *Aloetick*, belonging to Aloes; as Aloetick Pills. 1754 Smellie *Midwif.* I. 152 In which case all aloetic medicines ought to be avoided. 1831 Carlyle *Sart. Res.* (1858) 138 A perceptible smell of aloetic drugs. 1875 Wood *Therap.* (1879) 536 Salines, and not aloetic purgatives.

2. *Chem.* *Aloetic Acid*: a yellow amorphous powder, 2 $C_7H_2N_2O_5{\cdot}H_2O$, of acrid taste, forming purple-red solutions in boiling water and in alcohol.

1855 Pereira *Mat. Med.* i. ii. 196 By the action of nitric acid on aloes [Schunk] obtained..aloetic acid.

B. *sb.* An aloetic medicine.

1706 Phillips, *Aloeticks*, medicines that consist chiefly of Aloes. 1756 C. Lucas *Ess. Waters* II. 267 Some gross corpulent persons..will require aloetics. 1791 *Edin. New Disp.* 527 The general purposes of aloetics.

†**alo'etical,** *a. Obs. rare.* [f. prec. + -al¹.] = prec.

1734 R. Wiseman *Surgery* (J.) It may be excited by aloetical, scammoniate, or acrimonious medicines.

aloft (ə'lɒft), *adv.* and *prep.* Forms: 3 **o lofft,** 3–5 **o loft, o lofte,** 4–7 **a lofte,** 4– **a loft, aloft.** Also expanded: 3 **inne þe lofte,** 2–5 **on the lofte,** 4 **on þe loft,** 4–5 **on lofte,** 4–6 **on loft.** [a. ON. *á lopt* of motion, *á lopti* of position (EE. *o loft* and *o lofte*), f. *á*, in, on, to + *lopt*, air, atmosphere, sky, heaven, upper floor, loft (Dan. *lofts*), cogn. w. Goth. *luftus*, OHG. *luft*, OE. *lyft*, air, etc. (In Eng. the distinction of motion and position, *a loft* and *a lofte*, was lost with the mutescence of final *e*.) Really equivalent to OE. *on þá lyft*, *on þǽre lyfte*, ME. *on þe lufte*, *on þe lyft(e*, 'into, in the air,' but while the latter never acquired the merely local sense of 'on high, up,' this became from the first the special sense of *a loft*. Some mixture of forms is probable in the expanded *in the lofte*, *on the lofte*, *on lofte*.]

†**1.** In the atmosphere or space above the earth.

*c*1200 *Moral Ode* 83 He makede fisses in þe se and fuȝeles in þe lifte [*v.r.* inne þe lofte, on þe lofte, in þe lufte].

†**2.** In the visible sky, above the horizon, up, as a star. *Obs.*

*c*1340 *Alex. & Dind.* 122 And reed gan schine þat his lem on þe loft liȝht ȝaf aboute. *c*1400 *Epiph.* (Turnb. 1843) 118 For this day aloft was the sterre. 1577 B. Googe *Heresbach's Husb.* (1586) 53 b, The moone being aloft and not sette.

†**3.** *fig.* In the ascendant, ruling, prevailing, up. *Obs.*

*c*1400 *'Chaucer's' Test. Love* ii. (1560) 291/1 Kindely heaven, when merie weather is a lofte, appeareth..in Blewe. *c*1430 *How the good Wyf* 74 in *Babees Bk.* 39 If þou be in place where good ale is on lofte. 1601 Holland *Pliny* (1634) I. 24 The Sun raiseth..windes. At rising and setting hee causeth them to be aloft.

4. In heaven; 'on high.' *arch.* (cf. 12.)

*c*1386 Chaucer *Man of Lawes T.* 179 My souerayn plesance, Ouer alle thyng (out taken crist on lofte). 1577 *St. Augustine's Man.* 65 The day-spryng hath visited us from aloft. 1596 Chapman *Iliad* vii. 85 But conquest's garlands hang aloft, amongst th' immortal Gods. 1774 R. Lloyd *Hymn to Apollo*, Aloft in heaven imperial Juno sat. *c*1800 Dibdin, There's a sweet little cherub that sits up aloft, To keep watch for the life of poor Jack.

5. *gen.* High above the earth, on high; at a great elevation relatively; high up.

*c*1200 Ormin 11961 Wiþþuten o þe temmple..þær wass greȝȝþed sæte o lofft. *c*1325 *E.E. Allit. P.* B. 1183 For þe borȝ watȝ so bygge baytayled alofte. *c*1420 *Pallad. on Husb.* iv. 80 A sadder vyne a bigger stake olofte Mot holde. *c*1450 Henryson *Mor. Fables* 56 The Larke on loft with other birdes haill. 1535 Coverdale *Ps.* ciii. 8 Then are the hilles sene alofte. 1580 Lyly *Euphues* (Arb.) 221 A feather..sette a loft in a woemans hatte. 1663 Butler *Hudibr.* i. iii. 575 Thrice have they seen your Sword aloft Wav'd o're their Heads. 1711 Pope *Temp. Fame* 483 Fame sits aloft, and points them out their course. 1860 Tyndall *Glac.* ii. §8. 265 Vast masses of granite are thus poised aloft on icy pedestals.

†**b.** On horseback or in a vehicle; opposed to *afoot*. *Obs.*

*c*1400 *Ywaine & Gaw.* 2532 Than sighed Ywain wonder oft, Unnethes might he syt oloft. 1654 Ussher *Annals* v. (1658) 43 Besides those which fought aloft from the Chariots.

†**c.** Extant, standing; not thrown down. *Obs. rare.*

*c*1400 *Destr. Troy* ii. 349 To this souerayne Citie þat yet was olofte Iason aioynid.

†**6.** Above geographically; higher up on the same plane. *Obs. rare.*

1805 Nelson in Nicolas's *Disp.* VI. 477 The Frigates are ordered from aloft [*i.e.* the upper part of the Mediterranean] to join you.

†**7.** On the top, atop, on the surface. *Obs.*

*c*1420 *Pallad. on Husb.* i. 1088 So that the flamme upbende The celles forto chere and chaufe olofte. 1523 Fitzherb. *Husb.* cxxviii, They cast and lay grauell aloft. 1587 Holinshed *Chron.* I. 43/1 And aloft therevpon she had a thicke Irish mantell. 1667 H. More *Div. Dial.* iv. xxxiv. (1713) 387 Where's your Oil now..that floats aloft? 1718 Pope *Iliad* xxiv. 997 Forth to the pile was borne the man divine, And placed aloft.

8. *fig.* On high in rank, power, estimation, etc.

1377 Langl. *P. Pl.* B. Prol. 157 We myȝte be lordes aloft. *c*1400 *Rom. Rose* 5506 They saw hem set on loft, And weren of hem succoured oft. 1552–5 Latimer *Serm. & Rem.* (1845) 51 Bilney..was induced to bear a fagot..when the cardinal was aloft and bore the swing. 1851 Hussey *Papal Power* i. 20 A high and mighty personage seated aloft somewhere.

†**9.** In a lofty tone, loftily. *Obs.*

1613 PURCHAS *Pilgr.* I. VI. xii. 531 Speake aloft and prowdley.

10. Of direction: Into the air, or from the ground; up, upward, on high.

c **1200** ORMIN 11823 Crist þolede þe deofell To brinngenn himm heȝhe upp o lofft. **1330** R. BRUNNE *Chron.* 274 Þe erles of Scotlond had reysed baner oloft. **1430** LYDG. *Thebes* 33 in *Dom. Arch.* III. 111 To a chamber she led him vp alofte. *c* **1588** GREENE *Fr. Bacon* ii, A whirlwind .. mounted me aloft unto the clouds. **1667** MILTON *P.L.* I. 226 With expanded wings he stears his flight Aloft. **1725** DE FOE *Voy. round World* (1840) 207 Blow her aloft in the air. **1877** LYTTEIL *Landm.* II. ii. 88 A steep bluff crag .. towers aloft.

b. To heaven. *arch.* (cf. 12.)

1692 E. WALKER *Epictetus Mor.* (1737) Introd., His rich Soul aloft did soar. *c* **1800** DIBDIN *Tom Bowling*, For though his body's under hatches, His soul is gone aloft.

11. *fig.* Up in rank, estimation, feeling, etc.

c **1200** ORMIN 11849 Te laþe gast Aȝȝ eggeþ hise þeowwess, To draȝȝhenn hemm aȝȝ upp o lofft. **1300** *E.E. Psalter* lxxiv. 8 Þis mekes he ful ofte, And þis up-heves he o-lofte. **1567** JEWEL *Def. Apol.* (1611) 386 But afterward the Popes began to looke aloft. **1836** J. GILBERT *Chr. Atonem.* ii. (1852) 41 The very principles which bore aloft your spirits.

12. *Naut.* On or to a higher part of a ship; as the mast, the mast head, the rigging generally, in reference to the deck; or the deck as opposed to below.

1330 R. BRUNNE *Chron.* 169 Þe saile was hie o loft. **1509** BARCLAY *Ship of Fooles* (1570) 251 Our sayles are a loft, Our ship flyes swiftly. **1629** GAULE *Holy Madn.* 210 Come a loft Jack. **1762** FALCONER *Shipwr.* I. 697 Rous'd from repose, aloft the sailors swarm. **1813** SOUTHEY *Nelson* iii. 82 So cut up, that she could not get a topmast aloft during the night. **1836** MARRYAT *Midship. Easy* xiii. 47 The men had come from aloft, and Jack was summoned on deck.

†**B.** *prep.* On the top or summit of; above, over.

1509 HAWES *Past. Pl.* XXXVIII. iii, Alofte the basse toure foure ymages stode. **1595** SHAKS. *John* IV. ii. 139 But now I breath againe Aloft the flood. **1600** CHAPMAN *Iliad* XIX. 93 They bear her still aloft men's heads. **1613** CAMPION in Arber's *Garn.* III. 279 Aloft the trees .. Our silent harps we pensive hung.

aloge, alogge, variants of ALLODGE *v. Obs.*

alogh, aloȝ, variants of ALOW *adv. Obs.*

alogian (əˈləʊdʒɪən). [ad. med.L. *alogiān-ī*; f. Gr. ἀλόγι-οι (f. ἀ priv. + λόγος translated '*Word*' in *John* i. 1) + -AN; cf. *christian.*] One of an ancient sect who denied the divinity of the 'Logos.'

1675 S. COLVIL *Whigs Suppl.* (1751) 142 And some prove Maximinians .. Cerinthians and Alogians. **1753** CHAMBERS *Cycl. Supp.* s.v., The alogians made their appearance towards the close of the second century. **1849** W. FITZGERALD tr. *Whitaker's Disp.* 34 The Alogians .. would not acknowledge as God the Logos, whom John declares to be God.

†**aˈlogic,** *a. Obs.*—⁰ [ad. Fr. *alogique* (Cotgr.), f. Gr. ἀ priv. + λογικ-ός reasonable, f. λόγος speech, reason.] Illogical; 'unreasonable, inconsiderate.' Blount *Glossogr.* 1656.

alogical (eɪˈlɒdʒɪkəl), *a.* [f. A- 14 + LOGICAL *a.* Cf. F. *alogique.*] Non-logical; not based upon reason or formed by an act of judgement; opposed to logic. Also *absol.*, that which is alogical. Hence **aˈlogically** *adv.*; **ˌalogiˈcality.**

1694 MOTTEUX *Rabelais* V. xviii, Foreign Civilians .. have uncivily drawn alogical and unreasonable Consequences from it [*tiré à consequence alogicque, c'est à dire desraisonnable*]. **1881** G. S. HALL *Asp. German Culture* 43 There is an immanent teleology in his [Julius Bahnsen's] universe; but it is not merely alogical, but anti-logical, and even anti-causal. **1907** E. B. BAX *Roots of Reality* 19 Undoubtedly the *a*logical is .. a primary element in all experience. *Ibid.*, In ordinary consciousness .. the ultimate elements of a reality or thing are an alogical feeling or sensation, and a logical form or category. *Ibid.* 161 In every process of consciousness a contradiction lies embedded, based on the antithetic character of its two ultimate elements, the mark of which we have found to consist respectively in alogicality and logicality. *Ibid.* 173 The aim of art .. is to express the unity and harmony of experience .. in the world of immediate feeling—in a word, *alogically.* **1908** J. M. BALDWIN *Thought & Things* II. 386 The Logical and the A-logical. **1909** W. JAMES *Let.* in R. B. Perry *Tht. & Char. W. J.* (1935) II. 680, I am *a*-logical, if not illogical, and glad to be so. **1925** J. E. TURNER *Theory Direct Realism* 25 It is not surprising .. that this attitude .. should be regarded as instinctive non-rational, and alogical. **1957** P. LAFITTE *Person in Psychol.* xiv. 205 What was described as alogical thinking was quite logical thinking in a different frame of reference.

ˈalogism. In 7 all-. [f. Gr. ἀλογίζεσθαι to be irrational, as if ad. Gr. *ἀλογισμός; cf. λογισμός reason, argument.] †**1.** *Obs. rare*—¹. An illogical or irrational statement.

1679 EVERARD *Depos. Popish Plot* 14 The ground from which they took the occasion of this slanderous Allogisme.

2. The fact or quality of being alogical. *rare.*

1911 J. M. BALDWIN *Thought & Things* III. iv. 47 The 'alogism' of Bergson, which James cites as nearer his own, seems, however, .. in its outcome, nearer to that of Bradley, since it is a mode of higher intuition or immediacy to which Bergson makes appeal. **1935** R. B. PERRY *Tht. & Char. W. James* II. 681 An almost morbid alogism, or antipathy to the mode of thinking which employs definitions, symbols, and trains of inference.

alogotrophy (æləˈgɒtrəfɪ). *Med.* [ad. mod.L. *alogotrophia* (also used in Eng.), f. Gr. ἄλογος unreasonable + τροφ-ή nourishment + *-ia*: see -Y³.] Excessive nutrition of any part of the body, resulting in deformity.

1753 CHAMBERS *Cycl. Supp.* s.v., If the bones of the vertebræ of the back receive too much nutriment on one side .. an incurvation necessarily ensues, which, as Charleton expresses it, is produced by an *alogotrophia.* **1853** MAYNE *Exp. Lex.* s.v., Done by alogotrophy according to Charlton.

†**ˈalogy.** *Obs.* [ad. med.L. *alogia*, a. Gr. ἀλογία unreasonableness, f. ἄλογ-ος unreasonable; f. ἀ priv. + λόγος reason.] Absurdity, unreasonableness.

1646 SIR T. BROWNE *Pseud. Ep.* 372 The Alogie of this opinion consisteth in the illation. *Ibid.* 113 The error therefore and Alogy in this opinion, is worse then in the last. **1775** ASH, *Alogy* (not much used).

aloha (əˈləʊə, ɑːˈləʊhə), int. (*sb.*) Also **aroha.** [Hawaiian *aloha*, Maori *aroha* love, affection, pity.] **1.** *Hawaii* and *S. Pacific.* A greeting or valediction: 'welcome', 'greetings', 'farewell', etc. Also ***aloha 'oe*** ['*oe* (to) you], and as *sb.*

[**1798** G. VANCOUVER *Voy. N. Pacific Ocean* II. III. v. 139 The man instantly replied 'arrowhah,' meaning that he pitied him.] **1825** W. ELLIS *Jrnl. Tour Hawaii* v. 109 When they designed to leave us, they would .. give us their parting *aroha* as we passed. **1847** H. BINGHAM *Residence Twenty-one Years Sandwich Islands* vi. 135, I saluted him with a kiss and a hearty *aloha.* **1898** M. H. KROUT *Hawaii & Revolution* xxv. 317, I was greeted with friendly smiles and gestures and the kindly '*Aloha*'. **1914** R. BROOKE *Let.* Mar. (1968) 566 The anchor's up & the folk on shore sing 'Good-bye, my flenni!' or 'Aloha oe!' **1937** D. & H. TEILHET *Feather Cloak Murders* i. 12 Jeffrey Preacher raised his glass. 'Aloha! Better have one with us.' **1963** *Times* 31 Dec. 12/7 Aloha .., a word that survives from old Hawaii .. means both farewell and greeting, friendship and love, hope and promise. So, as the English church bells ring out, I shall be thinking 'Plenty Aloha, 1964'. **1972** J. POTTER *Going West* 38 Half an hour out of Honolulu the arrival of yet another printed form roused him... Midnight local time and a temperature of seventy-four degrees. 'Aloha,' the airport tower announced in neon lights .. Aloha meant welcome. **1978** *Islands* Aug. 13 Please offer my warmest *aroha* to Miss Gilhooly, and thank her for looking after you so well.

2. *attrib.* passing into *adj.*, esp. as ***aloha shirt*** (see quot. 1951). Cf. *Hawaiian shirt* s.v. HAWAIIAN *a.* II. Chiefly *U.S.*

1918–19 *T. Eaton & Co. Catal.* Fall & Winter 369/1 Hawaiian Records... Aloha Oe Waltzes. **1951** *Amer. Speech* XXVI. 19 *Aloha* .. is often heard in compounds such as *aloha party* or *aloha shirt*—for a bright sport garment now winning favor in continental United States. 'Aloha Week' is the annual gala season about the end of October. **1954** *Ellery Queen's Mystery Mag.* Oct. 9/2 David was dressed casually in a red *aloha* shirt. **1967** M. DAVIS *Strange Corner* (1968) vi. 50 She chose jade and ivory trinkets, teatimers, dolls and aloha shirts. **1972** J. POTTER *Going West* 48 Tourist housewives .. wore Polynesian shifts in patterns matching their husbands' Aloha shirts... Open cars passed... The number plates proclaimed Hawaii the Aloha State.

aloid (ˈæləʊɪd), *a.* [f. ALOE + *-id* for -OID.] Resembling aloes.

1853 in MAYNE *Exp. Lex.* **1879** in *Syd. Soc. Lex.*

aloin (ˈæləʊɪn). *Chem.* [f. ALOE + -IN.] The bitter purgative principle in aloes, $C_{17}H_{18}O_7$, which crystallizes in prismatic needles of a pale yellow colour, and has a taste, at first sweet, and then intensely bitter.

1841 T. & H. SMITH in *Jrnl. Med. Sc.* Feb., To the new crystalline substance we have given the name of Aloine. **1863** WATTS *Dict. Chem.* I. 148 Caustic and carbonated alkalis dissolve aloïn with a bright yellow colour.

alom(e, obs. form of ALUM.

alomancy, variant of HALOMANCY.

alond(e, obs. form of ALAND.

alone (əˈləʊn), *a.* and *adv.* Forms: 3–4 **al on, al one,** 4 **alle on,** 4–5 **alle one, al oon, all one, (ylone),** 6– **alone;** *north.* 4 **alan,** 4–7 **allane,** 5–9 (*mod. Sc.*) **alane.** [orig. a phraseological comb. of ALL *adv.* 'wholly, quite,' + ONE; emphasizing *oneness* essential or temporary, 'wholly one, one without any companions, one by himself.' App. not earlier than end of 13th c., and long treated as two words. Aphetized in north. dial. to LONE.]

I. As an objective fact.

1. *lit.* Quite by oneself, unaccompanied, solitary. **a.** as extension of predicate.

c **1300** *Beket* 59 Heo wende alone heo nuste whoderward. *c* **1330** *Assumpcion* 456 Al one I hanged on þe tree. *c* **1385** CHAUCER *L.G.W.* 1777 And al a-lone his weye hathe he nome. *c* **1420** *Chron. Vilod.* 120 And in a preveye place all one he lay. **1601** SHAKS. *Jul. C.* III. ii. 60 Good Countrymen, let me depart alone. **1611** BIBLE *Lev.* xiii. 46 He shall dwell alone. **1712** STEELE *Spect.* No. 491 ¶2 She was left alone with him. **1807** CRABBE *Par. Reg.* II. 409 Apart she lived, and still she lives alone. **1845** FORD *Handbk. Spain* i. 43 It is almost impossible to travel alone. **1852** H. ROGERS *Ecl. Faith* 204 It stands alone like the peak of Teneriffe.

b. as compl. to vb. *be.*

1382 WYCLIF *Gen.* ii. 18 It is not good man to be alone. *c* **1440** *Gesta Rom.* lxix. 262 *Ve soli*! Wo be to him that is alle one. **1526** TINDALE *Mark* iv. 10 When he was alone [*so* **1611**; WYCLIF, bi hym self.] **1609** SKENE *Reg. Maj.* 10 Gif the forester is allane: he sall mak ane crosse in the earth. **1646** HOWELL *Lett.* (1650) II. 121, I am never less alone, than when I am alone. **1711** ADDISON *Spect.* No. 12 ¶1 To keep me from being alone. **1798** COLERIDGE *Anc. Mar.* IV. iii, Alone, alone, all, all alone, Alone on a wide wide sea! **1851** RUSKIN *Mod. Paint.* II. III. II. iii. §28 No man's soul is alone: Laocoon or Tobit, the serpent has it by the heart or the angel by the hand.

2. *fig.* **a.** Alone of its kind; having no equal, or fellow; being the sole example; unique; *sui generis. Obs.* exc. as extension of 1.

1535 COVERDALE *Ps.* lxxxii. 18 That thou art alone, that thy name is the Lorde. **1591** SHAKS. *Two Gent.* II. iv. 167 All I can, is nothing, To her, whose worth, make other worthies nothing; Shee is alone. **1712** BUDGELL *Spect.* No. 404 ¶4 Tully would not stand so much alone in Oratory.

b. Alone in action or feeling, having no sharer in one's action, or position.

1297 R. GLOUC. 38 Cunedag was þo al one kyng, & þe kyndom to hym nom. **1382** WYCLIF *John* viii. 16, I am not aloone, but I and the fadir that sent me [*so in* **1611**]. **1752** J. GILL *Trinity* v. 97 Nor am I alone in the sense of this text. **1800** G. TREVYLLION in Trevelyan *Macaulay* (1876) I. i. 10 The young Overseer was not alone in his scruples. **1853** THACKERAY *Engl. Hum.* i. 32 Through life he always seems alone, somehow. *Mod.* You are not alone in that opinion.

†**3.** Formerly often strengthened by a pronoun prefixed, *me al-one* (or *al me one*: see ONE), afterw. esp. in north. dial. (like *me self, my self*) *mine alone, my alone, my* LONE. Now only *dial.*

c **1360** *E.E. Poems* (1862) 119 Ful stille i stod . my self al on. **1375** BARBOUR *Bruce* II. 146 All him alane the way he tais. **1393** GOWER *Conf.* I. 148 He made his mone Within a gardin all him one. **1533** BELLENDENE *Livy* III. (1822) 273 Thus stude Virginia hir allane. **1535** STEWART *Cron. Scotl.* I. 528 At the Hunting, quhair he was him alane. **1578** in *Scot. Poems 16th c.* II. 206 Leif mee not All my Lone, leif mee not Thus mine allone. *a* **1575** *Murning Maidin* in *Laneham's Let.* (1871) Pref. 151, I yow find In this wod walkand your alone. **1588** A. KING *Canisius' Catech.* II. 35 b, I ame myne alane and poore. **1733** RAMSAY *Tea-T. Misc.* (ed. 9) I. 79, I get the other to my lane.

4. To **let** or **leave alone**: *lit.* to leave to himself; to leave persons or things as they are, or to their own efforts; to abstain from interfering or having to do with.

1366 MAUNDEV. xxix. 294 So he let hem allone. *c* **1394** *P. Pl. Crede* 827 Lat the loseles alone. **1413** LYDG. *Pylgr. Sowle* I. i. (1859) 2 Lete me alone to do that my ryght is. **1535** COVERDALE *1 Kings* xx. 6 Shal I go vnto Ramoth to fighte, or shal I let it alone? **1589** *Pasquil's Return* D ij b, Let the Court alone. **1601** SHAKS. *Twel. N.* III. iv. 201 Let me alone for swearing. **1611** BIBLE *Job* xiii. 13 Let me alone that I may speake. **1712** F. T. *Meth. Shorthand* 41 Which Persons may either follow or let alone, as they please. **1850** MRS. STOWE *Uncle Tom's C.* xx. 211 Topsy soon made the household understand the propriety of letting her alone; and she was let alone accordingly.

5. *attrib.* Said of that of which there exists no other example, or whose action is unshared in: Sole, only, unique, exclusive. Now *rare.*

1547 *Homilies* I. ii. II. (1859) 22 He is the alone Mediator between God and man. **1564** BECON *Common-pl. H. Script.* (1844) 299 To know [thee] the alone God. **1569** *Bury Wills* (1850) 155 Whome I make my sole and alone executor. **1633** G. HERBERT *Aaron* in *Temple* 169 Christ is my onely head, My alone onely heart and breast. **1656** SANDERSON *Serm.* (1689) 60 Son of God and alone Saviour of the World. **1668** HOWE *Bless. Right.* (1825) 131 Had this been the alone folly. **1873** GOULBURN *Pers. Relig.* iii. 20 Christ is .. the alone source of sanctification. **1874** BLACKIE *Self-Cult.* 11 The alone keystone of all sane thinking.

6. Taken or acting by itself; of itself, without anything more. †**a.** preceding the sb.: Solitary, isolated, unattended. *Obs.*

1663 *Flagellum, O. Cromwell* (1672) 103 Ascribes it .. to the alone wisdome of God. **1683** GADBURY *Pref. Sir G. Wharton's Wks.*, By this alone Example, the Non-conformist should learn to be obedient. **1772** J. FLETCHER *Log. Genev.* 212 For the alone sake of Christ's atoning blood.

b. following the sb.

1382 WYCLIF *Matt.* iv. 4 A man lyueth not in breed aloon [**1388** oonli; so TINDALE, *Genev.*; **1611** by bread alone]. **1756** C. LUCAS *Ess. Waters* III. 67 This can not be done by the acid alone. **1757** JOHNSON *Rambl.* No. 159 ¶9 He that hopes by philosophy and contemplation alone to fortify himself against that. **1857** BUCKLE *Civiliz.* I. ii. 118 This fact alone must have produced a considerable effect. **1872** YEATS *Techn. Hist. Comm.* 430 Material progress alone will not suffice. **1879** B. TAYLOR *Germ. Lit.* 51 Form, alone, gives us a waxen doll, heartless and brainless.

†**c.** qualifying a possessive. *Obs.*

1611 BIBLE *Rom.* iv. 23 It was not written for his sake alone. **1683** tr. *Erasmus, Moriæ Enc.* 7 Plutus .. at whose alone beck Religion and Civil Policy have been successively undermined and re-established. **1689** *Apol. Fail. Walker's Acc.* 17 These Gentlemen, whose alone Commands could qualifie Mr. Walker to plead.

d. separated from sb. and tending to become adv.

c **1540** *Pract. Cyrurg.*, The flesshe and bone wyl heale alone by nature. **1849** MACAULAY *Hist. Eng.* II. 160 The appointment of a ruined gambler would alone have sufficed to disgust the public. **1863** KEMBLE *Resid. Georgia* 19 Whose .. perfect foliage would alone render it an object of admiration.

7. In all the prec. senses used also of a group or number: By themselves, without other companions.

c **1440** *Morte Arth.* (1819) 34 To the bote they yede with oute stynte, They two allone. **1591** Shaks. *Two Gent.* i. ii. 1 Say Lucetta (now we are alone) Would'st thou then counsaile me to fall in loue? **1824** Byron *Don J.* ii. clxxxviii, They were alone, but not alone as they Who shut in chambers think it loneliness.

II. As a subjective limitation.

8. With no one else in the same predicament; as distinct from any one else; only, exclusively. ***he alone*** came = he came, and no one else did.

a. immed. following the sb.

1330 R. Brunne *Chron.* 138 Not to þe fader alle on, bot tille his heir. *c* **1340** Hampole *Pr. Consc.* 24 For never na God was bot he alan. *c* **1449** Pecock *Repr.* i. ii. 10 Holi Scripture al oon ȝeueth the sufficient kunnyng. **1548** Udall etc. *Erasm. Paraphr. Luke* i. 69 By hym alone and onely. *Ibid.* ii. 30 That he alone and onely might pourge all mankinde. *a* **1600** *King & Barker* in Ritson *Anc. P.P.* 62 The tanner thowt, the Kyng ylone thes be. **1611** Bible *Dan.* x. 7, I Daniel alone saw the vision. **1729** Burkitt *On N.T.* Matt. xxv. 45 Man, and man alone, is the cause of his own destruction. **1788** Franklin *Autobiog.* Wks. 1840 I. 165 The citizens alone should be at the expense of it. **1790** Burke *Fr. Rev.* 11 Not of the affairs of France alone, but of all Europe. **1849** Macaulay *Hist. Eng.* I. 223 Clifford, who, alone of the five, had any claim to be regarded as an honest man. **1854** Thackeray *Newc.* I. xxi. 197 It is not youth alone that has need to learn humility.

b. preceding or separated from the sb. (hence tending to *adv.*)

c **1400** *Apol. for Loll.* 110 Alon he vsiþ ministry. Alon he chalangiþ to him all þingis. Alon he assoyliþ oþer partyes. **1602** Shaks. *Haml.* i. ii. 77 'Tis not alone my Inky Cloake, (good Mother). **1702** Pope *Sapho* 14 Music has charms alone for peaceful minds. **1817** Coleridge *Sib. Leaves* (1862) 125 That malignity of heart, which could alone have prompted sentiments so atrocious. **1878** Seeley *Stein* III. 515 Always and alone he blames the Reaction.

9. *adv.* Referring to vb., adj., phr. or clause: Only, solely, merely, simply, exclusively.

a **1300** *Cursor M.* 451 Hetlik he lette of ilk fere To godd self wald he be pere; Noght pere allan, bot mikul mare, For vndur him he wald all ware, And be him self þair comandur. **1661** Heylin *Hist. Ref.* II. iii. 74 These prayers..were not alone thought necessary for all sorts of people..but used both by Priest and People. **1697** Dryden *Virg. Georg.* ii. 515 Whose Leaves are not alone foul Winter's Prey, But oft by Summer Suns are scorch'd away. **1850** Tennyson *In Mem.* cxiii, Wisdom..Which not alone had guided me, But served the seasons that may rise.

10. *Comb.* **alone-liver**, one who lives alone.

1553 Grimald *Cicero's Offices* (1556) 77 Even to the alone-liver, and one that leades his life in the feeldes.

† **alonely** (əˈləʊnlɪ), *a.* and *adv. Obs.* Forms: 3–5 **al only**, 3–6 **allonly**, 3–7 **all only**, 4 **al onli, al oonly, alonlich**, 4–5 **aloonly**, 4–7 **allonelye**, 5–6 **alonly, -lie**, 5–7 **alonely**, 6 **alonelie, al(l)onlye, all onelie**, 6–7 **all onely**, 9 **alonely**. [phraseol. comb. of all *adv.* 'wholly, quite, altogether' + only; hence, orig., emphatic form of *only*. Not in use bef. end of 13th c., OE. using the simple *ánlíc*, (only). Obs. in 17th c., though used by Lamb. Aphetized in north. dial. to lonely.]

1. *adv.* restricting vb., adj., adv. or predication: Only, solely, exclusively, merely.

1303 R. Brunne *Handl. Synne* 6826 Ȝyve..nat allonely largely, But wyþ loue. *c* **1360** Wyclif *De Eccl.* Pref. 32 Not al oonly in defaut of cornys but in beestis & oþer good. **1366** Maundev. *Voy.* i. 6 Alle only summe Contrees. **1484** Caxton *Chyualry* 27 Nat al only contrarye to the ordre and offyce of Chyualrye but also, etc. *a* **1564** Becon *New Year's Gift* Wks. 1843, 342 Alonely walk before me, and be perfect. **1577** H. Bull tr. *Luther's Comm. Ps. Grad.* 233 Our life resteth wholly and alonely in the Remission of Sins. **1600** Fairfax *Tasso* xvi. xlvii. 289 All only let me goe with thee.

2. *adv.* Solitarily, by himself.

1525 Ld. Berners *Froissart* II. cxx. 344 And so rode but alonely with his page. **1608** *Commun. Sick*, In time of Plague ..upon speciall request of the diseased, the Minister may alonely communicate with him.

3. *adv.* (or *adj.*) restricting the subj. or obj. of a predication: Only, solely; (such a person or thing) and no other; without any one (or any thing) else. **a.** separate from sb.

1366 Maundev. i. 8 He hathe lost alle, but Grece, and that Lond he holt alle only. *c* **1440** *Gesta Rom.* xxvii. 355 In the house alle only of Jonathas he founde fire and watir. **1480** Caxton *Chron. Eng.* iii. (1520) 24/1 Beloved of God and man, and not alonely with good men, but evyll men also. **1541** Barnes *Wks.* (1573) 227/2 The lambe hath alonely dyed for vs: The lambe hath alonely shed his bloud for vs: The lambe hath alonly redeemed vs. *a* **1617** Hieron *Wks.* I. 13 The grand guide, whose directions are alonely to bee looked vnto. **1823** Lamb *Elia* Ser. ii. viii. (1865) 290 The sole and single eye of distemper alonely fixed upon itself.

b. following the sb.

1382 Wyclif *2 Chron.* xxiii. 6 Thei aloonly commen in, that ben halowed. *c* **1450** *Merlin* 49 Merlin, whiche is the wysest man that is in all the worlde, saf god al only. **1483** Caxton *Cato* B viij b, For many to gyder seen more clerely thenne doth one allonelye. **1494** Fabyan vi. clxxix. 177 London alonely excepted. **1564** Bauldwin *Mor. Philos.* (ed. Palfr.) ix. (1595) 4 The truth alonely among all things is priviledged. **1625** *Gonsalvio's Sp. Inquis.* 197 Faith, wherewith alonely he encourageth and emboldneth man before the face of God.

c. preceding the sb.

c **1325** *E.E. Allit. P.* A. 778 Al only þyself so stout and styf. *c* **1440** *Gesta Rom.* 49 [He] asked no thing with here, but alonly here bodie, and here clothing. **1494** Fabyan vi. cxlvii. 133 Promysynge to hym not allonely victory, but also the lond. **1587** Fleming *Contn. Holinshed* III. 1291/1 And this alonelie word was heard: Here comes the pearle of grace. **1634** *Malory's Arthur* (1816) II. 454 All the lords were right glad..save all only sir Gawaine.

4. *adj. attrib.* **a.** Sole, only; beside which there is no other.

1494 Fabyan vii. 438 Isabell the allonly doughter & chylde of Phylyppe le Beawe. **1604** *Suppl. Masse-Priests* § 1 The Catholike Romaine faith, the all onely meane of saving our soules. **1612** Wither *Pr. Hen. Obseq.* in *Juven.* (1633) 303 The alonely comfort of his own.

b. Unparalleled in degree, unequalled, unique.

1567 Jewel *Def. Apol.* (1611) 341 Your High and alonely Bishop, and the Bishop of all Bishops. **1571** —— *Exp. 2 Thess.* ii. 42 This is the alonely mysterie aboue all other mysteries. **1587** Fleming *Contn. Holinshed* III. 316/1 Know yee therefore alonelie princesse.

c. Exclusive, singular. *rare.*

1567 Jewel *Def. Apol.* (1611) 357 The speciall and alonely office of Loue, of things common to make things peculiar.

d. Solitary, lonely. *rare.*

a **1622** H. Ainsworth *Annot. Psalms* xxii. 21 My alonely soule, which is one alone, solitary, and desolate.

aloneness (əˈləʊnnɪs). [f. alone + -ness.]

1. The quality or state of being alone or solitary; solitariness, solitude, loneliness.

1382 Wyclif *Joel* ii. 3 After hym aloonenesse [**1388** wildirnesse] of desert. **1564** Haward *Eutropius* vii. 74 Every manne had bewailed his owne private losse and alonenesse. **1625** Bp. Mountagu *App. Cæsar* 61 (T.) God being sibi solus..did communicate himself out of his Alonenesse euerlasting unto somewhat else. **1675** T. Brooks *Gold. Key* Wks. 1867 V. 588 Don't talk of thy solitariness and aloneness. **1866** *Cornh. Mag.* Aug. 134 A sharp, sudden thorn of aloneness and utter forlornness. **1877** J. Legge *Life Confucius* 44 Watchful over his aloneness.

along (əˈlɒŋ), *a.*[1] *arch.* and *dial.* Forms: 1 **ȝelang, ȝelong**, 2–4 **ilong**, 4 **ylong**, 4–5 **alonge**, 4– **along**, 6– **all long, 'long**. [OE. *ȝelang*, cogn. with OS., OHG. *gilang*. The prefix sank by 14th c. to *ă-*, which from 16th onwards was frequently dropped: see long.] In prep. phr. *along of* (formerly 1–5 *on*, in OE. *æt*): (*a*) pertaining, belonging, chargeable, attributable, owing to; on account of; common in London, and southern dialects generally); (*b*) (together) with; cf. along *adv.* 3.

c **880** K. Ælfred *Oros.* iv. x. § 9 Ðæt wæs swiðor on ðam ȝelang. *a* **1000** Ælfric *Gen.* xlvii. 25 Æt þé is úre lýf ȝelang. *a* **1000** *Gúðlac* 223 On heofonum sind láre ȝelonge. *c* **1175** *Lamb. Hom.* 195 Vor o ðe is al ilong mi lif. *c* **1300** *Beket* 1644 The strif is on the Ilong. *c* **1374** Chaucer *Troylus* ii. 1001 On me is not along thin evil fare. *c* **1380** *Sir Ferumb.* 4292 Hit ys no þyng on hymen ylong þat y ne hadde y-lost Rolond. **1489** Caxton *Faytes of Armes* i. viii. 19 Whome it is alonge or causeth. **1530** Palsgr. 427/2, I am longe of this stryfe: *je suis en cause de cest estrif.* *c* **1570** Thynne *Pride & Lowl.* (1841) 56 The villain sayth it is all long of me. **1602** *Return fr. Parnass.* (Arb.) Prol. 3 Its all long on you. **1611** Shaks. *Cymb.* v. v. 271 Oh, she was naught; and long of her it was That we meet heere so strangely. **1767** H. Brooke *Fool of Qual.* (1792) II. 88 'Tis all along of you that I am thus haunted. **1805** Scott *Last Minstr.* v. xxix, Dark Musgrave, it was long of thee! **1848** Dickens *Dombey* 496 An't my heart been heavy and watchful along of him and you? **1872** Black *Adv. Phaeton* xxii. 312 That was all along of Bell. **1881** *Atlantic Monthly* June 742/2 'Pears to me ez ye mought hev brought him hyar ter eat his supper along of us, sidelin' a-leavin' him a-grievin' over his dead wife. **1886** Baumann *Londinismen* 3/1 Being friendly along o' you..He sleeps along o' me. **1906** Kipling *Puck of Pook's Hill* 252 A present from the Gentlemen, along o' being good! **1929** Galsworthy *Exiled* ii. 78 There's a good few round 'ere wantin' your blood, along o' closin' pits. **1940** J. Cary *Charley is my Darling* xxx. 177 You come along a me, Ginger, and we'll get another cave. **1963** N. Marsh *Dead Water* (1964) vii. 178 'The trouble I've had along of that lady's crankiness,' he confided, 'you'd never credit.'

along (əˈlɒŋ), (*a.*[2]), *adv.* and *prep.* Forms: 1 **and-, ond-, -lang, -long**, 1–3 **on-, an-long**, (3 **on longen**), 4–5 **allonge**, 4–6 **alonge**, 4– **along**. *Aphetic* 4–7 **long**. [OE. *and-lang*, f. *and-* against, facing, in a direction opposite + *lang* long. At first an *adj.* (cf. *eást-lang* extending eastward) = 'extending away in the opposite direction, far-stretching, extended, continuous,' then used with gen. case as 'the lengthened or continuous extent of,' 'the whole length of,' 'the long way of,' or *absol.* 'the long way,' 'lengthwise.' To some extent mixed with the ON. cogn. *end-lang*, adopted in north. dial. (see endlong).]

† **A.** *adj.* (only in OE.) Extending lengthwise, long-extended, livelong. Afterwards merged in *all long*: as *andlonge niht, al-longe night*, now *all night long*; cf. all day *over*, all the year *through*.

a **1000** *Andreas* 1276 Wæs andlangne dæȝ swungen. *c* **1000** *Gúðlac* 1261 Andlonge niht. *c* **1300** *Beket* 403 Al alonge day. *c* **1300** *St. Brandan* 595 Oure Maister ous hath i turmented so grisliche allonge niȝt. *c* **1325** *E.E. Allit. P.* B. 476 Dreȝly alle alonge day þat dorst neuer lyȝt.

B. *prep.* Orig. the adj. used absol. or advb. with a dependent genitive. Cf. *ahead of*, etc. Through gradual disappearance of the genitive ending the dependent word appears at length as a true *object*.

1. Through the whole or entire length of; from end to end of (whether *within*, as a valley, or *by the side of*, as a river). Afterwards strengthened ***all along***: all through the course of.

935 *Charter* in *Cod. Dipl.* V. 220 Upp andlang Ocerburnan tó hálelan mærscæ éasteweardan andlang brócæs. *c* **1000** Ælfric *Lev.* i. 15 Læte yrnan ðæt blod nyðer andlang ðæs weofudes. **1205** Layam. 19677 þas swiken þer heo sæten on longen þere streten. **1483** Caxton *Gold. Leg.* 439/4 He swete blood allonge his body. **1660** South *Serm.* (1843) II. 67 Christ's design all along the Evangelists. **1726** Thomson *Winter* 186 The whirling Tempest raves along the plain. **1808** Scott *Marm.* i. v, Along the bridge Lord Marmion rode. **1827** Keble *Chr. Year* 6 Sprinkled along the waste of years.

2. This passes imperceptibly into an indication of *direction* rather than *space traversed*: Through any part of the length of, lengthwise through or parallel to, as distinguished from *across*; following the line of (a road, wall, river, sea-shore, etc.)

887 *O.E. Chron.*, Her for se here up..andlang Siȝene oþ Mæterne. **1509** Hawes *Past. Pleas.* xx. i, They sayled Alonge the haven. **1600** Fairfax *Tasso* i. lxxviii. 4 The armed ships, coasting along the shore. **1611** Bible *1 Sam.* vi. 12 The kine..went along the high way, lowing as they went. **1751** Johnson *Rambl.* No. 187 ¶ 9 Stealing slow and heavy laden along the coast. **1818** Hallam *Mid. Ages* (1841) I. 367 Before..the first lances of France gleam along the defiles of the Alps. *c* **1858** R. Hoyt *Snow*, 'Tis winter, yet there is no sound Along the air Of winds along their battle ground. **1879** Tennyson *Lover's T.* 80 We roam'd along the dreary coast.

3. Lying or placed parallel to the length of.

1205 Lay. 138 Muche lond he him ȝef..an long þare sea. **1667** Milton *P.L.* vii. 328 Each fountain side, With borders long the Rivers. **1697** *Lond. Gaz.* mmmccccxviii/3 The biggest, a Ship of 60 or 64 Guns, came along our side. **1877** Lytteil *Landm.* iii. iii. 110 Along the line of which there are still several out-standing pikes or spink-rocks.

C. *adv.* [The prep. with the object not expressed.]

1. a. In a line with the length, parallel to the longest dimension or course (of something understood); lengthwise, longitudinally. Now only with *by*, and as in 2.

1366 Maundev. v. 45 The contree is sett along upon the ryvere of Nyle. *c* **1420** *Anturs Arth.* xxxvii, Thay sette listes on lenthe olong on the lawnde. **1541** R. Copland *Guydon's Quest. Cyrurg.*, He ought to open it alonge and ouerthwart this way and that. **1556** *Chron. Grey Friars* 61 The gardyns that was made a longe by the walles of the citte. **1611** Bible *Numb.* xx. 17 We will not turne into the fields..but we will goe along by the kings high way. *Mod.* We found plenty of primroses along by the hedge.

b. Some way on (in the progress of time). *U.S.*

1870 'Mark Twain' *More Distinction* in *Sketches* (1872) 282 In the one case, you start out with a friend along about eleven o'clock. **1883** —— *Life Mississippi* xxviii, Far along in the day, we saw one steamboat. **1886** *Harper's Mag.* Oct. 808/1 He come to the house 'long in the first part of the evenin'. **1897** 'Mark Twain' *Following Equator* xxi. 290 He was along toward fifty. **1902** *N.Y. Tribune* 26 Apr. 82 The afternoon was well along by this time.

c. *along back*: at or for some time in the past. *U.S.*

1851 N. Kingsley *Diary* (1914) 165 Worked as usual to-day, took out 50 ounces and 4 dollars, which gains on our days along back. **1880** *Harper's Mag.* Dec. 85/1 She's had an easy time along back, but she's seen the last on't.

d. *right along*: continuously; without interruption. *U.S.*

1856 *Mich. Agric. Soc. Trans.* VII. 806 His corn grew right along, for it could not help it. **1936** Wodehouse *Laughing Gas* xiv. 150 'And you come from England?' 'Yes.' 'London?' 'Yes.' 'Lived there right along, I guess?'

2. a. With vbs. of motion: Onward in the course or line of motion, progressively on. Also *fig.* in phr. ***to get along***: to get on, advance in any business, or in life. ***get along!***: 'pass on! be off!'

c **1300** *K. Alis.* 3410 Ten myle they yeode alang. **1601** Shaks. *Jul. C.* iv. ii. 33 Speak the word along. **1610** —— *Temp.* iv. i. 233 Let's along [*v.r.* alone] And doe the murther first. **1664** Butler *Hudibr.* ii. iii. 389 No porter's Burthen past along But serv'd for Burthen to his Song. **1767** Fordyce *Serm. Yng. Wom.* I. vii. 298 The shallow stream runs babbling along. **1821** Keats *Isabel* xxv, As he to the court-yard pass'd along. **1830** S. Smith *Sel. Lett. J. Downing* (1834) 34, I wish you'd write me..whether you think I could get along with the business [of Governorship]. **1837** [see get *v.* 59 b]. **1837** Dickens *Pickw.* xiv. 135 Get along with you, you wretch, said the handmaiden. **1850** Mrs. Stowe *Uncle Tom's C.* xvi. 153 But she'll get along in heaven better than you or I. *a* **1884** *Colloq.* That's enough; go along with you!

b. *to be along*, to come to a place, to call, to arrive.

1831 Mrs. Holley *Texas* (1833) 21 The captain..sent word that he would be along for us about sun-set. **1892** 'Mark Twain' *Amer. Claimant* xvi. 162 They'll be along as soon as it's done. **1951** 'J. Wyndham' *Day of Triffids* i, Any time now they'd be along with pneumatic drills. **1959** N. Kneale *Quatermass Exper.* iv. 114 The official pathologists' report should be along in half an hour.

3. ***along with.*** **a.** orig. with vb. of motion: Onward *with*, on the way *with*, in company *with*.

1592 Shaks. *Rom. & Jul.* i. i. 106 You, Capulet, shall go along with me. **1596** —— *Merch. V.* ii. viii. 2 With him is Gratiano gone along. **1615** Bedwell tr. *Moham. Imp.* i. § 40 Go along with vs on our iourney. **1712** Addison *Spect.* No. 494 ¶ 5 The spies bringing along with them the clusters of grapes. *c* **1800** Dibdin, Then I must lug you along with me, Says the saucy Arethusa. **1879** Froude *Cæsar* x. 115 Too shrewd to go along with them upon a road.

b. Together *with*, in association *with*. (Here *along* attaches to *with* rather than to the vb.)

1711 ADDISON *Spect.* No. 29 ¶11 This Inclination of the Audience to sing along with the Actors. **1768** STERNE *Sent. Journ.* (1778) I. 86, I would rejoice along with them. **1859** GEN. P. THOMPSON *Audi Alt. Part.* II. App. 97 A hunger for news of killed and wounded, along with shrimps, at breakfast. **1876** FREEMAN *Norm. Conq.* IV. xvii. 64 Wiltshire had most likely submitted along with Hampshire and Berkshire.

c. Side by side *with*, in conjunction *with*.

1817 JAS. MILL *Brit. Ind.* II. v. iv. 467 Along with this he was mild and equitable. **1840** GLADSTONE *Ch. Princ.* 6 Recognising along with, though subordinately to, the Scriptures, the authorised interpretations of primitive Christian antiquity. **1868** G. DUFF *Pol. Surv.* 1, I must ask all..to read what I shall say to-night, along with what I said on the 19th December last.

4. *ellipt.* (*with* omitted, but the force it has imparted to *along* retained.) In company, as a companion, with (some one).

1590 SHAKS. *Mids. N.* v. i. 123 Demetrius and Egeus go along: I must imploy you in some business. **1668** PEPYS *Diary* 5 Nov., We did all along conclude upon answers. **1682** N. O. tr. *Boileau's Le Lutrin* II. 182 The Knave had wit in's Anger, And wisely took along his rusty Hanger.

[*Amer. colloq.* **1882** HOWELLS *Lady of Aroostook* 137 'Our Captain's wife..was not along,' said Lydia. 'Not along?' repeated Mrs. Erwin..'Who were the other passengers?']

5. all along: during the whole course of any proceeding, throughout, continuously.

1670 BAXTER *Cure Ch.-div.* 280 The same all along I may say about the Relicts of Martyrs. **1674** MARVELL *Reh. Transp.* II. 257 To have to do with such a man all along and thorow. *c* **1680** BEVERIDGE *Serm.* (1729) I. 76 The Bishops..have..continued all allong from the apostles. **1712** ADDISON *Spect.* No. 463 ¶8, I have all along declared this to be a Neutral Paper. **1861** HOOK *Lives Abps.* I. vi. 310 The Church..had been all along, the point of centralisation. **1876** FREEMAN *Norm. Conq.* II. vii. 123 This impost was all along felt to be a great burthen.

6. Lengthwise, in regard to a thing itself; at full length. Often strengthened with *all*. *Obs.*

1413 LYDGATE *Pilgr. Sowle* III. ix. (1483) 55 These were leyd a long vpon a table. **1483** CAXTON *G. de la Tour* civ b, He began to drawe it oute a long with his teeth. **1535** COVERDALE *2 Kings* iv. 35 [Elisha] went up, and layed him selfe a longe vpon him. **1592** SHAKS. *Rom. & Jul.* v. iii. 3 Vnder yond young Trees lay thee all along. **1637** GILLESPIE *Eng.-Pop. Cerem.* IV. vi. 29 The usuall table gesture of the Iewes, was lying along. **1670** T. BROOKS *Wks.* (1867) VI. 441 He that foots it best may be sometimes found all along, and the neatest person may sometimes slip into a slough. **1761** SMOLLETT *Gil Blas* (1802) II. VII. xvi. 330 My nurse laid me all along again.

†**7.** *fig.* At length, in full. (? Confused with Fr. *au long.*) *Obs.*

1461 *Past. Lett.* 409 II. 38, I enformyd hem the mater along. **1481** CAXTON *Myrr.* I. xiii. 42 We shal declare a litil our matere a longe. **1485** —— *Paris & Vienne* 56 And redde it al allonge. **1506** *Ord. Cryst. Men* (W. de Worde) IV. iv. 173 And this mater declareth ryght a longe saynt Bernarde. **1588** J. MELLIS *Briefe Instr.* E vij b, You shal make the marchandise or goods Debitor..with all the particular parcels, along.

†**8.** At a distance, afar. (Perh. confused with Fr. *au loin.*) *Obs.*

a **1300** *E.E. Psalter* ix. 22 Wherto, Lord, wentist thou awei along? [WYCLIF, fer awei]. **1580** TUSSER *Husb.* xix. 25 Exceptions take of the champion land, from lieng alonge from that at thy hand.

9. *Comb.* (with object), as †**along-board**, along-side (of a ship); **along-ships**, lengthwise to the ship, directed fore and aft. Also ALONG-SIDE, -SHORE, q.v.

1548 HALL *Chron.* 534 The Regent crappeled with her along boord. **1687** *Lond. Gaz.* mmcclvi/4 His Men on his Bowsprit and his Sprissel-yards along Ships, all ready to Board us.

†**a'long,** *v.*[1] *Obs.* [OE. *alangian* (f. A- *pref.* 1 intens. + *langian* to last, endure; cf. OHG. *arlangen*); only used impersonally. The pa. pple. *alonged* seems to represent the OE. *of-langed* afflicted with longing, wearied with desire, f. *of-langian*. See LONG *v.*]

1. *impers.* To seem long to, to affect with longing.

a **1000** *Departed Soul* (Grein) 154 Me alangaþ, þæs þe ic þe on þissum hýndum wát. **1393** GOWER *Conf.* II. 237 This worthy Jason sore alongeth, To se the straunge regions.

2. *pass.* To be afflicted with longing, to long.

c **1325** *Cœur de L.* 3060 Afftyr pork he alongyd is. *a* **1400** *Leg. Rood* (1871) 23 He was alonged sore After þe Oyle of Milce. *c* **1400** *Gamelyn* 630 He was sore alonged after a good meel.

†**a'long,** *v.*[2] *Obs. rare.* [f. ALONG *adv.* 8, probably by form-assoc. with Fr. *éloigner*, to remove: cf. ALOYNE.] To put at a distance, remove far.

1506 *Ord. Cryst. Men* (W. de Worde) v. vii. 419 The bodye gloryous may not along hym from the presence of god.

alongshore (ə'lɒŋ'ʃɔə(r)), *adv. phr. Naut.* [f. ALONG *prep.* + SHORE.]

1. Along by the shore; on the water 'in a course which is in sight of the shore and nearly parallel to it.' Adm. Smyth.

1779 T. FORREST *Voy. N. Guinea* 50 In steering along-shore, the island..that makes the harbour, may be easily perceived. **1849** GROTE *Greece* (1862) V. II. lvii. 118 The Syracusans..rowed close along-shore. *Ibid.*, Seamanship was of no avail in this along-shore fighting.

2. Along and *on* the shore. (See the aphetic 'LONG-SHORE.)

alongside (ə'lɒŋ'saɪd), *adv.* and *prep.* [properly a phrase, ALONG *prep.* + SIDE.]

A. *adv.* Along or parallel to the side (*of* something expressed or understood). **a.** *simply*, Close to the side of the ship.

1707 *Lond. Gaz.* mmmmccclxxx/2 The Enemy would not come up a long Side. **1769** DOUGLAS in *Phil. Trans.* LX. 41 A case, filled with water from along-side. **1798** COLERIDGE *Anc. Mar.* III. 13 The naked hulk alongside came. **1833** MARRYAT *Pet. Simp.* (1863) 207 'I thought, Mr. Simple, that you knew by this time how to bring a boat alongside.' **1851** DIXON *Will. Penn* xvii. (1872) 149 The boat-men..used their oars as if they had been ordered to come alongside.

b. with *of*: Parallel to or close by the side of, side by side with; also *fig.*

1781 *Westm. Mag.* IX. 167 We chased, and at noon got along-side of her. **1822** T. JEFFERSON *Writ.* (1830) IV. 347 A new authority, marching independently along-side of the government. **1870** HAWTHORNE *Eng. Note-Bks.* (1879) I. 264 Alongside of a sheet of water. **1870** YEATS *Nat. Hist. Comm.* 74 And the fig attains perfection almost alongside of the oak and fir. **1876** FREEMAN *Norm. Conq.* I. v. 264 Alongside of him stood his maternal uncle. *Ibid.* V. xxiv. 385 Alongside of reliefs and wardships, the Danegeld was duly levied.

B. *prep.* [*of* omitted.] In a position parallel to; side by side with.

1793 SMEATON *Edystone L.* §100 A boat..lying alongside the rock. **1866** G. MACDONALD *Ann. Q. Neigh.* xxvi. 448 She only bowed and kept alongside her companion. **1875** BUCKLAND *Log-Bk.* 90 Hauled up alongside a barge.

†**a'longst,** *prep.* and *adv. Obs.* or *dial.* [orig. *alonges*, f. ALONG with advb. genitive *-es* (see also ENDLONGS); but very early corrupted to *alongest*, *alongst*, as if it were a superlative form, which perhaps also led to its being considered more emphatic. Cf. *against*, *amongst*, *amidst*, *betwixt*, etc.]

A. *prep.*

1. Down or through the length of (in contrast to *across*, *athwart*).

1250 LAY. 19677 þar isete in langes [**1205** on longen] þane strete. **1470** HARDING *Chron.* ccxlii, Passe alongest the brydge. **1533** WRIOTHESLEY *Chron.* (1875) I. 21 Fower other tables alongest the hall. **1587** TURBERVILLE *Trag. T.* (1837) 30 Alongst the lawnde he kest his eye. **1600** CHAPMAN *Iliad* IV. 227 The herald flew From troop to troop along'st the host. *c* **1630** DRUMM. OF HAWTH. *James II*, Wks. 1711, 29 At a horse's tail, is dragg'd alongst the streets.

2. By the side of, close by, parallel to.

1580 C. HODDESDON in T. Wright *Q. Eliz.* (1838) II. 115 The malecontents..alongest the frontiers. **1588** CAVENDISH in Beveridge *Hist. Ind.* (1858) I. I. ix. 210 Alongst the coast of Chili. **1598** SYLVESTER *Du Bartas* I. i. (1641) 2/1 But 'longst the shore..must coast. **1614** RALEIGH *Hist. World* I. 129 Should send Gallies alongst the Coast of the Red Sea. **1633** H. COGAN *Pinto's Voy.* liv. 212 By Land alongst the Rivers side. **1839** STONEHOUSE *Axholme* 68 Alongst both sides screens, formed of reeds, are set up.

B. *adv.*

1. In the direction of the length of anything, onwards by the side of something.

1550 NICOLL *Thucyd.* 68 (R.) To sayle alongest by the lande. **1575** TURBERVILLE *Bk. Venerie* 156 They follow a furrow, rowting and worming all alongst by some balke. **1599** HAKLUYT *Voy.* II. II. 329 And plied vp alongst till we came within seuen or eight leagues to Cape Trepointes. *Ibid.* II. 105 This coast all alongst is very lowe.

2. Lengthwise (in contrast to *athwart*).

1562 BULLEYN *Dial. Sorenes* 14 b, Thinsisscion must be made..alongest. **1737** OZELL *Rabelais* I. I. xliii. 297 Striking athwart and alongst, and every way.

3. In company; side by side, together *with*: cf. ALONG *adv.* 3.

1773 MONBODDO *Lang.* I. I. vi. 58 Thus far the brute goes alongst with us. *c* **1817** HOGG *Tales & Sk.* V. 27 The unaccountable monster actually tried to get in alongst with them.

4. On to, or as far as, a place otherwise indicated.

1650 DUNDAS in Carlyle *Cromw.* (1871) III. 94 Such I hope you will permit to come alongst at the first opportunity.

5. *Comb.* **alongst-ships** = along-ships: see ALONG *adv.* 9.

1628 DIGBY *Voy. Medit.* (1868) 5 Brought her spritsaile yarde alongst shippes.

aloof (ə'luːf), *adv.* (orig. *phr.*), *a.* and *prep.* Forms: 6 **a loofe, a luf, alowfe, aloufe,** 6–7 **a loof, aloofe, alooff,** 6– **aloof.** [f. A *prep.*[1] + LOOF, luff, weather-gage, windward direction; perh. immed. from Du. *loef*, in *te loef* to windward, *loef houden* to keep the luff, etc.; cf. Dan. *luv*, Sw. *lof*, perh. also from Du. The orig. meaning of Du. *loef*, and connexion with ME. *lof, loof*, some kind of rudder or apparatus for steering (see Sir F. Madden, notes to Layamon, III. 476), are not clear: see Skeat s.v. *Aloof* and *Luff*. From the idea of keeping a ship's head to the wind, and thus *clear of* the lee-shore or quarter towards which she might drift, came the general sense of 'steering clear of,' or 'giving a wide berth to' anything with which one might otherwise come into contact. See also LUFF.]

A. *adv.*

†**1. a.** *phr. Naut.* The order to the steersman to turn the head of the ship towards the wind, or to make her sail nearer the wind. *Obs.*; now LUFF.

1549 *Compl. Scotl.* vi. 41 Than the master cryit on the rudir man, mait keip ful and by, a luf. **1587** GASCOIGNE *Wks.* 165 Aloofe, aloofe then cryed the master out. **1620** J. TAYLOR (Water P.) *Praise of Hempseed* 12 Aluffe; clap helme a lee. **1678** PHILLIPS, *Aloofe*, a term used in conding the Ship, when she goes upon a Tack, commonly spoken by the Condoy unto the Steersman, when he doth not keep so near the wind as she may ly. **1867** SMYTH *Sailor's Word-bk.*, *Aloof*, The old word for 'Keep your luff' in the act of sailing to the wind.

b. *fig.*

1775 SHERIDAN *Duenna* I. iii. 319, I thought that dragon's front of thine would cry aloof to the sons of gallantry.

2. *adv. Naut.* Away to the windward. *to spring aloof*: see LUFF.

1532 MORE *Confut. Barnes* VIII. Wks. 1557, 759/2 This anker lyeth to farre aloufe fro thys shyppe. **1592** WYRLEY *Armorie* 33 A looffe to winde-ward all our Nauie wride [= wry-ed], To view the turne right goodlie was the sight. **1725** POPE *Odyss.* IX. 635 With all our force we kept aloof to sea. **1762** FALCONER *Shipw.* II. 817 Whene'er loud thund'ring on the leeward shore, While yet aloof, we hear the breakers roar. *Ibid.* II. 189 She springs aloof once more.

3. Hence *gen.* Of position: Away at some distance (*from*), with a clear space intervening, apart; *esp.* with the vbs. *hold, keep, sit, stand.*

c **1540** J. CROKE *Ps.* cii. (1844) 20 No frende draweth nere, I syt alowfe. **1548** UDALL, etc. *Erasm. Paraphr., Mark* xiv. 54 Howbeit he folowed Jesus aloofe. **1611** BIBLE *Ps.* xxxviii. 11 My louers and my friends stand a loofe from my sore [COVERDALE a farre]. **1614** RALEIGH *Hist. World* III. 100 With troups of the light-armed shot and slingers, compelled the enemie to lie a-loof. **1647** CORBETT *Iter Bor.* 270 Wee care not for those glorious lampes aloofe. **1791** COWPER *Iliad* V. 562 They stand aloof Quaking. **1849** MACAULAY *Hist. Eng.* I. 328 He quitted his seat, and stood aloof. **1878** EMERSON *Sov. Ethics* in *N. Amer. Rev.* CXXVI. 406 Heat is not separate, light is not massed aloof.

4. Of action: From a distance; not at close quarters.

a **1547** EARL SURREY *Æneid* IV. (R.) The stricken hinde..which chasing with his darte Aloofe the shepheard smiteth. **1568** *Like will to Like* in Hazl. *Dods.* III. 311 Then speak aloof, for to come nigh I am afraid. **1600** HOLLAND *Livy* XXXVIII. xxi. 996 k, Certaine speares to use aloofe [*eminus*]. **1622** BACON *Henry VII*, 105 Untill he had first aloofe seene the Crosse set up. **1671** MILTON *P.R.* v. 310 The lion and fierce tiger glared aloof. **1830** TENNYSON *Ode to Mem.*, Purple cliffs, aloof descried.

5. *fig.* Without community of action or feeling. *esp.* in phr. **to stand, keep, hold aloof** (*from*): to hold back, keep clear; to take no part in, show no sympathy with.

1583 BABINGTON *Wks.* 399 [Lying]..maketh them hang aloofe, suspect, and bee strange one to another. **1602** SHAKS. *Ham.* v. ii. 258, I stand aloofe, and will no reconcilement. **1781** COWPER *Charity* 59 God stood not, though he seemed to stand, aloof. **1790** BURKE *Fr. Rev.* 132 We felt for them as men; but we kept aloof from them. **1838** THIRLWALL *Greece* V. xliii. 287 Sparta it seems kept aloof from this struggle. **1859** MASSON *Milton* I. 635 The English Puritans held aloof at this time from the poor sectaries. **1879** FARRAR *St. Paul* I. 236 Peter was not the man to stand coldly aloof.

†**6.** In senses 3, 4, 5, 7, formerly strengthened by *off*. (Cf. clear off, far off.) *Obs.*

1571 DIGGES *Geomet. Pract.* I. xxx, You desire with shotte to beat the enemie aloofe of. **1579** TOMSON *Calvin's Serm. Tim.* 130/2 He withdraweth him selfe, and keepeth him selfe a loofe off. **1618** *Hist. P. Warbeck* in *Harl. Misc.* (1793) 82 A true woman's part..in standing a-loof off from what I most desire. **1665** BOYLE *Occas. Refl.* (1675) 345 Those that gaze at them aloof off. **1674** N. FAIRFAX *Bulk & Selv.* 106 He could not feel himself, whilst playing aloof off, to have wheeled about into the selfsame snare.

7. As *compl.* or *pred.*: At a distance; distant; hence, detached, unsympathetic.

1607 BACON *Ess., Empire* (Arb.) 298 Solid and grounded Courses to keepe them [dangers] aloofe. **1642** ROGERS *Naaman* 548 When he is aloofe to others, they shall haue familiar accesse. **1789** MRS. PIOZZI *France & It.* I. 78 To keep infection aloof. **1845** TRENCH *Huls. Lect.* Ser. I. vi. 96 Psalms become our own which before were aloof from us. **1872** GEO. ELIOT *Middlem.* III. VI. lviii. 287 What that cleverness was—what was the shape into which it had run as into a close network aloof and independent. **1934** H. NICOLSON *Curzon: Last Phase* 8 His public manner..created the legend of a man, conceited, reactionary, unbending and aloof.

B. Hence *attrib.* as *adj.* Distant (*obs. rare*), also, detached, unsympathetic.

1608 CHAPMAN *Byron's Trag.* Wks. 1873 II. 271 These aloofe abodes. **1642** ROGERS *Naaman* 8 A Prophet not to vouchsafe to come..but to send an aloofe message. **1893** A. J. BALFOUR in *Daily News* 27 Apr. 6/7 Democracy..perhaps required the cold and aloof reasoning of a statesman like Lord Derby. **1913** *Stage Year Book 1913* 19 The imported 'yes' and 'no' of an aloof and distant Censor. **1948** LD. D. CECIL *2 Quiet Lives* I. 14 She..hid her true self behind the shield of an aloof formality.

†**C.** *prep.* [short for *aloof from.*] Away from, clear of, apart from. *Obs. rare.*

1643 MILTON *Divorce* II. iv. (1847) 141/1 Rivetus..would fain work himself aloof these rocks and quicksands. **1667** —— *P.L.* III. 577 Where the great Luminarie Alooff the vulgar Constellations thick..Dispenses Light from farr.

aloofly (ə'lu:flɪ), *a.* and *adv.* [f. ALOOF *a.* + -LY[1, 2].] **A.** *adj.* Characterized by aloofness; 'distant', unsympathetic. *rare.* **B.** *adv.* So as to keep, or as if keeping, aloof.

1901 F. CAMPBELL *Love* 118 His cold justice and aloofly Christianity. **1921** *Chambers's Jrnl.* Mar. 203/1 A tall moon rode aloofly across the sky. **1924** *Blackw. Mag.* Oct. 514/1 This aloofly displeased person now came and spoke to us. **1963** *New Statesman* 24 May 806/3 In case I sound aloofly virtuous.

aloofness (ə'lu:fnɪs). [f. ALOOF *adv.* + -NESS.] The state of being aloof; withdrawal from common action or feeling; lack of sympathy.

1642 ROGERS *Naaman* 242 Aloofenesse and carrying of things afarre off. **1817** COLERIDGE *Biogr. Lit.* 153 The alienation, and, if I may hazard such an expression, the utter aloofness of the poet's own feelings. **1849** THOREAU *Concord & Merr. Riv.* 59 The wary independence and aloofness of his dim forest life. **1878** DOWDEN *Studies* 420 The same aloofness, the same hauteur.

† **a'loose**, *v. Obs. rare*[−1]. [f. A- *pref.* II + LOOSE *v.*] To loosen.

1562 BULLEYN *Bk. Compds.* 17b, This doeth mitigate all aches . . it doeth alose, and not binde.

a-lop (ə'lɒp), *adv.*, prop. *phr.* [A *prep.*[1] + LOP.] Hanging over on one side.

1865 A. CARY *Ballads* 81 Mildewed hay-stacks, all a-lop.

‖ **alo'pecia.** *Med.* [L. *alōpecia*, a. Gr. ἀλωπεκία fox-mange, also baldness in man, f. ἀλώπηξ a fox.] A medical term for baldness.

1398 TREVISA *Barth. De P.R.* v. lxvi. (1495) 184 By that euyll callyd Allopicina nourysshynge of heer is corrupte and fayllyth, and the fore party of the heed is bare, suche men fare as foxes. **1585** LLOYD *Treas. Health* B viij, Burne the heade of a great Ratte and myngle it wyth the droppynge of a Beare or of a hogge and anointe the head, it heleth the desease called Allopecia. **1862** H. MACMILLAN in *Macm. Mag.* 462 Alopecia or baldness is much more common now than it used to be.

† **alo'pecian**, *a. Obs.*[−0] [f. prec. + -AN.] 'Belonging to alopecy.' Coles 1692.

a'lopecist. [f. ALOPECIA + -IST.] One who undertakes to cure or prevent baldness.

alopecoid (æləʊ'pi:kɔɪd), *a.* and *sb. Zool.* [f. Gr. ἀλώπηξ fox: see -OID.] Belonging to the division of the genus *Canis* of which the fox is the type; vulpine. As *sb.*, an animal of this division.

1880 [see THOOID *a.* (*sb.*)].

a'lopecy. *rare*[−0]. An adaptation of ALOPECIA, in Blount *Glossogr.* 1656, and in mod. Dicts.

† **alopicke**, 'One that hath no haire on his head.' Cockeram 1623.

alorcinic (ˌælɔ:'sɪnɪk), *a. Chem.* [f. AL(OE) + ORCIN + -IC.] In *alorcinic acid*, $C_9H_{10}O_3$, produced by the action of melting potash upon aloes.

1875 WATTS *Dict. Chem.* 2nd Supp. VII. 53 Alorcinic acid is resolved by fusion with potash into acetic acid and orcin.

alose (ə'ləʊs), *sb.* [a. Fr. *alose*:—L. *alōsa*, *alausa.*] A fish of the Herring family (*Alosa communis*), commonly called ALLICE, or *Allice shad.*

1591 PERCIVALL *Sp. Dict.*, *Alosa*, an Alose or shad. **1620** VENNER *Via Recta* iv. 75 The Allowes is taken in the same places that Sammon is. **1674** RAY *Catal. Fishes* 102 Alose: called in other places Shads. **1854** BADHAM *Halieut.* 6 Greasy Alose sputtering from the Stall.

† **a'lose**, *v. Obs.* [a. OFr. *alose-r*, *all-*, to praise, f. *à* to + *los*:—L. **laudis* for *laus* praise.]

1. To praise. Chiefly in pa. pple.: Praised, renowned.

c **1314** *Guy Warw.* 64 As knight that wele alosed is. *c* **1374** CHAUCER *Troylus* IV. 1474 He shal som Greke so preyse and wele alose. *c* **1440** *Morte Arth.* 3882 Ffore he was lyone allossede in londes i-newe. *c* **1448** in *R. Glouc. Chron.* 450 *note*, These ij bisshoppes . . were the most alosed bisshoppes.

2. *refl.* To renown oneself.

1340 *Ayenb.* 183 To ssewy his strengþe ine tornemens oþer ine viȝtinges him uor to alosi. *Ibid.* 199 Inþe viȝtinge . . huer þe knyȝt lierneþ, ham proueþ and aloseþ.

3. In a bad sense: To fame, report.

c **1325** *E.E. Allit. P.* B. 274 For her lodlych laykeȝ alosed þay were. **1389** *E. Eng. Gilds* 11 If any of the bretheren be alosed of thefte . . they be put out of the bretherhede.

‖ **alouatte** (ælu:'æt). *Zool.* [a. Fr. *alouate*, ? ad. *araguato* native name.] The Howling Monkey, *Mycetes seniculus* of Iliger, a native of S. America.

1778 CAMPER in *Phil. Trans.* LXIX. 156 The very extraordinary organ of voice of the *alouate* or *hurleur de Cayenne*, the *Simia Capucina* of Linnæus. **1852** T. ROSS tr. *Humboldt's Trav.* I. viii. 273 The monotonous howling of the alouate apes, which resembles the distant sound of wind when it shakes the forest. **1860** GOSSE *Rom. Nat. Hist.* 31 The alouattes or howling monkeys.

aloud (ə'laʊd), *adv.*; also 4–6 **aloude**, 6 **alowd**, [A *prep.*[1] of manner + LOUD *a.* Cf. *alow*, *ahigh.*]

1. In a loud voice; with great noise; loudly.

c **1374** CHAUCER *Troylus* II. 401 The kinges foole is wont to crie aloud. **1393** LANGL. *P. Pl.* C. VII. 23 Lauhynge al a-loude. *c* **1400** *Destr. Troy* xv. 6251 He . . on lowde saide. **1539** BIBLE ('great') *Gen.* xlv. 2 (R.) He wepte alowde. **1593** SHAKS. *2 Hen. VI*, v. i. 3 Ring Belles alowd, burne Bonfires. **1603** —— *Meas. for M.* II. iv. 153 Ile tell the world aloud, What man thou art. **1767** FORDYCE *Serm. Yng. Wom.* I. vi. 252 One of the Company would often read aloud. **1821** KEATS *Isabel* xxxiii, In dreams they groan'd aloud.

b. doubtfully *attrib.*

1509 HAWES *Past. Pleas.* XLII. iii, Open thine eares unto my song aloude. **1806** W. TAYLOR in Robberds' *Mem.* II. 137 The only serious poem that is resorted to for aloud reading.

2. *fig.* (*colloq.*)

1872 *Daily News* 28 Feb., The stuff, to quote the trenchant expression of an on-looker, 'stank aloud.'

† **a'lout**, *v. Obs.* Forms: 1 alút-an, 2–3 alute, 4–5 aloute, 5 alowte. [*Alout* as a weak. vb. represents formally OE. *lútian* to lurk, but in sense it answers to the strong *alútan* to stoop: see LOUT. In either case the *a-* is A- *pref.* I intensive.]

1. *intr.* To stoop, to bow down; to fall over.

c **1000** *Ags. Gosp.* Luke xxiv. 12 And alútende he ȝeseah þa lin-wæda. *c* **1160** *Hatton G.*, ibid., And alutede, he ȝeseah þa linwæde. **1297** R. GLOUC. 476 The thridde . . ther after smot anon, & made him a loute al adown. *c* **1480** CAXTON *Life of our Ladye* (R.) He [statue of Romulus] alowted vpon the same nyght Whan Cryst was bore of a pure virgyne.

2. *esp.* To bow in deference or worship *to.*

a **1260** *Hymn* in *Rel. Ant.* I. 101 That child . . to me alute lowe. *c* **1340** HAMPOLE *Pr. Consc.* 1182 All men that to him wol allowte. *c* **1450** J. RUSSELL *Bk. Nurt.* in *Babees Bk.* 139 Kutt þe vpper crust, for youre soueravne, & to hym alowt. *a* **1500** *St. Katherine* (Halliw.) 8 All they schall alowt to thee, Yf thou wylt alowte to me.

b. (When the cases were levelled, the *indirect* object appeared as *direct*, and the verb as if *transitive.*)

c **1300** *Alisaunder* 851 þe ludes in þe lond alouten him shal. **1413** LYDG. *Pylgr. Sowle* IV. xxix. (1859) 62 Alle folke the alouteth, and obeyeth. *c* **1440** *Arth.* 117 Heyest & lowest hym Loved & alowte.

‖ **à l'outrance**: see OUTRANCE.

1837 J. F. COOPER *Recoll. Europe* I. ix. 310 There was a famous quarrel, *à l'outrance*, about it. **1860** *Once a Week* 20 Oct. 476/2 Francis II. will be called upon to make his choice between casting in his lot with the defenders *à l'outrance* of Gaeta, or making his escape by sea.

alow (ə'ləʊ), *adv.*[1] (and *prep.*), orig. *phr.* Forms: 3–7 alowe, 4 aloȝ, a-logh, a-loughe, (5 *north.* a-lawe) 6 alowe, 5– alow. [A *prep.*[1] + LOW *a.* Cf. *on high*, *afar.*] Contrasted with *aloft.*

1. Of position: Low down, below.

c **1260** *E.E. Poems* (1862) 14 Hit nas no wonder þoȝ ȝo wep for hir swet child alowe. **1377** LANGL. *P. Pl.* B. XII. 234 His mouth . . Rather þan his lykam a-low [*v.r.* aloȝ]. **1430** LYDG. *Chron. Troy* I. vii, The corps is layde in earth alowe. **1578** LYTE *Dodoens* 324 A lowe, even by the ground. **1611** SPEED *Hist. Gt. Brit.* IX. xviii. (1632) 903 The Queene her selfe sate alone alow on the rushes. *a* **1733** NORTH *Lives of Norths* (1826) II. 344 The reason given for the sun's absence a-low. **1867** J. INGELOW *Lily & Lute* II. 146 Floating of the film aloft, Fluttering of the leaves alow.

2. Of direction: Downwards, towards the ground.

a **1423** JAMES I. *Kingis Q.* II. xvi, As I beheld, and kest myn eyen alawe. *a* **1528** SKELTON *Image Hypoc.* I. 91 They may not stoop alowe. **1700** DRYDEN *Cymon & Iph.* 370 Toss'd and retoss'd, aloft and then alow.

3. *Naut.* In or into the lower part of a vessel, *i.e.* the deck as opposed to the rigging, the cabin or hold as opposed to the deck.

1509 BARCLAY *Ship of Fooles* (1570) 177 Within this ship a lowe or els a hye. **1630** J. TAYLOR (Water P.) *Wks.* 65/2 Downe, downe alow, into the hold. **1863** C. READE *Hard Cash* I. 268 With studding sails alow and aloft.

4. *fig.* In low condition or estate.

1377 LANGL. *P. Pl.* B. XII. 222 Why somme be alowe [*v.r.* alouȝ] and somme alofte. **1535** COVERDALE *Deut.* xxviii. 43 Thou shalt come downe alowe and lye euer beneth.

†**5.** In a low voice, quietly: opposed to *aloud.*

c **1325** *E.E. Allit. Poems* B. 670 þou laȝed a-loȝ. **1482** *Monk of Evesham* (1869) 23 Sykyng alow in his breste.

†**B.** *prep.* ellipt. for *alow in* or *on. Obs. rare.*

1533 TINDALE *Answ. Frith* in Southey *Bk. Ch.* 112 (R.) Creep alow the ground. **1591** HARINGTON *Orl. Fur.* II. xii, Alow the vale a hermit she did find.

alow (əlɔ:'ʊ, əlaʊ), *adv.*[2], *north. dial.* [A *prep.*[1] in, on + LOW flame.] Ablaze, in flame.

c **1200** ORMIN 16185 Teȝȝ alle þrenngdenn ut Of all þatt miccle temmple, All alls itt wære all oferr hemm O loȝhe. **1818** SCOTT *Hrt. Midl.* xlv. 350 To speak to him about that . . wad be to set the kiln a-low.

† **a'low**, *v. Obs.* Also **allow**. [f. A- *pref.* II + LOW: cf. ALOW *adv.*, and *abase.*] To lower, bring down, lessen. *lit.* and *fig.*

1530 PALSGR. 414/1, I abate, or lay downe, or beate downe, or alowe one in his accompt. *Je abas.* *a* **1541** WYATT *Ps.* cii. (R.) Whereby he . . gynneth to alowe his payne and penitence. *c* **1576** TURBERVILLE *Fall of Pride* (R.) They may most plainely see how pride hath beene allowde.

alowe, aloye, obs. forms of ALLOW, ALLOY.

† **aloyn(e**, *v. Obs.* [a. OFr. *aloigne-r*, *-ier*, AFr. *aloyner*, f. *à* to + *loin*:—L. *longe* far.] To remove far off, to carry away.

1303 R. BRUNNE *Handl. Synne* 9358 þe vessel þat was of ryche metalle . . he dyde aloyne. *c* **1325** *E.E. Allit. P.* A. 892 þay arn boȝt fro þe vrþe aloynte. **1464** *Past. Lett.* 493 II. 166 Such goods as were . . deseitfully aloyned out of the possession and knowlech of the seid John Paston.

Alp[1] (ælp). [In pl. *Alps*, a. Fr. *Alpes*:—L. *Alpēs* name of a mountain system in Switzerland and adjacent countries; said by Servius to be of Celtic origin, and variously explained as meaning 'high' (cf. Gaelic *alp* a high mountain, Irish *ailp*) and 'white' (cf. L. *albus*).]

1. *pl.* Proper name of the mountain range which separates France and Italy, etc. *sing.* A single peak. (Applied in Switzerland to the green pastureland on the mountain side.)

1551 TURNER *Herbal* II. (1568) 64 The alpes that depart Italy and Germany. **1827** M. WILMOT *More Lett.* (1935) 276 An Alpe . . is a cottage and little establishment to which a shepherdess conducts a certain number of flocks and herds in the spring. **1857** B'NESS VON TAUTPHŒUS *Quits* I. xvi. 253 Is this Peissenberg what you call an alp or alm . . is it one of those pasture-grounds on the mountains where . . the people send their cattle in summer? **1860** TYNDALL *Glac.* I. §3. 27 After a rough ascent over the Alp we came to the dead crag. **1922** W. G. KENDREW *Climates of Cont.* xi. 54 Between the forests and the cap of perpetual snow is a zone of alp, pasture land with drought-resisting bushes.

2. Any high, especially snow-capped, mountains.

1598 HAKLUYT *Voy.* I. 112 Certaine Alpes or mountaines directly Southward. **1667** MILTON *P.L.* II. 620 O're many a Frozen, many a Fierie Alpe. **1856** RUSKIN *Mod. Paint.* IV. v. xx. §3 A great Alp, with its purple rocks and eternal snows above.

3. *fig.*

1645 MILTON *Tetrach.* Wks. 1847, 182/1 This adamantine alp of wedlock. **1709** POPE *Crit.* 232 Hills peep o'er hills, and Alps on Alps arise. **1854** J. ST. JOHN *Nemesis of Power* 156 The loftiest minds, which tower like intellectual Alps.

4. *Comb.*, as ***alp-horn.***

1864 ENGEL *Mus. Anc. Nat.* 10 Consisting of pieces of wood fixed tightly together, like the Swiss Alp-horn.

alp[2] (ælp). Also **alpe**: see AWBE, OLP. [Origin unknown.] A bullfinch.

c **1400** *Rom. Rose* 658 Alpes, fynches, and wodewales. **1440** *Promp. Parv.*, Alpe, a bryde, *Ficedula*. **1678** RAY *Ornith. Willughby* 247 The Bulfinch, Alp or Nope, *Rubicilla seu Pyrrhula.* **1843** YARRELL *Brit. Birds* I. Index 13 Alp, a name for the Bull-finch.

† **alp**[3]. *Obs.* [variant of ELP.] Elephant. Hence, ***alpes-bone***: ivory.

c **1220** *Leg. St. Kath.* (in Halliw.) Thai made hir bodi blo and blac, That er was white so alpes-bon.

‖ **alp**[4] (ælp). [a. Ger. *alp* night-mare, demon.]

1836 *Blackw. Mag.* XL. 146 Those alps and goblins, those nixies and wood-nymphs.

alpaca (æl'pækə). Formerly **alpaco**. [a. Sp. *alpaca* or *al-paco*, f. *al* Arab. article often prefixed to names + *paco*, prob. a native Peruvian name.]

1. a. A Peruvian quadruped, a species of llama, having long fine woolly hair.

[**1604** E. G. *D'Acosta's Hist. W. Ind.* xli. 319 Pacos, or sheep bearing wooll. **1753** CHAMBERS *Cycl. Supp.*, *Pacos* . . the name of a species of camel . . known among many by the name of the *Indian sheep*, or *Peruvian sheep*.] **1811** *Arcana* (*of Nat. Hist.*) The Acalpa [*sic*] is another animal of Peru. **1827** GRIFFITH *Cuvier* IV. 57 The Paco or Alpaca was first clearly described by M. Frederick Cuvier in 1821. **1830** *Gard. & Menag. Zool. Soc.* I. 278 Early travellers in America speak vaguely of the Llama, the Guanaco, the Paco or Alpaco, and the Vicugna. **1848** T. SOUTHEY *Colon. Wools* iv. 289 The Alpaca is about 4 feet high.

b. *attrib.*

1836 *Bradford Observer* June (*Advt.*) L'pool Wool Sales . . 400 bags of Alpacca wool, just landed.

2. = alpaca wool.

1792 J. TOWNSEND *Journ. Spain* II. 417 in *N. & Q.* Ser. IV. VI. 133 A gentleman from Peru gave me samples of wool . . one called Alpaca . . very fine and excellent for hats. **1877** *Birm. Weekly Post* 22 Dec. 1/3 His [Mr. Titus Salt's] eye fell upon a huge pile of dirty-looking bales of alpaca.

3. The fabric made of alpaca wool. Often *attrib.*

1838 *Monthly Rev. Worsted Tr.* July, The Alpaca figure has for the present become a decided trade. **1859** *Lady's Tour M. Rosa* 7 A dress of some light woollen material, such as carmelite or alpaca. **1869** E. BLAKEY in *Eng. Mech.* 13 Aug. 466/1 Alpaca umbrellas are made of alpaca weft and cotton warp.

4. A garment, as a coat, made of alpaca or of a fabric resembling this.

1853 [see VICUÑA, VICUNA 2]. **1868** A. D. WHITNEY *Patience Strong's Outings* 187 A merino gown, or a poplin alpaca, isn't much. **1900** J. K. JEROME *Three Men on Bummel* v. 110 Poor little woman! I see her now in the shabby grey alpaca, with the inkstains on it.

alpargata (alpar'gata). Also 9 **alpargate**. [Sp.] A type of sandal (see quot. 1897).

A form in earlier use was *alparca*: see Stanford Dict. Anglicised Words.

1827 J. P. HAMILTON *Trav. Int. Prov. of Columbia* I. 217 They had not a pair of shoes and stockings in the whole battalion; the officers wearing alpargátes. **1845** R. FORD *Handbk. Trav. Spain* I. i. 35 The *caleseros* on the eastern coast wear.. the ancient Roman sandals, made of the *esparto* rush, with hempen soles, '*alpargatas*'. *Ibid.* II. xii. 926 In dry weather they prefer the sandal *Alpargata*, which, however, will not stand much wet. **1897** GADOW *In Northern Spain* iv. 63 My companions wore *alpargatas*, namely, canvas shoes with thick soles of plaited hemp or grass. **1909** BELLOC *Pyrenees* v. 169 Remember that, in Alpargatas, you will always end the day with wet feet. **1920** *Glasgow Herald* 6 Mar. 3 Spinning, and twisting heavy jute yarns for alpargatas. **1940** HEMINGWAY *For whom Bell Tolls* i. 12, I wonder if he has a pair of boots or if he rides in those *alpargatas*.

alpeen ('ælpiːn). *Anglo-Ir.* Also -ine. [Ir. *ailpín*.] A cudgel, stout-headed stick.
1828 BANIM *Anglo-Irish* II. 188 The..alpeens of the primitive Irish. **1844** THACKERAY *Box of Novels* in *Wks.* (1900) XIII. 411 Here comes Rory O'More thundering down with his big alpeen. **1847** TROLLOPE *Macdermots* xiii, Thady had an alpine in his hand, and was preparing to strike a blow at the Captain.

alpenglow ('ælpənɡləʊ). [Partial tr. G. *alpenglühen*, less freq. *alpenglut*, f. *alpen*, gen. pl. of *alp* + *glühen*, *glut* fire, flame, glow (see GLEED *sb.*).] The rosy light of the setting or rising sun seen on high mountains.
1871 TYNDALL *Fragm. Sci.* 282 On August 23, 1869, the evening Alpenglow was very fine. **1880** *Scribner's Monthly* XX. 346/2 The whole picture stood revealed in the full flush of the alpenglow.

alpenhorn ('ælpənhɔːn). Also **alphorn**. [Both G., f. *alpen* (see prec.) + HORN *sb.*] (See quot. 1879.) Also *attrib.*
1864 [see ALP[1] 4]. **1879** GROVE *Dict. Mus.* I. 56 *Alpenhorn*, or *Alphorn*, an instrument with a cupped mouthpiece, of wood and bark, used by the mountaineers in Switzerland. **1895** *Westm. Gaz.* 13 Aug. 2/3 The time-honoured Alphorn melodies.

alpenrose ('ælpənrəʊz). *Bot.* [G., f. as prec. + ROSE *sb.*] = *Rose of the Alps* (see ROSE *sb.* 3 b).
1914 *Gardening Illustr.* 24 Jan. 49/2 R. hirsutum had disappeared while R. ferrugineum was abundant... They are the two varieties of the well-known Swiss Alpenrose, which looks handsome in large sheets of colour. **1924** 'L. MALET' *Dogs of Want* i. 17 Bilberries and dwarf thickets of juniper and *alpen-rose* grew in the shelter of outcrops of rock and scattered boulders. **1960** *Times* 5 Mar. 9/1 Alpenroses, gentians, and other alpine plants may often be found.

alpenstock ('ælpənstɒk). [mod.Ger.; *Alpen* (gen. pl.) of the Alps + *stock* stick.] A long staff pointed with iron, used in climbing the Alps, whence it has passed into general use in mountain climbing.
1829 C. LATROBE *The Alpenstock; or Sketches of Swiss Scenery* Advt. 5 The *Alpenstock* is the name of the long iron-spiked pole, in common use on the Alps, in the hands of the chamois-hunter and the pedestrian traveller. **1871** TYNDALL *Fragm. Sci.* (ed. 6) I. vii. 232 The handle of a pitchfork doing, in my case, the duty of an alpenstock.

alpenstocker ('ælpən,stɒkə(r)). *rare*[−1]. [f. prec. + -ER[1].] One who uses an alpenstock; a mountain-climber.
1864 BURTON *Cairngorm* 54 The most enthusiastic of the Alpenstockers..get a little tired of snow.

†**Al'pestral**, *a.* and *sb. Obs. rare.* [f. L. *alpestr-is* belonging to the Alps + -AL[1]. A more analogical form would be *alpestrial* like *terrestrial*.]
A. *adj.* Alpine. **B.** *sb.* An Alpine species.
1664 EVELYN *Silva* (1776) 316 Flanked by the Alpestral hills. **1675** —— *Terra* (1776) 22 Monstrous trees as Firs, Pines, and other Alpestrals.

Alpestrian (æl'pɛstrɪən). [f. L. *alpestri-s* alpine + -AN. Cf. *pedestrian*.] An Alpine climber.
1861 *Peaks, Passes, etc.* I. 148 My companion was..an Alpestrian known to most Swiss readers. **1863** *Macm. Mag.* Sept. 393 It has become a proverb with alpestrians that impracticable means unattempted.

Alpestrine (æl'pɛstrɪn), *a. Bot.* [f. L. *alpestr-is* + -INE: cf. *lacustrine*.]
1880 GRAY *Bot. Text-bk.* 395, *Alpestrine*, Growing on mountains below an alpine region or one unwooded from cold.

†**Al'pestrious**, *a. Obs.*[−0] [f. Fr. *alpestre*, or L. *alpestri-s*: cf. *illustrious*.] = ALPINE.
1623 MINSHEU, Alpestrious, mountainous, craggie, hillie, [Fr.] *Alpéstre, dict. de Alpibus.*

alpha ('ælfə). In technical, as in general, contexts frequently written α. [a. L. *alpha*, a. Gr. ἄλφα name of the first letter *A*; ad. Heb. or Phœnician *āleph*, meaning 'ox' or 'leader,' name of the first letter of the Phœnician and Hebrew alphabet, orig. formed from the hieroglyph of an ox's head.]
1. Name of the letter *A*, α, in the Greek alphabet.
1626 COCKERAM, *Alpha*, the first letter of the Greekes. **1751** CHAMBERS *Cycl.* s.v., The Greek alpha answers to what in English we call simply A.
2. Hence, The beginning; *esp.* in phr. **alpha and omega**, 'the beginning and the end,' originally of the divine Being.
1382 WYCLIF *Rev.* i. 8, I am alpha and oo, the bigynnyng and endyng, seith the Lord God. **1526** TINDALE, **1582** *Rhem.*, and **1611** *ibid.*, I am Alpha and Omega. **1633** COWLEY *Piramus & Thisbe* Ded., But if you smile, if in your gracious Eye She an auspicious Alpha can descry. **1830** SIR J. HERSCHEL *Stud. Nat. Phil.* 114 The alpha and omega of science. **1865** CARLYLE *Fredk. Gt.* VIII. XIX. v. 183 This Siege of Dresden is the alpha to whatever omegas there may be.
3. Used also to indicate the first in numerical sequence. *esp.* **a.** *Astr.* The chief star in a constellation, the letters of the Greek alphabet being used for the first 24 stars in succession. **b.** *Chem.* The first of two or more isomerous modifications of the same organic compound. **c.** The first subspecies or permanent variety of a species in Nat. Hist.
1626 COCKERAM *Alpha*..also used for the first or chiefe in a thing. **1751** CHAMBERS *Cycl.*, *Alpha* is also used as a letter of order, to denote the *first*. **1863** WATTS *Fownes' Chem.* (1877) II. 578 The α-acid is converted by heat into the β-acid. **1869** DUNKIN *Midn. Sky* 123 A line drawn through these three stars leads..nearly to Alpha and Beta Capricorni. **1880** FRISNELL in *Jrnl. Soc. Arts* 445 The sulphonic acid of alpha naphthol.
d. *Metallurgy.* (*a*) Applied to the first of a series of allotropic forms of a metal, as ***alpha iron***. (*b*) Applied to a solid solution in a range of alloys, as ***alpha brass***, the first of a series of alloys of copper and brass: that in which there is the highest proportion of copper.
1885 *Jrnl. Iron & Steel Inst.* II. 618 The author [Osmond] believes..that there are two..varieties of iron, α and β. The crystalline iron α is obtained by tempering at a red heat, followed by a slow cooling. This is transformed into the β variety (which the structure of tempered steel shows to be amorphous) either by a permanent alteration at a low temperature, or by rapid cooling from a red heat..in the presence of carbon, or some other body (manganese, tungsten) exercising the same influence on the..steel. **1902** *Encycl. Brit.* XXIX. 572/2 We must recognize the further complication in the constitution of iron, due to its having at least three distinct allotropic modifications, α, β, and γ, each corresponding to a distinct range of temperature. α iron is the weak, ductile, magnetic variety.., β iron is the non-magnetic variety, [etc.]. **1914** W. ROSENHAIN *Physical Metallurgy* viii. 167 Iron is capable of existing in at least three diverse or 'allotropic' conditions. These are generally known as the γ, β and α forms of iron. **1957** *Encycl. Brit.* XII. 669/2 Pure iron or ferrite at room temperature consists of tiny crystals of so-called alpha iron, crystallized in body centred arrangement.
1904 HEYCOCK & NEVILLE in *Phil. Trans. R. Soc.* A. CCII. 9 Crystals of five different types, which we designate α, β, γ, δ, η... The α crystals are solid solutions, apparently isomorphous with pure copper. They may contain any percentage of tin not greater than 9 per cent. The β crystals are also solid solutions, perhaps isomorphous with the α. **1919** *Jrnl. Inst. Metals* XXII. 370 (*heading*) Thermal expansion of Alpha and Beta Brass between 0° and 600° C. **1923** GLAZEBROOK *Dict. Appl. Physics* V. 223/1 As the α solution becomes more and more saturated the tensile strength of the alloys increases... The αβ alloys cannot be worked cold, but are always rolled, or extruded, hot.
e. *Physics.* ***alpha radiation***, the first of three types of radiation emitted by radio-active substances, and consisting of positively charged particles. So ***alpha particle*** (identified with the helium nucleus: see quot. 1908), ***ray***.
1899, **1902** [see BETA 2 f]. **1903** RUTHERFORD in *Phil. Mag.* V. 184 The α rays are complex, and probably consist of particles projected with velocities lying between certain limits. **1903** —— in *Nature* 20 Aug. 366/2 The determination of the mass of the α body..supports the view that the α particle is in reality helium. **1908** —— & GEIGER in *Proc. R. Soc.* A. LXXXI. 172 We may conclude that an α-particle is a helium atom, or, to be more precise, the α-particle, after it has lost its positive charge, is a helium atom. **1925** F. SODDY in *Evol. Light Mod. Knowl.* x. 371 The radiant α- and β-particles expelled by the radio-elements. **1938** R. LAWSON tr. *Hevesy & Paneth's Man. Radioactivity* (ed. 2) ix. 94 The α-particle..a kind of 'molecule' of the 'nuclear atoms' possessing especial stability, and arising from the union of 2 protons and 2 neutrons.
Hence ellipt. for ***alpha particles*** in ***alpha decay***, ***emission***, ***emitter***; ***alpha-emitting*** adj.
1936 *Physical Rev.* L. 977 The radioactive α-decay is discussed as a many-body problem. *Ibid.*, The probability of α-emission consists therefore of two parts. **1937** *Ibid.* LI. 818/2 Possible evidence for the existence of a new alpha-emitting isotope of uranium. **1949** W. E. SIRI *Isotopic Tracers & Nucl. Radiations* iv. 95 It is assumed that the nuclear radius is nearly constant for all alpha emitters. **1962** *Newnes Conc. Encycl. Nucl. Energy* 25/1 Spontaneous α-emission takes place with many of the nuclei heavier than lead, each species decaying with its characteristic half-life.
f. ***alpha rhythm***, ***waves***, the normal rhythmic activity of the brain recorded in an electroencephalogram, having a frequency of eight to thirteen cycles per second.
[**1930** H. BERGER in *Jrnl. f. Psychologie & Neurol.* XL. 162 Der Kürze halber werde ich im folgenden die Welle erster Ordnung als Alphawellen = α-W., die Wellen zweiter Ordnung als Betawellen = β-W., bezeichnen.] **1935** [see BETA 2 h]. **1936** *Archives Neurol. & Psychiatry* XXXVI. 1215 Most prominent is a rhythm of approximately 10 a second..variously known as the 'Berger rhythm', the 'alpha waves' or the '10 cycle rhythm'. *Ibid.* 1220 There is a group of persons in whom the alpha rhythm is rarely visible in the spontaneous record, although it may usually be found for a second or two shortly after the subject has closed his eyes. **1941** P. BARD *Macleod's Physiol. in Mod. Med.* xix. 238 The most prominent rhythm is one which ranges from 8 to 13 and averages 10 waves a second. This is sometimes called the 'Berger rhythm', but has more generally come to be known as the *alpha rhythm*.
4. a. An examiner's first-class mark. Also *transf.* and in *fig.* use, first-class, excellent.
1902 S. T. in *Oxford Mag.* 22 Jan., And what I deemed an α rules (Like markets) flat as β+. **1907** A. D. GODLEY *Ibid.* 23 Jan., One who to all Experience gave An Alpha or Epsilon. **1923** *Times Lit. Suppl.* 25 Oct., The critic (who can hardly help feeling on this occasion like an examiner with prize competition papers before him) must give the *alpha* here to Mr. Sichel. **1929** *Ibid.* 2 May, Nor can we give an alpha mark to [etc.]. **1958** *Oxf. Mag.* 13 Mar. 361/1 Is there now a painter of Oxford portraits as good as Richmond was? .. Gunn has at Trinity a colossal Lord Chief Justice Goddard..at L. M. H. he has an alpha picture of Miss Grier, true, affectionate and discerning, and wonderfully painted. **1962** C. S. LEWIS *Let.* 10 Aug. (1966) 305 Yes, I.. have read Gombrich and give him alpha with as many plusses as you please. **1966** [see sense b below]. **1980** *Nature* 24 Apr. 653/1 Britain's Science Research Council has been forced to reject £2.2 million worth of 'alpha' quality applications for university research, a spokesman said last week.
b. ***alpha minus***, a mark approaching (or in the lower range of) first-class; ***alpha plus***, an excellent mark; one in the higher range of first-class. Freq. *fig.* (also as *adj. phr.*), nearly (or superlatively) excellent or first-rate. Cf. MINUS 2 a, PLUS 1 c.
1903 E. THOMAS *Oxford* iv. 107 He will be frivolous to the extent of remarking, about a pretty face, 'Oh, she is *alpha plus*!' *a* **1930** [see PLUS 1 c]. **1940** H. NICOLSON *Let.* 11 July (1967) 101 He is seeing the Alpha Plus people all day and I am seeing the Beta Plus people whom he throws on to me. **1958** *Listener* 12 June 987/2 On the literary side, *The Sweeniad* rates only an alpha minus: pleasant light reading, nothing more. **1966** 'W. COOPER' *Mem. New Man* I. iv. 43 He's got edge, and flair—alpha quality for certain. And if he has luck he may turn out alpha plus.

alphabet ('ælfəbɪt), *sb.* [ad. L. *alphabētum* (Tertull.), f. *Alpha, Beta* = Ἄλφα, Βῆτα, the first two Greek letters taken as a name for the whole, as in our 'ABC.' Cf. Fr. *alphabet* (not in Cotgr. 1611).]
1. a. The set of letters used in writing the Greek language; extended to those used by the Romans; and thence to any set of characters representing the simple sounds used in a language or in speech generally.
1580 BARET *Alv.* A., This common vsuall order in our Alphabet or crosrowe. **1611** COTGR., (R.) Touching the French *abece*, for alphabet I will not call it, according to the vulgar error, that word being peculiar only to the Greek tongue [*not in ed.* 1632]. **1751** JOHNSON *Rambler* No. 141 ¶8 The lexicographer at last finds the conclusion of his alphabet. **1781** COWPER *Convers.* 11 As alphabets in ivory employ, Hour after hour, the yet unlettered boy. **1857** MAX MÜLLER *Chips* (1880) I. x. 261 The Chinese alphabet was never intended to represent the sound of words.
†**b. in alphabet**: in alphabetical order. *Obs.*
1699 GARTH *Dispens.* I. 5 Here Phyals in nice discipline are set, There Gally-pots are rang'd in Alphabet.
c. A series of symbols used to represent an alphabet (sometimes including numerals), differing from it in the form of the symbols or in their order.
1838 *N.Y. Observer* 3 Feb. 18/6 The Electro-Magnetic Telegraph..can..furnish the *copy*, ready for the hands of any printer who understands the telegraphic alphabet. **1852** E. HIGHTON *Electric Telegraph* 63 The following represents Professor Morse's alphabet, composed..of long and short marks. **1939** [see *polyalphabetic* adj. s.v. POLY- 1]. **1974** *Encycl. Brit. Macropædia* V. 326/1 The Gronsfeld cipher is identical with a Vigenère system with direct standard alphabets, except that only the first ten alphabets are used in conjunction with a numerical key.
d. *Computing.* (See quot. 1962.)
1962 *Gloss. Terms Automatic Data Processing* (*B.S.I.*) 15 *Alphabet* (*character set, character repertoire*), an agreed set of representations..from which selections are made to denote and distinguish data... For example, an alphabet may include the numerals 0 to 9, the letters A to Z, a space, specified punctuation marks and functional characters. **1973** H. HELLERMAN *Digital Computer System Princ.* (ed. 2) ii. 25 The alphabet of APL, showing all its atomic symbols as they appear on the terminal keyboard, is illustrated. **1984** J. SCRIVEN *Working Electron* ii. 58 (*heading*) Defining your own alphabet.
e. *attrib.*
1513 W. DE WORDE (*title*) The Flores of Ovide..with theyr Englysshe..and Two alphabete Tables. **1636** COGAN *Haven Health* (ed. 2) The Table containing the principall points of the whole booke in Alphabet order.
f. Special Comb. **alphabet book**, a book for teaching the alphabet; **alphabet soup**, a clear soup containing pieces of paste or biscuit shaped like letters of the alphabet.
1922 JOYCE *Ulysses* 49 One of the alphabet books you were going to write. **1907** *Black Cat* June 15 Alphabet soup—that thin, clear soup, with little noodle or cracker letters in it.
2. *fig.* The key to any study or branch of knowledge; the first rudiments.
1588 SHAKS. *Tit. A.* III. ii. 44, I (of these) will wrest an Alphabet, And, by still practice, learne to know thy meaning. *a* **1652** J. SMITH *Sel. Disc.* iv. 101 Our senses.. first taught us the alphabet of this learning. **1837** WHEWELL *Induct. Sc.* I. I. i. 27 The alphabet in which nature writes her answers to such inquiries.
†**3.** An index in alphabetical order. *Obs.*
1552 HULOET, Alphabet of a boke, *Elenchus*. **1578** BIBLE (Genev.) Pref., These two Alphabets of directions..in maner of a briefe Concordance. **1666** PEPYS *Diary* 25 Dec.,

Reducing the names of all my books to an alphabet. **1825** *Bro. Jonathan* II. 159 Where's the alphabet? Find Harwood.

4. *fig.* A long or complete series.

1592 NASHE *P. Penilesse* (ed. 2) 8 b, Small beere, that wold make a man..runne through an Alphabet of faces. **1600** HOLLAND *Livy* XXII. vii. 436 i, An alphabet of faces [*varios vultus*]. **1727** POPE *Dunc.* IV. 217 While tow'ring o'er the Alphabet like Saul. **1923** G. B. SHAW in *Nation* 10 Feb. 715/1 The soldiers would have to be inoculated with a whole alphabet of microbes.

alphabet ('ælfəbɪt), *v.* [f. the sb.; cf. to *index.*] 'To range in the order of the alphabet.' J.

c **1700** PEPYS *Mem.* in *Catal. Bks. Geog. & Hydrogr.*, To collect and alphabet the particulars. **1848** [See ALPHABETED]. [In regular use with Librarians, etc., in U.S.]

alphabetarian (ˌælfəbɪ'tɛərɪən). [f. mod.L. *alphabētāri-us* + -AN: see -ARIAN. Cf. *abecedarian.*]

One learning his alphabet, or the mere rudiments of any subject; a beginner; an abecedarian; *also*, one who studies alphabets.

1614 SELDEN *Tit. Honor* Pref., They cesse to be Doctors, nay, are scarce Alphabetarians. *a* **1693** SANCROFT *Serm.* 30 (T.) Every alphabetarian knowing well that the Latin of [a city] is *urbs* or *civitas.* **1864** A. J. ELLIS in *Reader* No. 88, 303/3 [Which] all subsequent alphabetarians should study.

† '**alphabeˌtary**, *a.* and *sb. Obs.* [ad. mod.L. *alphabētāri-us*: see prec. Cf. *abecedary.*]

A. *adj.* Of or pertaining to the (or an) alphabet, alphabetic; *hence*, rudimentary.

1569 J. SANFORD tr. *Agrippa's Van. Artes* 62 That Alphabetarie, and Arithmantical diuinitie, which Christ secretely shewed to his Apostles. **1605** CAMDEN *Rem.* (1637) 169 Alphabetary revolution, which they will have to be Anagrammatisme. **1681** MANTON *Serm. Ps.* cxix. 162 Wks. 1872 IX. 180 An alphabetary knowledge fit for beginners.

B. *sb.* = ALPHABETARIAN.

1656 TRAPP *Exp. Gal.* iv. 2 Those under the law were but alphabetaries in comparison of those under the gospel.

alphabeted ('ælfəbɪtɪd), *ppl. a.* [f. ALPHABET *v.* + -ED.] Arranged alphabetically; also *fig.*

1845 *Bachel. Albany* 192 A pigeon-holed, alphabeted mind.

alphabetic (ælfə'bɛtɪk), *a.*; also 7 **alphabetique**. [perh. ad. Fr. *alphabétique* (not in Cotgr. 1611); cf. It. *alfabetico* (Florio 1598), Sp. *alphabetico* (Minsheu 1623): see ALPHABET and -IC.]

†**1.** Arranged in order of the alphabet. *Obs.*

1642 HOWELL *For. Trav.* 23 In reading hee must couch in a faire Alphabetique Paper-book the notablest occurences.

2. Of, pertaining to, or by means of an alphabet; or by letters representing simple sounds.

1736 H. COVENTRY *Phil. Conv.* iv. (T.) The author probably had his eye upon alphabetick writing in his own time. *c* **1799** K. WHITE *Childhood* I. 66 Enur'd to alphabetic toils. **1858** MARSH *Lect. Eng. Lang.* ii. 31 The visible language of written alphabetic characters. **1864** H. SPENCER *Illust. Progr.* 19 It is alleged that the Egyptians never actually achieved complete alphabetic writing.

alphabetical (ælfə'bɛtɪkəl), *a.* [f. prec. (or *alphabetico* in Romance langs.) + -AL[1].]

1. Of, pertaining to, or in order of the alphabet.

1567 MAPLET *Greene Forest* 56 b, All the whole kind of bruite Beastes..with the Alphabetical order. **1577** tr. *Bullinger's Decades* (1592) 253 That Alphabeticall Psalme.. the hundred and nineteenth. **1622** MALYNES *Anc. Law-Merch.* 341, I made an alphabetical register of them. **1703** MOXON *Mech. Exerc.* 109 Alphabetical Table of Terms. **1837** WHEWELL *Induct. Sc.* XVI. iii. §1 Arabian writers.. adopting an alphabetical arrangement [of plants].

†**2.** *fig.* Literal, strict. *Obs. rare.*

1643 MILTON *Divorce* I. xiv, An alphabetical servility.

3. = ALPHABETIC 2.

1806 *Adm. Off. Rep.* 19 Aug. 22 The Lords Commissioners of the Admiralty gave a decided preference to the alphabetical mode [of telegraphing]. **1848** A. J. ELLIS *Fonetics* 106 The history of alphabetical writing would lead us to conclude this.

alpha'betically, *adv.* [f. prec. + -LY[2].]

1. In alphabetical order.

1567 MAPLET *Greene Forest* 68 b, Let us begin Alphabetically..with the Adder. **1682** *Lond. Gaz.* mdcclxxxii/1 The Entries are to be made Alphabetically, according to the first Letter of the Sirname. **1780** BURKE *Econ. Ref.* Wks. III. 305 To avoid all suspicion of partiality and prejudice, we must take the pensions alphabetically.

2. By means of an alphabet.

1667 *Phil. Trans.* II. 574 Then count Alphabetically to E. *Mod.* The symbolization of spoken sounds, whether alphabetically or syllabically.

alphabetics (ælfə'bɛtɪks). [ALPHABETIC *a.* used subst. in pl.: see -ICS.] The science of the expression of spoken sounds by letters or alphabetic characters.

1865 A. J. ELLIS in *Reader* No. 136. 155/2 Alphabetics as a science.

alphabetiform (ælfə'bɛtɪfɔːm), *a.* [See -FORM.] Resembling the letters of an alphabet.

1901 G. SERGI *Mediterranean Race* xiv. 296 The alphabetiform signs in megalithic inscriptions. **1908** A. J. EVANS in R. R. Marett *Anthropol. & Classics* 12 Linear signs which..present a truly alphabetiform character.

alphabetism ('ælfəbɪˌtɪz(ə)m). [f. ALPHABET + -ISM.]

1. Symbolization of spoken sounds by means of an alphabet.

1879 *Encycl. Brit.* I. 602/1 Alphabetism, in which the syllable is no longer denoted by an indivisible symbol, but is resolved into vowel and consonant.

2. Employment of certain letters of the alphabet as a signature or assumed indication of authorship.

1867 O. HAMST *Martyr to Bibliogr.*, Alphabetism, as A.B.C., X.Y.Z., frequently used.

alphabetist ('ælfəbɪtɪst). [f. as prec. + -IST.] A student of alphabets; a deviser of an alphabet.

1860 HALDEMAN *Analyt. Orthogr.* ii. 22 Some alphabetists take credit to themselves.

alphabetization (ˌælfəbɪtaɪ'zeɪʃən). [f. ALPHABETIZE *v.* + -ATION.] The process of arranging words in alphabetic order; the result of this, an alphabetic series or list.

1889 H. B. WHEATLEY *How to Catalogue* 203 In the alphabetization of a catalogue. **1902** *Academy* 19 July 76/2 The index to the completed work, covering under one alphabetization the ninth edition and the new volumes.

alphabetize ('ælfəbɪtaɪz), *v.* [f. ALPHABET + -IZE.]

1. To express or symbolize by alphabetic letters; to reduce to (alphabetic) writing.

1867 A. M. BELL *Vis. Speech* 91 Languages also which have never been reduced to writing may now be alphabetized.

2. To arrange alphabetically.

1880 *N.Y. Nation* 12 Aug. 2 (*Advt.*) Schools.. alphabetized, first by States, second by Towns, third by Initial Letters. **1882** *Artist* 1 Feb. 62 Nor is the list always correctly alphabetized.

alphameric (ælfə'mɛrɪk), *a.* Contraction of ALPHA-NUMERIC *a.*

1956 BERKELEY & WAINWRIGHT *Computers* II. i. 29 This is ..*alphameric coding*, a system of coding or abbreviation such that information for the machine to handle may be reported not only in digits but also in letters.

alphametic (ælfə'mɛtɪk), *sb.* (and *a.*) [f. ALPHA(BETIC *a.* + ARITH)METIC *sb.*] A type of mathematical puzzle in which an arithmetical proposition is expressed using a different letter for some or all of the ten digits, the task being to find what digit each letter stands for. Also *attrib.* or as *adj.*

1955 J. A. H. HUNTER in *Globe & Mail* (Toronto) 23 Dec. 13/7 These alphametics seem set to take the place of crosswords as a new craze... Don't forget that each letter stands for a particular figure. **1965** [see PANGRAM]. **1970** [see PUZZLIST]. **1978** *Creative Computing* Nov.–Dec. 110/1 Why not write a single program which accepts as input an alphametic and then solves the alphametic? *Ibid.* 110/3 What follows is a description of a simplified version of an additive alphametic solver.

alphanumeric (ˌælfənjuː'mɛrɪk), *a.* and *sb. pl.* Also **alpha-numeric**. [f. ALPHA(BET *sb.* + NUMERIC(AL *a.*] **A.** *adj.* Consisting of or employing both letters and numerals; applied esp. to a system of coding in computers. Also **alpha-numerical**.

1955 BRADSHAW & NEWMAN in M. J. Dooher *Electronic Data Processing in Industry* i. 18 Typical methods of classifying, as to both type of classification and examples, are: (*a*) alphanumeric codes, commonly used for customer accounts where it is desirable to have the ease of numeric filing coupled with the advantages of alphabetic reference. **1959** *Brit. Standard 3174* (*title*) Alpha-numeric punching codes for data processing cards. **1961** *Times* 3 Oct. (Computer Suppl.) p. viii (Advt.), It has a built-in parity check on all alpha-numeric input information. **1962** *B.S.I. News* Apr. 15/1 Mixed alpha-numerical systems..caused many mistakes in transcription.

B. *sb. pl.* Alphanumeric characters.

1970 *Publishers Weekly* 8 June 152 There is a strong effort under way to bring pictures within the compass of the computer, thereby making possible the combination of text —or, to say it in computer language, alphanumerics—with pictures. **1975** *Physics Bull.* July 325/2 In the experimental array there is a display area of 6 cm × 5 cm, sufficient for 8 rows of 16 characters (each character built up from a 7 × 5 block of cells in the usual way for alphanumerics). **1978** *Nature* 19 Oct. p. xvi/2 Data can be presented graphically in point or histogram mode, and alphanumerics are presented in upper and lower case, normal, underlined, bold face, and video reverse.

† **al'pharion**. *Obs. rare*[−1]. A little-known stringed musical instrument.

1610 GWILLIM *Displ. Heraldry* IV. v. (1660) 282 The second sort [of Musical Instruments] consisteth in Strings ..as are Harps..Alpharion, Citterne, etc.

alphenic (æl'fɛnɪk). *Pharm.* Also 7 **-ix.** [a. Fr. *alphenic* (Sp. *alfeñique*, Pg. *alfenim*), according to Devic, corrupted from Arab. *alfānīd*, i.e. *al* the + Pers. *fānīd* refined sugar. Other adaptations of the same word were Fr. *pénide* and med.L. *penidium.*] White barley sugar, or sugar candy.

1657 TOMLINSON *Renou's Disp.* 172 To be retained in the mouth like so much Alphenix. **1775** ASH, *Alphenic*, White barley sugar. **1811** HOOPER *Med. Dict.*, *Alphanic, Alphenic*, an Arabian word for barley-sugar, or sugar-candy.

† **al'phitomancy**. *Obs.* [ad. Fr. *alphitomantie* (Cotgr. 1611); f. Gr. ἀλφιτόμαντις 'a diviner by barley-meal,' of which the abst. sb. would be ἀλφιτομαντεία. Probably in med.L. before adoption into mod. langs.] Divination by means of barley-meal.

1652 GAULE *Magastr.* 165 Alphitomancy, divining by meal, flower, or branne. **1693** URQUHART *Rabelais* III. xxv, Fully and amply disclosed unto you..by alphitomancy. **1721** in BAILEY; and in mod. Dicts.

alphitomorphous (ˌælfɪtəʊ'mɔːfəs), *a.* [f. Gr. ἄλφιτον barley-meal + μορφ-ή form + -OUS.] Having the appearance of barley-meal; 'applied to pulverulent microscopic fungi, parasitical on plants.' *Syd. Soc. Lex.* 1879.

alphonsin (æl'fɒnsɪn). *Surg.* [see below.] A surgical instrument having three elastic branches for the extraction of bullets from the body.

1751 CHAMBERS *Cycl.*, The *Alphonsin*, so called from its inventor Alphonsus Ferrier, a physician of Naples [in 1552] consists of three branches, which are closed together by means of a ring. **1839** in HOOPER *Med. Dict.*

Alphonsine (æl'fɒnsɪn), *a.* Of Alphonso the Wise, King of Castile; applied to astronomical tables invented by him in 1252, etc.

1678 PHILLIPS, *Alphonsin Tables*, certain Astronomical Calculations, invented by Alphonsus King of Aragon. **1797** *Encycl. Brit.* II. 420/2 He likewise corrected the tables of the planets..because the Alphonsine tables were very faulty in this respect. **1880** M. PATTISON *Milton* xiii. 180 The old Ptolemaic or Alphonsine system..explained the phenomena on the hypothesis of nine (or ten) transparent hollow spheres wheeling round the stationary earth.

‖ **alphos** ('ælfɒs). *Path.* [L. *alphos, alphus*, a. Gr. ἀλφός a dull-white leprosy.] (See quot.)

1706 PHILLIPS, *Alphos*, a kind of Morphew or White Specks on the Skin. **1751** CHAMBERS *Cycl.*, *Alphos*.. described by Celsus under the name of *vitiligo*; wherein the skin is rough, and becomes sprinkled as it were with drops of white. *c* **1870** MURPHY *Comm. Lev.* xiii. 39 It is *alphos.* This is a convenient word instead of the phrase 'non-contagious leprosy.'

alphyn, obs. variant of ALFIN.

† **alpi**, *a. Obs.* Also **ælpi**, **elpi**, an early reduced form of *anlepi*: see ONELEPY *a.*, only.

† '**Alpian**, *a. Obs. rare*[−1]. [f. L. *Alpes, Alpi-um*, the Alps + -AN.] = ALPINE.

1607 TOPSELL *Four-footed Beasts* (1673) 193 Alpian, Wilde or Rock-goat.

† '**Alpic**, *a. Obs. rare*[−1]. [ad. L. *alpic-us*, f. *Alpes* Alps.] = ALPINE.

1611 COTGR., *Chercée*, a kind of earth-Alpicke.

† **al'pieu**. *Obs.* [a. Fr. *alpiou*, a. It. *al più* 'for the more, for most.'] In the game of basset, a mark put on a card to indicate that the player doubles his stake after winning.

1693 SOUTHERNE *Maid's Last Pr.* III. i. (1721) II. 46 You have discretion enough to win all our money; I'll take your word for any thing but an Alpieu. **1768** LADY M. MONTAGUE *Poems* (1785) 13 Ah! madam, since my Sharper is untrue, I joyless make my once ador'd alpieu.

Alpigene ('ælpɪdʒiːn), *a.* [ad. assumed L. *alpigenus*, f. *Alpes* Alps + *-genus* born.] Produced on the Alps or in Alpine regions.

1847 in CRAIG.

Alpine ('ælpaɪn), *a.* and *sb.* [ad. L. *alpīnus*, f. *Alpes* Alps: see -INE.] **A.** *adj.* **1.** Of or pertaining to the Alps; hence, of any lofty mountains.

1607 TOPSELL *Four-footed Beasts* (1673) 405 The Alpine Mouse taketh her name from the Alpes.. The Italians call it Marmota. **1759** B. STILLINGFLEET *Econ. Nat.* in *Misc. Tracts* (1762) 69 Alpine plants..ripen their seeds very early. **1845** DARWIN *Voy. Nat.* xvi. (1858) 359 This animal [Vicuna] is pre-eminently alpine in its habits. **1847** GROTE *Greece* III. xxv. 8 Mountains which rise..to an alpine height. **1861** PRATT *Flower. Pl.* IV. 90 Alpine Speedwell.. is found only on the Highland mountains. **1861** HOOK *Lives Abps.* I. vii. 402 He..perished in the Alpine snows.

2. Designating a physical or racial type (see quots.).

1899 W. Z. RIPLEY *Races of Europe* (1900) iv. 72 The great central highland seemed indeed to constitute a veritable focus of this peculiar physical type... This geographical characterization of the broad-headed variety entitled it, in our opinion, to be called the Alpine type, in distinction from the two others above mentioned [*sc.* the Teutonic and the Mediterranean]. **1921** E. SAPIR *Language* x. 225 The mass of the German-speaking population..belong to..the shorter, darker-complexioned, short-headed Alpine race... The distribution of these 'Alpine' populations corresponds in part to that of the old continental 'Celts'. **1934** R. BENEDICT *Patterns of Culture* (1935) i. 11 The so-called race line..is held to divide the people of Baden from those of Alsace, though in bodily form they alike belong to the Alpine sub-race.

3. *Comb.* **Alpine anemone**, a small blue flower indigenous to mountain areas in N.E. America and Europe, now widely introduced elsewhere;

Alpine club, one for alpinists; **Alpine fir**, a tall tree (*Abies lasiocarpa*), indigenous to the mountains of western North America; **Alpine hat**, a soft felt hat with a brim and low crown, often sporting a feather or other ornament, typically worn in the Alpine regions; **Alpine rose**: see ROSE *sb.* 3 b and cf. ALPENROSE.

1892 C. M. YONGE *Old Woman's Outlook* 49 The garden shows their blue brother, the Alpine anemone. **1859** Alpine Club [see CLUB *sb.* 14]. **1864** TROLLOPE *Can you forgive Her?* I. v. 33 What fine fellows those Alpine club men think themselves. **1900** W. ROBINSON *Eng. Flower Garden* (ed. 8) 407/1 *A. Lasiocarpa* (Alpine Fir)—A beautiful spire-like tree 150 feet high with white bark, and very small cones, purple, 2 to 3 inches long, and red male flowers.. Alaska, B. Columbia. **1901** G. B. SHAW *Capt. Brassbound's Conversion* I. in *Three Plays for Puritans* 232 Drinkwater comes from the house with an Italian dressed in a much worn suit of blue serge, a dilapidated Alpine hat, and boots laced with scraps of twine. **1967** 'T. WELLS' *What should you know of Dying?* ix. 99 Dolph parked his Alpine hat on a chair.

B. *sb.* **1.** (Also with small initial.) An Alpine plant, or one that grows on high ground; also, such a plant grown in rock-gardens, etc. So *alpine frame, garden, house*.

1830 B. MAUND *Bot. Gard.* III. No. 234 *Onosma taurica.* A plant of it may also be kept in a pot amongst the alpines. **1841** MRS. LOUDON *Ladies' Comp. Fl. Gard.* (1846) 257 Of such plants as Saxifrages or other Alpines. **1881** *Encycl. Brit.* XII. 250/1 Many of the little alpines may be brought into the front line planted between suitable pieces of stone, or they may be.. placed on an artificial rockery. *Ibid.* 290/1 Give abundance of air to the greenhouse, conservatory, and alpine frame in mild weather. **1907** R. FARRER *My Rock-garden* 26 *Arenaria gothica* justly heads the list of our alpines. **1925** E. F. NORTON *Fight for Everest 1924* viii. 162 As we descended, the lichens, starveling grasses and dwarf alpines rapidly succeeded each other and in turn gave way to larger growths. **1933** *Jrnl. R. Hort. Soc.* LVIII. 223 With the development of the alpine house.. it would be possible to grow numbers of them. **1951** *Dict. Gardening* (*R. Hort. Soc.*) (ed. 2) I. 86/1 Alpine Garden.

2. A racial type. (Cf. *adj.* 2.)

1916 MADISON GRANT *Passing of Great Race* (1917) iv. 120 The Alpines are of stocky build and moderately short of stature. **1922** A. J. TOYNBEE *Western Question in Greece & Turkey* vi. 113 The Central Asian 'Mongoloid' type is found in Anatolia, but it is rare, and the great mass of the Turkish-speaking peasantry are 'Alpines'. **1935** HUXLEY & HADDON *We Europeans* v. 152 The Alpines (Eurasiatics), who are of medium build, rather dark, and broad-headed.

alpinism ('ælpɪnɪz(ə)m, -pɪn-). [ad. F. *alpinisme*: see ALPINE *a.* and -ISM.] Climbing of the Alps or of high mountains.

1884 *Standard* 5 July, Alpenism is, in this country at least, a relaxation, not a pursuit more serious than the nature of it demands. **1888** *Ibid.* 9 July 5/4 For these members of the upper crust of Alpinism, Switzerland is ceasing to have its old attractions. **1892** *Ibid.* 24 May 5/2 The Geographical Society has.. admitted 'Alpinism' to be geography. **1960** KOESTLER *Lotus & Robot* II. vii. 190 Sporting activities such as skiing or alpinism, which are of recent origin.

Alpinist ('ælpɪnɪst). [a. Fr. *alpiniste.*] One devoted to Alpine climbing.

1881 *Times* 4 Aug. 3/1 The 'Zermatt Pocket book'.. just the thing an Alpinist wants. **1881** *N. Y. Nation* XXXII. 133 The indefatigable Alpinist.

† **'Alpish**, *a. Obs. rare.* [f. ALP + -ISH.] = ALPINE.

1598 FLORIO, *Alpestre*, alpish, mountainous, craggie. **1623** MINSHEU, *Alpish*, as Alpestrious.

alpist ('ælpɪst). ? *Obs.* Also **alpia**. [a. Fr. *alpiste*, a. Sp. *alpiste*, supposed to be a *Guanche* word.] The seed of the Canary Grass (*Phalaris Canariensis*) given to cage birds; sometimes applied to other grass-seeds.

1597 GERARD *Herbal* 81 In the Ilands of Canarie *Alpisti.* **1802** REES *Cycl.* s.v., The alpiste seed is of an oval figure, of a pale yellow, inclining to an isabel colour. **1859** WORCESTER, *Alpist* or *Alpia.*

† **'Alpsian**, *a. Obs.* [f. ALPS + -IAN; cf. *Alpian.*] = ALPINE.

a **1610** FLETCHER *Faithf. Shep.* II. i. 218 The Alpsian Snow.

‖ **alquifou** (ælkɪ'fuː). [Fr. *alquifoux* (*arquifoux*), ad. Sp. *alquifol*, ad. Cat. *alcofol* ALCOHOL (*f* repr. guttural *ḥ*, cf. *alforge* and Eng. *draft, draught*). In this form the word has more closely retained the original sense.] A lead ore, containing sulphide of lead, which when broken looks like antimony; it is found in Cornwall, and is used by potters to give a green glaze to coarse earthenware.

1819 in *Pantologia.* **1849** in WEALE *Dict. Terms.*

alreadiness (ɒl'rɛdɪnɪs). ? *Obs.* [f. ALREADY + -NESS.] State of complete preparation, anticipative eagerness or alacrity.

1640 BP. HALL *Medit.* xciii. 243 Heaven & earth obey him with alreadiness.

already (ɒl'rɛdɪ, ɔːl-), *adv.* [orig. phr. ALL *adv.* = fully, + READY.]

† **1.** *adj.* (*pred.* or *compl.*) Fully prepared, in a state of complete preparation. *Obs.*

c **1380** *Sir Ferumb.* 1117 Wanne þay come to þe castel 3ate: þe porter alredi was þer-ate. *c* **1386** CHAUCER *Wife's T.* 169 (Harl. MS.) Al redy was his answer [*other texts* and ready]. **1509** HAWES *Past. Pleas.* XXIX, And founde the basket at the grounde already.

¶ This sense can still be traced in

1584 POWEL *Lloyd's Cambr.* 21 A populous countrie Alreadie furnished with inhabitants. **1849** MACAULAY *Hist. Eng.* I. 594 The three Scotch regiments were already in England. **1865** R. W. DALE *Jew. Temple* viii. (1877) 86 The preparations.. are already around us.

2. a. *adv.* Beforehand, in anticipation; previously to some specified time; by this time, thus early.

[Not in WYCLIF.] *c* **1391** CHAUCER *Astrol.* II. §11 The howres of the clokke ben departid by 15 degrees al-redy. **1495** CAXTON *Vitas Patr.* (W. de Worde) I. i. 5 b/2 Thou arte alle redy a deuyll like to us. **1526** TINDALE *Rom.* iii. 9 We have all redy proved. **1541** ELYOT *Image Govt.* 96 Any more quietnesse, than I haue all readie. **1611** BIBLE *Eccles.* i. 10 It hath beene already of olde time. **1623** HEMING & CONDELL in *Shaks. Cent. Praise* 145 These Playes have had their triall alreadie. **1711** STEELE *Spect.* No. 140 ¶2, I have lost so much time already. **1860** TYNDALL *Glac.* I. §25. 177 The sunbeams had already fallen upon the mountain.

¶ Sometimes united by a hyphen to participles.

1831 CARLYLE *Sart. Res.* I. xi. 92 The first dim rudiments and already-budding germs of a nobler Era. **1862** H. SPENCER *First Princ.* II. ix. §77 (1875) 231 Already-fractured portions of the Earth's crust.

b. In non-standard idiomatic uses: (*a*) *U.S.* [tr. Yiddish *shoyn* (also Penn. G. *schu*(*u*)*n*)], in final position, to denote emphasis, exasperation, etc.; in Yiddish-influenced speech: freq. 'now', as 'Enough, already!' [tr. Yiddish *genug, shoyn!*]; (*b*) *S. Afr.* [tr. Afrikaans *al* already, yet], used finally (esp. for emphasis) or redundantly: freq. 'by that time'; 'a substandard particle marking or reinforcing "perfective"' (Branford et al. *Agterryer*, 1984).

(*a*) **1903** *McClure's Mag.* Dec. 219/1, I tole the conductor I wanted off right away at the corner already. **1943** M. SHULMAN *Barefoot Boy* (1944) 21 'Yes, young man, this story has helped a great many people, and I hope it will help you.' 'So tell it already,' I said. **1958** *Amer. Speech* XXXIII. 232 Contrast.. 'He has lost his respect for her already,' cited from Pennsylvania-German American speech.. with 'Finish up, already!' from Jewish American speech. **1962** *Ibid.* XXXVII. 204 Other syntactical idiosyncrasies have been moving beyond their usual circuit—from the *shoyn*-inspired *already*, as in, 'Enough, already!'.., which has been heard on the old Paul Winchell television show among others, to [etc.]. **1964** D. GREENBURG *How to be Jewish Mother* (1966) 27 Give me the watermelon already. **1975** *New Yorker* 11 Aug. 29/1 'And Mrs. Orfinger?' 'Dead, Ma. Last year already.'

(*b*) **1920** R. Y. STORMBERG *Mrs. Pieter de Bruyn* 47 If I were a man and your ma was fifty-five already I should still be mad for her. **1926** E. LEWIS *Mantis* II. viii. 131 The baboons having their Hesperean depression already so long —time we got along. **1959** J. MEIRING *Candle in Wind* 8 The old Baas had told her to pay for the sugar and coffee she had bought three weeks ago already! **1975** *Darling* (S. Afr.) 12 Feb. 119 'Smooching, hell,' he grins. 'This is the "Back to Nature" road we on already so soon.' **1984** J. PLATT et al. *New Englishes* vii. 123, I called you up but you weren't there *already.*

† **al'right**, *adv. Obs.* 2–3 **alriht, alrihtes**. [f. ALL *adv.* wholly, quite + *rihte* RIGHT.] Just, exactly.

c **1175** *Lamb. Hom.* 133 Alrihtes swa alse þe wise teolie.. nimeð 3eme of twam þingen. *c* **1230** *Ancr. R.* 92 And alriht so of þe oðre wittes.

alright, a frequent spelling of *all right.*

1893 *Durham Univ. Jrnl.* Nov. 186, I think I shall pass alright. **1897** *Westm. Gaz.* 16 Dec. 9/3 Witness said, 'Alright, come along.' **1924** H. W. FOWLER in *S.P.E. Tract* XVIII. 1 (*subtitle*) Open Court on 'Alright'. **1925** MARQUESS CURZON in Marq. of Zetland *Life* (1928) III. 378, I am sure I shall get through alright. **1926** H. W. FOWLER *Mod. Eng. Usage* 16/1 There are no such forms as *all-right, allright*, or *alright*, though even the last, if seldom allowed by the compositors to appear in print, is often seen.. in MS.

† **als**, *adv.* and *conj. Obs.* Also **alse, alce, alls.** [An intermed. form between the fuller *al-swa*, ALSO and the modern AS. Chiefly northern, though also in Wyclif, etc.] Used especially as:—

1. = ALSO, in its present sense, q.v.

2. = AS, antecedent, with following *as*: *Als* long *as.*

3. (In early times) = AS, relative or conjunctive, with antecedent *also, alse, als*: *Also* old *als* I.

alsa, obs. form of ALSO.

Alsatia (æl'seɪʃ(ɪ)ə). [L. form of *El-sasz*, i.e. foreign settlement, Fr. *Alsace.*]

1. A province west of the middle Rhine, which has formed a 'debatable ground' between France and Germany, whence,

2. Cant name for the precinct of White Friars in London, formerly a sanctuary for debtors and law-breakers; hence, an asylum for criminals.

1688 SHADWELL (*title*) The Squire of Alsatia. **1822** SCOTT *Nigel* xvi. (1878) 204 The lawless and turbulent society of Alsatia. **1865** *Daily Tel.* 22 Dec. 4/6 The two countries are so closely allied that one cannot possibly be turned into an Alsatia for the criminals of the other.

Alsatian (æl'seɪʃ(ɪ)ən), *a.* and *sb.* [f. prec. + -AN.] **1.** Of or belonging to Alsatia. Also *sb.*, an inhabitant of Alsatia; a debtor or criminal in sanctuary.

1691 LUTTRELL *Brief Rel.* (1857) II. 259 The benchers of the Inner Temple, having given orders for bricking up their little gate leading into Whitefryers.. the Alsatians came and pull'd it down. **1704** *Gentl. Instr.* (1732) 491 (D.) Here he struck up with sharpers, scourers, and Alsatians. **1822** SCOTT *Nigel* xvii. (1878) 209 The true Alsatian bully.

2. The registered Kennel Club name for the German Shepherd Dog (*deutscher Schäferhund*), formerly known as the ***Alsatian wolf-dog*** (occas. ***wolf-hound***).

The name *Alsatian* was adopted in order to avoid the associations of *German.* The dog does not belong to Alsace, nor is there a wolf strain in its composition.

1917 A. CROXTON SMITH in *Ladies' Field* 12 May 416/3 The French or Alsatian sheepdogs, which are now becoming familiarised to us. **1922** R. LEIGHTON *Compl. Bk. Dog* 119 The dogs lately introduced into Great Britain as the Alsatian Wolfdog and into the United States as the German sheepdog. *Ibid.* 120 The Alsatian was known in England before the war. **1923** [see WOLF-HOUND]. **1926** D. BROCKWELL (*title*) The Alsatian. *Ibid.* 25 The so-called Police Dog, or German Shepherd Dog,.. variously known as the Alsatian Wolf Dog, Belgian Police Dog, and French Police Dog. **1948** C. L. B. HUBBARD *Dogs in Britain* xviii. 197 The breed [German Shepherd Dog], on its re-importation during 1918–1919, was named Alsatian Wolfdog.

† **al'sauf**, *adv. Obs.* [phrase = all safe, quite safe.] Without fail.

1297 R. GLOUC. 391 Þe kyng.. bed hym alsauf to hym to Gloucestre wende.

‖ **al segno** (æl 'sɛnjəʊ), *phr. Mus.* [It., = to the sign or mark.] A direction to the performer to go back to the place marked 𝄋, and repeat the music from that point.

alsene, variant of ELSON, *Obs.* or *dial.*, awl.

a **1300** W. DE BIBLESWORTH in Wright *Voc.* 150 *Tru de subiloun*, a bore of an alsene.

alsike ('ælsɪk). [Named from *Alsike* near Upsala in Sweden, mentioned by Linnæus as a habitat of this plant.] A species of clover, *Trifolium hybridum.*

1852 LAWSON *Veg. Prod. Scotl.* 68 *Trifolium hybridum* is now well known as Alsike Clover. **1881** *Daily News* 17 Sept. 3/4 (*Seed-market*) Alsike, white, and trefoil continue exceedingly steady.

alsinaceous (ælsɪ'neɪʃəs), *a. Bot.* [f. L. *alsine* chickweed (a. Gr. ἀλσίνη an unidentified plant) + -ACEOUS.] Allied to, or resembling the chickweed.

1835 LINDLEY *Introd. Bot.* I. ii. (ed. 2) 141 The alsinaceous [corolla] has short distant [claws]. **1854** HOOKER *Himalayan Jrnls.* II. xxii. 137 The tufted alsinaceous one. **1879** *Syd. Soc. Lex.*, *Alsinaceous*, Having a polypetalous corolla with intervals between the petals.

alsnesien, early f. ASNESE, *v. Obs.* to pierce.

also ('ɔːlsəʊ, 'ɒlsəʊ), *adv.* Forms: 1 **all swa, al swá**, (WS. **eall swá, eal swá**), 2 **alswa**. *North.* 3–7 **alswa**, 5 **allswa, alsswa**, 5–6 **alsway**, 5–7 **alsua, alsuay**, 4–6 **alsa**. *South.* 2–3 **al swo**, 3–5 **al so**, 5–7 **all so**, 4– **also**. *Contr.* (north. and midl.) 4 **alse,** (**alce**), 3–7 **als**, (6 **alls**). [comb. of ALL = altogether, wholly + SO *sb.* (OE. *al* + *swá*). Cf. Ger. *also*, Du. *alzoo.* Orig. an emphasized expansion of *so* (cf. *al-though, all one, all the same, al-together*), and used in all the historical senses of SO *sb.*, demonstrative, antecedent, and relative. It was, first as a relative, and then as antecedent, shortened through *alsĕ* (*ase*), *als*, to AS, which now always fulfils the relative function, and shares with the original *so* the antecedent function; thus, *as* good *as* this, not *so* good *as* that. As a demonstrative, its force has been weakened from *wholly so, just so*, through *in the same way, likewise*, to *eke, too.* For this weakened sense there was in the 15th c. a tendency, developed in the north into an established usage, to employ the weakened form *alse, als*, but this has been resisted in standard English, where the full *also* is retained in this, now the only current sense. Not common in 16th c.; Shaks., according to Schmidt, has it only 22 times. See AS.]

A. Demonstrative.

† **1.** Wholly so, or quite so; just, or even so; in this or that very manner, even thus. *Obs.*

c **1200** *Trin. Coll. Hom.* 109 Alswo ure helende is almihtin god, and nis non oðer bute he. *c* **1220** *Hali Meid.* 13 Alswa deð meidenhad meidenes cwike flesch wiðute wemmunge halt. *c* **1230** *Ancr. R.* 24 Et alle þe oþre tiden, also biginnen & also enden. *c* **1305** *Judas* in *E.E. Poems* (1862) 111 Also he endede his lyfe. *c* **1425** WYNTOUN *Cron.* III. iii. 110 Hys Land callyd was Hunia, Hunys his Men was callyd alsua.

† **2.** In the very manner of something else; in like manner, in the same way, likewise, similarly (passing in later times into 3). *Obs.*

c **1175** *Lamb. Hom.* 5 Al þat folc eode þar ford to processiun..and in al swa. **1297** R. GLOUC. 319 An byleuede hym þer al nyȝt, & al hys ost al so. *c* **1380** *Sir Ferumb.* 474 Tak þou þanne my gode stede..& eke my scheld al-so. *c* **1400** *Apol. for Loll.* 29 And so it semeth al so to me. *c* **1425** WYNTOUN *Cron.* IX. xiv. 82 And upir Gentillis ..Of his Kyn and his House alswa. **1428** in Heath *Grocers' Comp.* 5 Alsoe the cres-table on the seide north syde of the halle was maad and layd on. **1513** WRIOTHESLEY *Chron.* (1875) I. 8 This yeare allso..Te Deum was sungen. **1535** COVERDALE *Job* ii. 1 When the seruauntes of God came & stode before the Lorde, Sathan came also amonge them, and stode before him. **1611** BIBLE *Mark* i. 38 Let vs goe into yᵉ next townes, that I may preach there also. **1710** STEELE *Tatler* No. 55 ¶5 Some Forces are also posted at Taloir.

3. As a further point, item, or circumstance tending in the same direction; further, in addition, besides, as well, too; taking the place of OE. *éac*, EKE.

a. † *a.* in form *als. Obs.*

c **1250** *Gen. & Ex.* 867 Ðat hird he folȝed als to ðan. **1330** R. BRUNNE *Chron.* 218 And Sir Hugh Bigote als with þe erle fled he. *c* **1325** *E.E. Allit. P.* B. 1377 Þe bourȝ watȝ so brod & so bigge alce. **1352** MINOT *Poems* 4 Thare was crakked many a crowne Of wild Scottes, and alls of tame. *c* **1386** CHAUCER *Frankl. T.* 870 The sorwe of Dorigen he tolde hym als [*v.r.* alse]. **1470** HARDING *Chron.* xxxi, Sixe temples he made, in Cambre & Logres als. **1596** SPENSER *F.Q.* I. ix. 18 Als Una earnd her traveill to renew. *c* **1603** JAMES I *Chorus Ven.* in Farr's *S.P.* 3 With viols, gitterne, cistiers als. **1642** H. MORE *Song of Soul* III. App. liv, Als see whose lovely friendship you decline.

β. in form *also* (northern *alswa*).

[**1382** WYCLIF *John* viii. 19 If ȝe wisten me, perauenture and ȝe schulden wite my father.] **1388** *ibid.*, Ȝe schulden knowe also my fadir [**1526** TINDALE, Ye shuld have knowen my father also]. *c* **1460** *Towneley Myst.* 186 Oure lantarnes take with us alsway. **1570** ASCHAM *Scholem.* I. (Arb.) 49 By his father and mothers also consent. **1582-8** *Hist. James VI* (1804) 87 They not only relaxt him, bot alswa my Lord Heries. **1588** A. KING *Canisius' Catech.* 37 Grante me alsua, o heauenlie father, thy grace. **1597** SHAKS. *2 Hen. IV*, II. iv. 459 Not in Words onely, but in Woes also. **1611** BIBLE *John* xii. 18 For this cause the people also met him. *c* **1720** PRIOR *Engl. Ballad* 53 With ekes and alsos tack thy strain. **1849** MACAULAY *Hist. Eng.* II. 213 The declaration of Charles dispensed only with penal laws. The declaration of James dispensed also with all religious tests. **1857** BUCKLE *Civilis.* i. 2 Great attention has been paid to the history of legislation, also to that of religion. *Ibid.* I. vii. 374 The opposition was not only futile, but it was also injurious.

b. In phr. ***also ran***, applied to horses in a race which do not get a 'place'; also *fig.* of any unsuccessful competitor or inferior person or thing.

1896 ADE *Artie* 21 They ain't even in the 'also rans'. **1904** *Enquirer* (Cincinnati) 6 Feb. 13/3 (*heading*) George B. Cox —He Heads The List Of Also Rans. **1908** G. H. LORIMER *Jack Spurlock* xi. 269 Sporty old three-bottle ancestors, with a genius for throwing deuces and picking also-rans. **1921** F. KLICKMANN *Trail of Ragged Robin* 73 Bella's name [in a list of scholarship winners] was not even among those who 'also ran'. **1924** B. PAIN in *Nash's Mag.* June 7 He is so hard that he puts the nether millstone among the also-ran. **1926** *Daily Gaz.* (Karachi) 11 Oct. 5 Karachi Autumn Meeting. Also ran: Teddy... Also ran: Sir Visto. **1934** *Bulletin* (Sydney) 2 May 25/2 As a football tipster, he is in the also-ran class. **1946** R. KNOX *Epistles & Gospels* 73 It is not enough that he should have put his name down as a candidate in the race for salvation; he may yet be found, if he is not careful, among the also-rans, the ἀδόκιμοι, the people who are 'counted out'. **1949** WODEHOUSE *Mating Season* xxiv. 209 Dobbs..was more laboured in his movements and to an eye like mine, trained in the watching of point-to-point races, had all the look of an also-ran.

B. Antecedent or correlative, with rel. *so, also, alse, als, as. Obs.*, represented by AS, SO, q.v.

†**1.** In the very way (in which something is done); so, as. *Obs.*

c **1250** *Gen. & Ex.* 3436 Als he redde, al-so gan it ben. **1256** *Procl. Henry III*, Al swo al se hit is biforen iseid.

†**2.** In the same degree (in which some other attribute is); so, as. *Obs.*

c **1250** *Gen. & Ex.* 1238 Al-so fer so a boȝe mai ten. *c* **1320** *Seuyn Sages* (W.) 569 Al so sone so he mighte. **1393** LANGL. *P. Pl.* C. XXII. 440 Trauaileþ..for a tretour al-so sore As for a trewe tydy man. *c* **1410** N. LOVE *Bonaventura's Mirr.* (Gibbs MS.) xl. 88 Also mykyll as þow may.

C. Relative and conjunctive. (In this use *alswá*, *also* took the place of OE. *swá*, and was very early weakened to *alse, als*, AS, q.v.)

†**1.** In what manner, in the way that (a thing is done); as. *Obs.* †**2.** To what extent, in the degree that (an attribute is); as. *Obs.*

c **1175** *Cotton Hom.* 217 Alswo sanctus augustinus cweð. **1205** LAYAM. 468 To libben al swa þat wilde swin [**1250** al so þe wilde swin]. *Ibid.* 69 Al swa þe boc spekeð [**1250** as þe bokes speke]. **1250** *Gen. & Ex.* 475 Al-so he mistaȝte, also he schet. *a* **1300** *Floriz & Bl.* 803 A kinedom Also long and also brod Also eure ȝet þi fader ibod. [*c* **1350** in *Dom. Arch.* II. 31 When it was wrought als it sould be. **1458** *Ibid.* III. 42 Werkemen als wise as they coude fynde any.]

†**3.** with *subjunct.* As though, as if. *Obs.*

a **1300** *Floriz & Bl.* 326 Ber wiþ þe square and schauntillun Also þu were a gud Mascun. *c* **1410** N. LOVE *Bonaventura's Mirr.* (Gibbs MS.) xxxix. 86, I haue ouercome þe world Alse who seyth And so schulle ȝe.

† **al'soon**, *adv. Obs.* Also **alsone**, **alsoone**. [= *als soon*, i.e. *as soon*, which is the modern form in sense 1; sense 2 is quite obs.] See also AS SOON.

1. Followed by *as*: As soon. Cf. Fr. *aussitôt que*.

1375 BARBOUR *Bruce* x. 368 Alsoyn As this deuisit wes. **1434** *Test. Ebor.* II. 41 Alson as yᵉ saule be out of yᵉ boddy. **1579** SPENSER *Shep. Cal.* July, Alsoone may shepheard clymbe to skye..As Goteheard prowd.

2. *absol.* As soon as possible, at once, immediately. (Fr. *aussitôt.*)

a **1300** *Cursor M.* 339 He..said wit word, and als son All his comament was don. **1340** HAMPOLE *Pr. Consc.* 4624 Þe grete dome sal noght be aftir alsone. **1375** BARBOUR *Bruce* v. 574 Iames of douglas..The presoners has tane alsone. *c* **1420** *Sir Amadace* lvii. (1842) 50 Alsone his lord he metes.

† **als'tite, als'tit**, *adv. Obs. north.* [= *als tite* = as quick: see TITE.] See also AS-TITE.

1. Followed by *as*: As quick, as soon.

1340 HAMPOLE *Pr. Consc.* 6460 Als tyte alsþe last dome es gyven.

2. *absol.*: As quick as possible, immediately, at once. Cf. ALSOON.

c **1325** *E.E. Allit. P.* B. 1099 What-so he towched also-tyd tourned to hele. *Ibid.* B. 64 Now turne I þeder als-tyd. **1375** BARBOUR *Bruce* v. 80 That we may haf don als-tit. *c* **1400** *Destr. Troy* XXVIII. 11693 Antenor alstite amet to speike. *c* **1420** *Sir Amadace* lvi, Go, Hasteli and alstite.

alstonite ('ɔːlstənaɪt). *Min.* [f. *Alston* in Cumberland, where found.] A double carbonate of lime and baryta, crystallizing in the prismatic or orthorhombic system; Dana prefers the name BROMLITE given by Thomson.

alstrœmeria (ælstrəʊ'mɪərɪə). [mod.L., f. the name of Claude *Alstrœmer*, Swedish naturalist (1736–96): see -IA[1].] A plant of the genus of tropical American amaryllidaceous plants so named, grown in hothouses for their flowers.

1791 *Bot. Mag.* IV. 125 Striped-Flower'd Alstrœmeria... We treat it, and successfully, as a stone plant. **1833** *Penny Cycl.* I. 447/2 Gaily-marked flowers called Alstromerias. **1882** *Garden* 30 Sept. 292/3 Alstrœmerias are real gems, and should be in every garden. **1961** *Amateur Gardening* 2 Dec. 4 Alstrœmerias..with their azalea-like colours and flower heads, are good middle-border plants.

† **al'swith(e, al'swyth(e**, *adv. Obs.* [= *als swith(e*, as quickly: see SWITHE, and cf. *alstite.*]

1. Followed by *as*: As fast, as quickly, as soon.

a **1300** *Cursor M.* 489 Alsuiþe als he was made.

2. *absol.* As fast as possible, with all speed, immediately. Cf. ALSOON.

1375 BARBOUR *Bruce* VIII. 153 His ansuer he tald alswith. *c* **1440** *Morte Arth.* 29 There the knight is dede as swithe. **1501** DOUGLAS *Palice of Hon.* I. lxvii. (1787) 31 Alswyth Do write the sentence.

† **alt**[1]. *Obs.* [a. 16th c. Fr. *alte*; or modification of the earlier ALTO after Fr.] A halt; only in phr. ***to make alt*** (Fr. *faire alte*).

1623 BINGHAM *Xenophon* 61 Cherisophus, that at other times vpon the receit of such messages made vsually Alt, made not Alt then. **1664** S. CLARKE *Tamerlane* 44 The Sultan made divers Alts with four thousand horse.

alt[2] (ælt). *Mus.* [a. Pr. *alt*:—L. *altum* high.] High tone (of voice or instrument); *spec.* in the phr. ***in alt***: in the octave above the treble stave beginning with G.

1535 STEWART *Cron. Scotl.* II. 627 Mony trumpet into sindrie tune, Sum into bas, and sum in alt abone. **1674** PLAYFORD *Skill of Mus.* I. i. 3 Those above E la are called Notes in Alt. **1719** D'URFEY *Pills* (1872) I. 52 In soaring Alts his grand ambition show. *a* **1794** COLMAN *Mus. Lady* I. (D.) Your ladyship's absolutely in alt... Yes, in alt: give me leave to tell your ladyship, that you have raised your voice a full octave higher. **1845** CARLYLE *Cromwell* (1871) IV. 60 Voice risen somewhat into Alt. **1864** BROWNING *Youth & Art* in *Dram. Pers.* 155 As I shook upon E in alt.

b. *fig.* ***in alt***: in an exalted or excited frame of mind; of 'high-flying' views.

1748 RICHARDSON *Clarissa* V. 145 The fair fugitive was all in alt. **1784** *Europ. Mag.* V. 425, I know you to be in alt, as to your religion.

Altaian (æl'teɪən), *a.* and *sb.* [a. Fr. *altaïen* f. *Altai* (mountains in Asia): see -AN.] A term applied by Castrèn to the peoples and languages lying between the Altai Mountains and Arctic Ocean; called by some ethnologists Ugro-Finnish.

1874 tr. *Peschel's Races of Man.* (1876) 377 This group of nations which Castrèn has named Altaians is closely allied to the Eastern and Southern Asiatics.

Altaic (æl'teɪɪk), *a.* and *sb.* [ad. Fr. *altaïque*, f. as prec.: see -IC.] **A.** *adj.* Of or pertaining to the Altai Mountains, or to a family of languages comprising Turkish, Mongol, and Tungus. **B.** *sb.* The Altaic family of languages.

1832 W. MACGILLIVRAY *Trav. Humboldt* xxviii. 415 Between the Altaic range and Teen-shan are Zungaria and the basin of the Ele. **1850** LATHAM *Var. Man.* 15 The term Altaic is taken from the Altai mountains in Central Asia. **1887** C. R. CONDER (*title*) Altaic hieroglyphs and Hittite inscriptions. **1905** *Dublin Rev.* Jan. 190 The Finns..belong rather to the Altaic group. **1933** BLOOMFIELD *Lang.* iv. 68 The Turkish (Turco-Tartar or Altaic) family of languages covers a vast main area, from Asia Minor, conquered, at the end of the Middle Ages, by the Ottoman Turks... These languages..are spoken by some 39 millions of people: Turkish, Tartar, Kirgiz, Uzbeg, Azerbaijani are the more familiar language-names. **1954** PEI & GAYNOR *Dict. Linguistics* 10 *Altaic*, a sub-family (also called Turco-Tartaric or Turkish) of the Ural-Altaic family of languages. It consists of three main branches: Turkic, Mongol and Manchu or Tungus... Some linguists consider Mongol and Manchu distinct sub-families of the Ural-Altaic family, and consider only the members of the Turkic group as the true Altaic languages; hence the alternative designation Turkish for the Altaic sub-family. **1959** *Chambers's Encycl.* I. 303/1 At one time the Altaic family was considered to be related to the Uralian languages, but this view is no longer held.

altaite (æl'teɪaɪt). *Min.* [f. *Altai* mountains, in Asia + -ITE.] A mineral analogous to hessite, a telluride either of silver, or of lead and silver.

‖ **altaltissimo** (æltæl'tɪsɪməʊ,). [It., redupl. comp. of *alto* high + *altissimo* highest.] The very highest summit.

1855 BROWNING *Pict. Flor.* in *Men & Wom.* II. 47 The Belltower's altaltissimo.

altar ('ɔːltə(r)). Forms: 1 **altar**, 1–6 **alter**, 3–6 **auter**, 3–7 **aulter**, 4 **altere**, **awtiere**, **awteer**, 4–5 **awtier**, 4–6 **awter**, **autere**, 5 **autir**, **auuter**, **awtare**, (**nawtyr**), 5–6 **aughter**, 6 **autre**, **awlter**, **alterr(e**, **-are**, **aultar**, 6–7 **altar**. [a. L. *altāre*, pl. *altāri-a*, prob. orig. a 'high place,' f. *alt-us* high. With OE. *altar*, cf. OS., OHG. and ON. *altari*, *alteri*, OFris. *altare*, *alter*. Side by side with the OE. form, the OFr. *au'ter* (earlier *autier*, *aultier*, *altier*:—L. *altāre*) was adopted *a* 1300, and both forms, with many intermediate ones, continued to 16th c., when the spelling *altar*, after L., prevailed.]

A. 1. a. A block, pile, table, stand, or other raised structure, with a plane top, on which to place or sacrifice offerings to a deity.

c **1000** ÆLFRIC *Matt.* v. 23 Læt þær þine lác beforan þam altare [*v.r.* wefode, *Lindisf. G.* wigbed, *Hatt.* weofede]. *c* **1200** *Trin. Coll. Hom.* 135 Ðe holi man sah þe heȝ engel atte alteres ende. *c* **1250** *Gen. & Ex.* 1325 Ysaac was leid ðat auter on. **1366** MAUNDEV. iii. 16 There is an Awtier upon his Toumbe. **1393** GOWER *Conf.* III. 250 From under thalter sodeinly An hideous serpent openly Cam out. **1535** COVERDALE *Ex.* xxxviii. 1 The altare of burnt offrynges. *Ibid.* *1 Macc.* iv. 49 The aulter of incense. **1611** BIBLE *Gen.* viii. 20 And Noah builded an Altar vnto the Lord. **1667** MILTON *P.L.* XI. 323 So many grateful Altars I would reare Of grassie Terfe. **1772** PENNANT *Tours in Scotl.* (1774) 180 An altar for sacrifices to the immortal gods. **1821** BYRON *Cain* I. i, I will build no more altars.

b. *fig.* with reference to the uses, customs, dedication, or peculiar sanctity of the altar.

1401 *Pol. Poems* (1859) II. 42 Datan and Abiron..with newe senceres ensencen the auters of synne. **1580** SIDNEY *Arcadia* I. 82 Where thoughts be the temple, sight is an aultar. **1601** SHAKS. *Twel. N.* v. i. 116 You vnciuill Ladie To whose ingrate, and vnauspicious Altars My soule the faithfull'st offrings haue breath'd out. **1635** HOWELL *Lett.* (1650) II. 41 Farewell my dear Tom..Yours to the altar, J.H. **1775** BURKE *Sp. Conc. Amer.* Wks. III. 94 The stones which construct the sacred altar of peace. **1857** HEAVYSEGE *Saul* (1869) 381 The stars shall sooner fall Each from its sacred altar in the heavens.

2. a. In those Christian Churches which celebrate the eucharist or communion service as a sacrifice, the raised structure consecrated to this celebration.

(*High Altar*, the chief altar in a cathedral or church.)

c **1200** ORMIN 1061 Att te minnstredure wass An allterr þær wiþþutenn. *c* **1340** *Gaw. & Gr. Knt.* 593 He herkneȝ his masse, Offred & honoured at þe heȝe auter. **1366** MAUNDEV. x. 112 A gret Awteer of a faire Chirche. *a* **1420** OCCLEVE *De Reg. Princ.* 381, I in the sacrament Of the autére fully beleve. *c* **1440** *Gesta Rom.* 261 The body of Crist liyng vpon the awter. *a* **1500** *Nominale* in Wright *Voc.* 230/2 *Hoc altare*, a nawtyr. **1553-87** FOXE *A. & M.* I. 456/2 Priests to offren in the auter thy flesh and thy blood. **1692** WASHINGTON tr. *Milton's Def. Pop.* ii. (1851) 68 He compell'd them to set up Altars, which all Protestants abhor. **1826** SCOTT *Woodst.* (1832) 175 The high altar had been removed.

b. As applied to the 'holy table' of the English Prayer-book, which occupies the place of the altars removed after the Reformation.

[In the Prayer Book of 1549 *altar* occurs side by side with 'God's board, Lord's table, Holy table,' the two latter of which at length displaced it in authoritative use (exc. in the Coronation Service). The word was the subject of much controversy in 17th c. In common parlance it is now used to a great extent indifferently with 'Communion-table' (Lord's table, Holy table) sometimes literally, sometimes figuratively; but controversially, one or the other is used according to the doctrine of the Eucharist held or sought to be emphasized.]

1549 *1st Prayer Bk. Edw. VI* (1852) 298 These wordes before rehersed are to be saied, turning still to the Altar, without any eleuacion or shewing the sacrament to the people. [Also called p. 266 *Lord's Table*, p. 302 *God's Board*, and p. 273 *Holy Table.*] **1625** LAUD *Diary* Wks. (1853) III. 181, I returned and offered them [the regalia] solemnly at the altar in the name of the king. *a* **1626** BP. ANDREWES *Answ. Cdl. Perron* 6 The Holy Eucharist being considered as a Sacrifice, the same is fitly called an altar: which again is as fitly called a Table, the Eucharist being considered as a Sacrament. **1635** BRERETON *Trav.* (1844) 82 It was not to be accounted an altar but the communion-table. **1637** (14 June) LAUD *Sp. in Star-Ch.* 54 The placing of the Holy Table Altarwise (since they will needs call it so). *a* **1638** MEDE *Wks.* II. 386 [*Marg. title*] Of the name Altar anciently given to the Holy Table. **1641** LD. BROOKE *Episc.* 18 Placing the Communion Table Altar-wise, Railing it in, Bowing to it, etc. **1641-74** CLARENDON *Hist. Reb.* I. i. (1843) 39/1 [anno 1635] Those Disputes brought in new words, and terms (Altar, Adoration, and Genuflexion, and other expressions). **1660** STILLINGFLEET *Irenicum* I. ii. (1662) 66 The Altar, as they metaphorically called the Communion-Table. **1742** BAILEY *Dict.* s.v., The Christians call the Communion Table their *Altar*, because they offer up thereon a Sacrifice of Thanksgiving, in Memory of the Death and Passion of Jesus Christ. **1791** BOSWELL *Johnson* (1831) I. 484 We went and looked at the church..and walked up to the altar. **1831** *Eng. Coron. Service*, Then the Archbishop takes the sword from off the altar, and..saith:—Receive this kingly sword brought now from the altar of God. **1883** *Daily News* 27 Mar. 7/2 Disturbing the congregation of St. Paul's Cathedral..[and] breaking certain ornaments on the altar.

c. In phr. '*to lead a bride to the altar*,' as the place at which the marriage service in a church is concluded; whence 'hymeneal altar.'

1820 COMBE (Dr. Syntax) *Consolation* VI. 236 The indissoluble tie Which hallow'd Altars sanctify. *a* **1842** TENNYSON *Lord of Burl.* 11 Leads her to the village altar. **1883** *Daily News* 9 Mar. 3/2 Mr. — is about to lead to the hymeneal altar a charming young lady now resident in Paris.

3. *fig.* A place consecrated to devotional observances. ***family altar***: the place or scene of family devotions.

1693 O. HEYWOOD (*title*) The Family Altar, erected to the honour of the Eternal God.

4. A metrical address or dedication, fancifully written or printed in the form of an altar. *arch.*

1680 BUTLER *Rem.* (1759) II. 120 As for *Altars* and *Pyramids* in Poetry, he has outdone all Men. **1682** DRYDEN *Mac Fleckn.* 206 Some peaceful province in Acrostic land, Where thou may'st wings display, and altars raise.

5. A southern constellation, also called *Ara*.

1556 RECORDE *Cast. Knowl.* 270 Vnder the Scorpions tayle, standeth the Altar. **1868** LOCKYER *Heavens* (ed. 3) 334 The Altar and the Southern Triangle..bring us back to Argo.

6. Each of the steps or ledges up the sloping sides of a graving-dock. [Suggested by *altar-step*: see B. II.]

1840 *Civil Engin. & Arch. Jrnl.* III. 27/2 The object of these altars is for the convenience of placing the shores against the hull of a vessel at any height, and for resting the ends of spars for staging. **1885** VERNON-HARCOURT *Harbours & Docks* I. 457 The sides of a graving dock..are constructed with steps, or altars, for receiving the timber props which support the vessel in an upright position.

B. altar- in *comb.* **I.** General syntactic relations.

1. *objective gen.* with n. of agent or action, as ***altar-adorer, -building, -worship***.

1641 in Rushw. *Hist. Coll.* III. (1692) I. 553 A notable Arminian and an Altar-adorer. **1705** HICKERINGILL *Priest-cr.* IV. 231 Cold Formality, and Altar-Worship. **1831** CARLYLE *Sart. Res.* III. iii. 256 Were this an altar-building time.

2. *instr.* & *locative* with pa. pple., as ***altar-vowed***.

1748 RICHARDSON *Clarissa* (1811) II. 72 Some new breach of an altar-vowed duty.

3. *attrib.* Of or belonging to an altar or its appurtenances, as ***altar-cross, -pile, -place, -side, -top***; ALTAR-CLOTH, -PIECE, -STONE; and most of those in II.

1816 BYRON *Darkness* 58 The dying embers of an altar-place. **1871** F. T. PALGRAVE *Lyr. Poems* 34 From the altar-top Strewing her golden hair with ashes hoar.

4. *attrib.* Of or connected with the use of an altar, as ***altar-boy, -god, -servant, -service, -taper***; ***altar-bread, -thane***.

1552-5 LATIMER *Serm. & Rem.* (1845) 260 Their white idol (I should have said their altar-god). **1610** HEALEY *St. Aug., City of God* 281 The altar-servant, or sacrificer. **1772** *Hist. Friar Gerund* I. 150 Idiots who are not fit to be made altar-boys. **1860** G. M. HOPKINS *Escorial* in *Poems* (1930) 129 The Altar-tapers flar'd in gusts.

II. Special combinations (with quotations in alphabetical order). **altar-bread**, the bread used in celebrating the Communion; **altar-card**, any of a set of three cards placed on the altar (one in the middle, and one at either end), containing certain portions of the Eucharistic prayers to assist the priest's memory; **altar-fire**, the fire on an altar, *fig.* religious rite; **altar-front, -frontal, -facing**, a movable frame, or a hanging of silk, etc., placed in front of an altar, the *antependium*; **altar-plate**, the plate used in the communion service; **altar-pyx**, a pyx or box for holding the consecrated elements; **altar-rails**, the rails separating the sacrarium from the rest of the chancel; **altar-screen**, the reredos wall or screen at the back of a (church-) altar; **altar-slab**, the slab forming the top of an altar; **altar-stair**, a flight of steps ascending to an altar; **altar-stead**, the place where an altar stands; **altar-step**, a step ascending to an altar; **altar-table** (= **altar-slab**); †**altar-thane**, the priest serving an altar, a mass-priest; **altar-tomb**, a raised monument resembling a solid altar; **altar-ways** (= ALTARWISE).

1849 ROCK *Ch. Fathers* I. ii. 144 *Altar-Bread was unleavened. *Ibid.* 149 Irons for baking *Altar-Breads. **1849** T. GRANT *Let.* 4 July in 'G. Ramsay' *Thomas Grant* (1874) v. 85 A subscription for publishing on stone a set of illuminated *altar cards. **1884** ADDIS & ARNOLD *Cath. Dict.* s.v. *Altar*, Under the crucifix there ought to be an altar-card, with certain prayers which the priest cannot read from the Missal without inconvenience. **1905** *Church Times* 30 June 842/2 A 'wooden altar card' of the 18th century. It is a thick wooden panel, about 2 ft. by 18 in., painted to imitate a book, bearing the words, 'The Lord Jesus after He was betrayed,' etc., from the prayer of Consecration in the English liturgy; it stood on the altar of Redbourn Church, Herts, until about 1850. **1850** TENNYSON *In Mem.* xli. 3 Mounts the heavenward *altar-fire. **1876** GEO. ELIOT *Dan. Der.* III. xxxvii. 129 To Daniel the words Father, Mother had the *altar-fire in them. **1566** in *Eng. Ch. Furn.* (1866) 56 Item an *altar ffront sold to Sir Richard thoryld. **1867** LADY HERBERT *Cradle L.* iii. 80 A beautiful silver *altar-front. **1859** GULLICK & TIMBS *Paint.* 308 A more important class of panel picture—viz. the *altar-frontals or *antependia*. These *altar-facings were moveable. **1856** FROUDE *Hist. Eng.* III. II. xiii, The desecration of the abbey-chapels and *altar-plate. *a* **1683** OLDHAM *Wks.* 1697, 79 (JOD.) Yon *altar-pyx of gold is the abode, And safe repository of their god. **1860** W. CLARK *Vac. Tour* 53 An aged priest, standing within the *altar rails. **1866** PEACOCK *Eng. Ch. Furn.* 21 The *altar-slabs thus used as fire-backs and bridges. **1856** MRS. BROWNING *Aur. Leigh* IV. 802 The topmost *altar-stair. **1868** MORRIS *Earthly Par.* I. 94 Hung up as relics nigh the *altar-stead. **1846** KEBLE *Lyra Innoc.* (1873) 7 With pure heart to fall Before His *Altar-step. **1566** in *Eng. Ch. Furn.* (1866) 42 On *alter table broken by Mr. Vycar. **1753** CHAMBERS *Cycl. Supp.*, **Altar-thane* in our ancient law-books, denotes a priest or parson of a parish. **1739** F. BLOMEFIELD *Hist. Norfolk* I. 227 Under this, is an *Altar-Tomb cover'd with a Black Marble. **1769** GRAY *Let.* in *Wks.* (1775) 368 There is an altar-tomb of one of them dated 1577. **1879** G. SCOTT *Lect. Archit.* I. 180 The marble altar-tomb of Queen Eleanor. **1641** in Burton *Diary* (1828) III. 89 Caused the Communion-Table..to be removed, and set *altar-ways.

altarage ('ɔːltərɪdʒ). Also 5 **awterage**. [a. OFr. *auterage, autelage*: see ALTAR and -AGE.]

1. The revenue arising from oblations at an altar.

1478 *Paston Lett.* 819 III. 232 The parson had all the awterage and oder profytes. **1661** J. STEPHENS *Procurations, etc.* 108 Altaragies, that is, offerings made upon the Altar. **1778** T. BATEMAN *Agistm. Tithe* (ed. 2) 83 The Vicar..is excluded from every Tithe—Altarage and Emolument.

2. A fund or provision for the maintenance of an altar and a priest to say masses thereat.

1634-46 J. ROW (father) *Hist. Kirk* (1842) 27 That all formerlie pertaining to freirs, preists, monks, altarages, etc., be employed for schools. **1851** *Orig. Paroch. Scot.* I. 461 Between 1329 and 1371 John Spottiswood..founded an altarage in this church.

'altar-cloth. [ALTAR- 3.] *prop.* The linen cloth used at the Communion or the Mass; but frequently applied to the silk frontal and super-frontal.

c **1200** *Trin. Coll. Hom.* 163 His alter cloð is great and sole. *c* **1440** *Lay-Folks Mass-Bk., B.P.* iii. (1879) 71 Awterclath or towel, or any other anourment. *a* **1500** *Nominale* in Wright *Voc.* 231/1 *Hoc lurthium*, a nawtyr-cloth. **1522** in *Bury Wills* 117, I bequethe to Fryers of Babbewell an aughter clothe of diaper. **1641** MILTON *Ch. Discip.* II. (1851) 47 Rich Coaps, gorgeous Altar-clothes. **1856** R. A. VAUGHAN *Hours w. Myst.* (ed. 2) I. 222 He covers his table with an 'altar-cloth.'

altared ('ɔːltəd), *ppl. a.* [f. ALTAR + -ED.] **a.** Furnished or honoured with an altar. **b.** Treated as an altar.

1641 *Armin. Nunnery* 6 The east end, where the altered table stood. **1652** in *Benlowe's Theophila* Pref., Altar'd Theophil, Incenst with sweet obedience.

†**'altarer.** *Obs.* In 5 **auterer.** [f. ALTAR + -ER[1]; cf. *waggoner*.] One who ministers at an altar.

1413 LYDG. *Pylgr. Sowle* I. i. (1859) 1, I sawe also the Auterer, that clepyd is dame prayer.

†**al'tarian,** *a. Obs. rare*$^{-1}$. [f. ALTAR + -IAN.] Of, or connected with, an altar.

1642 SIR E. DERING *Sp. on Relig.* 111 Our Papall misleaders and Altarian innovators.

altarist ('ɔːltərɪst). [a. Fr. *altariste*:—late L. *altarista*.] (See quot.)

1753 CHAMBERS *Cycl. Supp.*, *Altarist* properly denotes the vicar of a church. **1882** W. HENDERSON *Process. Eccl. Sarum* Pref. 10 Altarists had to see that everything necessary for the service of the altars was ready for the priest.

altarless ('ɔːltəlɪs), *a. poet.* [f. ALTAR + -LESS.] Without any altar.

1878 B. TAYLOR *Deukalion* II. iv. 78 Go, altarless yet worshipped!

altarlet ('ɔːltəlɪt). [f. ALTAR + -LET.] A small altar.

1829 SOUTHEY *All for Love* Wks. VII. 281 Of how small dimensions..may better be collected from the measure of the altarlet itself.

'altar-piece. [ALTAR- 3.] A painting or sculpture placed behind and over an altar; a reredos.

1644 EVELYN *Mem.* (1857) I. 127 The altar-piece of St. Michael being of Mosaic. **1762** H. WALPOLE *Vertue's Anecd. Paint.* (1786) I. 81 A much admired work of Mabuse was an altar-piece at Middleburgh. **1859** GULLICK & TIMBS *Paint.* 305 Altar-pieces were originally portable.

'altar-stone. [ALTAR- 3.] A stone forming part of an altar; especially, the slab forming the top or table; the super-altar; also (in *R.C. Ch.*) a portable slab used by priests when mass is said at 'stations.'

c **1325** *Cœur de L.* 41 At Cantyrbury at the awterston, Wher many myraclys are idon. **1566** in *Eng. Ch. Furn.* (1866) 37 The aulter stones—Broken in peces by the aboue named church wardens. **1814** SCOTT *Ld. of Isles* II. xxiv, Murder done Even on the sacred altar-stone! **1870** BRYANT *Homer* I. II. 50 A frightful serpent From beneath the altar-stone Came swiftly gliding.

altarwise ('ɔːltəwaɪz), *adv.* [f. ALTAR + WISE.] After the manner of an altar; in the position of an altar in a church.

1562 in Strype *Ann. Ref.* (1824) I. I. xxvii. 475 That the table from henceforth stand no more altarwise. **1637** LAUD *Sp. in Star-Ch.* (T.) The holy table ought to stand at the upper end of the quire, north or south, or altarwise. [See also ALTAR 2 b.] **1697** DRYDEN *Virgil* (1806) III. 161 In altar-wise, a stately pile they rear. **1859** MASSON *Milton* I. 629 Fixing the communion-table altarwise at the east end of the chancel.

altazimuth (æltˈæzɪmʌθ). [f. *alt.* for ALTITUDE + AZIMUTH.] An instrument, invented by Prof. Airy, for determining the altitude and azimuth of a heavenly body.

1860 DUNKIN *Handbk. Astron.* §49 The Greenwich altazimuth instrument. **1868** LOCKYER *Elem. Astron.* §523 To make an observation with the altazimuth. **1876** CHAMBERS *Astron.* 640 A form of altazimuth mounting for Newtonian Reflectors.

†**'altel.** *Obs. rare*$^{-1}$. [a. MFr. *altel* (mod. *autel*) altar.] = ALTAR 2.

a **1555** BRADFORD *Wks.* II. 314 (D.) Hear mass devoutly, and take altel holy bread.

alter ('ɔːltə(r)), *v.* Forms: 4-5 **altere**, 6 **altar**, 6-7 **altre**, 4- **alter**. [a. 14th c. Fr. *altére-r* (Pr. or It. *alterar*) ad. med.L. *alterā-re*, f. *alter* other.]

1. a. To make (a thing) otherwise or different in some respect; to make some change in character, shape, condition, position, quantity, value, etc. without changing the thing itself for another; to modify, to change the appearance of.

c **1374** CHAUCER *Troylus* III. 1787 Love..alterid his spirit so withynne. **1398** TREVISA *Barth. De P.R.* VIII. x. (1495) 314 The ouer bodyes of heuen altere and chaunge thyse nether thynges. **1509** FISHER *Fun. Serm.* Wks. 1876, 304 [The body] anone begynneth to putrefye..The ayre dothe alter it. **1596** SHAKS. *Merch. V.* IV. i. 219 No power in Venice Can alter a decree established. **1605** CAMDEN *Rem.* 14 The English-Saxon conquerors altred the tongue. **1691** LUTTRELL *Brief. Rel.* (1857) II. 301 Several of the Irish forces that intended at first to goe for France, have alter'd their minds. **1756** BURKE *Vind. Nat. Soc.* Wks. I. 25, I am obliged to alter my design. **1833** LYELL *Princ. Geol.* III. 373 The heat which alters the strata. **1872** YEATS *Techn. Hist. Comm.* 164 Fashion in shoes..was quite altered after the Crusades.

b. *transf.* To geld or spay (an animal). *U.S.* and *Austral.*

1821 T. B. HAZARD *Nailer Tom's Diary* (1930) 555/2 Worner Knowles oltered my four Boar Piggs. **1895** *Australas. Pastoralists' Rev.* 15 Aug. 295 For this reason bulls were rarely altered (castrated) till they were four or five years old.

2. *intr.* (for *refl.*) To become otherwise, to undergo some change in character or appearance.

1590 GREENE *Mourning Garm.* (1616) Pref. 4 Such as alter in a moment, win not credit in a moneth. **1611** BIBLE *Dan.* vi. 12 The law of the Medes and Persians which altereth not. **1769** *Junius Lett.* xxxv. 154 Human nature..is greatly altered for the better. **1879** LUBBOCK *Sci. Lect.* i. 30 Both insects and flowers are continually altering in their structure.

†**3.** *trans.* To affect mentally; to disturb. *Obs.* (Cf. the dial. *to put about.*)

1542 HENRY VIII *Declar.* in *Compl. Scotl.* 194 We..suffered our selfe to be somewhat altred by his wordes and fayre promyses. **1615** CHAPMAN *Odyss.* IX. 96 Then began the bitter Fate of Jove To alter us unhappy. *a* **1674** MILTON (in Webster), I suppose them..not a little altered and moved inwardly in their minds.

†**4.** *intr.* To administer alterative medicines. *Obs.*

1656 RIDGLEY *Pract. Physic* 331 Afterwards we must purge, alter, and that often. **1684** tr. *Bonet's Merc. Compit.* XIX. 764 Some practitioners..always alter and never Purge.

alter ('ɔːltə(r), 'æltə(r)), *sb. Psychol.* [L., another.] Something (esp. another person) regarded as existing outside the self; the objects and experience of the world viewed as distinct from and interacting with oneself. Cf. ALTER EGO and EGO 4.

1897 J. M. BALDWIN *Social & Ethical Interpretations in Mental Devel.* i. 11 All the things I hope to learn..are now, before I acquire them, possible elements of my thought of others, of the social alter, or of what considered generally we may call the 'socius'. **1909** W. M. URBAN *Valuation* ix. 267 The dramatic tendency in the characterisation of the self and the alter. **1934** H. C. WARREN *Dict. Psychol.* 10/2 *Alter*, the individual's conception of other beings as distinct from himself. **1977** A. GIDDENS *Stud. in Social & Polit. Theory* x. 336 Ego may try to control the 'situation' in which alter is placed, or try to control alter's 'intentions'.

alterability (ˌɔːltərəˈbɪlɪtɪ). [f. ALTERABLE: see -BILITY. Cf. Fr. *altérabilité*.] = ALTERABLENESS.

[Not in JOHNSON 1755, TODD 1818, RICHARDSON 1836.] **1847** in CRAIG. **1851** RUSKIN *Mod. Paint.* III. IV. xii. §10 The difference..is, on the whole, chiefly in this point of alterability. **1862** F. HALL *Hindu Philos. Syst.* 192 Neither to Brahma, nor to any part of him, has there ever attached..the least ignorance or alterability.

alterable ('ɔːltərəb(ə)l), *a.* [a. Fr. *altérable*: see ALTER and -ABLE.]

†**1.** Liable to alter or vary, variable, changeable.

1526 FRITH *Disput. Purg.* 193 His justice and mercy are ever one, and not alterable. 1696 WEDDERBURN *David's Test.* iv. 28 His peace, his joy..are indeed moveable and very alterable things.

2. Capable of being altered or changed.

1574 WHITGIFT *Def. Answ.* ii. Wks. 1851 I. 284 Which, being external matters and alterable, are to be altered and changed. 1630 PRYNNE *Anti-Armin.* 114 It is contingent and alterable at mans pleasure. 1744 LD. LYTTELTON *Sp. Scotch Bill* Wks. 1776 III. 5 The laws that concern publick right, policy and civil government..are declared to be alterable by Parliament. 1802 PLAYFAIR *Illustr. Hutton. Th.* 278 Substances alterable by fire. 1840 CARLYLE *Heroes* v, The manner of it is very alterable: the matter and fact of it is not alterable by any power under the sky.

†**3.** Capable of producing alteration, or change of state in something else. *Obs. rare.*

1594 CAREW tr. *Huarte's Exam. Wits* (1616) 283 There are some men whose generatiue facultie is vnable, and not alterable for one woman, and yet for another is apt & begetteth issue.

alterableness (ˈɔːltərəb(ə)lnɪs). [f. prec. + -NESS.] The quality of being alterable; capability of being altered; alterability.

1655 GOUGE *Comm. Hebr.* xii. 27 III. 373 The Apostle giveth us to understand..1. The alterablenesse of the Law. *Ibid.* 381 The alterableness of the law is implied in this word, *removing*. 1755 in JOHNSON; and in mod. Dicts.

alterably (ˈɔːltərəblɪ), *adv.* [f. ALTERABLE + -LY².] In an alterable manner; so as to be capable of alteration.

1755 in JOHNSON; and in mod. Dicts.

†ˈ**alterage**. *Obs. rare*⁻¹. [f. L. *altor* a foster-father, agent-noun f. *al-ĕre* to nourish + -AGE. Cf. *porterage*.] Fostering, rearing.

1612 SIR J. DAVIES *Why Ireland etc.* (1747) 180 In Ireland, where they put away al their children to Fosterers, the potent and rich men selling, the meaner sort buying, the alterage of their children.

†ˈ**alterance**. *Obs. rare*⁻¹. [f. ALTER + -ANCE, as if a. Fr. **altérance*.] Alteration.

1559 BP. SCOT in Strype *Ann. Ref.* I. App. x. 27 But maketh fourther earneste request for alteraunce, yea, for the clear abolysshinge of the same.

alterant (ˈɔːltərənt), *a.* and *sb.* [a. Fr. *altérant* pr. pple. of *altérer* to ALTER.]

A. *adj.* Producing alteration or change.

1626 BACON *Sylva* §800 Whether the Body be Alterant, or Altered, evermore a Perception preceedeth Operation. 1879 WHITNEY *Sansk. Gram.* 57 The vowels that cause the alteration of s to ṣ may be called..'alterant' vowels.

B. *sb.*

1. Anything which alters, or changes the state of another.

1750 *Leonardus's Mirr. Stones* 41 Both from the water and the sun, and from extrinsic alterants. 1879 G. GLADSTONE in *Cassell's Techn. Educ.* I. 76 Importance of mordants consists in their so fixing the colours..and that of alterants in their bringing out or changing the tint.

†**2.** *spec.* An alterative medicine. *Obs.*

17.. QUINCY in *Phil. Trans.* XXXI. 75 We frequently meet with..many of this sort mention'd, as Alterants. 1737 BRACKEN *Farriery Impr.* (1756) II. vi. 221 Then Vomits, Purgatives, and proper Alterants take place. 1753 CHAMBERS *Cycl. Supp.*, *Alterants* are supposed to exert their power chiefly on the humours of the body.

†ˈ**alterate**, *ppl. a. Obs.* [ad. late L. *alterāt-us* pa. pple. of *alter-āre* to ALTER.] = ALTERED.

c1450 HENRYSON *Test. Cres.* 195 (R.) She was dissimulate ..And sodainly chaunged and alterate. 1470 HARDING *Chron.* cvi, With sickenes he was so alterate He dyed then. 1531 ELYOT *Governour* II. ix. (R.) His excellent lawes beinge stablyshed shulde never be alterate.

†ˈ**alterate**, *v. Obs.* [f. prec., or on analogy of vbs. so formed.] A by-form of ALTER.

c1475 *Pol. Poems* II. 287 That theyre pover levyng..May be altratyd unto welth. 1530 PALSGR. 421/1, I alterate, I alter, I chaunge, *Je altere*. 1549 CHALONER tr. *Erasm. Moriæ Enc.* T ij b, Those holy men shall be altogether transformed and alterated. a1618 SYLVESTER *Myst. Mysterie* 24 (1880) II. 316 No outward Force..Can Thy drad Essence alterate. 1655 CULPEPER *Riverius* VII. i. 152 Expectorating Medicines, and the rest are to be alterated for the same reason. 1693 W. ROBERTSON *Phraseol. Gen.*, To Alter, alterate or change.

alteration (ɔːltəˈreɪʃən). [a. Fr. *altération* (14th c.), ad. med.L. *alterātiōn-em*, f. *alterā-re* to ALTER.]

1. The action of altering or making some change in a thing.

1482 *Monk of Evesham* 58 Of these alteracyons of tymes.. ther was non ende. 1579 in Heath *Grocers' Comp.* (1869) 81 A mistrust and great dowte of alteracion of religion. 1585 ABP. SANDYS *Serm.* (1841) 238 To attempt alteration and change in the church of God. 1605 SHAKS. *Lear* v. i. 3 He's full of alteration. a1674 CLARENDON *Hist. Reb.* I. 55 The inconveniencies that might attend any alteration. 1769 BURKE *State Nat.* Wks. 1842 I. 106 Good men..take advantage of the opportunity of such derangement in favour of an useful alteration. a1884 *Mod.* The alteration of the house was a tedious business. 1922 JOYCE *Ulysses* 487 To alteration one pair trousers eleven shillings.

2. A change in the character or appearance of anything, viewed as a fact; an altered or changed condition.

1532 W. THYNNE in *Animadv.* Pref. 24 The contraricties and alteracions founde by the collacion of the one [edition] with the other. 1606 G. W[OODCOCKE] *Hist. Justine* 95 Reioycing in this happy alteration. 1667 MILTON *P.L.* IX. 599 Ere long I might perceave Strange alteration in me. 1796 MORSE *Amer. Geog.* II. 5 Any known alterations from this statement will be noticed. 1878 HUXLEY *Physiogr.* 187 Movements of elevation or depression which produce permanent alterations of level.

†**3.** A distemper. *Obs.*

1621 BURTON *Anat. Mel.* I. ii. II. iii. (1651) 77 Strange meats..cause notable alterations and distempers. 1653 URQUHART *Rabelais* I. xxiii, By which medicine he cleansed all the alteration and perverse habitude of his braine. 1663 BUTLER *Hudibr.* I. i. 575 Death of Great Men, Alterations, Diseases, Battels, Inundations.

†**4.** *Music.* (See quot.) *Obs.*

1597 T. MORLEY *Introd. Mus.* 24 The note which is to be altered is commonly marked with a pricke of alteration. 1609 DOULAND *Ornithop. Microl.* 57 Alteration..is the doubling of a lesser Note in respect of a greater, or..it is the doubling of the proper value.

5. *attrib.*: **alteration hand**, one who alters or remakes ready-made clothes to suit customers' requirements, or renovates old or second-hand garments.

1901 *Daily Chron.* 9 Sept. 9/4 Mantles.—Wanted a good alteration hand. 1961 *Evening Standard* 21 Aug. 17/6 Alteration Hand (female)..C. & A. Modes Ltd.

alterative (ˈɔːltərətɪv), *a.* and *sb.* [f. late L. *alterāt-* ppl. stem of *alterāre* to ALTER, as if ad. L. **alterātīvus* prob. used in med. or mod.L. Cf. Fr. *altératif, -ive*.] **A.** *adj.*

1. Having the tendency to produce alteration; *esp.* applied to medicines which alter the processes of nutrition, and reduce them to healthy action.

1605 BACON *Adv. Learn.* II. x. §5 (1873) 138 Cannot be removed by medicine alterative. 1621 BURTON *Anat. Mel.* II. iv. I. ii, Simples are alterative or purgative. 1775 JOHNSON in *Boswell* xlix. (1847) 451 My opinion of alterative medicine is not high, but *quid tentasse nocebit?* 1855 GARROD *Mat. Med.* (ed. 6) 23 Iodine has a powerful alterative action.

†**2.** *passively*, Liable to be changed. *Obs.*

1656 BLOUNT *Glossogr.*, *Alterative*, changed, or that may be changed.

B. *sb.* An alterative medicine or treatment.

1398 TREVISA *Barth. De P.R.* VII. xxi. (1495) 239 The cure is with hote alteratiues. 1621 BURTON *Anat. Mel.* II. iv. I. i, Of alteratiues and Cordials, no man doubts. 1720 GIBSON *Dispens.* App. I. i. (1734) 47 Alteratives..have a power of changing the Constitution, without any sensible increase or decrease of the natural evacuations. 1807 CRABBE *Libr.* 59 Here alt'ratives, by slow degrees controul The chronic habits of the sickly soul. 18.. H. S. WILSON *Alpine Asc.* ii. 29 Alterative and excitement are best got in Switzerland.

†**altercand**, *ppl. a. Obs. rare*⁻¹. [? ad. L. *altercant-em* pr. pple. of *altercā-ri* (see next) with northern ppl. ending.] Disputing; quarrelsome.

1330 R. BRUNNE *Chron.* 314 Þe parties wer so felle altercand on ilk side, þat non þe soth couth telle, whedir pes or werre suld tide.

altercate (ˈæltəkeɪt, ˈɔːl-). [f. L. *altercāt-* ppl. stem of *altercā-ri* to dispute with another, wrangle, f. *alter* another.] To dispute vehemently, warmly, or angrily; to contend in wordy warfare; to wrangle.

1530 PALSGR. 421/1, I altercate, I moultiply langage or stryve in wordes. 1632 QUARLES *Div. Fancies* I. xl, Never fight Nor wrangle more, nor altercate agin. 1778 B. LINCOLN in Sparks *Corr. Amer. Rev.* (1853) II. 241 The hard necessity of altercating with the civil power. 1810 *Ann. Reg.* 333/2 To altercate with the Landlady about some threepence or fourpence. 1837 LYTTON *Athens* II. 208 It becomes us not..to altercate on the localities of the battle.

altercation (æltəˈkeɪʃən, ˌɔːl-). Forms: 4–5 **altercacioun**, 4–6 **-cion**, **-cyon**, 5 **-tyown**, **altircacioune**, 6 **altri-**, **altrycacion**, **altérication**, 6– **altercation**. [a. Fr. *altercation*, ad. L. *altercātiōn-em*, n. of action f. *altercā-ri*; see prec.]

1. The action of disputing in warmth or anger; wordy strife, wrangling.

c1386 CHAUCER *Merch. T.* 229 As alday fallith altercacioun [*v.r.* altercacion(e] Bitwixe frendes in dispitesoun. 1480 CAXTON *Chron. Eng.* ccliii. 327 Therof arose a grete altercacyon among wryters of this mater pro and contra. 1509 BARCLAY *Ship of Fooles* (1570) 2 Not to fall in altrication. 1541 PAYNELL *Catiline* liv. 77 Cesar & Cato, being at altercation togyther touching the peyn & punishment of the conspirators. 1651 BAXTER *Inf. Bapt.* 241 A Judicious Reader..looks for Arguments, and loathes altercation. 1773 FRANKLIN *Lett.* Wks. 1840 VI. 379, I have an extreme aversion to public altercation on philosophic points. 1856 E. BOND *Russia in 16th C.* Introd. 21 This monopoly..was a pregnant cause of altercation between the two courts.

b. The conduct of a case in a court of justice by means of question and answer. (L. *altercātio* Quint.)

1779 JOHNSON *K. of Prussia* Wks. 1787 IV. 553 In the discussion of causes, altercation must be allowed; yet to altercation some limits must be put. There are therefore allowed a bill, an answer, a reply, and a rejoinder. 1875 POSTE *Gaius* IV. (ed. 2) 497 An oral pleading or altercation.

2. A vehement or angry dispute, a noisy controversy, a wrangle.

1552 HULOET, Altricacion, *Rixa*. 1582 N.T. (Rheims) *Jude* 9 When Michael..made altercation for the body of Moyses. 1665 GLANVILLE *Sceps. Sci.* 74 Which excites men to endless bawlings and altercations. 1753 RICHARDSON *Grandison* (1781) II. xxv. 241 An altercation cannot end in your favour. 1840 MACAULAY *Clive* 42 Stormy altercations at the India House and in Parliament. 1856 MISS MULOCH *J. Halifax* 293 Which produced a warm altercation among the children.

ˈ**altercative**, *a.* ? *Obs. rare.* [f. ALTERCATE + -IVE; cf. *alternative*.] Characterized by altercation, full of wrangling.

1731 FIELDING *Grub St. Op.* Wks. 1784 II. 51 You have made additions..to the altercative or scolding scenes. 1737 —— *Tumble-Down Dick* III. 397 The true altercative, or scolding style of the ancients.

altered (ˈɔːltəd), *ppl. a.* [f. ALTER + -ED.]

1. Made otherwise, changed in some particulars.

a1400 *Chester Plays* I. 6 Not altered in many poyntes from the olde fashion. 1549 *Compl. Scotl.* vii. 70 It vas baytht altrit in cullour ande in beaulte. 1699 DRYDEN *Pal. & Arc.* I. 562 And gazing there, beheld his alter'd look. 1725 POPE *Odyss.* x. 529 Shame touch'd Eurylochus's alter'd breast. 1866 G. MACDONALD *Ann. Q. Neighb.* xviii. 356, I have been an altered character ever since I knew you. 1870 JEVONS *Elem. Logic* xxvii. 235 We can see the stars in slightly altered positions.

†**2.** Thirsty. (Cf. Fr. *altéré* 'dry, athirst, almost dried up,' Cotgr. 1611; and see quot. dated 1605 under ALTERING *ppl. a.* 2. In this sense Diez suggests a confusion with med.L. *arteriātus*.) *Obs.*

1602 WARNER *Alb. Eng.* XII. lxx. (1612) 295 And here mine altred Muse this theame surceaseth to pursue. 1653 URQUHART *Rabelais* II. vii, So altered, and a dry with drinking these flat wines, that they did nothing but spit.

alter ego (ˈɔːltər ˈiːgəʊ, ˈæltər ˈɛgəʊ). [L. (Cicero), *alter* another, *ego* I. Cf. Gr. ἄλλος ἐγώ, ἕτερος ἐγώ.] A second self; an intimate and trusted friend; a confidential agent or representative. Hence ˌ**alter-ˈegoism**, altruism; ˌ**alter-egoˈistic** *a.*, altruistic.

1537 R. LAYTON *Let.* 4 June in *Lett. Suppress. Monast.* (1843) 156 Ye muste have suche as ye may trust evyn as well as your owne self, wiche muste be unto yowe as *alter ego*. 1622 MABBE tr. *Aleman's Guzman d'Alf.* I. ii. 24 She would tell him, that I was his *alter ego*, that he and I were one. 1650 TRAPP *Comm. Gen.* ii. 18 One..that may be to him as an *Alter-ego*, a second-self. 1652 N. CULVERWEL *Lt. Nature* 10 We use to call a friend *Alter ego*. 1872 GEO. ELIOT *Middlem.* v. ii. 148 These people might not take that high view of you which I have always taken, as an *alter ego*, a right hand. 1880 MEREDITH *Trag. Comedians* I. v. 93 The pleasure she had of the sensational comparison was in an alteregoistic home she found in him, that allowed of her gathering a picked self-knowledge. 1886 *Law Times Rep.* LIV. 856/1 He who makes the contract agrees to the condition that it shall not be binding on the person whose *alter ego* or representative he is if he has made any misrepresentation, or has been guilty of any concealment. 1901 M. F. LIBBY in *Amer. Jrnl. Psychol.* XII. 470 The social affections in Shaftesbury generally mean the alteregoistic affections. *Ibid.* 485 His tendency to see patriotic and cosmic affections as an expansion of the narrower forms of alteregoism, as shown in love, family, and party relations. 1926 D. H. LAWRENCE *Plumed Serpent* i. 10 'Isn't that fun!' 'No,' said Kate, her little *alter ego* speaking out for once. 1936 *Mind* XLV. 72 The wider forms of alter-egoism (so-called altruism, which is really *égoïsme à deux, à trois*, etc.). 1939 A. J. TOYNBEE *Study Hist.* VI. 44 The One True God whose *alter ego* Allāh was now proclaimed to be. *fig.* 1856 S. DOBELL *Eng. in time of War* 80 Methinks the fruit But alter ego of the root.

alterer (ˈɔːltərə(r)). [f. ALTER + -ER¹.] He who or that which alters.

1583 GOLDING *Calvin on Deut.* cxcv. 1214 They themselues were the alterers of Gods order. 1683 SALMON *Dor. Med.* I. 115 If it be an alterer only. 1781 *Ann. Reg.* 168/2 He was the alterer of *Antony and Cleopatra* acted at Drury Lane.

altering (ˈɔːltərɪŋ), *vbl. sb.* [f. ALTER + -ING¹.] The action of changing in some respect; alteration. (Now mostly gerundial.)

1513 DOUGLAS *Æneis* XIII. iii. 39 O how grete mocioun, quhat altering vnstabill. 1628 GAULE *Practique The.* 107 The many and strange alterings and happenings to Men. 1697 LUTTRELL *Brief Rel.* (1857) IV. 282 Accused of altering an exchequer bill from £10 to £100.

altering (ˈɔːltərɪŋ), *ppl. a.* [f. ALTER + -ING².]

1. Changing in some respect: **a.** Making otherwise; **b.** Becoming otherwise.

1611 SHAKS. *Wint. T.* IV. iv. 410 Is he not stupid With Age, and altring Rheumes? 1646 SIR T. BROWNE *Pseud. Ep.* 208 Every seventh year [is] conceived to carry some altering character with it, either in the temper of body, minde, or both. 1856 FROUDE *Hist. Eng.* I. 81 The altering issue proved the altering nature of the conditions.

†**2.** *Med.* = ALTERATIVE *a. Obs.*

1605 TIMME *Quersit.* II. iii. 115 It is become hote, and of a drying quality..which is altogether the vertue and facultie of an altering medicine. 1684 tr. *Bonet's Merc. Compit.* VI. 162 To resist the Fever onely by..altering remedies. 1720 BLAIR in *Phil. Trans.* XXXI. 35, I have distributed the Plants into such as are Altering and Evacuating.

alterity (ælˈtɛrɪtɪ, ɒl-). [a. Fr. *altérité*, ad. med.L. *alteritāt-em* a being otherwise, f. *alter* other: see -ITY.] The state of being other or different; diversity, 'otherness.'

1642 H. MORE *Song of Soul* I. I. i, Psyche! from thee they spring O life of Time, and all Alterity! 1660 STANLEY *Hist. Philos.* (1701) 377/2 The Maker of all things took Union, and Division, and Identity, and Alterity, and Station, and Motion to compleat the soul. 1827 COLERIDGE *Table T.*

(1851) 45 In the Trinity there is, 1. Ipseity; 2 Alterity; 3. Community. **1849** —— *Notes on Shaks.* II. 295 Outness is but .. alterity visually represented.

altern (æl'tɜːn, ɒl-; 'æltən, 'ɔːl-), *a.* [ad. L. *altern-us*, every other, one after the other, f. *alter* the other, the second; cf. mod.Fr. *alterne.*]

1. Alternate.

1644 RIDER *Hor. Od.* III. xxviii, With altern share We Neptune will extoll. **1644** QUARLES *Sheph. Orac.* ix, 'Tis best to be altern; For mutuall language works a faire conclusion. **1868** GEO. ELIOT *Sp. Gipsy*, When with obliquely soaring bend altern She seems a goddess quitting earth again.

2. *Crystallog.* Exhibiting upper and lower faces which correspond in form, but alternate with each other in the position of their sides and angles.

3. *Math.* ***altern base***: in an oblique-angled triangle, the difference or sum of the segments formed by a perpendicular falling from the vertex according as it cuts the base or base produced.

1727–51 CHAMBERS *Cycl.* s.v., The true base is either the sum of the sides; in which case, the difference of the sides is called the *altern* base: or the true base is the difference of the sides; in which case, the sum of the sides is called the *altern* base.

4. quasi-*adv.* In turns, one after the other.

1667 MILTON *P.L.* VII. 348 The greater to have rule by Day, The less by Night alterne. **1757** DYER *Fleece* (1807) 95 Which open to the woof, and shut altern. **1792** D. LLOYD *Voy. Life* 141 Who sang altern Of nature, and accordant providence.

†**altern**, *v. Obs.* [a. OFr. *alterne-r*, ad. L. *alternā-re*: see ALTERNATE *a.*] = ALTERNATE *v.*

1447 BOKENHAM *Lyvys of Seyntys* 48 Eftsonys she low .. And aftyr wept ageyn .. She alte[r]nyd the tyme mervelously. **1811** FERNANDEZ *Sp. Dict.*, *Alternar*, to altern.

alternacy (æl'tɜːnəsɪ, ɒl-). ? *Obs.* [f. ALTERNATE: see -ACY.] Alternate condition; alternateness; alternation.

1731 HALES *Stat. Ess.* I. 122 As any liquor in a thermometer rises and falls with the alternacies of heat and cold. **1782** GILPIN *Observ. Wye* (1789) 22 A kind of alternacy takes place: what is, this year, a thicket; may, the next, be an open grove. **1795** H. WALPOLE *Corr.* (1837) III. 467 The softening alternacy of vowels and consonants.

†**al'ternal**, *a. Obs. rare.* [f. L. *altern-us*: see ALTERN and -AL[1] I. 3.] = ALTERNATE *a.*

1571 T. N[EWTON] *Lemnie's Touchst. Complex.* (1633) 91 That thing that lackes alternall rest, continue cannot long. **1611** FLORIO, *Vicissitudinale*, according to an alternall or enterchangeable course. [Not in J.; but in TODD, etc.]

†**al'ternally**, *adv. Obs. rare*$^{-1}$. [f. prec. + -LY[2].] = ALTERNATELY.

1627 MAY *Lucan* IV. 7 Their men obey'd Alternally both Generales commands. [Not in JOHNSON; but in TODD, etc.]

alternance ('ɔːl-, 'æltənəns). [Fr.: cf. ALTERNATE *a.* and *sb.* and -ANCE.] Alternation, variance. Chiefly in *Philol.*

J. Baudouin de Courtenay *Versuch einer Theorie phonetischer Alternationem* (1895) uses the German word *Alternation* in the sense illustr. by quots. 1934, 1935.

1921 *Times Lit. Suppl.* 20 Oct. 676/2 There are .. two tendencies or groups of tendencies which alternately dominate literature... His book .. is the most coherent essay we have seen to attach this alternance to a psychological reality. **1934** J. R. FIRTH in *Le Maître phonétique* XLVI. 45 Kruszewski, however, extended the term phoneme to include sound alternances associated with changes of morphological categories. **1935** —— in *English Studies* XVII. 11 Vowel alternance is also a very important morphological instrument in the strong conjugation of verbs. There are thirty vowel alternances for our babies to learn. **1957** C. L. WRENN in West & Kimber *Deskb. Correct English* p. vi, Doubt-provoking alternances in spelling or in grammatical usage. *Ibid.*, The alternance of spellings and usages of all kinds has struck me very forcibly.

alternant (æl'tɜːnənt, ɒl-), *ppl. a.* and *sb.* [a. Fr. *alternant*, pr. pple. of *alterner*, ad. L. *alternāre* to ALTERNATE.] **A.** *adj.*

1. Alternating, changing from one to the other.

a **1640** JACKSON *Creed* x. xlii. Wks. IX. 492 Whatsoever is mutably good, or mutably evil .. hath its alternant motions from God's decree.

2. *Min.* Consisting of alternating layers or laminæ.

1847 in CRAIG.

B. *sb.* **1.** An alternating quantity.

1882 *Academy* 21 Oct. 298/2 Chap. iii. .. gives in a concise form an account of continuants, alternants, symmetric determinants.

2. *Logic.* An alternative proposition or term; one of the components in an alternation (see ALTERNATION 7 b); = DISJUNCT *sb.*

1892 W. E. JOHNSON in *Mind* I. 237 The alternants of the alternative synthesis *a·b*. **1912** *Mind* XXI. 263 The argument .. proves that there are *alternants* of universals like isosceles and scalene with respect to triangularity. **1921** W. E. JOHNSON *Logic* I. iii. 31 In the alternative function 'Either *p* or *q*' *p* and *q* are alternants. *Ibid.* 36 It may very well be the case that the alternants in an alternative proposition are .. 'exclusive' to one another. **1957** J. G. BRENNAN *Handbk. Logic* vi. 95 If at least one of the alternants must be true, then if one of them is false, the other is true.

3. *Philol.* The name given to any one of the possible variants found within any particular feature of speech or language. Cf. ALTERNANCE.

1926 L. BLOOMFIELD in *Language* II. 160 Absence of sound may be a phonetic or formal alternant. **1942** BLOCH & TRAGER *Outl. Ling. Analysis* 57 We call the three forms /-ez, -z, -s/ alternants of the same morpheme. **1949** C. E. BAZELL in *Archivum Linguisticum* I. 2 There are variant expressions of the morpheme (the so-called morpheme-alternants) which may resemble the expressions of distinct morphemes in so far as they have no phonemes in common.

alternate (æl'tɜːnət, ɒl-), *a.* and *sb.* [ad. L. *alternāt-us* pa. pple. of *alternā-re* to do one thing after the other; f. *altern-us* ever the other, every second; f. *alter* the other of two, the second.]

A. *adj.* Done or changed by turns, coming each after one of the other kind.

1. Said of things of *two* kinds, so arranged that one of one kind always succeeds, and is in turn succeeded by, one of the other kind; occurring by turns; as alternate day *and* night, red stripes alternate *with* the blue ones, alternate layers of stone *and* (layers of) timber.

1513 MORE *Rich. III*, Wks. 1557, 70/2 Alternate proofe, as wel of prosperitie as aduers fortune. **1647** CRASHAW *Poems* 157 Alternate shreds of light Sordidly shifting hands with shades and night. *a* **1704** T. BROWN *Sat. agst. Wom.* Wks. 1730 I. 56 Alternate smiles and frowns, both insincere. **1790** BURKE *Fr. Rev.* 12 The most opposite passions .. mix with each other in the mind; alternate contempt and indignation; alternate laughter and tears; alternate scorn and horror. **1879** FROUDE *Cæsar* xix. 315 Walls, built of alternate layers of stone and timbers.

2. a. Said of a series, or whole, constituted by such alternate members.

1650 DAVENANT *Gondib.*, Pref., Nor doth alternate rhyme .. make the sound less heroic. **1762** FALCONER *Shipwr.* Proem. 39 Alternate change of climate has he known. **1807** CRABBE *Village* I. 9 No shepherds now, in smooth alternate verse, Their country's beauty or their nymph's rehearse. **1875** BENNETT & DYER *Sachs' Bot.* 524 If the members of a whorl fall between the median lines of those of the next whorl above or below, the whorls are alternate.

b. alternate generation (*Biol.*): genealogical succession by alternate processes; as in one generation by budding, or division, and in the next by sexual reproduction; and so on.

1858 LEWES *Sea-side Stud.* 293 The doctrine of Alternate generations has been persistently denied. **1861** HULME *Moquin-Tandon's Med. Zool.* II. I. 49 The existence of two modes of reproduction in the same species constitutes Alternate Generation.

3. a. Said of things of the same kind taken in two numerical sets, so that one member of each set always succeeds one of the other. = Alternately taken; —— about; as, 'He and I go on alternate days, or *day about*,' i.e. his days and my days are alternate with each other.

1809 J. BARLOW *Columb.* IV. 237 Alternate victors bid their gibbets rise. **1858** GLADSTONE *Homer* I. 134 Castor and Pollux .. revisited the earth in some mysterious manner on alternate days. *Mod.* The minister and the people read alternate verses.

b. alternate proportion: see quot.

1660 BARROW *Euclid* v. def. 12 Alternate Proportion is the comparing of antecedent to antecedent and consequent to consequent. **1827** HUTTON *Course Math.* I. 324 Alternate proportion .. As, if 1:2::3:6; then, by alternation, or permutation, it will be 1:3::2:6.

4. Said (elliptically) of the members of either set as above constituted, taken by themselves apart from the other set, thus: of the series 1, 2, 3, 4, 5, 6, 7, 8, 9, etc., either 1, 3, 5, 7, 9, 11, etc. or 2, 4, 6, 8, 10, 12, are the alternate members = Alternate with others not taken in; every other, every second.

1697 DRYDEN *Virg. Georg.* I. 107 Both these unhappy Soils the Swain forbears, And keeps a Sabbath of alternate Years. *Mod.* The drawing-master comes on alternate days.

5. a. Said of things of the same kind occurring along the course of an axial line, first on one side and then on the other and so on; = Alternately placed. *esp.* in *Bot.* of *leaves*, and in *Geom.* of *angles*. (The latter are doubly alternate, being situated also on the alternate sides of the successive lines which make angles with the axial line.)

1570 BILLINGSLEY *Euclid* I. xxvii. 38 This worde alternate is .. taken sometimes for a kind of situation in place. **1660** BARROW *Euclid* I. xxvii, If a right line falling upon two right lines make the alternate angles equal. **1770** WARING in *Phil. Trans.* LXI. 375 Some of the stalks .. have their leaves singly at the joints, alternate. **1827** HUTTON *Course Math.* I. 293 When a line intersects two parallel lines, it makes the alternate angles equal to each other. **1880** GRAY *Struct. Bot.* iv. § 1. 119 Alternate leaves are those which stand singly, one after another, that is, with one leaf to each node or borne on one height of stem.

b. *Electr.* ***alternate current*** = alternating current (see ALTERNATING *ppl. a.*).

1858 WHEATSTONE *Brit. Pat. 1241* 8 No contrivance is .. required to invert or to stop out the alternate currents. *a* **1877** KNIGHT *Dict. Mech.* I. 781/2 Alternate currents of opposite character are generated in each set of bobbins, the polarity being changed at the moment of polar passage. **1878** *Design & Work* 23 Feb. 234/2 In each revolution .. there will have been induced 16 alternate currents.

6. Alternately performed by two agents, reciprocal.

a **1716** SOUTH (J.), Mutual offices, and a generous strife in alternate acts of kindness. **1829** U.K.S. *Nat. Phil.* I. II. xiii. § 104. 53 These [motions] may be divided into continued and alternate, or reciprocating.

†**7.** Interchanged, exchanged for the other (of two). *Obs. rare.*

1590 GREENE *Arcadia* (1616) 36 As if .. Bacchus, forsaking his heauen-borne deitie, should delude our eies with the alternate form of his infancie.

8. = ALTERNATIVE *a.* 3. *U.S.*

1961 in WEBSTER. **1962** *Amer. Speech* XXXVII. 109 Only the *PDAE* records [ɱ], and this as an alternate end to four words.

9. quasi-*adv.* One after the other, in turns, by turns.

1712 POPE *Temp. Fame* 486 Or wane and wax alternate like the moon. **1762** FALCONER *Shipwr.* I. 202 Egyptian, Thracian gales alternate play. **1808** SCOTT *Marm.* II. x, Massive arches broad and round That rose alternate row and row.

10. *Comb.* **alternate-leaved** (see 5); **alternate-pinnate** (*Bot.*): having the pinnæ or leaflets of a compound leaf alternate upon the midrib or petiole.

1861 PRATT *Flower. Pl.* VI. 214 Alternate-leaved Spleen-wort.

B. *sb.* [the adj. used *absol.*] **1.** That which alternates with anything else; a vicissitude, an alternative. Now chiefly *U.S.*

1718 POPE *Iliad* XVIII. 117 'Tis not in Fate the alternate now to give. *a* **1733** NORTH *Examen* III. vi. ¶ 106. 498 The King having done all that was possible .. about Alliances, and claimed the Alternate. **1915** L. M. PHILLIPPS *Form of Colour* iv. 70 On the completion of Santa Sophia an alternate confronted the Byzantine architects. **1952** *Times* 27 Oct. 7/5 Their official reasons for proposing an extension of Gatwick were that it was required .. as an 'alternate' to London Airport. **1962** J. GLENN in *Into Orbit* 37 In the interests of safety all the major systems had to be studded with alternates or stand-by components.

2. One who is appointed to act in place of a delegate who is unable to be present; a substitute. *U.S.*

1848 *N.Y. Weekly Tribune* 26 Feb. 4/1 *Resolved*, That the Chair appoint a Committee .. to report to this Convention thirty-six delegates to the National Convention; also an alternate to each delegate. **1888** BRYCE *Amer. Commw.* II. III. lxix. 542 To every delegate there is added a person called his 'alternate', .. to replace him in case he cannot be present .. ; if from any cause the delegate is absent, the alternate steps into his shoes. **1895** *Denver Times* 5 Mar. 2/7 Each precinct is entitled to delegates and alternates as follows.

3. A person who alternates with another in the occupation, or performance of the duties, of an office.

Cf. F. *alternat* (used also in Eng. context), the arrangement according to which rotation of office is maintained among persons of equal rank, etc.

1898 *Westm. Gaz.* 21 Apr. 4/3 When sitting at our Board as an alternate in London for Mr. Rhodes. **1908** *Ibid.* 21 July 5/2 In 1903 he was appointed alternate to the Chief of the Admiralty Staff.

alternate ('æltəneɪt, ɔːl-), *v.* [f. prec., or on analogy of vbs. so formed; formerly accented *al'ter-nate.*]

1. *trans.* To arrange, do, or perform (two sets of things) each after the other continuously; to do (a thing) in two ways alternately; to cause to occur or succeed in alternation.

1599 SANDYS *Europ. Spec.* (1632) 239 Their Liturgy is intermedled much with singing .. grave, alternated, and braunched with divers parts. **1667** MILTON *P.L.* v. 657 Who in their course Melodious Hymns about the sovran Throne Alternate all night long. *a* **1711** GREW (J.), The most High God .. alternates the disposition of good and evil.

2. To interchange (one thing) by turns *with*, or to cause (a thing) to succeed and be succeeded *by*, another continuously.

1850 MERIVALE *Rom. Emp.* IV. xxxviii. 317 The Envoys of Maroboduus were instructed to alternate a tone of respect and deference .. with the boldest assertions of equality. **1859** MRS. SCHIMMELPENNINCK *Princ. Beauty* I. xi. 39 Always alternating an Active by a Passive style.

†**3.** To change the other way, to reverse. *Obs. rare.*

1595 MARKHAM *Sir R. Grinvile* xliii, Yet may thy power alternat heauens doome.

4. *intr.* Of two or more things: To succeed each other by turns, in time or space.

1700 DRYDEN *Pal. & Arc.* III. 882 Good after ill, and after pain, delight, Alternate, like the scenes of day and night. **1705** J. PHILIPS *Blenheim* v. 339 (T.) Rage, shame and grief alternate in his breast. **1850** LYNCH *Theoph. Trin.* ii. 23 Great souls in whom dark and bright alternated. **1875** STUBBS *Const. Hist.* II. xiv. 1 The fortunes of parties alternate.

5. *intr.* Of a whole: To consist of alternations, to vary in two directions by turns. Const. *between*.

1823 LAMB *Elia* (1860) 294 The scene [shall] only alternate between Bath and Bond Street. **1847** DISRAELI *Tancred* III. vii. (1871) 229 A land which alternates between plains of sand and dull ranges of monotonous hills.

6. *intr.* Of one thing, or class of things: To come or appear in alternate order *with* another, in time or space.

1831 CARLYLE *Sart. Res.* (1858) 47 Thus does famine of intelligence alternate with waste. **1858** LEWES *Sea-side Stud.*

87 Alternating with these are placed others of similar structure. **1876** FREEMAN *Norm. Conq.* II. vii. 76 Those periods of decay..alternate with periods of regeneration.

alternately (æl'tɜːnətlɪ, ɒl-), *adv.* [f. ALTERNATE *a.* + -LY².]

1. In alternate order; one after the other by turns, by alternation, time about.

1552 HULOET, Alternatelye, or by turne. *Subalternatim.* **1646** SIR T. BROWNE *Pseud. Ep.* 96 Parallels or like relations alternately releeve each other. **1661** *Grand Debate* 68 Singing Psalmes alternately. **1781** GIBBON *Decl. & F.* II. xliii. 617 The sea alternately advanced and retreated. **1849** MACAULAY *Hist. Eng.* I. 620 Lumley and Portman had alternately watched the Duke. **1880** GEIKIE *Phys. Geog.* iii. xviii. 154 The current runs alternately east and west.

2. By taking the alternate terms; by permutation.

1695 ALINGHAM *Geom. Epit.* 18 If *A:B::C:D*, then alternately compar'd it will be as *A:C::B:D*.

3. In alternate positions, on each side in turn. ***alternately-pinnate***: see ALTERNATE *a.* 10.

1751 CHAMBERS *Cycl.* s.v. *Alternate*, There are also two external angles, alternately opposite to the internal one. **1821** S. GRAY *Nat. Arr.* I. 72 Alternately disposed.. Leaflets alternate, instead of being opposite and in pairs.

†**al'ternateness.** ? *Obs.*—⁰ [f. as prec. + -NESS.] The quality or state of being alternate, or of following by turns.

1731 in BAILEY; and in mod. Dicts.

alternating ('æltəneɪtɪŋ, 'ɔːl-), *ppl. a.* [f. ALTERNATE *v.* + -ING².] **a.** Succeeding each other by turns. **b.** Occurring in alternation to something else. **c.** Consisting of alternations.

1837 W. HOWITT *Rur. Life* III. iii. (1862) 230 A land of alternating ridge and hollow. **1841** TRIMMER *Pract. Geol.* 180 Large masses which occupy extensive districts.. without any other alternating rock. **1855** BAIN *Senses & Intell.* I. ii. §18 (1864) 50 An alternating movement is thus kept up. **1862** TRENCH *Mirac.* xxix. 415 Alternating ebbs and flows.

d. ***alternating current*** (abbrev. A.C., a.c.): an electric current which reverses its direction at regular intervals. So ***alternating machine***, etc.

1839 *Ann. Electr., Magn., & Chem.* III. 389 The alternating currents, from the semi-revolutions of the armatures, are converted into a current of the same direction, by the application of my pole changer. **1869** *Brit. Pat.* No. 3196 A foot motion..is employed to generate a rapid succession of alternating currents. **1879** G. PRESCOTT *Sp. Telephone* xiv. 491 Alternating magneto machine. **1884** F. KROHN tr. *Glaser de Cew's Magn.- & Dyn.-Electr. Mach.* 249 The Ferranti alternating current generator. **1888** E. ATKINSON tr. *Mascart & Joubert's Electr. & Magn.* II. 289 Use of the Electrodynamometer with Alternating Currents. **1903** *Electr. Times* 31 Dec. 962/1 (*heading*) The Ferranti A.C. Meter. **1910** *Hawkins' Electr. Dict.* 2/1, a.c., abbreviation for *alternating current*. **1922** GLAZEBROOK *Dict. Appl. Physics* II. 30/2 The potentiometer is then thrown on to the A.C. supply. **1931** *Times Trade & Engin. Suppl.* 24 Jan. p. iv/3 The Mooltan has British Thomson-Houston a.c. generators.

alternatingly ('æltə'neɪtɪŋlɪ, 'ɔːl-), *adv.* [f. prec. + -LY².] In an alternating manner; alternately.

1881 R. WATSON in *Jrnl. Lin. Soc.* XV. 395 They appear alternatingly as stronger and finer.

alternation (æltə'neɪʃən, ɔːl-). [a. Fr. *alternation*, ad. L. *alternātiōn-em*, n. of action f. *alternāre*: see ALTERNATE *a.*]

1. a. The action of two things succeeding each other by turns; alternate succession or occurrence.

1611 COTGR., *Alternation*, an alternation, a succession by turne. **1646** SIR T. BROWNE *Pseud. Ep.* 147 Hares may exchange their sex, yet..not in that vicissitude or annuall alternation as is presumed. **1766** GOLDSMITH *Vic. Wakef.* (1857) 242 My spirits were exhausted by the alternation of pleasure and pain. **1866** G. MACDONALD *Ann. Q. Neighb.* xxi. 394 She behaved with strange alternations of dislike and passionate affection. **1880** H. JAMES *Benvolio* I. 345 To take the helm in alternation.

b. alternation of generations: = *alternate generation*; see ALTERNATE *a.* 2 b.

1858 LEWES *Sea-side Stud.* 287 The solitary Salpa produces the chain-Salpa by 'budding'; and the chain-Salpa by 'alternation of generations' (the phrase is Chamisso's [1819]) produces the solitary Salpa by ova. **1875** BENNETT & DYER *Sachs' Bot.* I. iii. 203 When alternation of generations occurs, in certain cases all the alternate generations may be asexual. **1881** LUBBOCK in *Nature* No. 618. 404 In 1842, Steenstrup published his 'Alternation of Generations.'

2. The action of taking the individuals of a series alternately.

1695 ALINGHAM *Geom. Epit.* 100 For if *A:a::B:b*, Then by Alternation *A:B::a:b*.

3. Successive change in a scene or action by the alternate occurrence of phenomena.

1633 T. ADAMS *Comm. 2 Pet.* i. 19 (1865) 196 By the vicissitude of time, and alternation of the wheeling heavens. **1791** HAMILTON tr. *Berthollet's Dyeing* I. Introd. 35 Inequalities in the alternation of the action of the liquor. **1845** FORD *Handbk. Spain* i. 46 Love is..an alternation of the agrodolce. **1868** G. DUFF *Pol. Surv.* 75 Some of these provinces consist almost entirely of alluvial plains, but the greater number exhibit an alternation of fertile river valleys.

4. The position or state of being in alternate order.

1830 LYELL *Princ. Geol.* (1875) I. I. iii. 53 Alternations were rare, of marine strata, with those which contain marshy and terrestrial productions. **1841** TRIMMER *Pract. Geol.* 182 Rarely met with..without the alternation of other rocks. **1860** MAURY *Phys. Geog. Sea* ii. §128 Streak after streak of warm and cool water in regular alternations.

5. The doing of anything by two actors by turns, alternate performance; reading or singing antiphonally.

1642 MILTON *Apol. Smect.* (1851) 313 Such alternations as are there [in the Liturgy] us'd must be by severall persons. **1795** MASON *Ch. Mus.* 130 (T.) The words are not confused by perplexing alternations.

6. *erron.* 'Sometimes used to express the divers changes, or alterations of order, in any number of things proposed.' (Chambers.) Permutation.

1751 CHAMBERS *Cycl.* s.v., How many changes or alternations can be rung on six bells.

7. a. *Logic.* The truth-function that has the value 'true' whenever at least one of its components is true, or that has the value 'false' only when every component is false; the function that is usually symbolized by 'v' (L. *vel*) and corresponds to the inclusive sense of the word 'or' that is sometimes rendered by 'and/or'.

1874 W. S. JEVONS *Princ. Science*: *Treat. Logic* I. v. 81 We require a sign of the alternative or disjunctive relation, equivalent to one meaning at least of the little conjunction *or* so frequently used in common language... In my first logical Essay I..adopted the common sign +; but this sign should not be employed unless there exists exact analogy between mathematical addition and logical alternation. **1890** E. E. C. JONES *Elem. Logic* 120 Mill, and Jevons..insist upon the non-exclusiveness of alternation. **1940** QUINE *Math. Logic* i. 12 Alternation—composition of statements by means of the connective 'or'. **1955** A. N. PRIOR *Formal Logic* i. 8 Writers who use 'disjunction' in this way generally call the non-exclusive 'Either *p* or *q*', the 'alternative' function or 'alternation' of its arguments... The alternation of two propositions is also often called their logical sum.

b. A compound statement or formula formed by joining two or more statements or formulas by the connective symbol 'v' or the word 'or'.

1894 J. N. KEYNES *Formal Logic* (ed. 3) II. ix. 231 To deny an alternation is the same thing as to affirm a conjunction. **1950** QUINE *Methods Logic* (1952) i. 19 'Either' and 'or' may be used to mark the boundaries of the first component of an alternation.

alternative (æl'tɜːnətɪv, ɒl-), *a.* and *sb.* [ad. med.L. *alternātīv-us*, f. L. *alternāt-* ppl. stem of *alternāre*: see ALTERNATE *a.* and -IVE.]

A. *adj.* **1.** Stating or offering the one or the other of two things of which either may be taken.

1590 SWINBURN *Testaments* 252 b, The alternatiue or disiunctiue speech of the testator..I make A. or B. my executors. **1753** CHAMBERS *Cycl. Supp.* s.v., An alternative, or disjunctive proposition is true, if one side or part of it be true.

2. Of two things: Such that one or the other may be chosen, the choice of either involving the rejection of the other. (Sometimes of more than two.)

1861 A. B. HOPE *Engl. Cathedr.*, I feel bound..to recapitulate the alternative possibilities. **1876** FREEMAN *Norm. Conq.* I. App. 746, I accept the statements as alternative statements.

3. *ellipt.* The other (of two), which may be chosen instead.

1838 DE QUINCEY *Mod. Greece* Wks. XIV. 290 The alternative supposition presumed him..the merchant. **1877** KINGLAKE *Crimea* IV. iv. 50 Who had ready an alternative plan.

4. Having an alternative bearing, purport, or use.

1753 CHAMBERS *Cycl. Supp.*, *Alternative* promise is where two or more are engaged to do a thing..though if either of them discharge it, both are acquitted. **1818** COLEBROOKE *Obligations* I. 107 To constitute an alternative obligation, two or more acts or things must be promised disjunctively. **1863** BAIN *Eng. Gram.* 65 The alternative conjunctions are either—or, whether—or, neither—nor.

†**5.** Characterized by alternation; alternate. *Obs.*

1601 HOLLAND *Pliny* (1634) I. 3 He ordereth the seasons in their alternatiue course. **1682** *Lond. Gaz.* mdclxxxviii/3 Churches where the Collation is alternative between the Bishops and the Chapters. **1716** PRIDEAUX *Connect. O. & N. Test.* I. v. (R.) A direction both to the reader and to the interpreter where to make their stop at every alternative reading and interpreting. **1880** GRAY *Bot. Text-bk.* 395 *Alternative*, In æstivation, with an inner whorl alternating with an outer one.

6. ***Alternative Service Book***, a book containing the public liturgy of the Church of England in modern English, published in 1980 for use as the alternative to the Book of Common Prayer (1662); abbrev. *A.S.B.* (see A III.); ***alternative vote***, a system of voting in which the voter places the names of the candidates in the order in which he supports them. Cf. PREFERENCE *voting*.

[**1979** *PN Review* XIII. 40/1 The General Synod of the Church..now has the power to create new liturgies and even an Alternative Services Book.] **1980** (*title*) Alternative Service Book. **1981** *Ripon College Cuddesdon Newslet.* 3 Our staple diet of daily offices and daily..eucharist..continues, but now with the Alternative Service Book providing the forms of service. **1983** M. DUGGAN *Runcie* iii. 39 The synod agenda ranged over a wide variety of subjects. There was revision of some of the new services to go in the *Alternative Service Book*. **1910** *Rep. R. Comm. Elect. Systems* (*Cmd.* 5163) 3 *The Alternative Vote.* Here the voter is invited to arrange the candidates in the order of his choice by placing the figures 1, 2, 3..against their names. **1926** HOAG & HALLETT *Proport. Represent.* x. 483 (*heading*) The Alternative Vote (The Single Transferable Vote as a Majority System). *Ibid.*, Such a preferential ballot is provided under the single transferable vote used as a majority system, known in Australia simply as 'preferential voting', in Great Britain and Canada as the 'alternative vote'.

7. Purporting to represent a preferable or equally acceptable alternative to that in general use or sanctioned by the establishment, as ***alternative*** (i.e. non-nuclear) ***energy, medicine, radio***, etc.; ***alternative society***: see SOCIETY 3 e. Cf. FRINGE *sb.* 2 b, UNDERGROUND *a.* 4 d.

1970 in A. Sampson *New Anat. Brit.* (1971) xxi. 401 *Cyclops* has died. *Strange Days* has died. *Grass Eye* and *Zig Zag* ail. The alternative Press is in trouble all round. **1971** [see PARTICIPANT *sb.* 1]. **1973** *Times* 18 May 4/5 An "alternative" prospectus produced by a group of students at Cambridge University has led to a demand by Professor Alec Deer, the vice-chancellor, that it should be withdrawn. **1975** *Sunday Times* 30 Nov., There are all the signs of Alternative Energy burgeoning into a big business. **1978** *Peace News* 1 Dec. 4/3 The Lucas workers have produced an 'Alternative Corporate Plan' demanding the right to work on socially useful products as an alternative to redundancy and to the production of armaments. **1982** I. GORDON in *N.Z. Listener* 29 May 67 There is another non-rigid non-school with what in today's language we could call an alternative life-style. Its members cheerfully write 'Faced with these four alternatives, he chose the third.' **1983** *Brit. Med. Jrnl.* 30 July 307/1 One of the few growth industries in contemporary Britain is alternative medicine. **1984** *Listener* 14 June 31/4 The demand for 'alternative' radio, an alternative to the services offered by the BBC and IBA contractors, has been clearly demonstrated by the persistence of pirate stations.

B. *sb.* [the adj. used *absol.*] That which is alternative; an alternative statement, course, etc.

1. *strictly*, A proposition containing two statements, the acceptance of one of which involves the rejection of the other; a statement or offer of two things of which either may be agreed to, but not both; permission to choose between two things.

(This is the only use of the word in Johnson, the following three being unknown to dictionaries till very recently.)

1624 BEDELL *Lett.* iii. 71 A long compasse of a sentence.. with I know not how many ampliations and alternatiues. **1719** YOUNG *Revenge* II. i. Wks. 1757 I. 128 My lord, you know the sad alternative, Is Leonora worth one pang, or not? **1794** GODWIN *C. Williams* 123, I could not endure to think ..of that side of the alternative as true. **1817** JAS. MILL *Brit. Ind.* II. IV. iii. 107 In the opinion of Clive there was but one alternative: that of embracing the neutrality, or instantly attacking Chandernagore. **1853** H. ROGERS *Ecl. Faith* 422 The brief, simple alternative of Mahomet, death or the Koran.

2. *loosely*, Either of the two 'sides' or members of the alternative proposition, called in this use 'the two alternatives'; either of two courses which lie open to choose between. In this use we find 'no other alternative.'

1814 MISS AUSTEN *Lady Susan* xxxviii. (1879) 282 It is impossible to submit to such an extremity while another alternative remains. **1858** BUCHANAN *Message to Congr.* 6 Dec., I could make no better arrangement, and there was no other alternative. **1864** J. H. NEWMAN *Apol. Life* 329 There are but two alternatives, the way to Rome, and the way to Atheism.

3. *esp.* The other or remaining course; thing which may be chosen instead. In this use we find 'no alternative' (which may also = no choice; see 1).

[**1760** STERNE *T. Shandy* (1802) IX. ii. 211 There was no alternative in my uncle Toby's wardrobe.] **1836** J. GILBERT *Chr. Atonem.* i. (1852) 19 Yet law was never so repealed but that it still remained as the alternative. **1860** TYNDALL *Glac.* I. §2. 19 We had therefore no alternative but to pack up. **1867** BUCKLE *Civilis.* III. iii. 146 A fate compared to which death would have been a joyful alternative.

4. Extended to, A choice between more than two things; or one of several courses which may be chosen.

1848 MILL *Pol. Econ.* (1865) I. 404 The alternative seemed to be either death, or to be permanently supported by other people, or a radical change in the economical arrangements. **1857** GLADSTONE *Oxf. Ess.* 26 My decided preference is for the fourth and last of these alternatives.

†**5.** Alternate course; alternation. *Obs.*

1732 BERKELEY *Min. Philos.* I. 69 The actual enjoyment is very short, and the alternative of Appetite and Disgust long. **1782** WEDGWOOD in *Phil. Trans.* LXXII. 317 They bear sudden alternatives of heat and cold.

al'ternatively, *adv.* [f. prec. + -LY².]

1. In an alternative manner, in a way that offers a choice between two. Now freq. = as or by way of an alternative.

1590 SWINBURN *Testaments* 249 When the testator dooth appoint executors..alternatiuely, or disiunctiuely, as I make A. or B. my executor. **1726** AYLIFFE *Parerg.* 75 An appeal alternatively made may be tollerated by the Civil Law as valid. **1877** LYTTEIL *Landm.* I. iv. 34 The name of MacCamalain is used alternatively with Ballantyne. **1884** *Law Rep. Queen's Bench* XIII. 674 The defendants claimed 30,000 *l.* in respect of their counter-claim, and alternatively 30,000 *l.* damages. **1912** *Times* (weekly ed.) 4 Oct. 794 Mr. Paul Taylor imposed the full penalty of £5, or, alternatively, sentenced the prisoner to one month's imprisonment. **1921**

Act 11 & 12 Geo. V c. 13 §1 Liable..to a fine not exceeding [25 *l.*], or alternatively or in addition thereto to be imprisoned..for a term not exceeding three months. **1927** *Sunday Express* 8 May 4 What you do..is to secure a photograph of the hall... Alternatively, you may make an exact drawing of the hall.

†**2.** Alternately, by turns. *Obs.*
1581 SAVILE *Ende of Nero* (1591) 53 Six [tribunes] executing their charge alternativelie, two at one time for two months. **1601** HOLLAND *Pliny* (1634) II. 627 Hieracites changeth colour all whole alternatiuely by turns. **1686** *Lond. Gaz.* mmcxcv/1 The Dyet should meet Alternatively in Poland and Lythuania. **1751** STACK in *Phil. Trans.* XLVII. 87 The muscle..was contracted and relaxed alternatively. **1869** MRS. WOOD *Rol. Yorke* I. 101 Striking his two forefingers alternatively on the table's edge.

†**3.** On two sides alternately. *Obs. rare.*
1725 BRADLEY *Fam. Dict., Aristolochy*, a Plant..cloathed at certain Distances, or alternatively, with Leaves.

†**4.** Reciprocally. *Obs. rare.*
1667 MARVELL *Corr.* 78 Wks. 1872–5 II. 222 The impositions which ly alternatively upon the importations of each others commodityes.

al'ternativeness. ? *Obs.*$^{-0}$ [f. as prec. + -NESS.]
1. The quality of being alternative, or of offering a choice between two.
1847 in CRAIG.
†**2.** The quality of being alternate; alternateness. *Obs.*
1731 BAILEY, *Alternativeness*, a succession by course.

alternator ('ɔːltəneɪtə(r)). *Electr.* [f. ALTERNATE *v.* + -OR]. A dynamo giving an alternating current.
1892 *Sci. Amer.* 16 Apr. 246/1 (*heading*) 250-Kilowatt 'Mordey-Victoria' Alternator. *Ibid.*, The electromotive force of the alternator varies only about five per cent, even if the full load is thrown on or off. **1893** G. KAPP *Dynamos* 10 The alternator, in which mechanical energy of rotation is converted into the energy of an alternating current. **1919** R. STANLEY *Wireless Telegr.* (ed. 2) I. 86 An alternator is a machine in which the difference of potential, or voltage, induced has not a constant value, as in an ordinary direct current generator, but rises and falls and reverses in direction many times per second. **1962** *Newnes Conc. Encycl. Electr. Engin.* 337/2 The turbo-alternator is essentially a high-speed construction..for coupling to steam or gas turbines..the salient-pole alternator is suited to..lower speeds and may therefore be driven by water turbines or internal-combustion engines.

alterne ('ɔːltən, æl-). *Ecology.* [Cf. F. *alterne* adj. alternate and ALTERN *a.*] A contrast, often sharply defined, shown by vegetation in adjoining areas; an area exhibiting such a contrast.
1916 F. E. CLEMENTS *Plant Succession* 115 Significance of alternation. Alternation is the consequence of disturbed or incomplete zonation. Such areas produce *alternes*, which it now seems can always be related to more primary zones. **1920** —— *Plant Indicators* 73 Communities show general structural features, such as zones, alternes, layers... Alternes are due to the interruption of zonation through any cause whatsoever, but they are especially typical where disturbed..areas are found. **1926** TANSLEY & CHIPP *Study of Vegetation* iv. 53 When there is no such regular spatial or temporal change, different communities *alternate* with one another, and the different areas occupied by these may be called *alternes* in contrast to zones. **1929** WEAVER & CLEMENTS *Plant Ecology* 7 Where conditions change abruptly instead of gradually and zonation is disturbed or incomplete, vegetation exhibits *alternes*.

†**al'ternement.** *Obs. rare*$^{-1}$. [a. OFr. *alternement*, n. of action f. *alterner*, ad. L. *alternāre*: see ALTERNATE *a.*] = ALTERNATION.
1413 LYDG. *Pylgr. Sowle.* v. vi. (1859) 77 None alternementes of dayes, neyther of monethes; but one contynuell day.

al,terni-, combining form of L. *altern-us* (see ALTERN); = ALTERNATE or ALTERNATELY, as in **alterni-foliate**, alternate-leaved, **alterni-pinnate, -sepalous**, etc.
1857 HENFREY *Bot.* §95. 59 If the leaflets are not in pairs, but alternate with each other, the leaf is alterni-pinnate.

alternity (æl'tɜːnɪtɪ, ɒl-). *rare.* [f. L. *altern-us* (see ALTERN) + -ITY. Cf. *eternity.*]
†**1.** Alternateness, alternation. *Obs.*
1646 SIR T. BROWNE *Pseud. Ep.* III. i. 105 In a continuall motion, without..alternity and vicissitude of rest. **1755** in JOHNSON; and in mod. Dicts.
2. In Welsh prosody:
1856 J. WILLIAMS *Gram. Edeyrn* §1758 What is alternity? The counterchange of vowels, and correspondency of consonants, occurring in the rhymes of the systich..When an alternity ends in vowels not followed by consonants, the same is called semi-alternity.

†**'alternize**, *v. Obs. rare*$^{-1}$. [f. ALTERN + -IZE: cf. *modernize.*] To alternate.
a **1840** MDME. D'ARBLAY *Diary* VII. 355 (D.) I only saw him once, but that was in a tête-à-tête, alternized with a trio by my son that lasted a whole afternoon.

†**al'tess.** *Obs. rare*$^{-1}$. [a. Fr. *altesse* highness.] Highness, nobility.
1660 WATERHOUSE *Arms& Arm.* 25 Standing dishes of altess..are not to be touched.

‖**alteza** (al'teθa), ‖**altezza** (al'tɛttsa). *Obs.* [Sp. and It.] Highness. (Used also as an Italian title.)
1599 NASHE *Lenten Stuffe* (D.) To chaunt and carroll forth the alteza and excelsitude of this monarchall fludy induperator. **1616** BEAUM. & FL. *Faithf. Friends* IV. iv, The altezzas and their souereigns, Must this night do you service.

‖**Althæa** (æl'θiːə). *Bot.* [L. *althæa*, a. Gr. ἀλθαία marsh mallow, f. ἄλθειν to heal.] A genus of plants (N.O. *Malvaceæ*) of which the Marsh Mallow and Hollyhock are species; by florists often extended to the genus *Hibiscus*.
1669 W[ORLIDGE] *Syst. Agric.* (1681) 125 Grafting is principally used in..Gessamins, Althea-frutex, and such like. **1785** COWPER *Task* VI. 170 Althæa with the purple eye. **1866** MASTERS in *Treas. Bot.* 46 Several species of *Althæa* are in cultivation, but the gay flowering shrub commonly called *Althæa frutex* is, properly speaking, a *Hibiscus* (*H. syriacus*). **1882** *Contemp. Rev.* Jan. 8 Althæas of many colours.

†**'altheodi**, *a.* and *sb. Obs.* 1–3; in 1 ælþeódiȝ. [f. æl- foreign + *þeód* nation, people + *-iȝ*: see -Y[1]. Cf. OHG. *alithiotic.*] Foreign; a foreigner.
c **880** K. ÆLFRED *Boeth.* xxvii. §3 On ælþeódiȝ folc. *c* **1000** *Ags. G.* Matt. xxiii. 15 Ȝe don anne æl-þeodiȝne. *c* **1160** *Hatton G.* ibid., Ænne ealðeodiȝene. *a* **1200** *Gloss.* in Wright *Voc.* 89 *Peregrinus*, alþeodi. **1205** LAYAM. 2327 Heo nolden iþolian: for alþeodene gold, þat þeos laððe weore.

†**'altheodisc**, *a. Obs.* 2–3. [f. OE. *æl-þeód*: see prec. and -ISH.] Of a foreign nation, alien.
1205 LAYAM. 79 Elene was ihoten, alðeodisc wif. *Ibid.* 2301 Þu..bi-leafest..mine dohter Guendoleine for alþeodisc meiden.

alther, var. *aller*, gen. pl., 'of all': see ALL D 3.

althing. *Obs.* Everything. See ALL A 3, C 2 b.

‖**Althing** ('ɔːlθɪŋ). [ON. *al-þing* whole assembly.] (See quot.)
1875 STUBBS *Const. Hist.* I. iii. 57 The general assembly of the island [Iceland] was called the Althing.
Comb. **althing-man**: a member of the Icelandic parliament.
1863 BARING-GOULD *Iceland* Introd. 35 The interests of the people are invested in Althingmen.

althionic (ælθɪ'ɒnɪk), *a. Chem.* [f. AL(COHOL) + Gr. θεῖον sulphur + -IC.] In *althionic acid*, $C_2H_4SO_4$, produced, according to Regnault, by heating alcohol with an excess of strong sulphuric acid.
1858 in *Penny Cycl.* 2nd Supp. 126/2. **1863** WATTS *Dict. Chem.* I. 149 The barium-salt of althionic acid.

althorn ('ælthɔːn). *Mus.* [G.: cf. ALT[2].] A high-pitched instrument of the saxhorn family; an alto or tenor saxhorn.
1859 C. MANDEL *Treat. Instrumentation Milit. Bands* 38 The Tenor Horn or Baryton (Alt-Horn in B Flat). **1879** GROVE *Dict. Mus.* I. 57/2 *Althorn*, an instrument of the Saxhorn family... It is exclusively used in military music. **1939** A. CARSE *Mus. Wind Instr.* xx. 296 Tenor Horn, E Flat Saxhorn... The earliest of these various alto or tenor instruments was probably the German *Althorn* or *Altkornett* which appeared in Berlin round about 1830. *Ibid.* 299 Instruments in C or B flat have also been called 'althorns'.

although (ɔːl'ðəʊ), *conj.* Forms: 4 **al þaȝ, al þauȝ, al þeȝ,** 4–5 **al thogh, al though(e, al they, al thouh,** 4–6 **althogh,** 5 **alle thoȝe, all þaw, alle, þawe,** 5–6 **althof, althow,** 4– **although.** [Orig. two words, see ALL C 10. *All though* was originally more emphatic than *though*, but by 1400 it was practically only a variant of it, and *all* having thus lost its independent force, the phrase was written as one word. See also THOUGH.] Even though, though..even; though; be it that, granting that, supposing that.
c **1325** *E.E. Allit. P.* A. 758 My dere destyné Me ches to hys make alþaȝ vnmete. [**1330** R. BRUNNE *Chron.* 23 Þof alle þat he werred in wo.] *c* **1360** *Mercy* in *E.E. Poems* (1862) 123 Al þauȝ i kouþe, yf þat i wolde. *c* **1386** CHAUCER *Prol.* 737 He may not spare, although he were his brother [*v.r.* al thogh, althogh, al they, al though, al þouhe]. *c* **1420** *Chron. Vilod.* 883 All þaw þay hadde þis gold þus y stole. **1440** SHIRLEY *Dethe of James* 7 Althofe he fonde colourabill wais to serve his entent. **1577** VAUTROULLIER *Luther's Ep. Gal.* 7 Although I am a sinner by the lawe..yet I despaire not. **1676** HALE *Contemp.* I. 87 Although that this was the very end for which he came into the World. **1692** E. WALKER *Epictetus Mor.* xlii, Your Head but weak, altho' your Lungs be strong. **1795** SOUTHEY *Joan of Arc* iii. 474 Wks. I. 47 Although thy life Of sin were free. **1881** N.T. (revised) *Mark* xiv. 29 Although all shall be offended, yet will not I.

alti-, comb. form of L. *alto-, alta-,* (*altus*) high, and *alte* highly; occurring as first element in many derivatives.

alticomous (æl'tɪkəməs), *a. rare*$^{-0}$. [f. late L. *alticom-us* (f. *alti-* high + *coma* head of hair or foliage) + -OUS.] Having leaves on the higher parts only.
1879 in *Syd. Soc. Lex.*

†**,altifi'cation.** *Obs. rare*$^{-1}$. [f. L. *alti-* high + -FICATION making.] Making high; ?sublimation. (?Mispr. for *albification.*)
1652 in Ashm. *Theat. Chem.* 97 Notably serving for Seperation Of dividents, and for Altification.

†**'altify**, *v. Obs.* ? *nonce-wd.* [f. L. *alti-* high + -FY, after *magnify.*] To make high, exalt.
1662 FULLER *Worthies* I. 217 Every County is given to magnify (not to say altify) their own things therein.

†**'altigrade**, *a. Obs.*$^{-0}$ [ad. L. *altigrad-us* high-stepping, f. *alti-* high + *grad-i* to step.] 'Going on high, ascending aloft.' Bailey 1731: whence in J.

†**,alti'latitude.** *Obs. rare*$^{-1}$. (Prob. in jest.)
1628 SHIRLEY *Witty Fair One* II. i, These circles, degrees, and altilatitudes, you speak of.

altiloquence (æl'tɪləkwəns). [f. next; see -NCE.] 'High speech, pompous language.' J.
1731 in BAILEY. **1755** in JOHNSON. **1808** J. MACDONALD *Telegr. Comm.* 59 Its elegant archaisms..containing an altisonant altiloquence.

†**al'tiloquent**, *a. Obs.*$^{-0}$ [f. L. *alti-* high, loftily + *loquent-em* speaking, pr. pple. of *loqui* to speak, on analogy of *altiloquium*: see ALTILOQUY.] Using high or pompous language.
1656 in BLOUNT *Glossogr.* **1721** in BAILEY. [Not in JOHNSON.]

†**alti'loquious**, *a. Obs.*$^{-0}$ [f. late L. *altiloqui-um* (see next) + -OUS.] 'Talking loud; also of high matters.' Bailey 1731.

†**al'tiloquy.** *Obs.*$^{-0}$ [ad. late L. *altiloqui-um* sublime diction, f. *alti-* high, loftily + *-loqui-um* speaking, f. *loqui* to speak. Cf. *soliloquy.*] 'Loud talk; also of high things.' Bailey 1731.

altimeter ('æltɪmiːtə(r), æl'tɪmɪtə(r)). [f. L. *altimeter* (quoted by Ducange from Papias), f. L. *alti-* high + Gr. μέτρον a measure.] **1.** 'An instrument for taking altitudes geometrically.' Craig 1847.
2. A form of aneroid barometer which indicates the altitude reached, esp. in aviation. Also *attrib.* See also *radio altimeter*.
1918 'BOYD CABLE' *Air Men o' War* 179 His altimeter showed him to be a bare couple of hundred feet up. **1923** *Blackw. Mag.* July 10/1 His altimeter needle crawled down from nine to eight thousand feet. **1950** *Gloss. Aeronaut. Terms* (*B.S.I.*) I. 40 *Altimeter calibrator*, an apparatus for measuring the instrument errors of an altimeter. *Contacting altimeter*, an instrument in which electrical contacts are made or broken at a predetermined height. *Ibid.* 41 *Recording altimeter*, an instrument by which variation in height is recorded against time.

altimetric (,æltɪ'mɛtrɪk), *a.* [f. ALTIMETRY + -IC[1].] = ALTIMETRICAL *a.*; relating to or concerning altimetry. Spec. ***altimetric frequency curve***: in morphological analysis, a graph constructed to show the distribution of areas of a certain height, or of the highest or lowest points, in a given area.
1900 *Geogr. Jrnl.* Oct. 472 He proposed to carry a chain of altimetric observations to Kara-koshun and Chaklik. **1935** H. BAULIG *Changing Sea Level* 42 (*caption*) Altimetric curves (from frequency of spot heights) for peninsular Brittany, [etc.]. **1937** WOOLDRIDGE & MORGAN *Physical Basis Geogr.* xvii. 266 Altimetric frequency curves... If the map is divided into small uniform squares, we may estimate the elevation of the highest point in each square, or use simply the spot heights shown on the map, providing that these, in general, mark elevated points. A curve may then be constructed showing altitudinal distribution of such points over the region. **1948** *Jrnl. Inst. Navig.* I. 57 It would be unlikely that altimetric determinations of drift over the Adriatic Sea would be reliable at levels below 5000 feet. **1952** MONKHOUSE & WILKINSON *Maps & Diagrams* ii. 89 Two altimetric frequency curves of Cornwall and Devon. **1958** F. E. ZEUNER *Dating the Past* (ed. 4) vii. 225 Resting on an irregular rock-floor..a beach conglomerate is found which, on altimetric evidence, can be correlated with the Late Monastirian phase of the Last Interglacial.

,alti'metrical, *a. rare*$^{-0}$ [f. ALTIMETER + -ICAL. Cf. *meter, metrical.*] 'Pertaining to the measurement of heights or altitudes.' Blount *Glossogr.* 1681.

altimetry (æl'tɪmɪtrɪ). [ad. med.L. *altimetria*, f. L. *alti-* high + Gr. -μετρία measuring: see -METRY. Cf. Fr. *altimétrie.*] 'The art of taking or measuring heights, whether accessible or inaccessible, generally performed by a quadrant.' J.
1696 PHILLIPS, *Altimetry*, the first part of Geometrical Practise, which reaches the measuring of Lines. **1706** *Ibid.*, *Altimetry*, that part of Geometry, which teaches the Method of taking and measuring of Heights. **1778** B. DONN (*title*) An Essay on the Elements of Plane Trigonometry with their application to Altimetry and Longimetry. **1815** *Encycl. Brit.* I. 750 *Altimetry*, the art of measuring altitudes, or heights.

‖**altincar** (æl'tɪŋkə(r)). [a. (ult.) Arab. *al-tinkār*, f. *al* the + Pers. and Hind. *tinkār*, Mal.

tingkal:—Skr. *ṭankaṇa*.] = TINCAL; crude borax.

1753 CHAMBERS *Cycl. Supp.*, Altincar is a sort of flux powder.

† **'altion.** *Obs.*—⁰ [n. of action f. L. *alt-* ppl. stem of *al-ĕre* to nourish.] 'A nourishing.' Bailey 1721.

altiplanation (ˌæltɪplə'neɪʃən). *Geol.* [f. ALTI- + PLANATION.] (See quot.)

1916 H. M. EAKIN *Yukon-Koyukuk Region* 78 The author has suggested the term 'altiplanation' to designate a special phase of solifluction that, under certain conditions, expresses itself in terrace-like forms and flattened summits and passes that are essentially accumulations of loose rock materials.

‖ **altiplano** (æltɪ'plɑːnəʊ). Also Alti-. [Sp., f. *alto* high (f. L. *altus*) + *plano* flat (f. L. *plānus*).] The high tableland between the Western and Eastern Cordilleras of the Andes, extending some 200,000 km² from Peru through Bolivia to Argentina.

1914 B. MIALL tr. *Walle's Bolivia* ii. 45 Those who should judge Bolivia only by the *altoplano* [sic]..would form a melancholy idea of the country. 1921 G. McC. MCBRIDE *Agrarian Indian Communities Highland Bolivia* 1 Bolivia consists of three great natural divisions: the eastern lowland; the long valleys reaching westward..and the highland plateau, or *altiplano*, and its bordering ranges. 1939 *Trans. Linn. Soc.* I. 27 The Altiplano forms a trough of undulating ground 3600 to 4200 metres above the sea. 1957 K. A. WITTFOGEL *Oriental Despotism* iii. 56 Cuzco, the capital of the *altiplano*. 1966 *Economist* 2 Apr. 33 The old boiler plates piled before the doors to keep the piercing *altiplano* wind from reaching families of nine sharing two beds in one room. 1978 *Nature* 6 Apr. 486/2 The average yield is about 800 to 1,000kg per ha on the altiplano.

altisonant (æl'tɪsənənt), *a.* [f. L. *alti-* comb. form of *alt-us* high + *sonant-em* sounding, pr. pple. of *sonā-re* to sound. L. has the analogous *altison-us*: cf. *altitonant-em* and *altiton-us*, both found.] High-sounding, lofty, pompous, loud.

1620 SHELTON *Don Quix.* (R.) He should alter likewise his denomination, and get a new one, that were famous and altisonant. 1664 EVELYN *Silva* (1776) Pref., Altisonant phrases. 1837 *Old Commodore* i. 2 Does he not, I say, arrest it ere it fall with the altisonant Zounds?

† **al'tisonous,** *a. Obs.*—⁰ [f. L. *altison-us* (f. *alti-* high + *-son-us* sounding) + -OUS.] = prec.

1731 in BAILEY; whence in JOHNSON and mod. Dicts.

‖ **altissimo** (al'tɪssɪmo). *Mus.* [It. *altissimo* very high, superl. of *alto* high.] In the phr. *in altissimo*: in the second octave above the treble stave, beginning with G.

1819 *Pantol.* s.v., *Altissimo*..applied to all notes situated above F in alt. 1838 *Penny Cycl.* XII. 54/1 The compass.. reached five [octaves] from double F below the base to F in altissimo. 1845 E. HOLMES *Mozart* 63, I could not have conceived it possible to sing to C in altissimo.

† **al'titonant,** *a. Obs.* [ad. L. *altitonant-em*, f. *alti-* high + *tonant-em* pr. pple. of *tonā-re* to thunder.] 'Thundering from on high.' Bailey 1721.

a 1627 MIDDLETON *World Tossed* Wks. V. 175 Altitonant, Imperial crown'd, and thunder-armèd Jove. 1641 COWLEY *Guardian* II. i, Hear, thou altitonant Jove, and Muses three. 1656 in BLOUNT *Glossogr.*

altitude ('æltɪtjuːd). Also altytude. [ad. L. *altitūdin-em* height, f. *alti-* (*altus*) high: see -TUDE. Cf. mod.Fr. *altitude*, not in Palsg. or Cotgr.]

1. *gen.* Vertical extent or distance; the quality of being high or deep, as one of the dimensions of space; height or depth.

c 1420 *Pallad. on Husb.* IV. 791 Her sydes longe, her altitude aboundे [= abundant]. 1509 HAWES *Past. Pl.* I. viii, This goodly picture was in altitude Nyne fote and more. 1605 SHAKS. *Lear* IV. vi. 53 The altitude, Which thou hast perpendicularly fell. 1794 SULLIVAN *View Nat.* I, The gravity of the fluid..will be always proportional to the altitude or depth. 1821 CRAIG *Drawing* ii. 63 It has neither form nor colour, nor altitude nor dimensions, and yet it is a flower.

2. *Geom.* The height of a triangle or other figure, measured by a perpendicular from the vertex to the base or base produced.

1570 BILLINGSLEY *Euclid* VI. def. 4. 154 Figures to have one altitude and to be contayned within two equidistant lines, is all one. 1751 CHAMBERS *Cycl.* s.v., Triangles of equal bases and altitudes are equal. 1810 HUTTON *Course Math.* I. 286 A triangle is equal to half a parallelogram of the same base and altitude.

3. Height of the mercurial column in a barometer. ? *Obs.*

1664 POWER *Exp. Philos.* II. 91 Its wonted pitch and altitude of 29 inches, or thereabouts. 1753 CHAMBERS *Cycl. Supp.* s.v., The different altitudes of the mercury may arise from the different states of the air.

4. Height above the ground, or, *strictly*, above the level of the sea; height in the air, loftiness.

1535 STEWART *Cron. Scot.* II. 146 Ane grit montane..of greit altitude. 1583 STANYHURST *Æneis* II. (Arb.) 58 Theare was a toure..that in altitud euened Thee stars. 1727 SWIFT *Gulliver* II. i. 97 Trees so lofty, that I could make no computation of their altitude. 1773 BRYDONE *Sicily* xxii. (1809) 225 The degree of altitude in the atmosphere. 1880 HAUGHTON *Phys. Geogr.* ii. 43 The Himalaya chain..has a mean altitude of about 18,000 feet.

5. *Astr.* The height of a body in the heavens expressed by its angular distance above the horizon.

c 1391 CHAUCER *Astrol.* I. §14, I wol clepe the heyhte of any thing that is taken by thy rewle, the altitude, with-owte mo wordes. 1594 BLUNDEVIL *Exerc.* II. (ed. 7) 117, 55 degrees, 56′ and 21″..is the Meridian altitude of the Sunne for that day. 1678 R. HOLME *Acad. Arm.* II. i. §77 Altitude is the height or elevation of the Pole or any other thing above the horizon. 1764 MASKELYNE in *Phil. Trans.* LIV. 371, I fixed the equal altitude instrument..against a strong post. 1849 MRS. SOMERVILLE *Connex. Phys. Sc.* xviii. 172 The apparent altitude of the heavenly bodies is always greater than their true altitude.

6. a. *sing.* A point or position at a height above the ground or sea-level; a height. **b.** *pl.* Elevated regions; great heights.

1432-50 tr. *Higden* (1865) I. 112 Þer was a towre in the altitude of the mownte of Syon. 1704 SWIFT *T. Tub* iii. Wks. 1760 I. 49 Should immediately deliver himself up to ratsbane or hemp, or from some convenient altitude. 1853 KANE *Grinnell Exp.* xv. (1856) 107 No mountain altitudes to furnish forth the increments of ice growth.

7. *fig.* **a.** High degree or eminence of any quality or attribute. **b.** High or exalted position in the scale of being, rank, power, etc.; hence ***His altitude*** = his Highness.

a 1400 *Cov. Myst.* 288 O! thou altitude of al gostly ryches! 1596 BELL *Surv. Popery* III. v. 279 Euen in the altitude of popedome. 1601 DENT *Pathw. Heaven* 217 Oh the profoundnesse and altitude of Gods mercy! 1612 CHAPMAN *Widdowe's Teares* Plays 1873 III. 11 He comes armed with his altitudes letters. 1672 SIR T. BROWNE *Let. to Friend* §27 (1881) 145 He that hath taken the true altitude of things. 1704 SWIFT *T. Tub* (R.) He has exalted himself to a certain degree of altitude above them. 1850 MRS. BROWNING *Poems* I. 74 Rise, woman, rise To thy peculiar and best altitudes. 1858 (20 May) BRIGHT *Speeches* 39 Men of that altitude.

† **8.** *fig.* in *pl.* Lofty mood, ways, airs, phrases. *Obs.*

1616 BEAUM. & FL. *Laws of Candy* II, This woman's in the altitudes. *a* 1733 NORTH *Examen* 258 (D.) If we would see him in his altitudes, we must go back to the House of Commons..there he cuts and slashes at another rate. 1748 RICHARDSON *Clarissa* (1811) V. 232 From the nature of their conversation, there was no room for altitudes. 1782 JOHNSON *Lett.* 293 (1788) II. 252 While you were in all your altitudes, at the Opera. 1803 *Lett. Miss Riversdale* III. 7 You are getting into your English altitudes.

9. *attrib.* as ***altitude table***; **altitude chamber** *Aeronaut.*, a chamber in which the air pressure, temperature, etc., can be regulated to simulate conditions at different altitudes; **altitude control** (see quots.); **altitude sickness**, sickness brought on by ascent to a high altitude.

1935 *Jrnl. R. Aeronaut. Soc.* XXXIX. 909 A full-scale engine (Curtis D. 12) working in an altitude chamber. 1911 R. M. PIERCE *Dict. Aviation* 23 *Altitude-control*, the controlling-apparatus by which the altitude of an airship is regulated; the control by the manipulation of which the altitude-rudder is operated. 1919 W. B. FARADAY *Gloss. Aeronaut. Terms* 49 *Altitude control*, a device fitted to a carburettor or other part of induction system to obtain a correct mixture of the fuel gas at high levels. 1932 *Flight* 5 Feb. 111/2 Limitation of the movement of the altitude control in aircraft might well be discontinued. 1920 W. H. WILMER *Aviation Med. in A.E.F.* 226 The euphoria which accompanies altitude sickness..robs the pilot of the opportunity of recognizing that he is in danger. 1907 F. BALL (*title*) Altitude tables..designed for the determination of the position line at all hour angles without logarithmic computation.

altitudinal (æltɪ'tjuːdɪnəl), *a.* [f. L. *altitūdin-em* (see prec.) + -AL¹.] Relating to height, or to degree of elevation above the surface of the earth, the horizon, or the sea-level.

1778 HUTTON in *Phil. Trans.* LXVIII. 716 The altitudinal difference between the two given points. 1861 H. MACMILLAN *Footn. Page Nat.* 8 The immense altitudinal range of these plants. 1883 TROMHOLT in *Nature* XXVII. 395 Altitudinal measurements..for fixing the parallax of the aurora borealis.

altitudinarian (ˌæltɪtjuːdɪ'nɛərɪən), *a.* and *sb.* [f. ALTITUDE, after *latitude*, *latitudinarian*: see -ARIAN.] **A.** *adj.* Pertaining to, or reaching to, the heights (of fancy, doctrine, etc.). **B.** *sb.* One who is given to lofty thoughts or plans.

1850 LYNCH *Theoph. Trin.* xii. 242 The wise latitudinarian is also an altitudinarian: his thought spreads broadly, but it is also high-rising, and strikes deep. 1871 MISS BOWMAN *Th. Chr. Life* (1877) 13 Sermons are.. altitudinarian, latitudinarian, or platitudinarian.

altitudinous (æltɪ'tjuːdɪnəs), *a.* [f. L. *altitūdin-*, *altitūdo* ALTITUDE.] Used affectedly for: high, lofty.

1868 H. T. TUCKERMAN *Collector* 55 The confined and altitudinous cells into which so many of the complacent victims of these potentates are stowed. 1890 *Cornhill Mag.* Feb. 146 The keen air of this altitudinous city exhilarated him. 1921 *Public Opinion* 15 June 57/3 Enveloped in the mists of his altitudinous thoughts.

al'tivolant, *a.* [ad. L. *altivolant-em*, f. *alti-* (comb. form of *alt-us*) high + *volant-em* flying; cf. *altitonant*.] 'Flying on high' (Blount).

1656 in BLOUNT (whence in Bailey, J., etc.). 1833 W. E. WALL in *Fraser's Mag.* VIII. 659 Bore him altivolant from Salem's towers. 1960 *Aeroplane* XCIX. 565/1 Another altivolant classification was for altitude sustained by an aircraft for 15-25 km. or 90 min.

† **'alto,** *sb.*¹ *Mil. Obs.* Also 6 alta. [a. Sp. *alto* in phr. *alto hacer*, an adaptation of Ger. *halt machen* to make a stop, f. *halt* hold-on, stop, stand. Soon changed to ALT (perh. after Fr. *faire alte*, also from Ger.) and HALT.] A halt.

1591 GARRARD *Art of Warre* 168 When the Armie makes Alta to rest. 1598 BARRET *Theor. Warres* 34 How to make their Alto or stand, and how to double their ranks. *Ibid.*, How to plant his pike in the ground, at any stand or Alto. 1622 F. MARKHAM *Decades War* v. iii. §4. 171 To make stands (which some call *Altoes* or *Hallts*)..whereby the souldier may be refresht when he is weary with travell.

alto ('ɑːltəʊ, æ-), *sb.*² and *a. Mus.* [a. It. *alto* high (sc. *canto* singing).] **A.** *sb.*

1. *strictly*, The highest male voice, the counter-tenor; formerly considered as restricted in compass to a sixth above and a sixth below the 'middle C'; also, the musical part for this voice.

1819 *Pantol.*, *Alto*, in music, the highest natural tenor voice. 1883 C. WOOLSON in *Harper's Mag.* Mar 567/2 He could join in with his soft little alto.

2. Extended also to, The female voice of similar range, or the musical part sung by it, more strictly known as *contralto*.

1881 A. HOPKINSON *Waiting* vi. 129 The Count takes the accompaniment, Anne and Dolly the treble and alto. 1883 *Harper's Mag.* Feb. 443/1 Their..voices serving only as a foil to her powerful alto.

3. One who has an alto voice.

1784 *Europ. Mag.* V. 324 Altos,—Rev. Mr. Clark..and 48 assistants. 1850 *Illustr. Lond. News* XVII. 368 The entire Choir..is not here, there are..ten altos, six tenors, etc.

4. = ALT².

1862 T. MARTIN *Horace* (1870) 265 From C in alto down to double D.

5. The Italian name for a tenor violin.

1833 *Penny Cycl.* I. 404 *Alto*..called in England the Tenor, and by the Italians, the Viola.

6. *ellipt.* for **alto saxophone.** Also *attrib.* Hence **'altoist, 'alto-man,** an alto saxophonist.

1876 STAINER & BARRETT *Dict. Mus. Terms* 385/2 *Saxophones*..are six in number, the high, soprano, alto, tenor, baritone and bass. 1927 *Melody Maker* June 553/3 Lionel Clapper..trots out the 'hottest' extemporisations on his alto. 1928 *Ibid.* Feb. 184/2 The 'hot' alto chorus by Breed. 1949 L. FEATHER *Inside Be-Bop* ii. 12 Charlie Parker offers inspired alto solos. 1952 B. ULANOV *Hist. Jazz in Amer.* (1958) xxi. 276 Alto-men of course—they all imitated Bird. 1956 M. STEARNS *Story of Jazz* (1957) xviii. 242 Altoist Julian 'Cannonball' Adderley from Florida.

B. *attrib.* as *adj.* **a.** Belonging to the alto; also, applied *gen.* to the second highest member of a family of musical instruments: high, tenor. **alto clef**: the C clef when placed on the third line of the stave. **alto-ripieno** [f. It. *ripiéno* that which fills up]: a tenor part, instrumental or vocal, used only occasionally in a grand chorus.

Whether *alto* in such contexts is an adjective or a combining form (i.e. ALTO- 1) is not certainly determinable, and the presence or absence of a hyphen is an uncertain guide. Many of the examples given below could be placed with equal justification s.v. ALTO- 1.

1845 E. HOLMES *Mozart* 347 It was sung by his visiters.. himself taking the alto part. 1802, 1856 [see ALTO- 1]. 1871 HAWEIS *Mus. & Mor.* ix. 353 A quiet alto song, full of solemn pathos. 1879 CURWEN *Mus. The.* 23 The Alto or Contralto Clef is..a C Clef but it is placed in the middle line. 1939 [see ALTHORN].

b. *spec.* **alto saxophone**, the third highest member of the saxophone family, usually pitched in E flat. Abbrev. **alto sax.** Hence (often written with hyphens) **alto saxist, saxophonist**, one who plays the alto saxophone.

1869 C. MANDEL *Mandel's Syst. Mus.* xvi. 68 There are various kinds of Saxophones. The smallest..is in B flat; the next, or Alto Saxophone, is in E flat. 1889 GROVE *Dict. Mus.* IV. 780/2 A. Adam gives an effective solo to the E♭ Alto Saxophone in his opera 'Hamlet'. 1927 *Melody Maker* Aug. 785/2 The best features are the alto saxophone in the third chorus and the 'hot' fiddle in the first half of the last chorus. 1955 KEEPNEWS & GRAUER *Pict. Hist. Jazz* iii. 40 Cobb himself could play trumpet, clarinet, alto sax and banjo. 1958 S. TRAILL in P. Gammond *Decca Bk. of Jazz* vi. 82 Alto-saxophonist Boyce Brown and pianist Floyd Bean both play in real Chicago style. A. MORGAN *Ibid.* xii. 143 The resultant band..contained..alto-saxist Lee Konitz.

c. alto-horn, (*a*) = ALTHORN; (*b*) *U.S.*, an alto saxophone.

1934 WEBSTER, *Alto horn*, the althorn. 1940 C. SACHS *Hist. Mus. Instrum.* 429 The *alto horn*, called *Altkornett*..is coiled either in the shape of a trumpet, or upright as a tuba, or circular as a horn. Its usual pitch is E♭ or F. 1946 R. BLESH *Shining Trumpets* (1949) vii. 161 To some extent, the alto horns and piccolos dropped out of the march band during this period. 1957 W. C. HANDY *Father of Blues* v. 64, I had bought a tenor sax for myself, but W. N. P. Spiller, our alto horn player, appropriated it mostly for his own use.

‖ **alto-** ('ɑːltəʊ, æ-), It., = high-, used in various comb.

1. *Mus.* as **alto-clarinet, -fagotto, -viola,** musical instruments similar to, but higher in pitch than, the clarinet, fagotto, viola. See also ALTO *a.*

1856 BERLIOZ *Instrument.* 114 The alto-clarinet is no other than a clarinet in F or in E♭. 1802 REES *Cycl.* s.v., *Alto viola*, the tenor violin, in opposition to the bass viol.

2. *Sculpt.* (See ALTO-RELIEVO.)

alto-cumulus (ˌæltəʊ'kjuːmjʊləs). *Meteorol.* [mod.L. *alto-*, f. L. *altus* high + CUMULUS.] A cloud-formation made up of rounded masses similar to cumulus clouds but at a higher altitude; a cloud of this kind. Similarly **alto-'stratus**, a cloud-formation consisting of a more or less uniform continuous layer or veil resembling stratus or cirro-stratus clouds but lying in the middle-cloud region. So **alto(-) cloud**, an alto-cumulus or alto-stratus cloud; also *alto* ellipt.

1894 *Nature* 8 Feb. 344/2 Clouds having altitudes from 3000 to 6000 metres... Alto-cumulus... Alto-stratus. **1898** *Jrnl. Sch. Geogr.* (U.S.) Oct. 297 The development of alto-cumulus and heavy cumulus clouds over the land, while out to sea only small cumuli were visible. **1905** CLAYDEN *Cloud Studies* 59 From cirro-cumulus and cirro-stratus we pass through almost insensible gradations to the denser forms classed together in the alto group. *Ibid.* 62 The simplest alto cloud is alto-stratus.

altogether (ɔːltə'gɛðə(r)), *a.*, *adv.*, and *sb.* [comb. of ALL and TOGETHER. Orig. a mere strengthening of *all*, but, like *all* itself, gradually becoming adverbial, in which sense alone it is now used when written in combination.]

A. *adj.* A strengthened form of ALL *a.*

†**1.** The whole together, the entire; everything, the whole, the total. (Often *absol.*; cf. ALL A II.) *Obs.*

1154 *O.E. Chron.* (Laud MS.) an. 1137 §4 & brenden sythen þe cyrce & al te gædere. *c* **1200** ORMIN 9581 Issraæle þeod..all togeddre att Drihhtin Godd. **1526** TINDALE *1 Cor.* vii. 19 Circumcision is nothynge..but the keppynge of the commaundmentes of god is altogether. **1528** MORE *Heresyes* IV. Wks. 1557, 285/1 Ananias & Saphyra..made semblance as though they brought to the apostles altogether. **1611** BIBLE *Ex.* xix. 18 And mount Sinai was altogether on a smoke. *Ibid. Ps.* cxxxix. 4 There is not a worde in my tongue: but lo, O Lord, thou knowest it altogether.

†**2.** *pl.* All united, all in a company; all inclusively; all without exception. Now written separately *all together*.

1330 R. BRUNNE *Chron.* 264 Bot alle þei were forholn, & failed þam alle togider. *c* **1400** *Ywaine & Gaw.* 2955 Cumes forth, he said, ye altogeder. **1535** COVERDALE *Ezek.* xxxiv. 13 Proude wordes agaynst me, which I haue herde altogether. **1590** SHAKS. *Com. Err.* v. i. 245 Then altogether They fell vpon me. **1663** GERBIER *Counsel* 102 Solidity, Conveniency, and Ornament, altogether to be observed in true Building. [*Mod.* They came separately, but went away all together.]

B. *adv.* [by gradual transference from the sb. to the predicate; cf. ALL C 1.]

1. Everything being included; in all respects, in every particular; entirely, wholly, totally, quite.

c **1200** *Trin. Coll. Hom.* 19 Here fifealde mihte was altegeder attred. *c* **1330** *Kyng of Tars* 601 Whon he hedde altogedere ipreyd, And al that evere he couthe iseyd. **1534** MORE *On the Passion* Wks. 1557, 1373/1 Were he as bad as Judas altogiter. **1611** BIBLE *John* ix. 34 Thou wast altogether born in sins. **1712** ADDISON *Spect.* No. 441 ¶9 Scenes and Objects, and Companions that are altogether new. **1782** PRIESTLEY *Nat. & Rev. Relig.* I. 30 The idea of chance is altogether excluded. **1857** BUCKLE *Civilis.* I. ii. 125 In Greece, we see a country altogether the reverse of India. **1881** TROLLOPE *Ayala's Angel* III. lvi. 163 That kept me from being altogether wretched.

2. Uninterruptedly, without deviation or admixture. (Cf. ALL C 4.)

1700 *Lond. Gaz.* mmmdcix/4 A dark Iron-grey Horse.. Paces altogether. **1709** *Ibid.* mmmmdcviii/4 A Bay Mare,.. Trots altogether.

3. for altogether: for all time to come, as a permanent arrangement, finally, definitely, permanently, 'for good.' (*For* is sometimes omitted.)

1548 UDALL etc. *Erasm. Paraphr. Luke* xxiv. 44 Did he not once for altogether..take awaie all autoritie from the priestes? **1580** NORTH *Plutarch* (1676) 311 Perswading themselves he was fled for altogether. **1674** SCHEFFER *Lapland* xxvi. 121 Most of them then were baptized very late ..some deferred it for altogether. **1825** *Bro. Jonathan* II. 40 Walter and Edith were not in a humour..for separating.. altogether.

4. In all, in total amount.

1797 H. COX *Jrnl. Resid. Burmhan Emp.* (1821) 93 We were in the palace tent altogether about an hour and a half. **1811** JANE AUSTEN *Sense & Sens.* I. ii. 24 Altogether, they will have five hundred a-year amongst them. **1871** S. T. HALL *Morning Studies* III. xii. 158 Debt amounting altogether to not much more, perhaps, than twenty pounds. **1928** H. W. FREEMAN *Joseph & His Brethren* xxx. 259 Altogether they did not spend as much on the whole meal as some of his other customers on drink alone.

5. On the whole, taking everything into account.

a **1817** JANE AUSTEN *Persuasion* (1818) IV. xi. 256 Though we could have wished it different, yet altogether we did not think it fair to stand out any longer. **1888** W. R. INGE *Society in Rome* 44 Altogether, Roman slavery at this time contrasts favourably in many ways with the negro slavery of Christian nations. **1927** W. E. COLLINSON *Contemp. Eng.* 43 Altogether I cannot think of any modern writer who has exercised so far-reaching an influence on our every-day speech.

C. *sb.* **a.** A whole, a *tout ensemble*.

1667 WATERHOUSE *Fire of Lond.* 141 Her Congregations, Her Citizens, Her altogether has been as orderly, etc. **1674** N. FAIRFAX *Bulk & Selv.* 33 We only call..Gods All-fillingness an altogether, to loosen it from any thing of sundership. **1865** *Pall Mall G.* 26 June 9 American fingers ..impart a finish and an altogether (this is much better than to steal *tout-ensemble* from the wicked Emperor).

b. the altogether (colloq.): the nude.

1894 DU MAURIER *Trilby* I. 185, I have sat for the 'altogether' to several other people. **1908** *Daily Chron.* 16 Apr. 5/7 Mme. Sarah Bernhardt frankly says she sees nothing wrong in the 'altogether'. **1947** N. BALCHIN *Lord, I was Afraid* 52 *Should* I get a kick out of just seeing a girl in the altogether?

attrib. **1896** *Punch* 25 Jan. 45/2 O, Röntgen..Your worse than 'altogether' state Of portraiture we bar *in toto*!

c. *pl.* A set of tights for the whole body.

1927 *Observer* 24 July 13/2 Sokolova impersonated Death in scarlet altogethers.

¶ There is a common tendency to write *altogether* where *all together* is logically preferable. Cf. sense A. 2.

1765 MRS. GLASSE *Art of Cookery* p. iv, Put all the ingredients together again,..strain it off well,..and give it a boil altogether. **1837** T. BACON *First Impr. Nat. in Hindostan* I. 243 Of infinitely greater importance to the creation than the sun, moon and stars altogether. **1861** TROLLOPE *Orley F.* I. xxix. 225 In that field the dogs were now running, altogether, so that a sheet might have covered them. **1880** GROVE *Dict. Mus.* II. 574/2 The pipes of the early organs are said to have sounded at first altogether. **1930** E. RAYMOND *Jesting Army* I. iii. 45 A medical officer.. and the whole of his Sick Parade ran altogether.

altogetherness (ɔːltə'gɛðənɪs). *rare.* [f. prec. + -NESS.] Wholeness, unity of being.

1674 N. FAIRFAX *Bulk & Selv.* 60 So Gods All-fillingness is in the world..in an indivisible altogetherness. **1824** J. GALT *Rothelan* II. III. viii. 67 His courteous mildness, his altogetherness of fraud and smiles.

†**alto'gethers**, *adv. Obs.* [f. ALL + TOGETHERS a variant of TOGETHER, with genitival ending: cf. *afterward, -s, elsewhere, -s.*] = ALTOGETHER.

c **1175** *Lamb. Hom.* 81 Þe an is aquenched al to geðeres. *c* **1450** LONELICH *Grail* xxxvii. 842 Now Altogederis we ben present. **1569** J. ROGERS *Glasse of Godly Love* 180 Christe only is her comfort all togethers. **1586** J. HOOKER *Giraldus's Hist. Irel.* in *Holinshed* II. 114/1 The present state of all Ireland, altogethers deuoured with robberies, murders, riots.

alto-relievo (ˌæltəʊ, rɪ'liːvəʊ). Pl. -os. [It. *alto-rilievo* high relief; this spelling is sometimes used in Eng.] High relief; sculpture or carved work in which the figures project more than one half of their true proportions from the wall or surface on which they are carved. Hence *concr.* A sculpture or carving in high relief.

1717 BERKELEY in Fraser *Life* (1871) 550 The infinite profusion of alto-relievo. **1762** H. WALPOLE *Vertue's Anecd. Paint.* (1786) I. 276 A fine bust of queen Elizabeth on onyx, alto relievo in profile. **1773** BRYDONE *Sicily* xix. (1809) 199 The representation of a boar-hunting in alto relievo, on white marble. **1878** LADY HERBERT tr. *Hübner's Round the World* II. v. 342 There are no alto-relievos.

alto-stratus: see ALTO-CUMULUS.

altricate, -tion, obs. ff. ALTERCATE, -TION.

altricial (æl'trɪʃ(ɪ)əl), *a. Ornith.* [f. mod.L. *Altrices* division of birds, f. L. *altric-*, *altrix*, fem. of *altor* nourisher (*alĕre* to nourish) + -AL.] = NIDICOLOUS *a.*: opp. PRÆCOCIAL *a.*, q.v.

1872 COUES *N. Amer. Birds* 224 Pigeons are altricial, and monogamous. **1884** *Ibid.* (ed. 2) II. §3. 88 Altricial birds such as are reared by the parents in the nest. **1885** *Athenæum* 1 Aug. 146/2 The altricial herons. **1902** [see PRÆCOCIAL *a.*]

altruism ('æltruːɪz(ə)m). [a. Fr. *altruisme* formed by Comte on It. *altrui* (Fr. *autrui*) of or to others, what is another's, somebody else, f. L. *alteri huic* 'to this other,' the dative afterwards passing into a general oblique case. See -ISM. *Altruisme* was apparently suggested by the Fr. law-phrase *l'autrui*, standing according to Littré for *le bien, le droit d'autrui*. Introd. into Eng. by the translators and expounders of Comte.] Devotion to the welfare of others, regard for others, as a principle of action; opposed to egoism or selfishness.

1853 LEWES *Comte's Philos. Sc.* I. xxi. 224 Dispositions influenced by the purely egotistic impulses we call popularly 'bad,' and apply the term 'good' to those in which altruism predominates. **1865** MILL in *Westm. Rev.* July, To make altruism (a word of his [Comte's] own coining) predominate over egoism. **1871** FARRAR *Witn. Hist.* iv. 144 Is altruism a sweeter, or better word than charity? **1876** —— *Marlb. Serm.* xvi. 157 A good and wise modern philosopher summed up the law and duty of life in Altruism—*Vive pour autrui*—'Live for others.' **1877** C. ROW *Bampt. Lect.* (1881) 106 The religion of humanity, whose great moral principle is altruism. **1879** GEO. ELIOT *Theophr. Such* viii. 147 The bear was surprised at the badger's want of altruism.

altruist ('æltruːɪst). [f. ALTRUISM: see -IST. Cf. Fr. *altruiste* adj.] One who professes the principles of altruism.

1868 NETTLESHIP *Browning's Poetry* vi. 167 His development as a great altruist. **1881** *Daily News* 27 Aug. 5/1 If they were thorough altruists, a sweet reasonableness would induce them to avoid inflicting..distress.

altruistic (æltruː'ɪstɪk), *a.* [f. Fr. *altruiste* (adj. f. *altruisme*) + -IC. Earlier than ALTRUIST.] Of or pertaining to altruism; actuated by regard for the well-being of others; benevolent.

1853 LEWES *Comte's Philos. Sc.* I. xxi. 221 The noble termination of the emotional series by the group of social or altruistic instincts. **1862** HINTON *Let.* in *Life* (1878) 194 The word altruistic I borrow from Comte. Is it not a capital word? I am resolved to naturalise it. **1873** H. SPENCER in *Contemp. Rev.* Feb., Up to a certain point altruistic action blesses giver and receiver, beyond that point it curses giver and receiver.

altruistically (æltruː'ɪstɪkəlɪ), *adv.* [f. prec. + -AL[1] + -LY.] In an altruistic manner; benevolently.

1874 H. SPENCER *Sociol.* viii. 186 A means to furthering the general happiness altruistically. **1879** —— *Data of Eth.* xi. 197 The most altruistically-natured leave no like-natured posterity.

altruize ('æltruːaɪz), *v. nonce-wd.* [f. It. *altrui* some one else + -IZE; suggested by ALTRUISM.] To change into some one else.

1878 T. SINCLAIR *Mount* 300 Etherealised or converted, altruised, or..artisticised into a third world of thought.

†'**altry.** *Obs. rare*[−1]. [f. ALTER + -Y; purely imitative: cf. *enter, entry*.] Alteration, change.

1527 *Acct. of Gibson, Master of Revels*, Payd to John Skut, y[e] quenys tayler for makynge of y[e] ladies aparell by altry.

†'**altumal**, *a. Obs.* ? *slang.* [f. L. *altum* the deep, *i.e.* the sea + -AL[1].] (See quot.)

1711 *Medleys* 29 Jan. (1712) 186 His Altumal Cant, a Mark of his poor Traffick and Tar-Education. **1753** CHAMBERS *Cycl. Supp.*, *Altumal*, a term used to denote the mercantile style, or dialect. In this sense, we meet with altumal cant, to denote the language of petty traders and tars.

†'**alture.** *Obs.* [ad. It. *altura* height; f. *alto*:—L. *altum* height: see -URE.] Height, altitude.

a **1547** EARL SURREY *Ps.* lv. 29 From that the sun descends, Till he his alture win. **1598** BARRET *Theor. Warres* v. i. 127 Casamats..so low that they arriued not vnto the alture of the ditch.

‖'**altus.** *Mus. Obs.* [L. *altus* high (sc. *cantus* singing).] = ALTO *sb.*[2]

1609 DOULAND *Ornithop. Microl.* 86 The Base requires a third below, and the Altus the same aboue. *a* **1659** CLEVELAND *Comm. Place* (1677) 163 A Deep Base that must reach as low as Hell to describe the Passion, and thence rebound to a joyful *Altus*, the high-strain of the Resurrection.

†**a'luco.** *Obs. rare.* [f. L. *alūcus* an owl.] A book-name given by some to the White, by others to the Tawny, Owl.

1753 CHAMBERS *Cycl. Supp.*, *Aluco*, the name by which authors have called the common white owl. **1785** LATHAM *Synopsis* 134 Tawny Owl, *Syrnium Stridula*, Aluco Owl.

aludel ('æl(j)uːdɛl). *Chem.* [a. Fr. *aludel*, in 13th c. *alutel*, ad. Arab. *al-uthāl* (quoted by Dozy with this sense in 9th c.), i.e. *al* the + *uthāl*, prob. variant of *ithāl* pl. of *athla* utensil, apparatus.] A pear-shaped pot of earthenware or glass, open at both ends, so that a series could be fitted one above another; used by the alchemists in sublimation.

1559 MORWYNG *Evonym.* 6 Putting wull of wode, or bombice into the upper hoole of the aludel. **1610** B. JONSON *Alchem.* II. iii. (1616) 624 Let your heat, still, lessen by degrees, To the Aludels. **1677** HARRIS tr. *Lemery's Chem.* (1686) Introd. 44 Aludels..are Pots without a bottom, joyned together and are placed over another Pot with a hole in the middle to serve for Sublimations. **1731** HALES *Stat. Ess.* I. 201 We luted a German retort to two or three large alodals. **1881** RAYMOND *Gloss. Mining Terms*, *Aludel*, an earthen condenser for mercury.

a-luff, obs. form of ALOOF.

alula ('æljʊlə). Pl. alulæ. [mod.L. dim. of *āla* wing.]

1. *Ornith.* The bastard wing of a bird (see BASTARD *a.* 5 c).

1772 [see BASTARD *a.* 5 c]. **1959** VAN TYNE & BERGER *Fund. Ornith.* iii. 82 The group of feathers borne by the 'thumb' or 'pollex' is called the alula. *Ibid.* 83 Alula quills should be numbered from the innermost to the outermost.

2. *Ent.* A small scale-like appendage at the base of each wing of many *Diptera*, above the halteres. Also, a similar appendage beneath the elytron in some water-beetles.

1817 KIRBY & SPENCE *Entomol.* II. 359 (*Diptera*) Their winglets (*Alulæ*). **1877** *Encycl. Brit.* VI. 127 In certain water beetles (Dytiscidæ) a pair of *alulæ*, or winglets, are developed at the inner angle of the elytra. **1899** D. SHARP in *Camb. Nat. Hist.* VI. vii. 447 On the hind margin of the wing, near the base, there is often a more or less free lobe.. called the 'alula'.

alum ('æləm), *sb.* Forms: 4 alem, 4–5 alym, 4–8 alom, 5–7 alume, alome, 6 alme, 6–7 allume, 6–8 allom(e, allum, 4– alum. [a. OFr. *alum*:—L. *alūmen*, the same substance: cf. *alūta* tawed skin.]

1. A whitish transparent mineral salt, crystallizing in octahedrons, very astringent, used in dyeing, tawing skins, and medicine, also for sizing paper, and making materials fire-proof; chemically a double sulphate of aluminium and potassium ($AlK(SO_4)_2$ + $12H_2O$ water of crystallization).

burnt alum, A. deprived of its water of crystallization so as to become a white powder; ***rock*** or ***Roman alum***, that prepared from the alum-stone in Italy; ***saccharine alum***, an artificial composition of alum, rosewater, and egg albumen, boiled to a paste, which hardens when cold.

c **1325** *E.E. Allit. P.* B. 1035 As alum & alka[t]ran, that angré arn boþe. **1366** MAUNDEV. ix. 99 About that see growethe moche Alom. *c* **1386** CHAUCER *Chan. Yem. Prol.* 260 Tartre, alym, glas [*v.r.* alum, alumglas(se, alem]. **1436** *Pol. Poems* II. 172 Coton, roche-alum, and gode golde of Jene. **1453** in Heath *Grocers' Comp.* (1869) 422 Alum, foyle or rooch, yᵉ bale..iiij*d.* **1551** TURNER *Herbal* II. (1568) 123 Layed to with honey and allome. **1585** JAMES I *Ess. Poesie* 16 Cleare and smothe lyke glas or alme. **1587** HOLINSHED *Chron.* III. 1199/1 A mightie great hulke, laden with wood & allume. **1601** HOLLAND *Pliny* (1634) II. 559 Alume brought from Melos, is the best. **1622** HEYLYN *Cosmogr.* I. (1682) 75 Well furnished with Allom, Sulphur, and Bitumen. **1660** R. COKE *Power & Subj.* 208 The Pope had excommunicated all persons whatsoever, who had bought alume of the Florentines. **1671** SALMON *Syn. Med.* III. xxii. 437 A lotion with Honey, Alome, and White wine. **1703** MOXON *Mech. Exerc.* 238 A fat Earth full of Allom. **1718** MRS. EALES *Receipt* 38 Put in a good piece of Roach-Allum. **1718** QUINCY *Compl. Disp.* 106 Alum is dug out of the earth as we find it in the Shops. **1768** BOSWELL *Corsica* i. (ed. 2) 52 There are also mines of allum. **1815** BAKEWELL *Introd. Geol.* 201 The sulphuric acid uniting with the alumine, forms the well-known salt called alum. **1855** TENNYSON *Maud* I. i. x, While chalk and alum and plaster are sold to the poor for bread. **1875** URE *Dict. Arts* I. 105 [Alum] seems to have come to Europe in later times as *alum of Rocca*, the name of Edessa; but it is not impossible that this name was an Italian prefix, which has remained to this day under the name of *Rock Alum, Allume di Rocca*.

2. *Mod. Chem.* (with *pl.*) A series of isomorphous double salts, including the foregoing, consisting of aluminium sulphate in combination with the sulphate of a monatomic metal, as potassium, sodium, ammonium, silver, etc., with general formula $Al'''M(SO_4)_2$ + 12 H_2O; all of which crystallize in octahedrons: distinguished as ***common*** or ***potash alum, soda alum, ammonia alum, silver alum***, etc.

1868 WATTS *Dict. Chem.* V. 580 Argento-aluminic sulphate or Silver alum. Potassio-aluminic sulphate or Potash-alum: this is the salt to which the name alum is most generally applied. **1873** WILLIAMSON *Chem.* §185 These alums cannot be separated by crystallization; and a crystal of one of them grows regularly in a solution of another alum. **1873** FOWNES *Chem.* 373 Sodium alum is much more soluble. **1875** URE *Dict. Arts* I. 107 The composition of potash-, soda-, and ammonia-alums found ready formed in nature.

3. *Mod. Chem.* (with *pl.*) Extended to a family of compounds analogous to and including the preceding series, in which the alumina itself is absent, and replaced by the isomorphous sesquioxide of iron, chrome, or manganese; whence ***iron alum*** (potassio-ferric sulphate), ***manganese alum*** (potassio-manganic sulphate), ***chrome alum*** (potassio-chromic sulphate), ***chrome-ammonia alum*** (ammonio-chromic sulphate), etc.

1868 WATTS *Dict. Chem.* V. 578 The dodecahydrated double sulphates of the alkali-metals and triatomic metals constitute the true alums. The sulphates of ammonium, potassium, and sodium are capable of forming alums with the aluminic, ferric, chromic, and manganic sulphates. **1874** ROSCOE *Elem. Chem.* 247 Chromium sulphate forms a series of alums with potassium and ammonium sulphates, which have a deep purple tint, and are isomorphous with common alum.

4. *Min.* Applied to various native minerals, which are chemically alums proper, as ***native alum*** or kalinite; also to others (pseudo-alums), which are compounds of aluminium sulphate with the sulphate of some other base, as ***magnesia alum*** (magnesio-aluminic sulphate) or pickeringite; or with the protoxides of iron, manganese, etc., as ***feather*** or ***plume alum*** (ferroso-aluminic sulphate) or halotrichite, ***manganese alum*** or apjohnite, ***manganoso-magnesian alum*** or bosjemanite.

The name *feather alum* has been applied also to *magnesia alum* and *alunogen*.

a **1661** HOLYDAY *Juvenal* (1673) 122 Plume-alume burns the skin..rock-alume dissolves metals, shrivels the skin, loosens the teeth. **1868** DANA *Min.* 655 Hallotrichine is a silky alum from the Solfatara near Naples. **1868** WATTS *Dict. Chem.* V. 583 Manganoso-aluminic sulphate, or *manganese alum*..occurs in snow-white silky fibres at Lagoa Bay.

5. *Comb.*, in which *alum* stands in obj. relation to pr. pple. or vbl. sb., as ***alum-bearing, -maker, -making, -manufacture***; in instrumental relation to pa. pple., as ***alum-steeped***; in simple attrib. relation, as ***alum-crystal, -house, -liquor, -water***; or attrib. relation of material, as ***alum-styptic***.

1578 LYTE *Dodoens* VI. xxx. 697 Soked, or delayed in allom water. **1587** HARRISON *Engl.* I. II. xxiii. 348 A tast much like to allume liquor. **1656** DU GARD *Lat. Unlocked* §443 Hee wetteth with allom-water every sheet of thinner paper. **1674** RAY *Coll. Words* 139 The Liquor..is conveyed to the Allom-house. **1711** POPE *Rape Lock* II. 131 Alom-stypticks with contracting pow'r Shrink his thin essence like a rivelled flow'r. **1830** G. COLMAN *Random Rec.* I. vi. 187 Most readers will pardon me for not taking them into the Alum-House, to explain the several methods of crystallization &c. **1837** SYD. SMITH *Let.* Wks. 1859 II. 277/1 Let him drive his alum-steeped loaves a little further. **1869** ROSCOE *Elem. Chem.* 215 Ammonium Sulphate is largely employed for alum making. **1870** YEATS *Nat. Hist. Comm.* 381 The chief localities of alum manufacture in this country. **1875** URE *Dict. Arts* I. 117 *Alum Liquors*,—In the alum works on the Yorkshire coast, eight different liquors are met with.

Also **alum cake**, a massive and porous sulphate of alumina, mixed with silica, manufactured from fine clay; **alum earth**, applied to various earthy or loose substances yielding alum; †**alum-farmer**, one who farmed the royal alum-works; †**alum-flower**, alum calcined and powdered; †**alum-glass**, crystallized alum; **alum-mine**, raw material from which alum is obtained; **alum-rock, -schist, -shale, -slate**, thin-bedded rocks found in various formations, from which alum is manufactured; **alum-stone**, the mineral ALUNITE, from which the rock or Roman alum is made; **alum-works**, the place and apparatus for making alum. Also ALUM-ROOT, q.v.

1611 SPEED *Theat. Gt. Brit.* xli. 81/1 An allum-earth of sundry colours. **1641** in *4th Rep. Hist. MSS.* (1874) 71/1 Account of the sums for which the Allom farmers left Morgan engaged. **1730** SWIFT *Lady's Dress. Room* Wks. 1755 IV. I. 114 Allum-flower to stop the steams. **1386** [See under I.] *a* **1500** *E.E. Misc.* (1856) 78, j *di*, of alome glas molte into clere water. **1612** W. STRACHEY *Travaile into Virginia* (1849) I. i. 33 We doe already heare the Indians talke both of allam mines and copper. **1758** *Phil. Trans.* L. 688 What we call allum-rock, a kind of black slate that may be taken up in flakes. **1875** URE *Dict. Arts* I. 111 At Whitby, the alum-rock. **1872** NICHOLSON *Palæont.* 513 Beds of so-called 'alum-schist,' which are of Upper Cambrian age. **1875** URE *Dict. Arts* I. 111 Such alum-shales as contain too little bitumen for the roasting process. **1805** *Edin. Rev.* VI. 237 He also classes the alum-slate..among the transition rocks. **1875** URE *Dict. Arts* I. 111 The ustulation of alum-slate. **1833** LYELL *Princ. Geol.* III. 223 Hot sulphureous vapours, which convert the trachyte into alum-stone. **1875** URE *Dict. Arts* I. 109 The alum-stone appears to be confined to volcanic districts. **1868** DANA *Min.* 659 Alunite was first observed at Tolfa, near Rome, in the 15th c. by a Genoese, who had been engaged in the manufacture of alum, from an alum-stone or 'Rock-alum' found near Edessa in Syria. **1617** BACON in *Fortescue Pap.* 34 The offers made..to your Majestie of his allome workes. **1641** in *4th Rep. Hist. MSS.* (1874) 42/2 William Turnor, and others, who farmed the alum works of his late Majesty. **1875** URE *Dict. Arts* I. 119 Boiling the scum of the alum works.

alum ('æləm), *v.* [f. prec. sb.] To treat or impregnate with alum.

? *a* **1500** in *Middle Eng. Dict.* **1598** FLORIO *Worlde of Wordes* 14/3 *Allumare*..to allume silkes..before they can be died into any light colour. **1735** J. BARROW *Dict. Polygraphicum* II. s.v. *silk*, How to alum the boiled silk. **1791** HAMILTON *Berthollet's Dyeing* I. I. I. i. 19 Having alumed as completely as possible a pound of wool. **1877** W. GREY in Mackail *W. Morris* (1899) I. 356 Silks were alumed for to-morrow's dyeing. **1889** *Internat. Ann. Anthony's Photogr. Bull.* II. 108 The plate should be alumed before and after the operation.

‖**Alumbrado** (ˌalum'braðo). [Sp. *alumbrado* illuminated, enlightened; pa. pple. of *alumbrar*:—L. *allūmināre*: see ALLUMINE.] One of the Spanish *Illuminati* or Perfectionists, who arose about 1575, and were suppressed by the Inquisition; hence sometimes applied to any one claiming special spiritual illumination.

1671 GLANVILL *Further Disc. M. Stubbe* 33 Worthless Fanaticks, Alumbradoes in Religion. **1749** LAVINGTON *Enthus. Methodists* II. 114 The Alumbrado's or Illuminati of Spain, who were stiff Maintainers of Perfection. **1847** BUCH *Hagenbach's Hist. Doct.* II. 197 The question whether he stood in connection with the Alumbrados.

alumed ('æləmd), *ppl. a.* [f. ALUM *v.* + -ED.] Treated or impregnated with alum.

? *a* **1425** in *Middle Eng. Dict.* **1580** BARET *Alv.* A 330 Alumde, or mixed with alum, *aluminatus*. **1725** BRADLEY *Fam. Dict.* s.v. *Muzzle*, If it be allom'd Leather. **1893** *Pall Mall Gaz.* 30 Jan. 7/3 These harmful alumed baking powders. **1896** *Kodak News* Aug. 29/1 During development, fixing and aluming, it showed no sign of blistering... Using an alumed fixing bath..improved matters.

†**alu'mere.** *Obs. rare*⁻¹. [a. OFr. *alumere* (:—L. **adlūminātōr*), f. *alumer* to light:—L. **adlūmināre*: see ALLUMINE.] An illuminator, lighter up.

c **1300** in Wright's *Lyric P.* xxv. 68 Ihesu, nothing may be suettere,..Then thou so suete alumere.

alumian (ə'l(j)u:mɪən). *Min.* [mod. (1858) f. ALUMINA.] A white, sub-translucent mineral, a native sulphate of aluminium; classed by Dana among the Anhydrous Sulphates.

alumic (ə'l(j)u:mɪk). Rare variant of ALUMINIC.

1869 *Eng. Mech.* 19 Mar. 585/3, I have obtained alumic sulphate neutral often.

alu'miferous, *a.*; a variant of ALUMINIFEROUS.

1853 T. ROSS tr. *Humboldt's Trav.* III. xxvi. 118 The alumiferous rocks of Parad.

alumina (ə'l(j)u:mɪnə). [mod.L.; formed, along with its Fr. equivalent *alumine* (also used in Eng.) on L. *alūmen, alūmin-*, alum, on the type of *soda, potassa, magnesia*, by the Fr. chemical nomenclators of 1787; its character as the *earth of alum* (*alaun-erde*) having been proved by Marggraf in 1754. Other proposed names were *arga, argil*.]

a. One of the earths, a white, insoluble, tasteless, amorphous substance; the only oxide (Al_2O_3) of the metal aluminium, the basis of alum, the chief constituent of all clays, and found crystallized as the sapphire.

c **1790** J. BLACK *Elem. Chem.* II. 150 The French chemists have given a new name to this pure earth; *alumine* in French, and *alumina* in Latin. I confess I do not like this *alumina*. **1801** CHENEVIX in *Phil. Trans.* XCI. 197, I could..discover iron, silica, alumina, and carbonic acid. **1802** —— *Chem. Nomencl.* 116 In the chapter upon Earth, we find..Argil for Alumina. **1813** SIR H. DAVY *Agric. Chem.* 156 Alumina exists in a pure and crystallized state in the white sapphire. **1871** TYNDALL *Fragm. Sc.* (ed. 6) I. xii. 362 These masses of slate contain silica, alumina, potash, soda, and mica.

b. *attrib.*

1908 *Chem. Abstr.* 735 Process of producing alumina solutions compounded with plant extracts. **1909** *Cent. Dict.* Suppl., *Alumina cream*, freshly precipitated aluminium hydrate held in suspension in water. **1951** R. MAYER *Artist's Handbk.* ii. 40 *Alumina hydrate*, aluminium hydroxide, artificially produced. A white, fluffy, light-weight powder which becomes virtually colourless and transparent when it is ground in oil. **1963** *Lancet* 5 Jan. 13/1 The management of the isotope on an alumina column has proved quite easy and the expense not unreasonable.

aluminate (ə'l(j)u:mɪneɪt), *sb.* [f. prec. + -ATE.] A compound in which alumina acts the part of an acid; 'a compound of alumina with one of the stronger bases.' Watts.

1841 TRIMMER *Pract. Geol.* 68 They have therefore by some chemists been named aluminates. **1869** PHILLIPS *Vesuv.* x. 286 Aluminates are equally limited. **1873** FOWNES *Chem.* 372 Spinell is an aluminate of magnesium.

aluminate (ə'lju:mɪneɪt), *v.* [f. L. *alūmināt-us* pa. pple.; f. *alūmin-* ALUM] To treat or impregnate with alum; to combine with alumina. (Commonly in pa. pple. **aluminated.**)

1731 BAILEY, *Aluminated*, done with alum. **1833** FYFE *Chem.* (ed. 3) 474 The solution called aluminated potass is transparent and colourless.

alumine ('æl(j)u:maɪn). *Chem. arch.* [a. Fr. *alumine*: see ALUMINA.] = ALUMINA.

1791 HAMILTON *Berthollet's Dyeing* I. I. I. i. 22 They unite with acids..and some earths, principally alumine. **1798** *Phil. Trans.* LXXXVIII. 16 The absorbent earths were distinguished into calcareous, magnesia, and alumine or clay. **1805** SIR H. DAVY *ibid.* XCV. 232, I have separated the alumine by solution of potash. **1852** T. ROSS tr. *Humboldt's Trav.* I. ii. 78 The alumine, magnesia, soda, and metallic oxides gradually disappear. **1854** F. BAKEWELL *Geol.* 47 Carbonate of lime..combined with alumine.

aluming ('æləmɪŋ), *vbl. sb.* [f. ALUM *v.* + -ING¹.] The act of treating or impregnating with alum.

1791 HAMILTON *Berthollet's Dyeing* I. I. I. ii. 35 Tartar is not used in the aluming of silk and thread. **1862** C. O'NEILL *Dict. Calico Printing & Dyeing* 15/1 By aluming the silk is considered to take the dye better. **1896** [see ALUMED *ppl. a.*].

aluminic (æl(j)u:'mɪnɪk), *a.* *Chem.* [f. ALUMINIUM + -IC.] Of or containing aluminium, as ***Aluminic chloride***, also called *Aluminium chloride* and *Chloride of aluminium*.

1873 WILLIAMSON *Chem.* §185 The double salt containing aluminic sulphate, combined with potassic sulphate, has long been known by the name of alum. **1876** HARLEY *Mat. Med.* 369 The ash is chiefly composed of aluminic phosphate. **1880** *Athenæum* 27 Nov. 713/1 Two new aluminic compounds.

aluminiferous (əˌl(j)u:mɪ'nɪfərəs), *a.* [f. L. *alūmin-* ALUM + -(I)FEROUS.] Alum-bearing, yielding alum.

1849 MURCHISON *Silur.* viii. (1867) 154 These rocks, anthracite and aluminiferous, are charged with graptolites and annelides. **1853** T. ROSS tr. *Humboldt's Trav.* III. xxxii. 396 The aluminiferous slates of Chaparuparu.

aluminiform (ə'l(j)u:mɪnɪˌfɔ:m, ˌæl(j)u:'mɪnɪ-), *a.* [f. L. *alumin-* ALUM + -(I)FORM.] Having the form of an alum.

1864 WEBSTER cites CHAPTAL.

alu'minilite. *Min.* [f. L. *alūmin-* alum + Gr. λίθος stone.] A mineral called more commonly ALUNITE, q.v.

aluminio- (ˌæl(j)u:'mɪnɪəʊ), combining form of ALUMINIUM, as in *Aluminio-silicate*, a salt in which the combined oxides of Aluminium and Silicon are supposed to act as an acid.

†**a'luminish,** *a.* *Obs. rare.* [f. L. *alūmin-* ALUM + -ISH.] = ALUMISH.

1641 FRENCH *Distill.* v. (1651) 167 There will distill over a certain acid alluminish water.

aluminite (ə'l(j)u:mɪnaɪt). *Min.* [mod. (Ger. *aluminit* 1807) f. L. *alūmin-* ALUM + -ITE min. form.] An opaque, whitish mineral, a native hydrosulphate of alumina, called also WEBSTERITE[1].

1868 WATTS *Dict. Chem.* (1871) V. 579 The tribasic sulphate [of aluminium], $3Al_2O_3.SO_3.9H_2O$, occurs native as aluminite, a white, opaque earthy mineral.

aluminium (,æl(j)uː'mɪnɪəm). [a modification of ALUMINUM, the name given by its discoverer, Sir H. Davy *c* 1812 (for which he had first of all used ALUMIUM), f. ALUMINA. The termination *-ium* now preferred harmonizes best with other names of elements, as *sodium, potassium, magnesium, lithium, selenium*, etc. Both *alumium* and *aluminum* lived for some time.] **a.** A metal, white, sonorous, ductile, and malleable, very light, not oxidized in the air, used for instruments, ornaments, and as an alloy. In *Chem.* it has the symbol Al., is tetratomic, has *alumina* as its oxide, and the *alums* as its chief salts.

1812 *Q. Rev.* VIII. 72 Aluminium, for so we shall take the liberty of writing the word, in preference to aluminum, which has a less classical sound. **1835** HOBLYN *Dict. Med.* 6 Aluminium, the metallic base of alumina. **1845** *Vest. Creation* ii. (ed. 3) 34 Aluminium..is another abundant elementary substance. *c* **1860** FARADAY *Forces of Nat.* i. 195 *note*, Aluminium is $2\frac{1}{2}$ times heavier than water. **1869** *Eng. Mech.* 14 May 187/3 Some Belgian manufacturer has just had a bell cast of aluminium. **1876** C. GEIKIE *Life in Woods* xxv. 399 Science got the beautiful metal aluminium out of the clay which ignorance trod under foot.

b. *attrib.* in chem. compounds, as ***aluminium chloride*** (also chloride of aluminium, and aluminic chloride), ***aluminium fluoride, sulphate*** (sulphate of alumina), ***silicate***, etc. Also in ***aluminium brass***, an alloy of aluminium and brass; ***aluminium-bronze***, a beautiful and important alloy (or chemical compound) of aluminium and copper; ***aluminium foil***, paper-thin sheet aluminium, used as wrapping material, etc.; ***aluminium hydroxide***, a compound used in medicine and industry.

1862 *Morn. Star* 21 May The specimens of aluminium-bronze, as it is called, have a fine golden hue, which appears to especial advantage in combination with the pure metal. **1863** WATTS *Dict. Chem.* (1879) I. 154 General character and reactions of Aluminium compounds. **1866** ROSCOE *Elem. Chem.* xx. 181 Aluminium chloride, Al_2Cl_6, is a volatile yellow solid body..; it is used in the manufacture of the metal. *Ibid.*, The soluble aluminium sulphate, Al_23SO_4, is prepared..for the use of the dyer by decomposing clay by acting upon it with sulphuric acid. **1871** *Ibid.* (ed. 3) xvii. 188 The hydroxides..may be represented as six molecules of water in which half of the hydrogen is replaced by a hexad group, thus: Aluminium hydroxide..(or Hydrate of Alumina). **1873** FOWNES *Chem.* 372 Aluminium Sulphate crystallises in thin pearly plates, soluble in 2 parts of water. *a* **1875** KNIGHT *Dict. Mech.* I. 70/2 The uses to which aluminium bronze is applicable are various... For certain parts, such as journals of engines..it has proved itself superior to all other metals. **1892** *Photography Ann.* II. 71 Aluminium foil is easily ignited and gives no smoke. **1907** G. S. NEWTH *Inorg. Chem.* (ed. 12) III. viii. 618 Aluminium hydroxide unites with many soluble organic colouring-matters, and precipitates them from solution as lakes. **1909** *Cent. Dict.* Suppl., Aluminium brass. **1934** *Discovery* June 162/2 It [*sc.* Alucol, a patent medicine] was aluminium hydroxide, and was given in doses of 1 grm. from three to six times a day. **1958** A. D. MERRIMAN *Dict. Metall.* 8/1 *Aluminium Bronze*, this is the name conferred on a series of copper-aluminium alloys which may or may not also contain additions of iron, manganese, nickel, tin and zinc... It has been used for making imitation gold cigarette cases and trinkets. **1959** *Engineering* 20 Feb. 250/1 The heat transmission properties of aluminium brass are good, and the material is remarkably resistant to corrosion. **1962** *House & Garden* Jan. 54/2, 2 pieces of aluminium foil to cover breasts of chicken. **1964** N. G. CLARK *Mod. Org. Chem.* 546 Aluminium chloride, $AlCl_3$, is a pale yellow, fuming, hygroscopic solid, which hydrolyses in contact with water.

aluminize (ə'l(j)uːmɪnaɪz), *v.* [f. L. *alūmin-* alum + -IZE.] **1.** To treat or impregnate with alum, to alum. *rare.*

1857 *Nat. Mag.* I. 390 Our bread was alumenised if not worse.

2. *trans.* To spray or coat with aluminium. Hence **a,lumini'zation; a'luminized** *ppl. a.*; **a'luminizing** *vbl. sb.*

1934 *Sci. Amer.* Feb. 81/3 With aluminized mirrors and quartz prisms and lenses, the stellar spectrum between 3400 and 3000 angstroms should now be easily observable. *Ibid.*, The construction of an aluminizing apparatus big enough to hold a good-sized mirror..and provided with the necessary devices for..volatizing the aluminium, involves considerable time and cost. **1938** *Times* 2 June 4/5 The cost of aluminizing the mirror has been found to be prohibitive, and the observatory will have to be content with a silvered mirror. **1940** *Jrnl. Iron & Steel Inst.* CXLII. 114 A This process is usually known as 'aluminising', and the coating may be said to consist of three layers. **1946** W. LEWIS *Thin Films & Surfaces* vii. 60 Another advantage of aluminized mirrors as compared with silvered mirrors..is that aluminium films do not scatter light. *Ibid.* 61 Aluminization improves the reflectivity of speculum metal gratings. **1957** AMOS & BIRKINSHAW *Television Engin.* I. 301 Aluminised Cathode-ray Tube Screen. **1960** *Metallurgia* Jan. 15/1 The coatings were of the hot-dipped aluminium, aluminised (aluminium sprayed and subjected to a diffusion heat treatment), and chromised types.

alumino- (ə'l(j)uːmɪnəʊ), combining form of the words ALUMINA, ALUMINUM, used in compound names implying the union of these with another element, as ***alumino-magnesian silicate***, a double silicate of aluminium and magnesium.

1864 *Reader* 18 June 784/1 An alumino-magnesian silicate allied to chlorite in composition.

alumi'nography. Fuller form of ALGRAPHY.

1909 in WEBSTER.

aluminose (ə,l(j)uːmɪ'nəʊs), *a.* [ad. L. *alūminōs-us*: see ALUMINOUS.] = ALUMINOUS.

1879 in *Syd. Soc. Lex.*

alumino-silicate (ə,l(j)uːmɪnəʊ'sɪlɪkət). [f. ALUMINO- + SILICATE.] A natural compound which occurs in many minerals, esp. feldspars, forming the basis of all clays and used industrially as a constituent of strengthened glass. Also *attrib.*

1907 *Chem. Abstr.* 2547 The action of free humus acids on alumino-silicates is identical with that of water. **1934** W. H. TAYLOR in *Proc. R. Soc.* A. CXLV. 80 (*title*) Nature and Properties of Aluminosilicate Framework Structures. **1935** *Chem. Abstr.* 7550 The clays should therefore be considered aluminosilicates. **1946** *Electronic Engin.* XVIII. 299 Experiments with new aluminosilicate glasses..are giving interesting results. **1962** *Aeroplane* 29 Mar. 43/2 Windscreens for supersonic transports incorporating alumino-silicate..are to be produced by Triplex.

aluminosity (ə,l(j)uːmɪ'nɒsɪtɪ). *rare*[−1]. [f. L. *alūminōs-us* + -ITY.] Aluminous quality.

1678 R. R[USSELL] *Geber* III. II. I. viii. 159 You will find a manifest Substance of Aluminosity to distill from them.

aluminothermy (ə,l(j)uːmɪnəʊ'θɜːmɪ). [ad. G. *aluminothermie* (H. Goldschmidt 1900, in *Zeitschr. Ang. Chem.* 919).] A process by means of which high temperatures are produced by the combination of aluminium and oxygen. So **a,lumino'thermic** *a.*, of or pertaining to aluminothermy; **a,lumino'thermics**, a collective name for processes involving aluminothermy.

[**1900** *Engineering Mag.* Aug. 755/2 An important new industry, to which the name 'Aluminothermie' has been given.] **1904** H. GOLDSCHMIDT in *Electro-chem. Ind.* II. 145 Production of pure metals free from carbon by the aluminothermic method. **1904** *Railroad Gaz.* I. 111 (*title*) Alumino-thermics and its use for welding and metallurgical purposes. **1909** *Cent. Dict.* Suppl., Aluminothermy. **1916** *Chambers's Jrnl.* Apr. 270/1 In the preparation of the cobalt for combination with the steel, what is known as the alumino-thermic process is practised. **1958** *Chambers's Techn. Dict.* 955/1 Aluminothermic process..also known as the thermite process, is used especially for the oxides of metals which are reduced with difficulty. **1958** A. D. MERRIMAN *Dict. Metallurgy* 8/2 Aluminothermy..is used for welding certain articles *in situ*.

aluminous (ə'l(j)uːmɪnəs), *a.* [a. Fr. *alumineux*, ad. L. *alūminōs-us*: see ALUM and -OUS.]

1. Of the nature of alum, containing alum. **aluminous cake** = ALUM cake.

1541 R. COPLAND *Guidon's Form.* Uj, Wasshyng with wyne and aluminous water with good and artefycyall lygature. **1652** FRENCH *Yorksh. Spa* iii. 34 *Astringing* waters, as Alluminous, and Vitrioline almost everywhere. **1725** BRADLEY *Fam. Dict.* II, Add a little burnt Allom..to give it a discernable alluminous Taste. **1845** *Blackw. Mag.* LVIII. 488 Aluminous perspiration stood thick upon us, the alum being deposited from the walls and atmosphere of the place.

2. Of the nature of or containing alumina; clayey.

1802 *Edin. Rev.* I. 208 A chaotic collection of flinty sand and aluminous and magnesian mud. **1812** SIR H. DAVY *Chem. Philos.* 49 Margraaf..distinguished accurately between the silicious, calcareous, and aluminous earths. **1841** TRIMMER *Pract. Geol.* 22 Aluminous, or clayey soils, retain too much moisture. **1872** NICHOLSON *Palæont.* 8 The Argillaceous or Aluminous Rocks. **1930** *Engineering* 14 Feb. 238/1 The net effect..is..to avoid the use of either salt [sodium chloride or calcium chloride] in the preparation of reinforced concrete or with aluminous cements. **1940** *Chambers's Techn. Dict.* 26/1 The aluminous cements.. possess rapid-hardening qualities.

aluminum (ə'l(j)uːmɪnəm). *Chem.* = ALUMINIUM; being the name given by Davy in 1812, and the usual form in the U.S.

1812 SIR H. DAVY *Chem. Philos.* I. 355 As yet Aluminum has not been obtained in a perfectly free state. **1833** *Penny Cycl.* I. 406 *Alumina*, the earthy oxide of aluminum sometimes called argil or the argillaceous earth. **1855** in *Proc. Am. Phil. Soc.* VI. 141 Mr. DuBois laid upon the table specimens of the metal aluminum. **1879** C. CAMERON in *Cassell's Techn. Educ.* I. 170 Aluminum is a white malleable metal.

alumish ('æləmɪʃ), *a.* [f. ALUM + -ISH.] Having somewhat of the character or taste of alum.

1562 TURNER *Baths* 7 The water of this bath is alumish. *a* **1682** *Hist. Royal Soc.* IV. 196 (T.) Tasting something alumish, and being found near some places which afford alum.

† **'alumite.** *Min.* Obs. form of ALUNITE.

1853 T. ROSS tr. *Humboldt's Trav.* III. xxvi. 118 The alumite of Tolfa, which..I have examined on the spot.

† **alumium** (ə'l(j)uːmɪəm). *Chem. Obs.* The name first suggested by Davy for the metal which he finally called ALUMINUM, a name eventually further changed to ALUMINIUM.

1808 SIR H. DAVY in *Phil. Trans.* XCVIII. 353 Had I been so fortunate as..to have procured the metallic substances I was in search of, I should have proposed for them the names of silicium, alumium, zirconium, and glucium. **1815** W. PHILLIPS *Outl. Min. & Geol.* (ed. 3) 22 Alumine consists of Oxygen united with a base Alumium the nature of which has not been completely ascertained. **1854** PEREIRA *Mat. Med.* (L.) Aluminum, aluminium, or alumium, is the metallic base of the earth alumina.

alumna (ə'lʌmnə). Pl. **alumnæ**. [L., fem. of *alumnus*.] A female graduate or former student of a school, college, or university. Chiefly *U.S.*

1882 M. HARLAND *Eve's Daughters* 177 The Alumnæ and Alumni of Oberlin. **1896** *Century Mag.* LI. 798/1 The average salary of the alumna teacher would be below rather than above $1000 a year. **1939** A. HUXLEY *After Many a Summer* vi. 69 Successive generations of the College's Alumni and Alumnæ.

† **a'lumnate**, *v. Obs.*[−0] [f. L. *alumnāt-* ppl. stem of *alumnā-re* to bring up; f. ALUMNUS.] 'To nourish or feed.' Blount *Glossogr.* 1656.

† **alum'nation.** [n. of action f. prec.] 'Fostering, feeding.' Coles 1692.

alumner, probably error for ALMONER.

1401 *Pol. Poems* II. 110 The releef of Cristis feeste..That his alumners the postlis gaderid togidere.

alumniate (ə'lʌmnɪət). *rare.* [irreg. f. ALUMNUS, by form-assoc. with words like *noviciate*, where the affix is really only -ATE.] The period of pupillage.

1879 BARING-GOULD *Germ.* II. 134 When the alumniate is over, the seminarist goes forth.

‖ **alumnus** (ə'lʌmnəs). Pl. **-i**. [L., = a foster-child; f. *al-ĕre* to nourish, with ending akin to Gr. *-όμενος*; cf. *Vert-umnus*, etc.] The nurseling or pupil of any school, university, or other seat of learning. Also, a graduate or former student (chiefly *U.S.*, esp. in *pl*).

1645 EVELYN *Diary* (1827) I. 212 We saw an Italian comedy acted by their alumni before the Cardinals. **1696** SEWALL *Diary* 12 Oct. (1878) I. 435 Lt. Govr...promised his Interposition for them, as become such an Alumnus to such an Alma Mater. **1823** J. & R. C. MORSE *Traveller's Guide* 320 The number of alumni, that is, the number who have been educated at each college since its establishment. **1843** HOPKINS in B. H. Hall *College Words* (1851) 7 So far as I know, the Society of the Alumni of Williams College was the first association of the kind in this country... It was formed September 5th, 1821. **1846** LYTTON *Lucretia* x. (1853) 93 The poorer and less steady alumni of the rising school. **1872** MINTO *Eng. Lit.* II. ix. 598 An alumnus of Glasgow, and travelling tutor. **1890** *Harper's Mag.* Apr. 799/1 The associated alumni of a college organized into a club preserve..the old feeling of comradeship.

attrib. **1843** HOPKINS in B. H. Hall *College Words* (1851) 8 Last year, for the first time, the voice of an Alumnus orator was heard at Harvard. **1851** *Ibid.*, An Alumni Society was formed at Columbia College in the year 1829. **1895** *Century Mag.* Sept. 794/2 How often at an alumni banquet is intellectual supremacy in college life praised? **1906** *Springfield* (Mass.) *Weekly Republ.* 28 June 10 Tuesday was alumni day at Yale, when hundreds of old graduates.. gathered in alumni hall.

alumocalcite (ə,l(j)uːməʊ'kælsaɪt). [f. ALUM + *calc-em* lime + -ITE.] A milk-white mineral, a variety of opal with an addition of lime and alumina.

'alum root. A name given to the astringent roots of various plants.

1818 NUTTALL *Gen. N. Amer. Plants* I. 174 *Heuchera*, Allum-root. **1830** LINDLEY *Nat. Syst. Bot.* 140 The root of *Geranium maculatum* is considered a valuable astringent in North America, where it is sometimes called Alum root. **1866** *Treas. Bot.* 588 The root of *Heuchera americana* is so astringent that it is called Alum root.

alundum (ə'lʌndəm). [f. ALU(MINIUM + COR)UNDUM.] The proprietary name of a hard material produced by fusing alumina in an electric furnace, used chiefly as an abrasive agent.

U.S. Patent by C. B. Jacobs, 1900, but the word *alundum* was not used in it.

1904 *Sci. Amer.* Suppl. 24 Sept. 24018/2 *Alundum*, the trade name for artificial corundum, is an abrasive made by a process due to C. B. Jacobs and others. **1905** *Trans. Faraday Soc.* I. 301 Artificial corundum, or, as the Americans call it, 'alundum', also deserved notice..as, in addition to being highly refractory, it was of extreme hardness. **1906** *Westm. Gaz.* 27 Dec. 2/1 The advent of the electric furnace has brought about a revolution by the introduction of alundum. **1918** *Nature* 4 July 350/2 The fusion of bauxite gives another abrasive, alundum, which has practically superseded other materials for the grinding of steel.

alu'niferous, *a.* [f. Fr. *alunifère* (f. *alun* alum + L. *-(i)fer-us* bearing) + -OUS.] = ALUMINIFEROUS.

1879 in *Syd. Soc. Lex.*

alunite ('æl(j)uːnaɪt). *Min.* [mod. f. Fr. *alun* alum + -ITE min. form.; see quot. 1868.] A mineral, also called Alum-stone and Aluminilite (consisting of common alum together with normal hydrate of aluminium (Al $K(SO_4)_2$.2 Al H_3O_3), found in the volcanic districts of Italy, etc.), which is the source of the Roman alum.

1868 DANA *Min.* 659 It was named *Aluminilite* by Delametherie in 1797, a long name well changed to *Alunite* by Beudant in 1824. **1875** URE *Dict. Arts* I. 109 The alum-stone or alunite is a mineral of limited occurrence, being found in moderate quantity at Tolfa (near Civita Vecchia).

alunogen (ə'l(j)uːnədʒɪn). *Min.* [mod. (Fr. *alunogène* 1832) f. Fr. *alun* alum + -GEN, taken as = producing.] A mineral, also called Keramohalite, a hydrous sulphate of alumina, occurring as a feathery efflorescence, to which, among other substances, the names *hair-salt* and *feather-alum* are applied. (*Halotrichite*, sometimes used as a synonym, is applied by Dana to a distinct mineral.)

1868 DANA *Min.* 650 This species was made known by Beudant, and by him first named Alunogen. **1868** WATTS *Dict. Chem.* V. 579 The normal or neutral sulphate [of aluminium] $Al_2(SO_4)_3$..is known mineralogically as *alunogen, hair-salt, feather-alum*, and *halotrichite*. **1878** LAWRENCE *Cotta's Rocks Class.* 43 Alunogen is sometimes the product of volcanic action, sometimes a result of the decomposition of pyrites in coal districts.

'alure, *sb.* Now *rare.* Also 3-4 **alour, alur**, 4 **aler**, 5 **allure**. [a. OFr. *aleure*, later *alure*, now *allure*, walk, gait, going; a place to walk in, a gallery; f. *aller* to go: see -URE.] A place to walk in, a gallery; *esp.* **a.** a walk or passage behind the parapets of a castle, or round the roof of a church; **b.** a covered passage, a cloister; **c.** *rarely* a walk in a garden, a passage between the seats in a church, an alley or 'aisle.'

1297 R. GLOUC. 192 Vpe þe alurs of þe castles þe ladyes þanne stode. *c* **1300** *K. Alis.* 7210 The touris to take, and the torellis, Vawtes, alouris. *c* **1314** *Guy Warw.* 85 At the alours thai defended hem. **1382** WYCLIF *1 Kings* vii. 2 Foure aluris betwixe the cedre pilers [L. *deambulacra*; **1388** aleis]. **1388** —— *2 Kings* i. 2 Ocozie felde thorou the aleris of his soler [L. *per cancellos cœnaculi sui*; **1382** wyndowes]. **1430** LYDG. *Chron. Troy* II. xi, Freshe alures with lusty hye pynacles.. That called were deambulatoryes. *c* **1430** —— *Stor. Thebes* 1267 In this gardyn.. In the allures walking to and fro. **1440** *Promp. Parv.*, Alure or alurys of a towre or stepylle, *Canal.* [*Test. Ebor.* 197 In allura inter fontem et introitum chori.] **1776** T. WARTON *Eng. Poetry* (1840) II. xxiii. 300 The sides of every street were covered with fresh alures of marble, or cloisters. **1851** TURNER *Dom. Archit.* i. 8 And alures of stone were to be raised above the roof timbers. **1878** M'VITTIE *Chr. Ch. Cath.* 63 Round north and south transepts and on to the alure of choir. **1919** *Proc. Soc. Antiq. Scot.* LIII. 38 Its base in the ditch must have been visible from the allure on the curtain.

†**alured**, *ppl. a. Obs.* In 5 **alourde**. [f. prec.] Furnished with an alure or alures.

1412 *Catterick Contr.* Parker *Gl. Archit.* III. 128 The ele sall be alourde accordant with the quere.

†**aluring**, *vbl. sb. Obs.* [f. as prec. + -ING[1].] Provision or construction of alures; alure-work.

1412 *Catterick Co.* (as above) A botras rising into the tabill that sall bere the aloryng. *ibid.* The hight of the walles of the quere sall be..xx fote with a naluryng abowne.

a'lurk, *adv.*, prop. *phr.* [A *prep.*[1] + LURK.] †**1.** *Obs.* Out of place, awry.

1572 LAWSON *Orchet, MS. Lansd.* No. 208, 4 His heed in shappe as by natures worke, Not one haire amisse, or lyeth a loorke.

2. Lurking. *rare.*

1895 F. THOMPSON *Sister-Songs* 20 And whitest witchery, a-lurk in that Authentic cestus of two girdling arms.

alutaceous (æl(j)uː'teɪʃəs), *a.* [f. L. *alūtāci-us* (f. *alūta* soft leather) + -OUS: see -ACEOUS.] Of the quality or colour of tawed leather.

1873 *Trans. Amer. Phil. Soc.* XIII. 122 Striæ coarsely punctured, intervals flat, finely alutaceous.

†**alu'tation.** *Obs.*[−0] [f. L. *alūta* prepared leather + -ATION; as if f. a L. **alūtā-re* to prepare leather.] 'A tanning or dressing of leather.' Cockeram 1623; whence in Blount, Bailey, etc.

‖**alva'rado.** *Obs.* [Sp. *alvorada, alborada*, 'musicke giuen at the breake of day' (Minsheu) f. *albor, alvor*, dawn, f. L. *albus* white.] (See quot.)

1598 BARRET *Theor. Warres* 249 *Alvarado*, a Spanish word, and is the discharging of the morning watch, by the sound of the drumme.

†'**alvary.** *Obs. rare*[−1]. [f. L. *alvus*, womb + -ARY.] Womb; lap; bed.

1595 BARNFIELD *Cassandra* (Arb.) 71 From his softe bosom (th' aluary of blisse).

alveary ('ælviːərɪ). [ad. L. *alveāri-um* a range of bee-hives; f. *alveus* a tub or hollow vessel, *hence* a bee-hive: see -ARY.]

1. A bee-hive; a title given to an early Dictionary of English, Latin, French, and Greek.

1580 BARET *Alv.* To Reader, Within a yeere, or two, they had gathered together a great volume, which (for the apt similitude betweene the good Scholers and diligent Bees in gathering their waxe and honie into their Hiue) I called then their Alvearie. **1660** HOWELL *Parly of Beasts* 137 (D.) Ther's not the least foulness found in our alvearies or hives. **1669** W[ORLIDGE] *Syst. Agric.* 321 Alveary, a Hive of Bees.

2. *Anat.* The hollow of the external ear; 'so called because the cerumen or wax is found there.' *Syd. Soc. Lex.* 1879.

? **1719** WEBSTER cites QUINCY. **1751** CHAMBERS *Cycl.*, *Alvearium*, the bottom of the concha, or hollow of the auricle, or outer ear.

†'**alveate**, *v. Obs.*[−0] [f. L. *alveāt-us* ppl. adj. 'hollowed out in the form of a channel'; f. *alveus* a channel, etc.] 'To cut into the form of a trench or chanel.' Bullokar 1676.

alveated ('ælviːeɪtɪd), *ppl. a.* [ad. L. *alveātus* (see prec.) with ppl. ending -ED.] (See quot.)

1623 COCKERAM, *Alueated*, trenched, chanelled. **1656** BLOUNT *Glossogr.*, *Alveated*, hollow like a hive, vaulted, or trenched. **1864** WEBSTER, *Alveated*, having a prismatic cellular structure, like a honey comb.

alveolar (æl'viːələ(r), 'ælviːələ(r)), *a.* and *sb.* [f. mod.L. *alveol-us* the socket of a tooth, in cl. L. a little channel or hollow, dim. of *alveus* a channel, etc. + -AR. Cf. Fr. *alvéolaire.*] **A.** *adj.*

1. a. Of or pertaining to the sockets of the teeth, or to that part of the upper jaw, the *alveolar arch*, in which the teeth are placed.

1799 CORSE in *Phil. Trans.* LXXXIX. 216 Both the fangs and the alveolar processes begin to be absorbed. **1872** NICHOLSON *Palæont.* 366 The alveolar border of the upper jaw. *Mod.* The English *t* and *d* are not strictly *dental*, they are *alveolar*.

b. Pertaining to or resembling an alveolus in a membrane, air-cell of the lungs, etc. Cf. ALVEOLUS senses d, e, f.

1848 *Quain's Anat.* (ed. 5) I. p. cclxxxi, This peculiar character of the mucous membrane, which might be called 'alveolar', is seen very distinctly in the gall-bladder;..still more minute alveolar recesses with intervening ridges may be discovered..on the mucous membrane of the stomach. **1882** *Ibid.* (ed. 9) 228 The flattened cells which compose the basement-membrane may send delicate lamellar processes between the alveolar cells. **1885** E. A. SCHAEFER *Essent. Histology* xxv. 123 Section of injected lung, including several contiguous alveoli... Between the capillaries is seen the homogeneous alveolar wall with nuclei of connective-tissue corpuscles. **1889** *Cent. Dict.* s.v., *Alveolar passages*, the passages into which the respiratory bronchial tubes enlarge. **1927** HALDANE & HUXLEY *Anim. Biol.* vii. 153 This, which is called the alveolar air, can be obtained at the end of a deep breath out.

2. Socket-shaped, having a cylindrical hollow.

1858 T. JONES *Aquar. Nat.* 278 On the other hand, when cylindrical or alveolar it appears to be always more brittle.

B. *sb. pl.* **1.** The alveolar processes of the maxillary bone, in which the teeth are fixed.

1874 DAWKINS *Cave Hunt.* vi. 192 The alveolars short, but rather projecting.

2. *Phonetics.* An alveolar sound or letter. Cf. *apico-alveolar* sb.

1895 P. GILES *Man. Compar. Philol.* I. v. 68 The sounds called dentals—*t, d, th, dh*, where *th* represents not the sound in *then* or *thin* but *t* followed by breath—are in English pronunciation not dentals but alveolars, being produced by the pressure of the tongue against the roots of the teeth. **1910** *Encycl. Brit.* VII. 725/1 The English *d*..in phonetic terminology is called an alveolar. In the languages of India..both true dentals and alveolars are found. **1961** R. B. LONG *Sentence & its Parts* xix. 430 This obstruction [in the flow of air] can occur..in the front of the mouth above the teeth, as for the alveolars.

Hence **alveo'larity**, the quality of being alveolar; an instance of this.

1952 A. COHEN *Phonemes of English* ii. 36 If now we put 'normal' [t] against [þ] we find: alveolarity v. labiality. **1964** R. H. ROBINS *Gen. Linguistics* iv. 155 The nine separate phonemes..are maintained as distinctive units by six features: plosion, voice, nasality, bilabiality, alveolarity, and velarity.

alveolariform (ˌælviːəʊ'lærɪfɔːm), *a.* [f. prec. + -(I)FORM.] Having the form of the cells of a honey-comb.

1879 in *Syd. Soc. Lex.*

alveolary (æl'viːələrɪ, 'ælviːələrɪ), *a.* [f. L. *alveol-us* (see ALVEOLE) + -ARY.] = ALVEOLAR.

1847 in CRAIG. WORCESTER cites LOUDON.

alveolate (æl'viːəleɪt, 'ælviːəleɪt), *a.* [ad. L. *alveolāt-us*, f. *alveolus*: see ALVEOLE.] Honey-combed; pitted with little cavities.

1839 HOOPER *Med. Dict.*, *Alveolatus*, Alveolate, having small cavities. **1846** DANA *Zooph.* (1848) 508 Corallum profoundly alveolate. **1870** HOOKER *Stud. Flora* 266 *Digitalis purpurea*..seeds alveolate.

alveole ('ælviːəʊl). [a. Fr. *alvéole*, ad. L. *alveolus* a little hollow, dim. of *alveus* a hollow channel.] = ALVEOLUS (which is more often used).

1845 *Penny Cycl. Suppl.* I. 364/1 The receptacle naked, alveolate, the alveoles with elevated dentate margins.

alveoliform (æl'viːəlɪfɔːm, ælviː'ɒlɪfɔːm), *a.* [f. L. *alveol-us* + -(I)FORM.] 'Celled like a honey-comb, as in the case of certain corals.' Craig 1847.

1847-9 TODD *Cycl. Anat. & Phys.* IV. 65 Alcyonellum.. polygonal, alveoliform.

alveolite (æl'viːəlaɪt, 'ælviːəlaɪt). *Zool.* [f. mod.L. *alveolites*, f. L. *alveol-us* + -ITE.] A genus of fossil Zoophytes found in the chalk.

1846 DANA *Zooph.* (1848) 537 Lamarck's name Alveolites might be extended to the Stenoporæ. **1847** in CRAIG.

alveolo- (æl'viːələʊ), combining form of ALVEOLUS: Of or pertaining to the sockets of the teeth or to the alveolar arch; as **al'veolo-condy'lean plane**, the plane bounded by the central point of the upper alveolar arch and the base of the occipital condyles, sometimes called the natural plane of the base of the skull; **alveolo-dental**; etc.

1878 BRYANT *Surg.* I. 558 The alveolo-dental membrane.

alveolo-palatal ('ælviːələʊ'pælətəl), *a.* *Phonetics.* [f. ALVEOLO- + PALATAL *a.*] Designating sounds formed by placing the tongue against the alveolar arch and the palate; of or relating to this position.

1942 A. H. MARCKWARDT *Introd. Eng. Lang.* i. 33 The tongue-tip is fairly well back on the alveolar ridge, and the blade of the tongue..against the extreme front portion of the hard palate; this forms the lengthened trough or channel, *alveolopalatal* in position, through which the breath stream must escape. *Ibid.* 40 The shift of the tongue from the alveolar to palatal position has resulted in the establishment of the alveolopalatal affricate. **1950** D. JONES *Phoneme* p. xiii, Alveolo-palatal fricatives (Polish *ś, ź*).

‖**alveolus** (æl'viːələs). Pl. **-i.** [L. *alveolus*, dim. of *alveus* a cavity.] A small cavity; *hence* **a.** The socket of a tooth; **b.** The cell of a honey-comb; **c.** The conical chamber of a Belemnite, or the conical body found in it.

1706 PHILLIPS, *Alveolus*, any wooden Vessel made hollow; a Tray. Among Anatomists, *Alveoli dentium* are the Holes in the Jaws in which the Teeth are set. **1746** DA COSTA in *Phil. Trans.* XLIV. 398 This conic Cavity is..filled with a regular jointed conic Body, called by Lithologists the *Alveolus* of the Belemnites. **1753** CHAMBERS *Cycl. Supp.*, *Alveoli*, waxen cells in the combs of bees..The *alveoli* are all of a hexagonal figure. **1799** CORSE in *Phil. Trans.* LXXXIX. 229 The alveoli or sockets of the two grinders. **1881** MIVART *Cat* 27 Each alveolus closely invests the fang contained within it.

d. A small depression on the mucous membrane of the stomach.

1848 *Quain's Anat.* (ed. 5) II. 1025 The gastric mucous membrane..is seen to be marked..with little depressions or cells, named *alveoli*. **1858** GRAY *Anat.* 605 The entire surface of the mucous membrane [of the stomach] is covered with small shallow depressions or alveoli.

e. An air-cell of the lungs.

1859 A. T. H. WATERS in *Proc. R. Soc.* X. 17 Structure.. of the human lung... Here and there circular orifices exist, leading to smaller air-sacs, sometimes only to a small group of 'air-cells', or *alveoli*. **1873** T. H. GREEN *Introd. Path.* (ed. 2) xxxvii. 295 Minute spots of a more decidedly yellow colour..which are very common in capillary bronchitis, are merely alveoli containing mucus and purulent matter which has been drawn in by the act of inspiration. **1909** *Practitioner* Dec. 859 The alveoli themselves are distended with a mixture of gases.

f. An acinus of a compound gland.

1867 *Quain's Anat.* (ed. 7) I. p. clxxxvii, [The trabeculæ] are mostly lamellar in form, and divide the space into small compartments, *alveoli*, from $\frac{1}{60}$ to $\frac{1}{30}$ of an inch wide. **1880** E. KLEIN *Atlas of Histology* xxiv. 192 The alveoli of all salivary glands..are surrounded by a dense network of capillary blood-vessels. **1920** *Gray's Anat.* (ed. 21) 1087 Each lobule [in compound racemose glands] consists of the ramification of a single duct, the branches ending in dilated ends or alveoli. *Ibid.*, (*caption*) Surface view of alveolus. **1953** *Faber Med. Dict.*, 7/1 *Acinus*, one of the minute berry-like beginnings of the excretory ducts of a racemose gland. Syn. alveolus.

‖'**alveus.** [L.] The bed or channel or a river; the trough of the sea.

1695 WOODWARD *Nat. Hist. Earth* I. (1723) 182 This mass of Water fell back again..into the Alveus of the Ocean.

alviducous (ˌælvɪ'djuːkəs), *a. Med.* [f. L. *alv-us* belly + *duc-ĕre* to lead + -OUS.] Purgative.

1839 in HOOPER *Med. Dict.*

alvine ('ælvaɪn), *a.* [ad. L. *alvīn-us*, f. *alvus* the belly.] Pertaining to the abdomen or its contents.

1754 *Phil. Trans.* XLVIII. 581 As to the natural excretions, the alvine were easy and proper. **1871** TYNDALL *Fragm. Sc.* (ed. 6) II. xii. 286 Sanguinolent alvine evacuations.

alvish, obs. f. ELVISH.

alvite ('ælvaɪt). *Min.* [f. L. *alvus* belly + -ITE.] A reddish-brown mineral, a complex hydrous silicate, containing besides silica, alumina, and glucina, yttria, thoria, zirconia, and iron sesquioxide.

alway ('ɔːlweɪ, archaic ˌɔːl'weɪ), *adv.* Forms: 1-2 **alne weȝ** (WS. **ealne weȝ**), 3-4 **alne way**, 4-5 **alle wey, al wey**, 5-6 **allewaye, allwaye, alwaye**, 5- **alway**. [orig. two words ALL and WAY, in the accusative of space or distance, = *all the way*, *the whole way*, probably at first in reference to space traversed, but already in the oldest Eng. transferred to an extent of time, *all along*, *all the time*, *continually*. Afterwards confused with the genitive form, ALWAYS, which has superseded it in prose, *alway* surviving only in poetry or as an archaism.]

1. All along, all the time, perpetually, throughout all time.

c **885** K. ÆLFRED *Boeth.* xxxviii. §5, & þæt ealne weȝ siofodest þæt hi ealne weȝ næron on wite, & ic þe sæde ealne weȝ þæt hi næfre ne bioþ buton wite. **1340** *Ayenb.* 136 Þe wel couaytouse wrechche þet alneway heþ þet eȝe to þe guodes þet oþre habbeþ and doþ alneway and makeþ alneway semblont þet he ne heþ naȝt. *c* **1374** CHAUCER *Anel. & Arc.* 236 For to love him Alweye [*v.r.* alwey, alway] never the lesse. **1398** TREVISA *Barth. De P.R.* v. xx. (1495) 126 Yf lyfe duryd a thousande yere alwaye shold growe teeth more and more. **1611** BIBLE *Matt.* xxviii. 20 And Loe, I am with you alway, even unto the end of the world. **1845** NEALE *Hymns for Sick* 36 Whoso receiveth them, receiveth Thee, With them alway. *a* **1858** MUHLENBERG *Hymn*, I would not live alway I ask not to stay.

2. = ALWAYS 1; every time, at all times, on all occasions. Opposed to *sometimes*, *occasionally*.

c **1410** *Sir Cleges* 221 Wethyr wee have les or more, All-waye thanke we God therefore. **1473** WARKW. *Chron.* 4 Al-wey he promysed he wuld do. **1513** MORE *Edw. V* (1641) 7 Not alway for ill will, but oftner for ambition. **1535** COVERDALE *2 Sam.* xv. 2 Absalom gat him vp allwaye early in the mornynge, and stode in the waye by the porte. **1611** BIBLE *John* vii. 6 My time is not yet come: but your time is alway ready. **1851** TRENCH *Poems* 46 And boldly use the children's prayer alway. **1868** MISS J. E. BROWN *Lights thro' Lattice* 56 For he [the foe] doth mark each open door alway.

†**3.** In any case, after all, still. = ALWAYS 3. *Obs.*

a **1400** in Hallam *Mid. Ages* (1872) III. 91 Savyng alwey to our liege lord his real prerogatif. **1413** LYDG. *Pylgr. Sowle* IV. xx. (1483) 67 He a disciple is, thou arte a lord Thou al awey art greter than he is. **1475** *Bk. Noblesse* 34 Notwithestanding so oft tymes trewes and alliaunces taken and made . . alle waye whan the Frenshe partie coude have and fynde any avauntage or coloure . . they did make new werre.

† **'alwayness.** *Obs.* [f. prec. + -NESS.] Everlastingness, eternal existence, sempiternity.

1674 N. FAIRFAX *Bulk & Selv.* 165 The alwayness of the soul. *Ibid.* 155 The alwayness of him who is unbounded.

always ('ɔːlweɪz, -wɪz), *adv.* Forms: 3 **alles weis**, 4 **alleweyes**, 5–7 **alwayes**, 6 **alwaise**, **allweyz**, 6–7 **alwaies**, **allwaies**, 6– **always**. [genitive case of *all way*, prob. conveying the distributive sense 'at every time.' Cf. *once* = at one time, the Ger. *eines Morgens*, and Eng. '*of* a morning, *of* a Sunday'; and compare *sometimes*, of separate occasions, with *some time*, of duration. But eventually this distinction between *alway* and *always* was lost, and the latter is now used in both senses.]

1. At every time, on every occasion, at all times, on all occasions. Opposed to *sometimes*, *occasionally*.

c **1230** *Ancr. R.* 4 Ye schullen alles weis, mid alle mihte . . wel witen þe inre, & þe uttre vor hire sake. **1375** BARBOUR *Bruce* II. 92 James off dowglas, that ay-quhar All-wayis befor the byschop schar. *c* **1400** *Rom. Rose* 919 A bachelere, That he made alleweyes with hym be. *c* **1425** WYNTOUN *Cron.* VII. vi. 10 In justice lawchful he wes allwayis. **1584** POWEL *Lloyd's Cambr.* 91 And alwaise returned with great spoils. **1593** SHAKS. *3 Hen. VI*, IV. iii. 45 Edward will alwayes beare himselfe as King. **1600** THYNNE *Epigr.* in *Animadv.* Pref. 57 Thy wife allwaies is but a needfull ill, And beste is bad. **1611** BIBLE *Rom.* i. 9, I make mention of you, alwayes in my prayers. **1711** ADDISON *Spect.* No. 7 ¶4 She is always seeing Apparitions. **1732** POPE *Ess. Man* I. 92 Man never is, but always to be blest. **1751** JOHNSON *Rambl.* No. 165 ¶6 He that indulges hope will always be disappointed. **1860** TYNDALL *Glac.* II. §24. 355 Water always holds a quantity of air in solution.

2. = ALWAY; all along; through all time, without any interruption; ever, continually, perpetually. Opposed to *for a time*.

1375 BARBOUR *Bruce* VII. 60 He ran on fut alwayis hym by, Till he in-till the wod wes gane. **1513** MORE *Edw. V* Ded., Laudable custome that hath alwaies been observed. **1667** MILTON *P.L.* III. 704 Pleasant to know, and worthiest to be all Had in remembrance always with delight. **1711** STEELE *Spect.* No. 2 ¶5 Having always had a very easy fortune, Time has made but little Impression. **1862** TRENCH *Mirac.* 50 They were done once, that they might be believed always.

3. In any or every circumstance; whatever the circumstances; whatever happens, whatever one may do or say; in any event, anyhow. (Cf. ALGATE, and Fr. *toujours*.) Formerly chiefly northern.

1490 CAXTON *Eneydos* xxi. 76 How be it that he had grete pyte and compassyon of her . . alwayes he determyned hymself and went his way. **1533** BELLENDENE *Livy* I. 81 Alwayis he had ane brothir, eldare of yeris than he. [*c* **1460**, **1488**] **1600** [see PROVIDED *ppl. a.* 5, 5 b]. **1649** H. GUTHRY *Mem.* (1702) 57 Always, having done that Business he came for, his Grace return'd next day to Court. **1663** BLAIR *Autobiogr.* v. (1848) 74 Always we thanked God for what was done. **1778** F. BURNEY *Evelina* xxxvii, You will always make my respects to the hospitable family to which we are so much obliged. **1846** DICKENS *Dombey* viii. 78 Never so distressed as by the company of children—Florence alone excepted, always. **1872** GEO. ELIOT *Middlem.* III. xxiii. 5 Fred had always (at that time) his father's pocket as a last resource. *a* **1884** *Mod.* It is told in the north of a modern representative of the ancient Σχολαστικός, that being dismissed from his employment in the depth of winter, he said, 'I don't care, I can *always* shear' (= reap). **1888** MRS. H. WARD *R. Elsmere* xxx, Always supposing there were no risk in the matter. **1910** *Punch* 9 Feb. 104/3 It don't look as if I'm goin' to 'ave a job this arternoon. 'Owever, no matter. There's always the work'us.

4. *Comb.* Qualifying an adj. or ppl. adj. used attributively.

1855 WHITMAN *Leaves of Grass* 27 Sea of unshovelled and always-ready graves! **1902** *Academy* 16 Aug. 183/1 The spirit who is not weighed down with the cares of an always-ageing body. **1952** C. DAY LEWIS tr. *Virgil's Aen.* VI. p. 134 Giving no rest to the always-replenished vitals. **1955** P. LARKIN *Less Deceived* 39 Bargains, suffering, and love, Not this always-planned salute.

alwhat, variant of ALLWHAT.

† **'alwise**, *adv.* *Obs.* 5–6; also 5 **allewyse**, 5–6 **alwyse**. [contr. of *in all wise*: see WISE; perhaps influenced by *always*.] In every way; in any way.

1440 *Partenope* 2570 Cursid he ys and covetous in allewyse. *c* **1449** PECOCK *Repr.* 472 Nile ȝe swere alwise. **1466** MARG. PASTON in *Lett.* 560 II. 290 In alwyse I avyse you for to be ware. **1559** in *Misc. Wodr. Soc.* (1844) 275, I sall be alwyse reddy to answer.

aly ('eɪlɪ), *a.*; also 8 **aley**. [f. ALE + -Y. For the spelling cf. *scaly*.] Of or characterized by ale.

a **1624** N. BRETON in *Heliconia* I. 213 Whose Aly nose . . Would kill an honest wench to view. **1630** J. TAYLOR (Water P.) *Wks.* I. 126/1 To conclude this drinking Alye tale. **1742** *Lond. & Country Brew.* I. (ed. 4) 22 Its mild aley Taste.

alyaunte, obs. form of ALIEN.

alym, obs. form of ALUM *sb.*

† **a'lyne**, *v.* *Obs.* *rare*$^{-1}$. [perh. a confusion of *ali-en* (ALIE *v.*²) = *elien* to oil, anoint, and L. *allinĕre* to besmear.] To anoint.

c **1315** SHOREHAM 13 Hi beethe eke atte fount Mid oylle and creyme alyned.

alypin (ə'laɪpɪn). *Med.* Also **-ine**. [G. (E. Impens 1905, in *Deut. Med. Wochenschrift* XXXI. 1154/2), f. Gr. ἄλυπος painless + -IN¹.] A proprietary term for a glycerin derivative, used as a local anæsthetic.

1905 *Lancet* 29 July 321/2 A new anæsthetic compound termed 'alypin'. **1908** *Practitioner* Jan. 143 A 5 per cent. solution of cocaine and alypine. **1917** *Calif. State Jrnl. Med.* XV. 268 (*title*) Two cases of poisoning from the use of alypin in the urethra. **1928** *New Eng. Jrnl. Med.* CXCIX. 267 (*title*) Deaths from alypin poisoning.

† **a'lypum, -us.** *Obs.* [for *alypon*, a. Gr. ἄλῡπον painless.] An unidentified plant, so called by Dioscorides from its anodyne virtue.

1611 COTGR., *Turbit blanc* . . the reddish hearbe *Alypum*, or *Alypia*; talked of, but not otherwise named, by our English Herbarist. **1621** BURTON *Anat. Mel.* II. iv. II. i, But these are very gentle, alypus, dragon root, centaury, ditany.

alyssum (ə'lɪsəm). *Bot.* [mod.L. for *alysson* (Pliny), a. Gr. ἄλυσσον name of a plant, perh. neut. of adj. ἄλυσσος 'curing (canine) madness,' f. ἀ priv. + λύσσα madness.]

1. *Bot.* A genus of Cruciferous plants, a yellow-flowered species of which (*A. saxatile*) popularly known as Gold-dust, is a favourite spring flower in English gardens. The early herbalists used the name very vaguely.

1551 TURNER *Herbal* (1568) 21 Alysson is an herbe lyke vnto horehounde. **1578** LYTE *Dodoens* 107 Alysson . . groweth upon rough mountaynes. **1731** BAILEY, *Alysson*, comfrey. **1753** CHAMBERS *Cycl. Supp.* s.v., The species of alysson enumerated by Mr. Tournefort . . The alysson is a medicinal plant. **1876** B. TAYLOR *Echo Club* 30 Such cakes of myrrh or fine alyssum seed.

2. *pop.* **sweet alyssum** (or '*alison*), (*Königa maritima*), A small cruciferous plant with white flowers.

1822 *Hortus Angl.* II. 150 *A. maritimum*, Sweet Alyssum. *c* **1840** CAMPBELL *Dead Eagle* 91 Fields white With alasum, or blue with bugloss. **1866** J. SYME in *Treas. Bot.* 536 The Sweet Alyssum of gardens is found in some places of Britain, but only imperfectly naturalized where escaped from gardens. **1873** LONGF. *Rhyme St. Christ.* 40 A modest flower-bed thickly sown With sweet alyssum and columbine.

† **'alytarch.** *Obs.* [ad. L. *alytarcha* a superintendent of the games, ad. Gr. ἀλυτάρχης, f. ἀλύτ-ης police-officer + -ἀρχης ruler.]

1646 J. G[REGORY] *Notes & Observ.* (1650) 48 To bear the Alytarcha's part, and be a May-king, or Mock-Jupiter in these Revels. **1656** BLOUNT *Glossogr.*, *Alytark*, he who seeth that good rule be kept at common Games and Exercises. **1692** COLES, *Alytarch*, keeper of order at publick sports.

alythe, variant of ALITHE *v.* *Obs.*, to dissolve.

Alzheimer's disease ('æltshaɪməz dɪ'ziːz). [f. the name of Alois *Alzheimer* (1864–1915), German neurologist.] A grave disorder of the brain which manifests itself in premature senility.

1912 S. C. FULLER in *Jrnl. Nervous & Mental Dis.* XXXIX. 440 (*title*) Alzheimer's Disease (*senium præcox*): the report of a case and review of published cases. **1930** *Lancet* 19 July 138/2 Two cases of Alzheimer's disease. . . In one typical case, that of a woman aged 51, there was a gradual failure of mental power. **1952** *Ibid.* 27 Sept. 635/1 The characteristic changes of Alzheimer's disease could be designated . . disseminated paramyloidosis of the brain. **1955** H. H. MERRITT *Textbk. Neurology* vi. 417 The microscopic changes in Alzheimer's disease are somewhat similar to those which occur with senility. There is a diffuse loss of cells in all layers of the cortex, secondary gliosis, argentophile plaques (Alzheimer plaques) and neurofibrillar degeneration.

A.M., a.m. *contr.* for

1. L. *ante meridiem* before noon (in which sense it is familiarly read and spoken ˌeɪ'ɛm). Also (*colloq.*) in sense of 'morning'. Cf. ANTE MERIDIEM.

1762 BORLASE in *Phil. Trans.* LII. 507 At ten A.M. the driver of a plough . . laden with tin . . found himself and the plough, on a sudden, surrounded by the sea. **1776** A. R. ROBBINS *Jrnl.* (1850) 6 Exercised and walked around with the officers in A.M. **1839** G. W. M. REYNOLDS *Pickwick Abroad* i. 3 At about ten o'clock A.M., [etc.]. **1889** *Cent. Dict.* s.v., I arrived here this A.M. . . that is, this morning or forenoon. **1925** E. F. NORTON *Fight for Everest 1924* I. iv. 81 Overcast and warm, light snow in early a.m. **1955** *Times* 9 May 5/5 At 2.50 a.m. . . the stolen car approached.

2. L. *anno mundi* in the year of the world.

3. L. *artium magister* Master of Arts (now usually M.A., in England).

am (æm, əm, (ə)m, m), *v.*, 1st sing. pres. ind. of vb. BE. *Am*, and its inflections *art*, *is*, *are*, are the only parts of the original substantive vb. (Skr. *as-*, Gr. ἐσ-, L. *es-*, Goth. *is-*, *i-*) now left in Eng.; the pa. t. ind. and subj. being supplied from a different vb. (stem *wis-*, *wes-*, Skr. *was-* to remain, abide: see WAS); and all the other parts from a third vb. BE Skr. *bhū-*, Gr. φυ-, L. *fu-*, *fy-* to become). As the latter, although its association with the substantive vb. is very recent, supplies the infinitive, the vb. is now usually as a whole called the vb. *to* BE, under which its forms and uses will be found.

‖ **ama** ('ama). [Jap., lit. 'sea'.] A Japanese woman diver, who dives for shellfish and edible seaweed, usu. without breathing apparatus.

1954 F. HAAR *Mermaid of Japan* 2 Every living *ama* is the daughter of an *ama*, their mothers were daughters of *ama*, as were their mothers' mothers. **1962** *New Scientist* 10 May 274/1 There have been Japanese women 'ama' who have dived for over 2½ minutes and to depths of 30 metres. **1971** *Nat. Geographic* July 122/1 The ama dive for food—shellfish and edible seaweeds—never for pearls.

amability (æmə'bɪlɪtɪ). [ad. L. *amābilitas*, n. of quality f. *amābil-is* lovely; or perh. a. Fr. *amabilité*, OFr. *amableté*. Usefully distinct from AMIABILITY.] The quality of being lovable; lovableness.

1604 WRIGHT *Passions of Mind* v. §4. 209 A sweete grace and motive to amabilitie. **1635** J. HAYWARD *Banished Virg.* 131 The amability of his conditions and carriage. **1636** HEYWOOD *Love's Mistress* Prol., Shee, The very soul of amabilitee. **1655** JER. TAYLOR *Unum Necessar.* viii. §5. 31 There may be the apprehension of two amabilities. **1659** *Gentlem. Calling* xviii. §24. 449 There being such a venerable amability in it. **1775** in ASH. [**1791** MRS. DAMER in *Miss Berry's Corr.* I. 348 My *amabilité* I suppose was so great that one of them proposed to embrace me.]

† **'amable, -ile**, *a.* *Obs.* *rare.* [a. OFr. *amable*:—L. *amābil-em* lovely, f. *amā-re* to love. Gale apparently formed it afresh from L.; cf. It. *amabile*.] Lovely, lovable.

c **1430** LYDG. *Min. Poems* (1840) 25 Face of Absolon, moost fayre, moost amable! **1677** GALE *Crt. Gentiles* II. IV. 338 The Divine Essence is most amabile and appetible for itself.

amabyr, variant of AMOBER. *Obs.*

amacratic (æmə'krætɪk), *a.* [improp. for *hamacratic*, f. Gr. ἅμα together + -κράτ-ος strength, power + -IC.] Uniting the actinic rays of the solar speculum into one focus, as an amacratic lens.

Mod. Dicts. cite SIR J. HERSCHEL.

amacrine ('æməkrɪn), *sb.* and *a.* *Histol.* Also (*rare*) **-in**. [f. A- 14 + Gr. μακρός MACRO- + ἶς, ἰν-ός sinew, strip (cf. INO-).] **A.** *sb.* An amacrine cell (see B below).

1900 DORLAND *Med. Dict.* 34/2 *Amacrine*, any one of a group of branched retinal structures regarded as modified nerve-cells. **1901** *Gray's Anat.* (ed. 15) 816 (*caption*) Large amacrine with thick processes ramifying in second stratum. **1930** MAXIMOW & BLOOM *Text-bk. Histol.* xxxv. 746 The diffuse amacrins send out a bundle of branching processes which permeate all parts of the inner reticular layer. **1964** [see MULTIPOLAR *a.* a].

B. *adj.* Designating a type of small nerve cell in the inner nuclear layer of the retina which has neurites with characteristics of both axons and dendrites.

1901 *Gray's Anat.* (ed. 15) 816 At the innermost part of this inner nuclear layer is a stratum of cells, which are named by Cajal amacrine cells, from the fact that they have no axis-cylinder process. **1923** A. DUANE tr. *Fuchs's Text-bk.*

Ophthalmol. (ed. 7) v. 42 (*caption*) Layer of amacrine cells (spongioblasts). **1974** D. & M. WEBSTER *Compar. Vertebr. Morphol.* x. 212 These are the horizontal cells and the small amacrine nerve cells that connect distal portions of the bipolar cells.

†**a'mad**, *ppl. a. Obs.* Also 3 **amadde**, (**amed**). [prob.:—OE. *ʒemǣd* for *ʒemǣded* pa. pple. of *ʒemǣdan* to madden, Goth. **gamaidjan* f. *gamaid-s* bruised, crazed (ON. *meiddr* from *meiða* to hurt, maim), OHG. *gameit*, OS. *gamêd* foolish, of which the OE. cogn. *ʒemád* adj. was apparently replaced by this pple. *ʒemǣd*. The vowel was shortened as in *clad*, OE. *ʒeclád* for *ʒeclǣðod*. See also MAD.] Demented, distracted; mad.

1205 LAYAM. 4438 Of witten heo were amadde. *c* **1220** *Hali Meid.* 37 Mare amad ʒif ha mei beo; þen is madschipe self. *c* **1230** *Ancr. R.* 324 Nis he more þen a-med. *c* **1315** *Pol. Songs* 156 Heo wendeth bokes unbrad Ant maketh men a moneth a-mad.

‖**amadavat** (ˌæmədəˈvæt). Also **avadavat**. [The name in various Indian langs.] An Indian song-bird (*Estrilda amandava*), brown in colour with white spots.

1777 SHERIDAN *Sch. Scan.* v. i, A few presents now and then..congou tea, avadavats, and Indian crackers. **1813** J. FORBES *Orient. Mem.* I. 47 Amadavats and other songsters are brought thither [Bombay] from Surat. **1871** DARWIN *Desc. Man* II. xiii. 49 The Bengali baboos make the pretty little males of the amadavat..fight together.

amadelphous (æməˈdɛlfəs). *a.* [improp. for *hamadelphous*, f. Gr. ἅμα together + ἀδελφός brother, brotherly + -OUS.] 'Living in society or in flocks.' *Syd. Soc. Lex.* 1879.

Amadis (ˈæmədɪs). Also **amadis**. [Name of the hero of a romance of chivalry, and title of one of Quinault's operas (1684).] A close-fitting sleeve buttoned at the wrist, which became fashionable from the costume of Amadis as worn in the opera of the name. Also, an embroidered edging on a bodice.

1835 *Court Mag.* VI. p. xxi/1 An attempt has been made to bring up again the Amadis sleeve. **1898** LADY MARY LOYD tr. *O. Uzanne's Fashion in Paris* ii. 38 Their bodices.. were known as 'canezous', a scalloped embroidery called 'amadis' was carried round the edges and wrists.

‖**amado** (ˈamado). [Jap., f. *ame* rain + *to* door.] One of a set of shutters on the outer side of a Japanese house. Freq. *collect.*

1880 I. BIRD *Unbeaten Tracks in Japan* I. xiii. 135 They rise at daylight..open the *amado*—wooden shutters which ..box in the whole house at night. **1890** B. H. CHAMBERLAIN *Things Japanese* 24 The sides of the house, composed at night of wooden sliding doors, called *amado*, is stowed away in boxes during the day-time. **1899** M. C. FRASER *Custom of Country* 89 You must get him to come inside then shut the amados. **1938** D. T. SUZUKI *Zen Buddhism* II. i. 210 The falling leaves striking shower-like against the roof and *amado*. **1959** R. KIRKBRIDE *Tamiko* xix. 152 A cabin whose face was blind with locked amado.

‖ˈ**amadot**, **amaˈdetto**. [a. Fr. *amadote*, according to Littré a corruption of *d'amoudot* or rather of *Dame Oudet*, name of the first grower.] A kind of pear.

1706 PHILLIPS, *Amadetto*, a sort of Pear. **1755** [JOHNSON has *Amadetto* and *Amadot*.] **1763** MILLER *Gard. Dict.*, *Pyrus sativa..L'Amadote*, i.e. the Amadot Pear.

amadou (ˈæmədu:). [mod.Fr. f. *amadouer* to allure, found in many forms in the north. Fr. dialects, but of doubtful origin; considered by Diez and Littré to be f. ON. *mata* (Dan. *made*) to feed, as if to attract with a bait: see Littré.] German tinder, prepared from species of fungus *Polyporus* and *Boletus*, that grow on trees, employed as a match and a styptic.

1815 *Encycl. Brit.* I. 761 Some give to the amadow the name of pyrotechnical sponge. **1863** TYNDALL *Heat* i. 14 Tinder or dry amadou, may be ignited by this syringe. **1869** LORRAIN in *Eng. Mech.* 22 Oct. 137/2 Amadou, punk or German Tinder, is made from a kind of fungus that grows on the trunks of old oaks, ashes, beeches, &c. **1878** BRYANT *Pract. Surg.* I. 35 Cushions of amadou and well-adjusted pads of cotton wool or spongio-piline.

amaffised, corrupt form of AMETHYST.

c **1325** *E.E. Allit. P.* B. 1470 Amaraunȝ & amaffised stones.

†ˈ**amafrose**. *Obs.* [a. Fr. *amafrose* (Cotgr. 1611) for *amaurose* or *amavrose*, ad. mod.L. *amaurōsis*, a. Gr. ἀμαύρωσις.] = AMAUROSIS.

1598 SYLVESTER *Du Bartas* II. i. (1641) 98/2 Th' Amafrose and Cloudy Cataract, That..clean puts out the eye. **1731** BAILEY, *Amafrose*, a disease in the sinews of the sight.

‖**amah** (ˈɑːmə). [Anglo-Indian a. Pg. *ama* nurse.] A name given in the south of India, and elsewhere in the East, to a wet-nurse.

1839 *Lett. fr. Madras* 294 House-keeper-like bodies, who talk only of *ayahs* and *amahs*. **1857** TOMES *Americ. in Japan* viii. 179 Either maid-servants or women of Macao called Amahs or Ayahs were employed.

amain (əˈmeɪn), *adv.* Also 6-7 **amayn(e**, **amaine**. [f. A *prep.*[1] in, on, at + MAIN, OE. *mæʒn*, power, force. Apparently not preceded by an earlier full *on mæʒn*, *on main*, but formed in 16th c. after words in *a-*, as *afoot*.]

1. *lit.* In, or with, full force; with main force, with all one's might; vehemently, violently.

1540 *Four P.P.* in Hazl. *Dodsl.* I. 375 God save the devil, quoth I, amain. **1556** ABP. PARKER *Psalter* xliv, As sheepe we see, to slaughter driven amayne. **1611** CORYAT *Crudities* 215 Two dayes after it rained amaine. **1678** BUNYAN *Pilgr.* I. 61 Apollyon therefore followed his work amain. **1743** WESLEY *Wks.* 1872 I. 417 The colliers..began shouting amain. **1829** HOOD *E. Aram* xviii, But when I touch'd the lifeless clay The blood gush'd out amain. **1841** LONGF. *Hesperus* vii, Down came the storm, and smote amain the vessel.

b. In full force of numbers.

1601 HOLLAND *Pliny* (1634) I. 243 The Tunies to auoid it, goe alwaies amaine in whole flotes, toward the cape. **1663** *Flagellum, O. Cromwell* (1672) 22 New-England, a receptacle of the Puritans, who flocked thither amain.

2. Hence, with reference to motion. At full speed.

1563 B. GOOGE *Eglogs* (Arb) 82 He rounes amayne, to gase on Beauties cheare. **1587** HOLINSHED *Chron.* I. 176/2 Then without respect of shame they fled amaine. **1636** HEYLIN *Hist. Sabbath* 54 Laban..pursued after him amayn. **1640** BASTWICK *Lord Bishops* ix. I iiij b, The Tower of Babel went up a maine, till God confounded their worke. **1725** POPE *Odyss.* XI. 150 But vengeance hastes amain. **1851** LONGF. *Gold. Leg.* III. ii, Here comes a third who is spurring amain.

b. Without delay, in all haste; at once.

1600 HAKLUYT *Voy.* III. 568 The gentlemen came and repaired to the garden amaine. **1821** JOAN. BAILLIE *Met. Leg.*, *Calum.* xxvi. 11 Housewives left amain Their broken tasks.

†**a main gallop**: at full gallop. *Obs.* See MAIN.

1553 BRENDE *Curtius* IX. 57 Straightways the horsemen returned amaine gallop.

3. Exceedingly, greatly. (Cf. L. *valde*, f. *valēre*.)

1587 TURBERVILLE *Epit. & Sonn.* (1837) 333 Who so doth runne a race, Shall surely sweate amaine. **1616** SURFLET *Country Farm* 541 Too much drinesse doth disaduantage the husbandman amaine. **1671** MILTON *P.R.* II. 429 They whom I favour thrive in wealth amain. **1820** KEATS *St. Agnes* xxi, The maiden's chamber..Where Porphyro took covert, pleased amain.

†**a'main(e**, *v. Obs.* [a. Fr. *amene-r* to draw towards, in naval phr. *amener pavillon*, or absolutely *amener*, to strike flag, to surrender.]

1. *trans.* To lower (a sail, etc., *esp.* the topsail).

1593-1622 R. HAWKINS *Voy. S. Sea* (1847) 224 He called to us to amaine our sayles, which we could not well doe. **1627** SMITH *Seaman's Gram.*, vii. 33 When you let anything downe into the Howle, lowering it by degrees, they say, Amaine; and being downe, Strike. *Ibid.* ix. 40 When you would lower a yard so fast as you can, they call *Amaine*.

2. *fig.* To lower, lessen, abate.

1578 T. N. *Conq. W. Ind.* 257 They somewhat amayned their furie for their princes sake.

3. *intr.* To lower the topsail in sign of yielding; to yield.

1593-1622 R. HAWKINS *Voy. S. Sea* (1847) 33 Wished that the gunner might shoote at her, to cause her to amaine. **1628** DIGBY *Voy. Medit.* (1868) 77 Then the Swallow bad them 'Amaine for the King of England!' **1751** CHAMBERS *Cycl.*, *Amain*, or *Amayne*, a sea term, used by a man of war, to his enemy; and signifying, *yield*. **1867** SMYTH *Sailor's Word-Bk.* s.v., When we used to demand the salute in the narrow seas, the lowering of the topsail was called *striking amain*.

4. To conduct, guide. (A former sense of Fr. *amener*; cf. *amenée*, 'action de conduire.') *rare.*

1553 in Strype *Eccl. Mem.* II. II. xxi. 418 That his majesty may have..the ameyning of the matters.

a'maist, *adv. Sc.* [f. A *adj.*[3] + *maist*, *mast*, OE. *mást*, most.] = ALMOST.

1733 RAMSAY *Tea-T. Misc.* (ed. 9) I. 25, I had amaist forgot. **1862** in Hislop's *Sc. Proverbs* 15 'Amaist' and 'Very near' hae aye been great liars.

†**a'maister**, *v. Obs.* 3-5. Also **ameistre**, **amayster**. [a. OFr. *amaistre-r*, *-ier*, to master, to teach, f. *à* to + *maistrer*, *-ier*:—L. *magist(e)rā-re* to direct, rule, f. *magister* master.] To master, control, subdue; to teach.

c **1230** *Ancr. R.* 282 Schal flesches fondunge..ameistre þe neuer. **1340** *Ayenb.* 129 Þe guode leche þet amaystreþ his ziknesse. **1362** LANGL. *P. Pl.* A. VII. 200 Hou I mihte A-Maystren hem · and maken hem to worche. **1393** —— C. III. 167 For we han mede a-maistrid · þorw oure myrye tonge. *c* **1400** *Test. Love* I. (1560) 274/1 Disease shall no more hereafter thee amaistre.

[**1876** MISS JACKSON *Shropsh. Gloss.* s.v., An old man near Leintwardine, speaking of his schoolmaster, said "E used to amaister me, Sir.' Now rarely heard.]

Amal (əˈmɑːl, ‖ˈamal), *sb.* (*a.*) [a. Arab. *amal* hope; in full *Ḥarakat al-Amal* Movement of Hope. Also said to represent an acronym (as unvocalized *'ml*) of *afwāj al-muqāwama al-Lubnāniyya* detachments of the resistance of the Lebanese.] A Shiite Muslim political and paramilitary organization founded in Lebanon by Imam Musa Sadr in 1975. Also *attrib.* or as *adj.*

1979 *Middle East Jrnl.* XXXIII. 449 The Shīʿī *imām*, Musa al-Sadr,..organized a political movement called *Amal* (Hope). **1980** *N.Y. Times* 11 June A6/6 Mr. Berry, the Amal militia leader, blames Libya and particularly Iraq for provoking the recent clashes between Shiites and Palestinians. **1982** *Washington Post* 30 Aug. A10/5 The biggest militia force outside the Movement is Amal, the militia of Lebanon's..Shiite Moslem community. **1983** *Facts on File World News Digest* 18 Nov. 870 A/2 U.S. officials privately accused Islamic Amal and its leader..of providing personnel, explosives [etc.]. **1985** *Ann. Reg. 1984* 195 The Lebanese temporarily withdrew..after Israel had arrested men of the Amal movement. **1986** *Lebanon News* 31 Oct. 3/2 The Shiite Amal Movement launched an aggressive shelling campaign on the Christian Kesrouwan province.

amalette, obs. form of AMULET.

amalgam (əˈmælgəm), *sb.* Forms: 5 **malgam**, **amalgame**, (7 **amalgama**), 5-9 **amalgama**, 5- **amalgam**. [a. Fr. *amalgame* (15th c. in Litt.), and, in the formerly common *amalgama*, of med.L., in which the word was in regular alchemical use in 13th c. Usually taken as a perversion of L. *malagma* (in Pliny and the physicians) a mollifying poultice or plaster, a. Gr. μάλαγμα an emollient, f. μαλάσσ-ειν (stem μαλακ-) to soften; or of an Arabic adaptation of μάλαγμα with prefixed *al-* (as in *al-chemy*, *al-embic*, etc.): see the form (of the vb.) *almalgamynge* in one MS. of Chaucer, and *algamala* in Du Cange. Bacon's spelling *amalagma* was refashioned after *malagma*. Other early writers associated it with Gr. ἅμα together, and γάμος marriage. Devic (Littré *Suppl.*) suggests a direct Arabic derivation, taking an early variant *algame* as ad. Arab. *al-jamʿa* (orig. *al-gamʿa*) union, conjunction, f. *jamaʿa* to unite, and conjecturing for *amalgame* *ʿamal al-jamʿa* 'the operation of conjunction,' or *al-mojāmʿa* marriage union. But no instance of the use of these, as chemical terms, is cited from Arabic writers.]

1. *orig.* A soft mass formed by chemical manipulation, *esp.* a soft or plastic condition of gold, silver, etc. produced by combination with mercury; *hence*, *now*, any mixture of a metal with mercury, a mercurial alloy, as ***gold amalgam***, ***copper amalgam***, etc.

1471 RIPLEY *Comp. Alch.* in Ashm. *Theatr. Chem.* 1652 IX. 174 When the Medcyn as wax doth flowe, Than uppon Malgams loke thou hyt throw. *Ibid.* 191 Many Amalgame dyd I make. **1599** A. M. *Gabelhouer's Bk. Physic* 380/1 Beete a Ducket verye thinne..put therof j *dr.* to j *oz.* of Quicksiluer..The Amalgama must you wash with Saulte and Vineger. **1664** *Phil. Trans.* I. 23 An Amalgama of Gold and Virgin-Mercury. **1757** LEWIS *ibid.* L. 156 An amalgam of one part of platina and two of gold with a suitable quantity of mercury. **1782** KIRWAN *ibid.* LXXII. 217 An amalgama of lead and mercury decrepitates when heated. **1869** ROSCOE *Elem. Chem.* 214 An amalgam of ammonium can easily be prepared.

native amalgam, an amalgam of mercury with silver or gold, found crystalline, massive, or semi-fluid in various countries.

1875 URE *Dict. Arts* I. 133 A native amalgam of mercury and silver occurs in fine crystals in the mines of Moschellandsberg, in the Palatinate..A gold amalgam is obtained from the platinum region of Columbia.

2. Extended to, An intimate (plastic) mixture or compound of any two or more substances.

1626 BACON *Sylva* §99 The Body of the Wood will be turned into a kind of Amalagma. **1650** ASHMOLE *Arcanum* (ed. 3) 252 Let three weights of Red Earth..Water and Aire, well beaten, be mixt together: let an Amalgama be made like Butter, or Metalline Paste. **1828** KIRBY & SPENCE *Entomol.* I. xv. 497 The bees sometimes mix wax and propolis and make an amalgam.

3. *fig.* A complete combination of various elements. Also *attrib.*

1790 BURKE *Fr. Rev.* 274 They have attempted to confound all sorts of citizens into one homogeneous mass; and then they divided this their amalgama into..republics. **1823** HONE *Anc. Myst.* 187 Custom is an amalgam of sense and folly. **1841** CATLIN *N. Amer. Ind.* II. lvi. 210 [They] go by the familiar appellation of the amalgam name of 'Sacs and Foxes.' **1863** MRS. C. CLARKE *Shaksp. Char.* ii. 60 Touchstone's philosophy,—a choice and rich amalgam of sweet temper and untiring humour.

4. An ingredient in an amalgam; an 'alloy.'

1840 CARLYLE *Heroes* (1858) 315 Few men were without quackery; they had got to consider it a necessary ingredient and amalgam for truth. **1873** BURTON *Hist. Scotl.* I. iii. 119 No tin or other amalgam.

a'malgam, *v. arch.* [a. Fr. *amalgame-r* (14th c. in Littré); f. *amalgame*: see prec. Now repl. by AMALGAMATE *v.*]

†**1.** *trans.* To soften by combination with mercury; to alloy with mercury. *Obs.*

c **1386** CHAUCER *Chan. Yem. Prol. & T.* 218 The care and wo That we hadde in amalgamynge [*v.r.* almalgamynge, a malgamynge] and calcenynge Of quyksilver. **1471** RIPLEY *Comp. Alch.* in Ashm. *Theatr. Chem.* 1652 IX. 174 They Amalgam ther Bodys wyth Mercury lyke papp. **1610** B. JONSON *Alchem.* II. iii, What is some three ounces Of gold, t' Amalgame with some six of Mercury?

†**2.** *intr.* To enter into combination with mercury.

1583 PLAT *Jewel-ho.* III. (1594) 79 If you put Mercurie therein it will amalgame with it. *a* **1691** BOYLE *Wks.* I. 638 (R.) Quicksilver easily amalgams with metals.

3. *trans.* To coat or cover with amalgam.
1789 NICHOLSON *Electr.* in *Phil. Trans.* LXXIX. 272, I pasted a piece of leather upon a thin flat piece of wood, then amalgamed its whole surface.
4. *fig.* To combine.
1827 HARE *Guesses at Tr.* II. 254 They transferred the intelligence to human forms instead of amalgaming it as we do with the material objects themselves.

amalgamable (əˈmælgəməb(ə)l), *a.* [f. prec. + -ABLE.] Capable of amalgamation.
a **1691** BOYLE *Wks.* I. 632 (R.) A mineral body.. amalgamable with gold. **1835** *Lond. Jrnl.* 4 Feb. 33 Things not only far from incompatible, but thoroughly amalgamable.

amalgamate (əˈmælgəmət), *ppl. a.* [? ad. med.L. **amalgamāt-us*, pa. pple. of *amalgamā-re*, f. *amalgama*: see AMALGAM *sb.* Used also as pa. pple. of AMALGAMATE *v.*]
1. Combined or alloyed. (Said of mercury and another metal.)
1642-7 H. MORE *Poems* 262 Nimble quicksilver that doth agree With gold.. or with what ere it be Amalgamate.
2. Combined, coalesced; *spec.* of languages (see quot. 1862).
1849-52 TODD *Cycl. Anat. & Phys.* IV. 1346/2 The Amalgamate type, of which the classical languages are the most perfect example. **1850** MRS. BROWNING *Gerald. Courtsh.* lxviii. 3, I felt self-drawn out, as man, From amalgamate false natures. **1862** SPENCER *First Princ.* (1870) 321 Out of these [agglutinate languages] by further use, arose the 'amalgamate' languages, or those in which the original separateness of the inflexional parts can no longer be traced.

amalgamate (əˈmælgəmeɪt), *v.* [f. prec., which also continues in occasional use as its pa. pple., instead of *amalgamated.*]
1. *trans.* To soften or dissolve (a metal) by combination with mercury; *hence*, to combine mercury with another metal.
1660 BOYLE *Exper. Phys. Mech.* (R.) Amalgamating mercury with a convenient proportion of pure tin. **1706** PHILLIPS, *Amalgamate*, to mix Mercury or Quicksilver with Gold, or some other noble Metal; so as to reduce it into a kind of Paste. **1753** CHAMBERS *Cycl. Supp.* s.v. *Amalgamation*, The amalgamating mercury with copper is a very difficult process. **1875** URE *Dict. Arts* III. 806 The chloride of silver thus formed.. is amalgamated with the quicksilver.
2. *intr.* To enter into combination with mercury.
1751 CHAMBERS *Cycl.* s.v. *Amalgamation*, All metals, except iron and copper, spontaneously unite and amalgamate with mercury. **1804** WOLLASTON in *Phil. Trans.* XCIV. 424 On the surface of mercury a metallic film was precipitated, but did not appear to amalgamate.
3. By extension, To mix any substances so as to form a uniform compound.
1821 SCOTT *Kenilw.* (1867) 53 Wayland.. mixed, pounded, and amalgamated the drugs.
4. *fig.* To unite together (classes, races, societies, ideas, etc.) so as to form a homogeneous or harmonious whole. (Used either of combining two elements, or one element *with* another.) **a.** *trans.*
1802 T. JEFFERSON *Writ.* (1830) III. 489 It remains to amalgamate the comptroller and auditor into one. **1833** COLERIDGE *Table T.* 239 [The Romans] were ordained by Providence to conquer and amalgamate the materials of Christendom. **1868** M. PATTISON *Academ. Organ.* §5. 157 To amalgamate Merton with Corpus Christi College. **1872** MINTO *Eng. Lit.* I. i. 63 The four sentences of the original are amalgamated into two.
b. *intr.*
1797 *Anti-Jacobin* No. 5 Liberty's friends thus all learn to amalgamate. **1848** LYTTON *Harold* I. ii. 12 These turbulent invaders had amalgamated amicably with the native race. **1862** MARSH *Eng. Lang.* ii. 31 The Celtic words in English .. have never amalgamated with it. **1866** CRUMP *Banking* ix. 200 Two banks of issue had amalgamated.

aˈmalgamated, *ppl. a.* [f. prec. + -ED.]
1. Combined or alloyed with mercury; covered with amalgam.
1827 FARADAY *Chem. Manip.* xvii. 427 The same amalgamated silk. **1849** MRS. SOMERVILLE *Connex. Phys. Sc.* §xxv. 271 Placing an amalgamated copper plate upon it.
2. *fig.* Combined, united into one body.
a **1797** BURKE (T.) Ingratitude is indeed their four cardinal virtues compacted and amalgamated into one. **1864** *Daily Tel.* 11 Oct., The Birmingham branch of the Amalgamated Engineers. **1880** ADYE in *19th Cent.* 703 Why not give promotion to the.. officers in an amalgamated regimental list?

amalgamating (əˈmælgəmeɪtɪŋ), *vbl. sb.* [f. as prec. + -ING[1].] *lit.* The process of alloying with mercury; *hence*, of intimately combining different elements into one. (Mostly gerundial or *attrib.*)
1753 [See AMALGAMATE *v.* 1.] **1789-96** MORSE *Amer. Geog.* II. 301 Quicksilver.. sent over to America for the purpose of amalgamating. **1859** SEVIN *Mexico* in *Jrnl. R.G.S.* XXX. 48 Smelting and amalgamating works.

amalgamating (əˈmælgəmeɪtɪŋ), *ppl. a.* [f. as prec. + -ING[2].] **a.** Combining different elements into one, uniting.
1809 SOUTHEY in *Q. Rev.* II. 34 The amalgamating spirit of polytheism. **1869** *Daily News* 2 Sept., These ten offices were merged in the Albert.. a great amalgamating interest.

b. Of a language: inflexional; characterized by the use of inflexions to express the grammatical relations of words.
1877 J. PEILE *Philology* (ed. 2) 51 But you must not suppose that any one language is so absolutely 'isolating', 'agglutinative', or 'amalgamating', as to exclude all traces of the other methods. *Ibid.* 54 The second great group of amalgamating languages is called Indo-European. **1908** T. G. TUCKER *Introd. Nat. Hist. Lang.* 87 Languages commonly spoken of as 'inflexional', sometimes as 'organic'. We shall prefer to call them 'amalgamating'. These modify the sense and relation of words by variations of the terminating elements.

amalgamation (əˌmælgəˈmeɪʃən). [n. of action f. AMALGAMATE: see -ATION. Cf. mod.Fr. *amalgamation*, which may be the earlier.]
1. a. The softening of metals, etc. by union with mercury; the action or process of combining with mercury; and *by extension*, the intimate combination of two metals into an alloy. Often *attrib.*
1612 WOODALL *Surg. Mate* Wks. 1653, 268 Amalgamation is the putting together, solution, or calcination of familiar metals, by *Argentum vivum*, etc. **1794** SULLIVAN *View Nat.* I. 474 Metals by amalgamation shall be confounded and entirely concealed within each other. **1869** ROSCOE *Elem. Chem.* 271 For the extraction of silver from the other ores, a process termed amalgamation is employed, in which mercury is used to dissolve the metallic silver. **1875** URE *Dict. Arts* III. 808 Details of the Amalgamation Process.
b. (See quot.)
1753 CHAMBERS *Cycl. Supp.*, *Amalgamation* is also applied, in a less proper sense, to a solution of sulphur with mercury. In this sense amalgamation amounts to the same as mollification or softening; in which sense the word is used by some ancient chemists.
2. *fig.* The action of combining distinct elements, races, associations, into one uniform whole.
1775 DE LOLME *Constit. Eng.* I. ii. (1784) 24 The amalgamation of the Saxons and Normans. **1824** COLERIDGE *Aids to Refl.* 226 The forced amalgamation of the Patriarchal tradition with the incongruous scheme of Pantheism. **1837** *Baltimore Com. Transcript* 8 June 2/1 (Th. Suppl.), *Amalgamation*. A black man and a white woman were lately brought before the Police Court in Boston charged with unlawfully marrying. **1868** M. PATTISON *Academ. Organ.* §2. 45 The amalgamation of County, City, and University police into one Corps. **1905** *N. Y. Even. Post* 11 Oct. 4 If the white race are permeated with race consciousness, there is no danger of amalgamation.
3. The state or condition of being united with mercury; and *by extension*, a mixture or union of metals generally.
1753 CHAMBERS *Cycl. Supp.* s.v., According to these rules, there will always be an amalgamation made. **1874** BOUTELL *Arms & Arm.* ii. 38 Bronze or hardened brass, an amalgamation, that is, of copper with tin.
4. *fig.* A homogeneous union of what were previously distinct elements, societies, etc.
1828 MACAULAY *Hallam, Ess.* I. 51 The two hostile elements of which it consists have never been known to form a perfect amalgamation. **1850** GLADSTONE *Gleanings* V. lii. 204 Reasons.. for a close amalgamation between ecclesiastical and civil authority.

amalgamative (əˈmælgəmeɪtɪv, -ətɪv), *a.* [f. AMALGAMATE *v.*: see -IVE.] Tending to, or characterized by, amalgamation.
1841 *Blackw. Mag.* XLIX. 632 The metropolis is a gregarious, social, or amalgamative region.

†aˈmalgamatize, *v. Obs. rare*[−1]. [f. **amalgamat-* assumed stem of AMALGAMA + -IZE. An affectation of a more scholarly form than AMALGAMIZE. Cf. *dramatize, stigmatize.*] = AMALGAMATE.
c **1610** BACON *Physiol. Rem.* (Spedding) III. 813 Quest. touching Minerals:—Sublimation; Precipitation; Amalgamatizing, or turning into a soft body; Vitrification.

amalgamator (əˈmælgəmeɪtə(r)). Rarely -er. [f. AMALGAMATE *v.*: see -OR, -ER.] One who, or that which, amalgamates: *spec.* **a.** One who arranges an amalgamation between public companies; **b.** The apparatus used for extracting silver from its ore by combining it with mercury.
1838 P. PARLEY *Tales ab. Christm.* xxxii. 293 A great blazy fire.. the great amalgamater of the age and sex. **1862** *Lond. Rev.* 23 Aug. 156 The professional amalgamators who conduct the negotiations. **1875** URE *Dict. Arts* III. 807 The amalgamators.. are usually cast-iron pans.

aˈmalgamed, *ppl. a.* ? *Obs.* [f. AMALGAM *v.* + -ED.] Coated with amalgam.
1789 NICHOLSON *Electr.* in *Phil. Trans.* LXXIX. 265 The cylinder was then excited by applying an amalgamed leather.

aˈmalgaming, *vbl. sb.* ? *Obs.* [f. as prec. + -ING[1].] The process of forming amalgams.
c **1386** & **1827** [See AMALGAM *v.*]

†aˌmalgamiˈzation. *Obs. rare*[−1]. [n. of action f. next: see -ATION.] = AMALGAMATION.
1753 CHAMBERS *Cycl. Supp.* s.v. *Amalgamation*, This shews the general method of amalgamizations.

†aˈmalgamize, *v. Obs. rare.* [f. AMALGAM *sb.* + -IZE.] To reduce to a soft mass; *esp.* to soften or alloy with mercury.
1599 A. M. *Gabelhouer's Bk. Physic* 2/2 Take Persickernells.. and amalgamize the same verye well til it be like a salve. **1674** GODFREY *Inj. & Abus. Physic* 39 Having Amalgamiz'd many pounds worth of Gold with Mercury.

†aˈmalgamized, *ppl. a. Obs.* [f. prec. + -ED.] Reduced to a soft mass.
1599 A. M. *Gabelhouer's Bk. Physic* 5/2 The whyte of one Egge, and oyle of Poppyes, amalgamized with water.

†aˈmalgamy. *Obs. rare*[−1]. [f. AMALGAM, by form-assoc. with *-y* in *alchemy*, *pharmacy*, or -GAMY in *poly-gamy*, etc.] Amalgamating process or action.
1788 *New Lond. Mag.* 525 Foote deemed the crimes and follies of individuals convertible into advantage by the amalgamy of wit.

amalic (əˈmælɪk), *a. Chem.* [f. Gr. ἀμαλ-ός weak, feeble + -IC.] In ***amalic acid***: $C_4(CH_3)_4N_4O_7 + H_2O$, a product of the decomposition of caffeine by chlorine; so named from its feeble acid reaction.
1863 WATTS *Dict. Chem.* I. 161 Amalic acid.. with baryta, potash, and soda, forms compounds of a deep violet colour. **1876** HARLEY *Mat. Med.* 705 Amalic acid.. stains the skin pink.

amall, variant of AMEL, *Obs.*, enamel.

amamon, obs. form of AMOMUM.

†aˈmand, *v. Obs.* [ad. L. *āmandā-re* to send away, f. *ā* = *ab-* off + *mandā-re* to order.] To send off, dismiss.
? *a* **1600** *MS. Rawl.* No. 437, 11 (Halliw.) Opinion guideth least, and she by faction Is quite amanded. **1611** SPEED *Hist. Gt. Brit.* IX. x. 15 Who.. was amanded, and sent Prisoner to Shrewesburie. *c* **1665** R. CARPENTER *Prag. Jesuit* 64, I will amand.. thee to some vast and horrid Desert. **1795** WYTHE *Decisions* 86 A court of equity which would rather amand the plaintiff to his remedy at common Law.

amand, *sb. Sc. Law.* See AMENDS.

†amanˈdation. *Obs.*[−0] [ad. L. *āmandātiōn-em* a sending away, n. of action f. *āmandā-re*: see prec.] The action of sending off or dismissing.
1656 BLOUNT *Glossogr.*, *Amandation*, a sending away, or removal. **1755** JOHNSON, *Amandation*, the act of sending on a message or employment.

amandin(e (əˈmændɪn). [a. Fr. *amandine*; f. *amande* almond + -IN(E.] **a.** An albuminous substance contained in sweet almonds. **b.** A kind of cold cream prepared from the same.
1845 *Bachel. of Albany* (1848) 123 Explaining that the candles were 'patent amandines.' **1861** SALA *Tw. Round Clock* 197 They would want you to buy amandine for your hands, kalydor for your hair.

amandine, obs. form of ALMANDINE.

amang, obs. and north. dial. form of AMONG.

amanitine (æməˈnaɪtaɪn). [f. Gr. ἀμανῖτ-αι a sort of fungi, mentioned by Dioscorides + -INE.] The active narcotic principle of poisonous fungi.
1847 in CRAIG. **1861** H. MACMILLAN *Footn. Page Nat.* 248 When extracted by water and alcohol, a brown solid substance called amanitine is obtained. **1878** KINGZETT *Anim. Chem.* 302 Harnack has found in the red fungus which yields muscarine another alkaloid which he terms amanitine.

†aˈmanse, *v. Obs.* Forms: 1 **amánsumi-an**, ? **amánsi-an**, 2-3 **amansi-en, amansi**, 4 **amonsi.** [f. A- *pref.* 1 out, away + *mánsum* familiar, intimate + *-i-an* verbal formative; *lit.* to dis-familiarize, to put out of intimacy. (Has been erroneously said to be derived from *somnung*, *samnung*, congregation.) The contraction to *amansi-an* app. began in OE. as one MS. of Cnut's *Secular Laws* has pa. pple. *amánsod* = *amánsumod.*] To excommunicate, anathematize.
c **800** BÆDA iv. §17 (Bosw.) We amansumiaþ mid heortan & mid muþe ða ðe hi amansumedan. *c* **1175** *Lamb. Hom.* 45 Amansed beo þe mon þe sunne-dei nulle iloken. *a* **1250** *Owl & Night.* 1307 Heo were ifurn of prestes muþe Amansed. **1297** R. GLOUC. 474 He amansede alle thulke, that such vnriȝt adde ido. *c* **1308** *Pol. Songs* 196 To extredite and amonsi al That lafful men doth robbi.

†aˈmansed, *ppl. a. Obs.*; also 1 **amansumod.** [see prec.] Excommunicated, anathematized.
c **1000** *Cnut's Sec. Laws* §67 (Bosw.) Gif hwá amánsodne [*MS.* B. amánsumodne] oððe útlahne hæbbe and healde. *c* **1220** *Leg. St. Kath.* 2101 And tine mix maumeȝ alle beon amansed.

†aˈmansing, *vbl. sb. Obs.* Forms: 1 **amánsumung**, 3 **amanzinge, manzinge.** [f. *amánsumi-an* AMANSE + -ING[1].] Excommunication, anathema.
c **1000** ÆLFRIC *Josh.* vii. 12 Besmiten mid þære amánsumunge. **1340** *Ayenb.* 189 þanne ssel he keste his greate manzinge as þe heȝe bissop.. þe ilke amanzinge sel by ope alle þo volke þet ssole by a left half.

† **'amant.** *Obs.* [a. Fr. *amant* lover:—L. *amant-em*, pr. pple. of *amā-re* to love.] A lover, partisan.

1493 *Festivall* (W. de Worde 1515) 107 The nyght before eyther Johans appeyred to theyr amantes.

amantadine (ə'mæntədi:n). *Pharm.* [f. alteration of ADAMANTANE + AM)INE.] A derivative, $C_{10}H_{17}N.HCl$, of adamantane which inhibits the action of some viruses, and is used prophylactically against influenza type A2 and also in the treatment of Parkinsonism. Also ***amantadine hydrochloride.***

1964 *Science* 15 May 862/1, 1-Adamantanamine (amantadine), a stable, colorless, crystalline amine with an unusual symmetrical structure, reproducibly and selectively inhibits influenza viruses in tissue culture, chick embryos, and mice. **1977** *Lancet* 23 Apr. 904/1 It is difficult to know whether to prescribe levodopa, bromocriptine, or amantadine for patients with Parkinson's disease who also have heart-disease, because all these drugs may be cardiotoxic. **1977** *Martindale's Extra Pharmacopoeia* (ed. 27) 855/2 Amantadine hydrochloride is an antiviral agent which probably inhibits penetration of the virus into the host cell. It has no virucidal actions. **1983** *New Scientist* 10 Mar. 644/1 The third anti-viral drug available now is a cage-like hydrocarbon amine molecule called amantadine.

amanu'ense, *v.* To act as an amanuensis, to write from dictation.

1849 SOUTHEY *Comm.-Place Bk.* Ser. II. 359 Brought up to the trade of copying books or rather of amanuensing.

amanuensis (ə,mænju:'ɛnsɪs). Pl. **-es** (i:z). [L. (in Suetonius) adj. used subst., f. denominative phrase *a manu* a secretary, short for *servus a manu* + *-ensis* belonging to.] One who copies or writes from the dictation of another.

1619 SCLATER *Expos. Thess.* (1627) I. To Reader 6 An Amanuensis to take my Dictates. **1621** BURTON *Anat. Mel.* Democr. 11 Allowing him six or seven amanuenses to write out his dictates. **1714** *Spect.* No. 617 ¶4 Our Friend.. by the help of his Amanuensis, took down all their Names. **1765** TUCKER *Lt. Nat.* II. 446 Cæsar could dictate to three amanuenses together. **1860** SMILES *Self-Help* ii. 38 For many years after their marriage, she acted as his amanuensis.

Amapondo (æmə'pɒndəʊ). Also **Amaponda.** = PONDO; the tribe of the Pondos. Also *attrib.*

1824 BROWNLEE *Let.* in G. Thompson *Trav. & Adv. in S. Afr.* (1827) I. xviii. 209 A tribe called Amaponda, who live on the coast to the eastward of the Tambookies. **1837** F. OWEN *Diary* (1926) 15 Faku, the chief of the Amapondas. **1838** *Ibid.* 120 The Amaponda country—Faku's tribe—beyond the Umzimvubu between Port Natal and Caffraria. **1871** C. M. YONGE *Pioneers & Founders* x. 258 The next tribes, the Amapondas, were scrupulously honest. **1876**, **1884** [see PONDO].

† **a'mar,** *v. Obs.* Forms: 1 amyrr-an, 1-2 amerr-an, 2-5 amerr-e(n, 3-5 amer, 3-5 amærr-e, amarr-e. [f. A- *pref.* 1 intens. + MAR, OE. *merr-an, myrr-an,* to spoil, destroy.] To destroy, spoil, mar, squander; hurt, injure.

c **885** K. ÆLFRED *Boeth.* xxxii. §1 Ðæs andwearða wela amerþ and læt ða men. *c* **1000** *Ags. Gosp.* Luke xv. 14 Ða he hiȝ hæfde ealle amyrrede. *c* **1160** *Hatton G.* ibid., Ða he hyo hæfde ealle amerde. **1205** LAYAM. 19469 Ne mihte heo.. mid hare strengðe: þene wal amærre. **1399** LANGL. *Rich. Redeless* Prol. 15 Thus tales me troblid.. And amarride my mynde. *a* **1400** *Octouian* 1307 He ran with a drawe swerde.. And all hys goddys ther he amerrede. *c* **1440** *Gesta Rom.* (1879) 253 Not a litle mevid, & amarryd in mynde.

‖ **amaracus** (ə'mærəkəs). Adapted in 5 as amarac. [L. *amăra-cus*, a. Gr. ἀμάρακος, applied to same plant.] An aromatic plant, the Dittany of Crete (*Origanum dictamnus*), by some made the type of a distinct genus (*Amaracus*).

c **1420** *Pallad. on Husb.* I. 1017 Eke amarac and other fresshed floures. **1601** HOLLAND *Pliny* (1634) II. 92 That Amaracus or Marjeram which they call the Phrygian. **1830** TENNYSON *Œnone* 95 Violet, amaracus, and asphodel.

† **ama'rantal,** *a. Obs. rare*$^{-1}$. [f. Gr. ἀμάραντ -ος (see AMARANT(H) + -AL[1].] Unfading, everlasting.

1674 J. B[RIAN] *Harv.-Home* Postsc. 56 A Kingdom that Is apthartal, amiantal, Amarantall.

amarant(h) ('æmərænt, -ænθ). Also 6-7 **amaranthe.** [a. Fr. *amarante*, f. L. *amarant-us*, a. Gr. ἀμάραντ-ος, used as name of a flower, but properly adj. 'everlasting,' f. ἀ not + *-μαραντ-ος fading, corruptible, f. μαρ-αν- stem of μαραίν-ειν to wither, decay (root *mar-, mor-* die). Long used in the L. form *amarantus*, corruptly written (by form-assoc. with *polyanthus*, etc.) *amaranthus*, as if containing the Gr. ἄνθος flower; *amarant* (now commonly *amaranth*) being at first only poetic.]

1. An imaginary flower reputed never to fade; a fadeless flower (as a poetic conception). Also *attrib.*

1616 DRUMM. OF HAWTH. in Farr's *S.P.* (1848) 285 Vpon her head shee ware Of amaranthes a crowne. *c* **1630** —— *Wks.* 1711, 17/1 Th' immortal amaranthus. **1637** MILTON *Lycidas* 149 Bid amaranthus all his beauty shed. **1667** —— *P.L.* III. 353 Thir Crowns inwove with Amarant and Gold, Immortal Amarant. **1815** SOUTHEY in *Q. Rev.* XIII. 274 His laurels are entwined with the amaranths of righteousness. **1827** KEBLE *Chr. Y.* St. Barn., The genial amarant wreath to wear.

2. A genus of ornamental plants (*Amarantus*, N.O. *Amarantaceæ*) with coloured foliage, of which the Prince's Feather and Love-lies-bleeding are species.

1551 TURNER *Herbal* 22 Amaranthus of Pliny.. is rather a purple eare then a floure. **1579** LANGHAM *Gard. Health* (1633) 258 The hearbe called purple veluet flower, or Amaranthus. **1596** SPENSER *F.Q.* III. vi. 45 Sad Amaranthus, in whose purple gore Me seemes I see Amintas wretched fate. **1626** BACON *Sylva* §512 (R.) Some Plants Blood-Red, Stalke and Leafe, and all; as Amaranthus. **1725** BRADLEY *Fam. Dict., Amaranthus,* Flower Gentle, called by some, Princes Feathers. **1794** MARTYN *Rousseau's Bot.* xvi. 207 The Crested Amaranth.. is commonly called Cock's-comb. **1847** LINDLEY *Veg. Kingd.* (ed. 2) 510 Amaranths grow in crowds or singly.

3. A purple colour, being that of the foliage of *Amarantus.*

1690 *Lond. Gaz.* mmdlv/4 One amarant and green Mantua and Petticoat. **1858** PLANCHE *Fairy Tales* 74 Her dress was of amaranth satin.

4. globe amaranth: *Gomphrena globosa* (N.O. *Amarantaceæ*).

5. yellow amaranth: A composite plant (*Helichrysum Stœchas*).

1551 TURNER *Herbal* 23 The herbe.. called of Galene amaranthus.. hath a little white branche.. the tope is al yelowe. **1578** LYTE *Dodoens* 89 *Ageratum Aurelia*.. of some *Amaranthus Luteus.* **1731** BAILEY, *Amarantus luteus,* flower maudlin, or baltazar with a yellow flour. **1875** MISS BIRD *Hawaii* 134 Roses, pohas, yellow amaranth.

6. = PURPLE-HEART 1 a and (*rare*) b. Chiefly *U.S.*

1909 in *Cent. Dict.* Suppl. **1924** RECORD & MELL *Timbers Tropical Amer.* II. 234 *Peltogyne*... *Common names*: purple heart.. amaranth. **1930** [see PALISANDER]. **1931** *Tropical Woods* XXV. 1 (*heading*) Use of amaranth for interior trim and flooring. **1947** [see PURPLE-HEART 1 a].

amarant(h)aceous (,æmərən'teɪʃəs), *a. Bot.* [f. AMARANT(H) + -ACEOUS.] Of the nature of amarant(h).

1836 *Penny Cycl.* VI. 408/1 *Celosia,* a genus of amarantaceous plants. **1879** *Syd. Soc. Lex., Amarantaceous,* and *Amaranthaceous.*

amarant(h)ad (æmə'ræntəd). *Bot.* [f. as prec. + -AD.] A plant of the N.O. *Amarantaceæ*, an ally of the genus Amarant(h).

1866 *Treas. Bot.* 244 *Celosia,* a genus of amaranthads.

amarant(h)ine (æmə'ræntɪn, -θɪn), *a.* In Milton **amarantin.** [f. AMARANT(H) + -INE; in mod.L. *amarantinus.*]

1. Of or pertaining to amarant(h), of everlasting flowers, fadeless.

1667 MILTON *P.L.* XI. 78 Thir blissful Bowrs Of Amarantin Shade. **1713** SWIFT *Caden. & Van.* Wks. 1755 III. II. 8 She plucks in heav'n's high bow'rs A sprig of amaranthine flow'rs. **1858** LONGF. *The Two Angels* viii, The angel with the amaranthine wreath, Pausing, descended.

2. Fadeless, immortal, undying.

1781 COWPER *Hope* 164 Hope Plucks amaranthine joys from bowers of bliss. **1847** H. ROGERS *Ess.* I. v. 240 To bloom for ever in amaranthine loveliness.

3. Amarant(h)-coloured.

1874 HARDY *Madding Crowd* II. i. 15 Promontories of coppery cloud which bounded a green and pellucid expanse in the western sky; amaranthine glosses came over them.

amarant(h)oid (æmə'ræntɔɪd, -θɔɪd), *a.* and *sb.* [f. as prec. + -OID.] **A.** *adj.* Resembling amarant(h). **B.** *sb.* An ally of amarant(h).

1741 *Compl. Fam.-Piece* II. iii. 357 Make hot Beds for your tender annual Flowers.. such as Amaranthus's, Amaranthoides. **1879** *Syd. Soc. Lex., Amaranthoid.*

amarantite (æmə'ræntaɪt). *Min.* [ad. G. *amarantit* (A. Frenzel 1888, in *Min. und Petrogr. Mittheilungen* IX. 398), f. AMARANT(H): see -ITE[1].] A hydrous ferric sulphate of brownish-red colour (see quot. 1938).

1890 *Amer. Jrnl. Sci.* XL. 199 *Amarantite.* The crystallization is triclinic. *Ibid.* 201 Amarantite occurs associated with, and sometimes imbedded in a finely fibrous orange-colored mineral, probably sideronatrite. **1938** [see HOHMANNITE]. **1938** M. C. BANDY in *Amer. Mineralogist* XXIII. 745 *Amarantite group.* .. The members of this group are brownish red basic hydrous iron sulphates, in one of which, amarantite, dehydration data indicate that the water is given off in three stages... The formulae are, accordingly, written to indicate these various kinds of water.

amaraunt, obs. form of EMERALD.

c **1325** *E.E. Allit. P.* B. 1470 Amaraunȝ & amaffised stones.

† **a'maricate.** *v. Obs. rare*$^{-1}$. [f. late L. *amāricāt-* ppl. stem of *amāricā-re* to make bitter, f. *amārus* bitter.] To embitter, irritate.

1651 N. BIGGS *New Dispens.* ¶80. 47 How doth Opium amaricate?

amarine (ə'mɛəraɪn), *sb. Chem.* [f. L. *amār-us* bitter + -INE[4].] A name proposed for various bitter vegetable principles; *spec.* applied to the alkaloid ($C_{21}H_{18}N_2$) resulting from the action of ammonia on essence of bitter almonds, which has also been called BENZOLINE.

1839 HOOPER *Med. Dict.* 77 *Amarine,* a name given by some to the bitter principle of vegetables. **1863** WATTS *Dict. Chem.* I. 162 Amarine becomes strongly electrical by friction.

† **'amarine,** *a. Obs. rare*$^{-1}$. In 7 **amerine.** [f. L. *amār-us* bitter + -INE[1]. Cf. med.L. *amarina*, a morello cherry.] Bitter, sour.

1601 HOLLAND *Pliny* (1634) I. 440 The Amerine Apples doe keepe good long, whereas the honie Apples will abide no time.

† **a'maritude.** *Obs.* [a. OFr. *amaritude*:—L. *amāritūdo* bitterness, f. *amār-us* bitter.] Bitterness.

1490 CAXTON *Eneydos* xxvi. 94 Thou haste absorbed me and reclosed in the grete see of amarytude. **1599** A. M. *Gabelhouer's Bk. Physic* 18/1 Adde thervnto a little Suger, that heereby the amaritude may somewhat be diminished. **1611** SPEED *Hist. Gt. Brit.* IX. viii. (1632) 576 With much more bleeding amaritude of spirit. **1666** G. HARVEY *Morbus Angl.* (J.) What amaritude or acrimony is deprehended in choler. **1755** in JOHNSON; and in mod. Dicts.

Amarna (ə'mɑ:nə). In full *Tell el-Amarna*, the modern name of Akhetaten, the site of a city in ancient Egypt built by Amenophis IV in the 14th century B.C. on the east bank of the Nile near Mallawi; used *attrib.* to designate remains found in this city, esp. certain tablets discovered in 1887 (see quots.).

1888 E. A. W. BUDGE in *Proc. Soc. Biblical Archæol.* X. 554 On the Tell el-Amarna tablets Amenophis III is addressed by his prenomen. **1893** C. R. CONDER *Tell Amarna Tablets* p. xi, The Hebrews.. appear for the first time in monumental history in the Tell Amarna letters. **1901** J. HUTCHISON tr. *Niebuhr's Tell el Amarna Period* ii. 8 Ai, called Haya in the Amarna letters, received golden honours. **1923** E. S. BRISTOWE *Oldest Lett. in World* i. 7 With the Amarna Tablets we come up against the mystery of the Hebrew race. **1960** K. M. KENYON *Archaeol. in Holy Land* viii. 206 The Amarna letters.. provide contemporary evidence for the break-up of the Asiatic empire re-established by Thotmes III. **1962** J. GRAY *Archaeol. & O.T. World* iv. 85 The Amarna Tablets, the correspondence of the native chiefs and Egyptian deputies in Palestine and Syria with the suzerain power in the reigns of Amenhotep III (1411–1375 B.C.) and his son the 'heretic' Akhnaten (1375–1358 B.C.). **1962** *Listener* 19 July 106/3 The curious lack of confidence which Amarna art sometimes displays.

† **a'marous,** *a. Obs.*$^{-0}$ [f. L. *amār-us* bitter + -OUS.] 'Bitter, sharp, froward, hard to be appeased, spightful, sour.' Blount *Glossogr.* 1656.

† **a'marstled,** *ppl. a. Obs. rare.* ? Stuffed full.

c **1300** in Wright *Lyric P.* xxxix. 111 Hupe forth, Hubert, hosede pye, ichot thart a-marstled in to the mawe.

† **a'martyr,** *v. Obs. rare*$^{-1}$. [f. A- *pref.* 1 or 11 + MARTYR, ME. *martr-en.*] To martyr.

? *a* **1300** *MS. Laud* No. 108. 165 (Halliw.) And amartrede so thane holie man.

† **a'marulence.** *Obs.*$^{-0}$ [f. next: see -NCE.] 'Bitterness.' J.

1731 in BAILEY; whence in JOHNSON.

† **a'marulent,** *a. Obs.* [ad. L. *amārulent-us*, f. *amār-us* bitter: see -ULENT.] Full of bitterness.

1583 STUBBES *Anat. Abuses* (1836) 181 Al other pleasures and delightes of this life set a parte as amarulent and bitter. **1656** BLOUNT *Glossogr., Amarulent,* very bitter, spightful, envious. **1742** BAILEY, *Amarulent,* bitter, froward.

† **a'marvel,** *v. Obs.*; also 4-5 **amerveil(e, -vail(e,** 5 **-veyl(le, -vel, amarvail(e, -vel, admerveyll(e, -vayll(e,** 5-6 **amervayl(le.** [a. OFr. *amerveillie-r*, earlier *émerveillier, esmerveillier*, to strike with wonder, f. *es-*:—L. *ex-*, out, utterly + *merveiller* to surprise, f. *merveille* wonder, marvel:—L. *mirābilia.* The prefix *a-* was subseq. erroneously refashioned as *ad-* in MFr., which was also introduced into Eng. by Caxton: see ADMERVEYLLE and AD-.] To strike or fill with wonder; almost always in the passive, To be surprised, astonished.

a **1330** *Sire Degarré* 1046 The Fader amerueiled wes Whi his swerd was point les. *c* **1350** *Will. Palerne* 3857 Many were ameruailed of here douȝti dedes. *c* **1400** *Epiph.* (Turnb. 1843) 1694 He was amerveld of that syght. *c* **1430** LYDG. *Bochas* I. xv. (1554) 31 a, As he that was amerueyled in his thought. *c* **1440** *Gesta Rom.* II. xxxvii. 392 He was amarvailede of her fairenesse. **1470** HARDING *Chron.* lxxvi, The knightes.. Amarueled were of it doutelesse. **1483** CAXTON *Gold. Leg.* 218/1 Thenne were they admerueylled of the beaute of the reson. *c* **1530** LD. BERNERS *Arth. Lyt. Bryt.* (1814) 100 Arthur.. mette wyth much people.. whereof he was gretly ameruayled.

amaryllid (æmə'rɪlɪd). *Bot.* [a. L. *amaryllid-* stem of AMARYLLIS.] A plant of the same order as the genus *Amaryllis*; an amaryllidaceous plant.

1830 LINDLEY *Nat. Syst. Bot.* 260 Amaryllids show themselves in countless numbers in Brazil. **1880** S. HIBBERD in *N. & Q.* Ser. VI. I. 412/2 The daffodils of the garden are amaryllids; and between these and lily-worts there is a world of difference.

amaryllidaceous (æmə,rılı'deıʃəs), *a. Bot.* [f. prec. + -ACEOUS.] Of or pertaining to the *Amaryllidaceæ*, a Nat. Ord. of plants, of which Amaryllis, Narciss, and Snowdrop are examples.

1837 W. HERBERT *Amaryllidaceæ* 5 Newly introduced Amaryllidaceous plants. **1866** T. MOORE in *Treas. Bot.* 48 Amaryllis, the type of the amaryllidaceous family.

amaryllideous (,æmərı'lıdi:əs), *a. Bot.* [f. as prec. + -EOUS.] = prec.

1830 LINDLEY *Nat. Syst. Bot.* 260 The genuine Amaryllideous genera *Phycella* and *Placea*.

‖**amaryllis** (æmə'rılıs). *Bot.* [adopted by Linnæus, from L. *Amaryllis*, a. Gr. Ἀμαρυλλίς, name of a country-girl in Theocritus, Ovid, and Virgil.] A genus of autumn-flowering bulbous plants, typical of the N.O. *Amaryllidaceæ*, species of which are cultivated as garden or hot-house flowers; applied also by florists to allied genera.

1794 MARTYN *Rousseau's Bot.* xviii. 246 *Amaryllis*; known by its superior, bell-shaped corolla of six petals. **1834** PRINGLE *Afric. Sketches* vi. 209 The large purple flowers of a species of amaryllis. **1855** TENNYSON *Daisy* iv, Here and there, on sandy beaches A milky-bell'd amaryllis blew. **1866** T. MOORE in *Treas. Bot.* 48 Most of the plants called *Amaryllis* in gardens are now referred to *Hippeastrum*.

†**a'masked**, *ppl. a. Obs. rare.* [f. MASK *v.* with A- *pref.* 11 or ? 6.] Covered with a mask; blindfolded.

a **1571** JEWEL *Holy Script.*, Philosophy is darke, Astrology is dark, and Geomatry is darke. The professors thereof oftentimes runne amasket: they leese themselues, and wander they know not whither. **1697** *Let. in MS. Lansd.* No. 1033. 2 (Halliw.) To go a masked, To wander or be bewildered.

amass (ə'mæs), *v.* [a. Fr. *amasse-r* (12th c.) f. *à* to + *masser*, f. *masse* MASS.]

1. *gen.* To collect into a mass or masses, to heap together, pile up, collect. †**a.** things material. *Obs.*

1594 CAREW tr. *Huarte's Trial of Wits* vi. (1596) 83 The water, with which the other elements are amassed. **1644** BULWER *Chirol.* 26 By the joyning of his Hands together, he doth amasse them into one. **1695** WOODWARD *Nat. Hist. Earth* IV. (1723) 196 They are amass'd into Balls, Lumps, or Nodules. **1775** BARKER in *Phil. Trans.* LXV. 256 [Ice] by being collected and amassed into a large body is thus preserved.

b. things immaterial. *Obs.* or *arch.*

a **1619** DONNE *Biathan.* (1644) 177 This last lesson, in which hee amasses and gathers all his former Doctrine. **1638** *Penit. Conf.* vii. (1657) 123 That ridiculous pack of heresies amassed by the Council of Constance. **1756** BURKE *Subl. & B.* Wks. I. 177 With what severity of judgement, has Virgil amassed all these circumstances. **1833** I. TAYLOR *Fanat.* viii. 311 By amassing to a prodigious height the evidences of sanctity.

c. men, troops, etc. *Obs.* or *arch.* (Cf. to *mass.*)

1658 CLEVELAND *Rustic Ramp.* Wks. 1687, 415 Why they had amassed such Swarms of the People. **1660** BLOUNT *Boscobel* 7 Cromwell had amass'd togither a numerous Body of Rebels. **1745** H. WALPOLE *Lett. to Montagu* 12 Lady Granville and the dowager Strafford have their At-home's and amass company. **1802** J. BARLOW *Columb.* VII. 309 Her gallant Stuart here amass'd from far The veteran legions of the Georgian war.

2. *intr.* To gather, assemble. *arch.*

1572 O. KING in Froude *Hist. Eng.* (1881) X. 276 The soldiers were amassing from all parts of Spain. **1881** D. ROSSETTI *Bal. & Sonn.* 181 Billowing skies that scatter and amass.

3. *esp.* To heap up for oneself, collect, or accumulate as one's own. Said of wealth and resources of all kinds. (The earliest, now the ordinary sense.)

1481 CAXTON *Myrr.* I. iv. 14 Peple that will suffer payne and trauaylle.. for to amasse grete tresours. **1483** —— *G. de la Tour* f v b, Erthely good that he hath gadred and amassed. *a* **1546** SURREY *Eccles.* iii. (R.) The heire shall waste the whourded gold amassed with muche payne. **1712** HUGHES *Spect.* No. 554 ¶4 [He] had amassed to himself such stores of knowledge. **1725** POPE *Odyss.* III. 385 Amassing gold, and gath'ring naval stores. **1769** ROBERTSON *Charles V*, V. II. 228 The great sums of money which his father had amassed. **1860** SMILES *Self Help* iv. 84 Addison amassed as much as three folios of manuscript materials before he began his 'Spectator.' **1872** BLACK *Adv. Phaeton* iv. 44 He has been able to amass a fortune.

†**a'mass**, *sb. Obs.* [a. OFr. *amasse*, f. *amasser*: see prec. Cf. mod.Fr. *amas.*] A gathering, accumulation, collection; a massing of forces.

1592 WYRLEY *Armorie* 120 At Eureux then I made my chiefe amasse, And found I had full seauen hundred speares. **1603** DANIEL *Def. Rhime* (1717) 20 This great Amass of Eloquence. **1624** WOTTON *Archit.* (1672) 25 This Pillar is nothing in effect, but a medly, or an amasse of all the precedent Ornaments. **1734** EAMES in *Phil. Trans.* XXXVIII. 246 An Amass of Heterogeneous Parts diffused in the Æther.

amassable (a'mæsəb(ə)l), *a. rare.* [f. AMASS *v.* + -ABLE.] Capable of being amassed.

Mod. A sum not so easily amassable in those days.

amassed (ə'mæst), *ppl. a.* [f. AMASS *v.* + -ED.] Gathered into a mass, accumulated, massed.

1673 RAY *Journ. Low Countr.* 117 Shells amassed together into great Stones. **1725** BRADLEY *Fam. Dict.* s.v. *Distillation*, All the Taste and Smell of its amassed Simple. *a* **1763** SHENSTONE *Elegies* vii. 49 Gold in heaps amast. **1881** in *Jrnl. Educ.* 35/2 Amassed riches serve or sway every man.

amasser (ə'mæsə(r)). [f. AMASS *v.* + -ER¹.] One who amasses; an accumulator.

1697 EVELYN *Numism.* viii. 289 The great Amasser of this ..useful Curiosity. **1861** *Cornh. Mag.* Sept. 355 The amasser of colossal wealth.

amassing (ə'mæsıŋ), *vbl. sb.* [f. AMASS *v.* + -ING¹.] The action of heaping up or accumulating. (Mostly gerundial.)

1674 COLES, An Amassing, *Coacervatio.* **1716** BP. OF ELY *Charge* 7 Aug. 5 There is little need of amassing the Passages together. **1824** DIBDIN *Libr. Comp.* 279 His ruling passion was amassing state papers.

amassment (ə'mæsmənt). [a. OFr. *amassement*, f. *amasser*: see AMASS *v.* and -MENT.] The action of amassing; an accumulation into a mass.

1665 GLANVILL *Sceps. Sci.* xiii. 76 An amassment of imaginary conceptions, ungrounded opinions, and infinite impostures. **1741** WATTS *Improv. Mind* i. 10 A mere amassment of what others have written. **1863** KINGLAKE *Crimea* (1877) V. i. 273 That famous amassment of troops.

amaster: see AMAISTER *v. Obs.*

amasthenic (æməs'θɛnık), *a. rare*⁻⁰. [improp. for *hamasthenic*, f. Gr. ἅμα together + σθέν-ος strength + -IC.] = AMACRATIC.

1859 in WORCESTER.

†**amate** (ə'meıt), *v.*¹ *Obs.* or *arch.* [a. OFr. *amate-r*, and *amati-r*, f. *à* to + *mater*, *matir*, f. *mat* dejected, downcast. Obs. bef. 1700, but used by Lytton (as archaic) and Keats.] To dismay, daunt, dishearten, cast down.

c **1320** *Bevis of Hampt.*, There myght men sorow see Amatud that there had be. **1530** PALSGR. 421 [see also 633], I amate, I forwery or astonisshe, *Jamatte.* **1562** J. HEYWOOD *Prov. & Epigr.* (1867) 14 All mirth was amated. *a* **1586** SIDNEY *Ps.* cxxix, Terror shall your mindes amate. **1611** COTGR., *Matter*, to quell, mate, amate; subdue, pull vnder, take lower. **1642** CHARLES I *Answ. Declar.* 19 May 3 The great labour and skill hath beene used to amate and afright Our good Subjects. **1693** W. ROBERTSON *Phraseol. Gen.* 79 *Amate*, to discourage or daunt. *a* **1821** KEATS *Rem.* I. 12 (1848) A half-blown flow'ret which cold blasts amate. **1843** LYTTON *Last of Bar.* II. iii. 136 It amates me much,.. that thou leavest the court in this juncture.

†**a'mate**, *v.*² *Obs.* [f. A- *pref.* 11 intens. + MATE *v.*] To be a fellow or mate to; to be a match for, to match, equal.

1596 SPENSER *F.Q.* II. ix. 34 Many a iolly paramoure, The which them did in modest wise amate. **1642** ROGERS *Naaman* 128 To amate and equall even true selfedeniall.

†**a'mate**, *a. Obs.* Also **amat.** [a. OFr. *amat* overwhelmed, beaten down, f. *amater* or *amatir*: see AMATE *v.*¹] Overwhelmed, dejected, dismayed.

a **1400** *Cov. Myst.* 294 Beth ryht [*pr.* ryth] ware he make you not amat. **1430** LYDG. *Chron. Troy* I. i, Awhaped and a mate, Comfortles of any creature. **1558** W. FORREST *Grysilde Sec.* (1875) 95 Being blanked, as one all amate.

†**a'mated**, *ppl. a. Obs.* [f. AMATE *v.*¹ + -ED.] Dismayed, overwhelmed, confounded.

1592 GREENE *Groatsw. Wit* (1874) 15 He that tamed monsters, stoode amated at beauties ornaments. **1600** FAIRFAX *Tasso* XI. xii. 197 Stood husht and still, amated and amased. **1656** TRAPP *Expos. Matt.* x. 19 (1868) 154/1 Demosthenes.. was.. sometimes so amated that he had not a word to say.

amateria'listic *a. rare.* [f. Gr. ἀ privative + MATERIALISTIC.] Opposed to (philosophic) materialism.

1878 J. FISKE in *N. Amer. Rev.* CXXVI. 33 It is intensely amaterialistic for us to speak of the table as if it had some objective existence.

amates, obs. form of AMETHYST.

amateur (æmə'tɜ:(r), 'æmətjʊə(r), -tə(r)). [a. Fr. *amateur* ad. L. *amātōr-em*, n. of agent f. *amā-re* to love. Occ. pron. as Fr.; often with (ɜ:) for Fr. *eu*; some who say (jʊə) still keep the stress on last syllable. So with the derivatives.]

1. One who loves or is fond *of*; one who has a taste for anything.

1784 *Europ. Mag.* 268 The President will be left with his train of feeble Amateurs. *a* **1797** BURKE (T.) Those who are the greatest amateurs or even professors of revolutions. **1801** MISS EDGEWORTH *Irish Bulls* xiv. (1832) 266 The whole boxing corps and gentlemen amateurs crowded to behold the spectacle. **1817** CHALMERS *Astron. Disc.* i. (1852) 40 The amateurs of a superficial philosophy. **1863** MRS. ATKINSON *Tartar Steppes* 89, I am no amateur of these melons.

2. a. One who cultivates anything as a pastime, as distinguished from one who prosecutes it professionally; hence, sometimes used disparagingly, as = dabbler, or superficial student or worker. See also quot. 1861.

1786 *European Mag.* Dec. 421/1 Dr. Percival.. writes on philosophical subjects as an amateur rather than as a master. *c* **1803** REES *Cycl.*, *Amateur*, in the Arts, is a foreign term introduced and now passing current amongst us, to denote a person understanding, and loving or practising the polite arts of painting, sculpture, or architecture, without any regard to pecuniary advantage. **1807** *Edin. Rev.* X. 461 It was not likely that an amateur.. should convict these astronomers of gross ignorance. **1827–39** DE QUINCEY *Murder* Wks. 1862 IV. 15 Not amateurs, gentlemen, as we are, but professional men. **1861** B. HEMYNG in Mayhew *London Lab.* Extra vol. (1862) 221/2 This class [of prostitutes] have been called the 'amateurs', to contradistinguish them from the professionals, who devote themselves to it entirely as a profession. **1882** *Boy's Own Paper* IV. 807 Our amateurs are improving, and the interval between them and the professionals is growing beautifully less.

b. Often prefixed (in apposition) to another designation, as ***amateur painter***, ***amateur gardener***.

1805 *Wynne Diaries* 8 May (1940) III. vii. 166 The Amateur performers were Mrs. W. Jerningham on the Harp, myself on the Piano. **1818** E. BLAQUIÈRE tr. *Panant's Narr. Res. Algiers* xiv. 266 There are, also, many amateur performers, but these always practice at home. **1822** DE QUINCEY *Confess.* 7 The number of *amateur* opium-eaters (as I may term them) was, at this time, immense. *a* **1855** C. BRONTË *Emma* in *Cornhill Mag.* (1860) Apr. 496 Any secret quest was to his taste; perhaps there was something of the amateur detective in him. **1863** BURTON *Bk. Hunter* 101 Amateur purchasers do not, in the long run, make a profit. **1866** GEO. ELIOT *Felix H.* 38 He's a sort of amateur gentleman. **1953** B. GORDON-CUMMING *Gentle Rain* 160 I've appointed myself amateur detective and am trying to discover a few things.

3. a. Hence *attrib.* almost *adj.* Done by amateurs. Cf. *amateur gardener* with *amateur gardening*.

a **1828** J. BERNARD *Retrosp. of Stage* (1830) I. iv. 78 A party of ladies and gentlemen, who were going to get up an amateur play at Poole. *Ibid.* II. iii. 73 This was.. the best piece of amateur acting I ever saw. **1848** MARIOTTI *Italy* II. iii. 84 Not merely a subject for amateur discussion. **1849** SIR J. STEPHEN *Eccles. Biogr.* (ed. 2) I. 442 The evening closed with amateur theatricals. **1862** HELPS *Organiz. Daily Life* 64 The getting-up of an amateur play. **1873** C. M. YONGE *Pillars of House* III. xxv. 42 He dabbled in everything that was *not* his proper occupation—concerts, amateur theatricals, periodical literature. **1882** *St. Nicholas* II. 717 Amateur Newspapers. **1882** *Boy's Own Paper* IV. 415 Amateur running records. **1892** *Pall Mall Gaz.* 27 Feb. 6/2 The judge: Was this an amateur company?—Yes; they took money out of it.—The judge: Oh, then, I don't call that amateur. **1962** 'S. NASH' *Killed by Scandal* i. 21 Young men who had wasted their time on amateur theatricals.

b. Used disparagingly. Cf. sense 2.

1814 M. EDGEWORTH *Patronage* I. vi. 183 Sir Amyas talked a great deal of amateur nonsense. **1903** KIPLING *Five Nations* 194 'Ow we're sugared about by the old men ('Eavy-sterned amateur old men!) That 'amper an' 'inder an' scold men. **1950** T. S. ELIOT *Cocktail Party* I. i. 37 *Peter.* I met her here, about a year ago. *Edward.* At one of Lavinia's amateur Thursdays? *Peter.* A Thursday. Why do you say amateur? *Edward.* Lavinia's attempts at starting a salon.

amateurish (æmə'tjʊərıʃ, 'æm-), *a.* [f. prec. + -ISH.] Such as characterizes an amateur rather than a professional worker; having the faults or deficiencies of amateur work.

1864 MISS BRADDON *H. Dunbar* III. i. 6 Fond of pictures, in a frivolous amateurish kind of way. **1865** DICKENS *Mut. Fr.* I. x. 72 He goes in a condescending amateurish way, into the city. **1868** *Pall Mall G.* 19 Sept. 12 As a work of literary art it is what painters call 'amateurish.' **1881** *Athenæum* No. 2810, 310/3 Written in a more amateurish style.

ama'teurishly, *adv.* [f. prec. + -LY².] In an amateurish manner.

1882 *Jrnl. Educ.* No. 155. 171 Those.. who dabbled amateurishly in useful work.

ama'teurishness. [f. as prec. + -NESS.] The quality of being amateurish; the appearance of being an amateur, and not a professional worker.

1865 *Pall Mall G.* 1 May 11 Making allowances for a certain amateurishness which time will cure. **1881** *Standard* 9 May, The amateurishness of the gentleman and the self-consciousness of the lady.

amateurism ('æmətjʊərız(ə)m). [f. AMATEUR + -ISM.] The characteristic practice of an amateur.

1868 *Tomahawk* 5 Dec., Amateurism is the curse of the nineteenth century. **1882** *Field* 7 Oct. 506 [Either] to keep within the bounds of honest amateurism, or turn professional.

amateurship ('æmətjʊəʃıp). [f. as prec. + -SHIP.] The quality or character of an amateur; **a.** of being fond of, having a liking for, something; **b.** of dabbling in matters for which one has no professional training, dilettantism.

1827 DE QUINCEY *On Murder* in *Blackw. Mag.* XXI. 209/2 Wearied with the frigid pleasures.. of mere amateurship, he had quitted England. **1834** —— *Caesars* Wks. 1862 IX. 106 The cool and cowardly spirit of amateurship in which the Roman.. sat looking down upon the bravest of men.. mangling each other for his recreation. **1834** MISS EDGEWORTH *Helen* II. 2 Horace [thinking] most of himself and his amateurship **1875** HAMERTON *Intell. Life* III. v. 100 Napoleon III indulged in.. a dangerous kind of amateurship. He had a taste for amateur generalship.

Amati (a'ma:ti). The name of a celebrated Italian family of violin makers of Cremona (*c* 1550–*c* 1700), applied *absol.* and *attrib.* to violins, violas, etc., of their manufacture.

1833 T. FARDELY tr. *Otto's Treat. Violin* II. 16 An Amati . . has a very beautiful *high* model, very fine wood and highly finished workmanship... The Amatis possess a *brilliant silvery* tone. **1885** G. B. SHAW *How to become Mus. Critic* (1960) 93 Take a Stradivarius or Amati fiddle. **1887** [see STRADIVARIUS]. **1945** 'E. CRISPIN' *Holy Disorders* ii. 19 Geoffrey felt . . like a man who while brandishing an Amati is suddenly confronted with a Strad. **1976** *Early Music* Oct. 473/3 From the 17th century the collection owns an anonymous Italian spinet from about 1600 . . : an Amati violin and a tromba marina that might, however, come from the 18th century. **1986** *Times* 28 May 19 His silver-toned Amati violin . . sounded crisply responsive to his touch.

†**a'mating**, *vbl. sb. Obs.* [f. AMATE *v.*[1] + -ING[1].] The action of dismaying, casting down, or quelling.

1607 HIERON *Wks.* I. 373 This doctrine is of great vse to the amating of this humor, which is the very height of pride.

†**a'mating**, *ppl. a. Obs.* [f. AMATE *v.*[1] + -ING[2].] Dismaying, daunting.

1600 FAIRFAX *Tasso* XIII. xxii. 238 Vpon their faces pale well might you note A thousand signes of hart amating feare.

†**a'mation.** *Obs.*—[0] [ad. L. *amātiōn-em*, n. of action f. *amāre* to love.] 'Wanton loue.' Cockeram 1623.

amatist, amatites, obs. forms of AMETHYST.

amative ('æmətɪv), *a.* [f. L. *amāt-* ppl. stem of *amā-re* to love + -IVE, as if ad. L. **amātīvus*.] Disposed to loving.

1636 EARL MANCHESTER *Contempl. Mort.* 33 [The soul's] amative vertues unite her to God. *a* **1678** WOODHEAD *Holy Living* (1688) 174 The affectionate and amatiue powers. **1850** KINGSLEY *Alt. Locke* ii. (1876) 32 Amative and combative organs small—a general want of healthy animalism.

amativeness ('æmətɪvnɪs). *Phren.* [f. prec. + -NESS.] Propensity to love, or sexual passions.

1815 SPURZHEIM *Physiogn. Syst.* Pref. 9 In the nomenclature of the propensities . . I have therefore adopted amativeness, like destructiveness. **1828** COMBE *Constit. Man* ii. §5 Amativeness is a feeling obviously necessary to the continuance of the species. **1869** SWINBURNE *Ess. & Stud.* (1875) 210 The Satyrs . . retain their natural amativeness.

amatol ('æmətɒl). [irreg. f. AM(MONIUM + *-tol-* in TRINITROTOLUENE.] A high explosive consisting of a mixture of trinitrotoluene (T.N.T.) and ammonium nitrate.

1918 E. COLVER *High Explosives* 252 In England these mixtures [trinitrotoluene and ammonium nitrate] are designated amatol. **1922** H. F. MOULTON *Life Ld. Moulton* vii. 191 Finally in February 1915 Lord Kitchener . . gave his casting vote on the side of big production, and A. 6 were told that they might proceed with the production of amatol.

†**ama'torculist.** *Obs.*—[0] [f. L. *amātōrcul-us* a pitiful lover, dim. of *amātor* + -IST.] 'A trifling sweetheart, a general lover.' Bailey 1731; whence in J.

amatorial (æmə'tɔərɪəl), *a.* [f. L. *amātōri-us* pertaining to a lover + -AL[1].]

1. Of or pertaining to a lover, or to love-making.

1603 J. DAVIES *Microcosmos* (1876) 66 The fourth and last by Venus governed, Is called the Fury amatoriall. **1774** T. WARTON *Eng. Poetry* (1840) I. Diss. ii. 118 Epigrams, amatorial verses, and poems. **1829** JESSE *Jrnl. Naturalist* 271 Various amatorial and caressing language. **1841** D'ISRAELI *Amen. Lit.* (1859) I. 308 The amatorial poet even designates the spots hallowed by his passion.

2. Epithet of the oblique muscles of the eyes, 'which give them a cast sideways, and assist in that particular look by some called *ogling*.' Chambers *Cycl.* 1751.

ama'torially (æmə'tɔərɪəlɪ), *adv.* [f. prec. + -LY[2].] In an amatorial manner.

a **1859** WORCESTER cites DARWIN.

ama'torian, *a.* ? *Obs. rare.* [f. L. *amātōri-us* + -AN.] Amatorial, amatory.

1779 JOHNSON *L.P., Smith,* Wks. 1787 II. 456 After the manner of Horace's Lusory or Amatorian Odes. [Not in Johnson's Dict.]

ama'torious, *a.* [f. as prec. + -OUS.] Relating to love, amatory. Also, inclined to love, amorous. Hence **ama'toriousness**.

1601 HOLLAND *Pliny* (1634) II. 40 This root had an amatorious propertie to win loue. **1603** —— *Plutarch's Mor.* 27 These and such like amatorious words. **1649** MILTON *Eikonokl.* 12 The vaine amatorious Poem of Sir Philip Sidneys *Arcadia*. **1746** FRANCIS tr. *Horace, Ep.* I. iii. 31 Sure to gain, for amatorious Lays, The Wreaths of Ivy, with unenvied Praise. **1887** *Longman's Mag.* Nov. 108 A fine balance between domestic and 'amatorious' interest on one hand, and romance on the other. **1893** *National Observer* 1 Apr. 489/1 Girls and boys . . jostle and jest at one another with a certain violence of amatoriousness. *Ibid.* 23 Sept. 482/1 The divagations of amatorious poets with fragile women. **1897** W. E. HENLEY in *Poetry R. Burns* IV. 249 It was natural and honourable in a young man of this lusty and amatorious habit to look round for a wife.

amatory ('æmətərɪ), *a.* and *sb.* [ad. L. *amātōri-us* of or pertaining to *amātor* a lover.]

A. *adj.* Of or pertaining to a lover, to love-making, or to sexual love generally.

1599 A. M. *Gabelhouer's Bk. Physic* 183/1 When any person hath eaten any amatorye fascinations. **1772** SIR W. JONES *Poems & Ess.* Pref. 11 The form of those little amatory poems. **1846** H. ELLIS *Elgin Marbles* II. 109 The urn contained the ashes of some amatory poet. **1858** THACKERAY *Virgin.* xxii. (1878) 175 To say that she confessed this amatory sentiment.

B. *sb.* A love-potion, a philtre. [L. *amatōrium*.]

1635 HEYWOOD *Hierarch.* IX. 615 Magicke vanities, Exorcismes, Incantations, Amatories. **1652** GAULE *Magastrom.* 268 Exorcisms, and incantations, and amatories. **1721** BAILEY, *Amatory*, a philter to cause love. [Not in JOHNSON.]

†**a'maugrey,** *prep. Obs.* [a. OFr. *à mal gré, à maugré*, more common in Fr. and Eng. without *a-*: see MAUGRE.] In spite of, despite.

c **1449** PECOCK *Repr.* 52 He schal consente in his witt . . wole he nyle he, amaugrey his heed.

‖**amaurosis** (æmɔː'rəʊsɪs). *Med.* [mod.L., a. Gr. ἀμαύρωσις, n. of action f. ἀμαυρό-ειν to darken, f. ἀμαυρ-ός dark, dim.] Partial or total loss of sight arising from disease of the optic nerve, usually without external change in the eye.

1657 *Phys. Dict., Amaurosis, gutta serena,* a disease in the eyes, viz. when the sight is gone, and no fault to be seen. **1704** *Lond. Gaz.* mmmmlix/4 Forerunner of an Amaurosis or Gutta Serena. **1843** CARLYLE *Past & Pres.* (1858) 81 Thick serene opacity, thicker than amaurosis. **1876** *Athenæum* 16 Dec. 806/3 An attack of amaurosis had suspended his labours.

amaurotic (æmɔː'rɒtɪk), *a. Med.* [f. prec., as if ad. Gr. *ἀμαυρωτικ-ός.] **a.** Affected with amaurosis.

1839 HOOPER *Med. Dict.* 78 There is moreover something very characteristic in the appearance of an amaurotic eye. **1839–47** TODD *Cycl. Anat. & Phys.* III. 722/1 After a time he became amaurotic and comatose.

b. Applied to an extreme type of hereditary imbecility, with the symptoms of amaurosis.

1896 B. SACHS in *N.Y. Med. Jrnl.* LXIII. 703/1 It will be better . . to find a clinical designation, and I would propose the name *amaurotic family idiocy*. **1900** *Pediatrics* X. 9 Sachs has suggested and applied the name 'amaurotic family idiocy' to the condition. In view of the blindness that invariably follows, the term 'amaurotic' is distinctive and correct. **1937** I. H. PAGE *Chem. of Brain* iii. 93 (*heading*) Tay-Sachs amaurotic familial idiocy.

†**a'may,** *v. Obs.* [a. ONFr. *amaier* = OFr. *esmaier* (whence also Eng. form *esmay*; cf. Pr. *esmaiar*, It. *smagare*), f. *es*:—L. *ex* out + *-magare*, according to Diez, ad. OHG. *magan, -en*, to be powerful or strong: see DISMAY.] *trans.* and *refl.* To dismay.

c **1380** *Sir Ferumb.* 485 þou ne miȝt noȝt me amaye. *c* **1425** *Seven Sages* (P.) 1536 Sire, ne amay the nouȝt. **1485** CAXTON *Chas. the Gt.* 142 Lordes, esmaye you nothyng.

†**amay'ed,** *ppl. a. Obs.* [f. prec. + -ED.] Dismayed.

c **1300** *K. Alis.* 1748 His knyghtis amayed buth. *c* **1374** CHAUCER *Troylus* IV. 641 Whereof ertow . . þanne amayed? **1393** GOWER *Conf.* I. 110 Wherein he wold ride amaied.

amaze (ə'meɪz), *v.* Also, 3–7 **amase**. [f. A- *pref.* 1 ? intensive + MAZE.]

†**1.** To put out of one's wits; to stun or stupefy, as by a blow on the head; to infatuate, craze. *Obs.*

c **1230** *Ancr. R.* 270 Nis he witterlich amased & ut of his witte. **1509** HAWES *Past. Pleas.* XXX. xii, It was no wonder that I was amased, My herte and minde she had so tane in cure. **1530** PALSGR. 421/1 You will amase hym with beatyng of hym thus aboute the heed. He was so amased with the stroke that he was redy to fall downe. **1553** UDALL *Roister Doister* IV. vii, To be amased with the smoke. **1642** ROGERS *Naaman* 44 The Lord . . smote him to the ground, and amazed him.

†**2.** To drive one to his wit's end, bewilder, perplex. *Obs.*

1563 *Homilies* II. ii. III. (1640) 70 They dull and amaze the understanding of the unlearned. **1603** DRAYTON *Heroic. Ep.* xi. 136 Let not the Beames, that Greatnesse doth reflect, Amaze thy Hopes. **1609** C. BUTLER *Fem. Mon.* (1634) 135 The Snow amazeth them, and, dazzling their eyes, causeth them presently to fall. **1642** H. MORE *Song of Soul* II. App. lxxix, That which well amazen may The wisest man and puzzle evermore.

†**3.** To overcome with sudden fear or panic; to fill with consternation, terrify, alarm. *Obs.*

1530 PALSGR. 421/1, I amase, I fray sodenly, *Jesgare*. **1603** DRAYTON *Odes* xvii. 27 Though they to one be ten, Be not amazed. **1653** WALTON *Angler* 109 The sight of any shadow amazes the fish. **1706** tr. *Dupin's Eccl. Hist. 16th C.* II. III. ii. 35 Besides it is the Duty of a Preacher to amaze a Sinner.

4. To overwhelm with wonder, to astound or greatly astonish.

1592 SHAKS. *Ven. & Ad.* 634 Crystal eyne, Whose full perfection all the world amazes. **1766** H. BROOKE *Fool of Quality* (1859) II. 9 You amaze me greatly—is this all the notice and care they take of such a treasure? **1824** DIBDIN *Libr. Comp.* 185 Would startle the sensitive, and even amaze the incredulous. **1849** MACAULAY *Hist. Eng.* II. 33 A young man, whose eccentric career was destined to amaze Europe.

†**5.** *refl.* To bewilder, puzzle, or drive oneself stupid. *Obs.*

1645 MILTON *Colast.* (1851) 357, I amaze me. **1653** WALTON *Angler* 98, I might easily amaze my self, and tire you in a relation of them. *a* **1678** MARVELL *Poems* Wks. 1776 III. 412 How vainly men themselves amaze, To win the palm, the oak, or bays.

6. *intr.* To be astounded or stupefied. *arch.*

1589 PUTTENHAM *Eng. Poesie* (1869) 240 It would so make the chast eares amaze. **1593** PEELE *Edw. I*, 79 Madam, amaze not. **1875** B. TAYLOR *Faust* I. i. II. 5 Eye is blinded, ear amazes. *Ibid.* IV. i. II. 236 Men amaze thereat.

amaze (ə'meɪz), *sb.* [f. the vb.] = AMAZEMENT. (*Amaze* and *a maze* were often identified.)

†**1.** Loss of one's wits, mental stupefaction, craze. *Obs.*

1430 LYDG. *Chron. Troy* I. v, To gape and loke as it were in a mase. **1586** LUPTON *Thousand Notable Things* (1675) 281 The gentleman was stricken in amaze, fell sick, and died.

†**2.** Bewilderment, mental confusion. *Obs.*

1593–1622 R. HAWKINS *Voy. S. Sea* 52 Heaving the lead in fourteene fathoms, wee had ground, which put us all into a maze. **1616** *Trav. Eng. Pilgr.* in *Harl. Misc.* I. 351, I was in amaze, and knew not what to do. **1671** MILTON *P.R.* II. 38 Soon our joy is turn'd Into perplexity and new amaze. **1754** MRS. DELANY *Lett.* 278 Our god-daughter is pretty well, still in a whirl and an amaze.

†**3.** Loss of presence of mind through terror, panic. *Obs.*

1601 WEEVER *Mirr. Martyrs* E viij, What forme most terrour and amaze will show. **1665** MANLEY *Grotius's L. Countr. Wars* 811 Thus once more brought into an amaze, they fled absolutely. *a* **1703** POMFRET *Poet. Wks.* (1833) 97 Strike the affrighted nations with a wild amaze. **1718** POPE *Iliad* v. 35 Struck with amaze and shame, the Trojan crew Or slain or fled, the sons of Dares view. **1766** GOLDSMITH *Vic. Wakef.* xi. (1857) 63 The whole rout was in amaze.

4. Extreme astonishment, wonder. (Now chiefly poetical, AMAZEMENT being usual in prose.)

1579 LYLY *Euphues* (1868) 251 A Cathedrall Church, the very Maiestie whereoff, stroke them into a maze. **1588** SHAKS. *L.L.L.* II. 246 His faces owne margent did coate such amazes, That all eyes saw his eies inchanted with gazes. **1647** MAY *Hist. Parl.* III. v. 100 An amaze, that the besieged should continue in such an height of resolution. **1713** ADDISON *Cato* IV. iii. 58 With pleasure and amaze, I stand transported! **1741** RICHARDSON *Pamela* I. 64 She stood all in Amaze, and look'd at me from Top to Toe. **1880** HOWELLS *Undisc. Country* v. 85 He stared at Ford in even more amaze than anger.

amazed (ə'meɪzd), *ppl. a.* [f. AMAZE *v.* + -ED.]

†**1.** Driven stupid; stunned or stupefied, as by a blow; out of one's wits. *Obs.*

c **1230** *Ancr. R.* 284 Nai, seið sum amased þing. **1393** GOWER *Conf.* II. 21, I wot neuer, what I am . . But muse as he, that were amased. **1447** BOKENHAM *Lyvys of Seyntys* 14 As a man amasyd he sodeynly dede abreyde. **1551** TURNER *Herbal* (1568) 9 Leopardes bayne layd to a scorpione maketh hym vtterly amased and num. **1586** T. B. *La Primaudaye's Fr. Acad.* 491 She strake hir head so hard against the wall, that she fell downe amazed. *a* **1604** HANMER *Chron. Irel.* (1633) 20 The other gave Starcuterus such a blow, that he stood a great while amazed. **1683** LADY RUSSELL *Lett.* I. v. 14 A woman amazed with grief. **1704** POPE *Windsor For.* 109 Sudden they seize th' amaz'd defenceless prize.

†**2.** Bewildered, confounded, confused, perplexed. Of things: Thrown into confusion. *Obs.*

c **1450** *Merlin* xiii. 199 Thei were so a-masid that thei wiste not what to do. **1513** MORE *Rich. III* (1641) 249 The poore, amased, and desolate commons of this Realme. **1598** YONG *Diana* 215 One, that is amazed in minde, Not knowing whether he doth dreame or no. **1608** *Yorksh. Trag.* I. iv. 207 All his studies amazed. **1651** JER. TAYLOR *Serm.* I. xxvii. 343 The contradiction is multiplyed and the labyrinths more amazed.

†**3.** Struck with sudden terror; terror-stricken, terrified, alarmed. *Obs.*

c **1386** CHAUCER *Chan. Yem. Prol. & T.* 383 Be ye no thyng amased [*v.r.* amazed, a-mased, amasud]. **1430** LYDG. *Chron. Troy* III. xxvii, To the kinge she ran So amased in her mortall wo. **1611** BIBLE *Judg.* xx. 41 When the men of Israel turned againe, the men of Beniamin were amased. **1640** FULLER *Abel Rediv., Luther* (1867) I. 67 Amazed not so much for her own as for her children's preservation.

4. Lost in wonder or astonishment.

1583 STANYHURST *Æneis* I. (Arb.) 32 With woonder amazed. **1590** SHAKS. *Mids. N.* III. ii. 220, I am amazed at your passionate words. **1659** HAMMOND *On Ps.* Pref. 16 Admiring and glorifying God as he stands amazed. **1782** COWPER *J. Gilpin* xli, The callender, amazed to see His neighbour in such trim. **1855** MAURY *Phys. Geog. Sea* §741 We are utterly amazed at the offices which have been performed . . by the animalcula.

amazedly (ə'meɪzɪdlɪ), *adv.* [f. prec. + -LY[2].] In amazed manner; with stupidity, bewilderment, consternation (*obs.*); with astonishment, or wonder.

1590 SHAKS. *Mids. N.* IV. i. 153 My Lord, I shall reply amazedly, Halfe sleepe, halfe waking. **1605** —— *Macb.* IV. i. 126 Why Stands Macbeth thus amazedly? **1640** BP. HALL *Chr. Moder.* 17/1 Looked somewhat amazedly upon the mass of plate and treasure. **1879** MISS BRADDON *Vixen* III. 29 To stare amazedly at the passing carriage.

amazedness (ə'meɪzɪdnɪs). [f. as prec. + -NESS.] The state or quality of being amazed;

literally, loss of one's wits or of self-possession from any cause.

†**1.** The state of being out of one's wits; infatuation, stupefaction. *Obs.*

1576 T. NEWTON tr. *Lemnie's Touchst. Complex.* (1633) 112 Of it springeth madnesse, losse of right wits, amazednesse, raving dotage. **1581** GOSSON *Playes Confut.* (1869) 202 Glutte..with the clubbe of amasednesse strikes such a pegge into the heade of Life, that he falles downe for dead vpon the Stage.

†**2.** Loss of presence of mind, bewilderment, confusion. *Obs.*

1611 SPEED *Hist. Gt. Brit.* IX. iv. (1632) 475 Through amazednesse not knowing how to shift. **1624** CAPT. SMITH *Virginia* v. 174 Extreme ioy, euen almost to amazednesse. **1751** CHAMBERS *Cycl.* s.v. *Amble*, Checking him in the cheeks when in a gallop; and thus putting him into an amazednesse, between gallop and trot.

†**3.** Loss of self-possession through fear; consternation, panic. *Obs.*

1557 BARCLAY *Jugurtha* (Paynell) 63 b, Thinhabitantes expelled their amasednes remembryng themselfe. **1587** FLEMING *Contn. Holinshed* III. 311/1 A sudden earthquake ..caused such an amazednesse among the people as was wooonderfull for the time. **1598** SHAKS. *Merry W.* IV. iv. 55 Vpon their sight We two, in great amazednesse will flye. **1641** PRYNNE *Antipathie* 15 By reason of his trembling and fearful amazednessé.

4. Overwhelming astonishment.

1607 HIERON *Wks.* I. 349 We may well with a kind of astonishment and amazednesse admire it. **1863** KINGLAKE *Crimea* (1877) II. xxiii. 357 Before their amazedness ceased, they found themselves—marshalled and governed.

†**a'mazeful**, *a. Obs.* [f. AMAZE *sb.* + -FUL.]

1. *actively*, Causing amazement; driving one out of his wits; distracting.

1530 PALSGR. 305/1 Amasefull, *effraieux.* **1581** SIDNEY *Astr. & Stella* xcvi. 9 Amazefull solitarinesse.

2. *passively*, Struck with amazement; distracted, infatuated, stupefied.

1598 SYLVESTER *Du Bartas* II. iv. II. (1641) 216/2 The Queen, nigh sunk in an amazeful swoon. **1600** CHAPMAN *Iliad* XVII. 658 Who at length Put all the youth of Greece besides in most amazeful rout.

amazement (ə'meɪzmənt). [f. AMAZE *v.* + -MENT. (An early instance of this suffix added to a Teutonic vb.)] *orig.* Loss of one's wits or of self-possession through any cause whatever.

†**1.** The condition of being mentally paralyzed, mental stupefaction, frenzy. *Obs.*

1606 SHAKS. *Tr. & Cr.* v. iii. 85 Behold, destraction, frenzie, and amazement, Like witlesse Antickes, one another meete. **1671** MILTON *P.R.* IV. 561 Satan, smitten with amazement, fell. **1746** W. COLLINS *Ode to Fear* Wks. 1771, 45 The Maids and Matrons, on her awful Voice, Silent and pale, in wild amazement hung.

†**2.** Loss of presence of mind; bewilderment, perplexity, distraction (due to doubt as to what to do). *Obs.*

1595 SHAKS. *John* v. i. 35 Wilde amazement hurries up & downe The little number of your doubtfull friends. **1641** BAKER *Chron.* (1679) 333/1 This answer was but to hold her in amazement, while some mischief was practising against her. **1690** J. NORRIS *Beatitudes* (1694) I. 50 A thing that can hardly be thought of without Confusion and Amazement. **1722** DE FOE *Plague* (1756) 198 This Amazement of the Magistrates proceeded rather from want of being able to apply any Means successfully, than from any Unwillingness.

†**3.** Overwhelming fear or apprehension, consternation, alarm. *Obs.*

1596 SPENSER *F.Q.* (L.) Adding new Fear to his first amazement. **1611** BIBLE *1 Pet.* iii. 6 Not afraid with any amazement [WYCLIF, *Rhem.* perturbation; TINDALE, shadow; CRANMER, *Genev.* terror]. **1641** MILTON *Ch. Govt.* vii. (1851) 132 To cast amazements and panick terrors into the hearts of weaker Christians. **1756** BURKE *Subl. & B.* Wks. I. 159 Do not the French *étonnement* and the English astonishment and amazement point out as clearly the kindred emotions which attend fear and wonder?

4. Overwhelming wonder, whether due to mere surprise or to admiration.

1602 SHAKS. *Haml.* III. ii. 339 Your behauior hath stroke her into amazement, and admiration. **1611** BIBLE *Acts* iii. 10 They were filled with wonder and amazement at that which had happened vnto him. **1624** LD. KENSINGTON in Ellis *Orig. Lett.* II. 302 III. 178 But the amasment extraordinary to finde her..the sweetest creature in France. *a* **1742** BENTLEY *Serm.* (L.) To raise unprofitable amazement. **1866** G. MACDONALD *Ann. Q. Neighb.* xii. (1878) 237, I saw to my amazement..Miss Oldcastle struggling against the wind.

†**amazia** (ə'meɪzɪə). *Med.* [mod.L., repr. a possible Gr. *ἀμαζία, n. of state f. ἀ priv. + μαζος breast, pap.] Non-development of the breasts in a female, with consequent want of provision for suckling offspring.

1874 [See AGALACTIA.]

amazing (ə'meɪzɪŋ), *vbl. sb.* [f. AMAZE *v.* + -ING[1].] The action of causing amazement. (Now only gerundial.)

1530 PALSGR. 194/1 Amasynge, *stupefaction.* **1580** HOLLYBAND *Treas. Fr. Tong.*, *Effray*, or *effroy*, feare, astonying, abashing, amasing. **1597** T. MORLEY *Introd. Mus.* 156 To the amasing of the young singer. *a* **1617** HIERON *Wks.* I. 16 To the appalling and amasing of a Christian. **1674** COLES, An Amazing, *Stupefactio, consternatio. Mod.* After so amazing friends and foes.

amazing (ə'meɪzɪŋ), *ppl. a.* [f. as prec. + -ING[2].]

†**1.** Causing distraction, consternation, confusion, dismay; stupefying, terrifying, dreadful. *Obs.*

1593 SHAKS. *Rich. II*, I. iii. 81 Let thy blowes..Fall like amazing thunder on the Caske Of thy amaz'd, pernicious enemy. **1659** HAMMOND *On Ps.* cvii. 23–30 They meet with terrible amazing tempests. **1705** STANHOPE *Paraphr.* III. 542 The amazing Prospects of an angry God and a gaping Hell. **1781** GIBBON *Decl. & Fall* III. 93 A dreadful and amazing prodigy.

2. Astounding, astonishing, wonderful, great beyond expectation.

1704 J. TRAPP *Abra-Mulé* v. i. 1981 Such amazing Generosity Exceeds Belief. **1717** LADY M. MONTAGUE *Lett.* II. xlvi. 37 To turn round with an amazing swiftness. **1769** BURKE *State Nat.* Wks. II. 85 The author's amazing assertion. **1822** IMISON *Sc. & Art* I. 4 To observe to what an amazing extent the actual division of matter may be carried. **1849** MACAULAY *Hist. Eng.* I. 335 Great as has been the change in the rural life of England since the Revolution, the change..in the cities is still more amazing.

3. quasi-*adv.* Wonderfully, astonishingly.

1824 W. IRVING *T. Trav.* I. 54 All of whom laughed, and took it in amazing good part.

a'mazingly (ə'meɪzɪŋlɪ), *adv.* [f. prec. + -LY[2].] In an amazing manner. Now often hyperbolically in colloquial use for: Exceedingly, very.

1673 *Ladies Call.* I. i. § 15 There is no noise on this side hell can be more amazingly odious. **1744** H. WALPOLE *Lett. to H. Mann* 98 (1834) I. 332 My father has exerted himself most amazingly. **1794** SULLIVAN *View Nat.* II. 178 The thigh bones of some amazingly large animal. **1801** MISS EDGEWORTH *Good Fr. Gov.* (1852) 99 She speaks English amazingly well for a Frenchwoman. **1873** BLACK *Pr. Thule* viii. 121 He is an amazingly clever fellow.

amazingness (ə'meɪzɪŋnɪs). [f. AMAZING *ppl. a.* + -NESS.] The state or condition of being amazing.

1860 PUSEY *Min. Proph.* 562/1 The surpassing amazingness of it [*sc.* God's goodness] in the work of our redemption.

Amazon ('æməzən). Also 5 **Amysone**, 7 **Amason.** Pl. **Amazons**; also 4–7 **Amazones.** In 6–7 often accented *a'mãzon.* [a. L. *Amazon*, a. Gr. Ἀμαζών, -όνα; explained by the Greeks from ἀ priv. + μαζ-ός a breast (in connexion with the fable that they destroyed the right breast so as not to interfere with the use of the bow), but prob. pop. etym. of an unknown foreign word.]

1. *pl.* A race of female warriors alleged by Herodotus, etc. to exist in Scythia.

1398 TREVISA *Barth. De P.R.* xv. xii. (1495) 492 They were callyd Amazones, that is vnderstonde wythout breste. *c* **1400** *Destr. Troy* XXVII. 10804 Of Amysones auntrus atlet the qwene. **1653** COGAN *Diod. Sic.* 100 The Amazones inhabited..near to the river of Thermodon. **1753** CHAMBERS *Cycl. Suppl.* s.v., The existence of the Amazons was called in question by Strabo. **1847** TENNYSON *Princess* II. 110 Glanc'd at the legendary Amazon As emblematic of a nobler age.

2. Hence, A female warrior. *lit.* and *fig.*

1578 T. N. tr. *Conq. W. Ind.* 14 There were Amazons women of warre, in certaine Ilandes. **1593** SHAKS. *3 Hen. VI*, IV. i. 106 Belike she minds to play the Amazon. **1702** *Lond. Gaz.* mmmdcccxl/2 About 200 Virgins in two Companies richly attired, many of them like Amazons, with Bows and Arrows. **1777** ROBERTSON *Amer.* (1783) III. 86 An opinion that..Amazons were to be found in this part of the New World. **1866** B. TAYLOR *Continents* 394 When Europe rose a stately Amazon.

3. *transf.* A very strong, tall, or masculine woman.

1758 JOHNSON *Idler* No. 6 ¶2, I am far from wishing..the amazon..any diminution..of fame. **1767** FORDYCE *Serm. Yng. Wom.* I. iii. 105 To the men an Amazon never fails to be forbidding. **1853** KANE *Grinnell Exp.* xlvi. (1856) 425 Extremes meet in the Esquimaux of Greenland and Amazons of Paris.

†**4.** The queen in chess. *Obs.*

1656 F. BEALE *Biochimo's Chesse-play* 2 The Queen or Amazon is placed in the fourth house from the corner of the field by the side of her King, and alwayes in her owne colour.

5. *fig.* in reference to the sexual habits of the Amazons.

1860 *Vac. Tour.* 137 These hinds are amazons, not vestals.

6. = AMAZON-ANT.

1880 HUNTER in *Cassell's Dict.* s.v., These when hatched become a kind of pariah caste in the habitation of the Amazons.

7. *Comb.*, as ***Amazon-dress***, ***Amazon-like.*** Also AMAZON-ANT, -STONE, q.v.

1580 SIDNEY *Arcad.* (1622) 142 Her sword, which (Amazon-like) she euer ware about her. **1599** STORER *Wolsey* (1826) 28 Her handmaids, in Amazon-like attire. *c* **1630** DRUMM. OF HAWTH. *Poems* Wks. 1711, 50/1 A country maid Amazone like did ride. **1711** SHAFTESB. *Charac.* (1737) II. 252 Whom you admire..in her amazon-dress, with a free manly air becoming her.

Amazon-ant. [AMAZON 2.] A species of red ant, of which the neuters capture and enslave the young of other species; sometimes applied to the neuters alone.

1824 GRIFFITH *Cuvier* XV. 501 Huber is erroneous in supposing that the amazon ants have a sting. **1868** WOOD *Homes without Hands* xxiv. 459 The Ant which employs forced labour is called the Amazon Ant, and is tolerably common on the Continent.

Amazonian (æmə'zəʊnɪən), *a.* and *sb.* [f. L. *amazoni-us* + -AN.] **A.** *adj.*

1. Of, pertaining to, resembling, or befitting the Amazons or an Amazon; warlike, or masculine, as a woman.

1594 *2nd Pt. Contention* (1843) 131 To triumph like an Amazonian trull Vpon his woes. **1609** C. BUTLER *Fem. Mon.* (1634) 64 These Amazonian dames begin to wax weary of their mates. **1711** STEELE *Spect.* No. 104 ¶3 This Amazonian Hunting-Habit for Ladies. **1837** W. HOWITT *Rur. Life* III. vi. (1862) 285 His amazonian lady, half the head taller than himself. **1844** *Blackw. Mag.* LVI. 214 Caps were dragged off, and nails shown with amazonian spirit.

2. Of the river Amazon (so called from the female warriors there seen by the Spaniards), or its basin.

1863 BATES *Nat. on Amazons* i. 10 The only Amazonian species. **1875** *Blackie's Pop. Encycl.* 133/1 The Amazonian water system.

B. *sb.* An Amazon (fabulous).

a **1704** T. BROWN *Drunkenness* Wks. 1730 I. 37 His Hydra, and Amazonians, and the hellish Cerberus.

Amazonic (æmə'zɒnɪk), *a.* Also **amazonic.** [f. L. *Amāzonic-us* (see AMAZONICAL *a.*).] = AMAZONIAN A. 1.

1889 *Cornhill Mag.* Aug. 179 Amazonic war, the war of female relatives armed to the teeth. **1920** D. H. LAWRENCE *Lost Girl* iii. 45 Her curious Amazonic power left her again. **1927** *Times* 13 Feb. 9 Miss Davies was neither a scholar nor a student. Nor was there anything amazonic about her, as there undoubtedly was about her friend, George Eliot.

†**Ama'zonical**, *a. Obs. rare*[−1]. [f. L. *Amāzonic-us* (a. Gr. ἀμαζονικ-ός) + -AL[1].] = AMAZONIAN.

1582 STANYHURST *Æneid* I. (Arb.) 33 Theare wear Amazonical wommen with targat, an haulfmoone Likning.

Amazonism ('æməzəˌnɪz(ə)m). [f. AMAZON + -ISM.] Amazonian character or condition; a condition in which women have the supremacy. Also **Ama'zonianism.**

1873 E. J. M. COLLINS *Transmigr.* II. xv. 247 A world in which women were analytical..would result in absolute Amazonism. **1903** L. F. WARD *Pure Sociol.* xiv. 338 It might be supposed that woman would prove the dominant sex in primitive hordes... The..most striking form of evidence pointing this way consists in a class of facts that may be roughly grouped under the general head of *amazonism.* **1909** W. J. LOCKE *Septimus* ii, She had done with men... In that she prided herself on her Amazonianism.

Amazonite ('æməzənaɪt). [f. AMAZON + -ITE.]

†**1.** One of the race of Amazons. *Obs.*

1601 HOLLAND *Pliny* (1634) I. 108 Smyrna, built by an Amazonite. **1630** BRATHWAIT *Eng. Gentl.* 94 The Amazonites being women expert above all people of the world in shooting.

2. *Min.* = AMAZON-STONE.

'Amazon-stone. *Min.* [named from river *Amazon.*] A mineral; a 'bright verdigris-green and cleavable' variety of orthoclase, worn as an amulet by the Indians of the Rio Negro.

1836 MACGILLIVRAY tr. *Humboldt's Trav.* xviii. 266 Those green pebbles known by the name of Amazon-stones and worn as amulets. **1862** RAWLINSON *Anc. Mon.* I. vi. 474 They are cut upon serpentine, amazon-stone, and Lapis-lazuli.

ambage ('æmbɪdʒ). Pl. **ambages** ('æmbɪdʒɪz, or as L. æm'beɪdʒiːz). [a. 14th c. Fr. *ambages*, a. L. *ambāges* circuits, circumlocutions, f. *amb-* about + *ag-ĕre* to drive. Thoroughly naturalized in 16th c. as *'ambages*, with sing. *'ambage* (as in Fr.) in sense I, but owing to the coincidence of the spelling with the original L., there has been a growing tendency to look upon it as merely L., and to use it accordingly, thus restricting the sense and altering the pronunciation.]

I. Of language (from Fr.; pron. *'ambages*; with *sing.*) Roundabout or indirect modes of speech.

1. For deceit: Equivocation, quibbles, ambiguities. *Obs.* or *arch.*

c **1374** CHAUCER *Troylus* v. 897 If Calkas lede us with ambages, That is to seyn, with dowble wordes slye. **1553–87** FOXE *A. & M.* (1596) 666/1 Without ambages and sophistication of wordes. **1669** GALE *Crt. Gentiles* I. III. x. 108 An Ambages of words is very deceitful. *a* **1733** NORTH *Exam.* I. ii. ¶26. 43 Factious polemic Tricks, Ambages, and treacherous Counsels. **1857** SIR F. PALGRAVE *Norm. & Eng.* II. 415 He commenced by a few politic ambages, or—to speak more plainly—lies.

†**2.** For concealment: Dark or obscure language, ambiguity. *Obs.*

1520 WHITTINTON *Vulgaria* (1527) 2 Tendre wyttes with suche derke ambage be made dull. **1664** H. MORE *Myst. Iniq.* 211 That Prophecies are delivered in obscure Ambages. **1713** BERKELEY *Hylas & Phil.* iii, To use some ambages, and ways of speech not common.

†**3.** For delay: Circumlocutions, beating about the bush. *Obs.* exc. as a case of II. 6.

1567 DRANT *Horace Ep.* vii. D vj, For to make the ambage shorte, And not to draw it on. **1568** C. WATSON *Polybius* To Reader, With any tedious ambage or painted preamble. **1607** DEKKER *Wh. Babylon* 240 Vmh: ya're ful of Ambage: I answere as my spirits leade me, thus. **1678** MRS. BEHN *Sir P. Fancy* v. i. 303 Without more ambages, Sir, I have considered your former desires, and have consented to marry him.

†**4.** *Rhet.* (in *sing.*) Periphrasis. *Obs.*

1589 PUTTENHAM *Eng. Poesie* (1869) 203 Periphrasis, or the Figure of ambage. *Ibid.* 24 Tedious ambage and long periods.

II. Of paths, ways. [A later adoption from L., and in recent times as a L. word *ambāges*.]

5. Circuits, windings, circuitous paths. *arch.*

1615 SANDYS *Trav.* 99 [The river] running from South to North (besides in ambages) aboue one and forty degrees. **1677** GREW *Anat. Plants* IV. III. vii. §2 (1682) 191 The Elongation of the seed-vessels, sometimes directly, as in Plums and Nuts, and sometimes by several Ambages before they shoot into the Seeds, as in Tulip. **1796** PEGGE *Anonym.* (1809) 373 You will find it, through the windings and ambages, eight, or perhaps nine miles. **1823** LAMB *Elia* Ser. II. xxiv. (1865) 409 After hunting and winding through all the possible ambages of similar sounds.

6. *fig.* Circuitous, indirect, or roundabout ways or proceedings; delaying practices.

1546 LANGLEY *Polyd Verg.* IV. iv. 87 b, When a Byshop was consecrated ther was used no other rytes or ambages. **1605** BACON *Adv. Learn.* II. 33 He shall, by Ambages of diets, bathings, anointings, etc. prolong life. **1657** AUSTEN *Fruit Trees* I. 38 Meat and drink work upon the spirits by ambages and length of time. **1726** AYLIFFE *Parergon* 65 The Ambages of Law Suits.

†**7.** Dark, secret, or mysterious ways of action. *Obs.* (Cf. Livy I. 56.)

a **1626** BACON *Theol. Wks.* (1838) I. 337 The ways and ambages of God. **1704** SWIFT *T. Tub* Wks. 1768, 141 The other cost me so many strains and traps and ambages to introduce. *a* **1797** H. WALPOLE *George II* (1847) II. iv, He would not enter into all the ambages of the *Corps Diplomatique*.

†**am'bagical**, *a. Obs. rare*$^{-1}$. [f. prec. + -IC + -AL[1].] = AMBAGIOUS.

1652 GAULE *Magastrom.* 142 To trouble his own answer, and confound his own sentence, through an ambagicall circumlocution of words and termes.

am'baginous, *a. rare.* [f. L. *ambāgin-em* = AMBAGES + -OUS.] = AMBAGIOUS.

a **1859** in WORCESTER.

ambagiosity (æmbeɪdʒɪ'ɒsɪtɪ). *rare*$^{-1}$. [f. L. *ambāgiōs-us* (see next) + -ITY.] Circuitousness.

1824 SOUTHEY *Lett.* (1856) III. 419 Without any delay, let, hindrance, impediment, ambagiosity, circumlocution, or needless, superfluous and unnecessary roundabout forms of speech.

ambagious (æm'beɪdʒəs), *a.* [ad. Fr. *ambagieux*, ad. L. *ambāgiōs-us*: see AMBAGE and -OUS.] Full of ambages: **a.** Circumlocutory, roundabout; **b.** Winding, circuitous.

1656 BLOUNT *Glossogr.*, *Ambagious*, full of idle circumstances of speech, or of deceitful words. **1678** H. MORE *Annot. Glanvill's Sadducismus* I. (1726) 60 All those ambagious Windings and Meanders of feigned Abstraction. **1682** —— *Annot. Glanvill's Lux Orient.* 176 A more operose and ambagious inference. **1731** BAILEY, *Ambagious*, full of far-fetch'd speeches. **1870** SMITH *Syn. & Antonyms*, *Devious.. Syn.* Tortuous, ambagious, roundabout.

am'bagiously, *adv. rare.* [f. prec. + -LY[2].] In a roundabout manner; circuitously, indirectly.

1678 CUDWORTH *Intell. Syst.* I. iii. xxxvii. 157 The medicinal art..doth its work ambagiously, by the use of such medicaments as do but conduce..to help that which is nature indeed.

am'bagiousness. *rare.* [f. as prec. + -NESS.] The quality of being circuitous or circumlocutory.

1870 SMITH *Syn. & Antonyms, Anfractuosity.. Syn.* Ambagiousness, angularity, tortuousness.

†**am'bagitory**, *a. Obs. rare.* [f. L. *ambāges* (see AMBAGE) by form-assoc. with *dilatory*, *transitory*, etc., but not etymologically defensible.] Circumlocutory, ambagious.

1814 SCOTT *Wav.* xxiv, Partaking of what scholars call the periphrastic and ambagitory, and the vulgar the circumbendibus. **1826** —— *Woodst.* I. v. 115 All the ambagitory expressions they made use of.

ambara's, obs. form of EMBARRAS.

1676 ETHEREDGE *Marr. à la Mode* III. ii. (1684) 34 An Ambara's of chairs and couches at your Door.

ambari (æm'bɑːrɪ). Also -ee. [Urdu *ambārā*, *ambārī*.] The fibre of an Indian plant, *Hibiscus cannabinus*, used for making ropes and coarse cloth; brown Indian hemp (also ***ambari hemp***); the plant itself.

1855 in *Imp. Dict.* Suppl. **1873** H. DRURY *Useful Plants of India* (ed. 2) 243 Hibiscus cannabinus..Ambaree... The bark of this species is full of strong fibres which the inhabitants of the Malabar coast prepare and make into cordage. **1887** MOLONEY *Forestry W. Afr.* 282 The plant is largely grown in Western India, both as a pot-herb and for its fibre, known as 'Ambari', which much resembles jute. **1910** *Encycl. Brit.* XIII. 263/1 Deccan or Ambari hemp,.. an Indian and East Indian malvaceous plant.

†**ambassade, embassade** ('æm-, 'ɛmbəseɪd). *Obs.* or *arch.* Forms: 5 **ambaxade**, 5–9 **ambassade**; also 5 **am'bassiad(e**, 5–6 **-'bassad**, 6 **-'bassed**, **-'basset**; and with *e-* as **embassade**, **enbassade**, etc. [a. Fr. *ambassade*, 15th c. *ambaxade*, ad. OSp. *ambaxada* (mod. *em-*), cogn. w. Pr. *ambaissada*, It. *ambasciata*, OFr. *ambassée*, (superseded by this form in -ADE: see AMBASSY):—L. **ambactiāta* (found in med.L. as *ambaxiāta*, *-asciāta*, *-assiāta*, *-asiāta*), ppl. derivative of **ambactiāre* to go on a mission, f. *ambactia*, *ambaxia* (in Salic and Burgundian Laws) 'charge, office, employment,' n. of office f. *ambactus* a servant (? vassal, retainer). The OFr. form *ambassée* was also adopted in Eng. as AMBASSY, EMBASSY; as was also the med.L. as AMBASSIATE, etc., the forms of which appear to have been quite mixed up with those of the present word, leading to the pronunciation in 5–6 *am'bassiade*, *am'bassade*, and the spellings in *-ad*, *-ed*, *-et*. But Shakspere and subseq. writers have *amba'ssade* or *'ambassade*.

The origin and meaning of *ambactus* have given rise to much discussion. According to Festus '*Ambactus* apud Ennium lingua Gallica *servus* appellatur'; and Caesar (*B.G.* VI. 15) applies it to the vassals or retainers of a Gallic chief. Hence Zeuss and Glück identify it with Welsh *amaeth*, *ammaeth*, (for **ambaeth*) 'husbandman, tiller of the ground,' perh. orig. 'tenant, retainer,' or even 'goer about, footman.' Grimm finds the origin in OHG. *ambaht*, Goth. *andbahts* servant, retainer, OE. *ambeht*, ON. *ambótt* (cf. AMBOHT), variously explained as f. *and* against, towards + *bak* BACK, or **bah* to do, or **baht* = Skr. *bhakta* devoted, and assumed to have been adopted in Gallic, or erroneously taken as Gallic by Festus. But the majority of etymologists consider the Teut. word to be an adaptation or refashioning of the Lat. or original Celtic. For the latter, Mahn (*Etym. Unt.* 145) has also proposed *ambi(amb-*, *amm-*, *am-*) about + Breton *aketuz*, *akeduz* 'busy,' hence 'one employed about (his lord).']

1. The mission or function of an ambassador.

c **1450** in *3rd Rep. Comm. Hist. MSS.* (1872) 280/1 Whan he was at Toures in ambassiad. **1489** CAXTON *Faytes of Armes* II. i. 91 Dyde sende..as by manere of ambaxade. **1494** FABYAN VI. clxxxi. 179 He sent hym in ambassade. **1535** *Facsimiles Nat. MSS.* II, Monsieur de Brion, Admyral of Fraunce, nowe here in Ambassiade. **1549** EDWARD VI. *Rem.* 239 Sir Philip Hobbey, lately cum from his ambassad in Flaundres. **1602** CAREW *Cornwall* 60 a, Sent by him also in diuers Ambassades. **1727** WODROW *Corr.* III. 321 A sort of ambassade from the Kirk to the King. **1843** LYTTON *Last of Bar.* III. v. 172 Power to resign the ambassade and trust.

2. A body of persons (or a single person) sent on a mission, or as a deputation, to or from a sovereign; an ambassador and his suite.

c **1450** in *3rd Rep. Comm. Hist. MSS.* (1872) 280/1 As large power as any was gevyn to any ambassad. **1489** CAXTON *Faytes of Armes* I. vii. 17 An ambassade cam to hym. **1523** LD. BERNERS *Froissart* I. xxvi. 37 The Kyng of Ingland sent his ambassad to the kyng of Scottis. **1576** GASCOIGNE *Compl. Phil.* xvi, He shewde the cause, which thither then Did his ambassade bring. **1709** STRYPE *Ann. Ref.* I. xl. 455 It was thought convenient to stay the ambassade, and to condole only.

β. **1502** ARNOLD *Chron.* (1811) 282 Now was sent an other enbassade to Caleis. **1580** LYLY *Euphues* (Arb.) 459 Ye Kings of Assiria, who aunswere Embassades by messengers.

3. The message borne by an ambassador.

1560 J. DAUS *Sleidane's Comm.* 139 a, He came to Rome, declareth his Ambassade. **1589** BP. COOPER *Admon.* 224 The state of an ambassade or message.

ambassador, embassador (æm-, əm'bæsədə(r)). Forms: *α.* 4–6 **ambassiatour**, 5 **-dour**, **ambaxadour**, **-tour(e**, **-tor**, **ambassatour**, **-tor**, 5–8 **-dour**, 6–9 **-dor**. *β.* 4–5 **embassatour**, **-etour**, **-adour**, **embasitour**, 5 **enbassatour**, **-itour**, **-ytour**, **enbasetore**, 5–6 **embassitour(e**, 6 **-iator**, **-eatour(e**, **-ytor**, **-ader**, **enbassadoure**, 6–7 **embassadour**, **-ore**, 6–9 **embassador**. *γ.* 5 **imbassadore**, **inbassetour**, 5–6 **imbassator**, 6 **-etor**, **-itor**, **-otor**, **-ador**, **imbasodor**. [The actual *ambassador*, *-our*, is a. Fr. *ambassadeur* (15th c. also *ambaxadeur*), ad. OSp. *ambaxador* (now *emb-*) and Pr. *ambassador*, cogn. w. It. *ambasciatore*, *-dore*, and OFr. (superseded by this adopted form) *ambasseur* (*ambaseor*, *-asseor*, *-axeur*, etc.). The innumerable early variants are chiefly adoptions or adaptations of the med.L. prop. **ambactiātor* (agent-noun f. **ambactiāre*; see AMBASSADE), but found as *ambaxi-*, *ambasci-*, *ambassi-*, *ambasi-ator*, *-itor*; also with initial *e* and *i*, *embassiator*, *imbassiator*, etc.; varied with crosses between these and the Fr., and phonetic forms like *embassader*. Of these variants *embassador*, supported by *embassy*, was much more common than *ambassador* in 17–18th c., and was still the common spelling in United States in 19th c.

'Our authors write almost indiscriminately *embassador* or *ambassador*, *embassage* or *ambassage*; yet there is scarce an example of *ambassy*, all concurring to write *embassy*.' JOHNSON.]

1. a. An official messenger sent (singly, or as one of a party) by or to a sovereign or public body; an envoy, commissioner, or representative. *esp.* **b.** A minister of high rank sent by one sovereign or state on a mission to another. (In the general sense (mostly in plural) now only historical; and when used as in b., commonly qualified as ***Ambassador Extraordinary***, to distinguish it from sense 2.)

α. *c* **1374** CHAUCER *Troylus* IV. 145 Thambassiatours hem answerd for final. *c* **1425** WYNTOUN *Cron.* IX. ix. 119 Swilk request Of swilk Ambassatoures. *c* **1460** FORTESCUE *Abs. & Lim. Mon.* (1714) 49 Ambassators sent from Kyngs and Princis. *c* **1465** *Eng. Chron.* 48 The king sente ambassiatours ayen to king Charlis. **1489** CAXTON *Faytes of Armes* II. xxxv. 149 The ambaxatoures of the cytee went and came for to treatte of peas. *Ibid.* I. v. 11 His ambassiadours auctorised to the duc of lancastre. *Ibid.* II. v. 99 That thise ambassadours shulde not sprede suche wordes abrode. **1531** ELYOT *Governour* 8 But a feble answere to an ambassador. **1602** SHAKS. *Haml.* IV. vi. 10 Th' Ambassadours that was bound for England. **1768** BLACKSTONE *Comm.* I. I. vii. 189 The privileges of ambassadors are determined by the law of nature and nations. **1844** THIRLWALL *Greece* VIII. lxiv. 300 Ambassadors from Philip were also present.

β. *c* **1386** CHAUCER *Pard. T.* 275 Stilbon, that was a wis embasitour [*v.r.* embassadour^{-3}, -atour, ambassatour]. **1398** TREVISA *Barth. De P.R.* XVII. clxxv. (1495) 716 Embassatours: messengers and herdes. **1443** *Pol. Poems* II. 210 Mediacioun of wise enbassitoures. *a* **1450** *Knt. de la Tour* 16 Whanne the king..sawe the embassitours. **1464** *Mann. & Househ. Exp.* 250 My mastyr rode to mete the enbasetore. **1480** CAXTON *Chron. Eng.* VII. (1520) 130/1 Ther came solempne enbassatours fro the pope. *Ibid.* ccxlix. 319 Our enbassatours came home ageyne. **1523** MORE in Ellis *Orig. Lett.* I. 69 I. 198 Th' Embassiator hath requyred his Grace to send his advice. **1526** TINDALE *Hebr.* iii. 1 The embasseatour and hye prest of ourre profession. **1529** MORE *Comf. agst. Tribul.* III. Wks. 1557, 1223/1 He hadde bene diuers times Embassiator. **1535** COVERDALE *2 Macc.* iv. 44 Yᵉ embassitours were thre. **1542** BRINKLOW *Compl.* xxiv. (1874) 69 Thei be also embassytors for princes. **1544** *Suppl. Hen. VIII*, 14 Which also haue done to them good seruice as enbassadoures. **1599** SHAKS. *Hen. V*, I. i. 91 The French Embassador, vpon that instant Crau'd audience. *a* **1617** P. BAYNE *Ephes.* (1658) 2 Kings dispatch Lords Embassadours into other countries. *a* **1631** DONNE *Poems* (1650) 47 My tongue to Fame; to Embassadours mine eares. **1644** MILTON *Areop.* (Arb.) 37 Comming Embassadors to Rome. **1779** JOHNSON *Drake* Wks. 1787 IV. 445 Our general received two embassadors from the King of the country. **1824** NARES *Herald. Anom.* 74 Advising the Embassador speedily to return to his Imperial master.

γ. **1430** LYDG. *Chron. Troy* I. iv, In haste hath sent his imbassadore unto Jason. *c* **1450** GREGORY *Chron.* 106 Inbassetours fro the Duke of Orlyaunce. **1472** SIR J. PASTON in *Lett.* 703 III. 59 Imbassators of Bretayne shall come to London to morawe. **1544** *Plumpton Corr.* 248 The French Imbasodor is gon to the Emporor. **1556** *Chron. Grey Friars* 61 Proclamyd in the curte by ane imbassitor of France. **1662** J. BARGRAVE *Pope Alex. VII* (1867) 51 Only a Cardinal of this family and of that have place..with imbassadors.

2. (= *Ordinary* or *Resident Ambassador*, formerly *Ambassador Leger*.) A minister at a foreign court, of the highest rank, who there permanently represents his sovereign or country, and has a right to a personal interview with the sovereign or chief magistrate of the country in which he resides.

1603 SHAKS. *Meas. for M.* III. i. 58 Intends you for his swift Ambassador, Where you shall be an euerlasting Leiger. **1667** PEPYS *Diary* (1877) V. 167 The French Embassador in Holland. **1753** RICHARDSON *Grandison* (1781) II. xxxvii. 353 The English Embassador at the Porte. **1814** WELLINGTON in Gurwood's *Desp.* XI. 681 That I should be the ambassador at Paris. **1880** W. CORY *Mod. Eng. Hist.* I. 158 An Ambassador, unlike other ministers, has a right to a personal interview with the Sovereign of the country in which he resides.

3. An appointed or official messenger generally. (Formerly in common use, but now only *fig.*, with distinct reference to the literal sense.)

1483 CAXTON *G. de la Tour* B ij b, [He] wente with his embassatours that is to saye his messageres. **1535** COVERDALE *Prov.* xiii. 17 A faithful embassitoure is wholsome. —— *Isa.* lii. 7 How bewtiful are the fete of the Embassitoure, yᵗ bringeth the message from the mountayne. **1587** GOLDING *De Mornay* xxvii. 434 The Ambassadour whome God meant to send afore him to prepare his wayes. **1596** SHAKS. *Merch. V.* II. ix. 92 Yet I have not seen So likely an Embassador of loue. **1611** BIBLE *Transl. Pref.* 1 The Embassadors and Messengers of the great King. **1796** PEGGE *Anonym.* x. lxix. (1809) 465 The fame of a man is his representative when absent, or his embassador. **1836** MARRYAT *Japhet* III. 204 I require no embassador from the ladies in question. **1847** YEOWELL *Anc. Brit. Ch.* Pref. 11 The honoured ambassador of Christ that first laboured in this vineyard.

4. ***Ambassador Leger*** (***legier, lieger***) (see sense 2); ***Ambassador Extraordinary*** (see sense 1); ***Ambassador Plenipotentiary***: one with full power to sign treaties, and otherwise act for his sovereign.

1603 *Eng. Mourn. Garm.* in *Harl. Misc.* (Malh.) II. 489 The ambassador-lieger of Spain..did plot and confederate with native traitors of this land. **1630** WADSWORTH *Sp. Pilgr.* i. 2 His Majesty sent him with his first Ambassador Legier ..into Spaine. **1655** MRQ. WORC. *Cent. Inv.* lvi, Two Extraordinary Embassadors accompanying His Majesty. **1663** MARVELL *Corr.* 44 Wks. 1875 II. 93 My Lord of Carlisle being chosen by his Majesty, Embassadour Extraordinary to Muscovy. **1753** HANWAY *Trav.* (1762) II. VIII. iv. 202 Nominated as embassador-plenipotentiary to the court of Russia.

5. ***ambassador-at-large*** (U.S.), an ambassador appointed to perform special duties, and not accredited to any one government or sovereign. Also *transf.*

1908 *Busy Man's Mag.* Sept. 122/1 If he ever does get his deserts, he will be designated as ambassador-at-large for the Canadian Pacific Railway. **1933** *U.S. Naval Inst. Proc.* May 740/2 Conversations in London..between Premier MacDonald and Norman H. Davis, President Roosevelt's ambassador-at-large.

ambassadorial (æm,bæsəˈdɔːrɪəl), *a.* [mod. f. prec., by form-assoc. with adjs. in *-orial* formed by suffix -AL¹ on L. adjs. in *-ōrius*, f. sbs. in *-or*; as *senator, senatori-us, senatori-al*: see -ORIAL.] Of or pertaining to an ambassador.

1759 H. WALPOLE *Lett.* 343 (1834) III. 320 To prepare your ambassadorial countenance. **1778** LAURENS in Sparks *Corr. Am. Rev.* (1853) II. 117 Our Ambassadorial Commissioners.. are unhappily divided in sentiments. **1866** J. MARTINEAU *Ess.* I. 366 They recognize the ambassadorial credentials of Conscience. **1881** *Echo* 16 Feb. 3/4 The Ambassadorial Affront at Rome.

ambassaˈdorially, *adv.* [f. AMBASSADORIAL *a.* + -LY².] According to the capacity or manner of an ambassador; as an ambassador.

1889 *Clergyman's Mag.* V. 165 St. Paul, directing an offender to be restored, says, 'I forgive the offence in the person of Jesus Christ'—ambassadorially. **1960** *Times* 27 Aug. 3/2 She was ambassadorially non-committal about tomorrow evening.

ambassadorship (æmˈbæsədəʃɪp). [f. AMBASSADOR + -SHIP.] The office, position, or function of an ambassador.

1837 *Blackw. Mag.* XLI. 610 Something for ambassadorship to do. **1838** *Ibid.* XLIV. 370 The marshal's ambassadorship-extraordinary. **1882** *Pall Mall G.* 27 May 1 Ten years of successful ambassadorship.

ambassadress (æmˈbæsədrɪs). Also emb-. [f. AMBASSADOR + -ESS. Varied with forms in *-drice, -drix, -trice, -trix.*]

1. A female ambassador or messenger.

[**1577–87** HOLINSH. *Chr.* III. 910/1 The two ladies ambassadors of the king of England, sitting in great estate.] **1594** CAREW tr. *Tasso* (1881) 53 Dawnyng th' Embassadresse was ris'ne from bed, Tydings to beare, how now grey morne annies. **1600** CHAPMAN *Iliad* III. 126 Iris, the Rainbow, then came down, ambassadress from heaven. **1703** ROWE *Fair Penit.* I. i. 213 Well, my Embassadress, what must we treat of? **1755** CROKER *Ariosto's Orl. Fur.* XXXII. cx, Near to her th' embassadress did rise. **1761** SMOLLETT *Gil Blas* (1802) I. IV. ii. 331 She..bad her ambassadress retire into another room. **1847** TENNYSON *Princess* III. 187 Are you ambassadresses From him to me?

2. The wife of an AMBASSADOR (*leger*) 2.

1716 LADY M. MONTAGUE *Lett.* I. xxxi. 107 The French Ambassadress agreed with me as to his good mien. **1777** GIBBON *Misc. Wks.* (1814) II. 209, I cannot quite determine whether I shall sup at Madame Necker's or the Sardinian Ambassadress's. **1880** DISRAELI *Endym.* I. xxxiii. 305 Not only an ambassador, but an ambassadress..had been asked to meet them.

†amˈbassadrice. *Obs.* [a. mod.Fr. *ambassadrice*, fem. of *ambassadeur*: see -RICE.] An ambassador's wife.

1683 TEMPLE *Mem.* Wks. 1731 I. 452 The Evening Entertainments..in the Apartments of the several Ambassadrices. **1687** *Lond. Gaz.* mmccxciii/4 The Ambassadrice intends to continue at Bagnania near Rome till the ceremony is over.

amˈbassadrix. *rare*⁻¹. [irreg. f. AMBASSADOR: see -RIX.] = AMBASSADRESS I.

1846 *Blackw. Mag.* LX. 456 The sweetest messenger and ambassadrix in the world; so exact in her messages—so brisk on her errands.

†amˈbassadry. *Obs.* Forms: 4–5 **ambassatrye, -trie, -drie, embassadrye,** 5–6 **embassadrie.** [a. Fr. *ambassaderie*; f. *ambassadeur*: see -RY.] The office or function of an ambassador; ambassadorship.

*c***1386** CHAUCER *Man of Lawes' T.* 135 By tretys and ambassatrye [*v.r.* embassadrye, -drie] They ben acordid. *c***1450** HENRYSON *Mor. Fab.* 35 The Wolfe is better in Ambassadrie than I. **1538** LELAND *Itin.* III. 120 Cumming from his Embassadrie out of Italie.

†amˈbassady, ? mistake for preceding, or confusion between it and *ambassade*.

1693 LUTTRELL *Brief Rel.* (1857) III. 65 His arrears due on his ambassady to Spain.

ambassage, embassage (ˈæm-, ˈɛmbəsɪdʒ). Also imb-. [At first accented *am-, emˈbassage* (Sidney, Marlowe, Drayton, Sandys, Quarles, Colvill, Marvell), but *ˈembassage* in Shakspere. Of Eng. formation, not found (like *passage, message*) in Fr. or any Rom. lang., but not formed on a word already in Eng. (like *parentage, breakage*): see -AGE. May have been formed on Fr. *ambasse* (:—L. *ambaxia, ambactia*), or med.L. vb. *ambassāre, ambassiāre*, or by simple analogy on *ambass-iate* (cf. *vicariate, vicarage*), or by taking *ambass-* as a verb stem (as if *amˈbassate, -et, -ed* were pa. pple.). The spelling EMBASSAGE is more common.]

†1. The sending or dispatch of ambassadors; a mission. *Obs.*

1569 GOLDING tr. *Heminge's Postill.* 27 The Ambassage of Christ..when he sayth 'Go and preache.' **1596** DRAYTON *Leg.* i. 785 Who on Ambassage to the Emperor sent. **1598** HAKLUYT *Voy.* I. 150 One deceased by the way,..and the other remained sick..so that ambassage took none effect. **1640** YORKE *Union of Hon.* 39 Knowing his troubles to arise from his Ambassage to the Lady Bona.

2. The message conveyed by an ambassador; the business entrusted to him.

1548 LATIMER *Ploughm.* (1868) 26 Troubeled wyth Lordelye lyuynge..burdened with ambassages. **1580** SIDNEY *Arcad.* III. 275 Sent this ambassage in versified music. *c***1600** SHAKS. *Sonn.* xxvi, To thee I send this written ambassage. **1628** WITHER *Brit. Rememb.* v. 1490 Let not my person hinder my Ambassage. **1676** HOBBES *Iliad* IX. 167 That our Ambassage may successful be. **1860** TRENCH *Serm. Westm. Ab.* xii. 135 He sends the ambassage of his submission.

3. The position, or tenure of office, of an ambassador; ambassadorship.

1577–87 HOLINSHED *Chron.* III. 1245/2 This man..being yet after his ambassage treasuror. **1622** BACON *Hen. VII* (1860) 385 Urswick, upon whom the king bestowed this ambassage. **1632** PORY in Ellis *Orig. Lett.* II. 273 III. 273 His lordship had ended his ambassage with the King of Denmark. **1653** HOLCROFT *Procopius* I. 15 Rufinus is coming in Ambassage.

4. A body of men sent on a mission, or as a deputation, to or from a sovereign, etc.

1605 *Play of Stucley* (1878) 216 To my royal master Hath honorable ambassage been sent. **1611** BIBLE *Luke* xiv. 32 Hee sendeth an ambassage [WYCLIF, a messanger; TINDALE, etc., embasseatours; *Rhem.* a legacie], and desireth conditions of peace. **1612** BACON *Ess.* (Arb.) 473 Yonder Men, are too Many for an Ambassage, and too Few for a Fight.

β. [See more fully under EMBASSAGE.]

1558 BP. WATSON *Seven Sacram.* xiv. 85 Vsynge as it were hys embassage to exhort you to be reconciled to him. **1663** GERBIER *Counsel* C iv a, Embassages and Negotiations in the Court of forraign Princes. **1860** MOTLEY *Netherl.* (1868) I. vii. 443 Except your embassages have better success.

γ.

1593–1620 R. HAWKINS *Voy. S. Sea* 194 Ransoming of prisoners, bringing of presents, and other imbassages.

ambassate, variant of AMBASSIATE.

ambassator, -atour, obs. ff. AMBASSADOR.

†amˈbassatrice. *Obs. rare*⁻¹. [f. AMBASSATOR; with Fr. fem. ending -RICE.] An early variant of AMBASSADRICE.

*a***1641** FINET *For. Ambass.* (1656) 199, I answered that I had brought the Ambassatrice a liberty of election from my Lord Chamberlain whether she would be pleased to sit with the great Ladies or apart.

†amˈbassatrix. *Obs. rare*⁻¹. [mod.L. fem. of AMBASSATOR: see -RIX. *Ambassiatrix* occurs in med.L.] = prec.

1638 BAKER *Balzac's Lett.* (1654) III. 13, I have not yet seene the Ambassatrix.

ambassed, -et, variants of AMBASSADE, -IATE.

†amˈbassiate. *Obs.* Also 5 **ambacyat, -assite, -assat(e, -asset,** 5–6 **-axat, -assiat;** also **embassiate, embasset, imbasset.** [ad. med.L. *ambassiata*, also *-asciata, -asiata, -asseata, -axiata, -assata, -axata*, for **ambactiāta*: see AMBASSADE, a doublet of this word through Sp. and Fr., with which the later forms of this were at length blended; also AMBASSY from the cognate Fr. form.]

1. The business or message of an ambassador.

*a***1400** *Cov. Myst.* 77 Now myn imbasset I have seyd to yow thus. **1417** HEN. V in Ellis *Orig. Lett.* III. 26 I. 61 Thambassiatours of oure Brothir the Duc of Baire have been here with us and doon theire Ambassiat. **1419** ASSHETON *ibid.* II. 22 I. 73 When that he comes on his Ambassate. **1430** LYDG. *Chron. Troy* II. xvi, Of one assent to make ambassyat. *c***1430** —— *Bochas* v. xv. (1554) 133 a, In this Ambasset.. had none audience. **1440** SHIRLEY *Dethe K. James* (1818) 23 Beyng in Scotteland, upon his ambassite. **1447** BOKENHAM *Lyvys of Seyntys* 52 b, Whan the aungel thus his ambacyat Had brefly doon. **1461** WYNDESORE in *Paston Lett.* 416 II. 52 Goyng uppon an ambassate to the Frenshe Kyng. **1513** DOUGLAS *Æneis* VIII. iii. 108 Nowthir by ambassiat, message, nor writingis. **1548** HALL *Chron.* 847 Ambassiates, excuses, allegacions.

2. A body of men sent on a message by a sovereign or other authority; an embassy.

1461 *Paston Lett.* 416 II. 52 We shall have a gret ambassate out of Scotland. **1513** DOUGLAS *Æneis* XI. lvi. 27 The ambassiat that was returnit agane. **1529** RASTELL *Pastyme* (1811) 101 They sende an embasset to Aecias. **1535** STEWART *Cron. Scotl.* II. 221 Ane greit ambaxat suddantlie he send. **1580** NORTH *Plutarch* (1676) 140 Twenty persons of this Ambassiate.

3. A single envoy or ambassador. [Fr. *ambassade* (masc.), Pr. *ambaissat*. Cf. -ADE³.]

1470 HARDING *Chron.* lxxxi, He..sent his letters with his Ambassatis. *c***1520** *State Let.* in Burnet *Hist. Ref.* II. 95 The French king hath sent hither an Ambassiate, Monsieur de Langes. **1535** STEWART *Cron. Scotl.* I. 55 The ambaxat tuke leve and passit hame.

ambassy, embassy (ˈæm-, ˈɛmbəsɪ). [a. OFr. *ambassée* (*ambaxée, embascée, enbasée*), cogn. w. Pr. *ambaissada*, OSp. *ambaxada*, It. *ambasciata*:—L. **ambactiāta*: see AMBASSADE. In Fr. the native *ambassée* was afterwards superseded by *ambaxade* (15th c.), *ambassade*, ad. Sp. (see -ADE), whence also our *ambassade*. (*Ambassée, ambassy*, is not:—L. *ambactia, ambaxia*, which gave OFr. *ambasse*, not adopted in Eng.) Commonly written EMBASSY; Johnson considered the spelling *ambassy* quite obs.; see note under AMBASSADOR.]

1. The mission, function, or office of an ambassador.

1600 HOLLAND *Livy* VII. xxx. 269/1 The people of Capua hath sent us in ambassie [*legatos*] unto you. **1664** MARVELL *Corr.* Wks. 1875 II. 148 Having destinated him for this Ambassy. *c***1690** TEMPLE *Pop. Discont.* Wks. 1731 I. 264 During my Ambassies abroad. **1732** BERKELEY *Min. Philos.* II. 38 The Son of God, upon an ambassy from Heaven.

2. The message brought by an ambassador.

1606 WARNER *Alb. Eng.* XIV. lxxxii. 342 None better aunswerd Ambasies in whatsoeuer tongue. **1738** GLOVER *Leonidas* VII. 128 Here, Persian, tell thy ambassy.

3. A body of men sent as ambassadors; an ambassador and his suite or surroundings.

1732 LEDIARD *Sethos* II. vii. 25 He even thought of sending an ambassy to him. **1851** HELPS *Friends in C.* I. 32 An Eastern man, one of the people attached to their ambassies. **1863** KINGLAKE *Crimea* (1876) I. viii. 116 In the case of Sovereigns and their ambassies.

β. [See more fully under EMBASSY.]

1588 SHAKS. *L.L.L.* (1623) I. i. 135 Here comes in Embassie the French king's daughter. **1742** YOUNG *Nt. Th.* II. 199 Sent On his important embassy to man. **1839** KEIGHTLEY *Hist. Eng.* I. 447 A joint embassy was then sent to the King of Navarre to demand his neutrality.

ambatch (ˈæmbætʃ). Also **ambach, ambash.** [app. of Ethiopic origin.] A leguminous tree or shrub, *Æschynomene elaphroxylon*, of tropical Africa, with very light spongy wood; also called *pith-tree*.

1864 J. A. GRANT *Walk across Africa* p. xv, Ambadj; native name for the pith-tree. **1884** J. COLBORNE *With Hicks Pasha in Soudan* 100 Here, too, we came across the famous ambatch.., one of the most extraordinary growths of African vegetation. **1887** [see *pith-tree*, PITH *sb.* 8]. **1889** H. M. STANLEY in *Daily News* 4 Dec. 3/1 A..sand bank overgrown with sedge and ambatch. **1935** C. S. FORESTER *Afr. Queen* ix. 169 On either bank now appeared broad fringes of reeds—papyrus and ambash. **1957** BANNERMAN *Birds Brit. Isles* VI. 91 Not until the nose of the canoe was pushed into the ambatch bushes did the brooding birds leave their nests.

ambaxade, -at, obs. var. AMBASSADE, -IATE.

‖**ambe** (ˈæmbiː). [Gr. ἄμβη, Ion. for ἄμβων a projecting lip or edge.] **1.** *Surg.* (see quot.)

1711 in *Lond. Gaz.* mmmmdccclvii/4 This [reduction of fractures] is not effected either by the Ambe or Comander. **1743** ZOLLMAN in *Phil. Trans.* XLII. 387 Among the Machines which Art has invented for the performing of it, the Ambe of Hippocrates is one of the most antient and most famous. **1811** HOOPER *Med. Dict.*, *Ambe*, an old chirurgical machine for reducing dislocations of the shoulder, and so called, because its extremity projects like the prominence of a rock.

2. *Anat.* 'A superficial crest or eminence of a bone.' *Syd. Soc. Lex.* 1879.

ˈambeer, -ia, -ier. ['probably from *ambre*, denoting its colour.' Bartlett.]

1763 *Brit. Mag.* IV. 464 Sprinkle strong ambeer over it, made from tobacco trash. **1871** JOAQUIN MILLER in *Athenæum* 3 June 681 The bronzed mate..Spirted a stream of ambier wide Across and over the ship side.

amber (ˈæmbə(r)), *sb.*¹ and *a.* Forms: 4 **ambra,** 5 **aumber, -ur, ambyr,** 5–7 **ambre,** 6 **awmer,** 5– **amber.** Also 5–6 **lamber, -re, lammer.** [a. Fr. *ambre*, cogn. w. Pr. *ambre*, Pr. and It. *ambra*, Sp. *ambar*, med.L. *ambar, -are, -er, -ra, -re, -rum*, a. Arab. *ꜥanbar*, 'ambergris,' to which the name orig. belonged; afterwards extended, through some confusion of the substances, to the fossil resin 'amber.' In Fr. the two are distinguished as grey, and yellow amber, *ambre gris* ('*ambre proprement dit*'), and *ambre jaune* (*succin*); in mod.Eng. as *amber-gris* and *amber*. In the north. dial. the latter was formerly distinguished as LAMBER, a. Fr. *l'ambre* with article attached.]

A. *sb.* **I.** A product of the whale.

†1. a. *orig.* = AMBERGRIS. (In 17th c. *greece of amber, gris ambre, gray amber*.) *Obs.*

1398 TREVISA *Barth. De P.R.* XIII. xxvi. 463 The whale haþ gret plente of sperme..and yf it is gaderid and dryeþ, it turneþ to þe substaunce of ambra [**1535** ambre]. **1477** NORTON *Ord. Alch.* in Ashm. (1652) v. 70 Amber, Narde, and Mirrhe. **1587** HARRISON *England* I. II. xx. 330 Induing the fruits with the savour of muske, ambre, etc. **1662** FULLER *Worthies* I. 194 It is called Ambra-gresia, That is, Gray Amber, from the Colour thereof. **1670** COTTON *Espernon* III. IX. 447 Some pieces of Amber-gris, (or rather black Amber, for it was of that colour). **1693** in BLOUNT *Nat. Hist.* 14 Great variety of Opinions hath there been concerning Amber. Some think it to be a Gum that distils from Trees: Others tell us, it is made of Whales Dung; or else of their Sperm or Seed, (as others will have it,) which being consolidate and harden'd by the Sea is cast upon the Shore. **1718** LADY M. MONTAGUE *Lett.* I. xxxvii. 146 Slaves ..with silver censers..perfumed the air with amber, aloes-wood, and other scents.

b. *attrib.*

1634 HABINGTON *Castara* (1870) 85 A mighty showre Of Amber comfits it sweete selfe did powre Vpon our heads. **1671** MILTON *Samson* 720 An amber scent of odorous perfume.

†2. white amber (med.L. *ambra alba*): Spermaceti. [Confused with prec., as the 'sperm' of a whale.] *Obs.* (See also 6.)

[Cf. **1598–1611** FLORIO, *Ambra*, amber, also amber greece, also the sperme of a Whale called Spermaceti. **1611** COTGR., *Ambre blanc*, white Amber.]

II. The resin.

3. a. A yellowish translucent fossil resin, found chiefly along the southern shores of the Baltic. It is used for ornaments; burns with an agreeable odour; often entombs the bodies of insects, etc.; and when rubbed becomes notably *electric* (so called from its Greek name ἤλεκτρον). (See also LAMBER.)

c **1400** *Destr. Troy* v. 1666 Bourdourt about all with bright Aumbur. *c* **1450** *Bk. Curtasye* III. 481 The wardrop he herbers, and eke of chambur Ladyes with bedys of coralle and lambur. **1463** in *Bury Wills* 15 A peyre bedys of ambyr with a ryng of syluir. *a* **1529** SKELTON *Elynour Rummyng* 603 But my bedes of amber, Bere them to my chamber. **1552** HULOET, *Ambre* called *lambre* or yelow Ambre. **1556** *Richmond. Wills* (1853) 89 One paire of long beads of awmer. **1602** SHAKS. *Haml.* II. ii. 200 Thicke Amber, or Plum-Tree Gumme. **1658** SIR T. BROWNE *Hydriot.* ii. 18 That Romane Urne.. wherein were found an Ape of Agate, an Elephant of Ambre. **1735** POPE *Ep. Arbuthnot* 169 Pretty! in amber to observe the forms Of hairs, or straws, or dirt, or grubs, or worms! **1794** SULLIVAN *View Nat.* II. 27 Amber, when rubbed, was observed to attract bits of straw, down, and other light bodies. **1847** BLACKWELL *Malet's North. Antiq.* 374 Byron caught him up, and.. preserved him, like a fly in amber, for future generations to wonder at. **1865** CARLYLE *Fredk. Gt.* I. II. ii. 54 Amber, science declares, is a kind of petrified resin, distilled by pines that were dead before the days of Adam.

b. *oil of amber*: obtained by its dry distillation. *spirit of amber*: old name of succinic acid.

1551 ROBINSON *More's Utopia* (1869) 80 Fine linnen cloth dipped in oyle of [*printed* or] ambre. *a* **1700** [see SPIRIT *sb.* 22]. **1737** GRAY *Let.* in *Poems* (1775) 23 Not hartshorn, nor spirit of amber, nor all that furnishes the closet of an apothecary's widow. **1879** *Syd. Soc. Lex.*, *Amber*.. is used to prepare oil of amber and succinic acid.

†**4.** A piece of amber used as an amulet to attract lovers. *Obs.*

1604 DEKKER *Honest Wh.* 51 Pearles and Ambers, Shall not draw me to their Chambers. **1691** *Bagford Bal.* I. 122 The fair Queen of Egypt she wore a Commode, On the top of it was a lac'd Amber.

5. *fig.* **a.** Referring to the property of amber as enclosing and preserving insects of past ages.

1863 MRS. C. CLARKE *Shaks. Char.* xii. 314 Full-fledged specimens of your order, preserved for all time in the imperishable amber of his genius.

b. Referring to colour: Amber-coloured substance or appearance.

1735 SOMERVILLE *Chase* III. 173 In the full Glass the liquid Amber smiles, Our native Product. **1830** TENNYSON *Margaret* i, The tender amber round, Which the moon about her spreadeth. **1879** —— *Lover's T.* 32 The loud stream Ran amber toward the west. **1862** TYNDALL *Mountaineer.* i. 4 The amber of the western sky.

III. Extensions of prec.

6. An alloy of four parts of gold with one of silver (L. *ēlectrum*, Pliny, Gr. ἤλεκτρον, f. ἠλέκτωρ bright, beaming as the sun, considered by some to be the original sense in Gr. See Liddell & Scott. Used also by the LXX to translate Heb. *khashmal*, whence in Vulg. and A.V.)

c **1400** *Destr. Troy* xv. 6203 A chariot full choise.. the whelis full wheme, all of white aumber. **1430** LYDG. *Chron. Troy* II. xii, Like a foole.. That aumber yelowe cheseth for the white. **1611** BIBLE *Ezek.* i. 4 Out of the midst thereof as the colour of amber [WYCLIF electre], out of the midst of the fire.

7. = LIQUIDAMBAR. (The poets vaguely confuse this with senses 1 and 3. See *amber-dropping*, *-weeping*, etc. in C 1; *amber-varnish* in C 2.)

1569 J. SANFORD *Agrippa's Van. Artes* 15 The gumme called Amber, groweth out of a tree. **1850** MRS. BROWNING *Comfort* Poems I. 328 Let my tears drop like amber.

8. A local name of the plant called St. John's-wort.

1861 PRATT *Flower. Pl.* II. 14 *Hypericum perforatum*.. In N. Kent, one of the common names of the species is Amber.

9. *Theatr.* An amber-coloured spotlight. Also *attrib.*

1913 A. BENNETT *Regent* ix. 260 The curtain rose... 'What about that amber, Cosmo?' Mr. Marriner cried. **1921** G. B. SHAW in *Times Lit. Suppl.* 17 Mar. 178/2 Take your ambers out of your number one batten. **1933** P. GODFREY *Back-Stage* vii. 90 'What's in your perches?' 'Ambers, sir.' *Ibid.* i. 18 The amber circuits in No. 1 batten.

B. *adj.* [orig. attrib. use of sb. Cf. *rose*, *pink*, *orange*, etc.; also Fr. *ambré*.] **a.** Of the colour and clearness of amber (sense 3), amber-coloured; of a clear yellowish brown.

c **1500** *Almanak 'for* 1386' 27 Uryne.. þat semes aumbre. **1594** GREENE *Orl. Fur.* (1861) 111 Where Phœbus dips his amber tresses oft. **1599** —— *George a Greene* 63 Those hairs of amber hue. **1610** *Histrio-mast.* ii. 6, I crush out bounty from the amber grape. **1632** MILTON *L'Allegro* 61 Robed in flames and amber light. **1671** —— *P.R.* III. 284 Choaspes, amber stream. **1713** *Lond. & Country Brew.* I. (1742) 25 Pale and amber Ale. **1853** C. BRONTË *Villette* xvi. (1876) 164 Warm in its amber lamp-light. **1877** BRYANT *Sella* 96 The sun Stooped towards the amber west. **1879** MISS BRADDON *Vixen* III. 132 The Duchess's amber drawing-rooms. **1879** TENNYSON *Lover's T.* 10 Days Of dewy dawning, and the amber eves.

b. Designating the intermediate cautionary light in road traffic signals, between red (= stop) and green (= go). Also, as *sb.*, the amber-coloured light itself; hence *fig.*, an indication of approaching change or danger.

1929 *Min. Transport Roads Dept. Mem.* No. 297 The signal indications should be given in the following order: (1) Red, (2) Red and Amber together, (3) Green, (4) Amber... The purpose of the Amber is to give warning to drivers of vehicles of an impending change from Red to Green or Green to Red. **1933** *Traffic Signs (Size, Col. and Type) Prov. Regs.* §27 (a) Three lights shall be used facing the stream of traffic which the signal is intended to control, one red, one amber and one green. **1937** AUDEN & MACNEICE *Lett. fr. Iceland* 32 And always need a noise, the radio or the city, Traffic and changing lights, crashing the amber. **1956** *Ann. Reg. 1955* 421 The increase from 3 to 3½ per cent... was described as an 'amber light' of general warning. **1961** A. WILSON *Old Men at Zoo* iii. 136 In view of Godmanchester's remarks, I regard this as the amber warning. I'm afraid you must make it a must.

C. *comb.* (chiefly in sense 3, sometimes 1 or 6).

1. General relations: **a.** *attrib.* of material or source, as ***amber beads, studs, mouthpiece***, etc.; **b.** *obj. genitive*, and *obj.* of pple. or vbl. sb., as ***amber-fishing***, ***-dropping***, ***-weeping***, ***-yielding***; **c.** *similative*, as ***amber-clear***, ***-like***, ***-solid***, ***-yellow***; **d.** *instrumental* with pa. pple., as ***amber-headed***, ***-tinged***, ***-tinted***, ***-tipped***, ***-toned***; passing into **e.** *synthetic derivatives*, as ***amber-coloured*** (of amber colour) ***-foaming***, ***-hued***, ***-locked*** (having amber locks), ***-sanded***.

1449 in *Test. Ebor.* (1855) II. 156 A peir of awmbur bedis. **1596** SHAKS. *Tam. Shr.* IV. iii. 58 With Amber Bracelets, Beades, and all this knau'ry. **1711** 'J. DISTAFF' *Don Sacheverellio* 4 The Amber-Head has dropt from his Cane. **1865** MISS BRADDON *Only a Clod* iii. 15 The amber mouthpiece of his pipe. **1620** *Swetnam Arraigned* (1880) 12 Their very breath Is sophisticated with Amber-pellets, and kissing causes. **1637** MILTON *Com.* 863 Thy amber-dropping hair. **1596** FITZ-GEFFREY *Sir F. Drake* (1881) 88 Th' amber-weeping Pegase-hoofe-made fount. **1647** CRASHAW *Poems* 2 (T.) The soft gold, which Steals from the amber-weeping tree. **1850** MARG. FULLER *Woman in 19th C.* (1862) 207 When thoughts flow through the mind amber-clear and soft. **1949** S. SPENDER *Edge of Being* 15 The sense felt behind darkened walls, An amber-solid world. **1667** H. MORE *Div. Dial.* v. x. (1713) 434 This pure amber-like or transparent Gold. **1817** COLERIDGE *Sib. Leaves* (1862) 226 They're amber-like to me. **1748** SMOLLETT *Rod. Rand.* xxxiv. (1804) 225 An amber-headed cane hung dangling from his wrist. **1866** G. M. HOPKINS *Jrnl.* 3 May (1959) 134 Swallows.. shewing their amber-tinged breasts. **1895** *Daily News* 20 Dec. 2/3 Allusion was also made to his amber-tinted hair. **1878** A. NESBITT *Catal. Glass Vessels S. Kens. Mus.* 120 Amber-toned glass. **1588** SHAKS. *L.L.L.* IV. iii. 88 An Amber coloured Rauen. **1713** *Lond. & Country Brew.* I. (1742) 12 The amber-coloured Malt. **1881** WILDE *Panthea* in *Poems* 178 The hot and amber-foaming must. **1729** SAVAGE *Wanderer* III. (Jod.) Yon amber-hued cascade. **1831** CARLYLE *Sart. Res.* I. v. 26 Thy own amber-locked, snow-and-rose-bloom Maiden. **1939** A. E. HOUSMAN *Coll. Poems* 192 Oh, the pearl seas are yonder, The amber-sanded shore.

2. Special combinations: **amber-bush**, a head of amber-coloured hair, a youthful head; **amber-crowned** *a.* crowned or covered with amber hair; **amber-drink**, drink of amber colour and transparency; **amber fauna**, the animals of which the remains are found in amber; **amber fishing**, fishing or dredging at the bottom of the sea for amber; **amber flora**, the plants of which specimens are found in amber; **amber-forest**, the primeval forest from the trees of which amber exuded; **amber oil** (see A 3); **amber pear**, a pear with the odour of ambergris, an AMBRETTE; **amber-plum**, a variety of yellow plum; **amber shell**, **snail** = SUCCINEA; **amber-varnish**, made of liquid amber or copal. Also AMBER-SEED, AMBER-TREE, q.v.

1605 SYLVESTER *Du Bartas* 471 A gray-beards wisedom in an amber-bush. **1580** SIDNEY *Arcad.* (1622) 425 Bending her amber-crowned head ouer her bedside. *a* **1626** BACON (J.), All your clear amber-drink is flat. **1880** *Cope's Tobacco Pl.* Oct. 531/1 Treating of the Amber Flora and the Amber Fauna. **1828** CARLYLE *Misc.* (1857) I. 94 The savage Prussians with their amber-fishing. **1854** T. R. JONES in *Q. Jrnl. Geol. S.* X. II. 4 Twigs of *Thuia occidentalis* (found in the Amber-flora). *Ibid.* X. II. 3 A similar extension in former times of the Amber-forests. **1741** *Compl. Fam.-Piece* II. iii. 388 Amber Pear, Muscat Robine, Poir sans Peau. **1629** PARKINSON *Parad.* III. xiii. 578 The Amber plum is a round plum, as yellow on the outside almost as yellow waxe. **1718** MRS. EALES *Receipt* 25 Take the green Amber Plum, prick it all over with a Pin. **1835** W. KIRBY *Creat. Anim.* I. ix. 291 The amber shells, as least one species, is [*sic*] stated to swim occasionally on the surface of the water. **1858** W. BAIRD *Cycl. Nat. Sci.* 528/1 *Succinea*, Amber Snail. **1867** J. HOGG *Microsc.* I. ii. 155 The wood having been previously lightly inked with printers' ink or amber-varnish.

†**'amber**, *sb.*[2] *Obs.* [OE. *amber*, *omber*, *-or*, earlier *ámbær*, cogn. w. OS. *émbar*, *-ber*, OHG. *einpar*, *eimpar*, *eimber*, *eimer* (mod.G. *eimer*); according to Grimm, f. *án* one + *-ber* from *beran* to bear; though perh. orig. an adaptation of L. *amphora*, f. Gr. ἀμφορεύς, assimilated to a Teut. form and meaning. App. not used in Eng. since 1100; but preserved in old documents in L. form *ambra*, and hence in Spelman, Blount, and other Dicts.]

1. 'A vessel with one handle'; a pail, bucket, pitcher, urn.

c **700** *Epinal Gl.* (O.E.T. 106) *Urna*, ambær; *Erfurt Gl.* ombar; *Corpus Gl.* amber. *c* **950** *Lindisf. Gosp.* Mark xiv. 13 Ombor full wætres [Vulg. *laguenam aquæ*; *Ags. Gosp.* wæter-flaxan]. *Ibid.* Luke xxii. 10 Ombor full wætres [Vulg. *amphoram aquæ*; *Ags. Gosp.* wæter-buce].

2. A liquid measure; a pitcher, a cask.

804-29 *Cod. Dipl.* No. 460, xxx ómbra gódes Uuelesces aloþ, ðæt limpnað to xv mittum. *c* **950** *Lindisf. Gosp.* Luke xvi. 6 Hundteantih ombras oeles [Vulg. *cados*; *Ags. Gosp.* sestra; *Hatton* sestres]. *c* **1000** ÆLFRIC *Gloss.* in Wright *Voc.* 24/2 *Batus*, amber.

3. A dry measure of four bushels. (See *Introd. to Domesday* I. 133.)

c **885** K. ÆLFRED *Oros.* I. i. §15 Tyn ambra feðra. **1691** BLOUNT *Law Dict.*, *Ambra*, a Vessel among our Saxons.. I have seen in an old Deed, mention of *Ambra Salis.* **1872** E. ROBERTSON *Hist. Ess.* II. 68 The amber.. was a measure of 4 bushels in the 13th century by the London Standard.

†**'amber**, *sb.*[3] Obs. form of AMBRY. [Cf. OFr. *armaire*, *aumaire*.]

1593 *Rites & Mon. Ch. Durham* (1842) 2 The severall lockers or ambers for the safe keepinge of the vestments.

amber ('æmbə(r)), *v.* *rare* exc. in pa. pple. **ambered**. [f. the sb. Cf. Fr. *ambrer*, pa. pple. *ambré*.]

1. To perfume with ambergris.

1616 BEAUM. & FLET. *Cust. Country* III. ii, Be sure The wines be lusty, high, and full of spirit, And amber'd all. *a* **1648** DIGBY *Closet Opened* (1677), You may strew Ambred Sugar upon it.

2. To make amber-coloured.

1809 J. BARLOW *Columb.* IV. 548 The sand-sown beach, the rocky bluff repays The faint effulgence with their amber'd rays.

3. To preserve in amber.

1882 H. MERIVALE *Faucit of B.* II. II. ii. 155 Like the ambered fly.. incessantly wondering why he was anywhere.

amber-days: see EMBER-DAYS.

'amber-fish. [AMBER *sb.*[1]] A brightly coloured fish of the genus *Seriola*, found esp. in warm parts of the Atlantic.

1674 JOSSELYN *Two Voy.* 107 The Sea-bream, Dorado, or Amber-fish, they follow ships.. and are good meat. **1706** PHILLIPS *New World of Words* (ed. 6), *Dorado*.. a Fish otherwise call'd the Sea-bream; or Amber-fish, the Head of which in the Water is Green, and the Body as Yellow as Gold. **1799** A. ELLICOTT in C. V. Mathews *Life & Lett.* (1908) 186 A great abundance and variety of fish.. such as.. Amber-fish. **1888** GOODE *Amer. Fishes* 232 The Amber-fish, *Seriola carolinensis*, is quite common off the West Florida coast. **1897** *Outing* (U.S.) XXIX. 330/2 Not inferior to the kingfish for sport is the amber-fish, or 'amberjack'.

ambergris ('æmbəgri:s). Forms: 5 **imbergres**, 6 **ambar-**, **-ber-gris(e**, **amber-de-grece**, 6-8 **amber-greece**, 7 **amber-greice**, **ambre-gris**, **ambragresia**, 7-8 **ambergrise**, **-griese**, **-greese**, 7-9 **ambergrease**, 7- **ambergris**. Also 7 **greece of amber**, **gris-amber**. [a. Fr. *ambre gris*, 'gray amber,' as sometimes transl. To this substance the name AMBER originally belonged; after its extension to the resin, *ambre jaune* or *succin*, the *amber* proper was distinguished as *ambre gris*, which has become in Eng. its regular name. The spelling variants are due to attempts to explain *gris*, as *grease*, *Greece* (usual in 17th c.), etc.]

A wax-like substance of marbled ashy colour, found floating in tropical seas, and as a morbid secretion in the intestines of the sperm-whale. It is odoriferous and used in perfumery; formerly in cookery.

1481-90 *Howard Househ. Bks.* (1841) 202 Imber-gres j. lb. price xij. d. **1533** ELYOT *Cast. Helth* (1541) 68 Confortatives of the Harte hotte.. Ambergrise, etc. **1542** BOORDE *Dyetary* viii. (1870) 249 Perfumed with amber-degrece. **1576** BAKER *Gesner's Jewell of Health* 85/1 Adde both musk and amber greece. **1604** DEKKER *Honest Wh.* 49 He smells all of Muske and Amber greece. **1612** DRAYTON *Poly-olb.* xx. (1748) 337 Their lips they sweet'ned had with costly ambergrease. **1614** W. BARCLAY in *James I's Counterbl.* (Arb.) 116 Is not Amber-greese coastly? **1616** R. C. *Times' Whistle* III. 978 His beard, perfumde with greece of amber. **1624** B. JONSON *Neptune's Triumph*, Why do you smell of amber-grise, Of which was formed Neptune's niece? **1654** LESTRANGE *Charles I*, 136 They perfumed this respect with presenting to [their Majesties] a massive piece of Ambre Gris. **1657** S. COLVIL *Whigs Suppl.* (1751) 36 Why devils music do not please? What sort of thing is Ambergrease? **1662** H. STUBBE *Ind. Nectar* III. 45 Spicery (under which I comprise Amber-griese, and Musk). **1671** MILTON *P.R.* II. 341 In pastry built, or from the spit, or boiled, Gris-amber-steam'd. **1673** *Phil. Trans.* VIII. 6115 Amber-Greece is not the Scum or Excrement of the Whale, etc. **1680** MORDEN *Geog. Rect.* (1685) 407 There is also found.. Amber-greice. **1687** SEDLEY *Bellam.* IV. i, Breakfast.. upon new laid eggs, ambergrease and gravy. **1711** SHAFTESB. *Charac.* (1737) III. 207 Some wonderful rich dainty, richer than amber-greese. **1712** tr. *Pomet's Hist. Drugs* I. 19 Everybody now rejects Musk and Ambergriese. **1713** DERHAM *Physico-Theol.* IV. iv. 138 A piece of Amber-greece suspended in a pair of scales, lost nothing of its weight in 3½ days. *c* **1720** POPE in *Swift's Wks.* (1841) I. 837 Praise is like ambergris; a little whiff of it, by snatches, is very agreeable; but when a man holds a whole lump of it to his nose, it is a stink and strikes you down. **1774** GOLDSM. *Nat. Hist.* II. 228 Discovering the manner of preparing ambergrease. **1783** *Phil. Trans.* LXXIII. 226 Ambergrise, or properly speaking *Grey Amber*, is a solid, opaque, inflammable substance. **1791** *Ibid.* LXXXI. 47, I think amber-gris most likely to be found in a sickly fish. **1849** MACAULAY *Hist. Eng.* I. 442 Something had been put into his [Chas. II] favourite dish of eggs and ambergrease. **1874** HARTWIG *Aerial W.* ii. 24 Some papers perfumed with a grain of amber-gris still retained a strong odour after 40 years.

ambering ('æmbərɪŋ), *vbl. sb.* [f. AMBER *v.*] **1753** CHAMBERS *Cycl. Supp.*, *Ambering* is used by some writers to denote the giving a scent or perfume of amber to anything.

'amberjack. Also **amber jack.** [AMBER *sb.*[1]] A species of amber-fish, esp. *Seriola dumerili.* **1893** *Funk's Stand. Dict.*, *Amber-jack*, an amber-fish (*Seriola lalandi*). **1897** [see prec.]. **1960** *Catal. Names Fishes Medit.* (Gen. Fish. Council Medit.) 161 Seriola dumerili.. Amber jack.

amberoid, var. AMBROID.

'amber-seed. [f. AMBER *sb.*[1] in reference to their agreeable odour and use.] An old name for the seeds of *Abelmoschus moschatus*, also called Musk-seed, and Ambrette, used to perfume hair-powder, pomatum, etc. **1727-51** CHAMBERS *Cycl.*, *Amber-seed* or *Musk-seed*.. gives a grateful scent to the breath.

'amber-,tree. [f. AMBER *sb.*[1] in reference to the fragrant odour of its leaves.] A common name of the genus *Anthospermum*, consisting of evergreen shrubs with leaves fragrant when bruised. **1847** CRAIG, *Anthospermum*, the Amber-tree, a heath-looking shrub from the Cape of Good Hope.

ambery ('æmbərɪ), *a.* [f. AMBER *sb.*[1] + -Y[1].] Of the nature or colour of amber. **1862** THORNBURY *Turner* I. 89 A landscape-painter.. admired for a rich ambery tone he knew how to give.

ambery, obs. form of AMBRY.

ambes ace, ambes-as, obs. ff. AMBS-ACE.

ambi- (æmbɪ), repr. L. *ambi-* both, on both sides (*ambo* both), in various (chiefly scientific) terms (see words in *ambi-*). **ambiciliate** (-'sɪlɪət), *a. Ichth.*, having the scales on both sides of the body minutely toothed along the edges; **ambicolorate** (-'kɒlərət, -'kʌl-) *a. Ichth.*, applied to flat-fishes abnormally coloured on both sides instead of having the under side white; so **ambicolo'ration.** **1894** *Proc. Zool. Soc.* 439 Ambicolorate fish appear to be always what one may call 'ambiciliate' also. *Ibid.* 435 Why Cyclopean examples should be ambicolorate. *Ibid.* (*heading*) 432 On an Adult Specimen of the Common Sole.. with Symmetrical Eyes, with a Discussion of its bearing on Ambicoloration.

†**'ambiate**, *v. Obs. rare*$^{-1}$. [irreg. f. L. *ambī-re* (see AMBITION) + -ATE[3].] To desire earnestly, be ambitious of, ambition. **1652** SPARKE *Prim. Devotion* (1663) 162 You few that wisdom above treasure prize, And ambiate the title of the wise.

ambidexter (,æmbɪ'dɛkstə(r)), *a.* and *sb.* Also 6-8 **ambodexter.** [a. med.L. *ambidexter* (used in senses 2, 3), f. *amb(i)-* both, on both sides + *dexter* right-handed. In 17th c. generally spelt *ambodexter*, after L. *ambo* both.] **A.** *adj.*

1. *lit.* Right-handed on both sides, able to use the left hand as well as the right. **1646** SIR T. BROWNE *Pseud. Ep.* 191 So may Aristotle say, that only man is Ambidexter. **1751** SMOLLETT *Per. Pic.* (1779) IV. xcix. 292 Being ambi-dexter, he raised.. a clatter upon the turnkey's blind side. **1880** BLACKMORE *M. Anerley* II. xvi. 283 With his left hand, for he was ambidexter.. he caught up a handspike.

2. Double-dealing; practising on both sides. **1613** SIR H. FINCH *Law* (1636) 186 To call.. an Attornie Ambodexter, or to say that he dealeth corruptly. **1624** E. S. in *Shaks. Cent. Praise* 154 These ambi-dexter Gibionites. **1705** HICKERINGILL *Priest-cr.* I. (1721) 44 Nor Ambodexter Lawyers take a Fee On both sides. **1856** DOVE *Logic Chr. Faith* I. ii. II. §2. 94 Tortuous and ambidexter sophistries.

3. Of or belonging to both hands or sides; two-sided. **1806** W. TAYLOR *Ann. Rev.* IV. 228 Posted by double entry with the ambidexter formality of an Italian ledger. **1839** SIR J. STEPHEN *Ess. Eccl. Biog.* (1850) II. 37 An ambidexter controversialist, the English Church warred at once with the errors of Rome and of Geneva.

B. *sb.* [The adj. used *absol.*]

1. One who uses the left hand as well as the right; hence *fig.* a man of unusual dexterity. **1598** FLORIO Ded. 1 If we be not ambidexters, vsing both handes alike. **1615** CROOKE *Body of Man* 732 A woman, saith Hipocrates, cannot be an ambidexter. **1753** CHAMBERS *Cycl. Supp.* s.v., Surgeons and oculists are of necessity obliged to be Ambidexters.

2. *Law.* One who takes bribes from both sides. (The earliest sense in Eng.) **1532** *Use of Dice Play* (1850) 17 Any affinity with our men of law?.. Never with those that be honest. Marry! with such as be ambidexters, and use to play in both the hands. **1652** BENLOWE *Theoph.* XIII. xviii. 238 From costly bills of greedy Emp'ricks free, From plea of Ambo-dexters fee. **1691** BLOUNT *Law Dict.*, *Ambidexter*.. in the legal acception.. That Juror or Embraceor who takes Money on both sides for giving his Verdict. **1809** [So in TOMLINS.]

3. A double-dealer, a two-faced actor, generally. *a* **1555** RIDLEY *Wks.* 27 They may be called neutrals, ambi-dexters, or rather such as can shift on both sides. **1599** PEELE *Sir Clyomon* Wks. III. 44 Such shifting knaves as I am the ambodexter must play. **1628** WITHER *Brit. Rememb.* IV. 825 In this Battell I espy'd Some Ambodexters, fight on either side. **1703** DE FOE *Ref. Manners* 93 Those Ambo-Dexters in Religion, who Can any thing dispute, yet any thing can do. **1864** SIR F. PALGRAVE *Norm. & Eng.* III. 278 An Ambidexter, owing fealty to both Counts and not faithful to either.

ambidexterity (,æmbɪdɛk'stɛrɪtɪ). [f. prec. + -ITY, after *dexterity.*]

1. The power of using both hands alike. *a* **1652** BROME *Court Beggar* I. i. 191 Some Tellers Clearke to teach you Ambo-dexterity in telling money. **1753** CHAMBERS *Cycl. Supp.* s.v., Plato enjoins Ambidexterity to be observed and encouraged in his republic. **1881** *Times* 2 Feb. 10/5 The single-stick play.. was remarkable for its ambidexterity.

2. *fig.* Superior dexterity or cleverness; shiftiness or general readiness; manysidedness. **1760** STERNE *Trist. Shandy* III. xxxvii. 103 Speculative subtilty or ambidexterity of argumentation. **1804** W. TAYLOR *Ann. Rev.* II. 278 The idiomatic ambidexterity of a patriot of both countries. **1858** DE QUINCEY *Autobiog. Sk.* Wks. II. ii. 76 Presence of mind, and a general ambidexterity of powers for facing all accidents.

3. Double-dealing. **1755** in JOHNSON. **1841** D'ISRAELI *Amen. Lit.* (1859) I. 362 That intricate net of general misery, spun out of his own crafty ambidexterity.

ambidextral (,æmbɪ'dɛkstrəl), *a. rare.* [f. L. *ambidexter* + -AL[1].] Belonging to both sides. **1871** EARLE *Philol. Eng. Tong.* §84 What may be called the ambidextral adjective.. Thus Chaucer:—'I say the woful day fatal is come.'

ambidextrous, -erous (,æmbɪ'dɛkstrəs), *a.* [f. med.L. *ambidexter* + -OUS.] = AMBIDEXTER.

1. Able to use both hands alike. **1646** SIR T. BROWNE *Pseud. Ep.* 188 Not considering ambi-dextrous and left handed men. **1751** CHAMBERS *Cycl.* s.v., Women, according to the observation of Hippocrates, are never ambidextrous. **1878** BRYANT *Pract. Surg.* I. 340 Every ophthalmic surgeon should.. become ambidextrous.

2. *fig.* More than usually dextrous, or clever. **1682** SIR T. BROWNE *Chr. Mor.* (1756) 117 Many, who are sinistrous unto good actions, are ambi-dexterous unto bad. **1844** *Blackw. Mag.* LVI. 54 O many-sided, ambidextrous Goethe.

3. Acting in two opposite directions; and in a bad sense: Double-dealing; humouring both parties. **1654** GATAKER *Disc. Apol.* 77 An ambidextrous Trick.. of divers persons in the same familie adhering some to one partie and some to another. *a* **1768** STERNE *Pol. Romance* (1774) 316 A little, dirty, pimping, pettifogging, ambidextrous fellow. *a* **1847** CHALMERS *Posth. Wks.* I. 22 Rebuking Peter for his ambidextrous policy between Jews and Gentiles. **1858** J. MARTINEAU *Stud. Chr.* 279 It would be hypercritical to complain of the antithesis of understanding and feeling, sense and soul. But to an exact thinker.. an ambidextrous intellect is no intellect at all.

,ambi'dextrously, -erously *adv.* [f. AMBIDEXTROUS, -EROUS *a.* + -LY[2].] In an ambidextrous manner; with both hands; with more than usual dexterity; cunningly. **1791-1823** D'ISRAELI *Cur. Lit.* 459 To prove himself not to have been the author, [he] ambidexterously published another. **1837** *Blackw. Mag.* XLI. 439 Ambidexterously plying her knitting-needles.

,ambi'dextrousness. [f. as AMBIDEXTROUSLY *adv.* + -NESS.] The quality of being ambidextrous; ambidexterity. **1721** in BAILEY. **1881** *Sat. Rev.* No. 1323. 301 The remarkable ambidextrousness which he shows.

†**,ambi'dextry.** *Obs. rare*$^{-1}$. In 7 ambo-. [ad. med.L. *ambidextria*, f. *ambidexter.*] Double-dealing. Cf. AMBIDEXTER B 2. **1611** *Brief* in *3rd Rep. R. Comm. Hist. MSS.* (1872) 58/1 For ambodextry and disturbing the King's service, and threatening the jurors.

ambience ('æmbɪəns). Also ‖**ambiance** (ɑ̃biɑ̃s). [f. AMBIENT *a.*: see -ENCE; cf. F. *ambiance.*] Environment, surroundings; atmosphere.

The Fr. form *ambiance* is used in *Art* for the arrangement of accessories to support the main effect of a piece.

1889 *Harper's Mag.* Sept. 500/2 The form which we discern in the dreamy ambience is of supreme elegance. **1902** W. WATSON *Ode on Coronation of King Edward VII* 5 Slowly in the ambience of this crown Have many crowns been gathered. **1923** R. H. MYERS *Mod. Music* iv. 47 No other composer has ever reproduced in music with such complete success the very perfume and ambiance of a literary text. **1944** *Burlington Mag.* June 156/1 But the present picture was never meant to be microscopically dissected thus, for it is.. an impression, a single figure in its *ambiance*, which is vaguely suggested as reflections in a mirror. **1952** *Ballet Ann.* VI. 25 The costumes and sets.. have such a suggestion of space that they give the Sadler's Wells stage the *ambiance* of Covent Garden. **1957** *London Mag.* Jan. 52 For some writers the urban ambience may provide just the kind of stimulus they need. **1961** *Listener* 5 Oct. 527/2 The Zoo provides a colourful ambience for this Administrative Novel [*sc.* Angus Wilson's 'Old Men at the Zoo']. **1965** *N. & Q.* CCX. 15/1 The way in which the poet by the use of the traditional vocabulary gives the impression that he was introducing his heroine into a Germanic ambience.

ambiens ('æmbɪɛnz). *Ornith.* [pres. pple. of L. *ambīre* to go round, surround, f. *ambi-* around + *īre* to go.] A muscle in the thigh of certain birds, so called from the way in which it winds in passing from the hip to the foot. **1873** A. H. GARROD in *Proc. Zool. Soc.* 630 The ambiens and the accessory femoro-caudal are absent. **1884** COUES *N. Amer. Birds* (ed. 2) 193 The ambiens arises from the pelvis about the acetabulum, and passes along the inner side of the thigh.

ambient ('æmbɪənt), *a.* and *sb.* [ad. L. *ambientem* pr. pple. of *ambīre* to go about, f. *amb-* on both sides, round, about + *ī-re* to go. Cf. It. *ambiente* bef. 1600.] **A.** *adj.*

†**1.** Turning round, revolving. *Obs. rare.* **1614** CHAPMAN *Odyss.* I. 28 The point of time wrought out by ambient years. **1620** —— *Homer's Hymns* Ep. Ded., Of all arts ambient in the orbe of Man.

2. Moving round, circling about (something). *rare.* **1655-60** STANLEY *Hist. Philos.* (1701) 64/1 The ambient æther.. by the swiftness of its Motion, snatcheth up Stones from the Earth. **1692** BENTLEY *Boyle Lect.* 234 That the planets should naturally attain these circular revolutions.. by impulse of ambient bodies. **1834** DISRAELI *Rev. Epick* I. xxx. 15 Ye ambient Winds, That course about the quarters of the globe.

3. Lying round, surrounding, encircling, encompassing, environing. **1596** BELL *Surv. Popery* I. I. xvi. 69 As well for the ambient restraint. **1658** SIR T. BROWNE *Gard. Cyrus* i. 103 The tree of knowledge was placed in the middle of the Garden, what ever was the ambient figure. *c* **1750** SHENSTONE *Elegy* IX. 38 Exalted to yon ambient sky. **1784** BOSWELL *Johnson* (1816) IV. 428 A captive in thy ambient arms. **1850** BLACKIE *Æschylus* II. 37 With echoing groans the ambient waste bewails Thy fate. **1928** E. A. WILCOX *Electric Heating* vi. 128 Tank temperatures are constantly maintained at 100° F. above surrounding (or *ambient*) temperatures. **1958** *Engineering* 28 Mar. 393/3 The air pressure within the dome is maintained at the not uncomfortable figure of 2 lb per sq in above the ambient pressure.

4. *esp.* Surrounding as a fluid; circumfused. **1605** BACON *Adv. Learn.* (1640) 201 Consumption is caused by.. Depredation of innate Spirit, and Depredation of ambient Aire. **1667** MILTON *P.L.* VI. 481 Opening to the ambient light. **1711** POPE *Temp. Fame* 26 Whose tow'ring summit ambient clouds conceal'd. **1806** VINCE *Hydrost.* xi. 110 If the plate be cold, and the ambient fluid be warm. **1866** KINGSLEY *Herew.* v. 104 It diffused a delicate odour through the ambient air.

5. Rounded like a solid body. *rare.* **1801** FUSELI *Lect. Art* i. (1848) 360 He who decided his outline with such intelligence that it appeared ambient, and pronounced the parts that escaped the eye.

†**6.** Ambitious, aspiring. (A Latinism.) *Obs. rare.* **1647** N. BACON *Hist. Disc.* iii. 12 The Clergy.. soon began to be ambient and conceipt a new Idea of deportment.

¶ As an epithet of the air, often ignorantly put for 'limpid,' or otherwise misused.

B. *sb.* [The adj. used *absol.*]

†**1.** A canvasser, suitor, or aspirant. *Obs. rare.* **1649** BP. HALL *Confirmation* (1651) 16 What Fair-like confluences have we there seen of zealous ambients?

2. An encompassing circle or sphere. **1624** WOTTON *Elem. Archit.* (1672) 7 The aire.. being a perpetual ambient and ingredient. **1657** TOMLINSON *Renou's Disp.* 547 They are broad, asperated about their ambient. **1864** MACVICAR in *Reader* IV. 679/1 Atoms or molecules have extensive atmospheres or ambients of some kind.

3. *Astrol.* The ambient air or sky. **1686** GOAD *Celest. Bodies* III. iii. 472 ♄ and ♂, by the Repetition of the Aspect, may sometimes disturb the Ambient above a year. **1868** GEO. ELIOT *Sp. Gypsy* 193 For the ambient. Though a cause regnant, is not absolute.

‖**ambiente** (æmbɪ'ɛnteɪ). [It. and Sp., f. L. *ambient-em*: see AMBIENT *a.* and *sb.*] = AMBIENCE. **1926** D. H. LAWRENCE *Plumed Serp.* xii. 197 He was utterly still.. soft and unroused, within his own *ambiente*. **1927** —— *Lett.* (1962) II. 988 So with the mind. One's *ambiente* matters awfully. **1965** *House & Garden* Dec. 37/1 Within the entertaining ambiente of this decoratively practical kitchen/dining-room. **1966** M. STEEN *Looking Glass* iv. 75, I couldn't afford it, but I liked the *ambiente*.

†**ambi'farious**, *a. Obs.*$^{-0}$ [f. L. *ambifāri-us* two-sided, of double meaning + -OUS.] 'Double, or that may be taken both ways.' Blount *Glossogr.* 1656; whence in Bailey 1721.

†**'ambiform**, *a. Obs.*$^{-0}$ [ad. L. **ambiform-is* (in adv. *ambiformiter*), f. *amb(i)-* both + *-formis* -shaped.] 'Having a double form.' Bailey 1721.

†**'ambigate**, *v. Obs. rare*$^{-1}$. [irreg. f. L. *ambigĕre* to go round (taken as = *ambīre*: see AMBITION) + -ATE[3].] = AMBIATE. **1633** T. ADAMS *Exp. 2 Pet.* i. 6 There are some things, wherein it is no godliness to ambigate a likeness to God.

ambigenal (æm'bɪdʒɪnəl), *a.* [f. (by Newton) L. *ambigen-us* of two kinds, mongrel (f. *amb(i)-* both + *-gen-us* -born, -natured: see -GENOUS) + -AL[1]. Absurdly referred by some to *genu* a knee!] Of two kinds, hybrid. (Used by Newton to describe one kind of hyperbola.) **1727-51** CHAMBERS *Cycl.* s.v. *Hyperbola*, Ambigenal Hyperbola is that which has one of its infinite legs inscribed and the other circumscribed.

ambigenous (æm'bɪdʒɪnəs), *a.* [mod. f. L. *ambigen-us* (see prec.) + -OUS.] Of two kinds; *spec.* applied, after Mirbel, to a multifoliate calyx, externally leaf-like and internally petaloid.

1850 HENSLOW *Dict. Bot., Ambigenus.* **1879** in *Syd. Soc. Lex.*

†**'ambigu.** *Obs.* [a. mod.Fr. in same sense: prop. adj. = AMBIGUOUS.] An entertainment at which the viands and dessert are served together; or at which a medley of dishes are set on.

1688 *Lond. Gaz.* mmccclxxi/3 They were all entertain'd to their Satisfaction, at a very splendid Ambigu. *a* **1695** WOOD *Life* (1848) 287 This ambigu or banquet cost the University £160. **1753** CHAMBERS *Cycl. Supp., Ambigu* denotes a kind of mixed entertainment, wherein both flesh and fruit are served together.

†**am'bigual,** *a. Obs. rare*$^{-1}$. [f. L. *ambigu-us* AMBIGUOUS + -AL[1].] = AMBIGUOUS.

1683 CHALKHILL *Thealma & Cle.* 163 Wherefore he By some ambigual discourses thought It best to let him know the news he brought.

†**ambigue,** *a. Obs. rare*$^{-1}$. [ad. L. *ambigu-us*, or ? Fr. *ambigu.*] = AMBIGUOUS.

a **1733** NORTH *Examen* II. v. ¶ 19. 327 A clear Explication of '*running down*,' an ambigue Term of the Author's.

ambiguity (æmbɪ'gjuːɪtɪ). Also 5-6 **ambyguyte**, etc. [? a. Fr. *ambiguïté* (16th c. in Littré) ad. med.L. *ambiguitāt-em*, n. of state f. *ambigu-us* AMBIGUOUS.]

†**1.** Subjectively: Wavering of opinion; hesitation, doubt, uncertainty, as to one's course. *Obs.*

c **1400** *Beryn* 2577 Dout, pro, contra, and ambiguite. **1426** *Pol. Poems* II. 131 To put away..Holy the doute and the ambyguyté. **1502** ARNOLD *Chron.* (1811) 10 If deficultye or ambyguyte and dout were vpon ony artycle. *c* **1534** tr. *Polyd. Verg., Eng. Hist.* I. 160 Hee beganne to stande in great ambiguitee of his saftie. *c* **1590** MARLOWE *Faustus* i. 78 Shall I make spirits fetch me what I please, Resolve me of all ambiguities?

†**2.** *concr.* An uncertainty, a dubiety. *Obs.*

1598 BARCKLEY *Felic. Man.* (1631) 369 Here riseth an ambiguity of no small importance. **1658** BRAMHALL *Consecr. Bps.* iv. 99 And this was the onely question or ambiguity which was moved.

3. a. Objectively: Capability of being understood in two or more ways; double or dubious signification, ambiguousness.

c **1430** LYDG. *Bochas* VI. ii. (1554) 148a, To auoide al ambiguitie, To declare the summe of mine entent. **1549** *Compl. Scotl.* x. 83 Appollo gaue..ane doutsum ansuere of ambiguite. **1675** BAXTER *Cath. Theol.* I. I. 57 The Schoolmens contention whether the Son be freely begotten, and the Holy Ghost freely procceed, ariseth from the ambiguity of the word *free.* **1768** BLACKSTONE *Comm.* II. 71 The king..took a handle from the ambiguity of this expression to claim them both. **1849** MACAULAY *Hist. Eng.* II. 665 To clear the fundamental laws of the realm from ambiguity. **1866** ARGYLL *Reign of Law* ii. (ed. 4) 99 Confusion of thought arising..out of the ambiguity of language.

b. *spec.* in *Literary Criticism* (see quots.).

1930 W. EMPSON *Seven Types of Ambiguity* i. 1 An ambiguity, in ordinary speech, means something very pronounced, and as a rule witty and deceitful. I propose to use the word in an extended sense, and shall think relevant to my subject any consequence of language, however slight, which adds some nuance to the direct statement of prose. [ed. 3, 1953: I..shall think relevant to my subject any verbal nuance, however slight, which gives room for alternative reactions to the same piece of language.] **1962** W. NOWOTTNY *Lang. Poets Use* vii. 146 The term 'ambiguity' now has wide currency as a means of referring to diverse ways in which the language of poetry exhibits a charge of multiple implications and fits itself to contain within the form of discourse aspects of human experience whose difference or distance from one another might seem such as not easily to permit their coherent assembly in linguistic form. *Ibid.* 172 'Ambiguity' in its current critical sense of the manysidedness of language.

4. *concr.* A word or phrase susceptible of more than one meaning; an equivocal expression.

1591 HORSEY *Trav.* (1857) 207 This Emperowr reduced the ambiguities and uncertainties of their lawes..into a most plain forme. **1668** DRYDEN *Evenings Love* 56 Give me your hand, and answer me without Ambages or Ambiguities. **1699** BENTLEY *Phal.* 298 What a wretched Ambiguity would be here..unworthy of so elegant a Poet? **1871** MARKBY *Elem. Law* 415 Those plausible ambiguities which not infrequently occur in English law.

ambiguous (æm'bɪgjuːəs), *a.* [f. L. *ambigu-us* doubtful, driving hither and thither (f. *ambigĕre*, f. *amb-* both ways + *ag-ĕre* to drive) + -OUS.] The objective meanings, though second in Latin, seem earliest in Eng.

I. Objectively.

1. Doubtful, questionable; indistinct, obscure, not clearly defined.

1528 MORE *Heresyes* IV. Wks. 1557, 247/2 If it wer nowe doutful & ambiguous whether the church of Christ wer in the right rule of doctrine or not. **1573** MURRAY *Let.* in *Wodrow Soc. Misc.* (1844) 289 Cairfull for the gude ordour of the Kirk in thingis ambiguous. *c* **1800** K. WHITE *Contempl.* 133 Faint ambiguous shadows fall. **1851** RUSKIN *Mod. Paint.* I. II. 2. v. § 10 Even the most dexterous distances of the old masters..are ambiguous.

2. Of words or other significant indications: Admitting more than one interpretation, or explanation; of double meaning, or of several possible meanings; equivocal. (The commonest use.)

1532 MORE *Confut. Tindale* Wks. 1557, 437/1 This englishe word knowledge is ambiguous and doubtfull. **1589** PUTTENHAM *Eng. Poesie* (1869) 267 The ambiguous, or figure of sence incertaine, as if one should say *Thomas Tayler saw William Tyler dronke*, it is indifferent to thinke either th'one or th'other dronke. **1671** MILTON *P.R.* I. 435 Answers..dark, Ambiguous, and with double sense deluding. **1752** JOHNSON *Rambl.* No. 192 ¶ 8 The gentlemen ..irritated me with ambiguous insults. **1853** MAURICE *Proph. & Kings* xvii. 288, I do not rest anything upon tenses. Every reader of the prophets must feel how ambiguous they are. **1867** A. J. ELLIS *E.E. Pron.* I. i. 25 The Welsh alphabet ..having only one ambiguous letter, *y*.

3. Of doubtful position or classification, as partaking of two characters or being on the boundary line between.

1603 FLORIO *Montaigne* (1634) 294 Mungrell and ambiguous shapes. **1667** MILTON *P.L.* VII. 473 Ambiguous between sea and land The river-horse and scaly crocodile. **1756** HUME *Hist. Eng.* II. xx. 20 His character became fully known. and was no longer ambiguous to either faction. **1839** MURCHISON *Silur. Syst.* 418 Stratified rocks of ambiguous character.

II. Subjectively.

†**4.** Of persons: Wavering or uncertain as to course or conduct; hesitating, doubtful. *Obs.*

1550 NICOLS *Thucyd.* 175 (R.) People that be ambiguous or doubtefulle. **1649** MILTON *Eikonok.* 239 Thus shall they be too and fro, doubtfull and ambiguous in all thir doings.

5. Of things: Wavering or uncertain in direction or tendency; of doubtful or uncertain issue.

1612 SHELTON *Don Quix.* I. II. v. 90 That she do favour and protect him in that ambiguous Trance which he undertakes. **1813** SCOTT *Rokeby* I. xii, The eddying tides of conflict wheeled Ambiguous. **1850** MRS. BROWNING *Prom. Bd.* Poems I. 184 Do not cast Ambiguous paths, Prometheus, for my feet.

6. Hence, Insecure in its indications; not to be relied upon.

1756 BURKE *Subl. & B.* Wks. 1842 I. 26 The taste, that most ambiguous of the senses.

7. Of persons, oracles, etc.: Using words of doubtful or double meaning.

1566 KNOX *Hist. Ref.* Wks. 1846 I. 370 To no point wald sche answer directlie; bot in all thingis sche was..ambigua. *a* **1700** DRYDEN (J.) Th' ambiguous god, who rul'd her lab'ring breast. *a* **1725** POPE *Odyss.* I. 490 Antinous.. Constrain'd a smile and thus ambiguous spoke. **1864** SWINBURNE *Atalanta* 1500 What mutterest thou with thine ambiguous mouth.

ambiguously (æm'bɪgjuːəslɪ), *adv.* [f. prec. + -LY[2].] In an ambiguous manner: †**a.** Hesitatingly, doubtfully (*obs.*); **b.** With doubtful issue (*obs.*); **c.** Indistinctly, obscurely, questionably; **d.** In terms susceptible of more than one meaning.

1579 W. FULKE *Heskin's Parl.* 151 Hee vseth the name of bloud figuratiuely, and ambiguously. **1606** in *Misc. Scot.* I. 32 Valiantly and ambiguously was it foughten on both sides. **1652** *Seas. Expost. Netherl.* 5 Promises of Neutralitie drawn up so ambiguously, as if they had come from jugling Delphos. **1695** LD. PRESTON *Boeth.* v. 222 This Prophet used to speak ambiguously. **1813** SCOTT *Rokeby* II. xxiii, 'Where's Bertram? Why that naked blade?' Wilfred ambiguously replied, 'Bertram is gone.' **1823** LAMB *Elia* Ser. II. xxiv. 433 One that you conceived worse than ambiguously disposed towards you.

ambiguousness (æm'bɪgjuːəsnɪs). [f. as prec. + -NESS.] The quality of being ambiguous; capability of being understood in various ways.

1679 *Animadv. Speeches Jesuits* 2 Mental equivocation, not on the account of ambiguousness in the words..but because of a double sense in some Proposition. **1837** HALLAM *Hist. Lit.* III. ii. §26 Close reasoning which..yields to no ambiguousness of language. **1861** GOSCHEN *Foreign Exch.* 95 The ambiguousness of the term 'favorable exchanges.'

ambilævous, -levous (,æmbɪ'liːvəs), *a. rare*$^{-1}$. [f. L. *amb(i)-* both + *læv-us* left + -OUS.] As it were, left-handed on both sides; the opposite of *ambidexter*.

1646 SIR T. BROWNE *Pseud. Ep.* 191 Againe, some are.. Ambilevous or left handed on both sides. **1879** *Syd. Soc. Lex., Ambilævous*, Having left hands only; that is, clumsy.

ambi'lingual, *a.* and *sb.* [AMBI-, after *bilingual.*] (See quots.) Hence **ambi'lingualism**, the condition of being an ambilingual.

1959 J. C. CATFORD in Quirk & Smith *Teaching of English* vi. 164 In everyday speech the word 'bilingual' generally refers to a person who has virtually *equal* command of two or more languages. If a special term is required for such persons of equal linguistic skill (which is very difficult to measure) I should prefer to call them 'ambilinguals'. Ambilinguals are relatively rare. **1964** M. A. K. HALLIDAY et al. *Ling. Sciences* iv. 78 The endpoint where a speaker has complete mastery of two languages and makes use of both in all uses to which he puts either. Such a speaker is an 'ambilingual'. True ambilingual speakers are rare. *Ibid.*, Even those who approach or attain true ambilingualism are still usually unable to translate without instruction.

†**am'bilogy.** *Obs.*$^{-0}$ [f. L. *amb(i)-* both, on both sides + Gr. -λογία speaking.] 'Talk of ambiguous or doubtful signification.' J. (A needless hybrid for AMBILOQUY.)

1656 in BLOUNT *Glossogr.* **1731** in BAILEY; whence in J., etc.

†**am'biloquent,** *a. Obs.*$^{-0}$ [formed as next + -ENT, as in *magniloqu-ent*, L. *magniloqu-us.*] = next.

1656 BLOUNT *Glossogr., Ambiloquent*, that speaks doubtfully or two languages. [Not in JOHNSON.]

†**am'biloquous,** *a. Obs.*$^{-0}$ [f. med.L. *ambiloqu-us* (f. *amb(i)-* both, on both sides + *-loquus* speaking, *loqui* to speak) + -OUS.] 'Using ambiguous and doubtful expressions.' J.

1721 BAILEY, *Ambiloquous*, double-tongued. [In mod. Dicts.]

†**am'biloquy.** *Obs.*$^{-0}$ [ad. med.L. *ambiloquium* double-speaking: see prec. and -Y[3].] 'The use of doubtful and indeterminate expressions; discourse of doubtful meaning.' J.

1731 BAILEY, *Ambiloquy*, double-speaking. [In mod. Dicts.]

ambiparous (æm'bɪpərəs), *a. Bot.* [mod. f. L. *amb(i)-* both + *-par-us* producing: see -PAROUS.] 'Applied to a bud that contains the rudiments of both flowers and leaves.' *Syd. Soc. Lex.* 1879.

ambi'sextrous, *a. humorous.* [Blend of AMBIDEXTROUS *a.* and SEX *sb.*] = AMBISEXUAL *a.*

1929 M. LIEF *Hangover* vi. 96 The big scene..in which twenty or thirty young Apollos..paraded their ambisextrous charms all over the stage. **1960** *Spectator* 1 Apr. 475 She avoids ever producing her ambi-sextrous young publisher. **1976** T. SHARPE *Wilt* vii. 66 A lot of intellectual claptrap about Women's Lib and violence and the intolerance of tolerance and the revolution of the sexes and you're not fully mature unless you're ambisextrous. **1982** *Times Lit. Suppl.* 21 May 548/5 Painter argued for an ambisextrous Proust.

ambi'sexual, *a.* [f. AMBI- + SEXUAL *a.*] Of both sexes, bisexual; sexually attracted by or attractive to persons of either sex; of clothing, (that may be) worn by both men and women; not sexually distinctive, unisex. Cf. BISEXUAL *a.* 2.

1938 *Biol. Bull.* LXXV. 283 The activation of the male constituents of the primary ambisexual gonad always precedes the development of such secondary.. behaviouristic sexual characteristics. **1947** J. LEES-MILNE *Diary* 19 Feb. (1983) 136 Eddy stoutly denied the possibility of persons being ambisexual. **1969** *Daily Tel.* 29 May 16/5 The strip [*sc.* Sunset Boulevard] today is largely hippie record shops, ambi-sexual clothes stores, blue cinemas and psychedelic bars. **1975** MONEY & TUCKER *Sexual Signatures* (1976) i. 16 It is safe to say that every adult human being has, in fantasy, engaged in some sort of bisexual behavior..at some time in his or her life. 'Ambisexual' describes the human race more accurately than 'heterosexual', 'homosexual', or even 'bisexual', although the degree of ambisexuality varies in intensity from one person to the next. **1980** *Maledicta* IV. 59 The ancient Greeks, who gave us many of these synonyms, did not have a term for homosexuality, since they themselves were usually ambisexual.

So **ambisexu'ality**.

1924 H. ELLIS *Stud. Psychol. Sex* (ed. 3) II. iii. 81 Ferenczi, again..accepts 'the psychic capacity of the child to direct his originally objectless eroticism to one or both sexes', and terms this disposition ambisexuality. **1972** N. SAUNDERS *Alternative London* xxi. 225 Probably the ambisexuality of fashion has done more to bring about changes in attitude than any other single thing.

ambisinistrous (,æmbɪsɪ'nɪstrəs), *a.* [f. L. *amb(i)-* both + *sinister* left + -OUS.] = AMBILÆVOUS.

1863 LD. W. P. LENNOX *Biog. Remin.* I. 63 In wedlock, he [Prince of Wales]..was certainly more than ambi-sinistrous.

ambisonic (æmbɪ'sɒnɪk), *sb.* and *a.* [f. AMBI- + SONIC *a.*, SONICS *sb. pl.*] **A.** *sb. pl.* (const. as *sing.*) A system of (usu. high-fidelity) sound reproduction which uses two or more channels and four or more speakers in such a way that the effect of indirect sound can be reproduced in addition to other directional properties.

1973 P. FELGETT in *Hi-Fi News* July 1311/3 Ambisonics is quite a different matter from the offerings on most..so-called quadraphonic discs. **1973** *New Scientist* 20 Dec. 843/1 The new concept, called 'ambisonics', aims at giving the listener the experience not only of the spacial positioning of the performers, but also of the directional qualities of the reverberant sound. **1974** *Nature* 13 Dec. 537/2 Ambisonics is a complete system from the pick-up of the original sound field through encoding and decoding to the reconstruction of an approximation to the original sound-field in the listener's home. **1977** *Times* 14 June 5/5 The tests of the system, called ambisonics, will be part of Liverpool's jubilee celebrations. **1983** *Radio Times* 19 Mar. 12/1 *Gilgamesh*..is the first radio play to be recorded in ambisonics.

B. *adj.* Pertaining to or employing ambisonics.

1973 P. FELGETT in *Hi-Fi News* July 1311/1 There is still a need for a general term referring to either circular or spherical information, and for this purpose we can translate into Latin and say 'ambisonic'. **1973** *New Scientist* 20 Dec. 843/1 The CD4 system..is a method of frequency modulating the two channels of a conventional stereophonic LP record so as to provide four separate channels. This leaves open the way in which the channels are to be employed, and the 'ambisonic' system can use them optimally. **1976** *Gramophone* Sept. 501/2 The 'ambisonic' microphone system used imparts something of a bathroom quality in stereo. **1980** *New Scientist* 20 Mar. 929 Ambisonic master recordings are made in the full four-channel format. But the few which have so far been made available as discs or broadcasts have used three channels or less. **1983** *Radio Times* 19 Mar. 12/1 As yet..there are no ambisonic radio receivers.

Hence **ambi'sonically** *adv.*

1976 *Gramophone* Feb. 1398/2 QS must be compatible with ambisonic reproduction, since RM is itself ambisonically compatible. **1983** *Radio Times* 19 Mar. 12/4 No one can hear *Gilgamesh* ambisonically.

ambit ('æmbɪt). [ad. L. *ambit-us* a going round, a compass; f. *amb-* about + *-itus* going, f. *ī-re* to go.]

1. A circuit, compass, or circumference.

1597 J. KING *Jonah* (1864) 210 The very ambit of their walls and turrets. **1655** OUGHTRED in Rigaud *Corr. Sci. Men* (1841) I. 83 The area of the whole circle is equal to the half ambite multiplied by the radius. **1686** GOAD *Celest. Bodies* I. iii. 8 Prodigious Hailstones, whose ambit reaches five, six, seven Inches. **1713** DERHAM *Phys.-Theol.* 43 [The earth's] Ambit therefore is 24930 Miles. **1753** CHAMBERS *Cycl. Suppl.* s.v., A particular enquiry concerning the Ambit or circumference of antient Rome. **1794** T. TAYLOR *Pausanias* II. 38 The ambit of each of the parts above the prothysis is thirty-two feet.

2. *esp.* A space surrounding a house, castle, town, etc.; the precincts, liberties, 'verge.'

1398 TREVISA *Barth. De P.R.* XIX. cxxix. (1495) 938 Ambitus is a space bytwene place and hous of neighbours of two fote brode and an halfe ordeyned for a waye. **1753** CHAMBERS *Cycl. Supp.* s.v., It was frequent to inscribe the Ambit on it [a saint's tomb], that it might be known how far its sanctity extended. **1818** HALLAM *Mid. Ages* (1872) II. 428 Within the verge or ambit of the king's presence.

3. The confines, bounds, limits of a district.

1845 STEPHEN *Laws of Eng.* II. 745 Districts lying within the parochial ambit. **1851** SIR F. PALGRAVE *Norm. & Eng.* I. 240 Within the ambit of the ancient kingdom of Burgundy. **1876** K. DIGBY *Real Prop.* iv. §1. 178 Whose tenements are not within the ambit of the manor.

4. *fig.* Extent, compass, sphere, of actions, words, thoughts, etc.

1691 WOOD *Ath. Oxon.* II. col. 107 His great parts did not live within a small ambit. **1859** *Sat. Rev.* 19 Nov. 615/1 The ambit of words which a language possesses. **1882** *Times* 10 Apr. 7/1 Misconception as to the ambit of this legislation.

am'bitient. *Obs. rare*$^{-1}$. [ad. med.L. *ambitient-em* pr. pple. of *ambitīre* to solicit, fawn on.] (Used by confusion for) AMBIENT.

1657 TOMLINSON *Renou's Disp.* 331 Long leafs..whose ambitient is rotund.

ambition (æm'bɪʃən), *sb.* Also 4–5 -cion, -oun, ambitioun. [a. Fr. *ambition* (14th c. in Littr.), ad. L. *ambitiōn-em*, n. of action f. *ambī-re* to go round or about (see AMBIT), 1. going round, 2. going round to canvass for votes, 3. eager desire of honour, etc., 4. ostentation, pomp, 5. earnest desire generally. Of these, meaning 3 was first adopted in the modern languages; 2 is a later literary adoption directly from Latin.]

1. The ardent (in *early usage*, inordinate) desire to rise to high position, or to attain rank, influence, distinction or other preferment.

1340 *Ayenb.* 22 Ambicion, þet is kuead wilninge heȝe to clue. *c* **1449** PECOCK *Repr.* III. viii. 323 Vicis..as pride, ambicioun, vein glorie. **1593** NASHE *Christ's Teares* 41 a, Ambition is any puft vp greedy humour of honour or preferment. **1601** SHAKS. *Jul. C.* II. i. 22 Lowlynesse is young Ambition's Ladder Whereto the Climber vpward turnes his Face. **1613** —— *Hen. VIII*, III. ii. 441 Cromwel, I charge thee, fling away Ambition, By that sinne fell the Angels. **1621** FLETCHER *Isl. Princ.* III. i, Love and Ambition draw the devils coach. **1771** *Junius Lett.* xlix. 254 That kind of fame to which you have hitherto directed your ambition. **1821** BYRON *Cain* II. ii, Dust! limit thy ambition. **1866** W. ALGER *Solit. Nat. & Man* III. 120 Aspiration is a pure upward desire for excellence, without side-references; ambition is an inflamed desire to surpass others. **1883** GLADSTONE *Sp. in Parl.* 26 Apr., A seat in this House is to the ordinary Englishman in early life..the highest prize of his ambition.

†**2.** Ostentation, display of the outward tokens of position, as riches, dress; vain-glory, pomp. *Obs.*

1382 WYCLIF *Acts* xxv. 23 Agrippa and Bernyce camen with moche ambicioun, *or pryde of staat.* *a* **1631** DONNE *Serm.* lvii. 579 a, Costly and expensive ambitions at Court.

3. A strong or ardent desire of anything considered advantageous, honouring, or creditable. Const. *of* (rarely *for*) a thing, *to be* or *do* something.

1607 BACON *Ess., Ambition* (Arb.) 226 It is lesse harmefull, the Ambition to prevaile in great Things, then that other, to appeare in every thing. **1610** SHAKS. *Temp.* I. ii. 482, I haue no ambition To see a goodlier man. **1737** POPE *Lett.* Pref., A juvenile ambition of Wit, or affectation of Gayety. **1756** BURKE *Vind. Nat. Soc.* Wks. I. 22 The pitiful ambition of possessing five or six thousand more acres. **1770** LANGHORNE *Plutarch's Lives* (1879) II. 898/2 Some populous town which has an ambition for literature.

4. The object of strong desire or aspiration.

1602 SHAKS. *Haml.* III. iii. 55 My Crowne mine own Ambition and my Queene. **1798** FERRIAR *Illustr. Sterne* i. 21 To jest was the ambition of the best company. **1857** RUSKIN *Pol. Econ. Art.* 37 Their pleasure is in memory, and their ambition is in heaven.

†**5.** Canvassing, personal solicitation of honours. (L. *ambitio.*) *Obs.*

1531 ELYOT *Governor* III. xvi. (R.) Certayne lawes were made by the Romaynes..named the lawes of ambition. **1671** MILTON *Samson* 246, I, on the other side, Used no ambition to commend my deeds. **1677** *Houssaie's Govt. Venice* 13 This bartering and ambition of Office was forbidden.

ambition (æm'bɪʃən), *v.* [a. Fr. *ambitionne-r*, f. *ambition*; cf. *raisonner* to reason, f. *raison* reason.]

†**1.** To move to ambition, to make desirous. *Obs.*

a **1628** F. GREVILLE *Life of Sidney* Ded., Who hath ambition'd me to make this offering.

2. To be ambitious of, to desire strongly. **a.** Const. *simple obj.*

1664 MRQ. WORC. in Dircks' *Life* xvii. (1865) 270 Whatever I have or do ambition. **1776** H. WALPOLE in *Last Jrnls.* (1859) II. 51 The Bishop of Chester had ambitioned the Bishopric of Winchester. **1824** D'ISRAELI *Cur. Lit.* (1866) 365/1 Every noble youth..ambitioned the notice of the Lady Arabella. **1881** R. PIGOTT in *Macm. Mag.* Dec. 174/2 The Fenian leaders ambitioned not the extinction of landlordism, but rather the reconciliation of landlords and tenants.

b. Const. *inf.* or *clause.*

1688 CLAYTON in *Phil. Trans.* XVII. 979 Each ambitioning to engross as much as they can. **1818** T. JEFFERSON *Writ.* (1830) IV. 453 Who ambitioned to be his correspondent. **1871** H. SMART *Cecile* 5 Ambitioning that her lover should make his mark.

†**am'bitionat(e,** *ppl. a. Obs. rare*$^{-1}$. [f. prec. + -ATE (as if ad. L. **ambitiōnāt-us*), latinized upon Fr. *ambitionné* (cf. *moderate*, *modéré*), or Eng. AMBITIONED, cf. *destined*, *destinate*.] Sought with ambition; ambitiously desired.

1671 *True Non-Conf.* 30 The Garland of Martyrdom became a most Ambitionat Crown.

†**am'bitionate,** *v. Obs. rare*$^{-1}$. [f. prec., or latinized ad. Fr. *ambitionner*; cf. *compassionate*.] = AMBITION *v.* 2.

1659 GAUDEN *Tears of Ch.* 252 (D.) The petty Provinces of their Parochial and Independent Episcopacies which they so infinitely ambitionated.

ambitioned (æm'bɪʃənd), *ppl. a. rare.* [f. AMBITION *v.* + -ED.] Eagerly sought after or desired.

1651 R. BOYLE *Parthenissa* (1655) I. I. 5 My performing it has not onely produc'd the ambition'd effect of making you perceive your fault. **1670** G. H. *Hist. Cardinals* I. iii. 70 The most coveted and ambition'd dignity in the world. **1824** *New Monthly Mag.* XI. 555 A long-ambitioned and long-promised addition to her summer finery. **1873** C. M. YONGE *Pillars of House* III. xxix. 137 'I should not have thought it a woman's work.' This, the most ambitioned praise a woman can receive.

ambitioning (æm'bɪʃənɪŋ), *ppl. a. rare.* [f. as prec. + -ING^{2}.] Eagerly seeking or desiring.

1709 KENNET tr. *Erasm. Moriæ Enc.* 61 More the object of a commiserating pity, than of an ambitioning envy.

ambitionist (æm'bɪʃənɪst). *rare.* [f. AMBITION *sb.* + -IST.] One who is ruled by ambition.

1655 TRAPP *Marrow of Auth.* (1868) 812/1 Oh, therefore that our aspiring ambitionists would but measure themselves by their own model. **1657** —— *Comm. Esther* v. 5 Cæsar Borgia, that restless ambitionist. **1827** CARLYLE *Misc.* (1857) IV. 146 (D.) Napoleon..became a selfish ambitionist and quack.

†**ambitionize** (æm'bɪʃənaɪz), *v. Obs. rare.* [f. as prec. + -IZE. Cited only in pa. pple.] To make ambitious.

1600 TOURNEUR *Transf. Metam.* xix. 128 Their minds ambitioniz'd do seeke her fall.

ambitionless (æm'bɪʃənlɪs), *a.* [f. as prec. + -LESS.] Void of ambition.

1828 POLLOK *Course of Time* III. (1860) 64 The simple hind who seemed Ambitionless, arrayed in humble garb. **1829** GLEIG *Chelsea Pens.* 318, I am a poor ambitionless wretch.

†**ambiti'osity.** *Obs.* [f. L. *ambitiōs-us* + -ITY.] The state of being ambitious; ambitiousness.

1535 STEWART *Cron. Scot.* III. 358 Ouir greit desyre of ambitiositie Causis richt mony ressoun for to tyne. **1731** BAILEY, *Ambitiosity*, Ambitiousness.

ambitious (æm'bɪʃəs), *a.* Also 4–6 ambicious, cyous(e, etc. [ad. Fr. *ambitieux*, or its orig., L. *ambitiōs-us*: see AMBITION and -OUS.]

1. Full of ambition, thirsting after honour or advancement; aspiring to high position.

1382 WYCLIF *1 Cor.* xiii. 5 Not inblowyn..not ambicious, *or coueitous of worschipis* [Vulg. *ambitiosa*]. **1484** CAXTON *Curial* 6 Thambycious vanyte of the peple of the court. **1538** BALE *Thre Lawes* 1609 The first are ambycyouse prelates. **1601** SHAKS. *Jul. C.* III. ii. 95 Did this in Cæsar seeme Ambitious? **1667** MILTON *P.L.* I. 41 With ambitious aim Against the Throne and Monarchy of God. **1711** ADDISON *Spect.* No. 256 ⁋7 How few ambitious men are there, who have got as much Fame as they desired. **1876** MOZLEY *Univ. Serm.* iv. 79 An ambitious mind..wants success.

2. Strongly desirous (*of* something expected to bring credit or honour), eager. Const. *of* (*for* obs.) a thing; *to be* or *do* something.

1513 MORE *Rich. III*, Wks. 1557, 65/2 His owne ambicious minde and deuise, to..take himself the crown. **1600** SHAKS. *A.Y.L.* II. vii. 43 O that I were a foole, I am ambitious for a motley coat. **1651** HOBBES *Leviathan* I. xi. 48 Men that are ambitious of Military Command. **1653** WALTON *Angl.* (1877) 51 You are such a companion..as makes me ambitious to be your scholer. **1718** LADY M. MONTAGUE *Lett.* II. lvi. 86 An ambitious thirst after knowledge. **1855** H. REED *Lect. Eng. Lit.* iii. (1878) 100 The half educated are always most ambitious of long words.

3. *fig.* Erecting itself, as if aspiring to rise; rising, swelling, towering.

1601 SHAKS. *Jul. C.* I. iii. 7, I haue seene Th'ambitious Ocean swell. **1605** B. JONSON *Volpone* I. ii. (1616) 455 Hood an asse..So you can hide his two ambitious eares, And he shall passe for a cathedrall Doctor. *c* **1735** POPE *Mor. Ess.* iv. 59 Helps th'ambitious hill the heav'ns to scale.

4. Of works of art, etc.: Displaying ambition or aspiration on the part of the author; aspiring or pretending to take a high position.

1751 JOHNSON *Rambl.* No. 156 ⁋2 The simplicity is embarrassed by ambitious additions. **1846** MILL *Logic* II. vii. §4 Put off the ambitious phraseology. *Mod.* This ambitious attempt ended in failure.

†**5.** Circuitous, circumlocutory, ambagious. (A Latinism.) *Obs. rare.*

1656 *Vind. Jud.* in *Phenix* (1708) No. 24. 392 Your Worship cannot expect either prolix or polite discourses upon so sad a subject; for who can be ambitious in his own calamity?

†**6.** quasi-*sb.* An ambitious man. *Obs.*

c **1430** LYDG. *Bochas* VIII. i. (1554) 177 a, The proud ambicious called Domician. **1563** *Homilies* II. xxi. v. (1640) 307 A few ambitious, and malicious are the authours..of Rebellion.

ambitiously (æm'bɪʃəslɪ), *adv.* [f. prec. + -LY^{2}.]

1. In an ambitious manner; with eager desire of attaining to high position or gaining advantage.

1413 LYDG. *Pylgr. Sowle* III. vii. (1483) 54 They hauen set their hertes ambiciously for to kepen and assemblen sommes of tresour. **1561** T. N[ORTON] *Calvin's Inst.* III. 227 Nor ambiciously gape for honors. **1588** SHAKS. *Tit. A.* I. i. 18 Princes, that striue..Ambitiously for Rule and Empery. **1655** FULLER *Ch. Hist.* II. 70 Martyrdome, as it is not cowardly to be declined, so it is not ambitiously to be affected. **1781** GIBBON *Decl. & F.* III. 116 A croud of rivals, who ambitiously disputed the hand of the princess. **1805** WORDSW. *Waggoner* IV, Guide after guide Ambitiously the office tried.

2. With manifest effort to be something great; in bad sense, pretentiously.

1822 *New Monthly Mag.* V. 332 Scenic description..laboriously and ambitiously worked up. *a* **1884** *Mod.* An address ambitiously worded. Ambitiously conceived, but unsuccessfully carried out.

†**3.** By personal canvassing; fawningly. *Obs. rare.*

1598 GREENWEY *Tacitus Ann.* IV. i. 89 Neither did he abstaine from ambitiously courting the Senators.

ambitiousness (æm'bɪʃəsnɪs). [f. as prec. + -NESS.] The quality of being ambitious; eagerness to attain a high position; pretentiousness.

1477 NORTON *Ord. Alch.* in Ashm. 1652 i. 13 It [Alchemy] voydeth [*i.e.* nullifies] Ambitiousnesse. **1548** UDALL, etc. *Erasm. Paraphr. Mark* Pref. 6 To litle to satisfie his ambiciousnes. **1610** HEALEY *St. Aug., City of God* 218 Yet let the love of righteousnesse suppresse the thirst of ambitiousnesse. **1845** SHAW in *Blackw. Mag.* LVIII. 34 Those who measure the value of a poem..by the pretension and ambitiousness of its form.

ambitty (æm'bɪtɪ), *a. Glass-making.* Also **ambetti, ambetty, ambitti.** [app. ad. F. *ambité*, of obscure origin.] Designating glass which becomes devitrified while it is being worked. Also *absol.*

1883 H. CHANCE *Crown & Sheet Glass* in H. J. Powell et al. *Glass-Making* 104 Glass made with sulphate of soda is less liable to devitrify or as it is termed, become 'ambitty' in the pot during the time of working. **1885** F. MILLER *Glass-painting* 52 A beautiful make of glass is anbetti [*sic*]. **1885** *Spon's Mechanic's Own Book* 630 'Ambilti' [*sic*] (single and double) is a sheet glass, originally of Italian manufacture. **1902** SUFFLING *Art of Glass Painting* 63 Ambetty sheet. **1953** *Glass for Glazing (B.S.I.)* 20 *Ambetti, antique venetian*, [etc.]..translucent 'antique' glasses used chiefly for leaded lights and decorative purposes.

†**'ambitude.** *Obs.*$^{-0}$ [ad. L. *ambitūdo*, f. *ambitus*: see AMBIT and -TUDE.] 'A circuit or compassing round; also ambition.' Blount *Glossogr.* 1681.

ambivalence, -ency (æm'bɪvələns, -ənsɪ). [ad. G. *ambivalenz* (Bleuler 1910–11, in *Psychiatr.-neurol. Wochenschrift* Nos. 18–21), after EQUIVALENCE, EQUIVALENCY.] The coexistence in one person of contradictory emotions or attitudes (as love and hatred) towards a person or thing.

The examples in *β* illustrate the diverse applications of the word in literary and general works: a balance or combination or coexistence of opposites; oscillation, fluctuation, variability, etc. Quot. 1948 shows a *spec.* techn. sense.

a. In *Psychology.*

1912 *Lancet* 21 Dec. 1730 'Ambivalency', a condition which gives to the same idea two contrary feeling-tones and invests the same thought simultaneously with both a positive and a negative character. **1913** *Amer. Jrnl. Insanity* 880 This ambivalency leads, even with normal people, to difficulties of decision and to inner conflict. **1916** C. E. LONG tr. *Jung's Analytical Psychol.* vi. 200 The author [*sc.* Bleuler] presents us with a new psychological conception.. viz. the concept of ambivalency... This must not be taken as meaning that every positive psychic action simply calls up its opposite. **1924** A. A. BRILL tr. *Bleuler's Textbk. Psychiatry* xiii. 382 The synchronous laughing and crying are a partial manifestation of schizophrenic ambivalence. **1927** HENDERSON & GILLESPIE *Text-Bk. Psychiatry* ix. 197 In Bleuler's opinion, ambivalence is simply one aspect of the not yet fully understood disorder of association which he supposes to be the fundamental defect in schizophrenic thinking.

β. **1939** L. TRILLING *M. Arnold* iv. 123 Rousseau's *Confessions* had laid the ground for the understanding of emotional ambivalence. **1948** M. JOOS *Acoustic Phonetics* 23 The principle of ambivalence, which states that any thing which is capable of emitting acoustic power linearly will also absorb acoustic power according [to] the same rules that govern its behavior as an emitter. **1953** *Times Lit. Suppl.* 9 Oct. 645/2 What social anthropologists call 'plural belonging', what literary critics call ambivalence of attitude, and what the proverb calls having your cake and eating it, is a common human phenomenon. **1956** A. L. ROWSE *Early Churchills* p. vii, There is much to be said for a certain judicious ambivalence. **1959** *Times Rev. Industry* Mar. 4/3 There is an ambivalence in the claims on promotional moneys, for the furtherance of distribution on the one hand and for the extension of advertising on the other. **1963** *Oxf. Mag.* 6 June 353/1 The ambivalence of Arnold's attitude to the Romantics.

ambivalent (æm'bɪvələnt), *a.* [f. AMBIVALENCE, after EQUIVALENT *a.*] Of, pertaining to, or characterized by ambivalence; having either or both of two contrary or parallel values, qualities or meanings; entertaining contradictory emotions (as love and hatred) towards the same person or thing; acting on or arguing for sometimes one and sometimes the other of two opposites; equivocal.

(*a*) In *Psychology*.

1916 C. E. LONG tr. *Jung's Analytical Psychol.* vi. 200 Tendencies, under the stress of emotions, are balanced by their opposites—thus giving an ambivalent character to their expression. **1920** P. M. BLANCHARD *Adolescent Girl* (1921) v. 125 A second case where the falsehoods were.. the result of ambivalent desire for and fear of the erotic life. **1922** J. RIVIERE tr. *Freud's Introd. Lect. Psycho-Analysis* II. xv. 194 The coincidence of opposites in the dream-work is analogous to what is called the antithetical sense of primal words in the oldest languages. The philologist, R. Abel.. begs us not.. to imagine that there was any ambiguity in what one person said to another by means of ambivalent words of this sort. **1924** A. A. BRILL tr. *Bleuler's Textbk. Psychiatry* ii. 126 It is chiefly ambivalent complexes that influence pathology. **1954** *Listener* 30 Sept. 523/2 Our deeper urges are strangely ambivalent, ready to spend themselves on love or hate, altruism or destruction.

(*b*) In literary and general use.

1929 B. RUSSELL *Marriage & Morals* xiii. 140 Christianity .. has always had an ambivalent attitude towards the family. **1939** L. TRILLING *M. Arnold* iv. 123 The story of ambivalent love is a characteristic one of the 19th century. **1947** C. S. LEWIS *Miracles* xiv. 151 Death is.. what some modern people would call 'ambivalent'. It is Satan's great weapon and also God's great weapon; it is holy and unholy; our supreme disgrace and our only hope. **1957** D. J. ENRIGHT *Apothecary's Shop* 196 Where Rilke is concerned .. Auden's attitude in his poetry is ambivalent. He cannot help disapproving the application, but.. he cannot help praising the technique. **1958** A. E. DYSON in *Ess. & Stud.* 53 Irony is.. the most ambivalent of modes, constantly changing colour and texture. **1958** J. PRESS *Chequer'd Shade* v. 93 Some readers obviously derive from poetry which they do not comprehend a peculiar, ambivalent pleasure. **1963** *Times Lit. Suppl.* 15 Feb. 103/2 Ambivalent-seeming relations with his brilliant Eton tutor. **1965** *Camb. Rev.* 20 Feb. 273/1 A Ph.D. is a somewhat ambivalent acquisition: it is not always clear whether it is mentioned as a positive desideratum or a last resort.

ambiversion (æmbɪ'vɜːʃən). *Psychol.* [f. AMBI- + L. *versiōn-em*, n. of action f. *vertĕre* to turn; cf. EXTROVERSION 3, INTROVERSION.] A mental condition characterized by a balance of extravert and introvert features. Hence **'ambivert**, a person whose mind is so formed. Also **'ambiverted** *a.*

1927 K. YOUNG *Source Bk. Social Psychol.* III. xv. 399 People who.. are both extroverted and introverted... I shall .. call them *ambiverted*. *Ibid.* 401 These I have called ambiverts. *Ibid.* 402 The definition of ambiversion.. is to be stated as a condition of development in which attention is controlled by either objective or subjective conditions of attention and in which the content of the subjective conditions is so varied as to make possible.. prolonged periods of either extroversion or introversion. **1930** R. S. WOODWORTH *Psychol.* (ed. 8) xiii. 558 People fall into the two opposed types of *introvert* and *extrovert* with an intervening group of ambiverts.

†**'amblant**, *ppl. a. Obs.* [a. Fr. *amblant* pr. pple. of *ambler*, perh. identified with *ambland*, north. form of pr. pple.: see AMBLING *a.*] Ambling.

c **1300** *K. Alis.* 3462 Mony fat palfray amblant, And mony armed olifant. **1393** GOWER *Conf.* I. 210 Upon a mule white amblaunte.

amble ('æmb(ə)l), *v.* [a. Fr. *amble-r*:—L. *ambulā-re* to walk.]

1. *intr.* Of a horse, mule, etc.: To move by lifting the two feet on one side together, alternately with the two feet on the other; hence, to move at a smooth or easy pace.

c **1386** CHAUCER *Clerkes T.* 332 An hors snow-whit and wel amblyng. *c* **1400** *Beryn* 940 As hors that evir trottid, trewlich I yew tell, It were hard to make hym after to ambill well. **1553** T. WILSON *Rhet.* 66 Trotte sire and trotte damme, how should the fole amble? that is, when bothe father and mother were noughte, it is not like that the childe wil prove good. **1587** HOLINSHED *Chron.* II. 20/1 They amble not, but gallop and run. **1600** SHAKS. *A.Y.L.* III. ii. 328, I will tell you who time ambles withal; who time trots withal; who time gallops withal; and who he stands withal. **1650** B. *Discollim.* 5 She ambles with one leg, trots with another. **1690** *Lond. Gaz.* mmdxc/4 [The Mare] hath all her Goings, but ambles most. **1703** STEELE *Tender Husb.* II. i, A chariot drawn by one horse ambling, and t'other trotting. **1812** COMBE (Dr. Syntax) *Picturesque* VIII. 27 Grizzle, all alive and gay, Ambled along the ready way.

2. Of a person: To ride an ambling horse, to ride at an easy pace.

c **1386** CHAUCER *Wife's Prol.* 838 What? amble, or trotte, or pees, or go sit doun. **1568** *Jacob & Esau* IV. iv. in Hazl. *Dodsl.* II. 235, I will amble so fast, that I will soon be there. **1676** WYCHERLEY *Plain-Dealer* IV. i. 55 Are all my hopes frustrated? shall I never.. see thee amble the Circuit with the Judges? **1742** FIELDING *Jos. Andr.* Wks. 1784 V. II. ii. 109 A grave serjeant at law condescended to amble to Westminster on an easy pad. **1856** T. TROLLOPE *Cath. de Medici* 246 [The] little ladies, as they ambled on side by side, at the head of their gay cavalcade. *a* **1859** MACAULAY *Hist. Eng.* V. 306 William was ambling on a favourite horse.. through the park of Hampton Court.

3. Hence, To move in a way suggesting the motion or pace of an ambling horse. Said of dancing, of the gait of an elderly person, or *fig.* of any easy motion.

1596 SHAKS. *1 Hen. IV*, III. ii. 60 The skipping King, hee ambled vp and downe. **1612** DRAYTON *Poly-olb.* i. 7 The Tawe.. easely ambling downe through the Deuonian dales. **1713** ROWE *Jane Shore* (J.) Make him amble on a gossip's message. **1714** *Spect.* No. 623 ¶16 A pretty young creature who closed the Procession came ambling in. **1715** ADDISON *Drummer* I. i, She has.. play'd at an Assembly, and ambled in a Ball or two. **1765** H. WALPOLE *Otranto* ii. (1798) 31 How fast your thoughts amble. **1812** COMBE (Dr. Syntax) *Picturesque* XVII. 67 You shall soon Be ambling to some pretty tune. **1850** MRS. STOWE *Uncle Tom's C.* xi. 92 A good-natured but extremely fidgetty and cautious old gentleman, ambled up and down the room.

amble ('æmb(ə)l), *sb.* Also 4–5 **aumble**, 5 **ambil**, **ambel**. [a. Fr. *amble*, f. vb. *ambler*: see prec.]

1. The pace described in prec. (sense 1) and *loosely*, an easy pace.

c **1386** CHAUCER *Sir Thopas* 174 His steede was al dappul gray, It goth an ambel [*v.r.* ambil, aumble] in the way. **1598** B. JONSON *Ev. Man in Hum.* (J.) Out of the old hackney-pace to a fine easy amble. **1751** CHAMBERS *Cycl.* s.v., An Amble is usually the first natural pace of young colts.. There is [now] no such thing as an Amble in the manage; the riding-masters allowing of no other paces, beside walk, trot, and gallop. **1840** DICKENS *Barn. Rudge* (1866) I. xiv. 65 The grey mare.. breaking from her sober amble into a gentle trot. **1859** JEPHSON *Brittany* viii. 111 The usual pace of these animals [mules] is an amble, which consists in lifting both legs on the same side at once.

2. Of persons: A movement in dancing or walking suggesting an amble; an artificial or acquired pace.

1607 TOURNEUR *Rev. Trag.* III. v. 84 Put a Reueller Out of his Antick amble. **1632** MASSINGER *Maid of Hon.* I. ii, To teach him his true amble and his postures When he walks before a lady. **1819** SCOTT *Ivanhoe* I. xii. 177 There is many one of them upon the amble in such a night as this.

ambleocarpous (ˌæmbliːəʊ'kɑːpəs), *a. Bot.* [mod. f. Gr. ἀμβλό-εσθαι to miscarry, come to nought + καρπ-ός fruit + -OUS: the *e* in the second syllable is not etymological.] Having the seeds entirely, or in great part, abortive.

1847 in CRAIG. **1879** in *Syd. Soc. Lex.*

ambler ('æmblə(r)). Also 4–5 **amblere**, **aumbelere**, 5 **ambuler**. [f. AMBLE *v.* + -ER[1].] One that ambles; hence,

1. An ambling horse or mule.

c **1386** CHAUCER *Prol.* 469 Vp on an amblere [*v.r.* aumbelere] esily sche sat. *c* **1449** PECOCK *Repr.* v. viii. 525 A man holdith vp with the bridil the heed of his ambuler. **1464** *Mann. & Househ. Exp.* 184, Ij. hawmbelerres koltes in Wensche parke. **1470–85** MALORY *Arthur* II. xxviii. (1817) II. 47 He mounted vpon a softe ambuler and rode to Kynge Marke. **1591** PERCIVALL *Span. Dict.*, *Amblador*, an ambler, *Gradarius equus*. **1630** HOWELL *Lett.* 5 June, An ambler is proper for a lady's saddle, but not for a coach. **1725** BRADLEY *Fam. Dict.* s.v. *Horse*, The Ambler is a little unapt to it [galloping], because the motions are both one.

2. One who rides an ambling horse.

1737 BRACKEN *Farriery Impr.* (1756) I. xix. 164 The Ambler had rid the Horse into the cold Water.

3. One who 'ambles' in dancing or walking.

1865 DICKENS *Mut. Fr.* I. xi, The ambler took Miss Podsnap for a furniture walk. *Ibid.*, Georgiana having left the ambler up a lane of sofa.

†**am'blere.** *Obs. rare*[−1]. [prob. a. OFr. *ambleure*:—L. *ambulātūra* act of pacing, f. *ambulāre*: see AMBLE *v.*] An amble or ambling pace.

c **1380** *Sir Ferumb.* 344 Dvc Oliuer him rideþ out of þat plas: in a softe amblere, ne made he non oþer pas.

ambligon, obs. variant of AMBLYGON.

ambling ('æmblɪŋ), *vbl. sb.* [f. AMBLE *v.* + -ING[1].]

1. Of a horse: Motion in an amble.

1580 BARET *Alv.* A 344 The pleasant pase or ambling of a horse, *Glomeratio*. **1646** SIR T. BROWNE *Pseud. Ep.* IV. vi. 193 They move *per latera*, that is two legs of one side together, which is Tollutation or ambling. **1725** BRADLEY *Fam. Dict.* s.v. *Horse*, Ambling; which is chosen for Ease, Great Men's Seats, or long Travel, is a Motion contrary to Trotting. **1847** YOUATT *Horse* ii. 19 As for trotting, cantering, or ambling, it would be an unpardonable fault were he ever to be guilty of it.

2. Of persons: Dancing or walking in an amble; tripping, gliding, walking affectedly.

1592 SHAKS. *Rom. & Jul.* I. iv. 11, I am not for this ambling; Being but heavy, I will beare the light. **1748** RICHARDSON *Clarissa* (1811) I. x. 65 What.. your uncle Antony means by his frequent amblings hither. **1810** CRABBE *Borough* xix. 35 Their wanton ambling and their watchful wiles. **1828** SCOTT *F.M. Perth* xii, For all thy mincing and ambling.

3. *attrib.* (formally identical w. AMBLING *ppl. a.*)

a **1450** *Knt. G. de la Tour* (1868) 9 Sette a colte in aumblyng ringes, he wille use it whiles thei aren on. **1580** TUSSER *Husb.* XCV. ii, Least homelie breaker mar fine ambling ball. *a* **1635** CORBETT *Poems* (1807) 19 A wondrous witty ambling pace. **1842** TENNYSON *Lady of Shalott* II. 20 An abbot on an ambling pad. *a* **1845** HOOD *Paul Pry* vi, Thy pace, it is an ambling trot.

ambling ('æmblɪŋ), *ppl. a.* Also 4 **-ende**, 6 *north.* **-and**. [f. AMBLE *v.* + -ING[2].]

1. Of a horse: Moving in an amble.

1393 GOWER *Conf.* II 45 On faire amblende hors they set. *c* **1430** *Syr Gener.* 4031 Thei set him on an ambling palfray. **1535** LYNDESAY *Sat* 3363, I let ȝow wit, I am na fuill.. I ride vpon ane amland Muill. **1550** J. COKE *Debate* (1877) 118 Ambelynge hackeneys, and hobbes plentie. **1598** SHAKS. *Merry W.* II. ii. 320, I will rather trust.. a Theefe to walke my ambling gelding then my wife with her selfe. **1751** CHAMBERS *Cycl.* s.v., The ambling horse changes sides at each remove. **1822** W. IRVING *Braceb. Hall* xvi. 133 She rode her sleek ambling pony. **1836** HOR. SMITH *Tin Trump.* I. 28 To those elderly gentlemen.. an ambling nag has always been an equestrian beatitude.

2. Hence, Moving with the gait or pace of an ambling horse, whether with regard to alternacy, smoothness, or affectation.

1612 DRAYTON *Poly-olb.* xiv. 228 The ambling Streame. **1704** ROWE *Ulysses* I. i. 308 Easie ambling Speeches. **1850** BLACKIE *Æschylus* I. Pref. 14 Our own Anapæstic verse.. has.. a light, ambling, unsteady air about it.

†**3.** Walking. *Obs.*

1600 FAIRFAX *Tasso* IV. xxvii. 60 Of their night ambling dame, the Syrians prated.

ambling-communion: see AMBULING.

amblingly ('æmblɪŋlɪ), *adv.* [f. prec. + -LY[2].] 'With an ambling movement.' J.

‖**amblosis** (æm'bləʊsɪs). *Med.* [Gr. ἄμβλωσις abortion, n. of action f. ἀμβλό-εσθαι to come to nought, miscarry.] Miscarriage, abortion.

1706 PHILLIPS, *Amblosis*, Abortion or Miscarriage; an abortive Birth. **1839** in HOOPER *Med. Dict.*

amblotic (æm'blɒtɪk), *a. Med.* [ad. Gr. ἀμβλωτικ-ός pertaining to abortion: see prec.]

A. *adj.* (See quot.)

1839 HOOPER *Med. Dict.*, *Amblotic*, having the power to cause abortion. **1879** in *Syd. Soc. Lex.*

B. *sb.* A medicine causing abortion.

1706 PHILLIPS, *Ambloticks*, Medicines that cause Abortion. **1721** in BAILEY. [So in ASH, HOOPER, *Syd. Soc. Lex.*]

amblygon ('æmblɪgən), *a.* and *sb.*, also **ambligon**. [a. Fr. *amblygone*, or ad. its original, med.L. *ambligōni-us*, ad. Gr. ἀμβλυγών-ιος obtuse-angled, f. ἀμβλύ-ς blunt + γωνία corner, angle.]

†**A.** *adj.* Obtuse-angled. *Obs.*

1598 SYLVESTER *Du Bartas* (1621) 290 As the buildings ambligon May more receive than mansions oxigon. **1796** HUTTON *Math. Dict.* [see AMBLYGONAL].

B. *sb.* (at first used in L. form **amblygonium.**) An obtuse-angled figure, *esp.* triangle.

1570 BILLINGSLEY *Euclid* I. def. 28 An ambligonium or an obtuse angled triangle. **1623** COCKERAM, *Amblygone*, A flat Triangle. **1706** PHILLIPS, *Amblygon*, a Figure that has an obtuse or blunt Angle; any plain Figure, whose Sides make an obtuse Angle one with another. **1721** BAILEY, *Amblygon*, a Figure that has an obtuse Angle. [So in ASH, and mod. Dicts.]

amblygonal (æm'blɪgənəl), *a. rare.* [f. prec. + -AL[1].] Obtuse-angled.

1731 BAILEY, *Amblygonal*, pertaining to an amblygon. **1796** HUTTON *Math. Dict.* I. 105 *Ambligon*, or *Ambligonal*, signifies obtuse-angular. [Also in mod. Dicts.]

†**ambly'gonial**, *a. Obs.* Also **ambli-**. [f. med.L. *ambligōni-us*, a. Gr. ἀμβλυγών-ιος (see AMBLYGON) + -AL[1].] = prec.

1706 PHILLIPS, An *Ambligonial Triangle* is that which has one obtuse Angle. **1721** BAILEY, *Amblygonial* [later edd. *Ambligonial*], obtuse-angular.

amblygonite (æm'blɪgənaɪt). *Min.* [mod. f. (Ger. 1817) Gr. ἀμβλυγών-ιος obtuse-angled + -ITE.] A greenish white or sea-green translucent mineral, occurring in obtuse-angled rhombic prisms, and consisting of alumina, lithia, potash, soda, iron, and fluoric acid; made by Dana the type of a group.

1847 in CRAIG. **1868** DANA *Min.* 528 Phosphates, Arsenates, Antimonates: I. Anhydrous..VII. Amblygonite group.

†**am'blygonous**, *a. Obs.* [f. AMBLYGON + -OUS.] = AMBLYGONAL.

1751 CHAMBERS *Cycl.* s.v. *Triangle*, If one of the angles be obtuse, the triangle is said to be..amblygonous.

‖**amblyopia** (æmblɪ'əʊpɪə). *Path.* [mod.L., a. Gr. ἀμβλυωπία dimsightedness, n. of quality f. ἀμβλυωπός, f. ἀμβλύς dull, blunt + ὤψ, ὠπ- eye. Cf. AMBLYOPY.] Impaired vision, generally from defective sensibility of the retina, or cloudiness of the media; the early stage of *amaurosis*.

1706 PHILLIPS, *Amblyopia*, Dulness or Dimness of Sight, when the Object is not clearly discern'd at what distance soever it be placed. **1849–52** TODD *Cycl. Anat. & Phys.* IV. 1457/2 A bootmaker in Paris was attacked with amaurotic amblyopia. **1883** O. W. HOLMES in *Pall Mall G.* 15 Jan. 11/2 The candidate to be proved free from colour-blindness and amblyopia.

amblyopic (æmblɪ'ɒpɪk), *a.* [f. prec. + -IC.] Of or pertaining to amblyopia; of impaired vision.

1849–52 TODD *Cycl. Anat. & Phys.* IV. 1463/2 Compelled..to pursue their literary avocations..by the aid of a dim candle, and..myopic and amblyopic in consequence.

amblyopy ('æmblɪɒpɪ, æm'blaɪəpɪ). *rare.* Anglicized form of AMBLYOPIA. Cf. Fr. *amblyopie*.

1719 QUINCY *Lex. Phys.-Med.* 14 *Amblyopy* is the same disease as Amaurosis. **1815** *Encycl. Brit.* I. 780 Amblyopy among physicians, signifies an obscuration of the sight, so that objects at a distance cannot easily be distinguished.

ambo ('æmbəʊ). Pl. **ambos** (-əʊz), also in L. form **am'bōnēs**. [a. late L. *ambo* (*ambōn-em*), ad. Gr. ἄμβων: see AMBON.] Special name of the pulpit or reading-desk in early Christian churches; 'an oblong enclosure with steps usually at the two ends.' Gwilt.

1641 MILTON *Hist. Ref.* I. Wks. 1847. 10/1 The admirers of antiquity have been beating their brains about their ambones. **1673** CAVE *Prim. Chr.* I. vi. 123 The Ambo or reading pew. **1753** CHAMBERS *Cycl. Supp.* s.v., In some churches remains of the Ambos are still seen. **1864** W. GRIEVE in *Vac. Tour.* 427 In the centre is the ambo, marked sometimes only by a circle in the pavement, whilst at others it is a platform of one, two, or three steps. **1881** STANLEY *Chr. Inst.* iii 55 In England the huge reading-desk or 'pew' long supplied the place of the old ambo.

Ambo: see OVAMBO.

amboceptor ('æmbəʊ,sɛptɔː(r)). *Biochem.* [G. (Ehrlich & Morgenroth in *Berl. Klin. Wochenschr.* 11 Mar. 252/1), f. L. *ambo* both + RE)CEPTOR.] In Ehrlich's theory of immunization, a receptor having two combining or haptophoric groups of atoms, by which it unites both with the immunizing body and with the complement. Opp. UNICEPTOR.

1902 *Brit. Med. Jrnl.* 12 Apr. 920 There is no amboceptor as such, but the body consists of a zymophoric group. **1904** [see THERMOLABILE *a.*]. **1937** T. W. B. OSBORN *Complement or Alexin* i. 4 The 'preventive substance', 'immune body', 'antibody', or 'sensitizer' became the 'amboceptor'.

ambodexter, etc., obs. f. AMBIDEXTER, etc.

†'**amboht**. *Obs. rare.* [a. ON. *ambótt*, *ambátt*, a bondwoman, handmaid; cogn. w. Goth. *andbahts*, OHG. *ampaht*, OE. *ambeht* servant, attendant; L. *ambactus*: see under AMBASSADE.] A handmaid, bondwoman.

c **1200** ORMIN 2329 Icc amm ammbohht all bun To follȝhenn Godess wille. *Ibid.* 2527 ȝho seȝȝde þat ȝho wass Ammboht Drihhtin to þeowwtenn.

ambolic (æm'bɒlɪk), *a.* [ad. Gr. ἀμβολικ-ός contr. f. ἀναβολικ-ός throwing up, f. ἀνά up + βολ- throw.] 'Having the power to produce abortion.' *Syd. Soc. Lex.* 1879.

ambolife, -lyfe, var. EMBELIF *a. Obs.*, oblique.

ambon ('æmbən). [a. Gr. ἄμβων a rising, the raised edge or rim of a dish, a raised stage or pulpit; prob. f. ἀνα-βα- go up, rise.]

1. = AMBO.

1725 tr. *Dupin's Eccl. Hist. 17th C.* I. v. 69 They mounted the Ambon on *Juba*, which was betwixt the Choir and the Nave. **1794** *Archaeol.* XI. 320 Before this vault was also placed the choir, with the ambon. **1848** B. WEBB *Cont. Eccles.* vii. 208 A preacher..was discoursing from the ambon. **1959** E. POUND *Thrones* xcvi. 5 A stone in Modena by the ambon.

2. *Anat.* 'The margin or tip of the sockets in which the heads of the large bones are lodged.' Hooper *Med. Dict.* 1811. (So ἄμβων in Galen.)

am'bonoclast. [f. prec. after *iconoclast*.] *rare.* One who aims at the abolition of ambons. Also *attrib.*

1851 PUGIN *Rood Screens* 99 Modern ambonoclasts, unlike their predecessors, confine their attacks to strokes of the pen. **1916** W. H. A. VALLANCE in *Yorks. Archæol. Jrnl.* XXIV. 116 This phase of the ambonoclast movement. **1936** —— *Eng. Ch. Screens* ix. 79 Queen Elizabeth's Bishops, many of them more ardent ambonoclasts than their mistress.

†**ambo'sexous**, *a. Obs.*$^{-0}$ [f. L. *ambo* both + *sex-us* sex + -OUS.] Of both sexes; hermaphrodite.

1656 in BLOUNT *Glossogr.*

ambo'sexual, *a.* [f. L. *ambo* both + SEXUAL *a.*]

a. Of a group: composed of individuals of both sexes. *rare*$^{-1}$.

1788 *Columbian Mag.* Aug. 449/1 The next order of *social* beings which demands our attention, is the numerous and *ambosexual* order of *tatlers*.

b. *Biol.* Having characteristics of both sexes in a single individual; = INTERSEXUAL *a.* 2.

1935 in DORLAND *Med. Dict.* **1970** R. REINBOTH in Benson & Phillips *Hormones & Environment* 515 In an ambosexual animal both male and female characteristics are associated normally in a single individual—either simultaneously or in a temporal succession. **1978** *Japanese Jrnl. Ichthyol.* XXV. 101 Histological examination of gonads indicated that all individuals..are ambosexual as juveniles. **1982** *Gynécologie* XXXIII. 25 These may be found in the majority of gonadal endocrine tumours, conferring them with latent or patent ambosexual or adrenocortical possibilities.

amboyna (wood) (æm'bɔɪnə). [from the island of that name, one of the Moluccas.] The wood of the Asiatic tree *Pterospermum indicum* (N.O. *Sterculiaceæ*). *Treas. Bot.* 1866.

1879 *Cassell's Techn. Educ.* IV. 168/2 Amboyna-wood.. also called Vryabuca or Vryabooca-wood..is beautifully mottled and curled, of various tints from light red to dark yellow. **1882** *Daily Tel.* 23 Nov. (*Advt.*) Walnutwood chiffonnière, beautifully inlaid with amboyna and marqueterie.

†**ambra'can.** *Obs. rare*$^{-1}$. [a. It. *ambracane*.] Ambergris.

1599 HAKLUYT *Voy.* II. I. 274 With this they weigh amber, corall, muske, ambracan, ciuet, and other fine wares.

ambreada (ɑːmbriː'ɑːdə, æ-). [a. Sp. or Pg. *ambreada*, f. Pg. *ambre* amber: see -ADE[1].] (See quot.)

1815 *Encycl. Brit.* I. 784, *Ambreada*, thus they call the false or fictitious amber, which the Europeans use in their trade with the negroes on the coast of Africa.

ambreate ('æmbriːeɪt). *Chem.* [f. med.L. *ambre* amber + -ATE[4].] A salt of Ambreic acid.

1839 HOOPER *Med. Dict.* 81 (ed. 7). **1863–79** WATTS *Dict. Chem.* I. 165 Ambreate of potassium.

ambreic (æm'briːɪk), *a. Chem.* [f. as prec. + -IC.] Of or pertaining to ambreine or ambergris, as *Ambreic Acid.* (See also next.)

1831 URE *Dict. Chem.* 148 By this absorption of oxygen, it is converted into acid which has been called ambreic acid.

ambrein ('æmbriːɪn). *Chem.* [a. Fr. *ambréine*, f. *ambre* amber: see -IN.] A crystalline fatty substance forming the main constituent of ambergris.

1832 *Rep. Brit. Assoc.* (1835) 528 Ambreic [Acid. Discovered by] Pelletier and Caventou. By treating ambreine with nitric acid. **1863** WATTS *Dict. Chem.* I. 165 Ambrein is perhaps impure cholesterin.

ambrette (ɑːm'brɛt, æ-). [a. Fr. *ambrette*, in form a dim. of *ambre*: see -ETTE.]

1. A kind of pear with an odour of ambergris or musk.

1725 BRADLEY *Fam. Dict.* s.v. *Pears*, The Ambret is much esteemed. **1768** MILLER *Gard. Dict.* (ed. 8) 11 A, Ambrette ..so called from its musk flavour, which resembles the smell of the Sweet Sultan Flower, which is called Ambrette in France.

2. The seeds of a plant (*Hibiscus Abelmoschus*) grown in Egypt, Arabia, Martinique, etc., having an odour somewhat between musk and amber, used in perfumery.

1858 R. HOGG *Veg. Kingd.* 105 It is employed by perfumers in the preparation of pomatums, powders, and perfumes, by whom it is called Ambrette.

ambreve, var. of ENBREVE *v. Obs.*, to inscribe.

ambrite ('æmbraɪt). *Min.* [f. AMBER + -ITE, min. formative; ad. Ger. *ambrit* 1861.] A yellowish grey, sub-transparent fossil resin found in large masses in Auckland, New Zealand.

ambroid ('æmbrɔɪd). Also **amberoid** ('æmbərɔɪd). [f. AMBER *sb.*[1] + -OID.] A name used for a substance made by moulding pieces of amber by heat and pressure. Also *attrib.*

1899 *Sci. Amer.* 16 Sept. 188/2 The inferior pieces of amber are made into what is called ambroid. **1904** *Westm. Gaz.* 9 Aug. 4/1 The sale of amberoid, however, declined. **1913** *Daily Mail* 4 Feb. 5/6 Charged..with keeping the trimmings and selling them to be made into pressed amber, known in the trade as 'ambroid'. **1922** JOYCE *Ulysses* 62 I gave her the amberoid necklace she broke.

ambrology (æm'brɒlədʒɪ). [f. mod.L. *ambra* amber + -(O)LOGY.] The natural history of amber, its formation, flora, fauna, etc.

1879 in *Syd. Soc. Lex.*

ambrose ('æmbrəʊz). [a. Fr. *ambroise*:—L. *ambrosia* (see next.)]

1. *Herb.* An English plant: with some the Wood Sage (*Teucrium Scorodonia*); with others, *Chenopodium Botrys*; with both of which *Teucrium Botrys* seems to have been in name confused.

1440 *Promp. Parv.*, Ambrose herbe, *Ambrosia*, *Salvia silvestris*. **1530** PALSGR. 194/1 Ambrose, an herbe *ache champestre*. **1548** TURNER *Plant Names* (1881) 76 Stachys semeth to Gesner to be the herbe that we call in English Ambrose. **1578** LYTE *Dodoens* 253 It is called in English woodde Sage, wild Sage, and Ambros. **1853** *N. & Q.* Ser. I. VIII. 36/2 Herb Ambrose has a Greek origin, and is not indebted to the saint of that name.

†**2.** The mythical AMBROSIA. *Obs.*

1621 BURTON *Anat. Mel.* III. ii. (T.) Ambrose it selfe was not sweeter.

ambrosia (æm'brəʊzɪə, -ʒɪə). [a. L. *ambrosia*, a. Gr. ἀμβροσία, fem. of ἀμβρόσι-ος 'pertaining to the immortals' (f. ἄμβροτ-ος immortal, f. ἀ not + μβροτός = μροτός = μορτός mortal, root *mor-* 'die'); used in mythology for the food, etc. of the immortals, but applied by Dioscorides and Pliny to one or more herbs.]

1. a. In Greek mythology, The fabled food of the gods and immortals (as in Homer, etc.).

1590 T. WATSON *Poems* (1870) 169 Now Melibœus.. drinkes Nectar, eates diuine Ambrosia. **1603** FLORIO *Montaigne* (1634) 144 It is for Gods to mount winged horses, and to feed on Ambrosia. **1753** CHAMBERS *Cycl. Supp.*, The Ambrosia is commonly represented as the solid food of the gods. **1822** DE QUINCEY *Confess.* Wks. V. 194, I had heard of it as I had heard of manna or of ambrosia. **1877** BRYANT *Odyss.* v. 115 A table where the heaped ambrosia lay.

b. *fig.*

1610 G. FLETCHER *Christ's Vict.* II. xxix, But he upon ambrosia daily fed, That grew in Eden. **1629** MASSINGER *Picture* III. v, To feed His appetite with that ambrosia due And proper to a prince. *a* **1703** POMFRET *Poet. Wks.* (1833) 13 Ambrosia mixed with aconite may have A pleasant taste, but sends you to the grave.

2. The fabled drink of the gods (as in Sappho, etc.).

1567 MAPLET *Greene Forest* Ded., Whose bread is Nectar, and drink Ambrosia, a sugred and confect kinde of Wine. **1599** MARSTON *Scourge of Vill.* II. vii. 204 Eates Nectar, drinkes Ambrosia, saunce controule. *a* **1625** FLETCHER *Night Walker* I. 211 [A man that] cannot relish Braggat from Ambrosia.

3. The fabled unguent or anointing oil of the gods; also *fig.*

1667 MILTON *P.L.* V. 57 His dewie locks distill'd Ambrosia. **1718** POPE *Iliad* XIX. 375 And pour'd divine ambrosia in his breast. **1791** COWPER *Odyss.* XVIII. 236 Her lovely face She with ambrosia purified.

4. *transf.* A mixture of water, oil, and various fruits anciently used as a libation; also a perfumed draught or flavoured beverage.

1685 *Gracian's Courtier's Orac.* 201 Waters, which..smell of Physick, and they call them Ambrosia. **1725** BRADLEY *Fam. Dict.* s.v. *Juice*, This Juice being well fermented and prepar'd with Clove, Cinnamon, &c., would prove an Ambrosia, that would not be esteem'd indifferent, by those who do not care to drink Water. **1807** ROBINSON *Archæol. Græca* III. ii. 195 They..poured before it a libation called ambrosia, which was a mixture of water, honey, and all kinds of fruits.

5. *fig.* Something divinely sweet or exquisitely delightful to taste or smell.

1731 SWIFT *Streph. & Chloe* Wks. 1755 IV. I. 152 Venus-like her fragrant skin Exhal'd ambrosia from within. **1823** DE QUINCEY *King of Hayti* Wks. XII. 60 When a whole company had tasted the ambrosia of her lips. **1863** MARY HOWITT tr. *Bremer's Greece* II. xiii. 86 The flavour of the grapes is ambrosia, which I take it for granted was something divine.

6. Bee-bread.

1609 C. BUTLER *Fem. Mon.* i. (1623) B iij, They gather with the one Nectar, with the other Ambrosia. **1753** CHAMBERS *Cycl. Supp.*, The Ambrosia..if not speedily spent, corrupts and turns sowr. **1816** KIRBY & SPENCE *Entomol.* (1843) II. 149 Whether a bee had collected its ambrosia from one or more..species of flowers.

7. With the early herbalists a name of various plants: see AMBROSE.

1597 GERARD *Herbal* 950 The fragrant smell that this kinde of *Ambrosia* or Oke of Cappadocia yeeldeth, hath mooued the Poets to suppose that this herbe was meate and foode for the gods. **1601** HOLLAND *Pliny* (1634) II. 273 Ambrosia is a name that keepeth not to any one herb, but is common to many. **1605** TIMME *Quersit.* I. xiii. 64 The oyles of..ambrosia, of sage, and betony. **1753** CHAMBERS *Cycl. Supp.*, The Ambrosia of the moderns is not at all like the plant so called by the generality of the ancients.

8. *Mod. Bot.* A genus (N.O. *Compositæ*) consisting of weeds allied to Wormwood. *A. artemisifolia* is the 'Oak of Cappadocia' or 'of Jerusalem.'

1721 BAILEY, *Ambrosia*..an Herb called the Oak of Jerusalem.

9. A fungous substance which forms the food of certain N. American wood-boring beetles of various species (hence called **ambrosia beetles**).

1896 *Yearbk. U.S. Dept. Agr.* 421 Their food consists not of wood, but of a substance to which the name ambrosia has been given, and which is a coating formed by certain minute fungi and propagated on the walls of their galleries by the beetles. **1922** *Glasgow Herald* 16 Dec. 4 But some beetles that bore in fresh wood have discovered how to grow a mould that yields what is called 'ambrosia'. **1924** J. A. THOMSON *Sci. Old & New* xvi. 89 The burrows of the ambrosia beetles are practically confined to the sap-wood.

†**am'brosiac**, *a. Obs.* [ad. L. *ambrosiac-us*, a. Gr. ἀμβροσιακ-ός: see prec. Cf. Fr. *ambrosiaque.*] Of the nature of ambrosia; ambrosial.

1600 B. JONSON *Cynthia's Rev.* I. iii. 18 Here is most ambrosiacke water. **1611** —— *Catiline* I. i, This ambrosiac kiss, and this of nectar. **1662** COKAINE *Poems* (1669) 349 Which with Ambrosiack cream shall swell thy breast. **1731** in BAILEY. [Not in JOHNSON.]

ambrosiaceous (æm,brəʊzɪ'eɪʃəs), *a. Bot.* [f. AMBROSIA + -ACEOUS.] Akin to the genus *Ambrosia.* (Applied to a subdivision of Composite plants.)

1879 in *Syd. Soc. Lex.*

ambrosial (æm'brəʊzɪəl, -ʒɪəl), *a.* [f. L. *ambrosi-us*, a. Gr. ἀμβρόσι-ος (see AMBROSIA) + -AL[1].]

1. Immortal, divine, celestial, ethereal. **a.** *orig.* in the Greek mythology: Belonging to or worthy of the gods, as their food, anointing oil, locks, raiment, sandals, etc.

1596 DRAYTON *Leg.* iii. 118 Me with Ambrosiall Delicacies fed. **1718** POPE *Iliad* v. 460 Fed by fair Iris with ambrosial food. **1790** COWPER *Iliad* I. 685 The sovereign's everlasting head his curls Ambrosial shook. **1835** THIRLWALL *Greece* I. vi. 193 They need the refreshment of ambrosial food. **1866** FELTON *Greece* I. viii. 129 The Homeric father of gods and men, from whose head the locks ambrosial waved. **1870** BRYANT *Homer* II. XIV. 54 Rich oil, Ambrosial, soft and fragrant. **1877** —— *Odyss.* v. 57 The fair, ambrosial, golden sandals.

b. *transf.* Belonging to heaven or paradise.

1637 MILTON *Comus* 16, I would not soil these pure ambrosial weeds With the rank vapours of this sin-worn mould. **1647** CRASHAW *Poems* 206 The bright ambrosial nest, Of love, of life, and everlasting rest. **1671** MILTON *P.R.* IV. 586 Ambrosial fruits, fetched from the tree of life, And from the fount of life ambrosial drink. *c* **1746** HERVEY *Medit. & Cont.* (1818) 109 The trees of life and knowledge, whose ambrosial fruits we now may 'take and eat, and live for ever.'

c. *fig.* Divinely fragrant; perfumed as with ambrosia; balmy; *rarely*, Divinely beautiful.

1667 MILTON *P.L.* IX. 852 Fruit, that..ambrosial smell diffus'd. **1702** ROWE *Amb. Step-Mother* III. ii. 46 From thee ..Ambrosial Odours flow. **1719** YOUNG *Revenge* v. i. Wks. 1757 II. 173 Th' ambrosial rose, And breath of jess'min. **1781** COWPER *Expostul.* 11 Ambrosial gardens. **1815** MOORE *Lalla R.* (1824) 248 One of those ambrosial eves A day of storm so often leaves. **1847** TENNYSON *Princess* 87 The broad ambrosial aisles of lofty lime. **1857** HUGHES *Tom Brown* II. iii. 345 When any ambrosial colour spread itself.

2. Of the pollen of flowers, or of bee-bread. *rare.*

1816 KIRBY & SPENCE *Entomol.* (1843) II. 157 [It] covers itself with their ambrosial dust which it kneads into a mass and packs upon its hind legs.

am'brosially, *adv.* [f. prec. + -LY[2].] After the manner of ambrosia; with divine fragrance.

1833 TENNYSON *Œnone* 66 Dew of Heaven Ambrosially smelling. [*later ed.* A fruit of pure Hesperian gold, That smelt ambrosially.]

ambrosian (æm'brəʊzɪən, -ʒɪən), *a.*[1] [f. L. *ambrosi-us* (see prec.) + -AN.] = AMBROSIAL.

1. Of or pertaining to the immortal gods; divine.

a **1637** B. JONSON *Masques* (T.) Ambrosian hands and silver feet. **1676** HOBBES *Homer* 372 Ambrosian shoes, that over sea and land Bear him as swift and lightly as the winds. **1850** MERIVALE *Rom. Emp.* (1865) IV. xxxviii. 324 Unworthy..of the ambrosian blood of their parent Venus.

2. Of or like ambrosia; divinely fragrant or delicious.

1632 in *Shaks. Cent. Praise* 192 Fed with Ambrosian meate. **1647** H. MORE *Oracle* 60 Ambrosian streams sprung from the Deitie. **1661** HICKERINGILL *Jamaica* 32 A most ambrosian Dainty. **1697** DRYDEN *Virg.* XII. (R.) Venus.. brews Th' extracted liquor with ambrosian dews. **1823** LAMB *Elia* Ser I. xxiv. (1865) 193 One ambrosian result.

Ambrosian (æm'brəʊzɪən), *a.*[2] [ad. L. *Ambrosiān-us*, f. *Ambrosius* (same word as in prec., used as prop. name) St. Ambrose, bishop of Milan.] Of, pertaining to, or instituted by, St. Ambrose.

1609 DOULAND *Ornithop. Microl.* 27 A Song ending in *D lasolre*, or in *C fa ut*, is either an Ambrosian song, or corrupted with the ignorance of Cantors. **1753** CHAMBERS *Cycl. Supp.*, *Ambrosian* rite or office denotes a particular office or formula of worship used in the church of Milan, which is sometimes called the Ambrosian church..The public library at Milan is also called the Ambrosian Library. **1880** HELMORE in Grove *Dict. Mus.* I. 60 The Ambrosian chant was eventually merged, but certainly not lost..in that vast repertory of plainsong..which we now call Gregorian.

2. Of the Ambrosian Library: see prec.

1724 WATERLAND *Athan. Creed.* x. 148 Some words are wanting in the Ambrosian manuscript.

†**ambrosianie.** *Obs.* App. merely a capricious variant of AMBROSIA.

1600 TOURNEUR *Transf. Metam.* lxxxvii. 611 God's nectar; heav'n's sweet ambrosianie.

†**am'brosiate**, *a. Obs.* [f. AMBROSIA + -ATE; cf. *aureate*, *roseate*, etc.] Formed of or furnished with ambrosia.

1602 DEKKER *Satirom.* Wks. 1873 II. 252 Th' ambrosiate banquet of the Gods.

†'**ambrosie, -y.** *Obs.* [a. Fr. *ambrosie*, ad. L. *ambrosia.*] = AMBROSIA, in various senses.

1594 *Zepheria* XXIX. in Arber's *Garner* V. 80, I drew for wine, but found 'twas Ambrosie. **1612** J. DAVIES *Wittes Pilgrim.* (1876) 31 With Balme-breaths Ambrosie Shee it enaires in Prose, or Poesy. **1613** HEYWOOD *Braz. Age* II. ii. 229 The vnruly stalions fed with Ambrosy. **1676** BULLOKAR, *Ambrosie*, a sweet shrub, or little tree, wherewith some people were wont to make Garlands. In Poetry it usually signifieth the meat of the Heathen gods. It is sometime taken for Immortality.

ambrosin ('æmbrəʊsɪn). *Numism.* [ad. med.L. *ambrosīn-us* (sc. *nummus* coin), f. *ambrosius*: see AMBROSIAN *a.*[2]]

1753 CHAMBERS *Cycl. Supp.*, *Ambrosin*, in middle aged writers, denotes a coin..whereon was represented St. Ambrose on horseback.

ambrosine ('æmbrəʊsɪn). *Min.* [f. L. *ambrosius* ambrosial + -INE; or ? f. *amber.*] A resinous mineral of eocene age, related to amber, found in the phosphatic beds near Charleston, S.C., which gives off on fusion an agreeable balsamic odour. Dana *Suppl.* (1872).

ambrotype ('æmbrətaɪp). [? f. Gr. ἄμβροτος immortal (? imperishable), or perh. AMBER, + TYPE.] The name given in U.S. to a photograph on glass, in which the lights are produced by the silver, and the shades by a dark background showing through.

1855 *N. & Q.* 7 Apr. 270 *Ambrotype Likenesses.*—The Boston Atlas states that a most valuable improvement in the art of producing likenesses has been recently introduced. **1858** O. W. HOLMES *Aut. Breakf.* xi. 103 Willis touched this last point in one of his earlier ambrotypes. **1882** *Cent. Mag.* Oct. 852 An ambrotype taken at Springfield, Illinois, in 1860.

ambry, aumbry ('ɑːmbrɪ, æ-). Forms: *α.* 4 armary, 6 armorie; *β.* 4–6 almarie, 5 -arye, -erye, 5–6 -ary, 5–7 -erie, 5–9 almery; *γ.* 6 awmery, amrye, 6–7 aumery, 8–9 awmry, aumry, -ie, (amrie); *δ.* 6–7 aumbrie, -bray, 6–9 aumbry (-brye, ambery, -brey), ambry. [ad. L. *armārium*, in med.L. also *almārium* and *almāria* (cf. Pr. *armari*, Sp. and It. *armario*, It. *armadio*, Pg. *almario*, OFr. 12th c. *ar'marie*, *al'marie*, 13th c. *almaire*, *aumaire*, *aumoire*, 16th c. refash. after L., *armoire*) a closet, chest, place for implements, tools, etc., f. *arma* gear, tools, arms + *-ārium* depot, as in *herbarium*, *aquarium* (cf. also ARMOURY). The phonetic development was *armarium*, *almarium* (by dissimilation from following *r*, as in peregrinus, pelegrin, pilgrim), *almary*, *almery*, *aumery* (cf. palma, paulme, paume), *aumry*, *aumbry* (cf. slumere, slumber, numerus, number), *ambry* (cf. chaunt, chant); but *aumry*, without adscititious *b*, is retained in north. dial., in which alone the word is in living everyday use; see sense 2 a. *Obs.* in ordinary Eng. since *c*1600, but a familiar term in domestic and ecclesiastical antiquities, whence to some extent used as an archaism in various 16th c. spellings. In the form *almery*, corruptly confused with *almonry*, as if a place for *alms*. The same word has passed into Anglo-Ind. through Pg. *almario* and Urdu *almārī* as ALMIRAH.]

1. *gen.* A repository or place for keeping things; a storehouse, a treasury; a cupboard (either in the recess of a wall or as a separate article of furniture); a safe; a locker, a press.

1393 LANGLAND *P. Pl.* C. XVII. 88 Auarice haþ almaries and yre-bounden cofres. **1463** in *Bury Wills* (1850) 29 The same keye to be leyd in an almarye..the almerye where the seid keyes shal lyn in. **1534** in *Eng. Ch. Furn.* (1866) 187 Item a playne awmery with ij litill chambers wythin with too lockes. **1535** COVERDALE *Jer.* xxxviii. 11 Vnder an almery [WYCLIF celer, **1611** treasurie] he gat olde ragges & worne cloutes. **1564** in *Wills & Inv. N. Counties* (1835) 219 A littel paynted ambry with ij doores. **1571** *Ibid.* 361 Ij owld chystes ijs. vjd...ij armoires *jl.* **1583** STANYHURST *Aeneis* II. (Arb.) 44 In this od hudge ambry [*i.e.* the Trojan horse] they ramd a number of hardye Tough knights. **1591** PERCIVALL *Span. Dict.*, *Alhazéna*, a hole in a wal to set things in, an Ambrie ..*Almário*, an armorie, an ambrie, *Armarium*. **18..** WORDSWORTH in Myers *Life* (1881) 3, I possess..an almery, made in 1525, at the expense of a William Wordsworth. **1835** BECKFORD *Recoll.* 48 A press or ambery elaborately carved. **1842** GRESLEY *Forest of Ard.* 66 An almery or arched recess of compact brickwork, so constructed as to be impervious to fire. **1868** MORRIS *Jason* VIII. 444 A little aumbrye, with a door o'er-gilt.

b. Sometimes applied to a compartment of a cupboard, etc.; a 'pigeon hole.'

c **1530** *Furn. Hen. VIII.* in *Dom. Arch.* III. 135 A cupborde with ij smale ambries in yt. **1542** UDALL *Erasm. Apoph.* (1564) 5 A cupbourd full of almeries of joigners werke. **1570** DEE *Math. Præf.* 40 The Brasen Vessels, which in Theatres, are placed by Mathematicall order, in ambries, vnder the steppes. **1613** PURCHAS *Pilgr.* I. xviii. 97 This Moloch had seuen Roomes, Chambers, or Ambries therein.

†**c.** *fig.* = 'repository, treasury.' *Obs.*

1477 EARL RIVERS (Caxton) *Dictes* 115 The tunge is the dore of the almerye of sapience. **1628** LE GRYS tr. *Barclay's Argenis* 148 In what Chest or Almerie of heaven..that former faculty be stored up.

2. *spec.* The following are the chief uses: **a.** A place for keeping victuals; variously applied to a store-closet, pantry, or cupboard in a pantry; a wall-press; a dresser; a meat-safe, as in 'ambry of hair,' *i.e.* with sides of hair-cloth. *arch.* & *dial.*

1398 TREVISA *Barth. De P.R.* XVIII. cxii. (1495) 853 Noo token of meete founde in the almerye. **1440** *Promp. Parv.*, Almery of mete kepynge, or a saue for mete, *Cibutum.* **1553** *Midl. Counties Hist. Collec.* I. 232 Item, an ambrey of heare xijd. *a* **1564** BECON *Govern. Virtue* Wks. 1843, 468 Cursed shall thine almary be and thy store. **1580** TUSSER *Husb.* lxxv. ii, Some slouens from sleeping no sooner get vp, But hand is in aumbrie, and nose in the cup. **1590** *Three Lords & Ladies* in Hazl. *Dods.* VI. 412 Like two mice in an ambery, that eat up all the meat. **1622** DEKKER *Virg. Martir* II. i. 37 Full of the same meat out of my ambrey. **1655** MOUFFET & BENN. *Health's Impr.* (1746) 394 He baited at every Village ..and swept clean the Ambery in every Inn. **1674** RAY *N. Countr. Words* 3 An Aumbry or Ambry or Aumery, A pantry or Cupboard to set victuals in. **1693** W. ROBERTSON *Phraseol. Gen.* 82 An Ambry or Cupboards-head, *Abacus*, *armorium.* **1733** RAMSAY *Tea-T. Misc.* (ed. 9) II. 181 An ark, an ambry, and a ladle. **1800** A. CARLYLE *Autobiogr.* 440 Rummaging about in the awmry, however, I found at last about two pounds weight of cold roast veal. **1859** MRS. GASKELL *Round the Sofa* II. 98 The polished oaken awmry, or dresser, of the state kitchen. **1868** G. MACDONALD *Rob. Falc.* I. 203 Having escaped from his grandmother's aumrie.

b. In a church: A cupboard, locker, or closed recess in the wall, for books, sacramental vessels, vestments, etc. *arch.*

1440 in *Eng. Ch. Furn.* (1866) 183 Item an almerie to kepe his vestmentes and bookes in. **1555** *Fardle of Facions* II. xii. 301 Upon the right hande of the highe aulter, that ther should be an almorie, either cutte into the walle, or framed vpon it: in the whiche thei would haue the Sacrament of the Lordes bodye, the holy oyle for the sicke, and the Chrismatorie, alwaie to be locked. **1593** *Rites Mon. Ch. Durh.* (1842) 2 Three or four amryes in the wall pertaininge to some of the said altars. **1870** F. WILSON *Ch. of Lindisf.* 83 A lancet-arched aumbry or locker.

†**c.** A place for books; library; archives. *Obs.*

1382 WYCLIF *Ezra* iv. 15 Thou shall finde write in armaries [**1388** cronyclis]. —— *2 Macc.* ii. 13 These same thingis weren born in discripciouns, and the almeries of Neemye. **1483** CAXTON *Gold. Leg.* 240/3 A fisshar cast his hoke..and drewe up the bookes..without ony wetyng, lyke as they had ben kepte dylygently in an almarye. **1775** ASH, *Almaria*, The archives of a church.

†**d.** A hutch for live-stock. *Obs.*

1572–3 *Durh. Reg. Will of Eliz. Somner*, To Bessye Somer an almerie for keping of conyes.

¶**3.** Corruptly for ALMONRY; (*Almry* or *Ambry Close*, Westminster, was originally *Almonry Close.*)

1593 *Desc. Rites & Cust. Durh.* (1842) 77 Certayne poore children, called the children of the almery, which was brought upp in learninge and mantayned with the almose of the Howse, havinge dyett in a lofte on the north side of the Abbey gates. **1597** J. PAYNE *Royal Exch.* 11 Let your doores and portalls in lyfe tyme, and not the churche porche after death be your almeries. **1603** STOW *Surv.* (1842) 176/2 Called the Elemosinary, or Almonry, now corruptly the Ambry, for that the alms of the abbey were there distributed to the poor. **1693** W. ROBERTSON *Phraseol. Gen.* 185 An Aumbry or almonry, where the Almoner lives; *Eleemosynarium.* **1700** LESLIE *Right of Tithes*, They had amberies for the daily relief of the poor. **1773** *Gentlem. Mag.* XLIII. 480 The bell to call the poor people to the adjacent almery.

b. *fig.* Beneficence, bounty.

a **1638** MEDE *Wks.* I. xxiii. 88 Judge then..what account they make of God's Ambre.

ambs-ace (,æmz 'eɪs). Forms 3–4 **ambes as, -z as**, 4–5 **ambes aas**, 6–7 **ambes ace**, 6–9 **ambs ace.** Also 4 **amys ase**, 6 **aums ase**, 6–7 **aumes-, aums-, amnes-**, 6–9 **ames-**, 7 **alms-**, 8 **ams-, am's-, ame's ace.** [a. OFr. *ambes as*:—L. *ambas as*, both ace: see ACE *sb.*]

1. *lit.* Both aces, double ace, the lowest possible throw at dice; hence, *fig.* bad luck, misfortune; worthlessness, nought, next to nothing.

1297 R. GLOUC. 51 Ac he caste þer of ambes as. *c* **1300** *Beket* 450 Thu ert icome therto to late: thu hast icast ambez as. *c* **1400** *Beryn* 2955, I bare thre dise, in myne owne purs ..I kist hem forth al three, and too fil amys ase. *c* **1430** LYDG. *Minor Poems* (1840) 166 Whos chaunce gothe neyther on synk nor sice, But withe ambes aas encresithe his dispence. **1601** SHAKS. *All's Well* II. iii. 85, I had rather be in this choise, than throw Ames-ace for my life. **1611** COTGR., *Besas*, Aumes-ace, on the dice. *a* **1658** CLEVELAND *Clev. Vind.* (1677) 28 In whom Dame Nature tries To throw less than Aums Ace upon two Dice. *a* **1680** BUTLER *Rem.* (1759) VI. 81 Idly vent'ring her good Graces To be disposed of by Alms-Aces. **1721** MRS. CENTLIVRE *Gamest.* I. i. 136 My evil genius flings Am's Ace before me. **1722** WOLLASTON *Relig. Nat.* iii. 56 Nobody can certainly foretell, that sice-ace will come up upon two dies fairly thrown before ambs-ace. **1731** FIELDING *Lottery* (1755) I. 249 If I can but nick this time, ame's-ace I defy thee. **1870** LOWELL *Among my Bks.* Ser. I. (1873) 192 A lucky throw of words which may come up the sices of hardy metaphor or the ambs-ace of conceit.

2. The smallest point. ***within ambs ace of***, emph. form of 'within an ace of': on the very verge of. ? *Obs.*

1679 *Trial of Langhorn* 18 His Wife was but aumes ace turned from a Devil. **1698** VANBRUGH *Æsop* v. i, Reduced within ambs-ace of hanging or drowning. *a* **1733** NORTH *Examen* I. iii. ¶158 His Lordship was within Ams-ace of being put in the Plot. **1800** MAR. EDGEWORTH *Cast. Rackr.* 28 Within ames-ace of getting quit..of all his enemies.

†**'ambubey.** *Obs.* [ad. L. *ambubēia* (of unkn. origin), a herb mentioned by Celsus and Pliny. Florio 1611 has '*Ambubeia*, a kind of wild Endiue or common Cycorie. Also the Dandelion, the Priests-crowne, the Monks-head, or Dogs-teeth.'] Wild Succory or Endive (*Cichorium Intybus*).

1585 *Nomenclator* (Halliw.) A kinde of wild endive like ambubey.

‖**ambula'craire.** [Fr., prop. adj. 'belonging to the ambulacra.'] A group or series of the perforated coronal pieces in an echinus. (Also used in L. form pl. *ambulacraria*).

a **1837** *Penny Cycl.* IX. 260/2 The *ambulacraires* narrower and covered with very small, fine, close-set spines.

ambulacral (æmbjuː'leɪkrəl, -'ækral), *a.* [f. L. *ambulacr-um* + -AL[1].] Of or pertaining to the ambulacra of Echinoderms; avenue-like.

1836–39 SHARPEY in Todd *Cycl. Anat. & Phys.* II. 32/1 The ten ambulacral columns are disposed in five pairs. **1847** *Ibid.* III. 440/2 Hundreds of feet protrude through the ambulacral apertures. **1857** WOOD *Com. Obj. Seashore* vii. 128 These are the ambulacral organs..but I prefer to call them feet. These feet are in fact suckers.

ambulacriform (æmbjuː'leɪkrɪfɔːm, -'ækrɪ-), *a.* [f. as prec. + -(I)FORM.] Having the shape or appearance of ambulacra.

1837 *Penny Cycl.* IX. 259/2 Mouth subcentral..with five converging, ambulacriform furrows. **1879** in *Syd. Soc. Lex.*

‖**ambulacrum** (æmbjuː'leɪkrəm, -'ækrəm). Pl. **-a.** [L., a walk, avenue; f. *ambulā-re* to walk.] An 'avenue' or double row of pores for the protrusion of the ambulacral tubes or tube-feet, of which five series radiate from the apex of an echinoderm.

1837 *Penny Cycl.* IX. 259/1 Species [of *Echinidæ*] whose ambulacra are petaloid, going from a centre..This section is divided into subsections, according to the depth of the ambulacra. **1877** HUXLEY *Anat. Inv. An.* ix. 568 At its apical extremity the ambulacrum is composed of only two small ossicles which meet in the middle line.

ambulance ('æmbjʊləns). [a. mod.Fr. *ambulance* (formerly *hôpital ambulant* walking hospital); f. L. *ambulant-em* walking, as if ad. L. **ambulantia*: see -ANCE.] Not in Craig 1847; app. came into general use during the Crimean War.

1. A moving hospital, which follows an army in its movements, so as to afford the speediest possible succour to the wounded. Often *attrib.*

1809 *Ann. Reg. 1807* (Otridge) 14/1 They [*sc.* the wounded] were successively carried to the ambulance, or train of carriages. **1819** *Edin. Rev.* XXXI. 310 These *ambulances* in their most perfect form consist of a mounted corps of surgeons and inferior assistants..to remove them [the wounded] to other *ambulances* or temporary hospitals. **1833** *Penny Cycl.* I. 425 *Ambulance*, a French word applied to the moving hospitals which are attached to every French army. **1860** TRISTRAM *Gt. Sahara* i. 9 Ambulance waggons laden with sick and wounded. **1864** *Daily Tel.* 3 Mar., The ambulance men carrying the stretchers.

2. a. An ambulance waggon or cart; a covered vehicle on springs for conveying the wounded off the field of battle, etc. More recently, a vehicle for conveying sick or wounded persons.

1854 *Manch. Guard.* 25 Nov., The ambulances as fast as they came up received their load of sufferers. **1870** DISRAELI *Lothair* lviii. 312, I passed an ambulance this moment. **1922** *Home Service Ambulance Committee Rep.* (St. John & Brit. Red Cross Soc.) 1 The total number of patients carried in the Committee's ambulances..amounts to 103,655. **1931** N. C. FLETCHER *St. John Ambulance Assoc.* 24 There were treated 247 cases, of which 41 required removal by ambulance.

b. *attrib.* and *Comb.* as **ambulance (aero)plane**, an aeroplane equipped to carry the sick and wounded (cf. *air ambulance*, AIR *sb.*[1] III. 5); **ambulance-chaser** *U.S. slang*, a lawyer who makes a business of raising actions for personal injuries; **ambulance class**, a first-aid class; **ambulance service**, a service whereby ambulances are provided; also *fig.*

1925 *World's Health* July 282 Ambulance aeroplanes are at present rendering remarkable services in Morocco. **1939** *Times* 2 Nov. 8/2 Last week the State Department granted export licences for the shipment to Sweden of 15 Seversky aeroplanes and one ambulance aeroplane. **1897** *Congress. Rec.* 24 July 2961/1 In New York City there is a style of lawyers known to the profession as 'ambulance chasers', because they are on hand wherever there is a railway wreck, or a street-car collision..with..their offers of professional services. **1961** *Guardian* 14 Mar. 2/4 A new kind of 'ambulance chaser'—who were unscrupulous lawyers who collected details of casualties as they were taken to hospital in order to persuade the person concerned to bring action for damages. **1878** P. SHEPHERD *Handbk. Aids for Injuries* p. xiii, I have hurriedly arranged the following Manual for the use of..ambulance classes. **1921** *Flight* 2 June 382/1 American ambulance 'plane comes to grief. **1903** *Encycl. Amer.* I. s.v. *Ambulance*, The first city ambulance service was inaugurated by the Bellevue Hospital authorities in New York in December 1869. **1907** *Daily Chron.* 11 Feb. 4/6 London's 'ambulance service' for street accidents and sudden illness. **1962** *Daily Tel.* 15 June 26 The 'ambulance service' run by the Co-operative Wholesale Society to take over and rescue failing retail societies.

3. A touring caravan or similar vehicle. *U.S.*

1856 *N.Y. Herald* 9 Jan. 2/1 The vehicle..like most ambulances, or 'prairie wagons', as they call them here, proved rather airy. **1899** T. W. HALL *Tales* 95 Once in a while she caught sight of a muffled figure in an ambulance that stopped for water for its thirsty mules.

ambulancier (ˌæmbjʊlən'sɪə(r)). *rare.* [? a. mod.Fr. *ambulancier*, or f. AMBULANCE + -IER. Cf. *financier*.] A man in charge of, or attached to, an ambulance.

1871 *Standard* 16 Jan., Their ambulanciers are armed like other soldiers.

ambulando: see SOLVITUR AMBULANDO.

ambulant ('æmbjʊlənt), *a.* [ad. L. *ambulantem* pr. pple. of *ambulā-re* to walk about. Also in mod.Fr. *ambulant*.]

1. Walking, moving about.

1619 BACON *Let.* 20 Nov. in Spedding *Lett. & Life* (1874) VII. 61 Sir Edward Coke was at Friday's hearing, but in his night-cap; and complained to me he was ambulant and not current. **1654** GAYTON *Fest. Notes* iv. 8 (L.) A knight dormant, ambulant, combatant. **1837** CARLYLE *Fr. Rev.* III. IV. vi. 267 An ambulant 'Revolutionary Army'..shall perambulate the country at large. **1885** G. MEREDITH *Diana* II. ii. 58 The zealous Irishman might be trusted to become an ambulant advertizer.

2. Moving, shifting, unfixed. *rare.*

1810 COLERIDGE *Friend* I. xi. (1867) 44 Discriminating offence from merit by such dim and ambulant boundaries.

†**3.** *Path.* and *Med.* **a.** Of a disease: shifting from one part of the body to another; = WANDERING *ppl. a.* 2 g. *Obs.*

1879 *St. George's Hosp. Rep.* IX. 703 Such inquirers.. must bear in mind the existence of ambulant fever. **1881** A. B. BALL in *von Ziemssen's Cycl. Med.* Suppl. 682 Ambulant œdema.

b. Of a disease: allowing the patient to walk about, not confining him to bed; also of medical treatment in which the patient is allowed or ordered to walk about, and of a patient who is able to walk.

1913 DORLAND *Med. Dict.*, *Ambulant, Ambulatory*... Walking or able to walk; not confining the patient to bed. **1927** *Daily Tel.* 31 May 15/5 Additional provision for what was called ambulant treatment of those suffering from lupus. **1958** *Hosp. O. & M. Service Reports* I. 11 Patients who attend from a distance (and who have no private transport) are dependent either on public transport or, if non-ambulant, on the ambulance service.

ambulate ('æmbjʊleɪt), *v. rare.* Obs. pa. pple. **ambulate.** [f. L. *ambulāt-* ppl. stem of *ambulā-re* to walk.] To walk, move about.

1623 COCKERAM, *Ambulate*, To moue hither and thither. **1724** RAMSAY *Evergreen* II. 65, I haif ambulate on Parnasso the mountain [*orig.*, I perambulate]. **1794** SOUTHEY in *Life* (1849) I. 215 Burnett ambulated to Bristol with me. **1814** BYRON in Moore *Life* (1866) 246 Without once quitting the table except to ambulate home.

ambulating ('æmbjʊleɪtɪŋ), *ppl. a.* [f. prec. + -ING[2].] Walking, moving; fitted for walking.

1786 tr. *Beckford's Vathek* 89 These ambulating spectres. **1837** SWAINSON *Nat. Hist. Birds* II. 186 Legs lengthened; ambulating, but webbed. **1839** LADY LYTTON *Cheveley* (ed. 2) I. ii. 26 This ambulating lottery-office now advanced.

ambulation (æmbjʊ'leɪʃən). [ad. L. *ambulātiōn-em*, n. of action f. *ambulāre* to walk.]

1. The action of walking, moving about.

1574 T. NEWTON *Health of Mag.* 7 Persons which feede upon grosse meates..may use vehementer exercise and stronger ambulations. *a* **1770** AKENSIDE *The Poet* The door is free, And calls him to evade their deafening clang By private ambulation. **1839** *Blackw. Mag.* XLV. 779 A style of ambulation peculiarly crustacean!

†**2.** The spreading of a gangrene. *Obs.*

1541 R. COPLAND *Guydon's Formul.* Riv, To drye the rottennesse that is..blody, and vyrulent and after nede to deffende the ambulacyon. **1751** CHAMBERS *Cycl.*, *Ambulation*, in physic, is used by some for the spreading of a gangrene or mortification.

†**'ambulative**, *a.* ? *Obs.* [a. Fr. *ambulatif*, *-ive*; f. L. *ambulāt-um*: see AMBULATE and -IVE.] Characterized by constant walking or motion.

1543 TRAHERON *Vigo's Chirurg.* II. vi. 21 Every Formica is ambulative, and not every one corrosyve. **1611** COTGR., *Ambulatif*, ambulatiue, ever-walking. **1657** J. COOKE *Hall's Cures* 237 [He] had the ambulative Gout.

ambulator ('æmbjʊleɪtə(r)). [a. L. *ambulātor* a walker; f. *ambulā-re* to walk.]

1. One who walks about, a walker; hence applied to a tourist's guide-book.

1652 GAULE *Magastrom.* 237 Such a perigrinator, such an ambulator. **1782** (*title*) The Ambulator; or Stranger's Companion Round London.

2. An instrument for measuring distances on the road, also called *perambulator*.

[Not in CRAIG 1847.] **1859** in OGILVIE.

ambulatorial (ˌæmbjʊlə'tɔərɪəl), *a.* [f. L. *ambulātōri-us* (see next) + -AL[1].] **a.** Connected with ambulatory exercise. **b.** Adapted for walking; = AMBULATORY 2.

1874 COUES *Birds of N.-W.* 602 Legs decidedly ambulatorial, placed well forward.

ambulatory ('æmbjʊlətərɪ), *a.* [ad. L. *ambulātōri-us* of or pertaining to a walker, f. *ambulātor*, q.v.; cf. Fr. *ambulatoire*.]

1. Of or pertaining to a walker, or to walking.

1622 HEYLYN *Cosmogr.* III. (1682) 129 Being at his ambulatory Exercise. **1796** MORSE *Amer. Geog.* II. 83 The ambulatory life of herdsmen and shepherds. **1874** HELPS *Soc. Press.* iv. 63 When that man has an object, it is astonishing what ambulatory powers he can develop.

2. Adapted or fitted for walking.

1835 KIRBY *Habits & Inst. An.* II. xvi. 84 The thoracic legs..become also its ambulatory legs. **1852** DANA *Crustacea* I. 10 Feet ambulatory or prehensile. **1877** W. THOMSON *Voy. Challenger* I. ii. 133 Leaf-like sacs..which fringe the ambulatory disk.

3. Moving from place to place, having no fixed abode; movable.

1622 HOWELL *Lett.* 5 Mar., His council of state went ambulatory always with him. **1649** JER. TAYLOR *Gt. Exemp.* Pref. ¶25 They served the ends of God..by their ambulatory life. *a* **1703** BURKITT *On N.T.* Acts vii. 50 The tabernacle was an ambulatory temple. **1845** R. HAMILTON *Pop. Educ.* 191 Many [schools] are ambulatory, and..are held only during four or five months in farm houses. **1858** GEN. P. THOMPSON *Audi Alt. Part.* I. xxv. 96 While the ambulatory guillotine was doing its work in the provinces.

4. *fig.* Shifting, not permanent, temporary, mutable. (So in L. and Fr.) ***ambulatory will***: one capable of revocation.

1621–31 LAUD *Serm.* (1847) 73 Nor is this ceremony Jewish or ambulatory, to cease with the law. **1651** W. G. *Cowel's Instit.* 133 A mans will..according to the Civill Law is ambulatory, or alterable, untill Death. **1789** MRS. PIOZZI *Fr. & It.* II. 387 They learn to think virtue and vice ambulatory. **1832** J. AUSTIN *Jurispr.* I. xxi. 452 Every intention..which regards the future is ambulatory or revocable.

5. *Path.* and *Med.* = AMBULANT *a.* sense 3.

1857 DUNGLISON *Med. Lex.* s.v., A morbid affection is said to be 'ambulatory'..when it skips from one part to another. **1882** QUAIN *Dict. Med.* I. 38/1 *Ambulatory*, a term given to typhoid fever, showing that the patient is able to walk about during the attack. **1903** *Westm. Gaz.* 21 Feb. 6/1 That the cause of death was ambulatory typhoid. **1947** L. K. FERGUSON *Surg. Ambulatory Patient* (ed. 2) p. ix, Surgery of the ambulatory patient is the surgery performed more often by the younger men and general practitioners. *Ibid.* i. 1 (*heading*) A survey of the field of ambulatory surgery.

ambulatory ('æmbjʊlətərɪ), *sb.* [ad. med.L. *ambulātōrium* a place for walking; f. *ambulā-re*: see AMBULATE and -ORY.] A place for walking in; especially, a covered way; an arcade, a cloister.

1623 COCKERAM, *Ambulatorie, A place to walke in.* **1659** P. HEYLIN in *Biblioth. Reg.* 258 A stately portico..raised on Corinthian pillars to serve for an Ambulatory, or common gallery. **1759** MARTIN *Nat. Hist.* I. 253 Ambulatories within the Change. **1812** W. TAYLOR in *Month. Rev.* LXVII. 295 Sheltered Ambulatories for wet weather are too rare in London. **1855** MILMAN *Lat. Chr.* (1864) IX. XIV. viii. 281 Its succursal aisles and ambulatories and chapels. **1870** F. WILSON *Ch. of Lindisf.* 52 Open seats on either side of a central ambulatory.

†**'ambuling**, *ppl. a.* *Obs.* [refashioned on AMBLING after L. *ambulans*, Fr. *ambulant* walking.] Walking, moving about. ***Ambuling Communion***, an observance of the Lord's Supper while walking or moving about.

1603 BARLOW in *Phenix* I. 177 A word his Highness had us'd the day before..Ambling-communions. **1655** FULLER *Ch. Hist.* x. 21 The indecencie of ambuling Communions.

ambulomancy ('æmbjuːləʊˌmænsɪ). *rare.* [f. L. *ambulā-re* to walk + μαντεία divination: see -MANCY.] Divination by walking.

1816 in *Month. Mag.* XLII. 22 His Ambulomancy, and many other foolish observances.

†**ambu'lones**, *sb. pl.* *Obs.* [f. L. *ambulā-re* to walk, as if a. L. **ambulo* sb.; cf. *calcitro*, *erro*, *prædo*.] (See quot).

1635 HEYWOOD *Hierarch.* VIII. 505 The Ignes Fatui that appeare To skip and dance before us ev'ry where, Some call them *Ambulones* for they walke Sometimes before us, and then after stalke.

amburbial (æm'bɜːbɪəl), *a.* *Rom. Antiq.* [f. L. *amburbiāl-is* of the *amburbi-um* or expiatory procession round the city, f. *amb-* about + *urbi(urbs)* city: see -AL[1].] *lit.* Connected with the circuit of a city; *hence*, Of or pertaining to the expiatory procession round the city of Rome.

1656 BLOUNT *Glossogr.*, *Amburbial*, that goes about the city. *Amburbial Sacrifices* were, when the beast went about the City before he was sacrificed. **1731** in BAILEY.

ambury, variant of ANBURY.

ambuscade (ˌæmbə'skeɪd), *sb.* Forms: 6 **ambuscaid, imboscade,** 6– **ambuscade.** [a. Fr. *embuscade*, ad. It. *imboscata*, or Sp. *emboscada*,

Pg. *embuscada* (= OFr. *embuchée*), ppl. deriv. of *imboscare* (Sp. *emboscar*, Pg. *embuscar*, Fr. *embucher*): see AMBUSH *v.* and -ADE[1]. For spelling with initial *a*, see AMBUSH. Almost displaced in 17th c. by the quasi-Spanish form AMBUSCADO.]

1. = AMBUSH 1 (and now more formal as a military term).

1582-8 *Hist. James VI.* (1804) 163 Thair was men lying in ambuscaid to haue trappit him. **1591** GARRARD *Art of Warre* 77 In placing Imboscades. **1679** *Establ. Test.* 22 They post themselves as in a wood, and lie in Ambuscade. **1694** CROWNE *Regulus* IV. 35 Y' entice me into a dangerous ambuscade. **1697** DRYDEN *Eneid* VI. (J.) Rous'd the Grecians from their ambuscade. **1757** BURKE *Abridgm. Eng. Hist.* Wks. X. 176 They formed frequent ambuscades. **1811** WELLINGTON in *Gen. Desp.* VII. 280 They had been lying in ambuscade for the patroles..for some days; but he contrived to draw them to an ambuscade which he had laid. **1846** GROTE *Greece* III. xxx. 100 To fall into an ambuscade.

2. The force placed in ambush, the company of liers in wait; = AMBUSH 2.

a **1674** CLARENDON *Hist. Reb.* III. xv. 454 An Ambuscade in the woods..fell upon them with such fury, that disordered the whole Army. **1781** GIBBON *Decl. & F.* (1869) II. xliii. 611 They were assaulted on the flanks by two ambuscades. **1814** SCOTT *Ld. of Isles* V. xxvii, It waked the lurking ambuscade.

3. *fig.* = AMBUSH 4.

1794 S. WILLIAMS *Hist. Vermont* 143 All is then caution, stratagem, secrecy, and ambuscade. **1842** MRS. GORE *Fascination* 148 In spite of this ambuscade, Martha made other preparatives of defence. **1844** H. ROGERS *Ess.* I. ii. 84 Nothing but the ambuscade of a fallacy.

ambuscade (æmbə'skeɪd), *v.* [f. the sb.]

1. *intr.* To lie in ambuscade; to ambush.

1592 WYRLEY *Armorie* 118 In ruinous house sequestred from the way, We ambuscade. **1848** KINGSLEY *Saint's Trag.* V. iii. 33 How! ambuscading?

2. *trans.* To conceal in ambush.

1853 G. JOHNSTON *Nat. Hist. E. Borders* I. 141 The broom..was long enough to ambuscade warriors of yore.

ambuscaded (æmbə'skeɪdɪd), *ppl. a.* [f. prec. + -ED.] Placed in ambuscade; ambushed.

1685 TRAVESTIN *Siege of Newheusel* 4 Some Janizaries, who were ambuscaded in an Inclosure. **1881** A. GRANT *Bush Life* II. 276 The spears of the ambuscaded natives.

ambuscader (æmbə'skeɪdə(r)). [f. as prec. + -ER[1].] One who lies in ambush, a lier in wait to surprise a foe.

1775 ADAIR *Amer. Ind.* 258 The most artful ambuscaders, and wolfish savages, in America. **1825** MILLAR *Time's Telescope* 118 The corselet-armed ambuscaders [*i.e.* beetles] have perpetrated the mischief.

ambuscading (æmbə'skeɪdɪŋ), *vbl. sb.* [f. as prec. + -ING[1].] Lying in wait to attack.

1831 CARLYLE *Sart. Res.* (1858) 80 An ironic man, with his sly stillness, and ambuscading ways..a pest to society.

ambuscado (æmbə'skeɪdəʊ), *sb. arch.* Pl. **-os**, earlier **-oes**, **-o's**. [An affected refashioning of AMBUSCADE after Sp. Here Englishmen may have confused the Sp. pa. pple. *emboscado* ambushed, in *estar emboscado* to lie in ambush, with the fem. sb. *emboscada* ambuscade; but cf. the series of words in -ADO[2] for Fr. *-ade*, Sp. *-ada*. Much commoner than *ambuscade* in 17th c., but eventually displaced by it, and now only an archaic by-form.]

1. = AMBUSCADE 1, AMBUSH 1.

1592 SHAKS. *Rom. & Jul.* I. iv. 84 Then dreames he of cutting Forraine throats, of Breaches, Ambuscados, Spanish Blades. **1598** BARRET *Theor. Warres* IV. iii. 110 Ambuscados ..are to be done in places of couert; as woods, thickets, etc. **1607** CHAPMAN *All Fooles* Plays 1873 I. 141 To lye in Ambuscado to surprize him. **1650** BAXTER *Saints' Rest* (1662) IV. iii. 632 In vain doth the Enemy lay his Ambuscado's. **1755** *Gentl. Mag.* XXV. 132 He talk'd; and many a tale he told Of battles, and of ambuscadoes. **1819** J. HOGG *Flodden Field*, Till some English, like tornado, Rushed from deepest ambuscado.

†**2.** A force (*pl.* troops) lying in ambush; = AMBUSCADE 2, AMBUSH 2. *Obs.*

1598 BARRET *Theor. Warres*, Gloss., *Ambuscado*, a Spanish word, and signifieth any troupe or company of soldiers either foot or horse, lodged secretly in some couert, as in woods, hollow wayes, behind bankes, or such like; to entrappe the enemy secretly attending his comming. **1603** KNOLLES *Hist. Turks* vi. (1621) 72 Saladin..with certaine ambuscadoes charged the rereward. **1726** CAVALLIER *Mem.* III. 224 My Ambuscadoes and Troopers fired at them.

3. *fig.*

1640 BROME *Sparagus Gard.* IV. v. 185 Had you your ambuscado for me? **1691** WOOD *Ath. Oxon.* II. col. 284 The judicious reader may perceive such a reserve, tho it lay in ambuscado.

†**ambu'scadoed**, *ppl. a. Obs.* [f. prec. + -ED.] Placed in ambush; ambuscaded.

1635 J. HAYWARD *Banish'd Virg.* 27 A princesse, ambuscadoed between hunters and savage beasts. **1650** W. CHARLETON *Paradoxes* 76 There was a large stock of malignant science ambuscadoed in the forbidden fruit.

ambush ('æmbʊʃ), *sb.* Forms: 5-6 **enbusshe, embushe,** 6- **ambush.** Occas. weakened in 4- to **abush, 'bush.** [a. OFr. *embusche*, f. vb. *embuscher*: see AMBUSH *v.* Nearly equivalent words from the pa. pple. of Fr., Sp., It., are ENBUSCHY, AMBUSCADO, AMBUSCADE, EMBOSCATA, IMBOSCATA. The change from *em-* to *am-* (which appears to have begun with this word *c* 1550, and thence extended to its cognates, including even *embuscade* from Fr.) is not accounted for; it was perh. due to the influence of words like *ambages*.]

1. *strictly.* A military disposition consisting of troops concealed in a wood or other place, in order to surprise and fall unexpectedly upon an enemy. The *ambush* is the entire strategic arrangement or *trap*; but sometimes the *posture*, sometimes the *place*, sometimes the *troops*, are the prominent part of the idea. Often in phr. ***to make, construct, lay an ambush; lie in ambush.*** (As a formal military term AMBUSCADE is now used.)

[*c* **1380** *Sir Ferumb.* 2887 þan schullaþ our men..breken out of þe bossche.]

1489 CAXTON *Faytes of Armes* I. i. 4 And made an enbusshe for the better to vaynquisshe theym. **1560** BIBLE (Genev.) *1 Macc.* ix. 40 (1590) Then Ionathans men that lay in ambush rose vp. **1600** HAKLUYT *Voy.* III. 406 The inhabitants of this Isle..layed an ambush for him. **1653** HOLCROFT *Procopius* 109 He layd ambushes upon the way, to cut them off as they fled. **1776** MCINTOSH in Sparks' *Corr. Am. Rev.* I. 168, I placed..ambushes in the different roads leading to it. **1870** BRYANT *Homer* I. VI. 191 He chose..The bravest men to be in ambush for him.

†**2.** The force (*pl.* troops) so disposed, liers in wait. *Obs.*

1489 CAXTON *Faytes of Armes* I. xvi. 48 Sawted on the sydes by som embushe. **1587** *Myrr. for Mag., Albanact* xiii. 1 By night the ambushe..Came forth from woods. **1653** HOLCROFT *Procopius* III. 111 The Ambushes rose, and put themselves between them and the Town.

3. Any disposition of persons (or of a single person) lying in wait.

[*c* **1386** CHAUCER *Knts. T.* 659 This Palamon Was in a busshe [*v.r.* bosch] that no man myhte hym se.]

1573 TWYNE *Æneid* VII. (R.) In secret ambush I, in yonder wood..my selfe entend to hide. **1593** SHAKS. *Rich. II*, I. i. 137 Once I did lay an ambush for your life. **1747** GRAY *Ode to Eton Coll.* lviii, Show them where in ambush stand To seize their prey, the murth'rous band!

4. *fig.*

1592 GREENE *Groatsw. Wit* (1617) 13 That rich ambush of amber colored darts [a Lady's hair], whose points are leueld against his heart. **1633** HERBERT *Ch. Milit.* 66 in *Temple* 185 Who by an ambush lost his Paradise. **1642** FULLER *Holy & Prof. St.* I. ix. 22 Lest some unseen ambushes should surprise his conscience. **1751** JOHNSON *Rambl.* No 183 ¶6 He that perishes in the ambushes of envy. **1852** H. ROGERS *Ess* I vii. 395 To forewarn the mind itself of the points in which an ambush of error may be suspected.

¶ By confusion for AMBAGES.

1602 FULBECKE *1st Pt. Parall.* 76 For the more ful & forcible destruction of delayes & ambushes in pleading.

ambush ('æmbʊʃ), *v.* Forms: α. 4 **enbusse, inbuche,** 4-5 **enbusshe,** 5 **embuisshe,** 4-6 **enbusche,** 5-6 **embusshe,** 6-7 **embush,** 7- **ambush.** Also β. 4 **abusse, abusche;** γ. 4 **busse,** 6 **busche,** 7 **bush.** [a. OFr. *embusche-r*, *embuissier*, cogn. w. Sp. *embuscar*, It. *imboscare*:—late L. **inboscāre*, f. *in* in + *bosc-us* wood, BUSH, i.e. to place in a wood, or among the *bushes*. For change to *am-* bef. 1600, see prec. Accented *am'bush* as late as 17th c.; already in 14th the toneless *en-* was treated like OE. prefix *an-*, becoming *ă-*, and then falling away: *en'bush, ă'bush, 'bush*. In 16th c. there was a by-form IMBOSQUE, a. It. *imboscāre*.]

1. To dispose troops in concealment among bushes, or elsewhere, so as to take an enemy by surprise; to place in ambush; to lay in wait. *Obs.* or *arch.*, exc. in pa. pple. *ambushed.*

α. **1330** R. BRUNNE *Chron.* 187 Alle þat suerd mot bere, Were sette R[ichard] to dere, enbussed þorgh þe feld. *c* **1380** *Sir Ferumb.* 2879 Do þat þaye in-buched beo..In þe wode þat þow mi3t see. *c* **1450** *Merlin* xxii. 404 Sir Gawein and his felowes were enbusshed. **1483** CAXTON *G. de la Tour* F viij, The paynyms whiche nyghe were embusshed. **1513** DOUGLAS *Æneis* XI. x. 84 Thare lay ane vale in ane crukit glen, Ganand for slicht to enbusche armit men. **1580** SIDNEY *Arcadia* III. (1622) 250 [We] embushed his footmen in the falling of a hill. **1624** HEYWOOD *Gunaik.* IV. 207 These hee ambushes in divers places. **1725** POPE *Odyss.* IV. 602 Ambush'd we lie, and wait the bold emprize.

β. *c* **1300** *Beket* 1382 He him abussed there. *c* **1350** *Will. Palerne* 3634 A fersche ost..a-buschid þer bi-side.

γ. **1330** R. BRUNNE *Chron.* 187 Saladyn prively was bussed beside þe flom. **1535** STEWART *Cron. Scot.* I. 263 The Pechtis than was buschit neir hand by. **1623** DANIEL *Hymen's Tri.* II. i, Being closely bush'd a pretty distance off.

b. *refl. Obs.* exc. as in 1.

c **1300** *Beket* 1382 Seint Thomas was..in huding, as hit were, In the hows of Seint Bertin, for he him abussede there. **1375** BARBOUR *Bruce* VI. 396 Neir thar-by He him enbuschit preuely. *c* **1450** *Merlin* xvii, Ye and I shull go..and enbussh us there. *c* **1530** LD. BERNERS *Arthur Lyt. Bryt.* 177 Syr Isembartes cosyn embusshed him in a great forest. **1572** R. H. *Lavaterus's Ghostes* 86 That he shoulde embush himself behinde the wood. **1637** HEYWOOD *Dialogues* 287 Here on the top of the mount Ericine Ambush thy selfe. **1814** SCOTT *Ld. of Isles* V. xvi, To ambush us in greenwood bough.

2. *intr.* (refl. pron. omitted) To lie down in ambush; lie in wait, lurk.

1626 SHIRLEY *Brothers* IV. ii, Now you know where to ambush. **1742** YOUNG *Nt. Th.* V. 826 Behind the rosy bloom he loves to lurk, Or ambush in a smile. **1855** M. ARNOLD *Memory Pict.* 28 The archest chin Mockery ever ambush'd in. **1859** H. KINGSLEY *G. Hamlyn* II. 179 A wicked kitten, who ambushes round the corner of the flower-bed.

3. *trans.* To waylay, attack from an ambush.

1631 HEYWOOD *England's Eliz.* (1641) To Reader 1 The criticks of this age, who with their frivolous cavils..ambush the commendable labours of others. **1780** CLINTON in Sparks' *Corr. Am. Rev.* (1853) I. 135 This party were ambushed by the enemy, and defeated. **1881** *Daily News* 26 Mar. 2/5 It was admitted that Mr. L. had ambushed him at midnight.

ambushed ('æmbʊʃt), *ppl. a.* [f. prec. + -ED.]

1. Placed or lying in ambush.

1330 R. BRUNNE *Chron.* 288 Biside enbussed, was fiften hundred sped, In foure grete escheles. **1393** GOWER *Conf.* I. 260 This knight..Embuished upon horsebake. *c* **1450** *Merlin* XV. 246 Men enbusshed in that streite passage. **1481** CAXTON *Myrr.* II. vi. 77 The hunters that ben embusshed by. *c* **1590** MARLOWE *Faustus* 136 (Enter the ambushed Soldiers). **1667** DRYDEN *Indian Emp.* I. ii. (1725) 336 Swarming Bands of ambush'd Men. **1810** COLERIDGE *Friend* III. xv. (1867) 211 The ambushed soldier must not fire his musket. **1861** RUSSELL in *Times* 29 July, The ambushed rifleman.

2. *fig.* Concealed so as suddenly to burst forth, come in view, or take by surprise.

1647 R. STAPYLTON *Juvenal* 90 Her teares in troops still ambusht, waite to know What's her designe. **1798** S. ROGERS *Epist. Friend* 143 Tuneful echoes, ambushed at my gate. **1833** TENNYSON *Poems* 43, I wish I were her earring, Ambushed in auburn ringlets sleek. **1835** J. HARRIS *Gt. Teacher* 267 Murder, ambushed in an unbreathed and unsuspected thought. **1839** BAILEY *Festus* 35/1 Till in some ambushed eddy it is sucked down. **1875** LOWELL *Poet. Wks.* (1879) 462 Half-tamed hamlets, ambushed round with woods.

ambusher ('æmbʊʃə(r)). [f. AMBUSH *v.* + -ER[1].] One who makes an ambush.

1893 in *Funk's Stand. Dict.* **1920** *Glasgow Herald* 20 Nov. 7 The ambushers, he said, were all dressed in khaki.

ambushment ('æmbʊʃmənt, formerly ɛm'bʊʃmənt). *arch.* Forms: α. 4 **enbusse-, enbuschy-, enbuchy-, anbuschy-,** 4-6 **enbusche-, enbusshe-,** 5 **enbussh-, embusche-,** 5-6 **embusshe-, enbusch-, enbush-,** 6 **embush-, ambushe-,** 6- **ambushment.** Also β. (refash. after L. *in-*, *im-*, 5 **inbusshe-,** 5-6 **imbusshe-,** 6 **imbushment.** γ. (*Weakened*) 4 **abusse-, abuche-, abuchy-,** 4-6 **abusshe-,** 5-6 **abusch-, abushment.** δ. *Aphetic*, 4 **busse-, buche-, buchy-,** 4-6 **busshe-,** 5-6 **busch-, bushment.** [a. OFr. *embuschement* (med.L. *imboscāmentum*), n. of action f. *embuscher*: see AMBUSH *v.* and -MENT. As late as 1600 accented *am'bushment*, though *'embushment* is found in Sc. in 1513. In ME. the atonic *en-*, treated as OE. *an-*, was phonetically reduced to *ă-*, and then allowed to fall away: *en-'bushment, ăn-'bushment, ă-'bushment, 'bushment*. The uncontracted word was often Latinized as *imbushment* after the Renascence, but finally assimilated to AMBUSH.]

1. A disposition or arrangement of troops in a wood or other place of concealment so as to fall on an enemy by surprise; the trap so constructed; ambush, ambuscade.

α. **1330** R. BRUNNE *Chron.* 187 Ne man ne hors suld go þorgh þat enbussement. **1375** BARBOUR *Bruce* VIII. 45 Thai maid enbuschement all the nycht. *c* **1380** *Sir Ferumb.* 812 Of þys anbuschymenȝ þan brek out: Bruyllant..& Sorty-brant ..with hure rout. *Ibid.* 2989 þe Saraȝynȝ at arst brek out: þat were on þe enbuchyment. *c* **1386** CHAUCER *Melibeus* 354 Counterwayte embusshementz and alle espiaille. **1470-85** MALORY *Arthur* I. xi, Syre Kay came oute of an enbusshement. **1485** CAXTON *Paris & Vienne* 5 The enbusshement that was layed for them. **1513** DOUGLAS *Æneis* XI. x. 67 Ly at wate in quyet enbuschment. *c* **1530** LD. BERNERS *Arthur Lyt. Bryt.* (1814) 493 The Frensshe men lepte out from theyr enbusshementes. **1542** *Piteous Tr.* in *Harl. Misc.* (Malh.) I. 239 Falling amonge theyr embushmentes. **1577** HANMER *Eccl. Hist.* (1619) 30 Whence he might make an ambushment upon Jerusalem. **1582** N. T. (Rhem.) *Acts* xxiii. 30 Embushments that they had prepared against him. **1591** HARINGTON *Orl. Fur.* XXXVI. v, While in ambushment close they lay on land. **1597** DANIEL *Civ. Wars* VII. lxxxvi, Where round enclos'd by ambushments forelaid. **1676** I. MATHER *K. Philip's War* (1862) 166 He hath as it were set Ambushments against the Enemy. **1803** W. ROSE *Am. de Gaul* 93 Then from his ambushment shall Abyes rush.

β. *c* **1450** *Merlin* XV. 234 Comen all fressh of here inbusshement. **1523** LD. BERNERS *Froissart* I. ccxi. 254 Capitaynes of this imbusshement.

γ. [See also ABUSHMENT.] **1330** R. BRUNNE *Chron.* 242 Leulyn in a wod a bussement he held. *c* **1380** *Sir Ferumb.* 798 Y leuede ȝond on a buchyment. *Ibid.* 4340 Ȝe mote leue with ȝoure power On a-buchement..In a wode þat ys þer faste by. *a* **1450** *Knt. de la Tour* lxx. 92 She hadde hidde in a busshement for hym. **1557** *Arthur* (Copland) V. vi, Lefte in a busshement. **1612** MONIPENNIE in *Misc. Scot.* I. 94 [He] was inclosed with an abushment.

δ. [See also BUSHMENT. Early instances confound *abushment* and *a bushment*.] **1375** BARBOUR *Bruce* VI. 415 Quhill thai Fer by thar buschement war all past. **1387** TREVISA *Higden* Rolls Ser. IV. 73 þe consuls of Rome sette bussshementes for hym. *c* **1430** *Syr Generides* (1865) 64 The king was passed by his bushment. **1553** BRENDE *Q. Curt.* III. 18 For feare the enemyes should lye there in busshement. **1870** MORRIS *Earth. Par.* I. I. 54 The barbarous folk..from bushments on us broke.

†**2.** The troops so concealed; a force that actually is, has been, or is about to be placed in ambush. *Obs.*

1393 GOWER *Conf.* III. 208 Thembushements to-breken alle And him beclipt on every side. *c* **1440** *Morte Arth.* 1407 Thane þe embuschement of Bretons brake owte at ones. **1480** CAXTON *Chron. Engl.* II. (1520) 11/1 Then came Corin with the busshement. **1548** HALL *Chron.* 197 He with an Imbusshement of Englishemen laye in a Valley nye to the Fortresse. **1580** SIDNEY *Arcadia* (1622) 328 An ambushment broken forth from the houses behinde them. *a* **1581** CAMPION *Hist. Irel.* II. i. 63 Then stept out an ambushment of the Irish.

†**3.** A company of soldiers secretly deployed; a surprise party. *Obs.*

1387 TREVISA *Higden* Rolls Ser. VI. 251 He was assailled wiþ busshemente of Gaskyns. **1549** LATIMER 7 *Serm.* (1869) 184 Judas..was prouydyng among the byshoppes and preistes, to come with an imbushment of Iewes to take our sauiour Iesus Christ. **1655** GOUGE *Comm. Heb.* 105 Of Souldiers there useth to be a Van-guard, main Battalio, Reer, right and left Wings, and Ambushments.

†**4.** *fig.* Devices to entrap, or take by surprise. *Obs.*

1579 TOMSON *Calvin's Serm. Tim.* 346/2 All subtilties and ambushments that the diuell layeth against vs. **1580** (*title*) A Detection of damnable driftes practised by three Witches.. Set forthe to discouer the Ambushements of Sathan, whereby he would surprise vs. **1641** MILTON *Animadv.* (1851) 185 The close ambushment of worst errors.

ambusion, erron. var. (cf. prec. 1 γ) ABUSION.

†**am'bust**, *a. Obs.*⁻⁰ [ad. L. *ambūstus* f. *amb-* about + *ūstus* burnt.] 'Burnt round about.' Bailey 1731.

am'bustial, *a. rare*⁻⁰. [improp. f. L. *ambūstum* a burn, or *ambūstiōn-em* burning.] 'Produced by, or being in connection with, a burn.' *Syd. Soc. Lex.* 1879.

am'bustion (æm'bʌstɪən). ? *Obs.* [ad. L. *ambūstiōn-em*, n. of action f. *ambūr-ĕre*, f. *amb-* about + *ūrere* to burn.] 'A burn, a scald.' J.

1623 COCKERAM, *Ambustion*, scorching, scalding. **1684** tr. *Bonet's Merc. Compit.* XVIII. 662 Gun-shot Wounds, which are complicated with Ambustion. **1706** PHILLIPS, *Ambustion*, a Solution of the continuity of the Parts, caus'd by some outward Burning; a Burn, or Scald. **1755** in JOHNSON. **1879** in *Syd. Soc. Lex.*

ame, obs. form of AAM, AIM, AM.

amebean, variant of AMŒBÆAN.

amebiasis, var. AMŒBIASIS.

amebly. *Obs. rare*⁻¹. [?] 'Apparently means a simpleton.' Nares.

1651 CARTWRIGHT *Ordinary* (N.) Where is thylk amebly, Francklin, cleped Meanwel?

‖**âme damnée** (ɑm dane). [Fr., lit. 'damned soul'.] A devoted adherent; a tool.

1823 SCOTT *Pev. Peak* IV. xii. 288 He is the *ame damnée* of every one about my court—the scape-goat, who is to carry away all their iniquities. **1830** C. C. F. GREVILLE *Mem.* (1874) II. xiii. 96 He [*sc.* Sefton] is the *âme damnée* of Lord Grey, and defends everything of course. **1879** M. E. BRADDON *Vixen* III. vii. 185 Their *âmes damnées*, the men who hold their hods and mix their mortar. **1917** ASQUITH *Let.* 13 Nov. (1933) I. 46 We are having Col. House, the Head of the American 'Mission', to lunch; he is President Wilson's own particular *âme damnée*. **1938** S. BECKETT *Murphy* iv. 54 Neary..boarded the first train for Dublin, accompanied by his *âme damnée* and man-of-all work, Cooper.

amedoun, variant of AMYDON, *Obs.*, starch.

amee, obs. form of AMMI, bishopweed.

ameed (ə'miːd), *v. rare*⁻¹. [f. A- *pref.* 11 + MEED: a modern formation.] To reward.

1809 J. BARLOW *Columb.* VII. 611 An equal prize each gallant troop ameeds.

†**a'meek**, *v. Obs. rare*⁻¹. [f. A- *pref.* 1 or 6 + MEEK *v.*] To make meek; to soothe, appease.

c **1440** *Gesta Rom.* 224 Then the Emperour was amekid.

‖**ameer** (ə'mɪə(r)). Also amír. [a. Arab. (Pers. and Urdu) *amīr* commander, f. *amara* to tell, order, command. As a historical Saracen title commonly spelt EMIR; the spelling *amír, ameer*, is used of modern Indian and Afghan rulers.]

†**1.** = EMIR. *Obs.*

1614 SELDEN *Titles of Hon.* 49 In the Mahumedan state, they haue the name of *Ameras, Amir*, or *Amera* (applied to their great Sultan) which truly..may express *Dominus* or *Lord*. **1615** BEDWELL *Arab. Trudg.* s.v. *Amir.*, Foure lieutenants, (Amir's they call them). **1679** JENISON *Narr. Pop. Plot* 40 The Moorish Amir told the Embassadors, etc.

2. The title of various Mohammedan rulers in Scinde and Afghanistan; now specially of the latter.

1803 COLEBROOKE *Asiat. Res.* vii. 220 It will be sufficient to instance those of..Amīr Khān Anjām. **1870** KNIGHT *Crown Hist. Eng.* lxv. 898 Scinde..was, in 1842, under the rule of a body of despotic nobles, the Ameers. **1883** *Daily News* 4 Apr. 2/1 The Ameer of Afghanistan had expressed a wish to visit India.

ameership (ə'mɪəʃɪp). [f. prec. + -SHIP.] The position of an ameer.

1882 *American* No. 105. 277 The faithful ally of England, owing his Amirship to her armies.

ameistre(n, var. AMAISTER *v. Obs.* to subdue.

†'**amel**, *sb. Obs.* Forms: 4 **aumayl**, 5 **amall**, 5–7 **amell(e**, 6–7 **ammel**, **ammell**, 6–8 **amel**. Also, 6 **esmayle**, **anmayle**. [a. AFr. **amail*, **amal* (see A- *pref.* 9), OFr. *esmal, esmail*, cogn. w. Pr. *esmalt, esmaut*, Sp. and Pg. *esmalte*, It. *smalto*, med.L. *smaltum*; according to Diez, f. Teut. **smaltjan*, OHG. **smalzian, smelzan*, OE *smęltan*, to SMELT; OFr. *esmail* repr. Teut. *smalti*. (The *au-* in early instance is not accounted for: see it also in *enamel*.) Now superseded by the compound EN-AMEL. An (?) interm. ANMAILE, and a form ESMAYLE from Fr. also occur in 6.] Enamel.

c **1340** *Gaw. & Gr. Knt.* 236 Grene aumayl on golde lowande bryзter. *c* **1460** *Launfal* 270 An ern ther stod, Of bournede gold..Ifloryschеd with ryche amall. **1598** SYLVESTER *Du Bartas* I. iii. (1641) 26/1 The Lillie's snowe, and Pansey's various ammell. **1633** P. FLETCHER *Purple Isl.* X. xxxiii, Heav'ns richest diamonds, set on Ammel white. **1683** PETTUS *Fleta Min.* II. 5 The Lime..being well calcin'd ..makes the Amel. **1751** CHAMBERS *Cycl.*, *Enamel*, popularly *Amel*. **1819** *Pantolog.*, *Amel*, the matter with which the variegated works are overlaid.

b. *attrib.* and quasi-*adj.*

1578 T. N. tr. *Conq. W. Ind.* 199 They have skill also of Amell worke. **1625** W. LISLE *Du Bartas* I. 34 Gardens of delight Whose ammell beds perfume the skie.

†'**amel**, *v. Obs.* For forms see AMELED. [f. AMEL *sb.*; cf. Fr. *esmailler, émailler*, AFr. 1363 *aymeler*.] To enamel. (Chiefly in pa. pple. AMELED.)

1530 PALSGR. 425/1, I ammell as a goldesmyth dothe his worke, *Jesmaille*.

amel, obs. form of AMYL, starch, fine flour.

amelanchier (æmə'lænʃɪə(r)). *Bot.* [ad. Savoy *amelancier* the medlar tree.] A genus of small trees, natives of Europe and N. America, allied to the Medlar and Cotoneaster.

1741 *Compl. Fam.-Piece* II. iii. 374 Trees and Shrubs which are now in Flower..wild Service or Quickbeam, Amelanchier. **1866** JOHNS in *Treas. Bot.* s.v., The common Amelanchier has long been cultivated in England.

amelcorn ('æməlkɔːn). Also 6 amilcorne. [a. Ger. or Du. *amelkorn*, f. L. *amyl-um* starch + CORN.] An inferior variety of wheat, the larger spelt (*Triticum vulgare dicoccum*), called also French rice.

1578 LYTE *Dodoens* 456 This corne is called in high Douch *Ammelkorne*..in base Almaigne, *Amelcorne*, and in Latin *Amyleum frumentum*..it may be englished *Amelcorne*, or bearded wheate. **1611** COTGR., *Scourgeon*, Amell-corn, or Starch-corn; a wild or degenerate Wheat. **1627** SPEED *Eng. Abridg.* xi. §4 The fields bring forth a kinde of Rie or Amell-corne. **1762** tr. *Duhamel's Husb.* IV. v. 474 Amel, or starch-corn was cut on the 28th. **1879** *Syd. Soc. Lex.*, *Amel corn*, French rice, from which starch is made.

amelectic (æmə'lɛktɪk), *a.* [f. Gr. ἀμελ-ής indifferent + ἐκτικός habitual.] Careless.

1879 in *Syd. Soc. Lex.*

†'**ameled**, '**amelled**, *ppl. a. Obs.* Forms: 4 **amiled**, 5 **amelyd**, 6 **ammelyt**, **amelled**, **ameld**, **aumayld**, 7–8 **amell'd**. [f. AMEL *v.* + -ED; in AFr. 1363 *aymelet*.] Enamelled.

c **1400** *Rom. Rose* 1080 Knopes fine of golde amiled. **1513** DOUGLAS *Æneis* VII. xi. 77 With latit sowpyl siluer weyll ammelyt [*v.r.* annelit]. *a* **1564** BECON *Christ & Antichr.* (1844) 518 The cross of pride..well gilt and ameled. **1596** SPENSER *F.Q.* II. iii. 27 Gilden buskins..entayld With curious antickes, and full fayre aumayld. **1600** CHAPMAN *Iliad* (1857) XVI. 123 Achilles' arms, enlighten'd all with stars, And richly amell'd. **1710** PHILIPS *Pastorals* 2 Oh when shall I once more With ravished eyes review thine amell'd shore?

†'**amelet**, **amlet**. *Obs.* [a. OFr. *amelette* (see Littré), now *omelette*.] = OMELET *sb.*

1761 SMOLLETT *Gil Blas* (ed. 6) 10 When the amlet I had bespoke was ready I sat down to table. **1775** ASH, *Amelet*, a kind of pancake.

†'**ameling**, *vbl. sb. Obs.* Also 6 **ammellyng**. [f. AMEL *v.* + -ING¹.] Enamelling, inlaying.

1530 PALSGR. 194/1 Ammellyng, *esmaillevre*. **1571** in Campbell *Love-l. Mary Q. Scots* (1824) 47, I send you one sepulture of hard stone..The ameling that is about is black.

ameliorable (ə'miːlɪərəb(ə)l), *a.* [f. AMELIORATE: see -ABLE.] Capable of amelioration or improvement.

1807 W. TAYLOR in *Ann. Rev.* V. 274 In short, the execution, like the design, is ameliorable.

ameliorate (ə'miːlɪəreɪt), *v.* [a recent formation (not in Johnson 1773), after the earlier MELIORATE q.v., on Fr. *améliorer*, refashioned from OFr. *ameillorer* to make better, f. *à* to + *meillorer*:—L. *meliōrāre*, f. *melior* better.]

1. *trans.* To make better; to better, improve.

1767 [See AMELIORATING]. **1779** SWINBURNE *Trav. Spain* xxxvi. (T.) The probability of their lot being so much ameliorated. **1813** SIR H. DAVY *Agric. Chem.* 203 A sterile soil..may be ameliorated by the application of quick lime. **1849** MACAULAY *Hist. Eng.* I. 279 In every human being there is a wish to ameliorate his own condition. **1879** *Quatrefages' Hum. Spec.* 70 Gardeners and breeders.. ameliorate..the plants and animals in which they are interested.

2. *intr.* To grow better.

1789–96 MORSE *Amer. Geog.* I. 626 The state of things is rapidly ameliorating. **1882** GEIKIE in *Macm. Mag.* Mar. 365/2 [Man]..would find his way back as the climate ameliorated.

ameliorated (ə'miːlɪəˌreɪtɪd), *ppl. a.* [f. prec. + -ED.] Made better, improved.

1795 COLERIDGE *Plot Disc.* 9 Progressive reformation and ameliorated manners. **1829** I. TAYLOR *Enthus.* ii. (1867) 32 Ameliorated mysticism.

ameliorating (ə'miːlɪə'reɪtɪŋ), *ppl. a.* [f. as prec. + -ING².] Improving, making better.

1767 A. YOUNG *Farmer's Lett.* 112 Sow oats after a fallow or some ameliorating crop. **1864** GLADSTONE in *Daily Tel.* 12 Oct., Any man who proposes an ameliorating law becomes..a sort of object of suspicion.

amelioration (əˌmiːlɪə'reɪʃən). [a. mod.Fr. *amélioration*, or analogously formed on AMELIORATE. Quot. 1659 ought perh. to read 'a melioration.']

1. The action of making better; or the condition of being made better; improvement.

1659 MORRICE in Burton *Diary* (1828) IV. 355 The fruit receives amelioration by the second concoction. **1796** BURKE *Regic. Peace* (T.) These very robbers..are in a course of amelioration. **1813** WELLINGTON in Gurwood *Desp.* X. 475 We cannot hope for any permanent amelioration. **1813** SIR H. DAVY *Agric. Chem.* 260 Plants are capable of amelioration by peculiar methods of cultivation. **1875** WOOD *Therap.* (1879) 107 If recovery occur, it is by a gradual amelioration of the symptoms.

2. *concr.* A thing wherein improvement is realized; an improvement.

1776 ADAM SMITH *W.N.* IV. ix. (1869) 248 The buildings, drains, enclosures, and other ameliorations which they may either make or maintain.

ameliorative (ə'miːlɪəˌreɪtɪv), *a.* [f. AMELIORATE + -IVE; cf. *agglomerative*.] Tending to ameliorate; improving.

1809 *Edin. Rev.* XV. 95 There are other branches of ameliorative administration. **1861** SMILES *Engineers* I. 470 The ameliorative influence he exercised upon the condition of his countrymen.

ameliorator (ə'miːlɪəˌreɪtə(r)). [f. AMELIORATE + -OR, after L. analogies; cf. *arbitrator*.] He who, or that which, ameliorates.

1865 BUCKMAN *Sc. in Farm Cult.* xi. 74 The admixture of manures or ameliorators, such as guano. **1872** YEATS *Growth & Viciss. Comm.* 272 The ameliorator of agricultural distress was François. **1877** W. THOMSON *Voy. Challenger* I. ii. 121 Our beneficent ameliorator, the Gulf-stream.

†**amell(e**, *adv.* and *prep. Obs.* or *dial.* Also 4 **omelle**, 3–5 **emell(e**. [ad. Norse *á milli, á millum*, 'amid,' for *á miðli, miðlum* dat. sing. and pl. of *miðil* or *meðal* 'mid, middle'; or perh. of a later form **á meðli* from *meðal*, corresponding to OSw. *i mælli*, Dan. *imellum*, the direct cognate of which is the kindred IMELLE.]

A. *adv.* In the middle; between; in the interval.

a **1400** *Leg. Rood* (1871) 90 Two hundreth зeres war omell, Betwix þe tymes þat I of tell.

B. *prep.* Amid, among, betwixt.

a **1300** *Cursor M.* 23931 Þi eme leuedi vs light emell. *c* **1460** *Towneley Myst.* 55 A manner of men That make great mastres us emelle. *Ibid.* 56 Ther shuld a man walk us amelle. **1674** RAY *N. Countr. Words* 2 *Amell*, among, betwixt, contracted from a midle; some pronounce it *ameld*. **1686** G. STUART *Joco-Ser. Disc.* 59 Amell them twa was sik a league. **1863** ATKINSON *Whitby Gloss.*, *Amell*, between, in the middle. 'They came amell seven and eight o'clock.'

Comb. **amell-doors**, *dial.* 'doors between the outer door and that of an inner room.' Atkinson *Gloss.*

ameloblast (ə'mɛləʊblæst). *Zool.* [f. EN)AMEL *sb.* + -O + -BLAST.] A columnar cell which secretes enamel in the teeth of the higher vertebrates.

1882 J. L. WILLIAMS in *Dental Cosmos* XXIV. 229 Prof. Eames, of St. Louis, introduced the term ameloblast..as an appropriate one for the inner layer, or true enamel cells. **1886** W. X. SUDDUTH in W. F. Litch *Amer. Syst. Dentistry* I. III. 641 A slight layer of enamel has been formed... Between this layer of enamel and the layer of ameloblasts a space is noticed. **1942** E. S. HORNING in G. Bourne *Cytology & Cell Physiol.* vi. 178 The cells destined to become ameloblasts in the developing enamel organ were found to contain relatively large amounts of calcium and magnesium.

amen (ˌeɪ'mɛn, often ˌɑː'mɛn), *adv.*, *int.*, *sb.* [a. L. (or Fr.) *āmēn*, a. Gr. ἀμήν, a. Heb. *ā-mēn*, 'certainty, truth,' f. vb. *āman* to strengthen, confirm; used adverbially 'certainly, verily, surely' as an expression of affirmation, consent, or ratification of what has been said by another (*Deut.* xxvii. 26, *1 Kings* i. 36); adopted in Gr. by the LXX., whence in N.T., and in early Christian use, in Gr. and L., as a solemn expression of belief, affirmation, consent, concurrence, or ratification, of any formal utterance made by a representative; thus with prayers, imprecations, confessions of faith. App. not so used in OE., but transl. by *Sóðlice!*, *Swá hit ys* or *sý!* Added however as a concluding formula to Luke and John in the Ags. Gospels.]

A. *int.* or *adv.*

1. As a concluding formula (merely transferred from L.) = Finis.

c **950** *Lindisf. Gosp.* Luke xxiv. 53 Lofando & gebloedsando gód. Soðlice. *c* **1000** *Ags. G.* ibid., God herȝende & hyne eac bletsiȝende. Amen. [**1611** *Ibid.* Praising and blessing God. Amen.]

2. a. A solemn expression of concurrence in, or ratification of, a prayer, or wish; Be it so really! *c* **1230** *Ancr. R.* 430 He beo euer i-heied from worlde to worlde, euer on ecchenesse! Amen. *c* **1300** in Wright *Lyric P.* xv. 51 God us lene of ys lyht, That we of sontes habben syht, ant hevene to mede! Amen. **1382** WYCLIF *Matt.* vi. 13 But delyuere vs fro yuel. Amen, *that is so be it.* *a* **1400** *Relig. Pieces fr. Thornton MS.* 37 Say we Amen,þat es to say swa be it. **1535** COVERDALE *Ps.* lxxi. 19 Blessed be the name of his maiesty for euer.. Amen, Amen. **1605** SHAKS. *Macb.* II. ii. 28, I could not say, Amen, When they did say, God blesse vs. **1615** BEDWELL *Moham. Imp.* II. §90 To morrow if God Almighty say, Amen, we will meet. **1859** TENNYSON *Elaine* 1217 An end to this! A strange one! Yet I take it with Amen!

b. *attrib.* **amen corner, seat** *U.S.*, that part of a meeting-house occupied by persons who assist the preacher with occasional and irregular responses; also *transf.*; **Amen glass**, an eighteenth-century drinking-glass with part of the Jacobite version of 'God Save the King', concluding with the word 'Amen', engraved upon the bowl.

1860 *Harper's Mag.* Jan. 279/2 The Rev. Judson Noth, a local Methodist preacher,.. was one of the best 'scotchers' that occupied the 'Amen Corner'. **1868** *All Year Round* 31 Oct. 490/1 Sunday found them, judge and lawyers, seated in the 'amen corner'. **1877** HABBERTON *Jericho Road* xiv. 128 In an 'amen' seat sat an old half-breed. **1884** *Congress. Rec.* 24 Apr. 3207/1 When commiserated upon the fact that he was compelled to go to what is commonly known here as the amen corner, [he] frankly said that any seat in the Senate was better than none. **1894** *Ibid.* Jan. 1502/2 One of those saintly Republican monopolists who sit in the 'Amen corner' of protected privilege. **1904** HARBEN *Georgians* vii. 67 [They] were in their places in the 'amen corner', at the right of the crude pulpit.

[**1897** A. HARTSHORNE *Old Eng. Glasses* xxiv. 349 This glass also has on the bowl the first two verses of the song, and the crowned cypher with *amen* under it.] **1924** J. BLES *Rare Eng. Glasses XVII & XVIII Cent.* 98 This interesting goblet is engraved in diamond point with the crowned cypher JR, forward and reversed with the figure 8.. in the same manner as the majority of 'Amen' glasses. **1926** G. R. FRANCIS *Old Eng. Drinking Glasses* xvi. 167 Of this type are most of the 'Amen' glasses, which were all similar in the inscription; some ten or twelve are now known to exist. **1936** *Burlington Mag.* May xvii/1 An *Amen* Jacobite glass, with the full Jacobite National Anthem inscribed upon it, had realised as much as £300 last year.

3. Of concurrence in a formal statement, confession of faith, etc.: It is so in truth.

[*a* **1000** *Creed* in *Rel. Ant.* I. 35 Ic ȝe-lyfe on þone halȝan gast.. & þat éce lif. Sy it swa.] *c* **1220** *Creed* in Morris *E.E. Hom.* I. 217, Ibileue on ðe holi goste.. eche lif efter deað; amen. **1662** *Bk. Comm. Prayer, Nicene Creed*, I believe in.. the life of the world to come. Amen.

4. Retained in the Bible from the original Gr. or Heb.: Truly, verily.

c **1382** WYCLIF *2 Cor.* i. 20 Therefore and by him we seyn Amen to God, to oure ioye. **1582** N. T. (Rhem.) *John* viii. 34 *note*, The Reader may see great reason why vve also say Amen, Amen, and durst not translate it. **1611** BIBLE *2 Cor.* i. 20 The promises of God in him are Yea, and in him Amen.

B. *sb.*

1. The word *Amen!* at the end of a prayer, etc. *c* **1230** *Ancr. R.* 24 And efter þe amen, '*Per Dominum: benedicamus Domino.*' **1597** T. MORLEY *Introd. Mus.* 82, I finde no better word to say after a good praier, then Amen. **1711** ADDISON *Spect.* No. 285 ¶6, I have spoke the Assent to a Prayer with a long Amen. **1829** SOUTHEY *All for Love* IV. Wks. VII. 175 The Choristers, with louder voice, Intoned the last Amen!

2. An expression of assent; an assertion of belief.

1579 W. FULKE *Heskins's Parl.* 227 Be thou a member of the bodie of Christ, that thy Amen may be true. **1613** SHAKS. *Hen. VIII*, v. i. 24 *Gard.* I wish it grubb'd vp now. *Lov.* Me thinkes I could Cry the Amen. **1851** MRS. BROWNING *Casa Guidi Wind.* 119 False doctrine, strangled by its own amen.

3. *transf.* Concluding word or act; conclusion. (Cf. *Culorum* in *P. Pl.* A. III. 264.)

1677 HALE *Contemp.* II. 95 That such an act as this should be the Amen of my Life. *c* **1860** Chairman of Public Meeting (at Hawick): —'You must hear the speaker to Amen, and then ask your questions.'

4. Retained in the Bible from the original, as a title of Christ; = The faithful one.

1388 WYCLIF *Rev.* iii. 14 Thes things seith Amen the feithful witnesse. **1611** *ibid.*, These things saith the Amen, the faithfull and true witnesse. **1704** NELSON *Fest. & Fasts* II. ii. (1739) 478 Jesus, who is the Truth is called Amen.

amen (ˌeɪˈmɛn), *v.* [f. prec. sb.] *trans.* To say Amen to: hence **a.** To ratify solemnly. **b.** To conclude, say the final word to.

1854 THACKERAY *Newc.* II. 188 Is there a bishop on the bench that has not amen'd the humbug? **1812** SOUTHEY *Lett.* (1856) II. 281, I am come to the 'End'.. of my third year's 'Register';.. this very evening I have Amen'd the volume.

amenability (əˌmiːnəˈbɪlɪtɪ). [f. AMENABLE: see -BILITY.] The quality of being amenable.

1. The liability to answer (*to* a tribunal); responsibility.

1789 J. MADISON *Writ.* (1904) V. 373 A unity in each has been resolved on, and an amenability to the President alone, as well as to the Senate by way of impeachment. **1810** COLERIDGE *Friend* I. xv. (1867) 67 The mysterious faculty of free-will and consequent personal amenability. **1849** MILL *Ess.* (1859) II. 407 A moral responsibility, an amenability to the bar of public opinion.

2. Disposition to respond to; responsiveness, tractableness.

1851 HELPS *Comp. Solit.* xi. (1874) 206 His amenability to good reasoning. **1861** BUMSTEAD *Vener. Dis.* (1879) 629 The extent of the lesions and their amenability to treatment.

amenable (əˈmiːnəb(ə)l), *a.* Also 6-8 **amesnable**, 7-8 **amainable**. [apparently a. AFr. *amenable* (not in Godef.), f. *amener* to bring to or before, f. *à* to + *mener* to lead:—L. *mināre* to threaten, hence to drive cattle with minatory shouts. Cf. Sc. *ca'* = call and drive. The spelling *amesnable* is quite artificial, influenced by *mesne*, *demesne*, etc.]

1. Of persons: Liable to be brought before any jurisdiction; answerable, liable to answer, responsible (*to* law, etc., or *absol.*).

1596 SPENSER *State of Irel.* 100 Not amesnable to Law. **1662** FULLER *Worthies* II. 74 The inferiour sort of the Irish were.. not Amesnable by Law. **1691** BLOUNT *Law Dict.*, *Amenable*, others write it *amainable*, from the Fr. *main*, a hand.. is applied in our Law Books to a Woman that is supposed governable by her Husband. **1769** *Junius Lett.* Pref. 12 The sovereign of this country is not amenable to any form of trial. **1810** COLERIDGE *Friend* (ed. 3) II. 5 The sufficiency of the conscience to make every person a moral and amenable being. **1876** GRANT *Burgh. Sch. Scotl.* I. i. 6 The Abbots of Dunfermline, to whom only he was amenable.

2. Of things: Liable to the legal authority of. **1768** BLACKSTONE *Comm.* III. 413 Personal property, which is.. always amesnable to the magistrate. **1817** JAS. MILL *Brit. India* II. v. ix. 697 All offences against the act were rendered amenable to the courts of law.

3. Hence *loosely*. Liable (*to* a charge, claim, etc.).

1863 MRS. C. CLARKE *Shaks. Char.* xvii. 431 He is amenable to the charge of a host of vices. **1876** E. MELLOR *Priesth.* vii. 312 The next witness.. is amenable to the same imputation of uncandid.. quotation. **1844** DICKENS *Mar. Chuz.* (C.D. ed.) 270 Your property.. being amenable to all claims upon the company.

4. *fig.* Answerable at the bar of (any critical instrument): capable of being tested by. Const *to*.

1828 MILL *Autobiogr.* (1924) 298 Make them amenable to the general tribunal of the public at large. **1843** —— *Logic* I. II. i. 216 Such of them [*sc.* assertions].. as, not being amenable to direct consciousness or intuition, are appropriate subjects of proof. **1845** —— *Ess.* II. 220 Historical facts are hardly yet felt to be.. amenable to scientific laws. **1867** BUCKLE *Civilis.* III. v. 369 Amenable to the touch, but invisible to the eye.

5. Of persons and things: Disposed to answer, respond, or submit (*to* influence); responsive, tractable; capable of being won over.

1803 WELLINGTON in *Gen. Disp.* II. 417 A high spirited people.. by no means amenable to discipline. **1861** MILL *Utilitar.* iv. 60 Will.. is amenable to habit. **1874** SPURGEON *Treas. David* lxxxii. I. IV. 40 Oriental judges are frequently .. amenable to bribes. **1878** E. WHITE *Life in Christ* v. xxix. 496 Perplexed but amenable spirits whom sorrow and fear.. are drawing back to their Father.

a'menableness. [f. prec. + -NESS.] The quality or state of being amenable.

1849 J. HARRIS *Prim. Man* I. iv. ¶6. 83 This latent amenableness of the imagination to the majesty of law. **1876** MOZLEY *Univ. Serm.* v. 101 Of.. distinct nations.. each.. is a centre to itself, without any amenableness to a common centre.

amenably (əˈmiːnəblɪ), *adv.* [f. as prec. + -LY[2].] In an amenable manner.

1864 in WEBSTER.

†**ame'nage**, *v. Obs. rare*[−1]. [a. OFr. *amenage-r*, earlier *amesnagier*, to receive into a house, f. *à* to + *ménage*, *mesnage*, household establishment: see MANAGE.] To domesticate.

1596 SPENSER *F.Q.* II. iv. 11 Whoso will raging Furor tame, Must first begin, and well her amenage.

†**amenance, -aunce.** *Obs.* [a. OFr. *amenance*, action of bringing, conducting, f. Fr. *amener* to lead, bring to: see -ANCE.] Conduct, bearing, mien.

1591 SPENSER *Mother Hubb. T.* 781 For armes and warlike amenaunce. **1596** —— *F.Q.* II. viii. 17 Well kend him.. Th' enchaunter by his armes and amenaunce. **1633** P. FLETCHER *Purple Isl.* XI. ix, [He] with grave speech, and comely amenance Himself, his State, his Spouse, to them commended. **1739** MELMOTH *Fitzosb. Lett.* (1763) 290 One only impe he had.. Whose sweet amenaunce pleas'd each shepherd's eye.

amend (əˈmɛnd), *v.* Also 3-4 **amendie, -y**, 3-6 **amende.** [a. OFr. *amende-r*:—L. *ēmendā-re* to free from fault, correct, improve, f. *ē* = *ex* out + *mend-um*, *mend-a* fault. The change from *e-* to *a-* took place very early, being found in Pr. and It. as well as OFr. Already in 14th c. aphetized to MEND.]

1. To free (a person) from faults, correct, reform, turn from wrong, convert. †**a.** *trans. Obs.*

c **1220** *Prov. Alfred* in *Rel. Ant.* I. 188 Þuru þis lore & genteleri, he amendit huge companie. **1297** R. GLOUC. 73 Þo pope.. twei holy men hym sende.. hys soule for to amende. **1362** LANGL. *P. Pl.* A. III. 185 A sermun he made For to a-Mende meires. **1480** CAXTON *Chron. Engl.* III. (1520) 22/2 Lud governed well the lande.. and amended yll folk. **1588** SHAKS. *L.L.L.* IV. iii. 76 God amend vs, God amend, we are much out o' th' way. **1704-5** PENN in *Pa. Hist. Soc. Mem.* IX. 375 Till those unworthy people.. are amended.

†**b.** *refl. Obs.*

1297 R. GLOUC. 350 Þat hii.. Repenty mowe, & þer of hem amendy. *c* **1340** HAMPOLE *Pr. Consc.* 1569 God.. at þe last on þam will sende Veng[e]aunce, bot if þai þam here amende. *c* **1360** *E.E. Poems* (1862) 131 Ȝif þou art in synne i-bounde, Amende þe. **1481** CAXTON *Myrr.* III. x. 154 Yet for al that they amende them not. **1535** COVERDALE *Matt.* iii. 1 Amende youre selues the kyngdome of heuen is at honde.

c. *intr.* To reform oneself, abandon one's faults or evil ways.

c **1300** *Lay-Folks Mass-Bk.* B. (1375) 238, I trow.. of my synnes, forgyfnes If I wil mende. *c* **1400** *Apol. for Loll.* 15 Wan þe synnar wil not dewli obey ne a mend. **1535** COVERDALE *Jon.* iii. Argt., They amende, and God is mercifull to them. **1655** H. VAUGHAN *Silex Scint.* I. (1858) 83 If here One Sinner doth amend Strait there is Joy. **1727** DE FOE *Apparitions* x. 192 It gives advice to amend and reform. **1837** CARLYLE *Fr. Rev.* II. III. iv. 172 The bad Editors promise to amend, but do not.

2. *trans.* To free (a thing) from faults, correct (what is faulty), rectify. *arch.*

c **1280** 7 *Sins* in *E.E. Poems* (1862) 18 Ȝoure sinful lif to amendie to-dai ic wol ȝow teche. **1393** GOWER *Conf.* III. 226 The wrongfull lawes ben amended. *Ibid.* 241 Her olde sinnes to amende. **1477** EARL RIVERS (Caxton) *Dictes* 128, I may wele correcte and amende my thoughtis. **1596** SHAKS. *1 Hen. IV*, III. i. 180 You must needes learne, Lord, to amend this fault. **1611** BIBLE *Jer.* vii. 3 Amend your wayes, and your doings. **1757** BURKE *Abridgm. Eng. Hist.* Wks. X. 525 Made him swear to amend his civil government. **1879** FROUDE *Cæsar* iii. 29 A few things had gone wrong, but these had been amended.

b. *esp.* Of errors in the text of a book or document: To emendate.

1483 CAXTON *Cato* 3 [I] beseche alle suche that fynde faute or errour that.. they correcte and amende hit. **1611** BIBLE *Pref.* 9 To goe ouer that which hee had done, and to amend it where he saw cause. **1747** WARBURTON *Pref. Shaks.* (T.) Amending the corrupted text. **1753** CHAMBERS *Cycl. Supp.* s.v. *Amendment*, In cases of wrong returns.. that the returns be amended by the returning officer.

3. *Law.* To correct (an error committed in legal process), or rectify (a legal document). Also *absol.*

1429 *Act 8 Hen. VI*, xv. (Pulton 1632) The Iustices may in certaine cases amend defaults in Records. **1768** BLACKSTONE *Comm.* III. 409 They might.. have excused themselves from amending in criminal, and especially in capital, cases. **1809** TOMLINS *Law Dict.* I. Gij a/2 But a *mandamus* may not be amended after return.

4. To make professed improvements in (a measure before Parliament); *formally*, to alter in detail, though *practically* it may be to alter its principle, so as to thwart it. (See AMENDMENT 1 d.)

1777 BURKE *Aff. Amer.* Wks. III. 136 During its progress through the house of commons, it has been amended. **1879** McCARTHY *Own Time* II. xxiii. 176 There was no reason why the Government should not have amended their bill.

5. To repair or make good (what is broken or damaged); to restore. *arch.* Commonly replaced by the aphet. form MEND.

c **1230** *Ancr. R.* 420 Seouweð, and amendeð chirche cloðes. *c* **1305** *E.E. Poems* (1862) 44 þe toun also of wynchestre: he amendede ynouȝ. **1393** LANGL. *P. Pl.* C. IV. 65 Wyndowes ..ich wolle a-menden & glase. **1483** CAXTON *Gold. Leg.* 338/1 Amendynge & cloutynge poure mennes shoes. **1523** FITZHERB. *Husb.* cxxviii, How an hye way sholde be amended. *c* **1575** STILL *Gamm. Gurton's Needle* I. ii. 14 Dame Gurton these breeches amended. **1611** SPEED *Hist. Gt. Brit.* VII. xliv. (1632) 418 They fell to amending their shippes. **1721** PERRY *Daggenh. Breach* 130 Repair and amend all the said Walls. **1875** H. E. MANNING *Mission H. Ghost* xii. 324 Until the machine is either amended or destroyed.

†**b.** *fig. Obs. rare.*

c **1399** *Pol. Poems* II. 10 So stant the werre, and pes is noght amendid.

†**6.** *trans.* To heal or recover (the sick); to cure (a disease). *Obs.*

c **1305** *St. Lucy* 24 in *E.E.P.* (1862) 102 To þe tumbe of seint Agace: hire moder lyf to amende. *c* **1386** CHAUCER *Sqrs. T.* 460 If þat I verraily the cause knewe Of youre disese.. I wolde amenden it. **1388** WYCLIF *John* iv. 52 He axide of hem the our in which he was amendid. **1483** CAXTON *G. de la Tour* Fij b, Whan she was amended of her legges. **1548** COVERDALE *Erasm. Paraphr. Phil.* Argt., Epaphroditus was amended of his extreme daungerous sickenesse. **1653** MILTON *Ps.* vi. 4 Pity me, Lord.. heal and amend me. **1804** ABERNETHY *Surg. Observ.* 154 Although the sores were not amended.

†**b.** *intr.* (through *refl.*) To recover from illness. *Obs.*: see MEND.

1297 R. GLOUC. 8 Ac men of France in þilke vuel me syþ sone a mende. **1393** GOWER *Conf.* III. 316 She began somdele amende. **1610** SHAKS. *Temp.* v. i. 115 Th' affliction of my minde amends. **1611** BIBLE *John* iv. 52 The houre when he began to amend.

7. To bring into a better state, better, improve (anything implicitly imperfect). **a.** *trans.*

1384 CHAUCER *Ann. & Arc.* 84 In her ne myght no thing be amendid. **1496** *Dives & Paup.* (W. de Worde) VII. x. 289/2 Yf the seller be moche harmed by the sellynge, & the byer moche amended by the byenge. *c* **1500** *Merch. & Son* in Halliw. *Nug. P.* 23 Some fayre syens to amende wyth thy degree. **1597** SHAKS. *2 Hen. IV*, I. ii. 142 To punish you by the heeles, would amend the attention of your eares. **1796** MORSE *Amer. Geog.* I. 554 Sunday-schools..have a tendency to amend the morals and conduct of the rising generation. **1832** HT. MARTINEAU *Ella of Gar.* i. 11 Presently, however, his idea of her was amended.

†**b.** *refl. Obs. rare.*

1393 GOWER *Conf.* I. 16 Eche of hem him self amendeth Of worldes good.

c. *intr.* (Rare exc. as in 1 c.)

c **1530** LD. BERNERS *Arthur Lyt. Bryt.* (1814) 2 Thus amended this chylde frome daye to daye & grew so goodly. **1616** SURFLET & MARKH. *Countr. Farme* 378 Raisins or dried Grapes being wrapped in Figge leaues..amend and become better both in tast and smell.

†**d.** *absol.* To improve *on. Obs. rare.*

c **1314** *Guy Warw.* 4 The kirtel bicom him swithe wel, To amenden theron was neuer a del.

†**8.** *trans.* To better: passing from the idea of 'improve' to that of 'improve upon,' surpass. *Obs.*

c **1386** CHAUCER *Sqrs. T.* 89 With so heigh reuerence and obeisaunce..That Gawayn with his old curteisye..Ne koude hym nat amende. **1393** GOWER *Conf.* III. 363 Of women I sigh foure there, Whose name I herde most commended. By hem the court stode all amended. *c* **1500** *Merch. & Son* in Halliw. *Nug. P.* 22 He cowde hys gramer wonder wele, hys felows cowde hym not amende.

†**9.** To make amends, or give satisfaction for an offence. **a.** *trans. Obs.* but see MEND.

1297 R. GLOUC. 391 He wolde to Engelond..amende þat he adde mys do. *c* **1386** CHAUCER *Wife's T.* 241 What is my gult?..tel me it, And it schal be amendid. *c* **1400** *Destr. Troy* XXVIII. 11217 He is happy, þat a harme hastely amendes. **1513** DOUGLAS *Æneis* x. xiv. 61 Be all maner of torment and of pyne, For till amend my offensis. **1622** MALYNES *Anc. Law-Merch.* 119 If a Factor by errour of account doe wrong vnto a Merchant, hee is to amend and to make good the same. **1635** SWAN *Spec. Mundi* (1670) 368 In little medling is much rest; and 'nothing said is soonest amended.'

†**b.** *absol.* To make amends. *Obs. rare.*

c **1314** *Guy Warw.* 203 Gif Ich him haue ought misdo, Amenden Ichil wele therto.

†**c.** *trans.* To make amends to a person *of* the wrong. *Obs. rare.*

c **1380** *Sir Ferumb.* 1917 Amendie hem of þy wronge: of al þyng þou hym hast offent.

†**a'mend,** *ppl. a. Obs.* [contr. of AMENDED, like *send* for *sended.*] Amended.

1482 *Monk of Evesham* (1869) 68 Mekyll thyng was correcte and amende more than yt was wonte to be before. *c* **1560** *Proud Wife* in *Laneham's Let.* Pref. 115 Therfore, good lorde, let this be a-mende.

amend, *sb.*: see AMENDS.

amendable (ə'mɛndəb(ə)l), *a.* [f. AMEND *v.* + -ABLE.]

†**1.** *actively,* Able to amend; improving. *Obs.*

? *a* **1600** *MS. Ashmole* No. 60. 5 (Halliw.) That til oure lif is ful profitable, and to oure soule amendable.

2. *passively,* Capable of being amended, corrected, bettered, repaired, made amends for.

1589 PUTTENHAM *Eng. Poesie* (Arb.) 157 We finde in our English writers many wordes and speaches amendable. **1614** SELDEN *Titles of Hon.* 261 Before whom sometimes causes criminall and amendable by amercements or mulcts were heard. **1674** *Peace & Good Will* 27 Liturgies..are amendable, alterable, upon just occasions. **1740** *Prov. for Poor* 15 Roads not amendable by Act of Parliament. **1809** TOMLINS *Law Dict.* G ij a/2 The faults and mistakes of clerks are in many cases amendable.

a'mendableness. [f. prec. + -NESS.] The quality of being amendable.

1731 in BAILEY. [Not in JOHNSON.]

amendatory (ə'mɛndətərɪ), *a.* [f. AMEND *v.* as if on a L. ppl. stem **amendāt-*: see -ORY, and cf. L. *ēmendātōrius.*] Of or pertaining to amendment; tending to amend. (U.S.)

a **1859** WORCESTER cites HALE. **1854** BANCROFT *Hist. U.S.* (1876) VI. xlvi. 304 An amendatory bill was prepared. **1862** LINCOLN *Message to Congr.* in *Times* 17 Dec. 9/6 Articles amendatory of the Constitution of the United States.

amended (ə'mɛndɪd), *a.* [f. AMEND + -ED.] Freed from faults, repaired, recovered, improved.

1382 WYCLIF *Ezra* Prol., No thing it profitide to han amendid bokis. **1580** BARET *Alv.* A 354 Amended, repaired, *Sartus.* **1670** W. WALKER *Idiom. Anglo-Lat.* 23 The World's well amended with him. **1798** SOUTHEY *Lett.* (1856) I. 52, I found her somewhat amended by bleedings. **1831** GEN. P. THOMPSON *Exerc.* I. 416 These amended times.

‖**amende-honorable** (a'mɑ̃:d ɔnɔ'rabl). [Fr. = 'honourable compensation,' (*amende* being the sing. of the word adopted in Eng. as AMENDS) orig. a public and humiliating acknowledgement of crime, now *fig.* as in Eng. Now usually treated as Fr., but in 18th c. as Eng. The word *honorable* is occas. omitted.]

Public apology and reparation such as to re-establish the injured or offended honour of one who has been wronged. Cf. *honourable amends*; AMENDS 2 b.

[**1670** COTTON *Espernon* III. XII. 650 Honourable Satisfaction to his own Domesticks. (*Side-note, Amende honorable* signifies something more, but what cannot be intended by the Author in this place.)] **1703** DE FOE *Ref. Mann.* Pref., He promises to give Testimony to their Repentance, as an Amand Honourable in a manner as publick as possible. **1835** GEN. P. THOMPSON *Exerc.* (1842) III. 165 And make the *amende* to any of his youthful kindred he may have terrified into unhappiness. **1859** KINGSLEY *Misc.* I. 370 The 'Edinburgh Review'..made the amende honorable to Burns.

amender (ə'mɛndə(r)). [f. AMEND *v.* + -ER[1].] One who, or that which, amends. Const. usually *of.*

c **1386** CHAUCER *Wife's T.* 341 Poverte is..A gret amender eek of sapiens. **1532** MORE *Confut. Tindale* Wks. 1557, 402/2 Theyr amenders and punyshers, God hath maynteyned and fauoured. *a* **1776** LD. LYTTELTON *Wks.* 1776 I. 85 That it [his motion] will not be mended..and then objected to and thrown out by the amenders. **1870** *Daily News* 30 Mar., Ambitious of trying his hand as an amender of the Act.

†**a'mendful,** *a. Obs. rare.* [f. AMEND + -FUL; cf. *wasteful.*] Much-amending, correcting; improving.

1623 FLETCHER *Bloody Bro.* III. i. 437 Far flye such rigour your amendful hand. *Ibid.* III. i. 438 Your most amendful and unmatched fortunes.

amending (ə'mɛndɪŋ), *vbl. sb.* [f. AMEND + -ING[1].] The action of freeing from faults, correcting, reforming, repairing, making good; amendment. (Now mostly gerundial.)

c **1315** SHOREHAM *Ps.* xxiii. 4 Thy discipline and thyn amendyng conforted me. **1340** *Ayenb.* 180 After the ssrifte comþ ynoȝbote, þet is þe amendinge. **1435** in Heath *Grocers' Comp.* (1869) 417 Amendyng of banneres, and hire of barges ..iiijlb. vjs. iiid. **1570** ASCHAM *Scholem.* (Arb.) 28 Heedefull amending of faultes. **1620** VENNER *Via Recta* v. 85 For amending of a dry constitution..it is..of singular efficacy. **1622** CALLIS *Stat. Sewers* (1824) 110 The repairing and amending of bridges. **1656** *Artif. Beauty* (1662) 214 Concealings or amendings of what is..amiss. *Mod.* Prove your repentance by amending your life.

amending (ə'mɛndɪŋ), *ppl. a.* [f. AMEND + -ING[2].] Correcting, reforming, improving.

1641 MILTON *Ch. Govt.* vii. (1851) 133 The unsetl'd estate of a Church, while it lies under the amending hand. **1771** BURKE *Powers of Juries* Wks. X. 128 Blessed be the amending hand. **1873** STRATMANN *O.E. Dict.* Pref., Few lines in which the amending hand is not visible.

amendment (ə'mɛndmənt). Also 3-7 **amendement;** *aphet.* **mendment.** [a. OFr. *amendement* f. *amender*: see AMEND and -MENT.] The action of amending, whether in process, or as completed.

1. Removal of faults, correction, reformation.

a. of human conduct. *absol.* = self-reformation.

1297 R. GLOUC. 472 Ȝuf eni man in mansinge were ibrouȝt, & suþþe come to amendment. **1393** LANGL. *P. Pl.* C. IV. 122 A sarmon he made In amendement of meyres. *a* **1450** *Knt. de la Tour* 60 Withoute amendement thei be dampned. **1557** N. T. (Genev.) *Matt.* iii. 8 Ye fruites belongyng to amendement of life. **1596** SHAKS. *1 Hen. IV*, I. ii. 114, I see a good amendment of life in thee: from Praying, to Purse-taking. **1732** LAW *Serious Call* xxiii. (ed. 2) 467 Without any remorse of mind, or true desire of amendment. **1839** J. H. NEWMAN *Par. Serm.* IV. vii. 111 Men commonly think..that amendment is an expiation.

b. of faults or errors in things, as a book, a law, etc.

1599 THYNNE *Animadv.* 59 The former printe.. deseruethe amendemente. **1759** DILWORTH *Pope* 17 Mr. Pope promised to revise his poems..finding great room for amendment. **1762** GOLDSM. *Beau Nash* 57 This amendment of the law soon gave birth to new evasions. **1843** MILL *Logic* Introd. 2 Has adopted the above definition with an amendment.

c. *Law.* Correction of error in a writ or process.

1607 COWEL *Interpr.* (1637) Djb, *Amendment*..a correction of an errour committed in a Processe, and espied before judgement. **1768** BLACKSTONE *Comm.* III. xxv. (R.) Courts, where justice requires it, will allow of amendments. **1809** TOMLINS *Law Dict.* G ij b/2 The court gave leave to file a right bill..This was done as an amendment at common law.

d. The alteration of a bill before Parliament. Hence *concr.* A clause, paragraph, or words proposed to be substituted for others, or to be inserted, in a bill (the result of the adoption of which may even be to defeat the measure; see AMEND 4).

1696 LUTTRELL *Brief Rel.* (1857) IV. 149 The commons reason for disagreeing to the lords amendment. **1710** *Lond. Gaz.* mmmmdcciii/2 A Bill for the better securing the Liberty of the Subject..was agreed to with some Amendments. **1825** T. JEFFERSON *Autobiog.* Wks. 1859 I. 48 This should be..attempted only by way of amendment, whenever the bill should be brought on. **1883** *Daily News* 4 May 3/5 The House divided on the amendment by Sir R. Cross, that the bill be read a second time on that day six months.

e. *In a Public Meeting.* A proposed alteration in the terms of a resolution submitted to a meeting for adoption; *extended to* a resolution proposed instead of or in opposition to another; a countermotion.

(During the period from 1840 to 1848, it was the practice in some parts of the country where the Chartists were strong, to move 'The People's Charter' as an 'amendment' to every resolution proposed in Public Meeting on any subject whatever.)

†**2.** Repair, mending (of things damaged). *Obs.*

1602 FULBECKE *2nd Pt. Parall.* 52 The tenant may cut trees for the amendment of houses. **1682** *Lond. Gaz.* mdcclv/3 [The Engine] has daily forced up great quantities of Water..without the least error or amendment.

3. General 'improvement' of condition.

1297 R. GLOUC. 404 Non maner hope hii nadde, to amendement to come. **1393** GOWER *Conf.* III. 30 If there be amendement To gladde with this wofull king. **1576** LAMBARDE *Peramb. Kent* (1826) 261 A fair to be holden—for the amendment of the Towne. **1692** RAY *Creation* (J.) Her works are so perfect that there is no place for amendments. **1868** RUSKIN *Pol. Econ. Art* Add. 186 If the points that I want amended seem to you incapable of amendment, or not in need of amendment, say so.

4. Improvement in health, recovery from illness.

1303 R. BRUNNE *Handl. Synne* (1901) 9225 Ne never hadde þey amendement..at any corseynt, But at þe vyrgyne Seynt Edyght. **1526** TINDALE *Mark* v. 26 [She]..felte none amendment [WYCLIF, was no thing amendid] at all, But wexed worsse. **1601** SHAKS. *All's Well* I. i. 12 *Count.* What hope is there of his maiesties amendment? *Laf.* He hath abandon'd his Physitions, Madam. **1745** H. WALPOLE *Lett. to H. Mann* 121 (1834) II. 22 His recovery is now at such a pause..it is in vain to expect much further amendment. **1789** R. F. GREVILLE *Diaries* 17 Feb. (1930) 228 The King for some time past, had been in a State of Amendment &.. he was this day in a state of convalescence. **1814** JANE AUSTEN *Mansf. Park* III. xvi. 260 Tom's amendment was alarmingly slow.

†**5.** Amends-making, reparation. *Obs.*

1297 R. GLOUC. 54 þat he for ys neueu wolde..Do hey amendement. *c* **1386** CHAUCER *Reeves T.* 265 Syn I sal have nan amendement Agayn my los. *c* **1450** *Merlin* v. 79 Yef the pees and the a-mendement to the lady lay in me.

†**6.** 'Improvement' of the soil; *concr.* that which improves the soil, manure. *Obs.*

1413 LYDG. *Pylgr. Sowle* IV. x. (1483) 62 Yet sawe I neuer tree that wold nought saue hym seluen by moysture..yf hit myght be and receyuen tylthe and amendement. **1668** CHILD *Disc. Trade* (ed. 4) 241 If a man borrow five pounds, and bestow it on an acre of ground, the amendment stands him in ten shillings the year. **1699** EVELYN *Acetaria* (1729) 156 Chalk, Lime, and other sweet Soil and Amendments.

amends (ə'mɛndz). Also 3-7 **amendes,** 4-5 **amendis,** 5 **amendys,** (6 **amense**), 6 **mends.** [a. OFr. *amendes* pecuniary fine, penalties, pl. of *amende* reparation, f. *amender* to AMEND. The sing., common in Fr., is very rare in Eng., in which *amends* has been used as a collective sing. from the first, and is now always construed with sing. vb.]

†**1.** The moneys paid, or things given to make reparation for any injury or offence, = L. *pœnæ*; a fine. *Obs.*

1340 *Ayenb.* 37 Bedeles, and seruons, þet steleþ þe amendes, and wyþdraȝeth þe rentes of hire lhordes. *Ibid.* 38 Kueade lordes..þet be-ulaȝeþ þe poure men..be amendes. *a* **1618** RALEIGH *Ess.* (J.) Of the amends recovered, little or nothing returns to those that had suffered the wrong, but commonly all runs into the prince's coffers.

†**b.** in *sing. Obs. rare.*

1609 SKENE *Reg. Maj.* 127 He quha is persewer..sall pay ane amande arbitrall to the Lords. *c* **1834** J. HAMMER *E. Efendi.* in Southey *Comm.-Pl. Bk.* Ser. II. (1849) 451 The Pashaw fixed immediately an amend of fifty thousand piastres.

2. Reparation, retribution, restitution, compensation, satisfaction. *esp.* in phr. **to make amends.**

a. *pl.* in form, *collect.* in sense.

c **1314** *Guy Warw.* 156 Take the amendes after the gilt. **1330** R. BRUNNE *Chron* 291, I rede þou mak amendes of þat grete misdede. *c* **1450** *Merlin* v. 83 What amendes she required for the deth of hir lorde. *a* **1553** UDALL *Royster D.* IV. vii, Bee not at one with hir, upon any amendes. **1594** GREENE *Look. Glasse* (1861) 122 If I have wronged thee, seek thy mends at the law. **1611** BIBLE *Lev.* v. 16 Hee shall make amends for the harme that he hath done. *a* **1704** T. BROWN *Lett.* Wks. 1730 I. 183, I hope to make you amends the next post. **1768** BLACKSTONE *Comm.* III. 15 If tender of amends is made before any action is brought. **1783** COWPER *Lett.* 1 Aug., But to make amends we have many excellent ballads. **1870** BRYANT *Homer* II. XIX. 239 It dishonors not a king To make amends to one whom he has wronged.

b. *pl.* in form, distinctly *sing.* in use. (Cf. *a means.*)

c **1449** PECOCK *Repr.* I. xviii. 110 To make a sufficient amendis. **1624** MASSINGER *Parl. Love* III. iii, The ends I hope to reach shall make a large amends. **1650** EARL MONM. *Man Guilty* Ep. Ded., I have made an Amends by printing an Errata. **1712** ADDISON *Spect.* No. 530 ¶ 1 Very often make an honourable Amends. **1723** DE FOE *Col. Jack* (1840) 15 The warmth of the glass-house fires above was a full amends for all the ashes..we rolled in below. **1821** SOUTHEY *Corr.* V. 86, I looked forward to an honourable amends.

†**c.** *sing.* (See also AMENDE.) *Obs. rare.*

1489 CAXTON *Faytes of Armes* II. xiii. 115 To make peas with hym and to make hym amende and restitucion. **1668** MARVELL *Corr.* 103 Wks. 1872-5 II. 259 To make amend in time for this misscarriage.

†**3.** Means of obtaining satisfaction, or of amending; remedy. *Obs. rare.*

1606 DEKKER in *Knt's. Conjur.* (1842) Pref. 15 Yf his answers be.. bad, and like thee not, thou hast the amends in thine owne hands.

†**4.** Improvement, betterment, amendment. *Obs.*

1580 LYLY *Euphues* (Arb.) 351 What I now giue you in thankes, I will then requite with amends. **1699** BENTLEY *Phal.* 103 If our Examiner's Performance in the last Section was very poor.. we may expect an amends in this. **1709** STRYPE *Ann. Ref.* I. I. xxvi. 314 This was like to the former with this amends, that, etc.

†**b.** Improvement in health, recovery. *Obs.*

1596 SHAKS. *Tam. Shrew* Induct. ii. 99 Now Lord be thanked for my good amends. **1671** MILTON *Samson* 9 But here I feel amends.

5. *Comb.* **amends-making**.

1580 HOLLYBAND *Treas. Fr. Tong., Desdommagement*, a repayring, an amends making. **1581** MARBECK *Bk. Notes* 904 Satisfaction or amends making.. to mine neighbour whome I haue offended.

†**a'mendsful**, *a. Obs. rare*$^{-1}$. [f. prec. + -FUL.] Making compensation; giving satisfaction.

1600 CHAPMAN *Iliad* III. 83 His amendsful words did Hector highly please.

amene (ə'miːn), *a.* Also 6 amen, ameyne. [a. OFr. **amene*, ad. L. *amœnum* pleasant, connected with *amāre* to love. (Godefroi has the adv. *amenement* pleasantly.) Not uncommon in 15th c.; afterwards only in Sc. writers, with whom it was a favourite word; occasional in Eng. writers of present c.] Pleasant, agreeable.

c **1400** *Epiph.* (Turnb. 1843) 125 To thi son be for (h)us amene. *c* **1500** *Lancelot* 997 The morow blythfull and amen. **1535** STEWART *Cron. Scot.* II. 347 The da wes fair, the wedder richt and ameyne. **1578** *Ps.* li. in *Sc. Poems 16th C.* II. 112 In heuinly joy, fair and amene. *c* **1820** FUSELI *Lect. Art* xii. (1848) 550 Whatever is commodious, amene, or useful, depends in a great measure on the arts. **1863** R. BURTON *Abeokuta* I. 1 The amene delta of the lovely Niger.

amener, obs. form of ALMONER.

†**a'menge**, *v. Obs. rare.* [f. A- *pref.* 1 + MENG to mix.] To mix, mingle.

c **1440** in *Archæol.* XXX. 357 Amenge it with gres of a swyne. *a* **1500** *E.E. Misc.* (1855) 74 Thenne amenge it with thy fyngere.

amenity (ə'miːnɪtɪ, ə'mɛnɪtɪ). Also 5 -ite, 7 -itie, 7–8 amœnity, amænity. [? a. Fr. *amenité* (in Cotgr. 1611), or perh. direct ad. of its original L. *amœnitāt-em*, f. *amœn-us* pleasant: see AMENE and -ITY.]

1. The quality of being pleasant or agreeable: **a.** of places, their situation, aspect, climate, etc.

1432–50 tr. *Higden* (1865) I. 77 That place hath also amenite. **1611** CORYAT *Crudities* 448 For amenity of situation.. it doth farre excel all other cities. **1683** *Brit. Spec.* 17 The amœnity and Utility of its Seas, Rivers and Ponds. **1832** J. AUSTIN *Jurispr.* (1879) II. l. 858 The fiar may also cut and sell timber, so as not to injure the amenity. **1846** PRESCOTT *Ferd. & Is.* I. ii. 120 The superior amenity of the climate.

b. of persons, their habits, actions, etc.

1815 MAR. EDGEWORTH *Patron.* xvii. 279 His manners wanted amenity, gaiety, and frankness. **1824** DIBDIN *Libr. Comp.* 90 Who does not love the amenity of Erasmus? **1873** DIXON *Two Queens* I. I. vii. 46 In amenity of life, his Court had been a Moorish rather than a Gothic Court.

c. In mod. use (freq. in pl.) applied to the more 'human' and pleasurable environmental aspects of a house, factory, town, etc., as distinguished from the features of the house, etc., considered in or by itself. Also *concr.* (usu. in sing.), a particular advantageous or convenient feature of this kind. Also *attrib.* Also, **amenity bed** (see quots.). (See also sense 3 b.)

1908 *Royal Comm. Care Feeble-Minded, Min. Evid.* II. 63/1 *Social Amenities.* The experience we have gained emphasises the desirability of organised recreation. **1928** *Britain's Industr. Future (Liberal Ind. Inquiry)* IV. xxiv. §9. 336 Amenity woodland definitely uneconomic. **1929** *Oxford Times* 8 Feb. 13/4 The payment of £88 for the purchase of the land; the payment of £250 as compensation for the loss of amenities and disturbance of existing garden and grounds. **1936** *Times* 2 Apr. 10/3 Repairable cottages of amenity value.. could be acquired and sympathetically repaired by the local authorities. **1951** *Brit. Med. Jrnl.* 13 Oct. Suppl. 146/2 Amenity beds, for which the maintenance charge is almost negligible and medical service is given under the National Health Service Act. **1951** B. J. COLLINS *Devel. Plans Explained* 42 *Amenity*, the quality which makes a desirable residence desirable, a favoured locality favoured, or enchanting views in all directions enchanting. **1952** *Lancet* 2 Aug. 229/1 No privileges can be bought within the service (except the amenity bed, for which a relatively small charge has been made). **1957** *Times* 12 Dec. 18/4 Arrangements were made to provide an amenity centre for the labour on Effingham and Seventh Mile Estates, the centre comprising a clubroom with cinema and a playing field. **1958** *Times* 1 July 1/3 There are, of course, many holdings below 20 acres, especially those that are part-time or amenity holdings where the earning of an income from the holding is not of great importance. **1958** *Listener* 11 Sept. 368/2 Where the people themselves want a new amenity—a school, a meeting house, a road to link up with the outside world, [etc.]. **1964** G. L. COHEN *What's Wrong with Hospitals?* i. 23 'Amenity beds'.. were designated under the Act for patients who want more privacy and will pay extra for it.

†**2.** Joyousness, exhilaration. *Obs. rare.*

1627 FELTHAM *Resolves* II. lxx. (1677) 307 The Amœnity and Floridness of the warm and spirited bloud.

3. *concr.* in *pl.* †**a.** Pleasant places or scenes. (Cf. *pleasance.*) *Obs.*

1664 EVELYN *Silva* (1776) 604 Arboreous Amenities and plantations of woods. **1671** —— *Diary* (1827) II. 354 The suburbs are large, the prospects sweete, with other amenities. **1762** H. WALPOLE *Vertue's Anecd. Paint.* (1786) IV. 140 A country so profusely beautified with the amænities of nature.

b. Pleasant ways or manners; pleasant pursuits, pleasures, delights, agreeable relations, civilities.

1841 D'ISRAELI (*title*) Amenities of authors. **1860** MOTLEY *Netherl.* (1868) I. v. 234 This interchange of dainties led the way to the amenities of diplomacy. **1866** *Cornh. Mag.* Aug. 157 All the amenities of home life are wanting. **1883** *Scotsman* 12 May 9/7 Talking amenities with Sir Stafford Northcote.

‖**amenorrhœa** (ə,mɛnərìːə). *Med.* [mod.L. f. ἀ priv. + μήν month + -ροια flowing, f. ῥέ-ειν to flow. Cf. Fr. *aménorrhée.*] Absence or suppression of the menstrual discharge.

1804 *Edin. Rev.* III. 336 The women suffer much from amenorrhea. **1872** THOMAS *Dis. Wom.* 64 An inactive state of the ovaries which results in amenorrhœa.

ameno'rrhœal, *a. Med.* [f. prec. + -AL[1].] Of or pertaining to amenorrhœa.

1833 J. FORBES et al. *Cycl. Pract. Med.* I. 70/2 A torpid or amenorrhœal condition of the uterus. **1879** *Syd. Soc. Lex.*, Amenorrhœal Insanity.

†**a'menous**, *a. Obs. rare*$^{-1}$. [f. L. *amœn-us* pleasant (see AMENE) + -OUS.] Pleasant.

1567 W. SALESBURY in E. Evans *Spec.* 160 In the amenous varietie of over reading and revoluting many volumes.

‖**a mensa et thoro** (eɪ 'mɛnsɑː ɛt 'tɔərəʊ). *Law.* [L., lit. 'from table and bed'.] In the older English law (before 1857) = *judicial separation* (SEPARATION 3): see DIVORCE *sb.*

1600 [see SEPARATION 3]. **1628** COKE *Littleton* v.§36. 32 When the husband and wife are diuorced *à vinculo matrimonij*, as in case of precontract, consanguinitie, affinitie, &c. and not *à mensa & thoro* onely as for adulterie. *a* **1683** J. OWEN *Sermons* (1721) 572 This divorce *a mensa & thoro* only is no true divorce, but a mere fiction of a divorce. **1857** [see SEPARATION 3]. **1957** O. R. MCGREGOR *Divorce in Engl.* i. 3 The ecclesiastical court would only pass sentence of divorce *a mensa et thoro* (a divorce from bed and board), which had the effect of a modern judicial separation.

ament[1] (ə'mɛnt). [ad. L. AMENT-UM.]

†**1.** 'A thong, or string.' Cockeram 1623. *Obs.*

2. *Bot.* = AMENTUM.

1791 E. DARWIN *Bot. Gard.* II. 9 The scales in the ament in the *Salix rosea*, grow into leaves. **1874** COUES *Birds of N.-W.* 208 A Thistle-bird swinging under the globular ament of a button-wood.

ament[2] ('eɪmɛnt, ə'mɛnt). [ad. L. *āment-, āmens*: see AMENTY.] A person congenitally deficient in mind or intellect; a born idiot or imbecile.

1894 in GOULD *Dict. Med.* **1912** *Ch. Q. Rev.* LXXIII. 326 We will classify them all (idiots, imbeciles, or feeble-minded) under the name 'Ament', meaning people without mind in contrast to the class of Dement, which we will assume to mean all those who have been sane, but have lost their mind. **1935** W. DE LA MARE *Early One Morning* 552 Aments.. begin to talk late, have certain special defects, are sluggish of thought. **1952** A. F. & R. F. TREDGOLD *Mental Deficiency* (ed. 8) iv. 61 Aments vary very greatly in the degree of their defect.

amentaceous (æmən'teɪʃəs), *a. Bot.* [f. L. AMENTUM + -ACEOUS.] **a.** Of the nature of a catkin. **b.** Bearing catkins.

c **1737** MILLER (J.) The pine tree hath amentaceous flowers or katkins. **1852** T. ROSS *Humboldt's Trav.* I. vi. 213 Among amentaceous plants, the willows, oaks, and birch-trees.

amental (ə'mɛntəl), *a.*[1] (and *sb.*) *Bot.* [f. L. *ament-um* + -AL[1].] Bearing catkins; epithet of one of Lindley's alliances of Gymnogens.

1847 LINDLEY *V.K.* (ed. 2) 254 Amental Exogens. *Ibid.* 248 Natural Orders of Amentals. **1866** BALFOUR in *Treas. Bot.* 140 The amental or catkin-bearing alliance of Lindley.

a'mental, *a.*[2] *rare.* [f. Gr. ἀ priv. + MENTAL, intentionally analogous to *a-theistic.*] Denying or dispensing with the existence of mind or intelligence. Also, non-mental.

1877 E. CONDER *Basis of Faith* vii. 293 The strict parallel to the atheistic theory of creation would be an amental theory of any art,—say painting; showing how the art and its products were evolved by slow historic gradations from the scratches made by passing boulders on the rocks.. without any intervention of human intellect. **1938** S. BECKETT *Murphy* xi. 247 An amental pattern as precise as any of those that governed his chess.

amentia (eɪ'mɛnʃ(ɪ)ə, ə'mɛ-). [L., see AMENTY.]

1. Mental deficiency; feeble-mindedness, either congenital or resulting from damage to the brain in early childhood.

1398 TREVISA *Barth. De P.R.* (1535) VII. p. lxxxvii, Amentia and madnesse is all one, as Plato sayeth. **1800** tr. *W. Cullen's Nosology* II. iv. 131, I have brought Amnesia and Amentia under one genus,.. because they are in general conjoined. **1879** MAUDSLEY *Pathol. Mind* vii. 327 Amentia is .. used to denote idiocy, or the privation of mind occasioned by causes that have acted before or soon after birth. **1887** *Buck's Handbk. Med. Sci.* IV. 88/2 The word [*sc.* idiocy] was used until Esquirol first clearly applied it.. in connection with both amentia and the terminal stage of chronic insanity. **1914** A. F. TREDGOLD *Mental Deficiency* (*Amentia*) (ed. 2) xiii. 226 Secondary Amentia and its Clinical Varieties. Toxic, Inflammatory and Vascular Amentia. *Ibid.* 228 The fact that the onset of these cases is so often attended with convulsions causes them to be frequently designated 'epileptic' or 'eclampsic' amentia.

2. *Psychiatry.* A particular psychotic state (see quot.).

1924 J. RIVIERE et al. tr. *Freud's Coll. Papers* II. 252 In.. amentia, the acute hallucinatory confusion which is perhaps the most extreme and striking form of psychosis, the outer world is.. not perceived.

amentiferous (æmən'tɪfərəs), *a. Bot.* [f. L. AMENT-UM + -(I)FEROUS.] Bearing catkins.

1854 BALFOUR *Class-bk.* 1087 Plants having catkins are Amentiferous. **1870** BENTLEY *Bot.* 192 All plants with this kind of inflorescence are called amentaceous or amentiferous.

amentiform (ə'mɛntɪfɔːm), *a. Bot.* [f. as prec. + -(I)FORM.] Catkin-shaped.

1869 OLIVER *Less. Bot.* 239 Common Birch.. a deciduous tree, with.. amentiform inflorescence.

‖**amentum** (əmɛntəm). *Bot.* Pl. **-a.** [L. *amentum* a thong or strap. Cf. AMENT[1].] A catkin.

1770 MILNE *Bot. Dict.* A iij, Scales forming an amentum or catkin. **1870** H. MACMILLAN *Bible Teach.* iv. 77 Their [cedars'] fruit consists of an amentum, the pericarps of which.. are imbricated woody scales.

†**a'menty.** *Obs.* [ad. L. *āmentia* madness, f. *āment-em* mad, f. *ā* away from + *ment-em* mind. Now used in *Path.* in L. form AMENTIA.] Madness.

1623 COCKERAM, *Amentie* [ed. 1626 *amenty*], madnesse. **1650** CHARLETON *Paradoxes* 76 An Amenty or short alienation of the reason.

†**amenuse**, *v. Obs.* Also 5 **amenusy, -uyse, admenuse.** [a. AFr. *amenuse-r*, OFr. *amenuisier*, f. *à* to + *menuisier* to lessen, cogn. w. Pr. *menuzar*, It. *minuzzare*:—late L. **minūtiāre*, f. *minūt-us* lessened, MINUTE. Spelt in 15th c. with *ad-* after L., and ultimately refashioned as *amynysh*, AMINISH.]

1. *trans.* To make less, lessen, diminish.

c **1374** CHAUCER *Boeth.* I. 19 He amenusiþ þe secre of hys conscience. *c* **1386** —— *Pers. T.* 285 The dede.. amenuseth the loue that men sholde han to god. **1417** in *E.E. Wills* (1882) 24 Volle power to chaunge þis testament, oþer to mak hit more, oþer to amenusy hit. **1554** PHILPOT *Exam. & Writ.* (1842) 424 Which amenusing that majesty of Christ did diminish therewithal the.. mercy of our salvation.

2. *intr.* (through refl.)

c **1391** CHAUCER *Astrol.* I. §21 Thanne amenuseth his coldnesse. **1447** BOKENHAM *Lyvys of Seyntys* 262 And ych daye yt began to amenuse. **1481** CAXTON *Myrr.* II. xxvii. 120 The haylle.. cometh doun brekyng and amenuysyng in the fallyng.

†**amenusing**, *vbl. sb. Obs.* [f. prec. + -ING[1].] Lessening, diminishing.

c **1374** CHAUCER *Boeth.* II. 46 A voys al hool, þat is to seyn, wiþoute amenusynge. **1413** LYDG. *Pylgr. Sowle* IV. xxxviii. 63 Long tyme withouten admenusynge. *c* **1465** *Eng. Chron.* 103 Any thyng that may be or sowne.. to hurte or amenusyng of hys regne or dygnyte royalle.

amer, obs. form of EMBER.

amer(e, variant of AMAR, *v. Obs.*, to mar.

ameral, -aunt, -el, obs. forms of ADMIRAL.

Amerasian (,æmə'reɪʒ(ɪ)ən), *a.* and *sb.* orig. *U.S.* [f. AMER(ICAN + ASIAN.] **A.** *adj.* Of mixed American and Asian parentage; esp. fathered by an American serviceman stationed in Asia.

1966 *Sci. News* 27 Aug. 140/1 Efforts to help the Amerasian children of U.S. servicemen. **1977** *Guardian Weekly* 25 Dec. 16/2 Some 4,000 'Amerasian' children born of American GI fathers and Thai mothers. **1985** *N.Y. Times* 27 Oct. I. 46/1 They wanted to talk about public concerns —dioxin, Amerasian children, divided families and missing comrades.

B. *sb.* A person of mixed American and Asian parentage; esp. one whose father was an American serviceman.

1966 P. S. BUCK in Buck & Harris *For Spacious Skies* 166 We travel throughout the country telling Americans in all walks of life of the plight of these forsaken Amerasians. **1968** *N.Y. Times* 30 Apr. 6/1 Among the sociologists concerned with the problem, they are called Amerasians. **1983** *Listener* 1 Sept. 10/2 All these youngsters are the Amerasians—the children of war.

ameraud, obs. form of EMERALD, EMEROD.

amerce (ə'mɜːs), *v.* Also 4–5 **amercy**, 5 **-sy**, 5–6 **amercie**, 6 **amearse**, 8 **ammerce**. [orig. *amercy*, a. AFr. *amerci-er* (not in continental Fr.), f. *à* to, at + *merci*:—L. *mercēdem*, which passed through the senses of 'wages, remuneration, a gift in recompense, a gift generally, a gift offered gratuitously (already in Gregory the Great), a present, a favour, grace, MERCY.' From the phr. *estre à merci* to be at the mercy of any one, was formed *estre amercié*, at first always passive (as in Magna Carta), and then the active *amercier* (in Britton *c* 1292). Britton has *estre en nostre merci* synonymous with *estre amercié*. 'To be amerced' was thus orig. to be at the mercy of any one as to amount of fine, to 'come in his will,' be fined at his pleasure; hence the active 'to amerce,' to fine arbitrarily or according to one's own estimate. The *-y* was lost through being viewed as inflexional, or through phonetic identity of *amercied*, *-id*, *-ed*.

1215 *Magna Carta* xiv, Liber homo non amercietur pro paruo delicto nisi secundum modum delicti, et pro magno delicto amercietur secundum magnitudinem delicti, saluo contenemento suo. *French version*: Frans hom ne seit amerciez pour petit forfet, fors solon la maniere del forfait, et pour le grant forfait seit amerciez solonc la grandesce del forfait sauf son contenement. *c* **1292** BRITTON I. vii, A chescun murdre soit le hundred, ou le murdre sera trové fet, en nostre merci; et si le fet serra trove en deus hundrez, si soint ambideus amerciez. (Let the hundred where the murder shall have been done be 'amercied' [in our mercy]; and if the deed shall be found to have been done in two hundreds, let them both be 'amercied.') *Ibid.* I. iii. 7 Qe nul ne soit si hardi de amercier nul homme.]

1. *trans.* To punish by an arbitrary fine; to fine, mulct (a person). **a.** Of legal fines.

c **1375** WYCLIF *Antecrist* 143 To amercy þe cely puple wiþouten any mercy. **1377** LANGL. *P. Pl.* B. VI. 40 þowgh ȝe mowe amercy hem · late mercy be taxoure. **1444** *Paston Lett.* 42 I. 55, I should be amercied in the Kyngges Courte. *c* **1469** EARL OF OXFORD *ibid.* 597 II. 337 Shall at the said court be amersid. **1523** FITZHERB. *Husb.* §148 To be amerced in yᵉ courte or elles to make hym amendes or bothe. **1666** FULLER *Hist. Camb.* 84 The University have power to punish and amerce all forestallers, regraters, &c. **1768** BLACKSTONE *Comm.* I. 179 For this offence the borough was amerced. **1863** COX *Inst. Eng. Govt.* II. x. 533 Liable to be amerced to the Crown, or fined for his delay of justice.

b. *fig.* and *loosely*, To exact something from, make exactions on; to punish.

c **1570** THYNNE *Pride & Lowl.* 60 The vintener amercing them so deepe, That..Their wife and children oft for hunger weepe. **1652** EVELYN *Diary* (1827) IV. 4 For which presumption if you think fit to amerce me. **1821** BYRON *Cain* III. i, Thou shalt be amerced for sins unknown.

2. With the penalty or amount expressed; **a.** as a second object (obj. of value): To fine *so much*.

1500 ARNOLD *Chron.* (1811) 1 That the Sherefs be not amercyed ouer xx pond. **1633** G. HERBERT *Humilitie* iv. in *Temple* 62 They..amerc'd them, double gifts to bring at the next Session-day. **1725** BAILEY tr. *Erasm. Colloq.* 317 I'll be content to be amerc'd a Supper. **1762** HUME *Hist. Eng.* (1806) IV. lxv. 779 The person, in whose house the conventicle met, was amerced a like sum.

b. introduced by *in* (*at* obs.): To fine *in*.

1611 BIBLE *Deut.* xxii. 19 They shall amearse him [WYCLIF, *Genev.* condemne] in an hundred shekels of siluer. **1648** PRYNNE *Plea for Lords* 8 The Barony..shall be amerced at an hundred markes. **1783** MARTYN *Geog. Mag.* II. 240 He ammerced the inhabitants in the sum of twelve hundred thousand crowns. **1817** SCOTT *Rob Roy* (1855) 190 He would amerce him in half his wages.

c. introduced by *with* (*by* rare): To punish *with*.

1592 SHAKS. *Rom. & Jul.* III. i. 195 Ile Amerce you with so strong a fine. **1594** SPENSER *Sonnet* lxx, Shall be by him amearst with penance dew. **1648** MILTON *Tenure of Kings* (1650) 55 Amerce him with the loss of his Kingdom. **1850** BLACKIE *Æschylus* II. 111, I shall be Amerced with bitter loss. **1855** MILMAN *Lat. Chr.* (1864) V. IX. iv. 248 Any clerk ..is to be amerced by the loss of his benefices and his order.

d. introduced by *of*: To mulct, deprive *of*.

1667 MILTON *P.L.* I. 604 Millions of spirits for his fault amerced Of Heaven. **1791** COWPER *Iliad* XVI. 68 Amerce me of my well-earn'd recompense. **1844** LD. COCKBURN *Jrnl.* II. 61 St. Andrews, though amerced..of its ancient greatness.

amercement (əˈmɜːsmənt). Also 5 **amerciment, amercyment.** [a. AFr. *amerciment*, n. of action f. *amercier*; see AMERCE. Often aphet. in 16th c. to MERCIMENT, and in 15th varied with AMERCIAMENT after med.L.]

1. The infliction of a penalty left to the 'mercy' of the inflicter; hence the imposition of an arbitrary mulct or fine (originally lighter in amount than fines fixed for specific offences).

1513 MORE *Rich. III* (1557) 62/1 Amercements turned into fines, fines into ransomes. **1523** FITZHERB. *Surv.* xv. (1539) 33 Most commonly by fynes and mercimentes. **1641** MILTON *Ch. Govt.* II. iii. (1851) 159 [The church] wanting the beggarly help of halings and amercements in the use of her powerful Keies. **1768** BLACKSTONE *Comm.* III. 275 Liable to an amercement from the crown for raising a false accusation. **1849** GROTE *Greece* V. II. xliii. 299 The defeat, the humiliation, and the amercement of the Carthaginians.

2. The mulct or fine so inflicted.

c **1386** CHAUCER *Pers. T.* 678 Eek they taken of hire bonde men amercimentȝ [*v.r.* amercymentȝ, -cementis, -cementȝ, -sementes, -cymentes, -ciament] whiche myghten moore resonably ben cleped extorcions than amercimentȝ [mercymentȝ, -mentes]. **1483** *Plumpton Corr.* 43 Yt is necessary to aske, distreyne, and levie the sayd amerciments. **1580** HOLLYBAND *Treas. Fr. Tong.*, *Amende*, an amercement, a fine. **1591** PERCIVALL *Span. Dict.*, *Multa*, an amercement. **1641** *Termes de la Ley* 20 Amercement, most properly is a penalty assessed, by the Peeres or equals of the party amerced, for an offence done. **1757** BURKE *Abridgm. Eng. Hist.* Wks. X. 397 The fines and amercements were another branch [of the king's revenue, A.D. 1070]. **1855** SINGLETON *Virgil* I. 284 Nor is 't alone the Teucrians that pay Amercements with their blood.

b. *fig.*

1839 BAILEY *Festus* xix. (1848) 208 Earth Was its amercement made, its prison flesh.

†**3.** Penal deprivation of anything. *Obs.*

1659 MILTON *Civ. Power* Wks. 1851, 316 The amercement of their whole virilitie.

amerciable (əˈmɜːsɪəb(ə)l), *a.* Also 7 **amerceable.** [a. AFr. *amerciable*, f. *amercier*, see AMERCE *v.*] Liable to be amerced.

1611 COTGR., *Amendable*, amerceable, fineable. **1622** CALLIS *Stat. Sewers* (1647) 132 Fine in cases Fineable, and Amerce in cases Amerciable. *Ibid.* 138 If the same by his neglect be left undone..he is therefore amerceable. **1678** HALE *Hist. Plac. Coron.* (1736) II. 73 The hundred is amerceable for the escape. **1865** NICHOLS *Britton* I. 188 He shall be amerciable.

amerciament (əˈmɜːsɪəmənt). Also 5-6 **amercyament.** [Refashioned from AMERCEMENT, after med.L. *amerciāment-um*, f. *amerciāre*: see AMERCIATE. More freq. than *amercement* as techn. term.]

1. = AMERCEMENT 1.

1543 GRAFTON *Contn. Harding's Chron.* 508 Euery thyng was haunsed above the measure; amercyamentes turned into fines, fines into raunsomes. *c* **1550** SIR. J. BALFOUR *Practicks* (1754) 18 Gif ony of thame cumis not, he sall be in the Kingis amerciament. **1576** LAMBARDE *Peramb. Kent* (1826) 202 The amerciament of bloudshead. **1607** COWEL *Interpr.* (1637) Djb, *Amerciament*..signifieth the pecuniarie punishment of an offendor against the King or other Lord in his Court. **1714** SCROGGS *Courts-Leet* (ed. 3) 119 He was amerced, and by the Amerciament affeered to 10*s.* **1776** *Customs of Epworth* in Stonehouse *Axholme* (1839) 145 All amerciaments made to be the usual and customary amerciaments. **1860** FORSTER *Grand Remonstr.* 22 That such amerciaments..should be imposed by the oath of the good men of the neighbourhood.

2. = AMERCEMENT 2.

c **1425** CHAUCER *Pers. T.* (Lansd. MS.) 678 Elles take þei of her bondemen amerciament. **1473-4** *Act 12 & 13 Edw. IV* in *Oxf. & Camb. Enactmts.* 9 Fynes, amerciamentes and other profites. **1514** FITZHERB. *Just. Peas* (1538) 83 The parsons that shal be gatherers of the sayde amerciamentes. **1605** *Play of Stucley* (1878) 183 Theres your amerciaments. And give Jack Dudley this from me to pay his fees. **1783** MARTYN *Geog. Mag.* II. 400 He collects all public fines, distresses, and amerciaments. **1800** COLQUHOUN *Comm. & Pol. Thames* xi. 311 The emoluments..arise chiefly from fines and amerciaments.

†**aˈmerciate**, *v.* *Obs. rare.* [f. med.L. *amerciāre*, *-āt-um*, f. AFr. *amercier* to AMERCE.] = AMERCE.

1566 KNOX *Hist. Ref.* Wks. 1846 I. 345 Patrick Murray.. was amerciated for his non-appearance to underly the law.

amercing (əˈmɜːsɪŋ), *vbl. sb.* [f. AMERCE + -ING¹.] The action of punishing by fine; fining, mulcting. (Now chiefly gerundial.)

1580 HOLLYBAND *Tr. Fr. Tong.*, *Condemnation d'amende*, an amercing or putting to fine. **1611** COTGR., *Multation*, a fining, amercing, punishing by the purse. *Mod.* The right of amercing for offences.

†**aˈmere**, *a.* or *adv.* *Obs.* *rare*⁻¹. [a. Fr. *amère*:—L. *amār-us* bitter.] Bitter, bitterly.

c **1300** *K. Alis.* 4427 With sweord ryden he dud amere, In this strong fyghtyng cas, He mette with Dalmadas.

amere, variant of AMAR *v.* *Obs.*, to mar.

Amerenglish (ˌæməˈrɪŋglɪʃ). Also **AmerEnglish.** [f. AMER(ICAN + ENGLISH.] = *American English* s.v. AMERICAN *a.* 3.

1974 *Encounter* Oct. 56 He lives in a duplex in one of the citadels of Amerenglish, downtown Manhattan. **1975** *Ibid.* Oct. 41 (*heading*) A symposium: aspects of Amerenglish. **1978** *Sewanee Rev.* 427 The English of America is AmerEnglish. **1979** *Logophile* III. 1. 23/1 Both show some influence of Amerenglish.

amergent, obs. variant of EMERGENT.

†**Aˈmericall**, *a.* *Obs.* *rare*⁻¹. = AMERICAN.

1651 N. BIGGS *New Dispens.* ¶ 124 The New-found-land of Americall or Prester-John humours.

American (əˈmɛrɪkən), *a.* and *sb.* **A.** *adj.*

1. a. Belonging to the continent of America. Also, of or pertaining to its inhabitants.

1598 SYLVESTER *Du Bartas* I. iii. (1641) 25/1 Under the Empire of the Ocean, Atlantike, Indian, and American. **1633** HERBERT *Temple, Ch. Mil.* 235 Religion stands on tiptoe in our land, Readie to pass to the American strand. **1773** BARRINGTON in *Phil. Trans.* LXIII. 285, I have happened.. to hear the American mocking-bird. **1885** *Century Mag.* Apr. 953/2 To use an expression made popular, we believe, by General Hawley some years ago.., dynamiting is '*not the American way*'! **1937** HEMINGWAY *To Have & Have Not* III. xvi. 232 The Colt or Smith and Wesson..so well designed to end the American dream when it becomes a nightmare. **1960** *Observer* 17 Jan. 20/6 The spread of personal prosperity in America has led away from, rather than towards, the American Dream. *Ibid.* 20/7 The American Dream, the reasonable expectations of Americans, are by tradition that all men shall be equal. **1961** M. MCCARTHY *On the Contrary* (1962) I. 40 Apologists for the American Way of Life find themselves condoning injustices.

b. ***American language*** (usu. with *the*), (i) a language of American Indians; (ii) American English (see sense 3). Also ***American tongue.***

1643 J. LANGLEY in *R. Williams' Key into Lang. of Amer.* 200, I have read over these thirty Chapters of the American Language, to me wholly unknowne. **1689** I. MATHER *Brief Relation of State of New Engl.* 16 In an Indian Town..was an Englishman, who being skilful in the American Language, Preached the Gospel to them in their own Tongue. **1789** WEBSTER *Dissertations Eng. Lang.* i. 22 Numerous local causes..will introduce new words into the American tongue. **1800** in Mencken *Amer. Lang.* (1936) I. i. 11 (*title*) On the Scheme of an American Language. *Ibid.*, Grammars and dictionaries should be compiled by natives of the country, not of the British or English, but of the *American* tongue. **1839** *Penny Cycl.* XIII. 320 The singular congruity in structure between all the American languages, from the northern to the southern extremity of the continent. **1936** MENCKEN *Amer. Lang.* (ed. 4) I. iii. 23 This occasional tolerance for things American was never extended to the American language.

2. a. Belonging to the British colonies in North America (*obs.*). **b.** Belonging to the United States.

1647 WARD *Simple Cob.* 24 Divers make it an Article of our *American* Creed. **1775** JOHNSON (*title*) Taxation no Tyranny, an Answer to the Resolutions and Address of the American Congress. **1883** *Daily News* 14 May 5/8 The plain evening dress which bespeaks the American Minister everywhere.

c. *U.S. spec.* (See quot. *a* 1861.)

1837 *Diplom. Corr. Texas* (1908) I. 187 A large number of fine American horses..which there is no doubt had been stolen from citizens of Texas. **1846** E. BRYANT *What I saw in Calif.* (1849) iv. 37 Such [Indians] as rode ponies were desirous of swapping them for the American horses of the emigrants. *a* **1861** WINTHROP *John Brent* (1862) ii. 14 He was an American horse,—so they distinguish in California one brought from the old States. **1878** J. H. BEADLE *Western Wilds*, xvi. 253, I rode a good-sized American horse.

3. a. Special Combs. **American bar** [BAR *sb.*¹ 28], the name given (outside the U.S.) to a bar serving refreshments in allegedly American style; **American blight** = APPLE-*aphis*; **American cheese**, cheese of the Cheddar type, made in the U.S.; **American cloth**, (*a*) = AMERICANI; (*b*) also **American oilcloth**, see CLOTH *sb.* 9 c; **American dream**, the ideal of a democratic and prosperous society which is the traditional aim of the American people; a catch-phrase used to symbolize American social or material values in general; **American English**, the form of English used by the inhabitants of the U.S.; **American football**, a team game orig. based on Rugby football and played between two sides each with eleven players on the field; now the prevalent form of football in N. America; **American leather** (see LEATHER *sb.* 1); **American organ**, see ORGAN *sb.*¹ 3 c; **American plan**, 'the system of charging an inclusive price for room and board in a hotel' (see D.A.E.), contrasted with *European plan*; **American sheeting** = AMERICANI; **American Sign Language**, a sign language consisting of a system of manual gestures, developed for the use of the deaf in the U.S.; cf. *ASL* s.v. A III, AMESLAN; **American supper, tea**, a social function for raising funds to which the guests contribute by bringing or buying food and drink; **American tournament** *Sport*, a tournament in which each competitor plays each of the others in turn; opp. KNOCK-OUT *a.* 1, *sb.* 6.

1862 *American bar [see COBBLER 3]. **1869** B. J. SPEDDING *Ino* 25 Trio. Air, 'American Bar'. **1886** L. P. RICHARDSON *Dark City* ii. 20 If the English bar is a curiosity to an American, the American bar is still more so. **1913** G. W. HILLS *John Bull Ltd.* 229 [Many English hotels] proudly bear aloft the sign of relief yclept 'American Bar'; but sign and beverages are alike delusions. **1815** KIRBY & SPENCE *Introd. Entomol.* I. vi. 196 The greatest enemy of this tree, and which has been known in this country [England] only about twenty years, is the apple-aphis, called by some *Coccus*, and by others the **American blight*. **1882** American blight [see BLIGHT *sb.* 2 b]. **1804** *Guardian of Freedom* (Frankfort, Ky.) 10 Mar. 2/1 (D.A.), Cheese, *American per lb. 18. **1860** DICKENS *Uncomm. Traveller* vi, in *All Year Round* 24 Mar. 515/1 Your waiter..is carrying in seventeen pounds of American cheese. **1879** American cheese [see CHEDDAR]. **1860** J. A. GRANT in *Blackw. Mag.* (1865) XCVII. 107 The body sewed up in an *American cloth. **1889** J. C. WILLOUGHBY *East Africa & its Big Game* App. II. *Eng.-Swaheli Vocab.*, American cloth, *Amerikano.* **1896** C. T. C. JAMES *Yoke of Freedom* 85 Not a single ring of stickiness was to be found upon the American-cloth table-cover. **1896** H. G. WELLS *Wheels of Chance* iv, A neat packet of American cloth behind the saddle contained his change of raiment. **1904** E. NESBIT *Phoenix & Carpet* x. 190 The marble-patterned American oil-cloth which careful housewives use to cover dressers and kitchen tables. **1931** J. T. ADAMS *Epic of Amer.* 410 If the *American dream is to come true and to abide with us, it will, at bottom, depend on the people themselves. **1937**, etc. [see sense 1 above]. **1977** *Rolling Stone* 13 Jan. 45/2 When they die-cast the fins on the 1959 Cadillac, part of the American Dream blossomed. **1986** *Guardian* 18 Jan. 19/8 The American dream seems as far from reality as my Communist dream. Your faith is money and mine is politics, so we both have our burden. **1806** WEBSTER Pref., In fifty years from this time, the *American-English will be spoken by more people, than all the other dialects of the language. **1906** *Westm. Gaz.* 24 Dec. 16/3 It is..distinctly American-English in its tendency towards phonetic spelling. **1942** BLOCH & TRAGER *Outl. Linguistic Anal.* 52 The accentual features of the sentence in American English are as yet practically unknown. **1891** W. CAMP *Amer. Football* 19 One should also call attention to a menace which threatened *American football... I refer to the 'block game'. **1906** GALLAHER & STEAD *Compl. Rugby Footballer* p. xi, A comparison with modern American football. **1972** J. MOSEDALE *Hall of Fame Bk. Football* p. ii, Rugby evolved into American football, first played by colleges when Princeton met Rutgers in 1869. **1985** *Economist* 26 Oct. 6 It should be mandatory for all *Economist* correspondents in the United States to attend one game of American football. **1856** A. M. MURRAY *Lett. from U.S.* 56, I like one *American plan, of paying for inn accommodations.. at the rate of three or four dollars a-day, and there is an end of it. **1879** *Appleton's Guide to U.S. & Canada* 1 The [N.Y.] hotels conducted on the regular or American plan. **1914** *Maclean's Mag.* June 109/3 Windsor Hotel.. Rates: American Plan, $1.50–$2.50. European Plan, 75c. to $1.50. **1863** in Petherick *Trav. Central Africa* (1869) II. 179, I have already taken from your stores.. 96 yards of *American sheeting. **1960** W. C. STOKOE *Sign Lang. Structure* 29 The *American sign language, ultimately deriving from the French, has been extended to a larger population. **1977** D. M. RUMBAUGH et al. in D. M. Rumbaugh *Lang. Learning by Chimpanzee* iv. 89 Both in the American Sign Language used by the Gardners and in Premack's plastic sign language, word-concepts are the smallest units of expression. **1926** *Guild* Mar. 93/2 *American Supper at Cadby... The men provided the baskets containing supper for two, and the ladies bid for them... A good amount was raised. **1931** *Oxf. Times* 5 June 8/5 An *American tea was held on Saturday in the gardens of 158, Banbury-road. **1939** T. S. ELIOT *Family Reunion* I. i. 23, I should have been helping Lady Bumpus, at the Vicar's American Tea. [**1881** *Times* 2 May 12/2 An All-England tournament on the American principle.. was commenced on Saturday last at the Royal Aquarium.] **1896** W. BROADFOOT et al. *Billiards* i. 41 In 1876 D. Richards.. ran second to Cook in an *American tournament. **1976** *Cumberland News* 3 Dec. 19/1 On Thursday, December 16 .. a Christmas American tournament will take place.

b. In the names of various trees and plants native to North America, as **American arbor vitæ**, *Thuja occidentalis*; **American ash**, *Fraxinus americana*; **American aspen (tree)**, *Populus tremuloides*; **American Beauty (rose)**, a variety of cultivated rose; **American beech (tree)**, *Fagus grandifolia*; **American elm (tree)**, = WHITE ELM; **American plane (tree)**, the buttonwood or Virginian Plane (see PLANE *sb.*[1] 1).

1785 H. MARSHALL *Amer. Grove* 152 *Thuja adorata*. American sweet-scented Arbor Vitæ. **1892** A. C. APGAR *Trees Northern U.S.* 194 American Arbor-Vitæ.. Wild north, and extensively cultivated throughout under more than a score of named varieties. **1744** F. MOORE *Voy Georgia* 98 The trees in the grove are mostly bay,.. hickory, American ash. **1897** G. B. SUDWORTH *Arborescent Flora* 327 *Fraxinus americana*, White Ash.. Common names [include] .. American Ash (Iowa). **1785** H. MARSHALL *Amer. Grove* 107 American Aspen-tree. **1892** A. C. APGAR *Trees Northern U.S.* 168 American Aspen.. [is] common both in forests and in cultivation. **1887** *Columbus* (Ohio) *Hort. Soc. Jrnl.* II. 43 The American Beauty is one of the finest introductions of late years. **1904** *N.Y. Times* 24 Nov. 14 A box of thirty-nine American Beauty roses. **1785** H. MARSHALL *Amer. Grove* 46 American Beech Tree. The nuts are eaten by swine. **1955** *Nomencl. Commerc. Timbers* (*B.S.I.*) 42 *Fagus grandifolia*, Canada and Eastern U.S.A., American beech. **1785** H. MARSHALL *Amer. Grove* 156 American rough leaved Elm-tree.. rises to the height of about thirty feet. **1868** H. W. BEECHER *Norwood* 4 Of all trees, no other unites, in the same degree, majesty and beauty, grace and grandeur, as the American Elm! **1785** H. MARSHALL *Amer. Grove* 105 American Plane-Tree, or large Button Wood,.. is sometimes sawed into boards. **1848** A. GRAY *Man. Botany Northern U.S.* 433 American Plane or Sycamore.

B. *sb.*

1. An American Indian.

1578 G. BEST *Frobisher's Voy.* (1867) 284 The Americans .. which dwell under the equinoctiall line. **1632** MASSINGER *City Madam* III. iii, Worse Than ignorant Americans. **1711** ADDISON *Spect.* No. 56 ¶1 The Americans believe that all creatures have souls. **1777** ROBERTSON *Amer.* II. 417 Amazing accounts are given of the persevering speed of the Americans.

2. A native of America of European descent; *esp.* a citizen of the United States. Now simply, a native or inhabitant of North or South America (often with qualifying word, as *Latin American, North American*); a citizen of the United States.

1765 GALE in *Phil. Trans.* LV. 198 Paying quit-rents to monopolizers of large tracts of land, is not well relished by Americans. **1775** JOHNSON *Tax. no Tyr.* 13 That the Americans are able to bear taxation is indubitable. **1809** KENDALL *Trav.* II. lviii. 286 The Americans, that is the subjects of the United States. **1882** HOWELLS in *Cent. Mag.* Nov. 26 We Americans are terribly in earnest about making ourselves.

3. A ship belonging to America.

1817 SOUTHEY in *Q. Rev.* XVII. 2 He had sailed in an American to Manilla.

4. *pl.* Short for *American stocks* or *shares*.

1886 *Times Reg. Events in 1885*, p. cliii, People.. who.. had come to believe that 'Americans' would never advance any more. **1897** *Daily News* 7 Sept. 7/1 A further rise in Americans. **1905** *Daily Report* 22 Mar. 1/2 Yankees. As predicted yesterday, Americans have quickly recovered their reaction.

5. American English; the form of English spoken in the United States.

[**1782** CHASTELLUX *Voyages dans l'Amérique* (1786) II. 202 Vous parlez bien américain.] **1802** *Port Folio* 28 Aug. 266/2 [A Latin verse] which my schoolmaster has translated into American. **1803** J. DAVIS *Trav. U.S.* 139 What do you think of the style of *Johnson*, the Reviewer? It is not *English* that he writes, Sir; it is *American*. **1869** GILLMORE *Accessible Field Sports* 19 But it was evident I was not boss. [*Note*] American for 'master'. **1889** KIPLING *From Sea to Sea* (1899) xvii. 368 The American I have heard up to the present, is a tongue as distinct from English as Patagonian. **1908** *Daily Chron.* 10 June 6/7 English spoken; American understood. **1919** MENCKEN *Amer. Lang.* 26 American thus shows its character in a constant experimentation,.. a steady reaching out for new and vivid forms. **1966** *Listener* 2 June 810/3 We have tried.. to translate from French into American and vice versa.

Hence (in sense A. 2 or B. 2) **Americana** (-ˈeɪnə, -ˈɑːnə) *sb. pl.* [*see* ANA *suff.*]; **Americanese** (-ˈiːz) = AMERICAN B. 5 (see above); **A'mericaness**, an American woman; **Americanitis** (-ˈaɪtɪs) [see -ITIS], some characteristically American penchant (esp. *fig.*, over-weening or blatant national conceit in American achievements, etc.) or (*loosely*) related in some way to what is American (*e.g.* morbid fear of American competition or rivalry); **A'mericanly** *adv.*, in an American manner; **A'mericanness**, the quality of being American, of having or revealing American characteristics.

1841 J. G. LOCKHART *Let.* 24 June in *N. & Q.* (1944) 9 Sept. 114/2 In case of accidents—the Buckingham Americana have been done already by myself. **1926** *Chambers's Jrnl.* Aug. 513/1 The trade in Americana is no common huckstering of second-hand volumes. **1882** SALA *Amer. Revis.* II. xii. 160 A 'bull-fiddle'.. Americanese for a violoncello. **1927** *Observer* 10 July 18/7 At Speech Day at Uppingham School.. [the] Bishop of Peterborough, said.. They needed to retain their English tongue and preserve it from the pollution caused by Americanese and journalese. **1838** FENIMORE COOPER *Home as Found* I. vi. 93 Every true American and Americaness was expected to be at his or her post. **1883** LD. R. GOWER *My Reminiscences* II. 75 The American Minister.. Mr. Washbourn, and 'his lady', a pert little Americaness. **1891** ANNIE P. CALL *Power through Repose* ii. 13 Extreme nervous tension seems to be so peculiarly American, that a German physician coming to this country to practise became puzzled by the variety of nervous disorders he was called upon to help, and finally announced his discovery of a new disease which he chose to call 'Americanitis'. **1901** *Daily Chron.* 18 Oct. 4/6 We are not among those who are attacked by the disease of Americanitis in its extreme form. **1904** G. S. HALL *Adolescence* II. 411 Less perfervid Americanitis at games and in celebrating victories. **1832** F. A. BUTLER *Jrnl.* II. 64 Miss ——.. pronounces Italian very Americanly. **1866** HOWELLS in *Harper's Mag.* Jan. 325/1 For our novelists to try to write Americanly, from any motive, would be a dismal error. **1892** *Illustr. London News* Summer No. 3 Horribly, incredibly, Americanly rich. **1906** *Daily Chron.* 13 Apr. 4/7 Rather than 'expect' in this sense, let us Americanly 'calculate', or even 'guess'. **1885** *Sat. Rev.* 17 Oct. 517/2 In none of Mr. Howells' books is his Americanness more conspicuous than in his latest.. *The Rise of Silas Lapham*. **1959** *Listener* 30 July 177/2 The true masters of American literature, those in whose work the notion of Americanness is meaningful and definable, are not paltry imitators of European naturalism.

American Express. orig. *U.S.* [f. the name of the *American Express* Co., whose orig. function was to provide express mail services throughout N. America.] A proprietary name for an international organization which provides its members with the facility of a personal charge card, on payment of an initial entrance fee and annual subscription. *attrib.* as ***American Express card***, etc. Cf. AMEX.

1958 *Business Week* 16 Aug. 111/1 American Express will present its new credit card to society Oct. 1. **1959** *Official Gaz.* (U.S. Patent Office) 25 Aug. TM151/1 American Express Company, New York... Filed Feb. 18, 1959... American Express.. for credit card plan for extension of credit to customers who patronize subscribing establishments and making collections from said customers through a central billing system. First use Sept. 23, 1958. **1959** *Ibid.* 19 Nov. TM84/1, 688,103 Representation of gladiator on a shield and 'American Express'... Pub. 8-25-59. Filed 2-18-59. **1976** N. THORNBURG *Cutter & Bone* ix. 225 Fifty of which.. he had secreted in his wallet between his driver's license and a three-year-old American Express card. **1979** [see *Diners' Club* s.v. DINER 3]. **1981** *N.Y. Times* 20 Mar. A18/4 Caricatures were commissioned by American Express as part of a tie-in advertising campaign bolstering the New York theater as well as the credit card.

Americani (əmɛrɪˈkɑːniː). Also **Amerikani, Mer(c)kani.** [Swahili; also *Amerikano* (Madan, Steere), *Marekani* (Sucleur).] A kind of cotton cloth.

1863 SPEKE *Jrnl. Discov. Source Nile* App. B. 617 Merikani or American sheeting. **1872** BURTON *Zanzibar* II. App. I. 419 The Takah or piece.. of 'Merkani', American domestics, is generally of 30 yards. **1894** N. BELL tr. *L. von Höhnel's Discov. Lakes Rudolf & Stefanie* I. 12, 600 pieces (*djora*) of white cotton goods (Merckani).

1893 *Geogr. Jrnl.* Mar. 221 Their dress is a white cloth.. of broad Americani. **1900** GROGAN & SHARP *From the Cape to Cairo* 182 'Amerikani'. [*Note*] White trade cloth. **1910** ETHEL YOUNGHUSBAND *Glimpses E. Africa & Zanzibar* 34 Boys wear a cotton singlet, a loin cloth of 'Amerikani'. **1921** *Blackw. Mag.* Jan. 118/1 A venerable savage, with a yard of tattered and dirty americani round his loins. **1925** *Chambers's Jrnl.* Apr. 352/1 The rough *Americani* curtain.

Americanism (əˈmɛrɪkəˌnɪz(ə)m). [f. AMERICAN *a.* and *sb.* + -ISM.]

1. Attachment to, or political sympathy with, the United States.

1797 JEFFERSON *Let.* 24 June in *Wks.* (1854) IV. 190 The dictates of reason and pure Americanism. **1808** —— *Writ.* (1830) IV. 114, I knew your Americanism too well. **1853** MARY HOWITT tr. *Bremer's Homes N. World* I. 160 What constitutes noble republicanism and Americanism. **1861** H. KINGSLEY *Ravenshoe* xlii, The leaven of Americanism and European Radicalism.

2. Any thing peculiar to, or characteristic of, the United States.

1833 *Edin. Rev.* LVII. 451 The existence of some peculiar Americanism of character, and even language. **1870** EMERSON *Soc. & Sol.* ii. 232, I hate this shallow Americanism which hopes to get rich by credit. **1893** *Nation* (N.Y.) 2 Feb. 75/1 The spread of American influence and domination abroad, known as 'Americanism'. **1926** D. H. LAWRENCE *Plumed Serp.* ii. 46 Americanism is the worst of the two, because Bolshevism only smashes your house or your business or your skull, but Americanism smashes your soul. **1966** *Listener* 3 Nov. 644/2 There is already a generation of Englishmen who think of tinned beer as a normal part of life, and not any longer as a hideous Americanism.

3. *esp.* A word or phrase peculiar to, or extending from, the United States; (the common, and app. earliest, use of the word in Great Britain.)

1781 WITHERSPOON in *Pennsylvania Jrnl.* No. 1391. 1/2 The first class I call Americanisms, by which I understand an use of phrases or terms, or a construction of sentences, even among persons of rank and education, different from the use of the same terms or phrases, or the construction of similar sentences, in Great Britain. The word Americanism, which I have coined for the purpose, is exactly similar in its formation and signification to the word Scotticism. **1826** MISS MITFORD *Our Village* Ser. II. (1863) 352 Society has been progressing (if I may borrow that expressive Americanism) at a very rapid rate. **1833** GEN. P. THOMPSON *Exerc.* (1842) III. 470 There are many Americanisms which in the course of time will work their way into the language of England. **1891** *Daily News* 26 June 5/2 Americanisms are modes of expression which vary from the standard of good English, and which are either peculiar to America, or chiefly prevalent there. **1936** MENCKEN *Amer. Lang.* (ed. 4) I. i. 12 The period from the gathering of the Revolution to the turn of the century was one of immense activity in the concoction and launching of new Americanisms, and more of them came into the language than at any time between the earliest colonial days and the rush to the West. **1955** *Times* 6 June 7/4, I suspect that 'Mr. Mayor' is an Americanism and as applied to females it is obviously incorrect.

A'mericanist. [f. as prec. + -IST.] One who makes a special study of subjects pertaining to America, as its geology, natural history, ethnology, antiquities, history, or resources.

1881 *Athenæum* 3 Sept. 311/2 The Congress of Americanists.. is to open at Madrid on the 25th of this month.

Americanization (əˌmɛrɪkənaɪˈzeɪʃən). [f. next + -ATION.] The process of Americanizing.

1860 *Times* 12 Apr. 8/2 This Americanization is represented to us as the greatest of calamities. **1882** *Pall Mall G.* 23 Nov. 1 The partial Americanization of English journalism.

Americanize (əˈmɛrɪkəˌnaɪz), *v.* [f. AMERICAN *a.* + -IZE.]

1. *strictly*, To make American; to naturalize as an American, *esp.* as a citizen of the United States.

1816 PICKERING *Voc.*, *Americanize*, to render American. **1859** in WORCESTER.

2. *loosely*, To make American in character; to assimilate to the customs or institutions of the United States. (Chiefly a term of English party politics, intended to be opprobrious.)

1797 J. JAY *Corr. & Public Papers* 27 Oct. (1893) IV. 232, I wish to see our people more *Americanized*, if I may use that expression; until we feel and act as an independent nation. **1803** W. O. PUGHE *Cambrian Biogr.* 140 Him they found perfectly Americanized: before any answer was sent he must first know who would pay him for his trouble. **1824** *Blackw. Mag.* XVI. 595 His wish is to see Greece 'not Anglicized, but Americanized'. **1830** *Gentl. Mag.* Mar. 238 They take upon themselves to scout learning.. Americanize episcopacy and the liturgy. **1858** (27 Oct.) BRIGHT *Sp.* 289 They say we must not on any account 'Americanize' our institutions. **1898** *Library Jrnl.* June 229/2 The library should be wholly American, and its influence tend wholly toward Americanizing the foreign-born.

3. *intr.* To become American in character, etc.

1854 T. CHOLMONDELEY *U. Thule* xix. 324, I am convinced that society in such a colony as New Zealand must daily Americanise. **1875** HOWELLS *Foregone Concl.* 77 He was Americanizing in that good lady's hands as fast as she could transform him. **1882** —— in *Longm. Mag.* I. 42 They have Americanised in such degree that it is hard to know some of them from ourselves.

4. *intr.* To use Americanisms in language.

1839 *Q. Rev.* Oct. 311 The second example will satisfy Mr. Murray that Hood Americanizes not.

A'mericanized, *ppl. a.* [f. prec. + -ED.]

1. Made American; naturalized in America, *esp.* in the United States.

1864 MISS YONGE *Trial* II. xvi. 315 'And he is quite Americanized?' asked Leonard. **1866** *Spect.* 1 Dec. 1325 Arresting Americanized Irishmen, among others a Head Centre.

2. Made like the American; assimilated to the character of the United States.

1879 M. ARNOLD *Democr.* in *Mixed Essays* 23 To prevent the English people from becoming, with the growth of democracy, Americanised.

americium (æməˈrɪsiəm, æməˈrɪʃ(ɪ)əm). [f. *Americ(a* + -IUM.] A metallic radioactive transuranic element produced artificially by the

bombardment of uranium with high-energy helium nuclei. Symbol Am, atomic number 95.
Discovered by G. T. Seaborg, R. A. James and L. O. Morgan at Berkeley, California, in 1945.
1946 *N.Y. Times* 11 Apr. 15/4 Elements 95 and 96, the two newest trans-uranium elements to be created, have been named, respectively, Americium, after the Americas, and curium. **1946** *Times* 20 Nov. 3/3 The isolation in a pure form of americium, one of four newly discovered elements in the release of atomic energy, was announced last night before the American Chemical Society. **1952** *Sci. News* XXIV. 92 The two following elements, americium..and curium.. show similarity and difficulty of separation comparable to the rare-earths case.

A'merico-, combining form of AMERICA, as in **Americo-mania**, a craze for what is American.
1798 W. TAYLOR in *Month. Rev.* XXVI. 527 Their Americo-mania he seems to consider as a criminal heresy. **1882** *World* 11 Jan., Americomania has reached a point when a writer is gravely taken to task..for calling Transatlantic *meesses* 'eccentric.'

Amerika (ə'mɛrɪkkə). *slang* (orig. *U.S.*). Also **Amerikkka**. [a. G. *Amerika* America; var. form with the initial letters of *Ku Klux Klan*.] American society viewed as racist, fascist, or oppressive, esp. by Black consciousness.
1969 *Ann Arbor* (Mich.) *Argus* 18 Nov.-3 Dec. 5/2 (*heading*) Hayden on Amerika on Trial. **1970** *Ibid.* 9-23 Feb. 5/3 (*heading*) In Amerikkka. **1971** *Black Scholar* June 51/1 The oppressive contract cannot be broken as long as any sort of hierarchy exists to perpetuate the sensitized relationships of tribalism (in Amerikkka?). **1973** *Black Panther* 17 Nov. 2/2 The political situation which exists here in Nazi Amerikkka. **1977** C. MCFADDEN *Serial* (1978) xxii. 50/1 He wasn't up for another..rap session about macho in Amerika. **1985** *New Statesman* 27 Sept. 19/3 Exiled from Amerika (the spelling comes naturally) Beck..lived a nomadic existence in Europe.
So **A'merik(kk)an** *a.*
1969 *Ann Arbor* (Mich.) *Argus* 8-22 Oct. 4/1 The 'World Series of Amerikan Justice'—the Chicago Conspiracy vs. the Washington Kangaroos—opened to a full house in Cowtown on Sept. 24. **1971** *Black World* Apr. 85 All draw not only from our unique amerikkkan horror but also from the lush beauty of Mother Africa for inspiration. **1981** *Time* 9 Nov. 34/1 The Weather Underground proceeded to bomb 'symbols of Amerikan..injustice'.

Amerind ('æmərɪnd), **Amerindian** (æmə'rɪndɪən), *sbs.* and *adjs.*, contractions of *American Indian* (see AMERICAN B. *sb.* 1, INDIAN A. *adj.* 2, B. *sb.* 2).
1900 *Ann. Rep. Bur. Amer. Ethnol. 1897–98* I. p. xlviii, The tribal fraternities of the Amerinds. *Ibid.* II. 835 The four worlds of widespread Amerindian mythology. **1901** DELLENBAUGH *N.-Americans Yest.* 247 The communal principle of living had much to do almost everywhere with the size and character of the Amerind houses. **1902** *Man* II. 101 A group of Amerind tribes are known as Algonquians. **1921** *Edin. Rev.* Apr. 268 Crosses between Amerindians.. and Europeans. **1955** *Times* 22 June 11/6 In 1945 the district was declared a reserve for the 1,500 Amerindians living there. **1965** *Amer. N. & Q.* Apr. 122/2 Volume One: *Natural Environment & Early Cultures*, edited by Robert C. West, marks a turning point as well as a progression in Amerind anthropology.

amerous, obs. variant of AMOROUS.

amerveille, -aille, var. AMARVEL *v. Obs.*

‖**à merveille** (a mɛrvɛj). [Fr., lit. 'to a marvel'.] Admirably, wonderfully. Cf. ADMIRATION 2 b.
1762 STERNE *Let.* 19 Oct. (1935) 186 French speaking, in ..which she does *à marveille.* **1872** TROLLOPE *Eustace Diam.* (1873) I. xli. 199 You and Carbuncle get on à merveille. **1896** BEERBOHM in *Yellow Bk.* Oct. 26 It fitted *à merveille.* **1932** D. L. SAYERS *Have his Carcase* vii. 83 When the heart dances with the feet, then it will be *à merveille.*

ames ace, obs. form of AMBS-ACE.

†**a'mese**, *v. Obs.* [a. OFr. *amesir, amaisir*, also *amaisier, amaiser*, to calm, pacify, appease:—med.L. **admītī-āre*, f. *ad* to + *mīti-s* mild.] To appease, calm, render mild; to moderate, pacify.
1375 BARBOUR *Bruce* XVI. 134 Bot othyr lords that war hym by Ameyssyt the King. *c* **1400** *Destr. Troy* XXXII. 12842 Ames you of malice. *c* **1425** WYNTOUN *Cron.* V. iii. 49 Til amese all were and stryfe. *c* **1460** *Towneley Myst.* 194 Sir, amese you. **1529** LYNDESAY *Compl.* 42 The first men wer displesit. Bot he thame prudentlie amesit.

†**a'mesing**, *vbl. sb. Obs.* [f. prec. + -ING[1].] Mildness, moderation.
c **1325** *E.E. Allit. P.* C. 400 In his mylde amesyng he mercy may fynde.

Ameslan ('æməslæn). orig. *U.S.* [Acronym, f. the name *American Sign Language*.] = *American Sign Language* s.v. AMERICAN *a.* 3. Cf. *ASL* s.v. A III.
1972 L. J. FANT (*title*) Ameslan: an introduction to American Sign Language. **1976** *Sci. Amer.* Dec. 136/1 The deaf..use Ameslan fluently. **1977** SAVAGE & RUMBAUGH in D. M. Rumbaugh *Lang. Learning by Chimpanzee* xvi. 304 Apes are relatively facile in the learning of arbitrary representations (i.e., Ameslan signs, lexigrams, words). **1979** *Amer. Speech 1978* LIII. 273 Ameslan is..as much like a spoken language as it possibly could be.

amesnable, obs. form of AMENABLE.

amess, obs. form of AMICE.

amesure, earlier form of ADMEASURE.
a **1450** *Knt. de la Tour* xviii. 25 Here is a good ensaumple to amesure in this matere bothe herte and thought.

‖**Ametabola** (æmɪ'tæbələ), *sb. pl. Zool.* [prop. mod.L. adj. pl. neut. (sc. *insecta*), a. Gr. ἀμετάβολα pl. neut. of ἀμετάβολος, f. ἀ priv. + μετάβολος changeable.] A sub-class of Insects, consisting of those such as the Lice and Spring-tails, which do not undergo metamorphosis.
1870 NICHOLSON *Zool.* (1880) 341 Insects are divided into sections, called respectively *Ametabola, Hemimetabola*, and *Holometabola.*

ametabolian (ə,mɛtə'bəʊlɪən), *a.* and *sb. Zool.* [f. prec. + -IAN: cf. *agamian.*] **A.** *adj.* Belonging to the *Ametabola*. **B.** *sb.* An insect of this sub-class.
1835 KIRBY *Habits & Inst. An.* II. xiv. 18 Dr. Leach divides Insects into *Ametabolians* and *Metabolians.* **1875** BLAKE *Zool.* 243 Diœcious and ametabolian.

ametabolic (ə,mɛtə'bɒlɪk), *a. Zool.* [f. as prec. + -IC.] Not undergoing metamorphosis.
1870 NICHOLSON *Advd. Zool.* 162 The insects are said to be 'Ametabolic,' because they pass through no metamorphosis.

ametabolous (æmɪ'tæbələs), *a. Zool.* [f. as prec. + -OUS.] = prec.
1870 ROLLESTON *Anim. Life* xxxiv. 105 The fresh-water congeners of marine species which go through metamorphoses, are very frequently ametabolous in the sub-kingdoms of Mollusca. **1877** HUXLEY *Anat. Inv. An.* vii. 424 Of ametabolous insects, there are some with masticatory, others with suctorial mouths.

ametallous (ə'mɛtələs), *a. Chem.* [f. Gr. ἀ priv. + μέταλλ-ον mine (taken in sense of L. *metall-um* metal) + -OUS.] Not of the nature of a metal, non-metallic.
1879 in *Syd. Soc. Lex.*

†**ame'thodical**, *a. Obs.*[—0] [f. A- *pref.* 14 + METHODICAL (now replaced by UNMETHODICAL).] 'Out of method, without method, irregular.' J.
1721 in BAILEY. Also in mod. Dicts.

†**ame'thodically**, *adv. Obs. rare*[—1]. [f. prec. + -LY[2].] Without method; unmethodically.
1631 *Whimzies* 86 In a tempest you shall heare him pray, but so amethodically, as it argues that hee is seldome vers'd in that practice.

†**a'methodist**. *Obs. rare*[—1]. [f. A- *pref.* 14 + METHODIST.] One who follows no method; 'a physician who does not practise by theory, a quack.' Todd.
1654 WHITLOCK *Mann. Engl.* 89 (T.) It cannot be lookt for, that these empiricall amethodists should understand the order of art, or the art of order.

amethyst ('æmɪθɪst). Forms: 3 **ametist**, 4 **ame-, amatistus**, 4–6 **amatyst(e**, 5 **ametiste**, 5–7 **amatist**, 6 **amitist, amates**, 6–7 **amatites**, 6–8 **amethist**, 7 **amæthist**, 7– **amethyst**, (4 **amaffised**). [a. OFr. *ametiste, amatiste*, ad. L. *amethyst-us*, a. Gr. ἀμέθυστ -ος, prop. adj. 'not drunken' (f. ἀ priv. + *μέθυστος, verbal adjective f. μεθύσκ-ειν to intoxicate, f. μέθυ wine), applied subst. to this stone (as also to a herb), from a notion that it was a preventive of intoxication. In end of 16th c. the word began to be refashioned after the Latin, though the earlier *amatist* was still usual in early part of 17th.]
1. A precious stone of a clear purple or bluish violet colour, of different degrees of intensity, consisting of quartz or rock-crystal coloured by manganese, or, according to Heintz, by a compound of iron and soda.
c **1290** *Cokayngne* in *E.E.P.* (1862) 158 Ametist and crisolite. *c* **1325** *E.E. Allit. P.* A. 1015 Þe amatyst purpre with ynde blente. **1398** TREVISA *Barth. De P.R.* XVI. ix. (1495) 557 Amatistus is purpre red in colour medelyd wyth colour of uyolette. **1477** NORTON *Ord. Alch.* in Ashm. 1652 v. 65 The Amatist followeth the Ruby in dignity. **1535** STEWART *Cron. Scot.* II. 569 Rubeis reid..amates that courtlie war and cleir. **1580** SIDNEY *Arcadia* II. (1654) 141 The bloodie shafts of Cupids war, With amatists they headed are. **1596** LODGE *Marg. of Amer.* 79 The amethist staieth drunkennesse. **1611** BIBLE *Rev.* xxi. 20 The twelfth an Amethyst [WYCLIF, ametistus; TINDALE, *Genev.* amatist; *Rhem.* amethyste]. **1612** DRAYTON *Poly-olb.* xv. 241 The rich Ruby, Pearle, and Amatist. **1727** THOMPSON *Summer* 151 The purple streaming Amethyst is thine. **1874** WESTROPP *Prec. Stones* 41 The finest amethysts are brought from India, Persia, Ceylon, Brazil, and Siberia.
oriental amethyst: a rare violet or amethyst-coloured variety of Corundum or Sapphire.
1753 CHAMBERS *Cycl. Supp.* s.v., Oriental Amethysts are found in Calecut and Bisnagar. **1874** WESTROPP *Prec. Stones* 16 The violet variety of corundum is termed the oriental amethyst. It may be distinguished from the ordinary amethyst by its superior brilliancy.
2. *fig.*
1818 KEATS *Endym.* I. 27 Western cloudiness, that takes The semblance of gold rocks..palaces And towers of amethyst. *c* **1875** LONGF. *Palingen.* I, The rolling meadows of amethyst.
3. *Her.* The colour of the amethyst, purple violet.
1572 BOSSEWELL *Armorie* 105 He beareth on a wreathe 'Topaze' and 'Saphiere' an Alcian, volant, of the 'Amatist' mixte with 'Pearle.' **1725** BRADLEY *Fam. Dict.*, *Amethist*, a Term in Heraldry, signifying the Purple Colour in the Coat of a Nobleman.
4. *attrib.* quasi-*adj.*; = AMETHYSTINE 2.
1601 HOLLAND *Pliny* IX. xxxviii. (1634) 259 Rich Amethyst or purple violet colour. **1791** HAMILTON *Berthollet's Dyeing* I. Introd. 11 The amethyst purple had the colour of the stone so called. **1879** E. CLERKE in *Cornh. Mag.* June 724 The savage sculpture of their stony ribs accentuated by amethyst shadow.

amethystine (æmɪ'θɪstɪn), *a.* Also 7 **-istine**, 8 **-estyne**. [ad. L. *amethystinus*, a. Gr. ἀμεθύστιν-ος, f. ἀμέθυστ-ος: see prec. and -INE.]
1. Containing, or composed of, amethyst.
1670 E. BROWN in *Phil. Trans.* V. 1197 Amethysts or Amethystine mixtures in the clefts of the Rocks. **1695** WOODWARD *Nat. Hist. Earth* IV. (1723) 244 Gold grains, Amethistine Pebles, Amber. **1877** JEWITT *Half-hrs. Eng. Antiq.* 206 Beads of amethystine quartz.
2. Amethyst-coloured; violet-purple.
1671 J. WEBSTER *Metallogr.* xv. 211 Most elegant Amethystine flowers. **1772** PENNANT *Tours in Scotl.* (1774) 218 Crystalline kernels, of an amethestyne color. **1834** DISRAELI *Rev. Epick* I. i. 8 Bright beings like the morn, With amethystine wings. **1870** H. MACMILLAN *Bible Teach.* i. 2 The Pleiades..quivering with radiance in the amethystine ether.

‖**ametropia** (æmɪ'trəʊpɪə). *Path.* [mod.L., f. Gr. ἄμετρος irregular (f. ἀ priv. + μέτρον measure) + ὤψ, ὠπ-α, eye + -ια abst. ending.] Any abnormal condition of the refraction of the eye.
1875 WALTON *Dis. Eye* 617 Such deviation is sometimes called ametropia.

ametropic (æmɪ'trɒpɪk), *a. Path.* [f. prec. + -IC.] Pertaining to ametropia; with defective refraction.
1878 BRYANT *Pract. Surg.* I. 300 The ametropic eye differs from the emmetropic in two opposite directions.

ametrous (ə'miːtrəs), *a. Path.* [f. Gr. ἀ priv. + μήτρα womb + -OUS.] Having no uterus.
1879 in *Syd. Soc. Lex.*

†'**ametry**. *Obs. rare*[—1]. [ad. Gr. ἀμετρία immoderation, f. ἀ priv. + μέτρον measure + -ια abst. ending.] Immoderation; excess.
1541 R. COPLAND *Galyen's Terap.* 2 E j b, Ametrie, that is to saye..vncompetence and immoderacyon.

‖**a'meuble**, *v. Obs.* [a. Fr. *ameubl-ir* to render movable, f. *à* to + *meuble*:—L. *mōbil-em* movable.] To stir up, loosen (soil).
1725 BRADLEY *Fam. Dict.*, *Ameubling, Ameublir* in French, a Term peculiar to that Language, concerning the Culture of the Earth, which is grown hard..As we may say, to *ameuble* that Surface; *i.e.* to render it *moveable.*

ameve, variant of AMOVE *v. Obs.*, to move.

Amex ('æmɛks). orig. *U.S.* Also **AMEX**. [Blend f. the name of the *American Express* Co.] = AMERICAN EXPRESS. Chiefly *attrib.*, esp. as ***Amex card***. (Proprietary.)
Amexco was registered as a U.S. trademark for travel, shipping, and financial services by the American Express Co. on 21 Mar. 1950.
1970 *Trade Marks Jrnl.* 12 Aug. 1316/1 *Amex*..Paper, paper articles [etc.]. American Express Company. **1973** *Official Gaz.* (U.S. Patent Office) 25 Dec. 183 American Express Company, New York, N.Y. Filed Sept. 19, 1972... Amex. **1977** C. MCFADDEN *Serial* (1978) l. 106/2 Harvey watched one of them making a sale, cheerfully accepting an Amex credit card. **1979** *Washington Post* 3 June F4/4 American Express reports that the largest growth in AMEX card membership is among women. **1983** C. HYDE *Tenth Crusade* II. 100 'You take American Express?'.. 'Are you kidding? Aspen would be a ghost town without Amex.' **1985** *Financial Times* (Weekend Suppl.) 10 Aug. p. iv/1 Then there was the lottery winner in the U.S. who, after a $1.1m win, applied for an Amex card only to be rejected.

Amgot ('æmgɒt). Also **A.M.G.O.T., AMGOT.** The name formed from the initial letters of 'Allied Military Government of Occupied Territory', the title of an organization first set up in Sicily during the 1939–45 war. Abbrev. *A.M.G.*
1943 *Times* 19 July 4/4 Directly under him [*sc.* the Military Governor] a new organization called the Allied Military Government of Occupied Territory—and known as Amgot for short—has been set up and is already functioning. *Ibid.* 14 Aug. 4/4 An explanation that Amgot is concerned with enemy territory, and that any allied organizations in liberated countries will come to help and not direct, will set perturbed minds at rest. *Ibid.* 6 Sept. 3/4 'Amgot' officials came in with the landing this morning. Among the first signs erected in the little village of Gallico was the A.M.G.O.T. sign. **1943** *Amer. N. & Q.* III. 86/2 AMG. Not long after AMGOT (Allied Military Government of Occupied Territories) first appeared in print it was denounced as an unprintable Turkish word. Immediately the War Department shortened the form to AMG (Allied Military Governments).

Amharic (æm'hærɪk), *a.* and *sb.* [f. *Amhara*, name of a central province of Ethiopia + -IC.]

Of or pertaining to Amhara, its people, or its language; the language itself, the principal language of modern Ethiopia.

[**1600** J. Pory tr. *Leo's Hist. Afr.* i. 8 One kinde of language, called by them *Aquel Amarig*, that is, the noble toong.] **1813** *Q. Rev.* Oct. 258. **1835** *West of England Jrnl.* ii. 94 The Amharic language, which at first was supposed a dialect of the Gheez, and thus to be Shemitic, is now alleged ..to be of African pedigree. **1836** N. Wiseman *Connect. Sci. & Revealed Relig.* ii. 85 Another example may be drawn from the Amharic. **1907** *Camb. Univ. Press Bull.* Jan. 27 Every Amharic word is phonetically expressed in Roman letters as well as given in the Amharic character. **1923** *Blackw. Mag.* Aug. 245/2 Ancient Ge'z, the language of the Abyssinian Church and parent of the modern Amharic. **1935** *Discovery* Nov. 315/2 It is to be hoped that the fighting [in Ethiopia] will not lead to the destruction of existing monuments of the old Amharic civilisation. **1959** *Times* 29 June 11/6 The domination of a Christian Amharic minority over a number of other tribes.

†**ami, amy(e.** *Obs.* Also *fem.* ameye. [a. OFr. *amy*, *ami*:—L. *amīc-us* friend, and *amie*:—L. *amīca* female friend.] A friend, a lover.

a **1300** *Cursor M.* 20193 Quat es ti name þou suet ami [*v.r.* amy]. *c* **1300** *K. Alis.* 520 Scheo saide heo was ameye To Ammon the god of pleye. *Ibid.* 1834 He scholde come as amye. *c* **1330** *Arth. & Merl.* 9307 Arthour and Ban, and Bohort, his amis.

amiability (ˌeɪmɪəˈbɪlɪtɪ). [f. next: see -bility. App. a mod.Eng. formation, though the cognate *amiableté* common in OFr. was still in use in beg. of 17th c. See also amability.]

1. The quality of being amiable (in the modern sense); amiableness.

1807 *Edin. Rev.* X. 439 It is quite painful to look at such terms as *womanised, amiability*. **1817** Ticknor *Life* I. 111 Which in France is called amiability but which everywhere else would be called flattery. **1838** Dickens *Nich. Nick.* xiv. (C.D. ed.) 104 They were delighted with his amiability.

2. Lovableness (better expressed by amability).

1869 Goulbourn *Purs. Holiness* vii. 62 The amiability of God consists in his moral perfections.

amiable (ˈeɪmɪəb(ə)l), *a.* Forms: 4 **amiabul**, 4–6 **amyable**, 5 **aimiable**, **ameabill**, 5–6 **amyabil(l**, 6– **amiable**. [a. OFr. *amiable*:—L. *amīcābil-em* friendly, f. *amīc-us* a friend; afterwards confused with OFr. *amable* (mod. *aimable*):—L. *amābilem* lovable, f. *amāre* to love: see amicable and -ble. Occas. compared *-er*, *-est*.]

†**1.** (= Fr. *amiable*, L. *amīcābil-em*.) **a.** Of persons: Friendly, amicable; kind (in action). *Obs.*

c **1350** *Will. Palerne* 586 þat amiabul maide alisaundrine a hiȝt. *c* **1374** Chaucer *Boeth.* 61 Amyable fortune with hir flaterynges draweth mys wandrynge men fro the souereyne good. *c* **1400** *Beryn* 1657 He made hym chere, semeyng amyabill. **1491** Caxton *Vitas Patr.* i. xix. (1495) 22 a/1 One namyd Phylemon whyche was moche amyable and debonayr to the peple.

b. Friendly, kindly disposed, favourably inclined (*to* a thing). ? Only in U.S.

1875 Howells *Foregone Concl.* 72 That foreign eccentricity to which their nation is so amiable.

c. Of words, conduct, etc.: Friendly, kindly. (Now almost restricted to *temper*, *mood*, and so passing into 3.)

c **1386** Chaucer *Melibeus* 10 With amyable wordes hire to recomforte. **1443** *Pol. Poems* II. 210 Froward cheerys, pees makith amyable. **1598** Shaks. *Merry W.* ii. ii. 243 Lay an amiable siege to the honesty of this Ford's wife. **1712** Addison *Spect.* No. 459 ¶12 Giving us more amiable Ideas of the Supreme Being. *c* **1746** Hervey *Medit. & Cont.* (1818) 87 In vain we strive to behold the features of amiable nature. **1849** Macaulay *Hist. Eng.* I. 602 The rebels.. proceeded to Wells, and arrived there in no amiable temper.

†**d. amiable numbers**: see amicable 3 b.

†**2.** (= Fr. *aimable*, L. *amābilem.*) Worthy to be loved, lovable, lovely. **a.** of persons. *Obs.* (exc. as restricted in 3.)

1535 Coverdale *Jud.* x. 4 She was exceadinge amyable and welfauoured in all mens eyes. **1604** Shaks. *Oth.* iii. iv. 59 While she kept it, 'T would make her Amiable, and subdue my Father. *a* **1656** Bp. Hall *Invis. World* ii. vi, The infinitely amiable and glorious Deity. **1711** Addison *Spect.* No. 162 ¶4 We.. are amiable or odious in the Eyes of our great Judge. **1788** *New Lond. Mag.* 572 Not more amiable for the beauty of her person than the accomplishments of her mind.

†**b.** of things. *Obs.* or *arch.* exc. in regard to personal human actions, in which it approaches 3.

1382 Wyclif *Phil.* iv. 8 What euere thingis amyable, *or able to be loued* [Vulg. *amabilia*; *Rhem.* amiable; **1611** lovely]. —— *Amos* v. 11 ȝe shuln plante most amyable vyne ȝerdis. **1513** Douglas *Æneis* xii. Prol. 151 Mayst amyabil waxis the emerant medis. **1535** Coverdale *Ps.* lxxxiii. 1 How amiable are thy dwellinges, thou Lorde of hoostes? [Wyclif, looued; **1611** amiable]. **1578** Lyte *Dodoens* i. xcvi. 138 Of savour and smell more amiable or pleasant. **1615** Markham *Eng. Housew.* (1660) 101 Smoothing of the skinne, and keeping the face delicate and amiable. **1644** Howell *Lett.* (1650) I. 470 They keep their churches so cleanly and amiable. **1715** Burnet *Own Time* II. 297 It was no amiable thing to be a province to Spain. **1722** Steele *Consc. Lovers* ii. i. (1755) 35 To tear his amiable Image from my Heart. **1802** Miss Edgeworth *Moral T.* (1816) I. xvi. 133 He should appear in a more amiable light. **1877** M. Arnold *Heine's Gr. Poems* II. 258 This amiable home of the dead.

3. The ordinary modern meaning mixes senses 1 and 2, implying the possession of that friendly disposition which causes one to be liked; habitually characterized by that friendliness which awakens friendliness in return; having pleasing qualities of heart.

(A *lovable* person is viewed as wholly objective; an *amiable* person is the *subject* of friendly emotions, which make him the *object* of our friendly emotions.)

1749 Fielding *Tom Jones* iii. vii. (1840) 30/2 The amiable temper of pity. **1776** Gibbon *Decl. & F.* I. vi. 122 That amiable prince soon acquired the affections of the public. **1806–31** A. Knox *Rem.* I. (1844) 67 The Church of England has produced numberless specimens of.. the most amiable goodness. **1816** Crabbe *Synon.* 74 An *amiable* disposition, without a *lovely* person, will render a person beloved. It is distressing to see any one who is *lovely* in person to be *unamiable* in character. **1866** Carlyle *Remin.* I. 168, I remember her well, one of the amiablest of old maids.

amiableness (ˈeɪmɪəb(ə)lnɪs). [f. prec. + -ness.] The quality of being amiable.

1. The quality of being lovable; lovableness, loveliness. = amability. **a.** of persons. *Obs.* or *arch.*

1534 Whittinton *Tullyes Offices* i. (1540) 58 There be two maner of beauties, of the which.. we must applye amyablenesse to woman, dignyte to man. **1684** Baxter *Cath. Commun.* 32 Men must be loved.. every one according to the measure of his amiableness. *c* **1746** Hervey *Medit. & Cont.* (1818) 192 His amiableness, who is 'fairest among ten thousand, and altogether lovely.' **1837** J. Harris *Gt. Teacher* 74 The character of Christ is the conception of a being of infinite amiableness.

b. of things. *Obs.* or *arch.*

a **1652** J. Smith *Sel. Disc.* ix. 485 Let us inform our minds ..in the excellency and loveliness of practical religion.. beholding it in its own beauty and amiableness. **1753** Law *Lett. Import. Subj.* 163 The amiableness of any virtue, or the horrid nature of any vice.

2. Kindliness of character which wins friendship; pleasing quality of heart and behaviour. = amiability.

a **1719** Addison (J.) The natural gaiety and amiableness of the young man wears off. **1779** Johnson *L.P.* Wks. 1816 X. 202 The amiableness of his manners made him loved wherever he was known. **1846** *Blackw. Mag.* LX. 482 My national frigidity was doomed to be thawed into civility, if not into amiableness. **1849** Miss Porter *Scot. Chiefs* 133 If you knew all her goodness, all the amiableness that dwells in her gentle heart.

amiably (ˈeɪmɪəblɪ), *adv.* Also 5–6 **amyably**. [f. as prec. + -ly[2].] In an amiable manner.

†**1.** Amicably, in a friendly manner. *Obs.*

1489 Caxton *Fayt of Armes* iv. v. 243 Praying that amyably they wyl receyue his lettres. **1523** Ld. Berners *Froissart* I. ccxxix. 308 He was amyably alyed with the kynge of Grenada. **1692** R. Lestrange *Josephus Ant.* x. xi. (1733) 290 They.. look perhaps, less amiably upon it [their food].

†**2.** Lovably, agreeably, so as to attract love or admiration. *Obs.*

1605 Drayton *Man in Moone* 136 Her Cleere and dainty Skin, To the beholder amiably did show. **1634** T. Herbert *Trav.* (1677) 129 The Palaces rise so amiably. **1779** Johnson *Milton* 157 The solitary fidelity of Abdiel is very amiably painted.

3. Good-temperedly; with kindly disposition.

1826 Disraeli *Viv. Grey* iii. iii. 97 Amiably arrogant. **1841** Miall *Nonconf.* I. 3 He then very amiably remarks. **1851** Ruskin *Mod. Paint.* (1860) V. 151 Which we should be amiably grieved to think any human being had been so happy as to find before.

amiant(h (ˈæmɪænt, -ænθ). Also 5 **amyaunt**. [a. Fr. *amiante*, ad. L. *amiant-us*.] = amiant(h)us. (Now a poetic form.)

1420 *Siege of Rouen* in *Archæol.* XX. 372 The kyngis heraudis & pursuiauntis In cotis of armys amyauntis. **1601** Holland *Pliny* (1634) II. 589 The Amiant stone is like Alume. **1713** Angestein in *Phil. Trans.* XXVIII. 223 The Amiant part is of a light Gray or Lead colour. *c* **1815** Southey *Young Dragon* i. VI. 263 With amianth he lined the nest, And incombustible asbest.

†**ami'antal**, *a. Obs. rare*$^{-1}$. [f. Gr. ἀμίαντ-ος (see amiant(h)us + -al[1].] Undefiled, undefilable.

1674 J. B[rian] *Harv.-Home* Postsc. 56 A kingdom that Is apthartal, amiantal.

amiant(h)iform (æmɪˈæntɪfɔːm), *a.* [f. amiant(h)us + -(i)form.] Of the form or structure of amiant(h)us.

1801 Bournon in *Phil. Trans.* XCI. 181 This hematitic variety is found with the same diversity of colours as the preceding, or amianthiform variety [of Arseniate of Copper].

amiant(h)ine (æmɪˈæntɪn), *a.* [f. as prec. + -ine[1].] Of the nature or material of amiant(h)us.

1833 Brewster *Nat. Magic* xii. 309 A cap made of amianthine cloth.

ami'ant(h)inite. *Min.* [f. assumed L. **amiant(h)in-us*, f. amiant(h)us + -ite.] A mineral, a variety of actinolite.

1847 in Craig.

amiant(h)oid (æmɪˈæntɔɪd), *a.* and *sb.* [f. amianth-us + -oid.] **A.** *adj.* Having the appearance of amiant(h)us. **B.** *sb.* A mineral akin to amiant(h)us, also called Asbestoid.

1847 in Craig. [In Dana only as Fr.]

amian't(h)oidal, *a.* [f. prec. + -al[1].] Of the appearance of, or resembling, amiant(h)us.

1864 Ruskin in *Reader* IV. 678/1 The upper covering of fibrous and amianthoidal schist.

‖**amiant(h)us** (æmɪˈæntəs, -θəs). [L. *amiantus*, a. Gr. ἀμίαντος undefiled, undefilable; also *subst.* the mineral, because freed from all stains by being thrown in the fire, it being itself incombustible. Spelling corrupted by confusion with *polyanthus*, etc. The correct form *amiantus* should be used.]

1. A mineral, a variety of asbestos, splitting into long flexible pearly white fibres, which have been woven into a fabric.

1668 Wilkins *Real Char.* ii. iii. §2. 62 Middle Prized Stones.. Incombustible nature.. Amiantus, Asbestus. **1671** *Phil. Trans.* VI. 2167 That Lanuginous Stone, called Amianthus. **1725** Bradley *Fam. Dict.*, *Amianthus*, call'd by us sometimes Earthflax, and sometimes Salamander's Hair. **1750** *Leonardus's Mirr. Stones* 75 Amiantus or Amianthus.. is not to be destroyed by Fire. **1866** Ruskin *Ethics of Dust* 76 Here is amianthus, for instance, which is quite as fine and soft as any cotton thread you ever sewed with.

2. A fibrous kind of chrysolite of a greenish colour; the ἀμίαντος of Dioscorides.

1862 Dana *Man. Geol.* §18. 61 Serpentine.. also delicately fibrous, and then called amianthus or chrysolite.

amias, obs. form of amice[1].

amias. ? for amethyst.

1545 *Lanc. Wills* II. 63 My ryng of golde withe a ston of amias withe lettres in it of R and E.

amic (ˈæmɪk), *a. Chem.* [f. am(monia) or am(ide) + -ic.] Of or pertaining to ammonia, of the nature of an amide or amine; *esp.* in *amic acid*, a compound of the nature of an amide, an acid amide; e.g. *lactamic*, *carbamic*, *phosphamic* acid; ***amic ether***, the ether of an amic acid; ***amic base***, a compound of the nature of an amine, e.g. *anisamine*.

1863 Watts *Dict. Chem.* I. 168 Amic acids are distinct monobasic acids. **1877** —— *Fownes' Chem.* II. 381 Amic or Amidic acids.. They are also designated as a group by the name 'Alanines.'

amicability (ˌæmɪkəˈbɪlɪtɪ). [f. next: see -bility.] The quality of being amicable; friendliness, amicableness; *concr.* in *pl.* friendly relations.

1660 G. Fleming *Stemma Sacr.* 42 That amicability that we are now knit in. **1838** Dickens *Nich. Nick.* xii. (C. D. ed.) 87 Perfect amicability being thus restored. **1877** *Hon. Miss Ferrard* III. iii. 102 This abominable disestablishment has rather caused an interruption of amicabilities.

amicable (ˈæmɪkəb(ə)l), *a.* [ad. L. *amīcābil-is* (a word of Roman law), f. *amīc-us* friend, connected with *amā-re* to love. The earlier form was amiable through OFr.; cf. *appliable*, which preceded *applicable*.]

1. *gen.* Friendly.

1532 T. Audeley in Ellis *Orig. Lett.* i. 109 II. 24 The most joyous and amycable assemblie and meting of his Grace and the French Kinge. **1651** Baxter *Inf. Bapt.* Apol. 22 The most amicable expressions. **1717** Pope *Eloisa* 301 Each mild, each amicable guest. **1748** Anson *Voy.* iii. vi. (ed. 4) 468 We once more arrived in an amicable port. **1835** Sir J. Ross *N.-W. Pass.* v. 72 The amicable and good-tempered manner. **1860** Motley *Netherl.* (1868) I. vi. 355 She had frequently, by amicable embassies, warned her brother of Spain.

2. *esp.* Of mutual arrangements: Done in a friendly spirit, with mutual goodwill, or without quarrelling or employment of force; peaceable, harmonious. ***amicable suit***: an action instituted by mutual understanding between the parties concerned, in order to secure an authoritative decision on a point of law.

1609 Skene *Reg. Maj.* (Table) 65 Amicabill composition is ane aggreance be arbitrie, conforme to ane paction agreid betwixt the parteis. *c* **1680** in Somers *Tracts* II. 272 Their Insolence.. declares them to be above the humble Dispensation of an amicable Composure. **1780** Burke *Sp. Econ. Ref.* Wks. III. 247 Amicable arrangements with a friend in power. **1794** S. Williams *Hist. Vermont* 249 An amicable settlement of all differences. **1865** Livingstone *Zambesi* iii. 79 We entered into amicable relations with the chief.

†**3.** Of things: Kindly, benign, genial. *Obs.*

1684 tr. *Bonet's Merc. Compit.* iv. 127 Balsam of Peru.. its amicable and peculiar faculty in strengthening the Nerves. **1691** Ray *Creation* (1714) 214 No amicable verdure of Herbs.

b. amicable (or *amiable*) **numbers**: 'numbers which are mutually equal to the whole sum of each other's aliquot parts. Such are the numbers 284 and 220.' Chambers *Cycl.* (1727–51).

1796 Hutton *Math. Dict.* I. 104/2 F. Schooten.. I believe first gave the name of *amicable* to such numbers. **1816** T. Taylor (*title*) Theoretic Arithmetic.. together with some remarkable Particulars respecting Perfect, Amicable, and other Numbers.

'amicableness. [f. prec. + -ness.]

1. The quality of being amicable; friendliness.

a **1667** Jer. Taylor *Peacemaker* (R.) True friends to it [peace], and to that amicableness that attends it. **1868** Geo.

Eliot *Felix H.* 37 The conversation..ended with determined amicableness.

†**2.** Of things. Cf. AMICABLE 3. *Obs.*

1667 Boyle in *Phil. Trans.* II. 552 This Experiment..to shew the Amicableness of Volatil spirits to the Blood.

amicably (ˈæmɪkəblɪ), *adv.* [f. as prec. + -LY[2].] In an amicable or friendly manner, without quarrelling or use of force.

1699 *Lond. Gaz.* mmmcccclviii/3 It's hoped, that..the Affair of Elbing will be amicably adjusted. **1724** Swift *Drapier's Lett.* Wks. 1755 V. ii. 101 Honourable names very amicably joined with my own. **1796** Morse *Amer. Geog.* I. 487 Amicably disposed towards the English colonies. **1813** Southey *Nelson* vii. 264 The conference however proceeded amicably on both sides. **1867** Miss Broughton *Not Wisely* II. iii. 47 She and her cavalier toddled amicably along.

amical (ˈæmɪkəl), *a.* Now *rare* [a. Fr. *amical*, ad. L. *amīcāl-is* (rare in cl., frequent in med.L.), f. *amīc-us* friend: see -AL[1]. Cf. *inimical.*] Friendly.

1652 Gaule *Magastrom.* 86 Planets amicall, benevolous, auspicious. **1691** W. Watson (*title*) An Amical Call to Repentance, etc. **1789** H. L. Piozzi *Observ. & Refl.* I. 373 This pretty animal's amical disposition towards man. **1794** —— *Brit. Synon.* I. 26 Amical..is very lately come very much into favour, and one hears it now perpetually in fashionable and literary circles. [**1814** W. Taylor in *Month. Mag.* XXXVII. 118 *Amicable*..appears to have been originally either an impure word for *amical*, or a misprint for *amiable.*] **1832** Mme. D'Arblay *Mem. Dr. Burney* III. 132 In his amical career, he still possessed Mr. Twining. **1891** 'Q' *Blue Pav.* iv. 66 His conscience led him to exchange this country..for a soil more amical to his religious opinions.

Hence **amiˈcality**, friendliness. *rare*$^{-1}$.

1899 W. James *Let.* 7 June (1920) II. 88 The R.R. train seems to be great stimulus to the acts of the higher epistolary activity and correspondential amicality in you.

amice[1] (ˈæmɪs). Forms: 4 **amyse**, 6 **amis(e, ames, amyss(e, amys(e, amias, ammess, amyce,** 6- **amice.** [Earlier *amyt*, AMIT(E, a. OFr. *amit*:—L. *amict-us*. The form *amyse*, *amice*, is not satisfactorily accounted for; the *s* may be due to an early confusion of *amyte* with the next word (OFr. *aumusse*); to a med.L. *amicia* (see Ducange)? for *amitia*, f. OFr. *amit*; or to one of the OFr. forms (Burguy has '*amit, amict, amis,*' Littré '*amist*'). Wyclif translates *amictus* once *amyt*, once *amys*, but has also *amyt* for *capitium* 'hood,' where the sense seems to be *aumusse*, AMICE[2], showing already a confusion between the two words. In Caxton, and the 18th c. writers, we find AMICT.]

†**1.** *gen.* A cloth for wrapping round, a scarf, handkerchief, or other loose wrap. *Obs.*

1382 Wyclif *Isa.* xxii. 17 As an amyse, so he shal vnderreren thee [**1388** As a cloth so he shal reise thee; Vulg. *Quasi amictum sic sublevabit te*].

2. *Eccl.* An oblong piece of white linen, used in the Western Church in conjunction with the alb, originally enveloping the head and neck, now generally folded so as to lie round the neck and shoulders: often taken to symbolize 'the helmet of salvation'.

1532 More *Confut. Tindale* Wks. 1557, 641/2 He would haue the peple pull the priest from the aulter, and ye amis from his head. *Ibid.* 390/1 What signifyeth the albe, the ames, and stole, and so forth. **1533** Tindale *Answ. More* Wks. III. 73 The amice on the head is the kerchief that Christ was blindfolded with..now it may well signify that he that putteth it on is blinded, and hath professed to lead us after him in darkness. **1536** *Reg. Riches in Antiq. Sarisb.* 197 Divers Stoles and Fannons, some wanting an Ammess. **1539** *Bk. Cerem.* in Strype *Eccl. Mem.* I. App. cix. 285 First he putteth on the amyss, which as touching the mystery, signifieth the vail..And therfore he putteth that upon his head first. **1552-3** *Inv. Ch. Goods Staff.* 12, Iij albes, and ij ameses. *Ibid.* 48 One vestement of grene lynen clothe, with albe and amysse. **1558** Bp. Watson 7 *Sacr.* xiii. 76 As the Jewes dyd fyrst couer Chrystes face..so hath the Priest in memorye of that, an Amise put vpon his head. *a* **1564** Becon *Displ. Pop. Mass* (1844) 259 Ye first put on upon your head an head-piece, called an amice, to keep your brains in temper, as I think. **1570** B. Googe *Pop. Kingd.* (1880) 9 b, And then his amias and his albe. **1815** Scott *Ld. Isles* ii. xxiii, His wither'd cheek and amice white. **1847** Maskell *Mon. Rit. Eccl. Angl.* III. 25 For its ancient purpose it was a covering for the head; a square piece of linen embroidered ..upon one edge..But at that time..as now by the clergy of the church of Rome, the amice was only placed for an instant upon the top of the head, and then lowered upon the shoulders, to be left there, and adjusted round the neck. So that the use of it became merely symbolical. **1856** J. H. Newman *Callista* 262 The neck was bare, the amice being as yet unknown.

†**3.** Used to render the Roman *toga*. *Obs.*

1600 Holland *Livy* xxxiv. vii. 858 k, Shall we put on our rich amyces and copes [*prætextati*]?

4. Used *loosely* of other garments.

1641 Milton *Animadv.* (1851) 244 We have heard of Aaron and his linnen Amice, but those dayes are past. **1727** Pope *Dunciad* iv. 549 On some a priest [*i.e.* the cook], succinct in amice white, Attends: all flesh is nothing in his sight.

amice[2] (ˈæmɪs). Forms: 5 **amisse,** 6 **ammes, ammas, ammys, ames, amys, am(m)esse,** 6-7 **amis(e,** 7 **amysse,** 6, 9 **amos,** 6- **amice.** [ad. OFr. *aumuce, aumusse* (Pr. *almussa*, med.L. *almussa, almussia, almucia, almucium*, Sp. *almucio*, Pg. *mursa*, It. *mozzetta* dim. of *mozza*), of doubtful origin, but generally taken as ad. Ger. *mutse*, *mütze*, cap (Sc. *mutch*), with Arab. article *al*-prefixed, as in some other non-Arabic technical words. The earliest examples in Eng. show confusion with the prec. word, the likeness between the Eng. adaptations of Fr. *aumusse* and *amit*, being assisted by the apparent similarity of use between the two articles; and from the 17th c. this has been distinguished from the prec., only as the *grey amice*.]

1. An article of costume of the religious orders, made of, or lined with grey fur. It varied at different times in character and mode of wearing, being orignally (it is said) a cap or covering for the head; afterwards a hood, or cape with a hood; in later times a mere college 'hood' or badge, borne by canons in France on the left arm.

c **1430** Lydg. *Bochas* (1554) 222 Al my riches may me nought disport Amisse of gris..a surples and prebende. **1509** Barclay *Ship of Fooles* (1570) 256 Hange vp the scapler, the ames coule and frocke. **1523** Skelton *Garl. Laurell*, Those wordes his grace dyd saye Of an ammas gray. **1527** in Pocock *Rec. Reform.* I. xxvi. 54 Four of the doctors prebendaries..in coppes and grey amys. **1530** Palsgr. 194/1 Ammys for a channon, *aumusse*. **1541** *Lanc. Wills* (1857) I. 127 An old grey amesse and a rochet xs. **1556** *Chron. Grey Friars* (1852) 94, Iiij. prebenttes..in ther grey amos. *Ibid.* 94 Their gray ammes. *Ibid.* 59 Alle the gray ammesse..in Powlles ware put downe. **1564** *Wills & Inv. N.C.* (1835) 219 My gownes, my surpless, my ij furred amysis. **1587** Holinshed *Chron.* III. 1184/2 The prebendaries and petie canons commanded to weare no more their graie amises. **1634** Canne *Necess. Separ.* (1849) 103 The gray amice, and other popish garments. **1671** Milton *P.R.* iv. 427 Morning fair Came forth with Pilgrim steps in amice gray. **1803** Scott *Last Minstr.* ii. xix, A palmer's amice wrapped him round With a wrought Spanish baldric bound. **1868** Marriott *Vest. Chr.* 228 Of similar origin is the Amess, often confused with the Amice.

†**2.** The fur of the marten or grey squirrel with which the amice was lined or bordered. *Obs.*

1548 Hall *Chron.* 513 Bleu damask purfeled with ames grey. **1573** *Art of Limming* 3 You shall with a pencell made of graye amys or calliber tailes laye on thy syse. **1598** Stow *Surv.* (ed. Strype 1754) II. v. viii. 255/1 Those Knights that have borne the office of the Mayoralty ought to have their Cloaks furred with grey Amis.

†**amiˈcitial,** *a. Obs. rare*$^{-1}$. [f. L. *amīcitia* friendship (f. *amīc-us* friend) + -AL[1].] Of or pertaining to private friendship, friendly.

1653 Gauden *Hierasp.* 97 Communion..with all Christians..both private and publick, amicitial and political.

†**amicous,** *a. Obs. rare*$^{-1}$. [f. L. *amīc-us* friendly + -OUS.] Friendly, pleasing, congenial.

1675 Evelyn *Terra* (1729) 28 Each single species draws and assimulates that only to itself, which it finds most amicous and congruous to its Nature.

†**aˈmict,** *sb. Obs.* [in early use, a. Fr. *amict*, later ad. orig. L. *amict-us* something thrown round the body, a loose upper garment, f. *amict-us* pa. pple. of *amicīre* f. *am(b)*- about + *iacĕre* for *iacĕre* to throw: see AMICE and AMIT.]

†**1.** A kerchief or cloth tied round the head. *Obs.*

1480 Caxton *Ovid's Met.* xiii. xii, Hys hore heed..was envoluted in a whyte amicte.

2. = AMICE[1].

1753 Chambers *Cycl. Supp.*, The Amict is the first of the six garments which are common to bishops and priests: the others are *alba, cingulum, stola, manipulus*, and *planeta*.

†**aˈmict,** *v. Obs. rare*$^{-1}$. [f. L. *amict*- ppl. stem of *amicīre*: see prec.] To wrap round, surround, cover.

1657 Tomlinson *Renou's Disp.* 315 With..purpureous flowers amicting its cubital branches.

†**aˈmicted,** *ppl. a. Obs.* [f. prec. + -ED.] 'Cloathed or covered with a garment.' Blount *Glossogr.* 1656.

‖**amiculum** (əˈmɪkjuːləm). [L., f. *amicīre* (see AMICT *sb.*).] (See quot.)

1753 Chambers *Cycl. Supp.*, *Amiculum*, in antiquity, denoted an upper garment worn by the women, also in use among the men. **1850** Leitch *Müller's Anc. Art* §341 The *Amiculum*..was often very rich, and also ornamented with fringes.

amicus curiæ (əˈmaɪkəs kjuːrɪiː). *Law.* [mod.L., lit. 'friend of the court'.] A disinterested adviser (see quot. 1959).

1612 Bacon *Ess.* xxxvi. 219 Those that ingage Courts in quarrels of Iurisdiction, and are not truly, *Amici Curiæ*, but *Parasiti Curiæ*. **1837** Dickens *Pickw.* x. 95, I shall be happy to receive any private suggestions of yours, as *amicus curiæ*. **1959** Jowitt *Dict. Eng. Law* I. 114/1 *Amicus curiae*, a friend of the court, that is to say, a person, whether a member of the Bar not engaged in the case or any other bystander, who calls the attention of the court to some decision, whether reported or unreported, or some point of law which would appear to have been overlooked. **1960** *Times* 12 Feb. 5/5 The suit.. was adjourned for the assistance of legal argument by the Queen's Proctor as *amicus curiae*.

amid (əˈmɪd), *adv.* and *prep.* Forms: 1 **on middan,** 2 **on midden,** 2-3 **on midde,** 3-4 **amidden, a midde,** 4-5 **a-mydde, in mydde,** 5-6 **a-myd,** 3- **amid.** [orig. a phrase: *on* 'in,' *middan*, dat. sing. weak decl. of *midde* adj. 'MID, middle'; as if = *on þām middan* (*dǣle*), *on þǣre middan* (*stówe*) 'in the middle (place or part)'; hence either absolutely, or followed by a genitive, 'in the middle *of*——.' Cf. L. *in medio* and Gr. ἐν μέσῳ, in which also the orig. adj. came to be used subst., and followed by the genitive: *in medio montium*. But already in OE. the phrase began to be treated as a prep., and followed by the dative, and in 12-13th c. the case signs were gradually dropped, leaving the governed sb. as a simple object. So late as 15th c. *amid* was still occas. expanded to *in mid*; cf. *a-two, in two*; *a-live, in life.*]

†**A.** *adv.* In the middle, in the midst. *Obs.*

a **1000** *Sol. & Sat.* 262 Se fuȝol is on middan hwæles hiwes. **1205** Layam. 8154 Þe stæf tobræc amidden. **1297** R. Glouc. 14 A temple heo fonde fair y-now, and a mawmed amidde. *c* **1380** *Sir Ferumb.* 3265 On þat oþer stage amidde ordeynt he gunnes grete. *c* **1400** *Rom. Rose* 7008 Al amydde I bilde and make My hous. **1581** Lambarde *Eiren.* ii. vii. (1588) 274 Amid betweene the violent Robber..and the miching theefe..standeth the crafty cutpurse.

B. *prep.*

1. In the middle or centre *of*. Orig. (*a* 13th c.) with a *genitive*. Now only *poet.*

c **975** *Rushw. G.* Luke xxii. 55 On middum cæfertune.. wæs [Peter] in middum hiora. *c* **1000** *Ags. G.* ibid., Petrus wæs mid him on middan þam cafertune. *c* **1175** *Cotton Hom.* 221 Ane treowe þe stent on midden paradis. *c* **1175** *Lamb. Hom.* 87 On midden þere se. *c* **1220** *Leg. Kath.* 1478 Amid te burh. *c* **1300** *Pop. Sc.* (Wright) 132 A-midde the hevene as the streon a-midde theye. *c* **1440** *Morte Arth.* (1819) 66 In mydde the felde we shall hem byde. **1513** Douglas *Æneis* x. v. 10 Amyd his cours, thare as he went. **1667** Milton *P.L.* iv. 218 And all amid them stood the Tree of Life.

†**2.** Of two things: Between. *Obs.*

c **1230** *Ancr. R.* 62 Leste heo þes deofles quarreaus habbe amidden þen eien.

3. *more loosely*, Near the middle of (a place), surrounded on all sides by (objects). Chiefly *poet.* **a.** with *sing. sb.*: In the interior of (a place *obs.*), surrounded by (an extended body).

1340 *Ayenb.* 143 Þe play of children a-midde þe strete. *c* **1374** Chaucer *Compl. Mars* 79 In chambre amydde the paleys. **1430** Lydg. *Chron. Troy* i. vi, She kept it in full close Amyd her herte. **1600** Fairfax *Tasso* iv. iv, The Peeres of Plutoes Realme assembled beene Amid the Palace of their angry King. **1730** Thomson *Autumn* 1156 Amid the miry gulf. **1790** Cowper *Odyss.* xix. 347 Amid the billowy flood. **1840** Longf. *Voices of Nt.*, *Flowers* ix, Like Ruth amid the golden corn.

b. with *pl. sb.*: Surrounded by, among (objects).

c **1230** *Ancr. R.* 270 He..þet amidden his unwines lið him adun to slepen. *c* **1320** *Cast. Loue* 333 A-midden alle his fon. *a* **1732** Gay *Wks.* 1745 I. 90 Suffer me..Amid thy bays to weave this rural weed. **1747** Collins *Passions* (1830) 58 His hand..Amid the chords bewilder'd laid. **1859** Capern *Bal. & Songs* 55 She is sitting in her cottage, Amid the flowers of May. **1874** Blackie *Self-Cult.* 42 A certain part of his work ..must be done amid books.

4. *esp.* In relation to the circumstances which surround an action. **a.** with *sing. sb.* (indicating state or condition).

1513 Douglas *Æneis* vii. x. 77 Amyd this deray This hate fury of slauchter and fell affray. **1596** Shaks. *Tam. Shr.* iv. i. 206 Amid this hurlie, I intend, That all is done in reuerend care of her. **1667** Milton *P.L.* vii. 48 Amid the choice Of all tasts else to please thir appetite. **1790** Cowper *Iliad* ii. 68 Amid the stillness. **1805** Scott *Last Minstr.* iii. xxxi, Amid the broil. **1812** J. Wilson *Isle of Palms* i. 29 My spirit sleeps amid the calm. **1853** Kingsley *Hypatia* iii. (1869) 43 Keep her spirit pure amid it all. **1871** J. Macduff *Mem. Patmos* i. 12 The last voice heard amid the roll of apocalyptic thunders.

b. with *pl. sb.* (indicating actions or events).

1719 Young *Busiris* i. i. (1757) 9 How wanton sits she amid nature's smiles! **1728** —— *Love of Fame* iv. (1757) 110 Amid sublimer views, To listen to the labours of the muse. **1812** Miss Austen *Mansf. Pk.* (1847) 71 The carriage drove off amid the good wishes of the two remaining ladies. **1841** Brewster *Mart. Sc.* ii. iii. (1856) 130 Hope..still cheered him amid his labours. **1876** Freeman *Norm. Conq.* II. x. 472 Amid general shouts of dissent.

5. *Comb.* †**amid-heaps** (in 3 *amid-hep(p)es* for OE. *on middan heápes*), in midst of a heap or crowd; †**amidmong** (see MONG *sb.*[1]), in the midst of. Also AMID-SHIPS, q.v.

c **1230** *Juliana* 69 Heo stod unhurt þer amidheppes heriende ure healent. **1548** Udall, etc. *Erasm. Paraphr. Mark* xiv. 54 And there sate amidmong the lewde and ungracious companie of seruauntes.

amid-, combining form of AMIDE, sometimes used instead of AMIDO- before vowels; as in *amidacetic acid*, *amidazobenzene*, etc.

1873 Watts *Fownes' Chem.* 681 Amidacetic Acid is formed by the action of ammonia on bromacetic or chloracetic acid. **1877** *Ibid.* II. 467 Amidazobenzene.. forms the chief constituent of commercial aniline yellow.

amidated (ˈæmɪdeɪtɪd), *ppl. a. Chem.* Converted into an amide.

1878 Kingzett *Anim. Chem.* 31 The majority..consist of alcohols, acids, amidated acids, and amines.

amide ('æmaɪd, ə'maɪd; the latter always in comb.). *Chem.* [f. AM(MONIA) + -IDE.]

†**1.** *orig.* A name given to the first-discovered derivatives of ammonia (NH_3), in which one atom of H was exchanged for a metal or organic radical, acid or basic; these being viewed as compounds of the *metal*, etc. with a hypothetical radical *amidogen*, NH_2. (Since the discovery of the actual relations of these 'amides' to the 'imides' and 'nitriles,' the compound ammonias have been rearranged according to the nature of the replacing radical, as *amides*, *amines*, and *alkalamides*. The present sense of 'amide' is therefore at once wider and more restricted than the original. See next.)

1850 DAUBENY *Atom. The.* viii. (ed. 2) 237 Compounds of NH_2 have been hitherto called amides.. but this name will probably be now discarded. **1854** SCOFFERN in Orr *Circ. Sc.*, *Chem.* 503 Others believe it to be an amide of metallic silver. **1863** WATTS *Dict. Chem.* (1872) I. 169 [Potassamine] was regarded as a compound of NH_2 (*amidogen*) with potassium, NH_2K, and called *amide* of potassium, analogous to the cyanide CNK. In process of time, compounds came to be discovered.. in which 2 or 3 atoms of hydrogen were replaced by metals or compound radicles, to which the name amide in its original sense of a compound containing amidogen, NH_2, was plainly inapplicable; accordingly these compounds were designated by other names *imides*, *nitriles*, &c.

2. *Mod. Chem.* Generic name of the compound ammonias derived from one or more molecules of common ammonia (NH_3), by exchanging 1, 2, or all 3 hydrogen atoms for acid radicals of equivalent acidity.

According to the number of ammonia molecules represented, they are denominated *Monamides*, *Diamides*, *Triamides*, &c., all of which may be *primary*, *secondary*, or *tertiary*, according as ⅓, ⅔, or the whole of the hydrogen is replaced. The nature of the replacing radicals (or related acids) is shown by prefixing their names (contracted), as *Acet-amide*, *Tri-acet-amide*, *Ox-amide*, *Succin-amide*, *Cyan-amide*, *Phosph-amide*, *Phenyl-di-benz-amide*. *Primary* amides may be viewed as formed from organic acids by substituting one atom of amidogen (NH_2) for one of hydroxyl (HO); they form one half of the earlier 'amides' in sense 1, the other half being now AMINES. The *secondary* and *tertiary* amides are the acid members of the former 'imides' and 'nitriles.'

1863 WATTS *Dict. Chem.* (1872) I. 169 Ammonias in which 1 or more atoms of hydrogen are replaced by an *acid*-radicle: to this division we propose to confine the name of 'amides.' *Ibid.* 170 Primary amides are mostly solid and crystalline, easily fusible, neutral to test paper, volatile without decomposition. **1879** *Syd. Soc. Lex.* s.v., Most of the nitrogenous animal bases are amides.

3. Extended to compounds intermediate between amides proper and AMINES: see ALKALAMIDES.

4. *acid amide*: a body uniting the types of an amide and an acid, also called AMIC or *amidic acid*, and ALANINE, q.v. ***amide-base***: earlier name for a primary AMINE.

amidic (ə'maɪdɪk), *a. Chem.* [f. AMIDE + -IC.] Of or derived from an amide; as in ***amidic acid***, the same as acid amide, or amic acid.

1877 WATTS *Fownes' Chem.* II. 379 The acid amides thus formed [by replacement of the alcoholic hydroxyl] are called amic or amidic acids.

amidide ('æmɪdaɪd). *Chem.* [f. AMIDE + -IDE.] A simple compound of amidogen with another element or complex radical.

1854 PEREIRA *Mat. Med.* (ed. 4) I. 437 The amidide of hydrogen (ammonia). **1869** *Eng. Mech.* 19 Mar. 581/3 It was proposed to regard the two molecules.. as an amidide of ammonium NH_4, NH_2.

amidin ('æmɪdɪn). *Chem.* [f. *amid-* the common Romanic form of L. *amyl-um* starch (as in Fr. *amid-on*, etc.) + -IN.]

1. The soluble matter of starch found in the interior of the granules.

1833 *Penny Cycl.* I. 452 One hundred parts of potato starch.. yielded 17 of amidine, 30·4 of sugar, 17·2 of gum, and some unaltered starch.

2. Starch in a state of solution, gelatinous and transparent.

1839 HOOPER *Med. Dict.* 84 Caventou says that the amidine is formed at once by the action of the hot water on the starch. **1879** in *Syd. Soc. Lex.*

amidmost (ə'mɪdməʊst, -əst), *adv.* and *prep. poet.* [mod.f. *amid* or *midmost* (itself a modern word), perh. influenced by the app. superlative form of AMIDST. Nothing similar in ME.]

A. *adv.* In the very middle or centre. **B.** *prep.* (by elision) In the very centre of.

1870 MORRIS *Earthly Par.* II. iii. 37 He.. stopped amidmost of the hall. *Ibid.* III. IV. 52 A.. lake Amidmost which the fowl did take Their pastime.

amido- (ə'maɪdəʊ), combining form of AMIDE; used also in the phrases ***amido compounds***, ***amido derivatives***, i.e. those in which one atom of hydrogen is replaced by an atom of the radical amidogen NH_2, as ***amido-benzine*** (= ANILINE), ***amido-ethane*** (= ETHYLAMINE), ***amido-methane*** (= METHYLAMINE), ***amido-caproic acid***, etc.

For recent use see AMINO- and quot. 1949.

1854 PEREIRA *Mat. Med.* (ed. 4) I. 938 Amido-chloride of mercury. **1864** *Reader* 18 June 782/1 The fluorescence of two new substances—amidophthalic and amidoterephthalic acid. **1873** FOWNES *Chem.* 683 Alanine, or amidopropionic acid. *Ibid.* 760 It is converted into amidobenzene or aniline. **1877** WATTS *Fownes' Chem.* II. 446 Benzene group: amido derivatives. *Ibid.*, Only one nitro-group is obtained in the first instance, so that nitro-amido compounds are obtained. **1881** THUDICHUM *Ann. Chem. Med.* II. viii, On the Albuminous Substances, Amides, Amido-Acids, and Ammonium Salts as Sources of the Urea. **1949** S. & L. M. MIALL *New Dict. Chem.* 29/2 The prefix amido.. is now usually restricted to compounds containing the amide group (—$CO.NH_2$).

amidogen (ə'maɪdədʒɛn). *Chem.* [f. AMIDO- + -GEN[2] 'producer.'] A name for the combination of nitrogen with two equivalents of hydrogen NH_2 (equal to ammonia minus one of its hydrogen atoms), viewed as the hypothetical radical of the primary amides and amines.

1850 DAUBENY *Atom. The.* viii. (ed. 2) 248 Amidogen.. seems to have no real independent existence, but to be a name expressive only of ammonia, in which 1 of its hydrogen atoms is replaced by an equivalent of some hydrocarbon. **1880** CLEMENSHAW tr. *Wurtz, Atom. The.* 263 All attempts have as yet been unsuccessful to isolate double *amidogen*.

amidol ('æmɪdɒl). [f. AMIDE + -OL.] A trade name for a salt of diamidophenol, used as a developer in photography.

1894 *Brit. Jrnl. Photogr. Alm.* 830 Diamidophenol or amidol, both as the chlorhydrate and the sulphate, was originally prepared by T. Gauche in 1869. **1961** A. L. M. SOWERBY *Dict. Photogr.* (ed. 19) 20 Amidol gives very little fog, and has been recommended for tropical development.

amidone ('æmɪdəʊn). [f. AMI(NO- + D(IPHENYL + -ONE.] A synthetic analgesic, in action similar to morphine; = METHADONE.

1946 *Pharmaceutical Jrnl.* 16 Nov. 308/1 Amidone or Hoechst 10820 was five to ten times a better analgesic than morphine. **1947** *Lancet* 26 July 146/1 The latest synthetic analgesic, amidone, which is highly active, bears only a slight chemical resemblance to morphine. **1950** *Sci. News Let.* 4 Feb. 67/1 The five new drugs do not produce the vomiting or other stomach and intestinal disturbances of amidone and morphine. **1953** *Pharmaceutical Formulas* (ed. 12) I. 933 Methadone Tablets; Amidone Tablets.

amidships (ə'mɪdʃɪps), *adv.* [prop. a phrase, = 'in the ship's middle, in centre of the ship,' retaining the genitive which originally followed AMID, as in *amid-heaps*. The phr. must therefore be old though our instances begin late.] **a.** In the middle of a ship; *rarely*, to or towards the middle of the ship.

1692 SMITH *Seaman's Gram.* I. xvi. 76 He who cuns the Ship uses these terms to him at Helm, *Starboard, Larboard, Port, Helm a Midships.* **1755** SMOLLETT *Don Quix.* (1803) II. 185 The other.. took us amidships, and laid the side of the bark entirely open. **1833** MARRYAT *Pet. Simple*, The two sheep-pens amidships are full of pigs. **1837** —— *Perc. Keene* xl. (1863) 282 The vessel.. had parted amidships. **1859** M. SCOTT *Tom Cringle* xv. 372, I moved round more amidships. **1873** *Brit. Q. Rev.* Jan., The whole of the protected guns are carried amidships.

b. *transf.* (*colloq.*).

1937 PARTRIDGE *Dict. Slang* 12/1 *Amidships*, on the solar plexus; in or on the belly. **1961** *Times* 11 July 4/7 Buss hit him painfully amidships and he had to leave the field. **1963** BIRD & HUTTON-SCOTT *Veteran Motor Car* 15 A slow-running horizontal engine amidships.

amidst (ə'mɪdst), *prep.* and *adv.* Forms: α. 4 **imyddes, y myddes, emiddes, in myddes.** β. 4–6 **amyddes,** 5 **-is,** 6 **-ys, amiddes, amydes,** 6–7 **amids.** γ. 6 **amidest,** 6–7 **amiddest, amid'st,** (7 **immid'st**), 7– **amidst.** [f. AMID, *a-midde*, with genitive *-s*, added to many advb. phrases. Subseq. corrupted (in the south), by form-assoc. with superlatives, to *-st*. Cf. *amongst*, *against*, *betwixt*. The early variants *y myddes*, *in middes*, shew resolution into the two elements: cf. AMID. Also aphetized MIDST.] There is a tendency to use *amidst* more distributively than *amid*, e.g. of things scattered about, or a thing moving, in the midst of others.

A. *adv.*

1. In the middle or central part. †**a.** *absol. Obs.*

1509 HAWES *Past. Pleas.* XXXII. 158 The rofe was golde, and amiddes A carbuncle.

b. with *of*. (In prose usually *in* (*the*) *midst of*.)

c **1384** CHAUCER *H. of Fame* 714 Right even in myddes of the way. **1483** CAXTON *Gold. Leg.* 278/4 A right fayr sterre whiche shone amyddes of the celle. **1565** T. STAPLETON *Bede's Hist. Ch. Eng.* 66 Warme with a softe fyre burning amidest therof. *a* **1628** SIR J. BEAUMONT *Poems* Immid'st of flames, or through the raging tide. **1868** MORRIS *Earthly Par.* I. 141 Amidst of these. *Ibid.* II. 279 Amidst of spring.

B. *prep.*

1. In or into the middle or centre of. **a.** with *sing. sb.*

α. *a* **1300** *Cursor M.* 655 Yon a tre.. þat standis emiddes [*Cott.* in midward, *Trin.* amidde] paradis. *c* **1340** HAMPOLE *Pr. Consc.* 6451 Als þe yholk ymyddes þe egge lys.. Right swa es þe erthe.. Ymyddes þe hevens þat gas obout. **1393** LANGL. *P. Pl.* C. XI. 33 A man in a bot · in-myddes a brode water. *c* **1400** *Destr. Troy* XII. 4957 Ymyddes the halle Was a tre.. all of tru gold.

β. *c* **1400** *Destr. Troy* XXI. 8774 Þo maisturs gert make, amyddes his hede, A hole þurgh his herne-pon. *c* **1450** LONELICH *Grail* xiv. 619 Amyddes the Feld there it lay. **1480** CAXTON *Chron. Eng.* ccviii. 190 The Communers.. token the bisshop and led hym amyddes Chepe. **1509** HAWES *Past. Pleas.* XXIX. 141 She did him up wynde, Amiddes the wall, and left hym there.. fyve fadom and more from the grounde. **1607** TOPSELL *Four-footed Beasts* (1673) 131 They plunge amids the water and passe the stream with their pawes.

γ. **1595** EDWARDES in *Shaks. Cent. Praise* 18 Amid'st the Center of this clime. **1667** MILTON *P.L.* IX. 661 The fruit of this fair tree amidst The garden. **1692** E. WALKER *Epictetus* (1737) Prol., Pensive, amidst the bellowing throng. **1866** G. MACDONALD *Ann. Q. Neighb.* xxx. (1878) 526 And died amidst a circle of friends.

b. with *pl. sb.* (Often becoming less definite = Amongst, surrounded by.)

β. *c* **1450** LONELICH *Grail* xlvi. 167 Amyddes the stretes.. they maden ful gret hepes. *Ibid.* li. 122 Amyddis his bretherin twelve. **1614** CHAPMAN *Odyss.* XIII. 261 Lost, Amids the moving waters.

γ. *c* **1590** MARLOWE *Dido* I. i. 369 Build his throne amidst those starry towers. **1605** CAMDEN *Rem.* 100 A plaine amiddest woods. **1697** DRYDEN *Virg. Georg.* IV. 677 And dared amidst the trembling Ghosts to sing. **1709** STRYPE *Ann. Ref.* I. xx. 239 A noble woman.. who died amidst the tormentors hands. **1762** HUME *Hist. Eng.* (1806) III. 320 Amidst his friends and vassals. **1842** BORROW *Bible in Sp.* (1849) 59 The road.. winding amidst thickets of broom and brushwood. **1853** THACKERAY *Eng. Hum.* iv. 202 Amidst the fumes of tobacco.

2. Of state, condition, or surrounding circumstances: Amongst, in the course of. **a.** with *sing. sb.*

c **1386** CHAUCER *Monkes T.* 739 Yet was he caught amyddes al his pride. *a* **1541** WYATT *Poet. Wks.* (1861) 66 Unless I sterve, For hunger still amiddes my food. **1613** PURCHAS *Pilgr.* I. I. xiii. 61 Amiddest the which hee fell asleepe. **1620** BP. HALL *Hon. Marr. Clergie* Concl., It was written.. amids the heat of contention. **1756** C. LUCAS *Ess. Waters* III. Ded., To smile amidst adversity. **1849** MACAULAY *Hist. Eng.* I. 535 Amidst the splendour and festivity of a court. **1866** G. MACDONALD *Ann. Q. Neighb.* ii. (1878) 19 Amidst the downward sweep of events.

b. with *pl. sb.*

a **1604** HANMER *Chron. Irel.* 108 Amids the warres of France, Flanders, and England. **1659** *Gentl. Calling* (1696) 65 Amidst all the seducements of Wealth. **1711** ADDISON *Spect.* No. 7 ¶6 Amidst all the evils that threaten me. **1794** S. WILLIAMS *Hist. Vermont* 162 Which is never found amidst the refinements of polished societies. **1849** SIR J. STEPHEN *Ess. Eccl. Biogr.* I. 253 Amidst his ascetic follies. *Ibid.* 275 Amidst the funeral rites, the soldered coffin had been opened.

amidulin (ə'mɪdjʊlɪn). *Chem.* [f. Fr. *amid-on* starch + -ULE diminutive + -IN chem. formative.] A soluble preparation of starch, resembling sago.

1879 *Syd. Soc. Lex.*, *Amidulin* is slowly deposited in white flocculi.

†**a'midward**, *adv.* and *prep. Obs.* [f. AMID + -WARD, analogously to *after-ward*, *down-ward*. OE. had no *on middan weard* or *on midde weard*.]

A. *adv.* Towards or near the middle or centre.

c **1420** *Pallad. on Husb.* IV. 631 Choppe of that amydwarde in the tree. **1513** DOUGLAS *Æneis* V. vi. 9 Euin amydwart in his trone.. [he] takin has his sete.

B. *prep.* Towards or near the middle of.

c **1300** *K. Alis.* 690 An horn the forhed amydward. *c* **1380** *Sir Ferumb.* 1332 Þe chambre stod oppon þe se: amidward a roch of stone. *c* **1400** *Cursor M.* 655 (Fairf. MS.) Yonder tre .. þat standes amidwarde [*Cott.* in midward] paradyse.

‖**amigo** (ə'miːgəʊ). *colloq.* (chiefly *U.S.*). [Sp., friend.] Esp. in Spanish-speaking areas: a friend or comrade; freq. as a form of address.

1837 *N.Y. Mirror* 30 Dec. 209/1 An overworked, spavined, broken-down set—but adios, Amigo. **1880** *News & Press* (Cimarron, New Mexico) 26 Feb. 3/2 Our old amigo P. M. Davenport. **1910** [see KRAG-JØRGENSEN]. **1935** M. ANDERSON *Winterset* II. 107 Don't try using your firearms, amigo baby. **1962** 'K. ORVIS' *Damned & Destroyed* XV. 112 'Listen, amigo,' he said. **1984** *New Yorker* 23 Apr. 49/2 'Have a really wonderful time.' 'Thanks, amigo,' I said.

amil, variant of AMEL, *Obs.*, enamel.

amil, variant and more modern form of AUMIL.

1898 *Daily News* 15 Aug. 6/2 They kept the amils (native revenue officials) at bay. **1921** *Times Lit. Suppl.* 10 Feb. 84/4 The *amil* was exacting.. 66 per cent. more than the authorized revenue.

†**a-mi-la.** *Mus. Obs.* The note A which is *mi* in one hexachord and *la* in another.

1760 STILES *Anc. Grk. Mus.* in *Phil. Trans.* LI. 772 He.. affirming.. that the Dorian mode answered exactly to our A-mi-la with a minor third, and the Phrygian to our A-mi-la with a major third.

‖**amildar** ('æməldɑː(r)). [a. Pers. and Urdu *ʿamal-dār*, f. Arab. *ʿamal* work + Pers. *dār* holding, holder (a common agential formative).] A native factor, manager, or agent, in India; *esp.* a collector of revenue.

1799 WELLINGTON in Gurwood *Desp.* I. 47 Never to pass over any disrespect from the amildars to the officers. **1804** —— *ibid.* III. 38, I know the character of.. every Mahratta amildar.

†**a'minded**, *pa. pple. Obs.* [f. A *particle* = ȝe- and MINDED.] Minded.

1578 in *Test. Ebor.* xxiii, Amynded with myselfe to make my Will. **1608** in *Eccl. Proc. Bp. Durh.*, He was aminded to send to Duresme. *a* **1640** JACKSON *Creed* XI. xxxii. Wks. XI. 19 Thou art better aminded towards him.

amine ('æmaɪn, ə'maɪn; the latter always in comb). *Chem.* [f. AM(MONIA) + -INE.]

Generic name of the *compound ammonias*, in which one or more of the three hydrogen atoms in ammonia, NH_3, are exchanged for alcohol or other positive radicals, as methyl, ethyl, phenyl, or for a metal, as potassium, platinum, zinc.

They are distinguished as *Monamines, Diamines, Triamines*, according to the number of ammonia molecules represented in the molecule of the compound; each of which may be *primary, secondary*, or *tertiary*, according as ⅓, ⅔, or the whole of the hydrogen is replaced. The nature of the replacing radical or element is shown by prefixing its name, as in primary amines, *Methylamine, Ethylamine, Phenylamine, Platinamine, Potassamine, Zincamine*; or, in secondary and tertiary amines, in the case of two or three replacements by the *same* radical, *Di-ethylamine, Tri-potassamine*, or by *different* radicals as *Methyl-ethylamine, Di-methyl-ethylamine* (NH_3, in which 2 atoms of H are replaced by methyl, and 1 by ethyl), *Methyl-ethyl-amylamine* (containing one atom each of methyl, ethyl, and amyl, in union with the nitrogen of the original ammonia). *Primary* amines were originally included under AMIDES in the earlier sense; they may be represented as derived from the paraffins by substitution of amidogen, NH_2, for hydrogen, or from the alcohols by substitution of amidogen for hydroxyl.

1863 WATTS *Dict. Chem.* (1872) I. 169 Ammonias in which 1 or more atoms of hydrogen are replaced by base-radicles. This division we call 'amines.' **1869** ROSCOE *Elem. Chem.* 146 It is a true amine. **1879** *Syd. Soc. Lex.* s.v., The amines are basic compounds, capable of uniting with acids and forming salts.. The lower members of the group are gases, the higher oily liquids.

†**a'minish**, *v. Obs.* Forms: 5 **amynusshe, amenyshe**, 6 **amynysshe**. [Refashioned from earlier AMENUSE; cf. *diminish*.] To make less, lessen, diminish.

1477 EARL RIVERS (Caxton) *Dictes* 33 It is better to amynusshe that hurteth than to encresse that helpeth. **1493** in *Test. Ebor.* IV. 26 Not to amenyshe my wife's parte. **1530** PALSGR. 426/2, I amynysshe, I lessyn or make lesse, *Je amenuise*. I dare nat amynysshe it for feare I marre all togyther.

amino- ('æmɪnəʊ, ə'maɪnəʊ, ə'miːnəʊ), *Chem.*, combining form of AMINE, used *spec.* in names of compounds containing the group NH_2 combined with a non-acid radical (thus distinguished from AMIDO-, which in strict use denotes those with an acid radical). Also used without hyphen as a quasi-*adj.* Examples: **amin(o-)a'cetic acid** = GLYCINE; **amino-acid**, one of an important class of organic compounds represented by the general formula $NH_2{\cdot}R{\cdot}COOH$, in which R is an aliphatic radical, having both basic and acidic properties; **aminoben'zoic acid**, a crystalline acid, $NH_2{\cdot}C_6H_4{\cdot}COOH$, of which the name of the ortho-compound is anthranilic acid; **amino'phenol**, one of a group of aromatic compounds of the type $NH_2{\cdot}C_6H_4OH$, used as components of certain dyes; **amino'phyllin(e)**, a compound of theophylline and ethylenediamine, used as a diuretic and cardiotonic; **aminoplastic**, a plastic or synthetic resin derived from certain amino (or amido) compounds; also *attrib.* or *adj.* and in the shortened form '**aminoplast**; also ***amino resin***; **ami'nopterin** [shortened from *amino-pteroyl-glutamic* + -IN], also called *4-aminopteroyl glutamic acid*, a yellow crystalline compound used in the treatment of some kinds of leukæmia, as an insecticide, etc.

1887 A. M. BROWN *Anim. Alkaloids* 85 The modes of syntheses of glycocolle or aminacetic acid and cyanide. **1898** *Jrnl. Chem. Soc.* LXXIV. 845/2 Glycocine (*amino-acetic acid*), as the chief amino-acid of sugar-cane. **1901** *Jrnl. Chem. Soc.* LXXX. I. 190 The acidity of an amino-acid depends on the electrochemical character of the groups near to the amino-nitrogen atom. **1904** *Ibid.* LXXXVI. I. 664 Electrolytic preparation of p-Aminophenol and its derivatives. *Ibid.* 806 p-Aminobenzoic acid may be acetylated by heating its sodium salt with glacial acetic acid. **1904** GOODCHILD & TWENEY *Technol. & Sci. Dict.* 15/2 Benzene is C_6H_6; the compound $C_6H_5NH_2$ is amino-benzene, commonly called aniline. *Ibid.*, Amino compounds have the group NH_2 replaced by OH when acted on by nitrous acids. **1906** *Jrnl. Soc. Chem. Ind.* XXV. 585/1 Manufacture of Aminophenols. **1910** *Encycl. Brit.* III. 756/2 Ortho-amino-benzoic acid, $C_6H_4 \cdot NH_2 \cdot COOH$ (anthranilic acid), is closely related to indigo. *Ibid.* V. 305/1 By the reduction of nitro-phenols, the corresponding aminophenols are obtained, and of these, the meta- and para- derivatives are the most important. **1910** *Practitioner* June 823 Practically all proteins are broken down by hydrolysis into the various amino-acids, out of which they were originally formed. **1934** *Chem. Abstr.* 7364 Action of theophylline-ethylenediamine (aminophyllin, metaphyllin) varied considerably. **1936** *Mod. Plastics* Oct. 312/1 *Aminoplast*, general term for synthetic resins from amino or amido compounds. **1938** *Brit. Plastics* IX. 387 Amino-Plastics.. Increased attention [has been] given to amino- and other plastics. **1940** *Brit Jrnl. Exper. Path.* XXI. 89, *p*-amino-benzoic acid has high activity in antagonizing sulphanilamide inhibition.. . There is strong circumstantial evidence that the yeast factor may be *p*-aminobenzoic acid. **1940** *Jrnl. R. Aeronaut. Soc.* XLVI. 60 'Kaurit' synthetic resin glue was used, a glue which is based on aminoplastics. **1945** *New Biol.* I. 16 Another 1·5 per cent [of a potato] consists in the main of amino acids. **1948** *Lancet* 2 Oct. 540/1 Aminopterin is a folic-acid antagonist. **1953** *Sci. News.* XXIX. 70 As a result of the protein breakdown there is a great increase in the amino-acid content of the cheese. **1955** *Sci. News Let.* 14 May 313/3 Chemicals like colchicine and aminopterin prevent cell division. *Ibid.* 28 May 345/2 She was given penicillin, digoxin for the heart, sedatives, morphine, aminophylline and streptomycin. **1958** *Times Rev. Industry* Feb. 77/2 Aminoplastic resins.. showed a 20 per cent. increase on last year. **1958** *Times* 5 July 10/7 A number of *o*-amino-phenols are now known to induce cancer in the bladder. **1958** *Oxford Mail* 7 Oct. 1/1 The Pope's personal physician at one time administered aminophyllin and eupaperin when the signs of circulatory trouble in the brain set in. **1959** *Chambers's Encycl.* III. 361/1 The amino-acids, such as amino-acetic acid or glycine, $CH_2(NH_2).COOH$, are amphoteric substances, being both acidic and basic; they are of particular interest in biochemistry as the final products of the hydrolysis of proteins, such as egg-white, haemoglobin, collagen, and keratins. **1964** N. G. CLARK *Mod. Org. Chem.* xii. 233 The characteristic functional group of primary amines, $-NH_2$, is called 'amino-'; similarly, the simplest group characteristic of a tertiary amine, $(CH_3)_2N-$, is known as 'dimethylamino-'. *Ibid.* xxii. 446 A poly-functional derivative [of the aromatic amines], *p*-aminobenzoic acid, is widely distributed in nature in small amounts, and is an essential dietary factor for many bacteria and higher animals.

‖**'amiot.** *Obs.* [Fr. *amiot* 'a kind of Peare whereof most excellent perrie is made.' Cotgr.] (See quot.)

1616 SURFL. & MARKH. *Countr. Farme* 417 The Amiot Peare is commended aboue all the rest, whereof likewise is made the Perrie, called waxen Perrie.

amir, variant of AMEER.

amiral, -el, -eld, obs. forms of ADMIRAL.

Amish ('æmɪʃ, eɪ-), *a.* [app. ad. G. *amisch*, f. Jacob *Amen* or *Amman* or *Ammon*, a Swiss Mennonite preacher active at the end of the 17th cent. + -ISH[1].] Of, belonging to, or characteristic of, a strict sect of the Mennonite church in the United States. Also as *sb.*

1844 RUPP *Relig. Denom.* 560 [Account of the] Omish or Amish Church. **1880** [see HOOKER[1] 2]. **1884** *Schaff's Relig. Encycl.* III. 2404/1 The Mennonites and the Amish baptize by pouring. **1960** *Commentary* XXIX. 530/2 No one is guilty unless one follows a fundamentalist Amish point of view.

amiss (ə'mɪs), *adv.*, *pred. a.*, and *sb.* Forms: 3 **a mis, 4 a mysse, 4–5 a mys**, (4 **of mys**, 5 **of mysse, on mys**), 3–6 **amys**, 5–6 **amysse**, 6–7 **amisse**, 7– **amiss.** [prop. phrase, A *prep.*[1] of manner + MISS *sb.* failure, deficiency, shortcoming.]

A. *adv.*, *gen. sign.* Away from the mark, not up to the mark, out of course, out of order.

1. Erroneously, in a way that goes astray of, or misses its object.

a **1250** *Owl & Night.* 1363 3if me hit wile turne a mis. **1330** R. BRUNNE *Chron.* 164 þei red him alle a mysse, þat conseil gaf þerto. *c* **1374** CHAUCER *Boeth.* III. xi. 100 False proposicious that goon amys fro the trouthe. **1480** CAXTON *Chron. Eng.* ccxliv. 298 Our Archyers shet neuer arowe amys. **1535** COVERDALE *Job* xxxiv. 32 Yf I haue gone amysse [WYCLIF errid], enfourme me. **1627** MAY *Lucan* II. 439 Phæton amisse did guide The day. **1755** YOUNG *Centaur* iii. Wks. 1757 IV. 182 If he judges amiss in the supreme point. **1827** KEBLE *Chr. Year* Easter Day, Your wisdom guides amiss To seek on earth a Christian's bliss.

2. Faultily, defectively; in a way that falls short of its object, or with which fault may be found.

c **1386** CHAUCER *Manc. T.* 145 'By God,' quod he, 'I synge not amys.' **1393** LANGL. *P. Pl.* C. II. 174 þe same mesure þat ȝe meteþ · amys oþer ellys. **1579** *News fr. North* in *Thynne's Animadv.* Pref. 133, I am sure I cannot be lodged amisse in this house. **1654** GATAKER *Disc. Apol.* 49 The Doctor.. had miscarried in his suit by joining issu amiss. **1846** KEBLE *Lyra Innoc.* (1873) 67 That widow poor Who only offered not amiss.

3. Hence, *euphem.* Wrongly, in a wrong way.

c **1380** *Sir Ferumb.* 4103 Rayner, þou spekest al amys. *c* **1450** *Merlin* i. 5 Ye sey amysse, for god hateth no creature. **1550** CROWLEY *Epigr.* 682 For doubtlesse those goodes are gotten amisse. **1633** G. HERBERT *Self-Condemn.* ii. in *Temple* 165 He that doth love, and love amisse This world's delights before true Christian joy. **1833** HT. MARTINEAU *Briery Creek* vi. 123 Apt to see wrong, and speak amiss, and do the very reverse of what he ought to do.

4. to come or **happen amiss**: to come or happen out of order, untowardly, or contrary to one's wishes or expectations.

1666 EVELYN *Mem.* (1857) I. 252 Sometimes we shot at fowls and other birds: nothing came amiss. **1836** *Johnsoniana* I. 75 He chatted gaily..as if nothing had happened amiss. **1857** BUCKLE *Civilis.* vi. 282 Nothing came amiss to their greedy and credulous ears.

5. to do, deal, or **act amiss**: to act erroneously, to err; *euphem.* to do wrong.

1297 R. GLOUC. 54 My neuew, þat a lytel dude amys. *c* **1384** CHAUCER *H. of Fame* 269 A woman dothe amys To loue hym that vnknowe ys. *c* **1400** *Deo Gracias* (Turnb. 1843) 162 Amende that thou has done of mysse. *c* **1420** *Chron. Vilod.* 279 When ony mon dude on mys. **1535** COVERDALE *Ps.* cv. 6 We haue synned with oure fathers, we haue done amysse. **1612** DEKKER *If it be not good* 313 Looke not to prosper, if thou dealst amisse. **1792** *Anecd. Pitt* I. iv. 60 We are convinced that something has been done amiss. **1870** BRYANT *Homer* I. II. 44 And soon will punish those Who act amiss.

6. to take (a thing) **amiss**: *orig.* to miss its meaning, mistake (i.e. *(a)miss-take*); *now*, to misinterpret its *motive* or to interpret it in a bad sense, to take offence at.

c **1380** WYCLIF *3 Treat.* i. 18 þis dreem takun a mys turneþ upsedoun þe chirche. *c* **1538** STARKEY *England* i. 9 You take the mater amys. **1638** CHILLINGWORTH *Relig. Prot.* I. i. §5. 33 So might we justly take it amisse, that.. you are not more willing to consider us. **1780** JOHNSON *Lett.* 238 II. 139 You ..therefore cannot take it amiss that I have never written. **1865** TROLLOPE *Belton Estate* iii. 26 You will not take it amiss if I take a cousin's privilege.

b. So, **to think amiss.**

1635 SWAN *Spec. Mund.* v. §2 (1643) 133 To think otherwise were to think amisse. **1702** POPE *Jan. & May* 809 None judge so wrong as those who think amiss. **1714** FORTESCUE-ALAND *Fortescue's Abs. & Lim. Mon.* Ded. 3, I am persuaded, he would not think amiss of my conduct. **1770** GOLDSM. *Haunch Ven.* 123 So, perhaps, in your habits of thinking amiss, You may make a mistake, and think slightly of this.

B. quasi-*adj.* [In construction with vb. *to be*, *amiss*, which properly belongs to the vb., is referred to the subject, and treated as an adj.; and hence extended to more distinct adjectival constructions. Cf. *matters went far amiss*; *matters were somewhat amiss*; *I found matters amiss*; *it would not be amiss to do so.* Never used *attrib.*]

1. Out of order: not in accord with the recognized good order of morality, society, custom, nature, bodily health, etc. etc.; deficient, faulty.

c **1315** SHOREHAM 144 3ef he..couthe and dede hyȝt nouȝt, Hyt were a-mys. **1473** WARKW. *Chron.* 12 He schulde ..amende alle manere of thynges that was amysse. **1580** SIDNEY *Arcadia* II. (1590) 223 Saying still the world was amisse. **1605** SHAKS. *Macb.* II. iii. 102 *Don.* What is amisse? *Macb.* You are, and doe not know't. **1754** RICHARDSON *Grandison* IV. ii. 19, I hear something very much amiss of this man. **1871** NAPHEYS *Prev. & Cure Dis.* III. ii. 625 The taste is nearly always amiss in illness.

2. *esp.* negatively, ***not amiss***: not beside the mark, not improper, quite in keeping with the object in view.

1513 MORE *Edw. V*, Ded., I have thought it not amisse to put to my helping hand. **1651** HOBBES *Leviath.* III. xlii. 314 It will not be amisse to lay open the Consequences. **1756** BURKE *Subl. & B.* Wks. I. 180 However it may not be amiss to add to these remarks. **1778** JOHNSON *Lett.* 198 II. 41 It is good to speak dubiously about futurity. It is likewise not amiss to hope. **1855** TENNYSON *Maud* I. xix. 82 Kind to Maud? That were not amiss.

b. Of the quality of objects.

1860 HAWTHORNE *Marble Faun* (1879) II. xxiv. 243 She was not amiss..but her companion was far the handsomer figure. *Ibid.* (1860) I. xxiii. 253 As an angel, you are not amiss.

†**C.** *sb.* [The *adv.* or *adj.* used subst. *quasi* 'a doing *amiss*' or 'a thing which is *amiss*'; perhaps partly due to formal confusion between *a miss* 'an error,' and *a-miss* 'in error.'] An error, fault, or misdeed; hence *euphem.* an evil deed. *Obs.*

1477 NORTON *Ord. Alch.* in Ashm. (1652) v. 65 Without amisse. **1590** LODGE *Gold. Leg.* in Halliw. *Shaks.* VI. 43 He [shall] receive meed for his amisse. **1602** SHAKS. *Haml.* IV. v. 18 Each toy seemes Prologue, to some great amisse. **1643** *Actors' Remonstr.* (1869) 265 We will..reforme all our disorders, and amend all our amisses. *c* **1700** *Rich. II* in Evans *Old Bal.* (1784) No. 410. 300 The nobles of England their prince's amiss, By parliament soon did rebate.

amissibility (ə,mɪsɪ'bɪlɪtɪ). *rare.* [a. Fr. *amissibilité*, f. *amissible*: see next and -BILITY.] Possibility of being lost; liability to lose.

1636 FEATLY *Clavis Myst.* ii. 16 The amissibility of justifying faith. **1657** BAXTER *Saints' Persev.* 36 The Amissibility of a state of Infant Justification, or rather the cessation of it. **1837** HALLAM *Hist. Lit.* III. iv. §41 The amissibility of sovereign power for misconduct.

amissible (ə'mɪsɪb(ə)l), *a.* [a. Fr. *amissible*, ad. L. *āmissibil-em*, f. *āmiss-* ppl. stem of *āmitt-ĕre* to lose.] Liable to be lost.

1672 JACOMB *Comm. Rom.* viii. (1868) 59 The same grace now..is not amissible as that was. **1777** WESLEY *Wks.* 1872 XI. 442 It [entire Sanctification] is amissible, capable of being lost. **1852** I. TAYLOR *Wesley & Method.* 213 That release from guilty fears which the Gospel affords should be thought of..as amissible.

amissing (ə'mɪsɪŋ), *ppl. a.* [the phrase *a-missing* (see A *prep.*[1] 12, 13) erroneously taken as a single word, as if from a vb. to *amiss*; chiefly in Scotch writers.] = MISSING; wanting.

1634–46 J. ROW (father) *Hist. Kirk* (1842) 131 The Kirk-Register being amissing. **1680** KID in *Spirit of Popery* 7 A Publick Spirit in contending for God..is much amissing amongst us. **1753** *Stewart's Trial* App. 84 The deponent.. does not know by what means the said lock..now amissing, was lost. **1854** H. MILLER *Sch. & Schm.* (1858) 10 Only his sloop was amissing. **1873** BURTON *Hist. Scotl.* V. lvii, Examined as to what he had done with the valuables amissing.

†a'mission. *Obs.* [a. Fr. *amission*, ad. L. *āmissiōn-em* loss, losing, n. of action f. *āmitt-ĕre* to lose, f. *ā* off + *mittĕre* to send, let go.] Loss.
1623 AILESBURY *Serm.* 11 In amission, the act is necessarie; in emission, voluntary. **1650** BULWER *Anthropomet.* xiii. 138 [Their] speech hath been very much impaired by the amission of their Fore teeth. **1677** GALE *Crt. Gentiles* III. 8 Again, the amission of God has taken up the name of sin. **1755** in JOHNSON; and in mod. Dicts.

†a'missive, *a. Obs.* [f. *āmiss-* ppl. stem of *āmitt-ĕre* to lose + -IVE, as if ad. L. **āmissīv-us*.] Characterized by, or tending to, loss or deterioration.
1633 T. ADAMS *Exp. 2 Pet.* ii. 9 It [God's Sovereignty] is either amissive, or perfective. **1677** GALE *Crt. Gentiles* II. IV. 260 God cannot change himself. For such a mutation would be either perfective or amissive.

a'missness. ? *Obs. rare*⁻¹. [f. AMISS *a.* + -NESS.] The state of being or doing amiss.
1648 *Brit. Bellman* in *Harl. Misc.* VII. 626 (D.) God forgive us our amissnesses!

amit, earliest form of ADMIT.

†a'mit, *v. Obs.* [a. L. *āmitt-ĕre* to lose: see AMISSION.] To lose. (Rarely with *of*.)
1525 *State Papers Hen. VIII*, IV. 399 It is not thought.. that she [the Queen] shulde amitte or loose any parte of her autorite. **1609** SKENE *Reg. Maj.* 30 The wife may tine and amit her Dowrie. **1664** POWER *Exp. Philos.* III. 157 If a Magnet itself be made red hot in the fire, it.. amits the Magnetical vigour. **1756** C. LUCAS *Ess. Waters* II. 10 The water amits of its pellucidity.

†amit(e, *sb. Obs.* Also 4-9 **amyt(e,** 5 **amitt,** 7 **ammit.** [a. OFr. *amit* (now *amict*, pron. *ami*):—L. *amict-um*: see AMICT and AMICE, the latter of which became the common form in 14th c.]

1. *gen.* A cloth for wrapping round, a handkerchief, scarf, etc.
1382 WYCLIF *Heb.* i. 12 Thou schalt chaunge hem as an amyte [**1388** cloth; Vulg. *amictum*] *or girdyng aboute*, and thei schulen be chaungid. **1451** in Gardner *Hist. Dunwich* (1754) 148 Cloth for Amyts and Girdelys.

2. *Eccl.* The white amice worn by priests.
1330 R. BRUNNE *Chron.* 319 Of preste þou has no merke, albe ne non amite. *c* **1470** *Lib. Dom. Edw. IV* in *Househ. Ord.* (1790) 85 The surplyces of singers of chapelles, and awbes, amittes. **1496** *Dives & Paup.* (W. de Worde) VIII. viii. 331/2 The amyt on his hede at the begynnynge betokneth the cloth that crystus face was hyled with in time of his passyon. **1683** OLDHAM *Wks.* (1686) 91 Their Motly Habits, Maniples, and Stoles, Albs, Ammits, Rochets, Chimers, Hoods, and Cowls. **1811** J. GRANT *Hist. Eng. Ch.* I. 159 Their appendages of albs, amyts, stoles, maniples, and girdles.

3. By confusion for *aumusse* AMICE²: A hood, upon a gown or cloak.
1382 WYCLIF *Ex.* xxxix. 21 And thei maden the coope coote [**1388** the coop coot *or aube*] al iacynctyne; and a hode [**1388** hood *or the amyt*; Vulg. *capitium*] in the ouerest parti.

amitotic (æmɪ'tɒtɪk, ˌeɪmaɪ'tɒtɪk), *a. Biol.* [ad. G. *amitotisch* (W. Flemming *Zellsubstanz* (1882) 376), f. A- 14 + MITOTIC *a.*] Of or pertaining to the division of a nucleus and hence of a cell without mitosis. So **amitosis** (-'əʊsɪs), amitotic division; **ami'totically** *adv.*
1888 ROLLESTON & JACKSON *Anim. Life* Introd. p. xxii, The.. division of the nucleus.. may be direct or amitotic... Or it may be indirect or mitotic. **1894** *Nat. Science* June 418 Amitosis is of frequent occurrence in the cells of pathological growths of all kinds. *Ibid.*, The sperm-mother-cells divide amitotically. **1946** *Nature* 23 Nov. 750/2 It has long been known that the micronucleus of ciliates divides mitotically while the macronucleus is amitotic. **1952** A. F. W. HUGHES *Mitotic Cycle* iv. 153 The clearest instances of the formation of binucleate cells by amitosis are seen in glandular tissues of Arthropods.

amitriptyline (æmɪ'trɪptɪliːn). *Pharm.* [f. AMI(NO + TRI- + *he*)*ptyl* s.v. HEPTANE + -INE⁵: cf. PROTRIPTYLINE.] A tricyclic antidepressant drug with sedative properties, $C_{20}H_{23}N$, given as the hydrochloride.
1961 *Lancet* 10 June 1287/2 Amitriptyline hydrochloride ('Tryptizol'), a new antidepressant drug recently released to hospitals. **1963, 1965** [see PROTRIPTYLINE]. **1979** *Daily Tel.* 27 Nov. 12/7 A third of the prescriptions were for imipramine and amitriptyline, and two-thirds of these were for branded products. **1981** *Approved Names* (Brit. Pharmacopœia Comm.) 4 *Amitriptyline*, 3-(10,11-dihydro-5*H*-dibenzo[*a,d*]cyclohepten-5-ylidene)propyldimethyl amine. **1982** *Sci. Amer.* Mar. 112/3 Many of the antidepressant drugs employed in psychiatry, such as amitriptyline (Elavil), block the reuptake of neurotransmitters, but they are not stimulants and they do not induce euphoria.

†'amiture. *Obs. rare*⁻¹. [? a. OFr. **amiture*, repr. L. **amictūra*, or OFr. **amitoire*, ad. L. *amictōrium*, f. *amict-* ppl. stem of *amicīre* to clothe: see AMICT.] Clothing, dress.
c **1300** *K. Alis.* 3975 Yursturday thow come in amiture, Y-armed so on of myne.

amity ('æmɪtɪ). Forms: 5-6 **amytie, -tye, -te, -tey, amite,** 6 **amytee, -itee, -itye,** 6-7 **amitie,** 6- **amity.** [a. Fr. *amitié*, 13th c. *amistié, amisté*, 11th c. *amistet*:—pop. L. **amīcitāt-em* (= L. *amīcitiam*), f. *amīc-us* friend; cf. *mendīcitāt-em* f. *mendīc-us*: see -TY.] Friendship, friendliness; friendly relations; especially of a public character between states or individuals. **a.** *sing.*
? **1450** in *3rd Rep. Comm. Hist. MSS.* (1872) 279/2 The Frenshemen.. enlarge their amite and their aliage to suche as were beste. **1474** CAXTON *Chesse* 80 Amytie is founded vpon honeste. **1483** —— *Gold. Leg.* 137/4 Why wilt thou not abyde in our amyte? **1597** CECIL in Ellis *Orig. Lett.* I. 234 III. 44 The auncient amitie betweene Spain and him. **1631** HEYWOOD *England's Eliz.* (1641) 45 Two brothers.. knit and joyned together in amitie. **1759** ROBERTSON *Hist. Scotl.* I. IV. 290 She declared her resolution to live in perpetual amity with England. **1782** PRIESTLEY *Corr. Chr.* I. Pref. 8 Hostility.. will give place to the most perfect amity. **1868** G. DUFF *Pol. Surv.* 101 Treaties of amity and commerce.

b. *pl. arch.*
1477 SIR J. PASTON in *Lett.* 786 III. 173 The preservacion off the amyteys taken late.. with Fraunce. **1534** LD. BERNERS *Gold. Bk. M. Aurel.* viii. E iv b/1 Suche.. as should be admytted to strait amitees. **1605** BACON *Adv. Learn.* II. ix. §2 (1873) 130 All leagues and amities consist of mutual intelligence and mutual offices. **1739** MELMOTH *Fitzosb. Lett.* (1763) 43 Those little jealousies and rivalships that shoot up in the paths of common amities. **1815** T. JEFFERSON *Writ.* (1830) IV. 264 The less we have to do with the amities or enmities of Europe, the better. **1826** DISRAELI *Viv. Grey* VIII. i. 461 Ancient amities.

amlet, obs. form of OMELET.

amlette, obs. form of AMULET.

‖**amma** ('æmə). *Surg.* [med.L. for Gr. ἅμμα a tie, f. ἅπ-τ-ειν to tie.] A band or truss.
1706 PHILLIPS, *Amma*, A Tying, Knitting, a Band; among Surgeons a Truss us'd in Ruptures. **1719** QUINCY *Lex. Phys.-Med.* 14. **1874** DUNGLISON *Med. Dict.*, *Amma*, Truss.

ammel(l, variant of AMEL, *Obs.*, enamel.

ammelide ('æmɪlaɪd). *Chem.* [f. AM(MONIA) + MEL(AM) + -IDE.] A white powder, $C_6N_9H_9O_3$, or $3\,CyH_2N.CyHO$, produced by the action of concentrated sulphuric acid on melam, melanine, or ammeline; regarded as acid amide of cyanuric acid.
1846 in *Penny Cycl.* 1st Supp. 336/2. **1863** WATTS *Dict. Chem.* II. 287 Ammelide boiled for some time with acids or alkalis is converted into cyanuric acid.

ammeline ('æmɪlaɪn). *Chem.* [f. as prec. + -INE⁴.] A white powder, $2\,CyH_2N.CyHO$, produced by boiling melam with dilute sulphuric acid or with caustic potash; an amic base of cyanuric acid.
1846 *Penny Cycl.* 1st Supp. 336/2 Ammeline.. is composed of very fine silky needles. **1863** WATTS *Dict. Chem.* II. 287 Ammeline is a weak base, forming crystalline salts, which are partially decomposed by water.

‖**'ammeos, ameos.** *Bot. Obs.* [a. Gr. ἄμμεως gen. of ἄμμι, ammi, here taken as nom.] = AMMI.
c **1000** *Sax. Leechd.* II. 192 Oþer swilc hwites cweodowes & ameos. **1585** LLOYD *Treas. Health* N vj, Ameos.. dryueth forth yᵉ stone broken. **1631** MARKHAM *Way to Wealth* I. i. Gloss., Ameos, Comin royal, is a Herb of some called Bulwort, Bishops-weed, or Herb-William. **1712** tr. *Pomet's Hist. Drugs* I. 3 Ameos.. has Leaves like Dill. **1751** CHAMBERS *Cycl.* s.v., According to Lemery, the plant takes its name *ammeos* from αμμος, its seed being very like grains of sand.

ammer, obs. form of EMBER.

ammer ('æmə(r)). *Ornith.* (See quot.)
1843 YARRELL *Brit. Birds* (1856) I. 518 [Yellow Hammer] I have ventured to restore to this bird what I believe to have been its first English name, Yellow *Ammer*.. The word *Ammer* is a well known German term for Bunting.

ammeter ('æmɪtə(r)). [f. AM(PERE) the unit of electric current + -METER measurer.] An instrument for estimating the force of electric currents.
1882 *Nature* 2 Mar. 426 The efficiency [of the battery] was got by measuring the power put in.. by means of Perry and Ayrton's voltameter and ammeter.

ammi ('æmɪ). *Bot.* Also 6 **ami.** [a. L. *ammi*, a. Gr. ἄμμι, connected by some with ἄμμος sand.] A genus of umbelliferous plants, with aromatic leaves; Bishop-weed.
1551 TURNER *Herbal* (1568) 25 Ami hath muche smaller sede, then Cumin; and resembleth organe in taste. **1621** BURTON *Anat. Mel.* III. ii. VI. i, Those opposite meats.. wood-bine, ammi, lettuce, which Lemnius so much commends. **1725** BRADLEY *Fam. Dict.*, *Ammi*, one of the four hot Seeds. The best Ammi is brought out of Candia or Alexandria. **1866** *Treas. Bot.* 51 Common Bishop-weed, *Ammi majus*.

†'ammic, *a. Obs. rare*⁻¹. [f. Gr. ἄμμ-ος sand + -IC, perh. confounded with *ammoniac*.] In **sal ammic,** an old name for sal ammoniac.
1611 COTGR., *Selammoniac*, Salt Ammicke; a medicinable drug resembling stone Allum, and found in long flakes vnder the Cyrenian sand.

ammine ('æmaɪn). *Chem.* [a. G. *ammine* (A. Werner 1897, in *Zeitschr. f. anorg. Chem.* XIV. 23), f. AMM(ONIA + -INE⁵.] A co-ordination compound formed from ammonia and a metallic compound.
1897 *Jrnl. Chem. Soc.* LXXII. II. 263 The ammonia group is designated by the word *ammine* to distinguish it from the *amine* of organic compounds. **1927** N. V. SIDGWICK *Electr. Theory* vii. 111 Platinous chlorine gives a similar series of ammines.

ammiolite ('æmɪəlaɪt, ə'maɪə-). *Min.* [f. Gr. ἄμμιον 'cinnabar in its sandy state, minium,' (f. ἄμμος sand) + -LITE.] A scarlet earthy powder found in Chili, classed by Dana among the Anhydrous Antimonates, containing also copper and mercury.

ammiral, -ant, obs. forms of ADMIRAL.
1623 FAVINE *Theat. Hon.* II. xiii. 236 The Ammirant of Affrica.

‖**a'mmites, a'mites.** *Min. Obs.* [a. Gr. ἀμμίτης sandstone, f. ἄμμος sand.] An obsolete name for Oolite, in reference to its granular structure.
1750 *Leonardus's Mirr. Stones* 75 Amites, is a Stone of the Colour of Alumn or Nitre, but harder than either. **1753** CHAMBERS *Cycl. Supp.*, The Ammites appears to the eye as a composition of large sand.

ammo ('æməʊ). Colloq. abbrev. of AMMUNITION (used esp. of ammunition for small arms). Also *attrib.*
1917 A. G. EMPEY '*Over the Top*' 282 'Ammo'. Rifle ammunition. **1925** FRASER & GIBBONS *Soldier & Sailor Words* 6 *Ammo*, ammunition, e.g., Ammo depot, Ammo store, etc. **1944** *Hutchinson's Pict. Hist. War* Oct. 78 Then you must leave it to the law of averages that the individual tanks, guns, ammo-dumps.. and so on are directly hit. As the bomb strikes rush across the target area you see the petrol and ammo.. bursting into flames. **1946** R. CAMPBELL *Talking Bronco* 28 And we'll hand in our Ammo and Guns As we handed them in once before.

ammo-, comb. form of AMMONIUM, implying conjunction of that basyl with an element, as in *Ammopalladium, Ammopalladammonium.*
1873 FOWNES *Chem.* 430 Ammopalladammonium chloride.

ammocœte ('æməʊsiːt). [ad. mod.L. *Ammocœtes* (formerly thought to be a distinct genus), f. Gr. ἄμμο-ς sand + κοίτη bed.] The larval form of any of various lampreys.
1859 YARRELL *Brit. Fishes* (ed. 3) I. 25 An organ.. becomes the suctorial muscle that distinguishes the Lampern from its Ammocœte. **1926** J. S. HUXLEY *Ess. Pop. Sci.* 209 The lamprey starts independent life as a larva, the so-called ammocoete or lampern. **1959** *Chambers's Encycl.* IV. 313/1 Lampreys undergo a metamorphosis. The larva, or Ammocoete, lives in mud or fine sand. It is toothless, with a transverse lower lip and a hood-like upper lip.

ammodyte ('æmədaɪt). *Zool.* [ad. L. *ammodytes*, a. Gr. ἀμμοδύτης a sand-burrower; f. ἄμμος sand + δύτης diver, f. δύ-ειν to dive.]

†1. A venomous snake, the Sand-Natter, a species of Viper found in Southern Europe. *Obs.*
1607 TOPSELL *Serpents* (1653) 763 By the same means that the poyson of the Viper, the Ammodyte and Horned-serpent is cured withal. **1627** MAY *Lucan* IX. 822 Sand-colour'd Ammodytes, the horned snakes. **1774** GOLDSM. *Nat. Hist.* IV. 131 The Surinam serpent, which some improperly call the *ammodytes*.

2. The Sand-eel, *Ammodytes* of modern zoologists.
1698 SIBBALD in *Phil. Trans.* XX. 266 The Women that catched the Sand Eels (Ammodites). **1748** SIR J. HILL *Hist. Anim.* 225 (JOD.) Ammodytes, the sandeel, or grig. **1847** CARPENTER *Zool.* §577 The *Ammodytes* or *Launces* are remarkable for their habit of burrowing in the sand.

ammole, var. AMOLE.

ammonal ('æmənæl). [f. AMMON(IUM + AL(UMINIUM.]
A high explosive composed of three parts of ammonium nitrate and one part of aluminium.
1903 *Westm. Gaz.* 30 Oct. 11/1 Ammonal is being manufactured at the works of Messrs. G. and J. Roth at Felixdorf, Austria. **1922** C. E. MONTAGUE *Disenchantment* v. 70 They could talk lyddite and ammonal well enough.

ammonia (ə'məʊnɪə). [a. mod.L. *ammonia*, invented by Bergman, in 1782, as a name for the gas obtained from *sal ammoniac*: see next.]

1. A colourless gas with pungent smell and strong alkaline reaction, chemically a compound of three equivalents of hydrogen with one of nitrogen, NH_3, which at a pressure of $6\frac{1}{2}$ atmospheres, at 50° Fahr., is condensed to a colourless liquid. Called also *spirit of hartshorn*, in allusion to one of its early sources, the dry distillation of nitrogenous matter, as the hoofs and horns of animals; and *volatile* or *animal alkali*, in contradistinction to the 'fixed' alkalis, potash or 'vegetable' alkali, and soda or 'mineral' alkali.
1799 A. AIKIN *Syllabus Lect. Chem.* 7 *Ammonia*, or Volatile Alkali. **1801** HATCHETT in *Phil. Trans.* XCII. 50 Ammonia formed a yellow flocculent precipitate. **1810** DALTON *Syst. Chem. Philos.* II. v. §6. 415 It has been long known to chemists as an important element, and under various names,.. namely, volatile alkali, hartshorn, spirit of sal ammoniac, etc., but authors at present generally distinguish it by the name of ammonia. **1822** J. FLINT *Lett. fr. Amer.* 62 A chemical manufactory in which ammonia,

copperas..and various acids, are prepared. **1855** BAIN *Senses & Int.* II. ii. §1 In smelling salts, ammonia is the substance given forth.

2. *pop.* *ammonia*, or specifically **liquid ammonia**: a solution of ammonia in water, being the form in which it is commercially used.

c **1850** J. GRIFFIN in Ure *Dict. Arts* I. 140 To judge at a glance of the money value of any given sample of ammonia. **1863** WATTS *Dict. Chem.* (1872) I. 184 Solution of ammonia, Aqueous ammonia, or simply Ammonia, Spirits of hartshorn.

3. *Chem.* Extended to a large series of compounds, analogous to ammonia, in which one or more of the three hydrogen atoms of NH_3 are replaced by a basic metal or radical (AMINES), or by the oxygenized radical of an acid (AMIDES), or by both at once (ALKALAMIDES).

1863 WATTS *Dict. Chem.* (1872) I. 169 Ammonias in which 1 or more atoms of hydrogen are replaced by an acid-radicle. **1869** ROSCOE *Elem. Chem.* xxix. 312 Each alcohol also forms a series of compound ammonias.

4. *Comb.* in which *ammonia* stands chiefly in attrib. relation, as ***ammonia gas***, ***compounds***, ***process***, ***solution***, ***substitution compound***, ***works***, etc. Also ***ammonia alum***, ***amalgam***, ***carbonate***, ***salts***, etc., in which AMMONIUM is now used in more systematic nomenclature.

ammonia-meter, an instrument for measuring the percentage of ammonia in an aqueous solution.

1873 FOWNES *Chem.* 156 Ammonia gas is colourless. **1879** *Athenæum* 30 Aug. 277/3 The 'ammonia process'—which has been developed by M. Ernest Solvay, of Brussels. **1864** *Reader* 9 April 464 The pale reddish amethystine colour of ammonia-iron-alum. **1849** MRS. SOMERVILLE *Connex. Phys. Sc.* xxiv. 227 Paper prepared with the ammonia-citrate of iron. **1875** URE *Dict. Arts* I. 140 Mr. J. J. Griffin has constructed a useful instrument called an Ammonia-meter.

ammoniac (əˈməʊnɪæk), *a.* and *sb.* Forms: 4–5 **armoniak, -yac,** 4–8 **-iac,** 5 **-yak(e, ammonyak, amoniak,** 7 **-ac,** 7–8 **armoniack(e, ammoniack(e,** 7– **ammoniac.** [a. Fr. *ammoniac*, *armoniac*, ad. L. *ammōniac-um*, a. Gr. ἀμμωνιακόν, belonging to *Ammon* or *Ammonia*; applied subst. to a salt, and a gum, both obtained from the Libyan region of Ammonia near the shrine of Jupiter Ammon; f. Ἄμμων, Gr. form of the name of the Egyptian Deity *Amûn*. The corruption to *armoniac* found in med.L., Fr., and Eng., was perh. due to an association with the Gr. ἁρμονία fastening or joining, from the use of gum ammoniac as a cement, or of sal ammoniac in the joining of metals.]

A. *adj.*

1. in ***sal ammoniac*** (L. *sal ammoniacus*, Fr. *sel ammoniac*) i.e. Salt of Ammon, a hard white opaque crystalline salt, supposed to have been originally prepared from the dung of camels near the temple of Jupiter Ammon, as it still is in Egypt; chemically Ammonium Chloride NH_4Cl, formerly called ***muriate of ammonia***; used in tinning iron, in pharmacy, and for the manufacture of Ammonium Alum for the dyer.

c **1386** CHAUCER *Chan. Yem. Prol. & T.* 245 Arsenik, sal armoniak [*v.r.* armonyak], and brimston. *c* **1420** *Pallad. on Husb.* I. 605 Hony, myxt with salt armonyake. **1470** *Bk. Quintess.* 9 If ȝe wole dissolue þe gold to watir. putte þanne yn þe watir corosyue. Sal armoniac. **1601** HOLLAND *Pliny* (1634) II. 415 This Ammoniacke salt is corrupted and sophisticate..with the pit salt of Sicily called Cocanicus. **1605** TIMME *Quersit.* I. v. 20 Sal armoniac is of nature spirituall. **1753** CHAMBERS *Cycl. Supp.* s.v. *Ammoniacum*, The liquor will be scentless, and of the taste of *sal armoniac*. **1873** WILLIAMSON *Chem.* viii. §53 The hydrochlorate can be obtained in crystals..mixed with sal-ammoniac.

2. in ***gum ammoniac***, i.e. 'gum of Ammon,' a gum-resin, of peculiar smell, and bitterish taste, the inspissated juice of an umbelliferous plant (*Dorema Ammoniacum*) found wild from North Africa to India, and perhaps of some of its congeners. Employed in medicine, and as a cement.

1627 PEACHAM *Gentl. Exerc.* I. xxi. (1634) 67 Take Gumme Armoniacke, and grinde it with the juyce of Garlicke as fine as may be. **1714** *Fr. Bk. Rates* 92 Gum Armoniack per 100 Weight. **1844** T. GRAHAM *Dom. Med.* 31 [Tartar emetic]..will operate as an expectorant, when combined with squill, gum ammoniac and camphor.

3. Of the nature of ammonia, ammoniacal.

1646 SIR T. BROWNE *Pseud. Ep.* 322 Also a volatile or Armoniac Salt. **1767** MONRO in *Phil. Trans.* LVII. 511, I saturated some of it with the volatile ammoniac salt. **1869** *Eng. Mech.* 30 Apr. 133/2 Samples of Ammoniac Sulphate.

B. *sb.*

1. = gum ammoniac: see A 2. Also in L. form, **ammoniacum.**

c **1420** *Pallad. on Husb.* I. 1120 White wex, hardde pitch, remysse ammonyak Thees three comixt. **1563** T. GALE *Antidot.* II. 62 The..Hammoniacum dissolued in Vineger must be boyled. **1591** PERCIVALL *Sp. Dict.*, *Armoniaque*, Armoniake, *Armoniacum*. **1601** HOLLAND *Pliny* (1634) II. 180 Since we are fallen into the mention of Gums, it will not be amisse to treat of Ammoniack. **1712** tr. *Pomet's Hist. Drugs* I. 193 The Fennel bearing Ammoniack grows plentifully in the Deserts of Lybia. **1751** CHAMBERS *Cycl.* s.v., The good ammoniac is of a pale colour. **1875** WOOD *Therap.* (1879) 529 The influence of ammoniac upon the general system is very slight. **1876** HARLEY *Mat. Med.* 601 Ammoniacum resembles the Persian drug.

†**2.** = ammonia. [mod.Fr. *ammoniaque*.] *Obs.*

1791 HAMILTON *Berthollet's Dyeing* I. I. iii. 46 The colour may be restored by means of chalk or ammoniac (volatile alkali). **1802** CHENEVIX *Chem. Nomencl.* 55 Ammoniac is a term, which Mrs. Fulhame..has expressed a desire to see changed. I agree with her in preferring Ammonia.

¶ in **bole Armoniac (amoniak)**, it is a corruption of *Armeniac*. '*Bole Armoniac* or the *Armenian Bole* is a soft friable fatty earth, usually of a pale red colour.' Chambers *Cycl.*

c **1386** CHAUCER *Chan. Yem. Prol. & T.* 238 As bol armoniak [*v.r.* armonyak, -yac, amoniak], verdegres, boras. **1585** H. LLOYD *Treas. Health* O iij, Take of..Mastycke, Dragons bloud, bole Amonike new, of eche like quantitee. **1586** COGAN *Haven Health* (1636), Coriander, Ginger, Bole Armoniacke, of each a dram. **1627** PEACHAM *Compl. Gent.* xiii. (1634) 139 Margaritone was..the first that devised laying Gold or Gilding upon Bole Armoniacke to be burnished. **1751** CHAMBERS *Cycl.* s.v., This popularly, though corruptly called in English *Bole Armoniac*, is called by the naturalists *Armenia terra*, or Armenian clay.

ammoniacal (æməˈnaɪəkəl), *a.* [f. prec. + -AL[1].] Of, pertaining to, or of the nature of ammonia.

1732 ARBUTHNOT *Rules of Diet* 268 Jellies made of the solid parts of Animals contain a sort of ammoniacal Salt. **1798** *Phil. Trans.* LXXXVIII. 20 The mixture..emitted ammoniacal gaz. **1813** SIR H. DAVY *Agric. Chem.* 301 A bitter extract, which affords Ammoniacal fumes. **1818** FARADAY *Exp. Res.* vii. 19 They gave off much ammoniacal gas. **1833** BREWSTER *Nat. Magic* v. 113 A solution of the ammoniacal carbonate of copper. **1869** ROSCOE *Elem. Chem.* 75 The ammoniacal liquors of the gasworks.

ammoniaco- (æməˈnaɪəkəʊ), combining form of AMMONIAC or AMMONIACAL, as in **ammoniaco-calculus**, a form of urinary calculus; also = AMMONIA +, as in ***ammoniaco-magnesian phosphate***.

1804 WOLLASTON in *Phil. Trans.* XCIV. 420 The ammoniaco muriate of platina. **1807** MARCET *ibid.* XCVII. 308 No doubt an ammoniaco-magnesian carbonate. **1849–52** TODD *Cycl. Anat. & Phys.* IV. 1291/2 A deposit occurs in the urine composed of the monobasic ammoniaco-magnesian phosphate.

ammoˈniacum: see AMMONIAC B 1.

†**aˈmmonial.** *Chem. Obs.* [f. AMMONIA + -AL[1].] = AMMONIACAL.

1818 ACCUM *Chem. Tests.* 227 The ammonial solution.

ammoniˈameter. (See AMMONIA 4.) = AMMONIA-METER. *Syd. Soc. Lex.* 1879.

†**ammoniate** (əˈməʊnɪeɪt). *Chem. Obs.* [f. AMMONIA + -ATE[4].] A combination of ammonia with a metallic oxide, as Ammonio-cupric oxide, formerly ***ammoniate of copper***. See AMMONIDE.

1844 T. GRAHAM *Dom. Med.* 355 Antispasmodics and alteratives, of which the best are, the flowers or acetate of zinc, quinine, ammoniate of copper.

ammoniated (əˈməʊnɪeɪtɪd), *ppl. a.* [f. prec. + -ED.] Combined with ammonia, ammoniuretted.

1822 DE QUINCEY *Confess.* Wks. V. 274, I derived no benefit from any medicine whatever, except ammoniated tincture of valerian. **1874** LOMMEL *Light* 176 A solution of the ammoniated oxide of copper is transparent.

ammonic (əˈmɒnɪk), *a. rare.* [f. AMMONIUM + -IC: cf. *potass-ic*, *sod-ic*, etc.] Of or derived from ammonium (or ammonia).

1869 *Eng. Mech.* 19 Mar. 581/3 To name one chemist who considers the solution ammonic hydrate. **1876** HARLEY *Mat. Med.* 111 Ammonic Carbonate is only known in solution.

aˈmmonical, *a. Chem. rare*$^{-1}$. = prec.

1869 *Eng. Mech.* 19 Mar. 585/3 Vapour Volumes of Ammonical Salts.

ammonide (ˈæmənaɪd). *Chem.* [f. AMMONI-UM + -IDE.] A combination of ammonium with a metallic or other oxide; called also *ammoniuret*, and formerly, as an ammonia salt, *ammoniate*. (Little used; these being now viewed as metallic (or other) salts of ammonium; as ***carbonic ammonide*** = Ammonium carbonate.)

1876 HARLEY *Mat. Med.* 107 Dry carbonic anhydride and dry gaseous ammonia combine directly to form carbonic ammonide.

ammonification (əˌməʊnɪfɪˈkeɪʃən). [Noun of action f. as next.] The chemical process by which ammonia is produced. Also, impregnation with ammonia; saturation with ammonia.

1886 *Sci. Amer.* Suppl. XXII. 8789/3 Ammonification [of the soil of Japan] can be performed only to a depth of 60 centimeters. **1910** C. G. HOPKINS *Soil Fertility* xiv. 195 Plant food is made available by chemical and biochemical processes, of which ammonification and nitrification are.. best understood. **1911** *Centr. Bakt. Par.* XXXI. 53 Ammonia production in different lengths of time..was studied with a view toward shortening the ammonification period. **1932** FULLER & CONARD tr. *J. Braun-Blanquet's Plant Sociology* viii. 237 *Bacterium mycoides* plays a major rôle in ammonification, especially in cultivated soils.

ammonify (əˈməʊnɪfaɪ), *v.* [f. AMMONIA + -FY.] *trans.* and *intr.* To produce or undergo or subject to ammonification; to infuse or impregnate with ammonia. Hence **aˈmmonifying** *ppl. a.* and *vbl. sb.*

1910 C. G. HOPKINS *Soil Fertility* xiv. 196 The ammonifying bacteria serve only to convert organic nitrogen into ammonia nitrogen. **1911** *Centr. Bakt. Par.* XXXI. 64 It might be supposed, therefore, that the..nitrogen in the 3 gms. of corn meal would be ammonified more thoroughly. *Ibid.*, The organic nitrogen was, to a great extent, ammonified. *Ibid.*, Soy bean meals showed themselves capable of being rapidly decomposed by ammonifying bacteria. **1912** E. J. RUSSELL *Soil Conditions & Plant Growth* 86 The ammonia produced after four days at 20° is taken as a measure of the 'putrefactive power' or, as it is often called, the 'ammonifying power' of the soil. **1921** *Ibid.* (ed. 4) vii. 263 Dried blood is ammonified more rapidly than cotton-seed meal. **1932** FULLER & CONARD tr. *J. Braun-Blanquet's Plant Sociology* viii. 237 The undecomposed organic matter first goes through an ammonifying process wherein both bacteria and fungi participate.

ammonio- (əˈməʊnɪəʊ), combining form of the word AMMONIUM, indicating the presence of that basyl or its salts in a compound; thus ***ammonio-chloride*** of silver, ***ammonio-cupric*** sulphate, ***ammonio-magnesian*** phosphate = magnesium and ammonium phosphate.

1853 *Family Her.* 3 Dec. 510/2 The solution of ammonio-nitrate of silver. **1876** HARLEY *Mat. Med.* 207 Ammonio-chloride of Iron was discovered by Basil Valentine in the 14th cent.

ammonite (ˈæmənaɪt). [f. mod.L. *ammōnītes* (after *ætītes*, *asphaltītes*, etc.: see -ITE), f. by Bruguière on the med.L. name *Cornu Ammonis* 'Ammon's horn,' given to these fossils from their resemblance to the involuted horn of Jupiter Ammon. At first used as L., with pl. *Ammonitæ*.]

1. A fossil genus of Cephalopods, consisting of whorled chambered shells, containing many species; once supposed to be coiled snakes petrified, and hence called *Snake-stones*. (Scott *Marmion* II. xiii.)

1758 *Phil. Trans.* L. 786 In this rock..the Ammonitæ, or Snake-stones, as they are commonly called, are found. **1798** *La Perouse's Voy. round World* III. 299 A very close analogy between the ammonite and nautilus. **1816** W. SMITH *Strata Ident.* 1 The Muscles and Ammonites found in Ironstone. **1847** TENNYSON *Princess* Prol. 15 Huge Ammonites, and the first bones of Time. **1854** H. MILLER *Sch. & Schm.* viii. 77 In a nodular mass of bluish-gray limestone..I laid open my first-found ammonite.

†**2.** Formerly used for AMMITES, i.e. oolite. *Obs.*

1706 PHILLIPS, *Ammonites*, a sort of stone call'd the lesser Spawn-stone. **1753** CHAMBERS *Cycl. Supp.*, *Ammites* is the same with what is otherwise called *Ammonites*.

ammonitiferous (ˌæmənaɪˈtɪfərəs), *a.* [f. prec. + -FEROUS bearing.] Containing fossil ammonites.

1830 LYELL *Princ. Geol.* I. 126 The ammonitiferous limestones of the Southern Apennines. **1860** WRIGHT in *Q. Jrnl. Geol. S.* XVI. I. 375 The ammonitiferous beds of the Lias.

ammonium (əˈməʊnɪəm). *Chem.* [a. mod.L. *ammōnium*, formed by Berzelius, 1808, on AMMONIA, after analogy of *soda*, *sodium*, *magnesia*, *magnesium*, and the names of the recent metals generally.] The radical supposed to exist in the salts of ammonia, a compound of 4 equivalents of hydrogen with 1 of nitrogen, NH_4, which behaves in composition as a monatomic alkaline metal, replacing, and presenting close analogies to, sodium and potassium.

1808 SIR H. DAVY in *Phil. Trans.* XCVIII. 364 From platina to potassium there is a regular order of gradation as to physical and chemical properties, and this would probably extend to ammonium, could it be obtained in the fixed form. **1850** DAUBENY *Atom. The.* ix. 295 The atomic volume which these lighter metals, viz. ammonium, barium, calcium..have. **1875** URE *Dict. Arts* I. 142 Although it may be objected..that the metal ammonium is not known, yet a curious metallic compound of this metal with mercury has been obtained.

b. *attrib.* In names of compounds in which *ammonia* was formerly, and is still often, used, as ***ammonium salts***, ***carbonate***, ***chloride***, ***phosphate***. Also **ammonium alum** (see ALUM *sb.* 2); **ammonium amalgam**, a soft solid metallic substance, an amalgam of ammonium and mercury, analogous to the sodium and potassium amalgams.

1863 WATTS *Dict. Chem.* (1872) I. 188 Ammonium-salts are isomorphous with potassium salts. *Ibid.* 195 Spoken of as *ammonium-bases* in contradistinction to the *amine-* or *ammonia-*bases. **1869** ROSCOE *Elem. Chem.* 214 *Ammonium Chloride*, or sal-ammoniac. **1873** WILLIAMSON *Chem.* viii. §52 The ammonium amalgam very rapidly decomposes when removed from the liquid.

†**a'mmoniuret.** *Chem. Obs.* [f. AMMONIA + -URET.] = AMMONIDE, AMMONIATE.

1839 HOOPER *Med. Dict.* 89 *Ammoniuret*, a compound of ammonia and a metallic oxide; as *ammoniuret* of gold, silver, zinc, etc. **1879** in *Syd. Soc. Lex.*

a'mmoniuretted, *ppl. a.* ? *Obs.* [f. prec. + -ED.] Combined with ammonia (or, according to later views, ammonium); as 'ammoniuretted oxide of gold,' now 'aurate of ammonium.'

1854 SCOFFERN in *Orr's Circ. Sc.* Chem. 503 Ammoniuretted Oxide of Silver. *c* **1865** J. WYLDE in *Circ. Sc.* I. 374/1 An explosive compound of silver is produced by adding liquid ammonia to the oxide of silver; forming what is termed the ammoniuretted oxide.

ammonoid ('æmənɔɪd). [f. mod.L. *Ammonoidea*, f. *Ammōnites* AMMONITE: see -OID.] A fossil cephalopod of the order *Ammonoidea*, comprising the ammonites and related genera.

1884 A. HYATT in *Proc. Boston Soc. Nat. Hist.* XXII. 303 The ventral sutures are interrupted by the funnels as in Ammonoids. **1889** NICHOLSON & LYDEKKER *Palæont.* (ed. 3) I. 849 The septal 'necks' of the Ammonoids are variable in their development. **1912** *Brit. Museum Return* 169 The collection of Austrian Triassic Ammonoids.

ammophilous (æ'mɒfɪləs), *a.* [f. Gr. ἄμμος sand + φίλος loving, fond.] Sand-loving; applied to plants or insects which inhabit sandy places.

1879 in *Syd. Soc. Lex.*

ammunition (æmju:'nɪʃən), *sb.* Also 7–8 **amu-**. [a. 16–17th c. Fr. *a(m)munition*, vulgarly *amonition*, an army corruption of *munition* (also vulgarly *monition*). H. Estienne (1578) says 'le peuplier grossier prononce *monition* (*amonition*, selon autres) pour *munition*'; and Ménage (1672), 'les soldats disent *pain d'amonition*; mais les officiers disent *pain de munition*' — Thurot *Pron. Franç.* 1881, p. 275. Apparently caused by taking *la munition* as *l'amonition* through confusion of the novel *munition* with the familiar *a(d)monition* a 'warning' legal or ecclesiastical. Cf. *noix d'Acajou* for *noix de Cajou*. Subseq. rejected in Fr. (exc. as a vulgarism), but retained in Eng. with *amm-*, assimilated to words from L. in *imm-*, *comm-*, *ann-*, etc. L. *adm-* does not become *amm-* in Fr. or Eng.]

1. Military stores or supplies; *formerly*, of all kinds (as still *attrib.*: see 3); *now*, articles used in charging guns and ordnance, as powder, shot, shell; and by extension, offensive missiles generally.

a **1626** BACON *Adv. Villiers* (J.) Convenient arms and a[m]munition for their defence. **1642** *Declar. Lords & Comm.* 7 Jan. 6 Horses, Armes, and Amunition. **1671** MILTON *Samson* 1277 He all their ammunition And feats of war defeats. **1692** LUTTRELL *Brief Rel.* (1857) II. 413 A French prize of 180 tunns, laden with ammunitions. **1703** MAUNDRELL *Journ. Jerus.* (1732) 54 The Amunition used in Battering the City. **1710** *Lond. Gaz.* mmmmdccvi/2, 25000 Fire-locks, with a suitable Proportion of Ammunition. **1769** MRS. HARRIS in *Priv. Lett. Ld. Malmesb.* I. 177 The ammunition of these rioters consisted chiefly of dirt, but many stones were seen to be thrown. **1870** KNIGHT *Crown Hist. Eng.* xl. 519 At seven in the evening their ammunition was nearly exhausted.

2. *fig.*

1645 BP. HALL *Content.* 103 This spirituall Ammunition shall sufficiently furnish the soul for her encounter with her last enemy. **1833** MARRYAT *Pet. Simp.* (1863) 70, I had finished my meal, which did not take long, for want of ammunition.

3. *attrib.* as ***ammunition-boots***, ***-bread***, ***-hat***, ***-loaf***, ***-shoes***, etc., those supplied to soldiers as equipment or rations; **ammunition-face**, a warlike one; **ammunition-house**, one used for the storage of ammunition; **ammunition-wag(g)on**, one used to convey the ammunition for a force.

a **1658** CLEVELAND *Clev. Vind.* (1677) 96 So much for his Warlike or Ammunition Face. **1663** BUTLER *Hud.* I. i. 314 Lin'd with many a piece Of ammunition bread and cheese. **1691** in *Hist. MSS. Commission 14th Rep.*, App. III (1894) 123 We had all our ammunition in the greatest hazard of blowing up upon Saturday night last by the treacherous fireing of two bombs..in the very center of our ammunition waggons. **1692** LUTTRELL *Brief Rel.* (1857) II. 471 An ammunition loafe of bread was sold for 18 soals. **1693** W. ROBERTSON *Phraseol. Gen.* 1320 A ammunition whore, *scortum castrense.* **1697** *Lond. Gaz.* mmmccxcvi/4 Deserted ..Thomas Stone..took away with him his Ammunition Hat. **1703** LUTTRELL *Brief Rel.* (1857) V. 356 Whose ammunition house at Turin is blown up by some incendiaries. **1720** DEFOE *Mem. Cavalier* II. 192 We took five Ammunition Waggons, full of powder. **1844** *Regul. & Ord. Army* 152 The Men are entitled to their Ammunition Boots or Shoes, with the rest of their Clothing. **1858** FROUDE *Hist. Eng.* IV. 275 Ammunition waggons were prepared and loaded.

ammunition (æmju:'nɪʃən), *v.* [f. sb.: cf. Fr. *amunitionner.*] To supply with ammunition.

1644 PRYNNE & WALKER *Fiennes's Trial* 19 Why did he fortifie and ammunition the City?

ammunitioned (æmju:'nɪʃənd), *ppl. a.* [f. prec. + -ED.] Supplied with ammunition.

1653 J. TAYLOR (Water P.) *Journ. Wales* (1859) 13 If it be well mand, victualled and ammunitioned, it is invincible. **1870** *Daily News* 17 Dec., The remaining forty, well armed, ammunitioned, and in good condition, established themselves in two or three private houses.

amnemonic (æmnɪ'mɒnɪk), *a. Path.* [f. Gr. ἀ priv. + μνημονικός of memory: see MNEMONICS; cf. Gr. ἀμνήμων forgetful.] Characterized by loss of memory.

1879 in *Syd. Soc. Lex.*

amner, obs. (regular 16th c.) f. ALMONER.

amnesia (æm'ni:sɪə, -zɪə). *Path.* [mod.L., a. Gr. ἀμνησία forgetfulness.] Loss of memory.

[**1674** J. FLAVEL *Token for Mourners* 11 There is a perfect ἀμνησία forgetfulness and insensibleness.] **1786** B. RUSH *Influence of Phys. Causes* in *Med. Inquiries & Observations* (1793) II. 5 The loss of memory has been called'amnesia'. **1829** *Lond. Encycl.* II. 127/1 *Amnesia*, in medicine, loss of memory; sometimes the consequence of febrile diseases, when it generally recedes as the patient gains strength. **1878** A. HAMILTON *Nerv. Dis.* 130 In place of there being simply a difficulty in expressing a clearly originated idea, there may be a condition of amnesia. **1880** BASTIAN *Brain* xxix. 621 An ordinary case of Amnesia..in which the 'volitional' and 'associational' recall of names was impossible.

amnesiac (æm'ni:sɪæk, -z-). [f. AMNESIA + -AC.] One who is afflicted with amnesia.

1913 in DORLAND *Med. Dict.* (ed. 7) 56/1. **1946** 'P. QUENTIN' *Puzzle for Fiends* (1947) iii. 21 The run-of-the-mill amnesiac didn't come back to such an ideal existence as this. **1954** MAURETTE & BOLTON *Anastasia* I. in J. C. Trewin *Plays of Yr.* IX. 174 What was your name before that—the name you was born with? I don't remember. Oh, so you're an amnesiac?

amnesic (æm'ni:sɪk, -'ɛzɪk), *a. Path.* [f. AMNESIA + -IC.] Of or pertaining to amnesia.

1868 OGLE in *Lancet* 21 Mar. 370/2 The inability to speak, is not..occasioned by forgetfulness of words—in other words, not amnesic. **1880** BASTIAN *Brain* xxix. 662 A grave Amnesic condition as regards Speech.

amnestic (æm'nɛstɪk), *a. Med.* [f. Gr. ἀμνηστία forgetfulness + -IC.] Causing loss of memory. (Said of diseases, poisonous agents, etc.)

1879 in *Syd. Soc. Lex.*

amnestied ('æmnɪstɪd), *ppl. a.* [f. AMNESTY *v.* + -ED.] Admitted to amnesty, having past (political) offences overlooked or forgiven.

1809 *Edin. Rev.* XIII. 440 Of this class are the amnestied emigrants. **1879** *Daily News* 29 Oct. 5/4 The amnestied Communards.

amnesty ('æmnɪstɪ), *sb.* [a. Fr. *amnestie* (16th c. in Litt.), or ad. its original, L. *amnēstia*, a. Gr. ἀμνηστία oblivion, f. ἄμνηστος not remembering. Used occas. in 16–17th c. in L. and Gr. form.]

1. Forgetfulness, oblivion; an intentional overlooking.

1592 SIR T. SMITH in T. Wright *Q. Eliz. Orig. Lett.* (1838) I. 456 To treade all underfoote that hath gone heretofore, with a perpetuall ἀμνηστία, and to begyn a new lyfe. **1605** BACON *Adv. Learn.* II. xxiii. §6. (1873) 223 Reconcilement is better managed by an amnesty, and passing over that which is past. **1624** SANDERSON *Serm.* Ad. Pop. v. (1674) 242 Quite forgotten, and buried in a perpetual Amnesty. **1647** HOWELL *Lett.* III. vi, I did not think Suffolk waters had such a lethæan quality in them, as to cause such an *amnestia* in him of his friends. **1724** WATTS *Logic* I. iv. §2. (1822) 60 Amnesty, an unremembrance. **1880** *Contemp. Rev.* XXXVII. 474 By mutual amnesty men avoid seeing the real drift of each other's statements.

2. a. An act of oblivion, a general overlooking or pardon of past offences, by the ruling authority.

1580 NORTH *Plutarch* (1676) 1020 A law that no man should be called in question nor troubled for things that were past..called *Amnestia*, or law of Oblivion. **1693** *Mem. Count Teckely* II. 105 He should grant them in due form an Amnesty for all that was pass'd. **1782** BURKE *Penal Laws agst. Irish Cath.* Wks. VI. 274 An act of amnesty and indulgence. **1787** MADISON in Sparks' *Corr. Am. Rev.* (1853) IV. 167 The insurgents decline accepting the terms annexed to the amnesty. **1849** MACAULAY *Hist. Eng.* I. 174 An amnesty was granted, with few exceptions, to all who, during the late troubles, had been guilty of political offences.

b. *spec.* **Amnesty International**, an international organization, founded in 1961, whose principal purpose is to uphold and campaign for the human rights of prisoners of conscience; freq. abbrev., as *Amnesty*; formerly the *(Appeal for) Amnesty Campaign.*

1961 *Observer* 28 May 21/1 Peter Benenson..conceived the idea of a world campaign, Appeal for Amnesty, 1961. *Ibid.* 21/7 The success of the Amnesty Campaign depends on how sharply..it is possible to rally public opinion. **1962** *Listener* 26 Apr. 731/2 The international movement known as Amnesty..has drawn particular attention to the plight of the prisoners of conscience in different countries. **1963** *Amnesty* IV. 9/1 Amnesty International (our new name) starts the New Year with the appointment of a young secretary. **1973** *Athens News* 1–2 Apr. 3 The West German branch of Amnesty International..called for an investigation into..inhuman torture of political prisoners. **1977** *Guernsey Weekly Press* 21 July 6/6 At a meeting of the Guernsey Branch of Amnesty International in St. Peter's recently members discussed a variety of topics covering their international activities. **1982** *Observer* 21 Feb. 9/3 There is an amnesty within Amnesty.

amnesty ('æmnɪstɪ), *v.* [f. prec. sb.] To give amnesty to, to admit to amnesty; to proclaim the overlooking of the past offences of (rebels).

1809 [See AMNESTIED.] **1837** CARLYLE *Fr. Rev.* II. v. iii. 294 And so hereby all is amnestied, and finished? **1851** MARIOTTI *Italy* i. 33 It was, in fact, the pope himself, or the papacy that was amnestied. **1869** *Echo* 13 Dec., Mr. Gladstone..won't be bullied into amnestying the Fenian convicts.

†'**amnic(ke**, *a.*[1] *Obs.*$^{-0}$ [ad. L. *amnic-us*, f. *amn-is* a river: see -IC.] Of or belonging to a river.

1623 in COCKERAM. **1656** in BLOUNT *Glossogr.*

'**amnic**, *a.*[2] [f. Gr. ἀμνί-ον + -IC.] = AMNIOTIC *a.*

1855 RAMSBOTHAM *Obstet. Surg.* 16 It contains..a free acid known as amnic acid.

†**am'nicolist.** *Obs.*$^{-0}$ [f. L. *amnicola* dwelling by a river (f. *amn-is* river + *-cola* inhabitant + -IST.] 'One that dwells by a river.' Bailey 1731; in J.

†**am'nigenous**, *a. Obs.*$^{-0}$ [f. L. *amnigen-us* river-born (f. *amn-is* + *-gen-us* born) + -OUS.] 'Born or bred in, of, or near a river.' Bailey 1731; in J.

amniocentesis (,æmnɪəʊsɛn'ti:sɪs). *Obstetrics.* Pl. **-centeses** (-'i:si:z). [f. AMNIO(N + Gr. κέντησις pricking (f. κεντεῖν to prick).] A prenatal diagnostic technique in which a sample of amniotic fluid is withdrawn from the uterus through a hollow needle and examined for information about the fœtus; an examination by means of this technique.

1958 H. M. PARRISH et al. in *Amer. Jrnl. Obstetr. & Gynecol.* LXXV. 724 The term 'transabdominal amniocentesis' is introduced as being descriptive of the procedure and is suggested in lieu of previous terminology including: amniotomy, abdominal paracentesis..and paracentesis uteri. **1971** *Nature* 31 Dec. 506/3 Foetal cells removed by amniocentesis can also be cultured and assayed for enzymatic deficiencies in cases where inborn errors of metabolism are suspected. **1972** *Daily Colonist* (Victoria, B.C.) 25 June 2/1 Amniocentesis will reveal the sex of the baby. **1977** P. B. & J. S. MEDAWAR *Life Sci.* vii. 62 When an older woman conceives a child her physician will often recommend the procedure of amniocentesis. **1977** *Lancet* 23 July 201/2 We analysed records of amniocenteses from four New York hospitals. **1984** *Sunday Tel.* 8 Jan. 9/5 Pregnant women over the age of 35 are now routinely offered amniocentesis tests to detect foetal abnormality. **1986** P. D. JAMES *Taste for Death* vii. 67 It's a boy. Barbara had an amniocentesis.

amnion ('æmnɪən). *Phys.* [a. Gr. ἀμνίον the caul, dim. of ἀμνός lamb.] The innermost membrane enclosing the fœtus before birth.

1667 *Phil. Trans.* II. 511 The Fœtus is nourished only from the Amnion by the Mouth. **1764** SMELLIE *Midw.* I. 114 The Chorion is on the inside lined with another membrane called Amnion. **1863** BARING-GOULD *Iceland* 127 The clerestory windows covered with the amnion of sheep.

b. *attrib.*

1879 tr. *Haeckel's Evol. Man* II. xviii. 133 All known Amnion Animals, coincide in many important points of organization and development.

amnios ('æmnɪɒs). [a variant of AMNION, founded upon an erroneous form of the Greek.]

1. *Phys.* = AMNION.

1657 *Phys. Dict.*, *Amnios*, the inner skin that compasseth the child round in the womb. **1660** BOYLE *New Exp. Phys.-Mech.* 374 The upper part of the involving Amnios. **1797** *Phil. Trans.* LXXXVII. 193 The two membranes..the chorion and amnios. **1828** KIRBY & SPENCE *Entomol.* IV. xliv. 236 Regarded as fœtuses in their amnios rather than eggs. **1845** NOEL *Richter's Flower etc. Pieces* II. ix. 37 A little hidden creature, which has past from the fœtus-slumber into the sleep of death, out of the amnios-skin of this world into the shroud, the amnios-skin of the next.

2. *Bot.* 'The fluid that is produced within the sac which receives the embryo-rudiment and engenders it.' *Treas. Bot.* 1866.

1816 KEITH *Physiol. Bot.* II. 293 The amnios had just made its appearance in the upper region of the chorion. **1830** LINDLEY *Nat. Syst. Bot.* Introd. 33 The amnios always surrounds the embryo in an early state.

‖**amniota** (æmnɪ'əʊtə), *sb. pl.* [mod.L. formed anomalously, after AMNIOTIC.] The vertebrates, comprising reptiles, birds and mammals, which possess in embryonic life an allantois and an amnion.

1879 tr. *Haeckel's Evol. Man* II. xviii. 137 Man is a true Amnion Animal, and, in common with all other Amniota, has descended from the Protamnion.

amniotic (æmnɪ'ɒtɪk), *a.* [mod. form. on the non-Gr. form AMNIOS (prob. first in Fr. which has *amnios*, *amniotique*) after *chaotic*, *Nilotic*, *demotic*: see -OTIC. The Gr. form from ἀμνίον would have been ἀμνιακός, *amniac.*] Of or pertaining to an amnion; of the nature of, or characterized by, an amnion. **a.** *Phys.*

1822 IMISON *Sc. & Art* II. 140 The amniotic acid is found in the liquor of the amnios of a cow. **1863** WATTS *Dict. Chem.* I. 128 The amniotic liquid contains albumin, pyin.. and in some instances glucose. **1877** HUXLEY *Anat. Inv. An.* vii. 445 A more or less complete amniotic investment.

b. *Bot.*

1870 HOOKER *Stud. Flora* 13 *Nymphæaceæ*.. embryo enclosed in the enlarged amniotic sac.

‖**a'mober, -br, -byr.** Also amabyr. [Welsh *amobr* (*-byr, -ber*); f. *am*(*bi* + *wobr*, *gwobr* a reward, fee.] Technical term in the Welsh Laws for the 'maiden-fee' formerly payable to a lord on the marriage of a maid of his manor.

1727 CHAMBERS *Cycl.* s.v. *Chevage*, Coke observes there is still a kind of Chevage subsisting in Wales called Amobyr, paid to the prince of Wales for the marriage of daughters.

†**a'mobrage.** *Obs.* [f. prec. + -AGE; perh. orig. in AFr. Also latinized as *amobragium*.] The payment or proceeds of the Amober.

1750 CARTE *Hist. Eng.* II. 338 The fines usually paid to the lord by his tenants for the marriage of their daughters, called *Amobragium*, were moderated.

†**a'mobreship.** *Obs.* [f. as prec. + -SHIP.] The right or title to receive the Amober.

1495 *Act II Hen. VII*, xxxiii, Thamobreship of the Counties of Caernervan and Anglesey with Reglorshippes and Raglorshippes of thadvoures of the same Counties.

†**a'modere,** *v.* *Obs.* [a. OFr. *amodére-r*, ad. L. *admoderā-ri*; f. *ad* to + *moderāri*: see MODERATE.] To moderate, restrain.

a **1450** *Knt. de la Tour* xciv. 122 Where as there be riottis and debatys and striff, the wisdom of gode counsaile.. amoderithe suche thinges. **1483** CAXTON *Cato* B iij, One may .. amodere or restreyne in hym self all illycite cogytacions.

amœba (ə'miːbə). *Zool.* Pl. amœbæ, amœbas. [ad. Gr. ἀμοιβή change, alternation.] A microscopic animalcule (class *Protozoa*) consisting of a single cell of gelatinous sarcode, the outer layer of which is highly extensile and contractile, and the inner fluid and mobile, so that the shape of the animal is perpetually changing.

1841 T. R. JONES *Anim. Kingd.* 52 The Proteus (*Amœba E.*).. affords a singular example of an acrite animal. **1855** H. SPENCER *Psychol.* (1872) I. III. iv. 307 The Amœba, a speck of jelly having no constant form, sends out.. prolongations of its substance. **1878** MACALISTER *Invertebr.* 22 These amœbæ.. are little masses of protoplasm, moving and taking food by means of pseudopodia.

b. *Comb.* as *amœba-like*.

1864 H. SPENCER *Illust. Progr.* 398 Immense numbers of Amœba-like creatures.. in a framework of horny fibres, constitute sponge.

amœbæan (æmiː'biːən), *a.* Also amebean. [f. L. *amœbæ-us* (a. Gr. ἀμοιβαῖ-ος interchanging, f. ἀμοιβή change) + -AN.] Alternately answering, responsive.

1658 PHILLIPS, *Amœbæan Verses* are such as answer one another by course; as in some of Virgil's Eclogues. **1810** COLERIDGE *Friend* VI. i. (1876) 279 Those contests or Amoibean eclogues, between workmen for the superior worth and dignity of their several callings. **1861** *Sat. Rev.* 25 May 526 That amœbean exchange of witticisms between the Bench and the Bar. **1883** *Cornh. Mag.* Jan. 80 Spring and Winter.. sing an amœbean ode.

amœbiasis (æmiː'baɪəsɪs). *Path.* Also (*U.S.*) amebiasis. [f. AMŒB(A + -IASIS.] A disease caused by amœbæ, esp. amœbic infection of the colon.

1905 *Jrnl. Amer. Med. Assoc.* XLV. 836/2 Intestinal amebiasis (amebic dysentery) manifests itself in a much broader.. clinical picture than is generally allotted to it. **1961** *Lancet* 19 Aug. 441/2 The inhabitants of Karachi designate the condition 'Karachi tummy', and some link it up with the inevitable amœbiasis. **1962** *Ibid.* 8 Dec. 1209/2 Juniper points out that amœbiasis is considered uncommon in the United States.

amœbic (ə'miːbɪk), *a.* [f. AMŒB(A + -IC.] Pertaining to, of the nature of, or caused by an amœba or amœbæ.

1891 GERRY & FITZ in *Boston Med. & Surg. Jrnl.* CXXV. 592/1 (*title*) A case of amœbic dysentery. *Ibid.* 593/1 Lösch experimented with the amœbic stools. **1902** *Encycl. Brit.* XXXI. 536 A form [of dysentery] has been described which is said to be due to an animal parasite—amœbic dysentery or amœbic enteritis. **1951** *New Biol.* X. 28 Occasionally.. it starts to invade the walls of the intestine and feed on red blood corpuscles, when it causes ulcers and the well-known disease of amoebic dysentery.

amœbiform (ə'miːbɪfɔːm), *a.* [f. AMŒB-A + -(I)FORM.] Amœba-like; *also*, having many varying shapes, proteiform.

1859 J. GREENE *Protozoa* 31 Smaller portion of Grantia showing ciliated amœbiform particles. **1872** NICHOLSON *Palæont.* 67 Sponges may be defined as Rhizopoda composed of numerous amœbiform masses of sarcode. **1876** M. FOSTER *Phys.* (1879) Introd. 1 Merely amœbiform phases in the lives of certain animals or plants.

amœbocyte (ə'miːbəsaɪt). *Zool.* [Fr. (L. Cuénot, 1888), f. AMŒB(A + -O + -CYTE.] A cell having amœboid shape or properties; esp. a type of corpuscle in the cœlomic fluid of certain echinoderms, etc.

1892 *Q. Jrnl. Microsc. Sci.* XXXIII. 111 Cuénot.. advances a theory that certain granules contained in 'amibocytes' [*sic*] consist of an 'albuminogenous' ferment. **1900** F. A. BATHER et al. in E. R. Lankester *Treat. Zool.* III. 22 In it float various bodies.. amoebocytes.. capable of wandering through all the tissues.. and containing refringent granules, proteids, [etc.]. **1911** *Encycl. Brit.* XXV. 727/1 Amoebocytes.. are amoeboid cells closely resembling the leucocytes or white blood corpuscles of higher animals. **1951** *New Biol.* X. 9 The wandering cells of the blood.. are often called amoebocytes.

amœboid (ə'miːbɔɪd), *a.* *Biol.* [f. AMŒB-A + -OID.] Of the character of the amœba; amœba-like.

1861 J. GREENE *Cœlent.* 52 Such amœboid particles occasionally become detached. **1872** HUXLEY *Phys.* vii. 157 The amœboid movements of the white corpuscles of the blood. **1878** MᶜNAB *Bot.* 16 The protoplasm escapes forming uniciliate zoospores which soon lose the cilia and become amœboid.

amoibite (ə'mɔɪbaɪt). *Min.* [mod. f. (Ger. 1844) Gr. ἀμοιβή change + -ITE.] A mineral, classed as a variety of Gersdörffite, or Nickel glance.

1837–68 DANA *Min.* 73 Von Kobell's amoibite.. occurs at Lichtenberg in the Fichtelgebirge in light steel-gray octahedrons.

†**a'moinder,** *v.* *Obs. rare.* [a. Fr. *amoindr-ir* to lessen, f. *à* to + *moindre*:—L. *minor* less.] To lessen, diminish.

1601 BP. BARLOW *Serm. Paules Crosse* 29 Doth rengrege or amoinder, that is, make greater or lesse the faults committed. *a* **1631** DONNE *Aristeas* (1633) 74 Which might cause damage or losse to the Revenues of their Prince, amoyndring and diminishing his Tributes.

amok (ə'mɒk), *a.* and *adv.* Also amock, amuck. [ad. Malay *amoq* adj., 'engaging furiously in battle, attacking with desperate resolution, rushing in a state of frenzy to the commission of indiscriminate murder... Applied to any animal in a state of vicious rage'; Marsden *Malay Dict.* Cf. AMOK(E *v.*]

1. a. *adj.* or *sb.* A name for a frenzied Malay. (Found first in Pg. form *amouco*, *amuco*.)

[*c* **1516** BARBOSA transl. by Ld. Stanley (Hakl. Soc. 1866) 194 There are some of them [the Javanese] who.. go out into the streets, and kill as many persons as they meet.. These are called Amuco.] **1663** H. COGAN *Pinto's Trav.* I. 199 That all those which were able to bear arms should make themselves Amoucos, that is to say, men resolved either to dye, or vanquish. *Ibid.* lxiv. 260 These same are ordinarily called Amucos. **1772** COOK *Voy.* (1790) I. 288 To run amock is to get drunk with opium.. to sally forth from the house, kill the person or persons supposed to have injured the Amock, and any other person that attempts to impede his passage. **1947** *Straits Times* (Malaysian ed.) 11 Oct. 1/2 The amok.. stabbed four B.O.R.s, a Malay and a Tamil. **1966** [see PARANG]. **1977** *Globe and Mail* (Toronto) 17 Sept. 36/2 An apparently friendly Malay woman turns out to be an amok.

b. A murderous frenzy; the act of running amok.

1849 *Jrnl. Indian Archipelago* III. 463 These amoks result from an idiosyncrasy or peculiar temperament common amongst Malays. **1893** F. A. SWETTENHAM *About Perak* 47 It is this state of blind fury, this vision of blood, that produces the amok. **1947** *Straits Times* (Malaysian ed.) 11 Oct. 1/2 It was feared that the man.. would.. begin a second amok. **1952** W. H. J. SPROTT *Social Psychol.* III. xi. 245 Men .. are the victims of the type of seizure known as 'amok', which also occurs in Malay.

2. to run amok: to run viciously, mad, frenzied for blood. (Here *amok* was orig. adj.)

1672 MARVELL *Reh. Transp.* I. 59 Like a raging Indian.. he runs a mucke (as they cal it there) stabbing every man he meets. **1772** COOK *Voy.* (1790) I. 289 Jealousy of the women is the usual reason of these poor creatures running amock (or amuck). **1833** SOUTHEY *Nav. Hist. Eng.* I. 21 The same pitch of fury which the Malays excite in themselves by a deleterious drug, before they run amuck. **1858** GEN. THOMPSON *Audi Alt. Part.* I. xxii. 81 If the laborious ox.. was seen.. running amuck and sending man, woman and child to the hospital by dint of horn or hoof. **1879** L. LINDSAY *Mind in Lower An.* 45 Thus the running amok (or amuck).. is a peculiar form of human insanity. **1933** L. AINSWORTH *Confessions Planter in Malaya* vii. 75 The reason for the headlong retreat was a Bengali who had run 'amok'... He had already killed two persons outright. **1972** *Straits Times* (Malaysian ed.) 4 May 9/8 A 27-year-old man ran amok with a meat-chopper and attacked a 62-year-old woman. **1980** S. NAIPAUL *Black & White* II. ii. 133 'Here,' an acquaintance said to me, 'you either reach for the stars or you crack up and run amok with a chainsaw.'

3. *fig.* Wild or wildly, headlong or heedlessly. (Very rarely with any other verb than *run*.) Const. *on*, *at*, *against* (*with*, *of*).

1689 HICKERINGILL *Modest Inq.* i. 2 Running a Muck at all Mankind. **1735** POPE *Hor. Sat.* II. i. 70 I'm too discreet To run a muck, and tilt at all I meet. **1827** HARE *Guess. Tr.* Ser. I. (1873) 259 If we could banish our wits to grin amuck with savages and monkies. **1859** THOREAU *Walden* viii. (1863) 186, I might have run 'amok' against society, but I preferred that society should run 'amok' against me. **1870** DISRAELI *Lothair* xxx. 145 Ready to run a muck with any one who crossed him. **1880** W. R. SMITH in *Manch. Guard.* 29 Oct., In their alarm they were determined to run amuck of everything.

¶ It has been erroneously treated as *muck* sb.

1687 DRYDEN *Hind & P.* III. 1188 And runs an Indian muck at all he meets. **1824** BYRON *Don Juan* x. lxix, Thy waiters running mucks at every bell.

a'mok(e, *v. rare.* [see AMOK *a.*] To run amuck.

1866 C. BROOKE *Saráwak* I. 29 On our return to Saráwak, we found a boy only sixteen years old had amoked in the town. *Ibid.* 27 Such causes in most instances lead to the Malay amoking.

amole (ə'məʊleɪ). Also ammole. [Mexican Sp.] The root or bulb of any one of several plants found in Mexico and California, used as a detergent; also any of such plants, esp. *Chlorogalum pomeridianum*, called also *soap-plant* (see SOAP *sb.* 6 b). Also *attrib.*

1831 BEECHEY *Voyage* II. 43 A very useful root called in that country [California] *amoles*. **1845** FRÉMONT *Exped.* (1846) 269 Great quantities of *ammole* (soap plant), the leaves of which are used in California for making.. mats for saddle-cloths. **1884** *Encycl. Brit.* XVII. 401/2 *Yucca filamentosa*, commonly called amole or soap-weed. **1886** *Proc. U.S. Nat. Mus.* VIII. 518 Lechuguilla is the most important of the soap or 'amole' plants of Southwestern Texas and Northern Mexico. **1927** *Chambers's Jrnl.* 227/1 Soap grows for him.. in the bulbs of the curious Amole. **1928** D. H. LAWRENCE *Woman Who Rode Away* 96 They.. washed her all over with water and the amole infusion.

†**a'molify,** *v.* *Obs.* [App. a confusion between *amolysh* (AMOLLISH), a common word in Caxton, and *mollify*, Fr. *mollifier* (16th c. in Litt.); but perh. only a misreading of *amolysh*, in MS.]

1483 CAXTON *Gold. Leg.* xxix/1 The holy ghoost.. amolyfyeth and softeth hard thynges by the yefte of pyte.

†**a'molish,** *v.* *Obs.* [a. *amoliss-* pr. stem of Fr. *amolir* 'to remove or put away hardly, with pain, or much adoe' Cotgr., ad. L. *āmōlī-ri*: see next. Cf. *demolish*.] To remove forcibly, do away with.

1624 BP. MOUNTAGU *Gagg* 286 Purgatory.. is utterly amolished before the general Judgment finished. *a* **1640** JACKSON *Creed* x. Wks. IX. 283, I have yet one thing to do, and that is to amolish the suspicion.

†**amo'lition.** *Obs. rare*⁻¹. [ad. L. *āmōlitiōn-em*, n. of action f. *āmōlīri* to remove with an effort, f. *ā* away + *mōlīri* to exert oneself upon, f. *mōles* a heavy mass.] Removal, displacement.

1673 BP. WARD *Apol. Myst. Gosp.* 4 (L.) We ought here to consider a removal or amolition of that supposal; the grounds and reasons of this amolition.

†**a'mollish,** *v.* *Obs.* Also 5 amolish, -ysh. [a. *amoliss-* pr. stem of OFr. *amolir* (mod. *amollir*) to soften, f. *à* to + *molir*:—L. *mollīre* to soften.] To soften, mollify, appease.

1474 CAXTON *Chesse* 10 Deboneyrte amolissheth and makyth softe the hertes of his enemyes. **1480** —— *Ovid's Metam.* x. viii, The mayde, whom love overcam.. and lyttil and lytyl amollyshyd. **1483** —— *G. de la Tour* A viij b, Cortosye.. amolysshyth thyre and wrathe of euery creature.

†**a'mollishment.** *Obs. rare.* In 7 amolish-. [a. Fr. *amollissement* softening, f. *amollir*: see prec.] Softening down, mitigation.

c **1612** DONNE *Lett.* Wks. VI. 356 These of which we speak at this present are capable of no Excuse, no amolishment.

†**a'mome.** *Obs. rare*⁻¹. [a. Fr. *amome*:—L. *amōm-um*.] = AMOMUM.

1382 WYCLIF *Rev.* xviii. 13 Marble, and canel, and amome, *that is, a swete saueringe tree* [Vulg. *cinnamomum*].

amomeous (ə'məʊmɪəs), *a.* [f. AMOM-UM + -EOUS.] Of the nature of amomum.

1853 in MAYNE *Exp. Lex.* **1879** in *Syd. Soc. Lex.*

†**a'momous,** *a.* *nonce-wd.* [f. Gr. ἄμωμ-ος blameless + -OUS.] Blameless.

1683 E. HOOKER *Pref. Pordage's Myst. Div.* 11 That it [the Church] shold be holi and without blemish, or rather Amomous.. that is irreprehensible, safeguarded from the bitings of Momus, one of the feined Gods among the Gentils.

‖**amomum** (ə'məʊməm). Rarely in 7 amomus. [L. *amōmum*, a. Gr. ἄμωμον applied to some, perhaps several, oriental spice plants.] An odoriferous plant. The *Amomum* of the ancients not being certainly identified, the word was used with uncertain denotation by earlier writers; it is now appropriated to a genus of aromatic plants (N.O. *Zingiberaceæ*) including the species which yield Cardamoms and Grains of Paradise.

1398 TREVISA *Barth De P.R.* XVII. viii. (1495) 607 Amomum hath that name for it smellyth as Canell dooth: that hyghte Cynamun. **1551** TURNER *Herbal* (1568) 26 Amomum is a small bushe.. Some call it a christenmase rose. **1637** NABBES *Microcosm.* in Dodsl. IX 140 Perfumes, no Persian aromats, Pontic amomus, or Indian balsam Can imitate. *a* **1719** ADDISON *Dial. Medals* xxiv. (1727) 140 Let Araby extol her happy coast Her Cinnamon and sweet Amomum boast. **1769** SIR J. HILL *Fam. Herbal* (1812) 8 The common amomum [*Sison Amomum*] otherwise called bastard stone parsley. **1855** SINGLETON *Virgil* I 21 And prickly brier amomum yield.

amoner, amonerer, obs. forms of ALMONER.

among (ə'mʌŋ), *adv.* and *prep.* Forms: 1 on ȝemonge, on ȝemang(e, 1–2 onmang(e, 1–6 amang(e (north. after 3), 2–6 amonge, 2– among, 6– 'mong. *North.* 4 omang, 4– amang. Also 2 enmang, 4–5 emang, 5 in mange, emonge, 5–6 emong. See I-MONG. [orig. a phrase, *on* in + *ȝemang* mingling, assemblage, crowd (f. *ȝemengan* to mingle, combine: see MENG); hence, with a sb. in the genitive, 'in the assemblage or company *of*,' then used prepositionally with dat. or acc. Bef. 1100, the full *on ȝemang(e* was reduced to *onmang*, whence by regular phonetic gradation *amang*, *among*. The simple *ȝemang* was also used prepositionally without *on*, giving later *ymong*, I-MONG, MONG. Between *among* and *imong*, thus used side by side, arose *emong*. Modern poets also abbreviate *among* to *'mong*. There was a parallel BIMONG.]

A. *prep.*

Prim. sign. In the mingling or assemblage of; *hence*, surrounded by and associated with.

(Cf. *amid*, *-st*, sometimes loosely used instead.)

Passage from phrase to preposition:—

a **1000** *Elene* (Grein) 105 On feonda ȝemang [= in the company *of* the enemies]. *c* **1000** *Metr. Ps.* lxxxi. 1 God mihtiȝ stód godum on ȝemonge [= the good among, in company *with* the good].

I. Of relation between object and objects.

1. Of the local relation of a thing (or things) to several surrounding objects with which it is grouped: Surrounded by locally. (With *pl. sb.*)

a **1000** *Metr. Ps.* xxv. 9 Ne forleos mine sawle onȝemang þam arleasum. *c* **1000** *Ags. Gosp.* Matt. x. 16 Swa sceap ȝemang wulfas [*Lindisf.* in middum *vel* inmong; *Rushw.* in midde]. *c* **1160** *Hatton G.* ibid., Swa scep onmang wulfen. *c* **1200** *Trin. Coll. Hom.* 195 Alse shep amang wulfes. **1250** LAY. 17742 Com vt..among alle his cnihtes. *c* **1300** *Pop. Sc.* (Wright) 133 Among all the planetes the sonne a-midde is. *c* **1374** CHAUCER *Troylus* IV. 697 The body sate amange hem there. **1382** WYCLIF *Matt.* xiii. 7 Other seedis felden amonge thornis. **1535** COVERDALE *Gen.* iii. 8 Amonge the trees of the garden. **1605** VERSTEGAN *Dec. Intell.* i. (1628) 6 To run up and downe one among another like madmen. **1613** SHAKS. *Hen. VIII*, v. ii. 18 To make me wait at doore ..'Mong Boyes, Groomes, and Lackeyes. **1711** STEELE *Spect.* No. 6 ¶6 The Lacedemonians rose up..and.. received him among them. **1842** LONGF. *Slave's Dream* iii, He saw once more his dark-eyed queen Among her children stand. *c* **1842** —— *Bridge* vi, Like those waters rushing Among the wooden piers.

β. (See also EMONG.)

1375 BARBOUR *Bruce* x. 709 He emang his fayis al Defendit him full douchtely. *c* **1460** *Towneley Myst.* 22 Emang both more and myn. **1592** DAVIES *Astræa* in Chalmers' *Eng. Poets* V. 101/2 Fair month..Emong thy days her birthday is.

b. ***among the hands of***: under the charge of, while being treated or attended to by, (Fr. *entre les mains de*). *Obs.* or *dial.*

1483 CAXTON *Gold. Leg.* 97/3 He deyed sodaynly emong the handes of the sergeans. **1534** LD. BERNERS *Gold. Bk. M. Aurel.* (1546) E vj b, They that haue the charge of a prince.. haue amonge theyr handes, hym that afterwarde oughte to gouerne. **1535** COVERDALE *Jer.* xviii. 4 The vessel that the Potter made off claye brake amonge his hondes. *Mod. north.* The work that we have among our hands, *i.e.* with which we are engaged.

2. Of the relation of a thing (or things) to the whole surrounding group or composite substance: Surrounded by the separate components or particles of. (With *collectives*, and *sing.* names of substances; with the latter *in* is often substituted.)

c **1175** *Lamb. Hom.* 43 þe leit a-monge þunre. *c* **1200** ORMIN 15367 Siþþen don þeȝȝ falls annd flærd Amang þe gode lare. *c* **1300** *Pop. Sc.* (Wright) 135 Whan hit cometh among the fur. *c* **1384** CHAUCER *H. of Fame* 1687 A potful of bawme..Amonge a basket ful of roses. **1535** FISHER *Wks.* (1883) 437 This multitude, amonge whiche our sauiour Christe was. **1697** DAMPIER *Voy.* (1729) I. 235 Vinello's.. are much used among Chocolate to perfume it. **1712** STEELE *Spect.* No. 431 ¶3 A..Stone, which I found among the gravel. **1810** SCOTT *Lady of L.* III. xi, Among the bubbling blood. **1851** LONGF. *Gold. Leg.* 165 We were among the crowd that gathered there.

3. Of the relation of anything in a local group to the other members of the group, although these do not actually surround it; as of an individual to the other members of the same community: In company, association, communion, or residence with or beside; in the house, city, or country of. (= L. *apud*, Fr. *chez*, Ger. *bei*.)

c **1175** *Lamb. Hom.* 19 He com among us. *c* **1200** ORMIN 299 Hæfedd preost Amang Iudisskenn þeode. *c* **1230** *Ancr. R.* 158 Ich wunie among men. *c* **1250** *Gen. & Ex.* 700 Cristes helpe be us amonge! **1387** TREVISA *Higden* Rolls Ser. VII. 45 Otho regnede among Duchesmen [*apud Teutonicos*]. **1535** COVERDALE *Judg.* i, The Cananites dwelt among them at Gaser. **1711** STEELE *Spect.* No. 156 ¶3 We have several of these irresistible Gentlemen among us when the Company is in Town. **1756** BURKE *Vind. Nat. Soc.* Wks. I. 32 The whim and caprice of one ruling man among them. **1807** CRABBE *Par. Reg.* I. 478 Susan..had some pride Among our topmost people to preside.

4. Of the relation of a thing to others in the same nominal or logical group: In the number or class of.

1297 R. GLOUC. 393 Roberd Courtehese þuderward hys herte caste..among oþere gode knyȝtes. **1340** *Ayenb.* 103 Amang alle þe heȝe names of oure lhorde þis is þe uerste. *c* **1340** HAMPOLE *Pr. Consc.* 6551 Omang alle þat þar has bene sene, I fynde wryten paynes fourtene. **1398** TREVISA *Barth. De P.R.* XIII. i. (1495) 438 Amonge all elementes water is prouffytablest. **1477** EARL RIVERS (Caxton) *Dictes* 1 Among other ther was..in my companye a worshipful gentylman. **1665** MANLEY *Grotius's L.-Countr.-Warrs* 297 Many were wounded, among whom was Count William. **1777** HUME *Ess. & Treat.* I. 86 Among the other excellencies of man. **1792** G. WAKEFIELD *Mem.* I. 529 My poetical taste is among the most fastidious. **1849** SIR J. STEPHEN *Eccl. Biog.* I. 111 It is among the mysteries which we are bound to revere.

b. *esp.* of things distinguished in kind from the rest of the group: Preeminent among, as distinguished from, in comparison with, above the others.

c **1230** *Ancr. R.* 2 Moni cunne riwle beoð, auh tuo beoð among alle þet ich chulle speke of. *c* **1375** in *Rel. Ant.* I. 40 As the male..among trees of wodes, So is my derlyng among sones. **1382** WYCLIF *Luke* i. 28 Blessid be thou among wymmen! [*Ags.* on wifum]. *a* **1450** *York Myst. Pewterers* F j, In mange al othir ane bare I. **1523** LD. BERNERS *Froissart* I. cccli. 564 Your folkes haue brent my house, the whiche I loued among all other. *c* **1590** MARLOWE *Faustus* 149 Mong which, as chief, Faustus, we come to thee. *Mod.* She is one among many. He is a Saul among the people.

II. Of the relation of a predicable (attribute, action, event) to things or circumstances.

†**5.** Of the relation of a fact or event to the circumstances which surround it; *esp.* (in early usage) to the time *during* or *in course of* which it happens. *Obs.*

c **1075** *O.E. Chron.* (Laud. MS.) an. 1002 On ȝemang þysum ofsloh Leofsiȝ..þæs cynges heah ȝerefan. *Ibid.* an. 1052 þa amang þison þa wearð Godwine eorl ȝewarnod. **1131** *Ibid.* an. 1127 Ofslaȝen on ane circe..amang þane messe. **1154** *Ibid.* an. 1135 En-mang þis was his nefe cumen to Engle-land. **1250** LAY. 18174 Amang þis motinge Merlyn atwende. *c* **1340** HAMPOLE *Pr. Consc.* 2240 Omang his grete anguys, Hym þai sal tak. **1475** CAXTON *Jason* 12 b, Among these thinges during these triews the king of sklauonye sente his propre messager. **1483** —— *Gold. Leg.* 155/1 Saynt ambrose..gaue up his ghoost emonge the wordes of his prayers. **1528** GARDINER in Pocock *Rec. Ref.* I. lii. 137 Among all which requests nothing certain is proponed. *a* **1691** BAXTER in Tulloch *Eng. Purit.* iii. 306, I never went to any place among all my life..which I had before.. thought of.

†**b.** Hence *conj. phr.* **among that**: during the time that, whilst. *Obs.*

a **1075** *O.E. Chron.* (Laud. MS.) an. 1046 Amanȝ þam þe hi ridon. *c* **1123** *Ibid.* an. 1105 Onmang þam þe he þær wunode. *c* **1200** *Trin. Coll. Hom.* 183 Among þat þe sowle witeð . þe licame worpeð hewe.

6. Of the relation of any action or attribute pervading a group to the members of the group: With or by (the members of a group) generally.

c **1200** ORMIN 2350 Nass þatt næfre fundenn ær Amang wimmenn onn eorþe. **1250** LAY. 29590 Amang the king his cnihtes me cleope[de] heom moglynges. **1297** R. GLOUC. 50 Ac þer was among hem deol ynow. **1481** CAXTON *Reynard* (Arb.) 4 Vsed..emonge marchantes and other comone peple. **1483** *Act 1 Rich. III*, i. §1 Grevous vexacions daily growen among the King's Subgiettis. **1535** COVERDALE *1 Cor.* v. 1 There goeth a commen reporte, that there is whordome amonge you. **1611** BIBLE *1 Sam.* xvii. 12 The man went among men for an old man in the dayes of Saul. **1711** ADDISON *Spect.* No. 131 ¶7, I pass among some for a disaffected Person. **1807** SYD. SMITH *Plymley's Lett.* i. Wks. III. 62 To render the military service popular among the Irish. **1877** LYTTEIL *Landm.* III. iv. 118 The strife of ages may have blotted out their remembrances from among men.

7. Of the relation of distribution or division to the various partakers: Divided between, in portions to each of, to be shared by severally.

1297 R. GLOUC. 23 þis lond was deled a þre among þre sones. *c* **1300** *K. Alis.* 4677 He nam Daries tresour, And pertid hit among his kynne. **1382** WYCLIF *John* vi. 9 What ben thes thingis among so many men? **1611** BIBLE *ibid.*, What are they among so many? **1712** ADDISON *Spect.* No. 507 ¶5 The scandal of a lie..when diffused among several thousand. *Mod.* That leaves five shillings among us.

8. Of the relation of joint action to the various actors: By the joint action of.

1597 SHAKS. *2 Hen. IV*, v. iv. 19 The man is dead that you and Pistoll beate among you. **1599** —— *Much Ado* v. i. 194 You haue among you kill'd a sweet and innocent Ladie. **1869** FREEMAN *Norm. Conq.* III. xii. 100 His first sojourn at Fécamp, his hermit life, his abbacy at Florence..might well take up 24 years among them. *Mod.* Do it among you.

9. Of the relation of reciprocal action between the members of a group.

1340 *Ayenb.* 65 Huanne þe dyeuel yziȝþ loue and onynge among uolke. **1535** COVERDALE *John* x. 19 Then was there discension amonge the Iewes for these sayenges. **1591** SHAKS. *1 Hen. VI*, v. i. 14 That such bloody strife Should reigne among Professors of one Faith. **1682** NORRIS *Hierocles* 34 Hence come wars among Relations, treacheries among Friends. **1711** ADDISON *Spect.* No. 70 ¶4 Whether they quarrelled among themselves, or with their neighbours. **1874** FARRAR *Christ* II. 303 The uncertainty as to what He meant carried the disciples once more to questions among themselves.

B. *adv.* [The prep. used *ellipt.*]

†**1.** During this (period), meanwhile, all the while, at the same time. *Obs.*

1250 LAY. 5110 þar was gleomenne songe, þar was piping among. *a* **1300** *Cursor M.* 88 Of hir to mak bath rim and sang, And luue hir suette sun amang. *c* **1340** HAMPOLE *Pr. Consc.* 3370 Wreth es dedly syn omang, If it be halden in hert lang. **1387** TREVISA *Higden* Rolls Ser. VII. 7 Elsynus bisshop of Wynchestre evere among fondede to have þe see. *c* **1400** *Court of Love* xi, So than apace I journied forth amonge. *c* **1440** *Morte Arth.* (1819) 98 Hys fader dred he euyr among. *c* **1550** BALE *Johan* (1838) 11, I am his gostly father and techear amonge. **1597** SHAKS. *2 Hen. IV*, v. iii. 21 Lustie Lads rome heere, and there; So merrily, and euer among so merrily. **1598** GREENWEY *Tacitus Ann.* I. xi. 20 Fortune ruled the rest, and some honest men were slaine among.

†**2.** Betweenwhiles, at intervals, from time to time, now and then. ***ever among***: every now and then; rarely of *place*, every here and there. *Obs.*

a **1250** *Owl & Night.* 6 Sum wile softe, and lud among. *a* **1300** *Floriz & Bl.* 431 Floriz siȝte and weop among. *c* **1420** *Pallad. on Husb.* IX. 86 Ere amonge ther be Welles wel colde. *c* **1449** PECOCK *Repr.* II. xii. 221 He schal seelde among be occupied of us. **1489** CAXTON *Faytes of Armes* I. xiii. 35 By suche a way hath many an oost suffred emonge grete honger. **1567** MAPLET *Greene Forest* 69 To eate Flies, and now & then among to eate crummie and dry earth. **1606** HOLLAND *Suetonius* 26 Admonishing his soldiers ever and among, to observe and have an ey unto him.

†**3.** Of place: Together, among *something else*.

1602 WARNER *Alb. Eng.* XI. lxi. (1612) 271 Yeat interlace we shall among the loue of her and him. *a* **1613** OVERBURY *A Wife* (1638) 67 She travels to and among, and so becomes a woman of good entertainment. **1624** BEDELL *Lett.* xi. 143 Here is..some truth mingled among.

C. *Comb.* **among-hands** (*north.*): see A 1 b.

1855 ATKINSON *Whitby Gloss.*, *Amang hands*, work done conjointly with other things. 'We can do't amang hands,' or 'all under one.'

amongst (əˈmʌŋst), *prep.* Forms: 3-4 **amanges**, (**amongus**), 4-6 **amonges**, 5 **-is**, **-ys**, 5-7 **amongs**, 6 **amongest(e**, 6- **amongst**, **'mongst**. *Northern* 3-6 **amanges**, 5-7 **amangs**, 7 **amangst**. Also 5 **emanges**, **-ez**, **emongis**, 6 **emonges**, **emongs**, **emongest(e**. [f. AMONG (*amang*, *emong*) with adverbial genitive *-es*, as in *besides*, *betimes*, in 16th c. corrupted to *-st*, by form-assoc. with superlatives, cf. *agains(t*, *amids(t*.]

Less usual in the primary local sense than *among*, and, when so used, generally implying dispersion, intermixture, or shifting position.

1. = AMONG 1.

a **1400** *Sir Perc.* 604 So commes the rede knyghte inne Emangez thame. **1559** in Strype *Ann. Ref.* I. App. vi. 9 Did he place himself amongest the prestes? *c* **1590** MARLOWE *Faustus* 51 Faustus is feasted mongst his noblemen. **1652** ASHMOLE *Theatr. Chem. Brit.* 217 Amongs the Wormys smale. **1851** HELPS *Friends in C.* I. 4 Red brick houses, with poplars coming up amongst them. **1866** G. MACDONALD *Ann. Q. Neighb.* x. (1878) 172, I walked about amongst them.

2. = AMONG 2.

c **1384** CHAUCER *H. of Fame* 1633 They amonges al the pres Shul thus be shamed. **1556** LAUDER *Tractate* 78 Amangs the heuinlie companye.

3. = AMONG 3.

c **1250** *Gen. & Ex.* 1619 Godes hus, Her heuenegate amongus us. **1258** *Procl. Hen. III*, We senden ȝew þis writ ..to halden a manges ȝew ínehord. **1366** MAUNDEV. xix. 211 Thei hadde no pore men amonges hem. **1556** ROBINSON *More's Utopia* 22, I spende almost al the day abrode emonges other. **1583** STUBBES *Anat. Abus.* (1877) 22 A God amongest men. **1633** P. FLETCHER *Purple Isl.* XI. iv, As those holy Fishers once amongs Thou flamedst bright with sparkling parted tongues. **1816** J. WILSON *City of Plague* I. iv. 23 'Tis the first death Hath been amongst us. **1851** HELPS *Friends in C.* I. 116 To live amongst those with whom one has not anything like one's fair value.

4. = AMONG 4.

c **1386** CHAUCER *Merch. T.* 784 Amonges other of his honest thinges, He had a gardin walled all with ston. *c* **1460** FORTESCUE *Abs. & Lim. Mon.* (1714) 44 The kepyng of the See I rekyn not amongs the Ordynarye chargs. **1551** RECORDE *Pathw. Knowl.* Ep. Ded., Amongest them all, I wyll take the exaumples of kyng Phylippe of Macedonie, and of Alexander his sonne. **1586** T. B. *La Primaudaye's Fr. Acad.* II. 41 Amongest terrestrial creatures..God hath created none with two legges onely..but man. **1605** BACON *Adv. Learn.* II. §14 (1873) 83 The opinion of plenty is amongst the causes of want. **1711** STEELE *Spect.* No. 2. ¶3 Frugal Maxims, amongst which the greatest Favourite is 'A Peny Saved is a Peny got.' **1785** C. WILKINS *Bhagvat* vii. 52 A few amongst ten thousand mortals strive for perfection. **1840** HOOD *Up Rhine* 4 Amongst other memorials, there is an old family watch.

5. = AMONG 6.

1366 MAUNDEV. xviii. 195 The more worschipe he hath amonges hem. **1536** BEERLEY in *Four Cent. Eng. Lett.* 34 Fowll vycys don amonckst relygyus men. **1588** A. KING *Canisius' Catech.* H ij b, Ye sonday being yairefter amanges ye Christians callit ye day of our lord. **1599** THYNNE *Animadv.* (1875) 1 One anciente and gretlye Estemed Custome emongeste the Romans. **1676** HOBBES *Iliad* I. 100 Nor will the sickness 'mongst the People cease. **1802** SCOTT *Minstr. Scot. Bord.* i. 39 This original miscellany holds a considerable value amongst collectors.

6. = AMONG 7-8.

c **1460** *Townley Myst.* 217 Emanges us alle I red we kest To bring this thefe to dede. **1527** in *Bury Wills* (1850) 118 Delte emongeste the poore people. *a* **1569** KYNGESMILL *Man's Estate* xiii. (1580) 110 Thei parted my garmentes emongest them. **1607** DEKKER in *Shaks. Cent. Praise* 74 Dispersing his giftes, amongst none but his honest breathren. **1640** *Bk. War-Comm. Covenanters* 2 The divisione of the said troupe horss amangst the parochess.

7. = AMONG 9.

1509 FISHER *Wks.* (1876) 296 Yf ony faccyons or bendes were made secretely amongest her hede Officers. **1543** (24 Dec.) HENRY VIII *Parl. Speech*, What Charity and Love is amongst you, when one calleth the other Heretick and Anabaptist? **1558** Q. ELIZ. in Strype *Ann. Ref.* I. App. iii. 3 Whereupon riseth amonges the common sort..unfruteful dispute. **1756** BURKE *Subl. & B.* Wks. I. 213 How are the partisans of proportional beauty agreed amongst themselves?

amontillado (əmɒntɪˈjɑːdəʊ, -tɪˈlɑːdəʊ). [Sp.; f. *Montilla*, a town in Spain + *-ado* -ATE².]

Formerly, a wine of the sherry type produced in Montilla; now, a matured sherry in which the 'flor' has developed.

1825 HENDERSON in *Q. Jrnl. Sci. & Arts* XVIII. 130 The driest species of Sherry is the Amontillado. **1833** C. REDDING *Mod. Wines* 190. *a* **1845** POE *Cask Amont.* in *Wks.* (1864) I. 347, I was silly enough to pay the full Amontillado price without consulting you in the matter. **1886** RUSKIN *Præterita* II. ix. 325 A certain quantity of the drier Amontillado, from the hill districts of Montilla. **1961** *Times* 16 Jan. 13/5 There are three main types of sherry..*finos*, which are dry, light, and pale; *amontillados*, which are softer, fuller, and less dry; and *olorosos*, which are sweet, rich dessert wines.

b. *attrib.* in fig. sense.

1862 THACKERAY *Philip* xvii, 'By the housekeeper, do you mean Mrs. Baynes?' I ask, in my *amontillado* manner. **1921** *Spectator* 22 Jan. 109/1 We will take as our next example of what we might call Mr. Max Beerbohm's Amontillado style 'Hosts and Guests'.

†**a'moped**, *ppl. a. Obs. rare*$^{-1}$. [f. MOPE, after the apparent analogy of *acold, ahungered, afeard*, etc.] Dispirited.

1573 TWYNE *Æneid* XI. H h iij b, All this citie great With mourninge sits amoapte.

†**amo'rado.** *Obs. rare*$^{-1}$. [ad. Sp. *enamorado* one that is in love, the Sp. prefix *en-* being perhaps confounded with Eng. 'indef. article' *an*: see also INAMORATO.] One in love.

1608 DAY *Hum. out of Breath* (1881) 74 What, hath he chang'd your shepheards hooks to swords? Of Amoradoes made you armed knights?

a'moral (ˌeɪ'mɒrəl), *a.* [f. A- *pref.* 14 + MORAL.] Not within the sphere of moral sense; not to be characterized as either good or bad; non-moral. So **a'moralism, a'moralist, amo'rality.**

1882 R. STEVENSON in *Longm. Mag.* I. 70 There is a vast deal in life and letters both, which is not immoral, but simply a-moral. **1892** S. WEIR MITCHELL in *Century Mag.* July 343/2 You are amoral, not immoral. **1910** *Westm. Gaz.* 19 Mar. 3/2 He argued..that Nature was a-moral, ethically neutral. **1915** A. S. NEILL *Dominie's Log* v. 56, I have no morals, I am an a-moralist, or should it be a non-moralist? **1917** KIPLING *Divers. Creatures* 176 He's the Absolutely Amoral Soul. I've never met one yet. **1920** *Glasgow Herald* 27 Nov. 6 Dada..leads to amoralism. **1923** *Observer* 10 June 8/3 Stupidity, brutality, and general amorality. **1926** *British Weekly* 16 Sept. 487/4 That great sceptic and amoralist [Anatole France]. **1927** R. A. TAYLOR *Leonardo* II. ii. 103 The bright amoral virtue of courage. **1962** J. GRAY *Archaeol. & O.T. World* v. 112 The fertility-cult of Canaan may have been quite amoral.

amorce (ə'mɔːs). ? *Obs.* [ad. F. *amorce* (OF. *amorse*) bait, lure, priming, f. OF. *amordre*, f. *à* + *mordre* to bite.] A charge of fine-grained powder for priming a small fire-arm; a cap for a toy pistol.

1802 C. JAMES *Milit. Dict.*, *Amorce*, an old military word for fine-grained powder, such as is sometimes used for the priming of great guns, mortars or howitzers; as also for small-arms, on account of its rapid inflammation. A port fire, or quick match. **1883** *B'ham Weekly Post* 15 Dec. 7/5 Summoned for having in his possession a small quantity of manufactured amorces, he not having a license for the sale of explosives... These toy pistol caps..were made of a very dangerous explosive. **1889** *Standard* 2 Dec. 4/8 To restrain Mr. Cadwell from making amorces for toy pistols.

†**'amoret.** *Obs.* Forms: 4–6 **amorette**, 5–6 **amourette**, 6 **amouret**, 6–8 **amoret**, 9 AMOURETTE. [a. OFr. *amorete, -ette, amourete, -ette*, dim. of *amour* love:—L. *amōr-em*. The Eng. form *amoret* having become obs., the word has recently been re-adopted from Fr. in sense 5, as AMOURETTE.]

1. A sweetheart, an amorous girl; a paramour.

c **1400** *Rom. Rose* 4758 Eke as well by amorettes In mourning blacke, as bright burnettes. **1483** CAXTON *G. de la Tour* C iv, That thought more to complaire and plese their amourettes..than to plese God. **1590** T. WATSON *Poems* (1870) 171 Bestow no wealth on wanton amorets. **1794** J. WARTON *Sappho's Advice* (R.) When amorets no more can shine And Stella owns she's not divine.

2. = AMORETTO.

1598 FLORIO *Amoretto*, an amoret, a little loue, a wanton, a paramour.

3. A love-knot.

c **1400** *Rom. Rose* 892 Nought clad in silk was he, But alle in floures & in flourettes, Painted alle with amorettes. *a* **1423** JAMES I *King's Q.* II. xxvii, Spangis bright as gold, Forgit of schap like to the amorettis.

4. A love sonnet or song.

1590 LODGE *Euphues' Gold. Leg.* in Halliw. *Shaks.* VI. 37 Rather passe away the time heere in these woods with wryting amorets. **1594** J. DICKENSON *Arisbas* (1878) 71 Where sweete Amorets were chaunted.

5. *pl.* Looks that inspire love, love-glances; 'love tricks, dalliances.' Cotgr. (See AMOURETTE.)

c **1590** GREENE *Friar Bacon* ix. 177 How martial is the figure of his face Yet lovely and beset with amorets. *Ibid.* xii. 8 Should..Phœbus scape those piercing amorets That Daphne glanced at his deity? **1590** —— *Never too late* (1600) 82 Shee alluring him with such wilie amorettes of a curtizan. **1651** *Life of Sarpi* (1676) 90 My amorets and wantonness.

‖**amoretto** (æmɒ'rɛtəʊ, It. amo'rɛtto). [It. *amoretto* a 'little love,' dim. of *amore* love; cf. prec. Formerly naturalized, with pl. *amorettoes*, *amoretto's*, but now treated as It. with pl. *amoretti.*]

†**a.** A lover (*obs.*) †**b.** A love-sonnet (*obs.*) †**c.** A love-trick (*obs.*) **d.** A little love, a cupid.

1596 SPENSER (*title* of Love-sonnets) Amoretti. **1646** J. HALL *Poems* 35 In each line lie More Amorettoe's then in Doris eye. **1654** GAYTON *Fest. Notes* 47 (T.) The amoretto was wont to take his stand at one place, where sate his mistress. **1710** PALMER *Proverbs* 139 The amoretto's of Bedlam..were always weak silly people, and were us'd to the conversation of ballad & romance. **1873** SYMONDS *Grk. Poets* x. 335 A painting, in which *amoretti* are plentiful.

†**amo'revolous**, *a. Obs. rare*$^{-1}$. [f. It. *amorevole* loving + -OUS.] Loving, affectionate.

a **1670** HACKET *Abp. Williams* I. 161 To shew her cordial and amorevolous affections.

†**a'moring**, *vbl. sb. nonce-wd.* Love-making.

1675 COTTON *Burlesque upon Burl.* 213 (D.) On Carian Latmus loudly snoaring, Insensible of thy amoring.

‖**amorino** (ɑːmɒ'riːnəʊ, æ-). Pl. -i. [It. *amorino*, dim. of *amore*: cf. *amoretto*.] A little love, a cupid.

1859 GULLICK & TIMBS *Paint.* 182 Chubby little *Amorini*, or, as they are popularly called, 'Cupids.' **1880** WARREN *Book-plates* v. 36 Frames most heavily adorned with angels, term-figures, amorini, or satyrs' heads.

amorism ('æmərɪz(ə)m). [f. as AMORIST + -ISM.] The disposition or practice of amorists; amorous sentiment or intrigue.

1897 *Star* 30 Mar. 1/7 We were in the land of romantic amorism. **1903** *Athenæum* 17 Jan. 77/1 Half old-world Spanish, half topsy-turvy Oriental in its fatalism and passionate amorism.

amorist ('æmərɪst). Also 7–9 **amourist.** [f. L. *amor* or Fr. *amour* love + -IST.] **1.** One who professes love, a professed lover. **a.** *usually*, A votary of (sexual) love, a gallant.

1581 SIDNEY *Sonnet* i, Faint amorist! what, dost thou think To taste love's honey, and not drink One dram of gall? **1620** SHELTON *Don Quix.* III. xxxii. 222 Tho' I be enamoured, yet I am not of those vicious Amourists, but of your chaste Platonicks. *a* **1652** BROME *Court Beggar* I. i, An extreame Amorist desperately devoted Unto the service of some threescore Ladies. **1798** LAMB *Lett.* I. (1841) 28 Like some hot amourist with glowing eyes. **1880** WEBB *Goethe's Faust* I. ii. 67 One clings to earth, like some fond amorist, With strong organic clutch.

b. *rarely* of other than sexual love.

1635 A. STAFFORD *Fem. Glory* (1869) 115 You who have lived spirituall Amourists. **1660** BOYLE *Seraph. Love* 92 Surely the Divine Amorist had cause to say that 'herein is the love, not that we loved God, but that he loved us.'

2. One who treats of love; a writer of amatory literature. Also *attrib.*

1641 MILTON *Reason Ch.-Govt.* II. 41 A work not..like that which flows..from the pen of some vulgar Amorist, or the trencher fury of a riming parasite. **1824** *Blackw. Mag.* XVI. 191 Our most eminent amorist..Tom Moore. **1882** PALGRAVE in Grosart *Spenser's Wks.* IV. p. lx, Amourist literature. **1905** *Athenæum* 1 Apr. 390/3 The poet..is imagined as a mild and amiable amorist. **1909** JUSSERAND *Lit. Hist. Eng. People* III. 468 The..amourist writers of Elizabethan times.

amoristic (æmə'rɪstɪk), *a. rare*$^{-1}$. [f. prec. + -IC.] Treating of love, amatory.

1881 R. ELLIS in *Academy* 9 Apr. 256 The sweetness of Mr. Butler's amoristic Muse.

Amorite ('æməraɪt), *sb.* and *a.* [ad. Heb. *'ᵉmōrî* (Akkadian texts called the lands which these people inhabited *Amurru(m)*, lit. 'West'; cf. Sumerian *martu*): see -ITE[1].] **A.** *sb.* A member of any of a group of Semitic tribes who dwelt in Mesopotamia, Palestine, and Syria in the second and third millenium B.C., and who are described in Biblical texts as inhabiting the land of Canaan before the arrival of the Israelites; their language.

1535 BIBLE (Coverdale) *Ezek.* xvi. 3 Thy father was an Amorite. **1788** *Encycl. Brit.* I. 625/2 The Amorites first of all peopled the mountains lying to the west of the Dead Sea. **1845** *Encycl. Metrop.* IX. 466/2 The Amorites derived their name from Amorrhæus, the fourth son of Canaan. **1914** T. E. LAWRENCE *Let.* 6 Feb. (1938) 165 We are digging up well preserved Amorites who were buried naked and headless. **1935** [see MESOPOTAMIAN *a.*]. **1958** W. F. ALBRIGHT in J. B. Pritchard *Anc. Near East* xii. 261 This expression is always in Amorite, transcribed in cuneiform *hayaram qatulum*. **1981** *Word 1980* XXXI. 222 Languages with *h* (Amorite, Hebrew, [etc.]).

B. *adj.* Of or pertaining to the Amorites or their language.

1875 *Encycl. Brit.* I. 747/2 Five of the most powerful of the Amorite kings..formed a confederacy. **1956** A. TOYNBEE *Historian's Approach to Relig.* iv. 45 Examples of marchmen empire-builders are the Amorite rulers of Hammurabi's reconstituted 'Empire of Sumer and Akkad'. **1965** H. B. HUFFMON (*title*) Amorite personal names in the Mari texts. **1973** M. LIVERANI in D. J. Wiseman *People of Old Testament Times* v. 108 The general linguistic unity of the Semites in Syria during Amorite times.

†**a-'morning**, *adv. phr. Obs.* [A *prep.*[1] on + MORNING: cf. *a-morrow*.] In the morning.

1480 CAXTON *Chron. of Eng.* iii. 8 Amornyng in the dawenynge brute went oute of the castel.

†**a-'mornings**, *adv. phr. Obs.* [f. as prec. with genitival *-s*: cf. *a-days*, and mod. 'He comes of a morning.'] In the morning, every morning.

1377 LANGL. *P. Pl.* B. XI. 7253 Males drowen hem to males · a mornynges bi hem-self. *a* **1541** WYATT *Poet. Wks.* (1861) 98 A mornings then when I do rise. **1572** MASCAL *Govt. Cattle* (1627) 13 Squirt thereof a mornings into his nostrils. **1633** EARL MANCH. *Al Mondo* (1636) 27 The brightest dayes dye into dark nights, but rise againe a mornings.

‖**amo'rosa.** *Obs.* [Sp. and It. *amorosa*, fem. of AMOROSO.] A female lover; a wanton, a courtesan.

1634 T. HERBERT *Trav.* (1677) 191, I took them for *Amorosa's*, and violators of the bounds of Modesty.

amorosity (æmə'rɒsɪtɪ). ? *Obs.* Also 5 **amorouste**, 7 **amourosity.** [a. OFr. **amouroustè* (cf. *pousté*); afterwards refashioned after mod. words in -OSITY.] The quality of being amorous; love, fondness. (Not confined to sexual love.)

1485 CAXTON *Paris & V.* 3 Parys as yet knewe nought of amorouste. **1611** CHAPMAN *May Day* Plays 1873 II. 382 Come away, you'll be whipt anone for your amourosity. **1677** J. WEBSTER *Witchcr.* xvi. 309 The soul may have a far greater amorosity to stay in some body that is lively, sweet and young. **1742** in BAILEY. **1830** GALT *Laurie Todd* (1849) VII. viii. 338 He whispered to me the warmth of his amorosity.

‖**amo'roso**, *sb.* [Sp. and It. *amoroso* a lover:—L. *amōrōs-um*: see AMOROUS.] †**1.** A lover, a gallant. *Obs.*

1616 *Rich Cabinet* (Wright) Though his wives amoroso have been at home all day. **1654** GAYTON *Festiv. Notes* III. ii. 72 This slut recites the dream false, and in her owne person, when it was her Amorosos. **1706** PHILLIPS, *Amoroso* (It.), an Amorous Man, a Lover, a Gallant, a Spark.

2. (usu. with capital initial). A type of sweetened Oloroso sherry.

c **1870** in H. W. Allen *Number Three St. James's St.* (1950) 184/1 Sherry..Amoroso—72/-. **1875** *Collier & Co.'s Price List* 6 (Advt.), Especially Selected Wines... 'Amoroso', *very pale, soft and delicate.* **1917** *Harrods Gen. Catal.* 1284 Sherry... Amoroso, with good flavour and colour. **1920** G. SAINTSBURY *Notes on Cellar-Bk.* ii. 20 One might jangle a long time on Montillas and Olorosos, Amorosos and the so vilely traduced Vino de Pasto itself. **1967** A. LICHINE *Encycl. Wines* 495/1 Brown Sherry is a very dark, sweet Amoroso, likely to be cheaper than East India. **1980** M. BROADBENT *Gt. Vintage Wine Bk.* 405/2 Amoroso. Bottled 1948... A most attractive wine.

‖**amoroso** (æmə'rəʊsəʊ), *a.* and *adv. Mus.* [It., loving(ly).] As a musical direction: (to be played) lovingly, tenderly.

1770 J. HOYLE *Dict. Mus.* 3 *Amoroso*, this word is seldom used; but when it is, it signifies that you must play in an amorous and gallant manner. **1775** 'J. COLLIER' *Mus. Trav.* (ed. 2) 80, I was playing in a strain somewhat *amoroso*. **1876** STAINER & BARRETT *Dict. Mus. Terms* 25/2 *Amoroso* (*It.*), in a loving style. **1922** JOYCE *Ulysses* 266 *Amoroso ma non troppo*. **1962** *Times* 16 Jan. 5/1 Liszt's strongest vein of fire-and-brimstone, relieved by an *amoroso* episode..of melting sweetness and remarkable originality. **1985** *Guardian Weekly* 23 June 20 It obeyed not only the adjective of the title but..those of the six individual movements as well—giovale, amoroso, [etc.].

amorous ('æmərəs), *a.* Forms: 4–5 **amorouse**, **-rows, amirous**, 4–6 **amorus, amerous**, 5 **-us, -ouse, -ose, amourous(e**, 6–7 **amarous(e**, 7 **amorose**, 4– **amorous.** [a. OFr. *amorous* (mod.Fr. *amoureux*):—L. *amōrōs-um*, f. *amōr* love: see -OUS.]

I. *actively.*

1. Of persons: Inclined to love; habitually fond of the opposite sex. Also *fig.* of things: Loving, fond.

1303 R. BRUNNE *Handl. Synne* 7988 Þys was a prest ryȝt amerous, And amerous men are leccherous. **1393** GOWER *Conf.* I. 304 Whiche of the two more amorous is Or man or wife. **1483** CAXTON *Gold. Leg.* 90/1 Therfore saith the holy ghoost to the sowle that is amerouse. **1607** TOPSELL *Four-footed Beasts* (1673) 341 The hairs layed to Womens lips, maketh them amorous. **1610** GWILLIM *Displ. Herald.* III. vii. (1660) 133 The Woodbine is a loving and amorous plant, which embraceth all that it growes near unto. **1616** R. C. *Times' Whistle* vi. 2583 Doth captive the hart Of amorous ladies. **1728** YOUNG *Odes to King* Wks. 1757 I. 177 Beneath them lies, With lifted eyes, Fair Albion, like an amorous maid. **1807** CRABBE *Par. Reg.* II. 405 Sir Edward Archer is an amorous knight.

†**b.** with *unto. Obs. rare.*

c **1400** *Destr. Troy* VIII. 3926 Troilus was..amirous vnto Maidens & mony hym louyt.

2. Affected with love towards one of the opposite sex; in love, enamoured, fond. Also *fig.* of things (both as subject and object of love). **a.** *absol.*

c **1314** *Guy Warw.* 37 Namore wostow of armes loue..So amerous thou were anon right. *c* **1385** CHAUCER *L.G.W.* 1189 This amerous quien. *c* **1440** *Gesta Rom.* II. v. 285 The thirde knyght is wondir amerous, and lovethe you passyng well. **1596** SHAKS. *Tam. Shr.* III. i. 63 Our fine Musitian groweth amorous. **1647** COWLEY *Bathing* iii. in *Mistress* (1669) 79 The amorous Waves would fain about her stay. **1711** STEELE *Spect.* No. 78 ¶4 The young Lady was amorous, and had like to run away with her Father's Coachman. **1822** W. IRVING *Braceb. Hall* xix. 164 The amorous frog piped from among the rushes.

†**b.** with *on. Obs.*

c **1386** CHAUCER *Frankl. T.* 764 This squier On Dorigen that was so amorus. **1477** EARL RIVERS (Caxton) *Dictes* 146 He was amerous on somme noble lady. **1599** SHAKS. *Much Ado* II. i. 161 Sure my brother is amorous on Hero. **1625** MILTON *Death Fair Inf.* i, Being amorous on that lovely dye That did thy cheek envermeil.

c. with *of.*

a **1450** *Knt. de la Tour* (1868) 168 There came another knyght which was also amerous of that lady. **1606** SHAKS. *Ant. & Cl.* II. ii. 202 And made The water to follow faster, As amorous of their strokes. **1692** DRYDEN *St. Euremont's Ess.* 212 One must be very amorous of a Truth, to search after it at that Price. **1821** KEATS *Isabel* xix, Thy roses amorous of the moon.

†**d.** with *in*: Delighting in. *Obs. rare.*

a **1674** CLARENDON *Hist. Reb.* II. VIII. 392 He was amorous in Poetry, and Musick, to which he indulged the greatest part of his time.

3. Of action, expression, etc.: Showing love or fondness; fond, loving. **a.** (sexual.)

c **1385** CHAUCER *L.G.W.* 1102 Many an Amorouse [*v.r.* amorous, amorows] lokynge & devys. **1493** *Petronylla* (Pynson) 123 Nightyngalys with amerous notys clere Salueth Esperus. **1525** LD. BERNERS *Froiss.* II. xxvi. 72 His eyen gray and amorous. **1605** SHAKS. *Lear* I. i. 48 France & Burgundy, Great Riuals in our yongest daughters loue, Long in our Court, haue made their amorous soiourne. **1750** JOHNSON *Rambl.* No. 182 ¶7 Not being accustomed to amorous blandishments. **1863** B. TAYLOR *Poet's Jrnl.* (1866) 54 Earth in amorous palpitation Receives her bridegroom's kiss.

b. (general): Loving, affectionate, devoted, ardent.

1677 GALE *Crt. Gentiles* II. III. 64 Those amorose impetuosities that are in men and tend to pietie or impietie. *Ibid.* 145 An amorous vehemence against sin. **1784** J. BARRY *Lect. Art* v. (1848) 187 With attention and amorous assiduity. **1856** R. VAUGHAN *Ho. w. Mystics* (1860) I. 65 The amorous quest of the soul after the Good.

4. Of or pertaining to (sexual) love.

c **1385** CHAUCER *L.G.W.* 2616 Fful is the place.. Of songis amerous, of maryage. **1483** CAXTON *Gold. Leg.* 31/2 The holy institucion of this amerous sacrament shold be the more honourably halowed. **1567** DRANT *Horace Ep.* To Reader, So greate a scull of amarouse Pamphlets. **1592** SHAKS. *Rom. & Jul.* III. ii. 8 Louers can see to doe their Amorous rights, And by their owne Beauties. **1635** SWAN *Spec. Mundi* vi. §4 (1643) 266 Sow-bread..is a good amorous medicine, and will make one in love. **1741** H. WALPOLE *Lett. to H. Mann* 7 (1834) I. 23 The poor Princess and her conjugal and amorous distresses. **1809** W. IRVING *Knickerb.* 75 To manhood roused, he spurns the amorous flute. **1846** PRESCOTT *Ferd. & Is.* I. viii. 373 Offered up his amorous incense on the altar of the Muse.

†**II.** *passively*, Of persons and things: Lovable, lovely. *Obs.*

c **1400** *Rom. Rose* 2901 It is thyng most amerous, For to aswage a mannes sorowe, To sene his lady by the morowe. **1535** STEWART *Cron. Scot.* II. 37 His wyfe.. buir to him ane virgin amorus. **1557** *Primer Sarum* D iij, O mother of God moste glorious, and amorous. **1567** *Trial of Treas.* in Hazl. *Dodsl.* III. 288 O she is a minion of amorous hue. **1611** DEKKER *Roaring Girle* 213, *J.* Here's most amorous weather, my Lord. *Omnes. Amorous* weather! *J.* Is not *amorous* a good word?

†**B.** quasi-*sb.* A lover; one in love. *Obs.*

a **1440** *Sir Degrev.* 655 Sir Degrivaunt that amerus Had joye of that syȝth. **1491** CAXTON *Vitas Patr.* (W. de Worde) I. xli. 62/2 How ofte she hath..made fayre herself for to playse her amourouse or loues.

amorously (ˈæmərəslɪ), *adv.* [f. prec. + -LY².] In an amorous manner; in the way of love; lovingly, fondly, affectionately.

c **1386** CHAUCER *Merch. T.* 436 So that ye please hir not to amorously. **1430** LYDG. *Chron. Troy* I. viii, Nightingales Full amorously did welcome in their songe The lusty season. **1525** LD. BERNERS *Froissart* II. xxvi. 72 He was of good and easy acquayntance with euery man, and amorously wolde speke to them. **1634** HABINGTON *Castara* (1870) 38 The Larke..amorously courts her [Aurora's] beames. **1821** KEATS *Isabel* lxii, Asking for her lost Basil amorously. **1830** TENNYSON *Madeline* iii, If my lips should dare to kiss Thy taper fingers amorously.

amorousness (ˈæmərəsnɪs). [f. as prec. + -NESS.] The quality of being amorous or inclined to love; fondness of the opposite sex; lovingness.

1580 SIDNEY *Arcadia* (1622) 160 Iealousie of his amourousnesse. *a* **1631** DONNE *Select.* (1840) 30 What doth thy holy amorousness, thy holy covetousness..most carry thy desire upon? **1665** BOYLE *Occas. Refl.* v. ix. (1675) 332 Lindamor has Wit and Amorousness enough..to defend fair Ladies. **1755** in JOHNSON; and in mod. Dicts.

‖**amorpha** (əˈmɔːfə), *sb.*¹ *pl.* [Gr. ἄμορφα adj. pl. neut. (sc. ζῷα) shapeless (animals).] = AMORPHOZOA.

1835 KIRBY *Habits & Inst. Anim.* I. iv. 149 [Infusories also called] amorpha or without form.

amorpha (əˈmɔːfə), *sb.*² *Bot.* [f. Gr. ἄμορφ-ος shapeless.] A genus of N. American deciduous shrubs, with long spiked clusters of purple flowers.

1753 CHAMBERS *Cycl. Supp., Amorpha*..a genus of plants of the papilionaceous kind. **1847** LONGF. *Evang.* II. iv. 13 Prairies..Bright with..purple amorphas. **1866** JOHNS in *Treas. Bot.* 53 The two pairs of petals, termed severally the wings and keel, are absent, the only representative of petals being the standard or vexillum, and hence its name *Amorpha*, 'deformed.'

amorphism (əˈmɔːfɪz(ə)m). [f. Gr. ἄμορφ-ος, + -ISM.] Want of regular form: *esp.* want of crystalline structure, as in amorphous minerals.

1852 PEIRCE tr. *Stockhardt's Exp. Chem.* (Index), Amorphism. **1882** *Times* 16 Feb. 9/3 While the Session is yet young, one day is pretty much like another, and the week as a whole shows a distinct tendency to amorphism.

amorpho- (əˈmɔːfəʊ), comb. form [Gr. ἀμορφο-] of AMORPHOUS; as in **amorphogranular**, consisting of amorphous granules.

amorphophyte (əˈmɔːfəfaɪt). *Bot.* [f. AMORPHO- + Gr. φυτόν plant.] A name given (after Necker) to plants having flowers of irregular or anomalous form.

1879 in *Syd. Soc. Lex.*

amorphose (əˈmɔːfəʊs), *a. rare*⁻¹. Irregular form of next word.

1834 GOOD *Bk. Nature* I. 116 Grey-wacke and grey-wacke slate may be distinguished by the terms amorphose and schistose killas.

amorphous (əˈmɔːfəs), *a.* [f. mod.L. *amorphus*, a. Gr. ἄμορφ-ος shapeless (f. ἀ priv. + μορφή form) + -OUS. Cf. mod.Fr. *amorphe.*] Not in J.

1. Having no determinate shape, shapeless, unshapen; irregularly shaped, unshapely.

1731 BAILEY, *Amorphous*, without form or shape, ill-shapen. **1791** D'ISRAELI *Cur. Lit.* (1866) 148/1 An amorphous hat, very much worn. **1831** CARLYLE *Sart. Res.* (1858) 178 The enormous, amorphous Plum-pudding, more like a Scottish Haggis. **1870** LOWELL *Among my Bks.* Ser. I. (1873) 203 That quality in man which..gives classic shape to our own amorphous imaginings. **1878** BLACK *Green Past.* xxxviii. 301 All three wore heavy and amorphous garments.

b. Belonging to no particular type or pattern; anomalous, unclassifiable.

1803 *Phil. Trans.* XCIV. 38 This kind of attraction is either regular, irregular, or amorphous. **1845** CARLYLE *Cromwell* (1871) I. 63 A morose, amorphous, cynical Law-pedant.

2. *Min.* & *Chem.* Not composed of crystals in physical structure; uncrystallized, massive.

1801 BOURNON *Arseniates* in *Phil. Trans.* XCI. 171 The matrix..siliceous; sometimes crystalline; and sometimes in an amorphous mass. **1842** W. GROVE *Corr. Phys. Forces* (ed. 6) 84 An opaque amorphous state, as graphite or charcoal. **1870** TYNDALL *Heat* xiii. §639 A fragment of almost black amorphous phosphorus. **1879** RUTLEY *Stud. Rocks* x. 123 Augite often contains inclosures of amorphous glass.

3. *Geol.* Occurring in a continuous mass, without stratification, cleavage, or other division into similar parts.

1830 LYELL *Princ. Geol.* I. 346 An amorphous mass passing downwards into lava, irregularly prismatic. **1853** PHILLIPS *Rivers, etc. Yorksh.* iv. 124 These perishing cliffs show at the bottom the amorphous boulder-clay.

4. *Biol.* Without the definite shape or organization found in most higher animals and plants.

1848 DANA *Zoophytes* 711 The structure was completely amorphous. **1868** WRIGHT *Ocean W.* iv. 74 A sort of animated jelly, amorphous and diaphanous. **1877** ROBERTS *Handbk. Med.* I. 51 Coagulated fibrin, either amorphous or fibrillated.

5. *fig.* Ill-assorted, ill-digested, unorganized.

1837 CARLYLE *Fr. Rev.* (1872) III. III. v. 121 An amorphous Sansculottism taking form. **1869** LECKY *Europ. Mor.* I. i. 247 [Rome's] population soon became an amorphous, heterogeneous mass.

aˈmorphousness. [f. prec. + -NESS.] Amorphous condition, shapelessness.

1870 SMITH *Syn. & Ant., Configuration..Ant.* Shapelessness, Amorphousness. **1880** *Scribn. Mag.* July 331 The amorphousness that is unavoidable when one works from the parts to the whole instead of from within outward.

‖**amorphozoa** (əˌmɔːfəˈzəʊə), *sb. pl. Zool.* [mod.L., f. AMORPHO- + Gr. ζῷα animals.] A collective appellation given by Blainville to those protozoa, such as sponges, and their allies, which have no regular form.

1857 PAGE *Advd. Text-bk. Geol.* (1876) 341 The amorphozoa or spongiform bodies, which seem to have crowded the waters.

amorphoˈzoary. *Zool.* [f. prec. + -ARY collective.] A compound or polypiform amorphozoic organism, as a mass of sponge.

1879 in *Syd. Soc. Lex.*

amorphoˈzoic, *a. Zool.* [f. as prec. + -IC.] Of or pertaining to the amorphozoa.

amorphoˈzoous, *a. Zool.* [f. as prec. + -OUS.] Related to or resembling the amorphozoa.

1879 in *Syd. Soc. Lex.*

amorphy (əˈmɔːfɪ). ? *Obs.* [a. Fr. *amorphie*, ad. Gr. ἀμορφία shapelessness, f. ἄμορφ-ος AMORPHOUS.] Shapelessness. (Used in jest by Swift.)

1704 SWIFT *T. of Tub.* v. (1750) 74 His epidemical diseases being Fastidiosity, Amorphy, and Oscitation. **1775** in ASH. **1879** *Syd. Soc. Lex., Amorphy*, same as *Amorphia.*

†**a-morrow,** *adv. phr. Obs.* Forms: 1 on **morȝenne,** 1–3 **on morȝen,** 3 **on morwen, a morwen, a-moreȝe,** 3–4 **amorewe,** 3–5 **a morwe, amorow(e.** [A *prep.*¹ on + MORROW: cf. *a-morning.*]

1. In the morning.

c **1000** *Ags. Gosp.* John xx. 1 Maria cóm on morȝen ær hit leoht wære. *c* **1230** *Ancr. R.* 22 A morwen oþer a niht.. siggeð Commendacium. *c* **1384** CHAUCER *H. Fame* 2106 Come we amorowe or on eve. *c* **1430** LYDG. *Chichev. & Bycorne* in Dodsl. XI. 335 A good repast A morwe to breke with my fast.

2. On the morrow after, next morning.

a **855** *O.E. Chron.* an. 755 Ða on morȝenne ȝehierdun þæt þæs cyninges þeȝnas. *c* **1230** *Ancr. R.* 122 Me ledde him amorwen uorte hongen. *a* **1300** *Floriz & Bl.* 67 Amoreȝe, so sone so hit was day, He tok his leue. *c* **1386** CHAUCER *Knt's T.* 763 Thus they ben departed til a-morwe [*v.r.* amorwe, a morowe, on morwe]. **1480** *Cambriæ Epit.* 411 Yet a-morow that stone Was seyne erly in Mon.

amort (əˈmɔːt), *adv.* and *pred. a.* [a. Fr. *à mort* at or to death; but it appears that the Fr. *à la mort* 'to the death' was orig. adopted, and corrupted to *all amort*, the Fr. *à mort* excusing the change, and leading to the use of *amort* without *all.*]

In the state or act of death; lifeless, inanimate; *fig.* spiritless, dejected. **a.** with *all.* (See also ALAMORT, the original form.)

c **1590** GREENE *Friar Bacon* I. i, Shall he thus all amort live malcontent? **1591** SHAKS. *1 Hen. VI*, III. ii. 124 Now where's the Bastards braues, and Charles his glikes? What all amort? **1600** HOLLAND *Livy* XXXIV. xxvi. 868 i, They were all amort [*obpressam*] for feare. **1659** BURROUGHS *Beatitudes* (1867) 128 If God do not answer thee presently, thou art all-a-mort and discouraged. **1839** BAILEY *Festus* xxx. (1848) 343 Why look ye all amort?

b. without *all* (suggested however in first quot.).

1619 H. HUTTON *Follie's Anat.* (1842) 24 She counts him but a nazard, halfe a-mort. **1667** WATERHOUSE *Fire of Lond.* 62 Without it [Gods allowance] all is abortive and amort. **1840** BROWNING *Sordello* VI. Wks. 1863 III. 435 Untasked of any love, His sensitiveness idled, now amort, Alive now.

†**aˈmortify,** *v. Obs.*⁻⁰ [ad. med.L. *a(d)mortificāre*, a purely L. equivalent of *admortizāre*; f. *ad* to + *mort-em* death + *-ficāre* to do, make: see -FY.] = AMORTIZE.

1742 BAILEY, *Amortization*..the Act of Amortifying.

amortizable, -isable (əˈmɔːtɪzəb(ə)l), *a.* [f. AMORTIZE + -ABLE. Cf. Fr. *amortissable.*] Capable of being cleared off as a liability; extinguishable.

1880 *Daily Tel.* 4 Dec., Spain has three classes of public debt..The Two per Ct. Exterior and Interior, is amortisable in about 12 years. **1881** *Daily News* 19 Mar. 5/5 Until the amortissable milliard was issued.

amortization, -isation (əˌmɔːtɪˈzeɪʃən). [ad. med.L. *a(d)mortizātiōn-em*, n. of action f. *amortizā-re*: see next.]

1. The action of alienating lands in mortmain; 'that is to some community that never is to cease.' J. ? *Obs.*

1672 MANLEY *Interpr., Amortization*..est prædiorum translatio in manum mortuam. **1726** AYLIFFE *Parergon* 88 After the Laws of Amortisation were devised. **1756** NUGENT *Montesquieu* (1758) II. XXI. xvi. 57 This confiscation was a species of the right of amortisation.

2. The extinction of a debt, or of any pecuniary liability, especially by means of a sinking fund. Also *concr.* the sum paid towards such extinction.

[Not in CRAIG 1847, WORCESTER 1859.] **1864** WEBSTER cites SIMMONDS. **1866** *Daily Tel.* 23 Jan. 6/1 The half-yearly three per cent. dividend and three per cent. amortisation fund. **1867** *Lond. Rev.* 28 Sept. 344/1 Every available resource for the amortization of the debt. **1883** *Pall Mall G.* 17 Mar. 5/2 An annual sum of 67,662*l.* for interest, and 11,277*l.* as amortization.

amortize, -ise (əˈmɔːtɪz), *v.* Forms: 4 **amorteise,** 5–6 **amortyse, -eyse, -ysse,** 4 **amortise,** 7– **amortize.** *Aphet.* 5 **mortayse.** [orig. a. Fr. *amortiss-* extended stem of *amort-ir* to bring to death, cogn. w. Pr. *amortir*, OCat. *amortir*, It. *ammortire*:—possible late L. **admortīre*, f. *ad* to + *mort-em* death. The etymological spelling of the last syllable would be *-ise* or rather *-iss*, *-ish*; *amortize* follows the med.L. *a(d)mortizā-re*, formed on the mod. languages: see -IZE 2.]

†**1.** *trans.* To deaden, render as if dead, destroy.

c **1386** CHAUCER *Pers. T.* 173 (Hengwrt MS.) The goode werkes that men don whil thay ben in good lif ben al amortised [*other texts* al mortefied] by synne folwyng. **1656** BLOUNT *Glossogr., Amortize*, to deaden, kill, or slay.

†**2.** *intr.* To droop, hang as dead. *Obs. rare.*

1480 CAXTON *Ovid's Metam.* XI. xix, With thys rayne wente the sayle amortyssynge and hanging hevy.

3. To alienate in mortmain, *i.e.* to convey (property) to a corporation.

1377 LANGL. *P. Pl.* B. xv. 315 And auyse hem..Or þei amortesed to monkes · or chanouns her rentes. **1393** —— C. XVIII. 54 Er thei amorteisede. *c* **1430** LYDG. *Min. Poems* 207 Let mellerys and bakerys..a litil chapelle bylde, The place amorteyse, and purchase liberté. **1487** PRIOR in *Paston Lett.* 893 III. 332 The seide annuyte schulde be mortaysed in perpetuyte. **1530** *Proper Dyaloge* (1863) 37 To amorteyse secular lordshippes to the state of the clergye. **1622** BACON *Hen. VII*, 74 Did in effect amortize a great part of the Lands of the Kingdome unto the Hold and Occupation of the Yeomanrie. **1750** CARTE *Hist. Engl.* II. 452 Lands amortised without licence. **1875** STUBBS *Const. Hist.* III. xviii. 245 To render inalienable or, so to speak, amortize the crown lands.

4. To extinguish or wipe out (a debt or other liability), usually by means of a sinking fund, which eventually redeems it.

1882 *St. James' Gaz.* 3 Feb., They would introduce economies in order to amortise the Egyptian Debt.

amortized, -ised (ə'mɔːtɪzd), *ppl. a.* [f. prec. + -ED.]

†**1.** Rendered dead, destroyed. *Obs.*

1617 J. RIDER *Dict., Mortuus*, amortised, killed.

2. Held in, or as in, mortmain; held in commission.

1628 *Reliq. Wotton.* (1672) 565 The Vice-Chamberlainship, which yet lyeth amortized in your Noble Friend. **1881** *Contemp. Rev.* Mar. 444 The sale or lease of such amortized property.

amortizement, -ise- (ə'mɔːtɪzmənt). [a. Fr. *amortissement*: see AMORTIZE and -MENT.] = AMORTIZATION.

1618 PULTON tr. *Act 27 Edw. I* (1632) 78 There to make fine for the amortisements. **1881** *Contemp. Rev.* Mar. 444 The future amortizement of land by corporations.

amortizing, -ising (ə'mɔːtɪzɪŋ), *vbl. sb.* [f. AMORTIZE *v.* + -ING[1].] The conveying to mortmain.

c **1377** WYCLIF *Poor Priests* Wks. xix. (1879) 278 þe sotil amortasynge of seculer lordischipis. **1530** *Proper Dyaloge* (1863) 26 So after the amortesyenge occupyeth yᵉ clarcke. **1618** PULTON tr. *Act 27 Edw. I* (1632) 78 Enquests impanelled for the amortizing Lands or Tenements.

amorwe, variant of AMORROW, *adv. Obs.*

amos, obs. form. of AMICE.

amosite ('æməsaɪt). *Min.* [f. *Amosa*, formed from the initial letters of *A*sbestos *M*ines *o*f *S*outh *A*frica + -ITE[1].] A form of asbestos found only in certain areas of South Africa. Also *attrib.*

1918 A. L. HALL *Asbestos in S. Africa* 12 *Amosite*, chemically characterized by high percentage of iron with variable amounts of aluminium, magnesium, and calcium. *Ibid.* 13 Amosite..the special variety of monoclinic iron amphibole from the Lydenburg and Pietersburg Districts. **1928** *Observer* 1 July 3 Four years later [in 1895] the chrysolite deposits of the Carolina district began to be exploited, followed by the discovery of amosite fibre in the Transvaal. **1961** *Engineering* 2 June 770 Marinite is a homogenous pressed lime-silica board having an amosite asbestos fibre content.

†**a'motine,** *v. Obs. rare*⁻¹. [ad. Sp. *amotinar* to raise in mutiny, f. *a* to + *motin* mutiny, uproar.] To raise in mutiny, rouse to arms.

1578 T. N. tr. *Conq. W. India* 245 Who had comen to Vera Crux to amotine the Towne.

amotion (ə'məʊʃən). *arch.* [ad. L. *āmōtiōn-em* a putting away, n. of action f. *āmōt-* ppl. stem of *āmovē-re*: see AMOVE *v.*[2]]

1. The action of removing a person or thing from a position; removal; ousting; *esp.* removal of a person from office.

1641 BAKER *Chron.* (1679) 190/2 A general amotion of corrupt officers. **1659** FULLER *App. Inj. Innoc.* (1840) 649, I could heartily have wished that an amotion of such devoted treasure had never been done. **1726** AYLIFFE *Parergon* 205 The Admission and Amotion of them do usually belong to the Bishop and Archdeacon both. **1835** *Q. Rev.* No. 103. 7 The amotion or transposition [of Shakspere's words] will alter the thought.

2. Removal of property from its owner; deprivation of possession.

1653 WATERHOUSE *Apol. Learn.* 91 Amotion of church honours and preferments. **1768** BLACKSTONE *Comm.* III. 174 Restitution or delivery of possession to the right owner; and..damages also for the unjust amotion.

†**a'mound,** *v. Obs. rare*⁻¹. [app. for rime: but cf. *amount*, *mound*, and L. *accumulāre*.] To accumulate, amount.

1642 H. MORE *Song of Soul* I. II. xxiv, So infinite..that it me confounds To think to what a vastnesse it amounds.

amount (ə'maʊnt), *v.* Also 3 **amunt, a-mounti, -ty,** 4 **amont,** 5 **amowynt,** 6 **admount.** [a. OFr. *amonte-r*, *amunter*, *amounter*, f. *amunt*, *amont*, upward, lit. *à mont*:—L. *ad montem* to the hill, hill-ward, upward. In earlier usage occas. aphetized to *mount*, and then not distinguished from the simple MOUNT, a. Fr. *monter*. This is probably the reason why *mount* is now used in all the literal senses.]

Gen. sign. To go up, rise; ascend (a hill); rise to, attain to; come up in rank, quantity, value, meaning, or practical effect to.

†**1.** *intr.* (*simply*, or with *prep.* defining relation to an object.) To go up, ascend, rise, mount. *Obs.*

c **1250** *O. Kent. Serm.* in *O.E. Misc.* 28 Ase se smech..goth upward..Swo amuntet si gode biddinge to gode. **1470** HARDING *Chron* cii, Death alone [to his corps] amounted, Dryuyng his soule out fro the worldly nest. **1470-85** MALORY *Arthur* x. iii, My lord..amounted vpon his horse. **1577** H. PEACHAM *Gard. Eloq.* 106 When the Larke doth fyrst amounte on high. **1596** SPENSER *F.Q.* I. IX. liv, So up he rose and thence amounted streight. **1631** MARKHAM *Way to Wealth* VI. III. x. (1668) 34 When any bough or spray shall amount above the rest.

†**2.** *trans.* To ascend, climb, mount. *Obs. rare.*

c **1325** *E.E. Allit. P.* B. 395 þay cryed vchone, þat amounted þe masse.

†**3.** *intr.* To ascend or go back in time. *Obs. rare.*

1704 HEARNE *Ductor Hist.* I. 398 Their earliest Observations..amounted no higher than 1903 Years before that Time.

†**4.** *intr.* To rise, mount up, increase. **a.** in quantity or amount; **b.** in value. *Obs.*

1599 HAKLUYT *Voy.* II. I. 173 This shippe lading the same commodity will cause it to amount in price. **1677** *Houssaie's Govt. Venice* 177 They have a certain allowance, which with their other Fees..amounts, and makes their Revenue very considerable. **1706** PHILLIPS, *Amount*, to rise up in Value, or Tenour.

5. To rise in number or quantity so as to reach; to come to (a specified number or quantity). †**a.** *trans.* with simple obj. *Obs.*

c **1300** *K. Alis.* 6020 Thes kyngis ost..amounted fyve hundred thousand Knyghtis. *c* **1391** CHAUCER *Astrolabe* I. §16 þat amonteth 360 degres. **1480** CAXTON *Chron. Eng.* ccv. 186 The som amounted v thousand pounde. [**1630** WADSWORTH *Sp. Pilgr.* iii. 14 The number..ordinarily neither amounts above or under an 100.]

†**b.** with quasi-advb. obj. *Obs.*

a **1325** *Metr. Hom.* 3 For [all than] sall we yeld acount Quat that wisdom mai amount. **1366** MAUNDEV. xix. 213 Now may men wel rekene, how moche that it amountethe.

c. *intr.* with *to.*

1546 LANGLEY *Polyd. Verg.* I. 111 The multitude admounted to suche infinitee of numbre. **1590** SHAKS. *Com. Err.* IV. i. 30 Which doth amount to three odde Duckets more Than I stand debted to this Gentleman. **1696** WHISTON *Th. Earth* III. (1722) 250 The Posterity of Jacob..amounted to six hundred thousand Males. **1704** *Lond. Gaz.* mmmmxlvi/2 They amount now to above 11000. **1852** MᶜCULLOCH *Taxation* II. x. 366 The entries for consumption amounted to 1,733,816 imperial gallons. **1863** COX *Inst. Eng. Govt.* II. ii. 312 The debt amounted to less than forty shillings.

†**6.** *intr.* To arise as the result of addition; to be the sum; to result. *Obs.*

1542 RECORDE *Gr. Artes* (1575) 118 Write that that amounteth, vnder the lowest line. **1571** DIGGES *Geom. Pract.* III. vi, Whervnto if ye adioyn 126..there amounteth 302. **1647** FULLER *Good Th. in Worse T.* xiv, The aforesaid number will amount of infants and old folk. **1650** —— *Pisgah Sight* Ded. 2 A constellation..the lustre thereof amounting from many stars together.

7. To come up to in meaning, effect, or substance; to be equivalent to. †**a.** *trans.* with quasi-advb. obj.: To mean, signify. *Obs.*

1297 R. GLOUC. 497 The erchebissop nolde come, vor it ne ssolde amounti noȝt. *a* **1300** *Leg. Rood* 240 (1871) 38 Wat þis somounce amounty [*v.r.* amounti] schal..Ich wene þe quene enqueri wole. *c* **1386** CHAUCER *Sqr's T.* 100 Thus much amounteth al þat euere he mente. **1393** GOWER *Conf.* III. 54 The more that he his sweven accompteth, The lasse he wot, what it amounteth. **1440** *Promp. Parv.*, Amowyntyn, or sygnifyyn, *Denoto, significo.* **1460** *Lybeaus Disc.* 1471 Tell me, mayde chast, What amounteth thys.

b. *intr.* with *to.* To be equivalent when taken in its full force or significance, to come practically *to*, be tantamount *to.*

1393 GOWER *Conf.* III. 281 Though I had her love wonne, It might into no prise amounte. **1533** MORE *Debell. Salem* Wks. 1557, 994/2 The verye whole sum [of the reason] amounteth to no more, but that it mai somtime happen, that an innocent may take harme therby. **1695** LUTTRELL *Brief Rel.* (1857) III. 486 The late disorder..made by the Jacobites amounts to high treason. **1712** ADDISON *Spect.* No. 494 ¶4 The proofs of it do not amount to a demonstration. **1865** TROLLOPE *Belton Estate* xv. 178 Such a speech..seemed to her almost to amount to insult.

†**8.** *causal.* To cause to rise, to raise or elevate, in quality, rank, or estimation. *Obs.*

1563 T. HOWELL *Arb. Amitie* (1879) 97 Right thus thou mayst thy praise amount on hie. **1599** *Broughton's Lett.* vii. 21 [They] amounted him to bee the *Chiefe professor* in Diuinitie. **1655** FULLER *Ch. Hist.* IX. 110 Here no Papists were arraigned to amount it to a Popish miracle.

amount (ə'maʊnt), *sb.* [f. prec. vb.]

1. The sum total to which anything mounts up or reaches: **a.** in quantity.

1710 *Act* 8 *Anne* in *Lond. Gaz.* mmmmdcci/3 Shall forfeit double the Amount of the said Drawback. **1852** MᶜCULLOCH *Taxation* II. i. 156 A greater amount of revenue. **1879** WRIGHTSON in *Cassell's Techn. Educ.* IV. 108/1 A smaller amount of straw as litter.

b. in number.

1801 STRUTT *Sports & Past.* III. vi. 221 A number of little birds, to the amount I believe of twelve or fourteen. **1849** ALISON *Hist. Eur.* VIII. liv. §28. 489 Fame had magnified the amount of the forces. **1859** B. SMITH *Arith. & Alg.* 4 The Sum or Amount of the several numbers so added.

c. *spec.* The sum of the principal and interest due upon a loan.

1796 HUTTON *Math. Dict.* I. 638/1 The sum of the Principal and Interest is called the Amount.

2. *fig.* The full value, effect, significance, or import.

1732 POPE *Ess. Man* IV. 307 The whole amount of that enormous fame. *a* **1748** THOMSON (J.) Ye lying vanities of life, Where are you now, and what is your amount? **1844** LINGARD *Anglo-Sax. Ch.* (1858) II. App. 362 What the real amount of that statement may be. **1881** *Times* 24 Dec. 5/3 (*American*) The amount of it is that you have too much to say in this case.

3. A quantity or sum viewed as a total.

1833 I. TAYLOR *Fanat.* ii. 32 Each [appetite] must observe its due amount of force. **1876** FREEMAN *Norm. Conq.* IV. xviii. 162 The amount of resistance which William met with. **1882** *Daily Tel.* 30 Jan., This year the National ought not to take a great amount of winning.

4. In colloq. phr. ***any amount*** (*of*), a great deal (of) (cf. ANY *a.* 2 b); ***no amount of***, not even the greatest possible amount of (orig. *U.S.*).

1893 G. B. SHAW *Widowers' Houses* II. iii. 41, I have any amount of letters for you. **1914** M. SINCLAIR *Three Sisters* lxiii. 369 And he had spent any amount of money on it. **1921** E. O'NEILL *Emperor Jones* v. 185 Capable of any amount of hard labor. **1925** F. SCOTT FITZGERALD *Great Gatsby* v. 116 No amount of fire or freshness can challenge what a man can store up in his ghostly heart. **1952** G. SARTON *Hist. Sci.* I. xiv. 363 It takes a surgeon to appreciate the fine points of Hippocratic surgery, and no amount of explanation would help other readers to judge them correctly. **1961** N. D. GILL *People of Way* v. 55 Many people wake up tired of a morning and no amount of rest seems to make any difference. **1961** D. BLACK *Foot of Rainbow* xxviii. 199 There was any amount of drink on board. **1968** *Listener* 10 Oct. 472/3 'Did you encounter opposition in the early stages?' 'Oh, any amount.' **1973** E. F. SCHUMACHER *Small is Beautiful* I. ii. 33 The disease having been caused by allowing cleverness to displace wisdom, no amount of clever research is likely to produce a cure. **1985** *N.Y. Times* 18 Dec. D27/6 When you can get five goals on thirteen shots, that pretty much makes up for any amount of mistakes.

†**a'mountance.** *Obs. rare*⁻¹. [prob. a. OFr. **amontance* (not in Godef., though *amontant* is): see AMOUNT *v.* and -ANCE. More commonly MOUNTANCE.] Amount, total extent.

c **1380** *Sir Ferumb.* 5601 þe A[meral] was heȝere þan Charlys was þe amountance of a fotes spas.

amounting (ə'maʊntɪŋ), *ppl. a.* [f. AMOUNT *v.* + -ING[2].] †**a.** *simply*, Forming a total, resulting (*obs.*). **b.** ***amounting to***: equalling in sum total, value, or practical effect.

1571 DIGGES *Geom. Pract.* II. xxiii, The amounting summe. *Mod.* To charge fees amounting to 100*l.* or more was an act amounting to simple robbery.

†**a'mountment.** *Obs. rare*⁻¹. [a. OFr. *amontement*, n. of completed action f. *amonter*: see AMOUNT *v.*] Amount, sum total.

1330 R. BRUNNE *Chron.* 248 þei brouht..þe olde chartres & titles..Of ilk a bisshop se, & ilk a priourie..Examend þam & cast ilk amountment.

amour[1] (ə'mʊə(r), Fr. a'mur). Also 4 **amoure,** 6-7 **amor.** [a. OFr. *amur*, *amour*:—L. *amōr-em* love, f. *amā-re* to love. In 13-15th c. accented *a'mour*, but thoroughly naturalized; hence duly became *'amour* in 15-17th (cf. *e'namour*); in 16-17th often written *amor* after L. But by 17th the good or neutral sense of the word became obs.; and being retained only in senses 3-4, it came to be treated more or less as a euphemistic employment of mod.Fr., and hence again accented *a'mour* (Milton, Butler, Pope, etc.).]

†**1.** *gen.* Love, affection, friendship. *Obs.*

c **1300** *K. Alis.* 4573 Alisaunder..wolde him, with gret honour, Have y-fonge in his amour. *c* **1330** *Florice & Bl.* 521 Tho spak Clarice to Blauncheflour Wordes ful of fin amour. *c* **1386** CHAUCER *Knts. T.* 297 For par amour I loved hire first or thou. **1660** R. BURNEY *Κέρδιστον Δῶ ρον* (1661) 133 The great City in homage to the Kings Majesty, the Kings Majesty in Amour with the City of London, is the holy bands of Matrimony. **1742** YOUNG *Nt. Thoughts* IV. 350 Oh love of gold! thou meanest of amours!

†**2.** *pl.* The tender affections, love towards one of the opposite sex (L. *amores*, Fr. *amours*). ***in amours*** (with): in love (*with*). *Obs.*

1375 BARBOUR *Bruce* VIII. 498 Than mycht he weill ask ane lady Hir amouris and hir drowry. *c* **1425** WYNTOUN VII. 99 Hyr amowris þus til my Hart rynnys. **1523** LD. BERNERS *Froissart* I. lxxvii. 98 The kyng of Englande was in amours with the countesse of Salisbury. *Ibid.* cccxliv. 543 In true amours togyder eche of other. **1590** GREENE *Arcadia* (1616) 11 He could not bridle his new conceiued amors. **1625** SHIRLEY *Love-tricks* V. iii, Out of mere amors and affections. **1727** ARBUTHNOT *John Bull* (1755) 48 There is nothing so obstinate as a young lady in her amours.

3. A love-affair, love-making, courtship. (Now only humorously of honourable love-making.)

1567 DRANT *Horace, Arte Poet.* A iij, The Musies taughte in lyrike verse..Amors of youth and banquets francke On instruments to sing. **1665** PEPYS *Diary* 15 Aug., To leave the young people together to begin their amours. **1678** BUTLER *Hudibr.* III. i. 913 In all amours a lover burns With frowns as well as smiles, by turns. **1791** HAMILTON *Berthollet's Dyeing* II. II. iii. 169 The life of the cochineal insect terminates by its amours. **1814** SCOTT *Wav.* xxiii. 104 You cannot expect me to disturb him in his amours. **1828** KIRBY & SPENCE *Entomol.* III. xxxii. 313 These gentlemen may have mistaken a battle for an amour.

4. *usually*, An illicit love affair, an intrigue.

a **1626** BACON *Q. Eliz.* Wks. 1860, 481 King Henry the Eighth was engaged in a new amour. **1673** DRYDEN *Marr. à la Mode* II. i, Intrigue, Philotis, that's an old phrase; I have laid that word by: amour sounds better. **1678** BUTLER *Hudibr.* III. i. 679 Few of either sex dare marry, But rather trust, on tick, t'amours. **1790** MISS GRAHAM *Lett. on Educ.* 144 Criminal amours are in general censured in these works. **1876** FREEMAN *Norm. Conq.* I. iv. 252 The amours or doubtful marriages of the Norman Dukes.

†**a'mour**². *Obs.* [a. OFr. *ameor*, *ameour*:—L. *amātōr-em* lover; mod.Fr. *aimeur*.] A lover.

c **1300** *K. Alis.* 951 Mony child was faderles: Mony lady les hire amoúre.

‖**amour courtois** (amur kurtwa). [F.] Courtly love (see COURTLY *a.* 2 b).

1907 CHAMBERS & SIDGWICK *Early Eng. Lyrics* 262 This poetry [*chanson d'amour* or *chanson courtois*] .. has practically but one theme, that of the *amour courtois*. **1950** N. COGHILL in *Ess. & Stud.* III. 10 Its sentiments are those of *amour courtois*. **1963** *Medium Ævum* XXXII. 59 The alleged resemblances between Andreas Capellanus' 'system' and the actual poetry of *amour courtois* break down at every point.

amourette (amu'rɛt). [a. mod.Fr. *amourette*, a restoration in Fr. dress of Eng. AMORET obs. since 17th c.]

1. A petty amour or love-affair: cf. AMORET 5.

1825 SCOTT *Betrothed* II. xi. 187 This comes of meddling with men's *amourettes*. **1826** DISRAELI *Viv. Grey* I. viii. 53 Master Vivian entered into all these amourettes in very beautiful style. **1865** CARLYLE *Fredk. Gt.* II. VII. ii. 161 A curious story, about one of Prince Fred's amourettes. **1871** *Pall Mall G.* 7 Feb. 11 Youthful amourettes more or less scandalous.

2. The Love-grass or Quaking-grass (*Briza media*).

1702 PETIVER in *Phil. Trans.* XXIII. 1257 Each squamose head resembling those of the common Amourets. [**1866** *Treas. Bot.*, *Amourette* (Fr.) *Briza media*.]

3. A cupid, an *amoretto*.

1860 ADLER *Fauriel's Prov. Poetry* iii. 50 Little amourettes, perched here and there upon the branches.

amourist, obs. form of AMORIST.

‖**amour propre** (æmʊə 'prɒprə). Also with hyphen. [mod.Fr., but in common use.] Self-love which is ready with its claims, and sensitive to causes of offence; good opinion of oneself, self-esteem.

1775 I. MOORE *Let.* 12 June in Duke of Argyll *Int. Soc. Lett. of 18th Cent.* (1910) II. 390 He is not found of the Company of his Superiours either in Rank or Understanding. The first put him under Restraint, and the others offend his *amour propre*. **1818** SCOTT *Ht. Midl.* xlviii. 365 When this unwonted burst of *amour propre* was thoroughly subdued. **1855** H. SPENCER *Psychol.* (1872) I. IV. viii. 487 A proof of power which cannot fail agreeably to excite the *amour propre*. **1865** TYLOR *Early Hist. Man.* iii. 35 His *amour propre* seems flattered. **1955** *Times* 27 July 9/2 Mr. Malcolm MacDonald .. has returned to the scene to counsel caution and soothe wounded amour-propre.

amovability (əˌmuːvə'bɪlɪtɪ). *rare*⁻¹. [f. next: see -ABILITY.] Capability of being removed or dismissed; liability to dismissal.

1816 T. JEFFERSON *Writ.* (1830) IV. 288 Let us retain amovability on the concurrence of the executive and legislative branches.

amovable (ə'muːvəb(ə)l), *a.* Also 9 **amovible**. [a. mod.Fr. *amovible* removable: see AMOVE *v.*² and -ABLE.] Capable of being removed from a situation or position; removable.

1851 SIR F. PALGRAVE *Norm. & Eng.* I. 154 A civil Hierarchy of Dukes or Counts, amovible perhaps by prerogative.

amoval (ə'muːvəl). ? *Obs. rare*⁻¹. [f. AMOVE *v.*² + -AL².] Removal, putting away.

1664 EVELYN *Silva* (1776) 342 The amoval of these unsufferable nuisances would infinitely clarify the air.

†**a'move**, *v.*¹ *Obs.* Also 4–5 **amoeve**, 4–6 **ameve**, 6 **amoove**. [a. OFr. *amov-er*, *amouv-oir*, accented stem *ameuv-*:—L. *admovē-re* to move to, excite to, f. *ad* to + *movē-re* to move. App. confounded to some extent with OFr. *esmover*, mod.Fr. *émouvoir*:—L. *exmovēre*.]

1. To set in motion, stir, stir up, excite (any action, a person to action, the heart, the blood, etc.).

a **1330** *Sir Otuel* (1836) 33 Suiche tydings thei herden, That a-moeuede al here blod. *c* **1425** WYNTOUN *Cron.* VIII. xxxiii. 118 He walde amowe were in Frawns. **1541** PAYNELL *Catiline* lii. 75 b, The commons were excedingly amoued agaynst the Senatours. *c* **1590** GREENE *Poems* 136 At all these cries my heart was sore amoved.

2. *esp.* To move the feelings of (a person), to move inwardly, cause emotion to. (Fr. *émouvoir*.)

a. *trans.* (usually *pass.*)

c **1374** CHAUCER *Boeth.* I. i. 6 Sche was a lytel ameued and glowed wiþ cruel eyen. **1494** FABYAN II. xlviii. 32 When the knowlege of yᵉ deth of Irreglas was brought vnto the kynge, he was therwith greatly amoued. **1513** DOUGLAS *Æneis* IX. iii. 40 How art thou thus agane the fatis amouit? **1596** SPENSER *F.Q.* I. iv. 45 She .. him amoves with speaches seeming fit.

b. *refl.*

1530 PALSGR. 425/2 Kepe your pacyence and amove you not.

c. *intr.*

c **1280** *Signs bef. Judg.* in *E.E.P.* (1862) 11 Þer nis no seint in heuen abow .. þat þer of ne sal amoue. *c* **1386** CHAUCER *Clerkes T.* 442 Whan she had herd al this she noght ameued [*v.r.* amoued] Neyther in word, in cheer, or countenaunce.

3. *trans.* To arouse (from sleep, etc.).

1595 SPENSER *Daphnaida* 545, I, stepping to him light, Amooved him out of his stonie swound.

amove (ə'muːv), *v.*² [ad. L. *āmovē-re* to remove, move out of the way; f. *ā* = *ab* off + *movē-re* to move; prob. as a legal term directly f. Fr. *amoever*, in this sense in Act 9 Hen. VI. (quoted by Godefr.).]

1. To remove (a person or thing) from a position; to dismiss (a person) from an office. (Now only in legal phraseology.)

1494 FABYAN VII. 486 The sayde persones were from the kynge amoued. **1524** *State Papers Hen. VIII*, IV. 110 Amoving and expellyng him from all auctorite. **1642** H. MORE *Song of Soul* II. I. II. xxxvi, Claws, horns, hoofs they use the pinching ill t'amove. **1800** COLQUHOUN *Comm. & Pol. Thames* xi. 319 These Harbour-Masters may be suspended or amoved. **1832** J. AUSTIN *Jurispr.* (1879) II. 1098 An abortive attempt to amove it [an object of theft].

†**2.** To remove, put away (things immaterial). *Obs.*

1536 BELLENDENE *Cron. Scotl.* I. 35 Al hatrent for that time beand amovit. **1611** SPEED *Hist. Gt. Brit.* IV. x. 13 To amoue the note of ingratitude, and turbulency from them. **1664** H. MORE *Myst. Iniq.* v. 12 Zeal .. in amoving this grand errour out of the Church.

†**a'moved**, *ppl. a. Obs.* [f. AMOVE *v.*¹ + -ED.] Stirred, aroused, excited.

c **1374** CHAUCER *Boeth.* I. v. 23 Sche .. no þing amoeued wiþ my compleyntes seide þus. **1470** HARDING *Chron.* cxix, To Flaundres she fled, full sore amoued. **1596** SPENSER *F.Q.* II. I. 12 Therewith amoved from his sober mood.

†**a'movement.** *Obs. rare*⁻¹. [f. AMOVE *v.*² + -MENT.] Removal, putting away.

1613 DANIEL *Eng. Hist.* 134 Who had often before laboured their amoouement, as held to be corrupt Councellors.

amoving (ə'muːvɪŋ), *vbl. sb.* [f. AMOVE *v.*² + -ING¹.] Removing, removal. (Only in *Law.*)

1618–29 in Rushw. *Hist. Coll.* (1659) I. 25 The Writ concerning amoving a Leper. **1688** *Lond. Gaz.* mmmmccccxvi/1 An Act for the Amoving Papists .. from the Cities of London and Westminster.

amoxycillin (əˌmɒksɪ'sɪlɪn). *Pharm.* [f. AM(INO- + OXY- + PENI)CILLIN (in the chemical name).] A broad-spectrum synthetic penicillin, closely related to ampicillin and with similar properties, but better absorbed when taken orally; amino-*p*-hydroxybenzylpenicillin, $C_{16}H_{19}N_3O_5S$.

1971 *Approved Names* (Brit. Pharmacopœia Comm.) Suppl. III, *Amoxycillin*, 6-[(-)-α-Amino-4-hydroxyphenyl acetamido]-penicillanic acid. **1975** *Sunday Times* 4 May 63/4 Amoxycillin has been sold on the Continent only during the past two years. **1977** *Lancet* 7 May 1013/1 The *S. liquefaciens* was also sensitive to sulphonamide and amoxycillin. **1979** *Daily Tel.* 29 Nov. 8/8 Amoxycillin is seen as a genuine advance because it is better absorbed orally than ampicillin. **1984** *Brit. Nat. Formulary* VIII. 187/2 Dental procedures .. special risk (patients with a prosthetic heart valve or who have had endocarditis), i/m amoxycillin 1 g + i/m gentamicin 120 mg before induction, then oral amoxycillin 500 mg 6 hours later.

Amoy (ə'mɔɪ). The conventional western name for the island of Xiamen in Fujian province, south-east China, used *attrib.* and *absol.* to designate the southern Fujian (Minnan) dialect of Chinese spoken by the people of Amoy.

1851 *Chinese Repository* July 475 The diacritical marks in the Amoy dialect show the tone, or *shing*, of each word. **1911** *Encycl. Brit.* V. 216/2 We pass in succession the following dialects: .. Amoy .. Foochow, [etc.]. **1917** S. COULING *Encycl. Sinica* 143/1 The Amoy dialect, spoken by some ten millions of people, differs very widely from the book-language. **1948** R. A. D. FORREST *Chinese Lang.* xi. 232 Hainanese has a basis in common Min, and seems to build its peculiar features on the traits of Amoy and Swatow where these diverge from the rest of the group. **1979** *Sci. Amer.* May 34/3 The most endearing .. seems the greeting spoken in Amoy, a language of the Chinese coast.

amp.¹, abbreviation of AMPERE.

1886 O. HEAVISIDE in *Electrician* 29 Jan. 227/2 But ampère shortened to am or amp is abominable. **1907** *Install. News* July 8/2 Suction gas plant and 200 amp. dynamo. *Ibid.*, A private plant supplying 100 amps.

amp² (æmp), colloq. abbrev. of AMPLIFIER 4.

1967 *Boston Globe* 21 May 2/3, I mean, like my ol' man won't buy me a new amp because he thinks he needs a new car. **1969** N. COHN *Pop from Beginning* xviii. 164 They worked between great fortresses of amps. **1975** J. PIDGEON *Flame* i. 9 He sat on his amp and wiped his face on his sleeve, his body heaving with each gasp for breath. **1977** G. SCOTT *Hot Pursuit* ii. 15 Next to the phone is the tape deck and on shelves above that the amp and the tuner and the turntable. **1986** *Making Music* Apr. 36/1 Taking the lead from your guitar and .. connecting it to an amp, then miking the resulting noise.

ampair, ampayr, *v.* 3–4. [a. OFr. *ampeire-r*] the earliest form of the word afterwards reduced to *apayr*, *apair*, *pair*, and erron. spelt APPAIR.

†**am'pare.** *Obs. rare*⁻¹. [ad. Sp. *amparo* defence, protection, f. *ampar-ar* to defend, fortify, cogn. w. Pr., Pg. *amparar*, Fr. *emparer*, It. *imparāre*, as if from a common late L. **imparāre*, f. *im*, *in*, into, towards (a purpose) + *parāre* to furnish, fit.] Defence, protection, guard.

1598 YONG *Diana* Ded., I humbly beseech your good Lordship to entertaine this booke vnder your Hon. ampare.

ampassy, phonetic corruption of AND *per se*, the old name of the character &; still in common use in the dialects from Cumberland to Cornwall: see AMPERSAND.

1706 *Harl. MS.* in Strutt *Sports & Past.* (1876) 507 *XY* wyth *Esed And* per se—Amen. **1878** DICKINSON *Cumberl. Gl.* 125 *Ampassy*. **1880** COUCH *E. Cornw. Gl.*, *Ampassy*.

ampelideous (æmpɪ'lɪdɪəs), *a. Bot.* [f. mod.L. *ampelīdeæ* the vine family (f. Gr. ἀμπελ-ος vine) + -OUS: see -IDEOUS.] Belonging to the vine family; resembling the vine.

1879 in *Syd. Soc. Lex.*

ampelite ('æmpɪlaɪt). *Min.* [ad. L. *ampelītis*, a. Gr. ἀμπελῖτις of the vine (f. ἄμπελ-ος vine; see -ITE), in ἀμπελῖτις γῆ an earth sprinkled on the vine to destroy insects.] A bituminous earth; perhaps cannel coal.

1751 CHAMBERS *Cycl.*, *Ampelites*, cannal coal, in natural history, a black, bituminous substance that dissolves in oil. **1852** T. ROSS *Humboldt's Trav.* I. xv. 490 The talcose slate contains small layers of soft and unctuous graphic ampelite.

ampelitic (æmpɪ'lɪtɪk), *a. Min.* [f. prec. + -IC.] Of the nature of ampelite.

1849 MURCHISON *Siluria* xvii. 410 Subordinate ampelitic schists containing graptolites.

ampelography (æmpɪ'lɒgrəfɪ). [a. mod.Fr. *ampélographie*, f. Gr. ἄμπελ-ος vine + -γραφία: see -GRAPHY.] The scientific description of the vine.

1879 in *Syd. Soc. Lex.*

Ampelopsis (æmpɪ'lɒpsɪs). *Bot.* [mod.L., f. Gr. ἄμπελος vine + ὄψις appearance.] A genus of climbing plants allied to the vine; (with small initial) a plant of this genus, as one of the various species of Virginia creeper.

1807 J. DONN *Hort. Cantab. or Catal. of Plants* (ed. 4) 49 Ampelopsis. heart-leaved. N. America. **1829** LOUDON *Encycl. Plants* 176 Ampelopsis .. is commonly employed for covering old walls, for which the rapidity of its growth renders it very suitable. **1843** *Florist's Jrnl. 1842* III. 148 The honeysuckle, the jasmine, the ampelopsis, .. may be made to contribute largely to the general appearance of a garden. **1866** [see *pepper-vine*, PEPPER *sb.* 7]. **1900** *Echo* 25 Sept. 1/3 The crimsoning leafage of ampelopsis. **1914** COMPTON MACKENZIE *Sinister Street* III. vii. 646 The tea-tray gothic of Balliol, and Trinity with its municipal ampelopsis. **1961** *Amateur Gardening* 30 Sept. Suppl. 3/2 Most of the ampelopsis are hardy climbers related to the Virginia Creepers.

†**'amper.** *Obs.* or *dial.* 1–2 **ampre**, 7 **amper**. A tumour or swelling; a blemish. (Cf. ANBURY.)

a **700** *Epinal Gl.* (O.E.T. 106) *Varix*, ampræ; *Erfurt Gl.* ompræ. *c* **1175** *Cott. Hom.* 237 Þri ampres were an mancyn ær his [Christ's] to-cyme. **1674** RAY *S. & E. Countr. Words* 57 An Amper: a fault or flaw in linnen or woollen cloath, *Suss.* Skinner makes it to be a word much used by the common or countrey-people in Essex to signifie a tumour, rising or pustule. **1693** W. ROBERTSON *Phraseol. Gen.* 85 An Amper or Ampor; *Tumor, phlegmone.* **1753** CHAMBERS *Cycl. Supp.*, *Amper*, a local term used in Essex for a *tumor*, or *phlegmon*. **1875** PARISH *Sussex Dial.* 13 [From RAY].

amperage (æm'pɛərɪdʒ, 'æmpərɪdʒ). *Electr.* [f. AMPERE + -AGE, after *voltage*.] The strength of an electric current expressed in amperes. Also *fig.*

1894 *Work* 17 Mar. 139/2 The longer the length of wire you use on any armature, the higher will be the voltage, but the lower the ampèrage. **1924** MÉGROZ *Walter de la Mare* 105 The living poet's 'Sunk Lyonnesse' in which each word has a far higher amperage of power. **1941** *Illustr. London News* 18 Feb. 191/1 Ordinary X-ray pictures are taken by long exposure to rays generated by high voltage and low amperage current.

ampere (‖ɑ̃ː'pɛr, 'æmpɛə(r)). *Electr.* Also **ampère**. [a. *Ampère*, name of a Fr. electrician; a designation adopted by the Paris Electric Congress in 1881.] (See quot. 1963). **ampere-hour**, the quantity of electricity equal to a current of one ampere flowing for one hour; abbrev. Ah; **ampere-turn**, a unit of magneto-motive force, expressed as the product of the number of turns in a coil and the current in amperes; abbrev. A.T.

1881 *Q. Rev.* Oct. 457 The unit of current is called the 'Ampère.' It is the current that one volt can send through one ohm. **1883** A. GREY in *Nature* XXVII. 321 The current flowing in a wire of resistance one ohm, between the two ends of which a difference of potentials of one volt is maintained, has been adopted as the practical unit of current and called one ampere. **1884** J. T. SPRAGUE *Electricity* xii. 526 To equally magnetize different sized cores, the 'ampere-turns' must be in the proportion of the square root of the cube of the diameters. **1885** *Electrician* 27 Nov. 49/1 Secondary cells .. giving 280 ampere hours. **1912** G. KAPP *Electricity* vi. 166 The excitation produced by a coil may be conveniently expressed by the product of amperes and turns, or 'ampere-turns'. **1919** R. STANLEY *Wireless Telegr.* I. 452 A proper check .. of the number of ampere-hours' charge and discharge. **1963** JERRARD & MCNEILL *Dict. Sci. Units* 17 The 9th Meeting of the International Weights and

Measures Congress in 1948 defined the ampere as the intensity of the constant current which, when maintained in two parallel straight conductors of infinite length and of negligible cross section placed one metre apart in a vacuum, produced between them a force equal to 2 × 10^{-7} M.K.S. units of force per metre length. This unit, known as the absolute ampere, replaced the international ampere which had been defined in 1908.

amperesse, obs. form of EMPRESS.

Amperian (æm'pɛərɪən), *a.* Pertaining to the French physicist André-Marie *Ampère* (1775–1836) or his theory of electromagnetic currents.
1866 E. ATKINSON *Ganot's Elem. Treat. Physics* (ed. 2) x. iv. 674 At the north pole of a magnet the direction of the Amperian currents is opposite that of the hands of a watch, and at the south pole the direction is the same. **1879** G. PRESCOTT *Sp. Telephone* xiv. 496 The Amperian currents in the inducing magnet.

amperometer (æmpə'rɒmɪtə(r)). *Electr.* [f. AMPER(E + -(O)METER. A shortened form is AMMETER.] (See quot. 1882.) Hence **ampero'metric** *a.*, esp. ***amperometric titration***, titration by electromagnetic methods.
1882 *Catal. Electr. Exhib.* 46 Patent amperometer for measuring electrical work, applicable to electro-plating, to show the work done or doing in a vat. **1941** KOLTHOFF & LINGANE *Polarography* VIII. xxxiii. 448 As it is the current which is measured during the titration, we prefer to call this type of titration 'amperometric titration'. **1960** *Jrnl. Iron & Steel Inst.* CXCV. 374/1 Amperometric titrations may be conducted with an indicator electrode in combination with a reference electrode, or by means of two indicator electrodes.

ampersand (æmpə'sænd, 'æmp-). Also **ampassy-, ampussy-, ampus-**. Corruption of '*and* per se—*and*', the old way of spelling and naming the character &; i.e. '& by itself = and;' found in various forms in almost all the dialect Glossaries. See *A per se* (under A IV 1) *I per se*, *O per se*, etc.
1837 HALIBURTON *Clockm.* (1862) 399 He has hardly learned what Ampersand means, afore they give him a horse. **1859** GEO. ELIOT *Adam Bede* xxi, He thought it [Z] had only been put there to finish off th' alphabet like, though *ampusand* would ha' done as well. **1869** *Punch* 17 Apr., Of all the types in a printer's hand Commend me to the Amperzand. **1881** MRS. PARKER *Oxf. Gl.*, '*Amsiam*, the sign &.' **1882** FREEMAN in *Longm. Mag.* I. 95 'Ampussy and,' that is, in full '*and* per se, *and*,' is the name of the sign for the conjunction *and*, &, which used to be printed at the end of the alphabet.

amperur, obs. form of EMPEROR.

†'**ampery**, *a. Obs. or dial.* [f. AMPER + -Y.] 'Weak, unhealthy. *Also*, beginning to decay, especially applied to cheese.' Parish *Sussex Dial.* 1875.

amphetamine (æm'fɛtəmaɪn, -ɪn). [f. *a*lpha*m*ethyl-*phe*ne*t*hyl*amine*.] A synthetic drug which stimulates the heart and respiration, constricts blood-vessels, and induces sleeplessness.
1938 *Amer. Jrnl. Psychiatry* XCV. 371 (*title*) The effective use of phenobarbital and benzedrine sulfate (amphetamine sulfate) in the treatment of epilepsy. **1939** W. BLOOMBERG in *New Engl. Jrnl. Med.* 26 Jan. 129/1 Amphetamine (Benzedrine) sulfate was introduced into therapeutics in 1935 by Prinzmetal and the author as an effective agent in the prevention of symptoms in narcolepsy. **1946** *Lancet* 14 Dec. 865/1 Amphetamine is a powerful stimulant of the central nervous system, an action which it owes to its ability to increase cerebral respiration. **1955** *Sci. News Let.* 9 Apr. 235/3 Amphetamine, popularly known as an ingredient of 'pep pills', has been reported one of the drugs used in brain washing by the Communists. **1959** *Times* 29 May 14/6 The use of amphetamine drugs in sport. **1962** *Lancet* 15 Dec. 1282/2 Hypertensive patients receiving amphetamine in addition to reduce obesity.

amphi- (æmfɪ), *prefix*. [a. Gr. ἀμφι- both, of both kinds, on both sides, about, around.] Used in many derivatives and compounds. **amphidiarthrosis** (ˌæmfɪdaɪɑː'θrəʊsɪs) *Anat.*, a form of articulation (see quots.); **amphidromic** (-'drɒmɪk), *a.*[2] [Gr. ἀμφίδρομος running both ways] (see quots.); **amphikaryotic** (-kærɪ'ɒtɪk), *a. Biol.* [Gr. κάρυον nut, kernel], of a nucleus, having two haploid sets of chromosomes; **amphimixis** (æmfɪ'mɪksɪs), *Biol.* [mod.L. (A. Weismann, 1891), f. Gr. μίξις mingling: cf. ἀμφιμιγνύναι to mix up thoroughly] (see quot. 1949); **Amphineura** (-'njʊərə), *sb. pl. Zool.* [mod.L. (H. von Jhering, 1876, in *Jahrb. d. deut. Malacozool. Ges.* III. 128): cf. Gr. νεῦρον nerve], a group of bilaterally symmetrical molluscs containing the chitons and related forms; '**amphiodont** (-əʊdɒnt), *a. Ent.* [Gr. ὀδούς, ὀδοντ- tooth], applied to a form of the mandibles in stag-beetles intermediate between the priodont and teleodont; **amphipneustic** (-'(p)njuːstɪk), *a. Zool.* [f. as AMPHIPNEUST + -IC], having breathing-pores at both ends of the body, as certain dipterous larvæ; ˌ**amphi-pro'stylar** *a.*, of or pertaining to an amphiprostyle; **amphirhine** ('æmfɪraɪn), *a. Zool.* [ad. mod.L. *Amphirhinus*, neut. pl. *Amphi-rhina*, f. Gr. ῥίν- nose], belonging to the *Amphirhina*, a division (comprising the large majority) of skulled vertebrates, having the nasal orifice double; two-nostrilled; opp. MONORHINE *a.*
1842 DUNGLISON *Dict. Med. Sci.* (ed. 3), *Amphidiarthrosis*, a name given by Winslow to the temporomaxillary articulation, because, according to that anatomist, it partakes both of ginglymus and arthrodia. **1890** BILLINGS *Med. Dict.*, *Amphidiarthrosis*, joint having characteristics of two classes, both hinge and gliding, as articulation of lower jaw. **1909** *Cent. Dict.* Suppl., Amphidromic. **1938** *Nature* 11 June 1067/1 The effect of uniting the two waves which will have the higher part of their crests on opposite shores is to produce a set of amphidromic points. These are points at which there is no tidal rise and fall of the water level. **1947** *Sci. News* IV. 92 In the northern hemisphere the tidal oscillation will appear to rotate in an anticlockwise direction round such a point, and cotidal lines, joining points which have high water at the same time, will radiate from it. The point is called an amphidromic point. *Ibid.*, The rotation of the tide-producing forces round the sea also operates so as to produce an amphidromic system. **1909** J. W. JENKINSON *Experim. Embryol.* 267 One blastomere has a male and a female nucleus, and therefore 2 *n* chromosomes (amphikaryotic), while the other has only a female (thelykaryotic). **1893** PARKER & RÖNNFELDT tr. *Weismann's Germ-Plasm* 20 Amphimixis..consists in the mingling of two individuals or of their germs, and owing to its constant connection with reproduction in multicellular organisms it is usually spoken of as 'sexual reproduction'... Amongst unicellular organisms..amphimixis is widely spread..in the form of conjugation. **1909** SORLEY *Interpr. Evolution* 23 It throws off certain cells which have the power of reproducing organisms like itself—this result being dependent in all the higher organisms upon amphimixis. **1913** Amphimixis [see APOMIXIS]. **1949** DARLINGTON & MATHER *Elements Genetics* 377 *Amphimixis*, reproduction by the fusion of two gametes in fertilization. As opposed to Apomixis. **1889** *Cent. Dict.*, Amphineura. **1906** G. BOURNE tr. *Pelseneer's Mollusca* ii. 40 When *Chaetoderma* and *Neomenia* were investigated from an anatomical point of view, von Jhering united them..in a division of 'Worms', which he called Amphineura. **1922** *Chambers's Encycl.* I. 238/2 Amphineura are primitive gasteropods. **1945** STEP & WELLS *Shell Life* 181 The orders [of Gastropoda] are only four, but several..have been divided into sub-orders. The first of these orders (Amphineura) consists of the Mail-shells. **1883** Amphiodont [see PRIODONT *a.*]. **1932** J. S. HUXLEY *Probl. Rel. Growth* vii. 209 A specimen is classified as Amphiodont if a gap is present which is considered larger than the normal gap between two teeth, Prionodont if it is considered not to exceed this size. **1891** H. M. & M. BERNARD tr. *A. Lang's Compar. Anat.* I. 482 This amphipneustic tracheal system is found in many parasitic or half-parasitic *Diptera* larvæ. **1899** *Camb. Nat. Hist.* VI. 450 Other larvæ have a pair of stigmata placed at the termination of the body, and another pair near the anterior extremity..; these larvæ are said to be 'amphipneustic'. **1957** RICHARDS & DAVIES *Imms's Textbk. Ent.* (ed. 9) I. 134 *Amphipneustic.*—Only the prothoracic and the posterior abdominal spiracles are open. This type is a common one among larval Diptera. **1875** *Encycl. Brit.* II. 459 A temple with a portico at each end is said to be amphiprostylar. **1871** T. H. HUXLEY *Anat. Vert.* 147 The other amphirhine fishes.

amphiarthrodial (ˌæmfɪɑː'θrəʊdɪəl), *a. Anat.* [mod. f. AMPHI- + Gr. ἀρθρώδ-ης well-articulated + -IAL.] Characterized by amphiarthrosis.
1859 TODD *Cycl. Anat. & Phys.* V. 121/2 The sacrum.. is united to the last lumbar vertebra..by an amphiarthrodial joint. **1879** MORRIS *Anat. Joints* 5 Connecting fibro-cartilages occur only in amphiarthrodial joints.

amphiarthrosis (ˌæmfɪɑː'θrəʊsɪs). *Anat.* [mod. f. AMPHI- of both kinds + ARTHROSIS 'articulation,' repr. a possible Gr. *ἄρθρωσις, n. of action f. ἀρθρόειν to articulate.] A form of jointing partaking of the characters both of diarthrosis and synarthrosis, the two bones being united by a cartilage of some elasticity, which prevents one surface sliding on the other, but admits of a certain amount of movement; as in the joints of the vertebral column, the carpus, etc.
1836 TODD *Cycl. Anat. & Phys.* I. 225/1 The amphiarthrosis possesses a manifest, although certainly a very limited degree of motion. **1874** ROOSA *Dis. Ear* 202 The articulation between the short process of the incus and the posterior tympanic wall is an amphiarthrosis.

amphiaster (æmfɪ'æstə(r)). [f. AMPHI- + ASTER 4.] **1.** *Biol.* [Fr. (H. Fol 1877, in *Arch. des Sci. Phys. et Nat.* Apr. 441).] A spindle-shaped formation in a developing ovum, with radiations at each end, thus resembling two star-shaped figures conjoined. Hence **amphi'astral** *a.*, pertaining to or involving an amphiaster.
1885 *Q. Jrnl. Microsc. Sci.* XXV. 131 In Echinoderms the germinal vesicle and spot are not directly but only partially transformed into the 'Amphiaster de rebut' or 'directive spindle'. **1901** G. N. CALKINS *Protozoa* 82 A central or 'astral' granule..which in some cases has been seen to divide..and to form an amphiaster. **1925** E. B. WILSON *Cell* (ed. 3) ii. 150 As far as the history of the chromosomes is concerned the anastral types of mitosis..do not differ in any important way from the amphiastral. **1952** G. H. BOURNE et al. *Cytol. & Cell Physiol.* (ed. 2) iv. 179 The importance of ..amphiaster formation in mitosis and cell division.
2. *Zool.* A sponge-spicule with rays at each end.
1887 SOLLAS in *Encycl. Brit.* XXII. 417/2 The sigmaspire becoming spined produces the spiraster;..this..by simultaneous concentration of its spines into a whorl at each end [becomes] the amphiaster. **1934** L. W. SHARP *Introd. Cytology* (ed. 3) xi. 155 In animal cells the amphiastral figure commonly develops essentially as follows.

amphibe. *rare*[−1]. [ad. Gr. ἀμφίβιος: see next.] = AMPHIBIAN.
1831 GEN. P. THOMPSON *Exerc.* (1842) I. 336 The veritable amphibes, or such as serve amphibiously by land or sea, videlicet Marines.

‖**amphibia** (æm'fɪbɪə), *sb. pl.* [L. *amphibia* (sing. *amphibium*), a. Gr. ἀμφίβια, sing. ἀμφίβιον, living in both, and subst. (sc. *animal*, ζῷον) an animal that lives in both elements; f. ἀμφί both + βίος life. The sing. forms *amphibion*, *amphibium*, were formerly in use, for which, in sense 4, AMPHIBIAN is now used.]
I. *sing. amphibium*, *-on*, with pl. *-a*, *-ums*.
1. A being that lives either in water or on land, or is equally at home in either element.
1609 HOLLAND *Amm. Marcell.* XXII. xv. 212 Some live on land and water both, whereupon they are named Amphibia. **1631** *Whimzies* 85 A Sayler is..an amphibium that lives both on land and water. **1655** FULLER *Ch. Hist.* IV. 136 Like an Amphibion, He was equally active on water, and land. **1667** *Phil. Trans.* II. 579 Could stay a great while under water, as Amphibiums use to do. **1865** ESQUIROS *Cornwall* 172 The boat can travel both on land and sea like Amphibia.
2. *fig.* A being of doubtful or ambiguous position.
1645 WHALY *Serm.* in Southey *Comm.-Pl. Bk.* II. (1849) 6 Ask these amphibia what names they would have. What, are you papists? no..are you protestants? no. *c* **1670** MARVELL *Unfort. Lover* Wks. III. 243 He both consumed, and increas'd: And languished with doubtful breath Th' amphibium of life and death.
3. A being having a double existence. *rare.*
1823 LAMB *Elia, Child Angel* 472 Humility and Aspiration went on even-paced in the instruction of the glorious Amphibium.
II. *pl.* only.
4. *Zool.* **a.** Applied by Linnæus to Reptiles in the wider sense (including Reptiles and Amphibia of mod. naturalists). *Obs.* **b.** By Cuvier to a tribe of Mammals including seals and their allies. **c.** By modern zoologists since Macleay (*c* 1819) to the fourth great division of Vertebrata, intermediate between reptiles and fishes, which in their early state breathe by gills like fishes, as frogs, newts, etc.
a. 1753 CHAMBERS *Cycl. Supp.*, *Amphibia*..a class of animals, whose essential characters are, that they have either a naked, or else a scaly body..their teeth being all sharp and pointed, and without radiated fins.
b. 1833 SIR C. BELL *Hand* 109 In the true Amphibia..we have the feet contracted..and the fingers webbed and converted into fins.
c. 1825 J. GRAY (*title*) Synopsis of the Genera of Reptiles and Amphibia. **1841** *Penny Cycl.* XIX. 407/1 Gray.. considers the Reptiles, or scaly-skinned group, and the Amphibia, or naked-skinned group, as distinct classes. **1859** CARPENTER *Anim. Phys.* ii. (1872) 90 Many Zoologists range the Frogs and their allies in a separate class under the name of Amphibia. **1870** ROLLESTON *Anim. Life* Introd. 61 Amphibia..cold-blooded Vertebrata..provided with gills for aquatic in addition to lungs for aerial respiration.

amphibial (æm'fɪbɪəl), *a.* and *sb. rare.* [f. prec. + -AL[1].] = AMPHIBIAN.
1834 GOOD *Bk. Nature* I. 185 Mammals, birds, amphibials, fishes. **1879** *Syd. Soc. Lex.*, *Amphibial*, capable of living in water or air.

amphibian (æm'fɪbɪən), *a.* and *sb.* [f. as prec. + -AN.] **A.** *adj.*
1. Having two modes of existence; *fig.* of doubtful nature.
1637 GILLESPIE *Eng. Pop. Cer.* III. viii. 195 A certaine Amphibian brood, sprung out of the stem of Neronian tyranny.
2. Of or pertaining to the Amphibia.
[**1847** Not in CRAIG.] **1862** DANA *Man. Geol.* 751 Amphibian Reptiles. **1878** BELL *Gegenbauer's Comp. Anat.* 425 The Reptilia, which so far approach the old Amphibian phylum.
3. Of, pertaining to, or designating an amphibian (sense B. 3).
1920 *Glasgow Herald* 26 June 7 A service employing flying boats or 'Amphibian' machines or a mixed service of sea and land aircraft. **1931** R. N. LIPTROT in *Handbk. Aeronaut.* (*R. Aeronaut. Soc.*) ii. 55 Where amphibian gear is provided add 4 per cent. of the flying weight. **1935** H. G. WELLS *Things to Come* v. 33 In the foreground a smooth-flowing river, or lake, that reflects the scene—suddenly the mirror is broken as enormous amphibian tanks crawl up out of the water. **1939** *War Illustr.* 21 Oct. 186 An interesting development made by the Soviet army is the amphibian tank.
B. *sb.* **1.** An animal of the division Amphibia.
1835 KIRBY *Habits & Inst. Anim.* II. xvii. 137 If we go from the Cetaceans to the Amphibians, we see a further metamorphosis of the organs of motion. **1873** DAWSON *Earth & Man* vi. 144 In my younger days frogs and toads and newts used to be reptiles; now we are told that they are more like fishes, and ought to be called..Amphibians.
2. *fig.* A person having two modes of existence or a double character.
1902 *Daily Chron.* 5 May 4/3 These quiet, undistinguished amphibians of Sunwich. **1903** *Ibid.* 7 Jan. 4/4 Such is the natural logic of the amphibian.

3. A seaplane, tank or other vehicle able to operate both on land and on water.

1920 *Glasgow Herald* 2 Aug. 6 The land tests for seaplanes (amphibians). **1923** *Sci. Amer.* May 306/1 A Man-Made Amphibian..a successful boat that would also travel on its bottom, or on its own wheels rather, upon dry land. **1933** *Jane's Fighting Ships 1933* 507/3 Aircraft in operation, 11 seaplanes, 2 UO seaplanes, 1 Viking Flying Boat, 3 Douglas amphibians. **1937** L. HART *Europe in Arms* iii. 31 There are great numbers of two-men light tanks which can 'swim' rivers and are based on the Carden-Lloyd amphibian. **1957** R. WATSON-WATT *3 Steps* 350 Tests in a *Walrus* amphibian on the slipway showed a useful surface-to-surface range.

‖**am'phibii**, *sb. pl. Obs.* [L. *amphibii*, a. Gr. ἀμφίβιοι, pl. masc. of the adj. of which AMPHIBIA is neut.] Amphibious men.

a **1678** MARVELL *Applet. Ho.* (1776) 224 How tortoise like, but not so slow, These rational amphibii [salmon-fishers] go!

†**'amphibille**, *a. Obs. rare*⁻¹. [for *amphibole*, a. Fr. *amphibole*: see AMPHIBOLE[1].] Ambiguous.

? **1450** in *3rd Rep. Comm. Hist. MSS.* (1872) 280/2 That amphibille demaunde that the seid Duke seith in his article to demaunde the cause of the losse of Normandie.

amphibiolite (æm'fɪbɪəlaɪt). [f. AMPHIBION + -LITE.] 'The remains of an amphibious animal found in the fossil state.' Craig 1847.

amphibiolith (æm'fɪbɪəlɪθ). [f. as prec. + Gr. λίθος stone.] = prec. *Syd. Soc. Lex.* 1879.

amphibiological (æmˌfɪbɪə'lɒdʒɪkəl), *a.* [f. next + -ICAL.] Of or pertaining to amphibiology.

1847 in CRAIG.

amphibiology (æmˌfɪbɪ'ɒlədʒɪ). [f. AMPHIBIA + -(O)LOGY.] A scientific treatise on the Amphibia; that part of zoology which treats of amphibious animals.

1840 EATON & WRIGHT *N. Amer. Bot.* (ed. 8) 569 *Amphibiology*, the department of zoology, embracing animals which are capable of suspending respiration for a long time without injuring the action of the arterial system.

amphibion, [Gr.] sing. form of AMPHIBIA.

amphibious (æm'fɪbɪəs), *a.* [f. AMPHIBIA + -OUS.]

1. Living both on land and in water. **a.** of animals.

[**1609** B. JONSON *Silent Wom.* I. iv, Captain Otter, sir;..he has had command both by sea and land... O, then he is *animal amphibium*?] **1654** LESTRANGE *Charles I*, 87 The..Admiral..being scanted in Mariners..was enforced to take in two thousand two hundred land men, who should be amphibious, serving partly for sea-men, and partly for land-souldiers. **1697** DAMPIER *Voy.* I. (1729) 57 Guano's..lay Eggs as most of those amphibious creatures do. **1735** SOMERVILLE *Chase* IV. 364 On him Th' amphibious Otter feasts. **1833** SIR C. BELL *Hand* 138 Buffon tried to make a dog amphibious.

b. of plants.

1716 BRADLEY in *Phil. Trans.* XXIX. 486 Plants..are either Terrestrial, Amphibious, or Aquatick. **1813** C. MARSHALL *Gardening* (ed. 5) 120 The amphibious tribe as willow, sallow, withy, osier, etc.

2. a. Of, pertaining to, suited for, or connected with both land and water.

1646 SIR T. BROWNE *Pseud. Ep.* 138 Not only to swim in the water, but move upon the land, according to the amphibious and mixt intention of nature. **1663** BUTLER *Hudibr.* I. i. 27 So some Rats of Amphibious Nature Are either for the Land or Water. **1713** C'TESS WINCHELSEA *Misc. Poems* 246 The fatal Goodwin..that dangerous Sand, Amphibious in its kind, nor Sea nor Land. **1805** WORDSW. *Prel.* III. 69 A floating island, an amphibious spot.

b. Of a vehicle, aeroplane, etc.: = AMPHIBIAN A. 3; of a military operation: involving both land and sea forces; of soldiers: trained or used for amphibious warfare.

1915 *Illustr. War News* 7 Apr. 17 A new and ingenious amphibious automobile..constructed for the Austrian Army..the invention combines..features both of a boat and of a motor-car. **1928** H. ROWAN-ROBINSON *Artillery* vi. 46 Even if amphibious tanks can be built, rivers will be normally crossed at the bridges. **1931** *Illustr. London News* 31 Oct. 675/2 The Carden-Loyd Amphibious Tank has all the fighting qualities of the latest light Tank, and, in addition, can navigate deep water as easily as it can cross the roughest country. **1941** *New Statesman* 15 Feb. 151/2 There remains the possibility of 'amphibious' warfare. **1943** W. S. CHURCHILL in *Hansard Commons* ser. v. CCCXC. 563 Amphibious operations of peculiar complexity and hazard. **1945** *Ann. Reg. 1944* 56 'Ducks', amphibious lorries which were equally at home on land and in the water. **1945** *Daily Tel.* 17 May 5/6 Vice-Adml. Barbey, Commander of Amphibious Forces in the South-West Pacific.

3. Having two lives; occupying two positions; connected with or combining two classes, ranks, offices, qualities, etc.

1643 SIR T. BROWNE *Relig. Med.* (1656) I. §34 We are onely that amphibious piece between a corporall and spirituall essence. **1712** ADDISON *Spect.* No. 435 ⁋5 Such an Amphibious Dress [*i.e.* belonging to both sexes]. **1756** NUGENT *Montesquieu* (1758) II. XXVIII. xxxix. 312 Formed an amphibious code, where the French and Roman laws were mixed. **1817** COLERIDGE *Biog. Lit.* I. i. 24 An amphibious something..half of image, and half of abstract meaning. **1843** CARLYLE *Past & Pr.* 178, I have considered this amphibious Pope.

am'phibiously, *adv.* [f. prec. + -LY[2].] In an amphibious manner; like an amphibious being.

1821 BYRON in Moore *Life* (1866) 498 Land tortoises..amphibiously crawled along the bottom. **1871** *Daily News* 7 Sept., There are few people so amphibiously constituted as to take unmixed delight in a straight downpour of rain.

am'phibiousness. *rare*⁻⁰. [f. as prec. + -NESS.] The quality of being amphibious; life in, or connexion with, two elements.

1731 in BAILEY; whence in JOHNSON, etc.

amphibium, [L.] sing. form of AMPHIBIA.

amphibole[1] ('æmfɪbəʊl). [a. Fr. *amphibole*, 1. adj. 'ambiguous, of a double sense' (Cotgr. 1611), 2. the mineral; ad. L. *amphibol-um* ambiguous, a. Gr. ἀμφίβολ-ον thrown or hitting on both sides, ambiguous, f. ἀμφί on both sides + βολ-, βαλ- stem of βάλλ-ειν to throw.]

†**1.** An ambiguity; = AMPHIBOLY. *Obs.*

1606 HOLLAND *Suetonius* Notes 34 There is not onely an Homonyme in the word..but an Ampibole also in the sentence. **1668** WILKINS *Real Char.* II. i. §6. 48 *Æquivocation*, Ambiguous, Amphibole.

2. A mineral, hornblende. So named by Haüy 1801, in allusion to the protean variety in composition and appearance, assumed by the mineral genus to which he gave the name, and which Dana takes as the type of his first group of Bisilicates, including under it many species and varieties, as Actinolite, Asbestos, Hornblende, Tremolite, etc. (The pronunciation æm'fɪbəlɪ is quite erroneous.)

1833 LYELL *Elem. Geol.* (1865) 592 Amphibole is a general term under which hornblende and actinolite may be united. **1868** DANA *Min.* 233 The varieties of amphibole are as numerous as those of pyroxene. **1869** PHILLIPS *Vesuv.* x. 296 Hornblende, or Amphibole in ejected blocks and scoriæ on Somma and Vesuvius.

‖**amphibole**[2] (æm'fɪbəliː). *Gr. Antiq.* [Gr. ἀμφιβολή a casting-net, f. ἀμφί on both sides, around + -βολή a throw, cast.] An ancient casting-net.

1854 BADHAM *Halieut.* 24 Whether the net employed by Vulcan, on a memorable occasion..was an amphibole.

amphibolic (ˌæmfɪ'bɒlɪk), *a. rare.* [f. AMPHIBOLE + -IC. Cf. *symbolic.*]

1. Of the nature of amphiboly; ambiguous, equivocal.

1873 *Daily News* 11 Aug., I turn from this amphibolic pleading to a more succinct opinion. **1876** tr. *Wagner's Gen. Pathol.* 621 A variably long period of irresolution with irregular fluctuations of temperature..the so-called amphibolic stage.

2. Of, or of the nature of, the mineral amphibole.

1852 T. ROSS *Humboldt's Trav.* II. xxiv. 512 The decomposition of some amphibolic or chloritic strata. **1865** TYLOR *Early Hist. Man.* viii. 202 A greenish amphibolic stone.

†**amphi'bolical**, *a. Obs.* [f. as prec. + -ICAL.] = AMPHIBOLIC 1.

1652 GAULE *Magastrom.* 321 Œnigmaticall, obscure, amphibolicall, ambiguous, and æquivocating speeches. **1656** BLOUNT *Glossogr.*, *Amphibolous*, *Amphibolical*, *Amphibological*, doubtful or doubtfully spoken.

amphiboline (æm'fɪbəlɪn), *a.* [f. as prec. + -INE; cf. *amethystine.*] = AMPHIBOLIC 2.

1875 J. DAWSON *Dawn of Life* vii. 187 A similar alternation occurs in amphiboline-calcitic marbles.

amphibolite, -yte (æm'fɪbəlaɪt). *Min.* [f. as prec. + -ITE.] = Hornblende-rock or Diabase.

1833 LYELL *Elem. Geol.* (1865) 593 Amphibolite—is a trap of the basaltic family. **1868** DANA *Min.* 240 *Hornblende-rock* or *amphibolyte*, consists of massive hornblende of a dark greenish-black or black colour, and has a granular texture. *Ibid.* 343 If the hornblende and labradorite constitute a homogeneous fine-grained compact mass, the rock is called amphibolyte or diabase.

am'phibolize, *v. nonce-wd.* [f. Gr. ἀμφιβολή a cast-net + -IZE.] To envelop with a net.

1854 BADHAM *Halieut.* 192 The..thunny..leap, without looking, into its [the net's] folds, and are thus completely 'amphibolized' and caught.

amphibological (æmˌfɪbə'lɒdʒɪkəl), *a.* [f. AMPHIBOLOGY + -ICAL; perh. f. Fr. *amphibologique* 14 c.] Ambiguous: *prop.* of a sentence or phrase of ambiguous construction; equivocating, quibbling.

1577 HOLINSHED *Chron.* (1587) III. 1245/2 He that..wrote the amphibologicall epistle for the death of the king. **1587** GREENE *2nd Pt. Tritameron* Wks. 1882 III. 127 Needles Allegories that haue such an amphibologicall equivocation. **1621** BURTON *Anat. Mel.* III. iii. I. ii. (1651) 607 [He] ingratiates himself with an amphibological speech. **1836** HOR. SMITH *Tin Trum.* 30 An apology which he gave in the following amphibological terms—'I called you a liar,—it is true. You spoke truth. I have told a lie.'

amphibo'logically, *adv. rare*⁻⁰. [f. prec. + -LY[2].] 'Doubtfully, with a doubtful meaning.' J.

amphi'bologism. *rare.* [f. next + -ISM; cf. *neologism.*] An amphibolous construction or phrase.

1813 T. JEFFERSON *Writ.* (1830) IV. 223 Paring off the amphibologisms into which they have been led.

amphibology (ˌæmfɪ'bɒlədʒɪ). [a. Fr. *amphibologie*, ad. late L. *amphibologia* (Isidore), for earlier *amphibolia* (Cic.), a. Gr. ἀμφιβολία ambiguity, with the ending *-logia*, Gr. -λογία speech, by form-assoc. with *tautologia*, etc. Also found in the Latin form.]

1. = AMPHIBOLY 1.

c **1374** CHAUCER *Troylus* IV. 1406 For goddes speken in amphibologies, And for o soth, they tellen twenty lyes. **1552** LATIMER *Serm. Lord's Prayer* vii. II. 112 It is an *amphibologia*, and therefore Erasmus turneth it into Latin with such words. **1665** GLANVILL *Sceps. Sci.* 115 That the mind be not misled by amphibologies. **1751** CHAMBERS *Cycl.* s.v., The English language..is not so capable of any amphibologies of this kind. **1864** J. H. NEWMAN *Apol. Vita* App. 86 Nothing is adduced..for the lawful use of Amphibologies.

2. = AMPHIBOLY 2.

1589 PUTTENHAM *Eng. Poesie* (Arb.) 267 Such ambiguous termes they call Amphibologia, we call it the ambiguous, or figure of sence incertaine. **1646** SIR T. BROWNE *Pseud. Ep.* 13 The fallacie of Æquivocation and Amphibologie. **1654** LESTRANGE *Charles I*, 71 Giving him a quaint wipe with the amphibology, the double-mindednesse of the word 'dux.' **1870** JEVONS *Elem. Logic* XX. 172 The fallacy of Amphibology consists in an ambiguous grammatical structure of a sentence which produces misconception.

amˌphibolo'stylous, *a. Bot.* [f. Gr. ἀμφίβολ-ος (see AMPHIBOLE) + στῦλ-ος column + -OUS.] Applied, after Wachendorff, to plants in which the style is not apparent. *Syd. Soc. Lex.* 1879.

amphibolous (æm'fɪbələs), *a.* [f. L. *amphibolus* (a. Gr. ἀμφίβολ-ος: see AMPHIBOLE) + -OUS.]

†**1.** Ambiguous, of double or doubtful character.

1644 *England's Tears* in *Harl. Misc.* (Malh.) V. 447 Never[was] such an amphibolous quarrel, both parties declaring themselves for the King. **1660** HOWELL, *Crocodile*, a kind of amphibolous creture, partly aquatil, partly terrestrial.

2. Of language: Ambiguous in sense.

1641 MARCH *Actions for Slander* 5 The law, in actions of Slander, admits that they shall be taken in the best sense where the words are amphibolus. **1656** BLOUNT *Glossogr.*, *Amphibolous*, doubtful or doubtfully spoken.

3. *Path.* Spreading on both sides.

1880 LEGG *Bile* 86 Animals in whom an amphibolous biliary fistula had been made.

amphiboly (æm'fɪbəlɪ). Also 6–7 -ie. [a. OFr. *amphibolie*, ad. L. *amphibolia*, a. Gr. ἀμφιβολία ambiguity. See AMPHIBOLE.]

1. Ambiguous discourse; a sentence which may be construed in two distinct senses; a quibble. (See AMPHIBOLOGY, which is the earlier and more popular word.)

1610 HOLLAND *Camden's Brit.* I. 307 What a crafty Amphibolie or Æquivocation. **1632** B. JONSON *Magn. Lady* II. i, Come, leave your schemes, And fine amphibolies, parson. **1682** EVATS *Grotius, War & Peace* 199 If a sentence will admit of a double sence, they term it an Amphiboly. **1803** *Edin. Rev.* I. 271 The amphibolies..etc. of which Kant speaks, are impossible.

2. A figure of speech: Ambiguity arising from the uncertain construction of a sentence or clause, of which the individual words are unequivocal: thus distinguished by logicians from equivocation, though in popular use the two are confused.

1588 FRAUNCE *Lawiers Log.* I. iv. 27 b, Amphiboly, when the sentence may bee turned both the wayes, so that a man shall be uncertayne what waye to take. **1660** STANLEY *Hist. Philos.* (1701) 247/1 Sophisms in the Word are six..2. By Amphibolie. **1681** HOBBES *Rhet.* 162 Now of those fallacies that are joyned together. It is either *Amphibolia* or the doubtfulness of speech: or etc. **1803** *Edin. Rev.* I. 262 The perplexing controversies on the divisibility of matter, are the product of a double amphiboly.

amphibrach ('æmfɪbræk). Also -us, -ys, -ee. [ad. L. *amphibrachus*, *-ys*, a. Gr. ἀμφίβραχυς short at both ends, and *subst.* the foot so called, f. ἀμφί on both sides + βραχύς short. Long used in the L. forms; *amphibrachee* seems due to form-assoc. with *spondee*, *trochee*. In Eng. form in Craig 1847.]

In Gr. and L. prosody, a foot consisting of a long between two short syllables, as *ămātă*. Sometimes applied in modern prosody to an accented syllable between two unaccented, as *con'sented*, *dra'matic*.

1589 PUTTENHAM *Eng. Poesie* (Arb.) 134 For your foote *amphibracchus*..ye haue these wordes and many like to these [*rĕsīstĕd*] [*dĕlīghtfŭll*]. **1749** *Power of Numb. in Poet. Comp.* 19 Amphibrachys ◡–◡ is an Iambic ◡– and half Pyrrhic ◡. *a* **1771** GRAY *Corr.* (1843) 260 A free verse of eleven or twelve syllables, which may consist of four Amphibrachees ..so Prior: 'As Chlŏē cāme īntŏ thĕ rōom t'ŏthĕr dāy.' **1807** COLERIDGE, One syllable long, with one short at each side, *Amphĭbrăchy̆s hāstes wĭth ă stātely̆ strīde.* **1858** MARSH *Lect. Eng. Lang* xxiv. 524 Theoretically we may consider the prosody of the Ormulum as composed of verses of six iambics and an amphibrach.

amphibrachic (-ˈbrækɪk), *a. Prosody.* [f. AMPHIBRACH + -IC.] Consisting of amphibrachs.

1822 *Blackw. Mag.* XI. 441 The amphibrachic verses of French poetry. **1874** *Chambers's Encycl.* VI. 428/2 In the opening of Byron's *Bride of Abydos*.. each of the three lines is in a different metre, the first dactylic, the second amphibrachic, the third anapæstic.

amphibryous (æmˈfɪbrɪəs), *a. Bot.* [f. Gr. ἀμφί about + βρύ-ειν to swell + -OUS.] (See quot.)

1866 GRAY *Introd. Bot.* 522 *Amphibryous*, growing by additions over the whole periphery. [**1880** —— *Bot. Text-bk.* 395 *Amphibrya*, equivalent to monocotyledones.]

amphicarpous (æmfɪˈkɑːpəs), *a. Bot.* [f. Gr. ἀμφί both + καρπ-ός fruit + -OUS.] Having fruit of two kinds, either as to form, or time of maturation.

1866 GRAY *Introd. Bot.* 522 *Amphicarpous* or *amphicarpic*: producing two kinds of fruit.

amphichroic (æmfɪˈkrəʊɪk), *a.* [f. Gr. ἀμφί both + -χρο-ος coloured (f. χρό-α, χρο-ιά colour) + -IC. (In 1. c. erroneously printed *amphicroitic*.)] Having a double action upon test colours in chemistry.

1876 M. FOSTER *Phys.* (1879) I. ii. 63 A living muscle at rest.. tested by litmus paper.. is frequently amphicroitic, *i.e.* it will turn blue litmus red and red litmus blue.

amphicœlian (æmfɪˈsiːlɪən), *a. Phys.* [f. as next + -IAN.] = AMPHICŒLOUS; also, possessing or characterized by amphicœlous vertebræ.

1855 OWEN *Skel. & Teeth* 42 Vertebræ of this amphicœlian type.. existed in the teleosaurus. **1870** ROLLESTON *Anim. Life* Introd. 56 Amphicœlian vertebræ are found in the *Geckotidæ*.

amphicœlous (æmfɪˈsiːləs), *a. Phys.* [f. Gr. ἀμφί on both sides + κοῖλ-ος hollow + -OUS.] Concave on both sides, double concave. Applied to vertebræ, as in the backbone of a fish.

1869 HUXLEY in *Jrnl. Geol. S.* XXVI. 33 Amphicœlous centra. **1879** LE CONTE *Elem. Geol.* 470 Their vertebræ were amphicœlous or biconcave, as in fishes and many extinct reptiles.

† **ˈamphicome.** *Obs.* [ad. Gr. ἀμφίκομ-ος, f. ἀμφί about + κόμη hair.] 'A kind of figured stone, of a round shape, but rugged, celebrated on account of its use in divination.' Chambers *Cycl. Supp.* 1753.

amphictyonian (æmˌfɪktɪˈəʊnɪən), *a.* = next.

1711 SHAFTESB. *Charac.* (1737) III. 138 Those which constituted the Amphictonian councils.

amphictyonic (æmˌfɪktɪˈɒnɪk), *a.* [ad. L. *amphictyonic-us*, a. Gr. ἀμφικτυονικ-ός: see next and -IC.] Of the Amphictyons; also *transf.*

1753 CHAMBERS *Cycl. Supp.* s.v., The Phocæans.. were restored to their seat in the Amphictyonic council. **1835** THIRLWALL *Greece* I x. 375 The affairs of the whole Amphictyonic body were transacted by a congress. **1882** *Pall Mall G.* 18 Sept. 12 The Conference will wait till England.. herself convokes the Amphictyonic Council of Europe.

amphictyons (æmˈfɪktɪənz), *sb. pl. Gr. Hist.* [ad. Gr. ἀμφικτύονες, 'orig. ἀμφικτίονες, they that dwelt round or near, next neighbours' (Liddell and Scott).] Deputies from the different states of ancient Greece composing an assembly or council.

1586 T. B. *La Primaudaye's Fr. Acad.* 629 The sacred councell of the Amphictions. **1602** L. LLOYD *Confer. Lawes* 43 They might appeale from the Areopagites in Athens.. to the Amphictions at Trozæna. **1869** RAWLINSON *Anc. Hist.* 192 Sentence of the Amphictyons against Phocis, B.C. 357.

amphictyony (æmˈfɪktɪənɪ). *Gr. Hist.* [ad. Gr. ἀμφικτυονία, abstr. sb. f. prec.] A confederation of Amphictyons; an association of neighbouring states for the common interest.

1835 THIRLWALL *Greece* I. x. 374 The term amphictyony ..more properly written amphictiony, denotes a body referred to a local centre of union. **1846** GROTE *Greece* II. ii. 28 There was an Amphiktyony of seven cities at the holy island of Kalauria. **1869** RAWLINSON *Anc. Hist.* 122 These leagues, known as Amphictyonies, were not political alliances.

amphiˈcyrtous. [f. Gr. ἀμφίκυρτ-ος convex on both sides, gibbous (f. ἀμφί + κυρτός curved) + -OUS. Badly spelt *amphicurtous*.] Curved on both sides, gibbous.

1879 *Syd. Soc. Lex.*, *Amphicurtous.*

† **amphid(e** (ˈæmfɪd). *Chem. Obs.* [mod. f. Gr. ἀμφί both + -IDE 'derivative.'] A name applied by Berzelius to salts, which he viewed as compounds of two oxides, sulphides, selenides, or tellurides, and which actually contain three elements (as sulphate of potash $SO_3.K_2O$), as distinct from the *haloid* salts (as common salt, chloride of sodium, NaCl) which contain only two.

1842 *Proc. Am. Phil. Soc.* II. 220 An amphide salt is one consisting of an acid and a base, each containing an amphigen body. **1863** WATTS *Dict. Chem.* (1872) I. 201 The so-called *amphid* salts are those which belong to the *water-type*.. whereas the haloid-compounds belong to the type HH or HCl.

amphidiploid (ˌæmfɪˈdɪplɔɪd), *a.* and *sb. Biol.* [f. AMPHI- + DIPLOID *a.*] Having a diploid set of chromosomes derived from each of its parents; double diploid; = ALLOTETRAPLOID *a.* Also as *sb.*, a hybrid of this kind. Hence ˌamphiˈdiploidy, the state of being amphidiploid.

1930 *Univ. Calif. Publ. Agric. Sci.* VI. 84 An amphidiploid *C. capillaris-C. dioscoridis* hybrid obtained by M. Nawashin.. was smaller. *Ibid.*, Amphidiploids.. involve two species of the same genus. **1932** N. I. VAVILOV in *Proc. VI Internat. Congress Genetics* I. 341 The phenomenon of amphidiploidy of sterile hybrids proved to be rather frequent... Several cases of amphidiploidy were produced in hybrids of wheat and Aegilops. **1936** *Nature* 23 May 874/1 An amphidiploid wheat. The plant.. had 42 chromosomes, and the evidence indicates that it was an amphidiploid produced by the parthenogenetic development of an egg... The amphidiploids are highly fertile.

amphidisc (ˈæmfɪdɪsk). *Zool.* [f. Gr. ἀμφί on both sides + δίσκος a round plate.] Peculiar asteroid spicules, resembling two toothed wheels united by an axle, which form a layer surrounding the gemmules of sponges. (Nicholson.)

1867 J. HOGG *Microsc.* II. ii. 389 Remains of the dead sponge, empty gemmule-cases with their amphidiscs. **1877** HUXLEY *Anat. Inv. An.* iii. 118 Nothing is left but the envelope of keratose, with imbedded amphidisks, disposed perpendicularly to its surface.

amphiˈdromic, *a.*—⁰ The mod. form of the next, if used.

† **amphiˈdromical,** *a. Obs.* [f. Gr. ἀμφιδρομία, f. ἀμφίδρομος running about or around + -ICAL.] Pertaining to the ancient Amphidromia ('an Attic festival at the naming of a child, so called because the parents' friends carried it round the hearth, and then gave it its name.' Liddell and Scott).

1658 SIR T. BROWNE *Gard. Cyrus* II. 561 At the Amphidromicall Feasts, on the fifth day after the Childe was born, presents were sent from friends. **1681** BLOUNT *Glossogr.*, *Amphidromical*, pertaining to the fifth day from the birth, when the child was purified, by carrying it round the fire, and having its name given.

amphigam (ˈæmfɪgæm). *Bot.* [a. Fr. *amphigame*, f. Gr. ἀμφί on both sides + γάμος marriage.] A name given by De Candolle to the lowest order of plants, supposed to have no distinct sexual organs, also called *Agamæ*.

1845 LINDLEY *Sch. Bot.* (1858) ix. 151 *Amphigams*, plants having neither air vessels nor stomates.

amphigamous (æmˈfɪgəməs), *a. Bot.* [f. AMPHIGAM + -OUS.] Of or pertaining to Amphigams.

1841 LINDLEY *Elem. Bot.* 90 Amphigamous.. that is, destitute of stomates and entirely cellular. **1880** GRAY *Struct. Bot.* ix. §2. 340 *Amphigamous*: destitute of sexual organs and of other than cellular tissue.

‖ **amphigastria** (æmfɪˈgæstrɪə), *sb. pl. Bot.* [mod.L. f. Gr. ἀμφί about, around + γαστρ- (γαστήρ) the belly.] Scale-like leaves, resembling stipules, developed on the under side of some Liverworts.

1842 *Penny Cycl.* XXIV. 278 Stipulæ or amphigastria. **1857** BERKELEY *Cryptog. Bot.* §489 There are ventral leaves, called amphigastra. **1875** BENNET & DYER *Sachs' Bot.* 306 Three rows of leaves, one being developed on the under or shaded side, hence termed Amphigastria.

amphigean (æmˈfɪdʒɪən), *a. rare.* [mod. f. Gr. ἀμφί on both sides of, about + γῆ earth + -AN.] Extending all over the earth from the equator to both poles.

1864 WEBSTER cites DANA.

amphigen¹ (ˈæmfɪdʒɛn). *Bot.* [a. Fr. *amphigène*, f. Gr. ἀμφί on both sides, around + -γενή-ς born, f. γεν- to produce: see -GEN¹.] A synonym of THALLOGEN, applied (after Brongniart) to those Cryptogams, which grow round a central point, including Seaweeds, Lichens, and Fungi.

1879 in *Syd. Soc. Lex.*

† **amphigen**² (ˈæmfɪdʒɛn). *Chem. Obs.* [mod. f. Gr. ἀμφί both + -GEN², taken as = 'producing.'] Name given by Berzelius to an element capable of forming in combination with metals, both acids and bases. He included as amphigens, or *amphigen bodies*, oxygen, sulphur, selenium, and tellurium.

1842 [See AMPHID(E].

amphigene (ˈæmfɪdʒiːn). *Min.* [a. Fr. *amphigène*, f. Gr. ἀμφιγενής of both kinds, of doubtful kind; f. ἀμφί both + γένος kind, nature.] A synonym of LEUCITE, rejected by Dana.

1803 *Edin. Rev.* III. 53 Now we see its [leucite's] place supplied by the word amphigene. **1868** DANA *Min.* 335 Haüy's name, Amphigene, is.. in allusion to the existence of cleavage in two directions (which is not a fact), and to his inference therefrom of 'two primitive forms' (which is only a notion of his); and it has therefore the best of claims for rejection. **1869** PHILLIPS *Vesuv.* x. 292 Leucite or Amphigene, frequent in the lavas of Somma.

amphigenite, -yte (æmˈfɪdʒɪnaɪt). *Min.* [f. AMPHIGENE + -ITE.] Name sometimes given to a lava containing much 'amphigene' or leucite.

1868 DANA *Min.* 335 At Vesuvius [leucite] is thickly disseminated through the lava in grains, and the name *leucitophyr* and also *amphigenyte* has been given to such lavas.

amphigenous (æmˈfɪdʒɪnəs), *a.* [f. AMPHIGEN + -OUS.]

1. *Bot.* Of or pertaining to the Amphigens; growing all round a central point.

1835 LINDLEY *Introd. Bot.* (1848) II. 380 *Amphigenous*; growing all round an object. **1857** BERKELEY *Crypt. Bot.* §392 Fructifying surface inferior or amphigenous.

2. *Chem.* Of the nature or class of an amphigen.

1879 *Syd. Soc. Lex.* s.v. *Amphide*, They are due to the composition of compounds produced by amphigenous bodies.

amphigonic (æmfɪˈgɒnɪk), *a. rare.* [f. Gr. ἀμφί on both sides + γονικός parental, f. γεν-, γον- bear, produce. The Gr. would be ἀμφίγονος.] Of the nature of amphigony; bisexual.

1876 tr. *Haeckel's Hist. Creat.* I. 195 Sexual or amphigonic propagation.. is the usual method.. among all higher animals and plants.

amphigonous (æmˈfɪgənəs). [f. Gr. *ἀμφίγονος (see prec.) + -OUS.] Pertaining to both parents.

1876 tr. *Haeckel's Hist. Creat.* I. 210 Law of mixed or mutual (amphigonous) transmission.

amphigony (æmˈfɪgənɪ). [mod.f. Gr. ἀμφί both + -γονία, f. -γονος producing, engendering.] A term for sexual reproduction.

1876 tr. *Haeckel's Hist. Creat.* I. 183 Those phenomena of Propagation.. seen universally in the higher plants and animals, the processes of Sexual propagation, or Amphigony.—The processes of Non-sexual Propagation, or Monogony, are much less generally known.

amphiˈgoric, *a.* [ad. Fr. *amphigourique*, f. *amphigouri* + -IC.] Of the nature of an amphigouri.

1869 *N. & Q.* Ser. IV. III. 224 *Amphigoric*, a term applied to nonsense verses, a rigmarole, or, more literally, a *round-about*, with semblable meaning enough to put one on finding it out.

‖ **amphigouri, -gory** (ˌæmfɪˈgʊərɪ, ˈæmfɪgərɪ). [mod.Fr.; orig. unknown. According to Litt. first used in 18th c.; referred by some to Gr. ἀμφί about + γῦρος circle, or -ἀγορία speech, cf. *allegory*, *category*.] A burlesque writing filled with nonsense; a composition without sense, as a Latin 'nonsense-verse.'

1809 *Q. Rev.* I. 50 The work must.. be considered as a kind of overgrown *amphigouri*, a heterogeneous combination of events. **1851** SIR F. PALGRAVE *Norm. & Eng.* II. 55 We do not like to confess we are beaten even by an *amphigouri* nonsense verse. **1869** *N. & Q.* Ser. IV. III. 145 The remaining verses.. of the following amphigory.

amphilogism (æmˈfɪlədʒɪz(ə)m). *rare.* [f. Gr. ἀμφίλογ-ος + -ISM.] A circumlocution.

1866 *Morn. Star* 18 Dec. 4/6 A youth this who.. when he is angry says, with no amphilogisms, 'I will shoot you.'

amphilogite (æmˈfɪlədʒaɪt). *Min.* [f. Gr. ἀμφίλογ-ος doubtful, disputed + -ITE.] A mineral of doubtful or disputed character, according to Dana, 'probably only a mica schist.'

† **amˈphilogy.** *Obs.*—⁰ [ad. Gr. ἀμφιλογία, f. ἀμφίλογ-ος uncertain, disputed, f. ἀμφί on both sides + -λογ-ος -speaking.] 'Equivocatiaon; ambiguity.' J.

1731 BAILEY, *Amphilogy*, an ambiguity of speech.

amphimacer (æmˈfɪməsə(r)). [ad. L. *amphimacrus*, a. Gr. ἀμφίμακρος long at both ends, *subst.* the foot so called; f. ἀμφί on both sides + μακρός long. Cf. Fr. *amphimacre*.] In Greek and Latin prosody, a foot consisting of a short between two long syllables, as *cārĭtās*. Sometimes applied in modern prosody to words like *multitude*, *runaway*.

1589 PUTTENHAM *Eng. Poesie* (Arb.) 134 For your *amphimacer* that is a long a short and a long ye haue these wordes and many moe [*excellĕnt*] [*īmĭnēnt*]. **1807** COLERIDGE, Fīrst ănd lāst bēĭng lōng, mīddlĕ shōrt, Amphĭmācer Strīkes hĭs thūndĕrĭng hōofs lĭke ă prōud hīgh brĕd rācer. **1869** MAX MÜLLER *Rig Veda* I. 190 Who is meant by *asmân*, which is here used as an *amphimacer*?

‖ **Amphioxus** (æmfɪˈɒksəs). *Zool.* [mod.L. f. Gr. ἀμφί on both sides + ὀξύς sharp, *i.e.*

sharpened or tapering at both ends.] A genus of fishes, consisting of a single species, called also the Lancelet, which is placed at the very bottom of the series, and has even been denied to be a vertebrate animal.

1836 YARRELL in *Penny Cycl.* 1st Supp. 233/1 The Lancelet, *Amphioxus lanceolatus*. **1847** CARPENTER *Zool.* §585 The most imperfectly formed of all Fish is, probably, the Amphioxus or Lancelet. **1881** *Athenæum* 15 Jan. 98/2 We cannot regard Amphioxus as a fish.

amphipneust (ˈæmfɪpnjuːst). *Zool.* [mod. f. Gr. ἀμφί both + -πνευστ-ος breathing, f. πνέ(υ)-ειν to breathe. *Pl.* *-s*, or collectively *amphipneusta*; first applied by Merrem 1790–1820.] An animal that breathes both by lungs and by gills; a name given by some to the lowest order of the Amphibious animals, including the Proteus and Siren, which retain their gills all their lives.

1841 *Penny Cycl.* XIX. 408/2 quoting J. A. GRAY (1831) In the second section (*Amphipneusta*) are placed the *Protei*. **1847** in CRAIG.

amphipod (ˈæmfɪpɒd), *sb.* and *a.* [f. AMPHIPODA.]

A. *sb.* An animal of the order *Amphipoda*.

1835 KIRBY *Habits & Inst. Anim.* II. xv. 41 Amphipods. Head distinct. Eyes sessile. **1836** TODD *Cycl. Anat. & Phys.* I. 755/2 In the Amphipods the want of resemblance between the different rings of the body becomes more remarkable.

B. *adj.* = AMPHIPODOUS.

1852 DANA *Crustac.* I. 11 The abdomen..partakes of the Amphipod character. **1877** W. THOMSON *Voy. Challenger* I. ii. 129 A very large amphipod crustacean.

‖**Amphipoda** (æmˈfɪpədə), *sb. pl.* *Zool.* The sing. is supplied by AMPHIPOD. [mod.L. *amphipoda* prop. adj. (sc. *animalia*); f. Gr. ἀμφί both + -ποδα (πούς) foot, -footed.] An order or sub-order of the sessile-eyed Crustacea, having feet of two kinds (in which they differ from the Isopoda), of which the common sand-hopper is an example.

1837 *Penny Cycl.* VIII. 197/2 The *Edriophthalmia* contain three orders, the *Amphipoda*, etc. **1874** WOOD *Nat. Hist.* 728 The first order of the Sessile-eyed Crustaceans is termed the Amphipoda.

amˈphipodan, *a.* *Zool.* [f. prec. + -AN.] Of or pertaining to the *Amphipoda*.

1877 HUXLEY *Anat. Inv. An.* vi. 369 The organisation of the Stomatopoda is more Edriophthalmian (and especially Amphipodan) than Podophthalmian.

amphipodiform (æmfɪˈpɒdɪfɔːm), *a.* *Zool.* [f. as prec. + -(I)FORM.] Of the form of the *Amphipoda*; resembling the sand-hopper.

1828 KIRBY & SPENCE *Entomol.* III. xxix. 169 The jumping amphipodiform Crustacea.

amphipodous (æmˈfɪpədəs), *a.* *Zool.* [f. as prec. + -OUS.] Of or pertaining to the *Amphipoda*; having feet of two kinds.

1862 ANSTED *Channel Isl.* II. ix. (ed. 2) 234 The isopodous and amphipodous species. **1870** ROLLESTON *Anim. Life* 111 An amphipodous..Crustacean.

amphiprostyle (æmˈfɪprəstaɪl). *Arch.* [a. Fr. *amphiprostyle*, ad. L. *amphiprostȳl-us*, a. Gr. ἀμφιπρόστυλ-ος, f. ἀμφί on both sides + πρόστυλος PROSTYLE.] 'A temple having a portico in the rear as well as the front, but without columns at the sides. This..never exceeded the use of four columns in the front, and four in the rear.' Gwilt.

1706 PHILLIPS, *Amphyprostylos* or *Amphyprostyle*, a kind of Temple of the Ancients, which had four Columns or Pillars in the Front, and as many in the Face behind. [So in BAILEY, etc. *Amphip-*.] **1850** LEITCH *Müller's Anc. Art* §288 Temples are divided into..*prostyle*, with porticoes on the front, and *amphiprostyle*, at the two ends.

‖**amphisarca** (æmfɪˈsɑːkə). *Bot.* [mod.L. f. Gr. ἀμφί about + σάρκα- flesh.] (See quot.)

1854 BALFOUR *Class-bk. Bot.* 1087 *Amphisarca*, an indehiscent multilocular fruit with a hard exterior, and pulp round the seeds **1880** GRAY *Bot. Text-bk.* 395 *Amphisarca*, a hard-rinded berry, or fruit succulent within and woody or crustaceous without, as a calibash.

‖**amphisbæna** (æmfɪsˈbiːnə). Also 4–5 amphibena, 6 -bene. [L., a. Gr. ἀμφίσβαινα, f. ἀμφίς both ways + βαίν-ειν to go. Cf. Fr. *amphisbène*.]

1. A fabled serpent of the ancients, with a head at each end, and able to move in either direction: retained by the moderns as a poetical conception.

1398 TREVISA *Barth. De P.R.* XVIII. ix. (1495) 758 Some serpentes hath two heedys as the adder Alphibena [*sic*]. **1572** BOSSEWELL *Armorie* II. 63 The fielde is Sable, an Amphibene, heade to heade reflexed. **1627** FELTHAM *Resolves* II. i. (1677) 159 A corrupt Book is an Amphisbæna: A Serpent headed at either end: one bites him that reads, the other stings him that writes. **1667** MILTON *P.L.* x. 524 Complicated monsters head and taile, Scorpion, and Asp, and Amphisbæna dire. **1728** POPE *Dunciad* III. (1736) 201 *note*, Thus Amphisbæna (I have read) At either end assails; None knows which leads, or which is led, For both Heads are but Tails. **1788** PASQUIN *Childr. Thespis* (1792) 49 Like the vile Amphisbæna, his verses assail, For none can discover their head from their tail. **1878** TENNYSON *Q. Mary* III. iv. 116 For heretic and traitor are all one: Two vipers of one breed—an amphisbæna, Each end a sting.

2. *Zool.* A worm-like genus of lizards found in America, having the two extremities so much alike that it is difficult to distinguish between the head and the tail.

1833 *Penny Cycl.* I. 467/2 In the amphisbæna..the upper jaw is fixed to the skull..as in birds and mammals. **1847** CARPENTER *Zool.* §501 The Amphisbæna bores in the soft earth like a worm, working its way with considerable despatch; and it lives principally on Ants..and their larvæ.

amphisˈbænian, *a.* *Zool.* [f. prec. + -IAN.] Of or belonging to the amphisbæna.

1872 MIVART *Anat.* 190 Amphisbenian group of Reptiles.

amphisbænic (æmfɪsˈbiːnɪk), *a.* [f. as prec. + -IC.] Of the nature of an amphisbæna.

1820 SHELLEY *Prom. Unb.* III. iv. 119 Yoked to it by an amphisbenic snake.

amphisbænous (æmfɪsˈbiːnəs), *a.* [f. as prec. + -OUS.] 'Walking equally in opposite directions.' *Syd. Soc. Lex.* 1879.

Amphiscians (æmˈfɪʃɪənz), *sb. pl.* [f. med.L. *Amphiscii* (æmˈfɪʃɪaɪ) more commonly used unchanged in Eng. (a. Gr. ἀμφίσκιοι, f. ἀμφί on both sides + σκία shadow) + -AN.] A name given to inhabitants of the torrid zone, whose shadows at one time of the year fall northward, at another southward.

1622 HEYLIN *Cosmogr.* (1674) Introd. 20/1 *Amphiscii*..so called, because their shadows are both ways. **1623** COCKERAM *Eng. Dict.* 111, *Amphisceans*, people whose shadow is sometime to the North, and sometime to the South. **1652** URQUHART *Jewel* Wks. 1834. 259 Whether Periscians, Hetroscians, or Amphiscians. **1656** BLOUNT *Glossogr.*, *Amphyscyans* [ed. 1672 *Amphiskians*] such people as live under the burning zone, near the equinoctial line. **1751** CHAMBERS *Cycl.* s.v., The *amphiscii* are called also *ascii*. **1788** PASQUIN *Childr. Thespis* (1792) 145 The wandering Amphiscii, whose singular state, Made sceptics to question the wisdom of Fate.

amphistome (ˈæmfɪstəʊm). *Zool.* [ad. mod.L. *amphistoma*, f. Gr. ἀμφί on both sides + στόμα mouth.] A genus of minute parasitic worms, having mouth-like openings at both ends of the body.

1880 *Athenæum* 20 Nov. 678/2 The worm..appears to be an aberrant Amphistome furnished with a singular central disc.

amphistomoid (æmˈfɪstəmɔɪd), *a.* *Zool.* [f. prec. + -OID.] Like or akin to the Amphistomes.

1880 *Athenæum* 20 Nov. 678/2 Doubts are thrown on its [the *Gastrodiscus*] amphistomoid affinities.

amphistylic (æmfɪˈstaɪlɪk), *a.* [f. Gr. ἀμφί on both sides + στῦλ-ος pillar + -IC.] Having pillars or piers on both sides: applied to the skulls of certain sharks, having piers supporting both upper and lower mandibular arches.

1876 HUXLEY in *Proc. Zool. Soc.* 41 A condition of the cranium which tends to connect the two by a middle form, which may be termed amphistylic. **1881** F. BALFOUR *Comp. Embryol.* II. 476 Skulls in which the mandibular arch has this double form of support have been called amphistylic.

amphitheatral (ˌæmfɪˈθiːətrəl), *a.* [a. Fr. *amphithéatral*, ad. L. *amphitheātrāl-em*: see next, and -AL[1].]

1. Of or belonging to an amphitheatre; performed in an amphitheatre.

1654 GAYTON *Festiv. Notes* IV. i. 178 Those Amphitheatrall Butcheries.

2. Resembling the arrangement of the seats in an amphitheatre; rising all round.

1615 SANDYS *Trav.* 278 (D.) Which..erect A Round amphitheatral. **1812** MISS PLUMTRE *Lichtenst. S. Africa* II. 162 Vast masses of rock rise one above the other in an amphitheatral form. **1863** BATES *Nat. on Amazon* i. 2 The City of Pará..affords no amphitheatral view from the river.

amphitheatre, -ter (ˌæmfɪˈθiːətə(r)). [ad. L. *amphitheātrum*, a. Gr. ἀμφιθέᾱτρον, f. ἀμφί on both sides + θέᾱτρον THEATRE. The 17–18th c. spelling *-theater* is common in U.S.; *-theatre* follows Fr.]

†1. *etymol.* A double theatre. *Obs.*

1615 SANDYS *Trav.* 270 An Amphitheater consists of two ioyned Theaters, and is thereof so called. **1628** DONNE *Serm.* cxxxiv. V. 396 An amphitheatre consists of two theatres. Our text hath two parts in which all Men may sit and see themselves acted. *a* **1631** —— *Select.* (1840) 99 A tragedy in the amphitheatre, the double theatre, this world, and the next too. **1807** ROBINSON *Archæol. Græca* I. i. 17 Amphitheatres, which had the form of two theatres united, were oval.

2. Hence (as the theatres of the ancients were semicircles or half-ovals): An oval or circular building, with seats rising behind and above each other, around a central open space or arena.

1546 LANGLEY *Polyd. Verg.* III. ix. 75 b, An Amphitheatre which was a round scaffold full of benches of diuerse heightes. **1589** PUTTENHAM *Eng. Poesie* (Arb.) 52 Their theaters..somptuously built with marble and square stone in forme all round..were called Amphitheaters. *a* **1661** HOLYDAY *Juvenal* 70 The theaters being for stage-plays.. but the amphitheaters for fights of men with men, and of men with beasts. **1703** *Lond. Gaz.* mmmdcccxci/1 An Ancient Amphitheater, called the *Coliseo*. **1866** KINGSLEY *Herew.* x. 160 The amphitheatre of Arles. **1883** TALMAGE in *Chr. Her.* 9 May 256/1 The students gathered in the amphitheatre to see a painful operation.

3. With reference to its ancient Greek and Roman uses: A place of public contest, an arena.

1640 BROME *Antipod.* I. v. 245 An Amphitheater Of exercise and pleasure. **1735** SOMERVILLE *Chase* II. 450 A listed Field..An Amphitheatre more glorious far Than ancient Rome could boast. **1875** HELPS *Ess.*, *Aids to Contentm.* 9 Many unhappy persons seem to imagine that they are always in an amphitheatre, with the assembled world as spectators.

4. A semicircular rising gallery in a theatre, containing part of the seats for spectators.

1859 G. A. SALA *Twice round Clock* 253 The dwellers in the high-up amphitheatre or gallery. **1882** C. DICKENS *Dict. Lond.* 96/1 Evening dress is indispensable in every part except gallery and amphitheatre stalls. **1883** *St. James's G.* 11 Apr. 1/2 First circle, 2*s.* 6*d.*; amphitheatre, 1*s.* 6*d.*; gallery, 1*s.*

†5. *fig.* Surrounding scene. *Obs.*

c **1630** DRUMM. OF HAWTH. *Wks.* 1711. 3 Look how Prometheus..wondred at this world's amphitheater. **1711** ADDISON *Spect.* No. 315 ¶11 All the Wonders in this immense Amphiteatre that lies between the Poles of Heaven.

6. *transf.* A natural situation consisting of a level surrounded in whole or part by rising slopes.

1772 PENNANT *Tours in Scotl.* (1774) 40 On every side mountains close the prospect, and form an amphitheatre almost matchless. **1812** BYRON *Childe Har.* II. li, Nature's volcanic amphitheatre. **1849** W. IRVING *Mahomed & Succ.* v. (1853) 19 Bounded by an amphi-theatre of hills.

7. *Gardening.* An arrangement of shrubs and trees rising behind each other like the seats of an amphitheatre, whether upon a natural slope or not.

1753 CHAMBERS *Cycl. Supp.*, *Amphitheatres* are also sometimes formed of slopes on the sides of hills.

amphitheatred (ˌæmfɪˈθiːətəd). *ppl. a.* [f. prec. + -ED[2].] Formed into, or provided with, an amphitheatre.

1857 *Nat. Mag.* II. 314 Those amphitheatred heights. **1859** MISS MULOCH *Romantic T.* 22 Deep Vale, amphitheatred by forest and mountain.

amphitheatric (ˌæmfɪθiːˈætrɪk), *a.* [ad. L. *amphitheātric-us*, a. Gr. ἀμφιθεᾱτρικ-ός; see prec.]

1. Of or pertaining to an amphitheatre.

1601 HOLLAND *Pliny* (1634) I. 392 Next in goodnesse to them was reputed the paper Amphitheatricke, which name was giuen vnto it of the place where it was made.

2. Rising all round like the rows of seats in an amphitheatre.

c **1811** FUSELI *Lect. Art* v. (1848) 464 The disposition is amphitheatric, the scenery a spacious hall. **1850** B. TAYLOR *Eldorado* xxxi. (1862) 317 The town and its amphitheatric hills.

ˌamphiˈtheatrical, *a.* [f. as prec. + -AL[1].]

1. Of or pertaining to an amphitheatre; performed in an amphitheatre.

1607 TOPSELL *Serpents* (1653) 783 The amphitheatricall fights of the Romans. **1654** GAYTON *Festiv. Notes* IV. xxi. (T.) Amphitheatrical gladiatures. **1752** HUME *Polit. Disc.* x. 165 Who can read the accounts of the amphitheatrical entertainments without horror? **1833** *Penny Cycl.* I. 470 Games of the circus or amphitheatrical shows.

2. Resembling an amphitheatre (in situation).

1724 DE FOE, etc. *Tour Gt. Brit.* (1769) II. 292 It lies in a great Valley, surrounded with an amphitheatrical View of Hills. **1845** DARWIN *Voy. Nat.* xix. (1873) 439 Valleys and great amphitheatrical depressions. **1858** HAWTHORNE *Fr. & It. Jrnls.* II. 74 Amphitheatrical ranges of wooden seats.

ˌamphiˈtheatrically, *adv.* [f. prec. + -LY[2].] After the manner of the ascending rows of seats in an amphitheatre.

1716 *Town Talk* No. 4 (1790) 41 Seats for the audience amphitheatrically built. **1881** *Chr. Treas.* 434 Beyond the white walls of the Seraglio..rise amphitheatrically..the houses of Stamboul.

amphithere (ˈæmfɪθɪə(r)). *Palæont.* [ad. mod.L. amphithērium (also in Eng. use), f. Gr. ἀμφί both, on both sides + θηρίον a beast; in reference to its disputed position in the animal series.] An extinct genus of small opossum-like quadrupeds, found in the Oolite.

1859 OWEN *Classif. Mammalia* 55 The nearest living analogue to the amphitheres..of our oolitic strata. **1864** —— *Power of God* 50 The marsupial analogues of the amphitheria.

amˈphitoky. [f. Gr. ἀμφί both + -τόκ-ος bringing forth + -Y.] 'The production in Parthenogenesis of both male and female forms.' *Syd. Soc. Lex.*

amphitropal (æmˈfɪtrəpəl), *a.* *Bot.* [mod. f. Gr. ἀμφί on both sides, about + -τρόπ-ος turning + -AL[1]. Cf. mod.Fr. *amphitrope*.] Of an embryo: So curved as to have both apex and radicle presented to the hilum.

1847 in CRAIG. **1870** HOOKER *Stud. Flora* 64 *Portulaceæ*.. ovules 2 or more.. amphitropal, ascending.

amphitropous (æm'fɪtrəpəs), *a. Bot.* [f. as prec. + -OUS.] = prec.

1841 LINDLEY *Elem. Bot.* 55 When [the ovule is] attached by its middle, so that the foramen is at one end and the base at the other, it is *amphitropous*. **1870** HOOKER *Stud. Flora* 47 *Frankeniaceæ*.. ovules.. amphitropous with the micropyle below.

‖**Amphitryon** (æm'fɪtrɪən). [From the comedy of Molière, in which Amphitryon (foster-father of Hercules) gives a great dinner.] A host, an entertainer to dinner.

[MOLIÈRE *Amphitryon* III. v, Le véritable Amphitryon est l'Amphitryon où l'on dîne.] **1862** AIDÉ *Carr of Carlyon* I. 113 He excused himself, when.. asked.. to dinner; and.. the would-be Amphitryon had pride enough not to renew the invitation. **1878** LADY HERBERT *Hübner's Round the World* II. ii. 521 My noble amphitryon made me sit down.

†**'amphitype.** *Obs.* [f. Gr. ἀμφί both + τύπος a stamp.] A photographic process, producing both negative and positive portraits at once.

1844 HUNT *Man. Photogr.* 64 Sir John Herschel, at the meeting of the British Association at York.. says.. 'I have designated the process thus generally sketched out, by the term "Amphitype"; a name suggested by Mr. Talbot.'

amphivorous (æm'fɪvərəs), *a.* [f. Gr. ἀμφί both + L. *-vorus* devouring, eating; cf. *omnivorous*.] Eating both animal and vegetable food; omnivorous.

a **1870** MAPOTHER *Anim. Phys.* 6 Animals, according to their food, may be divided into herbivorous, like the cow; carnivorous, like the lion; and amphivorous, like man.

amphodarch ('æmfədɑːk). *Gr. Ant.* [ad. Gr. ἀμφοδάρχ-ης, f. ἄμφοδον a quarter of a town, *orig.* a block of houses surrounded by streets + -αρχης ruler.] One exercising authority over a quarter of a town.

1878 *N. Amer. Rev.* CXXVII. 502 The new town [Jerusalem] was divided [by Hadrian] into seven quarters, each directed by an amphodarch.

amphodelite (æm'fɒdɪlaɪt). *Min.* [a. Ger. *amphodelit* (1832), formed, according to Dana, on Gr. ἀμφί on both sides + ὀδελ-ός = ὀβελ-ός a spit + -ITE.] A variety of Anorthite found in Finland.

1868 DANA *Min.* 338.

‖**amphora** ('æmfərə). Pl. **-æ**. [L., ad. Gr. ἀμφορεύς, shortened from ἀμφιφορεύς, f. ἀμφί on both sides + φορεύς bearer, f. φέρ-ειν to bear, descriptive of its two handles.]

1. *Cl. Antiq.* A two-handled vessel, of various shape, used by the ancients for holding wine, oil, etc.

c **1465** *Bk. Quintess.* 5 Putte it into a glas clepid amphora, with a long necke. **1857** BIRCH *Anc. Pottery* (1858) I. 35 The amphoræ or two-handled vases in the collections of the Museum. **1879** J. YOUNG *Ceram. Art* 24 Amphoræ—the Greek two-handled, oval-bodied vases with pointed base, which have been found wherever Greek commerce extended.

2. A liquid measure, containing, with the Greeks, about 9 gallons; with the Romans, containing 6 gals. 7 pts., and also called quadrantal.

1607 TOPSELL *Four-footed Beasts* (1673) 54 A horn brought out of India to Ptolemy the second, which received three Amphoraes of water. **1753** CHAMBERS *Cycl. Supp.* s.v., The Attic Amphora was one third part bigger than the Italic. **1820** MAIR *Tyro's Dict.* (ed. 10) 5 *Amphoralis*, containing an amphora or rundlet.

3. *Bot.* Sometimes applied to the lower or permanent part of the capsule called pyxidium, which remains attached to the flower stalk in the form of an urn, as in *Hyoscyamus*.

1821 S. GRAY *Arr. Brit. Pl.* I. 184 *Amphora*, the lower valve [of the pyxis] attached to the peduncle. **1880** GRAY *Bot. Text-bk.* 395 *Amphora*.. the lower part of a pyxis.

amphoral ('æmfərəl), *a.* [ad. L. *amphorāl-is*, f. *amphora*: see -AL[1].] Of, pertaining to, or resembling an amphora.

1656 BLOUNT *Glossogr.*, *Amphoral*, containing or pertaining to *amphora*. **1874** VIZETELLY *Rep. Wines at Vien. Exhib.* IV. 134 The amphoral shaped jars, in which it is the custom to keep the wine.

†**amphore.** *Obs.* Also 4 **amfore, amfer**. [a. Fr. *amphore*, ad. L. AMPHORA, now in Eng. use.]

1. = AMPHORA 1.

1382 WYCLIF *Zech.* v. 6 This is an amfer, *or a vessel that sum men clepen a tankard*. **1388** —— *1 Sam.* i. 24 An amfore, *ether a pot* of wyn.

2. = AMPHORA 2.

1382 WYCLIF *Dan.* xiv. 2 There weren spendid in it by alle days.. fourty sheep, and of wijn sixe amphoris. **1601** HOLLAND *Pliny* (1634) I. 405 The same Vine yeeldeth one yeare with another a dozen Amphores of good new wine yearely. *Ibid.* 259 To euery Amphore, (*i.* which containeth about eight wine gallons) they put one hundred pound and a halfe.

amphoric (æm'fɒrɪk), *a.* [ad. mod.L. *amphoricus*, f. *amphora*: see -IC. Cf. mod.Fr. *amphorique*.]

1. Of the character of an amphora. *rare*[—0].

2. *Med.* Like the sound produced by blowing or speaking into an amphora, or other large vessel with small mouth, as in *amphoric resonance, cough, echo, voice*, etc.

1839 HOOPER *Med. Dict.* 236 The Metallic tinkling, of which the Amphoric resonance is a modification. **1849** O. W. HOLMES *Stethoscope Song* in *Poems* 274 Five doctors took their turn to hear; 'Amphoric buzzing,' said all the five. **1877** ROBERTS *Handbk. Med.* I. 385 The percussion-note is.. of tubular or even amphoric quality.

amphoricity (æmfə'rɪsɪtɪ). [f. prec. + -ITY.] The quality of being amphoric; the condition in which an amphoric resonance is heard.

1879 in *Syd. Soc. Lex.*

amphoteric (æmfəʊ'tɛrɪk), *a. rare*[—0]. [f. Gr. ἀμφότερ-ος both, compar. of ἀμφώ + -IC.] Partaking of both characters; neutral, neither acid nor alkaline.

1849 in SMART. **1879** in *Syd. Soc. Lex.*

amphtrac(k), var. AMTRAC.

ampicillin (æmpɪ'sɪlɪn). *Pharm.* [f. AM(INO- + P(EN)ICILLIN.] A broad-spectrum semi-synthetic penicillin: see PENBRITIN.

1961 *Brit. Med. Jrnl.* 28 Oct. 1145/2 Ampicillin is a new synthetic penicillin... It is 6[D-(-)α-aminophenylacetamido] penicillanic acid. **1964** M. HYNES *Med. Bacteriol.* (ed. 8) x. 140 Ampicillin and adicillin.. differ from other penicillins in being effective against *E. coli, Proteus*, [etc.]. **1968** [see PENBRITIN]. **1970** *New Scientist* 25 June 612/1 Ampiclox (a preparation containing ampicillin and cloxacillin). **1974** M. C. GERALD *Pharmacol.* xxvii. 465 With the exception of ampicillin and carbenicillin, most penicillins have a narrow spectrum of antibacterial activity. **1977** *Lancet* 14 May 1060/1 Widespread tetracycline resistance may necessitate ampicillin or furoxone chemotherapy for shigellosis.

ample, obs. form of AMPUL.

ample ('æmp(ə)l), *a.* [a. Fr. *ample*:—L. *ampl-us* large, capacious, abundant. Compared *ampler, -st*, also with *more, most*.]

1. Extending far and wide; broad, wide, spacious. (Now always *eulogistic*: abundantly, excellently wide.) **a.** Of large superficial dimensions. Of persons: of large proportions; esp. in euphemistic use, of stout or well-covered women.

1548 HALL *Hen. VIII*, an. 31 (R.) All busshes and fyrres cutte downe, and a large and ample waye made. **1605** SHAKS. *Lear* I. i. 82 This ample third of our faire Kingdome. **1667** MILTON *P.L.* VIII. 258 And gazed a while the ample sky. **1751** GRAY *Elegy* xiii, But knowledge to their eyes her ample page.. did ne'er unroll. **1769** ROBERTSON *Charles V*, II. II. 111 The order acquired ample possessions in every catholic country. **1814** BYRON *Corsair* III. xv, An ampler canvass woos the wind from high. **1826** SCOTT *Woodst.* 179 The depths of some ample and ancient forest. **1860** WHYTE-MELVILLE *Mkt. Harb.* 60 Mrs. Dove, an ample lady, with the remains of considerable beauty. **1900** 'SARAH GRAND' *Babs* (1901) iii, She was already more ample than a woman of thirty-eight need be in active life. **1959** *Times* 23 Feb. 12/3 Drawings of.. blowsily ample girls undressing.

b. of the wide range of an action.

1485 CAXTON *Chas. the Gt.* 214 To gyue hym bataylle more ample & large. **1599** SHAKS. *Hen. V*, I. ii. 226 There wee'l sit, Ruling in large and ample Emperie. **1815** SCOTT *Ld. of Isles* VI. vii, This ample right o'er tower and land Were safe in Ronald's faithful hand. **1837** DISRAELI *Venetia* I. xi. (1871) 53 At one ample swoop.

2. Of large capacity or volume, roomy, capacious; copious.

1596 SPENSER *F.Q.* III. xi. 49 All the people in that ample hous. **1605** SHAKS. *Lear* IV. iii. 14 Now and then an ample tear trill'd down Her delicate cheek. **1718** POPE *Iliad* II. 10 To Agamemnon's ample tent repair. **1815** SOUTHEY *Roderick* III. 192 Where Minho rolled its ampler stream. **1847** J. WILSON *Chr. North* (1857) II. 13 All assembled in the ample kitchen. **1857** H. REED *Brit. Poets* v. 170 A high patriotic fervour kindling and filling each true and ample heart.

3. Of things immaterial: Large in extent or amount, extensive, abundant, excellent.

1481 CAXTON *Myrr.* I. xiii. 42 Ther is ynough here of tofore made ample mencion. **1542** HENRY VIII *Declar.* in *Compl. Scotl.* 196 The ambassadours.. vpon pretence to send for a more ample and large commission.. obteined a delay. **1611** SHAKS. *Wint. T.* IV. iv. 415 He has his health, and ampler strength, indeede, Then most haue of his age. **1756** BURKE *Vind. Nat. Soc.* Wks. I. 16 A very ample and very pleasing subject for history. **1850** LONGF. *Sonnet*, Leaving us heirs to amplest heritages Of all the best thoughts of the greatest sages. **1858** NEALE *Bern. de Morlaix* 20 The fouler was the error, The sadder was the fall, The ampler are the praises Of Him Who pardoned all.

4. a. *esp.* Large enough to satisfy all demands, abundant, full, complete.

1592 tr. *Junius on Rev.* xxi. 10 A type of that Church which is one, ample, or Catholike. **1671** J. WEBSTER *Metallogr.* i. 15 Doth give most ample and full satisfaction. **1719** YOUNG *Revenge* I. i, I.. groan'd for an occasion Of ample vengeance. **1770** *Junius Lett.* xli. 208 Ample justice has been done. **1820** W. IRVING *Sketch Bk.* I. 40 She had, it is true, no fortune, but that of my friend was ample. **1834** HT. MARTINEAU *Demerara* vi. 66 The ample provision of meat, bread and vegetables he had stored at hand. **1825** MACAULAY *Milton*, *Ess.* (1851) I. 17 Ample apologies indeed for 15 years of persecution. **1849** —— *Hist. Eng.* I. 43 Ample securities had been provided against despotism.

b. *Hence*, Liberal, unsparing, unstinted.

1536 LATIMER *1st Serm. bef. Convoc.* I. 33 He.. giveth unto us in most ample wise his benediction. **1607** SHAKS. *Timon* I. i. 45 A man, Whom this beneath world doth embrace and hugge With amplest entertainment. **1738** WESLEY *Hymn 'To Thee, O Lord,'* iv, With ample Blessings still reward The labour of your Love. **1846** KEBLE *Lyra Innoc.* (1873) 48 Till He with ampler grace their youthful hearts endow.

5. Of a writing or speech: Treating of matters at full length; copious.

1592 tr. *Junius on Rev.* i. 5 A most ample and grave commendation of Christ first from his offices. **1623** B. JONSON in *Shaks. Cent. Praise* 147 Am I thus ample to thy Booke, and Fame? **1670** G. H. *Hist. Cardinals* I. iii. 67 An ampler description, to satisfie.. the curiosity of the Reader. **1771** FRANKLIN *Autobiog.* Wks. 1840 I. 39 The Governor gave me an ample letter. **1807** CRABBE *Newsp.* 316 That ample list the Tyburn herald gives. **1833** I. TAYLOR *Fanat.* vi. 179 The subject.. well deserves more ample treatment.

†**6.** quasi-*adv. Obs.*

1549 *Compl. Scotl.* xiv. 116 Send ane of thy maist familiaris, to communicat mair ample of this byssynes. **1607** SHAKS. *Timon* I. ii. 136 You see, my Lord, how ample y' are belou'd.

7. *Comb.* in synthetic adjs., as ***ample-eyed***, etc.

1624 CHAPMAN *Hymn to Hermes* (1858) 52 Apollo's ample-foreheaded herd. **1790** COWPER *Iliad* I. 711 Him answered then the goddess ample-eyed.

†**'ample, amply**, *v. Obs. rare.* [a. OFr. *ampli-er, ample-er*, ad. L. *ampliā-re* to make ample.] = AMPLIATE, AMPLIFY.

1413 LYDG. *Pylgr. Sowle* v. vi. (1859) 77 An huge assemble.. ben comen.. for to amplye this feste with ioye. **1533** BELLENDENE *Livy* IV. (1822) 312 Thare power is ekit and amplit ilk day mair and mair.

†**am'plect**, *v. Obs.* [ad. L. *amplect-i* to embrace, clasp, f. *amb-* about + *plect-ĕre* to plait, twine.] To embrace, clasp; = AMPLEX.

1525 *State Papers Hen. VIII*, V. 417 If this matier.. shuld not be duely amplected, embraced and folowed. **1542** BECON *Christm. Banq.* (1843) 66 With how valiant courage should we amplect and embrace virtue! **1612** WOODALL *Surg. Mate* Wks. 1653, 401 To bestride the limb to be amputated; and to amplect the member. **1657** TOMLINSON *Renou's Disp.* 258 And with many involutions amplect them like Briony.

'ampleness. *arch.* [f. AMPLE *a.* + -NESS.]

1. Of extension in space: Largeness, breadth, extent.

1553-87 FOXE *A. & M.* (1596) 150/1 To defend and conserue fullie and wholie in all amplenesse.. all the lands. **1635** PAGITT *Christianogr.* I. ii. (1636) 36 The Protestants in strength and amplenesse of Territorie much exceed the Papists. **1652** NEEDHAM tr. *Selden's Mare Cl.* 16 The Sea.. for the ampleness and extreme distance thereof from the Land was not possible to bee governed. *Mod.* A skirt of greater ampleness.

2. Of things immaterial: Extent, greatness, magnitude, grandeur.

1570 DEE *Math. Præf.* 13 A Science of such dignitie and amplenes. **1692** SOUTH *Serm. to Mayor & Ald.* Pref. (1697) I. 43 The Ampleness of the Body you represent. **1762** B. STILLINGFLEET tr. *Linnæus' Oration* in *Misc. Tracts* 4 Whether i consider the ampleness of the place, or the dignity of the audience.

3. Sufficiency for its purpose, completeness, fullness.

1566 T. STAPLETON *Ret. Untr. Jewel* iv. 87 The greatnesse and amplenesse of the worke. **1607** HIERON *Wks.* I. 72 The largenesse and amplenesse of the word of God extending and stretching it selfe to all the spirituall occasions of all God's people. **1668** PEPYS *Diary* 6 Apr., The ampleness of his revenge. *Mod.* The ampleness of the apology.

4. Copiousness, fullness, diffuseness.

1803 W. TAYLOR in *Ann. Rev.* I. 429 The ampleness of his diction oftener results from throng of thought than plenty of words.

†**am'plex**, *v. Obs.* [f. L. *amplex-* ppl. stem of *amplect-i*: see AMPLECT.] To embrace; = AMPLECT.

1543 T. BASIL in Strype *Eccl. Mem.* I. I. l. 383 How many amplexed Christ for their sufficient Mediator and Advocate? **1542** BECON *Pathw. Prayer* (1843) 141 The truth of God's wisdom.. is ever amplexed and received joyfully. **1657** TOMLINSON *Renou's Disp.* 264 Branches, which climbe up the adjoyning bushes, amplexing and implicating them.

amplexatile (æm'plɛksətɪl), *a. Bot.* [a. mod.Fr. *amplexatile*, f. L. *amplexāt-*: see next, and cf. *versatile*.] An epithet applied by L. C. Richard to a radicle that envelops the embryo.

1879 in *Syd. Soc. Lex.*

amplexation (æmplɪk'seɪʃən). *rare.* [n. of action f. L. *amplexāt-* ppl. stem of *amplexā-ri* to embrace, as if ad. L. **amplexātiōn-em*.]

†**1.** Embracing. *Obs.*

1615 BP. HALL *Contempl.* IV. xxxiii. (1833) 517 An humble amplexation of those sacred feet.

2. *Surg.* 'A method of treating fracture of the clavicle.' *Syd. Soc. Lex.*

amplexicaudate (æm,plɛksɪ'kɔːdeɪt), *a. Ent.* [mod. f. L. *amplex-us* embrace + *cauda* tail + -ATE.] Having the tail entirely enveloped in the interfemoral membrane. (Said of certain insects.)

1879 in *Syd. Soc. Lex.*

amplexicaul (æm'plɛksɪkɔːl), *a. Bot.* [ad. mod.L. *amplexicaul-is* (Linn.), f. *amplex-us* embrace, embracing + *caulis* stem.] Embracing or clasping the stem; said of sessile leaves, the hollow base of which clasps the stem.

1760 J. LEE *Introd. Bot.* 187 *Amplexicaul*, embracing the stalk. **1830** LINDLEY *Nat. Syst. Bot.* 284 The Screwpine Tribe.. Leaves imbricated, in three rows.. amplexicaul. **1851** RICHARDSON *Geol.* vii. 203 Amplexicaule, stem-clasping, as in many umbelliferous plants. **1881** *Gard. Chr.* No. 413. 685 Leaves tapering at the base into a short broad amplexicaul stalk.

amplexicauline (æm,plɛksɪ'kɔːlaɪn), *a. Bot.* [f. as prec.; assimilated in form to CAULINE.] = prec.

1879 *Syd. Soc. Lex.*, *Amplexifoliate*, having amplexicauline leaves.

amplexifoliate (æm,plɛksɪ'fəʊlɪət), *a. Bot.* [f. mod.L. *amplexifolius* (f. *amplex-us* embracing + *folium* leaf) after L. *foliāt-us*, leaved.] Having leaves which clasp the stem.

1879 in *Syd. Soc. Lex.*

†**am'plexion.** *Obs.* [a. ? Fr. *amplexion*, n. of action f. L. *amplex-* (see AMPLECT), as if ad. L. **amplexiōn-em*.] Embracing.

1474 CAXTON *Chesse* 16 The amplexions.. of her husbond.

†**'ampliate,** *v. Obs.* [f. L. *ampliāt-* ppl. stem of *ampliā-re* to widen, f. *ampl-us* AMPLE. Preceded in use by AMPLE *v.* from Fr.] To enlarge, extend, increase in size, amount, or dignity; to amplify.

1513 BRADSHAW *St. Werburge* (1848) 148 Kyng Marius.. ampliat and walled strongly Chestre cite. **1548** UDALL, etc. *Erasm. Paraphr.* (1551) I. 206 Others would ampliate and enriche theyr natiue language with moe vocables. **1643** JESSOP *Angel of Eph.* 57 The Bishops power came afterwards to be ampliated. **1684** tr. *Bonet's Merc. Compit.* XI. 385 To ampliate and open the passages of the Messentery. **1686** GOAD *Celest. Bod.* II. xiv. 341 So ampliating the Serene Day preceding by an Illustrious Close.

'ampliate, *ppl. a.* [ad. L. *ampliāt-us*: see prec.] 'Enlarged or dilated.' Gray *Bot. Text-bk.* 1880.

†**'ampliated,** *ppl. a. Obs.* [f. AMPLIATE *v.* + -ED.] Enlarged, amplified.

1553-87 FOX *A. & M.* 1173 (R.) Confessions, cases reserued, restricted or ampliated for our gaine. **1653** GAUDEN *Hierasp.* 92 In ways of ampliated communion, and Catholike correspondencies.. by Synods and General Councils.

†**'ampliating,** *vbl. sb. Obs.* [f. as prec + -ING[1].] Enlarging, amplifying.

1541 ELYOT *Image Govt.* 2 Almost fatigate with the longe studie about the correctyng and ampliatyng of my Dictionarie. **1678** CUDWORTH *Intell. Syst.* 695 That besides this Power of Compounding things together, the.. Soul hath also another Ampliating, or Increasing and Improving Power.

ampliation (æmplɪ'eɪʃən). *arch.* Also 6 -iacion, -yacion. [a. Fr. *ampliation*, ad. L. *ampliātiōn-em*, n. of action f. *ampliā-re*: see AMPLIATE *v.*]

1. Enlarging, extending, amplification.

1509 HAWES *Past. Pleas.* VIII. xi, Wyth amplyacion more connyng to get, By the laboure of inventyfe busynes. **1630** LORD *Banians* 86 Meditating unjust ampliations of government. **1671** GREW *Anat. Plants* I. iv. §19 (1682) 33 The due spreading and ampliation of a Tree or other Plant. **1726** AYLIFFE *Parerg.* 157 Odious Matters admit not of an Ampliation, but ought to be.. interpreted in the mildest sense. *a* **1857** SIR W. HAMILTON *Logic* (1866) II. App. 273 This quantity [Extension] alone admits of ampliation or restriction.

2. That which is added in the process of enlarging; an enlargement or extension.

1590 SWINBURN *Testaments* 191 b, Which conclusion is accompanied with no smal traine of ampliations & limitations. **1624** BEDELL *Lett.* iii. 71 A long compasse of a sentence.. with I know not how many ampliations and alternatiues. **1671** GREW *Anat. Plants* I. iv. (1682) 29 The Skin of the Leaf, is only the ampliation of that of the Branch.

3. *Law.* Deferring of judgement till a case has been more fully examined.

1656 BLOUNT *Glossogr.*, *Ampliation*, a deferring or prolonging of Judgment or Trial, till the Cause be better certified. *a* **1661** HOLYDAY *Juvenal* (1673) 244 Which delay of the cause was called ampliation. **1708** MOTTEUX *Rabelais* IV. xxvii, [The Judges of the Areopagus] signifying.. by *A.* Ampliation or a Demur, when the Case was not sufficiently examined. **1809** TOMLINS *Law Dict.*, *Ampliation*.. in law a referring of judgment, till the cause is further examined.

ampliative ('æmplɪətɪv), *a. Logic.* [f. L. *ampliāt-* (see AMPLIATE *v.*) + -IVE.] Having the function of enlarging or extending a simple conception, or adding to what is already known.

1842 ABP. THOMSON *Laws of Th.* §81. (1860) 142 Judgments which attribute to the subject something not directly implied in it, have been called ampliative, because they enlarge or increase our knowledge. **1852** SIR W. HAMILTON *Disc.* 273 Philosophy.. is a transition from absolute ignorance to science, and its procedure is therefore ampliative.

†**'amplicative,** *a. Obs. rare*$^{-1}$. [f. med.L. *amplicāt-* ppl. stem of *amplicā-re* = *ampliā-re* + -IVE.] Characterized by increase or extension.

1604 T. WRIGHT *Passions of Mind* V. iv. 271 The rootes and groundes whereupon amplicative perswasions must be built.

Amplidyne ('æmplɪdaɪn). *Electr.* Also a-. [Trade-name (General Electric Co., U.S.A.), f. AMPLI(FIER + *-dyne* as in METADYNE.] A direct-current generator in which the output is controlled by small changes in the input.

1940 *Electronics* Apr. 54 Dr. E. F. W. Alexanderson.. of the General Electric Company revealed a new type of generator known as the Amplidyne... The Amplidyne generator responds almost instantaneously to changes in power input. **1943** F. FELIX in *Jrnl. Amer. Soc. Nav. Engin.* LV. 775 One of the most important developments of recent years is the amplidyne, a product of G-E engineering... The amplidyne is an externally-driven d-c generator, outwardly similar to a conventional motor. **1945** *Jrnl. R. Aeronaut. Soc.* XLIX. 540/1 In recent years developments have taken place in quick response electrical systems having a high ratio of output power to input control, typical methods being known as the 'Amplidyne' or the 'Metadyne'. **1958** *Guided Missiles* vii. 388/1 Power amplification is obtained by electronic means or by using a dynamotor-type amplifier such as a motor-generator set or an amplidyne.

†**'amplificate,** *v. Obs.*$^{-0}$ [f. L. *amplificāt-* ppl. stem of *amplificā-re*: see AMPLIFY.] 'To amplify, augment, or enlarge.' Bailey 1731; J. etc.

amplification (,æmplɪfɪ'keɪʃən). Also 6 -cion. [ad. L. *amplificātiōn-em*, n. of action f. *amplificā-re*: see AMPLIFY and -TION.] The action of amplifying, extending or enlarging.

1. Of things material: enlargement. Also *concr.* that which is added, or causes enlargement.

1546 LANGLEY *Pol. Verg. De Invent* VI. iii. 116 b, The preseruacion and amplificacion of fruictes, ordeyned for y[e] sustenaunce of man. **1615** CROOKE *Body of Man* 560 This amplification or inlargement hapneth because al the spirits doe assemble themselues vnto the eye which is open. **1705** *Col. Records Penn.* II. 218 Allowing one penny per line for Emplyfications. **1763** REID *Inq. Hum. Mind* (T.) This amplification of the visible figure of a known object. **1830** GEN. P. THOMPSON *Exerc.* (1842) I. 247 The reprinting and amplification of the 'Catechism on the Corn Laws.'

2. Of things immaterial: augmentation in extent, importance, significance, etc. Also *concr.* an enlarged or extended representation.

1569 in Strype *Ann. Ref.* I. liii. 567 That his studies and labours.. might be.. to the glory of God, and the amplification of the whole University. **1664** H. MORE *Myst. Iniq.*, A more full Amplification of his enormous Pride. **1687** *Assur. Abby Lands* 133 The Pope sent an Amplification of His Powers. **1874** SAYCE *Comp. Philol.* vii. 282 To regard the dual as an amplification of the plural forms.

3. *esp.* Of words and phrases: extension of meaning. ***amplification of the predicate***, in Grammar, = extension or enlargement of the predicate.

1551 ROBINSON *More's Utopia* (1869) 105 Those rules of restrictions, amplifications and suppositions, verye wittelye inuented in the small Logicalles. **1578** TIMME *Calvin on Gen.* 195 This saying [in this generation].. is added for Amplification. **1656** HARDY *Serm. 1 John* (1865) XXX. 185/2 An amplification of the proposition. **1870** SPURGEON *Treas. David* XVI. I. I. 217 The intercession recorded in John xvii is but an amplification of this cry.

4. *Rhet.* The extension of simple statement by all such devices as tend to increase its rhetorical effect, or to add importance to the things stated; making the most of a thought or circumstance.

1553 T. WILSON *Rhet.* 64 No one [figure] so muche helpeth forwarde an Oracion, and beautifieth the same with suche delitefull ornamentes as dooeth amplificacion. **1651** HOBBES *Rhet.* (1840) 438 An orator in praising, must also use the forms of amplification. **1727** POPE *Art of Sinking* 89 Amplification.. is the spinning-wheel of the *bathos*, which draws out and spreads it into the finest thread. **1829** I. TAYLOR *Enthus.* viii. 191 Modern writers.. have expatiated with disproportionate amplification upon the corruptions.

5. The particulars by which a statement is amplified or an account exaggerated; the amplified or exaggerated statement itself.

1567 JEWEL *Def. Apol.* 104 (R.) By sutche amplifications and outrage in speache, it would appeare, Christe were Peters vicare. **1605** BACON *Adv. Learn.* I. 2 No amplification at all, but a positiue and measured truth. **1779** JOHNSON *L.P.*, *Pope* Wks. 1787 IV. 65 The essay [on Man] abounded in splendid amplifications. **1841** T. TROLLOPE *West. France* II. xxxiv. 166 To exercise the novices.. in writing amplifications on the lives of the saints. **1869** PHILLIPS *Vesuv.* i. 6 The story is given with amplifications by Plutarch.

6. *Electr.* The action of amplifying (see AMPLIFY *v.* 2 b). Also *attrib.*

1915 *Year-Bk. Wireless Telegr.* 665 Amplification (Magnification). The ratio of the useful effect obtained by the employment of the amplifier to the useful effect obtained without that instrument. **1919** J. A. FLEMING *Thermionic Valve* vii. 249 Method.. for Measuring the Amplification Factor. **1920** H. J. VAN DER BIJL *Thermionic Vacuum Tube* vii. 160 The constant μ.. can therefore be referred to as the amplification constant. **1935** *Discovery* Sept. 278/2 Special valves are being developed suitable for direct signal amplification at the ultra-high frequencies. **1942** *Electronic Engin.*, XV. 127/3 Existing formulæ for the amplification factor of the three electrode valve.. assume.. that the distance between the grid and anode is large. **1943** *Gloss. Terms Telecomm.* (*B.S.I.*) 32 *Amplification factor*, the voltage factor of the anode and the control electrode, the anode current remaining unchanged. **1962** *Newnes Encycl. Electr. Engin.* 825/2 It [*sc.* the transistor] can be used.. to give current or voltage amplification as desired.

†**'amplifi,cator.** *Obs. rare*$^{-1}$. [a. L. *amplificātor*, n. of agent f. *amplificā-re*: see AMPLIFY and -TOR.] One who amplifies or enlarges.

1661 BOYLE *Style Script.* 190 These (oftentimes as Tedious as Servile) Amplificators, with all their Empty Multiplicity of Fine words.

amplificatory ('æmplɪfɪ,keɪtərɪ), *a. rare*$^{-1}$. [f. L. *amplificātōr* (see prec.) + -Y.] Of the nature of enlargement or extension.

1849 CURETON *Corp. Ignat.* 316 The former [additions] are principally illustrative or amplificatory.

amplified ('æmplɪfaɪd), *ppl. a.* [f. AMPLIFY *v.* + -ED.]

1. Enlarged, extended, augmented, in space, capacity, fullness of particulars, dignity, etc.

1580 TUSSER *Husb.* 159 The poynts of Huswifery.. newly corrected and amplified. **1876** E. MELLOR *Priesth.* viii. 393 The 'Kiss of Peace,' bears the following amplified title—'or, England and Rome at one on the Doctrine of the Holy Eucharist.'

2. Enlarged in representation, exaggerated.

1580 BARET *Alv.* A 369 Words uttered by Hyperbole, amplified words, *Verba superlata*. **1607** SHAKS. *Cor.* V. ii. 16, I haue beene The booke of his good Acts, whence men haue read His Fame vnparalell'd, happely amplified. **1865** LIVINGSTONE *Zambesi* ii. 56 This hint, a little amplified, saved us from the usual exactions.

3. *Electr.* (See AMPLIFY *v.* 2 b.)

1922 GLAZEBROOK *Dict. Appl. Physics* II. 856/1 Energy coming in on either [telephone] line will in part go into R, which.. sends out amplified energy to both lines.

amplifier ('æmplɪfaɪə(r)). [f. next + -ER[1].] One who amplifies or enlarges.

1. One who enlarges, who adds to the extent, capacity, or dignity of anything. *arch.*

1546 BALE *Eng. Votaries* II. (1550) 3 Y[t] great cytie Rome, wherof they were the fyrst amplyfyers. **1625** tr. *Camden's Hist. Eliz.* IV. (1688) 536 The Queen was always both a Favourer and an Amplifier of Essex his Honour.

2. One who enlarges or expands a statement or narrative; *also*, an exaggerator.

1580 SIDNEY *Arcadia* (1622) 121 Dorilaus could need no amplifiers mouth for the highest point of prayse. **1727** POPE *Art of Sinking* 89 There are amplifiers, who can extend half a dozen thin thoughts over a whole folio. **1857** GLADSTONE *Oxf. Ess.* 28 All the reasonings.. of the amplifiers.

3. A lens which enlarges the field of vision.

1866 *Intell. Observ.* No. 54. 419 An achromatic concave amplifier.

4. *Electr.* An appliance or circuit which amplifies. (See AMPLIFY *v.* 2 b.)

1914 *Electrician* 12 June 402/2 After developing the Audion as detector, amplifier and oscillator, Dr. Lee de Forest has recently described.. the small-sized $3\frac{1}{2}$ volt amplifier bulb. **1918** in J. A. Fleming *Thermionic Valve* (1919) 274 Where the de Forest valve acts as an amplifier it is outside any claim on the Fleming patent of 1904. **1933** *Boys' Mag.* XLVII. 108/1 The complete amplifier could be housed in any average existing gramophone, or could be converted, with the addition of a tuned circuit, into a radio receiver. **1941** *B.B.C. Gloss. Broadc. Terms* 3 *Amplifier*, apparatus used to increase the volume of a programme output by means of energy drawn from an external source, such as the supply mains.

amplify ('æmplɪfaɪ), *v.* [a. Fr. *amplifie-r*, f. L. *amplificā-re* to enlarge (cf. *amplific-us*), f. *ampl-us* large + *fic-* = *fac-* make: see -FY.] *gen.* To make large; in space, amount, capacity, importance, or representation.

†1. To enlarge or extend in space or capacity. *Obs.*

1432-50 tr. *Higden* (1865) I. 111 Aelya.. whom he amplifiede with more circuite of walles. **1576** LAMBARDE *Peramb. Kent* (1826) 379 Having amplified the buildings. **1636** DACRES *Machiavel's Disc.* I. Table, Republiques have taken three particular courses to amplify and inlarge their states.

2. a. To augment in volume or amount. *Obs.*

1580 NORTH *Plutarch* (1676) 984 A continual reading of all sorts of good Authors.. to amplifie his collections. **1626** BACON *Sylva* §140 All concaves that proceed from more narrow to more broad do Amplify the sound at the Coming out.

b. *Electr.* To increase the strength of (an electrical current, signal, etc.).

1915 *Proc. Inst. Radio Engin.* III. 282 By connecting the pliotron as an amplifier, as shown in Figure 10, the high frequency currents received from the grid may be amplified from 100- to 600-fold. **1928** *Daily Chron.* 9 Aug. 4/1 The Archbishop's voice was heard, amplified loudly, but indistinctly, telling us of the sacredness of Ypres. **1931** *B.B.C. Year Bk.* 279 On arrival at the Brookmans Park control room, the music is amplified to the correct strength and is then passed to the sub-modulators in the main transmitters. **1953** AMOS & BIRKINSHAW *Television Engineering* I. i. 17 In the present BBC television system vision and sound signals are transmitted over separate links but it is common practice for the aerial and early stages of receivers to accept and amplify vision and sound transmissions together. **1955** *Oxf. Jun. Encycl.* VIII. 470/1 The transistor can be used in the same way as a thermionic triode valve to amplify weak electric currents.

†3. To increase or augment (a number). *Obs. rare.*

1593 FALE *Dialling* 27, I amplifie 46226 the Sine thereof by the whole Sine.

†**4.** *intr.* (*refl.*) To become larger. *Obs. rare.*

1600 FAIRFAX *Tasso* x. xxxiii. 186 Strait was the way at first ..But further in did further amplifie.

5. To extend or increase (anything immaterial) in amount, importance, dignity, etc.

1549 COVERDALE *Erasm. Paraphr. Phil.* i. 11 In amplyfyinge of good dedes, the rewarde of immortalitie is amplyfyed also. 1590 MARLOWE *Edward II.* v. ii. 267 Let no man comfort him..But amplify his grief with bitter words. 1681 MANTON *Serm. Ps.* cxix. Wks. 1872 VIII. 9 This wisdom is amplified, by comparing it with the wisdom of others. 1767 T. HUTCHINSON *Hist. Prov. Mass. Bay* iii. 329 The house discovered.. a desire to amplify their jurisdiction. 1838 SIR W. HAMILTON *Log.* iii. (1866) I. 44 Logic cannot extend, cannot amplify, a science by the discovery of new facts.

6. To enlarge (a story or statement) by telling it more diffusely or fully, or by adding fresh details, illustrations, or reflections; to expand; make much of.

a 1400 *Chester Plays* Proem. 4 And you, worthy marchantes..Amplifye the storie of those wise Kinges three. 1594 PLAT *Jewell-ho.* I. 3 To amplifie the same by some of those manifest experiments. 1625 COOKE *Pope Joan* in *Harl. Misc.* (Malh.) IV. 34 You know..how he amplifies every point, and sets it out with all the circumstances. 1751 CHAMBERS *Cycl.* s.v. *Amplification*, Instead of saying merely, that Turnus died, he amplifies his death. 1879 C. GEIKIE *Life of Christ* li. 602 A parable, which I amplify, for its clearer understanding.

7. *intr.* To make additional remarks; to speak largely in many words; to lay oneself out in diffusion; to enlarge, expatiate, or dilate. **a.** *simply.*

1590 GREENE *Never too Late* (1600) 12 He tooke his Bible in his hand, whereupon leaning his arme, he amplified thus. 1670 G. H. *Hist. Cardinals* II. iii. 192 In his discourses..he would amplifie so much, he would often lose his way. 1751 WATTS *Improv. Mind* (1801) 35 Where he is too brief and concise, amplify a little. 1879 G. SCOTT *Lect. Archit.* I. vi, When I wished to amplify, I have done so by notes.

b. with *on, upon. arch.*

1692 R. L'ESTRANGE *Josephus* xi. (1733) 412 While he was amplifying upon the Story of his good Fortunes. 1748 RICHARDSON *Clarissa* (1811) I. 185, I..am the less solicitous ..to amplify upon the contents of either. 1808 SCOTT *Marm.* IV. Introd., Not even that clown could amplify, On this trite text, so long as I.

8. To enlarge (a thing) in representation; to magnify, exaggerate, make too much of.

1561 T. N[ORTON] *Calvin's Inst.* I. 23 The Prophet..doth amplifie ye madnesse of them. 1589 BP. COOPER *Admon.* 9 Thus odiously to amplifie and paint foorth their discredite. 1619 *Let.* in *Engl. & Germ.* (Camd. Soc.) I, The amplifying of the number of the horsemen slayne. 1831 BREWSTER *Nat. Magic* iii. 46 The descriptions are neither heightened by fancy, nor amplified by invention.

amplifying (ˈæmplɪfaɪɪŋ), *vbl. sb.* [f. prec. + -ING¹.] The action of enlarging, extending, increasing, exaggerating, etc. (Now mostly gerundial.)

1553 T. WILSON *Rhet.* 7 To the encrease and amplifying of his honour. 1589 BP. COOPER *Admon.* 89 Much amplifying of small offences. 1619 [See AMPLIFY 8.] 1655 GOUGE *Comm. Heb.* ii. 6, 152 The excellency of Christ's humane nature: in amplifying whereof, he continueth to the end of this chapter. 1765 R. LOWTH *Let. Warburton* 86 He sets out with a formed design of amplifying his subject.

amplifying (ˈæmplɪfaɪɪŋ), *ppl. a.* [f. as prec. + -ING².] **1.** Enlarging, magnifying.

1867 J. HOGG *Microsc.* I. ii. 40 An amplifying lens..by which the field of view is enlarged.

2. *Electr.* (See AMPLIFY *v.* 2 b.)

1920 *Chambers's Jrnl.* X. 274/1 The Boche listening apparatus or amplifying telephone. 1922 GLAZEBROOK *Dict. Appl. Physics* II. 888/2 Amplifying valves differ from those used for transmitting purposes in more than mere dimensions and power.

amplitude (ˈæmplɪtjuːd). [a. Fr. *amplitude*, ad. L. *amplitūdo, -inem*, breadth, f. *ampl-us*: see AMPLE and -TUDE.] The quality of being ample.

1. Extension in space, extent, largeness; *chiefly*, width, breadth.

1599 NASHE *Lenten Stuffe* (1871) 81 It cuts out an Island of some amplitude. 1671 GREW *Anat. Plants* I. i. (1682) 9 Growing to a three-four-five-fold amplitude above their primitive size. 1823 LAMB *Elia* Ser. I. xv. (1865) 121 An amplitude of form and stature, answering to her mind. 1833 CHALMERS *Constit. Man.* (1835) I. v. 208 Throughout the amplitudes of savage and solitary nature.

2. Of things immaterial: width, breadth, fullness; copiousness, abundance.

1605 BACON *Adv. Learn.* II. §2 (1873) 76 All works are overcommen by amplitude of reward..and by the conjunction of labours. 1664 H. MORE *Myst. Iniq.* 248 The amplitude of that Jurisdiction to which they belong. 1794 PALEY *Nat. Theol.* xxvi. (1879) 412 It is in those things.. that the amplitude of the Divine benignity is perceived. 1850 LYNCH *Theoph. Trin.* viii. 138 The blue of day shall image for us the amplitude of the divine charity. 1864 *Sat. Rev.* 31 Dec. 813/2 [He] arrays all the facts before the reader in their original amplitude.

3. Of mental capacity: breadth, wide range.

1575 LANEHAM *Let.* (1871) 48 Az for the Amplitude of his Lordship's mynde. *a* 1652 J. SMITH *Select Disc.* IX. iii. (1821) 423 Religion..does work the soul into a true and divine amplitude. 1746 HERVEY *Medit. & Contempl.* (1818) 139 The amplitude of a generous heart. 1814 CARY *Dante, Par.* x. 110 Endowed With sapience so profound..That with a ken of such wide amplitude No second hath arisen. 1828 MACAULAY *Hallam, Ess.* I. 52 His mind is.. distinguished by the amplitude of its grasp.

4. Excellence, dignity, grandeur, splendour.

1549 *Compl. Scotl.* 2 Ȝour honorabil amplitude of verteouse dignite incressis daly. 1655 FULLER *Ch. Hist.* I. 10 This was conceived to conduce to the state and amplitude of their Empire. 1660 R. COKE *Power & Subj.* 180 To the greater amplitude and glory of God. 1834 FOSTER *Pop. Ignor.* 456 Religion, believed and felt, is the amplitude of our moral and intellectual nature.

5. *Astr.* The space by which a celestial body rises wide of due east, or sets wide of due west; its angular distance at rising or setting from the eastern or western point of the horizon.

When reckoned from the eastern and western points as shown by the compass, the *Amplitude* is *Magnetic.*

1627 SMITH *Seaman's Gram.* xv. 83 To obserue the.. Amplitude. 1658 PHILLIPS s.v., The Amplitude of the Sun and Stars is an Arch of the Horizon, comprehended between the true East and West Point of it, and the Center of the Sun, Moon, or any Star, at its Rising or Setting. 1697 DAMPIER *Voy.* (1729) I. 531 Taking the Suns Amplitude mornings and evenings. 1779 FORREST *Voy. N. Guinea* 107 To day found the variation of the compass, by the medium of several amplitudes taken ashore. 1834 U. K. S. *Nat. Phil.* III. xiii. 256/2 Amplitude..differs from the azimuth merely in being counted from the east and west points, instead of from north and south.

6. Extent of motion in space.

1880 DARWIN *Movem. Plants* 3 The great sweeps made by the stems of twining plants..result from a mere increase in the amplitude of the ordinary movement of circumnutation.

Hence **a.** in *Gunnery*, The range of a projectile.

1727–51 CHAMBERS *Cycl.*, *Amplitude* of the range of a projectile denotes the horizontal line subtending the path in which it moved.

b. *esp.* in *Physics.* ***amplitude of a vibration***: the distance which an individual particle moves from side to side in performing a complete vibration.

1837 BREWSTER *Magnetism* 222 The diurnal oscillations have a small amplitude between the tropics. 1869 TYNDALL *Light* §220 The intensity of the light depends on the distance to which the ether particles move to and fro. This distance is called the amplitude of the vibration. The intensity of light is proportional to the square of the amplitude. 1876 BLASERNA *Sound* iii. 48 The loudness of a sound is represented by the amplitude of the vibrations causing it.

c. *Electr.* The maximum departure of the value of an alternating current or wave from the average value. Also *attrib.*, as ***amplitude distortion.***

1895 S. P. THOMPSON *Elementary Less. Electr. & Magn.* x. 487 The impressed electromotive-force follows a sine law.. where D is the maximum value or amplitude attained by E. 1931 *B.B.C. Year-Bk.* 436/1 *Amplitude Distortion*, in electrical apparatus, the variation in response at different amplitudes with an input of constant frequency. 1945 *Electronic Engin.* XVII. 640 Either the amplitude or the frequency of the sweep may be increased. 1953 AMOS & BIRKINSHAW *Television Engin.* I. i. 28 All the components of the vision signal must be reproduced at the correct amplitude to avoid distortion in the reproduced image.

d. Electr. ***amplitude modulation***, modulation of a wave by variation of its amplitude; also, the system using such modulation (abbrev. A.M.). Cf. FREQUENCY MODULATION.

1921 [see MODULATION 7]. 1922 [see FREQUENCY MODULATION]. 1932 F. E. TERMAN *Radio Engin.* x. 357 In all the commonly used systems of radio communication the intelligence is transmitted by varying the amplitude of the radiated waves.... Communication carried on in this way is said to take place by means of amplitude modulation. 1942 *Electronic Engin.* XIV. 630 The action of the limiter largely prevents the frequency distortion effect present with amplitude modulation. 1944 *Ibid.* XVII. 58 An A.M. transmitter. 1962 A. NISBETT *Technique Sound Studio* 240 *Amplitude modulation* (AM), a method whereby the information in an audio signal is carried on the much higher frequency of a radio wave. The envelope of the amplitude of the radio wave in successive cycles is equivalent to the wave form of the initial sound. Historically, AM is the method which was used first and such transmissions now crowd the short, medium and long wave bands.... For high quality transmission AM has largely given way to FM (frequency modulation).

amplitudinous (æmplɪˈtjuːdɪnəs), *a.* [f. L. *amplitūdin-em* (see AMPLITUDE) + -OUS.] Ample, capacious.

1904 *Daily Chron.* 9 Sept. 4/7 What monsters there be; Huge, amplitudinous, endless, and ravenous, Serpents that people the sea. *a* 1913 F. ROLFE *Desire & Pursuit* (1934) v. 38 His gesture was as amplitudinous as his drawl and deep guffaw. 1930 *Times Lit. Suppl.* 3 July 547/1 The well-known statuettes of amplitudinous female forms.

Hence **ampliˈtudinously** *adv.*, amply.

1921 JOYCE *Lett.* (1957) 164 Struggling with the acidities of Ithaca..to prepare for the final amplitudinously curvilinear episode Penelope.

†**amˈplivagant**, *a. Obs.*^{−0} [f. L. *ampl-us* (see AMPLE) + *vagānt-em* pr. pple. of *vagāre* to roam.] 'That stretcheth far, or hath a large scope.' Blount *Glossogr.* 1656.

†**amˈplivagous**, *a. Obs.*^{−0} [f. as prec. + *-vag-us* roaming + -OUS.] = prec.

1731 in BAILEY.

amply (ˈæmplɪ), *adv.* [f. AMPLE *a.* + -LY².] In an ample manner.

1. Widely, broadly, extensively.

1600 CHAPMAN *Iliad* xv. 279 Before whom, amply-pac'd, March'd Hector. 1755 *Songs & P. on Costume* (1849) 237 Let it keep her bosom warm, Amply stretched from arm to arm. 1859 CAPERN *Bal. & Songs* 71 A shady bonnet, Plaited, brown, and amply broad.

2. Of things immaterial: To a great extent, in large amount, largely.

1557 N. T. (Genev.) Ep. Ded. 4 The same promesse was more amply renued to Abraham. 1606 SHAKS. *Tr. & Cr.* II. iii. 203 His merit, As amply titled as Achilles is. *c* 1744 *Parl. Bill* in Hanway *Trav.* (1762) I. v. lxxi. 324 [He] shall.. enjoy, all the..privileges..as largely, fully, and amply..as any other member. 1781 J. MOORE *Italy* (1790) I. xxxvi. 382 To indulge our own curiosity very amply.

3. *esp.* With sufficient fullness to satisfy all demands; fully, abundantly.

1586 LD. BURGHLEY in Ellis *Orig. Lett.* I. 219 III. 5 Naw hath amply confessed. 1596 CHAPMAN *Iliad* v. 259 Amply-wise Athenia. 1605 *Lond. Prodigal* I. i. 223 Whom, God willing..I will see amply satisfied. 1751 JOHNSON *Rambl.* No. 162 ¶8 He..saw his care amply recompensed. 1855 MACAULAY *Hist. Eng.* III. 227 The food taken from the enemy would be amply sufficient. 1873 BLACK *Pr. Thule* x. 161 The prophecy was amply fulfilled.

b. *Hence*, Liberally, without stint.

1632 HEYWOOD *Iron Age* I. II. i. 289 Priam..Could not afford Her god-head more applause, Then amply wee bestow on Helena. 1667 MILTON *P.L.* VIII. 362 So amply, and with hands so liberal, Thou hast provided all things. 1714 *Spect.* No. 624 ¶2 A Course of Virtue will in the End be rewarded the most amply. 1852 MISS YONGE *Cameos* II. xxx. 319 He amply rewarded the faithful men who had aided him.

4. With fullness of expression, copiously; at large.

1651 HOBBES *Leviathan* IV. xlvi. 372 As I have elsewhere more amply expressed. 1702 W. J. *Bruyn's Voy. Levant* lxiii. 234 The Prophet Ezekiel speaks also very amply of the power of the Tyrians. 1741 H. WALPOLE *Lett. to H. Mann* 7 (1834) I. 23 Amply commented upon in Parliament. 1860 MAURY *Phys. Geog. Sea* x. §474 That such is the case..has been amply shown in other parts of this work.

ampoule (ˈæmpuːl), var. of AMPUL. Also **ampule**. **a.** A small sealed (glass) vessel used for storing sterilized materials prepared for injection. **b.** A similar vessel or phial containing other materials.

[1644 EVELYN *Diary* (1827) I. 108 The Monkes shew'd us the Holy *Ampoule*. 1750 CARTE *Hist. Eng.* II. 643 The vial or *ampoulle* kept at Reims.] [1886 S. LIMOUSIN in *Archives de Pharmacie* I. 145 (*title*) Ampoules hypodermiques; nouveau mode de préparation des solutions pour les injections hypodermiques.] 1907 *Chemist & Druggist* 1 June 843/2 The method of storing hypodermic and other liquids in closed glass bulbs or ampoules has long been in vogue in France. 1909 *Ibid.* 30 Jan. 169/1 M. Limousin..introduced the ampoule as a convenient method of preserving hypodermics. 1909 *Lancet* 8 May 1365/2 An ampoule filler. 1922 *Nature* CIX. 252/1 An apparatus for the routine standardisation of ampoules containing radium compounds and emanation by the γ-ray ionisation method was installed recently at the Institut Curie. 1930 *Discovery* Sept. 290/2 [A] device for detecting carbon monoxide [in mines]. This consists of an easily crushed cotton-covered ampoule filled with a solution which changes colour when exposed to air containing carbon monoxide. 1937 *Nature* 27 Feb. 380/1 Anahaemin..is issued as a solution in ampoules and rubber-capped vials. 1945 *Times* 7 Aug. 10/2 Special ampoules for time fuses. 1947 J. STEINBECK *Wayward Bus* xix. 239 A little ampule [containing poison] to wear around his neck. 1959 *Observer* 3 May 4/6 Messengers scurried in every direction to retrieve the condemned ampoules [of polio vaccine].

ampster (ˈæmpstə(r)). *Austral. slang.* Also **amster**. [Perh. abbrev. of *Amsterdam*, rhyming slang for 'ram' = a trickster's accomplice, with intrusive *p*.] The helper of a showman or trickster, 'planted' in the audience to start the buying of tickets, goods, etc. Hence as *v. intr.*, to act as an ampster.

1941 K. TENNANT *Battlers* xiii. 143 Mr. Fosdick was agreeable, provided the busker would 'ampster' for him. *Ibid.* 144 The ampster rushes eagerly up to the ticket-window. 1945 BAKER *Austral. Lang.* vii. 138 Terms for various sharpers, tricksters and others who live by their wits: *spieler*,..*amster* (or *ampster*), [etc.] . 1955 *Overland* (Melbourne) IV. 10 Holdens rub hubs with old four-wheelers; So do the amsters and their shielas. 1957 D. NILAND *Call me when Cross turns Over* (1958) iv. 101 Barbie, playing ampster, went up and bought a bottle... Others followed to buy. 1967 *Parade* (Austral.) Oct. 8/3 Niland roamed Australia working in jobs that ranged from circus hand to ampster and gee-man in travelling boxing shows. 1975 H. PORTER *Extra* 244 A shady Soho club patronised by dips, amsters, off-duty prostitutes.

ampte, amte, obs. forms of ANT.

amptman: see AMTMAN.

ampul (ˈæmpəl). *arch.* Forms: 3 **ampuile**, 3–6 **ampulle**, 4 **-olie, -olle**, 5 **ampole, -ull**, 5–6 **ample**, 6 **ampell, -ul**, (9 **ampul**). [a. OFr. *ampole, ampoule*:—L. *ampulla* (see next word), now commonly used instead; *ampul* having been obs. since the Reformation, exc. as Fr., or as an ecclesiastical revival; but see also AMPOULE.]

†**1.** A small bottle or flask; a phial. *Obs.* in general sense.

1205 LAY. 14993 þa ampulle heo ut droh. *Ibid.* 19770 Six ampullen [1250 ampulles] fulle. *c* 1230 *Ancr. R.* 226 þe tale of his ampuiles. *a* 1325 *Metr. Hom.* 148 Boystes on himsele he bare, And ampolies, als leche ware. 1474 CAXTON *Chesse* III. v. G vj, An ample or a boxe with oynementis in his lyft hand..and by the ampole ben signefyed the makers of pygmentaries.

2. *esp.* A vessel for holding consecrated oil, or for other sacred uses. (In this sense *ampulla* is now commonly used.)

1362 LANGL. *P. Pl.* A. vi. 11 An hundred of ampolles · on his hat seeten. **1483** CAXTON *Gold. Leg.* 111/3 Thenne a doue descended fro heuen whyche brought the crysme in an ampull. **1523** LD. BERNERS *Froissart* I. ccclxix. 606 He was sacred and anoynted, by tharchbysshop of Reynes, with the holy ampell. **1536** in *Antiq. Sarisb.* (1771) 195 An Ampul of chrystal..containing a Toe of St. Mary Magdalene. [**1644, 1750**: see AMPOULE. **1872** O. SHIPLEY *Gloss. Eccl. Terms* 394 *Ampuls*, standing transparent vials mounted in metals.]

‖**am'pulla.** *Pl.* -æ. [L. *ampulla* a small nearly globular flask or bottle, with two handles; of doubtful derivation; according to some f. *amb-* about, or both + *olla* pot; according to others, a modified dim. of *amphora* quasi *ampholla*. Preceded in use by the adapted form AMPUL.]

1. *Rom. Antiq.* The ancient vessel mentioned above.

1398 TREVISA *Barth. De P.R.* xix. cxxviii. (1495) 933 Ampulla is a lytyll mesure of lycoure and hath that name as it were Amplabulla, a large bulle, and is lyke in roundnesse to bolk that comyth of the fome of water by entrynge of wynde. **1857** BIRCH *Anc. Pottery* (1858) II. 318 The ampulla, a kind of jug, was used for bringing wine to table.

2. = AMPUL 2.

1598 STOW *Surv.* (ed. Strype 1754) I. i. xx. 121/1 The Ampulla or Eaglet of Gold, contained the holy oil. **1838** *Coron. Serv.* in Maskell *Mon. Rit. Eccl. Ang.* III. 108 The Dean of Westminster taking the Ampulla and spoon from off the Altar, holdeth them ready, pouring some of the Holy Oil into the Spoon, and with it the Archbishop anointeth the Queen in the Form of a Cross. **1868** STANLEY *Westm. Ab.* ii. 92 Busby carried the ampulla.

3. *Biol.* Any vessel shaped like the ancient ampulla; the dilated end of any vessel, canal, or duct in an animal; the spongiole of a root in plants.

1821 S. GRAY *Arr. Brit. Pl.* I. 49 *Ampullæ*, Hollow globular bodies found in the roots of some water-plants. **1845** TODD & BOWMAN *Phys. Anat.* II. 74 Each semicircular canal of the osseous labyrinth of the ear is dilated..into an *ampulla* of more than twice the diameter of the tube. **1879** CALDERWOOD *Mind & Brain* iii. 73 These enlarged spaces are known as the ampullæ of the canals.

ampullaceous (æmpəˈleɪʃəs), *a.* [f. L. *ampullāce-us* (f. *ampulla*) + -OUS: see -ACEOUS. Cf. mod.Fr. *ampullacé*.] Having the form or character of an ampulla; bottle-shaped, inflated, swelling.

1776 M. DA COSTA *Conchol.* 81 (JOD.) Ampullaceous, or bellied. **1815** KIRBY & SPENCE *Entomol.* (1843) I. 98 It wounds us with..a simple incurved mucro terminating an ampullaceous joint. **1880** GRAY *Bot. Text-bk.* 395 *Ampullaceous*, in the form of a bladder or short flask.

ampullar (ˈæmpələ(r)), *a.* [ad. mod.L. *ampullār-is*: see AMPULLA and -AR. (The L. was *ampullāri-us*, of which the Eng. ad. is AMPULLARY.) Cf. Fr. *ampullaire*.] = AMPULLARY.

1856 TODD & BOWMAN *Phys. Anat.* II. 74 Its ampullar extremity is close to that of the superior vertical canal. **1877** BURNETT *Ear* 129 Each of the canals has a dilated portion, its ampullar enlargement.

ampullary (ˈæmpələrɪ), *a.* [ad. L. *ampullāri-us*: see AMPULLA and -ARY.] Of the form or character of an ampulla.

1836–39 TODD *Cycl. Anat. & Phys.* II. 531/1 There are thus three ampullary dilatations.

ampullate (ˈæmpəleɪt), *ppl. a.* [ad. med.L. *ampullāt-us*: see AMPULLA and -ATE.] Furnished with or shaped like an ampulla; inflated, bellied.

1877 HUXLEY *Anat. Inv. An.* vii. 381 These glands are..aciniform, ampullate, aggregate, tubuliform, and tuberous.

ˈampullated, *ppl. a.* [f. prec. + -ED.] = prec.

1856 TODD & BOWMAN *Phys. Anat.* II. 82 The ampullated extremity of each canal.

ampulliform (æmˈpʌlɪfɔːm), *a.* [f. AMPULLA + -FORM.] Flask-shaped, bulging, dilated.

1870 HOOKER *Stud. Flora* 51 *Silene conica*..calyx ½ in., ampulliform. **1880** GUNTHER *Fishes* 117 The ampulliform ends of the semi-circular canals. **1881** BAKER in *Jrnl. Lin. S.* XVIII. 273 Capsule ampullæform, glabrous.

ampullosity (æmpəˈlɒsɪtɪ). *rare*$^{-1}$. [f. med.L. *ampullōs-us* (see next) + -ITY.] Swollen or pretentious inanity; turgidity of language, bombast.

1868 BROWNING *Ring & Bk.* IV. xii. 643 Didst ever touch such ampollosity [*after Ital.*] As the man's own bubble?

†**ˈampullous,** *a. Obs.* [f. med.L. *ampullōs-us* turgid, inflated, f. *ampulla* a flask, *also* turgid talk. Cf. It. *ampolloso*, in Florio 1598.] Boastful, vain-glorious; inflated, or turgid in language.

1622 PEACHAM *Compl. Gent.* (1661) 42 That same ampullous and scenical pomp, with empty furniture of phrase. **1656** BLOUNT *Glossogr.*, *Ampullous*, pertaining to, or empty as a bottle or such like vessel; also proud, swelling, or gorgeous.

ampus-and, ampussy: see AMPASSY.

amputate (ˈæmpjuːteɪt), *v.* [f. L. *amputāt-* ppl. stem of *amputā-re* to cut off or away, f. *am-* = *amb-* about + *putā-re* to prune, lop.]

1. *gen.* To cut or lop off, *e.g.* the branches of trees in pruning. *Obs.* exc. as a fig. use of 2.

1638 *Penit. Conf.* xii. (1657) 335 'Tis not impossible for a quick and fruitful branch to be amputated and cut off. **1731** BAILEY, *Amputate*, to cut off; in gardening, to lop or prune. **1864** BURTON *Scot Abr.* II. 268 The Government..finding this or that damaged part of the population, and immediately amputating it for removal.

Hence, by specialization, the proper term for,

2. To cut off a limb or other part of an animal body. Also *absol.*

1639 [See AMPUTATING.] **1670** G. H. *Hist. Cardinals* I. i. 19 Members amputated and divided from the Body. **1676** WISEMAN *Chirurg. Treat.* VI. v, It was complained, that their surgeons were too active in amputating fractured members. **1764** WOOLCOMB in *Phil. Trans.* LX. 97 It was not now practicable to amputate. **1809** WELLINGTON in *Gen. Disp.* IV. 328 Paget..was wounded in the right arm, which was amputated. **1826** H. COLERIDGE *Six Months in W. Ind.* 275 Two..sharks who would have amputated a baby's arm as soon as looked at it.

amputated (ˈæmpjuːteɪtɪd), *ppl. a.* [f. prec. + -ED.] Cut off, as a limb, etc.

1713 CHESELDEN *Anat.* (1726) III. viii. 221 A limb that has had part amputated. **1749** WESLEY *Prin. Physic* (1765) 38 This will stop the Bleeding of an amputated Limb. **1865** CARLYLE *Fredk. Gt.* II. VI. iii. 158 Lame of a foot, foot lately amputated of two toes.

b. *fig.* Pruned, excised.

1824 DIBDIN *Libr. Comp.* 66 An octavo edition of them appeared in a very amputated and imperfect state.

amputating (ˈæmpjuːteɪtɪŋ), *vbl. sb.* [f. as prec. + -ING^1.] The action of cutting off; amputation. (Mostly gerundial or *attrib.*)

1639 WOODALL in Rees *Cycl.* (1803) The amputating of any member in the mortified part. **1775** GOOCH in *Phil. Trans.* LXV. 374 It was the best stump he had ever seen, which he ascribed to the manner of amputating. **1856** KANE *Arct. Exp.* II. xxv. 251 My amputating-knives. **1883** WINSLOE in *Pall Mall G.* 6 Apr. 4/2 The patient..lay on the amputating table.

amputation (æmpjuːˈteɪʃən). [ad. L. *amputātiōn-em* (or a. Fr. *amputation* 16th c. in Litt.), n. of action f. *amputā-re*: see AMPUTATE.]

1. *gen.* A cutting or lopping off, as of branches of trees in pruning; *also*, the cut end. *Obs.* exc. as fig. use of 2.

1611 COTGR., *Amputation*, An amputation, or cutting away: or paring about; a ridding, or taking away. **1664** EVELYN *Kal. Hort.* (1729) 204 Cover the wound or Amputation with a Mixture of Bees-wax. **1727** POPE *Art of Sinking* 113 Yon' luminary amputation needs [*i.e.* the candle needs snuffing]. **1813** MARSHALL *Garden.* viii. (ed. 5) 103 Some amputations are necessary to help the sooner to new roots.

2. *esp.* The operation of cutting off a limb or other projecting part of the body. Also *attrib.*

1612 WOODALL *Surg. Mate* Wks. 1653, 156 Amputation or Dismembring is the most lamentable part of Chirurgery. **1646** SIR T. BROWNE *Pseud. Ep.* 187 The Amazones in the amputation of their right breast. **1743** tr. *Heister's Surg.* 345 Amputations of the Thigh. **1769** WHITE in *Phil. Trans.* LIX. 40, I had sawn it off with a common amputation-saw. **1878** MARKHAM *Gt. Frozen Sea* xii. 172 Some of the frost-bites were so severe as to render amputation necessary.

3. *fig.* Excision, *e.g.* of words or sentences from a speech or writing; pruning, retrenchment.

1664 BUTLER *Hudibr.* II. i. 364 'Twas he..Made those that represent the nation Submit and suffer amputation. **1741** RICHARDSON *Pamela* (1824) I. 6 In her own words, without amputation or addition. **1850** H. ROGERS *Ess.* II. iv. 188 The suppression or amputation of sundry compound prepositions and conjunctions.

amputator (ˈæmpjuːteɪtə(r)). [a. L. **amputātor*, n. of agent f. *amputā-re*: see AMPUTATE and -OR.] One who amputates. *lit.* and *fig.*

1810 COLERIDGE *Friend* I. vi. (1866) 26, I might..have referred our hurrying enlighteners and revolutionary amputators to the gentleness of nature. **1882** *Pall Mall G.* 4 July 2 A successful amputator of dogs' tails.

†**amˈpute,** *v. Obs.*$^{-0}$ [a. Fr. *ampute-r* (16th c.), ad. L. *amputā-re*.] = AMPUTATE.

1623 in COCKERAM.

amputee (æmpjuˈtiː). [f. AMPUT(ATE *v.* + -EE^1.] One who has lost a limb or other part of the body by amputation.

1910 *St. Barts. Hosp. Jrnl.* XVII. 90/1 Please put the patient *both* to bed, and then, perhaps, we'll see Which is the amputated part and which the amputee. **1939** *Lancet* 14 Oct. 837/2 In place of endless gadgets we now have a few standard 'set ups' round which limbs to suit any particular amputee can be constructed. **1945** *N.Y. Times* 28 Sept. 23/6 A permanent lodge where vacationing members of the Bilateral Leg Amputee Club of America may spend their vacations. **1958** *Oxford Mail* 11 Feb. 3/2 Loose lino. chairs and rugs were all snares for the unwary amputee.

‖**ampyx** (ˈæmpɪks). [Gr. ἄμπυξ.] A broad band or plate of metal worn on the forehead of ladies of rank among the Greeks (Fairholt); *also*, the headband of horses.

amrel, -te, obs. forms of ADMIRAL, -TY.

‖**amrita** (æmˈriːtə). Also **amreeta**. [ad. Skr. *ámṛita*, *ám'rta* (= Gr. ἄμ(β)ροτος) immortal, f. *a* priv. + *m'rta* dead, f. *m'r* die. (The vowel is erroneously lengthened in the anglicized adaptation of Southey and Moore.)] Immortal, ambrosial. (See Notes to Southey's *Kehama* xxiv. (1850) 626.)

1810 SOUTHEY *Kehama* XXIV, The Amreeta-cup of immortality. **1815** MOORE *Lt. Harem* 333 The divine Amrita tree, That blesses heaven's inhabitants With fruits of immortality.

amry, obs. form of AMBRY.

†**ˈamsel, amzel.** *Obs.* or ? *dial.* [app. a. Ger. *amsel*:—OHG. *amisala*, cogn. w. OE. *ósle*, now *ouzel*.] A name of the Blackbird and Ring Ouzel.

a **1705** RAY *Synops. Meth. Avium* (1713) 65, *Merula torquata*, The Ring-Ouzel or Amzel. **1802** MONTAGU *Ornith. Dict.* s.v. *Blackbird*, Amsel, a 'provincial' name. [Not in any of the Glossaries of the Eng. Dial. Soc., and perhaps only a dealer's adoption of the German name, erroneously considered dialectal. *Amsla* became *ósle* in OE. in prehistoric times.]

‖**amtman** (ˈamtman). *Obs.* Also 6–8 **amptman**. [Ger. *amtmann*, OHG. *ampahtman*, f. *ampaht(i*, Goth. *andbahti* service, ministry, charge, f. *andbahts*: cf. AMBASSADE and AMBOHT.] One in charge; a bailiff, steward, magistrate, or officer (in Germany, Netherlands, and Scandinavia).

1587 FLEMING *Cont. Holinshed* III. 337/1 Monsieur the amptman read the same oth to his highnesse in French. **1709** *Lond. Gaz.* mmmmdlii/2 Monsieur Rosencrans..is made Bailiff, or *Amptman*, of the District of Copenhagen. **1863** BARING-GOULD *Iceland* Introd. 35 Iceland is..divided into three amts. Over two of the amts is placed an Amtman, who is subject to the Governor General.

amtrac (æmtræk). *U.S.* Also **amphtrac(k, amtrack, amtrak.** [f. AM(PHIBIOUS *a.* + TRAC(TOR.] An amphibious tracked vehicle used esp. for landing assault troops on a shore.

1944 *Birmingham* (Alabama) *News-Age-Herald* 2 Apr. 9 A small American force..moved ashore..in amtracs (amphibious tractors) and boats. **1944** *Newsweek* 7 Aug. 29/3 Now amphtracks (amphibious tractors) thrashed through the water toward us. **1960** B. COCHRELL *Beaches of Hell* ii. 69 He was..riding ashore in a cargo amtrac to see how fighting was done. **1967** *Observer* 8 Jan. 1/4 Eight of 10 amtraks which moved into the swamps were bogged down. **1980** *Washington Post* 27 Jan. A3/1 They jumped out of the amphibious armored vehicle (Amtrac). **1983** *Observer* 30 Oct. 10/7 Throughout the morning the amtracks and tanks grunted and growled round Queen's Park.

Amtrak (ˈæmtræk). *U.S.* Also **Amtrack.** [f. AM(ERICAN *a.* + TRA(C)K *sb.*] A proprietary name for a Government-controlled railway service in the U.S., also called the National Railroad Passenger Corporation.

1971 *N.Y. Times* 20 Apr. 86/7 The corporation's new official nickname..is Amtrak. **1972** *Ibid.* 31 May 19 (Advt.), Amtrak announces two kinds of savings for New York train travelers... Call your Amtrak Travel Agent. **1973** *Official Gaz.* (U.S. Patent Office) 20 Mar. TM183/1 National Railroad Passenger Corporation, Washington, D.C. ..*Amtrak*, for rail transportation services... First use on or about Apr. 21, 1971. **1976** *New Yorker* 5 Jan. 20/3 The winner of a Hudson Valley Railroad society fund-raising raffle..won an all-expense-paid Amtrak trip to Montreal. **1984** *Guardian Weekly* 16 Dec. 8/4 Among the subsidies to go are those for the railway system, Amtrack. **1985** *Financial Times* 14 Jan. I. 2/7 Subsidies for Amtrack train service.

amty, obs. form of EMPTY.

amuck, var. of AMOK.

amulet (ˈæmjʊlɪt). Also 5 **amalett, amlett,** 7 **amulete, -ett, ammulett,** 8 **amulette**. [perh. in 15th c., a. Fr. *amulette*; but app. not in reg. use till after 1600, when adapted from L. *amulētum* (Pliny), a word of unknown origin, which has been conjecturally compared with mod.Arab. *ḥimālah*, *-at*, lit. 'a carrier, bearer,' now applied *inter alia* to a shoulder-belt or cord frequently used to secure a small Koran or prayer-book on the breast, regarded as an 'amulet'; but the history of this word shows that the resemblance between it and L. *amulētum* is purely fortuitous, and there exists no ground for ascribing the latter to an Arabic origin.]

1. Anything worn about the person as a charm or preventive against evil, mischief, disease, witchcraft, etc. (The 15th c. instances are doubtful.)

[**1447** BOKENHAM *Lyvys of Seyntys* 151 Specyally for there ladyis sake They baladys or amalettys lyst to make. **1481** *Howard Househ. Bks.* 49 Item, for claspis and amlettes *jd. ob.*] **1601** HOLLAND *Pliny* (1634) II. 229 A countercharm against al witchcraft and sorceries which kind of defensatiue is called properly Amuletum. **1605** CAMDEN *Rem.* (1657) 187 The onely amulet used in that credulous warfaring age. **1646** SIR T. BROWNE *Pseud. Ep.* 272 For amulets against Agues wee use the chips of Gallowes and places of Execution. **1774** BRYANT *Mythol.* II. 445 Teraphim..were lunar amulets. **1865** LIVINGSTONE *Zambesi* xxv. 523 A horn or rude image is worn..as an amulet.

†**2.** *Med.* 'Sometimes also applied...to all medicines, whether internal or external, whose virtue or manner of operation is occult.' Chambers. *Obs.*

1718 QUINCY *Compl. Disp.* 132 Some pretend it is an Amulet. **1753** CHAMBERS *Cycl. Supp.*, *Amuletic* in medicine, is used by some writers for what is more frequently called an Amulet.

3. *fig.* A preservative, protection, or charm.

1621 BURTON *Anat. Mel.* I. ii. III. xv. (1651) 140 He is our Amulet, our Sun, our sole comfort and refuge. **1684** *Lady's Call.* I. ii. §8. 15 A better amulet against delusion then the reading whole tomes of disputations. **1877** FARRAR *Days of Youth* iii. 28 Righteousness will give you love..but it will not give you an invincible amulet against misfortune.

amuletic (æmjuːˈlɛtɪk), *a.* and *sb. rare.* [f. L. *amulēt-um* (see prec.) + -IC, as if ad. L. **amulēticus*.] **A.** *adj.* Of or pertaining to amulets.

1742 [see PROPHYLACTIC *a.*]. **1775** in ASH. **1855** E. RICH in Smedley et al. *Occult Sciences* 359 The amuletic medicine which cured disease. **1932** *Times Lit. Suppl.* 17 Mar. 198/2 Although referred to as 'seals'..their purpose may be amuletic.

B. *sb.* An amuletic medicine; one that was believed to operate by occult means, or otherwise than by its physical properties. *Obs.*

1753 CHAMBERS *Cycl. Supp.*, *Amuletics* are chiefly used of late times to stop bleedings. Digby's sympathetic powder is one of the principal Amuletics in cases of hæmorrhages; and with many the *ancora sacra*.

†**amurˈcosity.** *Obs.*$^{-0}$ [f. next + -ITY.] 'The quality of lees or mother of anything.' J.

1731 BAILEY, *Amurcosity*, the having lees, dregginess.

amurcous (əˈmɜːkəs), *a.* ? *Obs.*$^{-0}$ [f. L. *amurca* lees of oil, ad. Gr. ἀμόργη + -OUS.] 'Full of dregs, foul.' Ash 1775.

(Also in mod. Dicts.)

†**aˈmurder, aˈmurther,** *v. Obs.* [In OE. *amyrðran*, f. A- *pref.* 1 intensive + *myrðran* to MURDER. Cf. OHG. *ermörden*.] To murder.

c **1000** *Cnut's Sec. Laws* 57 (Bosw.) Ðæt man sý amyrdred. **1205** LAY. 16147 Hafde alle heore hæfdmen mid cniuen amurðerd. **1297** R. GLOUC. 144 In fense of the lond, they were amorthered so.

amusable (əˈmjuːzəb(ə)l), *a.* [a. Fr. *amusable*: see AMUSE *v.* and -ABLE.] Capable of being amused.

a **1832** SIR J. MACKINTOSH in Colquhoun *Wilberforce* 445 He was the most amusable man I ever met with. **1875** MISS BRADDON *Hostages to Fort.* II. xi. 230 Flatterers have found their lord and master less amusable than of old.

†**aˈmusatory.** *Obs. rare*$^{-1}$. [f. AMUSE *v.* by form-assoc. with words like *accuse, accusatory*: see -ATORY.] A thing which tends to amuse; a diversion (*i.e.* of the attention from another matter).

1613 DANIEL *Hist. Eng.* 149 As an amuzatory to make the ill-governed people thinke they are not forgotten.

amuse (əˈmjuːz), *v.* Also 6–8 **amuze**, 7 **ammuze**, **-muse**. [a. OFr. *amuse-r* to cause to muse, to put into a stupid stare, f. *à* to, here with causal force + *muser* to stare stupidly. The simple MUSE was in earlier use, and in sense 1, *amuse* is perhaps an Eng. derivative, with A- *pref.* 1 intensive, or even ad. It. *amusare*. The word was not in reg. use bef. 1600, and was not used by Shakspere.]

†**1.** *intr.* To muse intently, gaze in astonishment. *Obs.*

c **1532** *Chaucer's H. of Fame* (Thynne) v. 1287, I amused a long while Upon this wall of berile [*early MSS.* mused]. **1611** FLORIO, *Amusare*, to ammuse or plod vpon. **1681** LEE *Jun. Brutus* (T.) In some pathless wilderness amusing.

†**2.** *trans.* To cause to 'muse' or stare; to confound, distract, bewilder, puzzle. *Obs.*

1606 CHAPMAN *M. D'Olive* Plays 1873 I. 216, I am amused, or I am in a quandarie, gentlemen. **1611** COTGR., *Amuser*, To amuse; to make to muse, or think of, wonder or gaze at: to put into a dumpe. *a* **1670** HACKET *Serm. Incarn.* iv, A glorious splendor filled the mountain where Christ was transfigured and it did amuse Peter, James, and John. **1665** J. SPENCER *Prodigies* 111 To amuze and scare us with one Prodigy or other perpetually. **1704** SWIFT *Mech. Oper. Spirit* (1711) 284 To..stupify, fluster, and amuse the senses. **1741** RICHARDSON *Pamela* III. 135, I would not amuse her too much.

†**3.** To engage, arrest, or occupy the attention of. (Const. *upon, with, about, to.*) *Obs.*

a. *actively.*

1603 FLORIO *Montaigne* (1634) 302 That he should not ammuse his thoughts about matters above the clowds. **1672** SIR T. BROWNE *Let. Friend* (1881) 135 Hairs which have most amused me have not been in the face or head, but on the back. **1712** *Spect.* No. 524 ¶1 It will..amuse the imagination of those who are more profound. *a* **1716** SOUTH *Serm.* vii. (T.) Sad and solemn objects to amuse and affect the pensive part of the soul.

b. esp. *refl.* and *pass.*

1601 HOLLAND *Pliny* XVIII. xxvii, Why art thou amused upon the course of the stars? **1641** MILTON *Animadv.* (1851) 186 The ingenuous Reader without further amusing himselfe in the labyrinth of controversall antiquity. **1689** BURNET *Tracts* I. 20 The Women are so much amuzed with the management at home. **1734** WATTS *Reliq. Juv.* (1789) 2 We are so amused and engrossed by the things of sense, that we forget our Maker.

4. To divert the attention of any one from the facts at issue; to beguile, delude, cheat, deceive. (The usual sense in 17–18th c.) *arch.*

1480 CAXTON *Ovid Metam.* XII. iii, I never amused my husbonde, ne can not doo it. **1569** CECIL in Strype *Ann. Ref.* I. liv. 582 He was secretly employed to amuse her, and render her the more secure. **1673** MARVELL *Reh. Transp.* II. 263 And all to amuse men from observing. **1693** *Mem. Count Teckely* II. 132 Teckeley..made these offers only to amuse the Council at Vienna. **1728** DE FOE *Magic* I. vii. 190 Tools of the Devil, to cheat and amuse the world. **1732** BERKELEY *Min. Philos.* II. 100 Alciphron, be not amused by Terms, lay aside the word Force. **1756** BURKE *Subl. & B.* Wks. I. 155 Leave us in the dark, or, what is worse, amuse and mislead us by false lights. **1817** COBBETT *Year's Resid. Amer.* (1822) 230 It becomes the people of America to guard their minds against ever being, in any case, amused with names.

5. *esp.* in military tactics: To divert the attention of the enemy from one's real designs. *arch.*

1670 COTTON *Espernon* I. IV. 179 He..thought it sufficient by charging, and amusing the Enemies Van, to win time. **1722** DE FOE *Mem. Cavaliers* (1840) 232 This I did to give [the enemy] an alarm and amuse them. **1775** MONTGOMERY in Sparks *Corr. Am. Rev.* (1853) I. 494 To amuse the enemy, and blind them as to my real intention. **1796** NELSON in Nicolas *Disp.* (1845) II. 1796 It is natural to suppose their Fleet was to amuse ours whilst they cross from Leghorn.

6. a. 'To draw on from time to time, to keep in expectation' (J.); to entertain with expectations not to be fulfilled; to divert, in order to gain or waste time. *arch.*

[**1611** COTGR., *Amuser*..to stay, hold, or delay from going forward by discourse, questions, or any other amusements.] **1639** EARL NORTHUMB. in *3rd Rep. Hist. MSS.* (1872) 79/1 They will no longer be amused with the King's neutrality. **1777** ROBERTSON *Amer.* I. II. 72 He had been amused so long with vain expectations. **1817** JAS. MILL *Brit. India* II. IV. vii. 241 The Rohillas had amused him with only deceitful promises. **1850** MERIVALE *Rom. Emp.* V. xliii. 179 Silanus was directed to amuse and negotiate with both powers, and avoid an open rupture by all the arts of diplomacy.

†**b.** ? To keep up for a purpose, detain. *Obs.*

1615 BACON *Lett.* Wks. 1870 V. 173 To retrench and amuse the greatness of Spain for their own preservation. **1693** EVELYN *Compl. Gard.* II. 25 They must be cut off Stump-wise, to amuse a little Sap in them during two or three Years.

7. a. To divert the attention of (one) from serious business by anything trifling, ludicrous, or entertaining; *passing into* **b.** To divert, please with anything light or cheerful; **c.** *esp.* (in mod. sense) To excite the risible faculty or tickle the fancy of. *Const.* To amuse one *with* an anecdote, *by* telling him a story; to amuse oneself *with* a puzzle, *with, by,* or *in* sketching; to be amused *with* a toy or whimsical person, *by* a story told me, *at* an incident, the self-complacency of another.

a **1631** DONNE *Septuag.* 96 (T.) Amusing themselves with no other things but pleasures. *a* **1667** COWLEY *Royal Soc.* ii, That his own Business he might quite forget, They amus'd him with the Sports of wanton wit. *a* **1677** BARROW *Folly of Sland.*, What do men commonly amuse themselves in so much, as in carping? *a* **1687** WALSH (J.) To amuse himself with trifles. **1716–18** LADY MONTAGUE *Lett.* I. xxxii. 110, I am careful..to amuse you by the account of all I see. **1756** J. WARTON *Ess. Pope* ix. (1782) II. 68 Representations of..artless innocence always amuse and delight. **1810** COLERIDGE *Friend* (1865) 4 To amuse though only to amuse our visitors is wisdom as well as good-nature. **1853** H. ROGERS *Ecl. Faith* 167 Twelve guests, who all had the misfortune to squint, amused their host with their ludicrous cross lights. **1876** M. DAVIES *Unorth. Lond.* 312 The three schoolboys..amused themselves with shooting light missiles into the young ladies' faces. *Ibid.* 313 Amusing themselves by trying the effect of stopping and unstopping their ears.

8. To cause (time) to pass pleasantly, to entertain agreeably; to 'beguile,' while away, enliven.

a **1771** SMOLLETT, He did this to amuse their concern. **1791** MRS. INCHBALD *Simp. Story* I. vii. 66 Every new pursuit that might amuse the time. **1849** MACAULAY *Hist. Eng.* i, Who live by amusing the leisure of others.

†**aˈmuse,** *sb. Obs. rare*$^{-1}$. [f. prec. vb.] Pre-occupation; musing, meditation.

1608 MACHIN *Dumb Knt.* IV. i, Orewhelm'd with thought, with darke amuze And the sad sullennesse of griev'd dislike.

amused (əˈmjuːzd), *ppl. a.* [f. AMUSE *v.* + -ED.]

†**1.** Put into a muse; mentally arrested or distracted; absorbed, occupied, diverted from the point, cheated. *Obs.*

1600 HOLLAND *Livy* VII. xix. 262 The cittie was earnestly amused upon[*intentus*] the Tuscane war. **1611** COTGR., *Amusé*, amused; put into a muse, driven into a dump. **1640** G. ABBOTT *Job Paraphr.* 142 But art as a man under water amused in these thy afflictions. **1667** MILTON *P.L.* VI. 581 While we suspense, Collected stood within our thoughts amus'd. **1670** T. BROOKS *Wks.* (1867) VI. 146 Terrified, amused, amazed, astonished, and dispirited in the late dreadful fire.

2. Diverted, entertained, tickled (in fancy).

1727 POPE *Dunc.* II. 87 Amus'd he [Jove] reads, and then returns the bills. **1784** COWPER *Task* v. 878 Amused spectators of this bustling stage.

amusedly (əˈmjuːzɪdlɪ), *adv.* [f. AMUSED *ppl. a.* + -LY^2.] As being amused; with amusement.

1844 *Fraser's Mag.* XXX. 63/1 He looked amusedly at the baggage. **1864** MEREDITH *Emilia in England* xv, Leaning back and contemplating him amusedly. **1901** W. J. LOCKE *Usurper* iii. 29 He wandered amusedly around the baccarat tables. **1955** T. W. THOMAS in *Ess. in Crit.* V. 78 The phrase is..Lou's but reported to hold her amusedly at a distance.

amusee (əmjuːˈziː). *rare.* [f. AMUSE *v.* + -EE.] The person amused, or for whom amusement is provided.

1838 *Blackw. Mag.* XLIV. 367 The whole tribe of amusers and amusees expressed their pleasure. **1840** CARLYLE *Heroes* iii. 251 Given the amuser, the amusee must also be given.

amusement (əˈmjuːzmənt). [a. Fr. *amusement*, n. of action f. *amuser*: see AMUSE and -MENT.] *gen.* The action of amusing, or a thing done to amuse.

†**1.** Musing, mental abstraction, reverie. *Obs.*

1611 COTGR., *Amusement*, an amusing, or amusement. **1712** FLEETWOOD *Lay Bapt.* Pref. (T.) Here I..fell into a strong and deep amusement revolving in my mind with great perplexity the amazing change of our affairs.

†**2.** Distracting bewilderment, distraction. *Obs.*

1648 JOS. BEAUMONT *Psyche* XXII. cxv, A strange Amusement on all hearts did seize. **1663** *Aron-bimn.* 69 Absur'd allusions, designed on purpose to raise up amuzements and jealousies in the people. **1690** LOCKE *Hum. Underst.* IV. ix. 353 This..if well heeded, might save us a great deal of useless Amusement and Dispute. **1699** R. LESTRANGE *Erasm. Colloq.* 238, I give no heed to what men do when they are under the Amusements of Death.

3. Distraction or diversion of the attention from the point at issue; beguiling, deception. *esp.* in military tactics, diversion of the enemy's attention from the real aims of the other side. *arch.*

1692 DRYDEN *St. Euremont's Ess.* 367 Too frequent Comparisons turn'd men from the Application to true Objects, by the Amusement of Resemblances. **1693** *Mem. Count Teckely* IV. 53 The Trumpets and Kettle-drums, which by way of Amusement had been sent out of that place the Night before. **1759** FRANKLIN *Ess.* Wks. 1840 III. 446 What he says..was mere sophistry and amusement.

†**4.** A trifling with the attention or time of any one; a diversion to gain or waste time. *Obs.*

1685 tr. *Bossuet's Doctr. Cath. Ch.* xii. 24 If there be any Sense in these Words, if they be not an useless sound, and a vain amusement. **1696** PHILLIPS, *Amusement*..the making of vain Promises to gain Time. **1696** LUTTRELL *Brief Rel.* (1857) IV. 83 The French offer the allies peace..which they take to be meer amusement to gain time. **1710** *Ibid.* VI. 553 This affair is look't upon only as a French amusement.

5. The pleasurable occupation of the attention, or diversion of the mind (from serious duties, etc.); *passing from* **a.** (*in early use*) Idle time-wasting diversion, or entertainment; *through* **b.** (*generally*) Recreation, relaxation, the pleasurable action upon the mind of anything light and cheerful; *to* **c.** (*esp.*) Pleasant excitement of the risible faculty by anything droll or grotesque, tickling of the fancy.

1698 ATTERBURY *Disc. Death of Lady Cutts* 11 Pieces of pure Diversion and Amusement. *c* **1720** POPE in *Swift's Wks.* (1841) I. 838 Amusement is the happiness of those that cannot think. **1735** HANWAY *Trav.* (1762) I. 10 We seldom profit by writings that do not afford amusement. **1771** *Junius Lett.* xlix. 257 The remainder of the summer shall be dedicated to your amusement. **1824** COLERIDGE *Aids to Refl.* 221 The same craving for amusement, i.e. to be away from the Muses for relaxation. **1855** THACKERAY *Newc.* xxvii. 262 Giving a new source of amusement to these merry travellers. **1865** RUSKIN *Sesame* 100 When men are rightly occupied, their amusement grows out of their work. *Mod.* He paints only for his own amusement. To provide for the amusement of the children. Much amusement was excited by the recital of his misadventures. To the growing amusement of the House, the honourable gentleman proceeded to complain that he had been called a 'blockhead.'

6. *concr.* Anything which lightly and pleasantly diverts the attention, or beguiles the time; a pastime, play, game, means of recreation. (Orig. used *depreciatively*.)

1673 TEMPLE *United Prov.* (R.) Pleased with the pomp and splendour of a government..as it is an amusement for idle people. **1696** PHILLIPS, *Amusement*, any idle employment to spin away time. **1706** *Ibid.* a trifling business to pass away the time, a Toy. **1711** ADDISON *Spect.* No. 10 ¶6 Their amusements seem contrived for them, rather as Women, than as..reasonable Creatures. **1712** SWIFT *Let. Eng. Tongue* Wks. 1755 II. I. 189 Monstrous productions, which under the name of trips, spies, amusements, and other conceited appellations, have over-run us for some years past. **1753** HANWAY *Trav.* (1762) II. I. ix. 48 They have plays, and other amusements. **1837** J. H. NEWMAN *Par. Serm.* (ed. 2) III. xx. 329 To take..pleasure in our families rather than to seek amusements out of doors. **1859** HELPS *Friends in C.* Ser. II. I. 8 The commonplace despotic amusement of war.

7. Frequent in *Comb.* in senses 5 and 6, as ***amusement-lover*** (***-loving***), ***-mad***, ***-seeker*** (***-seeking***); also ***amusement arcade, centre, hall, park.***

1870 D. J. KIRWAN *Palace & Hovel* (1963) xvii. 154 The cheap amusement halls of London are of the very lowest kind to be found anywhere. **1898** *Daily News* 8 Sept. 5/1 It may surprise old amusement lovers to learn that one of the original troupe of Christy Minstrels..is still alive. **1904** *Westm. Gaz.* 31 Dec. 16/3 The average amusement-seeker has a limited amount to spend. **1906** *Bungalow* Dec. 4/2 The Tivoli..caters for the amusement-loving people. **1906** 'O. HENRY' *Four Million* (1916) xxv. 252 [He] hied himself to play pennies in the slot machines at the Amusement Arcade. **1907** *Westm. Gaz.* 10 May 12/1 London in particular..is 'amusement mad'. **1908** *Daily Chron.* 9 Dec. 4/7 He would secure to the amusement-seeking public a far more genuine and substantial benefit. **1909** *N.Y. Even. Post* 13 June 4 This is, or was to have been, the year of the amusement park. **1923** R. D. PAINE *Comrades Roll. Ocean* ix. 161 It had been picked up empty in one of the amusement parks outside the city. **1924** *The Studio* (1925) Autumn no., 76 (Advt.), Advertising in the Amusement Park at Wembley. **1935** 'J. GUTHRIE' *Little Country* xxi. 330 Ernest..clung to the sides of his boat and wondered why they called the place amusement park. **1936** *Discovery* Sept. 267/1 All the resources of amusement that a great amusement-centre [*sc.* Blackpool] can offer. **1937** *Ibid.* June 816/2 Amusement halls, a club, swimming baths, parks and other comforts. **1947** *Min. Town & Country Planning Bull. Selected Appeal Decisions* I. 11 (*heading*) Amusement arcade in holiday resort. *Ibid.*, An amusement caterer purchased three small single storey lock-up shops. *Ibid.*, He opened two of the shops in succession, as an amusement arcade. **1958** *Times* 23 Aug. 8/6 A lady who also runs an amusement arcade and whose eyes flicker in time with the lights of her pin-ball machine.

amuser (ə'mjuːzə(r)). [f. AMUSE *v.* + -ER[1].] One who amuses.

†**1.** One that puts people in a muse; that arrests or distracts attention, *esp.* with things trifling; that trifles with people's attention or expectations; a trifler, deceiver, cheat. *Obs.*

1583 WHITGIFT in Fuller *Ch. Hist.* IX. 153, I doubt not but your Lordship will judge those amusers to deserve just punishment. **1603** HOLLAND *Plutarch's Mor.* 457, I take him [the musician] to be a great amuser of men in a small matter. **1611** COTGR., *Amuseur*, an amuser of people; one that holdeth people at gaze, or putteth them into dumpes. *a* **1733** NORTH *Examen* I. iii. ¶24 (1740) 137 The French are the greatest Amusers in the World. If Propositions are made which they resolve not to accept, they will not directly say so, but suspend. **1775** ASH, *Amuser*..one that deceives.

2. One that provides diversion; a diverter, entertainer.

1796 W. TAYLOR in *Month. Rev.* XX. 382 The amusers of our leisure, the artists of our pleasures. **1841** *Mann. & Cust. Japan.* 192 In their capacity of amusers, they indulge in extravagant buffoonery. **1864** *Nat. Rev.* in Bagehot *Lit. Stud.* (1879) II. 136 Mere amusers are never respected.

†**amusette** (æmjuː'zɛt). *Obs.* [a. Fr. *amusette*, dim. f. *amuse*, a little amusement, a plaything, toy, a light gun.] A light field-cannon, invented by Marshal Saxe, formerly used in mountain warfare.

1761 *Ann. Reg.* 172/1 A new piece of artillery was tried lately in Dublin, after the manner of Marshal Saxe's amusette. **1776** C. LEE in Sparks *Corr. Am. Rev.* (1853) I. 202, I am furnishing myself with four-ounced rifle-amusettes, which will carry an infernal distance. **1816** C. JAMES *Mil. Dict.* (ed. 4) 13 Amusette, a species of offensive weapon..found of considerable use in the late war, especially among the French.

amusing (ə'mjuːzɪŋ), *vbl. sb.* [f. AMUSE *v.* + -ING[1].] The action of the vb. AMUSE; amusement. (Now mostly gerundial.)

1603 FLORIO *Montaigne* I. li. (1632) 165 See how much our mind troubleth this ridiculous ammuzing [chess]. *Mod.* Clever at amusing the children.

a'musing, *ppl. a.* [f. AMUSE *v.* + -ING[2].]

†**1.** Beguiling; cheating. *Obs.*

1597 DANIEL *Civ. Wares* II. v, Th' amuzing shadowes that are cast upon The state of Princes, to beguile the sight.

2. Engaging the mind or attention in a pleasing way; interesting. *arch.*

1712 ADDISON *Spect.* No. 463 ¶2 These several amusing Thoughts having taken possession of my Mind. **1714** POPE *Let. Jervas* Wks. 1737 V. 224 The amusing power of Poetry. **1794** GODWIN *Cal. Williams* 290 The project which had formerly proved amusing to my imagination.

3. Pleasantly entertaining or diverting; exciting the risible faculty, tickling the fancy. Also, as a vogue-word in trivial applications. Also *absol.*

1826 DISRAELI *Viv. Grey* I. vi. 15 My dear Sir! you are pleased to be amusing this morning. **1855** MACAULAY *Hist. Eng.* IV. 147 His objections are highly curious and amusing. **1866** GEO. ELIOT *F. Holt* (1868) 25 She found ridicule of Biblical characters very amusing. **1925** A. HUXLEY *Along Road* III. 200 The great invention of more recent years has been the 'amusing'... All bad art, whose badness is a positive..quality..may be said to be amusing. **1929** D. L. MOORE *Pandora* ix. 168 'Amusing'..is at the moment the first favourite..'an amusing pair of shoes', 'amusing little sandwiches', 'an amusing kind of lipstick'. **1934** C. LAMBERT *Music Ho!* II. 79 The scrapbook taste which is considered so modern and 'amusing' when applied to interior decoration. **1939** O. LANCASTER *Homes Sweet Homes* 62 Steel-engravings and wax fruit enjoy a come-back on an 'amusing' basis. **1960** *Times* 15 Sept. 15/3 The cult of the 'amusing'. This lethal word has been applied during the past 30 years to one art after another. From ballet to interior decoration, from the Parisian music of 1920 to *objets trouvés*, clever people in search of high fashion have turned amusing.

amusingly (ə'mjuːzɪŋlɪ), *adv.* [f. prec. + -LY[2].] In an amusing manner.

1812 *Examiner* 3 May 282/2 Our minds should be..impressed with the immorality of the habit, otherwise so amusingly depicted. **1854** KINGSLEY *Alexandria* i. (1857) 18 Alas! the Muses..are hard to tempt into a gilded cage, however amusingly made. **1867** FREEMAN *Norm. Conq.* I. App. 789 The narrative is so amusingly coloured. **1881** *Athenæum* 15 Jan. 104/1 In the boy's dress..she is amusingly ill at ease.

amusingness (ə'mjuːzɪŋnɪs). [f. as prec. + -NESS.] The quality of being amusing.

1823 *Blackw. Mag.* XIV. 641/2 Touching the reality (as well as the amusingness) of spectral appearances, I protest..against being put down as a scoffer. **1859** KINGSLEY *Plays & Pur.* in *Misc.* II. 127 Depending for his amusingness on his quaint antiquated language. **1886** R. BROUGHTON *Dr. Cupid* I. iii. 26 Thoughts..that augur but ill for the amusingness of his dinner. **1959** *Times* 11 Sept. 16/5 Our entertainment is made to depend on..the general amusingness of the dialogue.

amusive (ə'mjuːzɪv), *a.* [f. AMUSE *v.* + -IVE; by form-assoc. with *abus-ive, diffus-ive*, etc., which appear to be f. vbs. *abuse, diffuse*, but are really f. L. ppl. stems *abūs-, diffūs-*; thus *abut-i, abūs-um, abūsī v-, abusive*: see -IVE.] Such as to amuse.

†**1.** Deceitful, illusive. *Obs.*

1728 THOMSON *Spring* 215 Beholds th' amusive arch before him fly, Then vanish quite away. **1760** BEATTIE *Poems* (1831) 165 Th' amusive dream of blameless fancy born.

†**2.** Fitted to afford relaxation from graver concerns; recreative. *Obs.*

c **1750** SHENSTONE *Wks.* 1764 I. 112 Some for amusive tasks design'd, To sooth the certain ills of life. **1753** HERVEY *Theron & Asp.* I. 149 A cool refreshment and an amusive gloom.

3. Affording pleasing entertainment: **a.** engaging the attention, interesting; **b.** *esp.* (in later usage) fitted to tickle the fancy or excite the risible faculty.

1760 BEATTIE *Hope* II. ii, Prattling amusive in his accent meek. **1774** WHITE in *Phil. Trans.* LXV. 265, I have regarded these amusive birds with great attention. *a* **1824** CAMPBELL *View fr. St. Leonard's* 74 The earth-circling sea Has spires and mansions more amusive still—Men's volant homes. **1842** *Blackw. Mag.* LI. 423 An article for the Edinburgh Review, more spicy and amusive. **1865** *Reader* 25 Feb. 221/1 Abridging from a larger work so as to retain its most amusive features.

4. Tending to, aiming at amusement; whose object is amusement. *rare.*

1781 HAYLEY *Trium. Temper* II. 96 Curiosity's amusive wings. **1810** COLERIDGE *Friend* I. i. (1867) 5 Urania must..leave the sons of verse to more amusive patronesses.

a'musively, *adv.* [f. prec. + -LY[2].] In an amusive manner.

1776 CHANDLER *Trav. Greece* 12 (T.) A south easterly wind..murmuring amusively among the pines. **1858** BAILEY *Age* 20 An air acquired, to speak of it amusively, By looking into millstones too exclusively.

a'musiveness. [f. as prec. + -NESS.] The quality of being amusive.

1805 W. TAYLOR in *Ann. Rev.* III. 544 Of the amusiveness ..of these volumes, we are disposed to think favourably. **1812** —— in Robberds' *Mem.* II. 387, I know..no other which equals it in amusiveness, but 'Oberon.'

a-mutter (ə'mʌtə(r)), *adv. phr.* [A *prep.*[1] of state + MUTTER.] In a muttering state, muttering.

1856 MRS. BROWNING *Aur. Leigh* 28 All The dark a-mutter round him.

†**a'muzle**, *v. Obs. rare*[−1]. [a. OFr. *amuselle-r* to muzzle; *fig.* to dupe; or, ? fanciful diminutive of *amuse.*]

1795 H. WALPOLE in *Miss Berry's Corr.* I. 466, I thought I could amuze or amuzle myself better by sitting and thinking of you than by going out.

amyctic (ə'mɪktɪk), *a. Med.* [ad. L. *amyctic-us*, a. Gr. ἀμυκτικ-ός scratching, pricking, f. ἀμύσσ-ειν to tear, prick.] Excoriating, irritating, vellicating.

1853 in MAYNE *Exp. Lex.* **1879** in *Syd. Soc. Lex.*

†**'amydon, -oun.** *Obs.* 4–7. Also 4 **amedoun**, 5 **amydone**. [a. Fr. *amidon* starch, cogn. w. Pg. *amidão*, Sp. *almidon*, augmentative forms of Pg. and It. *amido*:—late L. *amidum, amydum*, for cl. L. *amylum* starch: see AMYL[1].] (See quot.)

[**1306** in Rogers *Agric. & Prices* I. xxv. 630 'Amedoun,' 2½ lbs. of which are bought at Elham in 1306.] *c* **1420** *Liber Cocorum* (1864) 8 Lay hit anone With myed bred, or amydone. *c* **1440** *Anc. Cookery* in *Househ. Ord.* (1790) 439 With saunders and saffron, and another with amydoun. *c* **1475** *Noble Bk. Cookry* Holkham MS. (1882) 101 Alay it with flour or whit amydon. **1616** SURFLET & MARKH. *Countr. Farm* 572 Amydon or Amylon..the best wheat meal, put into water several times so that all the bran, etc., may float to the top and be skimmed off, the heavy meal being dried in the sun, broken into gobbets, and so made into fine meale.

amyelencephalic (ə,maɪəlɛnsɪ'fælɪk), *a. Phys.* [f. mod.L. *amyelencephalia* absence of the brain and spinal cord (f. Gr. ἀμύελ-ος without marrow + ἐγκέφαλ-ος brain) + -IC.] Having the central nervous system wanting.

1875 HUYDEN *Dis. Heart* 59.

amyelotrophy (ə,maɪə'lɒtrəfɪ). *Path.* [mod. f. Gr. ἀ priv. + μυελ-ός marrow + -τροφία nourishment; f. τρέφ-ειν to nourish.] 'Atrophy of the spinal cord.' *Syd. Soc. Lex.* 1879.

amyelous (ə'maɪələs), *a. Phys.* [f. Gr. ἀμύελ-ος without marrow + -OUS.] Wanting the spinal cord.

a'mygdal. ? *Obs.* [ad. L. *amygdal-a*, a. Gr. ἀμυγδάλη an almond; probably continued and extended to sense 2, through the OFr. *amygdale* and med.L. *amygdala* a tonsil.]

†**1.** An almond. *Obs.*

c **940** *Sax. Leechd.* I. 104 And ȝewyll hy wel mid amigdales ele. *c* **1250** *Gen. & Ex.* 3840 It [Aaron's rod] was grene and leaued bi-cumen, And nutes amigdeles ðor-onne numen.

2. *pl.* **a.** The tonsils. **b.** The almonds of the ears.

1541 R. COPLAND *Guydon's Quest. Cyrurg.*, The amygdales and faulses..are set behynde the tongue towarde the palays. **1601** HOLLAND *Pliny* (1634) II. 59 It restraineth the mumps or inflamation of the Amygdales. **1612** WOODALL *Surg. Mate* Wks. 1653, 10 Great swellings in the face, or in the amygdals and throat. [**1843** WILKINSON tr. *Swedenb. Anim. Kingd.* I. ii. 67 The *amygdalæ* are 2 glandular bodies of a reddish color.]

amygdalaceous (ə,mɪgdə'leɪʃəs), *a. Bot.* [f. mod.L. *amygdalāceæ*, f. *amygdala* almond: see -ACEOUS.] Akin to the almond. (Applied to those plants of the Rosaceous order, which produce stone-fruits; made by some a distinct natural order.)

1852 T. ROSS tr. *Humboldt's Trav.* II. xvi. 52 The milky emulsions that the fruits of the amygdalaceous plants yield.

amygdalate (ə'mɪgdəleɪt), *a.* and *sb.* [f. L. *amygdala* + -ATE; as if ad. L. **amygdalātum.*]

A. *adj.* 'Made of almonds,' J.

B. *sb.* †**1.** = ALMOND-MILK. *Obs.*

1657 TOMLINSON *Renou's Disp.* v. ix. 163 The Amygdalate is obdulcorated with sugar. **1706** PHILLIPS, *Amygdalate*, an Artificial Milk or Physick-drink, made of blanch'd Almonds and other Ingredients. **1721** BAILEY [and mod. Dicts.].

2. *Chem.* A salt of Amygdalic acid.

1863 WATTS *Dict. Chem.* I. 201 Amygdalate of ethyl.

amygdalic (æmɪg'dælɪk), *a. Chem.* [f. L. *amygdala* + -IC.] Of or pertaining to almonds. ***amygdalic acid***, $C_{20}H_{26}O_{12}$, derived from amygdalin by boiling with an alkali.

1857 PEREIRA *Mat. Med.* II. ii. 246. **1863** WATTS *Dict. Chem.*

amygdaliceous, *a.* for AMYGDALACEOUS.

1731 BAILEY; see AMYGDALINE.

amygdaliferous (ə,mɪgdə'lɪfərəs), *a.* [f. L. *amygdala* almond + -(I)FEROUS.] Almond-bearing; having an almond-like kernel. (Mod. Dicts.)

amygdalin (ə'mɪgdəlɪn). *Chem.* Formerly **-ine**. [f. L. *amygdala* almond + -IN chem. form.] $C_{20}H_{27}NO_{11}$ + $3H_2O$; a peculiar substance found crystalline in the kernels of almonds and other stone fruit, and amorphous in the leaves of the cherry-laurel, etc. It is one of the GLUCOSIDES.

1651 N. BIGGS *New Dispens.* ¶303 Whatsoever swims a top, is of the essentiall oyle; but the rest Amygdaline. *c* **1865** J. WYLDE in *Circ. Sci.* I. 351/1 The principle of almonds (amygdalin). **1875** WOOD *Therap.* (1879) 58 Amygdalin.. is nearly, if not quite, without effect upon the organism.

amygdaline (ə'mɪgdəlɪn, -aɪn), *a. rare.* [ad. L. *amygdalin-us*, a. Gr. ἀμυγδάλιν-ος of almonds: see AMYGDAL and -INE.] 'Relating to almonds; resembling almonds.' J.

1731 BAILEY, *Amygdaline*, the same as *Amygdalicious*, i.e. of or pertaining to almonds. [Also in mod. Dicts.]

amygda'lineous (-'ɪnɪəs), *a.* [f. mod.L. *amygdaline-æ* (plants) of the almond tribe + -OUS: see -INEOUS.] Belonging to the almond tribe or sub-order of the *Rosaceæ*.

1879 in *Syd. Soc. Lex.*

‖**amygdalitis** (-'aɪtɪs). *Med.* [f. med.L. *amygdala* a tonsil + -ITIS.] Inflammation of the tonsils.

1876 tr. *Wagner's Gen. Pathol.* 619 Thus it is in measles, scarlatina..amygdalitis, erysipelas.

amygdaloid (ə'mɪgdəlɔɪd), *a.* and *sb.* [f. Gr. ἀμυγδάλη almond + -OID. Cf. mod.Fr. *amygdaloïde.*]

A. *adj.* Almond-shaped; having almond-shaped nodules.

1836 TODD *Cycl. Anat. & Phys.* I. 583/1 The amygdaloid lobe. **1852** T. ROSS *Humboldt's Trav.* II. xvii. 79 The clay which separates these amygdaloid concretions. **1858** BEVERIDGE *Hist. Ind.* I. Introd. 7 Basaltic trap..globular, tabular, porphyritic, and amygdaloid. **1870** HOOKER *Stud. Flora* 323 Sea Buckthorn..embryo amygdaloid.

B. *sb. Geol.* An igneous rock, usually trappean, containing almond-shaped nodules or geodes of some mineral, as agate, chalcedony, or calc spar.

1791 BEDDOES in *Phil. Trans.* LXXXI. 69 The crystals often occurring in the cavities of the amygdaloides rocks. **1802** PLAYFAIR *Illust. Hutton. The.* 67 The common basalt.. and the amygdaloid, are comprehended under the name of whin. **1833** LYELL *Princ. Geol.* III. 361 Converting porous lava into amygdaloids. **1847** TENNYSON *Princess* III. 343 Chattering stony names Of shale and hornblende, rag and trap and tuff, Amygdaloid and trachyte. **1876** PAGE *Advd. Text-bk. Geol.* v. 105 Amygdaloids, having their vesicular cavities filled with agate, carnelian, etc.

amygdaloidal (əmɪgdəˈlɔɪdəl), *a.* [f. prec. + -AL[1].] Pertaining to, or of the nature or character of, the rock amygdaloid.

1813 BAKEWELL *Introd. Geol.* 28 Amygdaloidal.. when composed of a compact ground with cavities which have been filled up with another mineral substance. **1858** GEIKIE *Hist. Boulder* xii. 241 The same rocks may be likewise vesicular or amygdaloidal.

amygdule (əˈmɪgdjuːl). *Geol.* [f. L. *amygd(ala)* almond + -ULE, after *nodule*, etc.] (See quot.)

1877 LE CONTE *Elem. Geol.* (1879) 211 Sometimes the filling has taken place very slowly by successive additions of different coloured material. Thus are formed the beautiful agate pebbles, or more properly, amygdules. **1882** GEIKIE *Text-bk. Geol.* II. II. ii. 62 Secondary minerals (amygdules) such as calcite, calcedony, quartz, and zeolites.

†**aˈmyke.** *Obs. rare*[−1]. [ad. L. *amīc-us* a friend. Cf. early spellings of *opaque*.] A friend.

c **1495** *Digby Myst.* v. 70 O Worthy Spouse.. O swete amyke, oure Joye, oure blisse!

†**ˈamyl**[1]. *Obs.* [ad. L. *amyl-um*, a. Gr. ἄμυλ-ον starch, fine meal; prop. neut. of adj. ἄμυλ-ος not ground at the mill, f. ἀ priv. + μύλ-ος mill.] Starch; finest flour. Cf. AMYDON.

1572 B. GOOGE *Heresbach's Husb.* (1586) 27 b, Of wheate is made amyl. **1579** LANGHAM *Gard. Health* (1633) 14 Almonds.. taken in with fine amill. **1601** HOLLAND *Pliny* II. 171 They haue a property to stanch bleeding, mixed with Amylfloure and mints. *Ibid.* I. 562 Starch-floure called Amylum.. called it is in Greek Amylum, because it neuer came into the mill.

amyl[2] (ˈæmɪl). *Chem.* Formerly **-yle**. [f. L. *am(ylum)* starch + -YL(E = Gr. ὕλη matter, stuff, substance. So named, because its alcohol was first obtained from the Fusel oil separated in purifying or 'rectifying' ordinary spirits distilled from potato or grain *starch*. The name was not appropriate, as Fusel oil occurs in unrectified spirit of wine from any source (as from the grape or from sugar), and yields *propyl*, and *butyl*, as well as *amyl* alcohol; and it was unfortunate as seeming to connect this radical with the *amyloses* and *amylaceous* substances.]

The monatomic alcohol radical of the pentacarbon series C_5H_{11}, also called *pentyl* or *quintyl*.

(There are eight isomeric modifications of PENTYL, of which amyl proper is the second = isopentyl, $CH.2CH_3.C_2H_4$.)

1850 DAUBENY *Atom. The.* vii. 227 We regard this [fusel oil] as the alcohol of the supposed radical.. assigning to it the name of Amyle. **1870** *Daily News* 16 Sept., Professor Humphry.. looked forward to nitrate of amyle becoming a cure for.. lockjaw and hydrophobia. **1870** TYNDALL *Heat* xv. §745 The light of the sun also effects the decomposition of the nitrite of amyl vapour. **1875** URE *Dict. Arts* I. 522 Acetate of amyl, commercially known as jargonelle pear essence.

2. *attrib.* = of amyl, amylic: as in ***amyl compounds, series, group***; also ***amyl acetate, chloride, oxide, sulphide***, etc.; and esp. in **amyl alcohol**, also called *isopentyl alcohol*, and *isobutyl carbinol*, $CH.2CH_3.(C_2H_4)OH$, a burning acrid oily liquid of fetid odour, the chief constituent of Fusel oil, produced along with vinic alcohol in the manufacture of brandy; **amyl hydride**, another name for *pentane*; **ethyl-amyl-acetate**, the essence of jargonelle pears.

1863 WATTS *Dict. Chem.* (1872) I. 203 Amyl alcohol is difficult to set on fire, and burns with a white smoky flame. **1872** *Ibid.* VI. 107 The amyl-compounds obtained from fusel-oil.

3. As formative in names of compounds containing amyl: as *amylacetate, amylacetic, amylaniline, amyl-arsine, amyl-phosphine*.

1850 DAUBENY *Atom. The.* viii. 240 Amylaniline, a similar compound, into which amyle, as well as aniline, appears to enter, its composition being $C_{12}H_5.C_{10}H_{11}.HN$. **1863** WATTS *Dict. Chem.* (1872) I. 205 Sulphide of Amyl and Hydrogen: *Amyl-mercaptan*.

amylaceous (æmɪˈleɪʃəs), *a.* [f. L. *amyl-um* starch + -ACEOUS. Cf. mod.Fr. *amylacé*.] Of the character or nature of starch; starchy.

1830 LINDLEY *Nat. Syst. Bot.* 333 An amylaceous substance analogous to gelatine.. exists in the form of pure starch or amylaceous fibre.. in *Cetaria islandica*. **1881** MIVART *Cat* 166 Oleaginous and amylaceous substances, sugar, starch, and gum, are the two sets of non-nitrogenous foods.

amylamine (ˈæmɪləˌmaɪn). *Chem.* [f. AMYL[2] + AMINE.] An amine in which one of the hydrogen atoms of the ammonia is replaced by amyl; the compound ammonia of the amyl series.

1850 DAUBENY *Atom. The.* viii. 239 Amylamine—$C_{10}H_{11} + H_2N$, where it [1 atom of hydrogen] is replaced by amyle. **1881** *Athenæum* 14 May 658/3 The Active and Inactive Amylamines corresponding to the Active and Inactive Alcohols of Fermentation.

amylase (ˈæmɪleɪs, -z). *Biochem.* [f. AMYL[2] + -ASE.] An enzyme or organic catalyst which disintegrates starch, present in animals and plants; = DIASTASE.

1893 *Jrnl. Chem. Soc.* LXIV. II. 587 The dried, as well as the fresh, organism contains an enzyme 'amylase', similar to the diastase of malt. **1899** J. R. GREEN *Soluble Ferments* ii. 15 (*heading*) Diastase (Amylase, Ptyalin). **1910** *Practitioner* June 823 The hydrolysis is brought about by means of enzymes, such as ptyalin, amylopsin or amylase, lactase and glucase.

amylate (ˈæmɪleɪt). *Chem.* [f. AMYL[2] + -ATE.] A salt of the radical amyl, in which amyl takes the place of the oxygenated group in a metallic salt; as ***potassium amylate*** $C_5H_{11}.O.K$, compared with potassium nitrate $NO_2.O.K$.

amylate of amyl, = amyl ether $(C_5H_{11})_2O$, in which the potassium of potassium amylate is also replaced by amyl.

1869 ROSCOE *Elem. Chem.* xxx. 332 Potassium and sodium can replace the typical hydrogen of this [amyl] alcohol, forming potassium or sodium amylate.

amylene (ˈæmɪliːn). *Chem.* [f. AMYL[2] + -ENE.] The diatomic hydrocarbon, or olefine, of the pentacarbon series, C_5H_{10}, also called *pentene* or *quintene*, formed by the removal of one atom of water from amyl alcohol, and bearing the same relation to amyl that ethylene does to ethyl. It is a colourless very thin fluid with anæsthetic properties.

1858 *Penny Cycl.* 2nd Supp. 680/2 Dr. Snow found that amylene was capable of producing the same effects as chloroform. **1880** CLEMENSHAW *Wurtz' Atom. The.* 292 All known amylenes present the character of non-saturated compounds.

b. *attrib.* ***amylene-alcohol*** or ***-glycol***. $C_5H_{10}.2OH$, the glycol of the Amyl series; 'a colourless, very syrupy liquid, having a bitter taste with aromatic after-taste.' Watts.

amylic (əˈmɪlɪk), *a. Chem.* [f. AMYL[2] + -IC.] Of or pertaining to amyl; = AMYL[2] attributively, as *amylic* or *amyl alcohol, amylic ether*, etc.

1858 *Penny Cycl.* 2nd Supp. 127/1 Hydrated Oxide of Amyle = Amylic Alcohol = Fusel Oil.. This fermentation in which it is produced is called the amylic. **1863** WATTS *Dict. Chem.* (1872) I. 203 Amylic alcohol is a transparent colourless liquid having a peculiar odour (the peaty smell of whisky is due to its presence in small quantities).

amyliferous (æmɪˈlɪfərəs), *a. rare.* [f. L. *amyl-um* starch + -(I)FEROUS bearing.] Producing starch, starch-bearing.

1865 *Reader* No. 143. 355/2 The production of amyliferous plantules.

†**aˈmyllier.** *Obs.* [prob. corruption of OFr. *mellier*, f. Norm. *meille*, in various Fr. dialects *mêle, merle, mesle*:—L. *mespilus* medlar. The *a-* is prob. 'indef. article' first prefixed in sing: *a mellier, amellier*.] ? A medlar-tree.

a **1400** *Pistill of Sw. Susane* vii, On olyves and amylliers, and al kynde of trees The popejayes perken.

amylo-, comb. form of AMYL, in both senses, as:

1. amylo-cellulose, a name applied to a supposed constituent of starch granules, which is coloured copper-red by iodine.

2. amylo-methylic *a.* of amyl-methyl; as in ***amylo-methylic ether***, also called *methyl-amyl ether*. So ***amylovinic ether***, also called *ethyl-amyl ether*; ***amylonitrous ether***, etc.

1873 WILLIAMSON *Chem.* xxxix. §272 Amylomethylic ether is obtained by the action of methylic iodide on potassic amylate.

amylogen (əˈmɪlədʒɛn). [f. L. *amyl-um*, Gr. ἄμυλ-ον starch + -GEN.] That part of granulose which is soluble in water; soluble starch.

1879 in WATTS *Dict. Chem.* 3rd Supp.

amyloid (ˈæmɪlɔɪd), *a.* and *sb.* [G. (Vogel and Schleiden 1839, in *Ann. Phys. & Chem.* XLVI. 327), f. L. *amylum* (see AMYL[1]) + -OID.] **A.** *adj.*

1. Having the form or nature of starch, starch-like.

1857 HENFREY *Elem. Bot.* §671 Semi-gelatinous layers of thickening met with in.. certain seeds (called amyloid). **1877** *Athenæum* 1 Dec. 703/1 These yellow cells contain not oil but amyloid substances.

2. *Path.* Applied to a form of degeneration of various organs, or to the albuminoid substance (formerly supposed to be akin to starch) produced in this; = LARDACEOUS *a.*

1859 J. PAGET *Let.* 14 June in *Mem. & Lett.* (1901) 224, I have only a very imperfect knowledge.. of what has been done.. on amyloid degeneration. **1872** THUDICHUM *Chem. Phys.* 5 The term amyloid is perfectly correct as applied to this particular degeneration. **1873** [see LARDACEOUS *a.*]. **1879** *Syd. Soc. Lex.* s.v., Late observations clearly show that amyloid substance is not a starch, but a nitrogenous body; its exact composition is not known. **1881** [see CHOLESTERIN].

B. *sb.*

1. A substance akin to starch; any member of the group of carbohydrates including starch and related substances, as cellulose.

1872 HUXLEY *Phys.* vi. 134 Amyloids are substances which also consist of carbon, hydrogen, and oxygen only. **1873** LE CONTE in Stewart *Conserv. Force* vii. 177 The plastic matters of which vegetable structure is built are of two kinds—amyloids and albuminoids.

2. *Chem.* The substance formed in amyloid degeneration, also called LARDACEIN.

amyloidal (æmɪˈlɔɪdəl), *a.* [f. prec. + -AL[1].] Of the nature of an amyloid.

1872 HUXLEY *Phys.* v. 128 Whenever.. amyloidal matters, are being converted into the more highly oxidated waste products.. heat is evolved.

amyloidosis (ˌæmɪlɔɪˈdəʊsɪs). *Path.* [mod.L., f. AMYLOID *a.* and *sb.* + -OSIS.] Amyloid degeneration.

1900 in GOULD *Pocket Med. Dict.* (ed. 4). **1961** *Lancet* 9 Sept. 599/1 Amyloidosis in typhoid fever.

amylolysis (æmɪˈlɒlɪsɪs). *Biochem.* [f. AMYLO- + LYSIS; cf. AMYLOLYTIC *a.*] The conversion of starch into soluble products by the action of enzymes.

1890 BILLINGS *Med. Dict.* **1909** *Practitioner* Dec. 818 The contents [of the stomach] showed deficient amylolysis.

amylolytic (ˌæmɪləʊˈlɪtɪk), *a. Phys.* [mod. f. Gr. ἄμυλ-ον starch + λυτικ-ός solvent, f. λύ-ειν to dissolve.] Effecting the conversion of starch into dextrine and sugar.

1876 FOSTER *Phys.* II. i. (1879) 217 The amylolitic action of Saliva. **1881** *Athenæum* 14 May 658/2 The Amylolytic and Proteolytic Activity of Pancreatic Extracts.

amyˈlometer. [f. L. *amyl-um* starch + Gr. μέτρον a measure: see -METER.] An instrument for testing the amount of starchy matter, in potatoes, etc.

1876 *S. Kens. Mus. Catal.* No. 2737 Demby's Amylometer (potato-tester).

amylopectin (ˌæmɪləʊˈpɛktɪn). *Chem.* [ad. F. *amylopectine* (Maquenne and Roux 1905, in *Comptes Rendus* CXL. 1305), f. AMYLO- + PECTIN.] A mucilaginous constituent of starch.

1905 *Jrnl. Chem. Soc.* LXXXVIII. I. 511 The second constituent [of starch] is amylopectin. **1957** *Sci. News* XLV. 83 A branched-chain molecule such as the amylopectin component of starch.

amyloplast (ˈæmɪləʊplɑːst, -æ-). *Bot.* [ad. F. *amyloplaste* (L. Errera *L'Épiplasme des Ascomycètes* (1882) x. 74), f. AMYLO- + -PLAST.] A colourless granule in a plant-cell, around which a starch-grain is formed.

1886 S. H. VINES *Lect. Physiol. Plants* x. 180 Schimper has observed that the formation of starch-grains is commonly effected, in parts of plants not exposed to light, by certain specialised portions of the protoplasm which are termed starch-forming corpuscles or amyloplasts. **1955** *New Biol.* XIX. 90 The amyloplasts, the specific sites of starch formation.

amylopsin (æmɪˈlɒpsɪn). *Biochem.* Also **-ine**. [f. AMYLO-, after *pepsin*: cf. STEAPSIN.] The amylolytic ferment of the pancreatic juice.

1881 *Syd. Soc. Lex.* s.v., *Amylopsine*, a name given by Defresne to that ferment of the pancreatic juice which converts starch into sugar. **1886** *Buck's Handbk. Med. Sci.* II. 452/1 A third ferment, *amylopsin*, acts on starch as ptyalin does. **1894** *Jrnl. Chem. Soc.* LXVI. II. 103 The production of ferments by the pancreatic cell is successive; it is an operation of two acts, of which the first is the formation of amylopsin, the second of trypsin. **1937** *Thorpe's Dict. Appl. Chem.* I. 690/1 The proteolytic enzyme (trypsin), and the amylolytic enzyme (amylopsin).

amylose (ˌæmɪˈləʊs). *Chem.* [f. L. *amyl-um* starch + -OSE.] One of the three subdivisions of the *Carbohydrates*, or compounds containing 6 or 12 atoms of carbon, united by oxygen and hydrogen in the proportion to form water, the others being *Glucose*, and *Saccharose*. The Amyloses are dextrin, starch, inulin, glycogen, cellulose, tunicin, and gum; all of which have the composition $C_6H_{10}O_5$, or a multiple thereof.

1877 WATTS *Fownes' Chem.* II. 202 Oxygen-ethers or anhydrides of the polyglucosic alcohols—Amyloses.

ˌamyloˈsynthesis. (See quot.)

1882 T. HICK in *Naturalist* Mar. 124 For the formation of starch by what has hitherto been called the process of assimilation, I propose the name *amylosynthesis*.. From these we get at once *amylosynthetic* and *amylosynthetically*.

amyosthenic (əmaɪəsˈθɛnɪk). *Med.* [f. mod.L. *amyosthenia* want of muscular power (f. Gr. ἀ priv. + μῦς, μυ-ός muscle + -σθένεια strength) + -IC.] A medicine which depresses muscular action.

1879 *Syd. Soc. Lex.* s.v., Divisible into general and special amyosthenics; to the former belong belladonna, opium, etc.

amyotrophic (əmaɪəˈtrɒfɪk), *a. Path.* [f. next + -IC, after Gr. τροφικ-ός feeding.] Pertaining to amyotrophy.

1879 *Syd. Soc. Lex.*, *Amyotrophic* paralysis is paralysis which is due to muscular atrophy.

amyotrophy (æmɪˈɒtrəfɪ). *Path.* [mod. f. Gr. ἀ priv. + μῦς, μυ-ός muscle + -τροφία nourishment.] 'Atrophy of muscle.' *Syd. Soc. Lex.* 1879.

amyous (ˈæmɪəs), *a. Path.* [f. Gr. ἄμυ-ος wanting muscle + -OUS.] Wanting in muscle.
1879 in *Syd. Soc. Lex.*

amyral, -awnt, -ayl(e, obs. forms of ADMIRAL.
c **1450** LONELICH *Grail* xlii. 61 An amyrawnt, and with hym bothe princes and knyhtes.

amyrin (ˈæmɪrɪn). Also **-ine.** [ad. F. *amyrine* (S. Baup 1851, in *Jrnl. de Pharm.* XX. 323), AMYR(IS + -IN[1].] A resin obtained from a Mexican species of *Amyris* (*A. elemifera*).
1876 *Jrnl. Chem. Soc.* II. 423 Amyrin is found in elemi in the form of microscopic prisms. **1889** *Chambers's Encycl.* IV. 288/1 When treated with cold alcohol, it [*sc.* Elemi] partly dissolves, leaving about 20 per cent. of a white resinous substance called Amyrine.

‖**amyris** (ˈæmɪrɪs). *Bot.* A genus of tropical trees and shrubs, yielding resinous products.
c **1865** J. WYLDE in *Circ. Sci.* I. 86/2 The natives of British Guiana selected the wood of an amyris.

amys(e, obs. form of AMICE.

amyt, obs. form of AMICT and AMIT.

Amytal (ˈæmɪtəl). Also **amytal**. Trade-name of a white crystalline powder used as a sedative.
1926 *Jrnl. Pharmacol.* XXVI. 379 Isoamyl ethyl barbituric acid (Amytal). **1928** *Chem. Abstr.* 460 (*caption*) The effect of insulin on the metabolism of dogs under amytal anesthesia. **1930** *Trade Marks Jrnl.* 26 Mar. 484/1 *Amytal*, a medicated preparation in tablet form for human use as a sedative and hypnotic. Eli Lilly and Company. **1930** *Lancet* 14 June 1302/1 Amytal is the trade-name of iso-amyl-ethyl barbituric acid, and it has now been employed as an anæsthetic in a fair number of cases. *Ibid.*, It appears that amytal, if used without risk, is rather a hypnotic than a true anæsthetic. **1938** J. STEINBECK *Long Valley* 118 Here's some sodium amytal. One of these capsules will calm him down.

amzel, variant of AMSEL.

†**an,** *a.*[1] Earlier form of the numeral ONE; retained in the north. The OE. *án* began *c* 1150, to be reduced bef. a cons. to *a*; in the south, *ān*, *ā* were, bef. 1300, regularly rounded to *ōn* (*oon*, *one*), *ō* (*oo*) in the full original sense of the numeral; but when the sense was weakened to that of the 'indef. article' (see next) they continued to be written *an*, *a* (*ăn*, *ă*). In the north, the spelling *an*, *a*, was retained in both senses, the stress alone (as in Ger. *ein*, Fr. *un*) distinguishing the numeral from the article; and *an* was at length commonly written *ane*, which spelling, though proper to the numeral (*ane* = *ān*, with *e* mute indicating long vowel), was, especially by Sc. writers, used for the article also. See ANE, a *adj.*[2], and, for the senses, ONE; the following instances illustrate the form only.

1. OE. and early ME.: in all dialects.
c **950** *Lindisf. Gosp.* Mark xii. 29 Drihten God user God an is. *c* **1000** *Ags. G.* Matt. x. 29 An of ðám. **1131** *O.E. Chron.*, Næ be læf þær noht an. *c* **1220** *Hali Meid.* 23 Bi hu muchel þe an passed þe oþre. *Ibid.* 25 Nimeð an after an. *c* **1230** *Ancr. R.* (MS. C.) Pref. 23 Of anes cunnes fuheles. **1297** R. GLOUC. 223 Anne stroc he ȝef hym.

2. Late ME. and modern: northern. (*Thet an—thet other* were here written *the tan—the tother.*)
a **1300** *Cursor M.* 19339 All als an þai gaf ansuer. *Ibid.* 20860 þe tan was blisced and te toþer. **1340** HAMPOLE *Pr. Consc.* 4085 An sal come þat sal hald þe empire. *Ibid.* 259 Ane of þer four. *c* **1400** *Destr. Troy* IX. 4062 Archisalus was an.. And Protheno.. þat other. *c* **1430** *Syr Gener.* 1337 Not an word ageyn he yaf. *c* **1620** A. HUME *Brit. Tong.* 7 Distinguished the ane from the other.

an (toneless ən; emph. æn), *a.*[2], '*indef. article.*' The older and fuller form of *a*, now retained only before a vowel sound, as *an* orator, *an* honour, *an x*, *an* 'M.P.'; also by most writers before *h*, and by some even before *eu*, *ū* (= *yū*), in unaccented syllables, as *an hyæna*, *an euphonic change*, though many writers, and most speakers, now use *a* in such positions. *An* originated as a lighter or stressless pronunciation of the numeral *án* 'one'; see above: already by 1150, in midl. dial. it was reduced before a cons. to *a*; but in the south, the fuller *an*, even retaining part of its earlier inflected cases, is found as late as 1340. *An* was often retained before *w* and *y* in 15th c., as *an wood*, *an woman*, *an yere*, *such an one*, and was regular before *h* down to 17th c., as *an house*, *an happy*, *an hundred*, *an head* (1665). Its history thus shows a gradual suppression of the *n* before consonants of all kinds, and in all positions. For illustrations, and signification, see A *adj.*[2]

an, *v.*[1], var. *han*, obs. or dial. f. *haven*, inf. of HAVE.
1448 MARG. PASTON in *Lett.* I. 69 He myth an had mony to an holpyn hym self wyth.

†**an,** *v.*[2] *Obs.* 1 & 3 sing. pres. of UNN-EN, to grant.
a **1250** *Owl & Night.* 1737 Ich an wel, cwað the niȝtegale.

an, *adv.* 'only,' obs. form of ONE.

an, an' (ən, (ə)n), *conj.* [weakened from AND.]
1. = AND B. (L. *et.*)
In this sense the weak form *an* appears soon after 1100, and is not uncommon in ME., esp. northern, but very rare after 1500, till it reappears in modern times in the representation of dialect speech, in which it is printed *an'* with the apostrophe, recognizing the dropped letter. But *and* is almost always so pronounced in conversation, and even in reading, though this is conventionally considered a fault.
1154 *O.E. Chron.* (Laud. MS.) an. 1135 Mone an sterres abuten him at middæi. *c* **1250** *Gen. & Ex.* 647 Of Noe siðen an is ðre sunen. *c* **1400** *Apol. for Loll.* 15 Charitable pacience of þe martir, an vnriȝtwisnes of þe persewar. *c* **1400** *Destr. Troy* VI. 2328 Be sent from your seluon.. An aioynet to þis Jorney. *c* **1449** PECOCK *Repr.* II. ii. 140 An whi not thanne? **1606** G. W[OODCOCKE] *Hist. Justine* 39 Up an down in euery corner. **1859** TENNYSON *North. Farmer* 2 Doctor's abean an' agoan.
2. = AND, C. = *if.* (L. *si.*) *arch.* and *dial.*
In this sense *an*, *an'*, is rare bef. 1600, when it appears occasionally in the dramatists, esp. before *it*, as *an' 't please you*, *an' 't were*, etc. As the prec. sense was not at this time written *an*, modern writers have made a conventional distinction between the two forms, *an'* for 'and,' L. *et*, being dialectal or illiterate, but *an'* or *an* for 'and,' L. *si*, archaic, or even literary. Except in *an' 't*, *an* is found only once in the 1st Folio of Shakspere (see below); but modern editors substitute it for the full *and* usual in Shakspere and his contemporaries. Dialectally the two senses are alike *an'*; the intensified *and if*, *an if*, common in 17th c., remains in the s.w. dial. as *nif*.
[*a* **1300** *Havelok* 2861 And thou will my conseil tro. *c* **1386** CHAUCER *Doctor's T.* 86 Now kepe hem wel, for and [*v.r.* if] ye wil ye can.] **1542** BOORDE *Dyetary* viii. (1870) 246 An nede shall compell a man to slepe. **1588** SHAKS. *L.L.L.* v. ii. 584 There, an't shall please you. *Ibid.* v. ii. 232 Nay then two treyes, an if you grow so nice. **1687** T. BROWN *Saints in Uproar* Wks. 1730 I. 74 An't please your highness. **1749** FIELDING *Tom Jones* II. ii. (1840) 154 If an she be a rebel. **1775** SHERIDAN *Rivals* III. iv, An' we've any luck. **1817** COLERIDGE *Sib. Leaves* (1862) 273 But an if this will not do. **1821** COMBE (Dr. Syntax) *Search of Wife* I, An' please your Reverence, here we are. **1859** TENNYSON *Gar. & Lyn.* 251 But an it please thee not.

†**an,** *prep. Obs.* [cogn. w. Goth. and OHG. *ana* (MHG. *ane*, mod.G. *an*), OS., OFris. *an*, ON. *á*; Gr. ἀνά.] The orig. form of the prep. which, in prehistoric Eng., in accordance with the regular phonetic history of short *a* before nasals, was rounded to ON, a form, unlike the parallel *ond*, *hond*, *lomb*, *monn*, ever after retained. In Anglo-Saxon, but not in Anglian, *on* also absorbed the prep. *in*. As to its history in combination, see AN- *pref.* 1 below. After 11th c. when *on-* in comb. was generally reduced to *ă-* bef. cons., *ăn-* bef. vowel, the same befell *on* prep. to some extent, esp. in familiar phrases, as *an edge*, *an end*, *an erthe*, *an even* (at eve), *an high*, *an hand*, *an horseback*: see A *prep.*[1] But in course of time all these were altered back to *on*, or changed to *in*; *an* being retained only in those in which its prepositional character was no longer apparent, as to go *an* (now *a*) hawking, twice *an* hour. The following quotations illustrate the forms; for the various uses, see A *prep.*[1] See also AN-AUNTER, AN-END, AN-ERTH.
984 *O.E. Chron.*, An þara twegra apostola dæge. *c* **1175** *Cotton Hom.* 219 Me scel sigge an oðre stowe. *Ibid.*, He.. cweð an his hérto. *c* **1250** *Moral Ode* 270 in *E.E.P.* (1862) 30 An helle for-don. **1297** R. GLOUC. 537 Vpe the tour an hei. *c* **1300** *Beket* 2093 Seint Thomas nom a croice anhonde. *Ibid.* 1236 Lettres.. that thus an Englisch were. *c* **1320** *Cast. Loue* 1177 þe felynge he schal leosen an ende. **1340** *Ayenb.* 168 þis berþ away þane ssepe aneuen. **1377** LANGL. *P.Pl.* B. xx. 143 And armyd hym an [*v.r.* in] haste. *c* **1380** *Sir Ferumb.* 863 And said til hym an haste. *Ibid.* 3552 To þe ryuer an haukyng fare. *c* **1440** LONELICH *Graal* II. 221 And an horsbak setten hym. **1557** N. T. (Genev.) *John* iii. 31 He that commeth from an hye, is aboue all. **1580** LYLY *Euphues* (Arb.) 270 They make the teeth an edge. **1602** SHAKS. *Haml.* I. v. 19 Each particular haire to stand an end, Like Quilles vpon the fretfull Porpentine. **1611** —— *Wint. T.* IV. iii. 7 Set my pugging tooth an edge. **1741** RICHARDSON *Pamela* 64 Your hair will stand an end.

an-, *prefix*, from various sources.
1. OE. and ME. **an-**, = AN *prep.* (see prec.) In OE. the orig. *an-* remained only under the stress, i.e. in sbs.; otherwise, it was, like the separate preposition, rounded to *on-*; thus ˈ*angin* beginning, *onˈginnan* to begin, *onˈbútan* about. An example of the former remains in ANVIL. In ME. *on-* was regularly levelled to *ă-* (A- *pref.* 2); before a vowel (rarely bef. cons.) *ăn-*, as in *anelen*, *aninne*, *anoven*, *anunder*, *anuppe*, *anhigh*, *anblow*, *anlike*. Most of these are now obs.; a few remain with *an-* conformed to the prep. *on*, as *on high*; levelled to *a-* as *alike*; or assimilated to Fr. *en-*, as (?) *enamel*. Only where the individuality of the prefix has been lost, does *an-* remain, in *anon*, *anent*, *an(n)eal* (OE. *on-ǽlan*, ME. *an-ele(n)*.
2. ME. **an-**, reduced f. OE. *and-* 'against, towards, in return for': see AND-.
3. ME. **an-**:—OE. *án* one, retained in early ME., and subseq. in north. dial., in words now written with *on-*, *one-*, or obs.; as *ankenned*, *anfald*, *anhad*, *anlepy*, *anly* (= ONLY), *anmod*, *anred*, *anwill*.
4. ME. **an-**, = Anglo-Norm. *an-*, OFr. *en-*:—L. *in-*, = 'in, into,' as ANOINT (L. *inunctum*), AN(N)OY; *anhaunse*, *anjoin*, *anvenime*, where subsequently spelt *en-*; *andetted*, subseq. *endetted*, *indebted*; *anpayre*, subseq. *apayre*, also *enpayre*, *empayre*, *impair*.
5. ME. **an-**, for earlier *a-* = OE. *a-* (A- *pref.* 1), or OFr. *a-*:—L. *ab-*, *ad-*, *ex-*, *ob-*, which, being phonetically identified with No. 1 above, was like it expanded to *an-* bef. vowels, and occas. bef. consonants: as in *a(n)chesoun* = oc-casion, *a(n)ferm* af-firm, *a(n)ired*, *a(n)oure* ad-ore, *a(n)orn* ad-orn, *a(n)tempered* at-tempered; *a(n)s-aumple* ex-ample. Such of these as survived were either refashioned after L., as *adorn*, or changed *an-* to *en-*, *in-*, as *inorn*; *example*, *ensample*, shows both processes.
6. ME. **an-**, a later spelling of earlier *a-*, = OFr. *a-*:—L. *an-* assimilated form of *ad-* 'to,' when followed by *n-*, after L. forms or supposed analogies, as in *a(n)nounce*. This doubling of the *n* began in 14th c. Fr. and extended to Eng. in 15th c. In 16th c. it was ignorantly extended even to words containing *an-* from other sources, from which it has generally been again ejected exc. in ANNEAL, ANNOY, See AD-.
7. **an-**, repr. L. *an-* = *ad-* before *n-*, in words derived from L. directly, or indirectly through later Fr., and in words formed on the analogy of them, as *an-nex*, *an-nul*, *an-nunciation*.
8. **an-**, repr. L. *an-* before certain consonants, for *am-*, *amb-*, *ambi-*, 'on both sides, about.' Through OFr. in *an-(h)ele*; directly from L. in *an-cipitous*, *an-fractuous*.
9. **an-**, repr. Gr. ἀν- for ἀνά 'up, upwards, back, etc.' (see ANA-) bef. vowel, as in ANAGOGE, Gr. ἀναγωγή; also in ANCHOR *sb.*[2], ANCHORET.
10. **an-**, repr. Gr. ἀν- privative, 'not, without, wanting' (reduced before consonants to ἀ-: see A- *pref.* 14), cognate w. Skr. *an-*, L. *in-*, Eng. *un-*, 'not, non-.' In words already formed in Greek as *an-archy*, *an-arthrous*; whence common in modern scientific words as *an-allagmatic*, *an-alphabetic*, *an-antherous*, *an-isomerous*.

-an, *suffix*. **I.** Derivative. **1.** repr. L. *-ānus*, *-āna*, *-ānum* 'of, or belonging to'; as *castellān-us*, *oppidān-us*, *pāgān-us*, *urbān-us*, *silvān-us*, *Africān-us*, *Rōmān-us*, *Sullān-us*, *Justiniān-us*. In OFr. this became *-ain*, or (after *i*) *-en*, as *chastelain*, *Romain*, *payen*, *Italien*; and so originally adopted in ME., but subseq. refashioned after L. as *-an*, and so in all words formed in Eng. direct, or adopted from the mod. langs. (It. Sp. Pg. *-ano*, Fr. *-ain*, *-en*.). Esp. added to proper names; 'belonging to a place' as *American*, *Chilian*, *Russian*, *Oxonian*; 'following a founder,' as *Arminian*, *Lutheran*, *Muhammadan*, *Linnæan*, or 'a system,' as *Episcopalian*, *Presbyterian*, *Anglican*, *Gallican*; and, in Zoology, to names of divisions, 'belonging to a class or order,' as *mammalian*, *reptilian*, *crustacean*, *arachnidan*, *acalephan*. Primarily these are all adjs., but as in L. etc., all may be used subst., and with some this is the more frequent use. The zoological words supply singulars to the collective plurals in *-a*, as *a crustacean* = a member of the *Crustacea*. Already in L. this termination was often added to others, to *-i-us* so commonly that *-iānus*, -IAN, is in use merely a euphonic variety of *-an*; cf. *Corinth-i-an*, *Rom-an*, *Christ-i-an*, *Muhammad-an*.
2. in *Chem.* for *-ane*, arbitrary ending proposed by Davy for names of chlorides

containing one atom of chlorine, as in *azotan* obs. In some words *-an* is a meaningless formative as *allox-an*.

†**II.** Inflexional. **1.** In OE., ending of oblique cases, and nom. pl. of weak declension. Both became in ME. *-en*, now rarely preserved in pl., as *ox-en*:—OE. *ox-an*. Hence (dat. or loc. sing.) in advb. or prep. forms like *ut-an*, *abut-an*, *befor-an*, ME. *uten*, *abuten*, and *ute*, *abute*. Now obs.

2. In OE., ending of pres. inf. of vbs., levelled in ME. to *-en*, *-e*, and now lost, as OE. *writ-an*, *send-an*; ME. *writ-e(n*, *send-e(n*; mod. *write*, *send*.

ana ('eɪnə, 'ɑːnə), *suff.* and *sb.* [a. L. *-āna* in neut. pl. of adjs. in *-ānus* (see -AN *suffix* 1), as in (*Dicta*) *Virgiliāna* Sayings of Virgil, used in Fr. in 16–17th c. as sb. sing. *un Virgiliana*, and extended to collections of the notable sayings or 'table-talk' of modern authors as *un Huetiana* (Littré); whence also the simple termination was taken substantively *un ana*; both usages were known to Eng. in beginning of 18th c., and subseq. extended or transferred to anecdotes, scraps of information, or gossip *about* persons or places of note.]

A. *suffix*. Appended orig. to proper names, and subsequently also to nouns denoting hobbies, activities, etc. with sense of: **a.** Notable sayings of a person, literary trifles, society verses, items of gossip etc. of a place, as *Walpoliana*, *Tunbrigiana*; **b.** Anecdotes of, notes about, or publications bearing upon, as *Shaksperiana*, *Burnsiana*; **c.** Artefacts and other collectable items associated with a place, period, person, or activity, as AFRICANA, CHURCHILLIANA, CRICKETANA, VICTORIANA 2 etc.; **d.** A style or fashion reminiscent of, or associated with, a particular period, as VICTORIANA.

[**1666** (*title*) Scaligeriana, sive Excerpta ex ore Josephi Scaligeri (*ed.* 1667 Scaligerana).] **1741** (*title*) Caribeeana.. chiefly wrote by several Hands in the West Indies. **1796** PEGGE *Anonymiana*. **1814** (*title*) Frostiana; or the History of the River Thames in a frozen State. **1863** H. BOHN *Lowndes' Bibliogr.* VIII. Pref. 4 The volumes written respecting him, commonly called Shakespeariana.

B. *sb.* **1.** *coll. sing.* (with *pl.*) A collection of the memorable sayings or table-talk of any one.

1727–51 CHAMBERS *Cycl.*, *Ana's*, or books in ana, are collections of the memorable sayings of persons of learning and wit. **1796** PEGGE *Anonym.* (1809) 140 Those observations of the Dutchess's that follow those of her husband are not of the nature of *Anas*, because they are her own. **1834** SOUTHEY *Doctor* ccxxxi. (1862) 623 Boswell's Life of Johnson, which..for its intrinsic worth, is the *Ana* of all *Anas*.

2. *coll. pl.* Clever sayings or anecdotes of any one; notes and scraps of information relating to a person or place; literary gossip.

?*a* **1755** ? G. WEST *to Gray* (T.) They were pleased to publish some Tunbrigiana this season, but such ana! **1842** TENNYSON *Will Waterpr.* xxv, Ere days, that deal in ana, swarm'd His literary leeches. **1881** *Sat. Rev.* No. 1320. 214 To sweep *ana* and gossip out of..biographies.

‖**ana** ('ænə), *adv.* Often written *āā* or *ā*. [med.L. a. Gr. ἀνά (see next), in its advb. sense.] Used in recipes in the sense of *throughout*, *of each*, *of every one alike*, in specifying a quantity applicable to every ingredient; hence sometimes in older literature for 'an equal quantity or number.'

a **1500** *MS. Linc. Med.* 293 (Halliw.) Tak ȝarow and waybrede ana. **1579** LANGHAM *Gard. Health* (1633) 226 Make a tent of Euphorbium, mastick and French sope ana like much. **1651** CLEVELAND *Mixt Assembly* 2 An Assembly brew'd Of Clerks and Elders *ana*. *a* **1667** COWLEY *My self* Wks. 1710 II. 786 In the same Weight Prudence and Innocence take, Ana of each does the just Mixture make. *a* **1700** DRYDEN (J.) He'll bring an apothecary with a chargeable long bill of anas. **1879** *Syd. Soc. Lex.*, *Ana*, of each.

ana- *pref.*, repr. Gr. ἀνά 'up, in place or time, back, again, anew,' in derivatives from Gr., through late or med. L. and Fr., and in mod. words from Gr. direct.

ana. Abbreviated for ANASTOMOSING.

1871 *Athenæum* 27 May 660 The Loddon district is called the County of Gunbower, which means, it is said, an ana branch.

ana, var. of ANNA, an Indian money of account.

anabaptism (ænə'bæptɪz(ə)m). [ad. L. *anabaptism-us* (Aug.), a. Gr. ἀναβαπτισμός, f. ἀνά- over again + βαπτισμός baptism. Cf. Fr. *anabaptisme*.]

1. A second baptism, re-baptism. (The orig. sense in L. from 4th c. onwards.) Also *transf.*

1645 PAGITT *Heresiogr.* (1661) 48 Concerning the Anabaptism of elder people. **1753** CHAMBERS *Cycl. Supp.*, *Anabaptism*..denotes the repetition of baptism, practised on those who had been baptized by heretics. **1826** H. COLERIDGE *Six Months in W. Ind.* 165 They have to undergo a forcible anabaptism in salt water.

2. The doctrine of the Anabaptists; also applied, by opponents, to that of modern 'Baptists.'

1577 tr. *Bullinger's Decades* (1592) Pref., A booke of sermons—without Poperie, Anabaptisme..or any other heresie. **1641** MILTON *Ch. Govt.* vi. (1851) 126 That schisme..would be Brownisme and Anabaptisme indeed. **1856** FROUDE *Hist. Eng.* II. 16 [Wicliffe's] theory of property ..had led him to the near confines of Anabaptism. **1879** BARING-GOULD *Germ.* II. 125 Methodism, Anabaptism, and other forms of Dissent have made no way in Germany.

Anabaptist (ænə'bæptɪst). [ad. mod.L. *anabaptista*: see prec. and -IST. Cf. Fr. *anabaptiste*.]

1. *lit.* One who baptizes over again, whether *frequently* as a point of ritual, or *once* as a due performance of what has been ineffectually performed previously. Hence:

2. *Ch. Hist.* Name of a sect which arose in Germany in 1521.

1532 MORE *Confut. Tindale* Wks. 1557, 656/2 Those abominable heresies..yᵉ Anabaptistes haue added. **1645** PAGITT *Heresiogr.* Ep. Ded., The illuminated Anabaptists, who blasphemously affirm the Baptism of Children to be the mark of the Beast. **1790** BURKE *Fr. Rev.* 225 The Anabaptists of Munster..had filled Germany with confusion by their system of levelling and their wild opinions concerning property. **1856** FROUDE *Hist. Eng.* I. 364 An anarchical Germany..seething with fanatical anabaptists.

3. Applied (more or less opprobriously) to the Protestant religious body called BAPTISTS; formerly also, somewhat loosely, to other rejecters of Anglican doctrine as to the sacraments and 'holy orders.' *arch.* or *Obs.*

1586 H. BARROWE in *Harl. Misc.* (Malh.) II. 30 *Q.* Do you hold it lawful to baptise children? *A.* Yea; I am no anabaptist I thanke God. **1641** MILTON *Ch. Govt.* v. (1851) 115 But is not the type of Priest taken away by Christs comming? No, saith this famous Protestant Bishop of Winchester; it is not, and he that saith it is, is an Anabaptist. **1644** (*title*) The Confession of Faith of those Churches which are commonly (though falsely) called Anabaptists. *a* **1680** BUTLER *Rem.* (1759) II. 385 An Anabaptist is a Water-Saint, that, like a Crocodile, sees clearly in the Water, but dully, on Land. **1809** KENDALL *Trav.* I. xii. 132 The baptists, more properly called anabaptists. **1883** DR. J. ANGUS (in *let.*) Baptists never called themselves *ana*baptists; as they did not admit that immersion even was *baptism*, unless accompanied with an intelligent concurrence, practically, an avowal of faith, on the part of the recipient.

4. *attrib.*

1708 SWIFT *Sacram. Test.* Wks. 1755 II. I. 131 A presbyterian or anabaptist preacher. **1808** SYD. SMITH *Wks.* 1859 I. 106/2 Missions of Anabaptist dissenters. **1858** FROUDE *Hist. Eng.* IV. xxiii. 488 To check Anabaptist and Puritan excesses.

Anabaptistic (ˌænəbæp'tɪstɪk), *a. arch.* [f. prec. + IC.] Of Anabaptists; = ANABAPTIST 4.

1651 BAXTER *Inf. Bapt.* 140 The Church was afterward at more peace from the Anabaptistick fury. **1774** T. WARTON *Eng. Poetry* II. 415 The barbarous reformations of the anabaptistick zealots.

ˌ**Anabap'tistical**, *a.* [f. as prec. + -ICAL.] Connected with or attributed to Anabaptists; according to the opinions or practice of Anabaptists.

1549 LATIMER *7 Serm. bef. Edw. VI* (1869) 48 Pernitious and annabaptisticall opinions. **1589** BP. COOPER *Admon.* 36 An Anabaptisticall equalitie and communitie. **1643** PRYNNE *Sov. Power Parl.* III. 68 Intoxicated with an Anabaptisticall spirit, condemning all kind of warre. **1665** *Surv. Aff. Netherl.* 24 Anabaptistical outrages, such as that in Munster. **1861** MOTLEY *Dutch Rep.* I. 72 As little sympathy with anabaptistical as with Roman depravity.

ˌ**anabap'tistically**, *adv.* [f. prec. + -LY².] In accordance with the practice or doctrines of Anabaptists.

a **1555** BRADFORD *Wks.* 329 To the..scriptures I..do appeal, and not anabaptistically to the Spirit without the scriptures. **1691** WOOD *Ath. Oxon.* II. 412 He being anabaptistically inclin'd, was forced to leave.

Ana'baptistry. ? *Obs.* [f. ANABAPTIST + -RY.]

1. The doctrine or system of Anabaptists.

1553–87 FOXE *A. & M.* (1596) 1888/1 Called before the Margraue, and charged with Anabaptistry. **1651** BAXTER *Inf. Bapt.* 143 Anabaptistry..set out neer the same time and place with Luther's Reformation. **1709** CHANDLER *Effort agst. Bigotry* 14 'Tis not the espousing the Interest of Diocesan Episcopacy..Independency or Anabaptistry, that will make a good Man of a bad.

†**2.** Repetition of baptism, or *transf.* of any ceremony. *Obs.*

1659 HEYLIN *Animadv.* in Fuller *Appeal* (1840) 461 King Henry..would not be twice married to the same woman; that being a kind of bigamy, or Anabaptistry in marriage.

anabaptize (ˌænəbæp'taɪz), *v.* [ad. med.L. *anabaptīzā-re*, ad. Gr. ἀναβαπτίζ-ειν to baptize repeatedly or over again, f. ἀνά- over again + βαπτίζειν to baptize.] To baptize over again, re-baptize, re-christen; *hence*, to re-name.

1637 POCKLINGTON *Sunday no Sabb.* 6 And anabaptizing of it after the mind of some Jew..call it the Sabbath. **1663** BUTLER *Hudibr.* I. iii. 40 As Achilles dipt in Pond, Was Anabaptiz'd free from wound. **1799** SOUTHEY in C. Southey *Life* II. 31 The Dom Daniel romance is rechristened, anabaptized Thalaba the Destroyer. **1848** H. COLERIDGE *North. Worth.* I. 82 Marvell..now anabaptized Dr. Turner as Mr. Smirke.

anabaptizing (ˌænəbæp'taɪzɪŋ), *vbl. sb.* [f. prec. + -ING¹.] A baptizing over again; re-baptizing.

1660 FELL *Hammond* § 1 The anabaptizing of infants.

anabaptizing (ˌænəbæp'taɪzɪŋ), *ppl. a.* [f. as prec. + -ING².] That baptizes over again.

1642 FULLER *Holy & Prof. St.* v. xi. 399 Heare the Anabaptizing sing the same note.

‖**anabas** ('ænəbæs). [mod.L. (Cuvier), a. Gr. ἀναβάς, pple. of ἀναβαίν-ειν to walk up.] A genus of acanthopterygian fishes, which sometimes leave the water, and even ascend trees.

1845 in *Penny Cycl.* 1st Supp. 106/1. **1859** CARPENTER *Anim. Phys.* vi. (1872) 273 The Anabas or climbing-perch of Tranquebar which climbs bushes and trees in search of its prey.

‖**anabasis** (ə'næbəsɪs). [a. Gr. ἀνάβασις ascent, going up, f. ἀνα-βαίν-ειν to go or walk up; cf. βάσις going, walk.]

1. A going up, a march up, a military advance; the special title of the advance of Cyrus the Younger into Asia, as narrated by Xenophon; also transferred to other expeditions.

1706 PHILLIPS, *Anabasis*, an ascending or getting up, an Ascent or Rise. **1840** DE QUINCEY *Style* Wks. XI. 245 The most..productive year throughout his oriental anabasis, was the year 333 before Christ. **1864** *Spect.* 31 Dec. 1491 General Sherman's great anabasis, which the *Times* has at last ceased to call a retreat.

†**2.** The course of a disease from the commencement to the climax. *Obs.*

1706 PHILLIPS, *Anabasis*..in the Art of Physick, the growth or encrease of a disease. **1853** MAYNE *Exp. Lex.*, 'An old term.' **1879** *Syd. Soc. Lex.*, 'Used by Galen.'

‖**a'nabathrum.** *Obs.* Adapted by Cockeram as **anabather.** [L., a. Gr. ἀνάβαθρ-ον an elevated seat, f. ἀνά up + βάθρον a base, step, bench, f. βα-go.] A raised seat or platform; a pulpit.

1623 COCKERAM, *Anabather*, a pulpit. **1759** MARTIN *Nat. Hist.* I. 261 The Anabathrum, whereon the Communion Table is placed.

anabatic (ænə'bætɪk), *a.* [ad. Gr. ἀναβατικ-ός pertaining to ἀναβάτης 'one who ascends': see ANABASIS.] **1.** *Med.* Of or belonging to anabasis; augmenting, increasing (as a fever).

1811 HOOPER *Med. Dict.*, *Anabatica*. **1853** MAYNE *Exp. Lex.*, *Anabaticus*..augmenting, increasing, anabatic; applied formerly to a continued fever, the symptoms of which gradually increase in severity. **1879** in *Syd. Soc. Lex.*

2. *Meteorol.* Of a wind: caused by the (local) upward motion of warmed air. Cf. KATABATIC *a.*

1918 *Meteorol. Gloss.* 29 *Anabatic*, referring to the upward motion of air due to convection. **1919** FARADAY *Gloss. Aeronaut. Terms* 31 A local wind is called anabatic if it is caused by the convection of heated air, as, for example, the breeze that blows up valleys when the sun warms the ground.

anabiosis (ˌænəbaɪ'əʊsɪs). *Biol.* [mod.L., ad. Gr. ἀναβίωσις, f. ἀναβιόειν: see ANABIOTIC *a.*] A coming to life again; revival, resuscitation; see also quot. 1963.

1890 BILLINGS *Med. Dict.*, *Anabiosis*, the power which certain organisms possess of regaining vital activity after being dried and heated. **1913** J. G. FRAZER *Belief in Immortality* I. III. 85 John Hunter, supported by his experiments on *anabiosis*, hoped to prolong the life of man indefinitely by alternate freezing and thawing. **1926** *Chambers's Jrnl.* 1 May 349/2 From latent life there can be a protoplasmic resurrection, learnedly called 'Anabiosis'. **1963** *Times* 28 Feb. 8/2 Spacemen might one day be put in a state of anabiosis—in which the body functions are greatly slowed down and food is not necessary—for long space journeys, and then revived as they neared their destination.

anabiotic (ˌænəbaɪ'ɒtɪk), *a. Med.* [f. Gr. ἀνά again + βιωτικ-ός pertaining to life; cf. ἀναβιό-ειν to come to life again.] Acting as a stimulant or tonic.

[Not in MAYNE 1860.] **1879** in *Syd. Soc. Lex.*

anabolic (ænə'bɒlɪk), *a. Biol.* [f. Gr. ἀναβολή (*lit.* a throwing up), ascent, etc. + -IC.] Pertaining to, involving, or exhibiting anabolism; constructively metabolic: opp. to CATABOLIC.

1876 [see CATABOLIC *a.*]. **1885** *Encycl. Brit.* XIX. 13/2 An upward series of changes (*anabolic* changes). **1889** GEDDES & THOMPSON *Evol. Sex* ii. 26 The males live at a loss, are more katabolic... The females..live at a profit, are more anabolic —constructive processes predominating in their life, whence indeed the capacity of bearing offspring. *a* **1901** F. W. H. MYERS *Hum. Pers.* (1903) II. 514 The katabolic as well as the anabolic forces, the output as well as the intake of the bodily frame, are amenable..to subliminal control. **1962** *Lancet* 12 May 986/2 The second, or anabolic, phase in the newborn child also resembles the anabolic state after injury.

anabolism (ə'næbəlɪz(ə)m). *Biol.* [f. as prec. + -ISM.] The 'ascending' process in metabolism, in which simpler substances, as nutritive matter, are transformed into more complex ones, and thus built up into the living structure of the organism; constructive metabolism: opp. to CATABOLISM.

1886 W. H. GASKELL in *Jrnl. Physiol.* VII. 46 In other words, metabolism includes the two opposite processes of destruction and construction, or as they may be called of katabolism and anabolism. **1889** GEDDES & THOMSON *Evol. Sex* x. 122 These upbuilding, constructive, synthetic processes are summed up in the phrase anabolism. **1897** WILLIS *Flower. Pl.* I. 206 Metabolism .. may be divided into anabolism, the building up, and katabolism, the breaking down, of complex materials. **1959** *Chambers's Encycl.* II. 318/1 Growth, and all other processes involving chemical synthesis, are processes in which energy is consumed, and all such are grouped together under the title of anabolism. *Ibid.* IX. 309/1 Processes which lead to an increase in chemical complexity making up anabolism. *Ibid.*, Only the energy of their food can be put to service for anabolism, muscular movement and so on.

anabranch ('ænəbrɑːn(t)ʃ, -æ-). *Physical Geogr.* [f. ANA(STOMOSING *ppl. a.* + BRANCH *sb.*] Esp. in Australia: a branch stream which turns out of a river and re-enters it lower down.

1834 J. R. JACKSON in *Jrnl. R. Geogr. Soc.* IV. 79 Thus, such branches of a river as after separation re-unite, I would term anastomosing-branches; or, if a word might be coined, ana-branches. **1847** LEICHHARDT *Jrnl.* ii. 35 The river .. divided into ana-branches which .. made the whole valley a maze of channels. **1849** STURT *Central Austr.* I. 93 To ascertain how high the back-waters of the Murray had gone up the Ana-branch of the Darling. **1907** H. LAWSON *Send round the Hat* in *Prose Wks.* (1948) 649 He rode round the outside track and came in on to the river just below where the anabranch joins it.

‖**ana'brosis**. *Med. Obs.* [Gr. ἀνάβρωσις eating up, f. ἀνα-βρω- stem of ἀναβιβρώσκ-ειν to eat up.] Corrosion or ulceration of the soft parts of the body.

1721 in BAILEY. **1751** CHAMBERS *Cycl.*, *Anabrosis* .. the issuing of blood at a hole worn in a vein by corrosion. **1853** MAYNE *Exp. Lex.*, *Anabrosis*, used by Galen for a corrosion or exesion of the soft parts.

†**ana'brotic**, *a. Med. Obs.* [ad. Gr. ἀναβρωτικ-ός corrosive: see prec. and -IC.] 'A term formerly applied to corrosive agents.' *Syd. Soc. Lex.* 1879.

‖**ana'campserote**. *Obs.* [Fr., ad. L. *anacampserōs*, *-ōtem*, a. Gr. ἀνακαμψέρως, -έρωτα, f. ἀνακάμπ-τ-ειν to bend back + ἔρως love.] A herb feigned to restore departed love.

[**1611** COTGR., *Anacampserote*, a certain herb whose touch reneweth decayed love.] **1708** MOTTEUX *Rabelais* v. xxxi, Let's taste some of these Anacampserotes that hang over our heads.

‖**anacampsis** (ænə'kæmpsɪs). [Gr. ἀνάκαμψις bending back, n. of action f. ἀνακάμπ-τ-ειν: see next.] Reflection; reaction.

1879 *Syd. Soc. Lex.*, *Anacamptic*, pertaining to anacampsis.

anacamptic (ænə'kæmptɪk), *a.* [mod. f. Gr. ἀνακάμπ-τ-ειν to bend back (f. ἀνά back + κάμπ-τ-ειν to bend) + -IC; cf. Gr. καμπτικ-ός liable to bend.] Causing or suffering reflection; chiefly in reference to sound.

1706 PHILLIPS [see ANACAMPTICAL]. **1751** CHAMBERS *Cycl.*, *Anacamptic* signifies as much as reflecting; and is frequently used in reference to echoes. **1847** CRAIG, *Anacamptic sound*, an echo; *anacamptic hill*, a hill that produces an echo.

†**ana'camptical**, *a. Obs.* [f. as prec. + -ICAL.]

1706 PHILLIPS, *Anacamptical* or *Anacamptick*, Reflecting, Turning or Bowing back or again, a Word often used with respect to Echoes, which are Sounds produced *Anacamptically* or by Reflection.

ana'camptically, *adv.* [f. prec. + -LY².] By way of anacampsis or reflection.

1706 PHILLIPS [see prec.]. **1727** CHAMBERS *Cycl.* (1741) s.v. *Anacamptic*, Echoes .. are said to be sounds produced anacamptically, or by reflexion. **1796** HUTTON [see next].

†**anacamptics** (ænə'kæmptɪks), *sb. pl. Obs.* [ANACAMPTIC *a.* used in pl., after *acoustics*, *politics*, etc.: see -ICS.]

1. The branch of Optics now called CATOPTRICS.

1696 PHILLIPS, *Anacamptics*, a branch of Opticks call'd Catopticks. **1755** JOHNSON, *Anacampticks*, the doctrine of reflected light, or catoptricks.

2. The branch of Acoustics, that relates to reflection of sound.

1796 HUTTON *Math. Dict.*, *Anacamptics*, or the science of the reflections of sounds, frequently used in reference to echoes, which are said to be sounds produced anacamptically, or by reflection.

anacard ('ænəkɑːd). [a. Fr. *anacarde*, ad. mod.L. *anacardus* and *anacardium*, f. Gr. ἀνά according to + καρδία heart, in reference to shape of the fruit. Now commonly used in L. form.]

1. The Cashew-nut; the fruit of *Anacardium occidentale*, a West Indian tree; applied by Lindley to any plant of N.O. *Anacardiaceæ*.

1541 R. COPLAND *Guydon's Quest. Cyrurg.*, Some .. maketh scarres as lyme and sope and anacardus. **1657** TOMLINSON *Renou's Disp.* 78 Anacardian Honey is expressed out of small and young Anacards. **1712** tr. *Pomet's Hist. Drugs* I. 133 Anacardium is a kind of large Fruit like a Chesnut. **1753** CHAMBERS *Cycl. Supp.* s.v., The pith or medullary part of the Anacardium is extremely pungent and acrimonious. **1833** *Penny Cycl.* I. 484/2 The Cashew, or Acajou nut, anacardium. **1847** LINDLEY *Veg. Kingd.* 465 *Anacardiaceæ*, Anacards, or Terebinths.

ana'cardate. *Chem.* See ANACARDIC.

anacardiaceous (æna,kɑːdɪ'eɪʃəs), *a. Bot.* [f. mod.L. *anacardi-um* (see above) + -ACEOUS.] Belonging to the family *Anacardiaceæ*, to which the Cashew-nut belongs, as well as the trees that produce mangos, pistachios, mastic, and fustic.

1853 in MAYNE *Exp. Lex.*

†**ana'cardian**, *a. Obs.* [f. as prec. + -AN.] = next.

1657 [See ANACARD].

anacardic (ænə'kɑːdɪk), *a.* [f. as prec. + -IC.] Of the Anacardium or Cashew-nut; as in *anacardic acid*, $C_{44}H_{64}O_7$, extracted, together with cardol, by the action of ether on the pericarps of the cashew-nut. Its salts are **anacardates**.

1863 WATTS *Dict. Chem.* I. 209 From the solution of anacardate of ammonium .. the anacardic acid is liberated by the addition of sulphuric acid.

†**ana'cardine**, *a. Obs. rare*⁻¹. [f. as prec. + -INE¹.] = prec.

1585 H. LLOYD *Treas. Health* X viij, Take of Hierologodion .. of honye Anacardine .. mengle them together, and mele pilles. **1751** CHAMBERS *Cycl.* s.v. *Confection*, The anacardine confection .. is composed chiefly of anacardiums.

anacathartic (,ænəkə'θɑːtɪk), *a.* and *sb. Med.* [f. Gr. ἀνά upward + CATHARTIC.]

A. *adj.* Causing *anacatharsis*, i.e. vomiting or expectoration.

1696 PHILLIPS, *Anacathartic*, purging by the upper parts; as provoking to vomit, sweat or salivation. **1753** CHAMBERS *Cycl. Supp.* s.v., Blancard .. extends anacathartic medicines to all those which work upwards. **1853** in MAYNE *Exp. Lex.*

B. *sb.* An anacathartic medicine or drug. (Now commonly written ANOCATHARTIC.)

‖**anacephalæosis** (,ænəsɛfəliː'əʊsɪs). *rare.* [Gr. ἀνακεφαλαίωσις, n. of action f. ἀνακεφαλαιό-ειν to recapitulate, f. ἀνά back + κεφαλή head. Cf. Fr. *anacephaléose*.] 'Recapitulation, or summary of the principal heads of a discourse.' J.

1650 BULWER *Anthropomet.* Pref., A through-description .. being indeed an Anacephaliosis of the whole book. **1666** J. SMITH *Old Age* 248 (T.) As hath been said and is resumed in the following Anacephalæosis. **1721** in BAILEY.

anacephalize (ænə'sɛfəlaɪz), *v.* ? *Obs.* [f. Gr. ἀνά up, back + κεφαλή head + -IZE.] To recapitulate.

1654 GAYTON *Fest. Notes* IV. xv. 252 Mr. Licentiat .. succinctly, and concisely Anacephalyz'd, Analyz'd and Epitomiz'd the long story. **1701** BEVERLEY *Praise of Grace* 4 In this Text, he Anacephalizes, and sums up all the great Acts of God. [Not in JOHNSON.]

‖**anacharis** (ə'nækərɪs). [mod.L. f. Gr. ἀνά up + χάρις grace.] A North American water-weed (*A. Alsinastrum*, also called *Elodea Canadensis*) the only species of its genus, remarkable for its unexplained appearance in Britain in 1842, and the rapidity with which it filled canals, ditches, and ponds, all over the country.

1848 *Phytol.* III. 30 A specimen of the Leicestershire Udora or Anacharis. *Ibid.* 390 The force of the current detached small sprigs of the Anacharis. **1852** W. MARSHALL *New Water Weed* 6 Last year the Anacharis was noticed by myself and others in the river at Ely. **1855** KINGSLEY *Glaucus* (1878) 205 *Anacharis alsinastrum*, that magical weed which, lately introduced from Canada among timber, has multiplied self-sown.

anachoret(e, anachorite, var. ANCHORITE. (*Anachoret*, literally representing Gr. ἀναχωρητ-ής, is sometimes spec. applied to the primitive Anchorets of Egypt and the East.)

†**anacho'retal**, *a. Obs.*⁻⁰ [f. L. *anachōrēt-a*, ad. Gr. ἀναχωρητ-ής a recluse (see ANCHORITE) + -AL¹.] Pertaining to an anchoret; = ANCHORETIC.

1656 BLOUNT *Glossogr.* [see next].

anacho'retical, *a. rare.* [f. Gr. ἀναχωρητικ-ός of the nature of an ANCHORITE + -AL¹.] After the manner of an anchoret. (See ANCHORETICAL.)

1656 BLOUNT *Glossogr.*, *Anachoretical*, *Anachoretal*, belonging to solitariness or Hermites. **1845** G. PETRIE *Eccles. Archit. Irel.* 113 He betook himself to an anachoretical life.

anachorism (ə'nækərɪz(ə)m). *nonce-wd.* [formed, to match *anachronism*, on Gr. ἀνά back + χωρίον country, place: see -ISM.] Something out of place in, or foreign to, the country.

1862 LOWELL *Bigl. Papers* Ser. II. 55 Opinions [that are] anachronisms and anachorisms, foreign both to the age and the country.

†**a'nachorist**. *Obs. rare.* [f. Gr. ἀναχωρέ-ειν to retire + -IST.] An anchoret. (See ANCHORIST.)

a **1604** HANMER *Chron. Irel.* 90 An Abbot of Irish birth that became a recluse or an anachorist.

anachronic (ænə'krɒnɪk), *a.* [f. Gr. ἀνά up, against + χρόν-ος time + -IC: cf. *chronic*.] Erroneous in date; out of right chronological position or order; characterized by anachronism.

1807 W. TAYLOR in *Ann. Rev.* V. 502 The unconnected, the anachronic, the dissonant circumstances. **1819** COLERIDGE *Lect. Shaks.* I. 276 The anachronic mixture .. of the Roman republican .. with his James-and-Charles-the-First zeal for legitimacy of descent .. is amusing. **1879** G. MEREDITH *Egoist* I. Prel. 8 Better .. have held stubbornly to all ancestral ways, than have bred that anachronic spectre.

anachronical (ænə'krɒnɪkəl), *a. rare.* [f. prec. + -AL¹.] = prec.

1859 in WORCESTER. **1880** *Spect.* 25 Dec. 1655, I had a great, though anachronical, love of verse.

ana'chronically, *adv.* [f. prec. + -LY².] Erroneously as to date; out of correct chronological position or order; by anachronism.

1813 W. TAYLOR in *Month. Rev.* LXX. 133 Anachronically given after the alteration of the calendar. **1866** *Songs & Bal. Cumbld.* 439 *note*, Friends of the author introduced here anachronically.

†**ana'chronicism**. *Obs.*⁻⁰ [f. ANACHRONIC + -ISM; cf. *scepticism*.] = next.

1656 in BLOUNT *Glossogr.*

anachronism (ə'nækrənɪz(ə)m). [a. Fr. *anachronisme*, ad. L. *anachronism-us*, a. Gr. ἀναχρονισμ-ός, n. of action f. ἀναχρονίζ-ειν to refer to a wrong time, f. ἀνά up, backwards + χρόν-ος time.]

1. An error in computing time, or fixing dates; the erroneous reference of an event, circumstance, or custom to a wrong date. Said *etymologically* (like *prochronism*) of a date which is too early, but also used of too late a date, which has been distinguished as *parachronism*.

a **1646** J. G[REGORY] *De Æris et Ep.* (1650) 174 An error committed herein [in a Synchronism] is called Anachronism. **1669** GALE *Crt. Gentiles* I. III. viii. 85 This error sprang from Anachronisme, and confusion of Histories. **1704** HEARNE *Duct. Hist.* (1714) I. 7 Virgil making Dido and Æneas Co-temporaries, whereas they lived at Three Hundred Years distance .. committed an Anachronism. **1798** FERRIAR *Eng. Histor.* 249 An anachronism of thirty or forty years .. is easily overlooked. **1856** MRS. STOWE *Dred* (1856) I. Pref., Some anachronisms with regard to the time of the session of courts have been allowed. **1876** E. MELLOR *Priesth.* iv. 172 The so-called literal interpretation involves an anachronism, inasmuch as it antedates the death of our Lord upon the cross.

2. Anything done or existing out of date; *hence*, anything which was proper to a former age, but is, or, if it existed, would be, out of harmony with the present; also called a *practical anachronism*. Also *transf.* of persons.

1816 COLERIDGE *Lay Serm.* 329 If this one-eyed experience does not seduce its worshipper into practical anachronisms. **1859** JEPHSON *Brittany* ix. 145 A pilgrimage now seems an anachronism. **1864** *Round Table* 18 June 4/3 She gives them phrases and words which .. had their beginning long since that period, and are in fact linguistic anachronisms. **1871** *Daily News* 15 Apr. 2 [The Benchers] would be living anachronisms in this age of progress, were it not that they are extremely fond of good eating. **1899** B. HARRADEN *Fowler* I. vii, 'Sentiment,' she repeated. 'It is absurd to try and hustle sentiment off the scenes.' .. 'You are always an anachronism,' he said, quietly. **1952** M. MCCARTHY *Groves of Academe* iii. 37 She herself was a smoldering anachronism, a throwback to one of those ardent young women of the Sixties, Turgenev's heroines.

a,nachronis'matical, *a.* [f. prec.; cf. *schismatical*.] Anachronistic.

1847 BARHAM *Ing. Leg.* (1877) 182 The author has introduced many .. anachronismatical interpolations.

anachronist (ə'nækrənɪst). *rare*⁻¹. [f. ANACHRON-ISM + -IST.] One who commits or supports an anachronism; one out of harmony with his own time.

1842 DE QUINCEY *Pagan Oracles* Wks. VIII. 194 Modern appraisers of the oracular establishments are too commonly in all moral senses anachronists.

anachronistic (ə,nækrə'nɪstɪk), *a.* [f. as prec. + -ISTIC.] Of the nature of, or involving, anachronism.

1775 T. WARTON *Eng. Poetry* (1840) II. xxiii. 303 The anachronistic improprieties, which this poem contains. **1876** G. MEREDITH *Beauch. Career* II. xi. 199 He glanced contemptuously at his uncle Everard's anachronistic notions of what was fair in war. **1882** *Daily News* 4 May 5/3 The position of the Church of England is anachronistic and cannot last.

anachronitism (Blount *Glossogr.*), erron. f. ANACHRONISM.

anachronize (ə'nækrənaɪz), *v. rare*⁻¹. [ad. Gr. ἀναχρονίζ-ειν to confound time: see ANACHRONISM.] To put into a wrong chronological position; to transfer to a different time.

1870 LOWELL *Among my Bks.* Ser. I. (1873) 198 One of his contemporaries who endeavoured to anachronize himself.

anachronous (ə'nækrənəs), *a.* [f. Gr. ἀνά up + χρόν-ος time + -OUS.] Involving anachronism; out of proper chronological position, out of date.

1854 *Illustr. Lond. News* 30 Sept. 317 His impressions.. were after all a mass of anachronous entanglement and historical confusion. **1880** C. HERFORD *Romant. & Class. Styles* 25 Beguiled by the affected archaism of Spenser into the use of stanzas as anachronous as his language.

anachronously (ə'nækrənəslı), *adv. rare.* [f. prec. + -LY².] In a way which involves an anachronism; without regard to correct chronology.

1828 W. TAYLOR *Germ. Poetry* I. 179 It is more convenient, therefore, somewhat anachronously to marshal in groups those writers who acted on one another.

†**anack.** *Obs.* (See quot.)

1615 G. MARKHAM *Eng. Hous-wife* 177 With this small meal Oat-meal is made.. six severall kinds of very good and wholsome bread, every one finer than another, as your Anacks, Janacks, and such like. **1725** BRADLEY *Fam. Dict.* s.v. *Oatmeal*, They make good and wholsome Bread thereof in several Counties.. as Anacks, Sanacks [*sic*]. **1750** W. ELLIS *Countr. Housewife* 205 [as in Markham].

‖**anaclasis** (ə'nækləsıs). *Pros.* Also -klasis. Pl. -ases. [mod.L., a. Gr. ἀνάκλασις bending back (see ANACLASTIC *a.*).] In Ionic verse: an interchange of the final long syllable of the first metron with the opening short syllable of the second.

1784 J. B. SEALE *Anal. Gr. Metres* 25 In the intermediate places a second Pæon is occasionally joined to a second or third Epitrite, so that the two Feet together are equal in time to two Ionic Feet. This is called an Ανακλασις. **1830** J. SEAGER tr. *Hermann's Doctrine of Metres* xxxviii. 98 This method is termed ἀνάκλασις, and the verses themselves ἀνακλώμενοι, because the change in the numbers is not made in one Ionic foot, but in two, the end of the one, and the beginning of the other being changed. **1900** [in def. of GALLIAMBIC *a.*]. **1901** T. D. GOODELL *Chapt. Gr. Metric* v. 144 Not only were ionic kola extended to eighteen lines, with or without anaklasis, but also the plain iambic and trochaic. **1938** G. D. THOMSON tr. *Aeschylus: Oresteia* II. 327 A rearrangement of the opening syllables (anaclasis). **1949** *Oxf. Classical Dict.* 567/1 The view.. that the anacreontic is derived from the ionic dimeter by the interchange of the final long of the first metron with the opening short of the second ('anaclasis').

anaclastic (ænə'klɑːstık, -æ-), *a.* and *sb.* [f. Gr. ἀνάκλαστ-ος refracted (f. ἀνα-κλά-ειν to refract, bend back, f. κλά-ειν to break) + -IC.] **A.** *adj.*

1. *Opt.* Pertaining to refraction; produced by refraction through a medium of different density.

1796 HUTTON *Math. Dict.*, *Anaclastic Curves*, a name given by M. de Mairan to certain apparent curves formed at the bottom of a vessel full of water.. or the vault of the heavens, seen by refraction through the atmosphere. **1879** *Syd. Soc. Lex.*, *Anaclastic*, applied to that point where a luminous ray is refracted.

2. Springing back with a crackling sound; as in *anaclastic glasses* (see quot.).

1753 CHAMBERS *Cycl. Supp.*, *Anaclastic glasses* are a low kind of phials with flat bellies, resembling inverted funnels, whose bottoms are very thin.. and.. a little convex. But upon applying the mouth to the orifice, and gently.. sucking out the air, the bottom gives way with a horrible crack, and of convex becomes concave. On the contrary upon.. breathing gently into the orifice, the bottom with no less noise bounds back to its former place. **1815** *Encycl. Brit.* II. 166 Anaclastic Glasses, a kind of sonorous phials or glasses, chiefly made in Germany.

3. *Pros.* Of, pertaining to, or involving anaclasis.

1889 in *Cent. Dict.* **1912** J. W. WHITE *Verse Gr. Comedy* viii. 185 Normal and anaclastic metres may correspond in strophe and antistrophe. **1949** *Oxf. Classical Dict.* 566/2 The *hypodochmius*, or 'anaclastic' dochmius, inverts the first two elements, -⏑-⏑-. **1957** W. BEARE *Latin Verse & Europ. Song* vii. 83 Ionic Verse (a minore ⏑⏑--, a maiore --⏑⏑).. is.. highly emotional, particularly in its 'anaclastic' or 'broken' form (⏑⏑-⏑-⏑--).

B. *sb.* [Cf. *acoustics*.] The part of optics which treats of refraction; dioptrics.

1696 PHILLIPS, *Anaclatics*, a part also of Opticks which by the Lines of the Stars, and other visual Objects, refracted in a medium of a different thickness, measures their figures, magnitudes, distances, etc. [So spelt and defined in BAILEY, JOHNSON, ASH.] **1789** HOWARD *Encycl.*, *Anaclastics*.

anaclete ('ænəkliːt). *rare.* [ad. Gr. ἀνάκλητ-ος recalled, f. ἀνα-καλέ-ειν to call back, f. stem κ(α)λε- call; cf. *paraclete*.] (See quot.)

1817 COLERIDGE *Own Times* (1850) III. 356 The Heathen Priests and Philosophers hailed him [Julian the Apostate] the divine *Anaclete* (the Recalled), the re-ascending Apollo.

anaclinal (ænə'klaınəl), *a. Geol.* [f. Gr. ἀνά back + κλίν-ειν to bend + -AL.] Of a valley, river, etc.: descending in a direction opposite to the dip of the underlying rocks.

1875 J. W. POWELL *Explor. Colorado River* xi. 160 Transverse valleys.. three varieties are noticed.. (*c*) anaclinal, valleys that run against the dip of the beds. **1941** C. A. COTTON *Landscape* iv. 25 Those flowing in the reverse direction are 'anti-dip' or 'anaclinal' streams.

anaclitic (ænə'klıtık), *a. Psychol.* [f. Gr. ἀνάκλιτ-ος for reclining (ἀνακλίνειν to lean back, recline) + -IC.] Orig. in phr. *anaclitic type* (tr. G. *Anlehnungstypus* (Freud), lit. 'leaning-on type'), a person whose choice of a 'love object' is governed by the dependence of the libido on another instinct, e.g. hunger; also in extended use, characterized by dependence on another or others (see quots.).

1922 J. RIVIERE tr. *Freud's Introd. Lect. Psycho-Analysis* III. xxvi. 356 The anaclitic type (*Anlehnungstypus*) in which those persons who become prized on account of the satisfactions they rendered to the primal needs of life are chosen as objects by the Libido also. **1922** J. STRACHEY tr. *Freud's Group Psychol.* vii. 60 The boy has begun to develop a true object-cathexis towards his mother according to the anaclitic type. **1930** W. HEALY et al. *Struct. & Meaning of Psychoanalysis* II. 106 These attachments are likely in the beginning to be strongly anaclitic in nature; the child will turn first to those who assist it in its helplessness and gratify its self-preservative needs. **1934** H. C. WARREN *Dict. Psychol.* 12/1 *Anaclitic object-choice*, taking one's earliest attachments (to mother or nurse) as a model for the selection of the first love object. Contr. w. *narcissistic object-choice*.

‖**anacœnosis** (,ænəsiː'nəʊsıs). *Rhet.* [med.L., a. Gr. ἀνακοίνωσις, n. of action f. ἀνακοινό-ειν to communicate, f. ἀνά back + κοινό-ειν to make common, f. κοιν-ός common.] 'A figure in rhetoric, by which the speaker applies to his hearers or opponents for their opinion upon the point in debate.' T.

1589 PUTTENHAM *Eng. Poesie* (Arb.) 235 *Anacœnosis* [printed *Anachinosis*] or the Impartener. **1657** J. SMITH *Myst. Rhet.* 152 Anacœnosis.. is elegantly used with such as are (1) Dead: (2) with the Judge: (3) with the Hearers: (4) with the Opponent: (5) with such as are absent: (6) with sensitive or inanimate things. **1753** CHAMBERS *Cycl. Supp.*, *Anacœnosis*.. when we consult the adversary, or appeal to the judges.

‖**anacoluthia** (,ænəkəʊ'l(j)uːθıə). [L., a. Gr. ἀνακολουθία want of sequence.] A want of grammatical sequence; the passing from one construction to another before the former is completed.

1856 G. WOODS *Madvig's Lat. Gr.* 434 This want of strict grammatical coherence is called Anacoluthia.

anacoluthic (,ænəkəʊ'l(j)uːθık), *a. rare.* [f. ANACOLUTH-ON + -IC.] Of or pertaining to anacolutha; lacking grammatical sequence.

1859 WORCESTER cites LANE. **1873** tr. *Buttman's Gram. N.T.* 379 The great number of anacoluthic thoughts, sentences, periods, in all the writers of the N.T. *Ibid.* 382 In similar anacoluthic style we read, John xv. 5.

anaco'luthically, *adv.* [f. prec. + -AL¹ + -LY².] In anacoluthic manner.

1873 tr. *Buttman's Gram. N.T.* 381 Participles used anacoluthically in the Greek writers.

‖**anacoluthon** (,ænəkəʊ'l(j)uːθən). *Gram.* Pl. -a, (-ons). [a. L., a. Gr. ἀνακόλουθ-ον wanting sequence, f. ἀν priv. + ἀκόλουθ-ος following, f. ἀ copul. + κέλευθ-ος a road, or march.] An instance of anacoluthia, a phrase or series of words in which it appears.

[Not in JOHNSON 1755, CRAIG 1847.] **1706** PHILLIPS, *Anacolython*, a Rhetorical Figure, when a Word that is to answer another is not express'd. **1753** CHAMBERS *Cycl. Supp.*, *Anacoluthon* among antient grammarians denotes an incoherence, or a construction which does not hang together. **1860** JOWETT *Ess. & Rev.* (ed. 2) 397 The verbal oppositions and anacolutha of St. Paul. **1876** SWEET *Anglo-Sax. Reader* i. 1 The style is of the rudest character.. abrupt, disconnected, obscure and full of anacoluthons.

anaconda (ænə'kɒndə). Also -o. [Occurs in Ray, in a List of Indian Serpents from the Leyden Museum, as '*anacandaia* of the Ceylonese, i.e. he that crushes the limbs of buffaloes and yoke beasts,' but not now a native name in Ceylon, and not satisfactorily explained either in Cingalese or Tamil. (Cf. however Tamil ānaik'k'*on*ḍa 'having killed an elephant,' Col. Yule.)] A name (*a*) originally applied (by English writers) to a 'very large and terrible snake' of Ceylon (? *Python reticulatus*, or *P. molurus* Gray); but (*b*) made by Daudin (? through erroneous identification, or mistake as to the source of a specimen) the specific name of a large South American Boa (*Boa murina* Linn., *B. aquatica* Neuwied., *B. anacondo* Daud., *Eunectes murinus* Wagler, Gray), called in Brazil *sucuriù*, or *sucuriuba*, to which it is now attached in the British Museum Catalogue, and London Zoological Gardens. (*c*) *loosely* applied to any large snake which crushes its prey.

(*a*) [**1693** RAY *Synop. Method.* 332 Serpens Indicus Bubalinus, *Anacandaia* Zeylonensibus, id est *Bubalorum aliorumque jumentorum membra conterens*.] **1768** *Scots Mag.* Append. 673 *Description of the Anaconda*, a monstrous species of Serpent [a fictitious 'Letter' founded on Ray]. The Ceylonese seemed to know the creature well; they call it *Anaconda*. **1797** *Encycl. Brit.*, *Anacondo*, a name given in the isle of Ceylon to a very large and terrible snake which often devours the unfortunate traveller alive. **1808** *Lady's Monthly Mus.* V. 121 An account of the Anocondo, a monstrous serpent in the East Indies, and of the manner of its seizing and managing its prey. **1810** *Encycl. Lond.* IV. 61 s.v. *Ceylon*, The vast boa the Anacændaia of the Ceylonese is common here. **1849** PRIDHAM *Ceylon* II. 750 *Pimbeva* or *anaconda* is of the genus Python, and is known in English as the Rock Snake[*P. molurus*]. **1859** TENNENT *Ceylon* (ed. 2) I. 196 The great python [*P. reticulatus* Gray] the 'boa' as it is commonly designated by Europeans, the 'anaconda' of Eastern story, which is supposed to crush the bones of an elephant, and to swallow the tiger, is found.. in the cinnamon gardens. **1859** D. KING in *Jrnl. R.G.S.* XXX. 181 The skins of anacondas offered at Bangkok come from the northern provinces.

(*b*) **1836** *Penny Cycl.* V. 27 This.. according to Cuvier, is the *Boa aquatica* of Prince Maximilian and the Anaconda according to the same authority. Mr. Bennett observes.. that the name of *Anaconda*, like that of *Boa Constrictor*, has been popularly applied to all the larger and more powerful snakes. He adds that the word appears to be of Ceylonese origin, and applies it to the *Python Tigris*. **1849** J. GRAY *Brit. Mus. Cat. Snakes* 102 The Anacondo, *Eunectes murinus*.. Brazil.. Tropical America.

(*c*) **1826** DISRAELI *Viv. Grey* III. vi. 113 The lurid glare of the anaconda's eye. **1849** W. IRVING *Bonneville* 304 Having .. completely gorged himself, he would wrap himself up, and lie with the torpor of an anaconda. **1864** SALA in *Daily Tel.* 23 Nov., The circle of the general's admirers was growing every moment more anaconda-like. **1879** *Daily News* 13 June 2/2 A marvellous dress, which, aided by the supple form of the fair owner, conveyed the idea of an anaconda.

Anacreontic (ə,nækriː'ɒntık), *a.* and *sb.* [ad. L. *anacreontic-us*, f. Gr. Ἀνακρέων prop. name; cf. mod.Fr. *anacreontique*.]

A. *adj.* Of, or after the manner of, the Greek poet Anacreon. **a.** Having the structure or metre of Anacreon's lyrics.

1706 PHILLIPS, *Anacreontick Verse*, consists of seven syllables, without being tied to any certain Law of Quantity. **1749** *Power of Numb. in Poet. Comp.* 65 Anacreontic Verse.. is usually divided into Stanzas, each Stanza containing four Lines which Rime alternately to each other; and every Line consists of three Troches and a long syllable, *e.g.* Cease, Trelawney, cease to teize me, Mirth and Music are but vain; Wine and Laughter now displease me, And thy Rules increase my Pain.

b. Convivial and amatory.

1801 MISS EDGEWORTH *Belinda* (1832) I. vii. 121 He laughed and sang with Anacreontic spirit. **1839** HALLAM *Hist. Lit.* III. III. v. §29. 250 His amatory and anacreontic lines.

B. *sb.* A poem in imitation of, or after the manner of Anacreon's; an erotic poem.

a **1656** COWLEY (*title*) Anacreontiques; or some copies of verses translated paraphrastically out of Anacreon. **1878** T. SINCLAIR *Mount* 74 Moore and Burns's anacreontics are the first true step in the lyrical.

a,nacre'ontically, *adv.* [f. prec. + -AL¹ + -LY².] After the manner of Anacreon; in a convivial fashion.

1830 DE QUINCEY *Kant* Wks. III. 108 The decanters of wine were placed, not on a distant sideboard.. but anacreontically on the table, and at the elbow of every guest.

anacrotic (ænə'krɒtık), *a.* [f. Gr. ἀνά up + κρότος striking, clapping + -IC; cf. ἀνακροτέ-ειν.] Pertaining to, or exhibiting, anacrotism; dicrotic in the rise of the pulse. (More fully called *anadicrotic*.)

1879 *Syd. Soc. Lex.* s.v. *Anacrotism*, An anacrotic elevation may be obtained by compression of the artery beyond the point at which a sphygmograph is applied.

anacrotism (ə'nækrətız(ə)m). *Phys.* [f. as prec. + -ISM.] A secondary oscillation or notch occurring in the upward portion of the curve obtained in a sphygmographic or pulse-recording tracing; dicrotism occurring in the *rise* of the blood-wave.

1879 in *Syd. Soc. Lex.*

‖**anacrusis** (ænə'kruːsıs). *Pros.* [L. translit. of Gr. ἀνάκρουσις, f. ἀνακρού-ειν, f. ἀνά up + κρού-ειν to strike.] 'A syllable at the beginning of a verse before the just rhythm' (Kennedy).

1833 *Edin. Rev.* LVI. 372 The Iambus.. in technical language is said to consist of *anacrusis* and *arsis*. **1844** BECK & FELTON *Munk's Metres* 8 A *thesis* with which a rhythm begins is called *anacrusis*, or 'an upward beat.'

anacrustic (ænə'krʌstık), *a. Pros.* [ad. Gr. ἀνακρουστικ-ός, f. ἀνακρούειν: see ANACRUSIS.] Characterized by anacrusis.

1878 G. M. HOPKINS *Let. to Bridges* 30 May (1935) 53 The rhythm is anacrustic or, as I should call it, 'encountering'.

anadem ('ænədım). *poet.* [ad. L. *anadēm-a*, a. Gr. ἀνάδημα a band to tie up the hair, a headband, f. ἀνα-δέ-ειν to bind up.] A wreath for the head, usually of flowers; a chaplet, a garland.

1604 DRAYTON *Owle* 1168 Drest this Tree with Anadems of flowers. **1613** W. BROWNE *Brit. Past.* II. iii. (1772) 135 Sweet anadems to gird thy brow. *c* **1800** K. WHITE *Poems* (1837) 52 No more our nobles love to grace Their brows with anadems by genius won. **1821** SHELLEY *Adonais* xi, Another clipt her profuse locks, and threw The wreath upon him, like an anadem.

†**'anadesm.** *Obs.* [ad. Gr. ἀναδέσμη: see prec.]

1658 PHILLIPS, *Anadesme*, a Band or Tie: among Surgeons a Swathe or Bandage to bind up Wounds. **1742** in BAILEY. **1879** *Syd. Soc. Lex.*, *Anadesma*, a bandage for wounds.

anadi'crotic, a fuller form of ANACROTIC.
1879 in *Syd. Soc. Lex.*

‖**anadiplosis** (ˌænədɪ'pləʊsɪs). *Rhet.* [L., a. Gr. ἀναδίπλωσις, n. of action f. ἀναδιπλό-εσθαι to be doubled back, f. ἀνά back + διπλό-ειν to double, f. διπλό-ος double.] Reduplication; the beginning of a sentence, line, or clause with the concluding, or any prominent, word of the one preceding.
1589 PUTTENHAM *Eng. Poesie* (Arb.) 210 As thus: Comforte it is for man to haue a wife, Wife chast, and wise ..The Greeks call this figure *Anadiplosis*, I call him the *Redouble.* **1681** HOBBES *Rhet.* IV. iv. 148 A Redoubling called Anadyplosis as, 'The Lord also will be a refuge to the poor, a refuge, I say in due time.' *a* **1791** WESLEY in *Wks.* 1872 XIII. 524 In an anadiplosis the word repeated is pronounced the second time louder and stronger than the first.

anadrom ('ænədrəm). *Zool. rare.* [a. mod.Fr. *anadrome*, ad. Gr. ἀνάδρομ-ος: see next.] An anadromous fish.
a **1859** OGILVIE cites MORIN.

anadromous (ə'nædrəməs), *a.* [f. Gr. ἀνάδρομος running up (a river) (f. ἀνά up + δρόμος running) + -OUS.]
1. *Zool.* Of fishes: Ascending rivers to spawn.
1753 CHAMBERS *Cycl. Supp.*, *Anadromous*.. denoting such [fishes] as have their times of going from the fresh water to the salt, and afterwards returning. **1843** *Blackw. Mag.* LIII. 640 The salmon is undoubtedly the finest..of our fresh-water fishes, or rather of those anadromous kinds which.. seek alternately the briny sea and the 'rivers of water.' **1880** *Times* 31 Dec. 6/1 The artificial propagation of Anadromous Fish other than the Salmon.
2. *Bot.* (See quot.)
1881 J. BAKER in *Nature* XXIII. 480 Milde's classification of ferns into a catadromous and anadromous series, according as to whether their lowest secondary branches originate on the posterior or anterior side of the pinnæ.

anæmia (ə'niːmɪə). *Path.* [a. mod.L., a. Gr. ἀναιμία want of blood, f. Gr. ἀν priv. + αἷμα blood.] Lack of blood; a condition of unhealthy paleness and feebleness, resulting either from diminution of the amount of blood in the body, or from a diminished proportion of red corpuscles in the blood. The 1807 example cited in the *Stanford Dict. of Anglicized Words* is not certainly the same word.
[**1761** J. LIEUTAUD *Précis de la Médecine Pratique* (1765) I. I. 81 L'Anemie. Cette maladie (anemia) qu'on peut regarder comme l'épuisement des vaisseaux sanguins.] **1824** *Trans. Med. Chir. Soc. Edin.* 202 A disease, under the title of Anæmia, has been described by Becker. **1836** TODD *Cycl. Anat. & Phys.* I. 416/2 The state of anæmia, or a deficiency in the quantity of circulating blood. **1854** BADHAM *Halieut.* 215 In a state of acute suffering from exhaustion and anæmia. **1876** HOLLAND *Seven Oaks* ii. 32 Anemia is the normal condition of the pauper.

anæmial (ə'niːmɪəl), *a. Path. rare.* [f. prec. + -AL[1].] = next.
1853 MAYNE *Exp. Lex.*, *Anæmicus*..anemial, anemic.

anæmic (ə'niːmɪk, ə'nɛmɪk), *a.* [f. as prec. + -IC.] Characterized by anæmia.
1. a. Bloodless; ill-supplied with blood, or having blood of poor quality.
1839–47 TODD *Cycl. Anat. & Phys.* III. 720 c/2 The brain of the ill-nourished strumous child is generally an anæmic brain. **1879** H. SPENCER *Data of Eth.* vi. §37. 94 Anæmic, flat-chested school girls, bending over many lessons and forbidden boisterous play.
b. *transf.* and *fig.* Lacking in vigour, strength, or spirit. *colloq.*
1898 *Daily News* 16 Sept. 4/5 The Americans..are not anæmic. They are overflowing with vigour and enterprise. **1899** *Ibid.* 21 Oct. 7/7 Some of the tweeds are made in rather anæmic, sickly tones. **1906** *Westm. Gaz.* 1 Dec. 20/3 [He] must indeed have made an anæmic diamond declaration. **1941** N. COWARD *Australia Visited* iv. 28 Far too much anæmic nonsense was put forward by the young intelligentsia.
2. Of, or pertaining to, anæmia.
1858 THUDICHUM *Urine* 3 Chlorosis and other anæmic conditions. **1861** GRAHAM *Pract. Med.* 725 There is an anæmic murmur in the ascending aorta.

anæmotrophy (æniː'mɒtrəfɪ). *Path.* [f. Gr. ἀν priv. + αἷμα blood + -τροφία nourishment.] Deficient nourishment of the blood.
1860 in FOWLER *Med. Voc.*

anæretic (æniː'rɛtɪk). *Med.* [f. Gr. ἀναιρετικός taking away, destructive: see -IC.] An agent which tends to destroy tissue.
1879 *Syd. Soc. Lex.*, *Animal anæretics*, the gastric juice and vaccine lymph.

anaerobe (ə'neɪərəʊb, ə'nɛərəʊb). *Biol.* [ad. F. *anaérobie* (Pasteur 1863, in *Comptes Rendus* LVI. 1192), f. AN- 10 + AEROBE.] A micro-organism of the group *Anaerobia*, which can live without free oxygen. So **anae'robian, anaerobic** (-'ɒbɪk), **anae'robious** *adjs.*, of the nature of or pertaining to anaerobes; capable of living without free oxygen; **anae'robically** *adv.*; **aˌnaerobi'osis**, life in a medium devoid of free oxygen; **aˌnaerobi'otic** (-'ɒtɪk) *a.*, pertaining to or characterized by anaerobiosis, anaerobic.
1879 FAULKNER & ROBB tr. *Pasteur's Ferment.* iv. 116 We may divide living beings into two classes, aërobian..and anaërobian. **1884** KLEIN *Micro-Org.* vi. 34 Some bacteria require free access of oxygen, and are called aërobic (Pasteur); others grow without free oxygen, and are anaërobic (Pasteur). **1884** W. STIRLING tr. *L. Landois' Physiol.* I. IV. 374 This fungus [*sc.* Bacillus butyricus]..is a true anaërobe, and grows only in the absence of O[xygen]. **1885** VINES in *Encycl. Brit.* XIX. 51/2 It is just the anaerobiotic plants which are most highly endowed with the property of exciting fermentation. **1887** Anaerobically [see AEROBE]. **1891** LINSLEY tr. *Fraenkel's Bacteriol.* 115 That the anaërobia in particular distinguish themselves by generating gases is already known. **1894** *Pop. Sci. Monthly* June 278 With special reference to anaerobiosis and gas production among bacteria. **1914** G. B. SHAW *Misalliance* 15 There was a regular terror of a countess with an anaerobic system [of drainage]. **1931** *Discovery* Sept. 303/2 The distinction, seldom made, between anaerobic respiration and fermentation is pointed out. **1949** H. W. FLOREY *Antibiotics* I. I. i. 32 He isolated two anaerobes, one of which,..had apparently no direct effect in inhibiting the growth of any of a considerable number of organisms. **1958** *New Biol.* XXV. 87 Where the lagoons are not too deep, i.e. where the surface area is sufficiently large in relation to the volume of sewage, it is possible to dissolve, by diffusion at the surface, sufficient oxygen from the air to prevent anaerobiosis and consequent odour. **1959** J. CLEGG *Freshwater Life* (ed. 2) 68 The decomposition of the organic remains by anaerobic bacteria results in the formation of sulphuretted hydrogen. **1961** *Lancet* 22 July 210/2 The cells..are proliferating under virtually anaerobic conditions.

anaerophyte (ə'neɪərəʊfaɪt). *Bot.* [f. ἀν priv. + ἀηρ, ἀέρο-ς air + φυτόν plant; cf. *aerophyte.*] A plant which does not need a direct supply of air.
1876 tr. *Wagner's Gen. Pathol.* 101 The so-called anäerophytes, which do not need the direct influences of the air.

anæsthesia (ænɪs'θiːzɪə, -'θiːsɪə, -'θiːʒ(ɪ)ə). [mod.L., a. Gr. ἀναισθησία want of feeling, f. ἀν priv. + αἴσθησι-ς sensation, f. stem αἰσθε-, to feel, perceive. Cf. mod.Fr. *anesthésie.* In this and the following derivatives of αἰσθε-, the *æ* is by some pronounced (iː, ɪ) according to place of accent.]
a. Loss of feeling or sensation, insensibility. Also, **local anæsthesia**, anæsthesia of a limited area of the body; opp. to **general anæsthesia**, anæsthesia of the whole body. Cf. *basal anæsthesia*, BASAL *a.* 3.
1721 BAILEY, *Anæsthesia*, a Defect of Sensation, as in Paralytic and blasted Persons. **1846** O. W. HOLMES *Let. to W. T. G. Morton* 21 Nov. in E. Warren *Letheon* (ed. 2, 1847) 79 The state should, I think, be called 'Anæsthesia'. This signifies insensibility... The adjective will be 'Anæsthetic'. Thus we might say the state of Anæsthesia, or the anæsthetic state. **1848** SIR J. Y. SIMPSON in *Pharm. Jrnl.* VII. 517 The state of anæsthesia lasted for two or three minutes. **1848** *Monthly Jrnl. Med. Sci.* July 48 He could produce thus *local* anæsthesia in the worm. **1867** *Times* 14 Mar. 12/6 He [*sc.* Dr. Richardson] next demonstrated the principle and practice of the local method by ether spray... In veterinary surgery this local anæsthesia is, Dr. Richardson said, applicable to all operations. **1877** ERICHSEN *Surg.* I. 15 To induce anæsthesia by the inhalation of vapours. **1900** *Lancet* 21 Apr. 1125/2 (*title*) The production of local anaesthesia in the ear. **1910** *Encycl. Brit.* I. 909/1 *Local Anaesthesia*..The discovery of methods by which the insensibility may be confined to the area of operation and the loss of consciousness avoided... It is only lately that it has been successfully applied to the severer [operations]. It is very doubtful whether local anaesthesia will ever replace general in the latter class. **1936** *Discovery* Nov. 357/2 One who has had some personal experience of anaesthesia, both general and local.
b. *fig.*
1865 MRS. WHITNEY *Gayworthys* xliii, In that mysterious anæsthesia, he had left sense and certainty behind him.

anæsthesiant (ænɛs'θiːsɪənt), *a.* and *sb.* [f. prec. + -ANT, after *stimul-ant* etc.]
A. *adj.* Producing anæsthesia. **B.** *sb.* An agent of this nature; an anæsthetic.
1879 in *Syd. Soc. Lex.*

anæsthesimeter (əˌnɛsθɪ'sɪmɪtə(r), ə'niː-). [f. as prec. + Gr. μέτρον measure: see -METER.] An instrument for determining the amount of an anæsthetic administered.
1860 in FOWLER *Med. Voc.*

anæsthesiology (ænɪsθiːzɪ'ɒlədʒɪ) [f. ANÆSTHESI(A + -OLOGY.] The study and practice of anæsthesia and anæsthetics. So **anæsthesi'ologist**, a person versed in anæsthesiology.
1914 *Stedman's Med. Dict.* 46/1 Anesthesiology. **1947** DORLAND & MILLER *Med. Dict.* 101/1 Anesthesiologist. **1955** *Sci. News Let.* 28 May 351/2 Resident anesthesiologists can quickly learn the techniques so as to reinforce the hypnosis daily. **1959** *Times Suppl. Rubber Industry* 27 Apr. x/6 Anaesthesiology, a branch of the medical sciences of ever-increasing importance.

†**anæsthesis** (ænɪs'θiːsɪs). *Obs. rare.* [f. ANÆSTHESIA, after Gr. αἴσθησις, *æsthesis.*] = ANÆSTHESIA.
1848 SIR J. SIMPSON in *Pharm. Jrnl.* VII. 516 The brief period which elapses before the state of complete anæsthesis is induced.

anæsthetic (ænɪs'θɛtɪk, -'θiːtɪk), *a.* and *sb.* [f. Gr. ἀναίσθητ-ος without feeling, insensible (f. ἀν priv. + αἰσθητ-ός sensible; f. αἰσθε- perceive) + -IC. Cf. mod. Fr. *anesthétique*, and ÆSTHETIC.]
A. *adj.*
1. Insensible, deprived of sensibility.
1846 [see ANÆSTHESIA]. **1848** SIR J. SIMPSON in *Jrnl. Med. Sc.* IX. 220 The anæsthetic state must be made adequately deep. **1853** MAYNE *Exp. Lex.*, *Anæstheticus*, Applied specially of late to the state of persons rendered insensible by inhalation of ether or chloroform: anesthetic. **1879** TIMBS in *Cassell's Techn. Educ.* IV. 106/2 The possibility of setting patients into an anæsthetic state.
2. *fig.* Unfeeling, unemotional. *rare.*
1860 A. WINDSOR *Ethica* vii. 338 In his judgment of character this cold anæsthetic temperament displays itself perhaps more prominently.
3. Producing, or connected with the production of, insensibility.
1847 SIR J. SIMPSON in *Jrnl. Med. Sc.* VIII. 415 At the first winter meeting of the Edinburgh Medico-Chirurgical Society (10th November) I directed the attention of the members to a new respirable anæsthetic agent.. Chloroform, Chloroformyle, or Perchloride of Formyle. **1848** —— in *Jrnl. Med. Sc.* IX. 220 The results of anæsthetic midwifery. **1859** BAIN *Emot. & Will* i. §21. 34 Exercise or action is itself anæsthetic. **1870** SIR J. SIMPSON *Anæsthesia* Wks. 1871 II. 23 The first case of an anæsthetic operation under sulphuric ether occurred at Boston [U.S.A.] on the 30th September 1846. The first case of an anæsthetic operation under chloroform occurred at Edinburgh on the 15th of November 1847.
B. *sb.* [The adj. used *absol.*] An anæsthetic agent; an agent which produces insensibility. **local anæsthetic**, a substance which by application or injection induces local anæsthesia; opp. to **general anæsthetic**, a substance which induces general or total anæsthesia. Cf. *basal anæsthetic*, BASAL *a.* 3.
1848 SIR J. SIMPSON in *Pharm. Jrnl.* VII. 518 None of the five anæsthetics which I have mentioned..are..comparable with chloroform. **1851** J. ARNOTT *Neuralgic Affections* 20 It is very natural that the disappointment from the exaggerated statements..should indispose the surgeon to put trust in any local anæsthetic, without such corroborative evidence. **1876** BARTHOLOW *Mat. Med.* (1879) 360 The term *anæsthetic*, proposed by Dr. Oliver Wendell Holmes, means an agent capable of producing *anæsthesia*, or insensibility to pain. **1876** DUNGLISON *Dict. Med. Sci.* 47/2 The ethers, rhigolene and other agents, when applied to a part in the form of spray, by their evaporation benumb it; and thus act as local anæsthetics. **1878** LECKY *Eng. in 18th C.* I. iv. 551 Vivisection..before the introduction of anæsthetics, was often inexpressibly horrible. **1879** *Syd. Soc. Lex.* s.v., General anæsthetics are commonly employed in the form of vapour. **1910** *Encycl. Brit.* I. 909/1 The earliest local anaesthetic was cold, produced by a mixture of ice and salt. In place of this cumbersome method, the skin is now frozen by means of a fine spray of ether or ethyl chloride directed upon it. **1955** *Oxf. Jun. Encycl.* XI. 4/2 A patient to whom a general anaesthetic is administered loses consciousness, while a local anaesthetic affects only the area of operation, the patient remaining fully conscious. Cocaine..the most commonly used local anaesthetic, was introduced in 1879.

anæs'thetically, *adv.* [f. ANÆSTHETIC *a.* and *sb.* + -AL[1] + -LY[2].] As, or in the way of, an anæsthetic; so as to produce anæsthesia.
1847 SIR J. SIMPSON in *Mem.* (1873) viii. 262 As one who knows..what operations were to the patients before æther or chloroform was employed anæsthetically.

anæsthetist (ænɪs'θiːtɪst). [f. ANÆSTHET-IZE: see -IST.] One who administers anæsthetic agents.
1882 *Daily Tel.* 23 Mar. 5 Anæsthetist to the Dental Hospital of London.

anæsthetization (əˌnɛsθɪtaɪ'zeɪʃən). [f. next: see -ATION.] The process of rendering insensible; subjection to the action of anæsthetics.
1860 in FOWLER *Med. Voc.* **1875** WOOD *Therap.* (1879) 287 The condition of the pupil cannot be considered a safe guide in anæsthetization. **1876** tr. *Wagner's Gen. Pathol.* 180 That certain painful operations be undertaken..only after preceding local anæsthetization.

anæsthetize (ə'nɛsθɪtaɪz, ə'niː-), *v.* [f. Gr. ἀναίσθητ-ος (see ANÆSTHETIC) + -IZE.] To render insensible.
1848 SIR J. SIMPSON in *Jrnl. Med. Sc.* IX. 216 The patients were thus only partially..anæsthetized. **1871** LOWELL *Study Wind.* 25 Gratuitous hearers are anæsthetized to suffering by a sense of virtue. **1872** THOMAS *Dis. Women* 141 The doctor anæsthetizes his patient.

anæsthetized (ə'nɛsθɪtaɪzd), *ppl. a.* [f. prec. + ED.] Rendered insensible.
1848 SIR J. SIMPSON *Jrnl. Med. Sc.* IX. 219 Dangerous symptoms..in an anæsthetized patient. **1876** GROSS *Dis. Urin. Organs* 151 The thoroughly anæsthetized patient.

anagenesis (ænə'dʒɛnɪsɪs). *Biol.* [mod.L., f. Gr. ἀνά up + γένεσις origin: see GENESIS.] Progressive or 'upward' evolution of species (opp. CATAGENESIS). So **anagenetic** (ˌænədʒɪ'nɛtɪk) *a.*
1889 A. HYATT *Genesis of Arietidae in Mem. Museum Comp. Zool.* XVI. II. 71 (*title*) Anagenesis, or the Genesis of Progressive Characteristics. *Ibid.* 74 The law of succession in anagenesis, therefore, is that progressive species..were the direct descendants of progressive varieties or forms. **1893** E. D. COPE in *Monist* III. 637 The process of evolution may be either progressive (Anagenesis) or retrogressive (Catagenesis). **1896** —— *Organ. Evol.* ix. 475, I have termed

these classes the Anagenetic, which are exclusively vital... The anagenetic class tends to upward progress in the organic sense. **1953** J. S. HUXLEY *Evolution in Action* iii. 75 Bernhard Rensch, the German biologist.. separated evolutionary processes into cladogenesis, or branching evolution.. and anagenesis, or upward evolution.

‖**anagennesis** (ænədʒɪ'ni:sɪs). [Gr. ἀναγέννησις regeneration, f. ἀνα-γεννά-ειν to regenerate.] A reproduction or regeneration of structure.
1879 in *Syd. Soc. Lex.*

anaglyph ('ænəglɪf). [ad. Gr. ἀναγλυφή work in low relief, f. ἀνά up + γλύφ-ειν to hollow out, carve. Cf. Fr. *anaglyphe*, perh. earlier.] **1.** An embossed or chased ornament, worked in low relief.
1651 N. BIGGS *New Dispens.* ¶98 The *Anaglyphe* or exterior Cortex and figure of things. **1753** CHAMBERS *Cycl. Supp.*, *Anaglypha*, in antient writers, denote vessels, or other things, adorned with sculpture in *basso relievo*. **1843** PRESCOTT *Mexico* I. iv. (1864) 30 The mysterious anaglyphs sculptured on the temples of the Egyptians.
2. *Photogr.* A composite stereoscopic picture printed in superimposed complementary colours.
1897 E. J. WALL *Dict. Photogr.* (ed. 7) 30 *Anaglyph*, a means of producing stereoscopic effect due to MM. Louis Ducos du Hauron and D'Almeida. *Ibid.* 31 The principle of the anaglyph is applicable to the stereoscopic projection with the magic lantern. **1910** *Lancet* 5 Nov. 1366/2 The method of anaglyphs—i.e. the projection of the right stereoscopic image in red and the left in green, the composite image being viewed through spectacles furnished with red and green glasses. **1925** *English Mechanics* 13 Mar. 123/1 The anaglyph is a composite picture consisting of the two pictures forming a stereoscopic pair, one being printed in red, and the other in green; the two pictures are not quite superimposed, but a small amount of lateral displacement is given to one. This composite 'anaglyph' is viewed through a mask, containing two ocular apertures, the left one being covered with a red transparent screen and the right with a green one. Each eye, therefore, sees only the picture taken with the corresponding lens of the stereo camera, with the result that the two views are merged and stereoscopic relief obtained.

anaglyphic (ænə'glɪfɪk), *a.*, *sb.* [f. prec. + -IC.] **A.** *adj.* Of or pertaining to anaglyphs; anaglyptic.
1836 [See ANAGLYPTIC]. **1836** *Edin. Rev.* LXIV. 92 Hieroglyphics.. tropical and anaglyphic. **1854** FAIRHOLT *Dict. Art* 24 Anaglyphic is that process of machine ruling on an etching ground which gives to the subject the appearance of being raised.
B. *sb. pl.* **anaglyphics** = ANAGLYPTICS.
a **1864** in BRANDE.

ana'glyphical, *a. rare*$^{-0}$ = prec.
1859 in WORCESTER.

anaglypta (ænə'glɪptə). [a. L. *anaglypta* work in bas-relief; cf. ANAGLYPTIC *a.*] A proprietary term for a special type of thick embossed wallpaper. Also *attrib.*
1887 *Trade Marks Jrnl.* 12 Oct. 1142 Anaglypta.. Thomas John Palmer.. Decorative Material in the Nature of a Covering, sold in the Piece, for Application to Walls, Ceilings, or other Surfaces. **1905** *Daily Chron.* 9 June 9/7 (Advt.), Paperhanger wants work, high-class or commons, anaglypta, lincrusta, &c., a speciality. **1920** *Punch* 30 June 505/1 You can stare at the anaglypta ceiling. **1934** *Times* 15 Feb. 17/5 Has he not, paperhanger and decorator too, hung lincrusta and anaglypta, as well as other papers difficult to hang?

anaglyptic (ænə'glɪptɪk), *a.* and *sb.* [ad. L. *anaglyptic-us*, a. Gr. ἀναγλυπτικός: see ANAGLYPH.]
A. *adj.* Of or pertaining to anaglyphs, or to the art of carving in low relief, embossing, etc.
1656 BLOUNT *Glossogr.*, *Anaglyphick* or *Anaglyptick*, pertaining to the Art of Carving, Embossing, or Engraving. **1662** EVELYN *Sculptura* (1755) 32 Plastica.. and the anaglyptic art. **1847** in CRAIG, etc.
B. *sb. pl.* **anaglyptics**: the art of carving in low relief, chasing, embossing, etc.
1662 EVELYN *Sculptura* (1755) 16 They rather concern the statuary art—though we might yet safely admit some of the Greek anaglyptics. **1818** in TODD.

anaglyptograph (ænə'glɪptəgraf). [see ANAGLYPTOGRAPHY and -GRAPH.] A machine for producing representations in relief, of coins, medals, etc.
1876 *Catal. Sci. Appar. S. Kens.* 275.

anaglyptographic (ænə,glɪptəʊ'græfɪk), *a.* [f. ANAGLYPTOGRAPH-Y + -IC.] Of, pertaining to, or according to anaglyptography. (In mod. Dicts.)

anaglyptography (ænəglɪp'tɒgrəfɪ). [f. Gr. ἀνάγλυπτος embossed + -γραφία writing.] (See quot.)
a **1871** *Art Journal*, quoted in RINGWALT *Encycl. Print.* 34 *Anaglyptography*, the art of so engraving as to give the subject an embossed appearance, as if raised from the surface of the paper; used in representing coins, bas-reliefs, etc.

‖**anagnorisis** (ænəg'nɒrɪsɪs). [L., a. Gr. ἀναγνώρισις, f. ἀνα-γνωρίζ-ειν to recognise, discover.] Recognition; the *dénouement* in a drama.
a **1800** BLAIR is cited in WEBSTER. **1833** *Blackw. Mag.* XXXIV. 464 He, aged man, ignorant of the anagnorisis, is overcome by the catastrophe. **1846** DE QUINCEY *Antigone* Wks. XIII. 220 Some dreadful discovery or anagnorisis (*i.e.* recognition of identity) takes place.

anagnost ('ænəgnɒst). ? *Obs.* [ad. L. *anagnōst-es*, a. Gr. ἀναγνώστ-ης a reader, f. ἀναγιγνώσκ-ειν to read.] A reader, a prelector; one employed to read aloud; the reader of the lessons in church.
1601 HOLLAND *Pliny* (1634) II. 231 (*note*) Lay the fault.. vpon Plinies Anagnosts or Readers, who either read wrong, or pronounced not their words distinctly. **1702** tr. *Le Clerc's Prim. Fathers* 201 They.. would both be Anagnostes, or read the Holy Scriptures in the Church. **1708** MOTTEUX *Rabelais* IV. Ded., Carefully and distinctly read to him by the most learned and faithful Anagnost in this Kingdom.

†**anag'nostian.** *Obs.*$^{-0}$ [f. L. *anagnōst-es* (see prec.) + -IAN.] = prec.
1626 MINSHEU *Duct.*, *Anagnostian*, a curate that serueth onely to reade, or a clarke or scoller that readeth to a writer.

†**anag'nostic.** *Obs.*$^{-0}$ [ad. Gr. ἀναγνωστικ-ός fitted for reading.] = prec.
1623 COCKERAM, *Anagnosticke*, a curate seruing onely to reade.

‖**anagoge** (ænə'gəʊdʒi:). [L. *anagōgē*, a. Gr. ἀναγωγή elevation, religious or ecstatic elevation, mystical sense; f. ἀν-άγ-ειν to lead up, lift up, elevate. See also ANAGOGY.]
†**1.** Spiritual elevation or enlightenment, esp., to understand mysteries. *Obs.*
1706 PHILLIPS, *Anagoge*, a raising of the mind to search out the hidden Meaning of any Passage; especially the Mystical Sense of the Holy Scriptures. **1721** So in BAILEY. **1751** in CHAMBERS: see ANAGOGY. Not in J.
2. Mystical or spiritual interpretation; an Old Testament typification of something in the New.
1849 FITZGERALD tr. *Whitaker's Disp.* 407 We should form a like judgment of the type or anagoge.

†**anago'getical**, *a. Obs. rare*$^{-1}$. [f. prec., by form-assoc. with *apology*, *apologetical*.] A badly-formed equivalent for ANAGOGICAL.
1731 in BAILEY. **1794** SULLIVAN *View Nat.* II, There is a grammatical and an anagogetical or moral sense.

anagogic (ænə'gɒdʒɪk), *a.* and *sb.* [? ad. med.L. *anagōgic-us*, a. Gr. ἀναγωγικ-ός mystical: see prec. and -IC. Cf. Fr. *anagogique*.]
A. *adj.* **1.** Of or pertaining to anagoge; mystical, spiritualized.
1388 WYCLIF *Isa.* Prol., Anagogik[vndurstondyng of hooli scripture] techith what we owen to hope of euerlastyng meede in heuene. **1677** GALE *Crt. Gentiles* II. III. 118 The papists make their anagogic sense of Scripture correspondent to the Judaic Cabala. **1849** FITZGERALD tr. *Whitaker's Disp.* 403 The mystic or spiritual.. he says is either tropological, or anagogic, or allegorical.
2. *Psychol.* (See quots.)
1917 S. E. JELLIFFE tr. *Silberer's Probl. Mysticism & Symbolism* III. i. 241 Anagogic interpretation.. is a form of functional interpretation. *Ibid.* 242 The true functional phenomenon, as I have so far described it, pictures the actual psychic state or process; the anagogic image appears on the contrary to point to a state or process that is to be experienced in the future. **1934** H. C. WARREN *Dict. Psychol.* 12/1 *Anagogic*, a term applied by Silberer and Jung to the moral, spiritual, allegorical, or uplifting trends of the unconscious. **1940** HINSIE & SHATZKY *Psychiatric Dict.* 29/1 Silberer believes that dreams are susceptible of two different interpretations. One is.. [the] infantile sexual interpretation. The other is related to the spiritual, idealistic, non-sexual forces of the unconscious; hence, the expression anagogic interpretation. The latter is of the kind stressed by Jung. **1954** R. F. C. HULL tr. *Jung's Coll. Wks.* XVI. 9 The synthetic or anagogic view.. asserts that certain parts of the personality which are capable of development are in an infantile state.
B. *sb.* [The adj. used *absol.*]
†**1.** 'One skild in explaining the Scriptures.' Cockeram 1623. *Obs.*
2. *pl.* **anagogics**: anagogic studies, or practice; 'mysterious considerations.' T.
1675 L. ADDISON *State of Jews* 248 (T.) That the Misna Torah was composed out of the cabalisticks and anagogicks of the Jews.

anagogical (ænə'gɒdʒɪkəl), *a.* [f. prec. + -AL[1].] Of words and their sense: mystical, spiritual, having a secondary spiritual sense, allegorical.
1528 TINDALE *Obed. Chr. Man* Wks. I. 303 They divide the scripture into four senses, the literal, tropological, allegorical, and anagogical.. The allegory is appropriate to faith; and the anagogical to hope, and things above. *a* **1652** J. SMITH *Sel. Disc.* vi. 192 To discern the true mystical and anagogical sense of them. **1753** CHAMBERS *Cycl. Supp.* s.v., The rest of the Sabbath, in the anagogical sense, signifies the repose of everlasting blessedness. **1857** MAURICE *Mor. & Metaph. Philos.* III. v. §71. 218 The anagogical, whereby we learn how to adhere to God.
¶ *catachr.* of persons.
1841 D'ISRAELI *Amen. Lit.* (1859) II. 251 These anagogical children of reverie. **1851** S. JUDD *Margaret* II. i. (1871) 165 You are very 'anagogical' as my Master says; strange and mysterious, I mean.

ana'gogically, *adv.* [f. prec. + -LY[2].] In an anagogical manner; with a hidden spiritual sense.
1553-87 FOXE *A. & M.* I. 870/2 Anagogically some part thereof [Prophecy] may also be referred.. unto the Pope. **1875** *Blackie's Pop. Encycl.* I. 151/1 To explain anagogically, means to apply the literal sense of the text to heavenly things.

anagogy ('ænəgəʊdʒɪ). [f. Gr. ἀναγωγή ANAGOGE, as if ad. Gr. *ἀναγωγία, n. of quality f. ἀναγωγός soul-raising, sublime; but not used in this sense in Gr. A better Eng. form than *anagoge*; cf. Fr. *anagogie*.]
†**1.** Spiritual elevation or enlightenment, esp. to understand mysteries. *Obs.*
1727-51 CHAMBERS *Cycl.*, *Anagogy*, *Anagoge*, a rapture or elevation of the soul to things celestial, and eternal.
2. Mystical interpretation, hidden 'spiritual' sense of words.
1519 HORMAN *Vulgaria* 98 Let no man call hym selfe a diuyne: that knoweth nat.. allygoris, and tropologies, and anagogies, for scripture is full of them. **1659** HAMMOND *On Ps.* Pref. ¶18. 8 Some kind of accommodation, or Anagogy, or Figure. **1753** CHAMBERS *Cycl. Supp.*, *Anagogy*.. denotes the application of the types and allegories of the Old Testament to subjects of the New. **1847** CRAIG, *Anagogy*, a mystical meaning applied to the language of Scripture.

anagram ('ænəgræm). Also 6-7 **anagrame, -gramm(e.** [a. Fr. *anagramme*, or ad. mod.L. *anagramma* (16th c.), f. Gr. ἀνα-γράφ-ειν, to write up, write back or anew. 'Ανάγραμμα was not in Greek, though the grammarians had ἀναγραμματίζ-ειν to transpose the letters of a word, and ἀναγραμματισμός transposition of letters.]
1. A transposition of the letters of a word, name, or phrase, whereby a new word or phrase is formed.
1589 PUTTENHAM *Eng. Poesie* (Arb.) 115 Of the Anagrame, or poesie transposed. **1609** B. JONSON *Silent Wom.* IV. iii. (1616) 572 Who will.. make anagrammes of our names. **1632** HOWELL *Lett.* (1650) I. 261 This *Gustavus* (whose anagram is *Augustus*) was a great Captain. **1705** HICKERINGILL *Priest-Cr.* II. iii. 36 The true Anagram of *Jesuita*, is *Sevitia*, Cruelty. **1865** CARLYLE *Fredk. Gt.* II. VI. ii. 14 Monsieur Arouet Junior (*le Jeune*, or *l. j.*), who, by an ingenious anagram.. writes himself *Voltaire* ever since.
†**2.** *loosely* or *fig.* A transposition, a mutation. *Obs.*
1634 HEYWOOD *Maidenh. well Lost* XI. 119 What meane these strange Anagrams? *a* **1659** CLEVELAND *Comm. Place* (1677) 167 Heaven descends into the Bowels of the Earth, and, to make up the Anagramm, the Graves open and the Dust ariseth. **1678** BUTLER *Hudibr.* III. i. 772 His body, that stupendous frame, Of all the world the anagram.

†'**anagram**, *v. Obs. rare.* [f. prec. sb. after Fr. *anagrammer*, f. *anagramme*.]
1. *trans.* To ANAGRAMMATIZE.
1630 J. TAYLOR (Water P.) *Wks.* II. 114/1 To Anagram my Art into a Vermine [i.e. *art* into *rat*]. **1682** BUNYAN *Holy War* To Reader, Witness my name, if anagram'd to thee, The letters make 'Nu hony in a B.' **1751** WARBURTON *Pope's Wks.*, *Dunciad* III. 21 (JOD.) Some of these anagrammed his name Benlowes into Benevolus.
2. *intr.* To make anagrams.
1646 SHIRLEY *To C'tess Ormond*, I never learned that trick of court, to.. anagram upon her name.

†'**anagramize**, *v. Obs. rare*$^{-1}$. [f. ANAGRAM *sb.* + -IZE.] = ANAGRAMMATIZE.
1636 W. SAMPSON *Virtus post Fun. vivit* 47 William Farrington Which Anagramizde by conversion even, (Farwell I am gon) from Earth to Heaven.

anagrammatic (,ænəgrə'mætɪk). [f. mod.L. *anagrammat-*, stem of *anagramma* (see ANAGRAM) + -IC. Cf. Fr. *anagrammatique*.] Of or pertaining to an anagram; anagrammatical.
1814 *Month. Mag.* XXXVII. 47 Alcuinus is the anagram of Calvinus; and this is the earliest modern instance of the adoption of an anagrammatic device. **1881** ROUTLEDGE *Science* ix. 207 Huyghens published his discovery in the anagrammatic form which was the fashion of the time.

,**anagra'mmatical**, *a.* [f. as prec. + -ICAL.]
1. Of or pertaining to an anagram; performed or produced by transposition of letters.
1605 CAMDEN *Rem.* (1657) 175 This was by transposition anagrammatical, framed out of the name of the Earl of Worcester: *Edwardus Somerset*, *Moderatus sed Verus*. *a* **1745** SWIFT *Barb. Denom. Irel.*, Some have contrived anagrammatical appellations, from half their own and their [ladyes'?] names joined together. **1825** SOUTHEY in *Q. Rev.* XXXIII. 5 We cannot leave the author's name in that obscurity which the anagrammatical title seems intended to throw over it.. Merlin is only the representative of Dr. Milner.
†**2.** *fig.* Performed by the displacement and rearrangement of things. *Obs. rare.*
1678 CUDWORTH *Intell. Syst.* 744 The Generations, and Corruptions or Deaths of Animals, according to this Hypothesis, are nothing but an Anagrammatical Transposition of Things in the Universe.

,**anagra'mmatically**, *adv.* [f. prec. + -LY[2].] In the manner of an anagram; with a different arrangement of the same letters.
1605 CAMDEN *Rem.* (1657) 351 Which also contained his name anagrammatically. **1660** *Charac. Italy* 10 Whatsoever

he parrot (or if you will have it anagrammatically) prater-like twattles. **1751** CHAMBERS *Cycl.* s.v. *Anagram*, The question put by Pilate to Jesus Christ: *Quid est veritas?* which anagrammatically makes, *Est vir qui adest.* **1847** *Blackw. Mag.* LXI. 754 We tried them anagrammatically, but in vain: there was nought to be made of *Omoo*; shake it as we would, the *O's* came uppermost.

anagrammatism (ænə'græmətız(ə)m). [a. Fr. *anagrammatisme*, ad. (perh. through mod.L.) Gr. ἀναγραμματισμ-ός: see ANAGRAMMATIZE and -ISM.] The formation of anagrams; the transposition of letters so as to form a new word or words.

1605 CAMDEN *Rem.* (1657) 169 Names consisting of alphabetary revolution, which they will have to be anagrammatism. **1669** GALE *Crt. Gentiles* I. II. iii. 26 By the artifice of anagrammatisme, *Syna* is made *Nysa*. **1862** H. WHEATLEY *Anagr.* 74 The practice of anagrammatism was by no means uncommon among the Greeks.

anagrammatist (ænə'græmətıst). [f. ANAGRAMMATIZE: see -IST. Cf. mod.Fr. *anagrammatiste*, perh. earlier than Eng.] A maker of anagrams. Also applied to, A book of anagrams.

1613 GAMAGE *Epigrams* xviii. (T.) Mr. W. Aubrey, an ingenious anagrammatist. **1634** F. LENTON (*title*) The Inns of Court Anagrammatist, or, The Masquers Masqued in Anagrams. **1711** ADDISON *Spect.* No. 60 ¶4 When the Anagrammatist takes a Name to work upon, he considers it at first as a Mine not broken up. **1834–43** SOUTHEY *Doctor* clxxix. (1862) 467 Louis XIII appointed the Provençal Thomas Billen to be his Royal Anagrammatist.

anagrammatize (ænə'græmətaız), *v.* [ad. (? mod.L. *anagrammatizā-re* ad.) Gr. ἀναγραμματίζ-ειν to transpose the letters of a word, f. ἀνά back + γράμμα(τ-) letter + -ίζειν (see -IZE); cf. Fr. *anagrammatise-r*.] To transpose so as to form an anagram; to change into another word or phrase by a different arrangement of letters.

1591 NASHE *Introd. Sidney's Astroph.* in *P. Penilesse* Pref. 29 That seeke .. to anagrammatize the name of Wittenberge. **1630** J. TAYLOR (Water P.) *Wks.* II. 114/1, I doe anagrammatize *Water-rat* to bee *a true Art.* **1637** W. AUSTIN *Hæc Homo* 182 Others .. anagrammatize it from *Eva* into *væ*, because (they say) she was the cause of our woe. **1862** *Macm. Mag.* Nov. 23 Calvin .. anagrammatized his name, 'Rabelæsius' into *Rabie Læsus* [Afflicted with madness].

ana'grammatized, *ppl. a.* [f. prec. + -ED.] Transposed so as to form an anagram.

c **1590** MARLOWE *Faustus* iii. 9 Jehovah's name, Forward and backward anagrammatis'd. **1796** PEGGE *Anonym.* (1809) 95 The name anagrammatized was not Elizabeth, but Isabel. **1814** SOUTHEY in *Q. Rev.* XII. 77 The names of his numerous dedicatees laboriously anagrammatized.

† **'anagrammist.** *Obs. rare*⁻¹. [f. ANAGRAM + -IST. Cf. *anagramize*.] = ANAGRAMMATIST.

1613 HOBY *Counter-snarle* 21 Would hee not prove a good Anagrammist? **1727–51** CHAMBERS *Cycl.* s.v. *Anagram*, The Cabbalists among the Jews are professed anagrammists.

† **'anagraph**, *Obs.*⁻⁰ [ad. Gr. ἀναγραφή a writing up, a record, f. ἀνά up + γραφή writing.]

1656 BLOUNT *Glossogr.*, *Anagraph*, a registring or recording of matters, an Inventory. **1721** BAILEY, *Anagraphe*, a Description, a Registring or Recording of Acts: an Inventory, a Breviate. [So in mod. Dicts.] **1879** *Syd. Soc. Lex.*, *Anagraph*, used by Hippocrates for a physician's prescription or recipe.

† **a'nagraphy.** *Obs. rare*⁻¹. = prec.

1606 WARNER *Alb. Eng.* XIV. 332 Nor sleepeth [= neglects] your *Anagraphie* The sensuall Follies of the Hie.

† **ana'grapsis.** *Obs. rare*⁻¹. [f. Gr. ἀναγράφ-ειν to write up, rewrite, on analogy of *synopsis*, etc. See ANAGRAM.] Anagrammatism.

1669 GALE *Crt. Gentiles* I. II. iii. 30 *Maira* .. by an easie Anagrapsis, resolves into *Maria*, or Miriam.

† **'anagre.** *Obs. rare*⁻¹. [Used in Topsell, as ad. L. *anagy̆ros* a. Gr. ἀνάγυρος, f. ἀνά back + γῦρος a circle, γυρός round.] A leguminous shrub, bearing recurved pods; the bean-trefoil.

1608 TOPSELL *Serpents* 619 Conyza, strewed, the haunt of serpents spills; The nettle-crops, thorny anagres, stay their mood.

['**anagriph, anagrip.** In Spelman for Du Cange, who quotes it from the Laws of the Longobards! = OHG. *anagrif* rape.]

† **a,naitio'logical**, *a. Obs. rare*⁻¹. [f. Gr. ἀν priv. + αἰτιολογία cause assigned + -ICAL. The reg. form would be *anætiological*.] (See quot.)

1652 GAULE *Magastrom.* 81 Astrologicall [predictions] .. being (as is their own word) anaitiologicall, or not having any naturall cause at all.

anal ('eınəl), *a.* [ad. mod.L. *ānāl-is*, f. ANUS.]

1. a. Of or pertaining to the anus, or excretory opening.

1836 TODD *Cycl. Anat. & Phys.* I. 209/1 In the vicinity of the anal aperture. **1877** HUXLEY *Anat. Inv. An.* ii. 103 An anal region, which gives exit to the refuse of digestion. **1878** BRYANT *Pract. Surg.* I. 25 Anal fistula.

b. *anal eroticism* (or *erotism*) [cf. G. *analerotik* (Freud 1908, in *Psychiatrisch-Neurologische Wochenschr.* IX. 465)], erotic gratification from stimulation in the anal region; so *anal-erotic* adj., of, or pertaining to, anal eroticism; *anal-erotic* sb., a person who seeks anal-erotic gratification.

1913 E. JONES in *Papers on Psycho-Analysis* (1918) xxxi. 540 (*title*) Hate and Anal Erotism in the Obsessional Neurosis. **1917** C. R. PAYNE tr. *Pfister's Psychoanalytic Method* I. x. 201 The young man .. was analerotic to a high degree. *Ibid.*, His father .. is still deeper in analeroticism than he. **1924** *Freud's Coll. Papers* II. iv. 47 Anal erotism is .. useless for sexual aims. *Ibid.* xvi. 169 A wish for a child, in which .. an anal-erotic and a genital impulse .. coincide. **1931** *Amer. Jrnl. Orthopsychiatry* Oct. 515 Eventually poor Pons fell victim to gall-bladder disease, an occurrence of some significance in an anal erotic.

2. Situated near, or in the region of, the anus.

1769 PENNANT *Brit. Zool.* III. 133 The anal fin was white. **1835** KIRBY *Habits & Inst. Anim.* I. xii. 336 Leeches .. first fix themselves by their anal sucker. **1874** LUBBOCK *Orig. & Metam. Insects* v. 91 A many-jointed abdomen, often with anal appendages.

analcite, -ime (ə'nælsaıt, -aım). *Min.* [mod. f. (Fr. *analcime*, Ger. *analzim*) Gr. ἀν priv. + ἄλκιμ-ος strong, given by Haüy 'in allusion to its weak electric power.' For this Dana substitutes the more analogous form *analcite*, f. Gr. ἀναλκής weak + -ITE.] A mineral belonging to Dana's Zeolite section of Hydrous Silicates, consisting mainly of silica, alumina, and soda, usually with lime and potash, occurring in trap rocks.

1803 *Edin. Rev.* III. 50 Many mineralogists .. will be .. amazed to find zeolite subdivided into mesotype, stillbite, analcime and chabasite. **1831** BREWSTER *Optics* xvii. 155 In analcime there are several planes, along which if the refracted ray passes, it will not suffer double refraction. **1868** DANA *Min.* 432 Analcite .. gelatinizes with muriatic acid.

† **'analect**, *sb. Obs. rare*⁻¹. [ad. Gr. ἀνάλεκτος, -ον, 'gathered up,' also 'choice, select, *recherché*': see next.] The select part, the choice essence; the 'cream' or marrow.

a **1650** R. MASON *Let.* in *Bulwer's Anthropomet.*, Man, the Analect of all their perfections.

analects ('ænəlɛkts), *sb. pl.* [ad. L. *analecta*, a. Gr. ἀνάλεκτα things gathered or picked up, f. ἀναλέγ-ειν, f. ἀνά up + λέγ-ειν to gather, pick up. Often used in L. form when applied to extracts from the classical authors.]

† **1.** Crumbs that fall from the table; pickings up, gleanings. *Obs.*

1623 COCKERAM, *Analects*, crums which fall from the table. *a* **1643** CARTWRIGHT *Ordinary* III. v. in Hazl. *Dodsley* XII. 269 No gleanings, James? No trencher-analects? **1721** BAILEY, *Analects*, *Analecta*, fragments gathered from Tables.

2. Literary gleanings; collections of fragments or extracts. (Usually as a title.)

1658 PHILLIPS, *Analects*, .. is taken for Collections or Scraps out of Authors. **1770** G. CAREY (*title*) Analects in Verse and Prose. **1843** LIDDELL & SCOTT *Gr. Lex.* Pref. xi, Antipater Sidonius: in Brunck's Analecta. **1861** *Sat. Rev.* 30 Nov. 563 A few of the sage's sayings, selected from thousands .. to be found in the Confucian Analects.

† **'analem.** *Obs.*⁻⁰ [a. Fr. *analème*, ad. L. ANALEMMA.] = next.

1656 BLOUNT *Glossogr.*, *Analem*, a Mathematical Instrument, whereby is found out the elevation of any Planet or the height of any other thing.

‖**analemma** (ænə'lɛmə). [L. *analemma* the pedestal of a sun-dial, *hence* the sun-dial itself, a. Gr. ἀνάλημμα a prop or support, f. ἀναλαμβ-άν-ειν to take up, resume, repair.]

† **1.** *orig.* A sort of sun-dial. *Obs.* (and perh. never in Eng.)

1753 CHAMBERS *Cycl. Supp.*, *Analemma* in ancient writers denotes those sort of sun-dials which shew only the height of the sun at noon, every day, by the largeness of the shadow of the gnomon.

2. An orthographical projection of the sphere made on the plane of the meridian, the eye being supposed to be at an infinite distance and in the east or west point of the horizon; used in dialling, etc.

1652 R. AUSTIN in Rigaud *Corr. Sci. Men* (1841) I. 74 The triangles, either in your Analemma or perspective, which serve for the last propositions in your astronomical operations. **1693** E. HALLEY in *Phil. Trans.* XVII. 881 Fig. 10 .. is the Analemma projected on the Plain of the Meridian.

3. A gnomon or astrolabe, having the projection of the sphere on a plate of wood or brass, with a horizon or cursor fitted to it, formerly used in solving certain astronomical problems.

1667 *Phil. Trans.* II. 436 A good Globe or Planisphere .. that is, the Analemma, contrived into a form of Instrument for the use of the publick. **1685** J. TWISDEN (*title*) Use of the great Planisphere called the *Analemma* in the resolution of some useful Problems of Astronomy. **1796** HUTTON *Math. Dict.* I. 106 The oldest treatise we have on the analemma, was written by Ptolemy.

4. A scale of the sun's daily declination drawn from tropic to tropic on artificial terrestrial globes.

The *Analemma* is drawn either as a double line, a long ellipse, or as an elongated 8 crossing the equator, and is placed in the Pacific Ocean where it least interferes with geographical features.

1832 *Terrestrial Globe* by MARDINS, has *The Analemma*. **1876** CHAMBERS *Astron.* 910 *Analemma*, a scale painted on globes, and having reference to the motion of the sun.

'analepsy. *Med.* ? *Obs.* [ad. med.L. *analepsia* (also used unchanged), f. Gr. ἀνάληψις a taking up or back.]

1. 'Epilepsy arising from disorder of the stomach.' *Syd. Soc. Lex.* 1879.

1398 TREVISA *Barth. De P.R.* VII. x. (1495) 229 That manere euyl that hyghte Analempsia .. comyth of replycyon of the stomak and moost of indygestyon and of bolkynge.

2. 'The support given in the treatment of a fractured limb.' Fowler *Med. Voc.* 1860.

analeptic (ænə'lɛptık), *a.* and *sb. Med.* [ad. mod.L. *analēptic-us*, a. Gr. ἀναληπτικ-ός restorative, f. ἀναλαμβάν-ειν to take up, restore: see ANALEMMA. Cf. mod.Fr. *analeptique*.]

A. *adj.* Restorative, strengthening.

1661 LOVELL *Hist. Anim. & Min.* 443 The strength is to be repaired by analeptick and pleasant diet. *c* **1720** QUINCY (J.) Analeptick medicines cherish the nerves, and renew the spirits and strength. **1805** *Edin. Rev.* VII. 109 He .. informs us, that sage is analeptic.

B. *sb.* An analeptic medicine or aliment.

1671 SALMON *Syn. Med.* I. xlvii. 108 By Analepticks to repair the Strength. **1758** *Phil. Trans.* L. 672 Such analeptics are required. **1853** SOYER *Pantroph.* 314 Chocolate .. is an agreeable analeptic.

† **ana'leptical**, *a. Obs.* [f. prec. + -AL¹.] = prec.

1615 DANIEL *Queen's Arcad.* (1717) 187 Apply Some analeptical Elexipharmacum. **1657** TOMLINSON *Renou's Disp.* 523 The resumptive Syrupes .. may be referred to all analepticall and restorative ones.

analetical, obs. form of ANALYTICAL.

‖**analgesia** (ænæl'dʒiːsıə). *Med.* [mod.L., a. Gr. ἀναλγησία painlessness, f. ἀν-άλγητ-ος painless, f. ἀν priv. + ἀλγέ-ειν to feel pain.] Insensibility to pain; painlessness. Distinguished from *anæsthesia* or total insensibility.

1706 PHILLIPS, *Analgesia*, Indolency, a being free from Pain or Grief. **1876** DUHRING *Dis. Skin* 525 The condition known as 'analgesia' or 'anodynia,' in which there is a loss of sensibility to pain. **1878** FOSTER *Phys.* III. v. §3. 484 There is analgesia but no anæsthesia.

anal'gesic, *a.* and *sb. Med.* [f. prec. + -IC. A better formation would be *analgetic*: cf. *anæsthetic*.]

A. *adj.* Tending to remove pain. **B.** *sb.* A medicine that removes pain.

1875 WOOD *Therap.* 213 In the class Analgesics, are placed those drugs whose chief clinical use is in the relief of pain.

† **a'nalgesy.** *Obs.*⁻⁰ [ad. mod.L. *analgesia* (now used instead): cf. mod.Fr. *analgésie*.]

1731 BAILEY, *Analgesy*, an indolency, a being free from pain or grief. **1847** CRAIG, *Analgecy*, indolency, apathy.

analgetic (ænæl'dʒɛtık), analogical equivalent of *analgesic*.

† **a'nalie, analy, annaly**, *v. Obs. Sc.* [Apparently formed on L. *ali-us* other, but actual structure unexplained. It has the appearance of a variant of an earlier **enalie*, repr. Fr. **enalier*, L. **inali-āre*, f. *in* into, to + *alium* another. But no such antecedent forms appear.] To alienate, or abalienate.

1452 *MS.* in P. Tytler *Hist. Scotl.* (1864) II. 387 All maner of maills, goods spendit, taken, sould or analied be him. **1533** BELLENDENE *Livy* v. (1822) 464 Misereis and troubil .. had analyit [*abalienaverant*] thair hartis and mindis fra all respect that thay had to thare awne gudis. **1609** SKENE *Reg. Maj.* 112 Na husband of any woman may annaly the heritage of his wife.

† **a'nalier.** *Obs. Sc.* [f. prec. + -ER¹.] One who alienates a possession.

1609 SKENE *Reg. Maj.* 120 The house perteining to the analier, or seller.

anallagmatic (,ænælæg'mætık), *a. Math.* [f. Gr. ἀν not + ἄλλαγμα(τ-) something given in exchange, lit. a change (f. ἀλλάττ-ειν to change) + -IC.] Not changed in form by 'inversion': applied to the surfaces of certain solids, as the sphere.

1869 CLIFFORD *Brit. Assoc. Rep.* 8 On the Umbilici of Anallagmatic Surfaces. **1874** SALMON *Geom. Three Dimens.* §516 A surface which is its own inverse with regard to any point has been called an anallagmatic surface.

anallantoidian (,ænælæn'tɔıdıən), *a.* and *sb. Zool.* [f. AN- 10 + ALLANTOIDIAN.] **A.** *adj.* Having no allantois in the embryo, as the lower vertebrates. **B.** *sb.* An animal thus characterized. (Opp. to ALLANTOIDIAN.)

1861 R. T. HULME tr. *Moquin-Tandon's Elem. Med Zool.* II. I. 62 Anallantoidians—Batrachia, Pisces, Myelairia.

analog, U.S. variant of ANALOGUE.

†**a'nalogal**, *a. Obs.* [f. L. *analog-us* ANALOGOUS + -AL[1].] = ANALOGOUS. (Common in 17th c.)
a **1631** DONNE *Select.* (1840) 41 As may be analogal, proportionable, agreeable to the articles of our faith. **1677** HALE *Prim. Orig. Man.* I. i. 22, I see many analogal motions in Animals.

†**a'nalogally**, *adv. Obs. rare*$^{-1}$. [f. prec. + -LY[2].] = ANALOGOUSLY.
a **1619** DONNE *Biathan.* (1644) 29, I presume them to speak proportionally and analogally to their other Doctrine.

analogate (ə'nælәgәt). [f. ANALOG(OUS *a.* + -ATE[1].] A thing, concept, etc., shown to be analogous; an analogue.
1884 *Dublin Rev.* Apr. 307 *Being* cannot be predicated univocally of God and the creature, but by analogy of attribution of the second class, wherein God is the primary analogate. **1949** E. L. MASCALL *Exist. & Analogy* v. 100 The way in which it has being depends in the last resort upon its relation to the self-existent Being which is the prime analogate of all.

†**a'naloger**. *Obs. rare*$^{-1}$. [f. ANALOGY + -ER[1]. Cf. *astrologer, philologer*.] = ANALOGIST.
1606 FORD *Honor Trivm.* (1843) 24 Fictions and nugatory invectiues of deseruingly abused poets, or repulsed annalogers.

analogic (ænә'lɒdʒɪk), *a.* [ad. L. *analogic-us*, a. Gr. ἀναλογικ-ός pertaining to analogy, f. ἀναλογ-ία: see ANALOGY and -IC. Cf. Fr. *analogique*.] Of or belonging to analogy. †**a.** Constituted by the use of analogy; figurative (*obs.*). **b.** Of analogy.
1677 GALE *Crt. Gentiles* III. 198 Gods preceptive wil is only in an analogic, figurative, improper sense termed the wil of God. **1864** BROWNING *Sludge the Medium* 823 By all analogic likelihood. **1878** GEO. ELIOT *Coll. Breakf.-Party* 160, I will put your case In analogic form.

analogical (ænә'lɒdʒɪkәl), *a.* [f. L. *analogic-us* (see prec.) + -AL[1].]
†**1.** *Math.* Proportional; in exact ratio. *Obs.*
1570 DEE *Math. Præf.* 17 The perfect Analogicall description of the Ocean Sea coastes.
2. Of the nature of analogy; consisting in, constituted by, in accordance with analogy.
1609 E. HOBY *Let. Mr. T. H.* 41 Far more Analogicall is Saint Chrysostoms exposition. **1678** CUDWORTH *Intell. Syst.* 5 To spell out future events, by making such analogical interpretations as they use to do in augury. **1763** PRICE in *Phil. Trans.* LIII. 372 The strength of analogical or inductive reasoning. **1842** DICKENS *Amer. Notes* (1850) 29/1 Some of the analogical signs which (guided by his faculty of imitation) he had contrived. **1873** H. ROGERS *Superh. Orig. Bible* App. (ed. 3) 438 In any 'type' it is only analogical resemblance that is pretended.
3. Expressing an analogy, naming a thing after something else to which it has an analogy, metonymic; as the *heart* of an apple; the *apple* of the eye; the *mouth* of a cave; a man's *signature*.
1623 LISLE *Ælfric on O. & N. Test.* Pref. 18 Affecting too much the analogicall Latine, he leaves many times untold the true sense of our Saxon. **1724** WATTS *Log.* (J.) When a word..is attributed to several other objects, not by way of resemblance, but on the account of some evident reference to the original idea, this is peculiarly called an analogical word. **1843** MILL *Logic* III. xx. §1 When a country which has sent out colonies is termed the mother country, the expression is analogical.
†**4.** So called by analogy; figurative. *Obs.*
a **1638** MEDE *Wks.* I. xlii. 235 The food wherewith Spirits are fed is analogical, spiritual and not corporal.
5. Of analogy; = ANALOGIC.
1854 H. MILLER *Sch. & Schm.* xviii. 411 Argument in the analogical field. **1872** MINTO *Eng. Lit.* I. i. 47 The activity of his analogical faculty.
6. = ANALOGOUS. *arch.*
1644 BULWER *Chiron.* 15 Analogicall to this is that symboll of the Cynique. **1664** POWER *Exp. Philos.* III. 156 Some Parallel and Analogical effects. **1666** *Phil. Trans.* I. 144 Being Analogical to our Moon, it is most likely they are moved in like manner. **1839** HALLAM *Hist. Lit.* IV. IV. viii. 348 Zootomy has been suggested as a better name [than Animal Anatomy] but it is not quite analogical to anatomy.

analogically (ænә'lɒdʒɪkәlɪ), *adv.* [f. prec. + -LY[2].] In an analogical manner.
†**1.** *Math.* Proportionally. *Obs.*
1570 DEE *Math. Præf.* 17 Chorographie..teacheth Analogically to describe a small portion or circuite of ground.
2. In accordance with, or by the use of, analogy.
[**1635** PERSON *Varieties* I. 39 *Analogice* they may be said to be alike, that is, in some respect.] **1656** COWLEY *Pind. Odes* (1684) 67 Some new kind of Creature, called analogically by an old known name. **1667** H. MORE *Div. Dial.* I. §6 (1713) 14 Not only in Man, but analogically in the rest of Animals. **1732** BERKELEY *Min. Philos.* IV. §21 A prince is analogically styled a pilot, being to the state as a pilot is to his vessel. **1807** W. TAYLOR in *Ann. Rev.* V. 276 Children learn to speak analogically in two years. **1822** IMISON *Sc. & Art* I. 441 Reasoning analogically from the circumstances with which we are acquainted.
3. In an analogical sense, figuratively.
a **1638** MEDE *Wks.* I. li. 292 An Offering therefore is taken properly or analogically. **1677** J. WEBSTER *Witchcr.* xvii. 344 [Syllables] may analogically, and by way of similitude, be said to be measured. **1843** MILL *Logic* I. ii. §8 A name used analogically or metaphorically.

ana'logicalness. *rare.* [f. as prec. + -NESS.] 'The quality of being analogical; fitness to be applied for the illustration of some analogy.' J.
1731 BAILEY, *Analogicalness*, the being proportional. **1873** F. HALL *Mod. Eng.* 193 Popularity..is no guaranty of skill in neoterizing, with reference to need, analogicalness, or harmony.

†**a'nalogism.** *Obs. rare.* [ad. Gr. ἀναλογισμ-ός proportionate calculation, f. ἀναλογίζ-εσθαι f. ἀνάλογος: see ANALOGON, and -ISM.]
1. *Math.* The constitution of a proportion.
1656 HOBBES *Philos.* II. xiii. §4 Eng. Wks. I. 146 When four magnitudes are to one another in geometrical proportion, they are called proportionals; and by some, more briefly, analogism. **1677** BAKER in Rigaud *Corr. Sci. Men* (1841) II. 29, I work all..by analogism, bringing them to be wrought geometrically, he only arithmetically.
2. 'An argument from the cause to the effect,' J.; *à priori* reasoning.
1656 BLOUNT *Glossogr.*, *Analogism*, a forcible argument, from the Cause to the Effect, implying an unanswerable necessity. [Whence in PHILLIPS, BAILEY, JOHNSON, etc.]
3. *Med.* The judgment of diseases by similar appearances; diagnosis by analogy.
1706 PHILLIPS, *Analogism*, In the Art of Physick, a Comparison of Causes relating to a Disease. **1753** CHAMBERS *Cycl. Supp.* s.v., A discourse on the Analogism of fevers.

†**a'nalogist**[1]. *Obs.*$^{-0}$ [ad. med.L. *analogista*, used app. in error for *alogista* = an alleged Gr. *ἀλογιστής one who does not render an account, f. ἀ priv. + λόγος account.]
1656 BLOUNT *Glossogr.*, *Analogists*, Tutors who are not bound to give account of those whom they have under tuition: as Guardians and Protectors of Wards.

analogist[2] (ə'nælәdʒɪst). [f. ANALOGIZE, -ISM: see -IST.]
1. One who occupies himself with analogies, either in searching for them, pointing them out, or arguing from them.
1836 EMERSON *Nature* 35 Man is an analogist and studies relations in all objects. **1856** —— *Eng. Traits* xiv. 239 Bacon, in the structure of his mind, held of the analogists, of the idealists, or (as we popularly say, naming from the best example) Platonists. **1860** FARRAR *Orig. Lang.* 139 The Universe itself..is a mighty emblem, and man is the analogist who, by the Word that lighteth him, is enabled to decipher it.
2. A philosopher who saw in words images or analogues of the things expressed by them.
1860 FARRAR *Orig. Lang.* i. 7 The philosophers who held these views [that language was innate] were called Analogists, while those who leaned to the conventional origin of language were styled Anomalists.

analogistic (a,nælә'dʒɪstɪk), *a.* [f. prec. + -IC.] Of or pertaining to (linguistic) analogists.
1882 *Trans. Vict. Inst.* 321 Errors of the Conventional (anomalistic) and Connexional (analogistic) Theories of Language.

analogize (ə'nælәdʒaɪz), *v.* [f. ANALOGY + -IZE. Perh. immediately from Fr. *analogiser* (in Cotgr. 1611), f. same elements.]
1. *intr.* To employ analogy; to speak or reason analogically; (*orig.*) by proportion or ratio.
1655 *Let.* in Hartlib. *Ref. Commonw. Bees* 34 My Receipt would be contemptible, if I should analogize by proportion. **1849** J. WILSON in *Blackw. Mag.* LXVI. 253 Try to render 'State' by any other word, and you will be put to it. You may analogise. **1881** G. MACDONALD *M. Marston* xliii, Shall I analogise yet a little farther?
2. *trans.* To represent by analogy, to figure.
a **1743** CHEYNE (J.) We have systems of material bodies, diversely figured..: they represent the object of the desire, which is analogized by attraction or gravitation.
3. *trans.* To make, or show to be, analogous.
1802 E. PALMER *Princ. Nature* vi. (1826) 52 We cannot analogize these facts with the planetary system.
4. *intr.* (for *refl.*) To show itself analogous, to be in general harmony.
1733 CHEYNE *Eng. Mal.* I. x. §2 (1734) 91 Light..where it finds proper Organs, concurs and analogises in these Organs, with the established Laws of Bodies. **1872** F. HALL *False Philol.* 66 Exceptions, so called..analogize with special providences in the mundane order.

analogizing (ə'nælәdʒaɪzɪŋ), *vbl. sb.* [f. prec. + -ING[1].] The perception of analogies, reasoning by analogy.
1832 J. AUSTIN *Jurispr.* (1879) II. 1040 The analogising of several analogous objects: that is to say, the considering the several objects as connected by the analogy between them. **1875** EMERSON *Lett. & Soc. Aims* i. 18 All thinking is analogizing, and 'tis the use of life to learn metonymy.

‖**analogon** (ə'nælәgәn). *Pl.* **-a.** [a. Gr. ἀνάλογον that which is analogous, neut. sing. of adj. ἀνάλογ-ος according to due ratio, proportionate, conformable, f. ἀνά up to + λόγος account, ratio, proportion.] = ANALOGUE.
1810 COLERIDGE *Friend* VI. ii. (1867) 340 It has neither coordinate nor analogon. **1851** J. NICHOL *Archit. Heavens* 232 Would we seek an analogon amid phenomena of the earth, to alternations thus stupendous? **1869** FARRAR *Fam. Speech* iv. (1873) 116 This was the nearest analogon to such a conception as the natives could find.

analogous (ə'nælәgәs), *a.* [f. L. *analog-us* (a. Gr. ἀνάλογ-ος: see prec.) + -OUS.]
1. Having, or characterized by, analogy; similar in certain attributes, circumstances, relations, or uses; having something parallel. (Const *to*.)
1646 SIR T. BROWNE *Pseud. Ep.* 96 Analogus relations concerning other plants, and such as are of neare affinity unto this. **1736** BUTLER *Anal.* VII. iii. 101 We are in a state of trial..analogous or like to our moral and religious trial. **1832** J. AUSTIN *Jurispr.* (1879) I. v. 171 Two resembling objects are said..to be analogous, when one of them belongs to some class expressly or tacitly referred to and the other does not. **1847** GROTE *Greece* (1862) III. xliii. 562 The rest of Sicily had experienced disorders analogous in character to those of Syracuse.
b. *esp.* in *Nat. Hist.*
1664 POWER *Exp. Philos.* I. 55 The bristles and quils in other Animals..are analogous to the hairs in a man. **1751** CHAMBERS *Cycl.* s.v. *Analogy*, The gills of fishes are said to be analogous to the lungs in terrestrial animals. **1854** WOODWARD *Man. Mollusca* (1856) 47 Parts which correspond in their real nature (their origin and development) are termed 'homologous'; those which agree merely in appearance or office are said to be 'analogous.'
2. Expressing an analogy; = ANALOGICAL 3. *rare.*
1671 J. WEBSTER *Metallogr.* iii. 42 An analogous, if not an univocal generation. **1860** ABP. THOMSON *Laws of Th.* §58 Nouns are either Univocal, Equivocal, or Analogous. In analogous nouns one meaning is extended to new sets of objects from some proportion or resemblance between them.

a'nalogously, *adv.* [f. prec. + -LY[2].]
1. In a manner analogous (*to*, *with*, something else).
1646 SIR T. BROWNE *Pseud. Ep.* 106 Quadrupedes oviparous..have their joynts and motive flexures more analogously framed unto ours. **1853** T. ROSS tr. *Humboldt's Trav.* III. xxv. 41 This word formed analogously with the words *Tamanacu, Otomacu*, etc.
2. By, or in accordance with, analogy.
1749 P. SKELTON *Deism Rev.* vi. (T.) His unity or omnipresence, which you conceive but analogously and imperfectly. **1857** M. HOPKINS *Handbk. Average* 354 Freight, which has been called *the mother of wages*, and, therefore, analogously, of those expenses which are incidental to the production of freight.

a'nalogousness. [f. as prec. + -NESS.] The quality of being analogous; similarity in regard to relations or attributes; = ANALOGY 3.
Mod. The analogousness of objects constitutes their connexion in thought.

analogue ('ænәlɒg), *sb.* and *a.* [a. Fr. *analogue*, f. Gr. ἀνάλογ-ον ANALOGON, which was in earlier use.]
A. *sb.* **1.** An analogous word or thing; a representative in different circumstances or situation; something performing a corresponding part.
1837 WHEWELL *Induct. Sc.* (1857) III. 438 Identifying..the strata with their foreign analogues. **1839** HALLAM *Hist. Lit.* IV. IV. v. §12. 228 Boileau is the analogue of Pope in French literature. **1874** SAYCE *Compar. Philol.* viii. 324 'Renard the Fox' has its analogue among the Kafirs.
2. *esp.* in *Nat. Hist.* **a.** A part of an animal or plant which in function answers to a different part in another animal or plant; a representative or corresponding organ. Strictly said of organs of different origin.
1826 KIRBY & SPENCE *Introd. Entomol.* III. 566 In Vespa &c. a small subtriangular piece just below the base of the upper wing is probably its analogue. **1870** H. MACMILLAN *Bible Teach.* vii. 137 The green cells which clothe the veins of the leaf..may be regarded as the analogues of the green leaves which clothe the branches. **1878** FOSTER *Phys.* I. iv. §5. 158 Such a vasometer centre has an analogue in the intrinsic ganglia of the heart.
b. A species or tribe in one region, or at one period of the earth's history, which represents or occupies the place of a different species or tribe in another country, or at a different epoch; a foreign representative, an ancient or modern representative.
1830 LYELL *Princ. Geol.* I. 28 Steno had compared the fossil shells with their recent analogues. **1870** YEATS *Nat. Hist. Comm.* 105 The Arctic vegetation has no analogue in the southern hemisphere.
c. A species or group of animals or plants which occupies in relation to the division to which it belongs a position similar to that of another species or group in relation to its division; a representative in a different class or group; as the newt is among amphibians the analogue of the lizard among reptiles.
1835 KIRBY *Habits & Inst. Anim.* I. ii. 71 Humming birds, like the butterflies, whose analogues they are, suck the nectar of the flowers. **1858** T. R. JONES *Aquar. Nat.* 253 This sipunculus, however, would appear to be of a less changeable disposition than its crustacean analogue. **1879** G. ALLEN *Colour Sense* iii. 25 The fishes, marine analogues of flying creatures.
3. *Chem.* An organic compound with a molecular structure closely similar to another (typically differing in one atom or group).
1939 *Jrnl. Org. Chem.* IV. 366 The synthesis of the true pyridine analog of thiamine is under way. **1941** *Jrnl. Biol. Chem.* CXXXIX. 975 The sulfonic acid analogue of

pantothenic acid. **1953** FRUTON & SIMMONDS *Gen. Biochem.* x. 251 In general, substances that exert a competitive inhibitory effect on a given enzyme are closely related in chemical structure to the substrate of that enzyme. One of the classical cases of such inhibition by structural analogs is the inhibition, by malonic acid..of the action of the enzyme that catalyzes the conversion of succinic acid..to fumaric acid. **1957** [see *iron-monticellite* s.v. IRON *sb.*[1] 15 b]. **1969** *Nature* 29 Mar. 1225/2 Non-toxic concentrations of amino-acid analogues when fed to *Drosophila* larvae reduced the longevity of adults. **1975** *Sci. Amer.* Jan. 84/1 If this were the case, then analogues of the toxin (molecules with structural similarities) might interfere with the production of runners by the toxin. **1985** *Chem. Week* 29 May 15/2 Synthetic human calcitonin and its analogues isolated from nonhuman sources currently are used therapeutically.

4. A synthetic food product that is made to resemble a natural food in taste and texture, so as to serve as a substitute for it.

1970 *Jrnl. Agric. & Food Chem.* Nov.–Dec. 1007/2 In the preparation of the meat analogs, fat as well as other ingredients is added. **1973** *New Scientist* 2 Aug. 277/1 They're tinkering with analogues of scallops, prawns, and, one gets the impression, a good many other products. **1974** A. J. HUXLEY *Plant & Planet* (1978) xxx. 405 Similar analogues have been made by spinning protein from field and soya beans. **1977** *Washington Post Mag.* 3 July (Potomac Suppl.) 18/5 Stay away from processed cheeses and the 'analogs,' those synthetic products that pretend to be cheese substitutes.

B. *adj.* ***analogue*** (U.S. ***analog***) ***computer***, a computer which operates with numbers represented by some physically measurable quantity, such as weight, length, voltage, etc. (cf. DIGITAL *a.* 4). Also, ***analogue device, machine***, etc. Hence ***analogue computing***, computing by this process.

1946 D. R. HARTREE in *Nature* 12 Oct. 500/1 The American usage is 'analogue' and 'digital' machines. **1947** *Electronic Engin.* XIX. 178/1 Electrical analogue computing. **1948** G. R. STIBITZ *Function Unit Theory of Counting Computers* i. 2 The ordinary desk calculator is a digital machine. If the numbers are not broken down into digits, but are represented by physical quantities proportional to them the computer is called 'analog'. A slide rule is an 'analog' device. **1948** *Electronics* July 116 The REAC (Reeves Electronic Analog Computer) can solve such problems, and more complex ones. **1949** *Jrnl. R. Aeronaut. Soc.* LIII. 628/1 Electrical and electronic analogue computers have recently been developed on a commercial scale, and have been found useful in problems of aeroplane dynamics, heat transfer, and so on. *Ibid.*, The analogue machine is not strictly a computing machine, but rather a direct physical analogue of the system being studied. **1952** J. DIEBOLD *Automation* ii. 25 Analogue computers, especially the electrical ones, are very useful for the construction of models, or analogues, of industrial processes and systems. **1960** E. DELAVENAY *Introd. Machine Transl.* 130 The analog computer..simulates the problems it is asked to solve, the digital computer..works out numerical solutions to problems, by calculations made with and on digits.

analogy (əˈnælədʒɪ). Also 6 -gye, 6–7 -gie, (7 annalogy). [ad. L. *analogia*, a. Gr. ἀναλογία equality of ratios, proportion (orig. a term of mathematics, but already with transf. sense in Plato), f. ἀνάλογ-ος adj.: see ANALOGON. Cf. mod.Fr. *analogie*.]

1. *Math.* Proportion; agreement of ratios.

1557 RECORDE *Whetst.* C ij, If any one proportion be continued in more then 2 numbers, there maie be then a conference also of these proportions..that conference or comparison is named Analogie. **1570** BILLINGSLEY *Euclid* v. Introd. 126 This booke..entreateth of proportion and Analogie, or proportionalitie. **1660** BARROW *Euclid* v. def. 4 That which is here termed Proportion is more rightly called Proportionality or Analogy. **1742** BAILEY, *Analogy* [in the *Mathematicks*] the Comparison of several Ratio's of Quantities or Numbers one to another. **1855** H. SPENCER *Psychol.* (1872) II. vi. viii. 112 An analogy is 'an agreement or likeness between' two ratios in respect of the quantitative contrast between each antecedent and its consequent.

†**2.** Hence, Due proportion; correspondence or adaptation of one thing to another. *Obs.*

1577 tr. *Bullinger's Decades* 1018 Analogie is an aptnes, proportion and a certaine conuenance of the signe to yᵉ thing signified. *a* **1626** BP. ANDREWES *Serm.* (1856) I. 429 If there be an analogy of faith, so is there of hearing also. **1684** tr. *Bonet's Merc. Compit.* vi. 204 This bastard Pleurisie..arose from a pituitous matter gathered in the Bloud through Analogy with Winter. **1774** GOLDSM. *Nat. Hist.* I. 143 Some philosophers have perceived so much analogy to man in the formation of the ocean, that they have not hesitated to assert its being made for him alone.

3. Equivalency or likeness of relations; 'resemblance of things with regard to some circumstances or effects' (J.); 'resemblance of relations' (Whately); a name for the fact, that, the relation borne to any object by some attribute or circumstance, corresponds to the relation existing between another object and some attribute or circumstance pertaining to it. Const. *to, with, between.*

This is an extension of the general idea of proportion from quantity to relation generally, and is often expressed proportionally, as when we say 'Knowledge is to the mind, what light is to the eye.' The general recognition of this analogy makes *light*, or *enlightenment*, or *illumination*, an *analogical* word for *knowledge*.

1550 VERON *Godly Sayings* (1846) 28 Marke well, good reader, the analogye of the old and new sacramentes. **1605** BACON *Adv. Learn.* II. viii. §3 (1873) 122 Which three parts active [experimental, philosophical, magical] have a correspondence and analogy with the three parts speculative. **1658** PHILLIPS, *Analogy*, Like Reason, Relation, Proportion, Agreement, Correspondency. **1675** BAXTER *Cath. Theol.* II. I. 13 We can think no otherwise of the Divine Conceptions and Volitions, but as we are led by the analogy of humane acts. **1765** TUCKER *Lt. Nat.* II. 466 Analogy is the similitude or correspondence of particulars between things. **1785** REID *Intell. Powers* 65 Some conceived analogy between body and mind. **1833** BREWSTER *Nat. Magic* viii. 195 There is still one property of sound, which has its analogy also in light. **1860** TYNDALL *Glac.* II. 10. 285 The analogy between a river and a glacier moving through a sinuous valley is therefore complete. **1879** LUBBOCK *Sci. Lect.* iv. 137 There seem to be three principal types [of ants] offering a curious analogy to the three great phases: the hunting, pastoral, and agricultural stages, in the history of human development.

4. *more vaguely*, Agreement between things, similarity.

1605 TIMME *Quersit.* I. iv. 18 A great analogie or conuenience is found in this contrarietie of beginnings. *a* **1682** SIR T. BROWNE *Tracts* 45 Who from some analogy of name conceive the Ægyptian Pyramids to have been built for granaries. **1712** ADDISON *Spect.* No. 416 ¶1 Places, Persons, or Actions in general which bear a Resemblance, or at least some remote Analogy, with what we find represented. **1806** SYD. SMITH *Elem. Mor. Phil.* (1850) 359 There is a certain analogy to this in drunkenness. **1839** MURCHISON *Silur. Syst.* I. xxvii. 358 The trilobites..bear so strong an analogy to those described by M. Brongniart.

†**5.** As a figure of speech: The statement of an analogy, a simile or similitude. *Obs.*

a **1536** TINDALE *Wks.* 473 (R.) Fetching his analogie and similitude at the naturall bodie. **1570** DEE *Math. Præf.* 21 Parables and Analogies of whose natures, etc. **1651** HOBBES *Leviath.* III. xxxiv. 213 According to the same Analogy, the Dove, and the Fiery Tongues..might also be called Angels.

6. = ANALOGUE.

1646 SIR T. BROWNE *Pseud. Ep.* 158 Many have nostrills which have no lungs, as fishes, but none have lungs or respiration, which have not some shew, or some analogy of nostrills. **1661** in Heath *Grocers' Comp.* (1869) 486 Man..is the worlds analogy, And hath with it a Co-existency. **1837** LYTTON *Athens* I. 296 The child is the analogy of a people yet in childhood. **1877** LYTTEIL *Landm.* I. iii. 28 We readily find many analogies to such a name as Kairguin.

7. *Logic.* **a.** Resemblance of relations or attributes forming a ground of reasoning. **b.** The process of reasoning from parallel cases; presumptive reasoning based upon the assumption that if things have some similar attributes, their other attributes will be similar.

1602 in *Thynne's Animadv.* Pref. 107 By true Annalogie I rightly find. **1692** BENTLEY *Boyle Lect.* iv. 127 He hath made out from Example and Analogy. **1736** BUTLER *Anal.* Introd. 4 Analogy is of weight..towards determining our Judgment. **1832** J. AUSTIN *Jurispr.* (1879) II. 1040 Analogy denotes an inference or a reasoning or argumentation, whereof an analogy of objects is mainly the cause or ground. **1843** MILL *Logic* III. xx. §1 The word Analogy as the name of a mode of reasoning is generally taken for some kind of argument supposed to be of an inductive nature but not amounting to a complete induction. **1853** ROBERTSON *Serm.* Ser. IV. xxx. (1863) 231 Analogy is probability from a parallel case. We assume that the same law which operates in the one case will in another, if there be a resemblance between the relations of the things compared. **1871** C. DAVIES *Metric Syst.* III. 176 The analogy of all experience warrants the conjecture. **1875** STUBBS *Const. Hist.* I. i. 11 Analogy, however, is not proof, but illustration.

8. *Language.* Similarity of formative or constructive processes; imitation of the inflexions, derivatives, or constructions of existing words, in forming inflexions, derivatives, or constructions of other words, without the intervention of the formative steps through which these at first arose.

Thus the new inflexion *bake, baked, baked* (instead of the historical *bake, book, baken*) is due to analogy with such words as *rake, raked, raked*, etc. When the formative steps are not only absent, but could not have been present, the process is often called *False Analogy*; as when *starvation* was formed to bear the same relation to *starve*, that *vexation* does to *vex*. *Vexation* being historically due to the existence of *vexāt-* the ppl. stem of a L. vb. *vexā-re*, whence through Fr. *vexe-r* we have *vex*, there could be no such formative steps in the case of the Teut. vb. *starve*. But as all mere analogy, even that of vex-*es*, vex-*ed*, vex-*ing*, is in this sense 'false,' the term *form-association* is now commonly used of an analogical process which considers the mere *forms* of existing words, apart from their history.

1659 B. WALTON *Consid. Considered* 264 There [is]..a particular Grammar analogy in each particular tongue, before it be reduced into rules. **1706** PHILLIPS, *Analogy*..in Grammar, the Declining of a Noun, or Conjugating of a Verb, according to its Rule or Standard. **1747** JOHNSON *Plan of Dict.* Wks. 1787 IX. 178 To our language may be with great justness applied the observation of Quintilian, that speech was not formed by an analogy sent from heaven. **1751** CHAMBERS *Cycl.* s.v. *Analogy*, In matters of language, we say, new words are formed by Analogy. **1874** MORRIS *Hist. Eng. Gram.* 95 The *th* in *farther* has crept in from false analogy with *further*. **1878** SWEET in *Trans. Philol. Soc.* (1877–9) 391 Paul goes on to protest against the epithet 'false' analogy, remarking that it is really 'correct,' working as it does with unerring psychological instinct.

9. *Nat. Hist.* Resemblance of form or function between organs which are *essentially* different (in different species), as the analogy between the tail of a fish and that of the whale, the wing of a bat and that of a bird, the tendril of the pea and that of the vine.

1814 SIR H. DAVY *Agric. Chem.* 62 Linnæus, whose lively imagination was continually employed in endeavours to discover analogies between the animal and vegetable systems, conceived 'that the pith performed for the plant the same functions as the brain and nerves in animated beings.' **1854** WOODWARD *Man. Mollusca* 55 Resemblances of form and habits without agreement of structure..are termed relations of..analogy. **1857** BERKELEY *Cryptog. Bot.* §25 We understand by analogy those cases in which organs have identity of function, but not identity of essence or origin. **1870** HOOKER *Stud. Flora* 13 *Nymphæaceæ*..Affinities. With Papaveraceæ, but not close; presents analogies with Hydrocharideæ and Villarsia.

a'nalphabet, *a.* and *sb. rare.* [ad. L. *analphabēt-us*, a. Gr. ἀναλφάβητ-ος not knowing one's ABC, f. ἀν priv. + ἀλφάβητ-ος alphabet.] **A.** *adj.* = ANALPHABETIC *a.*

1670 LASSELS *Voy. Italy* I. 123 Which [books] being shipped and taken by the Turks, were many of them thrown over-board by those analphabet rogues. **1961** C. WINSTON *Hours Together* (1962) vii. 140 She had..been..barely able to trace her name on those infrequent documents..which entered their analphabet domain.

B. *sb.* Also **analphabete.** [after F. *analphabète*, G. *analphabet*, etc.] One who is totally illiterate or unable to read.

1881 *Encycl. Brit.* XIII. 460 As late as..1861..[in Italy] in a population of 21,777,331 there were..16,999,701 'analphabetes', or persons..absolutely unable to read. **1914** *N.Y. Times Current History* 12 Dec. 79 There are no analphabets to be found among them. **1938** S. BECKETT *Murphy* x. 205 The skill is really extraordinary with which analphabetes..circumvent their dread of verbal commitments.

analphabetic (ænˌælfəˈbɛtɪk), *a.* and *sb.* [f. Gr. ἀναλφάβητ-ος (see prec.) + -IC.] **A.** *adj.* **1.** Not knowing the letters; totally illiterate. *rare.*

1876 R. BURTON *Gorilla Land* II. 226 They have relapsed into the analphabetic state of their ancestors. **1940** E. POUND *Cantos* lv. 49 Tartar Yuen ruled as protector Cut down taxes, analphabetic.

2. *Phonetics.* Of or pertaining to a system of phonetic transcription whereby sounds are represented not by single letters or single signs, but by composite symbols made up of a number of individual signs each representing a feature of the sound.

1889 JESPERSEN *Articulations of Speech Sounds Repr. Analphabetic Symbols* i. 8 The next step will be an ultra-alphabetic or *analphabetic* system of writing, symbolizing not sounds, but elements of sounds. **1937** —— *Analytic Syntax* i. 13 In phonetics my own Antalphabetic (formerly called Analphabetic) system provides analogous means for symbolizing the formation of speech-sounds. **1967** D. ABERCROMBIE *Elem. Gen. Phonetics* 112 Analphabetic notations..represent each segment by a composite symbol made up of a number of signs put together.

B. *sb.* = ANALPHABET *sb. rare.*

1947 I. A. RICHARDS in *Ess. & Stud.* XXXII. 8 Two-thirds of us on this planet are..analphabetics.

†**analpha'betical**, *a. Obs.*$^{-0}$. = prec.

1681 BLOUNT *Glossogr.*, *Analphabetical*, unlearned, unlettered.

analysability (ˌænəlaɪzəˈbɪlɪtɪ). [f. ANALYSABLE *a.* + -ILITY.] The quality of being analysable.

1925 A. N. WHITEHEAD *Sci. & Mod. World* (1926) x. 232 The complexity of an eternal object means its analysability into a relationship of component eternal objects. **1932** A. H. GARDINER *Theory of Speech & Lang.* iv. §58. 216 The analysability of utterances into subject + predicate cannot be made the touchstone of the sentence. **1965** N. CHOMSKY *Aspects of Theory of Syntax* i. 56 If the structural analyses that define transformations are restricted to Boolean conditions on Analyzability..it will be impossible to formulate many 'structure-dependent' operations as transformations.

analysable, -zable (ˈænəˌlaɪzəb(ə)l), *a.* [f. ANALYSE *v.* + -ABLE.] Capable of being analyzed.

1851 H. SPENCER *Soc. Statics* Introd. 31 Where motives are readily analyzable. **1868** *Sat. Rev.* 19 Dec. 794/2 One of the most curious and least analysable things in human life ..[is] force of character. **1879** WHITNEY *Sanskr. Gr.* §99 The inflected forms are analysable into inflective endings.. and inflected stems.

analysand (əˌnælɪˈzænd). *Psycho-analysis.* [f. ANALYSE *v.* + -AND[2].] The subject of, or patient in, psycho-analysis; one whose psycho-analysis is being attempted.

1933 H. CRICHTON-MILLER *Psycho-anal.* i. 105 'The transference'. By this is denoted the relation of the analysand to the analyst. **1949** *Brit. Jrnl. Psychol.* Sept. 8 The risks of failure might plunge both analyst and analysand into very deep waters. **1953** R. F. C. HULL tr. *Jung's Coll. Wks.* VII. 136 Every analysand starts by unconsciously misusing his newly won knowledge in the interests of his abnormal, neurotic attitude. **1962** *Listener* 29 Mar. 568/2 Psycho-analysis is primarily historical and reductive, deducing the analysand's present situation from his past history.

analysandum (əˌnælɪˈzændəm). *Philos.* [f. ANALYSE *v.* + *-andum* (L. neut. gerundive termination, 'thing fit to' undergo the action of the verb: see -AND[2]).] The proposition or concept to be analysed; in a philosophical analysis, the expression to be clarified, or that which is signified by the expression to be clarified.

1907 S. H. HODGSON in *Proc. Arist. Soc.* VII. 117 But in whichever way we define apperception..we have by no means surmounted the difficulty of distinguishing, in that universal panorama which is our *analysandum*, what is due to conation from what is due to perception. **1932** *Proc. Arist. Soc.* XXXIII. 77 The kind of analysis that is possible.. depends upon the kind of combination, or complex, which the analysandum is. **1944** [see next]. **1956** J. O. URMSON *Philos. Analysis* iv. 53 To say '*p* is equivalent to *q*' where *p* is the analysis and *q* the analysandum is to utter a tautology if true. **1960** in —— *Concise Encycl. Western Philos.* 18/1 An analysis.. is a sort of definition, a kind of equation with the puzzling expression, the *analysandum*, on the left-hand side and the new expression, sometimes called the *analysis*, sometimes the *analysans*, on the right.

analysans (əˌnælɪˈzænz). *Philos.* [f. ANALYSE *v.* + *-ans* (L. pres. pple. termination).] The clarifying expression, in a philosophical analysis; the concept signified by such an expression.

1944 *Mind* LIII. 73 He suspects that the statement of an analysis must, in some sense, be about the *expressions* used for the analysandum and the analysans, as well as about these concepts. **1960** [see ANALYSANDUM].

analysation, -zation (ˌænəlaɪˈzeɪʃən). [a. actual or possible Fr. *analysation*, n. of action f. *analyser* to ANALYSE: see -ATION.] The action of analyzing; analysis.

1742 PERRY in *Phil. Trans.* XLII. 53 The Phænomena which appear'd upon Analysation. **1765** TUCKER *Lt. Nat.* II. 666 The analyzation of action. **1842** *Blackw. Mag.* LII. 114 Analyzation cannot be vague, although it may be inexact. **1881** J. INGRAM *Mem.* in *Poe's Wks.* I. 49 The admirable analyzation of his prose writings.

†**ˈanalyse**, *sb. Obs.* Also 8 -ise. [a. Fr. *analyse* (not in Cotgr. 1611; cf. It. *analísi*, Florio 1598), f. med.L. *analysis*.] = ANALYSIS.

a **1638** MEDE *Wks.* I. ii. 4 The words..are few, and therefore shall need no other Analyse than what their very number presents unto us. **1642** ROGERS *Naaman* 293 The Analyse I gave of the contents of this Verse. **1664** H. MORE *Myst. Iniq.* 276 Without any further Analyse I shall guide my exposition by the order of the verses. *c* **1730** BOLINGBROKE *Fragm.* (1777) lii, To begin this analise.

analyse, -ze (ˈænəlaɪz), *v.* Also 7–9 analize, 8 analise. [a. mod.Fr. *analyse-r* (= *faire l'analyse*), f. *analyse* ANALYSIS; see prec. (It might also have been formed in Eng. itself on the prec. sb.) On Greek analogies the vb. would have been *analysize*, Fr. *analysiser*, of which *analyser* was practically a shortened form, since, though following the analogy of pairs like *annexe*, *annexe-r*, it rested chiefly on the fact that by form-assoc. it appeared already to belong to the series of factitive vbs. in *-iser*, Eng. -IZE, = L. *-īzāre*, f. Gr. *-ίζ-ειν*, to which in sense it belonged. Hence from the first it was commonly written in Eng. *analyze*, the spelling accepted by Johnson, and historically quite defensible. The objection that this assumes a Gr. ἀναλύζ-ειν itself assumes that *analyse* is formed on Gr. ἀναλύσ-ειν, which is etymologically impossible and historically untrue.]

Prim. sign. To take to pieces; to separate, distinguish, or ascertain the elements of anything complex, as a material collection, chemical compound, light, sound, a miscellaneous list, account or statement, a sentence, phrase, word, conception, feeling, action, process, etc.

I. Generally.

†**1.** Of things material: To dissect, decompose. *Obs.* in general sense.

1601 B. JONSON in *Chester's Loves Mart.* 186 (*title*) The Phœnix Analysde. **1655** GOUGE *Comm. Hebr.* Pref. Verses, Its clear Analysis the Text unties: 'Twas sad that death did th'Author analyze. **1794** SULLIVAN *View Nat.* I. 96 The elements of the fruit itself, after having analyzed and dissected it.

2. Of things immaterial: (see *prim. sign.* above.)

1758 JOHNSON *Idler* No. 18 ⁋4 Careful to analyze their enjoyments. **1794** BURKE *Wks.* 1842 II. 476 Otherwise we should dispute all the points of morality.. we should analyze all society. *a* **1832** SIR J. MACINTOSH *Bacon & Locke* Wks. 1846 I. 327 That incapacity of being analyzed, in which they agree with all other simple ideas. **1843** MILL *Logic* (1868) Introd. 12, I shall attempt to analyse the process of inference. **1860** TYNDALL *Glac.* II. §24. 358 Means of analysing the internal constitution of a glacier. **1871** DARWIN *Desc. Man* I. iii. 79 No one, I presume, can analyse the sensations of pleasure and pain. **1873** BAIN *Logic* II. 400 The use of the Syllogism may be expressed as analyzing or separating..the three parts of a step of reasoning. **1881** *Med. Temp. Jrnl.* No. 49. 23 If we analyse these returns for England and Wales, we find no rule.

3. a. Hence, to examine minutely, so as to determine the essential constitution, nature, or form, apart from extraneous and accidental surroundings.

1809 SYD. SMITH *Wks.* 1859 I. 178/1 If by a simple pleasure is meant one, the cause of which can be easily analysed. **1817** COLERIDGE *Biog. Lit.* I. x. 213 Having first explicitly defined and analized the nature of Jacobinism. **1833** MARRYAT *Pet. Simple* I As well as I can recollect and analyse my early propensities. **1854** HODGSON in *R. Inst. Lect.* 283 Exchange..is, in all cases, when analyzed, simply each man's giving something that he wants less, for something else that he wants more.

b. Short for PSYCHOANALYSE *v.*

1909 A. A. BRILL tr. *Freud's Sel. Pap. Hysteria* (1912) 122 In those patients whom I have analyzed there existed psychic health until..there appeared an experience..that the person decided to forget. **1919** M. K. BRADBY *Psycho-analysis* x. 126, I have had no nightmare..since I was analysed. **1921** ROSE MACAULAY *Dangerous Ages* v. §4, I think you'd be awfully wise to get analysed. **1958** *Times Lit. Suppl.* 28 Mar. 173/4 (*heading*) The Analysts Analysed.

4. a. *to analyse away*: to get rid of by a process of analysis.

1877 R. H. HUTTON *Ess.* (ed. 2) I. 43 This attempt to analyse away the positive additions of creative power.

b. *to analyse out*: to discover or isolate by a process of analysis. Hence, *colloq.* to work out the elements of (a situation): see quot. 1952.

1890 W. JAMES *Princ. Psychol.* I. xiii. 503 If any single quality or constituent..of such an object, have previously been known by us isolatedly,..then that constituent..may be analysed out from the total impression. **1952** M. MCCARTHY *Groves of Academe* (1953) ix. 169 'It's a dead give-away, Domna,' he expatiated. 'Analyse it out for yourself.' **1954** *Brit. Jrnl. Psychol.* May 146 It is possible to isolate *g* [*sc.* factor in intelligence], and progressively to analyse out the verbal, spatial and other content factors. **1958** *Spectator* 30 May 692/1 The author of our study would need to look into these and analyse out some common factors.

II. Specifically.

5. *Chem. & Physics.* To ascertain the elements (proximate or ultimate) of any compound; *hence*, to ascertain whether it contains any extraneous substances. To separate light into its prismatic constituents.

1667 BOYLE *Orig. Forms & Qual.*, Analiz'd by Distillation. *a* **1691** —— (J.) Chymistry enabling us to depurate bodies, and..to analyze them. **1793** SMEATON *Edystone L.* §192 He taught me how to analyze limestones. **1831** BREWSTER *Optics* xxi. 184 The plate B is called the *analysing* plate, because its use is to analyse, or separate into its parts, the light transmitted. **1874** SCHORLEMMER *Chem. Carb. Comp.* 16 If the body to be analysed contains nitrogen. *Mod.* Samples of water from these wells have been analyzed.

6. *Literature.* To examine critically so as to bring out the essential elements, or give the essence of (a treatise or any part of it).

a **1619** FOTHERBY *Atheomast.* II. xiii. §2. 350 Logicke teacheth the Preacher, to Analize and diuide his Text. **1646** *Burd. Issachar* in *Phenix* (1708) II. 264 The first analyseth, interpreteth, and taketh away the doubts of his Text. **1815** MOORE *Veiled Proph.* Epil. (1824) 126 He then proceeded to analyse the poem. **1868** ARBER *Milton's Areop.* Introd., Its [a book's] contents may be analysed as to their intrinsic truthfulness or falsity.

7. *Gram.* To distinguish the grammatical elements of a word, phrase, or sentence; *esp.* (since 1852) To resolve a sentence into elements performing distinct functions in the expression of thought.

1724 [See ANALYSIS 6.] **1750** JOHNSON *Rambl.* No. 88 ⁋2 The employment..of analysing lines into syllables. **1867** MORELL *Eng. Gramm.* 46 Method of analysing Simple Sentences. **1870** *Daily News* 16 Apr., She will take rhetoric ..and also attempt to 'analyse' Milton's 'Paradise Lost' into subjects and predicates.

8. *Mus.* To provide an analysis of (ANALYSIS 10).

1885 G. B. SHAW *How to become Musical Critic* (1960) 110 When the work analyzed is a familiar one..the analysis..is a stereotyped reprint. **1890** *Ibid.* 189 A calm confidence in his power..to 'analyze' the last movement of the Jupiter Symphony. **1935** D. F. TOVEY *Ess. Mus. Analysis* I. 1 If the defects of the works analysed are too notorious to be ignored, he must [etc.].

9. *Philos.* To subject to logical or philosophical analysis (see ANALYSIS 9).

1910, 1958 [see ANALYSIS 9 b].

analysed, -zed (ˈænəlaɪzd), *ppl. a.* [f. prec. + -ED.] Resolved or reduced to its elements or essential constituents.

1601 CHAPMAN in *Chester's Loves Mart.* 180 She was to him th'Analisde World of pleasure. **1768** *Phil. Trans.* LIX. 498 They had recourse to the analysed characters [of the Chinese]. **1794** J. HUTTON *Philos. Light, etc.* 4 Comparing that analised fact with every other event with which it should agree.

analyser, -zer (ˈænəlaɪzə(r)). [f. as prec. + -ER[1].]

1. He who or that which analyzes.

1627 BP. HALL *Apol. agst. Brownists* §52, I need no better analyser than your selfe. **1759–67** STERNE *Tr. Shandy* (1802) III. xxxviii. 377 Thou faithful analyzer of my Disgrazias. **1823** J. HARRISON (*title*) Etymological Enchiridion or Practical Analyzer shewing the Etymon or Root of all the Words in the English Tongue. **1869** J. MARTINEAU *Ess.* II. 10 Bacon—the great analyzer of common sense.

2. *Chem. & Physics.* He who analyzes; = ANALYST 2.

1756 C. LUCAS *Ess. Waters* III. 305 Our new analysers.. make it..to suit their different purposes. **1865** *Pall Mall G.* 25 Aug. 9/2 The Calcutta analyzers call it an impure peat. **1875** EMERSON *Lett. & Soc. Aims* i. 12 The hardest chemist, the severest analyzer.

3. In the polariscope, an apparatus employed to exhibit the fact that the light has been polarized.

1863 ATKINSON *Ganot's Physics* §638 Every instrument for investigating the properties of polarised light consists essentially of two parts, one for polarising the light, the other for ascertaining the fact of light having undergone polarisation The former part is called the polariser, the latter the analyser. **1867** SIR J. HERSCHEL *Fam. Lect. Sc.* (1871) 382 The tourmaline plate between the eye and the crystal, which we shall call the 'analyzing plate,' or the 'analyzer.'

analysing, -zing (ˈænəlaɪzɪŋ), *vbl. sb.* [f. as prec. + -ING[1].] The resolving of anything into its elements; resolution; analysis. (Now mostly gerundial.)

1750 HARRIS *Hermes* I. i. (1786) 2 These different Analysings or Resolutions constitute what we call Philosophical or Universal Grammar. **1808** PIKE *Sources of Mississippi* III. App. 18 In analysing the mineral and extracting the metals.

analysing, -zing (ˈænəlaɪzɪŋ), *ppl. a.* [f. as prec. + -ING[2].] That analyzes; practising or performing analysis.

1831 BREWSTER *Optics* xxiii. 202 Without the aid either of a polarising or an analysing plate. **1849** MRS. SOMERVILLE *Connex. Phys. Sc.* xxii. 210 One of these [pencils] it absorbs, and transmits the other; it is, therefore, called the analyzing plate. **1863** C. READE in *All Y. Round* 3 Oct. 125/1 A famous analysing chemist in London.

analysis (əˈnælɪsɪs). *Pl.* **analyses** (-iːz). [a. med. (or early mod.) L. *analysis* (found *c* 1470), a. Gr. ἀνάλυσις, n. of action f. ἀναλύ-ειν to unloose, undo, f. ἀνά up, back + λύ-ειν to loose: see -SIS.]

I. Generally.

1. The resolution or breaking up of anything complex into its various simple elements, the opposite process to *synthesis*; the exact determination of the elements or components of anything complex (with or without their physical separation).

†**a.** of things material. *Obs.*, exc. as fig. from spec. uses.

1667 H. STUBBE in *Phil. Trans.* II. 501, I tryed some Analysis of Bodies by letting Ants eat them. **1867** SIR J. HERSCHEL *Fam. Lect. Sc.* 70 A mechanical analysis of the contents of your basket.

b. of things immaterial.

1581 KIRKE *Spenser's Sheph. Cal.* Argt., Which difinition albe..it agree with the nature of the thing, yet no whit answereth with the analysis and interpretation of the worde. **1590** NASHE in *Greene's Arcad.* Pref. 7 These men..doe bound their base humours in the beggerly straights of a hungry Analysis. **1753** CHAMBERS *Cycl. Supp.*, *Analysis* is most proper for the discovery of truth, and synthesis for teaching and explaining it in a systematical way. **1797** GODWIN *Enquirer* I. vi. 46 The habits of investigation and analysis. **1825** MACAULAY *Ess.*, *Milton*, Analysis is not the business of the Poet. His office is to portray, not to dissect. **1866** G. MACDONALD *Ann. Q. Neighb.* 470 A time favourable to the analysis of feeling. **1873** H. SPENCER *Sociol.* 322 Analysis has for its chief function to prepare the way for synthesis.

c. *in the last* (or *final*) *analysis* [after F. *en dernière analyse*], when reduced to its fundamental elements; at the conclusion of the investigation or examination involved; all things duly considered and weighed.

[**1791** J. MACKINTOSH *Vindiciae Gallicae* i. 89 Corporate property is here as sacred as individual, because in the ultimate analysis it is the same. **1844** E. A. POE in *Chambers's Jrnl.* 30 Nov. 345/2 Now this mode of reasoning in the schoolboy, whom his fellows termed 'lucky',—what, in its last analysis, is it?] **1877** *Independent* 29 Mar. 13/2 In the last analysis there will be a painless universe! **1885** *Harper's Mag.* Mar. 648/1 The loveliest doll in the last analysis is merely sawdust. **1902** W. H. FITCHETT *Let.* 18 Oct. in D. P. Hughes *Life H. P. Hughes* (1904) xix. 535, I have always felt that, in the last analysis, the question of union was a religious one. **1918** B. RUSSELL *Logic & Knowl.* (1956) 194 Analysis ..always depends, in the last analysis, upon direct acquaintance with the objects which are the meanings of certain simple symbols. **1957** L. F. BROSNAHAN *Genes & Phonemes* 12 The total experience incorporated in a language, in the vocabulary, morphology and syntax, must, in the last analysis, have been gained through the senses. **1963** V. NABOKOV *Gift* iii. 188 In the final analysis all girls aspire to be beauties.

2. *concr.* A tabular statement or other form embodying the results of the above process; an abridgement exhibiting the essential heads; a synopsis or conspectus; as an analysis of a text-book, of a General Charges account. ***bowling analysis***: in *Cricket*, a register of the result of each ball bowled.

1668 WILKINS *Real Char.* II. i. §1. 22 A Scheme or Analysis of all the Genus's or more common heads of things belonging to this design. **1816** *Gentl. Mag.* LXXXVI. I. 11 So good an analysis of Mr. Park's 'History of Hampstead.' **1854** F. W. LILLYWHITE *Guide to Cricketers* 22 The analysis of the Bowling is given of all those matches possessing the most interest. **1862** ROBERTSON (*title*) Analysis of Mr. Tennyson's In Memoriam. **1882** *Daily Tel.* 27 May, The fielding of the Australians..was as nothing compared with the bowling, the analysis of which we append below. **1904** WARNER *How we recovered Ashes* iii. 57 His [*sc.* Rhodes's] analysis—two wickets for seventy-eight runs—is misleading, as analyses very often are.

II. Specifically.

3. *Chem.* The resolution of a chemical compound into its *proximate* or *ultimate* elements; the determination of the elements of which it is composed; or, in the case of a substance of known composition, such as water, of the foreign substances which it may contain.

When the analysis determines only *what* the elements are, it is *qualitative*; when it determines the quantity of each present, it is *quantitative*; the latter is *gravimetrical* or *volumetrical* according as the weights or the volumes of the elements are measured.

a **1655** *Let.* in Hartlib. *Commonw. Bees* 27 Manna..hath [not] the like nature as Honey, which in its Analysis more easily is apparent. **1686** W. HARRIS *Lemery's Chem.* II. xxii. 621 Let us examine now whether any such thing can probably be found in opium by the Analysis I have made of it. **1791** HAMILTON *Berthollet's Dyeing* I. I. I. iii. 51 The quantity of charcoal which they yield by analysis. **1831** T. P. JONES *New Convers. Chem.* xxviii. 282 Sugar, starch, and gum are proximate principles, and these we obtain by proximate analysis. **1878** HUXLEY *Physiogr.* 83 A large number of analyses of air from various localities.

4. *Optics.* The resolution of light into its prismatic constituents.

1831 BREWSTER *Optics* xxiii. 205 The polarisation of the incident light, and the analysis of the transmitted light. **1860** TYNDALL *Glac.* II. §6. 253 A delicate prismatic analysis of white light.

5. *Literature.* The investigation of any production of the intellect, as a poem, tale, argument, philosophical system, so as to exhibit its component elements in simple form.

1644 E. HUIT (*title*) The whole Prophecie of Daniel Explained by a Paraphrase, Analysis and Briefe Comment. **1789** BELSHAM *Ess.* II. xxxiv. 244 Of these [theories] I shall not descend to a particular analysis. **1860** MOTLEY *Netherl.* (1868) I. vi. 357 Such, in brief analysis, was the memorable Declaration of Elizabeth. **1862** STANLEY *Jew. Ch.* (1877) I. v. 105 The critical analysis of the text.

6. *Gram.* The ascertainment of the elements composing a sentence or any part of it. *esp.* (since 1852) ***logical, syntactic,*** or ***sentence analysis***: the resolution of the sentence into elements performing distinct functions in the expression of thought, and thus having definite relations to the whole sentence and to each other, as *subject* and *predicate* with their respective *enlargements*.

1612 BRINSLEY *Lud. Lit.* viii. (1627) 104 Of the analysis or resolving a sentence. **1724** WATTS *Logic* IV. i. Wks. 1813 VII. 511 The word analysis has three or four senses..When a sentence is distinguished into the nouns, the verbs, pronouns, and other particles of speech which compose it, then it is said to be analysed grammatically. When the same sentence is distinguished into subject, predicate..then it is analysed logically, and metaphysically. **1852** *Min. Comm. Council* I. 23 Geography, history, the analysis of language, arithmetic. **1852** MORELL (*title*) Analysis of Sentences explained. **1869** FARRAR *Fam. of Speech* i. 31 The name for grammar in Sanscrit means analysis.

7. *Math.* ***ancient analysis***, the proving of a proposition by resolving it into simpler propositions already proved or admitted. ***modern analysis***, the resolving of problems by reducing them to equations.

1656 HOBBES *Elem. Philos.* (1839) 309 Analysis is continual reasoning from the definitions of the terms of a proposition we suppose true..and so on, till we come to some things known. **1660** STANLEY *Hist. Philos.* (1701) 162/2 Analysis as defined by the Scholiast upon Euclid, is a sumption of the thing sought, by the consequents (as if it were already known) to find out the truth. **1753** CHAMBERS *Cycl. Supp.* s.v., Simple Analysis is that employed in solving problems reducible to simple equations. **1798** HUTTON *Course Math.* (1827) I. 3 *Analysis* or the *Analytic Method*.. is that which is commonly used in Algebra. **1879** THOMSON & TAIT *Nat. Phil.* I. I. 171 Spherical harmonic analysis, has for its object the expression of an arbitrary periodic function of two independent variables in the proper form for a large class of physical problems involving arbitrary data over a spherical surface. **1902** E. T. WHITTAKER (*title*) A Course of Modern Analysis. *Ibid.* Pref., The first half of this book contains an account of those methods and processes of higher mathematical analysis, which seem to be of greatest importance at the present time;..it is chiefly concerned with the properties of infinite series and complex integrals, and their applications to the analytical expression of functions. **1959** G. & R. C. JAMES *Math. Dict.* 10/2 *Analysis*, that part of mathematics which uses, for the most part, algebraic and calculus methods—as distinguished from such subjects as synthetic geometry, number theory, and group theory.

8. *Logic.* The tracing of things to their source, and the resolution of knowledge into its original principles; the discovery of general principles underlying concrete phenomena.

a **1680** GLANVILL (J.) We cannot know any thing of nature but by an analysis of its true initial causes. **1724** WATTS *Logic* IV. i. (1822) 372 Analysis finds out causes by their effects. **1877** CAIRD *Philos. Kant* vii. 319 Analysis..is simply going back on the path which the mind has already travelled, proceeding from the more to the less determinate.

9. *Philos.* **a.** The resolution into their elements, as a philosophical procedure, of complex things, facts, propositions, and concepts. Freq. with defining word, as *logical* (cf. also sense b), *philosophical analysis*.

1828 J. S. MILL in *Westm. Rev.* IX. 144 To perform the logical analysis of an argument, in the manner pointed out by the doctrine of the syllogism, is not the best means of discovering whether it contain a flaw. *Ibid.* 171 The philosophical analysis of Predication, the explanation of what is the immediate object of belief when we assent to a proposition, is yet to be performed. **1883** F. H. BRADLEY *Logic* I. ii. 95 It is wholly unjustifiable to take up a complex, to do any work we please upon it by analysis, and then simply predicate as an adjective of the given these results of our abstraction. **1901** W. JAMES *Mem. & Stud.* (1911) vii. 169 Some psychologists are fascinated..by the dissecting out, whether by logical analysis or by brass instruments, of whatever elementary mental processes may be [in living action]. **1903** B. RUSSELL *Princ. Math.* iv. 42 The correctness of our philosophical analysis of a proposition may..be usefully checked by..assigning the meaning of each word in the sentence expressing the proposition. *Ibid.* vii. 83 A less complete analysis of propositions into subject and assertion has also been considered. *Ibid.* liii. 466 A distinction is made..between conceptual analysis and real division into parts. **1918** —— *Logic & Knowl.* (1956) 192 The analysis of apparently complex things..can be reduced ..to the analysis of facts which are apparently about those things.

b. (Freq. in recent Philos.) The procedure or the result of finding an expression exactly equivalent to a given word, phrase, or sentence, for the purposes of clarification.

At first an analysis was intended simply to reveal the logical structure of the analysandum, but later was often intended as leading to, or justifying, the metaphysical claim that an element eliminated by the analysis was not real, or was not fundamental: then sometimes called ***reductive analysis***, etc. (see quot. 1956).

1910 WHITEHEAD & RUSSELL *Principia Mathematica* iii. 69 In all such cases, the proposition must be capable of being so analysed that what was the grammatical subject shall have disappeared. Thus when we say 'the round square does not exist', we may, as a first attempt at such analysis, substitute 'it is false that there is an object *x* which is both round and square'. **1912** RUSSELL *Probl. Philos.* v. 91 The fundamental principle in the analysis of propositions containing descriptions is this: Every proposition which we can understand must be composed wholly of constituents with which we are acquainted. **1949** *Mind* LVIII. 46 A later and more radical form of reductive analysis is characterised by the complete repudiation of 'consciousness' and the replacement of mental 'acts' as the constituents of mind by events which are common to both mental and physical complexes. **1956** J. O. URMSON *Philos. Analysis* iii. 39 The elimination of logical constructions..is then another sort of analysis. It was variously called new-level (as opposed to same-level), or philosophical (as opposed to logical), or directional, or reductive, analysis. Different names were patronized by different analysts. **1958** G. J. WARNOCK *Eng. Philos. since 1900* ii. 27 Moore involved both himself and others in difficulties resulting from the unquestioned assumption that any analysis must be of a standard pattern. It was always to consist in providing a verbal paraphrase of what was to be analysed, in the form of a longer, more explicit, but strictly synonymous phrase or sentence. **1960** [see ANALYSANDUM].

c. ***philosophical analysis***: as a branch of Philosophy, that conducted by means of, or understood as consisting in, analysis (senses a or b); philosophy concerned with the clarification of existing concepts and knowledge, by a method of reformulation, rather than with conceptual revision or addition to knowledge; *esp.* the analytic movement associated with Bertrand Russell, Moore, Wittgenstein and others.

1843 MILL *Logic* I. II. ii. 238 Philosophical analysis confirms the indication of common sense, that the function of names is but that of enabling us to *remember* and to *communicate* our thoughts. **1887** S. H. HODGSON *Let.* 8 Apr. in R. B. Perry *Tht. & Char. W. James* (1935) I. 642 What *is* 'the mind'?.. I suspect it is a mere *façon de parler*..which has a basis neither in psychological construction nor in philosophical analysis. **1936** AYER *Lang., Truth & Logic* ii. 62 The possibility of philosophical analysis is independent of any empirical assumptions. **1943** *Mind* LII. 275 The subject [*sc.* mathematical logic].. may claim an important place in the corpus of philosophical analysis. **1956** J. O. URMSON (*title*) Philosophical Analysis: Its development between the two world wars.

10. *Mus.* A critical description of a musical work, designed to make clear its structure.

1885 [see ANALYSE *v.* 8]. **1935** D. F. TOVEY *Ess. Mus. Analysis* I. 1 Some of the analyses..were written on occasions where there was no opportunity for musical quotations.

11. *Psychol.* The mental process of discrimination, by separate attention, of the separable elements in a totality of simultaneous sensory impressions, or in any other complex experience.

1890 W. JAMES *Princ. Psychol.* I. xiii. 502 Our first way of looking at a reality is often to suppose it simple, but later we may learn to perceive it as compound. This new way of knowing the same reality may conveniently be called by the name of *Analysis*. It is manifestly one of the most incessantly performed of all our mental processes. **1938** R. S. WOODWORTH *Exper. Psychol.* xxv. 645 To judge the lines and angles of a figure requires analysis which is difficult because the observer is engrossed in the appearance of the figure as a whole.

12. *Psychiatry.* Short for PSYCHOANALYSIS.

1907 *Brain* XXX. 179 In hysteria with very little trouble the complex may be revealed by analysis, and with a good prospect of therapeutic advantage. **1912** A. A. BRILL tr. *Freud's Sel. Papers on Hysteria* (ed. 2) iv. 76 It is very difficult to examine a case of neurosis before it has been subjected to a thorough analysis. **1913** *Lancet* 10 May 1345/2 Analysis might record some latent content having nothing to do with hunting and would perhaps show Dr. Brown that he no more fears hunting in dreams than he does awake. **1916** C. E. LONG tr. *Jung's Analytical Psychol.* vii. 208 An attempt has..been made to compare analysis with the reasoning method of Dubois, which is in itself a rational process. This comparison does not..hold good, for the psychoanalyst strictly avoids argument and persuasion with his patients. **1958** *Spectator* 1 Aug. 160/1 He [*sc.* Freud] was always attracted by telepathy (so much so that he alarmed his English followers, who feared that it would give their enemies an excuse to sneer at analysis as occultism).

analyst ('ænəlɪst). [a. Fr. *analyste*, f. *analyser*, by form-assoc. w. vbs. in *-iser* (= L. *-īzāre*, Gr. *-ίζειν*, Eng. -IZE), which have agent-nouns in *-iste* (L. *-ista*, Gr. *-ιστης*, Eng. -IST). See ANALYSE. *Analyser*, *analyste*, were thus formally analogous to *latiniser*, *latiniste*.] One who makes an analysis.

1. A mathematician skilled in modern algebraical geometry. (The only sense in 17–18th c., but now rarely used without qualification.)

1656 HOBBES *Elem. Philos.* III. xx. Eng. Wks. I. 307 The analyst that can solve these problems without knowing first the length of the arch..shall do more than ordinary geometry is able to perform. **1675** COLLINS in Rigaud *Corr. Sci. Men* (1841) I. 212 A learned analyst, and a person fit to labour in discovering canons for the surd roots of equations. **1748** HARTLEY *Observ. Man* I. iii. §2 ¶87 Till the Analyst obtains the true Root. **1841** J. R. YOUNG *Math. Dissert.* Pref. 7 [Berkeley] charged analysts with changing, at the close of the reasoning, the hypothesis upon which that reasoning commenced. **1869** J. MARTINEAU *Ess.* II. 136 A skill like that of the geometrical analyst.

2. *spec.* One skilled in chemical analysis; one whose profession it is to ascertain the chemical constitution of substances. (The common use now.)

1800 HENRY *Epit. Chem.* (1808) 424 The correct analyst ought to be well grounded in general chemical information. **1869** *Daily News* 11 Aug., In the stomach and liver of the child the analyst to whom they were committed found distinct traces of the same poison. **1873** *Ibid.* 7 Nov. 5/5 Public Analyst for Bethnal-green.

3. *gen.*

[**1753** CHAMBERS *Cycl. Supp.*, *Analyst*, a person who analyzes a thing, or makes use of the analytical method. (See I.)] **1809** COLERIDGE *Friend* I. i. (1867) 4 Some pleasant analyst of taste. **1851** H. SPENCER *Soc. Statics* xxii. §3 Unobserved, perhaps, by the many, but sufficiently visible to the analyst. **1859** BUCKNILL *Psychol. Shaks.* 3 Preeminently the most truthful analyst of human action.

4. *Mus.* One who carries out analysis (ANALYSIS 10) of a musical work.

1885 G. B. SHAW *How to become Musical Critic* (1960) 109 The false estimates into which the analyst has been led by the necessity of judging the score by eye instead of by ear. **1893** [see STREPITOUS *a.*].

5. *Psychiatry.* Short for PSYCHOANALYST.

1914 EDER & MOLTZER tr. *Jung's Theory Psychoanalysis* in *Psychoanal. Rev.* I. 425 Transference to, and dependence upon the analyst could be considered as a sufficient end, with a definite therapeutic effect, if the analyst were in every respect a great personality, capable..to guide the patients. **1920** *Internat. Jrnl. Psycho-anal.* I. 128 The ideal situation for analysis is when someone, otherwise master of himself, is suffering from an inner conflict which he is unable to resolve alone, so that he brings his trouble to the analyst and begs for his help. **1952** V. GOLLANCZ *My Dear Timothy* 55 In moneyed circles with a tinge of culture people talk of 'my analyst' as glibly as our grandmothers used to talk of 'my grocer'.

6. *Philos.* A practitioner of philosophical analysis (ANALYSIS 9c); an adherent of the analytic movement in philosophy.

1936 AYER *Lang., Truth & Logic* ii. 52 The majority of those who are commonly supposed to have been great philosophers were primarily not metaphysicians but analysts. **1941** *Mind* L. 166 Metaphysical propositions are indeed nonsense, as the Analysts say, but only if taken literally; and it is unfortunate that many of the Analysts have been only too literal-minded. **1945** *Mind* LIV. 194 Philosophical analysts can do either of two things; they may undertake what one could call case studies or they may engage in the construction of systems.

analytic (ænə'lɪtɪk), *a.* and *sb.* [ad. med.L. *analytic-us*, a. Gr. ἀναλυτικ-ός analytic, f. ἀνάλυτ-ος dissolved, dissolvable, f. ἀναλύ-ειν: see ANALYSIS. Cf. Fr. *analytique*, perhaps earlier.]

A. *adj.*

1. a. Of, pertaining to, or in accordance with analysis; consisting in, or distinguished by, the resolution of compounds into their elements. esp. in *Math.* and *Philos.*: cf. ANALYSIS 7 and 9 a, b, c.

1601 B. JONSON *Poetaster* v. i. Wks. 1616. 332 A direct, and analyticke summe Of all the worth and first effects of artes. **1724** WATTS *Logic* IV. i. (1813) 511 Natural method is ..two-fold, viz. *synthetic* and *analytic*. Analytick method takes the whole compound as it finds it..and leads us into the knowledge of it by resolving it into its first principles. **1750** JOHNSON *Rambl.* No. 54 ¶ 4 They are..understood without skill in analytick science. **1789** BENTHAM *Princ. Legisl.* vi. §46 Of the several circumstances..to give some sort of analytic view. **1802** WOODHOUSE in *Phil. Trans.* XCII. 95 In the present state of analytic science, there is no certain and direct method of integrating differential equations. **1837–8** SIR W. HAMILTON *Logic* xxiv. (1866) II. 7 The words analytic and synthetic..are, like most of our logical terms, taken from Geometry. **1865** MILL *Exam. Hamilton* xx. 405 Mr. Mansel expressly limits the province of Logic to analytic judgments—to such as are merely identical. **1870** —— in *Fortnightly Rev.* VIII. 123 Taine.. in the case of the axioms of geometry,..classes them among 'analytic propositions'—that is, truths latently included in the ideas which are the subject of them, to be proved by evolving them out of the ideas. **1902** E. T. WHITTAKER *Course Mod. Analysis* iii. 47 If $f(z)$ is an analytic function, regular at all points in the interior of a contour, then $\int f(z)dz = 0$, where the integration is taken round the contour. **1936** E. NAGEL in *Jrnl. Philos.* XXXIII. 5 (*title*) Impressions and Appraisals of Analytic Philosophy in Europe. *Ibid.* 9 Analytic philosophy *is* ethically neutral *formally*. **1938** HARDY & WRIGHT *Theory of Numbers* p. v, Thus Chs. XII–XV belong to the 'algebraic' theory of numbers,..Ch. XXII to the 'analytic' theories. **1946** AYER *Lang., Truth & Logic* (ed. 2) iv. 78 A proposition is analytic when its validity depends solely on the definitions of the symbols it contains, and synthetic when its validity is determined by the facts of experience. *Ibid.*, Analytic propositions are devoid of factual content. **1946** *Mind* LV. 339, I do not think that either Prof. Moore or most of the other adherents of Contemporary British Analytic Philosophy are ready to draw the consequences from this fact. **1948** *Ibid.* LVII. 292 Analytic philosophy consists at least partly, in replacing a concept, or a set of concepts, by another concept, or set of concepts. **1959** G. & R. C. JAMES *Math. Dict.* 11/1 (*heading*) Analytic continuation of an analytic function of a complex variable.

b. ***analytic psychology***, the branch or school of psychology mainly based on the work of Locke, which endeavours to analyse ideas and trace them to their origins.

a **1854** MILL *Draft Autobiog.* (1961) 76 [= 1873 *Autobiog.* iii. 68] Under my father's direction my studies were carried into the higher branches of analytic psychology. **1889** W. JAMES *Coll. Ess. & Rev.* (1920) 311 The widely prevalent notion that analytic psychology has proved the space-perceptions of the eye to be but reproduced experiences of touch and locomotion.

c. *Mus.* ***analytic programme***, a concert programme containing analyses (ANALYSIS 10) of the works performed.

1885 G. B. SHAW *How to become Musical Critic* (1960) 77 The analytic program..costs an additional shilling.

2. Concerned with, or addicted to the use of, analysis; analytical.

1805 WORDSW. *Prel.* II. (ed. 2) 40 A toil, Than analytic industry to me More pleasing. **1876** FARRAR *Gk. Syntax* 2 Few languages are more analytic than English. **1880** *Contemp. Rev.* XXXVII. 480 Analytic education makes against the creative search of beauty, which defies analysis.

3. Short for PSYCHOANALYTIC *a.*

1912 A. A. BRILL tr. *Freud's Sel. Papers on Hysteria* (ed. 2) viii. 178 The analytic therapy..concerns itself with the genesis of the morbid symptoms. **1959** *Times Lit. Suppl.* 13 Mar. 148/2 Certain analytic terms (which they profess to avoid) such as 'acting-out'.

B. *sb.* mostly *pl.* **analytics**, transl. L. *analytica*, a. Gr. ἀναλυτικά, adj. pl. neut., used subst. by Aristotle as title of his treatises on Logic.

1. *gen.* 'The science or doctrine and use of analysis.' Chambers.

1641 HOBBES *Lett.* Wks. 1845 VII. 462 A better philosopher in my opinion then De Cartes, and not inferior to him in the analytiques. **1857** SIR J. STEPHEN *Lect. Hist. France* xvii. II. 154 Skill in the science of moral analytics.

2. *spec.* **a.** That part of logic which treats of analysis.

c **1590** MARLOWE *Faustus* i. 6 Live and die in Aristotle's works. Sweet Analytics, 'tis thou hast ravish'd me. **1607** TOPSELL *Four-footed Beasts* (1673) 353 Aristotles first book of Analyticks. **1663** BUTLER *Hud.* I. i. 66 He was in Logick a great Critick, Profoundly skill'd in Analytick. (*Annot.* Analytique is a part of Logick that teaches to decline and construe Reason, as Grammar does Words.) **1837–8** SIR W. HAMILTON *Logic* xii. (1866) I. 218 His [Aristotle's] Prior Analytics, the treatise in which he develops the general forms of reasoning. **1846** (*title*) *ibid.* II. App. 251 A New Analytic of Logical Forms.

†**b.** The algebraical branches of pure mathematics; the application of algebra to geometry. *Obs.*

1656 HOBBES *Elem. Philos.* (1839) 309, I should there have spoken of the analytics of geometricians. **1685** *Phil. Trans.* XV. 1104 My design being to trace this of the *Analyticks* (as the Greeks call'd it) or *Algebra* (as the Arabs). **1751** CHAMBERS *Cycl.* s.v., To the modern Analytics, principally, belongs algebra.

ana'lytical, *a.* [f. med.L. *analytic-us* (see ANALYTIC *a.* and *sb.*) + -AL[1]. The earliest spelling is *analeticall*, and in 15th c. L. *analeticus* is of freq. occurrence.]

1. a. Of or pertaining to analytics; employing the analytic method or process.

c **1525** SKELTON *Replyc.*, Maister Porphiris problemes..in his thre maner of clerkly workes, analeticall, topicall, and logycall. **1591** PERCIVALL *Sp. Dict.* A iij b, Marke my first analytical table. *a* **1652** J. SMITH *Sel. Disc.* VII. i. (1821) 308 The principles of true religion..are all so clear and perspicuous, that they need no key of analytical demonstration to unlock them. **1750** HARRIS *Hermes* (1841) 119 We shall postpone the whole synthetical part..and confine ourselves to the analytical; that is to say, universal grammar. **1873** SYMONDS *Grk. Poets* i. 14 Homer was never analytical. He described the world without raising a single moral or psychological question.

b. *Lang.* Expressing the various notions and relations into which a proposition or complex notion may be analyzed, by distinct words, instead of combining several into one word; as, *they shall be sent out* for *ē-mitt-ē-nt-ur*; *with a sword* for *gladio*; *plus fort* for *fortior*; *of man* for *man's*.

1873 FARRAR *Fam. of Speech* ii. 74 The Swedish and Danish..have become more analytical than Old Norse. **1874** SAYCE *Comp. Philol.* ix. 368 The analytical character of the modern European languages, of which English is the most extreme example.

c. *Math.* Applied to geometry treated by means of algebra, in the Cartesian representation of curves and surfaces by equations.

1826 H. P. HAMILTON *Princ. Analytical Geom.* 2 Algebra may be applied to investigate the Theorems, and to resolve the Problems of Geometry... Application of these elementary branches of Mathematics forms the Science of Analytical Geometry. **1845** *Encycl. Metrop.* I. 709 This branch of the subject is usually distinguished by the name of Algebraic, or Analytical, Geometry. **1881** J. M. DYER (*title*) Exercises in Analytical Geometry.

d. *Math.* Pertaining to ANALYSIS (sense 7).

1902 [see ANALYSIS 7]. **1902** E. T. WHITTAKER *Course Mod. Analysis* iii. 46 The definition of functionality must now be translated into analytical language.

2. a. Of analysis. = ANALYTIC *a.* 1.

1656 HOBBES *Elem. Philos.* I. vi. §10 Eng. Wks. I. 79 There is need partly of the analytical and partly of the synthetical method. **1802** WOODHOUSE in *Phil. Trans.* XCII. 105, I shall now shew, by a purely analytical process, what are the divisions of $x^n \pm a^n$. **1847** WHEWELL *Philos. Induct. Sc.* I. 144 Having succeeded in this analytical process, we may invert it. **1854** J. COULTHARD tr. *C. W. von Humboldt's Sphere & Duties of Govt.* viii. 105 It is the analytical philosopher alone..who is able to arrive at his results through the calm, but cold processes of reason. **1865** MILL *Exam. Hamilton* xviii. 354 This doctrine ignores the famous distinction..between Analytical and Synthetical judgments. Analytical judgments are supposed to unfold the contents of a concept. **1945** *Mind* LIV. 194 My concern is exclusively with analytical philosophy. *Ibid.*, Both the casuist and the systematist, if they are analytical philosophers, are interested in the individual clarifications that are peculiar to this kind of philosophising. **1956** J. HOLLOWAY in A. Pryce-Jones *New Outl. Mod. Knowl.* 30 The philosophy of analysis thus tends to have two somewhat different branches: the analysis of *a priori* or analytical propositions..as represented by what Russell and Wittgenstein had to say about formal logic and mathematics; and the analysis of propositions which are expressed in words, which can occur in the ordinary layman's thinking... On the whole, modern analytical philosophy has developed most in this second field.

b. ***analytical psychology*** = ANALYTIC *psychology*; also applied to the psychology of C. G. Jung, as distinguished from that of Freud (psychoanalysis), esp. the practical procedure of psychological analysis laid down by Jung.

1835 MILL *Diss. & Disc.* (1859) I. 114 Of Locke's Essay, the beginning and foundation of the modern analytical psychology, we cannot speak but with the deepest reverence. **1916** C. E. LONG tr. (*title*) C. G. Jung. Collected Papers on Analytical Psychology. **1945** H. CRICHTON-MILLER *Psycho-analysis* (ed. 2) i. 13 If we respect the history of terms, no system which diverges from the Freudian can correctly be called psycho-analysis. For purposes of differentiation Jung uses the term Analytical psychology (which happens to be a plagiarism from Stout). **1962** A. M. DRY *Psychol. of Jung* p. xi, The International Association for Analytical Psychology has been formed.

c. ***analytical programme*** = ANALYTIC *programme*.

1885 G. B. SHAW *How to become Musical Critic* (1960) 57 A careful analytical program.

3. ***analytical chemistry***, the branch of chemistry concerned with analysis (ANALYSIS 3).

1879 A. J. BERNAYS (*title*) Skeleton notes on analytical chemistry, for students in medicine. **1938** R. W. LAWSON tr. *Hevesy & Paneth's Man. Radioactivity* (ed. 2) xxii. 220 The ..large domain of the analytical chemistry of the radio-elements.

ana'lytically, *adv.* [f. prec. + -LY[2].]

1. By analytic method or process; by way or means of analysis. By the analytical method; by the methods of analytical geometry.

1656 HOBBES *Six Lessons* Wks. 1845 VII. 248 Has he not proceeded analytically in a hundred problems? **1748** HARTLEY *Observ. Man* I. iii. §2 ¶88 To determine these Associations, both analytically and synthetically. **1872** *Daily News* 3 Oct. 2 Conic sections treated both geometrically and analytically. **1878** HUXLEY *Physiogr.* 109 Proving the composition of water analytically. **1879** *Encycl. Brit.* X. 408/1 It would be possible, analytically, or by the method of coordinates, to develop the truths of geometry in a systematic course.

2. After an analytical fashion; with an analytical tendency. *rare.*

1778 JOHNSON in *Boswell* (1831) IV. 114 To be distinct, we must talk analytically. **1855** H. SPENCER *Psychol.* (1872) I. IV. viii. 478 To persons analytically inclined.

analyticity (ˌænəlɪ'tɪsɪtɪ). *Philos.* [f. ANALYTIC *a.* + -ITY.] The property, in propositions or statements, of being analytic.

1939 *Mind* XLVIII. 76 Moreover, on the basis of the analyticity of (*a*) alone absolutely nothing can be known about a consequence-relation involving '*p* v*p*.⊃. *p*' as a first member. **1953** W. V. O. QUINE *From a Logical Point of View* ii. 21 Kant's intent, evident more from the use he makes of the notion of analyticity than from his definition of it, can be restated.

analytico-, combining form of Gr. ἀναλυτικό-ς analytic, prefixed to an adj. to denote **a.** 'pertaining to analytical...' as *analytico-chemical*; **b.** 'analytical and ...', as *analytico-synthetic*.

1920 T. P. NUNN *Education* xiii. 173 Thus the function of the nervous system is never purely integrative nor purely analytic, but always analytico-synthetic. **1938** R. W. LAWSON tr. *Hevesy & Paneth's Man. Radioactivity* (ed. 2) xxiii. 230 This analytico-chemical difference. **1961** T. LANDAU *Encycl. Librarianship* (ed. 2) 81/2 Attempts have been made..to build up classification schemes inductively from certain fundamental concepts which may be combined in various ways to form a synthesized concept for a whole book. Then groups of books in these analytico-synthetic schemes may be arranged into classes.

analyze, -able, etc.: see ANALYSE, -ABLE.

anamal, -el, obs. forms of ENAMEL.

†**a'name**, *v. Obs. rare.* [OE. *anemnan*, f. A- *pref.* 1 + *nemnan* to NAME.] To mention, name.

a **1000** *Guthlac* 13 Godes spel-bodan..eal anemdon. *c* **1305** *St. Christoph.* in *E.E.P.* (1862) 60 His iugelour adai: to-fore him pleide faste & anemnede in his rym: þe deuel atte laste. *c* **1425** WYNTOUN *Cron.* VIII. xl. 104 In the abbay of Hexhame All þare folk þai gert aname.

anamesite (ə'næmɪsaɪt). *Min.* [ad. G. *anamesit* (K. C. von Leonhard *Die Basalt-Gebilde* (1832) I. 150), f. Gr. ἀνάμεσος intermediate + -ITE[1].] A fine-grained variety of basalt.

1876 P. H. LAWRENCE tr. *B. von Cotta's Rocks Classified* II. i. 135 Basaltic Rocks..a fine-grained dark grey to black mass, in which we are unable to distinguish between labradorite and augite. This fine-grained variety has been specially named by von Leonhard as *Anamesite*. *Ibid.* 136 The different stages of compactness of texture may be typified by the three names Dobrite, Anamesite, Basalt. **1879** RUTLEY *Stud. Rocks* xiii. 253 Those [basalts] in which the constituents are too small to be recognised without a magnifying power, but in which a crystalline texture is yet clearly discernible, are styled anamesites. **1937** A. JOHANNSEN *Petrography* III. 291 The name *anamesite* was given by von Leonhard to those rocks of the basalt family which, in texture, stand between the dense basalts and the coarse dolerites... It is seldom used at the present time.

‖**anamnesis** (ænəm'niːsɪs). [Gr. ἀνάμνησις remembrance, n. of action f. ἀναμνα- stem of ἀνα-μι-μνή-σκ-ειν to remember, f. ἀνά back + μνα- call to mind, f. μέν-ος mind.] **a.** The recalling of things past; recollection, reminiscence.

1657 J. SMITH *Myst. Rhet.* 249 Anamnesis is a figure whereby the speaker calling to mind matters past, whether of sorrow, joy, &c. doth make recital of them. **1876** tr. *Wagner's Gen. Path.* 11 Diagnosis from the Anamnesis, that is, from the story which the patient tells of his illness. **1876** M. DAVIES *Unorth. Lond.* 22 The doctrine of *anamnesis*, in Plato, according to which the soul had pre-existed in a purer state, and there gained its ideas.

b. *Liturgiology.* That part of the Eucharistic canon in which the sacrifice of Christ is recalled and pleaded.

1894 H. LUCAS in *Dublin Rev.* CXIV. 123 The Anamnesis, a prayer commencing with the words Μεμνημένοι οὖν, and answering more closely to the Roman *Unde et memores* than to any Gallican *Post Secreta* or Mozarabic *Post Pridie.* **1912** A. FORTESCUE *Mass* ii. 103 The next prayer (*Post pridie* or *Post mysterium*) contains the Anamnesis and Epiklesis of the Holy Ghost. **1945** G. DIX *Shape of Liturgy* vii. 205 It was precisely the institution-narrative which would need amplifying and the *anamnesis* section which would have to be supplied.

anamnestic (ænəm'nɛstɪk), *a.* and *sb.* [ad. Gr. ἀναμνηστικ-ός able to recall to mind, f. ἀναμνηστ-ός vbl. adj. f. ἀναμνσ-: see prec.]

A. *adj.* Recalling to mind; aiding the memory or recollection.

1753 CHAMBERS *Cycl. Supp.*, *Anamnestic* is applied by Blancard to remedies proper for restoring or strengthening the memory. **1879** *Syd. Soc. Lex.*, *Anamnestic Symptoms*, Phenomena occurring in a previous stage..by the remembrance of which the present condition is made more manifest.

B. *sb.*

†**1.** An anamnestic medicine or symptom.

1706 PHILLIPS, *Anamneticks*, medicines that serve to restore the Memory. **1753** CHAMBERS *Cycl. Supp.*, *Anamnestics*, in medicine, are used by some writers to denote those signs which help to discover the past state of a patient's body. **1775** ASH, *Anamnestic*, a medicine to help the memory.

2. A proposed equivalent for *mnemonic-s*.

1836–7 SIR W. HAMILTON *Metaph.* (1877) I. vii. 123 Anamnestic, the art of Recollection or Reminiscence.

anamorphic (ænə'mɔːfɪk), *a.* [f. ANAMORPH(ISM + -IC.] **1.** *Geol.* Applied to a zone characterized by anamorphism (see ANAMORPHISM 3).

1904, 1914 [see ANAMORPHISM 3].

2. *Cinemat.* (See quot. 1960.)

1954 *New Internat. Yr. Bk. 1953* 326/1 The anamorphic lens used in CinemaScope was invented by Professor Henri Chretian, a French scientist who has been working on the lens for the past twenty-five years. **1958** *Engineering* 21 Mar. 384/1 Anamorphic lenses are also available to provide wide-screen pictures in the home. **1960** O. SKILBECK *Film & TV Working Terms* 9 *Anamorphic*, type of lens which 'squeezes' the width of an Angle, compared with its height, in a camera and does the converse in a Projector.

anamorphism (ænə'mɔːfɪz(ə)m). [f. ἀνά up + μορφή form + -ISM.]

1. Distorted projection or perspective.

1836 *Edin. Rev.* LXIII. 105 Emblazoning on a separate tablet..the anamorphisms in which it [the form of his brother] had been drawn.

2. Progression from a lower to a higher type.

1852 HUXLEY in *Phil. Trans.* CXLIII. i. 63 If, however, all Cephalous Mollusks..be only modifications by excess or defect of the parts of a definite archetype, then, I think, it follows as a necessary consequence, that no anamorphism takes place in this group.

3. *Geol.* Metamorphism below oxidation level resulting in the formation of complex minerals from simpler ones.

1904 VAN HISE *Treat. Metamorphism* iv. 169 The lower zone may therefore properly be called the zone of anamorphism, or anamorphic zone. *Ibid.* 170 The zone of anamorphism may be defined as the zone in which alterations of rocks result in the production of complex compounds from simple ones. **1914** RIES & WATSON *Engin.*

Geol. iii. 204 *Anamorphic zone.* The zone of anamorphism corresponds to the zone of flowage, in which there is great pressure in all directions. It is a zone of *reconstruction*, and is especially characterized by silication involving decarbonation, dehydration, and deoxidation.

anamorphoscope (ænəˈmɔːfəskəʊp). [f. ANAMORPHO(SIS + -SCOPE.] A device, usually in the form of a vertical cylindrical mirror, made so as to give a correct image of an anamorphosis (see ANAMORPHOSIS 1).

a **1884** in KNIGHT *Dict. Mech.* Suppl. **1932** *Times Educ. Suppl.* 12 Nov. p. iv/1 The exhibits in the historical section will include the 'Anamorphoscope', a set of 12 designs showing distorted figures in perfect formation in a cylindrical mirror (date about 1635).

anamorphose (ænəˈmɔːfəʊs, -əs), *v. rare.* [f. next (or its Gr. elements) on model of METAMORPHOSE.] To represent by anamorphosis; to distort into a monstrous projection.

1876 J. A. H. MURRAY in *Mill Hill Mag.* IV. 79 Shakspere might have seen this very picture, or, if not, some other in which a skull was thus anamorphosed; in which 'looking awry,' a 'shape of grief' was found. [Cf. *Rich. II*, II. ii. 22.]

anamorphosis (ænəˈmɔːfəsɪs). [a. Gr. ἀναμόρφωσις transformation, n. of action f. ἀναμορφόειν to transform, f. ἀνά back, again + μορφό-ειν to form, f. μορφή form. Still by some pronounced *anamorphōsis*, after the Gr. ω. Cf. *metamorphosis*.]

1. A distorted projection or drawing of anything, so made that when viewed from a particular point, or by reflection from a suitable mirror, it appears regular and properly proportioned; a deformation.

1727–51 CHAMBERS *Cycl.* s.v., To draw the *Anamorphosis*, or deformation of an image, upon the convex surface of a cone. **1816** T. JEFFERSON *Writ.* (1830) IV. 273 It was to correct their anamorphosis of the Deity, that Jesus preached. **1846** JOYCE *Sci. Dial.* xiv. 306 These images are called anamorphoses. **1873** *Athenæum* 25 Jan., This bewildering object is undoubtedly an anamorphosis of a human skull.

2. *Bot.* Such a degeneration or change in the habit of a plant from different conditions of growth, as gives it the appearance of a different species or genus; abnormal transformation. Chiefly said of cryptogams, as fungi, lichens, and sea-weeds.

1830 LINDLEY *Nat. Syst. Bot.* 55 The state of anamorphosis, or..that remarkable distension or increase of the cellular tissue of vegetables, from which the name of succulent is derived. **1857** BERKELEY *Cryptog. Bot.* §446 That genus [*Chroolepus*] may be a mere anamorphosis of the crust of Lichens.

3. Repetition of the same form at a later stage of development; return to an earlier form. *rare.*

1862 LATHAM *Elem. Comp. Philol.* (L.) There is not such a thing as a true anamorphosis in language.

4. = ANAMORPHISM 2.

1852 HUXLEY in *Phil. Trans.* CXLIII. i. 63 Whether true anamorphosis ever occurs in the whole animal kingdom.

anamorphous (ænəˈmɔːfəs), *a. rare.* [f. ANAMORPH-ISM + -OUS.] Distorted, out of shape.

1833 BREWSTER *Nat. Mag.* iv. 93 The original figure must have been a deformed or anamorphous drawing, in order to give a reflected image of just proportions.

anamoured, obs. form of ENAMOURED.

anan, obs. form of ANON.

anan (əˈnæn), *int. Obs.* and *dial.* Also 6– **anon**. The quot. from Udall and Shaks. show that this is the same word as ANON *adv.* orig. in response to a call = 'In one moment; presently; coming!'; hence a waiter's response to express that he was paying attention, or awaiting commands; thence a general mode of expressing that the auditor was at the speaker's service, or begged him to say on; and in later use, a mode of expressing that the auditor has failed to catch the speaker's words or meaning, but is now alert and asks him to repeat; = I beg your pardon! What did you say? Sir? Eh? [See the whole passage in *1 Hen. IV*. II. iv. 1–126.]

a **1553** UDALL *Royster D.* IV. iii. (1869) 65 *C.* What hough! come forth Trupenie! *I.* Anon! What is your will mistresse? dyd ye call me? **1596** SHAKS. *1 Hen. IV*, II. iv. 71 *Poines.* Francis! *Fran.* Anon, anon! *Prince.* 'Anon,' Francis? No, Francis: but to morrow Francis: or, Francis, on thursday: or, indeed, Francis, when thou wilt. **1728** VANBRUGH & CIBBER *Provok'd Husb.* I. i. 30 *Man.* A right English Academy for younger Children! *J. Mood.* Anon, Sir. [*Not understanding him.*] **1751** SMOLLETT *Per. Pic.* (1779) III. lxxxv. 322 A stare of infinite stolidity, accompanied with the word Anan! **1856** LEVER *Martins of Cro' M.* 159 'Such little events are not unfrequent down here, then?' 'Anan!' said she, not understanding his question. **1863** *Whitby Gloss.* s.v. *Anon* or *Non?* the enquiry 'Sir?' or 'What do you say?' to a question or remark not heard or understood.

ananas (əˈneɪnəs, -ˈɑːnəs). Also **anana**. [So in most of the languages of Europe; app. from a native Peruvian name *Nanas*, it having been first seen by Europeans in Peru, and described under the name *Nanas* by André Thevenet, a monk, in 1555. Through mistaking the final *-s* for a plural sign, some have made the sing. *anana*.]

1. The pine-apple plant (*Ananassa sativa*) or fruit.

1613 PURCHAS *Pilgr.* I. v. xii. 431 Of their fruits Ananas is reckoned one of the best: In taste like an Apricocke, in shew a farre off like an Artichoke, but without prickles, very sweet of sent. **1714** MANDEVILLE *Fab. Bees* (1733) II. 219 The first ananas, or pine-apple, that was brought to perfection in England, grew in his [Sir M. Decker's] garden at Richmond. **1727** THOMSON *Summer* 685 Witness, thou best anâna, thou the pride Of vegetable life. **1811** T. BALDWIN (*title*) Short Practical Directions for the Culture of the Ananas, or Pine-apple Tree. **1841** D'ISRAELI *Amen. Lit.* II. 229 [Rawleigh] had given..England the Virginian tobacco, and perhaps the delicious ananas.

2. An allied West Indian fruit, the Penguin (*Bromelia Pinguin*). J.

anandrious (æˈnændrɪəs), *a. Med.* [f. Gr. ἀνανδρία want of manliness or virility (see next) + -OUS.] Without virility; impotent.

1879 in *Syd. Soc. Lex.*

anandrous (æˈnændrəs), *a. Bot.* [f. Gr. ἄνανδρ-ος husbandless, without males (f. ἀν privative + ἀνδρ- male) + -OUS.] Having no stamens; said of the females of diœcious, or the female flowers of monœcious plants.

1847 in CRAIG. **1872** BRITTEN in *Jrnl. Bot.* X. 47 Anandrous state of *Erica cinerea*.

†**aˈnanger**, *v. Obs. rare.* [f. A- *pref.* 1 (here confused with A- *pref.* 2, and expanded bef. vowel into *an-*) + ANGER *v.*] To anger exceedingly.

c **1380** *Sir Ferumb.* 634 Ferumbras was an-angred sore þat O[liuer] hym stod [so longe]. ?*a* **1500** *Virgilius* (Thoms) When the emperoure herde this, he was..sore anangered.

anangular (æˈnæŋgjʊlə(r)), *a. rare*$^{-0}$. [f. AN- *pref.* 10 + ANGULAR.] Not angular.

a **1859** WORCESTER cites GOOD.

Ananias (ænəˈnaɪəs). Name of a man who, 'with Sapphira his wife, sold a possession and kept back part of the price' (Acts v. 1, 2); used allusively for a liar.

1876 in Sperber & Trittschuh *Amer. Polit. Terms* (1962) 15/1 It is a matchless product of Uriah Heep 'harmony', or of Ananias 'harmony'. **1890** *Harper's Mag.* Apr. 795/1 Since Locke's time newspaper Ananiases have not been infrequent. **1948** 'J. TEY' *Franchise Affair* xxiii. 266 The report [of the trial] was printed under a heading which read: Ananias Also Ran.

ananters, ananthers: see ANAUNTERS.

anantherate (æˈnænθəreɪt), *a. Bot.* [f. as next + -ATE.] Not furnished with anthers.

1879 in *Syd. Soc. Lex.*

anantherous (æˈnænθərəs), *a. Bot.* [f. AN- *pref.* 10 + ANTHER + -OUS.] Destitute of anthers.

1866 GRAY *Introd. Bot.*, *Anantherous*, destitute of anthers.

ananthous (æˈnænθəs), *a. Bot.* [f. Gr. ἀνανθής flowerless (f. ἀν priv. + ἄνθ-ος flower) + -OUS.] Destitute of flowers.

1866 GRAY *Introd. Bot.* 523 *Ananthous*, without flowers.

ananthropism (æˈnænθrəpɪz(ə)m). [f. Gr. ἀν priv. + ἀνθρωπισμ-ός humanity, f. ἄνθρωπ-ος man.] A lack of fellow-feeling or humanity.

1882 SEELEY *Nat. Relig.* 50 Science cannot easily destroy our feeling for human beings..If it were otherwise we should want a word—Ananthropism—to answer to Atheism.

ananym (ˈænənɪm). *rare.* [loosely formed on Gr. ἀνά back + ὄνυμα, ὄνομα name, which properly gives ANONYM (pre-occupied by another meaning).]

1867 O. HAMST *Mart. Bibliogr.*, *Ananym*, the real name written backwards, as John Dralloc (Collard).

anapæst (ˈænəpɛst, -piːst). *Pros.* [ad. L. *anapæstus*, a. Gr. ἀνάπαιστος 'struck back, reversed,' f. ἀνά back + παί-ειν to strike.]

1. A reversed dactyl, a metrical foot, consisting of two short syllables followed by a long one.

[**1589** PUTTENHAM *Eng. Poesie* (Arb.) 133 For your *anapestus* of two short and a long ye haue these words but not many moe, as *mănĭfōld, mŏnĭlēsse, rĕmănēnt, hŏlĭnēsse.*] **1678** PHILLIPS, *Anapæst.* **1789** BELSHAM *Ess.* I. xii. 222 French heroic verse, which consists of four regular anapests. *a* **1849** H. COLERIDGE *Ess.* II. 116 [The L'Allegro, Il Penseroso, etc.] owe their delightful variety to the judicious intermixture of trochees, spondees, and even anapæsts.

2. A verse composed of, or containing, such feet.

1846 GROTE *Greece* II. II. vii. 572 The scanty fragments remaining to us of his elegies and anapæsts. **1861** GEN. P. THOMPSON *Audi Alt.* III. cxliv. 129 What did the poet laureate know about it? He should have kept to his anapæsts.

anapæstic (ænəˈpɛstɪk, -ˈiːstɪk), *a.* and *sb.* [ad. L. *anapæstic-us*, a. Gr. ἀναπαιστικός: see prec. and -IC.]

A. *adj.* Composed of anapæsts.

1699 BENTLEY *Phal.* III. (T.) I had started a new observation about the measures of the anapestick verse. **1749** *Numbers in Poet. Comp.* 58 To make the whole Line purely Anapæstic, thus: *ĭn thĕir trĭplĕ Dĕgrēes; ănd thĕ Rĕgiŏns, tŏ whĭch.* **1847** GROTE *Greece* III. xxix. 66 Tyrtæus ..employed the Anapæstic metre.

B. *sb.* Verses containing anapæstic feet.

1699 BENTLEY *Phal.* III. (T.) Several seeming examples where an anapestick is terminated with a trochee. **1749** *Numbers in Poet. Comp.* 58 The rapid Flow of Anapæstics, is ..most contrary to the stately Movement of Iambics.

anaˈpæstical, *a.* [f. prec. + -AL^{1}.] = prec.

1841 FRANCK in *Hood's Mem.* (1860) II. 92 To treat the version more frequently anapæstical than is done in the original.

anaˈpæstically, *adv. rare*$^{-0}$. [f. prec. + -LY^{2}.] In anapæstic rhythm.

1859 in WORCESTER.

anapaganize (ænəˈpeɪgənaɪz), *v. rare*$^{-1}$. [f. Gr. ἀνά back, over again + PAGANIZE.] To make pagan or heathen again.

1831 SOUTHEY in *Q. Rev.* XLV. 416 The church of St. Geneviève was..anapaganized by its absurd name of the Pantheon.

anapeiratic (ˌænəpaɪˈrætɪk), *a. Path.* [irreg. f. Gr. ἀναπειρά-εσθαι to exercise; cf. πειρατικ-ός.] 'A term applied by Dr. Hammond to paralysis resulting from the habitual use of certain muscles for a long time, such as *writer's paralysis*.' *Syd. Soc. Lex.* 1879.

†**a-ˈnapes.** *Obs.* In *Fustian a napes* = o Napes, of Naples. ('The product of that city became so firmly established in public repute that the term became corrupted, and needed explanation.' *Drapers' Dict.* 141.)

[**1463** *Act 3 Edw. IV*, v, Que null homme..use ne were en araie pur son corps..ascun fustian, bustian, ne fustian de Napuls.] **1575** LANEHAM *Lett.* 38 His doobled sleeuez of blak woorsted..a wealt towards the hand of fustian anapes. **1611** COTGR., *Tripe de velours*, Valure, Mock-velvet, Fustian an Apes. *a* **1627** MIDDLETON *Wks.* IV. 425 One of my neighbours..set a-fire my fustian and apes breeches. [**1660** *Act 12 Chas. II*, iv, in *Schedule of Rates*, Naples fustians tript, or velure plaine, the peece containing 15 yards.]

anaphase (ˈænəfeɪz). *Biol.* [a. G. *anaphase* (E. Strasburger 1884, in *Arch. f. mikrosk. Anat.* XXIII. 260), f. ANA- + PHASE.] The stage in cell division, between metaphase and telophase, during which the daughter chromosomes move apart towards the opposite poles.

1887 W. HILLHOUSE tr. *E. Strasburger's Bot.* xxxii. 363 The further phases of the separation of the sister-segments, which appertain to the receding phases of division, the anaphases. **1901** CALKINS *Protozoa* 263 Late anaphase. **1946** *Nature* 17 Aug. 239/1 The birefringence disappears at fertilization and reappears during the anaphase of the first mitosis.

‖**anaphora** (əˈnæfərə). [L. *anaphora*, a. Gr. ἀναφορά a carrying back, f. ἀνά back + φέρειν to bear.] **1. a.** *Rhet.* The repetition of the same word or phrase in several successive clauses.

1589 PUTTENHAM *Eng. Poesie* (Arb.) 208 Anaphora, or the Figure of Report..as thus: To thinke on death it is a miserie, To think on life it is a vanitie: To thinke on the world verily it is, To thinke that heare man hath no perfit blisse. **1655** GOUGE *Comm. Hebr.* xi. 24 Three times by an elegant Anaphora is this phrase, 'by faith,' used. **1751** CHAMBERS *Cycl.*, *Anaphora*..such is this of the psalmist: The voice of the Lord is powerful: the voice of the Lord is full of majesty: the voice of the Lord shaketh the wilderness. **1880** in ROBY *Sch. Lat. Gram.* §946.

b. *Gram.* The use of a word which refers to, or is a substitute for, a preceding word or group of words.

1933 BLOOMFIELD *Language* xvi. 266 The word *one*.. replaces *a* with anaphora of the noun when no other modifier is present (Here are some apples; take one). **1964** M. A. K. HALLIDAY et al. *Linguistic Sciences* viii. 248 In English these [*sc.* non-structural features] include grammatical anaphora, grammatical substitution and lexical anaphora; the first is reference back by personal pronouns and by deictics such as 'the', 'this' and 'his'; the second is the use of 'do' and 'one' in the verbal and nominal groups, as in 'I might do' and 'a big one'; the third is the repetition of a lexical item, or occurrence of a second item from one lexical set. **1964** R. H. ROBINS *Gen. Linguistics* vi. 248 Membership of these gender classes also governs the lexical relationship of anaphora or back reference which may hold across sentence boundaries. *Boy*, *girl*, and *snake* are referred to by *he*, *she*, and *it*, respectively.

2. [late Gr., f. Gr. ἀναφορά offering.] *Liturgiology.* That part of the Eucharistic service which includes the consecration, oblation, and communion; in the Western Church, the canon of the mass. Hence **aˈnaphoral** *a.*

1744 *Anc. Liturgy Ch. Jerus.* Pref. p. iii, All that Part, both of this and the other ancient Liturgies, which precedes the Anaphora, is a latter Addition to the Service of the Church. *Ibid.* p. v, The proper Anaphora, or Eucharistical Service, *viz.* from the Sursum Corda..to the Ite in Pace. **1832** W. PALMER *Orig. Liturg.* I. 27 Omitting..any comparison of the introductions of these two liturgies, I will compare their *Anaphoræ*, or solemn offices. **1859** NEALE *Liturgies of S. Mark* p. xi, The Anaphoral portion has these four divisions: The great Eucharistic Prayer: The Consecration: The Intercession for quick and dead: and The Communion. **1930** A. G. HEBERT tr. *Brilioth's Euch. Faith* ii. 20 The following versicle and response, in the anaphora of Hippolytus. **1938** *Theology* XXXVII. 265 Early anaphoral traditions of Syria and Egypt.

anaphoric (ænəˈfɒrɪk), *a.* (and *sb.*). [f. ANAPHORA + -IC.] Of, pertaining to, or constituting anaphora (sense 1 b); referring to or standing for a preceding word or group of words. Hence as *sb.*, an anaphoric word.

1914 JESPERSEN *Mod. Eng. Gram.* II. I. x. 247, I propose to apply the word *anaphoric* to *one* (or any other word) if it refers to some word already mentioned, while I say *independent* if there is no such contextual reference. **1933** BLOOMFIELD *Language* xv. 251 Anaphoric substitutes.. say only that the particular form which is being replaced (the antecedent) has just been mentioned. **1934** PRIEBSCH & COLLINSON *German Lang.* vi. 315 Anaphoric expressions (e.g. *the former, he, this*) placed ahead of new matter. **1957** R. W. ZANDVOORT *Handbk. Eng. Gram.* III. vii. 177 Anaphoric *one* after a definite article or an adjective is usually called a *prop-word*. **1960** S. STUBELIUS *Balloon* 28 While *machine* was from the outset the standard anaphoric for the aeroplane in the press, *apparatus* was only occasionally used.

anaphorical (ænəˈfɒrɪkəl), *a.* [f. ANAPHORIC *a.* + -AL.] = prec. Hence **anaˈphorically** *adv.*

1914 JESPERSEN *Mod. Eng. Gram.* II. I. x. 247 *The little one* is used anaphorically if it means 'the little flower' or whatever it is that has just been mentioned. **1924** —— *Philos. Gram.* xviii. 237 When the prop-word *one* is anaphorical (i.e. refers to a word mentioned already). **1933** BLOOMFIELD *Language* xv. 251 In English, finite verb expressions are anaphorically replaced by forms of *do, does, did*, as in *Bill will misbehave just as John did.* **1947** H. JACOB *Planned Aux. Lang.* iv. 82 The adjective is used anaphorically with the plural -s.

anaphrodisiac (ænˌæfrəʊˈdɪzɪək), *a.* and *sb. Med.* [f. Gr. ἀν priv. + ἀφροδισιακ-ός venereal.] **A.** *adj.* That diminishes sexual appetite. **B.** *sb.* A drug having this tendency; an antaphrodisiac.

1823 PARIS & FONBL. *Med. Jurispr.* I. 209 The anaphrodisiac powers of camphor were long believed. **1865** FARRE *Mat. Med.* 587 Drastic cathartics act as anaphrodisiacs. **1875** WOOD *Therap.* (1879) 146 Stadion claims that digitalis.. may be regarded as a true anaphrodisiac.

anaphroditic (ænˌæfrəʊˈdɪtɪk), *a. Biol.* [f. Gr. ἀναφρόδῑτ-ος without love + -IC. Cf. Fr. *anaphroditique.*] Developed without concourse of sexes.

1879 in *Syd. Soc. Lex.*

anaphroditous (ænˌæfrəʊˈdaɪtəs), *a.* [f. as prec. + -OUS.] Without sexual appetite.

1879 in *Syd. Soc. Lex.*

anaphylaxis (ænəfɪˈlæksɪs). *Path.* [mod.L., ad. F. *anaphylaxie* (Portier and Richet 1902, in *Compt. Rend. Soc. de Biol.* 170), f. ANA- + Gr. φύλαξις watching, guarding. Cf. PROPHYLAXIS.] Extreme sensitivity of tissues to the reintroduction of an antigen. Also *transf.* So **anaphyˈlactic** *a.*, esp. in ***anaphylactic shock***, a rapid physical reaction to such reintroduction.

1907 *Jrnl. Med. Research* XVI. 143 (*heading*) On Serum Anaphylaxis in the Guinea-Pig. Animals may react to certain toxic or foreign substances.. by an increased susceptibility or anaphylaxis. *Ibid.* 174 It is important to consider certain general relations which exist between the anaphylactic serum and the affected organism... Sera of animals other than the horse have an anaphylactic power against the guinea-pig. **1909** *Arch. Int. Med.* III. 519 Anaphylaxis.., also called hypersusceptibility, supersensitiveness, is a condition of unusual or exaggerated susceptibility of the organism to foreign substances. **1910** *Lancet* 9 July 84/1 Deep ether narcosis.. modifies anaphylactic shock. **1913** J. M. BLIGH tr. *Richet's Anaphylaxis* i. 1 Anaphylaxis is the opposite condition to protection (phylaxis). **1925** C. H. BROWNING *Bacteriology* x. 232 A similar phenomenon is that of anaphylaxis in which a parenteral injection of foreign serum, which is quite harmless to a normal individual, may cause serious symptoms in one who has received a previous injection of serum; this result follows only when both injections consist of serum of the *same* foreign species. **1939** *Nature* 6 May 767/2 Anaphylactic phenomena in the rhesus monkey after intravenous injection of horse serum. *Ibid.* 768/1 Fatal anaphylaxis usually occurred within six minutes of the injection of egg-white. **1953** HINSIE & SHATZKY *Psychiatric Dict.* (ed. 2) 571/1 In psychic anaphylaxis.. the reaction is.. a response to the sensitizing agent rather than to the activating agent. **1955** *Sci. News Let.* 9 Apr. 234/3 These severe sting reactions, and similar severe reactions to bites of biting insects, are what scientists call anaphylactic shocks. **1959** *Listener* 24 Dec. 1115/2 Anaphylactic shock, allergy, and hypersensitivity are all aberrations or miscarriages of the immunological process.

anaplastic (ænəˈplɑːstɪk, -æ-), *a. Surg.* [f. as next + -IC; cf. Fr. *anaplastique.*] Of or pertaining to anaplasty.

1879 in *Syd. Soc. Lex.*

anaplasty (ˈænəplɑːstɪ, -æ-). *Surg.* [a. Fr. *anaplastie*, f. Gr. ἀνάπλαστ-ος, vbl. adj. f. ἀναπλάσσ-ειν to form anew: see -Y³.] Reparation of external lesions by the use of adjacent healthy tissue.

1879 in *Syd. Soc. Lex.*

‖**anaplerosis** (ˌænəplɪˈrəʊsɪs). [mod.L., a. Gr. ἀναπλήρωσις, f. ἀνα-πληρό-ειν to fill up.] The filling up of a deficiency.

1680 H. MORE *Apocal. Apoc.* 258 Respecting the voices of the three Angels, and Anapleroses of them. **1706** PHILLIPS, *Anaplerosis*.. in Surgery, that part of the Art, which restores what either Nature has denied, or is otherwise decayed. **1853** MAYNE *Exp. Lex.*, *Anaplerosis*.. filling up of parts that have been destroyed, as in wounds, cicatrices, etc.

anaplerotic (ˌænəplɪˈrɒtɪk), *a.* and *sb. Med.* [ad. assumed Gr. *ἀναπληρωτικός: see prec. and -IC.] **A.** *adj.* Tending to supply deficiencies of tissue.

1721 BAILEY, *Anaplerotick Medicines*, such that fill up Ulcers with Flesh. **1748** *Vegetius' Distemp. Horses* 165 You put an anaplerotick Medicine upon the Wound. **1853** in MAYNE *Exp. Lex.*

B. *sb.* (in *pl.*) An anaplerotic substance.

1706 PHILLIPS, *Anapleroticks*. Medicines that help to fill Ulcers with Flesh. **1751** CHAMBERS *Cycl.*, *Anaplerotics* are the same with what we otherwise call incarnatives.

†**anapleˈrotical**, *a. Obs.* = prec.

†**anapleˈroticalness.** *Obs.* [f. prec. + -NESS.]

1731 BAILEY, *Anapleroticalness*, the quality of filling up.

anapnograph (əˈnæpnəgrɑːf, -æ-). [f. Gr. ἀναπνοή respiration (f. ἀνά again + πνέ-ειν to breathe) + -γραφ-ος writing.] An instrument for registering the movements and amount of expiration and inspiration.

1870 S. GEE *Auscult. & Percuss.* ii. §2 ¶1 Whether the anapnograph will be more useful remains to be seen.

anapnoic (ænəpˈnəʊɪk), *a.* [f. as prec. + -IC.] Pertaining to respiration.

1879 in *Syd. Soc. Lex.*

anapnometer (ænəpˈnɒmɪtə(r)). [f. as prec. + μέτρον a measure: see -METER.] An instrument for measuring the force of respiration; a spirometer.

1860 in FOWLER *Med. Voc.*

anapodeictic (ænˌæpəʊˈdaɪktɪk), *a. rare*⁻⁰. [f. Gr. ἀν priv. + ἀποδεικτικ-ός demonstrable, f. ἀπό off, away + δεικ-νύ-ναι to show.] Incapable of being shown by argument, undemonstrable.

†**anapoloˈgetical**, *a. Obs.*⁻⁰ [f. Gr. ἀναπολόγητ-ος inexcusable (f. ἀν priv.: see APOLOGETIC) + -ICAL.]

1656 BLOUNT *Glossogr.*, *Anapologetical*, inexcusable.

anapophysial (ˌænəpəʊˈfɪzɪəl), *a. Phys.* [f. next + -AL¹.] Of or pertaining to an anapophysis.

1866 HUXLEY *Preh. Rem. Caithn.* 89 Anapophysial tubercles.. strong and well developed. **1875** BLAKE *Zool.* 16 The little development of the metapophysial and anapophysial processes.

anapophysis (ænəˈpɒfɪsɪs). *Phys.* [f. Gr. ἀνά back + ἀπόφυσις offshoot, f. ἀπό off + φύσις growth.] A small bony process, springing in a backward direction from the neural arch of the vertebræ, between the metapophysis and diapophysis.

1854 OWEN in *Orr's Circ. Sc.* Org. Nat. 169 The exogenous parts are the diapophysis.. [and] the anapophysis. **1881** MIVART *Cat* 39 The posterior process which projects backwards as much as any other part of the vertebra, is called the accessory process, or Anapophysis.

†**aˈnapped**, *pa. pple. Obs. rare*⁻¹. [f. A- *pref.* 1 (or 6) + OE. *hnæppian* to NAP.] Sleepy.

c **1305** *E.E. Poems* (1862) 78 Anapped he was sore. He lynede adoun vpon his boc þo he ne miȝte studie nomore.

anapsid (æˈnæpsɪd), *a.* and *sb. Zool.* [ad. mod.L. *Anapsida* (S. W. Williston 1917, in *Jrnl. Geol.* XXV. 419), f. AN- + Gr. ἀψίς, ἀψιδ- arch: see -ID³.] **A.** *adj.* Of or pertaining to the reptilian subclass Anapsida, which comprises turtles, tortoises, and extinct groups all characterized by a skull with no temporal openings; having or being such a skull. **B.** *sb.* A reptile of the subclass Anapsida. Cf. DIAPSID *a.*, SYNAPSID *a.* and *sb.*

1933 A. S. ROMER *Vertebr. Paleont.* vi. 128 Truly primitive forms must have possessed a completely roofed skull like that of their amphibian ancestors, and for this condition the term 'anapsid' was coined. **1956** —— *Osteol. Reptiles* II. 473 The Chelonia are considered as true anapsids. **1969** A. BELLAIRS *Life of Reptiles* I. ii. 25 (*caption*) Cross-section through reptilian skull behind orbits showing anapsid condition. **1971** E. C. OLSON *Vertebrate Paleozool.* III. viii. 305 This classification associated many reptiles that are now placed in separate categories and did not entirely follow its own criteria (e.g., placing anapsids as synapsids). **1982** I. F. SPELLERBERG *Biol. Reptiles* i. 7 (*caption*) Examples of extinct anapsid reptiles.

anaptotic (ænəpˈtɒtɪk), *a.* [f. Gr. ἀν(ά) again + ἄπτωτ-ος indeclinable + -IC: see APTOTIC. (Or ? f. ἀνά back + πτωτικ-ός belonging to case.)] Falling back from inflexion, again uninflected. Applied, by some, to languages, in which most of the inflexions have disappeared by phonetic decay, their place being supplied by relational words and rules of position.

1850 LATHAM *Varieties of Man* 12 Languages of the English type, Anaptotic. **1858** *Penny Cycl.* 2nd Supp. 378/1 The languages of the great European races are never aptotic. They are mostly anaptotic, or [else] having amalgamate inflections. **1862** H. SPENCER *First Princ.* II. xiv. §112 (1875) 322 There have grown out of the amalgamate languages the 'anaptotic' languages.

anaptyxis (ænəpˈtɪksɪs). *Phonetics.* [mod.L., a. Gr. ἀνάπτυξις unfolding.] (See quot. 1895¹.) So **anapˈtyctic, -ical** *adjs.*, pertaining to anaptyxis.

1885 *Athenæum* 18 July 76/1 The irregular appearance of the anaptyctic vowel. **1895** P. GILES *Man. Compar. Philol.* 169 Anaptyxis.. the development of a vowel between two consonants. **1895** *Athenæum* 14 Sept. 347/2 ['Cycular' is] formed from 'cycle' on the analogy of 'circular' from 'circle' (more correctly from *circulus*). The irregular anaptyxis cannot be defended on historical grounds. **1953** *Archivum Linguisticum* V. 83 The introduction of an anaptyctic vowel next to *H* is a logical step where contiguous consonants in zero grade forms, including *H*, impede the speaker. **1955** *Sci. Amer.* Aug. 79/3 The insertion of an extra vowel in the body of a word, giving rise to an additional syllable, is called 'anaptyxis'. Note athaletic, ellum, fillum, siggunel,.. and 'he ran thataway'.

anarch (ˈænək), *sb.* and *a.* [ad. Gr. ἄναρχ-ος without a chief or head; cf. Fr. *anarche* in Cotgr. 1611. But the Eng. use is conformed to that of other derivatives in *-arch*, as *monarch, tetrarch*, etc.]

A. *sb.* **1.** An author of anarchy; a leader of revolt.

1667 MILTON *P.L.* II. 988 Thus Satan: and him thus the Anarch old.. answer'd. **1728** POPE *Dunc.* III. 339 Lo! the great Anarch's ancient reign restor'd. **1818** BYRON *Childe Har.* II. xlv, Imperial anarchs doubling human woes. **1848** H. MILLER *First Impress.* xvii. (1857) 283 The old anarch of Infidelity is sure always to effect a transitory lodgment.

2. An advocate of anarchy, an anarchist.

1884 W. CORY *Lett. & Jrnls.* (1897) 508 We occupied the Delta in 1882 to prevent anarchs from hindering trade on the Canal. **1885** R. L. & F. STEVENSON *Dynamiter* 194, I recognise in you the marks of an accomplished Anarch. **1966** *New Statesman* 26 Aug. 299/2 The self-righteousness of a sour young anarch.

B. *adj.* [The sb. used *attrib.*] *rare.*

a **1822** SHELLEY *Triumph of Life*, The anarch chiefs, whose force and murderous snares Had founded many a sceptre-bearing line.

anarchal (əˈnɑːkəl), *a. rare.* [f. as prec. + -AL¹.]

1. Without government; anarchic.

1824-9 LANDOR *Imag. Conv.* (1846) I. 135 Calling those bodies of men anarchal which are in a state of effervescence.

2. Tending to, or involving, anarchy; anarchical.

1824-9 LANDOR *Imag. Conv.* I. 36 The anarchal doctrines of the popish priesthood.

3. = ANARCH *a.*

1840 *Blackw. Mag.* XLVII. 528 High-sated wealth, decorous pride of place, Mankind's anarchal kings.

anarchial (əˈnɑːkɪəl), *a.* [f. ANARCHY + -AL¹. Cf. *antimonial, arterial.*] Of the nature of anarchy or confusion; disorderly, unregulated; anarchical.

1710 'G. LOVEWHIG' *Last Will & Test. of C-h of E-d* 9 All other like Republican, Anarchial, and Factious Innovators. **1775** in ASH. **1823** BENTHAM *Princ. Legisl.* (ed. 2) i. §14 Whether it [the mere averment of his own unfounded sentiments] is not anarchial. **1831** *Blackw. Mag.* XXIX. 49 That anarchial and revolutionary spirit which had shewn itself. **1848** *Tait's Mag.* XV. 479 Thence two civilizations, two distinct societies: one Moldo-Wallachian and aristocratic; the other Illyrian and Mahometan; in Bosnia, anarchial; in Bulgaria, uncertain; in Servia, democratic. **1879** LEWES *Psychol.* i. 5 Each worker brings his labours as a contribution to a common fund, not as an anarchial displacement of the labours of predecessors.

anarchic (əˈnɑːkɪk), *a.* [f. Gr. ἄναρχ-ος (see ANARCH) + -IC; after ἀρχικός. Cf. Fr. *anarchique*, Cotgr. 1611.] **a.** Of or belonging to anarchy; without rule or government, lawless.

1790 BURKE *Fr. Rev.* Wks. V. 234 The barbarous anarchick despotism of Turkey. *Ibid.* 401 They expect that they shall hold in obedience an anarchic people by an anarchic army. **1850** CARLYLE *Latter-d. Pamph.* viii. (1872) 260 The whole world risen into anarchic mutiny. **1869** SEELEY *Ess. & Lect.* iv. 118 Culture itself has become anarchic.

b. Pertaining to ANARCHY 1 b.

1889 W. DONISTHORPE *Individualism* 256 Under a truly anarchic system.

anarchical (əˈnɑːkɪkəl), *a.* [f. as prec. + -ICAL.]

1. = ANARCHIC.

1597 HOWSON *Serm.*, 24 Dec., 29 That state was not anarchicall, or without authoritie. **1660** C. BOND *Scutum Reg.* 68 Then might the king make the acting of his people against him Treason.. which would bring all to Anarchical confusion. **1766** tr. *Beccaria, Crimes* xiii. 49 Formalities.. which will place anarchical impunity on the throne of justice. **1860** MOTLEY *Netherl.* (1868) I. i. 19 That powerful, turbulent, but most anarchical little commonwealth.

2. Connected with, tending to, or involving anarchy.

1649 C. WALKER *Hist. Indep.* II. 149 Who under colour of Merchandise vent Antimonarchicall and Anarchicall Tenents. **1797** *Hist. Europe* in *Ann. Reg.* 107/2 The propagation of their anarchical doctrines. **1847** LEWES *Hist. Philos.* II. 31 Anarchical efforts have ended in universal despotism.

a'narchically, *adv.* [f. prec. + -LY².] In an anarchic or anarchical manner or condition; in defiance of existing order, lawlessly.

1872 LIDDON *Elem. Relig.* iv. 152 It [the earth] cannot plunge anarchically through space.

anarchism ('ænəkɪz(ə)m). [f. Gr. ἄναρχ-ος (see ANARCH) + -ISM.] The principles or practice of anarchy, or anarchists.

1642 SIR E. DERING *Sp. on Relig.* 153 This Bill..will prove the mother of absolute Anarchisme. **1656** BLOUNT *Glossogr.*, *Anarchism*, the Doctrine, Positions or Art of those that teach anarchy; also the being itself of the people without a Prince or Ruler. **1882** SIR C. DILKE in *Daily News* 3 July 2/6 Russian Nihilism, German Social Democracy, and French Anarchism were, in a high degree, the children of Protection. **1893** G. B. SHAW (*title*) The Impossibilities of Anarchism. **1913** J. A. ESTEY *Revolutionary Syndicalism* v. 128 The 'veritable abyss', which separates the ideal of Anarchism (i.e. philosophic Anarchism) from the ideal of Syndicalism. **1962** *New Statesman* 7 Sept. 287/1 His method is to examine the 'Family Tree' of anarchism, with its roots in Lao-Tse, Zeno and the Essenes.

anarchist ('ænəkɪst). [f. as prec. + -IST. Cf. mod.Fr. *anarchiste.*] One who admits of no ruling power; an advocate or promoter of anarchy; one who upsets settled order.

1678 CUDWORTH *Intell. Syst.* 319 That the Egyptians were universally Atheists and Anarchists, such as..resolved all into Senseless Matter as the first and highest Principle. **1791** BENTHAM *Anarch. Fallac.* Wks. 1843 II. 498 The anarchist ..denies the validity of the law..and calls upon all mankind to rise up in a mass, and resist the execution of it. **1862** H. SPENCER *First Princ.* I. i. §2 (1875) 10 The anarchist who denies the right of any government..to trench upon his individual freedom. **1889** S. WEBB in Shaw *Fabian Ess. Socialism* 44 The complete freedom preached by..the scientific Anarchists of to-day.

b. *attrib.* quasi-*adj.*

1812 SOUTHEY in *Q. Rev.* VIII. 346 That some of the anarchist writers are in the pay of France.

anarchistic (ænɑː'kɪstɪk), *a.* [f. ANARCHIST + -IC: see -ISTIC.] Belonging to, characteristic of, or adhering to anarchists or anarchism. Hence **anar'chistically** *adv.*

1884 *Standard* 5 Dec. 5/5 The seizure of Revolutionary and Anarchistic prints. **1900** H. G. WELLS *Love & Mr. Lewisham* xxiii, That Honesty is essentially an anarchistic and disintegrating force in society. **1932** *Times Lit. Suppl.* 29 Dec. 990/3 They live at the expense of the society they anarchistically reject.

anarchize ('ænəkaɪz), *v.* [f. Gr. ἄναρχ-ος (see ANARCH) + -IZE; cf. *monarchize* and mod.Fr. *anarchiser.*] To render anarchic, reduce to anarchy; to destroy the settled order of.

1800 COLERIDGE *Own Times* I. 263 That Suwarrow, though he had rescued the North of Italy from its invaders, should have pillaged and anarchised it. **1815** T. JEFFERSON *Writ.* (1830) IV. 248 To anarchize by gold the government he could not overthrow by arms.

anarcho-syndicalism (æ,nɑːkəʊ 'sɪndɪkəlɪz(ə)m). [comb. form. of ANARCHY + SYNDICALISM.] = SYNDICALISM. So **a,narcho-'syndicalist** *sb.*, = SYNDICALIST; also as *adj.*

[**1913** J. A. ESTEY *Revolutionary Syndicalism* i. 31 Jaurès.. was throwing them back into Anarchist-Syndicalism.] **1934** in WEBSTER. **1937** A. KOESTLER *Spanish Test.* I. ii. 49 The party and Trades Union of the Anarchists and Anarcho-syndicalists. **1938** *Ann. Reg. 1937* 241 Anarcho-syndicalist opposition was forced underground. **1940** H. READ *Philos. Anarchism* iv. 28 Whatever may be the merits and demerits of the anarcho-syndicalist system, it can and does work. **1949** J. S. SCHAPIRO *Liberalism* xiv. 362 Proudhon has been exalted as the father of anarchosyndicalism. **1955** H. HODGKINSON *Doubletalk* 12 Anarcho-syndicalism, or direct action by anarchist factory workers, is equally anathema. *Ibid.*, The anarcho-syndicalists carry their treacherous activities under the banner of the 'protection of the rights of the individual and his free development'.

anarchy ('ænəkɪ). Also 6–7 -ie. [ad. Gr. ἀναρχία, n. of state f. ἄναρχ-ος without a chief or head, f. ἀν priv. + ἀρχός leader, chief. The word was also adopted in med.L. *anarchia*, and Fr. *anarchie* (Cotgr. 1611), from one or other of which the Eng. may have been immediately taken.]

1. a. Absence of government; a state of lawlessness due to the absence or inefficiency of the supreme power; political disorder.

1539 TAVERNER *Erasm. Prov.* (1552) 43 This unleful lyberty or lycence of the multytude is called an Anarchie. **1605** BACON *Adv. Learn.* II. xxiii. §36 (1873) 241 Pompey.. made it his design..to cast the state into an absolute anarchy and confusion. **1664** H. MORE *Myst. Iniq.* 219 A Polity without an Head..would not be a Polity, but Anarchy. **1796** BURKE *Corr.* IV. 389 Except in cases of direct war, whenever government abandons law, it proclaims anarchy. **1840** CARLYLE *Heroes* (1858) 277 Without sovereigns, true sovereigns, temporal and spiritual, I see nothing possible but an anarchy; the hatefullest of things. **1878** LECKY *Eng. in 18th C.* I. i. 12 William threatened at once to retire to Holland and leave the country to anarchy.

b. A theoretical social state in which there is no governing person or body of persons, but each individual has absolute liberty (without implication of disorder).

1850 *Eclectic Rev.* XCI. 167 Confessions of an Anarchist. .. Proudhon proceeds..that 'all men are equal and free. Society is, therefore, by nature and destination, autonomic ..there is no government'... We see nothing a-head that warrants us in supposing that man is about to be regenerated; and, for the present, must pronounce *anarchy* to be a delightful dream! **1884** RAE *Contemp. Socialism* vii. 281 This idea of a 'genial anarchy'..has always been the favourite social remedy of the Russian revolutionary party. **1889** W. DONISTHORPE *Individualism* 282 Scientific anarchy is..the end towards which society is moving. **1892** *Daily News* 27 Apr. 5/8 Anarchy means the placing in common of all this world's riches to allow each to consume according to his needs. Anarchy is a great family where each will be protected by all and will take whatever he requires.

2. *transf.* Absence or non-recognition of authority and order in any sphere.

a. *gen.*

1667 MILTON *P.L.* x. 283 The waste Wide Anarchie of Chaos. **1821** BYRON *Sardan.* I. ii. (1868) 356 The satraps uncontroll'd, the gods unworshipped, And all things in the anarchy of sloth. **1831** BREWSTER *Newton* (1855) II. xix. 205 Some of the provincial mints were in a state of anarchy. **1959** *Daily Tel.* 23 Feb. 10/5 The spirit of anarchy today current in the visual arts. *Ibid.*, A form of emotional anarchy even more destructive of talent than the slovenly disregard of technique.

b. Non-recognition of moral law; moral disorder.

1656 COWLEY *Chronicle* ix, Thousand worse Passions then possest The Inter-regnum of my Breast. Bless me from such an Anarchy! **1713** STEELE *Englishm.* No. 7. 44 The Licentious are in a State of barbarous Anarchy. **1875** HAMERTON *Intell. Life* VI. ii. 203 A moral anarchy difficult to conceive.

c. Unsettledness or conflict of opinion.

a **1661** FULLER (in WEBSTER) There being then..an anarchy, as I may term it, in authors and their reckoning of years. **1719** YOUNG *Revenge* IV. i, No more I'll bear this battle of the mind, This inward anarchy. **1754** CHESTERF. in Boswell *Johnson* (1816) I. 237 Our language is, at present, in a state of anarchy. **1842** W. GROVE *Corr. Phys. Forces* 3 An anarchy of thought,—a perpetuity of mental revolutions.

†**a'nareta.** *Obs. Astrol.* [Incorrect f. *anæreta*, Latinized ad. Gr. ἀναιρέτης destroyer, murderer.] 'The killing Planet threatning Death in a Nativity.' Phillips 1696. Hence **anaretic** *a.*

1647 LILLY *Chr. Astrol.* civ. 529 The Anareta, or Interficient Planet, is he who is placed in the eighth house. **1819** J. WILSON *Dict. Astrol.* 2, *Anareta*, the planet that destroys life. *Ibid.* 3 Violent deaths are caused when both the Malefics have dignities in the Anaretic place.

†**a'narmed,** *ppl. a. Obs.* [variant of ENARMED: see AN- *pref.* 4.] Armed, in arms.

c **1500** *Lancelot* 615 Rather I shall..Resaue my deith anarmyt wnder sheld. *Ibid.* 2219 Al anarmyt they Come to the King. *Ibid.* 2499 Al enarmyt both with spere and scheld.

†**a'narrow,** *v. Obs. rare*⁻¹. [f. A- *pref.* 1 + OE. *narwian* to NARROW, also to trouble, afflict. Cf. L. *angustus.*] To cramp, crush, dishearten.

c **1300** *K. Alis* 3346 He makith heom way with scharpe launce; Thy men anarwith thy continaunce.

anarthria (æ'nɑːθrɪə). [mod.L., ad. G. *anarthrie* (see below), f. Gr. ἀναρθρία want of vigour (ἄναρθρος without strength, f. ἀν- (AN- 10) + ἄρθρον joint): see -IA¹.] Defective articulation in speech. Hence **a'narthric** *a.*, of or pertaining to anarthria (*Cent. Dict.*, 1889).

First used in G. by E. Leyden 1867, in *Berl. klin. Wochenschr.* 25 Feb. 78/1, adopting a suggestion of Dr. Tobias.

1881 *Syd. Soc. Lex.*, *Anarthria*, disjointed speech, an impairment of the articulation usually dependent upon bulbar paralysis. **1897** H. T. PERSHING in T. L. Stedman *20th Cent. Practice* X. ix. 779 Stammering, syllable-stumbling, and scanning... The word anarthria may be used to designate any of these defects. **1915** C. B. CRAIG in *Jrnl. Amer. Med. Assoc.* LXIV. 51/2 Where this area is the site of disease, the resultant symptom is designated by Marie [1906 *La Semaine Médicale* 23 May 243/3] anarthria, and is the simple motor aphasia of the older writers. **1926** *Contemp. Rev.* CXXIX. 96 We have seen a number of hopelessly incurable general paralytics mumbling unceasingly through their anarthria—'Every day and in every way, I am getting better.' **1961** *Brit. Med. Dict.* 92/1 *Anarthria*, the loss of the power of articulating words, the condition being caused by a local lesion.

anarthrous (æ'nɑːθrəs). [f. Gr. ἀν priv. + ἄρθρ-ον joint, (in grammar) the article, + -OUS.]

1. Of Greek sbs.: Used without the article.

1808 MIDDLETON *Grk Article* (1841) 102 When it [πᾶς] is employed to denote that every individual of that species is spoken of, then the Substantive is anarthrous. **1879** FARRAR *St. Paul* II. 185 Γραφαί ἅγιαι..a proper name for the Scriptures, and therefore anarthrous.

2. *Phys.* Jointless; or so fat as to appear so.

1879 in *Syd. Soc. Lex.*

anarthrously (æ'nɑːθrəslɪ), *adv.* [f. prec. + -LY².] Without the (Greek) article.

1852 ALFORD *Grk. Test.* II. 308 Νόμος..is never thus anarthrously used as = ὁ νόμος except where usage will acount for such omission of the article.

a'narthrousness. [f. as prec. + -NESS.] Omission of the (Greek) article.

1879 FARRAR *St. Paul* II. 516 *note*, The spread of Christianity is naturally marked by the increasing anarthrousness (omission of the article) of its commonest terms.

anartic, obs. rare form of ANTARCTIC.

anasarca (ænə'sɑːkə). *Path.* [f. Gr. ἀνά up + σάρξ (σάρκα) flesh; perh. orig. a phrase, or adj. sing. fem., but at length taken as sb.] A dropsical affection of the subcutaneous cellular tissue of a limb or other large surface of the body, producing a very puffed appearance of the flesh.

1398 TREVISA *Barth. De P.R.* VII. lii. (1495) 265 The dropesye that hyghte Yposarca other Anasarca. **1681** tr. *Willis' Rem. Med. Wks.*, Anasarca, the watry dropsy swelling up the whole flesh. **1732** ARBUTHNOT *Rules of Diet* 391 When the Lymph stagnates, or is extravasated, under the Skin, it is called an Anasarka. **1836** TODD *Cycl. Anat. & Phys.* I. 425/2 Symptoms of sea-scurvy..with anasarca of the lower limbs.

b. *transf.* and *fig.*

1807 *Edin. Rev.* XI. 83 A similar fanciful analogy has induced him to give the name of Anasarca to the redundant moisture that is perceived in vegetables during wet weather. **1841** D'ISRAELI *Amen. Lit.* (1859) I. 316 An aged power dissolving in its own corruption, which..looked with complacency on its own unnatural greatness, its political anasarca. **1873** *Treas. Bot.* (ed. 2) 61 *Anasarca*, a condition of plants analogous to dropsy.

anasarcous (ænə'sɑːkəs), *a.* [f. prec. + -OUS.] Of the nature of, or showing signs of, anasarca.

1676 WISEMAN *Chirurg.* I. xxiii (R.) I found..his legs anasarcous, and his back and hips excoriated, with lying in bed. **1738** D. BAYNE *Gout* 100 Rheumatick anasarcous tumors or swellings. **1836** TODD *Cycl. Anat. & Phys.* I. 63/1 Anasarcous dropsy is the only disease in which the fat of the adipose membrane is entirely consumed.

ana'seismic, *a.* [f. Gr. ἀνά up + σεισμ-ός earthquake + -IC.] (See quot.)

1881 J. MILNE in *Nature* No. 632. 126 Anaseismic shocks, or those where vertical motion is prominent.

†**ana'staltic,** (*a.* and) *sb. Obs.* [ad. Gr. ἀνασταλτικ-ός tending to check (f. ἀνά back + στέλλ-ειν to send) + -IC.] (See quot.)

1775 ASH, *Anastaltics*, medicines of a restringent quality. **1860** FOWLER *Med. Voc.*, *Anastaltic*, synonym of 'styptic.'

anastate ('ænəsteɪt). *Biol.* (*Disused.*) [f. ANA- + Gr. στατός placed.] A substance formed in the process of anabolism in a living organism: opp. to KATASTATE.

1885 M. FOSTER in *Encycl. Brit.* XIX. 19 The substances or mesostates appearing in the former [*sc.* the anabolic series of processes] we may speak of as anastates, those of the latter we may call katastates. *Ibid.*, In the animal-cell the initial anastates seem..generally more complex than the final katastates. **1889** GEDDES & THOMSON *Evol. Sex* vii. 88.

anastatic (ænə'stætɪk), *a.* [f. Gr. ἀνάστασις resurrection; cf. στατικ-ός causing to stand.] Of the nature of revival; *spec.* applied to a printing process, in which facsimiles of writing, drawings, or letter-press are produced by a transfer process from zinc plates.

1849 *Rep. Brit. Assoc.* 120 On Anastatic Printing and its various combinations by H. E. Strickland, M.A. **1859** *Athenæum* 12 Feb., The anastatic process has two advantages over lithography.

anastigmat (ænə'stɪgmæt). *Photogr.* [a. G. *anastigmat* (Miethe), back-formation from *anastigmatisch* adj.: see next.] An anastigmatic lens or system of lenses.

1890 *Brit. Jrnl. Photogr.* 19 Sept. 604/2 Doublet Anastigmat, No. 102, by Carl Zeiss Jena. **1894** *Amer. Ann. Photogr.* 100 The Anastigmat..is the most rapid lens I have tried. **1902** *Westm. Gaz.* 23 June 8/2 All scientists have declared it impossible to construct a true Anastigmat lens without the aid of the Jena glass. **1908** *Ibid.* 6 June 14/2 The best lens for copying purposes is..one of the flat field anastigmats. **1957** AMOS & BIRKINSHAW *Television Engineering* I. ix. 187 For lens combinations it [*sc.* elimination of curvature of field] can be achieved, if the lenses are separated, by correct choice of lens constants. A lens combination thus corrected is termed an anastigmat.

anastigmatic (ænəstɪg'mætɪk), *a.* [f. AN- 10 + ASTIGMATIC *a.*; cf. G. *anastigmatisch* and STIGMATIC *a.* 9.] Not astigmatic; free from astigmatism: applied to a compound lens so constructed as to correct the astigmatic aberration.

1890 P. RUDOLPH *Brit. Pat. 6028* 1 It is..necessary to choose the ratios of the single lenses..in such a manner that the opposed astigmatic differences are of the same magnitude, in view of attaining compensation of this astigmatism, or anastigmatic correction of the entire objective. **1893** *Year-Bk. Photogr.* 10A (Advt.), Zeiss' Patent Anastigmatic Lenses..are the result of calculations with the new Jena Glass. **1897** *Outing* (U.S.) XXX. 340/2 The lens must be one of the almost faultless anastigmatic type. **1901** *Brit. Jrnl. Photogr.* 22 Nov. 744/1 The anastigmatic flatness of field. **1902** [see STIGMATIC *a.* 9]. **1953** *Electronic Engin.* XXV. 138/1 Anastigmatic lenses are employed in this unit so that a high degree of optical accuracy is obtained.

anastomasis, -atic, obs. ff. ANASTOMOSIS, -OTIC.

anasto'mosant, *ppl. a. rare*⁻⁰. [a Fr. *anastomosant*, pr. pple. of *anastomoser*: see next.] Anastomosing.
1879 in *Syd. Soc. Lex.*

anastomose (ə'næstəməʊz), *v.* [a. Fr. *anastomose-r*, f. *anastomose*, f. mod.L. *anastomōsis*, f. Gr. ἀναστόμωσ-ις: see ANASTOMOSIS.] **a.** *trans.* To connect by anastomosis (? *obs.*). **b.** *intr.* To communicate by anastomosis, to intercommunicate, inosculate. Said of blood-vessels, sap-vessels, rivers, and branches of trees.
1697 in *Phil. Trans.* XIX. 465 The Umbilical Arteries which are anastomosed with the Veins of the Matrix. **1788** ANDERSON in *Phil. Trans.* LXXIX. 158 An elongation of the sword-like cartilage.. having anastomosed with that bone at the symphysis. **1830** LINDLEY *Nat. Syst. Bot.* Introd. 22 The veins of their leaves.. anastomosing in various ways, so as to form a reticulated plexus of veins of unequal size. **1858** GEIKIE *Hist. Boulder* v. 75 The ribs not straight, but irregularly anastomosing, that is, running into and coalescing with each other. **1881** R. BURTON in *Academy* 21 May 367/1 The Libu and the Lungo-é-ungo influents have anastomosed to form the Liambai-zambese.

a'nastomosed, *ppl. a.* [f. prec. + -ED.] Connected by anastomosis.
1789 ANDERSON in *Phil. Trans.* LXXIX. 66, I found the chasms or divisions anastomosed through every part of it. **1868** WRIGHT *Ocean W.* v. 119 Substance of the skeleton cartilaginous, fibres anastomosed in all directions.

anastomosing (ə'næstəməʊzɪŋ), *vbl. sb.* [f. as prec. + -ING¹.] = ANASTOMOSIS.
c **1810** ABERNETHY *Surg. Wks.* (1827) II. 49 A slight hæmorrhage.. from the anastomosing of the vessels. **1836** TODD *Cycl. Anat. & Phys.* I. 15/1 This artery.. terminates by anastomosing with the internal mammary.

a'nastomosing, *ppl. a.* [f. as prec. + -ING².] Communicating by anastomosis; inosculating.
1795 HAIGHTON in *Phil. Trans.* LXXXV. 198 The anastomosing nervous filaments. **1842** *Blackw. Mag.* LII. 170 A Flemish landscape, irrigated by anastomosing ditches. **1854** CARPENTER *Comp. Phys.* v. 223 The arteries.. terminate in a complex system of anastomosing tubes.

‖**anastomosis** (əˌnæstə'məʊsɪs). *Pl.* -'oses. Also 7–8 **-asis.** [mod.L., a. Gr. ἀναστόμωσις, n. of action f. ἀναστομό -ειν to furnish with a mouth or outlet.] Intercommunication between two vessels, channels, or distinct branches of any kind, by a connecting cross branch. Applied originally to the cross communications between the arteries and veins, or other canals in the animal body; whence to similar cross connexions in the sap-vessels of plants, and between rivers or their branches; and now to cross connexions between the separate lines of any branching system, as the branches of trees, the veins of leaves, or the wings of insects.
1615 CROOKE *Body of Man* 379 By Anastomosis.. or apertion and opening of two vessels one into another. **1630** MAY *Contn. Lucan* I. 200 As they through each other glide Make many knots, as if they tooke a pride In these strange foldings, and themselves did please In those admired Anastomoses. **1769** in *Phil. Trans.* LIX. 201 The lymphatics of the stomach.. have very numerous anastomoses. **1856** H. MILLER *Test. Rocks* 446 We sometimes find cases of anastomosis among the stems of the higher plants. **1859** R. BURTON in *Jrnl. R. G. S.* XXIX. 234 The African name for a central lake is Tanganyika, signifying an anastomosis, or a meeting-place. **1879** DRESSER in *Cassell's Techn. Educ.* I. 151/2 Much of the Celtic ornament.. consisted of an anastomosis, or net-work of often grotesque creatures.

anastomotic (əˌnæstə'mɒtɪk), *a.* (and *sb.*) [ad. L. *anastomōtic-us*, a. Gr. ἀναστομωτικ-ός pertaining to opening, f. ἀναστομό-ειν: see prec. In sense 1 often written *anastomatic*, with reference to Gr. στοματικός pertaining to the mouth.]
†**1.** (As in Latin) Applied to medicines designed to open the mouths of vessels. Also used *subst. Obs.*
1657 *Physical Dict.*, *Anastomaticum*, medicine opening obstructions. **1706** PHILLIPS, *Anastomoticks*, medicines that open and widen the Orifices of the Vessels, so as to cause the Blood to circulate freely and pass easily out of the Arteries into the Veins: or Medicines which serve to open the Pores and Passages. **1721** BAILEY, *Anastomaticks*.. as Purgatives, Sudorificks, and Diureticks. **1839** HOOPER *Med. Dict.* 101 *Anastomotic*, a term anciently applied to medicines which were supposed to open the mouths of vessels.
2. Pertaining to or forming anastomosis; providing intercommunication.
1836 TODD *Cycl. Anat. & Phys.* I. 97/2 By.. the enlargement of the anastomotic branches, the whole system of the circulation is gradually being altered. **1847–9** *Ibid.* IV. 450/2 The anastomotic distribution of the bile-ducts.

‖**anastrophe** (ə'næstrəfiː). *Rhet.* [Gr. ἀναστροφή a turning back, f. ἀνά back + στρέφ-ειν to turn.] Inversion, or unusual arrangement, of the words or clauses of a sentence.
1577 H. PEACHAM *Gard. Eloq.* (T.) *Anastrophe*, a preposterous order, or a backward setting of words, thus: *All Italy about I went*, which is contrary to plain order, *I went about all Italy*. **1785** WALKER *Rhet. Gram.* (T.) Anastrophe.. by which we place last, and perhaps at a great distance from the beginning of the sentence, what, according to the common order, should have been placed first. **1871** in *Pub. Sch. Lat. Gram.* 446.

anatase ('ænəteɪs). *Min.* [a. Fr. *anatase*, ad. Gr. ἀνάτασ-ις extension, f. ἀνά up + τα- stem of τείνειν to stretch.] Haüy's name (in reference to the length of its crystal) for the native oxide of titanium, for which Dana prefers De Saussure's OCTAHEDRITE.
1843 HUMBLE *Dict. Geol.*, *Anatase*, pyramidal titanium.. a pure octahedral oxyde of titanium. **1878** GURNEY *Cryst.* 82 Anatase and Rutile have an identical composition, both being titanium dioxide.

† **'anathem,** *sb. Obs.* [a. Fr. *anathème* (12th c. in Littré), ad. L. *anathema*: see next. Rhymes with *them* in Sylvester, with *dream* in Drummond.]
1. One accursed. = ANATHEMA 1. *rare.*
c **1555** HARPSFIELD *Divorce Hen. VIII* (1878) 149 Pope Julius was an anatheme and accursed for dispensing with the same.
2. A sentence of damnation, a curse, = ANATHEMA 2.
c **1555** HARPSFIELD *Divorce Hen. VIII* (1878) 61 Terrible anathems and excommunications. **1598** SYLVESTER *Du Bartas, Captaines* 386 The voice divine.. [had] choicely armed them 'Gainst Jericho, with his owne anathem. *c* **1630** DRUMM. OF HAWTH. *Poems* (1711) 10/2 My voice, now cleave the earth with anathems.. Till.. life a slumber is of fearfull dreams. **1648** GAGE *West. Ind.* iii. (1655) 8 Excommunicated with an Anathem.

anathema (ə'næθɪmə). *Pl.* **anathemas**; also, in sense 3, **ana'themata.** [a. L. *anathema* an excommunicated person, also the curse of excommunication, a. Gr. ἀνάθεμα, orig. 'a thing devoted,' but in later usage 'a thing devoted to evil, an accursed thing' (see *Rom.* ix. 3). Orig. a var. of ἀνάθημα an offering, a thing set up (to the gods), n. of product f. ἀνατιθέναι to set up, f. ἀνά up + τιθέναι (stem θε-) to place. Cf. prec., and ANATHEME.]
I. From eccl. Greek and Latin.
1. Anything accursed, or consigned to damnation. Also quasi-*adj.* Accursed, consigned to perdition.
1526 [See ANATHEMA MARANATHA]. **1625** BACON *Ess., Goodness* (Arb.) 207 He would wish to be an Anathema from Christ, for the Salvation of his Brethren. **1634** CANNE *Necess. Separ.* (1849) 162 Delivered over unto Satan, proclaimed publicans, heathens, anathema. **1765** TUCKER *Lt. Nat.* II. 299 Saint Paul wished to become anathema himself, so he could thereby save his brethren.
2. The formal act, or formula, of consigning to damnation. **a.** The curse of God. **b.** The great curse of the church, cutting off a person from the communion of the church visible, and formally handing him over to Satan; or denouncing any doctrine or practice as damnable. *Hence* **c.** Any denunciation or imprecation of divine wrath against alleged impiety, heresy, etc. **d.** A curse or imprecation generally.
(The weakening of the sense has accompanied the free use of *anathemas* as weapons of ecclesiastical rancour.)
a. *a* **1619** DONNE *Biathan.* (1644) 192 Which Anathema.. was utter damnation, as all Expositors say. **1756** BURKE *Vind. Nat. Soc.* Wks. I. 64 The divine thunders out his anathemas. **1877** MOZLEY *Univ. Serm.* ii. 37 To strike with His anathema those who made a gain of their virtues.
b. 1590 SWINBURN *Testaments* 60 Vnlesse he be excommunicate with that great curse, which is called Anathema. **1642** FULLER *Holy & Prof. St.* v. xi. 404 The Donatists, whilest blessing themselves, cared not for the Churches Anathema's. **1726** AYLIFFE *Parerg.* 256 An Anathema.. differs from an Excommunication only in respect of a greater kind of Solemnity. **1769** ROBERTSON *Charles V*, III. VIII. 71 Against all who disclaimed the truth of these tenets, anathemas were denounced. **1844** GLADSTONE *Gleanings* V. xlv. 114 The Pope.. has condemned the slave trade—but no more heed is paid to his anathema than to the passing wind.
c. 1782 PRIESTLEY *Nat. & Rev. Relig.* II. 80 The Mohammedans denounce anathemas against unbelievers. **1850** GLADSTONE *Gleanings* V. xiv. 182 To deliver over to anathema the memories of our forefathers in the Church.
d. 1691 NORRIS *Pract. Disc.* 90 Willing rather to err with the Multitude.. than incur the great Censure, the heavy Anathema of Singularity. *a* **1757** CIBBER in Dilworth *Pope* 16 How then could you thunder out such anathema's on your own enemies? **1827** LYTTON *Pelham* lxvii. (1840) 294 'Confound the man!' was my mental anathema. **1867** LYD. CHILD *Romance Repub.* xx. 237 The Signor.. succeeded in smothering his half-uttered anathemas.
II. From the earlier sense of ἀνάθεμα or ἀνάθημα. (In this sense better pronounced ænə'θiːmə)
3. A thing devoted or consecrated to divine use.
1581 MARBECK *Bk. of Notes* 39 Anathema (saith Chrisostome) are those things which being consecrated to God, are laied up from other things. **1608** TOPSELL *Serpents* 779 Will not permit a [spider's] web—the very pattern, index, and anathema of supernaturall wisdome—to remain untouched. **1857** BIRCH *Anc. Pottery* (1858) I. 178 The little figures, in the shape of animals.. may have been votive offerings to the gods, such anathemata being offered by the poor.

anathema maranatha (mærə'neɪθə). [Gr. ἀνάθεμα a thing accursed; Μαρὰν ἀθά = Syriac *māran ethā* 'the Lord hath come.' (The pron. ought to be məˌrænə'θɑː)] These words occur together in *1 Cor.* xvi. 22. According to modern criticism, *maran atha* is a distinct sentence having no connexion with *anathema*; but in earlier texts of the Greek it was connected with it and the connexion variously explained; hence *anathema maranatha* has been taken as a portentously intensified form of *anathema* in its various senses.
1526 TINDALE *1 Cor.* xvi. 22 Yf eny man love not the lorde Jesus Christ, the same be anathema maranatha. [WYCLIF, Be he cursid, mara natha. **1611** Let him bee Anathema Maranatha. **1881** (*Revised*) Let him be Anathema. Maranatha.] **1753** CHAMBERS *Cycl. Supp.* s.v., Others will have Anathema maranatha to have answered to the third and highest degree of excommunication among the Jews. **1856** MRS. STOWE *Dred* II. ii. 23, I don't see the sense of such an anathema maranatha as we got to-day.

† **a'nathemate,** *v. Obs. rare*⁻¹. [f. med.L. *anathemāt-* ppl. stem of *anathemā-re* to anathematize, f. ANATHEMA.] To anathematize, to accurse.
1615 G. SANDYS *Trav.* 145 A countrey.. anathemated, for the death of Christ.

anathematic (ˌænəθiː'mætɪk), *a. rare.* [ad. Gr. ἀναθηματικ-ός, f. ἀνάθημα a votive offering: see ANATHEMA II.] Of the nature of, or pertaining to, an anathema or offering.
1850 LEITCH *Müller's Anc. Art* §361 The so-called Bathyllus of Samos.. and the anathematic reliefs there mentioned.

aˌnathe'matical, *a.* and *sb. rare* [f. Gr. ἀναθεματικ-ός (see ANATHEMA and -IC) + -AL¹.] **A.** *adj.* Of the nature of an anathema. † **B.** *sb.* = ANATHEMA. *Obs.*
1583 *Exec. Treason* (1675) 32 [Also in FLEMING *Contn. Holinshed* III. 1365/2] Their Curses, their Excommunications, their Sentences, and most solemn Anathematicals. **1775** ASH, *Anathematical*, relating to an anathema. **1882** *Li-quor Christmas Ann.* I. 27/1 To profane my lips with an anathematical expression. **1927** *Scots Observer* 22 Jan. 15/1 The tenets of militarism were fathered upon Carlyle and his name made anathematical.

aˌnathe'matically, *adv. rare*⁻⁰. [f. ANATHEMATICAL *a.* + -LY².] In anathematical manner; by means of solemn cursing.
1775 in ASH.

† **a'nathematism.** *Obs.* [ad. Gr. ἀναθεματισμός cursing, excommunication, f. ἀναθεματίζ-ειν: see ANATHEMATIZE and -ISM. Cf. Fr. *anathématisme*.] The formal statement or declaration of an anathema, an ecclesiastical denunciation.
1565 HARDING in Jewel *Def. Apol.* (1611) 269 Theodorites reprehension of the eleuenth Anathematisme against Nestorius. **1660** JER. TAYLOR *Duct. Dubit.* III. iii. §13 A law of Justinian, forbidding anathematisms to be pronounced against the Jewish Hellenists. **1699** BURNET 39 *Art.* Introd. 3 With Anathematisms against the contrary Doctrines. **1753** CHAMBERS *Cycl. Supp.* s.v., The decrees of councils are commonly guarded by anathematisms.

anathematization (əˌnæθɪmətaɪ'zeɪʃən). [ad. med.L. *anathematīzātiōn-em*, n. of action f. *anathematīzā-re* to ANATHEMATIZE. Cf. Fr. *anathématisation* in Cotgr. 1611.] The action of anathematizing, or (formally) pronouncing accursed.
1593 BILSON *Govt. Ch.* 26 Anathematization from the people of God. **1645** CALAMY *Indictm. Eng.* 16 From this hatred followeth Excommunications, Anathematizations, etc. **1865** DICKENS *Mut. Fr.* I. 11 Venerable parent promptly resorts to anathematization, and turns him out.

anathematize (ə'næθɪmətaɪz), *v.* [a. Fr. *anathématise-r*, ad. L. *anathematīzā-re* (Augustine, Jerome), f. Gr. ἀναθεματίζ-ειν, f. ἀναθεματ-, stem of ἀνάθεμα: see ANATHEMA and -IZE. By-forms neglecting the Gr. stem were ANATHEMIZE and ANATHEMATE = med.L. *anathemā-re*.]
1. *trans.* To pronounce an anathema against, to consign to Satan, to curse. Properly of formal cursing by ecclesiastics, whence extended to imprecation or malediction generally.
1566 T. STAPLETON *Ret. Untr. Jewel* iv. 137 Unlesse within ten dayes.. he doe anathematise and accurse.. his wicked preaching and doctrine. **1611** COTGR., *Anathematiser*, to anathematize, devote unto the devill. **1641** MILTON *Animadv.* (1851) 205 Gold hath been anathematiz'd for the idolatrous use. **1699** BURNET *39 Art.* xix. 185 He was anathematized by several of the succeeding Popes. **1796** MORSE *Amer. Geog.* II. 422 'All heresies.. anathematised by the church, I do likewise condemn, reject, and anathematise.' **1838** DICKENS *Nich. Nick.* x. (C.D. ed.) 79 Mr. Mantalini anathematising the stairs with great volubility. **1850** KINGSLEY *Alt. Locke* i. (1879) 9 Clergymen,

who anathematize us for wandering into Unitarianism—you, you have driven us thither.

2. *absol.* To utter anathemas, to curse.

1837 CARLYLE *Fr. Rev.* II. III. I. vi. 160 Well may mankind shriek, inarticulately anathematising as they can. **1847** BARHAM *Ingol. Leg.*, How some begin to bless—some anathematize.

anathematized (ə'næθɪmətaɪzd), *ppl. a.* [f. prec. + -ED.] Pronounced to be accursed.

1605 BACON *Adv. Learn.* II. xx. §7 (1873) The elected saints of God have wished themselves anathematized.. in an ecstasy of charity. **1705** HICKERINGILL *Priest-cr.* IV. (1721) 239 Perhaps the Anathematized Sinner will not pay the Knave a Groat. **1858** R. VAUGHAN *Ess. & Rev.* I. 55 Their sermons commonly exhibited, not a Saviour crucified, but a heretic anathematized.

anathematizer (ə'næθɪmə,taɪzə(r)). [f. as prec. + -ER[1].] One who pronounces an anathema.

1647 HAMMOND *Works* (1684) iv. 470 The censorious anathematizer, that breathes out woes and damnations. **1649** BP. HALL *Cases of Consc.* III. v, How many famous churches.. have been less guilty than their anathematizers.

a'nathema,tizing, *vbl. sb.* [f. as prec. + -ING[1].] The pronouncing of an anathema or curse.

1753 CHAMBERS *Cycl. Supp.*, *Anathematizing* amounts to the same with excommunicating. **1880** RUSKIN *Our Fathers Have Told Us* I. i. 26 Without any oratorizing, anathematizing, or any manner of disturbance, we find the Roman Knight made Bishop of Tours.

a'nathema,tizing, *ppl. a.* [f. as prec. + -ING[2].] Uttering or pronouncing anathemas.

1653 BAXTER *Chr. Concord* 4 Delivering up to Satan, and the great Anathematizing Excommunication. **1709** STRYPE *Ann. Ref.* I. lvi. 613 This anathematizing bull. **1833** I. TAYLOR *Fanat.* viii. 303 An anthematizing Deity.

anatheme ('ænəθiːm). [a. Fr. *anatheme* (Cotgr.), ad. L. *anathēma* a dedicated offering, a. Gr. ἀνάθημα a thing set up: see ANATHEMA 3.] An offering dedicated to God.

1654 LESTRANGE *Charles I*, 71 Colours taken forty four, hung up as An[a]themes.. in the Church of Nostre Dame. **1850** LEITCH *Müller's Anc. Art* §286 The pillars.. upon which were destined to be placed cauldrons, tripods and other anathemes.

anatheme, variant of ANATHEM, *Obs.*, anathema.

†**a,nathemi'zation.** *Obs. rare.* [f. ANATHEMIZE + -ATION.] = ANATHEMATIZATION.

1549 CHALONER *Erasm. Moriæ Enc.* Pija, They sticke hardily to theyr.. anathemisacions and peincted pictures. *a* **1555** GARDINER in Foxe *A. & M.* (ed. 1) 751/2 A solemne anathemization of all those that woulde call an image an idol.

a'nathemize, *v. rare.* [f. ANATHEM or ANATHEMA + -IZE, the Gr. stem *anathemat-* being neglected; cf. ANATHEMATE.] = ANATHEMATIZE.

1674 MARVELL *Gen. Counc.* Wks. 1875 IV. 132 Would you anathemize, banish, imprison, execute us, and burn our books? **1689** HICKERINGILL *Modest Inq.* iii. 29 They might Anathamize, and Curse, till their Hearts should ake. **1837** *Blackw. Mag.* XLI. 837 To anathemize the horrors of the anti-Poor Law bill.

†**a'natical.** *Obs. rare*⁻¹. [f. ANA *adv.* + -ICAL, with imitative *-t-*; cf. *identical*, *enneatical*, etc.] Containing equal quantities of each ingredient.

1671 J. WEBSTER *Metallogr.* xi. 154 The four Elements are in Gold, joyned together in an equal and anatical proportion.

†**ana'tiferous,** *a. Obs. rare*⁻¹. [f. mod.L. *anatifer-us* (f. *anas* (*anati-*) duck + *-ferus* producing) + -OUS.] Producing ducks or geese; *i.e.* producing barnacles, formerly supposed to grow on trees, and dropping off into the water below, to turn to 'Tree-geese' (Pennant II. 238), whence also the trivial name of the Barnacle *Lepas anatifera*. (Blount erron. refers the word to L. *anās*, defining it 'that brings the disease or age of old women.')

1646 SIR T. BROWNE *Pseud. Ep.* 133 Anatiferous trees, whose corruption breaks forth into Bernacles.

anatine ('ænətaɪn), *a.* and *sb.* [ad. L. *anatīnus*, f. *anat-*, *anas* duck: see -INE[1].] **A.** *adj.* Of or pertaining to, resembling or characteristic of, a duck. **B.** *sb.* A bird of the duck family.

1862 H. G. ADAMS *Wild Fl., Birds, & Insects* 274 Those [birds] of the Anatine group. **1875** *Encycl. Brit.* III. 712/2 The Anserines and Anatines. **1893** NEWTON *Dict. Birds* 543 Their [*sc.* the Merganser's] structure does not much depart from the Anatine or rather Fuliguline type.

anato, anatto, variants of ANATTA.

anatocism (ə'nætəsɪz(ə)m). *arch.* [ad. L. *anatocism-us*, a. Gr. ἀνατοκισμ-ός compound interest, f. ἀνατοκίζ-ειν to take interest upon interest, f. ἀνά again + τοκίζ-ειν to lend on interest, f. τόκος interest, *lit.* something produced, f. τίκ-τ-ειν (τεκ-) to produce.] Compound interest.

1656 BLOUNT *Glossogr.*, *Anatocism*, a yeerly revenue of usury, and taking usury for usury. **1704** *Phil. Trans.* XXV. 1700 Arithmetick.. with its application to Anatocism, Compound Interest, and Annuities. **1767** HEBERDEN *ibid.* LVII. 462 By the rule of anatocism, they [the inhabitants] have increased at the rate of 1·0082 per cent. per annum. **1842** *Blackw. Mag.* LII. 727 Researches on the questions of Nautical Interest.. of Anatocism, etc.

Anatolian (ænə'təʊlɪən), *a.* and *sb.* Also 6 **Natolian.** [f. *Anatolia* (cf. Gr. ἀνατολή east), Asia Minor + -AN.] **A.** *adj.* Of or pertaining to Anatolia or its inhabitants. **B.** *sb.* An inhabitant of Anatolia.

1590 MARLOWE *2nd Pt. Tamburl.* I. i, Natolians, Sorians, blacke Egyptians. *Ibid.* ii, The Natolian king. *Ibid.* II. ii, With full Natolian bowles Of Greekish wine. **1679** [see ORTHODOX A. 4]. **1788** [see THEME *sb.* 7]. **1888** *Encycl. Brit.* XXIII. 655/2 The cause of national education is seldom forgotten in the legacies of patriotic Anatolian Greeks. **1926** *Spectator* 17 Apr. 693/2 Groups of Anatolians whom I found assembled at the various stations. **1934** *Times Lit. Suppl.* 10 May 331/2 Curzon had prepared a memorandum.. arguing that Turkey.. must be maintained in her Anatolian homeland. **1958** *Listener* 18 Dec. 1034/2 It would be unwise to assume that the Mycenaean Greek was exactly like his Anatolian contemporary at Hattusas.

Anatolic (ænə'tɒlɪk), *a.* [f. Gr. ἀνατολικός eastern: see prec. and -IC.] = ANATOLIAN *a.*

1853 G. FINLAY *Hist. Byzantine Empire* I. i. 14 Seven great themes are particularly prominent in Asia Minor, Optimaton, Opsician, the Thrackesian, the Anatolic, [etc.].. and the Armeniac. **1886** *Amer. Jrnl. Archæol.* II. 124 A vast change had come over the Anatolic Theme: great parts of it, including the eastern and southern and much of the central regions, had been occupied by the Seljuk Turks. **1934** A. J. TOYNBEE *Study Hist.* II. D. iii. 79 In the central and north-eastern parts of the Anatolian Plateau or, in the administrative terminology of the day, in the Anatolic and Armeniac army corps districts.. of the East Roman Empire.

†**'anatome** (3 syllables). *Obs. rare.* [ad. Gr. ἀνατομή: see ANATOMY.] By-form of ANATOMY (in various senses).

1658 COKAINE *Obstin. Lady* Poems (1669) 393 And wear my body to an Anatome. **1676** *Phil. Trans.* XI. 743 An Anatome of a Tortoise, shewing, that what the ribs are in other Animals, the upper-shell is in Tortoises.

anatomic (ænə'tɒmɪk), *a. rare.* [a. L. *anatomic-us* (or its Fr. ad. *anatomique* 16th c. in Littré), a. Gr. ἀνατομικ-ός skilled in anatomy, f. ἀνατομή: see ANATOMY and -IC.] Of or pertaining to anatomy. Also *fig.*

1712 BLACKMORE *Creation* (1786) 228 The learned, who with anatomic art Dissect the mind. **1762** H. WALPOLE *Vertue's Anecd. Paint.* (1786) III. 195 The anatomic figure commonly seen in the shops of apothecaries. **1801** FUSELI *Lect. Art*, The mere anatomic verdict of Benvenuto Cellini. **1858** THACKERAY *Virgin.* ix. 69 To know culinary anatomic secrets.

ana'tomical, *a.* [f. as prec. + -ICAL.]

1. Belonging to, or connected with, the study or practice of anatomy or dissection.

1586 T. B. *La Primaudaye's Fr. Acad.* To Reader, To make this use of the anatomicall consideration of our bodies. **1665** *Phil. Trans.* I. 75 Many considerable Medical and Anatomical inquiries. **1724** WATTS *Log.* (J.) An anatomical knife, which dissects an animal body. **1753** HOGARTH *Anal. Beauty* i. 16 The superior anatomical knowledge.. of the ancients. **1821** W. CRAIG *Drawing* i. 40 A celebrated anatomical draftsman. **1878** BRYANT *Pract. Sur.* I. 68 *Anatomical* or *Pathological Tubercle* is a chronic skin affection.. met with on the hands of those constantly engaged in making post-mortem examinations.

2. Of anatomy; structural, anatomic; also *transf.*

1627 HAKEWILL *Apol.* (1630) 244 The perfiting of the anatomical.. art in this latter age. *a* **1704** LOCKE (J.) The minute anatomical parts of matter. **1840** DICKENS *Barn. Rudge* xxxix. (C.D. ed.) 185 Putting his fingers.. on Hugh's throat.. as if he were studying the anatomical development of that part of his frame. **1863** RAMSAY *Phys. Geogr.* iii. (1878) 36 The anatomical structure or existing Physical Geography of our island. **1880** BASTIAN *Brain* 29 The anatomical elements of nervous tissues.

ana'tomically, *adv.* [f. prec. + -LY[2].] In an anatomical manner; according to anatomy; by means of dissection.

1646 SIR T. BROWNE *Pseud. Ep.* 111 While some affirmed it had no gall, intending onely thereby no evidence of anger or fury, others have construed it anatomically, and denied that part at all. **1737** H. BRACKEN *Farriery Impr.* (1756) II. vi. 186 Let any one take the Trouble of enquiring into the Thing anatomically. **1831** CARLYLE *Misc.* III. 15 Anatomically studied, that it may be medically aided. **1873** A. FLINT *Phys. Man* i. 13 The nervous system is anatomically distinct.

anatomico- (ænə'tɒmɪkəʊ), comb. form of ANATOMIC or ANATOMICAL, as in **anatomico-physiological,** at once anatomical and physiological.

1790 SWAINSTON (*title*) Thoughts Physiological.. with some Cases and Anatomico-Practical Observations. **1882** *Nature* XXVI. 385 The different systems are examined.. rather in their anatomico-physiological than in their zoological aspects.

anatomiless (ə'nætəmɪlɪs), *a. rare*⁻¹. [f. ANATOMY + -LESS.] Devoid of, or not showing knowledge of, anatomy.

1853 RUSKIN *Stones of Ven.* II. vi. §14. 163 Ugly goblins, and formless monsters, anatomiless and rigid.

†**a'natoming,** *vbl. sb. Obs. rare.* [f. ANATOM-Y + -ING[1].] Anatomizing, dissecting.

1580 HOLLYBAND *Treas. Fr. Tong.*, *Incision*, an anatoming.

anatomism (ə'nætəmɪz(ə)m). [a. Fr. *anatomisme*, f. *anatomie* ANATOMY: see -ISM.]

1. Analysis or display of anatomic structure or features.

187. *Spectator*, The stretched and vivid anatomism of their [i.e. the French] great figure-painters.

2. The doctrine that the phenomena of life are accounted for by the anatomical structure of living organisms. (Cf. ANIMISM.)

1860 in FOWLER *Med. Voc.* **1879** in *Syd. Soc. Lex.*

anatomist (ə'nætəmɪst), *a.* and *sb.* [a. Fr. *anatomiste* (16th c.), prob. ad. med.L. **anatomista*, f. *anatomizā-re*: see ANATOMIZE and -IST.]

†**A.** *adj.* Anatomic. *Obs. rare.*

1569 J. SANFORD *Agrippa's Van. Artes* 153 The Anotomist Arte or cuttinge of menne by Phisitions.

B. *sb.* One who practises, or is skilled in, the art of dissecting bodies, *esp.* (when no qualifying word is prefixed) the human body.

1594 T. B. tr. *La Primaudaye's Fr. Acad.* II. 394 These skinnes which are three in number as some Anatomistes say. **1594** CAREW *Huarte's Exam. Wits* xii. 176 Many Phisitions, learned in the Greke and Latine tongue, and great Anotomists. **1610** HEALEY *St. Aug., City of God* XXII. xxiv. (1620) 848 Some butcherly Surgeons, (*Anatomists*, they call them) haue often cut vp dead men. **1658** COKAINE *Poems* (1669) 111 The skilfullest Anatomist that yet Vpon an humane body e're did sit. **1777** HUME *Ess. & Treat.* II. 8 The anatomist presents to the eye the most hideous and disagreeable objects. **1863** KINGLAKE *Crimea* (1876) I. xiv. 219 The relations between an anatomist and a corpse.

b. (The adjectives *vegetable*, *comparative*, *morbid*, etc. prefixed to *anatomist*, define the special department of *anatomy* in which he is skilled.)

1830 LYELL *Princ. Geol.* 3 A comparative anatomist may derive some accession of knowledge from the bare inspection of the remains of an extinct quadruped. **1845** TODD & BOWMAN *Phys. Anat.* I. 316 The researches of the morbid anatomist.

2. *fig.* A dissecter of anything, an analyzer.

1587 GOLDING *De Mornay* Pref. 9 Interpreters, and Anatomists or Decipherers of nature. **1828** MACAULAY *Hallam, Ess.* (1851) I. 52 The latter is an anatomist; his task is to dissect the subject.. and to lay bare before us all the springs of motion and all the causes of decay. **1848** H. ROGERS *Ess.* I. vi. 327 So keen an anatomist of human nature.

anatomization (ə,nætəmaɪ'zeɪʃən). [n. of action f. L. *anatomizā-re*: see ANATOMIZE and -ATION.]

1. The action or process of anatomizing; dissection; analysis of anatomic structure. Also *fig.*

1675 EVELYN *Terra* (1729) 28 Those elaborate Anatomizations, which the World will shortly admire. **1863** GROSART *Small Sins* 102 Nor do I advise a morbid anatomisation of ourselves, or a joyless dwelling upon our 'frames.' *a* **1865** T. HUDSON *Cork Leg* in *Comic Song Bk.* 95 He wanted a limb for anatomization.

†**2.** Anatomic structure. *Obs.*

1664 EVELYN *Silva* (1776) 504 A curious and rational account of their [*i.e.* plants'] Anatomization.

anatomize (ə'nætəmaɪz), *v.* Also 6–7 **anathom-, anotom-.** [ad. med. or early mod.L. *anatomizā-re* (or its Fr. ad. *anatomiser*, 16th c. in Litt.), f. *anatomia*, as if on a Gr. *ἀνατομίζ-ειν: see ANATOMY and -IZE.]

1. *trans.* To dissect or cut up; *esp.* To dissect a human body, or an animal, for the purpose of displaying the position, structure, and relations of the various parts; to make a dissection of.

1541 R. COPLAND *Guydon's Quest. Cyrurg.*, By experyence in deuysynge and Anathomysynge the deade corpses. **1593** NASHE *4 Lett. Confut.* 5 Who but a Foppe wil labour to anatomize a Flye? **1596** C. FITZ-GEFFREY *Drake* (1881) 99 Anatomize me into atomies. **1621** BURTON *Anat. Mel.* Democr. 5 The carkasses of many seuerall beasts, newly by him cut vp and Anatomised. **1696** *Phil. Trans.* XIX. 270 When I was Anatomizing of Eeels. **1716** CIBBER *Love makes a Man* v. iii. 81 Take you no Care about the Surgeons, you shall not be anatomiz'd. **1863** SALA *Capt. Dang.* II. vii. 224 Surgeon's Hall, where malefactors were anatomised after execution.

b. To dissect (plants).

1686 W. HARRIS *Lemery's Chem.* Introd. 21 Anatomize the Plant how you think fit, without using fire. **1830** LINDLEY *Nat. Syst. Bot.* Introd. 15 A botanist.. prefers to examine the stem, or the leaf.. and does not find it necessary to anatomise the seed.

2. *absol.*

1870 LOWELL *Among my Bks.* (1873) 308 When he should have been anatomizing. **1873** BROWNING *Red Cott. N.-Cap C.* 231 Cut, hack, slash, anatomize, Till peccant part be found.

3. *fig.* To lay open minutely; to analyse.

1553–87 FOXE *A. & M.* III. 879 Thus was the Mass anatomized, with the abominations thereof. **1588** THYNNE *Let.* in *Animadv.* Pref. 92, I will not anotomyze every perticular default of everye manne. **1589** GREENE *Menaph.* (Arb.) 51 To anatomize wit. **1601** SHAKS. *All's Well* IV. iii. 37, I would gladly haue him see his company anathomiz'd, that hee might take a measure of his owne iudgements. **1642** HOWELL *For. Trav.* 12 All the Topographers that ever anatomiz'd a Toun or Countrey. **1673** *Lady's Call.* I. §4 ¶ 10 (1683) 29 They anatomise every part of her dress, her meen, her dialect. *a* **1733** NORTH *Lives of Norths* II. 206 He found that tones and chords might be anatomized. **1777** BURKE *Let. Sheriffs Brist.* Wks. III. 183 People, who have split and anatomised the doctrine of free government. **1859** in GULLICK & TIMBS *Paint.* 175 In knowing how to 'anatomize light and shade in endless gradation.'

†**b.** To analyze chemically. *Obs.*

1612 WOODALL *Surg. Mate* Wks. 1653. 210 Paracelsus, who had truly anatomized that salt [Copperas]. **1652** FRENCH *Yorksh. Spa* iv. 40 If water were accurately anotamized.

anatomizer (ə'nætə,maɪzə(r)). [f. prec. + -ER[1].] One who anatomizes; a dissecter.

1873 SYMONDS *Grk. Poets* viii. 265 An insignificant anatomizer of fleas and gnats.

anatomizing (ə'nætə,maɪzɪŋ), *vbl. sb.* [f. as prec. + -ING[1].] The process of dissecting; anatomization. (Now mostly gerundial.)

1594 PLAT *Jewell-ho.* I. 17 In the anatomizing of their bodies. **1677** GALE *Crt. Gentiles* II. III. 32 Al their anatomisings of Natures bowels.

anatomy (ə'nætəmɪ). Forms: 4–5 **anothomia**, 6 **anothomy**, **-amie**, 6–7 **anathomy(e**, **(nathomy(e)**, **anatomie**, **-otomie**, **-my**, 6– **anatomy**. Also 6– **atomy**. [a. Fr. *anatomie*, ad. L. *anatomia*, a. Gr. ἀνατομία (quoted by Cælius Aurelianus *c*420 'apertionem quam Græci *anatomiam* dicunt'), abstr. sb. = ἀνατομή, a cutting up, a dissection, f. ἀνά up + τεμ-, τομ-, cut; cf. λιθοτομία stone-cutting. By confounding the initial syllable with the indef. article *a*, *an*, the Eng. word was erroneously divided as *a natomy*, *an atomy*; the latter of which became in senses 4–7 an established form: see ATOMY.]

I. The process, subjects, and products of dissection of the body.

1. The artificial separation of the different parts of a human body or animal (or more generally of any organized body), in order to discover their position, structure, and economy; dissection.

1541 R. COPLAND *Guydon's Quest. Cyrurg.*, Anathomy is called ryght dyuysyon of membres done for certayne knoweleges. **1543** TRAHERON *Vigo's Chirurg.* (1586) 430 *Anatomie*..signifieth the cutting up of a mans bodie, or of some other thing. **1667** MARVELL *Corr.* 203 Wks. 1872 II. 403 As if a man should dissect his own body, and read the anatomy lecture. **1688** J. CLAYTON in *Phil. Trans.* XVII. 990 Dr. Moulin and my self..made our Anatomies together.. we shew'd to the Royal Society, that all Flat-bill'd Birds.. had three Pair of Nerves. **1712** ADDISON *Spect.* No. 275 ¶1 Curious observations which he had lately made in an anatomy of an human body.

†**b.** with *quick*, *live*: Vivisection. *Obs.*

1651 N. BIGGS *New Dispens.* Pref. 7 Where have we constant reading upon either quick or dead Anatomies? **1651** *Life of Father Sarpi* (1676) 16 He had formerly cut in pieces a number of living Creatures with his own hands to make Anatomies. **1668** CULPEPPER & COLE tr. *Bartholinus' Anat.* II. vi. 101 In Live Anatomies we can hardly perceive that the one is hotter then the other.

†**2.** *concr.* **a.** A body (or part of one) anatomized or dissected, so as to show the position and structure of the organs. Hence **b.** A body or 'subject' for dissection. *Obs.*

1540 T. RAYNALD *Birth of Mankinde* (1634) Prol. 3 As though yee were present at the cutting open of Anatomy of a dead woman. **1598** B. JONSON *Every Man in his Humour* IV. vi, They must ha' dissected, and made an Anatomie o' me. **1602** DEKKER *Satirom.* 197 Carving my poore labours, Like an Anotomy. **1611** TOURNEUR *Ath. Trag.* v. ii. 146 His body when 'tis dead For an Anatomie. **1611** DONNE in Coryat *Crudities*, Worst malefactors..Doe publique good cut in Anatomies. **1691** WOOD *Ath. Oxon.* II/610 He intended to have her made an Anatomy. **1751** CHAMBERS *Cycl.*, *Anatomy* is sometimes used to denote the subject to be anatomized.

3. A model of the body, showing the parts discovered in dissection.

1727–51 CHAMBERS *Cycl.* s.v., An human anatomy in plaster of Paris, representing a man standing upright, with his skin flea'd off. **1753** —— *Cycl. Supp.*, Who has not seen the waxwork Anatomy?

4. *pop.* A skeleton. [In this and the allied senses the word was often reduced to ATOMY.] *arch.*

1594 T. B. tr. *La Primaudaye's Fr. Acad.* II. 57 As it were a drie anatomy, which is a body consisting onely of bones. **1595** SHAKS. *John* III. iv. 25–40 Death, death, O amiable louely death, Thou..fell Anatomy. **1600** HORTOP in Arber *Eng. Garner* (1882) V. 324 He carried with him, in his ship, to be presented to the king of Spaine the anatomy of a giant which was sent from China. **1605** VERSTEGAN *Dec. Intell.* iv (1628) 106 The bones or anatomie of a sea Elephant. **1662** FULLER *Worthies* (1840) I. 496 The anatomy of a man lying in the tombe abovesaid, onely the bones remaining. *a* **1823** D'ISRAELI *Cur. Liter.* (1866) 455/1 Death in the Gothic form of a gaunt anatomy parading through the universe.

b. *fig.*

1589 *Pappe with Hatchet* (1844) 36 So like the verie Anatomie of mischiefe, that one might see through all the ribbes of his conscience. **1636** HEYWOOD *Loves Mistr.* III. i, What bare anotomy of griefe is this? **1821** SHELLEY *Epipsych.* 122 Incarnate April, warning..Frost the anatomy Into his summer grave.

5. A skeleton with the skin left; a corpse shrunken or dried to skin and bone; a mummy.

1586 T. B. tr. *La Primaudaye's Fr. Acad.* 192 The Egyptians..used in the midst of their bankets to bring in the anatomy of a dead body dried. **1611** COTGR., *Aridelle*..an Anatomie, or bodie whereon there is nought left but skin and bone. **1669** PENN *No Cross, etc.* Wks. 1782 II. 319 The Egyptians, who..in the full of their greatest Cheer caused the Anatomy of a Dead Man to be brought before them. **1826** SOUTHEY *Q. Rev.* XXXIII. 407 More like an anatomy than a living person. **1861** SALA *Twice Round Clock* 9 Myriads of dried sprats and cured pilchards—shrunken, piscatorial anatomies.

b. *fig.* The withered lifeless form of anything.

1605 VERSTEGAN *Dec. Intell.* iv. (1628) 99 The winde and the raine having long since beaten away the earth from them, may thus haue left them to appeare the very true anatomies of themselves. **1867** FROUDE *Short Stud.* (1872) I. 31 What lean and shrivelled anatomies the best of such descriptions would seem!

6. A living being reduced to 'skin and bone'; a withered or emaciated creature, a 'walking skeleton.'

1590 SHAKS. *Com. Err.* v. 238 One Pinch: a hungry leane-fac'd Villaine, A meere Anatomie, a Mountebanke. **1633** FORD *Love's Sacr.* II. i, Passion, and the vows I owe to you, Have chang'd me to a lean anatomy. **1824** W. IRVING *T. Trav.* I. 269 This withered anatomy would read about being 'stayed with flagons.' **1862** CARLYLE *Fredk. Gt.* II. VII. ix. 342 The thread-paper Duchess of Kendal..poor old anatomy.

b. *fig.* Applied to things. *rare.*

1607 DEKKER *Knt's Coniuring* (1842) 35 Made their countrey a pointing stocke to other nations, and a miserable anatomie to themselves. **1667** *Answ. West to Quest. North* 3 Ruine of Trade..hath brought the Land to a meer Anatomy.

7. Applied depreciatively to the bodily frame.

1592 SHAKS. *Rom. & Jul.* III. iii. 106 Tell me, In what vile part of this Anatomie Doth my name lodge? **1837** LOCKHART *Scott* (1839) VI. 240 Brown leathern gaiters buttoned upon his nether anatomy. *a* **1857** JERROLD *Wks.* (1864) II. 101 The aperture was too small for his big, burly anatomy.

II. The science of bodily structure; structure as discovered by dissection.

8. The body of facts and deductions as to the structure of organized beings, animal or vegetable, ascertained by dissection; the doctrine or science of the structure of organized bodies.

(Special divisions are ***Animal Anatomy*** or ***Zootomy***; ***Vegetable Anatomy***; ***Human Anatomy***; ***Comparative Anatomy*** which compares the structure of different classes or groups of animals.)

[**1398** TREVISA *Barth. De P.R.* v. xlii. (1495) 158 *Anothomia* is a craft and a scyence to knowe how the membres and lymmes of the body ben sette ordred and dystyngued.] **1541** R. COPLAND *Guydon's Quest. Cyrurg.*, The scyence of the Nathomy is nedefull and necessaryе to the Cyrurgyen. **1547** BOORDE *Brev. Health* Pref. 4 That they [Chierurgions] be sure in Anothomy. **1615** H. CROOKE *Body of Man* 189 There can no reason be giuen but onely from Anatomy. **1675** GREW (*title*) Comparative Anatomy of the Trunks of Plants. **1753** CHAMBERS *Cycl. Supp.*, Anatomy is of use in painting, designing, statuary, etc. **1877** HUXLEY *Anat. Inv. An.* xii. 687 A large and thorough acquaintance with anatomy and embryology.

b. A treatise on this science.

1528 PAYNELL *Salerne Regim.* 2 A iiij, There is in man CCClxv. veynes, as appereth in the anothamie. **1674** R. GODFREY *Inj. & Abuses in Physick* 115 All the Anatomies or histories I ever could meet with.

9. Anatomical structure or organization, arrangement of the parts of the body of animals or plants.

1579 GOSSON *Schoole of Ab.* (Arb.) 38 The anotomy of man [is] set out by experience. **1607** TOPSELL *Four-footed Beasts* (1673) 383 The inward proportion and anatomy of their bodies is like unto a man. **1868** DUNCAN *Insect World* Introd. 1 To investigate the anatomy of insects.

b. *transf.* Of machines, etc.: Structure.

1879 C. HIBBS in *Cassell's Techn. Educ.* IV. 299/2 Each article has an iron screw or spike as a part of its anatomy.

III. Tropical. (Already by Aristotle ἀνατομή was used for logical dissection or analysis.)

10. The dissection or dividing of anything material or immaterial, for the purpose of examining its parts; detailed examination, analysis.

a **1569** KINGESMYLL *Godly Advise* (1580) 15 Make an Anotamie of the suter you have in hand, make no confusion of wealthe, witte, bodie and soule. *a* **1593** H. SMITH *Wks.* (1866) I. 73 Let thy question be, 'What have I done?' and make thy anatomy of thyself. **1621** BURTON (*title*) The Anatomy of Melancholy: what it is, with all the kinds, causes, symptoms, prognostickes, and seuerall cures of it. **1641** MILTON *Animadv.* (1851) 191 Such an unripping, such an Anatomie of the shiest, and tenderest particular truths. **1764** REID *Inq. Hum. Mind* i. §1 It must be by an anatomy of the mind that we can discover its powers and principles. **1815** MOORE *Parad. & Peri* Epil., He proceeded to the anatomy of the short poem just recited.

†**11.** Chemical analysis. *Obs.*

1621 MOLLE *Camerarius' Liv. Lib.* I. xii. 35 A certaine Anatomie of siluer. **1686** W. HARRIS *Lemery's Chem.* II. xxii. 620 They who have made the Anatomy of this mixt do know very well that it is almost all of it sulphur.

anatopism (ə'nætəpɪz(ə)m). *rare.* [f. Gr. ἀνά up + τόπ-ος a place + -ISM.] A putting of a thing out of its proper place, a faulty arrangement.

1812 COLERIDGE *Rem.* I. 317 In arranging which [books] the puzzled librarian must commit an anachronism in order to avoid an anatopism. **1850** DE QUINCEY *Wks.* XVI. 72 Geographical blunders, or what might be called anatopisms.

anatreptic (ænə'trɛptɪk), *a.* [ad. Gr. ἀνατρεπτικ-ός turning up, overturning; f. ἀνατρέπ-ειν to turn up, to upset in argument; f. ἀνά up + τρέπ-ειν to turn.] Overturning, overthrowing; one of the subdivisions of Platonic Discourse.

1655–60 STANLEY *Hist. Philos.* (1701) 175/1 Agonistick [discourse is] Endeictic [or] Anatreptick. **1859** in WORCESTER.

anatriæne ('ænətraɪ,iːn). *Zool.* [f. Gr. ἀνά up, back + TRIÆNE.] In sponges, a triæne with recurved prongs.

1887 [see PROTRIÆNE].

anatrip'sology. *Med.* [f. Gr. ἀνάτριψις rubbing, friction (see next) + -OLOGY. *Syd. Soc. Lex.* gives also *Anatriptology*.] The scientific consideration of the remedial use of friction.

1839 HOOPER *Med. Dict.* 102 *Anatripsology*, A treatise on the use of friction. **1853** in MAYNE. **1879** in *Syd. Soc. Lex.*

anatriptic (ænə'trɪptɪk), *a.* *Med.* [f. Gr. ἀνάτριπτ-ος rubbed up (f. ἀνατρίβ-ειν to rub up) + -IC. Cf. mod.Fr. *anatriptique*.] Belonging to friction, characterized by friction. (Applied to some medicines.)

1879 in *Syd. Soc. Lex.*

†**anatron.** *Obs.* [a. Sp. *anatron*, ad. Arab. *an-naṭarûn*, i.e. *an* = *al* the + *naṭrûn*.] Native carbonate of soda: see NATRON.

1706 PHILLIPS, *Anatron* or Natron, a kind of Salt drawn from the water of the River Nile. **1753** CHAMBERS *Cycl. Supp.*, *Anatron* is of a cineritious colour, and bitter taste.

anatropal (ə'nætrəpəl), *a.* *Bot.* [f. as next + -AL[1].] = ANATROPOUS.

1835 LINDLEY *Introd. Bot.* (1848) I. 397 Such ovules as these Mirbel terms anatropal..examples may be found in the almond, the apple. **1854** BALFOUR in *Encycl. Brit.* II. 141 In orthotropal seeds the embryo is said to be inverted.. while in anatropal seeds it is erect.

anatropous (ə'nætrəpəs), *a.* *Bot.* [f. mod.L. *anatrop-us*, a. assumed Gr. *ἀνάτροπος turned upside down (f. ἀνά up + -τροπος, f. τρέπειν to turn) + -OUS.] Said of the ovule of phanerogamous plants when its nucleus, with its integuments, is inverted, so that its apex points to the base of the ovule. Opposed to *orthotropous*, in which the nucleus is erect within the ovule.

1847 in CRAIG. **1857** HENFREY *Bot.* 130 The anatropous ovule is only an orthotropous ovule with a long funiculus confluent with the outer coat. **1875** BENNET & DYER tr. *Sachs's Bot.* 501 The usual form of the ovule of angiosperms is the anatropous.

anatropy (ə'nætrəpɪ). *Bot.* [f. Gr. type *ἀνατροπία, f. *ἀνάτροπος: see ANATROPOUS *a.*] The condition of being anatropous.

1848 [see ORTHOTROPY].

anatta, anatto (ə'nætə, ə'nætəʊ). Also 7–9 **arnotto**, 8 **annotta**, 8–9 **arnatto, anotta, annotto, annatto.** [? a. native American name.] An orange-red dye, procured in Central America from the waxy pulp surrounding the seeds of the *Bixa orellana*; used in dyeing, and for colouring cheese.

a **1682** SIR W. PETTY in Sprat *Hist. R. Soc.* 299 (T.) Arnotto dyeth of itself an orange-colour. **1697** DAMPIER *Voy.* (1729) I. 226 Otta or Anatta, is a red sort of Dye. **1753** CHAMBERS *Cycl. Supp.*, *Annotto*, in commerce, a kind of red dye, brought from the West Indies. **1770** W. GUTHRIE *Geog.* (T.) Arnatto is mixed up by the Spanish Americans with their chocolate. **1784** TWAMLEY *Dairying* 64 Spanish-Annatto..is much the best for Cheese-colouring. **1791** HAMILTON *Berthollet's Dyeing* I. Introd. 20 Substances.. useful in dyeing..anotta, logwood. *Ibid.* II. 130 Annotta. **1850** HAWTHORNE *Scarlet Let.* (1851) 25 Pepper-bags, and baskets of anatto. **1852** T. ROSS tr. *Humboldt's Trav.* I. ix. 308 His skin besmeared with annatto. **1863** H. BATES *Nat. on Amazons* vi. 138 The red [tints are made] with the seeds of the Urucú, or Anatto plant. **1866** *Treas. Bot.*, *Anotta* or *Arnotto*. **1870** YEATS *Nat. Hist. Comm.* 212 Good arnotto is of the colour of fire.

†**a'naunter,** *phr. comb.* *Obs.* or *dial.* [= AN *prep.* + *aunter*: see ADVENTURE *sb.* 1 c.] In risk or peril; on the chance, in case, lest.

1297 R. GLOUC. 311 Þy loue ych abbe wel dere aboȝt, & my lyue anaunter ydo. **1377** LANGL. *P. Pl.* B. XIII. 71, I wil nouȝt write it here On englisch, an auenture it sholde be reherced to ofte. **1387** TREVISA *Higden* Rolls Ser. II. 295 Anaunter leste þe olde man schulde be holde a lecchour. **1855** ATKINSON *Whitby Gloss.*, *Ananthers*, *Anthers*, or *Enanthers*. 'I'll take my cloak, ananthers it should rain.'

a'nauntrins, *adv. phr.* *Obs.* or *dial.* [f. prec. + *-ins*, -INGS, advb. ending.] In case, in the event that.

1691 RAY *N. Countr. Words*, *Anauntrins*; If so be. I know not what the Original of this should be, unless it be from *An*, for *if*, and *Auntrins* contracted from Peradventure.

anautotomic (ænɔːtəʊ'tɒmɪk), *a.* *Geom.* [f. AN-10 + AUTOTOMIC *a.*] Of a curve: not intersecting itself; having no multiple point: opp. to AUTOTOMIC *a*.

1901 A. B. BASSET *Cubic & Quartic Curves* Pref. p. vii, I have..introduced the words *autotomic* and *anautotomic* to designate curves which respectively do and do not possess multiple points.

anauxite (æ'nɔːksaɪt). *Min.* [ad. G. *anauxit* (A. Breithaupt 1838, in *Jrnl. f. Prakt. Chem.* XV. 325), f. Gr. ἀναυξής not increasing, so named 'because the mineral does not swell up before the blowpipe' (Chester): see -ITE[1].] A pearly-white translucent variety of CIMOLITE.

1850 J. D. DANA *Syst. Min.* (ed. 3) 288 Anauxite, *Breithaupt*..pearly; greenish-white; translucent. **1883** *Encycl. Brit.* XVI. 424/2 Anauxite..Granular..Translucent, pearly.

Anaxagorean (ænæk,sægə'riːən), *a.* and *sb.* [f. *Anaxagoras*, prop. name + -EAN.]

A. *adj.* Of or pertaining to Anaxagoras, a Greek philosopher who taught the eternity of matter, but the agency of a supreme intelligence in combining it into bodies. **B.** *sb.* A follower of Anaxagoras.

1586 BRIGHT *Melanch.* ii. 6 After an Anaxagorian manner. **1678** CUDWORTH *Intell. Syst.* 35 The Anaxagorean Hypothesis. *Ibid.* 199 All of them except the Anaxagoreans. **1845** LEWES *Hist. Philos.* I. 137 Anaxagorean system.

Ana'xagorize, *v. rare*[−1]. [f. as prec. + -IZE.] To hold or teach the principles of Anaxagoras.

1678 CUDWORTH *Intell. Syst.* 35 The other ancient Physiologers..did not Anaxagorize, as Empedocles.

Anaxi'mandrian, *a.* and *sb.* [f. *Anaximander*, + -IAN.] **A.** *adj.* Adhering to the opinions of Anaximander. **B.** *sb.* An adherent of Anaximander.

1678 *Phil. Trans.* XII. 938 The most ancient Atheistick Hypothesis..the Hylopathian or Anaximandrian. **1678** CUDWORTH *Intell. Syst.* 141 Pliny..maintained against the Anaximandrians..the Worlds Eternity and Incorruptibility. *Ibid.* 136 Those Atheists who derive all things from Dead and Stupid Matter..are the Anaximandrian Atheists.

†**an'belȝen**, *v. Obs.* [for ABELȜEN: see AN- *pref.* 5.] To be enraged.

1205 LAY. 26359 þa an-bælh [*v.r.* a-balh] Walwain, swulc an iburst þein. *Ibid.* 1696 Brutus wes on-bolȝen [*v.r.* abolȝe] swa bið þa wilde bær.

†**an'blow**, *v. Obs.* [f. AN- *pref.* 1 + BLOW; = OE. *onbláwan*; cf. ABLOW, which in sense 1 is prob. weakened from this, while in 2 it contains A- *pref.* 1.] To blow on or into, breathe upon, inspire.

c **1175** *Cotton Hom.* 223 He worhte þa þane man..and him anbléow sáwle.

†**an'burst**, *v. Obs.* [f. AN- *pref.* 5 (for A- *pref.* 1) + BURST *v.* Cf. ABURST.] To burst out.

1205 LAY. 25241 Cnihtes an burste [*v.r.* a-borst] weoren. *Ibid.* 25831 He an-bursten agon [*v.r.* a-borst iwarþ], swulc weore a wilde bar.

anbury, amb- ('ænbərɪ, 'æm-). Forms: 6–7 **anburie**, 7– **anbury, ambury**; also **anberry, nanberry**. [Deriv. doubtful; *ambury* has been assumed by some to be the earlier form, and taken as a corrupt descendant of OE. *ampre, ompre*; but the latter regularly survives in the dialects as AMPER, app. quite unconnected in sense with this. *Ambury* appears to be a phonetic variant of *anbury* (as in *im-brue, em-balm, Stam-ford*), and this perhaps = *ang-berry*, f. OE. *ang-* 'pain, suffering,' as in *ang-nail* (AGNAIL), and OE. *ang-seta* carbuncle, pimple. For *berry* cf. *strawberry* applied to a birth-mark. In It. associated in name with 'mulberry.' Cf. ANGLEBERRY.]

1. A soft tumour or spongy wart on horses and oxen.

1598 FLORIO, *Moro*..a mulberie tree; also a wart in a horse called an Anburie. [Also at *Selfo.*] **1607** TOPSELL *Four-footed Beasts* (1673) 327 Of an Anbury. **1614** MARKHAM *Husb.* (1623) 82 The Anbury is a bloody wart on any part of a Horses body. **1617** —— *Caval.* VII. 84 Anbury. **1631** —— *Way to Wealth* (1668) I. lxii. 66 Anbury. **1670** *MS. Acct. Bk. of G. Norton of Disforth*, P[d] for takeing of 3 anberryes of 2 oxen, 3*s*. **1696** PHILLIPS, *Ambury*, a Disease in Horses, which causes 'em to break forth in spungy Tumors full of hot Blood and Matter. *c* **1720** W. GIBSON *Farrier's Guide* II. l. (1738) 192 Anburies and other encysted Tumors require a peculiar treatment. **1725** BRADLEY *Fam. Dict.*, *Anbury*, a kind of Wen. or spungy Wart, growing upon any Part of a Horse's Body, full of Blood. **1775** T. WALLIS *Farrier's Dict.*, *Anbury* or *Ambury*. **1783** AINSWORTH *Lat. Dict.* (Morell) The ambury (in horses), *Verruca spongiosa sanguine plena*. **1785** *Sportsman's Dict.*, *Anbury* or *Ambury*. **1816** JAMES *Mil. Dict.* 13 Anbury. **1882** E. PEACOCK (*in letter*) Our farriers and farmers here [North-west Lincolnshire] always call these things *Nanberrys*.

2. A diseased affection of the roots of turnips and allied plants.

1750 W. ELLIS *Mod. Husb.-man* IV. i. 27 That common destructive turnip disease..in the sandy grounds of Norfolk ..there called Anbury. [Also called] Fingers-and-toes. **1815** KIRBY & SPENCE *Entomol.* (1843) I xiv. 383 From the knob-like galls on turnips called in some places the ambury I have bred another of these weevils. **1833** *Penny Cycl.* I. 504/2 Cabbages or turnips whose roots are infected with anbury. **1839** REES *Encycl. Agric.* 861 The forked excrescences [in turnips] known as fingers and toes in some places, and as the anbury in others. **1878** R. THOMPSON *Gard. Assist.* (ed. Moore) x. 279/2 The anbury has been attributed to the agency of insects, but these are now generally considered to be a consequence, and not the cause, of the malformation.

ancar: see ANCHOR *sb.*[2] 3.

-ance, *suffix*; a. Fr. *-ance*:—L. *-ānt-ia, -ēnt-ia, -ent-ia* (see -ENCE), all of which in words that survived into Fr., or were formed in Fr. as nouns of action, on the pres. pple., were levelled under *-ance*. But other L. words of this form, subseq. adopted in Fr., took *-ence* or *-ance*, according to L. spelling. Thus of popular preservation or formation, *aidance, assistance, complaisance, nuisance, parlance, séance*; of later learned adoption from L., *absence, clémence, différence, diligence, providence, prudence*, as well as *élégance, tempérance*. Words of both classes were adopted in Eng. in their actual Fr. forms, which they still generally retain. But, since 1500, various words orig. in *-ance* from Fr. have been altered back to *-ence*, after L.; and all words recently adopted from L., directly or through mod.Fr., or formed on L. analogies, have taken *-ence* or *-ance* according to the L. vowel. Hence, mod.E. words in *-ance* partly represent L. *-āntia*, but largely L. *-entia, -ēntia*, through OFr. *-ance*; partly also mod.Fr. *-ance* from vbs. of various origin. On the other hand, OFr. *-ance*:—L. *-entia, -ēntia*, is, in consequence of refashioning, partly represented by Eng. *-ence*. For the confusion and inconsistency which this causes in current spelling, as in *dependance, -dence, resistance, subsistence*, see -ENCE. As, in many cases, the OFr. vbs. themselves, as well as their derivatives in *-ance*, were adopted in Eng. (e.g. *appear -ance, assist -ance, purvey -ance, suffer -ance*), the suffix became to a certain extent a living formative, and was occas. used to form similar nouns of action on native vbs., as *abid-ance, abear-ance, forbear-ance, further-ance, hinder-ance, ridd-ance*, etc. For meaning, see -ENCE; and cf. -ANCY.

ance, north. dial. form of ONCE.

ancel, var. AUNCEL *Obs.*, a kind of steelyard.

ancelle, var. of ANCILLE, *Obs.*, a maid-servant.

ancenned, var. ANKENNED *ppl. a.*, only-begotten.

ancestor ('ænsɪstə(r)), *sb.* Forms: 3–4 **ancestre**, 4 **aun-**; 3–5 **auncetre**, 4–5 **-ceter, -setre, -sestre, accessour, aun-**; 5 **ancetor, aunsetter**, 5–6 **aunciter, -cetour, ansetor**, 6 **ancytour, -sitor, auncetur, -sytor**, 6–7 **-citor, auncester, -our, -or, ancester, -our**, 6– **ancestor**. [a. OFr. *ancestre*, nom.:—L. *ante'cēssor*, and *ancesor, ancessor, -ur, -our*, acc. (Pr. *ancessor*):—L. *antecēs'sōrem*, a foregoer, predecessor, agent-noun f. *antecēd-ĕre* to precede, f. *ante* before + *cēd-ĕre, cēss-um*, to go. The distinction of nom. and acc. was lost before their adoption in Eng., so that they were, as in contemporary Fr., mere synonyms. In Eng., *ance'ssour* soon became obs.; *an'cestre* became phonetically *an'cetre, 'aunceter*, of which the regular mod. form, now dialectal, is *'anceter* or *'anster*; but this was disturbed, on the one hand, by writing the termination (after late AFr.) *-our*, latinized in 16th c. to *-or*; and on the other, by spelling with *-s-*, after later Fr., *auncestre*. A combination of both gave the 16th c. spelling *auncestour, -or*, now *ancestor*, in which the *-s-* has come to be pronounced; *'auncitor* survived to 17th c. After *ancestre* became restricted in Fr. to the sense of 'progenitor', *ancessour, -eur*, was refashioned after L. as *antécesseur* in the general sense, whence also Eng. ANTECESSOR, and a mixed form ANTECESTRE.]

1. a. One from whom a person is descended, either by the father or mother; a progenitor, a forefather. (Usually said of those more remote than a grandfather.) Also, of animals, and *fig.* as 'spiritual ancestor.'

1297 R. GLOUC. 193 Vor þyn auncetres dude al, þat we þe hoteþ do. *c* **1300** *Beket* 428 Bi the kyng Henries dai, that oure ancestre was. **1330** R. BRUNNE *Chron.* 166 The lond..that thin ancessour So wele kept biforn. **1393** GOWER *Conf.* III. 182 That her auncestre brake the lawe. *c* **1400** *Rom. Rose* 391 Tyme, that eldith our auncessours. **1447** BOKENHAM *Lyvys of Seyntys* 64 Oure aunsetrys us beforn. *a* **1450** *Knt. de la Tour* (1868) 4 Stories, the whiche hathe ben wretin bi oure aunsetters. **1475** *Bk. Noblesse* (1860) 10 Geffrey Plantagenet youre noble auncetour. *c* **1535** LD. LA WARR in Ellis *Orig. Lett.* Ser. II. II. 134 There lyethe many of my aunsytorys. **1579** GOSSON *Sch. Abuse* (Arber) 26 The Trophees and Triumphes of our auncestours. **1596** BP. BARLOW *3 Serm.* i. 19 Our auncestors were woont to say. **1597** SHAKS. *2 Hen. IV.* IV. iv. 61 When I am sleeping with my Ancestors. **1601** HOLLAND *Pliny* (1634) II. 152 Our auncitors..haue giuen vs counsell. **1614** RALEIGH *Hist. World* II. 284 Hercules..the Ancester of the Macedonian Kings. **1667** MILTON *P.L.* II. 894 Eldest Night and Chaos, ancestors of Nature. **1756** BURKE *Vind. Nat. Soc.* Wks. I. 12 We owe an implicit reverence to all the institutions of our ancestors. **1793** —— *Discuss. Trait. Corresp. Bill*, The wisdom of our ancestors. **1855** MILMAN *Lat. Chr.* (1864) I. II. i. 106 St. Peter..the spiritual ancestor of the Bishop of Rome. **1849** MACAULAY *Hist. Eng.* I. 315 The ancestors of the gigantic quadrupeds [*i.e.* dray-horses]..were brought from the marshes of Walcheren. [**1881** EVANS *Leicestersh. Wds.* 91 *Ancetor* var. of ancestor.]

b. *attrib.*

1854 *Wesleyan Methodist Mag.* X. 623 Ancestor-worship ..has linked and attached itself most powerfully to the heart of every Chinese. **1883** MISS SIMCOX in *Academy* 14 Apr. 249/3 A real domestic ancestor cult. **1883** MAINE *Early Law & Custom* iii. 55 Ancestor-worship, the worship of father, grandfather, and great-grandfather, has among the Hindus a most elaborate liturgy and ritual. **1928** H. C. DAWSON *Age of Gods* iii. 47 The churingas or 'ancestor stones' of the modern Australian natives. **1936** C. DAY LEWIS in Day Lewis & Stebbing *Imag. & Thinking* 11 The profound desire for a feeling of continuity, to which some of us young poets have applied the expression 'ancestor-worship'. **1957** V. W. TURNER *Schism & Cont. in Afr. Soc.* p. xxi, The misfortunes of life..are attributed to the punitive action of ancestor spirits.

c. *Law.* A person who precedes another in the course of inheritance, and from whom an inheritance is derived, whether in the direct line of descent or not: correlative to ***heir***. ***collateral ancestor***: see COLLATERAL *a.* 4.

1628 COKE *Littleton* 380 b, If lands had beene giuen to the husband and wife and their heires, and the husband had made a Feoffement to another, to whom a Collaterall Ancester of the wife had released and died. **1651**, **1767** [see HEIR *sb.* 1]. **1768**, **1809** [see ANCESTRAL *a.* 1 b.] **1959** JOWITT *Dict. Eng. Law* I. 116/2 Under the law as it stood before the Law of Property Act, 1925, an ancestor meant any person from whom real property was inherited.

2. *Biol.* An organized being of a lower or earlier type, whence others of a higher type subsequently existing are, according to the Evolution theory, inferred to have been 'developed.'

1863 RAMSAY *Phys. Geol.* (1878) 359 *Elephas antiquus*, the ancestor of the African elephant. **1882** GEIKIE *Text-bk. Geol.* VI. IV. i. §1 They [*Anchitheria*] were about the size of small ponies, had three toes on each foot, and are regarded as ancestors of the horse.

Hence **'ancestor** *v. trans.*, to be the ancestor of; also *transf.*; **'ancestored** (-əd) *ppl. a.*, having an ancestor or ancestors (of a specified kind); **'ancestorship**, the position of an ancestor.

1776 H. WALPOLE *Let.* 9 Sept. (1904) IX. 412 Few men are so well ancestored in so short a compass of time. **1853** *Tait's Mag.* XX. 604 The thorough-bred, orientally ancestred horse. **1883** MAX MÜLLER *India, What can it teach Us?* vii. 239 Ancestorship as a natural ingredient of religion among all savage nations. **1921** *Times Lit. Suppl.* 10 Feb. 92/2 Their younger brother ancestored the well-known family of Howard-Vyse, of Stoke Place, Slough. **1940** BRYANT & AIKEN *Psychol. of English* iv. 33 The *Ursprache* which ancestored our own English.

ancestorial (ænsɪ'stɔərɪəl), *a.* [f. prec., after words like *media'torial*, f. L. adjs. in *-ōri-us*: see -ORIAL.] = ANCESTRAL.

1659 *Harl. Misc.* (1810) VI. 88 Neither the foundation-men nor ancestorial gentry being educated so as to be serviceable to the publick. **1827** POLLOK *Course of Time* IV. (1860) 105 Not content with ancestorial name Or to be known because his fathers were. **1846** GROTE *Greece* (1862) I. xiv. 216 Thebes in Egypt, his ancestorial seat.

ance'storially, *adv. rare*[−1]. [f. prec. + -LY[2].] In an ancestorial or ancestral manner, by inheritance from one's ancestors.

1825 SYD. SMITH *Wks.* 1859 II. 63/2 A nation.. ancestorially bound by foolish and improvident treaties.

†**'ancestory**, *a. Obs. rare*[−1]. [f. ANCESTOR *sb.* + -Y, after words like *intercessor-y*, due to L. forms in *-ōri-us*. Cf. ANCESTORIAL.] = ANCESTRAL.

1650 ELDERFIELD *Right of Tythes* 291 The former may have been our ancestory principles and rules.

ancestral (æn'sɛstrəl), *a.* Forms: 6 **auncetrell**, 6–7 **-cestrell**, 6 **-cestrall**, 6–9 **ancestrel**, 8– **ancestral**. [a. OFr. *ancestrel, ancêtrel*, AFr. *auncestrel*, f. *ancestre*: see ANCESTOR *sb.* and -AL[1].]

1. Of, belonging to, or inherited from ancestors.

1579 J. STUBBES *Gaping Gulf* D iv, A faultor prince of Rome..that may be warranted to vs and our heyres for an enemy auncestrell. **1644** HOWELL *Lett.* IV. xi. (R.) History is the great looking-glass thro' which we may behold with ancestral eyes..actions of ages past. **1797** COLERIDGE *Kubla Khan*, Kubla heard from far Ancestral voices prophesying war. **1857** H. REED *Lect. Brit. Poets* iii. 85 The ancestral position of Chaucer in the annals of our poetry. **1879** O'CONNOR *Beaconsfield* 235 The extent of their ancestral acres and the splendour of their ancestral halls.

b. *esp.* in *Law.* (Often written *ancestrel* as in OFr.)

1523 FITZHERB. *Surv.* 12 These tenauntes maye holde their landes by dyuers tenures..as by..franke almoyne, homage, auncetrell. *c* **1570** THYNNE *Pride & Lowl.* (1841) 16 His cause was good, his title auncestrell. **1768** BLACKSTONE *Comm.* III. 186 Another ancestrel writ..to establish an equal division of the land..on the death of an ancestor. **1809** TOMLINS *Law Dict.* 4 L a/1 Homage ancestrel is where a man and his ancestors have time out of mind held their land of the lord by Homage.

2. *Biol.* Of, pertaining to, or constituting the original type, or any earlier type, whence existing forms are supposed to have been 'developed.'

1862 DARWIN *Orchids* vii. 288 All homologous parts or organs, however much diversified, are modifications of one and the same ancestral organ. **1880** HAUGHTON *Phys. Geog.* vi. 282 Oreodon is the type of a family of ancestral pigs. **1881** FLOWER in *Nature* No. 619. 438 The generalised or ancestral characters of a race.

ancestrally (æn'sɛstrəlɪ), *adv.* [f. ANCESTRAL *a.* + -LY[2].] By or in respect of ancestry.

1882 G. ALLEN *Colin Clout's Calendar* xvii. 97 Ancestrally, yellow-rattle is a near relation of the pretty little blue veronicas. **1886** *Athenæum* 6 Mar. 328/3 Whether the vertebrate eye..will turn out..to be ancestrally derived from a number of modified ancestral gills. **1923** R. FROST *New Hamp.* (1924) 50 With something of the baby grip Acquired ancestrally in just such trees.

ancestress ('ænsɪstrɪs). Also 6 **auncestrese.** [f. ANCESTOR *sb.* + -ESS; of Eng. formation, there being no analogous word in Fr.] A female ancestor.

1580 T. NORTON in Wright *Q. Eliz. Orig. Lett.* (1838) II. 124 An Englishe treatise..wherein her Majestie's auncestrese is termed base in contempt. **1826** SCOTT *Woodst.* (1832) I. xii. 227 What if the soul of an ancestress of hers and yours were now addressing you? **1874** HELPS *Soc. Press.* ix. 132 The ladies of the present day..suffer much more waste in their households, than their ancestresses did.

ancestrial (æn'sɛstrɪəl), *a. rare.* [f. ANCESTRY + -AL[1]; cf. *industry, industrial.*] Of or pertaining to ancestry; = ANCESTRAL.

a **1641** BP. MOUNTAGU *Acts & Mon.* 488 Desert..ancestriall, or derived titles from grandsires long agone. **1659** HOWELL *Lex. Tetragl.*, Naturall Children..legitimated by prescription and long Tract of Ancestriall Time. **1806** W. TAYLOR in *Ann. Rev.* IV. 261 If ancestrial persecutions were to be visited on posterity.

ancestrian (æn'sɛstrɪən), *a.* ? *Obs. rare.* [f. as prec. + -AN; cf. *Italy, Italian.*] = prec.

1756 *Gentl. Mag.* XXVI. 82 We find this ancestrian enthusiasm breathing through all their noblesse.

ancestry ('ænsɪstrɪ). Forms: 4 **ancestrie, -istry, aunceterye, -cetre, -setre,** 4–6 **awncestry(e, auncetrie, -etry(e,** 4–7 **-estrie,** 5–6 **auncestrye, ancestrye,** 6 **auncetrye, -itrie,** 6–7 **-estry,** 5– **ancestry.** [An Eng. modification (due to the survival of *ancestre* and not *ancessour*, as the Eng. form) of OFr. *anceserie, ancesserie*, f. *ancesor* ANCESTOR *sb.* + *-ie* (see -Y), as if:—late L. **antecēssōrī-a.*]

1. The relation or condition of ancestors; progenitorship; ancestral lineage or descent. *Hence*, distinguished or ancient descent.

1330 R. BRUNNE *Chron.* 14 What þorgh lowe of lond, & olde auncestrie, Wan he þe regne of Westsex. *c* **1386** CHAUCER *Reeves T.* 62 His purpos was for to bistowe hire hye In to som worthy blood of Auncetrye [*v.r.* -trie, -terye, -cestrie]. *c* **1400** *Destr. Troy* xv. 6319 Þe proud kyng, was full pure ryche, Of aunsetre old. *c* **1425** WYNTOUN *Cron.* IX. xxvii. 45 Mychty lordis of ancestry. **1513** BRADSHAW *St. Werburge* (1848) 10 Blessed Saynt Werburge..Descended by auncetry and title famous. **1591** SHAKS. *Two Gent.* v. iv. 139 Now, by the honor of my Ancestry. **1697** DRYDEN *Æneid* XI. 82 A Son, whose Death disgraced his Ancestry. *a* **1719** ADDISON (J.) Title and ancestry render a good man more illustrious. **1836** HOR. SMITH *Tin Trum.* I. 28 They who on length of ancestry enlarge.

2. *collect.* The persons who stand to us in the above relation; the line or body of ancestors. (Cf. the similar passage from abst. to concrete in *tenantry, chivalry, gentry, majesty, knighthood, peerage.*)

1330 R. BRUNNE *Chron.* 81 His auncestrie whilom when left it þorgh folis. **1483** CAXTON *Gold. Leg.* 423/3 Thys place is belongyng to me by myn owne herytage comyng fro myn auncestrye. **1514** BARCLAY *Cyt. & Uplondyshm.* 27 Theyr patrymony, Whiche was to them lefte by theyr olde auncestry. *c* **1625** R. JAMES in *Shaks. Cent. Praise* 164 You are descended of Noble Auncestrie. **1780** COWPER *Table Talk* 372 Our ancestry, a gallant Christian race. **1825** *Bro. Jonathan* III. 419 A powerful nation, whose large ancestry had peopled..all that part of the earth.

anchanteor, obs. form of ENCHANTER.

anchentry, obs. form of ANCIENTRY.

†**anchesoun.** *Obs.* 3–4. Also **ancheisun, -esun. -eysone, -eaysoun.** [refashioning of ACHESOUN, a. OFr. *acheson, acheison*:—L. *occāsiōn-em*, after words in *a-* for earlier *an-, en-*. This began in AFr., where *enchesoun* is commoner than the orig. *achesoun.* See also ENCHEASON, the common later form in Eng.] Occasion, cause, reason, motive.

c **1230** *Ancr. R.* 158 And seið þe ancheisun hwi. *Ibid.* 234 Þe þridde anchesun is. **1340** *Ayenb.* 47 Vor be þe ancheysoun of ham byeþ uorlore manye zaules.

anchithere ('æŋkɪ'θɪə(r)). *Palæont.* [ad. mod.L. *anchithērium* (also in Eng. use), f. Gr. ἄγχι near + θηρίον wild beast.] A fossil animal as large as a small pony, having three toes on each foot, found in the Eocene and Miocene strata; regarded evolutionally as an ancestor of the horse, and as forming a link between carnivora with toes and herbivora with hoofs.

1879 LE CONTE *Elem. Geol.* 509 The Miohippus of the United States and the nearly allied Anchithere of Europe, more horse-like than the last. **1881** LUBBOCK in *Nature* No. 618. 403 Huxley has traced up the genealogy of the horse to the Miocene Anchitherium.

anchoate ('æŋkəʊeɪt). *Chem.* [f. next + -ATE[4].] A salt of anchoic acid.

1863 WATTS *Dict. Chem.* I. 290 Anchoate of ammonium is an amorphous mass.

anchoic (æŋ'kəʊɪk), *a. Chem.* [f. Gr. ἄγχ-ειν to throttle, suffocate (+ *o*) + -IC.] In *anchoic acid*: a dibasic acid, $C_9H_{16}O_4$, emitting suffocating fumes, obtained by the action of nitric acid on Chinese wax, or the fatty acids of cocoa-nut oil.

1863 WATTS *Dict. Chem.* I. 290 Anchoic acid..at a stronger heat sublimes..emitting white inodorous vapours, which produce a suffocating effect, when inhaled.

anchor ('æŋkə(r)), *sb.*[1] Forms: 1 **ancor, -er, oncer,** 1–7 **ancre,** 2–7 **anker,** 4–5 **-yr,** 4–6 **-re, -ir,** 6 **ancour, anchore, (anger),** 7 **ankor, ancker, anchour,** 6– **anchor.** [OE. *ancor*, a. L. *ancora* (sometimes erron. spelt *anchora*), ? cogn. w. or adoption of Gr. ἄγκῡρα, f. stem αγκ-, *anc-*. 'bend, crook, hook,' whence Eng. *angle.* Cf. OHG. *anchar* (LG., MHG. *anker*) directly cogn. w. OE.; also ON. *akkeri* (Sw. *ankare*, Da. *anker*) from L. independently. The ME. form with final *-e* is probably influenced by OFr. *ancre*:—L. *ancora.* The current spelling *anchor* is a pedantic corruption, imitating the erroneous L. *anchora.*]

1. An appliance for holding a ship, etc., fixed in a particular place, by mooring it to the bottom of the sea or river; now consisting of 'a heavy iron, composed of a long shank, having a ring at one end to which the cable is fastened, and at the other branching out into two arms or flukes, tending upwards, with barbs or edges on each side.' J.

Anchors are of various sizes. The largest is the SHEET-anchor; next in size are the BOWER-anchors, hung in the bows of the ship; the smallest is the KEDGE-anchor. *foul anchor* is when the anchor becomes in any way entangled.

c **880** K. ÆLFRED *Boeth.* x. 30 Ðin ancor is ȝit on eorþan fæst..Eala wæran þa ancras swa trume! *c* **1205** LAY. 25517 Wind wex an honde, ankeres [**1250** ancreas] heo up droȝen. *c* **1230** *Ancr. R.* 142 Ase ancre under schipes borde, uorte holden þet schip. *c* **1325** *E.E. Allit. P.* B. 418 Kable, oþer capstan to clyppe to her ankreȝ. **1382** WYCLIF *Acts* xxvii. 40 Thei hadden takun vp the ancris. **1480** CAXTON *Chron. Eng.* II. (1520) 10 b/2 He lete the ancres wynde up and sayled into the hye see. **1513** DOUGLAS *Æneis* III. iv. 128 Of oure foreschip ankirris lete vve doun. **1594** SHAKS. *Rich. III*, I. iv. 26 Wedges of Gold, great Anchors, heapes of Pearle..All scattred in the bottome of the Sea. **1692** in *Smith's Seaman's Gram.* I. xvi. 75 The Anchor is foul, that is, the Cable is got about the Fluke. **1694** *Lond. Gaz.* mmmxxiii/1 As soon as they could get up their Anchors they sailed away. **1709** *Ibid.* mmmmdxxi/2 One of the Flukes of the Spare-Anchor [was]..shot off. **1727** SWIFT *Gulliver* I. v. 59 Not a ship would stir..too fast held by their anchors. **1779** COOK *Voy.* (1790) V. 1818 We had lost our kedge anchor. **1807** ROBINSON *Archæol. Græca* IV. xv. 392 The most ancient anchors were only large stones bored through the middle. **1835** SIR J. ROSS *N.-W. Pass.*, Let go the bower-anchor. **1864** TENNYSON *Enoch Ard.* 18 Anchors of rusty fluke.

2. *fig.* That which gives the feeling of stability or security; a ground or source of abiding confidence.

1382 WYCLIF *Heb.* vi. 19 The which as an ankir we han sikir to the soule [**1611** Which hope we haue as an anker of the soule. (So in all other versions.)] *c* **1400** *Rom. Rose* 3780 So farith Love, that selde in oon Holdith his anker. *a* **1536** TINDALE *Wks.* 166 (R.) The roote and grounde of all, and the ancre that neuer fayleth. **1593** SHAKS. *3 Hen. VI*, V. iv. 13 Say Warwicke was our Anchor: what of that? **1699** BENTLEY *Phal.* 303 One Passage more..his last Anchor, to prove his notable point. **1754** CHATHAM *Lett.* iv. 27 Hold fast..by this sheet-anchor of happiness, Religion. **1781** COWPER *Hope* 167 Hope as an anchor, sure and firm, holds fast. **1864** TENNYSON *Enoch Ard.* 222 Cast all your cares on God; that anchor holds.

¶ From the passage in *Heb.* vi. 19, quoted above, an *anchor* is used as the symbol of *hope*, as a *cross* is of *faith*, and a *heart* of *love* or *charity*.

3. a. *transf.* Any contrivance or instrument which fulfils a similar purpose to that of an anchor, by holding fast or giving security; *also*, an anchor-shaped appendage, as the spicules on the skin of Holothuroids.

1855 GOSSE *Mar. Zool.* I. 114 In *Lerneoma* the head..being furnished with a prong on each side curving backwards, forms a powerful anchor by which the parasite is firmly moored to its hapless prey. **1860** TYNDALL *Glac.* I. §22. 157 In some places, however, the anchor [axe] had but a loose hold. **1870** NICHOLSON *Zool.* (1880) 221 In *Chirodota* the skin is provided with microscopic calcareous wheels, in the place of anchors. *Ibid.*, The *Synaptæ*..have the skin furnished with innumerable anchor-shaped spicules attached to special 'anchor-plates' in the integument. **1906** *Westm. Gaz.* 29 Aug. 2/1 The tram lines that corrugate most freely are those which are laid on the concrete foundation without anchors. **1951** *Gloss. Terms Plastics* (*B.S.I.*) 44 *Anchor.* In injection moulding. An undercut extension to the feed. It is usually located on an ejector pin to facilitate the removal of the stalk from the mould.

b. *Billiards.* A stroke in which the two object-balls are kept close to or against the cushion so that a series of cannons can be made without disturbing their position; in full ***anchor cannon, shot, stroke.*** Also ***anchor baulk-line***: one of four lines drawn on a billiard table to form spaces in which the number of cannons allowed is restricted; hence ***anchor-space.***

1901 *World of Billiards* 25 Sept. 460/2 When the two object balls are at rest in any one of the eight spaces, one or both of the object balls must be driven out... The same condition applies to the anchor. **1904** S. A. MUSSABINI *Billiards Expounded* i. 20 The greatest thing known to close-cannon play is the 'anchor stroke'. **1907** *Daily Chron.* 15 Mar. 8/5 T. Reece..went on with his 'anchor' cannon until he had reached an item of 1,825. **1907** T. REECE in *Ibid.* 27 Mar. 5/5 To the ordinary, everyday billiard player..I would not recommend a cultivation of this 'anchor'. **1910** *Encycl. Brit.* III. 939/1 The 'anchor baulk-lines' form a tiny compartment, 6 in. by 3, and are drawn at the end of a baulk-line where it touches the rail and so divides the compartment into two squares. Only one shot is allowed in this 'anchor-space', unless a ball be driven out of it. **1911** C. ROBERTS *Compl. Billiard Player* xx. 146 (*caption*) Position of balls in the famous anchor cannon, from which T. Reece made 499,135 in 1907. **1922** *Westm. Gaz.* 16 Oct., The push-stroke and the anchor-cannon were eliminated when the need for their elimination became obvious.

c. *Athletics.* The end member of a tug-of-war team, who secures the rope by looping it round his body; = *anchor-man* (below).

1909 T. A. COOK et al. *4th Olympiad* 92 Tug of War..The Americans were magnificent athletes, but were not aware how to tie an anchor or how to place their men. **1911** *Encycl. Brit.* XXVII. 365/1 When a tug-of-war takes place out of doors the men, or at least the 'anchors', are allowed to dig holes in the ground for their feet.

d. *Athletics.* The person who runs the last section of a relay race; also *attrib.*

1934 in WEBSTER. **1958** *Observer* 27 July 22/2 On the anchor leg, M. C. Spence..finished first by ten yards for his team. *Ibid.* 3 Aug. 16/1 M. Spence..held off Britain's J. E. Salisbury on the anchor stage to win by a long yard. **1961** *Sunday Times* 16 July 20/7 He must surely be our best prospect as an anchor runner for the relay against America next week.

e. *pl.* Brakes. *slang.*

1936 *Daily Herald* 5 Aug. 8/4 List of busmen's slang phrases..Anchors (Brakes). **1965** PRIESTLEY & WISDOM *Good Driving* vii. 55 There is more to it..than just putting on the brakes—or, to use the colourful language of the sporting motorist, 'clapping on the anchors'.

4. A compère of a radio or television programme, esp. the host presenter of a news programme; = *anchor-man*, avoiding reference to sex. Chiefly *U.S.*

1965 *Guardian* 20 Sept. 4/8 'Panorama' will continue... Richard Dimbleby remains the anchor. **1976** *National Observer* (U.S.) 16 Oct. 10/3 Network television's highest paid..news-show anchor. **1978** *Americana Ann.* 482 NBC moved David Brinkley to Washington, as permanent anchor there for the news of the nation's capital. **1984** *New Yorker* 13 Aug. 22/3 Nine hundred thousand dollars—about what it would cost to buy a second-string anchor in commercial television.

5. †**a.** From its action: the pin or 'chape of a buckle; a buckle is usually described with its "tongue and anchor."' T. *Obs.*

b. *Arch.* 'An ornament shaped similarly to an anchor or arrow-head; used with the egg ornament to decorate or enrich mouldings. Used in all the orders but only applied to the moulding called the Echinus or quarter round.' Gwilt 1876.

1663 GERBIER *Counsel* 70 Small Beads with round and long ones at one peny and..the edges and housings at foure pence per foot. **1751** CHAMBERS *Cycl.*, *Anchor*, in architecture and sculpture, denotes an ornament in form of an anchor, or arrow's-head.

6. Phrases from sense 1. *lit.* and *fig.*

a. at anchor, †**at an, the, anchor,** in OE. *on ancre*: anchored, held by the anchor.

a **1000** *Beowulf* 3771 Sæ-genga [*i.e.* the ship] se þe on ancre rád. *Ibid.* 611 Scip on ancre fæst. **1393** GOWER *Conf.* II. 27 His ship on anker rode. *c* **1530** LD. BERNERS *Arth. Lyt. Bryt.* (1814) 250 Manye shyppes, some vnder sayle..some lienge at the anger. **1598** BARRET *Theor. Warres* v. ii. 129 The enemies fleet riding easily at an anker. **1633** P. FLETCHER *Purple Isl.* XII. lii, Whilst I in vale of tears at anchour ride. **1666** PEPYS *Diary* 4 June, We found the Dutch fleet at anchor. **1740** WOODROOFE in Hanway *Trav.* (1762) I. IV. lix. 273 It is always found the best method to lie at single anchor. **1850** TENNYSON *In Mem.* ciii. 20 A little shallop lay At anchor in the flood.

b. to come to (an) anchor: = ANCHOR *v.* 2, 4.

1590 *Pasquil's Apol.* I. D iij b, But to come to anker..let them..become of one hart with vs. **1595** T. MAYNARD

Drake's Voy. (1849) 7 On Friday..we came to anchor. **1790** BEATSON *Nav. & Mil. Mem.* I. 156 All the ships had come to an anchor.

c. to cast anchor: to let down or 'drop' the anchor; *hence*, to bring the ship to rest, to take up a position. Also of the ship: *she* cast anchor.

a **1300** *K. Horn* 1014 Hi strike seil and maste And ankere gunne caste. *c* **1450** LONELICH *Grail* xx. 122 Heren ancres they casten þere anon, Forto abyden there that nyht. **1526** TINDALE *Acts* xxvii. 29 They caste iiii ancres out of the sterne [WYCLIF, sendinge foure ancris; **1611** cast foure ancres]. **1719** DE FOE *Crusoe* (1865) 39 We dropped our little anchor, and lay still all night. **1780** W. COXE *Russ. Discov.* 31 They were driven to the other side of the same island, where they cast anchor.

d. to weigh anchor: to take up the anchor so as to sail away.

c **1325** *E.E. Allit. P.* C. 103 Wiȝt at þe wyndas weȝen her ankres. *c* **1440** *Morte Arth.* 493 Þey weyde up þeire ankyrs. **1583** STANYHURST *Aeneis* III. (Arb.) 78 We weyed the anchors. **1814** SCOTT *Ld. of Isles* III. iv, And Cormac Doil in haste obey'd, Hoisted his sail, his anchor weigh'd.

e. the anchor comes home: *i.e.* is dragged from its hold. So, a ship ***drags her anchor***. To ***slip the anchor***, to let it go by letting the cable slip.

1694 *Lond. Gaz.* mmmxxiii/1 The Wind blowing very hard..riding in deep Water, his Ankors came home. **1719** DE FOE *Crusoe* (1865) 30 We thought once or twice our anchor had come home.

7. *Comb.* chiefly attrib., as **anchor-ball** (see quot.); **anchor bolt** (see quots.); **anchor-chocks** (see quot.); **anchor escapement** = *recoil escapement*; **anchor-frost**, a miller's term for the clogging of a mill-wheel with ice below the water-surface; † **anchor-gable**, an anchor cable; **anchor-ground**, anchorage ground; **anchor-hoops**, iron hoops binding the stock to the shank of the anchor; **anchor-ice**, ice formed at the bottom of lakes and rivers, ground-ice; **anchor-line**, a line attached to or serving as an anchor (see also quot. 1909); also *transf.* and *fig.*; **anchor-lining** = BILL-BOARDS; **anchor-man**, † (*a*) he who has charge of the anchor; (*b*) *transf.* and *fig.* the person at the end of a group tugging a rope, roped together, etc.; (*c*) a compère of a radio or television programme; cf. sense 4 above; † **anchor-master** = *anchor-man* (*a*); **anchorperson** = sense 4 above; see PERSON *sb.* 2 f; **anchor-plate**, a heavy piece of timber or metal, serving as a point of support (*e.g.* for the cables of a suspension-bridge); see also 3; **anchor-ring**, (*a*) the great ring for attaching the cable; (*b*) *Geom.*, = ANNULUS 2; **anchor-shackle**, an iron loop used instead of an anchor-ring; **anchor-smith**, a maker of anchors; **anchor-tow**, the cable of an anchor; **anchor-watch**, a detachment of seamen kept on deck to perform any duties depending on the ship's position while she lies at anchor; **anchorwoman**, a female presenter of a radio or television news programme; cf. sense 4 and *anchorperson* above.

Also ***anchor-like***, ***-shaped***, ***-wise***; and ANCHOR-HOLD[1], -STOCK, q.v.

1867 SMYTH *Sailor's Word-bk.*, *Anchor-ball, a pyrotechnical combustible attached to a grapnel for adhering to and setting fire to ships. *a* **1875** KNIGHT *Dict. Mech.* I. 96 **Anchor bolt* (Machinery), one having an expanded shank to prevent its drawing out. **1957** *Gloss. Terms for Stone used in Building (B.S.I.)* 21 *Anchor bolt*, a T-shaped bolt for attaching fascia and similar stones to a supporting R.S.J. **1867** SMYTH *Sailor's Word-bk.*, **Anchor-chocks*, pieces indented into a wooden anchor-stock where it has become worn or defective in the way of the shank; also pieces of wood or iron on which an anchor rests when it is stowed. **1854** E. B. DENISON in *Encycl. Brit.* VII. 8/1 The '*anchor' escapement..appears to have been invented by the celebrated Dr. Hooke as early as the year 1656. **1867** WHYTE MELVILLE in *Fortn. Rev.* Nov. 588 Bright enough to thaw an *anchor-frost on the mill-wheel. **1609** HOLLAND *Amm. Marcell.* XIV. ii. 4 Creeping on all foure among the *anchor-gables. **1815** *Niles' Reg.* IX. 201/1 On the same day the *anchor-ice began to run a little. **1877** GREEN *Phys. Geol.* iii. §2. 109 Anchor-ice forms sometimes..at the bottom of lakes and rivers while the rest of the water remains unfrozen. **1793** SMEATON *Edystone L.* 195 The *anchor-like piece of iron by which the main tackle blocks are hung. **1906** *Westm. Gaz.* 29 Sept. 13/3 The first thread spun [by a spider] is secured to the ground as an *anchor-line. **1909** *Cent. Dict. Suppl.*, *Anchor-line*, a line attached to a small buoy and to one fluke of an anchor: used in towing a raft of logs and to free the anchor when fast to rocks or snags. (U.S.) **1910** BELLOC *Verses* 47, I stand at home and slip the anchor-line. **1598** *anchor-maker [see *anchor master* below]. **1831** J. HOLLAND *Manuf. Metal* I. 95 Different anchor-makers have their respective rules of proportion. **1870** [See 3]. *a* **1200** in Wright *Voc.* 88/2 *Proreta*, *ankermon. **1911** *Encycl. Brit.* XXVII. 365/1 Some rules allow the 'anchor-men', who hold the ends of the rope, to fasten it to their persons. **1955** E. HILLARY *High Adv.* ix. 173 Ang Temba went first..; then Tom Bourdillon; and finally Charles Evans as anchor-man. **1957** L. P. HARTLEY *Hireling* i. 9 The driver..[had] been the anchorman in many a tug-of-war. **1958** *Spectator* 29 Aug. 278/2 Mr. Williams is almost always there on this kind of occasion as a tubby anchor-man. **1958** *Observer* 28 Dec. 3/1 Its [*sc.* a television programme's] remarkable compère or anchor-man, Cliff Michelmore. **1598** FLORIO, *Ancoraio*, an *anchor master or an *anchor maker. **1973** *Newsweek* 2 July 50/2 In her new job—which she will share with co-*anchorperson Hughes Rudd—Quinn hopes to achieve a tone that is 'comfortable and relaxed.' **1982** *Amer. Banker* 31 Mar. 11/4 Individual interviews..will include questions from different anchorpersons. **1883** W. CONANT in *Harper's Mag.* 932/1 At the bottom..are imbedded four massive *anchor-plates of cast iron, one for each of the cables. **1863** FROST & WOLSTENHOLME *Solid Geom.* xiv. 213 An *anchor ring, supposed to be generated by the revolution of a circle about an axis in its plane not intersecting the circle. **1862** ANSTED *Channel Isl.* II. ix. (ed. 2) 238 Small, *anchor-shaped calcareous plates. **1870** [See 3 above]. **1662** PEPYS *Diary* 27 Apr., Visited the Mayor, Mr. Timbull, our *anchor-smith. **1703** MOXON *Mech. Exerc.* 14 Chosen by Anchor-Smiths, because it abides the Heat better than other Iron. **1637** RUTHERFORD *Lett.* 107 (1862) I. 271 The *anchor-tow abideth fast within the vail: the end of it is in Christ's ten fingers. *c* **1860** LONGF. *Dutch Pict.* ix, A ship that..tugs at her anchor-tow. **1876** DAVIS *Polaris Exp.* viii. 219 The tidal observations were made by..the *anchor-watch during the remaining nine hours. **1976** *People Weekly* 26 Apr. 18/1 She would be the first *anchorwoman ever on national television. **1985** *N.Y. Times* 15 Dec. XI. 2/4 She was a correspondent and anchorwoman in New York for the NBC Radio Network News.

† **'anchor**, *sb.*[2] *Obs.* Forms: 1 **ancra**, 3–6 **ancre**, 4–5 **ankre**, 4–7 **anker**, 5 **ankyr**, **aunker**, 5–6 **anchor(e.** *Pl.* **-s**; 1 **ancran**, 3 **-en**, 3–6 **-es**, 5–6 **anker(e)s**, **anchor(e)s**. [OE. *ancra*, *ǫncra*, for *ancora*, **ancoro*, shortened f. L. **anchōrēta*, *anachōrēta*: see ANCHORITE. App. made *áncora* by 'popular etymology' after *án* 'one, alone'; the similarly transformed OS. *ênkoro*, OHG. *einchoran* (cf. OHG. *einsidilo*, mod.G. *einsiedel*, *-ler*), were according to Sievers, prob. adaptations of the OE. ME. again had *a* short before two cons. OE. had prob. *ancra* masc., *ancre* fem., though the latter is not recorded; in ME. *ancre* was of common gender; the fem. *ancress*, *ankeress*, ANCHORESS, appeared in 14th c., and an extended masc. ANKERER in 16th; but Fr. *anachorète*, modified to *anchoret*, ANCHORITE, has superseded the earlier forms, *anchor* appearing last (as current wd.) in Shaks.]

1. An ANCHORITE.

a **1000** ÆLFRIC *Gloss.* in Wright *Voc.* 42 *Anachoreta*, ancra. *c* **1230** *Ancr. R.* 10 Powel þe erest ancre, Antonie, & Arsenie. *c* **1300** *St. Brand.* 330 The threteoth fram the to the Ylle of Ankres schal wende. **1362** LANGL. *P. Pl.* A. Prol. 28 Ancres and Hermytes þat holdeþ hem in heore celles. **1387** TREVISA *Higden* Rolls Ser. VI. 149 He lyvede anker his lyf. **1432–50** tr. *Higden* ibid., Lyvede after as an ankre in yle of Farne. **1496** *Dives & Paup.* (W. de Worde) VI. xiii. 253/1 Whan men take them to be ankeres and recluses. *c* **1500** *Robt. Deuyll* in *E.E. Pr. Rom.* 1858 I. 23 We have robbed and kylled nonnes, holy aunkers, preestes. **1529** MORE *Comf. agst. Tribul.* III. Wks. 1557, 1247/1 Ancres and ancresses most especiallye. *a* **1536** TINDALE *Exp. Matt.* Wks. II. 42 Monks..whether obseruant or ancre. **1553–87** FOXE *A. & M.* (1596) 113/1 To Crowland, where he led the life of an Anker. **1599** BP. HALL *Satires* IV. ii. 103 Sit seauen yeares pining in an anchores cheyre. **1604** SHAKS. *Haml.* III. ii. 229 (2nd Q°.) And anchors cheere [*i.e.* chair] in prison be my scope. **1872** [See ANCHORAGE[2]].

2. An ANCHORESS. Well known in the book-title *Ancren Riwle*, the 'Rule of Nuns.'

c **1230** *Ancr. R.* 4 Nu aski ȝe hwat riwle ȝe ancren schullen holden? **1297** R. GLOUC. 380 An ancre..þat nolde vor non þyng fle out of hyre house. **1393** LANGL. *P. Pl.* C. IV. 144 In þe castel of corf ich shal do þe [womman] close Ther as an ancre. *c* **1400** *Rom. Rose* 6351 Now lyk an anker in an hous ..And now a nonne, and now abbesse. **1466** *Past. Lett.* 549 II. 267 To the Prioress of Carow, *vis.* viiid. To a maide that came with her, xxd. To the anchors xld.

¶ At an early period fancifully associated with ANCHOR *sb.*[1]

c **1230** *Ancr. R.* 142 For þi is ancre icleoped ancre, & under chirche iancred, ase ancre under schipes borde.

3. *Comb.* **anchor-house**, an anchorite's cell; also, a monastery or nunnery; **anchor-settle**, **-saidell**, an anchorite's seat or cell, also applied to the occupant, an anchorite.

c **1230** *Ancr. R.* 88 From smiðe, & from ancre huse, me tiðinge bringeð. **1086** *O.E. Chron.*, Twegen hâliȝe menn.. on ancersettle wuniende. **1516** *Diurn. Occur.* (1833) 6 Thair was ane woman..ane anarcadell inclosit in the Grenesyid. **1603** *Philotus* cxxiv, I charge the..Thow neyther girne, gowl, glowme, nor gaip, Lyke Anker saidell, like vnsell Aip.

anchor ('æŋkə(r)), *v.* Also 3–7 **ancre**, **-ker**, 7 **-kor**. [? a Fr. *ancre-r*, f. *ancre*; cf. med.L. *ancorāre*. (There may have been an OE. *ancrian*, unrecorded.)]

1. *trans.* To secure (the ship) with an anchor; to place at, or bring to, anchor.

c **1230** *Ancr. R.* 142 For þi is ancre..under chirche iancred. **1489** CAXTON *Faytes of Armes* I. xvii. 49 They must be ancred within the watre that they may be stedfast. **1513** DOUGLAS *Æneis* VII. iii. 8 At the schore..Thare nauy can thay anker fast and hank. **1813** SOUTHEY *Nelson* ix. 348 It was not possible to anchor the fleet. **1851** SIR F. PALGRAVE *Eng. & Norm.* I. 517 (L.) He there anchored his bark.

2. *intr.* To cast anchor, to come to anchor. (Said either of the crew or the ship.)

1578 T. N. tr. *Conq. W. Ind.* 37 Cortez..anckred at the rivers mouth. **1667** MILTON *P.L.* II. 289 Sea-faring men.. whose Bark by chance Or Pinnace anchors in a craggy Bay. **1718** LADY M. MONTAGUE *Lett.* II. xlix. 52 We anchored in the Hellespont. **1813** SOUTHEY *Nelson* v. 147 The Vanguard was the first that anchored.

3. *fig. trans.* To fix as with an anchor, to fix firmly or abidingly.

1594 SHAKS. *Rich. III*, IV. iv. 231 Till that my Nayles were anchor'd in thine eyes. **1663** GERBIER *Counsel* 44 The doore-cases, well ankered into the wall. **1855** OWEN *Comp. Anat.* xiii. 275 (L.) The feet..permanently anchor the parasite to its prey. **1860** TYNDALL *Glac.* I. §22. 157 My first care was to anchor it [ice-axe] firmly in the snow.

4. *fig. refl.* and *intr.* To fix oneself, one's attention, thought; take up a position.

1581 SIDNEY *Astroph.* (T.) [She] will'd me these tempests of vain love to fly, And anchor fast myself on virtue's shore. **1603** SHAKS. *Meas. for M.* II. iv. 4 Whilst my Inuention, hearing not my Tongue, Anchors on Isabell. **1797** GODWIN *Enquirer* II. v. 238 He..advances..up the province upon which he anchors.

5. *trans.* To present (a radio or television news programme); *intr.*, to act as an anchorperson.

1961 *Sunday Times* 26 Feb. 48/5 They employed Mr. John Freeman to anchor an hour of absorbing recapitulation. **1976** *Time* 31 May 39/2 Barbara Walters.. will be the highest-paid woman ever to anchor a national news program. **1977** *New Yorker* 11 Apr. 104/2 Her ambition is simple and straightforward—'to anchor in a top-ten market'. **1986** G. PRIESTLAND *Something Understood* ix. 248 The prestige programme of radio talks and documentaries department was Analysis, then anchored by Ian McIntyre.

anchor, obs. form of ANKER.

† **'anchorable**, *a.* *Obs. rare*[−1]. [f. prec. + -ABLE.] Fit for anchorage.

1634 SIR T. HERBERT *Trav.* 40 (T.) The sea everywhere twenty leagues from land anchorable.

anchorage[1] ('æŋkərɪdʒ). Also 6 **ankarage**, 7 **-erage**, **-orage**, **anchrage**. [f. prec. + -AGE, cf. Fr. *ancrage*.]

1. The action or process of anchoring; the condition of lying at anchor.

1611 COTGR., *Anchraige*, ankorage, ankoring. **1634** W. WOOD *New Engl. Prosp.* I. i, There is roome for the Anchorage of 500 Ships. **1687** *Lond. Gaz.* mmcclxxxii/6 A Duty imposed upon Anchrage. **1855** (7 June) BRIGHT *Sp.* 257 The position and duration of the anchorages of ships between the Mediterranean and the Black Sea.

2. Conditions admitting of anchoring; *esp.* a place for anchoring; anchorage-ground.

1706 PHILLIPS, *Anchorage* or *Anchoring*, ground fit to hold the Ship's Anchor, so that she may ride it out safely. **1744** ANSON *Voy.* II. iv. (ed. 4) 218 Where a ship might come to an anchor..though the anchorage is inconvenient. **1779** T. FORREST *Voy. N. Guinea* 311 Many bays..affording good anchorage. **1835** SIR J. ROSS *N.-W. Pass.* ix. 127 The floe which had been our anchorage. **1878** MARKHAM *Gt. Frozen Sea* iii. 39 The scenery as we approached the anchorage was truly magnificent.

3. a. *transf.* A position affording support, a hold.

1860 TYNDALL *Glac.* I. §11. 70, I crossed the fissure, obtained the anchorage at the other side, and helped the others over. **1883** W. CONANT in *Harper's Mag.* 930/1 The anchorages are solid cubical structures of stone masonry.

b. *spec.* in *Dentistry*.

1912 *Catal. Dental Manuf. Co. Ltd.* G. 71 Sufficient anchorage must be made to withstand the force of mastication, and to provide for firm retention of the inlay within the cavity. **1917** *Recalled to Life* Sept. p. xx, They have platinum anchorages baked in the teeth and large, strong pins soldered to the anchorages after baking of the porcelain is complete.

4. *fig.* A point of support or rest for the mind or feelings; something on which to depend or repose.

1677 YARRANTON *Eng. Improv.* 21 Suppose all the houses in Lombard-street to be put into a Register..let them be the Credit, Anchorage, Fund and Foundation to build your Bank upon. **1746** HERVEY *Medit. & Cont.* (1818) 80 Here they enjoy safe anchorage; are in no danger of foundering amidst the waves of prevailing iniquity. **1856** FROUDE *Hist. Eng.* IV. xix. 151 The Church anchorage no longer tenable in the change of wind, and the new anchorage in the Bible as yet partially discovered and imperfectly sounded.

5. A toll or charge for anchoring; anchorage-dues.

1516 *Churchw. Acc. St. Marg. Westm.* (1797) 8 For 24 ton of barnestone with the pylage, ankarage, stallage..£11. **1661** MARVELL *Corr.* 29 Wks. 1872 II. 68 Mr. Porter..hath giuen order to stop the Primage, loadage, &c.: and will the anchorage as soon as he has seen your charter. **1755** MAGENS *Insurances* II. 210 Extraordinary Pilotage and Anchorage.. shall appertain to common Average.

6. 'The set of anchors belonging to a ship.' Smyth *Sailor's Word-bk.* 1867.

1588 SHAKS. *Tit. A.* I. i. 73 The Barke..Returnes with precious lading to the Bay, From whence at first she weigh'd her Anchorage.

7. *Comb.* **anchorage-ground** = anchorage 2, 4.

1824 W. IRVING *T. Trav.* I. 272, I had no longer an anchorage-ground for my heart.

anchorage[2] ('æŋkərɪdʒ). Also 6 **anchoridge**, 9 **ankrage**. [f. ANCHOR *sb.*[2] + -AGE. Cf. *hermitage*, *parsonage*.] The cell or retreat of an anchorite.

1593 *Mon. & Rites Ch. Durh.* (1842) 15 At the east end.. of the Quire..was the goodlyest faire porch which was called the anchoridge. **1598** STOW *Surv.* (ed. Strype 1754) I. III. xii. 712/1 Build her a Recluse or Anchorage. **1852** ROCK *Ch. of Fathers* III. 115 His ankrage or house, in which he [the ankret] was solemnly shut up. **1872** E. CUTTS *Scenes Mid. Ages* 128 There was also an anchorage in St. Ethelred's churchyard..and an anchor continually dwelt there till the Reformation.

† ˈ**anchoral**, *a. Obs.*$^{-0}$ [f. ANCHOR *sb.*[1] + -AL[1].] ‘Pertaining to the Anchor or Cable.’ Blount *Gl.*

anchored (ˈæŋkəd), *ppl. a.* [f. ANCHOR + -ED.] **1. a.** With the anchor let down to the ground; **b.** Held fast, secured by the anchor; **c.** Firmly fixed, fixed so as to obtain support, or be at rest.

1611 COTGR., *Ancré*, ankored, having cast ankor, at an ankor. *a* **1687** WALLER (L.) Like a well-twisted cable, holding fast The anchor'd vessel. *a* **1725** POPE *Odyss.* IV. 485 There, anchor'd vessels safe in harbour lie. **1837** WHEWELL *Hist. Induct. Sc.* (1857) II. 248 Each ear of grain is anchored by its stalk. **1878** SEELEY *Stein* II. 30 Stein wore the look of one anchored and secure.

2. Furnished with anchors; by extension, *esp.* in *Her.*, Furnished with anchor-like appendages, having two spreading points.

1611 COTGR., *Ancré*, ankored.. made or fashioned like an ankor. **1642** H. MORE *Song of Soul* II. I. II. xxix, With scornfull hisse, shooting her anchor'd tongue. **1661** S. MORGAN *Sph. Gentry* II. i. 13 *Anckred* is that form of cross whose points are made sharp like unto an ancker. **1725** BRADLEY *Fam. Dict.*, *Ankred*.. so they call one of their Crosses in a Coat of Arms.

anchorer: see ANKERER.

anchoress, ancress (ˈæŋkərɪs, ˈæŋkrɪs). Forms: 4–6 **ankres**, 5 **-keras, -korasse, (angoras)**, 5–7 **ancresse**, 6 **ankresse, -isse, anckres, anchorisse**, 6–7 **-esse**, (9 *arch.* **ancress, -kress**), 7– **anchoress.** [f. *ancre*, ANCHOR *sb.*[2], with Fr. fem. ending *-esse*, *-ess*; cf. *anchresse* in Palsgr. 1530. In ME. *ancre* was used for both sexes. A rarer fem. was ANCHORITESS.] A female anchorite, a nun.

1393 *Test. Ebor.* IV. 186, Xijd. to the Ankres of Thurgransby, and vjd. to Alison hir mayden. *c* **1420** *Chron. Vilod.* 308 To sytte upon a matte of the angoras. **1450** MYRC 1355 Yef ho were ankeras or nonne. **1549** LATIMER 7 *Serm. bef. Edw. VI* (Arb.) 127 Ladye faieth.. is no Anckres, she dwells not alone. **1565** JEWEL *Def. Apol.* (1611) 280 The Reuelation of Dame Eue the Anchorisse. **1600** FAIRFAX *Tasso* XI. ix. 197 Ancresses that dwell, Mewed vp in walles. **1625** FLETCHER *Fair Maid* III. i, I will.. wall up my girle, wife, like an anchoresse. *c* **1800** WORDSW. *Misc. Sonn.* xxi, There a saintly anchoress she dwelt. **1869** MRS. PALLISER *Hist. Lace* xxii. 251 This Lady Ancress, or Anchoress, being some worn-out old nun. **1876** ROCK *Text. Fabr.* ii. 11 Ankresses are forbidden to make purses.

anchoret, -etish, vars. of ANCHORITE, -ITISH.

anchoretic (æŋkəˈrɛtɪk), *a.* Also 9– -itic. [f. *anchoret*, ANCHORITE + -IC, after Gr. ἀναχωρητικός.] Of or pertaining to an anchorite.

1661 *Origen's Opin.* in *Phœnix* (1721) I. 6 A Monastick and Anchoretick Life. **1829** I. TAYLOR *Enthus.* viii. 203 In an enumeration of the natural causes of the anchoretic life, the influence of scenery should not be overlooked. **1862** LATHAM *Channel Isl.* III. xiii. (ed. 2) 326 Their discipline was, essentially, anchoritic and recluse.

anchoˈretical, *a. rare* Also 7 -itical; and see ANACHORETICAL. [f. prec. + -AL[1].] Resembling, or after the manner of, an anchorite.

a **1667** JER. TAYLOR *Serm.* I. 278 (L.) Those severe and anchoritical and philosophical persons. **1844** LINGARD *Anglo-Sax. Ch.* (1858) II. xii. 240 Leading an anachoretical life amid the ruins of some deserted abbey.

anchoretish, -itish (ˈæŋkəˌrɛtɪʃ, -ˌaɪtɪʃ), *a. rare.* [f. ANCHORITE, -ET + -ISH.] Partaking of the character or practice of an anchorite; reclusive, hermit-like.

1830 JAMES *Darnley* (1846) 4 A solitary duck.. passing its anchoritish hours in fishing. **1877** LYTTEIL *Landm.* III. vii. 134 Time.. spent in anchoretish devotions.

anchoretism, -it- (ˈæŋkərɪtɪz(ə)m, -aɪt-). [f. as prec. + -ISM.] The practice or life of an anchorite.

1652 SPARKE *Prim. Devot.* (1663) 491 Hermitage, or sullen anchoretisme. **1862** R. PATTERSON *Ess. Hist. & Art* 347 The peaceful and humble Anchoritism of the first centuries.

ˈ**anchor-hold**[1]. [ANCHOR *sb.*[1] + HOLD.]

1. The hold or grip that an anchor takes; also, the ground that it grips, = ANCHORAGE[1] 2.

1527 GARDINER in Pocock *Rec. Ref.* I. xxxix. 75 Being compelled to experiment whether anker-hold will serve us. **1628** DIGBY *Voy. Medit.* (1868) 25 If our anchor hold and ground tackle had failed, no industrie could haue preserued vs. **1725** DE FOE *Voy. round World* (1840) 111 They found good anchor-hold in about thirty-six fathom. **1867** SMYTH *Sailor's Word-bk.*, *Anchor-hold*, the fastness of the flukes on the ground.

2. *fig.* Firm hold; point clung to; chief ground of trust, expectation, argument, etc.

1533 MORE *Ans. Poys. Bk.* Wks. 1557, 1100/1 In these woordes is the very ankerhold. **1581** MARBECK *Bk. of Notes* 28 Their chiefest anker hold, was these words of Christ. **1611** SPEED *Hist. Gt. Brit.* VIII. vii. 403 The Norman Duke, who made that the anker-hold of his claime. **1855** I. TAYLOR *Restor. Belief* (1856) 120 Good anchor-hold in the roadstead of apostolicity. **1883** W. GIBSON in *Harper's Mag.* Jan. 192 Hope's anchor-hold on golden grounds of Faith.

anchor-hold[2]. *Hist.* [f. ANCHOR *sb.*[2] + HOLD *sb.*[1]] An anchorite ‘hold’, abode, or retreat; the cell of an anchorite; = ANCHORAGE[2].

1631 WEEVER *Anc. Funeral Mon.* 150 Their solitarie little cells.. carrie still the name of.. Anchor-holds. *a* **1666** WOOD *City of Oxford* (1889) I. 356 The Anchorhold of S. Giles Church. **1802** FOSBROKE *Brit. Mon.* (1843) 372 The *Destina* (for so these anchor-holds or stalls, affixed to larger buildings were called), occupied by Dunstan soon after he became a Monk. **1922** *Times* 22 Apr. 9/4 Both the church and its ‘anchorhold’, or anchorite's cell, are more than once mentioned in documents of the college [*sc.* Merton].

anchoring (ˈæŋkərɪŋ), *vbl. sb.* [f. ANCHOR *v.* + -ING[1].]

1. The action or condition of lying at anchor, or the means of doing so; anchorage.

1593–1622 R. HAWKINS *Voy. S. Sea* (1847) 178 Under which is good anchoring, cleane ground. **1690** *Lond. Gaz.* mmdix/3 A very violent Storm of Wind.. forced the Frigat from her Anchoring. **1724** DE FOE, etc. *Tour Gt. Brit.* (1769) III. 215 Good Anchoring in six or eight Fathom of Water.

2. *transf.* The action or method of fixing securely.

1767 ELLIS *Actinia* in *Phil. Trans.* LVII. 432 Like the anchoring of muscles [*i.e.* mussels], by their fine silken filaments, that end in suckers. **1883** W. CONANT in *Harper's Mag.* 930/1 The mode of anchoring the cables [of a suspension-bridge] will be described.

3. *Comb.* **anchoring-ground, -place**, ground, or a position, used or suited for anchoring; **anchoring-room**, space for anchoring; **anchoring-stone**, a stone used instead of an anchor.

1740 WOODROOFE in Hanway *Trav.* (1762) I. IV. lix. 273 On the south side there is good anchoring-ground. **1667** *Phil. Trans.* II. 497 In the ankoring places it [the Sea] was Blue. **1796** NELSON in Nicolas *Disp.* II. 309 Not one anchoring place from Genoa to Ventimiglia was accessible. **1865** *Morn. Star* 1 Feb., The anchoring room being too contracted. **1846** GROTE *Greece* I. I. xiii. 329 The Argonauts had left their anchoring-stone on the coast of Bebrycia.

ˈ**anchoring**, *ppl. a.* [f. ANCHOR *v.* + -ING[2].]

a. Coming to anchor; lying at anchor. **b.** Holding firm like an anchor.

1605 SHAKS. *Lear* IV. vi. 18 Yond tall Anchoring Barke. **1879** *Wild Life in S.C.* 29 The wrench at its anchoring roots.

† ˈ**anchorism.** *Obs. rare*$^{-1}$. [f. ANCHOR *sb.*[2] + -ISM.] An anchorite's manner of life.

1633 G. HERBERT *Ch. Mil.* 186 in *Temple* 189 He took fiue vizards to conceal his crimes: From Egypt Anchorisme and retiredness.

† ˈ**anchorist.** *Obs.* Also 7 **ancorist**; and see ANACHORIST. [f. ANCHOR *sb.*[2] + -IST.] = ANCHORITE, including ANCHORESS. Also *attrib.*

1651 *Churchw. Acc. St. Marg. Westm.* (1797) 60 The Anchorist house near the vestry. **1662** FULLER *Worthies* III. 193 A woman lately turn'd an Ancorist, and renowned for her holiness.

anchorite, -et (ˈæŋkəraɪt, -ɪt). Forms: 5 **ancorite**, 6–7 **anachorete**, 6–8 **-it(e**, 7–8 **-et**, 7 **anch'rit(e, anchorete**, (9 *arch.* **ankret**), 7– **anchoret, -ite.** [The forms *anachoret(e*, *anachorit(e* were a. Fr. *anachorète* and L. *anachōrēta*, med.L. *anachōrita*, ad. Gr. ἀναχωρητ-ής, n. of agent f. ἀναχωρέ-ειν to retire, retreat, f. ἀνά back + χωρέ-ειν to give place, withdraw. Under infl. of the earlier Eng. *ancre*, *anker* (ANCHOR *sb.*[2]), this has been modified to *anchrit*, *ancorite*, *anchoret*, *anchorite*, of which the last is now usual. Appeared *c* 1450, and superseded ANCHOR *c* 1600.]

1. a. A person who has withdrawn or secluded himself from the world; usually one who has done so for religious reasons, a recluse, a hermit. (Appl. to both sexes, though the special fem. is ANCHORESS.)

1460 CAPGRAVE *Chron.* 65 Thelophorus [was] mad Pope, which was first a ancorite. **1538** LELAND *Itin.* V. 116 A Chapel of a woman Anachorete. **1608** BP. HALL *Epistles* I. v, He had wilfully mur'd up himselfe as an Anachoret. **1634** HABINGTON *Castara* (1870) 18 The Vowes of recluse Nuns, and th' An'chrits prayer. *a* **1680** BUTLER *Rem.* (1759) I. 47 A solitary Anchorite that dwells, Retir'd from all the World in obscure Cells. **1741** JOHNSON *L.P.*, *Morin* Wks. 1787 IV. 473 The ostentation of a philosopher, or the severity of an anchoret. **1816** SCOTT *Antiq.* xxxv. (1829) 239 No anchoret could have made a more simple and scanty meal. **1852** ROCK *Ch. of Fathers* III. 115 Not always did the ankret live beneath the church's roof. **1869** GOULBOURN *Purs. Holiness* i. 1 Elijah was a sort of anchorite or hermit.

b. *attrib.*

1847 LONGF. *Evan.* II. iv. 25 The grim, taciturn bear, the anchorite monk of the desert. **1929** C. DAY LEWIS *Transitional Poem* II. 29 Then life's pistons.. Begin to tickle the most anchorite ear.

2. *Ch. Hist.* The recluses of the East in the early Christian centuries. (In this application the Gr. form *anachoret* (əˈnækərɪt) is often retained.)

1553–87 FOXE *A. & M.* (1596) 138/1 Moonks.. were divided into heremits or anachorits, and into Cœnobits. **1650** W. CHARLETON *Paradoxes* Prol. 29 The Faune.. desired the mediatory Prayers of Anthony, the Anachoret. **1781** GIBBON *Decl. & F.* II. xxxvii. 354 The holy man was followed by a train of two or three thousand anachorets. **1844** LINGARD *Anglo-Sax. Ch.* (1858) I. v. 204 The same contempt for riches which distinguished the anachorets of Egypt. **1867** LADY HERBERT *Cradle L.* v. 154 Endless caverns.. where the Anchorites, in the early days of the Church, lived.

3. *fig.* Any one of solitary secluded habits.

1616 DRUMM. OF HAWTH. *Sonnet* xxi. Wks. 1711, 4/2 Framed for mishap, th' anachorit of love. **1848** DICKENS *Dombey* (C. D. ed.) 117 Even amongst those absorbed young anchorites Paul was an object of interest. **1864** I. TAYLOR in *Good Wds.* 787 The individual reader, the fireside anchoret.

4. *Comb.*, as ***anchorite-like, -window.***

1657 TRAPP *Comm. Nehem.* vi. 10 He was thus (Anchoret-like) pent up. **1865** *Athenæum* No. 1960. 849/2 Considered the opening to be an anchorite-window.

† ˈ**anchoritess.** *arch.* [f. ANCHORITE + -ESS.] A rare fem. of ANCHORITE; = ANCHORESS.

1655 FULLER *Ch. Hist.* II. 96 Pega his sister, an Anchoritesse, led a solitary life, not far from him. **1872** E. CUTTS *Scenes Mid. Ages* 131 An Anchoritess in the hermitage of St. Brendon, in Bristol.

anchorless (ˈæŋkəlɪs), *a.* [f. ANCHOR *sb.*[1] + -LESS.] Devoid of an anchor; *fig.* without firm hold, having nothing to repose upon; drifting.

1832 *Fraser's Mag.* VI. 739/2 With all my anchorless thoughts adrift. **1853** C. BRONTË *Villette* I. vi. 94 My homeless, anchorless, unsupported mind. **1863** J. MORISON *St. Bern.* 69 The same anchorless insecurity as to what the invisible world would next do. **1914** R. BROOKE *Let.* 7 Mar. in *Coll. Poems* (1929) p. cxii, I really do feel a little anchorless. I shall be glad to be back among you all, and tied to somewhere in England. **1945** P. A. LARKIN *North Ship* 17 Then would the moon go raving, The moon, the anchorless Moon go swerving Down at the earth.

ˈ**anchor-stock.** [ANCHOR *sb.*[1] + STOCK.] **a.** A bar which crosses the top of an anchor, at right angles to the shank, and also to the plane of the arms, the use of which is to cause one or other arm to strike the ground.

c **1302** *Pipe Roll 30 Ed. I. lm. 2b* In vj Anchoris, vj ankerstokes. **1346–1688** [see STOCK *sb.*[1] 24 a]. **1825** H. GASCOIGNE *Nav. Fame*, An anchor-stock in ready halves they find, To fit the rudder head now well inclin'd.

b. *Comb.* **anchor-stock fashion** (see quot. 1867). Hence also **anchor-stock** *v.*

c **1850** *Rudim. Nav.* (Weale), *To anchor-stock*, To work planks in a manner resembling the stocks of anchors, by fashioning them in a tapering form from the middle, and working or fixing them over each other, so that the broad or middle part of one plank shall be immediately above or below the butts or ends of two others. This method.. is.. used where particular strength is required, as in the spirketings under ports. **1867** SMYTH *Sailor's Word-Bk.* 40 *Anchor-stock fashion*, the method of placing the butt of one wale-plank nearly over the middle of the other; and the planks being broadest in the middle, and tapered to the ends, they resemble an anchor-stock.

anchovy (ænˈtʃəʊvɪ, ˈæntʃəvɪ). Forms: 6–8 **anchoue, -ove**, 7 **-oua, -oveye**, 7–8 **-ova, -ovie**, 7– **anchovy.** [a. Sp., Pg. *anchova*, *anchoa* (It. *acciuga*, dial. *anciova*, *ancioa*, *anciua*), of disputed origin; Diez took the It. as the typical form, deriving it from a L. **apya* for *aphya*, ad. Gr. ἀφύη, name of some kind of small fish, with suffix *-ug*; Mahn considers the Sp., Pg., and It. dial. form to be an adoption of the Basque name *anchoa*, *anchua*, which he identifies with *antzua* adj. ‘dry,’ as if ‘dried fish.’]

1. A small fish of the Herring family (*Engraulis encrasicholus*) found on the European coasts, especially in the Mediterranean, where it is extensively caught, and pickled for exportation.

1596 SHAKS. *1 Hen. IV*, II. iv. 588 Item, Anchoues, and Sacke after Supper, ijs. *vid.* **1620** VENNER *Via Recta* iv. 78 Anchoua's, the famous meat of Drunkards, and of them that desire to haue their drinke oblectate the pallate. **1657** COLVIL *Whigs Suppl.* (1751) 16 Which to the pallat pleasing proves, Like Adriatic gulph anchoves. **1674** FLATMAN *Belly God* 100 To quicken appetite it will behoove ye To feed courageously on good Anchovie. **1774** GOLDSM. *Retal.* 14 Full certain I am, That Ridge is anchovy, and Reynolds is lamb. **1796** MRS. GLASSE *Cookery* v. 53 Have ready an anchovy minced small. **1854** SOYER *Cookery* §411 Add two tablespoonsful of essence of anchovies.

2. *Comb.* and *attrib.*, as ***anchovy-barrel, essence, paste***; **anchovy butter**, a paste made of anchovies mixed with butter, used as a filling for sandwiches, savoury biscuits, etc.; **anchovy-cullice, -sauce**, savoury broth, and sauce, made with anchovies; **anchovy-toast**, toast spread with anchovy, used as a whet to appetite for wine.

1741 *Compl. Fam.-Piece* I. iii. 210 Take an *Anchovy-barrel, or a deep glazed Pot. **1845** E. ACTON *Mod. Cookery* (ed. 2) iv. 127 *Anchovy Butter. (*Excellent.*) **1959** *Listener* 13 Aug. 263/1 Mashed liver sausage, or anchovy butter, or any other favourite paste. **1725** BRADLEY *Fam. Dict.* s.v., *Anchovie-Cullices are frequently made and put into several Ragoos. **1846** ‘A LADY’ *Jewish Man. Cookery* ii. 35 Pound it [*sc.* fish].. with a couple of anchovies, or a little *anchovy essence. **1856** DICKENS *Out of Season* in *Househ. Words* 28 June 555/2 *Anchovy Paste.. and the whole stock of luxurious helps to appetite. **1674** N. FAIRFAX *Bulk & Selv.* 180 Such a *Hoghen moghen* Leviathan that.. the one of Mr. Hobbes would never be enough to make *Anchovy-sauce for it. *c* **1771** S. FOOTE *Maid of Bath* I. 11 Get me an *anchovy toast. **1826** DISRAELI *Viv. Grey* v. xiii. 238 An after-dinner anecdote.. as piquant as an anchovy toast.

anˌchovy-ˈpear. A West Indian fruit, pickled and eaten like the mango; also the tree (*Grias cauliflora*) which bears it.

1696 [see *river pear*, RIVER *sb.*[1] 7]. **1725** SLOANE *Nat. Hist. Jamaica* tab. 207. fig. 12 Anchove pear tree. **1866** A. BLACK in *Treas. Bot.* 552 The Anchovy Pear of Jamaica has long been cultivated in plant stoves for the sake of its magnificent foliage.

anchusic (æŋ'kjuːzɪk), *a. Chem.* [f. as next + -IC.] In *anchusic acid*: = next.

1863 WATTS *Dict. Chem.* I. 290 Anchusin or Anchusic acid.

anchusin ('æŋkjuːsɪn). *Chem.* [f. L. *anchūsa* generic name of the Alkanets + -IN.] The colouring principle of alkanet root; an amorphous resinoid substance of a deep red colour.

1863 WATTS *Dict. Chem.* I. 290 Nitric acid transforms anchusin into oxalic acid and a bitter substance.. Alkalis form with anchusin blue compounds.

anchylose, ank- ('æŋkɪləʊz), *v.* [f. ANCHYLOSIS, after *anastomose*, *metamorphose*, etc., mod.Fr. *ankyloser*, f. *ankylose* sb., perhaps supplying a model.]

1. *trans.* To stiffen a joint by consolidation of the articulating surfaces; to consolidate two distinct bones; *usually* in *pass.* To be solidly united bone to bone.

1787 HUNTER in *Phil. Trans.* LXXVII. 383 In the Porpoise, four of the vertebræ of the neck are anchylosed. **1836** TODD *Cycl. Anat. & Phys.* I. 281/2 In the Ostrich the last rib abuts against the ilium, to which it is anchylosed. **1875** BLAKE *Zool.* 2 Teeth.. not anchylosed with the substance of the jaw.

2. *intr.* Of a joint: To grow stiff. Of two bones: To grow together.

1833 *Penny Cycl.* I. 508/1 It is very important to keep the fingers bent, because, if they anchylose in that position, the hand will be more useful. **1872** MIVART *Anat.* 99 The two parietals anchylose at a very early period into a single median bone.

anchylosed, ank- ('æŋkɪləʊzd), *ppl. a.* [f. prec. + -ED.] Of two bones: Grown together, so firmly united as no longer to move upon each other. Hence of a joint: Stiffened.

1812 H. BROWNE *Apothec. Vade Mec.* 8 The restored action of an anchylosed joint. **1849** MURCHISON *Siluria* x. 241 The jaws and anchylosed teeth of some small fish. **1875** BLAKE *Zool.* 88 The anchylosed lumbar and sacral vertebræ.

b. *fig.* Cramped, rigid.

1860 W. WEBB in *Med. Times* 15 Sept. 266/1 Mind and body, too, grow so anchylosed, that they will work only in one direction.

‖**anchylosis, ank-** (æŋkɪ'ləʊsɪs). Also 8 ancylosis. [Gr. ἀγκύλωσις stiffening of the joints, f. ἀγκυλό-ειν to crook, f. ἀγκύλ-ος crooked. The reg. transliteration of the Gr. is *ancylosis*; to preserve the hard *c* this has been spelled with *ch*, for which some substitute *k.* Cf. Fr. *ankylose.*]

The formation of a stiff joint by consolidation of the articulating surfaces; the coalescence of two bones originally distinct.

1713 CHESELDEN *Anat.* I. i. (1726) 8 When these cartilages are destroyed.. [the bones] very readily unite; this distemper is called Ancylosis. **1765** STERNE *Tr. Shandy* (1802) VII. xxi. 42 The abbess.. being in danger of an anchylosis, or stiff joint. **1875** HOLMES *Surg.* 6 The utility of joints is destroyed by soft ankylosis. **1880** *Syd. Soc. Lex.*, *Ankylosis.* **1881** MIVART *Cat* 60 The number of bones.. decreases with age, by anchylosis.

b. *fig.*

1853 H. ROGERS *Ecl. Faith* 35 Impossible that any man could have made so many and such violent turns.. without incurring the danger of a 'universal anchylosis.'

anchylotic, ank- (æŋkɪ'lɒtɪk), *a.* [f. Gr. ἀγκυλωτ-ός vbl. adj. f. ἀγκυλό-ειν (see ANCHYLOSIS) + -IC.] Of or pertaining to anchylosis.

1859 in WORCESTER. **1880** *Syd. Soc. Lex.*, *Ankylotic.*

ancianitie, variant of ANCIENTY.

†'**anciency.** *Obs.* Forms: 6 **aunciencie**, 6–7 **anciencie**, 7 **anciancie**, 7–8 **anciency.** [corruption of earlier ANCIENTY, due to the erroneous assimilation of ANCIENT, orig. *a(u)ncien*, to ppl. adjs. in -ENT, whose abstracts are in -ENCY; cf. *decent*, *decency*.] The quality of being ancient; ancientness, oldness, antiquity.

1548 COVERDALE *Erasm. Paraphr. Jude* 21 It hathe ben taken worthye authoritie both for the auncienci e and use of it. **1587** HOLINSHED *Scot. Chron.* (1806) I. 36 Esteeming it a glorie to fetch their beginning of great anciencie. **1608** TOPSELL *Serpents* 639 In regard of their gravity, hoariness, and anciency. **1661** *Jura Cleri* 42 The Bishops follow him.. according to the Dignity and Anciancies of their Respective Sees. **1759** ROBERTSON *Hist. Scotl.* II. App. ix. 153 The anciency of his house.

‖**ancien régime** (ɑ̃sjɛ̃ reʒim). [Fr., lit. 'old rule'.] See RÉGIME 2 b.

1794 MORRIS in *Amer. State Papers* (1832) *For. Relat.* I. 404 If once that terror were, by superior force, to receive a counter direction, the *Ancien Régime* or any other régime, would, I think, be submitted to without the slightest struggle. **1839** F. A. KEMBLE *Jrnl. of Residence Georgia Plant.* (1863) 82 Two little filthy children, however, seemed to be still under the *ancien régime* of non-ablution. **1856** C. M. YONGE *Daisy Chain* II. xviii. 539 An old French Marquis .. a dear old man, quite of the *ancien régime*. **1864** MRS. GASKELL *French Life* i, in *Fraser's Mag.* Apr. 436/2 She received the homage of the ladies and gentlemen of the ancien régime. **1944** A. L. ROWSE *Eng. Spirit* ii. 25 The oldest and greatest monarchy in Europe, the French *ancien régime*. **1961** *Guardian* 7 Mar. 7/6 The *ancien* (pre-Nasser) *régime* Egyptian politicians.

ancient ('eɪnʃənt), *a.* and *sb.*[1] Forms: 4 **auncien, -ian,** 4–5 **-yen,** 5 **-yenne, -ienne, -iand, auntceaunt,** 5–6 **auncyent(e, awncient, -yent,** 5–7 **auncient,** (6 **aunchent**), 6– **antient, ancient.** [a. Fr. *ancien* (= Pr. *ancian*, Sp. *anciano*, It. *anziano*):—late L. *antiān-um* for **anteān-um* former, previous, f. *ante* before + *-ān-us*: see -AN. In 15th c. the genuine *auncien -an* was corrupted to *aunciand*, *auncient*, by form-assoc. with ppl. forms in *-nd*, *-nt*, which sometimes lost final *-t* or *-d*; in the reaction against this, the supposed correct ending was extended also to *auncien*, as to *peasan(t)*, *pheasan(t)*, *tyran(t)*, etc. The great phonetic advance from *auncient* ('aʊnsjɛnt) to *ainshent* ('eɪnʃənt) is seen also in *change*, *chamber*, *gauge*. The spelling *antient* was due to form-assoc. with words like *patient*, *mention*, previously *pacient*, *mencioun*, aided perhaps by reminiscences of *antiquus*.]

A. *adj.*

I. Referring to date.

1. a. Of or belonging to time past, former, earlier, bygone. *arch.*, exc. when approaching sense 2.

1490 CAXTON *Eneydos* xi. 43 The delycyouse traces of myn auncyent loue. **1593** SHAKS. *Rich. II*, II. i. 248 The Nobles hath he finde For ancient quarrels. **1678** BUNYAN *Pilgr.* I. (1862) 93 Thy ancient kindness. **1702** ROWE *Amb. Step-Moth.* I. i. 165 Tyes of ancient Love. **1792** T. JEFFERSON *Writ.* (1859) III. 347 Congress would take it off your hands, in compliance with an ancient vote of that body. **1793** *Ibid.* (1859) IV. 54 Profound arguments.. entitle him really to his ancient signature.

†**b.** Hence, with titles of office or position formerly occupied: sometime, whilom, *ex-*. Cf. Fr. *ancien gouverneur* = ex-governor; and *old* in *Old Etonian, old soldier*. *Obs.*

1681 G. VERNON *Life of Heylin* 8 An Ancient colonel and excellent commander in the army of King Charles. *Ibid.* 26 He had been himself an ancient clerk in the old Convocations. **1692** LUTTRELL *Brief Rel.* (1857) II. 344 An ancient alderman of London, who was mayor in 1655. **1718** POPE *Iliad* II. 863 They mourn'd their ancient leader lost.

2. *esp.* Which existed in, or belonged to, times *long* past, or early in the world's history; old.

1366 MAUNDEV. viii. 93 An Ymage of.. old auncyen Werk. **1477** EARL RIVERS *Dictes* 129 If thou can not atteyn to the wysedom of auncient men, at the lest studye ther bookis. **1551** ROBINSON *More's Utop.* 165 The olde and auncient cosmographers. **1562** G. LEIGH *Armorie* (1597) Pref. A ij, Out of the holie Scriptures, as of other most antientest Authors. **1594** HOOKER *Eccl. Pol.* IV. (1617) 132 The reuerend simplicitie of ancienter times. **1632** in *Shaks. Cent. Praise* 190 To raise our auncient Soveraynes from their herse. **1673** RAY *Journ. Low Countr.* 6 In the most antient times.. these places were Firm Land. **1777** DALRYMPLE *Trav. Sp. & Port.* xl, Many antient weapons of war. **1836** MACGILLIVRAY *Humboldt's Trav.* xx. 296 Traces of ancient civilisation. **1860** TYNDALL *Glac.* I. §23. 163, I.. traced the action of ancient glaciers. **1877** LYTTEIL *Landm.* I. v. 42 The grave of Ossian.. and those of other Ancient worthies.

3. a. Specifically applied to the period of history before the fall of the Western Roman Empire. In this sense contrasted with *modern*, and *mediæval*.

1605 BACON *Adv. Learn.* I. iv. §2 (1873) 28 The ancient authors.. began to be read. **1704** ADDISON *Italy* Pref., Statuary and Architecture both Ancient and Modern. **1754** EDWARDS *Freed. Will* IV. §6. 227 The antient Greek and Roman Philosophers. **1808** Z. PIKE *Exp. Sources Mississippi* III. App. 69 Perfect master of the antient languages. **1846** ELLIS *Elgin Marbles* I. 1 The remains of antient art at Athens. **1875** SCRIVENER *Text of N.T.* 3 The decline of ancient literature.

b. Concerning or relating to ancient times. ***ancient history***: see HISTORY *sb.* 3.

1595 ROBINSON (*title*) A Record of Auncient Histories, intituled in Latine, Gesta Romanorum. **1740** JOHNSON *L.P.*, *Barretier* Wks. 1787 IV. 463 Antient or modern geography. *c* **1850** (*title*) The Edinburgh Academy's Ancient Geography.

II. Of length of existence. (Distinguished by Bacon from I.)

4. a. Of early origin or formation, going far back in history, of ancient date.

1475 *Bk. Noblesse* 2 The noble auncient bloode of Troy. **1535** COVERDALE *Baruch* iv. 5 Thou people of God, o thou awncient Israel. **1561** DAUS tr. *Bullinger on Apocal.*, The auncientest and noblest title, which the fathers.. haue used. **1586** COGAN *Haven Health* ii. (1612) 20 The Harpe of all instruments is the most auncient. **1653** HOLCROFT *Procopius* IV. 124 To them ever the ancienter the things are, the truer they seem. **1667** E. CHAMBERLAYNE *St. Gt. Brit.* I. III. i. (1743) 152 The meeting of Sufferings is one of the ancientest assemblies they have. **1751** JOHNSON *Rambl.* No. 177 §10 The seal of an antient corporation. **1845** CARLYLE *Cromwell* (1871) II. 191 One of the ancientest seats belonging to the Lord of Ormond. **1855** H. REED *Lect. Eng. Hist.* ii. 71 Contending for no new-born freedom, but for ancient rights.

b. ***ancient lights***: see LIGHT *sb.* 13.

c. ***ancient monument***: a monument made or set up long ago; *spec.*, a monument or other edifice scheduled as being of historical, architectural, or archæological interest and protected by Act of Parliament from damage or destruction. Also *attrib.* and *transf.*

1593 (*title*) Discription.. of all the Ancient Monuments, Rites, and Customes.. within the Monastical Church of Durham (1842, Surtees Soc.). **1873** *House of Commons Papers, Reports from Committees* XI. 54 [= 950] A Memorial from the Committee for the Conservation of Ancient Monuments. **1877** *Encycl. Brit.* VII. 308/1 His [*sc.* Döbrentei's] great work is the *Ancient Monuments of the Magyar Language* (*Régi Magyar Nyelvemlékek*). **1880** C. P. KAINS-JACKSON *Our Ancient Monuments* 1 We give below a list of the ancient monuments of the United Kingdom as scheduled in the bill repeatedly introduced into the House of Commons by Sir John Lubbock, Bart, [etc.]. *Ibid.* 6 Then it [*sc.* Wayland Smith's Forge] became a relic simply, a 'monument' in the sense of the framers of the Ancient Monuments Bill. **1911** *Encycl. Brit.* XVIII. 797/1 There are four acts: the Ancient Monuments Protection Acts of 1882, 1900 and 1910, and the Ancient Monuments Protection (Ireland) Act 1892. **1958** *Listener* 23 Jan. 150/2 The Ancient Monuments Department of the Ministry of Works has set out to preserve what remains.

5. a. Hence: having existed long, and now, in consequence, possessing the attributes of lengthened existence; long-established; time-worn; hoary.

1586 LUPTON 1000 *Notable Things* (1675) 102 [It doth] help the ancient pain of the Head. **1605** BACON *Adv. Learn.* I. v. §1 These times are the ancient times, when the world is ancient, and not those which we account ancient.. by a computation backward from ourselves. **1607** SHAKS. *Cor.* IV. v. 102 Thy Ancient Malice. **1719** YOUNG *Busiris* I. i. (1757) 8 This antient city, Memphis the renown'd. **1744** HARRIS 3 *Treat.* III. II. (1765) 224 An ancient wood. **1769** ROBERTSON *Charles V*, III. VII. 29 To strengthen its antient attachment to France. **1849** MACAULAY *Hist. Eng.* I. 378 Before the ancient front of All Souls College.

b. Of old renown, long known to fame.

1819 HEBER *Hymn, From Greenland's..* From many an ancient river, From many a palmy plain.

6. Of living beings: that has lived many years; aged, old; of great age. *arch.*

c **1340** *Gaw. & Gr. Knt.* 1001 Þe olde auncian wyf heȝest ho syttes. **1475** CAXTON *Jason* 46 Mirmidone yet liueth.. but he is moche auncient. **1592** SHAKS. *R. & J.* II. iv. 150 Farewell, auncient Lady. **1598** STOW *Surv.* xli. 431 Neyther the yong men of the City.. nor the auncient persons. **1621** BURTON *Anat. Mel.* I. ii. IV. vii. (1651) 168 A young Gentlewoman.. was married.. to an ancient man against her will. **1682** *Lond. Gaz.* mdccl/4 An antient Man in the Habit of a Seaman. **1704** LUTTRELL *Brief Rel.* (1857) V. 426 Sir Samuel Astry (being very antient) has resigned his place of clerk. *a* **1718** PENN *Life* Wks. 1726 I. 90 This A.M.C. aforesaid, is an Ancient Maid. **1795** SEWEL tr. *Hist. Quakers* I. Pref. 10 Things, which some ancient people had yet remembrance of. **1849** MACAULAY *Hist. Eng.* I. 663 An ancient matron of the Anabaptist persuasion.

7. Having the experience and wisdom of age, venerable. *arch.*

c **1460** *Bk. Curtasye* in *Babees Bk.* 323 An naunciande squier, or ellis a knyȝt, þo towelle down tase by fulle good ryȝt. **1564** BECON *Princ. Chr. Relig.* (1844) 521 The duty of old women is.. to be sober, sage, and ancient. **1596** SHAKS. *Tam. Shrew* V. i. 75 You seeme a sober, ancient Gentleman by your habit. **1685** BAXTER *Paraphr. 1 Tim.* v. 19 An accusation against a grave ancient Person. **1752** JOHNSON *Rambl.* No. 190 ⁋6 The precepts of ancient experience. **1875** STUBBS *Const. Hist.* III. xviii. 238 Henry wished to be .. counselled by the wise and ancient of the kingdom.

8. Savouring of age, old-fashioned, antique. *rare.*

1598 B. JONSON *Ev. Man in Hum.* IV. iii, I am glad no one was hurt by his ancient humour. **1820** KEATS *St. Agnes* xxxiii, He play'd an ancient ditty, long since mute.

9. That has been many years in some rank, position, or capacity. (Now commonly replaced by *old.*)

1413 LYDG. *Pylgr. Sowle* IV. xxxiii. (1483) 81 Auncyen trauayled men that ben experte in dedes of armes. **1598** BARRET *The. Warres* V. iii. 180 Respect to be had to graue and ancient souldiers. **1628** DIGBY *Voy. Medit.* 48 Seuerall of our ancientest seamen.. were sea sicke. **1663** KILLIGREW *Parson's Wedd.* in Dodsl. (1780) XI. 377 A soldier ancienter than thyself. **1715** BURNET *Own Time* (1766) I. 247 The ancientest and most eminent of the former Bishops. **1807** T. JEFFERSON *Writ.* IV. 68 My Dear and Antient Friend.

10. *Comb.*, as ***ancient-customed, ancient-looking.***

1681 *Lond. Gaz.* mdcxv/4 The antient Customed Inn, known by the name of the White Hart and Antelope. **1848** DICKENS *Dombey* (C.D. ed.) 24 He presently returned with a very ancient-looking bottle.

III. *Law.* (See quot.)

1607 COWEL *Interpr.* (J.) Ancient tenure is that whereby all the manours belonging to the crown in St. Edward's or William the Conqueror's days, did hold. **1768** BLACKSTONE *Comm.* II. 99 Antient demesne consists of those lands or manors, which, though now perhaps granted out to private subjects, were actually in the hands of the crown in the time of Edward the confessor, or William the conqueror.

B. *sb.*[1]

1. a. One who lived in ancient times. Commonly in pl. ***the Ancients***: *esp.* the ancient Greeks, Romans, and other civilized nations of antiquity. (Orig. adj. '*the ancient*,' like '*the learned.*')

1541 COPLAND *Galyen's Terap.* 2 F ij b, All the auncyentes apply the sayd suppuratyfe medycynes. **1597** HOOKER *Eccl. Pol.* V. lxi. §1 The ancient it may be were too severe. **1611** BIBLE *Transl. Pref.* 2 Neither is there any likelihood that enuie and malignity died and were buried with the ancient. **1665** MANLEY *Grotius's L.-Countr. Wars* 287 The famoust Engine of War now used, of whose use, the Antients were utterly ignorant. **1751** WATTS *Improv. Mind* ii. (1801) 21 The doctrines of the antients. **1880** HAUGHTON *Phys. Geog.*

v. 211 To the Ancients the Nile appeared almost miraculous.

b. *esp.* The ancient authors of Greece and Rome; the ancient classics. *Hence*, an ancient classic.

1615 G. SANDYS *Trav.* 210 In fame it [Sidon] contendeth with Tyrus..and is more celebrated by the Ancient. *a* **1633** HALES in *Shaks. Cent. Praise* 198 If Mr. Shakespear had not read the Antients. **1749** FIELDING *Tom Jones* III. iii. (1840) 26 He was deeply read in the ancients. **1763** J. BROWN *Poetry & Mus.* §6. 135 The same respectable Ancient [Plutarch] assures us, that, etc. **1777** SIR W. JONES *Poems, etc.* Pref. 14 We always return to the writings of the ancients. **1870** LOWELL *Study Wind.* 222 The only method by which a poet may..reckon on ever becoming an ancient himself.

2. ***the Ancient of Days.*** **a.** a scriptural title of the Almighty.

1560 BIBLE (Genev.) *Dan.* vii. 9, I beheld till the thrones were set vp, and the Ancient of dayes did sit. [So 1611; WYCLIF elde, COVERDALE olde aged.] **1833** ROBERT GRANT in *Bickersteth's Christian Psalmody* 17 Our Shield and Defender—the Ancient of Days Pavilioned in splendour, and girded with praise.

b. *transf.* A very old person or thing. *jocular.*

1935 T. E. LAWRENCE *Let.* 5 Apr. (1938) 867 I've only ridden the ancient-of-days twice this year. **1937** KIPLING *Something of Myself* i. 10, I was shown an Ancient of Days who, I was told, was the Provost of Oriel.

3. An old or aged man (or animal); a patriarch.

1502 *Ord. Crysten Men* (W. de Worde) II. viii. (1506) 107 Those the whyche mocketh with these auncyentes. **1603** *Philotus* clxviii, Let countenance accord with ȝour gray hairis ȝe auncients all. **1661** LOVELL *Hist. Anim. & Min.* 15 [Beavers] gnaw down trees to build with, and draw them on the bellies of their antients. **1753** RICHARDSON *Grandison* (1781) VI. ix. 32 Incomparable woman! If I were such an excellent ancient, I would no more wish to be young. **1790** COWPER *Odyss.* IV. 517 Then, hero, loose the ancient of the deep [Proteus]. **1814** SOUTHEY *Roderick* iii. Wks. IX. 28 A venerable ancient, by his side A comely matron. **1837** DICKENS *Pickw.* (1847) 160/2 'My father, sir,' replied Mr. Weller. 'How are you, my ancient?'

†**4.** An ancestor. *Obs. rare.*

1540 HYRDE *Vives' Instr. Chr. Woman* (1592) D vij, The auncient of his stocke is before the making of the Worlde. **1603** H. CROSSE *Vertues Commw.* (1878) 21 Can a man.. brag of the Vertues of his auncients, if his owne life be vitious? **1649** *Motion to Parl.* 6 Our Ancients were Gyants, and we are Dwarfs.

†**5.** A senior, a superior in age; usually with possessive, ***his ancient.*** Cf. Fr. *son ancien. Obs.*

1548 UDALL, etc. *Erasm. Paraphr. Mark* ix. 34 They sawe howe Peter had the preeminence..yet sum of theim were his auncients. **1553-87** FOXE *A. & M.* (1596) 767/1 Gower was a great deale his [Chaucer's] ancient. **1628** MEDE in Ellis *Orig. Lett.* I. III. 279 Justice Jones being the ancient on the bench. **1640** FULLER *Abel Rediv., Reinolds* (1867) II. 220 Reinolds was..bred up in the same college..with Jewel his ancient and R. Hooker his contemporary. **1659** LESTRANGE *Alliance Div. Off.* 105 To these evidences out of Jerome and Chrysostom, let me add that of Gregory Nazianzen antient to them both.

6. As a title of dignity: An 'Elder.' *arch.*

1534 MORE *On the Passion* Wks. 1557. 1299/1 Than gathered there together the prynces of the priestes and the auncientes, into the Palyce of..Caiphas. **1587** FLEMING *Contn. Holinshed* III. 342/1 The wardens, the ancients of the handicrafts. **1611** BIBLE *Jer.* xix. 1 Take of the ancients of the people, and of the ancients of the Priestes. **1654** USSHER *Annals* vi. (1658) 378 Conferring with some of the Ancients of the Town. **1708** *New View Lond.* II. 480/2 The Vestry.. is..composed of the Ancients of the Parish, who have passed Churchwarden. **1769** HOME *Fatal Discov.* IV, I go to meet the ancients of the land, The hoary counsellors.

7. *Law.* One of the senior members forming the governing body of the Inns of Court and of Chancery. (More or less *Obs.* in use.)

1563 *Act 5 Eliz.* i, As well Utter barresters, as Benchers, Readers, Auncients in any house or houses of Court. **1570** ASCHAM *Scholem.* 62 When he was Auncient in Inne of Courte, certaine yong Ientlemen were brought before him, to be corrected for certaine misorders. **1685** *Lond. Gaz.* mmx/6 From the Principal, Antients, and the rest of the Gentlemen of the Society of Bernards-Inn, London. **1691** BLOUNT *Law Dict., Ancient*, In Grey's-Inn the Society consists of Benchers, Ancients, Barrasters, and Students under the Bar. **1751** CHAMBERS *Cycl.* s.v, Here [Gray's-inn] the ancients are the elder barristers. **1860** FORSTER *Grand Remonstr.* 120 On going into commons at the Temple, he found himself, lad as he was, 'ancient' to above two hundred elder Templars.

ancient ('eɪnʃənt), *sb.*^{2} *arch.* Forms: 6 **ancyent, ansyant, ancientt, auncient(e, -chient,** 6–7 **antesign,** 6–8 **antient,** 7 **auncyent,** 8 **anshent,** 6– **ancient.** [a corruption of ENSIGN *sb.*, early forms of which, like *ensyne, enseygne*, were confounded with *ancien, ancyen*, the contemporary forms of *ancient*, with which they thus became formally identified from 16th to 18th c. Also spelt by pseudo-etymology *antesign.*]

1. An ensign, standard, or flag: *pl.* insignia, colours.

1554 *Chron. Grey Friars* 87, I know that theys be Wyettes ancienttes. **1569** *Rising in North* 105 in Percy *Rel.* I. 293 Erle Percy there his ancyent spred. **1578** T. N., tr. *Conq. W. India* 23 The devise of this ensigne or auncient was flames of fire. **1587** GOLDING *De Mornay* xxii. 331 When Osyris led his people to Battell, he had diuers Antesignes..as in one a Dog, in another an Ox. **1610** *Chesters Triumph* Particulars 1, A Man..carying an Auncient of our colours of S. George. **1622** F. MARKHAM *Dec. Warre* II. ix. 73 This Ensigne we corruptly call Antient, and I haue seene it written Antesigne. **1629** *S'hertogenbosh* 48 To let flye all their Ancients as well vpon the gates, as the walles. **1725** DE FOE *Voyage round World* (1840) 34 Hang out a signal, viz., a red ancient, on the mizen-top. **1727-51** CHAMBERS *Cycl.*, *Ancient* in the naval armament is the flag or streamer, borne in the stern of a ship. **1834** H. MILLER *Scenes & Leg.* xv. (1857) 223 Her ancient suspended half-way over the deck.

2. A standard-bearer, an 'ensign.' (The full name was ***ancient-bearer***: see below.)

1596 SHAKS. *2 Hen. IV*, II. iv. 120 Welcome, ancient Pistoll! —— *Hen. V*, III. vi. 20 (*Flu.*) Hee is call'd aunchient Pistoll. **1598** STOW *Surv.* (ed. Strype 1754) II. v. xxxi. 572/2 Their first elected Auntient or Ensign bearer. **1642** FULLER *Holy & Prof. St.* III. xv. 191 To see the flesh of our Ancient as torn as his colours. [**1830** JAMES *Darnley* xxxviii. 170 The banner of their company by their own ancient.]

3. *Comb.* †**ancient-bearer** = prec. sense.

1579 *Churchw. Acc. St. Marg. Westm.* (1797) 19 Paid to the soiers, the ansyant-bearer, and to him that played upon the drome £1 7s. 4d. **1591** PERCIVALL *Sp. Dict.*, *Alférez*, an ancient-bearer, *Signifer.* **1606** *Act 3 Jas. I*, v, No Recusant conuict..shall beare any Office or Charge, as Captaine, Lieutenant, Corporall, Sergeant, Ancient-bearer.

†'**ancienter.** *Obs. rare*$^{-1}$. [app. a confusion between *ancient*, and *anceter*, 16th c. form of ANCESTOR *sb.*] Ancestor, elder.

1654 GAYTON *Fest. Notes* III. vii. 115 What if my Ancienters were John of Cumber, If I no worth have.

anciently ('eɪnʃəntlɪ), *adv.* [f. ANCIENT *a.* + -LY^2.]

1. In ancient times, of old time, of yore.

1502 *Ord. Cryst. Men* (W. de Worde) I. iv. (1506) 43 Auncyently foure maner of people all onely be anoynted with the holy unccyon **1576** LAMBARDE *Peramb. Kent* (1826) 153 At Folkstone should auncientlly stande one of those Turrets which the Romanes planted. **1635** HEYWOOD *Harb. Health* 293 Mars..was antiently figured an angry man sitting in a Chariot. **1660** R. COKE *Power & Subj.* 36 The state of man most anciently was never anarchy, but monarchy. **1728** NEWTON *Chronol. Amended* i. 45 The Philosophers anciently delivered their Opinions in Verse. **1833** I. TAYLOR *Fanat.* ix. 394 The anciently recorded dishonours of the nation.

†**2.** With less idea of remoteness: Formerly. *Obs.*

1624 BEDELL *Lett.* iii. 58 This is not onely denied by Protestants, but..anciently..by the Spanish. **1734** tr. *Rollin's Anc. Hist.* (1827) VIII. XIX. §7. 206 Such as were anciently tributaries to me. **1737** *Col. Rec. Penn.* IV. 214 Those who had anciently settled by mistake in the limits of either Province. **1774** BURKE *Amer. Tax.* Wks II. 432 Leave the Americans as they anciently stood.

†**3.** From ancient times, of long standing. *Obs.*

1628 COKE *On Litt.* (1633) Pref., A Gentleman anciently descended. **1667** MILTON *P.L.* v. 723 We mean to hold what anciently we claim Of Deitie or Empire. **1686** RAVENSCROFT in *Sh. Cent. Pr.* 404 Some anciently conversant with the Stage.

†**4.** After the manner of an ancient or elder, old-fashionedly. *Obs. rare.*

1588 GREENE *Pandosto* (1607) 33 Taking a great hooke in his hand..he went verie anciently to find out the mistresse of his affection.

5. In an ancient manner, like something old. *rare.*

1870 HAWTHORNE *Eng. Note-Bk.* (1879) I. 49 They smelt anciently and disagreeably.

ancientness ('eɪnʃəntnɪs). Also 6 **auncientnesse,** 6–7 **antientness.** [f. as prec. + -NESS.]

1. The quality of being ancient or old; antiquity (by which word it is now almost superseded).

1537 ? TINDALE *Expos. St. John* 92 He alleged..ye author therof, and hys auncientnesse. **1538** LELAND *Itin.* IV. 106, I asked a merchant there of the Antientnesse of the Towne. **1610** HOLLAND *Camden's Brit.* II. 64 In comparison of them, the Antientnesses of all other nations is but novelty. **1621** AINSWORTH *Annot. Pentat.* Gen. x. 15 Sidon..a city renowned..for ancientnes and fame. **1813** SHELLEY *Q. Mab* vii, Chronicles of untold ancientness. **1882** FARRAR *Early Chr.* I. 204 Another important consideration is the ancientness of this Epistle.

†**2.** Ancient estate or condition. *Obs. rare.*

1602 FULBECKE *1st Pt. Parall.* 22 Certain honours..which be not of the ancientnes of the crowne. **1657** SCOTT in Burton *Diary* (1828) II. 383 If you resort to the ancientness of Parliaments, you will find it as that gentleman said.

†**3.** Seniority, priority. *Obs.*

1598 FLORIO, *Priorita*, prioritie, eldership, ancientnes, senioritie. **1619** *Treas. Anc. & Mod. Times* II. 513/2 The rest take their places according to the ancientnesse of their elections. **1628** COKE *On Litt.* 94 a, Next to him the Bishop of Winchester, and then all other Bishops of both Prouinces after their ancientnesse.

ancientry ('eɪnʃəntrɪ). *arch.* Also 6 **aunchent-,** 7–8 **antient-.** [f. ANCIENT + -RY. Cf. *pageantry.*]

1. The quality or estate of being ancient or very old; ancientness, antiquity; old-fashioned style; seniority, priority.

1580 NORTH *Plutarch* (1676) 92 The Nobility and ancientry of their Houses. **1599** SHAKS. *Much Ado* II. i. 80 The wedding manerly modest, as a measure full of state and aunchentry. **1661** S. MORGAN *Sph. Gentry* IV. iii. 52 A Baron must go after the ancientry of his Creation. **1742** WEST *Let.* in *Gray's Poems* (1775) 144 They contain not one word of antientry. **1789** H. WALPOLE in *Miss Berry's Corr.* I. 175, I allow my ancientry and that I am an old fond, jealous and peevish husband. **1866** J. INGELOW *Poems* 26 It could not fail to find Much proof of ancientry. **1877** DIXON *Diana* I. IV. i. 257 An air of stateliness, reserve, and ancientry. **1913** KIPLING *Songs from Books* 21 Witness hereby the ancientry Of Oak and Ash and Thorn! *a* **1954** F. BRETT YOUNG *Wistanslow* (1956) i. 7 Not merely venerable to me in its ancientry but also impressive as a work of art.

†**2.** Ancient lineage or descent; ancestry, origin.

1596 SPENSER *State Irel.* 32 The Irish thinke to enoble themselves by wresting their Auncientry from the Spaniard.

†**3.** *collect.* Ancients, elder people, elders. *Obs. rare.*

1548 UDALL, etc. *Erasm. Paraphr. Rev.* xvii. 4 The florishing and bewtiful rayment wherwith they and theyr auncientries haue garnished and annowrned this whore. **1589** R. HARVEY *Plaine Perc.* 7 To be infourmed..by the Auncientry of the Parish. **1611** SHAKS. *Wint. T.* III. iii. 63 Wronging the Auncientry, stealing, fighting.

4. The ancient or olden time; antiquity.

1755 CROKER *Ariosto's Orl. Fur.* XIV. lxxxi, Once they were there; but 'twas in antientry. **1839** *Blackw. Mag.* XLV. 271, I love those tales of ancientry. **1855** BAILEY *Mystic* 63 Ere all, in ancientry æterne, was God.

5. *pl.* or *collect.* Ancient things or relics, antiquities. *rare.*

1866 E. WAUGH *Eawr Folk* in *Lanc. Lyrics* 201 There connot be Another pate like his, It's o crom-full o' ancientry, An' Roman haw-pennies! **1904** H. JAMES *Golden Bowl* I. I. vi. 111 Small florid ancientries, ornaments, pendants, lockets.

†'**ancienty.** *Obs.* Forms: 4 **anciente,** 5 **-yaunte, aunciente,** 5–6 **-yente, -ientee, -ientye, -yauntye, ancianitie,** 6–7 **aunc-, ant-, ancientie,** 6–8 **ancienty.** [a. AFr. *ancienté* for OFr. *ancienneté*, f. *ancien* ANCIENT, cogn. w. Pr. *ancianetat*, It. *anzianità*, Sp. *ancianidad.* (Of Romanic formation: if the word had been L., the OFr. would have been *ancienté*: see -ITY.) The erroneous association of *ancien(t)* with ppl. forms in *-ent*, finally caused *ancienty* to be corrupted to ANCIENCY. Only in Scotch did the regular *ancianitie* (cf. *christianity*, etc.) appear in 16th c.] *gen.* The quality of being ancient, ancientness, antiquity.

1. Remoteness in past time; distance back from the present.

1485 CAXTON *Chas. Gt.* 25 the Romans whyche of grete ancyaunte were of grete apporte. **1563** PILKINGTON *Burning of Pauls* (1841) 586 We know what ancienty and authority they be of. **1579** W. FULKE *Heskins's Parl.* 281 No one writer of like auncientie sayth it is not the verie bodie.

2. The time long past; the ancient or olden time; antiquity.

1489 CAXTON *Faytes of Armes* III. v. 175 That the lande were bounde so to doo of auncyente. *c* **1525** SKELTON *Ph. Sparowe* 767 These poetes of auncyente. **1602** CAREW *Cornwall* 236 Their Wooll..hath (from all auncientie) beene transported, without paying Custome.

3. *concr.* The people of old times; the ancients.

1556 VERON *Godly Saiyngs* (1846) 15 We do synne no lesse ..than the auncyauntye dyd synne in the Arke of the Lordes covenante.

4. The quality of having existed since a remote period, or of extending back from the present to a time long past; old standing.

1524 *Suppl. for Beggers* (1845) 12 For the..auncientie of your kyngdome whiche was bifore theyrs. *a* **1572** KNOX *Hist. Ref.* Wks. 1846 I. 281 The ancianitie of the blood of my Hous. **1592** GREENE *Quip for Upst. Courtier* in *Harl. Misc.* (Malh.) II. 228 To preach, and shew the antiquitie and antientie of his house. **1623** SANDERSON *Serm.* Ad. Mag. ii. 106 We may not deny them the ancienty of their descent; ..*semen serpentis*, the spawn of the old Serpent.

5. The quality of being aged; agedness, oldness.

1375 BARBOUR *Bruce* VI. 252 A gret stane..That throw the gret anciente Was lowsyt, reddy for to fall. **1483** CAXTON *Gold. Leg.* 426/1 He, fylled with benewred auncyente of dayes..rendred hys sowle. **1569** T. NEWTON *Cicero De Senect.* 17 a, My gray heares, and my auncientie of yeres.

6. Seniority; priority of birth or appointment.

1549 W. THOMAS *Hist. Italy* 39 The Cardinalls bestowed themselfes after their auncientee in certaine stalles. *a* **1604** HANMER *Chron. Irel.* 194 For the eldest can demand..the chiefe mease by reason of her auncienty. **1775** ASH, *Ancienty* (a law term), Seniority, priority of birth.

‖**ancile** (æn'saɪliː). [L. *ancile* (of doubtful etymol.), pl. *ancilia*, a small oval shield, and *spec.*] The sacred shield of the ancient Romans, said to have fallen from heaven; on the preservation of which the prosperity of the city was supposed to depend.

1600 HOLLAND *Livy.* I. xx. 15/1 Certaine scutcheons or bucklers that fell from heaven, called Ancilia. **1674** BREVINT *Saul at Endor* 385 (T.) The Trojans secured their palladium: the Romans their ancile. **1855** SINGLETON *Virgil* II. 171 And in his left hand the ancile bare.

‖**ancilla** (æn'sɪlə). [L. *ancilla* handmaid, dim. of *ancula*, dim. fem. of early L. *ancus, anca*, servant; cf. also ANCILLE.] A maidservant, handmaid.

1871 M. COLLINS *Inn of Strange Meetings* 27 The pert ancilla flutters foolish feet.

ancillary ('ænsɪlərɪ, æn'sɪlərɪ), *a.* and *sb.* [ad. L. *ancillāri-us* (more correctly *ancillār-is*) of or pertaining to a handmaid, f. *ancilla*: see prec.]

A. *adj.* **1.** Subservient, subordinate, ministering (*to*).

1667 WATERHOUSE *Fire of Lond.* 60 God makes every thing ancillary hereunto. **1768** BLACKSTONE *Comm.* III. vii. (R.) It is beneath the dignity of the king's courts to be merely ancillary to other inferior jurisdictions. **1836** H. TAYLOR

Statesm. viii. 49 It will be rather ancillary than essential. **1848** ARNOULD *Mar. Insur.* II. II. v. 652 Warlike stores.. directly ancillary to warlike purposes. **1869** RAWLINSON *Anc. Hist.* 8 Geography, the other ancillary science to History.

2. *lit.* (after L.) Of or pertaining to maid-servants. *rare* and *affected.*

1852 THACKERAY *Esmond* III. ix. (1876) 404 The ancillary beauty was the one whom the Prince had selected. **1854** BADHAM *Halieut.* 399 Ancillary reformation has not yet begun to be thought of; cats are not more detrimental to mice.. than these smashing wenches to.. Sèvres teacups.

3. Designating activities and services that provide essential support to the functioning of a central service or industry; also, of staff employed in these supporting roles. Now used esp. of non-medical staff and services in hospitals.

1948 B. NEWMAN *Baltic Background* vi. 139 Sixty-five per cent of the Estonians are directly engaged in agriculture, and many more in its ancillary occupations. **1955** *Times* 10 May 9/2 There were inadequate ancillary services such as laundries, kitchens, bathrooms, and lavatory accommodation. **1957** *Encycl. Brit.* XVIII. 948/1 The Transport act.. nationalized the railways, together with their ancillary services—docks, steamers, road vehicles, hotels and canals. **1962** *Lancet* 26 May 1114/1 *Ancillary workers.*—An ample complement of ancillaries is essential. We would suggest one psychiatric social worker for each consultant team. **1976** *Daily Tel.* 20 July 2/4 Ancillary and other staff from five trade unions are to stage a 24-hour strike from midnight tonight. **1982** *Financial Times* 7 July 12/6 The Government was not prepared to improve on its latest offer of 7.5 per cent for nurses and 6 per cent for ancillary staff and other grades.

B. *sb.* **1.** †**a.** One who acts as an assistant or servant. *Obs.*⁻¹

1867 G. MEREDITH in *Fortn. Rev.* 1 Sept. 294 They were yoked before the glad youth by his sister-ancillaries.

b. An ancillary worker. See sense 3 of the adj.

1962 [see sense A. 3 above]. **1982** *Financial Times* 17 Aug. 12/1 Bank staff can hardly expect.. the kind of public support enjoyed by the low-paid hospital ancillaries. **1985** *Ibid.* 15 Nov. 24/8 Local authority manual workers have settled..; health service ancillaries are expected to secure a similar deal.

2. Something which is ancillary; an auxiliary or accessory.

1929 *Morning Post* 2 Oct. 10/4 Aircraft must be regarded only as a very useful and necessary ancillary to the main fleet. **1942** W. S. CHURCHILL *Secret Session Speeches* (1946) 63 He had expected to meet the three Kongos and perhaps two aircraft carriers together with ancillaries. **1972** *Proc. Inst. Electr. Engineers* CXIX 189 A design of great simplicity has been developed in which the vacuum-interrupter circuit-breakers and all ancillaries are housed in one modular enclosure. **1980** *Daily Tel.* 23 Apr. 3 (Advt.), Cave Tab are *the* specialists in ancillaries, equipment and supplies for all DP and WP operations. **1986** *New Yorker* 27 Jan. 47/1, I thought I might as well do some air tests. That involves two stages: first the airframe and its ancillaries, then the engine.

†**'ancillate,** *v. Obs. rare*⁻¹. [f. L. *ancillāt-* ppl. stem of *ancillā-ri* to be a handmaid, or slave.] To be subservient.

1659 SIR S. D'EWES in Rushw. *Hist. Coll.* III. I. 314 So forward with his Arms to ancillate to the Emperor's Designs.

†**ancille.** *Obs.* Also 4 an'celle, 4–6 'ancelle, 5 ancylle. [a. OFr. *ancelle, ancele*:—L. ANCILLA.] A maid-servant or handmaid.

c **1365** CHAUCER *A.B.C.* O, Ffrom his ancille [*v.r.* ancelle, ancile] he made þe maistresse Of heuene & eerþe. *c* **1430** LYDG. *Min. Poems* 37 Do trewe service, as ancille.. Unto hir lord. **1474** CAXTON *Chesse* 148 In the olde lawe the faders had dyuerse wyues and ancellis. **1483** —— *Gold. Leg.* 151/1 She callid herself ancylle or handmayde and not lady. *c* **1500** *Partenay* 6456 Glorius virgin, Mayden, moder off god, Doughter and Ancelle.

ancipital (æn'sɪpɪtəl), *a. rare.* [f. L. *ancipit-* (*anceps*) two-headed (f. *an* (= *ambi*) both + *capit-* head) + -AL¹.] Having two sharp edges.

1794 MARTYN tr. *Rousseau's Bot.* xxv. 372 It has an ancipital, or two edged stem. **1864** WEBSTER cites GRAY.

ancipitate (æn'sɪpɪteɪt), *a.* [f. as prec. + -ATE², after Fr. *ancipité*; cf. L. *capitāt-us.*] = prec.

1879 in *Syd. Soc. Lex.*

ancipitous (æn'sɪpɪtəs), *a.* [f. as prec. + -OUS.] †**1.** Uncertain, doubtful. *Obs.*

1652 GAULE *Magastrom.* 86 Planets amicall, benevolous.. as also ancipitous, and indifferent to both. **1657** TOMLINSON *Renou's Disp.* 263 Which is the true turbith is yet ancipitous.

2. *Bot.* = ANCIPITAL.

a **1859** WORCESTER cites BRANDE. **1866** *Treas. Bot.* 62/1 *Ancipitous*, two-edged, as the stem of an *Iris.* **1882** BAKER in *Jrnl. Bot.* No. 231. 70 A large tree with branchlets ancipitous and obscurely pilose towards the tip.

ancistroid (æn'sɪstrɔɪd), *a.* [ad. Gr. ἀγκιστροειδής hook-shaped, f. ἄγκιστρον hook: see -OID.] Hook-shaped.

1879 in *Syd. Soc. Lex.*

ancle, variant spelling of ANKLE *sb.*

anclose, obs. form of ENCLOSE.

ancloy, earlier form of ACCLOY *v.*

†**'ancoly.** *Herb. Obs.* [a. Fr. *ancolie*, for *accolie*, corrrupt f. med.L. *aquilēja, aquilegia.*] Columbine.

1561 HOLLYBUSH *Hom. Apoth.* 26b, Take the sede of Ancolie or Accolie beaten to pouder. **1578** LYTE *Dodoens* 166 It is called in English Columbine.. in French *Ancoly*, in high Douch *Agley*, and *Ageley*: in base Almaigne *Akeley.*

†**'ancome.** *Obs.* or *dial.* Forms: 6–7 **uncome,** 6–8 **ancome,** 7 **ancombe,** 8 **andicomb.** [Of somewhat doubtful formation; expl. by Elyot, Baret, etc. as '*adventitius* morbus'; thus evidently viewed by them as a derivative of COME (cf. *income* revenue). Hence prob. a variant of northern Eng. *on-come* (14th c.) 'visitation, access of disease,' perh. a partially translated adaptation of Norse *ákoma*, 'arrival, visitation, eruption on the skin.' *On-come* would also easily yield the 16th c. variant *uncome*; the mod.Sc. and north Eng. *in-come*, used in a similar sense, shows a further refashioning of the prefix; cf. *amid, among*, with their variants *on mid, in mid, o mong, on mong, in mong.* The later spellings *ancombe, andicomb*, show that the word was no longer understood.] 'An ulcerous swelling rising unexpectedly' (Wright); a boil; an imposthume; by some later authors applied to a whitlow.

[*a* **1300** *Cursor Mundi* 5910 (Cott. MS.) Hard on-come sal i send him [Pharaoh] sere, Bath on him and his kingrike.] **1538** ELYOT (in *Prom. Parv.* 154 note), *Adventitius morbus* sycknes that cometh without our defaute, and of some men is called an uncome. **1544** *Act 34–5 Hen. VIII*, viii, Vncomes of hands, scaldings, burnings. **1580** BARET *Alv.* F 382 A fellon, vncomme, or cattes haire; a bile or sore that riseth in mans bodie, *furunculus. Ibid.* A 380 An Ancome, *Aduentitius morbus.* **1605** MARSTON etc., *Eastw. Hoe* III. ii, I have seene a little prick, no bigger than a pins head, swel bigger and bigger till it has come to an ancome. **1660** HEXHAM *Dutch Dict.*, *Vijt*, an Ancombe, or a Sore upon ones finger. **1678** A. LITTLETON *Lat. Dict.*, *Clavus*.. a whitlow or andicomb. **1736** BAILEY *Househ. Dict.* 102 Betony.. will bring ancomes and impostumes to a suppuration.

†**'ancoming,** *vbl. sb. Obs. rare*⁻¹. [f. AN- *pref.* 1 (?) + COMING. (The use of this prefix as a formative, at so late a date, must have been due to some special cause. Did the writer think of Ger. *ankommen*?)] An approach, avenue, entrance.

1589 IVE *Fortif.* 8 The bulwarks.. should be placed.. where they may.. commaund ouer the ancomings to the Fort.

‖**ancon** ('æŋkən). *Pl.* **an'cones.** [L., a. Gr. ἀγκών a nook or bend, *spec.* the elbow.]

1. *Phys.* The elbow. (See quot.)

1706 PHILLIPS, *Ancon*.. the Elbow.. sometimes taken by Anatomists for the backward and larger shooting forth of the Bone of the Arm called Vlna. **1853** MAYNE *Exp. Lex.*, *Ancon*, term for the elbow; or the triangular surface of the olecranon process of the ulna.

2. *Arch.* **a.** The corner or quoin of a wall, cross-beam, or rafter. **b.** One of 'the trusses or consoles sometimes employed in the dressings or antepagmenta of apertures, serving as an apparent support to the cornice of them at the flanks.' Gwilt.

1706 PHILLIPS, s.v., In Architecture Ancones are the corners or coins of Walls.. Cross-beams or Rafters. **1753** CHAMBERS *Cycl. Supp.*, *Ancon*.. in the antient architecture, the brackets, or shouldering pieces, called consoles by the moderns. **1823** NICHOLSON *Pract. Builder* 583 Consoles are called, according to their form, ancones or trusses, mutules, and modillions.

3. ancon sheep: A race with long bodies, and very short legs, the fore-legs crooked; bred from a single lamb born with these peculiarities in 1791.

1819 LAURENCE *Phys.* (1848) 312 Where common ewes have had twins by ancon rams. **1852** T. ROSS tr. *Humboldt's Trav.* I. ix. 342 The sheep with very short legs, called ancon sheep in Connecticut.

Ancona¹ (æn'kəʊnə). [Name of a town in Italy.] A breed of domestic fowl characterized by black and white mottled plumage and leaden-grey shanks.

1853 WINGFIELD & JOHNSON *Poultry Bk.* 110 The *Ancona* is a first cousin to the Minorca, its sole point of difference being a mottled or splashed plumage, black and white, in about equal proportions. **1873** L. WRIGHT *Bk. Poultry* 357 We entertain scarcely any doubt that the origin of Anconas is to be found in accidental 'sports' of this colour from crossing Black and White Minorcas. **1960** *Farmer & Stockbreeder* 8 Mar. 135/1 One of my Ancona bantams lays eggs with blood spots.

‖**ancona**² (æn'kəʊnə). Pl. **ancone.** [It., = med.L. (Stat. Guild of Painters at Venice, A.D. 1271): etym. uncertain; perh. an alteration of Gr. εἰκόνα, acc. of εἰκών image, ICON.] An altar-piece, esp. one consisting of a group of pictures or painted panels connected by architectural structure.

1874 R. H. BUSK *Tirol* 146 A priceless work of Alb. Durer, an '*Ancona*', showing forth in its various compartments the history of the Passion. **1885** *Athenæum* 19 Sept. 377/2 The Van Eycks' 'Adoration of the Lamb'.. [is] a true representative of the Italian *ancona* or group of pictures included in a single altarpiece. **1887** *Ibid.* 20 Aug. 248/3 The work is neither more nor less than an ancona, which is different in kind as well as in scale from a triptych. 'Altar-piece' would be a correct term here, if the author fears to use 'ancona'. **1903** *Burlington Mag.* I. 309/2 This altarpiece now hangs on the north wall of the choir of the Collegiata. It is a Gothic *ancona* in which four scenes are represented. **1906** H. R. F. BROWN tr. *Molmenti's Venice, Mid. Ages* II. xii. 123 It is in these *ancone*, sacred images painted on wood, that we find the origin of Venetian painting.

attrib. **1900** *Speaker* 28 Apr. 116/1 The ancona form of composition.. was characteristic of the old Venetian school.

anconal ('æŋkənəl), *a. Phys.* [f. ANCON + -AL¹.] Of or pertaining to the ancon or elbow.

1803 *Edin. Rev.* III. 109 The atlantal extremities again are subdivided.. into anconal and thenal. *c* **1865** OWEN in *Circ. Sci.* II. 71/2 The humerus.. is strongly bent in a sigmoid form, with the anconal surface convex.

anconeal (æŋ'kəʊnɪəl), *a. Phys.* [f. med.L. *ancōne-us* of the elbow (f. ANCON) + -AL¹.] = prec.

1870 FLOWER *Osteol. Mamm.* 243 The olecranon or anconeal process [of the *ulna*].

anconeous (æŋ'kəʊnɪəs), *a. Phys. rare*⁻⁰. [f. as prec. + -OUS.] = prec.

1853 MAYNE *Exp. Lex.*, *Anconeus*.. applied to a triangular muscle of the elbow; anconeous.

anconoid ('æŋkənɔɪd), *a. Phys.* [ad. Gr. ἀγκωνοειδής curve-shaped, elbow-like: see ANCON and -OID.] Elbow-like; anconal.

1819 *Pantolog.*, *Anconoid Process*, a process of the cubit. **1835** HOBLYN *Dict. Med.*, *Anconoid*, Elbow-like, as applied to a process of the cubit. **1879** in *Syd. Soc. Lex.*

†**'ancony.** *Obs.* (See quot.)

1674 RAY *Iron Work* in *Collect.* 128 After two or three heats and working they bring it to an ancony, the figure whereof is in the middle a barr about 3 feet long of that shape they intend the whole barr to be made of it. **1751** CHAMBERS *Cycl.*, *Ancony*, a bloom wrought into the figure of a flat iron bar.. with two square rough knobs, one at each end. **1795** *Repert. Arts* in J. Holland *Manuf. Metal* (1831) I. 124 Draw them under the forge hammer into anconies.

ancor, obs. form of ANCHOR.

‖**ancora.** *Obs.* [It. *ancora* again.] Formerly used in same sense as Fr. ENCORE.

1712 ADDISON *Spect.* No. 323 ¶8 Mr. Froth cried out *Ancora.* **1712** BUDGELL *Spect.* No. 341 ¶3 The second Night the Noise of *Ancora's* was as loud as before.

ancoral ('æŋkərəl), *a. Zool. rare.* [ad. L. *ancorāl-is*, f. *ancora* ANCHOR.] Of or pertaining to an anchor; anchor-like, fitted to take hold like an anchor, like the feet of some parasitic crustacea.

1852 DANA *Crust.* II. 746 The feet are not all ancoral.

ancre, obs. form of ANCHOR.

ancress, earlier form of ANCHORESS.

-ancy, *suffix.* [ad. L. *-āntia*, forming abstr. sbs. on ppl. adjs. in *-ānt-em* (see -ANT).] A modern Eng. differentiated form of the earlier -ANCE, expressing more distinctly the sense of *quality, state*, or *condition*, often belonging to L. sbs. in *-ntia*, as in *ēlegāntia* 'elegant-ness,' *prūdēntia* 'prudentness,' as distinct from the sense of *action* or *process*, regularly expressed by the Fr. form *-ance*, as in *aid-ance, assist-ance, guid-ance, admitt-ance.* Partly used to form new words, partly to refashion earlier words in *-ance*, expressing quality. If the L. *diligentia, elegāntia, temperāntia, prūdēntia*, were now for the first time adopted as Eng., they would be made *diligency, elegancy, temperancy, prudency*; they owe their existing forms in *-nce*, to the fact that they were adopted from Fr., long before *-ncy* came into use. But many words, once like these, have been refashioned, and now appear with *-ncy*; e.g. *constancy, infancy, piquancy, vacancy*; the modern tendency being to confine *-nce* to action, and to express quality or state by *-ncy*; cf. *compliance, pliancy, annoyance, buoyancy.* For the formation see -ENCY, and cf. -ACY, -CY.

‖**ancyle.** *Obs.*⁻⁰ [Gr. ἀγκυλή the thong of a javelin, also, a stiff joint: see ANCHYLOSIS.] (Phillips transfers the Gr. senses to Eng.)

1706 PHILLIPS, *Ancyle*, a kind of Javelin or Dart, or the Leather thong with which it is thrown. In Anatomy, the bending of the Elbow or of the Ham; the Contraction or Drawing together of a Joynt. **1721** in BAILEY.

ancyloid ('ænsɪlɔɪd), *a. rare*⁻⁰. [f. prec. + -OID.] 'Resembling a clasp, noose or hook.' *Syd. Soc. Lex.* 1879.

ancyroid (æn'saɪrɔɪd), *a. Phys.* [ad. med.L. *ancyroīd-es*, a. Gr. ἀγκυροειδής anchor-shaped: see ANCHOR and -OID. Sometimes made *ankuroid.*] Anchor-shaped; applied to a process of the shoulder-bone, also called the *coracoid*, and to the middle cornu of the lateral ventricle of the brain.

[**1706** PHILLIPS has *Ancyroides*.] **1839–47** TODD *Cycl. Anat. & Phys.* III. 674/2 The posterior cornu is also named the digital, or ancyroid cavity.

and, *sb.* breath, animus: see ANDE.

and (ænd, ənd, *famil.* ən, (ə)n), *conj.*[1] formerly *prep.* Forms: 1- **and**; also 1 **end, ond,** 2–5 **ant,** 3–7 **an,** 8–9 *dial.* **an',** 3–4 *occas.* **a**; but usually expressed by the compendium for L. *et*, in OE. 7, later &, & ('*And* per se'), so that it is impossible to tell the full form intended. [OE. shows two forms: (1) *and, ǫnd*(:—OTeut. **anda*) OFris. *anda, and*, OS. *ant*, OHG. *ant*, Goth. *anda-, and*, ON. *and-*, prep. 'against, fronting'; (2) *ęnd*(:—OTeut. **andi*) OFris. *ande, and, an, end, en*, OHG. *anti, enti, inti, unti, endi, indi, unde*, MHG. *unde, und, unt*, mod.G. *und*, Du. *en*, conj.; cf. L. *ante* before, Gr. ἀντί against, Skr. (Vedic) *antí* over against, locative of *antá* 'end, boundary, vicinity,' hence 'on the frontier of, abutting on, fronting, facing.' From the idea of opposition, juxtaposition, or antithesis, the word was used in the Teut. langs. to express the mutual relation of notions and propositions. The general Teut. form of the conj. is **andi*, of the prep. **and(a*; in OE., with the early loss of *ęnd*, *and* (*ǫnd*) remained for both, but soon became obs. as prep., exc. in a few derivatives: see C. The levelling of OE. *ǫnd, ęnd*, under the single form *and* was no doubt helped by the fact that the conj. is nearly always unemphatic, so that the vowel is obscured and tends to sink to a mere voice glide ((ə)nd). From the same cause the final *d* has from early times been often dropped, as now universally in the dialects, and commonly in familiar speech: bread and butter = bread 'n butter. See also AN *conj.*]

†**A.** *prep.* (in OE. governing *dat.*) *Obs.*

†**1.** Of local relation: Before, in presence of.

a **1000** CÆDMON 13 Hæfdon gleám and dreám and heora ordfruman [*i.e.* joy *and* mirth *in presence of* their creator].

†**2.** Of logical relation: By the side of, besides, along with, in addition to.

a **1000** *Menol.* (Grein) 211 Emb eahta niht and feówerum. *Ibid.* 188 Ymb twentiȝ and fíf nihtum [cf. 161 Ymbe twá niht].

B. *conj. co-ordinate.* (Introducing a word, clause, or sentence, which is to be taken *side by side with, along with*, or *in addition to*, that which precedes it.)

I. Connecting words.

1. a. Simply connective.

c **700** *Epinal Gl.* (Sweet *O.E.T.* 42) *Adqueve*, ænd suilcæ. *c* **875** *Erfurt Gl.* (ibid.) *Atqueve*, end suilce. *c* **700** CÆDMON *Hymn* 2 Metudæs mæcti end his modgidanc. **871** *O.E. Chron.*, Æðeréd cyning ond [*MS.* 7] Ælfred his broður. *a* **1154** *Ibid.* (Laud. MS.) an. 1135 þa men..carl-men and wimmen. **1205** LAY. 5461 Sorwen an kare. *c* **1250** *Gen. & Ex.* 485 Twin-wifing ant twin-manslaȝt. *Ibid.* 647 Noe..an is ðre sunen. *c* **1300** *Dial. Sol. & Sat.* (Kemble) II. 270 Wyt ant wysdom. **1382** WYCLIF *Gen.* i. 1 Heuene and erthe. **1590** SHAKS. *Com. Err.* v. i. 169 My master and his man are both broke loose. **1711** STEELE *Spect.* No. 2 ¶1 Both in Town and Country. **1711** ADDISON *ibid.* No. 126 ¶2 We do in our Consciences believe two and two make four. **1846** GROTE *Greece* (1869) I. i. 45 The immortal food, nectar and ambrosia. **1859** TENNYSON *Elaine* 1185 The bond of man and wife.

b. It is used to connect the unit numbers with the tens when they precede, but not when they follow, as *one* and *twenty, twenty-one*; to connect (units or) tens to hundreds (or thousands), as *two hundred* and *one, three thousand* and *twenty-one, six thousand two hundred* and *fifty-six*; to connect fractions to wholes, as *four* and *a half, a pound* and *three quarters, an hour* and *twenty minutes*, also with shillings and pence, as *three* and *sixpence* (fam. *three* and *six*); but not usually with different denominations of weights and measures, as *two pound(s ten shillings* (or *two pound ten*); *four pound(s, six ounces*; *five foot, six inches*; nor in 'railway time,' *nine forty-eight* (48 minutes past nine).

c **950** *Lindisf. G.* John xxi. 11 Full mið miclum fiscum, hunteantiȝ 7 fiftiȝ 7 ðreo. **973** *O.E. Chron.*, Seofon and twentiȝ..ðusend a-úrnen. *Ibid.*, Niȝon and xx..wintra on woruld e. **1150** *Ibid.* an. 1137, xx winter & half ȝær & viij dæis. *c* **1250** *Gen. & Ex.* 657 Nine hundred ȝer and fifti told, Or or he starf, noe was old. **1340** HAMPOLE *Pr. Consc.* 4554 When þai haf liggen dede..Thre days and an half. **1382** WYCLIF *Gen.* v. 20 Al the daies of Jared ben maad nyne hundridȝeer and two and sixti. Enok lyued fyue and sixti ȝeer [**1611** Nine hundred sixtie and two yeeres;—sixtie and fiue yeeres]. **1398** TREVISA *Barth. De P.R.* xix. cxxix. (1495) 937 The Stadiall felde conteyneth syxe score pace and fyue, that is syxe hundryd fote and fyue, and twenty and eyȝte suche makyth a myle. **1535** COVERDALE *Ps.* xc. 10 The dayes of oure age are iij. score yeares & ten. **1673** RAY *Journ. Low Countr.* 3 We..at a League and halfs end came to a Lock. **1712** STEELE *Spect.* No. 431 ¶2, I am now entering into my One and Twentieth year. *Mod.* Six-and-eightpence, and costs. *Nursery Rime*, Four and twenty blackbirds baked in a pie.

c. Formerly, in expressing two dimensions of space, where we now use *by*.

1667 PRIMATT *City & Country Build.* 64 The principal Rafters being nine and seven inches.

d. and all: see ALL A 8 c.

2. Expressing continuous repetition: **a.** repetition of numerical groups; as in 'they walked two *and* two' = by twos, two and then other two and so on, two preceded and followed by two continuously.

c **1000** *Ags. Gosp.* Mark vi. 7 [He] agan hi sendan twam 7 twam. **1205** LAY. 24749 Æuer tweie and tweie · tuhte to-somne. *c* **1250** *Gen. & Ex.* 2323 He gan hem ransaken on and on. *c* **1460** *Towntl. Myst.* 296, I lefe it you bi oone and oone. **1596** SHAKS. *1 Hen. IV*, III. iii. 104 Must we all marche? Yea, two and two, Newgate fashion. **1630** WADSWORTH *Sp. Pilgr.* v. 38 Putting foure and foure to an oare. **1830** TENNYSON *L. Shalott* ii. 25 The knights come riding two and two.

b. repetition to an indefinite extent; as for ever *and* ever; miles *and* miles = miles and yet more miles, miles upon miles, miles without number.

1086 *O.E. Chron.*, A hit wyrsode swiðor and swiðor. *c* **1175** *Lamb. Hom.* 49 Heo delueð deihwamliche..deoppre and deoppre. *c* **1200** ORMIN 205 Ice amm Gabriæl þatt æfre and æfre stannde Biforenn Godd. *c* **1230** *Ancr. R.* 288 Deopeð into þe soule..furðre & furðre. **1597** SHAKS. *2 Hen. IV*, II. i. 35, I haue borne, and borne, and borne. **1606** —— *Tr. & Cr.* IV. v. 256 Ile kill thee euery where, yea, ore and ore. **1820** SHELLEY *Skylark* ii, Higher still and higher. *a* **1824** BYRON *Lett.* (M.) I have lived for months and months on shipboard. **1843** DICKENS *Chr. Car.* i, Many and many a day. *a* **1884** *Mod.* To roll over and over down hill. Wet through and through.

3. Emphatically. **a.** Opposed to *or*.

1837 CARLYLE *Fr. Rev.* (1872) I. VII. ix. 239 He can only answer Yes or No; would so gladly answer Yes and No.

b. Expressing a difference of quality between things of the same name or class; = and also, and other. (Commonly called a French idiom, and referred to Molière's 'il y a fagots et fagots': perhaps so in recent use, but found in Eng. a century before the production of *Le Médecin malgré lui* in 1666.)

a **1569** KINGESMYLL *Confl. w. Satan* (1578) 39 There is a sinne and a sinne: much oddes betweene the committing of sinnes in the reprobate and the elect. **1633** EARL MANCH. *Al Mondo* (1636) 86 A heart and a heart God cannot abide. **1855** BROWNING *Heretic's Trag.* Wks. 1863 I. 289 Alack, there be roses and roses, John! **1883** W. POLLOCK in *Harper's Mag.* 909/1 There are, in the first place, photographs and photographs.

c. and/or: a formula denoting that the items joined by it can be taken either together or as alternatives.

1855 *Law Jrnl. Reports* XXIV. II. Excheq. 199/2 The parties were to 'load a full and complete cargo of sugar, molasses, $\frac{\text{and}}{\text{or}}$ other lawful produce'..the words 'and' and 'or' being introduced into the charter-party. **1895** POLLOCK & MAITLAND *Hist. Eng. Law* I. I. v. 152 In medieval Latin *vel* will often stand for *and*..Often it is like the $\frac{\text{and}}{\text{or}}$ of our mercantile documents. **1916** H. BARBER *Aeroplane Speaks* ii. 85 The jamming of the rudder and/or elevator. **1929** *Penrose's Ann.* XXXI. 99 A good proportion of cotton and/or linen in the furnish of a paper. **1959** *Camb. Rev.* 2 May 454/2 The Press has rather plumped for the scholar as writer, and/or as bibliophile. **1960** E. BOWEN *Time in Rome* iii. 82 The young set-apart creature, waiting at home for her fifteenth birthday and/or the next vacancy in the Atrium.

4. Connecting two adjectives of which the former logically stands in (or approaches to) an adverbial relation to the latter; esp. in familiar language, and dialectally, after *nice, fine*. Cf. GOOD *adv.* d.

1575 R. LANEHAM *Let.* in *Leisure Hour* (1884) 631/1, I am ..jolly and dry of a mornings. [**1592** SHAKS. *Rom. & Jul.* II. ii. 8 Her Vestal liuery is but sicke and green. **1604** —— *Oth.* IV. ii. 56 His slow and mouing finger.] **1846** [see NICE *a.* 15 d]. *a* **1884** *Mod. fam.* That will make you nice and warm. Cut it nice and thin. The grass is fine and tall. **1887** T. DARLINGTON *Folk-Speech of S. Cheshire* 109 'Fine an' vexed' = exceedingly vexed.

†**5.** Before both words connected: = Both —— and ——. (L., Fr. *et* —— *et* ——.) *Obs.* (or only a Latinism.)

c **1175** *Cott. Hom.* 239 Forté isi and frend and fend. *c* **1340** HAMPOLE *Pr. Treat.* 30 þou sall be made and bryghte and clene. **1483** CAXTON *Gold. Leg.* 242/4 To thende that he wold not leue them and disheryted and orphanes he made his testament. *a* **1520** *Myrr. Our Ladye* 146 He ys now gloryfyed in heuen and in soulle and body.

6. When many notions (or clauses) are connected, *and* is in ordinary prose expressed only with the last. But formerly, and still in illiterate composition, it is used with every member; rhetorically, also, it may be so used, to emphasize the number of points, or length of the series.

1297 R. GLOUC. 4 Of Lyncolne, and of Chestre, and of Wircester. **1362** LANGL. *P. Pl.* A. III. 273 Loue and louhnesse and leute to-gedere. **1480** CAXTON *Chron. Eng.* cxcii. 168 Al tho that myghte trauaylle, as wel monkes and preestes and frerys and chanons and seculeres. **1601** SHAKS. *Jul. C.* II. ii. 80 Warnings and portents and evils imminent. **1805** SCOTT *Last Minstr.* v. xiii, Sorrow, and sin, and shame. **1846** GROTE *Greece* (1869) I. i. 46 Dance and song and athletic contests adorned the Solemnity.

II. Connecting co-ordinate clauses or sentences.

7. Simply connective. **a.** additive.

855 *O.E. Chron.* (Parker MS.) an. 534 Her Cerdic forþ ferde, 7 [? ond] Cynric his sunu ricsode. *c* **1000** *Ags. Gosp.* Matt. ii. 20 Aris ænd nim þæt cild, and his moder. *c* **1200** *Moral Ode* 159 þer men luȝen her ent stelen. *a* **1250** *Owl & Night.* 31 The niȝtingale hi i-seȝ..An thuȝte wel ful of thare hule. *a* **1300** *Havelok* 359 Him for to hoslon, an for to shriue. **1502** ARNOLD *Chron.* (1811) 223 He was howsled and anelid and soo died. **1751** JOHNSON *Rambl.* No. 165 ¶3 The brightest hours of prosperity have their clouds, and the stream of life..will grow putrid by stagnation. **1756** BURKE *Vind. Nat. Soc.* Wks. I. 9, I then thought, and am still of the same opinion. **1832** CARLYLE in *Remin.* (1881) I. 9, I often wondered and admired at this. **1879** TENNYSON *Lover's T.* 54 Love mourn'd long, and sorrow'd after Hope.

b. adversative.

c **1000** *Ags. Gosp.* Matt. xii. 7 Ic wille mild-heortnysse, and na onsæȝdnysse. **1366** MAUNDEV. 51 Thei wenen that thei han bawme, and thei have non. **1481** CAXTON *Reynard* (Arb.) 69 He complayneth and I playne not. **1611** BIBLE *Matt.* xxii. 30 Hee said, I goe sir, and went not.

8. Introducing a consequence: **a.** the historical sequel or consequence of a fact.

c **1000** ÆLFRIC *Gen.* i. 3 God cwæþ þa · ȝeweorþe leoht: and leoht wearð ȝeworht. **1382** WYCLIF *ibid.*, God seide, Be maad liȝt: and maad is light. **1611** *ibid.*, God said Let there be light: and there was light. —— *Luke* vii. 8, I say vnto one Goe, and he goeth; and to another Come, and hee commeth. **1667** PEPYS *Diary* 30 June, A pretty young woman, and I did kiss her. **1821** KEATS *Lamia* 441 You have dismiss'd me, and I go From your breast houseless. **1879** A. CLARK tr. *Rydberg's Rom. Days*, A few paces from the *trattoria*, and I stood on the Forum Romanum. *Mod.* He spoke, and all was still.

b. the predicted consequence or fulfilment of a command, or of a hypothesis put imperatively, or elliptically.

c **1000** *Ags. Gosp.* Matt. viii. 8 Cweð þin án word, and mine cnapa bið ȝehæled. **1386** CHAUCER *Miller's T.* 344 Werke by counseil, and thou schalt nat rewe. **1388** WYCLIF *John* xvi. 16 A litil, and thanne ȝe schuln not se me. **1557** (Genev.) *ibid.*, A litle whyle, and ye shal not see me. **1611** BIBLE *Luke* x. 28 This do, and thou shalt liue. **17..** *Sc. Paraphr.* xxxv, My broken body thus I give For you, for all—take, eat, and live. **1799** ALLINGHAM *Fort. Frol.* I. iii, Gee' us a buss, and I'll tell thee. **1826** DISRAELI *Viv. Grey* VI. ii. 296 Five minutes more, and our son must have reigned in Little Lilliput. *a* **1884** *Mod.* Give him an inch, and he will take an ell. Speak one word, and you are a dead man! **1896** A. AUSTIN *Eng. Darling* III. i. 63 Face a head gust and it will steady you. **1933** D. L. SAYERS *Murder must Advertise* iv. 72 Spray with Sanfect and you're safe.

9. Introducing an explanatory, amplificative, or parenthetic clause or phrase.

996 *Cod. Dipl.* III. 295 ȝesyllan ælce ȝeare xv leaxas, and ð a ȝode. **1205** LAY. 2360 Makian an eorð-hus..& þæt inne swiðe feire stude. *c* **1386** CHAUCER *Prol.* 43 A knyght ther was, and that a worthy man. *c* **1460** *Towntl. Myst.* 259 Into this dongeon depe I soght, And alle for luf of the. **1610** SHAKS. *Temp.* II. i. 317, I heard a humming (And that a strange one too). **1710** ROWE *J. Shore* I. i, Yet there is one, and he amongst the foremost. **1818–1884** [see MISTAKE *sb.* 2 c]. **1843** DICKENS *Christm. Car.* i, Scrooge signed it: and Scrooge's name was good upon 'Change. **1853** [see WONDER *sb.* 6 e]. **1855** MACAULAY *Hist. Eng.* III. 323 He and he alone has done all this. **1869** A. MORRIS *Open Secret* xi. 194 To think that *we* are, and we only are, to blame. *a* **1884** *Mod.* You doubt his capacity, and with reason. **1890** F. GOLDIE *Ven. Ed. Arrowsmith* (C.T.S.) 2 Robert Arrowsmith's father ..was often thrown into gaol—and we know what gaols were in those days. **1914** S. A. HIRSCH in A. G. Little *R. Bacon* v. 128 Another large portion of the Greek Grammar is taken up by Bacon's treatment of accentuation and prosody (pp. 95–144), and no wonder! **1930** G. K. CHESTERTON *Resurr. Rome* v. 202 The French would certainly have recovered the stolen French provinces whenever they could; and quite right too.

10. Connecting two verbs the latter of which would logically be in the infinitive, *esp.* after *go, come, send, try*; familiarly and dialectally after various others.

[**1526** TINDALE *Acts* xi. 4 Peter began and expounde the thinge.] **1671** MILTON *P.R.* I. 224 At least to try and teach the erring soul. **1780** MRS. THRALE *Let.* 10 June (1788) II. 150 Do go to his house, and thank him. **1819** MOORE in *N.Q.* Ser. I. (1854) IX. 76/1 Went to the theatre to try and get a dress. **1878** JEVONS *Prim. Pol. Econ.* 42 If every trade were thus to try and keep all other people away. *Mod.* You will come and see us sometimes, won't you?

III. Introductory.

11. Continuing the narration: **a.** from a previous sentence, expressed or understood.

855 *O.E. Chron.* (Parker MS.) an. 855 Ond þa fengon Æþelwulfes suna tweȝen to rice. *a* **1154** *Ibid.* (Laud. MS.) an. 1140 And te eorl of Angæ u wærd ded, & his sune Henri toc to þe rice. *c* **1449** PECOCK *Repr.* 140 An whi not thanne Crist schulde allowe and approve men for to have and use a Graven Ymage of the Emperour in hevene? **1595** SHAKS. *John* IV. i. 40 *A.* Must you with hot Irons burne out both mine eyes? *H.* Yong Boy, I must. *A.* And will you? *H.* And I will. **1611** BIBLE *John* xxi. 21 Peter seeing him saith to Jesus, Lord, and what shall this man do? **1846** GROTE *Greece* (1869) I. i. 29 And thus she remained a whole year. **1853** KINGSLEY *Hypatia* v. (1869) 69 And why could not you run away, boy? **1861** LYTTON *Pilgr. Rhine* (beginning) And the stars sat each upon his ruby throne and looked with sleepless eyes upon the world.

b. from the implied assent to a previous question or opinion, = Yes! and; as 'Will you go?' 'And take you with me.' 'This applies to all men, I suppose?' 'And to women too.'

1847 HELPS *Friends in C.* Ser. I. I. 284 *E.* 'It gives new life to politics.' *M.* 'And not to politics only.' **1853** KINGSLEY *Hypatia* v. 61 'You are now to obey me.' 'And I will.'

12. In expressing surprise at, or asking the truth of, what one has already heard.

a **1788** W. J. MICKLE *Nae Luck aboot the House*, And are ye sure the news is true? And are ye sure he's weel? *c* **1800** *Jolly young Waterman*, And have you not heard of that jolly young waterman, That at Blackfriars' Bridge used for to ply? **1844** DISRAELI *Coningsby* III. iii. 96 'And you walked here!' said Lady Everingham. *a* **1884** *Mod.* O John! and you have seen him! And are you really going?

IV. Quasi-adverbially.

†**13.** Also; even. (A Latinism.) *Obs.* (or *arch.*)

1382 WYCLIF *John* xv. 23 He that hatith me, hatith and [**1388** also] my fadir. [Vulg. *Qui me odit, et patrem meum odit*]. —— *Wisd.* xviii. 20 Thanne forsothe touchede and [**1388** also] riȝtwismen the temptacioun of deth. *c* **1449** PECOCK *Repr.* 519 If thin answere now mad to my questiouns is good, and such thanne a lijk answere schal be good..to thi Questioun. **1558** BP. T. WATSON 7 *Sacr.* xvi. 98 b, He that hath promysed pardone vnto vs, whensoeuer we conuerte, dothe not promise vnto vs longe lyfe and to lyue whyle to morowe.

C. *conj. conditional*, = if. [This was a common use of MHG. *unde*; the ON. *enda* (which Vigfusson thinks 'probably identical' with *and*, while Sievers would see in it a reduced form of *enn þó*, even though) approached this use, in the latter clause of a conditional premiss, as 'ef þú þorir, enda sér þú nokkut at manni..' 'if thou darest, and (supposing that) thou art something of a man..' (Vigf.). It has been suggested that the Eng. use was derived from that of Norse *enda*, but this is very doubtful. More probably the idiom arose in Eng. independently, as in MHG. It may have originated from ellipsis, as in the analogous use of *so*, e.g. 'I'll cross the sea, *so* it please my lord' (Shaks.); cf. 'and it please'; or it may be connected with the introductory *and* in 'And you are going?' A direct development from the original prepositional sense, though *à priori* plausible, is on historical grounds improbable. Modern writers, chiefly since Horne Tooke, have treated this as a distinct word, writing it *an*, a spelling occas. found *c*1600, esp. in *an' 't* = *and it*. See AN *conj.*]

1. a. If; suppose that, provided that, on condition that.

1205 LAY. 8313 And þu hit nult ileuen..ich hit wulle trousien. **1250** *Ibid.* 3524 Help him nou an þou miht. *a* **1300** *Havelok* 2861 And þou wile my conseil tro, Ful wel shal ich with þe do. *c* **1300** *Harrow. Hell* 11 Ant he were at this worldes fyne. *c* **1314** *Guy Warw.* 12 Leuest thing me were to dye And Ich wist bi wiche weye. **1330** R. BRUNNE *Chron.* 69, I salle..Help þe..& euer I se þat day. **1483** CAXTON *G. de la Tour* D vj b, For and she be wyse she ought to thynke, etc. **1526** TINDALE *Matt.* xix. 17 But and thou wilt entre into lyfe. **1529** MORE *Comf. agst. Trib.* II. Wks. 1557, 1170/2 Gesse her and you can. **1540** HYRDE *Vives' Instruct. Chr. Wom.* I vj, Let her chaunge her place..and need be. **1547** *Homilies* I. (1859) 108 And it please your grace, you did once promise me. **1590** SHAKS. *Com. Err.* I. ii. 94 And you will not, sir, Ile take my heeles. **1612** SHELTON *Quix.* I. III. viii. 183 They may tell it and they please. **1625** BACON *Ess.* (1862) 97 They will set an House on Fire, and it were but to roast their Egges. **1711** J. GREENWOOD *Eng. Gram.* 163 Sometimes And is used for If: As, and you please, for, if you please. See also AN *conj.*

b. Strengthened with following *if*: 'and if,' 'an' if,' in same sense.

The common s.w. dial. form of *if* is now *nif* = *'n if, an if*. (See Elworthy *West-Somerset Gram.* p. 93.)

c **1394** *P. Pl. Crede* 17 þerfor lerne þe byleue leuest me were And if any werldly wiȝt wisse me couþe. *a* **1400** *Chester Pl.* 27 We shoulde dye..and yf we touch that tree. **1523** LD. BERNERS *Froissart* I. xxviii. 41 He wolde haue had his right, and yf he wyst how. **1526** TINDALE *Matt.* vi. 14 For and yff ye shall forgeve other men there treaspases. —— *ibid.* xxiv. 48 But and yf that evill servaunt shall saye [so CRANM., *Genev.*, 1611; WYCL. and *Rhem.* But if]. **1591** SHAKS. *Two Gent.* I. i. 75 A Sheepe doth very often stray, And if the Shepheard be awhile away. **1673** *Lady's Call.* I. §1. ¶27 But and if on the other side they meet with one of too much sagacity. **1859** TENNYSON *Enid* 1402 An if he live, we will have him of our band.

2. Concessive: 'Even if,' passing into 'although.'

c **1325** *E.E. Allit. P.* B. 864 And ȝe ar iolyf gentylmen your iapes ar ille. *c* **1400** *Apol. for Loll.* 40 And He was riche, He was mad nedy for vs. **1526** TINDALE *Mark* vi. 56 Thatt they myght touche and hit wer but the edge off hys vesture. [So CRANM., *Genev.*; *Rhem.* & 1611, If it were.] *a* **1553** UDALL *Royster D.* I. ii, He shall go without hir and he were my brother. *a* **1593** MARLOWE *Jew of Malta* II. ii, I must have one that's sickly, An't be but for sparing victuals. **1658** T. WALL *Enemies of Ch.* 33 Religious they will be and 't be but for the benefit they receive thereby.

†**3.** = 'As if,' 'as though.' *Obs.*

a **1423** JAMES I *King's Q.* v. x, A maner smylyng make And sche were glad. **1590** SHAKS. *Mids. N.* I. ii. 86, I will roar you an 'twere any Nightingale. **1606** —— *Tr. & Cr.* I. ii. 139 O he smiles valiantly..Oh yes, and 't were a clow'd in Autumne.

†**4.** *indirect interrog.*: If, whether (L. *an*). *Obs. illiterate*, or *dial.*

1590 SHAKS. *Mids. N.* v. i. 195 To spy an I can heare my Thisbys face. **1598** B. JONSON *Ev. Man in Hum.* IV. i, To feel an there be any brain in it. **1602** —— *Poetaster* I. i, Ask him an he will clem me.

¶ Used *subst.* An expression of condition or doubt.

1513, **1613** [see IF *sb.*]. **1638** CHILLINGWORTH *Relig. Prot.* I. vii. §10. 395 Whence without all Ifs and Ands, that appeares sufficiently which I said in the beginning. **1678** CUDWORTH *Intell. Syst.* 723 Absolutely, and without any ifs and ands. **1683** HOOKER *Pordage's Myst. Div.* 137 An absolute approbation..without any cautions, qualifications, ifs or ands. *Proverb*, If ifs and an's were pots and pans, there'd be no trade for tinkers. **1823** tr. *J. Campan's Mem. M. Antoinette* (ed. 2) I. x. 259 Five different requests—such an office, *or* such a mark of distinction, *or*..and so on... The *ors* were changed into *ands*.

D. As *sb.* and *adj.* A Boolean function of two or more variables that has the value unity if and only if each variable has this value. Usu. *attrib.* and in capitals, esp. designating devices for realizing this function.

[**1938**: see OR *conj.*[2] (*adv.*[3]) 8.] **1946** J. P. ECKERT in *Theory & Techniques Design Electronic Digital Computers* (Univ. Penn.) (1947) II. xv. 9 In an 'and' circuit, when an impulse A and an impulse B are received on a set of terminals, an output will be given. **1950**, etc. [see NOT *adv.* and *sb.* 14]. **1960** M. G. SAY et al. *Analogue & Digital Computers* viii. 165 The 'and' and 'or' operations may be performed by the diode gates. **1967** *Electronics* 6 Mar. 157/2 Utilogic is a line built around a basic AND and a basic NOR circuit. **1971** J. H. SMITH *Digital Logic* iv. 51 The AND function, like the OR, is used for simplifying circuit arrangements but does not form the basis for a complete logic system. **1984** J. HILTON *Choosing & using your Home Computer* 51/1 Combinations of AND, OR and NOT allow all decisions based on conventional logic to be made.

†**and**, *conj.*[2] *after comparatives. Obs.* An erroneous literary expansion of northern dial. *'an, en* 'than' [perhaps a. ON. *an, en, enn* (Da. *end*) apocopate form of the same word as Eng. *than*], formally confused with *an'*, dialectal and familiar form of the preceding word. After *other, otherwise*, it may however literally render L. *alius, aliter ac*.

1463 MARG. PASTON in *Lett.* 480 II. 142 Bettyr and ye have be befor thys tyme. *c* **1500** *Cock Lorell's Bote* 7 Fayrer and euer the halfe strete was. **1554** PHILPOT *Exam. & Writ.* 339 Otherwise and ye suppose. **1565** *Eccl. Proc. Durh.* (1857) 597 Likned togither more and 2 yere. **1599** SHAKS. *Hen. V*, II. iii. 12 Hee's in Arthurs Bosome, if euer man went to Arthurs Bosome: a made a finer end, and went away and it had beene any Christome Child.

†**and-**, *pref. Obs.* The prep. AND in comb., Goth. *anda-, and-*, OHG. *ant-, ent-*, 'against, in return, opposite, fronting, toward.' In OE. the full form (often labialized to *ǫnd-*) remained only under the stress, i.e. in sbs. and adjs.; as *'and-git* apprehension, *'andsǽte* opposed, hostile, *'andswaru* answer, *'andweard* present. When proclitic, as in vbs., it was weakened to *ǫn-* as *ǫn'gitan* to apprehend. The former still remains as *an-* in *answer* (see AN- *pref.* 2); the latter, like *ǫn-* for *an-*, afterwards fell to *a-*, as in *along* (see A- *pref.* 4).

-and, *suffix*[1]. Ending of pr. pple. in northern dial., representing OE. *-ende*, early ME. midl. and south. *-ende, -inde*, later ME. and modern *-ing*; as in OE. *writende*, ME. north. *writand*, early south. *writende, -inde*, later *writinge*, modern *writing* (thus identified with vbl. sb. or gerund). In some north. dialects, the pple. and vbl. sb. are still distinguished as *-ănd, -ing*, or at least *-ăn', -in'*. As ppl. adjs. from Fr. ended in *-ant, -aunt*, these were often interchanged with *-and* in 15th c., as in sembl*ant*, sembl*and*; ambl*ant*, ambl*and*; cf. warr*ant*, warr*and*; tyr*ant*, tirr*and*; gi*ant*, gy*and*; merch*ant*, march*and*, and the like.

-and, *suffix*[2]. A formative element representing the termination *-andus, -a, -um* of the gerundive of Latin verbs in *-āre*. Examples of words in *-and* are *analysand, confirmand, educand, graduand, multiplicand, operand, ordinand*. The meaning of these words is passive, thus *ordinand* 'person to be ordained'. This element has never been a living suffix, having no separate existence apart from the Latin gerundive form from which it is derived. The gerundial endings are sometimes retained in their Latin (neut.) form (with pl. *-a*), as in *avizandum, memorandum, notandum*.

†**andaba'tarian**, *a. Obs. rare*[−1]. [f. L. *andābata* (see next) + -ARIAN.] Pertaining to, or of the nature of, an andabate; struggling blindfold.

1624 BP. MOUNTAGU *Gagg* 299 This andabatarian fencer fighteth with his owne shadow.

†**andabate.** *Obs. rare.* [ad. L. *andābata* a Roman gladiator who fought on horseback in a helmet without eye-holes; of unkn. orig., but generally assumed to be ad. Gr. ἀναβάτης a rider.] A hoodwinked gladiator. Hence *fig.* One who is hoodwinked or blindfolded.

a **1564** BECON *New Year's Gift* Wks. 1843, 331 With what eyes do these owls and blind andabates look upon the holy scriptures?

†**an'dabatism** *Obs.* [f. prec. + -ISM.] The practice of an andabate; struggling in the dark; contention or debate with no certain end in view.

c **1630** DRUMM. OF HAWTH. *Irene* Wks. 1711, 169 To trouble an estate, be authors of divisions, insurrections, andabatism, uproars. **1635** SHELFORD *Disc.* 121 (T.) To state the question that we might not fall to andabatism.

Andalusian (ændə'lu:ʃ(ɪ)ən, -zɪən), *a.* and *sb.* Forms: 7–9 **Andalucian, Andaluzian.** [f. *Andalusia* (see below) + -AN.] **A.** *adj.* Of or pertaining to Andalusia, a southern province of Spain, or its inhabitants or speech. **B.** *sb.* **a.** A native or inhabitant of Andalusia. **b.** The variety of Castilian spoken in Andalusia. **c.** A Mediterranean breed of domestic fowl, rabbit, etc.

1612 SHELTON *Quix.* (1619) I. ii. 12 The Oast thought he had called him a Castellano, or Constable,..whereas he was indeede an Andaluzian. **1615** *Ibid.* (1617) II. i. 10 A famous Andaluzian Poet wept, and sung her teares: and another famous and rare Poet of Castile her beauty. **1740** P. PINEDA *New Spanish Dict.* (s.v. *Andalùz*), The Castilians, who have no good opinion of the Andaluzians. **1823** BYRON *Don Juan* XII. lxxv. p. 42 She cannot step as does an..Andalusian girl from mass returning. *Ibid.* XIII. xxiii. p. 66 And Juan, like a true-born Andalusian, Could back a horse. **1839** G. DENNIS *Summer in Andalucia* II. xvi. 385 This failing of the Andalucians betrays itself in many ways. **1854** *Poultry Chron.* I. 101 Several so-called Andalusians, bred by a Minorca cock out of a Maltese hen... The Andalusian fowls were introduced to the notice of amateurs by Mr. Taylor, of Shepherd's Bush. **1862** G. BORROW *Wild Wales* III. xxiv. 275 The place upon the whole put me very much in mind of an Andalusian village overhung by its sierra. **1868** DARWIN *Var. Anim. & Plants under Domestication* I. iv. 105 Various allied sub-breeds [of rabbit] are reared on the Continent, such as the so-called Andalusian, which is said to have a large head with a round forehead, and to attain a greater size than any other kind. **1879** *Cassell's Fam. Mag.* Apr. 274/2 The experiment was once tried of fattening a youthful Andalusian [rabbit] entirely on clover hay. **1882** CAULFEILD & SAWARD *Dict. Needlework* 6/2 Andalusian Wool..is also called Victoria Wool, and is a fine soft warm make of woollen thread or yarn... It is the same wool as the Shetland, but is thicker. **1887** *Encycl. Brit.* XXII. 351/1 The word 'dialect' is still more appropriately applied to Andalusian than either to Asturian or Navarrese-Aragonese. **1900** J. D. M. FORD in *Studies & Notes in Philol. & Lit.* VII. 1 Andalusian and other dialect peculiarities are only incidentally concerned. **1911** —— *Old Sp. Readings* p. vii, Andalusian does not differ radically enough from Castilian to oblige us to regard it as a separate dialect. **1920** *Discovery* July 200/2 This form of fowl is bluish-black with black lacing, and is called the Blue Andalusian. **1924** KIPLING *Debits & Credits* (1926) 229 The fifth bull rushed out—an unthinking black Andalusian. **1927** *Blackw. Mag.* Sept. 313/1 A sky of Andalusian azure. **1936** W. J. ENTWISTLE *Sp. Lang.* vi. 220 Since 1600..there has been no 'correct' Andalusian, and the dialect has gathered to itself all current vulgarisms.

andalusite (ændə'l(j)u:saɪt). *Min.* [f. *Andalusia* a province of Spain, where first found + -ITE.] A very hard silicate of alumina, found in rhombic crystals of various colour.

1837–80 DANA *Min.* 371 Andalusite..color whitish, rose-red, flesh-red, violet, pearl-gray, reddish-brown, olive-green. **1843** HUMBLE *Dict. Geol.*, *Andalusite*, occurs in gneiss in England.

Andaman ('ændəmən), *a.* and *sb.* [f. *Andaman* Islands in the Bay of Bengal.] **A.** *adj.* Of or belonging to the Andaman Islands, or pertaining to their inhabitants or language, esp. in ***Andaman islander***. **B.** *sb.* The language of the Andaman people.

1848 J. CRAWFURD in *Jrnl. Indian Archipelago* II. 206 On comparing the native portion of the language of Wageou with that of the Sámang, and the words of the Andaman, no resemblance can be found between them. **1860** MAYNE REID *Odd People* 412 We trace in the Andaman islander the true physiognomy of a negro. *a* **1873** MILL *Ess. Relig.* (1874) 193 It is to suppose that God could not, in the first instance, create anything better than a Bosjeman or an Andaman islander. **1936** J. R. KANTOR *Obj. Psychol. Gram.* xv. 208 An animate and inanimate division is also found in Andaman, the language of the Andaman Islands in the Bay of Bengal. **1952** *Jrnl. R. Anthrop. Inst.* LXXI. 17/1 An analysis of the non-totemic Andaman Islanders. **1955** *Nomencl. Comm. Timbers* (*B.S.I.*) 66 *Pterocarpus dalbergioides*, Andaman padauk; Andaman redwood (U.S.A.).

Andamanese (ˌændəmə'ni:z). [f. as prec. + -ESE.] An aboriginal of the Andaman Islands; also the language of the Andaman people; also *attrib.* or as *adj.* Hence ˌ**Andama'nesian** *a.* Also **Anda'maner**, an Andaman islander.

1727 A. HAMILTON *New Acc. E. Ind.* II. xxxviii. 68 The Andemaners have no Notions of a Deity. **1833** *Penny Cycl.* I. 513/2 The Andamaners eat rats, guanas, and snakes. **1862** *Andamanese Vocab. & Phraseol.* 1 Those words marked thus * are strongly suspected to be Hindostanee, or words from some other language picked up by the Andamanese. **1875** *Jrnl. Anthrop. Inst.* IV. 464 The larger shed was filled with 110 Andamanese of all ages. **1887** M. V. PORTMAN (*title*) A Manual of the Andamanese Languages. Part I.—Dictionary, English-Andamanese. **1907** *Indian Antiquary* XXXVI. 220 For the purpose of an adequate presentation of Andamanese..I gradually framed a Theory of Universal Grammar. **1922** *Blackw. Mag.* June 787/2 A keen-sighted Andamanese saw two men on a little hill. **1932** W. L. GRAFF *Language & Languages* xi. 416 The Andamanesian dialects spoken by the natives of the Andaman Islands. *a* **1942** B. MALINOWSKI *Scientific Theory of Culture* (1944) vi. 61

Among the..Andamanese, we can not speak of the political organization of the tribe, since this does not exist.

‖**andante** (an'dante, æn'dæntɪ), *a.* and *sb. Mus.* [It., pr. pple. of *andare* to go.]

A. *adj.* Of musical movement: Moderately slow and distinct. Also used advb.

1742 BAILEY, *Andante*, chiefly respects the thorough Base, and signifies that in playing, the Time must be kept very just and exact, and each note made very equal and distinct from one to the other. **1784** *Europ. Mag.* V. 322 Haydn's celebrated Andante movement. **1868** GEO. ELIOT *Sp. Gypsy* I. 63 Not angular jigs..but action curved to soft andante strains. **1880** E. PROUT in Grove *Dict. Mus.* I. 65/1 Andante is a quicker rate of movement than larghetto, but..is slower than allegretto.

B. *sb.* A movement or piece in andante time.

1784 COWPER *Task* II. 351 [He] sells accent, tone..and gives to prayer The *adagio* and *andante* it demands. **1845** E. HOLMES *Mozart* 30 An Andante in one of them [sonatas] is of especial taste.

‖**andantino** (andan'tino), *a.* and *sb. Mus.* [It. *andantino*, dim. of prec.]

A. *adj.* Of musical movement: *orig.* Rather slower than andante; but often taken to mean: With less of andante, *i.e.* rather quicker.

1819 *Pantolog.*, *Andantino*, in music, gentle, tender, and somewhat slower than andante. **1833** *Penny Cycl.* I. 514 It ..seems to be agreed, that andantino now shall signify a movement quicker than andante—that it shall be the medium between the latter and allegretto.

B. *sb.* A movement or piece of this description.

1845 E. HOLMES *Mozart* 166 To this succeeds an andantino in the form of an entr'acte.

†**ande**, *sb. Obs.* Forms: 1–2 **anda, onda,** 2–5 **ande,** 2–4 **onde,** 3 **ond,** 3–4 **aand,** 4 **honde,** 4–5 **and, hand,** 5 **aande, oonde.** *Sc.* 4–6 **aynd,** 6– **aind.** [OE. *anda*, cogn. w. OS. *ando*, OHG. *anado, ando, anto*, mental emotion, ON. *andi, önd*, breath. The reg. south. form after 1200 was ONDE, *oond*; but the word became obs. in the south *a* 1500; in north. dial. *and, aand, aynd, aind*, has continued to the present day.]

1. (from OE.) Emotion or tendency of the mind against; enmity, rancour, hatred; 'animus.'

c **1000** *Ags. Gosp.* Matt. xxvii. 18 He wiste sōþlice þæt hiᵹ hyne for ándan him sealdon. *c* **1160** *Hatton G.* ibid., For ánden hym sealden. *a* **1175** *Cotton Hom.* 223 Þa nam he muclene gramen and andan to ðan mannum. *c* **1175** *Lamb. Hom.* 65 Þurh nið and onde com deð into þe worlde.

¶ Later only in southern form ONDE in this sense.

2. (from ON. *andi*; chiefly northern, and after 1500 Scotch). Breath.

a **1300** *Cursor Mundi* 531 Þis aand þat men draus oft. *Ibid.* 580 Of four elementes wroght; O watur his blod..hijs and [*v.r.* ande, ond, honde] of air. **1340** HAMPOLE *Pr. Consc.* 775 His nese ofte droppes, his hand stynkes. **1375** BARBOUR *Bruce* IV. 199 He na mocht His aynd bot with gret panys draw. **1440** *Promp. Parv.*, Oonde or brethe, *Anhelitus*. *c* **1460** *Towneley Myst.* (1836) 154 Myn and is short, I wante wynde. **1513** DOUGLAS *Æneis* IV. xii. 122 With ane puft of aynd the lyfe out went. **1536** BELLENDENE *Cron. Scot.* (1821) I. 117 Thay wer out of aind, or evir thay come to any straikis.

†**ande**, *v. Obs.* or *north. dial.* Also 4–5 **onde,** 4–6 **aynd,** 6 **eand,** 6– **aind.** [f. ANDE *sb.* Cf. ON. *anda* to breathe. Mostly northern.] To breathe, blow.

1393 LANGL. *P. Pl.* C. XVI. 257 Be sobre · of syght, and of tounge boþe, In ondyng, in handlyng · in alle þy fyue wittes. **1440** *Promp. Parv.*, Ondyn, or brethyn, *Aspiro, anelo.* **1483** *Cathol. Angl.*, To Ande, *Afflare, asspirare.* **1536** BELLENDENE *Cron. Scotl.* (1821) I. Pref. 42 Gif thai [bustards] find thair eggis aindit or twichit be men, thay leif them. **1540** ABP. HAMILTON *Catech.* 133 b (JAM.) He eandit on thame and said: Ressaue ye the haly spreit. *a* **1575** *Ress. betw. Knox & Crosraguel* E ij a (JAM.) *Spirat, ergo vivit*, as I wald say, he aindes, *ergo* he lives.

Andean ('ændiːən), *a.* [f. *Andes* name of the principal mountain range of S. America + -AN.] Of, pertaining to, or resembling the Andes.

1839 BAILEY *Festus* (1848) 39/1 Some Andean chain Of shadowy rolling mountains, based on air. **1861** L. NOBLE *After Icebergs* 69 Sketched the surrounding scenery..for the sake of comparison with some of his Andean pencillings.

andelong, obs. form of ENDLONG.

anderoon (ændə'ruːn). Also **anderun.** [Pers. *enderūn* prop. internal, interior, f. *ender* within.] The apartments of a (Persian) harem; also, any inner room of a house.

1840 SAVILE in *New Monthly Mag.* LVIII. 189 In the anderoon..sat Khodadad, in sweet converse with his beloved Semira. **1842** THACKERAY *Sultan Stork* (1887) 7 The ladies they kept so secretly in the anderoon. **1900** *Westm. Gaz.* 20 July 2/1 The household gathering outside the *anderoun* till the Shah emerges. **1934** F. STARK *Valleys of Assassins* iii. 213 An inner *anderun* where the women slept.

†'**anders-meat, aunders-.** *Obs.* [Prob. mod. form of OE. *undern-mete* dinner, with sense altered.]

1598 FLORIO, *Merenda*, a repast betweene dinner and supper, a nunchin, a beuer and andersmeate. **1611** COTGR., *Gouster*, a nunchion, drinking, aunders-meat, afternoones collation, mouthes-recreation.

Anderson ('ændəsən). *Anderson shelter*, a small prefabricated air-raid shelter devised by Mr. (later Sir) William Paterson, a Scottish engineer, and adopted while Sir John Anderson was Home Secretary (1939–40). Also *ellipt.*

1939 *New Statesman* 3 June 860/2 Goats sheltered from high explosive in Anderson shelters were claimed to be quite unhurt. **1939** *War Illustr.* 29 Dec. 535 An Anderson shelter erected in a kitchen because there is no garden space available. **1940** *New Statesman* 9 Nov. 465/2 Where's my rabbits?..Kept 'em in the Anderson. **1944** *Modern Reading* x. 87 'Cold?' Dad asked her. 'No. Like toast. That's the best of Andersons, you can get warm in them.' **1952** *Oxf. Jun. Encycl.* X. 89/1 Anderson shelters were small, curved, steel huts, partially buried in people's gardens and covered with 2 or 3 feet of earth to protect them from the effects of explosion.

andesine ('ændizɪn). *Min.* [f. *Andes* (see ANDEAN) + -INE.] = next.

1862 DANA *Man. Geol.* 56 Andesine is another lime and soda feldspar. **1879** RUTLEY *Stud. Rocks* x. 90 Regarding labradorite, oligoclase, and andesine as admixtures..of.. albite and anorthite.

andesite ('ændɪzaɪt). *Min.* [f. as prec. + -ITE.] A silicate of alumina, lime, and soda, found at Marmato in the Andes and elsewhere; perhaps only a mixture of labradorite with soda-felspar.

1850 DANA *Geol.* xiii. 565 This albitic rock appears to be allied to the Andesite described by Mr. Darwin. **1879** RUTLEY *Stud. Rocks* xii. 234 The name andesite was first used by L. von Buch.

andesith, var. ENDESITH *adv. Obs.*, formerly.

andesitic (ændɪ'zɪtɪk), *a. Min.* [f. ANDESITE + -IC.] Of the nature of, or containing, andesite.

1876 JUDD in *Q. Jrnl. Geol. S.* XXXII. 308 The andesitic lava of the Schemnitz district.

andetted, obs. form of INDEBTED.

andevile, obs. form of ANVIL.

andȝet, -ness: see ANGET, -NESS.

Andine ('ændaɪn), *a.* [f. *Andes* + -INE[1].] = ANDEAN *a.*

1900 *Daily Chron.* 23 Aug. 3/4 The explorations carried out..for the Argentine Government in the Andine region. **1924** *Chambers's Jrnl.* Mar. 188/2 A vast ancient crater of the Andine range.

†'**anding**, *vbl. sb. Obs.* in north. dial. **aynding.** [f. AND(E *v.* + -ING[1].] Breathing, breath.

1375 BARBOUR *Bruce* XI. 615 Sic ane stew..Of aynding, bath of hors and men. **1513** DOUGLAS *Æneis* V. xii. 136, I feile the aynding of his horsis blaw.

andiron ('æn,daɪən). Forms: 4 **aundyre,** 3–4 **aundyrne,** 4 **-iren,** 5 **awndyryn, aundeiren, -ryn, andyron,** 5–6 **awnderne,** 6 **andyar, awndyrn, aundyern, -yron, aundernn, handern, -iron,** 7 **handyron, landyron,** 5– **andiron.** [a. OFr. *andier* (mod.Fr. *landier*, i.e. *l'andier*), cf. med.L. *andena, anderia, anderius*, mod.Fr. dialects *andier, andi, andian.* Its remoter history is unknown: see Diez, Skeat, and Wedgwood *Contested Etymol.* In Eng. the termination was at an early date identified with the word *yre, yren* iron, whence the later illusive spellings *and-iron, hand-iron.* Instances also occur of *land-iron* after later Fr.]

A utensil, consisting of an iron bar sustained horizontally at one end by an upright pillar or support usually ornamented or artistically shaped, at the other by a short foot; a pair of these, also called '*fire-dogs*,' being placed, one at each side of the hearth or fire-place, with the ornamental ends to the front, to support burning wood. Sometimes 'in a kitchen fire-place the upright support carried a rack in front for the spit to turn in' (Wedgwood).

a **1300** W. DE BIBLESWORTH in Wright *Voc.* 171 *Forgé de fers*, aundyrnes [*v.r.* in *Rel. Ant.* II. 84 *Furchez de ferz*, aund hirnes]. *c* **1314** *Guy Warw.* 250 An aundiren he kept in his honden. *c* **1400** *Metr. Voc.* in Wright *Voc.* 176 Stipes ut andēna (*glossed* a aundyre) sustentus deperit ardens. [The reading of the MS. is clear.] **1440** *Promp. Parv.*, Awnderne [*v.r.* awndyryn, **1499** awndyrn], *Andena, ipoporgium.* **1442** in *Reg. Test. Ebor.* I. 56 a, Duo ferra nominata aundeiryns pro supportatione foci in aula. **1447** *Par. Accts. Ludlow* in *Shropsh. Word-bk.*, Item, a pare of andirons. **1480** CAXTON *Ovid's Met.* XII. xii, Threwe..an hevy andryon agenst his Enemyes. **1483** *Act 1 Rich. III*, xii. §1 Andyrons Cobbardes Tongges Fireforks Gredyrons &c. **1493** in *Bury Wills* (1850) 82 A speete wᵗ an aundeiren. **1519** HORMAN *Vulg.* (in *Pr. Parv.* 19), I lacke a fyre pan and andyars to bere up the fuel. **1522** in *Bury Wills* (1850) 115 A payer of handerns. **1590** in *Midl. Count. Hist. Coll.* II. 31 Item..ij landyrons one fire shovell. **1591** FLORIO *Sec. Frutes* 159 Set that firebrand vpon the handiron. **1609** *Acc. Feoffees of Rotherham* 8 For mending of a handyron in the chamber, 8*d.* **1616** *Ibid.*, For mendinge the Scowll house landyron, 8*d.* **1611** SHAKS. *Cymb.* II. iv. 88 Her Andirons..were two winking Cupids Of Siluer. **1626** BACON *Sylva* §178 If you strike..an Andiron of brass, at the top, it maketh a more treble sound. **1650** FULLER *Pisgah Sight* III. vi. 390 Like brazen andirons in great mens chimnies. **1789** MRS. PIOZZI *Fr. & It.* I. 93 Ashes raked out from between the andirons. **1826** SCOTT *Woodst.* (1832) 187 The andirons, or dogs..for retaining the blazing firewood on the hearth. **1878** MRS. STOWE *Poganuc People* xiii. 111 The social sit-down in front of the andirons.

†'**andless**, *a. Obs. Sc.*; also 4 **handles, ayndlesse,** 6 **aindles.** [f. ANDE *sb.* + -LESS.] Breathless, out of breath.

1375 BARBOUR *Bruce* x. 609 Thai war handles [*ed.* 1620 ayndlesse] and wery: And thair abad thair aynd to ta. **1533** BELLENDENE *Livy* II. (1822) 152 Thay war ouresett and aindles, throw thair lang rinning.

andlet, var. ANLET *Obs.*, a small ring.

Andorran (æn'dɒrən), *a.* and *sb.* Also 9 **Andorrian.** [f. *Andorr(a*, a small independent state in the eastern Pyrenees, and its capital: see -AN, -IAN.] **A.** *adj.* Of or pertaining to Andorra. **B.** *sb.* A native or inhabitant of Andorra.

1837 J. E. MURRAY *Summer in Pyrénées* (ed. 2) I. v. 99 The leader of our little band was a considerable proprietor in the valley, who was well known to the Andorrians. *Ibid.* 117 This Andorrian piscator..was a labourer. **1856** *Chambers's Jrnl.* 12 Apr. 235/2 It was not difficult to recognise in the cavalier an Andorran of the upper class. **1865** M. EYRE *Over the Pyrenees* iv. 118 The Andorrans are passionately fond of dancing. *Ibid.* 123 An Andorran peasant..always carries arms. **1906** H. BELLOC *Hills & Sea* vi. 36 In the further Andorran valley. **1909** —— *Pyrenees* v. 268 The Andorrans have all the vices and virtues of democracy clearly apparent. **1967** *Chambers's Encycl.* I. 420/1 Each of the two suzerains ..has a court..for Andorran affairs.

‖**an'douille.** ? *Obs.* [Fr.:—L. *inductilia* pl. neut. of *inductilis* (f. *indūcĕre* to lead or put in, insert, introduce), rendered *boudin* in an early glossary.] 'A big hogges gut stuffed with small guts (and other intrailes) cut into small pieces, and seasoned with pepper and salt.' Cotgr. 1611.

1605 in *Archæol.* XIII. 371 Table of necessarie provisions for the whole yeare..Andulees, potatoes, kidshead, colflorry, etc. **1653** URQUHART *Rabelais* I. xxi, He began his meale with..Andouilles or sauciges. **1706** PHILLIPS, *Andouille*, a kind of Chitterling, made either of Hogs or Calues Guts. **1796** MRS. GLASSE *Cookery* v. 84 This sort of andouilles or puddings must be made in summer when hogs are seldom killed.

andouillere, obs. (or Fr.) form of ANTLER.

‖**andoui'llet** (ɑ̃dujɛ). Also **andouillette** (ɑ̃dujɛt). [a. Fr. *andouillette* (in Littré), dim. of *andouille*] (See quot.)

1611 J. DONES *Paneg. Verses* in T. Coryat *Crudities* sig. f5ᵛ [Rabelais] Whose *Papagants, Andoüilets*, and that traine Should be such matter for a Pope to curse. **1706** PHILLIPS, *Andouillet*, minced Veal with Bacon and other Ingredients roll'd into a Paste: Andouillets for Fish-days are also made of Eels and Carp's-flesh, chopt small or pounded in a Mortar. **1725** BRADLEY *Fam. Dict.* s.v. *Veal*, These *Andouillets* are to be roasted on a Spit between Slices of Bacon. **1736** in BAILEY *Househ. Dict.* 285. **1775** in ASH. **1877** *Kettner's Book of Table* 30 We know little of the andouillette in England. **1906** I. BEETON *Househ. Managem.* xxiv. 737 Andouillettes of game. **1958** R. GODDEN *Greengage Summer* ix. 106 Andouillette is a kind of sausage. **1965** *House & Garden* Jan. 60/1 *Andouillette.* This sausage, similar to andouille but fresh, is usually cooked slowly in white wine or champagne and served with crisp potatoes and watercress.

andradite ('ændrədaɪt). *Min.* [f. *d'Andrada* (see quot. under ALLOCHROITE) + -ITE.] A variety of lime-irongarnet.

1868 DANA *Syst. Min.* (ed. 5) 268 Named *Andradite* by the author after the Portuguese mineralogist d'Andrada, who described and named the first of the included subvarieties, Allochroite. The included kinds vary so widely in color and other respects that no one of the names in use will serve for the group. **1903** F. RUTLEY *Mineralogy* (ed. 13) II. 114 The Iron-lime garnets are included under the name Andradite. **1914** *Brit. Mus. Return* 227 Garnet (andradite) from China.

andranatomy (ændrə'nætəmɪ). ? *Obs.* [f. Gr. ἀνδρ- (ἀνήρ) man + ANATOMY.] (See quot.)

1811 HOOPER *Med. Dict.*, *Andranatomia, Andranatome*, the dissection of the human body, particularly of the male. **1847** CRAIG, *Andranatomy*.

'**Andrew.** [A man's name, used in specific senses.]

†**1.** A broadsword, an 'Andrea Ferrara.' *Obs. rare.*

1618 FLETCHER *Chances* viii, Here's old tough Andrew.

†**2.** A valet, gentleman's servant. *Obs. rare.*

1698 CONGREVE *Way of Wld.* v. i, Abigails and Andrews.

3. See MERRY-ANDREW.

4. *Naval slang.* Also ***Andrew Millar*** or ***Miller.***

†**a.** A ship, esp. of war. Also ***Andrew Millar's lugger.*** *Obs.*

[**1596** s.v. DOCK *v.*[2] 2.] **1812** VAUX *Flash Lang.*, *Andrew Miller's lugger*, a king's ship or vessel. **1864** HOTTEN *Slang Dict.* 67 *Andrew Millar*, a ship of war.

b. The Royal Navy; also (obs.), a government department or authority.

1867 SMYTH *Sailor's Word-Bk.* 40 *Andrew*, or *Andrew Millar*, a cant name..for government and government authorities. **1916** 'TAFFRAIL' *Carry On!* 29 Terms..heard every day in 'Andrew', as the bluejacket calls the Navy. **1955** G. FREEMAN *Liberty Man* I. iv. 62 That's 'ow it is in the Andrew... That's what we call the navy. *Ibid.*, A press man called Andrew Miller..forced so many blokes to join, that it got known as Andrew's navy. Then they shortened it to the Andrew.

5. St. Andrew is regarded as the patron saint of Scotland. From him are named—**St. Andrew's Day**: the 30th Nov., on which the festival in his honour is held, formerly also called *St. Andrew-mass*; and **St. Andrew's Cross**: an oblique cross, or one shaped like the letter X.

1641 BEST *Farming* (1856) 76 The best time for frost and snowe is about a weeke afore St. Andrewmasse. **1727–51** CHAMBERS *Cycl.*, *Andrew's Cross* is a badge wore in the hat, by the people of Scotland, on the day of the feast of that saint. It consists of blue and white ribbands, disposed into a cross, or saltier. **1771** BAXTER in *Phil. Trans.* LXXVII. 45 Directly opposite to the sun was a luminous cross, in the shape of a St. Andrew's Cross.

Andrewsite (ˈændru:zaɪt). *Min.* [f. the name of Thomas *Andrews* + -ITE[1].] A bluish-green hydrous phosphate of iron and copper.

1871 *Chem. News* XXIV. 99 A mineral recently found in Cornwall..has been analysed in the Museum Laboratory, and Professor Maskelyne named it Andrewsite, in honour of the distinguished President of the Chemical Section of the British Association, Dr. Andrews, of Belfast.

andro- (before a vowel **andr-**), repr. Gr. ἀνδρο-, combining form of ἀνήρ man, male. **androcentric** (ændrəʊˈsɛntrɪk) *a.*, having man, or the male, as its centre; so **androcenˈtricity**; **androcracy** (ænˈdrɒkrəsɪ) [-CRACY], the rule of man or the male, male supremacy; **androcratic** (-ˈkrætɪk) *a.*, pertaining to or involving androcracy; **andromonœcious** (-məˈni:ʃ(ɪ)əs), *a. Bot.* [MONŒCIOUS *a.*], having male and hermaphrodite flowers on the same plant; **andromonœcism** (-məˈni:sɪz(ə)m) *Bot.*, the condition of being andromonœcious.

1903 L. F. WARD *Pure Sociol.* xiv. 292 The *androcentric theory is the view that the male sex is primary and the female secondary in the organic scheme, that all things center, as it were, about the male. **1959** *Guardian* 6 Nov. 6/5 The Fathers of the Church accepted from their cultural environment the androcentric standpoint. **1954** *Theology* LVII. 326 Do we see anything of this *androcentricity in the Christian ministry? **1903** L. F. WARD *Pure Sociol.* xiv. 376 The stage of gynæcocracy was succeeded by the stage of *androcracy, and the subjection of woman was rendered complete. **1893** *Athenæum* 7 Oct. 494/1 Marital relations among tribes in the enjoyment of an *androcratic government being generally far more satisfactory. **1903** L. F. WARD *Pure Sociol.* xiv. 399 The androcratic régime, during which woman had no voice in the selecting process. **1877** *Andromonœcious [see ANDRODIŒCIOUS *a.*]. **1888** G. HENSLOW *Origin Floral Struct.* 227 *Andromonœcism signifies that the same plant bears both male and hermaphrodite flowers.

androconium (ændrəʊˈkəʊnɪəm). *Zool.* [mod.L., f. Gr. ἀνδρο- male + κονία dust.] Usu. in pl. *androconia*, scales on the wings of certain male Lepidoptera from which the attractive scent of the male is diffused; = PLUMULE 3 b. Hence **androˈconial** *a.*

1877 S. H. SCUDDER in *Proc. Amer. Acad. Arts & Sci.* XII. 157 These peculiar scales [on a male butterfly], or androconia, as they may be called in reference to their masculine nature, were first noticed by Bernard Deschamps... Deschamps called them plumules. **1914** T. B. FLETCHER *Some Indian Insects* v. 49 The flocculent yellow androconial hairs which line the interior of the pocket and which doubtless emit a smell attractive to the female. **1937** *Nature* 13 Feb. 265/2 The androconial scale and its development in the genus *Erebia*. **1957** E. B. FORD *Butterflies* (ed. 3) v. 96 The attractive scent of the male is scattered by the androconia, usually situated on the upper side of the fore-wings.

andro-diœcious (ˌændrəʊdaɪˈi:ʃəs), *a. Bot.* [f. Gr. ἀνδρο- male + DIŒCIOUS, f. δι- (DI-[2]) twice + οἰκία house + -OUS.] 'With flowers on one plant hermaphrodite, and on the other staminate only.' Gray *Bot. Text-bk.* 1880. Hence **androdiˈœcism**, the state of being androdiœcious.

1877 C. DARWIN *Different Forms Flowers* i. 13 There are plants which produce hermaphrodite and male flowers on the same individual, for instance, some species of Galium, Veratrum, &c.; and these might be called andro-monœcious. If there exist plants, the individuals of which consist of hermaphrodites and males, these might be distinguished as andro-diœcious. **1888** G. HENSLOW *Origin Floral Struct.* xxiv. 277 Androdiœcism signifies that the same species has both male and hermaphrodite plants.

androdynamous (ˌændrəʊˈdɪnəməs), *a. Bot.* [mod. f. Gr. ἀνδρο- male + δύναμ-ις strength + -OUS.] 'A name proposed by Fries for those dicotyledonous plants, in which there is a more than ordinary development of stamens and petals.' Craig.

‖**andrœcium** (ænˈdri:ʃɪəm). *Bot.* [mod.L., f. Gr. ἀνδρο- male + οἰκίον house.] A name given to the whole of the male organs of a flower.

1839 in LINDLEY *Introd. Bot.* 172. **1857** HENFREY *Elem. Bot.* §196 The stamens collectively constitute the andrœcium. **1870** BENTLEY *Bot.* 208 The andrœcium constitutes the whorl or whorls of organs situated on the inside of the corolla.

androgen (ˈændrəʊdʒən). *Biol.* [f. ANDRO- + -GEN.] A substance, as a male sex hormone, capable of developing and maintaining certain male sexual characteristics (cf. ŒSTROGEN). Hence **androˈgenic** *a.*

1936 *Jrnl. Amer. Med. Assoc.* 18 July 212/2 The Nomenclature of 'Male Hormones'..*Androgen* to designate substances possessing masculinizing activity. **1939** I. F. & W. D. HENDERSON *Dict. Sci. Terms* (ed. 3) 16/2 *Androgenic*, stimulating male characters; masculinising; *appl.* hormones; *appl.* tissue capable of elaborating an androgenic hormone. **1939** *Lancet* 22 Apr. 948/1, 50 mg. of testosterone is equivalent to 3500 I.U. of androgenic activity. **1946** *Nature* 24 Aug. 276/2 The significance of androgen and œstrogen excretion in the urine in relation to ageing. **1962** *Lancet* 1 Dec. 1166/1 The action of the œstrogens is far less specifically related to precise molecular structures than is that of the androgens or corticoids.

androgenesis (ændrəʊˈdʒɛnɪsɪs). *Biol.* [mod.L. f. ANDRO- + -GENESIS; cf. G. *androgenese* (M. Verworn 1891, in *Pflüger's Archiv ges. Physiol.* LI. I. 81).] (See quot. 1925.) Hence **androgeˈnetic** *a.*, pertaining to androgenesis.

1916 B. D. JACKSON *Gloss. Bot. Terms* (ed. 3) 21/1 *Androgenesis*, the growth of an individual from a male cell. **1918** C. PACKARD in *Biol. Bull.* XXXV. 50 The inference is that these embryos have developed under the influence of the sperm nucleus and are therefore androgenetic. **1925** E. B. WILSON *Cell* (ed. 3) v. 464 Androgenesis. By this term we may designate the activation of the egg by the sperm followed by development without the participation of the egg nucleus. *Ibid.* 465 The nuclei of the embryo are solely of paternal origin, *i.e.*, descendants of the sperm-nucleus alone. This process is designated as 'androgenetic'.

androgynal (ænˈdrɒdʒɪnəl), *a. rare.* [f. L. *androgyn-us* + -AL[1].] = ANDROGYNOUS.

1646 SIR T. BROWNE *Pseud. Ep.* 149 We must acknowledge this Androgynall condition in man. **1839** LADY LYTTON *Cheveley* II. ix. 303 An androgynal abortion, combining all the coarseness of the one sex with all the weakness of the other.

anˈdrogynally, *adv. rare*[−1]. [f. prec. + -LY[2].] After the manner of hermaphrodites.

1646 SIR T. BROWNE *Pseud. Ep.* 148 The examples hereof have undergone no reall or new transexion, but were Androgynally borne. **1755** in JOHNSON; also in mod. Dicts.

androgynary (ænˈdrɒdʒɪnərɪ), *a. Bot.* [mod. f. L. *androgyn-us* (see ANDROGYNE *sb.*) + -ARY, after mod.Fr. *androgynaire*.] Applied, after De Candolle, to flowers in which both stamens and pistils are developed into petals, as in the double narcissus.

1879 in *Syd. Soc. Lex.*

androgyne (ˈændrədʒɪn), *sb.* [a. Fr. *androgyne* (14th c.), ad. L. *androgyn-us*, a. Gr. ἀνδρόγυνος male and female in one, f. ἀνδρο- male + γυνή woman, female. Sometimes used in 17th c. in the L. form *androgynus* and (erron.) *androgyna*.]

1. A being uniting the physical characters of both sexes; a hermaphrodite.

1552 HULOET, *Androgine*, whiche bene people of both kyndes, both man and woman. **1601** HOLLAND *Pliny* (1634) I. 157 Children of both sexes, whom wee call Hermophrodites. In old time they were knowne by the name of Androgyni. **1677** HALE *Prim. Orig. Man.* 316 As if Adam had been Androgyna, or one double Person.. consisting of both Sexes. **1795** T. MAURICE *Hindostan* I. i. 66 The fabulous tales of the Androgynes.. warring against the gods.

†**2.** An effeminate man; a eunuch. *Obs. rare.*

1587 J. HARMAR *Beza's Serm. Canticles* 173 (L.) These vile and stinking androgynes, that is to say, these men-women, with their curled locks. **1706** PHILLIPS, *Androgynus* ..a Scrat or Will Jill, an effeminate Fellow. **1742** BAILEY, *Androgyne*, an Hermaphrodite, or one..that is castrated and effeminate.

3. *Bot.* An androgynous plant.

1785 HOWARD *Cycl.*, *Androgyna*, in botany, plants which bear on the same root male and female flowers. **1837** WHEWELL *Hist. Induct. Sc.* XVII. iv. §2 Zaluzian, a botanist who lived at the end of the 15th century, says that the greater part of the species of plants are androgynes.

androgyne (ˈændrəʊdʒaɪn), *a.* [f. the sb.] = ANDROGYNOUS *a.* Also *absol.*

1848 *Tait's Mag.* XV. 703/2 The planets being androgyne, like plants, *copulent avec eux-memes* and with the other planets. **1958** J. G. BENNETT *Subud* viii. 164 The force of sex..reunites the separated parts to produce the androgyne fourth gradation of the human essence. **1962** *Listener* 8 Mar. 415/2 The symbolists' fascination with the unnatural in Byzantium—in a taste for the androgyne and the perverse.

androgynic (ˌændrəʊˈdʒɪnɪk), *a. rare*[−0]. [mod. f. ANDROGYNE *sb.* + -IC.] Of androgynous nature or character.

1879 in *Syd. Soc. Lex.*

androgynism (ænˈdrɒdʒɪnɪz(ə)m). *Bot.* [f. as prec. + -ISM.] 'Change from the diœcious to the monœcious condition.' Masters *Veg. Terat.* 1869.

androgynous (ænˈdrɒdʒɪnəs), *a.* [f. L. *androgyn-us* (see ANDROGYNE *sb.*) + -OUS.]

1. Uniting the (physical) characters of both sexes, at once male and female; hermaphrodite.

1651 BIGGS *New Disp.* ¶69 Nature.. contenteth herself with that which is androgynous and promiscuous. **1751** CHAMBERS *Cycl.* s.v., Many of the rabbins are of opinion that Adam was created androgynous. **1828** KIRBY & SPENCE *Entomol.* IV. xlii. 167 To suppose these insects are truly androgynous, as strictly uniting both sexes in one. **1844** *For. Q. Rev.* XXXIII. 273 Madame Sand has been known to travel in an androgynous costume. **1878** BESANT & RICE *Celia's Arb.* I. xiii. 185 A woman without the mystical veil is no woman, but a creature androgynous.

†**2.** Hence, of men: womanish, effeminate. *Obs.*

1628 PRYNNE *Love-Lockes* 49 Clemens condemnes all such for androginous and effeminate persons.

3. *Astrol.*

1652 GAULE *Magastrom.* 86 Planets masculine, feminine, androgynous. **1751** CHAMBERS *Cycl.* s.v., The astrologers also give the appellation androgynous to such of the planets as are sometimes hot, and sometimes cold. **1819** *Pantolog.* s.v., Mercury is reckoned androgynous, being hot and dry when near the Sun, cold and moist when near the moon.

4. *Bot.* Bearing both stamens and pistils in the same flower, or on the same plant.

1760 J. LEE *Introd. Bot.* I. xxi. 64 Androgynous, Male and Female, such as upon the same Root bear both male and female Flowers. **1793** MARTYN *Lang. Botany*, Androgynous plant. **1821** S. GRAY *Arr. Brit. Pl.* I. 44 *Androgynous*, having male and female organs on the same root, but not in the same flowers. **1837** WHEWELL *Hist. Induct. Sc.* XVII. iv. §2 The florets of composite flowers [are] formed on the type of an androgynous flower. **1881** BENTHAM in *Jrnl. Lin. S.* XVIII. 366 Spikelets..collected in androgynous heads.

androgyny (ænˈdrɒdʒɪnɪ). *Biol.* [f. as prec. + -Y.] Union of sexes in one individual; hermaphroditism.

1849–52 TODD *Cycl. Anat. & Phys.* IV. 1425/2 Instances of androgyny..depend upon an excessive development of this structure.

android (ˈændrɔɪd). [f. mod.L. *androīdes* (also used), f. Gr. ἀνδρο- man + -ειδης -like: see -OID.] An automaton resembling a human being. Also *attrib.*

1727–51 CHAMBERS *Cycl.* s.v., Albertus Magnus is recorded as having made a famous *androides*. **1819** *Pantolog.* s.v., M. de Kempelen..constructed an androides capable of playing at chess. **1847** CRAIG, *Android*. **1951** C. SIMAK *Time & Again* (1956) i. 1 Human gossip as well as android and robot gossip. **1958** *Spectator* 19 Sept. 379/1 Today SF must be more than a blood-and-sex day-dream spattered with words like androids (robots made of flesh and bone).

androidal (ænˈdrɔɪdəl), *a. rare*[−0]. [f. prec. + -AL[1].] 'Like an automaton.' Craig 1847.

ˈandrolepsy. *Obs. rare.* [ad. Gr. ἀνδροληψία seizure of men.] A custom whereby according to Athenian law, if a citizen were killed abroad, and his death unatoned for, three subjects of the offending country were seized as reprisals.

1727–51 in CHAMBERS *Cycl.*

Andromed(e (ˈændrəmɪd), *Astr.* A system of meteors which appear to radiate from a point in the constellation of Andromeda.

1876 CHAMBERS *Astron.* 799 Designating other meteor showers by the constellations in which their radiant-points are situated; so that we have the *Leonids* and the *Andromedes* of November 14 and 27.

Andromeda (ænˈdrɒmɪdə). [Gr., prop. name of the mythical daughter of Cepheus and Cassiopeia, who, when bound to a rock and exposed to a sea-monster, was delivered by Perseus.]

1. One of the constellations of the northern hemisphere, figured to represent the mythical Andromeda.

1706 PHILLIPS, *Andromeda*, a Northern Constellation, consisting of 27 Stars. **1883** *Whitaker's Almanac* 60 An irresolvable Nebula on the right foot of Andromeda may be observed this month [November].

2. *Bot.* A genus of shrubs (N.O. *Ericaceæ*), of which one dwarf herb-like species is native to Britain, and others to North America.

1760 [see ROSEMARY 3]. **1765** J. BARTRAM *Jrnl.* 30 Dec. (1769) 8 The..dwarf-myrtle, andromeda..and other evergreens. **1794** MARTYN *Rousseau's Bot.* xix. 268 Andromedas..& a few others, have regular monopetalous corollas. **1856** KANE *Arct. Expl.* I. v. 50 Filling up the interstices with..sods of andromeda and moss. **1960** *Oxf. Bk. Wild Flowers* 118/2 Bog Rosemary or Marsh Andromeda.

Andromedid (ænˈdrɒmɪdɪd). *Astr.* [f. ANDROMEDA 1 + -ID[2]: cf. LEONID, PERSEID.] = ANDROMED(E.

1898 *Pall Mall Gaz.* 21 Nov. 2/3 The Leonids are remarkably swift; the Andromedids strikingly slow. **1904** *Westm. Gaz.* 17 Nov. 12/1 The Andromedids form part of the débris of Biela's Comet.

andromedotoxin (ænˌdrɒmɪdəʊˈtɒksɪn). [a. G. (P. C. Plugge 1882, in *Pharm. Weekblad* 1 Oct.), f. ANDROMEDA 2 + TOXIN.] A poisonous crystalline substance found in various ericaceous plants, esp. the genus *Andromeda.*

1883 *Jrnl. Chem. Soc.* XLIV. 349 The poisonous principle of *Andromeda japonica* has been examined with similar results by P. C. Plugge, who calls it Andromedotoxin. **1902** *Westm. Gaz.* 16 July 2/2 A chicken fed for four days on increasing doses of the andromedotoxin from this plant [sc. *Kalmia latifolia*]. **1956** *New Gould Med. Dict.* (ed. 2) 70/1 Andromedotoxin,..has potent hypotensive action.

andromorphous (ˌændrəʊˈmɔːfəs), *a. rare.* [f. Gr. ἀνδρο- male + -μορφ-ος -form + -OUS.] Having the form of a male, masculine-looking.
1865 *Reader* No. 142. 326/2 An andromorphous female.

andropetal (ˈændrəʊˌpɛtəl). *Bot. rare.* [f. Gr. ἀνδρο- male + PETAL *sb.*] 'A petal produced from a metamorphosed stamen, as in the rose and other double flowers.' *Syd. Soc. Lex.* 1879.

androˈpetalar, *a. Bot. rare.* [f. prec. + -AR, after mod.Fr. *andropetalaire* (De Candolle).] = next.
1879 in *Syd. Soc. Lex.*

androˈpetalous, *a. Bot.* [f. as prec. + -OUS.] Made double by having the stamens changed into petals, as in the ranunculus, etc.
1847 in CRAIG.

androphagous (ænˈdrɒfəgəs), *a. rare.* [f. Gr. ἀνδροφάγ-ος man-eating (f. ἀνδρο- man + -φαγ-ος eating + -OUS.] Man-eating, anthropophagous.
1865 *Athenæum* No. 1978. 408/3 Androphagous Massagetæ.

androphore (ˈændrəfɔə(r)). [ad. mod.L. *androphor-um* (Mirbel), f. Gr. ἀνδρο- male + φόρος bearing, f. φερ- bear.]
1. *Bot.* A name applied by some to the column formed by the united filaments in monadelphous plants, or a more or less columnar portion of the receptacle bearing several anthers.
1821 S. GRAY *Arr. Brit. Pl.* I. 142 *Androphore, Androphora,* Filaments soldered together in one or more bundles. **1870** BENTLEY *Bot.* 250 When the union takes place so as to form a tube or column, the term androphore has been applied to the column thus formed.
2. *Zool.* The male gonophore of certain of the *Physaphoridæ*.
1861 J. GREENE *Cœlent.* 53 Androphore of the same Condylophora, its contents escaping. **1877** HUXLEY *Anat. Inv. An.* iii. 143 The groups of male and female gonophores . . (androphores and gynophores).

androsphinx (ˈændrəʊsfɪŋks). [a. Gr. ἀνδρόσφιγξ, f. ἀνδρο- male + SPHINX.] A man-sphinx; a sphinx whose human portion is male.
1607 TOPSELL *Four-footed Beasts* (1673) 15 In the porch of Pallas . . he placed such great colosses and Andro-sphinges that it was afterwards supposed he was buried therein. **1850** LEITCH *Müller's Anc. Art* §228 Sphinxes or androsphinxes are lions with human heads.

androspore (ˈændrəʊspɔə(r)). *Bot.* [ad. mod.L. *androsporus*, f. (by Pringsheim) Gr. ἀνδρο- male + σπόρος SPORE, seed.] The zoospore which in certain fucoid *Algæ* produces the male reproductive organs.
1864 in WEBSTER. **1875** BENNET & DYER *Sachs' Bot.* 229 In many species (of Œdogonieæ) the female plant produces peculiar swarm-spores (Androspores) out of which proceed very small male plants.

androsterone (ænˈdrɒstərɒn, ˌændrəʊˈstɪərəʊn). *Biochem.* [f. ANDRO- + *ster*(*ol* as in CHOLESTEROL + -ONE.] A male sex hormone.
1934 *Brit. Chem. Abstr.* A. 1221/2 (*title*) Synthesis of the testicular hormone (androsterone and stereoisomerides thereof). **1935** *Ann. Reg. 1934* 53 The conversion by Ruzicka of cholesterol into the male sex hormone . . gave promise that the three sex hormones (androsterone, progestin, and oestrin) will be available for clinical use in chemically pure crystalline form. **1935** *Lancet* 13 July 77/1 Solutions of the crystalline male hormone androsterone injected into rats will maintain normal prostate and seminal vesicles after adult castration.

androtomous (ænˈdrɒtəməs), *a. Bot.* [f. Gr. ἀνδρο- male + -τομ-ος cut + -OUS.] Having the filaments of the stamens divided into two parts.
1879 in *Syd. Soc. Lex.*

†**anˈdrotomy.** *Obs. rare*[−1]. [f. Gr. ἀνδρο- male, man + -τομία cutting.] The dissection of human bodies; more accurately denominated *anthropotomy*.
a **1691** BOYLE *Wks.* I. 68 (R.) Androtomy, as some of the moderns call the dissection of man's body, to distinguish it from zootomy, as they name the dissection of the bodies of other animals. **1755** in JOHNSON; and in mod. Dicts.

-androus, *Bot. suffix* of adjs., f. mod.L. *-andr-us* (a. Gr. -ανδρος adj. ending, f. ἀνδρ- stem of ἀνήρ man) + -OUS. Used as = 'having . . male organs or stamens'; as in *tri-androus* having three stamens, *polyandrous* having many stamens, *gynandrous* having stamens situated on the pistil.

†**ˈandsech.** *Obs. rare.* [OE. *andsæc* denial, cf. *andsaci-an* to deny, refuse, f. *and-* against + *sæc* contention, strife.] Denial, abjuration.
a **1000** *Laws of Ina* 41 (Bosw.) Be borȝes andsæce. *a* **1000** *Elene* (Gr.) 472 þæs unrihtes andsæc. *c* **1200** *Trin. Coll. Hom.* 147 Mid swiche teares lauede Seint peter þe hore of þe fule sinne of ure helendes andseche.

†**ˈandsete, ˈansete,** *a.* and *sb. Obs.* [OE. *andsǽte*, f. *and* against + *-sǽte* from *sitt-an* to sit.]
A. *adj.* Hostile, hateful, odious.
c **1000** ÆLFRIC *Gram.* xxxiii. §3 *Exosus* and *perosus*, andsæte oððe onscuniȝendlic. *c* **1175** *Lamb. Hom.* 107 Idelȝelp is him ansete. *c* **1200** ORMIN 16070 He wass Godd anndsæte & all unnewene.
B. *sb.* An enemy, foe.
c **1200** *Trin. Coll. Hom.* 115 þe king was cumen fro fehte and hadde his andsete ouercumen.

andswere, obs. form of ANSWER.

andvile, obs. form of ANVIL.

andweald, bad f. *anwald*: see ONWALD.

†**ˈandwurde, -wyrde,** *v. Obs.* [OE. *andwyrd-an, -werdan, -wirdan*, cogn. with OHG. *antwurtan* (mod.G. *antworten*), OS. *andwordian*, Goth. *andwaurdjan*; formed on the sb., Goth. *andawaurdi*, OS. *andwordi*, OHG. *antwurti*, MHG. *antwürte* (mod.G. *antwort*), OE. *andwyrde* an answer; f. *anda-, and-*, against, back + *word* (Goth. *waurd*) 'word.' The sb. *andwyrde* (in King Ælfred) was displaced by *andswaru* before the end of the OE. period; the vb. also was usually replaced by *andswerian*, ANSWER, in late OE., and did not survive 12th c.] To answer.
c **885** K. ÆLFRED *Oros.* I. x. §1 Hý him andwyrdon and cwædon. *c* **1000** ÆLFRIC *Gen.* iii. 2 Ðæt wíf andwirde. *Ibid.* xvi. 6 Abram hire andwerde. *c* **1000** *Ags. Gosp.* Matt. xxvii. 14 He ne andwerde mid nanum worde [*v.r.* andswarede; *Lind.* ondsuarede, *Rushw.* andwyrde, *Hatt. G.* andswerede]. *c* **1175** *Lamb. Hom.* 91 Ða and-wurde Petrus, hit is underted. *Ibid.* Ða and-wrde Petrus.

†**ane**, *a. Obs.* or *dial.* [representing sundry parts and uses of the adj. ONE, OE. *án*.]
1. *án-e*: Various inflected forms of *án* 'one': in OE. the acc. sing. fem., nom. and acc. pl. of indef. decl., and nom. and acc. sing. fem. and neut. of def. decl.; in early ME. representing other earlier inflections, esp. dat. sing. m. and n., but used chiefly as the def. form, and after the sb. = 'only': see ONE.
879 *O.E. Chron.*, Aþiestrode sió sunne áne tíd dæȝes. *a* **1000** CÆDMON *Gen.* 2134 Nymðe feá áne. *c* **1000** *Andreas* 492 Is þys áne má. *c* **1175** *Lamb. Hom.* 35 Bi-foren þam preoste ane. *c* **1220** *Hali Meid.* 7 Serue Godd ane. *Ibid.* 25 Al . . oðer ane deale.
2. In ME., north. dial., common variant of *an* (*ane* = *ān*, with mute *e* indicating long vowel), the full form of the numeral used absol. or attrib. bef. a vowel (bef. a const. reduced to *a*); also occas. of the weakened numeral or 'indef. article' bef. a vowel, the stress alone distinguishing the two senses (as in Ger. *ein* and Fr. *un*). See AN *adj.*[1]
1340 HAMPOLE *Pr. Consc.* 3109 þe body with flesshe and bane Es harder þan þe saul by it ane. *c* **1340** —— *Prose Treat.* 8 Ane es þat sche es neuer ydill. **1375** BARBOUR *Bruce* v. 24 Rouit alwayis in-till ane. *c* **1425** WYNTOUN *Cron.* VII. v. 98 This is ane of my Ladyis Pynnys.
3. In 16th c. Sc., the literary representative of earlier *ane*, *an*, and *a*, in all positions, alike as numeral and indefinite article. = One, an, a.
c **1425** WYNTOUN *Cron.* II. ix. 8 Ane honest man and of gud fame. ? *a* **1530** *Peebles to Play* 51 Ane young man . . With ane bow and ane bolt. **1535** STEWART *Cron. Scotl.* I. 3 Ane profound clerk is he. **1578** *Ps.* li. in *Sc. Poems 16th C.* II. 120 Ane sweit humble hert. **1588** A. KING *Canisius' Catech.* 124 Sic a ane as makis nocht ane man gods enimie.
4. In mod.Sc. and north dial., the *absolute* form of the numeral one (pron. en, in, i(ə)n, jɪn, jen, jɛn, jæn, jan); the adj. form bef. either vowel or const. being *a*, *ae* (pron. e, ɪ, i(ə), ji, je, jɛ, jæ, ja). One.
c **1620** A. HUME *Orthog. Brit. Tong.* (1865) 33 Ane is a noun of number. **1782** CLUNZEE in BURNS *Wks.* I. 364, I loe nae a laddie but ane. *a* **1796** BURNS *Wks.* (Moxon) 476 Oh, let me in this ae night, This ae, ae, ae night. **1826** J. WILSON *Noct. Ambr.* Wks. 1855 I. 177 At ane and the same time.

ane, obs. form of AWN and of ONE *v.*

-ane, *suffix.* **1.** Occas. Eng. ad. L. *-ānus*, perh. orig. a. Fr. *-ain*; used, chiefly for sake of distinction, in words that have a parallel form in *-an*, as *germane*, *humane*, *urbane*, also in *mundane*.
2. *Chemical formative.* †**a.** Arbitrary ending proposed by Davy for names of *monochlorides*, now obsolete. (See Watts *Dict. Chem.* IV. 121.)
b. *Organic Chem.* In the systematic nomenclature proposed by Hofmann 1866, the formative of the names of the saturated hydrocarbons of composition C_nH_{2n+2}, also called *paraffines*; as *Methane* CH_4 (formerly *Methyl hydride*), *Ethane* C_2H_6, *Propane* C_3H_8, *Butane* or *Quartane* C_4H_{10}, *Pentane* C_5H_{12}, *Hexane* C_6H_{14}, etc. [The formation is purely imitative; the Greek feminine patronymic endings *-ene, -ine, -one*, (-ήνη, -ίνη, -ώνη) were already in partial use in naming hydrocarbon derivatives. Hofmann proposed the adoption of the entire vowel series *-ane, -ene, -ine, -one, -une*, and the strict application of these to hydrocarbons of the types C_nH_{2n+2}, C_nH_{2n}, C_nH_{2n-2}, C_nH_{2n-4}, C_nH_{2n-6}, or their analogues, respectively. So far as concerns the first three members this has been generally adopted.]

†**aneabil**, *a. Sc. Obs. rare*[−1]. [f. ANE one + -ABLE, here used somewhat indefinitely as an adj. formative; cf. *double, treble.*] Single, unmarried.
1609 SKENE *Reg. Maj.* 30 Ane aneabil or singill woman.

aneal, obs. form of ANELE, ANHELE, ANNEAL.

aneanst, obs. form of *anenst*, ANENT.

aneantize, adapted spelling of the earlier *anentise*, ANIENTISE *v. Obs.*, to reduce to nothing, conformed to mod.Fr. *anéantir*.

anear (əˈnɪə(r)), *adv.* and *prep.* [cf. *anew*, *afar*.]
A. *adv.*
1. Nearly, well-nigh, almost, to a nearness.
1608 SHAKS. *Per.* III. Introd. 51 The lady shrieks, & well a-near Does fall in travail with her fear. **1669** WORLIDGE *Syst. Agric.* (1681) 241 They know anear in what parts they [water-fowl] most usually frequent. **1850** MRS. BROWNING *Poems* II. 10 Your wisdom may declare That womanhood is proved the best By golden brooch . . Yet is it proved, and was of old, Anear as well . . By truth, or by despair.
2. Near, as opposed to *afar*.
1798 COLERIDGE *Anc. Mar.* V. v, And soon I heard a roaring wind, It did not come anear. **1805** SCOTT *Last Minstr.* v. xxxi, Now seems it far, and now a-near. **1870** MORRIS *Earth. Par.* I. I. 283 And timidly the women drew anear.
B. *prep.* Near, near to.
a **1732** ATTERBURY *Lett.* I. (T.) To fright the clergy . . from coming anear me. **1850** BLACKIE *Æschylus* I. 117 While anear thee Pours this sorrow-stricken maid The pure libation. **1879** LONG *Æneid* IX. 889 Anear some river's bank.

anear (əˈnɪə(r)), *v. arch.* Also 6 anere, -eer, -erre, 7 annear. [f. A- *pref.* II + NEAR *v.*]
†**1.** *intr.* **a.** To draw near, or approach *to*. *Obs.*
1534 *State Papers, Henry VIII*, II. 200 Diverse husbandmen aneryth un to hym. **1583** STANYHURST *Aeneis* II. (Arb.) 54 Such troups as neauer too citty Troian aneered.
†**b.** To be near or close *to*. *Obs.*
1583 STANYHURST *Aeneis* II. (Arb.) 66 A tumb to Troytowne and mouldy tempil aneereth.
2. *trans.* To approach, come or be near to; to near. *arch.*
1586 J. HOOKER *Giraldus's Hist. Irel.* in *Holinsh.* II. 94/2 If they durst anerre the coast. *a* **1687** P. WALSH quoted in *Q. Rev.* XXXVIII. 543 Never has any other nation . . anneared the Milesian race . . in the most unnatural . . destructive feuds. **1850** MRS. BROWNING *Poems* II. 52 The castle . . to-night anears its fall. **1875** MYERS *Poems* 2 Yet not in solitude if Christ anear me.

aneath (əˈniːθ, *Sc.* əˈnɛθ), *prep.*[1] [f. A *prep.*[1] + NEATH, for *beneath*; cf. *afore*, *ahind*, the northern forms of *before*, *behind*.] Beneath.
c **1801** H. MACNEILL *Poems* (1844) 116 Aneath thy sheltering wing I flee. **1813** HOGG *Queen's Wake* 175 Ane lovlye land anethe her laye. **1825** J. WILSON *Noct. Ambr.* I. 6 Aneath the marbled roof of clouds.

anecdotage (ˈænɪkdəʊtɪdʒ). [f. ANECDOTE *sb.* + -AGE.]
1. Anecdotes collectively; anecdotic literature.
1823 DE QUINCEY in *Lond. Mag.* Mar. (*title*) Anecdotage. **1832–4** —— *Cæsars* Wks. 1862. 23 So minute and curious a collector of anecdotage as Suetonius. **1876** J. DAVIES in *Academy* 25 Nov. 515 His biography . . a repertory of anecdotage to the critics.
2. *Humorously* (attributed to John Wilkes; suggested by *age* and *dotage*), garrulous old age.
1835 *Blackw. Mag.* XXXVII. 112 The disgusting perversions of their anile anecdotage. **1870** DISRAELI *Lothair* xxviii. 124 When a man fell into his anecdotage it was a sign for him to retire from the world. **1880** M. COLLINS *Th. in Gard.* I. 151 A man who has reached his anecdotage—to use a pun which Disraeli the younger has conveyed from Wilkes.

anecdotal (ˈænɪkdəʊtəl), *a.* [f. ANECDOTE *sb.* + -AL[1].] **a.** Of, pertaining to, or consisting of, anecdotes.
1836 *Chamb. Jrnl.* 2 Apr. 74 A few anecdotal notices, if they may so be termed, respecting such animals. **1840** *Blackw. Mag.* XLVIII. 123 A certain sense of anecdotal vivacity. **1882** *Ch. Times* 28 Jan. 36 The weakest part of the work . . has been the anecdotal portion.
b. In extended use in *Art* (cf. ANECDOTE *sb.* 2 c).
1933 C. H. C. BAKER *Brit. Painting* xxii. 219 Forbes' *Fish Sale*—a vivid out-of-door piece, is his least anecdotal picture. **1937** S. SITWELL *Narr. Pictures* i. 3 These [paintings] are as full of anecdotal detail as any painting by Hogarth.

anecdotalism (ænɪkˈdəʊtəlɪz(ə)m). [f. ANECDOTAL *a.* + -ISM.] A propensity for telling anecdotes. Also *spec.* in *Art*.
1901 E. H. FOWLER *World & Winstow* xiii. 320 'Admiral Kingston tells a great many very prosy stories,' continued Major Trayne. 'Anecdotalism is his besetting sin.' **1928** *Sunday Express* 6 May 12/2 The Royal Academy . . is full of vitality, experiment, and imaginative creativeness. There is

hardly a trace of sickly sentimentalism and sugary anecdotalism. **1961** W. H. SALTER *Zoar* iii. 28 Defects such as these..brought on them the stigma of 'anecdotalism'.

So **anec'dotalist**, a person given to or adept in telling anecdotes.

1911 *Daily News* 25 Aug. 7/1 Maupassant as well as Mr. Kipling was included by Mr. Moore among the anecdotalists. **1960** *Spectator* 12 Feb. 228 He is a superb anecdotalist, endowed with vast self-confidence and the gift of imagery ten times the size of life.

anecdotard (ænɪk'dəʊtəd). *rare.* [Jocular blend of ANECDOTE and DOTARD *sb.*] A dotard given to recounting anecdotes. Cf. ANECDOTAGE 2.

1894 *World* 14 Mar. 24/2 The anecdotard..is busying himself in smoking-rooms and other centres of 'the latest intelligence'. **1937** KIPLING *Something of Myself* v. 145 Americans are too much anecdotards; the French too much orators for this light-handed game.

anecdo'tarian. ? *Obs.* [f. next + -ARIAN; cf. *abecedarian.*] One who publishes anecdotes.

a **1733** NORTH *Examen* III. viii. ¶79. 644 Our ordinary Anecdotarians make use of Libels but do not declaredly transcribe and ingraft them into their Text.

anecdote ('ænɪkdəʊt), *sb.* [a. Fr. *anecdote*, or ad. its source, med.L. *anecdota* (see sense 1), a. Gr. ἀνέκδοτα things unpublished, f. ἀν priv. + ἔκδοτ-ος published, f. ἐκ-διδόναι to give out, publish: applied by Procopius to his 'Unpublished Memoirs' of the Emperor Justinian, which consisted chiefly of tales of the private life of the court; whence the application of the name to short stories or particulars.]

1. *pl.* Secret, private, or hitherto unpublished narratives or details of history. (At first, and now again occas. used in L. form *anecdota* (ə'nɛkdətə).)

1676 MARVELL *Mr. Smirke* Wks. 1875 IV. 71 A man.. might make a pleasant story of the *anecdota* of that meeting. **1686** F. SPENCE (*title*) Anecdotes of Florence, or the secret History of the House of Medicis [a translation of Varillas' *Anecdotes de Florence*]. **1727** SWIFT *Gulliver* III. viii. 230 Those who pretend to write anecdotes, or secret history. **1727-51** CHAMBERS *Cycl.*, *Anecdotes, Anecdota*, a term used by some authors, for the titles of Secret Histories; that is, of such as relate the secret affairs and transactions of princes; speaking with too much freedom, or too much sincerity, of the manner and conduct of persons in authority, to allow of their being made public. **1769** BURKE *State Nat.* Wks. II. 157 Professing even industriously, in this publick matter, to avoid anecdotes, I say nothing of those famous reconciliations and quarrels which weakened the body. **1882** *Pall Mall G.* 23 Oct. 5 To dispel by means of 'anecdota' the common impression that Mdme. de Staël and her mother did not get on very well together.

2. a. The narrative of a detached incident, or of a single event, told as being in itself interesting or striking. (*At first*, an item of gossip.)

1761 YORKE in Ellis *Orig. Lett.* II. 483 IV. 429 Monsieur Coccei will tell you all the anecdotes of London better than I can. **1769** *Junius Lett.* xxix. 133 The anecdote was referred to, merely to show how ready a man, etc. **1789** BOSWELL *Lett.* (1857) 311 It [life of Johnson] will certainly be..full of literary and characteristical anecdotes (which word, by the way, Johnson always condemned, as used in the sense that the French, and we from them, use it, as signifying particulars). **1806** MAR. EDGEWORTH *Forester* (1832) 160 Telling little anecdotes to his disadvantage. **1832** HT. MARTINEAU *Demerara* i. 12 He told some anecdotes of Alfred's childhood. *Mod.* An after-dinner anecdote.

b. *collect.*

1826 DISRAELI *Viv. Grey* III. ii. 95 A companion who knew everything, everyone, full of wit and anecdote.

c. spec. in *Art*, used of a painting, etc., that depicts a small incident.

1933 C. H. C. BAKER *Brit. Painting* xviii. 188 His [*sc.* Mulready's] *Last In*..is typical of his concessions to anecdote, at the expense of design and unity of rhythmic control. **1937** S. SITWELL *Narr. Pictures* ii. 28 Truth to life ..he [*sc.* Hogarth] achieved..by every detail in his anecdote, by the aptness of every small incident that he depicted. *Ibid.* 29 The utmost detail of anecdote has been lavished upon every incident depicted.

3. *Comb.*, as ***anecdote-book, -loving***; **anecdote-monger**, a retailer of anecdotes.

1862 BURTON *Bk.-hunter* II. 125 Irish bulls.. manufactured for the..anecdote-books betray their artificial origin. **1836** *Edin. Rev.* LXIII. 364 By no means so explanatory as his anecdote-loving master could desire. **1807** *Ibid.* X. 43 The large tribe of anecdote-mongers. **1850** MAURICE *Mor. Philos.* 164 The gossiping anecdote-mongers of later Greece.

anecdote ('ænɪkdəʊt), *v. rare.* [f. the sb.] **a.** *intr.* To tell anecdotes. **b.** *trans.* To tell anecdotes to; to entertain with anecdotes; also, to make (a person) the subject of an anecdote or anecdotes.

1786 H. MORE *Let.* in W. Roberts *Mem. of H.M.* (1834) II. ii. 34, I left Mrs. Boscawen to anecdote with them. **1867** HOWELLS *Ital. Journ.* 170 It is a story they tell in Rome, where everybody is anecdoted. **1900** *Academy* 28 Apr. 347/2 His wish not to be interviewed, anecdoted, or otherwise disturbed.

anecdotic (ænɪk'dɒtɪk), *a.* [f. ANECDOTE *sb.* + -IC; cf. mod.Fr. *anecdotique.*]

1. a. Of, pertaining to, or consisting of anecdotes.

1786 'P. PINDAR' *Poet. Ep. to Boswell* 18 Amidst the anecdotic mine, Thou labour'st hard to bid thy Hero shine. **1816** H. C. ROBINSON *Diary* II. 10 His conversation is only intelligent and anecdotic and gentlemanly. **1829** CARLYLE *Misc.* II. 6 The peculiar talent of the French in all.. anecdotic departments. **1856** LEVER *Martins of Cro' M.* 237 That taste for story-telling—that anecdotic habit is quite vulgar.

b. spec. in *Art.*

1933 C. H. C. BAKER *Brit. Painting* xxi. 208 We notice.. a steady revulsion from anecdotic 'period' pictures. The pity is that so habitual had become the yearning to tell a story that the anecdotic spirit persisted even in the modern realistic genre of the '70's.

2. Addicted to anecdote, ready to tell stories.

1870 HAWTHORNE *Eng. Note-bks.* (1879) II. 67 The Captain is..very talkative and anecdotic. **1881** *Athenæum* 5 Feb. 192 Dr. Stevens, however, is not an anecdotic biographer.

anec'dotical, *a.* [f. as prec. + -ICAL.]

1. Of the nature of *anecdota* or anecdotes.

a **1744** BOLINGBROKE *To Pope* (L.) Particular anecdotical traditions, whose authority is unknown or suspicious. **1850** MERIVALE *Rom. Emp.* IV. xxxvii. 267 The anecdotical gossip of Suetonius. **1877** *Daily News* 26 Dec. 3/3 The anecdotical and more secret parts of the late events.

2. Gossiping; story-telling.

a **1744** POPE *Wks.* 1751 VIII. 212 (Jod.) If the graver historians hereafter shall be silent of this year's events, the amorous and anecdotical may make posterity some amends. **1861** DICKENS *Lett.* (1880) II. 143 He was talkative, anecdotical, and droll.

anec'dotically, *adv.* [f. prec. + -LY[2].] In an anecdotic manner; with use of anecdotes.

1836 *New Monthly Mag.* XLVII. 416 They may be thrown in *anecdotically*, or conundrum-wise. **1871** *Lit. World* 6 Jan. 6 They do not talk epigrammatically enough for one kind of reporters, nor anecdotically..enough for another.

anecdotist ('ænɪkdəʊtɪst, ə'nɛkdətɪst). [f. ANECDOTE *sb.* + -IST.] A relater of anecdotes or *anecdota*.

1837 CARLYLE *Diamond Neckl.* xvi, To the astonishment of..all Quidnuncs, Journalists, Anecdotists, Satirists. **1850** MERIVALE *Rom. Emp.* (1865) I. viii. 332 A mere invention of the Roman anecdotists. **1855** KINGSLEY *Glaucus* 161 Waterton and Jesse..are rather anecdotists than systematic or scientific enquirers.

anecdotive ('ænɪkdəʊtɪv), *a. rare*[−1]. [irreg. f. as prec. + -IVE; cf. *talkative.*] = ANECDOTIC 2.

1881 M. LEWIS *2 Pretty Girls* II. 174 Mr. Palmer grew very anecdotive.

†**anecdo'tographer.** *Obs. rare*[−1]. [f. med.L. *anecdot-a* (see ANECDOTE *sb.*), after *biographer.*] One who publishes *anecdota* or secret histories.

1686 F. SPENCE *Anecd. Florence* Ded., The ushering in of such are the prerogative of the Anecdoto-grapher.

anechoic (ænɛ'kəʊɪk), *a.* [AN- 10 + ECHO *sb.* + -IC.] Free from echo.

1948 *Electronics* Nov. 106/1 The usual method of obtaining the sound field by the use of free-field or anechoic chambers was felt to be too expensive. **1959** *Engineering* CLXXXVIII. 65 (*title*) Anechoic chamber for noise research.

†**a'nedged**, *ppl. a. Obs. rare*[−1]. [f. phrase *an edge* 'on edge' (see AN *prep.*) + -ED.] Set on edge.

1579 LANGHAM *Gard. Health* (1633) 510 Teethach, and anedged, chew it [purslaine].

anefald, anefauld, early forms of AFALD.

anehede, obs. north. f. ONEHEAD, -HOOD, unity.

c **1340** HAMPOLE *Prose Treat.* 13 The Anehede of Godd with mannis saule. *a* **1400** *Rel. Pieces Thornt. MS.* 45 It behouede nede þat anehede and manyhede bathe ware in Godd.

anelace (anelate in Blount), var. ANLACE.

anele (ə'ni:l), *v. arch.* Forms: 4 aneli, -ye, 4-6 aneyle, 5 enele, 6 aneil, -eele, anneyle, -el, 6-7 aneal(e, anneal, 4- anele. [orig. *aneli-en*, f. AN- *pref.* 1 on + *eli-en* to oil, f. OE. *ele, æle*, oil:—**oli*, ad. L. *oleum.* Cf. ANOIL.]

1. To anoint (chiefly as a religious rite).

c **1315** SHOREHAM 44 Me schel the mannes lenden anelye. **1642** JER. TAYLOR *Episcop.* (1647) 205 Dispensation..*vt baptizatos Vnguant*, to aneale baptized people. **1649** —— *Gt. Exemp.* xv. §11 Mary Magdalen thought it not good enough to anneal his sacred feet. **1875** FARRAR *Sil. & Voices* x. 171 The love of Mary..led her to..anele with precious spikenard her Saviour's feet.

2. *spec.* To give the last anointing or extreme unction to the dying. (See ANELING.)

1303 R. BRUNNE *Handl. Synne* 11269 Many..seye, Anele hem nat but þey shulde deye. **1483** CAXTON *Gold. Leg.* 337/4 He dyde doo calle his Abbot and dyd hym to be eneled or enoynted. **1494** FABYAN VII. 318 Chyldren were crystened ..& men houselyd & anelyd. **1530** PALSGR. 431/1, I aneele a sicke man..*Jenhuylle.* **1558** BP. WATSON *7 Sacr.* xxx. 193 Priestes or Priest..to praye ouer you, and to aneyle you. **1853** ROCK *Ch. of Fathers* III. II. 79 For aneling those whose sickness threatened them with speedy death.

anele, obs. form of ANNEAL, ANHELE.

anelectric (ænɪ'lɛktrɪk), *a.* and *sb.* [f. AN- *pref.* 10 + ELECTRIC.]

A. *adj.* †**a.** Non-electric (*obs.*). **b.** Parting rapidly with any electricity developed in it.

1830 *Brewster's Cycl.* II. 69/2 *Anelectric*, a word employed by the French to denote those bodies that are non-conductors of Electricity. **1853** MAYNE *Exp. Lex.*, *Anelectric*, having no electric properties.

B. *sb.* †**a.** A non-electric body; a substance which does not become electric when rubbed (*obs.*). **b.** A body, such as a metal, which being a good conductor parts rapidly with electricity.

1863 ATKINSON *Ganot's Physics* (ed. 3) 585 Bodies were formerly divided into..those which become electrical by friction, and anelectrics, or those which do not possess this property.

anelectrode (ænɪ'lɛktrəʊd). [f. ἀνά up + ELECTRODE (f. ἤλεκτρον amber, taken as = 'electricity' + ὁδός way, path.] The positive pole of a galvanic battery; the point at which the electric current enters the fluid to be electrolyzed.

1864 WEBSTER cites FARADAY.

anelectrotonic (ænɪ,lɛktrəʊ'tɒnɪk), *a. Phys.* [f. next. + -IC.] Of or pertaining to anelectrotonus.

1877 ATKINSON *Ganot's Physics* (ed. 7) §804 The excitability of the nerve is diminished in the anelectrotonic region. **1878** FOSTER *Phys.* I. ii. 61 The nerve is said to be in an anelectrotonic condition.

‖**anelectrotonus** (,ænɪlɛk'trɒtənəs). *Phys.* [mod. f. ἀν = ἀνά up + ἤλεκτρον amber (see ELECTRIC) + τόν-ος strain, tension.] A state of depressed irritability produced in a nerve in the vicinity of the positive pole of an electric current which traverses it.

1873 A. FLINT *Phys. Man* iii. 116 Near the anode, the excitability of the nerve is diminished, and this condition has been called anelectro[to]nus. **1878** FOSTER *Phys.* I. ii. §2. 61 The changes in the region of the anode are spoken of as anelectrotonus.

a'neled, *ppl. a.* [f. ANELE *v.* + -ED.] **a.** Anointed; **b.** *spec.* Having received extreme unction.

1557 NORTH *Diall of Princes* (1568) 12a, The goodlye Faustina in 4 daies dyed..of a burnynge feuer, and so annealed was caried to Rome. **1558** BP. WATSON *7 Sacr.* xxx. 191 Christ inwardly worketh the inuisible grace..in the soule of the party aneyled. [**1602** SHAKS. *Haml.* I. v. 77 Vnhouzzled, disappointed, vnnaneld.]

anelepy, early form of ONELEPY: see ANLEPI.

†**a'neler.** *Obs. rare*[−1]. In 7 **annealer.** [f. ANELE *v.* + -ER[1].] One who anoints, *spec.* who administers extreme unction.

1656 TRAPP *Comm. Matt.* xxv. 9 As if God should say.. Go to your indulgencers, pardon-mongers, annealers.

aneli, -ly, north. forms of ONLY.

a'neling, *vbl. sb. Arch.* For forms see ANELE *v.* [f. ANELE *v.* + -ING[1].] The action of anointing, *usually* as a religious rite; unction; and *spec.* the last anointing or extreme unction of the dying.

1303 R. BRUNNE *Handl. Synne* 11234 þese clerkys kalle hyt oynament, On englys hyt ys aneylyng. *c* **1315** SHOREHAM 40 Sacrament of aneliinge, Nou her ich wolle telle. **1483** CAXTON *Gold. Leg.* 34/1 The last unction or enelyng. **1529** MORE *Comf. agst. Trib.* I. Wks. 1557, 1164/1 Somme that lie adiynge saye full deuoutely..prayers wyth the Prieste at theyr anneylinge. **1558** BP. WATSON *7 Sacr.* xxx. 191 The outwarde sacrament of Aneiling. **1650** JER. TAYLOR *Holy Dying* iv. §9 (1727) 178 It is..an excellent anealing us to burial. **1853** [See ANELE *v.* 2.]

anelytrous (ə'nɛlɪtrəs), *a. Ent.* [f. Gr. ἀνέλυτρος sheathless, f. ἀν- priv. + ἔλυτρον a covering.] Not having the anterior wings converted into elytra or wing-cases as in beetles, but all membranous as in bees, etc.

1847 in CRAIG.

anemious (ə'ni:mɪəs), *a. rare.* [f. Gr. ἀνέμι-ος windy + -OUS.] Of plants: Windy, *i.e.* growing in windy and exposed situations.

1879 in *Syd. Soc. Lex.*

anemne, early form of ANAME *v. Obs.*, to name.

anemochord (ə'nɛməkɔ:d). *rare.* [mod. f. Gr. ἄνεμος wind + χορδή a string (of a lyre, etc.); cf. Fr. *anémocorde*, and *harpsi-chord.*] A species of harpsichord, in which the strings were moved by the wind; an æolian harp.

1801 W. TAYLOR in *Month. Mag.* XII. 423 The Anemochord was invented by John James Schnell.

anemocracy (ænɪ'mɒkrəsɪ). *nonce-wd.* [f. Gr. ἄνεμος wind + -(O)CRACY, Gr. κρατεία rule; cf. *theocracy.*] A government by the wind.

1808 SYD. SMITH *Plymley's Lett.* Wks. 1859 II. 165/1 The miserable and precarious state of an anemocracy, of a people who put their trust in hurricanes, and are governed by wind.

anemogram (ə'nɛməgræm). [f. Gr. ἄνεμος wind + γράμμα what is written; cf. *telegram.*] An automatically-marked record of wind-pressure, a prepared sheet marked by an anemograph.

1875 *Chamb. Jrnl.* No. 133. 7 Self-recording observatories ..from which issue anemograms, barograms, and thermograms. **1881** C. BURTON in *Nature* No. 622. 511 A machine intended for the mechanical reduction of anemograms.

anemograph (əˈnɛməgrɑːf, -æ-). [f. as prec. + -γραφ-ος -writing, -writer; cf. *telegraph.*] An instrument for recording on paper the direction and force of the wind.

1865 *Reader* 7 Oct. 408/1 The Anemograph, by means of which winds..record their own direction and force in the form of a diagram on paper. **1881** W. LEY in *Nature* XXIV. 8 The anemographs of our..inland stations.

anemographic (əˌnɛməʊˈgræfɪk), *a.* [f. prec. + -IC.] Of or pertaining to anemography; produced by an anemograph.

1881 W. LEY in *Nature* XXIV. 8 Comparing anemographic records from stations at our different coasts.

anemography (ænɪˈmɒgrəfɪ). *rare*$^{-0}$. [f. Gr. ἄνεμος wind + -γραφία description; cf. *geography.*]

1. Description of, or a treatise on, the winds. **1755** in JOHNSON.

2. The art of recording the direction and force of the wind.

anemological (əˌnɛməʊˈlɒdʒɪkəl), *a. rare.* [f. next + -ICAL.] Of or pertaining to anemology.

1870 LAUGHTON *Phys. Geogr.* i. 6 A description of the various parts of the world from an anemological point of view.

anemology (ænɪˈmɒlədʒɪ). [f. Gr. ἄνεμος wind + -(O)LOGY.] The doctrine or science of the winds.

1791 E. DARWIN *Bot. Gard.* I. 93 *note,* This imperfect sketch of Anemology.

anemometer (ænɪˈmɒmɪtə(r)). [f. Gr. ἄνεμος wind + -(O)METER; cf. *barometer.*]

1. An instrument for measuring the force of the wind; a wind-gauge.

1727–51 CHAMBERS *Cycl., Anemometer,* a machine wherewith to measure the strength of the wind. **1818** *Art of Preserv. Feet* 36 They act as living..anemometers to ascertain the direction of the wind, especially when it is easterly. **1838** in *Proc. Amer. Phil. Soc.* I. 3 Drawings of a self-registering anemometer. **1860** MAURY *Phys. Geog. Sea* ii. §88 The sea-weed..serves the mariner as a sort of marine anemometer.

2. An apparatus for indicating the wind-pressure in an organ.

1876 HILES *Catech. Organ* viii. (1878) 55 A wind-gauge, or anemometer..is a small curved glass tube into which a little water is poured, and it is then placed in one of the pipe holes on the sound board.

anemometric (əˌnɛməʊˈmɛtrɪk), *a.* [f. ANEMOMETRY + -IC.] Of or pertaining to anemometry.

1881 W. LEY in *Nature* XXIV. 8 The comparison of anemometric records. **1882** *Athenæum* 5 June 703/1 Anemometric variations, and hydrometric alternations.

aˌnemoˈmetrical, *a.* = prec.

1842 PHILLIPS *Rep. Brit. Assoc.* 340 A complete anemometrical register should give..the direction of the wind, and its pressure or velocity. **1865** *Athenæum* No. 1979. 439/2 Anemometrical observations.

anemometrograph (əˌnɛməʊˈmɛtrəgrɑːf, -æ-). [f. ANEMOMETER + -γραφος writer.] = ANEMOGRAPH.

1847 in CRAIG.

anemometry (ænɪˈmɒmɪtrɪ). [f. Gr. ἄνεμος wind + -μετρία: see -METRY.] The measurement of the force or velocity of the wind.

1847 PHILLIPS *Rep. Brit. Assoc.* 340 Anemometry..is a process of recording certain effects of the (horizontal) pressure or movement of the atmosphere. **1881** in *Nature* XXIV. 96 The present state of anemometry.

anemonal (əˈnɛmənəl), *a. rare*$^{-1}$. [irreg. f. Gr. ἀνεμ-ος wind, with ending due perh. to *anemone,* or to assoc. with *diagon-al, phenomen-al, longitudin-al,* etc.] Of or pertaining to the wind.

1851–9 BIRT *Atmosph. Waves* in *Man. Sc. Enq.* 185 The third kind of anemonal movement.

anemone (əˈnɛməniː, *Bot.* L. ænɪˈməʊniː). Also 7 **enemony,** 7–9 **anemony.** [a. L. *anemōnē,* a. Gr. ἀνεμώνη the wind-flower, lit. 'daughter of the wind,' f. ἄνεμ-ος wind + -ώνη fem. patronymic suff. The anglicized *anemony* was common last century.]

1. *Bot.* A genus of plants (N.O. *Ranunculaceæ*) with handsome flowers, widely diffused over the temperate regions of the world, of which one (*A. nemorosa*), called also the Wind-flower, is common in Britain, and several brilliantly-flowered species are cultivated.

1551 TURNER *Herbal.* (1568) 30 Anemone hath the name ..because the floure neuer openeth it selfe, but when the wynde bloweth. **1657** S. PURCHAS *Pol. Flying Ins.* II. xv. 94 Bees gather of these flowers following..In March.. Enemony. **1728** THOMSON *Spring* 533 From the soft wing of vernal breezes shed, Anemonies. **1759** B. STILLINGFLEET in *Misc. Tracts* (1762) 149 Linnæus says, that the wood-anemone blows from the arrival of the swallow. **1763** STUKELY *Palæogr. Sacra* 13 The wild anemone is called pasque flower, from the Paschal solemnity of our Saviour's death. **1873** SYMONDS *Grk. Poets* xii. 403 Scarlet and white anemones are there, some born of Adonis' blood, and some of Aphrodite's tears.

b. *attrib.*

1731 BRADLEY *Gardening* 149 Choice Anemony roots. **1760** MRS. DELANEY *Autobiog.* (1861) III. 598, I have not grounded any part of the anemony pattern.

2. *Zool.* **sea anemone**: (when understood from the subject or context '*sea*' is omitted;) the popular name of various Actinoid Zoophytes, especially of the genera *Actinia, Bunodes,* and *Sagartia.*

1773 *Phil. Trans.* LXIII. 371, I clipped all the limbs of a purple Anemone. **1775** *Ibid.* LXV. 217, I have seen an anemony of a moderate size swallow a smelt at least six inches long. **1855** GOSSE *Mar. Zool.* I. 15 The extensive group known popularly as Sea-anemones or Animal flowers, from the blossom-like appearance of their expanded disks and tentacles, and their gorgeous colours. **1881** H. MOSELEY in *Nature* XXIII. 515 The mouth of the sea-anemony.

anemonic (ænɪˈmɒnɪk), *a. Chem.* [f. prec. + -IC.] Derived from the anemone.

1842 FOWNES *Chem.* 1150 Anemonic acid.

anemonin (əˈnɛmənɪn). *Chem.* [f. as prec. + -IN.] An acrid crystalline substance, obtained from several species of anemone.

1842 FOWNES *Chem.* 1150 Anemonine occurs in *Anemone pulsatilla.* **1863** WATTS *Dict. Chem.* I. 291 By the action of alkalis, anemonin is transformed into anemonic acid.

anemony, see ANEMONE.

anemophilous (ænɪˈmɒfɪləs), *a. Bot.* [f. Gr. ἄνεμος wind + φίλ-ος loving, fond of + -OUS.] Wind-loving; assisted by the wind in fertilization, wind-fertilized.

1874 LUBBOCK *Wild Fl.* i. 9 The pollen is wind-borne, whence they have been termed anemophilous. **1876** DARWIN *Cross-fertil.* x. 405 The amount of pollen produced by anemophilous plants, and the distance to which it is often transported by the wind, are both surprisingly great.

anemophily (ænɪˈmɒfɪlɪ). *Bot.* [f. Gr. ἄνεμος wind + -PHILY.] Pollination with the assistance of the wind.

1883 D'ARCY W. THOMPSON tr. *H. Müller's Fert. Flowers* IV. 591 In a few cases reversion to anemophily has taken place. **1896** G. HENSLOW *How to study Wild Flowers* 105 The flowers are purple..with the usual tufted stigma characteristic of anemophily.

anemoscope (əˈnɛməʊskəʊp). ? *Obs.* [mod. f. Gr. ἄνεμος wind + -σκοπος watching, a watcher; also mod.Fr.] An instrument for showing the direction of the wind, or foretelling a change of weather.

1706 PHILLIPS, *Anemoscope,* a Device invented to foreshew the Change of the Air, or the Shifting of the Wind. **1727–51** CHAMBERS *Cycl.* s.v., Hygroscopes made of cat's gut, etc., proved very good anemoscopes. **1744** PICKERING in *Phil. Trans.* XLIII. 9 The Anemoscope is a Machine four Feet and a Quarter high, consisting of a broad and weighty Pedestal, a Pillar fastened into it and an iron Axis, of about half an Inch Diameter, fastened into the Pillar. Upon this Axis turns a wooden Tube, at the Top of which is placed a Vane. **1812** *Edin. Rev.* XX. 184 This whimsical piece of mechanism, under the name of anemoscope.

anemotropism (əˌnɛməʊˈtrɒpɪz(ə)m). [f. Gr. ἄνεμος wind + TROPISM.] Tropism in response to wind.

1899 W. M. WHEELER in *Archiv f. Entwicklungsmechanik* VIII. 373 This peculiarity [in the flight of Diptera]..is an orientation of the body with respect to the wind. As it appears to be a true tropism I shall call it anemotropism. **1938** J. R. CARPENTER *Ecol. Gloss.* 21 *Anemotropism,* tropic response of organisms to wind and air currents.

anemps, -t, anen, -ce, obs. forms of ANENT.

anencephalic (æˌnɛnsɪˈfælɪk), *a. Phys.* [f. Gr. ἀνεγκέφαλ-ος + -IC.] = ANENCEPHALOUS.

1839–47 TODD *Cycl. Anat. & Phys.* III. 720/2 Anencephalic fœtuses. **1848** SIR J. SIMPSON *Month. Jrnl. Med. Sc.* IX. 241 The anencephalic child born at Dundee. **1960** *New Scientist* 4 Aug. 335/2 Some anencephalic infants do survive briefly after delivery.

anencephaloid (ænɪnˈsɛfəlɔɪd), *a. Phys.* [f. as prec. + -OID, like.] Partially, or tending to be, anencephalous.

1879 in *Syd. Soc. Lex.*

anencephalous (ænɪnˈsɛfələs), *a. Phys.* [mod. f. Gr. ἀνεγκέφαλ-ος in Galen (f. ἀν priv. + ἐγκέφαλος brain, prop. adj. 'within the head,' f. ἐγ = ἐν in + κεφαλή head) + -OUS. Cf. Fr. *anencéphale.*] Brainless; wanting, or bereft of, the brain.

1836–39 TODD *Cycl. Anat. & Phys.* II. 471/2 Congenital malformations, such as acephalous and anencephalous states. **1855** BAIN *Senses & Intell.* I. ii. §20 (1864) 58 The Automatic actions..we have seen to go on in the decapitated or anencephalous animal.

anencephaly (ænɪnˈsɛfəlɪ). *Physiol.* Also (formerly) in mod.L. form **anencephalia.** [ad. mod.L. *anencephalia*; cf. ANENCEPHALOUS *a.*] The condition of being anencephalous.

1832 tr. G. BRESCHET in *Meckel's Man. Anatomy* II. 495 The following terms have been proposed..anencephalia, absence of the encephalon. **1835–36** TODD *Cycl. Anat.* I. 744/1 *False acephalia* and *anencephalia.* **1889** in *Cent. Dict.* **1954** *New Biol.* XVII. 115 Anencephaly is a fatal defect rather common in man, in which the skull and skin over the top and back of the head are missing and so is the major part of the brain. **1960** *New Scientist* 4 Aug. 335/2 Among such [congenital] defects is anencephaly, the absence of a large part of the brain.

an-ˈend, *phr. arch.* [see AN *prep.,* and END.]

†1. At last, in the end, in fine. *Obs.*

c **1320** *Cast. Loue* 1224 And hou he hit ouer-com an ende.

2. To the end, right through; straight on, constantly; continuously, consecutively. *arch.*

c **1420** *Pallad. on Husb.* IV. 138 Hele hem light: eke weede hem ofte anende. **1591** SHAKS. *Two Gent.* IV. iv. 66 A slaue, that still an end, turnes me to shame. **1624** QUARLES *Job Milit.* (1717) 181 Some lag, whilst others gallop on before; All go an-end, some faster, and some slower. **1748** RICHARDSON *Clarissa* VII. 220 [He] would ride an hundred miles an end to enjoy it. **1785** MRS. THRALE in *Johnsoniana* (1845) I. 75 He would follow the hounds fifty miles an end.

†3. *most an end*: almost uninterruptedly, almost always, mostly, for the most part. *Obs.*

1570–87 HOLINSHED *Scot. Chron.* (1806) II. 257 An armie ..which lay must an end at Douglasse. **1658** J. R. *Mouffet's Theat. Ins.* 1074 In Europe they are most an end black ones. **1678** BUNYAN *Pilgr.* II. 115 Knew him! I was a great Companion of his, I was with him most an end. **1691** *Clandest. Marr.* in *Harl. Misc.* I. 372 But, most an end, they are not ministers of parishes, but indigent curates.

4. On end, in an upright position. *arch.*

1593 SHAKS *2 Hen. VI,* III. ii. 318 Mine haire be fixt an end, as one distract. **1703** MOXON *Mech. Exerc.* 149 The whole number of Boards are set an end. **1817** COLERIDGE *Zapolya* IV. i, His steed, which proudly rears an-end. *c* **1850** *Rudim. Nav.* (Weale) 92 The topmasts are said to be an-end when they are hoisted up to their usual stations.

5. In the direction of the length; directly ahead. Chiefly *Naut.*

1601 DEACON & WALKER *Spirits & Diuels* 68 You must not be haled hedlong an end with an ineuterate opinion. **1769** FALCONER *Dict. Marine* (1789), *Avoir vent de bout,* to have the wind right an-end, or a-head. **1801** ADML. HYDE PARKER *Let.* 15 Apr. in *Ann. Reg. 1801* (1802) Chron. 82/1 They were riding with two cables an end. **1867** SMYTH *Sailor's Word-bk.* s.v., To strike a spar or plank *an-end* is to drive it in the direction of its length. *Ibid., Every rope an end,* the order to coil down the running rigging, or braces or bowlines, after tacking, or other evolution. Also, the order, when about to perform an evolution, to see that every rope is clear for running.

anent (əˈnɛnt), *prep.* and *adv.* Forms: α. 1 **on efen, on efn, on emn,** 2–3 **onefent, oneuent,** 2–4 **onont,** 3 **onond,** 3–5 **anont,** 4 **anen,** 4– **anent.** β. with *-e*: ? 2–3 **anonde, ononde,** 3 **onnente,** 4 **anende,** 5–6 **-ente.** γ. with *-es, -s*: 2 **anundes,** 4 **anendez, anemptes, -emtis, -entys, -yntes, enence, onence,** 4–5 **anentes, -ens, -ence(s,** 4–6 **-entis,** 5 **aneentes, anentz, -emps,** 5–6 **-endes.** δ. with *-t*: 4 **anentist, anenist,** 4– **-enst,** 5 **-emste, -enste,** 5–6 **annenst,** 5–6 **anempst,** 6 **annempst, aneinst, enenst, anendest.** [The form-history of this wd. presents several points not fully explained; the primitive form is the OE. phrase *on efen, on efn, on emn,* with the dative = 'on even (ground) with, on a level with,' whence later *side by side with, beside, face to face with, opposite, against, towards, in view of,* etc.; cogn. w. OS. *an eban,* MHG. *eneben, neben,* and (with phonetic *-t*) *nebent.* In Eng. also a final *-t* had been developed by 1200, interchanging with *-d,* perhaps by form-assoc. with some other word. At the same time this extended form occurs with final *-e* and *-es,* after datival and genitival words like *on-bute(n, on-ȝeanes.* Following the latter class also, the final *-s* became in 14th c. *-st,* giving *anentist, anentst, anenst,* as the midl. form, in literary use in 17th c., and still dialectal. The north preserved the earlier *anent,* still common in north. dial., and in literary and legal Scotch, whence not unfrequent in literary Eng. during the present century. The early form *anende* may have been influenced by the prec. phr. AN-END; *anont, anond(e,* are not explained. The development of meaning is largely parallel to that of *again, against.*]

A. *prep.*

I. In line or company with.

†1. In a line with, side by side with, in company with, beside. *Obs.* or *dial.*

a **800** *Beowulf* 2903 Him on efn liȝeð ealdorȝewinna. *a* **1000** *Byrht* 181 þá on emn hyra freán feorh ȝesealdon. [**1883** EASTHER *Dial. Huddersfield* 4 A cricket-ball in a line with the wicket is anent it.]

†2. On a level with in position, rank, or value; equal to, on a par with. *Obs.* or *dial.*

1220 *Hali Meid.* 9 The poure...þat nabbeð hwerwið buggen ham brudgume onont ham. *c* **1230** *Wohunge of ure Lord* in *Cott. Hom.* 285 ȝif ich michte a þusandfald ȝiue þe me seluen, nere hit nowt onont te þat ȝef þe seluen for me. [**1883** EASTHER *Dial. Huddersf.* 4 A lass striving to rival a lady in the fashion dresses anent her.]

†3. In the company of, with, among, beside, by (L. *apud,* Fr. *chez,* Ger. *neben*). *Obs.* or *dial.*

1382 WYCLIF *Gen.* xxxi. 32 Anentist [**1388** at] whom euer thow fyndist the goddis, be he slaw. **1382** —— *Gal.* i. 18, I cam to Jerusalem, for to se Petre, and dwellide anentis [**1388** with] him fifteene dayes. **1387** TREVISA *Higden* Rolls Ser. VII. 107 Gretter enence þe kyng [*apud regem*]. **1432–50** tr.

Higden (1865) I. 37 þer were viij. maneres to calcle yeres; iij. anendes men of Ebrewe, thre anendes the Grekes, etc. [**1883** EASTHER *Dial. Huddersf.* 4 When one man works in company with another, he works anent him.]

†**4.** With (figuratively), according to the way or manner of (L. *apud*). *Obs.*

1382 WYCLIF *Mark* x. 27 Anentis men it is impossible, but not anemptis God; for all thingis ben possible anemptis God. *c* **1449** PECOCK *Repr.* I. xii. 63 Accepcioun of persoones is not anentis God.

II. In front of.

†**5.** Before the face of, in the sight or presence of (L. *coram*). *Obs. rare.*

1382 WYCLIF *Gen.* xii. 15 The princis..preyseden hir anentys hym. —— *1 Cor.* vi. 6 A brother with brothir stryueth in dome, and that anentis vnfeithful men.

†**6.** In the mental eyes or sight of; in the consideration, opinion, or reckoning of; before. *Obs.*

1340 HAMPOLE *Pr. Consc.* 1353 Worldes wysdome.. Onence God es bot foly. **1382** WYCLIF *Prov.* iii. 7 Ne be thou wis anent thiself. **1469** MARG. PASTON in *Lett.* 601 II. 340 And a nemps God, ye arn as gretly bownd to her as ye were maried. **1483** CAXTON *Gold. Leg.* 280/1 Thou haste founde grace anenste oure lord Jhesu Cryst.

III. Facing, against, towards.

7. Of position: fronting, opposite, over against, close against, close to. *arch.* or *dial.*

In this sense many northern dialects have now *fore-nent*.

c **1325** *E.E. Allit. Poems* A. 1135 A wounde ful wyde..Anende hys hert. **1366** MAUNDEV. vii. 80 Anen that Vale of Josaphathe..is the Chirche of seynt Stevene. **1450** MYRC 1961 Bere thyn ost a-nont thy breste. **1513–75** *Diurn. Occurr.* 164 Wardane of the eist Merchis anentis Ingland. **1610** HOLLAND *Camden's Brit.* I. 542 The shelves or barres of sand be every where anenst the land. **1857** E. WAUGH *Lanc. Life* 201 O'er anent this biggin. **1864** HEAVYSEGE *Dark Huntsm.* 7 The huntsman..Anent me a moment, tall, tarried behind.

†**8.** Of motion: against, towards. *Obs.*

1340 HAMPOLE *Pr. Consc.* 5130 He sal come doun..Even onence [*v.r.* ageyns] þe mount of Olyvet. **1366** MAUNDEV. xxix. 298 Wylde Bestes..that slen and devouren alle that comen aneyntes hem. **1375** BARBOUR *Bruce* XIX. 512 Tharfor thair ost but mar abaid Buskyt, and ewyn anent thaim raid. **1587** *Misfort. Arthur* III. iv. in Hazl. *Dodsl.* IV. 313 My slender bark shall creep anenst the shore.

†**9.** Towards (expressing the bearing of actions, etc.: L. *erga*). *Obs.*

c **1200** *Pater N.* in *Lamb. Hom.* 55 Uwilc mon hes undernim, to halden wel anundes him. *c* **1320** *Seuyn Sages* (W.) 2871 Thou wirkis to thi reproue, Onence thi son that thou sold loue. **1417** HEN. V. in Ellis *Orig. Lett.* III. 26 I. 62 How Duc Johan..governeth him anenst us. **1470** HARDING *Chron.* clxx, Anentes Kyng Bruys to execute his treason. **1513** BRADSHAW *St. Werburge* (1848) 100 Why suffer ye suche wyckednes done for to be Anendes our felawe? **1525** *State Papers, Hen. VIII*, VI. 457 Anenst Whom that loue was engendyrd in his hert when ye wer to gedyr.

†**10.** In respect of, as regards, as to (limiting or confining the bearing of a statement: L. *quoad*). *Obs.*

c **1230** *Wohunge of ure Lord* in *Cott. Hom.* 273 Onont ti monhad born þu wes of Marie. *c* **1230** *Ancr. R.* 164 Auh hit, anonde [*v.r.* onefent] meidelure, mei leosen his holinesse. *c* **1449** PECOCK *Repr.* Prol. 1 Correccioun..longith oonli to the ouerer anentis his netherer. **1579** *Wardrobe Warr.* in Nichol. *Prog. Q. Eliz.* II. 297 These our lettres..shall be your sufficient warraunte and dischardge in this behalf annempst us, our heires and successors.

†**b.** In this sense strengthened with *as*. *Obs.*

c **1320** *Cast. Loue* 1076 þu noldest holden hem as a-nont þe. *c* **1380** WYCLIF *Sel. Wks.* (1869) I. 33 Jesus..was an alien as anentis his godhede. **1390** SWINDERBY *Protest.* in Foxe *A. & M.* (1562) I. 538/1 As anences taking away of Temporalities..I say thus. *c* **1410** N. LOVE *Bonavent. Mirr.* (Gibbs MS.) xviii. 46 As anempst sothen deth, hit is spedeful for many men for to haue suche deth. **1463** *Plumpton Corr.* 7 As anent Scatergood I hafe yett taken a longer continuance.

11. In respect or reference to, respecting, regarding, concerning, about. (Common in Scotch law phraseology, and affected by many English writers.)

c **1325** *E.E. Allit. Poems* A. 696 Anende ryȝtwys men, ȝet saytȝ a gome Dauid in sauter. *c* **1380** *Sir Ferumb.* 5877 God for-beode þat y anentes þilke neode Any-þyng sayde a-gayne. **1549** *Compl. Scotl.* 9 He vas speikand victht hym self anent his auen byssynes. **1609** C. BUTLER *Fem. Mon.* i. (1623) 2 Anent the age of Bees there are divers opinions. **1723** WODROW *Corr.* (1843) III. 43 The process at Glasgow anent Mr. Hervey. **1820** SCOTT *Abbot* xvii. 132 Nor is it worth while to vex oneself anent what cannot be mended. **1845** MIALL *Nonconf.* V. 8 The order anent the surplice. **1875** HELPS *Anim. & Masters* iii. 63, I do not like to make any violent assertion anent the sayings of philosophers.

†**B.** *adv.* (obj. understood). Opposite. *Obs.* or *dial.*

1520 WHITTINTON *Vulgar.* (1527) 16 b, Upon the other syde anendest be fysshemongers. **1837** R. NICOLL *Poems* 82 Anent was sair-toiled father's chair. **1863** MRS. TOOGOOD *Yorksh. Dial.*, All yon meadows ower anent belong to grandfather.

anenterous (æ'nɛntərəs), *a. Zool.* [mod. f. Gr. ἀν priv. + ἔντερα bowels + -OUS. The name *Anentera*, mod.L., was given by Ehrenberg to certain infusoria having no intestinal canal.] Destitute of an intestine; belonging to the *Anentera*.

1847–9 TODD *Cycl. Anat. & Phys.* IV 4/1 Animal polygastric, anenterous. **1855** OWEN *Comp. Anat.* ii. 24 (L.) Such species have no intestine, no anus, and are said to be anenterous.

anentise, -ish, variant of ANIENTISE *v. Obs.*

anepiploic (æˌnɛpɪ'pləʊɪk), *a. Phys.* [mod. f. Gr. ἀν priv. + ἐπίπλοον EPIPLOON + -IC.] Having no epiploon, or omentum.

1879 in *Syd. Soc. Lex.*

anerd, var. ENHERD *v. Obs.*, to adhere to.

anerithmoscope (ænə'rɪθməskəʊp). [f. Gr. ἀνήριθμ-ος countless (f. ἀν priv. + ἀριθμός number) + -σκοπ-ος observing; cf. *kaleidoscope*.] (See quot.)

1882 *Catal. Electr. Exhib.* 86 Patent Anerithmoscope—a magic lantern for displaying pictorial..advertisements, changing them automatically by means of electricity.

†'**anerly,** *adv. north. Obs.* [Formed on ANE one; the *-er* is not accounted for; but cf. *formerly*, *latterly*, *utterly*; and the compd. ALLENARLY.] Only, alone; merely, only just.

1375 BARBOUR *Bruce* VII. 59 Quhen he saw his lord swa stad, That he wes left swa anerly. *Ibid.* x. 608 Ane place thai fund so braid That thai mycht syt on anerly. *c* **1425** WYNTOUN *Cron.* v. x. 352 Wes in hys begynyg Bot anerly of Brettane Kyng. *a* **1500** *Lancelot* 1476 The strenth of victory ..cummyth not of man, bot anerly Of hyme, the wich haith euery strinth. **1513** DOUGLAS *Æneis* IX. iv. 124 Thy maist reuthfull moder..Quhilk anerlie..Has followit the hir louit child about.

aneroid ('ænərɔɪd), *a.* and *sb.* [a. mod.Fr. *anéroïde*, f. Gr. ἀ priv. + νηρ-ός wet, damp: see -OID.]

A. *adj.* Specifying a barometer, in which the pressure of the air is measured, not by the height of a column of mercury or other fluid which it sustains, but by its action on the elastic lid of a box exhausted of air.

1848 *Mechan. Mag.* 19 Aug. ['Aneroid' does not occur in the description of 'the new French barometer,' but in the index to the volume.] **1849** DENT (*title*) The Construction and Uses of the Aneroid Barometer. **1863** ANSTED *Ionian Isl.* 88 To take with me an aneroid barometer, as I desired to check the various statements..as to the height.

B. *sb.* [Short for 'aneroid barometer.']

1849 DENT in *Athenæum* 27 Jan., The Aneroid of M. Vidi. **1875** BEDFORD *Sailor's Pocket Bk.* iv. (ed. 2) 93 In the aneroid, atmospherical pressure is measured by its effect in altering the shape of a small, hermetically sealed, metallic box. **1879** C. KING in *Cassell's Techn. Educ.* IV. 114/2 The pocket aneroid..resembles a watch in size and appearance.

b. *attrib.*

1859 L. OLIPHANT *China & Japan* I. xii. 225 A precipice 1000 feet high by aneroid measurement.

aneroidograph (ænə'rɔɪdəʊgrɑːf, -æ-). [f. ANEROID *a.* and *sb.* + -O: see -GRAPH.] An instrument for recording the reading of an aneroid barometer (cf. BAROGRAPH).

1918 *Meteorological Gloss.* (*Met. Office*) 30 *Aneroidograph*, a self-recording aneroid. An aneroid-barometer provided with mechanism for recording the variations of pressure of the atmosphere.

anerre, obs. form of ANEAR *v.*

†**an-'erthe,** *advb. phr. Obs.* [See AN- *pref.* 1 and EARTH.]

1. Of motion: To or into the earth.

1297 R. GLOUC. 441 Our Loruerd anerþe com. *Ibid.* 311 Me greyþede þys gode kyng..An broȝte hym vayre anerþe. *c* **1305** *St. Edm.* 594 in *E.E.P.* (1862) 86 þer he was ibroȝt an vrþe, and also ischryned is.

2. Of position: On or in the earth.

a **1300** *Leg. Rood* (1871) 24 An vaire welle Of wan alleþe wateres þat beþ anerþe comeþ. *c* **1305** *St. Kath.* 99 in *E.E.P.* (1862) 92 God almiȝtie deþ an vrþe þolede.

anes, earlier f. ONCE, retained in the north.

anes, var. ANNESSE, *Obs.*, oneness.

‖**anesis** ('ænɪsɪs). [Gr. ἄνεσις remission, vbl. sb. f. ἀνιέναι to send or let back, remit.] The abatement of the symptoms of a disease.

1811 in HOOPER *Med. Dict.*

anesthetic, variant of ANÆSTHETIC.

anet ('ænət). Also 3–6 **anete,** 4–6 **annet(t, ennet.** [a. Fr. *anet*, *aneth*:—L. *anēthum*, a. Gr. ἄνηθον, dial. form of ἄνισον dill, anise; the two carminatives being originally confounded. See ANISE.] The herb Dill (*Anethum graveolens*).

c **1265** in Wright *Voc.* 140 *Anetum*, anete, dile. **1382** WYCLIF *Matt.* xxiii. 23 Woo to ȝou, scribis and Pharisees.. that tithen mente, anete [*v.r.* anese] and comyn. **1398** TREVISA *Barth. De P.R.* XVII. lxxi. (1495) 645 The sede of Ferula is lyke to Annet. **1533** ELYOT *Cast. Helth* (1541) 76 Oyle of camomyll, oyle of anete, and other lyke. **1540** R. WISDOM in Strype *Eccl. Mem.* I. App. cxv. 317 To tyth mint & annett. **1617** MINSHEU, *Anet*; *Vide* Dill. **1736** BAILEY *Househ. Dict.*, *Anet* or Dill, a plant much resembling fennel. **1811** HOOPER *Med. Dict.*, *Anethum*, Fennel, dill, anet.

b. *Comb.* **anetseed,** the seed of Anet or Dill (sometimes confounded with ANISEED).

1549 *Compl. Scotl.* vi. 67 Ennetseidis that consumis the ventositeis of the stomac. **1549** LATIMER 7 *Serm. bef. Edw. VI.* (Arb.) 165 Their doctrine was vnsauery, it was but of Lolions, of decimations of Anets seade, and Cummyn and suche gere. **1571** *Wills & Inv. N. Count.* (1835) II. 363, Ij lb. of annetseedes xvjd.

anethated ('ænɪθeɪtɪd), *ppl. a.* [f. L. *anēthum* dill + -ATE + -ED.] Prepared or mixed with dill.

1879 in *Syd. Soc. Lex.*

anethene ('ænɪθiːn). *Chem.* [f. L. *anēth-um* anise + -ENE.] The most volatile part of the essential oil of dill, fennel, etc.; composition $C_{10}H_{16}$.

1874 FLÜCKIGER & HANB. *Pharmacogr.* 292 A hydrocarbon, to which [Gladstone] gave the name Anethene. **1876** HARLEY *Mat. Med.* 583 Oil of Dill is chiefly composed of a fluid hydro-carbon, anethene, isomeric with oil of turpentine.

†**a'nether, a'nither,** *v. Obs.* [f. A- *pref.* 1 + OE. *niðerian* to lower: see NETHER. Cf. Ger. *erniedrigen*.] To bring down, lower, reduce, humiliate.

a **1121** *O.E. Chron.* (Laud MS.) an. 675 Aniðrod mid Iudas and mid ealle deofle on helle. **1205** LAY. 14861 þus we scullen an ure daȝen: aniðeri [**1250** a-neoþeri] Hengestes laȝen. **1250** *Ibid.* 25235 Aneþered [**1205** iniðered] worþe þe ilke man: þat nele þar to helpe. **1297** R. GLOUC. 217 þoru þys cas þe compaynye aþes half muche aneþered was.

anethes, variant of UNETHES *adv.*, scarcely.

†**a'nethine.** *Obs. rare*⁻¹. [f. L. *anēth-um* anise + -INE.] = ANISE.

1700 SEDLEY *Past. Virg.* Wks. 1722 I. 268 Leaves of the sweet smelling Anethine [L. *bene olentis anethi*].

anethol ('ænɪθɒl). *Chem.* [mod. f. L. *anēth-um* (see ANET) + -OL = *alcohol*.] An essential principle of the oils of anise, fennel, and allied plants; composition $C_{10}H_{12}O$.

1863 WATTS *Dict. Chem.* I. 297 Oil of anise..appears to consist of two distinct oils, one of which solidifies at temperatures below 10°, while the other remains fluid at all temperatures. The former is generally known as *anethol* or *anise-camphor*. **1876** HARLEY *Mat. Med.* 578 Anethol exists in both a fluid and crystalline form.

anetic (ə'nɛtɪk), *a. Med.* [ad. L. *anetic-us*, a. Gr. ἀνετικός fitted to relax, f. ἀνιέναι, see ANESIS.] Assuaging the severity (of a disease), soothing.

1853 in MAYNE *Exp. Lex.*

aneuch, north. form of ENOUGH.

aneuploid ('ænjuːplɔɪd), *a. Biol.* [a. G. (G. Täckholm 1922, in *Acta Horti Berg.* VII. 234), f. AN- 10 + EUPLOID *a.*] Not euploid. Hence as *sb.* So **'aneuˌploidy** [G. *aneuploidie* (Täckholm)], the condition of being aneuploid.

1931 S. H. YARNELL in *Genetics* XVI. 455 (*title*) A study of certain polyploid and aneuploid forms in Fragaria. *Ibid.* 464 The chromosome number falls within the polyploid series and..its appearance is that of an aneuploid type. **1932** C. D. DARLINGTON *Rec. Advances in Cytology* 494 *Aneuploid*, having an uneven multiple of the basic number of chromosomes through purely numerical aberration—therefore an unbalanced polyploid. **1934** WEBSTER Aneuploidy. **1937** *Nature* 28 Aug. 368/2 Three aneuploid species [of the grass *Poa*] have chromosome numbers suggestive of a 9*n* origin. **1939** *Ibid.* 14 Oct. 649/1 The various peculiar arrangements seen in meiosis..in all sorts of species hybrids,..aneuploids, and auto- and allo-polyploids. **1946** *Ibid.* 12 Oct. 520/1 Reduced fertility in autotetraploids depends primarily on irregular chromosome distribution in meiosis, leading to the formation of aneuploid micro- and macrospores and consequently to pollen abortion. **1956** *Ibid.* 25 Feb. 376/2 Males with average litter sizes of nine or more were not examined cytologically. This may result in the loss of small translocations which do not cause lethal aneuploidy of the zygote.

aneurin, -ine (ə'njʊərɪn). *Biochem.* [f. A(NTI- + POLY)NEUR(ITIS + VITAM)IN.] Vitamin B_1; = THIAMIN(E.

1935 B. C. P. JANSEN in *Nature* 16 Feb. 267/2, I propose to call the present vitamin B_1 in the future aneurin... Dr. Donath and I were the first to obtain this vitamin in a crystalline state. **1945** *New Biol.* I. 16 Aneurine (the anti-beri-beri vitamin, B_1)..and riboflavine..are present in appreciable quantities. **1946** *Nature* 31 Aug. 306/1 A conditioned pyridoxine deficiency in rats receiving a diet of high aneurin content.

aneurysm, -ism ('ænjʊrɪz(ə)m). [mod. ad. (in Cotgr. 1611) Gr. ἀνεύρυσμα or ἀνευρυσμός dilatation, f. ἀνευρύνειν to widen out, f. ἀνά up, back + εὐρύν-ειν to widen, f. εὐρύ-ς wide. The spelling with *y* is etymological; but that with *i*, by form-assoc. with the ending *-ism*, is more frequent.]

1. *Path.* A morbid dilatation of an artery, due to disease in the arterial coats, or to a tumour caused by their rupture. Also *attrib.*

1656 RIDGLEY *Pract. Physic* 7 New Aneurisms may be cured, but old not. **1728** in *Phil. Trans.* XXXV. 436 An Aneurysm, without Doubt, is a Tumour arising from some Disorder in an Artery. **1743** tr. *Heister's Surg.* 290 A true Aneurism has always a Pulsation. **1836–39** TODD *Cycl. Anat. & Phys.* 225/1 After which the ligature is to be carried round it [the artery] by means of a blunt aneurism-needle. **1859** CARPENTER *Anim. Phys.* v. (1872) 229 Arteries are liable to a peculiar disease termed Aneurism which consists in a thinning-away or rupture of the tough fibrous coat. **1880** LEGG *Bile* 92 Aneurysm of the hepatic artery.

2. *transf.* and *fig.* An abnormal enlargement.

1880 T. HODGKIN *Italy & Invad.* I. I. iv. 23 The Eastern half of the Empire..had suffered the dangerous aneurism of the Gothic settlement south of the Danube. **1881** TAIT in *Nature* XXV. 92 There is another peculiarity of the Challenger thermometers..at the lower end of each of the two vertical columns there is an aneurism on the tube.

aneurysmal, -ismal (ænjʊˈrɪzməl), *a. Path.* [f. prec. + -AL¹. Also in mod.Fr.] Of, pertaining to, or due to aneurysm; affected with aneurysm.
1757 WARNER in *Phil. Trans.* L. 367 Rules for infallibly distinguishing aneurismal tumors. **1794** HOME *ibid.* LXXXV. 22 The aorta taking on diseases of different kinds, as being ossified, or becoming aneurismal. **1861** RAMADGE *Cur. Consumpt.* 45 Aneurysmal tumours are powerful antagonists to consumption. **1877** ROBERTS *Handbk. Med.* (ed. 3) I. 44 The veins..assume a varicose or aneurismal aspect.

aneurysmatic, -ismatic (ˌænjʊrɪzˈmætɪk), *a. Path. rare.* [f. Gr. ἀνευρύσματ- stem of ἀνεύρυσμα (see ANEURYSM) + -IC; cf. mod.Fr. *aneurysmatique.*] Characterized or affected by aneurysm.
1836 TODD *Cycl. Anat. & Phys.* I. 235/1 An aneurismatic limb. **1839** *Ibid.* II. 590/1 This greater tendency to aneurismatic dilatation.

†**ˌaneuryˈsmatical,** *a. Obs.* = prec.
1753 CHAMBERS *Cycl. Supp.* s.v. *Aorta,* The Aorta is found in divers states..aneurysmatical, polypose, etc. **1761** PULTENEY in *Phil. Trans.* LII. 347 The whole heart might be said to be entirely aneurismatical.

†**aneuˈrysmous, -ismous,** *a. Path. Obs. rare* ⁻¹. [f. ANEURYSM + -OUS.] = ANEURYSMAL.
1728 NICHOLLS in *Phil. Trans.* XXXV. 443 The internal Coat will soon burst, and the external form itself into aneurismous Tumors.

†**aneus,** *sb. pl. Obs.* Also 5 **anewis.** [a. OFr. *aniau,* earlier *anel* (mod.Fr. *anneau*):—L. *ānellus* a ring, prop. 'a little ring,' dim. of *ānulus* (incorrectly spelt *annulus*): see ANNULAR. In OFr. *aniaus* had received the sense of 'chains, fetters,' in which it was introduced into Eng.]
1. Links of a chain; fetters, irons.
1330 R. BRUNNE *Chron.* 278 Þei sent tueye & tueye In aneus for doute, ilk on his hakneye. In kartes oþer were sent with aneus on þer fete. *Ibid.* 167 Now er his aneus wrouht, of siluere wele ouer gilt.
2. Wreaths.
a **1423** JAMES I. *King's Q.* v. ix, A chapellet with mony fresch anewis Sche had upon hir hede.

aˈneusance, var. of ANNUISANCE. *Obs.*

†**an-ˈeven,** *phr. Obs.* [see AN- *pref.* 1 and EVEN. Cf. *a-morwen, a-morrow.*] At eve, in the evening.

anew (əˈnjuː), *adv.* Forms: α. 1 of-niowe, 4–6 of newe, 5– **of new.** β. 4–6 **of the new(e,** 7 **of anew.** γ. 4–6 **on new.** δ. 4 **onew,** 5 **anewe,** 6– **anew.** [*Anew,* earlier *o-new,* prob. for *of new*: cf. *of old,* and see A- *pref.* 3. OE. had *ˈedniwan, ˈedniwe* (with stress on *ed-* which would not give *aˈnew*); also simple adv. *niwan,* 2–3 *neowen, neowe,* 3–4 *newe,* still in compounds *new,* as *new-laid.* For *edniwan* the Rushw. gloss has *of niowe,* and *of newe* is the common form from 14th to 16th c. The occasional *on new* is probably only bad form of *oˈnew.* Cf. also the Fr. equivalents *de nouveau à nouveau,* and *à neuf.*]
1. A second time as a new trial or action, over again, afresh, once more.
α. [*c* **1000** *Ags. Gosp.* John iii. 7 Eow ȝebyraþ þætte ȝe beon acennede edniwan.] *c* **975** *Rushw. ibid.* Bihofaþ iow alle (*nasci*) of-niowe. *c* **1430** LYDG. *Bochas* I. ii. (1544) 5 a, Nimrod..in his errour procedeth forth of new. **1509** BARCLAY *Ship of Fooles* (1570) ¶¶j, It was expedient that of newe some lettered man..shoulde awake and touche the open vices of fooles. **1636** RUTHERFORD *Lett.* 66 (1862) I. 174, I find old sores bleeding of new. **1653** URQUHART *Rabelais* (1859) I. 116 Should take good heart of new. **1865** MᶜLENNAN *Prim. Marriage* viii. 228 The threads of legal history..began to unwind themselves, of new, after..a social revolution.
β. *c* **1449** PECOCK *Repr.* 378 Therfore y wole not thilk processe here aȝen of the newe reherce. **1535** COVERDALE *1 Kings* xx. 22 The kynge of Syria shall come agaynst the of the New. **1535** STEWART *Cron. Scot.* II. 624 He..occupyit all Ingland of the new. **1653** H. MORE *Conject. Cabbal.* (1713) 95 He now creates nothing of anew.
γ. *c* **1380** WYCLIF *Three Treat.* 27 Newe customs..bi whiche thei spuylen on new the puple. **1535** STEWART *Cron. Scot.* I. 382 And stoutlie straik with greit curage on new.
δ. *c* **1340** *Gaw. & Gr. Knt.* 65 Nowel nayted o-newe, neuened ful ofte. **1494** FABYAN IV. lxx. 49 Nat longe after, the sayd Octauius gaderyd anewe people of Britons and Norways. **1535** COVERDALE *Jer.* xviii. 4 So he beganne a new, and made another vessell. **1604** SHAKS. *Oth.* IV. i. 85 For I will make him tell the Tale anew. **1696** WHISTON *Th. Earth* IV. (1722) 325 The Sun would anew hide himself in a thick Mist. **1770** BURKE *Pres. Discont.* Wks. II. 229 The power of the crown almost dead and rotten..has grown up anew. **1846** KEBLE *Lyra Innoc.* (1873) 50 Then died away, then rose and moaned anew. **1866** KINGSLEY *Herew.* vi. 125 They sped him forth to begin life anew.
2. In a new or different way from the previous.
c **1386** CHAUCER *Clerk's T.* 882 Ther kan no man..been half so trewe As wommen been, but it be falle of newe. *c* **1400** *Rom. Rose* 5174 If I hate men of newe, More than love it wole me rewe. **1632** *Shaks. Cent. Praise* 191 To steere th' affections, and by heavenly fire Mould us anew. **1712** ADDISON *Spect.* No. 447 ¶1 Custom is a second Nature. It is indeed able to form the Man anew. **1807** CRABBE *Par. Reg.* II. 253 Now clothed himself anew, and acted overseer. **1843** J. MARTINEAU *Chr. Life* 77 The system is edited anew.
†**3.** Newly, freshly, recently; in opposition to *of old.*
c **1380** WYCLIF *Three Treat.* 3 Thes synnen not of the newe but purgen her olde synnes. *c* **1400** *Rom. Rose* 3875 His falsenesse is not now anew, It is too long that he him knew. *c* **1449** PECOCK *Repr.* 532 Religiosite foundun of newe bi men ..sett and joyned with the al hool lawe of Crist. **1509** HAWES *Past. Pleas.* xxix. iii, He wente to lande..And wedde there one that was comen anewe. **1535** STEWART *Cron. Scot.* II. 609 Sic aventure wes hapnit of the new. **1728** *Col. Records Penn.* III. 294 They had of new visited the said ship.
†**4.** Newly, as something new, in opposition to what has existed long and is now old. *Obs.*
c **1543** W. CLEBE *MS. Addit.* No. 4609 Hath made..a new halle with a squillery, saucery, and surveyng place, al of new. **1570** HOLINSHED *Scot. Chron.* (1806) I. 357 He restored the other two to their former beauties, and furthermore erected two other of new. **1582** *Durh. Wills & Inv.* (1860) 88 One cundithe of leade, which was made of new.

†**aˈnew,** *v. Obs.* [perh. represents OE. *edniwian,* f. *ed* again + NEW; perh. a later formation with A- *pref.* 1. Cf. OHG. *irniuwôn,* mod.G. *erneuen.*] To renew.
[*a* **1000** *O.E. Psalms* (Sp.) ciii. 31 Þú edniwast ansíne eorþan.] **1399** *Rich. Redeless* III. 24 [The hart] ffedith him on the venym his ffelle to a-newe. ?*a* **1500** *MS. Lincoln Med.* 284 Tak May butter and comyne..and thane laye it on the eghe, and ofte anewe it. **1579** FULKE *Heskins's Parl.* 503 Hee anueth also a saying of Oecumenius. **1690** LADY R. RUSSELL in *Four Cent. Eng. Lett.* 130 You must anew in practice that submission you have so powerfully tried.

†**aˈnewst, aneust,** *adv. Obs.* [OE. *on neáhwest, neáwest* in the neighbourhood or vicinity (cf. OHG. *nâhwist*); *hence,* near, nigh.]
1. Of place: Near, hard by.
c **1000** *Elene* 874 Brohton þa on bære..on neáweste ȝingne gástlease. **1205** LAY. 25752 Forð þe king wende: þat he com aneuste [**1250** þat he anewest com]. **1598** FLORIO, *Arente,* aneust, anenst, very near, hard by.
2. Of manner and degree: Very nearly, well-nigh, closely.
1589 R. HARVEY *Pl. Perc.* 19, I know a newst what Circuit you are in. **1674** RAY *S. & E. Countr. Words* 58 *Anewst,* nigh, almost, near hand, about, *circiter.* **1881** *Isle of Wight Gloss., Aneust,* nearly alike.

[**aneye, -aye,** *v.* mispr. for AVEYE (Shoreham).]

aneyle, obs. form of ANELE *v.,* to anoint.

anfald, earlier f. AFALD, *a. Obs.,* single, simple.

anfeld, -felt, obs. forms of ANVIL.

†**anˈferme,** *v. Obs.* [a. OFr. *enfermer* = *afermer.*] = AFFIRM.
1340 *Ayenb.* 152 Wel to deme be-longeþ þet me naȝt ne anfermi, bote me hit habbe wel of-acsed.

†**ˈanfract.** *Obs. rare.* [ad. L. *anfract-us* (also occas. used), a breaking round, a bending, f. *anfring-ĕre,* f. *an-* = *am-, amb-* about + *frangĕre* to break.] A winding, a circuitous route; a sinuosity.
1567 MAPLET *Greene Forest* 86 The Fleck..goeth with rowling foote, and hath often anfractes or turnings. **1611** CORYAT *Crudities* 576 The numerous anfracts and intricate windings thereof. **1714** DERHAM *Astro-theol.* 6 Anfractus or Roughnesses on the Concave part of the enlighten'd Edge.

anfractuose (ænˌfræktjuːˈəʊs), *a. rare.* [ad. L. *anfractuōs-us* winding, roundabout, f. *anfract-us*: see prec. and -OSE.] Winding, sinuous.
1691 RAY *Creation* II. (1701) 272 Behind this drum are several vaults and anfractuose [*ed.* 1704 anfractuous] cavities in the ear bone. **1830** LINDLEY *Nat. Syst. Bot.* 35 *Bombaceæ*..Anthers 1-celled, linear, reniform or anfractuose.

anfractuosity (ænˌfræktjuːˈɒsɪtɪ). Also 7 amf-. [a. Fr. *anfractuosité,* f. L. *anfractuōs-us*: see prec. and -ITY.] The quality of being anfractuous.
1. *lit.* Sinuosity, circuitousness; usually *concr.* in *pl.* winding or tortuous crevices, channels, passages.
1596 LOWE *Art Chirurg.* (1634) 241 The vayne goeth aboue the artier, but not right lyne as other parts doe, but in anfractuosities, like unto a Woodbine. **1656** BLOUNT *Glossogr., Amfractuosity.* **1835** KIRBY *Hab. & Inst. Anim.* I. v. 182 Upon the bottom of the sea following its curvatures, declivities and anfractuosities. **1875** H. JAMES *Rod. Hudson* vii. 233 Chance anfractuosities of ruin in the upper portions of the Coliseum. **1877** *Havard's Pict. Holland* 406 The quarry is usually entered by an anfractuosity of the mountain.
b. *spec.* The sinuous depressions separating the convolutions of the brain.
1687 *Phil. Trans.* XVI. 373 The Anfractuosities of the Brain. **1839–47** TODD *Cycl. Anat. & Phys.* III. 383/2 The principal anfractuosities sink more than a line's depth into the substance of the hemisphere.
2. *fig.* Involution, intricacy, obliquity; *concr.* in *pl.*
1652 URQUHART *Jewel* Wks. 1834. 231 The sweet labyrinth and mellifluent anfractuosities of a laciuious delectation. **1780** JOHNSON in *Boswell* (1831) IV. 336 Sir, among the anfractuosities of the human mind I know not if it may not be one, that there is a superstitious reluctance to sit for a picture. **1879** *Cornh. Mag.* Nov. 592 Subtle hints of the various anfractuosities of their minds.

anfractuous (ænˈfræktjuːəs), *a.* Also 7–8 amf-. [a. Fr. *anfractueux* (16th c.), ad. L. *anfractuōsus*: see ANFRACTUOSE.] **1.** Winding, sinuous, involved; roundabout, circuitous; spiral.
1621 BURTON *Anat. Mel.* I. i. II. iv, Two common anfractuous eares..the one to hold blood, the other aire. **1646** SIR T. BROWNE *Pseud. Ep.* 167 That famous [horn].. hath anfractuous spires, and cochleary turnings about it. **1667** H. MORE *Div. Dial.* ii. §1 (1713) 88 So intricate, so anfractuous, so unsearchable are the ways of Providence. **1684** tr. *Bonet's Merc. Compit.* XVIII. 655 Oftentimes wounds..are anfractuous and oblique. **1763** *Brit. Mag.* IV. 130 This astonishing amfractuous passage, over rocks and precipices. **1836** *Penny Cycl.* s.v. *Botany, Anfractuous,* doubled up abruptly in several different directions. **1953** C. Day Lewis *Ital. Visit* iv. 49 A gorge of a street, anfractuous, narrow.
2. [After F. *anfractueux* craggy.] Rugged, craggy.
1920 T. S. ELIOT *Sweeney Erect* in *Ara Vus Prec* 22 Paint me the bold anfractuous rocks Faced by the snarling and yelping seas.
3. *slang* (*jocular*). Fractious, irritable.
1932 KIPLING *Limits & Renewals* 140 If they've been hoicked out of bed, *ad hoc,* they're apt to be anfractuous.

anˈfractuousness. ? *Obs.*⁻⁰ [f. prec. + -NESS.] 'Fulness of windings and turnings.' J.
1731 BAILEY, whence in J., etc.

†**anˈfracture.** *Obs. rare.* [f. L. *anfract-us* (see ANFRACT) + -URE.] 'A turning; a mazy winding and turning.' J.
1657 *Phys. Dict., Anfractures,* turning and winding. **1657** TOMLINSON *Renou's Disp.* 576 Its gyres and anfractures.

†**ˈangard,** *sb. Obs.* 4–5; also 4 **ongart,** 5 **ogart, angerd.** [Of uncertain derivation. It looks like a perversion of ON. *ágjarn* ambitious, insolent, *ágirnd,* ambition, insolence; cf. also mod.Icel. *gort,* 'brag, vainglorious boast,' not in ON., and of unknown origin.] Brag, boastfulness, arrogance.
a **1325** *Metr. Hom.* 49 Her may ye alle ensampel tak Ongart and rosing to forsak. *c* **1340** *Gaw. & Gr. Knt.* 681 For angardeȝ pryde. *c* **1400** *Destr. Troy* XXIV. 9745 If vs auntrid, Vlyxes, thurgh angard of pride..Hit was folly, by my faith. *c* **1440** *Morte Arth.* 1661 Ane erle þane in angerd answeres hym sone. *c* **1470** HENRY *Wallace* x. 155 For thi ogart othir thow sall de, or in presoun byd.

†**ˈangard,** *a. Obs. rare.* [Cf. ON. *ágjarn,* ambitious, insolent, greedy: see prec.] Proud, arrogant. (App. sometimes confused with ANGERED.)
c **1400** *Destr. Troy* XII. 5015 Angers me full euyll your angard desyre. ?*a* **1450** *MS. Ashmole* No. 44. 40 (Halliw.) Thire athils of Atenes, ther angard clerkis..red over the pistille.

†**ˈangardly,** *adv. Obs. rare.* [Cf. ON. *ágjarnliga* insolently, greedily. Perh. confused in sense with ANGERED, ANGERLY.] Impetuously, eagerly, exceedingly.
c **1400** *Destr. Troy* XIX. 7994 Achilles was angret angardly sore. *Ibid.* XXII. 9104 Achilles..angardly dissiret The Citie for to se. *Ibid.* XVII. 7470 Þen Vlixes & Arest angurdly faght.

angareb, -eeb, -ep (ˈæŋgəreɪb). Also -er-, -ib. [Native name.] A stretcher or light bedstead used by the Arabs, and in Egypt and the Sudan.
1867 S. W. BAKER *Nile Trib. Abyssinia* viii. 182 The angareps, or native bedsteads,..are simple frameworks upon legs, covered with a network of raw hide. **1885** *Daily News* 3 July 5/4 Camels..heavily laden with angerebs transversely placed and resting on the flank upon a huge box. **1900** CONAN DOYLE *Green Flag* 329 He lay upon his angareeb still debating it. **1925** *Blackw. Mag.* Sept. 424/2 The harassed native Bimbashi sought his angerib.

†**anˈgariate,** *v. Obs. rare*⁻¹. [f. L. *angariāt-* ppl. stem of *angariā-re,* to constrain to service, f. *angarīa* forced service, a. Gr. ἀγγαρεία the office of the ἄγγαρος (a Persian word), a courier, a messenger (liable to be impressed on the King's business). *Angaria, angariāre,* and their deriv. were very common in med.L. in reference to feudal burdens. Cf. Fr. *angarier* in Cotgr. 1611.] To exact forced labour from; to press into service; to impress.
1676 MARVELL *Mr. Smirke* Wks. 1875 IV. 24 It is not wisdom in the Church to pretend to..that power of angariating men further than their occasions will permit.

†**angariˈation.** *Obs.* [f. prec.: see -ATION. Prob. already in med.L. or Fr.] The exaction of forced service; impressment to labour or service.
1611 SPEED *Hist. Gt. Brit.* IX. ix. (1632) 613 The Popes continuall angariations and extortions. *a* **1656** BP. HALL *Rem. Wks.* (1660) 153 This leading of God's Spirit must neither be a forced angariation, nor some sudden protrusion to good. *a* **1670** HACKET *Cent. Serm.* 336 There are violence, injustice, a thousand angariations in the kingdoms of the world.

angary (ˈæŋgərɪ). [ad. F. *angarie,* ad. L. *angaria*: see ANGARIATE *v.*] In full ***right of angary*** (F. *droit d'angarie*): the right of a belligerent to use and destroy, if necessary, the property of neutrals.

1880 HALL *Internat. Law* 655 The most recent cases of the exercise of the right of angary occurred during the Franco-German War of 1870–71. **1902** *Encycl. Brit.* XXXI. 129.

†**ange.** *Obs. rare.* [a. ON. **anga*, in pl. *öngur* straits, anguish; cf. OE. *ang-* in comb., pain, painful, and L. *ang-ĕre* to trouble, vex.] Trouble, affliction, anguish.

c **1200** ORMIN 11904 þatt himm wass waȝȝ & ange. *Ibid.* 19804 Dide hemm mikell ange.

angeio-, see ANGIO-.

angekok ('æŋgɪkɒk). [Eskimo.] An Eskimo sorcerer or medicine-man.

1767 J. GAMBOLD tr. *Cranz's Hist. Greenland* I. 206 When a dearth befalls them [*sc.* Greenlanders] at sea, an Angekok must undertake a journey thither. **1819** *Edin. Rev.* XXXI. 345 Their conjurors or angekoks are merely a superior order of jugglers. **1837** [see CONJURE *v.* 5 a]. **1842** MOFFAT *Mission. Labours S. Africa* 305 The angekoks of the Greenlanders.. and the greegrees of Western Africa. **1895** KIPLING *2nd Jungle Bk.* 147 The *angekok*, the sorcerer, frightened them into the most delightful fits.

angel ('eɪndʒəl), *sb.* Forms: 1–3 engel, 2–3 ængel, ængle, 3 enngell, -gle, angil, eangel, 3–7 angle, 4–5 aungel(e, -ell(e, -il, 4–7 angell, 5–6 angelle, 6 angele, 2– angel. *Pl.* 1–2 englas, 2–3 engles, 3–7 angles, 2– angels (4–5 -is, -ys, 4–6 -es). [An early Teut. adoption from L., (or, in Goth., from Gr.), afterwards influenced in Eng. by OFr. and L. With OE. *ęngel:—angil*, cf. OS. *engil*, OFris. *angel*, *engel*, ON. *engill*, OHG. *angil*, *engil*, Goth. *aggilus* for *angilus*; a. L. *angelus*, or Gr. ἄγγελ-ος a messenger, used by the LXX to translate Heb. *mal'āk*, in full *mal'āk-yĕhōwāh* 'messenger of Jehovah'; whence the name and doctrine of angels passed into L. and the modern langs. All other uses of the word are either extensions of this, or taken from the Gr. in the primary sense of 'messenger.' The OE. form *engel*, with *g* hard, remained to 13th c., but eventually, under influence of OFr. *angele*, *angle* (with *g* soft), and L. *angelus*, initial *a* prevailed; the forms in *au-* in 14–15th c. show Fr. influence.]

I. 1. a. A ministering spirit or divine messenger; one of an order of spiritual beings superior to man in power and intelligence, who, according to the Jewish, Christian, Mohammedan, and other theologies, are the attendants and messengers of the Deity.

c **950** *Lindisf. Gosp.* Matt. xxii. 30 Sint suelce englas godes in heofnum [*c* **1000** *Ags. G.*, Godes englas. *c* **1160** *Hatton G.*, Godes engles]. *Ibid.* John v. 4 Engel uutudliche Drihtnes.. of-dune astaȝ. *c* **1175** *Cott. Hom.* 227 þa sende he his ængel to áne mede. *c* **1200** *Trin. Coll. Hom.* 31 Ðo cam on angel of heuene to hem. *c* **1200** *Moral Ode* 94 Hwat sulle we seggen oðer don þar ængles beð of dradde. *c* **1200** ORMIN 3914 Godess enngless wærenn þa Well swiþe glade wurrþenn. *c* **1230** *Ancr. R.* 92 Ure Lefdi mid hire meidenes, & al þe englene uerd. *c* **1260** *Signs bef. Judg.* 153 in *E.E.P.* (1862) 11 þat þan sal quake seraphin and cherubin, þat beþ angles two. þer nis in heuen angil iwis þat to oþer sal hab spech. **1388** WYCLIF *Ps.* viii. 6 Thou hast maad hym a litil lesse than aungels. [*Coverd.* lower then the angels.] **1393** LANGL. *P. Pl.* C. XXII. 150 Aungeles & archaungeles..Comen kneolynge. **1485** CAXTON *Chas. Gt.* 239, I saw the aungellys mounte into heuen on hye. **1526** TINDALE *Matt.* xxvi. 53 Moo then xii legions of angelles. **1605** SHAKS. *Macb.* IV. iii. 22 Angels are bright still, though the brightest fell. **1607** HIERON *Wks.* I. 392 'Mahanaim'; because there the angles met him. **1712** POPE *Spect.* No. 408 ¶4 Man seems to be placed as the middle Link between Angels and Brutes. **1742** BLAIR *Grave* 589 Its visits, Like those of angels, Short and far between. *a* **1842** TENNYSON *May Q.* III. 25 All in the wild March-morning I heard the angels call. **1858** TRENCH *Parables* xxiii. (1877) 389 The tears of penitents are the wine of angels. **1865** R. W. DALE *Jew. Temple* ii. (1877) 24 An angel strengthened Christ in Gethsemane.

b. One of the fallen or rebellious spirits, said to have been formerly angels of God.

c **950** *Lindisf. Gosp.* Matt. xxv. 41 Fýr ècce seðe foreȝeȝearuuad is diwle & englum his. *c* **1160** *Hatton G.* ibid., Deofle and hys englen ȝegarewað. **1382** WYCLIF *Rev.* ix. 11 The aungel of depnesse. *c* **1400** *Destr. Troy* x. 4354 þere onswaret opunly the aungell of helle. **1611** BIBLE *Matt.* xxv. 41 Euerlasting fire, prepared for the deuill and his angels. —— *Rev.* IX. 11 The Angel of the bottomelesse pit. **1667** MILTON *P.L.* I. 125 So spake th' Apostate Angel.

c. A guardian or attendant spirit: *lit.* in sense 1; but also *rhet.* without implying any belief in their reality, as 'her good angel,' 'my evil angel triumphed,' 'angel of innocence, repentance.'

1382 WYCLIF *Acts* xii. 15 Forsoth thei seiden, It is his aungel. **1588** SHAKS. *L.L.L.* I. i. 78 There is no euill Angell but Loue. **1594** —— *Rich. III*, IV. i. 93 Go thou to Richard, and good Angels tend thee. **1717** POPE *Eloisa* 340 Bright clouds descend, and Angels watch thee round. **1875** FARRAR *Sil. & Voices* ii. 43 Though the Angel of Innocence have long vanished, the Angel of Repentance takes him gently by the hand. **1879** TENNYSON *Lover's T.* 29 I to her became Her guardian and her angel.

d. *fig.* A person who resembles an angel either in attributes or actions; (*a*) a lovely, bright, innocent, or gracious being; (*b*) a minister of loving offices.

1592 SHAKS. *Rom. & Jul.* II. ii. 26 O, speake againe, bright Angell, for thou art As glorious..As is a winged messenger of heauen. **1660** STANLEY *Hist. Philos.* (1701) 87/2 Looked upon as Angels for Wit and Eloquence. *a* **1687** PETTY *Pol. Arith.* i. (1691) 10 Many..do so magnifie the Hollanders.. making them Angels. **1808** SCOTT *Marm.* VI. xxx, When pain and anguish wring the brow, A ministering angel thou. **1819** S. ROGERS *Hum. Life*, A guardian angel o'er his life presiding, Doubling his pleasures, and his cares dividing. **1858** LONGF. *M. Standish* II. 58 The angel whose name is Priscilla. *Mod.* Not quite such an angel as he looks.

II. from the literal sense of Gr. ἄγγελος.

2. Any messenger of God, as a prophet, or preacher. [A Hellenism of the Bible and theological writers; sometimes an affected literalism of translation.]

1382 WYCLIF *Gal.* iv. 14 ȝe resceyueden me as an aungel of God. [So in all versions.] *c* **1400** *Apol. Loll.* 31 He [þe prest] is þe aungel of þe Lord of hostis. *c* **1560** *Prayer* in *Phenix* (1708) II. 232 Our Lord Jesus Christ, that Great Angel of Thy counsel. **1860** PUSEY *Min. Proph.* 606 The priest of God is called angel, i.e. messenger, because he.. announces the things of God to the people. **1879** FARRAR *St. Paul* I. 148 The last utterance of the Angel Malachi.

3. Title of the pastor or minister of a church, in the apocalypse, Eccles. Hist., and in some modern sects, as the Catholic Apostolics.

1382 WYCLIF *Rev.* ii. 8 To the aungel of the chirche of Smyrna, wrijte thou. **1526** TINDALE *ibid.*, The angell of the congregacion of Smyrna. **1611** *ibid.*, The Angel of the Church in Smyrna. **1660** STILLINGFLEET *Iren.* II. vi. (1662) 289 The publick Minister of the Synagogue, called the Angel of the Congregation. **1831** E. IRVING in Mrs. Oliphant *Life* II. iv. 204, I fulfil the part of the pastor or angel of the church. **1839** YEOWELL *Anc. Brit. Ch.* iv. (1847) 37 To act in the Presbyterial College..as President, Angel, or very soon by the exclusive title of Bishop.

4. *poet.* A messenger generally; *fig.* in ***angel of death***, formerly used literally in sense 1.

1574 tr. *Marlorat's Apocalips* 30 An Angell (that is too say, a Messenger) is one that is sent of an errand. **1600** CHAPMAN *Iliad* XXIV. 189 An angel I have seen, Sent down from Jove. *a* **1637** B. JONSON *Sad Sheph.* II. vi. (T.) The dear good angel of the spring, The nightingale. **1648** JOS. BEAUMONT *Psyche* XV. cxxxv, They should be The Angels of this News as well as He. **1815** BYRON *Destr. Sennach.* 9 For the Angel of Death spread his wings on the blast. **1853** *Arab. Nts.* (Rtlg.) 455 My father..hath been summoned away by the angel of death.

III. *transf.*

5. A conventional representation of the celestial ministers, figured with wings.

1536 *Reg. Riches* in *Antiq. Sarisb.* (1771) 203 Another cope of green cloth of gold, with images and Angels of Jesse. **1855** TENNYSON *Maud* I. VIII An angel watching an urn Wept over her, carved in stone. **1877** *Athenæum* 3 Nov. 571/3 The heads of the countesses lie on cushions which have angels at the corners.

6. An old English gold coin, called more fully at first the ANGEL-NOBLE, being originally a new issue of the Noble, having as its device the archangel Michael standing upon, and piercing the dragon.

The angel copied the device of the Fr. *angelot* or *ange*, a gold coin of France struck by Louis XI. It was first coined in 1465 by Edward IV when its value (like that of the earlier noble) was 6*s.* 8*d.* In 1 Henry VIII it was 7*s.* 6*d.*, 34 Henry VIII 8*s.*, and 6 Edw. VI 10*s.*; it was last coined by Chas. I. (This was the coin always presented to a patient 'touched' for the King's Evil. When it ceased to be coined, small medals having the same device were substituted for it, and were hence called *touch-pieces*.)

1488 *Inv. Jewels* in Tytler *Hist. Scot.* (1864) II. 390 Twa hundreth four score and v angellis. **1494** FABYAN VII. 655 He ordeyned the seconde coyne of golde, and namyd it the angell, whiche was and yet is in value of vis. viiid. **1526** WRIOTHESLEY *Chron.* (1875) I. 15 The Kinge enhaunsed his coyne, that is to saye, the riall at 11*s.* 3*d.*, the angell 7*s.* 6*d.* *a* **1593** H. SMITH 3 *Serm.* (1624) 6 To fill a coffer full of Angels. **1598** SHAKS. *Merry W.* I. iii. 60 She has all the rule of her husbands Purse: he hath a legend of Angels. **1623** MASSINGER *Dk. Milan* III. ii, His stripes washed off With oil of angels. **1719** D'URFEY *Pills* (1872) III. 325 An angel of money you must me bring. **1808** SCOTT *Marm.* I. x, As Lord Marmion crossed the Court, He scattered angels round. **1883** *Leisure Ho.* 247 Chief Justice Hall, so long as he practised at the Bar, persisted in charging only the angel in ordinary matters.

7. ***angels on horseback*** (see quot. 1900).

1888 MRS. BEETON *Bk. Househ. Managem.* §2078 Angels on Horseback. (Fr. — Anges à Cheval). **1900** 'SARAH GRAND' *Babs* (1901) xv Angels on Horseback, now—those delicious little morsels of oysters rolled in bacon, and served on crisp toast.

8. *slang.* A financial backer of an enterprise, esp. one who supports a theatrical production. orig. *U.S.*

1891 J. MAITLAND *Amer. Slang Dict.* 18 *Angel*..One who possesses the means and inclination to 'stand treat'. **1900** G. ADE *More Fables* 190 There was no more Capital coming from the Angels. **1921** WODEHOUSE *Jill the Reckless* xi. 161 Ike hasn't any of his own money in the thing... The angel is the long fellow you see jumping around. **1948** *Times Lit. Suppl.* 17 Apr. 218/5 In the United States there is more money, more paper..the magazines are fatter, the 'angels' are richer. **1953** *Economist* 28 Mar. 853/1 That increasingly rare being, the 'angel' who will risk his money in a theatrical venture.

9. *R.A.F. slang.* Height; *spec.* a height of 1,000 feet. Usu. in *pl.*

1943 P. BRENNAN et al. *Spitfires over Malta* i. 18 'Gain your angels quickly...' We continued to climb. *Ibid.* iii. 71 We climbed into sun, Woody advising us to get as much angels as possible. **1943** HUNT & PRINGLE *Service Slang* 11 '20 M.E.s at Angels one owe' means '20 Messerschmitts at 10,000 ft.' **1946** J. IRVING *Royal Navalese* 23 *Angels*, a measurement of one thousand feet in height, used in the air combat code.

10. An 'unexplained' mark on a radar screen.

1947 W. B. GOULD in *Proc. Inst. Radio Engineers* XXXV. 1105/1 Radar equipment..has given fairly consistent unexplainable echoes at altitudes between approximately 300 and 3000 yards. For want of a better term, these echoes have been dubbed 'Angels' by Signal Corps personnel. **1958** *Listener* 30 Oct. 691/1 New radar sets of much higher power, on which the display was sometimes covered with small echoes, called 'angels' by the operators. *Ibid.*, A Swiss biologist, working with British radar equipment at Zurich airport, proved that 'angels' were the echoes from small birds on migration. **1962** *New Scientist* 12 Apr. 23/3 A substantial proportion of angel echoes are indeed attributable to birds.

11. = *hell's angel* s.v. HELL *sb.* 12.

1969 *Listener* 1 May 624/1 His climactic sequence in church, in which an Angel's funeral degenerates into an orgy, is no more than a picturesque trifling with the perverse. **1970** [see FRAIL *sb.*[3]]. **1976** *Southern Even. Echo* (Southampton) 18 Nov. 8/5 There is little dramatic tension in the book until the introduction of the scientist whom three Angels are sent to rescue/kidnap. **1977** *Rolling Stone* 16 June 11/3 Another 20 Angels and maybe twice that number of Dead friends freely wander around in the wings.

B. *Comb.* and *Attrib.*

1. General relations (freq. in poetic use): **a.** appositive, as ***angel-goddess***, ***-guardian***, ***-messenger***, ***-mother***, ***-power***, ***-stranger***, ***-vampire***, ***-warder***, ***-woman***. **b.** objective with pr. pple. or vbl. sb., as ***angel-worship***, ***-worshipper***, ***-ing***. **c.** instrumental with pa. pple., as ***angel-borne***, ***-builded***, ***-guarded***, ***-heralded***, ***-infested***, ***-loosened***, ***-warned***. **d.** similative, as ***angel-bright***, ***-fair***, ***-seeming***, ***-wise***. **e.** attrib. (of, or as of, or pertaining to, an angel or angels; = ANGELIC), as ***angel appearance***, ***choir***, ***-evening***, ***-event***, ***face***, ***form***, ***grace***, ***infancy***, ***music***, ***psalm***, ***trumpet***, ***visit***, ***voice***.

1858 SEARS *Athan.* VI. 50 The *angel-appearances were not the same to all the witnesses. **1742** YOUNG *Nt. Th.* (1751) 144 Talents *angel-bright. **1839** BAILEY *Festus* xix. (1848) 226 The fragments of that *angel-builded fane. **1929** E. BLUNDEN *Near & Far* 41 The tender amaranthine domes Of *angel-evenings. *Ibid.* 49 The bright *Angel-event of sunset's fresh creation. **1833** J. H. NEWMAN *Bk. Praise* (1862) 432 And with the morn those *angel faces smile. **1878** GLADSTONE *Prim. Homer* 74 Iris, the messenger or *angel-goddess. **1611** HEYWOOD *Gold. Age* I. i, So full of *Angell grace. **1917** D. H. LAWRENCE *Look! We have come Through!* 101 But we storm the *angel-guarded Gates of the long-discarded Garden. **1940** G. BARKER *Lament & Triumph* 31 The Seven Seas with their *angel-infested crests. **1938** W. DE LA MARE *Memory* 26 The noon sun's *angel-loosened archery. **1830** T. HAMILTON *Cyr. Thornton* (1845) 121 You may yet see and embrace your *angel-mother. **1711** POPE *Rape Lock* I. 33 Virgins visited by *Angel-Powers. **1856** R. VAUGHAN *Ho. w. Mystics* (1860) II. 97 The floating tones of some distant *angel-psalm. **1738** WESLEY *Ps.* No. 47, v, Shout the *Angel-Quires aloud. **1748** THOMSON *Cast. Indol.* xlv. 402 These same guileful *angel-seeming sprites. *c* **1630** MILTON *At Sol. Music*, The bright seraphim..Their loud uplifted *angel-trumpets blow. **1936** W. H. AUDEN *Look, Stranger!* 41 The white *angel-vampires flit. **1799** CAMPBELL *Pleas. Hope* II. 386 *Angel visits, few and far between. **1879** G. M. HOPKINS *Poems* (1918) 44 Frowning and forefending *angel-warder. **1871** C. PEARSON *Sarum Seq.* 29 *Angel-warned, no word they bring Back to Herod. **1918** W. DE LA MARE *Motley* 54 The Shape who hoofs applause..Hoots—*angel-wise—'the Cause!' **1863** JEAFFRESON *Sir Everard's Dau.* xiii. 235 Bernard thought of an *angel-woman..his boyhood's love. **1577** tr. *Bullinger's Decades* (1592) 744 Augustine..naming them Angelici, *angel-worshippers.

2. Special combinations: †**angel-beast**, an old game at cards; †**angel-bed**, 'a sort of open bed without bed-posts,' Phillips 1706; †**angel-bread**, a kind of purgative cake, made of oatmeal and flour, with ginger and spurge; **angel-cake** (orig. *U.S.*), a variety of sponge-cake; **angel-cornice**, one decorated with figures of angels; **angel dust** *slang* (orig. *U.S.*), = PHENCYCLIDINE, used as a hallucinogen; **angels' eyes**, the plant, germander speedwell; **angel-face**, used, esp. as a term of address and freq. ironically, for a person with an 'angelic' or innocent face (cf. quot. 1833, sense B. 1; see also quot. 1925); †**angels'-food**, a term for strong ale; **angel('s)-food (-cake)**, (orig. *U.S.*), angel-cake; †**angel-gold**, standard or 'guinea' -gold; **angel-kind**, the race of angels (cf. *mankind*); †**angel-piece**, = ANGEL 6; †**angel-proof**, the gold standard of the angel; **angel skin** [tr. F. *peau d'ange*], a fabric with a smooth waxy face; **angel sleeve**, a long loose sleeve.

Also ANGEL-FISH, -LIKE, -NOBLE, -SHOT, -WATER, q.v.

1668 SEDLEY *Mulb. Gard.* IV. i, Offering to play at *Angel-beast with them, tho' he scarce know the cards. **1886** *Good Housek.* (N.Y.) 10 July 127/2, I always use the pan sold as an '*angel cake pan'. **1904** *N.Y. Times* 13 June 8 To have angel cake would be sacrilegious. **1905** *N.Y. Even. Post* 4 Aug. 7 Angel cake, sponge cake, and ice-cream cake have conspired to relegate the seed cake to practical oblivion. **1909** J. MASEFIELD *Tragedy of Nan* II. p. 28 None but angel-cakes 'd be fit eating for you, Miss Nan. **1956** 'N. SHUTE' *Beyond Black Stump* vii. 201 He would usually take with him an enormous peach pie or an angel cake. **1862** RICKMAN *Goth. Archit.* 371 Another peculiar ornament is the *angel cornice.

1969 *Rolling Stone* 28 June 4/1 Parsley can give a more powerful high on marijuana. The garden herb, says Olas Hendrickson, is the basic ingredient in a new psychedelic substance called '*Angels' Dust'. **1973** [see PHENCYCLIDINE]. **1978** J. WAMBAUGH *Black Marble* ix. 189 My nephew was arrested because he was holding this angel dust for somebody else. **1985** *Sunday Times* 24 Mar. 12/2 PCP or 'angel dust', a strong anaesthetic which came after LSD in 1960s drug fashions.. has recently emerged anew. Now they call it 'rocket fuel' in Chicago and mix it with peanut butter. **1863** GOSSE *Dartmoor* in *Intell. Obs.* 318 The sweet germander speedwell.. here, most poetically, named by the peasantry, '*angels' eyes.' **1913** WODEHOUSE *Little Nugget* I. i. 14 'Ogden, darling.. stay by me, *angel-face.' 'Oh, shush!' muttered angel-face. **1925** FRASER & GIBBONS *Soldier & Sailor Words* 6 *Angel face*, Air Force slang for any young, or boyish looking, Probationary Flight Officer. **1932** E. WALLACE *When Gangs Came* xxi. 181 I've finished talking about it, angel-face. **1577** HARRISON *Engl.* II. xviii. (1877) 295 There is such headie ale & beere in most of them [markets], as for the mightinesse thereof.. is commonlie called huffecap, the mad dog.. *angels food, dragons milke. **1881** MRS. OWENS *Cook Bk.* 161 *Angel's food. In other words, White Sponge Cake. **1920** SINCLAIR LEWIS *Main St.* vii. 88 They distributed.. stuffed olives, potato salad, and angel's-food cake. **1951** *Good Housek. Home Encycl.* 335/1 *Angel Cake* (*Angel Food Cake*), an extremely light, feathery cake of the sponge type. **1583** STUBBES *Anat. Abus.* 53 Gilt .. with good *angell gold. **1676** H. PHILLIPS *Purch. Pattern* 223 Angel-Gold is worth somewhat more, and Sovereign Gold somewhat less. *a* **1300** *Cursor M.* 362 First þan wroght he *angel kind. **1874** R. MORRIS tr. *Blickling Homilies* vii. 92 All angel-kind shall look through the aperture on mankind. **1688** *Lond. Gaz.* mmccccxliii/4 Suspected to have stolen an *Angel piece. **1607** DEKKER *Wh. Babylon* 270 Head all the speares With gold of *Angell-proofe. **1935** *Times* 13 Nov. 15/5 The short jacket is of white *angel skin with blue sleeves. **1951** F. STARK *Beyond Euphrates* 186 A white evening gown of a satin they call angel-skin. **1862** CHESNUT *Diary* (1905) 204 She saw them coming in *angel sleeves, displaying all their white arms. **1887** E. B. CUSTER *Tenting on Plains* (1889) v. 174 The sting was inflicted.. in the far back days of 'angel sleeves', which fell away from the arm to the shoulder. **1906** *Daily Chron.* 19 Sept. 5/6 Capes of fur with large 'angel' sleeves.

angel (ˈeɪndʒəl), *v.* [f. the sb.] **1.** *trans.* To finance or back (an enterprise, esp. a theatrical production). *slang* (chiefly *U.S.*).

1929 M. LIEF *Hangover* 235 He's trying to get me to angel one of his plays. **1948** LAIT & MORTIMER *New York: Confid.* (1951) xxi. 194 A revue angeled by gangster dough. **1949** *Newsweek* 16 May 60/2 Last week.. Aunt Anita agreed to angel a new Manhattan morning tabloid.

2. *intr.* To gain height. Cf. ANGEL *sb.* 9. *R.A.F. slang.*

1941 *Reader's Digest* Feb. 54 The boys of Britain's R.A.F. have developed a language all their own. A fighter pilot is told to 'scramble', instead of take off; then he 'angels upward'.

angelate (ˈændʒəleɪt). *Chem.* [f. ANGEL-IC *a.*² + -ATE⁴; cf. *oxal-ic*, *oxal-ate.*] A salt of angelic acid.

1863 WATTS *Dict. Chem.* I. 293 The angelates of the alkali-metals are soluble in water and in alcohol.

† **'angeled,** *ppl. a. Obs. rare*⁻¹. [f. ANGEL *sb.* + -ED.] = ANGELIZED.

a **1628** F. GREVILLE *Mustapha* v. Cho. (1633) 158 So Blest be they, so Angel'd, so Eternized.

† **'angelence.** *Obs. rare*⁻¹. [irreg. f. ANGEL *sb.* + -ENCE.] Angelic condition or quality.

1652 BENLOWE *Theoph.* I. xi, The organs to my optick sense Are dazled at the Blaze of so bright Angelence.

Angeleno (ˌændʒəˈliːnəʊ). [a. American Sp. *Angeleño* (also used), f. the name of (Los) *Angeles* in California + *-eño*, suffix forming name of inhabitants from some place-names.] A native or inhabitant of Los Angeles.

1888 W. LINDLEY in Lindley & Widney *California of South* II. 79 Governor Pico is still a resident of Los Angeles, and any Angeleño will cheerfully point him out to the inquiring stranger. **1922** *Chambers's Jrnl.* Apr. 223/1 A true Angelenos [*sic*] will hardly ever admit the fact. **1934** WEBSTER, Angeleno. **1948** *Los Angeles Times* 10 May 1/6 Angelenos upheld summer traditions and went to the beach yesterday. **1968** *Listener* 29 Aug. 268/1, I think.. that some fundamental Angeleno psychology is involved. Anything less than perfection they cannot stand. **1978** J. HYAMS *Pool* ix. 126 The Pacific beaches were crowded with Angelenos and visitors alike. **1984** *USA Today* 6 Apr. 1D/1 Angelenos will be preening.. over *L.A. Is A Lady*. The musical paean to their previously unsung city will soon be recorded.

angelet (ˈeɪndʒəlɪt). Also 5-6 -elett, 5-7 -ellet. [a. OFr. *angelet* = It. *angeletto*, dim. of *angelo* ANGEL *sb.*; cf. *eaglet.*]

† **1.** A gold coin, half the value of the angel. *Obs.*

1481-90 *Howard Househ. Bks.* 284 My Lord sent home to my Lady in angelletes.. x *li.* **1551** *Procl. Edw. VI* in Wriothesley *Chron.* II. 59 The third peece called an angelett of fine gould of fiue shillinges. **1608** W. YONGE *Diary* (1848) 18 Flear's wife offered one of them one hundred angeletts to let him escape. **1707** FLEETWOOD *Chron. Precios.* 21 It appears that Angelets were the same with Half-Angels. **1834** *Penny Cycl.* s.v. *Angel*, The Angelets of Edward IV.. have on the reverse, *O crux ave spes unica.*

2. A little angel, a cherub; *fig.* a pretty child.

1823 LAMB *Elia* Ser. II. xxii. (1865) 387 The Angelet sprang forth, fluttering its rudiments of pinions. **1868** G. MACDONALD *Rob. Falc.* III. 133 Smiling, as if she rejoiced in the idea of taming the little wild angelets.

angel-fish. A fish of the *Squalidæ* or Shark family, found on the British coasts, having also an affinity to the Rays. It receives this name from the wing-like expansion of its pectoral fins; also called Monk-fish, Fiddle-fish, and Shark-ray. Also applied to various other fish, such as *Pterophyllum scalare* and some species of the family Chætodontidæ or Ephippidæ (mainly those in N. and Central American Atlantic waters).

1668 WILKINS *Real Char.* II. v. §3. 133 Of fish.. Viviparous.. 5. Scate, Angel-fish. **1784** ANDRE in *Phil. Trans.* LXXIV. 274 Slender flexible teeth in the chætodontes, or angel-fishes. **1862** ANSTED *Channel Isl.* II. ix. 213 Of fish not eaten, the sword-fish.. and the angel-fish, are the most remarkable among large species. **1873** T. GILL *Catal. Fishes East Coast N. Amer.* 24 *Chaetodontidae*.. angel-fish (*Berm.*) West Indies; occasional northwards. *Ibid.* 29 *Ephippidae*.. Moon-fish; angel-fish (South Carolina). **1888** GOODE *Amer. Fishes* xviii. 146 The Moon-fish, *Chætodipterus faber*, is.. abundant... In the northern parts of Mexico it is called 'Spade-fish'; from Florida to Charleston the Angel-fish. **1905** D. S. JORDAN *Stud. Fishes* II. xxiii. 404 The angel-fish or isabelita (Holacanthus ciliaris), orange-red, sky-blue, and golden, as though gaudily painted, is the best known species [of the family Chætodontidæ]. **1931** J. R. NORMAN *Hist. Fishes* ii. 16 The beautiful Angel-fish (*Pterophyllum*) of the rivers of South America, a familiar object in aquaria, has a very much compressed and almost circular body. **1962** *Listener* 22 Nov. 852/2 My black-and-silver lace angel fish was a most appealing wide-eyed beauty.

angelhood (ˈeɪndʒəlhʊd). [f. ANGEL *sb.* + -HOOD.]

1. The state or condition of an angel.

1839 BAILEY *Festus* xix. (1848) 215 That all might in Him Be one; and full and holy equalness Belong humanity as angelhood. **1858** MISS MULOCH *Th. ab. Wom.* 35 'Womanhood,' the most heavenly thing next angelhood.

2. Angelic nature embodied; an angelic being; *collect.* a company or brotherhood of angels.

1850 MRS. BROWNING *Poems* I. 7 'Twas then I knew How ye could pity, my kind angelhood! **1862** —— *Last Poems* 30 English children pass in bloom.. Such rose angelhoods, emplumed In such ringlets of pure glory.

angelic (ænˈdʒɛlɪk), *a.*¹ and *sb.* Forms: 5-6 angelyk(e, 6 aungelyke, 6-7 angelike, -ique, 6-8 -ick, 7 angellike, 7- angelic. [ad. Fr. *angelique*, ad. L. *angelic-us*, a. Gr. ἀγγελικ-ός, f. ἄγγελ-ος ANGEL *sb.*] **A.** *adj.*

1. Of or pertaining to angels; of angel kind.

1485 CAXTON *St. Wenefr.* 20 This said the angelyk visyon vanysshed away. **1635** A. STAFFORD *Fem. Glory* (1869) 136 Th' Angellike Quire did greet their New-Borne King. **1667** MILTON *P.L.* x. 18 From Paradise in hast Th'angelic guards ascended, mute and sad. **1711** STEELE *Spect.* No. 6 ¶3 His [Satan's] Wit and Angelick Faculties. **1865** R. DALE *Jew. Temp.* ii. 24 Angelic messengers conversed with Abraham.

2. Like an angel; *hence*, of superhuman nature, intelligence, innocence, purity, sweetness.

c **1510** MORE *Picus* Wks. 1557. 4/2 Many noble bokes, whiche well testifie his angelike wit. *c* **1520** W. DE WORDE *Treat. Galaunt* (1860) 15 Our aungelyke abstynence is nowe refused. **1550** J. COKE *Debate* (1877) 109 England is a holy and angelique grounde, blyssed of God. **1667** MILTON *P.L.* v. 74 Happy creature, fair angelic Eve. **1712** POPE *Spect.* No. 408 ¶4 As a Man inclines to the angelick or brute Part of his Constitution. **1855** MACAULAY *Hist. Eng.* IV. 550 His profligacy and insolence united had been too much even for the angelic temper of Tillotson.

3. ***angelic doctor***: title given to Thomas Aquinas; ***Angelic Salutation***, the words addressed to the Virgin Mary by the angel Gabriel (Luke i. 28), the *Ave Maria.*

1657 S. COLVIL *Whigs Suppl.* (1751) 115 Aquinas new modell'd the school-Divinity; wherefore he was call'd the Angelic Doctor. **1843** MARIOTTI *Italy* I. 130 Dante was as wild as any of the angelic or seraphic doctors that preceded him. **1868** R. MORRIS *Chaucer's Boeth.* Introd. 1 'The angelic' Thomas Aquinas commented on him.

† **B.** *sb.* A worshipper of angels. *Obs. rare.*

1554 PHILPOT *Exam. & Writ.* (1842) 420 Men which were called Angelicks, because they worshipped Angels.

angelic (ænˈdʒɛlɪk), *a.*² *Chem.* [f. next.] Of or derived from angelica; as in ***angelic acid*** $C_5H_8O_2$, a monatomic monobasic acid of the acrylic series, obtained from the root of *A. archangelica* (and other plants); with a corresponding aldehyde C_5H_8O.

1863 WATTS *Dict. Chem.* I, Angelic acid crystallises in large long prisms and needles. **1869** ROSCOE *Elem. Chem.* 390 Angelic acid [occurs] in the archangel root, while angelic aldehyde is contained in the essential oil of chamomile.

‖ **angelica** (ænˈdʒɛlɪkə). [med.L. = *herba angelica* the 'angelic herb,' or 'root of the Holy Ghost,' so named (when or by whom does not appear—used by Brunfells in 1530) on account of its repute against poison and pestilence, prob. from the fragrant smell and aromatic taste of its root.]

1. a. An aromatic umbelliferous plant (*A. archangelica*, or *Archangelica officinalis*) indigenous to Europe, and cultivated (since 1568) in England, for culinary or medicinal purposes, and for preparing a confection, 'Candied Angelica.' **b.** in *Bot.* The genus, of which the prec. plant is, or was considered, the type; of which several species are diffused over the northern hemisphere, one being wild in Britain.

1578 LYTE *Dodoens* 297 The rootes of Angelica are contrarie to all poyson. **1598** SYLVESTER *Du Bartas* I. iii. (1641) 27/1 Angelica, that happy counterbane, Sent down from heav'n. **1601** R. CHESTER *Love's Mart.* 92 There is *Angellica* or Dwarfe Gentian. From death it doth preserue the poysoned man. **1630** J. TAYLOR (Water P.) *Wks.* I. 60/1 Angelicaes distastfull roote is gnawed. **1794** MARTYN *Rousseau's Bot.* xvii. 234 Angelica has large globose umbels. **1813** MARSHALL *Gardening* xvi. (ed. 5) 262 Angelica is cultivated for the large ribs of its leaves, cut in May or June to make a candied preserve.

2. *attrib.*

1641 FRENCH *Distill.* ii. (1651) 53 A pint of the best Angelica-water. **1652** —— *Yorksh. Spa* ix. 84 Elecampany root candied, or for want thereof Angelica root. **1827** NUTTALL *Introd. Bot.* 82, *Aralia*, two of the native species called spikenard and Angelica-tree. **1863** BARING-GOULD *Icel.* 112 The beautiful angelica leaf starred the black soil.

3. Short for **a.** Angelica water (cf. ANGEL-WATER). **b.** Candied angelica root.

1653 URQUHART *Rabelais* I. lv, Spirit of roses, orange-flower-water and Angelica. **1676** BEAL in *Phil. Trans.* XI. 587 The Thymes.. do make a sprightful.. infusion in Angelico, against Contagions. **1801** MAR. EDGEWORTH *Angelina* iv. (1832) 63 What was it you pleased to call for —angelica, ma'am, did you say? **1874** MISS ROSSETTI *Speaking Liken.* 39 Two melons.. and about four dozen sticks of angelica.

4. *fig. rare.*

1592 G. HARVEY *New Letter* 18 Converting the wormwood of just offence into the angelica of pure attonement.

angelical (ænˈdʒɛlɪkəl), *a.* Also 6 aungellical, 6-7 angelycall, etc. [f. ANGELIC + -AL¹: see -ICAL.]

1. Of or pertaining to angels; of angel kind. *arch.*

1509 HAWES *Past. Pleas.* xxiii. ii, Yet have they nature whych is angelycall. **1577** *St. Aug. Manuell*, This aungellical ditie: Holy, Holy, Holy, Lord God of hostes. **1699** EVELYN *Acetaria* (1729) 146 Our Paradisian Bard introduces Eve dressing of a Sallet for her Angelical Guest. **1718** CHAMBERS *Cycl.* s.v., The Angelical Salutation is called by the Romanists *Ave Maria.* *a* **1834** COLERIDGE *Notes Theol. & Pol.* 364 The mighty kingdoms angelical.. sounding forth their blessedness.

2. Angel-like, resembling an angel; hence, of superhuman nature, intelligence, holiness, disposition, beauty, etc.

1577 tr. *Bullinger's Decades* (1592) 569 We are by baptisme purged into an Angelicall life. **1592** SHAKS. *Rom. & Jul.* III. ii. 75 Beautifull Tyrant, fiend Angelicall: Rauenous Doue-feather'd Rauen. **1635** A. STAFFORD *Fem. Glory* (1869) 31 The Angellicall Innocency of God's Owne Mother. *a* **1687** PETTY *Pol. Arith.* i. (1691) 16 Such Angelical Wits and Judgments, as some attribute to the Hollanders. **1805** WORDSWORTH *Prel.* III. (1850) 67 A boy, no better, with his rosy cheeks Angelical. **1847** J. WILSON *Chr. North* (1857) II. 20 Angelical indeed was his temper.

3. An attribute of the Carthusians, and of Thomas Aquinas: Spiritual as an angel.

c **1555** HARPSFIELD *Divorce Hen. VIII* (1878) 286 The very Turk would have reverenced.. the angelical Carthusians. **1560** J. DAUS *Sleidane's Comm.* 3 b, [Aquinas] commonly called thangelical doctor, for the subtiltie of his witte. **1837** WHEWELL *Hist. Induct. Sc.* (1857) I. 378 The Angelical Doctor had systematized it.

4. Of or pertaining to a divine messenger, or pastor. Cf. ANGEL *sb.* 2 and 3. *rare.*

1678 in Heath *Grocers' Comp.* (1869) 524 Religion in a sable robe.. bearing a buckler in one hand.. in the other hand a banner on an angelical staff. **1864** BURTON *Scot. Abr.* II. i. 96 The angelical office of godly pastors.

5. ***angelical stone***: a fancy of the alchemists.

1652 ASHMOLE *Theat. Chem. Brit.* Prol. 8 Lastly, as touching the Angelicall Stone, it is so subtill.. that it can neither be seene, felt, or weighed.

an'gelically, *adv.* [f. prec. + -LY².]

1. By the instrumentality of angels. *rare.*

1635 WITHER *Lord's Prayer* (1665) 14 Revelations that seem to be.. Angelically inspired.

2. After the manner of, or like, an angel.

1740 GRAY *Let.* in *Poems* (1775) 86 La Diamantina.. played on the violin divinely, and sung angelically. **1814** CARY *Dante* 5 With gentle voice and soft Angelically tun'd. **1824-5** WIFFEN *Tasso's Jerus. Deliv.* IX. lxxxi, His favourite page, angelically fair.

† **an'gelicalness.** *Obs. rare.* [f. as prec. + -NESS.] The quality of being like an angel; angelic character or nature.

1664 H. MORE *Apol.* 493 The Lucidity and Angelicalness of our Saviour's Body after the Resurrection. **1667** —— *Div. Dial.* v. xi. (1713) 445 The Angelicalness of this last and best state of the Church. **1755** in JOHNSON; and in mod. Dicts.

angelicize (ænˈdʒɛlɪsaɪz), *v.* [f. ANGELIC *a.*¹ + -IZE.] *trans.* To make angelic; = ANGELIZE. Also *intr.*, to act in an angelic manner.

1825 *Blackw. Mag.* XVII. 52/1 The better half.. will be for ever on the wing.. not merely coquetting but *angelicising* with men—floating and flying literally. **1838** *Fraser's Mag.* Feb. 148/2 His notions of gentlemanly conduct so completely *angelicised* the mode of its exhibition. **1852** MISS MULOCH *Agatha's Husb.* (1858) 196 Brian.. in fact strongly resembled his father angelicised into childhood. **1902** *Academy* 8 Feb. 149/1 He [Thackeray] had to 'angelicise' the old gentleman at the club. **1948** W. DE LA MARE *Chardin* 24/1 His children, never belittled, prettified or angelicized.

angelico, = angelica-water: see ANGELICA 3.

†**an,gelifi'cation.** *Obs. rare*⁻¹. [n. of action f. ANGELIFY: see -FICATION.] The making, or being made, into or like an angel.

1629 DONNE *Serm.* xlix. 494 b, Such a Purification, such an Angelification, such a Deification in this Life.

†**an'gelified,** *ppl. a. Obs. rare.* [f. next + -ED.] Made into, or like, an angel; made angelic.

1636 S. WARD *Serm.* (1862) 64 A spiritual, an angelified body, made apt and obsequious to all divine services. **1678** CUDWORTH *Intell. Syst.* I. v. 797 Tertullian himself [styled the Resurrection-body] *angelificatam carnem*, 'angelified flesh.' **1728** EARBERY tr. *Burnet's State of Dead* I. 194 Tertullian [says] that it is an angelify'd Substance.

†**an'gelify,** *v. Obs. rare.* [ad. L. *angelificā-re* (Tertull.), f. *angelus* ANGEL *sb.* + *-ficāre*: see -FY.] To make into or like an angel; = ANGELIZE.

1653 T. ADAMS *Pract. Wks.* (1861) III. 295 Angels.. singing those raptures.. which did in a manner angelify him.

angelina (ændʒə'liːnə). *Bot.* Also 7 angelin. [f. ANGEL *sb.*: see -INA.] A genus of *Leguminosæ*, native chiefly to tropical America, comprising trees of moderate height, with showy purple flowers.

1663 H. COGAN tr. *Pinto's Trav.* xlviii. 188 A world of Angelin-wood, Chestnuts, Trees, Oak, and Cedar, wherewith thousands of Ships may be made. **1783** HOWARD *Encycl.*, *Angelina*, in botany, a tree growing in the rocky and sandy places in Malabar, in the East Indies. **1879** *Syd. Soc. Lex.*, *Angelina*, the *Andira inermis*.

†**angelique.** *Obs. rare*⁻¹. [Fr. *angelique* angelical, also a musical instrument.] A species of guitar; = ANGELOT 3.

1660 PEPYS *Diary* 23 June, He showed me.. an instrument he called an Angelique.

angelist ('eɪndʒəlɪst). [f. ANGEL *sb.* + -IST.] One who held heretical or peculiar opinions concerning angels.

1651 CARTWRIGHT *Cert. Relig.* I. 49 Nazianzen [was] an Angelist.

angelite ('eɪndʒəlaɪt). [ad. L. *angelīta*, said to be f. *Angelium*, a place in Alexandria where their assemblies were held.] A sect of ancient heretics, which arose A.D. 494.

1753 CHAMBERS *Cycl. Supp.* s.v. *Angelite*, The distinguishing tenets of the *Angelitæ* were, that the several parts of the Trinity had no distinct essence, substance, or deity; but only a substance or deity in common, or indivisible among them.

†**an'gelity.** *Obs. rare*⁻¹. [f. L. *angel-us* or Eng. ANGEL *sb.*, after *de-ity, human-ity*: see -ITY.] The estate of angels; angels as an order of being.

1652 BENLOWE *Theoph.* v. xxxii. 71 Oft, my rapt soul, ascending to the eye Peept through upon Angelitie.

angelize ('eɪndʒəlaɪz), *v. arch.* [f. as prec. + -IZE.]

1. *trans.* To convert into an angel, render angelic.

1633 T. ADAMS *Exp. 2 Pet.* ii. 10 That sin.. would have deified angels, and angelized men. **1633** EARL MANCH. *Al Mondo* (1636) 190 Such like thoughts.. will Angelize thy body, and Emparadise thy soule. **1796** W. TAYLOR in *Month. Rev.* XX. 520 It ought not to be our object to angelize, nor to brutalize, but to humanize man.

†**2.** *intr.* To belong or lean to the Angelists. *Obs.*

1605 T. BELL *Motives conc. Rom. Faith* Ded. 1 If Tertullian.. erred montanizing.. if Nazianzen angelizing, if Eusebius arrianizing.

'**angelized,** *ppl. a.* ? *Obs.* [f. prec. + -ED.] Made into or like an angel, rendered angelic.

1598 SYLVESTER *Du Bartas, Fathers* 268 Illuding Sathan cannot shine so bright, Though Angelliz'd. **1648** STERRY *Serm. Clouds* 39 Angels Spiritualized, Bodies Angelized. **1653** GAUDEN *Hierasp.* 232 Gifted Hypocrites, devout devils, angelized Satans.

angel-like, *a.* (*adv.*) ? *Obs.* Like or resembling angels; angelic.

c **1385** CHAUCER *L.G.W.* 236 And aungellych[*v.r.* aungelyke, -lik, Aungell lyke, angelyke, -llike] hyse wengis gan he sprede. **1561** T. N[ORTON] *Calvin's Inst.* III. xii. (1634) 362 Job.. seeth that very Angell-like holiness cannot appease God. **1611** SHAKS. *Cymb.* IV. ii. 48 How Angell-like he sings? **1660** G. NEWTON *John* xvii. (1867) 135 Their life is angel-like, they walk with God.

angel-noble. [*i.e.* NOBLE, bearing the device of an angel: cf. *spade-guinea*.] The fuller name of the gold coin ANGEL (see ANGEL *sb.* 6); it being really the representative in value (6*s.* 8*d.*) of the earlier *noble*, coined by Edward III, but with a device adopted from the Fr. *angelot*; while the new nobles, called *rose-nobles*, or *rials*, passed for 10*s.*

1474 WARKW. *Chron.* (1839) 4 Also he [made] angelle noblys of vjs. viijd. **1552** in *Bury Wills* (1850) 142 To haue for his payunes too aungell nobles. **1587** HOLINSHED *Chron.* III. 893/2 In this season the angell noble was iust the sixt part of an ounce Troie. **1686** *Cerem. for King's Evil* in *Reader* (1866) 3 Mar. 227/2 The King.. crossing the sore of the sick person with an Angel Noble. [**1834** *Penny Cycl.* II. 14/1 When first introduced, the angel was rated in value at 6*s.* 8*d.*, and being of the same value as the noble, was sometimes called the noble angel.]

angelocracy (eɪndʒə'lɒkrəsɪ). ? *Obs. rare*⁻¹. [f. Gr. ἄγγελος ANGEL *sb.* + -κρατία government: see -CRACY.] A government by angels.

1685 J. SCOTT *Chr. Life* (1700) II. II. vii. 320 Those angelocracies or angelical governments of countries and nations.

angelography (-'ɒgrəfɪ). *rare*⁻¹. [ad. mod.L. *angelographia*; f. Gr. ἄγγελος ANGEL *sb.* + -γραφία writing.] A descriptive treatise on the angels.

1753 CHAMBERS *Cycl. Supp.* s.v., Casmannus and Manitius have published Angelographies.

angelolatry (-'ɒlətrɪ). [f. Gr. ἄγγελος + λατρεία service, worship: see -LATRY.] Angel-worship.

1847 BUCH *Hagenbach's Hist. Doctr.* I. 342 The prohibition of the worship of angels (angelolatry) by the synod of Laodicea. **1879** M. CONWAY *Demonol.* II. IV. xiv. 158 The theory that man could get along without any Angelolatry or Demon-worship.

angelology (-'ɒlədʒɪ). [ad. mod.L. *angelologia*, f. Gr. ἄγγελος + -λογία discourse.] Doctrine as to angels; that part of theology which treats of angels.

[**1753** CHAMBERS *Cycl. Supp.*, *Angelologia*, the doctrine or science of angels.. Gerhard has published a sacred *Angelologia*.] **1846** GEO. ELIOT tr. *Strauss's Life of Jesus* I. 106 The manner in which this interpreter [*sc.* Olshausen].. treats of angelology and demonology. **1847** in CRAIG. **1855** MILMAN *Lat. Chr.* (1864) IX. XIV. ii. 54 The same vast mythology commanded the general consent; the same angelology. **1874** H. REYNOLDS *John Bapt.* ii. 91 Some opponents.. urge that the angelology of the New Testament was a Persian tradition.

†**ange'lomachy.** *Obs. rare*⁻¹. [f. Gr. ἄγγελος + -μαχια fighting.] A war between angels.

1635 HEYWOOD *Hierarch.* VI. 341 The Weapons, Engines, and Artillerie Used in this great Angelomachy.

angelophany (-'ɒfənɪ). [f. as prec. + -φανία or -φάνεια appearance, manifestation.] The appearing or visible manifestation of angels.

1846 GEO. ELIOT tr. *Strauss's Life of Jesus* I. 67 The Theophany and Angelophany of the Old and New Testament. **1858** SEARS *Athan.* vi. 47 It has been asserted.. that in the angelophanies both of the Old and New Testament, the angels assumed a material body. **1874** H. REYNOLDS *John Bapt.* ii. 89 All these angelophanies were anticipations of the ultimate adoption of our humanity by the Eternal Logos.

angelot ('ændʒələt). *arch.* [a. Fr. *angelot*, dim. of OFr. *angele*:—L. *angel-us* ANGEL *sb.*]

†**1.** A French gold coin struck by Louis XI, bearing the image of St. Michael with the dragon under his feet; also a piece coined at Paris by the English under Henry VI. *Obs.*

1525 *State Papers, Hen. VIII*, VI. 505 The money lent at his first transporting.. forty thousand angelottes. **1753** CHAMBERS *Cycl. Supp.*, *Angelot*, an antient English gold coin, struck at Paris, while under the English subjection. It was thus called from the figure of an angel supporting the scutcheon of the arms of England and France.

†**2.** A small rich cheese, made in Normandy. [Littré says because stamped with the coin.] *Obs.*

1611 COTGR., *Angelot*, the cheese called an Angelot. **1655** MOUFFET & BENN. *Health's Impr.* (1746) 221 The Angelots of Normandy are counted restorative. **1674** T. DUFFETT *Amorous Old. Wom.* I. ii, As mellow as an Angelot Cheese, that has been mortifi'd Fifteen Months in Horse-dung. **1719** *Accompl. Fem. Instr.* (N.) To make angelots. **1753** in CHAMBERS; and in mod. Dicts.

3. A musical instrument.

1678 PHILLIPS, *Angelot*.. a sort of Musical Instrument somewhat like a Lute. **1863** BROWNING *Sordello* II. Wks. III. 306 How to twirl His angelot, plaything of page or girl Once. *Ibid.* IV. III. 382 For elegance he strung the angelot, Made rhymes thereto.

angelry ('eɪndʒəlrɪ). *rare*⁻¹. [f. ANGEL *sb.* + -RY, as in *tenantry, yeomanry*.] A body of angels.

1805 W. TAYLOR in Robberds' *Mem.* II. 99 To surround the vine-planter of Ararat with a more racy and autochthonous machinery than his Miltonic angelry.

'**angelship.** *rare.* [f. ANGEL *sb.* + -SHIP; cf. *lordship*.] The condition of being an angel; a mock title for an angel.

1648 JOS. BEAUMONT *Psyche* XVII. cvi, Give Their Angelships the lie. **1802–12** [see MOUSESHIP]. **1907** J. H. MCCARTHY *Needles & Pins* i. 8 Two human beings.. are transmuted from their humanity into an angelship of intimate bliss.

angel-shot. [called also in Fr. *ange*; in reference to the wing-like position of the segments on each side of the central disk, in its flight through the air.] A species of chain-shot used to destroy the rigging of ships, etc., consisting of the (2 or 4) segments of a hollow ball, attached by chains to a central disk; these appendages being packed inside, the whole was fired as a ball, which spread asunder in its course.

1731 BAILEY, *Angel shot*, chain-shot, being a cannon bullet cut in two, and the halves being joined together by a chain.

‖**angelus** ('ændʒələs). [L., so called from its opening words '*Angelus domini nuntiavit Mariæ.*']

1. A devotional exercise commemorating the mystery of the Incarnation, consisting of versicles and responses, and the Angelic Salutation three times repeated, said by Roman Catholics, at morning, noon, and sunset, at the sound of a bell rung for that purpose.

1727 CHAMBERS *Cycl.* [Incorrectly explained.] **1847** LONGF. *Ev.* I. iv. 127 Sweetly over the village the bell of the angelus sounded. **1849** ROCK *Ch. of Fathers* III. ix. 340 The 'Angelus' did not come into use before the beginning of the XVIth century, and seems to have commenced in France. **1866** NEALE *Seq. & Hymns* 131 The Angelus at Compline shall sweetly close the day.

2. Short for *angelus-bell*.

1847 LONGF. *Ev.* I. i. 30 Softly the Angelus sounded. **1867** LADY HERBERT *Cradle L.* iv. 121 When the Angelus summons us.. to dwell for a few moments on the mystery of the Incarnation. **1881** *Atl. Monthly* XLVII. 176 'Tis the set of sun, The angelus must ring.

†'**angel-water.** *Obs.* [for angelica-water: see ANGELICA 2.] A perfumed liquid of which angelica once formed a chief constituent; afterwards containing ambergris, rose, myrtle, and orange-flower waters.

1687 SEDLEY *Bellam.* I. i, I met the prettiest creature in new Spring-garden!.. angel-water was the worst scent about her. **1719** *Accompl. Fem. Instr.* (N.), *Angel-water*, an excellent perfume: also a curious wash to beautify the skin.

anger ('æŋgə(r)), *sb.* Also 4–5 angyr, -gir, 4–6 angre, 5 angar. [a. ON. *angr* trouble, affliction, f. root *ang* strait, straitened, troubled: see ANGE.]

†**1.** That which pains or afflicts, or the passive feeling which it produces; trouble, affliction, vexation, sorrow. *Obs.*

c **1250** *Gen. & Ex.* 972 ȝhe held hire hard in ðralles wune, And dede hire sorȝe and anger mune. **1340** HAMPOLE *Pr. Consc.* 3517 Na man may to heven ga, Bot-if he thole here anger and wa. **1375** BARBOUR *Bruce* III. 321 Thir angrys may I na mar drey. **1393** LANGL. *P. Pl.* C. XXII. 291 To suffren al þat god sente · syknesses and angres. *c* **1440** *Gesta Rom.* 243 Deliuer me from this anger þat I dwelle in. **1475** CAXTON *Jason* 76 b, For the deth of whiche childe the anger and sorow was moche the more.

2. a. The active feeling provoked against the agent; passion, rage; wrath, ire, hot displeasure.

c **1325** *E.E. Allit. P.* B. 572 þe anger of his ire þ at arȝed monye. *c* **1386** CHAUCER *Frankl. T.* 825 Neuere eft ne was ther Angre [*v.r.* angyr, -er] hem bitwene. **1393** GOWER *Conf.* I. 282 Ne couth I after that be wroth, But all min anger overgoth. **1483** CAXTON *Gold. Leg.* 185/4 In an angre [he] toke his swerde and smote of the heed of thys holy man. **1548** UDALL, etc. *Erasm. Paraphr. Eph.* iv. 26 (R.) Restrayn your angre, whan it would barst out. **1552** LATIMER *Serm. Lord's Prayer* iv. II. 57 A man slain openly of another man in an anger. **1613** SHAKS. *Hen. VIII*, III. ii. 92 May be he heares the King Does whet his Anger to him. **1621** BURTON *Anat. Mel.* I. i. II, Anger, which is a desire of revenge; Hatred, which is inveterate anger. **1657** J. SMITH *Myst. Rhet.* 168 Anger is a vehement heat of the minde, which brings palenesse to the countenance, burning to the eyes, and trembling to the parts of the body. **1690** LOCKE *Hum. Underst.* II. xx. (1695) 122 Anger is uneasiness or discomposure of the Mind upon the receit of any Injury, with a present purpose of Revenge. **1754** CHATHAM *Lett. Nephew* v. 39 Anger, that dæmon, that destroyer of our peace. **1875** H. E. MANNING *Mission H. Ghost* xiv. 393 Anger has its proper use. Anger is the executive power of justice.

b. As a literary nonce-use (quot. 1937). Later with overt or implicit reference to J. Osborne's play *Look Back in Anger* (first performed 1956). Cf. ANGRY *a.* 3 c.

1937 H. G. WELLS *Brynhild* vii. 100 It brings my Anger back. I am an Angry Man... Almost professionally. You don't know my books? **1957** J. HOLLOWAY in *Hudson Rev.* Autumn 424 Notes on the 'School of Anger'. *Ibid.* 426 The anger of Sassoon's war poem was not, of course, the kind.. of Amis, Wain, Osborne, etc. **1958** *Spectator* 4 July 17/3 Students here have become sceptical about protest campaigns, petitions and the Anger Cult.

3. Physical affliction or pain; inflammatory state of any part of the body. (Still dial.)

1377 LANGL. *P. Pl.* B. XIII. 335, I cacche.. an ague in suche an angre, and some tyme a feure. *a* **1500** *MS. Lincoln* A i. 17. 305 (Halliw.) Anoynte hym fyrste with popilione if he hafe anger in his lyver. **1659** HAMMOND *On Ps.* lviii. 9 Rawness and anger (in that dialect, wherein we call a sore angry). *a* **1698** TEMPLE (J.) Where the greatest anger and soreness still continued.

4. *Comb.* (mostly *poet.*) **a.** attrib., as *anger-glow*; **b.** objective, as *anger-kindling*; **c.** instrumental, as *anger-boiling, -coddled, -lined, -swollen*.

1851 H. MELVILLE *Whales* xxxvi. 181 My heat has melted thee to anger-glow. **1634** W. WOOD *New Eng. Prosp.* II. vii, Anger-boyling blood. **1651** CLEVELAND *Miser* 29 Ajax with his anger-codled brain. **1879** *Spect.* 6 Sept. 1128/2 The sea had scarcely a wrinkle on the salt face which but a night or two before had looked anger-lined and wind-worn. **1839** BAILEY *Festus* vii. (1848) 70 Through anger-swollen wave or sparkling spray.

anger ('æŋgə(r)), *v.* Also 3 anngre, 4 angrye, 4–6 -re, 5 -ar, -ur. [a. ON. *angr-a* to grieve, vex, f. *angr*: see ANGER *sb.*]

†**1.** To distress, trouble, vex, hurt, wound. *Obs.*

c **1200** ORMIN 432 Nan þing .. þatt mihhte ohht anngrenn oþre. **1340** HAMPOLE *Pr. Consc.* 799 [The ald man] is ofte angerd, and ay pleynand. **1377** LANGL. *P. Pl.* B. XIV. 244 þough auarice wolde angre [**1393** angrye] þe pore. *c* **1400** *Rom. Rose* 3526 Is it youre ese Hym for to angre or disese? *c* **1440** *Gesta Rom.* I. lii. 183 To be turmentide, angride, and bete for oure defavtis.

2. Hence, through the idea of *irritate*: To excite to wrath, make angry, enrage. **a.** *trans.*

1377 LANGL. *P. Pl.* B. v. 117 Who-so hath more þan I, þat angreth me sore. **1494** FABYAN II. xxxvii. 26 Lyghtly he slewe all men yt hym tened or angred. **1530** PALSGR. 431/2, I angre, I chafe or bringe out of pacience. *Je courrouce.*—Beware howe you anger hym. **1592** SHAKS. *Rom. & Jul.* II. iv. 215, I anger her sometimes, and tell her that Paris is the properer man. **1662** FULLER *Worthies* (1840) III. 130 A person free from passion, whom none could anger out of his ordinary temper. **1758** JOHNSON *Idler* No. 9 ¶1 You have both pleased and angered me. **1841** MIALL *Nonconf.* I. 9 It would be difficult to anger the people just now. **1882** *Athenæum* No. 2831. 121 He angered every body who was affected by the project.

b. *impers.*

c **1400** *Destr. Troy* XI. 4571 Hit angris to abide, Or tary .. when tulkes ben redy. *c* **1440** *Morte Arth.* 1662 Me angers at Arthure. **1592** SHAKS. *Rom. & Jul.* II. i. 22 T'would anger him To raise a spirit in his Mistresse circle. *c* **1735** POPE *Epil. Sat.* II. 150 It anger'd Turenne .. To see a footman kick'd that took his pay. **1809** SOUTHEY *Lett.* II. 165 It angers me when people .. depreciate the Spaniards.

†**c.** *refl.* To vex oneself, become angry. *Obs.*

c **1400** *Destr. Troy* VI. 2236 Angurs you noht. *Ibid.* XVI. 7329 He angurt hym full euyll. *a* **1450** *Knt. de la Tour* (1868) 20 Anger you not .. of that that he saithe.

d. *intr.* (refl. pron. omitted.) *rare.*

c **1400** *Destr. Troy* XV. 6911 Vlixes .. angrit full sore. **1786** BURNS *Sc. Drink* xiii, When neebors anger at a plea.

†**3.** To irritate or inflame a sore. *Obs.* or *dial.*

a **1626** BACON (J.) He .. maketh the wound bleed inwards, and angereth malign ulcers. *c* **1735** POPE *Donne Sat.* IV. 119 Itch most hurts when anger'd to a sore. **1760** STERNE *Tr. Shandy* II. iv. 108 Uncle Toby, perceiving that [it] .. angered his wound, left off the study of projectiles.

angered ('æŋgəd), *ppl. a.* [f. prec. + -ED.] †**a.** Grieved, troubled (*obs.*). **b.** Provoked to wrath, irate; *lit.* and *fig.* **c.** Irritated, inflamed. **d.** Flushed as with rage.

c **1300** *Leg. Rood* (1871) 124 þis son of chosdroas .. euill angerd was. **1340** HAMPOLE *Pr. Consc.* 302 þe prophet .. was angred, in thoght. *c* **1400** *Destr. Troy* XIX. 7994 Achilles was angret angardly sore. **1606** SHAKS. *Ant. & Cl.* II. vi. 21 The anger'd ocean fomes. *c* **1830** TENNYSON *Madeline* iii, The flush of anger'd shame. **1830** —— *Dream Fair Wom.* 255 Those dragon eyes of anger'd Eleanor. **1878** B. TAYLOR *Deukalion* I. vi. 47 Every nightly crag .. Is angered with the glory. **1881** *Daily News* 11 Aug. 2/2 A somewhat angered controversy took place across the table. **1883** *Harper's Mag.* Feb. 483/1 The young man became angered.

†'**angerful**, *a. Obs. rare.* Also 3 ancreful, angresful. [prob. orig. a. ON. *angr-fullr* full of trouble, f. *angr* trouble: see ANGER. Analysed in 13th c. as *angres-full*, with *angres* in genitive. In its later use prob. a new formation on Eng. ANGER *sb.* (in sense 2) + -FUL.]

1. Full of trouble; careful, anxious.

c **1230** *Ancr. R.* 244 Inward, & meðlease, & angresfule bonen biwinneð sone sucurs. *Ibid.* 370 Forto beon so angresful þerefter nis nout God icweme: and ancreful nomliche uor swuch religiun nis nout God icweme.

2. Wrathful.

1598 SYLVESTER *Du Bartas* II. ii. (1641) 115/1 Repentant, jealous, fierce, and angerful.

angering ('æŋgərɪŋ), *vbl. sb.* [f. ANGER *v.* + -ING¹.] Making angry, enraging. (Now gerundial.)

1393 GOWER *Conf.* III. 175 In angring of the king. **1594** CAREW *Tasso's Godfr. Bulloigne* (1881) 26 Angring eneigres. **1692** BP. OF GLOUC. *Vindic.* Pref. A ij b, The angering of the Vicious Part of the Kingdom. *Mod.* Nothing will be gained by angering him.

'**angering**, *ppl. a.* [f. as prec. + -ING².] Enraging, provoking.

1602 WARNER *Alb. Eng.* II. lxvii. (1612) 286 The Amorous with the sea-Crabs gaet do angring Amours flie.

angerless ('æŋgəlɪs), *a.* [f. ANGER *sb.* + -LESS.] Free from anger.

1580 SIDNEY *Arcadia* (1622) 198 With an angerlesse brauery, and an vnabashed mildenesse, in this manner spake vnto them. **1598** SYLVESTER *Du Bartas* II. ii. (1641) 115/1 A judge self-angerless. **1839** DICKENS *Nich. Nick.* v. (C.D. ed.) 27 The termination of every angerless dispute brought them nearer .. to the close of their slight preparations.

angerly ('æŋgəlɪ), *adv. arch.* Forms: 4–5 angerliche, -irly, -yrly, -rely, 5 -arely, 6 -erlye, -erlie, 4– angerly. [f. ANGER *sb.* + -LY². This supposes an earlier use of *angerly*, *angerlic* as adj., as in ON. *angrligr* sad, painful.]

†**1.** With trouble or pain; hurtfully, painfully. *Obs.*

1327–1485 in Wright *Pol. Poems* I. 323 The kings law wol no man deme Angerliche without answere. **1393** GOWER *Conf.* I. 292 For that he with anger wrought His anger angerliche he bought. *c* **1400** *Rom. Rose* 3511 Gret wrong ye do To worche this man so mych woo, Or pynen him so angerly.

†**b.** Furiously. (Somet. intensive, like mod. 'terribly, awfully.') Cf. ANGARDLY, and ON. *ágjarnliga*. *Obs.*

1375 BARBOUR *Bruce* VIII. 486 Thai so angirly on thame socht, That of thame all eschapit nane. *c* **1400** *Destr. Troy* XI. 6483 Armyt at all peces, angarly mony. *Ibid.* XV. 6998 Issit out of þe ost angarely fast.

2. With anger or resentment. (Since 17th c. replaced by ANGRILY; but used as an archaism by some 19th c. poets.)

c **1386** CHAUCER *Pars. T.* ¶510 Than wol he be angry and answere hokerly and angerly [*v.r.* angrily, -yrly, -rely]. *c* **1450** HENRYSON *Mor. Fables* 78 Then angerly the Wolfe vpon him cryes. **1557** N. T. (Genev.) *Mark* iii. 5 He loked rounde about on them angerly. **1591** SHAKS. *Two Gent.* I. ii. 62 How angerly I taught my brow to frowne. *a* **1631** DONNE *Serm.* xxvi. 263 Fathers will speak loudest .. and look angerliest, that intend not the severest correction. **1641** *Vind. Answ. Humb. Rem.* §6. 89 Let him take it never so angerly. **1721** MRS. CENTLIVRE *Gamester* ii. 149, I am not to be us'd so angerly. **1856** MRS. BROWNING *Aur. Leigh* i. 14 A mother never is afraid Of speaking angerly to any child.

¶ as adj.: Angry.

1814 BYRON in Moore *Life* (1866) 244 Was angerly, but tried to conceal it.

†'**angerness.** *Obs. rare*⁻¹. [f. ANGER + -NESS: see prec.] Trouble, affliction.

a **1300** *Hymn to Virg.* in Warton *Eng. Poetry* (1840) II. 109 Heyl inocent out of angernesse.

†'**angersome**, *a. Obs.* [f. ANGER *sb.* + -SOME.] Troublesome, irritating.

1650 EARL MONM. *Man Guilty* 28 These Tyrants do not allways vex their subjects with angersome Commands. **1656** —— *Advt. fr. Parnassus*, Being hindred from growing fat in good pastures by angersome vexations.

†**an'get**, *v. Obs.* Forms: 1 **onȝit-an**, 1–2 **onȝet-an**, 3 **anȝet-en, anndȝæt-en.** [f. OE. *on* -proclitic form of *ond-*, *and-* (see AN *pref.* 2) + *git-an*, *ȝitan* to GET, acquire. The opposite of FOR-GET. The reg. form was *on-* or *a-get*; *and-get* in Orm. is assimilated to the sb.]

1. To comprehend, catch the sense of, understand, recognize.

c **975** *Rushw. Gosp.* Matt. xv. 17 Ne onȝetað ȝe þætte ȝ ehwæt þæs þe in muðe ingæð in wombe gangeð? *c* **1000** *Ags. Gosp.* ibid., Ne onȝyte ȝe? *c* **1175** *Lamb. Hom.* 223 þa onȝeat se deofel þat adam and eua weron toði ȝesceapene. **1250** LAY. 15726 þo anȝete [**1205** anȝæt] ich at þan ende: þat ich was mid childe.

2. To acknowledge, confess. *rare.*

c **1200** ORMIN 13633 Opennliȝ biforenn mann Anndȝæteþþ hiss missdede.

†**an'getness, and-.** *Obs. rare.* [f. prec. + -NESS.] Acknowledgement, confession.

c **1200** ORMIN 2762 To clennsenn aȝȝ hiss lif, þurrh soþfasst anndȝætnesse.

†**an'getting, and-**, *vbl. sb. Obs.* [f. as prec. + -ING¹.] Acknowledging or confessing.

c **1200** ORMIN 18027 Missdedess anndȝætinnge.

Angevin ('ændʒɪvɪn), *a.* and *sb.* [a. F. *Angevin*:—med.L. *Andegavin-us*, f. *Andegavum* Angers, capital of Anjou (*Andegavia*).] **A.** *adj.* Of or pertaining to Anjou, a former province of France, or any sovereign, government, etc., derived thence; *spec.* in *Eng. Hist.*, belonging to or characteristic of the Plantagenet kings (beginning with Henry II) descended from Geoffrey, count of Anjou, and Matilda, daughter of Henry I; pertaining or relating to their descendants, the period of history which they cover, etc. **B.** *sb.* A native of Anjou; an Angevin ruler.

1653 T. URQUHART *Pantagruel* II. xxvi. 170 One hundred and fifty thousand whores .. whereof some are Amazons, some Lionnoises, .. Angevines, [etc.]. **1737** MRS. THOMSON tr. *M. Baudier's Hist. Marg. Anjou* 4 Henry .. complained of the Angevin's Escape. **1769** G. LYTTELTON *Hist. Hen. II* (ed. 3) I. 162 The Angevin family had been long very powerful and illustrious. **1834** *Penny Cycl.* II. 35/1 The Angevin prince invaded Italy with an army of 30,000 men. **1874** GREEN *Short Hist.* ii. §7. 94 To understand the history of England under its Angevin rulers, we must first know something of the Angevins themselves. **1887** KATE NORGATE *Eng. under Angevin Kings* I. 3 Those wonderful Angevin counts who .. grew into a sovereign house. **1887** *Encycl. Brit.* XXII. 27/2 The Angevin conquest of Sicily. **1924** J. S. C. BRIDGE *Hist. France* II. 173 Charles had vindicated his Angevin claims. **1935** T. S. ELIOT *Murder in Cath.* I. 32 Let the Angevin Destroy himself, fighting in Anjou.

angico (an'dʒiko). [Pg.] A Brazilian name applied to the gum, etc., of the tropical S. American tree *Piptadenia rigida*, which yields a hard durable timber, and an astringent bark and a gum both used medicinally.

1867 SIMMONDS *Dict. Trade* Suppl., *Angico Gum.* **1897** WILLIS *Flowering Pl.* II. 298 P[iptadenia] rigida .. yields Angico gum used like gum-arabic.

†'**angild.** *Obs.* [OE. '*angild*, cogn. w. *an-*, *ǫngildan* to pay for, atone for; f. AN- *pref.* 1 + *gildan* to pay.] In O.E. law, payment in composition or atonement for injury. (Erroneously taken by later writers as meaning 'single payment,' as if OE. were *ángild*.)

a **940** *Laws of Athelst.* v. §8. 4 Forgylde ðæt yrfe angylde. **1706** PHILLIPS, *Angild*, the bare single Valuation or Satisfaction made for a Man or Thing. **1775** ASH, *Angild*, a mulct, a fine.

†'**angin.** *Obs.* 1–2. (g hard) Also **anginn, -gun** (Y). [cogn. w. OE. *an-*, *ǫn-ginn-an* to begin.] A beginning.

c **1000** ÆLFRIC *Gen.* i. 1 On anginne ȝescéop God heofenan and eorþan. *c* **1160** *Hatt. Gosp. Jo.* i. 1 On anginne (*Ags. G.* frymðe) ærest wæs word. *c* **1175** *Cott. Hom.* 237 Fram midden-ardes anginn. *c* **1200** *Trin. Coll. Hom.* 107 Ech iuel þonc · and speche · and dede .. sam it haue angun of þe mannes lichames wille, sam it haue þe biginning of the deules fortuhting.

‖**angina** ('ændʒɪnə, æn'dʒaɪnə). *Path.* Also 6–7 **angine.** [L. *angina* quinsy: cf. *ang-ĕre* to choke, strangle, and Gr. ἀγχόνη strangling. The L. was until recently supposed to be *angīna*, whence the erroneous pronunciation prevalent in English. Fr. *angine* (Cotgr.) was also in Eng. use.]

1. Quinsy.

1590 *Pasquil's Apol.* I. C b, A daungerous *Angina* in your throate. **1598** SYLVESTER *Du Bartas* II. i. (1641) 83/2 Knew the cold Cramp, th' Angine and Lunacy. **1645** EVELYN *Diary* (1827) I. 341 Afflicted with an angina and sore throat. **1751** CHAMBERS *Cycl.*, *Angina* is the same with that we popularly call quinzy. **1832** THOMPSON *Ann. Influenza* 57 In February 1738 coughs and anginas were very common amongst horses. **1876** tr. *Wagner's Gen. Pathol.* 13 Scarlet fever and angina .. often occur spontaneously.

2. (More fully, ***angina pectoris.***) A dangerous disease, the paroxysms of which are characterized by sudden and severe pain in the lower part of the chest, towards the left side, with a feeling of suffocation and alarm of impending death; they are brought on by over-exertion when the heart is diseased; called also *breast-pang*, *heart-stroke*, and *spasm of the chest*.

1768 W. HEBERDEN in *Med. Trans.* (1772) II. 59 Angina pectoris. **1811** HOOPER *Med. Dict.* 51 Angina pectoris is attended with a considerable degree of danger. **1833** J. FORBES in *Cycl. Pract. Med.* (ed. 3) I. 83 Angina occurs in both sexes. **1877** ROBERTS *Handbk. Med.* II. 24 Some cases of sudden death are due to angina. **1883** *Daily News* 6 July 5 The death of the Duke of Marlborough .. from an attack of angina pectoris.

anginal ('ændʒɪnəl, æn'dʒaɪnəl), *a.* [f. ANGINA + -AL.] Pertaining to angina, i.e. quinsy, or *angina pectoris*; = ANGINOUS. Also **anginic** (æn'dʒɪnɪk) *a.* So **an'giniform, 'anginoid** *adjs.*, resembling *angina pectoris*.

1811 LETTSOM in Pettigrew *Life* (1817) III. 4 The anginal stridula may make its onset without that exudation in the throat. **1882** J. D. HOOKER in L. Huxley *Life* (1918) II. 260, I have had a ten days' bout of my Anginic pains. **1889** *Cent. Dict.*, Anginoid. **1891** *Lancet* 14 Feb. 371/2 A series of anginoid attacks. *Ibid.* 371/1 Such cases might be termed 'anginous' or 'anginal'. **1906** *Westm. Gaz.* 27 Sept. 4/2 Tea .. gave me an awful pain, almost anginiform. **1910** W. JAMES *Let.* 25 May (1920) II. 337, I have a dilatation of the aorta, which causes anginoid pain of a bad kind whenever I make any exertion.

anginous ('ændʒɪnəs), *a. Path.* [f. ANGINA + -OUS; cf. mod.Fr. *angineux*.] Of or pertaining to *angina pectoris*.

1833 J. FORBES in *Cycl. Pract. Med.* (ed. 3) I. 87 The anginous symptoms being feebly manifested .. The anginous paroxysms seem to be the direct consequence of organic disease of the heart.

angio-, first element in many compounds, representing Roman transliteration of Gr. ἀγγεῖο-ν a vessel, receptacle, dim. of ἀγγε- (ἄγγος) a chest, box. Now used chiefly in terms relating to seed- and blood-vessels. Sometimes spelt *angeio-*; but Roman *ī* is the true equivalent of Gr. ει. Except where the stress falls on the *o* (ændʒɪ'ɒ-), the pronunciation ought to be (æn'dʒaɪəʊ) for (æŋ'gaɪəʊ-) but ('ændʒɪəʊ-) is in common use.

angiocardiography (,ændʒɪəʊkɑːdɪ'ɒgrəfɪ). [f. ANGIO- + CARDIOGRAPHY.] X-ray examination of the thoracic vessels and the heart after the intravenous injection of a substance opaque to X-rays. Hence **,angio'cardiogram**, a cardiogram taken during and immediately after such an injection.

1938 *Lancet* 24 Dec. 1476/2 Method of radiography of the heart and great vessels after the intravenous injection of opaque fluid. Angiocardiography is mainly applicable to congenital malformations in children, and can be used after death where a full post-mortem examination is refused. **1948** *Brit. Jrnl. Radiology* XXI. 381/1 The normal angiocardiogram. After injection of 20 c.c. of contrast agent local venous pressure is rapidly raised. **1951** *Brit. Encycl. Med. Practice* VI. 235 The size and shape of the various chambers of the heart and the great vessels arising from it may be studied during life by means of angiocardiography. A radio-opaque substance is injected rapidly intravenously and X-ray films are taken at frequent intervals to enable the course of the dye to be followed through the heart chambers and lungs.

angiocarpian (,ændʒɪəʊ'kɑːpɪən). *Bot.* [f. mod.L. *angiocarp-us* (see next) + -IAN.] An angiocarpous plant; a member of Mirbel's second class of fruits.

1839 LINDLEY *Introd. Bot.* (ed. 3) 232 *Angiocarpians*, fruit seated in envelopes not forming part of the calyx.

angiocarpous (-'kɑːpəs), *a. Bot.* [f. mod.L. *angiocarp-us* (f. ANGIO- + καρπ-ός fruit) + -OUS. Cf. Fr. *angiocarpe.*] Having the fruit in an envelope not constituting part of the calyx. Also, having the apothecium enclosed within the thallus, as certain lichens.

1836 *Penny Cycl.* s.v. *Botany, Angiocarpous*, having seeds enclosed in a pericarp. **1851** W. A. LEIGHTON (*title*) The British Species of Angiocarpous Lichens. **1875** *Sachs' Bot.* 268 The apothecium of Angiocarpous Lichens is.. similar in its mode of development.

angiogenesis (ændʒɪəʊ'dʒɛnɪsɪs). *Med.* [f. ANGIO- + -GENESIS.] The development of new blood-vessels.

1899 in GOULD *Pocket Med. Dict.* (ed. 3). **1935** *Contrib. Embryol.* XXV. CXLVI. 51/1 Early stages of angiogenesis [in the macaque embryo] are still present in the form of isolated, solid, multicellular strands without intercellular boundaries. **1975** *Nature* 18 Sept. 224/1 Folkman's work on tumour angiogenesis has emphasised the importance of vascularisation and blood supply in growth processes. **1983** *Sci. Amer.* Jan. 24 Large amounts of these factors are needed for research that may lead to the development of drugs for regulating angiogenesis.

angiogram ('ændʒɪəʊgræm). [f. ANGIO- + -GRAM.] A radiogram of blood vessels, made after injection of a contrast medium.

1933 A. EGAS MONIZ in *Lancet* 18 Nov. 1147/1 The speed of circulation is very different in the brain as compared with other parts of the head... We have ascertained this fact by studying the arteriograms and phlebograms of diverse cases, but confirmation was obtained by a series of angiograms, taken from second to second, after the injection of thorotrast in the common carotid and the external and internal carotids.

angiograph ('ændʒɪəʊgrɑːf, -æ-, æn'dʒaɪəgrɑːf, -æ-). [f. ANGIO- + Gr. -γραφος writer: see -GRAPH.] A special kind of sphygmograph or instrument for recording on paper the movements of the pulse.

1880 in *Syd. Soc. Lex.*

angiography (ændʒɪ'ɒgrəfɪ). [f. ANGIO- + -γραφία writing about: see -GRAPHY.]

1. A description of instruments, vessels, etc., used by any nation.

1727-51 CHAMBERS *Cycl.*, *Angeiography* also includes the consideration of the weights, measures, &c. used by the several nations.

2. A description of the blood-vessels. Recently extended to denote the examination of the blood vessels by radiography. Hence **angio'graphic** *a.*, of or pertaining to angiography.

1731 BAILEY, *Angeiography.* **1847** CRAIG, *Angiography.* [**1933** EGAS MONIZ & ALVES in *Rev. Neurologique* XL. I. 375 Dans le domaine radiologue nous obtenons non seulement l'artériographie du cerveau mais aussi les angiographies du passage du thorotrast par les capillaires et par les veines du cerveau.] **1933** *Lancet* 18 Nov. 1157/2 By taking a series of radiograms at intervals of one second, it has been found possible to display the cerebral veins and sinuses as well as arteries, and Moniz has therefore changed the name of the procedure from arteriography to angiography. **1950** P. ALMEIDA LIMA *Cerebral Angiography* vii. 156 The localization of aneurysms in the arterial region is almost always clear and well defined in the angiographic images. *Ibid.* x. 212 The angiographic method lends itself to application in physiological studies of the cerebral circulation. **1955** *Gloss. Terms Radiology* (*B.S.I.*) 56 *Angiography*, the radiological examination of blood vessels following direct injection of a contrast medium. **1956** *Acta Radiologica* XLVI. 480 (*title*) Angiographic Appearances in Transtentorial Herniation of the Brain.

angiology (ændʒɪ'ɒlədʒɪ). [f. as prec. + -λογία discussion: see -LOGY.] That part of anatomy which relates to the vessels in the human body.

1706 PHILLIPS, *Angiology*, a Discourse or Treatise of the Vessels of a Humane Body; as of the Veins, Arteries, Sinews, &c. **1737** BRACKEN *Farriery* (1756) I. x. 92 Angiology, or the Anatomy of the Veins and Arteries. **1843** WILKINSON *Swedenb. Anim. Kingd.* I. xii. 372 To explain the nature of the spirit of the blood belongs to.. psychology; to explain the nature of the body thereof, to angiology.

angioma (ændʒɪ'əʊmə). *Path.* Pl. **-ata.** [mod.L., f. Gr. ἀγγεῖον vessel + -OMA.] A tumour produced by dilatation or new formation of blood-vessels. Hence **angi'omatous** *a.*

1871 T. H. GREEN *Introd. Path.* xxiv. 186 The angiomata, or vascular tumours, are tumours consisting of blood-vessels held together by.. connective tissue. **1897** *Trans. Amer. Pediatric Soc.* IX. 154 Angiomatous tumours. **1962** *Lancet* 1 Dec. 1136/2 A man of 53 had an angioma of the spinal cord and a neurogenic bladder.

angiomono'spermous, *a. Bot.* [f. ANGIO- + MONOSPERMOUS.] Bearing solitary seeds, and these each in a pod or vessel of its own.

1731 BAILEY, *Angiomonospermæous.* **1847** in CRAIG.

angioneurosis (ˌændʒɪəʊnjʊ'rəʊsɪs). [ad. G. *angioneurose* (H. Quincke 1882, in *Monatshefte f. Prakt. Dermatologie* I. 130), f. ANGIO- + NEUROSIS.] Neurosis of the blood vessels. So **ˌangioneu'rotic** *a.*, characterized by angioneurosis.

1887 *Lond. Med. Rec.* 33/1 (*heading*) Strübing on Acute (Angioneurotic) Œdema. **1889** *Cent. Dict.*, Angioneurosis. **1908** *Practitioner* LXXX. 824 Colcott Fox, Quincke, and Walker put urticaria as an angioneurosis, while Pepper.. calls angioneurotic œdema, 'giant urticaria', with symptoms of heat, swelling, itching. **1964** S. DUKE-ELDER *Parsons' Dis. Eye* (ed. 14) xxxi. 490 An intermittent and acute œdematous condition due to unstable vasomotor reactions, frequently determined on an allergic basis, is relatively common in the lids (angioneurotic œdema).

angioscope ('ændʒɪəʊskəʊp, æn'dʒaɪəskəʊp). [f. ANGIO- + -σκοπος viewing: see -SCOPE.] An instrument for the minute examination of the capillary vessels of animals and plants.

angiosperm ('ændʒɪəʊspɜːm). *Bot.* [ad. mod.L. *angiosperm-us* (Hermann 1690), f. Gr. ἀγγεῖον vessel, receptacle + -σπερμ-ος, adj. formative from σπέρμα, σπέρματ-, seed. (Gr. has also -σπέρματ-ος; cf. πολύ-σπερμος or πολυ-σπέρματ-ος many-seeded; whence *angiospermous* and *-spermatous.*)] A plant which has its seeds inclosed in a seed-vessel, as the *poppy*, *apple*, *beech*, etc.; opposed to *gymnosperms* or plants with naked seeds, as the *pine*.

1852 ANSTED *Man. Geog. Sc.* 320 Phanerogamous plants are therefore either Gymnosperms (naked seeded) or Angiosperms (covered-seeded). **1861** G. BENTHAM *Flora Hong-Kong* Introd. 23 The seed is enclosed in the pericarp in the majority of flowering plants, called therefore angiosperms.

angio'spermal, *a. Bot.* [f. as prec. + -AL[1].] = ANGIOSPERMOUS.

1847 A. LINCOLN *Lect. Bot.* App. 189 *Angiospermal*.. Plants whose seeds are enclosed or covered.

angio'spermatous, *a. Bot.* [See ANGIOSPERM.] = ANGIOSPERMOUS.

1853 in MAYNE *Exp. Lex.*

angiospermous (-'spɜːməs), *a. Bot.* [f. mod.L. *angiosperm-us* (see above) + -OUS.] Having the seeds enclosed in a pericarp or seed-vessel.

1731 BAILEY, *Angiospermous* [as ANGIOMONOSPERMOUS]. **1760** LEE *Bot.* v. (Jod.) The fruit angiospermous. **1854** BALFOUR in *Encycl. Brit.* V. 237 The Tertiary period is characterized by the abundance of Angiospermous Dicotyledons.

angiosporous (ændʒɪ'ɒspərəs), *a. Bot.* [f. ANGIO- + σπόρ-ος sowing, seed + -OUS.] Having spores enclosed in a hollow receptacle, like the puff-ball and other fungi.

1847 in CRAIG. **1857** HENFREY *Bot.* 436 Angiosporous, Flowerless Plants producing spores.

angiostomous (ændʒɪ'ɒstəməs), *a. Conch.* [f. ANGIO- + -στομ-ος mouthed (f. στόμα mouth) + -OUS. But the sense seems to be taken from L. *angere* to compress.] Having a narrow opening. (Applied to certain univalve shells.)

1880 in *Syd. Soc. Lex.*

angiotenic (ˌændʒɪəʊ'tɛnɪk), *a. Med.* [f. ANGIO- + τεν- stem of τείνειν to stretch + -IC; cf. Fr. *angiotenique.*] *lit.* Tending to stretch the blood-vessels; applied, after Pinel, to inflammatory fevers.

1840 in Tweedie *Cycl. Pract. Med.* II. 162.

angiotomy (ændʒɪ'ɒtəmɪ). [f. ANGIO + Gr. -τομία cutting: see -TOMY.] (See quot.)

1706 PHILLIPS, *Angiotomy*, a Cutting open of those Vessels [of the Body]: as in opening of an Artery or Vein. **1753** CHAMBERS *Cycl. Supp.*, *Angeiotomy* may be divided into phlebotomy and arteriotomy. **1839** HOOPER *Med. Dict.*, *Angiotomy*, the anatomy of the sanguiferous and absorbent vessels.

†**'angiport.** *Obs. rare.* [ad. L. *angiport-us* a narrow lane or alley, f. *ang-ĕre* to compress + *portus* a harbour, *orig.* an entrance, passage.] A narrow passage or opening in a wall, either to fire from, or as an easily-commanded entrance.

1647 WARD *Simple Cob.* 72 They are the cursed Countermures, dropt Portcullises, scouring Angi-ports. **1652** URQUHART *Jewel* Wks. 1834. 267 Secret angiports and dark postern-doors.. so narrow that few of them could get in.

†**'angit.** *Obs.* 1-2. Also **and-, ond-, -ȝyt, -ȝite.** [OE. *andȝit*, f. AND- *pref.* + *ȝitan* to get; cf. ANGET.] Perception, understanding, intelligence.

*c*950 *Lindisf. Gosp.* Matt. xv. 16 Buta ondȝet aro ȝie. *c*1000 *Ags. G.* ibid., Butan andȝyte. *c*1160 *Hatton G.*, Buton andȝytte. *c*1175 *Lamb. Hom.* 99 He onlihte ure mod.. mid wisdom . and anȝite.

angle ('æŋg(ə)l), *sb.*[1] *arch.* Forms: 1 angul, ongul, 1-2 angel, 4 angil, 5 -ell, -ylle, (hangul), 5- angle. [OE. *angul*, cogn. w. OS. and OHG. *angul* (mod.G. *angel*), ON. *öngull*:—**angulr*; cf. L. *unc-us*, *angulus*, and Aryan root *ank-* to bend.]

1. A fishing-hook; often, in later use, extended to the line or tackle to which it is fastened, and the rod to which the latter is attached. *arch.*

*c*880 K. ÆLFRED *Boeth.* xx, Swa swa mid angle fisc ȝefangen biþ. *c*950 *Lindisf. Gosp.* Matt. xvii. 27 Gae to sæ & sende ongul *vel* hóc. *c*1160 *Hatton G.* ibid., Wirp þinne angel ut. [TINDALE, *Genev.* angle; WYCLIF, *Rhem.*, **1611** hook.] **1440** *Promp. Parv.*, *Angylle* to take wyth fysche, *Piscale, fistuca.* **1496** *Bk. St. Alban's* (title of ed. 2) Treatyse perteynynge to Hawkynge, Huntynge and Fysshynge with an Angle. **1535** COVERDALE *Job* xl. 20 Darrest thou drawe Leuiathan with an angle? **1606** SHAKS. *Ant. & Cl.* II. v. 10 Giue me mine Angle, weele to 'th' Riuer. **1611** BIBLE *Isa.* xix. 8 They that cast angle upon the brookes shall lament. **1653** WALTON *Angler* 120 You will be pleased too, if you find a Trout at one of our Angles. **1764** GOLDSM. *Trav.* 187 With patient angle trolls the finny deep. **1829** J. CLARE *Autumn* in *Anniv.* 76 On which the shepherd crawls astride, to throw His angle clear of weeds.

†**2.** *fig.* A person or thing that catches like a hook. *Obs.*

1535 COVERDALE *Eccles.* vii. 26 A woman is bytterer then death: for she is a very angle, hir hert is a nett. **1537** ? TINDALE *Exp. St. John* 45 He can not.. hyde the angle of his poysoned heresye vnder a bayte of true doctrine. **1598** SYLVESTER *Du Bartas* I. i. (1641) 6/2 Yea Faith it selfe, and Zeale, be sometimes Angles, Wherewith this Juggler heav'n-bent souls intangles.

3. *Comb.* †**angle-head**, the barbed head of an arrow; †**angle-taster**, an Arctic bird; **angle-worm**, a worm for bait. Also ANGLE-HOOK, -ROD, -TWITCH, q.v.

*c*1470 HENRY *Wallace* IV. 554 Ane angell hede to the hukis he drew, And at a schoyt the formast sone he sleu. **1743** in *Phil. Trans.* XLII. 612 Greenland produces Maws, Redshanks.. Angle-tasters, Snipes, &c. **1875** B. TAYLOR *Faust* I. i. 26 Digs with eager hand for buried ore, And, when it finds an angle worm, rejoices.

4. [f. ANGLE *v.*[1]] An act of angling. Here *fig.*

1874 HARDY *Madding Crowd* II. i. 5 She forgot for a moment her thoughtless angle on that day in February.

angle ('æŋg(ə)l), *sb.*[2] Also 4-5 **aungel**, 4-7 **angel**, 5-6 **-ule, -yll.** [a. Fr. *angle*:—L. *angul-um* (nom. *-us*) corner, a dim. form, of which the prim. **angus* is not in L.; cf. Gr. ἄγκος a bend, a hollow angle, and L. *ang-ĕre* to compress in a bend or fold, to strangle; Aryan root *ank-* to bend.]

1. a. The indefinite space included between two meeting lines or planes, the shape of which depends upon their mutual inclination; hence in *Geom.* the degree of inclination of two lines to each other, or of one line to a horizontal or vertical base-line.

The angle is measured by the portion of the circumference of a circle described from the intersection of the lines as centre, which is intercepted between the two lines. The inclination of two lines in the same plane is a plane angle, which may be *rectilineal* or *curvilineal*, as it is formed by straight or curved lines; the inclination of two lines on the surface of a sphere is a *spherical* angle; the space included by more than two plane angles meeting at a point is a *solid* angle.

*c*1386 CHAUCER *Sqrs. T.* 222 By compositions of angles and of slie reflections. **1570** BILLINGSLEY *Euclid* I. def. 9 There are of angles thre kindes, a right angle, an acute angle, and an obtuse angle. **1571** DIGGES *Geom. Pract.* I. Bj, A Playne Angle is the inclination of two lines lying in one playne Superficies, concurring or meeting in a poynt. **1594** BLUNDEVIL *Exerc.* III. I. (ed. 7) 272 Sphericall, that is to say, round Angels, which consist of two circular lines drawn upon a Sphericall superficies. **1646** SIR T. BROWNE *Pseud. Ep.* IV. vi. 193 With man.. in natation they [legs and arms] intersect and make all sorts of Angles. **1690** LOCKE *Hum. Underst.* I. iv. (1695) 37 The three Angles of a Triangle are equal to two Right ones. **1878** HUXLEY *Physiogr.* 60 The slope or inclination which one face [of a crystal] has to another; in other words the angle made by two neighbouring faces.

¶ Measurement by angle is used in many departments of physics, mechanics, etc., to estimate the position of bodies, the direction of forces, etc. Hence such phr. as ***angle of application, approach, attack, depression, deviation, elevation, entry, incidence, inclination, position, reflection, refraction, repose, rest, traction, trail, vision***; and the vbl. phr. ***to take the angle.***

1626 etc. [see INCIDENCE 4]. **1638** WILKINS *Discov. New World* I. (1684) 44 Where the Angel of Reflexion is Equal to the Angel of Incidence. **1790** RAY in *Phil. Trans.* LXXX. 154 By the means of this piece of mechanism in the eye-end of the telescope.. small angles of elevation or depression may be determined with great accuracy. **1805** FLINDERS *ibid.* XCV. 190 Endeavoured to take the angles on shore with a.. theodolite. **1812** WOODHOUSE *Astron.* viii. 58 When through a Star great circles are drawn respectively from the poles of the equator and ecliptic, they form at the Star an angle called the Angle of Position. **1831** BREWSTER *Optics* iv. §35. 29 The angular change of direction or the angle of deviation as it is called. **1831** —— *Nat. Magic* iv. 87 A prism with a small refracting angle. **1849** WEALE *Dict. Terms* 17 *Angle of application*, the angle which the line of direction of a power gives the lever it acts upon. *Angle of inclination*, the angle an inclined plane makes with the horizon. *Angle of traction*, the angle which the direction of a power makes with the inclined plane. **1869** PHILLIPS, *Vesuv.* vii. 180 The usual angle of rest in loose materials. **1908** *Westm. Gaz.* 30 May 7/3 The angle at which the plane is inclined to the direction of motion, the technical term for that angle being the angle of attack. **1910** R. FERRIS *How it Flies* xx. 454 *Angle of Entry*, the angle made by the tangent to the curve of the aeroplane surface at its forward edge, with the direction, or line, of travel. *Ibid.*, *Angle of Incidence*, the angle made by the chord of the arc of a curved 'plane', or by the line of a flat plane, with the line of travel. *Ibid.*, *Angle of Trail*, the angle made by the tangent to the rear edge of a curved plane with the line of travel. **1932** H. NICOLSON *Public Faces* II. 29 Even the angles were so diffcult: the angles of approach: the actual moment of initiation: the excruciating angle of continuance. **1948** *Jrnl. R. Aeronaut. Soc.* LII. 441/2 Approaches at a constant angle could be made by means of an 'angle of approach light', which was a light having three coloured sectors arranged one above the other, so that the pilot saw a red light if the aircraft was too low, a green light if the aircraft was approaching at the correct angle, and a yellow light if the aircraft was too high. **1962** *Gloss. Aeronaut. Terms* (*B.S.I.*) IV. 1 *Angle of incidence, angle of attack*, the angle between the chord of a wing or the reference line in a body and the direction of the undisturbed flow in the absence of sideslip. *Ibid.* v. 4 *Rigging angle of incidence*, the angle between the chord of the main or tail plane and the horizontal when the aeroplane is in the rigging position.

b. ***at angles with***: so placed as to form an angle with, in opposition to *parallel* (and, unless qualified by *right*, to *perpendicular*) to. ***on the angle***: obliquely.

1753 HOGARTH *Anal. Beauty* iii. 19 The painter, if he is left to his choice, takes it on the angle rather than in front. **1779** J. MOORE *Soc. in France* II. 169 Others which go off at right angles from that. **1862** LYTTON *Str. Story* II. 11 Behind the portico of a detached house at angles with the street.

c. The point or direction from which one views or approaches an object, circumstance, event, subject of inquiry, etc.; standpoint; hence (loosely) = ASPECT 9; (*slang*) scheme, illegal method. Freq. with defining word. Cf. SLANT *sb.*[1]

1872 GEO. ELIOT *Middlem.* III. xxiii. 13 Tacit expectations of what would be done for him by Uncle Featherstone determined the angle at which most people viewed Fred Vincy in Middlemarch. **1922** H. WALPOLE in S. Lewis *Babbitt* p. viii, Mr. Lewis turns the figure round and allows us to view it from every possible angle. **1928** A. WAUGH *Nor Many Waters* (1930) vi. 241 The account of the cricket from an Australian angle. **1935** *Proc. Prehist. Soc.* I. 10 The study and appreciation of a culture from this angle imposes fresh obligations upon the archaeologist. **1936** *Punch* 14 Oct. 430/1 Let us approach the subject from a mathematical or statistical angle. **1942** *World Rev.* May 6/1 The right type of advertising man might be better as an adviser on the propaganda angle. **1942** A. CHRISTIE *Body in Library* xviii. 157 The selection of the poor child, Pamela, the approach to her from the film angle. **1944** 'N. SHUTE' *Pastoral* v. 116 The old stagers.. the men who knew all the angles, who had great experience. **1958** S. ELLIN *Eighth Circle* (1959) II. ix. 103 His angle was to sell off tapes and pictures to the dirt magazines. **1958** *Spectator* 22 Aug. 259/3 This collection of essays.. feels obliged to use such a selling angle to persuade America that a favourable attitude to colonialism can be held without giving hostages to Marxist criticism.

d. *Squash Rackets.* In full *angle shot*: a shot struck at the side wall so that it rebounds directly to the front wall without touching the floor.

1926 C. ARNOLD *Squash Racquets* ii. 12 The angle shot can be made from either court, forehand or backhand. **1933** *Times* 4 Dec. 6/6 In the fourth game Elsmie set an even faster pace by means of cleverly played angle shots. **1934** *Times* 13 Jan. 4/5 He played the angles cleverly and showed a delicate touch when using the drop.

e. *Photogr.* In full ***camera angle***: the direction or viewpoint from which a photograph is taken. So ***angle shot***, esp. in *Cinemat.*, a shot taken with the camera at an angle to the horizontal.

1928 *Amer. Speech* III. 352 Directors are obsessed with camera angles. **1937** *Mod. Encycl. Photogr.* I. 70/2 The angle shot is now extensively employed in order to give emphasis and dramatic force. **1959** HALAS & MANVELL *Technique Film Amination* 336 For variety of continuity a different angle is often used in long shots, medium shots and close-ups of the same subject.

2. The meeting-point of two lines not in the same direction. Also *fig.*

1605 BACON *Adv. Learn.* II. v. §2 (1873) 105 Several lines that meet in one angle, and so touch but in a point. **1677** HALE *Prim. Orig. Man.* 362 He is *nexus utriusque mundi*, the common Angle wherein the highest and noblest of Material and Corporeal Nature is joyned to the Spiritual. **1870** FLOWER *Osteol. Mamm.* 122 The angle of the jaw is the point at which the vertical hind edge of the ramus, descending from the condyle, meets the horizontal inferior border.

3. A corner viewed internally or as a receding space; a retreating corner, a corner into which one may withdraw, a coign. Also *fig.*

c **1384** CHAUCER *H. of Fame* 1959 Alle the houses Angles [*v.r.* aungelys] Ys ful of rovnynges and of Iangles. **1430** LYDG. *Chron. Troy* I. vi, Not openly as ypocrytes praye In dyuers angels ioyning on the waye. **1509** FISHER *Wks.* (1876) 171 We be thraste downe into a very streyght angyll. **1607** TOURNEUR *Rev. Trag.* III. i, Some darken'd blushless angle. **1655** DIGGES *Compl. Ambass.* 321 For truth will seek no angles. **1826** SCOTT *Woodst.* 187 In each angle of the ascent was placed.. the figure of a Norman foot-soldier.

4. A spot lying out of the direct way, an outlying spot or 'corner,' without reference to shape; a nook. Also *fig. arch.*

1447 BOKENHAM *Lyvys of Seyntys* 2 For this the[y] soun Throwyn it [this book] in the angle of oblyvyoun. **1480** CAXTON *Descr. Brit.* 3 Anglia hath that name as it were an angle and a corner of the world. **1563** GRINDAL *Rem.* (1843) 256 That little angle where I was born, called Cowpland. **1610** SHAKS. *Temp.* I. ii. 223 Whom I left.. In an odde Angle of the Isle. **1641** MILTON *Ch. Govt.* II. iii. (1851) 171 To search the tenderest angles of the heart. **1656** S. HOLLAND in *Shaks. Cent. Praise* 302 The fire of Emulation burnt fiercely in every angle of this Paradise.

5. A corner viewed externally or as a projection, a projecting corner (of a building, etc.). Also *fig.*

1532 MORE *Confut. Barnes* VIII. Wks. 1557. 783/1 That corner stone that is layed in the hed of the angle. **1589** PUTTENHAM *Eng. Poesie* (Arb.) 111 The Roundell hath no bonch nor angle, Which may his course stay or entangle. **1624** WOTTON *Archit.* (1672) 20 That the Angles be firmly bound, which are the Nerves of the whole Edifice. **1756** BURKE *Subl. & B.* Wks. I. 184 There is nothing more prejudicial to the grandeur of buildings than to abound in angles. **1842** E. WILSON *Anat. Vade M.* 18 The superior angle is received into the interval formed by the union of the posterior and superior angles of the parietal bones.

6. An angular or sharp projection; *hence* an angular fragment. Also *fig.*

1684 DRYDEN *Ovid's Met.* (R.) Though but an angle reach'd him of the stone. **1844** KINGLAKE *Eothen* ii. (1878) 21 The angle of the oriental stirrup is a very poor substitute for spurs. **1850** TENNYSON *In Mem.* lxxxix. 40 We rub each other's angles down. **1853** KANE *Grinnell Exp.* xxviii. (1856) 229 We trod on the fractured angles of upturned ice.

7. *Astrol.* A name given to the four astrological 'houses,' at the cardinal points of the compass.

c **1386** CHAUCER *Sqrs. T.* 263 Phebus hath laft the Angle [*v.r.* angel] meridional. **1594** BLUNDEVIL *Exerc.* IV. xxxvi. (ed. 7) 493 Of which 12 houses the foure principall are foure points of the Zodiaque, whereof two do fall upon the Horizon, and the other two upon the Meridian, and are called principall points, Poles, or Angles. **1727–51** CHAMBERS *Cycl.* s.v., The horoscope of the first house is termed the angle of the East. **1819** J. WILSON *Dict. Astrol.* 6 Ptolemy gives the preference to the south angle.

8. *Comb.*, chiefly *attrib.*: **a.** of shape (= ANGULAR), as ***angle-leg***, ***-piece***, ***-taper***; **b.** of position (at or in an angle), as ***angle-bracket***, ***-column***, ***-niche***, ***-rafter***, ***-rib***, ***-stone***, ***-tower***, ***-turret***. Also **angle-bar**, the upright bar at the angle of a polygonal window, *also* (= **angle-iron**); **angle-bead**, a vertical bead, usually of wood, fixed to an exterior angle, flush with the surface of the plaster; **angle-brace**, a piece of timber fixed to the adjacent sides of a quadrangular framing; **angle-bracket**, (*a*) (see above); (*b*) *Typogr.*, etc. (unhyphened), either of the symbols < or > used, alone or in pairs, as a bracket in various scientific and general editorial contexts (see quots.); **angle-brick** (see quot. *a* 1884); **angledozer, angle-dozer** ('æŋg(ə)l ˌdəʊzə(r)) [cf. BULLDOZER], a type of bulldozer on which the blade can be set at an angle; **angle-iron**, an **L**-shaped piece of iron, used to secure or strengthen all kinds of framework; **angle-meter**, an instrument for measuring angles, esp. for ascertaining the dip of geological strata, a CLINOMETER; **anglepoise, angle-poise** [proprietary term] *a.*, designating a type of swivelled reading-lamp; also *ellipt.*; **angle shades** [cf. SHADE *sb.* 3 c], collectors' name for a species of moth, *Phlogophora meticulosa*; **angle-staff** (= *angle-bead*); **angle-tie** (= *angle-brace*). Also ANGLE-WISE, q.v.

1842 GWILT *Encycl.* 1181 *Angle beads of wood round the intradosses of circular arches are difficult to bend without cutting or steaming them. *a* **1875** KNIGHT *Dict. Mech.* I. 103/1 **Angle-bracket* (*Carpentry*), one beneath the eave at the corner of a building, and projecting at an angle of 45° with the face of each wall. **1940** *Chambers's Techn. Dict.* 34/2 *Angle bracket* (*Eng.*), a bracket consisting of two sides set at right-angles, often stiffened by a gusset. [**1954** T. W. CHAUNDY et al. *Printing of Math.* ii. 33 Two further sorts of brackets can be made available..'double' brackets ⟦ ⟧ and 'angular' brackets < >... Angular brackets have already been conventionalized in Physics, in connexion with Dirac's 'bra' and 'ket' vectors, and elsewhere.] **1956** F. H. COLLINS *Authors' & Printers' Dict.* (ed. 10) 15/1 Angle brackets < >. **1978** *N. & Q.* Feb. 90/1 The editors' preliminary announcement of policy together with..angle brackets for doubtful readings, removes the necessity for most textual footnotes. **1982** *Giant Bk. Electronics Projects* vi. 246 An angle bracket is a satisfactory mounting. *a* **1884** KNIGHT *Dict. Mech.* Suppl. 36/2 **Angle-brick*, bricks specially formed to enable other than square angles to be turned. **1937** *Discovery* Sept. 289/2 Angle-bricks and half-sized bricks have been found. **1880** J. MIDDLETON in *Academy* 21 Aug. 139/3 The *angle columns have the least weight to bear. **1940** *Gloss. Highway Engin. Terms* (*B.S.I.*) 54 *Bulldozer*, **Angledozer*, a power operated machine of the grader type employed for spreading and levelling by pushing loose excavated material. **1942** *Times* 9 Oct. 2/2 There are..machines for levelling—motor propelled scrapers—tractors, dumpers, angle-dozers and bulldozers. **1958** J. S. SCOTT *Dict. Civ. Engin.* 8 *Angle dozer*, a bulldozer with the mouldboard set at an angle so that it pushes earth sideways instead of straight ahead. **1862** SMILES *Engineers* III. 422 Cells formed of boiler-plates riveted together with *angle-iron. **1869** E. REED *Ship-build.* ii. 25 The vertical flanges of the angle-irons were bolted through all. **1881** GREENER *Gun* 415 A wooden frame..strengthened by an angle-iron facing. **1649** LOVELACE *Lucaste*, Like flyes Caught by their *angle-legs. **1793** SMEATON *Edystone L.* §295 Sixteen *angle pieces of iron..in the nature of knee timbers of a ship. **1940** GRAVES & HODGE *Long Week-end* xx. 350 *Angle-poise reading-lamps that would swing and bend in any desired direction. **1949** *Trade Marks Jrnl.* 22 June 548/2 Angle-poise... Electric lamps embodying adjustable brackets or supports. Herbert Terry & Sons Limited.. Redditch; Manufacturers—5th February, 1947. **1961** I. MURDOCH *Severed Head* vi. 52 He switched off the centre lights and turned on a single anglepoise lamp on the work table which he swung round towards the pedestal. *Ibid.* 56 Alexander..had turned the anglepoise back to shine upon his unfinished head. **1879** G. SCOTT *Archit.* II. 185 The *angle ribs of the outer half meet the transverse ribs of the inner half of the vault. **1843** J. DUNCAN in W. Jardine *Naturalist's Libr.* XL. 235 (*heading*) The *Angle Shades. *Phlogophora Meticulosa*... Angle-Shades Moth. **1938** C. A. HALL *Pocket-Bk. Brit. Butterflies* 86 The Angle-Shades..is on the wing in June and again in the autumn. **1961** R. SOUTH *Moths Brit. Isles* I. 294 (*heading*) The Small Angle Shades.. The pale reniform mark on the outer edge of the blackish central area is the prominent feature of this pinkish or purplish brown moth. *Ibid.* 295 The Angle Shades... In this position [*sc.* with the wings folded] the moth is very like a crumpled decaying leaf. **1649** BLITH *Eng. Improver Impr.* (1653) 131 The other two run towards an *Angle-taper, declining from twelve Inches in the But or bottom, to six Inches at the mouth. **1782** in *Phil. Trans.* LXXII. 368 From the place into which this holdfast was driven to the outer end of the *angle-tie. **1911** T. E. LAWRENCE *Let.* 8 June (1938) 110 No one knows how the outwork at Gaillard was breached: I fancy..that the *angle tower was mined over the filled up moat. **1958** *Listener* 9 Oct. 558/1 Telephone wires, aerials, angle towers, and sub-stations. **1867** A. BARRY *Sir C. Barry* iv. 110 The elevated *angle-turrets.

Angle ('æŋg(ə)l), *sb.*[3] [ad. L. *Angl-us*, pl. *Angl-i* (Tacitus), a. OTeut. **angli-*, in OE. regularly *ęngle* (occas., after L., *Angle*), the people of *Angul, -ol, -el*, ON. *Öngull* ('illa patria quæ *Angulus* dicitur,' Bæda) a district of Holstein, so called from its shape, the word being the same as ANGLE *sb.*[1]; whence also *Angul-cynn, Angul-þeod*, orig. 'the race or people of Angul'; afterwards, the race of this and kindred descent in Britain, the 'English' race.]

1. *pl.* One of the Low-German tribes that settled in Britain, where they formed the kingdoms of Northumbria, Mercia, and East Anglia, and finally gave their name to the whole 'English' people.

c **885** K. ÆLFRED *Bæda* IV. xxvi, þæt land, ðætte Angle ǽr hæfdon. **1794** SULLIVAN *View Nat.* V. 116 The Angles, from whom the majority of the English derive their blood, and the whole their name. **1867** FREEMAN *Norm. Conq.* I. 24 North of the Thames lay the three great Kingdoms of the Angles.

2. *pl.* Rhetorically for: The English.

1823 BYRON *Juan* XIV. xxxviii, All foreigners excel The serious Angles in the eloquence Of pantomine.

angle ('æŋg(ə)l), *v.*[1] [f. ANGLE *sb.*[1]; cf. to *hook.*]

1. To use an angle; to fish with a hook and bait. **a.** *intr.* Const. *for* (*to* obs.).

1496 *Bk. St. Alban's* in *Eng. Home* (1861) 66 [The most] stately ffyssh that ony may angle to in freshe water. **1530** PALSGR., 431/2 It is but a sory lyfe and an yuell to stand anglynge all day to catche a fewe fysshes. **1593** NASHE *4 Lett. Confut.* 5 Let them not..angle for frogs in a cleare fountaine. **1653** WALTON *Angler* 52 The fish which we are to Angle for. **1741** *Compl. Fam.-Piece* II. ii. 338 Always angle in black or dark-colour'd Cloaths. **1850** MERIVALE *Rom. Emp.* (1865) IV. xxxviii. 324 He would..listlessly angle in the placid waters.

b. *trans.* To angle (a stream, etc.). *rare.*

1866 ROGERS *Agric. & Prices* I. xxiv. 610 Fishermen licensed either to angle or net parts of the piscary.

2. *fig.* To use artful or wily means to catch a person or thing, or elicit an opinion; to lay oneself out for, to 'fish.' **a.** *intr.* Const. *for.*

1589 *Pappe w. Hatchet* Pref. 3, I doo but yet angle with a silken flye, to see whether *Martins* will nibble. **1601** SHAKS. *All's Well* v. iii. 212 She..did angle for mee, Madding my eagernesse with her restraint. **1750** CHESTERF. *Lett.* 255 III. 19 Modesty is the only sure bait, when you angle for praise. **1799** SOUTHEY *Love Eleg.* iii. II. 125 The subtile line Wherewith the urchin angled for my Heart. **1867** DISRAELI in *Morn. Star* 12 Feb., We are not angling for a policy; we have distinct principles which will guide us.

†**b.** *trans.* with the thing wanted as object. *Obs.*

a **1586** SIDNEY (J.) If he spake courteously, he angled the people's hearts. **1597** DANIEL *Civ. Wares* VIII. xlvi, To angle the benevolence And catch the love of men with curtesies. *a* **1683** OLDHAM *Wks. & Rem.* (1686) 85 Shooes which.. angled their Charity, that pass'd along.

†**c.** *trans.* To angle *one on*: to draw him onward by holding out a bait. *Obs. rare.*

1653 WALTON *Angler* 38 You have Angled me on with much pleasure to the thatcht House.

angle ('æŋg(ə)l), *v.*[2] [f. ANGLE *sb.*[2]]

†**1.** *intr.* To run into a corner. *Obs.*

1575 TURBERVILLE *Venerie* 194 To make the vermine eyther start or angle.

2. *refl.* To move in angles, wind, twist. Also *intr.* = *refl.*

1863 W. H. GOODE *Outp. Zion* II. xvii. 381 Thence angling across the country, we..entered the Lane road. **1876** MRS. WHITNEY *Sights & Ins.* xx. 198 The road angles itself up the precipitous hillside. **1883** *Century Mag.* Oct. 923/2 He.. once more alters his direction, and so twists off, 'angling' across the meadow. **1953** A. UPFIELD *Murder must Wait* xx. 177 She wondered why he didn't walk direct to the.. boulders, why he angled this way and that.

3. a. *intr.* To turn or move at an angle, diagonally, or obliquely; to lie in an oblique direction.

1741 *Boston Rec.* 274 They have computed the charge of fixing piers..set angling cross the channel. **1835** *Fraser's Mag.* XI. 39 The circuitous route you are obliged to take —angling off at an infinite variety of points. **1869** *Rep. U.S. Comm. Agric.* 1868 258 About half the saplings may be laid along outside one stake, then inside of the next, and thence angling across to the other row. **1881** MAYNE REID *Free Lances* II. xxxii. 116 [The road] angles abruptly to the right. **1897** *Times* 5 Feb. 14/5 The Majestic..broke her starboard quarter rope, which caused her to angle across the entrance and to become jammed. **1942** R. CHANDLER *High Window* (1943) xxix. 189 Two davenports angled across the corners of the room and there was one gold chair.

b. *trans.* To strike, put, or drive at an angle.

1920 *Westm. Gaz.* 16 Oct. 2/2 She attracted the returns to her by cleverly angling the ball. **1953** A. UPFIELD *Murder must Wait* xxv. 222 Bony had walked like a white man, angling his feet at twenty-five minutes to five.

4. *trans.* To present (a story, description, subject of inquiry, etc.), esp. in journalism, so as to suit a particular point of view. Cf. ANGLE *sb.*[2] 1 c.

1937 *Harper's Mag.* Dec. 54/2 The good communist editor to-day turns a news story..over to his copy-writer and says: 'Class-angle that, Jim.' **1951** M. DICKENS *My Turn to make Tea* ii. 13 You..almost never see the proprietor, although you feel his presence, because you have to angle your writing his way. **1959** C. MACINNES *Absol. Beginners* 132 The leader columns are angled at the more intelligent portions of the population.

angleberry, anle-. [? variant of ANBURY, or earlier *ang-berry*.] 'A fleshy excrescence resembling a very large hautboy strawberry, found growing on the feet of sheep, cattle, etc.' Jamieson.

a **1600** A. MONTGOMERIE in Watson's *Coll.* III. 13 Overgane with Angleberries as thou grows ald. **1711** *Lond. Gaz.* mmmmdccclxxix/4 A bushy bob Tail, and has had a little Anleberry taken off of his Breast. **1844** H. STEPHENS *Bk. Farm* II. 156 Warts and angle-berries are not uncommon excrescences upon cattle. **1914** P. MACGILL *Children of Dead End* vi. 32 One of the horses was spavined and the other was covered with angle-berries.

angled ('æŋg(ə)ld), *ppl. a.* [f. ANGLE *v.*[2], *sb.*[2] + -ED.]

†**1.** Driven into, or stationed in, a corner. *Obs.*

1575 TURBERVILLE *Venerie* 193 The vermine is Angled (which is to say, gone to the furdest parte of his chamber to stand at defence). **1598** SYLVESTER *Du Bartas* 514 The angry beast to his best chamber flies, And (angled there) sits grimly intergerning.

2. Placed angularly, or at angles with each other. ***angled deck***, a flight deck on an aircraft carrier on which the landing path is inclined to the ship's fore-and-aft axis.

1852 D. MOIR *Seton Chapel* ii. Poet. Wks. I. 188 The angled bones, the sand-glass, and the scythe. **1952** *Flight* 21 Nov. 636/2 The angled deck has the effect of increasing the operational length of the carrier by 40 per cent... Preliminary trials..have been conducted by the Royal Navy and the U.S. Navy—where it is known somewhat misleadingly as the 'canted deck'. **1955** *Ann. Reg. 1954* 12 Three aircraft carriers with angled flight decks would be completed..within the year.

3. a. Having an angle or angles; having an outline marked by angles.

1612 DRAYTON *Poly-olb.* I. 5 Her hauen angled so about her harb'rous sound That in her quiet Bay a hundred ships may ride. **1699** J. JONES in *Misc. Cur.* (1708) III. 381 Two or three other sorts of Seeds..one is black and angled. **1788** *Edin. New Disp.* I. ii. (1797) 55 A crucible which is angled at the top for the conveniency of pouring out. **1825** H. GASCOIGNE *Naval Fame* 50 The angl'd Jib with speed they hoist away. **1870** HOOKER *Stud. Flora* 195 *Tussilago Farfara*; leaves..angled or lobed toothed.

b. ***angled bracket*** = *angle-bracket* (b) s.v. ANGLE *sb.*[2] 8 b.

1976 J. B. HOOPER *Introd. Natural Generative Phonol.* viii. 159 The material in angled brackets is not used. **1979** *Trans. Philol. Soc.* 106 The umlaut changes by which back vowels are fronted and front vowels raised, at first sight separate processes, can be collapsed into one change by the use of braces or angled brackets.

4. -angled: having (such or so many) angles, as *acute-angled*, *three-angled*, *many-angled*, etc.

1597 BP. HALL *Sat.* III. i. (T.) The thrice three-angled beech-nut shell. *a* **1637** B. JONSON *Neptune's Tri.* (T.) Fifty-angled custards. **1660** BARROW *Euclid* I. def. 28 An Oxygonium, or acute-angled Triangle, is that which has three acute angles. **1811** HUTTON *Course Math.* III. 77 A right-angled spherical triangle has one right angle.

5. Of a story, description, question, etc.: presented so as to suit a particular point of view; distorted, biased (see ANGLE *v.*[2] 4).

1958 *Manchester Guardian* 29 Jan. 6/5 'Pravda' carried 370 words on Mr. Macmillan's reply... It contained some direct quotation but in the main it was angled comment. **1958** *Times* 10 Oct. 8/3 A great deal of unwholesome, often erotically angled, American rubbish. **1960** J. FINGLETON *4 Chukkas* i. 1 The journalist..has to look for what is known as the 'angled' story.

†**'angle-hook.** *Obs.* [f. ANGLE *sb.*[1], when that word (orig. = *hook*) had been extended to the line, or rod and line.] A fish-hook. Also *fig.*

c **1374** CHAUCER *Compl. Mars* 238 And lyke a fissher.. Bateth hys angle-hoke [*v.r.* angil hooke, anglise hewkis] with summe plesaunce. **1382** WYCLIF *Isa.* xix. 8 Fissheres, and alle into the flod puttende the angil hoc. *c* **1449** *Pol. Poems* (1859) II. 222 The Fisshere hathe lost his hangulhooke. **1604** JERILO *Fr. Bacon's Proph.* 231 in *E.P.P.* IV. 276 Then love went not by lookes..Nor words were Angle-hookes.

angler[1] ('æŋglə(r)). [f. ANGLE *v.*[1] + -ER[1].]

1. a. One who angles or fishes with a hook and line.

1552 HULOET, Angler or fysher with an angle, *Hamota.* **1597** BP. HALL *Sat.* v, Seest thou the wary angler trayle along his feeble line? **1653** WALTON *Angler* 8 The Primitive Christians..were (as most Anglers are) quiet men and followed peace. **1722** DE FOE *Moll Flan.* (1840) 147, I played with this lover as an angler does with a trout. **1867** F. FRANCIS *Angling* iii. (1880) 78 When the angler essays his skill upon the wily old veterans of the pond.

b. *fig.*; *spec.* in *Thieves' Cant*: see quot. 1673. *Obs.* Also in extended use (see quot. 1903) in U.S.

1567 T. HARMAN *Caveat* 16 These hokers or Angglears be peryllous and most wicked knaues. **1592** NASHE *P. Penilesse* (ed. 2) 28 b, Noble Lord Warden of the Wenches and Anglers. [*i.e.* 'the Diuell.'] **1612** DEKKER *O per se O* sig. N4ᵛ, Hee is an Angler for Duds, who hath a Ferme in the Nab of his Filch. **1673** R. HEAD *Canting Academy* 68 Anglers are so called, because they have a Rod or Stick with an Iron hook at the end of it, with which they Angle in the night at Windows or any other place in which they cannot convey their hand. **1823** 'JON BEE' *Dict. Slang* 4 *Anglers*, thieves who with a hook at the end of a mop-stick drag to them the ends of cloth which may lie exposed, and so pull out entire pieces. **1930** CLAPIN *New Dict. Americanisms* 19 *Angler*, in thieves' slang, a street prowler, generally belonging to a gang of petty thieves, and who is always on the lookout for opportunities to commit small larcenies.

2. *Zool.* In full ***angler-fish.*** A British fish, called also Sea Devil, Frog Fish, Toad Fish, and Fishing Frog (*Lophius piscatorius* Linn.), so named from its preying upon small fish, which it attracts by the movement of certain wormlike filaments attached to the head and mouth. Also applied to other pediculate fishes having a free dorsal spine, as in the family Antennariidæ.

1653 [see SEA-ANGLER]. **1766** PENNANT *Zool.* III. 122 (JOD.), I have changed the old name of fishing frog to the more simple one of angler. **1845** [see TOAD-FISH]. **1867** F. FRANCIS *Angling* i. (1880) 1 The Angler or Fishing-frog has ..a rod, line, and bait appended to its nose. **1884** GOODE *Nat. Hist. Aquatic Anim.* 173 Marbled Angler, *Pterophryne histrio.* **1889** *Cent. Dict.*, Angler-fish. **1902** *Westm. Gaz.* 28 Jan. 1/3 An enormous specimen of the rare and curious angler-fish (*Lophius piscatorius*) known as the 'Fishing Frog'. **1951** R. CAMPBELL *Light on dark Horse* xix. 274 The fishing frog or angler-fish.

†**'angler**[2]. *Obs. rare*[−1]. [f. ANGLE *sb.*[2] + -ER[1].] One who occupies an angle.

1726 AMHERST *Terræ Filius* App. 295 To desert one place, which he then enjoy'd for life, and the well-grounded expectation of another, in order to become a precarious angler in your hall. [Dr. Richard Newton, principal of Hart Hall, Oxford, 1710–53, incorporated in 1740 as Hertford College, among his rules for its reform, prescribed, 'One tutor is to lodge in the middle room of the middle staircase in each angle of the College court.']

†**'angle-rod.** *Obs.* [ANGLE *sb.*[1]] A fishing-rod.

1523 LD. BERNERS *Froissart* I. ccccvi. 706 He had bene more vsed to fisshe with an angle rod. **1653** WALTON *Angler* 170 Before you undertake your tryal of skil by the Angle-Rod. **1711** ADDISON *Spect.* No. 108 ¶3 He makes a May-fly to a Miracle; and furnishes the whole Country with Angle-Rods. **1775** in ASH; and in mod. Dicts.

anglesite ('æŋglɪsaɪt). *Min.* [f. *Anglesea* (where first found at Parys mine) + -ITE.] The native sulphate of lead, called also lead vitriol, a beautiful crystalline mineral.

1837–68 DANA *Min.* 624 Sardinian is distorted anglesite from Monteponi..white and like anglesite in lustre.

anglet ('æŋglɪt). *rare*[−0]. [a. Fr. *anglet*, dim. of *angle*: see -ET[1].] A little angle or corner.

1611 COTGR., *Anglet*, An Anglet, or Angle, a corner. **1816** C. JAMES *Mil. Dict.* (ed. 4) 16 *Anglet* (Fr.), an anglet, a corner; also a small right-angled cavity.

†**'angletwitch, -touch.** *Obs.* or *dial.* Forms: 1 **-twæcca, -twicce,** 2 **-twæcche,** 4–6 **-twytche, -twitche,** 5–6 **angle-twache,** 5–7 **-towch, -touch.** [? f. ANGLE *sb.*[1] + OE. **twæcca*, **twicce*, app. connected with vb. *twiccean*, TWITCH, of which the OHG. cognate *zwickan*, MHG. *zwicken* (also *zwacken*) had orig. the sense 'to pierce or transfix as with a nail,' f. *zwec* 'nail, peg, pin.' Halliw. gives *twachel* in east. dial. = dew-worm.] A worm used as bait in fishing; an earth-worm. (Not mentioned by Izaak Walton, but still used in various south. dialects.)

c **940** *Sax. Leechd.* II. 44 Genim angeltwæccean ȝehalne, leȝe on þa stowe. *c* **1000** ÆLFRIC *Voc.* in Wright *Voc.* 24 *Lumbricus*, ren-wyrm, *vel* angeltwicce. [*MS. c* **1150** *ibid.* 90/2 *Lubricus*, ongel-twæcche.] **1398** TREVISA *Barth. De P.R.* XVIII. cxv. (1495) 856 Wyth angyltwytches fysshe is taken..Molles hunte Angyltwytches vnder erthe. **1513** STANBRIDGE *Voc.* in *Promp. Parv.* 12 Angletwache, *lumbricus.* [*ed.* 1615 Angle-touch]. **1562** BULLEYN *Sorenes* 22 b, Rosed oile, wherin Angletwitches, or yearth Wormes haue been sodden. **1602** CAREW *Cornwall* 26 a, His baites are ..Tag-wormes, which the Cornish English term Angle-touches. **1864** CAPERN *Devon Provinc.*, *Angle-Twitch*, the common earth-worm.

angle-wise ('æŋg(ə)lwaɪz), *adv.* [f. ANGLE *sb.*[2] + -WISE, OE. *wise* manner.] After the manner of an angle; angularly.

1604 EDMONDS *Observ. Cæsar's Comm.* 44 Fishes..haue heads for the most part sharpe, and thence Anglewise are inlarged into the grossenesse of their bodie. **1632** J. HAYWARD *Eromena* 150 Two timber-beams, joyning anglewise. **1727** BRADLEY *Fam. Dict.* s.v. *Chimney*, The lowermost Part of which [funnel] will descend anglewise into the Pipe. **1880** R. JEFFERIES *Gr. Ferne Farm* 282 Long clay pipes, stacked anglewise.

Anglian ('æŋglɪən), *a.* and *sb.* [f. L. *Anglī* (see ANGLE *sb.*[3]) + -AN.] Of or pertaining to the Angles. Often in combination, as ***East Anglian***, of East Anglia or the East Angles, the Teutonic occupants of Norfolk and Suffolk; also used in reference to the same district in modern times.

The OE. adj. f. *Engle* was *Englisc*, now *English*, but as this was in course of time used of all the Teutonic occupants of Britain (and afterwards extended also to Danish, Norman-French and other immigrants), *Anglian* is conveniently used by modern writers to translate *Englisc*, in its early restricted sense, as distinct from *Saxon*.

1726 TINDAL *Rapin's Hist. Eng.* (1757) I. 192 Both the East-Anglian kings being slain. **1871** EARLE *Philol. Eng. Tong.* §23 That the whole Anglian vernacular literature should have perished. **1875** SWEET in *Philol. Soc. Trans.* 561 There seem to have been three dialects, Anglian, Kentish, and Saxon. **1875** *Bibliogr. List of Eng. Dial.* 50 On the principal characteristics of East Anglian pronunciation.

Anglic ('æŋglɪk), *a.* [ad. med.L. *anglic-us* (in Bæda), f. *Anglī* the Angles or English. See prec. and -IC.] Of or pertaining to the Angles; Anglian.

1868 SKENE *4 Bks. Wales* I. 62 Ida the Anglic king..The Anglic kingdom of Bernicia. **1880** A. FRYER *Cuthb. of Lindisf.* 144 The teaching of the Anglic Church.

Anglic ('æŋglɪk), *sb.* [f. ANGL(O- + -IC.] A simplified form of English spelling devised by the Swedish philologist R. E. Zachrisson (1880–1937), and intended for use as an international auxiliary language.

1930 ZACHRISSON *Anglic: A New Agreed Simplified English Spelling* 12 Anglic, which is based on an analysis of all English words in general use, supplies the demand for an agreed method of simplified spelling without adding new letters to the alphabet, and at the same time keeps the continuity with the conventional English orthography. **1935** A. LLOYD JAMES *Broadc. Word* iii. 125 The result is the system known as Anglic, which, based on the foundations laid by Professor Zachrisson, of Uppsala, is what English spelling will probably be when the English-speaking world decides that the moment has come for spelling reform. **1937** J. R. FIRTH *Tongues of Men* vi. 79 Anglic simplifies the spelling, Basic English the vocabulary.

Anglican ('æŋglɪkən), *a.* and *sb.* [ad. med.L. *Anglicān-us* (Magna Carta), f. *Anglic-us*; see prec. and -AN.] **A.** *adj.*

1. Of or peculiar to the English ecclesiastically; of the reformed Church of England, and other churches in communion therewith. Cf. '*Pananglican* Synod.' Also used as *Gallican* is, in opposition to *Roman*; and to indicate moderate High Church opinions, as distinguished from those said to be 'Romanizing.'

[**1215** *Magna Carta* in Stubbs *Sel. Ch.* v. 288 Quod Anglicana ecclesia libera sit.] **1635** HOWELL *Lett.* (1650) II. 23 They all concur in opposition to the Roman Church; as also they of the Anglican, Scotican, Gallic..and Belgick Confessions. **1660** FELL *Hammond's Life* in Wks. (1684) I. 12 The sober Principles and old establishment of the *Anglicane* Church. **1840** GLADSTONE *Ch. Princ.* 228 Many members of the Papal communion have maintained the validity of Anglican orders. **1849** MACAULAY *Hist. Eng.* II. 91 [To] force the Anglican clergy to become his agents for the destruction of the Anglican doctrine and discipline. *Mod.* 'An Anglican Sisterhood, styled "The Society of the Holy Trinity."'

2. English (in the general sense).

1860 MARSH *Eng. Lang.* 15 All who use the Anglican speech. **1871** RUSKIN *Fors Clav.* I. iii. 19 The quite Anglican character of [King] Richard, to his death.

B. *sb.* An adherent of the reformed Church of England; *esp.* one holding High Church principles, or who approves of Catholic doctrine and ritual, while claiming for the English Church a national independence of Rome, and repudiating certain popular tenets of Rome as corruptions.

a **1797** BURKE *Let. to R. Burke* (L.) Whether Catholicks, Anglicans, or Calvinists. **1844** PUGIN *Gloss. Eccl. Orn.* 75 Copes were among the chief ornaments retained by the Anglicans. **1858** FROUDE *Hist. Eng.* III. xvi. §4. 361 Secondly there were the Anglicans..content to separate from Rome, but only that they might bear Italian fruit more profusely and luxuriantly when rooted in their own soil. **1882** *Church Q. Rev.* XV. 159 The loyal Anglican's grief.

'Anglicanism. [f. prec. + -ISM.]

Adherence to the doctrine and discipline of the reformed Church of England (and other churches in communion therewith), as the genuine representative of the Catholic Church.

1838 [see ANGLO-CATHOLICISM]. **1846** KINGSLEY *Lett.& Mem.* I. 143 Decent Anglicanism..having become the majority is now quite Conservative. **1856** FROUDE *Hist. Eng.* I. 336 The famous theory of high church Anglicanism—the notion that the English Church could and should subsist as a separate communion, independent of foreign control, self-governed, self-organized, and at the same time adhering without variation to catholic doctrine. **1864** J. H. NEWMAN *Apol.* 231 Anglicanism claimed to hold that the Church of England was nothing else than a continuation in this country ..of that one Church of which in old times Athanasius and Augustine were members. **1865** LECKY *Rational.* (1878) II. 325 Anglicanism has always been singularly free from the taint of fanaticism.

'Anglicanize, *v.* [f. ANGLICAN *a.*] *trans.* **1.** To Anglicize.

1904 L. O. BRASTOW *Repres. Mod. Preachers* 50 Although in remote lineage he may have been Scotch, he had become thoroughly Anglicanized.

2. To make Anglican (in doctrine, character, etc.).

1919 N. HILL *Story Sc. Church* vii. 143 Events..were destined to interrupt for some years James' policy of seeking to strengthen his position by Anglicanising the Scottish Church. 1962 *Observer* 20 May 31/3 Many of our cathedrals, having duly 'Anglicanised' the chancel more and more through three centuries, have destroyed the *raison d'être* of the basilican plan.

‖**Anglice** (ˈæŋglɪsiː), *adv.* Also **anglice**. [med.L., adv. corresp. to *anglicus*: see ANGLIC *a.*] In English; in plain English.

1602 [see WINDFALL 1]. 1665 R. HEAD *Eng. Rogue* xxxix. 139 An old Comrade..had lately *heav'd a Booth, Anglice* broken open a Shop. 1718 J. OZELL tr. *Pitton de Tournefort's Voy. Levant* I. i. 36 Here we lay at the Sign of the Moon and seven Stars (*anglicè* in the open Air). 1760 STERNE *Tr. Shandy* I. xx. 132 Baptism shall..be administered..by injection—*par le moyen d'une petite Canulle*,—Anglicé *a squirt*. 1828 H. STEUART *Planter's Guide* (ed. 2) 465 The workmen objected to the execution of three spits deep, at the same price per Fall (anglicè pole), as had been paid for two spits. 1848 H. W. HAYGARTH *Bush Life Austral.* xii. 135 A set of the veriest 'Russians' (Anglicè, wild things) *he* ever had anything to do with. 1908 'IAN HAY' *Right Stuff* iii. 44, I handed him a quarter's salary in advance, gave him two days' holiday wherein to 'make his arrangements'—*Anglicè*, to replenish his wardrobe.

Anˈglicify, *v. rare*⁻⁰. [f. L. *Anglic-us* English + -FY. Cf. *Frenchify*.] = ANGLICIZE.

1859 in WORCESTER.

Anglicism (ˈæŋglɪsɪz(ə)m). [f. ANGLICIZE: see -ISM.]

1. Anglicized language, such as the introduction of English idiom into a sentence in another language; *hence*, a peculiarity of the English language, an idiom specially English.

1642 HOWELL *For. Trav.* (Arb.) 65 An odde kind of *Anglicisme*..as to say Your Boores of Holland, Sir; Your Iesuites of Spaine, Sir. 1679 DRYDEN *Tr. & Cr.* Ep. Ded. Wks. 1725 V. 11 False Grammar, and Nonsense couch'd beneath that specious Name of Anglicisme. 1699 BENTLEY *Phal.* §xi. 318 Dr. B. has abundance of pure Anglicisms in his Latin. 1755 T. CROKER *Ariosto's Orl. Fur.* Pref. 8 Low familiar anglicism, quite inconsistent with the dignity of the divine original. 1839 HALLAM *Hist. Lit.* IV. IV. vii. §37. 319 The anglicism of terminating the sentence with a preposition.

2. An English characteristic or fashion; English character, the quality of being English; also, imitation of or support for what is English.

1781 JOHNSON *Lives Eng. Poets* II. 86 If his language had been less idiomatical, it might have lost somewhat of its genuine Anglicism. 1787 BECKFORD *Italy* II. 90 The short jacket of the postilion and other anglicisms of the equipage. 1810 JEFFERSON *Writ.* XII. 373 The Anglicism of 1808..is a longing for a King, and an English King rather than any other. 1818 M. BOUCHER *Let.* 1 Oct. in Lady Morgan *Memoirs* (1862) 146 Frenchmen..have adopted the opposite mania of Anglicism, down to the most trifling fashions. 1827 LAMB in W. Hone *Table Bk.* I. 302/1 Christianism; and true hearty Anglicism of feelings, shaping that Christianism; shine throughout his beautiful writings. 1831 *Blackw. Mag.* XXIX. 519 Among other allegorical emblems of nations, as the representative and express image of Anglicism, he drew a naked man. 1871 LOWELL *Study Windows* iii. 62 She [*sc.* England] has a conviction that whatever good there is in us is wholly English, when the truth is that we are worth nothing except so far as we have disinfected ourselves of Anglicism. 1876 *Dublin Rev.* July 103 Mr. Carlyle, whom nobody will suspect either of narrow Anglicism or of unreasoning antipathy to other nations.

3. English political principles or methods of administration.

1873 GLADSTONE in *Daily News* 20 Aug. 2/2 The most unfortunate policy which sent Englishmen into the country for every purpose of civil as well as of religious life..to propagate what I may call Anglicism in the teeth of the feelings of the country. 1878 *N. Amer. Rev.* CXXVII. 185 Those elements of political Anglicism.

Anglicist (ˈæŋglɪsɪst). [f. ANGLICISM: see -IST.]

1. An advocate or favourer of Anglicism, in any sense; in quots., one who advocated the use of English in Indian schools.

1867 P. M. MEHTA *Speeches & Writings* (1905) 6 Two parties, who may be conveniently denominated as the Vernacularists and the Anglicists. 1878 G. SMITH *Life John Wilson* xvi. 529 Dr. Duff, Macaulay, and the Anglicists under Lord William Bentinck. 1892 *Athenæum* 24 Sept. 411/3 The controversy between the 'Orientalists' and the 'Anglicists', which evoked Macaulay's famous minute.

2. (See quot. 1930.)

1930 K. MALONE in *English Jrnl.* XIX. 642 In various papers I have used *Anglicist* in the technical sense 'worker in Anglistics', and this practice of mine seems to have given the term a certain currency. 1959 *Brno Studies* I. 23, *i* (termed '*i* impurum' by the older generations of Anglicists).

Anglicity (æŋˈglɪsɪtɪ). *rare*⁻⁰. [ad. mod.L. *Anglicitāt-em*, f. *Anglic-us*, after *Latinus*, *Latinitāt-em*, *Latinity*: see -ITY.] English quality, as of speech or style; English idiom.

Anglicization (ˌæŋglɪsaɪˈzeɪʃən). [f. next + -ATION.] The action or process of making English.

1878 W. ADAMS *Latter-d. Lyr.* 377 The new movement for the Anglicisation of French metres. 1883 *St. James's Gaz.* 13 Feb. 3 It will soon be seen how shallow is the Anglicization of India.

Anglicize (ˈæŋglɪsaɪz), *v.* [f. L. *Anglic-us* English + -IZE.]

1. To make English in form or character; to english.

1710 SEWALL *Letter-book* (1886) I. 401 The best thing we can do for our Indians is to Anglicize them. 1748 T. EDWARDS *Can. Crit.* 275 (T.) In all Greek words anglicised as *system, hypocrite*. 1795 COLERIDGE *Plot Disc.* 47 Let me be pardoned, if the actions are too much anglicized. 1831 SCOTT *Cast. Dang.* iv, William Longlegs, having refused, on any terms, to become Anglocised. 1837 HALLAM *Hist. Lit.* I. 275 The glaring affectation of anglicising Latin words.

2. *intr.* (refl. pron. omitted.) *rare.*

1857 GEN. P. THOMPSON *Audi Alt. Part.* I. ix. 30 Are they allowed to *Anglicise* if they like, as the Scottish Highlanders were? 1882 HOWELLS in *Longm. Mag.* I. 60 England Americanises in some respects, in some respects America Anglicises.

ˈ**Anglicized**, *ppl. a.* [f. prec. + -ED.] Made English in form or character.

1774 PENNANT *Tour Scotl.* (ed. 3) 69 John of Sterling, with his army of Anglicised Scots, sat down before it. 1862 MRS. CROSLAND *Mrs. Blake* II. 214 The Anglicised residence of an English lady. 1881 *Athenæum* 27 Aug. 266/3 The secondary Anglicized education of Bengal. 1883 E. INGERSOLL in *Harper's Mag.* Jan. 195/1 Fort Ross—an anglicized abbreviation of *Fuerte de los Rusos*.

Anglification (ˌæŋglɪfɪˈkeɪʃən). *rare.* [f. ANGLIFY: see -FICATION.] The act or process of making anything English, or conforming it to English modes.

1867 LD. STRANGFORD *Selection* (1869) II. 99 A thorough Anglification of the public service [in the Ionian Isles].

Anglified (ˈæŋglɪfaɪd), *ppl. a.* [f. next + -ED.] Made English, put into English form; englished.

1816 *Q. Rev.* XV. 139 Through the dark dialect of Anglified Erse. 1845 DARWIN *Voy. Nat.* xxi. 483 Calais or Boulogne was much more Anglified. 1865 W. ANDERSON *Geneal. & Surn.* 136 The Anglified form of the name.

Anglify (ˈæŋglɪfaɪ), *v.* [f. L. *Angli* the English (see ANGLIAN) + -FY.] To make English, put into English form; = ANGLICIZE. (Rather out of use.)

1751 FRANKLIN *Ess.* Wks. 1840 II. 320 Aliens, who will shortly be so numerous as to Germanize us instead of our Anglifying them. 1853 LYTTON *My Novel* I. ix. 23 Giacomo shall be Anglified into Jackeymo.

angling (ˈæŋglɪŋ), *vbl. sb.*¹ [f. ANGLE *v.*¹.]

1. The action or art of fishing with a rod.

1496 *Bk. St. Albans, Fysshynge* 1, Fysshynge, callyd Anglynge wyth a rodde. 1580 LYLY *Euphues* 396 The ende of fishing is catching, not anglyng. 1606 SHAKS. *Ant. & Cl.* II. v. 16 When You wager'd on your Angling. 1653 WALTON *Angler* 246 Hate contentions, and love quietnesse, and vertue, and angling. 1796 MORSE *Amer. Geog.* I. 479 Amusing to those who are fond of angling. 1823 BYRON *Juan* XIII. cvi, Angling too, that solitary vice, Whatever Izaak Walton sings or says.

2. *fig.* (see ANGLE *v.* 2.)

1674 N. FAIRFAX *Bulk & Selv.* 91 Jet and straw, loadstone and iron, with some others of that hooking kind: where, setting aside their angling and groping one for another, etc. 1828 CARLYLE *Misc.* (1857) I. 113 Such juggleries, and uncertain anglings for distinction.

3. *Attrib.* and *Comb.*, as in ***angling books***, ***literature***, etc.; †**angling-hook**, a fish-hook; **angling-rod**, †**angling-wand**, a fishing-rod.

1867 F. FRANCIS *Angling* i. (1880) 2 The stock of angling literature. 1883 *Athenæum* 3 Mar. 274/3 Every collector of angling books..can thus..hanker after the many prizes of angling bibliomania. 1549 COVERDALE *Erasm. Paraphr. James* iii. 8 It hydeth under the bayte of pleasure, the very angling hoke of death. 1552 HULOET, Angling gad, or rodde, *Pertica*. 1598 FLORIO, *Lungagnola*, a fishing rod, a fishing pole, an angling rod. 1814 WORDSW. *Excurs.* II. 662 A broken angling-rod. 1834 BANCROFT *Hist. U.S.* (1876) IV. xxxv. 573 They brought angling-rods. 1565 *Letter* in NARES s.v., You will use a long anglyng-wand to catch some knowledg.

†ˈ**angling**, *vbl. sb.*² *Obs. rare.* [f. ANGLE *v.*²] The action of making angles *with* (anything).

1570 DEE *Math. Præf.* 42 Certaine..Sterres..their Coniunctions, and Anglynges with the Planetes, etc.

Anglish (ˈæŋglɪʃ), *a. rare*¹. [f. ANGLE *sb.*³ + -ISH.] = ANGLIAN (which is the common word).

1865 CARLYLE *Fredk. Gt.* V. XIX. ix. 636 Of Jutish or Anglish type.

Anglist (ˈæŋglɪst). [a. G. *Anglist*, f. L. *Anglus* English (see ANGLE *sb.*³): see -IST.] A student of English, or scholar versed in English language or literature.

1888 *Jrnl. Educ.* Jan. 32 The 'Anglist' is warned that he has yet stricter duties to fulfil than the 'Germanist'. Most Anglists, it appears, in Germany conceive that they have done their duty if they have studied thoroughly Gothic, German, and English. 1930 K. MALONE in *English Jrnl.* XIX. 640 On the Continent our subject is known as *Anglistics*..and a worker in it is called an *Anglist*.

Hence **Anˈglistics** *sb. pl.*, the study of English language or literature.

1930 [see ANGLICIST]. 1936 *Amer. Speech* XI. 101/1 *ELH*, the only American journal devoted exclusively to *anglistics*. 1947 *Eng. Studies* XXVIII. 129 English studies or Anglistics (the usual Continental term) is a discipline which deals with the speech and writings of the whole Anglo-Saxon world.

†ˈ**Anglize**, *v. Obs. rare*⁻¹. [f. L. *Angl-i* (see ANGLIAN) + -IZE.] = ANGLICIZE, ANGLIFY.

1655 FULLER *Ch. Hist.* III. xii. 31 These Norman Lords..wedding with English wives, became so perfectly Anglized.

Anglo (ˈæŋgləʊ), *sb.* (and *a.*) *colloq.* (chiefly *N. Amer.*). [f. ANGLO-.] **1.** *Canad.* [Cf. *Anglo-Canadian*, ANGLOPHONE *sb.* and *a.*] An English-speaking (as opp. to a French-speaking) Canadian. Also *attrib.* or as *adj.*

1800 *Upper Canada Gaz.* (York, Ontario) 22 Feb. 3/2 The inference to be drawn, is the closest union between the Anglo and trans-atlantic Anglos. 1959 *Maclean's Mag.* 14 Feb. 41/1 The scientific, technical and commercial faculties, areas once left to the 'Anglos', are booming. 1968 *Listener* 1 Aug. 131/1 The Conservatives attempted vaguely to..qualify their traditionally Anglo party to pick up some Quebec seats. 1977 *Maclean's Mag.* 4 Apr. 18/2 Whether Quebec separates or not, there is a feeling among Anglos that things will never be the same for them as the province moves to 'francicize' business and restrict the right to English-language education for newcomers.

2. a. A person of English (or non-Latin European) origin, esp. one resident in the United States, an Anglo-American; orig. in South-west U.S., distinguished from a Mexican-American.

1941 E. FERGUSSON *Our Southwest* 70 Los ricos accepted the incoming Anglos as friends, as wives or husbands. 1948 *New Mexico Q. Rev.* Spring 67 Most non-Spanish city dwellers, the Anglos, so-called..are too busy. 1958 CARROLL & CASAGRANDE in S. Rogers *Children & Lang.* (1975) III. xiii. 193 The test was also administered to 28 'Anglos' (as they are called in the Southwest) consisting of 12 adults of a comparable degree of education in a rural New England community and 16 graduate students at Harvard. 1966 MRS. L. B. JOHNSON *White House Diary* 2 Apr. (1970) 380 Joe Frantz..began to weave together the story of the place..the westward thrust of the Anglos, wild tales of Pancho Villa. 1971 J. WAMBAUGH *New Centurions* (1972) iv. 47 Serge couldn't..think of another family on his street with only three children except the Kulaskis and they were Anglos, at least to the Chicanos they were Anglos, but now he thought how humorous it was to have considered these Polacks as Anglo. 1979 *Tucson* (Arizona) *Daily Citizen* 20 Sept. 9C/1 In Tucson, such recollections would show persistently good relations between Anglos and Mexican-Americans. 1984 *Observer* 19 Aug. 13/4 Earlier this year the Anglos were for the first time tipped into the minority by accumulated Blacks, Hispanics and Asians.

b. *attrib.* or as *adj.*

1968 *Economist* 8 June 53/2 As they are basically without power, the radical leaders must take their cues from the people with power, the white, or 'Anglo', majority. 1973 *Newslet. Amer. Dial. Soc.* Nov. 11 Thirty Black and Anglo kindergarten children..were asked to respond. 1977 *New Yorker* 2 May 92/2 The entire city council of San Antonio was selected, from out of the same north-side Anglo neighbourhoods. 1981 *Economist* 11 Apr. 28/1 He even did well, although he did not win an outright majority, in the Anglo sections of town.

Anglo- (ˈæŋgləʊ), originally L., combining form of *Angl-us* English; in derivatives, as ANGLOPHOBIA; compounds, as ANGLO-SAXON; combinations, as *Anglo-Turkish*. For history see ANGLO-SAXON.

1. a. English, of England; as in ANGLO-CATHOLIC, ANGLO-SAXON; **Anglo-Danish**, pertaining to the Danes in England; **Anglo-French**, the French retained and separately developed in England; **Anglo-Latin**, Anglicised Latin; **Anglo-Norse** *a.*, pertaining to the Norse in England during the Anglo-Saxon period, esp. to their language; also as *sb.*; **Anglo-Scandinavian** *a.*, pertaining to England and Scandinavia, esp. to the Norsemen in England in the Anglo-Saxon period; also as *sb.*; ***Anglo-Judaic***, ***-Jewish*** (so ***Anglo-Jewry***), ANGLO-NORMAN. Also, **b.** Of English race, origin, descent (though now living temporarily or permanently elsewhere), as ***Anglo-American***, ***-Canadian***, ***-Hibernian***, ***-Indian***, ANGLO-IRISH.

a. [1584 FENNER *Def. Ministers* (1587) F iv, The Iesuites who dayly laugh at vs both, calling some *Anglo-puritani*.] 1791 BOSWELL *Johnson* (1831) I. 198 Sir Thomas Browne..was remarkably fond of Anglo-Latin diction. *Ibid.* 293 This Anglo-Latian word *procerity*. 1859 GEN. P. THOMPSON *Audi Alt. Part.* II. lxxxviii. 59 Rebuilt, whether in the Italo-Gothic or the Anglo-Gothic style. 1871 *Times* 7 July 5/2 An influential meeting..for the purpose of constituting the Anglo-Jewish Association of the Universal Israelitish Alliance. 1908 W. G. COLLINGWOOD *Scandinavian Britain* ii. 167 Edward's reign was disturbed throughout by a struggle between the Anglo-Scandinavians and the Franco-Scandinavians. 1910 *Westm. Gaz.* 9 Apr. 5/1 It may..be accepted that only books worthy of preservation are paid this compliment in Anglo-Jewry. 1924 MAWER & STENTON *Introd. Surv. Eng. Place-Names* ix. 183 The time has therefore not yet come for any general estimate of the character of Anglo-Scandinavian personal nomenclature in the phases which preceded its final disappearance. 1927 E. V. GORDON *Introd. O. Norse* 306 The change of Norse *w* to bilabial *v* had not taken place in Anglo-Norse. *Ibid.* 304 The Anglo-Norse form borrowed in English..shows no trace of the fronting of *g*. 1936 P. THORSON (*title*) Anglo-Norse Studies. An Inquiry into the Scandinavian Elements in the Modern English Dialects. 1961 *New Left Rev.* Jan.–Feb. 60/2 An official Anglo-Jewry, represented by such institutions as the Chief Rabbi.

b. 1789–96 MORSE *Amer. Geog.* I. 669 They never shed the blood of an Anglo American. 1842 *Penny Cycl.* s.v. *Texas*, Distrust between the Anglo-American colonists..and the settlers of Spanish descent. **1858** Gen. P. Thompson *Audi Alt. P.* I. xlvii. 183 That sensible men consider Nana Sahib as an Anglo-Indian myth. **1861** Swinhoe *N. China Camp.* 153 Called Bier by the Anglo-Indians. **1882** *Standard* 5 Dec. 5/5 Amongst Anglo-Egyptians..the prevailing feelings are very different.

c. Used separately. *rare.*

1844 A. Mallalieu *Buenos Ayres* 65 The federal system in the Anglo States of America.

2. English *and*; English in connexion with; as ***Anglo-Boer, -Chinese, -Egyptian, -French, -Soviet, Turkish***, etc. Cf. the similar *Franco-German, Græco-Roman*, and other modern combinations.

1900 *Westm. Gaz.* 4 May 11/3 A large proportion of the money hoarded up, as a consequence of the Anglo-Boer War, will be set into circulation so soon as peace shall be declared. **1961** *Times* 18 May 18/4 Events that led up to the Anglo-Boer war. **1855** *(title)* Diplomatic Mystifications and Popular Credulity; or, The Anglo-French Alliance. **1878** *N. Amer. Rev.* CXXVII. 396 The Anglo-Russian convention. **1924** *Glasgow Herald* 12 July 9/3 If an agreement which is at present being considered by the Anglo-Soviet Conference is finally approved it will have the effect of benefiting the Soviet Government. **1939** E. H. Carr *Propaganda in Internat. Politics* 19 The Anglo-Soviet Trade Agreement of March 1921. **1943** *Lancet* 26 June 818/2 The Anglo-Soviet Medical Council. **1878** *N. Amer. Rev.* CXXVII. 396 The Anglo-Turkish treaty.

ˌAnglo-A'merican, *sb.* and *a.* [f. Anglo- + American.] **A.** *sb.* **a.** An American of English origin.

[**1738** *Remarks on Trial of J. P. Zenger* i. 16 (*Signature of letter*), I am yours, &c. Anglo-Americanus.] **1787** S. S. Smith *Ess. Complexion* (1788) 194 The Anglo-Americans on the frontiers of the states, who acquire their sustenance principally by hunting. **1792** J. Morse *Amer. Geogr.* (ed. 2) 63 The greater part, however, are descended from the English; and for the sake of distinction, are called Anglo-Americans. **1856** Simms *Charlemont* 19 That sleepless discontent of temper, which, perhaps,..is the moral failing in the character of the Anglo-American. **1948** *Seventeen* June 4/4 We had a Chinese boy cheerleader, a Mexican girl cheerleader, and three Anglo-Americans.

b. In contrast to the non-English races in, or on the borders of, the United States.

1828 C. Sealsfield *Americans as they Are* xi. 132 The Anglo-Americans, however, treat their slaves throughout better than the French. **1842** *McDonogh Papers* (1898) 64 The Anglo-Americans, a term by which all Americans and strangers generally are called by the natives of Louisiana of French descent. **1858** *Texas Almanac* 114 The Anglo-Americans of Texas were threatened with subjection to military despotism.

B. *adj.* **a.** Of or pertaining to Americans of English origin.

1797 Pinckney in *State P.* (1819) III. 140, I should have made some observation on being termed Anglo-American, but, on inquiry, I found it was customary to call all my countrymen so, to distinguish us from the inhabitants of St. Domingo, and the other French West India Islands. **1841** H. S. Foote *Texas & Texans* I. 91 The heroic achievements of these three hundred Anglo-American soldiers. **1851** C. Cist *Cincinnati* 34 Destined to render the Anglo-American race paramount throughout this great continent. **1880** G. W. Cable *Grandissimes* liii. 402 A comparison of..Anglo-American and Franco-American conventionalities.

b. Of or belonging to both England and America.

1812 H. Marshall *Hist. Kentucky* 81 The Anglo-American army, then on its march to attack the French and Indians, posted in Fort Duquesne. **1843** *Knickerbocker* XXII. 90 The 'American Book Circular' recently put forth by Mr. Geo. P. Putnam, of the Anglo-American House of Wiley and Putnam. **1898** W. James *Coll. Ess. & Rev.* (1920) 436 The great Anglo-American alliance against the world, of which we nowadays hear so much. **1933** *Discovery* Dec. 359/1 An Anglo-American agreement has now been reached regarding a transatlantic air service.

Hence **ˌAnglo-A'mericanism.**

1803 *Christian Observer* II. Sept. 554 Occasional vulgarisms (possibly Anglo-Americanisms). **1841** H. S. Foote *Texas & Texans* I. 110 In the land [*sc.* England] whence what we now call Anglo-Americanism has derived its origin.

Anglo-'Catholic, *a.* and *sb.* [See Anglo-.] **A.** *adj.* Catholic of the Anglican communion, as distinguished from Roman Catholic.

1838 C. Seager *(title)* The Daily Service of the Anglo-Catholic Church, adapted to family or private worship. **1838** C. M. Le Bas in *Brit. Crit.* XXIV. 83 Both of them appeal to the Homilies and Formularies of the Anglo-Catholic Church. **1838** W. Palmer *Treatise on Church of Christ* I. p. vi, Many of the ancient errors against which the masters of Anglo-catholic theology contended in the sixteenth and seventeenth centuries, have been permitted to sink into oblivion. **1841** *(title of series of reprints)* Library of Anglo-Catholic Theology. **1859** *Lit. Ch.-man* V. 18 The price of the Anglo-Catholic Library.

B. *sb.*

1. *Hist.* An Englishman who, without wishing to sever the English from the Catholic Church, was in favour of its national independence of organization and working.

1858 Froude *Hist. Eng.* III. xvii. §1. 517 The Anglo-catholics did not intend to repeat the blunder of showing a leaning towards the Romanists.

2. *Modern.* A member of the Church of England who contends for its 'catholic' character, and repudiates the name 'protestant.'

1842 P. Gell *Sermon Preached at Visitation of Archdeacon of Derby* 33 The Anglo-Catholics consider it essential to be ordained by bishops receiving their appointment in regular succession from the apostles. **1849** C. Brontë *Shirley* i. 1 One [dish] that a Catholic—ay, even an Anglo-Catholic—might eat on Good Friday.

Anglo-Catholicism. [f. prec. + -ism.] Catholicism of Anglican type, or according to English ideas; the doctrine or constitution of the Anglican Church as a branch of the Church Catholic.

1838 J. H. Newman in *Brit. Crit.* XXIV. 61 The heroine ..after going through the phases of Protestantism..seeks for something deeper and truer in Anglicanism, or, as Mr. Palmer more correctly speaks in his recent work, Anglo-Catholicism. **1842** Pusey *Crisis in Eng. Ch.* 141 When Greek Catholicism..becomes well-disposed to Anglo-Catholicism.

Anglocentric (ˌæŋgləʊ'sɛntrɪk), *a.* [f. Anglo- + centric *a.*] Centring on England; centred in England. Hence **ˌAnglocen'tricity.**

1886 *Ann. Rep. U.S. Treas.* p. ix, An Anglo-centric monetary system. **1898** L. A. Tollemache *Talks with Gladstone* 114 A belief in the anthropomorphic and anthropocentric—I had almost said Anglo-centric—government of the physical world. **1960** *Times Lit. Suppl.* 7 Oct. 642/2 The excuses for such Anglocentric history are now wearing thin. *Ibid.* 642/4 A similar Anglocentricity of outlook..colours Mr. Watson's treatment..of the French Revolution. **1962** *Economist* 26 May 776/2 The Commonwealth has moved further and further away from being Anglocentric.

Anglocize, -fy, bad forms of Anglicize, -fy.

ˌAnglo-'Frisian, *sb.* and *a.* Also 9 **Anglo-Friesic.** [f. Anglo- + Frisian *a.* and *sb.*] **A.** *adj.* **1.** Pertaining to both English and Frisian. **2.** In the use of H. Sweet and some later writers: pertaining to a subdivision of the West Germanic branch of the Germanic group of languages, the hypothetical parent language of Anglo-Saxon and Old Frisian. **B.** *sb.* In senses of the adj.

1836 Halbertsma in J. Bosworth *Orig. Eng., Gmc. & Scand. Lang.* 75 Low-Saxon has all the appearance of German grafted on an Anglo-Friesic tree. The words are Anglo-Friesic with German vowels, as if the Friesians, in adopting the German, retained the consonants of the old language. **1877** H. Sweet in *Trans. Philol. Soc. 1875–6* 562 The language spoken by these tribes before the migration may be called Anglo-Frisian, and its characteristics may be ascertained with considerable certainty from a comparison of the oldest English and Frisian. **1888** —— *Hist. Eng. Sounds* 85 Within Low German English and Frisian again form a special group 'Anglo-Frisian'. **1907** H. M. Chadwick *Orig. Eng. Nation* 99 But have we any justification for believing that a language of Anglo-Frisian type was spoken beyond the sea to the north? **1913** P. Sipma *Phonol. & Gram. Mod. W. Frisian* 2 From time immemorial English and Frisian have had in common a certain number of peculiarities in their system of vowels and consonants: these must have been proper to the original Anglo-Frisian language. **1948** *Trans. Philol. Soc. 1947* 14 This view [in *T.P.S. 1939*]..attached over much weight to literary Old Saxon, a language highly divergent from Old Frisian, and assumed that we must postulate a stage in which there was an Anglo-Frisian unity rather closer than the loose unity of Frisian, English, and Saxon, i.e. non-High German West Germanic. **1958** A. S. C. Ross *Etymology* ii. 98 In Anglo-Frisian, initial and medial *k* before a front vowel > [ts] [tʃ].

ˌAnglo-'Gallic, *a.* [f. Anglo- + Gallic *a.*[1]] Pertaining, relating, or common to both England and France; *spec.* in *Numismatics* (see quot. 1962). Hence ***Anglo-'Gallicized*** adj.; ***Anglo-'Gallicism***, a French word or phrase adopted into English.

1757 A. C. Ducarel *(title)* A series of above 200 Anglo-Gallic..Coins of the antient Kings of England. **1821** *New Monthly Mag.* II. 310 Take then your new-fangled Anglo-gallicism *trait.* **1901** J. E. Moon *(title)* Catalogue of Anglo-Saxon, English and Anglo-Gallic Coins. **1926** Fowler *Mod. Eng. Usage* 476/2 *Purposive*..the Latin suffix *-ive* is unsuited to the delatinized & anglogallicized *pur-*. **1960** L. D. Stamp *Brit. Struct. & Scenery* (ed. 5) xii. 141 A partly enclosed sea, which has been called the Anglo-Franco-Belgian Basin or the Anglo-Gallic Basin, covered the south-east of England, the north-east of France and the greater part of Belgium. **1962** R. A. G. Carson *Coins* 249 The..term 'Anglo-Gallic' has been generally adopted to describe the coinage in the name of English rulers for the territories in France which they at different times controlled.

ˌanglo-hel'vetium. Earlier name for astatine. Cf. also alabamine. (*Disused.*)

1942 *Nature* CL. 768 As a tribute to the scientific work of our two countries, we propose to name the element 85 'anglo-helvetium'.

Anglo-Indian (ˌæŋgləʊ'ɪndɪən), *a.* and *sb.* [f. Anglo- 1 b + Indian.] **A.** *adj.* Of, pertaining to, or characteristic of India under British rule, or the English in India. **B.** *sb.* **a.** A person of British birth resident, or once resident, in India. **b.** A Eurasian of India.

1826 J. Malcolm *Polit. Hist. India 1784–1823* II. xi. 248 The mixed population of Calcutta, Madras and Bombay, made up of European Half Castes, or Anglo-Indians. **1842** *Ainsworth's Mag.* II. 63 He had been at Massorie, that sanatorium of Anglo-Indians. **1845** E. Acton *Mod. Cookery* (ed. 2) xiv. 288 We think..the proportion of onion and garlic by one half too much for any but well seasoned Anglo-Indian palates. **1847** *Howitt's Jrnl.* 30 Jan. 67/2 The transmission of the Anglo-Indian mails. **1861** Swinhoe *N. China Camp.* 153 The Chinese *Tsaou*, called Bier by the Anglo-Indians, is a somewhat cylindrically shaped fruit. **1907** *Westm. Gaz.* 11 Dec. 2/1 Calcutta..merits the epithet of Anglo-Indian better than anything else in India. **1929** *Cowley Evangelist* June 134 A congregation of Indian, Anglo-Indian and European people, all happily joining together. **1929** *Church Times* 14 June 726/4 The Archdeacon of Madras said that the Anglo-Indian, and particularly the lower class of Anglo-Indian, was the crux of the whole question. **1934** *S.P.E. Tract* xli. 21 The term 'Anglo-Indian' used to be applied to people of British birth who had lived long in India. In 1911 the Government of India decided to substitute 'Anglo-Indian' for 'Eurasian' as the official term for those of mixed descent. **1941** O'Malley *Mod. India & West* xv. 552 Anglo-Indian literature is really a subject in itself.

ˌAnglo-'Irish, *a.* and *sb.* [f. Anglo-.] **A.** *adj.* Of, pertaining to, or descended from both the English and the Irish.

1839 T. C. Croker *Pop. Songs of Ireland* p. vi, The Anglo-Irish settlers degenerated. **1905** *Daily Chron.* 8 Feb. 3/3 This Gaelic world..did immeasurably more for poetry than the Anglo-Irish spheres.

B. *sb.* **a.** Collectively, persons of English descent born or resident in Ireland, or descendants of mixed English and Irish parentage. **b.** The English language as spoken or written in Ireland.

1792 Burke *Let.* Wks. 1845 III. 507 Finding the Anglo-Irish highly animated with a spirit, which had shewn itself before. **1834** Bancroft *Hist. U.S.* (1876) III. iv. 350 The Anglo-Irish could not intermarry with the Celts. **1927** J. J. Hogan *Eng. Lang. in Ireland* 16 The Poems..present a full mirror of medieval Anglo-Irish as used about 1300, the time of its greatest extension. **1940** L. MacNeice *Last Ditch* 4 And the mist on the Wicklow hills Is close..As the Irish to the Anglo-Irish.

ˌAnglo-'Israelite. One who holds that the English-speaking peoples represent the 'lost' tribes of Israel. Also *attrib.*, as ***Anglo-Israelite theory, theorist***. So **ˌAnglo-'Israelitism**; also **ˌAnglo-'Israelism.**

1875 'Clericus' *Anglo-Israel Theory Refuted* 8 The other errors of Anglo-Israelite advocates (while holding some truth) is their ignoring any of these acts of God but *one.* **1876** J. C. McClellan *(title)* Anglo-Israelism: its pernicious Nature fully exposed. **1884** R. Roberts *(title)* Anglo-Israelitism refuted. **1886** *Brit. & For. Evang. Rev.* Jan. 65 The Anglo-Israelite Theory. *Ibid.* 72 The Anglo-Israelite theorists hold that they [*sc.* the Ten Tribes] were 'lost' first, and then their punishment and humiliation was changed to a brilliant future. **1897** *Westm. Gaz.* 22 Nov. 3/3 Anglo-Israelitism, which, judged on an historical theory, is simply a foolish craze, has yet no little importance as a sentiment. **1963** *Times* 20 Aug. 9/6 Busy advocates of..Anglo-Israelism.

†**'Angloman**[1]. *Obs. rare.* [f. Anglo- + ? man, but app. associated in sense with Fr. *anglomane*: see next.] A partisan or friend of English interests in America. (Understood to have been invented by Jefferson.)

1787 T. Jefferson *Writ.* (1859) II. 317 It will be of great consequence to France and England, to have America governed by a Galloman or Angloman. **1795** *Ibid.* IV. 124 A treaty of alliance between England and the Anglomen, against the Legislature and people of the United States.

'Angloman[2], **-e.** *rare.* [a. Fr. *anglomane*, f. *anglomanie* Anglomania.] = Anglomaniac.

1860 Mrs. P. Byrne *Undercurr. Overl.* II. 298 The most rampant Anglomane will admit that speaking is not exactly the forte of the English. **1880** Fagan *Panizzi* II. 191 To be looked upon as a crazy Angloman.

Anglomania (æŋgləʊ'meɪnɪə). Rarely adapted as **anglomany.** [f. Anglo- + Gr. μανία madness (see mania), imitating Fr. *anglomanie.*] A mania for what is English; an excessive admiration of English customs, etc.

1787 T. Jefferson *Writ.* (1859) II. 161 A little disposition to Anglomania. **1805** *Ibid.* (1830) IV. 33 Till Anglomany.. yields to Americanism. **1809** Coleridge *Friend* vi. ii. (1867) 297 Anglo-mania in France, followed by revolution in America. **1856** *Sat. Rev.* II. 237 Anglomania consisted chiefly in the adoption of frock-coats and top-boots as the national costume.

Anglomaniac (æŋgləʊ'meɪnɪæk), *sb. rare.* [f. Anglo- + maniac: after prec.] One possessed by Anglomania; a rabid partisan of what is English.

1837 Carlyle *Fr. Rev.* I. iii. ii. 85 There is not a dwarf jokei..or Anglomaniac horseman rising on his stirrups, that does not betoken change. **1882** *Society* 30 Dec. 5/2 [These terms] intersperse every Anglomaniac's conversation.

ˌAngloma'niacal, *a.* [f. Anglomaniac.] Of the nature of Anglomania.

1893 *Outing* (U.S.) XXII. 115/1 Bunker's utmost anglo-maniacal yearnings had never caused him to be taken for a Briton.

Anglomanist. *rare*$^{-1}$. [f. Fr. *anglomane* + -ist.] = prec.

1882 Turner in *Macm. Mag.* XLV. 475 Frequent visits to London had made his father a rampant anglomanist.

ˌAnglo-'Norman, *a.* and *sb.* [f. Anglo- + Norman *sb.*[1] and *a.*] **A.** *adj.* Of or pertaining to the Normans in England after the Norman Conquest, or to their descendants, or to the variety of Norman French spoken in England after the Conquest.

1767 A. C. DUCAREL (*title*) Anglo-Norman Antiquities considered, in a Tour through part of Normandy. **1767** LD. LYTTELTON *Hist. Hen. II* I. I. 158 It is from his reign we must date the first regular settlement of the Anglo-Norman constitution. **1801** G. ELLIS in *Spec. Early Eng. Poets* I. ii. 37 The Anglo-Norman jargon was only employed in the commercial intercourse between the conquerors and the conquered. **1811** SCOTT in *Sir Tristr.* Introd. 81 The Anglo-Norman Rimeur. **1847** F. MADDEN *Laȝ. Brut* I. p. xii, The Anglo-Norman metrical chronicle of the *Brut*. **1865** W. WHITE *Eastern England* I. xvii. 235 An Anglo-Norman church with its round arches, arcades, and zig-zag mouldings. **1874** PARKER *Introd. Goth. Archit.* I. ii. (ed. 3) 22 The French Archæologists..call our Norman style the Anglo-Norman style. **1923** J. VISING (*title*) Anglo-Norman Language and Literature. **1960** E. G. STANLEY *Owl & Nightingale* 34 It is..worth noting that similar use of proverbs is made in the Anglo-Norman debate, Chardry's *Petit Plet*.

B. Also as *sb.*

1735 M. SHELTON tr. *Wotton's Sh. View of Hickes's Treasury* 41 Hickes observes, that all the Charters which shine with guilt Crosses, and painted Images, (or Figures,) ..were spurious, and forged by Anglo-Normans long afterwards. **1758** J. RAYNER tr. *Anc. Dial. concerning Exchequer* I. 33 That division of the country in the time of the Anglo-Saxons, was called among the English *shire*, which was afterwards called county by the Anglo-Normans. **1847** F. MADDEN *Laȝ. Brut* III. 453 *Stal*, in A[nglo]-Norman, *estal*. **1953** A. J. BLISS in *Archivum Linguisticum* V. 22 (*title*) Vowel-quantity in Middle English Borrowings from Anglo-Norman.

So **ˌAnglo-Norˈmanic** *a.* and *sb.*

1707 FLEETWOOD *Chron. Prec.* iii. 36 Remember that the 120 are *Anglo-Saxonic* Shillings, and the 50 are Anglo-Normanic ones. **1796** MORSE *Amer. Geog.* II. 113 England is full of Anglo-Normanic monuments. **1845** STODDART in *Encycl. Metrop.* I. 73/1 The modern English Language is founded on the Anglo-Normannic, of which the two earliest specimens referred to by Hickes are the Life of St. Margaret and the Description of Cokaygne.

Anglophile (ˈæŋgləʊfaɪl), *a.* and *sb.* Also **-phil.** [ad. F. *anglophile*, f. ANGLO- + -PHIL, -PHILE.] **A.** *adj.* Friendly to England or to what is English. **B.** *sb.* One who is friendly to England. Hence **Angloˈphilia**, **ˈAnglophilism**, friendliness to England; **Angloˈphilic** *a.*, Anglophile.

1867 *Contemp. Rev.* IV. 88 The *Revue des deux Mondes*, a thorough 'Anglo-phile' periodical. **1883** *Chambers's Jrnl.* 13 Jan. 18/1 This telephone..was an Anglophile, and would only respond to the honoured name of Faraday. **1892** *Athenæum* 26 Mar. 400/3 When prudence dictated assistance to the Dutch, the Huguenots, or the 'Anglophile' party in Scotland. **1896** *Westm. Gaz.* 2 Oct. 2/1 To show how Anglophilia and Anglophobia counteract each other. *Ibid.* 5 Dec. 6/3 The New York *Evening Sun*..has frequently attacked Mr. Bayard for what it regards as his extreme Anglophilism. **1920** ROBB *Thre Prestis of Peblis* (S.T.S.) Introd. p. xxxv, The unpopularity he thus incurred as an anglophile. **1950** *Amer. Speech* XXV. 90 The large Anglophilic group in the city.

Anglophobe (ˈæŋgləfəʊb), *sb.* (and *a.*) [a. Fr. *anglophobe*: see -PHOBE.] One affected with Anglophobia, one who has a morbid dread of, or aversion to, England or the English. Also *attrib.* or as *adj.*

1866 LOCKYER *Heavens* (1868) 493 This climate of ours, which..is not so bad, astronomically speaking, as some Anglophobes would make it. **1882** *St. James's Gaz.* 12 Apr. 5 The Prince—the greatest ruffian and chief Anglo-phobe at the Mandalay Court. **1901** *Daily Chron.* 6 Aug. 3/1 The revival of Anglophobe reaction was further strengthened by the Parliamentary activity of Clericalism.

Anglophobia (æŋgləʊˈfəʊbɪə). [f. ANGLO- + Gr. -φοβία horror: see -PHOBIA.] Intense dread or fear of England.

1793 JEFFERSON *Writ.* (1895) VI. 250 We are going on here in the same spirit still. The Anglophobia has seized violently on three members of our Council. **1816** W. TAYLOR in *Month. Rev.* LXXX. 501 To propagate an Anglo-phobia in France. **1880** FAGAN *Panizzi* I. 200 An intimate feeling of Anglomisos (to coin a word somewhat milder than Anglophobia) materially influenced Thiers.

Anglophobiac (æŋgləʊˈfəʊbɪæk), *sb.* (and *a.*) [f. ANGLOPHOBIA after *mania*, *maniac*.] = ANGLOPHOBE. Also *attrib.* or as *adj.* So **Angloˈphobian** *a.*

1893 *N. Amer. Rev.* Aug. 170 The work of an Anglophobiac who labors to widen..the schism. **1894** *Pop. Sci. Monthly* XLV. 476 The Anglophobiac American who proposed cutting a canal through Yucatan. **1896** *Daily News* 11 Jan. 7/5 If..scurrilous little newspapers of Paris indulge in Anglophobian diatribes. **1902** *Daily Chron.* 26 May 5/1 The New York 'Sun', a violently Anglophobiac paper.

Anglophobic (æŋgləʊˈfəʊbɪk), *a.* [f. ANGLOPHOBIA + -IC.] Of or pertaining to Anglophobia.

1865 *Pall Mall G.* 28 July 10 The anglophobic phase may have begun again. **1894** *Westm. Gaz.* 1 June 3/1 Our old Anglophobic friend, M. Deloncle. **1907** *Ibid.* 6 May 11/1 The Anglophobic outbursts of the German Press. **1958** *Listener* 13 Nov. 786/2 On our side, there is a counterpart Anglophobic sentiment.

Anglophobist (æŋˈglɒfəbɪst). *rare.* [f. Fr. *anglophobe* + -IST.] = ANGLOPHOBE.

1854 *Blackw. Mag.* LXXV. 13/1 In all matters relating to the East he is an Anglophobist (to coin a word for the occasion). **1882** *Standard* 24 Aug., It represents the opposite camp of Anglophobists. **1904** *Westm. Gaz.* 24 Sept. 12/1 François Garnier, a bitter Anglophobist.

anglophone (ˈæŋgləʊfəʊn), *sb.* and *a.* Also with capital initial. [f. ANGLO- + -PHONE 2.] **A.** *sb.* An English-speaking person. **B.** *adj.* English-speaking.

1900 [see FRANCOPHONE *sb.* and *a.*]. **1965** *Punch* 24 Nov. 775/2 His intimate knowledge of affairs in Africa (Francophone as well as Anglophone)..equips him outstandingly to point out not only what has gone wrong in West Africa..but what should be done to put it right. **1967** *Saturday Night* (Toronto) Oct. 19 It is because our fizzy Canadian cocktail has intoxicating qualities, because a dazzling future lies in wait for francophones and anglophones..that we should hold together, along with the valuable New Canadians. **1971** *Times* 12 June 15/2 It is significant that the same development did not take place in Anglophone Africa. **1974** *Globe & Mail* (Toronto) 26 Feb. 1/1 Now it is the Anglophone spokesmen who have rushed to the political front lines to defend what they see as a fundamental right. **1978** *Nature* 23 Nov. 425/2 Occasional lapses grate a little to anglophones ('...the Protestant minister David Fabricius') and some analogy requires a good knowledge of Italian geography. **1984** *Newslet. Amer. Dial. Soc.* Sept. 6/1 Multilingual Switzerland is not an anglophone country.

ˌAnglo-ˈRoman, *a.* [f. ANGLO-.] **a.** English Roman Catholic. Hence **ˌAnglo-ˈRomanism**, English Romanism. **b.** Of or pertaining to England and Rome.

c **1840** A. W. PUGIN in E. S. Purcell *Life & Lett. A. Phillipps de Lisle* (1900) II. 218 The Oratory..fitted up..with a sort of Anglo-Roman altar. **1866** 'A LAYMAN' (*title*) Anglo-Romanism unveiled; or, Canon Oakeley and Dr. Newman at issue with the Catholic and Roman Church, and with one another. **1891** GLADSTONE in *Westm. Gaz.* (1898) 20 May 8/1, I share the dissatisfaction which many feel at the attitude in England of the *Anglo*-Roman body. **1895** *Ibid.* 12 Jan. 8/2 An essential part of that history [of the sixteenth and seventeenth centuries] is what I may term Anglo-Roman. **1913** C. G. BAYNE (*title*) Anglo-Roman Relations, 1558–1565.

Anglo-Saxon (ˌæŋgləʊˈsæksən), *sb.* and *a.* Forms: 1 **Angul-, Angel-, Ongol-seaxan** *sb. pl.*, 7– **Anglo-Saxon, -saxon**, 9 **Anglosaxon.** [Prob. in 9th c., as certainly in 17th, ad. L. *Anglo-Saxones, -Saxon-icus*, in which *Anglo-*, comb. form of *Anglus, -ī*, is used adverbially, as in similar L. and Gr. compounds, as *sacro-sanctus* sacredly sanctioned, Ἰνδο-σκυθία Indian Scythia, Scythia of the Indus, Συρο-φοῖνιξ, L. *Syrophœnix*, Phœnician of Syria. Cf. also *Gallo-græci*, and in later use *Mœso-Gothi* Goths of Mœsia. Hence *Anglo-Saxones, Angel-seaxan* = English Saxons, Saxons of England or of the Angul-cynn (*gens Anglorum*, Bæda), as distinguished from the *Ald-Seaxan* (*Antiqui Saxones*, Bæda) or Old-Saxons of the continent. The earliest L. forms were *Angli Saxones*, *Saxones Angli* (two words 'English Saxons'), whence *Angli-Saxones*, and finally *Anglo-Saxones, Anglosaxones.* App. of continental origin; in OE. use, rare in the Eng. form; not uncommon in Latin documents down to 1100.]

I. English Saxon, Saxon of England: *orig.* a collective name for the Saxons of Britain as distinct from the 'Old Saxons' of the continent. Hence, properly applied to the Saxons (of Wessex, Essex, Middlesex, Sussex, and perhaps Kent), as distinct from the Angles.

a. *sb.* (the only contemporary use).

[*c* **775** PAULUS DIACONUS IV. xxiii, Vestimenta..qualia Angli Saxones habere solent. *Ibid.* IV. xxxvii, E Saxonum Anglorum genere duxit uxorem. *c* **885** *Charter, Cod. Dip.* V. 134 Ego Ælfredus, gratia Dei, Angul-Saxonum rex.] **934** *Chart. C.D.* V. 218–9 Ic Æthelstán, Ongol-Saxna cyning and Brytænwalda eallæs þyses iȝlandes. **955** *Chart. C.D.* II. 303 He hafað ȝeweorðad mid cynedóme Angulseaxna Eádred cyning and cásere *totius Britanniæ*.

b. *adj. absol.* In this Dictionary, the language of England before 1100 is called, as a whole, 'Old English' (OE.); *Anglo-Saxon*, when used, is restricted to the Saxon as distinguished from the Anglian *dialects* of Old English; thus we may say that *eald* was the Anglo-Saxon (*i.e.* West Saxon and Kentish) form of the normal OE. *ald* (retained in Anglian), whence, and not from *eald*, we have mod.Eng. *old*.

II. Extended to the entire Old English people and language before the Norman Conquest.

For these there was apparently at first no collective name; subsequently, the name *Englisc* (Anglish, English) was extended from the dialect of the Angles (the first to be committed to writing) to all dialects of the vernacular, whether Anglian or Saxon; and *Angul-cynn* (Angle-kin, *gens Anglorum*), and later still, during the struggle with the Danes, 'English' and 'Englishman,' to all speakers of the vernacular in any dialect Angle or Saxon. After the Norman Conquest, the natives and the new incomers were at first distinguished as 'English' and 'French,' but, as the latter also became in a few generations 'English' politically and geographically, men's notions of 'English' changed accordingly, so that the 12th c. chroniclers could no longer apply the word distinctively to the people of Edward the Confessor and Harold, for whom therefore they recalled the name 'Saxon,' applicable enough to the West Saxon dynasty, but incorrect when extended to the whole Angle-kin over whom they ruled. At the hands of the Latin chroniclers, often foreigners, to whom the historical relations of Saxons and Angles were not very obvious, a similar extension of meaning had been given to *Anglo-Saxones*. But this name did not reappear in English till after 1600, when, with the revival of OE. learning, historians and philologists again felt the need of distinguishing English 'Saxon' from the Saxon of Germany. The modern use dates from Camden, who himself used *Anglo-Saxon-es, -icus*, in Latin, and *English Saxon* in his vernacular works. His translator adapted the Lat. as *Anglo-Saxon*, which gradually displaced 'English Saxon,' first as sb., and finally as adj. also. But it was applied, as *Saxon* had been for 500 years erroneously applied, to 'Old English' as a whole. This has led in turn to an erroneous analysis of the word, which has been taken as = *Angle* + *Saxon*, a union of Angle and Saxon; and in accordance with this mistaken view, modern combinations have been profusely formed in which *Anglo-* is meant to express 'English and..', 'English in connexion with..', as 'the Anglo-Russian war'; whence, on the same analogy, Franco-German, Turko-Russian, etc. See ANGLO-.

a. *sb.*

[**1586–1607** CAMDEN *Brit.* 94 Nunc..*Anglo-Saxones* ad differentiam eorum in Germania, vocatos. *Ibid.* 128 Maiores nostri Anglo-Saxones Wittena-ȝe-mott, .i. *Prudentum Conuentus*..vocârunt.] **1610** HOLLAND *Camden's Brit.* 177 The Anglo Saxons our ancestors termed it *Wittena-ȝe-mott*, that is, an assembly of the wise. *Ibid.* I. 127 (*title*) English Saxons; (*marg. title*) Anglo-Saxons. [**1605** CAMDEN *Rem.* (1614) 20 The English-Saxon tongue came in by the English-Saxons out of Germany.] **1726** TINDAL *Rapin's Eng.* (1757) I. I. 90 They were generally called Saxons, yet they had sometimes the compound name of Anglo-Saxons given them. **1735** THOMSON *Liberty* IV. (T.) Ere, blood-cemented, Anglo-Saxons saw Egbert and Peace on one united throne. **1846** WRIGHT *Mid. Ages* I. i. 2 Public attention..was first drawn to the writings of the Anglo-Saxons at the time of the reformation. *a* **1861** PALGRAVE *Norm. & Eng.* (1864) III. 596, I must..substitute henceforward the true and antient word English for the unhistorical and conventional term Anglo-Saxon, an expression conveying a most false idea in our civil history. **1867** FREEMAN *Norm. Conq.* (1877) I. 548, I speak therefore of our forefathers, not as 'Saxons,' or even as 'Anglo-Saxons,' but as they spoke of themselves, as Englishmen.

b. *adj.* (*absol.* The Old English language.)

[**1586–1607** CAMDEN *Brit.* 121 In Anglo-Saxonicis legibus nusquam comparet. **1610** HOLLAND *Camden's Brit.* 168 In the English-Saxon lawes, it is nowhere to be seene. **1605** CAMDEN *Rem.* (1614) 21 The English-Saxon conquerors, altred the tongue which they found here wholly. *Ibid.* 70 *Folc*, the English-Saxon woorde for people. **1715** E. ELSTOB (*title*) The Rudiments of Grammar for the English Saxon Tongue. **1726** AYLIFFE *Parerg.* 11 Under all the English Saxon Kings.] **1726** TINDAL *Rapin's Eng.* (1757) I. III. 157 The Anglo-Saxon kings were naturally very restless. **1783** BAILEY, *Anglosaxon*, the Saxon language as it was spoken in *England*. **1876** SWEET *Anglo-Sax. Reader* xi, The oldest stage of English before the Norman Conquest is now called 'Old English,' but the older name of 'Anglo-Saxon' is still very generally used. **1955** QUIRK & WRENN *O.E. Gram.* 1 In the eighteenth and nineteenth centuries the term *Anglo-Saxon*..was the commonest name for the language; but, although still sometimes used by scholars it has gradually been replaced in the last hundred years by the more scientific term *Old English*.

III. Used rhetorically for *English* in its wider or ethnological sense, in order to avoid the later historical restriction of 'English' as distinct from Scotch, or the modern political restriction of 'English' as opposed to American of the United States; thus applied to (1) all persons of Teutonic descent (or who reckon themselves such) in Britain, whether of English, Scotch, or Irish birth; (2) all of this descent in the world, whether subjects of Great Britain or of the United States.

a. *sb.*

1853 GEN. P. THOMPSON *Audi Alt. Part.* (1858) I. xv. 51 Sometimes they stand on the right and the necessity for the *European* to live by plunder; and sometimes..they concentrate their claim upon the *Anglo-Saxon*. **1904** CONRAD *Nostromo* II. vi. 180 It is part of the truth of things which hurts the—what do you call them?—the Anglo-Saxon's susceptibilities.

b. *adj.*

Quot. 1871 should perhaps be placed in sense II. B.

1832 R. CHOATE in *Deb. Congress* 13 June 3515 The whole circle of the..arts, trades, and branches of manufacture, which characterize the..industry of the Anglo-Saxon race of men. **1840** GEN. P. THOMPSON *Exerc.* (1842) V. 314 The chief reason stated for the recognition of the pirates, is that they are of the Anglo-Saxon race. **1846** *Spirit of Times* (N.Y.) 6 June 177/3 The Anglo-Saxon 'never can acknowledge the corn' to the cross of negro and Indian. **1855** MACAULAY *Hist. Eng.* III. 143 The Puritan part of the Anglosaxon colony had little right to complain. **1871** 'L. CARROLL' *Through Looking-Glass* vii, He's an Anglo-Saxon Messenger—and those are Anglo-Saxon attitudes. **1871** *Spect.* 22 Apr. 467 England's best alliance would be the free confederation of the English race in every part of the world. Change 'English' for 'Anglo-Saxon,' and in that sentence lies the policy of the future. **1875** W. JAMES *Coll. Ess. & Rev.* (1920) 16 But the thing which to our Anglo-Saxon mind seems so outlandish is that crowds of dapper fellows, revelling in animal spirits and conscious strength, should enroll themselves in cold blood as his [*sc.* Schopenhauer's] permanent apostles. **1888** KIPLING in *Lett. of Marque* (1891) xvi. 119 A snowy-bearded chowkidar..threw himself into Anglo-Saxon attitudes. **1924** R. GRAVES *Mock Beggar Hall* 63 Yet commonsense, the Anglo-Saxon flair Seems weakest on its vaunted practical side. **1956** ANGUS WILSON (*title*) Anglo-Saxon Attitudes.

IV. Used for 'the English language'. '(Of) the English language (of the modern period)' *U.S.*;

freq. with the implication 'plain, unvarnished, forthright'. *colloq.*

a. *adj.*

1859 'J. DOWNING' *Thirty Years out of Senate* 10 The best and truest exposition of the peculiar Yankee dialect of the Anglo-Saxon language that there is extant. **1863** C. LYELL *Antiquity of Man* xxiii. 466 Among the [Germans of Pennsylvania]..I found the newspapers full of terms half English and half German, and many an Anglo-Saxon word which had assumed a Teutonic dress, as 'fencen', to fence, instead of umzäunen. **1927** in *Amer. Speech* (1928) III. 376 Several Laborites were suspended in the House of Commons..to the accompaniment of..the hurling of bald Anglo-Saxon epithets traditionally classed as unparliamentary. **1927** *Sat. Rev. Lit.* 23 Apr. 772/4 All nine of the tabooed Anglo-Saxon monosyllables. **1958** *Spectator* 31 Jan. 133/2 The Bishop was reported in reputable newspapers as having said (and in more Anglo-Saxon terms) that he had been reliably informed of the truth of this fact.

b. *sb.*

1866 J. C. GREGG *Life in Army* xv. 137 Occasionally a word of honest, hearty Anglo-Saxon, or a 'bit of the brogue', to remind you that you are not in Naples, but in New Orleans. **1872** H. A. WISE *Seven Decades of Union* 141 He [*sc.* Senator Leigh of Virginia] was a purist in his Anglo-Saxon. **1917** in *Amer. Speech* (1929) IV. 271, I like your stilted style best Jack. When you descend to the Anglo Saxon you get too much in dead earnest. **1926** *Amer. Speech* I. 265/1 Specimens of the jargon daily spoken by witnesses believing they talk pure Anglo-Saxon. **1927** *Yale Rev.* Jan. 414 Tell me what you forget and I will tell you what you are, says the psycho-analyst. But I can do this, too, and in plain Anglo-Saxon. The man who insists on telling me what he forgets is a fool. **1947** K. MALONE in *Word Study* Oct. 2/2 In current speech *Anglo-Saxon* often means plain English. In this use, the word has *Latin* for antonym.

Anglo-'Saxondom. [f. prec. + -DOM; cf. *Christendom.*] The Anglo-Saxon domain or community; the collective body of Anglo-Saxons, the Anglo-Saxon race viewed as a whole; a rhetorical phrase for Great Britain and the United States.

1850 LYELL *Let.* in *Life* II. 168 A regard for the sacredness of truth is not a rare exception to the rule in Anglo-Saxondom at least. **1872** *Daily News* 25 Mar., Anglo-Saxondom is to have a wrangle royal at Geneva. **1881** BREWER *Eng. Stud.* 63 For the strictly orthodox spelling of Cuthberht he gives Cuthbert, not known in Anglo-Saxondom.

†**Anglo-Sa'xonic,** *a. Obs.* [f. ANGLO-.] = SAXONIC *a.* 2. Also as *sb.*

1672 PENN *Truth Vin.* 53 Besides, several other Languages, amongst others a Gothick and Anglo-Saxonick Testament. **1686** PARR *Life of Usher* 101 His great activity.. to advance the Restauration of our old Northern Antiquities, which lay buried in the Gothick, Anglo-Saxonick, and other the like obsolete Languages. **1739** J. LEWIS *Hist. Transl. Bible into Eng.* (ed. 2) i. 7 In his Observations on the Anglo-Saxonic Version of the Gospels. *Ibid.*, To note what Books of the Old Testament he translated into Anglo-Saxonic. **1796** *Ann. Reg. 1767* (ed. 5) 150/1 The heavy Gothic by Sir C. Wren is distinguished as Anglo-Saxonic, the lighter as Saracenic.

Anglo-'Saxonism. [f. ANGLO-SAXON + -ISM.]

1. Anything peculiar to the Anglo-Saxon race.

2. *esp.* A word, phrase, idiom, or habit of speech, belonging to, or derived from, the Old English, unaffected by Romanic or other foreign admixture.

3. The sentiment of being 'Anglo-Saxon' (in sense III.) or English ethnologically; a belief in the superiority or claims of the 'Anglo-Saxon' race.

1860 GEN. P. THOMPSON *Audi Alt. Part.* III. cxli. 121 The zeal for Anglo-Saxonism, will be found to be little but rogue calling upon rogue. **1867** BAGEHOT *Physics & Pol.* (1876) 36 In America and in Australia a new modification of what we call Anglo-Saxonism is growing.

,Anglo-'Saxonize, *v.* [f. ANGLO-SAXON + -IZE.] *trans.* To make Anglo-Saxon.

1883 MARQUIS OF LORNE in *Contemp. Rev.* Nov. 641 That great Anglo-Saxonizing amalgamation mill, the United States, would soon efface their [*sc.* French Canadians'] language. **1898** *Westm. Gaz.* 14 July 2/1 These silly efforts to Anglo-Saxonise the United States.

Anglo-'Saxony. *rare.* [f. ANGLO-SAXON + -Y[3].]. A rhetorical expression for 'Great Britain and the United States'.

1905 *Daily Chron.* 13 Mar. 3/7 Miss Annie Russell is artistically eager to render his 'Jinny the Carrier' all over Anglo-Saxony. **1937** WYNDHAM LEWIS *Blasting & Bombardiering* v. iv. 272 T. S. Eliot—need I say the premier poet of Anglo-Saxony?

,Anglo-ver'nacular, *a.* [f. ANGLO-.] Pertaining to or consisting of English and an Indian language.

1877 CALDWELL *Evangel. Work Tinnevelly* 2 Our S.P.G. Anglo-Vernacular School. **1888** KIPLING *Plain Tales fr. Hills* 269 He wound up with a six-shot Anglo-Vernacular oath. **1915** (*title*) A List of Educational Books..for Schools in India, Burma and Ceylon..(Vernacular, Anglo-Vernacular and English).

angnæȝl, -nale, -naylle, obs. ff. AGNAIL.

angola (æŋ'gəʊlə). **1.** A corruption of ANGORA; often used of the fabric made of Angora wool.

1827 GRIFFITH *Cuvier* IV. 327 Angola breeds. **1845** FORD *Handbk. Spain* I. i. 60 Shirts..good English angola or flannel ones. **1882** *Times* 12 Apr. 4 Tweed and angola trowsers.

2. *angola cat.* Also *ellipt.* (See ANGORA 1.)

1851 BORROW *Lavengro* i, The cheerful hum of the kettle and the purring of the immense angola. **1854** MRS. GASKELL *Let.* ? 15 May (1966) 285 We are going to have a little kitten ..with long hair... It is called an Angola or a Persian cat.

Angolan (æŋ'gəʊlən), *sb.* and *a.* [f. *Angola* (see below) + -AN.] **A.** *sb.* A native or inhabitant of Angola, a republic (formerly a Portuguese colony) in south-western Africa. **B.** *adj.* Of or pertaining to Angola or its inhabitants.

1600 J. PORY tr. *Leo Africanus, Geog. Hist. Afr.* 413 For first in the yeere 1582, a fewe Portugals in an excursion that they made, put to flight an innumerable companie of the Angolans. **1875** J. J. MONTEIRO *Angola* I. ii. 24 The character of the Angolan landscape is entirely different from that of the West Coast proper. **1922** J. C. B. STATHAM *Through Angola* p. v, It was at an Angolan port that Livingstone..ended his first great African journey in 1853. **1933** J. T. TUCKER *Angola* i. 11 His cunning artistry became proverbial among Angolan tribes. **1960** *Times* 30 May 9/6 Sitting at a pavement café..in the little Angolan fishing port of Mocamedes. **1976** *Daily Times* (Lagos) 12 July 9/4 President Neto, in refusing to commute the death sentences explained: 'Every Angolan remembers the vile and cruel behaviours of the mercenaries who have sown death and despair in African countries in return for pay.' **1980** *Amer. Speech* LV. 27 The Angolan slaves taken into Surinam by the Dutch seem to have carried the essentials of a Portuguese pidgin with them.

angon ('æŋgɒn). [med.L., ad. Gr. ἄγγων.] (See quot. 1893.)

1875 *Encycl. Brit.* II. 555/1 Iron head of Angon from a grave at Darmstadt. **1893** *Athenæum* 9 Sept. 361/3 Among the most curious of the weapons our ancestors used was the angon, a sort of long spear with a double barb—one tongue of which was longer than the other and flame-shaped. **1908** *Victoria Hist. Kent* I. 377 One of the rare iron weapons usually called angons. **1940** *Antiquity* XIV. 14 Through one of the drop-handles of the outer bowl the shafts of three iron angons had been thrust.

angor ('æŋgə(r)). Also 5 **angure,** 7 **angour.** [a. OFr. *angor, angour* :—L. *angōr-em* strangling, vexation, f. *ang-ĕre* to squeeze, strangle. Now only as a medical term, and more or less as Latin.]

†**1.** Anguish (physical or mental). *Obs.*

1440 *Promp. Parv.*, Angure or angwys, *Angor, angustia.* **1598** SYLVESTER *Du Bartas* II. i. III. (1641) 100/1 Man is loaden with ten thousand languors. All other Creatures onely feele the angors Of few Diseases. **1677** GALE *Crt. Gentiles* II. IV. 146 Inflamed with perpetual sparkes of fears, angors and agitations. *a* **1711** KEN *Psyche* Poet. Wks. 1721 IV. 261 Her Hours in silent Anguors now ran waste.

2. *spec.* A feeling of 'anxiety and constriction in the precordial region, which accompanies many severe diseases; nearly synonymous with *angina.*' Mayne *Exp. Lex.* 1853.

1666 HARVEY *Morb. Anglic.* (J.) If the patient be surprised with a lipothymous angour. **1753** CHAMBERS *Cycl. Supp.*, *Angor* is reputed a bad symptom. **1839** in HOOPER *Med. Dict.*

Angora (æŋ'gɔərə). [modern form of ancient Ἄγκυρα *Ancyra.*]

1. A town in Asia Minor, giving its name to a species of goat, and to its silk-like wool; also to a long-haired variety of cat. Also applied to a variety of rabbit having fine white fur and pink eyes; also ellipt. as *sb.*, a rabbit of this variety, its fur or a fabric made from it.

1819 T. HOPE *Anast.* II. i. 5 Of the things themselves whose appellations he had learnt, he seemed to have no more idea than the huge Angora cat which sat purring by his side. **1833** *Penny Cycl.* I. 511 The bright, silk-like wool of the Angora goat. **1838** *ibid.* X. 223 The Angora cat with its long silky hair. **1849** tr. *Wyss's Swiss Family Robinson* Ser. II. xvii. 152 Fritz has two magnificent Angora rabbits in his pouch. **1875** URE *Dict. Arts* I. 177 The first parcels of Angora wool were shipped from Constantinople for England in 1820. **1908** J. A. THOMSON *Heredity* x. §4. 365 Hurst paired white Angora rabbits..with 'Belgian hare' rabbits. **1927** E. V. KNOX *Awful Occasions* 58 The vexed topic of dandelions as a diet for half bred Angoras. **1960** *Which?* Jan. 19/2 *Angora*, hair from the angora rabbit. Very fine and soft. Angora sheds fibres easily. *Ibid.* Feb. 39/2 *Angora*..a fabric made from Angora rabbits' hair with the addition of up to 5 per cent wool to facilitate spinning.

2. The fabric manufactured from the wool of the Angora Goat, now commonly called ANGOLA.

1867 *Morn. Star* 12 Apr., Fancy boudoir mats in lambs'-wool and angora.

Angostura: see ANGUSTURA.

angre, -ful, variants of ANGER, -FUL.

Angrian, *a.* [f. *Angria* (see below) + -AN.] Of or pertaining to Angria, an imaginary African empire invented by the Brontë children (Charlotte, Branwell, Emily, and Anne) in stories that they composed. Also as *sb.*

1834 C. BRONTË *Twelve Adv.* (1925) 168 The wife of Northangerland, the prima donna of the Angrian Court. **1834** P. B. BRONTË in *Misc. Unpub. Writ.* (1936) I. 435 Sound the loud Trumpet o'er Afric's bright sea; Zamorna hath triumphed: the Angrians are free. **1936** *Times Lit. Suppl.* 3 Oct. 784/3 These Angrian games are the most curiously exciting ever played by children. **1954** K. TILLOTSON *Novels of Eighteen-Forties* I. 97 Recollected from Charlotte's early reading, through her own Angrian romances.

†**angrice.** *Obs. rare*[−1]. [? a confusion between Eng. ANGER *sb.* (in sense 1) and OFr. *anguise* ANGUISH: cf. ANGRISE.] Trouble, affliction.

1340 *Ayenb.* 147 Þe on leme þoleþ zuetliche of þe oþre þet he him deþ of angrice.

angrily ('æŋgrɪlɪ), *adv.* Also 4 **angryliche,** 5 **angryly.** [f. ANGRY *a.* + -LY[2]. Appears first as var. of earlier ANGERLY (blending with it in the spelling *angrely*), which it has since replaced.]

†**1.** Vexatiously, grievously. *Obs. rare.*

c **1425** WYNTOUN *Cron.* VI. vi. 30 Hir chyld ill al suddanly Travalyd hyr sa angryly.

2. In an angry or wrathful manner, with anger or open resentment.

c **1386** CHAUCER *Pars. T.* 510 (Ellesm. MS.) Thanne wole he be angry and answeren hokerly and angrily [*v.r.* angerly, -yrly, -rely]. **1393** LANGLAND *P. Pl.* C. XVII. 115 Al angryliche · and argueynge as hit were. **1597** DANIEL *Civ. Wars* II. (R.) Turns angrily about his grieved eyes. **1766** H. BROOKE *Fool of Qual.* I. 101 He..angrily called to know what was the matter. **1873** MISS BROUGHTON *Nancy* II. 66 Battling angrily with an angrier wasp.

angriness ('æŋgrɪnɪs). *rare.* [f. ANGRY + -NESS: see also earlier ANGERNESS.]

1. The quality of being angry; wrathfulness.

1553 GRIMALDE *Cicero's Offices* I. (1558) 40 They would not commende angrinesse. **1561** T. N[ORTON] *Calvin's Inst.* IV. xx. (1634) 739 If they must punish let them not be borne away with a headlong angrinesse. **1658** *Whole Duty of Man* x. §22 (1684) 86 Such an angriness of humour, that we take fire at everything. **1871** R. ELLIS *Catullus* xcix. 6 No portion of any Tears could abate that fair angriness.

†**2.** Inflamed condition of a sore or wound.

1612 BENVENUTO *Passengers' Dial.* (N.) Their sweate.. takes away the angrinesse and rednesse of skars.

†**angrise,** *v. Obs. rare*[−1]. [? confusion between Eng. ANGER *v.* 1, and OFr. *anguiser* to anguish, or with AGRISE.] To distress, afflict.

1340 *Ayenb.* 146 Þet me naȝt him misdo ne angrisi ne harmi.

angry ('æŋgrɪ), *a.* Forms: 4 **angre, (angerich),** 4–5 **angri,** 4–7 **angery,** 5 **angrye, (hangry),** 6 **anggre,** 6–7 **angrie,** 4– **angry.** [f. ANGER *sb.* + -Y[1]: cf. *hungry*. With senses 2 and 3 cf. Fr. *fâché de* and *fâché contre.* Comp. *-er, -est.*]

†**1.** Full of trouble actively; troublesome, vexatious, annoying, trying, sharp. *Obs.*

c **1360** *Gloss.* in *Rel. Ant.* I. 8 *Molestus*, angri. **1375** BARBOUR *Bruce* v. 70 Myne auenture heir tak will I, Quhethir it be eisfull or angry. *c* **1400** *Rom. Rose* 2628 To liggen thus is an angry thyng. *a* **1667** JER. TAYLOR *Serm.* III. 267 God had provided a severe and angry education to chastise the frowardness of a young spirit.

†**2.** Passively affected by trouble; vexed, troubled, grieved. *Obs.*

1375 BARBOUR *Bruce* III. 530 The hart is sorowfull or angry. *c* **1394** *P. Pl. Crede* 553 Angerich I wandrede the Austyns to prove. [*Skeat conjectures* angerlich.] **1485** CAXTON *Paris & V.* 42 Parys was moche angry bycause he sawe wel that it was moche peryllous.

3. a. Of persons: actively affected against the agent or cause of trouble; feeling or showing resentment; enraged, wrathful, irate.

c **1386** CHAUCER *Pers. T.* 510 Thanne wole he be angry [*v.r.* angery, hangry] and answeren hokerly. **1440** *Partonope* 2556, I am wroth and in my hert angry. **1440** *Promp. Parv.*, Angrye, *Iracundus, bilosus.* **1547** J. HEYWOOD *Prov. & Epigr.* (1867) 52 He that will be angry without cause, Must be at one without amendes. **1647** COWLEY *Dialogue* ix. in *Mistr.*, I'm angry, but my wrath will prove, More Innocent than did thy Love. **1718** LADY M. MONTAGUE *Lett.* I. xxii. 69 Very angry that I will not lie like other travellers. **1750** JOHNSON *Rambl.* No. 74 ¶4 Angry without daring to confess his resentment. **1864** BURTON *Scot. Abr.* I. iv. 191 Angry letters to his angrier mistress.

b. Const. (*of, for, upon*, obs.) *at, about,* the occasion; *at* a person when the subjective feeling is denoted, *with* a person when the anger is manifested; but the tendency is to use *with* for both.

c **1400** *Destr. Troy* XVIII. 7703 There-at Ector was angry, & out of his wit. *a* **1450** *Knt. de la Tour* (1868) 25 He was angri of her governaunce. **1483** CAXTON *G. de la Tour* E viij, God was therefore angry upon them. **1523** LD. BERNERS *Froissart* I. ccxxxii. 317 Y[e] prince..was in a maner angry of the honour y[t] sir Bertram of Clesquy had gotten him. **1556** *Chron. Grey Friars* (1852) 88 Some were very anggre wyth hym because he sayd soo. **1579** TOMSON *Calvin's Serm. Tim.* 115/2 Must they needes be angrie for it? **1599** SHAKS. *Hen. V*, IV. i. 217, I should be angry with you. **1607** —— *Timon* III. iii. 13 I'me angry at him. **1611** BIBLE *Ps.* vii. 11 God is angrie with the wicked euery-day. —— *Eccles.* v. 6 Wherefore should God be angrie at thy voyce? **1740** CHESTERF. *Lett.* 61 I. 173, I shall be very angry at you. **1778** BURKE *Corr.* (1844) II. 242 The people are angry with the ministry. **1875** *Fam. Her.* 21 Aug. 263/2 Major Porter is so awfully angry about it. **1883** SPOFFORD in *Harper's Mag.* June 130/1, I felt a little angrier with myself.

c. *spec.* Dissatisfied with and outspoken against the prevailing state of affairs, current beliefs, etc.; esp. in phr. *angry young man* (abbrev. A.Y.M.).

The expression 'angry young man' and variants of it became commonly used, esp. by journalists, after the production of J. Osborne's play *Look Back in Anger* (first performed 1956). The phrase did not occur in the play but was applied to Osborne by G. Fearon, a press reporter (see quot. 2 Oct. 1957), thence used particularly of young writers, usually of provincial and lower middle-class or working-class origin, who denounced or satirized the 'Establishment' (q.v.) and the abuses of the time; later applied by extension to any person, group, etc., in Britain and elsewhere who considered the times to be out of joint. For the formation, cf. 'bright young thing' (BRIGHT *a.* 7b).

(*a*) (General and nonce uses.)

1937 [see ANGER *sb.* 2b]. **1941** 'R. WEST' *Black Lamb* (1942) I. 157 Their [*sc.* the Dalmatians'] instinct is to brace themselves against any central authority as if it were their enemy. The angry young men run about shouting. **1951** LESLIE PAUL (*title*) Angry Young Man. **1954** J. B. PRIESTLEY *Magicians* vi. 132 Too much resentment, too much cheap cynicism. And he's expecting too much, in the wrong way. He's the contemporary Angry Little Man.

(*b*) With overt or implicit reference to Osborne's *Look Back in Anger*; also extended uses.

1956 *Reporter* (N.Y.) 18 Oct. 33/1 The angry young man is a stock character in literature. **1957** G. FEARON in *Daily Tel.* 2 Oct. 8/7, I had read John Osborne's play. When I met the author I ventured to prophesy that his generation would praise his play while mine would, in general, dislike it... 'If this happens,' I told him, 'you would become known as the Angry Young Man.' In fact, we decided then and there that henceforth he was to be known as that. **1957** *Times Lit. Suppl.* 4 Oct. 593/1 The 'angry young men' of England (who refuse to write grammatically and syntactically in order to flaunt their proletarian artistry). *Ibid.* 8 Nov. 674/1 *Declaration* is a volume of essays in which four of the 'angry' movement attempt to formalize their beliefs. **1958** *Times* 1 Feb. 7/5 The angry young man who feels that life is short, and that he must make his mark early by carping at established ideas and institutions. **1958** *Spectator* 11 July 67/2 A vigorous but implausible book about an AYM, *strictly* lower-class. **1958** *Listener* 4 Dec. 961/2 A fine, hard-bitten performance of an Angry Old Man. **1959** *Times* 1 Jan. 9/3 Mr. Forster..has been angry but never Angry.

d. ***Angry Brigade***, the name of an urban guerrilla organization responsible for a number of acts of terrorism in Great Britain, chiefly in the early 1970s.

1971 *Times* 14 Jan. 1/5 The handwritten letter, signed 'The Angry Brigade' had been posted before first collection yesterday. **1971** *Guardian* 15 Jan. 1/4 Detectives investigating the bomb attack on the home of Mr Robert Carr..regard a letter sent to the 'Guardian', signed by 'The Angry Brigade', as one of the most important leads in the case. **1975** G. CARR *Angry Brigade* iv. 71 The name.., thought up at a raucous, drunken Christmas party, would be 'The Angry Brigade'. The words were a rough translation of *Les Enragés*. The 'Brigade' bit smacked slightly of the Spanish Civil War. **1984** *Washington Post* 1 July (Book World Suppl.) 4/1 We learn that Effie has become a member of the Angry Brigade (or Baader-Meinhof), given to crimes of violence, urban revolution and ultimately, the murder of police.

4. Of mood or action: Moved or excited by anger.

1509 HAWES *Past. Pleas.* xxxiv. xxix, The spirite of pacience Doth overcome the angry violence. **1670** COTTON *Espernon* III. IX. 443 The angry trade of War. **1855** TENNYSON *Maud* I. VI. vii, A man's own angry pride Is cap and bells for a fool. **1859** GEO. ELIOT *A. Bede* 106 Even in his angriest moods.

5. Bearing the physical marks of anger, looking or acting as if in anger; as ***an angry countenance, an angry sky, angry billows***.

1393 GOWER *Conf.* I. 283 So bere I forth an angry snoute. **1595** SHAKS. *John* IV. iii. 149 Now..Doth dogged warre bristle his angry crest. **1611** BIBLE *Prov.* xxv. 23 An angrie countenance. **1687** DRYDEN *Hind & P.* III. 270 He sheathes his paws, uncurls his angry mane. **1756** BURKE *Subl. & B.* Wks. I. 197 The angry tones of wild beasts. **1860** TYNDALL *Glac.* I. §25. 185 Angry masses of cloud. **1878** R. STEVENSON *Inland Voy.*, The water, yellow and turbulent, swung with an angry eddy..and made an angry clatter along stony shores.

6. Having the colour of an angry face, red. *rare.*

1632 G. HERBERT *Vertue* in *Temple* 80 Sweet rose, whose hue angrie and brave. **1823** LAMB *Elia* Ser. I. xviii. (1865) 139 His waistcoat red and angry.

7. Habitually under the influence of anger; hot-tempered, irritable, choleric, passionate. *arch.*

1387 TREVISA *Higden* (1865) I. 427 As men in þis londe Beeþ angry. **1398** —— *Barth. De P.R.* XVIII. i. (1495) 736 Some beestes..be ryght wrathfull and angry. **1535** COVERDALE *Prov.* xxi. 19 A chydinge and an angrie woman. **1650** tr. *Bacon's Life & Death* 10 The Turkey-Cock..An Angry Bird, And hath exceeding white flesh. **1703** ROWE *Ulysses* IV. i. 1695 Honour, This busie, angry thing, that scatters Discord.

8. Inflamed, smarting, as a sore.

1579 GOSSON *Sch. Abuse* (Arb.) 21 Curst sores with often touching waxe angry. **1611** FLORIO, *Pedignoni*, angrie kibes, chilblanes, or bloodie falles. **1676** WISEMAN (J.) This serum ..grows red and angry. **1863** ATKINSON *Yorksh. Gloss.*, *Angry*, applied to a sore (1) that looks very red and inflamed, (2) or that is very irritable and painful. *Mod.* The gouty toe is very angry.

9. Sharp, acrid in taste. Sharp, keen, as appetite. *rare.*

c **1325** *E.E. Allit. P.* B. 1035 Alum & alka[t]ran that angré arn boþe. **1859** TENNYSON *Enid* 1082, I never ate with angrier appetite.

10. ***Comb.***, as ***angry-eyed, -looking***.

1865 DICKENS *Mut. Fr.* 34 That angry eyed, buttoned-up, inflammatory-faced old gentleman.

†**'angry**, *v. Obs. rare*$^{-1}$. [f. prec. Cf. to *weary*.] To make angry, anger, provoke.

1642 FULLER *Holy & Prof. St.* v. i. 358 Nothing angrieth her so much as when modest men affect a deafnesse.

angry ('æŋgrɪ), *sb.* [f. the adj.] An 'angry' person (see ANGRY *a.* 3c); an 'angry young man'.

1957 *Times Lit. Suppl.* 15 Nov. 689/3 Writers, such as Mrs. Lessing, who have never been called Angries at all. **1958** *Observer* 14 Sept. 4/5 The 'beat generation' is beginning to acquire the same kind of dubious place in American culture as the Young Angries in Britain. **1959** *Bookseller* 7 Mar. 1133/1 The 'beats' are represented by Anatole Broyard..and Carl Solomon; the 'angries' by John Wain, Colin Wilson, John Osborne, [etc.].

†**'angryable**, *a. Obs. rare.* [f. ANGRY + -ABLE.] Capable of being angry, irascible.

1662 J. CHANDLER *Van Helmont's Oriatrike* 165 Among angryable or wrathful Beings. *Ibid.* 304 The Schools do assign..the angryable or wrothful power to the heart.

‖**angst** ('æŋst). [G.] Anxiety, anguish, neurotic fear; guilt, remorse.

[**1849** GEO. ELIOT *Let.* 5 Aug. (1954) I. 293 'Die Angst' she says often brings on a pain at her heart. **1922** C. J. M. HUBBACK tr. *Freud's Beyond Pleasure Principle* ii. 9 Apprehension (*Angst*) denotes a certain condition as of expectation of danger..even though it be an unknown one. **1941** *Philosophy* XVI. 260 To Heidegger *Angst*, dread, is the fear of metaphysical insecurity.] **1944** 'PALINURUS' *Unquiet Grave* 22 Angst may take the form of remorse about the past, guilt about the present, anxiety about the future. **1950** A. HUXLEY *Themes & Variations* 202 To *acedia* and confusion, to nightmare and *angst*, to incomprehension and panic bewilderment. **1956** C. P. SNOW *Homecomings* viii. 65 Discussing other people whose lives were riven by angst—it domesticated her wretchedness a little to have that label to pin on. **1964** *New Statesman* 10 Apr. 574/1 Telly-angst is a natural corollary of architectural news-angst generally.

Comb., as ***angst-forming, -ridden, -wrought*** adjs.

1944 'PALINURUS' *Unquiet Grave* 43 There need be nothing angst-forming about the sexual act. **1958** *Times* 14 Feb. 6/1 (Advt.), The..contrast drawn between those years and our *Angst*-ridden era. **1958** *Observer* 27 Apr. 15/3 Petrushka is a tied-up angst-wrought neurotic.

Ångström (unit) (ɔːŋstrœm). Also **angstrom** ('æŋstrəm). [The name of A. J. *Ångström* (1814–74), a Swedish physicist.] A hundred-millionth of a centimetre (10^{-8} cm.), used in measuring the wavelengths of light, X-rays, etc. (also called *absolute Ångström*); the same unit used as a measure of the thickness of thin film. Abbrev. Å, Å.U.; also A.U.

The *International Ångström* (I.Å.) was defined in 1907 in terms of the wavelength of cadmium which in standard conditions is 6438·4696 I.Å. When the metre was defined in terms of the wavelength of krypton in 1960 the Ångström became exactly equal to 10^{-8} cm.

[**1887** *Phil. Mag.* XXIII. 258 As all observers so far seem to accept the measures of Ångström, I have decided that a table of my results would be of value.] **1892** *Nature* 29 Sept. 513/1 This width..is ·04 of an Ångström or Rowland unit..in the yellow part of the spectrum. **1897** *Rep. Brit. Assoc. Advancem. Sci.* 556 No lines were found to shift more than a fraction..of an Ångström unit. **1906** *Trans. Internat. Union Solar Research* I. VIII. 230 *Resolutions concerning standards of Wave-length.* The wave-length of a suitable spectroscopic line shall be taken as the primary standard of wave-length. The number which defines the wave-length of this line shall be fixed permanently and thereby define the unit in which all wave-lengths are to be measured. This unit shall differ as little as possible from 10^{-10} metres and be called the Ångström. **1911** KAYE & LABY *Phys. & Chem. Constants* 9, 1 Å.U. = 10^{-10} metre. **1916** ALLEN & MOORE *Text-Bk. Pract. Physics* III. vii. 300 Ångström Units (A.U.). **1921** *Discovery* Sept. 226 An X-ray of wave length equal to two-tenths of an Ångström Unit (100-millionth of a centimetre). **1933** S. W. COLE *Pract. Phys. Chem.* (ed. 9) x. 255 Ångström units (Å or A.U.). **1943** A. E. MIRSKY in Nord & Werkman *Advances in Enzymology* III. 18 Histone spreads to give a film 7–9 Å thick. **1951** *Engineering* 18 May 589/1 Dr. J. S. Courtney-Pratt has used interferometric methods to study the uniformity and thickness of thin films. .. He was able to measure the thickness correct to the nearest Ångstrom. **1957** *Technology* July 168/4 Those [fluorescing agents] emitting a visible blue light in the 4,000–4,400 angstrom range are commercially useful in detergents. **1957** H. BARRELL in *Nature* 21 Dec. 1388/1 The value λ_R = 6438·4696 A. was adopted as the spectroscopic reference standard in 1907 and thereby became the means of defining the international angstrom—the unit that has since served for all spectroscopic measurements of wave-length.

anguicular (æŋ'gwɪkjʊlə(r)), *a. rare.* [f. mod.L. *anguicula* (fem. dim. of *anguis* snake) + -AR.] Of or pertaining to *Anguiculæ* or microscopic 'eels.'

1755 B. MARTIN *Mag. Arts & Sc.* (ed. 3) 162 View 8 represents the Anguiculæ, or small microscopic eels in Vinegar or Paste..in all their natural motions and Anguicular Forms.

anguiform ('æŋgwɪfɔːm), *a.* [f. L. *angui-s* snake + -FORM; cf. mod.Fr. *anguiforme*.] Having the shape of a serpent or snake; snake-shaped.

1800 *Phil. Trans.* XC. 130 The anguiform motion suspected by Newton. **1835** KIRBY *Habits & Inst. Anim.* II. xvi. 68 The anguiform Chilognathans represent the living and moving Serpent.

†**an'guigenous**, *a. Obs.*$^{-0}$ [f. L. *anguigen-a* (f. *anguis* snake + *-genus* born) + -OUS.] 'Engendered or begotten of serpents.' Bailey 1731.

Anguillan (æŋ'gwɪlən), *sb.* and *a.* Formerly also **An'guillian**. [f. *Anguilla* (see below) + -AN.] **A.** *sb.* A native or inhabitant of the island of Anguilla in the West Indies. **B.** *adj.* Of or pertaining to Anguilla or its inhabitants.

1920 K. J. BURDON *Handbk. St. Kitts-Nevis* xxviii. 225 The Anguillians fought bravely. **1963** D. M. DOUGLASS *Saba's Treasure* vi. 96 The widespread cheerfulness of my fellow men could be as irritating as a streetful of grumpy Anguillans. **1967** *Guardian* 17 June 1/6 The Anguillans rebelled three weeks ago. *Ibid.* 19 June 8/1 Mr Peter Adams, the Anguillan leader, is now reported to have asked President Johnson to accept Anguilla as an associated state. **1972** D. E. WESTLAKE *Under English Heaven* (1973) iii. 43 As of February 1967, there were two Anguillan-owned airlines and many motor-driven fishing boats and launches. **1977** *Guardian* 3 Feb. 3/8 A new chief minister today replaced the Anguillan leader, Mr Ronald Webster. **1984** *Whitaker's Almanack 1985* 776/2 In 1967 the Anguillans repudiated government from St. Kitts.

†**anguille, anguelle.** *Obs.* [a. Fr. *anguille* eel:—L. *anguilla*, dim. of *anguis* snake.] 'A sort of small worms cast up by sick hawks.' Phillips 1658; whence in Bailey, etc.

a **1500** *Bk. Hawkyng* in *Rel. Ant.* I. 301 For wormys called anguilles.

anguilliform (æŋ'gwɪlɪfɔːm), *a.* [f. L. *anguill-a* eel + -(I)FORM.] Eel-shaped.

1693 *Phil. Trans.* XVII. 930 Our Author treats of Fishes, and begins with such as are Anguilliform. **1753** CHAMBERS *Cycl. Supp.* s.v., Membranes full of Anguilliform worms. **1858** CLARK *Van der Hoeven's Zool.* II. 144 *Zoarces*, Body elongate, anguilliform, with scales small.

anguillous ('æŋgwɪləs), *a. rare*$^{-1}$. [f. as prec. + -OUS.] Of the nature of an eel, eel-like.

1704 TYSON *Yellow Gurnard* in *Phil. Trans.* XXV. 1752 Even the Anguillous kind are Scaly.

anguillule (æŋ'gwɪljuːl). [mod. f. L. *anguill-a* eel + -ULE dim. suffix; cf. mod.Fr. *anguillule*.] A small eel-shaped creature; *esp.* one of the animalcules of the family *Anguillulidæ*, such as the 'eels' in sour paste or vinegar.

1860 *All Y. Round* No. 45. 387 One anguillule is found in wet moss, green slime, rain water.

anguine ('æŋgwɪn), *a.* [a. L. *anguīn-us* pertaining to a snake, f. *anguis* snake: see -INE.] Of or resembling a snake or serpent.

1657 TOMLINSON *Renou's Disp.* 241 Four sorts of cucurbites, the greater, the lesser..or the anguine. **1847** CARPENTER *Zool.* §501 The Anguine Lizard, also a native of South Africa. **1871** LE FANU *Tenants of Malory* xi. 54 Her beautiful eyebrows wore that anguine curve, which is the only approach to a scowl which painters accord to angels.

anguineal (æŋ'gwɪnɪəl), *a. rare*$^{-0}$. [f. L. *anguine-us* of the nature of a snake (f. *anguis*) + -AL[1].] = next.

1731 BAILEY, *Anguineal Hyperbola* [as CHAMBERS; see next]. **1847** in CRAIG.

anguineous (æŋ'gwɪnɪəs), *a. rare.* [f. as prec. + -OUS: see -EOUS.] Of the nature or appearance of a snake; as in *Anguineous Hyperbola*, a name given by Newton to four of his curves of the second order.

1656 BLOUNT *Glossogr.*, *Anguineous*, of or belonging to a Snake. **1727–51** CHAMBERS *Cycl.* s.v. *Curve*, That [hyperbola] which cuts its asymptote with contrary flexures, and is produced both ways into contrary legs, *anguineous* or *snake-like*. **1858** CLARK *Van der Hoeven's Zool.* II. 285 Body elongate, anguineous.

anguipede, -ped ('æŋgwɪpiːd, -pɛd), *a.* [ad. L. *anguipēs* (*-ped-*), f. *anguis* serpent + *pēs* foot.] Having feet or legs in the form of serpents, serpent-footed: an epithet of certain giants of ancient mythology.

1883 A. S. MURRAY *Gr. Sculpt.* II. 305 A winged anguipede giant. **1888** A. H. SMITH *Catal. Engr. Gems Brit. Mus.* 100 Athenè..treading down anguipede Giant.

anguish ('æŋgwɪʃ), *sb.* Forms: 3 anguise, -oise, 3–4 **anguisse, -uysse, -usse, -uis,** 3–5 **angus,** 4 **anguys, -wys(e, -wish(e, -uych,** 4–5 **anguisshe, -wisshe, uyssh, -wisch(e, -uysch(e,** 4–6 **anguysh,** 5 **angwich, -wysch, -wysshe,** 5–6 **anguyshe, -uysshe,** 4– **anguish.** [a. OFr. *anguisse, angoisse* (Pr. *angoissa*, It. *angoscia*) the painful sensation of choking:—L. *angustia* straitness, tightness, *pl.* straits, f. *angust-us* narrow, tight, f. root *angu-* in *ang(u)-ĕre* to squeeze, strangle, cogn. w. Gr. ἄγχ-ειν.] Formerly with *pl.*

1. Excruciating or oppressive bodily pain or suffering, such as the sufferer writhes under.

c **1220** *Hali Meid.* 35 Hwen hit þer to cumeð þat sar sorhfule angoise. *a* **1300** *Pop. Sc.* (Wright) 374 The bodi.. in strong anguisse doth smurte. *c* **1380** *Sir Ferumb.* 212 Hys wounde..for angwys gan to chyne. **1382** WYCLIF *Jer.* iv. 31 Anguysshes as of the child berere [**1388** angwischis as of a womman childynge; **1611** the anguish as of her that bringeth forth her first child]. *c* **1386** CHAUCER *Pers. T.* 139 The peyne of helle..is lik deth, for the horrible anguisshe [*v.r.* angwissh(e, -uysch, -uyssche, -wysshe]. **1485** CAXTON *Chas. Gt.* 238, I haue suffred many anguysshes of hungre. **1592** SHAKS. *Rom. & Jul.* I. ii. 47 One paine is lesned by anothers anguish. **1656** RIDGLEY *Pract. Physick* 150 If there be pain of the Stomach, anguish, heat. **1758** S. HAYWARD *Serm.* xvii. 520 His [Job's] body was full of anguish. **1880** CYPLES *Hum. Exp.* iii. 70 The anguish of corns and toothache.

2. Severe mental suffering, excruciating or oppressive grief or distress.

c **1230** *Ancr. R.* 234 In the muchel anguise aros þe muchele mede. **1297** R. GLOUC. 177 In gret anguysse and fere Wepynde byuore þe kyng. *c* **1325** *E.E. Allit. P.* C. 325 When þacces of anguych watȝ hid in my sawle. **1382** WYCLIF *Prov.* xxi. 23 Who kepeth his mouth and his tunge, kepeth his soule fro anguysschis. *c* **1450** *Merlin* 64 Grete angwysshe that he suffred for the love of Ygerne. **1583** STANYHURST *Aeneis* II. (Arb.) 46 With cholericque fretting I dumpt, and rranckled in anguish. **1611** BIBLE *Job* vii. 11, I wil speake in the anguish of my spirit. **1678** JENKINS in *Pepys* VI. 125 An honest man..full of Anguishes for his King and his Country. **1769** *Junius Lett.* xxiii. 105 You may see with anguish how much..authority you have lost. **1810** SCOTT *Lady of L.* II. xxxiv, The deep anguish of despair.

†**3.** ***anguish of weathering***: stress of weather. *Obs.*

c **1450** LONELICH *Grail* xxxv. 50 Angwisch of wedering made vs hider to go.

4. *Comb.*, as ***anguish-stricken, -torn.***

1810 COLERIDGE *Friend* IV. iii. (1867) 242 The anguish-stricken wife of Toxaris.

anguish (ˈæŋgwɪʃ), *v.* Forms: 4 anguise, anguisse, 4–5 anguysch(e, angwische, angwishe, 6 anghysshe, 6– anguish. [a. OFr. *anguissie-r, angoissie-r*:—L. *angustiā-re* to straiten, distress, f. *angustia*: see prec.]

1. To distress with severe pain or grief, excruciate.

c **1374** CHAUCER *Boeth.* III. viii. 80 Euery delit..anguisseþ hem wiþ prikkes þat vsen it. **1388** WYCLIF *Gen.* xxxi. 40 Y was angwischid in dai and nyȝt with heete and frost. **1560** J. HEYWOOD *Seneca's Thyestes* Argt. (1581) 21 Thiestes..knowing he had eaten his owne children, was wonderfully anguished. **1627** FELTHAM *Resolves* I. viii. (1677) 11 Sores are not to be anguish't with a rustic pressure. **1797** *Encycl. Brit.* IV. 341/1 s.v. *Charade*, My first..anguishes the toe of a man. **1855** CDL. WISEMAN *Fabiola* 338 It was..the making him doubly a fratricide, which deeply anguished her.

†**2.** *refl. Obs. rare.*

1538 LATIMER *Serm. & Rem.* (1845) 397, I will no longer anguish myself with a matter that I cannot remedy.

3. *intr.* (refl. pron. omitted.) To distress oneself, suffer severe pain or sorrow.

1330 R. BRUNNE *Chron.* 132 Kyng Henry..anguised greuosly, þat Thomas was so slayn. **1601** J. WEEVER *Mirr. Martyrs* D ij b, Whose soules with sin-empoisning hate did anguish. **1624** BARGRAVE *Serm.* 36 Thy bones anguish, thy limbes sinke under thee. **1820** KEATS *Isabella* vii, He had waked and anguished A dreary night of love and misery.

†**4.** ? To smother, quash, crush, put down. (Cf. OFr. *angoissier* = 'serrer fortement, presser, étreindre vivement, sans idée de souffrance.' Godef.) *Obs. rare.*

1502 *Ord. Cryst. Men* (W. de Worde) III. iii. 157 The .vii. maner of almesdede spyrytuall is to hyde, to couer, and to anghysshe yᵉ yll and defame of his neyboure.

†ˈ**anguish, -guis, -guissh,** *a. Obs. rare.* [a. OFr. adj. *anguis, angois*, cited by Godefroi in fem. *angoisse*: see ANGUISH *sb.*] Excruciating, exceedingly distressing.

c **1400** *Test. Love* II. (1560) 289/1 For badde thinges and anguis wretchednes been passed. **1475** CAXTON *Jason* 42 The moost anguisshyst dethe that ony man may endure.

anguished (ˈæŋgwɪʃt), *ppl. a.* Also anguisht. [f. ANGUISH *v.* + -ED.]

1. Distressed with severe pain or grief; tormented.

1382 WYCLIF *Jon.* ii. 8 My soule was angwishid in me. **1627** FELTHAM *Resolves* I. viii. (1677) 74 The spirits shrink inward, and retire to the anguisht heart. **1818** *Art of Preserv. Feet* 50 Anguished sufferers try these panaceas. **1857** MISS WINKWORTH *Tauler's Serm.* xxv. 391 The thorns of an anguished conscience.

2. Expressing pain, full of anguish, agonized.

c **1800** SOUTHEY *Race of Banquo* Wks. II. 155 The anguish'd shriek, the death-fraught groan. **1864** NEALE *Seaton. Poems* 7 The ocean with unwonted roar, And anguish'd moan, shall vex his shore.

anguishful (ˈæŋgwɪʃfʊl), *a. rare.* [f. ANGUISH *sb.* + -FUL.] Full of anguish, distressing.

1847 SARA COLERIDGE *Mem. & Lett.* II. 137 The..oft-repeated agonies and anguishful trials of the Romish heroine.

ˈ**anguishing,** *vbl. sb.* ? *Obs. rare.* [f. ANGUISH *v.* + -ING[1].] The action of afflicting with severe pain; affliction, torment.

1521 *St. Werburge* Prol., O cruell deth..Thou causest wo, languor, and anguissyng. *a* **1617** HIERON *Wks.* II. 204 This renting of the heart, and anguishing of the bones.

anguishing (ˈæŋgwɪʃɪŋ), *ppl. a.* [f. as prec. + -ING[2].] Deeply distressing or afflicting, agonizing.

c **1680** PORDAGE *Mystic Div.* (1683) 118 The Eternal Anguishing Fire-Spirit. **1761** LAW *Comf. Weary Pilgr.* (1809) 107 The anguishing terrors of thy soul. **1810** CAMPBELL *Poems* I. 128 Heaven's mercy relieving Each anguishing wound.

†ˈ**anguishment.** *Obs. rare.* [a. OFr. *angoissement*, f. *angoissier*: see ANGUISH *v.* and -MENT.] Torment, torturing; severe suffering.

1592 WYRLEY *Armorie* 129 When we are with anguishment distrest. **1655** H. VAUGHAN *Silex Scint.* I. (1858) 33 His Agonie And moving anguishments.

†ˈ**anguishness.** *Obs. rare*$^{-1}$. [f. ANGUISH *a.* + -NESS.] Sore distress, torment.

a **1564** BECON *Chr. Knt.* Wks. 1844, 628 Upon them which do service unto unrighteousness..anguishness shall come.

†ˈ**anguishous,** *a. Obs.* or *dial.* Forms: 3 anguisuse, -ussus, -uysous, 3–4 anguyssous, 4 angwisous, 4–5 anguisschous, -wischous(e, -uissous, -wissous, -wysshous, -uissheous, 5 anguisshous, -uysshous(e, -wisshous, -wyschschous, 4–6 anguishous. [a. OFr. *anguissus, -ussus, -uessous*, later *-oisseux*:—late L. *angustiōsum*, f. *angustia*: see ANGUISH *sb.* and -OUS.]

1. *actively*, Fraught with anguish, attended with much suffering; tormenting, distressing.

c **1230** *Ancr. R.* 112 þe anguisuse deaðe þ he schulde þolien. *c* **1374** CHAUCER *Troylus* III. 816 Ful angwysshous than is..quod she, Condicioun of veyn prosperite. **1481** CAXTON *Myrr.* IV. xviii. 107 [In helle] is the fyre so ouer moche ardaunt hote and anguysshous. **1554** PHILPOT *Exam. & Writ.* (1842) 415 The thing was..anguishous to his country, and grievous to all good men.

2. *passively*, Full of anguish, oppressed with pain or grief, sore distressed.

1297 R. GLOUC. 222 Kyng Arture was anguysous..þat þe luþer traytor adde of scaped hym. *c* **1386** CHAUCER *Pers. T.* 230 My soule was anguissheous withinne me [*v.r.* angwissous, -uissous, -uysshous, -wisshous]. *c* **1450** LONELICH *Grail* xlv. 93 He sawh..Oure lord ful angwischous and al torent. *c* **1450** *Merlin* xv. 232 Thei were full anguysshouse for the grete losse that thei hadden. **1875** *Gloss. Lanc. Dial.* s.v., He lookt quite anguishous, an aw felt sorry for him.

3. Anxious.

c **1230** *Ancr. R.* 240 Holie meditaciuns..anguisuse bonen. *a* **1300** *Floriz & Bl.* 366 Whanne þu lest him þe cupe iseo Wel angussus he wile beo. *c* **1314** *Guy Warw.* 75 Herhaud to nim angwisous thai were. **1503** *Sheph. Kal.* (1656) xlii, Feet flat and short, signifieth an anguishous person, of small wisedom.

†ˈ**anguishously,** *adv. Obs. rare.* [f. prec. + -LY[2]; answering to OFr. *anguissousement.*] Distressingly, grievously; with much suffering.

c **1450** LONELICH *Grail* xiv. 759 Angwisschously ascryed they were, And slayn, takyn, and maymed, many were there. **1475** CAXTON *Jason* 17 b, Alle were hurte, that one more angusshously thene that other. *c* **1500** *New Notbrowne Mayd* 46 He wyll not..hym applye My wordes to here, That bought hym dere, On crosse anguyously.

angular (ˈæŋgjʊlə(r)), *a.* [ad. L. *angulār-is*, f. *angul-us*: see ANGLE and -AR. Cf. Fr. *angulaire.*]

1. a. Having an angle or angles, sharp-cornered.

1598 FLORIO, *Triangolare*, three angular, hauing three corners, three cornered. *a* **1631** DONNE *Poems* (1650) 240 Enormous greatnesses, which are So disproportion'd and so angulare. **1664** POWER *Exp. Philos.* I. 55 Hairs..are none of them Cylindrical, but angular and corner'd. **1756** BURKE *Subl. & B.* Wks. I. 238 Perfectly beautiful bodies are not composed of angular parts. **1857** HENFREY *Elem. Bot.* §58 A stem is..angular when the section is polygonal. **1878** GREEN *Coal* ii. 55 Nearly all the grains of quartz are angular.

b. Of writing: having the turns angled instead of rounded, as in German handwriting.

1863 BURTON *Bk. Hunter* 41 His handwriting was clear, angular, and unimpassioned.

2. Of or pertaining to an angle: **a.** Constituting an angle, sharp corner, or apex; also *fig.*

1597 J. KING *Jonah* xxiii. (1864) 145 The night which followed the sabbath of the Jews was the angular night..for both it belonged to the Sabbath preceding, and must be ascribed again unto the Christian Sabbath. **1675** OGILBY *Brit.* Introd., The next Angular Point being at Ivy Bridg. **1699** NEWTON *Opticks* (J.), The angular point where the edges of the knives meet. **1831** BREWSTER *Optics* xi. 98 At the angular termination of bodies these fringes widen. **1835–6** Supra-angular [see SUPRA- 1 b]. **1836** W. BUCKLAND *Geol. & Min.* I. xiv. 176 Head of the Crocodile. In the lower jaw, *u*, marks the dental bone; *v*, the angular bone; *x*, superangular. **1855** OWEN *Skel. & Teeth* 18 In the cod there is a small separate bone, below the joint of the articular, forming an angle there, and called the 'angular piece.' **1866** R. OWEN *Anat. Vertebrates* I. ii. 141 The mandibular arch..the 'articular' piece; that beneath it, which develops the angle of the jaw, when this projects, is the ' angular' piece; the piece above..is the 'surangular'.

b. Placed in or at an angle.

1842 E. WILSON *Anat. Vade M.* 336 The frontal is continued downwards by the side of the root of the nose, under the name of the angular vein. **1874** BOUTELL *Arms & Arm.* v. 78 The space between the angular bands. **1880** *Syd. Soc. Lex.*, *Angular artery*..The terminal branch of the facial artery.

c. Measured by angle.

1674 PELLY *Disc. bef. R. Soc.* 129, I call..the motion of the Biasses..the Angular or Curve Motion. **1785** REID *Intell. Powers* 159 Astronomers call it angular distance. **1796** HUTTON *Math. Dict.* I. 116/2 Angular Motion, is the motion of a body which moves circularly about a point. Thus, a pendulum has an angular motion about its centre of motion; and the planets have an angular motion about the sun. **1819** PLAYFAIR *Nat. Phil.* (ed. 3) I. 67 The angular velocity with which the bodies will begin to revolve. **1835** M. SOMERVILLE *Connex. Physical Sciences* (ed. 2) 455 The angular velocity of the earth is at the rate of 180° in twelve hours. **1837** [see DISTANCE *sb.* 5 e]. **1858** SUTTON & WORDEN *Dict. Photogr.* 21 The angular aperture of a lens is the angle which its diameter subtends at its principal focus. **1867** J. HOGG *Microsc.* I. ii. 41 Having an angular aperture of 60°. **1870** [see MOMENTUM 4]. **1873** J. N. LOCKYER *Elem. Lessons in Astr.* viii. 292 The mean angular diameter of the Moon is 31′ 8″·8. *Ibid.*, Knowing the real and also the apparent angular diameter, we can at once determine the distance. **1880** GRAY *Bot. Text.-bk.* 396 The angular divergence, or distance of the axis of the first leaf from the second. **1883** *Encycl. Brit.* XV. 692/1 The angular accelerations about these axes are equal at that instant. **1885** RANKINE & MILLAR *Man. Appl. Mech.* (ed. 11) v. ii. 505 Angular momenta are compounded and resolved like forces, each angular momentum being represented by a line whose length is proportional to the magnitude of the angular momentum. **1895** P. G. TAIT *Dynamics* 254 Thus the linear acceleration of each of the masses is equal to *a* times the angular acceleration of the pulley. **1921** *Discovery* Sept. 237/1 Professor Eddington..made an estimate of the probable angular diameters of some of the brighter stars. **1929** RATCLIFFE *Physical Princ. Wireless* i. 3 The angular frequency will often be referred to as the frequency of the oscillation. **1940** *Chambers's Techn. Dict.* 35/2 *Angular aperture*, the ratio of the working diameter to the focal-length of a lens, i.e. reciprocal of the *f*-number. *Ibid.*, *Angular frequency*, the frequency of a steady recurring phenomenon expressed in radians per second. *Ibid.* 554/1 *Angular momentum* is the product of the moment of inertia and the angular velocity of a body. **1949** W. E. SIRI *Isotopic Tracers & Nucl. Radiations* i. 12 In any nuclear reaction, spin and angular momentum must be conserved as well as mass and energy. *Ibid.* xiii. 375 The angular distribution of beta particles from a point source of small mass is isotopic. **1952** *Sci. News* XXIII. 41 Many nuclei behave as though they have angular momentum—that is to say, part of the system is either spinning on its own axis or revolving around the centre in an orbit, or both.

3. Of personal appearance: having the joints and bony protuberances prominent, through deficiency of roundness and plumpness in the fleshy parts. Of action: Moving the limbs in angles, jerky, abrupt, ungraceful, awkward.

1850 BLACKIE *Æschylus* I. Pref. 45 Their movements were slow, their gesticulations abrupt and angular. **1858** HOLMES *Aut. Breakf. T.*, The angular female in black bombazine. **1880** MCCARTHY *Own Time* IV. I. 61 His gestures were angular and ungraceful.

4. Of character: stiff and formal; hard and wanting suavity; crotchety and deficient in *savoir faire*; unaccommodating; cantankerous.

1840 HAWTHORNE *Biog. Sk.* (1879) 180 Here follow many bows and a deal of angular politeness on both sides. **1851** RYLAND *Neander's Planting of Chr.* II. 204 Rugged and angular natures. **1870** DICKENS *E. Drood* 62 As a particularly angular man, I do not fit smoothly into the social circle.

5. *Astrol.* Of an 'angle': see ANGLE *sb.*[2] 7.

1643 MILTON *Divorce* I. x. (1847) 133/2 The supernal influence of schemes and angular aspects.

6. **-angular**, -angled, as in ACUTANGULAR, etc.

angular (ˈæŋgjʊlə(r)), **angulare** (æŋgjʊˈlɑːriː), *sb. Zool.* [ad. mod.L. *angulāre*, neut. of *angulāris* adj. (see ANGULAR *a.*).] In some vertebrates, the angular bone of the lower jaw.

1846 R. OWEN *Lect. Comp. Anat. Vertebrate Animals* v. 113 It sends upwards a pointed coronoid process to which..the masticatory muscles are attached; one short square plate downwards, to join with the angular. **1896** [see SUPRA- 1 b]. **1905** D. S. JORDAN *Study Fishes* xxxiv. 606 Each half of the lower jaw consists of..the articular, angular, dentary, and splenial (coronoid). Most of these bones are armed with teeth. **1928** G. R. DE BEER *Vertebrate Zool.* v. 71 The quadrate articulates with a bone of the lower jaw called the articular... The ventro-posterior part of the lower jaw is formed by the angular. *Ibid.* xx. 298 The angular becomes converted into the tympanic bulla..and the supra-angular is represented by the processus Folii.

angularity (æŋgjuːˈlærɪtɪ). [f. L. *angulār-is* ANGULAR + -ITY.]

1. The quality or state of being angular; the having sharp or prominent corners.

1642 H. MORE *Song of Soul* III. II. xxxviii, What body ever yet could figure show Perfectly perfect, as rotundity Exactly round, or blamelesse angularity? **1646** SIR T. BROWNE *Pseud. Ep.* 84 Glasse grossely or coursely powdered..by reason of its acutenesse and angularity..excoriates the parts through which it passeth. **1841** TRIMMER *Pract. Geol.* 173 Volcanic grits are distinguished by the angularity of the particles.

b. *concr.* in *pl.* Angular outlines, sharp corners.

1853 KANE *Grinnell Exp.* xxx. (1856) 259 Dried apples become one solid breccial mass of compacted angularities. **1859** OWEN *Mammalia* App. B. 84 The shaft of the humerus..is peculiarly rounded..and offers none of those angularities and ridges. **1880** HOWELLS *Undisc. Country* vi. 104 The bold angularities of the fashionable female scrawl.

2. Of personal appearance: Want of rounded outline. Of manner: Want of suavity, crankiness.

1848 DICKENS *Dombey* (C.D. ed.) 5 Miss Tox's dress..had a certain character of angularity and scantiness. **1878** SEELEY *Stein* I. 310 The angularity and combativeness of Stein's manner.

angularly (ˈæŋgjʊləlɪ), *adv.* [f. ANGULAR + -LY[2].] In an angular manner.

1. In or with angles; so as to form an angle.

1599 B. JONSON *Cynthia's Rev.* (T.), A labyrinthean face, now angularly, now circularly, every way aspected. *a* **1691** BOYLE (J.), Another part of the same solution afforded us an ice angularly figured. **1703** MOXON *Mech. Exerc.* 162 A piece of Timber growing angularly, or crooked. **1794** SULLIVAN *View Nat.* I. 467 A crystaline substance..angularly arranged. **1880** GUNTHER *Fishes* 54 Angularly bent, so as to consist of a vertical and horizontal limb.

2. At (acute) angles, obliquely, diagonally, from corner to corner. Also *fig.*

1471 CAXTON *Chesse* 150 Goyng cornerly or angularly sygnefyeth cautele or subtilytye. **1650** J. WEEKES *Truth's Confl.* Pref. A ij b, Look not in an oblique manner or angularly upon the persons. **1808** J. WEBSTER *Nat. Phil.* 18 If the plates be placed angularly, or touch each other at one of the ends. **1830** LYTTON *Paul Cliff.* i. 2 A blanket, stretched angularly from the wall to the chimney.

3. Of personal appearance: see ANGULAR 3.

1846 POE *Wks.* (1864) III. 35 He is about five feet seven inches high..angularly proportioned. **1849** DICKENS *Barn. Rudge* xxxv. (C.D. ed.) 165 Gashford..was angularly made.

ˈangularness. ? *Obs. rare*$^{-0}$. [f. as prec. + -NESS.] The quality of being angular; angularity.

1731 in BAILEY; whence in JOHNSON, etc.

†**ˈangulary,** *a. Obs. rare*$^{-1}$. [f. L. *angul-us* (see ANGLE) + -ARY: there was no L. *angulāri-us.*] Situated at the corners, being at angles.

1474 CAXTON *Chesse* IV. ii. (1860) 144 The quene foloweth vnto two angularye places after the maner of the alphyn.

angulate (ˈæŋgjʊlət), *a.* [ad. L. *angulāt-us* pa. pple. of *angulā-re*, f. *angul-us* an angle.] Formed with corners; angled, cornered.

1794 MARTYN *Rousseau's Bot.* xvi. 189 The stalk is hairy, angulate and unbranched. **1852** DANA *Crust.* I. 260 Carpus angulate at inner apex.

angulate (ˈæŋgjʊleɪt), *v.* [f. prec. or its L. source.] To make angulate, or cornered.

1880 J. WATSON in *Jrnl. L.S.* XV. 228 The upper carinal thread becomes much the most dominant and angulates the whorls.

angulated (ˈæŋgjʊleɪtɪd), *ppl. a.* [f. L. *angulāt-us* ANGULATE + -ED, by assimilation to Eng. pa. pples.] Made to have angles, cornered.

1486 *Bk. St. Albans* E v a, A cheeff pale angulatit [L. *angulatum*] of asure and golde. **1695** WOODWARD *Nat. Hist. Earth* IV. (1723) 198 Angulated Columns..of six Sides. **1769** SIR J. HILL *Fam. Herb.* (1812) 41 The stalks [of the Bramble] are..angulated. **1804** BEWICK *Brit. Birds* (1847) II. 183 The bill is..thick, strong, and angulated. **1857** *Nat. Mag.* I. 368 A curiously angulated chrysalis.

ˈangulately, *adv.* [f. ANGULATE + -LY^{2}.] In an angulate manner; with angles or corners.

1848 DANA *Zooph.* 503 Surface angulately rough, or covered with very irregular protuberances.

angulation (æŋgjuːˈleɪʃən). [n. of action f. L. *angulāt-us* (see ANGULATE), as if ad. L. **angulātiōn-em.*] A making angulate; angular or cornered formation, or position.

1869 HUXLEY in *Jrnl. Geol. Soc.* XXVI. 38 The acute angulation of the union of the scapula and coracoid. **1880** J. WATSON in *Jrnl. Linn. Soc.* XV. 90 Suture linear, but strongly marked by the angulation of the whorls.

angulato- (ˌæŋgjʊleɪtəʊ-), comb. f. L. *angulātus* used advb. = ANGULATELY; as in **angulato-gibbous**, gibbous with an angulate tendency; **angulato-sinuous**, sinuous or winding with the curves angled.

1852 DANA *Crust.* I. 352 Carapax angulato-gibbous. *Ibid.* 573 Finger..angulato-sinuous on outer margin.

anguliferous (æŋgjuːˈlɪfərəs), *a.* [f. L. *angulus* ANGLE + -(I)FEROUS bearing.] 'Applied to a shell which has the last whorl angulated.' Craig 1847.

†**anguliˈzation.** *Obs.* [f. L. *angul-us* after *crystallization.*] = ANGULATION.

1676 SHADWELL *Virtuoso* IV. Wks. 1720 I. 386 To Fluidity ..so to Angulization, then Christallization.

angulo- (ˌæŋgjʊləʊ-), combining form of L. *angulus* (see ANGLE *sb.*^{2}) used advb., as in **angulo-dentate**, angularly toothed.

1829 LOUDOUN *Cycl. Plants, Angulo-dentate.*

anguloa (æŋgjuːˈləʊə). *Bot.* [mod.L. (1794), named by Ruiz and Pavon, *Fl. Peruv.*, in honour of Francisco de *Angulo*, a Spanish naturalist.] A member of a genus of South American plants so called, belonging to the family Orchidaceæ.

1836 *Mag. Bot. & Gardening* III. 29/2 Anguloa Superba. Superb Anguloa..is found growing on trees in Peru, sucking their sap by insinuating its roots beneath the bark. .. It should be planted in pots filled with porous stones. **1882** *Garden* 11 Mar. 168/2 Anguloas of all the different species ought to be potted. **1962** *Amateur Gardening* 7 Apr. 6/1 The anguloas, or Cradle orchids, are so named from the movable lip which bears a fanciful resemblance to a rocking cradle.

angulometer (æŋgjuːˈlɒmɪtə(r)). *rare.* [f. ANGULO- + -METER.] An instrument for measuring external angles.

1859 in WORCESTER. **1880** KNIGHT *Dict. Mech.* I. 106 A try-square may be termed an angulometer, 'a bent measure.'

angulose (ˌæŋgjuːˈləʊs), *a. rare.* [ad. L. *angulōs-us*: see ANGULOUS and -OSE.] = ANGULOUS.

1699 *Phil. Trans.* XXI. 66 Indian Mallows..bring forth Seeds either angulose or round. **1853** MAYNE *Exp. Lex.*, *Angulosus*, Full of angles or corners, angulose or angulous.

†**anguˈlosity.** *Obs.*$^{-0}$ [f. L. *angulōs-us* + -ITY.] The quality of having angles, cornered character.

1706 in PHILLIPS. **1755** in JOHNSON; and in mod. Dicts.

anguloso- (æŋgjuːˌləʊsəʊ-), comb. f. L. *angulōsus*, used advb.; as in **anguloso-gibbous**, gibbous with the curved sides almost forming angles.

1848 DANA *Zooph.* 617 Lobules..anguloso-gibbous..

angulous (ˈæŋgjʊləs), *a.* ? *Obs.* [a. Fr. *anguleux*, ad. L. *angulōs-us*, f. *angulus*: see ANGLE and -OUS.] Having angles or corners; angular.

1656 STANLEY *Hist. Philos.* III. III. 28 As to figure they are infinite; angulous, not-angulous, strait and round. **1665** GLANVILL *Sceps. Sci.* vii. 37 Held together by hooks, and angulous involutions. **1725** BRADLEY *Fam. Dict.* s.v. *Sow-Thistle*, The Stem is angulous. **1853** [See ANGULOSE.]

‖**Anguria** (æŋˈgjʊərɪə). *Bot.* [mod.L., f. Gr. ἀγγούριον a water melon.] A genus of plants of the gourd family; also their fruit.

1611 CORYAT *Crudities* 258 Anguria, the coldest fruite in taste that ever I did eate. **1753** CHAMBERS *Cycl. Supp.* s.v., The black seeded *citrul* or *Anguria.* **1869** *Eng. Mech.* 6 Aug. 446/3 Anguria.. The plant now so called is a kind of gourd.

Angus (ˈæŋgəs). The name of a county in Scotland, applied *attrib.* to a breed of cattle. Also *absol.* Cf. ABERDEEN *Angus.*

1842 D. LOW *Breeds Dom. Animals* I. II. 13 The Polled Angus breed. *Ibid.* 14 The Angus is a good breed. **1844** [see DEVON]. **1882** MACDONALD & SINCLAIR *Hist. Polled Aberdeen or Angus Cattle* viii. 136 No stock but polled Angus was at Kinnaird until about 1834. **1956** J. HEARNE *Stranger at Gate* iv. 31 This was the problem..how to keep beef on the mixed Angus and shorthorn stock in a climate that never had any spring or autumn.

†**anˈgust,** *a. Obs.* [a. Fr. *anguste* (Cotgr. 1611), ad. L. *angust-us* narrow, f. *ang-ĕre* to choke, squeeze tight.] Strait, narrow, compressed.

1599 A. M. *Gabelhouer's Bk. Physic* 61/1 An angust neckede glasse. *Ibid.* 338/1 If so be the wounde weare anguste, or closed together. **1621** BURTON *Anat. Mel.* II. ii. III. (1651) 251 If..the aire be so angust, what proportion is there between the other three Elements and it? **1661** LOVELL *Hist. An. & Min.* Introd., A great intestine, like that of a dogge, angust, and of a long figure.

†**angustate,** *v. Obs. rare*$^{-1}$. [f. L. *angustāt-* ppl. stem of *angustā-re* to narrow, f. *angust-us* narrow.] To make narrow, contract.

1657 TOMLINSON *Renou's Disp.* 694 It angustates and constringes laxer parts.

angustate (æŋˈgʌsteɪt), *a.* [ad. L. *angustāt-us*: see prec. and ANGUST.] Narrowed. (Said of leaves narrowed at the base.)

1847 in CRAIG. *Mod.* Leaves lanceolate, angustate, sessile.

†**angustated,** *ppl. a. Obs. rare.* [f. as prec. with ppl. ending -ED.] Narrowed, contracted.

1615 CROOKE *Body of Man* 787 His Venter or Belly is angustated or straightned [*i.e.* straitened].

angustation (æŋgəˈsteɪʃən). ? *Obs.* [n. of action f. L. *angustā-re* to narrow: see -ATION.] The action of narrowing, straitening; contraction.

1651 tr. *Bacon's Life & Death* 8 There is simple Contraction and Angustiation or Straitning. **1676** WISEMAN (J.), Obstruction of the vein somewhere in its passage, by some angustation upon it. **1853** in MAYNE *Exp. Lex.*

angusti- (æŋˈgʌstɪ-), combining form of L. *angustus* narrow; as in **angustifoliate, -ous**, narrow-leaved, **angustirostrate**, with narrow beak.

‖**anˈgustia.** *Obs. rare*$^{-1}$. [L. *angustia* narrowness, in *pl.* *-æ*, straits.] Straits, difficulties.

1682 SIR T. BROWNE *Chr. Morals* (1756) 81 They everlastingly struggle under their angustia's.

†**anˈgustity.** *Obs. rare*$^{-1}$. [ad. late L. *angustitāt-em*, n. of state f. *angust-us.*] = next.

1599 A. M. *Gabelhouer's Bk. Physic* 103/1 Heerwith hath on bine curede whoe throughe the angustitye of his Brest oftentimes fell downe to the earth.

†**anˈgustness.** *Obs. rare*$^{-1}$. [f. ANGUST + -NESS.] Narrowness, tightness, contraction.

1599 A. M. *Gabelhouer's Bk. Physic* 101/2 Pilles..for the Coughe, and angustnes of the Brest.

Anguˈstura, Angostura. A town on the Orinoco, now called Ciudad Bolivar. It gives its name to a bark, valuable as a febrifuge and tonic, the produce of *Galipea* or *Cusparia febrifuga.* The word *Angostura* as a brand of aromatic bitters is a registered trade mark. It derives its name from the fact that it was originally made in the town of Angostura, but it is not made from the bark exported from Angostura.

1791 A. BRANDE (*title*) Experiments and Observations on the Angustura Bark. **1840** PEREIRA *Mat. Med.* 1204 Angostura bark..was first publicly noticed in the *London Medical Journal* for 1789. **1866** MASTERS in *Treas. Bot.* 517 The means, chemical and otherwise, of distinguishing the true from the false Angostura barks. **1879** MISS BRADDON *Vixen* III. 191 Propped up with sherry and Angostura bitters. **1879** WATTS *Dict. Chem.* 3rd. Suppl. 87 Sections of true Angustura bark. **1881** *Syd. Soc. Lex.*, Angustura.

anhad, obs. form of ONEHOOD, unity.

an-hand, on hand: see AN *prep.* and HAND.

†**anˈhang,** *v. Obs.* 3–5 Forms: α. *strong*: *Inf.* **anhon.** *Pa. t.* **anheng, -hong, -hunge.** *Pa. pple.* **anhongen, -hong(e, -hon.** β. *weak*: *Inf.* **anhonge(n, anhang.** *Pa. pple.* **anhonged, -od,** (5 **enhonged**). [app. a variant of AHANG:—OE. *ahón* (:—**ahahan*, **ahangan*) through confusion of AN- *pref.* 1 and A- *pref.* 1. The weak conjugation of the pa. pple. exemplifies the ultimate levelling of OE. *hón* trans. and *hangian* intr., and their respective compounds.] To hang. **a.** *trans.*

α. **1205** LAY. 1023 þat he sculde beon anhongen. *Ibid.* 22628 He wolde hine slæn oðer anhon. *Ibid.* 29358 And anheng alleþa munkes. **1297** R. GLOUC. 509 Harmles me him nom..& suþþe anhunge him. *c* **1380** *Sir Ferumb.* 2362 þan schulleþ þay þeues..Beo to-drawe and eke an-honge.

β. **1205** LAY. 13166 Swor..þat he hine wolde anhongen [**1250** anhonge]. *c* **1305** *Oxf. Stud.* in *E.E.P.* (1862) 40 What is þe man: þat ȝund anhongod is. **1340** *Ayenb.* 51 þanne he becomþ..þyef, and þanne me hine anhongeþ. *c* **1400** *Rom. Rose* 453 She shulde anhonged be. **1430** LYDG. *Chron.* III. xxiv, To be enhonged by the halse.

b. *intr.*

a **1300** *K. Horn* 328 Schame mote þu fonge And on hiȝe rode anhonge.

anharmonic (ˌænhɑːˈmɒnɪk), *a. Math.* [ad. Fr. *anharmonique*, f. Gr. ἀν- not + ἁρμονικ-ός HARMONIC.] Not harmonic. Applied to the *section* of a line by four points *A, B, C, D*, when their mutual distances are such that $\frac{AB}{CB}$ is unequal to $\frac{AD}{CD}$; the ratio between these two quotients is called the ***anharmonic ratio*** of *AC*.

1863 SALMON *Conic Sect.* 57 This ratio is called the Anharmonic ratio of the pencil. **1865** C. PRICE *Tril. Coordinates* 45 For a system of four points (or lines) there are but six different Anharmonic ratios. **1881** *Athenæum* 13 Aug. 205/1 Anharmonic section.

an-haste, in haste: see AN *prep.* and HASTE *sb.*

†**anhaunce, -anse,** *v. Obs.* [variant of ENHANCE: see AN- *pref.* 4.] To raise up; exalt, extol.

1297 R. GLOUC. 458 þanne ȝe noblemen an hansyeþ ȝoure þoȝt. *a* **1300** *Leg. Rood* (1871) 48 þe holi rode was ifounde.. in may, And anhansed [*Vernon MS.* honoured] was in septembre. *c* **1450** *Pol. Poems* 239 Idylnesse and thefte..On the galwys they scholde anhaunse. *c* **1450** LONELICH *Grail* liii. 31 Forto anhawncen there goddis name.

†**anˈheat,** *v. Obs.* [OE. *onhǽtan* to make hot: see AN- *pref.* 1 and HEAT *v.*] *trans.* To heat, inflame. *intr.* To become hot or inflamed.

c **1250** *O. Kent. Serm.* in *E.E. Misc.* 30 Wyn þat..an-het alle þo þet hit drinked: betokned alle þo þet bied an-héét of þe luue of ure lorde. **1340** *Ayenb.* 131 þise wordle þet ne is bote..a fornays anhet mid uer of zenne. *Ibid.* 108 þanne an-het þe guode herte and trewe and him wreþeþ to him-zelue.

†**anˈheave,** *v. Obs.* 2–3. *Inf.* **anhebben;** *Pa. t.* **anhof, anhefde.** [? OE. *onhebban*: see AN- *pref.* 1 and HEAVE *v.*; but perh. for AHEAVE (see AN- 5).] To lift up; *also*, to hold up, sustain.

c **1200** *Trin. Coll. Hom.* 177 Ðe water stormes an-hefden here stefne. **1205** LAY. 16699 Samuel þat sweord an-hof [**1250** vp heof]. *Ibid.* 12627 An oðer halue we habbeoð mare þene we maȝen an-hebben.

‖**anhedonia** (ænhiːˈdəʊnɪə). *Psychiatry.* [ad. F. *anhédonie* (Ribot, 1896), mod.L., f. Gr. ἀν- priv. + ἡδονή pleasure.] Inability to feel pleasure.

1897 tr. *T. A. Ribot's Psychol. of Emotions* iii. 53 *Anhedonia* (if I may coin a counter-designation to analgesia) has been very little studied..but there are cases of an insensibility relating to pleasure. **1902** W. JAMES *Var. Relig. Exper.* vi. 145 One can distinguish many kinds of pathological depression. Sometimes it is mere passive joylessness and dreariness, discouragement, dejection, lack of taste and zest and spring. Professor Ribot has proposed the name *anhedonia* to designate this condition. *Ibid.* 146 Prolonged seasickness will..produce a temporary condition of anhedonia. **1960** HINSIE & CAMPBELL *Psychiatric Dict.* (ed. 3) 44/1 *Anhedonia*..is seen often in schizophrenic patients.

anhedral (ænˈhiːdrəl, -ˈhɛdrəl), *a.* [f. AN- 10 + HEDRAL *a.*] Applied to crystals that are not bounded by plane faces; also called ALLOTRIOMORPHIC, *xenomorphic.* So **anˈhedron,** a crystal of this kind.

1896 L. V. PIRSSON in *Amer. Geologist* XVII. 94 Since the term *crystal*, when strictly used, means a body possessing not only a certain internal molecular structure, with definite physical properties, but more especially an outward symmetrical form with plane faces, it is evident that there is no good term for the rounded or formless masses in which minerals occur in rocks. Therefore, after consultation with Prof. E. S. Dana, the term *anhedron* (meaning without planes) is proposed for these formless masses which possess the internal structure of crystals; and such minerals may also be spoken of as having an anhedral development. **1898** *Amer. Jrnl. Sci.* V. 361 The rock..shows numerous tabular phenocrysts..and a few anhedra of augite. **1913** G. A. J. COLE *Outl. Min.* ii. 20 The individual crystal in such cases is sometimes said to be *anhedral*, because it has no good bounding planes, in opposition to the well-crystallised or *euhedral* forms. **1950** HARTSHORNE & STUART *Crystals & Polarising Microscope* (ed. 2) iii. 44 Crystals which are bounded by plane faces are described as *idiomorphic* or *euhedral*, and irregular ones as *allotriomorphic* or *anhedral*. **1961** J. CHALLINOR *Dict. Geol.* 7/2 'Anhedral', 'euhedral', and 'subhedral', in mineralogy, are probably to be preferred to 'allotriomorphic', 'idiomorphic', and 'hypidiomorphic' as avoiding any confusion between mineralogical terms and petrographical-textural terms.

†**an'helant**, *a. Obs. rare*$^{-1}$. [ad. L. *anhēlānt-em*, pr. pple. of *anhēlā-re*: see ANHELE.] Breathing, inhaling.

1764 *Ann. Reg.* 141/1 The anhelent tubes by which trees suck their nourishment from the earth.

anhelation (ænhɪ'leɪʃən). *arch.* [a. Fr. *anhélation*, ad. L. *anhēlātiōn-em*, f. *anhēlā-re*: see next.]

1. A breathing with difficulty, panting; shortness of breath, asthma.

1623 COCKERAM, *Anhelation*, the Tissique. **1655** CULPEPER *Riverius* VII. i. 148 In a Dispnœa, the breath is thick, without noise or anhelation. **1794** PALEY *Nat. Theol.* x. §5 (1819) 159 In a city-feast, for example, what deglutition, what anhelation! **1839** HOOPER *Med. Dict.* 547 A permanent difficulty of breathing or anhelation.

2. *fig.* Panting, aspiration (*after* an object of desire).

a **1631** DONNE *Serm.* vii. 73 Our Anhelation and panting after the Joyes of the Kingdom of Heaven. **1695** BLACKMORE *Pr. Arth.* I. 903 When his exhaling Soul to Heav'n aspires, In sacred Anhelations, and inflam'd Desires.

†**an'hele**, *v. Obs.* Also 4–5 **anele**. [a. OFr. *anele-r*, *anhele-r* to breathe, cogn. w. Pr. *anelar*, It. *anelare*:—L. *anhēlāre* to pant; f. *an-* = *ambi* on both sides, doubtfully + *hālāre* to breathe.]

1. ? To blow, puff.

c **1340** *Gaw. & Gr. Knt.* 723 He werreȝ..Boþe wyth bulleȝ & bereȝ..And etayneȝ, þat hym a-nelede, of þe heȝe felle.

2. *fig.* To pant *for*, aspire *to*.

c **1425** WYNTOUN *Cron.* v. x. 480 Constantynys sonnys thre Ðat anelyd to þat Ryawte. **1536** LATIMER *2nd Serm. bef. Conv.* I. 49 With most fervent desire, they anheale, breathe, and gape for the fruit of our convocation.

anhele, obs. form of ANNEAL.

†**an'heled**, *ppl. a. Obs. rare.* [f. ANHELE + -ED.] Breathing, or breathed out, with pain or effort.

1644 *England's Tears* in *Harl. Misc.* V. 452 The poor labourer, who useth to mingle the morning dew with his anheled sweat. **1656** BLOUNT *Glossogr.*, *Anheled*, which breatheth with pain or difficulty, puffed up, brokenwinded.

†**anhe'lose**, *a.* ? *Obs. rare.* [f. L. *anhēl-us* panting + -OSE, as if ad. L. **anhēlōs-us*.] = next.

1731 BAILEY, *Anhelose*, fetching breath quick and short; puffing and blowing. **1808** MACDONALD *Telegr. Comm.* 59 [It] rendered him so constantly anhelose.

†**an'helous**, *a. Obs.* [f. L. *anhēl-us* panting, puffing + -OUS; cf. Fr. *anhéleux*.] Short of breath, short-winded, panting.

1661 S. STONE *Deceiv. Deceiv'd* 12 Rude anhelous pantings, and interrupt breathings at Devotion. **1684** tr. *Bonet's Merc. Compit.* VI. 182 Anhelous or Short-breathed Fevers have their name from difficult and anhelous respiration. **1880** in *Syd. Soc. Lex.*

anhidrotic (ænhɪ'drɒtɪk), *a.* and *sb. Med.* [f. Gr. ἀν not + ἱδρωτικ-ός sudorific, f. ἱδρώς sweat.] **A.** *adj.* Tending to check perspiration. **B.** *sb.* A medicinal agent of this nature.

1880 *Syd. Soc. Lex.*, *Anhidrotics*..sponging the surface of the body with cold mineral or vegetable acids..internal administration of dilute phosphoric acid, etc.

an-high, **-hegh**, **-hey(e**, on high: see AN- *prep.* and HIGH.

†**an'high(e**, *v. Obs.* 4. Also **anheȝi**, **anheighe**. [prob. for *a-high* (see AN- *pref.* 5):—OE. **a-heán*, cogn. w. OHG. *irhōhan* (mod.G. *erhöhen*), Goth. *ushauhjan*; perh. a later formation on AN- *pref.* 1 + *hegh-en*, *high-en*, to exalt: see HIGH *v.*]

1. *trans.* To exalt, raise, advance, promote.

1340 *Ayenb.* 42 Huanne hi wylleþ..hare uryendes an heȝy ine dingnetes of holi cherch. *Ibid.* 23 To miszigge to ham þet he wyle harmi, him uor to anheȝi.

b. To lift up on the gallows, hang.

c **1330** *Arth. & Merl.* 2366 Told hem this vilanie And seyd he wold hom anheighe.

2. *intr.* To raise itself, mount up, increase.

1340 *Ayenb.* 49 Þis zenne anheȝeþ and loȝeþ be þe stat of þe persones þet hit doþ.

anhima ('ænhɪmə). Also **aniuma**. [Pg., f. Tupi.] The kamichi or horned screamer (*Palamedea cornuta*).

1773 [see SCREAMER 3 a]. **1774** GOLDSM. *Hist. Earth* V. v. v. 389 A bird..called the Anhima,..a native of Brasil. **1869–73** Aniuma [see SCREAMER 3 a].

anhinga (æn'hɪŋgə). [Tupi.] Any bird of the genus *Anhinga*, esp. the American snake-bird, *A. anhinga*.

1769 T. PENNANT *Indian Zool.* xii. 13/1 The black-bellied Anhinga. We give it this epithet, to distinguish it from an American species with a silvery belly. This kind is found in Ceylon and Java..neck extremely long; the bill strait, long, and sharp-pointed. **1816** TUCKEY *Narr. Exped. River Zaire* (1818) 82 Mr. Cranch shot some birds amongst which..an anhinga. **1838** [see SNAKE-BIRD 1]. **1872** COUES *N. Amer. Birds* 332 Few other birds, such as cormorants and anhingas, resemble the *Pygopodes* in this respect.

anhistous (æn'hɪstəs), *a. Biol.* [mod. f. Gr. ἀν priv. + ἱστ-όν web, tissue + -OUS; cf. Fr. *anhiste*.] Of tissue: Without recognizable structure.

1880 in *Syd. Soc. Lex.*

†**an'hit**, *v. Obs. rare.* [f. AN *pref.* 1 + HIT, ad. ON. *hitta*.] To hit, strike against.

1297 R. GLOUC. 185 Arture aȝen þe brest ys felawe uorst anhytte. *a* **1300** *K. Horn* 711 Wel sone bute þu flitte Wiþ swerde ihc þe anhitte. *c* **1325** *E.E. Allit. P.* C. 411 So hatȝ anger onhit his hert.

an-honest, for *on-honest*, north. f. UN-HONEST *a.*

anhungered (æn'hʌŋgəd), *ppl. a. arch.* [app. for earlier *a-hungred* (*an-* for *a-* before vowel: see AN- *pref.* 5):—*of-hungred*:—OE. *of-hyngrod* (cf. *a-thirst*, OE. *of-þyrsted*, *a-down*, OE. *of-dúne*): see A-HUNGERED, OF-HUNGERED. Later variants were EN-HUNGERED, IN-HUNGERED; the sequence being apparently *of-*, *a-*, *an-*, *en-*, *in-*.]

1. Overcome with hunger, hungry.

c **1300** *K. Alis.* 1229 The folk and the poraile weoren anhungred. **1377** LANGL. *P. Pl.* B. x. 59 (Oriel MS.) Bothe anhungred [*v.r.* afyngerd, a-hungred] and a-þrist. **1398** TREVISA *Barth. De P.R.* VI. ix. (1495) 195 The nouryce fedyth the childe whan it is an hungred. **1526** TINDALE *Matt.* xii. 1 His disciples wer anhongred. **1557** *Genev.*, anhongred. **1611** BIBLE, an hungred. [So **1881** *Revised*.]

2. *fig.* Eagerly desirous, longing.

1848 LOWELL *Poet. Wks.* 1879, 398 Anhungered for some joy untried. **1881** SWINBURNE *Mary Stewart* IV. i, My people seems in sooth Hot and anhungered on this trail of hers.

†**an-'hungry**, *a. Obs. rare.* [variant of A-HUNGRY, the *a-* or *an-* being due to assoc. with *a-hungered*, *an-hungered*, though perhaps meant to be intensive.] Hungry, in a hungry state.

1607 SHAKS. *Cor.* I. i. 209 They said they were an hungry: sigh'd forth Prouerbes; That Hunger broke stone wals: that, dogges must eate. **1681** R. KNOX *Hist. Ceylon* 123 Many times we were forced to remain an hungry.

anhurned, obs. form of ONE-HORNED *ppl. a.*

anhydric (æn'haɪdrɪk), *a.* [f. Gr. ἄνυδρ-ος waterless + -IC.] = ANHYDROUS.

1880 *Syd. Soc. Lex.*

anhydride (æn'haɪdraɪd). *Chem.* [mod. f. Gr. ἄνυδρ-ος waterless (f. ἀν priv. + ὕδωρ water) + -IDE.] A chemical compound formed by the union of oxygen with another element, without hydrogen, but which, on exposure to water, absorbs hydrogen and becomes an acid. Also called *anhydrous acids*, because they are produced by expelling the water (containing all the hydrogen) from oxy-acids.

1863 WATTS *Dict. Chem.* I. 295 Very few triatomic anhydrides are yet known. Phosphoric anhydride, P_2O_5, is the only well known member of this class. **1869** *Eng. Mech.* 9 Apr. 58/2 Sulphuric anhydride SO_3 when added to water, takes up the oxygen to form a new acid radical.

anhydrite (æn'haɪdraɪt). *Min.* [mod. f. Gr. ἄνυδρ-ος waterless + -ITE min. form.; so named by Werner.] Anhydrous gypsum, or sulphate of lime.

1831 BREWSTER *Optics* xxx. 252 Augite, Anhydrite, Axinite. **1842** T. GRAHAM *Elem. Chem.* II. v. 497 Sulphate of lime occurs in a crystalline form, without water, forming the mineral anhydrite. **1875** URE *Dict. Arts* I. 177 Anhydrite is frequently found in beds of rock-salt, where it is often associated with gypsum or hydrous sulphate of lime.

anhydro- (æn,haɪdrəʊ-), combining form of next, as in *anhydro-borate*, *-sulphate*, etc.

1873 FOWNES *Chem.* 325 Potassium forms..two acid sulphates, and an anhydrosulphate. **1883** *Nature* XXVII. 423 Benzoic sulphimide or anhydro-sulphamine benzoic acid.

anhydrous (æn'haɪdrəs), *a.* [mod. f. Gr. ἄνυδρ-ος waterless (f. ἀν priv. + ὕδωρ water) + -OUS.]

1. *Chem.* Having no water in its composition: said of *salts*, *crystals*, destitute of water of crystallization, etc. Cf. ANHYDRIDE.

1819 *Pantolog.* I. s.v., Anhidrous Sulphate of Lime. **1827** FARADAY *Chem. Manip.* xxiv. 610 Reduce the substance to an anhydrous state. **1833** *Penny Cycl.* I. 281 The vapour of anhydrous (waterless) alcohol. **1875** DAWSON *Dawn of Life* v. 108 An anhydrous silicate of lime and magnesia.

2. *transf.* Waterless, sapless, dried up.

1872 HOLMES *Poet Breakf. T.* ix. 294 That exsiccated and almost anhydrous organism. **1874** in COUES *Birds of N.-W.* 405 The sterile and anhydrous region of the central desert.

anhypostasia (,ænhaɪpəʊ'steɪsɪə). *Theol.* Also **anhy'postasis**. [mod.L., f. Gr. ἀνυποστασία, ἀνυπόστασις unsubstantiality, f. ἀν- priv. + ὑπόστασις substance, substantial existence (see HYPOSTASIS 5).] Lack of a substantial or personal existence. So **anhypo'static**, **-'statical** *adjs.*, having no independent or personal existence; describing the human nature of Christ which had no existence apart from the hypostatic union.

1862 D. W. SIMON tr. *Dorner's Person of Christ* (Div. II.) II. 92 Maintaining that Luther regarded the humanity of Jesus as the mere means of the manifestation of the person of the Logos, and taught most clearly that humanity was selfless or anhypostatical. **1863** *Ibid.* (Div. II.) III. 300 He describes the Logos..as the primal personality.., he holds the significance of the doctrine of the anhypostasis of humanity to be, that God is the essence of humanity. **1877** SCHAFF in Smith & Wace *Dict. Chr. Biogr.* I. 495/1 The anhypostasia, impersonality, or, to speak more accurately, the enhypostasia, of the human nature of Christ; for anhypostasia is a purely negative term, and presupposes a fictitious abstraction, since the human nature of Christ did not exist at all before the act of the incarnation, and could therefore be neither personal nor impersonal. **1941** *Jrnl. Theol. Stud.* XLII. 123 He sees no absurdity in Cyrilline anhypostatic manhood, with its corollary, the 'passionless suffering' of the Word. **1946** E. L. MASCALL *Christ, Christian & Church* 8 According to [the doctrine of *enhypostasia*], the humanity of Christ is neither *hypostatic* (that is, possessing a human person) nor is it *anhypostatic* (that is, without a person altogether), but it is *enhypostatic* (that is, it is constituted in the person of the divine Word). **1954** *Sc. Jrnl. Theol.* VII. 249 By *anhypostasia* classical Christology asserted that in the *assumptio carnis* the human nature of Christ had no independent *per se* subsistence apart from the event of the Incarnation, apart from the hypostatic union.

ani ('ɑːniː). [Sp. *aní* or Pg. *ani*, f. Tupi.] A bird of the genus *Crotophaga* (family Cuculidæ), of which several species are found in the warmer parts of America and in the West Indies.

1829 E. GRIFFITH et al. *Cuvier's Anim. Kingd.* VII. 476 The Ani, Crotophaga L. Are known by their thick bill. **1893** NEWTON *Dict. Birds* 191 There are other eggs, as those of the Anis, *Crotophaga*, the Grebes, *Podicipedidæ*, [etc.] which are more or less covered with a cretaceous film. **1918** W. BEEBE *Jungle Peace* (1919) iii. 45 Heavy-billed anis *whaleeped* and fluttered clumsily ahead of us. **1964** A. L. THOMSON *New Dict. Birds* 170/2 The anis are medium-sized non-parasitic cuckoos with almost black plumage, long and nearly square-ended tails, and extremely heavy hooked bills.

aniconic (ænaɪ'kɒnɪk), *a. Gr. Antiq.* Also **anik-**. [f. AN- 10 + ICONIC *a.*] Applied to simple material symbols of a deity, as a pillar or block, not shaped into an image of human form; also to the worship connected with these. Hence **aniconism** (æ'naɪkənɪz(ə)m), the use of, or worship connected with, such symbols.

1892 C. WALDSTEIN *Excav. Heraion Argos* I. 19 Clement of Alexandria..tells us that the aniconic σανίς was superseded by the iconic image, which he calls βρέτας. **1893** *Athenæum* 1 July 38/2 The various stages of development of her [*sc.* Hera's] *agalmata*: the rudest of all, the anikonic. ..A..pillar which may have been the actual aniconic image of the goddess. **1907** *Academy* 24 Aug. 818/1 Aniconism does not necessarily imply..anthropomorphism. **1912** L. R. FARNELL *Higher Aspects Gr. Relig.* i. 4 Certain aniconic sacred things that we may call fetishes—the hewn stock or pillar, the meteorite, the axe. **1956** I. A. RICHMOND in R. L. S. Bruce-Mitford *Rec. Archæol. Excav. in Brit.* 67 As often in religions which have sprung from Asia, there are iconic and aniconic traditions... The Zend-Avesta is a production of the second.

‖**'anicut**, **annicut**. [Anglo-Ind. ad. Tamil *Aṉai-kaṭṭu* dam-building.] 'In the Madras Presidency, the dam constructed across a river to fill, and regulate the supply of, the channels drawn off from it.' (Col. Yule.)

1784 *Desp. Crt. Direct.* in *Burke's Wks.* IV. 104 A supply of water..which can only be secured by keeping the Anicut and banks in repair. **1862** R. PATTERSON *Ess. Hist. & Art* 208 Vast dams or annicuts across the rivers take the place of the canals of the northern provinces.

anidio'matic, *a. rare*$^{-1}$. [f. Gr. ἀν priv. + IDIOMATIC.] A proposed substitute for *unidiomatic*.

1827 HARE *Guesses* (1859) 212 Even Landor recommends the adoption of *anidiomatic* as an English word; though our language does not acknowledge the Greek negative prefix, except in words like anarchy, introduced in their compound state, so that *anidiomatical* would exemplify itself.

anidio'matical, *a.* [f. prec. + -AL^1.] = prec.

1824–9 LANDOR *Imag. Conv.* II. 278 You would not say 'two times'; it is anidiomatical. [See also prec.]

†**ani'ente**, *v. Obs.* Also 4–6 **anyente**. [a. OFr. *aniente-r* to bring to nought (= Pr. and It. *anient-ar*), f. *à* to + *nient*, mod. *néant* nought (= It. *niente*):—late L. **neëntem* or **necentem*, f. *ne*, *nec* not + *entem* (nom. *ens*) being: see ENTITY.] = ANIENTISE (which is the commoner form).

1393 LANGL. *P. Pl.* C. xx. 267 How myghte he aske mercy ..That..wilfulliche wolde mercy anyente? *Ibid.* XXI. 389 So lyf shal lyf lete · þer lyf haþ lyf anyented. **1574** tr. *Littleton's Tenures* 140 b, The warraunte is anyented and defeated.

†**aniente**, *ppl. a. Obs.* [contr. pa. pple. of the preceding, for *aniented*.]

1641 *Termes de la Ley* 21 Aniente in our law language signifies as much as frustrated or made voyde.

†ani'entise, -ish, *v. Obs.* Forms: 4 **anientise, anyentise,** 4–5 **anientisse, anyntische, -esche, anentysch(e, -isch(e, annentissche,** 4–6 **anyntise,** 5 **anentise, -ish, -yssh, anyyntysch (enyyn-, enyntysch),** 6 **aneauntyse** (8 **aneantize**). *Aphet.* 4 **neentishe.** [a. OFr. *anientiss-* extended stem of *anientir* (later *aniantir, anaiantir, anéantir*) var. of *anienter*: see prec., and -ISH. *Aneantize,* in 18th c., is after mod.Fr.]

1. To bring to nought, annul, annihilate, destroy.

1382 WYCLIF *Rom.* iv. 14 If thei that ben of the lawe, ben eyris, feith is anentyschid, *or distroyed.* c**1386** CHAUCER *Melib.* 282 Ye han nat anientissed [*v.r.* anyntesched, anentisched] or destroyed hem. **1440** *Promp. Parv.* Anyyntyschyn or enyntyschyn, *Exinanio.* **1483** *Act 1 Rich. III,* ii. §1 Such memorialles as they had ordeigned..were anentised and anulled. **1791** J. BREE *Curs. Sketch* 324 (*modernizing petition of* **1430**) To great aneantizing and impoverishing of the persons of the same vessels.

2. To make of no account, to bring low, reduce.

1382 WYCLIF *Ecclus.* xiii. 8 To the tyme he neentishe [**1388** anyntische] thee twies or thries. **1398** TREVISA *Barth. De P.R.* v. x, Olde men þat ben anyntised..and wastid by elde oþer siknesse. **1496** *Dives & Paup.* (W. de Worde) VI. xv. 258/1 Cryste..anentysshed hymself and dysparyched hymselfe in to the lykenesse of a seruaunt. **1530** LOVE *Bonavent. Mirr.* xiii. (W. de Worde) H vj, In so moche he lowed hym and aneauntysed [*Gibbs MS.* anentysched] hymselfe, that, etc.

†ani'entisement. *Obs.* [a. OFr. *anientissement*: see prec. and -MENT. Cf. mod.Fr. *anéantissement.*] Annihilation, destruction.

1485 *Proclam.* in *Paston Lett.* 883 III. 319 The grettest anyntisshment, shame and rebuke that ever myght falle to this seid land. **1488** *Act 4 Hen. VII,* i, To decresse and destruccion of your lyvelode..and anyentesment of the same. **1495** *Act 11 Hen. VII,* xxxi, To the greet anyntissement of the value of thissues and profites.

†a'nigh, *v. Obs. rare*⁻¹. In 6 annie. [f. A- *pref.* 11 + NIGH.] To draw near, approach.

1594 CAREW *Tasso Godfr. Bulloigne* (1881) 53 Tydings to beare, how now grey morne annies.

anigh (ə'naɪ), *adv.* and *prep.* [mod. f. NIGH; app. intended as archaic by assoc. with *down, adown, far, afar,* etc. Cf. *near, anear.*]

A. *adv.* Nigh, near.

1868 MORRIS *Earth. Par.* I. Prol. 33 Ah, what a meeting as she drew a-nigh. **1870** *Ibid.* III. IV. 404 He came anigher to the sun. **1869** MRS. WHITNEY *Hitherto* xxxviii. 420 Worthy to dwell anigh.

B. *prep.* Nigh, near to.

1773 *Gentl. Mag.* XLIII. 399 So chang'd!—I hate to go a-nigh the place. **1860** READE *Cloist. & H.* IV. 173 They must not come anigh a dying bed. **1870** MORRIS *Earth. Par.* I. II. 532 No dart was cast, nor any engine bent Anigh him.

a-night (ə'naɪt), *adv.*, prop. *phr. arch.* [OE. *on niht,* reduced by common change of proclitic *on* to *a*: already in Chaucer MSS. it interchanges with the modern *at night.*] By night, at night.

c**1000** *Ags. Gosp.* John vii. 50 Nichodemus..se þe com to him on nyht. a**1300** *Floriz & Bl.* 24 Murie hi uerden þer aniȝt. c**1384** CHAUCER *H. of Fame* 42 To make folke to dreme a-nyght [*v.r.* on nyght]. c**1386** —— *Man of L.T.* 612 They moste take in pacience a-night [*v.r.* at nyght, at nyȝt, a nyht] Such maner necessaries. c**1440** *Partonope* 3113 They mete neuer but a nyght. **1600** SHAKS. *A.Y.L.* II. iv. 49, I..bid him take that for comming a night to Iane Smile. **1830** TENNYSON *Arab. Nights* ii, Anight my shallop..clove The citron-shadows in the blue.

†a-'nightertime, *advb. phr. Obs. rare*⁻¹. [A *prep.*[1] in, on + *nighter* (perh. = *nihte* or *nihta,* with *-er* for pronounced *-e*) + TIME.] At night time.

c**1430** LYDG. *Bochas* VI. iv. (1554) 151 b, Anyghtertyme his slepe ful oft he brake.

a-nights (ə'naɪts), *adv. arch.* [coalescence of the two OE. forms *on niht* (see A-NIGHT), and *nihtes* advb. gen. (cf. Where do you go *of a night?*), both = L. *noctu.* Thus simply = *a-night,* though the *-s* has often been taken as a plural sign, and has tended to give a more habitual sense.]

[**918** *O.E. Chron.*, þa bestælon hie hie þeah nihtes. a**1250** *Owl & Night.* 219 þu singest a niht. *Ibid.* 238 þu flihst nihtes.] c**1440** *Gesta Rom.* 61 The lady a-roose on nyghtes [*v.r.* rose a-nyghtes] for to here his songe. **1577** *Test. 12 Patriarchs* 72 Leachery and covetousness..walk abroad as well a nights as of days. **1601** SHAKS. *Jul. C.* I. ii. 193 Sleeke-headed men, and such as sleepe a-nights. **1647** R. STAPYLTON *Juvenal* 104 They lodged a-nights in hollow trees. **1673** SHADWELL *Epsom Wells* II. Wks. III. 221 To sit up a-nights late. **1838** H. C. ROBINSON *Diary* III. 152 She used to go out a-nights with her face hid up in her cloak.

†a-'night-times, *advb. phr. Obs. rare*⁻¹. [A *prep.*[1] in, on + NIGHT + *times* advb. gen.] In the night time; by night.

1583 GOLDING *Calvin on Deut.* vii. 40 a, A nighttimes he appeared to them as in a pillar of fyre.

anil ('ænɪl). Also 6 anele, -ill, 6–7 -ile, 7 anneill. [a. Fr. or Pg. *anil* = Sp. *añil,* ad. Arab. *an-nīl,* i.e. *al* the + *nīl,* Arab. and Pers. ad. Skr. *nīlī* indigo (and -plant), f. *nīla* dark blue.]

1. The Indigo shrub; the native name of the E. Indian species (*Indigofera tinctoria*); but in *Bot.* the trivial name of the W. Indian Indigo (*I. Anil*).

1712 tr. *Pomet's Hist. Drugs* I. 91 There is a Meal made of Anil..out of the entire Plant. **1753** *Phil. Trans.* XLVIII. 257 [Indigo] not of equal value with that made of the anil. **1866** *Treas. Bot.* 621/2 *Indigofera Anil*..has become naturalised in Asia and Africa.

2. The indigo dye.

1581 *Act 23 Eliz.* ix. (Pulton) Cloth..grounded with woad only, or with woad and a nele, *alias* blew Inde. **1594** BLUNDEVIL *Exerc.* v. xi. (ed. 7) 555 Merchandizes that come from Afrique..Gold, Ivory, Anill, feathers. **1599** HAKLUYT *Voy.* II. I. 262 They vse to pricke the skinne, and to put on it a kinde of anile or blacking, which doth continue alwayes. **1611** *Bk. Rates* 1 (Jam.) Anneill of Barbarie for litsters [*i.e.* dyers], the pound weight thereof—xviijs. **1625** PURCHAS *Pilgrims* II. 1415 Hispahan..vseth great store of Anil. **1852** T. ROSS tr. *Humboldt's Trav.* I. xv. 502 The anil, or indigo, of these provinces has always been considered..as equal..to that of Guatemala.

3. *Chem.* Formative (prefix or suffix) of names of aniline compounds or derivatives; as ANILIDE, **anilamic** = PHENYLAMIC, chloranil $C_6Cl_4O_2$.

anile ('ænaɪl), *a.* [ad. L. *anīl-is,* f. *anus* old woman: see -ILE.] Of or like an old woman, old-womanish; imbecile.

1652 GAULE *Magastrom.* 118 Puerile hallucinations and anile delirations. **1684** tr. *Bonet's Merc. Compit.* Ded. 1 But why do I recount those ancient and (I had almost said) anile things? **1803** SYD. SMITH *Wks.* (1867) I. 64 Not anile conjecture, but sound evidence of events. **1856** R. VAUGHAN *Ho. w. Mystics* (1860) II. 251 Romanticism..grew anile in its premature decrepitude.

'anileness. ? *Obs.*⁻⁰ [f. prec. + -NESS.] The quality of being anile; anility.

1731 in BAILEY; whence in JOHNSON and mod. Dicts.

anilepi, variant of ANLEPI, *a. Obs.*, single.

anilic (ə'nɪlɪk), *a. Chem.* [f. ANIL + -IC.]

1. Of or pertaining to anil; as in ***anilic*** (or ***indigotic***) ***acid,*** obtained by the action on indigo of boiling nitric acid and water.

1868 WATTS *Dict. Chem.* V. 158.

2. -anilic in comb. = of aniline; as in *anthranilic, chrysanilic.*

1863 WATTS *Dict. Chem.* I. 957 *Chrysanilic Acid.*

anilide ('ænɪlaɪd). *Chem.* [f. ANIL- + -IDE, = *anil(ine am)ide.*] A species of alkalamide, related to aniline as the amides are to the amines; hence called *phenylamide*; it may be viewed as ammonia NH_3 in which one atom of H is replaced, as in aniline, by phenyl, and another by an oxidized radical, the name of the latter being prefixed, as in ACET-ANILIDE (= *phenyl-acetamide*).

1863 WATTS *Dict. Chem.* (1872) I. 295 Anilides, synonym of Phenylamides.

aniline ('ænɪlaɪn). *Chem.* [f. (by Fritzche 1841) ANIL indigo + -INE.] A chemical base important in the arts as the source of many beautiful dyes; obtained originally by distilling indigo with caustic potash, but subsequently from many other sources, especially coal-tar.

A. is a colourless, oily, aromatic, volatile liquid, of constitution $C_6H_5(NH_2)$, which may be viewed as ammonia in which one hydrogen atom is replaced by the compound radical phenyl C_6H_5, hence also called *phenylamine*; or as benzol C_6H_6, in which one atom of H is replaced by amidogen NH_2, whence also called *amidobenzol* and *amidobenzene.* It forms crystalline salts with acids, e.g. ***aniline acetate, oxalate, sulphate, nitrate,*** etc., and ***compound anilines*** in which one or both the hydrogen atoms in NH_2 are replaced by radicals, as ***ethylaniline, diethyl-aniline,*** etc.

1850 DAUBENY *Atom. The.* viii. (ed. 2) 237 [Isatine] if heated along with potass, yields an organic base capable of neutralizing acids..which is called aniline. **1860** PIESSE *Lab. Chem. Wond.* 138 Obtaining a dye, Aniline, from the waste tar of gas works. **1861** *Lond. Rev.* 22 June 732 Aniline is a colourless liquid, with a strong aromatic odour, and a sharp burning taste..From this aniline chemists are now preparing every shade of blue and red.

2. *attrib.* in ***aniline dyes, colours, black, red, purple, yellow, green,*** etc., ***printing, process,*** etc.; and in *Chem.* in ***aniline series, compounds, acetate,*** etc.

1864 *Daily Tel.* 29 July, That exquisite purple tint which is due to the modern discovery of the aniline dyes. **1869** *Eng. Mech.* 2 July 340/3 Aniline colours derived from coal were discovered in 1856. **1869** ROSCOE *Elem. Chem.* xxxix. 411 Aniline acetate..on heating loses a molecule of water, yielding an amide called acetanilide. **1875** VOGEL *Chem. Light & Photog.* xv. 247 The aniline-printing invented by Willis. **1878** A. HAMILTON *Nervous Dis.* 21 The black anilin process of Herbert Major. *Mod.* An aniline copying pencil.

3. As final element in many names of aniline derivatives; as ***chrysaniline, leucaniline, rosaniline,*** etc.

1872 WATTS *Dict. Chem.* VI. 160 A considerable quantity of very pure hydrochloride of rosaniline. **1875** URE *Dict. Arts* I. 187 *Aniline-yellow*..The name of *Chrysaniline* has been given to this very beautiful yellow colour. Hofmann has shown that chrysaniline is intimately related to rosaniline and leucaniline.

anility (ə'nɪlɪtɪ). [ad. L. *anīlitāt-em,* f. *anīlis*: see ANILE and -ITY.] The state of being an old woman; old-womanishness; dotage, foolishness. *Fig.* used more contemptuously than *senility.*

1623 COCKERAM, *Anility,* Dotage. **1760** STERNE *Serm.* III. 277 This reformation..perfected and handed down, if not 'entirely without spot or wrinkle,' at least without great blotches or marks of anility! **1765** TUCKER *Lt. Nat.* II. 189 Youth can never be anility, nor beauty become ugliness. **1841** *Blackw. Mag.* L. 206 The fopperies and anilities of fashion. **1863** *Macm. Mag.* May 62 Müller..treats as an exploded anility the belief in Hebrew as the primitive language.

†a'nim, *v. Obs.* [f. A- *pref.* 1 away + OE. *nim-an* to take (see NIM *v.*): cogn. w. Goth. *usniman,* MHG. *ernëmen.*] To take away.

c**1000** *Ags. Gosp.* Matt. xxv. 28 Anymað þæt pund æt hym. c**1175** *Cott. Hom.* 229 Crist..to helle ȝewende, and þane deofel ȝewilde, and him of ánam adam and euam.

anima ('ænɪmə). *Psychol.* [L., 'mind, soul'.] Jung's term for the inner part of the personality or character, as opposed to the ***persona*** or outer part; also, the feminine component of a male personality. Cf. ANIMUS 2.

1923 H. G. BAYNES tr. *Jung's Psychol. Types* xi. 593, I term the outer attitude, or outer character, the ***persona***; the inner attitude I term the *anima,* or *soul. Ibid.* 595 If, therefore, we speak of the *anima* of a man, we must logically speak of the *animus* of a woman. **1926** W. MCDOUGALL *Outl. Abnormal Psychol.* ix. 198 The *Anima* is not to be regarded as the whole of the Collective Unconscious; it is only a selection from it. **1943** *Horizon* VIII. 262 A seductive mixture which fascinated the *anima* in Kierkegaard. **1962** A. M. DRY *Psychol. of Jung* iv. 96 In women the phenomena corresponding to the moods of the anima-ridden man are 'opinions'. **1962** R. MANHEIM tr. *J. Jacobi's Psychol. of C. G. Jung* (ed. 6) iii. 112 Typical anima figures in literature are Helen of Troy.., Beatrice in the *Divine Comedy,* [etc.].

animability (ˌænɪmə'bɪlɪtɪ). *rare*⁻¹. [f. next: see -BILITY.] Capacity of animation.

1814 W. TAYLOR in *Month. Rev.* LXXIV. 393 That an animability of body is acquired (if we may coin a word).

†'animable, *a. Obs.*⁻⁰ [ad. L. *animābil-is* vivifying, f. *animā-re* to give life: see -BLE.] 'That which may be put into life or receive animation.' J.

1656 in BLOUNT *Glossogr.*; whence in BAILEY, JOHNSON, etc.

†'animableness. *Obs.*⁻⁰ [f. prec. + -NESS.] = ANIMABILITY. Bailey 1731.

†ˌanimad'versal. *Obs. rare*⁻¹. [f. ANIMADVERT, -VERSION, after *reversal,* beside *revert, reversion.*] The faculty of perceiving or noticing; consciousness. = ANIMADVERSION 2.

1642 MORE *Song of Soul* II. II. xxxv. *note,* That lively inward animadversal; it is the soul itself; for I cannot conceive the body doth animadvert.

†ˌanimad'verse, *v. Obs. rare*⁻¹. [f. L. *animadvers-* ppl. stem of *animadvert-ĕre*: see below.] To notice, comment upon; = ANIMADVERT 1.

1642 SIR E. DERING *Sp. on Relig.* 148 All the Fathers might be revised and briefly animadversed.

animadversion (ˌænɪmæd'vɜːʃən). [ad. L. *animadversiōn-em,* n. of action f. *animadvert-ĕre*: see ANIMADVERT. Cf. Fr. *animadversion* 16th c. in Littré, which may have been the immediate model.] *gen.* The action or process of animadverting, or its embodiment in words.

I. The turning or directing of the attention.

†1. The action of turning the attention to a subject; the observation or consideration *of* anything. *Obs.*

1605 BACON *Adv. Learn.* I. iv. §1 (1873) 27, I have no meaning..to make any exact animadversion of the errors and impediments in matters of learning. **1677** HALE *Prim. Orig. Man.* 63 The due animadversion and inspection of their own Minds. **1738** J. KEILL *Anim. Œcon.* Pref. 30 Accurate Animadversion and Comparison of..the appearances. **1795** T. TAYLOR *Apuleius* (1822) 61 Returning to an animadversion of the present transactions.

†2. The faculty or habit of noticing or observing; attention, perception, conscious mental action. *Obs.*

1601 CHESTER *Love's Mart.* clxxxi, The vnsatiate Sparrow..Foretels true things by animaduertion. **1681** GLANVILL *Sad. Trium.* II. (1726) 464 For in an infinite Life as God is, there can be no distraction, his animadversion necessarily being infinite. **1682** RUST *Disc. Truth* 177 Food which without their intention or animadversion is concocted in their Ventricle.

†3. (with *pl.*) The action of calling the attention of others; notice, monition, warning. *Obs.*

1647 SPRIGG *Ang. Rediv.* III. vi. (1854) 174 His excellency had animadversions from the committee..of incursions made by the king's horse. *a* **1674** CLARENDON *Hist. Reb.* I. I. 42 They all knew Cæsar's fate, by contemning, or neglecting such animadversions. **1712** STEELE *Spect.* No. 443 ¶7 Another timely Animadversion is absolutely necessary.

II. Judicial or critical attention.

4. The action of taking judicial cognizance of offences, and of inflicting punishment; *concr.* with *pl.* a penal visitation. *arch.*

1646 H. LAWRENCE *Comm. & Warre w. Angels* 65 O wish rather the animadversion to fall upon your bodies and estates. **1726** AYLIFFE *Parerg.* 157 A [ecclesiastical] Censure has a relation to a Spiritual Punishment, but an [ecclesiastical] Animadversion has only a respect to a Temporal one, as Degradation, and the Delivering of a Person over to the Secular Court. **1750** WESLEY *Wks.* 1872 VII. 394 Of all divine animadversions, there is none more horrid..than this [an earthquake]. **1839–42** ALISON *Hist. Eur.* (1849) VIII. I. §73. 198 A power whose lightest measure of animadversion would be banishment.

5. The utterance of criticism, usually of a hostile kind; censure, reproof, blame.

1599 THYNNE *Animadv.* 68 Fyve especiall thinges, woorthye the animadversione. **1621** BURTON *Anat. Mel.* II. iii. VI, He hath done more worthy of dispraise and animadversion, then worthy of commendation. **1680** in Somers *Tracts* II. 84 Could not possibly escape the Animadversion of the House. **1751** JOHNSON *Rambl.* No. 155 ¶1 No weakness of the human mind has more frequently incurred animadversion. **1835** I. TAYLOR *Spirit. Desp.* iii. 107 A perfect liberty of animadversion upon clerical conduct. **1868** M. PATTISON *Academ. Organ.* §1. 5 Our temper at this moment should not be one of animadversion and cavil.

6. *concr.* A criticism, comment, observation, or remark (usually, but not always, implying censure).

1599 THYNNE *Animadv.* 2 My petye animaduersions vppon the Annotacions and Corrections..deliuered by master Thomas Speghte vppon the last editione of Chaucers Workes. **1677** GALE *Crt. Gentiles* III. 162 His incomparable animadversions on God's love to mankind. **1740–61** MRS. DELANY *Life & Corr.* (1861) III. 498 Our landlady and her maids making animadversions on our conduct. **1839** HALLAM *Hist. Lit.* II. II. vii. §23. 303 He made some sharp animadversions on this ode.

†**ˌanimadˈversive**, *a.* (and *sb.*) *Obs.* [f. L. *animadvers-* ppl. stem of *animadvert-ĕre* (see ANIMADVERT) + -IVE.] Having the faculty of animadversion; perceptive, percipient.

1642 H. MORE *Song of Soul* II. I. II. xxvi, Though trees have not animadversive sense. **1678** CUDWORTH *Intell. Syst.* 159 Attentive to its own actions, or animadversive of them. **1685** BOYLE *Free Enq.* 184 Perception..is the Prerogative of Animadversive Beings.

b. Used as *sb.* Percipient agent. *rare.*

1660 H. MORE *Myst. Godl.* VIII. xi. 404 [These] will take up the Animadversion of the Soul so much, that one Animadversive will not suffice for both these Provinces.

†**ˌanimadˈversiveness.** *Obs.*$^{-0}$ [f. prec. + -NESS.] 'The power of animadverting or making judgment.' J.

1731 in BAILEY.

ˌanimadˈversor. *Obs.* [a. L. *animadversor*, n. of agent f. *animadvertĕre*: see next and -OR.] One who animadverts; a critic; = ANIMADVERTER.

1651 HARTLIB *Legac. Husb.* (1655) 145 To the fourth Letter of the Animadversor. **1672** NEWTON in *Phil. Trans.* VII. 5089 They agree so justly with my Theory, that if the Animadversor think fit to apply them, he need not, on that account, apprehend a divorce from it.

animadvert (ˌænɪmədˈvɜːt), *v.* [ad. L. *animadvert-ĕre* to turn the mind to, take notice of, orig. two words *anim(um* mind, *advertĕre* to turn to, f. *ad* to + *vert-ĕre* to turn. Through the sense of 'take cognizance of' it passed in judicial language to that of 'chastise, or punish after examination.']

†**1.** *trans.* To turn the mind or attention to, pay attention or attend to, observe. *Obs.*

1637 GILLESPIE *Eng.-Pop. Cer.* III. ii. 24 Which Theodosius..animadverting, commanded to pull them downe. **1673** NEWTON in Rigaud *Corr. Sci. Men* (1841) II. 353 The weak light..shall in comparison not be strong enough to be animadverted. **1679** PRANCE *Add. Narr.* 25, I shall onely Animadvert Two things.

2. *intr.* To take note, observe, remark, consider, bethink oneself. Const. *simply*, and with *that*. *arch.*

1642 H. MORE *Song of Soul* (1647) 159/2, I cannot conceive the body doth animadvert. **1672** MARVELL *Reh. Transp.* I. 163, I cannot but animadvert that this too lies open to his Dilemma. **1749** FIELDING *Tom Jones* XV. v. (1840) 219 Animadvert that you are in the house of a great lady. **1837** *Blackw. Mag.* XLII. 235, I animadverted that all the oldest-looking shrivelled oak-apples..had contained pupæ.

3. *intr.* To turn the attention officially or judicially, take legal cognizance of anything deserving of chastisement or censure; *hence*, to proceed by way of punishment or censure. *arch.*

1671 *True Non-Conf.* 12 If Israel was to animadvert with the sword against any city turning aside to Idolatrie. **1768** BLACKSTONE *Comm.* II. 395 The law will animadvert hereon as an injury. **1771** J. MACPHERSON *Introd. Hist. Gt. Brit.* 290 They animadverted upon petty offenders with slighter punishments. **1817** JAS. MILL *Brit. India* III. ii. 69 It is for the tribunal before which he offends to animadvert upon his conduct.

4. To comment critically (*on*), to utter criticism (usually of an adverse kind); to express censure or blame.

1665 GLANVILL *Sceps. Sci.* 13, I see no reason why her modesty should..be so severely animadverted on. **1699** BENTLEY *Phal.* 29 The Examiner animadverts on it for ten Lines together. **1718** POPE *Let.* Wks. 1737 VI. 36 Your grace very justly animadverts against the too great disposition of finding faults. **1791** SIR J. MACINTOSH *Vind. Gall.* Wks. 1846 III. 92 To animadvert on this modest and courteous picture belongs not to the present subject. **1839** HALLAM *Hist. Lit.* II. II. vii. §22. 302 The academies began to animadvert on defects beyond the province of grammar. **1873** GOULBURN *Pers. Relig.* i. 8 The state of things on which we have been animadverting.

†**ˌanimadˈvertence.** *Obs. rare*$^{-1}$. [f. L. *animadvert-ĕre* + -ENCE, as if ad. L. **animadvertentia*.] A calling of the attention, a warning.

1549 *Compl. Scotl.* xix. 163 Al this veil considrit, suld be an animaduertens to gar ȝou be vigilant.

animadverter (ˌænɪmədˈvɜːtə(r)). [f. ANIMADVERT *v.* + -ER[1].]

1. One who animadverts; a censurer, fault-finder, unfavourable critic or commentator.

1642 MILTON *Apol. Smect.* (1851) 267 Therefore the Animadverter haunts Playhouses and Bordelloes. **1714** NELSON *Script. Doctr. Trin.* Pref. 11, I was thus invited by your and my animadverter..to defend Bishop Bull and myself. **1768** BLACKSTONE *Comm.* Pref., Such of these animadverters as have fallen within the author's notice. **1792** SCOTT *Let.* 10 Sept. (1932) I. 21 He will have many advisers and animadverters upon the naughtiness of his ways. **1958** *Times Lit. Suppl.* 13 June 322/3 The most censorious Republican (or Democratic) animadverter on the 'mess in Washington'.

†**2.** An inflicter of chastisement, a chastiser. *Obs.*

a **1716** SOUTH *Serm.* VIII. 279 God is..a severe animadverter upon such as presume to partake of those mysteries, without such a preparation.

ˌanimadˈverting, *ppl. a.* [f. as prec. + -ING[2].] Criticizing, fault-finding.

1625 *Camden's Hist. Eliz.* To Reader, Those animadverting Observations which the Grecians aptly term Ἐπιστασεῖς. **1632** B. JONSON *Magn. Lady* II. i, A man of a most animadverting humour.

†**ˌanimadˈvertisement.** *Obs. rare*$^{-1}$. [Cf. ANIMADVERSION 3 and ADVERTISEMENT 2, both in this sense.] A warning notice, an admonition.

1651 HARTLIB *Legac. Husb.* (1655) 302 An Animadvertisement to the City and Country.

†**animadvertiser.** *Obs. rare*$^{-1}$. A by-form of ANIMADVERTER, prob. due to the original identity of ADVERT and ADVERTISE.

1596 NASHE *Saffron Walden* 1 Thrice egregious and censoriall animaduertiser of vagrant moustachios.

animal (ˈænɪməl), *sb.* and *a.* [a. L. *animal* a living creature, prop. 'anything living,' for *animāle*, neut. of adj. *animāl-is* having the breath of life, f. *anima* air, breath. life: see -AL[1]. As sb. hardly in Eng. bef. end of 16th c.; not in Bible 1611. Cf. Fr. *animal*, *animau*, 16th c. in Littré.]

A. *sb.*

1. a. A living being; a member of the higher of the two series of organized beings, of which the typical forms are endowed with life, sensation, and voluntary motion, but of which the lowest forms are hardly distinguishable from the lowest vegetable forms by any more certain marks than their evident relationship to other animal forms, and thus to the animal series as a whole rather than to the vegetable series.

[**1398** TREVISA *Barth. De P.R.* XVIII. i. (1495) 735 All that is comprehendyd of flesshe and of spyryte of lyfe..is callyd *Animall*, a beest. **1513** DOUGLAS *Æneis* Comm. (1839) 1 As for *animal* and *homo*..undyr *animal* beyn contenyt all mankynd, beist, byrd, fowll, fisch, serpent, and all other sik thingis. **1594** T. B. *La Primaudaye's Fr. Acad.* II. 581 Many men, by reason of their ignorance in the Latine tongue, think that Animal is a beast, whereas it signifieth a liuing creature.] **1602** SHAKS. *Haml.* II. ii. 20 What a piece of work is a man!..the Parragon of Animals. **1667** MILTON *P.L.* IV. 621 Man hath his daily work..While other Animals unactive range. **1678** CUDWORTH *Intell. Syst.* 75 The Deity is generally supposed to be a Perfectly Happy Animal, Incorruptible and Immortal. **1736** BUTLER *Anal.* I. iii. 82 Man is the acknowledged governing animal upon the earth. **1860** OWEN *Palæont.* 4 When an organism receives nutritive matter by a mouth, inhales oxygen and exhales carbonic acid, and developes tissues, the proximate principles of which are quaternary compounds of carbon, hydrogen, oxygen, and nitrogen, it is called an animal. **1869** HUXLEY in *Fortn. Rev.* Feb. 138 An animal cannot make protoplasm, but takes it ready made from some other..animal..or from some plant.

b. The living body or soft fleshy part of a mollusc, crustacean, etc., as distinguished from its shell or other hard part.

1834 MCMURTRIE tr. *Cuvier's Anim. Kingd.* 248 These Mollusca are arranged in several families according to the form of their shell, which appears to bear a constant relation to that of the animal. **1868** DANA *Syst. Min.* (ed. 5) 677 Carbonaceous matters..derived from the animals of the shells, corals, etc. out of which the limestones were..made.

2. In common usage: one of the lower animals; a brute, or beast, as distinguished from man. (Often restricted by the uneducated to quadrupeds; and familiarly applied especially to such as are used by man, as a *horse*, *ass*, or *dog*.)

1600 SHAKS. *A.Y.L.* I. i. 16 For the which his Animals on his dunghils are as much bound to him as I. **1697** DRYDEN *Virg. Georg.* IV. 224 Of all the Race of Animals, alone The Bees have common Cities of their own. **1734** POPE *Ess. Man* III. 65 He..feasts the animal he dooms his feast. **1875** HELPS *Anim. & Masters* iii. 53 When I use the word 'animals' I mean all living creatures except men and women. **1879** FURNIVALL in *Rep. New Shaks. Soc.* 9 The Animal Similes in Henry VI. *Mod.* Kindness to animals; domestic animals; the animals at the 'Zoo'; we fastened our animals to trees round the camp-fire.

3. a. Contemptuously or humorously for: a human being who is no better than a brute, or whose animal nature has the ascendancy over his reason; a mere animal. (Cf. similar use of *creature*.)

1588 SHAKS. *L.L.L.* IV. ii. 27 His intellect is not replenished, hee is onely an animal, onely sensible in the duller parts. *a* **1704** T. BROWN *Table T.* Wks. 1730 I. 140 A physician is a grave formal animal. **1765** S. MACKENZIE in Ellis *Orig. Lett.* II. 509 IV. 481 There is no animal on the face of the earth that the Duke has a more thorough contempt for than Grenville. **1795** MARY WOLLSTONECR. *Lett.* xxxiii. (1879) 93 My animal is well; I have not yet taught her to eat, but nature is doing the business. I gave her a crust to assist the cutting of her teeth. **1851** RUSKIN *Stones of Ven.* (1874) I. App. 363 Above the reach of human animals.

b. With *the*. The animal nature in man: cf. BEAST *sb.* 1 c.

1809 C. SIMEON *Memoirs* (1847) 272 Less mixture of the *animal* I never expect to see in this world. **1907** H. A. VACHELL *Her Son* i, The animal in this girl was about to spring upon her. **1919** M. K. BRADBY *Psychoanalysis* 231 His fleshly desires were strong, and he was unmerciful to the animal in himself.

4. As in the *slang phr.* 'go the whole hog.'

1838 DICKENS *Nich. Nick.* iii, Opposing all half-measures and preferring to go the extreme animal. **1864** SALA *Twice round Clock* 62 Better pay first-class and go the entire animal.

†**5.** *ellipt.* in *pl.* for ANIMAL SPIRITS. *Obs. rare.*

1628 D. DENT *Serm. agst. Drunk.* 16 Diseases in all the regions of man's body; in the animalls, vitalls, and naturalls. **1647** LILLY *Chr. Astrol.* xliv. 284 The Disease is in the Animals, not in the Body.

6. *colloq.* A person, thing; esp. in phr. (***there is***) ***no such animal.***

1922 E. F. MURPHY *Black Candle* II. xxii. 322, I would like to ask these same 'old-timers' 'how many square shooting addicts have you found in your experience?' I can hear them roar and say 'There is no such animal'. **1963** *Camb. Rev.* 27 Apr. 386/2 Teachers must remember that they are dealing with learners, which is another animal altogether. **1963** *Times Rev. Industry* May 85/1 Computer makers would therefore have us believe that there is no such animal as a typical programmer.

B. *adj.* [In its introduction distinct from ANIMAL *sb.*, and more = Fr. *animal*, ad. L. *animāl-is*; but mixed up with attributive uses of the sb., so as now to be hardly separable as a whole. As L. *animālis* was treated sometimes as a deriv. of *anima*, sometimes of *animus*, the mediæval use of *animālis* varied from 'bestial' to 'spiritual,' and Eng. *animal* adj. had a similar wide range. Mod. usage connects it with the sb. *animal*, and not with *anima* or *animus*.]

†**1.** Connected with sensation, innervation, or will; sometimes = psychical. (Opposed to *vital* and *natural*; the *animal* functions being those of the brain and nervous system; the *vital* of the heart, lungs, etc.; and the *natural* those of nutrition and assimilation.) See ANIMAL SPIRITS. *Obs.*

1541 R. COPLAND *Guydon's Quest. Cyrurg.*, The skull..is that parte of the heade..wherin the anymal membres are conteyned. **1586** BRIGHT *Melanch.* i. 3 Our actions, whether they be animal or voluntarie, or naturall not depending upon our will. **1656** tr. *Hobbes's Elem. Philos.* (1839) 405 Certain motions proceeding from sense, which are called animal motions. **1668** CULPEPPER & COLE *Barthol. Anat.* I. v. 9 This Motion of the Muscles is sometimes called *Voluntary*, sometimes *Animal*, to distinguish it from the *Natural*, in Brutes *Spontaneous*. *Ibid.* II. vi. 99 The motion of the heart is no Animal motion, but a natural motion.

†**2.** Animate, living, organized, as opposed to *inanimate*. *Obs. rare.*

1651 W. G. tr. *Cowel's Inst.* 67 Animall things cannot be kept..without charge, which is otherwise in inanimate.

3. Of or pertaining to the functions of animals; or of those parts of the nature of man which he shares with the inferior animals. (Thus opposed to *intellectual* and *spiritual*).

1651 JER. TAYLOR *Course of Serm.* I. i. 3 The animal, or the naturall man. **1718** QUINCY *Compl. Disp.* 111 Acquainted with the Animal Œconomy. **1783** COWPER *Lett.* 3 June Wks. 1876, 132 The season has been most unfavourable to animal life; and I who am merely animal have suffered much by it. **1841** KINGSLEY *Lett.* (1878) I. 51 The Excitement of Animal Exercise. **1868** FREEMAN *Norm. Conq.* II. vii. 39 The mere animal courage of the soldier.

4. a. Carnal, fleshly, as opposed to *moral*, *spiritual*.

1633 HALES *Brevis Disq.* in *Phenix* (1708) II. 337 From the 24th Verse [he] shews wherein that diversity of Bodies consisteth, not in the Manners, but in the very Substance of them..these weak, those strong; these animal, those spiritual. *a* **1770** AKENSIDE *Epist. Curio* Wks. 324 Whose native strength of soul..Bursts the tame round of animal affairs. **1879** FROUDE *Cæsar* ii. 12 The animal nature had grown as strongly as the moral nature, and along with it the animal appetites. **1923** G. SANTAYANA (*title*) Scepticism and Animal Faith. **1947** *Mind* LVI. 336 We have..no reason for believing any of these inferences; they are all a matter of custom or habit, or, if one prefers more recent terminology, of 'animal faith'.

b. Characteristic of or resembling (that of) a lower animal. Also *Comb.*, as ***animal-bodied*** adj.

1922 D. H. LAWRENCE *England, my England* (1924) 216 The wild, bare, animal shoulders. **1924** HICHENS *After the Verdict* III. xv, Fine-souled and **animal-bodied** men.

5. Of or pertaining to animals, as opposed to vegetables. (Not separable from the sb. used *attrib.*) Cf. *animal pole* below and VEGETATIVE *a.* 1 d.)

1646 SIR T. BROWNE *Pseud. Ep.* 133 Whereas in Job, according to the Septuagint..we finde the word Phœnix, yet can it have no animall signification; for therein it is not expressed φοῖνιξ but στέλεχος φοίνικος, the truncke of the Palme tree. **1684** T. BURNET *Th. Earth* I. 197 This is not necessary in plant-eggs or vegetable seeds: but neither doth it seem necessary in all animal-eggs. **1732** ARBUTHNOT *Rules of Diet* I. 252 The Animal Oils, Cream, Butter, and Marrow. **1843** T. W. JONES in *Brit. & Foreign Med. Rev.* XVI. 547 In the rabbit's ovum..two layers of the blastodermic vesicle can be demonstrated; which Bischoff therefore from this time calls *serous* or *animal* and *mucous* or *vegetative*. *Ibid.* 552 The whole embryo is as yet composed only of the thickened central part of the animal layer; the vegetative layer lies quite smooth at its under surface. **1855** KINGSLEY *Glaucus* (1878) 186 That the animal and vegetable respirations might counterbalance each other. **1902** E. B. WILSON *Cell in Devel. & Inheritance* (ed. 2) viii. 379 The smaller cells of the upper hemisphere [*sc.* of the ovum] represent the 'animal layer', outer germ-layer or ectoblast from which arise the epidermis, the nervous system, and the sense-organs. This fact..led to the designation of the two poles as *animal* and *vegetative*.

C. *Comb.* and *phrases.* Here it is often impossible to separate the sb. and adj. (see prec.)

1. *attrib.* or *adj.* ***animal-lover, -name, -ornament***; **animal black**, that formed by the carbonization of animal substance (cf. BONE-*black*, IVORY-BLACK); **animal charcoal**, that formed by charring animal substance; **animal electricity**, that developed in certain animals, as the torpedo and electric eel; **animal food**, animal substances used as food; **animal flower**, one of the actinozoa, as the sea-anemone; **animal grab** [GRAB *sb.*[2] 5], a card game similar to 'snap'; **animal heat**, the constant temperature maintained within the bodies of living animals; **animal kingdom**, the whole species of animals viewed scientifically, as one of the three great divisions of natural objects; **animal liberation**, the act or process of freeing animals from exploitation (e.g. in laboratory experiments) by man; applied chiefly *attrib.* to groups dedicated to this, as ***Animal Liberation Front***; hence **animal liberationist**; **animal magnetism** = MESMERISM; **animal magnetist**, a mesmerist; **animal myth**, one founded upon the habits of animals; **animal painter**, a painter of animals as opposed to landscapes, portraits, or incidents of human action; so ***animal painting*** and ***animal piece***; **animal plant**, a zoophyte or polype, as coral; **animal pole** *Embryology* (see quots. and cf. POLE *sb.*[2] 7); **animal psychology**, the study of the behaviour of animals; hence ***animal psychologist***; **animal rights** [after *human rights*, etc.], the natural rights of animals to live free from exploitation, confinement, etc., by humans; esp. as the slogan of a movement seeking to achieve this end; **animal size** [SIZE *sb.*[2]], a size made from gelatine; **animal tree**, one cut into the outline of an animal; **animal (tub)-sized, tub-sizing** (see quot. 1937 and TUB *sb.* 10); **animal world**, the world of animals. Also ANIMAL SPIRITS, q.v.

a **1875** KNIGHT *Dict. Mech.* I. 106/2 **Animal black*, carbonaceous matter obtained by the calcination of bones in close vessels. **1957** E. POUND tr. *Rimbaud* 15 As factories of suet and animal-Black spread out the whiff and flavour from Grenelle. **1873** WILLIAMSON *Chem.* §56 The presence of the phosphate in this *animal charcoal enables the carbon to remove various colouring matters from liquids. **1793** R. FOWLER (*title*) Experiments and Observations relative to the Influence lately discovered by M. Galvani, and commonly called *Animal Electricity. **1836–39** TODD *Cycl. Anat. & Phys.* II. 81/2 It is in the mode of its development that the chief peculiarity of Animal Electricity consists. **1767** *Animal flower [see ACTINIA]. **1833** *Penny Cycl.* I. 102/2 The popular names of *animal flowers* and *sea anemonies*, usually applied to the various species of actinia. *Ibid.* 104/2 The purple animal-flower (*Actinia equina*). **1749** FIELDING *Tom Jones* I. I. i. 3 The several Species of *animal and vegetable Food. **1819** KEATS *Let.* 26 (?) Oct. (1958) II. 225, I have left off animal food. **1912** E. M. DELL *Way of Eagle* liii. 350, I can play *Animal Grab as well as anybody. **1941** J. CARY *House of Children* x. 38 The unexpected playmate who..forgot some pressing duty in order to play..animal grab, even more noisily than we. **1779** A. CRAWFORD *Experiments & Obs. on Animal Heat* iv. 81 *Animal heat depends, indirectly, upon a change which the blood undergoes in the course of the circulation. **1874** ROSCOE *Elem. Chem.* 441 The whole of the animal heat is derived from the combustion of the materials of the body. **1847** CARPENTER *Zool.* (*title*) The Principal Families of the *Animal Kingdom. **1973** *N.Y. Rev. Books* 5 Apr. 21/4 *Animal Liberation will require greater altruism on the part of mankind than any other liberation movement. **1975** P. SINGER (*title*) Animal liberation. **1978** *N.Y. Times Mag.* 31 Dec. VI. 20/4 In Great Britain..a clandestine group called the Animal Liberation Front conducts commando-style raids on laboratories, liberating animals and sabotaging research equipment. **1983** *Listener* 14 Apr. 13/1 The animal liberation movement..is *not* saying that all lives are of equal worth. *Ibid.*, Lecky has anticipated what the *animal liberationists are now saying. **1910** F. E. WHITE (*title*) The *animal lover's birthday book. **1928** R. CAMPBELL *Wayzgoose* ii. 43 The usual animal-lover's sloppiness which is popular everywhere. **1784** H. WALPOLE *Let.* in *Academy* (1882) 25 Feb. 139/1 *Animal Magnetism has not yet made much impression here. **1786** *Lounger* (1787) III. 286 The Animal Magnetism of the illustrious Dr. Mesmer. **1860** JEAFFRESON *Bk. ab. Doctors* II. 38 Animal magnetism, under the name of mesmerism, has been made familiar of late years to the ears of English people. **1792** *Looker-On* No. 20, 15 May 155 A great number of *animal magnetists were among this crowd of philosophers. **1809** COLERIDGE *Friend* (1818) I. 91, I must have forgotten the Animal Magnetists; the proselytes of Brothers, and of Joanna Southcot. **1931** C. L'E. EWEN *Hist. Surnames* xiii. 333 The Anglo-Saxons commonly bestowed *animal-names upon their children. **1937** *Burlington Mag.* Feb. 99/1 Intricate geometrically conceived *animal-ornament. **1711** SHAFTESB. *Charac.* III. 378 In *animal-pieces; where beasts, or fowl are represented. **1846** PATTERSON *Zool.* 14 The term Zoophyte, literally meaning *animal-plant. **1887** C. O. WHITMAN in *Jrnl. Morphol.* I. 108 The next step consists in the formation of four ectoblastic micromeres which eventually present the figure of a quarter-foil at the *animal pole. *Ibid.* 111 The macromeres..take no further part in the cleavage, if we except the budding off of ectoblastic micromeres at the animal pole. **1890** BILLINGS *Med. Dict.* I. 69/2 *A*[*nimal*] *pole*, pole of ovum at which there is least yolk, and where the polar globules are extruded; where, also, subsequent segmentation is most rapid. **1961** *Brit. Med. Dict.* 1134/2 *Animal pole*, that end of the early ovum which shows..greatest proliferation and metabolic activity, and which eventually forms the head end of the embryo. **1894** CREIGHTON & TITCHENER tr. *Wundt's Lects. Human & Animal Psychol.* xxiii. 342 The inclination of *animal psychologists to see the intellectual achievements of animals in the most brilliant light. *a* **1942** B. MALINOWSKI *Sci. Theory Cult.* (1944) ix. 89 The concept of drive is better omitted from any analysis of human behavior, unless..we understand that we have to use it differently from the animal psychologists or physiologists. **1881** G. J. ROMANES *Animal Intelligence* p. vii, If it is remembered that my object in these pages is the mapping out of *animal psychology for the purposes of a subsequent synthesis, I may fairly..receive credit for a sound scientific intention. **1879** E. B. NICHOLSON *Rights of Animal* p. x, My first two chapters bear the plain stamp of Herbert Spencer's *Social Statics*, but I know no other theory of right and wrong which would not equally allow a proof of *animal rights. **1928** D. HARWOOD *Love for Animals* iii. 166 Like other champions of animal rights, he took and rejected what he pleased. **1972** *Rep. Society for Animal Rights* Sept. 1/2 The Society for Animal Rights, formerly the National Catholic Society for Animal Welfare, has embarked on this program. We intend to bring about recognition of the rights of animals. **1986** *Washington Post* 29 Apr. B7/4 Animal rights activists set up camp on the grounds of the National Institutes of Health in Bethesda yesterday. **1887** *Animal size [see *tub-size*, TUB *sb.* 10]. **1882** *St. James's Gaz.* 1 Apr., This sketch represents an *animal-tree. *a* **1912** *Animal tub-sized [see A.T.S., A III]. **1937** LABARRE *Dict. Paper Terms* 98/1 **Animal tub-sizing*, abbr. A.T.S., same as tub-sizing. **1940** *Chambers's Techn. Dict.* 36/1 *Animal-sized*, paper which has been hardened by passing the sheet through a bath of gelatine. More costly than engine-sized. **1835** SWAINSON *Classif. Quadr.* §15 Aristotle, in his system of the *animal world, excludes man from his scheme.

2. *similative* and *synthetic deriv.*, as ***animal-minded***.

1871 R. H. HUTTON *Ess.* I. 28 The ignorant and animal-minded millions by whom the earth is mostly peopled.

animalcula, *sb. pl.*: see ANIMALCULE.

animalcular (ænɪˈmælkjʊlə(r)), *a. rare.* [f. L. *animalcul-um* (see next) + -AR.]

1. Of or pertaining to animalcules.

1765 TUCKER *Lt. Nat.* I. 481 Imagine animalcules to take their rise in measuring from the width of their tail..then reckon by animalcular miles. **1823** SOUTHEY in *Q. Rev.* XXX. 9 Dr. Dwight has a theory that the diseases..are produced by animalcular putrefaction. **1830** COLERIDGE *Ch. & State* 219 The moving fairy states of animalcular life.

†**2.** Of or pertaining to Animalculism. *Obs. rare.*

1753 CHAMBERS *Cycl. Supp.* s.v., Systems of physic, of pathology..founded on the animalcular principles. **1807** *Edin. Rev.* XI. 81 Of the Animalcular system.

animalcule (ænɪˈmælkjuːl). Also 6–7 **animalcle.** [ad. L. *animalcul-um*, dim. of *animal*: see -CULE. Cf. mod.Fr. *animalcule.* Formerly often used in the L. form, of which the pl. *animalcula* is still frequent in scientific use. (By the ignorant the latter is sometimes made a sing. with pl. *animalculæ*.)]

†**1.** A small or tiny animal; formerly applied to small vertebrates, such as mice, and all invertebrates.

1599 A. M. tr. *Gabelhouer's Bk. Physic* 131/1 For the Laske..Boyle the Liver of any animalcle, decocte the same, and cause him to eate therof. **1662** MORE *Antid. Ath.* II. xii. (1712) 79 The assault of Flies and Gnats, and such like bold Animalcula. **1691** RAY *Creation* I. (1704) 168 The catching of these Animalcules [Beetles]. **1718** J. CHAMBERLAYNE *Relig. Philos.* III. xxv. §10 The next biggest Animalculum or Insect. **1728** G. CARLETON *Mem. Eng. Officer* 234 The horrid Desolation which attended the Visitation of those Animalcula [locusts]. **1831** CARLYLE *Sart. Res.* (1858) 121 The basest of created animalcules, the Spider.

2. An animal so small as to be visible only with the aid of the microscope; applied chiefly to the *Rotifera* and *Infusoria.*

1677 *Phil. Trans.* XII. 821 These animalcula or living Atoms did move. **1713** DERHAM *Phys. Theol.* 9 The Animalcules in Pepper-Water. **1722** WOLLASTON *Relig. Nat.* v. 89 If the semina, out of which animals are produced, are (as I doubt not) animalcula already formed. **1745** T. NEEDHAM *Microsc. Disc.* Introd. 3 The minutest microscopical Animalcule. **1748** SIR J. HILL *Hist. Anim.* 2 (JOD.), I have added some unknown species to the animalcule kingdom. **1835** KIRBY *Hab. & Inst. Anim.* I. iv. 149 The infusories,..also called animalcules, microscopic animals. **1862** SIR H. HOLLAND *Ess.* 84 The appearance of animalcule life in various artificial compounds. **1876** PAGE *Advd. Text-bk. Geol.* iii. 67 The coral animalcule rears its polypidom.

animalculine (ænɪˈmælkjʊlɪn), *a. rare.* [f. L. *animalcul-um* + -INE.] = ANIMALCULAR.

1821 DWIGHT *Trav. New Eng.* I. xxxviii. 385 The nidus, in which the animalculine existence is formed. *Ibid.*, That animalculine putrefaction is the immediate cause of those diseases..which are justly attributed to standing waters.

animalculism (ænɪˈmælkjʊlɪz(ə)m). [f. as prec. + -ISM.] A theory which seeks to explain physiological or pathological phenomena by the agency of animalcules, as (1) that they are the germs of life, (2) that they are the cause of diseases.

[**1751** CHAMBERS *Cycl.* s.v. *Animalcule*, The system of generation *ab animalculo*.] **1874** DUNGLISON *Med. Dict.*, *Animalculism*, Spermatism. **1880** in *Syd. Soc. Lex.*

aniˈmalculist. [f. as prec. + -IST.]

1. An adherent of Animalculism.

1816 KEITH *Phys. Bot.* II. 362 The theory of the animalculists. **1879** tr. *Haeckel's Evol. Man* I. ii. 37 The animalculists, or the believers in sperm, looked upon the moving seminal threads as the real animal germs.

2. One who makes a special study of animalcules.

animalhood (ˈænɪməlhʊd). *rare*[−1]. [f. ANIMAL *sb.* + -HOOD.] The state or condition of the inferior animals.

1863 *Reader* Nov. 537 A creature almost lapsed from humanity into animalhood.

animalic (ænɪˈmælɪk), *a. rare.* [f. ANIMAL + -IC by form-assoc. with *angel-ic*, etc.] Of or belonging to animals.

1677 HALE *Prim. Orig. Man.* III. vi. 281 The Eggs of a perfect Animal..will lose their animalick [*printed* Animatick] Faculties, being frozen or concrete with cold. **1878** T. SINCLAIR *Mount* 171 Falling next to Drydenism, and finishing with the animalic lyre of innuendo.

animaliculture (ænɪˈmælɪˌkʌltjʊə(r), -tʃə(r)). [f. L. *animal*, after *horticulture*, *pisciculture*, etc.] The rearing of animals as a branch of industry.

1879 C. A. CUTTER in *Catalogue* of Winchester (Mass.) Town Library, and in *Libr. Journ.* IV. 237, as a collective title for works 'relating to the raising and care of animals for industrial purposes.'

†**animaˈlillio.** *Obs. rare*[−1]. [f. ANIMAL, with dim. ending, as in It. *-iglio*, Sp. *-illo* (*-ilyo*).] A tiny animal, an animalcule.

1639 HOWELL *Fam. Lett.* (1650) II. 64 The same proportion which those small animalillios bore with me..the same I held with those glorious spirits which are near the throne.

†**ˈanimalish**, *a. Obs. rare.* [f. ANIMAL *sb.* + -ISH.] Of the nature of an animal.

1678 CUDWORTH *Intell. Syst.* I. i. §29. 37 Anaxagoras..did not make any Animalish Atoms Sensitive and Rational. *Ibid.* 73 To think that there was any Animalish Nature before all these Animals.

animalism (ˈænɪməlɪz(ə)m). [f. as prec. + -ISM.]

1. The exercise of the animal faculties; **a.** in an honourable sense: Animal activity, physical exercise and enjoyment; **b.** in depreciation: Mere animal enjoyment, sensuality.

1831 CARLYLE *Sart. Res.* (1858) 110 Savage Animalism is nothing, inventive Spiritualism is all. **1848** KINGSLEY *Saint's Trag.* Introd. (1878) 6 The 'healthy animalism' of the Teutonic mind. **1856** R. VAUGHAN *Mystics* (1860) II. 204 That snug animalism which some men call happiness. **1868** *Less. Middle Age* 198 A face that expresses pure intellect, and feeling, without a vestige of animalism.

2. The doctrine which views men as mere animals.

1857 T. WEBB *Intell. Locke* i. 6 The Philosophy of Sensualism was developed..by Helvetius, into an Animalism, which acknowledged no characteristic difference between man and the lower animals.

3. An embodiment of the mere animal propensities; a wholly sensual being. *rare.*

1868 TENNYSON *Lucr.* 53 Girls, Hetairai, curious in their art, Hired animalisms. **1875** FARRAR *Seekers* III. i. 270 The scandalous bronze-lacquer age of hungry animalisms.

animalist ('ænɪməlɪst). [f. as prec. + -IST.]

1. One who takes the 'animal' side of a discussion.

1837 P. PARLEY *Sun, Moon, & Stars* liv. (ed. 2) 284 Vegetablists say that it is a fungous plant..but the animalists agree in affirming it to be the altered remains of dead frogs.

2. One who holds the doctrine of animalism; a sensualist.

1851 in *Kingsley's Lett. & Mem.* I. 282 A 'healthy animalist' who has gone through that course of profligacy which, etc.

3. The same as animalculist.

1874 DUNGLISON *Med. Dict., Animalculist, Animalist*, one who attempts to explain different physiological or pathological phenomena by means of animalcules.

4. An artist who makes figures of animals; an animal-painter or -sculptor; also, a writer of stories of animals.

1886 *Century Mag.* Feb. 484/1 [Barye] brought envy and malice on his head through the erection..in the Tuileries gardens of his colossal bronze lion and serpent. It was then the sneer of 'animalist' began. **1890** *Universal Rev.* 15 July 412 The animalists greatly repeat themselves. **1909** *Daily Chron.* 19 Jan. 4/4 The whole crowd of animalists, from Æsop to Mr. Jack London.

Hence **anima'listic** *a.*, of or pertaining to animalism.

1877 L. STEPHEN in *Cornhill Mag.* Apr. 427 One may see in him [*sc.* Kingsley] the type of character which, under other conditions, produces the 'diabolical' or rather the animalistic school of art and literature. **1955** *Bull. Atomic Sci.* Mar. 76/3 Should we regret having to abandon many poetic illusions of the vast, pantheistic or animalistic interpretation of the world?

animality (ænɪ'mælɪtɪ). [a. Fr. *animalité*, n. of quality f. *animal* adj.: see -ITY. Cf. *humanity*, also L. *æquālitās, carnālitās*.]

1. The sum of the qualities and functions which are the attributes of an animal; the animal nature, constitution, or system; vital power.

1615 CROOKE *Body of Man* 40 Then followeth presently a sencelesse dulnes, and a priuation of the Animality, if I may so speake. **1674** N. FAIRFAX *Bulk & Selv.* 111 Lifesomness or animality. **1796** W. TAYLOR in *Month. Rev.* XX. 567 Empedocles..had no doubt of the animality of the earth. **1829** E. JESSE *Jrnl. Natur.* 241 That portion of vital air which brisks up animality. **1840** *Blackw. Mag.* XLVIII. 490 The luxuriant fulness of blooming animality.

2. The quality or condition of the inferior animals; the merely animal nature, as distinguished from the moral and spiritual; animalhood.

1646 S. BOLTON *Arraign. Errour* 158 There is something of animality, of the beast in man. **1653** H. MORE *Conject. Cabbal.* (1713) 14 Every man..hath these two Principles in him..Divinity and Animality, Spirit and Flesh. **1667** —— *Div. Dial.* IV. iv. (1713) 294 To gratifie our corrupt Animality. **1836** *For. Q. Rev.* XVII. 166 In woman, humanity, as contradistinguished to animality..has attained its zenith. **1868** in F. Lee *Valid. Angl. Ord.* 494 Sunk in the lowest depths of ignorance and animality. **1878** DOWDEN *Stud. Lit.* 114 The development of the entire human race from animality and primitive barbarism.

3. Animal nature, animal life, as opposed to that of vegetables or of inorganic matter.

1647 H. MORE *Poems* 88 It's more plain in animalitie. **1794** G. ADAMS *Nat. & Exp. Phil.* I. x. 429 Without it [fire] there would be neither vegetation, nor animality. **1858** T. R. JONES *Aquar. Natur.* 137 Jussieu..at last declared his complete faith in the animality of these creatures [the Zoophytic races]. **1879** LEWES *Stud. Psychol.* 54 It passes from Vegetality to Animality, and through Animality to Humanity.

4. The animal series, the animal world.

1770 WESLEY *Nat. Phil.* (1784) IV. v. viii. §14. 190 [The polypus] is too much an animal to be the last term of animality. **1841** DOUGLAS in *Proc. Berw. Nat. Club.* I. ix. 245 In any class or kingdom of animality. **1869** *Eng. Mech.* 11 June 262/1 Animality has no principle of cohesion by its members.

animalization (ˌænɪməlaɪ'zeɪʃən). [n. of action f. next: see -ATION.]

1. a. The action of converting into animal substance.

1767 J. PRIESTLEY *Hist. & Pres. State Electr.* IV. 489 The processes of calcination, vegetation, animalization. **1800** HATCHETT in *Phil. Trans.* XC. 401 That part of the blood [fibrin] which has undergone the most complete animalization. **1836** TODD *Cycl. Anat. & Phys.* 29/2 The animalization of the chyle. **1859** L. SIMPSON *Handbk. Dining* vii. 61 To discover in vegetables those affinities in consequence of which they also became susceptible of animalisation.

b. The process of animalizing vegetable fibre.

1862 O'NEILL *Calico Printing & Dyeing* 14 The present view of animalisation is, that it is not possible to animalise a fabric in any other way than by actually depositing upon it the animal matter in question.

2. A rendering unspiritual or sensual; sensualization. *rare.*

1863 DRAPER *Intell. Devel. Eur.* viii. (1865) 192 An animalization of religion.

‖**3.** Distribution of animal existence; animal population. (Not yet naturalized.)

1840 SIR C. LEMON in *Jrnl. R. Agric. S.* I. IV. 414 What the French call the animalization of the departments is shown as follows:—Cattle, 2,628,924; Sheep, 6,764,107.

4. The action of making into or representing as an animal. (Cf. ANIMALIZE *v.* 1.)

1886 HUXLEY in *19th Cent.* Apr. 493 In the theology of both the Babylonians and the Egyptians there is abundant evidence..of..the deification of animals, and the converse animalisation of Gods.

animalize ('ænɪməlaɪz), *v.* [f. ANIMAL + -IZE.]

1. To make into an animal; to represent in animal form. *rare.*

1741 WARBURTON *Div. Legat.* II. IV. §6. 182 The polite Egyptian Priests who first animalized the Asterisms. **1835** [see ANIMALIZED *ppl. a.* 2]. **1886** [implied in ANIMALIZATION 4]. **1889** *Cent. Dict.* s.v., The Egyptians animalized their deities.

2. a. To convert into animal substance.

1770 WESLEY *Nat. Phil.* v. viii. §14 (1784) IV. 190 The Hand, which has formed the polypus..can, when necessity requires, animalize matter at a much less expence. **1772** HUNTER in *Phil. Trans.* LXII. 454 Something secreted in the coats of the stomach, which..animalises the food, or assimilates it to the nature of the blood. **1805** W. TAYLOR in *Ann. Rev.* III. 17 That the juice of the Indian fig may be animalized into a crimson die.

b. To convert (vegetable fibre) into a substance resembling animal fibre.

1862 [see prec. 1 b]. **1869** *Dict. Dyeing* in *Eng. Mech.* 28 May 229/3 It is not possible to animalise a fabric in any other way than by actually depositing upon it the animal matter. *a* **1875** KNIGHT *Dict. Mech.* I. 106/2 *Animalizing fiber*, the process of conferring upon vegetable fiber the physical characteristics of animal fiber.

3. To reduce to animal nature; to sensualize, rouse the sensual passions of.

1806–31 A. KNOX *Rem.* (1844) I. 81 Nine out of ten are too much animalised for this. **1841** ARNOLD *Lect. Mod. Hist.* (1878) 55 Has sensualized and animalized its character. **1842** *Blackw. Mag.* LI. 297 A bright-eyed poissarde well able to animalize a monastery.

'animalized, *ppl. a.* [f. prec. + -ED.]

1. Converted into animal substance or product.

1784 TWAMLEY *Dairying* 93 Milk..yields a nourishment partly vegetable and partly animalized. **1800** HENRY *Epit. Chem.* (1808) 290 The product of vegetables, and not an animalized substance. **1869** *Eng. Mech.* 30 July 412/1 Absorbency of the animalised gases.

2. Endowed with the attributes or appearance of an animal. *rare.*

1835 KIRBY *Bridgew. Treat.* (1852) I. 189 Seemingly insignificant creatures..which seem as little animalized as any animal can be. **1879** M. CONWAY *Demonol.* I. III. viii. 380 The animalised form of the Hydra [of Lernæa].

3. Reduced to the level of the lower animals; sensualized.

1849 ROBERTSON *Serm.* (1866) xii. 209 The soul of the Roman..became secularized, then animalized. **1858** BUSHNELL *Nat. & Supern.* viii. (1864) 227 The animalized condition which we now designate by the term *savage*.

'animalizing, *ppl. a.* [f. as prec. + -ING².] Reducing to the rank or character of an animal; sensualizing.

1824 COLERIDGE *Aids to Refl.* (1848) I. 102 The animalizing tendency of his own philosophy. **1847** BUSHNELL *Chr. Nurture* II. iii. (1861) 278 This same animalizing process.

animally ('ænɪməlɪ), *adv.* [f. ANIMAL *a.* + -LY².]

†**1.** Psychically, in respect of the *anima*, animal soul, or 'animal spirits.' *Obs.*

c **1600** *Timon* v. iv. (1842) 87 Hee's an asse logically and capitally, not phisikallie and animallie. **1678** CUDWORTH *Intell. Syst.* 582 Πάντα ψυχικῶς, all things animally—that is, self-movably, actively, and productively.

2. Physically, in respect of the animal as opposed to the intellectual faculties.

1866 GEO. ELIOT *F. Holt* III. xxxv. 10 A nature more subtly mixed..less animally forcible.

†**'animalness.** *Obs.*—⁰ [f. as prec. + -NESS.] = ANIMALITY.

Bailey 1731.

animal spirits (formerly, spirit). [See ANIMAL B 1.]

†**1.** *orig.* The supposed 'spirit' or principle of sensation and voluntary motion; answering to nerve fluid, nerve force, nervous action. *Obs.*

1543 TRAHERON *Vigo's Chirurg.* Interpr., Physitions teache that there ben thre kindes of spirites, *animal*, *vital*, and *naturall*. The animal spirite hath his seate in the brayne, and is spredde in to all the bodye by synnowes, gyuyng facultie of mouynge, and felynge. It is called *animal*, bycause it is the first instrument of the soule, whych the Latins call *animam*. **1549** *Compl. Scotl.* vi. 67 Al my spreitis vital ande animal. **1594** T. B. *La Primaud. Fr. Acad.* To Reader, The braine for the animall spirite, the heart for the vitall, and the liver for the naturall. **1607** TOPSELL *Four-footed Beasts* (1673) 272 Those conducts through which the spirits animal do give feeling and moving to the body. *a* **1652** J. SMITH *Sel. Disc.* iv. 124 That part of the brain from whence all those nerves that conduct the animal spirits up and down the body take their first original. **1667** MILTON *P.L.* IV. 805 If..he might taint Th' animal Spirits that from pure blood arise. **1732** BERKELEY *Min. Philos.* I. 134 Animal Spirits..are the Messengers, which running to and fro in the Nerves, preserve a Communication between the Soul and outward Objects. **1777** PRIESTLEY *Matt. & Spir.* (1782) xx. I. 259 The doctrine of animal spirits.

†**b.** *fig. pl.* Nerves, sinews (as in 'sinews of war').

1719 W. WOOD *Surv. Trade* 295 The Increase of our Foreign Trade..whence has arisen all those Animal Spirits, those Springs of Riches which has enabled us to spend so many millions for the preservation of our Liberties.

†**2.** Nerve, physical or 'animal' courage. *Obs.*

1700 HICKS in *Pepys Corr.* 372 Sights..which others of more passive tempers, and a less stock of animal spirits, could not so well endure. **1719** DE FOE *Crusoe* 39 That the Surprise may not drive the Animal Spirits from the Heart. *Ibid.* (1858) 548 The animal spirits sink.

3. *coll. pl.* Nervous vivacity, natural gayety of disposition, 'healthy animalism.'

1739 WESLEY *Wks.* 1830 I. 256 Saying it was only nature, imagination, and animal spirits. **1813** MISS AUSTEN *Pride & Prej.* ix. 39 She had high animal spirits. **1844** DISRAELI *Coningsby* I. v. 23 He..had great animal spirits, and a keen sense of enjoyment. *Mod.* A great flow of animal spirits.

‖**anima mundi** (ˌænɪmə 'mʌndaɪ). [med.L. (Abelard), = 'soul of the world'; app. formed to render Gr. ψυχὴ τοῦ κόσμου. Cf. WORLD-*soul*, -*spirit*.] The soul of the world; a power or spirit supposed to be diffused throughout the material universe, organizing and giving form to the whole and to all its parts, and regularizing the motions and alterations of the parts.

1678 CUDWORTH *Intell. Syst.* I. iv. 561 All the Perfection of a Mundane Soul, may perhaps be attributed to God in some sense, and be [*printed* he] called, Quasi Anima Mundi, As it were the Soul thereof. **1698** J. LOCKE *3rd Let. to Stillingfleet* in *Wks.* (1823) IV. 363 There might be added other senses, wherein the word φύσις may be found, made use of by the Greeks..; as particularly Aristotle, if I mistake not, uses it for a plastic power, or a kind of *anima mundi*, presiding over the material world, and producing the order and regularity of motions, formations, and generations in it. *a* **1748** WATTS *Improvement of Mind* II. v. §2 in *Wks.* (1753) V. 340 Take a Platonist, who believes an *anima mundi*, a universal soul of the world to pervade all bodies, to act in and by them according to their nature, and indeed to give them their nature and their special powers. **1890** W. JAMES *Princ. Psychol.* I. x. 346, I find the notion of some sort of *anima mundi* thinking in all of us to be a more promising hypothesis. **1948** *Mind* LVII. 240 Especially the belief in an *anima mundi* and in the comprehensive analogy between man and the universe are present in Herbert's discussion. **1957** G. BOAS *Dominant Themes of Mod. Philos.* viii. 280 This was not the first time that a correlation between the *anima mundi* and the Holy Spirit had been made; indeed Abelard had been condemned at the Council of Sens in 1140 for identifying the two. **1958** *Spectator* 17 Jan. 80/3 His [*sc.* Wordsworth's] belief in an *anima mundi* was encouraged by ideas taken from Cambridge authorities such as Newton himself.

†**'animant,** *a.* and *sb.* *Obs. rare.* [ad. L. *animānt-em* breathing, living, pr. pple. of *animāre*: see ANIMATE.]

A. *adj.* Having life, living; animated.

1678 CUDWORTH *Intell. Syst.* 514 *Ut sit Animans*, That it be Animant, or endued with Life, Sense, and Understanding. *Ibid.* 512 He that acknowledges no Animant God..acknowledges no God at all.

B. *sb.* A living creature, an animal.

1677 GALE *Crt. Gentiles* II. IV. 447 There is no other cause of life to us men and other Animants.

†**ani'mantative,** *a.* *Obs. rare.* [f. prec., by form-assoc. with *alimentative*, etc.; a clumsy variant of ANIMATIVE. Cf. *vegetative*, and see -ATIVE.] Connected with the production of living beings.

a **1655** *Let.* in Hartlib. *Ref. Commonw. Bees* 25 Out of any Wood-berry may, by an animantative fermentation (if I may so speak) be produced, first a small Worm, which growing bigger groweth husky, and at last becomes a Fly.

†**animastic** (ænɪ'mæstɪk), *a.* and *sb.* [ad. med.L. *animastic-us* pertaining to the soul, f. L. *anima* breath, life. A hybrid formation: cf. *onomastic*.]

A. *adj.* Possessed of mind or spirit, as opposed to what is purely material; spiritual; *sometimes* = ANIMATE.

1651 J. F[REAKE] *Agrippa's Occ. Phil.* 370 The order of Animastick, viz. of blessed souls. **1794** T. TAYLOR *Plotinus* 226 A life neither vegetable, nor sensitive, nor of any other animastic nature. **1816** —— *Pamphl.* VIII. 65 Of fables..some are theological, others physical, others animastic (or relating to soul). **1855** BAILEY *Mystic* 123 Stretched from the all essential infinite, To animastic orders and ourselves.

†**B.** *sb.* Psychology. *Obs.*

a **1857** SIR W. HAMILTON (L.) [Apprehension, judgement, and reasoning] belonged to Animastic, as they called it, or Psychology.

†**ani'mastical,** *a.* *Obs. rare*—¹. = prec.

1651 J. F[REAKE] *Agrippa's Occ. Phil.* 453 After the Quires of the blessed Spirits, the Animastical order is the next.

animate ('ænɪmət), *ppl. a.* and *sb.* [ad. L. *animāt-us* filled with life, *also*, disposed, inclined, f. *animā-re* to breathe, to quicken; f. *anima* air, breath, life, soul, mind.]

A. *pple.* and *adj.*

†**1.** *pple.* Animated, inspired. *Obs.*

a **1546** ELYOT *Let.* in *Governour* (1836) 289, I am animate to importune your good lordship with most hearty desires. **1640** *Canterbur. Self-Conv.* Pref. 11 That..your Honours [may be] the more animate to deny your power.

2. *adj.* Endowed with life, living, alive.

1605 TIMME *Quersit.* II. i. 102 Phylosophers..have affirmed the magnet or loadstone to be animate. **1610**

Healey *St. Aug., City of God* viii. xxiii. (1620) 312 Statues, quoth he? Doe you not see them animate? **1667** *Phil. Trans.* II. 580 Corruption of Bodies Inanimat and Animat. **1677** Hale *Prim. Orig. Man.* i. i. 34 Some of the Ancients..have ..thought that the World was Animate. **1751** Chambers *Cycl.* s.v., In mechanics, animate power is used to denote a man, or brute. **1830** Lyell *Princ. Geol.* (1875) I. i. ix. 147 The former history of the animate world. **1840** Carlyle *Heroes* (1846) 5 That men should have worshipped..stocks and stones, and all manner of animate and inanimate objects.

3. Lively, having the full activity of life.

1801 Southey *Thalaba* vi. iii. Wks. IV. 220 A courser More animate of eye, Of form more faultless never had he seen. **1833** I. Taylor *Fanat.* iii. 59 The enthusiasm of the very meanest member of a warrior-clan is tenfold more animate.

4. a. Pertaining to what is endowed with life; connected with animals.

1828 Kirby & Spence *Entomol.* I. iv. 94 Both animate diseases, but derived from two distinct species of animals.

b. *Gram.* Denoting living beings.

1902 *Amer. Anthropologist* Jan.–Mar. 27 The distinction between animate and inanimate gender is still preserved in both Penobscot and Abenaki. **1939** S. C. Boyanus *Spoken Russian* ii. 5 The Accusative of masculine animate nouns is identical with the Genitive in the singular and plural.

†**B.** *sb.* That which has life, a living thing. *Obs.*

1642 H. More *Song of Soul* iii. xxviii, Magnetick might doth so combine Earth, Water, Air, into one animate. **1669** Gale *Crt. Gentiles* i. i. i. 5 The animate serves the animal.

animate ('ænɪmeɪt), *v.* [f. prec., or on analogy of vbs. so formed.]

I. To give life to, make alive or active.

1. *trans.* To breathe life into, endow with life, give life to or sustain in life, quicken, vivify.

1542 Boorde *Dyetary* xvi. 275 [Venison] doth anymate hym to be as he is..stronge and hardy. **1667** Milton *P.L.* viii. 151 Male and Femal Light, Which two great Sexes animate the World. **1736** Butler *Anal.* i. i. 25 We may hereafter animate these same or new bodies. **1794** G. Adams *Nat. & Exp. Phil.* IV. lii. 448 When the coals are animated by a pair of bellows. **1870** H. Macmillan *Bible Teach.* viii. 156 The breath of God animates his frame.

2. To represent as alive, give the appearance of life to. *arch.*

1612 Brinsley *Lud. Lit.* xxi. (1627) 247 That we forget not to animate that which we remember by: that is, to conceive of it in our minde, as being lively and stirring. **1750** Johnson *Rambl.* No. 168 ¶5 Poetry, that force which.. animates matter. **1776** Reynolds *Disc.* vii. (1876) 408 That Promethean fire, which animates the canvass and vivifies the marble.

3. To impart liveliness, vividness, or interest to; to enliven.

1670 Flecknoe in *Shaks. Cent. Praise* 345 Much less inimitable Shakspears way, Promethian-like to animate a play. **1736** Butler *Anal.* ii. vii. 329 These might have animated a dull relation. **1737** Pope *Horace's Ode* iii. xxviii, Exalt the dance, and animate the song. **1833** I. Taylor *Fanat.* vi. 201 To have thrown off every sympathy with what animates the open world.

†**4.** To bring into active or legal operation. *Obs.*

1580 Sidney *Arcad.* (1622) 243 No small errour winkt at, least greater should bee animated. **1655** Lestrange *Chas. I*, 214 The Bill..having past both Houses was animated with the Royall assent.

II. To give spirit, inspiration, or impulse.

5. *trans.* To fill with boldness, courage, spirit; to encourage, inspirit.

1538 Coverdale *Ded. N.T.* Wks. II. 24 It doth even animate and encourage me now likewise to use the same audacity. **1584** Whitgift in Fuller *Ch. Hist.* ix. 158 Such as animate them in their disobedience. **1607** Topsell *Four-footed B.* (1673) 107 The Dogs are animated by the winding of horns, and voices of the hunters. **1623** Cockeram, *Animate*, to encourage or hearten on. **1700** Dryden *Mel. & Atal.* 161 The shouting animates their hearts. **1793** Smeaton *Edystone L.* §294 The progress we had made this season could not fail to animate our further proceedings. **1839** Yeowell *Anc. Brit. Ch.* iii. (1847) 29 The few moments which preceded the decisive battle were employed..in animating his soldiers.

†**b.** *refl. Obs.*

1547 Boorde *Brev. Health* clxxxiii. 65 Let every man, woman, or chylde animate them selfe upon God.

†**c.** *intr.* To become animated, brighten up. *Obs.*

1779 Miss Burney *Diary* (1842) I. 256 She..alternately softens and animates just like her. **1782** —— *Cecilia* i. vi. (1783) 79 Mr. Arnott, animating at this speech, glided behind her chair.

6. *trans.* To move mentally, to excite to action of any kind; to inspire, actuate, incite, stir up.

1583 *Exec. Treason* (1675) 4 To animate them to continue their..wicked purposes. *c* **1590** Marlowe *Massac. Paris* ii. vi, Animated by religious zeal. **1598** Greenewey *Tacitus, Ann.* i. vii. (1622) 12 He..was thought to animate Drusus against the souldiers. **1658** Cromwell (Carlyle 1871) V. 119 Designs which are animated every day from Flanders and Spain. **1743** J. Morris *Serm.* iii. 74 The same spirit of opposition and cruelty animated the Gentiles. **1833** I. Taylor *Fanat.* x. 467 Those exalted motives which should animate virtue. **1877** Mozley *Univ. Serm.* i. 14 The motives which animated that wonderful and mysterious man.

7. To actuate, move, or put in motion (a thing).

1646 Sir T. Browne *Pseud. Ep.* 59 That extreme which is next the earth is animated unto the North, and the contrary unto the South. **1659** Leak *Water-works* 33 The Syphon.. shall make the Air breath forth of it, and animate the two Organ Pipes. **1860** Tyndall *Glac.* ii. §1. 225 Motion.. which animates the bullet projected from the gun.

†**8.** To impart any physical quality or virtue. *Obs.*

1605 Timme *Quersit.* i. iv. 15 Mercurie, sulphur, and salt ..do animate and adorne it with their properties.

animated ('ænɪmeɪtɪd), *ppl. a.* [f. prec. + -ed.] Commonly used as pa. pple of vb. *animate*; but also as equivalent to adj. *animate*.

1. a. Endowed with life; living, alive. ***animated nature***: that portion of Nature which is alive; the animal world.

1534 More *On the Passion* Wks. 1557, 1324/2 Thys is.. not my deade body, but animated and lyuinge with my soule. **1615** Crooke *Body of Man* 608 It is a thing Animated or hauing a life of it owne. **1774** Goldsm. (*title*) History of the Earth and Animated Nature. **1784** Cowper *Task* i. 198 Nature inanimate employs sweet sounds, But animated nature sweeter still. **1858** R. Vaughan *Ess. & Rev.* i. 34 The belief that the heavenly bodies were animated natures.

b. Peopled or 'alive' with living beings.

1827 Montgomery *Pelican Isl.* ii. 106 The expanse of animated waters.

c. *fig.* Of things vividly figured: appearing alive.

1711 Pope *Temp. Fame* 73 Heroes in animated marble frown, And legislators seem to think in stone. **1813** *Theatr. Inquisitor* II. 184 Correct and animated pictures of existing manners..are always gratifying. **1826** Disraeli *Viv. Grey* vi. vi. 345 Mine are all animated pictures. See that cypress, waving from the breeze.

d. Of or pertaining to cinematographic animation or 'moving pictures', esp. to cinema cartoons.

[**1895** *Cassell's Fam. Mag.* Mar. 320/1 The handle is turned..so as to move the series of photographs rapidly past the eyes, and give the impression of a single animated portrait.] **1897** C. M. Hepworth *Animated Photogr.* xii. 93 For animated photograph work it [*sc.* the 'Stigmatic' lens] can be made with an aperture of *f*/2. *Ibid.* xiii. 94 On taking animated photographs. **1903** *Westm. Gaz.* 28 Aug. 8/2 The America Cup race will be shown by animated pictures. **1912** [see next]. **1915** *Harper's Wkly.* 11 Dec. 574/3 Even cartoons began to come in—'animated' cartoons, as they are called. **1921** A. C. Lescarboura *Cinema Handbk.* (1922) xiv. 435 The basis of animated cartoons, animated models or so-called mechanigraphs, animated sculpture and so on is the fact that one frame can be exposed at a time with the usual motion picture camera. **1934** *Discovery* Feb. 50/2 The animated picture is that of a continuously repeated cycle of effects. **1935** R. Macaulay *Pers. Pleasures* 135 There is a news reel on;..troops walk past with that jerky gait peculiar to animated photography. **1960** *Times* 11 Feb. 3/4 Up to about 1950 the animated film all over the world was dominated by the influence of Disney.

2. Full of the activity and motion of life; enlivened, quickened; spirited; lively, vivacious.

1585 Abp. Sandys *Serm.* (1841) 63 The little cubs perhaps are animated by reason of their wiliness. **1708** Pope *St. Cecilia's Day* 28 Warriors she fires with animated sounds. **1824** Dibdin *Libr. Comp.* 99 Barbier's animated and excellent account of it. **1855** Prescott *Philip II*, I. ii. x. 254 The discussion was animated. **1859** Reeve *Brittany* 236 The scene was one of the most animated we had met with.

3. Mentally moved or excited; inspired, actuated, incited, encouraged. (Now mostly participial.)

1532 More *Confut. Tindale* Wks. 1557, 512/1 Anymated and instructed..with his owne spirite. **1614** Raleigh *Hist. World* II. v. iv. §1. 502 They departed home rich, and well animated to returne agayne. **1660** Milton *Free Commw.* 445 The Menaces, the Insultings of our newly animated common enemies. **1740** Somerville *Hobbinol* ii. 194 Incens'd With animated Rage. **1816** Scott *Old Mort.* 100 Desperate men, animated by the presence of two or three of the actors in the primate's murder. **1850** Smiles *Self Help* ii. 41 He worked..animated by the determination to excel.

†**4.** Endowed with some active physical property. *Obs.*

1706 Phillips, *Animated needle*, is one touch'd with a Loadstone. **1751** Chambers *Cycl.*, *Animated mercury*, quicksilver impregnated with some subtile and spirituous particles, so as to render it capable of growing hot when mingled with gold.

†**5.** Pertaining to animated beings; animal. *Obs.*

1753 Chambers *Cycl. Supp.* s.v., A system of animated pathology.

'animatedly, *adv.* [f. prec. + -ly².] In an animated manner, with animation; vividly, vivaciously, keenly.

1784 J. Barry *Lect. Art* iv. (1848) 158 That beautiful variety of..love, and reverence, which are so animatedly expressed. **1836** *Blackw. Mag.* XL. 806 Animatedly descriptive and devotional. **1876** G. Meredith *Beauch. Career* I. xvii. 252 Watching the ship's progress animatedly. **1882** J. Hawthorne *Fort. Fool* i. xix, He was talking animatedly.

'animateness. ? *Obs.*—⁰ [f. animate *a.* + -ness.] 'The state of being animated.' J.

1731 in Bailey; whence in Johnson.

'animater. [f. animate *v.* + -er¹.] = animator.

1831 De Quincey *Klosterheim* (1855) 34 He had been the chief combiner and animater of the Imperial party.

animating ('ænɪmeɪtɪŋ), *ppl. a.* [f. as prec. + -ing².] Life-giving, quickening, vivifying; enlivening, inspiring, encouraging; rendering life-like.

1680 in *Roxb. Bal.* (1883) IV. 547 Bring me a man with animating stroaks, Whose pregnant Steel gives life to formless rocks. **1727** Thomson *Summer* 168 From him they draw their animating fire. **1782** Miss Burney *Cecilia* i. vii. (1783) 88 So animating are the designs of disinterested benevolence. **1860** Tyndall *Glac.* i. §25. 182 The talk was incessant and animating. **1869** Seeley *Lect. & Ess.* i. 18 No new animating principle.

'animatingly, *adv. rare.* [f. prec. + -ly².] In an animating manner; so as to give life, inspiration, enlivenment, or encouragement.

1850 Anderson *Regen.* (1871) 99 How tenderly and animatingly it consoles and encourages! **1871** Morley in *Athenæum* 1 Apr. 398 Whose words and ideas spring up incessantly and animatingly within us.

animation (ænɪ'meɪʃən). [ad. L. *animātiōn-em*, n. of action f. *animā-re*: see animate.] The action of animating, or state of being animated.

†**1. a.** The action of imparting life, vitality, or (as the sign of life) motion; quickening, vitalizing. *Obs.*

1597 J. King *Jonah* xxvi. (1864) 167 Such as are strengthened by the arm and animation of God, his waves. **1623** Howell *Lett.* I. xxix, The fourth act that goeth to make man, is called Animation. **1721** Bailey, *Animation*, the informing an animal body with a soul.

b. *fig.*

1605 Bacon *Adv. Learn.* ii. xxiii. §49 (1873) 251 The administration, and (as I may term it) animation of laws.

2. The state of being animate or alive, animateness, vitality. ***spirit of animation***: see animal spirits. *arch.*

1615 T. Adams *Leaven* 116 Men of our own flesh, of the same animation with ourselves. **1678** Cudworth *Intell. Syst.* 169 Aristotle himself held the Worlds Animation, or a Mundane Soul. **1733** G. Cheyne *Eng. Malady* i. x. §1 (1734) 90 Mere Mechanism..can never account for Animation, or the animal life even of the lowest Insect. **1794** E. Darwin *Zoon.* (1801) I. 37 The spirit of animation is the immediate cause of the contraction of animal fibres—it resides in the brain and nerves. **1818** Mrs. Shelley *Frankenst.* (1865) iii. 58 Capable of bestowing animation upon lifeless matter. **1837** *Penny Cycl.* IX. 159/2 A case of suspended animation in a seaman who had..fallen into the sea.

†**3.** Representation of things as alive. *Obs. rare.*

1681 Hobbes *Rhet.* iii. ix. 114 Animation is that expression which makes us seem to see the thing before our eyes.

4. The action of filling with liveliness, enlivenment; enlivening operation or influence.

1818 Scott *Rob Roy* 93 The animation of the chase and the glow of the exercise. **1820** Shelley *Prom. Unb.* iv. i. 322 Ha! the animation of delight Which wraps me.

5. Liveliness of aspect or manner; vivacity, sprightliness, brightness.

1790 Boswell *Johnson* xxiv. 213 Johnson was in high spirits..talked with great animation and success. *a* **1817** Miss Austen *Mansf. Pk.* (1851) 62 She discussed the possibility of improvements with much animation. **1839** Hallam *Hist. Lit.* i. viii. §28 The substitution of the anapæst for the iambic..gives them [ballads] a remarkable elasticity and animation. **1863** Mary Howitt tr. *Bremer's Greece* I. i. 15 Little fishing-boats on the water gave animation to the scene.

†**6. a.** The action of inspiring or filling with any impulse; inspiration. *Obs.*

1613 Daniel *Hist. Eng.* 135 [The legate] now by the Kings animation, presumes more peremptorily to vrge them. **1664** H. More *Myst. Iniq.* 286 She by her counsel and animation stirs up the Seven-headed Beast to this Murther.

†**b.** *esp.* Inspiration with courage, encouragement.

1616 R. C. *Times' Whistle* (1871) 111 A great animation of my subsequent endeavours. **1680** H. More *Apocal. Apoc.* 303 An intimation and animation to us to follow his example.

†**7.** The imparting of any physical quality or virtue. *Obs. rare.*

1605 Timme *Quersit.* ii. xli. 117 We are now speaking of the animation of gold. **1667** *Phil. Trans.* II. 604 The animation of the Voyce of Man by his Masculine and Generative power.

8. *Cinemat.* The production of 'moving pictures'; the technique by means of which movement is given, on film, to a series of drawings (*esp.* for an animated cartoon). (See quot. 1959.)

1912 F. A. Talbot *Moving Pictures* i. 7 What we describe as animated photography is not animation at all. All that happens is that a long string of snap-shot photographs..are passed at rapid speed before the eye. **1919** A. C. Lescarboura *Behind Motion-Picture Screen* xvi. 302 The animation of a picture calls for a large number of separate drawings. **1958** *Observer* 9 Mar. 8/5 Commercial television has brought a boom in animation, with comic men and goofy animals bouncing out from everywhere. **1959** Halas & Manvell *Technique Film Animation* 336 *Animation*, the art of giving apparent movement to inanimate objects. The word is also used for the sequence of drawings made to create the movement, and for the movement itself when seen on the screen.

animatism ('ænɪmətɪz(ə)m). [f. animat(e *a.* + -ism.] The ascription of psychic qualities to inanimate as well as animate objects. So **anima'tistic** *a.*

1900 R. R. Marett in *Folk-Lore* June 171 It is Animism in the loose sense of some writers, or, as I propose to call it,

Animatism. **1910** *Encycl. Brit.* II. 53/1 The term [animism] is often extended to include panthelism or animatism, the doctrine that a great part.. of the inanimate kingdom, as well as all animated beings, are endowed with reason.. identical with that of man. *Ibid.*, One portion of the savage explanation of nature may have been originally animistic, another part animatistic. **1940** HINSIE & SHATZKY *Psychiatric Dict.* 33/2 Animatism.. is vividly exemplified.. in schizophrenic subjects, who often personify the whole of the inanimate world, as if the latter possessed the same mental qualities as human beings do. **1941** R. R. MARETT *Jerseyman at Oxford* xi, It reminds me of an occasion long ago when Andrew Lang and Count Goblet d'Alviella were engaged in public and printed controversy over the meaning of my term 'animatism'—one of which, by the way, I am rather ashamed as a verbal impropriety though it has happened to become current. **1952** *Theology* LV. 75 The evidence as to the chronological sequence in which animatism precedes animism is conflicting.

animative ('ænımeıtıv, -ətıv), *a. rare.* [f. L. *animāt-* ppl. stem of *animā-re* (see prec.) + -IVE.]

1. Having the faculty of animating; enlivening, quickening.

1755 in JOHNSON. **1799** J. CORRY *Sat. View Lond.* (1803) 97 The animative inspiration of His Spirit will renovate the love of religion in the hearts of many.

†**2.** ? Relative to animate beings. *Obs. rare.*

1792 T. TAYLOR *Comm. Proclus* I. Introd. 94 There are five orders of numbers, the divine, the essential, the animative, the natural, and the mathematic.

†**animatograph** (ænı'mætəʊgrɑːf, -æ-). *Obs.* [Hybrid f. L. *animātus* ANIMATE *a.* + -GRAPH.] An early name for the cinematograph; also, a cinematographic camera. Also *fig.* in reference to literary description. Hence †**animatographic** (-'græfık) *a.*

1896 *Daily News* 26 Mar. 3/6 At a neighbouring house we have the 'cinematographe', and by way of varying the title Mr. Paul calls his pictures the 'Animatographe'. **1897** *Westm. Gaz.* 5 Feb. 7/1 Animatographic Records for British Museum.... Photographs taken for the purpose of the animatograph, or theatregraph, as it is variously called. **1897** *Ibid.* 25 Sept. 2/3 The animatographic fight between Fitzsimmons and Corbett. **1898** *Field* 12 Feb. 213/2, I noticed.. a man with an animatograph, and, as there was a good fence to start with, and I know one spill, the photos should not lack animation. **1902** *Westm. Gaz.* 3 Oct. 6/2 Animatograph scenes of life in the Royal Navy.

animator ('ænımeıtə(r)). [a. L. *animātor*, n. of agent f. *animā-re*: see ANIMATE.] **1.** He who, or that which, animates, quickens, enlivens, or inspires.

1635 HEYWOOD *Hierarch.* I. Argt. 3 Of all that liue sole Animator. **1646** SIR T. BROWNE *Pseud. Ep.* (1650) 44 Bodies .. conform themselves to situations, wherein they best unite unto their Animator. **1836** LANDOR *Per. & Asp.* Wks. 1846 II. 428 The nobler animators of this frame, the flesh and blood.

2. *Cinemat.* An artist who produces the original drawings for an animated film; sometimes applied to other persons concerned with the preparation of an animated film.

1919 A. C. LESCARBOURA *Behind Motion-Picture Screen* xvi. 306 After the master artist or animator has indicated the changes from one drawing to the next, his assistants work out the drawings. **1936** A. JENKINSON *America came my Way* xvii. 142 The 'originals' drawn by the animators are traced on to celluloid by the tracers.

‖**animé** ('anıme, 'ænımı), *sb.* [Fr., said to be so called because it often contains so many insects as to be, figuratively, *animé* or *animated*; but according to some a native name.] A name given to various resins; the original, obtained from a West Indian tree (*Hymenæa Courbaril*), much used in making varnish; the others from Africa.

1577 FRAMPTON *Joyfull Newes* II. (1596) 2 They do bring from the Newe Spaine 2 kinds of Rosine, that be both much alike.. the one is called Copall, and the other Anime. **1604** E. G. D'Acosta's *Nat. Hist. Indies* xxix. 288 New Spaine ..[hath] abundance of matter for perfume and physicke, as is the Animé whereof there comes great store. **1751** CHAMBERS *Cycl.*, The eastern gum anime is distinguished into three kinds.. white.. blackish.. pale. **1851** E. FORBES in *Art Jrnl. Catal. Exhib.* II. 6†/2 Many and curious are the gums and balsams of the family; among others, gum-Arabic, tragacanth, animé. **1875** URE *Dict. Arts* I. 190 Gum-animé is sometimes mistaken for amber.

‖**animé** ('anıme), *a. Her.* [Fr. *animé* animated, excited, roused.] In action and showing a desire to fight; having the eyes, etc. of a different tincture from the animal itself.

1731 in BAILEY. **1753** in CHAMBERS *Cycl. Supp.*

animine ('ænımaın). *Chem.* [f. ANIM(AL) + -INE, chem. form.] An organic base obtained from bone oil, and other animal oils.

1863 in WATTS *Dict. Chem.* I. 296.

animism ('ænımız(ə)m). [f. L. *anima* life, soul + -ISM.]

1. The doctrine of the *anima mundi*, upheld by Stahl 1720; the doctrine that the phenomena of animal life are produced by an immaterial *anima*, soul, or vital principle distinct from matter.

1832 *Edinb. Rev.* LV. 472 Discussing the Animism of Stahl. **1864** *Sat. Rev.* 10 Dec. 726/1 All spiritual belief came to be laughed at.. There was no more account of Stahl and 'animism.' Nothing but sheer materialism remained.

2. The attribution of a living soul to inanimate objects and natural phenomena.

1866 *Fortn. Rev.* 15 Aug. 84 The theory which endows the phenomena of nature with personal life might be conveniently called Animism. **1871** TYLOR *Prim. Cult.* I. 45 The animism of the ruder tribes of India. **1877** DAWSON *Orig. World* i. 15 Polytheism.. takes very largely the form of animism.

3. Extended polemically to: The belief in the existence of soul or spirit apart from matter, and in a spiritual world generally; spiritualism as opposed to materialism.

1880 J. RAE in *Contemp. Rev.* Oct. 615 The universality of what Mr. Tylor calls Animism, the belief in spiritual and unseen agencies.

animist ('ænımıst). [f. L. *anima* soul + -IST.]

a. One holding the animism of Stahl. **b.** One who attributes a living soul to natural objects and phenomena. **c.** (Extended polemically to) One who believes in the existence of the soul as distinct from the body, and in a spiritual world generally.

1819 LAWRENCE *Man* iii. (1844) 84 A tribe of animists.. maintained that the soul is the only cause of life. **1864** R. BURTON *Dahome* II. 157 Those rewards and punishments by which, according to the Semitic animist, the balance of good and evil in this life is to be struck. **1866** *Fortn. Rev.* 15 Aug. 84 The Animist may or may not be an idolater.

animistic (ænı'mıstık), *a.* [f. prec. + -IC.] Of or belonging to animism or animists. Hence **ani'mistically** *adv.*, in an animistic manner.

1871 TYLOR *Prim. Cult.* I. 268 Its animistic development [*i.e.* of mythology] falls within a broader generalization still. **1876** *Academy* 4 Nov. 451/1 The animistic religions of the *Naturvölker*, of the Mexicans and Peruvians, and of the Finns. **1880** GOLDW. SMITH in *Atl. Month.* No. 268. 213 The doctrine of the immortality of the soul has become so entangled with animistic fancies. **1881** HUXLEY in *Nature* No. 615. 344 The essence of modern, as contrasted with ancient, physiological science, appears to me to lie in its antagonism to animistic hypotheses and animistic phraseology. **1882** *Jrnl. Anthrop. Inst.* 373 The simple animistic belief in the continued existence of the spirit. **1884** *Brit. Q. Rev.* LXXIX. 439 The doctrine of transubstantiation in the Romish Church.. is the same thing, only that the new element is animistically imparted to the food, instead of being taken from it. **1942** *Mind* LI. 3 Speaking animistically, but obliged by the prestige of science to speak jokingly, 'My car goes when she chooses.'

†**ani'mose**, *a. Obs.*$^{-0}$ [ad. L. *animōs-us*: see ANIMOUS.] = ANIMOUS.

1731 BAILEY, *Animose*, couragious, also stomachful. **1755** in JOHNSON. **1775** ASH, *Animose*, full of spirit, hot, vehement.

†**ani'moseness.** *Obs.*$^{-0}$. = ANIMOSITY.

1731 in BAILEY. **1755** in JOHNSON. **1775** ASH, *Animoseness*, heat, spirit, vehemence of temper.

animosity (ænı'mɒsıtı). Also 5–6 **-te**, 6–7 **-tie**. [a. Fr. *animosité*, f. L. *animōsitātem*, n. of quality f. *animōs-us* spirited; see ANIMOUS.]

†**1.** Spiritedness, high spirit, courage, bravery. *Obs.*

1432–50 tr. *Higden* (1865) I. 61 The cause is for euery thynge is of more animosite and audacite in his vniversalle then his parte parcialle. **1589** PUTTENHAM *Eng. Poesie* (Arb.) 296 It was thought a decent countenance and constant animositie in the king to be so affected. **1658** SIR T. BROWNE *Hydriot.* iv. 66 Confirming his wavering hand unto the animosity of that attempt. *a* **1670** HACKET *Abp. Williams* I. (1692) 20 Such as are of a high-flown animosity affect *fortunas laciniosas*.

2. Excitement of feeling against any one; hostility of mind tending to break out into action, active hatred or enmity.

1605 BACON *Adv. Learn.* II. xxiii. §48 (1873) 249 The natures and dispositions of the people.. their animosities and discontents. **1664** HEYLIN *Laud* II. 349 To foment those animosities.. raised in that nation against the King. **1660** in Somers's *Tracts* II. 168 To forget what is past, and lay aside all Animosities for the future. **1674** OWEN *Holy Spirit* (1693) 204 Forming new Parties and reviving old Animosities. **1754** HUME *Hist. Eng.* ii, It is a just remark, that the more affinity there is between theological parties, the greater commonly is their animosity. **1852** MᶜCULLOCH *Taxation* I. ii. 84 The jealousies and animosities that formerly subsisted between the privileged classes and the mass of the people.

†'**animous**, *a. Obs. rare*$^{-1}$. [a. Fr. *animeux*, ad. L. *animōs-um* spirited, f. ANIMUS.] Spirited, courageous; *also*, hot-tempered.

1620 SHELTON *Don Quix.* II. IV. v. 58 Don Cirongilio of Thracia, who was so animous and valiant. **1775** in ASH.

animus ('ænıməs). No pl. [a. L. *animus* (1) soul, (2) mind, (3) mental impulse, disposition, passion.] **1.** Actuating feeling, disposition in a particular direction, animating spirit or temper, usually of a hostile character; *hence*, animosity.

[**1818** Not in TODD.] **1820** *Ann. Reg. 1819* 74/2 The original design.. was demonstrative of the *animus* of the projectors. **1831** GEN. P. THOMPSON *Exerc.* I. 424 The animus is to impress upon the British soldiery the duty of putting down the liberties of their country. **1840** THACKERAY *Paris Sk. Bk.* (1872) 212 The animus with which the case has been conducted. **1863** I. TAYLOR *Pentateuch* 16 Almost every page.. affords an instance.. of an intense feeling, or, as we say, animus; this is the word we use when a speaker or writer, who is labouring to substantiate a defamation, finds it more than he can do to repress emotions, that are not of the most amiable sort, and which he does not choose to avow. **1864** LOWELL *Biglow P.* Wks. 1879, 264/2 The animus that actuates the policy of a foreign country. **1953** L. EDEL *Henry James, Untried Years* IV. 195 Henry James expressed.. the starch that congealed the blood of some New Englanders, with an often ill-concealed.. animus.

2. *Psychol.* Jung's term for the masculine component of a female personality. Cf. ANIMA.

1923 [see ANIMA]. **1943** *Horizon* VIII. 262 The dominating *animus* peeping through the light-heartedness of the young girl. **1943** H. READ *Educ. through Art* iv. 95 According to Jung, the conscious aspect of the individual's personality.. is balanced.. by a contra-sexual counterpart —that individual's animus (the male counterpart in the case of a woman) or anima (the female counterpart in the case of a man). **1962** J. JACOBI *Psychol. of C. G. Jung* (ed. 6) iii. 111 The animus-possessed woman, opinionated and argumentative, the female know-it-all, who reacts in a masculine way and not instinctively.

†**an-inne**, *prep. Obs. rare*$^{-1}$. [f. AN *prep.* + *inne*, OE. *innan* inside. Cf. *a-bove*, *a-bout*.] Within.

1205 LAY. 5617 Ic inc habbe beiene an-inne mine benden.

anion ('ænaıən). *Electr.* [a. Gr. ἀνιόν (a thing) going up, neut. of pr. pple of ἀνι-έναι to go up, f. ἀνά up + ἰ- go.] An ion carrying a negative charge which moves towards the anode (positive electrode) during electrolysis. Opposed to *cation*. Hence **anion exchange**, ion exchange involving anions; also *attrib.*; so **anion exchanger**, a substance capable of anion exchange. Also **anion-active** *a.*, having an active anion.

1834 W. WHEWELL *Let.* 5 May in I. Todhunter *W. Whewell* (1876) II. 182 If you take *anode* and *cathode*, I would propose for the two elements resulting from *electrolysis* the terms *anion* and *cation*,.. and for the two together you might use the term *ions*. **1834** FARADAY *Res. Electr.* (1849) I. 198, I propose to distinguish such bodies by calling those anions which go to the anode of the decomposing body. **1870** FERGUSON *Electr.* 162 In acids, hydrogen forms the cation, and the acid radical the other constituent, the anion. **1931** S. MATTSON in *Soil Science* XXXI. 325 Cation exchange predominates at high pH values whereas anion exchange predominates at low pH values. **1941** *Industr. & Engin. Chem.* XXXIII. 1271/2 The high-capacity anion-exchange resin was Amberlite IR-4. *Ibid.*, Table I indicates that a practical equilibrium adsorption value is attained with both anion-exchangers after 6-hour contact with either hydrochloric or sulfuric acid. **1946** *Nature* 26 Oct. 585/2 It is well known that the addition of divalent metallic ions greatly enhances the surface-active properties of anion-active detergents. **1963** A. J. HALL *Textile Sci.* vi. 296 Surface active agents or surfactants can be usefully classified into three main groups —*anion-active*, *non-ionic*, and *cation-active*. *Ibid.* 297 All the above surface active types are *anion-active*, that is, the effective hydrophobic component is present in the anion when the substance is dissolved in water and ionises into anions and cations.

Hence **ani'onic** *adj.*, (*a*) of or pertaining to anions; (*b*) = *anion-active*.

1922 *Chem. Abstr.* 3417 Evidence of salt properties is further verified by identity of negative charges with the no. predicted for the periodic group in which the anionic metal is found. **1928** *Jrnl. Chem. Soc.* II. 906 It would.. be expected that the tendency to migration of different potentially mobile anions (X) contained in systems otherwise identical would follow the order of anionic stability. **1948** *Q. Rev.* (*Chem. Soc.*) II. 312 Although there are many examples of systems in which cationic exchange is known to take place, there are relatively few reports of the anionic exchange. These are almost all in the field of inorganic chemistry. The term 'anionic exchanger' is often applied, however, to materials which absorb acid molecules from aqueous solution. **1950** *Thorpe's Dict. Appl. Chem.* X. 800/1 The anion is the active part of the molecule, hence the term anionic agents. The best detergents are in this class. **1962** *Lancet* 26 May 1109/2 The drug slowly exchanges with cations (or anions in the case of anionic drugs) in the lumen of the alimentary tract and is then free to be absorbed.

anionoid ('ænıənɔıd, ə'naıənɔıd), *a. Chem.* [f. ANION + -OID.] Resembling an anion (see quots.).

1925 A. LAPWORTH in *Proc. Manch. Lit. & Philos. Soc.* LXIX. p. xix, Some ions.. are shown to have some properties in common and are termed 'cationoid'... [Some] have other properties in common and are termed 'anionoid'. *Ibid.*, The 'anionoid' properties of ethylenic hydrocarbons are held to be closely related to Thomson's observation that methyl is frequently observed in vacuum tubes with a positive charge, but never with a negative charge. **1936** *Discovery* May 162/2 The function of anionoid and kationoid reagents in ionic reactions. **1943** H. GILMAN et al. *Org. Chem.* (ed. 2) II. xxv. 1859 The terms cationoid and anionoid.. refer to the characteristic acceptor or donor activity of reactive cations or anions. **1953** C. K. INGOLD *Struct. & Mech. in Org. Chem.* v. 203 [Lapworth] likened all reagents either to anions or to cations: an 'anionoid' reagent was one which behaved analogously to an anion, or, as Robinson subsequently expressed it, to an 'active' anion; and a 'cationoid' reagent was one which behaved like a cation, or an active cation. **1958** PACKER & VAUGHAN *Org. Chem.* ii. 57, B is said to be electron-donating, anionoid (anionlike) or nucleophilic.

anio'notropy. *Chem.* [f. ANION + -O + Gr. -τροπία turning.] Tautomerism characterized by the movement of an anion. So **aniono'tropic** *a.*

1928 BURTON & INGOLD in *Jrnl. Chem. Soc.* I. 904 It can be seen in a general way that opposite conditions will prevail in mobile-anion tautomerism (anionotropy). *Ibid.* 905 The effect of groups in promoting anionotropic change. **1941** *Trans. Faraday Soc.* XXXVII. 721 (*heading*) Mechanism and Kinetics of Anionotropic Change. **1942** *Nature* 31 Jan. 128/2 Anionotropic change is, in some respects, similar to prototropic change... In anionotropy we are concerned with the movement of negative groups, and there is evidence that the interconversion may proceed through the intermediate formation of a positive mesomeric ion and a complementary negative ion.

anioyn, early form of ENJOIN: see AN- *pref.* 4.

1340 *Ayenb.* 172 Him penonce to anioynj be þe zenne.

anioynt, early form of ENJOINED, ADJOINED.

c **1325** *E.E. Allit. P.* A. 894 As newe fryt to god ful due & to þe gentyl lombe hit arn anioynt [*ed.* amoynt].

†**anir,** obs. variant of ANIL, indigo.

[**1611** COTGR., *Anir*, the name of an Indian hearbe, vsed much by Dyers.] **1613** *Voy. Guiana* in *Harl. Misc.* III. 173 They in New Spain..have cocheneal, anir, and cotton-wool.

†**a'nired,** *ppl. a. Obs. rare*[−1]. [pa. pple. of vb. **anire*, representing an earlier **a-ire* a. OFr. *aïre-r, -ier*:—late L. *adīrāre* to enrage, f. *īra* anger. See AN- *pref.* 5.] Enraged, angry.

1330 R. BRUNNE *Chron.* 151 He sauh Richard anired.

aniridia (ænaɪə'rɪdɪə, -ɪ'rɪdɪə). *Path.* [mod.L., f. Gr. ἀν- (AN- 10) + ἰριδ-, ἶρις IRIS + -IA.] Traumatic or congenital absence of the iris. Cf. IRIDEREMIA.

1860 in MAYNE *Expos. Lex.* Suppl. **1885** *Ophthalmic Rev.* IV. 247 *Congenital Aniridia.* Mr. Lang showed a mother and son in both of whom the iris on both sides was totally deficient. **1961** *Lancet* 22 July 170/2 Traumatic subtotal aniridia in which 60% of the iris is missing. *Ibid.* 171/1 This technique [for implanting an artificial iris] might be applicable not only to cases of *traumatic* aniridia but also to ..cases of *congenital* aniridia.

anis-, *Chem.* Comb. form of L. *anīs-um*, anise, forming names of numerous organic compounds derived from oil of anise, the derivation and meaning of which are usually readily apparent from those of their second element. As **'anisal,** short for *anisic aldehyde.* **'anisa,lyl,** the hypothetical radical of anisic alcohol. **'anisa,mate,** a salt of anisamic acid. **ani'samic** acid or **'anisa,mide,** an acid amide of anisyl, $C_8H_9NO_3$. **'anisa,mine,** an amic base of the same, $C_8H_{11}ON$. **,ani'sanilide** = *phenyl-anisamide.* **'anisate,** a salt of anisic acid. **anisic** (æ'nɪzɪk) *a.*, of or derived from anise, as in *anisic series, anisic acid* $C_8H_8C_3$, *anisic alcohol* $C_8H_{10}O_2$, *anisic aldehyde* $C_8H_8O_2$, etc. **'anisi,dine** = methyl-phenidine C_7H_9NO, a peculiar organic base. **'anisine** $C_{24}H_{24}N_2O_3$, an alkaloid formed by the action of ammonia upon hydride of anisyl. **'anisoate,** a salt of anisoic acid. **ani'soic** *a.* [modified f. *anisic*], of or derived from the star-anise (see ANISE 3), as in *anisoic acid*, 'a product of the oxidation of oil of star-anise' (Watts). **'anisoin,** a white inflammable solid, apparently isomeric with anise-camphor. **'anisol** [see -OL], a colourless very mobile liquid, C_7H_8O, with pleasant aromatic smell, formed by the action of caustic lime or baryta on anisic acid, also called *phenate of methyl*; whence **ani'solic** (acid), **'aniso,late, 'aniso,lide. 'anisyl,** the hypothetical radical, $C_8H_7O_2$, of the anisic series. **ani'sylic** *a.*, of anisyl.

1863 WATTS *Dict. Chem.* I. 303 Anisic alcohol, *hydrate of anisalyl. Ibid.* 296 The only anisamate that has been analysed is the *silver-salt. Ibid.* 297 Anisamine crystallises in small needles. *Ibid.* 300 The general formula of the anisates is $C_8H_7MO_3$. *Ibid.* 300 Cahours prepares anisic acid by boiling oil of anise with nitric acid. *Ibid.* 303 Anisic alcohol crystallises in hard white shining needles. *Ibid.* 304 Anisidine passes over in the form of an oil which solidifies on cooling. *Ibid.* 299 Anis-hydramide..is converted into an isomeric alkaloid, to which the name *anisine* has been given. *Ibid.* 305 Anisol is a colourless, very mobile liquid, with a pleasant aromatic smell..Fuming nitric acid acts energetically on anisol, forming three distinct nitro-compounds, Nitranisol, Dinitranisol, and Trinitranisol. *Ibid.* 306 Anisyl..may be regarded as salicyl, $C_7H_5O_2$, in which 1 atom of hydrogen is replaced by methyl. *Ibid.* 307 Hydride of Anisyl = Anisylous acid, Anisic aldehyde, Anisal..a yellowish liquid, with a burning taste, and an aromatic smell, somewhat like that of hay.

‖**anis** (aniː, a'niːs). [Fr. (Sp. *anís*), lit. 'aniseed': cf. ANISE.] A liqueur or wine flavoured with aniseed. Cf. ANISETTE.

[**1841** G. BORROW *Zincali* I. II. iv. 288 Bring the bottle of anise; the señor and the señora must drink a copita.] **1926** E. HEMINGWAY *Fiesta* (1927) xiv. 173 One booth advertised *Anis del Toro.* **1938** 'G. ORWELL' *Homage to Catalonia* ix. 145 Anis, the filthy Aragonese liqueur. **1939** L. MACNEICE *Autumn Jrnl.* vi. 28 A Cambridge don who said with an air 'There's going to be trouble shortly in this country,' And ordered anis, pudgy and debonair, Glad to show off his mastery of the language. **1956** O. WELLES *Mr. Arkadin* I. v. 50 Listening to the braying of donkeys and the songs of the children, drinking *anis* in the deep shadow thrown by a convent wall. **1972** *Bottlers' Year Bk.* 1972–73 291 *Anis*, alcoholic aniseed cordial, alcoholic but usually rather sweet.

anisanthous (,ænaɪ'sænθəs), *a. Bot.* [mod. f. Gr. ἄνισος unequal + ἄνθ-ος flower + -OUS.] Having perianths of different form.

1880 in *Syd. Soc. Lex.*

anisated ('ænɪseɪtɪd), *ppl. a.* [f. assumed vb. **anisate* + -ED: cf. Fr. *aniser, anisé* (Cotgr. 1611).] Mixed or flavoured with aniseed.

1880 in *Syd. Soc. Lex.*

anise ('ænɪs). Forms: 4–5 **anys, -eys, -eis, -ese,** 4–7 **anyse,** 5 **annys, -eys, -es,** 6–8 **annis,** 7 **anis,** 7–8 **annise,** 7– **anise.** [a. Fr. *anis*:—L. *anīsum*, a. Gr. ἄνῑσον, in var. dial. forms ἄνησον, ἄνηθον, ἄνητον, under which the Greeks seem to have included the two plants Anise and Dill. When these were discriminated, the variants *anīsum* and *anēthum* were utilized in Latin to distinguish them. See ANET.]

1. An umbelliferous plant (*Pimpinella Anīsum*), a native of the Levant, cultivated for its aromatic and carminative seeds. Confused by the ancients with the Dill (*Anēthum graveolens*), which was probably the 'anise' of the Bible of 1611, where Wyclif has 'anete' [*v.r.* anese].

oil of anise, the essential oil obtained from aniseed by distillation with water, the source of many important chemical derivatives; see ANIS-.

c **1300** in Wright *Lyric P.* v. 26 The primerole he passeth, the parvenke of pris, With alisaundre thare-to, ache ant anys. **1382** WYCLIF *Matt.* xxiii. 23 That tithen mente, anete [*v.r.* anese], and comyn. [**1526** TINDALE annyse, **1535** COVERDALE anyse, **1611** annise.] **1398** TREVISA *Barth. De P.R.* XVII. x. (1495) 608 Anyse hath the same vertue that Anetum hath and is more swete in sauour. *c* **1400** *Apol. for Loll.* 45 Mynt, aneis, & comyn. **1453** in Heath *Grocers' Comp.* (1869) 422 Comyn and Anneys, yᵉ bale.... iiijᵈ. **1551** TURNER *Herbal.* (1568) 33 Anyse..maketh the breth sweter, swageth payne. **1605** TIMME *Quersit.* I. xiii. 64 The oyles or sulphurs of annis..drive away windinesse. **1693** EVELYN *De la Quint. Compl. Gard.* II. 141 Anis, is propagated only by seed, which is pretty small, and..of a longish Oval Figure. **1861** DELAMER *Kitch. Gard.* 122 *Anise*..whose seeds are much used by distillers to give flavour to cordial liqueurs. **1863** WATTS *Dict. Chem.* I. 297 *Oil of anise* is a neutral, yellowish, somewhat syrupy liquid, possessing a peculiar aromatic smell and taste.

2. *fig.* in allusion to *Matt.* xxiii. 23.

1741 WATTS *Improv. Mind* xiv. §8 (1801) 111 The mint, anise, and cumming, the gestures and vestures, and fringes of religion. **1841** GEN. P. THOMPSON *Exerc.* VI. 288 Knowledge which settles the anise and cummin of Greek accents.

3. Chinese or **star anise,** or **aniseed tree**: a shrub, *Illicium anisātum* (N.O. *Magnoliaceæ*), the fruit of which has the odour, and is used instead, of anise.

1727 BRADLEY *Fam. Dict.*, *Anise* of China or Siberia, is a Seed of about the same Form and Bigness as *Coloquintida.* **1838** *Penny Cycl.* XII. 445 The aniseed tree of China, of which the fruit is..well known in commerce by the name of *Star anise.* **1858** R. HOGG *Veg. Kingd.* 23 The seed vessels are imported from China under the name of *Chinese Anise*.. and from it a great portion of..*Oil of Anise* is obtained.

4. *Comb.*, as ***anise-like***; **anise camphor,** also called Anethol, one of the two constituents of Oil of Anise (see 1), a resinous substance crystallizing at a low temperature in soft, white, lustrous laminæ. Also ANISEED, q.v.

1863 WATTS *Dict. Chem.* I. 297 Anethol or Anise-camphor. **1871** M. COOKE *Fungi* (1874) 86 *Agaricus fragrans* and *A. odorus* have a sweet anise-like odour.

aniseed ('ænɪsiːd). Forms as in prec.

1. a. The seed of the anise, used as a carminative, and in the preparation of Oil of Anise, Spirit of Anise, Anise water, and Anisette.

1398 TREVISA *Barth. De P.R.* XVII. lxxxi. (1495) 653 Some greyne and sede is gendred in plantis wythout coddys: as it faryth in Annes sede. **1440** *Promp. Parv.*, Aneys seede or spyce, *Anetum, anisum.* **1579** LANGHAM *Gard. Health* (1633) 30 For the dropsie, fill an old Cock with Polipody and Anni-seeds, and seethe him well, and drinke the broth. **1621** BURTON *Anat. Mel.* II. iv. I. iii, Such and such plants..have a peculiar vertue to such particular parts, as to the head, Anniseeds, foalfoot, etc. **1727** BRADLEY *Fam. Dict.* s.v. *Anise*, Spanish Aniseed..is the best. **1882** *Chem. & Drugg.* XXIV. 61/1 One pound bottle of oil of aniseed.

b. *attrib.*, as ***aniseed-tree, -water.*** **aniseed ball,** a round, hard sweet flavoured with aniseed.

1698 CONGREVE *Way of World* IV. v, I banish..all aniseed, cinnamon, citron and Barbadoes-waters. **1727–51** CHAMBERS *Cycl.* s.v., In distilling the anise-seed for the oil, there is procured a limpid water called anise-seed water, which has much the same virtues with the oil. **1838** [See ANISE 3]. **1924** 'R. CROMPTON' *William—the Fourth* viii. 125 'Have an aniseed ball?' said Ginger.

2. = ANISETTE. *rare.*

1756 NUGENT *Grand Tour* IV. 204 They sell a great quantity of comfits in Verdun, and particularly their aniseeds are in great reputation. **1855** COSTELLO *Stor. Screen* 122 The air was redolent of gin..but aniseed was preferred by some.

‖**anisette** (ani'zɛt, æ-). [Fr., more fully *Anisette de Bordeaux*, f. *anis* ANISE + *-ette* dim.] A liqueur flavoured with aniseed.

1837 *For. Q. Rev.* XIX. 11 To drink with them a glass of anisette. **1839** L. SARGENT *Temp. T.* 210 The inveterate sipper of anisette. **1860** *All Y. Round* No. 42. 367 Raki, a sort of fiery oily anisette..is drunk with great relish by the Greeks.

aniso-, also (before a vowel) **anis-,** combining form of Gr. ἄνισος unequal, a formative of technical terms, in many cases merely the negatives of corresponding terms in ISO-. The chief are:—

aniseikonia (æ,naɪsaɪ'kəʊnɪə) *Path.* [Gr. εἰκον-, εἰκών image], a defect of vision marked by the presence of unequal images in each eye; so **aniseikonic** (-'kɒnɪk) *a.*, characterized by aniseikonia; **anisobryous** (,ænaɪ'sɒbrɪəs), *a. Bot.* [Gr. βρύειν to swell] = *anisodynamous* below; **anisocoria** (-'kɒrɪə) *Path.* [Gr. κόρη pupil], inequality in the size of the pupils of the eye; **anisocytosis** (-saɪ'təʊsɪs) *Path.* [Gr. κύτος receptacle], abnormal variation in the size of cells, esp. of the red blood corpuscles; **anisodactylic** (æ,naɪsəʊdæk'tɪlɪk), *a. Zool.* [Gr. δάκτυλ-ος finger, toe], unequal-toed (said of those insessorial birds called by Temminck *Anisodactyles*); **anisodynamous** (-'dɪnəməs), *a. Bot.* [Gr. δύναμις strength], growing with greater strength on one side of the axis than the other; **ani'sogamete** *Biol.* [cf. ISOGAMETE], either of two unequal uniting gametes; so **ani'sogamous** *a.*, characterized by **ani'sogamy,** the union of two unequal gametes in reproduction; **anisogynous** (,ænaɪ'sɒdʒɪnəs), *a. Bot.* [Gr. γυν-ή female], having the carpels not equal in number to the sepals; **anisomeric** (æ,naɪsəʊ'mɛrɪk), *a. Chem.* [Gr. μέρ-ος part], not composed of the same proportions of the same elements; **anisomerous** (,ænaɪ'sɒmərəs), *a.* [see prec.], not having equal, or the same number of, parts, unsymmetrical; *esp.* in *Bot.* having unequal numbers of parts in different whorls; **anisometric** (æ,naɪsəʊ'mɛtrɪk), *a.* [Gr. μέτρ-ον measure], of unequal measurement, consisting of unequal or nonsymmetrical parts; **anisometropia** (-mɪ'trəʊpɪə) *Path.* [Gr. μέτρ-ον measure + ὤψ, ὦπα, eye], inequality in the refractive power of the two eyes; **anisometropic** (-mɪ'trɒpɪk), *a. Path.* [see prec.], characterized by anisometropia, unequally refractive; **anisopetalous** (-'pɛtələs), *a. Bot.* [Gr. πέταλον leaf], with unequal petals; **anisophyllous** (-'fɪləs), *a. Bot.* [Gr. φύλλ-ον leaf], with unequal leaves; **anisopterous** (,ænaɪ'sɒptərəs), *a.* [Gr. πτερόν wing], having unequal wings; *esp.* in *Bot.* of fruit, flowers, etc.; **anisostemonous** (æ,naɪsəʊ'stɛmənəs), *a. Bot.* [Gr. στήμων, -ονα, thread, filament, stamen], having the stamens unequal in number to the petals or sepals; **anisosthenic** (-'sθɛnɪk), *a.* [Gr. σθέν-ος strength], of unequal strength; **anisostomous** (,ænaɪ'sɒstəməs), *a. Bot.* [Gr. στόμα mouth], having unequal mouths, as in a calyx or corolla unequally divided; **anisotropal, anisotropous** (-'ɒtrəpəl, -əs) *a.* = ANISOTROPIC; **anisotropy** (-'ɒtrəpɪ), *sb.* [Gr. -τροπία turning], the quality of being anisotropic, æolotropy.

1934 *Dartmouth Coll. Dept. Res. Physiol. Optics*, (*title*) Iseikonic Lenses; lenses to correct *Aniseikonia. **1935** *Amer. Jrnl. Ophthalmol.* XVIII. 1014 (*title*) Aniseikonia—A Factor in the Functioning of Vision. **1961** *Lancet* 22 July 167/2 The patients are..examined on the space eikonometer..which is an ingenious instrument enabling one to test for aniseikonia. **1935** *Amer. Jrnl. Ophthalmol.* XVIII. 1018/2 *Aniseikonic patients who come to the clinic are being tested..after their aniseikonia has been measured and corrected on the ophthalmo-eikonometer. **1944** *Electronic Engin.* XVII. 189 The aniseikonic effect is introduced by using optical systems of different focal lengths. **1847** CRAIG, **Anisobryous.* **1902** *Lancet* 12 July 69/2 The *anisocoria met with in some cases of thoracic aneurysm might be sufficiently explained by unilateral alterations in blood-pressure. **1910** *Practitioner* Apr. 420 Wall and Ainley Walker..have come to the conclusion that the most common cause of anisocoria is unequal blood pressure in the ophthalmic arteries. **1904** STEDMAN *Dunglison's Dict. Med. Sci.* (ed. 23) 64/1 **Anisocytosis*, irregularity in size of associated cells, especially of red blood cells. **1956** *Nature* 17 Mar. 524/1 During the first two weeks of cortisone treatment, the degree of polychromasia and anisocytosis seen in the normal blood picture became increased. **1834** MUDIE *Brit. Birds* (1841) I. 186 Feet..zygodactylic, or yoke-toed, and ..*anisodactylic, or unequal-toed. **1847** CRAIG, **Anisodynamous.* **1891** *anisogamous [see ISOGAMY]. **1901** G. N. CALKINS *Protozoa* 221 No sharp line, however, can be drawn between conjugation in isogamous and anisogamous forms. **1891** HARTOG in *Nature* 17 Sept. 484/1 **Anisogamy*: the union of two gametes differing chiefly in size. **1880** *Syd. Soc. Lex.*, **Anisogynous.* **1864** WEBSTER, **Anisomeric.* **1866** *Treas. Bot.*, **Anisomerous.* **1870** BENTLEY *Bot.* 348 When the number is unequal, the flower is anisomerous. **1868** Dana *Min.* 362 Guarinite Group: Tetragonal. Titanite Group: *Anisometric. **1880** *Syd. Soc. Lex.*, **Anisometropia*, **Anisometropic.* **1880** Gray *Bot. Text-bk.* 396 *Anisopetalous. *Ibid.*, *Anisophyllous, Unequal-leaved; *i.e.* the two leaves of a pair unequal. **1880** *Syd. Soc. Lex.*, **Anisopterous.* **1857** Henfrey *Elem. Bot.* §209 When the number [of stamens] is different [from the number of petals] the flower is *anisostemonous. **1880** *Syd. Soc. Lex.*, **Anisosthenic*, **Anisostomous*, **Anisotropal*, **Anisotropous*, **Anisotropy*.

anisotropic (æˌnaɪsəʊˈtrɒpɪk), *a.* [mod. f. Gr. ἄνισος unequal + τροπικός belonging to turning, f. τρόπος a turning.] Acting in different ways on the ray of polarized light; possessing the power both of right- and left-handed polarization; æolotropic.

1879 Rutley *Stud. Rocks* ix. 77 Minerals..which exhibit double refraction or are anisotropic. **1881** Maxwell *Electr. & Magn.* I. 137 A heterogeneous anisotropic medium.

†**anistoresy.** *Obs. rare*⁻¹. [ad. Gr ἀνιστορησία ignorance of history, f. ἀν-ιστόρητ-ος; f. ἱστορέ-ειν to inquire into.] Inaccuracy as to historical facts.

1660 Stanley *Hist. Philos.* (1701) 92/2 The anistoresie of the unknown Writers of Aristotle's Life, who supposeth him in the seventeenth Year of his Age, to have heard Socrates three Years.

aniuma: see ANHIMA.

ankaramite (æŋkəˈreɪmaɪt). [a. F. *ankaramite* (Lacroix 1916, in *Comptes Rendus* CLXIII. 182), f. *Ankaramy* in Madagascar: see -ITE¹.] A melanocratic basaltic rock (see quots.).

1926 G. W. Tyrrell *Princ. Petrol.* vi. 129 Some basaltic types..need to be distinguished from basalts proper... When augite is the predominant mafic mineral the term *ankaramite* (Ankaramy, Madagascar) is applied. **1933** R. A. Daly *Igneous Rocks & Depth of Earth* xvi. 398 The ankaramites appear to be analogous mixtures of approximately basaltic liquid with concentrated crystals of pyroxene. **1939** *Geogr. Jrnl.* XCIV. 134 Other basic lavas of which ankaramite is one notable type. **1946** *Nature* 3 Aug. 172/1 The commonest rock-type is trachybasalt, accompanied by variations in the ultra-basic direction through olivine-rich trachybasalt and ankaramite to limburgite.

†**anˈkenned, ancende,** *ppl. a. Obs.* 1–2. [f. OE. *án* one + *cenned* born; cf. AKENNED.] Only begotten (L. *unigenitus*).

c **950** *Lindisf. Gosp.* John iii. 18 Forðon ne ȝelefde on noma ðæs ancende sunu Godes. *c* **975** *Rushw. G.* ibid., An-cenda sunu. [*Ags. & Hatton*, acennendan, akennedan.] *c* **1200** Ormin 17002 He wass himm sellf soþ Godd, And Godess Sune ankennedd.

anker (ˈæŋkə(r)). Also 7 **ankor**, 8 **anchor**. [a. Du. (and Ger.) *anker*, of uncert. origin; found also in med.L. as *anceria*, *ancheria*.]

1. A measure of wine and spirits, used in Holland, North Germany, Denmark, Sweden, and Russia. It varies in different countries; that of Rotterdam, formerly also used in England, contains 10 old wine gallons or 8⅓ imperial gallons.

1673 *Pennsylv. Arch.* I. 32 Recᵈ one halfe Ankor of Drinke. **1751** Smollett *Per. Pic.* (1779) I. ii. 10 A few anchors of right Nantz. **1753** Hanway *Trav.* (1762) I. vi. lxxxi. 371, 2 Stakans = 1 anchor; 6 Anchors = 1 hogshead [in Russia]. **1816** *Gentl. Mag.* LXXXVI. ii. 217 The infused water amounts to 2 or 3½ ankers in quantity.

2. A cask or keg holding the above quantity.

?*c* **1750** *Anc. Poems, Bal. etc.* (1846) 180 We'll drink it out of the anker, my boys. **1848** in H. Miller *Ramb. Geol.* x. 384 Wedging them all fast together, like staves in an anker. **1863** W. Baldwin *African Hunt.* 290 The little there was..we transferred most carefully to the anker.

†**3.** As a dry measure of capacity. *Obs.*

1597 Middleton *Wisd. Solom.* Wks. V. 336, I fear me that the acres of my field pass the ankers of my seed.

anker, -as, obs. forms of ANCHOR, -ESS.

†**ˈankerer.** *Obs. rare.*⁻¹. [extended f. earlier *anker*, ANCHOR *sb.*², of comm. gender, by addition of masc. formative -ER, to match the fem. *ankeress*, ANCHORESS.] An anchoret.

1407 N. Thorpe in Foxe *A. & M.* I. 618/1 Ankerers and strange beggers, are licensed..to beguile the people.

ankerite (ˈæŋkəraɪt). *Min.* [Named after Prof. Anker of Styria: see -ITE.] A mineral closely allied to Dolomite, with the magnesia largely replaced by iron, with or without manganese.

1843 Humble *Dict. Geol.*, *Ankerite*, Paratomous limestone ..found in the mines of Styria. **1878** Lawrence *Cotta's Rocks Class.* 50 Ankerite is particularly rich in iron.

ankh (æŋk). Also **ank.** [Egyptian, = life, soul.] A figure resembling a cross, with a loop or ring forming a handle instead of the upper arm: used in ancient Egyptian art as a symbol of life. Also called *crux ansata*. Cf. TAU 2 b.

1888 A. H. Smith *Catal. Engr. Gems Brit. Mus.* 49 In front, Uraeus; beneath, ☥ ānχ and Uraei. **1895** Elworthy *Evil Eye* 279. **1896** T. Wilson *Swastika* 766 The *Crux Ansata*..according to Egyptian mythology, was Ankh, the emblem of Ka, the spiritual double of man. **1910** A. Churchward *Signs & Symb. Primord. Man* xix. 409 The cross on the church of Amba Derho is a form of the Ank-cross. **1961** S. Lloyd *Art Anc. Near East* iv. 125 (*caption*) In his hand he carries two *ankh*, symbols of the resurrection.

ankle, ancle (ˈæŋk(ə)l), *sb.* Forms: 1 an-, oncleow, 2 oncleou, 4 **anclowe, ankel**, 3–5 **anclee**, 5 **ankyl(le**, 6–7 **anckle**, 3– **ancle**, 7– **ankle**, (dial. anclef, -cliff, ancley). [Two forms: (1) OE. *onclé ow* (cf. OFris. *onklef*, Du. *anklaauw*, *enklaauw*, rare OHG. *anchlao*), whence 14th c. *anclee*, and mod. dial. forms; (2) mod. *ankle*, *ancle*, earlier *ankyl*, *ankel* (= OFris. *ankel*, Du. *enkel*, ON. *ökkla* for **ankula*, Dan. and Sw. *ankel*, OHG. *anchala anchal*, *enchil*, MHG., mod.G. *enkel*), not recorded in OE. and prob. taken in ME. from Norse. The latter is the original Teut. form, from root *ank-*, L. *ang-*, to bend, crook; cf. L. *angulus*. The first form is derived from this, but is not completely explained: the Du *anklaauw* appears to assimilate the ending to *klaauw* claw, the OE. *ancléow* may be a weakened form of the same, or the ending may be assimilated to that of *cnéow* knee (*-éow* being a formative, cf. *láréow* teacher).]

1. The joint which connects the foot with the leg; the slender part of the leg between this joint and the calf.

c **1000** *Sax. Leechd.* II. 116 Læt þonne blod under ancleow. *c* **1000** Ælfric *Gloss.* 299 *Talus*, ancléow. *c* **1150** in Wright *Voc.* 87/1 *Talus*, oncleou. *a* **1300** W. de Biblesw. *ibid.* 148 *Kyvil*, ancle [*v.r.* in *Rel. Ant.* II. 79 *Keuil*, ankel]. *c* **1330** *Arth. & Merl.* 5206 In blod he stode..into the Anclowe. *c* **1386** Chaucer *Knt's T.* 802 Vp to the anclee [*v.r.* anclees, ancle⁻³, anches] foghte they in hir blood. **1440** *Promp. Parv.* Ankyl, *Cavilla, Verticillum.* **1535** Coverdale *Ezek.* xlvii. 3 He brought me thorow yᵉ water, euen to the ancles. **1541** R. Copland *Guydon's Quest. Cyrurg.*, The lesser pyt bone..with the other pyt bone makynge the outwarde ancle. **1602** Shaks. *Ham.* ii. i. 80 His stockings foul'd, Vngartred, and downe giued to his Anckle. **1621** Sanderson 4 *Serm.* Ad Pop. (1681) 214 It is never well when the Cobbler looketh above the Ankle. *a* **1732** Gay *Wks.* I. 144 Above her ancle rose the chalky clay. **1812** Henry *Camp. agst. Quebec* 21 Without other accident than the spraining of Lieutenant Steele's ancle. *a* **1821** Keats *Poet. Wks.* (1861) 203 The neatness Of thine ankle lightly turned. **1875** Lubbock *Orig. Civilis.* ii. 56 Hanging things round their necks, arms and ancles. [**1875** Parish *Sussex Dial.* 13 Ancley, ancliff: in East Sussex, 'I have put out my ancliff-bone' = I have sprained my ancle. **1875** *Gl. Lanc. Dial.* 10 'Yore Jack's knockt his anclef out wi' jumpin.' **1881** Mrs. Parker *Oxfordsh. Gl.* 74 Ankley.]

2. *transf.*

1866 Thoreau *Yankee in Can.* i. 6 The sugar maple is remarkable for its clean ankle.

3. *Comb.* and *attrib.*, as ***ankle-bone***, ***-joint***, ***-vein***; also **ankle-bands**, straps passing round the ankles to fasten low shoes or sandals; **ankle-boot**, (*a*) a boot reaching to or a little above the ankle; (*b*) a covering for a horse's ankle, used as a protection; **ankle-deep** *a.* (*adv.*), so deep as to cover the ankles; **ankle-gear**, anything worn round the ankles; **ankle-high** *a.* (*adv.*), so high as to cover the ankles; **ankle-jack**, a jack- boot reaching above the ankles (hence **ankle-jacked** *a.*); **ankle-jerk**, a reflex movement of the ankle-joint produced by tapping the Achilles tendon; **ankle-length** *a.*, of a garment, that reaches down as far as the ankles; **ankle-rings**, rings worn as ornaments round the ankles; **ankle-sock**, a sock reaching to just above the ankle; **ankle-straps** = *ankle-bands*; also low shoes secured by such straps; **ankle-tie** = *ankle-straps*.

1863 Atkinson *Whitby Gloss.*, **Ankle-bands*, strings for the sandals; leathern straps for the shoes. **1398** Trevisa *Barth. De P.R.* v. lvi. (1495) 171 The hele is bounde to the *ancle bone wyth nesshe bondes. **1526** Tindale *Acts* iii. 7 His fete and ancle-bones receaued strength. [So in **1611**.] **1840** *New Monthly Mag.* LVIII. 505 He has no stockings under his *ankle-boots. **1917** G. Frankau *City of Fear* 16 The ankle-boots and the puttees, caked stiff with the Flanders mud. **1936** *Discovery* July 228/2 Many parachutists wear special ankle boots. **1958** J. Hislop *From Start to Finish* 166 *Ankle-boots*, felt or cloth pads made to go round a horse's legs below the knee and fastened with straps. **1764** Harmer *Round Towers* i. xii. 35 The water was *ancle-deep, and in some places half way up the leg. **1784** Cowper *Task* i. 270 Hence, ancle deep in moss and flow'ry thyme, We mount again. **1860** Tyndall *Glac.* i. §18. 133 We stood ankle-deep in snow. **1855** Singleton *Virgil* I. 363 He first Binds to his feet his *ancle-gear of gold. **1757** Lisle *Husb.* 425 The sedgy grass comes up, and grows *ancle-high. **1848** Dickens *Dombey* (1870) I. xv. 313 He changed his shoes and put on an unparalleled pair of *ankle-jacks. **1874** Hardy *Madding Crowd* I. viii. 86 The laced-up shoes called ankle-jacks. **1861** Sala *Tw. round Clock* 203 Its red 'kerchiefed, corduroyed, and *ankle-jacked proprietor. **1888** A. L. Ranney *Lect. Nerv. Dis.* ii. 173 The **ankle-jerk*. If the muscles of the tendo-Achillis be put upon the stretch by flexion of the foot, a blow upon that tendon will cause a similar extension of the foot. **1962** *Lancet* 1 Dec. 1133/2 Ankle-jerks were absent and knee-jerks much reduced. **1836** Todd *Cycl. Anat. & Phys.* I. 151/1 The *ankle-joint, or tibio-tarsal articulation. **1903** *Daily Chron.* 25 July 8/4 *Ankle-length ones [skirts] have gained votaries across the Channel. **1950** H. McCloy *Through Glass* (1951) ix. 89 An ankle-length housecoat. **1850** Layard *Nineveh* iv. 67 The silver *ankle-rings of his favorite wife. **1936** W. Holtby *S. Riding* iv. vi. 262 Her young body, partially covered by pink brassière, trunks, slippers and white *ankle-socks. **1962** V. Nabokov *Pale Fire* 123 In those days growing boys of high-born families wore on festive occasions..sleeveless jerseys, white ankle-socks with black buckle shoes, [etc.]. **1873** E. S. Phelps *Trotty's Wedding Tour* i. 3 Her little *ankle-ties swung tormentingly and carelessly to and fro against the wood-pile. **1923** Kate D. Wiggin *Gard. Memory* 5 Children with brief legs, white stockings, and ankle-ties. **1615** Crooke *Body of Man* 734 The *Saphena* or *ankle vaine.

ankle (ˈæŋk(ə)l), *v.* [f. the sb.] **1.** *intr.* To use the ankles to good effect in cycling (see quot. 1961).

1896 *C.T.C. Monthly Gaz.* July 323/1 How to learn to ankle is a question of some difficulty. **1961** F. C. Avis *Sportsman's Gloss.* 146/1 *Ankle*, to turn the pedal with the foot so that this pushes downwards with the forward stroke, and claws the pedal upwards from the rear, the ankle forming a kind of axis upon which the foot turns.

2. *intr.* To walk, go. *slang.*

1926 Maines & Grant *Wise-crack Dict.* 5/1 *Ankled by*, went by and not riding. **1930** 'I. Hay' & Wodehouse *Baa, Baa, Black Sheep* ii. 49 Let's ankle out of this. **1932** Wodehouse *Hot Water* xv. 243 Ankling into the hospital and eating my grapes with that woman's kisses hot upon your lips.

b. *trans.* To walk in. *poet.*

1949 Dylan Thomas in *Botteghe Oscure* IV. 399 The heron, ankling the scaly Lowlands of the waves.

ankled (ˈæŋk(ə)ld), *ppl. a. rare.* [f. prec. + -ED².] Furnished with ankles; commonly in synthetic compounds, as ***slender-ankled***.

1616 Beaum. & Fl. *Wit at 7 Weapons* i. i, Well ankled, two good confident calves.

anklet (ˈæŋklɛt). [f. ANKLE *sb.* + -LET, after *bracelet*, Fr. *bracelet*.] An ornament (or fetter) for the ankle; an ankle-ring.

1819 Shelley *Cyclops* in *Poet. Wks.* (1904) 795 She was bewitched to see The many-coloured anklets. **1832** Lander *Exped. Niger* III. xviii. 146 These women wore large ivory anklets. *c* **1850** *Christm. Stories* 292 The iron anklets to which our chains had been fastened. **1859** Tennent *Ceylon* II. ix. v. 514 Graceful limbs decorated with armlets, anklets and rings.

ankor, -re, -yr, obs. forms of ANCHOR.

ankorasse, ankress, obs. ff. ANCHORESS.

ankus (ˈæŋkəs). Also **ankush.** [Hindi *ankus*, Pers. *anguzh*, f. Skr. *aṅkuça*.] In India, an elephant-goad. Also *attrib.*

1886 Jacob & Hendley *Jeypore Enamels* 11 The pointed end of the goad..is termed *Ankas* or *Ankush*... It forms part of the *khillat* or 'dress of honour' given by the Maharajah of Jeypore. **1895** Kipling *2nd Jungle Bk.* 128 It was a two-foot ankus, or elephant-goad—something like a small boat-hook. **1951** J. Masters *Nightrunners* vii. 87 Each mahout..brandished his ankus. *Ibid.* 89 Oblivious of the ankus hook driven through her ear.

ankylosaurus (ˌæŋkɪləʊˈsɔːrəs). *Palæont.* [mod.L., f. Gr. ἀγκύλο-ς crooked + σαῦρος lizard.] A cretaceous dinosaur of the group including the genus so called.

1908 B. Brown in *Bull. Amer. Mus. Nat. Hist.* XXIV. 190 *Stereocephalus*..is probably ancestral to *Ankylosaurus*. **1934** *Discovery* July 210/1 The tank-like *Ankylosaurus*, 'the most ponderous animated citadel the world has ever seen', had only to squat tight to defy even *Tyrannosaurus*. **1962** E. Neaverson *Stratigr. Palaeont.* 572 The nodosaurs *Ankylosaurus*, *Dyoplosaurus*..are likewise recorded from both areas.

ankylose, -osis, variants of ANCHYLOSE, -OSIS.

ankylostomiasis (ˌæŋkɪləʊstəʊˈmaɪəsɪs). *Path.* Also **anchylo-**. [mod.L., f. *Ankylostoma* (see below) + -ASIS.] A disease, characterized chiefly by iron-deficiency anæmia, caused by a nematode worm (*Ankylostoma duodenale*, or some similar species) parasitic in the intestines; also called *hook-worm disease*, *tunnel-disease*.

1887 J. D. MacDonald tr. in *Papers Legislative Council Ceylon 1886* No. lvii. 19 By the term anchylostomiasis, we designate the various pathological conditions which arise from the presence of the parasite anchylostoma duodenale in the human intestines. **1889** *Brit. Med. Jrnl.* 21 Sept. 656/2 Sudden death from ankylostomiasis. **1897** *Allbutt's Syst. Med.* II. 1043 The essential symptoms of ankylostomiasis are those of a progressive anæmia associated with symptoms of intestinal catarrh. **1931** J. Arthur Thomson in W. Rose *Outl. Mod. Knowl.* 219 Hookworm disease, or ankylostomiasis.

anlace (ˈænləs, -ɪs). *arch.* Forms: 3 **aunlaȝ**, 4 **anlas, anlaas, anelas**, 5 **analasse**, 4–9 **anlace**, 9 **anelace.** [Used 5 times in Latinized form *anelacius*, *anelatius*, by Matthew Paris, as a vulgar, *i.e.* English word. No traces of it in any continental language. The OWelsh *anglas* (in *Gododin Poem*, Skene *4 Bks. Wales* II. 84, I. 399) is probably the same word, but nothing is known of its formation or origin.] A short two-edged knife or dagger, broad at the hilt and tapering to the point, formerly worn at the girdle. (Obs. bef. 1500, erron. defined in early Dicts., and used loosely by mod. poets.)

[*a* **1259** Matt. Paris (p. 274, in Du Cange) Genus cultelli, quod vulgariter anelacius dicitur.] **1297** R. Glouc. *Chron.*

(1887 Rolls Ser.) 82 þo hii were þoru out imengd·mid suerd & mid mace. Mid ax & mid anlas· so muche folc in þe place. *a* **1300** *Havelok* 2554 Hand-ax, sythe, gisarm, or spere, Or aunlaȝ, and god long knif. *c* **1380** *Sir Ferumb.* 5637 An anlas þo droȝ oute. *c* **1386** CHAUCER *Prol.* 357 An Anlaas [*v.r.* ane-, anlas]..Heeng at his girdel. *c* **1420** *Anturs of Arth.* xxx. 13 Opon his cheueroune be-forn Stode as a vnicorn Als scharpe as a thorn An nanlas of stele. *c* **1440** *Morte Arth.* 1148 Arthur with ane anlace egerly smyttez. [**1656** BLOUNT *Glossogr.*, *Anelate*, a Faulchion or wood-knife, which I gather out of M[atthew] Par[is]. **1678** PHILLIPS, *Anlace* (old word), a Falchion or Sith-fashioned Sword. **1775** ASH, *Anlace*, a short sword, a dagger, a wood-knife.] **1813** SCOTT *Rokeby* v. xv, And by his side an anlace hung. **1812** BYRON *Childe Har.* I. liv, The Spanish maid..the anlace hath espoused, Sung the loud song, and dared the deed of war. **1834** PLANCHÉ *Brit. Costume* 112 The anelace or anelas, a broad dagger tapering to a very fine point.

anlage ('anla:gə). Pl. **anlagen, anlages.** Also with anglicized pronunc. ('ænleɪdʒ) [G., = foundation, basis, f. *anlegen* to establish, f. *an-* on + *legen* LAY *v.*[1]] The rudimentary basis of an organ or organism; in *Embryology*, the first accumulation of cells recognizable as the beginning of a part or organ.

1892 MINOT *Human Embryol.* 432 Comparative anatomy renders it probable that every vertebra had ribs primitively, and most of them have still in the human embryo the anlages of ribs. **1907** DRIESCH *Sci. & Philos. Organism* (1908) I. 81 You will get a complete larva only from that part [of the gastrula] which bears the 'Anlage' of the endoderm. *Ibid.* 112 A leaf may be formed out of the Anlage of a scale, if all the leaves are cut off. **1962** *Lancet* 26 May 1129/1 This does not exclude its potential teratogenous effect in man, where the critical phases of determination of the various organ anlages are probably concentrated in distinct periods.

anlaut ('anlaʊt). *Philol.* [G., f. *an* on + *laut* sound.] The initial sound of a word. So **'anlauting** *ppl. a.*, serving as anlaut, initial.

1881 in *Imp. Dict.* **1884** EINENKEL *St. Kath.* p. xvii, [MS.] Z frequently softens the anlauting *f* to *u*, that is, *v*. Whenever this *u* is no more than a peculiarity of Z's,.. I gave it up for the *f*, which C always has as 'anlaut'. **1892** G. DUNN in *Classical Rev.* Feb. 2/2 This representation of *γ* by *ζ* only occurs with certainty as an anlaut. **1933** *Trans. Philol. Soc.* *1931–2* 28 Many philologists..distinguish between (1) absolute *Anlaut*.., (2) relative *Anlaut*... The first is the position of a sound at the beginning..of a phrase, the second is its position at the beginning..of a word within a phrase.

†**'anlepi,** *a. Obs.* [earlier, and subseq. north. repr. of OE. *ánlepiȝ*, which became in south *onelepi*. It was already in 12th c. reduced to *alpi*, *elpi*, and subseq., *a*, *an* being detached, to *lepiȝ*, LEPI. For full treatment see ONELEPI.] Only, sole, single.

c **1000** *Metr. Ps.* xiii. 2 Nis nan þe eallunga wel do, no forðon anlepe. *c* **1200** ORMIN *Introd.* 11 Þatt anlepiȝ treo þatt himm Drihhtin forrbodenn haffde. *c* **1220** *St. Kath.*, Ane kinges..anlepi dohter. *a* **1300** *Crede* in Maskell *Mon.* II. 240 Jhesu Krist [h]is anelepi sone, hure laverd. *a* **1400** *Rel. Pieces fr. Thornton MS.* 13 Be-twyx ane anlypy man and ane anlypy womane.

†**'anlet.** *Obs.* Also 6 **annlet,** 7 **andlet.** [for earlier *anelet, a. OFr. *anelet*, dim. of *anel* ring:—L. *ānell-us*, dim. of *ānulus*: see also ANNULET.] A small ring, as those used in ring mail.

1557 *Wills & Inv. N.C.* (1835) 415, Vij dosen mens bowstrings ijs.—viij pounde anletts vs. **1598** SYLVESTER *Du Bartas* (1611) 80 One Loadstone-touched annlet doth transport Another Iron-Ring. **1615** LATHAM *Falconry*, Jesses..are fastened to the Hawks legges, and so to the lease by varuels, anlets, or such like. **1660** *Act 12 Chas. II*, Andlets or Males, Babies, or Puppets for children.

†**'anleth.** *Obs.* Forms: 1 **and-, ond-wlita,** 2 **onlete,** 3 **ondlett, -læt, anleth, anneleth.** [OE. *andwlíta*, cogn. w. ON. *andlit* (Sw. *anlete*), OHG. *antluzi*, mod.G. *antlitz* (cf. Goth. *andawleizns*), f. *and* against, facing + *wlítan* to look, behold. The ME. *onlete*, *anleth*, represent the Norse form.] Countenance.

a **800** *Beowulf* 1382 Eorles andwlitan. *c* **975** *Rushw. Gosp.* Matt. vi. 17 Smere þin heafod & þine andwlitu þwah. *c* **1200** *Lamb. Hom.* 59 He makede mon i rihtwisnesse, Onlete on his onlichnesse. *c* **1200** ORMIN 12938 Ure Laferrd let hemm sen Hiss onndlæt. *a* **1300** *E.E. Psalter* xxvi. 9 Ne turne þine anleth me fra. *Ibid.* xliii. 24 Whi tornes þu þine Anneleth?

anli, anlich(e, early forms of ONLY.

†**'anlike,** *a.* and *sb. Obs.* Forms: 1 **anlíc,** 2–4 **anlich,** 4 **anlyk.** [OE. *anlíc*, f. AN- *pref.* 1, on, unto, to, + *líc* body, shape; cogn. w. Goth. *analeik*, ON. *álík*; the latter, with OE. *ȝelíc*, gave ALIKE, LIKE; *anlike* became obs. in 14th c.]

A. *adj.* Like, similar, alike.

c **1000** *Ags. Gosp.* Matt. xiii. 23 Forðam ys heofena rice ánlic ðam cyninge. *c* **1160** *Hatton G.* ibid., Forþam ys heofene riche anlich þan kyninge. **1340** *Ayenb.* 186 Þe oþre þet is him anlich ine kende. *Ibid.* 227 Þet stat makeþ þane þet hit wel lokeþ anlyke to þe angles of heuene.

B. *sb.* [The adj. used absol.; cf. mod. 'his like.'] A fellow-creature; *also*, a likeness or image.

1340 *Ayenb.* 145 Ech best ase zayþ salamouns [*Ecclus.* xiii. 19] loueþ his anliche. *Ibid.* 233 Ine zuyche manyere is Godes anlyche volveld ine manne.

†**an'liken,** *v. Obs. rare.* In 4 **anlykn-y.** [f. prec. adj., with neut. pass. ending -EN, OE. *-nan*, ON. *-na*, Goth. *-non*. Prob. formed analogously, the word not existing in OE. or Norse.]

1. *intr.* To be or become like, resemble.

1340 *Ayenb.* 101 Yef þou art ariȝt zone þou sselt him anlykny. *Ibid.* 91 Þe drope of deawe..anlykneþ to ane stone of pris.

2. In pa. pple. **anlikned:** Made like, likened.

1340 *Ayenb.* 232 The kingriche of heuene is anlikned to ten madines.

†**'anlikeness.** *Obs.* Forms: 1–3 **anlícnes(se, -nys(se,** 2 **onlich-,** 3 **on(n)lic-, anlich-,** 4 **anlik-, anlycnes(se.** [f. ANLIKE *a.* + -NESS.]

1. The quality of being like to; likeness, resemblance, similitude.

a **1000** CÆDMON *Gen.* 1529 (Bosw.) Mon wæs to Godes anlícnesse ǽrest ȝesceapen. *c* **1200** *Pater N.* 88 in *Lamb. Hom.* 59 He makede mon i rihtwisnesse, Onlete on his onlichnesse. *c* **1200** ORMIN 19012 Manness sawle iss lic Wiþþ Godd inn onnlicnesse. *c* **1340** *Ayenb.* 87 Oure riȝte uader..ssop þe zaule to his anlycnesse.

2. *concr.* Anything made in the likeness of some object; a likeness, portrait, image. *spec.* An image of a god, an idol.

c **1000** ÆLFRIC *Gloss.* 304 *Imago* vel *agalma*, anlícnys. *c* **1175** *Cott. Hom.* 227 Hi worhtan ham anlicnessen, sum of golde, sum of selfre. **1205** LAY. 21155 An on-licnes [**1250** anlichnisse] aleore! of drihtenes moder. *c* **1230** *Ancr. R.* 18 To þe oðer onlicnesses and to ower relikes cneoleð.

†**an'maile.** *Obs. rare*[−1]. [? intermed. form between AMEL, *amayle* and *an-amel* EN-AMEL; if not an error for *aumaile*, AMEL q.v.] Enamel.

1600 FAIRFAX *Tasso* xx. xlii. 371 She hit him, where with gold and ritch anmaile, His Diademe did on his helmet flame.

†**'anmod, onmod,** *a. Obs.* 1–3. [OE., f. *án* one + *mód* mood, mind.] Of one mind, unanimous.

a **1000** *Elene* 396 Hie þá ánmóde andswerodon. *c* **1175** *Lamb. Hom.* 101 Þet iferende is swa anmod swulc heom alle an weren on heorte. *c* **1200** *Trin. Coll. Hom.* 183 We ware onmode godes wille to done.

anna ('ænə). Also 8 **annoe,** 9 **ana.** [a. Hind. *ānā*.] An East Indian denomination of money; the 16th part of a rupee.

1727 A. HAMILTON *New Acc. E. Indies* II. App. 8 In Bengal their accounts are kept in Pice, 12 to an Annoe, 16 Annoes to a Rupee. **1770** *Treaty* in *Indian Rec.* (1870) 26 The annual stipend of Rupees thirty-one lakhs, eighty-one thousand, nine hundred, and ninety-one, and nine annas. **1804** COLEBROOKE *Husb. & Comm. Bengal* (1806) 98 The price of this labour may be computed..at two anas per diem. **1858** BEVERIDGE *Hist. India* II. v. vi. 412 These people ..extort the last anna from the ryot. **1959** *Chambers's Encycl.* VII. 448/2 On 1 April 1957 the decimal system came into use [in India] and the rupee was divided into 100 *noye paise* (new paisas) instead of into 16 annas as formerly.

¶ Among Anglo-Indians such expressions are common as 'a 6-anna share (i.e. $\frac{6}{16}$) in an indigo-concern'; '4 annas of dark blood,' (to denote a quadroon), etc.

annabergite (ænə'bɜ:gaɪt). *Min.* [named (in 1852) from Annaberg in Saxony, where found: see -ITE.] A hydrous arsenate of nickel, of a fine apple-green colour, occurring in capillary crystals or as an earthy mass.

1837–68 DANA *Min.* 560.

†**'annal,** *a. Obs. rare.* [ad. L. *annālis*: see ANNALS.] Annual, yearly.

1595 NORDEN *Spec. Brit.* Cornw. (1738) 38 Many votaries made annall pilgrimages vnto it. **1615** HEYWOOD *4 Prentises* I. xiii, Our annall Crownes revenues.

'annal, *sb.*, sing. form of ANNALS.

†**'annal,** *v. Obs. rare.* [f. ANNAL(S *sb.*; cf. to *chronicle*, *fable*.] *trans.* and *intr.* To compose annals, record events in annals, chronicle.

1606 WARNER *Alb. Eng.* XIV. To Reader 331, Stows late antiquarious Pen, That annald for vngratefull Men. **1670** MILTON *Hist. Brit.* Wks. 1738 II. 58 What..Kelwulf the West-Saxon is annal'd to have done against the Scots.

annalism ('ænəlɪz(ə)m). *rare*[−1]. [f. ANNALIST: see -ISM.] Annal-writing, chronicling.

1808 W. TAYLOR in Robberds' *Mem.* II. 222 It is philosophic history in the form of contemporary history, and unites the interest of coeval with the instruction of contemplated annalism.

annalist ('ænəlɪst). Also 7 **analyst, -ist.** [f. ANNAL *sb.* + -IST, or a. Fr. *annaliste*.] A writer of annals, a chronicler of events year by year.

1611 COTGR., *Annaliste*, an Annalist; a writer of yearely Chronicles. *a* **1623** SIR G. BUCK *Rich. III* (1646) 77 The weaker analysts and chroniclers. **1644** EVELYN *Mem.* (1857) I. 114 In it is buried Cæsar Baronius, the great annalist. *a* **1683** OLDHAM *Wks. & Rem.* (1685) 15 Of which dull Annalists in story tell. **1811** J. GRANT *Hist. Eng. Ch.* I. 296 The annalists wrote the records of the year. **1858** BUCKLE *Civil.* (1869) II. vii. 421 The historian sinks into the annalist ..instead of solving a problem, he merely paints a picture.

b. *ellipt.* and *transf.*

1642 HOWELL *For. Trav.* (Arb.) 23 The manner and method in reading of Annalists. **1660** (*title*) The Faithful Analist or Epitome of the English History..to this present Yeer 1660. **1748** HARTLEY *Observ. Man* II. ii. ¶24 Learned Men who had spent their Lives in the Study of Annalists.

annalistic ('ænəlɪstɪk), *a.* [f. prec. + -IC.] Of or proper to the annalist; characterizing annals.

1850 MERIVALE *Rom. Emp.* lix. VI. 560 The author [Tacitus] preserving strictly the annalistic form. **1860** ELLICOTT *Lect. Life of Our Lord* (1862) 6 The divine harmonies of our Master's life become lost in mere annalistic detail.

annalistically (ænə'lɪstɪkəlɪ), *adv.* [f. ANNALISTIC *a.*: see -ICALLY.] In annalistic order; by way of annals.

1881 FREEMAN in Stephens *Life & Lett.* (1895) II. 222 The years 1088–1093 are easy to tell, almost annalistically. **1894** *Academy* 24 Feb. 164/2 Chronologically and annalistically arranged.

†**'annalize,** *v. Obs. rare.* [f. ANNAL *sb.* + -IZE.] To record in annals, to chronicle.

1616 SHELDON *Rom. Miracles* 332 (T.) The miracle, deserving a Baronius to annalize it. **1629** GAULE *Pract. The.* 64 Jesus Christ..his Generation..annalized by Yeeres.

annals ('ænəlz), *sb. pl.* [ad. L. *annāl-es* the historical record of the events of each year, prop. masc. pl. (sc. *librī*) of *annālis* yearly, f. *annus* year. Occas. used in sing.]

1. A narrative of events written year by year.

1563 GRAFTON *Epist. to Cecil* (R.) Short notes in maner of Annales commonly called Abridgementes. **1607** SHAKS. *Cor.* v. vi. 114 If you haue writ your Annales true, 'tis there. **1622** HEYLIN *Cosmogr.* Introd. (1674) 17/2 Annals..are a bare recital only of the Actions happening every year. **1759** ROBERTSON *Hist. Scotl.* I. I. 1 Everything beyond that period to which well-attested annals reach is obscure. **1867** STUBBS *Benedict's Chron.* Pref. I. 12 The difference between chronicles and annals was..that the former have a continuity of subject and style, whilst the latter contain the mere jottings down of unconnected events.

b. *sing.* The record or entry of a single year, or a single item, in a chronicle.

1699 BENTLEY *Phal.* 282 Diodorus in the Annal of that year, says Phæon was Archon. **1814** SIR R. WILSON *Pr. Diary* II. 309 A modest inscription to record the act of restoration..an annal which the greatest anti-Buonapartist ought to respect. **1865** EARLE *Sax. Chron.* Introd. 10 Here and there may be seen an annal, expressed in riper language, which must be marked as the interpolation of a later Editor.

c. *attrib.* quasi-*adj.*

1670 MILTON *Hist. Eng.* IV. Wks. 1851, 175 Huntingdon, as his manner is to comment upon the annal Text, makes a terrible description of that fight.

2. Historical records generally.

a **1581** CAMPION *Hist. Irel.*, *Ep. Ded.* (1633) 1 Containing Annales and other worthy memorialls. *a* **1687** PETTY *Pol. Anat.* Ded., An Adventure that shall shine in the Annals of Fame. **1706** ADDISON *Rosamond* III. i, Whatever glorious and renowned In British annals can be found. **1750** GRAY *Elegy* viii, The short and simple annals of the poor. **1844** DISRAELI *Coningsby* VI. ii. 226 The glorious annals of their great country. **1878** C. STANFORD *Symb. Christ* i. 5 The first war recorded in the annals of the human race.

3. Masses said for the space of a year.

1536 LATIMER *2nd Serm. bef. Conv.* I. 52 No priest should sell his saying of tricennals or annals. **1726** AYLIFFE *Parerg.* 190 *Annals* are Masses said in the Romish Church for the Space of a Year, or for any other Time, either for the Soul of a Person deceas'd, or for the Benefit of a Person living.

Annamese (ænæ'mi:z), *a.* and *sb.* Also 9 **Anamese.** [f. *Annam* (see below) + -ESE.] **A.** *adj.* Of or pertaining to Annam, a province of Vietnam, or its inhabitants. **B.** *sb.* **a.** An inhabitant of Annam. **b.** The language of Annam.

[**1808** *Asiatick Researches* X. 267 The Anam language has neither genders, numbers, nor cases.] **1826** J. CONDER *Modern Traveller: Birmah* [etc.] 322 Adrian..was interred ..with all the pomp and ceremonies prescribed by the Anamese religion. *Ibid.* 332 The Anamese employ several sounds..which are incapable of being pronounced by a Chinese. **1862** R. G. LATHAM *Elem. Compar. Philol.* ix. 61 The collective name for them is Anam, or Annam; whence we get the adjectives Anamese or Anamitic. **1867** W. D. WHITNEY *Lang. & Study of Lang.* ix. 336 The principal nations of Farther India are the Annamese or Cochin-Chinese, the Siamese, and the Burmese... Annamese culture is of Chinese origin. **1875** —— *Life & Growth of Lang.* xii. 239 The various languages of Farther India—as the Annamese or Cochin-Chinese, the Siamese, and the Burmese. **1910** *Encycl. Brit.* II. 62/1 The Annamese language is composed of monosyllables. **1910** G. M. VASSAL *On & Off Duty in Annam* viii. 134 The birth of a son.. confers a celestial benediction on an Annamese. **1931** H. G. WELLS *Work, Wealth & Happiness of Mankind* (1932) vii. 278 It is a description of brutal compulsion and unhappiness, inflicted in this case upon Annamese victims. **1932** W. L. GRAFF *Lang. & Languages* xi. 417 Annamese, spoken along the eastern coast of Tonkin. **1933** H. G. WELLS *Bulpington* ix. 349 All these poor devils from the ends of the earth, Polynesians, Annamese, Coolies, Gurkhas.

Annamite ('ænæmaɪt), *a.* and *sb.* Also 9 **Anamite.** [f. as prec. + -ITE.] = ANNAMESE *a.* and *sb.* Hence (now rare) **Anna'mitic** *a.* [cf. mod.L. *Annamiticum* (A. De Rhodes, *Dictionarium Annamiticum* 1651)].

1838 P. S. DU PONCEAU *Diss. Nature & Char. Chinese Syst. Writing* I. vii. 87 Of one of them only, a dictionary and a short grammar exists in Europe. It is the Anamitic, or, as some write it, Annamitic, the language of the country of Anam. **1847** *Jrnl. Indian Archipelago* I. 112 The Anamite language is monosyllabic. *a* **1861** H. MOUHOT *Trav. Central Parts Indo-China* (1864) I. vii. 205 My Annamite was with me, and filled the office of interpreter. **1862** [see prec.]. **1877** *Trans. Philol. Soc. 1875–6* 83 Cambojan..has loan-words from Malay, Pali, Annamite, and Mon. *Ibid.* 84 Every town has at least four names, being known under a different combination of syllables by the Siamese, Annamites, Cambojans and Savage peoples. **1910** G. M. VASSAL *On & Off Duty in Annam* 1 The 'Annamitic Chain' expands in North Tongking, traverses Annam, where the highest peaks ..are to be found. **1921** E. SAPIR *Language* 205 Chinese has flooded the vocabularies of Corean, Japanese, and Annamite for centuries, but has received nothing in return. **1936** *Times Lit. Suppl.* 14 Nov. 915/4 The presence of black Senegalese and yellow Annamite troops.

† **'annary.** ? *nonce-wd.* [f. L. *ann-us* a year + -ARY; cf. *di-ary, itiner-ary.*] A history or record of the events of each year; an annual record.

1662 FULLER *Worthies* II. 111 Having since received an exact Annarie (as I may so say)..of his life.

annates ('æneɪts, -əts). Also 6 **annatys**, 6–8 **annats.** [a. Fr. *annate* (15th c.), ad. med. and late L. *annāta* a year's space, work, proceeds, the same word which in its primary sense became in Fr. *année.* See -ATA.] The first-fruits, or entire revenue of one year, paid to the Pope by bishops and other ecclesiastics of the R.C. Church on their appointment to a see or benefice.

At the Reformation the right to the annates of English benefices was transferred to the Crown; in the reign of Anne they were given up to form a fund for the augmentation of poor livings, known as Queen Anne's Bounty.

1534 *Act 25 Hen. VIII*, xx, It is ordained..that the paiments of the Annates or first fruits..[shall] vtterly cease. **1538** STARKEY *England* I. iv. §63 No just cause wy thes annatys schold be payd to Rome. **1621** HOWELL *Lett.* (1650) I. 55 These cardinals..have the annats of benefices to support their greatness. **1756** NUGENT *Grand Tour* IV. 11 The pope afterwards grants his bulls of consecration, and receives the annates or first fruits. **1856** FROUDE *Hist. Eng.* I. 334 The payment of annates..had originated in the time of the crusades, as a means of providing a fund for the holy wars.

2. *Sc. Law.* A half-year's salary, which, in addition to the ordinary stipend from his incumbency, is legally due to the executors of a deceased minister.

1571 *Act Jas. VI* (1814) 63 (JAM.) The annet thareaftir to pertene to thame, and thair executouris. **1708** CHAMBERLAYNE *St. Gt. Brit.* II. II. iii. (1743) 354 The widow, children, and nearest kin to the Defunct [minister] have a right by act of parliament to an annate, i.e. half a year's stipend over and above what is due for his Incumbency.

annatto, annotta, annotto, varr. ANATTA.

anneal (ə'niːl), *v.* Forms: 1 **onælan (anælan)**, 2 **onealen, anhelen,** 4–5 **anele,** 5 **enele,** 5–7 **aneal(e,** 6 **hanele,** 7 **anneile, eneal,** 7– **anneal.** *Aphet.* 8 **neal.** [In senses 1, 2, f. AN- *pref.* 1 on + OE. *ǽlan* to set on fire, burn, bake (tiles, etc.). There seems no reason why the later senses should not have sprung directly from this, the transition being simple from the baking of tiles, fusing of minerals (both senses of OE. *ǽlan*, and early ME. *anele*), to the burning of a glaze or enamel upon the surface of pottery, glass, or metals; and from this to the hardening, toughening, or tempering of the surface of such substances, as in modern use. But the former of these Mätzner derives from OFr. *neeler, nieler*, to enamel, originally to enamel in black upon gold or silver:—med.L. *nigellāre*, f. *nigellum*, dim. of *nigrum* black. Although there is no OFr. *a-neeler*, and no ME. *neele, nele*, so that the formal connexion of *neeler* and *anneal* is not established, it is possible that the native *anele* may have been viewed as the representative of Fr. *neeler*, and modified in sense accordingly.]

† **1.** To set on fire, kindle, inflame. *lit.* and *fig. Obs.*

a **1000** *O.E. Chron.* 694 (Bosw.) Mid andan þære rihtwisnesse anæld. *a* **1000** *Sol. & Sat.* 42 þæt Pater Noster ádwæsceð déofles fýr, dryhtnes onæleð. *c* **1175** *Lamb. Hom.* 97 He mid his bleade onealde eorðlichen monnan heortan. *Ibid.* 219 *Seraphim* birninde oðer anhelend.

† **2.** To subject to the action of fire; to alter in any way with heat; as, to 'fire' or bake earthenware, fuse ores, vitrify or glaze a surface. *Obs.*

1393 GOWER *Conf.* III. 96 So as the fire it hath aneled [vitrified] Lich unto slime, which is congeled. **1440** *Promp. Parv.*, *Anelyn*, or *enelyn* metalle, or other lyke. *c* **1465** *Bk. Quintess.* 7 Take þe calx of fyn gold..and putte it in a siluer spone, and anele it at þe fier. **1668** in *Phil. Trans.* III. 769 If they cannot cut the Rock, they use fire to aneale it.

3. To burn in colours upon glass, earthenware, or metal, to enamel by encaustic process. *arch.*

1580 BARET *Alv.* A 382 He that doth Aneale pottes or other vessels, *Inustor.* **1601** HOLLAND *Pliny* XI. xxxvii, Some paint and die them..others vernish and anneile them. **1633** G. HERBERT *Windows* ii. in *Temple* 59 When thou dost anneal in glasse thy storie. **1697** POTTER *Antiq. Greece* III. xv, Nor were they barely varnish'd over with them [colours], but very often anneal'd by Wax melted in the Fire.

4. a. To toughen anything, made brittle from the action of fire, by exposure to continuous and slowly diminished heat, or by other equivalent process.

1664 EVELYN *Sylva* 103 They use them amongst divers Artificers..to temper, and aneal their several Works. **1749** *Phil. Trans.* XLVI. 180 How comes it that the glass..when it has been nealed, it does not break? **1870** F. POPE *Telegraph* ii. (1872) 21 The iron cores, as they are termed, of electro magnets, should be annealed with great care. **1881** *Mechanic* §1439 It [steel] must be 'tempered' or partially annealed.

b. *loosely*, To cool down from a great heat.

1859 M. SCOTT *Cringle's Log* x. 220 You have been wasted one moment by the vertical rays of the sun and the next annealed hissing hot by the salt sea spray.

c. *transf.* Applied to the action of frost. *rare.*

c **1750** SHENSTONE *Econ.* iii. 106 From each branch, anneal'd, the works of frost Pervasive, radiant icicles depend.

5. *fig.* To toughen, temper.

1695 BLACKMORE *Pr. Arth.* I. 111 Had not our Mould been Æther, Pure and Fine, Labour'd with Care, anneel'd with Skill Divine. **1813** SCOTT *Rokeby* I. xxxi, To press the rights of truth, The mind to strengthen and anneal. **1842** B. SIMMONS in *Blackw. Mag.* LII. 401 Indomitable will Anneals those limbs to warrior purpose still.

6. *Microbiology.* (*trans.* and *intr.*) To combine to form double-stranded nucleic acid.

1961 *Proc. Nat. Acad. Sci.* XLVII. 147 A physical unit carrying both markers was formed by annealing a heated mixture of these two DNAs. *Ibid.* 149 S-C units do not form if the DNAs are mixed after heating and annealing. They must anneal together. **1965** *Biochim. & Biophys. Acta* XCV. 515 The denatured RNA anneals to give a ribonuclease-resistant form. **1978** *Sci. Amer.* Feb. 121/1 The DNA from SV40 virions was also separated into single strands by heating, and the resulting single strands were then 'annealed' with the cellular DNA at a lower temperature. **1983** *Biochem. & Biophys. Res. Communications* CXIV. 522 A duplex..cDNA transcript..can be synthesised..and..the transcription primer anneals to an internal sequence in the template.

anneal, obs. form of ANELE.

annealed (ə'niːld), *ppl. a.* [f. prec. + -ED.]

† **1.** Set on fire. *Obs.*

a **1000** CÆDMON *Gen.* 2922 Ad stód onæled.

† **2.** Fired, or baken, as earthenware; passing into the sense of 'glazed.' *Obs.*

1382 WYCLIF *Is.* xvi. 7 Vp on the walles of anelid [**1388** bakun] tyil. **1519** HORMAN *Vulgaria* 24 b, A new erthen potte that is not glassed or hanelydde.

3. Enamelled, having colours burnt in, 'stained' as glass. *arch.*

1552 *Ch. Goods Berksh.* 14 A crosse of wood, couered wt annyled plate. **1601** HOLLAND *Pliny* (1634) II. 596 Bricks or small tiles enealed with sundry colours. **1622** PEACHAM *Gentl. Exerc.* I. xxvii. 94 The old earth, that hath been scraped of the annealed work. **1633** G. HERBERT *Love-joy* in *Temple* 109, I saw a vine drop grapes with J and C anneal'd on every bunch. **1795** SOUTHEY *Joan of Arc* IV. 84 Conspicuous he In arms with azure and with gold anneal'd.

4. Toughened or tempered after fusion. Also *fig.*

1822 IMISON *Sc. & Art* I. 391 Annealed copper wire is the best. **1831** E. IRVING *Exp. Rev.* I. 95, I am not a hardened and annealed infidel. *a* **1865** J. WYLDE in *Circ. Sc.* I. 83/1 Annealed and unannealed glass.

annealer (ə'niːlə(r)). *rare.* [f. as prec. + -ER[1].] He who or that which anneals.

1656 DUGARD *Lat. Unl.* §478 Annealers, striking colours through glass with the fire. **1883** *Harper's Mag.* Aug. 327/1 Car wheels..swung still glowing into the dry-wells of a circular annealer.

annealing (ə'niːlɪŋ), *vbl. sb.* [f. as prec. + -ING[1].]

† **1.** The process of exposing to the action of fire; firing, burning, baking, etc. *Obs.*

1477 *Act 17 Edw. IV*, iv, True, seasonable, and sufficient making, whiting, and anealing of Tile, otherwise called Thaktile, Roofetile. **1753** CHAMBERS *Cycl. Supp.*, Annealing of tile is used in antient statutes for the burning of tile.

2. The burning of metallic colours into glass, etc.

1477 NORTON *Ord. Alch.* in Ashm. (1652) vi. 96 Tincture with anealing of Glasiers. **1657** EVELYN *Mem.* (1857) III. 92 Anealing in Glass, Enamelling. **1662** FULLER *Worthies* II. 97 Aneyling of Glass (which answereth to Dying in grain in Drapery)..is lost in our age. **1753** CHAMBERS *Cycl., Supp.*, *Annealing*..burning or fixing metalline colours on glass.

3. The tempering or toughening of glass, cast iron, etc. after fusion. Also *fig.*

1803 HATCHETT in *Phil. Trans.* XCIII. 137 An increase of specific gravity in the smaller coins, as a natural consequence of rolling, punching, annealing. **1822** IMISON *Sc. & Art* II. 237 Glass utensils require to be gradually cooled in an oven; this..is called annealing, and is necessary to prevent their breaking by change of temperature. **1841** *Lyra Apost., True Elect* xv. lv. 68, Lest our frail hearts in the annealing break. **1870** R. FERGUSON *Electr.* 150 Annealing improves conducting powers.

4. *attrib.*

1608 WITHALS *Dict.* (ed. Clerk) 136/2 The aneling place where pots and other things bee anneled. **1832** PORTER *Manuf. Glass* 173 A boy conveys it without loss of time to the annealing oven. **1875** BLACKMORE *Cl. Vaughan* vii. 24 From the fine temper of the metal, or some annealing process.

† **a'nnect,** *v. Obs.* [ad. L. *annect-ĕre*, f. *an-* = *ad-* to + *nectĕre* to tie, fasten; cf. *connect.*] = ANNEX (of which it was the earlier form).

1531 ELYOT *Governor* I. xix. (1557) 63 But annectethe it [dancing] with tyllyng and dyggynge. **1577** HANMER *Anc. Eccl. Hist.* (1619) 396 To Annect the Canon decreed in this behalfe vnto our present Historie. **1680** H. MORE *Apocal. Apoc.* 257 To this Line..all the rest of the visions..may some way be annected. **1737** WHISTON *Josephus, Hist.* III. vii. (R.) The like rings being annected to the ephod.

† **a'nnect,** *ppl. a. Obs. rare*[−1]. [for *annected*; cf. *affect, affected.*] Attached or close to.

1432–50 TREVISA *Higden* (1865) I. 321 Denmarke, is an yle contiguate or adnecte to the northe parte of Germayne.

annectent (ə'nɛktənt), *a.* [ad. L. *annectent-em* pr. pple. of *annectĕre*: see ANNECT *v.*] Joining on, connecting (one thing to another).

1826 KIRBY & SPENCE *Entomol.* (1828) IV, Three inferior groups, which he calls aberrant or annectent. **1841** OWEN *Rep. Brit. Foss.*, Transitional or annectent characters. **1875** BLAKE *Zool.* 18 In the lower baboons no trace can be found of any annectant link with such higher forms as the Gorilla.

annection, erron. form of ANNEXION.

anneile, obs. form of ANNEAL.

annelid(e ('ænəlɪd), *sb.* and *a. Zool.* [a. mod.Fr. *annélide*, f. as next: see -ID.]

A. *sb.* A member of the division of *Annelida*; a red-blooded worm.

1834 SIR C. BELL *Hand* 263 These annelides can creep and turn in every direction. **1857** WOOD *Obj. Sea-shore* 94 The commonest of the terrestrial annelids is the earth-worm.

B. *adj.* Of or pertaining to the *Annelida.*

1855 KINGSLEY *Glaucus* (1878) 113 Long Annelid worms of quaintest forms and colours. **1865** BRISTOW *Figuier's World bef. Del.* iv, [No] indications of life, except annelide-tracks, and burrows.

‖ **Annelida** (ə'nɛlɪdə), *sb. pl. Zool.* [mod.L. f. Fr. *annel-és*, (Lamarck's name for his first subd. of *Invertebrata*, 1801), 'ringed,' pa. pple. of *anneler* f. OFr. *annel* ring:—L. *annell-us* for *ānellus*, dim. of *ānulus* a ring + -IDA.] A class of animals (arranged by Cuvier under *Articulata*) comprising the Red-blooded Worms (including earth-worms, leeches, and sea-centipedes), with soft elongated bodies composed of numerous annular segments.

1834 *Penny Cycl.* II. 45/1 The annelida are for the most part oviparous. **1847** CARPENTER *Zool.* §834 The Annelida ..[are] usually furnished with a series of locomotive appendages in the form of bristles.

annelidan (ə'nɛlɪdən), *a.* and *sb. Zool.* [f. prec. + -AN.] **A.** *adj.* Of or belonging to the *Annelida.* **B.** *sb.* An annelid.

1835 KIRBY *Hab. & Inst. Anim.* II. xiv. 17 The Annelidans, which, though annulated, are not insected, and have no jointed legs. **1836** TODD *Cycl. Anat. & Phys.* I. 165/2 The colour of the blood is yellow and not red in some of the annelidans properly so called. **1877** HUXLEY *Anat. Inv. An.* v. 248 A mesotrochal Annelidan larva.

annelidian (ænə'lɪdɪən), *a.* = prec.

1837 *Penny Cycl.* VII. 205/1 The author regards them [Cirripeds]..as Annelidian crustacea.

annelidous (ə'nɛlɪdəs), *a. rare.* [f. as prec. + -OUS.] Of the nature of an annelid or worm.

1845 DARWIN *Voy. Nat.* iv. (1879) 66 Some kind of worm, or annelidous animal.

annelism ('ænəlɪz(ə)m). *rare*[−1]. [f. Fr. *annelé* ringed (see ANNELIDA) + -ISM.] Annelidan or ringed structure.

1860 HARTWIG *Sea* xii. 218 The great Band-worm is one of the most remarkable examples of this low type of annelism.

anneloid ('ænəlɔɪd). *Zool.* [f. as prec. + -OID.] An animal resembling the *Annelida.*

1869 W. BAIRD in *Eng. Mech.* 30 Apr. 123/2 The anneloids belonging to this group differ..from the *Aphroditacea.*

† **annerre,** obs. form, intermed. betw. ENHERDE, *annerde*, and ADHERE, INHERE. To adhere.

1536 BELLENDENE *Cron. Scotl.* (1821) II. 449 To annere to hir as his lauchful lady and wiffe. **1586** J. HOOKER *Giraldus's Hist. Irel.* in *Holinsh.* II. 90/2 Diuerse will annerre unto you to feed on you as crowes on carion.

† **'annes(se.** *Obs.* [OE. *án-nesse*, preserved in north. dial., while in south it became *on-nesse.* Obs. *c* 1300, and formed anew as ONENESS in 17th c.]

1. Oneness, unity.

c **885** K. ÆLFRED *Bæda* iv. 17 (Bosw.) We andettaþ þrýnesse in ánnesse, and ánnesse on þære þrýnesse. *c* **1175** *Lamb. Hom.* 99 He scal ileafan on þa halȝa þreomnesse, and on soðre annesse.

2. Loneliness, solitude.

a **1000** *Guthlac* iii. (Bosw.) Annys þæs wéstenes. *a* **1300** *E.E. Psalter* cii. 7 Like am I made to pellicane of annesse. *Ibid.* lv. 8 In anes I was wonand.

3. Oneness of kind, sameness; oneness of mind, concord, agreement.

1014 *O.E. Chron.*, Gewearð him and þam folce on Lindesiȝe anes. *c* **1175** *Lamb. Hom.* 93 Mid þere annesse and sibsumnesse þet heo sculen þolien. [*c* **1230** *Ancr. R.* 12 Me schal makien strencðe of onnesse of cloþes..þet te onnesse wiðuten bitocnie þe onnesse of o luue & of o wil.]

annet, obs. variant of ANET, dill.

annet, 'provincial name for the Kittywake.' Montagu *Ornith. Dict.* 1802.

annex (ə'nɛks), *v.* Also 4–6 **anex(e**, 5–7 **annexe**, 6 **adnex**. [a. Fr. *annexe-r* to join, f. *a(n)nexe*:—L. *annex-um*, pa. pple. of *annect-ĕre* or *adnect-ĕre* to tie to, f. *ad* to + *nect-ĕre* to tie, bind. In med.L. *annex-āre*, = Fr. *annexer*, was in common use in sense 3, in eccles. and legal language, and probably contributed to the same formal use in Eng.; hence also *annexātio*: see ANNEXATION.]

I. Without the idea of subordination.

1. To join, unite (*to*): **a.** things. *arch.*

1425 *E.E. Wills* (1882) 64 I haue annexed þis my wille with my testament..vnder my seal of myn armes. **1477** EARL RIVERS (Caxton) *Dictes* 12 To annexe the loue of god and of your feithe vnto sapience. **1538** LELAND *Itin.* II. 98 Whos Chirch was hard adnexid to the Est of the Paroch Chirch. **1598** BARCKLEY *Felic. Man.* (1631) 673 The soule that is annexed to the body. **1641** FRENCH *Distill.* iii. (1651) 86 The last crooked pipe, to which you must annex a receiver. **1866** ROGERS *Agric. & Prices* I. xx. 503 The windmill was probably turned to the wind by a pole annexed to an axle at the base.

†**b.** persons. *Obs.*

1526 SKELTON *Magnyf.* 200 Good fortune hath annexed us together. **1642** ROGERS *Naaman* 31 She will annexe and apply her selfe to Christ (after a fashion) for aide.

II. To join in a subordinate capacity. Const. *to*.

2. To join or unite materially, as an accessory. *arch.*

1605 BACON *Adv. Learn.* II. §10 Some places instituted for physic have annexed the commodity of gardens for simples. **1628** PRYNNE *Love-Lockes* 18 Ye annex I know not what enormities of Periwiges, and counterfeite Haire. **1671** J. WEBSTER *Metallogr.* x. 141 Having annexed to it some slates and other matter. **1863** KEMBLE *Resid. Georgia* 18 To each settlement is annexed a cook's shop.

3. To add as an additional part to existing possessions (with or without local contiguity).

1509 BARCLAY *Ship of Fooles* (1570) 202 Our marches marring as much as he [the Turk] may do, And much of them annexeth his vnto. **1534** tr. *Polyd. Verg., Eng. Hist.* (1846) I. 57 Julius Cæsar annexed Brittaine to the Romaine emperie. **1684** *Scanderbeg Rediv.* ii. 10 This Country..has now annext the Great Dukedom of Lithuania. **1768** BLACKSTONE *Comm.* II. 273 Appropriators may annex the great tithes to the vicarages. **1800** WELLINGTON in Gurw. *Disp.* I. 60 The whole country is permanently annexed to the British Empire.

4. To add to a composition or book, to append.

c **1450** *Merlin* xx. 327 That he dide write, he anexed to the booke that Blase wrote. **1592** tr. *Junius on Rev.* xx, This story of the Dragon must bee anexed unto that place. **1641** HINDE *Bruen* xxxviii. 117 He presently annexeth a note of remembrance. **1667** BOYLE in *Phil. Trans.* II. 601 To which he annexes a Disquisition of the Scurvey. **1799** S. TURNER *Anglo-Sax.* (1828) I. 312 He annexes almost invariably a lamentation of their festive indulgence. **1871** C. DAVIES *Metric Syst.* III. 145 To complete the system a vocabulary of new denominations was annexed.

5. To affix (a seal; *hence* a signature or other mark of sanction). *arch.*

1603 KNOLLES *Hist. Turks* (1638) 43 Nothing..was accounted of any force, except his [the emperor's] approbation were thereunto annexed. **1644** MILTON *Areop.* (Arb.) 59 Examin'd by an appointed officer, whose hand should be annext. **1659** BAXTER in Eedes *Christ's Exalt.* To Reader, Chearfully annex thy attestation that they are true. **1771** *Junius Lett.* xlviii. 252 What further sanction..will you annex to any resolution of the present house of Commons?

6. To join or attach as an attribute or qualification.

c **1386** CHAUCER *Wife's T.* 291 That genterye Is nought annexed [*v.r.* anexed] to possessioun. **1430** LYDG. *Chron.* II. x, Seying in hym most vertuous and good Mercye annexed vnto royall blode. **1537** ? TINDALE *Exp. John* 32 The dedes were unperfecte, and had synne annexed unto them. **1651** HOBBES *Leviath.* II. xviii. 91 It is annexed to the Soveraignty, to be Iudge. *a* **1778** *Anecd. Pitt* III. xxxix. 53 The privileges..which are annexed to the peerage. **1817** CHALMERS *Astr. Disc.* ii. 45 When we look back on the days of Newton, we annex a kind of mysterious greatness to him.

7. To add or attach as a condition.

1588 FRAUNCE *Lawiers Log.* I. xii. 53 b, Such conditions as were annexed to the first donation. **1628** MEADE in Ellis *Orig. Lett.* I. 348 I. 278 There was annexed to that Report that the Judges should sit at the Tower. **1754** HUME *Hist. Eng.* viii, He, though he granted him the commission, annexed a clause, that it should not empower him, etc. **1818** HALLAM *Mid. Ages* (1872) I. iv. 392 The cortes..having made a grant to Henry III, annexed this condition.

8. To attach as a consequence.

1538 STARKEY *England* 95 Thys thyngys folow, and be annexyd as commyn effectys. **1561** T. N[ORTON] *Calvin's Inst.* IV. xix. (1634) 723 Extreme annointing hath neither ordinance of God to be grounded on, nor promise of grace annexed. **1708** SWIFT *Sacram. Test* Wks. 1755 II. I. 126 It is not reasonable that revenues should be annexed to one opinion more than another. **1736** BUTLER *Anal.* II. v. 200 The future Punishment, which God has annext to Vice. **1876** M. ARNOLD *Lit. & Dogma* 7 Salvation is not annexed to a right knowledge of geometry.

annex(e ('ænɛks, ə'nɛks), *sb.* [a. Fr. *annexe* that which is joined:—L. *annex-um*: see prec. Obs. bef. 1700 exc. in Sc. Law, but lately re-adopted in Fr. form in senses 2 and 4; the tendency, however, is to drop the final *-e*, and treat the word as Eng.]

†**1.** Something annexed; an adjunct, accessory. *Obs.*

1541 R. COPLAND *Guydon's Quest. Cyrurg.*, Of naturall thynges, and of vnnaturall thynges, and also of theyr annexes. **1646** SIR T. BROWNE *Pseud. Ep.* I. x. (1686) 29 Satan hath assumed the annexes of Divinity. **1686** GOAD *Celest. Bod.* I. iv. 13 Which Dayes being Festival, or notable, for the Annex of some Mart, Fair, or other Solemnity.

2. *Sc. Law.* An appurtenance.

1540 *Acts James V* (1841) 361 (JAM.) The landis, lordschip, and baronie of Annendale..thare annexis and connexis and all thare pertinentis. **1814** SCOTT *Wav.* xix, With the manor-place thereof, tofts—crofts—mosses..annexis—connexis.

3. a. An addition to a document; an appendix.

1647 JER. TAYLOR *Lib. Proph.* i. 7 In the annexes of the several expressions such things are expressed. **1649** —— *Gt. Exemp.* x. §37 Moses did in other annexes of his law forbid fornication. **1667** *Decay Chr. Piety* xi. §1 (1683) 316 Not the testament of our dying Redeemer, but some codicils and annexes of our own. *Mod.* The annex to the Anglo-Turkish Convention of 1878.

†**b.** in *Logic*; (see quot.) *Obs. rare.*

1660 STANLEY *Hist. Philos.* (1701) 311/2 *Adnex* (which some reckon as a species of the connex)..an axiom connected by the conjunction *whereas*, beginning with an axiom, and ending with an axiom; as, *whereas it is day, it is light*.

4. From the mod.Fr. *annexe*, as applied to additional parts of an exhibition building: a supplementary building designed to supply extra accommodation for some special purpose; a wing.

1861 *Cornh. Mag.* July 94 In Paris you had to cross the road from the Annexe. **1862** *Times* 27 Mar., The western annexe for machinery is being rapidly completed. **1863** MARY HOWITT *Bremer's Greece* II. xvi. 149 A little metochi, or annex to the Jerusalem monastery. **1883** *Pall Mall G.* 20 Mar. 4/1 The success of Newnham and Girton, and of the Woman's Annex at Harvard.

annexable (ə'nɛksəb(ə)l), *a.* In 7 -ible. [f. ANNEX *v.*: see -BLE.] That can be attached.

1623 COCKERAM *Dict.* II, Which may be Knit, *Nexible, Annexible.* **1652** URQUHART *Jewel* Wks. 1834, 200 Adjectitious syllabicals annexible to nouns. **1875** POSTE *Gaius* III. 384 A Condition was not annexable to all dispositions.

†**'annexary.** *Obs. rare.* [f. L. *annex-* (see ANNEX *v.*) + -ARY.] A thing annexed, an adjunct.

1622 HEYLIN *Cosmogr.* Introd. (1674) 23/2 These particulars both of Earth and Water, which are considerable in Geography, and come within the compass of those Annexaries of each, which Ptolomy calleth τὰ συνημμένα. **1637** SANDYS *St. of Relig.* (T.) Unto which sundry of them are no other than annexaries and appurtenances.

annexation (ænɪk'seɪʃən). [ad. med.L. *annexātiōn-em*, n. of action f. *annexā-re*: see ANNEX *v.* and -ATION.] The action or process of joining to or uniting: **a.** of joining materially. *rare.*

1861 STANLEY *East. Ch.* iii. (1869) 109 He, performing the annexation in the dark and in haste, had fixed the heads on the wrong shoulders.

b. of adding or attaching as an attribute, condition, or consequence.

a **1660** HAMMOND (J.) All other christian virtues will, by way of concomitance or annexation, attend them. **1788** T. JEFFERSON *Writ.* (1859) II. 533 The annexation of a bill of rights to the Constitution. **1833** I. TAYLOR *Fanat.* x. 447 The annexation of the threatened punishment to vicious acts.

c. *esp.* of attaching as an additional privilege, possession, or territorial dependency; appropriation.

1634–46 J. ROW *Hist. Kirk* (1842) 142 That the act of annexation be dissolved. **1656** BP. HALL *Special. Life* 27 (T.) The Dean of Windsor, by an ancient annexation, is patron thereof. **1726** AYLIFFE *Parerg.* 87 How these Annexations of Benefices first came into the church. **1875** BRYCE *Holy Rom. Emp.* xx. 363 France..by the annexation of Piedmont, had overstepped the Alps.

†**2.** That which is annexed, an addition. *Obs.*

1611 COTGR., *Annexe*, an annexation, or thing annexed.

†**3.** Conjunction, combination, union. *Obs. rare.*

a **1626** BACON *Union Eng. & Scot.* (T.) To make one compounded annexation..out of the lands of both nations.

annexational (ænɪk'seɪʃənəl), *a.* [f. ANNEXATION + -AL[1].] Of, pertaining to, or relating to annexation. So **anne'xationism**, advocacy of, or a policy aiming at, annexation; **annexative** (ə'nɛksətɪv) *a.*, disposed to annex territory, given to annexation.

1850 CARLYLE *Latter-day Pamph.* (1872) iv. 127 A regular statistic of Annexationism. **1869** *Nation* 8 Apr. 267 They..are availing themselves of the strong annexational fever which now rages. **1918** A. GRAY tr. *R. Grelling's The Crime* II. i. 24 That a belligerent state..should..make known annexational intentions. **1921** *Contemp. Rev.* Dec. 723 A nation..insatiably aggressive and annexative. **1940** *Manch. Guardian Weekly* 19 Apr. 312/3 There assembled..in the Prussian Parliament on July 7 1915..about fifty persons who were concerned to oppose this mischievous annexationism.

annexationist (ænɪk'seɪʃənɪst). [f. ANNEXATION + -IST.] One who aims at or advocates annexation.

[*c* **1845** Used in U.S. of the 'annexation' of Texas.] **1860** W. RUSSELL *Diary in Ind.* II. 251 To regard with suspicion and dislike the policy of the Annexationists. **1860** *Sat. Rev.* No. 248. 98/1 The intrigues of French annexationists.

b. *attrib.* or *adj.*

1852 LUDLOW *Hist. U.S.* 209 The great annexationist majority were almost all pro-slavery men. **1880** *Daily Tel.* 19 June, We denounced the annexationist schemes of Greece.

annexed (ə'nɛkst), *ppl. a.* Also **annext**. [f. ANNEX *v.* + -ED.]

†**1.** Joined together without subordination of one to the other; united, conjoined, knit. *Obs.*

c **1400** *Rom. Rose* 4814 Love..is a sykenesse of the thought Annexed & kned bitwixe tweyne. **1526** TINDALE *Rom.* viii. 17 Heyres anexed with Christ. **1653** ROUS *Myst. Marr.* 57 A joynt-heir annexed with Christ.

†**b.** Adjoining, lying close to. *Obs.*

1703 MAUNDRELL *Journ. Jerus.* (1732) 100 Several large Vaults, annext to the Mountain. **1662** GERBIER *Princ.* 38 The Louver at Paris..with the delight of the annexed Tuilleries.

2. Added, attached, or appended as subordinate or supplementary; subjoined; rendered subject.

1509 HAWES *Past. Pleas.* v. xi, All the eyght partes [of speech]..Are Laten wordes, annexed properly To every speche. **1548** LD. SOMERSET in *Compl. Scotl.* 244 Howe holdeth the Frenche King Briteigne, now lately adnexed to that Croune. **1578** LYTE *Dodoens* 509 The roote is somwhat thicke, with many threddy stringes therunto annexed. **1667** MILTON *P.L.* XII. 99 Some fatal curse annext Deprives them of thir outward libertie. **1863** LYELL *Antiq. Man* 6 The annexed tabular view. **1883** *Observ.* 22 Apr. 5/3 It is England and not Queensland that must govern the annexed natives.

annexer (ə'nɛksə(r)). Also -or. [f. as prec. + -ER[1].] One who annexes (territory).

1845 *For. Q. Rev.* XXXIV. 500 The annexor of Scinde. **1872** *Daily News* 26 Mar., The annexers of Nice and Savoy.

annexing (ə'nɛksɪŋ), *vbl. sb.* [f. as prec. + -ING[1].] The action of joining or attaching; annexation. (Now mostly gerundial.)

1611 COTGR., *Attachement*, a tying, fastening, annexing. **1628** LAYTON *Sion's Plea* 20 Before the annexing of the right of Ecclesiastical jurisdiction to the Crown. **1736** BUTLER *Anal.* I. ii. 50 The annexing pleasure to some actions. **1860** MOTLEY *Netherl.* (1868) I. i. 4 He contemplated annexing..the kingdoms of France, of England and Ireland.

annexion (ə'nɛkʃən). *arch.* Also 7 **adnexion**, **annection**. [ad. L. *annexiōn-em*, n. of action f. *annex-* ppl. stem of *annect-ĕre*: see ANNEX *v.*]

1. The action of annexing; = ANNEXATION I.

1611 SPEED *Hist. Gt. Brit.* VII. v. 216 To seeke the annexion thereof to his owne Kingdome. **1670** G. H. *Hist. Cardinals* I. III. 69 The annection of several Provinces. **1667** H. MORE *Div. Dial.* v. x. (1713) 434 This signifies the adnexion of..Periods of Times to the Ministry of the Angelical Hosts. **1807** W. TAYLOR in *Ann. Rev.* V. 169 The use of the word *annexion* [by J. Gordon 1801], where *annexation* would be written by the slaves of usage..is unquestionably right.

†**2.** That which is annexed, attached, or appended; an addition, adjunct. *Obs.*

c **1600** ? SHAKS. *Lover's Compl.* 208 These talents of their hair..With the annexions of fair gems enrich'd. *a* **1641** BP. MOUNTAGU *Acts & Mon.* 418 Which traditions the Pharisees did not recommend as commentaries only..but as necessary annexions unto the Law. **1748** A. HILL in Mrs. Barbauld's *Richardson* (1804) I. 129 Every thing [is] unsimple that has foreign and unnatural annexions.

annexionist (ə'nɛkʃənɪst). [f. prec. + -IST.] One who aims at or advocates annexation; = ANNEXATIONIST. Often *attrib.*

1865 *Pall Mall G.* No. 371. 1248/2 The annexionist policy of Russia. **1882** in *Macm. Mag.* XLVI. 248/1 The annexionists are setting these good Palermitans by the ears.

annexive (ə'nɛksɪv), *a. Gram.* [f. L. *annex-* (see ANNEX *v.*) + -IVE.] Expressing annexation: = CONJUNCTIVE *a.* 3 b.

1853 EDWARDS & TAYLOR tr. *Kühner's Gram. Gr. Lang.* §321 A copulative coördinate sentence is either annexive or enhansive. **1913** J. M. JONES *Welsh Gram.* 440 Conjunctions are..i. annexive..ii. disjunctive.

annexment (ə'nɛksmənt). *rare.* [f. ANNEX *v.* + -MENT.] That which is annexed; an adjunct, or supplement.

1602 SHAKS. *Ham.* III. iii. 21 When it [majesty] falles, Each small annexment, pettie consequence, Attends the boystrous Ruine. **1824** COLERIDGE *Aids to Refl.* 174 Publishing it..as an Annexment to the 'Elements of Discourse.'

annexure (ə'nɛksjʊə(r), -ʃ(j)ʊə(r)). [f. L. *annex-* (see ANNEX *v.*) + -URE.] Something annexed; = ANNEX *sb.*, ANNEXMENT I.

1878 *Fraser's Mag.* XVIII. 85 A large and profitable annexure to our vast possessions on the Indian continent. **1902** *Westm. Gaz.* 7 July 5/4 The annexures to the petition. **1904** *Blue-bk. Papers Rel. to Thibet* 15, 17.

annie, variant of ANIGH *v. Obs.*

†**a'nniferous**, *a. Obs.*$^{-0}$ [f. L. *annifer* (f. *ann-us* year + *-fer* bearing, producing) + -OUS.] 'That bears fruit all the year.' Blount *Glossogr.*

†**a'nnihil**, *v. Obs.* Forms: 5 **anychile**, 6 **adnychell**, **adnihill**, **annihil**. [a. Fr. *annihile-r*, 14–16th c. *an(n)ichil(l)er*, *adnichil(l)er*, ad. late L. *annihilā-re*, *adnihilāre* (in Jerome), f. *ad* to +

nihil nothing. In med.L. commonly spelt *adnichilare*, whence the earlier Fr. and Eng. spellings.] = ANNIHILATE (being the earlier equivalent).

1490 CAXTON *Eneydos* xxii. 84 The grete loenge and good renommee of the..inventour of the first lettres neuer shal be extyncted nor anychiled. *c* **1525** SKELTON *Bk. of 3 Fools* 18 Thou wottest neuer in what maner thou mayst adnychell mine honour. **1591** HORSEY *Trav.* 168 To adnihill and frustrat all this. **1595** *Loves Owle* (Halliw.) Which els had been long since annihiled.

annihilability (əˌnaɪhɪlə'bɪlɪtɪ). *rare*⁻¹. [f. next: see -BILITY.] The capability of being annihilated.

1662 H. MORE *Immort. Soul* (1712) 228 The variety of degrees..in the Intellective faculties of the Soul..cannot at all argue her Mortality, no more than the different modifications of Matter the Annihilability thereof.

annihilable (ə'naɪhɪləb(ə)l), *a.* [f. L. *annihilāre* (see ANNIHIL) + -BLE.] Capable of being annihilated or blotted out of existence.

1677 J. WEBSTER *Witchcr.* x. 211 Seeing bodies, no more than spirits to be annihilable by second causes. **1791** T. PAINE *Rights M.* (ed. 4) 136 The rights of men in society, are neither deviseable, nor transferable, nor annihilable.

annihilate (ə'naɪhɪlət), *ppl. a. arch.* Forms: 4-7 adnichilat(e, 5-6 adnychyl-, 6 adnihil-, 6- annihilate. [ad. L. *annihilāt-us* pa. pple. of *annihilā-re*: see ANNIHIL. As in other instances (see -ATE) this ppl. adj. originated a vb. of same form, which eventually displaced the earlier ANNIHIL; of this vb., *annihilate* was for some time used as pa. pple., but was at length displaced by the regular *annihilat-ed*, retaining only its adj. use, which is now also arch.] = ANNIHILATED.

1. Reduced to nothing, blotted out of existence.

1388 *On 25 Art.* in *Wyclif's Wks.* (1871) III. 484 þat þai clepen adnichilat or brouȝt to nouȝt. **1491** CAXTON *Vitas Patr.* (W. de W.) III. xxiv. 325/1 Yf a brother Relygyous haue all his wyll mortefyed and adnychylate. *c* **1510** MORE *Picus* Wks. 1557, 18/2 If the world were adnihilate and turned to nought again. **1624** HEYWOOD *Gunaik.* II. 65 The sollace of life, is by such a restraint oppress, and by degrees adnichilate. **1795** SOUTHEY *Joan of Arc* I. 531 All sense of self annihilate, I seem'd Diffused into the scene. **1839** BAILEY *Festus* Proem. 7 Earth's Millennial foretaste, ill annihilate.

†**2.** Made null and void, of no effect. *Obs.*

1544 *Act 35 Hen. VIII*, i, I repute the same [othe] as vayne and adnichilate. **1553-87** FOXE *A. & M.* (1596) 78/1 Whereby all such errors and opinions..maie be made frustrat and adnihilat.

annihilate (ə'naɪhɪleɪt), *v.* For forms see prec. [f. prec., superseding the earlier ANNIHIL from Fr.]

1. To reduce to non-existence, blot out of existence

a. things material.

1599 A. M. *Gabelhouer's Bk. Physic* 112/2 Till the wormes be totally annihilatede or consumede. **1660** R. COKE *Just. Vind.* 22 God..can annihilate all the Universe in a moment. **1772** PENNANT *Tours Scotl.* (1774) 151 The vestiges of the Roman camp..are almost annihilated. **1855** MILMAN *Lat. Chr.* III. VI. ii. 387 The substance of the bread and wine was actually annihilated—nothing existed but the body and blood of the Redeemer.

b. things immaterial, actions, qualities, conditions of existence.

1586 T. B. *La Primaud. Fr. Acad.* 166 Idlenes annihilateth and corrupteth the goodnes of nature. **1603** HOLLAND *Plutarch's Mor.* Ded. 1 Who make profession in word.. but in deed and effect do annihilate..the power and efficacie thereof. **1727** POPE, etc. *Art of Sinking* 100 Ye Gods! annihilate but space and time, And make two lovers happy. **1813** WELLINGTON in Gurw. *Disp.* X. 473 That event has totally annihilated all order and discipline.

c. *Theol.* To destroy the soul (as well as the body).

1634 HABINGTON *Castara* (1870) 114 Death..not annihilates, but uncloudes the soule. **1702** tr. *Le Clerc's Prim. Fathers* 306 Justin Martyr and St. Irenæus believed that after a certain time they [the Wicked] should be annihilated. **1728** DE FOE *Magick* II. ii. 273 God can no more be the author of evil, than he can annihilate himself, and cease to be.

d. *spec.* in *Physics*, to convert (a sub-atomic particle) into radiant energy. Freq. in *pass.* Cf. ANNIHILATION 3.

1930 *Proc. Cambr. Philos. Soc.* XXVI. 362 It is easy to see from the laws of conservation of energy and momentum that an electron and proton cannot annihilate one another with the emission of only a single photon. **1938** *Physical Rev.* LIII. 126/1 The two quanta radiation produced when a positron is annihilated at rest. **1977** S. WEINBERG *First Three Minutes* iv. 80 Nuclear reactions, in which a fraction of the mass of atomic nuclei is annihilated. **1978** PASACHOFF & KUTNER *University Astron.* ix. 257 The most spectacular property of matter-antimatter pairs is that when a particle and its antiparticle come together, they annihilate each other, producing an energy $E = 2mc^2$, where m is the mass of each particle. That is, all their mass is converted into energy.

2. To make null and void, make of none effect, annul, cancel, abrogate (laws, treaties, rights, etc.).

1525 LD. BERNERS *Froiss.* II. cliii. 421 That shulde breke or adnychilate..the alyances that hath been sworne. **1579** W. FULKE *Confut. Sander* 558 To adnihilate the sacraments ministred by heretikes. **1665** GLANVILL *Sceps. Sci.* Addr. 5, To annihilate all such arguments. **1767** *Junius Lett.* xv. 65 These..rights..you can no more annihilate than you can the soil to which they are annexed. **1836** J. GILBERT *Chr. Atonem.* viii. 235 Annihilate law, and moral order is no more.

3. To treat as non-existent, set at nought. *arch.*

1542 BECON *Pathw. Prayer* Wks. 1843, 180 How were the singular merits of Christ's death..adnihilated and set at nought. **1599** *Broughton's Lett.* vii. 21 The effect and affection of men..Pharisaically ἐξουθενεῖν, to annihilate all others. **1755** SMOLLETT *Don Quix.* (1803) IV. 186 Who has thought proper to usurp your name, and annihilate your exploits. *a* **1843** SOUTHEY *Amat. Poems* Sonn. iii. Wks. II. 119 For Love annihilates the world to me!

4. To extinguish virtually; to reduce to silence, powerlessness, or humiliation.

1630 NAUNTON *Fragm. Reg.* (1870) 57 By a joynt conspiracy to ruine the House, and altogether to annihilate it. **1683** *Brit. Spec.* 226 An Omnipotent Power to create and annihilate Kings. **1771** BURKE *Corr.* (1844) I. 317 He has been not only ready, but earnest even, to annihilate himself. **1818** BYRON *Childe Har.* IV. lxxxiii, Thou who with thy frown Annihilated senates.

5. To destroy the collective or organized existence of anything, by reducing it to its elements; to put an army to utter rout, etc.

1808 WELLINGTON in Gurw. *Disp.* IV. 115 We only wanted a few hundred more cavalry to annihilate the French army. **1879** BARTLETT *Egypt to Pal.* iii. 50 Near the mouth of the Nile Nelson annihilated the fleet of Napoleon.

6. *intr.* To dwindle to nothing, become extinct.

1787 T. JEFFERSON *Writ.* (1859) II. 203 Their calling is, in fact, annihilating.

7. *intr. Physics.* Of a sub-atomic particle: to undergo annihilation; to combine with its antiparticle so that the mass of both is transformed into radiant energy.

1952 *Physical Rev.* LXXXVIII. 1435/2 This is the anticipated behavior if the original particles were positive electrons which annihilate in flight. **1962** *Newnes Conc. Encycl. Nucl. Energy* 32/1 Under appropriate conditions colliding positrons and electrons may not annihilate instantly but may form the system known as positronium. **1979** *Nature* 29 Mar. 406/1 It is assumed that in the collision an anti-quark of the ($q\bar{q}$) sea in one hadron annihilates with a quark in the other hadron resulting in the creation of a lepton pair.

a'nnihilated, *ppl. a.* [f. prec. + -ED.] Reduced to nothing, utterly destroyed.

1769 BURKE *Pres. St. Nat.* Wks. II. 82 The credit of France was low; but it was not annihilated. **1843** MILL *Log.* II. v. §6 Imagining a portion of matter annihilated.

annihilating (ə'naɪhɪleɪtɪŋ), *vbl. sb.* [f. as prec. + -ING.¹.] The action of reducing to nought, utter destruction, annihilation. (Now gerundial.)

1611 COTGR., An adnihilating, *annichilation, annullation.* **1667** MILTON *P.L.* VI. 347 Spirits..Cannot but by annihilating die. **1779** J. MOORE *View Soc. Fr.* II. 157 This would not be annihilating happiness, but only shifting the scene of the wretched.

a'nnihilating, *ppl. a.* [f. as prec. + -ING².] Reducing to nought, destroying; crushing.

1816 BYRON *Corinth* xxiv, That annihilating voice, Which pierces the deep hills through and through. **1865** *Cornh. Mag.* June 655 With that annihilating answer the major's daughter put up her parasol and walked back by herself.

annihilation (əˌnaɪhɪ'leɪʃən). [a. Fr. *annihilation*, 14th c. *anichilacion*, f. L. *adnihilāt-*: see ANNIHIL and -ATION. Not in Cotgr. 1611.]

1. The action or process of reducing to nothing, or of blotting out of existence. **a.** materially.

a **1638** MEDE *Paraphr. 2 Pet.* iii. 7 A destruction of the whole creature it self by utter annihilation. **1777** PRIESTLEY *Mat. & Spir.* vii. I. 79 Let any person..suppose the annihilation of all matter. **1856** DOVE *Log. Chr. Faith* IV. i. §1. 162 Creation and annihilation are absolute changes.

b. *Theol.* The destruction of soul as well as body.

1753 CHAMBERS *Cycl. Supp.* s.v., Christian writers, who, shocked with the horrible prospect of eternal torments, have taken refuge in the system of Annihilation..This *Annihilation* makes what they call the second death. **1876** MOZLEY *Univ. Serm.* iii. 61 When reason itself has opened a view into immortality, to put up contentedly with annihilation,—what a dreadful stupefaction of the human spirit!

c. Of conditions and circumstances: The bringing to an end; total abrogation.

1763 ERSKINE in Ellis *Orig. Lett.* II. 504 IV. 470 A total annihilation of Regal Authority. **1769** BURKE *Pres. State Nat.* Wks. II. 23 The annihilation of our trade, the ruin of our credit. **1796** MORSE *Amer. Geog.* I. 321 The annihilation of the credit of the paper bills.

d. Of collective and complex bodies: The action of destroying their combined or organized existence; effectual destruction.

1796 LD. SHEFFIELD in *Ld. Auckland's Corr.* (1862) III. 358 The annihilation of Jourdan's army is a great event. **1872** YEATS *Growth Comm.* 54 Their policy was, therefore, simply that of conquest, not annihilation.

2. The state of nothingness resulting from blotting out of existence.

1677 GALE *Crt. Gentiles* II. IV. 517 Cut off the dependence of a Creature from its Creator and what an..Annihilation would it fal into? **1794** SULLIVAN *View Nat.* I. 183 All nature would languish and fall into annihilation. **1851** MARIOTTI *Italy* in 1848, i. 8 Political annihilation had not yet brought with it mental prostration and degeneracy.

3. *Physics.* (See quot. 1962.)

1930 P. A. M. DIRAC in *Proc. Cambr. Philos. Soc.* XXVI. 361 The object of the present paper is to calculate the frequency of occurrence of these processes of annihilation of electrons and protons. **1938** R. W. LAWSON tr. *Hevesy & Paneth's Man. Radioactivity* (ed. 2) vii. 72 Processes in which the total energy of annihilation is emitted in a single quantum of energy 10^6e.V. **1942** J. D. STRANATHAN *Particles Mod. Physics* 374 (*heading*) Creation and Annihilation of Electron-Positron Pairs. **1962** *Gloss. Terms Nucl. Sci.* (*B.S.I.*) 9 *Annihilation*, a collision between a particle and its anti-particle..in which they both disappear, their energy being converted into annihilation radiation.

annihilationism (əˌnaɪhɪ'leɪʃənɪz(ə)m). *Theol.* [f. prec. + -ISM.] The doctrine of the total annihilation of the wicked after death.

1881 *Dubl. Rev.* Ser. III. V. 139 Others are preaching Annihilationism, or Conditional Immortality.

aˌnnihi'lationist. *Theol.* [f. as prec. + -IST.] One who maintains the eventual annihilation of the wicked. Often *attrib.*

1875 BALDW. BROWN in Minton *Life & Death* (1877) 66 These annihilationists are pitiless. **1880** *Academy* 23 Oct. 285/1 Objections..urged before by..Annihilationist controversialists—against the doctrine of eternal punishment.

annihilative (ɑː'naɪhɪlətɪv), *a.* [f. L. *annihilāt-* (see ANNIHIL) + -IVE.] Such as to annihilate; destructive, crushing.

1836 *Blackw. Mag.* XL. 255 Darkness [seems].. suppressive or annihilative of life. **1865** CARLYLE *Fredk. Gt.* VII. xviii. iii. 129 Victory at Prag considered to be much more annihilative than it really was.

annihilator (ə'naɪhɪleɪtə(r)). [f. ANNIHILATE *v.* + -OR, as if a. L. **annihilātor*.] He who, or that which, annihilates or utterly destroys.

1698 CONGREVE *Way of World* IV. ix. (Jod.) Witwood, you are an annihilator of sense. **1841** HOR. SMITH *Moneyed Man* III. xi. 325 Steam..the uniter of nations, the annihilator of distance.

¶ Occas. in comb., as ***smoke-annihilator***, etc.

†**a'nnihiled,** *ppl. a. Obs.* [f. ANNIHIL *v.* + -ED.] = ANNIHILATED.

1691 BLOUNT *Law Dict.*, *Adnichiled*, nulled or made void.

†**a'nnihiling,** *vbl. sb. Obs.* Also 6 **anniling.** [f. as prec. + -ING¹.] Annihilating, annihilation.

1593 NASHE *Lent. Stuffe* 22, I..put him not to the full anniling of me with any sound hammering persuasion.

†**a'nnihilment.** *Obs. rare*⁻¹. In 6 **anychyll-.** [f. Fr. *annihile-r* (see ANNIHIL) + -MENT. Prob. **anichillement* existed in OFr.] Annihilation.

1526 J. HACKET *To Wolsey* MS. Cott. Galba B. IX. 35 Comandment..for the anychyllment and destruccion of thys nywe bokes.

anniseed, obs. form of ANISEED.

'annist. *Hist.* A partisan of Queen Anne.

a **1745** SWIFT *Wks.* II. 117 Favouring none but..annists.

†**anni'versal,** *a. Obs.* [f. ANNIVERSE + -AL¹; cf. *universal.*] = ANNIVERSARY.

1753 CHAMBERS *Cycl. Supp.*, *Anniversary-Days*..In some authors we also find it written *anniversal.*

anniversarily (ænɪ'vɜːsərɪlɪ), *adv.* [f. as next + -LY².] By annual return, after the manner of an anniversary.

a **1631** DONNE *Serm.* xcii. IV. 173 Not only once but Anniversarily by a yearly Dedication. **1749** RICHARDSON *Clarissa* VIII. liii. 214 That fatal seventh which..I will never see anniversarily revolve but in sables. **1820** W. TAYLOR in *Month. Rev.* XCII. 44 The..slaughter of the idolatrous priests ordered by Darius..was anniversarily commemorated.

†**anni'versariness.** *Obs. rare.*⁻¹. [f. next + -NESS.] Anniversary character.

1676 W. ROW *Suppl. Blair's Autobiog.* xii. (1848) 386 Abstracting from the anniversariness of his birth-day.

anniversary (ænɪ'vɜːsərɪ), *a.* and *sb.* [ad. L. *anniversāri-us* returning yearly, f. *ann-us* year + *vers-us* turned, a turning + *-āri-us*: see -ARY. Cf. *advers-ārius*, f. *advers-us*. Used in med.L. subst. as *anniversāria* (sc. *dies*), and *anniversārium*, both ecclesiastical terms, whence also the subst. use is the earliest in Eng. Cf. Fr. *anniversaire.*]

A. *adj.*

1. 'Returning with the revolution of the year; annual; yearly' (J.); returning or commemorated at the same date in succeeding years.

The word was at first ecclesiastical: 'Anniversary days were of old those days, wherein the Martyrdoms or Deaths of Saints were celebrated yearly in the Church; or the days whereon, at every years end, Men were wont to pray for the Souls of their deceased Friends, according to the continued Custom of Roman Catholicks.' BLOUNT *Law Dict.* 1691.

1552 HULOET, Annyuersary, or that which yerlye runneth at one tyme, *Anniversarius.* **1591** G. FLETCHER *Russe*

Commonw. (1836) 113 This day (which they keep anniversarie). **1651** WITTIE *Primrose's Pop. Err.* IV. xvi. 271 Sick of an anniversary disease. **1666** *Phil. Trans.* I. 110 Of Periodical and Anniversary Winds and their Causes. **1696** J. AUBREY *Misc.* (1721) 7 On that day Anniversary his Father and Mother died. **1712** ADDISON *Spect.* No. 433 ⁋4 This Anniversary Carnival lasted a Week. **1858** CDL. WISEMAN 4 *Last Popes* 403 Commemorated by anniversary festivities.

†**2.** *loosely*, Annual, repeated each year. *Obs.*

1653 A. WILSON *James I* 156 Giving..anniversary stipends for connivency. **1685** STILLINGF. *Orig. Brit.* Pref. 60 Carrying away their anniversary Prey beyond the Seas. **1738** J. KEILL *Anim. Œcon.* Pref. 23 The anniversary Vicissitudes of the Sun.

†**3.** Enduring for or completed in a year. *Obs.* [So in med.L. *anniversārium* is used for *annāle.*]

1629 A. SYMMER *Spir. Posie* II. i. 32 The sunne by his anniversary revolution maketh the day and the yeare. **1660** BURNEY *Kerd. Doron* 20 Their applauded Government is like a Turn-coat, and is Anniversary. **1704** HEARNE *Duct. Hist.* (1714) I. 410 The anniversary Revolution of the Sun purifies the Air.

4. [attrib. use of sb.] Of or pertaining to the celebration of an anniversary.

1654 GAYTON in *Shaks. Cent. Praise* 299 A Goddard or an Anniversary Spice-Bowle. **1883** *Chr. World* 3 Aug. 515/2 The anniversary services..were held last Sunday.

B. *sb.* [for *anniversary day, service*, etc.]

1. The day in any year which agrees in date with a particular day in a former year; *hence*, the yearly return of any remarkable date, the day on which some event of ecclesiastical, national, or personal interest, is annually celebrated; formerly called *year-day*, *mind-day*, *mune-day*.

c **1230** *Ancr. R.* 22 Ine anniuersaries, þet is ine munedawes of ower leoue vreond. **1482** CAXTON *Chron. Eng.* ccxlvi. 311 Ones in the yere at his annyuersarye his terement to be holden in the moost honest wyse. **1561** VERON *Hunt. Purg.* 25 Yeares minds other wyse called anniversaries. **1660** R. COKE *Power & Subj.* 157 The day we have appointed, viz. the Anniversary of S. John Baptist beheaded. **1695** LUTTRELL *Brief Rel.* III. 460 This being the anniversary of King Williams coronation. **1860** *Sat. Rev.* No. 249. 136/1 Wear orange ribbons on the anniversary of the Battle of the Boyne.

2. The celebration which takes place at such annually recurring dates; *orig.* a mass or religious service in memory of some one on the day of his death, also called 'year's mind.'

1447 BOKENHAM *Lyvys of Seyntys* 33 That ye for me wil preyn specyally, And therto my annyversarye kepyn yerly. **1539** *Bury Wills* 138 My executors shall keape an yearelie obite or anniuersarie the space of v yeares. **1580** BARET *Alv.* A 427 To keepe an aniuersarie or yeares minde, *Exequi annua vota.* **1637** HEYWOOD *R. King* II. iv, This Anniversary doe we yeerely keepe In memory of our late victories. **1883** *Chr. World* 3 Aug. 515/4 Large collections in connection with Sunday-School anniversaries continue to be reported.

†**3.** *R.C. Ch.* Sometimes used for the *annale* or commemorative service performed daily for a year after the death of a person. *Obs.* See ANNALS 3.

1612 DEKKER *If not Good* Wks. 1873 III. 285 Chant Anthems, Aniuersaries, Dirges. **1726** AYLIFFE *Parerg.* 190 An Anniversary..is celebrated not only once, viz., at the end of the year..but ought to be said every day throughout the whole year for the soul of the deceas'd. **1753** CHAMBERS *Cycl. Supp.*, *Anniversary* is more particularly used for the *annale*, or mass rehearsed daily for the space of a year after a person's death.

†**4.** A magazine or review published annually; an 'annual.' *Obs. rare.*

1829 SOUTHEY *Lett.* (1856) IV. 140, I am sorry your anniversary has not answered..and indeed think the plan of a monthly much better than that of a yearly miscellany.

anniversary (ænɪˈvɜːsərɪ), *v. rare.* [f. prec. sb.; cf. to *fête.*] To celebrate the anniversary of.

1861 *Sat. Rev.* 23 Nov. 535 The kindred societies which came to be anniversaried on that day at Aylesbury.

†**'anniverse.** *Obs.* [f. L. *anni versus* the (re)turning of a year. Common in 17th c.] An anniversary.

1615 CORBET *Poems* (1807) 52 As Henryes vault, his peace, his sacred hearse, Are torne and batter'd by thine anniverse. *a* **1681** OLDHAM *Poems* (1698) 54 Only once a year, On the sad anniverse drop a remembering tear. **1817** W. TAYLOR in *Month. Mag.* XLIV. 234 The 7th of November was kept as a solemn Anniverse by Lorenzo dei Medici.

annivoler, corrupt variant of ANNUELLER.

†**a'nnobilize**, *v. Obs. rare*$^{-1}$. [f. Fr. *anoblir*, formerly *annoblir* (lengthened stem *annobliss-*); see -IZE².] To ennoble.

1730 MORTIMER in *Phil. Trans.* XXXVI. 401 He annobilized it by a Croud of Heroes, to whom he gave Birth.

‖**Anno Domini** (ˈænəʊ ˈdɒmɪnaɪ). *phr.* [L. 'in the year of (our) Lord'; usually written A.D.]

a. In the year of the Christian era; in the year since (the reputed date of) the birth of Christ.

1579 W. FULKE *Heskins's Parl.* 389 Whome M. Heskins.. affirmeth to haue liued *Anno Dom.* 511. **1818** MOORE *Fudge Fam.* iii. 68 Here toddles along some old figure of fun, With a coat you might date Anno Domini One.

b. *jocular colloq.* as *sb.* Advanced or advancing age. Also *attrib.*

1885 F. GALE *Hon. R. Grimston* xvi. 284 Whenever he felt less able to do things than formerly, he used to say he was afraid 'Anno Domini' was the cause. **1892** F. POLLOCK *Leading Cases* 93 Yet nothing mortal may deny The march of *Anno Domini* Not e'en the Senior Fellow. **1900** *Daily News* 3 Feb. 2/5, I suffer from an incurable complaint—the complaint of Anno Domini. **1906** E. V. LUCAS *Fireside & Sunshine* 186 When the time came for A. to take the bat he was unable to do so. *Anno Domini* asserted itself. **1921** *Times* 31 Mar., My resignation is due to what we call the *anno Domini* clause, which has come into operation.

annoie, annoious, obs. forms of ANNOY, etc.

annoisance, variant of ANNUISANCE.

annominate (əˈnɒmɪneɪt), *v. rare.* [variant of AGNOMINATE, after med.L. and Fr. spelling with *ann-*.] To name or call by some epithet or title.

1765 TUCKER *Lt. Nat.* I. 475 The vast Pacific Ocean, commonly..called, appellated, as the saying is, and annominated, the South-sea. **1834** SOUTHEY *Doctor* viii.§1 How then shall these chapters be annominated? Intercalary they shall not.

annomination (əˌnɒmɪˈneɪʃən). [variant of AGNOMINATION; cf. mod.Fr. *annomination.*]

1. Paronomasia.

1753 CHAMBERS *Cycl. Supp.*, *Annomination*, the same with what is otherwise called *paronomasia.* **1858** MARSH *Eng. Lang.* xxv. 566 Annomination consists in opposing to each other..words of similar sound but different signification.

†**2.** Alliteration. *Obs.*

1775 TYRWHITT *Ess. Chaucer* III. §1 *note*, Giraldus Cambrensis speaks of *Annomination*, the which he describes to be what we call *Alliteration.*

†**a'nnonary**, *a. Obs.* [ad. L. *annōnāri-us*, f. *annōna* provisions: see -ARY.] Of or pertaining to provisions.

1651 BIGGS *New Dispens.* 193 ⁋264 Their anonary or kitchin Physick.

‖**annonce** (aˈnɔ̃s). *rare.* [Fr. *annonce*, f. *annoncer*: see ANNOUNCE.] = ANNOUNCEMENT.

1807 *Edin. Rev.* XI. 215 We read the *annonce* of Mr. Wordsworth's publication with a good deal of interest. **1863** CHAMBERS *Bk. Days* 287 An over-flourishing family *annonce* in a newspaper.

annonciade, variant of ANNUNCIADE.

†**a'nnorm(e**, *v. Obs. rare*$^{-1}$. [f. L. *an-* = *ad-* to + *norma* rule.] To reduce to rule, normalize.

a **1644** QUARLES *Sheph. Ecl.* iii, Under Thee our Head, we did annorme Our Government, and made it uniforme.

annorn, -ourn, var. ANORN *v. Obs.*, to adorn.

†**a'nnosity.** *Obs. rare*$^{-1}$. [ad. L. *annōsitātem*, n. of quality f. *annōs -us* full of years, f. *annus* year.] Fullness of years, length of life, agedness.

1654 LESTRANGE *Chas. I.* 136 Robert Parr..the wonder of our times for annosity and long life. **1742** BAILEY, *Annosity*, Agedness. [Not in J. or mod. Dicts.]

annotate (ˈænəteɪt), *v.* [f. L. *annotāt-* ppl. stem of *annotā-re* or *adnotāre* to put a note to; f. *ad* to + *notā-re* to mark, f. *nota* a mark: see NOTE. An early by-form was ANNOTE.] (Not in Johnson's Dict., but used in explaining *Comment.*)

1. *trans.* To add notes to, furnish with notes (a literary work or author).

1755 JOHNSON, *Comment*, to annotate; to write notes; to expound. **1801** W. TAYLOR in *Month. Mag.* XII. 576 This translation is executed with exactness, and annotated with erudition. **1836** SOUTHEY *Lett.* IV. 462 His engagement to annotate 'Milton.' **1859** MASSON *Milton* I. 531 A copy of Aratus..which is annotated here and there by his hand.

2. *intr.* To add or make notes. Const. *on, upon.*

1733 ILIVE *Orat.* 26 (T.) Give me leave to annotate on the words thus. **1803** SOUTHEY in Robberds' *Mem. W. Taylor* I. 466 Examine what I and what Turner write..and annotate thereupon. **1882** *Blackw. Mag.* Jan. 108 It was Coleridge's habit to annotate with a pencil.

annotated (ˈænəteɪtɪd), *ppl. a.* [f. prec. + -ED.] Furnished with notes (by an editor).

1807 W. TAYLOR in *Ann. Rev.* V. 170 Then follows the journal of Bannatyne sparingly annotated. **1860** (*title*) The Annotated Paragraph Bible.

annotation (ænəʊˈteɪʃən). Also 6 **-cyon, anotacion.** [prob. a. Fr. *annotation* (16th c. in Littré), ad. L. *annotātiōn-em*, f. *annotāre* to ANNOTATE.]

1. The action of annotating or making notes.

1570 DEE *Math. Pref.* 28 And so finish my Annotation Staticall. **1583** T. WATSON *Poems* (Arb.) 78 So plainely..set downe..that it neede no further annotation to explaine it. **1870** *Daily News* 3 Oct., They do not need annotation or comment. Such revelations tell their own story.

†**2.** The action of marking by a particular date or era; chronological reckoning or notation. *Obs.*

1460 CAPGRAVE *Chron.* 36 In this same tyme began the annotacion of Olimpias. **1669** GALE *Crt. Gentiles* I. III. ii. 25 There was anciently no annotation of historie among them [the Grecians].

3. *concr.* (usually *pl.*) A note added to anything written, by way of explanation or comment.

1528 GARDINER in Pocock *Rec. Ref.* I. li. 129 The minute which master Fox bringeth with him, with annotations in the margin. **1563** J. SHUTE *Archit.* A iij a, Gulielmus Philander..wrote..Anotacions vpon Vitruuius. **1678** CUDWORTH *Intell. Syst.* 367 Where we have this Annotation of Servius. **1712** ADDISON *Spect.* No. 452 ⁋2 The Multitude of Annotations, Explanations, Reflexions, and various Readings. **1866** MOTLEY *Dutch Rep.* V. ii. 681 The letter.. was underlined by him..and furnished with the following annotation.

†**b.** *spec.* An inventory of goods seized by authority of justice. (So in Fr.) *Obs. rare.*

1616 BEAUM. & FL. *Scornf. Lady* I. ii, Fire off thy annotations and thy rent-books.

†**4.** *Med.* A sign, token, symptom, *and hence*, access of any illness. *Obs.*

1753 CHAMBERS *Cycl. Supp.*, *Annotation* in medicine, denotes the very beginning of a febrile paroxysm..This is called by the Greeks *episemasia.*

anno'tationist. ? *Obs. rare.* [f. prec. + -IST.] A professed annotator.

1672 J. WORTHINGTON *Mede's Life* in *Wks.* 7 If Mr. Mede's method of interpreting the Apocalyps be.. compared with the elder methods of any Annotationists whatsoever.

annotative (ˈænətɛ(ɪ)tɪv), *a.* [f. L. *annotāt-* (see ANNOTATE) + -IVE.] Of the nature of, or characterized by, annotation.

annotator (ˈænəteɪtə(r)). Also 7 **adn-.** [a. L. *annotātor*, n. of agent f. *annotāre* to ANNOTATE: see -TOR. Cf. mod.Fr. *annotateur.*] One who annotates or writes notes to a text; a commentator.

1663 SPENCER *Prodigies* 202 (J.) The speech of our learned and pious annotator. **1668** (*title*) Catalogue of our English Writers of the Old and New Testament..whether Commentators, Elucidators, Adnotators, Expositors. **1764** WILKES *Corr.* (1805) II. 92 All the author's friends shall be the friends of the annotator. **1808** COLEBROOKE *Vedas* in *Asiat. Res.* VIII. 481 A crowd of annotators whose works expound every passage in the original gloss.

annotatory (əˈnəʊtətərɪ), *a. rare*$^{-0}$. [f. ANNOTATOR + -Y, as if ad. L. **annotātōrius*, f. *annotātor.*] Of or pertaining to an annotator, or his work.

1859 WORCESTER.

†**a'nnote**, *v. Obs. rare.* Also 5 **anote.** [a. OFr. *anote-r*, ad. L. *annotā-re*; cf. *connote*, *denote.*]

1. To note against, lay to the charge of.

1494 FABYAN VII. 307 The lenger this contynuyd, yᵉ more disclaunder was anotyd to the iustyces.

2. = ANNOTATE.

1533 UDALL (*title*) Terentius, Flovres..with the Exposition..of such Latyne Wordes, as were thought nedefull to be annoted.

†**'annotine.** *Bot. Obs. rare*$^{-1}$. [ad. L. *annōtin-us* of a year's standing, f. *ann-us* a year + *-tinus* affix of time.] A tree of which the fruit does not ripen in a single season, but of which last year's fruit remains beside that of the present year; *e.g.* the fig.

1664 EVELYN *Silva* (1776) 460 We do not reckon trees to be sterile, which do not yield a fruitful burden constantly every year (as Juniper and some Annotines do).

annotinous (əˈnɒtɪnəs), *a. Bot. rare.* [f. L. *annōtin-us* (see prec.) + -OUS.] (See quot.)

1836 *Penny Cycl.* V. 251 *Annotinous*, a year old. [**1847** LINDLEY *Elem. Bot.*, *Rami annotini* are branches one year old.]

annotto, variant of ANATTA.

announce (əˈnaʊns), *v.* Also 5 **anounce, adnounce.** [a. OFr. *anonce-r*, earlier *anoncier*, *anuncier*:—L. *adnuntiā-re*, f. *ad* to + *nuntiāre* to bear a message, f. *nunti-us* bringing news. See AN- *pref.* 6.]

1. To make known as an official messenger; to deliver news; to make public or official intimation of, to proclaim (something of the nature of news). **a.** *simply.*

1485 CAXTON *Paris & V.* (1868) 7 Sente his heraulds in France and Englond to anounce. **1638** FEATLY *Lyndom.* I. 207 The Jesuits and Seminarie Priests at Doway and Rhemes..have fraught their English translation of the Bible, with so many affected harsh-sounding, and uncouth words to English eares, as *announce..euroclydon.* *a* **1721** PRIOR *Hymn of Callim.* (J.) Who model nations, publish laws, announce Or life or death. **1771** *Junius Lett.* I. 259 Your re-appointment to a seat in the Cabinet was announced to the public. **1809** W. IRVING *Knickerb.* 79 Announcing his determination of leading on his troops in person. **1860** TYNDALL *Glac.* II. §9. 272 He announces the fact, but gives no details.

b. with *subord. cl.*

1483 CAXTON *Gold. Leg.* 94/1, I adnounce and shewe to you that holy chirche shal haue peas. —— *G. de la Tour* I vj b, The angel which sayd and announced to them that he was rysen. **1857** MAURICE *Ep. St. John* ix. 139 Their first duty was to announce that that Jesus..was both Lord and Christ.

c. To make (a person) known *as* so-and-so; often *refl.*

1837 E. HOWARD *Old Commodore* II. xix. 184 Announcing himself as a magistrate made a considerable impression on the seamen. **1856** DE QUINCEY *Confess.* in *Wks.* V. 150, I announced myself as a passenger 'booked' for that night's mail. **1888** MRS. H. WARD *R. Elsmere* ii, He announced himself as safely installed at Oxford. **1891** HARDY *Group of Noble Dames* 125 She could not live without announcing herself to him as his mother. *Ibid.* 158 She..requested him to allow her to..announce him as having died of malignant ague.

2. *ellipt.* To intimate the approach or presence of.

1761 SMOLLETT *Gil Blas* (1802) II. IV. viii. 29, I stationed myself at the chamber door to announce and introduce the persons who arrived. **1802** MAR. EDGEWORTH *Moral T.* (1816) I. i. 4 Dinner was announced. **1845** FORD *Handbk. Spain* i. 59 Few take to their beds except to die and the doctor announces the undertaker.

3. To make known, intimate to the senses (without words).

1808 SCOTT *Marm.* VI. xxv, Nor martial shout, nor minstrel tone, Announced their march. **1848** L. HUNT *Jar of Honey* x. 131 Faint streaks of light..announced the approach of the great luminary. **1860** TYNDALL *Glac.* I. 124 A peal to the right announced the descent of an avalanche.

4. To declare or make manifest to the mind.

1781 GIBBON *Decl. & F.* II. xxvii. 59 His feeble efforts announced his degenerate spirit. **1794** SULLIVAN *View Nat.* II. 102 The successive beds of bitumens that are found in the bowels of the earth, announce them to have been deposited slowly. **1827** SCOTT *Highl. Wid.* I. 118 Gold buckles in his shoes, etc...announced him to be a domestic of trust and importance.

¶ App. confused with ANHAUNCE, q.v.

a **1533** FRITH *Disput. Purg.* (1829) 203 Behold, I pray you, whither my Lord of Rochester hath brought our Holy Father, in announcing his power so high.

†**announce**, *sb. Obs.* [f. ANNOUNCE *v.*; cf. ANNONCE.] **1.** = ANNOUNCEMENT.

1787 J. NICHOLS in Welsted *Wks.* p. xxvi, This friendly announce is somewhat premature. **1818** LADY MORGAN *Fl. Macarthy* III. iii. 106 The announce of the judges' carriages ..induced the whole party to rise. **1827** *Blackw. Mag.* XXI. 210/1 The baker..seemed to have been struck by catalepsy at my first announce.

2. announce bill, a poster advertising a theatrical performance or the like.

1824 R. HUMPHREYS in J. Decastro *Memoirs* 88 Here follows his announce bill for that night. **1866** M. MACKINTOSH *Stage Reminiscences* vi. 69 She [*sc.* Madame Vestris] then drove round to Fairbrother's, in Bow-street (the great playbill printer of those days), and ordered her 'announce' bills.

announced (ə'naʊnst), *ppl. a.* [f. ANNOUNCE *v.* + -ED.] Made publicly known; intimated.

1671 MILTON *P.R.* IV. 504 Of thy birth at length announced by Gabriel with the first I knew. **1867** DICKENS *Lett.* (1880) II. 319 All our announced readings are already crammed.

announcement (ə'naʊnsmənt). [a. Fr. *annoncement*: see ANNOUNCE and -MENT.] The action or process of announcing; public or official notification, intimation, declaration.

Not in J. 'In our old Dictionaries, *announcing* is found instead of this word, which is quite of modern use.'—TODD 1818.

1798 BELSHAM *Hist. Eng.* (L.) He made the announcement, and was received with cheers. **1847** C. BRONTË *Jane Eyre* xiv. 133 With this announcement he rose from his chair. **1859** B. POWELL *Ord. Nat.* iii. §2. 331 The sudden announcement of her husband's fate.

announcer (ə'naʊnsə(r)). [f. as prec. + -ER[1].] **a.** One who announces, tells news, or gives notice.

1611 COTGR., *Annonceur*, An announcer, declarer, proclaimer, signifier, advertiser. **1686** *Turkish Spy* (L.) The announcer of this good news was received with cheers. **1761** SMOLLETT *Gil Blas* (1802) II. IV. viii. 29 The announcer is a domestic who stands in the hall on visiting days, and pronounces aloud the names of the company as they come in. **1824–8** LANDOR *Imag. Conv.* (1846) I. 320 The sad announcer of your departure hence.

b. *Broadcasting.* The person who announces the subjects of a programme or the items of current news, etc.

1922 *Radio Broadcast* Dec. 138 You have heard the announcer say: 'This is XYZ, the Blankety Blank station at So-and-So.' **1923** *Radio Times* 28 Sept. 19 (Announcer) 'The Stock Exchange was very lively to-day.' **1929** G. N. CLARK in *S.P.E. Tract* XXXIII. 415 The professional announcers are not so dangerous as they seem. They belong to a class, very numerous under modern conditions, of what may be called persons of far-reaching insignificance. *Ibid.* 419 Coherence which is given..by the force of an individual personality... Those of us who value [this kind] of coherence regard with distaste the pure speech of the announcers. **1957** AUDEN & KALLMAN *Magic Flute* I. p. 57 For interruption is what we expect, Since that new god, the Paid Announcer, rose.

announcing (ə'naʊnsɪŋ), *vbl. sb.* [f. as prec. + -ING[1].] Making known, declaring. (Mostly gerundial.)

announcing (ə'naʊnsɪŋ), *ppl. a.* [f. as prec. + -ING[2].] Declaring, proclaiming.

1875 BROWNING *Aristoph. Apol.* 299 How say'st? What did I? Ill-announcing sire! **1878** T. SINCLAIR *Mount* 26 The announcing, almost prophetic, Emerson.

annoy (ə'nɔɪ), *sb.* Forms: 3 anui, 4 anuy(e, onnuy, 4–6 anoy(e, 4–7 annoye, 5 annoi, 6–7 annoie, 6– annoy. [a. OFr. *anoi, anui, enoi, enui* (mod. *ennui*), cogn. w. Sp. *enojo*, OSp. *enoyo* (Pg. and OIt. *nojo*), Pr. *enoi, enuoi*, OCat. *enutg*, OVenet. *inodio*, originating, according to Diez, in the L. phrase *in odio*, as *est mihi in odio* 'it is to me hateful,' whence *inodio* was at length taken as sb. 'hatred, dislike, annoyance': see Diez and Littré. The *n* was subsequently doubled in Fr. and Eng. by form-assoc. with compounds like *en-noble, an-nounce*; the aphet. form *noi*, NOY (cf. *noisome*) helping in Eng. to encourage an erroneous analysis of the word as *a-noy*, whence *an-noy*. ENNOY, after Fr., is occasional in 15–16th c. (Now mostly poetic, ANNOYANCE being the common prose equivalent.)]

1. A mental state akin to pain arising from the involuntary reception of impressions, or subjection to circumstances, which one dislikes; disturbed or ruffled feeling; discomfort, vexation, trouble. In earlier times often = mod. Fr. *ennui*; in later usage expressing more active feeling of discomfort.

c **1230** *Ancr. R.* 374 Þe þridde bitternesse is ine longunge touward heouene, & in þe anui of þisse worlde. *c* **1300** *Beket* 1618 Ich have ibeo in anuy. **1388** WYCLIF *Ps.* cxix. 28 Mi soule nappide for anoye [**1611** melteth for heauinesse]. **1483** CAXTON *Gold. Leg.* 104/3 And deyed in grete myserye of Annoye. **1534** LD. BERNERS *Gold. Bk. M. Aurel.* (1546) E e, They haue..greate annoy of theyr heyres. **1596** SPENSER *F.Q.* I. vi. 17 The lad n'ould after joy; But pynd away in anguish and selfe-wild annoy. **1675** T. BROOKS *Gold. Key* Wks. 1867 V. 147 His cross our comfort; his annoy our endless joy. **1700** DRYDEN *Pal. & Arc.* III. 1111 After past annoy To take the good Vicissitude of joy. **1812** W. TAYLOR in *Month. Rev.* LXVII. 143 His *ennui* amounted to *annoy*. **1870** EMERSON *Soc. & Solit.* xi. 243 He had better..have been defeated, than give her a moment's annoy. **1872** BLACKIE *Lays of Highl.* 121 A student toiling with annoy Through long dry tomes.

b. *phr.* **to work (do** *obs.*) **annoy**: to cause discomfort or trouble, to molest. *arch.*

a **1420** OCCLEVE *De Reg. Princ.* 1016 Writyng also dothe grete annoies thre. *c* **1450** *Merlin* xiii. 191 The heete that dide hem grete anoye. **1600** HOLLAND *Livy* XXXII. xxi. 822 The Romane navie by sea shall..do us all annoy. **1768** BEATTIE *Minstr.* II. xxxvii, Ere victory and empire wrought annoy. **1813** BYRON *Br. Abydos* I. v, Much I misdoubt this wayward boy Will one day work me more annoy.

2. That which causes the above feeling; a troubling thing, circumstance, or action; annoyance.

c **1305** *E.E. Poems* (1862) 97 Ech man þat haueþ mone In enie neode oþer anuy. **1375** BARBOUR *Bruce* III. 16 Auenturis that thaim befell, And gret anoyis. **1387** TREVISA *Higden* Rolls Ser. I. 239 [In the triumph] þis onnuy he hadde: a cherle was wiþ hym in his chare. **1594** SHAKS. *Rich. III*, v. iii. 156 Good Angels guard thee from the Boares annoy. **1624** WOTTON *Arch.* (1672) 42 The benefit of removing such annoies out of sight. **1827** KEBLE *Chr. Year* 3rd S. Trin., A newborn soul..yet wrapt in earth's annoy.

annoy (ə'nɔɪ), *v.* Forms: 3–4 anue, -uie, -uye, 4 anye, anuyȝe, 4–7 anoie, -oye, annoie, -oye, 5– annoy. Also aphetized to NOY, and written after Fr. ENNOY. [a. OFr. *anuie-r, enuier, anoier, enoier*, cogn. w. Pr. *enuiar, enoiar*, Sp. *enojar*, It. *annoiare*, pointing to a common Romanic *inodiāre* (found in OIt.), f. *inodio*: see prec. For spelling with double *n*, see AN- *pref.* 6.]

†**1.** *intr.* To be hateful, odious, offensive, or a cause of trouble (*to*, or with *dat.*) *Obs.*

c **1340** *Ayenb.* 162 To huam þet þe wordle anoyþ uor þe perils..huerof hi is al uol. *c* **1374** CHAUCER *Boeth.* I. v, Ne þe forsweryng ne þe fraude..ne a-noyeþ not to schrewes. *c* **1386** —— *Melib.* 31 As Motthes in the shepes flees anoyeth[*v.r.* annoyeþ, -oyen] to the clothes..so anoyeth [*v.r.* annoieþ, anoyþe] sorwe to the herte.

†**2.** *trans.* To be hateful or distasteful to; to trouble, irk, bore, weary. (= Fr. *ennuyer.*) In passive const. w. *of. Obs.*

a **1300** *Havelok* 1734 Þat is þe storie for to lenge, It wolde anuye þis fayre genge. *a* **1300** *Leg. Rood* (1871) 20 Of is lif he was anuyd [*v.r.* anuyȝed]. *a* **1400** *Rel. Pieces fr. Thornton MS.* 17 And sythen when þou has þam at þi will, þan erte þou of thaa thynges annoyede. **1534** LD. BERNERS *Gold Bk. M. Aurel* (1546) K ij, Ye all are anoyed and wery of all goodnes.

†**b.** *impers. it annoys me..*: it irks me. *Obs. rare.*

1382 WYCLIF *2 Cor.* i. 8 It anoyȝede [**1388** anoiede] vs, ȝhe, for to lyue. **1388** ——*Numb.* xxi. 4 It bigan to anoye the puple of the weie and trauel. *c* **1386** CHAUCER *Chan. Yem. Prol. & T.* 483 No thyng anoyeth me To lene a man a noble or two or thre.

3. *trans.* To affect (a person) in a way that disturbs his equanimity, hurts his susceptibilities, or causes slight irritation. (Refers to the feeling produced, rather than to the action producing it; hence commonest in the passive *to be annoyed*: to be ruffled in mind, troubled, vexed.)

1250 LAY. 2259 Corineus nas anued [**1205** un-eðe]. And wo on his mode. **1297** R. GLOUC. 487 King Philip was anuyd ..That ther nas of him word non, bote al of Richard the king. *c* **1315** SHOREHAM 36 Ȝef he the schel anoye aȝt, Hyt wyle of-thenche hym sore. *c* **1450** LONELICH *Grail* I. 324 Ȝif I wiste my lord not forto anoye. **1596** SHAKS. *Tam. Shrew* I. i. 189 She will not be annoy'd with suters. **1616** R. C. *Times' Whistle* vii. 3156 Soe overioyde That through excesse therof he is annoide. **1743** TINDAL *Rapin's Hist.* VII. XVII. 104 He did not want good-will to annoy Elizabeth. **1855** MACAULAY *Hist. Eng.* III. 532 He felt some..vindictive pleasure in annoying those who had cruelly annoyed him.

†**b.** *to be annoyed after* or *for*: to worry about, be anxious for. *Obs. rare.*

a **1400** *Rel. Pieces fr. Thornton MS.* 17 Þou erte anoyede eftire many thynges, and turment if þou hafe thaym noghte. **1616** R. C. *Times' Whistle* vii. 2949 The thing, for which he erst was soe anoyde.

†**c.** *refl.* To vex oneself, take offence, grieve. *Obs.*

c **1300** *K. Alis.* 876 Nicolas him anoyed: With wraththe to Alisaundre he saide.

†**d.** *intr.* (refl. pron. omitted.) *Obs.*

c **1374** CHAUCER *Boeth.* II. iv. 41 If þat þou anoie nat or forþenke nat of al þi fortune. *a* **1555** LATIMER *Serm. & Rem.* 332 To profit with learning, with ignorance not to annoy.

4. By transf. to the objective means: To molest, injure, hurt, harm; now *esp.* in military use.

c **1380** *Sir. Ferumb.* 364 Wyþ my werres y haue a-nyed muche of cristendome. *c* **1400** *Destr. Troy* xv. 6790 Theseus ..the troiens anoyet. **1593** SHAKS. *Hen. VI*, III. i. 67 Thornes that would annoy our Foot. **1607** TOPSELL *Four-footed Beasts* 530 Infested and annoyed with Lice. **1667** MILTON *P.L.* VI. 369 Nor stood unmindful Abdiel to annoy The atheist crew. **1759** MARTIN *Nat. Hist.* I. 41 A gallant Saxon, who annoyed this Coast. **1794** NELSON in Nicolas *Disp.* (1845) I. 368 The works on the hills would annoy the Town.

b. *absol.*

1382 WYCLIF *Is.* xi. 9 Thei shuln not noȝen [**1388** anoye] ..in al myn hoeli mounteyn. *c* **1420** *Pallad. on Husb.* II. 163 Yf Est or southeryn wyndes nought enaye. **1764** GOLDSM. *Trav.* 338 But foster'd e'en by Freedom, ills annoy. **1789–94** W. BLAKE *School Boy* 18 How can a child, when fears annoy, But droop his tender wing?

†**5.** To affect (a thing) in a way which interferes with its proper action; to interfere with detrimentally, affect injuriously. *Obs.*

c **1386** CHAUCER *Man of L.T.* 394 Who badde foure spiritz of tempest..Anoyen [*v.r.* annoyeþ] neyther londe, see, ne tree? *c* **1420** *Pallad. on Husb.* iv. 131 The molde, and other suche as diggeth lowe, Anoie hem not. **1596** SPENSER *F.Q.* II. vii. 15 Mucky filth his [the stream's] braunching armes annoyes. **1642** T. TAYLOR *God's Judgem.* I. I. xv. 42 The poysoned stinke and savour whereof so annoyed his stomacke that he never left vomiting. **1708** *Procl.* in *Lond. Gaz.* mmmmccccliI/2 So as to Annoy the Haling of Sayns in the usual Baiting Places. **1721** J. PERRY *Daggenh. Breach* 116 To annoy or choak the Harbour by any Drift.

annoyance (ə'nɔɪəns). Also 4–6 **anoyaunce**, (**anoysaunce**), 4–7 **anoyance**, (6 **innoyaunce**), 6–7 **anoiance.** [a. OFr. *anuiance, anoiance*, f. *anuiant* pr. pple. of *anuyer*: see prec. and -ANCE.]

1. The action of annoying, vexing, troubling, molesting, or injuring; molestation.

c **1386** CHAUCER *Pers. T.* 972 Nat to the anoyance [*v.r.* anoyaunce, -saunce, annoyance] of any man or womman. **1509** FISHER *Wks.* (1876) 304 [The risen body] shall perce thorowe the stone walles, without ony anoyance of them. **1605** SHAKS. *Macb.* v. i. 84 Looke after her, Remoue from her the meanes of all annoyance. **1789** G. WHITE *Selborne* xxi. (1853) 88 To secure these nests from the annoyance of sheperd boys. **1850–62** MERIVALE *Rom. Emp.* V. xlii. 34 [Germanicus] having thus crippled their means of annoyance, returned to the Rhine.

2. The state of feeling caused by what annoys; disturbance by what one dislikes; dislike, disgust, vexation, trouble.

1502 *Ord. Crysten Men* (W. de W.) I. vii. (1506) 54 Hauynge synne in hate, in anoyaunce. **1643** MILTON *Divorce* I. x. (1847) 134/1 The annoyance and trouble of mind [will] infuse itself into all the faculties..of the body. **1711** STEELE *Spect.* No. 20 ¶2 He..stands upon a Hassock ..to the great Annoyance of the devoutest Part of the Auditory. *a* **1716** SOUTH (J.) The greatest annoyance and disturbance of mankind has been from one of those two things, force or fraud. **1872** BLACK *Adv. Phaeton* xix. 270 She is put to the annoyance of refusing one of them.

3. Anything annoying or causing trouble, a nuisance. ***Jury of Annoyance***: one appointed to report upon public nuisances.

1502 ARNOLD *Chron.* 83 The corupte sauours and lothsom innoyaunces caused by slaughter of bestes within the cyte. **1622** CALLIS *Stat. Sewers* (1824) 211 Casting dirt, sand, ballast, or other annoyance, into the rivers or streams. **1663** GERBIER *Counsel* E vj a, The Kitchens may be..at hand; and yet not be an annoyance. **1754** *Act 29 Geo. II.* xxv. §12 The Jury of Annoyance..shall..enquire into..all bad pavements and all annoyances, obstructions and encroachments, upon any of the public ways. **1859** MRS. SCHIMMEL-PENNINCK *Princ. Beauty* I. xi. §34 An intrusive annoyance, like a succession of trifling visitors when we need to be alone.

annoyancer (ə'nɔɪənsə(r)). *rare.* [f. prec. + -ER[1]; cf. *conveyancer.*] He who, or that which, causes annoyance.

1632 D. LUPTON *Lond. Carbonad.* (1857) 307 There are three annoyancers of his Flocke, the Scab, Thieves, and a long Rotte. *a* **1834** LAMB in Colvin *Landor* (1881) 73, I knew all your Welsh annoyancers, the measureless Bethams.

annoyed (ə'nɔɪd), *ppl. a.* [f. ANNOY *v.* + -ED.]

1. Disturbed by what one dislikes; troubled, vexed, offended.

a **1300** *K. Alis.* 3310 Y am aschamed And sore anoyed, and agramed. **1388** WYCLIF *Bar.* iii. 1 A soule in angwischis and a spirit anoied crieth to thee. **1611** COTGR., *Molesté*.. offended, combered, vexed, annoyed. **1823** LAMB *Elia* (1860) 265 The actor who plays the annoyed man. *Mod.* She had an annoyed, harassed look.

†**2.** Of things: Detrimentally affected; incommoded, pestered. *Obs.*

1620 VENNER *Via Recta* Introd. 11 Them that haue their lungs annoyed with much moisture. **1658** EVELYN *Fr. Gard.* (1675) 105 A garden annoy'd with this plague.

annoyer (ə'nɔɪə(r)). [f. ANNOY *v.* + -ER[1].] One who, or that which, annoys; a disturber.

1577-87 HARRISON *Eng.* I. II. xi. 230 Our third annoiers of the common-wealth are roges. **1815** KIRBY & SPENCE *Entomol.* (1843) I. 83 One very prominent annoyer of our comfort and repose. **1846** DE QUINCEY *Wks.* (1859) XII. 269 These wretched annoyers of our peace.

†**a'nnoyful, anoyful,** *a. Obs. rare*[−1]. [f. ANNOY *sb.* + -FUL.] Full of annoyance; = ANNOYOUS.

c **1386** CHAUCER *Melib.* 66 For al be it so that alle tariyng be anoyful [*v.r.* a-noyeful, noyful].

annoying (ə'nɔɪɪŋ), *vbl. sb.* [f. ANNOY *v.* + -ING[1].] The giving of trouble or vexation; annoyance. (Now gerundial.)

c **1330** *Arth. & Merl.* 4470 No might do with hir wicheing In Inglond non anoiing. **1566** T. STAPLETON *Ret. Untr. Jewel* iii. 116 To whom euery light discorde is a great anoying. **1712** ADDISON *Spect.* No. 441 ¶2 Every Thing that is capable of annoying or offending us.

a'nnoying, *ppl. a.* [f. as prec. + -ING[2].] Troubling, disturbing, causing annoyance.

c **1374** CHAUCER *Boeth.* I. v. 22 Anoienge folk treden, and þat vnryȝtfully, in þe nekkes of holy men. **1593** T. WATSON *Poems* (Arb.) 187 Annoying sorrowes..Assaild my thoughts. **1753** HERVEY *Theron & Asp.* (1755) I. 94 Screened them from the annoying sun-beams. **1866** GEO. ELIOT *F. Holt* (1868) 37 He found Jermyn's manner annoying.

a'nnoyingly, *adv. rare.* [f. prec. + -LY[2].] In an annoying manner, disturbingly.

1851 H. SPENCER *Soc. Statics* xvii. §4 An unamiable little urchin..is perhaps annoyingly vociferous in his play.

a'nnoyingness. [f. as prec. + -NESS.] The quality of being annoying, vexatiousness.

Mod. The annoyingness of the incident is far greater than the actual damage done.

annoyment (ə'nɔɪmənt). *rare.* [? a. OFr. *anoiement, anuiement*: see ANNOY *v.* + -MENT.] The action of annoying; the state of annoyance.

c **1460** *Play Sacr.* 581, I warant she neuer fele annoyment. **1883** D. WINGATE *Lost Laird* xxxvi, McDougal..loved him too much to add to his annoyment.

†**a'nnoyous,** *a. Obs.* Forms: 4 **anious,** 4-5 **-oious, -oyus, annuyous, -noyus,** 6 **annoious, -yous.** Also aphet. NOYOUS, and, after Fr., ENNOYOUS. [a. OFr. *anuieus, anieus, anoios,* mod. *ennuyeux* (cogn. w. Pr. *enoios,* Sp., Pg. *enujoso*):—orig. Romanic **inodioso*: see ANNOY and -OUS.] Unpleasantly disturbing to the feelings; troublesome, vexatious, annoying; harmful, detrimental.

c **1340** *Gaw. & Gr. Knt.* 535 þen þenkkeȝ Gawan ful sone, Of his anious uyage. *c* **1386** CHAUCER *Melib.* 277 A gret multitude of poeple, ful chargeous and ful anoyous [*v.r.* annuyous, -noyus, noyous] for to hiere. *a* **1450** *Knt. de la T.* 128 Ansuerithe not with none anoyeus wordes of ungoodly speche vnto youre husbondes. **1548** GESTE *Pr. Masse* 125 Ye private masse supper is..annoyous to the practycioners therof. **1587** HARRISON *Eng.* I. II. xxiii. 348 Dispersing annoious oppilations.

2. Full of 'annoy'; troubled, grieved, vexed.

c **1440** LONELICH *Graal.* II. 156 The tothere Roses..fillen alle down pore and anoyows.

†**a'nnoyously,** *adv. Obs. rare*[−1]. In 4 **anoy-.** [f. prec. + -LY[2].] In a troublesome or hurtful manner; to one's annoyance or hurt; vexatiously.

c **1374** CHAUCER *Boeth.* III. viii. 80 Yif þou desiryst power, þou shalt..anoyously be cast vndir many periles.

annual ('ænju:əl), *a.* and *sb.* Also 4-7 **annuel(l.** [a. OFr. *annuel,* ad. later L. *annuāl-em* (= cl. *annāl-em*); refashioned after the L. *c* 1500.]

A. *adj.*

1. a. Of or belonging to the year; reckoned, payable, or engaged by the year; yearly.

1382 WYCLIF *Ecclus.* xxxvii. 14 The annuel werker [**1388** A werk man hirid bi the ȝeer]. *a* **1420** OCCLEVE *Male Regle* 51 Thy rentes annuel. **1602** SHAKS. *Ham.* II. ii. 73 Giues him three thousand Crownes in Annuall Fee. **1769** BURKE *Pres. St. Nat.* Wks. II. 73 That trade..is not of less annual value ..than 400,000*l.* **1852** McCULLOCH *Taxation* III. iii. 470 At an annual charge to the public of 30,174,364*l.*

b. Pertaining to a year's events: as ***annual stories, histories*** (obs.), *i.e.* yearly chronicles, annals; ***annual register.***

1502 ARNOLD *Chron.* (1811) 140 Titoleuoo that hath breuied all ye annuell storys of Rome. **1650** R. STAPYLTON *Strada's Low-C. Wars* I. 14 Inferiour princes, whose continued obsequies filled the Annual Register. **1789** (*title*) The New Annual Register, or General Repository of History, Politics and Literature for the year 1788. **1861** (*title*) The Annual Retrospect of Engineering and Architecture.

c. ***annual ring*** = RING *sb.*[1] 7 c.

1879 in R. HUNTER et al. *Encycl. Dict.* **1902** *Encycl. Brit.* XXV. 417/1 Annual rings. **1905** *Sci. Amer.* Suppl. 25 Mar. 24433/1 A partial or entire separation of two consecutive annual rings. **1928** *Forestry* II. 127 The term 'annual ring', originally used in describing the structure of European trees, was later expanded to include the zones of growth discernible..in the trunks of tropical trees.

2. a. Performed or recurring once every year; yearly. ***annual general meeting,*** the yearly meeting of shareholders or members, at which annual reports are read, officers elected, etc.; cf. *general meeting* s.v. GENERAL *a.* 2 a. Abbrev. *A.G.M.* s.v. A III.

1548 UDALL, etc. *Erasm. Par. Hebr.* xi. 28 (R.) Y annual vse or ceremonie to eate the Paschall Lambe. **1667** MILTON *P.L.* VII. 431 So stears the prudent crane Her annual Voiage. **1714** ADDISON *Spect.* No. 579 ¶7 Come up to the Temple with their annual Offerings. **1827** KEBLE *Chr. Year* S. bef. Adv. ii, The Church our annual steps has brought. **1879** *Tablet* 14 June 739/1 The annual general meeting of the Catholic Union of Great Britain. *a* **1884** *Mod.* The Annual Meeting of the association. **1908** NEVILL & JERNINGHAM *Piccadilly to Pall Mall* vi. 221 Up to 1892 there had been no general annual meeting of the members of Brooks's Club. **1937** *Discovery* Apr. 97/1 The annual general meeting of the [British] Association. **1985** *Washington Post* 29 Nov. D9/4 The annual general meeting of the 90-nation organization began Monday.

b. ***annual equation*** of the sun and moon: the determination of the difference between the theoretical and actual position of those bodies, due to the irregular orbital motions of the earth and moon.

1727-51 CHAMBERS *Cycl.* s.v., The annual equation of the mean motion of the sun depends upon the eccentricity of the earth's orbit..The greatest annual equation of the moon's mean motion is 11′, 40″, of its apogee 20′, and of its node 9′, 30″. **1849** MRS. SOMERVILLE *Connex. Phys. Sc.* v. 41 The Annual Equation [of the moon] depends on the sun's distance from the earth; it arises from the moon's motion being accelerated when that of the earth is retarded.

3. Repeated every year and occupying the whole year.

1635 N. CARPENTER *Geog. Del.* I. v. 112 The sunne, which is carried round about the earth in an Annual circuit. **1714** GROVE *Spect.* No. 588 ¶1 No more than the diurnal Rotation of the Earth is opposed to its Annual. **1879** FROUDE *Cæsar* xxv. 425 The annual course of the sun was completed in 365 days and six hours.

4. Existing or lasting for a year only; changed each year.

a. of an office or officer. ***annual priests***; see B 1.

1382 *Pol. Poems* (1859) I. 267 That frers shal annuel prestes bycome. **1460** CAPGRAVE *Chron.* 228 To paye this summe the annual prestis were compelled. **1659** MILTON *Let.* in Wks. 1738 I. 583 Whether the Civil Government be an annual Democracy or a perpetual Aristocracy. **1834** *Penny Cycl.* II. 286/1 The annual archons..to the time of Solon, were taken from the eupatridæ. **1877** STUBBS *Const. Hist.* II. xvi. 433 The commons pray that there may be annual parliaments.

b. of a plant.

a **1626** BACON (J.) The dying in the winter of the roots of plants that are annual. **1706** PHILLIPS, *Annual Leaves* are such as come up in the Spring, and perish in the Winter. **1720** SWIFT *To Stella* Wks. 1755 III. II. 185 Grafting on an annual stock That must our expectation mock. **1857** HENFREY *Elem. Bot.* §47 When a bulb flowers from its terminal bud, in its first season of growth, it is annual.

B. *sb.*

1. *R.C. Ch.* A mass said either daily for a year after, or yearly on the anniversary of, a person's death; *also,* the payment made for it.

1382 *Pol. Poems* (1859) I. 267 Suche annuels has made thes frers so wely and so gay. **1496** *Dives & Paup.* (W. de W.) VII. xxii. 310 Ye may for xx shellynges do synge a quarter of an annuell. **1502** ARNOLD *Chron.* 274 They cause masses to be songe or other annual or trental. **1646** J. ROW *Hist. Kirk* (1842) 34 The annuells, obits, and altarages within burghs. **1753** CHAMBERS *Cycl. Supp., Annual* is used in ecclesiastical writers to denote a yearly office, said for the soul of a person deceased on the day of his obit or anniversary.

2. An annual or yearly payment, tribute, allowance, etc. *Obs.* exc. in *Sc. Law,* where *annual* = quit-rent, ground-rent. Hence ***annual of annual*** = quit-rent of a quit-rent, or smallest possible return.

1622 BACON *Henry VII,* 111 Fiue and twentie thousand Crownes yearely..For which Annuall, etc. **1637** RUTHERFORD *Lett.* 119 (1862) I. 297 Had I but the annual of annual to give to my Lord Jesus, it would ease my pain. **1768** CHESTERF. *Lett.* 321 IV. 266, I will send your annual to Mr. Larpent..and pay the forty shillings a day quarterly. **1866** BELL *Conveyanc.* (1882) II. 1155 The ground-annual is a right of very early origin.

3. a. Anything that lasts only for a year.

1738 SWIFT *Polite Convers.* (R.) Oaths are the children of fashion; they are in some sense almost annuals.

b. *esp.* An annual plant; one that lives only for a year (perpetuating itself by seed, so that there is an annual succession of new plants). Also ***hardy annual*** (lit. and fig.): see HARDY *a.* 4 b. Less frequently applied to an animal.

1685 EVELYN *Diary* 6 Aug. (1955) IV. 462 The Apothecaries Garden of simples at Chelsey: where there ..[are] many rare annuals. **1710** SWIFT *Apol. T. of Tub* (Jod.) They are indeed like annuals, that grow about a young tree. **1726** DE FOE *Hist. Devil* II. iv. (1840) 212 Like an annual in a garden, which must be raised anew every season. **1767** ABERCROMBIE *Ev. Man his own Gardener* 49 To prepare for sowing some of the more curious forms of annuals. **1834** *Paxton's Mag. Bot.* I. 18 Treatment of Hardy Annuals. **1866** *Treas. Bot.* 966/1 Mignonette..is usually treated as an annual. **1883** DAY *Indian Fish* 31 The various modes in which the reproduction of these fishes is carried on... Whether the parents are monogamous, polygamous, or are annuals dying after the reproductive process has been accomplished. **1905** *Westm. Gaz.* 20 June 3/2 Presumably a time will come when even such a wonderfully hardy annual [as Sarah Bernhardt] will fail to reappear.

4. A book of which successive numbers are published once a year, usually at the same date; *esp.* one that conveys information for the year, or reviews the events of the past year; a year-book.

1689 *Answ. Two Papers* 37 Renowned in all the Histories of Europe, as well as in our Annuals. **1825** J. WILSON in Page *De Quincey* I. xii. 270 The volume..if an annual..can yield you fifty guineas. **1840** (*title*) Peter Parley's Annual. **1859** T. LEWIN *Invas. Brit.* 37 The rule laid down for the guidance of mariners in the annual referred to [Admiralty Tidal Tables].

annualist ('ænju:əlɪst). *rare.* [f. ANNUAL *sb.* + -IST.] A contributor to an annual publication.

1829 LAMB *Lett.* (1841) II. 73 The metropolis and its cursed annualists, reviewers, authors and the whole muddy ink press of that stagnant pool. *a* **1849** H. COLERIDGE *Ess.* (1851) II. 6 Carew and his contemporaries would have made excellent album contributors or annualists.

annualize ('ænju:əlaɪz), *v. rare*[−1]. [f. as prec. + -IZE.] To write for, or contribute to, an annual (publication). Hence **annualizing,** *vbl. sb.*

1805 SOUTHEY *Lett.* (1856) I. 310, I am still annualising. **1808** —— in C. Southey *Life* III. 189, I finish my annualising in a few days.

annualized ('ænju:əlaɪzd), *ppl. a.* [f. ANNUAL *a.*: see -IZE.] Of rates of interest, inflation, etc.: calculated on an annual basis, as a projection from figures obtained for a shorter period.

[**1957** E. L. KOHLER *Dict. Accountants* (ed. 2) 31/2 *Annualize,* (Federal income taxes) to expand to an annual basis.] **1969** *Daily Tel.* 31 Oct. 21/3 The..Society, which was the first in the assurance-linked field this March, said.. that its..contracts are already yielding annualised premiums of over £3/4 million. **1975** *Ibid.* 13 Nov. 18 By the late spring of next year we shall, if we are lucky,..have reduced the annualised rate of inflation to between 15 per cent. and 20 per cent. **1977** *Guardian Weekly* 6 Nov. 3/3 In September the..money supply rose 2.2 per cent for an annualised increase of nearly 13 per cent for 1977-78. **1985** *Daily Tel.* 3 Aug. 19/4 The 14 p.c. mortgage rate demanded by most societies at present, for instance, has a true rate—or an annualised percentage rate (APR) as it will be called—of about 15.5 p.c.

annually ('ænju:əlɪ), *adv.* [f. ANNUAL *a.* + -LY[2].] In annual order or succession; yearly, every year, year by year.

1598 FLORIO, *Annalmente,* annually, yeerely. **1633** MASSINGER *Guardian* III. vi, That day..In the remembrance of it annually..I have with pomp observed. **1664** H. MORE *Apol.* 483 The Earth is moved annually and diurnally about the Sun. **1781** GIBBON *Decl. & F.* III. 98 A phial of St. Stephen's blood was annually liquefied at Naples. **1849** MACAULAY *H.E.* I. 575 Parliaments should be held annually.

annuary ('ænju:ərɪ), *a.* and *sb.* [ad. Fr. *annuaire,* ad. L. **annuārius,* f. *annus* year: see -ARY.]

†**A.** *adj.* = ANNUAL *a. Obs.*

1646 J. HALL *Poems* I. 10 Supply anew With annuary cloakes the wandring Jew. **1651** N. BIGGS *New Disp.* Pref. 6 The annuary Registers of after-times.

B. *sb.* †**1.** A priest who says annual masses.

1550 BALE *Image both Ch.* I. (R.) There must be masses and dyrges, ther must be anuaries and bead men.

2. = ANNUAL B 4. (so Fr. *annuaire.*)

1856 (*title*) Annuary of the Kilkenny and S.E. of Ireland Archæological Society.

†**'annuate,** *v. Obs. rare.* [irreg. f. L. *annuĕre* to nod to + -ATE[3].] To nod to, give direction by signs.

1623 COCKERAM, *Annuate,* To nod with the head. **1705** HICKERINGILL *Priest-cr.* I. (1721) 52 To fast, and preach, and pray just as the *Hogen Mogen* States shall annuate and direct. *Ibid.* 62 He will kill and slay as the Priest annuates.

†**annueller.** *Obs.* 4-6. Also **annueler(e, annuler,** (**annivoler**). [Cf. AFr. *annueler* one who celebrates 'annuals,' f. *annuel*: see ANNUAL B 1.] A priest who celebrates annuals, or anniversary masses for the dead.

c **1386** CHAUCER *Chan. Yem. Prol. & T.* 459 In Londoun was a prest, an annueler [*v.r.* annuellere]. **1401** *Pol. Poems* (1859) II. 95 Al these annuellers that syngen for a tyme. **1496** *Dives & Paup.* VII. xviii. 305 He may..lette his trauayle to hyre by dayes and yeres, as annuelers done. *a* **1528** SKELTON *Image Hypocr.* Wks. IV. 97 Then be ther annivolers And small benivolers With chantry chapleynes.

annuent ('ænju:ənt), *a.* [ad. L. *annuent-em* pr. pple. of *annu-ĕre* to nod to.] Nodding; *spec.* applied to the muscles which nod the head.

[**1727-51** CHAMBERS *Cycl., Annuentes Musculi.*] **1849** SMART, *Annuent,* Adapted for nodding, as when one assents.

†**a'nnuisance.** *Obs.* Also 5-6 **anoysaunce,** 6-7 **annusance,** 7 **aneus-, anoys-, annuzance,** 8 **annoisance.** [a. AFr. *anuisance, anusance,* f. *anuire, anuisant,* f. Fr. *nuire* to hurt, perh. confused with *anuier* to annoy.] Nuisance, injury, hurt.

c **1435** *Chaucer's Pars. T.* 972 (Selden MS.) Nat to the anoysaunce of any man [*other MSS.* anoyance]. **1502** *Ord. Crysten Men* (W. de W.) V. vi. (1506) 411 The seconde imperfeccyon of glorye worldle is a maner of anoysaunce. **1514** FITZHERB. *Just. Peas* 96 Al maner of annusaunce of bridges broken in the hyghe wayes. **1641** *Termes de la Ley* 22 *Anoysance*..signifies no more than *Nusance,* and therefore see title *Nusance* afterward. **1649** W. BLITHE *Eng. Improver*

Impr. Ded., With many more annoyances and Annuzances. **1751** CHAMBERS *Cycl.*, *Annoisance*, or Nusance.

annuitant (əˈnjuːɪtənt). [f. next + -ANT, by form-assoc. with *accountant*, *attendant*, etc.]

1. One who holds, or is in receipt of, an annuity.

1720 MERES (*title*) The Equity of Parliaments, etc., in answer to the Crisis of Property, and addressed to the Annuitants. **1758** JOHNSON *Idler* No. 24 ⁋10 Materials for the meditation of the annuitant between the days of quarterly payment. **1823** LAMB *Elia* (1860) I A lean annuitant like myself. **1858** LD. ST. LEONARDS *Property Law* xvii. 130 An old servant who dies, as even annuitants some time must.

2. *fig.*

1811 W. SPENCER *Poems* 209 Annuitants of Fame, they took no care How ill their beggar'd successors might fare.

3. *attrib.* quasi-adj.

1792 A. YOUNG *Trav. France* 474 A variety of annuitant societies.

annuity (əˈnjuːɪtɪ). Also 5 -uitee, -ywyte, 5–6 -ytie, 6 anuyte. [a. Fr. *annuité*:—med.L. *annuitāt-em*, f. *annu-us* yearly: see -ITY.]

1. A yearly grant, allowance, or income.

a **1420** OCCLEVE *De Reg. Princ.* 821 Hathe to me grauntede an annuitee Of twenty mark, while that I have lives space. **1473** SIR J. PASTON in *Lett.* 732 III. 102, I praye yow doo for Berneye..that he maye be in sewerte for hys annywyte. **1628** EARLE *Microcosm.* xi. 25 If his annuity stretch so far, he is sent to the University. **1711** ADDISON *Spect.* No. 317 ⁋3 He had for several years last past lived altogether upon a moderate Annuity. **1838** DICKENS *Nich. Nick.* (C.D. ed.) x. 75 A decent annuity would have restored her thoughts to their old train.

†**b.** *fig. Obs. rare.*

1636 RUTHERFORD *Lett.* 70 (1862) I. 182, I think the very annuity and casualties of the Cross of Christ..better than the world's set-rent.

2. *Law.* The grant of an annual sum of money, for a term of years, for life, or in perpetuity; which differs from a rentcharge in being primarily chargeable upon the grantor's person, and his heirs if named, not upon specific land.

1439 *E.E. Wills* (1882) 122 That she claime no tenementes nor annuities wich he hath graunted to eny of his seruantez. **1502** ARNOLD *Chron.* (1811) 180 Grauntis of rentis charges and anuyte made by you [*i.e.* the King]..for terme of lyf or termes of yeres. **1558** *Wills & Invent. N.C.* (1835) 161 He shall haue one annuytie of sex poundes thirtene shillings and fourpence by yere duringe his naturall life to be taken fourthe of my lands of Ayslabie. **1632** MASSINGER *City Madam* I. ii, Lands..not encumbered, no annuity Or statute lying on them. **1809** TOMLINS *Law Dict.* s.v., An annuity granted by a bishop, with confirmation of dean and chapter, shall bind the successor of the bishop.

3. An investment of money, whereby the investor becomes entitled to receive a series of equal annual payments, which, except in the case of perpetual annuities, includes the ultimate return of both principal and interest; *also*, the annual (or, for convenience, quarterly) payment thus made.

In ***life annuities*** the payments cease at the death of the investor; in ***terminable annuities*** after a specified number of years; in ***perpetual annuities*** (such as government stock) only on repayment of the principal; in ***immediate annuities*** they commence at the end of the first interval of payment (year, quarter) after the investment, in ***deferred*** or ***reversionary annuities*** not till some considerable time has elapsed, or some specified event has taken place.

1693 HALLEY in *Phil. Trans.* XVII. 602 On this depends the Valuation of Annuities upon Lives. **1709** *Lond. Gaz.* mmmmdlxxvi/3 Lost five Annuity Orders..for 100*l.* per Annum. **1776** ADAM SMITH *Wealth of Nat.* I. II. ii. 321 The Bank [of England] pays the greater part of the annuities due to the creditors of the public. **1834** HT. MARTINEAU *Farrers* iv. 70 The money should be raised on terminable annuities. **1845** STEPHEN *Comm. Laws Eng.* (1868) II. 612 The form of the security held by the public creditors, in respect of the funded debt, is that of annuities..granted for the most part in perpetuity. **1882** A. WILSON *Nat. Budget* 35 This annuity [consolidated 3 per cent. stock] was first created in 1751 to consolidate a variety of petty annuities; hence its name.

annul (əˈnʌl), *v.* Forms: 5–6 anulle, adnull(e, 5–7 adnul, annulle, 7– annul. [a. OFr. *anulle-r*, *adnuller* (mod. *annuler*):—late L. *annullā-re* to make into nothing, f. *an-* = *ad-* to + *null-um* nothing, neut. of *nullus* none.]

1. To reduce to nothing, annihilate, put out of existence, extinguish.

c **1400** *Test. Love* III. (R.) Yᵉ crown of worship shal be taken from hem, with shame shul they be annulled. **1604** EDMONDS *Observ. Cæsar's Comm.* 21 They endeuour not to be adnulled, but to keepe themselues in being. **1671** MILTON *Samson* 70 Light..to me is extinct, And all her various objects of delight Annulled. **1843** MILL *Logic* III. vi. §1 If two causes..exactly annul one another.

2. To put an end or stop to (an action or state of things); to abolish, cancel, do away with.

1430 LYDG. *Chron. Troy* V. xxxvi, Grekes haue adnulled his fraunchyse. **1534** LD. BERNERS *Gold. Bk. M. Aurel.* (1546) B viij, Julius Cesar..adnulled and vndyd all that Sylla hadde made. **1795** NELSON in Nicolas II. 16 Signal to annul coming to the wind on the larboard tack. **1860** EMERSON *Cond. Life* i. (1861) 17 Intellect annuls Fate. So far as a man thinks, he is free. **1876** M. ARNOLD *Lit. & Dogma* 105 The saviour of Israel is he who makes Israel..conquer and annul his sensuality.

3. To destroy the force or validity of; to render void in law, declare invalid or of none effect.

1425 *Paston Lett.* 5. I. 19 His pretense of his title to the priourie of Bromholme is adnulled. **1506** *Bury Wills* (1850) 108, I anulle and revoke all the villes mad by for this date. **1531** *Dial. Laws Eng.* I. vi. (1638) 12 The first mariage was adnulled by that divorce. **1649** SELDEN *Laws of Eng.* II. i. (1739) 7 The pardon of the Earl of Arundel is adnulled. **1667** MILTON *P.L.* XII. 428 This God-like act..Annuls thy doom. **1786** T. JEFFERSON *Writ.* (1859) II. 70 It would be unjust to annul that contract. **1849** MACAULAY *Hist. Eng.* I. 175 A bill, which should at once annul all the statutes passed by the Long Parliament.

annular (ˈænjʊlə(r)), *a.* Also 6 anular. [ad. L. *annulār-is* (prop. *ānulār-is*) of or pertaining to a ring, f. *annul-us* ring: see -AR. Perh. immed. ad. Fr. *annulaire* (16th c. in Littré).]

1. Of or pertaining to a ring or rings; ring-like, ring-formed, ringed. ***annular space***: the space between an inner and an outer ring or cylinder.

1571 DIGGES *Geom. Pract.* II. xxii. P ij b, Diuide that anular Superficies into three other, euery one of them equall to the same inwarde circle. **1664** POWER *Exp. Philos.* I. 27 An Annular body like a Wasp, with some eight hoops or rims. **1766** SMITH in *Phil. Trans.* LVI. 92 She voided..a large annular worm. **1831** BREWSTER *Newton* I. xiii. 371 The annular system of Saturn. **1831** —— *Optics* xli. §197 Grinding an annular space on the plane surface. **1833** SIR J. HERSCHEL *Astron.* xii. 404 Annular nebulæ also exist, but are among the rarest objects in the heavens. **1874** *Lommel's Nat. Light* 7 The annular intervening space between the two tubes.

2. *esp.* in *Phys.* of ringed or ring-like structures. ***annular ligament***: a strong muscular band girding the wrist and ankle. ***annular process or protuberance*** (in the brain): the *Pons Varolii*; 'a process of the medulla oblongata; thus called by Dr. Willis [1664] in regard it surrounds the same, much like a ring.' Chambers *Cycl.* 1727–51.

1691 RAY *Creation* 2 The third coat of an artery..a muscular body composed of annular fibres. **1743** tr. *Heister's Surg.* II. 5 Three or four of its annular Cartilages. **1845** TODD & BOWMAN *Phys. Anat.* I. 128 The annular ligaments of the wrist and ankle.

3. *Astr.* ***annular eclipse*** of the sun: when the dark body of the moon is seen projected upon the sun's disk, so as to leave a ring of light visible all round; which happens when the moon is at such a distance from the earth, at the time of the eclipse, that its diameter appears smaller than the sun's.

1727–51 CHAMBERS *Cycl.*, *Eclipse* of the sun..is distinguished, like that of the moon, into ***total*** and ***partial***, to which must be added a third species called ***annular***. **1764** MURRAY in *Phil. Trans.* LIV. 171 About half an hour after 10, the eclipse was barely annular. **1849** MRS. SOMERVILLE *Connex. Phys. Sc.* v. 46 [He] would see a ring of light round the disc of the moon, and the eclipse would be annular.

4. *Arch.* ***annular vault***: a vaulted roof over an annular space between two concentric walls.

5. = ANNULARY 2.

1648 JOS. BEAUMONT *Psyche* v. 50 (D.) He pricks his annular finger, and lets fall Three drops of blood. **1727–51** CHAMBERS *Cycl.*, *Annular* is also an epithet given to the fourth finger; popularly called the *ring finger*.

annularity (ænjuːˈlærɪtɪ). [f. prec. + -ITY.] Annular quality, condition or form.

1851–9 AIRY in *Man. Sc. Enq.* 3 The times of beginning and end of the annularity can be obtained accurately. **1869** J. ROGERS in *Eng. Mech.* 18 June 286/1 The nebula in Lyra, the annularity of which was very apparent.

annularly (ˈænjʊləlɪ), *adv.* [f. as prec. + -LY².] In an annular manner; after the manner or form of a ring, or rings.

1718 J. CHAMBERLAYNE *Relig. Philos.* I. iv. §7 Other stronger Fibres encompass the stomach annularly. **1866** R. TATE *Brit. Mollusks* iv. 221 The tentacles are annularly wrinkled.

annulary (ˈænjʊlərɪ), *a.* and *sb.* [ad. L. *annulāri-us* relating to a ring, f. *annul-us*: see -ARY.]

†**1.** = ANNULAR 1, 2. *Obs.*

1646 SIR T. BROWNE *Pseud. Ep.* 142 Wormes and Leeches ..whose bodies consist of round and annulary fibers. **1691** RAY *Creation* (1714) 270 It [the windpipe] is made with annulary cartilages.

2. Bearing the ring. (Said of the fourth finger of the left hand.) Hence, with 'finger' understood.

1623 FAVINE *Theat. Hon.* I. v. 49 This Annulary finger becommeth Glandulous and swolne. **1855** *Labarte's Arts of Mid. Ages* iv. 144 The thumb and annulary crossed.

‖**Annulata** (ænjuːˈleɪtə), *sb. pl. Zool.* [L. adj. pl. neut. (sc. *animālia*) i.e. annulate or ringed animals.] The division of animals more commonly called ANNELIDA; sometimes used as a synonym of the larger division ANNULOSA: see ANNULATE 2.

1847 in CRAIG. **1856** W. CLARK *Van der Hoeven's Zool.* I. 219 *Annulata*, Animals elongate, living in waters or moist earth. **1874** WOOD *Nat. Hist.* 759 These creatures are technically called *Annulata*, or sometimes *Annelida*.

annulate (ˈænjʊleɪt), *a.* [ad. L. *annulāt-us*, f. *annul-us*: see -ATE.]

1. Furnished or marked with a ring or rings; *esp.* in *Bot.* Having an *annulus* or ring round the sporangium, as certain ferns and mosses.

1830 LINDLEY *Nat. Syst. Bot.* 313 The thecæ of various annulate ferns. **1880** GRAY *Bot. Text-bk.* 396 *Annulate*, marked with rings.

2. Consisting or formed of rings; composed of a series of ring-like segments united so as to form a tube. = ANNULATED 3. See prec. word.

1852 DANA *Crustac.* II. 801 Body narrow, fourteen-jointed, annulate. **1859** TODD *Cycl. Anat. & Phys.* V. 117/1 The class of Annulate Worms.

annulated (ˈænjʊleɪtɪd), *ppl. a.* [f. prec. + -ED.]

1. 'That weareth rings, ringed.' Blount *Glossogr.*

2. Furnished with rings; marked with ring-like lines, ridges or grooves.

1668 WILKINS *Real Char.* 122 Crustaceous..having generally eight legs, besides..two or more annulated horns or feelers. **1753** CHAMBERS *Cycl. Supp.* s.v. *Gazella*, The *Gazella Indica*..with very long horns, which are annulated only in that part near the head. **1796** MORSE *Amer. Geog.* I. 202 His tail annulated with alternate rings of black and brown. **1854** WOODWARD *Man. Mollusca* II. 242 Its cell, the interior of which is often annulated with furrows.

b. *Her.* Having a ring or annulet. ***annulated cross***, one having its extremities ending in annulets.

3. Composed of rings; consisting of a series of ring-like segments united so as to form a tube.

1748 SIR J. HILL *Hist. Anim.* 3 (JOD.) The enchelis with an annulated body small at each end. **1860** HARTWIG *Sea* xii. 216 The Annelides, or annulated worms. **1860** SAMUELSON *Honey Bee* ii. 11 [An insect] possesses six annulated legs.

b. ***annulated column*** in *Arch.*: 'Slender shafts clustered together or joined by bands of stone, sometimes of metal, to a central pier or to a jamb.' Gwilt 1842.

annulation (ænjuːˈleɪʃən). [n. of action f. ANNULATE.] The formation of rings or ring-like divisions; *concr.* a ring-like structure, a ring.

1829 ? JESSE *Jrnl. Natur.* 332 The whole body of the animal [hairworm] consists of numerous annulations. **1870** ROLLESTON *Anim. Life* Introd. 123 Their [worms'] bodies are..divided externally by annulation. **1872** NICHOLSON *Palæont.* 271 The walls of the shell are..surrounded with numerous thickened rings or annulations.

†**ˈannule.** *Obs.*—⁰ [ad. L. *annul-us.*] A by-form of ANNULUS or ANNULET.

1681 BLOUNT *Glossogr.*, *Annule* [*ed.* 1656 Annulet], a Ring, or anything like a Ring.

annulet (ˈænjʊlɪt). Also 6 annulette, 7–8 anulet. [f. L. *annul-us* ring + -ET¹; prob. refashioned on *annlet*, *andlet*, *anlet*, OFr. *annelet*, *anelet*, dim. of *anel*:—L. *ānell-us* dim. of *ānulus*.]

1. A little ring.

1598 SYLVESTER *Du Bartas* (1611) 80 In what sort One Loadstone-touched annlet doth transport Another Iron Ring. *c* **1602** *Lingua* in Hazl. *Dodsl.* IX. 426 Crosslets, pendulets..annulets, bracelets, and so many lets. **1647** R. STAPYLTON *Juvenal* 123 With summer annulets, and winter rings, He binds the poets fingers. **1699** *Lond. Gaz.* mmmccccclxxxix 4 Lost..two..Seals with 3 Laurel Leaves, and another with 6 Annulets. **1859** TENNYSON *Enid* 1107 Pluck'd the grass..And into many a listless annulet..Wove and unwove it.

2. *Her.* A small circle worn as a charge in coats of arms.

1572 BOSSEWELL *Armorie* II. 82 b, These annulettes, or.. rynges, are also certayne rounde signes or tokens borne in armes, to the great estimacion of the bearer. **1610** GWILLIM *Displ. Heraldry* IV. iv. (1660) 278 These are called Annulets in respect of their small quantity..and are supposed to be Rings of Maile. **1725** BRADLEY *Fam. Dict.*, *Anulet*..is the Mark of Distinction which the fifth Brother of any Family ought to bear in his Coat of Arms. **1877** JEWITT *Half-hrs. Eng. Antiq.* 128 A shield bearing six annulets.

3. *Arch.* A small fillet encircling a column. Usually applied to the three, four, or five fillets under the echinus.

1727–51 CHAMBERS *Cycl.*, *Annulets*..are small square members in the Doric capital, placed under the quarter round—also called Fillets, Listels, etc. **1823** P. NICHOLSON *Pract. Build.* 162 Fillets, which, when circular, or encompassing a column are called Annulets.

annulism (ˈænjʊlɪz(ə)m). [f. ANNUL(US + -ISM.] Annulate structure.

1841 [see RADIISM].

annullable (əˈnʌləb(ə)l), *a. rare.* [f. ANNUL + -ABLE.] Capable of being annulled.

1799 COLERIDGE *Own Times* I. 188 A legislature..whose acts are annullable *ad arbitrium*.

†**ˈannullate**, *v. Obs. rare.* Also 7 anul-. [f. late L. *annullāt-* ppl. stem of *annullā-re*: see ANNUL and -ATE.] = ANNUL.

1553–87 FOXE *A. & M.* I. 678/1 Annullating and reproving all the Acts and proceedings of the other Popes before. **1616** CHAMPNEY *Voc. Bps.* 76 Prohibiting the whole use of the orders so given..but not annullating the order it self. **1621** BP. MOUNTAGU *Diatribe* 474 Doe you suppose that a vow doth annullate..the otherwise generall right and use?

† **annu'llation.** *Obs.* Also 6 adn-. [a. Fr. *annulation*:—late L. **annullātiōn-em*, n. of action f. *annullā-re*: see ANNUL and -TION.]

1. The action of annulling or declaring void.

1495 *Act 11 Hen. VII*, xxxiii, This present acte of resumpcioun or adnullacioun. **1537** *Act 28 Hen. VIII*, vii, None appeale, repeale, revocation or adnullation thereof.. shall hereafter be had. **1670** G. H. *Hist. Cardinals* III. I. 230 The decree of annullation, published by Pope John.

2. The state of being annulled or reduced (as if) to nothing.

1603 FLORIO *Montaigne* (1632) II. xiii. 342 The generality of things doth in some sort suffer for our annullation.

annuller (ə'nʌlə(r)). *rare*$^{-1}$. [f. ANNUL + -ER[1].] One who annuls, abolishes, or revokes.

1853 MALDEN *Trans. Philol. Soc.* VI. 53 Acrisius.. in a mythical form the annuller of distinctions.

annulling (ə'nʌlɪŋ), *vbl. sb.* [f. ANNUL + -ING[1].] Doing away with; revoking; annulment.

c **1400** *Test. Love* I. (1560) 275/2 Fools thereof to enfourmen in adnulling of their erroures. **1653** A. WILSON *James I*, 270 The Anulling and breach of these two Treaties. **1839** JAMES *Louis XIV*, I. 71 That which he lost by the annulling of the king's will.

† **a'nnullity.** *Obs. rare.* [? f. ANNUL, after *nullity*.] = ANNULMENT.

1586 FERNE *Blaz. Gentrie* 338 This is not accounted a delaye, but rather an annullitie and auoyding of the combate for euer. **1641** STOCK *Comm. Malachi* (1865) 44 No sin dissolveth the bond, it makes not an annullity of the duty.

annulment (ə'nʌlmənt). [f. ANNUL + -MENT; prob. a. Fr. *anullement*, though neither Littré nor Godef. has the latter in 15th c.]

1. The action of reducing to nothing or putting an end to; abolition.

1491 CAXTON *Vitas Patr.* (W. de W.) III. xxiv. (1495) 325/2 Of humylyte procedeth mortyfycacyon, and anullement of his propre wyll. **1809** COLERIDGE *Friend* VI. v. (1867) 308 No better remedy for the overweening self-complacency of modern philosophy than the annulment of its pretended originality. **1862** F. HALL *Hindu Philos. Syst.* 32 Emancipation.. the annulment of the last subsisting misery.

2. The action of declaring void; invalidation.

1664 H. MORE *Myst. Iniq.* 107 Most impudent Annulments of the plain and express Laws and Doctrines of Christ. **1816** *Edin. Rev.* XXVII. 318 A letter meant as a revocation and annulment of that rescript. **1865** *Daily Tel.* 23 Aug., Hence the necessary annulment of the Richmond elections.

annuloid ('ænjʊlɔɪd), *a.* [mod. f. L. *annul-us* (see ANNULUS) + -OID.] Ring-like. In *Zool.* applied by Prof. Huxley to animals in which the division of the body into ring-like segments is less distinct than in the *Annulosa*: see next.

1855 H. SPENCER *Psych.* I. I. i. 6 The sluggish annuloid types.. contrasted with the energetic kinds of Annulosa. **1877** HUXLEY *Anat. Inv. An.* xii. 678 The Annuloid Series, is represented by the *Trichoscolices* and the *Annelida*.

‖ **Annuloida** (ænjuː'lɔɪdə), *sb. pl. Zool.* [mod.L. adj. pl. neut., prop. *annuloidea* (sc. *animālia*): see prec.] The Annuloid animals, one of Prof. Huxley's eight primary groups, placed by him between the *Annulosa* and *Infusoria*. Examples are the Flukes, Tapeworms, and Wheel animalcules.

1851 HUXLEY in *Penny Cycl. 2nd Supp.* 594/1 The Rotifera.. present a modification of the Annulose type—belong, in fact, to what I have called the Annuloida.

‖ **Annulosa** (ænjuː'ləʊsə), *sb. pl. Zool.* [mod.L. adj. pl. neut. (sc. *animālia*): see ANNULOSE.] The ANNULOSE animals, one of Prof. Huxley's primary groups, containing such as crustaceans, insects, and worms, which have a more or less firm external skeleton, composed of a series of rings. They comprehend the higher *Articulata* of earlier zoologists.

1855 H. SPENCER *Psych.* I. I. i. 3 The Sub-kingdom Annulosa shows us an immense difference between the slow crawling of worms and quick flight of insects.

annulosan (ænjuː'ləʊsən). *Zool.* [f. prec. + -AN.] A member of the *Annulosa*.

1835 KIRBY *Hab. & Inst. Anim.* I. xi. 319 Annulosans—with more propriety Condylopes.

annulose (ænjuː'ləʊs), *a.* [f. mod.L. *annulōs-us* characterized by rings: see ANNULUS and -OSE.]

1. Of a ringed or ring-like character.

1826 KIRBY & SPENCE *Entomol.* (1828) IV. xlvii. 394 Certain intestinal worms of an indistinct annulose structure.

2. *Zool.* Having the body formed of a series of rings or ring-like segments. (See ANNULOSA.)

1835 KIRBY *Hab. & Inst. Anim.* I. viii. 236 Their [Cirripedes'] nervous system.. approaches near to that of the Annulose animals. **1872** NICHOLSON *Palæont.* 29 The lower Annulose animals, such as Leeches, Earth-worms, and Errant Annelides.

‖ **annulus** ('ænjʊləs). *Pl.* -i. [L., erroneous mediæval spelling of *ānulus* a ring, dim. of rare *ānus* a rounding, a circular form (see Lewis and Short).]

1. A ring, or ring-like body (in various technical applications).

1563 J. SHUTE *Archit.* C j a, Thre of them ye shal geue to Echinus.. the fourth part geue to Annulus. **1713** DERHAM *Phys. Theol.* IV. xii. 223 These Rings have a Curious Apparatus of Muscles enabling those creatures.. to dilate or contract their Annuli. **1761** STERNE *Tr. Shandy* (1802) III. x. 275 By the return of the two ends of the strings thro' the annulus or noose made by the second implication of them. **1794** SULLIVAN *View Nat.* II, There is a prodigious annulus encompassing Saturn. **1853** KANE *Grinnell Exp.* xix. (1856) 143 An annulus of Arctic shrubs and trees.

2. *Geom.* 'The name of a ring, or solid formed by the revolution of a circle about a straight line exterior to its circumference as an axis, and in the plane of the said circle.' *Penny Cycl.* 1834.

1802 PLAYFAIR *Illustr. Hutton. The.* 508 If.. the ring is a solid annulus.. it may be so constituted that the attraction of Saturn.. may produce a force perpendicular to its surface.

3. *Bot.* **a.** In ferns: The ring of cells which partially surrounds the sporangia. **b.** In mosses: The elastic external ring of epidermal cells with which the brim of the sporangium is furnished. **c.** In fungi: Sometimes applied to the portion of the veil, which remains like a collar round the stalk.

1830 LINDLEY *Nat. Syst. Bot.* 313 The resemblance between the midrib of one of these scales and the annulus of a Polypodium. **1863** BERKELEY *Brit. Mosses* 311 *Annulus*, a little ring, which is often elastic, at the rim of the mouth of the sporangium. **1871** M. COOKE *Fungi* (1874) 19 The collar adherent to the stem falls back, and thenceforth is known as the annulus or ring.

4. *Astr.* A ring of light, as in an annular eclipse.

1871 SCHELLEN *Spectrum Anal.* §54. 256 Forming an annulus around the moon of about 8' in diameter.

annum, [L.] year, in phr. *per annum*: see PER.

† **a'nnumber,** *v. Obs. rare*$^{-1}$. [variant of ADNUMBER, f. NUMBER after L. *adn-*, *annumerāre*: see next. Cf. OFr. *anombrer*.] = ANNUMERATE *v.*

1687 *Death's Vis.* IX. (1713) 43 Whether the Leathern Bat .. be to be annumbered among Birds or Beasts.

† **a'nnumerate,** *ppl. a. Obs. rare*$^{-1}$. [ad. L. *annumerāt-us* pa. pple. of *annumerā-re* to reckon to, f. *an-* = *ad-* to + *numerāre* to number.] Reckoned or counted in.

1432-50 tr. *Higden* (1865) I. 165 If these iiij. yere, and xvi. yere of kynge Ioachim.. be annumerate.

† **a'nnumerate,** *v. Obs.* [f. prec., or on analogy of vbs. so formed.] To reckon as an addition *to*; to count in, add on.

1651 BAXTER *Inf. Bapt.* 255 All the church, whereto Infants also must be annumerated. **1775** PLANTA in *Phil. Trans.* LXVI. 136 This whole country.. could not but be annumerated to one of the provinces of the empire.

† **a,nnume'ration.** *Obs.* [ad. L. *annumerātiōn-em*, n. of action f. *annumerāre*: see above.] The action of adding to a number; reckoning in or up.

1604 T. WRIGHT *Passions of Mind* v. §4. 270 If he hath committed various offences, the conglobation and annumeration of them.. cannot but stirre vp.. the Auditors to abhorre him. **1646** SIR T. BROWNE *Pseud. Ep.* 297 They doe.. replenish the world with a new annumeration of others. **1693** OWEN *Holy Spirit* 179 The Annumeration of these Gifts.

† **a'nnunciable,** *a. Obs. rare*$^{-1}$. [f. L. *annuntiā-re*, as if ad. L. **annunciābilis*: see ANNUNCIATE *a.* and -BLE.] That may be announced or proclaimed; declarable.

1656 HARDY *Serm. 1 John* xx. (1865) 141/1 This propitiation, as it is applicable, so it is annunciable to every man.

¶ In this and the following words the erroneous med. spelling *annunciāre*, of L. *annuntiāre*, has determined the Eng. form.

annunciade (ənʌnsɪ'eɪd). [a. Fr. *annonciade*, ad. It. *annunziāta*, f. *annunziar*:—L. *annuntiāre* to announce: see -ADE.] A name given to: **a.** A military order founded by Amadeus VI of Savoy in 1362 under the title 'Knights of the true lover's knot,' and re-named, on the accession of Amadeus VIII to the Pontificate in 1439, in honour of the Annunciation of the angel Gabriel; **b.** A female religious order founded by Queen Jane of France; a nun of that order.

1706 tr. *Dupin, Eccl. Hist.* II. IV. xi. 459 Queen Jane, Daughter of King Lewis XI.. instituted the Order of the Annunciation or the Annonciades. **1711** *Lond. Gaz.* mmmmdclxxi/1 The Marquis de Tana, Knight of the Annunciade. **1712** *Ibid.* mmmmmli/1 All the Knights of the Annuntiade.. assisted at the Chapel [in Turin]. **1751** CHAMBERS *Cycl.* s.v. *Annunciate, Knights of the Annunciata, or Annuntiada*, was a military order.. at first called the order of the true lovers knots, in memory of a bracelet of hair presented to the founder by a lady.

† **a'nnunciate,** *ppl. a. Obs.* Also 4-5 anunciat. [ad. L. *annunciāt-us*, erroneous med. spelling of *annuntiātus*, pa. pple. of *annuntiāre*: see ANNOUNCE.] Announced, declared, proclaimed (especially beforehand).

c **1386** CHAUCER *Monkes T.* 25 Sampson, whiche that was annunciate [*v.r.* an(n)unciat] By thangel, long er his nativité. **1483** CAXTON *Gold. Leg.* 91/2 Her byrthe [was] anunciat and shewd by thaungel. **1509** HAWES *Past. Pleas.* viii. vi, By estimacion is made annunciate Whether the mater be long or brevyate.

annunciate, -tiate (ə'nʌnʃɪeɪt), *v.* [f. prec., or on analogy of vbs. so formed.]

1. To make known officially or publicly; to intimate, proclaim, declare. = ANNOUNCE 1.

a **1536** TINDALE *Supper of Lord* Wks. III. 255 'Preach the death of the Lord,' for so much signifieth *annunciate* in this place, until he come. **1659** HAMMOND *On Ps.* xcviii. 2 By God appointed to be annuntiated and proclaimed. **1705** BP. BULL *Corrupt Ch. Rome* (T.) Let my death be thus annunciated and shown forth. **1851** MRS. BROWNING *Casa Guidi W.* 123 The cause Which at God's signal, war-trumps newly blown Shall yet annuntiate to the world's applause.

2. To proclaim or intimate as coming, ready, etc.

1652 SPARKE *Prim. Devot.* (1663) 445 What here the angel annunciateth, Isaiah long before prophesied. **1659** PEARSON *Creed* 498 They who did annunciate unto the blessed Virgin the conception of the Saviour. **1883** J. MUNRO in *Gd. Words* May 315 The use of electricity for annunciating.

a'nnunciating, *ppl. a.* [f. prec. + -ING[2].] Bringing news, declaring, announcing.

1877 MRS. H. KING *Disciples* 73 The Annunciating Angel bows Before the Virgin.

annunciation (ə,nʌnsɪ'eɪʃən). Also 5 -cion(e, -cioun, 6 **annuntiation, annoncyacyon.** [a. Fr. *annonciation*, ad. L. *annuntiātiōn-em*, n. of action f. *annuntiā-re*: see ANNOUNCE and -TION.] The specific senses 2, 3, were the earlier in Eng.

1. The action of announcing, of proclaiming or declaring publicly or officially; the matter so announced, announcement.

1563 *Homilies* II. xv. I. (1859) 442 The memory of Christ, the Annunciation of his death. **1678** BARCLAY *Apol. Quakers* v. vi. 118 The Preaching of Christ.. truly termed the Gospel, or an Annunciation of Glad-Tidings to all. **1775** TOPLADY *Wks.* (1828) VI. 269 The annunciation of dinner occasioned a truce to debate. **1827** DE QUINCEY *Murder* Wks. (1862) IV. 60 The annunciation of some gigantic calamity.

2. *esp.* The intimation of the incarnation, made by the angel Gabriel to the Virgin Mary.

c **1440** *Gesta Rom.* I. lxvi. 243 The blesside Virgine, that conceivide by the annunciatione of the angille. *a* **1555** LATIMER in Foxe *A. & M.* III. 387 The Angel was sent to greet our Lady, and to annunciate and shew the good will of God towards her, and therefore it is called The Annunciation of our Lady. **1704** NELSON *Fest. & Fasts* xiv. (1739) 165 The Annunciation of the blessed Virgin, which the Church this Day celebrates. **1851** RUSKIN *Mod. Paint.* II. III. II. iii. §17 No subject has been more frequently treated by the religious painters than that of the Annunciation.

3. The church festival commemorating that event, observed on the 25th of March; Lady-day.

c **1400** *Epiph.* (Turnb. 1843) 80 Thre masses of Crystes nativite.. And thre of the annunciacion. **1479** CAXTON *Cordyale* Finis, Fiinisshed on the euen of thannunciacion of our said blissid Lady. **1537** *Bury Wills* (1850) 130 Owr Ladys daye the Annoncyacyon. *a* **1667** JER. TAYLOR (J.) Upon the day of the annunciation, or Lady-day, meditate on the incarnation of our blessed Saviour. **1863** R. CHAMBERS *Bk. Days* 417/2 Among the sermons of St. Augustine.. are two regarding the festival of the Annunciation.

4. *attrib.*: **Annunciation lily**, a Madonna lily such as is depicted in pictures of the Annunciation.

1877 LADY WOOD *Sheen's Foreman* I. 234 Clusters of annunciation lilies. **1899** *Daily News* 4 Feb. 6/3 The dress is white velvet, embroidered straight up the front with long sprays of Annunciation lilies. **1907** *Daily Chron.* 2 May 4/5 The large drawing room,.. decorated with tall Annunciation lilies.. and exquisite roses.

annunciative (ə'nʌnʃɪətɪv), *a. rare.* [f. L. *annuntiāt-* ppl. stem of *annuntiā-re* + -IVE.] Characterized by or proper to annunciation.

1659 *Gentl. Calling* v. §13. 418 Christ's words run not in an annunciative, but an exhortatory stile. **1821** *Q. Rev.* XXV. 153 A dream.. annunciative to the inspired Micah, of the murder of the King. **1851** MRS. BROWNING *Casa Guidi W.* 75 That, through all bursts and bruits Of popular passion.. Ye may not lack a finger up the air, Annunciative, reproving.

annunciator (ə'nʌnʃɪeɪtə(r)). [a. L. *annuntiātor*, n. of agent f. *annuntiāre* to ANNOUNCE.]

He who, or that which, announces, an announcer; *spec.* applied to: **a.** an officer of the Greek Church who gave notice of holy days; **b.** an indicator used in hotels, etc., to show in which direction the attendance summoned by bell or telephone is needed; **c.** various techn. uses (see quots.).

1753 CHAMBERS *Cycl. Supp.*, *Annuntiator*, in the Greek church, an officer whose business is to give notice of the feasts and holy days. **1845** PETRIE *Eccl. Archit. Irel.* 16 The annunciator, instructor, or proclaimer of the festivals. **1853** A. BUNN *Old Eng. & New Eng.* 39 There is an appendage to this office.. called an 'Annunciator', invented, we believe, by Jackson, of New York city, whereby all the bell-pulls of the house are brought within one focus. **1879** PRESCOTT *Sp. Telephone* 392 The annunciator disk and lever. **1883** J. MUNRO in *Gd. Words* May 317, Figs. 13, 14, and 15 represent a thoroughly reliable annunciator. **1886** *Marine Engin.* 1 Feb. 287/2 The Baird Annunciators..indicate in the pilot house or elsewhere..whether the engines of a ship are in motion and if so in what direction they are moving. **1904** *Daily Chron.* 25 Mar. 3/6 The annunciator is an electrical apparatus by means of which the name of the member [of Parliament] speaking is printed immediately he rises to his feet on a broad paper band which runs horizontally. **1905** *Ibid.* 7 Apr. 4/6 The 'Annunciator'.. announces to the smoking-room and libraries of the House of Commons the name of the Member addressing the Legislative Chamber. **1936** *Gloss. Terms Railway Signalling* (*B.S.I.*) 6 *Annunciator*, a device used to indicate audibly the passage of a train at a given point.

annunciatory (ə'nʌnʃɪətərɪ), *a.* [f. prec. + -Y: see -ORY.] Of or befitting an announcer; pertaining to announcing.

1834 W. ROBERTS *Memoirs Hannah More* III. xi. 161 That one of the most illustrious females..should have her tenderest feelings thus barbarously sported with..in annunciatory advertisements. **1885** *Chamber's Jrnl.* 19 Sept. 606/2 Before sundown their [*sc.* the mosquitoes'] annunciatory hum began.

‖**annus mirabilis** (ˈænəs maɪˈreɪbɪlɪs, mɪˈrɑːbɪlɪs). [mod.L., lit. 'wonderful year'.] A remarkable or auspicious year.

1667 DRYDEN (*title*) Annus Mirabilis: the year of wonders, 1666. *a* **1700** EVELYN *Diary* an. 1660 (1955) III. 239 Annus Mirabilis. **1767** LD. CHESTERFIELD *Let.* 1 June (1774) II. 518 This has been every where an *annus mirabilis* for bad weather. **1885** *Good Words* Jan. 63/1 The years of evil fame which followed the *annus mirabilis* of 1815. **1940** *19th Cent.* Feb. 157 In 1848, the *annus mirabilis* of European history, a movement arose which shook the core of Europe. **1959** *Listener* 13 Aug. 251/1 By then he [*sc.* Tennyson] was successful and famous, his *annus mirabilis* of 1850 already three years behind him.

ano- (ˌeɪnəʊ), comb. f. L. *ānus*, ANUS, as in anoperinæal, pertaining to both anus and perinæum.

1878 BRYANT *Pract. Surg.* I. 695 The exploratory anoperinæal operation.

ano- (ˌænəʊ), *pref.* a. Gr. ἄνω adv. 'upward'; in mod. scientific terms, as *anocarpous*, *anogenic*.

anoa (əˈnəʊə). [Native name.] An animal of the genus of the same name; a small wild ox of the Celebes.

1845 LORD DERBY 6 Nov. in J. E. Gray *Gleanings Menagerie Knowsley* (1850) II. 47, I have arranged our exchange for the *Anoa* and *Burchell's Zebra.* **1875** *Encycl. Brit.* II. 695/2 The singular ruminant, Anoa. **1888** *Athenæum* 1 Dec. 740/1 Prof. J. B. Steere [read a paper] on the 'tamaron', a bovine animal found in the island of Mindoro, Philippines, which he believed to be allied to the *anoa* of Celebes. **1930** *Times Educ. Suppl.* 27 Sept. p. iv/2 The Anoa, or dwarf buffalo, is confined to the island of Celebes.

anocarpous (ænəʊˈkɑːpəs), *a. Bot.* [mod. f. Gr. ἄνω upward + καρπ-ός fruit + -OUS.] Of ferns: Bearing fructification on the upper part of the frond.

1880 in *Syd. Soc. Lex.*

anocathartic (ˌænəʊkəˈθɑːtɪk), *a.* and *sb.* [mod. f. Gr. ἄνω upward + CATHARTIC = Gr. καθαρτικός purgative; formerly written *ana-*.] Emetic.

1853 MAYNE *Exp. Lex.*, *Anocathartic*, having power to purge upwards, or cause vomiting; emetic.

anoci-association (əˈnəʊsɪ-). *Surg.* [f. A- 14 + L. *noc-ēre* to hurt + -I- + ASSOCIATION.] Minimizing of operational shock by means of an anæsthetic routine introduced by the American surgeon G. W. Crile (1864–1943) in 1908.

1911 G. W. CRILE in *Jrnl. Amer. Med. Assoc.* LVII. 1814/1 The operation was done..under..anesthesia.. completely protecting the brain from all harmful associations—a state best designated by a new word, viz., *anoci-association.* **1913** *Lancet* 23 Aug. 557/1 Anoci-association involved the cutting out of all conditions inimical to brain areas. **1961** *Brit. Med. Dict.* 106/2 *Anoci-association*... The patient is kept free from fear by management and narcotics, remains in ignorance of the time of the operation, and is anaesthetized in such a way that no adaptive response is excited. The field of operation is completely blocked by local anaesthetics so that traumatic impulses do not reach the brain [etc.].

anodal (ˈænəʊdəl), *a.* [f. ANODE + -AL.] Pertaining to the anode; *anodal closure contraction*: see A.C.C. (s.v. A III).

1882 *Athenæum* 8 July 50/3 The character (anodal or kathodal) of the electric charge. **1886** BUCK *Handbk. Med. Sci.* II. 651/1 The second, anodal closure contraction, occurs when the anode is applied to the nerve or muscle.

anode (ˈænəʊd). *Electr.* [ad. Gr. ἄνοδος way up, f. ἀνά up + ὁδός way.] **a.** *strictly*, as applied by Faraday: The path by which an electric current leaves the positive pole, and enters the electrolyte, on its way to the negative pole. **b.** *loosely* used for: The positive pole. In both senses opposed to *cathode*, which is applied to the path of exit from the electrolyte, and to the negative pole.

a. 1834 W. WHEWELL *Let.* 25 Apr. in Todhunter *W.W.* (1876) II. 179, I have considered the two terms you [Faraday] want to substitute for *eisode* and *exode*, and recommend instead of them *anode* and *cathode.* **1849** RUSSELL & WOOLRICH in *Circ. Sc.* I. 220/1 A plate of Cadmium as an anode. **1875** URE *Dict. Arts* II. 221 The nickel anodes are connected to the..carbon plates of the battery; the articles to be coated with the zincs.

b. 1841 W. GROVE *Contrib. Sc.* 241 The anode of a voltaic combination. **1870** R. FERGUSON *Electr.* 161 The poles..are called electrodes, the + pole being called the anode.

c. *attrib.* and *Comb.*, as ***anode bend***, ***circuit***, ***current***, ***surface***, ***tap***; **anode mud**, the insoluble residue which forms on the anode during electrolytic refining.

1928 *Morn. Post* 26 Jan. 13/4 The best all-round results are often obtained when the rectifier is of the *anode bend type. **1940** *Chambers's Techn. Dict.* 37/2 *Anode bend*, the more or less abrupt curve in the anode-current versus grid-voltage characteristic of a triode, which occurs at small values of anode current. **1919** *Radio Rev.* Nov. 54 There are ..two sources of potential, the one in the *anode circuit being of fixed value, that in the grid circuit being variable. **1920** *Ibid.* Aug. 545 The values of the *anode-current..are then given. **1963** B. FOZARD *Instrumentation Nucl. Reactors* xi. 129 The production of positive ions in the residual gas due to collisions between anode-current electrons and molecules. **1922** J. W. MELLOR *Mod. Inorg. Chem.* xxi. 380 The anode is enclosed in filter cloth bags to facilitate the collection of the '*anode-mud'. Considerable amounts of silver and gold are obtained from the slimes or 'anode mud'. **1890** G. GORE *Art Electrolytic Separation Metals* II. G. 188 The amount of *anode surface per vat in different works therefore varies from 24 to 322 square feet. **1919** R. STANLEY *Textbk. Wireless Telegr.* v. 91 It will suffice to say here that an *anode tap may be usefully employed to increase the oscillating power and oscillating aerial current. **1929** J. A. RATCLIFFE *Physical Princ. Wireless* iii. 48 The anode lead.. should be connected to the aerial inductance by way of a movable contact known as the Anode Tap.

anodic (æˈnɒdɪk), *a.* [f. Gr. ἄνοδος way up (f. ἀνά up + ὁδός way) or directly f. ANODE + -IC.]

1. a. *Electr.* = ANODAL *a.*

1837 W. WHEWELL *Let.* 14 Oct. in S. P. Thompson *M. Faraday* (1898) iv. 164 As for positive and negative, I do not see why *cathodic* and *anodic* should not be used. **1844** NOAD *Lect. Electricity* (ed. 2) 200 The anodic division..will finally become colourless, owing to the separation of chlorine. **1853** in MAYNE *Exp. Lex.* **1889** [see *A.C.C.* s.v. A III]. **1890** BILLINGS *Med. Dict.* s.v., *A*[*nodic*]-*closure-contraction*,.. contraction of a muscle when circuit is closed by placing the anode over the motive-point. *A.-opening-contraction*,.. contraction when circuit is opened by removal of anode from over motive-point. **1943** *Electronic Engin.* XVI. 170 The operations involved are:..rinsing, anodising, modifying of the anodic film and plating.

b. ***anodic bath***, the electrolyte in the anodic oxidation process; ***anodic oxidation***, ***process***, ***treatment***, anodizing (see ANODIZE *v.*).

1924 BENGOUGH & STUART *Brit. Pat.* 223,995 The invention consists in subjecting a surface of aluminium or aluminium alloy to anodic treatment in an electrolytic bath. **1924** U. R. EVANS *Corrosion of Metals* xi. 185 In the anodic process the recesses always receive adequate covering—no matter where the cathodes are placed. **1926** *Engineering* 27 Aug. 274/1 The film produced by anodic oxidation in a bath containing a chromate, bichromate, or—best of all—chromic acid, protects the metal..against corrosion. **1932** *Jrnl. R. Aeronaut. Soc.* Jan. 15 Chromic acid from the anodic bath..might cause trouble. *Ibid.* 11 In modern anodic oxidation plants stainless steel cathodes are frequently used.

2. *Physiol.* Of nerve force: proceeding towards a nerve-centre; afferent. (Cf. CATHODIC *a.* 1.)

1852 M. HALL *Diastaltic Nerv. Syst.* 32 The influence which has induced this effect must have been anodic and cathodic in one and the same lumbar nerve.

3. *Bot.* (See quot. 1882 s.v. CATHODIC *a.* 2.) Hence **a'nodically** *adv.*

1905 J. MCCABE tr. *Haeckel's Wond. Life* 101 Most of the flagellate infusoria..are anodically sensitive or positively galvanotactic. **1932** *Jrnl. R. Aeronaut. Soc.* Jan. 18 The modern tendency was to make tanks of either duralumin or aluminium, and the Air Ministry required that these should be anodically treated.

anodize (ˈænədaɪz), *v.* [f. ANOD(E + -IZE.] To cover (aluminium or its alloys) with a protective layer of aluminium oxide by means of electrolysis. Hence **'anodizing** *vbl. sb.*, **'anodized** *ppl. a.*, covering, covered, with such a layer; **anodi'zation**, the process of anodizing; **'anodizer**, apparatus used for anodizing.

1931 *S.A.E. Jrnl.* XXIX. 148 Methods of protecting parts from exposure to corrosive influences are considered..in heat-treating, nitriding, anodising. **1933** *Archit. Rev.* LXXIV. 228/1 The wood doors are..fitted with anodized aluminium..handles. **1936** *Nature* 24 Oct. 708/1 The production of adherent oxide coatings on aluminium and its alloys by anodic treatment (anodizing). **1947** *Electronic Engin.* XIX. 170 Other controlling factors are indicated such as the concentration of the electrolyte and the nature of the alloy to be anodised. **1948** 'N. SHUTE' *No Highway* iv. 109 Scratches on the paint and anodising [of the tailplane]. **1952** *Electronic Engin.* XXIV. 282 In carrying out anodization by the sulphuric acid process, the acid strength used industrially is about 36 per cent by weight. **1958** *Times Rev. Industry* Feb. 68/1 Recently one London factory brought an automatic anodizer into operation.

anodon(t (ˈænədən, -ɒnt). *Zool.* [mod.L. *anodonta* (in which form the word usually occurs), f. Gr. ἀν priv. + ὀδόντ-α tooth.] A genus of bivalve molluscs, so called because they have no teeth on the hinge of their shell; e.g. fresh-water mussels.

1847 CARPENTER *Zool.* §949 The *Unio* resembles the Anodon in the structure of the shell..except that the hinge is more complicated. **1876** BENEDEN *Anim. Paras.* 39 The young anodonts have, not like the other acephala, vibratory wheels in order to move themselves. **1878** BELL *Gegenbauer* 342 The other posterior, as in Unio or Anodonta.

anodyne (ˈænədaɪn), *a.* and *sb.* Also 6–7 **-in**, **-ine**. [ad. L. *anōdyn-us* (Celsus, etc.), a. Gr. ἀνώδυν-ος painless, f. ἀν priv. + ὀδύνη pain. Cf. Fr. *anodin -e* (16th c. in Littré), whence also the obs. Eng. spelling in *-in*, *-ine*.]

A. *adj.*

1. Having the power of assuaging pain.

1543 TRAHERON *Vigo's Chirurg.* v. xv. 161 Anodyne remedyes, whych do swage payne. **1643** STEER *Exp. Chyrurg.* vi. 26 To ease paine apply this Anodine Medicine about the sore. **1712** tr. *Pomet's Hist. Drugs* I. 212 Tar and Bees-wax makes a Plaister that is discussive and anodine. **1758** JOHNSON *Idler* No. 40 ¶6 The anodyne necklace for.. toothing infants. **1859** G. WILSON *E. Forbes* iv. 127 The chief..sleep-producing..anodyne virtues of the opium.

2. *fig.* Soothing to the mind or feelings.

1790 BURKE *Fr. Rev.* 105 The anodyne draught of oblivion. **1831** CARLYLE *Sart. Res.* (1858) 69 Probably Imposture is of sanative, anodyne nature, and man's Gullibility not his worst blessing.

B. *sb.* (So Gr. ἀνώδυνον, L. *anodynum*, which were also in early use in Eng.)

1. A medicine or drug which alleviates pain.

1543 TRAHERON *Vigo's Chirurg.* (1586) 431 Things which are without griefe, are called in Greke, *Anodina.* Howbeit Vigo useth the word for things that remove paine. **1578** LYTE *Dodoens* VI. xc. 774 Softening playsters, anodines which take away payne and griefe. **1625** HART *Anat. Ur.* II. iv. 69 The injection of an anodine, or mitigating glister. **1641** FRENCH *Distill.* iii. (1651) 88 This liquor is a famous Anodynum. **1735** POPE *Moral Ess.* II. 111 The daily Anodyne, and nightly draught. **1856** DE QUINCEY *Wks.* V. Pref. 9 Amongst the most potent of anodynes, we may rank hemlock, henbane, chloroform, and opium.

2. *fig.* Anything that soothes wounded or excited feelings, or that lessens the sense of a misfortune.

c **1550** COVERDALE *Christ's Cross* iv. Wks. II. 245 The wicked..run from God to their anodynes, saints, and unlawful means. **1647** WARD *Simp. Cobler* 66 When multitudes sin, multitudes of mercy are the best Anodines. *c* **1670** BARROW *Serm.* (1686) III. xv. 170 An assured Anodynon, and infallible remedy. **1782** T. CHALMERS *Estimate* (1812) 272 Of public debts..the true anodyne is a sinking-fund. **1831** BREWSTER *Newton* (1855) I. xi. 280 Time..the only anodyne of sorrow.

anodynous (æˈnɒdɪnəs), *a.* [f. L. *anōdyn-us* (see prec.) + -OUS.] = ANODYNE *a.*

1657 TOMLINSON *Renou's Disp.* 130 Anodynous medicaments. **1662** CHANDLER *Van Helmont's Oriatr.* 331 It is an anodynous or sleepifying, and mad poyson. **1676** COLES, *Anodynous*, belonging to anodynes. **1904** 'O. HENRY' *Cabbages & Kings* v. 89 The prestige of drifting music on moonlit waters gave it an anodynous charm.

anoetic (ænəʊˈɛtɪk), *a.* [f. Gr. ἀνόητ-ος inconceivable (f. ἀ priv. + νοητός perceptible) + -IC.] **1.** Not able to be thought; unthinkable. *rare.*

1856 FERRIER *Inst. Metaph.* 93 The conversion of the incogitable (the anoetic) into the cogitable (the noetic).

2. *Psychol.* Relating to or characterized by **anoesis** (ænəʊˈiːsɪs), a hypothetical state of consciousness in which there is sensation but no thought.

1896 G. F. STOUT *Anal. Psychol.* I. 51 Objective reference supervening on purely anoetic experience would be a completely new psychical fact. **1902** *Encycl. Brit.* XXXII. 63 Such a consciousness has been happily named anoetic. Whether or no it actually exists is another matter... But relative anoesis suffices here. **1916** W. MCDOUGALL *Introd. Social Psychol.* (ed. 10) Suppl. i. 360 Anoetic sentience; a mere feeling or sentience involving no objective reference.

anogenic (ænəʊˈdʒɛnɪk), *a.* [mod. f. Gr. ἄνω upwards + -γεν-ης produced + -IC.] Developed or growing upwardly or inwardly.

1878 LAWRENCE *Cotta's Rocks Class.* 383 Hardinger has proposed the term *catogenic*, in contradistinction to the *anogenic* transmutations which proceed from the exterior towards the interior, under the influences of air and water.

anogh, anoȝ, obs. forms of ENOUGH.

†**a'noil**, *v. Obs.* Also 6 annoil, 6–7 anoyl(e, 7 annoyle. [modification of ENOIL, a. OFr. *enuiler*, mod.Fr. *enhuiler*, perh. influenced by the native synonym ANELE.] To anoint with oil (as a religious rite); *spec.* to administer extreme unction.

1303 [See ANOILING]. *a* **1520** *Myrr. Our Ladye* Pref. 57 And receyuynge the blessyd Bodye of oure Lorde [she] was anoylyd. **1577** HOLINSHED *Chron.* II. 302 Children were also christened, and men houseled and annoiled. **1582** *N.T.* (Rhem.) *James* v. 14 Let them pray over him, anoiling him with oile in the name of our Lord. **1688** HUDLESTON in Ellis *Orig. Lett.* II. IV. 79 Desired His Majesty [Chas. II], that.. he would give me leave to proceed to the sacrament of Extreme Unction..I then anoyled him.

†**a'noiling**, *vbl. sb. Obs.* Forms: 4–7 anoyling(e, 6 annoyling, -ynge, annoiling, 6–7 anoiling. [f.

prec. + -ING[1]: cf. ENOILING, ANELING.] The action of anointing (as a religious rite); unction.

1303 R. BRUNNE *Handl. Synne* 844 Holy watyr take of þe prestys hande, For anoylyng hyt wyl þe stande. **1340** *Ayenb.* 14 Þe holy ssrifte, and þe laste anoylinge. **1537** *Inst. Chr. Man* H vij, This maner of annoylynge of sycke persons. **1586** T. ROGERS 39 *Art.* (1607) 263 The Papists do take anoiling of the sick (which they call extreme unction) for a sacrament. **1627** BP. HALL *Apol. agst. Brownists* §45. 612 Their masses, their oblations..their anoylings, their exorcisings.

†a'noint, *ppl. a.* etc. *Obs.* 4-5. Also **enoynt**, **anoynt**. [a. OFr. *enoint*:—L. *inunct-um*, pa. pple. of *enoindre*:—L. *inung-ĕre*. The pref. *an-*, is an AFr., or Eng. modification; it varied with *en-* to 1485. After formation of the vb. *anoynt-en*, *anoynt* remained for some time as its pa. pple., and even contracted pa. t. (cf. *lift* for *lifted*, etc.), till superseded by the regular *anointed.*] Anointed.

a. *ppl. adj.*

1303 R. BRUNNE *Handl. Synne* 7417 Þe prest þat ys a noynt. **1382** WYCLIF *Numb.* vi. 15 Thinne cakys..anoynt with oyle. *c* **1386** CHAUCER *Knts. T.* 2103 Who wrastleth best naked, with oyle enoynt [*v.r.* anoynt(e]. *c* **1399** *Pol. Poems* (1859) II. 12 My worthi noble prince and kyng enoignt.

b. *pa. pple.* or *pa. t.* of vb.

c **1340** HAMPOLE *Prose Tr.* 7 He..anoynte hym, and swa he dyede. *c* **1400** *Rom. Rose* 1889 The God of Love it hadde anoynt With a precious oynement. *c* **1400** *Ywaine & Gaw.* 1779 She enoynt his heved wele. *c* **1450** LONELICH *Grail* xvii. 133 That wownde he..anoynt ful softely.

anoint (əˈnɔɪnt), *v.* Forms: 4-6 **enoynt(e**, 4-7 **anoynt(e**, 5 **ennoynt**, **-oint**, 5-6 **annoynt**, 6-7 **-oint**, 4- **anoint**. [f. prec., which see. Though etymologically, *an* + *oint*, it was treated phonetically as if *a* + *noint*, and thus aphetized to NOINT, and illusively spelt in 16-17th c. *annoint* (cf. *annoy*). Obs. by-forms: ENOINE, NOINT, OINT. *Anoint* has partially replaced OE. *smérian*, SMEAR, as a more refined and specialized synonym.]

I. To smear with an unguent.

1. To smear or rub over (medicinally or cosmetically) with oil or unguent; to oil, grease, apply ointment to. **a.** To anoint the body, etc. *with. arch.*

1366 MAUNDEV. ii. 11 Oyle of Mercy for to anoynte with his Membres. **1393** GOWER *Conf.* III. 67 Thanne first he hath anointed With sondry herbes that figure. **1430** LYDG. *Chron. Troy* I. vi, He was enoynted with an oyntement. **1483** CAXTON *Cato* C viij b, The scorpion and the honyflye the whyche anoynten before and prycken hard behynde. **1514** BARCLAY *Cyt. & Uplondyshm.* 11 With butter for to anoynt theyr necke. **1591** HARINGTON *Ariost. Orl. Fur.* 135 To noynt him selfe over with goates suet. **1611** BIBLE *Rev.* iii. 18 Anoint thine eyes with eye salue, that thou mayest see. [So in *Revised*.] **1697** DRYDEN *Virg. Georg.* IV. 599 With Nectar she her son anoints.

†b. With the unguent as object. *Obs.*

1599 A. M. *Gabelhouer's Bk. Physic* 357/1 Wash chilblanes when they breake..and anoynte Terebinthine thereon. **1655** MRQ. WORC. *Cent. Inv.* lxiv, The green Oile ..that was first anointed and used between the barrel [of the Cannon]..and the Engine [for loading].

†c. With the unguent as subject. *Obs.*

1697 DRYDEN *Virgil* (J.) Fragrant oils the stiffen'd limbs anoint.

d. *intr.* (refl. pron. omitted.)

1697 POTTER *Antiq. Greece* I. viii. (1715) 40 The Greeks usually Anointed before Meals.

2. *spec.* To apply or pour on oil, etc., as a religious ceremony: **a.** at baptism, or on consecration to an office, as those of priest or sovereign.

1330 R. BRUNNE *Chron.* 206 Enoynted he was als kyng. **1382** WYCLIF *Acts* iv. 27 Thi hooly child Jhesu, whom thou anoyntidest..for to do the thingis, that thin hond and thi counceil demiden for to don. **1450** MYRC 670 Wassche þe chylde ouer þe font þere he was anoynted in þe front. **1485** CAXTON *Chas. Gt.* 4 All kynges of fraunce ben enoynted at Raynes. **1611** BIBLE *Ex.* xxviii. 41 Thou..shalt annoint them, and consecrate them..that they may minister vnto mee in the Priests office. **1867** LADY HERBERT *Cradle L.* 168 Here David was anointed king over the house of Judah.

†b. in extreme unction; = ANELE, ANOIL. *Obs.*

1366 MAUNDEV. 19 Thei anoynte not the seke men.

†3. *fig.* **a.** To besmear with flattery; to 'butter.'

c **1400** *Rom. Rose* 1057 These losengeris hem preyse and smylen, And thus the world with word anoynten. **1483** CAXTON *G. de la Tour* H v b, More worthe is the frend whiche prycketh than the flateryinge frend whiche enoynteth.

b. ***to anoint the hand***: to bribe. (*Sc.* to creesh the luif.)

1566 KNOX *Hist. Ref.* Wks. 1846 I. 102 Yea, the handis of our Lordis so liberallie war anoynted.

II. To moisten or rub.

4. To moisten or rub a surface with any substance. (Const. as in 1.)

c **1325** *E.E. Allit. P.* B. 1446 Wyth besten blod busily anoynted. **1356** WYCLIF *Last Age of Ch.* (1840) 35 Wiþ his blood he anoyntide þe glas. *c* **1460** *Towneley Myst.* 23 Anoynt thi ship with pik. **1481** CAXTON *Myrr.* II. xvi. 102 Who someuer ennoynteth hym self with the blode. **1563** T. HYLL *Gardening* (1593) 73 The ashes of Dill..may profitably be annointed on moiste vlcers. **1611** BIBLE *John* ix. 11 Iesus made clay, and anointed mine eyes. **1653** WALTON *Angler* 139 The box in which he put those worms was anointed with a drop, or two..of the oil of Ivy-berries. **1868** HEAVYSEGE *Jezebel* I. 74 Neither for years shall be allowed to fall Dew to anoint the ground.

5. Hence *ironically*: To beat soundly, to 'baste.' (In the north they say humorously 'to anoint with the sap of a hazel rod.')

c **1500** *Partenay* 5653 The kyng away fly, Which so well was anoyted [Fr. *si bien oingt*] indede, That no sleue ne pane had he hole of brede. **1824** W. IRVING *T. Trav.* II. 287 Seize a trusty staff..and anoint the back of the aggressor.

anointed (əˈnɔɪntɪd), *ppl. a.* [f. prec. + -ED.]

1. Smeared or rubbed with any unctuous matter; *esp.* having had oil poured on, as a sacred rite.

c **1374** CHAUCER *Boeth.* II. iii. 36 Þise ben faire þinges and enoyntid wiþ hony swetnesse of rethorike and musike. *c* **1440** *Morte Arth.* 50 He..Mad of his cosyns kyngys ennoyntede. **1528** MORE *Heresyes* III. Wks. 1557, 222/2 Priest..in our owne tongue hath alway sygnified an enoynted parson. **1595** SHAKS. *John* III. i. 136 Haile you annointed deputies of heauen. **1727** POPE *Dunc.* III. 2 On Dulness' lap th' Anointed head repos'd. **1735** BOLINGBROKE *Parties* 14 That anointed Pedant. **1827** KEBLE *Chr. Year* S. Matthias x, By Thine anointed heralds duly crown'd.

2. *fig.* Consecrated, sacred. *rare.*

1597 DANIEL *Civ. Wars* III. xxiii, Barring th' Anointed Liberty of Laws.

3. *absol.* (formerly as *sb.* with pl.) A consecrated one. ***the Lord's Anointed***: Christ or the Messiah; also, a king by 'divine right.'

1529 FRITH *Epist. Chr. Reader* (1829) 467 False prophets and false Christs (that is to say, false anointed). **1535** COVERDALE *2 Sam.* i. 14 To laye thine hande vpon the Lordes anointed [WYCLIF, to slee the crist of the Lord]. **1602** T. FITZHERB. *Defence* 25 Thou art Messias, that is to say, the anoynted, or as we commonly say, Christ. **1611** BIBLE *Is.* xlv. 1 Thus saith the Lord to his Anointed, to Cyrus. *a* **1641** BP. MOUNTAGU *Acts & Mon.* 30 Christ carries royaltie upon the back, above all Anointeds. **1727** POPE *Hor. Ep.* II. i. 389 No Lord's anointed, but a Russian Bear. **1883** *Daily News* 14 Feb. 5/4 If he went through Western France, and was acclaimed..as the Lord's anointed.

anointer (əˈnɔɪntə(r)). [f. as prec. + -ER[1].]

1. One who anoints.

1591 PERCIVALL *Sp. Dict., Untador*, an annointer, *Vnctor*. **1655** MOUFFET & BENN. *Health's Impr.* (1746) 74 Perfumers, Anointers, and Bath-masters. **1752** J. GILL *Trinity* iii. 61 The Anointer is the Spirit of the Lord. **1845** *Eng. Saints, St. Aug.* iv. 37 Kings were anointed..and were soon afterwards put to death, without trial, by their anointers.

2. Applied to a religious sect of the 17th c.

1677 PLOTT *Oxfordsh.* xxxviii. (T.) At Watlington, in Oxfordshire, there was a sect called Anointers, from their anointing people before they admitted them into their communion.

anointing (əˈnɔɪntɪŋ). [f. as prec. + -ING[1].]

1. *gen.* The action of applying grease or oil to the surface of the body. (Often gerundial.)

1303 R. BRUNNNE *Handl. Synne* 11985 Anoyntyng ys gode for body sore. **1440** *Promp. Parv.*, Anoyntynge, or enoyntynge, *Inunctio*. **1635** HAKEWILL *Apol.* 390 (T.) Their bathings and anointings before their feasts. **1776** GIBBON *Decl. & F.* xxxvii, The salutary custom of bathing the limbs in water and of anointing them with oil.

2. *spec.* **a.** The application of oil, as a sign of consecration to a sacred office.

1382 WYCLIF *Ex.* xxx. 31 This oyle of anoyntyng holy it shal be to me. **1432-50** tr. *Higden* (Rolls Ser.) VI. 159 By the noyntynge of holy creame. **1529** RASTELL *Pastyme* (1811) 8 The crownyng and noyntyng of the kyng. **1692** WASHINGTON tr. *Milton's Def. Pop.* iv. (1851) 105 One that ..had wash'd off that anointing of his, whether Sacred or Civil, with the Blood of his own Subjects. **1820** A. TAYLOR (*title*) The Glory of Regality; an Historical Treatise of the Anointing and Crowning of the Kings and Queens of England.

†b. ***last anointing*** of the sick: extreme unction.

1340 HAMPOLE *Pr. Consc.* 3409 Last enoyntyng gyven to þe seke. *a* **1400** *Relig. Pieces fr. Thornt. MS.* 8 The fyfte sacrament es þe laste enoyntynge with oyle.

c. *fig.*

1382 WYCLIF *1 John* ii. 20, 27 ȝe han anoyntyng [*v.r.* unccioun] of the Holy Goost. His anoyntyng techith ȝou of alle thingis. **1611** The same anointing teacheth you of all things.

†3. An anointing material, ointment, unguent.

1382 WYCLIF *Ecclus.* xxxviii. 7 The oynement makere shal make pymentis of swotenesse, and enoyntingus [**1388** anoyntyngis] he shal make of helthe. **1561** J. DAUS *Bullinger on Apoc.* (1573) 144 b, Oyle is a resemblaunce of the holy Ghost, wherfore S. John calleth also the holy Ghost an annoyntyng.

4. *attrib.*

1611 BIBLE *Lev.* x. 7 The anointing oyle of the Lord is vpon you. **1636** HEALEY *Theophrast.* 46 Being at a Barbars shop or an anointing place.

a'nointment. *arch.* Forms: 5 **enoynte-**, 4-7 **anoynt-**, 6 **annoint-**. [f. ANOINT + -MENT.]

1. The action or process of anointing.

1494 FABYAN VI. cxciv. 198 The whiche penaunce durynge, he was kept from the sayd enoyntement. **1593** T. HYLL *Gardening* 139 The same annointment amendeth the foulenes or filthines of the skin. **1649** MILTON *Eikon.* xxviii. 519 Were that true, which is most fals, that all Kings are the Lords Anointed, it were yet absurd to think that the Anointment of God, should be as it were a charme against Law. **1813** W. TAYLOR in *Month. Rev.* LXXI. 127 The clergy awaited only the pretence of an anointment at Rheims. **1868** MILMAN *S. Paul's* 40 The dying yearned in vain for anointment with the blessed oil. **1887** HARDY *Woodlanders* I. iv. 59 As if your knee-jints were greased with very saint's anointment.

2. An anointing material; ointment, unguent, salve.

1398 TREVISA *Barth. De P.R.* VI. ix. (1495) 195 She batheth hym and anoynteth hym wyth noble anoyntments. *c* **1460** *Towneley Myst.* 262 Oure anoyntments fare and clere, That we have broght. **1580** SIDNEY *Arcadia* III. 315 Had given her soveraign anoyntment to preserve his body withall. **1626** COCKERAM, *Vnguent*, An anoyntment.

†a'noise. *v. Obs. rare.* [f. A- *pref.* 1 (or 6) + NOISE *v.*] To noise abroad, bruit, renown.

c **1400** *Destr. Troy* I. 220 By þi name þus anoisyt & for noble holden.

anoli, -is (əˈnəʊlɪ, -ɪs). *Zool.* Also 8 **annolis**, **anole**. [a. native name in the Antilles, *anoli*, *anoalli*; Fr. and mod.L. *anolis*.] A genus of lizards of the Iguana family, found in the West Indies and adjacent mainland.

1706 PHILLIPS, *Annolis*, a Creature in America, about the bigness of a Lizard, and of a yellowish Skin. **1753** CHAMBERS *Cycl. Supp.*, *Anole*..the name of a species of lizard. **1835** KIRBY *Hab. & Inst. Anim.* II. xxii. 430 They [the Guanas] are remarkable—as well as the Anolis, for the kind of goitre in their throat, which..they can inflate to a large size. **1847** CARPENTER *Zool.* §495 The Anolis is a small, slender, active, little animal, frequenting woods and rocky places.

anolyte (ˈænəlaɪt). [f. ANO(DE + ELECTRO)-LYTE.] That part of the electrolyte which adjoins the anode. Cf. CATHOLYTE.

1890 G. GORE *Art Electrolytic Separation Metals* II. E. 79 In the cases of electrolysis of two liquids, separated by a porous partition, it is sometimes convenient to call the liquid containing the anode the anolyte, and that containing the cathode the catholyte. **1903** W. MCA. JOHNSON in *Electrochem. Industry* I. 454 Whenever a current passes from the anode to the anolyte, or from the catholyte to the cathode, then chemical change ensues. **1949** F. A. LOWENHEIM in A. E. Knowlton *Stand. Handbk. for Electr. Engin.* (ed. 8) XX. 1926 The solution itself is the electrolyte; that surrounding the cathode is the catholyte, and that surrounding the anode the anolyte.

†a'nomal, *a.* and *sb. Obs. rare.* [a. Fr. *anomal*, ad. L. *anōmal-us*, a. Gr. ἀνώμαλ-ος irregular, uneven; f. ἀν priv. + ὁμαλ-ός even.]

A. *adj.* Irregular, anomalous.

1681 tr. *T. Willis' Rem. Med. Wks.*, *Anomal*, Irregular, out of order.

B. *sb.* Anything anomalous; an anomaly.

1569 J. SANFORD *Agrippa's Van. Artes* 107 Whiche things because they haue neither measure, nor rule, are called Anomals. [**1620** *Reliq. Wotton.* (1672) 261 Irregularitives of Fortune, who hath likewise her Anomola.] **1665** J. SPENCER *Prodigies* 131 A more faithful History of the Anomals in Nature.

†a'nomalar, *a. Obs. rare*$^{-1}$. [f. L. *anōmal-us* (see prec.) + -AR.] = ANOMALOUS.

1709 *Phil. Trans.* XXVI. 432 The Anomalar Blackness of the Girl's Face..is divided into a few dark, clowdy Specks.

anomaliflorous (əˌnɒməlɪˈflɔərəs), *a. Bot.* [f. L. *anōmal-us* + *-flōr-us* flowered + -OUS.]

1880 in *Syd. Soc. Lex.*

anomaliped (əˈnɒməlɪpɛd), *a.* and *sb. rare.* [a. Fr. *anomalipède*, f. L. *anōmal-us* (see ANOMAL) + *ped-* (*pes*) foot.] **A.** *adj.* Having an anomalous foot; 'applied to a bird, the middle toe of which is united to the exterior by three phalanges, and to the interior by one only' (Craig). **B.** *sb.* A bird having this structure of foot.

Craig 1847.

anomalism (əˈnɒməlɪz(ə)m). *rare.* [f. Gr. ἀνώμαλ-ος (see ANOMAL) + -ISM.] Anomalousness, irregularity, anomaly; an example of irregularity.

1668 WILKINS *Real Char.* 447 The vast multitude of Anomalisms and exceptions in the inflexions of Verbs. **1796** PEGGE *Anonym.* (1809) 310 This would breed no obscurity by the anomalism, as such modes of spelling would always be perfectly well understood. **1862** MRS. WOOD *Mrs. Hallib.* (1864) III. i. 313 She could not understand how so great an anomalism could be.

anomalist (əˈnɒməlɪst). *rare.* [mod. f. as prec. + -IST. (Farrar takes it from Ger. of Lersch.)] One who held that language was purely conventional or arbitrary in its origin, or without any natural analogy between names and the things named.

1860 FARRAR *Orig. Lang.* i. 7 Those who leaned to the conventional origin of language, were styled Anomalists. **1865** —— *Chapt. Lang.* 109 The Analogists who argued for the natural origin of language against the Anomalists.

anomalistic (əˌnɒməˈlɪstɪk), *a.* [mod. f. as prec. + -ISTIC. Cf. mod.L. *anōmalistic-us*, and Fr. *anomalistique* perh. earlier.] Connected with or pertaining to an anomaly.

1. *Astr.* Pertaining to the anomaly or angular distance of a planet from its perihelion. ***anomalistic year***: the time occupied by the earth (or other planet), in passing from perihelion to perihelion, or from any given value of the angular element called *anomaly* to the same again, which, owing to the slow eastward motion of the apsidal points of the orbit, is longer than a tropical or sidereal year, containing 365 d. 6 h. 13′ 49·3″. ***anomalistic month***: the time similarly occupied by the moon in passing from perigee to perigee, etc.

1767 HORSLEY in *Phil. Trans.* LVII. 179 The duplicate proportion of the periodic month to the anomalistic month. **1794** G. ADAMS *Nat. & Exp. Phil.* IV. xlv. 244 The anomalistic period of Saturn is increasing, at present, about a day in a century. **1833** J. NARRIEN *Hist. Astron.* 261 Her [the moon's] mean anomalistic velocity. **1874** MOSELEY *Astron.* xxx. (ed. 4) 116 The time intervening between two successive passages of the earth through an aphelion or perihelion, of its orbit, is called an Anomalistic Year.

2. Of or pertaining to a (linguistic) anomalist.

1882 *Trans. Vict. Inst.* 321 The Conventional (Anomalistic) and Connexional (Analogistic) Theories of Language.

† **a,noma'listical,** *a. Obs. rare.* = prec.

1727-51 CHAMBERS *Cycl.* s.v., The anomalistical or common year, is somewhat greater than the tropical year. **1796** HUTTON *Math. Dict.* I. 120 The *anomalistical year*, called also *periodical year*, is the space of time in which the earth, or a planet, passes through its orbit.

a,noma'listically, *adv. rare*$^{-0}$. [f. prec. + -LY^2.] In an anomalistic manner.

1775 in ASH; and in mod. Dicts.

anomalo- (ə,nɒmələʊ), comb. form of Gr. ἀνώμαλος, irregular; as in **anomalogonatous** (-'gɒnətəs), *a. Zool.* [Gr. γονατ- (γόνυ) knee], of or belonging to the *Anomalogonati*, an order of birds, including sparrows, woodpeckers, etc., so named by Prof. Garrod as lacking the *rectus femoris* muscle.

1882 *Athenæum* 27 May 671/1 The whole group of anomalogonatous birds.

anomaloscope (ə'nɒmələʊskəʊp). *Optics.* [ad. G. *anomaloskop*, f. ANOMALO- + -SCOPE.] An apparatus invented by W. A. Nagel (1870–1911) for measuring abnormality in colour vision.

Apparatus of this kind was first announced by Nagel in 1898 but he did not at first call it an 'Anomaloskop'.

1923 L. C. MARTIN *Colour* x. 150 Nagel's anomaloscope is a simple instrument similar to a direct-vision spectroscope, in which a yellow may be matched by a mixture of red and green. The brightness of the yellow and the ratio of red to green are indicated by the readings on two micrometer heads. The numerical divergences from the normal readings are taken as arbitrary measures of the 'anomaly'. **1929** W. D. WRIGHT *Re-det. Trichr. Mixture Data* 27 So-called anomalous matches made on the Nagel anomaloscope. **1962** *Lancet* 15 Dec. 1269/1 Anomaloscope examination.. reveals deviations from normal.

anomalous (ə'nɒmələs), *a.* [f. L. *anōmal-us* (see ANOMAL) + -OUS.]

1. With *to*: Unequal, unconformable, dissimilar, incongruous. *arch.*

1646 SIR T. BROWNE *Pseud. Ep.* 51 Neutralls and bodies anomalous hereto. **1652** GAULE *Magastrom.* 18 [The stars in the East] appeared and disappeared anomalous to ordinary starres. **1829** I. TAYLOR *Enthus.* x. 267 These [early missions].. were anomalous to the general feeling of Christians.

2. a. *simply*: Unconformable to the common order; deviating from rule, irregular; abnormal.

1655 LESTRANGE *Chas. I*, 137 These things.. being anomalous, innovations, and so severely urged, many.. separated themselves into factious sidings. **1667** *Phil. Trans.* II. 601 Some anomalous Feavers. **1789** BENTHAM *Princ. Legisl.* xviii. §10 Offences of this description may well be called anomalous. **1872** HOLMES *Poet Breakf. T.* xi. 347 Peculiar and anomalous in her likes and dislikes.

b. in *Nat. Hist.*

1655 *Let.* in Hartlib. *Ref. Commonw. Bees* 22 A third very anomalous Generation.. is of a sort of stinging Flies. **1737** P. MILLER *Gard. Dict.* s.v. *Viola*, It hath a polypetalous, anomalous Flower, somewhat resembling the papilionaceous Flower. **1845** DARWIN *Voy. Nat.* viii. (1879) 162 This beautiful and most anomalous structure is adapted to take hold of floating marine animals.

c. in *Gram.*

1659 B. WALTON *Consid. Considered* 263 The following Masorites, finding such anomalous punctuation, left all as they found them. **1706** PHILLIPS s.v., In Grammar there are four kinds of Anomalous Nouns, viz. Heterogeneal, Heteroclites, Difficients and Redundants. **1874** SAYCE *Compar. Philol.* ix. 349 The tendency of all linguistic progress is to reduce the number of anomalous forms.

d. ***anomalous dispersion***: the dispersion of light in the vicinity of an absorption band, where the refractive index changes rapidly with wavelength, being abnormally high on one side of the band and abnormally low on the other.

1883 R. T. GLAZEBROOK *Phys. Optics* x. 277 In ordinary dispersing media the refractive index increases as the wave-length and the period of vibration decrease;.. in media in which anomalous dispersion takes place this is not the case, for it is no longer true that waves of short period have a greater refractive index than waves of long period. **1899** A. S. PERCIVAL *Optics* viii. 179 Anomalous dispersion is best displayed in substances that have strongly marked absorption bands. **1904** J. WALKER *Analytical Theory of Light* xvii. 337 There is an intimate connection between anomalous dispersion and the absorptive power of a substance. **1936** *Discovery* June 198/1 Such molecular rearrangements as anomalous dispersion and dipole phenomena.

a'nomalously, *adv.* [f. prec. + -LY^2.] In an anomalous manner, irregularly, in a way at variance with due order.

1646 SIR T. BROWNE *Pseud. Ep.* v. v. (1686) 195 Eve anomalously proceeded from Adam. **1790** BURKE *Fr. Rev.* 91 It is better that the whole should be imperfectly and anomalously answered, than, etc. **1858** FROUDE *Hist. Eng.* III. xii. 80 The separate translations, still anomalously prohibited in detail, were exposed freely to sale in a single volume.

a'nomalousness. [f. as prec. + -NESS.] The quality of being anomalous.

1698 [R. FERGUSSON] *View Eccles.* 95 Objections fastened upon Persons, because of some Anomolousness in their Bodily Structure. **1865** PUSEY *Eiren.* 12 The temporary notoriousness which they [Essays and Reviews] gained shows the more their anomalousness.

anomalure (ə'nɒməl(j)ʊə(r)). *Zool.* [ad. mod.L. *Anomalūrus*, f. Gr. ἀνώμαλος ANOMALOUS *a.* + οὐρά tail.] An animal of the African genus *Anomalurus* of rodents resembling the flying squirrels, and having projecting scales on the tail which serve for assistance in climbing; a scale-tailed squirrel.

1876 *Proc. Zool. Soc. 1875* 88 In external appearance the Anomalures very closely resemble the larger Flying Squirrels. *a* **1886** *Cassell's Nat. Hist.* III. 96 Whilst in the Flying Squirrels this spur springs from the wrist.., in the Anomalures it projects from the elbow. **1920** *Brit. Museum Return* 102 An Anomalure.. from Sierra Leone.

anomaly (ə'nɒməlɪ). [ad. L. *anōmalia*, a. Gr. ἀνωμαλία, n. of quality f. ἀνώμαλ-ος: see ANOMAL.]

1. Unevenness, inequality, of condition, motion, etc.

1571 DIGGES *Pantom.* (1591) 178 The excesse wherby the Semidiameter of the Ringe or Cornice of the Head dooth exceed the Cornice of the Coyle [of cannon] I call the Anomalye. **1684** T. BURNET *Th. Earth* II. 98 The great shakings and concussions of our globe at that time, affecting some of the neighbouring orbs.. may cause anomalies and irregularities in their motions. **1837** WHEWELL *Hist. Induct. Sc.* I. III. ii. 175 The motions of the sun and moon.. had other anomalies or irregularities.

2. a. Irregularity, deviation from the common order, exceptional condition or circumstance. *concr.* A thing exhibiting such irregularity; an anomalous thing or being.

1664 POWER *Exp. Philos.* I. 78 To admire Nature's Anomaly.. in the number of Eyes, which she has given to several Animals. **1722** WOLLASTON *Relig. Nat.* ix. 217 Support him under all the anomalies of life. **1818** HALLAM *Mid. Ages* (1872) II. 213 Time changes anomaly into system. **1852** GLADSTONE *Gleanings* IV. xvi. 152 The intolerable anomaly of a state obeying in the civil sphere the dictates of the Church. **1870** DISRAELI *Lothair* l. 274 A capital without a country is an apparent anomaly.

b. *Nat. Sc.* Deviation from the natural order.

1646 SIR T. BROWNE *Pseud. Ep.* 135 They confound the generation of perfect animalls with imperfect.. and erect anomalies, disturbing the lawes of Nature. **1859** DARWIN *Orig. Spec.* v. (1873) 108 There is no greater anomaly in nature than a bird that cannot fly. **1860** MAURY *Phys. Geog.* xv. §669 A low barometer.. was considered an anomaly peculiar to the regions of Cape Horn.

c. *Gram.* Irregularity, exception to the prevailing form of inflexion, etc.

1612 BRINSLEY *Lud. Lit.* xx. (1627) 224 Most exceptions or Anomalies may be learned after. **1751** WATTS *Improvem. Mind* (1801) 57 Let but few of the anomalies or irregularities of the tongue be taught.. to young beginners. **1874** BLACKIE *Self-Culture* 34 Some anomalies, as in the conjugation of a few irregular verbs.

3. *Astr.* The angular distance of a planet or satellite from its last perihelion or perigee: so called because the first irregularities of planetary motion were discovered in the discrepancy between the actual and the computed distance.

1669 FLAMSTEAD in *Phil. Trans.* IV. 1109 The moons mean Anomaly is 0 s. 15 d. 10 m. 37 sec. **1706** PHILLIPS, *Anomaly of the Orbit* is the Arch, or Distance of a Planet from its Aphelion. **1867** E. DENISON *Astron.* 32 The distance of a planet from perihelion, or of the moon from perigee.. is called its true anomaly; and the distance it would have gone in the same time if it moved uniformly, or in a circle instead of an ellipse, is its mean anomaly; and their difference is called the *equation of the centre*. **1868** *Chambers's Encycl.* I. 280 The anomaly was formerly measured from the aphelion; but from the fact that the aphelia of most of the comets lie beyond the range of observation, the perihelion is now taken as the point of departure for all planetary bodies.

4. *Mus.* A small deviation from a perfect interval, in tuning instruments with fixed notes; a temperament. *Ed. Encycl.* 1830.

5. a. *Meteorol.* (See quots.)

1853 E. J. SABINE tr. *Dove's Distribution of Heat* 20 We require.. to exhibit the relation of the actual temperature of each place to the mean or normal temperature of its geographical latitude. I call the difference between the actual and normal temperature the 'thermic anomaly'. **1922** W. G. KENDREW *Clim. Cont.* I. i. 3 The 'anomaly of temperature' for that place, a positive anomaly if the place is warmer than the mean, a negative anomaly if it is colder.

b. *Geogr.* A local departure from the normal pull of gravity.

1924 H. JEFFREYS *Earth* 121 This anomaly is always negative. In other words, the gravity on a mountain top is less than elsewhere. **1944** A. HOLMES *Princ. Physical Geol.* xviii. 404 This band of what are called 'negative anomalies of gravity' implies that there is a corresponding deficiency of density in the materials of the crust beneath.

anomie, var. ANOMY.

anomo- (,ænəməʊ, ə,nɒmə), comb. form of Gr. ἄνομ-ος without law, f. ἀ priv. + νόμος law; first element in various compounds, chiefly modern, as:—

anomobranchiate (-'bræŋkɪət), *a.* and *sb. Zool.* [Gr. βράγχια gills], *adj.* having gills of irregular structure, *sb.* a crustacean having such gills. **anomocarpous** (-'kɑːpəs), *a. Bot.* [Gr. καρπός fruit], bearing unusual fruit. **anomodont** (ə'nɒməʊdɒnt), *a.* and *sb. Zool.* [Gr. ὀδοντ- tooth], having irregular or no teeth, applied to a genus of fossil reptiles. **anomophyllous** (-'fɪləs), *a. Bot.* [Gr. φύλλον leaf], having leaves irregularly placed. **anomorhomboid** (-'rɒmbɔɪd). *Cryst.* [Gr. ῥομβο-ειδής rhombus shaped], 'a name given to certain varieties of crystalline spars, of no determinate regular external form, but always fracturing into irregular rhomboids' (Craig). **anomorhomboidal** (-rɒm'bɔɪdəl), *a. Cryst.*, consisting of irregular rhomboids.

1852 DANA *Crust.* I. 8 In the Anomobranchiates the feet are in part two-branched or bifid. **1880** *Syd. Soc. Lex.*, *Anomocarpous.* **1881** *Athenæum* 19 Mar. 401/1 The Skeleton of an Anomodont Reptile. **1879** LE CONTE *Elem. Geol.* 410 The beaked Saurians, also called Anomodonts. **1880** *Syd. Soc. Lex.*, *Anomophyllous.* [**1753** CHAMBERS *Cycl. Supp.*, *Anomorhomboidia*.. pellucid crystalline spars.. composed of plates running both horizontally and perpendicularly thro' the masses.. There are five known species.] **1847** CRAIG, *Anomorhomboidal.*

Anomœan (ænəʊ'miːən), *a.* and *sb. Theol.* Also **Anomean.** [f. mod.L. *Anomœus*, ad. Gr. ἀνόμοιος unlike, dissimilar (f. ἀν- priv. + ὅμοιος like, similar) + -AN.] Belonging to, or a member of, an extreme sect of Arians who held that the Father and the Son are unlike in essence: = HETEROOUSIAN: opp. to HOMŒAN.

[**1526** R. WHYTFORD *Martiloge* sig. k1^r, Y^e heretykes called.. anomeyes.] **1683** CAVE *Ecclesiastici* 153 The Anomæan Heresie. *Ibid.* 224, The Head of the Homoiousian, against the Anomæans or Heterousian Sect. **1780** A. BUTLER *Lives Saints* V. 31 The Anomæans or rank Arians. **1840** MILMAN *Hist. Chr.* III. III. v. 47 The party of the Anomeans triumphed, while Aetius, its author, was sent into banishment. **1874** J. C. ROBERTSON *Hist. Chr. Ch.* II. vi. 63 The perpetual virginity of the Saviour's mother was denied by the anomœan Eunomius. **1882-3** [see HETEROOUSIAST].

anomœ'omery. *rare.* [f. Gr. ἀνομοιομερή-ς of dissimilar parts; cf. ὁμοιομέρεια HOMŒOMERY (f. ὅμοιος like + μέρος part).] The theory that the ultimate atoms of matter are dissimilar.

1678 CUDWORTH *Intell. Syst.* Pref. 7 The true and genuine Atomology of the Ancient Italicks.. was an Anomœomery, or doctrine of Dissimilar and Unqualified Atoms.

anomoural, -mural (ænəʊ'mʊərəl), *a. Zool.* [f. as next + -AL^1.] Having the character of the *Anomoura* (see next).

1852 DANA *Crust.* I. 56 These different Anomoural forms. *Ibid.* 399 The term Anomoural refers to the anomalous character of the abdomen.

anomouran, -muran (ænəʊ'mʊərən), *a.* and *sb. Zool.* [f. *Anom(o)ura* (mod.L. f. Gr. ἄνομ-ος irregular + οὐρά tail) + -AN.]

A. *adj.* Of the *Anomoura* or stalk-eyed crustacea, allied to the hermit-crab; so called from the want of any regular type in the abdomen or 'tail.'

1877 HUXLEY *Anat. Inv. An.* vi. 350 The Anomuran condition passes into that of the young Brachyuran.

B. *sb.* A member of the *Anomoura*.

anomourous (ænəʊmʊərəs), *a. Zool.* = prec.

1847 CARPENTER *Zool.* II. 251 Anomourous Decapods; Hermit-crabs.

anomphalous (ə'nɒmfələs), *a.* [f. Gr. ἀν priv. + ὀμφαλ-ός navel + -OUS.] Without a navel.

1742 BAILEY, *Anomphalous*, without a Navel, as it is supposed our first Parents were created, not wanting Nourishment in the Womb that way. **1853** in MAYNE *Exp. Lex.*

'anomy. [ad. Gr. ἀνομία, n. of quality f. ἄνομ-ος lawless.] † **1.** Disregard of law, lawlessness; esp. (in 17th c. theology) disregard of divine law. *Obs.*

1591 LAMBARDE *Archeion* (1635) 120 That were to set an Anomy, and to bring disorder, doubt, and incertaintie over all. **1683** E. HOOKER *Pref. Pordage's Myst. Div.* 23 Men's Lusts, animosities, enormities, Anomies. **1689** *Apol. Fail. Walker's Acc.* 15 You Presbyterians distinguish between the Action and the Anomy, or Irregularity of it. **1755** in JOHNSON.

2. Also commonly in French form **anomie.** [F. (Durkheim *Suicide*, 1897).] Absence of accepted social standards or values; the state or condition of an individual or society lacking such standards.

1933 E. MAYO *Human Probl.* vi. 130 We are facing a condition of *anomie*, of planlessness in living, which is becoming characteristic both of individual lives and of communities. **1938** R. K. MERTON in *Amer. Sociol. Rev.* III. 674 The integration of the society becomes tenuous and anomie ensues. **1951** SPAULDING & SIMPSON tr. *Durkheim's Suicide* II. v. 253 The state of de-regulation or anomy is.. further heightened by passions being less disciplined, precisely when they need more disciplining. **1959** *Guardian* 18 Sept. 8/5 An emphasis on order and stability (as opposed to anarchy or *anomie*). **1959** B. WOOTTON et al. *Soc. Sci. & Soc. Path.* ii. 69 Sociologists have thought it worth while to coin a special term—'anomie'—to describe the unorthodox social values, norms and attitudes to which 'underprivileged' children may be conditioned.

So **a'nomic** [ad. F. *anomique* (Durkheim, 1897)] *a.*, of, pertaining to, or characterized by such a state (see quots.).

1950 D. RIESMAN et al. *Lonely Crowd* III. xiv. 287 My use of anomic.. covers a wider range than Durkheim's metaphor: it is virtually synonymous with 'maladjusted'. **1951** SPAULDING & SIMPSON tr. *Durkheim's Suicide* II. v. 258 The third sort of suicide.. results from man's activity's lacking regulation and his consequent sufferings. By virtue of its origin we shall assign this last variety the name of *anomic* suicide. **1961** B. R. WILSON *Sects & Society* 8 It is the leisure time of the individual in which his anomic circumstances will be most acutely felt.

anon (ə'nɒn), *adv.* Forms: 1 on án, on áne, 2–3 anan, 3 anæn, 3–4 onon, onan(e, an-nane, in an(e, in oon, 4 on o(o)ne, 4–5 anoon(e, 4–7 anone, 5 onon(e, enon, onoon, 6 annon(e, 2– anon. *Aphet.* 4 noon. [OE. *on án* into one, *on áne* in one, *i.e.* in one body, mind, state, act, way, course, motion, movement, moment.]

†**1.** In (or into) one body, company, or mass; in one; together; in one accord; in unity. *Obs.*

a **1000** *Metr. Ps.* cxxxii. 1 Hú glædlic.. þætte bróður onán beȝen hicȝen. *a* **1000** CYNEWULF *Christ* 970 (Grein) Téonleȝ bærneð préo eall onán grimme togædre.

†**2.** In one (and the same) state or condition (without change); the same. *Obs. rare.*

c **1220** *Ureisun* in *Lamb. Hom.* 189 [He] halt euer anon wiþute sturunge. *a* **1300** *Cursor M.* 1852 þe streme it stud ai still in-an [*v.r.* in ane, on an, in oon].

†**3.** In one (and the same) course or direction, in a straight course, straight on, even. ***anon to***: even to, as far as to; = L. *usque ad*, Fr. *jusqu'à*, Ger. *bis zu*. *Obs.*

c **1200** ORMIN 1105 He wass all daȝȝ Unnclene anan till efenn. *c* **1305** *E.E. Poems* (1862) 49 Al þe lond biȝunde humber: anon into scotlonde. **1387** TREVISA *Higden* (1865) I. 85 From þe see þat is i-cleped Caspius anon to þe Rede see. **1399** *Rich. Redeles* II. 126 ȝe.. plucked and pulled hem anon to þe skynnes. *c* **1460** *Towneley Myst.* 156 Shalle I never rest .. Or I come ther anone?

†**4.** *strictly*, Straightway, at once, forthwith, instantly. *Obs.* (exc. when mod. writers have tried to revive the strict sense.)

a **1000** *Juliana* 69 (Grein) Heó me onán saȝað, þæt heó.. ne ȝyme. *c* **1175** *Cotton Hom.* 231 Gief he fend wére, me sceolde ánon eter gat [hine] ȝemete. *c* **1250** *Gen. & Ex.* 1067 He boden him bringen ut onon. **1330** R. BRUNNE *Chron.* 99 Roberd went to.. Sir Lowys on one, and told him þat greuance. **1375** BARBOUR *Bruce* IV. 364 Thai buskit thame on-ane. **1393** LANGL. *P. Pl.* C. XXI. 365 A-non vndo þe ȝates! **1398** TREVISA *Barth. De P.R.* VI. vi, þey risen oute of here bed and axen mete on oone [L. *subito* **1582** anone]. *c* **1400** *Destr. Troy* III. 813 Enon he lurkys to his loge. **1523** FITZHERB. *Surv.* xli. (1539) 61 [Though] the aduantage.. come nat anone, it will come at length. **1611** BIBLE *Matt.* xiii. 20 He that heareth the word, & anon with ioy receiueth it. **1862** TRENCH *Miracles* xvii. 281 The toiling rowers are anon at the haven where they would be.

†**b.** ***anon so*** or ***as***: once that, immediately as, as soon as ever (Fr. *aussitôt que*). *Obs.*

c **1175** *Cotton Hom.* 241 Ælc cristen mán ánon se stepð up of þe funte.. he maceð him þri ifon. **1205** LAY. 6369 Anan [**1250** wane] se he wes wrað wið eni mon. **1377** LANGL. *P. Pl.* B. XIX. 18 Kneolen and bowen, Anon as men nempned · þe name of god Ihesu. *c* **1400** *Sowdone* 1836 Ye shall be hanged ..Anoon as I have eten I-nowe. *a* **1520** *Myrr. Our Ladye* 178 Ioye to aungels anone as they were made. **1553–62** FOXE *A. & M.* I. 588/2 Anon as the word of the Sacrament is said.

†**c.** ***anon after***, ***after anon***: directly or immediately after. *Obs.*

c **1220** *Leg. Kath.* 1600 An se swiðe swote smal com anan þrefter. **1377** LANGL. *P. Pl.* B. XI. 45 Coueityse-of-eyghes conforted me anon after. *c* **1400** *Destr. Troy* I. 287 All entred into Argon after anon. **1473** WARKW. *Chron.* 6 Anone aftere that.. there was a grete insurreccyon. **1523** LD. BERNERS *Froiss.* I. xlvii. 65 Whan they were all assembled, anone after Easter. **1574** tr. *Marlorat's Apocalips* 4 He myght shew.. what was to come anone after.

†**d.** ***soon anon***: immediately, quickly. *Obs.*

c **1220** *Leg. Kath.* 1899 þis meiden sone anan onswerede. *a* **1300** *Cursor M.* 1435 Ful sone onane [*v.r.* an-nane, anoon], His saule it was til hell tane. *a* **1325** *Metr. Hom.* 124 He undid it sone on an.

5. Gradually misused (like *presently*, *immediately*, *by and by*, *directly*, *in a moment*) to express: Soon, in a short time, in a little while. (Cf. **d.** above.) ***till anon*** (obs.): until by and by, for a little.

1526 TINDALE *Rev.* xi. 14 The seconde woo is past, and beholde the thyrd woo wyll come anon [WYCL. soone; *Rhem.*, **1611**, quickly]. **1598** STOW *Surv.* (1603) xlix. 557 As it shall better appeare anone. **1606** SHAKS. *Ant. & Cl.* II. vii. 45 Forbeare me till anon. **1610** —— *Temp.* II. ii. 84 Thou do'st me yet but little hurt; thou wilt anon. **1656** COWLEY *Mistress* Wks. 1710 I. 124 Leading them still insensibly on By the strange Witchcraft of Anon. **1661** BOYLE *Spring of Air* I. ii. (1682) 3 The answering of this we shall suspend until anon. **1661** PEPYS *Diary* 15 Sept., To put things in order against anon for the buriall. **1719** D'URFEY *Pills* (1872) IV. 352 Take not the first Refusal ill, Tho' now she wont, anon she will. **1858** SEARS *Athan.* vii. 59 We dream now, we shall wake anon.

6. Now again. **a.** Now at this time, in contrast to *at that time*, presently again; here again.

1588 SHAKS. *L.L.L.* IV. ii. 6 Who now hangeth like a Iewell in the eare of Celo the skie.. and anon falleth like a Crab on the face of Terra. **1670** G. H. *Hist. Cardinals* III. II. 204 Contriving new designs, now for this Cardinal, anon for another. **1794** SULLIVAN *View Nat.* II. 369 Now it is a people with hats; anon with turbans. **1833** I. TAYLOR *Fanat.* viii. 347 Sometimes.. the sacred writers say too little; and anon too much! **1860** TYNDALL *Glac.* I §2. 11 The avalanche rushed, hidden at intervals, and anon shooting forth.

b. ***ever and anon***: ever and again, every now and then; continually at intervals.

1588 SHAKS. *L.L.L.* v. ii. 102 Ever and anon they made a doubt. **1647** WARD *Simp. Cobler* 7 They are sure to be hunted ever and anon. **1703** ROWE *Fair Penit.* I. i. 232 Then ever and anon she wrings her hands. **1820** SCOTT *Monast.* xi. 69 Looking ever and anon to Edward for assistance.

7. A response by a servant etc. called: 'Immediately! presently! coming!'; whence extended to an expression of attention, 'At your service! awaiting your orders!'; and finally implying that the auditor has failed to catch the speaker's words or meaning, and asks him to repeat = 'Beg your pardon! what did you say? eh?' See ANAN.

†**8.** *Comb.* **anon-right**, also (later) ***right anon***: straightway, forthwith, right off, immediately. *Obs.*

c **1175** *Cotton Hom.* 265 Hwer se eauer þe gast wule, þe bodi is anan riht. *c* **1200** ORMIN 2571 Allswa birrþ himm forrþrihht anan. *c* **1384** CHAUCER *H. Fame* 132, I sawgh anoon [*v.r.* anon(e, a non] ryght hir figure. *c* **1386** —— *Sqrs. T.* 391 Right anon she wiste what they mente. *c* **1430** LYDG. *Bochas* I. v. 8 To make a mariage, after anon right. **1480** CAXTON *Chron. Eng.* l. 34 He lete slee hem euerychone anon right.

†**b.** With adverbial genitive *-es*, *-s*. *Obs.*

c **1230** *Ancr. R.* 248 Herdi bileaue bringeð þene deouel a vlihte anon-rihtes. *c* **1300** *K. Alis.* 824 After mete, anon ryghtis, Theo kyng clepith gentil knyghtis. *c* **1460** *Launfal* 658 Syxty ladyes and fyf.. went hem doun anoon ryghtes.

anon (ə'nɒn). Also **anon.** (with full point), **Anon.** Abbrev. of ANONYMOUS *a.* Hence as *sb.*, a person (esp. a writer or composer) whose name is unknown or not given.

1736 POPE *Works* IV. 235 A compleat Key to the What d'ye call it. Anon. By Griffin a Player, supervis'd by Mr. Th——. **1815** *Gentl. Mag.* LXXXV. II. 539/2 Besides the great composers.. the Author has drawn his materials from the following: Anon, Baillot, Borri, [etc.]. **1902** J. M. BARRIE *Little White Bird* v. 55 She had sworn to hunt Mr. Anon down. **1947** *Punch* 5 Feb. 135 To-day I brought off a first-class scoop, An interview with Anon., The most prolific poet of us all. **1951** V. H. GALBRAITH *Hist. Research in Med. Eng.* 10 The medieval historians are dim figures. The vast majority would be classed in modern anthologies as 'anon'.

anonaceous (ænəʊ'neɪʃəs), *a. Bot.* [f. mod.L. *anōna* the pine-apple (cf. ANANAS) + -ACEOUS.] Of or pertaining to the pine-apple, and the N.O. *Anonaceæ*, to which it belongs.

1852 T. ROSS tr. *Humboldt's Trav.* I. vi. 213 Among anonaceous plants. **1863** H. BATES *Nat. on Amazons* vii. (1864) 188 Fruit-trees; some, belonging to the Anonaceous order, yielding delicious fruits large as a child's head, and full of custardy pulp.

anonad (ə'nəʊnəd). *Bot.* [f. L. *anōna* (see prec.) + -AD 1 d.] A plant allied to the pine-apple, or included in the N.O. *Anonaceæ*.

1847 LINDLEY *Veg. K.* (ed. 2) 421 Anonads are connected with Berberids through Bocagea. **1866** in *Treas. Bot.*

anonde, -des, anont, obs. forms of ANENT.

anonder, var. ANUNDER. *Obs.*, under.

an-oniwar, *adv. Obs.*, at UNAWARES.

anonxcion, var. ANUNCTION. *Obs.*, anointing.

anonym ('ænənɪm). [a. Fr. *anonyme*, ad. Gr. ἀνώνυμ-ος, or its L. a. *anōnym-us*, ANONYMOUS.]

1. A person whose name is not given, who remains nameless. (Often *anonyme*, as in Fr.)

1812 BYRON in Moore *Life* (1866) 166, I should hardly wish a contest with.. all the anonymes and synonymes of Committee Candidates. **1866** DE MORGAN *Budg. Parad.* 10 Among my anonymes is a gentleman who is angry at my treatment of the 'poor but thoughtful' man who, etc. **1878** H. H. GIBBS *Ombre* 78 Sir Anonym (as.. [Dr. Pole in *Macmillan* 1875].. calls the third player) being at Belinda's right hand, and the Baron at her left.

2. A fictitious designation, concealing the real name of a writer; a pseudonym. (Cf. *synonym*.)

1866 *Anti-Slavery Rep.* 2 July 169/1 The writer, who signs himself St. Jago de la Vega, is scarcely veiled under his anonym. **1882** *Nonconf.* 5 May 401/3 The critic crowing loudly behind his anonym sneers at Dr. Hutton.

3. An anonymous book. *rare.*

1867 O. HAMST *Mart. Bibliogr.*, *Anonym*, book without a name on the title.

anonyma (ə'nɒnɪmə). [mod.L., fem. of L. *anōnymus* (see ANONYMOUS *a.*).] †**1.** A woman of the demi-monde. *Obs.*

1864 SALA *Quite Alone* I. i. 2 Bah! there are so many Anonymas now-a-days. **1889** *Modern Society* 13 July 852 His mother-in-law mistakes his buxom laundress for a fair anonyma.

2. *Anat.* The innominate artery.

1871 T. H. HUXLEY *Anat. Vert.* viii. 380 The arteries arise from the arch of the aorta, as in Man, by an *anonyma*, a left carotid and left subclavian.

†**a'nonymal**, *a. Obs. rare.* [f. Gr. ἀνώνυμ-ος (or its L. a. *anōnym-us*) + -AL[1].] Anonymous.

1586 THYNNE in *Animadv.* Introd. 89 Other anonymall Chronicles. **1662** FULLER *Worthies* II. 155 And take the original thereof out of an anonymal croniclering manuscript.

anonymity (ænə'nɪmɪtɪ). [f. as prec. + -ITY; cf. *unanim-ity*, etc.] The state of being anonymous. (Used of an author or his writings.)

1820 *Blackw. Mag.* Oct. 98/2 An attempt was made to fasten anonymity on Blackwood's Magazine. **1829** CARLYLE *Misc.* (1857) II. 11 With a strange system of anonymity.. has Voltaire surrounded himself. **1880** GROSART *James I's Poems* Introd. 77 The anonymity of the poem on Felton and the semi-anonymity of the poem on Shakespeare. **1882** *Times* 14 Feb. 10/2 Academical dignitaries, writing.. under a disguise of transparent anonymity.

anonymous (ə'nɒnɪməs), *a.* [f. Gr. ἀνώνυμος (whence also in L. *anōnymos*, *anōnymus*), f. ἀν priv. + ὄνομα, in Æolic ὄνυμα, name; + -OUS. Often used in Gr. form early in 17th c.]

1. Nameless, having no name; of unknown name.

1601 HOLLAND *Pliny* (1634) II. 274 Anonymos, finding no name to be called by, got therupon the name Anonymos. A Plant this is brought out of Scythia to vs. **1631** *Whimzies* 22 Hee is *anonymos*, and that wil secure him. **1675** OGILBY *Brit.* 24 The confluence of an Anonimous Rill with the Tame. **1712** STEELE *Spect.* No. 546 ¶4 Amongst the crowd of other anonymous correspondents. **1794** PALEY *Evidences* II. vi. §41 These altars.. were called anonymous, because there was not the name of any particular deity inscribed upon them. **1866** G. MACDONALD *Ann. Q. Neighb.* xxxiii. 560 Clothed in the coat of darkness of an anonymous writer.

b. Hence *subst.* A person whose name is not given, or is unknown.

1603 HARSNET *Pop. Impost.* 49 Killico, Hob and a third *anonymos*, are booked downe for 3 graund Commaunders. **1654** WHITLOCK *Mann. Eng.* 208 It were.. wisdome it selfe, to read all Authors as Anonymo's, looking on the Sence, not Names of Books. **1832** MISS PORTER *Hungarian Bro.* 15 To become certain that my anonymous is a woman.

2. *transf.* Bearing no author's name; of unknown or unavowed authorship.

1676 EVELYN *Mem.* (1857) II. 111 An anonymous book, called Naked Truth. **1796** MORSE *Amer. Geog.* I. 576 Observations from an anonymous pamphlet. **1831** BREWSTER *Newton* (1855) II. xv. 65 The anonymous attacks upon Newton. **1841** MYERS *Cath. Th.* III. §17. 62 Many of the books which they [the Jewish Scriptures] contain are anonymous.

3. Unacknowledged, illegitimate. *rare.*

1881 *Daily News* 1 Feb. 5/8 The anonymous daughter of a King, who became enamoured of her mother while on a visit to Paris.

a'nonymously, *adv.* [f. prec. + -LY[2].] In an anonymous manner; without any name being given or attached.

a **1745** SWIFT (J.) I would know whether the edition is to come out anonymously. **1835** WORDSW. *Wks.* V. 347, I might avail myself of the periodical press for offering anonymously my thoughts.. to the world. **1880** CYPLES *Hum. Exp.* iii. 62 Experiences re-appear anonymously in the consciousness of the old man.

a'nonymousness. [f. as prec. + -NESS.] The quality or state of being anonymous; anonymity.

1802 SOUTHEY in Robberds *Mem. W. Taylor* I. 426, I, with all proper anonymousness, am printing an abridged 'Amadis.' **1859** MILL *Dissert.* I. Pref., Writings put forth under the screen of anonymousness.

anonymuncule (ə,nɒnɪ'mʌŋkjʊl). [f. L. *anōnym-us* (see ANONYMOUS), after L. *homunculus* a little man.] A petty anonymous writer.

1867 SWINBURNE *Let.* 25 Dec. (1962) VI. 263, I have always found that these 'anonymuncules' vanish or collapse as soon as one attempts to set foot on them. *a* **1869** C. READE in Swinburne *Ess. & Stud.* (1875) 3 Anonymuncules who go scribbling about. **1883** PROCTOR in *Knowl.* 25 May 313/2 Charles Reade is awfully hard on the criticasters and anonymuncules of the press.

†**a-'noon**, *advb. phr. Obs.* [A *prep.*[1] at + NOON. Cf. *a-day*, *a-night*, *a-morn*, etc.] At noon.

c **1386** CHAUCER *Merch. T.* 641 (Harl. MS.) The moone that a-noon was thilke day.. In tuo of Taure [6-*text MSS.* at noon, none].

anoon(e, obs. form of ANON.

anopheles (ə'nɒfɪli:z). *Ent.* [mod.L. (Meigen *Syst. Beschr. Eur. Zweifl. Ins.* (1818) I. 10), a. Gr. ἀνωφελής unprofitable, useless.] A mosquito of the genus *Anopheles*, which conveys the parasite of malaria. Also *attrib.* Hence **a'nopheline** *a.* and *sb.*

1899 *Daily News* 28 Sept. 3/4 We could kill most of the anopheles grubs here in a few hours with kerosene oil. **1902** *Encycl. Brit.* XXIX. 498/2 The parasite has now been found to live in the body of the Anopheles. **1915** G. B. SHAW *Doctors' Delusions* (1931) 133 Inoculation with anopheles vaccine. **1915** *Indian Jrnl. Med. Res.* July 180 The exact identity of Arabian anophelines has been for some time a matter of interest. **1920** J. RITCHIE *Animal Life Scot.* 511 Mosquitos,..I mean Anopheline, or..'spot-winged' Gnats. **1929** *Times* 10 Jan. 13/6 The anopheline mosquitoes, which spread malaria, breed chiefly in marshes and streams.

†**ano'physial**, *a. Obs. rare*⁻¹. In 6 ann-. [? f. Gr. ἄνω up, above + φύσι-ς nature + -AL¹.] ? Of heavenly nature; supernatural.

1559 MORWYNG *Evonym.* Pref., Calling it Psammurgicall, and misticall, and Annophysiall, and holy.

anophyte ('ænəfaɪt). *Bot.* [ad. mod.L. *anōphytum*, f. (by Endlicher) Gr. ἄνω upward + φυτόν growth, plant.] A name given by some to the non-vascular acrogens, or mosses and their allies.

1850 GRAY *Bot. Text-bk.* (ed. 3) 365 The Anophytes, represented by the Mosses. **1873** DAWSON *Earth & Man* vi. 122 The Anophytes or mosses and their allies, with stems and leaves, but no vessels.

anopisthograph (ˌænəʊ'pɪsθəʊgrɑːf, -æ-), *a.* [f. Gr. ἀν- (AN- 10) + ὀπισθόγραφος OPISTHOGRAPH.] Having no writing (or printing) on the back; inscribed only on one side. Also **ˌanopistho'graphic, -ical** *adjs.*; hence **ˌanopistho'graphically** *adv.*

1871 H. BRADSHAW in *Coll. Pap.* (1889) xiv. 263 If a fragment is found printed only on one side it has hitherto been described as 'a remarkably interesting specimen of anopisthograhic typography'. **1887** BIGMORE tr. *Bouchot's Printed Bk.* i. 15 Gutenberg..desired..that the leaves of his books should not be anopist[h]ograph, or printed only on one side. **1887** *Book-Lore* VI. 159 Two leaves were..pasted together, back to back, forming what is termed an anopist[h]ographical book. **1893** E. G. DUFF *Early Printed Bks.* 13 There must have been some reason for printing these books on one side only..or, as it is called, anopisthographically.

anoplothere (æ'nɒpləθɪə(r)). *Palæont.* [a. Fr. *anoplothère*, f. Gr. ἄνοπλ-ος unarmed (f. ἀν priv. + ὅπλον weapon) + θηρίον beast. Often in mod.L. form *anoplotherium*.] An extinct pachydermatous quadruped, found fossil in the Middle Eocene beds of Hampshire and the Paris basin; so named by Cuvier from its apparent want of organs of defence.

1815 W. PHILLIPS *Outl. Min. & Geol.* (1818) 89 Cuvier discovered the bones of 5 varieties of another extinct animal, which he calls the anoplotherium (..it had no canine teeth), varying in size from the horse to the ass. **1879** LE CONTE *Elem. Geol.* 496 The Anoplothere was a slender and graceful animal without snout, and possessing only two toes.

anoplotheroid (ænɒpləʊ'θɪərɔɪd), *a. Palæont.* [f. prec. + -OID.] Like or related to the anoplothere; also *subst.* An anoplotheroid animal.

1847 ANSTED *Anc. World* xiii. 295 The anoplotheroid animals of the older beds. **1863** RAMSAY *Phys. Geol.* (1878) 254 In the Bembridge beds there has also been found the Anoplotheroid mammal *Dichobune cervinum*.

anopluriform (ænəʊ'pl(j)ʊərɪfɔːm), *a. Zool.* [f. mod.L. *anoplūra* (f. Gr. ἄνοπλ-ος unarmed + οὐρά tail) + -(I)FORM.] Of the form of the *Anoplura* (wingless insects having no tail appendage, lice); louse-like.

1816 KIRBY & SPENCE *Entom.* (1828) III. xxix. 166 This animal in its general structure is anopluriform.

anopsia (æ'nɒpsɪə), var. ANOPSY. See also quot. 1842.

1842 DUNGLISON *Dict. Med. Sci.* (ed. 3) 49/2 *Anopsia*, a case of monstrosity in which the eye and orbit are wanting. **1880** *Syd. Soc. Lex.*, *Anopsia*..defect of sight, blindness. **1937** *Brit. Jrnl. Psychol.* Apr. 360 These people have developed a functional anopsia with regard to conditions obtaining in other parts or groups of their social environment.

'anopsy. ? *Obs.* [f. Gr. ἀν priv. + ὄψις sight; as if ad. Gr. ἀνοψία, not used in this sense.] Want of sight; sightlessness.

1646 SIR T. BROWNE *Pseud. Ep.* 174 Aristotle computeth the time of their [*i.e.* whelps'] anopsie or invision by that of their gestation. **1656** in BLOUNT *Glossogr.*

†**a'nopticall**, *a. Obs.* [f. Gr. ἄνοπτ-ος unseen + -ICAL, after *optical*.] Not in the field of vision.

1598 R. HAYDOCKE *Lomatius, Painting* (N.) As touching the shaddowes aboue our eie in the anopticall sight.

anorak ('ænəræk). Also ‖anoraq. [Greenland Eskimo.] A weatherproof jacket of skin or cloth, with hood attached, worn by Eskimos; a similar garment in countries other than Greenland.

1924 [see MUCKLUCK]. **1934** I. W. HUTCHISON *North to Rime-Ringed Sun* xvii. 191, I displayed..the gay beaded 'anorak' and scarlet embroidered trousers and boots of the Greenland Eskimo woman. **1936** *Discovery* Mar. 91/2 The [Greenland] bride was resplendent in her handsome national dress of scarlet boots, sealskin trousers, and *anoraq* with magnificent bead collar. **1937** E. A. M. WEDDERBURN *Alpine Climbing* ii. 17 A wind-proof 'Anorak' or glacier smock, with a hood and without zip-fasteners..is a life-saver in foul weather. **1950** tr. *Mountaineering Handbk.* ii. 24 In rain an Anorak worn over the shoulders is an excellent protection. **1952** MORIN & J. A. SMITH tr. *M. Herzog's Annapurna* iii. 50 We put on our nylon anoraks..which were both snow- and wind-proof. **1959** *Vogue* Oct. 180 Swiss ski clothes..poplin anorak with attached hood.

anorectic (ænɒ'rɛktɪk), *a.* and *sb. Med.* [f. Gr. ἀνόρεκτ-ος without appetite (f. ἀν- AN- 10 + ὀρέγειν to desire) + -IC.] **A.** *adj.* **1.** Characterized by a lack of appetite, *spec.* anorexia nervosa.

1894 in G. M. Gould *Illustr. Dict. Med.* 90/2. **1927** *Arch. Pediatrics* XLIV. 179 The anorectic child should not be overburdened with excessive school work. **1956** *Amer. Jrnl. Orthopsychiatry* XXVI. 751 The patient is..alternately bulimic..and 'self-starving' prior to the onset of the final full-blown progressive anorectic state. **1968** *Vet. Med. Small Animal Clin.* LXIII. 769 (*heading*) A new approach to feeding the anorectic and debilitated small animal patient. **1985** *Listener* 31 Jan. 12/3 This condition, which almost exclusively affects females, on average slightly older than the anorectic patient, comprises chaotic eating patterns with alternate bouts of carbohydrate bingeing.

2. Producing a loss of appetite.

1958 *Jrnl. Amer. Med. Assoc.* 24 May 434/1 Determinations of anorectic effect of 1-phenyl-2-aminopropane alginate..were made in dogs. **1966** DUNLOP & ALSTEAD *Textbk. Med. Treatm.* (ed. 10) 369 The prescription of an anorectic drug is never justified at the beginning of the dietary treatment of an obese person. **1972** *Brit. Med. Jrnl.* 26 Feb. 562/1 Both fenfluramine and diethylpropion have been shown in controlled clinical trials ..to have a significant anorectic effect and appear to be well tolerated and safe. **1983** *Oxf. Textbk. Med.* I. VIII. 41 Anorectic drugs have fallen into disrepute because one of the most effective agents, amphetamine, proved to be addictive.

B. *sb.* **1.** An anorectic agent.

1957 *Dorland's Med. Dict.* (ed. 23) 94/2 *Anorectic*, a substance which diminishes the appetite. **1958** *Jrnl. Amer. Med. Assoc.* 24 May 433 (*heading*) New anorectic. **1965** *Psychosomatics* Nov.–Dec. 410 (*heading*) How reliable are patients in judging anorectics? **1976** *Chem. Week* 1 Dec. 5/1 Gaylord Nelson's..Senate Monopoly Subcommittee has concluded five days of hearings on amphetamines and.. anorectics. **1978** *Nature* 19 Oct. 597/1 A variety of drugs active on the central nervous system, including neuroleptics (chlorpromazine),..anorectics (fenfluramine) and some barbiturates, also display maturational activity.

2. = ANOREXIC *sb.*

1977 *Times* 29 Nov. 20 The full-blown anorectic has totally rejected this fatness, together with the biological.. maturity that it heralds. **1983** *Brit. Med. Jrnl.* 17 Sept. 827/1 He is harsh with the parents of anorectics. **1986** S. ORBACH *Hunger Strike* 14 While the anorectic comes to fear taking in food herself, she feels the need to be near it.

anorectous (ænɒ'rɛktəs), *a. Med.* [f. Gr. ἀνόρεκτ-ος without appetite (see ANOREXIA) + -OUS.] Without appetite.

1880 in *Syd. Soc. Lex.*

anoretic (ænɒ'rɛtɪk). *Med.* [Alteration of ANORECTIC *a.* and *sb.*, after *pyretic*, etc.] = ANORECTIC *sb.* 1, 2.

[**1926** in *Gould's Med. Dict.* 89/1 as a misprint for *anorectic*.] **1961** in WEBSTER. **1976** *Maclean's Mag.* 23 Feb. 46/1 In 1965 only one anoretic was treated. **1976** *Daily Colonist* (Victoria, B.C.) 19 Mar. 2/3 Some of the reducing pills (anoretics) can have unpleasant side effects.

anorexia ('ænɒˌrɛksɪə). *Med.* Also **anorexy**.[a. mod.L. *anorexia*, a. Gr. ἀνορεξία, f. ἀν privative + ὀρέγ-ειν to reach after, desire. Cf. Fr. *anorexie*.] Want of appetite; 'inappetency.' **J. anorexia nervosa**, a condition marked by emaciation, etc., in which loss of appetite results from severe emotional disturbance.

1598 SYLVESTER *Furies* 450 (D.) Then the Anorexie, Then the Dog-hunger or the Bradypepsie. **1650** BAXTER *Saints Rest* IV. vi, These are sick of the anorexia, and apepsy, they have neither appetite nor digestion. **1864** R. BURTON *Dahome* I. 329 We bade adieu to anorexy, felt *hinc sanitas* now. **1873** W. W. GULL *Let.* 30 Apr. in *Trans. Clinical Soc.* (1874) VII. 26 The case appears to be an extreme instance of what I have proposed to call 'Apepsia hysterica', or 'Anorexia nervosa'. **1874** *Ibid.* 25, I used the term *Apepsia hysterica* but..*Anorexia* would be more correct. The want of appetite is, I believe, due to a morbid mental state... We might call the state hysterical... I prefer, however, the more general term 'nervosa'. **1939** *Psychosomatic Med.* I. 335/1 The syndrome of anorexia nervosa. **1963** P. H. JOHNSON *Night & Silence* xxiv. 173 He tried to eat it, but was taken by a terrible anorexia.

anorexiant (ænɒ'rɛksɪənt), *a.* and *sb. Pharm.* [f. ANOREXIA + -ANT¹.] **A.** *adj.* = ANORECTIC *a.* 2.

1957 *Jrnl. Amer. Med. Assoc.* 14 Sept. 137/2 In almost every instance a marked anorexiant effect was noted, and side-effects were minimal. **1966** *Ibid.* 11 Apr. 165 (*heading*) Evaluation of an anorexiant drug.

B. *sb.* = ANORECTIC *sb.* 1.

1957 *Jrnl. Amer. Med. Assoc.* 14 Sept. 135 (*heading*) Treatment of obesity with phenometrazine hydrochloride, a new anorexiant. **1969** *New Scientist* 24 Apr. 194/1 Certain drugs given in pregnancy—tranquillizers, anti-nausea agents, anorexiants. **1974** M. C. GERALD *Pharmacol.* vi. 120 The truly effective appetite suppressant or anorexiant does not merely depress appetite *per se*, but rather causes the individual to lose interest..in food.

anorexic (ænɒ'rɛksɪk), *a.* and *sb. Med.* [ad. F. *anoréxique*: see ANOREXIA, -IC.] **A.** *adj.* **1.** = ANORECTIC *a.* 1.

1907 P. JANET *Major Symptoms Hysteria* XI. 238 If food is introduced by force..into the stomach of the most anorexic hysterical..you will recognize that the digestion..comes to be completely effected. **1939** *Proc. R. Soc. Med.* XXXII. 158 When an anorexic patient begins to confide her troubles they are always associated with doubts of sexual potency. **1961** *Lancet* 22 July 185/2 He became listless, anorexic, and increasingly sleepy, refusing to stand or crawl. **1977** *Lancet* 29 Jan. 233/1 The affected animals have difficulty in walking, become anorexic, lose weight, and may die. **1982** *Daily Tel.* 16 Nov. 16/1 One newspaper writes of her 'apparent anorexic condition'.

2. = ANORECTIC *a.* 2.

1967 *Jrnl. Pharmacol. & Exper. Therap.* July 32 (*heading*) A new anorexic agent, WY-5244: cardiovascular actions and influence on sympathomimetic amines. **1970** *Jrnl. Gen. Psychol.* LXXXIII. 168 The anorexic action of the drug may have been exaggerated.

B. *sb.* A person with anorexia.

1913 S. E. JELLIFFE tr. *Déjérine & Gauckler's Psychoneuroses* i. 3 These patients are what are known as mental anorexics, who..have lost a quarter, a third, and sometimes a half of their weight. **1939** *Proc. R. Soc. Med.* XXXII. 157 The purpose of the anorexic to starve herself is of fundamental importance. **1975** *Daily Tel.* 6 June 13/7 Anorexics are by nature 'good' children. **1979** DALLY & GOMEZ *Anorexia Nervosa* vi. 90 When the mother has to go into hospital it is the anorexic who readily takes over the running of the home. **1983** *Listener* 10 Feb. 17/3 Compulsive runners share the same symptoms as anorexics.

anorexigenic (ˌænɒrɛksɪ'dʒɛnɪk), *a. Pharm.* [f. ANOREXI(A + -GENIC.] = ANORECTIC *a.* 2.

1948 *Ann. Internal Med.* XXIX. 510 We chose to decrease the desire for food by administering anorexigenic compounds of a type similar to 'Benzedrine'. **1961** L. MARTIN *Clinical Endocrinol.* (ed. 3) ii. 55 On general principles anorexigenic drugs should not be given [to obese children]. **1978** *Acta Endocrinologica* LXXXIX. 207 The food refusal peptide of human origin suggests itself as a biological anorexigenic agent.

anorganic (ænɔː'gænɪk), *a. rare.* [mod. f. Gr. ἀνόργαν-ος (see below) + -IC.] = INORGANIC.

1880 in *Syd. Soc. Lex.*

anorganognosy (æˌnɔːgə'nɒgnəsɪ). [f. as next + Gr. γνῶσις knowledge.] Scientific study of inorganic bodies. (*Syd. Soc. Lex.*)

anorganography (-'ɒgrəfɪ). [f. as next + Gr. -γραφία writing.] Description of inorganic bodies. (*Syd. Soc. Lex.*)

anorganology (-'ɒlədʒɪ). [mod. f. Gr. ἀνόργαν-ος without organs + -(O)LOGY; negative form (ἀν priv.) of ORGANOLOGY.] That one of the two great divisions of Natural Science which relates to inorganic objects, and phenomena explicable by mechanical and chemical principles.

1876 tr. *Haeckel's Hist. Creat.* I. 6 Anorganology, or the Science of *Anorgana* (Mineralogy, Geology, Meteorology, &c.) *Ibid.* I. v. 102 In the whole of Anorganology..all phenomena are said to be explicable merely by mechanism.

anormal (ə'nɔːməl), *a.* [a. Fr. *anormal*, variant of *anomal*, found as early as 13th c., ad. med.L. *anormalus* (sometimes 'rectified' to *anormālis*), a corruption of *anōmalus*, a. Gr. ἀνώμαλος (see ANOMALOUS), due to confusion with *norma* a rule, and explained as f. Gr. ἀ priv. + *norma*. In Eng. it has been taken as f. L. *ā* away from + *norma*, referred to L. *abnormis*, and refashioned after it as ABNORMAL.] = ABNORMAL. In recent use (eɪ'nɔːməl) as antonym of 'normal' when the associations of 'abnormal', *i.e.* 'unhealthy', 'unnatural', would be inappropriate.

1835 HOBLYN *Dict. Med.*, *Anormal*, without rule. **1836** *Penny Cycl.* VI. 476/1 Duméril and Bibron..consider the chameleons and the geckos as two groups absolutely anormal. **1850** *Nat. Encycl.* IX. 161 Upon a form so anormal [the *ornithorhyncus*] conjecture was busy. **1853** MAYNE *Exp. Lex.*, *Anormal*..the same as *abnormal*. **1936** *Mind* XLV. 504 An important distinction between 'normal' and 'anormal' series is defined. **1951** *Essays & Stud.* IV. 127 The collocations are unique and personal, that is to say, a-normal.

†**anormality** (ænɔː'mælɪtɪ). *Obs.* [f. prec. + -ITY.] = ABNORMALITY.

1836–39 TODD *Cycl. Anat. & Phys.* II. 695 Anormalities in developement. *Ibid.* 722/1 The doctrine of..anormality in the developement of the malformed parts.

†**a'norn**, *v. Obs.* Also 4–5 **aourn**, **anowrn(e**, **enourn(e**, 5 **aorne**, 4–6 **anourn**, 6 **annorn**. [a. OFr. *aörne-r*, *aöurne-r*:—L. *adornā-re*; in later Fr. *adorner*, ADORN. By identification of A- *pref.* 7 with A- *pref.* 2, of which the full form bef. a vowel was *an-* (see AN- *pref.* 1), *a-ourne* was erron. expanded into *an-ourne*, and this again after analogy of Fr. words in *en-* (often *an-* in AFr. and Eng.) was frequently made ENORN. *Anourn* was further confused with the infinitive *anour-en*, contr. *anour-n*, of vb. ANOURE 'adore, honour,' the confusion being facilitated by the fact that the senses come into contact, since to *adorn* is a common form of *honouring*. See

ANOURE, ADORN, and ADORE.] To deck, dress, trim; = ADORN.

c **1380** in *Rel. Ant.* I. 9/1 *Dextrotirium*, a ty of golde anornyng the ryght arme. **1382** WYCLIF *Gen.* xxiv. 47 Eer ryngis to anourne [*v.r.* honoure, ourne] the face of hir. **1413** LYDG. *Pylgr. Sowle* IV. xx. (1483) 66 He . . that aourned the with grene. *a* **1450** *Knt. de la Tour* (1868) 39 Suche pompe and pride to aorne suche a carion as is youre body. **1483** CAXTON *Gold. Leg.* 29/4 The holy ghoost hath aourned the hevenes. **1494** FABYAN VI. cxciv. 198 She anourned her in moste costly and shewynge aparayl. **1502** *Ord. Crysten Men* (W. de W.) I. iv. (1506) 44 The soule the whiche is annorned and ennobled with all vertues. **1530** PALSGR. 432/2, I anourne, I beautyfe or make more pleasaunt to the eye. *Je aorne*. . Whan a woman is anourned with ryche appareyle. **1558** BP. WATSON 7 *Sacram.* xxvii. 172 As the husbande anorneth and decketh his wyfe.

¶ By confusion with ANOURE: To worship, do reverence to.

1382 WYCLIF *Gen.* xxxiii. 1 Whanne the same maner þei hadden anowrned, the laste Joseph and Rachel anowryden [Vulg. *adorassent . . adoraverunt*; **1388** worschipid].

† **a'nornament.** *Obs.* Also 4 anournement, 5–6 -ament, 6 enournament, annourneament. See also ANOUREMENT. [f. prec. + -MENT.] Adornment, decoration, ornamentation.

c **1325** *E.E. Allit. P.* B. 1290 þe hous & þe anournementes. **1494** FABYAN VI. clxxvi. 174 Relyques and anournamentes or ornamentes belongynge to the same. **1541** *Richmond. Wills* (1853) 21 The reparacion of and annourneament of the quere. **1611** SPEED *Hist. Gt. Brit.* IX. xxi. (1632) 1033 Jowellys, Plate, and other anornaments of our Parish Churches.

† **a'norned,** *ppl. a.* *Obs.* Also 5 **aourned, anourned.** [f. as prec. + -ED.] = ADORNED.

1481 CAXTON *Myrr.* Prol. 1 Fair and Aourned volumes. **1513** DOUGLAS *Æneis* VI. x. 87 Thair lyfe illuminat and anornit cleir.

† **a'norning,** *vbl. sb.* *Obs.* Also **anourn-, anowrn-, enourn-, honournyng** (!). [f. ANORN + -ING[1].] Adorning, decking, decoration.

c **1382** WYCLIF *Gen.* ii. 1 Heuene and erthe and al the anowrnyng [**1388** ournement] of hem. —— *Esther* ii. 12 Alle thingus that to wymmenys enournyng [*v.r.* honournyng] pertende. **1529** *Reg. Test. Ebor.* IX. 444 To the anornyng of one litle chapell.

anorth (əˈnɔːθ), *adv.* prop. *phr.* *rare*[−1]. [f. A *prep.*[1] + NORTH.] On the north; northward.

1809 J. BARLOW *Columb.* I. 289 Anorth from that broad gulph . . A happier hemisphere invites thy view.

anorthic (æˈnɔːθɪk), *a.* *Cryst.* [mod. f. Gr. ἀν priv. + ὀρθ-ός straight, right + -IC.] Irregular in crystallization; applied to all crystals which do not fall under one of the more regular systems; called also *doubly oblique*, *triclinic*, *tetartoprismatic*.

1864 *Reader* 438/2 That the crystals included in the oblique and anorthic systems are formed by the combination of hemihedral and tetartohedral forms of the prismatic system. **1869** PHILLIPS *Vesuv.* x. 276 The sixth system, called anorthic, or doubly oblique, has its three axes unequal, and neither of them perpendicular to another.

anorthite (æˈnɔːθaɪt). *Min.* [f. Gr. ἀν priv. + ὀρθ-ός straight + -ITE; named by Rose in 1823.] 'Lime-feldspar,' a mineral placed by Dana in the Feldspar group of Unisilicates, and occurring in small triclinic or 'anorthic' glassy crystals.

1833 LYELL *Elem. Geol.* (1865) 590 Anorthite, so called from the oblique interfacial angles of its rhomboidal prisms. **1869** PHILLIPS *Vesuv.* x. 288 Christianite or Anorthite occurs in ejected blocks on Somma in cavities of dolomite.

‖ **anorthopia** (ænɔːˈθəʊpɪə). *Path.* [mod.L., f. Gr. ἀν priv. + ὀρθ-ός straight + -ωπία vision, f. ὤψ, ὦπ-α eye, face.] Obliquity of vision, squinting.

1849–52 TODD *Cycl. Anat. & Phys.* IV. 1462/2 Children who show evidences of anorthopia. **1880** in *Syd. Soc. Lex.*

anorthoscope (æˈnɔːθəʊskəʊp). [mod. f. as prec. + -σκοπ-ος observer.] An optical toy for viewing distorted figures drawn on a rotating disk.

1842 BRANDE *Dict. Sc.* (1865) I. 114 *Anorthoscope*, the name given by M. Plateau of Brussels, to an instrument . . intended to produce a peculiar kind of anamorphoses by means of two discs rotating rapidly one before the other.

anorthosite (æˈnɔːθəʊsaɪt). *Min.* [f. F. *anorthose* + -ITE[1].] A granular igneous rock composed mainly of a soda-lime feldspar. Hence **anortho'sitic** *a.*, of the nature of, or containing, anorthosite.

1863 T. S. HUNT in *Amer. Jrnl. Sci.* 2nd Ser. XXXVI. 222 A series of strata characterized by a great development of anorthosites. *Ibid.* 224 These anorthosite rocks are often compact, but more frequently granitoid in structure. **1925** J. JOLY *Surface-Hist. Earth* iii. 47 These rocks . . present to our view many varieties of structure and mineral composition; e.g. in the granites, gneisses, anorthosites, diorites. **1939** *Geogr. Jrnl.* XCIV. 104 A diorite . . so altered by movement and pressure that it has acquired a foliated structure. They want to call it 'anorthositic gneiss'.

‖ **anosmia** (æˈnɒsmɪə). *Path.* [mod.L., f. Gr. ἀν priv. + ὀσμή smell.] Loss of the sense of smell.

1811 HOOPER *Med. Dict.*, *Anosmia*, a loss of the sense of smelling. **1872** COHEN *Dis. Throat* 291 A case of anosmia occurring after a blow received upon the occiput.

anosphresy (æˈnɒsfrɪsɪ). *Path.* [ad. mod.L. *anosphrēsia*, f. Gr. ἀν priv. + ὄσφρησι-ς smell, f. vb. stem ὀσφρα-ιν- smell.] = prec.

[**1839** HOOPER *Med. Dict.*, *Anosphresia*, loss of the sense of smell.] **1853** MAYNE *Exp. Lex.*, *Anosphresia*, term for the absence or loss of the sense of smell: anosphresy.

anote, var. ANNOTE *v.* *Obs.*

another (əˈnʌðə(r)), *a.*, *pron.* (and *adv.*) [orig. separately *an other* (often *a nother*, rarely *a other*), and really two words, = *a second*, *a remaining*, *a different*. In OE. *án* not being yet weakened to the 'indef. article,' *óðer* was used by itself, as still in the plural *other*, absolutely *others*. See OTHER.]

I. A second, further, additional. (*Another* is distinguished from *the other*, in that, while the latter points to the remaining determinate member of a known series of two or more, *another* refers indefinitely to *any* further member of a series of indeterminate extent; it is not therefore applied to the determinate second of two.)

1. One more, one further; originally *a second* of two things; subsequently extended to anything additional or remaining beyond those already considered; *an additional*.

a. with sb. expressed. (Pl. *other*.)

c **1374** CHAUCER *Anel. & Arc.* 144 And sawe a noþere ladye proude and nuwe. c **1385** —— *L.G.W.* 594 And wolde algates han a nother [*v.r.* another, a-nothir, an othir] wif. c **1400** *Destr. Troy* xv. 7038 Anoþer brother of þo bold to þe buerne rode. c **1425** WYNTOUN *Cron.* VIII. vi. 302 Þis Alane . . Ane oþir Dowchtyr had. c **1440** *Gesta Rom.* I. i. 3 Nowe he takithe an other arowe, and wolle shete aȝen. **1594** SHAKS. *Rich. III*, I. i. 150 Clarence hath not another day to liue. **1604** HIERON *Wks.* I. 569 Shew me but one commandement To proue an other sacrament. **1711** STEELE *Spect.* No. 2 ¶2 The Gentleman next in esteem among us is another Batchelor. **1849** MACAULAY *Hist. Eng.* I. 528 Another fugitive was Richard Goodenough. **1870** JEVONS *Elem. Log.* xxiii. 194 Another example of this kind. *a* **1884** *Mod.* Try another pear. Discovery of another asteroid.

b. with sb. understood. (Pl. *others*.) ***you're*** (or ***you are***) ***another!***, a colloq. phrase properly used in retorting a charge upon the person who makes it (cf. TU QUOQUE); hence humorously as a meaningless or vaguely contemptuous retort.

1340 HAMPOLE *Pr. Consc.* 1685 Ane [manere of dede] es bodily ded . . Ane other gastely, þe thred endeles. **1377** LANGL. *P. Pl.* B. Prol. 185 Thouȝ we culled þe catte, ȝut sholde þer come another. *a* **1422** HENRY V in Ellis *Orig. Lett.* III. 32 I. 75 We send a Lettre to our Cosin ye Bysshop of Excetre . . and a noþer to ye Bysshop of Lincoln. **1553** UDALL *Roister D.* III. v, R. If it were an other but thou, it were a knaue. *M.* Ye are an other your selfe, sir. **1569** PRESTON *Cambyses* (1898) 786 And thou calst me knave, thou art another! **1590** SHAKS. *Com. Err.* III. i. 52 *Dro.* Haue at you with a Prouerbe, Shall I set in my staffe. *Luce.* Haue at you with another, that's when? can you tell? **1605** —— *Macb.* IV. i. 118 Another yet? a seaventh? Ile see no more. **1749** FIELDING *Tom Jones* IX. vi. (D.) 'You mistake me, friend . . I only said your conclusion was a non sequitur.' 'You are another,' cries the sergeant. **1836** DICKENS *Pickw.* xv, 'Sir,' said Mr. Tupman, 'you're a fellow.' 'Sir,' said Mr. Pickwick, 'you're another.' **1882** *Boston Lit. World* 3 June 184/3 The argument of it is simply 'You're another'—a retort in dignified manner to those British critics who, etc. **1887** LOWELL *Democracy* 10, I find little . . to edify me in these international bandyings of 'You're another'.

c. ***such another***: another of the same sort.

a **1300** *Cursor M.* 1942 For nakins chaunce Sal i ta suilk a noiþer wengance. **1553** UDALL *Roister D.* III. v, Pay the like hire, I will make you suche an other. **1599** SHAKS. *Much Ado* III. iv. 87 Yet Benedicke was such another, and now is he become a man. *a* **1884** *Mod.* I never saw such another.

2. *fig.* A second in effect, though not in name or intention; a second in likeness of character or attributes; a counterpart to.

c **1577** HELLOWES *Gueuara's Epist.* I. 113, I bewaile the death of my friend which is another my selfe. **1591** SHAKS. *Two Gent.* III. i. 119 A Ladder, quaintly made of Cords . . Would serue to scale another Hero's towre. **1599** —— *Much Ado* V. iv. 62 Another Hero! Nothing certainer. *a* **1884** *Mod.* That boy will be another Nelson some day.

II. Not this, not the same, a different.

3. By giving prominence to the fact that this is *not* that already considered: A different.

a. with sb. expressed. ***another place***: a traditional phrase used by members of parliament to designate the other House, i.e. the House of Lords or the House of Commons.

c **1225** *St. Margarete* (1866) 74 He was al out of rede As he wer in anoþer wordle. **1382** WYCLIF *2 Cor.* xi. 4 If he that cometh prechith anothir Crist . . or if ȝe taken anothir spirit. c **1400** *Destr. Troy* xv. 6628 Anon to anothir side naitly he dryuys. *a* **1520** *Myrr. Our Ladye* 8 The better wyll he be aduysed, or he blame an other mannes studdy. **1611** BIBLE *Prov.* xxvii. 2 Let another man praise thee, and not thine owne mouth. **1687** LADY RUSSELL *Lett.* I. lii. 127, I am glad you find cause to be of another mind. **1711** STEELE *Spect.* No. 96 ¶6 To go among quite another People. **1712** ADDISON *Spect.* No. 549 ¶3 Preparing . . for another world. **1789** [see PLACE *sb.* 5 d]. **1808** SCOTT *Marm.* VI. xx, Another sight had seen that morn . . And Flodden had been Bannockbourn! **1883** LD. GRANVILLE *Sp. in Parl.* 18 June 2/2, I hear that question is to be asked in another place [*circumlocution for* the House of Commons] by Mr. Warton. **1908** *Westm. Gaz.* 27 July 1/3 Lord Lamington, was a busy member of the House of Commons . . before he went to 'another place' on his father's death in 1890. **1927** *Observer* 10 July 15/7 Usually M.P.'s speak dispassionately of 'another place', but Mr. Baldwin the other day made it 'the other end of the passage', and Mr. Snowden 'the other end of the corridor'. **1960** *Guardian* 24 Nov. 18/6 Has a sovereign the ultimate right to unseat a member of Parliament and transfer him, against his will, to 'another place'?

b. with sb. not expressed.

a **1884** *Mod.* This towel will not do; give me another. Ask him to give you another for it.

c. *esp.* of persons: Another person, some one else, any one else. (In this sense *another* has *poss.* **another's**; *pl.* **others**, *poss.* **others'**.)

1340 *Ayenb.* 155 Huanne hi eft yzyeþ anoþrene þet ine anoþre stat deþ manie guodes. c **1400** *Apol. Loll.* 3 Þus seiþ an oþer. **1526** TINDALE *Col.* iii. 13 If eny man have a quarrel to a nother. —— *Matt.* xi. 3 Arte thou he that shall come: or shall we loke for another? **1605** BACON *Adv. Learn.* ii. (1873) 2 And blaze from . . the least spark of another's knowledge. **1632** SANDERSON *12 Serm.* 14 Taught him his lesson, not to despise anothers infirmity. **1752** J. GILL *Trinity* iv. 82 The Father has life in himself; he does not owe his being to another. **1879** TENNYSON *Lover's T.* 41 There, where I hoped myself to reign . . There, in my realm . . Another!

4. Different in effect; different in character, though the same in substance.

1382 WYCLIF *1 Sam.* x. 6 Thow shalt be chaungid into another man [so in all versions]. —— *Gal.* i. 6 Another euangelie, which is not another. **1611** *ibid.*, An other [Gr. ἕτερον] gospel which yet is not another [Gr. ἄλλο]. **1588** BERNARD *Terence* (N.) He is nowe become another man. **1877** BROCKETT *Cross & Cresc.* 87 From that time I became another man.

5. Const. *than* (*from* catachr.).

a **1656** USSHER *Serm.* in Southey *Commonpl. Bk.* Ser. II. (1849) 98 Neyther is the church reformed in our dayes, another church than that . . deformed in the dayes of our fore-fathers. **1867** FREEMAN *Norm. Conq.* I. 642 Either the Anlaf here spoken of was another person from Olaf or, etc.

III. With *one*.

6. Contrasted explicitly with *one*. (In both prec. main senses, but especially II.) With or without sb. expressed.

a. Of *two* things from an indefinite number.

1297 R. GLOUC. 379 A lond ygranted were To a man to bere þeruore a certeyn rente . . And anoþer com & bode more. **1377** LANGL. *P. Pl.* B. III. 256 A penyworth for an othre. **1528** PERKINS *Profit. Bk.* iv. §295 The exchange . . of one intire thing for an other intire thing. **1591** SHAKS. *Two Gent.* II. iv. 191 Euen as one heate, another heate expels, Or as one naile, by strength driues out another. **1713** *Lond. & Country Brew.* II. (1743) 114 One Man's Mistake is another's Gain. **1876** J. PARKER *Paracl.* II. xvii. 280 The infinity of God is one thing, and our knowledge of that infinity is another. *Provb.* One man's meat is another man's poison.

b. Of two things only, when their mutual position is undefined. In this case *the other* is now commonly used.

1398 TREVISA *Barth. De P.R.* IX. i. (1495) 345 Passynge fro one ende to a nother. **1413** LYDG. *Pylgr. Sowle* V. xiii. (1483) 104 Sette full of saphyres fro one ende to another. **1590** SHAKS. *Com. Err.* V. i. 425 Now let's go hand in hand, not one before another. **1615** CROOKE *Body of Man* 379 Apertion and opening of two vessels one into another. **1742** RICHARDSON *Pamela* III. 320 Sir Jacob sat aghast, looking at one, and at another, and at me, each in Turn.

c. Of a series taken two by two.

1413 LYDG. *Pylgr. Sowle* III. v. (1483) 54 This bocher lepte fro one to another. **1490** CAXTON *Eneydos* x. 39 Yolus made to come the foure windes to gyder one ayenst another. **1601** SHAKS. *All's Well* IV. i. 20 We must euery one be a man of his owne fancie, not to know what we speak one to another. **1673** CAVE *Prim. Chr.* III. ii. 281 Two or three stories one still under onother. **1711** ADDISON *Spect.* No. 8 ¶7, I plied her from one Room to another with all the Galantries I could invent. **1850** MAURICE *Mor. & Met. Phil.* I. iii. §239 He taught it to one and another. *a* **1884** *Mod.* They marched in Indian file, one after another.

d. ***one with another***: (*a*) added each to the others as they come; all together, all alike; (*b*) taken on the average, so that the excess of one supplies the deficiency of another.

1539 BIBLE ('Great') *Ps.* xlix. 2 High and Low, Rich and Poor, one with another. **1598** SHAKS. *Merry W.* II. i. 118 He loves . . both young and old, one with another. **1633** HOWELL *Lett.* (1650) I. 350 This gravity, reservedness and tergiversations of his, have turned rather to his prejudice than advantage, take one with another. **1677** YARRANTON *Eng. Improv.* 27 It is not worth sixteen years Purchase all England over, one place with another. *Mod.* Taken one with another, they may fetch thirty shillings a-head.

7. Hence, **one another**, as a compound reciprocal pronoun not separated by verb or prep. (Said of two or more). With *poss.* **one another's**, but in this case *each other's* is oftener used.

1526 TINDALE *Gal.* vi. 4 Beare ye one anothers burthen [WYCLIF, others charges] and so fulfill the lawe of Christ. **1598** SHAKS. *Merry W.* I. i. 257 When wee are married, and haue more occasion to know one another. **1667** MILTON *P.L.* IV. 506 These two Imparadis't in one anothers arms. **1711** ADDISON *Spect.* No. 3 ¶5 Bags of Money were piled upon one another. **1712** STEELE *Spect.* No. 400 ¶5 Such friendly Thoughts and Concerns for one another. **1756** BURKE *Vind. Nat. Soc.* Wks. I. 17 Such [actions] as tend to the destruction of one another. *Mod.* 'See how these Christians love one another!'

†**IV.** *adv.* (perhaps orig. neut. sing. of adj.)

†**8.** A different thing; differently, otherwise. *Obs.*

1205 LAY. 724 Ʒet ich ou sigge on oþer [**1250** an oþer]. **1297** R. GLOUC. 444 Þo þe Kyng was ded hys vncle, anoþer he þoȝte do. *a* **1300** *Havelok* 1395 Avelok thouthe al another. *c* **1300** *Beket* 540 That he scholde another do.

† **a'nother-gaines**, *a. Obs.* [A corruption of ANOTHERKINS or ANOTHER-GATES, or a mixture of the two.] Of another kind.

1580 SIDNEY *Arcadia* (1622) 152 If my father had not plaid the hasty foole..I might haue had another-gaines husband then Dametas.

† **a'nother-gates**, *a. Obs.* [orig. genitive case, 'of another gate,' i.e. of another way, manner, or fashion: see GATE.] Of another fashion or sort, of a different kind.

1594 LYLY *Moth. Bombie* I. (N.) Bringing up another-gates marriage. **1631** SANDERSON *21 Serm.* Ad Aul. i. (1673) 7 That, I ween, is another-gates matter. **1693** W. ROBERTSON *Phraseol. Gen.* 891 'Tis another-gates matter, than to mock and slight me so.

a'notherguess, *a. arch.* Also 7 -ghess, -gess. [a phonetic reduction of *anothergets* for ANOTHER-GATES: cf. *bless-* for *blets-ien*, *best* for *betst*, etc. The spelling *-guess* suggests a wrong derivation.] Of another sort or kind.

1625 HOWELL *Lett.* I. ix. §4, I wish you anothergets wife then Socrates had. **1644** *Ibid.* (1726) 90 Algiers is anothergess thing now than she was then. **1690** SHADWELL *Amor. Bigot* III. 268 She has made another guess choice. **1690** DRYDEN *Amphitr.*, The truth on't is, she's anotherghess Morsel than old Bromia. **1762** FOOTE *Orators* III. (1767) 61 This is anotherguess matter, because why, the head is concerned. **1837** T. HOOK *Jack Brag* 196 He was as they say 'quite another guess sort of man' from what he had been. **1868** BROWNING *Ring & Bk.* IV. 1498 Anotherguess tribunal than ours here.

† **a'notherguise**, *a. Obs. rare.* [a plausible but erroneous 'emendation' of ANOTHERGUESS, as if f. ANOTHER + GUISE.] Of another kind.

1727 ARBUTHNOT *John Bull* 92 It used to go another-guise manner in thy time.

† **a'notherkins**, *a. Obs.* or *dial.* [orig. genitive case 'of another kin or kind': cf. *alkins*, etc.] Of another or a different kind or character.

1863 ATKINSON *Whitby Gloss.*, *Anotherkins*, different, of another mould. 'He was anotherkins body to the other man.'

a'notherness. *nonce-wd.* [f. ANOTHER + -NESS: cf. *oneness*.] Difference, non-identity.

1587 GOLDING *De Mornay* vi. (1617) 84 Both a selfesamenesse and also an anothernesse (if I may so tearme them).

† **a'nother-while**, *phr. Obs.* [cf. *erewhile*.] At another time.

1648 SYMMONS *Vind. Chas. I*, 118 The poor innocent Bells..must be..turned into Guns, that they may be another while instruments of destruction.

anotta, anotto, variants of ANATTA.

anough, obs. form of ENOUGH.

† **a'nour**, *sb. Obs.* [Orig. a var. of *onour*, *honour*, a. OFr. *onor*, *anor*, *anur*; but influenced by the confusion between *onour-en* to honour, and *anour-en* to adore, worship. See ANOURE *v.* and HONOUR.] Honour, reverence, worship.

c **1314** *Guy Warw.* 149 God hath the don gret anour. *c* **1330** *Rol. & Vernagu* (1836) 3 Jhesu..bit the sende with michel anour After Charls.

† **a'noure**, *v. Obs.* Forms: 3-4 aoure, -ri, anuri, 3-5 anoure, 4-5 anowre. [repr. two OFr. vbs., 1. *anore-r*, *anure-r*, *onure-r*, *onoure-r*, also written *honore-r*, *honure-r*, *honour-er*:—L. *honōrā-re* to HONOUR. 2. *aöre-r*, *aüre-r*, *aoure-r*:—L. *adōrā-re*, later Fr. *adorer*, Eng. ADORE, of which the orig. adopted form *a-oure* was, by confusion of A- *pref.* 7 with A- *pref.* 2 (of which the full form was AN- *pref.* 1), expanded into *an-oure*; and, as the senses of *honour* and *adore* meet in that of worship, the two vbs. were completely identified in ME. For further confusion with ANORN, see that word. Before 1500 the Fr. forms were refashioned as *hono(u)rer*, *ado(u)rer*, and *ado(u)rner*, and the Eng. followed, as *honour*, *ado(u)re*, and *ado(u)rn*.] To ADORE, worship, reverence, or honour.

c **1250** *Kent. Serm.* in *O.E. Misc.* 26 Þet hi wolden gon for to hyne an-uri. *c* **1260** *A Sarmun* in *E.E.P.* (1862) 6 Anouriþ god and holi chirch. *c* **1305** *St. Kath.* 32 *ibid.* 90 Þat here godes noþing nere · þat hi aourede hem to. *c* **1315** SHOREHAM 96 Ʒif thou annourest God aryȝt. **1340** *Ayenb.* 135 Yef þou wilt lyerni God to bidde and to aouri ariȝte. *c* **1382** WYCLIF *Gen.* xix. 1 He..ȝede to mete with hem, and anourede [*v.r.* honowride; **1388** worschipide; Vulg. *adoravit*] bowide into the erthe. *a* **1400** *Relig. Pieces fr. Thornt. MS.* 21 O blyssed Godd..þay anourene þe.

¶ By confusion with ANOURNE: To adorn, to deck.

c **1440** LONELICH *Graal* I. 425 Ʒit was that schip.. Anoured with diuers ioweillis.

† **a'nourement.** *Obs.* Also 4-5 anour-, enour-, 5 enor-. [corruptly for *anournement* ANORNAMENT: see prec.] = ADORNMENT, ORNAMENT.

c **1382** WYCLIF *Esther* ii. 3 And take thei wymmen enourmentis [*v.r.* wymenus ournemens]. **1405** *Lay Folks' Mass-Bk.*, *B.P.* ii. 65 Boke or chales, vestiment, lyght or towelle, or any other anourment. *c* **1440** *Gesta Rom.* 383 My lecherouse anourement of myn heere. **1513** BRADSHAW *St. Werb.* 154 The people..Gaue diuers enormentes unto this place.

anourn(e, anowrne, obs. var. ANORN, ADORN.

anourous (ə'nuərəs, ə'naurəs), *a. Zool.* Also **anurous.** [f. Gr. ἀν priv. + οὐρ-ά tail + -OUS. The reg. transliteration of the Gr. is *anur-ous*, but *anour-ous* is in common use.] Tailless. Applied to Amphibia, like the frog and toad, and (less correctly) to brachyurous crustacea, like the crab.

1838 *Penny Cycl.* X. 487/1 The Anurous or Tailless Batrachians, having no tails except in their young state, including frogs and toads. **1875** *O. Schmidt's Doctr. Descent* iii. 57 The crabs, or anourous crustacea, are raised by sundry characteristics above their long-tailed congeners.

† **'anous**, *a. Obs. rare*[−1]. [f. L. *an-us* vent + -OUS.] = ANAL.

1684 tr. *Bonet's Merc. Compit.* VIII. 277 The anous Vessels allotted to the Spleen.

† **a'noven**, *adv. Obs.* Forms: 1 on ufan, 3 on-, anuven, 3-5 anoven. [f. AN *prep.* + *ufan* adv. 'up, above' (= Ger. *oben*), properly dative case of *uf-* (Goth. *uf*) 'up, upward.' *An-ufan*, *anoven*, was thus nearly a synonym of *b(e)-ufan*, *boven*, *a-bove*: cf. *on-foran*, *afore*, and *be-foran*, *before*. Superl. *anovenast*.]

1. Above, atop.

a **1000** *Judith* 252 Ær ðon ðe him se egesa on ufan sǽte. *a* **1300** *K. Horn* 624 On his swerde Anouen at þan orde. *c* **1320** *Cast. Love* 712 The thridde hue an ovenast Over wryeth all. *c* **1430** *Pol. Rel. & L. Poems* 188 Clappe we of the hevedes anoven o the grene.

2. Onward in time, after.

a **1230** *St. Juliana* 53 Neauer mare her on uuen. *c* **1230** *Ancr. R.* 236 Uorte tenten euermore on vuen swuch manere sunne.

† **a'novenon**, *prep.* and *adv. Obs.* 3-4. Also **anovenan, anuvenan, anufene.** [f. ANOVEN + *an*, ON: cf. *up-on*, and quot. *a* 1300 in ANOVEN 1. The form *anufene* is perh. a weakening of *anufen-an* through *anufen-en*, as in *abutan*, *abuten*, *abute*.]

A. *prep.* On from above, down upon.

1205 LAY. 26051 Þe eotend smat þer anouenan. *Ibid.* 16432 Þa cristine men cumen heom anufene. *c* **1300** *K. Alis.* 2233 Tholome smot Hardapilon, helm and basnet, on ovenon. *c* **1330** *Arth. & Merl.* 3430 Bohort hit king Glorion, His right schuldir anouen on.

B. *adv.* Up above.

a **1300** *Floriz & Bl.* 232 On þe tur auouenon Is a charbugle ston.

† **a'noveward**, *adv.* and *prep. Obs.* 3-4. Also **anoue-, anou-, ano-, anuward.** [f. AN *prep.* on + OE. *ufeweard* upward: cf. ANOVEN.]

A. *adv.* Towards the top, upward, away up.

c **1305** *St. Swithin* 111 Anoueward þer liþ a ston. *c* **1350** *Leg. Rood* (1871) 25 A-nowarde he sayh a ȝong smal child. *c* **1380** *Sir Ferumb.* 5581 To Gauter þanne a smot A strok.. Riȝt on þe heued anoueward, & clef ys helm.

B. *prep.*

1. Of position: Towards the top of, high upon.

a **1300** *Leg. Rood* (1871) 24 Þe child..þat þou iseiȝ a noueward þe tre. *c* **1305** *St. Kenelm* 331 A cold welle & fair þer sprong: anoueward þis doune. *c* **1330** *Arth. & Merl.* 3323 The hors hem lay anoward.

2. Of direction: Upon, on the top of.

1297 R. GLOUC. 186 Anowarde þe helm þen oþer he smot.

anovulant (æ'nɒvju:lənt), *sb.* and *a. Med.* [f. AN- 10 + OVUL(ATION + -ANT[1].] **A.** *sb.* A drug or other agent that suppresses ovulation. **B.** *adj.* Having the property of an anovulant; anovulatory.

1960 *Theol. Stud.* XXI. 599 (*heading*) Use of anovulants. **1965** J. T. NOONAN *Contraception* xiv. 461 In the discussion of the pill which took place among theologians from 1957 to 1964, it was regarded solely as an anovulant, that is, as an agent preventing conception by preventing ovulation. **1971** WEBSTER Add., Anovulant *adj.* **1975** *Irish Med. Jrnl.* LXVIII. 204/2 The results show the effectiveness of the anovulant agent in acne vulgaris. **1980** *Jrnl. Reproductive Med.* XXIV. 11/2 It is possible that the progestin supplied by these anovulants may offer some protection against endometrial neoplastic changes.

anovulatory (,ænɒvju:'leɪtərɪ), *a. Med.* [f. AN- 10 + OVULATORY *a.*] Of menstruation, etc.: not accompanied by ovulation.

1934 *Jrnl. Amer. Med. Assoc.* 10 Feb. 454/1, I have.. urged that anovulatory menstruation, so common in monkeys, is not nearly so rare in women as was once believed. **1964** L. MARTIN *Clinical Endocrinol.* (ed. 4) viii. 251 Anovulatory menstruation, which sometimes explains sterility in women, can also be detected by the absence of a temperature change during the menstrual cycle. **1971** *Nature* 22 Jan. 244/1 A higher percentage of anovulatory cycles were reported for college age women than for older women. **1976** J. WALKER et al. *Combined Textbk. Obstetr. & Gynaecol.* (ed. 9) xxxiv. 648/2 (*heading*) Anovulatory bleeding.

So **a'novular** *a.*, anovulatory; also, lacking an ovum.

1938 DORLAND & MILLER *Med. Dict.* (ed. 18) 110/1. **1970** *Sci. Jrnl.* June 30/1 Failure of ovulation, however, does not result in failure of menstruation..nor are anovular cycles necessarily shorter in length. **1973** *Nature* 27 July 244/3 Anovular and polyovular follicles are considered. **1976** *Path. Ann.* XI. 79 Anovular cycles appear to be associated with a paucity of progesterone production.

anoxæmia (ænɒk'si:mɪə). *Path.* [mod.L., f. Gr. ἀν- (AN- 10) + OX(YGEN + Gr. αἷμα blood + -IA[1]. Cf. F. *anoxémie*.] A deficiency of oxygen in the blood.

1890 BILLINGS *Med. Dict.* I. 74/1 *Anoxæmia* or *Anoxyhæmia.* **1919** *Proc. Physiol. Soc.* 25 Jan. p. lxiv, While..the accelerated output of adrenalin must be supposed to participate in the effect, the rise in blood sugar must be in the main due to a direct action of the anoxæmia upon the liver. **1920** [see ANOXIC *a.*]. **1922** *Encycl. Brit.* XXXI. 902/2 The chief sign of anoxaemia is cyanosis. **1931**, **1939** [see ANOXIA].

anoxia (æ'nɒksɪə). *Path.* [mod.L., f. Gr. ἀν- (AN- 10) + OX(YGEN + -IA[1].] Deficiency of oxygen in the tissues (see quot. 1931).

1931 PETERS & VAN SLYKE *Quant. Clin. Chem.* I. 577 Anoxia literally means oxygen lack. We shall use the term to cover *any condition which retards oxidation processes in the tissues*... The less specific word anoxia seems preferable as a general term to cover the condition defined, 'anoxemia' being limited to..oxygen deficit in the blood. **1939** *Nature* 15 Apr. 619/2 'Pressor episodes', that is to say, a narrowing of the small vessels with resulting deprivation of oxygen (*anoxia* or *anoxæmia*). **1957** *New Scientist* 20 June 16/1 In the thin upper atmosphere, lack of oxygen may result in a progressively intoxicated state... *Anoxia*, the aviator's most insidious and lethal enemy, is perhaps the most difficult to detect and counter.

Hence **a'noxic** *a.*, characterized by or causing anoxia.

1920 J. BARCROFT in *Lancet* 4 Sept. 487/1 The anoxic type of anoxæmia is the most serious. **1925** —— *Resp. Function Blood* (ed. 2) I. xii. 155 The same amount of exercise considerably reduces the oxygen content of the arterial blood in an animal which is already anoxic. **1955** *Sci. Amer.* Dec. 60/3 But equally we do not ignore the well-acclimated man accustomed to the low pressure of the mountain heights, who surely represents the maximum of adaptation to anoxic conditions.

anoy(e, obs. form of ANNOY.

anoysance, variant of ANNUISANCE.

anp-, in earlier spelling often used for AMP-.

† **an'peyn**, *v. Obs. rare.* [erroneous expansion of earlier *apeyne*, APAIN, a. OFr. *apeine-r*, f. *à* to + *peine* punishment, trouble:—L. *pœna* penalty: see AN- *pref.* 5.] *refl.* To put oneself to trouble, exert oneself, try with all one's might.

c **1380** *Sir Ferumb.* 665 Firumbras..anpeynedem þanne þorȝ al þyng: erle O[lyuer] þer to slee. *Ibid.* 2947 Anpeyny we ous our felawe to fette: þat ys among ys fos.

anpyre, obs. form of EMPIRE.

† **'anred**, *a. Obs.* 1-3. Also 1 ánrǽd, 3 anrad. [f. OE. *án* one + *rǽd* counsel, purpose.] Having a single aim or object, constant, steadfast.

c **1000** ÆLFRIC *Gen.* xli. 25 Ðis swefen ys ánrǽde. *c* **1175** *Lamb. Hom.* 115 He scal..been on erfeðnesse anred and edmod on stilnesse. *c* **1230** *Ancr. R.* 228 So treouliche and so ueste ilimed mid lim of anrad [*v.r.* ancre] luue.

† **'anredly, -liche**, *adv. Obs. rare.* [f. prec. + -LY[2].] With singleness of heart, steadfastly.

c **1200** *Trin. Coll. Hom.* 61 Bute we turnen to gode anradliche, he wile his swerd draȝen.

† **'anrednesse.** *Obs.* 1-3. Also 1 ánrǽd-, 3 onred-. [f. as prec. + -NESS.] Singleness of aim, unanimity; constancy, steadfastness.

c **885** K. ÆLFRED *Oros.* v. iii. §3 Hí heora ánrǽdnesse ȝeheoldan him betwenan. *c* **1175** *Lamb. Hom.* 107 *Instantia boni operis*, Þet is anrednesse godes werkes. *c* **1230** *Ancr. R.* 250 Hu god is onrednesse of luue, and onnesse of heorte.

‖ **ansa** ('ænsə). *Pl.* **ansæ.** Formerly anglicized (through Fr.) as **anse, -s.** [L. *ansa* handle (of a vessel, tool).] A name applied to the apparent ends of Saturn's ring seen projecting like two handles beyond the disk of the planet.

1665-6 *Phil. Trans.* I. 155 The present Figure of his Anses or Ring. **1721** BAILEY, *Ansae, Anses*, are the various positions of the ring of Saturn, which sometimes appear like Handles to the Body of that Planet. **1876** CHAMBERS *Astron.* 246 Saw both one ansa and the ball [of Saturn] flattened.

Ansafone, var. of ANSWERPHONE.

† **'ansal**, *a. Obs. rare.* [prob. ad. med.L. **ansālis* two-handled, *whence*, used both ways, double. Cf. Cotgr. 1611 '*un pot a deux anses*, an equivocation, a word, etc. of double meaning.'] Cutting both ways, two-edged.

1541 R. COPLAND *Guydon's Quest. Cyrurg.*, The other [cultelere] is [called] Ansall bycause it is made in maner of a swerde cuttynge on both sydes. *Ibid.*, Openynge made with a knyfe ansall to drawe out the rottennes.

ansate ('ænseɪt), *a.* [ad. L. *ansātus*, f. *ansa* handle.] = ANSATED *ppl. a.* Also in L. (fem.) form in ***ansata cross*** for *crux ansata* (= ANKH).

1891 KINNS *Graven in Rock* viii. 292 Iris and Horus are each holding the ansata cross or emblem of life. **1891** *Athenæum* 31 Oct. 591/1 Centurial stone, ansate, 17 in. by 8 in.

'ansated, *ppl. a.* [f. L. *ansāt-us* pa. pple. of *ansā-re*, f. ANSA.] 'Having handles, or something in the form of handles.' J.

1785 *European Mag.* VIII. 131 The Tau, or ansated Cross of the Egyptians. **1798** *Proc. Soc. Antiquaries* IV. 2 An ansated patera. **1891** *Athenæum* 16 May 644/1 [The stone has] well-cut letters .. in an ansated panel.

ansation (æn'seɪʃən). [f. L. *ans(a* handle + -ATION, after ANSATE *a.*] The provision of handles.

1859 *Jrnl. Brit. Archæol. Assoc.* XV. 69 There is rarely any attempt at ansation; the nearest approach to handles being heavy perforated knobs placed a little beneath the mouth.

‖**Anschauung** ('anʃaʊʊŋ). [G. = 'looking at', mode of view, f. G. *anschauen* to look at (MHG. *aneschouwen*); cf. SHOW *v.*] **1.** Sense-perception; *spec.* in Kantian philosophy = INTUITION 5c (see note).

[*a***1856** HAMILTON *Logic* (1860) I. vii. 127 We are .. in want of a general term to express what is common to the presentations of Perception, and the representations of Phantasy, that is, their individuality and immediacy. The Germans express this by the term *Anschauung*, which can only be translated by *intuition*, .. which literally means *a looking at*.] **1865** MILL *Exam. Ham.* xvii. 327 By intuitions Mr. Mansel means the Anschauungen of Kant, or what Mr. Mansel himself otherwise calls Presentations of Sense. *Ibid.* xviii. 352 It is the Anschauungen, the intuitions, the presentations of experience, which we in this case compare and judge. [**1889** E. CAIRD *Crit. Philos. of Kant* p. xi, *Anschauung* I have generally translated by 'Perception', rarely by 'Intuition', as the term Intuition seems in English to carry with it associations which are misleading. Sometimes I have used 'Pure Perception' where the context seemed to require it.] **1901** BALDWIN *Dict. Philos.* I. 569/1 High authorities have of late questioned the equivalence of intuition and the Kantian Anschauung.

2. An outlook, attitude, or point of view.

1907 G. B. SHAW *Major Barbara* Pref. 148 The Shavian *Anschauung* was already unequivocally declared. **1922** *Internat. Jrnl. Psycho-anal.* III. 377 In many respects however they .. are merely 'points of view' (*Anschauungen*).

‖**Anschluss** ('ænʃlʊs, 'an-). [G., 'addition, annexation, union', f. *anschliessen* to join, annex.] Annexation or union, *spec.* of Austria to Germany (either the actual union in 1938 or as proposed before that date).

1924 *Ann. Reg.* *1923* 192 This .. could be explained by the decline of interest in the *Anschluss* idea, due to the calamitous condition of Germany. **1929** *Social Sci. Abstr.* 3496 *Anschluss* would be disastrous to Austria and to the peace of Europe. **1939** J. N. L. BAKER *Atlas of War* 5/1 The Anschluss with Austria, proposed periodically since 1917 and forbidden by the treaty, was accomplished by force in March 1938. **1955** *Times* 9 May 11/2 A united Germany must not use an *anschluss* to extend her power into the Balkans and eastern Europe. **1958** *Economist* 18 Oct. 219/1 Ability to opt to join the Commonwealth might give certain states a valuable policy counter, when other forms of Anschluss seem to be in the offing.

Also **'anschluss** (rare) *v. trans.*, to annex, join.

1945 in *Amer. Speech* (1948) XXIII. 69/1 Hitler's next big coup was to anschluss Austria. **1945** *News Rev.* 29 Mar. 5/3 What would anschlussed Austria do?

ansegnie, ansenȝie, obs. Sc. ff. ENSIGN *sb.*

Anselmian (æn'sɛlmɪən), *a.* [f. St. *Anselm* + -IAN.] Of or pertaining to St. Anselm (1033–1109), Archbishop of Canterbury, the scholastic philosopher, and esp. to his ontological argument for the existence of God.

1884 W. JAMES in *Mind* IX. 283 Only the Anselmian proof can keep Fact out of philosophy. *a***1910** —— *Some Probl. Philos.* (1911) iii. 43 The anselmian or ontological proof of God's existence, sometimes called the cartesian proof, criticised by Saint Thomas, rejected by Kant, redefended by Hegel. **1943** E. L. MASCALL *He who Is* viii. 98 What we cannot imagine we can nevertheless conceive, as we saw in discussing the Anselmian definition of God.

Anselmic (æn'sɛlmɪk), *a.* [f. as prec. + -IC.] = ANSELMIAN *a.*

1872 G. S. MORRIS tr. *Ueberweg's Hist. Philos.* I. II. 379 The character of the Anselmic philosophy was not that of the whole period. **1932** *Times Lit. Suppl.* 18 Feb. 106/3 The objective or Anselmic theory, sometimes called the Satisfaction Theory. **1939** J. BAILLIE *Our Knowledge of God* iv. 151 Something that closely resembled the Anselmic proof which St. Thomas had condemned.

anserated ('ænsəreɪtɪd), *ppl. a. Her.* Of a cross: Having the extremities cleft and terminated (orig.) in the heads of serpents, (subseq.) of eagles, lions or other animals.

1678 R. HOLME *Armory* I. v. §90 He beareth Gules a Cross Anserated, Argent. **1859** WORCESTER, *Anserated cross.*

anserine ('ænsəraɪn), *a.* [ad. L. *anserin-us*, f. *anser* goose: see -INE.]

1. Of, pertaining to, or of the nature of a goose.

1839 *Blackw. Mag.* XLV. 689 The *paté de foie gras* is the diseased anserine liver stuffed with truffles. *a***1845** HOOD *Forge* I. xi, No anserine skin would rise thereat, It's the cold that makes Him shiver! **1855** OWEN *Skel. & Teeth* 65 The swan and other anserine birds.

2. As the goose is conventionally (though erroneously) a type of unintelligence: Stupid, silly.

1858 HOLMES *Aut. Breakf. T.* (1865) 91 If you expect me to hold forth in a 'scientific' way about my tree-loves .. you are an anserine individual.

anserous ('ænsərəs), *a.* [f. L. *anser* + -OUS; there was no L. *anserōsus*; cf. *piscōsus*, *silvōsus*, etc.] Gooselike, stupid, silly; = ANSERINE 2.

1826 SYD. SMITH *Wks.* 1859 II. 98/2 Can any be so anserous as to suppose, etc.? **1842** —— *Lett.*, He is anserous and asinine. **1879** *Truth* No. 125. 642/2 If people are sufficiently anserous to rely on the babble.

ansete, variant of ANDSÆT *a. Obs.* hostile.

‖**an sich** (an 'zɪç), *phr.* [G., = 'in itself'. Orig. taken from Ger. philos.] In itself; in the abstract; not in relation to anything else. Cf. DING AN SICH.

1846 J. D. MORELL *Hist. View Speculative Philos.* II. v. 142 An existence may be viewed in relation to itself, or in relation to the things around it; it may be existence *an sich* or existence *für andere*. **1909** W. JAMES *Pluralistic Universe* v. 215 Others, as Kant for example, have denied intellectualism's pretension to define reality *an sich* or in its absolute capacity. **1928** T. S. ELIOT in E. Pound *Sel. Poems* p. xvii, Not the matter *an sich*, which is unknowable, but the matter as we know it. **1956** A. HUXLEY *Adonis & Alphabet* 197 Much more widespread than the love of truth is the appetite for marvels, the love of the Phony *an sich*, in itself and for its own sweet sake.

†**'ansin(e.** *Obs.* Also 1 ansíon, -síen, -sín, -sýn. [f. AN- *pref.* 1 + OE. *sín, sýn*, sight, f. *séon* to see.]

1. Sight, face, aspect. (Only in OE.)

*c***1000** *Ags. Gosp.* Luke vii. 27 Beforan ðine ansýne.

2. A sight, a thing seen. (Only in OE.)

*c***885** K. ÆLFRED *Oros.* VI. vii, Seó ansín wearð mycel wundor Romanum.

3. A looking for, longing, desire, want.

*a***1000** *Metr. Ps.* cxlii. 6 Swá eorþan biþ ansýn wæteres. *a***1400** *Dame Sirith* MS. Digby No. 86. 167 (Halliw.) As povre wif that falleth in ansine.

anslaight. A variant of ONSLAUGHT. ? a misprint, supposed archaism, or affected form.

1619 FLETCHER *M. Thomas* II. ii, I do remember yet that anslaight, thou wast beaten, And fledst.

‖**anspe'ssade.** [Fr. *l'anspessade* erron. for *lanspessade, lancespessade*, ad. It. *lancia spezzata* broken lance; applied originally, it is said, to a cavalier, who, on his horse being killed under him, was made a petty officer in the foot. See Littré.]

1751 CHAMBERS *Cycl.*, *Anspessades* or *Lanspessades*, a kind of inferior officers in the foot, below the corporals. **1800** COLERIDGE *Wallenstein* II. iii. *note*, Anspessade .. a soldier inferior to a corporal but above the sentinels.

†**an'stand,** *v. Obs.* Also 1 **andstand-an.** [f. AND- against + STAND. OE. *and-, anstandan*, is cogn. w. Goth. *andstandan*, OHG. *intstantan*, mod.G. *entstehen*.] To withstand, resist.

*a***1000** *Rule of St. Ben.* 1 (Bosw.) Andstandende onȝean. **1297** R. GLOUC. 267 Aȝen þe Deneys to anstond.

†**'ansulary,** *a. Obs. rare*$^{-1}$. [f. L. *ansula*, dim. of *ansa* handle + -ARY.] Of or pertaining to handles, handle-like.

1664 POWER *Exp. Philos.* Pref. 4 The secondary Planets of Saturn and Jupiter and his ansulary appearances.

answer ('ɑːnsə(r), æ-), *sb.* Forms: 1 **and-, ondswaru, -suaru,** 2 **ondswore,** 2–3 **andsware, -swere,** 3 **ændswere, ænsware, enswere,** 3–4 **onswere,** 3–5 **answare,** 3–7 **answere, -uer(e,** 4 **answar, -suar, vnswere, (on-, ansquare, -quer),** 5 **on-, aunsware,** 5–6 **aunswer(e,** 6 **answeare,** 4– **answer.** [OE. *'andswaru*, cogn. with OS. *antswôr*, OFris. (*ontswer*) *ondser*, ON. *andsvar, annsvar*, Dan. and Sw. *ansvar*, OTeut. **andswarâ-*; f. *and-* against, in reply + **swarâ-* affirmation, swearing, f. OTeut. **swarjan*, Goth. *swaran*, OE. *swęrian* to affirm, swear. The original meaning was thus a solemn affirmation made to rebut a charge.]

1. A reply made to a charge, whereby the accused seeks to clear himself; a defence. *spec.* in *Law*, The counter-statement made in reply to a complainant's bill of charges.

1340 HAMPOLE *Pr. Consc.* 5779 Of whilk þai sal þan answer gyf. *c***1360** *Mercy* in *E.E.P.* (1862) 120 Let seo what vnswere constou make. *c***1385** CHAUCER *L.G.W.* 401 To dampne a man with-oute answere [*v.r.* aunswer, ansuere] or word. *a***1400** *Cov. Myst.* 18 Ded men xul rysyn .. And ffast to here ansuere thei xul hem dyth. **1580** BARET *Alv.* A 433 The answere of the defendant, *Intentionis depulsio.* **1593** SHAKS. *2 Hen. VI*, II. i. 203 Call these foule Offendors to their Answeres. **1611** BIBLE *2 Tim.* iv. 16 At my first answer no man stood with me. [So *Rhem.*; TINDALE, *Genev.*, answerynge; WYCLIF, *Revised*, defence.] **1694** W. BROWN (*title*) The Clerk's Tutor in Chancery, giving true Directions how to draw affidavits, petitions .. bills, answers. **1809** TOMLINS *Law Dict.* s.v. *Chancery*, An answer generally controverts the facts stated in the bill, or some of them. **1876** J. PARKER *Paraclete* I. xiii. 201 To the charge that Christianity takes a low view of human nature, the cross of Christ is the answer of God.

2. A reply to an objection rebutting its force; a reply in writing or debate, setting forth arguments opposed to those previously advanced.

1534 MORE (*title*) The Answer to the First Part of the Poysoned Booke. **1578** TIMME *Calvin on Gen.* 214 If any man object .. the aunswere is easy to be made. **1612** WOODALL *Surg. Mate* Wks. 1653 Pref. 13 A loving answer to all such as shall hereafter find fault with his Book. **1798** WOLCOTT (P. Pindar) *Tales of Hoy* Wks. 1812 IV. 425 An answer is inserted, he answers the answer with blacker inventions. **1846** L. LOCKHART (*title*) An Answer to the Protest of the Free Church. *a***1884** *Mod.* A sufficient answer to all your objections.

3. A reply (spoken, written, or otherwise given) to a question. (The most common use.)

*a***800** *Beowulf* 5713 Grim andswaru. *c***950** *Lindisf. Gosp.* John xix. 9 Se hælend ondsuare ne salde him [*Rushw.* ondswora]. *c***1000** *Ags. G.* ibid., Him ne sealde nane andsware. *c***1160** *Hatton G.*, Nane andswere. *c***1230** *Ancr. R.* 8 Him þuncheð wunder .. of swuch onswere. *c***1325** *Leg. Rood* (1871) 111 þe messagers him gaf ansquare. **1375** BARBOUR *Bruce* II. 60 Quhen thai hard nane mak ansuer, Thai brak the dur. **1580** J. FRAMPTON *Joyf. Newes*, in *James I's Counterbl.* (Arb.) 82 Geuing them continually doubtfull answeares. **1601** SHAKS. *All's Well* II. ii. 42, I will bee a foole in question, hoping to bee the wiser by your answer. **1714** *Spect.* No. 625 ¶1 The following Letter of Queries, with his Answers to each Question. **1850** LYNCH *Theoph. Trin.* 5 To this question there is no answer.

4. a. A reply to an appeal, address, remark, letter, etc.; anything said or written in reference to, or acknowledgement of, what another has said or written; a response, rejoinder.

*c***1200** ORMIN 12016 Alls iff þe Laferrd ȝæfe þuss Anndsware onnȝæn þe deofell. **1382** WYCLIF *Prov.* xv. 1 A nesshe onswere breketh wrathe. **1388** *Ibid.* A soft answere brekith ire. **1400** LD. GREY in Ellis *Orig. Lett.* II. i. I. 5 An other lettre that I have send to hym agayn of an Answare. *a***1450** *Knt. de la Tour* (1868) 106 So plesaunt of ansuere unto her husbonde. **1596** SHAKS. *Merch. V.* II. vii. 72 Had you beene as wise as bold .. Your answere had not beene inscrold. **1611** BIBLE *Job* xix. 16, I called my seruant, and he gaue me no answere. **1771** *Junius Lett.* liv. 281 His letter to me does not deserve an answer. **1859** TENNYSON *Enid* 995 He flung a wrathful answer back.

b. ***answer-back***: a rejoinder or repartee; also *fig.*

1924 J. A. THOMSON *Sci. Old & New* xvi. 90 First there is the gall—an answer-back which the plant makes to the irritation which follows when the gall-midge lays an egg in the soft tissue. **1925** —— *Sci. & Relig.* vi. §9. 194 The struggle for existence is a formula covering all the answers-back that organisms make to environing difficulties.

c. In catch-phr. ***—'s answer to*** (..): applied (often *iron.*) to something or someone promoted by one place, group, etc., as a rival to a celebrated example from elsewhere.

[**1940** B. I. EVANS *Short Hist. Eng. Lit.* xiii. 208 The *Quarterly Review* (1809) began publication as a Tory answer to the *Edinburgh*.] **1966** N. ROREM *Paris Diary* xi. 226 For years *she's* been Europe's answer to Louella Parsons. **1970** T. WOOD *Bright Side Billy Wilder* xv. 167 Erich Maria Remarque .. was then editor of *Die Dame*, Ullstein's answer to *Vogue Magazine*. **1973** *Times* 30 May 11/4 A ghastly talent-spotting show with smirking juveniles being mobilized by a Seattle's answer to Harry Lauder. **1974** *Maclean's Mag.* Apr. 94 Calling a magazine Success doesn't necessarily make it one, either. At last report, Canada's answer to Playboy and Penthouse was close to folding. **1986** *Daily Tel.* 29 Apr. 15/1 Norway has had enough of the man described .. as Norway's answer to Kim Philby.

5. The reply to an implied question; decision upon a point at issue.

1466 *Mercers' Accts.* in Blades *Caxton* 151 As for yor desire of aunsware of the lordes intent. **1599** SHAKS. *Mids. N.* IV. i. 143 Is not this the day That Hermia should giue answer of her choice? *a***1842** TENNYSON *Two Voices* 309 There must be answer to his doubt. **1875** MAINE *Hist. Inst.* ii. 42 The *Responsa Prudentum*—the accumulated answers (= judgments in Brehon law) of many successive generations of famous Roman lawyers.

6. a. The solution of a problem of any kind; and, by extension: Any work solving a problem or performing an exercise set to test knowledge.

1592 R. FIELD (*title*) Firste Booke of Arithmeticke; shewing the ingenius inventions and figurative operations by whiche to calculate the true Solution or Answers to Arithmeticall Questions. **1686** I. SPEIDEL (*title*) An Arithmetical Extraction; or, a Collection of 800 Questions with their Answers. **1742** BAILEY, *Answer* .. the Solution of a Mathematical Question, an Ænigma, &c. **1881** L. HENSLEY (*title*) The Scholar's Arithmetic, with Answers to the Examples.

b. ***to know all the answers***, to be fully knowledgeable or expert; to be worldly-wise or experienced. (Cf. similar colloq. phrases s.v. KNOW *v.* 15.)

1933 G. LAVEN *Rough Stuff* p. ix, *To know all the questions and answers*, to know your way about. To be clever in things relating to crime and law-breaking. **1935** G. & S. LORIMER *Heart Specialist* v. 128 'You may be one of these carefully reared dames,' he said with a trace of doubt in his voice, 'but you sure know all the answers.' **1937** C. BOOTHE *The Women* in *Famous Plays 1937* 622 *Miriam.* Getting wise, aren't you? *Mary.* Know all the answers. **1940** J. THURBER *Fables for Our Time* xii. 30 It is better to ask some of the questions than to know all the answers. **1955** A. L. ROWSE *Expansion Eliz. Eng.* x. 408 The positive old lady in the garden, who knew all the answers and could not be told anything, had not ceased to be a marvellous politician. **1956** A. WILSON *Anglo-*

Saxon Attitudes II. iii. 367 She'd been a glamour girl, but she knew all the answers.

7. A practical reply; anything done in return; a responsive, corresponding, or resulting action. In *Fencing*, the return hit.

1535 Coverdale *Gen.* xli. 16 God shall geue Pharao a prosperous answere. **1602** Shaks. *Haml.* v. ii. 280 If Hamlet give the first or second hit, or quit in answer of the third exchange. **1611** —— *Cymb.* v. iii. 79 Great the slaughter is Heere made by 'th' Romane; great the answer be Britaines must take. **1845** Darwin *Voy. Nat.* iv. 64 The answer was given by a volley of musketry.

8. A re-echoing or reproduction of sounds.

1869 Ouseley *Counterpoint, &c.* xix. 152 Essentially the answer may be regarded as a transposition of the subject. **1880** Grove *Dict. Mus.* I. 69/2 An answer in music is, in strict counterpoint, the repetition by one part or instrument of a theme proposed by another.

9. *Comb.* **answer-jobber**, one who makes a trade of writing answers; **answer print** *Cinemat.* (see quot. 1940).

1711 Swift *Barrier Treaty* (J.) This race of *answer-jobbers..have no sort of conscience in their dealing. **1940** *Chambers's Techn. Dict.*, **Answer print*, the first print from the edited negative, shown to the producers of the sound-film for final approval before release. **1959** Halas & Manvell *Technique Film Anim.* xix. 234 The studio manager..records deadline dates for line-tests, rough cuts and answer print screenings.

answer, *v.* Forms: 1 and-, ond-, -swarian, -suarian, -sworian, -swerian, 2 ænd- andswarien, -erien, 2–3 an- onswerien, 3 andswaren, -eren, ond- onswere(n, un- onsquare, 3–4 answere(n, 4 an- on- unswar(e, answer-n, ansuerye, 4–5 ansuere, aunswar(e, 4–7 answere, 5 unswer, 5–7 aun-, awnswer(e, 7 answeare, 4- answer. [OE. *andswar-ian*, direct deriv. of sb. *andswaru* (see prec.). Thus, orig. used of rebutting a charge or accusation; its extension to the common sense of *reply* is parallel to that of the Gr. ἀποκρίν-εσθαι, f. ἀπό off + κρίν-ειν to judge, condemn, i.e. to get oneself off from judgement; and the L. *re-spondēre*, f. *re-* back, undoing + *spondēre* to pledge oneself, undertake a liability, hence to rebut a liability or legal obligation.]

Gen. sign. I. To make a statement in reply to a legal charge; to meet a charge of any kind; to be liable so to do, or to suffer the consequences, to atone, pay the penalty. II. To speak (write) or act, in reply to a question, remark, or expression of will or opinion, or in response to a mere sound or sign. III. To act in response to an act, imitatively, suitably, consequently; to be so constituted as to imitate, fit, suit; to be in physical or mental conformity or logical consequence to anything. Originally *intr.*, with *dative*; but through various elisions and levelling of inflexions at length also used *trans.* in nearly every sense.

I. To answer to a charge.

1. *intr.* To speak in reply or opposition to a charge or accusation, to make a rebutting statement, defend oneself. **a.** *simply.*

c **950** *Lindisf. Gosp.* Luke xxi. 14 Ne ʒie fore-ðencʒæ huu ʒie ondsuariʒa [*Rushw.* ondsworiʒað]. *c* **1000** *Ags. G.* ibid., Hu ʒe andswarian. *c* **1160** *Hatton G.*, Andswerien. **1297** R. Glouc. 194 We þe setteþ day of þys nexte yere, At Rome uorto ansuerye. *c* **1400** *Beryn* 2092 Graunte me day til to morow, that I myȝt be avisid To answere forth. **1599** Shaks. *Much Ado* iv. ii. 25 How answer you for your selues? **1601** F. Tate *Househ. Ord. Edw. II*, §51 (1876) 35 He..shall aunswere before the steward..if any complaint be made. **1687** Luttrell *Brief Rel.* (1857) I. 403 Then he was ordered immediately to answer over. **1768** Blackstone *Comm.* III. 397 That the defendant do answer over, *respondeat ouster*; that is, put in a more substantial plea. *Mod.* To answer at the bar of public opinion.

b. with *for*. To answer charges in regard to; to be responsible or accountable for.

1384 Wyclif *De Eccles.* viii. Wks. III. 357 He shal answere for þes soulis þat his children leesen. **1582** Lyly in *4 Cent. Eng Lett.* 39 Before whome for my speache I shal aunswer. **1600** Shaks. *A.Y.L.* v. i. 13 We that haue good wits, haue much to answer for. **1711** Steele *Spect.* No. 263 ¶1, I have no outrageous Offence against my own excellent Parents to answer for. **1838** Lytton *Leila* i. 6, I answer alone to Allah for my motives.

2. *intr.* To speak or make a statement in behalf of another; to undertake responsibility *for*. *spec.* To stand sponsor (*for* a child).

c **1200** *Trin. Coll. Hom.* 17 Here godfaderes sullen for hem andswerie bifore þe prest ate fanstone. **1483** Caxton *G. de la Tour* iij b, How euery good woman ought to ansuere for her lord in al thinge. **1611** Bible *Gen.* xxx. 33 So shall my righteousnesse answere for me. **1762** H. Walpole *Vertue's Anecd. Paint.* (1786) IV. 71 The late king and queen, then prince and princess, answered for his son.

3. *intr.* To undertake a responsibility, to guarantee, give an assurance. Const. *for*.

1728 Pope *Dunc.* Advt., I cannot answer but some mistakes may have slipt into [this edition]. **1866** Mrs. Gaskell *Wives & D.* II. xxi. 326 'I'll answer for it Mrs. Goodenough saw Molly'..When Miss Browning 'answered for it' Miss Phoebe gave up doubting. **1881** *Daily Tel.* 27 Dec., A musical monarch, whose tunefulness is answered for by Mr. Henry Nordblom.

4. a. *trans.* To make a defence against (a charge); *hence*, **b.** To give a satisfactory answer for, to justify. *arch.*

1552 Huloet, Answer an action, or plaint, *Dicere causam.* *c* **1590** Marlowe *Faust.* (2nd vers.) 124 We were best look that your devil can answer the stealing of this same cup. *c* **1680** Beveridge *Serm.* (1729) I. 307 How they will answer it..at the last day I know not. **1793** Smeaton *Edystone L.* §125 The Proprietors could not answer it to the public..if they kept me in waiting.

5. To reply to, meet, or rebut an objection or argument. †**a.** *intr. Obs.* **b.** *trans.*

c **1305** *St. Kath.* (in *E.E.P.* 1862) 33 Mid oþer reisouns of clergie þat maide preouede also þat here godes noþing nere ..þemperour stod and ne couþe answerie in non wise. *c* **1374** Chaucer *Boeth.* v. iv. 161 Whan I haue..ansewered to þo resouns by whiche þou art ymoeued. *c* **1526** Frith *Disput. Purg.* (1829) 107 Let us see how he answereth the argument. **1581** Charke in *Confer.* iv. (1584) Ffb, You haue so often chalenged vs to answere you an argument. **1635** A. Stafford *Fem. Glory* (1869) 81, I determined to answeare his Forgeries. *Mod.* So far as I know, that protest has never been answered. No attempt has been made to answer my objections. Some theologians of Queen's College essayed to answer Locke.

6. To meet the charge in regard to (an act) practically; to suffer the consequences, atone for, make amends. **a.** *intr.* Const. *for* (*to* obs.).

1297 R. Glouc. 53 Ȝef ys neuew hadde mysdo..he scholde Onswere to eche mon. **1601** Shaks. *Jul. C.* iii. ii. 85 If it were so, it were a grieuous fault And grieuouslie hath Caesar answered for it. **1710** W. Mather *Yng. Man's Comp.* (1727) 122 The Husband must answer to his Wive's Faults; if she wrong another..he must make Satisfaction.

†**b.** *trans., esp.* with *it* as obj. *Obs.*

1594 Shaks. *Rich. III*, iv. ii. 96 Stanley looke to your Wife: if she conuey Letters to Richmond, you shall answer it. **1625** Donne *Serm.* cl. Wks. VI. 61 Whosoever is dead in that family by thy negligence, thou shalt answer the King that subject. **1754** Sherlock *Disc.* (1759) I. i. 31 If you receive not the Light you must answer it.

7. To satisfy a pecuniary claim. †**a.** *intr.* To be responsible for payment of the claim. Const. *of, for. Obs.*

1480 Caxton *Chron. Eng.* ccxxv. 230 The lordes of euery toun wher suche thyng shold be taxed..shold ansuere to the kyng therof. **1628** Coke *On Litt.* 54 a, Tenant in dower.. shall answer for the waste done by a stranger.

†**b.** *trans.* To account to or satisfy (a person) *of* or *for* the claim; to repay, recompense. *Obs.*

1413 Lydg. *Pylgr. Sowle* i. xvii. (1859) 18 By whiche caucyon he myght bynd hym self for to ansuere me yf that his accyon be desalowyd. **1523** Ld. Berners *Froiss.* I. cccviii. 467 We wolde demaunde good hostages and sufficient, to answere vs of our horses agayne. **1577** Holinshed *Chron.* II. 240 The emperour declared plainlie that he would be answered for such summes of monie as king Richard had taken. **1641** Baker *Chron.* (1679) 231/1 That King Richard should yearly pay and answer the Duke of all the revenues.

c. *trans.* To satisfy (the claim), discharge (a debt), pay (the sum legally demanded); *hence*, to be sufficient for, meet (a pecuniary liability).

1581 Lambarde *Eiren.* ii. iv. (1588) 177 Their armour and weapon shall be prised, and the same answered to the use of the Queenes Maiestie. **1596** Shaks. *1 Hen. IV*, i. iii. 185 This proud King, who studies..To answer all the Debt he owes vnto you. **1608** *Yorksh. Trag.* i. ii, His fortunes cannot answer his expense. *a* **1626** Bacon *Max. & Uses Com. Law* 60 The third part must descend to the heire to answer guardship. **1710** in *Lond. Gaz.* mmmmdclxxxiii/3 Officer for any refusal or neglect of his Duty, to answer Damages. **1770** Langhorne *Plutarch's Lives* (1879) I. 386/1 A fine which his circumstances could not answer. **1832** Ht. Martineau *Hill & Valley* i. 6 A few shillings..to answer any sudden occasion.

¶ In senses 8–11 the idea of *compensation* is linked with that of *correspondence*; cf. III.

†**8. a.** *trans.* To prove a satisfactory return or equivalent for (an expenditure); to repay, recoup. *Obs.*

1596 Bp. Barlow *3 Serm.* Ded. 81 Yet did they not answer either the threshers labour, or the owners measure. **1673** Ray *Journ. Low Countr.* Pref., Nothing..which might answer their trouble and expence. **1731** Swift *Corr.* II. 649 The maid will..sell more butter and cheese than will answer her wages. **1780** W. Coxe *Russ. Discov.* 7 No crop.. sufficient..to answer the pains and expence of raising it.

†**b.** To repay, pay (a person). *Obs. rare.*

1587 Fleming *Cont. Holinshed's Chron.* III. 415/1 The said countries, which with their riches by common estimation answered the emperour Charles equallie to his Indies.

c. *intr.* To be advantageous, or servicable *to*.

1850 Lytton *Wks.* II. viii. iii. 15 If Beatrice di Negra would indeed be rich, she might answer to himself as a wife. **1865** Carlyle *Fredk. Gt.* V. xiii. viii. 90 He was in the way of making such investments..and found them answer to him.

9. *trans.* To satisfy or fulfil (wishes, hopes, expectations, etc.).

1653 Walton *Angler* i. 2, I shall almost answer your hopes. **1673** Cave *Prim. Chr.* i. i. 3 This he well foresaw and the event truly answered it. **1765** Wilkes *Corr.* (1805) II. 137 Were you here with me, my fondest wishes would be answered. **1878** Bosw. Smith *Carthage* 126 The result answered his expectations.

10. a. *trans.* To fulfil or accomplish (an end); to suit (a purpose).

1714 Grove *Spect.* No. 588 ¶2 In both Cases the Ends of Self Love are equally answered. **1749** Fielding *Tom Jones* vii. xiii, I applied a fomentation..which highly answered the intention. **1790** Paley *Hor. Paul.* i. 8 My design will be fully answered. **1877** Mozley *Univ. Serm.* ii. 33 Less severity would not have answered his purpose.

b. *trans.* To fulfil, satisfy the requirements, etc. of (a person); to suit.

1816 Scott *Antiq.* xvi. (1829) 105 He offered him a beast he thought wad answer him weel eneugh.

11. *intr.* (*ellipt.*). To serve the purpose, attain the end, succeed, prove a success. Also (with suitable qualification): To turn out (well or ill).

1783 Cowper *Lett.* 19 Jan., Their labour was almost in vain before, but now it answers. **1785** T. Jefferson *Writ.* (1859) I. 488 If they find our timber answer. **1856** Froude *Hist. Eng.* I. 27 It answered better as a speculation to convert arable land into pasture. *c* **1865** J. Wylde in *Circ. Sc.* I. 314/1 Boxwood charcoal answers best for this purpose.

II. To answer a question, remark, etc.

12. To speak or write in reply to a question, remark, or any expression of desire or opinion; to reply, respond, rejoin; *also* To reply to an implied question, to solve a doubt.

Const. **a.** *simply*; **b.** *to* a person; **c.** a person as indirect (dat.) obj.; **d.** *to* or *unto* the question, etc.; **e.** the question, etc., as obj.; *spec.* in Horse-racing, ***to answer (the question)***: (of a horse) to respond to a call made by the jockey (cf. *to ask the question*, ask *v.* 2b); †**f.** (combining c and d) a person *to* his question; **g.** (combining c and e) a person his question; **h.** with the answer as subordinate objective sentence, or clause introduced by *that*; **i.** with the answer as simple obj., sb. or pron.; **j.** (combining b or c and h); **k.** (combining b or c and i); **l.** (combining d and h); **m.** (combining d and i).

a. *c* **1200** *Trin. Coll. Hom.* 129 He answerede þus, queðinde. **1375** Barbour *Bruce* i. 437 The byschop hard him swa ansuer. **1590** Shaks. *Com. Err.* ii. ii. 195 Why prat'st thou to thy selfe, and answer'st not? **1765** H. Walpole *Cast. Otranto* v. (1798) 79 Thou answerest from the point. *a* **1842** Tennyson *Miller's Dau.* 118 Will she answer if I call?

b. *c* **1230** *Ancr. R.* 10 O þisse wise answerieð to þeo þet askeð ou of ower ordre. *c* **1400** *Apol. Loll.* 68, I þe Lord schal ansuere to him. **1483** Caxton *G. de la Tour* iij b, No good woman ought to ansuere to her husbond whan he is wrothe. **1607** Shaks. *Cor.* iii. iii. 61 Answer to us. **1842** Tennyson *Love & Duty* 28 To that man My work shall answer.

c. *c* **950** *Lindisf. Gosp.* John xviii. 22 Ondsuærestu suæ ðæm biscobi. *c* **1000** *Ags. G.* ibid., Andswarast ðu swa ðam bisceope. *c* **1160** *Hatton G.* ibid., Ændswerest þu swa þam biscoppe. *a* **1300** *Cursor M.* 1304 Mildely he him þam vnsquerede. **1450** Myrc 930 Unsware thow me. **1601** Shaks. *Jul. C.* iv. iii. 78 Should I haue answer'd Caius Cassius so? **1611** Bible *Prov.* xxvi. 4 Answer not a fool according to his folly. **1791** Cowper *Iliad* iv. 490 Whom with a frowning brow, the brave Tydides answer'd. **1859** Tennyson *Elaine* 286 Lancelot spoke And answered him at full.

d. *c* **1400** *Destr. Troy* xxxiv. 13266 To all thing he answarit abilly. **1592** Shaks. *Rom. & Jul.* ii. v. 35 Is thy newes good or bad? answere to that. **1699** Bentley *Phal.* Pref. 68 Mr. B. here answers to a Question, that never was ask'd him. **1881** N. T. (Revised) *Luke* xiv. 6 They could not answer again unto these things.

e. **1722** De Foe *Plague* 67 To answer their question directly. **1864** Tennyson *Aylmer's F.* 465 My lady's cousin Answered all queries touching those at home. **1894** H. Custance *Riding Recoll.* vi. 88, I..asked 'King Lud' the question. He answered in the most generous manner possible,..and won. **1894** *Idler* June 545 The certain winner of the Derby—if he is able to answer the question I am going to put to him.

f. *c* **1385** Chaucer *L.G.W.* 2079 Ariadne in this manere Answerde [*v.r.* ansuerd] hym to his profre. **1526** Tindale *Luke* xiv. 6 They coulde not answer him agayne to that. **1611** Bible *Ibid.* They could not answere him againe to these things. **1605** Shaks. *Macb.* iv. i. 60 Answer me To what I aske you.

g. **1593** Shaks. *3 Hen. VI*, iii. iii. 238 Ere thou go, but answer me one doubt. *Mod.* Answer me this question.

h. *a* **1300** *Cursor M.* 1095 He onsquared [*v.r.* ansuerd, vnswerd]..Quen was I keper of þi childe. **1340** *Ayenb.* 190 He ansuerede þet he ne hedde bote þri pans. **1611** Bible *Acts* xxii. 8, I answered, Who art thou, Lord? **1733** Pope *Mor. Ess.* i. 84 Wks. 1735 II. ii. 5 The mighty Czar might answer, he was drunk. **1860** O. Meredith *Lucille* i. iv. xxi, Who can answer where any road leads to?

i. **1382** Wyclif *Matt.* xxvii. 12 Whanne he was acusid.. he answerid nothing. *c* **1460** *Towneley Myst.* 196 Fyrst wold I here, What he wold answere. **1860** Dickens *Uncomm. Trav.* xv. (1866) 109/1 Chips answered never a word.

j. *c* **1175** *Lamb. Hom.* 45 Paul him onswerde, Lauerd ic biwepe þas monifolde pine. *c* **1250** *Gen. & Ex.* 4107 God hem andswerede, 'iosue Ic wile ben loder-man after ðe.' **1596** Spenser *F.Q.* v. ii. 11 To whom he aunswerd wroth, 'loe there thy hire.' **1611** Bible *Acts* xxv. 16 To whom I answered, It is not the maner of the Romanes, etc.

k. *c* **950** *Lindisf. Gosp.* Mark xiv. 40 Ne wiston huæd scealdon onsuæreʒa him. *c* **1160** *Hatton G.* ibid., Nyston hwæt hyo him andswereden. *c* **1230** *Ancr. R.* 96 Ne answerie ȝe him nowiht. **1611** Bible *Job* xxiii. 5 The words which he would answere me. —— *Matt.* xxii. 46 No man was able to answere him a word.

l. **1382** Wyclif *Acts* xxv. 16 To whiche I answerid that, etc. **1756** Burke *Subl. & B.* Wks. I. 269 To this I answer that admitting, etc.

m. **1593** Shaks. *3 Hen. VI*, iv. vi. 45 What answeres Clarence to his Soueraignes will?

13. Coupled with *say*. Sometimes without preceding question. (A Hellenism of the N.T.) *arch.*

c **1000** *Ags. Gosp.* John iii. 9 Ða andswarode Nichodemus & cwæð. Hu maʒon þas þing þus ʒeweorðan? *c* **1160** *Hatton G.* ibid., Ða andswerede N. & cwæð. *c* **1220** *Hali Meid.* 3 Ho mei onsweren & seien. *c* **1420** *Chron. Vilod.* 466 Unswered þe monk, and sayde ryȝt þus. **1526** Tindale *Luke* xiii. 25 He shall answer and saye vnto you: I knowe you not. **1611** Bible

Mark xi. 14 And Jesus answered, and said vnto it, No man eate fruit of thee hereafter.

14. To make a rejoinder to anything authoritative or final, or where silence or acquiescence would be proper; to reply impertinently. Also, ***to answer back.***

1526 Tindale *Tit.* ii. 9 The servauntes exhort..to please in all thynges, not answeryng agayne. [So **1611**; Wyclif, aȝeinseiynge]. **1853** Lytton *My Novel* i. xiii. 53 Mrs. Hazeldean (observing Frank colouring, and about to reply).—Hush, Frank, never answer your father. *a* **1884** *Mod.* You should never answer back. **1904** Stanislaus Joyce *Dublin Diary* (1962) 52 She is obstinate and inclined to answer back a great deal. **1926** *Sat. Rev.* 20 Mar. 376/1 In dialogue the characters do not answer so much as answer back. **1929** H. G. Wells *King who was King* ii. §4. 66 The King receives him coldly and admonishes him with evident severity... Against all etiquette he answers back. **1937** F. Stark *Baghdad Sketches* 172 One who, after many years of patient trampling upon, suddenly answers back. **1948** *Daily Herald* 7 Aug. 2/2 This sort of person is compensating himself for not being allowed to Answer Back as a child.

15. *trans.* or *absol.* To solve a problem put in the form of a question; to perform the exercises or 'questions' set in an examination paper.

1742 Bailey, To *Answer*..to solve a Proposition or Question in Arithmetick or Geometry, &c. by declaring what the Amount is. **1868** M. Pattison *Acad. Organ.* 294 The student himself will tell you that he answered such a paper 'out of Grote,' and such another 'out of Maine' or 'Austin.' *Ibid.* 296 No candidate would be expected in three hours to answer all the thirteen [questions]. *a* **1884** *Mod.* You have answered very well.

16. to answer to a name: *lit.* to answer when addressed by that name, and thus to acknowledge it as one's own; to have the name of.

1599 Shaks. *Much Ado* v. iv. 73, I answer to that name, what is your will? **1607** —— *Cor.* v. i. 12 Coriolanus He would not answer to: Forbad all names. **1758** Johnson *Idler* No. 12 ⁋5 A spaniel..that answers to the name of Ranger.

17. To say or sing antiphonally.

1611 Bible *1 Sam.* xviii. 7 The women answered one another, as they played. **1697** Dryden *Virg. Ecl.* vii. 4 Both alike inspir'd To sing, and answer as the Song requir'd.

18. To make a responsive sound, as an echo.

c **1385** Chaucer *L.G.W.* 2193 The holwe rokkis answerden hire a-gayn. **1596** Spenser *F.Q.* ii. xii. 33 The rolling sea, resounding soft, In his big base them fitly answered. **1667** Milton *P.L.* x. 862 With other echo late I taught your Shades To answer. **1709** Pope *Summer* 16 The woods shall answer, and their echo ring. **1847** Tennyson *Princ.* Prol. 66 Echo answer'd in her sleep From hollow fields.

19. a. To reply favourably to (a petitioner), or conformably to (his petition). Cf. 9.

1593 Shaks. *Lucr.* 1606 At length addressed to answer his desire. **1611** Bible *Ps.* xxvii. 7 Haue mercie also vpon mee, and answere me. **1648** Milton *Ps.* lxxxvi. 24 Thou wilt.. Answer what I prayed. **1689** *Col. Records Penn.* I. 313 With reluctancy to answer my Request. **1864** Tennyson *Boad.* 22 The Gods have heard it, O Icenian!..Doubt not ye the Gods have answer'd.

†**b.** To give or administer (anything) in answer to petition. *Obs. rare.*

1586 J. Hooker *Girald. Irel.* in *Holinsh.* II. 151/2 Hir maiesties principall and high courts, to answer the law to all sutors throughout the whole realme.

20. To reply to what is practically a request, as a knock at the door, a bell, or other signal. **a.** *intr.*

1597 Shaks. *2 Hen. IV.* i. i. 6 Knock but at the gate, and he himself will answer. **1722** De Foe *Plague* 51 They knocked at the door, but nobody answered.

b. *trans.* To answer the door, the bell, etc.

1862 Mrs. Wood *Channings* II. 349 He answers all the rings at the yard bell. **1866** W. Collins *Armadale* III. 205 The woman had left us to answer the door. **1878** Halliwell *Dict.* s.v., At a farm-house near South Petherton, a maidservant was recently asked why she did not answer the door. The girl replied..' Why—why—why, if you plaze, mim, I—I—I did'n hear'n speak.'

21. To make a sign of any kind in response to, or acknowledgement of, any signal. **a.** *intr.* **b.** *trans.*

1805 Sir E. Berry in Nicolas *Disp.* (1846) VII. 117 At daylight I made the Private Signal which was not answered. *a* **1884** *Mod.* He gave a nod; I answered with a wink.

III. To answer in similarity, to correspond.

22. *trans.* To act in conformity with (any indication of will or law), to obey; *esp.* of a ship: ***to answer the helm.***

1610 Shaks. *Temp.* i. ii. 190, I come To answer thy best pleasure. **1637** Milton *Comus* 888 Bridle in thy headlong wave Till thou our summons answered have. **1738** J. Keill *Anim. Œcon.* Pref. 11 That the Indications..are right, or such as, if answered, would cure the Disease. **1854** G. Richardson *Univ. Code* v., 2578 = Will not answer her helm.

23. *intr.* To act in sympathy with, or in response (*to*), action on the part of another.

1684 R. Waller *Ess. Nat. Exper.* 6 The former immediately answer to the least change of the Air. **1697** Dryden *Virg. Georg.* i. 274 The Glebe will answer to the Sylvan Reign, Great Heats will follow, and large Crops of Grain. **1865** Dickens *Mut. Fr.* i. 2 The girl instantly answered to the action in her sculling.

24. *trans.* To repeat the action of, correspond to.

1599 Shaks. *Hen. V,* iv. Prol. 8 Fire answers fire. **1603** —— *Meas. for M.* v. i. 415 Haste still paies haste, and leasure answers leasure.

25. *trans.* To give back in kind, to return, render.

1576 Lambarde *Peramb. Kent* (1826) 231 They bee so ready..not to aunswere, but to offer, force and violence, even to Kings and Princes. **1596** Spenser *F.Q.* v. i. 24 Well did the squire perceive himselfe too weake To aunswere his defiaunce in the field. **1601** Cornwallyes *Seneca* (1631) 44 Able to answere feast with feast. **1793** Holcroft *Lavater's Physiog.* xxxi. 163 To answer wit with reason is like endeavouring to hold an eel by the tail. **1827** Keble *Chr. Y.* 24 S. Trin. iv. 2 Answering love for love.

†**26.** *trans.* To return the hostile action of (a person), meet in fight, encounter. *Obs.*

c **1400** *Destr. Troy* xx. 8274 Or hit auntrid hym to aunsware Ector agayne. **1468** J. Paston in *Lett.* 585 II. 317 My Lord the Bastard, took upon hym to answere xxiiij. knyts and gentylmen..at jostys of pese. **1586** J. Hooker *Girald. Irel.* in *Holinsh.* II. 155/1 His Gallowglasses were good men to incounter with Gallowglasses, and not to answer old souldiers.

27. *intr.* To correspond in number, shape, size, position, appearance, fitness, or other characteristics. Const. *to* (*against, with,* obs.).

c **1230** *Ancr. R.* 94 Euerichones mede þer scal onswerien aȝein þe swinc..þet heo her uor his luue edmodliche þolieð. *c* **1391** Chaucer *Astrol.* ii. §10. 22 Whiche bordure is answering to the degrees of the equinoxial. **1471** Ripley *Comp. Alch.* i. (in Ashm. 1652) 130 Every Burgeon answereth to his owne Seed. **1563** J. Shute *Archit.* D iij b, The Proiecture of Them doth answer iustly with the thicknes of the pillor. **1611** Bible *Gal.* iv. 25 This Agar.. answereth to Ierusalem, which now is. **1794** Paley *Nat. Theol.* xi. §1 (1819) 169 The right arm answers accurately to the left both in size and shape. **1878** Bosw. Smith *Carthage* 420 It answers to the description of Strabo.

†**28.** *trans.* To correspond with (as in prec.), come up to. *Obs.* or *arch.*

1577 Hanmer *Anc. Eccl. Hist.* (1619) 133 So many..as now the number of all sorts cannot answer. **1671** Milton *Sams.* 1090 If thy appearance answer loud report. **1690** Locke *Hum. Und.* iii. v. (1690) 241 The Terms of our Law ..will hardly find Words that answer them in the Spanish, or Italian. **1775** Sheridan *Duenna* ii. ii, I wish she had answered her picture as well. **1789** Smyth tr. *Aldrich's Archit.* (1818) 146 Opposite to these..the rooms for the wine presses answered the baths.

†**29.** *causal.* To cause to correspond or agree *to.*

1713 Swift *Caden. & Van.* Wks. 1755 III. ii. 18 He could not answer to his fame The triumphs of that stubborn dame.

answerability (ɑːnsərəˈbɪlɪtɪ, æ-). [f. Answerable *a.* + -ility.] = Answerableness 2.

1929 *Another Milestone* (Brit. & For. Bible Soc.) 18 The answerability of the Christian West for such a situation. **1949** *Sc. Jrnl. Theol.* II. 280 Terms like Responsibility and its Anglo-Saxon equivalent answerability, have become household words on the lips of those who have contrived to keep abreast of recent theological thought.

answerable (ˈɑːnsərəb(ə)l, æ-), *a.* Also 6 **aunswerable.** [f. answer *v.* and *sb.* + -able (an early instance of this as a living Eng. suffix).]

I. Liable to answer to a charge.

1. Liable to be called to account; under legal or moral obligation; responsible, accountable. **a.** *absol.* or with *subord. cl.*

1596 Shaks. *1 Hen. IV,* ii. iv. 571 If he haue robb'd these men, He shall be answerable. **1601** F. Tate *Househ. Ord. Ed. II,* §12 (1876) 12 He shalbe aunswerable if any peril happen. **1781** T. Pickering in Sparks *Corr. Am. Rev.* (1853) III. 419 He was answerable with his head, if the King's army were not duly supplied. **1828** Scott *F.M. Perth* I. 105, I will be answerable that this galliard meant but some Saint Valentine's jest.

b. *to* an authority.

1548 Udall, etc. *Erasm. Par. Hebr.* xii. (R.) You must nedes be answerable vnto your hie prieste and his lawe. **1640–1** *Kirkcudbr. War-Comm. Min. Bk.* (1855) 75 The Committie ordaines Barquhillantie..to be answerable to the Commissar Depute. **1775** Adair *Amer. Ind.* 239, I imagined I should be answerable to myself for every accident that might befal them. **1869** Freeman *Norm. Conq.* III. xiii. 277 For the good administration of which the magistrate..was answerable to the power which appointed him.

c. *for* an act or its results, a debt, or any implied duty or obligation.

a **1667** Jer. Taylor *Serm.* Ded., He is highly answerable for his talent. **1699** Bentley *Phal.* 378 Mr. B...at least is answerable for the Language of his Book. **1722** De Foe *Moll. Fl.* (1840) 178 She would be answerable for her on all accounts. **1768** Blackstone *Comm.* II. 459 The ship and tackle..are answerable (as well as the person of the borrower) for the money lent. **1837** J. H. Newman *Par. Serm.* (ed. 3) I. ii. 25 Both Scripture and conscience tell us we are answerable for what we do. **1863** Kemble *Resid. Georgia* 24 Slavery is answerable for all the evils.

II. Capable of answering requirements, purposes.

2. Such as responds to demands, needs, wishes; suitable, fitting, proper, becoming. **a.** *absol. arch.*

1571 Digges *Geom. Pract.* iv. xxiv. E e iij, Ye shall there in his answerable Chapiter, receiue rules for the inuention of his capacitie superficiall. **1594** Carew *Huarte's Exam. Wits* (1616) 102 If he who hath any answerable nature, giue himselfe to make verses. **1691** Wood *Ath. Oxon.* II/740 Attended with an answerable train, in rich Liveries. **1756** Burke *Vind. Nat. Soc.* Wks. I. 47 His reception was answerable. **1828** Carlyle *Misc.* I. (1857) 193 The most answerable things in the world.

b. with *to. arch.*

1575 Thynne in *Animadv.* Introd. 54 Thee performance wherof shall..bee..answerable unto your callinge, and profitable unto mee. **1628** tr. *Camden's Hist. Eliz.* ii. (1688) 228 A Guard answerable to his Royal Dignity. **1658** J. Rowland *Mouffet's Theat. Ins.* 907 A death answerable to his life. **1754** Richardson *Grandison* II. xxxii. 311 Her treatment..was not answerable to her merits.

3. Corresponding, correspondent, accordant, agreeable. **a.** *absol. arch.*

a **1586** Sidney (J.) A likeness..answerable enough in some features and colours, but erring in others. **1612** T. Taylor *Comm. Titus* ii. 12 (1619) 467 The Gospel bringeth saluation, but looketh for an answerable returne. **1673** Cave *Prim. Chr.* ii. i. 4 Humility—a mean estimation of ourselves and an answerable Carriage towards others. **1775** Adair *Amer. Ind.* 90 If the seasons have been answerable..the old women pay their reputed prophet. **1827** Hare *Gues. Truth* (1859) 264 It is a difficulty which presses on all such as have ever made a venture into the higher regions of thought, to discover anything like answerable realities,—to *atone* their ideas with their perceptions.

b. with *to. arch.*

1580 Lyly *Euph.* 252 If the courtesie of Englande be aunswerable to the custome of Pilgrimes. **1638** Chillingw. *Relig. Prot.* i. i. §1. 30, I feare your proceedings will be answerable to these beginnings! **1718** *Free-thinker* No. 80. 177 Some young Princess whose Birth is answerable to your own. **1869** A. Morris *Open Secret* i. 13 The themes..are.. too momentous to be introduced into common..talk in a manner answerable to their sacredness.

4. Corresponding in quantity or amount; proportional, commensurate. **a.** *absol. arch.*

1604 Edmonds *Observ. Cæsar's Comm.* 7 Eminent and extraordinarie attempts..are thought worthie their answerable rewards. **1622** Heylin *Cosmogr.* ii. (1682) 49 Stretched out in great length..but not of answerable breadth. *a* **1716** South *Wks.* 1717 VI. 400 But their success was answerable.

b. with *to.*

1617 J. Taylor (Water P.) *Lond. to Hamburgh* C, His post-like legges were answerable to the rest of the great frame which they supported. **1693** Evelyn *De la Quint. Compl. Gard.* 78 With a thickness answerable to their height. **1769** Sir J. Reynolds *Disc.* (1876) 314 Render your future progress answerable to your past improvement. **1844** Lingard *Anglo-Sax. Ch.* II. xiv. (1858) 300 The success of their labours was answerable to the purity of their motives.

5. Equivalent, equal; adequate, sufficient (*to*). *arch.*

1581 Marbeck *Bk. of Notes* 909 This word Reward..the schoolemen, doe fondly set it to be aunswerable to a deseruing which they call merite. **1594** Blundevil *Exerc.* i. xii. (ed. 7) 37 One whole Integrum, which being added to 2344, will be answerable to the second number of the Question. **1645** Rutherford *Trial & Tri. Faith* (1845) 5 An answerable number of men and angels. **1801** Wellington *Desp.* 613 The revenue of that Island will [not] be found answerable to its necessary expenditure.

†**6.** quasi-*adv.* Answerably; conformably. *Obs.*

1640–1 *Kirkcudbr. War-Comm. Min. Bk.* (1855) 61 That they may be..punished answerable to thair deservings. **1681** Manton *Serm. Ps.* cxix. 166 Wks. IX. 226 Live answerable to your hope.

III. *passively.*

7. Able to be answered. *rare.*

1697 J. Collier *Ess. Mor. Subj.* (L.) His best reasons are answerable; his worst are not worthy of being answered. **1881** *Spect.* 19 Nov. 1456/1 An Austrian statesman.. suggests solid, if answerable, reasons.

ˈanswerableness. [f. prec. + -ness.] The quality of being answerable.

1. Correspondency, conformity, adaptation. *arch.*

1583 Golding *Calvin on Deut.* xvi. 95 So as there may be a mutual answerablenesse on both sides. **1659** Hammond *On Ps.* cl. 3 The answerableness of the notes in Musick to those observed by nature. **1752** Law *Spir. Love* i. (1816) 45 There are but three forms of nature, in answerableness to the threefold working of the triune Deity.

2. Liability to be called to account; responsibility.

1850 Lynch *Theoph. Trin.* i. 15 To feel..our dependence upon God, and our distinct personality and answerableness.

answerably (ˈɑːnsərəblɪ, æ-), *adv. arch.* [f. as prec. + -ly².] In an answerable manner; correspondingly, proportionally, conformably, suitably, fittingly. **a.** *absol.*

1611 Speed *Hist. Gt. Brit.* vi. xxv. (1632) 129 Had his mind been answerably furnished with vertue. **1662** Fuller *Worthies* (1840) III. 317 Held the state of a bishop, answerably habited. **1713** Derham *Phys.-Theol.* v. iv. 333 If Beasts had been made answerably bigger, there would not have been Grass enough. **1748** Richardson *Clarissa* (1811) VI. 147 May I behave answerably!

b. with *to.* Conformably to, consistently with.

1658 Sir T. Browne *Gard. Cyrus* II. 504 Answerably unto the wisdom of that eminent Botanologer. **1698** [R. Fergusson] *View of Eccles.* Pref., He had acted but answerably to the Badge he wears, etc. **1728** Morgan *Algiers* I. iv. 114 Rewarded him answerably to his Demerits.

†**ˈanswerage.** *Obs. rare*⁻¹. [f. answer + -age; cf. *break-age.*] The action of answering.

1642 *Declar. House Comm.* 21 July 8 Rather inflict an exemplary punishment on the contriver of such a scandalous Pamphlet, then condescend unto the answerage of it.

answerer (ˈɑːnsərə(r), æ-). Also 6 **ansurer, aunswerer.** [f. as prec. + -er¹.] One who answers.

1. One who replies to a charge, objection, argument or statement.

1533 MORE *Debell. Salem* Wks. 1557, 987/1 This good answerer hath heere borne himself so wel. **1638** CHILLINGW. *Relig. Prot.* I. 22 Pref., Which the answerer..clearly demonstrated. **1714** SHAFTESB. *Charac.* v. ii. (1737) III. 270 Authors who subsist wholly by the criticizing or commenting Practice upon others..distinguish'd by the title of Answerers. **1838** HALLAM *Hist. Lit.* IV. iv. ii. §30. 38 The *Defensio* did not want answerers in England.

2. One who replies to a question or appeal.

a **1556** CRANMER *Wks.* I. 66 Your wise dialogue..between the curious questioner [and] the foolish answerer. **1666** *Phil. Trans.* I. 189 Inquiries that require Learning or Skill in the Answerer. **1796** MORSE *Amer. Geog.* II. 188 The best answerer..receives a premium of books. **1866** J. MARTINEAU *Ess.* I. 119 Such questions are sure to find answerers.

3. One who answers back, or makes impertinent retorts.

1552 LATIMER *Serm. Lord's Prayer* ii. II. 26 Servants.. shall not be murmurers, nor froward answerers.

†**4.** One accepting a challenge. *Obs.*

1511 in Ellis *Orig. Lett.* II. 60 I. 182 That every gentilman answerer doo subscribe his name to the Articles. **1525** LD. BERNERS *Froiss.* II. clvii. 435 The prise of the iustes of the aunswerers..was gyuen to the frenche kynge.

†**5.** One responsible. *esp.* The person answerable to the Court of Augmentation for the rents and profits. *Obs.*

? **1539** *Plumpton Corr.* 234 One farme hold..which..I did speake to the Ansurer for the use of the said children.

answering (ˈɑːnsərɪŋ, æ-), *vbl. sb.* [f. ANSWER *v.* + -ING¹.]

1. The action of replying or responding to a charge, inquiry, argument, etc.; answer, reply.

1375 BARBOUR *Bruce* IV. 235 Thai mak ay thair ansuering In-till dowbill vndirstanding. *c* **1450** LONELICH *Grail* xix. 168 Of al thing he ȝaf hem answeringe. **1579** FULKE *Heskins's Parl.* 374 As for Damascenes authoritie..it is not worth the aunswering. *Mod.* His answering in the examination was excellent.

†**2.** The action of meeting a liability. *Obs. rare.*

1658 CROMWELL *Sp.* 25 Jan. (Carl.) Let God move your hearts for the answering of anything that shall be due unto the nation.

†**3.** Correspondency, adaptation. *Obs. rare.*

1674 N. FAIRFAX *Bulk & Selv.* 2 The answerings or analogies of beings, have been hitherto but ill pitcht or adjusted. **1696** PHILLIPS, *Descant*..signifying the answering of quick Notes in one part unto a slower measure in the other.

4. Special Comb. **answering machine**, a machine which answers incoming telephone calls by repeating a pre-recorded message to the caller (and by recording a message left by the caller for subsequent audio playback); **answering service**, an agency that receives and answers telephone calls for its clients.

1961 *Daily Mail* 25 July 1/3 The quarterly rent for a coin box is to go up from 11s 3d to £1, but for an *answering machine it will go down from £10 to £8. **1985** *New Yorker* 18 Mar. 46/3 Then Kate remembers that she has to change the message on the answering machine. **1941** L. G. BLOCHMAN *See you at Morgue* (1946) xiv. 95, I was using the telephone *answering service. **1961** S. PRICE *Just for Record* i. 13 The phone hasn't rung all day because I've switched over to the answering service. **1984** *Listener* 1 Nov. 2/3 BT runs..radio phones and pagers, answering services, and recently has even gone into manufacturing its own slimphones.

ˈ**answering**, *ppl. a.* [f. as prec. + -ING².]

1. Making, giving, or constituting a reply or response.

1533 FRITH (*title*) A Book..answering to M. More's Letter. **1727** POPE *Dunc.* IV. 437 And answering gin-shops sourer sighs return. **1801** SOUTHEY *Thalaba* v. xliii, In awe the youth received the answering voice. **1849** MACAULAY *Hist. Eng.* II. 386 The boats which covered the Thames gave an answering cheer.

2. Corresponding, correspondent (*to*).

1801 SOUTHEY *Thalaba* XII. xxvii, Where the sceptre in the Idol's hand Touch'd the Round Altar, in its answering realm, Earth felt the stroke. **1845** TRENCH *Huls. Lect.* II. v. 223 The world's expectation..has an answering fact. **1857** BUCKLE *Civilis.* I. ix. 569 The French have never had anything answering to our yeomanry.

ˈ**answeringly**, *adv. rare.* [f. prec. + -LY².] Correspondingly.

c **1449** PECOCK *Repr.* 351 Ech man, which wole trowe that thilk voice was seid in the eir ouȝte answeringli trowe that thilk voice was spokun by the feend. **1865** RUSKIN *Sesame* 3 The answeringly wider spreading..of the irrigation of literature.

answerless (ˈɑːnsəlɪs, æ-), *a. rare.* [f. ANSWER *sb.* + -LESS.]

1. Without an answer, having no answer. **a.** Having no answer to give. **b.** Having received no answer. **c.** That is, or contains, no answer.

1533 MORE *Debell. Salem* Wks. 1557, 988/1 And then as you se this good man had ben quyt answerlesse. **1586** *Let. to Earle Leycester* 32 Excuse my doutefulnesse, and take in good part my answere answerelesse.

2. Having no possible answer, unanswerable. (Cf. *countless, endless.*)

1822 BYRON *Juan* VI. lxiii, Our ultimate existence? what's our present? Are questions answerless. **1870** SPURGEON *Treas. David* Ps. xviii. 19 Why Jehovah should delight in us is an answerless question.

ˈ**answerlessly**, *adv. rare*⁻¹. [f. prec. + -LY².] In an answerless manner; in a way that is no answer. (See ANSWERLESS 1 c.)

1620 BP. HALL *Hon. Maried Clergie* I. §1 Answered indeed; but, as he said, δοτα ανεκδοτα—answerlesly.

answerphone (ˈɑːnsəfəʊn, æ-). Also **Ansafone** (*proprietary*), **ansaphone**, etc. [f. alteration of ANSWER *sb.* or *v.* + PHONE *sb.*².] = *answering machine* s.v. ANSWERING *vbl. sb.* 4.

1963 *Official Gaz.* (U.S. Patent Office) 11 June TM67 Ansa Fone Corp., Inglewood, Calif. **1970** *Trade Marks Jrnl.* 11 Nov. 1897/1 *Ansafone*... Sound recording and sound reproducing apparatus, all for use with telephones. Ansafone Limited, Lyon Way, Frimley Road, Camberley, Surrey; Manufacturers and Merchants. **1973** *Official Gaz.* (U.S. Patent Office) 20 Mar. TM155/1 Dictaphone Corporation, Bridgeport Conn... Ansafone... For automatic telephone answering device. **1976** *Derbyshire Times* (Peak ed.) 3 Sept. 11/1 (Advt.), Answerphone service. **1977** *Oxf. Univ. Gaz.* 13 Oct. 147/1 (Advt.), After-hours ansaphone service with fast ansaback. **1978** *Jrnl. R. Soc. Arts* CXXVI. 270/1 Apart from the Ansaphone, some consultancies in Germany are already manning the telephone at weekends to discuss jobs with interested applicants. **1982** *Financial Times* 22 Dec. 6 The move by NEC..assures Ansaphone of a place in a market in which a number of British companies intend to compete. **1984** *Daily Tel.* 2 Feb. 3/3 Clients on the third line will hear an answerphone message asking them to try again five minutes later.

ant (ænt). Forms: 1 (*W. Sax.*) **ǽmete, -ette, -ytte,** 3–4 **amete (amote), amte,** 4–6 **ampte,** 5–6 **ante,** 5–7 **annt,** 6– **ant.** Also 1 (*Anglian*) ***émete,** 3–4 **emete (-atte),** 4–6 **emote,** 6 **emmette, -otte (-ont), amyte, emet,** 6–7 **emmot(t,** 6– **emmet.** *Pl.* **ants** (1 **ǽmetan,** 2–4 **ameten,** 4 **amptes**). [OE. *ǽmete, émete*, cogn. w. OHG. *âmeiza*, WGer. **âmaitjô*, f. *á-* (see Æ- *pref.*) off, away + *maitan*, ON. *meita*, OHG. *meizan* 'to cut,' as if 'the cutter or biter off.' (Graff.) The OE. became in 12–13th c. *āmete* or *ēmete* in different dialects; *āmete* has by suppression of medial vowel and bringing together of two consonants become *amte* (*ampte*), *ante* (cf. *account* for *accompte*), *ant*; *ēmete*, retaining the medial vowel, is now EMMET, q.v. *Ant* is the leading literary form.]

1. a. A small social insect of the Hymenopterous order, celebrated for its industry; an emmet, a pismire. There are several genera and many species, exhibiting in their various habits and economy some of the most remarkable phenomena of the insect world. (For other quotations see EMMET.)

c **1000** *Sax. Leechd.* I. 87 Æmettan ægru ȝenim. **1297** R. GLOUC. 296 As þycke as ameten crepeþ in an amete hulle. **1340** *Ayenb.* 141 Alsuo ase þe litel amote. **1382** WYCLIF *Prov.* xxx. 25 Amptis [**1388** amtis] a feble puple, that greithen in rep time mete to them. **1430** LYDG. *Chron. Troy* I. i, He sawe by the earthe lowe Of Antes crepe passing greate plente. **1533** ELYOT *Cast. Helth* III. xii. 66b, The lyttelle ant or emote helpeth up his felowe. **1547** BOORDE *Brev. Health* clxi. 58 Amytes, or Pysmars, or Antes. **1585** LLOYD *Treas. Health* B viij, Pouder of Amptes, myxte with Oyle. **1578** MASCALL *Planting* (1592) 58 For to destroy Emets or Antes, which be about a Tree. **1611** BIBLE *Prov.* vi. 6 Goe to the Ant [*Wycl.* ampte, amte, *Coverd.* Emmet], thou sluggard. **1633** G. HERBERT *Ch. Mil.* in *Temple* 184 The smallest ant or atome knows thy power. **1642** SIR T. BROWNE *Relig. Med.* 30 The wisdome of Bees, Annts and Spiders. **1733** POPE *Ess. Man* III. 184 The Ant's republic, and the realm of Bees. **1838** *Penny Cycl.* X. 372 Formic Acid, or acid of ants. **1861** HULME *Moquin-Tandon* II. IV. i. 213 When the Red Ant (*Formica Rufa*) crawls over a piece of litmus paper, it produces a red track.

b. In colloq. phr. ***to have ants in one's pants*** (orig. *U.S.*), to fidget constantly, esp. because of extreme agitation, excitement, nervousness, etc.; to be impatient or restless. Cf. ANTSY *a.*

[**1939** KAUFMAN & HART *Man who came to Dinner* I. ii. 62 'I'm in love.'..'I'll pull you out of this Miss Stardust..I'll get the ants out of those moonlit pants.'] **1940** 'C. WOOLRICH' *Bride wore Black* III. iii. 181 Wagner started to have ants in his pants. **1942** R. G. DEAN *Layoff* xvi. 158 You have ants in your pants tonight. **1954** E. MCLEOD tr. *Colette's Vagabond* I. i. 5 Once again I'm ready too soon. My friend..takes me to task..'You've always got ants in your pants.' **1967** *Listener* 30 Nov. 715/2 Notoriously, the American people have always had ants in the pants, or, as Mr Allsop puts it, an urge 'to soak up the zircon light of potluck adventure from the bordermen'. **1986** *Washington Post* 10 July B5/3 Uncle Milton has ants in his pants.

2. ant-eggs, ants' eggs, popular name of the larvæ of ants (a favourite food of young pheasants).

c **1000** [See 1]. **1398** TREVISA *Barth. De P.R.* XIX. xciii. 916 Yf amptes egges..ben remeuyd..the amptes gadreth theim and beeryth theym ayen to theyr neest. *c* **1420** *Pallad. on Husb.* I. 680 Annt eyron yeve hem [young pheasants] eke. **1585** LLOYD *Treas. Health* F vj, Stampe Amptes egges and strain them thorough a clothe. **1663** BUTLER *Hud.* I. iii. 325 Till purging Comfits and Ants Eggs Had almost brought him off his Legs. **1753** CHAMBERS *Cycl. Supp.* s.v., Little vermicles, as small as mites, commonly called Ants-eggs. **1879** LUBBOCK *Sci. Lect.* iii. 69 The larvæ of ants..when full grown, turn into pupæ..constituting the so-called 'ant-eggs.'

3. white ant: A very destructive social insect of the Neuropterous order, also called Termite.

[*c* **1328** JORDANUS 53 Est etiam genus parvissimarum formicarum sicut lana albarum, quarum durities dentium, etc. **1713** BLUTEAU *Port. Dict.*, Formigas biancas.] **1729** A. HAMILTON *New Acct. E. Indies* II. xlvii, The white ants, which are really insects, that..can do much mischief to cloth, timber, etc. **1842** *Penny Cycl.* XXIV. 233 The Termites, or white ants, as they are often called, though they have little affinity with the true ants, are chiefly confined to the tropics. **1857** LIVINGSTONE *Trav.* xxvii. 540 The white ants..are the chief agents employed in forming a fertile soil.

4. *attrib.* and *Comb.*, as ***ant-colony, -community, -man***; **ant-bird**, any bird of the ant-eating family Formicariidæ, ant-thrush; **ant-catcher** = ANT-THRUSH; **ant-cow**, a popular name for the aphides kept and tended by ants for the sake of the sweet fluid that they extract from them; **ant-eggs, ants' eggs**, properly, the eggs of ants; popularly applied to their larvæ or pupæ; **ant-guest**, an animal of any other species, that habitually lives in ants' nests; **ant-heap, ant-hillock,** = ANT-HILL; **ant-hive**, an artificial nest for ants; **ant-orchis**, a terrestrial Australasian orchid of the species *Chiloglottis gunnii* (Morris *Austral English*, 1898); **ant-rice** (see quot.); **ants' wood** = *saffron plum* (SAFFRON B. b); †**ant-wart** (see quot.); **ant-worm**, the larva of the ant; **ant-wren**, W. Swainson's name for a South American ant-eating bird of the genus *Formicivora*, included by P. L. Sclater in the subfamily Formicariinæ in his division of the family Formicariidæ, the ant-thrushes. Also obvious syntactic combinations, as ***ant-eating, -like.***

Also ANT-BEAR, ANT-EATER, ANT-EGG, ANT-FLY, ANT-HILL, ANT-LION, ANT-THRUSH q.v.

1858 SCLATER in *Proc. Zool. Soc.* 13 Apr. 202 Synopsis of the American *Ant-birds (Formicariidæ). **1868** CHAMBERS *Encycl.* s.v., The true *ant-catchers..are of comparatively sober plumage, live among the huge ant-hills, seldom fly. **1897** J. H. COMSTOCK *Insect Life* viii. 276 The workers are by far the most interesting portion of the *ant colony. **1909** H. C. MCCOOK (*title*) *Ant communities and how they are governed. **1924** J. A. THOMSON *Sci. Old & New* xii. 67 The success of the ant-community depends on a semi-repression of the workers. **1875** *Encycl. Brit.* II. 98/1 The Coccidæ in America take the place of the European aphides as *ant-cows. **1875** BLAKE *Zool.* 85 The *ant-eating forms of edentata. **1666** *Phil. Trans.* No. 23. 426 Upon opening of these Banks, I observe first a white substance, which..looks like the scatterings of fine white Sugar or Salt... This same substance..I finde in the Ants themselves, which I take to be the true *Ants Eggs. *Ibid.* 427 In the Morning they bring up those of their Young (that are vulgarly call'd Ants Eggs) towards the top of the Bank. **1834** *Penny Cycl.* II. 61/1 To collect the cocoons (popularly and erroneously called ants'-eggs) in quantity as food for nightingales and larks. **1879** LUBBOCK *Sci. Lect.* iii. 72 The majority of these *ant-guests are beetles. **1591** PERCIVALL *Sp. Dict., Hormiguero*, an *ant heape, *Formicarium, myrmicetum.* **1859** E. BURRITT in Smiles *Self-Help* 82 That plodding, patient, persevering process of accretion which builds the ant-heap. **1657** TRAPP *Comm. Ps.* cxiii. 4 He looketh on the earth as on an *Ant-hillock. *a* **1719** ADDISON (J.) Those who have seen ant-hillocks, have..perceived those small heaps of corn about their nests. **1826** KIRBY & SPENCE *Entomol.* (1828) II. xvii. 58 Huber invented a kind of *ant-hive. **1879** GEO. ELIOT *Theoph. Such* xvii. 302 Every petty *ant-like performance. **1901** H. G. WELLS *First Men in Moon* xxii. 272 These ant-like beings, these ant-men. **1949** E. SITWELL *Canticle of Rose* 254 But I saw the little *Ant-men as they ran. **1879** LUBBOCK *Sci. Lect.* iv. 109 A Texan ant..is also a harvesting species, storing up especially the grains of *Aristida oligantha*, the so-called *'ant rice.' **1884** *Ants' Wood [see SAFFRON B. b]. **1585** *Nomenclator* (N.) An *ant-wart, which, being deepe-rooted, broad below, and little above, doth make one feele, as it were, the stinging of ants. **1747** W. GOULD *Acc. Eng. Ants* 39 *Ant Worms can only a little turn or extend their Bodies. **1825** W. SWAINSON in *Zool. Jrnl.* (1826) II. 146 The *Formicivoræ*, or *Ant-Wrens, are all of them very small.

ant, obs. form of AUNT, and of AND.

an't (ɑːnt), contraction of *are n't, are not*; colloquially for *am not*; and in illiterate or dialect speech for *is not, has not* (*han't*). A later and still more illiterate form is AINT, q.v.

1706 E. WARD *Hud. Rediv.* (1711) I. I. 24 But if your Eyes a'n't quick of Motion, They'll play the Rogue, that gave the Caution. **1734** FIELDING *Old Man* 1007/1 Ha, ha, ha! an't we? no! How ignorant it is! **1737**—— *Hist. Reg.* I. i, No more I an't, sir. **1812** H. & J. SMITH *Rej. Addr.* (1873) 69 No, that a'nt it, says he. **1828** LYTTON *Pelham* lxii. (1853) 172 A'n't we behind hand? **1864** TENNYSON *North. Farm.* xiii, A mowt 'a taäken Joänes, as 'ant a 'aäpoth o' sense.

†**an't** (ənt). *Obs.* Variant of *on't*, properly 'on it,' but frequently, in 16th c. and still dialectally, as = *o't* 'of it.' See ON.

1589 *Pappe w. Hatchet* (1844) 23 At least three figures in that line, besides, the wit ant. ? **1589** SHAKS. *L.L.L.* (Q°.) v. ii. 460, I see the tricke ant!

ant-, *pref.*, short f. ANTI- 'against,' before vowels, and *h-*; in words already in Gr. as ἀνταγωνιστής antagonist, and occas. in mod. words, as *ant-acid* (less commonly *anti-acid*).

-ant¹, *suffix*, a. Fr. *-ant*, sometimes:—L. *-entem, -āntem, -ēntem*, ending of pres. pple. (see -ENT); sometimes a later adaptation of *-āntem* only. All the participial forms were in OFr. levelled under *-ant*, the sole ending of the pr. pple., as L. *amānt-, vidēnt-, sedēnt-, crēdent-em* in Fr.

amant, voyant, séant, croyant. But other words were subsequently adopted in their L. stem form, as *prudent, présent, élégant*. Hence Fr. words in *-ant* are of two kinds, one answering to L. *-ānt*, the other to L. *-ent, -ēnt*. All were adopted, in their actual Fr. forms, in Eng., where they subseq. became *-'aunt*; then again, with the change of stress, *-ant*, as L. *affīdent-em, diffī-dent-em, plicānt-em, servient-em, tenēnt-em*, OFr. *afiant, defiant, pliant, serjeant, tenant*, ME. *afi'a(u)nt, defi'a(u)nt, pli'a(u)nt, serje'aunt, te'naunt*. Most of them retain *-ant*, e.g. *claimant, pleasant, poursuivant, servant, suppliant, valiant*; but since 1500 some have been refashioned with *-ent* after L., wholly (as *apparaunt, -ent*), or partly (as in *pendant, -ent, dependant, -ent, ascendant, -ent*). Hence, inconsistency and uncertainty in the present spelling of many words, in which L. and Fr. analogies are at variance: see -ENT. Many new words of this class have been adopted from L. *-āntem* directly or through later Fr., or have been formed on L. analogies, or adopted from mod.Fr. and Romance *-ant, -ante*; as *concomitant, protestant, commandant, anæsthesiant*. For sense, see -ENT.

-ant[2], for -AND[1], an assimilation of the northern Eng. to the Fr. form of the pres. pple., as in *allwealdant, -ent*. More commonly the converse took place, the native *-and* being substituted by northern writers for *-ant*, as in *aboundand, sembland*.

-ant[3], a corruption of *-an* from various sources, due to confusion and assimilation of final *-an, -and, -ant*, as in *pagean(t, peasan(t, pheasan(t, truan(t, tyran(t*. Cf. *gyane, gyand*, obs. forms of *giant*.

‖**anta** ('æntə). *Arch.* Commonly in pl. **antæ**. [L. *antæ* (no sing.), perh. f. *ante* before. Cf. ANTES.] A square pilaster on either side of a door, or at the corner of a building.

1751 CHAMBERS *Cycl.* s.v., The projecture of the *Antæ* should always equal that of the ornaments. **1837** *Penny Cycl.* VII. 220/1 The Greeks never employed antæ, except at an angle or the extremity of a wall.. Sometimes the Doric anta has a simple kind of moulding and groove at its foot.

Comb. **anta-cap** (pl. **antæ-caps**), the capital or top of an anta.

1837 *Penny Cycl.* VII. 220/1 [The Greeks] purposely gave to such pilasters, bases and antæ-caps dissimilar from those of the columns.. The Doric anta-cap is very simple, and its abacus and other mouldings much narrower than those of the column-capital.

Antabuse ('æntəbju:z). Also **antabuse**. [f. ANTI- + ABUSE *sb.*] A proprietary name for disulfiram, a substance which causes a severe unpleasant reaction to the subsequent ingestion of alcohol and is given as tablets in the treatment of alcoholism.

1948 *Lancet* 25 Dec. 1002/1 We have further examined this peculiar effect of diethylthiuramdisulphide (trade name 'Antabuse'). **1950** *Official Gaz.* (U.S. Patent Office) 16 May 711/2 Ayerst, McKenna & Harrison Limited, New York and Rouses Point, N.Y... *Antabuse*... For medicinal preparation for the treatment of alcohol. **1959** *Observer* 1 Nov. 20/4 The cure..was done by kindness and re-education not antabuse. **1964** R. A. HEINLEIN *Farnham's Freehold* iii. 52 Antabuse doesn't stop the craving; it simply makes the patient deathly ill if he drinks. **1971** *Trade Marks Jrnl.* 10 Feb. 223/2 *Antabuse*... Pharmaceutical preparations and substances. A/S Dumex (Dumex Limited) .., Copenhagen, Denmark. **1976** SMYTHIES & CORBETT *Psychiatry* ix. 183 In some centers he is given a controlled antabuse reaction, but others consider it potentially too dangerous to use. **1984** *Listener* 22 Nov. 15/1 What Antabuse actually does is to interfere with the body's breakdown of alcohol and in so doing causes a build-up of the chemical acetaldehyde.

antacid (ænt'æsɪd), *a.* and *sb.* Also **antiacid**. [f. ANT- = Gr. ἀντί against + ACID.]

A. *adj.* Having the power of counteracting acidity, *esp.* in the stomach.

1732 ARBUTHNOT *Rules of Diet* 249 Carrots.. antiacid and fattening. **1875** WOOD *Therap.* (1879) 452 Magnesia and its carbonate act in the same manner.. being both antacid and laxative. **1880** *Times* 5 Oct. 4/6 The use of glucose, antacid finings, and more recondite drugs [by brewers].

B. *sb.* A remedy for, or preventive of, acidity.

1732 ARBUTHNOT (J.) Oils are anti-acids, so far as they blunt acrimony. **1753** CHAMBERS *Cycl. Supp., Antacids* are chiefly of the alcalious kind. **1861** HULME *Moquin-Tandon* II. III. ii. 87 The shell of the oyster.. was formerly extolled as a powerful absorbent and antiacid.

antacrid (ænt'ækrɪd), *a.* [f. ANT- + ACRID.]

1853 MAYNE *Exp. Lex., Antacrid*, applied to medicines which have power to correct an acrid condition of the secretions.

antæ: see ANTA.

antagonal (æn'tægənəl), *a. rare*[−1]. [irreg. f. stem of ANTAGON-ISM + -AL[1]; app. after L. *agōnāl-is*.] In antagonism; antagonistic.

1863 J. WOODFORD *Chr. Sanct.* 70 Whilst the antagonal principles of faith and sight fight out their contest.

antagonism (æn'tægənɪz(ə)m). [ad. Gr. ἀνταγώνισμα, n. of action f. ἀνταγωνίζ-εσθαι: see ANTAGONIZE. Cf. mod.Fr. *antagonisme*. Not in Johnson; in Todd 1818 without quot.]

1. a. The mutual resistance or active opposition of two opposing forces, physical or mental; active opposition to a force.

1839 *Blackw. Mag.* XLVI. 647 When this antagonism ceased to operate. **1859** MILL *Liberty* ii. (1865) 28/1 Opinions favourable.. to sociality and individuality, to liberty and discipline, and all the other standing antagonisms of practical life. **1880** ADYE in *19th Cent.* No. 38. 709 Mixing up castes and nationalities with a view to class antagonism.

b. *spec.* in *Phys.* and *Art.*

1853 MAYNE *Exp. Lex., Antagonism*, a term for the action of those muscles which are opposed to each other in their office. **1859** MRS. SCHIMMELPENNINCK *Princ. Beauty* III. ii. §26 Antagonism is the juxtaposition of opposing expressions in equally intense degree. **1872** DARWIN *Emotions* vii. 197 The central fasciæ of the frontal muscle would have contracted in antagonism. **1872** BLACKIE *Lays Highl.* Introd. 22 One of Beethoven's cunningly balanced antagonisms of sweet sound.

c. Const. Antagonism *between* two things, *to* or *against* a thing; to be or act in antagonism *to*; to be in, or come into antagonism *with*.

1838 *Blackw. Mag.* XLIV. 587 Consciousness is an act of antagonism against the modification of man's natural being. **1849** COBDEN *Speeches* 37 The Government had not placed itself in antagonism to them. **1855** H. REED *Lect. Eng. Hist.* iv. 443 The natural antagonism of a base to a noble nature. *a* **1862** BUCKLE *Civiliz.* (1869) III. iii. 171 This antagonism between the aristocratic and trading spirit. **1870** DISRAELI *Lothair* xlviii. 260 That the Church is in antagonism with political freedom. **1878** HUXLEY *Physiogr.* Pref. 7 In direct antagonism to the fundamental principles of scientific education. **1879** MCCARTHY *Own Times* II. 227 Russia.. was brought into chronic antagonism with Turkey.

d. *Biochem.* Inhibition of or interference with the action of a substance or organism (as a salt, microbe, mould, etc.) by another substance or organism.

1874 W. ROBERTS in *Phil. Trans. R. Soc.* CLXIV. 466 There was an antagonism between the growth of certain races of *Bacteria* and certain other races of *Bacteria*. **1938** *Ann. Reg. 1937* 349 Much research was done on synergism and antagonism of vitamins. **1949** H. W. FLOREY *Antibiotics* II. VIII. xv. 636 When a mixture of micro-organisms is grown together, certain bacteria or moulds will inhibit the growth of other bacteria or moulds. This phenomenon is known as 'bacterial antagonism'.

2. An opposing force or principle.

1840 CARLYLE *Heroes* (1858) 340 These two Antagonisms at war here, in the case of Laud and the Puritans, are as old nearly as the world. *a* **1859** DE QUINCEY in Page *Life* (1877) II. xix. 186 As if resulting from mighty and equal antagonisms. **1866** FERRIER *Lect. Grk. Philos.* I. xiv. 435 An antagonism put forth against the passions.

antagonist (æn'tægənɪst). [ad. (perh. through Fr. *antagoniste*, 16th c. in Litt.) L. *antagōnista* (in Jerome), ad. Gr. ἀνταγωνιστ-ής opponent, rival, n. of agent f. ἀνταγωνίζ-εσθαι: see ANTAGONIZE.]

1. One who contends with another in an athletic contest, a battle, or struggle for the mastery; an opponent, an adversary.

1599 B. JONSON *Cynthia's Rev.* v. ii, Your antagonist, or player against you. **1623** COCKERAM, *Antagonist*, an enemy. **1667** MILTON *P.L.* x. 387 Satan.. Antagonist or Heaven's Almightie King. **1790** BURKE *Fr. Rev.* 246 He that wrestles with us strengthens our nerves, and sharpens our skill. Our antagonist is our helper. **1855** PRESCOTT *Philip* I. ii. (1857) 31 Philip ran the first course. His antagonist was the Count Mansfeldt, a Flemish captain of great renown.

2. An opponent in any sphere of human action, as politics, controversy, etc.

1626 PORY in Ellis *Orig. Lett.* II. 333 III. 247 Potter and Godfrey, antagonistes to the Pope's supremacy here. **1628** PRYNNE *Cens. Cozens* 14 Marke what good vse our Antagonist makes of this conclusion. **1706** PHILLIPS, *Antagonist*.. one that in Disputation or Arguing opposes another. **1831** BREWSTER *Newton* (1855) II. xxiii. 307 This answer of Sir Isaac's.. called into the field a fresh antagonist.

3. An impersonal agent acting in opposition.

1711 ADDISON *Spect.* No. 10 ¶3 A well written Book compared with its Rivals and Antagonists, is like Moses's Serpent. **1794** SULLIVAN *View Nat.* II. 117 Fire and air act as antagonists in boiling. **1836** J. GILBERT *Chr. Atonem.* v. (1852) 136 Justice and mercy ought by no account to be considered as antagonists.

4. *Phys.* A muscle which counteracts another, contracting while the opposite one relaxes, and conversely.

1706 PHILLIPS, *Antagonista* or *Antagonist* (in Anat.) is taken for a Muscle of an opposite Situation or contrary Quality. **1751** CHAMBERS *Cycl.* s.v., We have some solitary muscles, without any Antagonists. **1880** *Syd. Soc. Lex.* s.v., The flexor muscles are the antagonists of the extensors.

5. Used *attrib.* as sb. in apposition, or adj.: = ANTAGONISTIC.

1671 MILTON *Sams.* 1628 None daring to appear antagonist. **1777** PRIESTLEY *Phil. Necess.* §4. 31 A limb is kept motionless by the equal action of antagonist muscles. **1789** T. JEFFERSON *Writ.* (1859) II. 588 The antagonist nation. **1830** COLERIDGE *Ch. & State* 141 Antagonist forces are necessarily of the same kind. **1830** SIR J. HERSCHEL *Stud. Nat. Phil.* 189 The quality of opacity is not a contrary or antagonist quality to that of transparency.

6. *Biochem.* A substance or organism that inhibits or interferes with the action of another substance or organism. Cf. ANTAGONISM 1 d. Freq. with defining word.

1889 SHOEMAKER & AULDE *Treat. Materia Med., Pharmacol.* I. I. 122 After the ingestion of a poison its physiological antagonist might be administered with the expectation that the effects of the first poison might be counteracted by the second. *Ibid.* 123 Morphine and atropine are well-known physiological antagonists. **1961** *Lancet* 12 Aug. 371/1 The adverse effects commonly produced by cytotoxic and cytostatic agents such as.. folic-acid antagonists. *Ibid.* 2 Sept. 512/2 Only one other patient with periodic paralysis has been treated with an aldosterone antagonist.

antagonistic (æn,tægə'nɪstɪk), *a.* [f. prec. + -IC.]

1. Of the nature of an antagonist; mutually opposed; actively opposed.

1632 B. JONSON *Magn. Lady* III. iv. (T.) Their valours are not yet so.. truly antagonistick as to fight. **1843** MILL *Logic* II. iv. §6 The antagonistic action of acids and alkalies. **1859** MILL *Liberty* 127 The progressive principle.. is antagonistic to the sway of Custom. **1875** WOOD *Therap.* (1879) 260 That opium and belladonna are, in their influence upon the system, antagonistic. **1881** M. WILLIAMS in *19th Cent.* No. 49. 505 Innumerable antagonistic forces which confront each other in eternal opposition.

2. *Phys.* Said of the muscles which counteract each other's action.

1845 TODD & BOWMAN *Phys. Anat.* II. 399 The action of the external and internal intercostals must be antagonistic.

antago'nistical, *a. rare.* [f. prec. + -AL[1].] Of antagonistic character or tendency.

1630 J. TAYLOR (Water P.) *Wks.* III. 76 There hath been an Antagonisticall repugnancy betwixt vs. **1842** POE *M. Roget* Wks. 1864 I. 230 Until the instances.. be sufficient in number to establish an antagonistical rule.

antago'nistically, *adv.* [f. prec. + -LY[2].] In antagonistic manner; in rivalry or active opposition.

1855 EMERSON in *Corr. Carlyle* (1883) II. 243 The solo sings the theme; the orchestra roars antagonistically. **1880** MACLEAN in *Standard* 11 Mar. (1882) 6/1 The people being so antagonistically inclined towards me.

antagonization (æn,tægənaɪ'zeɪʃən). *rare.* [f. next + -ATION.] The action of antagonizing.

1883 HOWELLS *Undisc. Country* II. 100 This question of antagonisation could be settled in a manner absolutely final.

antagonize (æn'tægənaɪz), *v.* [ad. Gr. ἀνταγωνίζ-εσθαι to struggle against, vie with, rival; f. ἀντί against + ἀγωνίζ-εσθαι to struggle, f. ἀγών a contest: see AGON.]

†**1.** *trans.* To compete with, vie with, rival. *Obs.*

1634 T. HERBERT *Trav.* 211 The Dodo which for shape and rarenesse may antigonize the Phœnix of Arabia.

2. To act in antagonism to, struggle against, contend with, oppose actively.

1742 BAILEY, *Antagonize*, to act the Part of an Opponent in arguing, to oppose, to contradict. **1773** in JOHNSON, and **1818** in TODD [only from Bailey]. **1818** KEATS *Endym.* (1851) 81 Like one huge Python Antagonising Boreas. **1865** MASSON *Rec. Brit. Philos.* 48 A so-called Scottish Philosophy of Common Sense to antagonize all this mass of English and imported Sensationalism.

b. In England, antagonizing forces must be of the same kind, but in the political phraseology of U.S. a person may antagonize (*i.e.* oppose) a measure.

1882 *Boston Evg. Transcr.* 4/3 Ex-Secretary Windom did not hesitate openly to antagonize ex-Secretary Sherman's bill. *Ibid.* 8/5 The Democrats on the committee have given notice of a determination to antagonize this and all other bills for the admission of Territories as States.

3. *Phys.* To counteract the action of (the opposite muscle).

1840 *Penny Cycl.* XVI. 65/1 These fibres.. have a constant tendency to antagonize the adductor muscle. **1860** LEWES *Phys. Com. Life* II. x. 280 The body is balanced by an incessant shifting of the muscles, one group antagonising the other. **1870** ROLLESTON *Anim. Life* 56 The ligament divaricates, when not antagonized by the adductor muscles.

4. Hence: To counteract or neutralize the action of (any force).

1833 SIR J. HERSCHEL *Astr.* viii. 285 Perpetual contest between conservative and destructive powers.. so antagonizing one another as to prevent the latter from ever acquiring an uncontrollable ascendancy. **1860** EMERSON *Cond. Life* (1861) i. 17 If Fate follows and limits power, power attends and antagonizes Fate. **1861** RAMADGE *Cur. Consump.* 49 The tumefaction of latent catarrh.. is sufficient to antagonize consumption.

5. *intr.* To act in antagonism.

1861 HULME *Moquin-Tandon* II. VI. i. 318 These organs.. act from above downwards, but without antagonizing.

6. *trans.* To render antagonistic, make an antagonist.

1882 *Echo* 20 Feb. 2/4 The very doing of this work.. antagonises certain sections of the people whose interests are supposed to be prejudiced by legislative changes.

an'tagonized, *ppl. a.* [f. prec. + -ED.] Rendered antagonistic, irreconcilably opposed.
1845 R. HAMILTON *Pop. Educ.* viii. (ed. 2) 189 Nobly standing aloof from all Sectarianism, but practically antagonised to all spurious latitude. **1877** A. SULLIVAN *New Irel.* xiv. 158 Protestant and Catholic were daily becoming more and more hopelessly antagonised.

an'tagonizer. *Phys. rare.* [f. as prec. + -ER[1].] A muscle that antagonizes another; = ANTAGONIST 4.
1879 MORRIS *Anat. Joints* 12 One set of muscles acting as antagonisers to the others.

an'tagonizing, *ppl. a.* [f. as prec. + -ING[2].] Acting in direct opposition; mutually opposing.
1810 BENTHAM *Packing* (1821) 231 To..reconcile..to each other the antagonizing ends of justice. **1817** JAS. MILL *Brit. India* II. v. v. 486 This step was vehemently opposed ..by the antagonizing party. **1848** MILL *Pol. Econ.* III. xv. §2 A complete equipoise between these antagonizing forces. **1855** BAIN *Senses & Int.* II. iv. §7 (1864) 268 The two antagonizing classes of muscles.

†**an'tagony.** *Obs. rare*[−1]. [ad. Gr. ἀνταγωνία, f. ἀντί against + ἀγωνία struggle.] Antagonism.
1643 MILTON *Divorce* viii. (1851) 42 The incommunicable antagony that is between Christ and Belial.

†**antal.** *Obs.* [ad. med.L. *antale, antalium, entalium*, of uncertain origin.] The gasteropod shell *Dentalium Entale*, or an allied species.
1657 TOMLINSON *Renou's Disp.* 461 Another Sea shell-fish, called an Antal, whose use in medicine is very frequent. **1678** PHILLIPS, *Antal*, a Sea Shell-fish of a little fingers length, streaked without, smooth and hollow within, like a little Tub[e] where the fish is contained.

antalgic (ænt'ældʒɪk), *a.* and *sb. Med.* [mod. f. ANT- + ἄλγ-ος pain + -IC.]
A. *adj.* Tending to prevent or alleviate pain.
1775 in ASH. **1839** in HOOPER *Med. Dict.* **1853** MAYNE *Exp. Lex.*, *Anodyne*, driving away pain, antalgic.
B. *sb.* A medicine or application having this tendency; 'that which softens pain, anodyne.' J.
1753 CHAMBERS *Cycl. Supp.*, *Antalgics* amount to the same with Anodynes.

antalkali (ænt'ælkəlɪ). *Med.* [f. ANT- + ALKALI.] Anything which counteracts the action of an alkali, *esp.* in the human body.
1834 *Penny Cycl.* II. 67/1 Antalkalies..are means of counteracting the presence of alkalies in the system.

antalkaline (ænt'ælkəlaɪn), *a.* and *sb. Med.* [f. prec.: cf. *alkaline.*]
A. *adj.* Counteracting the action of alkalis.
1853 MAYNE *Exp. Lex.*, *Antalkaline*, Having the power of neutralising alkalis: such are all the acids.
B. *sb.* An antalkaline substance or agent.
1811 in HOOPER *Med. Dict.*

antalphabetic (,æntælfə'bɛtɪk), *a. Phonetics.* [f. ANT- + ALPHABETIC *a.*] = ANALPHABETIC *a.* 2.
1933 JESPERSEN *Linguistica* Index 454/1 Antalphabetic symbols. **1937** [see ANALPHABETIC *a.* 2].

antambulacral (,æntæmbju:'leɪkrəl, -'ækrəl), *a. Zool.* Also **anti-amb-**. [f. ANT- + AMBULACRAL.] Opposite to what is ambulacral. (In Echinoderms it sometimes happens that the ambulacral zones do not extend from one pole of the body to the other. Where the ambulacral zone ends, the antambulacral begins, as in the apex of a sea-urchin, or the upper side of a star-fish.)
1870 ROLLESTON *Anim. Life* 142 The antiambulacral surface. **1877** HUXLEY *Anat. Inv. An.* 553 [In a Starfish] the ambulacral, and the opposite, or antambulacral faces are of equal extent.

‖**antanaclasis** (æntə'næklәsɪs). *Rhet.* ? *Obs.* [L., a. Gr. ἀντανάκλασις, f. ἀντανακλά-ειν to reflect, bend back; f. ἀντί against, in the opposite direction + ἀνακλά-ειν to break or bend back.]
1. A figure of speech, 'when the same word is repeated in a different, if not in a contrary signification; as *In thy youth learn some craft, that in thy old age thou mayest get thy living without craft.*' J.
1657 J. SMITH *Myst. Rhet.* 107 Antanaclasis, A figure when the same word is repeated in a divers if not in a contrary signification..also a retreat to the matter at the end of a long parenthesis. **1681** MANTON *Serm. Ps.* cxix. 123 Wks. 1872 VIII. 266 'That Abraham against hope believed in hope'..is an antanaclasis, an elegant figure, having the form of a contradiction. **1711** ADDISON *Spect.* No. 61 ¶3 He generally talked in the Paranomasia..but in his humble Opinion he shined most in the Antanaclasis.
2. 'A returning to the matter at the end of a long parenthesis; as *Shall that heart (which doth not only feel them, but hath all motion of his life placed in them) shall that heart, I say,* etc.' J.
1646 SIR T. BROWNE *Pseud. Ep.* 364 That mortall Antanaclasis, and desperate piece of Rhetorick. **1657** [See in 1.]

†**antana'goge.** *Rhet. Obs.* [f. ANT- + Gr. ἀναγωγή a leading or bringing up.] (See quot.)
1589 PUTTENHAM *Eng. Poesie* (Arb.) 224 Antenagoge, or the Recompencer, seemeth to make amends, for which cause it is called by the originall name in both languages, the Recompencer, as..I must needs say, that my wife is a shrevve, But such a husvvife as I knovv but a fevve. **1706** PHILLIPS, *Antanagoge*, in Rhetoric a figure; when, not being able to answer the Adversary's accusation, we return the charge, by loading him with the same Crimes. **1751** in CHAMBERS *Cycl.*; and in mod. Dicts.

antapex (ænt'eɪpɛks). *Astr.* Also **anti-apex.** [f. ANT- + APEX.] The point on the celestial sphere, situated in the constellation Columba, away from which the sun is moving; the point opposite to the apex of the solar way (cf. *solar apex* s.v. SOLAR *a.* 7).
1890 A. M. CLERKE *Syst. Stars* xxiii. 320 There would be the semblance of a general retreat from the 'apex' or solar *point de mire*, coupled with a thronging-in from all sides towards the opposite point, or 'anti-apex'. **1906** J. C. KAPTEYN in *Rep. Brit. Assoc. 1905* 258 If..we determine these lines of symmetry for several points of the sky and prolong them, they must all intersect in two points, which are no other than the apex and the antapex. **1911** *Encycl. Brit.* XXV. 791/1 The annual parallactic motion is equal to four times the parallax, for a star lying in a direction 90° from the solar apex; for stars nearer the apex or antapex it is foreshortened. **1923** *R. Astr. Soc., Monthly Notices* LXXXIII. 465 Two quantities are of fundamental importance—the angular distance of a star from the apex or ant-apex of the solar motion, and the position angle of the star relative to the apex or ant-apex. **1928** W. M. SMART *Sun, Stars & Universe* x. 171 The sun..is moving towards the solar apex with a speed of 12 miles per second, and therefore our group of stars will appear to us to move as a whole towards the solar antapex.

antaphrodisiac (,æntæfrəʊ'dɪzɪæk), *a.* and *sb.* Also **anti-aph-**. [mod. f. ANT- + Gr. ἀφροδισιακ-ός, f. ἀφροδίσιος venereal, f. 'Αφροδίτη Venus.]
A. *adj.* Tending to counteract venereal desire.
1742 BAILEY, *Antaphrodisiack*, a Term given to Medicines that extinguish Venereal Desires: also Antivenereal. **1830** LINDLEY *Nat. Syst. Bot.* 12 The whole of this order [the water lily tribe] has the reputation of being antiaphrodisiac.
B. *sb.* A medicine or application so used.
1753 in CHAMBERS *Cycl. Supp.* **1788** *Edinb. New Disp.* (1791) 119 These seeds have been celebrated as antiphrodisiacs.

antaphroditic (,æntæfrəʊ'dɪtɪk), *a.* and *sb.* [mod. f. ANT- + Gr. Ἀφροδίτη Venus + -IC.]
A. *adj.* Of use against venereal disease.
1755 in JOHNSON. **1853** in MAYNE *Exp. Lex.*
B. *sb.* **1.** A medicine so used.
1706 PHILLIPS, *Antaphroditicks*, Medicines that are us'd against the French Pox. [So in BAILEY, etc.]
†**2.** = ANTAPHRODISIAC *sb. Obs.*
1719 *Glossogr. Nova, Antiaphroditicks* are medicines that lay Lust.

anta'pology. *rare.* [f. ANT- + APOLOGY.] A reply to an apology.
1693 WETENHALL (*title*) The Antapology of the melancholy Stander-by: in answer to the Dean of St. Paul's late book. **1710** tr. *Dupin's Eccl. Hist. 16th C.* I. III. xvi. 427 [Petrus Sutor] wrote an Apology for the Vulgar Version: an Antapology Printed at Paris in 1523.

antapoplectic (,æntæpəʊ'plɛktɪk), *a.* and *sb. Med.* Also 8 **anti-**. [f. ANT- + APOPLECTIC.]
A. *adj.* Tending to prevent or cure apoplexy.
1697 *Phil. Trans.* XIX. 468 Bleedings, Purges, Diureticks, and Antapoplectick Medicines. **1720** BLAIR *ibid.* XXXI. 35 They are also Pectoral, Anti-Apoplectick. **1755** in J.
†**B.** *sb.* A medicine so used. *Obs.*
1753 CHAMBERS *Cycl. Supp.*, *Apoplectica*..a name used by some for what we more properly call Antapoplectics.

antarchism ('æntəkɪz(ə)m). *rare*[−0]. [mod. f. as ANTARCHY + -ISM.] Opposition to government in general. (In mod. Dicts. So the two next.)

'antarchist. *rare*[−0]. [f. as prec. + -IST.] One who is opposed to all government.

antar'chistic, *a. rare*[−0]. [f. prec. + -IC.] Opposed to all government.

†**'antarchy.** *Obs. rare*[−1]. [ad. mod.L. *antarchia* f. Gr. ἀντί against + -αρχία, f. ἀρχ- in ἄρχ-ειν to rule, ἀρχ-ή rule, government.] (See quot.)
1656 BLOUNT *Glossogr.*, *Antarchy*, an opposition to government. **1692** WASHINGTON tr. *Milton's Def. Pop.* ii. 56 (1851) That this word *Antarchy* and Monarchy are Synonymous, I cannot easily perswade my self to believe.

Antarctic (æn'tɑ:ktɪk), *a.* and *sb.* Forms: 4 **antartyk**, 4–7 **-ik(e**, **-ick(e**, 6 **-ique**, **antiartick**, 6–8 **antartic**, **-arctique**, 7–8 **antarctick(e**, (7 **anartic**), 6– **antarctic**. [a. OFr. *antartique* (= Pr. *antartic*, It. *antartico*), ad. L. *antartic-us*, *-arctic-us*, a. Gr. ἀνταρκτικ-ός opposite to the north, f. ἀντί against, opposite + ἀρκτικ-ός of the Bear, northern, f. ἄρκτος bear, the constellation of the Bear. The orig. Eng., phonetically modified by passage through Romance, has, like mod.Fr. *antarctique*, been since conformed to the Gr. spelling, though still often pronounced (æn'tɑ:tɪk).]
A. *adj.*
1. Opposite to the arctic; pertaining to the south polar regions; southern. ***Antarctic Pole***, the South pole of earth or heavens; ***Antarctic Circle***, the parallel of 66° 32′ South, which separates the South Temperate and South Frigid Zones.
1366 MAUNDEV. xvii. 181 In Lybye men seen first the sterre antartyk. *c* **1391** CHAUCER *Astrol.* II. §25 Than is the pol antartik bynethe the Orisonte. **1556** RECORDE *Cast. Knowl.* 27 The Antartike circle is equall and equidistant to the Arctike circle. **1594** BLUNDEVIL *Exerc.* iv. Introd. 433 The Pole Antartique, that is to say, the South Pole. **1601** HOLLAND *Pliny* (1634) I. 130 Canopus, a goodly great and bright star about the pole Antarcticke. **1645** HOWELL *Lett.* Addr., From the Anartic to the Artic skie. *a* **1649** DRUMM. OF HAWTH. *Poems* Wks. 1711, 38/2 Antarick parrots, Æthiopian plumes. **1777** ROBERTSON *Hist. Amer.* I. 453 It is probable that an open sea stretches to the Antartic pole. **1881** HOOKER in *Nature* No. 619. 447 There is no Antarctic flora except a few lichens and sea-weeds.
†**2.** *fig.* Directly opposite, contradictory, antipodean. *Obs.*
1644 CLEVELAND *Gen. Poems* (1677) 129 My Wit shall be on what side Heaven you please, provided it ever be Antarctick to yours. **1670** COTTON *Espernon* II. VIII. 362 So strange an alteration in them both, and so antartick to those good dispositions betwixt them. *a* **1711** KEN *Christophil* Poet. Wks. 1721 I. 501 Antarctick Wills in me for Empire vy'd; My Rational to Heav'n alone inclin'd, My Sensual with the World and Satan join'd.
B. *sb.* [The adj. used *ellipt.*]
1. The south pole, or the regions adjacent.
1366 MAUNDEV. xvii. 182 Thei that ben toward the antartyk. **1596** FITZ-GEFFREY *Drake* (1881) 20 From th' Artique to th' Antartique famosed. **1662** H. MORE *Enthus. Tri.* (1712) 31 The Axle-tree of the Antarctick. **1784** COWPER *Task* I. 620 Far into the deep Towards the Antarctic.
†**2.** *fig. Obs. rare.*
c **1640** JACKSON in Southey *Commonpl. Bk.* Ser. II. (1849) 77 *Antarcticks* they are, and think they can never be far enough from the *North Pole*, until they run from it into the *South Pole*, and pitch their habitation *in terrâ incognitâ*, in a world and church unknown to the ancients.
†**C.** as *v. intr.* ***antarctic it.*** *Obs.* [f. the sb.; cf. *lord it, tree it.*] To go to the opposite extreme.
1647 WARD *Simp. Cobler* 47 If it [*Majestas Imperii*] extends itself beyond its due Artique..*Salus Populi* must Antartique it, or else the world will be Excentrick.

†**an'tarctical,** *a. Obs. rare.* [f. prec. (B) + -AL[1].] Of or pertaining to antarctic regions.
1693 SIR T. BLOUNT *Nat. Hist.* 122 Others call it Antarctical Buglosse, Henbane of Peru.

†**an'tarctically,** *adv. Obs. rare.* [f. prec. + -LY[2].] In an antarctic or contrary way, in direct opposition.
a **1711** KEN *Hymns Ev.* Wks. 1721 I. 107 None God and Mammon can at once obey, They humane Wills Antarctically sway.

antarthritic (æntə'θrɪtɪk), *a.* and *sb. Med.* [f. ANT- + Gr. ἀρθρῖτικ-ός gouty: see ARTHRITIC.]
A. *adj.* Tending to prevent or relieve gout.
1775 in ASH. **1830** LINDLEY *Nat. Syst. Bot.* 73 The root is supposed by the Hindoos to possess..antarthritic virtues.
B. *sb.* A medicine so used.
1706 PHILLIPS, *Antarthriticks*, Remedies good against the gout. **1742** in BAILEY; and in mod. Dicts.

antasthmatic (æntæsθ'mætɪk), *a.* and *sb.* [f. ANT- + Gr. ἀσθματικ-ός ASTHMATIC.]
A. *adj.* Tending to prevent or relieve asthma.
B. *sb.* A medicine so used.
1681 tr. *Willis's Rem. Med. Wks.*, *Antasthmaticks*, Things good against the cough or asthma. **1706** PHILLIPS, *Antasthmaticks*, Medicines against the Ptisick or shortness of Breath. **1742** in BAILEY. **1775** in ASH. **1853** in MAYNE.

antatrophic (æntə'trɒfɪk), *a.* and *sb. Med.* [f. ANT- + Gr. ἀτροφία ATROPHY + -IC.]
A. *adj.* Tending to counteract atrophy. **B.** *sb.* Anything given with this purpose.
[**1811** HOOPER *Med. Dict.*, *Antatrophica*, Medicines which relieve or restore consumption.] **1853** in MAYNE *Exp. Lex.*

'ant-,bear. [from its remote likeness to a bear.]
1. The popular name in British Guiana of the Great Ant-eater, *Myrmecophaga jubata.*
1555 EDEN tr. *P. Martyr of Angleria's Hystorie of West Indies* in *Decades* fol. 189 There is also on the firme lande an other beaste cauled *Orso Formigaro*, that is, the Ante beare. **1691** RAY *Creation* (L.) Two sorts of tamanduas [live] upon ants, which therefore are called in English ant-bears. **1863** *Cornh. Mag.* Jan. 122 A huge ant-bear..his bushy tail curled over his back..and his long snout held close to the ground, as if in search of his insect prey.
2. The English name for the S. African aardvark. Also *attrib.*
1894 *Daily News* 8 Nov. 6/1 A poor little boy, who had tried to hide himself in an ant-bear hole. **1910** *Encycl. Brit.* I. 3/1 The typical form, *Orycteropus capensis*, or Cape ant-bear from South Africa. **1951** A. ROBERTS *Mammals S. Afr.* (1954) 239 Order Tubulidentata. Family Orycteropodidæ: Antbears. The family comprises the Antbears of the Old World, or Aardvarks (in Afrikaans now spelt Erdvarks), which are survivors of an ancient type of animal.

'antdom. *nonce-wd.* [f. ANT *sb.* + -DOM.] The estate or race of ants.
1883 in *Knowledge* 22 June 374/1 The skeletons of antdom were around that lonely one.

†'**ante**, *sb.*[1] *Obs.* [a. Sp. *ante*, also *dante*, ad. Arab. *lamt*, some animal of the antelope or buffalo kind, 'el Dante, que los Affricanos llaman *Lamt*' (Marmol, in Dozy). Its skin is called in Arab. *ad-daraca lamt*, corrupt. in Sp. *adaraga dante*, *adarga de ante*, whence *dante*, *ante*, for the animal.]

[**1598** FLORIO, *Ante*.. a wilde beast in India as big as an asse with round eares, with the neather lip like a trumpet, neuer going but by night.] **1625** PURCHAS *Pilgrims* II. 1029 Buffles, Badgers, Ante, Deere.

ante ('ænti:), *sb.*[2] Orig. and chiefly *U.S.* Also erron. anti. [a. L. *ante* before.] In *Poker*, a stake put up by a player (usually, the eldest hand) before the draw; similarly in other card games. Also *attrib.* in ***ante-man*** = AGE *sb.* 6 b.

1838 *Victims of Gaming* 86 The one next to the dealer [at brag] puts up into the pool.. any sum he may choose, unless the amount has been.. fixed by the company. This sum is called the ante. **1844** J. COWELL *Thirty Years* 94 The dealer makes the game, or value of the beginning bet, and called the anti. **1853** J. G. BALDWIN *Flush Times Alab.* 8 A negro *ante* and twenty on the call, was moderate playing. **1882** *Poker* 7 To begin the pool, the player next to the dealer, on his left, must put up money, which is called an 'Ante'. *Ibid.* 8 It is best generally for the ante-man to make good and go in.

b. *transf.* An amount paid in advance; price, subscription, means. Freq. in phr. ***to raise the ante.***

1890 *Harper's Mag.* Feb. 428/2, I raised the ante, and sold three hundred papers at ten cents each. **1934** *Bulletin* (Sydney) 1 Aug. 36/1 Weekly premiums are paid, and after a conviction a member pays a double ante, because his fine will be heavier next time. **1959** *Economist* 16 May 655/2 Raising the Ante... The problem for the News of the World was how it was to find the cash to make the purchase. **1964** *Wanganui Chronicle* 25 Mar. 1/9 Few people in Wanganui and district had the ante to go into the fishing industry.

ante ('ænti:), *v.* Orig. and chiefly *U.S.* Also erron. **anti.** [f. ANTE *sb.*[2]] *trans.* To put (an ante); also *transf.*, to bet, stake; to pay *off*, *up*; to hand over, surrender. Also *absol.*

1846 J. J. HOOPER *Adv. Simon Suggs* x. 129 Ante up! ante up, boys—friends I mean—don't back out! *Ibid.* xii. 144 Exsept.. 500 dollers I anteed off amongst the boys of a night, I couldn't git off a sent. **1854** in Thornton *Amer. Gloss.* (1912) 971 Playin' at billiards an' monte Till they've nary red cent to ante. **1857** *Knickerbocker* Jan. 43, I did hear that you anted off 1000 shares in trade for Texas lands. **1859** BARTLETT *Dict. Amer.* (ed. 2), To *Anti*, to risk; to venture a bet; as, 'I'll anti all I'm worth on that'. This term is derived from the game of poker. **1888** FARMER *Americanisms*, To *Ante up* is to pay, as well as to wager. **1889** R. GUERNDALE *Poker Bk.* ii. 13 The player after the dealer must Ante first, before the draw. *Ibid.* vii. 42 B Antes one, and the cards are dealt by A. **1896** H. A. VACHELL *Rom. Judge Ketchum* III. viii. 267 Death.. and I hev bin pardners many a time, an' when he passes the word, I'll ante up with a smile if I kin. **1900** H. LAWSON *On Track* 157 The man that doesn't ante gets the best of this world. **1904** 'G. B. LANCASTER' *Sons o' Men* vii. 98 Look here; you anti them [missing sheep] up, at once. **1919** W. H. DOWNING *Digger Dialects* 8 *Ante up*, to surrender anything. **1938** WODEHOUSE *Summer Moonshine* viii. 88 You pay as you enter. Can you ante up? **1945** D. WHEATLEY *Man who missed War* i. 13 The income tax payer would have to ante-up quite a bit more in the pound. **1948** V. PALMER *Golconda* v. 33 'Ante up for your union ticket..,' went on Mahony.

ante, obs. form of ANT and AUNT.

ante-, L. *prep.* and *adv.*, used in composition with vbs., as *antecēdere* to go before; vbl. sbs., as *antecēssor* a foregoer; other sbs. and adjs. derived from phrases, as *antecēnium* (from *ante cēnam*), *antetemplum*, *antemeridiānus* (f. *ante meridiem*), *antepænultimus* (f. *ante pænultimum*). Examples of all these have been adopted in Eng. directly or through Fr., and have, since 1600, served as models for the formation of others, especially of the last class, from which, as in *ante-temple*, *ante-nuptial*, *ante-* has acquired a separable character, and is prefixed to other words, as *ante-room*, *ante-Cuvierian*, *ante-date*. Adjectives of this type are formed at will, either with or without adj. endings, as *ante-baptismal*, *ante-Norman*, *ante-reformational*; and *ante-communion*, *ante-reformation*, *ante-war*. The latter are really attributive *phrases*, similar to the native *after-dinner* oration, *before-breakfast* lesson, *out-of-doors* employment, *up-stairs* room. The former, though formally compounds of *ante* + *adjective*, are in sense adj. formations on a phrase, as *ante-mundane*, logically (*antemund*)*um* + *ane*; cf. (*old-woman*)*ish*. Some of the more obvious of these combinations of *ante-* are grouped together here, as not needing separate treatment.

A. *sbs.* (Main stress on '*ante-*: '*antechapel*.)

1. Of position: in which *ante-* usually = A smaller introductory ——; as **ante-cavern, -closet, -garden, -hall, -porch, -portico, -stomach**; also **ante-bath**, an apartment opening into the bath; **ante-church** = ANTE-CHAPEL; **ante-nave**, the western part of a divided nave; **ante-number**, the preceding number. These begin after 1600.

1817 *Edin. Rev.* XXVIII. 331 The bathers first enter a vault or *antebath. *Ibid.*, The Georgian ladies employ the *ante-caverns as dressing rooms. **1874** MICKLETHWAITE *Mod. Par. Ch.* §27 If there is an *antechurch, they should be placed there. **1705** *Phil. Trans.* XXV. 2109 Its Entrance, first and second Galleries, *Anticlosets. **1861** *Gard. Chron.* 6 July 621/3 The spectator is supposed to stand in the *ante-garden. **1848** LYTTON *Harold* iv. 148 A low forlorn *ante-hall. **1829** SOUTHEY *All for Love* IV. Wks. VII. 173 Now before the Holy Door In the *Ante-nave they stand. **1626** BACON *Sylva* §106 Whatsoever Vertue is in Numbers, for Conducing to Concent of Notes, is rather to be ascribed to the *Ante-number than to the Entire Number. **1624** WOTTON *Archit.* (1672) 28 An *Atrium Græcum* (we may translate it an *Anti-Porch, after the Greek manner). **1838** BRITTON *Dict. Arch.* 13 *Antica*.. a door, a porch, or *ante-portico. **1691** RAY *Creation* (1714) 28 Swallowed into the crop.. or at least into a kind of *Ante-stomach.

2. Of time or order: in which *ante* = A previous or anticipatory ——, *or* A something previous or anticipatory to ——; as **ante-dawn, -disposition, -luminary, -occupation, -predicament, -spring, -taste**; also **ante-eternity**, the quality of having existed from all eternity; **ante-noon**, the fore-noon. These begin after 1600.

1841 *Blackw. Mag.* XLIX. 287 That mysterious *ante-dawn—that prelibation of the full daylight.. the Zodiacal light. **1611** FLORIO, *Antidispositione*, an *antidisposition, or precedent inclination. **1678** CUDWORTH *Intell. Syst.* 141 He .. maintained.. the Worlds *Ante-Eternity and Incorruptibility. **1684** CHARNOCK *Attrib. God* (1834) I. 367 The promise of eternal life is as ancient as God himself.. as it hath an *ante-eternity, so it hath a post-eternity. **1686** GOAD *Celest. Bod.* I. xv. 96 At other hours of the *Ante-Noon. **1656** BLOUNT *Glossogr.*, **Anteoccupation*, a preventing or seising first. **1706** PHILLIPS, **Antepredicaments* (in Logick) things necessary to be known before-hand, for the better understanding of the Predicaments; as Definitions of Terms, etc. **1881** G. MILNER *Country Pleas.* (ed. 2) 2 Our *antespring—our premonitory awakening. **1861** SHEPPARD *Fall of Rome* iv. 165 An *antetaste of those dire and bloody struggles.

B. *adjs.* (Main stress not on *ante*: *ante-'nuptial*, *ante-'war*. Mostly of 19th and 20th c.)

1. Of position: in which *ante* = Before, in front of ——; as **ante-cæcal**, before the *cæcum* or 'blind gut'; **anteconsonantal**, preceding a consonant; **antecubital** *Anat.*, pertaining to the inner surface of the forearm; **ante-initial**, before the beginning, prefatory; **ante-pectoral**, in front of the breast.

1861 HULME *Moquin-Tandon* II. I. 44 The small intestine or *anticæcal. **1909** WEBSTER, *Anteconsonantal. **1927** *Mod. Philology* Nov. 226 OHG *za-* is the anteconsonantal form of *zar-*. **1937** C. E. BAZELL in *Jrnl. Eng. & Ger. Philol.* Jan 6 Part of a plural system wherein *j* represented before a vowel the ante-consonantal *i* of the other cases. **1893** *Funk's Standard Dict.*, *Antecubital. **1908** *Practitioner* Sept. 486 The injection made into one of the large veins of the ante-cubital region. **1962** *Lancet* 29 Dec. 1372/2 In other cases an ante-cubital vein was used. **1834** SOUTHEY *Doctor* (1862) 2 The chapters *ante-initial and post-initial. **1826** KIRBY & SPENCE *Entomol.* IV. xxxviii. 38 The *antepectoral pair of the mole-cricket.

2. Of time or order: in which *ante* = Occurring or existing in the time before (a fact or condition, implied in the following adj., or definitely expressed by the following sb.); as **a.** with adj. ending: **ante-Babylonish, -baptismal, -Christian, -ecclesiastical, -Gothic, -historic, -human; ante-jentacular**, before breakfast; **ante-judiciary**, taking place before judgement; **ante-Justinianian, -metallic, -mortal, -Mosaical, -Norman, -nuptial; ante-patriarchal**, existing before the patriarchs; **ante-posthumous**, posthumous (professedly), but written before; **ante-reformational, -revolutional, -revolutionary.** **b.** with sb., forming attrib. phr.: ***ante-bridal, -communion, -reformation, -resurrection, -sunrise, -war.*** Cf. the L. *ante-mortem*, before-death. In this sense *ante-* varies with *pre-*.

1835 I. TAYLOR *Spir. Desp.* iii. 96 The *antebabylonish Jews. **1850** C. WORDSW. *Occas. Serm.* Ser. I. 104 *Ante-baptismal regeneration. **1847** L. HUNT *Men, Wom., & Bks.* II. x. 219 *Ante-bridal trepidation. **1858** SEARS *Athan.* III. iii. 270 What was the *ante-Christian doctrine respecting the condition of the dead? **1827** *Gentl. Mag.* XCVII. II. 487 This part of the *Ante-Communion Service is now so commonly omitted on Sundays. **1880** GUNTHER *Fishes* 16 Several of such *antecuvierian works must be mentioned. **1829** SOUTHEY in *Q. Rev.* XXXIX. 361 Its *ante-ecclesiastical history. **1834** H. COLERIDGE *Grk. Class. Poets* 99 This event.. is involved in the same thick mist of *ante-historic antiquity. **1860** FARRAR *Orig. Lang.* x. 214 Other languages also in an *ante-historical and embryonary state. **1861** TULLOCH *Eng. Purit.* ii. 264 He fills up the *ante-human space.. by an array of spiritual machinery. **1811** KNOX & JEBB *Corr.* II. 44 This *ante-jentacular hour. **1679** PRANCE *Addit. Narr.* 50 Purgatory, or *Antejudiciary and intermedial delivery of souls. **1880** MUIRHEAD *Gaius* Introd. 7 Any question of *Ante-Justinianian law. **1865** LUBBOCK *Preh. Times* 60 The Stone age.. the *ante-metallic period. **1827** HARE *Guesses* II. (1873) 556 If a spirit.. were to revisit this home of its *antemortal existence. **1883** *Standard* 16 May 5/2 The **ante-mortem* treatment of the brutes. **1684** T. BURNET *Th. Earth* I. 283, I look upon all other [books] that pretend to be *ante-Mosaical or patriarchal, as spurious and fabulous. **1863** COX *Inst. Eng. Govt.* I. iii. 11 As to the *ante-Norman councils. **1818** HALLAM *Mid. Ages* (1872) III. 75 To legitimate the duke of Lancaster's *ante-nuptial children. **1765** TUCKER *Lt. Nat.* II. 328 Primeval sages or *ante-patriarchal Saracens. **1855** WISEMAN *Fabiola* 220 The old *capsarius* as he had had himself rattlingly called in his *ante-posthumous inscription. **1852** S. MAITLAND *Essays* 165 They had never seen any *ante-reformation Waldenses. **1861** A. B. HOPE *Eng. Cathedr. 19th C.* iii. 73 Bishop Osmond, the regulator of the *ante-reformational English ritual. **1858** SEARS *Athan.* iv. 25 The *ante-resurrection period. **1839** W. IRVING *Wolfert's Roost* (1855) 164 An old gentleman, whose dress was decidedly *ante-revolutional. **1860** MILL *Repres. Govt.* (1865) 23/2 With Austria or *ante-revolutionary France. **1842** *Chamb. Jrnl.* 30 July 231 The dim *ante-sunrise light. **1878** *N. Amer. Rev.* CXXVII. 123 *Ante-war lightness of national taxation.

ante-, in earlier spelling often put for ANTI-.

†'**ante‚act.** *Obs.*$^{-0}$ [ad. L. *ante-actum*, pa. pple. of *ante-agĕre* (a questionable compound) to do before.] 'A former act.' J.

1721 in BAILEY, whence in JOHNSON, ASH, etc.

†‚**ante-'acted,** *ppl. a. Obs. rare.* [f. L. *ante-act-* (see prec.) + -ED.] Previously done, or spent.

1607 DEKKER *Knt's. Conjur.* (1842) 62 Shee begins to be sorie for her ante-acted euils. **1620** —— *Dreame* (1860) 22 A loathing of their anteacted life.

anteal ('ænti:əl), *a. rare.* [f. L. *ante* before + -AL[1].] Pertaining to what is in front.

1852 LANDSBOROUGH *Zooph.* 388 *Anteal*, in front of anything forward. **1859** in WORCESTER.

†**ante-'ambulate,** *v. Obs.*$^{-0}$ [f. L. *ante* before + *ambulāt-* ppl. stem of *ambulā-re* to walk; suggested by sb. ANTE-AMBULO.] To walk before, as an usher.

1623 COCKERAM, *Anteambulate*, To vsher. **1656** in BLOUNT.

†**ante-ambu'lation.** *Obs.*$^{-0}$ [n. of action f. prec.: see -TION.] The act of walking before.

1678 in PHILLIPS, whence in BAILEY, JOHNSON, etc.

‖**ante-'ambulo.** *Obs.* [L., f. *ante* before + *ambulāre* to walk; app. in familiar use in 17th c.] One whose business it is to walk in front, an usher.

1609 *Man in Moone* (1857) 95 [A serving-man] is the ante-ambulo of a gentlewoman, the consequent of a gentleman. **1641** MAISTERTON *Serm.* 18 An anteambulo to usher in a thousand pains. **1706** PHILLIPS, *Anteambulo*, A Sergeant of the Mace to a Prince, a Verger or Gentleman-usher.

'**ant-‚eater.** The popular name of several animals which feed upon ants (and termites).

1. A group of quadrupeds of the order *Edentata* having long thread-like viscous tongues which they thrust into ants' nests and retract into their mouths covered with ants. They consist of the Ant-eaters proper (*Myrmecophaga*) of S. America, the Scaly Ant-eaters (*Manis*) of the Old World, and the Cape Ant-eater or Aardvark (*Orycteropus*).

1764 WILLIAMS *Dict. Arts* s.v., The Ant-Eater.. is as long and as tall as a middle-sized dog. **1869** J. GRAY in *Guide Brit. Mus.* 4 The Shielded Beasts, as the Manis or Scaly Ant-eaters of India and Africa. **1870** SPURGEON *Treas. David* Ps. v. 9 Many human ant-eaters that with their long tongues covered with oily words entice and entrap the unwary.

2. The Aculeated, or Porcupine Ant-eater (*Echidna*) of the order *Monotremata*, found in Australia.

1868 CHAMBERS *Cycl.* s.v., The *Echidnæ* of New Holland are sometimes called Porcupine Ant-Eaters from their food, and their similarity to the true ant-eaters in their sharp muzzle and extensile tongue. **1880** HAUGHTON *Phys. Geog.* vi. 268 *Myrmecobius*, the living Australian Ant-eater.

3. A bird, also called ANT-THRUSH.

1827 GRIFFITH *Cuvier* VI. 399 The Ant-eaters.. are recognized by their long legs and short tail. *Ibid.* 403 The King of the Ant-eaters.. is about the size of a quail, and its grey plumage is agreeably variegated.

ante-baptismal, -bath, etc.: see ANTE-.

ante-bellum ('ænti 'bɛləm). [Lat. phr., 'before the war', used *attrib.* or as *adj.*] Previous to the war, i.e. *spec.* the American civil war (1861–5), the S. African war (1899–1902), or either of the wars of 1914–18 and 1939–45.

1862 M. B. CHESNUT *Diary* 14 June (1905) 188 Her face was as placid and unmoved as in antebellum days. **1879** TOURGÉE *Fool's Errand* xv. 82 Evidently thinking that his connection with this ante bellum barbarity had somehow increased his importance. **1882** *Rep. Ho. Repr. Prec. Met. U.S.* 306 One of the productive mines of antebellum days. **1905** *Westm. Gaz.* 4 Jan. 1/3 The ante-bellum negotiations. **1924** *Contemp. Rev.* Apr. 438 Deaths of infants from overlaying.. were also only one-third of the ante-bellum number. **1955** *Times* 28 May 7/5 In the particular case of our basic raw material, paper, the *ante-bellum* price for certain grades has actually trebled itself.

antebrachial, *a.*, more correct f. ANTIBRACHIAL *a.* So **antebrachium (anti-)** *Biol.* [med.L.], in mammalia, the part of the arm or fore-limb from the wrist to the elbow; the forearm.

1877 [see BRACHIUM]. **1880** [see ANTIBRACHIAL *a.*].

†**ˌanteceˈdane**, *a.* *Obs. rare*$^{-1}$. [ad. med.L. **antecēdāne-us*: see next.] = next.

1655 Bramhall *Answ. Hobbes* 207 (R.) He makes the willing..no willing at all, but onely some antecedane inclination.

antecedaneous (ˌæntɪsɪˈdeɪnɪəs). *a.* [f. med.L. **antecēdāne-us* (f. *antecēd-ĕre*: see ANTECEDE) + -OUS: see -ANEOUS.] Having the property or character of preceding or going before; of a preliminary or previous character.

1630 Preston *Breastpl. Faith* 12 As antecedaneous [*printed* -darious] and precedent to the pardon. **1684** tr. *Bonet's Merc. Compit.* vi. 165 Some antecedaneous weakness of the patient. **1692** *Cov. Grace* 58 The Promise is made..without any Condition in us Antecedaneous, as a moving cause. [Not in J.] **1818** in Todd.

ˌanteceˈdaneously, *adv.* ? *Obs.* [f. prec. + -LY^2.] In an antecedaneous manner; previously.

1668 Wilkins *Real Char.* 51 Those more special kinds of beings to be treated of Antecedaneously to the Predicaments. **1688** Norris *Theor. Love* (1694) 198 Neither is this latter..made only Practical by being put in Practice, but is so antecedaneously.

antecede (æntɪˈsiːd), *v.* Also 7 anteceed. [ad. L. *antecēd-ĕre*, f. *ante* before + *cēdĕre* to go.]

1. *trans.* To go before or in front of; to precede, in place, time, or rank; to surpass.

1624 Heywood *Gunaik.* iv. 207 In wealth and nobilitie ..[he] anteceded the best in the cittie. **1677** Hale *Prim. Orig. Man.* i. iii. 82 The Fabrick of the World did not long antecede its Motion. **1822** T. Taylor *Metam. Apuleius* 399 A particular negative antecedes either of the affirmative propositions. **1902** H. Spencer *Facts & Comments* 204 Recognizing the properties of Space..as anteceding all creation..and all evolution. **1914** C. A. Mercier *Astrol. in Med.* i Its origin is so remote as to antecede all written records.

2. *intr.* To go or come before, to come first.

1628 T. Spencer *Logick* 239 This Axiome..containes nothing that doth antecede, or follow. **1656** Baxter *Ref. Pastor* 100 Three daies prayer for him..should antecede. **1690** —— *Kingd. Christ* i. 4 Though the Embrio and Infancy anteceding, it was to be first in Execution.

antecedence (æntɪˈsiːdəns). [f. L. *antecēdentia* (see next), on analogy of sbs. in -ENCE through Fr. (mod.Fr. *antécédence* is a neologism, Littré).]

1. The action or fact of going before, precedence, priority: **a.** in time.

1677 Hale *Prim. Orig. Man.* i. iii. 77 A pre-existence of the simple Bodies..and an antecedence of their Constitution. **1830** Lyell *Princ. Geol.* (1875) I. i. x. 195 The Antecedence of a colder climate. **1871** Farrar *Witn. Hist.* iv. 134 Not that we claim a mere antecedence and originality for the separate precepts of Christianity.

b. in a causal relation.

1651 Hobbes *Lev.* i. xii. 52 Man..remembreth in them Antecedence and Consequence. **1830** Sir J. Herschel *Stud. Nat. Phil.* 151 Invariable antecedence of the cause and consequence of the effect.

†**2.** That which goes before or precedes: **a.** An antecedent, a premiss. (Cf. *antecedens* in ANTECEDENT *sb.* 1 b.)

1535 Joye *Apol. Tindale* 5 His antecedence may be true and consequence false.

b. The preceding part.

1593 Nashe *Lent. Stuffe* 7 The rest of the antecedence of the day worne out in disputations.

3. *Astr.* A motion from a later to an earlier sign of the Zodiac, or from east to west; retrograde motion; also a position more to the west.

1669 Flamstead in *Phil. Trans.* IV. 1109 Therefore she [the Moon] is in Antecedence of the Star 15 m. 25 sec. **1740** Winthrop *ibid.* XLII. 575 Mercury was in Antecedence of the Sun 3′ 57″. **1797** *Encycl. Brit.* (*Astronomy*) II. 508/1 A motion of the heavens in the order of the signs..is said to be a motion in *consequence*; and such are the true motions of all the planets; tho' their apparent motions are sometimes contrary, and then they are said to move in *antecedence*.

antecedency (æntɪˈsiːdənsɪ). [ad. L. *antecēdentia*, f. *antecēdent-em*: see ANTECEDENT *a.*]

1. The quality or condition of being antecedent, priority, precedence.

1598 Florio, *Antecedentia*, antecedencie, precedencie, superioritie. *a* **1617** Bayne *Ephes.* (1866) 32 An antecedency of faith before the act of electing. **1874** Whitney *Orient. Ling. Studies* 245 Those who believe in the antecedency of ideas to words.

†**2.** An antecedent condition or state of things; in *pl.* = ANTECEDENTS. *Obs.*

1682 Sir T. Browne *Chr. Morals* 55 Many things happen, not likely to ensue from any promises of antecedencies. **1748** Richardson *Clarissa* (1811) IV. iv. 12 Most of thy reflections..are fitter to come in as after-reflections than as antecedencies.

†**3.** Movement back to a former position. *Obs.*

1656 Hardy *1 John* (1865) xiv. 86/1 Some sudden emanations of the will as regenerate, antecedencies to the conflicts and lustings of the will as corrupt.

antecedent (æntɪˈsiːdənt), *sb.* [a. Fr. *antécédent* (see next), subst. use of the adj. Already in L. *antecēdens* was used subst. as a term of philosophy, and in this technical sense it first appeared in the modern languages.]

1. A thing or circumstance which goes before or precedes in time or order; often also implying causal relation with its *consequent*. **a.** generally.

1612 T. Taylor *Comm. Titus* i. 11 (1619) That there may be full content with it selfe, the antecedents and consequents. *c* **1680** in Somers *Tracts* II. 548 Consider the Antecedents to the calling the Convention. *a* **1716** South (J.) It is..the necessary antecedent..of a sinner's return to God. **1824** Coleridge *Aids to Refl.* (1848) I. 92 Conscience is the ground and antecedent of human (or self-) consciousness, and not any modification of the latter. *a* **1862** Buckle *Civilis.* (1869) III. iii. 130 Circumstances.. governed by a long chain of antecedents.

Hence, in various special applications, of which the *logical* and *grammatical* are the earliest uses of the word in Eng.

b. *Logic.* (Opposed to *consequent.*) The statement upon which any consequence logically depends; hence †(*a*) The premisses of a syllogism (*obs.*); (*b*) The part of a conditional proposition on which the other depends. †(*c*) By some early logicians the *subject* and *predicate* were called *antecedent* and *consequent*.

c **1400** *Test. Love* ii. (1560) 284 b/1 The consequence is false, needes the antecedent mote beene of the same condition. *c* **1425** Wyntoun *Cron.* viii. iii. 67 [I] grantis..þe Antecedens Bot I deny þe consequens. **1587** Fleming *Contn. Holinshed* III. 324/1 You have shewn us the antecedent, now let us have the *ergo*. **1628** T. Spencer *Logick* 161 Ramus doth call the *subiect*, and the *predicate*.. *antecedent*, and *consequent*: but very vnduely. *a* **1665** J. Goodwin *Filled w. Spirit* (1867) 191 Let the word person in the antecedent of the proposition be supposed to signify either something or nothing. **1870** Bowen *Logic* v. 128 All Hypothetical Judgments obviously consist of two parts, the first of which is called the Condition or Antecedent.

c. *Gram.* (*a*) The noun to which a following pronoun refers, and to avoid the repetition of which it is used. (*b*) *esp.* The substantive (word, clause, or sentence) to which a relative pronoun or adverb points back, and to which the relative clause stands in an attributive or adjective relation.

1393 Langl. *P. Pl.* C. iv. 364 Adjectif and substantif Acordeþ in alle Kyndes · with his antecedent. **1523** Whittinton *Vulg.* 2 The relatyue of substaunce shall accorde with his antecedent. **1655** Gouge *Comm. Hebr.* i. 10 This relative 'Thou' must have an antecedent. **1765** W. Ward *Eng. Gram.* 128 The connexion of a personal pronoun with its antecedent is very different from that of a relative pronoun. **1876** Mason *Eng. Gram.* 51 In the nominative and objective cases, *what* is never preceded by an antecedent.

d. *Math.* The first of two numbers or magnitudes between which a ratio is expressed; the first and third in a series of four proportionals.

1570 Billingsley *Eucl.* v. def. 3 The first Terme, namely, that which is compared, is called the antecedent. **1695** Alingham *Geom. Epit.* 14 In the Comparison of 7 to 3, 7 is named the Antecedent, and 3 the Consequent. **1862** Todhunter *Euclid* vi. iv, Those [sides] which are opposite to the equal angles are homologous sides, that is, are the antecedents or the consequents of the ratios.

e. *Music.* (See quot.)

1869 Ouseley *Counterp.* xv. 95 The leading part [in a Canon] is called the antecedent, the following part the consequent.

2. *pl.* The events of a person's bygone history (*usually*, as affecting the postion now to be accorded him); also used of institutions, etc.

1841 Gen. Thompson *Exerc.* VI. 237 They will..sift what the French call their antecedents, with the most scrupulous nicety. **1854** De Quincey *Selections* ii. 86 What modern slang denominates his antecedents. **1864** J. H. Newman *Apol.* 106 Froude and I were nobodies; with..no antecedents to fetter us. **1868** M. Pattison *Academ. Organ.* §4. 111 Young fellows unacquainted with the antecedents of the estates.

3. *concr.* A predecessor in the chain of development; an earlier form. *rare.*

1865 Lecky *Rational.* (1878) I. 254 A wind instrument which some have placed among the antecedents of the organ.

†**4.** *lit.* A person that walks in front; an usher, an ANTEAMBULO. *Obs.*

1608 Day *Hum. out of Br.* ii. ii, *Boy.* I say a seruingman is an antecedent. *Oct.* Because he sits before a cloakebag. **1632** Massinger *City Madam* ii. ii, My antecedent, or my gentleman-usher.

antecedent (æntɪˈsiːdənt), *a.* [a. Fr. *antécédent*, ad. L. *antecēdent-em*, pr. pple. of *antecēd-ĕre*: see ANTECEDE.]

1. Going before, preceding, in time or order.

1543 Traheron *Vigo's Chirurg.* 67 b/1 Apostemes..come sometymes of a primityue cause, but for the moost parte of a cause antecedent. **1588** Fraunce *Lawiers Log.* i. viii. 43 b, Some adjuncts bee antecedent or going before. **1646** S. Bolton *Arraign. Errour* 245 Whereuer the Antecedent duty was euer truly done, the consequent priviledge was never denied. **1830** Coleridge *Table T.* 91 Even in dreams nothing is fancied without an antecedent quasi cause. **1841** Gen. P. Thompson *Exerc.* (1842) VI. 275 Whose little finger was heavier than the loins of the antecedent tyranny.

b. with *to* (*unto* obs.).

1638 Chillingw. *Relig. Prot.* i. ii. 70 Antecedent to the act of seeing. **1745** Wesley *Answ. Ch.* 15 My Love to them was antecedent to any such Agreement. **1878** Bosw. Smith *Carthage* 2 A period antecedent to all contemporary.. records.

c. quasi-*adv.*; = ANTECEDENTLY 1 b.

1774 J. Bryant *Mythol.* II. 294 The name was imposed antecedent to his birth. **1804** Lauderdale *Publ. Wealth* (1819) 95 The same proportion which existed antecedent to the increase of production.

2. *ellipt.* Previous to investigation; presumptive, *à priori*.

1794 Paley *Evid.* iii. iv. §2 The cause..assigned for the rejection of Christianity by men of rank and learning among the Heathens, namely, a strong antecedent contempt. **1859** *Ecce Homo* i. ii. 9 If..the antecedent improbability of miracles is much diminished. **1876** Gladstone *Hom. Synch.* 271 The antecedent likelihood of Homer's possession of Egyptian knowledge.

antecedental (ˌæntɪsɪˈdɛntəl), *a.* ? *Obs.* [f. L. *antecēdent-ia* (see prec.) + -AL^1: cf. *incident-al.*] Of or pertaining to antecedents.

1796 Hutton *Math. Dict.* I. 121 *Antecedental Method*, a branch of general geometrical proportion..derived from an examination of the Antecedents of ratios having given consequents, and a given standard of comparison, in the various degrees of augmentation and diminution which they undergo by composition and decomposition..published in 1793.

anteˈcedently, *adv.* [f. ANTECEDENT *a.* + -LY^2.]

1. Previously, before, in time or causal relation.

1651 C. Cartwright *Cert. Relig.* i. 227 Sinne, as a cause antecedently moving Gods will. **1694** Slare in *Phil. Trans.* XVIII. 213 That the Air was antecedently there, we may reasonably believe. **1754** Sherlock *Disc.* (1759) I. v. 186 The Obedience..to which we are antecedently bound. **1863** Cox *Inst. Eng. Govt.* ii. iii. 347 Testimony as to facts which they had antecedently known. **1864** *Reader* No. 94. 471/3 Since the days of Charles VIII, if not antecedently.

b. with *to*.

1677 Hale *Prim. Orig. Man.* i. ii. 61 Notions..engraven in the Soul antecedently to any discursive Ratiocination. **1776** Campbell *Rhet.* I. 146 Testimony, antecedently to experience, hath a natural influence on belief. **1845** Stephen *Laws of Eng.* II. 300 Born antecedently to 14th August 1834.

2. *ellipt.* **a.** Not as a consequence, arbitrarily.

1682 Norris *Hierocles* 52 If by the divine sentence Riches were allotted to one, and Poverty to another antecedently and absolutely.

b. Previously to experience, presumptively, *à priori*.

1861 Maine *Anc. Law* (1874) 115 It would seem antecedently that we ought to commence with the simplest social forms. **1867** Froude *Short Stud.* 150 More evidence is required to establish a fact antecedently improbable.

anteˈceding, *ppl. a.* ? *Obs.* [f. ANTECEDE + -ING^2.] Going before, preceding; antecedent.

a **1619** Fotherby *Atheom.* Pref. 21 Both in the anteceding and succeeding passages. **1678** Cudworth *Intell. Syst.* 711 Such things..are [not] caused by things Natural Anteceding, but by some supernatural Power.

†**anteˈcell**, *v.* *Obs. rare.* [ad. L. *antecell-ĕre*, f. *ante* before + **cellĕre* to rise.] To excel, surpass.

1635 Heywood *Harb. Health* 299 Those that were before you..Equall you shall, although not antecell. **1638** —— *Port of Piety* 269 The dignity of merchants who can tell? Or how much they all Traders ante-cell? **1642** T. Taylor *God's Judg.* ii. vi. 87 Not to exceed those in virtue whom we antecell in place and dignity.

†**anteˈcellency.** *Obs. rare*$^{-1}$. [f. L. *antecellentem*: see prec. and -NCY.] The quality of excelling, superiority.

1657 Tomlinson *Renou's Disp.* 380 Turpentine from Chios..is most celebrated for its antecellency in odour and gust.

†**anteˈcession.** *Obs.*$^{-0}$ [ad. L. *antecēssiōn-em*, n. of action f. *antecēd-ĕre*: see ANTECEDE.] 'A going before or excelling.' Blount *Glossogr.* 1656.

antecessor (ˌæntɪˈsɛsə(r), ˈæntɪ-). Forms: 5–7 -cessour, 5 -owr, 5–6 -ur, -sessour, 7 -cesser, 6– antecessor. [a. MFr. *antécesseur*, a refashioning of earlier *ancesseur* ancestor, after L. *antecēssōr-em* in its L. senses of 'predecessor in office,' and 'professor of law': see ANCESTOR *sb.*]

1. One who goes before (*esp.* in office); a predecessor. (The latter word is more common.)

c **1425** Wyntoun *Cron.* viii. ix. 155 Hys Priwalagis..Ðat before hys Antecessowrys gat. **1494** Fabyan vi. clxi. 154 He shulde folowe the stablenes of his antesessours..and ponysshe mysdoers. **1502** Arnold *Chron.* 213 Our antecessurs and successours. **1636** Prynne *Unbish. Tim. & Tit.* (1661) 78 Before that he went up to the Apostles his Antecessors. **1789** Smyth tr. *Aldrich's Archit.* (1818) 54 The custom of all his antecessors in that profession. **1869** Gladstone *Juv. Mundi* viii. §1. 222 This deity [Zeus] has ancestors and antecessors.

†**b.** An ancestor, a progenitor (usually however when viewed as a *predecessor*). *Obs.*

c **1470** Henry *Wallace* i. 1 Our antecessowris, that we suld of reide..We lat ourslide. **1474** Caxton *Chesse* 53 Of his grauntsirs fader and of alle his antecessours. **1525** Ld. Berners *Froiss.* II. ccxxxvii. 736 Our fathers and Antecessours of olde tyme. *a* **1657** Sir J. Balfour *Ann. Scotl.* (1824) II. 223 Solemley interrid amongest his antecessers. **1660** R. Coke *Power & Subj.* 210 The Kings noble Progenitors and Antecessors of the Nobles of this Realm.

†**c.** A predecessor in the possession of property.

1574 tr. *Littleton's Tenures* 16 b, Writ of assise of the death of hys antecessoure at the common lawe. [**1628** COKE *On Litt.* 78 b, In Law .. *Antecessor* is applyed to a natural person .. but *Prædecessor* is applyed to a body Politique or Corporate. **1809** BAWDWEN *Domesd. Bk.* 624 Robert claims the land of Outi .. to be in the soke of his *Antecessor* Lepi.]

†**2.** A professor of civil law. *Obs.*

1751 CHAMBERS *Cycl.*, *Antecessor* .. is particularly used in some universities for a public professor, who teaches or lectures the civil law.

†**3.** *pl.* One of the advanced guard of an army. *Obs.*

1753 CHAMBERS *Cycl. Supp.*, *Antecessors*, in the antient art of war .. a party of horse dispatched before the agmen or body of an army .. also denominated Antecursores.

†**antecestre.** *Obs. rare*$^{-1}$. [A variant of *ancestre*, ANCESTOR *sb.*, partially assimilated to ANTECESSOR.] Ancestor, predecessor.

1549 *Compl. Scotl.* xx. 186 The thyng that his antecestres and forbearis hes conquiest be grite laubours.

antechamber ('æntiːtʃeɪmbə(r)), *sb.* In 7–8 **anti-chamber.** [a. Fr. *antichambre*, f. *anti* for *ante* before + *chambre* room, bedroom, after It. *anticamera.* 'It is generally written, improperly, *antichamber.*' Johnson 1755–83.]

1. A chamber or room leading to the chief apartment; an ante-room, in which visitors wait; *orig.* the room admitting into the (royal) bed-chamber.

1656 BLOUNT *Glossogr.*, *Antichambre*, any outward chamber which is next or near the bed-chamber. *a* **1667** COWLEY *Liberty* Wks. II. 679 He's besieg'd by two or three hundred suitors; and the Hall and Antichambers (all the outworks) possess'd by the Enemy. **1709** *Lond. Gaz.* mmmmdlviii/2 Her Majesty met them half-way of her Antichamber. **1789** SMYTH tr. *Aldrich's Archit.* (1818) 138 Beyond these ante-chambers were larger rooms or halls. **1855** MACAULAY *Hist. Eng.* IV. 39 He stayed long in the antechamber, and sent in his name by several servants.

2. *fig.*

1825 *Bro. Jonathan* II. 347 The ante-chamber of death. **1875** HAMERTON *Intell. Life* III. ii. 81 Grammars and dictionaries are antechambers.

3. *transf.* Any space forming the entrance to another.

1845 TODD & BOWMAN *Phys. Anat.* I. 434 The mouth, the ante-chamber to the digestive canal. **1862** DARWIN *Orchids* i. 21 The ante-chamber to the nectary .. is here small.

'**antechamber,** *v. intr.* and *trans.* To wait or wait for in or as in an antechamber: cf. ANTECHAMBERING *vbl. sb.*

1891 *Pall Mall Gaz.* 2 Oct. 1/3 All intriguing Paris was antechambering him. **1900** W. A. ELLIS *Wagner* I. II. ix. 291 My poor dog .. was antechambering in the street in wait for his more fortunate master, allowed to antechamber among men.

'**ante,chambering,** *vbl. sb. rare*$^{-1}$. [f. ANTECHAMBER *sb.* used as a vb. = Fr. *faire antichambre*; cf. *courting.*] Waiting in an antechamber; dancing attendance.

1879 *Pall Mall B.* 17 Oct. 12 To beguile the weariness of antichambering.

ante-chapel ('æntiːtʃæpəl). Also 8 **anti-.** [f. ANTE- + CHAPEL.] 'A term used in the Universities for the outer part at the west end of a chapel.' Parker *Gloss. Arch.* 1875.

1703 MAUNDRELL *Journ. Jerus.* (1721) 99 In a kind of Anti-Chappel to this Church. **1761** T. WARTON *Bathurst* 190 (T) The ante-chapel of Trinity College Chapel. **1814** WORDSWORTH *Excurs.* Wks. VIII. Pref. 10 The same kind of relation .. as the ante-chapel has to the body of a Gothic church.

ante-Christian, -church, etc.: see ANTE-.

antecian, var. ANTŒCIAN.

,**Ante-Co'mmunion.** In full *Ante-Communion Service* [ANTE- B. 2], a popular term for that part of the Communion Service in the Book of Common Prayer which extends from the beginning of the office to 'the end of the general Prayer "For the whole state of Christ's Church militant here in earth"' and is appointed to be said 'upon the Sundays and other Holy-days (if there be no Communion)'.

According to the American rite, the Ante-Communion ends with the Gospel.

1827 *Gentl. Mag.* XCVII. II. 487 There was no offertory, and no prayer for the church militant. I am not aware by what authority this part of the Ante-Communion Service is now so commonly omitted on Sundays. **1871** F. G. LEE *Dict. Ritual Terms, Ante-Communion.* (1) An Anglican term used to designate that portion of the Liturgy or Communion service which, commencing with the Introit, or the Lord's Prayer, closes with the end of the Nicene Creed. (2) This term is also used for the introductory part of the Eucharistic office, when it only, and nothing further, is intended to be used. **1899** *Westm. Gaz.* 2 Jan. 4/2 Those of you who feel that it is not necessary to hear the ante-Communion service twice on Sunday.

antecourt ('æntɪkɔət). [f. ANTE- + COURT, after Fr. *antécour.*] An outer or entrance court.

1691 NORRIS *Pract. Disc.* 201 One Day spent in these Ante-Courts of Heaven is better than a Thousand.

‖**ante'cursor.** *Obs.*$^{-0}$ [L. = forerunner.]

1656 BLOUNT *Glossogr.*, *Antecursor*, one that runs or rides before, a forerunner. [Whence in JOHNSON, ASH, etc.]

antedate ('æntɪdeɪt), *sb.* [f. ANTE- + DATE *sb.*]

1. A date affixed to a document, or assigned to an event, earlier than its actual date.

1580 HOLLYBAND *Treas. Fr. Tong.*, *Antidater une obligation*, to give an Antidate to an Obligation. **1609** ROWLANDS *Knave of Clubbes* 16 Ile frame a Bill that I am in thy debt, And to the same an Ante date will set. **1748** RICHARDSON *Clarissa* (1811) VI. 95, I posted away to the lady, intending to plead great affairs that I came not before, in order to favour your antedate. **1870** *Daily News* 31 Aug./2 Brevet-Colonel ——.. to be major-general, dated 6th March, 1868, such antedate not to carry back pay prior to 23rd July, 1870.

†**2.** *fig.* Anticipation. (Cf. ANTEDATE *v.* 6.) *Obs.*

1624 DONNE *Devotions* 10 (T.) Why hath not my soul these apprehensions, these presages .. those antedates .. those suspicions of a sin, as well as my body of a sickness?

antedate ('æntɪ,deɪt), *v.* Also 6–7 **anti-.** [f. prec. sb.; cf. *date* sb. and vb.]

1. *trans.* To affix an earlier than the true date to (a document).

1587 FLEMING *Contn. Holinshed* III. 953/1 Counterfeiting and antidating of the kings seale in a signet. **1682** SCARLETT *Exchanges* 56 He that Antidates an Endorsement is guilty of fraud and deceit. **1715** BURNET *Own Time* (1766) I. 343 He got the king to antedate it, as if it had been signed at Oxford. **1858** BEVERIDGE *Hist. India* II. VI. ii. 587 He drew up a letter which he antedated fifteen days.

2. To assign (an event) to an earlier date.

a **1631** DONNE *Poems* 4 Wilt thou then antedate some new-made vow? **1775** *Fielding's Life* in *Wks.* I. Pref. 19 Having often ante-dated, and sometimes post-dated, the matter which he found in the Spanish history. **1872** E. ROBERTSON *Hist. Ess.* 193 The struggle .. began in the reign of Edgar and was antedated long afterwards .. to throw odium upon Edwy.

3. To carry back to an earlier date or time.

a **1600** *Quaternio* 262 Wisedome .. could in some sort antidate their dayes, and giue them an essence and being with the holy Patriarkes. **1697** J. COLLIER *Ess. Mor. Subj.* II. (1702) 97 By Reading a Man does as it were Antedate his Life. *c* **1850** MRS. BROWNING *Vision of Poets* That rage Barbaric, ante-dates the age.

4. To bring about at an earlier date, accelerate.

1640 T. CAREW *Poems* Wks. 1824, 132 If you let her goe, she may Antedate the latter day. **1662** FULLER *Worthies* II. 67 A fright of his Mother .. accelerated, or rather ante-dated his nativity. **1712** *Spect.* No. 437 ¶1 Sorrow, and private Anxiety of Mind, which antedate Age and Sickness. **1813** SCOTT *Triermain* II. xxv, Seem'd .. that Fate Would Camlan's ruin antedate.

5. To come before (something) in date; precede.

1664 POWER *Exp. Philos.* Pref. 1 Neither do their Records furnish us with anything that does Antedate our late discoveries. **1703** DE FOE *Elegy on Annesley*, As if design'd by Instinct to be Great, His Judgment seem'd to antidate his Wit. **1867** DRAPER *Amer. Civ. War* I. ii. §1. 76 The Peruvian empire antedates that of Mexico.

6. To take in imagination before its actual occurrence, to anticipate.

1611 BEAUM. & FL. *Triumph Hon.* iii, Like an obedient servant, antedating My Lord's command. **1660** JER. TAYLOR *Duct. Dubit.* I. i. Wks. IX. 30 Shame does but antedate the divine anger. **1708** POPE *St. Cecilia's D.* 123 Our joys below it [Music] can improve, And antedate the bliss above. **1810** COLERIDGE *Friend* VI. xi. (1867) 343 Wisdom forbids her children to ante-date their knowledge, or to act and feel further than they know.

'**ante,dated,** *ppl. a.* [f. prec. + -ED.] Bearing an antedate, assigned to an earlier date; transferred to an earlier time; brought about at an earlier date, accelerated, anticipated.

1611 COTGR., *Antidaté*, Antidated. **1665** J. SPENCER *Prodigies* 375 An antedated and diseased old age. *a* **1711** KEN *Poet. Wks.* 1721 II. 83 Thou .. Apostates dost expel, Giving them here an antedated Hell. **1822** HAZLITT *Table T.* II. iv. 58 A file of antedated newspapers.

antedating ('æntɪ,deɪtɪŋ), *vbl. sb.* [f. as prec. + -ING^{1}.] The action of marking with or assigning to an earlier date; anticipating.

1587 [See ANTEDATE *v.* 1.] **1619** NAUNTON in *Fortesc. Papers* 96 The late entring and antedating of the Order. **1706** tr. *Dupin's Eccl. Hist.* II. v. 81 An Edict .. to reform Abuses, Frauds, Antedatings and Forgeries. **1879** FARRAR *St. Paul* II. 587 That ante-dating of the second Advent.

antediluvial (,æntɪdɪ'l(j)uːvɪəl), *a. rare.* [f. ANTE- + *diluvi-um* deluge + -AL^{1}.] Applied by Buckland to geological formations older than the 'diluvial' (then attributed to the Noachian deluge).

1823 BUCKLAND *Reliq. Diluv.* 2, I have felt myself fully justified in applying the epithet .. antediluvial to the state of things immediately preceding it [this great convulsion]. **1827** *Edin. Rev.* XLV. 317 The ante-diluvial rocks have a more compact stony aspect.

,**antedi'luvially,** *adv. rare*$^{-1}$. [f. prec. + -LY^{2}.] In times before the Flood.

1826 BEDDOES *To B. Procter, Poems* (1851) 168 Time's billows, swelling, Roll a deep, ghostly, and invisible sea Of melted worlds antediluvially Upon the sand of ever-crumbling hours.

antediluvian (,æntɪdɪ'l(j)uːvɪən), *a.* and *sb.* [f. ANTE- + *diluvi-um* the deluge + -AN.] **A.** *adj.*

1. Of or belonging to the world before the Noachian deluge; existing before the Flood.

1657 TRAPP *Comm. Job* xxii. 15 II. 200 Those Antediluvian Belialists. **1748** HARTLEY *Observ. Man* I. iii. §1 ¶83 Parts of the antediluvian Language. **1821** W. CRAIG *Drawing, etc.* ii. 109 The ingenious Dr. Burnet .. has made the antediluvian world a beautiful, smooth sphere, entirely covered with fine rich pasture land.

2. Concerning or referring to the period before the Flood.

1646 SIR T. BROWNE *Pseud. Ep.* 344 The antediluvian Chronology. *a* **1849** H. COLERIDGE *Ess.* II. 299 The antediluvian and postdiluvian history.

3. Of the sort which obtained before the Flood.

1698 NORRIS *Pract. Disc.* IV. 367 Could I then lengthen out my Span to an Antediluvian stretch. **1711** F. FULLER *Med. Gymn.* Pref., An Antediluvian Diet of Roots and Vegetables. **1846** H. ROGERS *Ess.* I. iv. 165 An antediluvian lease of life.

4. Belonging or proper to long past ages; very antiquated, primitive. (In a disparaging sense.)

a **1726** VANBRUGH & CIB. *Prov. Husb.* III. (1730) 334 Such primitive antediluvian notions of life. **1823** LAMB *Elia* Ser. I. xxiv. (1865) 188 The cottage, a sorry antediluvian make-shift of a building.

B. *sb.* [the adj. used absol.]

1. One who lived before the Flood; *fig.* one who attains to a very great age.

1684 T. BURNET *Th. Earth* I. 222 The long lives of the antediluvians. **1713** *Guardian* No. 101 (1756) II. 81 An antediluvian could not have more life and briskness in him at three-score and ten. **1823** SCOTT *St. Ronan's* xxxi, From what cursed old antediluvian, who lived before the invention of spinning-jennies, she learned this craft, Heaven only knows.

†'**antefact.** *Obs. rare.* [ad. L. *antefact-um*, pa. pple. of *ante-facĕre* to do before.] A thing done before, a previous act.

1623 COCKERAM, *Antefact*, a deed done before. **1655** FULLER *Ch. Hist.* III. 87 Being cleared and quitted from all ante-facts how hainous soever, by their entrance into Christianity. *Ibid.* x. 39 Confession was of antefacts, not post facts.

antefen, antefne, obs. forms of ANTHEM.

antefix ('æntɪfɪks). Usually in *pl.*; also in L. form, with *pl.* **-a.** [ad. L. *antefix-um* subst. use of pa. pple. of *ante-fīg-ĕre* to fix in front.] Ornamental tiles or other work on the eaves and cornices of ancient buildings, to conceal the ends of the tiles; also ornamental heads of animals, etc., making the spouts from the gutters.

1832 GELL *Pompeiana* I. viii. 174 Like the eaves of external roofs, with its ornamental antefixes. **1850** LEITCH tr. *Müller's Anc. Art* §249 Inverted antefixa or corner-ornaments of ancient sarcophagi are frequently to be found as decorations of pillars.

antefixal (æntɪ'fɪksəl), *a.* [f. prec. + -AL^{1}.] Of or pertaining to an antefix.

1857 BIRCH *Anc. Pottery* (1858) II. 7 This helix or antefixal ornament is the same as that which appears in the Doric entablatures. **1882** *Athenæum* 19 Aug. 248 The ornaments are more Asiatic than Egyptian; rosettes, chequers, antefixal ornaments, etc.

anteflexed ('æntɪflɛkst), *ppl. a. rare.* [f. ANTE- + *flex-* ppl. stem of *flect-ĕre* to bend + -ED.] Bent forward; *spec.* of the uterus.

1872 THOMAS *Dis. Wom.* 72 Anterior to the cervix [of the uterus] if it be in normal position or anteflexed.

anteflexion (æntɪ'flɛkʃən). *rare.* [f. ANTE- + L. *flexiōn-em*, n. of action f. *flect-ĕre* to bend.] A bending forward; *spec.* of the uterus.

1859 TODD *Cycl. Anat. & Phys.* V. 643/2 [This curvature] constitutes .. anteflexion of the uterus. **1872** THOMAS *Dis. Wom.* 72 Due to anteflexion or anteversion of the uterus.

‖**antefurca** (æntɪ'fɜːkə). *Ent.* [mod.L., f. L. *ante* in front + *furca* fork.] In cockroaches, an internal forked projection from the sternal wall of the anterior somite of the thorax, which helps to support the nervous cord; sometimes also applied to external forked projections on the ventral surface of the segments of some Arthropoda.

1826 KIRBY & SPENCE *Entomol.* (1828) IV. xliii. 185 The extensor of the anterior thigh to the antefurca. **1877** HUXLEY *Anat. Inv. An.* vii. 404 Forked or double apodemes, the antefurca, medifurca, and postfurca.

ante-garden, -hall, -human, etc.: see ANTE-.

†**ante'genital,** *a. Obs.*$^{-0}$ [ad. L. *antegenitāl-is* before birth, f. *ante* before + *genitāl-is* belonging to birth.] Previous to birth: (*erron.* 'Born before, elder born.' Blount *Glossogr.* 1656.)

†ante'gredient, *a. Obs. rare*$^{-1}$. [ad. L. *ante-gredient-em* pr. pple. of *ante-gred-i* to go before.] Preceding, going before.

1686 GOAD *Celest. Bod.* I. ii. 6 The antegredient part of the exhalation would give notice of the vehemency to be expected.

†ante'gression. *Obs.*$^{-0}$ [ad. L. **antegressiōn-em*, n. of action f. *antegredi*: see prec.] 'A going before.' Blount *Glossogr.* 1656.

ante-jentacular, -judiciary, etc.: see ANTE-.

†ante'lation. *Obs. rare.* [ad. med.L. *ante-lātiōn-em* prerogative, n. of action f. *ante-ferre* to carry before.] Precedence, preference, prerogative.

1553-87 FOXE *A. & M.* I. 790/2 The intrication of these prerogatives, antelations, and such other as do associate these expectative graces. **1623** MABBE *Aleman's G. d'Alfarache* II. 190 Alleaging the antelation of time, and priority of his debt.

antelope ('æntɪləʊp). Forms: 5-7 **antelop**, 5 **antyllope, antlop(e**, 6 **anteloppe**, 7 **antalope**, 6-9 **antilope**, 5- **antelope**. [a. OFr. *antelop* (also *antelu*), ad. L. *ant(h)alop-us* (Damianus, *a* 1072), Gr. ἀνθόλοψ, ἀνθόλοπ- (Eustathius of Antioch, *c* 336), original language and meaning unknown. Med.Latin forms were also *talopus, calopus*.]

The popular and literary name for the numerous species of the deer-like ruminant genus *Antilope* (Pallas), the limits of which have been variously extended or contracted by different zoologists. The most usual scientific characteristics of the genus are cylindrical, annulated horns, and the possession of a sub-orbital or 'lachrymal' sinus. They are sometimes grouped as *True* Antelopes, *Bush* A., *Capriform* or Goat-like A., and *Bovine* or Ox-like A. It is with the first of these, distinguished by extreme grace and speed of motion, that the name is now popularly associated.

This application of the word is recent. The Gr., L., and OFr. (*Trésor* of Brun. Lat.) notices describe a creature haunting the banks of the Euphrates, very savage, hard to catch, having long saw-like horns, with which they cut in pieces and broke all 'engines,' and even cut down trees. With these attributes the 'antelope' early became a heraldic animal. The modern denotation seems to begin with Topsell. The genus *Antilope* was constituted by Pallas *c* 1775.

c **1430** LYDG. *Min. Poems* (1840) 6 Twoo antelopis stondyng on outher syde, Withe the armys of Englond and of Fraunce. **1432** *Let.* in Riley *Liber Alb.* (1861) III. 459 In eadem pagina [i.e. pageant] erigebantur duo animalia vocata 'antelops.' **1440** *Promp. Parv.*, Antyllope, beste, *Tatula.* **1486** *Bk. St. Alban's*, *Arms* C viij b, As Lyon, Antlop, and other. **1596** SPENSER *F.Q.* I. vi. 26 The antelope and wolfe both fiers and fell. **1607** TOPSELL *Four-footed Beasts* (1673) 1 The Antalope called in Latin *Calopus*, and of the Grecians *Analopos*, or *Aptolos*. **1662** EVELYN *Diary* 9 June, Staggs, elks, antelopes. **1678** PHILLIPS, *Antilope*, a certain mongrel beast, begotten of an Hart and a Goat. **1774** GOLDSM. *Nat. Hist.* II. 47 The tenth variety of the gazelle is the antelope, so well known to the English, who have given it the name. **1821** SHELLEY *Epipsych.* 75 An antelope, In the suspended impulse of its lightness, Were less ætherially light. **1847** CARPENTER *Zool.* §265 The True Antelopes are remarkable for the graceful symmetry of their bodies, the length and slenderness of their limbs, and the lightness and agility of their movements... To the group of true Antelopes also belongs the Gazelle.

b. *attrib.*

1862 MRS. BROWNING *Last Poems* 8 Her throat has the antelope curve. **1872** BAKER *Nile Trib.* xviii. 318 At length we discovered a dangerous antelope-track.

†an'teloquy. *Obs.*$^{-0}$ [ad. L. *anteloquium*, f. *ante* before + *-loquium* speech.] (See quot.)

1623 COCKERAM, *Antiloquy*, a terme which stage-players use, by them called their cue. **1656** BLOUNT *Glossogr.*, *Anteloquy*, a Preface, or the first place or turn in speaking: also [as in COCKERAM].

‖ante'luca. *Obs. rare*$^{-1}$. [L. in form; app. f. *antelūcānus* (see next) after *noctilūca* the moon.] Used by Evelyn for the period before dawn (?).

1696 EVELYN *Corr.* (1846) 121 He brought the phosphorous and anteluca to the clearest light that ever any did.

antelucan (æntɪ'l(j)uːkən), *a.* [ad. L. *antelūcānus* before dawn; f. *ante* + *lūc-* (*lux*) light: see -AN.] Of or pertaining to the hours just before dawn.

1654 GAYTON *Fest. Notes* III. vi. 103 All manner of Antelucan Labourers. *a* **1656** BP. HALL *Rem.* 44 (T.) The Phosphorus of piety and antelucan devotion. *a* **1859** DE QUINCEY *Wks.* X. 259 This practice of crepuscular antelucan worship, possibly having reference to the ineffable mystery of the resurrection.

‖antelu'cano. *Obs. rare*$^{-1}$. [It. (:—L. *antelūcānus*) adj. used subst.] A hymn sung before dawn.

1656 TRAPP *Comm. Matt.* vii. 18 They sang antelucanos, hymns, psalms of praise, to God before break of day.

antelucidate, 'to work by Candle-light before day'; **anteluculated**, 'done before day light.' Bad formations in Cockeram 1623.

†'antelude. *Obs. rare*$^{-1}$. [ad. L. *antelūdium*, f. *ante* before + *lūd-us* play.] A prelude, short introductory play.

1667 H. MORE *Div. Dial.* (1713) 570 The part of the Puppet or Punchinello in the Antelude of the Pageant.

antem(e, obs. form of ANTHEM.

†'ante-man. *Obs.* [ANTE- A.] A valet, an usher.

1638 NABBES *Covent Gard.* II. ii, My Ladies Gentleman Vsher, her preambulator or her anteman.

antembletic (æntɪm'blɛtɪk), *a. rare*$^{-1}$. [a. Gr. *ἀντεμβλητικ-ός, f. ἀντεμβάλλ-ειν to throw in in return.] Making provision against or reparation for loss; as an insurance office.

1780 BENTHAM *Princ. Legisl.* xvi. §54 *note*, Offences against antembletic trust.

antemeridian (ˌæntɪmə'rɪdɪən), *a. rare.* [ad. L. *ante-merīdiān-us* of the fore-noon, f. phr. *ante merīdiem* before noon: see -AN.] Of or belonging to the forenoon or 'morning.'

1656 BLOUNT *Glossogr.*, *Antemeridian*, before noon, or mid-day. **1865** *Daily Tel.* 18 Apr. 3 Every[one] had come out in attire that was decidedly ante-meridian.

‖ante meridiem ('æntiː mɛ'rɪdɪɛm), *phr.* [Lat. phr., 'before midday'.] Before midday; applied to the hours between midnight and the following noon; abbreviated A.M. or a.m. (q.v.).

1563 DEE *Diary* 28 Sept. (1842) 2 Mr. John Ask ante meridiem, by York six myle on this syde. **1647** LILLY *Chr. Astrol.* iv. 41 If your hour of the day be in the morning, or as we say *Ante Meridiem*, or before noon.

ante-metallic, -mortal, etc.: see ANTE-.

antemetic (æntɪ'mɛtɪk), *a.* and *sb.* [mod. f. ANT- + EMETIC.] **A.** *adj.* Tending to check vomiting. **B.** *sb.* A medicine of this nature.

1706 PHILLIPS, *Antemeticks*, Medicines that are given against vomiting. **1853** MAYNE *Exp. Lex.*, *Antemetic*, opposed to or removing the inclination to vomit.

antemne, antempne, obs. forms of ANTHEM.

antempered, obs. form of ATTEMPERED.

antemundane (æntɪ'mʌndeɪn), *a.* [f. ANTE- + *mund-us* world + -ANE; after *mundane*, L. *mundānus*, belonging to the world.] Existing or occurring before the creation of the world.

1731 in BAILEY. **1742** YOUNG *Nt. Th.* v. 93 The supreme, Great, antemundane Father! **1823** LAMB *Elia* (1860) 102 Some probable insight into our ante-mundane condition.

ante'mural. ? *Obs.* [ad. L. *antemūrāle* a breastwork, f. *ante* before + *mūr-us* wall: see -AL[2].]

1774 T. WEST *Antiq. Furness* (1805) 369 A strong high wall with turrets, called the barbican or antemural.

antenatal (æntɪ'neɪtəl), *a.* [f. ANTE- + L. *nātāl-is* pertaining to birth, NATAL.] **1.** Happening or existing before birth.

1817 SHELLEY *Pr. Athan.* I, Memories of an antenatal life. **1848** KINGSLEY *Saint's Trag.* II. ix. 34 A heaven, my spirit's antenatal home. **1879** FARRAR *St. Paul* II. 242 The antenatal predilection for Israel and detestation of Esau.

2. Of, pertaining to, or concerned with the health and well-being of women during pregnancy.

1917 *Maternity & Child Welfare* (Local Govt. Board Rep.) p. xi, At Bradford there is an ante-natal clinic at the Maternity Hospital. *Ibid.* 19 There is a municipal ante-natal centre. **1930** *Lancet* 20 Dec. 1359/2 Many local authorities have already provided facilities for antenatal supervision.

†ˌantenata'litial, *a. Obs. rare.* [f. ANTE- + L. *nātālīci-us* belonging to a birthday + -AL[1].] Belonging to the condition before birth.

1708 J. KEILL *Anim. Secr.* Pref. 4 The ante-natalitial Ducts are stopp'd by breathing. **1717** —— *Anim. Œcon.* Pref. 12 Some of the ante-natalitial Ducts are expanded .. by breathing.

'ante-ˌnated, *ppl. a. Obs. rare*$^{-1}$. [f. ANTE- + L. *nāt-us* born + -ED.] Born before.

a **1670** HACKET *Abp. Williams* II. 48 Something of the Evangelical relish was in them, ante-nated, and in being, before the Gospels were written.

antenna (æn'tɛnə). *Pl.* **-æ**, rarely **-as**. [a. L. *antenna*, in ancient use 'a sail-yard'; usually referred to Gr. ἀνατείν-ειν to stretch out or forth. The modern use seems to begin with the L. transl. of Aristotle Περὶ ζῴων ἱστορίας, by Theodorus Gaza (died 1478) in which the Gr. κεραῖαι 'horns' of insects (*cornua, cornicula* Pliny) is rendered *antennæ*, which thence passed into subsequent entomological writers (many of whom cite Aristotle for it). As the projecting 'horns' or ends of sail-yards, in L. *cornua antennārum*, were also called κεραῖαι, *antennæ* was aptly employed to render the same word when meaning the horns of insects, which indeed often suggest the *cornua* of the long ascending *antennæ* or yards of lateen sails. Common in Lat. entomol. works during 16-17th c., but not found in the dict. of any mod. lang. bef. 1700.]

1. A sensory organ, occurring in pairs on the heads of insects and crustacea; popularly called *horns* or *feelers*.

[*a* **1478** THEOD. GAZA *Aristotle, Hist. Anim.* (1492) 18 b, Ad hæc antennæ nonnullis ante oculos prætenduntur, ut papilioni et fulloni [Gr. ἔτι κεραίας πρὸ τῶν ὀμμάτων ἔνια]. *a* **1600** U. ALDROVANDUS *De animalibus insect.* (1602) Prol. 7 Quædam cornicula gerunt in capite quæ antennas Aristoteles vocat. *Ibid.* II. 236 Aristoteles antennas iis ante oculos prætendi scripsit, idque ex eo repetiit Plinius, vocans istiusmodi antennas ignava cornicula. **1646** SIR T. BROWNE *Pseud. Ep.* III. xviii. 153 Insects that have *antennæ*, or long hornes to feele out their way, as Butter-flies and Locusts. [**1657** S. PURCHAS *Pol. Flying Ins.* I. iii. 4 The horns are called by Aristotle, *Antennæ*, because they hold them forth before them.] **1698** ALLEN *Death-Watch* in *Phil. Trans.* XX. 377 The Antennæ proceeded from under the Eyes. **1713** DERHAM *Phys. Theol.* (JOD.) Insects clean their eyes with their forelegs, as well as antennæ. **1826** KIRBY & SPENCE *Entomol.* (1828) II. xxiii. 303 This part looks like a jointed antenna. **1834** GOOD *Bk. Nat.* II. 21 The antennas of the butterflies. **1847** CARPENTER *Zool.* §788 The spiny Lobster .. is distinguished by the very large size of its lateral antennæ. **1879** LUBBOCK *Sci. Lect.* iii. 87 There are in the antennæ of ants certain curious organs which may perhaps be of an auditory character. **1880** HUXLEY *Cray-Fish* 24 The Antennæ are organs of touch.

2. *fig.* 'Feelers.'

1855 HOLMES *Poems* 214 Go to yon tower, where busy science plies Her vast antennæ, feeling thro' the skies. **1918** E. POUND *Pavannes & Divisions* 43 My soul's antennæ are prey to such perturbations. **1959** *Listener* 17 Dec. 1082/1 This is where an author with sound learning, a seeing eye, and sensitive 'antennae' can be of great assistance.

3. *Bot.* (by extension). A pair of long slender irritable processes in the male flower of certain orchids, by the excitement of which the pollinium is jerked out of the flower.

1862 DARWIN *Orchids* 225 When the right-hand antenna .. is touched, the pollinium is instantly ejected. **1874** LUBBOCK *Flowers & Insects* (1882) 175 Insects alight as usual on the lip of the flower, and it will be seen that in front of it are two long processes called antennæ.

4. A dorsal sense-organ in rotifers.

1886 A. G. BOURNE in *Encycl. Brit.* XXI. 5/2 A structure found in many Rotifers, and variously known as the 'calcar', 'siphon', 'tentaculum', or 'antenna'.

5. a. *Radio.* An aerial wire or other device for radiating or receiving radio waves, an aerial: see AERIAL *a.* 6 b.

1902 J. A. FLEMING in *Encycl. Brit.* XXXIII. 230/2 The great improvement introduced by Marconi was the employment of this vertical air-wire, aerial, antenna, or elevated conductor. **1904** *Physical Rev.* Sept. 197 In 1898 he [*sc.* Marconi] saw the importance of the direct grounding of the receiving antenna. **1915** A. E. SEELIG tr. *Zenneck's Wireless Telegr.* 150 Every radio station has an open oscillator, the 'antenna', that part of the antenna which is suspended in the air being called the'aerial'. **1922** GLAZEBROOK *Dict. Appl. Physics* II. 1044/1 Electric waves .. received on the antennae of wireless stations. **1960** *Daily Tel.* 22 Feb. 14 The radar antenna shown above .. has an 84-ft. 'dish'. **1961** *Word Study* Apr. 3/1 The biological scientist will insist that the creatures have *antennae*; an electronics technician writes about the *antennas* of a microwave installation. **1962** *Observer* 10 June 20/1 A huge 340-ton horn antenna at Andover, Maine, will beam signals at the satellite.

b. *attrib.* and *Comb.*

1906 J. A. FLEMING *Princ. Electr. Wave Telegr.* ix. 556 This is dissipated .. as heat in the antenna and antenna circuit. **1916** —— *Radiotelegr.* (ed. 3) 155 A single mast .. having two sprits attached to it by means of which an antenna wire is upheld in the form of a vertical rectangle. **1922** GLAZEBROOK *Dict. Appl. Physics* II. 1038/1 The condenser C is intended to represent the antenna capacity, and R .. the same power as is actually occasioned by the antenna resistance and radiation. **1940** *Chambers's Techn. Dict.* 39/1 *Antenna array*, a group of two or more antennae spacially arranged to have particular directional radiating and/or receiving properties. *Ibid.* 39/2 *Antenna system*, the whole of the equipment of a radio transmitter or receiver associated with the antenna-to-earth circuit. **1946** *Electronic Engin.* XVIII. 20 An automatic V.H.F. direction finder using a fixed .. antenna system. **1963** *Ann. Reg. 1962* 447 The U.S.S.R. built the highest tower in Europe .. a height of 1,383 feet with its antenna mast.

6. A 'feeler' attached to a naval mine. Also *attrib.*

1933 *Jane's Fighting Ships 1933* 461/1 Body of mine, spherical, 3 feet diameter. Form of detonation uncertain; said to consist of antennae fitted with .. magnetic pistol... Antennae said to consist of thin conducting wires and magnetic pistols. **1947** *10 Eventful Years* IV. 632 *Antenna mine*, a large naval mine .. exploding on contact with a metal object.

antennal (æn'tɛnəl), *a. Zool.* [f. prec. + -AL[1].] Of or belonging to antennæ.

1834 *Penny Cycl.* II. 92 The younger Huber has attributed to ants the use of certain signs made with those organs which he terms antennal language. **1861** HULME *Moquin-Tandon* II. VI. i. 318 The antennal pincers of the Spiders.

antennary (æn'tɛnərɪ, 'æntɪnərɪ), *a. Zool.* [f. mod.L. *antennāri-us*, f. ANTENNA: see -ARY.] Of, relating to, or of the nature of antennæ.
1836 TODD *Cycl. Anat. & Phys.* I. 776/1 The two antennary arteries. **1877** HUXLEY *Anat. Inv. An.* vi. 254 The very fine setæ..which abound on the antennary organs of Insecta and Crustacea.

antenniferous (æntɪ'nɪfərəs), *a. Zool.* [f. mod.L. ANTENNA + -FEROUS bearing.] Bearing or having antennæ.
1826 KIRBY & SPENCE *Entomol.* (1828) III. xxviii. 23 Their head and trunk are distinct, the former antenniferous. **1874** LUBBOCK *Orig. Ins.* i. 18 Hexapod antenniferous larvæ.

antenniform (æn'tɛnɪfɔːm), *a. Zool.* [f. as prec. + -(I)FORM.] Of the form or shape of antennæ.
1847 in CRAIG. **1856-8** W. CLARK *Van der Hoeven's Zool.* I. 239 Head with two very long antenniform tentacles. **1877** HUXLEY *Anat. Inv. An.* vi. 297 The first pair of swimming appendages..are converted into antenniform organs.

antennular (æn'tɛnjʊlə(r)), *a. Zool.* [f. ANTENNULE + -AR.] Of the nature of small antennæ.
1858 T. R. JONES *Aquar. Nat.* 318 The part representing the head is..furnished with eight antennular organs.

antennulary (æn'tɛnjʊlərɪ), *a. Zool.* [f. as prec. + -ARY.] = ANTENNULAR.
1877 HUXLEY *Anat. Inv. An.* vi. 282 Antennary and antennulary nerves.

antennule (æn'tɛnjʊl). *Zool.* [ad. mod.L. **antennula*, dim. of ANTENNA.] A little antenna; a tiny organ of the nature of an antenna.
1845 BAIRD in *Proc. Berw. Nat. Club* II. 156 Antennules of two branches of nearly equal size. **1872** NICHOLSON *Palæont.* 147 A pair of small jointed feelers..known as the 'lesser antennæ' or 'antennules.'

ante-orbital (æntiː'ɔːbɪtəl), *a. Phys.* Also antorbital. [f. ANTE- + ORBIT *sb.*, eyesocket + -AL[1].] Situated in front of the eyes.
1839-47 TODD *Cycl. Anat.* III. 269/1 The ant-orbital foramen. **1880** GUNTHER *Fishes* 36 The Eye divides the head into the ante-orbital and post-orbital portion. **1881** OWEN in *Nat.* XXIV. 499 These antorbital nostrils, as they are called.

antepagment (æntɪ'pægmənt). *Arch.* [ad. L. *antepagment-um* (also used unchanged, with pl. *-menta*), f. *ante* before + *pang-ĕre* to fasten.]
1678 PHILLIPS, *Antipagments*, garnishings in posts or doors, wrought in stone or timber. **1876** GWILT *Encycl. Arch.*, *Antepagmenta*, In ancient architecture the jambs or moulded architraves of a door.

ante-partum ('æntiː'pɑːtəm), *a.* [Lat. phr., 'before birth', used *attrib.* or as *adj.*] (Occurring) before birth, esp. of things affecting the mother immediately before or during the early stages of labour.
1908 *Practitioner* Mar. 358 Crédé's method..cannot prevent ante-partum infection. **1961** *Times* 26 Apr. 19/5 Antepartum haemorrhage.

antepaschal (æntɪ'pæskəl), *a. rare.* [f. ANTE- + *pascha* passover, Easter + -AL[1].] Coming before the Jewish Passover, or before Easter.
1660 JER. TAYLOR *Duct. Dubit.* III. iv. xiii. §17 Some did only observe three..out of the number of the seven ante-paschal weeks. **1704** NELSON *Fest. & Fasts* i. II. (1739) 445 Concerning the ending of the Ante-paschal Fast.

antepast ('æntɪpɑːst, -æ-). Also 6-7 anti-. [f. ANTE- + *pāst-us* food, f. *pāsc-ĕre* to feed; cf. *repast.*] Something taken before a meal to whet the appetite (*obs.*); a foretaste.
1590 *Eng. Rom. Life* in *Harl. Misc.* (Malh.) II. 182 The first messe, or antepast as they call it..is some fine meate to urge them to have an appetite. **1621** DONNE *Serm.* lxx. 713 An office is but an Antipast—it gets them an appetite to another office. **1778** H. WALPOLE *Last Jrnls.* Dec., A very unexpected blow..an antepast of the odium they were to incur. **1855** A. DE VERE *Poems* 208 Rich antepasts we have in thee Of glory and eternity.

ante-patriarchal, -pectoral, etc.: see ANTE-.

†'**antepend.** *Obs.* = ANTEPENDIUM.
1542 *Coll. Inventories* (JAM.) Item, ane antepend of blak velvot..item ane frontall of the samyn wark. **1555** *Inv. of Vestm.* (ibid.) Ane antipend for the Lady's altar of blew and yellow broig satin.

‖**antependium** (æntɪ'pɛndɪəm). Often anti-. [L., f. *ante* before + *pend-ēre* to hang: 'velum quod antependet.' Du Cange.] A veil or covering for the front of the altar, used in Roman Catholic and some Anglican churches; sometimes identified with a FRONTAL, which may be an ornamental panel.
1696 PHILLIPS, *Antipendium*, a large silver-skreen that covers the Front of a Popish Altar..hung on with skrews upon a high day. **1716** T. WARD *Eng. Ref.* 51 On Beds they Antipendiums laid, Of Sacred Vestments Cushions made. **1849** ROCK *Ch. of Fathers* I. iii. 236 The modern term for the frontal is 'antependium.' **1864** AINSWORTH *Tower Lond.* 158 The altar, covered with a richly-ornamented antipendium.

antepenult (,æntɪpɪ'nʌlt), *a.* and *sb.* [abbrev. of L. *antepænultima*: see next.]
A. *adj.* Preceding the penult; the last but two. Orig. a term of *Prosody*, but also used otherwise.
1585 JAMES I *Ess. Poesie* (Arb.) 57 Or *question* and *digestion*, It rymes in *ques* and *ges*, albeit they be bot the antepenult syllabis. **1597** T. MORLEY *Introd. Mus.* 76 Your penult and antepenult notes. **1852** DANA *Crust.* I. 631 Carapax..extending to antepenult thoracic segment.
B. *sb.* [The adj. used *absol.*, sc. syllable.]
c **1620** A. HUME *Orthogr. Brit. Tong.* 22 Never farther from the end then the third syllab, quhilk the grammareanes calls the antepenult. **1755** JOHNSON *Gram. Pros.*, Words in *ion* have the accent upon the antepenult.

‖**antepenultima** (,æntɪpɪ'nʌltɪmə). *Pros.* [L. (*syllaba*) *antepænultima* the last (syllable) but two, f. *ante* before + *pænultima* last but one, f. *pæne* almost + *ultima* last. Formerly with Eng. pl. in *-s.*] The last syllable but two of a word.
1581 SIDNEY *Def. Poesie* (1622) 529 The French..hath not one word that hath his accent in the last syllable sauing two, called Antepenultima. **1589** PUTTENHAM *Eng. Poesie* (Arb.) 92 In *altitude* and *heauinesse* the sharpe accent falles vpon *al* and *he* which be the antepenultimaes. **1874** SAYCE *Comp. Philol.* i. 19 The general rule [of Æolic dialect] which threw the accent back upon the *antepenultima*.

antepenultimate (-'ʌltɪmət), *a.* and *sb.* [f. L. *antepænultim-us* + -ATE, after *ultimate.*]
A. *adj.* The last but two. Orig. of syllables; but extended to order in place or time.
1730 NICHOLLS *Lobster* in *Phil. Trans.* XXXVI. 293 The antepenultimate Leg. **1775** WALKER *Rhym. Dict.* Pref. 19, I find every vowel in this antepenultimate syllable.. pronounced long. **1865** *Pall Mall G.* 20 Oct. 11 We have the antepenultimate Duke of Newcastle's authority for the dictum. **1870** ROLLESTON *Anim. Life* 12 Each succeeding vertebra up to the antepenultimate lumbar.
B. *sb.* [The adj. used *absol.*, sc. syllable, etc.]
1727 CHAMBERS *Cycl.* s.v., The Antepenultimate of a dactyle is long. **1871** *Athenæum* 10 June 725 In words of four syllables it [the accent] may be on the antepenultimate, as in *témérité*.

antephialtic (,æntɛfɪ'æltɪk), *a.* and *sb. Med.* [ad. mod.L. *antephialticus* (Hoffmann *a* 1740), f. Gr. ἀντί against + ἐφιάλτ-ης nightmare: see -IC.]
A. *adj.* Good against the nightmare. **B.** *sb.* A medicinal agent of this nature.
[**1811** HOOPER *Med. Dict.*, *Antephialtica*, medicines which prevent the night-mare]. **1853** MAYNE *Exp. Lex.*, *Antephialtic*, opposed to, or curative of ephialtes or night-mare.

antephne, obs. form of ANTHEM.

antepileptic (,æntɛpɪ'lɛptɪk), *a.* and *sb. Med.* Also 8 anti-ep-. [f. ANT- + EPILEPTIC.]
A. *adj.* Good against, or preventive of, epilepsy.
1656 RIDGLEY *Pract. Physick* 113 The Antepileptick Pill of the roots of Piony. **1757** PULTNEY in *Phil. Trans.* L. 73 Giving alexipharmics and anti-epileptic medicines. **1853** in MAYNE *Exp. Lex.*
B. *sb.* (sc. medicine.)
1742 BAILEY, *Antepilepticks.* **1753** CHAMBERS *Cycl. Supp.* s.v., The chief Antepileptics from the vegetable kingdom are, the roots of pæony, valerian, etc. **1864** in WEBSTER.

†**,antepi'leptical**, *a. Med. Obs.* = prec. adj.
1646 SIR T. BROWNE *Pseud. Ep.* II. v. (1686) 71 That Coral is Antepileptical we will not deny. **1667** *Phil. Trans.* II. 565 A Laxative Rosin, dissolved in an Anti-Epileptical Spirit.

antepiscopist: see ANTI-EPISCOPIST.

†**ante'pone**, *v. Obs. rare*[−1]. [ad. L. *antepōn-ĕre* to place before.] To set before, to prefer.
1656 BLOUNT *Glossogr.*, *Antepone*, to put or set before, to prefer. **1755** T. CROKER *Ariosto's Orl. Fur.* XLII. lxxxiii, Whose beauty, virtue, Rome should antepone To her she once so much did celebrate.

†'**anteport.** *Obs. rare.* [ad. It. *antiporta*, f. *anti* = L *ante* before + *porta* gate, door.]
1. An outer gate or door.
1644 EVELYN *Mem.* (1857) I. 126 Between the five large anti-ports are columns of enormous height.
2. A veil or hanging in front of a door.
1653 J. GREAVES *Grand Signour's Seraglio* 14 His Majestie's Bed-Chamber..The Anteporta's are cloth of gold of Bursia. **1669** T. SMITH *Mann. Turks* 75 (L.) If a Christian or Jew should but lift up the antiport and set one step into it.

ante-portico, -posthumous, etc.: see ANTE-.

anteposition (æntɪpəʊ'zɪʃən). *rare.* [n. of action f. L. *antepōn-ĕre*; cf. *position.*] The placing of anything in front: *esp.* **a.** of a word which in ordinary construction follows; **b.** in *Bot.* (see quot.).
1753 CHAMBERS *Cycl. Supp.*, *Anteposition*..as when in Latin the adjective is put before the substantive. **1775** ASH, *Anteposition*, a position of words contrary to their proper and natural order. **1880** GRAY *Bot. Text-bk.* 396 *Anteposition*, the opposition of successive (or apparently successive) whorls which normally alternate.

ante-post ('æntiːpəʊst), *a.* [f. ANTE + POST *sb.*[1] 2.] Of betting (see quot. 1902).
1902 *Encycl. Brit.* XXVI. 236/1 Betting is of two kinds: 'post', when wagering does not begin until the numbers of the runners are hoisted on the board; and 'ante-post', when wagering opens weeks or months before the event. **1914** *Daily Express* 19 Sept. 5/2 If there had been any important ante-post betting..many would have burnt their fingers badly.

anteprandial (æntɪ'prændɪəl), *a.* [f. ANTE- + *prandi-um* dinner + -AL[1].] Before-dinner.
1847 *Q. Rev.* No. 163. 66 The anteprandial fencing-bouts of the House of Lords. **1864** SALA in *Daily Tel.* 20 July, When he takes his anteprandial constitutional on deck.

anter, obs. form of ADVENTURE *sb.*

‖**ante rem** ('æntiː rɛm). *Philos.* [med.L. (Albertus Magnus), 'before the thing'.] Used as *phr.* and also *attrib.* Prior to the existence of a particular or physical thing; *spec.* of the philosophical theory (a form of REALISM 1) which holds that the universal is logically prior to, i.e. capable of existing independently of, the particular; also, of the universal so regarded.
c **1873** W. JAMES in R.B. Perry *Tht. & Char. of W.J.* (1935) I. 499 Our notion of a future time with its material content forms a sort of matrix *ante rem* into which in its time the *res* fits. **1904** —— *Coll. Ess. & Rev.* (1920) 446 Like empiricism, it is individualistic and phenomenalistic; it places truth *in rebus*, and not *ante rem*. **1927** C. R. S. HARRIS *Duns Scotus* I. vi. 215 The distinction of the threefold aspect of the universal *ante rem*, *in re*, and *post rem* forms the starting-point of the epistemological theory of Scotus no less than that of Albert or Aquinas. **1953** H. H. PRICE *Thinking & Exper.* ix. 266 Nothing in this world is a perfect instance of circularity, according to the *Ante Rem* theory. *Ibid.* x. 302 One might deny that there are subsistent and extra-mental universals, whether of the *Ante rem* or *In re* variety.

antergic (æn'tɜːdʒɪk), *a. Physiol.* [f. ANT- *pref.* + Gr. ἔργον work + -IC, after *synergic.*] Acting in opposition to the action of another part, as a muscle: = ANTAGONISTIC *a.* 2: opp. to SYNERGIC *a.*
1892 W. R. GOWERS *Man. Dis. Nerv. Syst.* I. 7 This antergic contraction is essential for the exertion of force.

anteriad (æn'tɪərɪæd), *adv.* [f. ANTERIOR + -AD.] Towards the anterior part or surface of the body.
1903 *Trans. Amer. Microsc. Soc.* Nov. 66 (Cent. D. Suppl.), The rudiment of the gall-bladder which in the previous stage..opens dorsad..in the present stage..opens anteriad.

anterior (æntɪərɪə(r)), *a.* [a. L. *anterior* fore, former, f. *ante* before; cf. Fr. *antérieur*, Cotgr.]
1. a. Of place: Fore, more to the front; opposed to *posterior*.
1611 COTGR., *Anterieur*, Anterior, fore, former..that goeth, or is set, before. **1626** BACON *Sylva* §115 Where the anteriour body giveth way, as fast as the posteriour cometh on, it maketh no noise. **1831** BREWSTER *Optics* xxxv. 288 The two parts into which the iris divides the eye are called the anterior and the posterior chambers.
b. *Anat.*, *Bot.*, and *Zool.* Situated in the front or nearer the head, fore-part, etc.: opp. to POSTERIOR A. 3. In *Bot.* also, below, inferior. In *Human Anat.* now usually (because of the erect posture of man) = VENTRAL *a.*; similarly for other animals having an upright posture.
1733 G. DOUGLAS tr. *Winslow's Anat.* I. 75 The Clavicle is divided into a Body or middle Part, and two Extremities, one anterior, inferior, and internal..; the other posterior, superior, and external. **1826** KIRBY & SPENCE *Entomol.* IV. 335 *Anterior*, the fore or upper wings. *Ibid.* 339 *Anterior* or *Exterior*, the outer margin of the wing, or that from the body. **1829** LOUDON *Encycl. Plants* 1094 *Anterior*, growing in front of some other thing. **1853** DARLINGTON *Flora Cestrica* (ed. 3) Gloss., *Anterior*, in front, or below,—as that part of a flower next to the bract, or farthest from the axis of inflorescence. **1875** W. TURNER *Hum. Anat.* I. v. 213 The anterior cerebral vesicle bends downwards from the middle vesicle. **1880** A. GRAY *Bot. Text-bk.* (ed. 6) I. 160 The portion of the flower which faces the subtending bract is the anterior. **1886** BUCK *Handbk. Med. Sci.* II. 507/2 The anterior oblique dislocation of Bigelow. **1893** H. MORRIS *Hum. Anat.* 1127 In front of the sterno-mastoid is the anterior triangle. **1897** D. H. SCOTT *Struct. Bot.* (ed. 4) I. 23 The two outer sepals are so placed that one lies next the axis (*posterior*), and the other remote from it (*anterior*). **1937** *Discovery* Jan. 16/2 The cortex of the hemispheres, the so called anterior brain.
c. *Phonetics.* = PALATAL A. 2.
1902 E. W. SCRIPTURE *Elem. Exper. Phonetics* xxiii. 316 The *n* contact involves an anterior occlusion. **1925** P. RADIN tr. *J. Vendryès's Lang.* I. i. 21 The vowels known as anterior or palatal. **1933** L. BLOOMFIELD *Lang.* vi. 99 One distinguishes, usually, between *anterior* or *palatal* position and *posterior* or *velar* position.
2. a. Of time and progress: Going before, preceding, former, earlier, prior.
1794 SULLIVAN *View Nat.* II, The memory of anterior ages. **1850** McCOSH *Div. Govt.* III. i. (1874) 271 The mind has not only the power of action, but the anterior..power of choice.
b. with *to.* (Like similar L. comparatives, *anterior* is, in Eng., comparative in sense, but not in construction; we do not say *anterior than.*)
1728 *M. Scriblerus* in Pope *Dunc.* (1736) 30 The first Dunciad was the first Epic poem..anterior even to the Iliad or Odyssey. **1856** DOVE *Log. Chr. Faith* v. i. §1. 243 Intuition is logically anterior to metaphysic.

anteriority (æntɪərɪ'ɒrɪtɪ). [f. L. *anteriōr-em* (see prec.) + -ITY. Cf. Fr. *antériorité.*] The quality of being anterior, in order of time or progress.

1720 POPE *Iliad* XIX. 93 *note* (R.) This anteriority of time makes this passage the more observable. **1754** *Phil. Trans.* XLVIII. 777 It has the anteriority of date with regard to Mr. Melvil's paper. **1869** PHILLIPS *Vesuv.* xii. 335, I was much impressed by..the anteriority of granite to greenstone.

an'teriorly, *adv.* [f. ANTERIOR + -LY[2].]

1. Of place: In an anterior position, in front.

1599 A. M. *Gabelhouer's Bk. Physic* 243/1 This Pessarye ..must she intrude anteriorlye into her bodye. **1774** GOLDSM. *Nat. Hist.* VI. I. i. (JOD.) The globe of the eye is more depressed anteriorly. **1855** MACGILLIVRAY *Nat. Hist. Dee Side* 387 The ears dusky, anteriorly edged with red.

2. Of time or logical order: Previously, antecedently. Const. *to*.

1839 J. ROGERS *Antipopopr.* III. iii. 163 Viewing the matter not as anteriorly probable. **1855** CDL. WISEMAN *Fabiola* 145 Anteriorly to the construction of catacombs.

an'teriorness. *rare*[−1]. = ANTERIORITY.

1870 J. GROTE *Exam. Util. Phil.* vi. 107 An anteriorness to any fixed conditions.

'antero- stem of assumed L. **anterus*, positive of ANTERIOR; used in Eng. as comb. form of the latter in modern technical adjectives = Front, fore; as **antero-external**, front outside or outer; **antero-frontal**, pertaining to the front part of the forehead; **antero-inferior**, lower front; **antero-lateral**, front side; **antero-parietal**, belonging to the front of the parietal or side plates of the skull; **antero-posterior**, front and back, forward and backward; **antero-spinal**, etc.

Also in advs., as **antero-posteriorly**, etc.

1852 DANA *Crust.* I. 362 The antero-external angle of the second joint. **1879** *Academy* 11 Jan. 35 Lesions of the antero-frontal region [of the brain]. **1849-52** TODD *Cycl. Anat. & Phys.* IV. 815/1 In the antero-inferior triangle of the neck. **1838** *Blackw. Mag.* XLIII. 653 The inferi- or antero-lateral extremity of the nose. **1864** *Reader* 23 Apr. 525/2 The outer surface [of this brain] has only the Sylvian fissure, and a faint trace of the antero-parietal. **1870** ROLLESTON *Anim. Life* 7 The anteroposterior movement of the lower jaw. **1878** A. HAMILTON *Nerv. Dis.* 221 Antero-spinal paralysis..is ushered in by fever. **1849-52** TODD *Cycl. Anat. & Phys.* IV. 1122/2 The tongue..is flattened antero-posteriorly.

ante-room ('æntɪruːm). [after Fr. *antichambre* or It. *anticamera*.] A room before, or forming an entrance to, another.

1762 H. WALPOLE *Vertue's Anecd. Paint.* (1786) II. 200 An anti-room at St. James's. **1854** BANCROFT *Hist. U.S.* (1876) VI. xli. 239 His ante-rooms were thronged with clients of all sorts. **1858** SEARS *Athan.* III. x. 338 Whatever our place, if we are doing its work well, it is the anteroom of heaven.

anterous, obsolete form of ADVENTUROUS.

antes ('æntɪz), *sb. pl. Arch.* [cf. Fr. *antes*, ad. L. *antas*, acc. of ANTÆ.] = ANTÆ.

1789 SMYTH tr. *Aldrich's Archit.* (1818) 102 Antes..are placed nowhere except in the angles, or at the junction of walls. **1813** HOGG *Queen's Wake* 292 Astounded and awed to the antes they clung.

antescript ('æntɪskrɪpt). *rare.* [suggested by *postscript*.] A note written in front or on the top of a letter, etc.; a prefatory note; *also*, The whole of a letter before the postscript.

1831 KNOX & JEBB *Corr.* II. 593 He has added an Antescript, which will indemnify you for the meagreness of this [letter]. **1844** MRS. BROWNING *Lett.* II. 164 There is a postscript scarcely proportionate to the antescript.

†**ante'signary.** *Obs. rare*[−1]. [ad. late L. *antesignārius*, for cl.L. *antesignānus*, a soldier fighting before the standard, f. *ante* before + *sign-um* standard: see -ARY.] *collect.* The picked soldiers who marched before and defended the standard.

1650 USSHER *Annals* VI. (1658) 220 Gave order to the Antesignary, i.e. those that stood next before the standard.

antesigne, obs. f. ENSIGN *sb.*, affiliating it to L. *antesignānus*. See prec., and ANCIENT *sb.*[2]

ante-spirant, -spring, etc.: see ANTE-.

†**antestature.** *Obs.* [a. Fr. *antestature*, Sp. *antestatura*, f. L. *ante* before + *statūra* a standing, f. *stat-* ppl. stem of *stā-re* to stand.] (See quot.)

1706 PHILLIPS, *Antestature*, a Traverse or small Intrenchment made of Pallisadoes, or of Sacks fill'd with Earth, and rais'd in haste, to dispute the rest of the Ground, when the Enemy has already gain'd part. **1816** [So JAMES *Mil. Dict.*]

†**'ante-supper.** *Obs. rare*[−1]. [f. ANTE- + SUPPER.] A course displayed but not partaken of, in anticipation of supper.

1658 OSBORN *K. James* (1673) 533 The Earl of Carlisle was one of the Quorum, that brought in the Vanity of Ante-Suppers, not heard of in our Fore-fathers time.

ante-temple ('æntɪtemp(ə)l). [ad. med.L. *ante-templum*, f. *ante* before + *templum* temple, transl. Gr. πρόναος PRONAOS.] The portico of an ancient temple or of a Christian church; also applied to the *ante-nave* of a church.

1703 MAUNDRELL *Journ. Jerus.* (1721) 136 The Temple is an oblong square..in length sixty-four [yards], of which eighteen were taken up by the Πρόναος or Anti-Temple. **1711** BINGHAM *Chr. Antiq.* (1840) III. VIII. §3. 394 The narthex or 'antetemple,' where the penitents and catechumens stood. **1876** GWILT *Encycl. Arch.* 1284 *Narthex*..an ante-temple or vestibule outside the church; it is thus used as synonymous with porch and portico.

†**'antethem(e.** *Obs.* 5-6. Also **antyteme, antithem, anthe- antetyme, antetewme.** [A derivative of THEME (earlier also *teme, tyme*), a. Fr. *thème, tesme, teme, teume*:—L. *thema*, in common mediæval use for 'subject proposed for discussion, text,' a Gr. θέμα, lit. 'the thing placed or laid down.' The prefix is doubtful, whether Gr. ἀντί, as if assuming a Gr. *ἀντίθεμα, from ἀντιτίθημι; or (more prob.) L. *ante* 'before,' as if = **antethema* 'text prefixed.' No corresponding word has yet been noticed in med.L. or OFr.]

The text prefixed to a sermon or discourse as its theme or motto.

1494 FABYAN VII. 306 He made vnto them Colacions or Exortacions, & toke for his anteteme, *Haurietis aquas in gaudio de fontibus saluatoris.* **1526** SKELTON *Magnyf.* 363 To preche..Without an antetyme. *a* **1529**—— *Merie Tales* vii. 78 As I said before in my antithem. **1530** PALSGR., Anthetyme, [Fr.] *thieme.* **1561** A. SCOTT *To Q. Mary* Protestandis takis the freiris auld Antetewme, Reddie ressauaris, bot to rander nocht.

antetype ('æntɪtaɪp). [f. ANTE- + TYPE, prob. by erron. analysis of ANTITYPE.] A preceding type; an earlier example.

1612 T. TAYLOR *Comm. Titus* i. 6 (1619) 99 Antetypes of Christ's puritie. **1844** MARG. FULLER *Wom. in 19th C.* (1862) 74 She is an antetype of a class to which the coming time will afford a field.

†**ante'vene**, *v. Obs.*[−0] [ad. L. *antevenī-re*, f. *ante* before + *venī-re* to come.] 'To come before, to anticipate, or prevent.' Blount, 1656; Bailey, etc.

antevenient (æntɪ'viːnɪənt), *ppl. a. rare*[−1]. [ad. L. *antevenient-em* pr. pple. of *antevenīre*; see prec.] Coming before, preceding.

1800 LAMB *Lett.* I. (1841) 49 Which..stupidly stood alone, nothing prevenient or antevenient.

anteversion (æntɪ'vɜːʃən). [ad. L. *anteversiōn-em*, n. of action f. *antevert-ĕre*: see next. Cf. mod.Fr. *antéversion*.] A turning forwards; *spec.* in *Surg.* = ANTEFLEXION.

1853 MAYNE *Exp. Lex.*, Anteversion of the womb. **1857** BULLOCK *Cazeaux's Midwif.* 327 Anteversion is very rare in the early stages of gestation.

antevert (æntɪ'vɜːt), *v.* [ad. L. *antevert-ĕre* to anticipate, prevent, f. *ante* before + *vertĕre* to turn.]

1. To avert beforehand, prevent, anticipate.

1649 BP. HALL *Cases of Consc.* iii. (1654) 421 To antevert some great danger. **1677** HALE *Cont.* II. 106 If Passion run before it [judgment]..and so antivert the use of Deliberation. **1914** *N. Amer. Rev.* Sept. 387 The Cossacks ..rode down the sidewalks..in an effort to antevert a meeting of the students.

2. To turn forward, displace. (See ANTEVERTED.)

1870 W. PLAYFAIR in *Lancet* 2 July 13/2 The uterus was anteverted, and the cervix exposed with difficulty.

anteverted (æntɪ'vɜːtɪd), *ppl. a.* [f. prec. + -ED.] Displaced; *spec.* in *Surg.* = ANTEFLEXED.

1860 TANNER *Pregn.* ii. 96 An anteverted uterus.

ante'verting, *vbl. sb.* [f. as prec. + -ING[1].] The action of averting beforehand, prevention (*obs.*).

1624-47 BP. HALL *Rem. Wks.* (1660) 157 It is high time to mourne for the anteverting of a threatened vengeance.

†**antevolate**, *v. Obs.*[−0] [f. L. *antevolāt-* ppl. st. of *antevolā-re*.] 'To fly before.' Cockeram 1623.

†**an'teyn.** *Obs. rare*[−1]. [a. OFr. *antaine, antienne*, an ANTHEM.] A by-form of ANTHEM.

c **1305** *E. E. Poems* (1862) 39 þis anteyn þat murie is: þat folc ihurde alle Hou þe harpe song al bi him silf.

'ant-fly. One of the winged ants, or perfect males and females, of an ant's nest; a favourite bait in angling.

1653 WALTON *Angler* 221 Take the blackish Ant-fly out of ..the Ant-hil. **1746** MILES in *Phil. Trans.* XLIV. 354 Winged Ants commonly known by the Name of Ant-Flies. **1787** T. BEST *Angling* (ed. 2) 117 The little Red and Black Ant-Flies come on about the tenth or twelfth of August. [**1867** F. FRANCIS *Angling* vi. (1880) 233 The Red and Black Ants are very favourite flies during July.]

anth-, Gr. ἀνθ, comb. form of ἀντί (see ANTI-) bef. an aspirate. Often, in mod. scientific words, written analytically *anti-*, as in *anthelix, anti-helix; anthypnotic, anti-hypnotic*.

anthelion (æn'θiːlɪən, ænth-). *Pl.* **-a.** [late Gr. ἀνθήλιον, neut. of ἀνθήλιος, earlier ἀντήλιος, opposite to the sun, f. ἀντί over against + ἥλιος sun.] A luminous ring or nimbus seen (chiefly in alpine or polar regions) surrounding the shadow of the observer's head projected on a cloud or fog bank opposite to the sun. As many as four such concentric rings have been seen, decreasing in brightness to the outer at 40° from the centre.

1670 *Phil. Trans.* V. 1072 The Anthelion, observed by M. Hevelius Sept. 6, 1661, in which there were two coloured Arches of a circle. **1760** SWINTON *ibid.* LII. 94 A very distinguishable Mock-Sun, opposite to the true one, which I take to have been an Anthelion. **1859** TENNENT *Ceylon* 72 Anthelia..may probably have suggested to the early painters the idea of the glory surrounding the heads of beatified saints.

anthelix: see ANTI-HELIX.

anthelminthic (ænθɪl'mɪnθɪk), *a.* and *sb. Med.* Also erron. **-mintic.** [mod. f. ANTH- + Gr. ἑλμινθ- (ἕλμινς) a worm + -IC.]

A. *adj.* Of use against intestinal worms.

1684 tr. *Bonet's Merc. Compit.* x. 365 All bitter things are Anthelminthick. **1830** LINDLEY *Nat. Syst. Bot.* 96 The Cochin-chinese consider that plant [*Ficus septica*] caustic and anthelmintic. **1871** KINGSLEY *At Last* xiii, Their bitter anthelminthic oil.

B. *sb.* An anthelmintic medicine.

1706 PHILLIPS, *Anthelminticks*, Medicines that destroy Worms in Humane Bodies. **1714** FULLER *Pharmacopœia* (ed. 2) 76 The Decoction called Sacrum..is a most noble.. Anthelminthic. *Ibid.* 203 Give Anthelminthics..to make the Worms weak and languishing. **1876** HARLEY *Mat. Med.* 407 Turpentine is chiefly employed internally as an anthelmintic.

anthem ('ænθɪm), *sb.* Forms: 1-4 **antefn(e**, 3-6 **-tempne** (3-4 **-tephne**, 5 **-thephne**), 4-6 **antem(e**, **-tim(e**, 5 **-tym**, 6 **-temne**, **-temme**, 6-7 **-theme**, 7 **-thym**, **-thymne**, **-themne**, 7- **anthem.** [OE. *antefn(e* a. early Romanic **antéfena*, **antéfna*:—late L. *antífona* (Isidore), for *antíphōna*, a. Gr. ἀντίφωνα: see ANTIPHON.

The Gr. accent was preserved in late L. *antíphōna, antífona*, whence It. *antífona*, Pr. *antifena, antiéfna*, OFr. **antievne*, later *antievre* and *antienne, antaine* (like OFr. *Estievre, Estienne* for **Estievne*, It. *Istéfano*:—L. *Stephanum*). The phonetic development in Eng. was *an'tefne, an'tevne, an'temne, 'antemn, 'antem, 'anthem.* Cf. (1) *efen, even, Stephen, Steven*; (2) *efn, emn, stefne, stemne, nefnian, nemnian*; (3) *hym(n, colum(n, autum(n*. For the subseq. corruption of *antem* to *anthem*, cf. *Ant(h)ony, amarant(h, amiant(h*; in 15th c. Fr. we also find *anthaine* for *antaine*; some Eng. spellings indicate an attempt to explain the word as *antihymn, ant'hymn*. A by-form ANTEYN, adopted from Fr. *antaine*, also occurs in 13-14th c.; in 16th *antiphona* was anew adopted as ANTIPHON.]

1. A composition, in prose or verse, sung antiphonally, or by two voices or choirs, responsively; an ANTIPHON. *Obs.* or *arch.*

a **1000** *Bæda* I. xxv. (Bosw.) Is ðæt sæd, ðæt hi ðysne letanían and antefn ȝeleóþre stæfne sungan. *c* **1230** *Ancr. R.* 42 Efter hire viue hexte blissen tel in þe antefnes [*v.r.* antempnes]. **1440** *Promp. Parv.*, Antym, *Antiphona.* *a* **1520** *Myrr. Our Lady* 95 After the Hympne cometh Antempnes and psalmes. Antem ys as moche to saye as a sownyng before, for yt ys begonne before the Psalmes; yt is as moche to saye as sownynge ageynste. **1555** *Fardle of Facions* II. xii. 272 The Anthemes..Damasus put ordre that the quiere should sing side aftre side. **1623** COCKERAM, *Anthemne*, a Song which Church-men sing by course one after another. **1654** LESTRANGE *Charles I* (1656) 114 The King and the Spanish Ambassador descended into the Chappell, continuing..untill an Anthymne was sung. **1782** PRIESTLEY *Corrupt. Chr.* II. VIII. 122 The method of singing by.. anthem..introduced.

2. A composition in unmeasured prose (usually from the Scriptures or Liturgy) set to music.

c **1386** CHAUCER *Prioress' T.* 208 And bad me for to synge This antym [*v.r.* -theme, -teme, -time, -thephene] verraily in my deyinge. **1530** PALSGR., Antemne, a song, *antiesme.* **1577** HOLINSHED *Chron.* 1005/2 In the meane time did the quier sing yᵉ antheme beginning '*Unxerunt regem.*' **1597** SHAKS. *2 Hen. IV*, I. ii. 213 For my voice, I haue lost it with hallowing and singing of Anthemes. **1712** ADDISON *Spect.* No. 405 ¶2 Those parts of the inspired Writings, which are proper for Divine Songs and Anthems. **1795** MASON *Ch. Music* ii. 108 The first Anthem set to English words after the Reformation..was that of Dr. Tye, beginning 'I will exalt thee.' **1855** TENNYSON *Wellington* 60 The sound of the sorrowing anthem roll'd Thro' the dome.

3. *loosely* in poetry: A song, as of praise or gladness. Also used of the English 'National' or 'Royal Anthem,' which is technically a *hymn*.

1591 SHAKS. *Two Gent.* III. i. 240 Breathe it in mine eare, As ending Antheme of my endlesse dolor. **1735** H. BROOKE *Univ. Beauty* III. (R.) The floods..tune their anthems. *a* **1821** KEATS *Nightingale* viii, Thy plaintive anthem fades

Past the near meadows, over the still stream. **1866** ENGEL *Nat. Music* i. 2 (Note to 'National Anthem') Anthem is musically an inappropriate title for this tune. It has, however, now been so generally adopted that it would be pedantic not to use it. **1880** GROVE *Dict. Music* I. 605 'God Save the King,' the so-called 'National Anthem' of England.

4. *Comb.* and *Attrib.*, as ***anthem-bell, -book***; **anthem-wise**, in manner of an anthem, antiphonally.

1611 COTGR., *Martinet*..a Saints bell, or Antham bell. **1625** BACON *Ess. Masques* (Arb.) 539 Seuerall Quires, placed one ouer against another, and taking the Voice by Catches Antheme-wise.

anthem (ˈænθɪm), *v.* [f. prec. sb.; cf. to *chant, hymn*.] *trans.* To celebrate or praise in an anthem, to sing to sacred music.

1628 FELTHAM *Resolves* I. xci. (1647) 285 He that had anthem'd the pureness of the God of Israel. *a***1821** KEATS *Fancy* 42 Sweet birds antheming the morn. **1877** LYTTEIL *Landm.* IV. ii. 193 The tips of the granite mountains.. antheming their hymn of praise.

antheming (ˈænθɪmɪŋ), *vbl. sb.* [f. prec. + -ING[1].] The action of singing anthems.

1829 A. HALLAM in Lockhart *Scott* (1839) IX. 331 And full-voiced anthemings the while Swelled from the choir. **1883** J. RYLANCE in *Homilet. Monthly* May 332 An eternity of antheming!

anthemion (ænˈθiːmɪən). Pl. **-mia**. [a. Gr. ἀνθέμιον flower.] = HONEYSUCKLE 4. Also *attrib.*

1865 J. K. COLLING *Art Foliage Sculpture & Decoration* I. iii. 25 Variations upon the Anthemion ornament may be seen upon Etruscan vases. **1899** R. GLAZIER *Man. Hist. Orn.* 17 The anthemion..is derived from the traditional lotus and bud of Egypt, Assyria, and India. **1912** R. FRY in H. G. Wells et al. *Socialism & Great State* 265 The chairs into the wooden seats of which some tremendous mechanical force has deeply impressed a large distorted anthemion. **1955** R. FASTNEDGE *Eng. Furn. Styles* 279 *Anthemion ornament*, of Greek derivation..popularized in England during the second half of the eighteenth century.

anthemize (ˈænθɪmaɪz), *v. rare*$^{-1}$. [f. ANTHEM *sb.* + -IZE; cf. *anagramize*.] To sing of or celebrate in an anthem.

1837 *Blackw. Mag.* XLI. 481 Do you think any piety.. proof against risibility, with such an ally as Lazarus anthemized with love in a church gallery?

anthemy (ˈænθɪmɪ). *Bot. rare.* [f. Gr. ἀνθε- (ἄνθος) flower; formation unexplained. Also in mod.L. *anthemia*.] 'A flower-cluster of any kind.' Gray *Bot. Text-bk.* 1880.

anther (ˈænθə(r)). *Bot.* [a. mod.Fr. *anthère*, and mod.L. *anthēra*, in cl.L. 'a medicine extracted from flowers,' a. Gr. ἀνθηρά, fem. of ἀνθηρός flowery, f. ἀνθε- (ἄνθος) flower. As these medicines often consisted of the internal organs of flowers (*e.g.* saffron, one of the chief *antheræ*, was the stigma), the name *anthēra* was specially applied by the early pharmacists to these parts, and at length confined by the herbalists, *c* 1700, to the pollen-bearing organ, known to earlier writers as *thēca, capsula*, or *apex*; which use was accepted and sanctioned by Linnæus. The following quotations illustrate these changes:

1551 TURNER *Herbal* II. 116 (*from Dioscor.*) [Dried rose petals] are mingled with medicines called *anthera* and preservatiue medicines for woundes. But the floure that is founde in the middes of the rose is good agaynst the reume or flowing of the gummes. **1657** *Phys. Dict., Anthera*, a compound medicine used for sore mouths. So in PHILLIPS **1678–96**; *ed.* **1706** *adds, Anthera*, the yellow seeds in the middle of a Rose..Among Herbalists *Antheræ* are taken for those little knobs that grow on the top of the *Stamina* of Flowers, and are oftner call'd *Apices*. **1727–51** CHAMBERS *Cycl.* s.v., *Anthera* in pharmacy, a term used by some authors for the yellow, or ruddy globules in the middle of certain flowers, as of lilies, saffron, etc. Some confine the *Anthera* to the yellowish globules in the middle of roses.. Other apply the name *Antheræ* to those little tufts or knobs which grow on the tops of the stamina of flowers; more usually called apices.]

That part of the stamen containing the pollen or fertilizing dust, which when mature is shed forth for the fertilization of the ovary; it is often supported on a slender pedicel called the *filament*.

1706–51 [See above]. **1759** B. STILLINGFLEET in *Misc. Tracts* Introd. (1762) 31 This anthera contains the male dust, which when ripe is scattered about by every breath of air. **1791** E. DARWIN *Bot. Gard.* I. 197 The bursting Anthers trust To the mild breezes their prolific dust. **1813** SIR H. DAVY *Agric. Chem.* 68 The essential part of the stamens are the summits or anthers. **1874** LUBBOCK *Wild Flow.* iii. 50 In the Buttercup the anthers commence to discharge their pollen, as soon as the flower opens.

b. *Comb.* and *Attrib.*, as ***anther-beak, -cell, -lobe***; **anther-dust**, pollen; **anther-valve**, the opening by which the pollen is shed.

1870 HOOKER *Stud. Flora* 356 *Ophrys apifera*..anther-beak hooked. *Ibid.* 285 *Salvia*..connective slender, bearing at one end a perfect anther-cell. **1875** tr. *Sachs' Bot.* 473 The anther consists of two longitudinal halves (anther-lobes). **1845** LINDLEY *Sch. Bot.* iv. (1858) 25 Flowers regular, with recurved anther-valves.

antheral (ˈænθərəl), *a. Bot.* [f. prec. + -AL[1].] Of or pertaining to anthers.

1795 ROXBURGH in *Asiat. Res.* IV. 406 The antheral glands give it a claim to the genus *Adenanthera*. **1847** in CRAIG.

antheridial (ænθəˈrɪdɪəl), *a.* [f. next + -AL[1].] Pertaining to, or of the nature of, an antheridium.

1848 DANA *Zooph.* v. 92 The union of a final cellule, with some other which is antheridial in its nature. **1875** tr. *Sachs' Bot.* 803 The antheridial branches of some Saprolegnieæ.

‖**antheridium** (ænθəˈrɪdɪəm). *Bot.* [mod.L., f. *anthēra* + Gr. -ιδιον dimin. ending.] Oblong or globular 'sperm' cells found in Cryptogams, answering to the anthers of flowering plants.

1854 BALFOUR *Bot.* 272 The antheridia were early noticed in the case of mosses. **1874** COOKE *Fungi* 169 An oblong cell, slightly curved,..an antheridium or organ of the male sex.

antheriferous (ænθəˈrɪfərəs), *a. Bot.* [f. L. *anthēra* + -(I)FEROUS bearing.] Anther-bearing.

1830 LINDLEY *Nat. Syst. Bot.* 212 The genuine antheræ, which he [Jacquin] calls antheriferous sacs. **1877** DARWIN *Diff. Forms Fl.* viii. 320 All five stamens are..antheriferous.

antheriform (ænˈθɛrɪfɔːm), *a. Bot.* [f. as prec. + -(I)FORM shaped.] Anther-shaped.

1847 in CRAIG.

†**ˈantherine.** *Obs.* 8. Also **anterne**. [? f. Gr. ἀνθηρ-ός flowery, bright-coloured + -INE.] A kind of poplin, now obsolete.

1710 *Lond. Gaz.* mmmmdcclxxxvii/4 A green strip'd Poplin Mantua and Petticoat, lined with a white Antherine. **1719** J. ROBERTS *Spinster* 346 Stuffs mixed with silk.. antherines and bombazines. **1739** in BECK *Drap. Dict.* (1882) 6 *Anterne*, a stuff of wool and silk mixed, or of mohair and cotton.

antherless (ˈænθəlɪs), *a. Bot.* [f. ANTHER + -LESS.] Without anthers.

1877 F. HULME *Wild Fl.* 6 Stamens..often antherless.

antherogenous (ænθəˈrɒdʒɪnəs). [f. Fr. *anthérogène* (De Candolle, f. L. *anthēra* anther + Gr. -γενης born) + -OUS.] Produced or developed from anthers, as most of the petals in a double rose.

1847 in CRAIG.

antheroid (ˈænθərɔɪd), *a. Bot.* [f. L. *anthēra* + -OID.] Anther-like in appearance or functions.

antherozooid, -zoid (ˌænθərəʊˈzəʊɔɪd, -ɪd). *Bot.* [mod. f. L. *anthēra* + ZOOID (f. Gr. ζωοειδής like an animal).] One of the minute moving bodies in the antheridia of cryptogams, analogous to the spermatozoa of animals.

1854 BALFOUR *Bot.* 272 In antheridia there have been detected cells containing moving filaments, *Phytozoa*, or *Spermatozoids* or *Antherozoids*. **1871** DARWIN *Desc. Man* I. viii. 274 The locomotive power of the antherozooids. **1875** tr. *Sachs' Bot.* 336 Antherozoids are..spirally coiled threads usually with a number of fine cilia on the anterior coils.

ˌantherozoˈoidal, -ˈzoidal, *a. Bot.* [f. prec. + -AL[1].] Of or pertaining to antherozooids.

1865 *Intell. Obs.* No. 37. 35 Antherozoidal cells.

‖**anthesis** (ænˈθiːsɪs). *Bot.* [Gr. ἄνθησις, n. of action f. ἀνθέ-ειν to blossom.] Full bloom.

1835 in LINDLEY *Introd. Bot.* **1870** BENTLEY *Bot.* 213 The term anthesis is sometimes used to indicate the period at which the flower-bud opens.

anthetyme, var. ANTETHEME, *Obs.*, a text.

ˈant-hill.

1. The mound or hillock raised over an ant's nest.

1297 R. GLOUC. 296 As þycke as ameten crepeþ in an amete hulle. **1527** L. ANDREW *Brunswyke's Distyll. Waters* B iij, Burye it in a pyssemer hyll that some call an antehyl. **1753** CHAMBERS *Cycl. Supp.* s.v. *Ant*, Ant-hills are little hillocks of earth, which the Ants throw up. **1813** SHELLEY *Q. Mab* II. 101 The thronging thousands to a passing view, Seemed like an anthill's citizens.

2. The sugar-loaf-shaped nests of the Termites.

1859 R. BURTON in *Jrnl. G. S.* XXIX. 177 The country is dotted with anthills, which, when old, become as hard as sandstone: they are generally built by the termite under some shady tree. **1860** *Hunt. Grounds O. World* I. xi. 172 [Ant-bears] at work scraping up the earth of the ant-hill.

3. *fig.*

1748 THOMSON *Cast. Indol.* I. 49 All things that do pass, Upon this ant-hill earth. **1856** KANE *Arct. Exp.* II. xi. 103 They [Esquimaux] soon crowded back into their ant-hill.

anthilly (ˈæntˌhɪlɪ), *a.* [f. ANT-HILL + -Y[1].] Full of or abounding in ant-hills.

1796 W. H. MARSHALL *Rural Econ. W. Eng.* II. 212 Rough anthilly land. **1892** *Field* 19 Nov. 766/2 Anthilly fields of grass.

†**ˈanthine**, *a.* and *sb. Obs.* [ad. L. *anthin-us*, a. Gr. ἄνθιν-ος, f. ἄνθος flower.]

A. *adj.* Derived from or flavoured with flowers.

1656 BLOUNT *Glossogr., Anthine*, That is ful of, or made of flowers, or of the hony-comb. **1775** ASH, *Anthine*, Medicated with the flowers of plants.

B. *sb.* (= L. *anthinum mel* or Gr. ἄνθινον ἔλαιον.) Honey, oil, or wine, flavoured with flowers.

1658 J. ROWLAND *Mouffet's Theat. Ins.* 910 If the Erycdan or Anthine appear reddish, it is accounted unwholesome. **1753** CHAMBERS *Cycl. Supp., Anthine*, among antient naturalists, is an appellation given to certain species of wine and oil.

anthobian (ænˈθəʊbɪən). *Ent.* [mod. f. Gr. ἄνθος flower + βίος life + -AN; cf. *amphibian*.] An animal living in or feeding on flowers; applied specially to certain minute beetles.

1835 KIRBY *Hab. & Inst. Anim.* II. xx. 365 Others [beetles]..devour the blossoms themselves, whence Latreille calls them Anthobians.

anthocarpous (ænθəʊˈkɑːpəs), *a. Bot.* [f. mod.L. *anthocarp-i* (f. Gr. ἄνθος flower + -καρπ-ος comb. adj. form of καρπός fruit) + -OUS.] Of or pertaining to the fruits called by Lindley *Anthocarpi*, composed of flowers and fruit proper blended into a solid mass, as in the pine-apple.

1835 in LINDLEY *Introd. Bot.* **1880** GRAY *Bot. Text-bk.* 396 *Anthocarpous*, Fruits in which some organ exterior to the pericarp is concerned.

anthocephalous (ænθəʊˈsɛfələs), *a.* [f. Gr. ἀνθο-ς flower + -κεφαλ-ος comb. adj. form of κεφαλ-ή head + -OUS.] Having a flower-like head.

1847 in CRAIG.

anthocyanidin (ˌænθəʊsaɪˈænɪdɪn). [a. G. *anthocyanidin* (R. Willstätter and A. E. Everest 1913, in *Ann. d. Chemie* CCCCI. 205); cf. next and CYANIDIN.] A plant pigment formed by the hydrolysis of an anthocyanin.

1914 *Chem. Abstr.* 335 The anthocyanidin reaction.. consists in extg. the fresh plant material. **1914** *Proc. R. Soc.* B. LXXXVII. 444 In no case could any trace of anthocyanidin be found. **1934** *Ann. Reg. 1933* 61 The widespread distribution in plants of a new class of colourless anthocyanidins was established.

anthoˈcyanin(e. Also **-cyan(e), -kyan.** [mod. f. Gr. ἄνθος flower + κύανος blue + -IN.] One of the blue, violet, or red pigments in plants. Also *attrib.*

1839 LINDLEY *Introd. Bot.* (ed. 3) 434 The blue matter [of chlorophyll] or anthocyane. **1894** F. W. OLIVER et al. tr. *Kerner von Marilaun's Nat. Hist.* I. 288 The under side of the leaf is coloured violet by a pigment called anthocyanin. **1902** *Encycl. Brit.* XXXI. 763/2 The red pigment anthocyan, which is found very commonly in young developing shoots, petioles, and mid-ribs. **1913** W. BATESON *Mendel's Princ. Hered.* I. iii. 38 The addition of various other factors produces anthocyan reds. **1918** A. W. STEWART *Rec. Adv. Org. Chem.* (ed. 3) 209 The anthocyanins. **1924** *Empire Review* May 583/1 The anthocyanin pigments belong to the great class of the glucosides. **1956** *Sci. News* XL. 42 The red and yellow pigments, the anthocyanins and the flavones, were all studied in Java.

anthodium (ænˈθəʊdɪəm). *Bot.* Pl. **-ia**. [mod.L., f. Gr. ἀνθώδης (see ANTHOID *a.*) + *-ium*.] A name for the flower-head or *capitulum* in Compositæ.

1858 in A. GRAY *Introd. Struct. & Syst. Bot.* 523/2. **1861** BENTLEY *Man. Bot.* 203 *The Capitulum, Anthodium, or Head.*—This kind of inflorescence constitutes the Compound Flower of Linnæus.

anthography (ænˈθɒgrəfɪ). *Bot.* [f. Gr. ἄνθο-ς flower + -γραφία writing.] The scientific description of flowers.

anthoid (ˈænθɔɪd), *a.* [f. Gr. ἄνθο-ς flower + -ειδής like. (The Gr. compound is ἀνθώδης.)] Resembling a flower, flower-like.

1859 TODD *Cycl. Anat. & Phys.* V. 17/1 Resemblance to the Polypes in their external anthoid appearance.

anthoˈleucin(e. ? *Obs.* [mod. f. Gr. ἄνθο-ς flower + λευκός white + -IN.] The white colouring matter in plants. (In mod. Dicts.)

antholite (ˈænθəlaɪt). [mod. f. Gr. ἄνθο-ς flower + λίθος stone.]

1. *Geol.* A name given by Brongniart to certain fossil plants having a resemblance to flowers, found in the Coal Measures; in mod.L. *Antholites*.

1847 in CRAIG.

2. *Min.* A variety of the mineral Amphibole.

anthologer (ænˈθɒlədʒə(r)). [f. ANTHOLOGY + -ER[1].] = ANTHOLOGIST.

1906 *Westm. Gaz.* 13 Oct. 11/3 These are far fewer than the examples..that have not yet found the anthologer. **1953** *Sat. Rev.* 7 Mar. 13/2 The anthologers set about their task with imagination and taste.

†**anthoˈlogic**, *a. Obs.*$^{-0}$ [f. ANTHOLOGY + -IC.] = next.

1656 in BLOUNT *Glossogr.*

anthological (ænθəʊˈlɒdʒɪkəl), *a. rare.* [f. prec. + -AL[1].]

1. Treating of flowers. ? *Obs.*

1691 WOOD *Ath. Oxon.* (R.) Robert Stafford..published a geographical and anthological description of all empires and kingdoms.

2. Of or relating to a literary anthology.
1796 W. TAYLOR in *Month. Rev.* XX. 512 What yet exist of anthological manuscripts in Rome. **1881** *Academy* 20 Aug. 131/1 The usual task of an anthological biographer.

anthologist (æn'θɒlədʒɪst). [f. ANTHOLOGY + -IST.] The compiler of an anthology.
1805 W. TAYLOR in *Ann. Rev.* III. 651 It ought not to be supposed that any anthologist can strip the garden of its flowers. **1883** *Sat. Rev.* 3 Feb. 150/2 The editors..had few or none of the virtues of the good anthologist.

anthologize (æn'θɒlədʒaɪz), *v.* [f. ANTHOLOGY + -IZE.] **a.** *trans.* To make an anthology of or from; to use in an anthology. **b.** *intr.* To make an anthology or anthologies; to compile as, or in the form of, an anthology; (of a large work) to yield suitable pieces for an anthology. Chiefly in *pa. pple.*, *vbl. sb.*, or *gerund.*
1892 *Sat. Rev.* 9 Apr. 426/2 The anthologized poet. **1892** *Daily News* 12 July 4/8 Where poets dead and gone are concerned,..the practice of selecting and anthologising is comparatively innocuous. **1923** *Times Lit. Suppl.* 4 Jan. 9/3 Many writers of verse are familiar to the public through an anthologized example. **1924** *Ibid.* 13 Nov. 724/2 The thirty-four lines..deserve to be rescued from Professor Macaulay's grim black covers and anthologized. **1928** *Manch. Guardian Weekly* 17 Aug. 133/2 The anthologising offences of Palgrave, Sir Arthur Quiller-Couch and Mr. J. C. Squire. **1959** *20th Cent.* June 612 One can get an idea of Huxley's own range..from a little book..anthologized from his works by his widow. **1965** *New Statesman* 24 Dec. 1006/3 *Private Eye* magazine does not anthologise well.

anthology (æn'θɒlədʒɪ). [ad. L. *anthologia*, a. Gr. ἀνθολογία (f. ἄνθο-ς flower + -λογια collection, f. λέγ-ειν to gather), applied to a collection of poems. Cf. mod.Fr. *anthologie*. Later Gr. had also the homonym ἀνθολόγιον applied to a hymnal.]

1. A collection of the flowers of verse, i.e. small choice poems, *esp.* epigrams, by various authors; originally applied to the Greek collections so called.
1640 CHILMEAD tr. *Ferrand's Love-Melanch.* 334 This clause..is found..both in Diogenes Laertius, in his life, and also in the anthology. **1756** J. WARTON *Ess. Pope* (1782) II. §14. 402 [The sepulchral inscriptions]..of Meleager on his wife, in the Greek Anthology. **1793** RITSON (*title*) The English Anthology. **1851** SIR F. PALGRAVE *Norm. & Eng.* I. 119 Anthologies are sickly things.

2. Extended to other literary collections. Also *transf.*, esp. of paintings, songs, etc., and other art forms.
1856 R. VAUGHAN *Mystics* I. Pref. 8 A kind of anthology from the writings of the leading mystics. **1878** GEO. ELIOT *Coll. Breakf.-Party* 410 Anthology of causes and effects. **1961** *Listener* 21 Dec. 1068/1 The quays..bore an anthology of western European coastal traffic: Bilbao, Stockholm, Hamburg, Glasgow. **1965** *Ibid.* 11 Nov. 760/1 Fry put on his second and even more demanding anthology of post-Impressionism. **1967** *Ibid.* 3 Aug. 129 Some of the LPs that Sinatra began bringing out in the mid-Fifties..are virtually anthologies of pop songs from the previous 20 years.

3. With some reference to the original meaning (in Greek) of a flower-gathering.
1755 JOHNSON, *Anthology*, a collection of flowers. **1822** DE QUINCEY *Confess.* Wks. V. 223 In the anthologies of earth..one flower beyond every other is liable to change, which flower is the countenance of woman.

4. A hymnal [= Gr. ἀνθολόγιον].
[**1727–51** CHAMBERS *Cycl.*, *Anthologion.*] **1775** ASH, *Anthology*, in the Greek Church, a collection of devotional pieces.

†**5.** A treatise on flowers. [A distinct use, on the analogy of *zoology*, *ornithology*, etc.: also in Fr.] *Obs.*
1678 PHILLIPS, *Anthologie*, a treating of flowers, also a florid discourse. **1706** —— *Anthology*, a Discourse or Treatise of Flowers, or of the Florist's Art. [So in BAILEY, etc.]

6. *anthology-piece.*
1935 *Scrutiny* IV. 168 A favourite anthology-piece *When the lamp is shattered.* **1965** *Listener* 2 Sept. 350/2 The ..'Battle of San Romano' by Uccello..is an anthology piece so familiar from countless small reproductions that its gigantic scale when one sees it again is breathtaking.

‖**antholysis** (æn'θɒlɪsɪs). *Bot. rare.* [mod.L., f. Gr. ἄνθο-ς flower + λύσις, n. of action f. λύ-ειν to loosen, undo.] 'A retrograde metamorphosis of a flower, in which normally combined parts are separated.' Gray *Bot. Text-Bk.* 1880.

anthomania (ænθəʊ'meɪnɪə). *rare.* [f. as prec. + Gr. μανία madness, passion.] An extravagant passion or fancy for flowers.
1775 ASH, *Anthomania*, an extravagant fondness for curious flowers. **1882** *Times* 8 June 8 A proof that anthomania is as real and potent as bibliomania.

anthomaniac (ænθəʊ'meɪnɪæk). *rare*$^{-1}$. [f. as prec. + MANIAC; cf. *bibliomaniac.*] One who is intensely fond of, or 'mad about,' flowers.
1841 HOR. SMITH *Moneyed Man* II. x. 321 The intense love of flowers that has procured for me the kindred title of an anthomaniac.

'anthonin. *rare.* [a. Fr. *Antonin*, ad. L. *Antonin-us*, f. *Antōnius*, Anthony; cf. *Capuchin*, *Austin*, etc.] A monk of the order of St. Anthony.
1536 *Pilgr. T.* 155 in Thynne *Animadv.* 81 There be other that be anthonyn, but he whom I salute was gylbertin. **1753** CHAMBERS *Cycl. Supp.*, The *Anthonins*, or monks of St. Anthony, are by some said to be of the begging kind.

Anthony Eden (ˌæntənɪ 'iːdən). [English politician, 1897–1977.] A black Homburg hat of the type often worn by Sir Anthony Eden (later Lord Avon). Also in shortened form **Eden.**
1940 GRAVES & HODGE *Long Week-End* xxi. 376 Anthony Eden, the Foreign Secretary, had reintroduced the black Homburg hat, known as the 'Eden' in Savile Row. **1956** D. DAVIN *Sullen Bell* II. iv. 128 Dark suit and Anthony Eden hat during the week, tweed jacket and flannels at the week-end. **1958** *Spectator* 31 Jan. 130/1 How did the soft black Homburg, with a bound, turned-up edge, come to be called an 'Anthony Eden'? **1959** S. GIBBONS *Pink Front Door* xv. 180 He was just off somewhere—white scarf, black Anthony Eden and all.

Anthony (St.), the patron saint of swineherds, to whom one of each litter was usually vowed. Hence *pop.* **Anthony** = the smallest pig of a litter.
1662 FULLER *Worthies* II. 56 (D.) He will follow him like a St. Anthony's Pig. St. Anthonie is notoriously known for the Patron of hogs, having a Pig for his Page in all pictures. **1753** CHAMBERS *Cycl. Supp.* s.v., In several places, they [Romanists] keep at common charges a hog denominated St. Anthony's hog. **1867** *Standard* 24 May, 'What is an "Anthony?"'..'The littlest pig, your honour. The little pig is always "Anthony."'

Anthony's or **St. Anthony's fire.** ['from the tradition that those who sought the intercession of St. Anthony recovered from the pestilential erysipelas called the *sacred fire*, which proved extremely fatal in 1089.' Brewer *Phr. & Fab.*] A popular name of erysipelas.
1527 L. ANDREW *Brunswyke's Distyll. Waters* A ij, Sorell water slaketh St. Anthonys fyre. **1607** TOPSELL *Serpents* 815 The disease called Erysipelas, commonly called St. Anthonies fire. **1657** *Phys. Dict.*, *Anthonies fire*, the shingles. **1693** LUTTRELL *Brief Rel.* III. 115 Symptoms of St. Anthony's fire appearing, she was let blood. **1834** *Penny Cycl.* II. 96/2 The cure of the distemper called the sacred fire, since that time called St. Anthony's fire.

anthood ('ænthʊd). [f. ANT + -HOOD; cf. *manhood.*] Ant nature; ants collectively.
1879 in Romanes *Anim. Intell.* (1881) 108 A mass of struggling anthood was piled up around the gate.

anthophilous (æn'θɒfɪləs), *a. Ent.* [f. Gr. ἄνθος flower + -PHILOUS.] Loving or frequenting flowers, as an insect (correlative to ENTOMOPHILOUS *a.*); *spec.* belonging to the division *Anthophila* of hymenopterous insects, comprising the bees.
1883 D'ARCY W. THOMPSON tr. *H. Müller's Fert. Flowers* 33 The larvæ of beetles which are anthophilous.

anthophore ('ænθəfɔə(r)). *Bot.* [mod. ad. (De Candolle) Gr. ἀνθοφόρος, f. ἄνθο-ς flower + -φορος bearing.] The stalk which in some flowers raises the receptacle above the calyx.
1839 LINDLEY *Introd. Bot.* (ed. 3) 211 In *Caryophylleæ* an internode below the receptacle is elongated, and bears on its summit the petals and stamens: De Candolle calls this *anthophore.* **1857** HENFREY *Elem. Bot.* §161 The stalk above the calyx of Silene, etc. is termed an anthophore.

anthophorous (æn'θɒfərəs), *a.* [see prec. and -OUS.] Flower-bearing.
1880 in *Syd. Soc. Lex.*

anthophyllite (ænθəʊ'fɪlaɪt, -'ɒfɪlaɪt). *Min.* [f. mod.L. *anthophyllum* clove + -ITE; from its clove-brown colour (Schumacher).] A variety of horn-blende found in Norway.
1843 HUMBLE *Dict. Geol.*, *Anthophyllite*..of a yellowish grey, or brownish colour..the prismatic schiller-spar of Mohs.

anthophy'llitic, *a. Min.* [f. prec. + -IC.] Of the nature of, or containing, anthophyllite.
1862 DANA *Man. Geol.* 71.

anthorism ('ænθərɪz(ə)m). *Rhet. rare*$^{-0}$. [ad. Gr. ἀνθορισμ-ός, f. ἀνθορίζ-ειν, f. ἀντί against + ὁρίζ- ειν to define.] A counter-definition; a description or definition differing from that given by one's opponent.
1846 in SMART.

†**'anthos.** *Obs.* [a. Gr. ἄνθος flower.] Formerly applied to Rosemary as 'the flower' *par excellence.*
1585 LLOYD *Treas. Health* I iiij, Basyll, Anthos, and suche whych comforteth the herte. **1727–51** CHAMBERS *Cycl.*, *Anthos*..signifies flower; but by way of excellency is appropriated to rosemary.

anthosiderite (ænθəʊ'sɪdəraɪt). *Min.* [f. Gr. ἄνθο-ς flower + σιδηρίτης iron-stone: see -ITE.] A hydrous silicate of iron occurring in fibrous tufts or feathery flowers.
1837–80 DANA *Min.* 407.

anthosperm ('ænθəʊspɜːm). *Bot.* [f. Gr. ἄνθο-ς flower + σπέρμα seed.] (See quot.)
1847 LINDLEY *Elem. Bot.* Gloss., *Anthosperm*, A little coloured concretion scattered in the tissue of certain Fucoids.

anthotaxy ('ænθəʊtæksɪ). *Bot. rare.* [f. as prec. + -ταξία arrangement, f. τάσσ-ειν to arrange.] Arrangement of flowers according to their inflorescence.
1880 GRAY *Bot. Text-bk.* 141.

antho'xanthin(e. ? *Obs.* [f. Gr. ἄνθο-ς + ξανθός yellow + -IN.] The colouring principle of yellow flowers; now called *xanthophyll.*
1839 LINDLEY *Introd. Bot.* (ed. 3) 434 The yellow matter or anthoxantine is an extractive resinous substance.

‖**Anthozoa** (ænθəʊ'zəʊə), *sb. pl. Zool.* ? *Obs.* [mod.L., f. Gr. ἄνθο-ς flower + ζῷα animals.] Another name for the Zoophytes called Actinozoa, including sea-anemones, coralline polypes, etc.
1851 RICHARDSON *Geol.* viii. 216 The calcareous skeletons of some Anthozoa. **1864** H. SPENCER *Illust. Progr.* 345 The wide range which the Anthozoa are known to have.

anthozoic (ænθəʊ'zəʊɪk), *a. Zool.* [f. prec. + -IC.] Of or pertaining to the *Anthozoa.*
1859 TODD *Cycl. Anat. & Phys.* V. 485/2 The minute creatures on which the Anthozoic polypes prey.

anthozooid (ænθəʊ'zəʊɔɪd). *Zool.* [f. Gr. ἄνθο-ς flower + ZOOID, ad. Gr. ζωοειδής like an animal.] An individual animalcule of a compound Zoophyte.
1877 HUXLEY *Inv. An.* iii. 159 The axial cavity of each anthozooid is in communication with a system of large canals.

anthra-. *Chem.* Abbreviation of ANTHRACENE (or stem *anthrac-*) forming compound names of the anthracene derivatives. The chief are:—
anthrachrysone (-'kraɪsəʊn) [Gr. χρυσός gold], one of the tetra-oxy-anthraquinones, obtained as a golden-yellow crystalline powder, by the dry distillation of dioxybenzoic acid. **anthraflavic** (-'flævɪk) acid, and **anthraflavone** (-'fleɪvəʊn) [L. *flāvus* yellow], two di-oxy-anthraquinones, isomeric with alizarine, the former crystallizing in bright yellow silky needles, the latter in small yellow needles; the salts of the former are **anthraflavates. anthra'nilic** [ANIL] acid, systematically called *Phenyl-carbamic*, $C_7H_7NO_2$, obtained from indigo. **anthraphenol** (-'fiːnɒl), a derivative of anthracene, in which one H atom is replaced by HO, having the two metameric modifications **'anthrol**, and **'anthranol. anthra'purpurin** [PURPURIN], a red colouring matter obtained from artificial alizarin. **anthraquinone** (-'kwɪnəʊn), $C_{14}H_8O_2''$, a compound related to anthracene as quinone is to benzene, produced by oxidation of anthracene, hence also called *oxy-anthracene*; it crystallizes in pale yellow needles, and is of great importance as the immediate source of artificial alizarin. It has numerous compounds, as *nitro-*, and *oxy-anthraquinones*, etc.
1875 WATTS *Dict. Chem.* VII. 86 Anthrachrysone dyes on iron-mordants a brown colour. *Ibid.* 87 Barium anthraflavate crystallises in reddish-brown hydrated needles. *Ibid.* Alkaline, as well as alcoholic solutions of anthraflavic acid, absorb the blue end of the spectrum very powerfully. **1879** *Ibid.* VIII. 107 Anthraflavone acts like a bibasic acid. **1881** ROSCOE in *Nature* XXIV. 228 By boiling indigo with soda and manganese dioxide, Fritzsche obtained ..as he then [1841] termed it, anthranilic acid. **1879** WATTS *Dict. Chem.* VIII. 97 α-Anthrol crystallises in brilliant yellow needles..β-Anthrol..in yellow prisms.—Anthranol crystallizes in yellowish needles. **1875** URE *Dict. Arts* I. 195 The anthrapurpurin reds being much purer and less blue, whilst the purples are bluer and the blacks more intense than those with alizarine. **1869** ROSCOE *Elem. Chem.* xxxix. 424 Both [alizarine and purpurine] are hydroxyl derivatives of anthraquinone, and they can both be reduced to anthracene by the action of zinc dust. **1881** *Athenæum* 17 Dec. 819/2 Artificial alizarine is prepared at the positive pole from a mixture of anthraquinone and caustic potash.

anthracene ('ænθrəsiːn). *Chem.* [f. Gr. ἀνθρακ-(-αξ) coal + -ENE.] **a.** A complex hydrocarbon, called in systematic nomenclature *Para-naphthalin*, obtained from coal-tar; discovered in 1832 in the heavy semifluid portion of the tar which comes over towards the close of the distillation. It belongs to the aromatic or Benzol group, has composition $C_{14}H_{10} = C_6H_2(C_4H_4)_2 = (C_6H_4)_2C_2H_2$, and passes under influence of light into the isomeric *paranthracene.*
1863 WATTS *Dict. Chem.* IV. 350 Crude commercial anthracene is distilled from an iron retort. **1873** COOKE *Chemistry* 325 Alizarine is manufactured on a large scale from the anthracene obtained from coal-tar. **1875** URE *Dict. Arts* I. 191 Pure anthracene appears in small, well-defined, lustrous crystalline laminæ of a clear white colour.

b. *attrib.* in ***anthracene colours, derivatives,*** etc. **anthracene red**, a name for artificial alizarine; **anthracene oil** (see quot. 1940).

1874 *Jrnl. Chem. Soc.* XXVII. 853 Red or anthracene oils and creasote oils. **1920** *Conquest* May 323/1 A final fraction above 270° C., when the anthracene oil or green oil is obtained. **1940** *Chambers's Techn. Dict.* 40/1 *Anthracene oil*, a coal-tar fraction boiling above 270° C., consisting of anthracene, phenanthrene, chrysene, carbazole, and other hydrocarbon oils.

anthracic (æn'θræsɪk), *a.* [mod. f. Gr. ἀνθρακ- (ἄνθραξ) coal, carbuncle + -IC.] Of or pertaining to the disease 'anthrax'.

1881 *Nature* No. 614. 328 Anthracic blood from a sheep that had died of the disease. **1882** *Manch. Guard.* 20 Mar., The protective influence of anthracic inoculation.

anthraciferous (ænθrə'sɪfərəs), *a. Min.* [f. as prec. + -(I)FEROUS.] Yielding anthracite.

1841 TRIMMER *Pract. Geol.* 209 The plants found in the anthraciferous rock of Baden. **1843** MURCHISON in Geikie *Life* II. 2 His own anthraciferous and slaty children.

anthraciform (æn'θræsɪfɔːm). *a.* [f. as prec. + -(I)FORM.] Having the form or appearance of anthrax.

1880 in *Syd. Soc. Lex.*

anthracin, a synonym of ANTHRACENE.

anthracite ('ænθrəsaɪt). [ad. L. *anthracītes*, a. Gr. ἀνθρακίτης coal-like, f. ἄνθρακ- (-αξ) coal.]

† **1.** A stone described by Pliny, supposed to be hydrophane. *Obs.*

1601 HOLLAND *Pliny* (1634) II. 617 There is found in Thesprotia a certaine minerall Rubie called Anthracitis, resembling coles of fire. **1750** *Leonardus's Mirr. Stones* 69 Antracites or Antracas, is a sparkling Stone of a fiery Colour.

2. The non-bituminous variety of coal called also glance coal, blind coal, and stone coal.

1812 SIR H. DAVY *Chem. Philos.* 313 The anthracite of Kilkenny.. has all the characters of well burned charcoal. **1833** LYELL *Princ. Geol.* III. 373 In the vicinity of some trap dikes, coal is converted into anthracite. **1856** BRYANT *Rhode-Island Coal* viii, Dark anthracite! that reddenest on my hearth. **1875** URE *Dict. Arts* I. 192 The term Culm is applied generally to anthracite in our parliamentary annals.

3. *attrib.*, as ***anthracite coal, stove***; **anthracite basin, bed**, in geology.

1837 CARLYLE *Fr. Rev.* (1872) III. VII. iii. 253 Anthracite coal, difficult to kindle, but which no known thing will put out. **1879** *Cassell's Techn. Educ.* I. 67 Anthracite coal.. is almost pure carbon. **1853** KANE *Grinnell Exp.* ii. (1856) 21 Three anthracite stoves. **1858** MOTLEY *Dutch Rep.* I. 2 That picturesque anthracite basin where now stands the city of Namur. **1851** DIXON *Penn* xxi. (1872) 182 Inexhaustible fields of coal; and anthracite beds of the same fossil.

anthracitic (ænθrə'sɪtɪk), *a.* [f. prec. + -IC.] Of, pertaining to, or resembling, anthracite.

1845 LYELL *Trav. N. Amer.* I. 88 The anthracitic coal-measures. **1858** CARLYLE *Fredk. Gt.* (1865) II. VII. vi. 305 The Duke.. blushed blue, then red.. at length settling into a steady pale, as it were, indicating anthracitic white-heat.

anthracitism ('ænθrəsaɪtˌɪz(ə)m). [mod. f. ANTHRACITE + -ISM.] The anthracitic condition (of coal).

1879 LE CONTE *Elem. Geol.* §4. 346 High heat is not necessary to produce anthracitism.

anthracitization (ˌænθrəsaɪtaɪ'zeɪʃən). [f. ANTHRACITE + -IZATION.] The process of becoming changed from bituminous coal into anthracite.

1903 *Progr. Geol. Surv. U.K. 1902*, 49 An investigation of the anthracitisation of the coals. *Ibid.* 190 The anthracitisation is more rapid in a north and south direction.

anthracitous ('ænθrəsaɪtəs), *a.* [f. as ANTHRACITISM + -OUS.] Containing, or characterized by, anthracite.

1860 *Edinb. Rev.* No. 225. 91 In Brecknockshire there are only 78 square miles of coal.. The whole is called anthracitous. **1857** PAGE *Advd. Text-bk. Geol.* xii. (1876) 204 Bands of anthracite and anthracitous shales.

anthracnose (æn'θræknəʊs). [a. F. *anthracnose* (Fabre and Dunal 1853, in *Bull. Soc. Centrale d'Agric. de l'Hérault* XL), f. ANTHRAX + Gr. νόσος disease.] A fungal disease of plants, esp. of vines and beans, characterized by dark spots or lesions.

1886 *Rep. Commissioner U.S. Dept. Agric.* (Mycology) 112 Anthracnose, *Sphaceloma ampelium DeBy*.. a comparatively new disease in this country... In Europe it has been known for many years.. as 'Charbon', 'Brenner', [etc.]. **1888** [see CHARBON 3]. **1938** *Nature* 12 Nov. 881/2 The fungus [*Colletotrichum lagenarium*] causes leaf spotting or anthracnose upon a wide range of varieties. **1950** *N.Z. Jrnl. Agric.* Oct. 325/1 Black spot or anthracnose appears on early spring growth [on grape-vines] and the most serious damage usually occurs before blossom time.

anthracoid ('ænθrəkɔɪd), *a. Biol.* [f. Gr. ἄνθρακ- (see ANTHRAX) + -OID.] Resembling, or having like nature to, anthrax.

1881 *Daily News* 19 Sept. 5/3 Of course the 'attenuated anthracoid microbe' is not a panacea. **1883** *Chamb. Jrnl.* 28 The germs of splenic fever called anthracoid microbes.

anthracomancy ('ænθrəkəʊˌmænsɪ). *rare*⁻⁰. [f. as prec. + μαντεία divination.] Divination by the inspection of burning coals. (In mod. Dicts.)

anthracometer (ænθrə'kɒmɪtə(r)). [f. as prec. + -(O)METER.] 'An instrument for determining the quantity of carbonic acid which exists in any gaseous admixture.' Craig 1847.

anthracometric (ˌænθrəkəʊ'mɛtrɪk). *a.* [f. as prec. + Gr. μετρικός: see -METRIC.] Of, or pertaining to the use of, an anthracometer.

anthraconite (æn'θrækənaɪt). *Min.* [mod. f. Gr. ἀνθρακ- coal + -ωνη female descendant, derivative + -ITE; so named by von Moll.] A name given to black varieties of limestone, as common black marble, and the black bituminous or fetid limestones called swinestones or stinkstones.

1843 HUMBLE *Dict. Geol.*, *Anthraconite*,.. on rubbing, yields a sulphureo-bituminous odour.

anthracosis (ænθrə'kəʊsɪs). *Med.* [mod.L., f. Gr. ἀνθρακ-, ἄνθραξ ANTHRAX + -OSIS.] Deposition of carbon particles in the lung; also, a severer form of such deposition, e.g. coal miner's pneumoconiosis. Hence **anthracotic** (-'ɒtɪk) *a.*, pertaining to or affected with anthracosis.

1838 T. STRATTON in *Edin. Med. & Surg. Jrnl.* XLIX. 490 Black infiltration of the whole lungs.. has been called the black lung of coal miners, and may more shortly be defined *anthracosis*. **1848** DUNGLISON *Med. Lex.* (ed. 7), Anthracosis. **1875** C. H. JONES & SIEVEKING *Path. Anat.* (ed. 2) 492 'Colliers' Phthisis', or as it has been called, anthrakosis. **1900** *Jrnl. Exper. Med.* V. 156 The cut section of the lungs, which were markedly anthracotic, was smooth. **1912** ADAMI & MCCRAE *Pathol.* 325 Section of an anthracotic lung. **1930** *Engineering* 25 Apr. 536/2 French experts consider that anthracosis, caused by coal-dust, is a form of silicosis.

anthracothere ('ænθrəkəʊˌθɪə(r)). *Palæont.* [ad. mod.L. *anthracothērium* (also used), f. as ANTHRACONITE + Gr. θηρίον beast.] A pachyderm quadruped whose remains occur in Tertiary lignites and coal.

1833 LYELL *Princ. Geol.* III. 222 Many entire jaws and other bones of an extinct mammifer, called by Cuvier Anthracotherium, have been found in the coal-beds. **1857** PAGE *Adv. Text-bk. Geol.* (1876) 373 The anthracothere stands intermediate between the river-hog and hippopotamus.

anthracoxen(e ('ænθrəkɒkˌsiːn). *Min.* [mod. f. Gr. ἄνθρακ- coal + ξέν-ος stranger, guest; so named by Reuss in allusion to its occurrence as a foreign substance in coal.] A brownish-black resin-like substance, occurring in amorphous masses which alternate with layers of coal, in the coal-beds of Brandeisl, near Schlan, in Bohemia.

1863 in WATTS *Dict. Chem.*

anthrax ('ænθræks). [a. L. *anthrax* a carbuncle, a. Gr. ἄνθραξ coal, a carbuncle.]

1. A carbuncle, or malignant boil.

1398 TREVISA *Barth. De P.R.* VII. lix. (1495) 275 Antrax is a postume whyche cometh of ful wood matere and venemous.. It is callyd also Carbunculus, for it brennyth as a cole. **1543** TRAHERON *Vigo's Chirurg.* II. xix. 29 Anthrax is a malygne pustle, havynge about it certayne lytle yelowe veynes of the coloure of the rayne bowe. **1706** PHILLIPS, *Anthrax*.. a Carbuncle-swelling.. that arises in several Parts surrounded with fiery, sharp, and painful Pimples. **1871** BRYANT *Pract. Surg.* I. 171 Anthrax of the lips has nothing in common with malignant pustule.

2. The 'splenic fever' of sheep and cattle, discovered by M. Pasteur to result from the introduction of minute organisms into the blood of the animal, and their rapid reproduction there. Also applied to the carbuncular disease, otherwise called *malignant pustule*, caused in man by infection from animals so affected.

1876 tr. *Wagner's Gen. Pathol.* 4 Infection.. from a diseased animal, e.g. glanders, anthrax, and hydrophobia. **1880** *19th Cent.* Nov. 858 Sheep of the very breed most liable to anthrax. **1882** *Standard* 29 Dec. 2/2 The third case was one of external anthrax in.. a.. wool-comber.

anthrone ('ænθrəʊn). *Chem.* [f. ANTHRA- + KET)ONE.] A colourless crystalline ketone, $C_{14}H_{10}O$.

1913 *Chem. Abstr.* 1872 Anthracene.. Derivatives of Anthrone. **1921** E. DE B. BARNETT *Anthracene* 96 Anthrone itself was first obtained by Liebermann. **1956** *Nature* 7 Jan. 38/1 A slightly modified anthrone method.. for the quantitative estimation of carbohydrate in chromatographic fractions.

anthropic (æn'θrɒpɪk), *a.* [ad. Gr. ἀνθρωπικ-ός human, f. ἄνθρωπ-ος man, human being.] **a.** Of or belonging to a human being; of a human sort. Also, concerned with or relating to human beings; in *Geol.* applied to the period of the deposits in which human remains are found.

1859 OWEN *Classif. Mamm.* App. B. 82 They impress that anthropic feature upon the face of the living gorilla. **1863** WATTS *Dict. Chem.* I. 310 This he at first supposed to be a peculiar acid (anthropic acid). **1884** HARRISON in *19th Cent.* Mar. 505 The conclusion that the future of religion is to be, not only.. anthropomorphic—but frankly anthropic. **1884** BLACKMORE *Sir Thomas Upmore* xiii, My dear little anthropic nautilus, I can do nothing. **1893** J. W. DAWSON *Salient Points* 465 The age of which we have been writing the history, is that which has been fitly named the Anthropic.

b. ***anthropic principle***: the principle that theories of the universe are constrained by the need to allow for man's existence in it as an observer.

1974 B. CARTER in *Internat. Astron. Union Symposium* No. 63 291 These predictions do require the use of what may be termed the *anthropic principle* to the effect that what we can expect to observe must be restricted by the conditions necessary for our presence as observers. **1981** *Sci. Amer.* Dec. 114/2 Not all cosmologists and philosophers of science assent to the utility of the anthropic principle, or even to its legitimacy. **1984** *Nature* 6 Dec. 525/1 In short, the anthropic principle seems to suggest that we should observe a universe of minimal order consistent with the existence of observers.

an'thropical, *a. rare.* [f. as prec. + -AL[1].] Connected with, or attached to, human nature.

1804-6 SYD. SMITH (1850) 238 A very strong anthropical party, who view all eulogiums on the brute creation with a very considerable degree of suspicion. **1845** *Blackw. Mag.* LVII. 523 By virtue of these anthropical elements—Homer, who happens to be a Greek, makes you one.

anthropinism (æn'θrəʊpɪnɪz(ə)m). *rare*⁻¹. [f. Gr. ἀνθρώπιν-ος human (f. ἄνθρωπ-ος man) + -ISM.] Consideration of things in their relation to man.

1880 G. ALLEN *Evol. at Large* 161 In our narrow anthropinism we should have refused to listen to him [Darwin] had he given us two volumes instead on the Descent of Walnuts.

anthropinistic (ænˌθrəʊpɪ'nɪstɪk), *a. rare*⁻¹. [f. prec.: see -ISTIC.] Of the nature of anthropinism; regarding things in their relation to man.

1880 G. ALLEN in *Academy* 23 Oct. 292 The primitive conception of beauty must have been purely anthropinistic —must have gathered mainly round the personality of man or woman.

anthropo-, repr. Gr. ἀνθρωπο- stem and comb. form of ἄνθρωπος man. In compounds formed in Greek itself, as *anthropopœia*, ἀνθρωποποιΐα; in others formed in L.; and in many of mod. formation. The pronunciation differs with the accent; and when the primary stress falls on the following syllable, the position of the secondary stress fluctuates from *anˌthrōpo-* in learned words, to *ˌanthropo-* in the more popular, as in *anˌthrōpo'logical*, *ˌanthropo'logical*.

anthropocen'trality. *rare.* [f. ANTHROPO- + CENTRALITY.] = ANTHROPOCENTRICISM.

1934 *Theology* XXVIII. 267 The humanist ethic.. leads us to the blind alley of anthropocentrality.

anthropocentric (ænˌθrəʊpəʊ'sɛntrɪk), *a.* [f. ANTHROPO- + Gr. κέντρ-ον centre + -IC.] Centring in man; regarding man as the central fact of the universe, to which all surrounding facts have reference.

1863 DRAPER *Intell. Devel. Eur.* iii. (1865) 42 In the most ancient records remaining, the Hindu mind is dealing with anthropocentric conceptions.. of the moral kind. **1876** tr. *Haeckel's Creat.* I. ii. 38 The anthropocentric error, that Man is the premeditated aim of the creation of the earth.

anthropo'centrically, *adv.* [f. prec. *a.* + -AL + -LY[2].] In an anthropocentric manner or way.

1953 *New Biol.* XIV. 16 Anthropocentrically minded observers have suggested [etc.]. **1963** *Times* 28 May 13/5 The second is that urban minds stop regarding agriculture anthropocentrically as if it always represented a human efficiency problem.

anthropocentricism, **anthropocentrism** (-'sɛntrɪsɪz(ə)m, -'sɛntrɪz(ə)m). [f. ANTHROPOCENTRIC *a.* + -ISM.] An anthropocentric view or doctrine.

1909 *Cent. Dict.* Suppl., Anthropocentricism. **1909** WEBSTER, *Anthropocentrism*, the assumption that man is the center of all things. **1912** J. H. MOORE *Ethics & Educ.* xvii. 141 There is a doctrine called Anthropocentricism... According to this theory, man is the centre of the universe. **1922** *Q. Rev.* July 97 The last shreds of anthropocentrism have been worn away. **1936** V. A. DEMANT *Chr. Polity* v. 103 To confine theological seriousness to God's redemptive work in man.. is a disguised form of the very anthropocentricism which this doctrine intends to oppose. **1941** A. HUXLEY *Grey Eminence* iii. 79 Theocentrism produces better ethical results than anthropocentrism and moralism. **1956** *Sc. Jrnl. Theol.* IX. 72 The anthropocentricism and moralism of Hebrew theology.

anthropogenic (-'dʒɛnɪk), *a.*

1. [f. ANTHROPOGENY + -IC.] Of or pertaining to anthropogeny.

1889 in *Cent. Dict.* **1952** GERTH & MARTINDALE tr. *Weber's Anc. Jud.* ix. 227 The cosmogonic and anthropogenic myths are of secondary importance in Yahwistic religiosity.

2. [f. ANTHROPO- + -GENIC.] Having its origin in the activities of man.

1923 A. G. Tansley *Pract. Plant Ecol.* iv. 48 Where he [*sc.* man] has introduced a more or less permanent modifying factor or set of factors, we have biotic (anthropogenic) climaxes or some stage of development towards them. **1939** —— *Brit. Islands & Vegetation* vi. 129 All the factors mentioned—felling, mowing, grazing, and fire—are sometimes loosely termed 'biotic factors', though they would be more properly called *anthropogenic factors*, and the climaxes they produce *anthropogenic climaxes*. Among the anthropogenic factors the grazing factor is biotic in the strict sense. **1947** *Nature* 11 Jan. 45/1 The virgin forest..and even the forest nursery are viewed as possible systems of this kind maintained either by natural or anthropogenic forces. **1960** N. Polunin *Introd. Plant Geogr.* vii. 200 Leaving aside the so-called 'anthropogenic relics' whose areas have become drastically reduced through the activities of Man.

anthropogeny (ænθrəʊˈpɒdʒɪnɪ). [f. as if ad. Gr. *ἀνθρωπογένεια, abstr. n. f. ἀνθρωπο-γεν-ής born of man.] The investigation of the origin of man.

1839 Hooper *Med. Dict.*, *Anthropogeny*, the study of the generation of man. **1879** tr. *Haeckel's Evol. Man* I. 2 The History of the Evolution of Man, or briefly 'Anthropogeny.'

anthropogeography (ænˌθrəʊpəʊdʒiːˈɒgrəfɪ). [f. anthropo- + geography, after G. *anthropogeographie* (F. Ratzel 1882).] That department of geography which treats of the relations of the earth to mankind as its inhabitants. So **anthropogeographer** (-ˈɒgrəfə(r)), one versed in anthropogeography; **anthropogeographic** (-əʊˈgræfɪk), **-ical** *adjs.*, pertaining to anthropogeography.

1652 *Hermeticall Banquet* 120 The new Anthropogeographicall Map. **1895** *Geogr. Jrnl.* Oct. 375 Biogeography..has three sections—phytogeography..zoogeography..and anthropogeography, or the geography of men. *a* **1899** Brinton *Basis Soc. Relat.* (1902) iv. 181 Even the most determined of the 'anthropo-geographers' will not deny that the power over the mind which they attribute to geographical features diminishes in proportion as culture increases. **1899** *Geogr. Jrnl.* Feb. 171 Anthropogeography is a convenient term under which to include all those aspects of geography that deal with the relations of humanity.. to the earth... 'Applied Geography' might be taken as an alternative term. **1939** *Jrnl. R. Anthrop. Inst.* 45 Anthropogeographical studies in Greenland. **1940** S. W. Boggs *Internat. Boundaries* ii. 27 The term 'boundary' as applied to any of the anthropogeographic types.

anthropoglot (ænˈθrəʊpəglɒt). [ad. Gr. ἀνθρωπόγλωττος speaking like a man, f. ἄνθρωπο-ς + γλῶττα, γλῶσσα, tongue.] An animal with a tongue like a man's, *e.g.* a parrot.

1847 Craig, *Anthropoglottis.* **1859** in Worcester.

anthropogony (ænθrəʊˈpɒgənɪ). [ad. Gr. ἀνθρωπογονία.] **a.** The origin of man. **b.** The investigation or an account of this.

a **1871** Mansel *Gnostic Heresies* (1875) 36 A scheme of cosmogony and anthropogony, running parallel to each other, man being regarded as the microcosm, or image in miniature of the world. **1874** J. W. Watson & M. J. Evans tr. *Van Oosterzee's Chr. Dogmatics* I. 361 A comparison with other Eastern Anthropogonies gives a result most favourable to the Mosaic.

anthropography (ænθrəʊˈpɒgrəfɪ). [f. anthropo- + Gr. -γραφία description: see -graphy.]

†**1.** A description of all the parts of the human body. *Obs.*

1570 Dee *Math. Pref.* 33 Anthropographie, is the description of the Number, Measure, Waight, Figure, Situation, and colour of euery diuerse thing, conteyned in the perfect body of Man. **1839** Hooper *Med. Dict.*, *Anthropography*..a description of the structure of man.

2. The branch of anthropology which treats of the geographical distribution of the races of mankind, and their local variations; ethnography.

1834 *Penny Cycl.* II. 97 A series of anthropographies, of different epochs, would form the true basis of ethnography.

anthropoid (ˈænθrəpɔɪd, ænˈθrəʊpɔɪd), *a.* and *sb.* [ad. Gr. ἀνθρωπο-ειδ-ής of human form: see -oid. Cf. mod.Fr. *anthropoïde.*]

A. *adj.* **a.** Of human form, man-like.

a **1837** Owen in *Penny Cycl.* VII. 69/2 The highest cultivation of which the anthropoïd apes are susceptible. **1862** D. Wilson *Preh. Man* iii. (1865) 31 The assumed anthropoid link between man and the brutes.

b. Shaped like a man.

1912 T. E. Lawrence *Home Lett.* (1954) 228 It [a sarcophagus] was white marble..anthropoid but Greek-featured. *Ibid.* 235 Anthropoid means human 'shaped': the sarcophagus is like the sort of mummy-coffin that has a face carved on it. **1920** *Brit. Mus. Return* 43 All the rectangular and anthropoid coffins..have been incorporated.

c. Of a human being: of ape-like form or character.

1930 *English Jrnl.* XIX. 608 Mr. Mencken watched with alert eyes the simian antics of the anthropoid rabble at the Dayton farce. **1939** C. K. Allen *Law in the Making* (ed. 3) 56 Some incalculably remote age when the life of anthropoid men was 'nasty, brutish, and short'.

B. *sb.* **a.** A being that is human in form only. **b.** An anthropoid ape.

1832 *Q. Rev.* XLVIII. 96 A race of Anthropoids,—neither Raleigh nor Sidney would have called them Men—has wormed itself into the dominion of the letter-press—not the literature of England. **1863** Huxley *Man's Place in Nat.* i. 23 There are four distinct kinds of anthropoids..the Gibbons and the Orangs..the Chimpanzees and the Gorilla.

anthropoidal (ænθrəʊˈpɔɪdəl), *a.* [f. prec. + -al[1].] Of anthropoid nature or structure.

1867 *Transmut. Species* x. 137 Our forefathers, the anthropoidal patriarchs of the tropical forests. **1882** Thompson in *Trans. Vict. Inst.* 238 The anthropoidal progenitor gradually became extinct.

anthropolatry (ænθrəʊˈpɒlətrɪ). *rare.* [ad. Gr. ἀνθρωπολατρεία man-worship, f. ἄνθρωπος man + λατρεία worship.] Man-worship; the giving of divine honours to a human being.

1658 Manton *Exp. Jude* 16 Wks. 1871 V. 319 We may admire the gifts of God in others..but not so as to be guilty of anthropolatry, or man-worship. **1813** W. Taylor in *Month. Rev.* LXXI. 477 The anthropolatry of the Greeks.

anthropolite, -lith (ænˈθrəʊpəlaɪt, -lɪθ). [f. anthropo- + Gr. λίθος stone: see -lite.] A petrified man; a fossil ascribed to the human species.

1848 tr. *Richter's Levana* 43 The ideal man comes upon the earth as an anthropolithe (a petrified man). **1863** G. Kearley *Links in Chain*, A veritable anthropolite, the petrified remains of one of the accursed race that was swept away by the flood.

anthropologic (-ˈlɒdʒɪk), *a.* *rare.* [ad. mod.L. *anthrōpologic-us* (1594), f. Gr. ἀνθρωπο-λόγ-ος: see anthropology and -ic.] Of anthropology.

1850 Kingsley *Misc.* I. 219 Such subtle anthropologic wisdom as the Ode on the Intimations of Immortality. **1878** *N. Amer. Rev.* CXXVI. 553 The vital principles of anthropologic science.

anthropological. (-ˈlɒdʒɪkəl), *a.* [f. as prec. + -al[1].] Of, pertaining to, or connected with, anthropology. **a.** Relating to the nature of man.

1825 Beddoes *Poems* (1851) Introd. 51 A series of anthropological experiments developed for the purpose of ascertaining some important psychical principle. **1834** *Penny Cycl.* II. 97 *Anthropological Didactic*, or instructions for learning both the Interior and Exterior of Man: *Anthropological Characteristic*, or the way to find out the Interior from the Exterior. **1869** Haddan *Apost. Succ.* i. 5 The anthropological side of Christianity.

b. Relating to the natural history of mankind.

1863 *Lond. Rev.* 7 Feb., The first meeting of the Anthropological Society will take place..on the 24th of this month. **1864** *Sat. Rev.* 27 Aug. 262/1 A weakness for an octogenarian Premier as an anthropological curiosity.

anthropoˈlogically, *adv.* [f. prec. + -ly[2].] In an anthropological manner or way.

1883 *Knowl.* 6 Jul. 7/1 The anthropologically-minded Africans had picked up more information about him than he had about them.

anthropologist (ænθrəʊˈpɒlədʒɪst). [f. anthropology: see -ist.] One who pursues the science of anthropology, a student of mankind.

1798 Willich *Elem. Crit. Philos.* 22 Plattner, that excellent Anthropologist,..has employed rational scepticism against the Kantian System. **1805** *Edin. Rev.* VI. 123 M. Peron..embarked in the capacity of anthropologist to the expedition. **1879** Wallace *Austral.* i. 6 The variety of human races..and the interesting problems which they present to the anthropologist.

anthropologize (ænθrəʊˈpɒlədʒaɪz), *v.* *colloq.* [f. anthropology + -ize, after *philosophize*, etc.] **a.** *trans.* To explain, treat, or study anthropologically. **b.** *intr.* To pursue anthropology.

1939 'M. Innes' *Stop Press* ii. v. 285 Modish enough to play at anthropologising an unknown culture. **1941** R. R. Marett *Jerseyman* xii. 178 To anthropologize in the field would have attracted me greatly. **1957** *Times Lit. Suppl.* 1 Nov. 656/3 But the more serious side of Mr. Speirs's anthropologizing is to be found, for instance, in his deep sense of the adjustment of medieval life..to the rhythms of the year.

anthropology (-ˈɒlədʒɪ). [f. Gr. ἄνθρωπο-ς man + -logy. Gr. had ἀνθρωπολόγος (Aristotle) treating of man, of which *ἀνθρωπολογία was analogically the abst. sb. *Anthropologia* occurs as mod.L. in 1595, and *anthropologie* as mod.Fr.]

1. The science of man, or of mankind, in the widest sense.

This seems to have been the original application of the word in Eng. but for two and a half cent., to *c* 1860, the term was commonly confined to the restricted sense b. Since that date, it has sometimes been limited, by reaction, to c.

1593 R. Harvey *Philad.* 15 Genealogy or issue which they had, Artes which they studied, Actes which they did. This part of History is named Anthropology. **1656** Blount *Glossogr.*, *Anthropology*, a speaking or discoursing of men.

b. The science of the nature of man, embracing Human Physiology and Psychology and their mutual bearing.

The sense in which ἀνθρωπολόγος was used by Aristotle, and *Anthropologia* by Otto Casmann 1594-5 in his *Psychologia Anthropologica*, sive *Animæ Humanæ Doctrina*; and *Anthropologia*: *Pars II. hoc est de fabrica Humani Corporis.* This author seems to have first used the term.

[**1706** J. Drake (*title*) Anthropologia Nova; or, A new System of Anatomy.] **1706** Phillips, *Anthropology*, a Discourse or Description of Man, or of a Man's Body. **1727-51** Chambers *Cycl.*, *Anthropology* includes the consideration both of the human body and soul, with the laws of their union, and the effects thereof, as sensation, motion, etc. **1810** Coleridge *Taste* in *Lect. Shaks.* II. 223 The analysis of our senses in the commonest books of anthropology. **1834** *Penny Cycl.* II. 97 Anthropology.. considers man as a citizen of the world, and has nothing properly to do with the varieties of the human race.

c. The 'study of man as an animal' (Latham). The branch of the science which investigates the position of man zoologically, his 'evolution,' and history as a race of animated beings.

1861 Hulme *Moquin-Tandon* Pref. 8 Natural History, or Anthropology..the principal characters of our species, its perfection, its accidental degradations, its unity, its races, and the manner in which it has been classified. **1881** Flower in *Nature* No. 619. 437 The aim of zoological anthropology is to discover a natural classification of man.

†**2.** A speaking after the manner of men; anthropomorphic language. [The sense in which ἀνθρωπολογέ-ειν was used by Philo.] *Obs.*

1727-51 Chambers *Cycl.*, *Anthropology* is particularly used in theology, for a way of speaking of God, after the manner of men, by attributing human parts and passions to him.

anthropomancy (ænˈθrəʊpəʊˌmænsɪ). [f. anthropo- + Gr. μαντεία divination: see -mancy. Cf. mod.Fr. *anthropomancie.* Cotgr. 1611 has '*Anthropomantie*: Divination by the raising of dead men.'] Pretended divination by the entrails of men.

1618 in Holyday *Technogamia.* **1652** Gaule *Magastrom.* 367 Anthropomancy, or predicting by intrailes of men, women, children. **1693** Urquhart *Rabelais* iii. xxv, Anthropomancy practised by the Roman emperor Heliogabalus. **1731** in Bailey; and in mod. Dicts.

†**anˌthropoˈmantic,** *a.* *Obs.* *rare*[−1]. [see prec.: cf. Gr. μαντικός prophetic.] Of or belonging to anthropomancy.

1652 Gaule *Magastrom.* 260 Such like anthropomanticke sacrifices were used by Mithridates.

†**anˈthropoˌmantist.** *Obs.* *rare*[−1]. [see prec.: and -ist.] One who practises anthropomancy.

1652 Gaule *Magastrom.* 369 Heliogobalus, an anthropomantist, [was] slain and cast into a jakes.

anthropometer (-ˈɒmɪtə(r)). [See -meter.] **a.** One who studies or practises anthropometry. *rare.* **b.** An anthropometrical instrument.

1883 *Ann. Rep. Smithsonian Inst. 1881* 499 Man is an animal..exhibiting in his adult form those characteristics which engage the attention of the anatomist, the physiologist, and the anthropometer. **1898** A. C. Haddon *Study of Man* xvi. 446 The rod of the Anthropometer should be held vertically in front of the face of the subject. **1951** *Notes & Queries on Anthropol.* (ed. 6) i. 12 In the field the anthropometer may be used, taking care to keep the instrument vertical.

So **anthroˈpometrist** = sense a above.

1883 *Pall Mall Gaz.* 3 Oct. 2 Surely the anthropometrists will do harm if they encourage the craze for tallness. **1904** G. S. Hall *Adolescence* I. 19 Anthropometrists think growth in height..antagonistic to growth in girth. **1956** *Antiquity* XXX. 123 Not all of the anthropometrists..could remember exactly how they had executed each of the measurements.

anthropometric (ænˌθrəʊpəʊˈmɛtrɪk), *a.* [f. anthropometry + -ic: see -metric.] Of or belonging to, skilled in, or given to, anthropometry.

1871 M. Collins *Marq. & Merch.* III. iv. 141 Given an hour of a man's life, and an anthropometric seraph could calculate all that he ever has been and all that he ever will be. **1882** *Athenæum* 18 Mar. 351/3 A complete series of anthropometric measurements of 111 individuals.

anˌthropoˈmetrical, *a.* [f. prec. + -al[1].] Relating or pertaining to anthropometry.

1878 C. Roberts *Anthropom.* 52 The principal object of.. anthropometrical observations is to ascertain the size of the body. *Ibid.* Introd. 5 The Anthropometrical Chart.

anˌthropoˈmetrically, *adv.* [f. prec. + -ly[2].] In regard to, or in the matter of, anthropometry.

Mod. Anthropometrically, the two races show important differences.

anthropometry (ænθrəʊˈpɒmɪtrɪ). [mod. f. anthropo- + Gr. -μετρία measuring: see -metry. Cf. Fr. *anthropométrie.*] The measurement of the human body with a view to determine its average dimensions, and the proportion of its parts, at different ages and in different races or classes.

1839 Hooper *Med. Dict.*, *Anthropometry*, The measurement of the dimensions of man. **1875** J. Baxter *Statistics Med. etc.* I. 62 An outline of the History of Anthropometry.

anthropomorph (ænˈθrəʊpəʊ-, ˈænθrəʊpəʊmɔːf). [ad. Gr. ἀνθρωπόμορφος: see anthropomorphous *a.*] A representation of the human form in art.

In quot. 1894 used with sarcastic application.

1894 *Daily News* 26 Nov. 6/5 Your fashionable and self-adoring man or 'anthropomorph'. **1895** A. C. Haddon *Evol. Art* 185 New Zealand is one of the places where anthropomorphs abound. **1913** J. Rendel Harris *Boanerges*

ii. 14 There was an ornithomorph, and..several theriomorphs, before the anthropomorph.

anthropomorphic (æn,θrəʊpəʊˈmɔːfɪk), *a.* [f. Gr. ἀνθρωπόμορφ-ος (see ANTHROPOMORPHOUS) + -IC.] **1.** Of the nature of anthropomorphism.

a. Treating the Deity as anthropomorphous, or as having a human form and character.

1827 HARE *Guesses* I. (1873) 67 Their anthropomorphic Religion..reacted powerfully upon them. **1851** WESTCOTT *Introd. Gosp.* i. (ed. 5) 80 The anthropomorphic language of the Pentateuch. **1878** GLADSTONE *Prim. Homer* 68 The anthropomorphic tracings are deepest upon the Zeus of Homer.

b. Attributing a human personality to anything impersonal or irrational.

1858 LEWES *Seaside Stud.* 255 As we are just now looking with scientific seriousness at our animals, we will discard all anthropomorphic interpretations, such as point to 'alarm.' **1872** BLACK *Adv. Phaeton* xxi. 294 The anthropomorphic abstractions which we call nations.

2. Having or representing a human form: = ANTHROPOMORPHOUS *a.*

1886 [see ZOOMORPHIC *a.* 2b]. **1905** A. S. GRIFFITH tr. *Capart's Prim. Art Egypt* iii. 59 The designs..borrowed from animals (zoomorphic designs), from the human figure (anthropomorphic), and occasionally from manufactured objects (skeuomorphic).

an,thropo'morphical, *a. rare.* [f. prec. + -AL^1.] Of anthropomorphic character or tendency.

1847 TORREY *Neander's Ch. Hist.* II. 307 Christ..employed fewer anthropomorphical images than the Old Testament. **1856** FERRIER *Inst. Metaph.* VIII. viii. 441 Our ontology would have been anthropomorphical and revolting.

an,thropo'morphically, *adv.* [f. prec. + -LY^2.] In an anthropomorphic manner or way.

1855 H. SPENCER *Psychol.* (1872) II. VIII. vii. 59 A power which he is prone to think of anthropomorphically. **1868** GLADSTONE *Juv. Mundi* xii. (1870) 454 The nymphs and other personages anthropomorphically conceived.

anthropomorphism (-ˈmɔːfɪz(ə)m). [f. ANTHROPOMORPHIZE: see -ISM. Cf. Fr. *anthropomorphisme.*] Attribution of human form or character.

a. Ascription of a human form and attributes to the Deity.

1753 CHAMBERS *Cycl. Supp.*, *Anthropomorphism*, among divines, the error of those who ascribe a human figure to the deity. **1781** GIBBON *Decl. & F.* II. xlvii. 742 Scandalized by the anthropomorphism of the vulgar. **1873** SYMONDS *Grk. Poets* i. 17 The anthropomorphism of the Greek Pantheon.

b. Ascription of a human attribute or personality to anything impersonal or irrational.

1858 LEWES *Seaside Stud.* 341 We speak with large latitude of anthropomorphism when we speak of the 'vision' of these animals [molluscs].

2. In language: The use of language applicable to men in speaking of God; anthropomorphology.

1833 COLERIDGE *Table T.* 293 The strong anthropomorphism of the Hebrew Scriptures. **1860** PUSEY *Min. Proph.* 433 Thou didst walk through the sea with Thine horses..Such anthropomorphisms have a truth, which men's favourite abstractions have not.

anthropomorphist (-ˈmɔːfɪst). [n. of agent f. ANTHROPOMORPHIZE: see -IST.] One who uses anthropomorphism, or attributes a human personality to God, abstract ideas, other animals, etc.

a **1617** BAYNE *Ephes.* (1866) 33 For to measure God by our scantling..is fitter for doating anthropomorphists than grave divines. **1834** *Penny Cycl.* II. 98 The Greeks were essentially anthropomorphists. **1878** EMERSON in *N. Amer. Rev.* CXXVI. 414 What anthropomorphists we are..that we cannot let moral distinctions be, but must mould them into human shape.

anthropomorphite (-ˈmɔːfaɪt), *sb.* and *a.* [ad. L. *anthrōpomorphītæ* (Aug.), a. Gr. ἀνθρωπομορφῖται: see ANTHROPOMORPHOUS and -ITE.]

A. *sb.* One ascribing (as an article of religious belief) a human form to God; *spec.* applied to **a.** A sect that arose in Egypt in the 4th century; **b.** A party in the Western Church in the 10th c.

1561 T. N[ORTON] *Calvin's Inst.* I. xiii. (1634) 43 The Anthropomorphites..which have imagined God to consist of a body. **1661** *Origen's Opin.* in *Phœnix* (1721) I. 8 Some unlearned Monks of Egypt..called by him [Origen] Anthropomorphites. **1872** O. SHIPLEY *Gloss. Eccl. Terms*, *Andæans*..were Anthropomorphites, attributing to God a human form, parts, and passions.

B. *attrib.* or as *adj.*; = ANTHROPOMORPHITIC.

1662 GLANVILL *Lux Orient.* iv. (1682) 43 The dull and coarse Anthropomorphite Doctrines. **1798** W. TAYLOR in *Month. Rev.* XXV. 516 For a mythology to be adapted to the purposes of the artist, it suffices that the religion be *anthropomorphite*.

anthropomorphitic (-mɔːˈfɪtɪk), *a.* [ad. late L. *anthrōpomorphitic-us*, f. *anthrōpomorphītæ*: see prec. and -IC.] Of or proper to anthropomorphites.

1861 W. MILL *Applic. Panth. Princ.* (ed. 2) 85 It is an unworthy anthropomorphitic conception..to surround the Almighty with a court like an earthly sovereign. **1875** *Fam. Herald* 13 Nov. 30/1 The instances of anthropomorphitic feeling in these legends.

†**anthropomor'phitical**, *a. Obs.* [f. as prec. + -AL^1.] = prec.

1678 J. J[ONES] *Brit. Ch.* 494 Men necessarily frame corporeal, anthropomorphitical sentiments to themselves of God. **1748** HARTLEY *Observ. Man* II. i. ¶ 11. 42 This method of speaking is not strictly literal and true, but merely popular and anthropomorphitical.

anthropomorphitism (-ˈmɒfɪtɪz(ə)m). [f. ANTHROPOMORPHITE + -ISM.] **a.** The doctrine of anthropomorphites. **b.** Anthropomorphism.

1664 H. MORE *Apol.* 489 A vindication of a certain passage in his Cabbala from the suspicion of Anthropomorphitism. **1748** HARTLEY *Observ. Man* I. iv. 508 How to put the Question in respect of God..without gross Anthropomorphitism. **1835** *Blackw. Mag.* XXXVIII. 27 To rob the deities of Homer and Ovid of their individuality, extending their anti-anthropomorphitism to all the Divinities of all known nations.

†**anthropo'morphitize**, *v. Obs. rare*$^{-1}$. [f. as prec. + -IZE.] *prop.* To make, or act as, an anthropomorphite; *improp.* = next.

1810 WATSON *Anecd.* (1818) II. 407 The doing of this I consider as anthropomorphitising in the worst sense the incomprehensible author of nature.

anthropomorphization (-mɔːfaɪˈzeɪʃən). [f. ANTHROPOMORPHIZE *v.* + -ATION.] = ANTHROPOMORPHISM 1 b.

1880 W. JAMES *Coll. Ess. & Rev.* (1920) 216 All such discussions rest on an anthropomorphization of outward force. **1963** *Punch* 2 Jan. 7/3 My..conviction..that anthropomorphisation, attributing to animals the characteristics of human beings, was a lot of rot.

anthropomorphize (-ˈmɔːfaɪz), *v.* [f. Gr. ἀνθρωπόμορφ-ος + -IZE.]

1. *trans.* To render, or regard as, anthropomorphous; to attribute a human form or personality to.

1845 FORD *Hand-bk. Spain* 107 The Deity was anthropomorphised. **1847** *Blackw. Mag.* LXI. 440 We spiritualise the material universe, and afterwards..anthropomorphise spirit.

2. *absol.*

1858 LEWES *Seaside Stud.* 365 Our tendency to anthropomorphise..causes us to interpret the actions of animals according to the analogy of human nature. **1870** LOWELL *Among my Bks.* I. (1873) 86 You may see imaginative children every day anthropomorphizing in this way.

anthropomorphological (-mɔːfəʊˈlɒdʒɪkəl), *a. rare.* [f. ANTHROPOMORPHOLOGY + -ICAL.] Using anthropomorphic language.

1863 W. JAMES *Let.* 13 Sept. (1920) I. 51, I send a photograph of Gen. Sickles... It is a part of a great anthropomorphological collection which I am going to make.

anthropomorpho'logically, *adv.* [f. prec. + -LY^2.] With anthropomorphic use of language.

1850 MCCOSH *Div. Govt.* IV. ii. (1874) 475 We are entitled to say, not metaphorically or anthropomorphologically..but literally and truly, that God hates sin.

anthropomorphology (-mɔːˈfɒlədʒɪ). [f. Gr. ἀνθρωπόμορφ-ος (see ANTHROPOMORPHOUS) + -λογία speaking.] The use of anthropomorphic language; = ANTHROPOMORPHISM 3.

†**anthropo'morphose**, *v. Obs. rare*$^{-1}$. [f. Gr. ἀνθρωπομορφό-ειν (see next) after *metamorphose.*] *lit.* To change into human shape. (In quot. wrongly used for, to change from human shape.)

1660 HOWELL *Parly of Beasts* 3 (D.) Some of those human cretures that you have anthropomorphos'd and transform'd to brute animals

anthropomorphosis (-mɔːˈfəʊsɪs, -ˈmɔːfəsɪs). [a. Gr. *ἀνθρωπομόρφωσις, analogical n. of action f. ἀνθρωπομορφό-ειν to clothe in human shape: see next.] Transformation into human shape.

1863 BARING-GOULD *Icel.* 275 A myth which has suffered ..anthropomorphosis. **1866** W. HENDERSON *Folk Lore N. Count.* 283 An ancient..goddess, who has fallen from her pedestal, and undergone anthropomorphosis and localization.

anthropomorphous (-ˈmɔːfəs), *a.* [f. Gr. ἀνθρωπόμορφ-ος of human form (f. ἄνθρωπο-ς man + μορφή form) + -OUS.]

1. Of human form, having the form of a man.

1753 CHAMBERS *Cycl. Supp.* s.v., Naturalists give instances of Anthropomorphous plants, Anthropomorphous minerals, etc. **1819** B. LAWRENCE *Man* i. (1844) 88 Their [monkeys'] forms are so much like the human, as to have procured for them the epithet Anthropomorphous. **1875** LUBBOCK *Orig. Civil.* vii. 345 The deities in this state are anthropomorphous.

2. = ANTHROPOMORPHIC.

1858 GLADSTONE *Homer* II. 148 Every thing..is made to conform to anthropomorphous ideas.

anthropo'morphously, *adv. rare.* [f. prec. + -LY^2.] In an anthropomorphous manner.

1839 I. TAYLOR *Anc. Chr.* I. 432 The divine modes of proceeding are spoken of anthropomorphously.

anthropo'nomical, *a.* ? *Obs. rare*$^{-1}$. [f. Gr. ἄνθρωπο-ς man + νόμ-ος law + -ICAL: Fr. has *anthroponomie.*] Concerned with the laws which regulate human action.

1734 BOLINGBROKE in *Swift's Wks.* (1819) XVIII. 216 Suppose that some Rochefoucault or other, some anthroponomical sage, should discover a multitude of similar instances.

anthroponymy (ænθrəʊˈpɒnɪmɪ). [f. ANTHROPO- + Gr. ὠνυμία, f. ὄνομα name: cf. TOPONYMY.] Personal names as a subject of study.

So **an'throponym**, a person's name.

1937 J. ORR tr. *I. Iordan's Introd. Romance Ling.* iii. 222 A special study of toponymy and anthroponymy. **1951** (*title*) Third International Congress of Toponymy and Anthroponymy..1949. Programme [etc.]. **1958** D. TAIT in Middleton & Tait *Tribes without Rulers* 170 Kitiak is therefore a toponym... Others are of the form Udzado or Gbiedo, these are anthroponyms.

anthropopathetic (-pəˈθɛtɪk), *a. rare*$^{-1}$. [f. as next, after *sympathetic.*] (See quot.)

1856 R. VAUGHAN *Mystics* (ed. 2) I. 47 The mystic..becomes not theopathetic, but anthropopathetic—suffers, not under God, but man.

anthropopathic (-ˈpæθɪk), *a. rare.* [f. Gr. ἀνθρωποπαθής having human feelings (f. ἄνθρωπο-ς man + πάθος feeling) + -IC.] Of or pertaining to anthropopathy.

[**1589** PUTTENHAM *Eng. Poesie* 44 To make him [God]..so passionate as in effect he shold be altogether *Anthropopathis.*] **1847** TORREY *Neander's Ch. Hist.* II. 308 The anthropopathic form of conception, which has its truth in the fact that man was created in the image of God. **1873** H. ROGERS *Superh. Orig. Bible* vii. (1875) 300 The daring anthropopathic imagery by which the prophets often represent God as chiding, upbraiding, threatening.

anthropo'pathically, *adv.* [f. prec. + -AL^1 + -LY^2.] In an anthropopathic manner.

1860 T. BALFOUR *Typ. Char. Nat.* 56 The earth is personified, or spoken of anthropopathically. **1880** J. RAE in *Contemp. Rev.* Oct. 626 The savage mind apprehends objects anthropopathically, thinking of them as gifted with life.

anthropopathism (ænθrəʊˈpɒpəθɪz(ə)m). [f. Gr. ἀνθρωποπαθ-ής (see above) + -ISM.] = next.

1847 TORREY *Neander's Ch. Hist.* II. 308 Christianity aimed at a transfigured spiritualised anthropopathism. **1867** RYLAND *Hengstenberg's Pentat.* II, There are two classes of Anthropomorphisms..those in which human affections are attributed to God, or anthropopathisms.

anthropopathy (-ˈpɒpəθɪ). [ad. med.L. *anthrōpopathīa*, a. Gr. ἀνθρωποπάθεια, n. of quality from ἀνθρωποπαθής: see above and -Y.] Ascription of human feelings and passions (to the Deity, etc.).

[**1578** TIMME *Calvin on Gen.* 176 He bringeth in God speaking after the manner of men, by a figure called *Anthropopathia.*] *a* **1647** BP. HALL *Rem. Wks.* (1660) 106 Two ways may the Spirit of God be said to be grieved..in Himself by an anthropopathie (as we call it), in his Saints by a sympathie. **1882** FARRAR *Early Chr.* I. 260 Expressions which spoke of God by what is called anthropopathy—that is, as subject to wrath, repentance, or other human emotions.

‖**anthropophagi** (-ˈpɒfədʒaɪ), *sb. pl.* Also 6 -ie, -y, 7 -ue. [L., pl. of *anthrōpophagus*, a. Gr. ἀνθρωποφάγ-ος man-eating, cannibal, f. ἄνθρωπος man + φαγεῖν to eat.] Men-eaters, cannibals. More rarely in sing. *anthropophagus*.

1552 B. GILPIN *Serm. bef. Edw. VI*, (T.) Histories make mention of a people called anthropophagi, men-eaters. **1598** MARSTON *Pygmalion* ii. (1764) 144 Take heede O world..Of these same damned Anthropophagy. **1604** SHAKS. *Oth.* I. iii. 144 The Canibals that each others eate, The Antropophague. **1624** in *Shaks. Cent. Praise* 159 (*title*) Anthropophagus: the Man-Eater. **1753** CHAMBERS *Cycl. Supp.*, M. Petit..disputes whether or no the Anthropophagi act contrary to nature. **1831** CARLYLE *Sart. Res.* (1858) 23 That same hair-mantled, flint-hurling Aboriginal Anthropophagus. **1837** J. LANG *New S. Wales* I. 386 A poor New Zealander, whose forefathers had from time immemorial been anthropophagi.

anthropophagic (æn,θrəʊpəʊˈfædʒɪk), *a. rare.* [f. Gr. ἀνθρωποφάγ-ος (see prec.) + -IC.] Of or connected with anthropophagy; cannibal.

1852 T. ROSS tr. *Humboldt's Trav.* I. vi. 200 The warlike anthropophagic Carib.

anthropo'phagical, *a. rare.* [f. as prec. + -ICAL.] Relating to anthropophagy. (Also for prec.)

1833 *Blackw. Mag.* XXXIV. 562 Some anthropophagical tribes of the Indian Seas.

†**anthropopha'ginian**. *Obs. rare*$^{-1}$. [f. L. *anthrōpophagi*, or Fr. *anthropophage*, app. after *Carthage*, *Carthag-inian.*] Used as a sing. to *Anthropophagi*; an anthropophagist, a cannibal.

1598 SHAKS. *Merry W.* IV. v. 9 Hee'l speake like an Anthropophaginian vnto thee.

anthropophagism (ænθrəʊˈpɒfədʒɪz(ə)m). *rare.* [f. Gr. ἀνθρωποφάγ-ος (see above) + -ISM.]

The practice of eating human flesh; cannibalism.

1813 *Q. Rev.* IX. 438 The fourth..reason for anthropophagism is hatred, contempt, and a thirst of revenge.

anthropophagist (-'pɒfədʒɪst). *rare*. [f. as prec. + -IST.] A habitual cannibal.

1881 *Nature* No. 625. 599 That during the Bronze period the inhabitants of this part were Anthropophagists.

anthropophagistic (-,pɒfə'dʒɪstɪk), *a. rare*. [f. as prec. + -IC.] Of or belonging to anthropophagists.

1826 Southey in *Q. Rev.* XXXIV. 109 They were all killed and eaten, except him who was converted into an anthropophagistic necklace.

anthropophagite (-'pɒfədʒaɪt). [f. as prec. + -ITE.] = ANTHROPOPHAGIST.

1602 Dekker *Satirom.* 234 Art not famous enough yet, but thou must eate men alive? thou Anthropophagite. **1822** W. Taylor in *Month. Mag.* LIII. 103 That bread is not human flesh, and that they will never turn Anthropophagites. **1857** Lytton *What will he do* III. VI. xvi, The thoroughbred Anthropophagite usually begins with his own relations.

anthropophagize (-'pɒfədʒaɪz), *v. rare*$^{-0}$. [f. as prec. + -IZE.] (See quot.)

1623 Cockeram, *Anthropophagize*, One man to kill and eate anothers flesh. **1656** Blount *Glossogr.*, *Anthropophagize*, To play the Canibal, to eat or feed on man's flesh.

anthro'pophagizer. *rare*$^{-1}$. [f. prec. + -ER[1].] A man-eater.

1854 Badham *Halieut.* 425 When they bathed in sharky localities, would surround themselves with a body-guard of Negroes as perquisites to these anthropophagizers.

anthropophagous (ænθrəʊ'pɒfəgəs), *a.* [f. L. *anthrōpophagus* (see ANTHROPOPHAGI) + -OUS.] Man-eating, cannibal.

1831 Carlyle *Sart. Res.* (1858) 24 Shame, divine Shame, as yet a stranger to the Anthropophagous bosom. **1842** *Blackw. Mag.* LI. 18 The anthropophagous banquet of Thyestes.

anthro'pophagously, *adv. rare.* [f. prec. + -LY[2].] In an anthropophagous manner; so as to eat men.

1854 Badham *Halieut.* 432 Whales have very small gullets, and are not anthropophagously disposed.

anthropophagy (ænθrəʊ'pɒfədʒɪ). [ad. Gr. ἀνθρωποφαγία, n. of quality f. ἀνθρωποφάγ-ος: see above.] The eating of men, cannibalism.

1638 Featly *Transubst.* 83 Which makes Anthropophagie or man eating so horrible a crime. **1753** Chambers *Cycl. Supp.* s.v., The Greek writers represent Anthropophagy as universal before Orpheus. **1882** *Athenæum* 7 Oct. 457 Although human sacrifices take place..anthropophagy, as usually understood, is not practised.

anthropophagy, -gie, obs. ff. ANTHROPOPHAGI.

anthropo'phobia. [f. ANTHROPO- + -φοβία fear; cf. *hydrophobia*.] Aversion to man.

1880 Swinburne *Study of Shaks.* iii. 200 Possibly a cynic himself in a nearly rabid stage of anthropophobia.

anthropophuism (ænθrəʊ'pɒfju:ɪz(ə)m). [f. Gr. ἀνθρωποφυ-ής of man's nature (f. ἄνθρωπος man + φυ-ή nature) + -ISM.] The ascription of a human nature to the gods.

1858 Gladstone *Homer* II. 175 At the time of Homer, anthropophuism had obtruded into the sphere of deity. **1878** —— *Prim. Homer* 65 The principle of anthropophuism ..through which they [the gods] reflect the image of a peculiar magnified humanity on a very grand scale.

anthropophuistic (æn,θrəʊpəʊfju:'ɪstɪk), *a.* [f. prec.: see -ISTIC.] Of or according to anthropophuism; **a.** ascribing a human nature to the gods; **b.** having such a nature ascribed.

1858 Gladstone *Homer* I. 561 They [Persians] did not consider..that the Gods were anthropophuistic. *Ibid.* II. 51 That introduction of the female principle into the sphere of deity, which the Greeks seem to have adopted after their anthropophuistic manner.

anthropopsychism (æn,θrəʊpəʊ'saɪkɪz(ə)m). [f. Gr. ἄνθρωπος man + ψυχή soul + -ISM.] The ascription of mental faculties or characteristics like those of man to the Divine Being or the agencies at work in nature. So **an,thropo'psychic,** *a.*, **an,thropo'psychically** *adv.*

1884 Duke of Argyll *Unity of Nature* v. 168 It is not the Form of Man that is in question. It is the Mind and Spirit of Man—his Reason, his Intelligence, and his Will... The question is of a..fundamental analogy..between the Mind which is in us and the Mind which is in Nature. The true etymological expression for this idea..would be, not Anthropomorphism, but Anthropopsychism. *Ibid.* viii. 289 Professor Tyndall himself cannot describe this System without using the most intensely anthropopsychic language: 'The continued effort of animated nature is to improve its conditions and raise itself to a loftier level.' **1884** *Edin. Rev.* Apr. 514 The Duke admits that much of the language which is anthropopsychically used, is of a metaphorical character. **1898** *Literary Guide* 1 Jan. 10, I desire to abstain from any thoughts about the Ultimate Reality which suggest anthropomorphism or anthropopsychism.

anthroposcopy (ænθrəʊ'pɒskəpɪ). *rare*$^{-0}$. [f. ANTHROPO- + Gr. -σκοπία looking.] The inspection of the physical features of a man with a view to judge of his mental and moral characteristics.

1847 in Craig.

an,thropo,soma'tology. *rare*$^{-0}$. [f. ANTHROPO- + SOMATOLOGY.] Human somatology; the scientific study of the structure of the human body.

1847 in Craig.

anthroposophist (ænθrəʊ'pɒsəfɪst). [f. ANTHROPO- + Gr. σοφιστής a professor of wisdom, a sophist.] One furnished with 'the wisdom of men.' (Cf. *1 Cor.* ii. 5, 13.)

1851 Kingsley *Yeast* xv. (1853) 296 The New Testament would be found a much simpler..book than the Theologians (Anthroposophists I call them) fancy.

anthroposophy (-'pɒsəfɪ). [f. ANTHROPO- + Gr. σοφία wisdom.] **1.** 'The knowledge of the nature of man.' Bailey 1742. *Also*, Human wisdom.

a **1841** T. Hook *Man of Many Fr.* (D.) Our boasted professor of anthroposophy. **1863** *N. & Q.* Ser. III. III. 304 (*title*) Theosophy and Anthroposophy.

2. A movement inaugurated by Rudolf Steiner (1861–1925) to develop the faculty of cognition and the realization of spiritual reality. So **anthropo'sophical** *a.*, of or pertaining to anthroposophy; **anthro'posophist**, an adherent of anthroposophy.

1914 tr. *Steiner's Spiritual Sci.* 26 This building will be for the use of the Anthroposophical Society. **1916** H. Collison *New Impulse* 19 The anthroposophist claims the ability to distinguish between subjective and objective phenomena. *Ibid.*, The object of anthroposophy is to enable man to work consciously on every part of his system, and be in full command of his own faculties. **1922** G. Kaufmann *Fruits of Anthroposophy* i. 4 While Natural Science is..*Anthropology*—the Spiritual Science..is *Anthroposophy*. *Ibid.* 6 The Anthroposophist comes forward with his claim. *Ibid.* ii. 39 The period of Rudolf Steiner's life-work when his teaching of Anthroposophical Science was to begin. **1927** tr. *Steiner's Anthroposophical Leading Thoughts* 11 Anthroposophy is a path of knowledge, to guide the Spiritual in the human being to the Spiritual in the universe. **1933** E. Bowen-Wedgwood tr. *Steiner's Anthroposophic Movement* 51 Robert Zimmermann wrote his book *Anthroposophy* [*Anthroposophie im Umriss*, 1882]. And from this *Anthroposophy* I afterwards took the name.

anthropotomical (æn,θrəʊpəʊ'tɒmɪkəl), *a.* [f. as next + -ICAL.] Of or in human anatomy.

1837 Whewell *Hist. Induct. Sc.* (1857) III. 555 A peculiarly anthropotomical coalesced congeries of bones. **1881** *N.Y. Nation* XXXII. 394 The inappropriateness of the current anthropotomical terms.

anthropotomist (ænθrəʊ'pɒtəmɪst). [f. next + -IST.] One who studies human anatomy.

1847–9 Todd *Cycl. Anat. & Phys.* IV. 731/1 In the Quadrumana..there is a proper abductor of the thumb, adductor as it would be called by the Anthropotomist. **1875** Blake *Zool.* Pref., A commissural mass, called by the old anthropotomists 'corpus callosum.'

anthropotomy (-'pɒtəmɪ). [f. Gr. ἄνθρωπο-ς man + -τομία cutting, f. τομ- a stem of τέμ-νειν to cut.] Anatomy of the human body.

1855 Owen *Skel. & Teeth* 19 The bones in anthropotomy are indicated only by special names..relating to the particular forms these bones happen to bear in man. **1870** Rolleston *Anim. Life* Introd. 18 The organisms of the lower animals give answers in simple language to what are difficult problems in Anthropotomy.

anthropurgic (ænθrəʊ'pɜ:dʒɪk), *a. rare*$^{-1}$. [f. Gr. ἀνθρωπουργ-ός man-making (but taken, on analogy of θεουργός, as = operating as man) + -IC.] *prop.* Man-making; but also used as: 'Wrought or acted upon by man.'

1838 Burton in *Bentham's Wks.* I. Introd. 16 Anthropurgic Somatology..the science of bodies so far as man, by his knowledge of the convertible powers of nature, is able to operate upon them.

anthurium (æn'θju:rɪəm). [mod.L., f. Gr. ἄνθ-ος flower + οὐρά tail.] A member of the large genus so called of tropical American perennial plants of the family Araceæ.

1839 in R. Sweet *Hort. Brit.* (ed. 3) 633. **1884** [see *tail-flower*, TAIL *sb.*[1] 14]. **1891** *Daily News* 14 May 6/2 A superb Goodyear bouquet of scarlet anthuriums and green wheatears. **1961** *Amat. Gardening* 30 Sept. Suppl. 3/3 There are also some very beautiful foliage plants among the anthuriums.

anthymne, obs. form of ANTHEM.

anthypnotic, anthysteric: see ANTI-HY-.

‖**anthypophora** (ænθɪ'pɒfərə). *Rhet.* Also **anti-hyp-**. [L., a. Gr. ἀνθυποφορά, f. ἀντ(ί against + ὑποφορά allegation.] A figure in which an objection is refuted by a contrary inference or allegation.

1589 Puttenham *Eng. Poesie* (Arb.) 214 Antipophora..is when we will seeme to aske a question to th'intent we will aunswere it our selues. **1657** J. Smith *Myst. Rhet.* 128 Anthypophora signifies a contrary illation or inference, and is when an objection is refuted or disproved by the opposition of a contrary sentence: as *Matt.* xxi. 23–25. **1753** Chambers *Cycl. Supp.* s.v., If the *hypophora* be 'grammar is very difficult to obtain'; the *Anthypophora* may be 'grammar is indeed a little difficult to attain, but then its use is infinite.'

anthypopho'retic, *a.* [f. prec.] Of the nature of an anthypophora.

1652 Urquhart *Jewel* Wks. 1834, 292 Figurative expressions..antipophoretick, cromatic, or any other way of figuring a speech by opposition.

anti ('æntɪ), *a.* and *sb.* [ANTI-[1] used as a word.]

A. *adj.* or quasi-*adj.* Against or antagonistic to some person or thing.

1857 Mundy *Antipodes* (ed. 4) xix. 209 The 'Anti' journals joined with them in coarse personalities. **1939** R. C. K. Ensor *Who Hitler Is* 6 The circumstances of Vienna made both schools anti-Semite; those of Austria made them both anti-Slav, and in particular anti-Czech. The 'anti' feelings were intense. **1948** 'J. Tey' *Franchise Affair* xii. 129 'Some letters on the correspondence page.'..'All anti, I suppose.' **1953** R. Lehmann *Echoing Grove* 299 'You were violently anti all that, weren't you?' 'You make me sound like a Hyde Park tub-thumper.'

B. *sb.* One who is against or antagonistic to some person or thing; *spec.* (U.S.) used as abbrev. of ANTI-FEDERALIST.

1788 *Columbian* July 414/1 It was agreed to raise the constitution that the anti's had burnt. **1801** *Spirit of Farmers' Museum* 56 There Feds shall cease to charge the Antis With making Frenchmen rule brave yankees. **1826** M. Edgeworth *Thoughts on Bores* in *Janus* 96, I invite every true friend of literature and of good conversation, *blues* and *antis*, to contribute their assistance. **1889** *Pall Mall Gaz.* 27 June 1 The 'antis' have no option but to take it up. **1963** *Times* 17 May 15/4 Our times are fertile of protestation; anything from new roads or buildings to the methods of national defence calls forth the campaigning of the 'antis'.

anti, erron. var. ANTE *sb.*[2], *v.*

anti-, *prefix*[1]; repr. Gr. ἀντι-, ἀντ-, ἀνθ- (see ANT-, ANTH-), 'opposite, against, in exchange, instead, representing, rivalling, simulating'; in Gr. combined *adverbially* with (1) *verbs*, as ἀντιλέγειν to speak against, contradict; (2) *vbl. adjs.*, as ἀντίλογος speaking against, contradictory, ἀντίλεκτος spoken against, disputed; (3) *vbl. sbs.* and *abstracts* from *vbl. adjs.*, as ἀντίλεξις speaking against, contradiction, ἀντιλογία contradictoriness, disputation; (4) other *sbs.*, forming *adjs.* and *sbs.*, as ἀντίβιος using force (βία) on the opposite side, ἀντιστράτηγος the general on the opposite side, the enemy's general; passing into the sense of 'counterfeit, false,' as ἀντίκλεις a key rivalling or simulating the true one, a counterfeit key. Less commonly combined *prepositionally* with *sbs.* in (5) *synthetic adjs.* as ἀντίθυρος opposite the door (from ἀντὶ θύρας), ἀντίθεος rivalling the gods (ἀντὶ θεῶν), ἀντίχριστος opposed to Christ, an opponent of Christ.

In English, used A. in compounds already formed in Greek, or others modelled on them. Also B. as a living formative, I. in words analogous to 4 above, as *anti-pope*, *anti-king*, *anti-climax*; II. mainly, in synthetic combinations, in which *anti-* governs a sb. expressed, or implied in its appropriate adj., as *anti-Jesuit*, *anti-English*, *anti-slavery*, *anti-friction*; III. in the derivatives of these, as *anti-royalist*, *anti-supernatural-ism*. The analogy for all these seems to have been given by *antichrist* and its adj. *antichristian*, which (with the analogous *antipope*) were almost the only examples in use bef. 1600. Shakspere has no *anti-* combinations.

A. *Derivatives.* Words in which *anti-* adverbially qualifies the vb. in vbl. sbs. or adjs., and their derivatives, in compounds already formed in Gr., as ANTILOGISM, ANTINOMY, ANTIPHONIC, ANTIPHONY, ANTITHESIS, ANTITHETIC, and mod. compounds modelled after them as ANTITROPOUS. All these appear in their alphabetic places hereafter.

B. *Combinations.*

I. Substantives, in which *anti-* attributively qualifies a sb. The main stress is on '*anti-* ('anti,king, 'anti,bishop, 'anti,growth).

1. a. Formed on the type of ANTICHRIST, and ANTI-POPE; with sense of 'Opposed, in opposition, opponent, rival,' whence 'pretended, spurious, pseudo-': as ***anti-apostle***, ***-balm*** (1559), ***-bishop***, ***-Cæsar***, ***-clergy***, ***-comet***, ***-creator***, ***-critic***, ***-deity*** (1602), ***-duke***, ***-emperor***, ***-king***, ***-martyr***, ***-Messiah***, ***-prophet***.

1642 F. Potter *Number* 666, 96 (T.) The cardinals of Rome..fitly stiled *anti-apostles. **1559** Morwyng *Evonym.* 261 Of trewe Balm and *Antibalm. **1865** Pusey *Truth Eng. Ch.* 74 Fortunatus was an *anti-bishop, consecrated in opposition to S. Cyprian. **1704** Hearne *Duct. Hist.* (1714) I. 80 Ludovicus of Bavaria, Emperor of Germany, 1314..is oppos'd by an *Anti-Cæsar, Frederick of Austria. **1658** Osborn *Adv. Son* (1673) 122 Stipendiaries or Lecturers, that signifie little less than an *Anti-clergy. *a* **1667** Cowley *To his Majesty* Wks. II. 572 The Flames of one triumphant Day, Which like an *Anti-Comet here Did fatally to that appear. **1642** Milton *Apol. Smect.* (1851) 262 The maker, or rather the *anticreator of that universall foolery. **1758** Warburton *Div. Legat.* (ed. 10) III. 149 All the reasonings of these *Anticritics. **1602** J. Davies *Mirum in Mod.* 23 (D.) Diu'lls incarnate, *antideities. *a* **1652** J. Smith *Sel. Disc.* ii. 29 Some of those *antideities that are set up against it. **1872** Yeats *Growth Comm.* 319 He was recalled, and later they set up an *anti-duke. **1880** T. Hodgkin *Italy & Inv.* I. I. 13 Eighteen emperors were recognised at Rome besides a crowd of *anti-emperors in the provinces. *a* **1617** Bayne *Dioces. Trial* (1621) 73 If one doe usurpe a kingly power in Kent onely, he were an *Anti-king to our Soveraigne. **1860** Pusey *Min. Proph.* 509 An *anti-king may..have set himself up in other parts of the kingdom. **1755** *Gentl. Mag.* 407 Amidst this army of *anti-martyrs I discern a volume of peculiar appearance. **1677** Gale *Crt. Gent.* II. III. 115 These Baalim brought in by Jezebel were an *Anti-Messias. *a* **1638** Mede *Apost. Later Times* 88 (T.) Well might St. John, when he saw so many *anti-prophets spring up, say.

b. The opposite or reverse of; an opponent of: as ***-luminary, -Paul, -priest, -wit.***

1714 *Spect.* No. 582 ¶5 The Nation has been a great while benighted with several of these *Antiluminaries. **1660** Fuller *Mixt Contempl.* (1841) 178, I might term many of these men *anti-Mephiboshets. *a* **1667** Cowley *Liberty* Wks. 1710 II. 676 An *Anti-Paul, who became all Things to all men, that he might destroy all. **1719** Waterland *Christ's Divinity* 28 Afraid of being guided by priests, they consent to be governed by *anti-priests. *a* **1688** Villiers (Dk. Buckhm.) *Poems* (1775) 167 Our brave *Anti-wits and great Ones.

2. With names of things: signifying **a.** a thing of the same kind placed opposite, or acting in opposition: = Opposed, opposing, opposite, opposition-, counter-; as in ***anti-association, -Bartholomew, -chorus, -climate, -conductor, -council, -critique, -decalogue, -ejaculation, -endowment, -extreme, -face, -faction, -fame, -fire, -growth, -hemisphere, -league, -mark, -narrative, -parliament, -part, -position, -prestigiation, -principle, -Rome, -school, -synod, -temple, -tone, -volition.*** (*antiface* occurs *c* 1599.)

1682 *Lond. Gaz.* mdcclxx/3 A very good *Anti-Association and Nursery of Loyalty. **1864** Burton *Scot Abr.* I. v. 274 Had the Huguenots ever possessed the opportunity for vengeance..they would have made an *anti-Bartholomew of it. **1863** Kinglake *Crimea* I. xxiv. 405 A chorus and an *anti-chorus engaged in a continual chant. **1635** N. Carpenter *Geog. Del.* I. ix. 216 To these they opposed so many towards the South, which they called *anticlimates. **1779** Swift in *Phil. Trans.* LXIX. 454 One particular addition I have made to the apparatus consists in what I call an *anti-conductor: it is exactly like the prime conductor. **1642** Fuller *Holy & Prof. St.* v. xi. 404 They called at Carthage an *Anti-councell of their own faction. **1805** W. Taylor in *Month. Mag.* XX. 41 Lessing published an *Anti-critique. **1861** Gen. P. Thompson *Audi Alt.* III. cliii. 153 If they dream of a 'Constitution' to support slavery, which honest men shall not alter, they might as well dream of an *Anti-Decalogue. **1765** Tucker *Lt. Nat.* II. 448 Those *anti-ejaculations..bear a great part in the ceremony. **1837** S. Maitland *Volunt. Syst.* 153 A sort of *anti-endowment of £20 per annum. **1647** Ward *Simp. Cobler* 49 If one Extreame should not constitute its *Anti-Extreame, all things would soon be in *extremo*. **1599** B. Jonson *Cynthia's Rev.* (T.) The third is your soldier's face..The *antiface to this is your lawyer's face. **1662** Fuller *Worthies* II. 8 Being of the *Anti-faction to Duke Dudley. **1642** —— *Holy & Prof. St.* III. xxiii. (D.) To set up an *antifame against it [a ridiculous report]. **1647** Ward *Simp. Cobler* 6 No divine Truth, but hath much Cœlestiall fire in it from the Spirit of Truth nor no irreligious untruth, without its proportion of *Antifire from the spirit of Error. **1818** J. Brown *Psyche* 30 This *antigrowth of words. **1684** T. Burnet *Th. Earth* I. 256 That antichthon, or *anti-hemisphere, which the ancients opposed to ours. **1844** *Blackw. Mag.* LV. 559 You make leagues and *anti-leagues for the sake of your morsel of bread. *a* **1658** Cleveland *Char. Diurn. Maker* (1677) 108 A Diurnal-maker is the *Antimark of an Historian. **1690** *Def. Dr. Walker* 2, I do not intend to set out an *Anti-Narrative, or to trouble my self with a Confutation. **1660** Milton *Dr. Griffith's Serm.* Wks. 1851, 396 All [laws] enacted without the King and his *Antiparlament at Oxford. *a* **1779** Warburton *Serm.* II. 64 (L.) There we shall find the *anti-part of this..truth. **1644** *Vind. Treat. Monarchy* iii. 17 He..sets up an *Antiposition, that..such a people ought to submit. **1656** Blount *Glossogr.*, **Antiprestigiation*, a contrary jugling, the diversity or opposition of Legerdemain. **1663** J. Spencer *Prodigies* 168 (T.) Besides one..source of good, there was an *anti-principle of evil. *a* **1628** F. Greville *Sidney* (1652) 201 Like a Remus, to leap over any wall of her new-built *Anti-Rome. **1875** Browning *Aristoph. Apol.* 156 He founds no *anti-school, upsets no faith. **1653** Ashwell *Fides Apost.* 272 Who ever and anon framed new Confessions in their Synods and *anti-Synods. **1876** A. Davidson *Hebr. Gram.* 23 To prevent this Emphasis or *anti-tone being lost. **1801** Darwin *Zoon.* IV. 233 A volition to wink, which by habit becomes stronger than the *antivolition not to wink.

b. A thing or process of the opposite or contrary kind: = The opposite, contrary, or reverse of; as anticlimax, ***anti-creation*** (1659), ***-holiday, -logic, -metaphysics, -method, -model, -music, -philosophy, -poison, -priestcraft, -religion, -romance, -science.***

1659 *Gentl. Call.* ix. §2. 452 By a kind of *anti-creation brought darkness out of light. **1868** Bain *Ment. & Mor. Sc.* IV. v. §5 The convict's yearly or half-yearly *anti-holiday would impart additional horror and gloom to his solitary reflections. **1866** *Spect.* 20 Oct. 1162/2 One of the most precise pieces of..*anti-logic ever invented by the mind of man. **1940** R. G. Collingwood *Essay on Metaphysics* viii. 81 In the second part I pass from metaphysics to *anti-metaphysics, by which I mean a kind of thought that regards metaphysics as a delusion and an impediment to the progress of knowledge, and demands its abolition. **1721** Amherst *Terræ Fil.* x. 47 If all societies took the same method, or rather the same *anti-method. **1825** Bentham *Ration. Reward* 98 Either as the models, or if the term may be admitted..the *anti-models of the remuneratory branch of procedure. **1697** Collier *Ess. Mor. Subj.* II. (1703) 24 Whether such *Anti-musick as this might not be of Service in a Camp. **1817** Coleridge *Own Times* (1850) III. 945 Had this anti-music been confined to the original band. **1818** Coleridge *Philos. Lect.* (1949) ii. 107 Materialism..is an *anti-philosophy arising out of a thorough coldness of the moral feeling. **1877** F. H. Laing *Ld. Bacon's 'Philosophy' Examined* xiv. 123 The Baconian view..might rather be called an *anti-philosophy* than a philosophy. *Ibid.* 125 The negative anti-philosophy of Bacon. **1812** Southey *Lett.* (1856) II. 266 As powerful an *anti-philtre as that fountain in the Forest of Arden which produced so many cross purposes between Angelica and her suitors. **1682** Sir T. Browne *Chr. Mor.* xxviii. (1756) 40 In venomous natures something may be amiable: poysons afford *antipoysons. **1772** Burke *Dorm. Claims Ch.* Wks. X. 146 Secure from Lay-bigotry and *Anti-priestcraft. **1710** Swift *Examiner* No. 20 Not properly atheism, but a sort of *anti-religion prescribed by the devil. **1653** J. Davies tr. *C. Sorel's The Extravagant Shepherd, (continuation of title)* The *anti-romance: Or, the history of the shepherd Lysis. **1911** G. B. Shaw *Doctor's Dilemma* p. xli, The medical profession is coming more and more to represent, not science, but a desperate and embittered *anti-science.

c. In recent use, of a form of art or literature seemingly opposed to the basic conventions or traditions of the form in question or to the form itself. Cf. anti-hero.

1935 D. Gascoyne *Short Survey Surrealism* ii. 35 The third review to appear was *Littérature* (which really meant Anti-literature). **1939** Dylan Thomas *Let.* 11 Sept. (1966) 236, I like the idea of Miller's anti-literature. [**1948** J.-P. Sartre in N. Sarraute *Portrait d'un Inconnu* (1956) 7 Un des traits les plus singuliers de notre époque littéraire c'est l'apparition, çà et là, d'œuvres vivaces et toutes négatives qu'on pourrait nommer des anti-romans.] **1955** J. Bazaine in A. C. Ritchie *New Decade* 12 The nature of painting is abstraction... It is not only 'anti-painting' that reminds us, in terms all too obvious, that a work of art exists only in the degree to which it denies itself, exceeds itself, blasphemes. **1958** *Archit. Rev.* CXXIV. 1/1 His [*sc.* Debord's] celebrated anti-film *Hurlements en Faveur de Sade* is chiefly notable for the fact that the uproar it creates is designed and predictable. **1958** M. Jolas tr. *J.-P. Sartre's Pref. to N. Sarraute's Portr. of Man Unknown* (1959) p. vii, These anti-novels maintain the appearance..of the ordinary novel... But..their aim is to make use of the novel in order to challenge the novel. **1958** *New Statesman* 25 Jan. 101/1 One of the cleverer heirs of that nineteenth-century tradition of playmaking against which M. Ionesco's anti-theatre is presumably directed is M. André Roussin. **1960** *Listener* 25 Feb. 368/1 Rag-time..flourished about the same time as Dada. It distorted and 'ragged' traditional melodies and rhythms into something like an anti-music. **1963** *Times* 11 Feb. 5/2 One begins to apply these doctrines to the anti-play, to Mr. Ionesco and to the other writers who seem to be ..in alliance with him.

Hence, of those who practise such a form of art or literature.

1935 D. Gascoyne *Short Survey Surrealism* ii. 30 [Picabia] was known to the others as the Anti-painter, just as Tzara was known as the Anti-philosopher. **1956** *Art News* Jan. 13/4 To be an anti-painter, as Appel clearly would like to be, one must first be a painter. **1959** *Listener* 5 Nov. 764/1 The anti-artists are those who in their work have attempted to deny or break with every conceivable canon of style, taste, or convention that may have been established by the practice of artists in the past. **1962** *Ibid.* 8 Mar. 406/1 The new French school of 'anti-novelists'.

d. ***anti-particle***: an elementary particle of the same mass as a given particle but having an opposite electrical charge, or (of an uncharged particle) differing in the direction of its magnetic moment (see also quot. 1962), etc. So ***anti-neutrino, -neutron, -nucleon, -proton*** (postulated earlier and called 'negative proton' but first discovered in 1955); also ***anti-matter***, matter composed of anti-particles.

1931 Dirac in *Proc. R. Soc.* A. CXXXIII. 61 We may call such a particle an anti-electron. **1934** *Chem. Abstr.* 2263 (*title*) Theoretical remarks on the..symmetry between particles and antiparticles. *Ibid.* 5327 (*title*) Tensorial fields accompanying the Dirac electron: neutrino and antineutrino. **1942** *Ibid.* 1235 Such a theory..demands the existence of antiprotons and antineutrons. **1946** *Nature* 24 Aug. 280/2 Since Dirac's treatment was able to predict the existence of the positron it is to be expected that anti-nucleons, produced by removing nucleons from negative energy states, also exist. **1953** *Sci. News Let.* 14 Mar. 169/1 The existence or creation of anti-matter, or the negative analogue of the proton..is theoretically possible. **1955** *N.Y. Times* 23 Oct. E9/6 (*heading*) Discovery of the Anti-Proton Ends a Long Search. **1958** *Chambers's Techn. Dict.* (ed. 3) 956/2 *Anti-neutron*, recently discovered particle which can mutually annihilate a neutron, with the evolution of vast energy. **1959** *New Scientist* 5 Nov. 854/1 The main ingredients of anti-matter—antiprotons, antineutrons and anti-electrons—can be set in the tables alongside the protons, neutrons and electrons of which ordinary matter is composed. **1962** *Newnes Conc. Encycl. Nuclear Energy* 33/2 *Anti-particle*, that particle (known or hypothetical) whose interaction with a given particle results in their mutual annihilation. Examples of particle-antiparticle pairs are electron-positron, proton-antiproton, and so on. *Ibid.* 521/1 The antineutrino..accompanies electron emission, whereas the neutrino is associated with positron emission.

II. Adjectives and attributive phrases, in which *anti-* prepositionally governs a sb. expressed, as ***anti-zealot, anti-slavery***, or implied in an adj. as ***anti-national***. The stress is *not* on *anti-* (anti-ˈcatholic, anti-ˈrent-, ˌantiminiˈsterial).

3. Adjectives, formed on the type of antichristian (pertaining to Antichrist), analysed as = Opposed to Christ, Christians, or what is Christian. These are formed on adjs. already existing, as ***anti-national***, or (rarely) on sbs. with simultaneous addition of an adj. ending, as ***anti-church-ian, anti-infant-al***. But when the sb. has no attendant adj., it is usually taken unchanged: see 4.

a. on adjs. derived from proper names of persons, parties, groups, or nations, as ***anti-Anglican, -Bolshevik, -British, -Calvinistic, -Comintern, -Darwinian, -English, -European, -German, -Humian*** (or ***-Humean***), ***-Jewish, -Judaic, -Nazi, -Negro, -Pelagian, -Platonic, -Radical, -Russian, -Soviet, -Stratfordian, -Wagnerian, -Zuinglian***, etc. (*anti-Platonic* occurs 1638.)

1809 Southey in *Q. Rev.* II. 337 Let not that *Anti-Anglican spirit be cherished. **1678** Cudworth *Intell. Syst.* I. iv. §36 The orthodox *anti-Arian Fathers. **1848** J. H. Newman *Loss & Gain* 190 *Anti-Athanasian views. **1860** Froude *Hist. Eng.* V. xxvii. 307 The older *anti-Austrian policy. **1919** *Spectator* 20 Sept. 360/1 Whether we should do good or harm by trying to help the *anti-Bolshevik Russians to a limited extent. **1845** Syd. Smith *Irish Ch.* Wks. 1859 II. 334/1 Such a piece of *anti-British villany. **1823** Lamb *Elia* (1860) 88 An order of imperfect intellects..essentially *anti-Caledonian. **1837** Hallam *Hist. Lit.* III. ii. §36 The *Anti-Calvinistic tenets of the fathers. **1936** *Times* 30 Nov. 12/4 (*Report of speech by H. Hess*) He [*sc.* Hitler] had lessened this grave, permanent danger to the nation by an act of such world-political significance as the *anti-Comintern alliance concluded between Germany and Japan. **1881** *Athenæum* 23 Apr. 562/1 An *anti-Darwinian manifesto. **1811** Southey in *Q. Rev.* VI. 338 *Anti-Dominican doctrines respecting the Virgin Mary. **1814** W. Taylor in *Month. Mag.* XXXVIII. 35 The *anti-Egyptian turn of the book of Exodus. **1808** Jane Austen *Let.* 1 Oct. (1952) 212 The Man describes well, but is horribly *anti-english. **1858** Froude *Hist. Eng.* IV. xxii. 467 The chief pillar of the anti-English policy. **1960** *Spectator* 30 Sept. 469 A republic would reduce slightly the anti-English feelings of the Afrikaners. **1948** B. G. M. Sundkler *Bantu Prophets S. Afr.* iii. 66 He was convinced that certain ministers of the African Methodist Episcopal Church were engaged in political *anti-European propaganda. **1900** *Daily News* 7 Sept. 5/2 The *anti-German nature of the recent official Russian enunciations. **1790** Boswell *Johnson* (1831) I. 112 With warm *Anti-Hanoverian zeal. **1879** W James in *Mind* IV. 330 In the second volume of Lewes's *Problems* we find this *anti-Humean view that the effect is the 'procession' of the cause. **1933** *Mind* XLII. 140 The more thoroughgoing and more famous anti-Humian arguments of Kant. **1817** M. Edgeworth *Harrington* iii. 57 When Jacob appeared in the school room, the *antijewish party gathered round him. **1956** A. H. Compton *Atomic Quest* 208 The anti-Jewish feeling that was being fomented here by the Nazis. **1885** Lightfoot *Apostolic Fathers* II. I. 371 Marcion was markedly *Anti-judaic. **1839** Thirlwall *Greece* VI. I. 189 The Spartan or *anti-Macedonian interest. **1877** Shields *Final Philos.* 64 The science [geology] having become so *anti-Mosaical. **1933** *Time* 20 Nov. 20/3 Last week an irate *anti-Nazi raiding party entered the cemetery. **1862** Greeley in J. A. Logan *Great Conspiracy* 432 The Rebels are everywhere using the late *Anti-Negro riots in the North ..to convince the Slaves that they have nothing to hope from a Union success. **1947** M. M. Lewis *Lang. in Society* x. 217 Books..have been..used to intensify anti-Negro attitudes. **1865** Pusey *Truth Eng. Ch.* 290 The *Anti-Pelagian statements of Faith. **1638** Suckling *Aglaura* Dram. Pers., Orsames, a young Lord *antiplatonique. **1860** Froude *Hist. Eng.* V. xxvii. 293 Having in his possession *anti-Protestant books. **1849** Macaulay *Hist. Eng.* I. 402 The spirit of the *Antipuritan reaction. **1866** Carlyle *Remin.* I. 152 A very fierce Radical and *anti-Radical time. **1856** Froude *Hist. Eng.* II. 12 The *anti-Roman policy was arrested. **1901** *Westm. Gaz.* 31 Oct. 2/1 *Anti-Russian political meetings. **1940** B. Ward *Russian Foreign Policy* 26 In the early days of 1939..Hitler himself still seemed determined to pursue his anti-Russian policy. **1698** Norris *Pract. Disc.* IV. 122 Learned *Anti-Socinian Writers. **1920** *Daily Herald* 22 Mar. 1/3 (*heading*) Smashing Reply to *Anti-Soviet Propaganda. **1939** *Ann. Reg. 1938* 182 To bring Poland into the anti-Soviet coalition. **1948** *N. & Q.* CXCIII. 111/2 We have enjoyed the three latest numbers of *Baconiana* and an *anti-Stratfordian brochure (from the same source): 'Was Shakespeare educated?' **1895** G. B. Shaw *Sanity of Art* (1908) 33 The old anti-Wagnerian confusion. **1674** Hickman *Hist. Quinquart.* (ed. 2) 197 To suppress the *Antizuinglian Doctrine.

b. on adjs. belonging to or formed on common nouns of every description, or when *anti-* simply reverses the adj., as ***anti-æsthetic, -angular, -aquatic, -art, -artistic, -astronomical, -authoritarian, -bacterial, -biblic, -bourgeois, -bridal, -caligraphic, -capitalistic, -carnivorous, -cholinergic, -churchian, -colonial, -commerical, -corrosive, -decadent, -depressant, -divine*** (1765), ***-dogmatic(al), -domestic, -episcopal, -evangelical, -everything, -feudal, -flatulent, -formal, -fuliginous, -grammatical, -hectic, -historical, -human, -humanitarian, -hydrophobic, -idolatrous, -infantal, -infective, -liturgical, -logical, -malarial, -materialistic, -melancholic, -mentalistic, -metaphysical, -microbial, -microbic, -military, -ministerial, -moral, -mythical, -nationalistic, -naturalistic,***

-nepotic, -neuritic, -nuclear (= opposed to nuclear weapons), *-ontological, -orthodox, -patriarchal, -philanthropic, -philosophic, -philosophical, -phylloxeric, -physical, -plethoric, -portable, -prelatic, -prudential, -psychological, -putrefactive, -quartan, -red* (see RED *a.*), *-reforming, -revolutionary, -rheumatic, -ritualistic, -royal, -sacerdotal, -scientific, -scrofulous, -sensational, -sensual, -sexual, -simoniacal, -snobbish, -soporific, -spiritual, -stimulant, -theological, -thyroid, -totalitarian, -traditional, -tubercular, -tuberculous, -usurious, -utilitarian, -venefic, -viral, -warlike, -western, -white.* Among these, medical terms relating to the prevention or cure of diseases are very frequent: the more important of them are treated separately in their alphabetical places. (*anti-prelatic* occurs 1641.)

1902 G. K. CHESTERTON *Twelve Types* 171 Savonarola could not have been fundamentally *anti-æsthetic, since he had such friends as Michael Angelo, Botticelli, and Luca della Robbia. **1841** CATLIN *N. Amer. Indians* xx. (1844) I. 193 A bold and prominent *anti-angular nose. **1814** SOUTHEY in *Q. Rev.* XI. 67 The people themselves never drink water..which would delight Dr. Lambe and his *anti-aquatic disciples. **1942** WYNDHAM LEWIS *Let.* 15 Sept. (1963) 337 Or is it just racial—that in Anglosaxon countries the Catholics like everybody else are a little *anti-art? **1896** G. B. SHAW *Let.* 20 Feb. (1965) 604 Your nature is radically *anti-artistic. **1947** M. LOWRY *Let.* 6 May (1967) 145, I take it you do not of course mean your own anti-artistic emotion of self-pity. **1747** COSTARD in *Phil. Trans.* XLIV. 484 Observations..burned by this *anti-astronomical Prince. **1937** A. KOESTLER *Spanish Testament* I. ii. 48 As a logical consequence of their *anti-authoritarian attitude, Anarchists proclaim their belief in the policy of direct action. **1897** *Lippincott's Med. Dict.* 67/2 *Anti-bacterial. **1903** *Med. Record* 28 Mar. 511/1 The leucocytes have a special antibacterial action. **1947** *New Biol.* II. 77 In the case of such a substance as penicillin at this stage of the research its only known property was its antibacterial effect. **1839** J. ROGERS *Antipopopr.* iv. §2. 174 Popery..its *anti-biblic origin. **1923** J. M. MURRY *Pencillings* 211 He had..a point of view which would have enabled him to see the comic side of Flaubert's *anti-bourgeois *emportement*. **1828** L. HUNT *Byron* (ed. 2) I. 70 Sandys..is anything but an *anti-bridal poet. **1865** TROLLOPE *Belton Estate* xxvii. 326 Confused and altogether *anti-caligraphic. **1887** S. MOORE & AVELING tr. *Marx's Capital* II. xxv. 798 How, then, to heal the *anti-capitalistic cancer of the colonies? **1828** SOUTHEY in *Q. Rev.* XXXVIII. 556 Vegetable Cookery, adapted to their *anti-carnivorous principles. **1950** WEBSTER Add., *Anticholinergic. **1962** *New Scientist* 26 Apr. 143/1 The effectiveness of the new anticholinergic drugs used in treating duodenal ulcers. **1853** MAYNE *Exp. Lex.* *Anticolic, opposed to the colic. **1952** *Atlantic Monthly* Aug. 10/2 *Anticolonial sentiments are strong in many South American republics. **1797** W. TAYLOR in *Month. Rev.* XXIII. 560 An *anti-commercial spirit of legislation. **1810** BENTHAM *Packing* (1821) 42 So much of the mischief of this institution as is confined to the *anticonstitutional abuse. **1824** COL. HAWKER *Instr. Yng. Sportsmen* (ed. 3) 469 A specification of a new '*Anti-corrosive' percussion powder. **1871** *Standard* 12 Apr. 2 Most people will associate the title of volta-electric with something anticorrosive. **1947** *New Biol.* III. 128 First it receives two or more coats of an anti-corrosive or protective paint, which prevents corrosion of the hull. **1760** GEO. LD. LYTTELTON *Dial. Dead* iv. Wks. 1776 II. 123 Apply his *Anticosmetick wash to the painted face of female Vanity. **1818** *Q. Rev.* XVIII. 534 Animated by *anti-covenanting zeal. **1673** *Lady's Call.* I. §2 ¶11 *Anticreative power, which reduces things to..chaos. **1916** H. G. WELLS *Mr. Britling sees it Through* iii. 75 'It's got its *anti-decadent side,' said Mr. Direck. **1849** GROTE *Greece* II. lxxiv. VI. 451 *Anti-democratical Sparta. **1962** *Lancet* 29 Dec. 1342/2 It is well known that *antidepressant drugs are of most use in the mild-to-moderate degrees of depression. **1765** TUCKER *Lt. Nat.* II. 448 Assemblies of such persons, all in the same way of..thoughtlessness, may be termed *anti-divine services. **1859** NEWMAN *Lect. & Ess. Univ. Subj.* iii. 75 In illustration and defence of the *anti-dogmatic principle in political and social matters. **1940** *Mind* XLIX. 423 Progressive, anti-dogmatic science is critical—criticism is its very life. **1846** J. D. MORELL *Hist. View Specul. Philos.* I. iii. 255 Simon Foucner..revived the spirit of the new academy, and with its *anti-dogmatical principles, firmly opposed the views of Descartes and Malebranche. **1861** R. PEACOCK *Gryll Gr.* xxxi. 271 Clubs..those *anti-domestic institutions. **1869** *Daily News* 29 Jan., Of purely *anti-dynastic men you would find..few in France. **1683** E. HOOKER *Pref. Pordage's Myst. Div.* 18 Is it not..an *Anti-Ecclesiastic, Anti-Fanatic..Age? **1828** SOUTHEY in *Q. Rev.* XXXVII. 217 This *anti-ecclesiastical partisan. **1642** SIR E. DERING *Sp. on Relig.* ix. 35 All that are..*Anti-Episcopall. **1734** RICHARDSON in Birch *Milton's Wks.* 1738 I. 60 He was always very Anti-Episcopal, and no Lover of our Establish'd Church. **1778** WESLEY *Wks.* (1872) XIII. 35 These are very frequently unevangelical, but they are not *Anti-evangelical. **1898** RIDER HAGGARD *Doctor Therne* v. 92 Mr. Strong was indeed *anti-everything. **1789** T. JEFFERSON *Writ.* (1859) II. 576 They are furiously *anti-federal. **1876** BARTHOLOW *Mat. Med.* (1879) 536 The *anti-fermentative properties of the essential oils. **1844** EMERSON *Misc.* (1875) II. 296 The new and *anti-feudal power of Commerce. **1848** BAILEY *Festus* (ed. 3) 111 The *antiformal spirit wants no word Whereby to mark its union with the soul. **1934** C. LAMBERT *Music Ho!* v. iv. 316 While romanticism is not specifically anti-formal it is specifically anti-symphonic. **1828** SOUTHEY *To A. Cunningham* Wks. III. 306 Thy laws *Antifuliginous; extend those laws Till every chimney its own smoke consume. **1801** W. TAYLOR in *Month. Mag.* XI. 291 The language of the law is at times *anti-grammatical. **1861** HULME tr. *Moquin-Tandon* II. III. v. 153 The *Antihæmorrhoidal ointment of Cullen. **1853** MAYNE *Exp. Lex.*, *Anti-hectic*, Having power to remove or assuage hectic fever. **1860** R. VAUGHAN *Mystics* (ed. 2) I. 246 The popular, *anti-hierarchical spirit of the day. **1937** J. ORR tr. I. *Iordan's Introd. Romance Linguistics* iv. 336 The Dutch scholar, C. de Boer..whose approach..is so definitely *anti-historical. **1854** GEO. ELIOT tr. *Feuerbach's Essence Chr.* p. xxxv, A superhuman, *i.e.*, *anti-human, anti-natural religion. **1965** *English Studies* Feb. 73 [The New Criticism]..is therefore both anti-historical and anti-human. **1945** POPPER *Open Society* I. vi. 76 His [*sc.* Plato's] political demands are purely totalitarian and *anti-humanitarian. **1880** *Syd. Soc. Lex.*, *Anti-hydrophobic*, Applied to remedies against hydrophobia. **1831** W. MILL *Christa Sangitá* Pref. 38 Its *anti-idolatrous tendency. **1659** GAUDEN *Tears of Ch.* 279 (D.) That *Anti-infantall Christ which they [Anabaptists] say is so predominant in them. **1899** *Daily News* 1 Dec. 3/4 The *anti-infective inoculation ..protecting the mucous membrane against the invasion of the microbe. **1933** *Discovery* May 158/1 Vitamin A has been called the 'anti-xerophthalmic' and 'anti-infective' vitamin. **1842** GEN. P. THOMPSON *Exerc.* VI. 418 The danger of *anti-liberal opinions on commerce. **1659** GAUDEN *Tears of Ch.* 90 (D.) *Antiliturgicall Preachers. **1821** *Blackw. Mag.* IX. 397 Its mode of reasoning is the most impudent and *antilogical that can be conceived. *a* **1834** COLERIDGE *Notes Theol. & Pol.* 142 'Makes' for 'produces,' a Gallo-barbarism not less anti-logical than anti-Anglican. **1893** *Funk's Stand. Dict.*, *Antimalarial. **1932** *Lancet* 9 Apr. 796/1 Atebrin, a new antimalarial preparation. **1758** BATTIE *Madness* (T.) With respect to vomits it may seem almost heretical to impeach their *antimaniacal virtues. **1882** W. JAMES *Let.* 8 Jan. in R. B. Perry *Thought & Char. W.J.* (1935) I. 737, I wanted to shew that physiology could send out an *anti-materialistic blast as well as she had been supposed to emit materialistic ones. **1942** A. KOESTLER in *Horizon* V. 391 Perhaps the common denominator we are looking for can best be described as an 'anti-materialistic nostalgia'. **1853** MAYNE *Exp. Lex.*, *Anti-melancholic*, Against or capable of dispelling melancholy. **1952** *Archivum Linguisticum* IV. 67 It may be doubted whether linguists and logicians, even those free from any *anti-mentalistic bias, will be satisfied. **1877** F. H. LAING *Ld. Bacon's 'Philosophy' Examined* vii. 74 Bacon..by his *anti-metaphysical, *i.e.*, anti-philosophical efforts, brought the whole study..into thorough disrepute. **1935** *Mind* XLIV. 108 The prevailing positivistic and anti-metaphysical philosophies of science. **1656** BLOUNT *Glossogr.*, *Antimetrical*, contrary or against the rule or order of Metre or Verse. **1910** *Lippincott's New Med. Dict.* 67/1 *Antimicrobic*, *-bial*, antagonistic to microbes. **1949** H. W. FLOREY et al. *Antibiotics* I. p. v, In this book plant products with antimicrobial properties have been included. **1901** DORLAND *Med. Dict.* (ed. 2) 53/2 *Antimicrobic*, checking the growth of microbes. **1850** R. HORT *Horse Guards* 100 For the advocates and friends of the service to successfully combat the *anti-military feeling abroad. **1653** GAUDEN *Hierasp.* 236 The *anti-ministeriall Adversaries. **1817** COLERIDGE *Biogr. Lit.* 101 That Journal..for many years continued Anti-ministerial. **1811** W. TAYLOR in Robberds *Mem.* II. 344 Calling their opinions *Anti-moral. **1830** MISS MITFORD *Village* Ser. IV. (1863) 266 Who rode a particularly *anti-musical, startlish blood-horse. **1846** GROTE *Greece* I. xvi. I. 506 The *anti-mythic vein of criticism. **1816** BYRON in Moore *Life* (1866) 311 A lady..fast asleep in the most *antinarcotic spot in the world. **1920** *19th Cent.* Aug. 204 *Antinationalistic class war. **1902** W. JAMES *Var. Relig. Exper.* xvi. 422 The mystic range of consciousness..is *anti-naturalistic. **1857** TREGELLES *Gesenius' Heb. Lex.* Introd. 9 These *anti-neologian remarks of mine. *a* **1845** SYD. SMITH *Let. Archd. Singleton*, They will be shamed into a more lofty and *anti-nepotic spirit. **1881** *Syd. Soc. Lex.* I, *Antineuritic*, term applied to remedies that prevent inflammation in nerves. **1934** *Times Lit. Suppl.* 22 Feb. 130/1 The potency of preparations containing the antineuritic vitamin B_1 has been tested. **1958** *Listener* 18 Dec. 1029/2 Switzerland who had forbidden an *anti-nuclear conference to be held on her soil. **1864** SELSS *Germ. Lit.* 176 A philosophical journal, in which..*anti-orthodox articles appeared. **1734** JORTIN *Milton's Lycid.* (T.) The most *antipapistical poets are inclined to canonize their friends. **1850** MRS. STOWE *Uncle Tom's C.* xiii. 118 The *anti-patriarchal operation of shaving. **1775** JOHNSON *Tax. no Tyr.* 4 These *antipatriotic prejudices. **1869** LECKY *Europ. Mor.* I. xi. 186 The anti-patriotic tendency of its [Epicureanism's] teaching. **1831** CARLYLE *Sart. Res.* (1858) 67 Teufelsdröckh had..expectorated his *antipedagogic spleen. **1850** J. S. MILL in *Fraser's Mag.* XLI. 26/1, I must first set my *anti-philanthropic opponent right. **1923** D. H. LAWRENCE *Ladybird* 13 So, her reckless, anti-philanthropic passion could find no outlet. **1818** COLERIDGE *Philos. Lect.* (1949) 72 The scheme..as delivered by Hesiod, is an *anti-philosophic Atheism. **1865** FARRAR *Chapt. Lang.* i. (1878) 6 An arbitrary and anti-philosophic hypothesis. **1877** *Anti-philosophical [see *anti-metaphysical* above]. **1881** *Daily News* 23 Aug. 5 An *anti-phylloxeric congress, to which all the great wine-growing countries will send representatives. *a* **1603** T. CARTWRIGHT *Confut. Rhem. N.T.* (1618) 511 We reiect not your Transubstantiation, because it is Metaphysicall, or aboue nature..but we refuse it as *Antiphisicall, or against nature. **1916** D. H. LAWRENCE *Twilight in Italy* iii. 124 Hamlet is far more even than Orestes..a mental creature, anti-physical and anti-sensual. **1679** PULLER *Moder. Ch. Eng.* (1843) 169 Those who are for a Spring Fast, are not only anti-christian, but *anti-physician. **1876** HARLEY *Mat. Med.* 189 The action of sulphate of Magnesia is..decidedly *antiplethoric and antiphlogistic. **1847** DISRAELI *Tancred* II. xiv, The *anti-poetic spirit of the age. **1825** SOUTHEY *Lett.* (1856) III. 475 The very ideal of an *Anti-portable volume. **1642** SIR. E. DERING *Sp. on Relig.*, The *Rooters*, the *Antiprelatick party, declaim against me. **1641** *Answ. Humb. Remonstr.* §18 He scoffes at the **Antiprelaticall Church*, and the *Antiprelaticall Divisions*. **1765** TUCKER *Lt. Nat.* II. 553 That *anti-prudential maxim..A short life and a merry one. **1890** W. JAMES *Princ. Psychol.* I. v. 141 The conception of consciousness as a purely cognitive form of being..is thoroughly *anti-psychological. **1933** *Mind* XLII. 262 Joad is uncompromisingly anti-psychological. **1814** SIR H. DAVY *Agric. Chem.* 255 The *antiputrescent quality of cold climates. **1825** SYD. SMITH *Wks.* (1859) II. 71 *Anti-rational Fallacies. **1840** GLADSTONE *Ch. Princ.* 317 The *anti-rationalistic handling of Christian truths. **1927** D. L. SAYERS *Unnatural Death* xix. 216 The 'Daily Yell' wrote *anti-Red leaders and discovered a plot. **1946** 'G. ORWELL' *Crit. Essays* vii. 122 He stays in Spain long enough to pick up a few anti-red atrocity stories. **1836** GEN. P. THOMPSON *Exerc.* (1842) IV. 77 Hostility to rail-roads..displayed by some of the *anti-reforming interest. **1831** CROKER in *Boswell's Johnson* I. 255 *note*, Hume's *anti-religious principles. **1828** J. S. MILL in *Westm. Rev.* IX. 295 Placing him under the protection of the *anti-revolutionary general Bouillé. **1830** GEN. P. THOMPSON *Exerc.* (1842) I. 241 Anti-revolutionary wars. **1817** *Anti-rheumatic [see ANTIBILIOUS *a.*]. **1867** *Ev. Standard* 6 Aug. 3 An *anti-ritualistic form of worship. **1681** NEVILE *Plato Rediv.* 18 The *Anti-royal Party in our late Troubles. **1855** MILMAN *Lat. Chr.* (1864) V. IX. viii. 378 A great *antisacerdotal movement. **1805** W. TAYLOR in *Ann. Rev.* III. 279 This *anti-sceptical writer. *a* **1834** COLERIDGE *Notes Theol. & Pol.* 264 Anselm, and the *anti-scholastic theologians. **1886** W. M. ROSSETTI *Pref.* to *Coll. Wks. D. G. Rossetti* I. p. xxi, Superstitious in grain, and *anti-scientific to the marrow. **1927** A. HUXLEY *Proper Stud.* 19 The prophets of the democratic-humanitarian religion have at all times, from the eighteenth century down to the present day, denounced the upholders of Christian orthodoxy as anti-scientific. **1846** J. D. MORELL *Hist. View Specul. Philos.* II. v. 18 The tendency of the Scottish philosophy..was clearly and decidedly *anti-sensational. **1916** *Anti-sensual [see *anti-physical* above]. **1890** W. JAMES *Princ. Psychol.* II. xxiv. 437 What might be called the **anti-sexual instinct*, the instinct of personal isolation, the actual repulsiveness to us of the idea of intimate contact with most of the persons we meet, especially those of our own sex. **1929** B. RUSSELL *Marriage & Morals* iv. 34 So far we have been considering pro-sexual elements in religion; anti-sexual elements, however, existed side by side. **1825** BENTHAM *Ration. Reward* 187 These *anti-simoniacal laws. **1890** W. JAMES *Princ. Psychol.* I. x. 293 Stiffen ourselves as we will by appealing to *anti-snobbish first principles, we cannot escape an emotion..of respect and dread. **1834** M. SCOTT *Cruise Midge* (1863) 107 Imminent peril is a beautiful *anti-soporific. **1827** —— in *Q. Rev.* XXXV. 204 Gross, earthly, and *anti-spiritual. **1869** *Eng. Mech.* 1 Oct. 43/1 The hydrochlorate is a..powerful *anti-stimulant. **1880** GOLDW. SMITH in *Atl. Month.* No. 268. 211 So fanatically *antitheological. **1908** H. MACKENZIE in Allbutt & Rolleston *Syst. Med.* (ed. 2) IV. I. 382 An *antithyroid serum, prepared by Merck from the blood of thyroidless sheep, has also been employed. **1962** *Lancet* 22 Dec. 1317/1 She was treated with antithyroid drugs, and later by subtotal thyroidectomy. **1941** 'G. ORWELL' in *Horizon* IV. 134 An attempted definition of fundamental human rights, of *anti-totalitarian tendency. **1860** *Wolff's Trav. & Adv.* I. xi. 339 Those who belong to the *anti-traditional party have their own pet traditions. **1946** *Nature* 30 Nov. 783/2 [France] has a special *anti-tubercular service for university students. *Ibid.* 14 Dec. 864/2 This compound..has very poor anti-tubercular power. **1904** T. L. STEDMAN *Dunglison's Dict. Med. Sci.* (ed. 23) 74/2 **Antituberculotic* or **antituberculous*, designed to arrest the progress of tuberculosis. **1958** *Times* 15 Oct. 19/1 Anti-tuberculous drugs. **1787** BENTHAM *Def. Usury* vi. 45 Mischiefs of the *anti-usurious Laws. **1861** J. S. MILL in *Fraser's Mag.* LXIV. 666/1 This is admitted even by *anti-utilitarian moralists. **1870** J. GROTE *Exam. Util. Phil.* xvi. 250 The anti-utilitarian principle of despising happiness. **1778** *Phil. Surv. S. Irel.* 390 Ireland got the appellation of *Sacra* from its *anti-venefic property. **1934** *Ann. Reg. 1933* II. 63 The development, in horse and baboon serum, of *anti-viral properties promises a means of immunising populations to yellow fever. **1806** W. TAYLOR in *Ann. Rev.* IV. 581 The *anti-warlike revolutionists of France. **1949** I. DEUTSCHER *Stalin* vi. 209 His '*anti-western' tone was vague enough not to cause any objection. **1906** *Westm. Gaz.* 2 Jan. 3/1 The contention that yellow labour is *anti-white labour he characterised as a 'foolish and atrocious falsehood'. **1935** G. GORER *Africa Dances* Itin. IV. 277 There is..anti-white feeling; at Accra I had..the experience of being hated by passers-by.

c. Many of these, like the simple adjectives, are also used as substantives, forming (1) party-names as ***anti-christian, anti-Arminian, anti-Catholic, anti-radical*** (see 5); (2) names of material agents as ***anti-corrosive, -perspirant,*** and esp. medical terms as ***anti-bacterial, -depressant, -diuretic, -malarial, -narcotic, -pyretic, -stimulant.*** Also ANTIBIOTIC, -COAGULANT, -CONVULSANT, -OXIDANT, -PRURITIC.

1944 *Lancet* 6 May 605/2 Such an influence is to be expected if natural antibiotics are involved in the interplay between plant and environment, and certain natural anti-bacterials appear to play such a part. **1962** *Ibid.* 29 Dec. 1341/2 The original assessment as to response to anti-depressants was judged almost entirely on the basis of double-blind trials. **1941** *Dorland's Med. Dict.* (ed. 19) 118/2 *Antidiuretic*, a drug which checks urinary secretion. **1935** *Discovery* Oct. 291/1 Two remarkable synthetic anti-malarials, plasmochin and atebrin. **1957** *Housewife* Sept. 88/3 Two deodorants and anti-perspirants make news.

d. *Advbs.* in *-ly* are formed on these adjs., when required: as ***anticalvinistically, anticonstitutionally.***

1674 HICKMAN *Hist. Quinquart.* 202 (ed. 2) [One who] preached Anticalvinistically in all the five Points under Controversie. *Mod.* They would act unconstitutionally, indeed altogether anticonstitutionally, in exluding a member personally disliked.

4. Attributive phrases, consisting of *anti-* governing a sb. Their origin is found in the mod. Eng. use of sbs. attributively, and the consequent combination of these with *anti-* in the same way as the adjectives to which they are equivalent; cf. the *episcopal* party, the *anti-episcopal* party, with the *church* party, the *anti-church* party. Thus they differ from the preceding group only in the absence of the adjective ending; and hence form the ordinary type, when the sb. has no appropriate derivative adj., as in most words of Teutonic and OFr. origin. But their widely extended modern use seems partly to be the result of an independent analysis of the phrase: thus, *anti-combination* laws = laws *anti* (i.e. *against*) *combination*; cf. the similar attrib. use of Latin phrases, as in *ante-mortem* fame, *ex tempore* discourse, *pro formâ* resolution, *post mortem* examination, and even the native *after-dinner* speech, *down-river* steamer, *underground* railway, *across-country* road, *off-hand* reply, *out-of-doors* life. So, *anti-* may here be considered as a naturalized preposition, equivalent to *against*, and taking its place in attributive phrases, in which *against* is never used. These may be formed *ad libitum*; they seem to have begun *c* 1650 with the **anti-court** party (cf. the *court* party); and notable instances are **anti-combination** (laws), **anti-corn-law** (league), **anti-rent** (agitation), **anti-slavery** (society), **anti-state-church** (association), **anti-vaccination** (league). Later used in senses: (i) Against or opposed to, as ***anti-apartheid***, ***-art***, ***-betting***, ***-Blimp***, ***-business***, ***-bus(s)ing***, ***-dumping*** (see DUMP *v.*^{1} 2c), ***-Establishment***, ***-litter***, ***-noise***, ***-pollution***, ***-poverty***, ***-reform***, ***-scrape***, ***-segregation***, ***-sex***, ***-theft***, ***-treat***, ***-union*** (= opposed to union; opposed to trade-unionism), ***-war***.

1961 *Daily Mail* 12 Sept. 11/5 *Anti-apartheid agitation was all right, but support for the committee was not. **1970** *Stand. Encycl. S. Afr.* I. 462/1 The Anti-Apartheid Movement.. was formed in 1960 for the specific purpose of opposing apartheid in South Africa. **1978** G. GREENE *Human Factor* III. iii. 126, I took you for one of those high-minded anti-apartheid sentimentalists. **1986** *Daily Tel.* 22 Aug. 24/5 Veteran British anti-apartheid campaigner Bishop Trevor Huddleston.. did not believe the South African authorities would allow him into the country. **1837** CARLYLE *Fr. Rev.* III. I. i. II. 131 Great is the fire of *Antiaristocrat eloquence. **1932** O. SITWELL *Dickens* 16 The genuine *anti-art bias which has possessed most English people since the triumph of Cromwell. **1837** CALHOUN *Wks.* III. 79, I am neither a bank man, nor an *anti-bank man. **1905** *Daily Chron.* 13 July 5/5 (*headline*) *Anti-Betting Campaign. **1941** *Horizon* III. 220 It is a magnificent *anti-Blimp pamphlet. **1817** MAR. EDGEWORTH *On Bores* (1831) 318 Well-bred persons, abhorring the pedantry of the Blues, are usually *anti-blue, or ultra-antis. **1938** *New Statesman* 15 Jan. 100/1 It [*sc.* the Wall Street market] had been depressed by the *anti-business speeches of the President and his lieutenants. **1968** *Economist* 16 Mar. 48/3 The *anti-busing groups' hysteria reached a peak early in January when some 1,500 white residents.. picketed a meeting of the Board of Education. **1977** *Time* 21 Nov. 30/3 In Boston, the voters tossed out of office a trio of the city's antibusing leaders. **1857** GEN. P. THOMPSON *Audi Alt.* I. 96 The Company stands therefore as a mere *Anti-Centralization bulwark. **1810** SOUTHEY in Robberds *Mem. W. Taylor* II. 300 My anti-Catholic opinions would.. clash with your *anti-church politics. **1882** J. HAWTHORNE *Fort. Fool* I. xxvii, The practice of dissipation and the formation of *anti-church-going societies. **1865** *Spectator* 14 Jan. 37 Re-establishing the old *anti-combination laws in a new and infinitely more stringent shape. **1873** WHITNEY *Ling. Stud.* 115 The case of the *anti-comment party. **1670** PENN *People's Lib.* Wks. 1782 I. 126 Jurors.. scared into an *anti-conscience verdict. **1828** SOUTHEY in *Q. Rev.* XXXVII. 567 The *anti-contagion philosophers. **1834** GEN. P. THOMPSON *Exerc.* (1842) III. 102 No thoroughly informed leader on the *Anti-corn-law side. **1838** *Morn. Herald* 7 Nov., At Manchester.. there has been formed an Anti-corn-law Association. **1843** NEALE *Ballads for People* 15, I am an English yeoman! And we yeomen know no change: Though anti-corn-law lecturers About the country range. **1654** GODDARD in *Burton's Diary* I. 67 It was ..moved by the *anti-court party, to adjourn the debate. *a* **1689** RERESBY *Mem.* (1734) 153 (T.) The anticourt party courted him at such a rate. [**1934** WEBSTER, *Antidumping.] **1948** *Ann. Reg. 1947* 198 In the cases where the exports of one country were assisted by dumping.. importing countries might impose anti-dumping duties. **1840** GEN. P. THOMPSON *Exerc.* V. 90 The same *anti-education devil that in America enters into a planter, in the old country enters into a bishop. **1958** *New Statesman* 12 July 37/2 An independent, basically '*anti-Establishment' tabloid with a deliberately mass appeal. **1859** *All Y. Round* No. 29. 58 A series of *anti-exporting acts of Parliament. **1857** GEN. P. THOMPSON *Audi Alt.* I. xxv. 97 We of the *anti-felon portion of society. **1832** —— *Exerc.* II. 15 The great *Anti-felony Association of modern times. **1876** BARTHOLOW *Mat. Med.* (1879) 520 The antiseptic and *anti-ferment properties of chlorine. **1839** GEN. P. THOMPSON *Exerc.* II. 466 An *Anti-Free-Trade orator, at that time of high consideration with his party. **1861** WHYTE-MELVILLE *M'kt. Harb.* 79 *Anti-hunting weather. **1882** *Sun* 14 May 6/5 It was intimated by *anti-lacrosse men yesterday that sterner repressive measures would be used. **1818** HAZLITT *Char. Shaks. Plays* (1838) 73 The principle of poetry is a very *anti-levelling principle. **1917** *Greater New York* 19 Nov. 11/3 The *Anti-Litter League. **1831** GEN. P. THOMPSON *Exerc.* I. 354 But if the steward.. had an *anti-machinery maggot in his head. **1865** *Public Opinion* 28 Jan. 96 A great *anti-malt-tax meeting was held at Leicester, on Saturday. **1860** MAURY *Phys. Geog. Sea* ii. 46 This *anti-mixing property in water. **1908** *Westm. Gaz.* 1 Aug. 3/2 New York has started an *anti-noise crusade. **1961** *B.S.I. News* Sept. 23 (*title*) Anti-noise regulations. **1840** GEN. P. THOMPSON *Exerc.* V. 328, I perceive.. further, that there is an *Anti-Opium Society. **1850** MAURICE *Mor. & Met. Phil.* (ed. 2) 141 In opposition to the *Antiplurality doctrine of Parmenides and Zeno. **1966** *Economist* 9 July p. xxv/3 The full application of this—or any other *anti-pollution measure—is going to have to wait until the older cars have been scrapped. **1979** *Jrnl. R. Soc. Arts* CXXVII. 406/2 The County Council appointed a specialist anti-pollution consultant. **1887** *Standard* (N. Y.) 7 May 2/1 The undersigned associate themselves together in an organization to be known as the *Anti-Poverty society. The object of the society is to spread.. a knowledge of the truth that God has made ample provision for the needs of all men during their residence upon earth, and that poverty is the result of.. human laws. **1976** *Billings* (Montana) *Gaz.* 24 June 3-A/1 Pope Paul Wednesday praised American Catholics for their 'sustained piety and generosity', singling out the church's domestic antipoverty effort and its overseas relief work. **1860** MAURY *Phys. Geog. Sea* vii. §368 The *Anti-radiating influence of clouds. **1835** J. S. MILL in *Lond. Rev.* I. 255 They.. will fight the battle of half-reform with *anti-reform artillery. **1840** GEN. P. THOMPSON *Exerc.* V. 233 The great probability of an *Anti-Reform war. **1879** *Pall Mall B.* 12 Sept., To applaud the *anti-rent agitation. **1865** *Ch. Times* 2 Dec., [The Bishop].. defends his *anti-ritual policy on arguments which he has expressly repudiated. **1877** W. MORRIS in J. W. Mackail *Life W. Morris* (1899) I. xi. 346 You have not yet joined our *Anti-Scrape Society. **1958** *New Statesman* 28 June 839/2 Churches, trade unions and professional organisations are being torn apart by the refusal of their members in the South to follow national *anti-segregation policies. **1936** *Discovery* Nov. 360/2 Headmasters with an *anti-sex bias. **1820** *Niles' Reg.* XIX. 127 An attempt.. to get up, what its projectors call, an '*anti-slavery' ticket. **1823** (9 Apr.) *Minute-bk. Brit. & For. Anti-Slavery Soc.*, At a Meeting of the Anti-Slavery Committee held at the King's Head Tavern, Poultry, it was resolved, etc. **1823** *N.Y. Observer* 17 May (*article*) Anti-Slavery Society. **1825** (*title*) Anti-Slavery Reporter. **1863** W. PHILLIPS *Speeches* iii. 36 Men undervalue the Antislavery movement. **1862** *Jrnl. R. Dublin S.* No. 25. 344 The *anti-squatting tendency of legislation in Victoria. **1845** MIALL *Nonconf.* V. 275 Great *Anti-state-endowment Meeting at Finsbury. **1858** GEN. P. THOMPSON *Audi Alt.* I. xlv. 177 Cockering up the *anti-tax-paying rich with the notion that the tax was to be put an end to. **1842** DICKENS *Amer. Notes* 98/1 The usual *anti-temperance recipe for keeping out the cold. **1959** *Observer* 12 Apr. 3/3 There are *anti-theft press-button latches on the ventilating panes. **1977** *Belfast Tel.* 28 Feb. 12/1 Car owners now have a legal obligation to ensure that their cars have a steering lock or some other anti-theft device. **1864** *Home News* 19 Dec. 6/1 Prosecuted at the instance of the *Anti-Tobacco Society. **1881** *Times* 28 Jan. 3/6 The *anti-torpedo gun adopted in the Royal Navy. **1860** GEN. P. THOMPSON *Audi Alt.* III. cxxix. 90 These *anti-trade tinkers are true to their kind; they make two holes, where they pretend to stop one. **1909** *Daily Chron.* 24 July 1/5 He has just turned them [*sc.* the saloons] into.. '*anti-treat' places, where no one will be allowed to get intoxicated or to treat a friend. **1813** *Niles' Reg.* V. 3/2 They may expose the British *anti-union demagogues. **1878** A. PINKERTON *Strikers, Communists* (1884) 206 (D.A.), The officers of the road secured a volunteer anti-union engineer and fireman to move the cars. **1905** *Daily Chron.* 24 Apr. 4 The anti-Union feeling in Norway grew. **1938** *Ann. Reg. 1937* 281 The 'independent' steel companies stuck to their anti-union policies. **1835** GEN. P. THOMPSON *Exerc.* III. 268 One great *anti-unjust-property-union. **1856** S. G. GOODRICH *Recoll. Lifetime* (1857) II. 51 The democrats were overjoyed that Colonel S. took pains to show his hatred and contempt for the *anti-war party. **1945** H. READ *Coat Many Colours* xv. 73 The spate of anti-war literature.

(ii) Commonly used in combinations denoting an agent, device, product, etc., that inhibits, limits, or counteracts a condition, effect, etc., as ***anti-crease***, ***-dazzle***, ***-drag***, ***-fallout***, ***-flash***, ***-foam***, ***-fouling***, ***-glare***, ***-halation***, ***-ice***, ***-knock***, ***-roll***, ***-shrink***, ***-skid***, ***-spin***. Also ANTI-FAT, ANTI-FREEZE. For combinations of this type used as sbs. (also *attrib.*) in *Biochem.*, etc., see sense 6 d.

1938 *Encycl. Brit. Bk. of Yr.* 636/2 New permanent finish substances, including anti-crease treatment with synthetic resin materials. **1920** *Flight* XII. 408/1 A large assemblage of cars of all types was brought together.. to test a variety of anti-dazzle devices, both British and foreign. **1963** *Times* 7 June 8/4 A two-position anti-dazzle driving mirror. **1918** H. J. STEPHENS *Gloss. Aeronaut. Words & Phr.* 40 Wires intended mainly to resist forces in the opposite direction to the drag are sometimes called 'anti-drag wires'. **1962** *Guardian* 9 July 14/3 Anti-fallout pills.. are thought to provide a resistance to radioactive iodine in the event of fallout. **1922** *Encycl. Brit.* XXX. 127/2 In order to reduce the flash on discharge of a gun *anti-flash charges* have been under experiment. **1960** *Times* 10 June 7/7 The wings painted in white anti-flash paint. **1934** WEBSTER, Antifoam. **1949** H. W. FLOREY et al. *Antibiotics* xvii. 695 The synthetic media were much more sensitive to antifoam reagents than corn steep liquor-lactose media. **1913** V. B. LEWES *Oil Fuel* iv. 91 Volatile spirit used in making up anti-fouling compositions. **1930** *Punch* 19 Feb. p. ix, Anti-glare head-lamps. **1905** *Westm. Gaz.* 8 Apr. 6/3 Orthochromatic non-curling and anti-halation films. **1959** W. S. SHARPS *Dict. Cinematogr.* 77/1 *Antihalation layer*, the layer interposed between the emulsion and base of film in order to prevent excessive halation. **1935** *Aircraft Engin.* Nov. 279/3 The application of anti-ice dopes.. is.. hardly a practical solution of the problem. **1921** *Flight* XIII. 412/2 Benzole and similar anti-knock fuels are, however, permitted. **1938** *Encycl. Brit. Bk. of Yr.* 426/1 As a rule, British cars prefer using a harder spring to obtain anti-roll characteristics. **1959** *Times* 16 Jan. 8/1 Her [*sc.* the liner's] anti-roll stabilisers ensure the utmost comfort at sea. **1946** *Nature* 19 Oct. 554/2 The unshrinkable finish is produced by means which differ from those suggested for the majority of other anti-shrink reagents. **1904** *Westm. Gaz.* 8 Dec. 10/2 A couple of chain bolts broken by catching against an anti-skid appliance had to be replaced. **1941** *Aeroplane Spotter* 29 May 195/3 Should the aeroplane develop a flat spin from which it cannot be pulled out the pilot releases the anti-spin parachute.

¶ Used as sbs. (see also sense 6).

1929 *Encycl. Brit.* V. 369 This substance [*sc.* lead tetra-ethyl] is of importance as an 'anti-knock' in petrol or gasoline. **1937** *Times* 13 Apr. x/3 About a year ago the regulations to deal with the lighting of road vehicles, and in particular with 'anti-dazzle', were issued. **1958** *Engineering* 21 Feb. 253/1 The development of suitable anti-foams to increase the utilisation of coil area of existing plant.

(iii) Employed or used for defence against enemy forces, weapons, etc., as ***anti-air-raid***, ***-airship***, ***-ballistic missile*** (also as sb.), ***-gas***, ***-missile***, ***-personnel*** (of bombs, mines, etc., designed to kill or injure human beings), ***-satellite***, ***-submarine***, ***-tank***, ***-torpedo*** (see sense 4 above), ***-U-boat***. Also ANTI-AIRCRAFT.

1934 J. HILTON *Good-bye, Mr. Chips* xiv. 95 The anti-air-raid blinds that had to be fitted on all the windows. **1939** *Ann. Reg. 1938* 184 Militia formations for anti-air-raid and coast defence. **1909** *Times* 13 July 13/4 Another 'Anti-airship' gun mounted on a motor car is exhibited. **1963** *Missiles & Rockets* 16 Sept. 14/1 The Soviet Union may be developing an anti-ballistic missile system capable of de-activating U.S. missiles in their silos. **1978** *Bull. Amer. Acad. Arts & Sci.* Feb. 4 The possible use of antiballistic missiles was soon to become a subject of lively debate. **1915** *Illustr. War News* 9 June 40/1 (*caption*) The anti-gas protective respirators which they are seen wearing. **1940** *Hutchinson's Pict. Hist. War* 7 Aug.—1 Oct. 25 Wearing respirators and anti-gas clothing, men of the Royal Marines engaged in anti-gas training on the West Coast. **1956** Anti-missile [see MISSILE *sb.*]. **1962** *Listener* 29 Mar. 546/2 The first-fruits of an anti-missile defence will be to deflect a small proportion of an attack. **1939** *Jrnl. R. Aeronaut. Soc.* XLIII. 909 Anti-personnel bombs must explode as soon as they touch the ground. **1945** *Lancet* 14 July 44/1 Anti-personnel mines are of many types but can be divided into three main groups—the 'S' mine, 'Schu', and the light Teller anti-tank mine adapted for anti-personnel use. **1961** *New Scientist* 20 July 140/3 To avoid interception and destruction by anti-satellite missiles, *Midas III* carries a number of small vernier rockets that enable its course to be changed. **1914** DOMVILLE-FIFE *Submarines, Mines & Torpedoes* ix, (*heading*) Anti-Submarine Tactics. **1942** *Ann. Reg. 1941* 272 The anti-submarine net guarding the harbour was open. **1916** W. S. CHURCHILL *Memorandum* 9 Nov. in *World Crisis, 1916–18* (1927) II. 564 Let me point out the need of establishing without delay an Anti-Tank Committee... We ought to have a complete anti-tank outfit by the spring. **1918** FARROW *Dict. Mil. Terms* 26 *Anti-tank Gun*, a gun especially designed and prepared to meet the onrush of the tank or mobile fort. **1944** *Return to Attack* (Army Board, N.Z.) 19/2 Then the staccato bark of the anti-tank guns could be heard as they were turned on the escaping vehicles. **1881** Anti-torpedo [see sense 4 above]. **1919** L. R. FREEMAN *Sea-Hounds* ix. 198 Probably some sort of patrol or anti-U-boat worker, for a guess, perhaps, a 'Q'. **1939** *War Illustr.* 2 Dec. 374/2 Our Navy is stronger. Our anti-U-boat forces are three times as numerous.

¶ For combinations of this type used as sbs., see 6 below.

III. Substantives uniform with, or formed on the preceding adjs. and attrib. phrases. Stress not on *anti-* (*anti-Calvinist*, *anti-fanatic*, *anti-friction*, *anti-moralism*).

5. Combinations in which *anti-* is prefixed to a personal appellation, or formed, as synthetic derivatives, on the adjs. and attrib. phrases in II, and used to designate a person or group of people; in -(I)AN, as ***anti-Arminian***, ***-Athenian***, ***-authoritarian***, ***-churchian***, ***-Dominican***, ***-puritan***, ***-surplician***, ***-theologian***, ***-utilitarian***, etc.; in -IST, as ***anti-abolitionist***, ***-aggressionist***, ***-alcoholist***, ***-atheist***, ***-Bolshevist***, ***-Calvinist***, ***-classicist***, ***-colonialist***, ***-episcopist***, ***-fascist***, ***-fedaralist***, ***-Gothicist***, ***-humanist***, ***-imperialist***, ***-Jansenist***, ***-materialist***, ***-militarist***, ***-moralist***, ***pædobaptist***, ***-rationalist***, ***-revolutionist***, ***-royalist***, ***-Sophist***, ***-suffragist***, ***-unionist***, ***-vivisectionist***, ***-Wycliffist***, etc.; with other endings, as ***anti-ascetic***, ***-Blimp***, ***Bolshevik***, ***cheator***, ***-covenanter***, ***everything***, ***-free-thinker***, ***-intellectual***, ***-Noahite***, ***-Stadtholder***, etc.

1835 *Southern Lit. Messenger* I. 772, I am both from conviction and expediency, a decided *anti-abolitionist. **1970** J. F. KIRKHAM et al. *Assassination & Polit. Violence* iv. 215 Abolitionists used violence to oppose slavery.. and anti-abolitionists resorted to violence to support slavery. **1882** *Sat. Rev.* 25 Feb. 225 All *Anti-Aggressionists present and future. **1862** *Cornh. Mag.* VI. 327 Our chemical *Anti-alcoholists. **1882** *Pall Mall G.* 28 Nov. 1 There are *Anti-annexationists in France as there are in England. **1651** BAXTER *Inf. Bapt.* 276 The highest *Antiarminian that ever had the happiness to be reputed orthodox. **1827** HARE *Guesses* I. (1873) 261 Neither the ascetics nor the *anti-ascetics seem to be aware that, etc. **1855** I. TAYLOR *Restor. Belief* (1856) 250 Our hostile friends—the antichristian *anti-atheists. **1849** GROTE *Greece* II. lxi. V. 337 The leading *anti-Athenians in the town. **1836** J. GILBERT *Chr. Atonem.* iii. (1852) 65 Maintained by the *anti-atonementists. **1910** *Encycl. Brit.* I. 916/2 After the names of 'Federalists' and '*Anti-authoritarians' had been used for some time by these federations the name of 'Anarchists'.. prevailed. **1662** FULLER *Worthies* II. 229 (D.) John of Oxford was.. a great *Anti-Becketist. **1941** 'G. ORWELL' *Lion & Unicorn* I. 49 The English intellectuals.. [were] purely *negative* creatures, mere *anti-Blimps. **1918** *New Statesman* 28 Dec. 250/1 Even the most enthusiastic of Russian *anti-Bolsheviks would be satisfied. **1921** G. B. SHAW *Ruskin's Politics* 32 Look at all that has been done, not only by Bolshevists, but by *anti-Bolshevists, by ourselves, and by all the belligerents! **1807** W. TAYLOR in *Month. Mag.* XXIV. 24 Whether Dr. Watkins, or the *Anti-Bucerist, has been the more attentive reader of English ecclesiastical history. **1814** SIR R. WILSON *Pr. Diary* II. 309 An annal which the greatest *anti-Buonapartist ought to respect. **1674** HICKMAN *Hist. Quinquart.* (ed. 2) 32 The *Anticalvinists or Arminians. **1819** (*title*) *Anti-Cathedralist,—exposition of the impropriety of expending £1,000,000 on National Churches. **1655** *Chym. Med. & Chyrurg. Addr.* 65, I have professed myself to be an *Anticheator. **1682** *2nd Plea Nonconf.* 49 The Bishops are *Anti-churchians (as against their Congregational Power). **1840** THACKERAY *Paris Sk. Bk.* (1872) 38 The *anticlassicists did not arise in France until about 1827. **1956** *Newsweek* 2 Apr. 41/1 Russia's new 'reasonableness' appeals to neutralist nations, to hotheaded *anticolonials and, dangerously, to our allies. **1960** *Times* 27 June 13/7 *Anti-colonialists say that the western countries dug themselves in commercially even in Siam. **1939** *Times* 26 Aug. 11/2 It [*sc.* the Russo-German agreement] has already produced a vigorous protest from Japan, where it is held that the pass has been sold by the leader of the *anti-Cominterns. **1865** PUSEY *Eiren.* 358 Probably *Anti-conceptionists will arise. **1865** *Daily Tel.* 9 Nov. 7/4 His place was taken by an *anti-confederationist. **1825** *Q. Rev.* XXXIII. 245 Are the *anti-contagionists ignorant of these facts? **1755** JOHNSON, *Anticourtier*, One that opposes the court. **1641** *Kirkcudbr. War-Comm. Min. Bk.* 120 To have the tymber maid worke..that perteinit to Mr. James Scott, *ante-covenanter. **1649** MILTON *Eikon.* xiv. (1851) 448 How to be a Covnanter and Anticovnanter, how at once to be a Scot, and an Irish Rebell. **1855** I. TAYLOR *Restor. Belief* (1856) 119 This *anticynic was too thoroughly cynical in soul and temper. **1751** CHAMBERS *Cycl.*, **Antiadiaphorists*.. the rigid Lutherans who disavowed the episcopal jurisdiction, and many of the church-ceremonies, retained by the moderate Lutherans. **1640** LD. DIGBY in *Rushw. Hist. Coll.* III. (1692) I. 35 An Argument..against *Antidisciplinarians, to stop their mouths withal. **1680** *Spir. Popery* 33 No society of Anti-scripturists, Antitrinitarians ..*Antidominicans (for I will not call them Antisabbatarians) Antipædobaptists, Antiepiscoparians of what Denomination soever. **1659** GAUDEN *Tears of Ch.* 283 (D.) The *Antidominicarians [might deny and overthrow] the Lords day. **1640** BP. HALL *Episcop.* II. §20. 200 What noyse is this I hear from our *Antepiscopists? **1659** GAUDEN *Tears of Ch.* 603 (D.) Of Episcopacy and *Anti-episcopalists. **1848** O. W. HOLMES in *Poems* (1851) 253 Lean, hungry, savage, *anti-everythings. **1882** *Pall Mall G.* 16 May 3 Not a single one..ventured to declare himself an *anti-evolutionist. **1660** MILTON *Griffiths' Serm.* Wks. 1851, 390 What Phanatic..could more presumptuously affirm whom the Comforter hath impowr'd, than this *Antifanatic, as he would be thought? **1926** *Sat. Rev.* 28 Aug. 228/1 Up to October, 1920, I have found the names of thirty-three *anti-Fascists who were killed by the Fascists. **1789** T. JEFFERSON *Writ.* II. 574 A vast majority of *anti-federalists have got into the Assembly of Virginia. **1851** J. B. EASTWICK *Dry Leaves* (ed. 3) xi. 186 All mere outward show!—says *Anti-formalist, who wears his hat in church, and talks during divine service louder than the minister. **1936** *Mind* XLV. 272 Leśniewski, an anti-formalist who has constructed a complete system of the foundations of mathematics. **1871** FRASER *Berkeley* iii. 58 He appears as a free-thinking *Anti-free-thinker. **1662** FULLER *Worthies* II. 450 (D.) The *anti-Friarists maintaining that such were Rogues. **1867** BARRY *Sir C. Barry* ix. 317 M. Hittorf is clearly a strong *Anti-Gothicist. **1741–70** MRS. CARTER *Lett.* (1808) 163 As soon as these *antiharmonists would consent to part with their card tables, we had a dance. **1640** BP. HALL *Episc.* I. § 11 39 This great *Antihierarchist. **1937** J. ORR tr. *I. Iordan's Introd. Romance Ling.* iv. 299 Such comparatists and *anti-historicists as Gilliéron and Vossler. **1904** W. JAMES in *Mind* XIII. 466 This is just another of those objections by which the *anti-humanists show their own comparatively slack hold on the realities of the situation. **1840** THACKERAY *Paris Sk. Bk.* (1872) 38 Your humble servant and other *anti-humbuggists. **1898** *Westm. Gaz.* 17 Dec. 1/3 The antithesis between imperialists and *anti-imperialists. **1870** *Eng. Mech.* 14 Jan. 422/2 Baker's *anti-incrustator for steam boilers. **1824** BENTHAM *Bk. Fallac.* Wks. 1843 II. 421 Is the *anti-innovationist mute? No. **1827** WHATELY *Logic* (1837) 249 The stronghold of bigoted *anti-innovators. **1937** V. GOLLANCZ in 'G. Orwell' *Road to Wigan Pier* p. xviii, Mr. Orwell..is at one and the same time an extreme intellectual and a violent *anti-intellectual. **1751** JORTIN *Eccles. Hist.* (1773) I. 158 The *Anti-Jansenists of the church of Rome. **1806** W. TAYLOR in *Ann. Rev.* IV. 713 The whole tribe of *Anti-jesuits. **1916** J. R. HARRIS & BURCH *Testimonies* I. 49 It is a very favourite quotation with the earlier *anti-Judaics. **1603** J. DAVIES *Microcosm.* 72 (D.) Mortal plagues to ev'ry Publike-weall; Right *anti-Kesars vndermyning thrones. **1882** *Sun* 14 May 6/5 The *anti-lacrossers cheered. **1659** GAUDEN *Tears of Ch.* 91 (D.) Our late *anti-liturgists thought forms of prayer might do well at sea. **1855** MILMAN *Lat. Chr.* XIV. iii. IX. 134 No Eastern *Anti-materialist ever guarded the primal Godhead more zealously. **1748** RICHARDSON *Clarissa* (1811) IV. 144 If she make a private purse, which we are told by *anti-matrimonialists, all wives love to do. **1948** L. SPITZER *Ling. & Lit. Hist.* i. 15 The *antimentalists who would suppress all expressions of opposition to their theories. **1896** *Academy* 1 Aug. 77/1 We godless ones and *anti-metaphysicians. **1941** *Mind* L. 187 The reactionary anti-metaphysician is primarily a reactionary in science and only secondarily a reactionary in metaphysics. **1905** *Daily Chron.* 27 Dec. 1/7 The trial of twenty-eight *anti-militarists was begun yesterday in Paris. **1790** BEATSON *Nav. & Mil. Mem.* I. 169 The *antiministerialists began now to perceive, etc. **1809** SOUTHEY in *Q. Rev.* I. 224 The *Anti-missionaries cull out from their journals and letters all that is ridiculous. **1809** —— *ibid.* I. 223 This madman, as it pleases the *anti-missioners to call him. **1824** COLERIDGE *Aids to Refl.* (1848) I. 106 In opposition to Hobbes and the *anti-moralists. **1938** *Encycl. Brit. Bk. of Yr.* 193/2 With Hitler's coming into power in Germany in 1933..the conflict between the Nazis and the *anti-Nazis in Danzig increased. **1810** LAMB *Lett.* I. (1841) 84 Hang temperance and he that first invented it!—some *Anti-Noahite. **1759** STERNE *Tr. Shandy* (1802) IV. 36 He can do nothing, replied the *Antinosarians. **1882** *St. James's Gaz.* 17 Mar. 5 The *anti-opiumists..must ask for the absolute prohibition..of opium culture. **1882** *Glasg. News* No. 2610. 4/2 Allegations made by the *anti-opiumites. **1651** BAXTER *Inf. Bapt.* 173 He might have called us *Anti-pædobaptists, as being against Infant-Baptism. **1703** E. STEPHENS *Dealings R.C. Mission.* 2 That the root of all our confusions and troubles did proceed from two opposite factions, of Papists and *Anti-papists. **1830** *Edin. Rev.* LI. 297 Hear, ye political economists and *anti-populationists! **1677** GALE *Crt. Gentiles* III. 214 We now procede to lay down the proper antithesis of the *Antipredeterminants. **1682** H. MORE *Annot. Glanvill's Lux Orient.* 14 This *Anti-Pre-existentiary is such a Trifler. **1789** HUBER in *Ld. Auckland's Corr.* (1861) II. 326 One of the clergy, a curate, strong *anti-prelate. **1673** BAXTER *Answ. Dodwell* 91 The *Antiprelatists..such as Beza, Gerson. **1650** J. COTTON *Sing. Psalms* 2 There be some *Anti-psalmists, who doe not acknowledge any singing at all with the voyce in the New Testament. *a* **1790** T. WARTON *Milton's Smaller P.* 501 (T.) Samuel Parker..now an *anti-puritan in the extreme. **1753** CHAMBERS *Cycl. Supp.* s.v., The rigid Calvinists..are denominated *Anti-rationalists. **1831** SYD. SMITH *Wks.* 1859 II. 219/1 The *Anti-Reformers cite the increased power of the press. **1852** SIR W. HAMILTON *Discuss.* 436 English Bishops have been always anti-reformers. **1847** *Secr. Soc. Mid. Ages* 267 The good old argument of *Anti-reformists, 'It works well.' **1898** *Westm. Gaz.* 26 Oct. 7 In view of probable trouble between revisionists and *anti-revisionists. **1828** J. S. MILL in *Westm. Rev.* IX. 272 The marquis de Ferrières,..a decided royalist and *anti-revolutionist. **1837** CARLYLE *Fr. Rev.* II. III. I. i. 133 Cashier of all the Anti-revolutionists of the interior. **1860** W. G. CLARK *Vac. Tour.* 72 Whether ardent *anti-romanists are wise in advocating the abolition of the temporal power. **1627** SIBTHORPE *Apost. Obed.* 16 To make use of *anti-royalists. **1648** PRYNNE *Plea for Lords* 25 The Duke of Gloucester..was the principall Anti-royalist. **1855** MILMAN *Lat. Chr.* IX. viii. V. 383 The simple *antisacerdotalists..repudiated the authority of the clergy. **1836** J. GILBERT *Chr. Atonem.* ii. 35 Crellius, the most subtle and elaborate of all the *anti-satisfactionists. **1806** W. TAYLOR in *Ann. Rev.* IV. 110 These *anti-savages sell their farms..to European emigrants. **1890** W. JAMES *Princ. Psychol.* II. xx. 252 A thorough-going *anti-sensationalist. **1850** GROTE *Greece* II. lxvii. VIII. 546 Sokrates deserves our admiration..not indeed as an *anti-Sophist. **1940** *Tablet* 4 May 419/2 That is why..a sop was conveniently thrown to the *anti-Soviets over the mysterious affair of the Soviet Embassy's plain language telegram. **1753** HANWAY *Trav.* (1762) II. I. ix. 50 The *anti-stadtholders, who wish to see the prince pulled out of his seat. **1940** *N. & Q.* CLXXIX. 181/1 *Anti-Stratfordians either do not make themselves acquainted with the facts recently discovered, or, knowing them, give them no place in their arguments concerning the authorship of the plays. **1897** *Westm. Gaz.* 7 July 1/2 We might have supposed that some satanic *anti-suffragist had contrived this thing. **1813** *Month. Mag.* XXXVI. 138 Selden was evidently an *anti-supernaturalist. **1842–4** BARHAM in *Life* II. ix. 139, I as one of the *anti-surplicians. **1878** *N. Amer. Rev.* CXXVII. 306 Theologians and *anti-theologians may argue the matter as they will. **1869** *Eng. Mech.* 24 Sept. 13/1 The *anti-tobacconists..attributing it to excess of smoking. **1959** *Times* 3 June 8/6 *Anti-Uglies at Peacehaven. **1803** W. TAYLOR in *Ann. Rev.* I. 282 The success of the *anti-unionists in the House of Commons. **1865** MILL *Exam. Hamilton's Philos.* 507 It is indifferent whether we are utilitarians or *anti-utilitarians. **1883** *Daily Tel.* 20 June 6/8 The *anti-vaccinationists will find it a difficult task to refute the statement. **1869** *Eng. Mech.* 8 Oct. 74/3 The *anti-vaccinators..[are] in a minority. **1822** *Blackw. Mag.* XII. 786 [He] treated with utter scorn..every hint of the *anti-vaccinist. **1882** BP. GOODWIN in *Macm. Mag.* XLV. 468 The extravagant views..of the extreme *anti-vivisectionists. **1908** *Practitioner* LXXXI. 479 Hostile agitation of the anti-vivisectionists. **1889** G. B. SHAW in *Star* 29 Nov. 2/4 He is by no means an *anti-Wagnerite. **1662** FULLER *Worthies* II. 297 (D.) John of Milverton..was a great *Anti-Wiccliffist. **1711** SHAFTESB. *Charac.* (1732) I. 91 What shou'd we say to one of these *anti-zealots, who, in the zeal of such a cool philosophy, shou'd assure us, etc.

¶ As combinations of the type *antichristian*, *anti-Catholic*, in which the preceding sense originated, were originally adjs. used substantively, so those of the type *anti-Jesuit*, *anti-Calvinist*, properly substantives, are occasionally used adjectively or attributively as ***anti-capitalist***, ***-colonialist***, ***-Communist***, ***-Fascist***, ***-historicist***, ***-humanist***, ***-imperialist***, ***-intellectualist***, ***-materialist***, ***-militarist***, ***-revisionist***, ***-sensationalist***, ***-substantialist***, ***-terrorist***, ***-vaccinist***; at other times an adj. ending is added, as the ***anti-Stadtholderian*** faction. Also ANTISOCIALIST.

1862 *Sat. Rev.* XIII. 648/1 This year's division list.. showed the *anti-abolitionist party in a majority. **1902** *Encycl. Brit.* XXVIII. 492/1 It was not a phase of the *anti-capitalist movement. **1949** I. DEUTSCHER *Stalin* iii. 56 A'bourgeois' (that is anti-feudal, but not anti-capitalist) revolution. **1955** *Times* 5 July 9/5 The Americans, who proclaim their *anti-colonialist spirit, are nevertheless paving the way for the British. **1958** *Ann. Reg. 1957* 179 Anti-colonialist speeches were made by a number of delegates and..resolutions were approved in which Western imperialism was condemned in all its forms. **1934** WEBSTER, *Anti-communist. **1938** *Encycl. Brit. Bk. of Yr.* 171/2 In 1936 an 'Anti-Communist Pact' was formed by Germany and Japan, and in Nov. 1937 this was joined by Italy. **1927** M. W. DAVIS *Pol. Handbk. Europe* 57 National Union Party: An *anti-Fascist organization. **1938** *Ann. Reg. 1937* 238 The loss of Málaga, due in no small measure..to the lack of cohesion between the anti-Fascist elements in the city. **1945** POPPER *Open Society* 201 From the *anti-historicist point of view, the question [whether the state originates through a conquest] is of no great importance. **1930** H. CRANE *Let.* 8 June (1965) 352 The *anti-humanist symposium. **1908** T. ROOSEVELT *Let.* 4 Mar. (1919) 222 This ought to be read before all the..*anti-imperialist societies of the present day. **1937** E. SNOW *Red Star over China* i. 20 Were the [Chinese] Reds really anti-imperialist? **1952** C. P. BLACKER *Eugenics* 276 The democratic anti-imperialist front. **1871** *Sat. Rev.* 29 Apr. 529 The *anti-infallibilist priests and laymen of the diocese. **1907** W. JAMES *Pragmatism* ii. 54 All these..are *anti-intellectualist tendencies. **1890** W. B. YEATS *Let. to K. Tynan* 28 Feb. (1953) 111 An article on Blake and his *anti-materialist Art. **1905** *Daily Chron.* 27 Dec. 5/6 *Anti-militarist placards. **1883** *Harper's Mag.* Jan. 315/2 A manifesto issued by the *Anti-Nihilist League. **1845** R. HAMILTON *Pop. Educ.* viii. 190 The Congregationalist and the *Anti-paedobaptist Denominations. **1845** CARLYLE *Cromwell* (1871) I. 103 To the horror of all *Anti-papist men. **1870** LOWELL *Among my Bks.* I. (1873) 325 These *anti-patriot flings of Lessing. **1881** MRS. PRAED *Policy & Pass.* I. 303 The wives of the *Anti-Railwayist Faction were decorously triumphant. **1866** *Ch. Times* 3 Feb., The *anti-reformist clergy. **1898** *Westm. Gaz.* 26 Oct. 1/2 No such deadly blow could have been aimed at the Government by any open opponent of revision as this.. open avowal of *anti-revisionist faith. **1931** *Times Lit. Suppl.* 22 Jan. 52/2 The Church, which was anti-revisionist. **1964** *Ann. Reg. 1963* 209 In the Communist Parties..pro-Chinese members broke away to form anti-revisionist groups. **1890** W. JAMES *Princ. Psychol.* II. xvii. 9 Such passages as the following abound in *anti-sensationalist literature: 'Sense is a kind of dull, confused, and stupid perception obtruded upon the soul from without.' **1765** *Ann. Reg.* 65/2 The *antistadtholderian faction in Holland. **1882** W. JAMES in *Princeton Rev.* July 62 *Anti-substantialist writers strangely overlook this function in the doctrine of substance. **1945** *Mind* LIV. 214, I do, in fact, like all positivists, hold views..greatly influenced by the anti-substantialist analyses of Berkeley and Hume. **1811** W. TAYLOR in *Month. Mag.* XXXI. 6 The *anti-supernaturalist christianity of..Eichhorn. **1949** KOESTLER *Promise & Fulfilment* viii. 95 Specially picked *anti-terrorist Haganah squads. **1976** *Scotsman* 15 Dec. 6/5 A senior officer of Rome's anti-terrorist police squad today narrowly escaped an assassination attempt. **1898** *Daily News* 20 Apr. 4/7 The *anti-vaccinist agitation.

6. Names of things of same form as the attrib. phrases in 4: **a.** of systems, etc., as ***anti-bibliolatry***, ***-bigotry***, ***-fouling***, ***-popery***, ***-restoration***, ***-romance***, ***-slavery***, ***-vivisection***; **b.** of material agents or appliances, as **anti-ferment**; **anti-erysipelas**, a plant so named from its use; **anti-huff**, a substance used to adulterate cheese; also ANTI-ATTRITION, -CORROSION, -FRICTION, -MACASSAR, q.v.; **c.** ***anti-horse***, ***-human***, etc., applied to, or pertaining to, an anti-serum prepared from the blood serum of the animal specified; **d.** of material agents that counteract or inhibit the effect of another substance; in *Biochem.*, spec. a substance that is an antibody (to the antigen to which it corresponds). Examples: ***anti-auxin***, ***-cholinesterase***, ***-coagulin***, ***-enzyme***, ***-hormone***, ***-metabolite***, ***-prothrombin***, ***-streptolysin***, ***-thrombin***, ***-trypsin***, ***-virus***, ***-vitamin***. Also ANTITOXIN; cf. ANTIBODY. Hence the names of specific agglutinins present in blood serum, as ***anti-A***, ***-B***, ***-globulin***, ***-Rh(esus)***; also ANTIHISTAMINE, ANTI-SERUM. (See also sense 4 ¶.)

1929 O. C. W. PRAUSNITZ *Standardisation Therapeutic Sera* 51 The designation [of diagnostic sera] should also indicate the blood corpuscle groups with which they reacted, thus: 'Test serum A (anti-B)' and 'Test serum B (*anti-A)'. **1932** L. W. H. BERTIE tr. *L. Lattes's Individuality of Blood* i. 17 The corresponding agglutinins are denoted by 'anti-A' and 'anti-B' respectively. **1955** *Sci. News Let.* 4 June 361/3 They can prevent the tar-extract effect on plants by adding a recently-discovered plant hormone, *antiauxin, to the tar at the time of application. The antiauxin is a crystalline substance extracted from the leaves of plants which are in flower. **1961** *Brit. Med. Dict.* 55/1 *Anti-A*, or *α, agglutinin*, the agglutinin in the serum corresponding to the agglutinogen A with which it will combine, causing clumping and haemolysis of the erythrocytes containing the latter... *Anti-B*, or *β, agglutinin*. **1824** COLERIDGE *Aids to Refl.* (1848) I. 122 Charged with Popish principles on account of their *anti-bibliolatry. **1851** CARLYLE *Sterling* III. iv. (1872) 204 An amount of..liberal *antibigotry that would surprise many. **1951** *Dorland's Med. Dict.* (ed. 22) 106/2 **Anti-cholinesterase*, a substance which inhibits the action of cholinesterase. **1951** *Proc. Soc. Exp. Biol.* LXXVI. 427/1 Phosphorus-containing anticholinesterase agents are currently in use in this country as agricultural insecticides. **1905** GOULD *Dict. New Med. Terms* 80/1 **Anticoagulin*, a substance formed in the body antagonistic in its action to that of a coagulin. **1952** *New Biol.* XIII. 86 The saliva [of the bed-bug] contains an anticoagulin which prevents the blood from clotting and so facilitates its passage through the narrow feeding channel. **1903** *Lancet* 4 Apr. 946/1 The human stomach wall contains an *anti-enzyme to its own ferment. **1958** *Times* 5 July 10/7 A group of patients who have been operated on for cancer of the bladder are now being given this anti-enzyme substance, in the hope that it may reduce the chance of new tumours developing. **1714** *Phil. Trans.* XXIX. 63 A Plant efficacious in curing Inflammations, whence they call it *Antierisypelas. **1876** HARLEY *Mat. Med.* 160 Dose.—½ to 1 drachm as *antiferment. **1869** SIR E. REED *Iron-Clad Ships* iv. 78 The superiority in point of *anti-fouling possessed by copper-sheathed wood ships. **1909** *Cent. Dict.* Suppl., *Anti-globulin. **1956** *Nature* 18 Feb. 329/2 Antiglobulin sera obtained by our technique contain antibodies against globulin denatured on the surface of red cells as a result of antigen-antibody reaction. **1934** F. E. D'AMOUR et al. in *Proc. Soc. Exp. Biol.* XXXII. 192 It seemed to us desirable to investigate the possibility of *anti-hormone production against estrin. **1940** *Biol. Rev.* XV. 27 The antihormones are specific in so far as, for instance, antigonadotrophic hormone does not antagonize the action of the thyrotrophic hormone and vice versa. **1949** I. F. & W. D. HENDERSON *Dict. Sci. Terms* (ed. 4) 26/2 *Antihormones*, substances which prevent the effect of hormones; chalones. **1909** W. D'ESTE EMERY *Immunity & Specific Therapy* xi. 317 The symptoms are present when not the slightest trace of *antihorse precipitin is demonstrable. **1964** M. HYNES *Med. Bacteriol.* (ed. 8) vii. 75 The horse-serum compound described above evokes the production of some anti-horse-serum antibodies in the rabbit. **1881** *Times* 19 Feb. 5/3 [Cheese] is adulterated ..by a commodity called *anti-huff. **1906** *Practitioner* Dec. 754 A powerful *anti-human serum may be injected intravascularly in man without necessarily producing the serum disease. **1946** *Nature* 5 Oct. 486/2 It was decided to find out if the test would give positive results only with rabbit anti-human serum, and not with rabbit anti-sera prepared with the serum of various animals. **1947** *Dorland's Med. Dict.* (ed. 21) 120/2 **Antimetabolite*, a closely similar but inactive compound which tends to replace an essential metabolite. **1956** *Nature* 14 Jan. 59/2 The abortifacient action of certain anti-metabolites which are related to nucleic acid metabolism. **1930** *Chem. Abstr.* 422 (*title*) Anti-complementary action of *antiprothrombin. **1879** G. Scott *Archit.* I. 177 In these days of *anti-restoration. **1941** Landsteiner & Wiener in *Jrnl. Exp. Med.* LXXIV. 310 The serum of these patients contained *anti-Rh iso-agglutinins. *Ibid.* 309 Certain *anti-*rhesus* immune sera contain agglutinins specific for the human agglutinogen M. *a* **1842** Arnold in *Life* I. 344 A man infected with the disorder of *anti-romance. **1951** *Dorland's Med. Dict.* (ed. 23) 1184/1 *Rh *antiserums* (*anti-Rh serums*), human serums containing Rh antibodies... Rh_o is also the original Rh factor discovered by Landsteiner and Wiener with the aid of immune anti-rhesus serum produced in animals. **1936** Stedman *Med. Dict.* (ed. 13) 71/2 *Antistreptolysin. **1949** *New Gould Med. Dict.* 79/2 *Antistreptolysin*, an antibody which operates against the hemotoxin of hemolytic streptococci. **1909** *Cent. Dict.* Suppl., *Antithrombin. **1910** *Encycl. Brit.* IV. 82/2 The body has been found to possess the power of making a substance, antithrombin, which can combine with thrombin forming a substance which is quite inactive as far as clotting is concerned. **1905** *Jrnl. Physiol.* XXXII. 394 The mixture of trypsin and *antitrypsin is kept at first at a low temperature. **1913** Dorland *Med. Dict.* (ed. 7), *Antitrypsin*, an antibody of blood-serum having an inhibitive action on trypsin. **1927** H. Plotz tr. *A. Besredka's Local Immunization* 53 The other [substance] is atoxic, thermostable..and antagonizes the former substance. For convenience, we will call this substance, '*antivirus'. **1949** H. W. Florey *Antibiotics* I. I. 45 Artificial immunity could be conferred locally on tissues by the use of what he termed an 'antivirus', which was prepared from old broth cultures of bacteria. **1942** *Chem. Abstr.* 5503 It is suggested that heated fats contain an *antivitamin A of undet[ermine]d nature. **1948** *Sci. News* VII. 56 Many substances are now known which antagonise the action of certain of the vitamins... These ' anti-vitamins' may occur in natural foodstuffs. **1948** *Ibid.* 67 A true anti-vitamin effect is shown by the fact that feeding nicotinic acid to the mice overcomes the deleterious action of the 3-acetyl-pyridine. **1881** *Times* 18 Nov., Ladies..interested in *anti-vivisection.

7. Abstract substantives, formed on the adjs. in 3, phrases in 4, or sbs. in 5–6, chiefly in *-ism*, as ***anti-anthropomorphism*** (opposition to anthropomorphic principles), ***-Arminianism***, ***-atheism***, ***-authoritarianism***, ***-Bolshevism***, ***-Calvinism***, ***-capitalism***, ***-colonialism***, ***-Communism***, ***-Darwinism***, ***-egotism***, ***-Fascism***, ***-foreignism***, ***-Germanism***, ***-ghostism*** (opposition to belief in ghosts), ***-historicism***, ***-imperialism***, ***-intellectualism***, ***-militarism***, ***-nationalism***, ***-negroism*** (opposition to negroes), ***-nominalism***, ***-pewism***, ***-pragmatism***, ***-rationalism***, ***-revolutionism***, ***-sensationalism***, ***-slaveryism***, ***-turnpikism***, ***-Wagnerism***, ***-westernism***. Also anti-Americanism, anti-clericalism.

1846 Sara Coleridge *Mem. & Lett.* II. 91 For other such *anti-anthropomorphisms my father has been set a mark against. **1674** Hickman *Hist. Quinquart.* (ed. 2) 169 If this be not Calvinism and *Antiarminianism, I know not what is. **1939** I. Berlin *K. Marx* ix. 203 The Swiss, Italian and Belgian sections [of the First International], bred on the *anti-authoritarianism of Proudhon and Bakunin. **1919** G. B. Shaw *Heartbreak House* p. xliv, By..calling the process *anti-Bolshevism. **1674** Hickman *Hist. Quinquart.* (ed. 2) 217 We have found *Anti-calvinism discountenanced by the Church, in Queen Elizabeth's Reign. **1934** Webster, *Anticapitalism. **1940** B. Ward *Russ. Foreign Policy* 4 The old fear of encirclement reappeared in the disguise of anti-capitalism. **1955** *Ann. Reg. 1954* 97 This cloud was the advent of the 'quit Africa' policy of *anti-colonialism. **1927** *New Statesman* 21 May 174/2 There seems to be an attempt to create a big issue of Communism versus *anti-Communism. **1840** Syd. Smith *Lett.* No. 438 That dreadful sin of *anti-egotism. **1923** *Time* 19 May 11/1 *Anti-Fascism. **1958** *Listener* 23 Oct. 656/2 The anti-fascism of the nineteen-thirties. **1926** *British Weekly* 18 Nov. 203/2 The bloodshed of May 30 in Shanghai carried *anti-foreignism to fever heat throughout the country. **1910** *Daily Chron.* 9 Apr. 1/3 For Great Britain *anti-Germanism is not merely a matter of ill-temper..nor even of dogma, but a view of world affairs which has grown up on historical and religious grounds. **1965** *New Statesman* 27 Aug. 281/2 Anti-Germanism in Britain is largely a prejudice of the middle-aged, the middle class and the intellectuals. **1819** Coleridge *Rem.* (1836) II. 213 Hume..could not but have had faith in this ghost..let his *anti-ghostism have been as strong as Samson. **1943** *Jrnl. Hist. Ideas* IV. 431 The *anti-historicism of Descartes and Malebranche expresses itself also in the fact that they failed to realize another essential aspect of history, namely, its social and cumulative character. **1899** *Daily News* 30 May 5/5 They champion *anti-Imperialism, free silver, and the rest of the doctrines dear to the Populists. **1909** *Anti-intellectualism [see fideism]. **1921** M. Ginsberg *Psychol. of Society* iii. 35 This anti-intellectualism is really open to much the same sort of objections as the 'intellectualism' which it attacks. **1906** J. Joyce *Let.* 19 Aug. (1966) II. 151 He was ridiculing ..*antimilitarism. **1907** *Daily Chron.* 16 Sept. 4/6 Socialists are entitled to say that Socialism is not anti-nationalism, anti-militarism in M. Hervé's sense, nor anti-patriotism. **1812** Coleridge *Rem.* (1836) I. 349 The *anti-moralism of Paley. **1851** Sara Coleridge *Mem. & Lett.* II. 434 The irrationality and antimoralism..involved in the popular religion. **1906** *Daily Chron.* 29 Sept. 5/7 The danger..was the growth of a spirit of what he could only call *anti-nationalism. **1863** E. Swifte *N. & Q.* Ser. iii. IV. 264 With veritable Northern *anti-negroism. **1897** W. James *Let.* 22 Dec. in R. B. Perry *Thought & Char. W. James* (1935) II. 419 *Anti-nominalism, categories [etc.]. **1960** *Encounter* Mar. 41/1 The two lines of anti-nominalism meet..in French existentialism. **1652** Tombes (*title*) *Anti-Pædo-Baptism. **1795** P. Edwards (*title*) Candid reasons for renouncing the principles of Antipedo-baptism. **1837** Carlyle *Fr. Rev.* v. vii. II. 330 Denouncing *Anti-patriotism. **1865** *Ch.-man* 14 Dec. 1405/2 *Anti-pewism has come out against Protestantism. **1907** W. James in *Jrnl. Philos.* IV. 465 If that be my friend Pratt's definition of a pragmatist, I can only concur with his *antipragmatism. **1909** A. O. Lovejoy *Let.* 27 Aug. in R. B. Perry *Thought & Char. W. James* (1935) II. 595, I mean the extreme of *anti-rationalism to which the book gives expression. **1936** *Mind* XLV. 272 By anti-rationalism is meant the rejection of any form of mystical intuition. **1855** H. Spencer *Psychol.* vii. xix. II. 491 *Anti-Realism..is open to the fatal criticism. **1930** *Anti-revolutionism [see *anti-Westernism* below]. **1702** *Lond. Gaz.* mmmdcccxvii/4 *Anti-Scepticism. **1909** W. James *Plur. Universe* vii. 277 To say nothing of your traditional Oxford devotion to Aristotle and Plato, the leaven of T. H. Green probably works still too strongly here for his *anti-sensationalism to be outgrown quickly. **1863** E. Dicey *Federal States* II. 188 Moderate *anti-slaveryism is obviously the correct thing. **1814** W. Taylor in *Month. Rev.* LXXIII. 66 The established Church of Prussia now teaches *anti-supernaturalism from the pulpit. **1856** Smyth *Rom. Fam. Coins* 191 The *anti-teetotalism of this stern reprover of others. **1843** Miall *Nonconf.* III. 446 The potentiality of *antiturnpikeism is proclaimed. **1895** G. B. Shaw *Sanity of Art* (1908) 33 The huge blunder of *anti-Wagnerism. **1930** L. Fischer *Soviets in World Affairs* II. xvii. 535 The elements of his *credo* were monarchy, anti-revolutionism and *anti-Westernism. **1959** *Economist* 14 Feb. 569/1 They have exploited Afro-Asian anti-westernism.

¶ Examples of the purposes to which *anti-* has been put are seen in the following:—***anti-contagious-diseasist***, ***anti-gigman-ic***, ***anti-money-an***, ***anti-pent-agonist***, ***anti-philippizing***, ***anti-street-musical***, ***anti-tintinnabularian*** (an enemy of bells), ***anti-tobacconal***.

1880 W. Wren in *Daily News* 28 Jan. 2/4 The Local Optionists, the *Anti-contagious-Diseasists. **1831** Carlyle in Froude *Life* II. 156 My visit to London is *antigigmanic from heart to skin. **1683** *Lond. Gaz.* mdccclxxxiii/4 A Confutation of the Whiggish Conspirators *Anti-Mony-an Principle. **1642** Sir E. Dering *Sp. on Relig.* xvi. 74 The point already warme between a reverend..Bishop and his *Anti-pent-agonists. **1853** Grote *Greece* ii. xc. XI. 617 Hegesippus, a strenuous *antiphilippising politician. **1865** *Pall Mall G.* 10 June 9 Mr. Mansfield, who has always been *anti-street-musical, sentenced them to pay a fine of 40*s*. **1818** J. H. Frere *Whistlecr. Nat. Poem* iii. xxxi, A prudent monk, their reader and librarian..Himself an *anti-tintinnabularian. **1862** *Cornh. Mag.* VI. 613 Excessive smoking is carried to a pitch that would make the hair of any *anti-tobacconal stand on end with horror.

IV. With reduplication of the prefix. Also *anti-anti* used *absol.*

1896 W. E. Gladstone in *Daily News* 29 May 6 Of course, I am strongly *anti*-anti-Semitism. **1900** M. Beerbohm *Around Theatres* (1924) I. 182, I gave them [i.e. my reasons] merely because they will explain equally why a play ought not to end on a high note, and will thus confute the anti-anticlimax party. **1951** R. Campbell *Light on Dark Horse* xiv. 200, I was dumbfounded by this anti-anticlimax, if I may coin such a word. **1953** *Times* 7 Dec. 24 A well-worn anti-anti-Communist technique; he denounced.. Brownell's handling of the White case as 'McCarthyism'. **1961** *New Statesman* 25 Aug. 234/2 It is not Communism that has been preoccupying Senators of the far right lately, but something called 'anti-anti-Communism', a barbarism coined by the intellectual wing of the McCarthy movement. **1962** *New Scientist* 15 Mar. 607/1 The weapons..include.. anti-missile and anti-satellite missiles, 'anti-antis' and decoys. *Ibid.* 22 Mar. 677 (*caption*) Satellite bombers ..'antis' and 'anti-antis'. *Ibid.* 677/1 There is every prospect of a major arms race in space, with the development of a variety of 'anti' and 'anti-anti' devices.

anti- *pref.*[2] A variant of ante- 'before,' being the form in It. and OFr., and occasionally in L., hence sometimes also in Eng. in words from these, as ***antibrachial***, ***anticamera***, ***antichamber***, ***anticipate***.

anti-acid, -aphrodisiac, -apoplectic, arthritic, -asthmatic: see antacid, etc.

‖**antiæ** (ˈæntiːː), *sb. pl. Zool.* [L., for *antiæ comæ* fore-locks, f. *anti-us* fore.] Forelocks.

1874 Coues *Birds of N.W.* 720 Frontal antiæ reaching beyond middle of nostrils.

anti-aircraft (ˌæntɪˈɛəkrɑːft, -æ-), *a.* [anti-[1] 4.] Used for defence against hostile aircraft; esp. ***anti-aircraft gun***, one for firing shells at a very high elevation. Hence *ellipt.* or as *sb.*, anti-aircraft defences, regiment, etc. Abbrev. *A.A.* (see A III); see also ack-ack.

1914 *Scotsman* 25 Sept. 5/4 An anti-aircraft gun of the Third Army Corps. **1919** *Athenæum* 23 May 360/2 The anti-aircraft force. **1939** *Times Weekly* 15 Feb. 8 Two Regular regiments of anti-aircraft artillery were being brought to London to give additional protection to the city. **1947** L. Hastings *Dragons are Extra* ix. 197, I had been passed A1 by the doctors in London and found myself back in uniform in anti-aircraft. **1959** *New Statesman* 3 Jan. 6/3 The Nike-Zeus anti-aircraft missile system. **1959** *Listener* 24 Dec. 1108/2 The anti-aircraft did its stuff.

anti-American (æntɪəˈmɛrɪkən), *a.* [f. anti-[1] 3 a + American.] Hostile to the interests of the United States, opposed to Americans. Hence **anti-Aˈmericanism**, a spirit of hostility towards Americans.

1773 in *Amer. Speech* (1945) XX. 269 The anti-American doctrine of the parliament's right in all cases. **1838** in J. S. Buckingham *America* (1841) I. ix. 173 Now our young men are rogues and fops, with extravagant anti-American notions. **1844** P. Hone *Diary* (1889) II. 238 Most of them seem to have escaped the foppery of foreign manners and the bad taste of anti-Americanism. **1932** H. Nicolson *Public Faces* xi. 301 Not only did he regard it [*sc.* the communication] as fresh in tone, but he regarded it as anti-American in substance..not merely against the Monroe Doctrine, but against the freedom of the seas. **1958** *Spectator* 1 Aug. 167/1 It is not anti-Americanism to feel that now, more than ever, we need to cultivate our own idiom and qualities. **1963** *Guardian* 21 Feb. 16/7 The Labour Party—which is anti-American without being pro-European.

‖**antiar** (ˈæntʃə(r), ˈæntɪə(r)). [a. Jav. *antjar*, *antschar.*] The Upas tree of Java, *Antiaris toxicaria*; also, the poison obtained from it. ***antiar resin***, a non-poisonous product of the same tree.

antiarin (ˈæntɪərɪn). *Chem.* [mod. f. prec. + -in.] The poisonous principle of the Upas tree.

1863 Watts *Dict. Chem.* I. 310 Antiarin..is employed by the Javanese for poisoning their arrows. **1866** Masters in *Treas. Bot.* 74 The Upas-tree, when pierced, exudes a milky juice, which contains an acrid virulent poison, called *Antiarin.*

anti-attrition (ˌæntɪəˈtrɪʃən). [anti- 6.] That which opposes or resists attrition. *spec.* Any compound applied to machinery to resist the effects of friction; as black lead mixed with grease, peroxide of iron, finely-divided hæmatite, etc. Also *fig.*

1833 Arnold in *Life* 349 It robs me of what is naturally my anti attrition. **1834** *Edin. Rev.* LVIII. 457 A deeper gratitude for the blessings of anti-attrition.

antibacchic (æntɪˈbækɪk), *a. Pros.* [f. L. *antibacch-us*, variant of *antibacchīus* + -ic.] Of the nature of the antibacchius.

1835 Scheller *Lex. tot. Latin.* s.v., *Versus antibacchius*, which consists of antibacchic feet.

‖**antibacchius** (ˌæntɪbəˈkaɪəs). *Pros.* [L., a Gr. ἀντιβάκχειος, f. ἀντί opposite to + βακχεῖος: see bacchius.] A reversed bacchius, a trisyllabic metrical foot of two long and one short syllable.

1589 Puttenham *Eng. Poesie* (Arb.) 134 For your foote *antibacchius*, of two long and a short ye haue these wordes [*fōrsākĕn*] [*impūgnĕd*].

antibilious (æntɪˈbɪlɪəs), *a.* [anti- 3.] Of use against biliousness.

1817 Jane Austen *Sanditon* (1954) ii. 373 The Sea air & Sea Bathing..were nearly infallible..; They were..anti-bilious & anti-rheumatic. **1835** T. Walker *Original* i. 2 Rejecting nothing as too trifling, provided it can excite in you an antibilious sensation. **1882** *Standard* 19 Sept. 4/3 Antibilious pills.

antibiosis (ˌæntɪbaɪəˈʊsɪs, -bɪ-). *Biol.* [mod.L., ad. F. *antibiose* (P. Vuillemin 1890, in *Compt. Rend. Assoc. Franç. Avanc. Sci. 1889* II. 525), f. anti-[1] 2 + sym)biosis.] A condition of antagonism between organisms, esp. micro-organisms (opp. *symbiosis*).

1899 H. M. Ward in *Ann. Bot.* XIII. 555 Extremes.. where one of the two associated organisms is injuring the other, as exemplified by many parasites... This state of affairs has been termed *Antibiosis.* **1949** H. W. Florey *Antibiotics* I. i. 73 Although much work has been done and considerable interest has been taken in antibiosis during the last 60 years it is only recently that it has reached its present intensity.

antibiotic (ˌæntɪbaɪˈɒtɪk), *a.* (*sb.*) [f. anti- 3 + Gr. βιωτικ-ός fit for life.] **1.** *rare.* Opposed to a belief in the presence or possibility of life.

1860 Maury *Phys. Geog. Sea* xiv. 604, I incline to the antibiotic hypothesis. **1877** W. Thomson *Voy. Challenger* I. i. 4 The antibiotic prejudice.

2. [ad. F. *antibiotique* (P. Vuillemin 1890, in *Compt. Rend. Assoc. Franç. Avanc. Sci. 1889* II. 526).] Injurious to or destructive of living matter, esp. micro-organisms. So ˌantibiˈotically *adv.*

1894 *Phil. Trans.* B. CLXXXV. 312 Production of a bactericidal, or at least antibiotic, substance. **1942** S. A. Waksman et al. in *Soil Science* LIV. 295 The most active antagonistic cultures were studied in detail, and several antibiotic substances were isolated. **1945** S. A. Waksman *Microbial Antagonisms & Antibiotic Substances* 271 *Antibiotic*, inhibiting the growth or the metabolic activities of bacteria and other microorganisms by a chemical substance of microbial origin. **1946** *Nature* 6 July 24/2 Antibiotically active cell-free watery extracts could be prepared from cultures on Dorset's egg medium.

3. Hence as *sb.*, an antibiotic substance: one of a class of substances produced by living organisms and capable of destroying or inhibiting the growth of micro-organisms; *spec.* any of these substances used for therapeutic purposes. Also used of synthetic organic compounds having similar properties.

1944 *Lancet* 18 Mar. 375/2 (*title*) The Mould Antibiotics. **1949** H. W. Florey et al. *Antibiotics* II. xlvii. 1438 The antibiotics comprise substances with diverse chemical structures and biological activities. They range in their action from those which inhibit the growth of certain strains of bacteria in a highly selective manner to those which are relatively toxic to all living cells. **1958** *Listener* 16 Oct. 620/1 The discovery of 'interferon', a sort of virus antibiotic.

Also in *Comb.*

1956 *Nature* 25 Feb. 368/1 The search for new antibiotic-producing organisms, particularly streptomyces, from Malayan soil continues. **1961** *Times* 17 Mar. 5/4 Of the antibiotic-resistant staphylococci.. 90 per cent were isolated from infants born in the hospital.

† **anti-Birmingham, -Bromingham.** *Eng. Hist.* [ANTI- 5.] An anti-Whig, a Tory; a nickname given to opponents of the Exclusion Bill in 1680; its supporters, who claimed to be 'true Protestants,' being ironically nicknamed by the Tories, 'Birmingham (*i.e* counterfeit) Protestants,' 'alluding to false groats counterfeited at that place'; whence at length *Birminghams* and *Anti-Birminghams*, terms finally merged in Whig and Tory. See North *Examen* (1740) II. v. ¶ 10. 321.

1681 DRYDEN *Abs. & Achit.*, *To Reader*, The longest chapter in Deuteronomy has not curses enough for an Anti-Bromingham. **1849** MACAULAY *Hist. Eng.* I. 256 Those who took the King's side were Antibirminghams, Abhorrers, and Tantivies.

antibody ('æntɪbɒdɪ). *Physiol.* [tr. G. *antikörper*: see ANTI-¹ 2 a.] Any of the proteins, naturally present in the body or produced in response to the introduction of an antigen, which react with specific antigens.

1901 HEKTOEN & RIESMAN *Pathol.* 231 Substances which appear during spontaneous or artificial infection or intoxication are known as antibodies (*Antikörper*) and antitoxins. **1921** R. A. FREEMAN in *Edin. Rev.* July 33 Those antibodies by which the existence of aggregates of the lower organisms is brought to an end. **1955** *Sci. News Let.* 8 Jan. 19/2 Antibodies are the substances formed in the body to fight off invading disease germs.. a different kind of antibody being formed for each different kind of disease germ.

Also *fig.*

1921 R. A. FREEMAN *Social Decay* 287 The Social Antibody is not Mechanism itself but the domination by it of human life and human activities. **1947** J. HAYWARD *Prose Lit. since 1939* 47 The writer himself creating the antibodies to protect his integrity.

antibrachial (æntɪ'brækɪəl), *a.* *Anat.* [f. med.L. *antibrachium* for *ante-brachium* (f. *ante* before + *brachium* arm) + -AL¹.] Of or pertaining to the forearm.

1836-39 TODD *Cycl. Anat. & Phys.* II. 369/2 The posterior superficial antibrachial region. **1880** HUXLEY in *Times* 25 Dec. 4/1 Complete, sub-equal antebrachial and crural bones.

ˌanti-ˈBritish (stress variable), *a.* [f. ANTI-¹ 3 a + BRITISH.] Hostile to the interests of Britain, opposed to the British. Hence **anti-Britisher**, one who is antagonistic to the British or British interests; **anti-Britishism**, a spirit of hostility towards the British.

a **1845** SYD. SMITH *Irish Ch.* in *Wks.* (1859) II. 334/1 Such a piece of anti-British villany. **1898** *Daily News* 4 Oct. 4/5 Germany has withdrawn her anti-British support from the Transvaal. **1902** *Daily Chron.* 10 Mar. 7/5 The result is that Dutch Reformed ministers are, as a rule, anti-British. *Ibid.* 15 Sept. 5/3 Commandant Wolmarans.. an extremely bitter anti-Britisher. **1909** H. G. WELLS *Tono-Bungay* III. iv, The captain helped him to express his own malignant Anti-Britishism. **1928** *Observer* 18 Mar. 17/4 There is no anti-Britishism here, but I am puzzled by the objection to our being pro-American.

antiburgher (ˌæntɪ'bɜːgər). [ANTI- 5.] A section of the Secession Church in Scotland (now merged in the United Presbyterian), which held it unscriptural to take the Burgess Oath, and in 1747 separated on this question from the other or 'Burgher' section; the two reunited in 1820.

[**1753** W. HUTTON *Calumny Rep. & Falsehood Det.* 55 You extoll the leniency of Mr. Gib, and his Antiburgess Presbyters, as you call them.] **1766** J. BROWN *Hist. Seceders* 67 Meanwhile the Antiburghers to support their cause, persecuted their Burgher brethren with deposition and excommunication. **1815** SCOTT *Guy M.* xxxii, Troth, sir, I am no free to swear—we aye gaed to the Antiburgher meeting.

antic ('æntɪk), *a.* and *sb.* Forms: 6-7 **antike, -cke,** 7-8 **-ick,** (7 **antique**), 6- **antic.** [app. ad. It. *antico*, but used as equivalent to It. *grottesco*, f. *grotta*, 'a cauerne or hole vnder grounde' (Florio), orig. applied to fantastic representations of human, animal, and floral forms, incongruously running into one another, found in exhuming some ancient remains (as the Baths of Titus) in Rome, whence extended to anything similarly incongruous or bizarre: see GROTESQUE. Cf. Serlio *Architettura* (Venice 1551) IV. lf. 70 a: 'seguitare le uestigie de gli *antiqui* Romani, li quali costumarono di far.. diuerse bizarrie, che si dicono *grottesche*.' Apparently, from this ascription of grotesque work to the ancients, it was in English at first called *antike, anticke*, the name *grotesco, grotesque*, not being adopted till a century later. *Antic* was thus not developed in Eng. from ANTIQUE, but was a distinct use of the word from its first introduction. Yet in 17th c. it was occas. written *antique*, a spelling proper to the other word.]

A. *adj.*

1. *Arch.* and *Decorative Art.* Grotesque, in composition or shape; grouped or figured with fantastic incongruity; bizarre.

1548 HALL *Chron. Hen. VIII.* an. 12 (R.) A fountayne of embowed woorke.. ingrayled with anticke woorkes. **1589** *Hawkins' 2nd Voy.* in Arb. *Garner* V. 126 To paint their bodies with curious knots or antike work, as every man, in his own fancy deviseth. **1598** FLORIO, *Grottesca*, a kind of rugged vnpolished painters worke, anticke work. **1603** —— *Montaigne* I. xxvii. (1632) 89 All void places.. he filleth up with antike Boscage or Grotesko workes. **1623** COCKERAM *Anticke Worke*, a worke in painting or caruing of diuers shapes of Beasts, Birds, Flowers, etc., vnperfectly mixt, and made one of another. **1624** WOTTON *Archit.* 97 Whether *Grotesca* (as the Italians) or Antique worke (as wee call it) should be receiued. **1703** *City & Country Build.* 5 Antick, or Antique-work.. a confused Composure of Figures of different Natures, and Sexes, etc. As of Men, Beasts, Birds, Flowers, Fishes, etc. And such like Fancies as are not *in Rerum Natura*... This Work which we call *Antick*, the Italians call *Grotesca*.. and the French *Grotesque*. **1826** J. ELMES *Dict. Fine Arts*, *Antick*, Odd, ridiculously wild.

2. Absurd from fantastic incongruity; grotesque, bizarre, uncouthly ludicrous: **a.** in gesture.

1590 MARLOWE *Edw. II.* I. i. 167 My men, like satyrs,.. Shall with their goat-feet dance the antic hay. **1602** SHAKS. *Ham.* I. v. 172 How strange or odde so ere I beare myselfe .. To put an Anticke disposition on. **1603** DRAYTON *Her. Epist.* xi. 13 A Satyres Anticke parts he play'd. **1645** MILTON *Colast.* Wks. 1851, 365 No antic hobnaile at a Morris, but is more hansomly facetious. **1660** H. MORE *Myst. Godl.* III. ix. 77 Their religious Rites and Ceremonies being uncouth and antick. **1719** DE FOE *Crusoe* 183 He came running to me.. making a many antic gestures. **1805** WORDSWORTH *Prel.* VII. (1850) 178 An antic pair Of monkeys on his back. **1878** G. MACDONALD *Phantastes* x. 149 Performing the most antic homage.

b. in shape.

1642 R. CARPENTER *Exper.* III. v. 53 To appeare in strange and antick shapes. **1788** *New Lond. Mag.* 17 Several antic figures in shapes of boys danced. **1861** *Tannhäuser* 20 The twilight troop'd with antic shapes.

c. in dress or attire.

1642 MILTON *Apol. Smect.* Wks. 1738 I. 125 It had no Rubric to be sung in an antic Cope upon the Stage of a High Altar. **1665** GLANVILL *Sceps. Sci.* 96 Their antick deckings with feathers. **1727** SWIFT *Gulliver* III. vii. 223 Two rows of guards.. dressed after a very antic manner. **1776** *Chron.* in *Ann. Reg.* 155/2 An ass.. with a fellow in an antick dress riding upon it. **1858** HAWTHORNE *Fr. & It. Jrnls.* I. 80 The papal guards, in the strangest antique and antic costume that was ever seen.

† **3.** Having the features grotesquely distorted like 'antics' in architecture; grinning. *Obs.*

1594 DRAYTON *Idea* 424 Making withall some filthy Antike Face. **1611** COTGR., *Gargouille*, The mouth of a Spowt, representing a Serpent, or the Anticke face of some other ouglie creature. **1620** QUARLES *Jonah* (1638) 41 Your mimick mouthes, your antick faces. *a* **1631** DONNE *Elegies* (R.) Name not these living death-heds unto me, For these not ancient but antique be. *a* **1659** CLEVELAND *Wks.* (1687) 31 The Antick heads which plac'd without The Church, do gape and disembogue a Spout. **1697** DAMPIER *Voy.* (1729) III. I. 406 The little Tame-Owl.. making divers antick faces.

4. *Comb.*, as † **antic-faced** (see 3).

1635 J. TAYLOR (Water P.) *Parr* in *Harl. Misc.* (Malh.) IV. 205 An antick-faced fellow, called Jack, or John the Fool.

B. *sb.*

† **1.** *Arch.* and *Decorative Art.* An ornamental representation, purposely monstrous, caricatured, or incongruous, of objects of the animal or the vegetable kingdom, or of both combined. **a.** Fantastic tracery or sculpture. *Obs.*

1548 HALL *Chron. Hen. VIII.* an. 18 (R.) Aboue the arches were made many sondri antikes and diuises. **1596** SPENSER *F.Q.* II. vii. 4 Woven with antickes and wyld ymagery. **1645** EVELYN *Mem.* (1857) I. 146 The walls and roof are painted, not with antiques and grotesques, like our Bodleian. **1653** URQUHART *Rabelais* I. viii, A faire Cornucopia or Horne of abundance, such as you see in Anticks. **1725** BRADLEY *Fam. Dict.*, *Grotesque* or *Grotesc*, a work, the same with what is sometimes called *Antick*. **1830** R. STUART *Dict. Archit.*: *Antics*, In architecture, Fancies having no foundation in nature, as sphinxes, centaurs, syrens, representations of different sorts of flowers growing on the same stem; grotesque ornaments of all kinds, as lions and pards with acanthus' tails, or any other tails but their own proper ones; human forms with similar ridiculous appendages. Ornaments, although strictly natural, in an unnatural situation; as, caryatidæ of all kinds.. The villa Palagonia, in Sicily, is an antic, from entrance gate to chimney top.

b. A caryatid, or (sculptured) human figure represented in an impossible position.

c **1590** MARLOWE *Faustus* (2nd vers.) 715 To make his monks.. stand like apes, And point like antics at his triple crown. **1615** BP. HALL *Contempl.* (1837) I. XVIII. iii. 395 Like some antic statue, in a posture of impotent endeavour. **1638** CHILLINGWORTH *Relig. Prot.* I. vi. §54, 374 Those crouching Anticks which seeme in great buildings to labour under the weight they beare. **1640** BP. HALL *Chr. Moder.* 20/1 Those antics of stone.. carved out under the end of great beams in vast buildings, which seem.. as if they were hard put to it with the weight. *c* **1656** HALES *Gold. Rem.* (1688) 167 Those that build houses make anticks that seem to hold up the beams. **1830** (See prec.).

c. A grotesquely figured representation of a face, such as are used in gargoyles.

1601 HOLLAND *Pliny* (1634) II. 552 To set vp Gargils or Antiques at the top of a Gauill end, as a finiall to the crest tiles. **1683** *Lond Gaz.* mdccclix/8 Three Gold Seals, one with an Old Man's Head, another with a Woman's Head, and the other with an Antick.

2. A grotesque or ludicrous gesture, posture, or trick; also *fig.* of behaviour. (Commonly in *pl.*)

1529 FOXE in *Supplic.* (1871) Introd. 9 In sothe it maketh me to laugh, to see yᵉ mery Antiques of M. More. **1572** SIR T. SMITH in Ellis *Orig. Lett.* II. 191 III. 20 Vaulting with notable supersaltes and through hoopes, and last of all the Antiques, of carrying of men one uppon an other which som men call *labores Herculis*. **1633** FORD *Love's Sacr.* III. iv, A pox upon your outlandish feminine anticks. **1823** LAMB *Elia* II. v. (1865) 266 This mortal frame, while thou didst play thy brief antics amongst us. **1843** LEVER *Jack Hinton* xxvii. 189 Performing more antics than Punch in a pantomine.

† **3.** A grotesque pageant or theatrical representation. *Obs.*

1588 SHAKS. *L.L.L.* V. i. 119 Some delightfull ostentation, or show, or pageant, or anticke, or fire-worke. *Ibid.* v. i. 154 We will haue, if this fadge not, an Antique. **1633** FORD *Love's Sacr.* III. ii, Performed by knights and ladies of his court, In nature of an antick. **1673** *Ladies Call.* II. iii. §26 How preposterous is it for an old woman.. to be at masks and dancings, when she is only fit to act the antics.

b. *Hence*, A grotesque or motley company. *rare.*

1589 WARNER *Alb. Eng.* (1612) 345 Heards-men, Sheapheards, Plow-men, and Hinds: this Anticke of Groomes.

4. A performer who plays a grotesque or ludicrous part, a clown, mountebank, or merry-andrew.

1564 *Cap* in *Thynne's Animadv.* App. 130 Thou wearest me.. sometime lyke a Royster, sometime like a Souldiour, sometime lyke an Antique. **1592** GREENE in *Shaks. Cent. Praise* 2 Those Anticks garnisht in our colours. **1618** BP. HALL *Serm.* v. 113 Are they Christians, or Antics in some Carnival? **1671** MILTON *Sams.* 1325 Jugglers and dancers, antics, mummers, mimics. **1719** DE FOE *Crusoe* (1858) 341 Dancing and hallooing like an antic. **1827** HOOD *Mids. Fairies* liv, How Puck, the antic.. Had blithely jested with calamity.

b. *transf.* and *fig.*

1593 SHAKS. *Rich. II*, III. ii. 162 There [death] the Antique sits, Scoffing his state, and grinning at his Pompe. [Cf. *a* 1631 in A 3. A death's head grins like an 'antic.'] **1606** G. W[OODCOCKE] *Hist. Justine* 10 b, There flocked a great throng of souldiers about him, wondering at this so mishapen an Anticke. **1823** LAMB *Elia* II. xxiv. (1865) 409 [A pun] is an antic which does not stand upon manners, but comes bounding into the presence. **1864** DICKENS *Mut. Fr.* II. i. 172 A little crooked antic of a child.

† **c.** phr. *to dance antics*. *Obs.*

1544 ASCHAM *Toxoph.* (Arb.) 47 Myght be thought to daunce Anticke very properly. *Ibid.* 147 Menne that shoulde daunce antiques. **1602** DEKKER *Satirom.* 245 Yet must we Dance Antickes on your Paper. [**1635** AUSTIN *Medit.* 208 Will Herod reward the Dance of an Antique with the Head of a Prophet? **1687** CONGREVE *Old Bachelor* III. x. Stage Direct., After the song a dance of Antics.]

5. *Comb.*, as **antick-cutter**, a carver of grotesques.

1660 H. BLOOME *Archit.* (title-page), Antick-Cutters.

antic ('æntɪk), *v.* Pa. t. **anticked, -ickt.** [f. prec. adj. and sb.; cf. to *caper* and *capers*.]

† **1.** *trans.* To make antic or grotesque. *Obs.*

1606 SHAKS. *Ant. & Cl.* II. vii. 132 The wilde disguise hath almost Antickt vs all.

2. *intr.* To perform antics, act as an antic. Also in phr. *to antic it.*

1589 NASHE in Greene *Menaph.* Ded. (Arb.) 17 They might have antickt it.. up and downe the countrey with the King of Fairies. **1606** WARNER *Alb. Eng.* XIV. xci. 367 Now Pincht they him, antickt about, and on, and off him lept. **1822** B. CORNWALL *Flood of Thessaly* II. 353 So, ere it slumber'd in entire repose, Antick'd the Ocean. **1829** HOOD *Epping Hunt* lxxiv, Some rolled about, And anticked as they rode. **1879** G. MEREDITH *Egoist* Prel. 7 Until he begins insensibly to frolic and antic, unknown to himself.

anticachectic (ˌæntɪkə'kɛktɪk), *a.* and *sb.* *Med.* [f. ANTI- 3 + Gr. καχεκτικός: see CACHECTIC.]

A. *adj.* Used against cachexy, or a bad state of the body. **B.** *sb.* (sc. medicine).

1719 *Glossogr. Nova*, *Anti-chachectics*, Remedies that correct the ill disposition of the blood. **1706** PHILLIPS, *Anticachecticks*. **1773** JOHNSON, *Antichachectick*. **1880** *Syd. Soc. Lex.*, *Anticachectic*, Opposed to what is cachectic.

antical (æn'taɪkəl), *a.* *Bot.* [f. L. *antīc-us* front (f. *ante* before) + -AL¹.] Fronting external objects, and thus remote from the axis.

1866 *Treas. Bot.* 75 The lip of an Orchis is antical.

† **anti'camera.** *Obs.* [a. It. *anticamera* (Sp. *antecamera*), f. *anti*:—L. *ante* before + *camera* chamber.] An antechamber.

1625 BACON *Ess.* (Arb.) 552 With Chambers, Bedchamber, Anticamera, and Recamera, ioyning to it. **1650** R. STAPYLTON *Strada's Low-C. Wars* x. 16 The priest, that said Masse in his Anti-Camera. *a* **1670** HACKET *Abp. Williams* I. 205 (D.) The Great Seal and the keeper of it waited two hours in the Anti-camera.

anticatarrhal (ˌæntɪkə'tɑːrəl), *a.* and *sb.* [ANTI-¹ 3.] **A.** *adj.* Of use against catarrh. **B.** *sb.* (sc. medicine).

1753 CHAMBERS *Cycl. Supp.* s.v., Anticatarrhal medicines, Anticatarrhal prescriptions, etc. **1853** in MAYNE *Exp. Lex.*

anticathode (ˌæntɪ'kæθəʊd). *Electr.* [ANTI-¹ 2.] The metal plate opposite the cathode in an X-ray tube, upon which the cathode rays impinge and produce X-rays.

1907 A. F. HERTZ in *Practitioner* Apr. 524 A pencil, which points directly towards the anticathode, is fastened behind the fluorescent screen. **1913** *Physical Rev.* II. 416 The anticathode..consists of a single piece of wrought tungsten, having at the end facing the cathode a diameter of 1·9 cm. **1923** GLAZEBROOK *Dict. Applied Physics* IV. 595/2 The electrons (cathode rays)..are directed on a heavy metal anticathode or target. **1951** J. R. PARTINGTON *Gen. & Inorg. Chem.* (ed. 2) viii. 191 When cathode rays strike a material target, which in the X-ray tube consists of a metal..plate called an anti-cathode, this emits a radiation which passes outside the tube.

anti-Catholic (æntɪˈkæθəlɪk), *a.* and *sb.* [ANTI-[1] 3, 5 ¶.] **A.** *adj.* Opposed to what is, or is called, catholic. **B.** *sb.* (sc. person).

1665 N. FRENCH *Let.* 19 Sept. in *Hist. Wks.* (1846) I. 136 A principal Leader in the Anti-catholick Ormonian Faction. **1780** H. WALPOLE *Let.* 6 Feb. (1904) XI. 125 Lord George Gordon..dresses..like the first Methodists; though I take the modern ones to be no anti-Catholics. **1819** S. PARR *Wks.* (1828) VII. 142 The Anti-Catholics have gone to the east and west, to the north and south, for recruits. **1823** SCOTT *Peveril* (1865) 168 The commercial and nautical interests of England were indeed particularly anti-catholic.

anticausotic (ˌæntɪkɔːˈsɒtɪk), *a.* and *sb. Med.* [f. ANTI-[1] 3 + Gr. *καυσωτικός, f. καυσό-εσθαι to be in a burning fever.] **A.** *adj.* Of use against a burning fever. **B.** *sb.* (sc. medicine).

1753 CHAMBERS *Cycl. Supp.*, An Anticausotic syrup. **1853** MAYNE *Exp. Lex.*, *Anticausotic*, Having power to remove or moderate an ardent fever; a medicine used for this purpose.

anticer (ˈæntaɪsə(r)). [Contraction of ANTI-ICER.] = ANTI-ICER.

1935 B. LOCKSPEISER in *Aircraft Engineering* Nov. 280/3 The anticer has been tested under ice forming conditions on ..aeroplanes. **1941** *Aeroplane Spotter* 23 Jan. 30/3 *Anticer*, a device for preventing the formation of ice on aircraft, usually in the form of a liquid paste. Should not be confused with De-icers, which are devices for removing ice when it has formed.

anticeremonial (ˌæntɪserɪˈməʊnɪəl), *a.* [ANTI-[1] 3 or 4.] Opposed to ceremonies.

1655 SANDERSON *21 Serm.* (1673) Pref. §7 These our Anticeremonial Brethren. **1668** *2nd Disc. Relig. Eng.* 29 Nothing appears to be done in favour of the Anticeremonial.

anticereˈmonialist. *rare.* [f. prec. + -IST.] One who is opposed to ceremonies.

1865 LITTLEDALE *North Side of Altar* 4 Nor would an anticeremonialist, if not exceptionally scrupulous, hesitate to comply with so harmless a custom.

†**anticereˈmonian**, *sb. Obs.* [ANTI-[1] 5.] = ANTICEREMONIALIST. Also *adj.* or *attrib.*

a **1644** QUARLES *Whipper Whipt* in *Chertsey Libr.* I. 166 Did not the Doctor..as good as confesse himself an enemy to Anticeremonians? **1657** SANDERSON *Serm.* (1674) Pref. §5 The usual..Objections of our Anti-ceremonian Brethren.

anti-chamber, obs. var. ANTECHAMBER *sb.*

antichlor(e (ˈæntɪklɔə(r)). *Chem.* [f. ANTI-[1] 6 + CHLOR(INE.] A substance used to obviate the injurious after-effects of chlorine in bleaching.

1869 ROSCOE *Elem. Chem.* 131 Sulphur dioxide is also employed as an antichlor. **1873** FOWNES *Chem.* 205 Much used as antichlores for removing the last traces of chlorine from bleached goods.

anti-choice (æntɪˈtʃɔɪs), *a. U.S.* Also **antichoice.** [ANTI-[1] 4.] Opposed to granting pregnant women the right to choose abortion. Cf. *pro-life* adj. s.v. PRO-[1].

1978 *Ms.* Oct. 8/1 What hypocrisy to call such anti-humanitarian people 'pro-life'. Call them what they are—antichoice. **1980** *Washington Post* 19 Jan. A3/1 If the anti-choice movement succeeds in defeating only a few of those who have had the courage to help lead the fight for woman's right to choose, [etc.]. **1983** *Ibid.* 16 June A10/2 The decision will simply convince anti-choice groups to intensify their efforts to restrict abortions. **1986** *Los Angeles Times* 9 Sept. I. 12/3 Zschau..got the anti-choice rating in 1985 because he opposed the use of U.N. funds to pay for abortions in China.

Antichrist (ˈæntɪkraɪst). Also 4-5 **ante-**, 4-7 **anticrist**, (4 **ancrist**, 5 **ancryst**), 6 **antycryst**, **antechriste.** [a. OFr. *antecrist(e*, ad. L. *antechrīstus*, a. Gr. ἀντίχρῑστος (1 John ii. 18), f. ἀντί against + χρῑστός CHRIST.]

1. An enemy or opponent of Christ.

1340 HAMPOLE. *Pr. Consc.* 4227 Fals anticristes he sal þam calle. **1382** WYCLIF *1 John* ii. 18 Now many antecristes ben made. *c* **1400** *Apol. Loll.* 54 Ilk one contrary to Crist is anticrist. **1579** FULKE *Heskins's Parl.* 255 He is defamed of more than heresie, and proued to bee an antichrist. **1646** GAULE *Cases Consc.* 20 A Witch is an Anticrist. **1751** CHAMBERS *Cycl.* s.v., Jews, Infidels, etc., may be said to be Antichrists. **1860** PUSEY *Min. Proph.* 587 The first Anti-Christ, Simon Magus, was said to have met his death in some attempt to fly.

2. The title of a great personal opponent of Christ and His kingdom, expected by the early church to appear before the end of the world, and much referred to in the Middle Ages.

a **1300** *Cursor M.* 22006 Nu sal yee her, i wil you rede, Hu þat anticrist [*v.r.* antecrist] sal brede. **1340** HAMPOLE *Pr. Consc.* 4065 Anticrist ar þat tyme sal noght com. *Ibid.* 3996 Of ancrist commyng, and his pousté. **1398** TREVISA *Barth. De P.R.* XIX. lxxx. (1495) 914 The egges of adders..ben wonder yelowe, slimy and gleymy: and of thyse egges comyth Cokatrice: and of the venemous juys shall come Antecrist. *a* **1500** in Wright *Voc.* 217 *Hic antechristus*, ancryst. **1509** FISHER *Wks.* (1876) 192 God shal make shorte the tyme of Antecryst. **1651** HOBBES *Leviath.* (1839) 552 He handleth the question, whether the Pope be Antichrist? **1753** CHAMBERS *Cycl. Supp.* s.v., Hippolitus and others held that the devil himself was the true Antichrist. **1791** D'ISRAELI *Cur. Lit.* (1834) VI. 247 There were to be three Anti-Christs, and..the last should be born..in the year 1790. **1856** R. VAUGHAN *Mystics* I. 143 The Franciscans think..that we live in, or near, the days of Antichrist.

b. Applied by some to the Pope or Papal power.

c **1370** WYCLIF *Agst. Begging Friers* (1608) 24 This false heresie and tyrantrie of Antichrist. **1566** *Let. Ch. Scot. to Eng. Ch.* 27 Dec. 91 The Bishops and Pastors of England, who have renounced the Roman Antichrist. **1641** MILTON *Ch. Govt.* vi. (1851) 123 That irreconcileable schisme of perdition and Apostasy, the Roman Antichrist. **1868** MILMAN *St. Paul's* x. 247 Against that antichrist the Pope. *fig.* **1728** POPE *Dunc.* II. 12 Rome in her capitol saw Querno sit, Thron'd on sev'n hills, the Antichrist of wit.

†**antiˈchristendom.** *Obs. rare*[−1]. [f. prec., after *Christendom.*] The dominion of Antichrist.

a **1638** MEDE *Wks.* v. 921 Blaspheming God by another Idolatrous worship, and warring at length against his Saints and overcoming them. This I would call Antichristendom.

antichristian (æntɪˈkrɪstɪən), *a.* and *sb.* Also 6 **antichristen.** [f. ANTICHRIST, after *Christian*; but often treated as f. ANTI- + CHRISTIAN, in which sense written in 17-18th c. with a hyphen.]

A. *adj.*

1. Of or pertaining to Antichrist.

1532 MORE *Confut. Tindale* Wks. 1557, 510/1 Tindales antichristen heresyes. **1533** TINDALE *Supper of Lord* Wks. III. 235 The authority of his antichristian synagogue. **1575-85** ABP. SANDYS *Serm.* (1841) 67 The head of the church antichristian is the pope. *a* **1680** BUTLER *Rem.* (1759) I. 354 More Protestant Blood..than ever was spilt either by Rome, Heathen, or Antichristian. **1860** FROUDE *Hist. Eng.* V. xxix. 475 Under no temptation would Knox have accepted an office which he believed to be antichristian.

2. Opposed to what is Christian or to Christianity. (Often *anti-christian.*)

1587 GOLDING *De Mornay* xxxiii. 531 With Mercurie, the Christian: and with Luna, the Antichristian. **1659** PEARSON *Creed* (1839) 145 This was the touchstone by which all men were tried, whether they were Christian or anti-Christian. **1679** PENN *Addr. Prot.* II. 150 All Christian Societies must uphold themselves upon the same free Bottom, or they turn Antichristian. **1865** LECKY *Rational.* II. 82 The greatest living antichristian writer was Hobbes. **1870** W. ROSSETTI in *Shelley's Wks.* Introd 41 Shelley's antichristian opinions.

B. *sb.* †**1.** A follower of Antichrist. *Obs.*

1531 LATIMER *Serm. & Rem.* (1845) 346 Neither pen nor tongue can divide the antichristians from their blind folly. **1561** DAUS *Bullinger on Apoc.* (1573) 120 Daniell attributeth prosperitie to the Antichristians. **1615** J. WRIGHT *Lady J. Grey* in *Phenix* (1708) II. 29 Him that call'd thee from Custom-gathering among the Romish Antichristians. **1753** CHAMBERS *Cycl. Supp.*, *Antichristians* properly denote the followers or worshippers of Antichrist.

2. An opponent of Christianity.

1621 AINSWORTH *Annot. Numb.* xvi. 37 Antichristians, which abuse and despise Christ's mediation. **1708** SWIFT *Abol. Chr.* Wks. 1755 II. I. 93 Toland, the great oracle of the anti-christians. **1801** W. TAYLOR in *Month. Mag.* XII. 577 The answerers of the French Antichristians.

†**antiˈchristian**, *v. Obs. rare*[−1]. [f. prec. adj.] To call, or denounce as, antichristian.

a **1718** PENN *Tracts* Wks. 1726 I. 609 How did they Antichristian all Force on Conscience, or Punishment for Nonconformity?

antiˈchristianism. [f. prec. adj. + -ISM.]

1. The system of Antichrist.

1588 *Marprel. Epist.* (1843) 22 The former poynt of Antichristianisme. **1659** MILTON *Civ. Power* Wks. 1851, 308 No less antichrist in this main point of antichristianism, no less a pope or popedom then he at Rome. **1701** R. FLEMING *Rise & F. Papacy* (1844) 36 When the reign of Antichristianism or the Papacy, began. **1849** W. FITZGERALD tr. *Whitaker's Disp.* 2 That..baneful and tedious night of popish superstition and antichristianism.

2. The quality of being opposed to Christianity; an antichristian act or belief.

1590 J. GREENWOOD *Answ. Gifford* 35 That the Church may professe *Christianisme* and *Antichristianisme*, both at a tyme. **1659** HARDY *1 John* (1865) xlvii. 302/2 Yea, which is the worst kind of antichristianism, Pseudochristianism is the brand of our times. **1717** DE FOE *Mem. Ch. Scot.* (1844) 5 Charg'd with so many Heresies, Errors, Schisms, and Antichristianisms. **1883** F. COOK in *Word & Wk.* 7 June 371/2 Corrupt Christendom possesses a large amount of the spirit of Antichristianism.

†**ˌantichristiˈanity.** *Obs.* [f. as prec. + -ITY, after *Christianity.*]

1. = ANTICHRISTIANISM 1.

1555 R. TAYLOR in Foxe *A. & M.* (1596) 1383/2, I did also affirme..poperie Antichristianitie. **1594** HOOKER *Eccl. Pol.* IV. (1617) 133 Popery being Antichristianity, is not healed but by establishment of orders thereunto opposite. The way to bring a drunken man to sobriety, is to carry him as farre from excesse of drinke as may be. **1670** BAXTER *Cure Ch. Div.* Pref. II. §6 To suspect them of Antichristianity.

2. = ANTICHRISTIANISM 2. 'Contrariety to Christianity.' J.

1661 BAXTER *Moral Prognost.* I. §91. 21 To call things lawful, by the name of Sin and *Anti-christianity.* **1687** *Good Advice* 19 Christianity should be propagated by the Spirit of Christianity, and not by Violence and Persecution, for that's the Spirit of Antichristianity. **1731** in BAILEY; whence in J. etc.

†**antiˈchristianize**, *v. Obs.* [f. as prec. + -IZE.] To act as an Antichrist; to oppose Christ.

1664 H. MORE *Myst. Iniq.* 110 That Polity..does therein notoriously Antichristianize, that is oppose Christ in his prophetick Office as much as any Antichrist can doe. **1701** BEVERLEY *Grand Apoc. Quest.* 32 During the true Christian Glory of the Christian Empire, Til it Antichristianiz'd.

†**antiˈchristianized**, *ppl. a. Obs. rare.* [f. prec. + -ED.] Become or made antichristian.

1701 BEVERLEY *Grand Apoc. Quest.* 24 Empire Lost as a Vengeance on an Antichristianiz'd State.

antiˈchristianly, *adv.* [f. ANTICHRISTIAN + -LY[2].] In an antichristian manner.

1596 J. NORDEN *Progr. Pietie* (1847) 121 Such as carry the titles of Christians, and will yet seek Antichristianly to impose themselves against him. **1664** H. MORE *Myst. Iniq.* 109 That expected eminent False-prophet who does Antichristianly oppose himself against the Spirit of Truth. **1701** BEVERLEY *Grand. Apoc. Quest.* 34 So Antichristianly Bitter. **1860** PUSEY *Min. Proph.* 77 That people might not use it [the name Jehovah] irreverently or anti-Christianly.

†**antiˈchronical**, *a. Obs.*[−0] [f. ANTI- 3 + Gr. χρονικ-ός (f. χρόνος time) + -AL[1].] Opposed to, or out of, proper chronological order.

1847 in CRAIG.

†**antiˈchronically**, *adv. Obs.*[−0] [f. prec. + -LY[2].] In wrong chronological order.

1847 in CRAIG.

†**anˈtichronism.** *Obs.* [ad. Gr. ἀντιχρονισμός, f. ἀντί against + χρόνος time: see -ISM.] Contradiction of true chronology; anachronism.

1612 DRAYTON *Poly-olb.* A 2 Intollerable Antichronismes, incredible reports, and bardish impostures. **1655** FULLER *Ch. Hist.* III. 96 This confounding so many Bacons in one, hath caused Anticronismes in many Relations. **1728** G. CARLETON *Mem. Eng. Officer* 179, I will..by an Antichronism in this Place, a little anticipate some Observations that I made.

‖**antichthon** (ænˈtɪkθəʊn). [Gr. ἀντίχθων, prop. adj. (sc. γῆ earth), f. ἀντί opposite to + χθών the earth, ground.] A (hypothetical) second Earth on the opposite side of the sun.

1655-60 STANLEY *Hist. Philos.* (1701) 391/2 The tenth is Antichthon, an Earth above, or opposite to ours. **1693** *Phil. Trans.* XVII. 805 Placing..the Moon as an Antichthone or opposite Earth enlightned by the Sun. **1753** CHAMBERS *Cycl. Supp.* s.v., Pythagoras and his disciples asserted an Antichthon. **1865** GROTE *Plato* I. i. 13 An hypothetical body, called the Antichthon or Counter-Earth.

‖**antichthones** (ænˈtɪkθəniːz). *Obs.* [L., a. Gr. pl. of ἀντίχθων (sc. 'men'): see prec.] The inhabitants of the opposite side of the earth.

1601 HOLLAND *Pliny* (1634) I. 129 Many haue taken it [Ceylon] to be the place of the Antipodes, calling it the Antichthones world. **1684** T. BURNET *Th. Earth* I. 255 Those two hemispheres were then as two distinct worlds.. this opposite earth being call'd by them antichthon, and its inhabitants antichthones. **1751** CHAMBERS *Cycl.*, *Antichthones*..much the same with what we more usually call Antipodes.

anticipant (ænˈtɪsɪpənt), *a.* and *sb.* [ad. L. *anticipānt-em*, pr. pple. of *anticipā-re* (see ANTICIPATE *a.*); or a. its Fr. repr. *anticipant.*]

A. *adj.*

1. Operating in advance, prevenient, 'preventing.'

1626 DONNE *Serm.* lxvii. 675 a, By antecedent and anticipant without concomitant and auxiliant grace. *c* **1828** SOUTHEY *Life & Corr.* (1850) V. 364 It was not forged by unseen hands, Anticipant of Jove's commands. **1854** B. TAYLOR *Poems of Orient* 171 Exercising power anticipant.

2. Apprehending beforehand, looking forward, expectant.

1798 SOUTHEY *Rose* Wks. VI. 107 The first pangs Of wakening guilt, anticipant of Hell. **1825** —— in *Q. Rev.* XXXII. 386 His mind..was retrospective rather than anticipant.

B. *sb.* One who anticipates; an anticipator.

1854 B. TAYLOR *L'Envoi* in *Poems of Orient* (1866) 396 The sweet anticipant of dawn. **1877** M. ARNOLD *Gipsy Child* Poems I. 55 O meek anticipant of that sure pain.

†**anˌticiˈparian.** *Obs. rare*[−1]. [irreg. f. L. *anticip-āre* + -ARIAN.] One given to anticipation.

1641 LESTRANGE *God's Sabb.* 31 Patrons of prolepsis.. anticiparians.

anticipatable (ænˈtɪsɪˌpeɪtəb(ə)l), *a.* [f. ANTICIPATE *v.* + -ABLE.] That can be anticipated or expected.

1872 GREG. *Enigm. Life* ii. 74 The utmost anticipateable moderation.

†**anˈticipate**, *ppl. a. Obs.* Also 6 **antecipet.** [ad. L. *anticipāt-us*, pa. pple. of *anticipā-re*, prop. *antecipā-re*, f. *ante* before + *-cipāre*, deriv. f. *cap-ĕre* (in comp. *-cip-ĕre*) to take.] Anticipated.

1549 *Compl. Scotl.* v. 36 The daye of iugement sal be antecipet.

anticipate (æn'tɪsɪpeɪt), *v.* [f. prec., or on analogy of vbs. so formed. Cf. Fr. *anticip-er* (ad. L.) found in 14th c.]

†**1.** To seize or take possession of beforehand. *Obs.*

1594 T. B. *La Primaud. Fr. Acad.* II. 576 To anticipate signifieth as much as to prevent and to take before. **1623** BINGHAM *Xenophon* 57 They feared the tops of the mountaines might be anticipated. **1783** COWPER *Task* v. 723 To soar, and to anticipate the skies.

2. To use in advance; to spend (money) before it is at one's disposal.

a **1674** CLARENDON *Hist. Reb.* I. II. 103 To carry on that vast Expence, the Revenue of the Crown had been Anticipated. **1725** DE FOE *Voy. round World* (1840) 171 That the men might have something to buy clothes.. without anticipating their wages. **1883** *Daily News* 8 Oct 5/5 Do not anticipate your income.

3. To take up or deal with (a thing), or perform (an action), before another person or agent has had time to act, so as to gain an advantage; to deal with beforehand, forestall (an action).

1605 SHAKS. *Macb.* IV. i. 144 Time, thou anticipatest my dread exploits. **1766** GOLDSM. *Vic. Wakef.* xxxix, He has anticipated the vengeance of heaven. **1864** D. MITCHELL 7 *Stories* 233 The Count anticipated their action.

4. To be before (another) in acting, to forestall.

a **1682** SIR T. BROWNE *Tracts* 55 The Barley, anticipating the wheat, might be in ear in February. *a* **1704** T. BROWN *Table T.* Wks. 1730 I. 143 Whenever he met a creditor, never gave him leave to dun him first, but was sure to anticipate him. **1796** C. MARSHALL *Gardening* xx. (1813) 423 Anticipate winter so as to put all in order. **1877** BROCKETT *Cross & Cresc.* 67 In many points on which the greatness of his reputation rests, he was anticipated by his predecessors.

5. To observe or practise in advance of the due date; to cause to happen earlier, accelerate.

1534 MORE *On the Passion* Wks. 1557, 1308/1 Christe dyd anticipate the tyme of eatynge his Paschall lambe. **1625** MEADE in Ellis *Orig. Lett.* I. 307 III. 190 The funerall.. is anticipated, and shall be on Thursday. **1751** CHAMBERS *Cycl.* s.v. *Anticipation*, Anticipating a payment means the discharging it before it falls due. **1818** SCOTT *Hrt. Midl.* (1873) 17 To anticipate by half an hour the usual time of his arrival. **1819** BYRON *Juan* II. lii, Some leap'd overboard.. As eager to anticipate their grave.

†**6.** *intr.* To occur earlier, to advance in time. *Obs.*

1588 A. KING *Canisius' Catech.* G viij, This calculation.. maid yᵉ æquinoxe of springe tyme to anticipat swa mony dayes. **1594** BLUNDEVIL *Exerc.* III. I. xli. (ed. 7) 356 It [the year] doth anticipate in the space of foure yeeres one whole day. **1646** SIR T. BROWNE *Pseud. Ep.* 219 The Equinoxes had anticipated.

b. *trans.* To occur earlier than, precede. *rare.*

1855 MILMAN *Lat. Chr.* (1864) IV. VII. vi. 172 They were eager.. if their death anticipated the Last Day, to die in the Holy Land.

7. To take into consideration before the appropriate or due time. **a.** *trans.*

1532 MORE *Confut. Tindale* Wks. 1557, 532/1 Here haue I, wel beloued readers.. to anticipate his woordes written in his other Chapiter. **1675** BAXTER *Cath. Theol.* II. I. 127 You shall not again tempt me to anticipate the question of effectual Grace. **1796** C. MARSHALL *Gardening* xii. (1813) 152 He is to anticipate consequences and provide for the future. **1859** *Ecce Homo* v. (ed. 8) 43 We have anticipated in a former chapter the means by which Christ avoided this result.

b. *absol.*

1700 DRYDEN *Fables* Pref. (Globe) 497, I find I have anticipated already. **1794** SULLIVAN *View Nat.* I. 31 Of this, more hereafter; we must not anticipate.

8. *trans.* To realize beforehand (a certain future event).

1643 SIR T. BROWNE *Relig. Med.* I. 41, I perceive I doe anticipate the vices of age. **1749** SMOLLETT *Regicide* v. vi, My fears Anticipate thy words! **1853** C. BRONTË *Villette* xxxvii. (1876) 421 Some real lives do.. actually anticipate the happiness of Heaven.

9. To look forward to, look for (an uncertain event) as certain. Const. *simple obj.* or *subord. cl.*

1749 SMOLLETT *Regicide* III. vii, How my fir'd soul anticipates the joy! **1751** HARRIS *Hermes* (1841) 149, I anticipate a like orderly and diversified succession.. in time future. **1839** KEIGHTLEY *Hist. Eng.* II. 38 Those, not in the secret, anticipated an acquittal. **1858** HAWTHORNE *Fr. & It. Jrnls.* II. 85 He appeared to anticipate that flying will be a future mode of locomotion.

anticipated (æn'tɪsɪpeɪtɪd), *ppl. a.* [f. prec. + -ED.]

1. Taken or occurring in advance or beforehand.

1611 COTGR., *Anticipé*, anticipated, prevented, forestalled. **1655** ORRERY *Parthen.* (1676) 21 The Heavens had put on anticipated Mourning. **1753** CHAMBERS *Cycl. Supp.*, *Anticipation*, or anticipated diseases. **1809** J. BARLOW *Columb.* III. 620 The waking stars [in an eclipse].. Peep out and gem the anticipated night.

2. Used beforehand, as money.

1781 COWPER *Ret.* 559 Anticipated rents, and bills unpaid.

3. Apprehended beforehand, looked for, expected.

1814 SOUTHEY *Roderick* xv, The anticipated meeting put to flight These painful thoughts. **1860** TYNDALL *Glac.* I. 185 The anticipated storm at length gave notice of its coming.

†**an'ticipately**, *adv. Obs.* [f. ANTICIPATE *a.* + -LY².] By anticipation; beforehand.

a **1677** BARROW *Pope's Suprem.* (L.) Our Lord did intend to bestow upon all pastors, that he did anticipately promise to Peter. *a* **1711** KEN *Poet. Wks.* 1721 IV. 81 Beneath his Wings secure I rest, And am anticipately blest.

an'ticipating, *ppl. a.* [f. ANTICIPATE *v.* + -ING².] Taking, apprehending, or occurring beforehand; forestalling.

1611 COTGR., *Anticipant*, anticipating, preventing, forestalling. **1711** SHAFTESB. *Charact.* (1737) III. 389 This natural Apprehension, or anticipating Sense of Unity. **1825** CARLYLE *Schiller* II. (1845) 75 His anticipating goodness.

an'ticipatingly, *adv.* [f. ANTICIPATING *ppl. a.* + -LY².] With anticipation.

1851 H. MELVILLE *Moby Dick* II. xxi. 158 That weapon must.. be anticipatingly tossed out of the boat. **1888** WALT WHITMAN in *Century Mag.* (1911) Dec. 250/1 His whole face would light up anticipatingly as he spoke. **1904** *Daily Chron.* 19 Mar. 7/5 The listeners.. tittered anticipatingly.

anticipation (æn,tɪsɪ'peɪʃən). [ad. L. *anticipātiōn-em*, n. of action f. *anticipāre* (see ANTICIPATE); or perh. a. Fr. *anticipation*, 16th c. in Littré.]

1. The action of taking into possession, actually or virtually, beforehand; the using of money before it is at one's disposal; the sum so dealt with in advance.

1548 HALL *Chron.* 672 This payment was called an Anticipation, which is to say a thing taken, or a thing commyng before his tyme. *a* **1674** CLARENDON *Hist. Reb.* I. II. 115 Had drawn assignments and anticipations upon the Revenue. **1691** LUTTRELL *Brief Rel.* II. 317 To speake to the lords of the treasury to give an account of all tallies of anticipation that are struck. **1769** BURKE *Pres. St. Nat.* Wks. II. 107 This deficiency arises.. from anticipation and from defective produce. **1858** LD. ST. LEONARD'S *Property Law* xvii. 118 Although she [a married woman] is restrained from anticipation by the settlement.

2. Prior action that meets beforehand, provides for, or precludes the action of another.

1553 T. WILSON *Rhet.* 100 Anticipacion is when we prevent those wordes that another would saie, and disprove them as untrue. **1602** SHAKS. *Ham.* II. ii. 304 So shall my anticipation preuent your discouery. **1815** SIR J. MACKINTOSH *Sp.* (27 Apr.) Wks. 1846 III. 342 Those whose flagitious policy they had by anticipation condemned. **1879** FROUDE *Cæsar* xv. 230 In anticipation of a riot the temples on the Forum were occupied with guards.

3. Assignment to too early a time; *hence*, observance in advance of the proper time.

1774 J. BRYANT *Mythol.* II. 106 Guilty of an unpardonable anticipation, in ascribing those conquests to the first king of the country. *c* **1854** STANLEY *Sinai & Pal.* xiv. (1858) 464 Easter Eve, which by a strange anticipation .. eclipses Easter Sunday.

4. Occurrence in advance of the expected time; *ellipt.* the amount of such earlier occurrence. *Obs.* in general sense.

1556 RECORDE *Cast. Knowl.* 277 The anticipation of the Equinoctiall tearmes. **1588** A. KING *Canisius' Catech.* Hj, Yᵉ anticipation being substractit. *a* **1697** HOLDER (J.) The golden number gives the new moon four days too late by reason of the aforesaid anticipation.

b. *Med.* (See quot.)

1753 CHAMBERS *Cycl. Supp.*, *Anticipation*, in a medicinal sense, may be understood of those diseases, which, having their accesses and remissions at stated hours, gain in point of time, and finish their period sooner than ordinary. **1853** MAYNE *Exp. Lex.*, *Anticipation*, The occurrence of certain phenomena, morbid or natural, before the customary period.

c. *Music.* The introduction beforehand of part of a chord which is about to follow.

1819 *Pantol.*, *Anticipation*, in music, is when a diminutive note lies between two other notes, and was invented with a view to vary the melody without altering the intention. **1880** POLE in Grove *Dict. Mus.* I. 73/2 Beethoven has many striking examples of anticipation.

5. Intuitive preconception; *à priori* knowledge, intuition; precognition, presentiment.

1549 LATIMER 7 *Serm. bef. Edw. VI* (Arb.) 47 Yᵉ Ethenickes, who wrought onely by naturall mocion and anticipations. **1594** T. B. *La Primaud. Fr. Acad.* II. 576 By these anticipations they understande those principles of knowledge and naturall informations, which.. wee have not learned of any masters. **1860** ABP. THOMSON *Laws of Th.* §115 (ed. 5) 229 Anticipation.. is the power of penetrating into the secrets of nature before the evidence is unfolded.

†**6.** The formation of opinions before examining the evidence; prepossession, prejudice. *Obs.*

1640 SANDERSON *21 Serm.* Ad Aul. xi. (1673) 160 Education and Custom commonly layeth such strong anticipations upon the judgment. *a* **1704** LOCKE *Cond. Underst.* §25 (R.) Men give themselves up to the first anticipations of their mind. **1711** SHAFTESB. *Charact.* (1737) III. IV. ii. 214 We cannot resist our natural Anticipation in behalf of Nature.

7. The action of representing to oneself or realizing a thing before it occurs; apprehension beforehand, preconception.

1711 SHAFTESB. *Charac.* III. 336 The Anticipation of high Titles, Honours, and nominal Dignitys.. may not prove beneficial or advantageous in the end. *a* **1764** R. LLOYD *Milk-Maid* Wks. II. 51 And when the thoughts on evil pore, Anticipation makes it more. **1816** MISS AUSTEN *Emma* I. xi. 77 First in anticipation and then in reality it became henceforth the chief object of interest.

8. The action of looking forward to, expectation.

1809 COLERIDGE *Friend* iv. (1837) I. 198 Had I not soothed my solitary toils with the anticipation of many readers. **1830** B'NESS BUNSEN in Hare *Life* I. ix. 342 We are in such a state of excitement in anticipation of political news. **1841** BREWSTER *Mart. Sc.* vi. (1856) 83 Looked forward to the arrival of her Father with the most affectionate anticipations.

anticipative (æn'tɪsɪpeɪtɪv), *a.* [f. L. *anticipāt-* (see ANTICIPATE) + -IVE, as if ad. L. **anticipātīvus*.]

1. Having the faculty or habit of anticipating.

a **1803** J. FOSTER *Life & Corr.* (1846) I. 188 The mind inspired with this enthusiasm asserts its grandeur. It expands toward eternity, anticipative of its destiny. **1834** LYTTON *Pompeii* 276 Anxious, fearful, anticipative, she resolved upon seizing the earliest opportunity.

2. Of the nature of anticipation.

1664 H. MORE *Myst. Iniq.* 304 Prophecie being nothing else but an anticipative History. **1848** MRS. JAMESON *Sacr. & Leg. Art* 219 Mary Magdalene, with the anticipative glory round her head.

an'ticipatively, *adv.* [f. prec. + -LY².] By way of anticipation.

1864 *Daily Tel.* 12 Apr., That simple and becoming costume with which all London had become anticipatively familiar. **1878** C. STANFORD *Symb. Christ* xii. 334 Holding anticipatively the complete knowledge of a later age.

anticipator (æn'tɪsɪpeɪtə(r)). Also -er. [a. L. *anticipātor*, n. of agent f. *anticipāre*: see ANTICIPATE and -OR.] One who anticipates.

1598 FLORIO, *Preuentore*, a preuentor, an ouertaker, an anticipator. **1753** RICHARDSON *Grandison* (1810) VI. xli. 271 He is such an anticipater, that he leaves not to me the merit of obliging him beyond his expectation. **1808** LD. GRENVILLE in Dk. Buckhm. *Crt. Geo. III*, IV. 284 The most confident anticipator of Bonaparte's downfall.

anticipatorily (æn'tɪsɪpətərɪlɪ), *adv. rare.* [f. next + -LY².] In anticipation, beforehand.

1878 RUSKIN *Notes* I. 71 Of these ten [drawings], he made anticipatorily four, to manifest what their quality would be.

anticipatory (æn'tɪsɪpətərɪ), *a.* [f. ANTICIPATOR + -Y: see -ORY.] Of or pertaining to an anticipator; of the nature of anticipation.

1669 H. MORE 7 *Churches* Pref. (T.) Prophecy, being an anticipatory history. **1855** H. SPENCER *Psychol.* (1872) I. III. iv. 315 Nascent vision.. amounts at first to little more than anticipatory touch. **1874** H. REYNOLDS *John Bapt.* iii. §3. 216 Anticipatory of a wider diffusion of the Holy Spirit.

anticivic (æntɪ'sɪvɪk), *a. rare.* [ad. mod.Fr. *anticivique*: see ANTI- 3 and CIVIC.] Opposed to citizenship, *esp.* to the doctrine of citizenship established in France at the Revolution of 1789.

1805 MAR. EDGEWORTH *Mdme. de Fleury* viii. (1832) 99 Bad citizens.. nourished in anticivic prejudices.

anticivism (æntɪ'sɪvɪz(ə)m). *rare*⁻¹. [a. mod.Fr. *anticivisme*: see ANTI- 7 and CIVISM.] Opposition to citizenship (as in prec.).

1837 CARLYLE *Fr. Rev.* II. III. I. ii. 138 Wo to him who is guilty of Plotting, of Anticivism, Royalism, Feuillantism.

anticize ('æntɪsaɪz), *v. rare.* [f. ANTIC *sb.* + IZE; cf. *critic-ize*.] To play antics, sport grotesquely.

1871 BROWNING *Pr. Hohenstiel* 1307 Could the orb sweep those puny particles.. from space They anticize in with their days and nights.

antick(e, obs. f. ANTIC, and of ANTIQUE.

†**'antick't**, *ppl. a. Obs.* [f. ANTIC *v.* + -ED.] Made fantastic; grotesquely dressed.

1612 WARNER *Alb. Eng.* IX. xlvii. 218 Some, by Arte, abusing Nature, heads of antick't hayre do frame.

anticlastic (æntɪ'klæstɪk), *a.* [formed as if ad. Gr. *ἀντικλαστικ-ός, f. ἀντικλά-ειν, f. ἀντί contrary + κλά-ειν to bend.] Applied to a double-curved surface, of which the two curvatures, transverse to each other, are in opposite directions; convex in its length, and concave in its breadth, or *vice versâ*.

1867 THOMSON & TAIT *Nat. Phil.* I. I. §128 We may divide curved surfaces into Anticlastic and Synclastic. A saddle gives a good example of the former class; a ball of the latter.. The outer portion of an anchor-ring is synclastic, the inner anticlastic.

anti'clerical, *a.* and *sb.* [ANTI-¹ 3 b.] Opposed to clericalism. Hence as *sb.*, a person who is opposed to clericalism.

1845 S. AUSTIN tr. *Ranke's Hist. Ref.* II. IV. v. 517 Here too, the inclinations of the council and citizens had received an anti-clerical bias from a great number of circumstances. **1881** *Times* 16 May 7/4 An anti-Clerical Congress.. closed to-day with a speech by M. Louis Blanc. *Ibid.* 19 July 5/1 When the anti-Clericals—for it would be absurd to call them Liberals—fail to obtain their provocation in one direction [etc.]. **1883** *Gd. Wds.* 204 The tide of anti-clerical reaction. **1906** J. E. C. BODLEY *Church in France* 51 The anti-Clericals were a minute and feeble minority. **1937** R. H. LOWIE *Hist. Ethnol. Theory* xi. 193 Anticlerical critics have suggested that the field work undertaken under Father Schmidt's auspices has been unduly coloured by Catholic or personal prejudices.

Hence **anti-'clericalism**.

1886 *Times* 31 Mar. 5/2 These measures may be regarded as the swing of the pendulum from clericalism to anti-clericalism. **1898** J. E. C. BODLEY *France* I. 141 Free-thinkers contravene the basis of their own profession in erecting anti-clericalism into a dogma.

anticlimactic (ˌæntɪklaɪˈmæktɪk), *a.* [f. ANTICLIMAX, after CLIMACTIC *a.*] Of the nature of an anticlimax. So ˌ**anticliˈmactically** *adv.*

1898 *Westm. Gaz.* 28 May 2/3 That sounds a little anticlimactic. **1915** W. J. LOCKE *Jaffery* xix, I urged, somewhat anticlima[c]tically after my impassioned harangue [etc.]. **1917** MCKENNA *Sonia* i. 37 He began valiantly enough, and then anticlimactically as he caught sight of me, 'What d'you want?' **1941** J. RANSOM *New Criticism* i. 100 When the artist works over the practical failures in human life, and the ambiguous anticlimactic half-successes.

anticlimax (ˌæntɪˈklaɪmæks). [ANTI- 2.]

1. *Rhet.* The opposite of climax: 'a sentence in which the last part expresses something lower than the first' J.; the addition of a particular which, instead of heightening the effect, suddenly lowers it or makes it ludicrous.

1727 POPE, etc. *Art of Sinking* 101 The *Anti-Climax* ..'And thou Dalhoussy the great God of war, Lieutenant colonel to the Earl of Mar.' **1791** BOSWELL *Johnson* (1816) III. 418, I objected also to what appeared an anticlimax of praise. **1842** DICKENS *Amer. Notes* (1850) 141/1 The stupendous silliness of certain stanzas with an anti-climax at the end of each.

2. By extension: A descent or fall in contrast to a previous rise.

1858 LEWES *Seaside Stud.* 42, I think of the Hunter's finale as merely an extra dish, and pronounce that to be an anticlimax to his day's work. **1879** MCCARTHY *Own Time* II. xviii. 35 The later years of his life were only an anticlimax.

anticlinal (æntɪˈklaɪnəl), *a.* and *sb.* [f. Gr. ἀντί against + κλίν-ειν to lean, slope + -AL[1]. Cf. Gr. ἀντικλίν-ειν to lean against (each other).] **A.** *adj.*

1. *Geol.* Applied to a line or axis from which strata slope down or dip in opposite directions; also said of the fold or bend in such strata, or of a ridge so formed. Opposed to SYNCLINAL.

1833 LYELL *Princ. Geol.* III. 287 The Hastings sands, forming an anticlinal axis, on each side of which the other formations are arranged with an opposite dip. **1848** MILLER *First Impress.* viii. (1857) 134 The strata shelve downwards on both sides from the anticlinal line a-top. **1875** J. W. POWELL *Explor. Colorado River* xi. 160 Longitudinal valleys ..three varieties (*a*) anticlinal, valleys which follow anticlinal axes. **1929** H. G. BUSK *Earth Flexures* ii. 7 An 'anticlinal bend' is any relatively sharp flexure in an anticlinal sense, that is, where the beds of the one limb dip gently towards the apex, and the beds of the other dip relatively steeply away from it.

2. *Anat.* (A vertebra) having an upright spine, towards which the spines on both sides incline.

1870 ROLLESTON *Anim. Life* 12 The tenth [dorsal vertebra of the Rabbit] is the anticlinal vertebra.

3. *Bot.* Applied to those cell-walls at a growing-point which have a direction at right angles to the surface: opp. to PERICLINAL *a.* 2. Also as *sb.*, an anticlinal wall or plane.

1882 VINES tr. *Sachs's Bot.* 951 The planes of the walls in a growing-point are classified thus: *a. Periclinal*... *b. Anticlinal*, those which intersect the surface and the periclinal walls at right angles... If the outline..of the growing-point is a parabola..the anticlinals being the orthogonal trajectories of the periclinals, constitute a system of confocal parabolas. **1960** I. F. & W. D. HENDERSON *Dict. Sci. Terms* (ed. 7) 33/2.

B. *sb.* [by ellipsis]. **1.** *Geol.* An anticlinal fold, axis, crest, or line; a line whence strata dip in opposite directions.

1849 MURCHISON *Siluria* v. 100 The same North and South anticlinal which is apparent in May Hill and Huntley Hill. **1869** PHILLIPS *Vesuv.* ix. 255 Anticlinals and synclinals, in the earth's crust.

2. (see A.3.)

Hence **antiˈclinally** *adv.*

1855 J. PHILLIPS *Man. Geol.* ii. 45 Thus in fig. 16 the strata are synclinally and anticlinally bent, but the cleavage is vertical, or nearly so. **1954** *New Biol.* XVI. 119 In the outer layer known as the tunica the cells divide anticlinally, that is by walls at right angles to the surface. **1965** G. J. WILLIAMS *Econ. Geol. N.Z.* xix. 349/2 The Ahaura basin at that time was but a shallow shelf or even anticlinally warped.

anticline (ˈæntɪklaɪn). *Geol.* [f. as prec., but assimilated to *incline*, etc.] An anticlinal fold.

1861 PAGE *Introd. Geol.* Index, *Anticline*, anticlinal. **1873** GEIKIE *Gt. Ice Age* xxi. 266 Diagrammatic view of synclines and anticlines. **1876** PAGE *Advd. Text-bk. Geol.* iv. 83 When strata dip..like the roof of a house..the strata are spoken of as forming an anticline or saddleback.

anticlinorium (ˌæntɪklɪˈnɔərɪəm). *Geol.* [mod.L., f. as ANTICLINAL + -ORIUM.] **1.** (See quot.)

1874 J. D. DANA *Man. Geol.* (ed. 2) IV. 752 An upward bend of the crust, or geanticlinal, is of itself an elevation; and such an elevation is an *anticlinorium*.

2. (See quot. 1893.) (The only current sense.)

1893 *13th Ann. Rep. U.S. Geol. Surv.* II. 220 It often happens that the result of the combination of many anticlines and synclines is to form a complex structure, which, regarded as a whole, is either synclinal or anticlinal. The former is called a synclinorium, the latter an anticlinorium. **1920** J. GEIKIE *Struct. & Field Geol.* (ed. 4) ix. 142 When a broad zone has bulged up under lateral pressure..we may have one great arch composed of numerous subordinate wrinkles or minor folds and flexures. A complex arch of this kind is termed an Anticlinorium. **1938** *Geogr. Jrnl.* XCI. 281 The whole San Carlos range is an arcuate anticlinorium trending east—west with convexity to the south.

Hence ˌ**anticliˈnorial** *a.*, of or pertaining to an anticlinorium.

1940 *Geogr. Jrnl.* XCV. 332 On the west Burma is separated from India by a complex anticlinorial fold of Alpine-Himalayan age.

anti-clockwise (ˌæntɪˈklɒkwaɪz), *a.* and *adv.* [f. ANTI-[1] 3 c + CLOCK *sb.* + -WISE.] = COUNTER-CLOCKWISE.

1898 G. WHERRY in *Lancet* 1 Jan. 24/1 Mathematicians often use the expression 'clockwise' or 'anti-clock-wise' to indicate the way of a spiral coil. **1914** DOMVILLE-FIFE *Submarines, Mines & Torpedoes* 163 A tiny three or four-cylinder engine which operates twin screws, moving 'clock-wise' and 'anti-clockwise'. **1917** 'CONTACT' *Airman's Outings* 153 A little left rudder again puts the needle into an anticlockwise motion. **1927** *Daily Express* 23 Sept. 3/3 A clockwork motor that is wound up anti-clockwise.

anticly (ˈæntɪklɪ), *adv. arch.* or *Obs.* [f. ANTIC *a.* + -LY[2].] In an antic manner, grotesquely.

1556 in *Macm. Mag.* XLV. 452 Twelve minstrels antickly disguised. **1599** SHAKS. *Much Ado* v. i. 96 Go antiquely, and show outward hideousnesse. **1671** *Lond. Gaz.* dxxxv/2 Frocks anticklly composed of White and Red pieces of Cloth.

†ˈ**anticness.** *Obs. rare.* [f. ANTIC *a.* + -NESS.] The quality of being antic; grotesqueness, oddity.

1638 FORD *Fancies* IV. ii, A port of humorous anticknesss in carriage. **1655** FULLER *Ch. Hist.* IX. 108 This Arch-Bishop was an excellent Antiquarie (without any Anticknesse).

anti-coagulant (ˌæntɪkəʊˈægjʊlənt), *a.* and *sb.* [ANTI-[1] 3 b.] **A.** *adj.* That retards or prevents coagulation, esp. of the blood. **B.** *sb.* Any substance that is antagonistic to coagulation.

1905 GOULD *Dict. New Med. Terms* 80/1 *Anticoagulant*, adj. and sb. **1909** *Jrnl. Physiol.* XXXVIII. 497 The large quantity of anti-ferment present in hirudin indicates that it also plays a part in the anti-coagulant action. **1920** *Discovery* Apr. 105/2 This effect is not spoilt by the admixture of citrate, though this is used as an anti-coagulant outside the body. **1958** *Observer* 2 Mar. 13/3 He takes anti-coagulants constantly. **1965** *New Scientist* 22 Apr. 245/2 The greatest advance in effective rodenticides was the development of the anti-coagulants such as dicoumarin.

anti-coˈincidence. *Physics.* [f. ANTI-[1] 4 + COINCIDENCE 7.] Applied *attrib.* to a device, or to a system employing a device, which rejects or discriminates against measurements of events which occur simultaneously or are separated by a predetermined time, used esp. in experiments with cosmic rays and in nuclear physics. Also, the indication of the occurrence of an ionizing particle in such a device.

1939 G. HERZOG in *Physical Rev.* LV. 1266/1 To investigate the nature of cosmic-ray particles a special anti-coincidence amplifying set was used to trip the cloud chamber only by those cosmic-ray particles whose further path lies below a given range. **1940** —— *Ibid.* LVII. 67/2 Anticoincidences can be used to suppress the recording of the discharges in a coincidence circuit when one additional G-M counter is fired simultaneously. **1948** L. JANOSSY *Cosmic Rays* iv. 40 If the background of coincidences, caused by the ionizing rays, could be eliminated, the arrangement would be vastly more sensitive for the detection of any non-ionizing rays. The solution of this problem was achieved by the important technique of *anti-coincidences*. *Ibid.*, By a suitable electrical arrangement the coincidence counters are made *insensitive* whenever the anti-coincidence counters register a particle. **1953** A. D. & K. H. V. BOOTH *Autom. Digital Calculators* vi. 42 The circuitry involves only standard coincidence and anti-coincidence units.

anticonvellent (ˌæntɪkənˈvɛlənt), *a.* and *sb. Med.* [f. ANTI- 3 + L. *convellent-em*, pr. pple. of *convell-ĕre* to convulse.] **A.** *adj.* Of use against convulsions. **B.** *sb.* An anti-convulsive.

1876 HARLEY *Mat. Med.* 348 Dr. Mitchell used it in convulsions in 1871, and advocated its use as an anticonvellent in eclampsia.

anti-convulsant (ˌæntɪkɒnˈvʌlsənt), *a.* and *sb.* [ANTI-[1] 3 b.] **A.** *adj.* That retards or prevents convulsions (*Lippincott's New Med. Dict.*, 1910). **B.** *sb.* A substance that is antagonistic to convulsions.

1943 *Lancet* 6 Nov. 578/2 Petit mal or slow-wave activity is less amenable to phenobarbitone and other anticonvulsants than are major fits. **1946** *Nature* 19 Oct. 541/2 Although the patient was under the influence of large doses of anticonvulsant drugs and was almost free from spontaneous attacks. **1966** *Lancet* 24 Dec. 1371/2 Phenobarbitone sodium and intramuscular paraldehyde in optimum doses, were used as anticonvulsants.

anticonvulsive (ˌæntɪkənˈvʌlsɪv), *a.* and *sb. Med.* [ANTI- 3.] **A.** *adj.* Of use against convulsions. **B.** *sb.* (sc. medicine).

a **1734** FLOYER (J.) Whatsoever produces an inflammatory disposition in the blood..as anticonvulsive medicines.

anticor (ˈæntɪˌkɔə(r)). Also 7 -core, 8 **antecor**, **-ticour** (**antocow**). [f. ANTI- + L. *cor* heart.] A disease amongst horses and cattle. (See quot.)

1607 TOPSELL *Four-footed Beasts* (1673) 335 An Anticor cometh of superfluity of evill bloud or spirit in the arteries, and also of inflamation in the liver. **1706** PHILLIPS, *Antocow* (among Farriers) a round Swelling about half as big as one's Fist, which breaks out in the Breast of a Horse, over against the Heart. [So in BAILEY 1721–1800.] **1737** BRACKEN *Farriery Impr.* (1756) I. xxii. 192 Of the Anticor. This Disease in Horses is called in French, *Anticœur*, on Account of its being over-against the Heart, or in the Breast. **1783** AINSWORTH *Lat. Dict.* (ed. Morell) s.v., The anticor [in horses], *Febris pestilens, phlegmone circa pectus stipata.*

anticorrosion (æntɪkəˈrəʊʒən). [ANTI- 6.] A substance which prevents corrosion; anticorrosive paint or varnish.

1851 *Ord. & Regul. R. Engineers* §19. 94 Iron Guns, Carriages, and Platforms, are to be coated with Anticorrosion, and not painted. **1862** F. GRIFFITHS *Artill. Man.* 58 Its first coat of anticorrosion.

anticous (ænˈtaɪkəs), *a. Bot.* [f. L. *antīc-us* front (f. *ante* before) + -OUS.] Fronting the axis of the whorl to which it belongs, as anthers whose line of dehiscence looks towards the pistils.

1870 HOOKER *Stud. Flora* 273 *Melampyrum*..Disk an hypogynous anticous gland. **1880** GRAY *Bot. Text-bk.* vi. §6. 253 An anther is..Introrse..or Anticous, when it faces toward the axis of the flower.

anticryptic (æntɪˈkrɪptɪk), *a. Zool.* [f. ANTI-[1] 3 c + CRYPTIC *a.* 3.] Applied to markings or coloration serving for concealment to the disadvantage of some other animal: distinguished from PROCRYPTIC *a.*

1890 E. B. POULTON *Colours Anim.* xvii. 336 Protective and Aggressive Resemblances are classed as Cryptic Colours (Procryptic and Anticryptic). *Ibid.* 337 Pseudepisematic colours..are special instances of Anticryptic colours. **1960** I. F. & W. D. HENDERSON *Dict. Sci. Terms* (ed. 7) 33/2.

anticyˈclometer. [ANTI- 5.] An opponent of squarers of the circle (humorously called by De Morgan *Cyclometers*).

1866 DE MORGAN in *Athenæum* 27 Oct. 534/2 Cyclometers have their several styles of wit; so have anticyclometers too, for that matter.

anticyclone (ˈæntɪˌsaɪkləʊn). *Meteor.* [ANTI- 2.] The rotatory outward flow of air from an atmospheric area of high pressure; also, the whole system of high pressure and outward flow.

1877 *Academy* 3 Nov. 435/1 The 'cirri'..cannot indicate the line of air motion from the cyclone to the anticyclone. **1880** GEIKIE *Phys. Geog.* ii. xi. 86 The outward flowing from a region of high pressure is called an anticyclone or anticyclonic movement. **1880** *Times* 11 Aug. 11/6 Owing to a sudden increase of pressure, a large anticyclone had been formed over France, England, and Ireland.

anticyclonic (ˌæntɪsaɪˈklɒnɪk), *a. Meteor.*

1. [f. ANTI- 3 + CYCLONIC.] Opposed to cyclones or cyclonic theories.

1860 MAURY *Phys. Geog. Sea* xix. §803 Espy maintains that they confirm his theory, and his is anti-cyclonic.

2. [f. ANTICYCLONE + -IC.] Of or pertaining to an anticyclone.

1871 in *Proc. Am. Phil. Soc.* XII. 64 The anticyclonic character of our winds and storms. **1882** W. MARRIOTT in *Standard* 26 Dec. 7/4 Nearly all British weather is cyclonic or anti-cyclonic. The wind in an anticyclonic system blows in the direction of the hands of a watch, but slightly outwards.

anticyˈclonically, *adv.* [f. prec. + -AL[1] + -LY[2].] After the manner of an anticyclone.

1882 E. ARCHIBALD in *Nature* No. 653. 10 Outside the annulus of high pressure surrounding a cyclone the air should move outwards anticyclonically.

anti-ˈdemocrat. [ANTI-[1] 5.] One who is opposed to democracy or to the principles of the Democratic party in the United States (see DEMOCRATIC *a.* 2).

1802 (*title*) The Republican; or, Anti-Democrat [cited in D.A.]. **1855** BRISTED in *Fraser's Mag.* LII. 521 Many of the Southern anti-Democrats..carried them [*sc.* some doctrines] to greater length than the Democrats themselves. *a* **1937** J. L. STOCKS *Reason & Intuition* (1939) vii. 112 The imposture of collective wisdom, of which anti-democrats talk. **1945** POPPER *Open Society* I. x. 161 He [*sc.* Thucydides] probably did not support the treacherous acts of the extreme anti-democrats.

So ˌ**anti-demoˈcratic** *a.*, **-deˈmocracy**.

1837 *U.S. Mag. & Democr. Rev.* Oct. 10 That extensive anti-democratic corruption of sentiment in some portions of our people. **1842** J. S. MILL *Let.* 6 Apr. in *Wks.* (1963) XIII. 514 Some of the opinions are likely to be considered ultra-liberal, although..rather anti-democratic. **1881** MAHAFFY *Old Grk. Educ.* xi. 140 The antidemocratic tone of the schools. **1909** G. K. CHESTERTON *Orthodoxy* ix. 281 These supernatural things are never denied except on the basis of anti-democracy or of materialist dogmatism. **1939** *War Illustr.* 9 Dec. 416/3 Fascism remains anti-Communist, but it also remains obstinately anti-democratic.

†**antideˈmoniac,** *a.* and *sb. Obs.* [ANTI- 3, 6.] **A.** *adj.* Opposed to demons. **B.** *sb.* Anything effective against evil spirits.

1603 HARSNET *Pop. Impost.* 90 The holy Stole..shewed itselfe an Antidæmoniack of special account. **1683** E. HOOKER *Pref. Pordage's Myst. Div.* 61 That famous Anti-Satanic Athleta, Anti-Dæmoniac Palestrita, and Hell's black Regiment's Antagonist.

antidicoˈmarian, *a.* and *sb.* [see next.] **A.** *adj.* Adverse to the Virgin Mary. **B.** *sb.* = next.

1532 MORE *Confut. Tindale* Wks. 1557, 489/1 Called them Antidychomarians, that is to saye Maryes aduersaryes.

antidico'marianite. [ad. med.L., ad. Gr. ἀντιδικομαριανῖται, f. ἀντίδικ-ος adversary + Μαρία Mary.] *pl.* Adversaries of Mary; a name applied to Oriental Christians, in the 4th c., who denied the perpetual virginity of the mother of Jesus.
a **1625** J. BOYS *Wks.* 1629, 21 Old Helvidians, New Antidicomarianits, holding it a point of zeale to disgrace this holy Virgin. **1751** CHAMBERS *Cycl.*, *Antidicomarianites*.. otherwise called *Antidicomaritæ*, and *Antidicomarites*, and *Antidicomarianists*, sometimes also *Antimariani*.

†**anti'dinic,** *a. Med. Obs.*—[0] [ad. med.L. *antidīnic-us*, f. ANTI- 3 + δῖν-ος whirl, dizziness: see -IC.] Acting as a remedy for giddiness.
1719 in *Glossogr. Nova.* **1853** in MAYNE *Exp. Lex.*

anti-dip (æntɪˈdɪp). *Physical Geogr.* [cf. DIP *sb.* 5.] Used *attrib.* (see quot. 1961).
1900 *Proc. Cotteswold Club* XIII. 178 It may be premised that dip streams are termed consequents..and anti-dip streams, obsequents. **1961** L. D. STAMP *Gloss. Geogr. Terms* 27/1 *Anti-dip stream*, a stream flowing in approximately the opposite direction to the regional dip.

,antidisestablishmen'tarianism. [f. ANTI-[1] + DISESTABLISHMENTARIAN + -ISM.] Properly, opposition to the disestablishment of the Church of England (*rare*): but popularly cited as an example of a long word. So **antidisestablishmentarian.**
1900 *N. & Q.* 25 Aug. 147/1 In the recent biography of Dr. Benson is an entry from the Archbishop's diary to the effect that 'the Free Kirk of the North of Scotland are strong antidisestablishmentarians'. **1923** in *Brewer's Dict. Phr. & Fable* (new ed.) s.v. *Long words.* **1960** *Amrita Bazar Patrika* 17 June 6/4 But then 'Antidisestablishmentarianism' contains three more letters, as pointed out by two readers. **1984** T. AUGARDE *Oxf. Guide Word Games* xxvi. 216 The longest words that most people know are *antidisestablishmentarianism*..and *supercalifragilistic expialidocious.*

†**'anti-di,vision.** *Obs.* [ANTI- 2.] (See quot.)
1655–60 STANLEY *Hist. Philos.* (1701) 308/1 There are three forms of division, anti-division, sub-division, partition. Anti-division is a distribution of the Genus into Species by the contrary; as for example, by negation, as, of things that are, some are good, others not good.

antidoron (æntɪˈdɔərɒn). *Eastern Church.* [Gr. ἀντίδωρον return-gift, f. ἀντι- ANTI-[1] + δῶρον gift.] = EULOGIA b, c.
1850 NEALE *Holy East. Ch.* I. 525 Before the people are dismissed, the Priest gives them the *antidoron*; i.e. a part of the bread blessed for the prothesis. **1892** A. J. MACLEAN & W. H. BROWNE *Catholicos of East* 209 The Syrian deacon.. may also make the holy loaves for consecration and for the *Antidoron.* **1957** *Oxf. Dict. Chr. Ch.* 1005/1 Among the E. Orthodox..the so-called 'antidoron'..i.e. what remains of the loaves from which the Eucharistic Bread is cut, is held to share in the liturgical offering, and is distributed as a consolation to those unable to receive Holy Communion.

antidotal (ˈæntɪdəʊtəl, ænˈtɪdətəl), *a.* [f. ANTIDOTE + -AL[1].] Of, pertaining to, or of the nature of, an antidote; alexipharmic. *lit.* and *fig.*
1646 SIR T. BROWNE *Pseud. Ep.* 168 None of the Ancients ascribed any medicinall or antidotall virtue unto the Unicornes horne. **1751** JOHNSON *Rambl.* No. 109 ¶2 Writings antidotal to levity and merriment. **1857** *Nat. Mag.* I. 285 The antidotal efficacy of a Honduras plant.

antidotally, *adv. rare.* [f. prec. + -LY[2].] After the manner of an antidote.
1646 SIR T. BROWNE *Pseud. Ep.* 102 Rather antidotally destroying, then seminally promoting its production.

†**an'tidotary,** *a.* and *sb. Obs.* [ad. med.L. *antidotāri-us*, f. *antidotum*: see ANTIDOTE and -ARY. Cf. Fr. *antidotaire.*]
A. *adj.* Of the nature of an antidote; antidotal.
1599 A. M. *Gabelhouer's Bk. Physic* 381/1 A verye excellent Antidotarye poudre. **1657** G. STARKEY *Helmont's Vind.* To Reader, Cured by killing the venome, by antidotary remedies.
B. *sb.*
1. An application of the nature of an antidote.
1583 STUBBES *Anat. Abus.* (1877) 96 Mariage an antidotarie against Whordome.
2. A practitioner who gives antidotes. *rare.*
1541 R. COPLAND *Guydon's Form.* R ij, I than Antydotary ordynary in the scyence of apostemes.
3. A book describing antidotes; sometimes extended to: A dispensary.
[*c* **1542** (*title*) in Hazlitt *Handbk.* 583/2 The Antidotharius.] **1543** TRAHERON *Vigo's Chirurg.* VIII. 199 The Antidotarie..conteyneth the description of Oyntmentes, Cerotes, Playsters, Oyles, Pilles. **1657** TOMLINSON *Renou's Disp.* Pref., The shop, or Antidotary divided into two Parts. **1727** BRADLEY *Fam. Dict.* s.v. *Honey*, Several others to be found in your Antidotaries..as the Buglossate made of Bugloss.

antidote (ˈæntɪdəʊt). [(? a. Fr. *antidote*,) ad. L. *antidotum*, a. Gr. ἀντίδοτον a remedy, prop. neut. sing. of ἀντί-δοτος given against. In 16–17th c. often used in Gr. or L. form, with pl. *-a.*]
1. A medicine given to counteract the influence of poison, or an attack of disease.
1543 TRAHERON *Vigo's Chirurg.* (1586) 431 Antidota, are medicines to be received within the bodie..some are geven against poison, some against the stinging of venemous beasts. **1598** B. JONSON *Ev. Man in Hum.* III. v. 64 An antidote, that had you taken the most deadly poysonous plant..it should expell it. **1604** JAMES I *Counterbl.* (Arb.) 101 The loathsome, and hurtfull vse of this stinking Antidote. **1633** G. HERBERT *Provid.* xxii. in *Temple* 112 Where are poysons, antidots are most. **1875** H. WOOD *Therap.* (1879) 45 [To] sulphate of copper..milk and eggs.. are the most efficient antidotes.
b. Const. *against*, *for*, *to*.
1515 in Froude *Hist. Eng.* II. viii. 241 Some say..that to find the antidotum for this disease is impossible. **1593** NASHE *Chr. Teares* 87 Him..that takes any antidote against it [the Plague]. **1653** WALTON *Angler* 145 A natural Balsome or Antidote against all Poison. **1752** HUME *Polit. Disc.* ii. 38 One poison may be an antidote to another. **1779** SHERIDAN *St. Patrick's D.* II. iv, He has antidotes for all poisons. **1843** MILL *Logic* III. ix. §1 Such examples are afforded by antidotes to these poisons.
2. *fig.* Const. as in prec.
1548 VERON (*title*) An Holsom Antidotus or counterpoysen agaynst the pestilent heresye and sect of Anabaptistes. **1635** QUARLES *Emblems* v. (1718) 333 To lend My wasting day, an antidote for night! **1656** BRAMHALL *Replic.* ii. 87 Adjuments of unity, and antidotes against Schism. **1656** H. MORE (*title*) Antidote against Atheisme. **1768** GOLDSM. *Good Nat. Man* I. i, His very mirth is an antidote to all gaiety. **1810** COLERIDGE *Friend* (1865) 118 The whole truth is the best antidote to falsehoods which are dangerous chiefly because they are half-truths. **1878** SEELEY *Stein* III. 433 To regard Reform as the best antidote against Revolution.

antidote (ˈæntɪdəʊt), *v.* [f. prec. sb., after med.L. *antidotā-re*, and Fr. *antidoter* (Cotgr. 1611).]
†**1.** *trans.* To furnish with an antidote; fortify against poison (a man or his system). Also *fig. Obs.*
1630 J. TAYLOR (Water P.) *Wks.* III. 98/1 She's antidoted, well perfum'd and painted. **1655** GURNALL *Chr. in Arm.* ix. (1669) 94/2 Be..careful to antidote thy Soul against receiving infection. *a* **1703** BURKITT *On N.T.* Matt. x. 31 To antidote our spirits against all distrustful fears.
2. To apply an antidote to, counteract (a poison, etc.). Also *fig.*
1661 BURNEY *Κέρδ. Δῶρον* 45 As the dearest Father, he has compassion to antidote extreams. **1742** RICHARDSON *Pamela* III. 238 Incapable of antidoting the Poison he has spread. **1869** H. USSHER in *Eng. Mech.* 3 Dec., Opium or belladonna taken internally antidote each other.

†**'antidoter.** *Obs. rare*—[1]. [f. as prec. + -ER.[1]] One who gives an antidote. (In the quot. the writer of a pamphlet entitled 'The Antidote.')
a **1709** SIR R. ATKINS *Parl. & Pol. Tracts* (1734) 376 The Opinion the Antidoter maintains.

†**anti'dotical,** *a. Obs. rare*—[1]. [f. Gr. ἀντίδοτ-ον (see ANTIDOTE) + -ICAL.] Pertaining to, or of the nature of, an antidote.
1607 TOPSELL *Serpents* (1653) 635 Within four hours after he perished, notwithstanding all his antidotical preservatives.

†**anti'dotically,** *adv. Obs.* [f. prec. + -LY[2].] By way of antidote.
1646 SIR T. BROWNE *Pseud. Ep.* 168 Antidotically used.. it is an insufferable delusion.

antidromal (ænˈtɪdrəməl), *a. Bot.* [f. Gr. ἀντί against + -δρομ-ος running + -AL[1]. Cf. Gr. ἀντιδρομέειν to run against.] = next.
1849 LINDLEY *Elem. Bot.* II. ix, *Antidromal*, when the direction of the spire of a lateral organ is the reverse of that on the central stem.

antidromous (ænˈtɪdrəməs), *a. Bot.* [f. as prec. + -OUS.] Running in an opposite direction round an axis.
1878 MASTERS *Henfrey's Bot.* 273 An inflorescence homodromous with the principal axis, antidromous with the leaf-bud. **1881** VINES in *Jrnl. Bot.* X. No. 217. 4 When the antidromous branch is developed, a system of alternating branches is produced.

antidysenteric (ˌæntɪdɪsɪnˈtɛrɪk), *a.* and *sb. Med.* [ANTI- 3.] **A.** *adj.* Of use against dysentery. **B.** *sb.* (sc. medicine.)
1853 T. ROSS *Humboldt's Trav.* III. xxv. 24 The febrifuge and antidysenteric bark of the Bonplandia.

antidysen'terical, *a.* = prec.
1775 in ASH.

antidysuric (ˌæntɪdɪˈsjʊərɪk), *a. Med.* [f. ANTI- 3 + Gr. δυσουρικ-ός, f. δυσουρία retention of urine.] Of use against dysury.

anti-emetic, -ephialtic, var. ANTEMETIC, -EPHIALTIC.
1830 LINDLEY *Nat. Syst. Bot.* 136 Employed..as a tonic, stomachic, and anti-emetic.

anti-ethnic (æntɪˈɛθnɪk), *a.* [f. ANTI- 3 + Gr. ἐθνικ-ός Gentile, f. ἔθνος (Gentile) nation.] Against the Gentiles, or nations other than the Jewish.
1861 W. MILL *Applic. Panth. Princ.* (ed. 2) 169 Their [the Rabbis'] own anti-ethnic prejudices.

anti-fat (ˈæntɪfæt), *a.* and *sb.* [ANTI-[1] 4, 7.]
A. *adj.* That counteracts the formation, or reduces the amount, of fat. **B.** *sb.* (*Disused.*) A substance used to counteract obesity.
1886 *Chambers's Jrnl.* III. 46/1 He must feed on either locusts or grasshoppers, which are both supposed to be anti-fat diet. **1887** BENTLEY *Man. Bot.* (ed. 5) 768 This Alga is the essential constituent in the nostrum termed Anti-Fat. **1909** *Brit. Med. Assoc., Secret Remedies* ix. 92 Anti-Fat..acts solely upon the food in the stomach.

†**antife'brific,** *a.* and *sb. Med. Obs.* [ANTI- 3. Through some error all the early works have *-febritick.*] = next.
1661 LOVELL *Hist. Anim. & Min.* 289 Their oile..is used in the antifebritick plaister. **1686** MOYLE *Sea Chyrurg.* I. 6 Greater quantities of Antefebritiques. **1694** WESTMACOTT *Scrip. Herb.* 156 This antifebrifick plaster was the secret of a great practitioner.

antifebrile (æntɪˈfɛbrɪl, -fiː-), *a.* and *sb. Med.* [ANTI- 3.] **A.** *adj.* Efficacious against fever. **B.** *sb.* A substance having this property.
1661 LOVELL *Hist. Anim. & Min.* 233 Some use them as an antefebrile. *a* **1734** FLOYER (J.), Antifebrile medicines check the ebullition. **1859** R. BURTON in *Jrnl. R.G.S.* XXIX. 184 Onions—an antifebrile which flourishes better in Central than in Maritime Africa.

anti-'fed, -'federal, -'federalist. *U.S.* [ANTI-[1] 5.] An opponent of federalism in the early years of American independence. Also **anti-'federal** *a.*, **-'federalism.**
1787 *Independent Gazetteer* (Philad.) 28 Sept., This anti-federalist should reflect that his name may yet be known and himself branded with infamy as an enemy to the happiness of the United States. **1788** R. KING in *Life & Corr.* (1894) I. 327 Of three thousand votes given..not more than two hundred were in favor of the antifederal Ticket. **1788** C. GORE in R. King *Life & Corr.* (1894) I. 348 Non-residence in one candidate..who was abhorred for his anti-federalism. **1788** *Maryland Jrnl.* 3 June (Th.), The famous Dr. Spring asked a lady on which side she was, fed, or antifed. **1800** *Aurora* (Philad.) 28 Nov. (Th.), By anti-federalist, the same is meant as by jacobin,..and the like. **1804** FESSENDEN *Orig. Poems* (1806) 55 And swears no anti-federal noddy Has half a soul to bless his body. **1805** —— *Democr. Unveiled* I. 13 As Torries many of you vex'd us As Antifederals then perplex'd us. *Ibid.* 112 Supported by the factious heads Of ever restless anti-feds.

anti-'feminist, *sb.* and *a.* [ANTI-[1] 5.] **A.** *sb.* One opposed to women or to feminism (sense 2); a person (usu. a man) who is hostile to sexual equality or to the advocacy of women's rights. **B.** *adj.* Of, pertaining to, or characterized by such views.
1924 G. B. SHAW *Saint Joan* Pref. p. x, If a historian is an Anti-Feminist, and does not believe women to be capable of genius in the traditional masculine departments, he will never make anything of Joan, whose genius was turned to practical account mainly in soldiering and politics. **1930** C. S. LEWIS *Let.* 10 June (1966) 141 His taking—what one expects to find mentioned only in anti-feminists—the Lilithian desire to be admired. **1936** H. NICOLSON *Let.* 2 Dec. (1966) 281 How I loathe and detest women... I am feeling very anti-feminist tonight. I *loathe* women. The only thing that will make them behave decently is to give them complete equality and no privileges. **1970** R. BARBER *Knight & Chivalry* II. viii. 131 Jean..is on the side of the clerks, when he is not being openly antifeminist. **1982** *N.Y. Times Mag.* 5 Sept. 46 Many points were valid and even antifeminists have seen the hopelessness of arguing against them.
Hence **anti-feminism.**
1954 J. A. C. BROWN *Soc. Psychol. Industry* vi. 175 Such attitudes as loyalty to a leader,..stress on authoritarian discipline, antifeminism, partriotism. **1981** *Amer. Speech* LVI. 87 Reactions against earlier epicene pronouns often reveal a spirit of antifeminism.

antiferromagnetic (ˌæntɪfɛrəʊmægˈnɛtɪk), *a.* and *sb.* [ad. G. *antiferromagnetisch* (L. Hulthèn 1936, in *Proc. Kon. Akad. Amsterdam* XXXIX. 190), f. ANTI-[1] 3 + FERROMAGNETIC *a.*] **A.** *adj.* Characterized by oppositely directed (or anti-parallel) alignment of electron spin. **B.** *sb.* A magnetic substance with these properties.
L. Néel 1932, writing in French in *Ann. Phys.* XVIII. 5f., introduced the idea of antiferromagnetism but did not use the words *antiferromagnétique*, *-magnétisme*.
1936 *Sci. Abstr.* A. XXXIX. 548 Cases where interchange action occurs, but with a positive coefficient, are indicated as antiferromagnetic. **1938** *Physical Rev.* LIV. 82/1 Manganese probably is an antiferromagnetic substance. **1949** *Ibid.* LXXVI. 1257/1 At absolute zero all of the atoms on one lattice have their electronic magnetic moments aligned in the same direction and all of the atoms on the other lattice have their moments antiparallel to the first. Above the Curie temperature the thermal energy is sufficient to overcome the tendency of the atoms to lock antiparallel... Materials exhibiting the characteristics described above have been designated 'antiferromagnetic'. **1955** *Sci. News* XXXVII. 36 In ferro-, antiferro-, or ferri-magnetics the alignment of atomic magnets is ordered and periodic.
Hence **,antiferro'magnetism,** the quality of being antiferromagnetic; the phenomena exhibited by antiferromagnetic bodies.
1938 F. BITTER in *Physical Rev.* LIV. 79 The proposed equations of state..may be regarded as an attempt to describe antiferromagnetism (i.e., the case in which oppositely directed spins on adjacent atoms have the lowest energy). **1961** *Encycl. Dict. Physics* I. 222/1 The state of complete antiferromagnetism (antiparallel alignment of spin vectors) will be attained only at absolute zero.

anti-fog'matic. *U.S.* [f. ANTI-[1] 6 + *fogmatic*, jocular formation on FOG *sb.*] An alcoholic liquor taken to counteract the effects of damp or wet.

1789 *Massachusetts Spy* 12 Nov. 4/2 Rum. Its great utility in preserving the planters from the effects of the damp and unwholsome air of the morning, has given it the medical name of an Antifogmatick. **1824** in HORRY & WEEMS *Life Marion* (1833) ix. 77 Now suppose you take a glass of peach ..they say it is good of a rainy morning..a mighty antifogmatic. **1852** *As good as a Comedy* (Philad.) 134 (Th.), Tom Nettles [was] mixing a couple of rosy anti-fogmatics.

anti-freeze (ˈæntɪfriːz), *a.* and *sb.* [ANTI-¹ 4, 7.] **A.** *adj.* That reduces the tendency (of a liquid) to freeze. **B.** *sb.* A chemical agent added to water to lower its freezing point.

1913 A. L. CLOUGH *Dict. Automobile Terms* 13 Anti-freeze solution. **1935** *Amer. Speech* X. 122/1 The material is.. limited by excluding the names of all products such as antifreezes which have neither a paraffin nor an asphalt base. **1937** D. ALDIS *Time at her Heels* i. 10 They kept the Ford out in the street in front of the house. It worked all right if they remembered to get it filled with anti-freeze. **1959** *Which?* Dec. 174 Most of the anti-freeze compounds sold in Britain are based on ethylene-glycol because methanol, though cheaper, has disadvantages.

antifriction (æntɪˈfrɪkʃən). [ANTI- 6.] That which prevents friction. Also *attrib.* and *fig.*

1837 CARLYLE *Diam. Neckl.* viii, Oil of flattery, the best patent antifriction known. **1869** *Eng. Mech.* 14 May 172/2 The block is kept in position by..anti-friction bowls.

anti-g (ˌæntɪˈdʒiː), *a.* [ANTI-¹ 2a + G III. b.] Designed to counteract the effects of high acceleration; ***anti-g suit***, = G-SUIT.

1945 *Flight* XLVII. 36/1 (*heading*) Anti-g suit for fighter pilots. A simple but effective means of protecting the fighter pilot from the effects of 'positive g' during violent manœuvres is now in general use with U.S.A.A.F. fighter pilots. **1961** *Ibid.* LXXX. 50/2 Ducts from the main air systems lead to..the pilot's anti-g trousers and air ventilated suit.

antigalactic (ˌæntɪgəˈlæktɪk), *a.* and *sb.* [f. ANTI- 3 + Gr. γαλακτικός, f. γάλακτ- milk.] **A.** *adj.* Of use in preventing the secretion of milk. **B.** *sb.* (sc. medicine, etc.)

1847 in CRAIG.

anti-Gallic (æntɪˈgælɪk), *a.* [f. ANTI- 3 + L. *Gallicus* of Gaul, 'French.'] = next.

1756 *Gentl. Mag.* XXVI. 512 That unequall'd zeal and Antigallic spirit.

anti-ˈGallican, *a.* and *sb.* [f. prec. + -AN.] **A.** *adj.* Opposed to what is French.

1765 SMOLLETT *Trav.* 56 Antigallican spirit enough to produce themselves in their own genuine English dress. **1817** COLERIDGE *Biogr. Lit.* (1817) 101 Far greater earnestness and zeal both anti-jacobin and anti-gallican. **1842** ALISON *Hist. Eur.* (1849) X. lxvi. §22. 135 The convulsion, as Wellington often observed, was anti-Gallican, not democratic.

B. *sb.* One opposed to the French.

1755 *Gentl. Mag.* XXV. 280 A..badge, given by the society of Antigallicans. **1826** MITFORD *Village* Ser. II. (1863) 331 The Anti-Gallicans retained Jacob. **1854** BANCROFT *Hist. U.S.* (1876) VI. xlvi. 302 Congress was divided between what the French envoy named 'Gallicans' and 'anti-Gallicans.'

anti-ˈGallicanism. [f. prec. + -ISM.] Opposition or aversion to the French.

1805 W. TAYLOR in *Ann. Rev.* III. 260 Anti-gallicanism is our habitual interest. **1810** COLERIDGE *Friend* VII. vi. (1867) 378 Translating their fanatical anti-Jacobinism into a well-grounded..anti-Gallicanism.

antigen (ˈæntɪdʒɛn). [a. G. *antigen*, ad. F. *antigène adj.* (L. Deutsch 1899, in *Ann. de l'Inst. Pasteur* XIII. 704), f. ANTI(BODY + -GEN.] A foreign substance which, when introduced into a living organism, stimulates the production of an antibody.

1908 PARK & BOLDUAN in Nuttall & Graham-Smith *Bacteriol. of Diphtheria* 628, v. Pirquet and Schick attribute the immediate or hastened reaction and indeed the serum disease as a whole to an interaction between the antigen and the antibody. **1911** *Jrnl. Chem. Soc.* C. II. 812 When an optimum dose of antigen (goat's or rat's blood) is injected intravenously into a dog. **1955** *Sci. News Let.* 16 Apr. 253/1 The test reaction is based on the body's ability to react to and destroy bacteria and foreign protein invaders. These foreign agents are called antigens, while the body's own destructive agents are referred to as antibodies. **1959** *Chambers's Encycl.* VII. 398/1 Most antigens are proteins or contain substantial amounts of protein, and they have a high molecular weight.

Hence **antiˈgenic** *a.*, of the nature of an antigen, **antiˈgenically** *adv.* So **ˌantigeˈnicity**, the condition or property of being antigenic.

1913 *Arch. Internal Med.* XI. 85 The 'antigenic' function of all the extracts resides solely in the lipoid fraction. **1916** OLITSKY & BERNSTEIN in *Jrnl. Infectious Diseases* XIX. 259 We have shown that organisms grown on serum media incorporate..those serum elements which possess serum antigenic properties. **1946** *Nature* 27 July 120/1 The hæmagglutinins are complexes of a phospholipid (probably lecithin) with an antigenically specific virus constituent. *Ibid.* 17 Aug. 239/1 The loss in antigenicity during preparation of the toxoid (measured by flocculation) was about half that usually found.

anti-god (ˈæntɪgɒd). [ANTI- 1.] He who or that which is opposed to God. *Hence* **b.** A rival deity; **c.** An evil demon or devil.

1684 CHARNOCK *Attrib. God* (1834) II. 567 It may be called..the spirit of anti-god. **1685** BAXTER *Paraphr. 1 John* ii. 18 It is not antichrist properly..but the anti-god, the Roman Idolatrous Emperor. **1720** WATERLAND *8 Serm.* 145 All Rival, or Anti-Gods, set up in opposition to God. **1856** R. VAUGHAN *Mystics* (1860) I. III. iv. 81 The malignant Dæmons, the Anti-gods (ἀντιθέους).

antigorite (ænˈtɪgəraɪt). *Min.* [f. *Antigorio*, the valley in Piedmont, where found + -ITE.] A mineral, a variety of Serpentine.

1862 DANA *Man. Geol.* §8. 82 Nickel and Chrome..occur also..in the antigorite of Piedmont.

†**ˈantigraph.** *Obs.*⁻⁰ [ad. med.L. *antigraphum*, a. Gr. ἀντίγραφον a duplicate copy: see ANTI- A. Cf. Fr. *antigraphe*.] A copy or transcript.

1656 BLOUNT *Glossogr.*, *Antigraph*, an example, a copy.

†**anˈtigrapher.** *Obs.*⁻⁰ [f. med.L. *antigraphus* (cf. Gr. ἀντιγραφεύς a check-clerk) + -ER¹.]

1656 BLOUNT *Glossogr.*, *Antigrapher*, a Comptroller..he that keeps the Accompts or Money received to the Prince's use, a maker or keeper of Counterpanes of Deeds.

anti-ˈgravity, *a.* and *sb.* [ANTI-¹ 2a.] **A.** *adj.* = ANTI-G *a.* **B.** *sb.* A hypothetical force opposed to that of gravity. Chiefly *attrib.* Also in shortened form (*colloq.*) **anti-grav.**

1945 in *Amer. Speech* (1946) XXI. 142/1 The anti-gravity pneumatic pants apply pressure to the pilot's abdomen and legs, preventing the blood from pooling in the lower extremities. **1946** A. C. CLARKE in *Across Sea of Stars* (1959) 155 The three explorers stepped out of the airlock and adjusted the antigravity fields of their suits. **1949** *Ibid.* 58 Antigravity..the ultimate secret that man had never learned. **1953** C. L. HARNESS *Flight into Yesterday* (1964) ii. 32 He had found a way to beat the tremendous solar gravity by..an anti-grav mechanism.

antiˈgropelos. [Said to be made up from Gr. ἀντί against + ὑγρός wet + πηλός mud (which should give *anthygroˈpēlos*)!] Coverings to protect the legs against wet mud; waterproof leggings. (Originally, a proprietary name.)

1848 KINGSLEY *Yeast* i. (D.) The surgeon of the Union in mackintosh and antigropelos. **1857** *Fraser's Mag.* LVI. 350 Would he not have stood aghast at the term 'antigropylos?' Would it not puzzle a Scaliger or Bentley? **1876** GEO. ELIOT *Dan. Der.* I. vii. 115 Her brother had on his antigropelos.

Antiguan (ænˈtiːgən), *sb.* and *a.* [f. the name of *Antigua* (see below), a. Sp. fem. of *antiguo*, lit. 'ancient, antique', + -AN.] **A.** *sb.* A native or inhabitant of the island of Antigua in the West Indies. **B.** *adj.* Of or pertaining to Antigua or its inhabitants.

1844 MRS. FLANNIGAN (*title*) Antigua and the Antiguans. *Ibid.* p. vi, Blinded by the many charms of..Antiguan society. **1876** W. G. PALGRAVE *Dutch Guiana* vii. 234 Some colonial Briton—Antiguan, it may be. **1896** M. BEERBOHM in *Yellow Bk.* IX. 169 The Antiguan was already on the brink of middle-age when he first trod the English shore. *Ibid.* 170 Emma..had cast a magic net about the warm Antiguan heart. **1952** *Jrnl. Polit. Econ.* Feb. LX. 101/1 That Antiguan workers sometimes reject classes of employment cannot be taken as clear evidence that they are satisfied with little income. **1973** *Advocate-News* (Barbados) 15 Jan. 6/2 On February 20, 1972, Antiguan sportman Clenceau Perry set out and organised a social and cricket club for less privileged Antiguans. **1985** *Washington Post* 12 June A30/4 A handful of Jamaicans, Barbadians or Antiguans, remnants of the U.S.-sponsored Caribbean Peace Force, are likely to remain on hand for a number of months to supervise Grenadian guards at the Richmond Hill prison.

anti-guggler (æntɪˈgʌglə(r)). [f. ANTI- 5 + *guggle* = GURGLE + -ER¹.] A small siphon inserted into the mouths of carboys, etc., when liquor is poured out, so as to admit the air without gurgling.

1794 G. ADAMS *Nat. & Exp. Phil.* I. ii. 58 The anti-guggler..formerly much used for the decanting of liquors liable to sediment. **1875** in URE *Dict. Arts.*

antihelix, anthelix (æntɪˈhiːlɪks, ˈænθɪlɪks). *Anat.* [a. Gr. ἀνθέλιξ, f. ἀντ(ί opposite + ἕλιξ the outer ear, *orig.* a spiral, curl, eddy.] The curved elevation within the helix or outer rim of the ear, which surrounds the central cavity or concha.

1721 BAILEY, *Anthelix*, The inward brink of the outward ear. **1836-39** TODD *Cycl. Anat. & Phys.* II. 550/2 The eminence within the helix is called anthelix. **1871** DARWIN *Desc. Man* I. i. 21 Various folds and prominences (helix and antihelix, tragus and anti-tragus) which in the lower animals strengthen and support the ear.

anti-hero (ˈæntɪˌhɪərəʊ). [ANTI-¹ 1b.] One who is the opposite or reverse of a hero; esp. a chief character in a poem, play, or story who is totally unlike a conventional hero. So **ˈanti-ˌheroine.**

1714 STEELE *Lover* (1720) 13 Every Anti-Heroe in Great Britain. **1897** W. P. KER *Epic & Romance* iv. 346 The ineffectual sorrows and good intentions of the anti-hero Fromont. **1907** F. W. CHANDLER *Lit. Roguery* I. ii. 68 A work of the Eulenspiegel type..its anti-heroes remain less roguish than Till. *Ibid.* iv. 148 Other women figured as anti-heroines in less literary tracts. **1958** *Listener* 14 Aug. 248/3 Anti-heroes and unpleasant young men are now so morbidly the fashion. **1959** *Sunday Times* 27 Dec. 6/4 It was the decade of..the new, shambling, oafish anti-heroes, flotsam of the Welfare State—Lucky Jim and his first cousin Joe Lampton. **1962** *Times* 26 Jan. 16/5 Miss Wendy Baldwin presented a drab, vulgar anti-heroine.

Hence **anti-heˈroic** *a.*

1876 E. HOPKINS *Rose Turq.* I. i. 27 A lame and impotent conclusion..and altogether Anti-heroic. **1959** *Times Lit. Suppl.* 20 Nov. 670/4 *Ulysses* was and remains the first great masterpiece of anti-heroic literature.

ˌantiˈhistamine, *a.* and *sb.* [ANTI-¹ 6d.] **A.** *adj.* That counteracts the effect of histamine. **B.** *sb.* A synthetic drug having this property, used esp. in the treatment of certain allergic conditions. So **ˌanti-histaˈminic** *a.* and *sb.*

1933 A. C. H. YEN & HSI-CHUN CHANG in *Proc. Soc. Exper. Biol.* XXXI. 338 The sensitivity to histamine in guinea pig and man may be accounted for by the absence of antihistamine activity in their blood. **1942** *Jrnl. Immunology* XLIV. 219 In a series of studies on the antihistamine activity of a number of derivatives of phenoxyethylamine ..(1571 F) prevented certain histamine effects. **1947** *Lancet* 17 May 678/1 (*title*) The Anti-histamine Drugs. **1950** *Chem. & Engin. News* XXVIII. 846/1 Opinion is divided on the use of antihistaminics as cold cures. **1955** *Sci. News Let.* 16 July 40/2 Many of the itch remedies used today..such as anti-histaminics..may depend for their results on a partial blocking of the proteinases, or itch enzymes. **1957** *N.Z. Listener* 26 July 15/1 The antihistamines, discovered to have a quietening effect and to act specifically against motion sickness. **1964** S. DUKE-ELDER *Parsons' Diseases of Eye* (ed. 14) xxii. 313 Treatment should consist of the administration of anti-histaminic or diuretic drugs in the early stages.

antihydropic (ˌæntɪhaɪˈdrɒpɪk), *a.* and *sb. Med.* [f. ANTI- 3 + Gr. ὑδρωπικ-ός f. ὕδρωπ-α (ὕδρωψ) dropsy.] **A.** *adj.* Tending to counteract dropsy. **B.** *sb.* (sc. medicine, etc.)

1742 SHORT *Dropsy* in *Phil. Trans.* XLII. 224 An anti-hydropic stomachic Mixture. **1853** in MAYNE *Exp. Lex.*

antihydropin (æntɪˈhaɪdrəpɪn). *Med.* [f. ANTI- + Gr. ὕδρωπ-α (see prec.) + -IN.] A crystalline principle obtained from the body of the cockroach, used in medicine as an antihydropic.

1875 H. WOOD *Therap.* (1879) 497 The dried bodies of.. cockroaches have long been popularly used in Russia as a remedy for dropsy, and under the name of antihydropin have been introduced into practical medicine.

antihygienic (ˌæntɪhaɪdʒɪˈɛnɪk, -ˈdʒiːnɪk), *a.* [ANTI- 3.] Adverse to health, insalubrious.

1876 tr. *Wagner's Gen. Pathol.* 143 The tendency to them in the affected localities can..be increased by anti-hygienic conditions.

antihypnotic (ˌæntɪhɪpˈnɒtɪk), *a.* and *sb. Med.* Also **anthypn-**. [f. ANTI- 3 + Gr. ὑπνωτικ-ός sleepy. The Gr. would have been ἀνθυπν-, *anthypn-*.] **A.** *adj.* Tending to prevent sleep. **B.** *sb.* A medicine, etc. so used.

1681 tr. *Willis's Rem. Med. Wks.*, Antihypnotics. **1693** SIR T. BLOUNT *Nat. Hist.* 110 Those who write of Coffee, do almost all reckon it amongst the Antihypnoticks. **1839** HOOPER *Med. Dict.* 135 *Anthypnotic.*

antihysteric (ˌæntɪhɪˈstɛrɪk), *a.* and *sb. Med.* [ANTI- 3.] **A.** *adj.* Of use against hysteria. **B.** *sb.* (sc. medicine, etc.)

1747 BERKELEY *Siris* 99 (T.) It..is an excellent antihysterick. **1879** P. BAYNE in *Lit. World* XIX. 137/1 A box of anti-hysteric pills.

anti-icer (æntɪˈaɪsə(r)). [f. ANTI-¹ 6 + ICE *sb.* + -ER¹.] A device for preventing the formation of ice on an aeroplane. Cf. ANTICER.

1935 *Aircraft Engineering* Nov. 281/2 Figures 7 and 8 are reproductions..illustrating the action of the anti-icer under ice forming conditions. *Ibid.*, The fin to which an anti-icer is fitted is also free from ice.

anti-icteric (ˌæntɪɪkˈtɛrɪk), *a.* and *sb. Med.* [f. ANTI- 3 + Gr. ἰκτερικ-ός, f. ἴκτερος jaundice.]

A. *adj.* Of use against jaundice. **B.** *sb.* (sc. medicine.)

1853 in MAYNE *Exp. Lex.*

anti-Jacobin (æntɪˈdʒækəbɪn), *a.* and *sb.* [ANTI- 3.] **A.** *adj.* Opposed to the Jacobins, one of the revolutionary parties in France in 1789; hence, opposed to the French Revolution, and to those who sympathized with it, or with democratic principles, who were nicknamed *Jacobins* by the partisans of Mr. Pitt's administration. **B.** *sb.* One opposed to the Jacobins, etc.; also name of a weekly paper started in 1797 in hostility to the French Revolution and democratic principles.

1809 *Hist. Eur.* in *Ann. Reg.* 93/1 The loudest of those anti-jacobin declaimers. **1826** MISS MITFORD *Village* Ser. II. (1863) 331 How my friend the cobbler came to be..so violent an Anti-jacobin. **1834** MACAULAY *Pitt* in *Biogr.* (1860) 201 Eager and intolerant Anti-jacobins. **1867** *Cornh. Mag.* Jan. 63 The neglect into which the wit and wisdom of the Anti-Jacobin have fallen.

anti-ˈJacobinism. [f. prec. + -ISM.] The practice and principles of the Anti-Jacobins.

1809 *Hist. Eur.* in *Ann. Reg.* 93/1 The cry of anti-jacobinism which had been set up with so much vigour. **1827** SCOTT in Lockhart *Life* (1839) IX. 106 The champion of antijacobinism.

antik(e, obs. f. ANTIC, and of ANTIQUE.

antilap'sarian. [f. ANTI- 5 + L. *laps-us* fall + -ARIAN.] A disbeliever in the Fall of man.
 1674 HICKMAN *Hist. Quinquart.* 74 The Writings of some Antelapsarians I have read.

Antilegomena (ˌæntɪlɪˈgɒmɪnə), *sb. pl.* [Gr. ἀντιλεγόμενα (Eus. Caes.), neut. pl. of pres. pple. pass. of ἀντιλέγειν to gainsay, pass. to be disputed.] (See quot. 1957.)
 [**1847** CRUSÉ tr. *Eusebius's Eccl. Hist.* (ed. 4) 247 He has given us abridged accounts of all the canonical Scriptures, not even omitting those that are disputed (The Antilegomenoi).] **1875** *Encycl. Brit.* II. 128/2 The following is a catalogue of the *Antilegomena.* **1957** *Oxf. Dict. Chr. Ch.* 62/1 *Antilegomena*, the word is used by Eusebius of Caesarea ..of those Scriptural books of which the claim to be considered a part of the NT canon was disputed. He subdivided them into (1) those 'generally recognized' (γνώριμοι), viz. Jas., Jude, 2 Pet., 2 and 3 Jn.; and (2) the 'spurious' (νόθοι), viz. the 'Acts of Paul', the 'Shepherd of Hermas', the 'Apoc. of Peter', the 'Ep. of Barnabas', the 'Didache', and (perhaps) the 'Rev. of St. John'.

antilibration (ˌæntɪlaɪˈbreɪʃən). *rare.* [f. ANTI-A. + L. *librātiōn-em* poising, balancing, n. of action f. *librāre* to balance.] The weighing of one thing against another; counterpoising.
 a **1858** DE QUINCEY *Whiggism* Wks. VI. 160 His artful antithesis, and solemn antilibration of cadences.

anti-life (ˈæntɪlaɪf), *a.* and *sb.* [ANTI-[1] 2 b, 4 + LIFE *sb.*] **A.** *adj.* Opposed to living fully and harmoniously with the natural order. **B.** *sb.* An alleged contrary principle to full and natural living; an attitude, or course of action, in accordance with this principle.
 1926 D. H. LAWRENCE *Plumed Serpent* vi. 112 But he, too, was widdershins, unwinding the sensations of disintegration and anti-life. **1929** —— *Let.* 12 June in F. Lawrence *Not I, But the Wind* (1935) 252 The real principle of Evil is not anti-Christ or anti-Jehovah, but anti-life. I agree with you, in a sense, that I am with the anti-Christ. Only I am not anti-life. **1938** 'N. BLAKE' *Beast must Die* III. xii. 214 Somewhere deep within her, thought Nigel, there is a stone core of lifelessness, an anti-life principle. **1956** C. WILSON *Outsider* iii. 47 The atmosphere of the Existentialist Outsider is unpleasant to breathe. There is something nauseating, anti-life, about it.

antilithic (æntɪˈlɪθɪk), *a.* and *sb. Med.* [f. ANTI-3 + Gr. λιθικ-ός, f. λίθ-ος stone.] **A.** *adj.* Tending to counteract stone in the bladder. **B.** *sb.* A medicine so employed.
 1853 in MAYNE *Exp. Lex.* **1869** *Eng. Mech.* 10 Dec. 312/2 Its medicinal properties are antacid, antilithic.

Antillean (ˌæntɪˈliːən, ænˈtɪlɪən), *a.* [f. *Antilles* + -AN.] Of or belonging to the Antilles, a group of islands in the West Indies, or their inhabitants.
 1876 A. R. WALLACE *Geogr. Distribution of Animals* II. xiv. 60 (*heading*) The West Indian Islands, or Antillean Sub-region. *Ibid.* 62 On the western group of islands..the chief pecularities of Antillean zoology are developed. **1888** A. AGASSIZ in *Bull. Mus. Compar. Zool.* XIV. 116 The deep soundings..do not lend much support to the theory of an Antillean continent. **1902** *Encycl. Brit.* XXV. 361/1 Central America, the West Indies, and various submarine ridges by which they are connected with one another and with the mainland to the west..all belong together in what has been termed the Antillean mountain system. **1961** L. D. STAMP *Gloss Geogr. Terms* 532 *Stratigraphical Terms*..Antillean. Miocene orogenesis of West Indies.

antilog, abbreviation of ANTILOGARITHM.
 1910 G. C. DOUGLAS (*title*) Douglas' Two Colour Logs & Anti-Logs. **1927** A. G. CRACKNELL (*title*) Elementary Practical Mathematics. With Tables of Logs and Antilogs. **1959** G. & R. C. JAMES *Math. Dict.* 16/2 *Antilogarithm*, the number whose logarithm is the given number; *e.g.* $\text{antilog}_{10}2 = 100$.

antilogarithm (æntɪˈlɒgərɪθ(ə)m). *Math.* [ANTI- 2. Cf. Fr. *anti-logarithme.*]
 †**1.** 'The complement of the logarithm of a sine, tangent, or secant; or the difference between that and the logarithm of ninety degrees.' Chambers *Cycl. Supp.* 1753. *Obs.*
 1796 HUTTON *Math. Dict.* I. 121.
 2. The number to which the logarithm belongs.
 1675 COLLINS in Rigaud *Corr. Sci. Men* I. 215 Between.. 1630 and 1640, Dr. Pell and one Mr. Warner..agreed to make a table of antilogarithms. **1834** *Penny Cycl.* II. 105 Antilogarithm, as used in this country, means *the number to the logarithm.* Thus in Briggs' system, 100 is the antilogarithm of 2, because 2 is the logarithm of 100.

antilogarithmic (-lɒgəˈrɪθmɪk), *a.* [f. prec. + -IC.] Of or pertaining to antilogarithms.
 1742 DODSON (*title*) The Antilogarithmic Canon. **1770** ROBERTSON in *Phil. Trans.* LX. 509 To illustrate the use of his Antilogarithmic Tables. **1850** SIR J. HERSCHEL *Ess.* (1857) 399 The exponential or antilogarithmic function.

antilogism (ænˈtɪlədʒɪz(ə)m). *Logic.* [f. Gr. ἀντιλογία contradiction + -ISM; the existence of late Gr. ἀντιλογισμός 'countercharge' was unkn. to the coiner.] An inconsistent triad, or set of three propositions which cannot all be true together, obtained by taking the premisses of any valid syllogism together with the negation of the conclusion. Hence **anˌtiloˈgistic** *a.*, **anˌtiloˈgistically** *adv.*
 The term, though implicit in earlier writers (see quot. 1962), was first used by Mrs. C. Ladd-Franklin.
 1902 MRS. C. LADD-FRANKLIN in *Baldwin's Dict. Philos. & Psychol.* II. 633/1 The three propositions taken together constitute an inconsistency, or an incompatibility, or, as it may perhaps be called, to distinguish it from the syllogism, an antilogism. **1922** W. E. JOHNSON *Logic* II. iv. 78 An antilogism may be defined as a formal disjunction of two, three, or more propositions, each of which is entertained hypothetically. *Ibid.* 80 From this single antilogistic dictum we construct the dicta for the first three figures of syllogism. **1962** W. & M. KNEALE *Devel. of Logic* iv. 278 Burleigh.. goes on to remark that Aristotle's procedure of indirect reduction depends on the principle that the premisses and the negation of the conclusion of any valid syllogism form together an inconsistent triad (or antilogism as it has sometimes been called).

antilogy (ænˈtɪlədʒɪ). [ad. Gr. ἀντιλογία, f. ἀντί against + -λογία speaking; directly, or through, Med.L. *antilogia*, or Fr. *antilogie.*] A contradiction in terms, or ideas.
 1614 BOYS *Wks.* (1630) 782 The replies and Antilogies of our accuratly learned Diuines. **1681** *Tears of Press* in *Harl. Misc.* (1745) IV. 426 Alas, How miserably is Truth torn by Antilogies! **1751** CHAMBERS *Cycl.* s.v., The seeming antilogies in the bible. **1855** SIR W. HAMILTON *Metaph.* App. (1877) I. 402 Speculation ends in a series of insoluble antilogies.

antilopine (ænˈtɪləpaɪn), *a.* Also **ante-**. [ad. mod.L. *antilopīn-us*, f. *antilope*: see ANTELOPE.] Of or pertaining to the antelope.
 1827 GRIFFITH *Cuvier* IV. 197 Another instance of wool on the skin of an antelopine species. **1870** HUXLEY in *Q. Jrnl. Geol. S.* XXVI. Addr. 55 Cameline, bovine, antilopine, cervine, and traguline Ruminants.

†**an'tiloquist.** *Obs.*[−0] [f. ANTI- A. + L. *-loqu-us* speaking + -IST.] 'A contradictor.' J.
 1742 in BAILEY; whence in JOHNSON, etc.

†**an'tiloquy.** *Obs.*[−0] [ad. med.L. *antiloquium* contradiction: see prec.] 'Contradiction, gainsaying or overthwarting.' Blount *Glossogr.* 1656.

antilyssic (æntɪˈlɪsɪk), *a.* and *sb. Med.* [f. ANTI-3 + Gr. λύσσ-α rage + -IC.] **A.** *adj.* Of use against hydrophobia. **B.** *sb.* (sc. medicine, etc.)

antim(e, obs. form of ANTHEM.

antimacassar (ˌæntɪməˈkæsə(r)). [f. ANTI- 6 + *macassar*, proprietary name of a kind of hair-oil.] **a.** A covering thrown over cushions, sofas, chairs, etc. to protect them from grease in the hair, or other soiling, or merely as an ornament.
 1852 *Lady's Newsp.* XI. 36 Anti-maccassar Materials.. crochet cotton..or pink and drab crochet twine. **1859** *All Y. Round* 11 June 157 The anti-Macassar on the arm-chair. **1879** MISS BRADDON *Vixen* III. 281 To sit alone by the fireside, and work antimacassars in crewels.
 b. *transf.* Applied *attrib.* to that which is typical of the period (chiefly the 19th cent.) when antimacassars were in general use.
 1913 *Eng. Rev.* Feb. 482 The Libraries..are largely swayed by the letters they receive, generally from old ladies (worthy, antimacassar people), who regard art with pious misgivings and..spend part of their leisure in denouncing it. **1938** *Scrutiny* VII. 397 Antimacassar evangelicanism and Sunday-school sanctimoniousness.
 Hence **ˌantimaˈcassared** [-ED[2]] *a.*, covered or adorned with an antimacassar. Also *transf.* (see b).
 1907 A. BENNETT *Grim Smile of Five Towns* 56 Seated in the antimacassared arm-chair. **1914** *Times* 13 May 11/5 The antimacassared ease of early Victorian times may have been too much of a good thing, but that was better than the excesses of the modern athletic girl. **1920** D. H. LAWRENCE *Lost Girl* vii. 137 A horse-hair antimacassar-ed sofa. **1928** *Daily Express* 31 July 8/3 The antimacassared chairs, the horse-hair sofa, and the picture of Queen Victoria's jubilee.

†**antimagi'stratical**, *a. Obs.* [ANTI- 3.] Opposed to the power or claims of civil magistrates.
 1645 *Presbyt. Let.* in *Plea Sacram. Test*, The Independents..with other Sects, sufficiently known to be Anti-Magistratical. **1669** *Surv. Naphtali* II. 88 Antimagistraticall clergy.

†**antima'gistrical**, *a. Obs. rare*[−1]. [f. ANTI- 3 + L. *magister* master + -ICAL.] = prec.
 1692 SOUTH *Serm.* V. 261 (T.) It would have been impossible for the Christian religion to have..gained any countenance from the civil power, had it owned such antimagistrical assertions.

Anti-'Mason. *U.S.* [ANTI-[1] 5.] One who is opposed to Freemasonry, used esp. (in the U.S.) of a member of the Anti-Masonic (political) Party.
 1828 in T. WEED *Autobiogr.* (1883) xxvi. 307 If under these multiplied difficulties the Anti-Masons incline to bestow their votes upon Mr. Southwick. **1838** *Congress. Globe* Apr., App. 275/1 Counterfeit Democrats, National Republicans, Antimasons and Abolitionists. **1878** J. H. BEADLE *Western Wilds* xii. 186 They parted and held their own, and they daresn't an anti-mason show hisself.
 So **Anti-Ma'sonic** *a.*; **Anti-'Masonry.**
 1826 (*title*) The Anti-Masonic Enquirer. **1827** in T. W. BARNES *Mem. T. Weed* (1883) 31 The subject of my communication was anti-Masonry. **1828–30** H. D. WARD (*title*) The Anti-Masonic Review and Magazine. **1841** EMERSON *Misc.* 219 Anti-masonry had a deep right and wrong, which gradually emerged to sight out of the turbid controversy. **1880** H. O'RIELLY (*title*) American Political-Antimasonry. **1899** A. H. QUINN *Pennsylv. Stories* 59 His grandfather..had been one of the local leaders of the Anti-Masonic party.

antimasque, -mask (ˈæntɪˌmɑːsk, -æ-). [ANTI-2.] A grotesque interlude between the acts of a masque, to which it served as a foil, and of which it was at first often a burlesque. (Sometimes made *antic-masque.*).
 1613 CHAPMAN *Inns of Court* Plays 1873 III. 107 A company of accomplisht Trauailers..excellent at Antemaskes. **1622** B. JONSON *Masque of Augurs*, We may be admitted, if not for a masque, for an antic-masque. **1625** BACON *Masques, Ess.* (Arb.) 540 Let Anti-masques not be long: they haue been commonly of Fooles, Satyres, Baboones..Antiques. **1761** *Lond. & Environs* IV. 73 (JOD.) The first antimask consisted of beggars and cripples. **1868** BROWNING *Ring & Bk.* x. 1903 The impatient antimasque treads close on kibe O'the very masque's self it will mock.

antimasquer, -ker (ˈæntɪˌmɑːskə(r), -æ-). [f. prec. + -ER[1].] A performer in an antimasque.
 1633 SHIRLEY *Tri. Peace* Introd., The Anti-masquers.. riding in coats and caps of yellow taffeta. **1669** COKAINE *Poems* 125 The Anti-masquers depart: then the Lar Familiaris speaks to the Satyre. **1761** *Lond. & Environs* IV. 73 (JOD.) After this noble troop came the antimasker.

†**ˌantimasque'rade.** *Obs. rare*[−1]. [f. ANTIMASQUE, after MASQUERADE.] The performance of an antimasque.
 1678 BUTLER *Hudibr.* III. III. 83 She order'd th' Antimasquerade, (For his Reception) aforesaid.

'anti-ˌmaximed, *ppl. a. rare*[−1]. [ANTI- 2.] Matched with 'anti-maxims' or counter-maxims.
 1647 WARD *Simp. Cobler* 52 There are some *Maximes* in Law, that would be..well *Anti-Maxim'd.*

antimere (ˈæntɪmɪə(r)). *Biol.* [f. Gr. ἀντί opposite + μέρος part.] Usually pl. *antimeres* or in L. form *antimera*: Opposite divisions or halves.
 1877 HUXLEY *Anat. Inv. An.* ix. 545 The metamorphosis of the mesoderm into radially disposed antimeres. **1879** tr. *Haeckel's Evol. Man.* I. 257 The whole body separates into two similar and symmetrical parts, the right and left halves ..called counterparts, or antimera.

antimeric (æntɪˈmɛrɪk), *a. Phys.* [f. prec. + -IC.] Of or characterized by antimeres.
 1880 *Syd. Soc. Lex.* s.v., An example of antimeric segmentation is to be found in the star-fish.

‖**antimetabole** (ˌæntɪmɪˈtæbəliː). *Rhet.* [L. a. Gr. ἀντιμεταβολή, f. ἀντί in the opposite direction + μεταβολή turning about.] A figure in which the same words or ideas are repeated in inverse order.
 1589 PUTTENHAM *Eng. Poesie* 217 Antimetauole or the Counterchange..as thus. If Poesie be, as some haue said, A speaking picture to the eye: Then is a picture not denaid, To be a muet Poesie. **1657** J. SMITH *Myst. Rhet.* 117 Antimetabole is a sentence inverst, or turn'd back, or it is a form of speech which inverts a sentence by the contrary.

‖**antimetathesis** (ˌæntɪmɪˈtæθɪsɪs). *Rhet.* [L. a. Gr. ἀντιμετάθεσις counterchange, f. ἀντί against + μετατιθέναι to transpose.] Inversion of the members of an antithesis.

ˌantimeta'thetic, *a. rare*[−1]. [f. prec. after Gr. analogies.] Of the nature of antimetathesis.
 1652 URQUHART *Jewel* Wks. 1834, 292 Antimetathetick commutations of epithets.

antimeter (ænˈtɪmɪtə(r)). [f. Gr. ἀντί, expressing equivalence, + μέτρον measure.] An obsolete instrument 'called also *Reflecting Sector*, invented by Mr. Garrard, for measuring small angles with greater accuracy than by the sextant or other instruments commonly used.' *Pantologia* (1819).

antimnemonic (ˌæntɪnɪˈmɒnɪk), *a.* and *sb.* [ANTI- 3.] **A.** *adj.* Prejudicial to the memory. **B.** *sb.* Anything having such a quality.
 1817 COLERIDGE *Biog. Lit.* I. iii. 50 The habit of perusing periodical works may be properly added to Averrhoes' catalogue of Anti-Mnemonics, or weakeners of the memory.

antimonachal (æntɪˈmɒnəkəl), *a.* [ANTI- 3.] Opposed to monkery or monastic usages.
 1864 *Realm* 29 June 8 Means to get married..expresses the most desperately anti-monachal sentiments.

†**'antimoˌnane.** *Chem. Obs.* [f. ANTIMONY + -ANE 2 a.] Obs. name of Antimony trichloride.
 1812 SIR H. DAVY *Chem. Philos.* 403 The only known compound of antimony and chlorine, antimonane, or butter of antimony.

†**antimo'narchial**, *a. Obs.* [ANTI- 3.] = next.
 1710 *Pro & Con* 23 To condemn the Antimonarchial Principles. **1749** BOLINGBROKE *Lett. Patriot.* 83 To think me antimonarchial, and in particular an enemy to the succession of kings by hereditary right.

antimo'narchic, *a.* [ANTI- 3.] = next.
 1660 ROSCOMMON *Poems* (1720) 67 Anti-monarchic heretics. *a* **1733** NORTH *Lives* II. 147 Their anti-monarchic insinuations and pamphlets. **1762** H. WALPOLE *Vertue's*

Anecd. Paint. II. 95 Hated and persecuted by the antimonarchic party.

antimonarchical (ˌæntɪməʊˈnɑːkɪkəl), *a.* [ANTI- 3.] Opposed to monarchy.
1625 *Reign K. Chas.* in Rushw. *Hist. Coll.* (1659) I. 157 The Presbytery, of whose Tyrannical and antimonarchical Principles, he had..experience. 1646 CHAS. I in *Clarend. State Papers* II. 260 The ground of their doctrine is anty-monarchical. 1832 H. COLERIDGE *North. Worthies* I. 25 The anti-monarchical prejudices of Milton. 1847 GROTE *Greece* III. xxxi. 150 The antimonarchical feeling has not perished.

antimoˈnarchically, *adv.* [f. prec. + -LY².] In an antimonarchical way or direction.
1659 in Rushw. *Hist. Coll.* I. 539 That opinion that we are Antimonarchically affected.

antimonarchist (æntɪˈmɒnəkɪst). [ANTI- 5.] A professed opponent of monarchs and monarchy.
a 1672 WOOD *Life* (1848) 82 Dennis Bond, a great Olivarian and Antimonarchist. 1844 DISRAELI *Coningsby* III. iii, Antimonarchists, and democrats.

†**antimonarˈchomachist.** *Obs.* [ANTI- 5.]
1753 CHAMBERS *Cycl. Supp.*, *Antimonarchomachists*, is used by some political writers to denote maintainers of monarchical or absolute power vested by divine right in the persons of princes.

antiˈmonarchy. [ANTI- 6.] Opposition to monarchy.
1648 C. WALKER *Hist. Indep.* I. 122 The predominant Principle is Anti-Monarchy.

antimonate (ˈæntɪməʊˌneɪt, -ˈməʊneɪt). *Chem.* [f. ANTI-MON-Y + -ATE⁴.] A salt of Antimonic acid. (This is the form used by Watts, and is analogous to *selenate*, *chromate*; ANTIMONIATE is preferred by many chemists.)
1854 SCOFFERN in *Orr's Circ. Sc.* Chem. 471 Two antimonates of potash are known. 1863 WATTS *Dict. Chem.* I. 325 The antimonates and metantimonates of the alkali-metals.

antimonial (æntɪˈməʊnɪəl), *a.* and *sb.* [ad. mod.L. *antimōniāl-is*, f. *antimōni-um*: see ANTIMONY and -AL¹.] **A.** *adj.*

1. Of or pertaining to antimony. ***antimonial cups***, made of glass of antimony, to communicate emetic qualities to wine.
1605 TIMME *Quersit.* I. xvi. 79 Spirits mercuriall, arsenical, and antimonial. *a* 1729 BLACKMORE (J.), Though antimonial cups prepar'd with art, Their force to wine through ages should impart. 1754 LEWIS in *Phil. Trans.* XLVIII. 688 It increases the hardness of zinc, and the antimonial semi-metal, but not of bismuth. 1865 *Daily Tel.* 8 July, If his wife died under the effects of antimonial poison.

2. Containing antimony in combination; as in the names of many minerals, e.g. *antimonial arsenic, copper, nickel, ochre.* ***antimonial wine***: sherry containing tartar emetic (tartarated antimony).
1771 SMOLLETT *H. Clinker* 827/2 To forward the operation of the antimonial wine. 1788 *Edinb. New Disp.* (1791) 97 The antimonial caustic of the shops. 1875 URE *Dict. Arts* I. 199 In the works where antimonial ores are smelted.

B. *sb.* A medicine containing antimony.
1727-51 CHAMBERS *Cycl.*, *Antimonials* are chiefly of an emetic tendency. 1754 *Phil. Trans.* XLVIII. 832 A physician, who prescrib'd antimonials, was expelled the faculty. 1875 H. WOOD *Therap.* 512 Antimonials act as diuretics.

antiˈmonian, *a. rare.* = ANTIMONIAL *a.*²
1836 *Blackw. Mag.* XL. 52 Efficient as antimonian wine.

antimoniate (æntɪˈməʊnɪeɪt). *Chem.* [f. mod.L. *antimōniāt-um*, f. *antimōni-um*: see ATE⁴.] A salt of antimonic acid. (Also called ANTIMONATE, q.v.)
1801 CHENEVIX in *Phil. Trans.* XCI. 378 A crystallized salt, which M. Berthollet terms an antimoniate of potash. 1869 ROSCOE *Elem. Chem.* 256 Antimony pentoxide forms salts with the alkalis, called antimoniates.

antimoniated (æntɪˈməʊnɪeɪtɪd), *ppl. a. Chem.* [f. as prec. + -ED.] Combined, tinged, or impregnated with antimony.
1729 WOODWARD *Eng. Fossils* I. 207 Striated or antimoniated lead ore. 1800 HENRY *Epit. Chem.* (1808) 371 The analysis of Antimoniated Silver Ore. 1880 *Syd. Soc. Lex.* (article) Antimoniated hydrogen.

antimonic (æntɪˈmɒnɪk), *a.* [f. L. *antimōn-ium* + -IC.] Of or pertaining to antimony. In *Chem.* applied to compounds of antimony in which it combines as a pentad; as ***antimonic chloride*** $SbCl_5$; ***antimonic acid*** (properly *a. oxide*), or ***antimony pentoxide*** Sb_2O_5.
1834 *Penny Cycl.* II. 106/2 When antimonic acid is subjected to a strong red heat, it loses oxygen and is reduced to antimonious acid. 1863 WATTS *Dict. Chem.* I. 324 The monobasic acid is called *Antimonic acid*; the dibasic acid, *Metantimonic acid.*

antimonide (ˈæntɪməʊˌnaɪd, -ˈməʊnaɪd). *Chem.* [f. as prec. + -IDE.] A compound of antimony with hydrogen, a metal, or an organic radical; also called STIBIDE, and formerly ANTIMONIURET.
1863 WATTS *Dict. Chem.* I. 322 Hydride of Antimony or Antimonide of Hydrogen, generally called Antimonetted or Antimoniuretted hydrogen. *Ibid.* 316 Antimonide of Gold. 1873 WILLIAMSON *Chem.* §143 A precipitate of argentic antimonide is formed.

ˌantimoniˈoso-, comb. form of ANTIMONIOUS, as in ***antimonioso-antimonic oxide***, a synonym of *antimony tetroxide* Sb_2O_4, regarded as consisting of antimonic acid, combined with antimonious acid.
1863 WATTS *Dict. Chem.* I. 324 The antimonioso-antimonates of the earth-metals..are insoluble in water.

antimonious (æntɪˈməʊnɪəs), *a.* [f. L. *antimōni-um* + -OUS.] Of the nature of, or containing, antimony. In *Chem.* applied to compounds of antimony in which it combines as a triad; as ***antimonious chloride*** Sb Cl_3; ***antimonious acid***, formerly applied to *antimony tetroxide*, afterwards to *antimonious oxide* or *antimony trioxide* Sb_2O_3.
1833 *Penny Cycl.* I. 87/2 Acids, Acetic, Antimonic, Antimonious, etc. 1876 HARLEY *Mat. Med.* 289 The antimonious oxyde sublimes with difficulty in needles.

antimonite (ˈæntɪməʊˌnaɪt, -ˈməʊnaɪt). [f. as prec. + -ITE.]

1. *Chem.* A salt of antimonious acid.
1834 *Penny Cycl.* II. 106/1 The antimonites are not an important class of salts. 1863 WATTS *Dict. Chem.* I. 324 *Ammiolite*, or (so-called) Antimonite of mercury occurs, mixed with clay..in the quicksilver mines.

†**2.** *Min.* Obsolete synonym of STIBNITE. (Dana.)

antimoniuret (æntɪˈməʊnjʊərɪt). *Chem.* [f. as prec. + -URET.] Older name for an *antimonide* or *stibide.*
1841 TRIMMER *Pract. Geol.* 109 Antimoniurets have a metallic lustre.

antimoniuretted (æntɪˈməʊnjʊərɛtɪd), *ppl. a.* [f. prec. + -ED².] Combined with antimony (in a gaseous state); as in ***antimoniuretted hydrogen***, SbH_3, also called *antimoniated hydrogen, antimonious hydride, antimony trihydride*, and *stibine.*
1854 SCOFFERN in *Orr's Circ. Sc.* Chem. 471 Antimoniuretted hydrogen is generated whenever hydrogen gas is developed in a liquid holding antimony in solution. 1873 WILLIAMSON *Chem.* §143 Antimoniuretted hydrogen is formed in a similar manner to arseniuretted hydrogen.

antiˈmonous, *a.*, variant of ANTIMONIOUS.
1868 DANA *Min.* 29 Sulphurous and antimonous fumes.

antimony (ˈæntɪmənɪ). [ad. med.L. *antimōnium*, of unknown origin, used by Constantinus Africanus of Salerno (Chaucer's 'cursed monk, daun Constantyn,' *Merch. T.* 566), in end of 11th c., whence also in all the mod. langs.
Prob., like other terms of alchemy, a corruption of some Arabic word, refashioned so as to wear a Gr. or L. aspect—perhaps, as has been suggested, of the Arabic name *uthmud, othmod*, itself, latinized as *athimodium, atimodium, atimonium, antimonium.* The earlier form of the Arab. is *ithmid*, in which Littré suggests an adaptation (quasi *isthimmid*) of Gr. στιμμίδ-α variant of στίμμι, whence also L. *stibium.* If this conjecture be substantiated, *antimonium* and *stibium* will be transformations of the same word. 'Popular etymology' has analyzed Fr. *antimoine* as ἀντί + *moine* against the monks ('monks'-bane'), and, as usual in such cases, supported the derivation by an idle tale (see Johnson), making the name originate (more than 400 years too late) with the chemist Basil Valentine, in end of 15th c.]

1. One of the elementary bodies, a brittle metallic substance, of bright bluish white colour and flaky crystalline texture. Its metallic characteristics are less pronounced than those of the metals generally; and it forms the fourth member of the natural series nitrogen, phosphorus, arsenic, antimony, bismuth, and some others, which are in different combinations triads and pentads. Symbol Sb (*Stibium*).

a. *Alchem.* and *Pharm.* Originally applied to the native trisulphide (called also *gray antimony*, or *Stibnite*; or when calcined and powdered, *crude* or *black antimony*), the στίμμι, στίβι, πλατυόφθαλ-μον, *stibium* of the ancients, and *al-koḥ'l* of the Arabs, used to stain the eyelids (see ALCOHOL); the *antimonium, proteus, leo ruber, plumbum nigrum, lupus metallorum* of the alchemists.
butter of antimony, an old name of the trichloride, 'a translucent fatty mass'; ***crocus of antimony***, an impure sulphide of antimony and sodium, formed as a scoria in smelting antimony; ***flowers of antimony***, crystals of the trioxide formed when the metal is sublimed; ***glass of antimony***, an oxy-sulphide fused; ***saffron of antimony*** = *red antimony* (see 2).
1477 NORTON *Ord. Alch.* in Ashm. 1652 iii. 39 Is Antimony, Arsenick, Honey, Wax and Wine. 1585 LLOYD *Treas. Health* D ij, A lyke vertue hath Antimonium, receyued wyth water. 1605 TIMME *Quersit.* xiii. 58 From this tree of Saturne springeth antimony, as the first branch of the stock which the phylosophers cal their magnesia. 1646 SIR T. BROWNE *Pseud. Ep.* 53 Stibium or glasse of Antimony, appears somewhat red in glasse, but in its powder yellow. 1689 *Gazophyl. Angl.*, *Antimony*, a famous Mineral amongst Chymists..It certainly comes from the Arab *Atimad*, signifying the same. 1751 CHAMBERS *Cycl.*, *Antimony* is what we properly call a semi-metal, being a fossil substance composed of some undertermined metal, combined with a sulphurous and stony substance. Sometimes there are veins of a red or golden colour intermixed, from which it is called *male antimony*; that without them being denominated *female.*

b. *Chem.* The simple element. (Called by earlier chemists ***regulus of antimony.***)
1788 HOWARD *Encycl.* 133 Pure regulus of antimony is a bright semi-metal resembling tin or dusky silver. It is one of the lightest of the metallic bodies. 1812 DAVY *Chem. Philos.* 400 Basil Valentine is the first chemist who has described the process of extracting antimony from the sulphuret, though it does not appear that he was the inventor of this process. 1866 RUSKIN *Ethics of Dust* 77 Sulphide of antimony..looks like mere purple wool, but it is all of purple needle crystals. 1875 URE *Dict. Arts* I. 196 *Native Antimony* is a mineral of a tin-white colour and streak, and of a metallic lustre. 1879 *Academy* 27 Dec. 467 [Wurtz] asserts that although antimony is usually regarded as a metal, it must, in a true chemical classification, find its place by the side of arsenic, phosphorus, and nitrogen.

2. with qualifications: **arsenical antimony**, the mineral *Allemontite*; **gray antimony**, the native sulphide of antimony, called as a mineral *Stibnite* or *Antimonite*; **red antimony**, the mineral *Kermesite*, a compound of the oxide and sulphide; **white antimony**, antimony trioxide, the mineral *Valentinite*; **sulphurated antimony**, the sulphide with a small admixture of the oxide, used in medicine; **tartarated antimony**, tartar emetic.

3. *attrib.*, as in ***antimony oxide, sulphide, ores***, etc. *spec.* **antimony blende** = red antimony; **antimony bloom** = white antimony; **antimony glance** = gray antimony (see 2); **antimony ochre**, the mineral *Cervantite*; **antimony vermilion**, a red pigment precipitated from an antimonial solution.
1860 PIESSE *Lab. Chem. Wond.* 80 The antimony mines are chiefly in Hungary, Transylvania and Germany. 1863 WATTS *Dict. Chem.* I. 311 Antimony is found in combination with oxygen, viz. as trioxide, in the form of antimony bloom, white antimony, or Valentinite, Sb_2O_3, and as tetroxide, antimony ochre or Cervantite, Sb_2O_4. 1875 URE *Dict. Arts* I. 195 *Antimony Glance*..sometimes occurs compact, but usually in very long prismatic or acicular crystals, or in a fibrous form.

antinational (æntɪˈnæʃənəl), *a.* Opposed to one's own nation, or to a national party.
1807 W. TAYLOR in *Ann. Rev.* V. 193 So selfish, so anti-national a feeling. 1840 GEN. P. THOMPSON *Exerc.* (1842) V. 208 What an anti-national church to this day denominates the Great Rebellion. 1858 BRIGHT *Sp.* 29 Oct. (1876) 466 My opinions are not..so anti-national as some..have sometimes assumed.

anti-natural (ˌæntɪˈnætjʊərəl, -tʃərəl), *a.* [f. ANTI-¹ 3 c + NATURAL *a.*] Contrary or antagonistic to nature; the reverse or opposite of natural.
a 1603 T. CARTWRIGHT *Confut. Rhem. N.T.* (1618) 228 Your Diuinity in the Supper is Anti-naturall..that is..contrary to nature. 1728 'MARTINUS SCRIBLERUS' *Art of Sinking* v. 19 This happy and antinatural way of thinking. 1897 *Daily News* 24 Nov. 9/5 Such wealth is represented as not only 'anti-social', but 'anti-natural'. 1947 C. S. LEWIS *Miracles* xiv. 144 The anti-Natural or pessimistic religions..such as Buddhism or higher Hinduism, tell us that Nature is evil and illusory. 1957 *Sc. Jrnl. Theol.* X. 230 Intellectually he [*sc.* modern man] often thinks of the supernatural as the preter- or anti-natural.

antinephritic (ˌæntɪnɪˈfrɪtɪk), *a. Med.* [mod. f. Gr. ἀντί against + νεφρῖτις disease of the kidneys (f. νεφρός kidney) + -IC.] **A.** *adj.* Of use against disease of the kidneys. **B.** *sb.* (sc. medicine.)
1678 PHILLIPS, *Antinephritic* medicines, such as cure the Distempers of the Reins. 1706 *Ibid.*, Antinephriticks or Antinephritick medicines. 1830 LINDLEY *Nat. Syst. Bot.* 306 The root is supposed..to have antinephritic virtues.

anting (ˈæntɪŋ), *vbl. sb.* [f. ANT + -ING¹, after G. *einemsen* (E. Stresemann 1935, in *Ornith. Monatsber.* XLIII. 138).] The action of birds in rubbing on their plumage ants or other insects that secrete acrid juices; also, a similar action of birds with various other objects (see quot. 1959). Hence (as back-formation) **ant** *v. trans.* and *intr.*, to act in this way.
1936 *Jrnl. Bombay Nat. Hist. Soc.* XXXVIII. 631 Dr. Stresemann suggests the use of a special term for this 'rubbing in' process..which may be translated into English..as 'anting',—e.g. a bird ants itself or its feathers, even when objects other than ants..are used in the process. 1944 *Ibis* July 404 Some birds..practise 'anting' more or less consistently, while others of related species do not 'ant' at all. 1959 *Observer* 1 Mar. 19/4 Starlings and rooks will 'ant', without ants, on smoking chimney-pots. Tame birds will ant with matches or cigarette ends.

anting-anting (ˈantɪŋˈantɪŋ). [Tagalog.] A supposed supernatural influence having the power of protecting its possessor from harm; also, an amulet or charm having the same qualities.
1890 FOREMAN *Philippine Isl.* 129 The most ignorant classes..believe that certain persons are possessed of a diabolical influence called *anting-anting*, which preserves them from all harm. 1898 *Daily News* 28 July 2/2

Supernatural qualities of anting-anting. **1900** F. H. SAWYER *Inhab. Philippines* 215 The famous Tulisanes or bandits, thoroughly believe in the power of the *Antin-Antin* or amulet to render them invulnerable to bullets.

antinode (ˈæntɪnəʊd). [f. ANTI-¹ 2 + NODE 6.] A point or line of maximum disturbance in a vibrating body, a region of maximum amplitude between nodes: for *spec.* applications see quots.
1882 J. D. EVERETT *Vibratory Motion & Sound* v. 51 Comparing together the four positions of the string.. points A, C, and A¹ remain permanently at rest, and the points B and D midway between them undergo the largest displacement... The points of permanent rest, A, C, and A¹ are called nodes and the points of maximum displacement, B and D, antinodes. **1889** *Cent. Dict.*, *Antinode*, a point of a vibrating string where the amplitude of vibration is greatest. **1910** *Hawkins' Electr. Dict.* 14/2 *Anti-nodes*, the points in wave motion which vibrate through the greatest amplitude, half-way between the points at rest, called *nodes*. **1926** *Gloss. Terms Electr. Engin.* (*B.S.I.*) I. 199 *Antinode*, in a system which has a non-uniform distribution of R.M.S. current or voltage, any point at which the R.M.S. value is at its maximum is called an antinode of current or of voltage respectively. **1930** *Engineering* 29 Aug. 255/2 Measurement of wavelength by noting successive current antinodes along the wires. **1959** *Chambers's Encycl.* VIII. 554/1 These points are called nodes. At the intermediate points.. the ether particles oscillate with maximum amplitude; these points are called antinodes.

antinome (ˈæntɪnəʊm). *rare.* [f. Gr. ἀντί against, opposite + νόμος law. Cf. ANTINOMY.] A logical contradiction or contrary.
1864 BURTON *Scot Abr.* 275 His notion of the real value of the precious metals was the antinome.. of his view that their cost prevented the supply of money in sufficient abundance.

antinomian (æntɪˈnəʊmɪən), *a.* and *sb.* [f. med.L. *Antinomi* the name of the sect (f. Gr. ἀντί against + νόμος law) + -AN.]
A. *adj.* Opposed to the obligatoriness of the moral law; of or pertaining to the antinomians.
1645 MILTON *Colast.* Wks. 1738 I. 295 Anabaptistical, Antinomian, Heretical, Atheistical Epithets. **1719** WATERLAND *Vind. Christ's Div.* Pref., Men.. bred up (during the great Rebellion) in the Predestinarian and Antinomian Tenets. **1863** H. ROGERS *Howe* x. 271 A fierce agitation of the whole Antinomian controversy.
B. *sb.* One who maintains that the moral law is not binding upon Christians, under the 'law of grace.' *spec.* One of a sect which appeared in Germany in 1535, alleged to hold this opinion.
1645 PAGITT *Heresiogr.* (1662) 120 The antinomians are so called, because they would have the law abolished. **1762** HUME *Hist. Eng.* (1806) IV. lx. 484 The antinomians even insisted that the obligations of morality and natural law were suspended. **1857** SPURGEON *Park St. Pulpit* II. 132, I am rather fond of being called an Antinomian.. the term is generally applied to those who hold truth pretty firm, and will not let it go.

antiˈnomianism. [f. prec. + -ISM.] The doctrine or practice of antinomians; avowed rejection of the moral law.
1643 MILTON *Divorce* xiv. (1851) 55 Anabaptism, Familism, Antinomianism, and other fanatick dreams. **1715** BURNET *Own Times* (1823) I. 451 False notions in religion, which led to Antinomianism. **1879** FARRAR *Paul* II. 146 The charge of antinomianism, which St. Paul sets aside in 1 Cor. ix. 21.

†**antiˈnomianize,** *v. Obs. rare.* [f. as prec. + -IZE.] To teach, or imbue with, antinomianism.
1692 *Christ Exalt.* §108. 87 He.. confronts his now self Arminianizing for Mr. Williams, by his then self Antinomianizing for Dr. Owen. **1707** HUMFREY *De Justif. Baxt.* 8 Who is a sober Preacher, and not Antinomianiz'd.

†**antiˈnomic,** *a.*¹ and *sb. Obs. rare*⁻¹. [f. L. *Antinom-i* (see ANTINOMIAN) + -IC.] = ANTINOMIAN.
1586 T. ROGERS 39 *Art.* 92 Islebius and his followers, the Antinomics, who will not have God's law to be preached.

antinomic (æntɪˈnɒmɪk), *a.*² *rare.* [ad. Gr. ἀντινομικός of the nature of an ἀντινομία: see ANTINOMY and -IC.] Of, pertaining to, or of the nature of, antinomy; involving a conflict of laws.
1849 KINGSLEY in *Lett. & Mem.* I. 196 Such an antinomic pair are those two great sayings 'He that loveth not knoweth not God,' and, 'If a man hate not father, mother, wife, he cannot be my disciple.'

antiˈnomical, *a. rare.* [f. as prec. + -AL¹.] Characterized by, or given to, antinomies.
1877 CAIRD *Philos. Kant* II. xvii. 590 Kant holds that reason is in itself antinomical, i.e. that it comes into contradiction with itself by a necessary illusion. **1878** BARING-GOULD *Orig. Rel. Belief* II. 22 Let us study that law.. in its antinomical conception.

†**ˈantinomism.** *Obs.* [f. as next + -ISM.] Opposition to or rejection of the moral law; antinomianism.
1658 MANTON *Exp. Jude* 19 Wks. 1871 V. 331 They turn.. antinomists, and antinomism is but sin licensed and privileged. **1672** JACOMB *Comm. Rom.* viii. (1868) 365 There is no Antinomism in this if it be rightly understood.

†**ˈantinomist.** *Obs.* [f. L. *Antinom-i* (see ANTINOMIAN) + -IST.] = ANTINOMIAN *sb.*
1632 SANDERSON *Serm.* Ad Pop. vii. (1674) 298 Antinomists who quite cancel the whole Law of God under the pretence of Christian Liberty. **1656** TRAPP *Exp. 2 Tim.* iii. 17 Controversies against.. Antinomists.

antinomy (ænˈtɪnəmɪ). [ad. L. *antinomia*, a. Gr. ἀντινομία, f. ἀντί against + νόμος law: cf. Fr. *antinomie* (16th c.).]
1. A contradiction in a law, or between two equally binding laws.
1592 DEE in *Chetham Misc.* I. 7 In antinomys, imagined to be in the law, I had good hap to finde out their agreementes. **1659** LESTRANGE *Alliance of Div. Off.* 239 An antinomy, a justle between the Canon laws of our Church and the law of the land. **1781** GIBBON *Decl. & F.* xliv, The antinomies or contradictions of the Code and Pandects. **1875** POSTE *Gaius* II. 220 We have here a case of Antinomy (contradictory laws) in Justinian's legislation.
b. A conflict of authority.
1842 DE QUINCEY *Cicero* Wks. VI. 224 The capital fault in the operative constitution of Rome had long been in the antinomies, if I may be pardoned for so learned a term, of the public service.
†**2.** A contradictory law, statute, or principle; an authoritative contradiction. *Obs.*
1643 MILTON *Divorce* II. iii. (1847) 139/2 That his holiest people might as it were by his own antinomy, or counter-statute, live unreproved. **1649** JER. TAYLOR *Gt. Exemp.* Add. iv. 48 The signes which the Angel gave.. are direct antinomies to the lusts of the flesh. **1656** —— *Deus Justif.*, An Antidote, and Antinomy of their great objection.
3. A contradiction between conclusions which seem equally logical, reasonable, or necessary; a paradox; intellectual contradictoriness. (After Kant.)
1802 H. C. ROBINSON *Diary* I. 144 The antinomies of pure reason. **1857** T. WEBB *Intell. Locke* ix. 175 The imagination was distracted on every side by counter inconceivabilities, the Mind was divided against itself; Antinomy was its very law. **1877** CAIRD *Philos. Kant* II. xvi. 566 Criticism must discover the nature and extent of the antinomies of reason, and must show that they are dogmatically insoluble; or that, whichever of the alternative solutions we adopt, we are led into absurdity and contradiction.

Antiochene (ænˈtaɪəkiːn), *a.* and *sb.* [ad. L. *Antiochēnus*, f. *Antiochia* Antioch.] **A.** *adj.* Of or pertaining to Antioch in Syria, esp. to the school of theology represented chiefly by the church at Antioch in the 4th and 5th centuries. **B.** *sb.* An adherent of this school.
1845 NEWMAN *Devel. Chr. Doctr.* i. 72 The Antiochenes and other heretics sometimes were Arians, sometimes Sabellians. **1884** *Encycl. Brit.* XVII. 355/2 The antagonism between the Alexandrian and Antiochene schools of theology. *Ibid.* 356/2 The Antiochenes continued to maintain for a considerable time an attitude of antagonism towards Cyril and his creed. **1894** RIVINGTON *Prim. Ch.* 192 To understand.. the Antiochene troubles of that century aright, it is necessary to bear in mind that St. Meletius entered upon his episcopate at Antioch under false pretences. **1939** *Burlington Mag.* Aug. 44/1 Authentic monuments of Antiochene art. **1939** P. HUGHES *Pop. Hist. Ch.* ii. 36 The Antiochenes, remaining obdurately aloof, were excommunicated too.
Also **Antiochian** (æntɪˈɒkɪən), *a.* and *sb.*, in the same senses.
1840 E. COX tr. *Döllinger's Hist. Ch.* I. ii. §7. 176 The Antiochian fathers. **1867** C. M. YONGE *Pupils S. John* xviii. 289 The Antiochans were satirizing his bearded figure. **1927** J. H. WILLEY *Early Ch. Portraits* v. 107 Hence came the famous skill of the Antiochians in coining names.

anti-odontalgic (ˌæntɪəʊdɒnˈtældʒɪk), *a.* and *sb. Med.* [ANTI- 3.] **A.** *adj.* Of use against toothache. **B.** *sb.* Anything so used.
1817 COLERIDGE *Own Times* (1850) III. 951 The famous anti-odontalgic teeth of St. Apollonia. **1821** BYRON *Wks.* 1837 V. 249 Tooth-powder, tooth-brushes, or any such anti-odontalgic.. articles. **1880** *Syd. Soc. Lex.*, *Antodontalgic*.

anti-orgastic (ˌæntɪɔːˈgæstɪk), *a. Med.* [f. ANTI- 3 + Gr. *ὀργαστικ-ός, f. ὀργά-ειν to be excited.] Allaying passion or excitement, sedative.
1880 in *Syd. Soc. Lex.*

anti-oxidant (ˌæntɪˈɒksɪdənt). [ANTI-¹ 3 b.] An agent which inhibits oxidation. Also *attrib.* or *adj.*, that inhibits oxidation.
1934 *Chem. Abstr.* XXVIII. 7504 The use of antioxidants in the stabilization of cracked gasolenes. **1943** *Jrnl. Biol. Chem.* CXLVII. 516 In all experiments reported.. on the effect of heat on antioxidant activity, the treatment involved moist heat under pressure. **1958** *Economist* 20 Dec. 1051/1 Antioxidants protect fats, oils and foods containing these products against development of off-flavour, unpleasant odour, or discolouration.

†**ˈantiˌpapacy.** *Obs.* [f. L. *antipāpa* ANTIPOPE, after *papacy*.] The position of antipope.
1670 G. H. *Hist. Cardinals* III. I. 238 The French, or Catalonian Anti-pope, renounc'd his Anti-papacy first.

anti-papal (æntɪˈpeɪpəl), *a.* [ANTI-¹ 3.] Opposed to popery and the pope.
1639 FULLER *Holy War* IV. xxv. (1840) 224 That all emperors would be possessed with an antipapal spirit. **1649** MILTON *Eikon.* xxvii. 214 He.. charges strictly his Son after him to persevere in that Anti-Papal Scisme. **1878** LECKY *Eng. in 18th C.* I. i. 5 If the Dissenters were more strongly anti-papal than the clergy. **1894** J. C. HEDLEY *Retreat* xxi. 257 The anti-Catholic, anti-Papal,.. and anti-spiritual literature. **1902** GAIRDNER *Eng. Ch. 16th Cent.* viii. 141 Some anti-papal measures.

antipape, early Eng. (and Fr.) f. ANTIPOPE.

antiparallel (æntɪˈpærəlel), *a.* and *sb.*
†**1.** Parallel, but opposed or contrary. *Obs. rare.*
a **1660** HAMMOND *Serm.* 646 (T.) To take the opposite course, and to provide our remedy anti-parallel to their disease.
2. *Geom.* ***antiparallel lines*** or ***antiparallels***: two lines which make with two other lines angles equal each to each, but contrary ways, one being exterior and the other interior.
1796 HUTTON *Math. Dict.* I. 122.
3. *Physics.* Parallel but moving or directed in opposite directions: used chiefly of vectors. Also as *adv.*
1927 C. G. DARWIN in *Proc. R. Soc.* A. CXVI. 230 When the electron *wave* is analysed by a Stern-Gerlach experiment, the associated *rays* (or particles) are polarised anti-parallel. **1938** F. BITTER in *Physical Rev.* LIV. 81/2 The case in which the internal forces are such as to make interacting spins antiparallel to each other. **1949**, **1961** [see ANTIFERROMAGNETIC, -MAGNETISM].

antiparalytic (ˌæntɪpærəˈlɪtɪk), *a.* and *sb. Med.* [ANTI- 3.] **A.** *adj.* Tending to prevent or counteract paralysis. **B.** *sb.* A medicine so used.
1755 in JOHNSON. **1880** in *Syd. Soc. Lex.*

†**antiparaˈlytical,** *a. Obs.* = prec.
1676 *Phil. Trans.* XI. 743 Fomentations made with the decoction of Emmets, very anti-paralytical.

†**ˈantiparle.** *Obs. rare.* [f. ANTI- + PARLE, f. Fr. *parler* to speak.] An exchange of words, a conference.
1602 F. VERE (*title*) Extremities urging the Lord General.. to offer the late Antiparle with the Archduke.

†**antiparliaˈmental,** *a. Obs.* [ANTI- 3.] Opposed to (the Long) Parliament.
1643 PRYNNE *Power of Parl.* II. Pref. A2 These Antiparliamentall Momusses. **1660** BOND *Scutum Reg.* 243 But is not Mr. Prynne the Anti-parliamental Momus and Viper?

antiparliamenˈtarian, *a.* (and *sb.*) [ANTI- 3, 5.] = ANTIPARLIAMENTARY 1.
1845 CAMPBELL *Chancellors* (1857) IV. xciv. 291 To make himself known at Court as an antiparliamentarian lawyer.

antiparliaˈmentary, *a.* [ANTI- 3.]
†**1.** Opposed to (the Long) Parliament or the parliamentary party. *Obs.* or *Hist.*
1643 MARSHALL *Lett.* 15 Champions of the Antiparliamentary cause. **1660** BOND *Scutum Reg.* 243 The books of the Royalists.. he calleth anti-Parliamentary Pamphlets.
2. Against parliamentary usage.
1656 BURTON *Diary* I. 207 Divers petitions were cast upon the table in a very confused way, and excepted unto.. as anti-parliamentary.

†**antiparliamenˈteer.** *Obs.* [Cf. *pamphleteer*.] A writer or speaker against (the Long) Parliament.
1643 PRYNNE *Open. Gt. Seal* Ep., Silenced the.. Tongues of most Anti-Parliamenteers.

antipasto (æntɪˈpæstəʊ, ‖antiˈpasto). [It., f. as ANTEPAST.] Hors d'œuvre. Also *fig.*
1934 in WEBSTER. **1939** C. MORLEY *K. Foyle* xxx. 300, I don't mean just what we got from the antipasto at Enrico's place. **1952** S. J. PERELMAN *Ill-Tempered Clavichord* (1953) 102 The gambol in the cupola.. is merely antipasto for a real shindig at the Praying Ghats, the sacred stairs fronting the Ganges. **1961** I. T. ROSS *Requiem for Schoolgirl* vi. 102, I demanded a large *antipasto* and a bottle of Valpolicella.

antipatharian (ˌæntɪpəˈθeərɪən), *a.* (*sb.*). *Zool.* [f. mod.L. *Antipatharia* (f. *Antipathes*, name of the typical genus) + -AN.] Belonging to the order *Antipatharia* of corals (the black corals); as *sb.*, a coral of this order. So **antipathid** (ænˈtɪpəθɪd), a coral belonging to the Antipathidæ, a family of this order.
1890 *Athenæum* 17 May 644/1 Prof. F. Jeffrey Bell [read a paper on] the antipatharian corals.. containing.. an account of a very remarkable antipathid from the neighbourhood of.. Mauritius. **1899** *Nat. Science* Jan. 90 Large numbers of hydroids, antipathids, and the crinoid *Antedon phalangium* were dredged. **1924** *Glasgow Herald* 1 Nov. 4 The black corals or antipatharians.

antipathetic (æntɪpəˈθetɪk), *a.* [ad. assumed Gr. *ἀντιπαθητικός, f. ἀντιπαθέ-ειν to have an aversion (see next); cf. παθητικός f. παθέ-ειν.] Having an antipathy or constitutional aversion; opposed in nature or disposition (*to*).
1640 *Canterbur. Self-Conv.* 95 The Scots humour.. is become naturally antipathetick to the masse. **1789** BENTHAM *Princ. Legisl.* vi. §35 Sympathetic and antipathetic sensibility are commonly stronger in her [the female]. **1831** ARNOLD in Stanley *Life* (1858) I. 250 Many.. are so antipathetic to it [cholera], that neither contagion nor infection will give it to them. **1865** TROLLOPE *Belton Est.* xxv. 296 The whole place and everything about it was antipathetic to her.

antipaˈthetical. [f. as prec. + -AL¹.] Of antipathetic nature or tendency. Const. *to.*
1601 CORNWALLYES *Ess.* II. xxxviii. (1631) 143 Able to resist things Antipatheticall. **1656** COWLEY *Davideis* I. (1669) 38 *note*, Serpents.. being the creatures most antipathetical and terrible to humane nature. **1869** LECKY

Europ. Mor. I. i. 18 Profoundly antipathetical to utilitarian morals.

antipa'thetically, *adv.* [f. prec. + -LY².] In an antipathetical manner; with antipathy.
1818 in TODD. **1882** *Athenæum* No. 2848. 673 Designed.. with care and somewhat antipathetically delineated, the lookers-on are but tame spectators.

antipa'theticalness. *rare*⁻⁰. [f. as prec. + -NESS.] The quality or state of being antipathetical, or 'of having a natural contrariety to anything.' J.
1731 in BAILEY; whence in JOHNSON, etc.

antipathic (æntɪ'pæθɪk), *a.* [ad. Fr. *antipathique*, f. *antipathie* ANTIPATHY: see -IC.] Of or belonging to antipathy; of contrary nature or character (*to*); *spec.* in *Med.* having or producing the contrary symptoms.
1830 *Edin. Rev.* L. 513 The antipathic [method].. opposes contrary to contrary. **1866** J. MARTINEAU *Ess.* I. 369 [These] were violently antipathic to those. **1868** W. GREG *Lit. & Soc. Judgm.* 24 They [Napoleon and Madame de Staël] were antipathic in their views. **1880** *Syd. Soc. Lex.*, *Antipathic*.. also applied to palliative medicines.

antipathist (æn'tɪpəθɪst). *rare.* [f. as ANTIPATHIZE: see -IST.] One possessed by an antipathy or constitutional aversion; a natural enemy.
1817 COLERIDGE *Sib. Leaves* II. 281 Sole Positive of Night! Antipathist of Light. *a* **1832** BENTHAM *Rationale Evid.* Wks. 1843 VII. 115 On the part of the antipathist, the profession of incredulity is but a pretence.

†**an'tipathite.** *Obs. rare*⁻¹. [See -ITE.] = prec.
1627 FELTHAM *Resolves* II. lvi. (1677) 274 As if nature had framed him an Antipathite to Virtue.

antipathize (æn'tɪpəθaɪz), *v.* ? *Obs. rare.* [f. ANTIPATH-Y + -IZE: the opposite of *sympathize.*]
1. *intr.* To feel the opposite; to show contrariety of feeling or disposition.
c **1633** T. ADAMS *Wks.* III. 157 (D.) That which antipathises against one thing sympathiseth with another. **1657** T. MAY *Satyr. Puppy* 18 Being moved to antipathize.. by my presuming insolence.
2. *trans.* To render antipathetic, to affect with contrariety or hostility of feeling.
1667 WATERHOUSE *Fire Lond.* 55 Had God antipathized and severed their conjunction, they had not done that complicated mischief. **1788** J. WILLIAMS *Childr. Thespis* (1792) 115 As venomous reptiles antipathized gaze.

an'tipa,thizing, *ppl. a.* ? *Obs.* [f. prec. + -ING².] Having contrary feelings or dispositions.
a **1640** JACKSON *Wks.* (1673) II. 522 Reconciliation of hostile and antipathizing natures.

†**an'tipathous**, *a. Obs. rare.* [irreg. f. ANTIPATH-Y or Gr. ἀντιπαθ-ής (see next) + -OUS.] Opposed in nature or disposition; antipathetic.
a **1616** BEAUM. & FL. *4 Plays in One* (R.) In this antipathous extreme. **1618** —— *Q. Corinth* III. i, As if she saw something antipathous Unto her virtuous life.

antipathy (æn'tɪpəθɪ). [ad. L. *antipathīa*, a. Gr. ἀντιπάθεια, n. of state f. ἀντιπαθής opposed in feeling, f. ἀντί against + πάθος, πάθε-, feeling. Cf. Fr. *antipathie*, in Cotgr. 1611.]
†**1.** Contrariety of feeling, disposition, or nature (between persons or things); natural contrariety or incompatibility. The opposite of *sympathy*. *Obs.*
1601 HOLLAND *Pliny* (1634) II. 430 The repugnancie and contrariety in nature which the Greeks call antipathie. **1605** SHAKS. *Lear* II. ii. 93 No contraries hold more antipathy, Then I, and such a knaue. **1692** BENTLEY *Boyle Lect.* 97 When occult quality, and sympathy and antipathy were admitted for satisfactory explications of things.
†**b.** Const. *with* a thing; *between* things. *Obs.*
1601 HOLLAND *Pliny* (1634) II. 227 Such a contrarietie in nature or Antipathie there is.. between them and this herb. **1626** BACON *Sylva* §983 The Sea Hare hath an Antipathy with the Lungs.. and erodeth them. **1655** GURNALL *Chr. in Arm.* ix. §2 (1669) 348/1 An Antipathy betwixt sinning and praying.
2. Feeling against, hostile feeling towards; constitutional or settled aversion or dislike.
1606 WARNER *Alb. Eng.* XIV. lxxxii. 344 Were other Rankes not free of Publique-weales *Antipathie.* **1663** BUTLER *Hud.* I. i. 208 A Sect, whose chief Devotion lies In odd perverse Antipathies; In falling out with that or this. **1734** tr. *Rollin's Anc. Hist.* (1827) I. 144 Mutual hatred and antipathy. **1853** C. BRONTË *Villette* viii. (1876) 67 To attempt to touch her heart was the surest way to rouse her antipathy.
b. Const. *against, to*; *between* persons.
1618 WITHER *Nec Habeo* Wks. 1633, 517, I no Antipathy (as yet) have had Twixt me and any Creature God hath made. **1667** PRIMATT *City & Count. Build.* 28 A kind of Antipathy against the thriving of any but themselves. **1712** ADDISON *Spect.* No. 440 ¶5 Having the same Natural Antipathy to a Pun, which some have to a Cat. **1858** MAX MÜLLER *Chips* (1880) II. xxvii. 324 A mutual antipathy between the white and the black man.
3. *concr.* †**a.** That which is contrary in nature (*obs.*). **b.** The object of antipathy or settled dislike.
1622 MASSINGER & DEKKER *Virg. Mart.* IV. iii, To go Where all antipathies to comfort dwell. **1691** NORRIS *Pract. Disc.* 205 Evil is the great antipathy of Human Nature.. her great and general Abhorrence. **1777** SHERIDAN *Trip to Scarb.* XI. i, Men that may be called the beau's antipathy, for they agree in nothing but walking upon two legs.

†**antipelargy.** *Obs. rare*⁻⁰. [a. Fr. *antipelargie* (Cotgr.), ad. med.L. *antipelargia*, a. Gr. ἀντιπελαργία mutual love, f. πελαργ-ός stork, a bird supposed to be peculiarly affectionate.] (See quot.)
1656 BLOUNT *Glossogr.*, *Antipelargy*, the reciprocal love of children to their parents, or (more generally) any requital or mutual kindness. **1731** BAILEY, *Antipelargy*, a mutual thankfulness or requital of a benefit; but especially a child's nourishing a parent in old age.

antipendium, incorr. form of ANTEPENDIUM.

antiperiodic (,æntɪpɪərɪ'ɒdɪk), *a. Med.* [ANTI- 3.] Destroying the periodicity of diseases that run a typical course.
1861 HULME *Moquin-Tandon* II. v. ii. 286 The poison of the Arachnida.. is at other times anti-periodic.

‖**antiperi'stalsis.** *Phys.* [mod.L., f. next, on Gr. analogies.] Antiperistaltic action.
1859 TODD *Cycl. Anat.& Phys.* V. 342/1 An abnormal antiperistalsis, by which they [i.e. the contents of the intestine] are propelled backwards towards the stomach.

antiperistaltic (,æntɪpɛrɪ'stæltɪk), *a. Phys.* [ANTI- 3.] Contrary to peristaltic motion; acting upwards. (See quot.)
1706 PHILLIPS, *Antiperistaltick* Motion, an irregular Motion of the guts. **1727-51** CHAMBERS *Cycl.* s.v., As the peristaltic motion is a contraction of the fibres of two intestines from above, downwards; the antiperistaltic motion is their contraction from below, upwards. *a* **1845** SYD. SMITH *Plymley Lett.* ix, They are nauseous, antiperistaltic, and emetical.

‖**antiperistasis** (,æntɪpə'rɪstəsɪs). *arch.* [L., a. Gr. ἀντιπερίστασις, f. ἀντί against + περίστασις a standing round, circumstance.] Opposition or contrast of circumstances; the force of contrast or contrariness; resistance or reaction roused against any action.
1598 SYLVESTER *Du Bartas* I. ii. (1633) 29 Tis doubtless this Antiperistasis (Bear with the word, I hold it not amiss). **1640** FULLER *Joseph's Coat* (1867) 29 Having their penury doubled by the antiperistasis of others plenty. *a* **1703** BURKITT *On N.T.* 2 Cor. iv. 16 The cold blasts of persecution.. did, by a spiritual antiperistasis, increase the heat of grace within. **1837** MACAULAY *Bacon, Ess.* I. 410/2 He tells us, that in physics the energy with which a principle acts is often increased by the antiperistasis of its opposite.

,antiperi'static, -al, *a. rare.* [f. prec., on Gr. analogies; see -IC, -AL¹.] Of the nature of antiperistasis; contrary or in opposition to its surroundings, heightened by force of contrast.
1601 CORNWALLYES *Ess.* II. xlv. (1631) 247 For in reason and discourse.. there is more then an Antiperistaticall Vertue. **1652** URQUHART *Jewel* Wks. 1834, 289 The antiperistatick faculty of a fountain or spring-well in the summer season, whose nature is to be the colder within itself the greater circumobresistance of heat be in the aire which surrounds it.

antiperi'statically, *adv. rare.* [f. prec. + -LY².] In an antiperistatic fashion; by force of contrast or contrariness.
1633 T. ADAMS *Exp. 2 Pet.* ii. 22 Like snow or ice in a vault or deep pit which antiperist[at]ically waxeth cold for the neighbouring heat.

†**antiperi'steze**, *v. Obs. rare*⁻¹. [irreg. f. ANTIPERISTASIS, for *-stase* or *-stasize.*] To strengthen by the force of contrast or contrariness.
1602 J. DAVIES *Mirum in Mod.* 15 (D.) Anteperistezing hir pow'rs with grace.

antipestilential (,æntɪpɛstɪ'lɛnʃəl), *a.* and *sb. Med.* [ANTI- 3.] **A.** *adj.* Of use against the plague and similar epidemics. **B.** *sb.* (sc. medicine).
1683 *Phil. Trans.* XIII. 104 Rare Antipestilentials, excellent Oyles, Liquors, etc. **1722** DE FOE *Plague* Wks. V. 23 Antipestilential pills. **1743** tr. *Heister's Surg.* 202 Certain hot Spirits or Waters, dignified with the Title of.. Antipestilential.

antipetalous (æntɪ'pɛtələs), *a. Bot.* [f. Gr. ἀντί opposite + πέταλ-ον petal + -OUS.] (See quot.)
1880 GRAY *Bot. Text-bk.* vi. §2. 178 *Antipetalous*, those stamens which stand before petals, whether adnate or free.

antipharmic (æntɪ'fɑːmɪk), *a. Med.* [f. ANTI- 3 + Gr. φάρμακ-ον poison: see ALEXIPHARMIC.] Antidotal, alexipharmic.
1853 in MAYNE *Exp. Lex.*

antiphlebo'tomical, *a.* [ANTI- 3.] Opposed to phlebotomy or bleeding.
1845 FORD *Handbk. Spain* II. 775 In rude and antiphlebotomical health.

antiphlogistian (,æntɪfləʊ'dʒɪstɪən), *a.* and *sb.* [f. ANTIPHLOGIST-ON + -IAN. See ANTI- 3.]
A. *adj.* Opposed to the theory of 'phlogiston,' or the existence of an element of pure fire. **B.** *sb.* An opponent of this theory.
1788 PRIESTLEY in *Phil. Trans.* LXXIX. 15 Sulphur is not that simple substance which the antiphlogistians suppose. **1791** W. NICHOLSON *Chem.* 185 The antiphlogistian philosophers. **1795** —— *Dict. Chem.* II. 642 The antiphlogistian theory. **1805** *Edin. Rev.* VI. 102 The antiphlogistians have nothing to dread.

antiphlogistic (,æntɪfləʊ'dʒɪstɪk), *a.* and *sb.* [f. as prec. + -IC; cf. *phlogistic.*] **A.** *adj.*
1. = prec. adj.
1788 PRIESTLEY in *Phil. Trans.* LXXVIII. 156 They cannot be simple substances, as the antiphlogistic theory makes them to be. *c* **1865** J. WYLDE in *Circ. Sc.* I. 88/2 His new theory of combustion, the Antiphlogistic.
2. *Med.* Counteracting or reducing inflammation.
1769 BUCHAN *Dom. Med.* xliii. (1826) 184 The plethoric state of the patient.. led to the employment of the antiphlogistic.. treatment. **1803** *Edin. Rev.* I. 471 The disease is.. to be treated by topical remedies and the antiphlogistic plan. **1877** ROBERTS *Handbk. Med.* I. 219 All antiphlogistic remedies are to be deprecated.
b. *fig.* Allaying excitement. *rare.*
1840 HOOD *Kilmansegg* cxxxvi, None more needs a Matthew to preach, A cooling antiphlogistic speech.
B. *sb.* A medicinal agent allaying inflammation.
1744 BERKELEY *Siris* 59 (T.) A powerful antiphlogistick, and preservative against corruption and infection. **1875** H. WOOD *Therap.* (1879) 50 As an antiphlogistic, nitrate of silver acts.. as an astringent.

antiphlogistin (,æntɪfləʊ'dʒɪstɪn). Also -ine. [f. ANTIPHLOGISTIC + -IN¹.] A proprietary form of kaolin poultice used as a convenient form of treatment for the relief of inflammatory lesions.
1901 DORLAND *Med. Dict.* (ed. 2). **1910** W. BENNETT in *Practitioner* June 750 The induction of hyperaemia is certainly sometimes beneficial and is most easily effected by the use of some such material as Antiphlogistine. **1965** G. MCINNES *Road to Gundagai* xi. 189 Some were in favour of.. antiphlogistine to 'draw the boil out'.

antiphlogiston (,æntɪfləʊ'dʒɪstən), *attrib. comb.* [ANTI- 4 + PHLOGIST-ON (Gr. φλογιστόν burnt, f. φλογίζ-ειν to set on fire, f. φλόγ-α flame).] = ANTIPHLOGISTIAN *a.*
1859 G. WILSON *E. Forbes* iv. 117 The partisans of the phlogiston and the antiphlogiston camp.

antiphon ('æntɪfən). Also 6-8 **antiphone.** [a. Fr. *antiphone*, or ad. med.L. *antiphōna*, an adaptation as a sb. fem. sing. of Gr. τὰ ἀντίφωνα sb. (prop. adj.) neut. pl., musical accords, things 'sounding in response,' of which the sing. τὸ ἀντίφωνον is used by Aristotle for 'an accord in the octave'; f. ἀντί in return + -φωνος sounding, f. φωνή vocal sound. *Antiphon* is thus a re-adaptation of the word which in earlier times became ANTHEM, after the latter had lost its etymological sense.]
1. A versicle or sentence sung by one choir in response to another.
a **1652** J. SMITH *Sel. Disc.* iv. 123 The responsals or antiphons wherein each of them catcheth at the other's part, and keeps time with it. **1661** T. F. S. (*title*) A Manual of Prayers and Litanies, Hymns with Antiphones. **1859** JEPHSON *Brittany* xvi. 269 The antiphons were sung by the choirboys alone.
2. A composition, in prose or verse, consisting of verses or passages sung alternately by two choirs in worship; = ANTHEM in the original sense, but passing also early into the modern sense of *anthem*.
c **1500** *Consecr. Nuns* in Maskell *Mon.* II. 318 Syngeng all together thys antiphone: *Ancilla Christi sum.* **1626** DONNE *Serm.* iv. 38 The whole Quire.. may joyne with old Simeon in this Antiphon, *Nunc Dimittis.* **1635** PAGITT *Christianogr.* I. ii. (1636) 70 In a certaine Antiphone or Hymn. **1876** GREEN *Short Hist.* i. §6. (1881) 52 Tones which the excited ears around frame into a joyous antiphon.
3. *techn.* 'A short piece of plain-song introduced before a psalm or canticle, to the Tone of which it corresponds, while the words are selected so as specially to illustrate and enforce the evangelical or prophetic meaning of the text.' Helmore in Grove *Mus. Dict.* 1879.
1775 T. WARTON *Eng. Poetry* II. 56 (T.) A sort of office.. consisting of an antiphone, versicle, response and collect.
4. *transf.* A response, answer.
1651 *Reliq. Wotton.* 376 (T.) The great synod of Protestant ambassadors that are to meet at Hamborough, which to me sounds like an antiphone to the other malign conjunctions at Colen. **1880** MRS. WHITNEY *Odd or Even* xxi. 228 A curious, fine ring in his tone, the antiphon, perhaps, to the clear, sweet pride that had been in Frances.

antiphonal (æn'tɪfənəl), *a.* and *sb.* [a. OFr. *antiphonal*, ad. ? med.L. *antiphōnāl-is*: see ANTIPHON and -AL¹.] **A.** *adj.*
1. Of the nature of an antiphon; sung alternately.
1719 BINGHAM *Orig. Eccles.* V. XIII. x. 336 By way of antiphonal or alternate Melody. *Ibid.* II. 111 (T.) Antiphonal singing was first brought into the church of Milan. **1859** *Sat. Rev.* 2 July 16 The antiphonal effect of the double choruses.. in 'Thy right hand, O Lord.'
2. Responsive in sound, or (*transf.*) other effect.
1848 MARIOTTI *Italy* I. i. 121 A peal of the organ is antiphonal to a flourish of trumpets. **1868** SWINBURNE *Ess.*

& Stud. 373 The dim floor-work in front.. is antiphonal to the wealth of water beyond.

B. *sb.* An antiphonal collection; an antiphonary.

1691 WOOD *Ath. Oxon.* I/572 [Warham] left all his.. Ledgers, Grayles and Antiphonals to Wykeham Coll. **1872** YEATS *Tech. Hist. Comm.* 379 The missals and antiphonals placed in churches exhibited magnificent exteriors.

an'tiphonally, *adv.* [f. prec. + -LY^2.] In an antiphonal manner, with responsive voices.

1753 CHAMBERS *Cycl. Supp.* s.v., The Greeks have a method of singing Antiphonally. **1865** *Reader* 19 Aug. 214 A 'dialogue chorus' where the two bodies of damsels answer each other antiphonally in successive couplets. **1876** M. DAVIES *Unorth. Lond.* 202 A hymn was sung antiphonally, the singers left inside taking one verse, and those outside the other.

†**an'tiphonar.** *Obs.* [ad. Fr. *antiphonaire*, later ad. L. *antiphōnārium*: see ANTIPHONER.] = ANTIPHONER, ANTIPHONARY.

[Not in JOHNSON 1755.] **1765** BURN *Eccles. Law* (T.) The antiphonar is that book which containeth the invitatories, responsories, verses, collects, and whatever is said or sung in the quire, called the seven hours or breviary.

antiphonary (æn'tɪfənərɪ). [ad. med.L. *antiphōnāri-um*, f. *antiphōna*: see ANTIPHON and -ARY. The earlier word was ANTIPHONER.] A book containing a set or collection of antiphons.

[**1295** *Visit. Dean Radulphus* in Dugdale *Hist. St. Paul's* (1668) 217 Antiphonarium Albrici est in duobus Voluminibus.] **1681** BLOUNT *Glossogr.*, *Antiphonary*, a book containing the antiphons and versicles sung by churchmen in the quire. *a* **1789** BURNEY *Hist. Mus.* (ed. 2) III. i. 9 This year all antiphonaries.. were called in and destroyed. **1859** JEPHSON *Brittany* viii. 105 An ugly reading-desk, with a great dogs-eared antiphonary lying open upon it. **1879** ROCKSTRO in Grove *Dict. Mus.* I. 615 This celebrated Antiphonary [of St. Gregory] was all but unanimously accepted.

antiphoner (æn'tɪfənə(r)). [a. OFr. *antiphonier*, f. med.L. *antiphōnārium*: see ANTIPHONAR, -ARY.] = ANTIPHONARY.

c **1370** WYCLIF *English Works* (1879) 194 Multitude of newe costy portos, antifeners, graielis, & alle oþere bokis. *c* **1386** CHAUCER *Prioresses T.* 67 He *O alma redemptoris* herde synge, As children lerned her antiphonere. **1483** CAXTON *Gold. Leg.* 144/1 The anthyphoner on whyche he lerned them is yet there. **1570** GRINDAL *Rem.* (1843) 135 That antiphoners, mass books.. be utterly defaced, rent, and abolished. **1727–51** CHAMBERS *Cycl.* s.v. *Antiphony*, Among the number of ecclesiastical books formerly used.. we meet with antiphoners or antiphonaries. **1823** SCOTT *Peveril* 202 Proper priest's trappings—antiphoners, missals, and copes.

antiphonetic (,æntɪfəʊ'nɛtɪk), *a. rare*$^{-1}$. [f. Gr. ἀντίφων-ος (see ANTIPHON) after Gr. φωνητικ-ός PHONETIC.]

1. Answering or matching in sound.

1840 BARHAM *Ingol. Leg.* 71 Moore and Tom Campbell themselves admit 'spinach' Is perfectly antiphonetic to 'Greenwich.'

2. Contrary or opposed to phonetic spelling.

antiphonic (æntɪ'fɒnɪk), *a. rare.* [f. Gr. ἀντίφων-ος + -IC.] Antiphonal, mutually responsive.

1847 BARHAM *Ingol. Leg.* (1877) 401 The knight and the maiden had rung their antiphonic changes on her fine qualities.

†**anti'phonical**, *a. Obs. rare*$^{-1}$. [f. as prec. + -ICAL.] = ANTIPHONAL.

1710 WHEATELY *Com. Prayer* 161 (T.) They sung in an antiphonical way.

anti'phonically, *adv.* [f. prec. + -LY^2.] In an antiphonic or antiphonal manner; antiphonally.

1846 MASKELL *Mon. Rit.* I. Introd. 34 Portions of the services.. sung.. antiphonically. **1851** *Q. Rev.* No. 177. 237 The singers, for their own ease, sang them antiphonically.

antiphony (æn'tɪfənɪ). [f. Gr. ἀντίφων-ος (see ANTIPHON) + -Y, as if repr. a Gr. *ἀντιφωνία, like συμφωνία SYMPHONY.]

The words *antiphon* and *antiphony*, are very indistinctly separated in use. It would be better to use *antiphon* of the actual responses, or alternately sung verses; and *antiphony*, in form an abstract sb. like *symphony*, *euphony*, of antiphonal composition, arrangement, or effect, and concretely of an antiphonal composition or anthem.

1. Opposition of sound; or harmony thereby produced.

1603 HOLLAND *Plutarch* 186 (R.) The harmony of music hath symphony by antiphony (that is to say) the accord ariseth from discord. *a* **1789** BURNEY *Hist. Mus.* I. 137 (JOD.) Antiphony is more agreeable than homophony. **1868** CHAMBERS *Encycl.* I. 297 *Antiphony*, a name given by the ancient Greeks to a species of musical accompaniment in the octave, by instruments or voices, in opposition to that executed in unison, which they called *Homophony*.

2. A musical response; a responsive musical utterance, the answer made by one voice or choir to another. = ANTIPHON 1.

1592 tr. *Junius on Rev.* xix. 3 The song of the Antiphonie or response. **1637** JACKSON *Creed* Wks. VI. 83 The antiphony unto it would have been 'No evil can come upon us.' **1751** CHAMBERS *Cycl.*, *Antiphony*, the answer made by one choir to another, when the psalm or anthem is sung between two. **1849** DE QUINCEY *Mail-coach* in *Misc.* II. 311 One after another, like the antiphonies in the choral service.

3. Alternate singing or chanting by a choir divided into two parts; antiphonal singing. Also *fig.*

1753 CHAMBERS *Cycl. Supp.*, *Antiphony* differs from *responsorium*, in that in this latter the verse is only spoke by one person, whereas in the former the verses are sung by the two choirs alternately. **1782** PRIESTLEY *Corrupt. Chr.* II. VIII. 122 Singing by antiphony or anthem. **1847** MRS. BROWNING in *Blackw. Mag.* LXI. 555 Life answering life across the vast profound In full antiphony. **1883** *Athenæum* 30 June 836/1 'Israel in Egypt'.. depends so largely.. upon the antiphony of double choruses.

4. *concr.* A composition in prose or verse, consisting of verses sung alternately by two choirs in worship; = ANTIPHON 2.

1868 CHAMBERS *Encycl.* I. 297 The dividing of the antiphonies into verses, with rules regarding the same, is attributed to Pope Cœlestin in 432.

†**5.** = ANTIPHON 3. *Obs.*

1753 CHAMBERS *Cycl. Supp.*

6. *transf.* A response or echo.

1657 TRAPP *Comm. Esth.* viii. 15 The joyful Jews then by way of antiphony answer. **1714** SHAFTESB. *Charac.* III. 300 The eccho or antiphony, which these elegant exclaimers hope.. to draw necessarily from their audience. **1841** DE QUINCEY *Rhet.* Wks. XI. 45 It is not.. any such bravura, that will make a fit antiphony to this sublime rapture.

‖**antiphrasis** (æn'tɪfrəsɪs). *Rhet.* [L., a. Gr. ἀντίφρασις, f. ἀντιφράζ-ειν to express by the opposite.] A figure of speech by which words are used in a sense opposite to their proper meaning.

1533 MORE *Debell. Salem* v. Wks. 1557, 939/1 The fygure of ironye or antiphrasis. **1589** PUTTENHAM *Eng. Poesie* 201 Antiphrasis or the Broad floute as.. to [say to] a Negro.. In good sooth ye are a faire one. **1650** CROMWELL *Lett. & Sp.* (Carlyle) (1857) ii. 110 You are pastors, but it is by an antiphrasis, *a minime pascendo*. **1734** tr. *Rollin's Anc. Hist.* (1827) VII. XVIII. i. 364 He was by antiphrasis surnamed Philopater. **1853** KANE *Grinnell Exp.* iv. (1856) 33 It was a bold antiphrasis that gave such a vernal title [Greenland] to this birth-place of icebergs.

antiphrastic (æntɪ'fræstɪk), *a.* [ad. Gr. ἀντιφραστικ-ός, f. as prec.] Of or pertaining to antiphrasis; opposed to the ordinary meaning.

1640 *Canterbur. Self-Conv.* Postscr. 3 Things are not alwayes correspondent to their names; Etymologies are sometimes antiphrastick. **1683** E. HOOKER *Pref. Pordage's Myst. Div.* 18 An Anti-phrastic and Anti-Christian.. Age.

†**anti'phrastical**, *a. Obs.*$^{-0}$.

1656 BLOUNT *Glossogr.*, *Antiphrastical*, that hath or gives a contrary meaning to words.

anti'phrastically, *adv.* [f. prec. + -LY^2.] In an antiphrastic manner.

1633 BP. MORTON *Discharge* 206 (T.) In his (antiphrastically so called) Sober Reckoning. **1657** G. STARKEY *Helmont's Vind.* 249 Medicines.. which deserve that name, and are not Ironically, or Antiphrastically named so. **1731** BAILEY, *Antiphrastically*, by way of Antiphrasis. **1818** in TODD.

antiphthisic (æntɪ'tɪzɪk), *a.* and *sb. Med.* [ANTI- 3.] **A.** *adj.* Tending to check phthisis or consumption. **B.** *sb.* [sc. medicine.]

1853 in MAYNE *Exp. Lex.*

†**anti'phthisical**, *a. Med. Obs.* = prec.

1719 *Glossogr. Nova*, *Antiphthisical Medicines*, such as withstand Consumption or Phthisick.

antiplastic (æntɪ'plæstɪk), *a. Med.* [f. ANTI- 3 + πλαστικ-ός plastic, f. πλάσσ-ειν to form.] 'Unfavourable to the process of healing or of granulation' (Mayne); 'also applied to medicines which impoverish the blood.' *Syd. Soc. Lex.*

antipleuritic (,æntɪplʊ'rɪtɪk), *a.* and *sb. Med.* [f. ANTI- 3 + πλευρῖτικ-ός suffering from πλευρῖτις pleurisy, f. πλευρά ribs.] **A.** *adj.* Of use against pleurisy. **B.** *sb.* [sc. medicine, application.]

1712 tr. *Pomet's Hist. Drugs* I. 88 A good Sudorifick, and Antipleuritick. **1736** BAILEY *Housh. Dict.*, *Burdock*.. is accounted a Diaphoretick and an Antipleuretick.

antipodagric (,æntɪpəʊ'dægrɪk), *a.* and *sb. Med.* [f. ANTI- 3 + Gr. ποδαγρικ-ός gouty, f. ποδάγρα gout.] **A.** *adj.* Of use against gout. **B.** *sb.* [sc. medicine, application.]

1712 tr. *Pomet's Hist. Drugs* I. 198 There is also prepar'd from it an excellent antipodagrick Plaister. **1853** in MAYNE.

†**antipo'dagrical**, *a. Obs.* = prec.

1676 *Phil. Trans.* XI. 744 Some Anti-podagrical remedies. **1682** *Weekly Mem.* 348 The antipodagrical moxa of the Chineses.

antipodal (æn'tɪpədəl), *a.* and *sb.* [f. ANTIPODES + -AL^1.]

1. Of or pertaining to the antipodes; situated on the opposite side of the globe.

1646 SIR T. BROWNE *Pseud. Ep.* 306 The Americans are Antipodall unto the Indians. **1831** CARLYLE *Sart. Res.* (1858) 46 The antipodal New Holland. **1877** SHIELDS *Final Philos.* 168 The Irish St. Virgilius in the ninth century, dared to advocate the theory of antipodal races.

2. *transf.* Diametrically opposite (*to* anything).

1664 H. MORE *Myst. Iniq.* iv. 10 So horrid and diabolical and so antipodal to both the Person and Spirit of Christ. **1846** HAWTHORNE *Mosses* II. xii. (1864) 251 There was nothing so antipodal to his nature as this man's cold, unimaginative sagacity. **1874** BLACKIE *Self-Cult.* 70 Two such antipodal characters as Coleridge and Thomas Carlyle.

3. *spec.* in *Bot.* Applied to cells at the base of the embryo sac, formed by division of the nucleus. Hence as *sb.*, a cell of this kind.

1876 *Encycl. Brit.* IV. 146/1 In some cases at the base of the embryo-sac a few cells are formed, which have been termed antipodal cells. **1898** *Nat. Science* June 375 The variety in the place of origin of the embryos from egg-cells, synergids, antipodal cells, or nucellus. **1946** *Nature* 10 Aug. 204/2 After fertilization, the antipodals also behave normally.

antipodeal, *a. rare.* Erroneous form of prec.

1881 *Cheq. Career* 63 A true tale of antipodeal vicissitudes.

Antipodean (æn,tɪpə'diːən), *a.* and *sb.* [irreg. f. ANTIPODE-S + -AN; perh. after *European*, but not analogous, a better form being the obs. ANTIPODIAN.]

A. *adj.* **1.** Of or pertaining to the opposite side of the world; *esp.* Australasian.

1861 SALA *Twice round Clock* 35 Antipodean legislators have a refreshment room they call 'Bellamy's.' **1877** HEATH *Fern W.* Introd. 4 The antipodean range of the Fern World.

2. *humorously*, Having everything upside down.

1852 DICKENS *Bleak H.* (1853) 621 A kind of Antipodean lumber room, full of old chairs and tables, upside down.

3. *fig.* Of or pertaining to direct opposition; diametrically opposed (*to*).

1651 BIGGS *New Disp.* Summ., All the medicines of the shops in Antipodæan position to our bodies. **1841** HOR. SMITH *Moneyed Man* I. ii. 32 We were Antipodean in all our tastes. **1881** *Scribn. Month.* XXII. 97 The writer who.. is most antipodean to Mr. Carlyle.

B. *sb.* In the senses of the adj.

1640 R. BROME *Antipodes* II. iv. sig. E 3^v, *Per.* And what are those? *Doct.* All Antipodeans. **1890** *Athenæum* 22 Feb. 239/2 The 'antipodeans'—the jugglers who work with their legs. **1890** A. P. MORTON tr. *H. Le Roux's Acrobats & Mountebanks* ix. 222 He.. rarely leaves the 'carpet'; he is a juggler or an antipodean. *Ibid.* 225 The crural muscles attain an extraordinary expansion and strength in the antipodeans. **1914** C. MACKENZIE *Sinister St.* II. IV. iv. 942 They were moral antipodeans to the magistrate or the legislator or the social reformer. **1921** *Glasgow Herald* 21 Jan. 8 The Englishmen.. are probably slightly weaker in Australia than the best side the Antipodeans can put on the field.

antipodes (æn'tɪpədiːz), *sb. pl.* Also **Antipodes.** [a. L. *antipodes*, a. Gr. (*οἱ*) ἀντίποδες (in sense 1 below), pl. of ἀντίπους having the feet opposite, f. ἀντί opposite + πούς foot (whence also a sing. ANTIPOS). Formerly (quite regularly) three syllables, *an-ti-pod(e)s*, and hence having a sing. *antipod*, *-pode* (cf. *apod*, *apode*, *decapod*), still in use in certain senses; cf. Fr. *antipode*, *-s*.]

†**1.** Those who dwell directly opposite to each other on the globe, so that the soles of their feet are as it were planted against each other; *esp.* those who occupy this position in regard to us. *Obs.*

1398 TREVISA *Barth. De P.R.* XV. lii. (1495) 506 Yonde in Ethiopia ben the Antipodes, men that haue theyr fete ayenst our fete. **1556** RECORDE *Cast. Knowl.* 93 People.. called of the Greeks and Latines also ἀντίποδες, Antipodes, as you might say Counterfooted, or Counterpasers. **1596** SHAKS. *Merch. Ven.* v. i. 127 We should hold day with the Antipodes, If you would walke in absence of the sunne. **1682** in *Phil. Collect.* XII. 181 These Antipodes.. indeavoured to begin a truck or Merchandize with the Yacht. **1788** V. KNOX *Winter Even.* I. III. vii. 275 Men, placed as the Antipodes are represented. **1837** WHEWELL *Hist. Induct. Sc.* (1857) I. 195 The existence of Antipodes, or persons inhabiting the opposite side of the globe.

†**2.** *fig.* Those who in any way resemble the dwellers on the opposite side of the globe. *Obs.*

1605 BACON *Adv. Learn.* I. 9 He will neuer be one of the Antipodes, to tread opposite to the present world. **1611** A. STAFFORD *Niobe* To Reader, My soul is an antipode, and treads opposite to the present world. **1642** FULLER *Holy & Prof. St.* I. ii. 32 Christians were forced to be Antipodes to other men, so that when it was night with others, it was day with them. **1688** in De Foe *Mem. Ch. Scotl.* IV. 99 Antipodes to all Mankind, Enemies to Government.

3. Places on the surfaces of the earth directly opposite to each other, or the place which is directly opposite to another; *esp.* the region directly opposite to our own.

1549 *Compl. Scotl.* vi. 50 The place that is direct contrar til our zenyth is callit antipodes. *Ibid.* 51 Lactantius firmien .. scornis the mathematiciens that effermis antipodos. **1599** SHAKS. *Much Ado* II. i. 273, I will goe on the slightest arrand now to the Antypodes. **1642** HOWELL *For. Trav.* (Arb.) 33 From the remotest parts of the Earth.. yea from the very Antipods. **1879** WALLACE *Austral.* i. 4 New Zealand, almost the antipodes of Britain.

4. a. *transf.* The exact opposite of a person or thing. (In this sense the sing. *antipode* is still used.)

1641 LD. DIGBY *Parl. Sp.* 19 Jan. 15 Would not one sweare that this were the Antipodes to the other? *a* **1667** COWLEY *Avarice* Wks. 1710 II. 754 Having nothing, he has all: This is just his Antipode, who, having all things, yet has nothing. **1682** SIR T. BROWNE *Chr. Mor.* (1756) 32 Fools.. are antipodes unto the wise. **1792** BURNS *Let.* Wks. (Globe ed.) 504 That antipode of folly.. the wise and witty Willie Nicol. **1809** KNOX & JEBB *Corr.* I. 515, I soberly believe, that selfishness is the very antipode of self-love. **1863** MRS.

CLARKE *Shaks. Char.* v. 120 Iago is the direct antipodes to Michael Cassio. **1867** G. MACDONALD *Alec Forbes* xviii. 77 Forbes he hated, for he was the very antipode to.. himself.

b. *phr.* **at antipodes**: in direct opposition.
1868 *Lessons Mid. Age* 232 When you feel that you are at antipodes with a man on almost all points.

†**5.** As adv. (orig. sb. in apposition) in phrases like ***to walk antipodes to***. *Obs.*
1643 *Char. Oxf. Incend.* in *Harl. Misc.* (1745) V. 474/2 The Man lives towards the Sun-setting, treads Antipodes of late to Victory. **1692** BENTLEY *Boyle Lect.* vii. 236 Two Vessels, placed there, Antipodes to each other. *a* **1718** PENN *Tracts* Wks. I. 493 He walkt Antipodes to the Genius of that Age.

6. *Chem.* (with pronunc. 'æntɪpəʊdz); *sing.* **antipode**. An enantio-morphic compound.
1897, 1951 [see *pseudoracemic* adj. s.v. PSEUDO-2.] **1918** J. B. COHEN *Org. Chem. Adv. Stud.* (ed. 2) II. iii. 169 The two complementary active forms are variously termed *active components, antipodes*, or *enantiomorphs*. **1947** A. J. MEE tr. *Karrer's Org. Chem.* (ed. 3) iv. 96 Two such isomerides, which differ neither in chemical nor in general physical properties, but which rotate the plane of polarization of light by the same amount, one to the right, the other to the left, are called *antipodes*, or *enantiomorphic* forms.

†**Anti'podian**, *a. Obs. rare*$^{-1}$. [f. ANTIPOD-ES + -IAN (cf. *Phœnices, Phœnician*).] = ANTIPODEAN.
1640 BROME *Antip.* 231 Hurried my Soule to the Antipodian strand.

antipodic (æntɪ'pɒdɪk), *a. rare*$^{-1}$. [f. ANTIPOD-ES + -IC.] = ANTIPODAL.
1881 RUSKIN *Bible of Amiens*, Some antithetic, antipathic, or antipodic point in the opposite hemisphere.

antipodist (æn'tɪpədɪst), *sb.* and *a.* [f. ANTIPOD-ES + IST.] **A.** *sb.* A believer in the antipodes (at a time when the belief was heresy).
1866 *Athenæum* 21 Apr. 532/2 Some maintain that the antipodist was a different person from the canonized bishop.
B. *adj.* = ANTIPODAL.
1844 MOZLEY *Arnold* in *Ess.* (1878) II. 52 A system like his was bound to.. thrust out such an antipodist one.

†**an'tipodite.** *Obs. rare.* [f. as prec. + -ITE; cf. *sybar-ite*.] An inhabitant of the antipodes.
1620 MELTON *Astrol.* 28 Those that in a peruerse order.. making the Day night.. liue.. like true Antipodites. *Ibid.* 29 The Antipodites haue their feete downwards.. and their heads upwards as well as wee.

antipole ('æntɪˌpəʊl). [ANTI- 2.] The opposite pole. *fig.* The direct opposite.
1822 DE QUINCEY *Conf.* (1862) 138 That determined pluralist and intense antipole of all possible sinecurists. **1876** GEO. ELIOT *Dan. Der.* v. xl. 372 That antipole of all enthusiasm called 'a man of the world.'

antipolemist (æntɪ'pɒlɪmɪst). *rare*$^{-1}$. [f. ANTI- 5 + Gr. πόλεμ-ος war, πολεμιστ-ής warrior.] A professed opponent of war.
1817 COLERIDGE *Biog. Lit.* 82 Sundry philanthropists and anti-polemists.

antipo'litical, *a. rare*$^{-1}$. [ANTI- 3.] Opposed to sound political principles; impolitic.
1791 T. PAINE *Rights M.* (ed. 4) 82 Let Mr. Burke continue to preach his antipolitical doctrine of Church and State.

†**anti'polliges**, *sb. pl. Obs.* [app. f. ANTI- 6 + *poll-ēre* to be powerful, on some erroneous analogy.] ? Opposing forces.
1652 GAULE *Magastrom.* 206 There are antipolliges, or occult qualities of actives and passives.

antipope ('æntɪpəʊp). Also 6–7 **antipape**. [orig. a. Fr. *antipape*, ad. med.L. *antipāpa*, formed on the analogy of *antichristus*. In 17th c. assimilated to *pope*.] A pope elected in opposition to one held to be canonically chosen; *spec.* applied to those who resided at Avignon during 'the great schism of the West.' (So called by adversaries; to those who upheld his claims he was the real pope.)
[*c* **1236** ROGER OF WENDOVER *Chron.* (1841) II. 194 Scisma orta est Romæ propter Gelasium antipapam.] **1579** FULKE *Conf. Sanders* 570 Interruption.. by meanes of.. Schismes and Antipapes. **1611** SPEED *Hist. Gt. Brit.* IX. vi. 31 He would forsake Pope Alexander, and ioyne with the Emperour, and Antipape. **1670** G. H. *Hist. Cardinals* I. II. 52 Novatianus the Roman was by faction created Antipope. **1781** GIBBON *Decl. & F.* lvi. III. 378 The antipope, Clement the third, was consecrated in the Lateran. **1855** MILMAN *Lat. Chr.* VI. iii. (1864) III. 454 Pope and Antipope waited their doom from the princes of the world.

antipophora, obs. form of ANTHYPOPHORA.

antipopular (æntɪ'pɒpjʊlə(r)), *a.* [ANTI- 3.] Adverse to the people, or popular cause.
1815 W. TAYLOR in *Ann. Rev.* III. 303 The constitutional laws passed during the present reign.. are innovations, in an anti-popular direction. **1837** LYTTON *Athens* II. 282 Servile generosity common to an anti-popular party.

anti-porch, obs. f. ANTE-PORCH: see ANTE- A I.

†**'antipos.** *Obs.* [ad. Gr. ἀντίπους, the regular Roman transliteration of which is *antipus*.] One diametrically opposed: see ANTIPODES 4.
1631 BRATHWAIT *Whimzies* 115 A Zealous Brother.. is an antipos to all church government.

†**'antipose**, *v. Obs. rare*$^{-1}$. [hybrid f. ANTI- A + -POSE (cf. *appose*).] To set in opposition.
1631 HEYWOOD *Engl. Eliz.* (1641) 7 The Pope sought by all means to antipose their opinions.

†**anti'practise**, *v. Obs.* [f. ANTI- A.] To practise on the other side, practise the opposite.
a **1670** HACKET *Abp. Williams* I. 95 (D.) Seldom anything but severity will make them anti-practise.

†**anti'præsulist.** *Obs. rare*$^{-1}$. [f. ANTI- 5 + L. *præsul* president, superintendent, in mod.L. 'bishop' + -IST.] One opposed to the government of the Church by bishops.
1640 BP. HALL *Episc.* II. §18. 190 Howsoever it pleaseth our Anti-præsulists to sleight the practice and judgement of all Churches.

†**anti'probabilism.** *Obs.*$^{-0}$ [ANTI- 7.] The doctrine or system of those who hold it unlawful to follow the more probable opinion in preference to the less probable one.
1753 CHAMBERS *Cycl. Supp.* s.v., F. Gisbert has a treatise express in favour of Antiprobabilism.

antipruritic (ˌæntɪprʊ'rɪtɪk), *a.* and *sb. Med.* [f. ANTI- 3 + L. *prūrītis* itching + -IC.] Tending to relieve itching. Hence as *sb.*, a substance tending to relieve itching.
1876 DUHRING *Dis. Skin* 92 Carbolic acid is the most valuable of antipruritic remedies. **1880** in *Syd. Soc. Lex.* **1894** in GOULD *Illustr. Dict. Med.* **1920** J. M. H. MACLEOD *Dis. Skin* vii. 119 Anti-pruritics allay irritation and itching, and act either directly on the sensory nerve terminations, or indirectly by evaporation or by astringing the blood-vessels.

antipsoric (æntɪp'sɒrɪk), *a.* and *sb. Med.* [f. ANTI- 3 + Gr. ψώρα itch, ψωρικ-ός of the itch.]
A. *adj.* Tending to prevent or cure the itch. **B.** *sb.* (sc. medicine, application.)
1853 in MAYNE.

‖**antip'tosis.** *Gram. Obs.* [med.L., a. Gr. ἀντίπτωσις, f. ἀντί in exchange + πτῶσις falling, case.] The use of one case for another.
1657 J. SMITH *Myst. Rhet.* 192 Antiptosis.. the putting of one case for another. **1659** PEARSON *Creed* (1839) 186 Ὁ κύριός μου καὶ ὁ Θεός μου.. In these words there is.. an antiptosis, the nominative case used for the vocative. **1751** in CHAMBERS.

antipyic (æntɪ'paɪɪk), *a.* and *sb. Med.* [ad. Fr. *antipyique*, f. Gr. ἀντί (ANTI- 3) + πύον pus, matter: see -IC.] **A.** *adj.* Tending to prevent suppuration. **B.** *sb.* (sc. medicine, application.)
1853 in MAYNE.

antipyretic (ˌæntɪpɪ'rɛtɪk), *a.* and *sb. Med.* [f. ANTI- 3 + Gr. πυρετός fever; cf. *pyretic*.]
A. *adj.* Tending to prevent or allay fever. **B.** *sb.* (sc. medicine.)
1681 tr. *Willis, Rem. Med. Wks., Antipyreticks*, medicines against burning feavers. **1719** in *Glossogr. Nova.* **1875** H. WOOD *Therap.* (1879) 74 All antipyretic remedies appear to act more strongly on children. *Ibid.* 74 Liebermeister.. has given some ten thousand doses of quinine as an antipyretic.

antipyrin (æntɪ'paɪərɪn). Also **-ine**. [f. ANTIPYR(ETIC + -IN^1.] The commercial name of a benzene derivative, $C_{11}H_{12}N_2O$, used as an antipyretic: discovered in 1884 by L. Knorr, professor at Jena.
1884 *Jrnl. Chem. Soc.* XLVI. 1378 By distillation with zinc-dust, antipyrine yields benzene. **1893** [see TOLYPYRIN]. **1902** *Encycl. Brit.* XXXIII. 271/1 Antipyrin belongs rather to the furfurol group.

antipyrotic (ˌæntɪpɪ'rɒtɪk), *a.* and *sb. Med.* [f. ANTI- 3 + Gr. πυρωτικ-ός burning, f. πυρό-ειν to burn, f. πῦρ fire.] **A.** *adj.* Tending to prevent or heal burns. **B.** *sb.* Anything so used.
1839 in HOOPER *Med. Dict.* **1853** in MAYNE *Exp. Lex.*

†**anti'quærer.** *Obs.* [f. next + -ER^1.] One who puts a counter-query. One whose opinions were expressed in the 'Antiquæries on Master Prin's 12 questions,' 1644.
1645 PAGITT *Heres.* (1661) 257 Some of the most foolishly zealous [Quakers] have burnt their goods to prevent pride, which the Antiquærers allow.

†**'antiquæry.** *Obs. rare*$^{-1}$. [ANTI- 2.] A counter-question.
1644 (*title*) Certain briefe Observations and *Antiquæries on Master Prin's 12 questions about Church Government.

antiquarian (æntɪ'kwɛərɪən), *a.* and *sb.* [f. L. *antīquāri-us* (see ANTIQUARY) + -AN.]
A. *adj.*
1. Of or connected with the study of antiquities.
1771 DUCAREL in *Phil. Trans.* LXI. 150 The antiquarian part of my subject. *a* **1779** WARBURTON *Let.* No. 213 (T.) You say your antiquarian taste drew you thither. **1872** YEATS *Tech. Hist. Comm.* 346 The antiquarian treasures of the British Museum. **1867** FREEMAN *Norm. Conq.* I. vi. 517 The axe, as antiquarian researches show, was in use almost everywhere.
2. Applied to a large size of drawing-paper.
1875 URE *Dict. Arts* III. 497 Antiquarian [size of paper], 53 by 31. **1879** SPON *Workshop Rects.* I Antiquarian [paper], 52 × 29 inches.

B. *sb.* [The adj. used *absol.*] One who studies or is fond of antiquities; an antiquary.
1610 HOLLAND *Camden's Brit.* (1627) 6, I referre the matter.. to the Senate of Antiquarians, for to be decided. **1778** JOHNSON in *Boswell* III. 61 A mere Antiquarian is a rugged being. **1856** MAX MÜLLER *Chips* (1880) II. xvi. 7 History.. appeals not only to the antiquarian, but to the heart of every man. **1872** HARDWICK *Trad. Lanc.* 220 A thoroughgoing antiquarian would call this a Druidical remain.

anti'quarianism. [f. prec. + -ISM.] The profession or pursuits of the antiquarian; taste for, or devotion to, antiquities.
a **1779** WARBURTON *Lett.* No. 221 (T.) I used to despise him for his antiquarianism. **1803** W. TAYLOR in *Ann. Rev.* I. 439 He views the earth, neither through the telescope of antiquarianism, nor the microscope of topography. **1849** FREEMAN *Archit.* 4 The first phase of ecclesiology was simple antiquarianism.

antiquarianize (æntɪ'kwɛərɪənaɪz), *v. colloq.* [f. ANTIQUARIAN; cf. *botanize, geologize*, etc.] To act as an antiquary; to 'play the antiquary.'
1828 LYELL in *Life* I. ix. 222 Have geologised and antiquarianised all day with much success. **1864** SALA in *Temple Bar* Jan. 189 Don't be afraid I am not about to antiquarianize.

antiquarianly (æntɪ'kwɛərɪənlɪ), *adv. rare*$^{-1}$. [f. ANTIQUARIAN + -LY^2.] After the manner of an antiquarian.
1772 H. WALPOLE *Lett. to C'tess Ossory* (1848) I. 37, I have just reflected antiquarianly, that *pale as ashes* must be one of our most ancient proverbs and in use before coals.

†**anti'quarious**, *a. Obs. rare.* [f. L. *antīquārius* (see ANTIQUARY) + OUS.] Given to, or connected with, antiquarian studies.
1606 WARNER *Alb. Eng.* XIV. To Reader 331 Adde Stows late antiquarious Pen.

†**antiquarism.** *Obs. rare*$^{-1}$. [f. ANTIQUARY + -ISM.] = ANTIQUARIANISM.
1658 SIR T. BROWNE *Hydriot.* iv. 41 Who were the Proprietors of these Bones.. were a Question above Antiquarism.

‖**antiquarium** (æntɪ'kwɛərɪəm). *rare.* [L., neut. of adj. *antīquārius* (see next); cf. *herbarium*, and see -ARIUM.] A repository of antiquities.
1881 *Athenæum* No. 2823. 747 It is rather an antiquarium containing chiefly statuettes and coins.

antiquark ('æntɪkwɔːk, -kwɑːk). *Particle Physics.* [f. ANTI- 1 d + QUARK.] The antiparticle of a quark.
1964 [see QUARK]. **1965** *New Scientist* 18 Mar. 703/1 There would be no physical law to prevent storing 'quarks' and 'anti-quarks' separately. **1977** *Dædalus* Fall 33 The observed strongly interacting particles such as neutrons, protons, and mesons are believed to be compound states, consisting of quarks, antiquarks, and gluons, but with no net color. **1978** PASACHOFF & KUTNER *University Astron.* ix. 262 Recent experiments have even indicated that an additional two quarks, bringing the total to six (plus six antiquarks) may be required. **1985** *Sci. Amer.* Jan. 66/1 Pairs of quarks and antiquarks might be created spontaneously in the wake of an escaping quark.

antiquary ('æntɪkwərɪ), *a.* and *sb.* [ad. L. *antīquāri-us* of antiquity, f. *antīqu-us*: see ANTIQUE and -ARY.]
A. *adj.* Of antiquity; ancient; antique. *rare.*
1606 SHAKS. *Tr. & Cr.* II. iii. 262 Here's Nestor Instructed by the Antiquary times. **1877** MRS. OLIPHANT *Carita* III. xli. 190 Some kind of antiquary courtship.
B. *sb.* [the adj. used *ellipt.*, sc. 'man,' 'thing.']
I. Of persons.
†**1.** A man of great age, an ancient. *Obs. rare.*
a **1581** CAMPION *Hist. Irel.* vii. (1633) 24 Had it beene my chaunce.. to meete and conferre with this noble Antiquarie [a man aged two thousand and forty one yeares]. **1635** J. TAYLOR (Water P.) *Parr*, He's in these times fill'd with iniquity, No antiquary, but antiquity; For his longevity's of such extent, That he's a living mortal monument.
†**2.** An official custodian or recorder of antiquities. (Bestowed as a title by Henry VIII upon Leland.) *Obs.*
1563 GRAFTON *Chron.* I. VII. (R.) The booke of the excellent antiquary John Leyland. **1601** HOLLAND *Pliny* (1634) II. 493 Annius Fæcialis (another antiquarie or herault at armes of Rome). **1753** CHAMBERS *Cycl. Supp.* s.v., The University of Oxford have still their Antiquary, under the denomination of *custos archivorum.* **1763** J. BROWN *Poetry & Mus.* §8. 161 The approved Songs of the ancient Bards were preserved in the Custody of the King's Antiquary.
3. A student (usually a *professed* student), or collector, of antiquities. (Formerly used, in a wide sense, of a student of early history; now tending to be restricted to one who investigates the relics and monuments of the more recent past.)
1586 THYNNE in *Animadv.* Introd. 80 It hath beene some question amongst the best antiquaries of our age, that, etc. **1602** WARNER *Alb. Eng.* Epit. (1612) 351 Our learned and studious Antiquarie Master Camden. **1762** H. WALPOLE *Vertue's Anecd. Paint.* (1786) I. 134 We antiquaries, who hold every thing worth preserving, merely because it has been preserved. **1830** HOR. SMITH *Tin Trump.* (1870) 28 Antiquary—too often a collector of valuables that are worth nothing, and a re-collector of all that Time has been glad to forget. **1851** D. WILSON *Preh. Ann.* (1863) I. iii. 86 Such evidences of primitive ages as have rewarded the researches

of Northern antiquaries. **1881** (*title of Magazine*) The Antiquary.

II. Of things.

†**4.** = ANTIC *sb.* 1. *Obs. rare.*

a **1603** in Nichols *Progr. Q. Eliz.* I. 378 Three bolles.. chased in the bottoms with antiquaries and fishes.

†**5.** = ANTIQUITY. *Obs. rare.*

1592 GREENE *Groatsw. Wit* 1 A Citie..the name is not mentioned in the Antiquary. **1612** WOODALL *Surg. Mate* Wks. 1653, 235 Of the antiquary, the first inventers, and worthinesse of the excellent Art of Alchymy.

antiquate ('æntɪkwət), *ppl. a. arch.* [ad. L. *antīquāt-us*, pa. pple. of *antīquā-re* to render old, f. *antīqu-us* ANTIQUE.] Rendered or grown old; obsolete through age; ANTIQUATED.

1537 ? TINDALE *Exp. 1 John* Wks. II. 174 It was antiquate, and clean out of knowledge. **1657** TOMLINSON *Renou's Disp.* 517 It abates the antiquate belly-flux. **1706** DE FOE *Jure Div.* XII. 274 Triumphant Vice grown antiquate and old. **1875** B. TAYLOR *Faust* I. xxi. 188 Who, now, a work of moderate sense will read? Such works are held as antiquate and mossy.

antiquate ('æntɪkweɪt), *v.* [f. prec.: see -ATE.]

1. To make old, or out of date; to make obsolete; to abolish as out of date.

1596 SPENSER *State of Irel.* 22 Now thorough change of time [they] are cleane antiquated. **1656** BLOUNT *Glossogr.* To Reader, Every.. Sciolist being at liberty, as, to antiquate and decry the old, so to coin and innovate new words. **1678** MARVELL *Growth Popery* Wks. 1875 IV. 254 He [the Pope] antiquates the precepts of Christ. **1859** G. WILSON *E. Forbes* iv. 106 Quickly-collected, yet trustworthy data, such as antiquated even modern text-books, with unheard-of rapidity.

2. To bring into conformity with the manner of earlier times; to make antique.

1821 *Edin. Rev.* XXXV 492 Familiar contemplation of them has..enabled him to antiquate his feelings. **1825** SCOTT in Lockhart *Life* VIII. 152 To disguise and antiquate as it were their names by spelling them after some quaint manner.

antiquated ('æntɪkweɪtɪd), *ppl. a.* [f. prec. + -ED; replacing as pple. and adj. ANTIQUATE *a.*]

1. Grown old, of long standing, inveterate.

1670 COTTON *Espernon* II. VIII. 384 Declaring he was sacrific'd to the Duke's antiquated hatred to those of his Countrey. **1770** BURKE *Pres. Discont.* Wks. II. 229 The offspring of antiquated prejudices. **1833** I. TAYLOR *Fanat.* viii. 333 Prejudice and antiquated jealousy did not freely yield themselves up.

2. Out of use by reason of age; obsolete.

1623 B. JONSON in *Shaks. C. Praise* 149 Neat Terence, witty Plautus now not please; But antiquated and deserted lye. *a* **1695** MRQ. HALIFAX in *Coll. Poems* (1705) 141 Reviving antiquated Laws. **1861** STANLEY *East. Ch.* i. (1869) 39 The languages by the lapse of years have become antiquated.

3. So old as to be unworthy to survive; obsolescent. (Often contemptuously = 'old-world.')

1692 BENTLEY *Boyle Lect.* iii. 106 Deride and explode the antiquated Folly. **1741** RICHARDSON *Pamela* (1824) I. xxvi. 41 No more, no more, said he, of these antiquated topics. **1860** MOTLEY *Netherl.* I. i. 5 The world had become tired of the antiquated delusion of a papal supremacy.

4. Old-fashioned, whether as surviving from, or as imitating, earlier usage.

1675 E. PHILLIPS in *Shaks. C. Praise* 359 The roughest, most unpolish't and antiquated Language. **1734** J. RICHARDSON in Birch *Milton's Wks.* 1738 I. 50 His antiquated Words were his Choice, not his Necessity. **1824** W. IRVING *T. Trav.* I. 327 Students..in their antiquated caps and gowns. **1867** FREEMAN *Norm. Conq.* I. App. 610 The antiquated phraseology which he uses.

5. Of persons: Advanced in age, incapacitated by age, superannuated. Also *fig.*

1678 C. HATTON in *Hatton Corr.* (1878) I. 164 Twisden was quite antiquated, and Wild very infirme. **1711** ADDISON *Spect.* No. 7 ¶4 A maiden Aunt..one of these Antiquated Sybils. **1802** WORDSW. *Sonn. Liberty* I. iii, The antiquated Earth, as one might say, Beat like the heart of Man.

'antiquatedness. [f. prec. + -NESS.] The quality of being antiquated or old-fashioned.

1731 in BAILEY; whence in JOHNSON, etc.

†**'antiquateness.** *Obs. rare*$^{-1}$. [f. ANTIQUATE *a.* + -NESS.] The quality of being antiquate; obsoleteness.

1672 *Mede's Life* in *Wks.* Introd. 41 That no man may pretend the Antiquateness of the Old Testament.

antiquating ('æntɪkweɪtɪŋ), *vbl. sb.* [f. ANTIQUATE *v.* + -ING^1.] A rendering antiquated or obsolete; antiquation. (Now gerundial.)

1669 HONYMAN *Surv. Naphtali* II. 125 The antiquating of former Laws. **1692** R. LESTRANGE *Josephus' Antiq.* XI. viii. (1733) 297 It look'd like a Step toward the antiquating of their Country's laws about Marriage.

antiquation (æntɪ'kweɪʃən). [ad. L. *antīquātiōn-em*, n. of action f. *antīquā-re*: see ANTIQUATE.]

1. The action of making antiquated, out of date, or obsolete; abolition, abrogation.

a **1643** W. CARTWRIGHT *To Queen* (R.) An antiquation of the salique law. **1828** SYD. SMITH *Wks.* (1867) II. 245 This silent antiquation of doctrines.

2. The production of an appearance of age.

1862 *Sat. Rev.* XIV. 476/2 A free use of acids and other tricks of 'antiquation'—as the artificial simulation of the appearance of age began to be called.

3. The state of being antiquated; antiquatedness; obsoleteness.

1659 HARDY *1 John* (1865) xxviii. 177/2 To take *new* not in opposition to *antiquity*, but *antiquation*. **1862** *Spectator* 29 Mar., Chaucer..would, in point of antiquation, be just as distant from the present language.

antique (æn'tiːk, 'æntɪk: see below), *a.* and *sb.* Forms: α. 6 **antyk(e, auntyke,** 6–7 **antik(e, -ick(e,** 6–8 **antick.** β. 6– **antique.** [ad. L. *antīqu-us, antīcus*, former, earlier, ancient, f. *ante* before (like *postīcus*, f. *post* after); or perh. immed. f. Fr. *antique* (16th c. ad. L., replacing OFr. *antif*). The modern ANTIC is a parallel form, which has always been distinct in sense in Eng., though both were spelt *antik(e, antick(e* in 16th c. For the present word the Fr. spelling *antique* has been concurrent from the first, and the only one since 1700. But the identity of pronunciation remained longer; Dr. Johnson says *antique* 'was formerly pronounced according to English analogy, with the accent on the first syllable; but now after the French, with the accent on the last, at least in prose; the poets use it variously.' In senses 1, 2 ('æntɪk) is still used in poetry; the prosaic 4–7 are always (æn'tiːk); 3 usually so. See also ANTIC.]

A. *adj.*

1. Belonging to former times, ancient, olden. (Now generally rhetorical = of the 'good old times.')

α. **1541** R. COPLAND *Galyen's Terap.* 2 Ciij b, And that this reason and maner were antyke. **1595** SPENSER *Sonn.* lxxix, The famous warriors of the anticke world. **1621** QUARLES *Esther* (1717) 141 Me list not ramble into antick days. **1678** BUTLER *Hud.* III. I. 43 And us'd the only Antick Philters Deriv'd from old Heroick Tilters.

β. **1538** STARKEY *England* 4 The old and antique phylosopharys. **1599** SHAKS. *Hen. V*, v. Prol. 26 The Senatours of th' antique Rome. **1664** BUTLER *Hud.* II. III. 902 Some say the Zodiack Constellations Haue long since changed their antique Stations. **1742** W. COLLINS *Ode* viii. 66 It is held of antique story. **1863** CLOUGH *Relig. Poems* ii. 31 The antique pure simplicity with which God and good angels communed undispleased.

2. Having existed since olden times; of a good old age, aged, venerable. *arch.*

α. **1536** *Pilgr. T.* 65 in *Thynne's Animadv.* App. 79 The old and antyk bulding. **1547** BOORDE *Introd. Knowl.* i. (1870) 120 The thyrd auntyke vniuersite of the worlde, named Oxford. **1664** BUTLER *Hud.* II. I. 792 Or Innovation introduce In place of things of antick use.

β. **1596** SPENSER *State Irel.* 28 A nation so antique, as that no monument remaines of her beginning. **1610** G. FLETCHER *Christ's Vict.* I. iv, Ye sacred writings in whose antique leaves. **1781** GIBBON *Decl. & F.* III. 138 Tempted them to neglect the care of their antique walls.

3. a. Old-fashioned, antiquated, such as is no longer extant.

α. **1647** N. BACON *Hist. Disc.* xxxii. 79 The Laws, though by their antick language darkned, yet plainly speak. **1680** BURNET *Rochester* (1692) 170 Vertue is thought an Antick piece of Formality.

β. **1734** tr. *Rollin's Rom. Hist.* III. VII. 364 Your integrity is of too antique a cast. **1756** C. LUCAS *Ess. Waters* II. 5 This antique expression has been..ridiculed by some moderns. **1847** LONGF. *Ev.* I. i. 74 There stood the broad-wheeled wains and the antique ploughs and the harrows. **1879** McCARTHY *Own Time* II. xxiii. 188 His loyalty to the Sovereign had something antique and touching in it.

b. Out of date, behind the time, stale. *rare.*

1755 H. WALPOLE *Lett. H. Mann* 261 (1834) III. 89 This will come to you as very antique news.

4. Of, belonging to, or after the manner of the ancients (of Greece and Rome).

1734 J. RICHARDSON in Birch *Milton's Wks.* 1738 I. 54 All his Images are pure Antique, so that we read Homer and Virgil in reading him. **1819** BYRON *Juan* II. cxciv, And thus they form a group that's quite antique, Half naked, loving, natural, and Greek. **1842** MRS. BROWNING *Grk. Chr. Poets* 160 The Apollo of the later Greek sculpture-school..placed in a company of the antiquer statues.

5. Of or after the manner of any ancient time, archaic.

1753 HOGARTH *Anal. Beauty* vi. §6. 37 The antique lappets belonging to the head of the Sphinx. **1855** C. BRONTË *Villette* i, Looking down on a fine antique street. **1870** F. WILSON *Ch. Lindisf.* 76 A stiff, stilted, modern bell-cot..breaks the antique charm.

6. *Bookbinding.* See ANTIQUE *v.* 1.

Mod. Bookseller's Catalogue, Æneids of Virgil..wants title, Antique calf extra.

7. *Typogr.* 'A popular style of display type in which all the lines are of uniform thickness.' Ringwalt *Encycl. Print.* 1871.

8. Applied to old furniture, pictures, china, and other articles of virtu, esp. as sought for and collected by amateurs (cf. sense B 4 below); *absol.* with *the*, antique articles collectively.

In practice 'old' with reference to antiques is frequently interpreted to mean 'more than 100 years old'.

1822 *P.O. London Directory* 17 Antique furniture and ornamental china dealer. **1851** (*title*) Antiquarian Gleanings in the North of England, being examples of antique furniture, plate,..etc. drawn and etched by William B. Scott. **1868** H. T. TUCKERMAN *Collector* 99 When an ancient dame..drew one [*sc.* a miniature] of her husband from an antique cabinet. **1877** *G. Shrimpton's Oxford Direct.* 33 Walford & Son, jewellers, and dealers in antique china. **1888** (*title*) Antique and Modern Point Lace. **1908** R. & E. SHACKLETON (*title*) The quest of the antique, being some personal experiences in the finding of old furniture.

9. Applied to a type of paper (see quot. *a* 1912).

1890 A. WATT *Art of Paper-Making* xiv. 157 Some descriptions of paper, as 'antique' and 'old style', for example, are surfaced with good cardboard instead of copper or zinc plates. *a* **1912** *Paper Terminol.* (*Spalding & Hodge*) ii. 1 *Antique*, a term originally applied to machine-made papers made in imitation of old handmade printings. It denoted colour and finish. It is now used to describe any good bulking paper with a rough surface. **1958** *Times Lit. Suppl.* 3 Oct. 567/4 To combine two qualities of paper in the same book, that is to print the text on antique paper and the plates on coated paper.

B. *sb.* [the adj. used *ellipt.*; sc. man, thing.]

†**1.** A man of ancient times; *pl.* the Ancients. *Obs.*

1563 J. SHUTE *Archit.* A iij a, Vitruuius one of the most parfaictest of all the Antiques. **1578** T. N. tr. *Conq. W. India* 170 The soles were tied to the upper parte with latchets, as is painted of the Antikes. **1598** W. PHILLIP *Linschoten's Trav. Ind.* (1864) 201 Their Shooes they weare like Antiques with cut toes.

2. A relic of ancient art, or of bygone days.

1530 PALSGR. 487/2 If this antique were closed in golde, it were a goodly thing. **1665** BP. PATRICK *Par. Pilgr.*, Consider that old Fashions are wont to come about again, and that we are much in love with Antiques. **1766** GOLDSM. *Vic. Wakef.* xx, His own business..was to collect pictures, medals, intaglios and antiques of all kinds. **1850** LEITCH *Müller's Anc. Art* §36 By far the greatest number of antiques, especially statues, were found between 1450 and 1550.

3. ***the antique***: ancient work in art, antique style.

1751 CHAMBERS *Cycl.* s.v., We say an antique building, or a building after the antique. **1859** GULLICK & TIMBS *Paint.* 312 The course of drawing from the 'antique' is then entered upon.

4. An article of old furniture, or a picture or piece of china, etc., esp. as sought after and collected by amateurs (cf. sense A 8 above. Freq. *attrib.* as in ***antique dealer, furnisher, shop***.

1771 J. WEDGWOOD *Let.* 13 Jan. (1965) 102 The first will enable us to make Tablets and figures &c without cracking, and the third to make *real Antiques* you know. **1884** *Eng. Illustr. Mag.* Dec. 210/1 Brass and copper vessels..many of them shapely as antiques. **1904** *Daily Chron.* 29 Jan. 8/1 A story told in the 'antique' shops shows the cunning of those concerned in the business. **1920** *19th Cent.* July 166 Morrison was staying with a little antique-dealer in the West of England.

antique, occas. spelling of ANTIC in 16–17th c.

antique (æn'tiːk), *v.* [f. the adj.] **1.** To bind (books) after an antique manner.

1753 CHAMBERS *Cycl. Supp.*, *Antiquing*, in book-binding, a method of ornamenting the edges of books with divers foliages and ramifications, by means of hot iron tools cut for the purpose.

2. *trans.* To give an antique appearance to (furniture, etc.) by artificial means. Hence **an'tiquing** *vbl. sb.*, **an'tiqued** *ppl. a.*

1923 *Daily Mail* 1 Mar. 8 Having completed the article, he proceeds to do the 'antiquing'. **1934** E. BOWEN *Cat Jumps* 212 The flat sprang into sight: 'art' distemper, six of the World's Best Pictures, the dark sharp angles of antiqued oak. **1959** F. ASTAIRE *Steps in Time* i. 3 Mr. Shipp claims I am aging him the way you antique furniture, at the rate of several years per week.

an'tiquely, *adv. rare.* [f. ANTIQUE *a.* + -LY^2.]

†**1.** Anciently, of old time. *Obs.*

1652 GAULE *Magastrom.* 72 Antiquely founded and grounded upon the idolatrous oracles of the pagans.

2. In an antique manner.

1675 OGILBY *Brit.* 76 In the Church-Yard an old Pyramidel Monument antiquely Graven.

an'tiqueness. [f. ANTIQUE *a.* + -NESS.] The quality of being antique; antiquity of style.

1655 FULLER *Ch. Hist.* II. 144 The modern Antiquenesse of his Apparell. *a* **1719** ADDISON (J.) We may discover something venerable in the antiqueness of the work. **1850** LEITCH *Müller's Anc. Art* §96 A female figure..in which grace is remarkably combined with antiqueness.

antiquish (æn'tiːkɪʃ), *a. rare.* [f. ANTIQUE *a.* + -ISH.] Somewhat antique or antiquated.

1838 FOSTER *Life & Corr.* (1846) II. 328 Language, a little of the antiquish.

antiquist ('æntɪkwɪst, æn'tiːkɪst). *rare.* [f. ANTIQUE + -IST.] †**a.** An antiquary (*obs.*). **b.** A collector or connoisseur of antiques.

1784 PINKERTON *Medals* II. §19 (R.) Such poor antiquists as Scotland..has produced. **1856** SMYTH *Rom. Fam. Coins* Introd. 28 These 'finds' have made many antiquists.

antiquitarian (æn,tɪkwɪ'tɛərɪən). [f. ANTIQUITY + -ARIAN; cf. *humanitarian*.] One attached to the practices or opinions of antiquity.

1641 MILTON *Reform.* 4, I shall distinguish..the hinderers of Reformation into 3 sorts, 1. Antiquitarians (for so I had rather call them then Antiquaries, whose labours are usefull and laudable). **1849** SARA COLERIDGE *Mem. & Lett.* II. 260 The Antiquitarian must shew the reasonableness of his creed, if he seeks to defend it.

† **an'tiquitated**, *ppl. a. Obs. rare.* [f. L. *antīquitāt-* + -ED; cf. *capacitated.*] ANTIQUATED.
1645 PAGITT *Heresiogr.* (ed. 4) 130 Pernicious and antiquitated heresies. **1652** *Persuasive* 7 Can you think he would have pretended antiquitated Oathes?

antiquity (æn'tɪkwɪtɪ). Forms: 4 antiquytee, 4–6 -iquite, 5 -yqwyte, 5–6 -yquyte, -yquytye, -iquitye, 6–7 -itie, 6– -ity. [a. Fr. *antiquité*, 11th c. *antiquitet*, ad. L. *antīquitāt-em*, n. of quality f. *antīqu-us*: see ANTIQUE and -ITY.]

I. As abstract sb.

1. The quality of being old (in the world's history) or ancient; long standing, oldness, ancientness.
c **1450** *Court of Love* lxxii, This statute was of old antiquite. **1532** MORE *Confut. Tindale* Wks. 1557, 707/1 Then be you Jewes of more antiquitie then they. **1687** T. BROWN *Saints in Upr.* Wks. I. 73 A rusty spear, and a cloak of antiquity. **1752** JOHNSON *Rambl.* No. 192 ⁋2 Every Man boasted the antiquity of his family. **1851** D. WILSON *Preh. Ann.* II. III. vi. 153 The geological antiquity of man.

†**2.** Old age (of human life); seniority. *Obs.*
1596 SHAKS. *2 Hen. IV*, I. ii. 208 Is not your voice broken? ..and euery part about you blasted with Antiquity. **1618** BOLTON *Florus* I. i. 7 Who for their authoritie should be called Fathers, and for their antiquitie, Senators, or Aldermen. **1677** *Act* in Marvell *Growth Popery* 30 Three.. to be placed in such Order as the said Prelates..think fit, without regard to dignity, antiquity, or any other form.

3. Ancient character or style.
1850 LYNCH *Theoph. Trin.* ix. 164 There is much novelty without hope, much antiquity without sacredness. **1867** MAX MÜLLER *Chips* (1880) III. xiii. 248 The air of antiquity which pervades that county [Cornwall].

II. Elliptical senses.

4. The time of antiquity, olden time. **a.** generally.
c **1380** *Sir Ferumb.* 1316 An old for-sake ȝeate! of þe olde antiquytee. **1580** BARET *Alv.* A 421 Historie is the reporter of antiquitie, or of things done in olde tyme. **1605** BACON *Adv. Learn.* II. ii. §7 Antiquity is like fame, *caput inter nubila condit*, her head is muffled from our sight. **1664** H. MORE *Myst. Iniq.* 473 The errours and Mistakes of dark Antiquity. **1712** *Spect.* No. 548 ⁋4, I cannot think of one real hero in all antiquity so far raised above human infirmities. *c* **1854** STANLEY *Sinai & Pal.* ii. (1858) 119 To what an antiquity does this carry us back! Ruins before the days of those who preceded the Philistines!

b. *spec.* The period before the middle ages, the time of the ancient Greeks and Romans.
c **1450** *Songs & Poems Costume* 53 Famous poetis of antyquyté, In Grece and Troye. **1594** T. B. *La Primaud. Fr. Acad.* II. 535 The writings of al antiquity. *a* **1704** T. BROWN *Comic. View* Wks. I. 157 Galen and other reverend blockheads of antiquity. **1874** BLACKIE *Self-Cult* 73 The coolest and most practical thinker of all antiquity.. Aristotle.

c. The early ages of the Christian era; the early centuries of the Church; more explicitly ***Christian antiquity***.
1564 HARDING *Answ. Jewel* 173 To see antiquitie for proufe hereof..Let him reade [etc.]. **1574** BRISTOW *Brief Treat. Diuerse Plain Waies* (1599) 54 All Antiquity is full of such practise. **1753** CHALLONER *Cath. Chr. Instr.* 77 This Custom..is as ancient as Christianity, as appears from the most certain Monuments of Antiquity. **1850** NEWMAN *Difficulties of Anglicans* ii. 34 He would..have given up the Establishment, rather than have rejected antiquity. **1860** A. P. DE LISLE in E. Purcell *Life* (1900) I. x. 185 Christian Antiquity.

5. The people (or writers, etc.) of ancient times collectively; 'the Ancients.'
1538 STARKEY *England* iii. 78 Aftur the opynyon of the wyse and auncyent antyquyte. **1598** BARRET *Theor. Warres* v. iii. 152 This manner of marching..we reade antiquitie to have vsed. **1641** MILTON *Prel. Episc.* (1851) 73 That indigested heap, and frie of Authors, which they call Antiquity. **1726** DE FOE *Hist. Devil* II. vi. (1840) 246 We have Antiquity on our side, we have this truth confirmed by the testimony of many ages. **1876** MOZLEY *Univ. Serm.* i. 3 We think we have excelled all antiquity. We have excelled a later antiquity, but not the earliest and first.

6. (Now *pl.* or *collect.*, formerly often *sing.*) Matters, customs, precedents, or events of earlier times; ancient records.
1557 NORTH *Diall of Princes* A ij b, Paulus Diaconus.. sheweth an antiquitie right worthy to remember. **1629** COKE *On Litt.* 69 a, Which Antiquity I cite for that it concurreth with the act of Parliament. **1660** BLOOME *Archit.* Title-page, Gathered with great diligence..out of Antiquities. **1782** PRIESTLEY *Corrupt. Chr.* I. I. 107 Whiston..was certainly well read in Christian antiquity. **1876** DIGBY *Real Prop.* ii. §8. 94 The subject belongs entirely to the antiquities of our law.

7. (Now usually *pl.*; formerly *sing.* or *collect.*) Remains or monuments of antiquity; ancient relics.
1513 MORE *Hist. Edw. V*, Ded. 1 The great care..that hath alwaies been observed..for the preservation of antiquities. **1605** BACON *Adv. Learn.* II. ii. §1 Antiquities are history defaced, or some remnants of history which have casually escaped the shipwreck of time. **1622** PEACHAM *Compl. Gentl.* xii. (1634) 112, I come to the last of our select Antiquities, Coynes. **1676** D'URFEY *Mad. Fickle* III. i, Rust adds to an Antiquity, 'tis our Friend. **1728** STUKELEY in *Phil. Trans.* XXXV. 430 At Paunton..I have heard of much Antiquity being found. **1787** T. JEFFERSON *Writ.* (1859) II. 133 The Pont du Gard, a sublime antiquity, and well preserved. **1869** RAWLINSON *Anc. Hist.* 2 Antiquities, or the actual extant remains of ancient times.

8. *Comb.* or *Attrib.*, as ***antiquity-hunting***, ***piece***.
1860 *Vac. Tour.* 119 The bishop of Ossory, who was antiquity-hunting in Sutherland. **1711** *London Gaz.* mmmmdccclv/4 A small Gold Ring, with an Antiquity Piece hanging to it.

anti-rabic (æntɪ'ræbɪk), *a.* [irreg. f. ANTI-[1] 3 b + RABIES + -IC.] Having the property of counteracting the virus of rabies; curing, or relating to the cure of, rabies. Also **anti-rabietic** (reɪbɪ'ɛtɪk) *a.*, **anti-rabific** (reɪ'bɪfɪk), *a.*; **anti-rabies** used *attrib.*
1887 *Science* IX. 186 The Russian antirabic inoculation institution [in Odessa]. **1888** *Nature* 22 Nov. 73/2 The anti-rabietic treatment of M. Pasteur. **1894** *Ibid.* 8 Mar. 437/2 The establishment in the chief town of each province of an antirabific laboratory. **1919** *Times Weekly* 25 Apr. 404 The treatment of patients with specific anti-rabic material. **1938** *Brit. Jrnl. Exp. Path.* XIX. 378 The successful cultivation of rabies virus in tissue cultures..has raised the possibility of simplifying antirabic immunization by the use of such cultures. **1961** *Times* 23 Dec. 9/2 He was the first human being to receive anti-rabies inoculation.

antirachitic (ˌæntɪrə'kɪtɪk), *a. Med.* [f. ANTI- 3 + Gr. ῥαχῖτ-ις spinal complaint, f. ῥάχις backbone.] Tending to cure spinal disease.
1853 in MAYNE *Exp. Lex.*

ˌanti-'resonance. [ANTI-[1] 2 a + RESONANCE.] The opposite of resonance in various senses (see quots.).
1923 *Bell System Techn. Jrnl.* II. 12 Series resonance and shunt anti-resonance coincide if both are included in an internal transmitting band. **1936** *Gloss. Acoustical Terms (B.S.I.)* 7 *Anti-resonance*, a condition resulting from a combination of the mass and stiffness reactances of a system in which a response to a sinusoidal stimulus of constant magnitude reaches a minimum at a particular frequency. **1948** M. JOOS *Acoustic Phonetics* 96 *Anti-resonance*, suppression of a narrow band of frequencies.

antireticular (ˌæntɪrɪ'tɪkjʊlə(r)), *a. Med.* [ANTI-[1] 3 b.] Acting against the reticulum cells of the reticulo-endothelial system; *spec.* in ***antireticular cytotoxic serum*** (abbrev. A.C.S.), a cytotoxic serum prepared from animal and human spleen and bone marrow, claimed to have a beneficial effect on the reticulo-endothelial system.
1942 tr. B. E. Linberg in A. A. Bogomolets *Therapeutic Action of the Antireticular Cytotoxic Serum 'ACS'* 154 Everywhere where a weakening of the physiological system of the connective tissue takes place it can be activized by means of ACS. **1943** *Brit. Med. Jrnl.* 14 Aug. 203/1 The favourable effect of antireticular cytotoxic serum on the course of infectious diseases of the nervous system.

antirrhinum (æntɪ'raɪnəm). *Pl.* **-s**. [a. L., a. Gr. ἀντίρρῑνον (also ἀνάρρῑνον), f. ἀντί opposite, counterfeiting + ῥιν-, (ῥίς) nose; from its resemblance to an animal's mouth.] A genus of Scrophulariaceous plants, also called Snapdragon.
1551 TURNER *Herbal* (1568) 36 Antirrhinum is an herbe like vnto pympernel. **1727** BRADLEY *Fam. Dict.* s.v. *Flower*, Sow Antirrhinum, or you may set it. **1741** *Compl. Fam.-Piece* II. iii. 386 Antirrhinum or Calves-snout. **1879** LUBBOCK *Sci. Lect.* i. 20 The Antirrhinum is especially adapted for fertilisation by humble-bees.

† **'anti-rumour**, *v. Obs.* [f. *anti-rumour* sb. See ANTI- 2.] To raise a contrary rumour.
1655 FULLER *Ch. Hist.* III. 105 The Queens party gave out that the King of France had sent over a vast Army for her assistance, and the Kings side Anti-rumoured..that the Pope had excommunicated all such who sides against him.

antisabbatarian (ˌæntɪsæbə'tɛərɪən), *a.* and *sb.* [ANTI- 3, 5.] **A.** *adj.* Opposed to the observance of the Sabbath by Christians. **B.** *sb.* One so opposed.
1645 PAGITT *Heresiogr.* (ed. 6) 159 These anti-sabbatarians hold the sabbath day, or that which we call the Lord's day, to be no more a Sabbath. **1656** TRAPP *Exp. John* ix. 16 (1868) 375/2 That late great Anti-sabbatarian prelate.

antiscian (æn'tɪʃɪən), *a.* and *sb.* [f. next + -AN.] **A.** *adj.* Of or pertaining to the Antiscii. **B.** *sb.* in pl. = ANTISCII.
1842 BRANDE *Dict. Sc., Antiscii, Antiscians.* **1864** WEBSTER *Dict.* s.v., Those who live north of the equator are *antiscians* to those on the south, and *vice versâ.*

‖ **antiscii** (æn'tɪsɪaɪ, -'ɪʃɪaɪ), *sb. pl.* [L. (in Amm. Marc.), a. late Gr. *ἀντίσκιοι, f. ἀντί opposite + σκιά shadow.] Those who live on the same meridian, but on the opposite side of the equator, so that their shadows at noon fall in opposite directions.
1706 in PHILLIPS; in CHAMBERS, JOHNSON, and mod. Dicts.

antiscion (æn'tɪʃɪən). *Astrol.* [f. as prec.] Applied to signs of the Zodiac at equal distances on opposite sides from Cancer and Capricorn.
1658 in PHILLIPS. **1706** *ibid.*, *Antiscion-Signs* are those which, with reference to each other, are equally distant from the two Tropical Signs Cancer and Capricorn, so that a Planet in such a Station is said to cast its *Antiscion*, i.e. to give Virtue or Influence to another Star or Planet, that is in the opposite Sign. **1819** J. WILSON *Dict. Astrol.* 304 To find the antiscions of any star, recourse must be had to tables of declination.

antiscolic (æntɪ'skɒlɪk), *a. Med.* [irreg. f. ANTI- 3 + Gr. σκώληξ worm + -IC.] Tending to prevent or expel worms, anthelmintic.
1880 in *Syd. Soc. Lex.*

antiscorbutic (ˌæntɪskɔː'bjuːtɪk), *a.* and *sb. Med.* [f. ANTI- 3 + SCORBUTIC, f. mod.L. *scorbūtus* scurvy.] **A.** *adj.* Of use against scurvy.
1725 BRADLEY *Fam. Dict.* s.v. *Scurvy*, Broths..into which you are to put antiscorbutick herbs. **1799** ROBERTSON *Agric. Perth.* 28 Pitcaithly is famous for its antiscorbutic waters. **1830** LINDLEY *Nat. Syst. Bot.* 17 The universal character of *Cruciferæ* is to possess antiscorbutic and stimulant qualities.

B. *sb.* (sc. agent.)
1696 PHILLIPS, *Antiscorbuticks*, medicines against the Scurvey. **1876** BARTHOLOW *Mat. Med.* (1879) 178 Lime-juice is the most important anti-scorbutic.

† **antiscor'butical**, *a. Med. Obs.* = prec.
1731 ARBUTHNOT *Ailments* (L.) Anti-scorbutical plants.

† **'antiscript.** *Obs. rare*[−1]. [f. ANTI- A + L. *script-um* written.] A writing opposite, or against.
a **1670** HACKET *Abp. Williams* I. 199 His Highness Read the Charges and admir'd at the Virulency; with the Antiscripts of the Keeper, which were much commended.

antiscriptural (æntɪ'skrɪptjʊərəl), *a.* [ANTI- 3.] Opposed to Holy Scripture.
1677 MARVELL *Growth Popery* 5 A new and Anti-scriptural Belief. **1856** R. VAUGHAN *Mystics* (1860) I. 72 Scriptural in phrase, and anti-scriptural in sense.

† **ˌantiscrip'turian**, *sb.* and *a. Obs.* [ANTI- 3, 5.] **A.** *adj.* Denying the authority of the Scriptures. **B.** *sb.* = ANTISCRIPTURIST.
1613 JACKSON *Creed* II. xxx. Wks. II. 107 Our anti-scripturian adversaries' importunity. **1645** PAGITT *Heresiogr.* (1661) 232 Antiscripturians. Among others, one wicked Sect denyeth the Scriptures both to the old and new Testament.

† **anti'scripturism.** *Obs.* [ANTI- 7.] The doctrine or practice of antiscripturists.
1661 BOYLE *Style H. Script.* 147 Now that Antiscripturism grows so rife.

† **anti'scripturist.** *Obs.* [ANTI- 5.] One who denies the truth and authority of Scripture.
1647 TORSHELL *Harmon. Bible* in *Phœnix* (1721) I. 96 The Majesty of it [the Bible] will triumph over the Attempts of all Anti-Scripturists. **1731** BLACKWALL *Sacr. Class.* II. 357 (T.) To confute the cavils of fanatical anti-scripturists.

antiscrofulous (æntɪ'skrɒfjʊləs), *a. Med.* [ANTI- 3.] Tending to prevent or cure scrofula.
1880 in *Syd. Soc. Lex.*

'anti-self. [ANTI-[1] 1 b + SELF C. 3.] (See quots.)
1917 W. B. YEATS *Wild Swans at Coole* 25 And look most like me, being indeed my double, And prove..The most unlike, being my anti-self. **1922** —— *Trembl. Veil* I. xviii. 58, I know very little about myself and much less of that anti-self. **1931** E. WILSON *Axel's Castle* ii. 45 The other self, the anti-self or the antithetical self. **1946** *Essays & Stud.* XXXI. 38 The Mask, the anti-self, the concrete image which is the opposite of the conscious normal Self. **1949** WELLEK & WARREN *Theory of Lit.* vii. 72 A work of art..may be the 'mask', the 'anti-self' behind which his real person is hiding.

anti-Semitism (æntɪ'sɛmɪtɪz(ə)m). [f. ANTI-[1] 7 + SEMITISM.] Theory, action, or practice directed against the Jews. Hence **anti-'Semite**, one who is hostile or opposed to the Jews; **anti-Se'mitic** *a.*
1881 *Athenæum* 3 Sept. 305/2 The author, apparently an anti-Semite. *Ibid.*, Anti-Semitic literature is very prosperous in Germany. **1882** *Athenæum* 11 Feb. 184/1 In these days of anti-Semitism. **1935** *Economist* 24 Aug. 366/1 The Nazi Party stalwarts..have all been leading an anti-Semitic, anti-Catholic, anti-Protestant..crusade. **1941** J. S. HUXLEY *Uniqueness of Man* ii. 50 Germanic nationalism on the one hand and anti-Semitism on the other.

antisepalous (æntɪ'sɛpələs), *a. Bot.* [f. Gr. ἀντί opposite + SEPAL + -OUS.] Placed opposite to the sepals or divisions of the calyx.
1878 MASTERS *Henfrey's Bot.* 228 A series of antisepalous scales which restore the symmetry. **1880** GRAY *Bot. Text-bk.* 178 *Antisepalous*, those stamens which stand before sepals.

antisepsis (æntɪ'sɛpsɪs). *Med.* [mod.L., f. Gr. ἀντί against + σῆψις putrefaction.] The principle of antiseptic treatment. Now the current word, superseding ANTISEPTICISM.
1875 H. WOOD *Therap.* (1879) 532 The discoveries concerning antisepsis.

antiseptic (æntɪ'sɛptɪk), *a.* and *sb.* [f. ANTI- 3 + Gr. σηπτικ-ός putrefying, f. σηπτός rotten, f. σήπ-ειν to rot.] **A.** *adj.*

1. Counteracting putrefaction; antiputrescent.
1751 *Gentl. Mag.* 557 Myrrh in a watery menstruum was 12 times more antiseptic than sea salt. **1774** PRIESTLEY *Observ. Air* 228 This remarkable antiseptic power of nitrous air. **1871** TYNDALL *Fragm. Sc.* (ed. 6) I. v. 155 He surrounds the wound..with antiseptic bandages.

2. *fig.* Preventing moral decay.
1820 SOUTHEY *Wesley* I. 204 In some such abominations Moravianism might have ended..where there was no antiseptic influence of surrounding circumstances to preserve it from putrescence. **1850** CARLYLE *Latter-d.*

Pamph. viii. (1872) 261 Not divine men, yet useful antiseptic products of their generation.

B. *sb.* **1.** (sc. agent.)

1751 *Gentl. Mag.* Dec. 557 Acids *per se* are most powerful antiseptics. **1871** NAPHEYS *Prev. & Cure Dis.* II. iv. 521 The charcoal poultice is an excellent antiseptic.

2. *fig.*

1825 BENTHAM *Ration. Reward* 175 A salary proportionate to the wants of the functionary operates as a kind of moral *antiseptic*, or preservative. **1849** H. ROGERS *Ess.* II. vi. 299 Johnson..speaks of an author's choosing a theme of enduring interest, if he would be remembered..Alas! we fear this is but an insufficient antiseptic.

anti'septically, *adv.* [f. prec. + -LY².] In an antiseptic manner, by means of antiseptics.

1881 *Standard* 20 May 3/3 The transplantation [of bone] must be conducted antiseptically. **1882** LD. WOLSELEY *ibid.* 15 Sept. 5/5 All treated antiseptically; the antiseptics sent will suffice.

anti'septicism (-sɪz(ə)m). Now *rare.* [f. ANTISEPTIC + -ISM.] The process or principles of the prevention or treatment of sepsis by antiseptic means. So **anti'septize** *v. trans.*, to treat antiseptically; to disinfect by means of an antiseptic.

1877 R. BARWELL in *Brit. Med. Jrnl.* 28 Apr. 506/1, I shall gather together the results of a number of major operations, and show you what effect antisepticism has had upon my practice. **1888** M. MACKENZIE *Illness Fredk. the Noble* 109 The Professor of Surgery, in the matter of antisepticism, attended to the letter rather than to the spirit. **1910** *Contemp. Rev.* Mar. 402 The bottle and its contents must be antiseptized at a heat of 123 degs. centigrade.

antisepticist (æntɪ'sɛptɪsɪst). [f. ANTISEPTIC + -IST.] A believer in antiseptic surgical treatment.

1881 L. TAIT in *Times* 25 Apr. 5/6 If germs could have had the unbounded influence..claimed for them by many antisepticists.

anti-serum, antiserum ('æntɪˌsɪərəm). *Biochem.* Pl. **-sera.** [ANTI-¹ 6 d.] **a.** A contraction of *antitoxic serum* (see ANTITOXIC *a.*); **b.** A serum containing a high level of antibodies, esp. one that can be used in the treatment of disease.

1901 NUTTALL in *Daily Chron.* 28 Dec. 3/7 No other bloods excepting those of monkeys give a reaction to the anti-serum for human blood. **1910** *Encycl. Brit.* III. 176/2 So far as bacterial immunity is concerned, the anti-serum exerts its action either on the toxin or on the bacterium itself; that is, its action is either antitoxic or anti-bacterial. **1948** *Endeavour* VII. 49 The assumption that most antibody molecules have two regions able to combine with antigen.. accounts for some of the properties of antisera. **1966** *New Scientist* 2 June 587/2 Blood serum obtained from the treated animal is known as the antiserum and the antibodies in it will combine specifically with the virus.

anti'siccative, *a.* [ANTI- 3.] Opposed to the tendency to dry.

1869 *Eng. Mech.* 19 Mar. 575/1 White lead itself, a siccative body, is anti-siccative with respect to linseed on metallic lead.

antisocial (æntɪ'səʊʃəl), *a.* and *sb.* [ANTI- 3.]

1. Opposed to sociality, averse to society or companionship.

1797 J. LAWRENCE in *Month. Mag.* XLVI. 113 Fanatical prejudices, antisocial antipathies and hatred.

2. Opposed to the principles on which society is constituted. Also, *spec.* in *Sociol.*, pertaining to a class of persons or actions devoid of or antagonistic to normal social instincts or practices.

1802 JAMES MACKINTOSH in *Memoirs* (1835) I. iv. 176 A collection of all the rebellious, antisocial, blasphemous.. books..published during..the Revolution. **1844** *Dublin Rev.* Mar. 34 The dark, malignant, atrocious, and utterly anti-social character, which the Republican party in its contest with the new government has exhibited. **1849** GROTE *Greece* II. lxvii. VI. 84 Doctrines openly and avowedly anti-social. **1862** MERIVALE *Rom. Emp.* (1865) VIII. lxv. 149 The earliest charge against the believers was that of perverse and antisocial usages. **1889** S. OLIVIER in G. B. Shaw *Fabian Ess. Socialism* 109 Some kinds of anti-social action are so unreasonable..that we brand them..as insane. **1896** GIDDINGS *Princ. Sociol.* iv. 72 The anti-social or criminal[class], in which the consciousness of kind is approaching extinction. **1904** *Westm. Gaz.* 7 Dec. 2/3 To insist on not paying when asked by the conductor is at once inconvenient and anti-social.

Hence as *sb.*, one who exhibits such tendencies.

1945 C. BURNEY *Dungeon Democracy* I. 14 The 'anti-socials'—that is..those who had been locked up for anti-social activity.

antisocialism (æntɪ'səʊʃəlɪz(ə)m). [f. ANTISOCIAL *a.* + -ISM.] **1.** = ANTISOCIALITY.

1867 *Catholic World* Apr. 1/1 A rampant, and apparently victorious, socialism, or more properly, anti-socialism, threatened the destruction of society itself. **1897** J. B. BURY *Gibbon's Decl. & F.* II. App. 543 [It] was converted into a charge of *odium generis humani* (a brief summary of the anti-socialism and other characteristics of Christianity).

2. Antagonism to socialism.

1905 *Daily Chron.* 26 June 5/3 Mr. Deakin declined on behalf of the Liberal Protectionists to accept Anti-Socialism as the issue at the next General Election.

anti'socialist. [f. ANTISOCIAL *a.* + -IST.]

1. One opposed to sociality. *rare.*

1775 T. SHERIDAN *Reading* 343 May justly be termed Antisocialists and..the worst company in the world.

2. One who is antagonistic to socialism. Also *attrib.* or as *adj.*

1862 J. S. MILL *Pol. Econ.* (ed. 5) II. IV. vii. 357 The vitality of these associations..enabled about twenty of them to survive..the antisocialist reaction. **1914** J. COLLINGS *Coloniz. Rur. Brit.* I. xv. 257 The well-to-do generally are alarmed, and are forming Property Defence Associations, Anti-Socialist Leagues, [etc.].

antisociality (ˌæntɪsəʊʃɪ'ælɪtɪ). [f. ANTISOCIAL *a.* + -ITY.] The quality or condition of being antisocial: **a.** aversion to social intercourse; **b.** antagonism to the laws of ordered society.

1818 T. L. PEACOCK *Nightmare Abbey* vii. 100 That amiable discontent and antisociality, which you reprobate in our present parlour-window literature. **1902** *Amer. Jrnl. Psychol.* Oct. 586 The anti-sociality of so many defectives is due to the arrest which so often takes place at the end of childhood. **1959** B. WOOTTON et al. *Soc. Sci. & Path.* x. 303 Investigators have made attempts..to restrict their category of 'delinquent' at least to those whose anti-sociality is both persistent and pronounced.

anti'socially, *adv.* [f. ANTISOCIAL *a.* + -LY².] In an antisocial manner.

1908 H. G. WELLS *First & Last Things* III. §29. 215 Sexual relations..tend to..set up a peculiar emotional partnership. It is a partnership that kept secret may work as anti-socially as a secret business partnership. **1943** J. L. BRIERLY *English Law* 39 If individual rights are in danger of being used anti-socially, it is for Parliament to re-define them in terms which will prevent their abusive use.

†**ˌantiso'cordist.** *Obs. rare*⁻¹. [f. ANTI- 5 + L. *socordia* sloth + -IST.] An opponent of sloth or stupidity.

a **1680** BUTLER *Rem.* (1759) II. 188 [The Virtuoso] calls himself an Antisocordist, a Name unknown to former Ages, but spawned by the Pedantry of the present.

anti-spadix (æntɪ'speɪdɪks). *Zool.* [ANTI-¹ 2.] A group of four tentacles situated opposite to the spadix in the male nautilus.

1883 E. R. LANKESTER in *Encycl. Brit.* XVI. 674/2 These four tentacles may be called the 'anti-spadix'. **1888** ROLLESTON & JACKSON *Anim. Life* 457. **1960** I. F. & W. D. HENDERSON *Dict. Sci. Terms* (ed. 7) 34/2.

antispasmodic ('æntɪspæz'mɒdɪk), *a.* and *sb.* *Med.* [ANTI- 3.] **A.** *adj.* Good against spasms. **B.** *sb.* A medicine so used.

1681 tr. *Willis' Rem. Med. Wks.*, *Antispasmodicks*, medicines against convulsions. **1763** WATSON *Tetanus* in *Phil. Trans.* LIII. 14 Antispasmodic remedies of various kinds. **1775** SCOTT in *Phil. Trans.* LXVI. 172 Laudanum, the most effectual and universal anti-spasmodic. **1842** RAMADGE *Cur. Consump.* (1861) 24 A soothing and antispasmodic power. **1868** A. B. GARROD *Mat. Med.* 393 The direct antispasmodics appear to give tone to the spinal cord and other parts of the nervous system. **1955** *Sci. News Let.* 2 Apr. 212 The Jamestown weed..whose alkaloids have been used in the manufacture of such sedatives and antispasmodics as atropine, hyoscyamine and scopolamine.

antispast ('æntɪspæst). *Pros.* [ad. Gr. ἀντίσπαστ-ος, f. ἀντισπά-ειν to draw in the contrary direction.] A metrical foot composed of an iambus and a trochee, as Ἀλέξανδρος.

1706 PHILLIPS, *Antispastus.* **1821** *Edin. Rev.* XXXV. 302 The lords of Antispast and friends to Double-dochmee.

antispastic (æntɪ'spæstɪk), *a.* and *sb.* [ad. Gr. ἀντισπαστικ-ός able to draw away: see prec. and -IC.] **A.** *adj.*

1. *Med.* Tending to divert or counteract.

1541 R. COPLAND *Guydon's Quest. Cyrurg.*, Blode lettynge ..is somtyme antyspatyc, that is to say dyuersyue..as the flux of blode at the nose of the ryght nosethrylle, is restraynte by the bledynge of the ryght arme. **1853** MAYNE *Exp. Lex.*, *Antispastic.*

2. *Pros.* Consisting of, or containing, antispasts.

1811 *Edin. Rev.* XVIII. 156 The first metre discussed is the Antispastic. **1860** J. W. DONALDSON *Lat. Gr.* (1867) §264 Antispastic rhythm..is not used by Latin poets.

B. *sb.* *Med.* An antispastic agent.

1719 *Glossogr. Nova*, *Antispasticks*, medicines that divert Distempers to other Parts.

antisplenetic (ˌæntɪsplɪ'nɛtɪk), *a.* and *sb.* [ANTI- 3.] **A.** *adj.* Good against disease of the spleen. **B.** *sb.* A medicine so used.

a **1734** FLOYER (J.) Antispleneticks open the obstructions of the spleen. **1847** in CRAIG.

anti-static (æntɪ'stætɪk), *a.* [ANTI-¹ 4.]

1. *Radio.* Designed to minimize 'static' (= ATMOSPHERICS).

1938 *Archit. Rev.* LXXXIII. 284 Antistatic aerials are provided for all flats for broadcast reception and separate aerials and wiring for television.

2. In various other specific applications: counteracting the effect of static electricity.

1952 *Jrnl. Textile Inst.* XLIII. P 212 The resistance of nylon can be reduced by as much as 10,000 times by treatment with a suitable anti-static agent. **1954** *Ibid.* XLV. P 253 The principle of the anti-static lubricant is that it shall provide a conducting coat on each filament. **1956** W. J. ROFF *Fibres, Plastics & Rubbers* III. 312 Surface resistivity is.. reduced by the presence of mould growth, and by application of 'anti-static' dressings. **1958** *Oxf. Mail* 19 Nov. (Suppl.) 14/4 A solution of anti-static fluid is used to moisten the pad, which then collects the dust and removes the static.

†**anti'stœchal,** *a.* *Obs. rare*⁻¹. [f. Gr. ἀντίστοιχ-ος in opposite rows (f. στοῖχ-ος row) + -AL¹.] Arranged in opposite ranks, arrayed against.

1680 H. MORE *Apocal. Apoc.* 267 If God had no more Servants but these only, then would they be Antistœchal to the Beast throughout.

antistrophal (æn'tɪstrəfəl), *a.* *rare.* [f. next + -AL¹.] Of or pertaining to antistrophe.

1878 T. SINCLAIR *Mount* 79 The passionate political music of strophal and antistrophal variety.

‖**antistrophe** (æn'tɪstrəfiː). [L., a. Gr. ἀντιστροφή a turning about, f. ἀντιστρέφ-ειν to turn against, f. ἀντί against + στρέφ-ειν to turn.]

1. The returning movement, from left to right, in Greek choruses and dances, answering to the previous movement of the strophe from right to left; *hence*, the lines of choral song recited during this movement; *and generally*, any choral response.

a **1619** FOTHERBY *Atheom.* II. xii. §5. 345 As euery Psalme beginneth with an *Allelu-iah*..by *Stropha*: so doth it likewise end, with an *Allelu-iah*..by *Antistropha.* **1671** MILTON *Samson* Pref., Strophe, Antistrophe, Epode..were a kind of stanzas framed only for the music then used with the chorus that sung. **1807** ROBINSON *Archæol. Græca* III. iv. 217 The sacred hymns, consisting of three stanzas..the first of which, called strophe, was sung in turning from east to west; the second, called antistrophe, in returning from west to east.

2. An inverse relation or correspondence.

1605 BACON *Adv. Learn.* II. ix. §3 The latter branch..hath the same relation or antistrophe that the former hath. **1611** COTGR., *Antistrophe*, An Antistrophe; or alternall conversion of two things, which bee somewhat alike. **1842** DE QUINCEY in *Blackw. Mag.* LI. 12 An inverse correspondency with the Nile (north and south, therefore, as the antistrophe to south and north).

3. *Rhet.* and *Gram.* **a.** The repetition of words in inverse order. **b.** The figure of retort, or turning an opponent's plea against him.

1625 tr. *Camden's Hist. Eliz.* I. (1688) 99 The renewing of the Contract is a flat Antistrophe, and may truly be retorted upon the French. **1727–51** CHAMBERS *Cycl.*, *Antistrophe* is a figure in grammar, whereby two terms or things, mutually dependent one on another, are reciprocally converted. As if one should say, the master of the servant, and the servant of the master.

4. *Cryst.* (See quot., and cf. METASTROPHE 2.)

1895 N. STORY-MASKELYNE *Crystallogr.* v. §80. 99 A solid figure..is [symmetrical] to a plane of symmetry when corresponding points equidistant from the plane would lie on any line drawn perpendicularly to the plane. Where the solid figure presents symmetry to only a single plane (and not to a centre also) the corresponding portions of its surface ..are to each other as either would be to its own image if seen reflected by the plane of symmetry as by a mirror. *Def.* —Such a correspondence of form will be termed antistrophe, and such figures will be said to be antistrophic to each other. **1899** W. J. LEWIS *Crystallogr.* 21.

antistrophic (æntɪ'strɒfɪk), *a.* and *sb.* [ad. Gr. ἀντιστροφικ-ός, f. ἀντιστροφή: see prec.]

A. *adj.* Of or pertaining to antistrophes.

1859 in WORCESTER. **1881** STANLEY *Chr. Inst.* iii. 65 An antistrophic hymn to Christ. **1882** M. DODDS *Genesis* 108 The answer is given in poetical form, in two couplets or antistrophic parallelisms.

B. *sb. pl.* **antistrophics** [Gr. ἀντιστροφικά]: the lyrical part of Greek dramas.

1811 *Edin. Rev.* XVIII. 176 Dr. Burney's disposition of the following..Antistrophics.

anti'strophically, *adv.* *rare.* [f. prec. + -AL¹ + -LY².] By antistrophe; in inverse order.

1842 DE QUINCEY in *Blackw. Mag.* LI. 12 The Danube.. is described as..corresponding rigorously, but antistrophically (as the Greeks express it), similar angles, similar dimensions, but in an inverse order, to the Egyptian Nile.

antistrophize (æn'tɪstrəfaɪz), *v.* *rare.* [f. ANTISTROPHE + -IZE.] To form an antistrophe.

1842 DE QUINCEY in *Blackw. Mag.* LI. 12 The particular instance of the Danube, as antistrophising with the Nile.

‖**antistrophon** (æn'tɪstrəfɒn). *Rhet.* [neut. sing. of Gr. ἀντίστροφ-ος turned in an opposite way, f. ἀντι-στρέφειν to turn to the opposite side.] An argument that is retorted upon an opponent.

1611 SPEED *Hist. Gt. Brit.* IX. xxiv. 55 But for the point wherein you touch vs..it is Antistrophon, and turneth a great deale better vpon you. **1642** MILTON *Apol. Smect.* Wks. 1851, 267, I turne his Antistrophon upon his owne head. **1818** in TODD; and in mod. Dicts.

antistru'matic, *a.* and *sb.* *Med.* [see next.] **A.** *adj.* = next. **B.** *sb.* A remedy for scrofula.

1676 WISEMAN (J.), I prescribed him a distilled milk with anti-strumaticks, and purged him.

antistrumous (æntɪ'struːməs), *a.* *Med.* [f. ANTI- 3 + L. *strūma* scrofula, + -OUS.] Tending to cure scrofula.

1861 BUMSTEAD *Ven. Dis.* (1879) 387 Scrofula..calls for preparations of iodine and other antistrumous remedies.

anti-sun ('æntɪsʌn). [ANTI-¹.] The point in the sky diametrically opposite the sun; *esp.* a point opposite the sun in azimuth, of the same altitude as the sun.

1902 *Encycl. Brit.* XXX. 705/2 Babinet located a neutral point or zone about as far from the anti-sun as was Arago's from the sun itself.

ˌantisy'mmetrical, *a.* *Math.* Also ˌantisy'mmetric. [ANTI-[1] 3 c.] The reverse or opposite of SYMMETRICAL *a.* in various senses (see quots.). Hence **anti-'symmetry**, the property of being antisymmetrical.

1913 L. SILBERSTEIN *Vectorial Mechanics* v. 96 The decomposition of the general operator into a symmetrical and a non-symmetrical part (the last being the so-called antisymmetrical part) can be effected in but one way. **1923** J. RICE *Relativity* vi. 126 If its components satisfy the relations $P_{\lambda\mu} = -P_{\mu\lambda}$ it [*sc.* the tensor] is called 'anti-symmetric'. *Ibid.* 127 So the anti-symmetry is preserved after transformation. **1926** P. A. M. DIRAC in *Proc. R. Soc.* A. CXII. 669 If there is interaction between the electrons, there will still be symmetrical and antisymmetrical eigen-functions... An antisymmetrical eigenfunction vanishes identically when two of the electrons are in the same orbit. **1939** *Mind* XLVIII. 113 The law of Fermi-Dirac for anti-symmetric wave-functions. **1948** E. A. MILNE *Vectorial Mechanics* iii. 40 A tensor *T* is said to be anti-symmetrical if its components in any triad satisfy the relation $T_{\beta\alpha} = -T^{\alpha\beta}$. **1950** E. SCHRÖDINGER *Space-Time Structure* ii. 16 Envisage a covariant antisymmetric tensor of the fourth rank T_{klmn}. By antisymmetric we mean that an exchange of *any* two subscripts should just merely produce a change of sign of the component. **1964** E. BACH *Introd. Transformational Gram.* vii. 156 Where *R*(*x*, *y*) and *R*(*y*, *x*) always imply identity of *x* and *y* the relation is called antisymmetric.

antisyphilitic (ˌæntɪsɪfɪ'lɪtɪk), *a.* and *sb.* *Med.* [ANTI- 3.] **A.** *adj.* Tending to cure syphilis. **B.** *sb.* A medicine so used.

1830 LINDLEY *Nat. Syst. Bot.* 106 The Jew Bush, or Milk plant, is used..as an antisyphilitic. **1878** BRYANT *Pract. Surg.* I. 318 Antisyphilitic remedies should be employed.

antisyzygy (æntɪ'sɪzɪdʒɪ). [f. G. ἀντισυζυγία, f. ἀντί opposite + συζυγία union, f. σύ(ν) together + ζυγ-όν yoke.] Union of opposites.

1863 F. HALE in *Reader* 24 Jan. 95 Zoroastrianism..fuses together—in what Clement of Rome would have denominated an antisyzygy—the Deity and Satan.

antitetanic (ˌæntɪtɪ'tænɪk), *a.* and *sb.* *Med.* [ANTI- 3.] **A.** *adj.* Good against tetanus or lockjaw. **B.** *sb.* A medicine so used.

1875 H. WOOD *Therap.* (1879) 233 It even acts as an antitetanic in the poisoning of codeia and of morphia.

antithalian (æntɪ'θeɪlɪən), *a.* [f. ANTI- 3 + *Thalīa*, the Muse of Comedy, the Grace of festivities.] Opposed to fun or festivity.

1817 PEACOCK *Nightm. Abbey* 106 As gloomy and antithalian a young lady as Mr. Glowry himself could desire.

antitheism (æntɪ'θiːɪz(ə)m). [ANTI- 7.] The doctrine of antitheists.

1833 CHALMERS *Bridgw. Treat.* II. iv. 405 Atheism might plead a lack of evidence within its own field of observation. But Antitheism pronounces upon the things which are, and the things which are not within that field. **1877** *Athenæum* 6 Oct. 430/2 Another theory justifying anti-theism.

antitheist (æntɪ'θiːɪst). [ANTI- 5.] One opposed to belief in the existence of a God.

a **1847** T. CHALMERS *Nat. Theol.* (1849) I. I. ii. 59 He is not an antitheist. **1855** GEO. ELIOT *Essays* (1884) 171 An antitheist—that is, one who deliberately..opposed and hated God. **1860** PUSEY *Min. Proph.* 533 The antitheist or anti-Christian world, which by violence, falsehood, sophistry, wars against the truth. **1881** SWINBURNE in *Fortn. Rev.* Feb. 142 If only he were a French antitheist.

antitheistic (ˌæntɪθiː'ɪstɪk), *a.* [f. prec. + -IC.] Of or pertaining to antitheists; opposed to God.

1860 PUSEY *Min. Proph.* 577 Petty, though Anti-theistic, wars of neighbouring petty nations, pitting their false gods against the True. **1880** *Athenæum* 20 Nov. 668 An antitheistic bias which obscures his vision.

antithem, var. ANTETHEME, text of a discourse.

antithesis (æn'tɪθɪsɪs). Pl. **antitheses**. [a. L. *antithesis*, a. Gr. ἀντίθεσις opposition, n. of action f. ἀντιτιθέναι, f. ἀντί against + τιθέναι (stem θε-) to place; already in Gr. a term of Logic and Rhetoric.]

1. *Rhet.* An opposition or contrast of ideas, expressed by using as the corresponding members of two contiguous sentences or clauses, words which are the opposites of, or strongly contrasted with, each other; as '*he* must *increase*, but *I* must *decrease*,' 'in *newness* of *spirit*, not in the *oldness* of the *letter*.'

1529 FRITH (*title*) Antithesis; wherein are compared togeder Christes actes and oure holye Father the Popes. **1674** *Govt. Tongue* iii. §17. 115 These are miserable antithesis's. **1728** POPE *Dunc.* I. 254 All arm'd with points, antitheses and puns. **1748** J. MASON *Elocution* 29 In an Antithesis, one contrary must be pronounced louder than the other. **1872** MINTO *Eng. Lit.* Introd. 9 When the balanced clauses stand in antithesis, it lends emphasis to the opposition.

2. The second of two such opposed clauses or sentences; a proposition opposed to a thesis; a counter-thesis or -proposition.

1533 FRITH *Answ. More* F ij, As the contrarye antithesis doth euidently expresse. **1677** GALE *Crt. Gentiles* III. Pref., Impossible..to discusse such an hypothesis without some opposition against such as defend the antithesis. **1678** OWEN *Mind of God* iii. 91 Given to disputing, or the maintaining of Antitheseses, or oppositions unto the Truth. **1833** COLERIDGE *Table T.* 264 The style of Junius is a sort of metre, the law of which is a balance of thesis and antithesis.

3. By extension: Direct or striking opposition of character or functions (between two things); contrast. Const. *of*, *between* (*with* obs.).

1631 PRESTON *Effec. Faith* 40 That Antithesis, that opposition that is made in that withdrawing of a mans selfe from God. **1850** KINGSLEY *Alt. Locke* xxxviii. (1879) 410 The antithesis of natural and revealed religion. **1872** DARWIN *Emotions* i. 5 Movements, so clearly expressive of affections..being in complete opposition or antithesis to the attitude and movements which are expressive of anger.

4. The direct opposite, the contrast. Const. *of*, *to*.

1831 MACAULAY *Moore's Byron, Ess.* I. 161 The reverse of a great dramatist, the very antithesis to a great dramatist. **1857** H. REED *Lect. Brit. Poets* vii. 244 Rhyme is sometimes taken as the antithesis of reason. **1879** FARRAR *Paul* II. 327 Is not the Pharisaic spirit..the antithesis of the Christian?

†**5.** (See quot.) *Obs.*

1591 PERCIVALL *Sp. Dict.* B ija, Antithesis, or Antistœchon: where if *l* follows immediately after *r*..they change *r* into *l*, to make the sound the pleasanter, as for *Dexarle, dexalle.* **1657** J. SMITH *Myst. Rhet.* 172 *Antithesis* is sometimes a figure, whereby one letter is put for another; and then it is the same with *Antistoichon*.

antithesism (æn'tɪθɪsɪz(ə)m). *rare*[−1]. [n. of result f. ANTITHESIZE: see -IZE and -ISM.] The production of antithesis, an antithetic sentence.

1816 GILCHRIST *Philos. Etym.* 214 His superfine antithesisms.

antithesistic (æn,tɪθɪ'sɪstɪk), *a.* *rare*[−1]. [f. as if on *antithesist* (n. of agent f. ANTITHESIZE) + -IC: see -ISTIC.] Of the nature of an opponent; opposing, contrary.

1801 E. DARWIN *Zoon.* IV. 234 The ideas..become exerted too violently for want of some antithesistic ideas.

antithesize (æn'tɪθɪsaɪz), *v.* *rare*[−1]. [f. ANTITHES-IS + -IZE; cf. *emphas-ize*.] To form antitheses; to put into antithesis.

1789 BURNS *Wks.* (Globe) 476, I can antithesize sentiment and circumvolute periods as well as any coiner of phrase.

an'tithesizer. *rare*[−1]. [f. prec. + -ER[1].] One who antithesizes or forms an antithesis.

1808 SOUTHEY *Lett.* II. 90 [Crabbe] is an imitator, or rather an antithesizer, of Goldsmith, if such a word may be coined for the occasion.

antithet ('æntɪθɛt). [ad. L. *antithet-on*, a. Gr. ἀντίθετ-ον, neut. of adj. ἀντίθετ-ος placed in opposition: see ANTITHESIS. Long used in Gr. and L. form *antitheton*, pl. *-a* (erron. *-as*).]

†**1.** The rhetorical figure of ANTITHESIS. *Obs.*

1580 NORTH *Plutarch* (1676) 702 A figure of Rhetorick called Antitheton: which is, opposition. **1610** HEALEY *St. Aug., City of God* 422 Contraposition, contention, or Antitheton is diversely used.

2. An instance of antithesis; an antithetic statement.

1605 BACON *Adv. Learn.* VI. iii. (1876) 261 The examples of antithets here laid down. *a* **1661** HOLYDAY *Persius* 297 In smooth antitheta's his fault he weighs. **1857** KINGSLEY *Two Y. Ago* xxvi, Sunshine comes after storm..Equally true is the popular antithet, that misfortunes never come single.

†**3.** *attrib.* or *adj.* Opposed, put forth in opposition.

a **1733** NORTH *Exam.* I. ii. ¶154 The antithet Topic used by the Plot-Mongers, when the Vility and Roguery of the Witnesses was made an objection, that only such could be privy to very bad Actions.

antithetic (æntɪ'θɛtɪk), *a.* and *sb.* [ad. Gr. ἀντιθετικός, f. ἀντίθετος: see prec. and -IC.]

A. *adj.* Of the nature of antithesis: **a.** *Rhet.*

1610 HEALEY *St. Aug., City of God* XI. xviii. 401 Making the worlds course like a faire poeme, more gratious by antithetike figures. **1778** BP. LOWTH *Isaiah* (ed. 12) 8 Parallel lines may be reduced to three sorts, parallels synonymous, antithetic, synthetic. **1817** COLERIDGE *Biogr. Lit.* 113 Which, in the antithetic form..of an adage or maxim, I have been accustomed to word thus: 'Until you understand a writer's ignorance, presume yourself ignorant of his understanding.'

†**b.** Opposing, controversial. *Obs.*

1753 CHAMBERS *Cycl. Supp.* s.v., In this sense [controversial] we meet with antithetic method, antithetic discourses, etc.

c. Contrasted, directly opposite.

1864 BURTON *Scot Abr.* I. v. 312 The more blasphemous and brutal the exhibition was, the more was a sort of antithetic holiness attached to it.

d. Consisting of two opposites.

1842 W. GROVE *Corr. Phys. For.* (ed. 6) 128 The dual or antithetic character of force involved in the term polarity.

B. *sb.* *rare.* **1.** A direct opposite.

1863 RUSSELL *Diary N. & S.* II. 84 The favorite resort of smokers and their antithetics, those who love the pure fresh air.

2. *collect. pl.* The doctrine of contrasts.

1852 M. STUART *Comm. Prov.* 31 Two *libelli*, one for antithetics and the other for synthetics.

anti'thetical, *a.* [f. prec. + -AL[1].]

1. Connected with, containing, or using antithesis.

1583 T. WATSON *Poems* (1870) 116 The whole piller..is by relation of either halfe to the other Antitheticall or Antisillabicall. **1795** MASON *Church Music* III. 179 Parallel antithetical expressions, are..substituted for Rhythm and cadence. **1853** ROBERTSON *Sermons* Ser. IV. ix. (1876) 112 The whole context is antithetical. Ideas are opposed to each other in pairs of contraries.

2. Characterized by direct opposition.

1848 MILLER *First Impressions* xvii. (1857) 283 To bring Revelation in direct antithetical collison with the inferences of the geologists. **1860** TYNDALL *Glaciers* II. §26. 372 Each of the snowy bands..contributed to produce an appearance perfectly antithetical to its own.

anti'thetically, *adv.* [f. prec. + -LY[2].] In an antithetic manner; in direct opposition.

1816 BYRON *Childe Harold* III. 36 Whose spirit antithetically mixt, One moment of the mightiest, and again On little objects with like firmness fixt. **1855** H. SPENCER *Psychology* II. i. (1872) I. 161 These outer activities.. become antithetically opposed in aspect.

antitoxic (æntɪ'tɒksɪk), *a.* (*sb.*) [ANTI-[1] 3 b.] Having the quality of counteracting the effect of a toxin; of the nature of an antitoxin. Also as *sb.*

1890 BILLINGS *Med. Dict.*, *Antitoxics*, antidotes. **1894** *Daily News* 1 Dec. 3/4 The anti-toxic serum treatment of diphtheria. **1894** *Liberal* 24 Nov. 41/2 Bacterial products being gifted with an antitoxic power. **1905** G. A. REID *Princ. Heredity* x. 124 'Passive' immunity which results from the injection of antitoxic sera. **1946** *Nature* 19 Oct. 557/1 Thus electrophoresis can serve as control of the various factors.. that govern the purification of antitoxic sera by means of enzyme digestion.

antitoxin (æntɪ'tɒksɪn). Also *erron.* **-ine**. [ANTI-[1] 6 d.] A substance which has the property of counteracting the effect of a toxin; one of the antibodies capable of neutralizing toxins. Also *attrib.*

1892 *Pop. Sci. Monthly* Sept. 629 Acquired immunity depends upon the formation of an antitoxine in the body of the immune animal. **1893** *Fortn. Rev.* Jan. 115 Antitoxin was used, and resulted in perfect recovery. **1895** *Pop. Sci. Monthly* Sept. 715 The principles..employed in the antitoxine treatment of diphtheria. **1904** [see TOXIN a, b]. **1941** *Nature* 26 Apr. 515/2 Antitoxin is stored in a sterile condition..in glass containers.

anti-trade ('æntɪˌtreɪd), *attrib. phr.* and *sb.* [ANTI- 2.] In *anti-trade wind*, also ellipt. *anti-trade, -s*: A wind that blows steadily in the opposite direction to the trade-wind, that is, in the northern hemisphere from S.W., and in southern hemisphere from N.W.

1853 SIR J. HERSCHEL *Pop. Lect.* iv. §19. (1873) 157 The great and permanent system of winds known as the 'trades' and 'anti-trades.' **1867** E. DENISON *Astron. without Math.* 40 This secondary or anti-trade wind prevails from about 30° to 60° latitude at sea. **1875** CROLL *Climate & Time* ii. 28 The south-west wind to which we owe so much of our warmth in this country, is the continuation of the anti-trade.

‖**antitragus** ('æntɪˌtreɪgəs, L. æn'tɪtrəgəs). [ANTI- 2.] A protuberance of the outer ear, the thicker part of the antihelix, opposite to the tragus.

1842 E. WILSON *Anat. Vade M.* 461 A tubercle opposite to this is the antitragus. **1877** BURNETT *Ear* 29 In the watershrew, the anti-tragus serves as an operculum to the auricle.

antitrinitarian (ˌæntɪtrɪnɪ'tɛərɪən), *a.* and *sb.* [ANTI- 3.]

A. *adj.* Opposed to the doctrine of the Trinity.

a **1665** GOODWIN *Filled w. the Spirit* (1867) 133 There is an anti-trinitarian spirit that hath broken prison of late. **1825** SYD. SMITH *Wks.* (1859) II. 206/2 Anti-Trinitarian Dissenters sit in the House of Commons.

B. *sb.* One who rejects the doctrine of the Trinity.

1641 BP. MOUNTAGU *Acts & Mon.* 452 The German and Polonian Anabaptists and Antitrinitarians. **1850** R. WALLACE (*title*) Sketches of the Lives and Writings of Distinguished Antitrinitarians.

antitrini'tarianism. [f. prec. + -ISM.] The doctrinal system of Antitrinitarians.

1860 PUSEY *Min. Proph.* 199 Anti-Trinitarianism denies to God His essential Being, Father, Son, and Holy Ghost.

antitropal (æn'tɪtrəpəl), *a.* *Bot.* [f. mod.L. *antitrop-us*, mod.Fr. *antitrope* (f. Gr. ἀντί against + -τροπ-ος turning) + -AL[1].] Of an embryo: Inverted, so as to have the radicle at the extremity of the seed opposite to the hilum.

1855 BALFOUR *Bot.* (ed. 3) §603 In an orthotropal seed the embryo is inverted or antitropal. **1866** in *Treas. Bot.*

antitropous (æn'tɪtrəpəs), *a.* *Bot.* = prec.

1830 LINDLEY *Nat. Syst. Bot.* 229 In Rhinanthaceæ it [the embryo] must be Antitropous or heterotropous.

anti-trust (ˌæntɪ'trʌst), *a.* *U.S.* [ANTI-[1] 4.] Opposed to trusts (TRUST *sb.* 7 b) or similar monopolistic combinations.

1890 *Congress. Record* 21 Mar. 2465/2 Will the senator inform me upon what ground the Missouri anti-trust bill was declared unconstitutional in his own State? **1938** *Ann. Reg. 1937* 277 A return to the old American policy of enforcing the 'anti-trust' laws forbidding all combinations 'in restraint of trade'. **1962** *Times* 9 Jan. 11/2 Under the anti-trust arrangements mergers can be disallowed.

anti-'tussient, *a. nonce-wd.* [f. ANTI- 3 + L. *tussient-em* coughing.] Good against coughing.
a **1704** T. BROWN *Comic. View* Wks. I. 161, I have been thirty years and upwards contriving my Anti-tussient pills.

antitypal ('æntɪtaɪpəl), *a. rare.* [f. next + -AL[1].] Of the nature of an antitype.
1851 KINGSLEY *Yeast* Epil. (D.) How am I to extricate my antitypal characters, when their living types have not yet extricated themselves?

antitype ('æntɪtaɪp). [ad. med.L. *antityp-us* a. Gr. ἀντίτυπ-ος, prop. adj. 'responding as an impression to the die,' f. ἀντί opposite to + τύπος stroke, stamp, type, f. stem τυπ- strike.] **1.** That which is shadowed forth or represented by the 'type' or symbol.
1613 ROBARTES *Rev. Gospel* vii. 55 If the order of Priesthood there spoken of be an eternall order, and yet such an order as to whome the tythes are due, then be the Priest, either Melchisedech the type, or Christ the antitype, yet the same thing is still euinced. **1635** PAGITT *Christianogr.* 68 The Bread and Wine after Consecration are called Antitypes. *a* **1652** J. SMITH *Sel. Disc.* vi. 191 In these types and shadows..to behold the antitypes themselves. **1704** SWIFT *T. Tub* Pref., The ship in danger is easily understood to be its old Antitype the Commonwealth. **1841** MYERS *Cath. Th.* III. §11. 42 The relation..of the Old Testament to the New..[is] that of Type to Antitype, of Porch to Temple, of Dawn to Day.
2. One of the opposite or contrary kind.
1926 G. K. CHESTERTON *Incredul. Father Brown* v. 146 An antitype; a sort of extreme exception that proves the..rule. **1937** 'M. INNES' *Hamlet, Revenge!* I. ii. 39 He looked lazily and amiably round his guests; the very anti-type..of King Claudius of Denmark.

antitypical (æntɪ'tɪpɪkəl), *a.* [f. prec. + -ICAL, after *typical.*] Of the nature of or pertaining to an antitype; fulfilling what is typical.
1641 BP. MOUNTAGU *Acts & Mon.* 493 Not any temporall, and therefore, but typicall, regality..but a spirituall, eternall, antitypicall regality. **1684** CHARNOCK *Attrib. God* (1834) II. 681 God smelled a sweet savour from Noah's sacrifice, not from the beasts offered, but the antitypical sacrifice represented. **1860** ELLICOTT *Life of our Lord* vii. 347 An antitypical reference to the ceremony of the Scape-Goat.

†**an'titypous**, *a. Obs. rare.* [f. Gr. ἀντίτυπ-ος force-resisting (f. ἀντί in opposition + -τυπος striking: see ANTITYPE) + -OUS.] Resisting force; material, substantial, solid.
1678 CUDWORTH *Intell. Syst.* 815 The Tenuity of their [Angels'] Bodies..as not..being so solid and Antitypous as those which we are now Imprisoned in. *Ibid.* 829 It is an Essential Property thereof [*Extensum*] to be Antitypous or Impenetrable.

antitypy (æn'tɪtɪpɪ). *rare.* [ad. Gr. ἀντιτυπία, n. of quality f. ἀντίτυπ-ος: see prec. and -Y.] The resistance of matter to force of penetration, compression, or motion.
1605 BACON *Adv. Learn.* (1640) 156 Motions of Antitypie, commonly called Motion opposing Penetration of Dimensions. **1846** SIR W. HAMILTON *Dissert.* in *Reid's Wks.* 847 Antitypy, a word in Greek applied not only to this absolute and essential resistance of matter, *quâ* matter, but also, etc.

antivariolous (,æntɪvə'raɪələs), *a. Med.* [ANTI- 3.] Good against smallpox.
1880 in *Syd. Soc. Lex.*

antivenereal (,æntɪvɪ'nɪərɪəl), *a. Med.* [ANTI- 3.] Tending to cure venereal disease.
1676 WISEMAN (J.) Antivenereal remedies. **1830** LINDLEY *Nat. Syst. Bot.* 314 Antivenereal and febrifugal virtues.

antivenin (,æntɪ'vɛnɪn). Also **-ine, -venene** (-vɪ'niːn). [f. ANTI-[1] 6 d + VENIN *sb.*[2]] Any anti-toxin used as an antidote to the venom of serpents. Also as *adj.*
1895 T. R. FRASER in *Brit. Med. Jrnl.* 17 Aug. 416/2 (*title*) The treatment of snake poisoning with antivenene derived from animals protected against serpents' venom. **1902** *Encycl. Brit.* XXXIII. 271/2 The serum is found to act as an anti-venin. **1904** *Brit. Med. Jrnl.* 10 Sept. 574 Polyvalent antivenenes. **1909** *Westm. Gaz.* 17 Aug. 6/3 The anti-venine treatment. **1912** ADAMI & MCCRAE *Pathol.* 168 By the repeated injection of minute quantities of venom into lower animals, antitoxins—or antivenins..can be obtained for all the animal poisons. **1959** *Times Lit. Suppl.* 3 Apr. 191/3 The main quarry is snakes..and his aim to bring them in alive—so that they can be milked of their venom to make antivenene.

antivermicular (,æntɪvə'mɪkjʊlə(r)), *a. Phys.* [ANTI- 3.] = ANTIPERISTALTIC.
1717 ST. ANDRÉ in *Phil. Trans.* XXX. 580 If the Vermicular Motion accelerates the Contents of the Intestins downwards; the Antivermicular..should force them upwards. **1880** in *Syd. Soc. Lex.*

antizymic (æntɪ'zɪmɪk), *a.* and *sb.* [f. ANTI- 3 + Gr. ζύμη leaven + -IC.] **A.** *adj.* Opposing fermentation. **B.** *sb.* A substance having this quality.
1804 T. TROTTER *Drunkenness* iii. 41 Hop..possesses no superior efficacy as an antizymic. **1839** HOOPER *Med. Dict.*, *Antizymic*, Applied to that which prevents fermentation.

antizymotic (,æntɪzɪ'mɒtɪk, -zaɪ'mɒtɪk), *a.* and *sb. Med.* [f. ANTI- 3 + Gr. ζυμωτικ-ός causing fermentation.] **A.** *adj.* = prec. **B.** *sb.* A substance that prevents fermentation or decomposition.
1875 H. WOOD *Therap.* (1879) 622 Antizymotics are used for the purpose of preventing decomposition.

antler ('æntlə(r)). Forms: 3 ? **antolier, auntolier,** 4–5 **auntelere, hauntelere,** 5–6 **auntler,** 6–8 **antlier,** 6– **antler.** [a. OFr. *antoillier* (i.e. antoʎer):—late L. **ant(e)oculār-em (ramum)* the 'branch' or tine of a stag's horn 'in front of the eyes'; cf. Ger. *augensprosze* 'eye-sprout.' *Antoillier* represented an earlier **antoglier* (cf. OFr. *avogle*, It. *avocolo* :—L. *abocul-um*, and OFr. *oill* for **ogl:—oculum*), later OFr. *andoillier*, now *andouiller* (see Dr. Bugge in *Romania* IV. 349). The original English form must have been *antolier, auntolier*, whence, by weakening and eventual loss of atonic *o*, *auntelere, auntler, antler*.]
1. *orig.* The lowest (forward-directed) branch of the horn of a stag or other deer; afterwards extended to any branch, the lowest being then called the *brow-antler*, and the next *bes-antler*.
1399 LANGL. *Rich. Redeles* II. 128 Ȝoure hauntelere dere were all y-takyn. *a* **1420** *Venery de Twety* in *Rel. Ant.* I. 151 Whan an hert hath fourched, and then auntelere ryall, and surryall, and forched on the one syde, and troched on that other syde, than is he an hert of .x. and of the more. *c* **1520** SKELTON *Speke Parrot* 481 So bygge a bulke of brow auntlers cabbagid that yere. **1583** STANYHURST *Aeneis* I. (1880) 23 Chiefe stags vpbearing croches high from the antlier hauted. **1608** NORDEN *Surv. Dial.* 183 What Deere hath the Lord of this Mannor in his Park, red and fallow: how many of Antler, and how many rascall? **1686** *Phil. Trans.* XVI. 225 The Andouilleres of a Staggs Horn. **1741** *Compl. Fam.-Piece* II. i. 289 The Fallow Hart or Stag doth bear his Head high..has small Beams, with long, slender, and ill-grown Antliers. **1727–51** CHAMBERS *Cycl.*, *Antler*, among hunters, the first of the pearls that grow about the bur of a deer's horn. There are also sur-antlers, brow-antlers, etc. **1849** MACAULAY *Hist. Eng.* vii, Huge stags with sixteen antlers. **1864** *Derby Merc.* 14 Dec., The curious articles made from the brow antler of a stag's horn.
2. Hence *popularly*: The branched horn of a stag or other deer.
1829 SCOTT *Demonol.* x. 395 A vaulted apartment garnished with stags' antlers. **1847** CARPENTER *Zool.* §260 The Deer tribe, distinguished by the possession of long deciduous horns, covered with a soft skin or *velvet*..and termed Antlers. **1851** D. WILSON *Preh. Ann.* II. III. vi. 164 The skull and antlers of a gigantic deer.

antlered ('æntləd), *ppl. a.* [f. prec. + -ED[2].]
1. Furnished with or bearing antlers: **a.** naturally.
a **1818** VERNON *Ovid's Met.* VIII. (T.) Sometimes a crested mare, or antler'd deer. **1870** BRYANT *Homer* XI. I. 355 Like a troop Of ravening jackals round an antlered stag.
b. Adorned with stags' horns.
1828 SCOTT in Lockhart *Life* (1839) IX. 227 We were surveying the antlered old hall.
2. *transf.* Branched as with antlers.
1870 DISRAELI *Lothair* xiii. 55 Sometimes a gorsy dell and sometimes a great spread of antlered fern.

antlerless ('æntləlɪs), *a.* [f. ANTLER + -LESS.] Without antlers.
1881 *Nature* No. 592. 417 These antlerless deer.

antler-moth. A noctuid moth (*Charæas* or *Cerapteryx graminis*), the larva of which is destructive in meadow lands. Also in shortened form **antler.**
1775 M. HARRIS *Eng. Lepidoptera* 9 Phalæna. English Names..Antler. **1832** T. BROWN *Bk. Butterfl. & M.* I. 75 The Antler Moth..devours a considerable variety of grasses. **1897** *Daily News* 13 Sept. 6/2 The grub of the antler moth..has been known to commit such havoc that..the meadows looked as if a fire had passed over them. **1961** R. SOUTH *Moths Brit. Isles* (ed. 4) Ser I. 196 *Antler Moth*..has the fore wings greyish brown or reddish brown, sometimes tinged with ochreous in the paler forms.

antlery ('æntlərɪ). *rare*[−1]. [f. ANTLER, after forms like *drapery, finery.*] Antlers collectively.
1849 J. WILSON in *Blackw. Mag.* LXVI. 9 An enormous fellow [a stag]..giving himself a shake of his whole huge bulk, and a *caive* of his whole wide antlery.

‖**antlia** ('æntlɪə). *Ent.* [L. *antlia*, an instrument for drawing up water, a. Gr. ἀντλία bilge-water, ἀντλίον a bucket.] The proboscis or haustellum of insects, with which they suck up juices.
1828 KIRBY & SPENCE *Entomol.* xliii. IV. 98 Extraordinary..irritability is exhibited by the antlia. **1869** NICHOLSON *Zool.* 211 These maxillæ adhere together by their inner surfaces, and thus form a spiral 'trunk,' or 'antlia.'

antliate ('æntlɪeɪt), *ppl. a. Ent.* [f. prec. + -ATE.] Furnished with sucking proboscis; haustellate.
1828 KIRBY & SPENCE *Entomol.* xlvii. IV. 390 Mouth antliate.

antling ('æntlɪŋ). *rare.* [f. ANT *sb.* + -LING.] A young or little ant.
1879 MCCOOK *Agric. Ant of Texas* 20 (D.) Within the formicaries antlings were found.

'ant-,lion. [a transl. of Gr. μυρμηκο-λέων, in the LXX.] A neuropterous insect, or genus of insects (*Myrmeleon*), the larva of which lies in wait for and devours ants.
1815 KIRBY & SPENCE *Entomol.* (1843) I. 304 The ant-lion was the stronger of the two and..dragged the object of contestation under the sand. **1880** H. ST. JOHN *Nipon* 157 One of the most ingenious insects I know of is the ant-lion.

antocow (in Miege 1688, Phillips 1706, Bailey 1721–83) = ANTICOR.

antocular (ænt'ɒkjʊlə(r)), *a. rare.* [mod. f. L. *ante* before + *oculāris* pertaining to the eye, f. *oculus* eye. Cf. ANTLER.] Situated in front of the eye.
1870 NICHOLSON *Zool.* (1880) 538 A layer of transparent epidermis covers the whole eye [of Serpents] and is termed the antocular membrane.

antodontalgic, variant of ANTI-ODONTALGIC.

‖**antœci** (æn'tiːsaɪ), *sb. pl.* [L., a. Gr. ἄντοικοι dwellers opposite, f. ἀντί opposite to + -οικος -dwelling.] The dwellers under the same meridian, on opposite sides of the equator, and at the same distance from it.
1622 HEYLIN *Cosmogr.* Introd. (1674) 20/1 Antœci are such as dwell under the same Meridian and the same Latitude or Parallel equally distant from the Æquator; the one northward, the other Southward; the days in both places being of a length; but the Summer of the one being the others winter. **1684** T. BURNET *Th. Earth* I. 255 Antichthones..comprehend both the antipodes and antœci, or all beyond the line. **1796** [See ANTŒCIAN].

antœcian (æn'tiːʃən), *a.* and *sb.* [f. prec. + -AN.]
A. *adj.* Of or belonging to the opposite latitude.
1860 MAURY *Phys. Geog. Sea* xx. §818 The westerly winds which prevail on the polar side of 40° S. are stronger and more constant than their antœcian fellows of the north.
B. *sb. pl.* = ANTŒCI.
1796 HUTTON *Math. Dict.* I. 121/1 Antecians or Antœci..have their noon, or midnight, or any other hour at the same time; but their seasons are contrary, being spring to the one, when it is autumn with the other.

Antonian (æn'təʊnɪən), *a.* and *sb.* [f. L. *Antoni(us* Anthony + -AN.] **A.** *adj.* Of or pertaining to St. Anthony of Egypt or St. Anthony of Padua (1195–1231).
1904 tr. *J. Rigauld's Life of St. Anthony of Padua* Introd. 11 A short account of the sources of Antonian history. *Ibid.* 12 The Antonian library of Padua. **1911** 'C. M. ANTONY' *St. Antony of Padua* p. xiii, For the present..Antonian studies are at a standstill. **1919** E. C. BUTLER *Benedictine Monachism* i. 12 The monachism that derived from St Anthony was eremitical in character. This type, which I shall call the Antonian, prevailed throughout northern Egypt. **1919** C. C. MARTINDALE *Upon God's Holy Hills* i. 12 Violent bodily penances, rarely read of in Antonian literature.
B. *sb.* Any of various communities claiming the patronage of, or continuity with the community of, St. Anthony of Egypt (*c* 251–356); = ANTHONIN.
1907 *Cath. Encycl.* I. 20/2 Some few houses..of the Antonians..are also under the direction of Abbots. **1932** *Pax* Oct. 161 There are also 771 monks who are neither priests nor deacons..divided as follows: Maronite Antonians..Chaldean Antonians.

Antonine ('æntənaɪn), *sb.* and *a.* Also 6 **Antonyne,** 7 **Antonin.** [f. L. *Antonīn(us* (see ANTHONIN) + -INE[1], or as variant of ANTHONIN.]
A. *sb.* **1.** A disciple or follower of St. Anthony of Egypt (*c* 251–356); = ANTHONIN.
a **1550** *Image of Ipocrysy* IV. 160 in Skelton *Poetical Wks.* (1843) II. 441/1 Some be Paulines, Some be Antonynes, Some be Bernardines. **1898** H. THURSTON *Life St. Hugh* IV. iii. 467 The Order of *Antonines* sprang into existence in 1090.
2. *pl.* The Roman emperors Antoninus Pius and Marcus Aurelius Antoninus who reigned in 138–161 and 161–180 respectively.
1686 G. BURNET *Some Lett.* iv. 209 Burying began in the times of the Antonins. **1770** H. WALPOLE *Let.* 6 May (1904) VII. 380 If we have the arts of the Antonines,—we have the fustian also. **1776** GIBBON *Decl. & F.* I. i. 8 The general system of Augustus was equally adopted and uniformly pursued by Hadrian and by the two Antonines. **1836** WISEMAN *Lect. Princ. Doctr. Cath. Ch.* I. i. 13 The study of philosophy..under the patronage of the Antonines..was become very prevalent. *Ibid.* II. xvi. 223 Prudent and philosophical men, like the Antonines. **1959** *Encycl. Brit.* XIX. 504/1 The internal tranquillity and the good government which have made the age of the Antonines famous.
B. *adj.* **1.** Of or pertaining to St. Anthony of Egypt or St. Anthony of Padua (1195–1231); = ANTONIAN *a.*
1898 H. THURSTON *Life St. Hugh* IV. iii. 469 The poor sufferers, and the Antonine monks who tended them. **1902** E. GUEST tr. *Lepitre's St. Antony of Padua* i. 3 The Antonine biographers of our own times. **1908** J. J. WALSH *Popes & Science* (1912) x. 276 The Antonine Congregation of Vienna, which was especially devoted to the care of patients suffering from the 'holy fire'.
2. Of or pertaining to the Antonines (sense A. 2 above) or their rule. ***Antonine Wall***: a Roman frontier-wall between the Forth and the Clyde, built for Antoninus Pius in A.D. 142.

1770 M. Folkes in *Archaeologia* I. 117 *(title)* On the Trajan and Antonine Pillars at Rome. [**1875** *Encycl. Brit.* II. 140/2 How many years Antonine's wall continued to be the boundary of the Roman territories in Britain it is impossible to say.] **1899** *(title)* The Antonine Wall Report, being an Account of Excavations, etc., made under the Direction of the Glasgow Archæological Society during 1890–93. **1900** *Daily News* 9 July 6/3 Another historical work dealing with the Flavian and Antonine periods. **1937** *Discovery* July 208/1 Antonine coins.

‖**antonomasia** (ˌæntənəʊˈmeɪzɪə, ænˌtɒnəʊ). [L., a. Gr. ἀντονομασία, f. ἀντονομάζειν to name instead, f. ἀντί instead + ὀνομάζειν to name, f. ὄνομα name.] The substitution of an epithet or appellative, or the name of an office or dignity, for a person's proper name, as *the Iron Duke* for Wellington, *his Grace* for an archbishop. Also, conversely, the use of a proper name to express a general idea, as in calling an orator *a Cicero*, a wise judge *a Daniel*.

1589 Puttenham *Eng. Poesie* (Arb.) 192 Antonomasia, or the Surnamer, as he that would say: not king Philip of Spaine, but the Westerne king. *a* **1638** Mede *Wks.* II. 332 That Capitolium by Antonomasia is put for a Gentile Temple in general. **1751** Chambers *Cycl.*, *Antonomasia*, a figure in rhetoric.. Thus we say, the philosopher, instead of Aristotle. **1759** Adam Smith *Mor. Sent.* (1797) II. 407 This way of speaking, which the grammarians call an antonomasia.

antonoˈmastic, *a.* *rare*[−0]. [f. prec. after Gr. ὀνομαστικ-ός.] Characterized by antonomasia.

antonoˈmastically, *adv.* *rare*[−1]. [f. prec. + -al[1] + -ly[2].] In antonomastic manner; by way of antonomasia.

1646 Sir T. Browne *Pseud. Ep.* 166 Although we single out one, and Antonomastically thereto assigne the name of the Unicorne, yet can we not be secure what creature is meant thereby. **1656** in Blount *Glossogr.*; and in mod. Dicts.

antonym (ˈæntənɪm). [See quot.] A term which is the opposite or antithesis of another, a counter-term.

1870 C. J. Smith *Syn. & Antonyms* Pref. 6 The Etymology of the word ἀντωνυμία merely expresses the idea of one word in *substitution for*, which in matters of verbal debate, is equivalent practically to *opposition to* another; a double force which, in addition to its analogy to Synonym, seemed to render Antonym a preferable word to *Counterterm*. **1881** *N. Y. Nation* No. 835. 464 The inevitable difficulty of choosing among synonyms and antonyms.

ˈAntony over. *U.S.* (See quot. 1872.)

1872 Schele de Vere *Americanisms* 579 *Antony over*, a game of ball played by two parties of boys, on opposite sides of a schoolhouse, over which the ball is thrown. Used in Pennsylvania. **1899** Ade *Doc' Horne* xi. 118 Why he and the alligator moved the dresser out from the wall and began to plan 'ant'ny over' with my eye.

antorbital, variant of ante-orbital.

antozone (ænt'əʊzəʊn). *Chem.* [f. (by Schönbein) ant- + ozone.] A gaseous product, supposed by Schönbein to be a permanently positive variety of oxygen, but subsequently shown to be hydrogen dioxide, H_2O_2. Hence **an'tozonide**.

1862 Faraday in *Proc. R. Inst.* 70 This substance he names antozone, and believes that it also enters into combination.. Hence there is not merely ozone and antozone, but also ozonide and antozonide compounds. **1868** Dana *Min.* 124 Its [Antozonite's] strong antozone odour is said often to produce headache and vomiting in the miners.

antozonite (ænt'əʊzəʊnaɪt). *Min.* [f. prec. + -ite.] A dark violet-blue variety of Fluorite.

1868 [See antozone].

antral (ˈæntrəl), *a.* [f. L. *antr-um* (see next) + -al[1].] Of the nature of, or pertaining to, an *antrum* or cavity.

1880 in *Syd. Soc. Lex.* **1955** K. F. M. Thomson in *Jrnl. Laryng. & Otol.* LXIX. 829 *(title)* Air-Embolism following Antral Lavage. **1962** *Lancet* 8 Dec. 1200/1 There was an overflow of acid on to the antral area.

antre (ˈæntə(r)). *poet.* [a. Fr. *antre*:—L. *antrum*, a. Gr. ἄντρον cave.] A cave, a cavern.

1604 Shaks. *Oth.* I. iii. 140 Antars vast, and Desarts idle. **1818** Keats *Endym.* II. 231 Out-shooting.. like a meteorstar, Through a vast antre. **1879** G. Meredith *Egoist* II. v. 109 She.. shunned his house as the antre of an ogre.

antrorse (ænˈtrɔːs), *a.* [ad. mod.L. *antrorsus*, f. L. **antero-* (see antero-) + *versus* turned, in imitation of *extrorsus*, etc.] Bent forward or upward.

1858 Gray *Bot. Text-bk.* 396 *Antrorse*, Directed upward or forward. **1877** Coues & Allen *N. Amer. Rodent.* 558 Stiffish, antrorse, adpressed hairs.

antroversion (æntrəʊˈvɜːʃən). [mod. f. *antro-*, for *antero-* (see prec.), + L. *versiōn-em* turning.] A turning forward; = anteversion.

1880 in *Syd. Soc. Lex.*

antrovert (æntrəʊˈvɜːt), *v. rare.* [mod. f. as prec. + L. *vert-ĕre* to turn.] To turn or bend forward.

1854 Owen in *Orr's Circ. Sc.*, *Org. Nat.* I. 248 The neural spines.. are antroverted in the last two dorsal vertebræ.

‖**antrum** (ˈæntrəm). Pl. -a. [L., a. Gr. ἄντρον cave.] A hollow place, a cavern; *spec.* applied in *Phys.* to cavities in the body.

1398 Trevisa *Barth. De P.R.* xiv. liii. (1495) 486 A derke caue hyghte Antrum. **1727–51** Chambers *Cycl.*, *Antrum Highmorianum* is a cavity discovered within the sinus of each maxillary bone. **1842** E. Wilson *Anat. Vade M.* 33 The.. antrum of Highmore. **1877** Huxley *Anat. Inv. An.* vii. 388 The nasal cavities and maxillary antra of Carnivores.

‖**antrustion** (ænˈtrʌstɪən). [a. Fr. *antrustion*, or med.L. *antrustiōn-em* (in Salic Law, etc.), f. OHG. *trôst* trust, protection, security, fidelity; latinized in Old Frankish documents as *trustis*. The prefix is prob. and- toward; but no Teutonic word so compounded is known.] A voluntary follower of the Old Frankish princes at the period of the national migrations.

1848 Hallam *Mid. Ages* (1878) I. ii. I. 156 *note*, In one of Marculfus's precedents, l. i. f. 18, we have the form by which an Antrustion was created. *Ibid.* I. ii. 306 Chilperic put this down by the help of his faithful Antrustions. **1875** Stubbs *Const. Hist.* I. ix. 254 None but the king could have antrustions.

an'trustionship. *rare.* [f. prec. + -ship.] The position of an antrustion.

1875 Stubbs *Const. Hist.* I. ix. 252 Roth.. goes further, connecting the antrustionship with the vassal relation.

antship (ˈænt-ʃɪp). *rare.* [f. ant *sb.* + -ship; cf. *lordship*.] *humorously* as title for: An ant.

1771 J. Cunningham *Poems* (Chalmers XIV. 434/2) 'Begone, you vile reptile,' his antship replied.

†**ˈantsigne.** [Obs. form of ensign *sb.*, intermed. between that and *antient*, ancient *sb.*, spelt as if f. *ante* before + *signum* sign, standard.]

1576 Lambarde *Peramb. Kent* 78 A flagge and antsigne of their owne pride. **1583** Golding *Calvin on Deut.* xii. 72 In such wise as wee may fight stoutly vnder his antsigne.

antsy (ˈæntsɪ), *a. colloq.* and *dial.* (chiefly *U.S.*). Also 9 **ancey**. [f. *ants*, pl. of ant (cf. the phr. *to have ants in one's pants* s.v. ant) + -y[1].] Agitated, impatient, restless; also, sexually eager. Also redupl. as **antsy-pantsy**.

1838 in *Dict. Amer. Regional Eng.* I. 71/2 Minard's talking & Peake's scribbling were enough to drive anyone ancey. **1950**, etc. in *Dict. Amer. Regional Eng.* **1962** K. Topkins *All Tea in China* vi. 141 'Well, now, what seems to be the trouble?' Daddy said. (That was what he always said to Marcie when she got antsy.) **1964** *Playboy* Oct. 48/2 Fascinating to watch are Richard Burton as the seedy Reverend T. Lawrence Shannon, Sue Lyon as an antsy-pantsy teenager, [etc.]. **1971** *Last Whole Earth Catal.* 123/3 Bert's rival, Norton, had been sucking on the laughing gas almost two minutes now, and Bert was getting antsy. **1972** W. A. Nolen *Surgeon's World* xvi. 159 Her husband got antsy and asked me to have Tom Lewis see her in consultation. **1982** *Verbatim* Autumn 14/2 Others who get my goat are antsy, crabby, pig-headed old buzzards.

ˈant-ˌthrush. [ant *sb.*] A bird of the Thrush family, which lives on ants and allied insects.

1863 Bates *Nat. on Amazons* i. 7 Ant-thrushes (a tribe of plainly-coloured birds intermediate in structure between flycatchers and thrushes). **1869** J. Gray in *Guide Brit. Mus.* 10 The Thrushes: some of these have long legs and short tails, such as the tropical Ant-thrushes.

Antwerp (ˈæntwɜːp). The Belgian city of that name, used *attrib.* in ***Antwerp edge, edging stitch***, an embroidery stitch used for decorating and finishing edges and hems; ***Antwerp lace***, a coarse-textured lace (see quot. 1960); ***Antwerp pigeon***, a variety of homing or carrier pigeon (ellipt. in quots. 1839 and 1876). Also ***Antwerp blue, brown, red*** (see quots.).

1835 G. Field *Chromatography* xi. 112 Antwerp Blue is a lighter-coloured and somewhat brighter Prussian blue. *Ibid.* xviii. 162 Antwerp Brown is a preparation of asphaltum ground in strong drying oil. **1839** *New Sporting Mag.* June 378 The Antwerps are a later introduction into our country. .. I believe little was known of them before the famous Antwerp match in July 1830. **1865** Mrs. F. B. Palliser *Hist. Lace* vii. 116 Antwerp lace would have disappeared from the scene had it not been for the attachment evinced by the old people for one pattern,.. generally known by the name of 'pot lace'. **1876** Fulton *Bk. Pigeons* 258 A few years ago, when Antwerp fanciers were few and far between. *Ibid.* 268 The bird now known as the Antwerp Carrier, Voyageur, or Homing Pigeon. **1882** Caulfeild & Saward *Dict. Needlework* 7/2 *Antwerp edge*, a needle point edging to braid on cordonnet. **1885** [see Haarlem]. **1885** J. Scott Taylor *Field's Chromatography Modernized* 187 *Antwerp Red*, a variety of Red Ochre. **1904** *Encycl. Amer.* XIV. 341 Two main types of the Belgian homer have been distinguished as the Antwerp and the Liege varieties, the former being larger but less graceful in form than the latter. **1934** M. Thomas *Dict. Embroidery Stitches* 138 *Knot stitch*, also known as Antwerp Edging Stitch, and Knotted Blanket Stitch. **1940** R. Mayer *Artist's Hand-Bk.* (1951) ii. 41 *Antwerp blue*, a pale variety of Prussian blue made by reducing pure Prussian blue with 75% of an inert pigment, usually alumina hydrate. **1960** H. Hayward *Antique Collecting* 15/2 *Antwerp lace*, pillow lace, strong and heavy looking, the patterns outlined in a *cordonnet* of thick untwisted thread and made at the same time as the *fond chant* ground.

antym(e, obs. form of anthem.

antyteme, var. antetheme, *Obs.*, a text.

anuf, obs. form of enough.

anufene, var. anovenon *adv. Obs.* on from above.

anui, obs. form of annoy *sb.* and *v.*

†**a'nunction, anonxcion.** *Obs. rare*[−1]. [a. OFr. *enonction*:—L. *inunctiōn-em*, n. of action f. *inungĕre*: see anoint *v.*] Anointing, unction.

1470 Harding *Chron.* lxxiv, This was their charge and verey dewe seruise, Of anonxcion tyme to don and excersise.

†**a'nunder**, *prep.* *Obs.* or *dial.* Also 3–4 **anundyr, anonder, -yr.** [f. an *prep.* + under; formed in the same way as *a-bove*, *a-round*, *a-fore*, etc. with the full *an-* before a vowel. Not in OE.]

1. Of local position: Under.

a **1300** *K. Horn* 567 Þer nis non betere anonder sunne. *c* **1325** *E.E. Allit. P.* A. 166 So schon þat schene anvnder schore. *a* **1400** *Octouian* 549 Fette water as hem was nede The roche anondyr. [Still used in northern dialect.]

2. Of condition: Under the rule of.

c **1220** *Orison* in *Lamb. Hom.* 193 Al is Godes riche anunder þine honden. *c* **1300** *St. Brand.* 1 A thousend monekes that alle anunder him were.

†**a'nuppe**, *prep. Obs.* Forms: 1 **an uppan, on uppan, 2 an uppen, on uppen, 2–3 anuppe, anoppe, onuppen;** also 2 **anuppon.** [f. an *prep.* + *uppan* dat. sing. of *up*: cf. *on-bufan*, *on-foran*.] On the top of, upon, both of position and direction.

c **1000** *Ags. Gosp.* Matt. xxi. 44 He tobrysð þone þe he on uppan fylð. *c* **1160** *Hatton G.* ibid., Þe he on uppen falð. *c* **1175** *Lamb. Hom.* 43 He walde anuppon his underlinges mid wohe motien. *Ibid.* 133 Sum of þe sede feol an uppe þe stane. *c* **1200** *Trin. Coll. Hom.* 107 Þat no man werpe þe gilt of his sinne anuppen god. **1250** Lay. 1916 Was þe cleue swiþe heh: ware anoppe hii fohte.

anura, -ous, variants of anoura, -ous.

anuran (əˈnʊərən, -jʊə-), *a. Zool.* [f. mod.L. *Anura* (J. Hogg 1839, in *Mag. Nat. Hist.* 270) + -an; cf. anourous *a.*] Of or pertaining to the Anura, an order of tailless amphibians. Hence as *sb.*

1900 *Amer. Naturalist* XXXIV. 689 The segmentation of several other anuran eggs that contain much yolk has not as yet been described. **1907** E. J. Bles in J. G. Kerr *Wk. of J. S. Budgett* xvi. 443 *(title)* Notes on Anuran Development. **1926** J. S. Huxley *Essays Pop. Sci.* 293 The different behaviour of the limbs and the tail in urodeles and anurans. **1932** —— *Probl. Rel. Growth* vi. 181 Even the normal growth of the Anuran tadpole's limbs is slightly heterogonic.

anuri, variant of anour *v. Obs.* to adore.

anuria (æˈnjʊərɪə). *Path.* [a. mod.L. *anūria* f. Gr. ἀν priv. + οὖρ-ον urine: see -y. Cf. Fr. *anurie*.] Absence or lack of urine.

1838 R. Willis *Urinary Diseases* I. ii. 28 The title under which this suspension or abolition of the secreting office of the kidney is usually spoken of in this century, is *Ischuria renalis*; but as ischuria means an impeded discharge of urine, I prefer adopting the title Anuria. **1876** Harley *Mat. Med.* 763 It is eliminated by the kidneys, and deposited in.. its straight tubules, producing anuria. **1894** *Lancet* 15 Dec. 1426/2 He mentioned the case of a man, now alive and well, who had twice had complete anuria for ten days. **1922** in F. W. Price *Textbk. Practice Med.* xv. 1097 *Anuria*, suppression, as opposed to retention of urine.

‖**anus** (ˈeɪnəs). [L.]

1. The posterior opening of the alimentary canal in animals, through which the excrements are ejected.

1658 J. R. tr. *Mouffet's Theat. Ins.* 1122 Take salt flesh.. and thrust that into the Anus. **1748** Hartley *Observ. Man* I. ii. §2. ¶37 The whole alimentary Duct, quite down to the Anus. **1872** Nicholson *Palæont.* 321 The fins.. are always placed far back, in the neighbourhood of the anus.

2. An opening at the base of a flower.

1730 Martyn in *Phil. Trans.* XXXVI. 380 These Flowers have no Anus at the Base. **1880** *Syd. Soc. Lex.*, *Anus*, in Botany, the inferior aperture of a monopetalous flower.

†**an'venom**, *v. Obs. rare.* [variant of envenom: see an- *pref.* 4.] To envenom, to poison.

1340 *Ayenb.* 27 Þe ilke zenne anuenymeþ alþeruerst þe herte of þe enuious. *Ibid.* 50 Þe eyr is anvenymed of þe dede. *a* **1400** *Cov. Myst.* 75 My synful steppys anvempnyd the grounde.

anvil (ˈænvɪl), *sb.* Forms: 1 **onfilti, onfilt(e, anfilte,** 4 **anfelt, -uylt, anefelt, -feld,** 4–5 **anfeld, -velt,** 5 **aneuelt, anuylde, anduell,** 5–6 **andfelde,** 6 **anvelde, anuilde, anuielde, (hanfeld), and(e)vile,** 6–7 **anfeeld, anvild, anvile, anvill,** 6– **anvil.** [Etymol. uncertain. OE. *ǫnfilti*, is prob. cogn. w. ODu. dial. *aenvilte* (Verdam I. 184), and OHG. *anafalz*; f. *an*, *on*, prep. + a possible **filt-an* to weld, cf. *felt*, Ger. *filz*, and *falz* in *falz-ambosz*. The *f* has become *v* as in *silver*, and the final *t*, passing through *d*, is lost, as is frequent in dialects.

Onfilti, anafalz, can hardly be distinct from synonymous forms with *b*: OHG. *anabolz*, LG. *anebolt, anebelte, ambult*, ODu. *aenbilt*, usually derived from **aen-billen* = '*aankloppen*, to strike upon' (Verdam 80); but more prob. an early variant of *aenvilte* above, due to some confusion. In OHG. *anabolz*, Sievers suggests a confusion of *anafalz* with the distinct *anabôz, anapôz*, MHG. *aneboz*, mod.G. *ambosz*, from *an* + *bôz-an*, Eng. BEAT. Mod.Du. *aanbeeld, ambeld*, seems assimilated to *beelden*, to form, fashion.]

1. The block (usually of iron) on which the smith hammers and shapes the metal which he is working.

a800 *Corpus Gl.* (Sweet *O.E.T.*) 1071 *Incuda*, onfilti. **c1000** ÆLFRIC *Gram.* ix. §33. 60 *Incus*, anfilt. **c1000** in Wright *Voc.* 286/2 *Cudo*, anfilte. **c1369** CHAUCER *Blaunche* 1165 As his brothers hamers ronge, Vpon his anuelt vp and downe [*v.r.* anuelet]. **c1380** *Sir Ferumb.* 1308 Anuylt, tange & slegge. **1388** WYCLIF *Ecclus.* xxxviii. 29 A smyth sittynge bisidis the anefelt. **1398** TREVISA *Barth. De P.R.* XVI. iv, Golde..bitwene þe anfelde [**1495** andfelde] and þe hamoure ..strecchep in to golde foyle. **1413** LYDG. *Pylgr. Sowle* IV. xxx. (1483) 78 Harder than the hamour or the aneuelt. **1483** CAXTON *Gold. Leg.* 358/1 They smyte on the stythye or anduell. **?a1500** *Virgilius* in Thoms *E.E. Pr. Rom.* II. 44 They smyte vpon a anuilde. **1530** PALSGR. 740 To stryke with his hammer upon his anvelde. **1543** TRAHERON *Vigo's Chirurg.* IV. 14d, A styth, or hanfeld. **1589** WARNER *Alb. Eng.* VI. xxx. (1612) 147 Vulcan..limping from the Anfeeld. **1607** HIERON *Wks.* I. 439 Wee be like the smiths dog, who, the harder the anuile is beaten on, lieth by, and sleepes the sounder. **1611** BIBLE *Isa.* xli. 7 Him that smote the anuill. **1808** SCOTT *Marm.* v. vi, The armourer's anvil clashed and rang.

2. a. *fig.* (the whole expression being usually metaphorical).

1534 LD. BERNERS *Gold. Bk. M. Aurel.* (1546) E ij, My spyrite is betwene the harde anuielde and the importunate hammer. **c1593** SPENSER *Sonnet* xxxii, The playnts and prayers with which I Doe beat on th' anduyle of her stubberne wit. **1605** CAMDEN *Rem.* 200 Hammering me vpon the anvild. **1677** R. GILPIN *Dæmonol. Sacr.* (1867) 214 Our present posture doth furnish him [Satan] with arguments; he forgeth his javelins upon our anvil. **1845** FORD *Handbk. Spain* i. 59 They have yet to learn that the stomach is the anvil whereon health is forged. **1864** BURTON *Scot Abr.* I. i. 34 Hardened on the anvil of a war for national freedom. **1883** SIR H. BRAND in *Standard* 18 May 3/3 Matters that, so to speak, are on the anvil of the House of Commons.

b. *phr.* **on or upon the anvil**: in preparation, in hand.

1623 HOWELL *Lett.* (1650) II. 29 Matters while they are in agitation and upon the anvill. **a1674** CLARENDON *Hist. Reb.* I. II. 110 The Earl of Strafford..whose destruction was then upon the anvil. **1755** *Mem. Capt. P. Drake* II. iii. 154 There was Rumours of a Peace being on the Anvil. **1785** BURKE *Nabob of Arcot* Wks. 1842 I. 319 He has now on the anvil another scheme.

3. a. *transf.* Anything resembling a smith's anvil in shape or use.

1678 BUTLER *Hud.* III. i. 340 When less Delinquents have been scourg'd, And Hemp on wooden Anvils forg'd. **1881** GREENER *Gun* 294 The anvil is shaped like an escutcheon, and is inserted in the cup of the cap, with the point against the detonating powder.

b. *esp.* in *Phys.* One of the bones of the ear; so called from its being struck by another bone called the 'hammer.'

[**1594** T. B. *La Primaud. Fr. Acad.* II. To Reader, Who hath fashioned the instruments of hearing in the head like to a hammer and an anvile.] **1687** *Death's Vision* iii. 21 When the Perceptive Hammer shall not..Consign Prescribed Blow Unto the Wonted Anvil. **1718** J. CHAMBERLAYNE *Relig. Philos.* I. xiii. §5 The Auditory Bones are four in Number, the Hammer, the Anvil, etc. **1879** CALDERWOOD *Mind & Brain* 71 The head of the hammer rests on the central bone known as the anvil.

c. In full ***anvil cloud*** (see quots.).

1894 W. C. LEY *Cloudland* v. 80 It is not difficult to understand the nature of the environment in which the Anvil cloud has its birth. **1903** S. BARBER *Cloud World* 108 *Anvil Cloud.* The 'Anvil' shape of a cloud is generally regarded as one of the best intimations of an approaching gale. **1920** G. A. CLARKE *Clouds* iii. 39 One special feature of cumulo-nimbus is the development above the domed portion of a mass of condensation which has a shape very closely resembling an anvil, if judged by its profile appearance, but which is really a tabular flat-topped mass, rounded in plan and widest at the top. The edges of this 'anvil' are frayed out into the fibrous form associated with the cirrus clouds.

4. *Comb.* and *Attrib.*, as ***anvil-block, -ding, -maker***, etc.; also **anvil-beater**, a smith; **anvil-headed** *a.*, having a head shaped like an anvil; **anvil-proof**, the standard of hardness of an anvil; **anvil rock** (see quot.); **anvil-smith**, a forger of anvils.

1677 *Cleveland's Poems* Ep. Ded. A iij b, Venus is again unequally yoaked with a sooty Anvile-beater. **1870** BRYANT *Homer* II. XVIII. 219 He spake, and from his anvil-block arose. **1876** G. M. HOPKINS *Wr. Deutschland* (1918) st. 10 With an anvil-ding And with fire in him forge thy will. **1851** MELVILLE *Whale* xlvii. 303 The anvil-headed whale. **1616** BEAUM. & FL. *Faithf. Fr.* II. iii, Though their scull-caps be of anvil-proof, This blade shall hammer some of 'em. **1862** DANA *Man. Geol.* 330 Above the twelfth [coal bed in Kentucky] there is the massive Sandstone..called the Anvil Rock, from the form of two masses of it in South-western Kentucky. **1831** J. HOLLAND *Manuf. Metal* I. 90 Some anvil-smiths..forge the upper part..out of one piece of iron.

anvil ('ænvɪl), *v.* [f. prec. sb.]

1. *trans.* To fashion on the anvil; chiefly *fig.*

1607 DEKKER *Wh. Babylon* F iij, Whilest our thunderbolts Are anuiling abroad. **c1700** *Gentl. Instr.* (1732) 303 You are now anvilling out some petty Revenge. **1748** RICHARDSON *Clarissa* (1811) VIII. 267 A roguery..ready anvilled and hammered for execution.

2. *intr.* To work at an anvil.

1882 *Manch. Guard.* 7 June, Thomas anvilled away at burning horse-shoes.

anvilling ('ænvɪlɪŋ), *vbl. sb. rare.* [f. ANVIL *v.* + -ING[1].] Hammering out; chiefly *fig.*

1662 PHILLIPS *Dict.* Ded., What Siftings, Anvelings, Traversings, there ought to be of Authours.

anwald, -weald, var. ONWALD, *Obs.*, power.

an'xietude. *rare*—⁰. [ad. L. *anxietūdo.*] = ANXIETY.

1864 in WEBSTER.

anxiety (æŋ'zaɪətɪ). [ad. L. *anxietāt-em*, n. of quality f. *anxi-us*: see ANXIOUS, and -TY.]

1. The quality or state of being anxious; uneasiness or trouble of mind about some uncertain event; solicitude, concern.

c1525 MORE *De Quat. Noviss.* Wks. 1557, 91 There dyed he without grudge, without anxietie. **a1631** DONNE *Select.* (1840) 25 Temporal prosperity comes always accompanied with much anxiety. **1714** *Spect.* No. 615 ¶1 It is the Business of Religion and Philosophy to free us from all unnecessary Anxieties. **1849** MACAULAY *Hist. Eng.* I. 200 The United Provinces saw with anxiety the progress of his arms.

2. Strained or solicitous desire (*for* or *to effect* some purpose).

1769 *Junius Lett.* i. 3 Anxiety..for the general welfare. **1833** I. TAYLOR *Fanat.* viii. 304 Every man's anxiety to obtain for himself the inestimable pearl of genuine knowledge.

3. *Path.* 'A condition of agitation and depression, with a sensation of tightness and distress in the præcordial region.' *Syd. Soc. Lex.* 1880.

1661 LOVELL *Hist. Anim. & Min.* 368 The paine and anxiety of the ventricle. **1732** ARBUTHNOT *Rules of Diet* 303 The Blood..pressing upon the heart creates great Anxieties. **1844** T. GRAHAM *Dom. Med.* 277 [Angina pectoris] is an acute constrictive pain..attended with anxiety, difficulty of breathing, and a sense of suffocation.

4. *Psychiatry.* A morbid state of mind characterized by unjustified or excessive anxiety, which may be generalized or attached to particular situations. Freq. *attrib.* and *Comb.*, as ***anxiety-producing, -ridden*** adjs.; **anxiety complex** (cf. COMPLEX *sb.* 3); **anxiety hysteria**, a form of anxiety neurosis (see quot. 1923); **anxiety neurosis** [tr. G. *angstneurose* (Freud 1895, in *Neurolog. Zentralbl.* XIV. 55)], **anxiety state**, names technically applied to such a condition of anxiety.

1904 G. S. HALL *Adolescence* I. iv. 285 The anxiety neurosis was relatively more common in women than in men. **1909** A. A. BRILL tr. *Freud's Sel. Papers on Hysteria* vi. 134, I call this symptom-complex 'anxiety neurosis' (Angstneurose) because the sum of its components can be grouped around the main symptom of anxiety. *Ibid.* vi. 136 A quantum of freely floating anxiety which controls the choice of ideas by expectation. **1912** *Ibid.* (ed. 2) xii. 210 We must slightly modify our procedure in anxiety-hysteria (phobias). **1913** *Lancet* 26 Apr. 1184/1 Anxiety dreams and anxiety neuroses represent a breaking down of this compromise. **1923** R. GABLER tr. *Stekel's Conditions of Nervous Anxiety* I. iii. 20 Freud..proposed to distinguish two sorts of anxiety neuroses: one with a pure somatic basis, Freud's genuine anxiety neurosis, and one with a psychical basis, which he terms 'anxiety hysteria'. **1926** W. McDOUGALL *Outl. Abnormal Psychol.* xiv. 269 The first factor in the production of the anxiety state is the bringing into activity of the instinct of flight. **1931** M. C. D'ARCY *Nature of Belief* ii. 39 Another cause for failure in reasoning is what has been called an anxiety state. Those who suffer from this are unable to make up their minds: they have had their balance upset by some shock to their old convictions, and as a consequence they oscillate to and fro. **1942** A. L. ROWSE *Cornish Childhood* 204 It undoubtedly produced an anxiety-complex, the combination of working hard with worry. **1958** *New Biol.* XXVII. 34 The tabu word which is presented subthreshold..is classified as an anxiety-producing word. **1960** C. DAY LEWIS *Buried Day* iv. 64, I went to school, entering..a world insulated, self-important, artificial, anxiety-ridden.

5. Phr. ***Age of Anxiety***: the title of W. H. Auden's poem applied as a catch-phrase to any period characterized by anxiety or danger.

1947 W. H. AUDEN (*title*) The Age of Anxiety. **1953** *Economist* 7 Nov. 413/1 The main change is to be found between the nineteenth and the twentieth century outlooks. .. A survey which ignores it..fails to achieve a complete relevance to the current Age of Anxiety. **1958** *Times* 11 Nov. 4/4 He [*sc.* Jackson Pollock] was very much an American product of the age of anxiety.

†an'xiferous, *a. Obs.*—⁰ [f. L. *anxifer* sorrow-bringing (f. *anxi-us* + *-fer* bringing) + -OUS.] 'Bringing sorrow, causing anguish.' Blount *Glossogr.* 1656.

anxious ('æŋkʃəs), *a.* [f. L. *anxi-us* troubled in mind (f. *ang-ĕre* to choke, distress) + -OUS.]

1. a. Troubled or uneasy in mind about some uncertain event; being in painful or disturbing suspense; concerned, solicitous.

1623 COCKERAM, *Anxious*, Carefull. **1636** RUTHERFORD *Lett.* vi, Often anxious, and cast down for the case of my oppressed brother. **1711** POPE *Rape Lock* II. 142 They wait, Anxious, and trembling for the birth of Fate. **1810** SCOTT *Lady of L.* II. xxxvii, Allan strained his anxious eye.

b. Const., *of* an issue dreaded (*obs.*); *for* an issue desired; *about* a thing or person involved in uncertain issues.

1711 STEELE *Spect.* No. 4 ¶1 It being the worst way in the world to Fame, to be too anxious about it. **a1735** GRANVILLE (J.) Anxious of neglect, suspecting change. **1849** MACAULAY *Hist. Eng.* I. 197 The counsellors of Charles..were anxious for their own safety.

2. a. Fraught with trouble or solicitude, distressing, worrying. (*Obs.* exc. where it can be explained as a transferred use of 1, as ***anxious cares***, i.e. such as anxious people cherish. So ***anxious seats, benches*** (*U.S.*): those set apart for anxious inquirers; see also quot. 1839).

1667 MILTON *P.L.* VIII. 185 Life, from which God hath bid dwell farr off all anxious cares. **1679** PENN *Addr. Prot.* II. iv. (1692) 117 That which is most of all Anxious is that Morality is denyed to be Christianity. **1744** HARRIS *3 Treat.* (1841) 52 Is not both the possession and pursuit of wealth, to those who really love it, ever anxious? **1832** F. TROLLOPE *Dom. Manners Amer.* I. vii. 111 The poor creatures..seated themselves on the 'anxious benches'. **1835** REED & MATHESON *Visit to Amer. Churches* I. 13, I was speedily led to conclude that..[the preacher] was about to try the anxious seat. **1837** HALIBURTON *Clockm.* (1862) 232 Settin' on the anxious benches. **1839** MARRYAT *Diary Amer.* II. xi. 184 In front of the pulpit there was a space railed off, and strewed with straw, which I was told was the *Anxious seat*, and on which sat those who were touched by their consciences or the discourse of the preacher. **1888** J. KIRKLAND *McVeys* 19 'Seekers' were sought for and urged forward to the 'anxious seat' or 'mourners bench' by zealous friends.

b. ***on the anxious bench*** or ***seat*** (fig.), in a state of anxiety. *U.S.*

1839 *Knickerbocker* XIII. 345 He did look as if he had been on 'the anxious seat', as he used to say, when things puzzled him. **1862** MRS. STOWE *Pearl Orr's Isl.* II. i. 159 What a life you did lead me in them days! I think you kep' me on the anxious seats a pretty middlin' spell. **1906** *N.Y. Even. Post* 23 Nov. 1 The entire diplomatic corps at Havana is..on the 'anxious bench'. **1910** W. M. RAINE *B. O'Conner* 25 That extra hour and a half cinches our escape, and we weren't on the anxious seat any without it.

3. Full of desire and endeavour; solicitous; earnestly desirous (*to effect* some purpose).

1742 R. BLAIR *Grave* 94 The gentle heart, anxious to please. **1794** NELSON in Nicolas *Disp.* I. 434 The General seems as anxious as any of us to expedite the fall of the place. **1843** CARLYLE *Past & Pr.* (1858) 171 Anxious no longer to be dumb. **1860** TYNDALL *Glac.* I. §13. 93, I was anxious to see many parts of it once more.

'anxiously, *adv.* [f. prec. + -LY[2].] In an anxious manner, with painful uncertainty; solicitously.

1673 *Lady's Call.* I. v. §45 To be very anxiously careful about her garments. **a1700** DRYDEN *Imit. Horace*, Thou.. what the Gallic arms will do, Art anxiously inquisitive to know. **1824** DIBDIN *Libr. Comp.* 233 Never was a history more anxiously expected. **1875** HOWELLS *Foregone Concl.* I He peered anxiously about him.

'anxiousness. *rare.* [f. as prec. + -NESS.] The quality of being anxious, anxiety.

1658 MANTON *Exp. Jude* Wks. 1871 V. 21 An anxiousness about their everlasting state. **1798** SOUTHEY *Occas. Pieces* xi. Wks. II. 241 A husband's love, a father's anxiousness. **1847** BUSHNELL *Chr. Nurt.* II. ii. (1861) 266 Where there is but little faith, there is apt to be great anxiousness.

any ('ɛnɪ), *a.* and *pron.* Forms: 1–3 **æniȝ, æni,** 2 **anyȝ, eini, eani,** 3 **ænij, anij, ænie,** 2–6 **eni,** 3–7 **ani,** 3–6 **anie, eny,** 4 **enye, anye,** 6 **anny,** 4– **any;** 4– **ony(e, onie.** Contracted: 2–3 **ei,** 3 **æi, eie, æie.** [OE. *ǽniȝ*, cogn. w. OS. *ênig*, OFris. *ênich, ienig*, OHG. *einîc*, mod.G. *einig.* Du. *eenig*, f. *án* one (in umlaut *ǽn*) + *-iȝ, -ig*, adj. ending (see -Y[1]), here perhaps diminutive; cf. L. *ullus* = *unulus*. Of the ME. forms, *eny, ei*, seem to have been southern, *any* midl., *ony* midl. and northern. The living word in mod.Eng. is *eny*. Fem. and pl. forms in *-e* existed in ME.; the word is now invariable, even pronominally.]

Primarily adj., but also from the earliest period used *absol.* or *pronominally* both in sing. and pl.

I. *simple adj.*

1. *gen.* An indeterminate derivative of *one*, or rather of its weakened adj. form *a, an*, in which the idea of unity (or, in plural, *partitivity*) is subordinated to that of indifference as to the particular one or ones that may be selected. In *sing.* = A —— no matter which; a —— whichever, of whatever kind, of whatever quantity. In *pl.* = Some —— no matter which, of what kind, or how many.

a. Its primary use is in interrogative, hypothetical, and conditional forms of speech, as 'Has any Englishman seen it?' *i.e.* an Englishman —— I care not which; 'if it do any harm,' *i.e.* harm, no matter of what kind.

c1000 *Ags. Gosp.* John iv. 33 Hwæðer æniȝ man him mete brohte. **c1175** *Lamb. Hom.* 33 ȝif eani mon bið inumen. *Ibid.* 121 Lokiað hweðer enies monnes sar beo iliche mine sare. *Ibid.* 201 Hwi luue ich ei þing bute þe one? **c1220** *Ibid.* 189 Al þet ich abbe..wiþ eini lim mis ifeled. **c1200** ORMIN 4423

Off aniȝ ifell wille. **1205** LAY. 4270 ȝef æi mon him liðere dude. *Ibid.* 8287 þurh æni cræft [**1250** eni craft]. *c* **1230** *Ancr. R.* 124 ȝif ei mon oðer ei wummon.. misdeð ou. **1340** *Ayenb.* 49 Huanne þe man heþ uelaȝrede myd enye wyfmane. **1366** MAUNDEV. 32 ȝif ony man do thereinne ony maner metalle. *c* **1449** PECOCK *Repr.* I. ii. 8 If eny man can be sikir for eny tyme. **1480** CAXTON *Chron. Eng.* ccxxxii. 251 By hym or by ony other. **1535** COVERDALE *Gal.* vi. 1 Yf eny man be ouertaken of a faute. **1590** SHAKS. *Com. Err.* I. i. 19 If any Siracusian borne Come to the Bay of Ephesus, he dies. **1611** BIBLE *Ps.* iv. 6 Who wil shew vs any good? **1849** MACAULAY *Hist. Eng.* I. 37 The best governed country of which he had any knowledge. **1860** GEN. P. THOMPSON *Audi Alt. Part.* III. cxvii. 54 Was there any the slightest indication?

b. With a preceding negative (explicit or implicit) it denies of a person or thing, without limitation as to *which*, and thus, constructively, of *every* being or thing of the kind. It thus becomes an emphatic negative, with its unqualified or uncompromising scope brought into prominence; = None at all; none of any kind, quantity, or number, even the minutest; not even one; as 'I could not think of any thing else,' 'he was forbidden to enter any house,' 'to prevent any loss.'

c **1000** *Ags. Gosp.* Mark xi. 16 He ne ȝeþafode þæt æniȝ man æniȝ fæt ðurh þam templ bære. **1205** LAY. 31209 Nas hit nauere iseid.. þat æuer ær weore æi swa muchel ferde ..þurh ænie king to-gadere. *c* **1449** PECOCK *Repr.* I. xix, Neuere save in late daies was eny clok telling þe houris. **1509** FISHER *Wks.* I. 2, I shall not declare vnto you ony parte of the epystle. **1658** SIR T. BROWNE *Hydriot.* Ded., We present not these as any strange sight. **1712** STEELE *Spect.* No. 503 ¶2 The Offence does not come under any law. **1790** BURKE *Fr. Rev.* 23 It ought not to be done at any time. **1870** NICHOLSON *Zool.* (1880) 463 In.. fish there is never any breast-bone.

c. In affirmative sentences it asserts concerning a being or thing of the sort named, without limitation as to which, and thus constructively of *every* one of them, since every one may in turn be taken as a representative: thus 'any chemist will tell you'; 'anything that I can do is at your service'; 'you may have anything almost for the asking.'

a **1300** *Cursor M.* 700 Þe nedder.. was more wise þen any beest. **1413** LYDG. *Pylgr. Sowle* v. xiv. 79 Hit is ful hard to ony creature to maken declaracion. **1592** SHAKS. *Rom. & Jul.* v. i. 67 Mantua's law Is death to any he that vtters them. **1598** —— *Merry W.* I. i. 11 Any time these three hundred yeeres. **1699** BENTLEY *Phal.* Pref. 67 The Director was consulted by him upon any Difficulty. **1798** FERRIAR *Illustr. Sterne* ii. 26 That enable any person to give an answer to any question. **1861** BUCKLE *Civiliz.* II. vi. 589, I challenge any one to contradict my assertion.

d. *at any rate, in any case*: whatever may be the circumstances; at all events.

1847 HELPS *Friends in C.* Ser. I. (1857) II. 53 Which they at any rate were not good enough for. **1831** CARLYLE *Sart. Res.* III. vii, But, in any case, hast thou not still Preaching enough?

e. ***any old***: any... whatever. ***any old how***: see ANYHOW. (Cf. OLD *a.*) *slang* (orig. *U.S.*).

1896 ADE *Artie* xviii. 171 Any old farmer.. could buy up him and a hundred more like him. **1911** R. W. CHAMBERS *Common Law* ii. 63 'Would you like to have a chance to study?'.. 'Study? What?' 'Sculpture—any old thing!' **1916** 'B. CABLE' *Doing their Bit* ii. 23 Mails take any old time to do their journey. **1918** W. J. LOCKE *Rough Road* v, Mate, Bill, Joe—any old name. **1940** *War Illustr.* 12 Jan. p. ii/2 It is just one man's reactions to circumstances of the moment and his thoughts on 'any old thing'. **1958** B. HAMILTON *Too Much Water* iv. 78 His steward.. just shoves some fruit in his cabin, any old time.

2. a. With a specially quantitative force = A quantity or number however great or small. (When unemphatic, expressed in French by the partitive article *du, de la, des.*) 'Have you any milk, any eggs?' But not in affirmative sentences, as 'any milk will do,' *i.e.* any *sort* of milk: see sense 3.

1526 TINDALE *Luke* xxiv. 41 Haue ye here eny meate? [So in *Cranmer, Genev.*, and **1611**; WYCLIF, ony thing that schal be eten, *Rhem.*, any thing to be eaten.] **1660** BOYLE *New Exper. Phys.-Mech.* i. 21 Whil'st there is any plenty of Air in the Receiver. **1711** *Lond. Gaz.* mmmmdccclxiii/4 Very little if any white about him. **1854** SCOFFERN in *Orr's Circ. Sc.*, Chem. 507 Whilst any lead.. remains to be removed.

b. A large or considerable (number, quantity, etc.). *colloq.*

1861 O. W. NORTON *Army Lett.* (1903) 26 In the woods near us we found any quantity of grapes and chinquapins. **1862** *Ibid.* 50 We cut down any number of the poles. **1876** *Coursing Calendar* 125 Irish Nell led any number of lengths.

3. With a specially qualitative force: Of any kind or sort whatever; = earlier ANYKINS. Often *depreciatory*: Any, however imperfect. Cf. ANYBODY 2 b, ANYTHING 2, ANYWAY 2.

1866 RUSKIN *Cr. Wild Olive* 98 This place.. this moorland torrent-bitten, snow-blighted; this any place where God lets down the ladder. **1868** M. PATTISON *Academ. Organ.* 2 The danger is.. that any reform should be adopted because some reform is required.

II. *absolutely*, etc.

4. a. *absol.* esp. when the substantive to which it refers has been already expressed, or when it is followed by *of*, as 'any of these books, any of the liquid.'

c **1175** *Lamb. Hom.* 65 ȝif eni us misdoð awiht. *Ibid.* 35 Ga .. þer eni of þine cunne lið in. *c* **1220** *Hali Meid.* 33 Eni of his limen. **1340** *Ayenb.* 5 Ine enie of þe ilke hestes. **1382** WYCLIF *James* i. 5 If ony of ȝou nedeth wisdom axe he of God. **1526** TINDALE, *ibid.*, If eny of you lacke wysdome. **1583** GOLDING *Calvin on Deut.* xlvi. 276 As excellent a lesson as a man shall read any. **1611** SHAKS. *Wint. T.* III. iii. 136 If there be any of him left, Ile bury it. **1711** STEELE *Spect.* No. 154 ¶2 How do you know more than any of us? **1883** *Scotsman* 11 July 5/3 The mean temperature of the month was lower than any recorded since 1879.

b. Colloq. phr. ***not having any*** (with verb 'to be'): to want no part in something; to turn down a proposition or to reject an overture of friendship. Also, more positively, to refuse to tolerate a situation.

1902 J. MILNE *Epistles of Atkins* ix. 166 A Boer cries to the trenches of the besieged, 'Have you any whiskey?' The cry back is 'Yes', and an invitation to call for it; but no, 'he isn't having any'. **1918** KIPLING *Land & Sea Tales* (1923) vii. 116 They tried to get into touch with the natives... But the natives weren't havin' any. They took to the bush. **1923** D. H. LAWRENCE *Studies in Classic Amer. Lit.* vii. 133 Hester urges Dimmesdale to go away with her, to a new country, to a new life. He isn't having any. **1943** J. B. PRIESTLEY *Daylight on Saturday* xxii. 177 They wanted me to be in it. But I wasn't having any, thanks. **1955** A. L. ROWSE *Expansion Eliz. England* v. 171 Lady Mary Hastings was thought of for promotion to the bed of Ivan the Terrible. She was not having any.

†**5.** One of *two* things indifferently; either. (*Obs.*, but still common in dialects, esp. north.)

c **1386** CHAUCER *Friar's T.* 233 If eny [*v.r.* any, ony] of us have more than other, Let him.. part it with his brother. *c* **1449** PECOCK *Repr.* 558 Eny of hem bothe. **1540** COVERDALE *Confut. Standish* Wks. II. 381 Doth any of both these examples prove that, etc.? **1585** THYNNE in *Animadv.* Introd. 78 Not at all.. benefited by anie of them both.

6. *pronominally.* = Any one, anybody; in *pl.* any persons.

c **950** *Lindisf. G.* Mark xi. 16 And ne ȝelefde þætte æniȝ ofer-ferede fæt ðerh þam tempel. **1220** ORMIN 9938 He nollde nohht þatt aniȝ shollde dwellenn. *c* **1230** *Cott. Hom.* 271 Is ani riccher þen þu? **1297** R. GLOUC. 376 ȝyf þat eny hym wraþþede. **1472** SIR J. PASTON in *Lett.* III. 65 Yit have I.. nott lefte any at hys most neede. **1562** J. HEYWOOD *Prov. & Epigr.* (1867) 89 Please they any, That serue many? Nay. **1611** BIBLE 2 *Pet.* iii. 9 The Lord is.. not willing that any should perish. **1705** ADDISON *Italy* Pref., [He] has wrote a more correct Account of Italy than any before him. **1821** KEATS *Lamia* 389 Unknown.. to any, but those two alone.

7. a. *adverbially*, esp. with comparative adjs., as ***any sooner, any better***: In any degree, to any extent, at all. (Cf. *somewhat* better, etc.) ***any more***: see MORE *adv.* 4 a.

c **1400** *Epiph.* (Turnb. 1843) 136 Or he come any nere [*i.e.* nearer]. **1490** CAXTON *Eneydos* xix. 72 To presse me wyth wordes ony more. **1598** SHAKS. *Merry W.* IV. ii. 128 You are not to goe loose any longer. *c* **1680** BEVERIDGE *Serm.* (1729) I. 503 Few that do any more than profess it. **1711** STEELE *Spect.* No. 154 ¶4 Before you go any farther. **1834** H. MILLER *Scenes & Leg.* xxx. (1857) 450 Having slept scarcely any all the night. *c* **1875** L. STEPHEN *Hours Libr.* Ser. I. 347 Few people.. would be any the worse for the study.

b. At all. (Without comparative adj. or adv.) *dial.* (occas. *slang*) and *U.S.*

1735 [see GENTLE *v.* 2 b]. **1780** S. HOLTEN *Jrnl.* in *Essex Inst. Coll.* (1920) LVI. 96, I have not traveled any this day on account of my horses. **1817** *Analectic Mag.* (Philad.) IX. 437 (Th.), If our readers are any like ourselves, we think they cannot help laughing. **1869** 'MARK TWAIN' *Innoc. Abroad* iv. 45 It is a good tune—you can't improve it any. **1886** R. E. G. COLE *Gloss. Words S.W. Linc.* 7 He's not worked any sin' June. She can't sit up any. **1890** KIPLING in *Harper's Wkly.* 22 Nov. 911/1 You don't want being made more drunk any. **1911** H. P. FAIRCHILD *Greek Immigr. to U.S.* 101 Costa was not used to springs, and he did not mind this any. **1937** A. CHRISTIE *Death on Nile* xxv. 245 We're used to responsibility. Doesn't worry us any. **1958** *Punch* 17 Sept. 386/1 This couldn't have helped the Yogi any.

8. any one. a. as *adj.* (ˌɛnɪˈwʌn). Any single or individual; **b.** *absol.* as in 'any one of them'; **c.** *pron.* (ˈɛnɪwʌn). Anybody, any person; as in, Has any one heard of it? Did you meet any one? ***any one's*** (or ***anyone's***) ***guess***, etc.: see ANYBODY 3.

c **1449** PECOCK *Repr.*, Any one person. **1577** *St. August. Manuell* 19 Neither soule, flesh, nor reason can in any one thyng please thee. **1690** W. WALKER *Idiom. Anglo-Lat.* 26, I understand not any one word. **1711** STEELE *Spect.* No. 104 ¶1 To be negligent of what any one thinks of you. **1833** HT. MARTINEAU *Vanderput & S.* i. 1 That any one district of Amsterdam was busier than another at any one hour. **1860** L. HARCOURT *Diaries G. Rose* I. 4 He never abuses any one. **1958** N. F. SIMPSON *Resounding Tinkle* I. ii, in *Observer Plays* 240 How close we're getting to the original tonight is anyone's guess.

9. In *comb.* with interrog. words, which then become indefinite: see ANYHOW, etc.

anybody (ˈɛnɪbɒdɪ, -bədɪ), *sb.* or *pron.*

1. comb. of ANY and BODY *sb.* in the sense of *person* (as in *nobody, somebody*): Any person, any one. It has all the varieties of use noted under ANY *a.* 1, as in 'Does anybody know? I do not see anybody. Anybody can do that.' Formerly written as two words: *any body*; but, when so written now, *body* has its ordinary sense: 'the velocity with which any body moves.'

1490 CAXTON *Eneydos* xxii. 81 Without to notyfye them to eny body lyuynge. **1598** SHAKS. *Merry W.* I. iv. 4 If he doe .. finde any body in the house. **1813** MISS AUSTEN *Pride & Prej.* vi. 194 Any body who would hear her. **1855** MACAULAY *Hist. Eng.* III. 13 Impossible to make an arrangement that would please every body, and difficult to make an arrangement that would please any body. **1876** J. PARKER *Paraclete* II. 385 Anybody can attach himself to a mob.

2. With qualitative force; sometimes made a regular substantive with *pl.*

a. In interrogative or hypothetical expressions, *laudatory*: A person of some rank or worth, 'a somebody' as opposed to 'a nobody.' **b.** In affirmative expressions, *depreciatory*: A person of any sort, an ordinary person, as opposed to 'a somebody.'

1826 DISRAELI *Viv. Grey* II. xv. 78 Everybody was there who is anybody. **1858** (Dec. 21) BRIGHT *Sp.* (1876) 306 Two or three anybodies. **1866** TROLLOPE *Last Chron.* v. 34 Everybody, who was anybody, knew that Mr. Walker was convinced of the man's guilt. **1961** *Harper's Bazaar* Dec. 47/2 Everybody who is anybody in the business world will be seeking the latest status symbol.

3. In colloq. phrs., as ***anybody's game, match, race***, designating a contest in which the competitors are so evenly matched that either side (any competitor) could win; also *fig.*; ***anybody's guess***, an unpredictable matter, a question to which no one knows the answer.

1840 *Spirit of Times* 4 Jan. 523/2 It was anybody's race yet! **1853** F. GALE *Public Sch. Matches* 58 Sixty-nine runs and six wickets down; anybody's match, by jingo! **1865** J. PYCROFT *Cricketana* vii. 152 Last year's match had been left unfinished, just in that interesting state in which it is called 'anybody's game'. **1898** *Forum* Jan. 576 In Greater New York, it was what is called 'anybody's race', till close upon the day of election. **1938** *Time* 21 Nov. 70/2 What this type of angry, incoherent prose will prove is anybody's guess. **1955** E. BOWEN *World of Love* x. 179 Anybody's game, she had thought... Though which of them, dead man and living girl, had been the player, and which the played-with? **1958** *Times* 27 Sept. 9/4 How many less serious accidents there were, is, therefore, anybody's guess.

any deal: see DEAL.

anyentise, -ish, variant of ANIENTISE *v. Obs.*

anyhow (ˈɛnɪhaʊ), *adv.* and *conj.* [See ANY 9.]

1. *adv.* Indefinite compound of *how*: In any way or manner whatever, or however imperfect; in random fashion, unmethodically. Also (*slang*) with insertion of *old*: *any old how* (cf. ANY *a.* and *pron.* 1 e).

1740 PINEDA *Eng. Span. Dict.* s.v., Anyhow, *de qualquiera manera que sea.* **1828** CARLYLE *Misc.* (1857) I. 192 Done anyhow, no profitable one. **1844** BROUGHAM *Brit. Const.* xvii. (1862) 258 Any law, anyhow made, provided it be made calmly. **1853** MRS. GASKELL *Ruth* II. iii. 64 Just try.. to think of all the odd jobs as to be done well.. not just slurred over anyhow. **1867** FREEMAN *Norm. Conq.* I. App. 747 Whether the two can anyhow be the same. **1896** *Pop. Sci. Monthly* Feb. 538 They are apt at first to be thrown in anyhow. **1933** *Punch* 23 Aug. 216/1 Scenes like a splash of confetti Hurled any old how. **1937** M. HILLIS *Orchids on your Budget* (1938) v. 79 The kind of woman who gets herself up any-old-how.. deserves just what she gets. **1949** F. SARGESON *I Saw in my Dream* xiv. 191 He was all dressed up in his Sunday best.. but his hair was any old how.

2. a. *advb. conj.* In any case, however it may be with what has been already said, at least.

1825 *Bro. Jonathan* I. 381, I was ready to go abroad, any how, then. **1842** NEWMAN *Ch. Fathers* 250 Any how, it must be acknowledged to be not a simple self-originated error. **1866** G. MACDONALD *Ann. Quiet Neighb.* xi. (1878) 220 They went, anyhow, whether they had to do it or not.

b. ***any old how***, in any case, at any rate. *slang.*

1924 P. CRESWICK *Beaten Path* xxxiii. 183 Oh, likes! Yes, she likes me. But liking's nothing. Well, any old how, I had to tell you. **1958** F. NORMAN *Bang to Rights* II. 34 Any old how.. he managed to get behind him..

†**any-kyn, -s.** *Obs.* [Orig. genitive phr., as 'any-kyns speech' = speech of any kind, afterwards with loss of *-s*, looking like an adj. 'anykyn speech,' as if = any kind of speech, *qualislibet locutio.*] Any kind or manner.

a **1300** *Cursor M.* 1941 Noe, for anikins chanse, Sal i noght take sli a noþer venganse. *c* **1315** SHOREHAM 95 ȝyf thy wyl rejo[isse] more In enyes kennes thynges. *a* **1400** *Sir Perceval* 2148 Fast he frayned that fre For any-kyns aughte. *a* **1400** *Relig. Pieces fr. Thornton MS.* 31 He moghte hafe made vs at his will anykyne oþer best. *c* **1420** *Lib. Cure Cocorum* 5 Hit wolde seme rawe by any-kyn way.

any-lengthian, *a. nonce-wd.* Ready to go any length, unscrupulous.

1798 TOOKE *Purley* 683 Disgust at the any-lengthian Lord with his numerous strings.

anyntise, -ische, variants of ANIENTISE *v. Obs.*

anyplace (ˈɛnɪpleɪs), *adv. U.S. colloq.* [f. ANY + PLACE *sb.*, after ANYWHERE *adv.*] Anywhere.

1934 in WEBSTER. **1936** *Punch* 25 Mar. 340/3 It's perfectly good American grammar. Why, you even say 'I can't find it any place'. **1948** J. STEINBECK *Russ. Jrnl.* (1949) v. 111 The tycoon.. makes it impossible for the correspondent to publish it anyplace else.

anything (ˈɛnɪθɪŋ), *pron., sb., adv.*

1. *pron.* **a.** A combination of ANY and THING, in the widest sense of the latter, with all the varieties of sense belonging to ANY *a.* Orig. always separated; separation now usually denotes stress upon *thing*, as 'any thing, but not any person.'

c **1000** *Ags. Gosp.* John i. 46 Mæȝ æniȝ þing godes beon of nazareth. [So in *Hatton.*] *c* **1230** *Ancr. R.* 64 Wheðer ei þing hermeð more. *c* **1370** WYCLIF *Wks.* xxvi. (1880) 388 More sikirnes.. may no man make of eny-þinge. *c* **1400** *Destr.*

Troy XXI. 8895, I haue not errit in anythyng. **1542** UDALL *Erasm. Apoph.* (1877) 32 Sweardes and kniues, beyng as sharpe as any thyng. **1611** BIBLE *John* xiv. 14 If ye shall ask any thing in my name, I will do it. **1677** YARRANTON *England's Impr.* 136 These Spouts convey the Corn into the Barges without anything of labour. **1711** ADDISON *Spect.* No. 1 ¶8, I would gratify my Reader in any Thing that is reasonable. **1741** RICHARDSON *Pamela* II. 57, I fear your girl will grow as proud as anything. **1793** SMEATON *Edystone Lightho.* §100 When there is any thing of a ground swell. *a* **1855** MISS MITFORD in L'Estrange *Life* (1870) I. v. 114 Anything in the remotest degree connected with Napoleon excites my curiosity. **1857** BUCKLE *Civil.* I. xii. 670 If the contest.. had been conducted with anything approaching to moderation. **1873** CARROLL *Through Looking-Glass* iv. 73 They wept like anything to see Such quantities of sand.

b. In various phrases: ***anything but***, by no means, not at all, the very reverse (of); (***he didn't do***) ***anything else***, (*U.S. colloq.*) phr. denoting a strong affirmation; ***anything goes***: see GO *v.* 19 d; ***if anything***: see IF; ***like anything***: see LIKE *adv.* 1 b; ***too...for anything***, extremely, excessively. *colloq.* (cf. TOO *adv.* 2 b.). See also HAPPEN *v.* 1 a.

1805-6 WORDSWORTH *Prelude* (1926) 376 Grief call it not, 'twas anything but that. *a* **1832** F. TROLLOPE *Notebks.* in *Dom. Manners Amer.* (1960) 428 Too hot for anything. Too bad for anything. *a* **1859** in BARTLETT *Dict. Amer.* 10 *Loco Foco.* Didn't Gen. Cass get mad at Hull's cowardice, and break his sword? *Whig.* He didn't do anything else. **1874** HARDY *Far from Madding Crowd* I. xxix. 320 His being higher in learning and birth than the ruck of soldiers is anything but a proof of his worth. **1897** *Westm. Gaz.* 1 Oct. 2/1 The anything-but-particular denominationalists. **1905** *Dial. Notes* III. 2 'He didn't do anything else', meaning he did just that. **1925** CHESTERTON *Tales of Long Bow* viii. 281 'Really,' she said, laughing, 'you are too ridiculous for anything.' **1933** *Times Lit. Suppl.* 16 Feb. 106/2 Richard Roe, the posthumous anything-but-hero. **1944** S. E. HICKS BEACH *A. & M. Verena* i. 12 'It sounds as if you were not altogether a Christian young gentleman.' 'Anything but.' **1960** *News Chron.* 27 July 4/2 The aspirin age needed its drugs largely because the fair sex tried so hard to look anything but.

2. as *sb.* Thing of any kind.

1596 SHAKS. *Tam. Shr.* III. ii. 234 She is my house.. My horse, my oxe, my asse, my anything. **1649** MILTON *Eikon.* Wks. 1738 I. 383 This was that terrible Any-thing from which his Conscience and his Reason chose to run rather than not deny. **1736** BUTLER *Anal.* Diss. i. 303 No Man, no Being,.. no Any-thing.

3. *adv.* Any whit, in any measure, to any extent.

a **700** *Epinal Gl.* 845 (Sweet) *Quoquomodo*, ængi þinga. *c* **1391** CHAUCER *Astrol.* II. §38. 47 Til that the schadwe.. passe ony-thyng owt of the cercle. **1480** CAXTON *Chron. Eng.* ccxv. 202 Yf my lady your wyf come ony thyng nyghe yowe. **1551** ROBINSON *More's Utopia* 16 Mine old good wil.. is not .. any thinge at all quayled. **1590** *Plain Perc.* 16 A Minister that hath any thing a fat benefice. **1656** H. PHILLIPS *Purchaser's Pattern* (1676) 22 If he be anything young. **1861** GEN. P. THOMPSON *Audi Alt. Part.* III. clxx. 196 Not furious anything, either for good or evil, no enthusiasts.

anythingarian (ˌɛnɪθɪŋˈɛərɪən). [f. prec. after *trinit-arian*, *unit-arian*, etc.] One who professes no creed in particular; an indifferentist. (A contemptuous term.)

a **1704** T. BROWN *Wks.* 1760 III. 97 (D.) Such bifarious anythingarians, that always make their interest the standard of their religion. **1738** SWIFT *Polite Conv.* i. Wks. III. 338 *Lady Smart.* What religion is he of? *Ld. Spark.* Why, he is an Anythingarian. **1850** KINGSLEY *Alton Locke* xxii. (D.) They made puir Robbie Burns an anythingarian with their blethers.

ˌanythingˈarianism. *rare*$^{-1}$. [f. prec. + -ISM.] The doctrine of an anythingarian.

1851 KINGSLEY in *Lett. & Mem.* I. 264 Schiller's 'Gods of Greece' expresses a tone of feeling.. which finds its vent in modern Neo-Platonism—Anythingarianism.

anyway (ˈɛnɪweɪ), *adv.* and *conj.* [cf. ANYWAYS, and the analogous pair *always*, *alway*.]

1. *adv.* In any way or manner, anyhow; to any degree or extent, in any measure.

1570 LEVINS *Manip.* 197 Any way, *quavis, ullo modo.* Least any way, *nequa.* **1593** BILSON *Ch. Govt.* To Reader 3 That anie waie touch the state. **1611** BIBLE *Transl. Pref.* 1 Any thing that sauoured any way of newnesse. **1642** ROGERS *Naaman* To Reader 4 That I may set my base heart on work any way to prevent sloth. **1712** ADDISON *Spect.* No. 529 ¶1 All those who are any way concerned in works of literature. **1842** TENNYSON *To J.S.* xv, How should I soothe you anyway?

2. In any way however imperfect; anyhow.

1660 STANLEY *Hist. Philos.* (1701) 183/1 Not he that speaketh any way speaketh rightly.

3. *advb. conj.* However the case may be; in any case; anyhow.

1859 HELPS *Friends in C.* Ser. II. (1869) I. 117 Anyway, I should soon be dispossessed of my lands. **1876** BLACK *Madcap V.* xiv. 124 That is how I look at it, anyway.

anyways (ˈɛnɪweɪz), *adv.* and *conj.* [ANY + *ways*, adverbial genitive, as in ALWAYS.]

1. *adv.* In any way, in any respect, at all.

c **1560** *Bk. Comm. Prayer*, All those who are any ways afflicted.. in mind, body, or estate. **1638** PRESTON *Mount Ebal* 10 As the Rudder of a ship, which turnes it any wayes. **1673** RAY *Jrny. thro' Low Countries* Ded., If either Catalogue or Observations prove any ways useful. **1794** SOUTHEY *Wat Tyler* III. i, Who may have been anyways concerned in the late insurrections. **1834** DE QUINCEY *Cæsars* Wks. X. 61 Nor was such an interference.. anyways injurious.

2. *advb. conj.* In any case, at all events, anyhow. *dialect.* or *illiterate.*

1865 DICKENS *Mut. Fr.* xii. 228 Anyways, I am glad, etc.

†**ˈanywhat,** *pron. Obs.* Indefinite compound of *what* (cf. *somewhat*): anything.

a **1400** *Cursor M.* (Tr.) 3629 If he any what myȝte gete.

anywhen (ˈɛnɪˌhwɛn), *adv.* [See ANY 9.] Indefinite compound of *when*: At any time, ever. *Rare* in literature, but common in southern dialects.

1831 CARLYLE *Sart. Res.* (1858) 159 And, simply by wishing that you were Anywhen, straightway to be Then! **1845** —— *Cromwell* Introd., There has been none braver anywhere or anywhen. **1878** BOSW. SMITH *Carthage* 333 Now, if anywhen, we might have expected that, etc.

†**ˈanywhence,** *adv. Obs. rare.* [See ANY 9.] Indefinite compound of *whence*: From anywhere.

a **1613** OVERBURY *Wks.* 1856. 171 (*title*) Newes from Any whence. **1671** BRANKER in Rigaud *Corr. Sci. Men* I. 167 As soon as I receive it anywhence, you shall have it presently returned.

anywhere (ˈɛnɪhwɛə(r), ˈɛnɪhwə(r)), *adv.* [See ANY 9; not in early use; the earlier *owhere*, *oughwhere*, and *aywhere*, came down to 1485.]

a. In any place. The indefinite compound of *where*. Formerly written separately.

c **1300** *Cursor M.* (Gött.) 3975 If he miht him aniquar ta. *c* **1450** *Song* in *Reliq. Ant.* II. 240 Tabberys gloson eny whare, And gode feyth comys all byhynde. **1587** GOLDING *De Mornay* xv. 234 How is it possible that they should be.. from aniwhere els than from aboue? **1673** RAY *Jrny. thro' Low Countries* 20 The best we have any where seen. **1766** GOLDSM. *Vic. Wakef.* xiv. (1806) 70 You'll do it at neighbour Jackson's, or anywhere. **1849** MACAULAY *Hist. Eng.* II. 208 Anywhere except in the high streets of royal burghs.

b. Used with *from...to*, to indicate limits of variation. *U.S.*

1897 *Outing* XXIX. 471/1 The tarpon will be anywhere from fifty to three hundred feet away when the boat is ready to follow him. **1909** 'O. HENRY' *Options* (1916) 13 I'll guarantee an increase of anywhere from ten thousand to a hundred thousand a year.

any while, any whit: see WHILE, WHIT.

anywhither (ˈɛnɪˌhwɪðə(r)), *adv. arch.* [See ANY 9; the earlier equivalent was OWHITHER, *oughwhither*.] Indefinite compound of *whither*. To or towards any place, in any direction whatever.

1611 BIBLE *1 Kings* ii. 36 Goe not forth thence any whither [WYCLIF & COVERDALE hidir and thider.] **1658** CROMWELL (Carl.) *Sp.* xv, To fly for Holland, New England, almost anywhither, to find liberty for their consciences. **1722** DE FOE *Hist. Plague* (1756) 69 There was no easy passing the Roads any whither. **1863** MRS. WHITNEY *Faith Gartney* xxx. 288 She would have fled—anywhither.

anywise (ˈɛnɪwaɪz), *adv.* [for *in any wise*, also used in full; OE. (*on*) *ǽniȝe wísan.*] In any manner, way, or case; in any degree, at all; anyhow.

a **1000** *Metr. Ps.* lxxiii. 9 On ǽniȝe wísan. [Cf. *Hymn* vii. 66 Aȝene wísan.] *c* **1200** *Moral Ode* 269 Alle þe þen aniȝewise doulen iquemde. *c* **1225** *Ste. Marherete* (1866) 13 Ȝef ich mahte eyweis makien ham to fallen. **1472** MARG. PASTON in *Lett.* III. 62 In any wyse.. labore to have an ende of your grete materes. **1563** MAN *Musculus' Comm. Places* 374 b, For all that, it is in any wise [*omnino*] necessarie. **1660** BARROW *Euclid* II. ii, If a right line be divided anywise into two parts. **1775** *Act 15 Geo. III*, liii. §1 in *Oxf. & Camb. Enactmts.* 85 Any law or usage to the contrary hereof in anywise not withstanding. **1783** BURKE *Affairs of India* Wks. 1842 II. 11 The only subject-matter of discussion, anywise important. **1870** HAWTHORNE *Eng. Note-Bks.* (1879) II. 11 Neither is it anywise essential.

Anzac (ˈænzæk). A word made up from the initials of *Australian and New Zealand Army Corps*, and used colloq. for a member of that corps, or to designate any Australian or N.Z. serviceman. Also *attrib.*, as ***Anzac Day***, the occasion (or anniversary) of the landing of the corps in the Gallipoli Peninsula on 25 April, 1915.

1915 *Sphere* 16 Oct. 55/3 The term, Anzac, which recent events on the Gallipoli Peninsula have rendered so prominent, is derived as follows [etc.]. **1916** W. R. BIRDWOOD in C. E. W. Bean *Anzac Book* p. ix, It may be of interest.. to hear the origin of the word 'Anzac'. When I took over the command of the Australian and New Zealand Army Corps in Egypt a year ago, I was asked to select a telegraphic code address for my Army Corps, and then adopted the word 'Anzac'. **1916** *Daily Mail* 1 Nov. 4/4 'Anzac'.. is a word that bids fair to be reckoned among the immortals. **1920** *Chambers's Jrnl.* June 374/2 The thing had been started by one of the Anzacs venturing the modest opinion that if Britain had had a million Australian troops, they.. would be.. in Berlin. **1920** *Glasgow Herald* 26 Apr. 9 Anzac Day. **1921** *Q. Rev.* CCXXXVI. July 18 This.. is.. the surest guide to an understanding of things Australian—that the Anzac, the 'Digger' in his best and worst qualities alike, is a fair type of his fellow countrymen. **1941** *Times Weekly* 23 Apr. 5 The Australian and New Zealand divisions fighting in Greece are to be known as the Anzac Corps. **1944** J. H. FULLARTON *Troop Target* xiv. 104 'What was wrong with being an Anzac?' demanded Peter Doe, whose father had died at Anzac Cove. 'Nothing,' said Robin. 'Except that to nine people out of ten Anzac means Australian.'

Anzus (ˈænzəs). Also **ANZUS.** [f. the initials of *Australia, New Zealand, United States.*] The combination of Australia, New Zealand, and the United States for the security of the Pacific, usu. *attrib.* in ***Anzus Alliance, Council, Pact***, etc.

1952 *Sydney Morning Her.* 18 July 3/4 The U.S. Secretary of State, Mr. Dean Acheson, yesterday suggested that the Pacific Council be called the 'Anzus Council'. *Ibid.* 9 Aug. 2/1 (*headline*) Anzus Alliance 'gets off to a good start'. **1952** *Times* 16 Oct. 5/6 Britain's Exclusion from A.N.Z.U.S. **1952** *N.Y. Times* 15 Dec. 1/6 The Alliance.. known as ANZUS, was devised to safeguard the Antipodes against a resurgence of Japanese militarism. **1959** *Times* 27 Oct. 12/5 Senior diplomatic and military officials of the United States, Australia, and New Zealand met.. to-day for the annual review of the Anzus defence pact.

‖**ao dai** (aʊ daɪ). [Vietnamese, f. *áo* jacket, tunic + *dài* to be long.] A Vietnamese woman's high-necked tunic with ankle-length panels at front and back, worn over trousers.

1961 J. K. GALBRAITH *Jrnl.* 17 Nov. in *Ambassador's Jrnl.* (1969) xiii. 259 The women are handsomely dressed in *ao dais*, these being high-waisted pajamas with flowing panels of white silk fore and aft. **1966** J. CLEARY *High Commissioner* iii. 46 The small Oriental woman in the yellow *ao dais.* **1968** R. WEST *Sk. Vietnam* ii. 34 A Vietnamese girl of about fifteen—in trailing *ao dai* dress and pantaloons. **1974** D. MORAES *Matter of People* viii. 130 The *ao-dai*, the long fluttery butterfly tunic of Vietnam. **1977** *Time* 9 May 21/1 A stroll along busy Tu Do Street [in Saigon].. remains one of the most fascinating city walks in the world, a gauntlet of boutiques, cafes and attractive women in *ao dai.*

A-OK (ˌeɪəʊˈkeɪ), *adj.* and *adv. phr. colloq.* (chiefly *U.S.*). Also **A-okay.** [Abbrev. of 'all (systems) OK': see O.K. *a.*] In perfect order or condition. Orig. *Astronaut.* (see quot. 1961[1]).

1961 *Flight* LXXIX. 615/1 The astronaut probably added a new phrase to the English language by his repeated use of 'A-OK' to report satisfactory conditions in flight. On the way back to Cocoa Beach Florida, six miles south of the Cape, newsmen were shouting 'A-OK' to one another, and many used the phrase in their stories. It means 'all OK'. **1961** *World-Herald* (Omaha) 8 May 12M/2 'A-okay', as everybody now knows, means all's well, everything functioning perfectly. **1963** K. PETERS *Mod. Tape Recording* v. 49 Always make a short test run before starting a dubbing session. This ensures that all systems are functioning A-O.K. **1970** N. ARMSTRONG et al. *First on Moon* i. 18 'A-OK', an expression coined by a public affairs announcer, and one which the astronauts.. never did use. **1978** *Daily Tel.* 8 Feb. 15 The blood sample proved A-OK, but a following ultrasound scan showed a discrepancy in the size of the foetus.

Aonian (eɪˈəʊnɪən), *a.* Of or belonging to Aonia, a region of ancient Bœotia, which contained the mountains Helicon and Cithaeron, sacred to the Muses or 'Aonian maids.'

1607 TOPSELL *Four-footed Beasts* (1673) 54 The Aonian oxen are of divers colours. **1667** MILTON *P.L.* I. 15 Above th' Aonian mount. **1741** POPE *Messiah* 4 The dreams of Pindus and th' Aonian maids.

aorist (ˈeɪərɪst). *Gram.* [ad. Gr. ἀόριστ-ος indefinite, f. ἀ priv. + ὁριστ-ός, f. ὁρίζ-ειν to limit, define.] One of the past tenses of the Greek verb, which takes its name from its denoting a simple past occurrence, with none of the limitations as to completion, continuance, etc., which belong to the other past tenses. It corresponds to the simple past tense in English, as 'he died.'

1581 CAMPION in *Confer.* II. (1584) N iiij b, What *tempus* is the verbe? *Camp.* I thinke it be the *Aoriste.* **1750** HARRIS *Hermes* I. vii. (1786) 123 Yet it seems agreeable to reason, that wherever Time is signified without any further circumscription, than that of Simple present, past or future, the Tense is an Aorist. **1865** R. W. DALE *Jew. Temp.* (1877) 297 In the Authorized Version the Greek aorist is very frequently represented by the English perfect.

aoristic (eɪəˈrɪstɪk), *a.* [ad. Gr. ἀοριστικ-ός, f. ἀόριστ-ος: see AORIST and -IC.]

1. Undefined, indeterminate.

1846 GROTE *Greece* (1854) I. 488 In the genuine Grecian epic, the theme was an unknown and aoristic past. **1876** G. MEREDITH *Beauch. Career* II. xv. 277 Like certain aoristic combinations in music, like tones of a stringed instrument swept by the wind, enticing, unseizable.

2. Of or pertaining to the aorist tense.

1860 ELLICOTT *Life of our Lord* vii. 334 The contested ἀπέστειλεν (*John* xviii. 24) is taken in its simple aoristic sense. **1876** FARRAR *Gr. Syntax* §124 The existence of the aoristic termination in such perfects as *vixi, scrip-si*, etc.

aoˈristical, *a.* ? *Obs. rare*$^{-1}$. [f. as prec. + -AL[1].] Of aoristic character, aorist-like; indefinite.

1750 HARRIS *Hermes* (1841) 153 [Here] the verb *walks* hath the like aoristical or indefinite application.

aoˈristically, *adv.* [f. prec. + -LY[2].] After the manner of, or as, an aorist.

1647 VINES *Lord's Supper* (1677) 85 Beza hints that ἐσθιόντων αὐτῶν may be Aoristically translated. **1860** G. P. MARSH *Lect. Eng. Lang.* xiv. 300 In most languages.. even the forms grammatically expressive of time are, in general propositions, employed aoristically, or without any reference to time. **1880** *Expositor* 381 There is no need to suppose these aorists used aoristically (as they would be in classic Greek).

†**a'orn(e, aourne**, *v. Obs.* Original form of ADORN, ANORN, q.v.

aorta (eɪˈɔːtə). [a. med. or mod.L. *aorta*, a. Gr. ἀορτή, applied by Hippocrates in pl. to the *bronchi*, *bronchia*, or branches of the windpipe, but subseq. by Aristotle to the great artery, as in modern use; *lit.* that which is hung (cf. ἀορτήρ a hanger, a strap), f. ἀείρ-ειν to raise, lift up.] The great artery or trunk of the arterial system, from its origin in the left ventricle of the heart to its division into the two iliac arteries. Also *fig.*

1594 T. B. *La Primaud. Fr. Acad.* II. 357 The great artery, called *Aorta* by the Physicions. **1621** BURTON *Anat. Mel.* I. i. I. iii, Aorta is the root of all the other [arteries], which serve the whole body. **1859** CARPENTER *Anim. Phys.* v. (1872) 226 From the arch of the aorta are given off the arteries which supply the head and upper extremities. **1882** *Society* 7 Oct. 8/2 London's great aorta, the Strand.

aortal (eɪˈɔːtəl), *a. rare.* [f. prec. + -AL[1].] Of, pertaining to, or of the nature of, an aorta.

1836–9 TODD *Cycl. Anat. & Phys.* II. 978/1 The thoracic or aortal portion of the heart. **1839** BAILEY *Festus* iv. (1848) 1 A wimpling streamlet ere its waters grow To size aortal. **1842** JOHNSON *Farmer's Cycl.* s.v., *Aortal Arteries* of vegetables. The large vessels destined to convey the elaborated juice..of plants..So denominated by Dr. Darwin.

aortic (eɪˈɔːtɪk), *a.* [ad. mod.L. *aortic-us*, f. AORTA: see -IC. Cf. mod.Fr. *aortique*.] Of or pertaining to the aorta.

1833 *Blackw. Mag.* XXXIII. 434 The balance preserved between the pulmonary and aortic circulation. **1872** HUXLEY *Phys.* v. 101 The aortic trunk enters the cavity of the abdomen.

aortitis (eɪɔːˈtaɪtɪs). *Path.* [f. AORT(A + -ITIS.] Inflammation of the aorta.

1842 in DUNGLISON *Dict. Med. Sci.* (ed. 3). **1906** *Practitioner* Nov. 581 Other causes of systolic aortic murmurs are aortitis and atheroma.

aoudad (ˈɑːuːdæd). Also **audad, udad.** [Fr. form of native name.] A species of wild sheep, *Ovis* or *Ammotragus tragelaphus* (often domesticated), found in N. Africa.

1861 *Proc. Zool. Soc.* 234 Additions to the Menagerie.. Aoudad, *Ovis tragelaphus*. **1864** J. ORMSBY *Autumn Rambles* 70 The maned moufflon of the Atlas,..the Aoudad of modern naturalists. **1886** *Encycl. Brit.* XXI. 785/1 The.. goat-like aoudad, *O. tragelaphus*. **1902** *Ibid.* XXXIII. 483/2 The magnificent udad or Barbary sheep.

aoul (ˈɑːuːl). Also **aoull, aul.** [Eastern Turkish *aul*.] A Caucasian or Tartar village or encampment.

1828 J. B. FRASER *Kuzzilbash* I. iv. 48 Men, women, and children, poured tumultuously from the nearer aouls. **1877** D. M. WALLACE *Russia* II. xxi. 39 The aoul consisted of about twenty tents..scattered about in sporadic fashion. **1884** *Leisure Hour* 461/1 One or two of the mounted young men are sent from the aul..to select a suitable spot for a new encampment. **1960** *Times* 27 July 11/7 The villagers coming down from their *auls* in the hills.

†**a'oure**, *v. Obs.* Original form of ADORE, ANOURE, q.v.

ap- *pref.*[1] assimilated form of L. *ad-* 'to,' bef. initial *p-*, as L. *ad-proba-*, *ap-proba-*. In OFr. this *ad- ap-* was, by regular phonetic law, reduced to *a-* (as in the separate word *ad*), and in this form the Fr. words were adopted in Eng., as *a-part*, *a-pere*, *a-ply*, *a-pose*, *a-prise*, *a-prove*. In imitation of the Latin forms, the scribes began to double the *p* in Fr. spelling in 14th c., and in Eng. in 15th, though, in speech, the prefix is still really *a-* (cf. əˈpɛnd, ˈæplɪkənt). By mistake *ap-* was also substituted for *a-* in several words where it had a different origin, as *appair*, *appeach*: see AD- *pref.* 2, A- *pref.* 10.

ap- *pref.*[2] in words of Greek origin, for ἀπ' the shortened form of ἀπό 'off, away,' bef. a vowel, as in ἀπ-αγωγή *ap-agoge*: see APO-.

ap-, *pref.*[3] [Welsh *ap*, from *map* son, used in pedigrees and a common prefix in surnames, as *Apjohn*, *Aprys*; cf. *Mac*.]

1647 CLEVELAND *Char. Lond. Diurn.* (1677) 108 It would tire a Welshman to reckon up how many *Aps* 'tis removed from an Annal.

apace (əˈpeɪs), *adv.* Forms: 4–5 **apaas, apas,** 4–6 **apase,** 4– **apace.** [orig. phr. *a pace*, like *afoot*, *ahead*, f. A *prep.*[1] of manner + PACE, formerly *pas*, *paas*.] *lit.* At a pace, *i.e.* at a considerable or good pace; *hence*, With speed; swiftly, quickly, fast.

a. *orig.* of the pace of men.

c **1350** *Rom. Athelston* in *Rel. Ant.* II. 98 Thorwȝout he went a pase. *c* **1374** CHAUCER *Troylus* IV. 465 He cometh to hym apaas. *c* **1400** *Rom. Rose* 3724 To Bialacoil she wente apas. **1549** COVERDALE *Erasm. Par. Gal.* v. 7 Ye dyd once runne apace, makyng hastye spede. **1611** BIBLE *Ps.* lxviii. 12 Kings of armies did flee apace. **1719** DE FOE *Crusoe* (1858) 486 They are coming towards us too, apace. **1837** DISRAELI *Venetia* I. xiv. (1871) 67 He..pushed on apace.

b. of motion generally, as flowing, gliding, sailing, flying; and hence of the flight of time.

1535 COVERDALE *Ps.* lviii. 6 Like water y[t] runneth a pace. —— *Jer.* xlviii. 14 The destruction off Moab commeth on a pace. **1665** MANLEY *Grotius's Low-C. Wars* 101 Autumn now coming on apace. **1702** POPE *Jan. & May* 783 The ready tears apace began to flow. **1762** FALCONER *Shipwr.* II. 35 Around before the squall she veers apace. **1813** SCOTT *Trierm.* I. xx, With lay and tale, and laugh, and jest, Apace the evening flew. **1878** BOSW. SMITH *Carthage* 260 The news..reached Rome apace.

c. of speed or progress in any action.

a **1423** JAMES I *King's Q.* IV. viii, The werk that first is foundit sure May better bere apace. **1530** PALSGR. 418 Thought maketh men age a pace. **1550** CROWLEY *Epigr.* 1020 Good Essay doeth cursse them apase. **1604** ROWLANDS *Looke to it* 8 Hoording wealth apace. **1611** COTGR., s.v. *Herbe*, An ill weed growes apace. **1628** DIGBY *Voy. Medit.* 9 My men begun to sicken apace. **1713** DERHAM *Phys. Theol.* 16 It rained a-pace. **1800** WELLINGTON in Gurw. *Disp.* I. 192 Dhoondiah's followers are quitting him apace. **1829** SOUTHEY *All for Love* III. Wks. VII. 166 The church Already fills apace. **1841** MISS SEDGWICK *Lett. fr. Abr.* I. 24 Our friendship ripens apace.

†**d.** of quickness in proceeding to act: At once, immediately. *Obs.*

c **1325** *Cœur de L.* 4041 Now leth in pes, lystenes apas! **1553** A. WILSON *Rhet.* 15 b, We hang theim a pace that offend a lawe. **1723** MRS. CENTLIVRE *Stolen Heiress* v. 371 Do not push me from thee..For I shall die apace, and go before.

Apache (əˈpætʃiː). Also 9 **Appache.** [Mexican Sp. (see quot. 1907).] **1.** A people of Athapascan Indians in New Mexico and Arizona; a member of this people; also their language. Also *attrib.*

1745 *H. Moll's Atlas Minor* Plate 46 (D.A.E.), Apaches. **1797** *Encycl. Brit.* I. 552/1 Many of those nations, as the Apaches, the Hiaquese,..are at least as tall as the tallest Europeans. **1834** A. PIKE *Prose Sk.* 126 He..overtook four Apaches. *Ibid.* 138 A filthy, ragged fellow with..Apache moccasins. **1907** F. W. HODGE *Amer. Indians* I. 63 Apache (probably from *ápachu*, 'enemy', the Zuni name for the Navaho, who were designated 'Apaches de Nabaju' by the early Spaniards in New Mexico)... They were first mentioned as Apaches by Oñate in 1598. **1921** E. SAPIR *Lang.* iv. 71 Such languages as Navaho, Apache, Hupa, [etc.].

2. (əˈpæʃ, ‖apaʃ) Also **apache.** [Fr., f. prec.] A ruffian of a type infesting Paris; also *gen.* a man of ruffianly behaviour.

1902 *Westm. Gaz.* 22 Oct 8/1 The leader of the band of roughs in Paris known as the 'Apaches'. **1909** *Times* 9 Feb. 4/4 Those *apaches* with which Brussels is haunted. **1920** *Times Lit. Suppl.* 10 June 363/2 Something a little more Bacchic than the calculated extravagances of the drawing-room *apache* would occasionally relieve the atmosphere. **1933** 'G. ORWELL' *Down & Out* iii. 20 He wore side whiskers, which are the mark either of an apache or an intellectual.

b. *attrib.*; **apache dance,** a violent dance in which the partners are dressed as apaches; so ***apache dancer***.

1914 G. W. YOUNG *From Trenches* i. 12 The apache element..was soon brought into order. **1918** H. G. WELLS *Joan & Peter* xi. 443 Huntley wanted to teach Joan an Apache dance. **1922** JOYCE *Ulysses* 469 In workman's corduroy overalls..and apache cap. **1928** *Punch* 30 May 602 *Friend* (referring to 'Apache' hat). I like that one, dear. You see, it's noticeable without being really fierce. **1945** H. L. MENCKEN *Amer. Lang.* Suppl. I. 186 During the [1914–18] war or soon afterward *apache-dancers* began to appear in the United States. **1962** J. D. SALINGER *Franny & Zooey* 57 It isn't enough to treat her with the doting brutality of an apache dancer towards his partner.

‖**apagoge** (æpəˈgəʊdʒiː). [Gr. ἀπαγωγή leading away, abduction, also used by Aristotle in the logical sense, f. ἀπ-άγειν to lead off.]

†**1.** *Logic.* The species of syllogism, or syllogistic reasoning, called ABDUCTION. *Obs.*

1727–51 CHAMBERS *Cycl.*, *Abduction* in logic, a kind of argumentation by the Greeks called *Apagoge*. **1872** GROTE *Aristotle* I. vi. 290 Another variety of ratiocinative procedure, which he calls Apagoge or Abduction.

2. A demonstration which does not prove a thing directly, but shows the absurdity or impossibility of denying it; a *reductio ad absurdum*.

a **1753** BERKELEY is cited in WORCESTER.

†**3.** *Math.* 'A progress or passage from one proposition to another, when the first having been once demonstrated, is afterwards employed to the proving of others.' Chambers *Cycl. Supp.* 1753. *Obs.*

apagogic (æpəˈgɒdʒɪk), *a. rare.* [ad. assumed Gr. *ἀπαγωγικ-ός, f. ἀπαγωγή: see prec. and -IC.] Of or pertaining to apagoge, or reduction to absurdity.

1671 *Phil. Trans.* VI. 2261 The Theorems may be demonstrated by the Apagogick way, or by reduction *ad absurdum*.

apa'gogical, *a.* [f. prec. + -AL[1].] Of the nature of apagoge; by *reductio ad absurdum*.

1706 PHILLIPS, *Apagogical* Demonstrations. **1734** BERKELEY *Analyst* §25. 41 Why any other apagogical Demonstration, or Demonstration *ad absurdum* should be admitted. **1860** FLEMING *Voc. Philos.* s.v. *Ostensive*, A proof ..is indirect, or apagogical when it evinces the truth of a thesis through the falsehood of its opposite, that is, mediately.

apa'gogically, *adv. rare.* [f. prec. + -LY[2].] In apagogical manner; by means of an apagoge.

1877 CAIRD *Philos. Kant* II. xvi. 568 An absolute Antinomy of reason, demonstrated apagogically on both sides.

apagogy (ˈæpəgəʊdʒɪ). *rare*[-0]. [a. Fr. *apagogie*.] Used as another form of APAGOGE, though, having the abstract ending -Y, it ought strictly to be: The use or practice of apagogical reasoning.

1847 in CRAIG.

apaid (əˈpeɪd), *ppl. a. arch.* Forms: 3–7 **apayed,** 4–7 **apaied, apayd,** 5 **apayede,** 5–6 **apayde,** 5–7 **apaide,** 5– **apaid;** also 4–7 **appaied, appayed,** 6 **appayde,** 6–7 **appayd, appaid.** [f. APAY *v.* + -ED. Only a poetic archaism since *c*1700.]

1. Satisfied, contented, pleased.

1297 R. GLOUC. 117 Mid al he was wel a payed. *c* **1374** CHAUCER *Boeth.* II. v. 47 With ful lytel þing nature halt hire appaied. *c* **1386** —— *Freres Prol.* 18, I pray that noon of yow be evel apayd [*v.r.* a-paide, apeide, ypayd, payd]. *a* **1450** *Knt. de la Tour* (1868) 35 Her husbonde was not best apaied with her for her outegoinge. **1565** GOLDING *Ovid's Met.* IV. (1593) 86 The sunne full ill appaid Did with his beames disperse the sand. **1675** T. BROOKS *Gold. Key* Wks. 1867 V. 189 They call me a devil, but be it so, so long as Christ is magnified, I am well a-payed. **1690** W. WALKER *Idiom. Anglo-Lat.* 28 Sufficiently apaid, *satisfactum*. **1867** C. CAYLEY *transl. Lucretius* in *Fortn. Rev.* Nov. 590 Well-appay'd [L. *placatum*] welkin brightens with an even effulgence.

†**2.** Repaid, requited, rewarded. *Obs.*

1598 YONG *Diana*, For euery pleasure then, with seuen folde paine I am now apaide. **1633** P. FLETCHER *Pisc. Eclogs.* III. xvii, My sick love (ah love full ill apay'd). **1748** THOMSON *Cast. Indol.* I. lxvi, Thy toils but ill apaid.

†**a'pain, apayne,** *v. Obs. rare*[-1]. [a. OFr. *apeine-r*, *apaine-r*, to punish, *refl.* to trouble oneself, exert oneself, f. *à* to + *peine* pain, trouble:—L. *pœna* penalty. Also expanded to AN-PEYN, by form-assoc. of pref. *a-* with A- *pref.* 2 = OE. *an, on*.] *refl.* To trouble oneself, exert oneself.

c **1315** SHOREHAM 146 Wel to donne apanyeth ueawe [*printed* neawe], Ach hym apayneth many a screwe To do amys.

†**a-'pain(e,** *advb. phr. Obs. Sc.* 4–5. Also **apayn, apane.** [a. Fr. *à peine* at or in trouble or difficulty; see prec.]

1. With difficulty; with much ado; hardly, unwillingly, scarcely.

1375 BARBOUR *Bruce* IX. 64 Folk for-outen Capitane, Bot thai the bettir be a-pane, Sall nocht be all so gud in deid. *Ibid.* 89 Ȝit sall thai fle a-payn. *c* **1470** HENRY *Wallace* VIII. 911 The toun to sege thaim thocht it was to lang And nocht a payn to wyn it be no slycht.

2. ***apain of***: under penalty or pain of.

c **1470** HENRY *Wallace* XI. 1313, I charge, apayn of loss of lywe, Nane be so bauld yon tyrand for to schrywe.

apair, apale, apall: see APP-.

apaise, apayse, obs. forms of APPEASE.

apan, obs. form of UPON.

apanage, appanage (ˈæpənɪdʒ). Also 7 **appannage, -onage, apennage,** 7–8 **appennage, -enage.** [a Fr. *apanage* (*appanage*, *appennage*), f. *apaner* to endow with the means of subsistence, Pr. *apanar*:—L. **appanāre*, *adpanāre* (common in med.L.), f. *ad* to + *pan-is* bread: see -AGE. The Fr. was often spelt *appanage* in 15–16th c, and regularly *appennage* in 17th (Cotgr.); whence also the same forms in Eng., where *appanage* is still equally common with *apanage*.]

1. The provision made for the maintenance of the younger children of kings, princes, etc.; it was originally a province, jurisdiction, or lucrative office, but the grant has also been made in money. ***in apanage***: in possession as an apanage.

1602 CAREW *Cornwall* 77 a, Belinus..had for his appannage (as the French terme it) Lœgria, Wales and Cornwall. **1605** CAMDEN *Rem.* 91 Valoys was but the Apponage..of Charles yonger sonne to Philip the second. **1645** HOWELL *Lett.* IV. 18 Monsieur hath for his apennage 100000 Liures. **1728** MORGAN *Hist. Algiers* II. i. 217 Abdalaziz..had the State of Bujeya..left him in appennage. **1847** DISRAELI *Tancred* II. iv. (1871) 70 Bishoprics..as appanages for the younger sons of great families. **1867** FREEMAN *Norm. Conq.* (1876) I. vi. 452 His son received, as usual, the apanage of Cumberland.

2. *loosely*, A specially appropriated possession; a perquisite.

1835 LYTTON *Rienzi* II. iv. 134 Its revenues and its empire will become the appanage of the hardy soldier. **1862** *Lond. Rev.* 26 July 71 The diplomatic service..must always remain the apanage of the wealthy.

3. A territory or property in the dependent condition of an apanage in sense 1; a dependency.

1807 SYD. SMITH *Plymley's Lett.* Wks. 1859 II. 166/2 Ireland..the most valuable appanage of our empire. **1872** YEATS *Growth Comm.* 187 The period when a 'New World' was the appanage of a European peninsula.

4. *transf.* A specially appointed, and hence, a natural or necessary, adjunct, accompaniment, endowment, or attribute.

1663 SIR G. MACKENZIE *Relig. Stoic* v. (1685) 36 One of the necessary Appanages of God's Omnipotency. **1731** SWIFT *To Gay* Wks. 1775 IV. I. 168 Had he thought it fit, That wealth should be the appennage of wit. **1844** DISRAELI *Coningsby* IV. viii. 146 Respect is not the appanage of such as I am. **1875** SWINBURNE *Ess. & Stud.* 249 This fretful and petulant appetite for applause, the proper apanage of small poets.

apanaged ('æpənɪdʒd), *ppl. a.* Also **appan-**. [f. prec. + -ED².] Endowed with an apanage.

1858 CARLYLE *Fredk. Gt.* (1865) I. II. xiv. 127 Sigismund, if apanaged with Brandenburg alone..might have done tolerably well there. **1875** *Blackie's Pop. Encycl.* 203/2 The descendants of the apanaged princes.

apanagist ('æpənɪdʒɪst). *rare.* Also **appan-**. [a. Fr. *apanagiste*: see prec. and -IST.] The holder of an apanage.

1834 *Penny Cycl.* II. 144/1 Towards the close of the thirteenth century the rights of the apanagist were still further circumscribed.

apanthropinization (æpæn,θrəʊpɪnaɪ'zeɪʃən). *rare*⁻¹. [n. of action f. assumed vb. *apanthropinize*: see AP- *pref.*² and ANTHROPINISM.] Withdrawal from preoccupation with what relates to man.

1880 G. ALLEN in *Mind* V. 451 The primitive human conception of beauty must..have been purely anthropinistic..All its subsequent history must be that of an apanthropinisation..a gradual regression or concentric widening of æsthetic feeling around this fixed point [man].

apanthropy (æp'ænθrəpɪ), *rare*⁻⁰. [ad. Gr. ἀπανθρωπία, n. of state f. ἀπάνθρωπ-ος away from men, solitary, f. ἀπ(ό) away from + ἄνθρωπος man: cf. mod.Fr. *apanthropie*.] (See quot.)

1753 CHAMBERS *Cycl. Supp.*, *Apanthropy*, in medicine, denotes a love of solitude. **1839** HOOPER *Med. Dict.*, *Apanthropy*..A species of melancholy characterised by a dislike to society. **1847** in CRAIG.

apar-: see under later spelling APPAR-.

aparail, aparceive: see APPAREL, APPERCEIVE.

†**apa'raunt.** *Obs. rare*⁻¹. [a. OFr. *aparant*, *-ent*, 'le pays qui dépend d'un autre, qui lui est soumis, les dépendances' (Godef.):—L. *adpārĕnt-em*, pple. of *adpārē-re*, in sense 'to appear as a servant, wait upon, attend': see APPEAR.] A dependency.

c **1325** *E.E. Allit. P.* B. 1007 An erde of erþe þe swettest As aparaunt to paradis þat plantted þe dryȝtyn.

†**a'pardon,** *v. Obs. Sc.* Also 6 **app-**. [f. PARDON *v.*: see A- *pref.* 11.] To pardon.

1535 STEWART *Cron. Scotl.* II. 91 Deir freind, I pray apardoun me. **1566** KNOX *Hist. Ref.* (1846) I. 235 He will apardoun thare formar offenses. **1586** JAMES VI in Ellis *Orig. Lett.* I. 224 III. 20 Appardon I pray you my free speaking.

aparejo (æpə'reɪhəʊ). *U.S.* Also **app-**. [Sp. *aparejo* preparation, harness, tackle.] A pack-saddle.

1844 J. GREGG *Commerce Prairies* I. 180 It is necessary too for the *aparejo* to be firmly bound on to prevent its slipping and chafing the mule's back. **1845** T. J. GREEN *Texian Exped.* xiv. 228 An aparejo, a kind of pack-saddle upon which is packed all kinds of produce. **1895** C. KING *Fort Frayne* ii. 22 Ten days rations were set aside in readiness to be packed on the apparejos the moment word should come. **1904** *Omaha Daily Bee* 6 July 4 The aparejo..as a valuable method of holding the cargo and protecting the animal's body from injuries, has never been improved upon.

‖**aparithmesis** (,æpərɪθ'miːsɪs). *Rhet.* [Gr. ἀπαρίθμησις, n. of action f. ἀπαριθμέ-ειν to count off.] 'A figure in rhetorick; enumeration.' Todd.

1753 CHAMBERS *Cycl. Supp.*, *Aparithmesis*, in rhetoric, denotes the answer to the protasis or proposition itself. Thus if the protasis be *appellandi tempus non erat*, the Aparithmesis is *at tecum anno plus vixi*.

apart (ə'pɑːt), *adv.* Also 5 **at part**. [Fr. *à part*, f. *à* to, *part* place, side; though formally identified with Eng. phrases like *a-side, a-head*, the various senses closely follow the Fr.]

1. To one side, aside, to a place removed from the general body. **a.** of motion.

c **1380** *Sir Ferumb.* 636 Adrow him apart þanne and saide. **1582** N. T. (Rhem.) *Matt.* xiv. 13 He retired..into a desert place apart. **1601** SHAKS. *Jul. C.* III. i. 282 Thy heart is bigge, get thee a-part and weepe. **1672** DRYDEN *Conq. Granada* I. I. i, I saw him ride a-part. **1827** KEBLE *Chr. Y.* 2nd S. Christm. ii, Then stole apart to weep and die.

b. of position.

1393 LANGL. *P. Pl.* C. VII. 384 Two..preysed þe penyworthes, apart by hem-selue. **1432** *Paston Lett.* 18. I. 34 Speche..had unto the King at part and in prive. **1528** MORE *Heresyes* III. Wks. 1557, 245/1 Our sauiour at tyme taught his apostles a part. **1611** BIBLE *2 Macc.* xiii. 13 Iudas being apart with the Elders. **1712** STEELE *Spect.* No. 498 ¶3 When they were apart, the impostor revealed himself. **1827** KEBLE *Chr. Y.* 3rd S. Epiph. ii, As I walk and muse apart.

2. Apart from each other, separately; asunder, parted. (Also of the parts of a thing.)

1399 LANGL. *Rich. Redeless* IV. 36 Comliche a clerk than.. pronouncid þe poyntis aparte to hem alle. **1728** NEWTON *Chronol. Amend.* i. 177 The Spartans lived in villages apart. **1816** J. WILSON *City of Plague* II. i. 41 They died three hours apart. **1829** HOOD *E. Aram* iv, His hat was off, his vest apart.

3. Separately in consideration; as a separate or distinct object of thought.

1577–87 HARRISON *Engl.* I. II. xxiv. 356 To deale with some of these antiquities apart. **1605** BACON *Adv. Learn.* II. ix. §3 The inquiry touching human nature entire, as a just portion of knowledge to be handled apart. **1756** C. LUCAS *Ess. Waters* II. 54 Let us view each ingredient apart. **1843** MILL *Logic* II. vi. §1 This is a case which merits examination apart.

4. Away from others in action or function; separately, independently, individually.

c **1400** *Test. Love* III. (R.) Ye han in your bodie diuers members..euerich aparte to his owne doing. **1597** HOOKER *Eccl. Pol.* v. (1632) 304 To make those things subsist a-part which haue the selfe-same generall Nature. **1649** SELDEN *Laws of Eng.* I. xvii. (1739) 34 Their power..was exercised either collectively, or apart and severally. **1794** SULLIVAN *View of Nat.* I. 97 All that they have each of them apart imagined. **1870** BRYANT *Homer* I. I. 30 When I form designs Apart from all the gods.

b. In this sense it often acquires by ellipsis of *being, standing, existing*, etc., an adjective force = Separate. (Cf. Fr. *c'est un homme à part.*)

1786 T. JEFFERSON *Writ.* (1859) II. 34 Qualities and accomplishments..which might form a chapter apart for her. **1849** MACAULAY *Hist. Eng.* I. 331 The London clergy were always spoken of as a class apart. **1868** MILL *Eng. & Irel.*, There is no other civilised nation which is so far apart from Ireland in the character of its history.

5. *fig.* Aside, away from all employment or consideration, as in *to set, lay, put apart*: to put away, dismiss. (Fr. *mettre, laisser à part.*) *arch.*

1477 EARL RIVERS (Caxton) *Dictes* 1 Whiche grace..hath compelled me to sette aparte alle ingratitude. **1558** KNOX *Regim. Wom.* (1878) 20 All shame laid a parte, they..learned the feates of warre. **1611** BIBLE *James* i. 21 Wherefore lay apart all filthinesse. **1827** KEBLE *Chr. Y.* East. Tues. viii, Let Pleasure go, put Care apart.

b. In absolute phrases, as 'jesting apart' (Fr. *raillerie à part*) = Laid aside, put out of question.

1732 BERKELEY *Min. Philos.* I. 52 But, Authority apart, what do you say to Experience? *a* **1744** POPE *Epil. J. Shore* 11 But let me die, all raillery apart. **1826** DISRAELI *Viv. Grey* I. ix. 20 However, jesting apart, get your hat.

6. Away from common use for a special purpose. **to set apart**: to separate, devote, consecrate. (Fr. *mettre à part.*)

1604 HIERON *Wks.* I. 492 Whom God did neuer set a part to that holy seruice. **1611** BIBLE *Ex.* xiii. 12 Thou shalt set apart [COVERDALE, sunder out] vnto the Lord all that openeth the matrix. *c* **1680** BEVERIDGE *Serm.* (1729) I. 13 If no places were set apart for the worship of God. **1711** ADDISON *Spect.* No. 10 ¶2 Families that set apart an Hour in every Morning for Tea. **1853** MAURICE *Proph. & Kings* ii. 22 A portion of the sacrifice was set apart for him.

7. *Const.* In all senses it may be followed by *from*.

1617 *Janua Ling.* 523 Let us be separated a-part from the company. **1833** HT. MARTINEAU *Loom & Lug.* I. v. 87, I see no crime in Elizabeth's taste apart from the means. **1860** TYNDALL *Glac.* II. §16. 312 What then can the viscous theory mean apart from the facts? **1862** LD. BROUGHAM *Brit. Const.* xiii. 184 The precise period at which the Commons first sat apart from the Lords is equally unknown.

¶ *From* is rarely omitted, leaving *apart* to act as a preposition = Away from. (Common in Fr.)

1615 CHAPMAN *Odyss.* I. 289 Apart this city, in the harbour.

†**a'part,** *v. Obs.* [f. prec.]

1. *trans.* To set aside, put away, remove, separate.

1563 SACKVILLE *Mirr. Mag.* Induct. xiv, When I sawe no ende that could aparte The deadly dewle. **1594** R. PARSONS *Next Succession* II. ix. 202 That al fansie and fonde opinion of the vulgar people be aparted, in this matter, from truth and substance. **1620** SHELTON *Quix.* III. vi. I. 157 We may very well cross the way, and apart ourselves from danger.

2. To depart (from), to quit. *Obs.*

1574 HELLOWES *Gueuara's Epist.* 239 To succour their necessities and to appart their conversations.

†**a 'part,** *advb. phr. Obs.* or *dial.* [A *prep.*¹ in + PART: cf. the earlier A-PARTY.] In part, partly.

1481 CAXTON *Reynard* (Arb.) 25 That causeth me a parte to be hevy in my herte. **1548** GESTE *Priuee Masse* 133 Which matere is..not a parte only but throughlie faultie.

apartheid (ə'pɑːtheɪt). [Afrikaans, lit. 'separateness', f. Du. *apart* (ad. F. *à part* APART *adv.*) + *heid* -HOOD.] Name given in South Africa to the segregation of the inhabitants of European descent from the non-European (Coloured or mixed, Bantu, Indian, etc.); applied also to any similar movement elsewhere; also, to other forms of racial separation (social, educational, etc.). Also *fig.* and *attrib.*

[**1929** J. C. DU PLESSIS in *Die N.G. Kerk in die O.V.S. en die Naturelle-Vraagstuk* 22 In hierdie grondbegrip van Sendingwerk en nie in rassevooroordeel nie, moet die verklaring gesoek word vir die gees van apartheid wat ons gedragslyn nog altoos gekenmerk het.] **1947** *Cape Times* 24 Oct. 7/7 Mr. Hofmeyr said apartheid could not be reconciled with a policy of progress and prosperity for South Africa. **1948** *Ibid.* 12 Aug. 1/1 Mr. P. O. Sauer..will explain the application of the apartheid policy on the railways. *Ibid.* 13 Aug. 8 It is always easy to discern the immediate benefits or comforts conferred on the *apartheid*-minded Europeans, but impossible to discern the benefits conferred on the non-Europeans. **1949** *Ibid.* 18 July 9/3 *Apartheid* is to be introduced at the Kimberley Post Office as soon as necessary structural alterations can be made. Separate counters will be provided for European and non-European customers. **1949** *Manch. Guardian* 13 July 4/6 Thus Dr. Malan's policy of 'Apartheid' for the non-Europeans, which is only the Dutch word for Field Marshal Smuts's policy of 'segregation', which in turn is only a pretty word for repression, is achieving a position of 'Apartheid', in the literal sense of isolation, for the nation as a whole. **1950** *Hansard Commons* CCCCLXXVI. 2020 It does not really justify making a sort of political *apartheid* as the basis of one's foreign policy. **1953** J. PACKER *Apes & Ivory* ii. 17 This residential and social *apartheid* is not artificial. It is in the very nature of life in South Africa. What *is* new in *apartheid* is the Immorality Act which forbids intimacy between White and Brown. **1955** *Times* 5 July 6/3 The Archbishop of Canterbury, Dr. Fisher, drew a parallel yesterday between the political *apartheid* which he had seen in South Africa, separating the nation, and ecclesiastical *apartheid* which prevented unity among the churches. **1958** *Times Lit. Suppl.* 21 Nov. 674/5 The tristichs deprived of their rhyming nexus suggest only a metrical *apartheid*. **1959** *Times* 28 Feb. 7/3 Some system of *apartheid* in Central Africa would result. **1959** *News Chron.* 13 Aug. 4/1 Without going to extreme lengths of apartheid, it should still be..possible to allow those who smoke to do so..on a bus top, reserving the lower deck to those who find the habit revolting. **1961** *Times* 15 Mar. 14/2 The South African Broadcasting Corporation said the word apartheid would now not be used except in direct quotation... It would use the word 'self-development' to describe the Government's race policies. **1963** *Listener* 25 Apr. 699/1 It was Sir Charles Snow who first put about the idea of cultural *apartheid*.

apartly, obs. variant of APERTLY *adv.*, openly.

apartment (ə'pɑːtmənt). Also 7–8 **app-**; 7 **appartment**. [a. Fr. *appartement*, ad. med.L. *appartīmentum*, f. *appartīre* to apportion, f. L. *ad* to + *partī-re* to divide, share.]

1. a. A portion of a house or building, consisting of a suite or set of rooms, allotted to the use of a particular person or party. *arch.*

1641 EVELYN *Mem.* (1857) I. 14 Our new lodgings..a very handsome apartment just over against the Hall-court. **1660** BLOUNT *Boscobel* I. (1680) 65 Mr. George Giffard who lived in an appartiment of the house. **1709** *Lond. Gaz.* mmmmcccxcv/2 The Great Hall of his Majesty's Apartment. **1751** CHAMBERS *Cycl.* s.v., A compleat Apartment must consist of a hall, a chamber, an antechamber, a closet, and a cabinet or wardrobe. *a* **1794** GIBBON *Autobiogr.* 27 My apartment consisted of three elegant and well-furnished rooms. **1883** *Standard* 10 May 8/4 To be let, furnished..a large and handsome Apartment, the residence of an English family leaving Genoa.

b. A set of rooms forming one dwelling-place in a building containing a number of these. Chiefly *N. Amer.* (Corresponding to *flat* in British use.)

1874 *Scribner's Monthly* VIII. 63/2 The apartments, some of six, others of ten rooms, including kitchen and servants' rooms, are designed for strictly independent house-keeping. *Ibid.*, Each of the family apartments includes a small ante-chamber or private entrance..a parlor,..a kitchen, three bed-rooms, and a bath-room. **1890** *Harper's Mag.* Jan. 327/1 Mr. and Mrs. Delancy Robinson reside in a cosy flat, or 'apartment', as they prefer to call it, in New York city. **1903** *N.Y. Even. Post* 12 Sept., The chief distinction between a flat and an apartment, according to the accepted definition, is that the apartment has an elevator. **1935** HOLT MARVELL *These Foolish Things* 5 A tinkling piano in the next apartment.

c. *attrib.*: **apartment house**, a building divided into residential suites of rooms (chiefly *N. Amer.*); so ***apartment block, building, hotel.***

1874 *Scribner's Monthly* VIII. 63/1 The pioneer apartment houses in New York are the well-known Stuyvesant Buildings, the first..having been opened in the fall of 1870. **1883** *Chicago Tribune* 4 May 9/3 To Rent..Flat in elegant apartment building, 7 rooms. **1909** EATON & UNDERHILL *Runaway Place* 238 The vast apartment hotels along the Park front. **1932** A. HUXLEY *Brave New World* v. 88 Henry's forty-story apartment house in Westminster. **1955** *Jrnl. Canadian Ling. Assoc.* Oct. 5 The classes into which Canadian English words commonly fall..(11). Everyday words formed into combinations unfamiliar abroad, such as *apartment block*. **1956** D. GASCOYNE *Night Thoughts* 24 Through streets of dwelling-houses and apartment-blocks.

2. A single room of a house; the original sense being expressed by the plur. *apartments*.

1715 in *Lond. Gaz.* mmmmmccccxxxviii/1 Apartments are fitting up in the..College..for Sig. Aldobrandi. **1815** SCOTT *Guy M.* xvi, I stole softly to the window of my apartment. **1824** MARY MITFORD *Our Village* Ser. I. (1863) 8 The curate's lodgings—apartments his landlady would call them. **1879** MISS BRADDON *Vixen* III. 186 Her morning-room was an airy apartment on the first-floor.

†**3.** Separate, proper, or special place of abode; quarters; place appropriated to any purpose. *Obs.*

1681 CHETHAM *Angler's Vade-mec.* xli. §6 Fish will..hide themselves in their private apartments. **1695** WOODWARD *Nat. Hist. Earth* IV. (1723) 205 No other Place or Apartment in the Globe, etc. **1719** DE FOE *Crusoe* 54 When I came down from my Appartment in the Tree.

†**4.** A separate division of any enclosure; a compartment. *Obs.*

1692 LUTTRELL *Brief Rel.* II. (1857) 397 In case a bullet peirce thro'..and the water come in, it shall come into but one apartment. **1703** MOXON *Mech. Exerc.* 127 What Apartments, or Partitions, to make on your Ground-plot. **1727** POPE, etc. *Art Sinking* 115 Every drawer shall be sub-divided into cells..The apartment for peace or war..may in a very few days be filled with several arguments perfectly new.

apartmental (əˌpɑːtˈmɛntəl), *a. rare.* [f. prec. + -AL^{1}.] Of or pertaining to an apartment.

1804 W. TAYLOR in *Ann. Rev.* II. 284 To personal would have succeeded apartmental decoration. **1881** *Daily News* 8 Nov. 5/1 Dwellings on the 'apartmental' principle.

apartness (əˈpɑːtnɪs). [f. APART used as adj. + -NESS.] The quality of being or standing apart, either locally or in character.

1858 HAWTHORNE *Fr. & It. Jrnls.* II. 24 A mild, benevolent coldness and apartness. **1879** STOPF. BROOKE *Milton* iii. 55 Its tone of apartness from strife was not long the tone of Milton.

†**a-ˈparty**, *adv. Obs.* Also 4–5 **a parti(e**. [prop. phr. *a party* in part: see A *prep.*^{1} and PARTY. Fr. *en partie*.] In part, partly; opposed to *in whole*.

1340 HAMPOLE *Pr. Consc.* 3272 Here haf I talde yhow aparty, Of sum payns of purgatory. **1388** WYCLIF *1 Cor.* xiii. 9 For a parti [**1382** of party] we knowun, and a parti we prophecien. *c* **1420** *Pallad. on Husb.* XI. 278 Swettest wynes hevy are, The white a partie salt is not to spare.

†**aˈpass**, *v. Obs.* [a. OFr. *apasse-r*, f. *à* to + *passer* to PASS.] *intr.*, rarely *trans.* To pass on or by (in space or time).

c **1330** *Arth. & Merl.* 2472 This beggar apasseing That dar so speke to a king. *c* **1374** CHAUCER *Boeth* II. v. 46 Whan þei [riches] ben apassed, nedys þei maken hem pore þat forgon þe rychesses. *c* **1400** *Beryn* 2827 [They] were a-passid & entrid in-to grete dispeyr.

†**aˈpassed, apast**, *ppl. a. Obs.* [f. prec. + -ED.] Past by. (Often, like *past*, used as *adv.* or *prep.*)

c **1314** *Guy Warw.* 148 Fort.. That Ich am apassed this hache. *c* **1325** *E.E. Allit. P.* A. 539 Þe day watȝ al apassed date. *c* **1380** *Sir Ferumb.* 2832 Hit is twelmonth and more apaste. *c* **1450** LONELICH *Grail* XX. 125 Þe nyht was wel apast.

†**aˈpassioned**, *ppl. a. Obs. rare*$^{-1}$. [f. OFr. *apassionné* or Sp. *apasionado*, with ppl. ending -ED. Cf. APPASSIONATE, -D, and IMPASSIONED.] Influenced by passion; biased, hostile.

1574 HELLOWES *Gueuara's Epist.* (1577) 157 The base Countrie people doe holde the words of their Lord for gospel, and of the officer [of justice] as apassioned.

apatelite (əˈpætəlaɪt). *Min.* [ad. F. *apatélite* (A. Meillet 1842, in *Revue Scientifique* XI. 255), f. Gr. ἀπατηλός illusive, deceptive + -ITE^{1}.] A hydrous ferric sulphate, found in yellow nodules in clay.

1844 DANA *Syst. Min.* (ed. 2) 617 *Apatelite*, a sulphate of the peroxyd of iron from Mendon and Auteuil, peculiar in containing but little water. **1883** *Encycl. Brit.* XVI. 401/2 Apatelite, reniform-earthy, yellow, from Auteuil near Paris.

apatetic (æpəˈtɛtɪk), *a. Zool.* [ad Gr. ἀπατητικός fallacious, f. ἀπατᾶν to deceive: see -IC.] Applied to markings or coloration deceptively resembling those of another species or of the environment.

1890 POULTON *Colours Anim.* xvii. 338 Apatetic Colours. **1926** *Contemp. Rev.* Sept. 369 Data affecting Epigamic colours have not been collected and examined to anything like the extent of those which concern Apatetic and Sematic colours.

apathaton, corruption of *epitheton*, EPITHET.

1588 SHAKS. *L.L.L.* I. ii. 14, I spoke it tender Juvenall, as a congruent apathaton, appertaining to thy young daies.

apatheia (æpəˈθiːə). Also **aˈpathia**. [ad. Gr. ἀπάθεια: see APATHY.] = APATHY I.

[**1887** *Encycl. Brit.* XXII. 567 This remarkable development of Stoic principles leads to the demand for the entire suppression of the affections (ἀπάθεια).] **1893** T. H. HUXLEY *Evol. & Ethics* 28 That 'apatheia' in which desire, though it may still be felt, is powerless to move the will. **1955** C. B. COX in *Essays & Studies* VIII. 77 The Stoic doctrine of *apatheia*, the principled refusal to experience more emotion than is forced upon one. **1956** S. BECKETT *Godot* I. 42 A personal God.. Who from the heights of divine apathia .. loves us dearly.

apathetic (æpəˈθɛtɪk), *a.* [f. APATHY, after PATHETIC.] Of, or pertaining to, apathy; insensible to suffering or emotion generally; unemotional; indifferent to what is calculated to move the feelings or excite attention.

1744 HARRIS *Happiness* (T.) I am not to be apathetick, like a statue. **1861** *Sat. Rev.* 23 Nov. 539 A sort of apathetic assent. **1863** FAWCETT *Pol. Econ.* II. ii. 131 A people so apathetic to gain. **1865** TROLLOPE *Belton Est.* xii. 138 He wept himself into an apathetic tranquillity.

apaˈthetical, *a. rare.* [f. prec. + -AL^{1}.] = prec.

1834 H. MILLER *Scenes & Leg.* vii. (1873) 87 The easy apathetical indolence of the mere country gentleman.

apaˈthetically, *adv.* [f. prec. + -LY^{2}.] Without emotion; with indifference, stolidly.

1831 *Crayons fr. Commons* 11 His tone was apathetically tame. **1842** EMERSON in *Corr. Carlyle, etc.* I. 366 Love him or hate him or apathetically pass by him. **1883** *Harper's Mag.* Mar. 563/1 Listening apathetically to the preacher.

aˈpathic. ? *Obs. rare*$^{-1}$. [ad. Fr. *apathique*: see APATHY and -IC.] Without sensation.

1836 TODD *Cycl. Anat. & Phys.* I. 107/2 Lamarck proposed three great divisions, the lowest of which comprehended the animals regarded by him as apathic or automatic.

apathist (ˈæpəθɪst). *rare.* [f. Gr. ἀπαθ-ής (see APATHY) + -IST. Cf. mod.Fr. *apathiste*.] One addicted to apathy, one sunk in stolid indifference.

1640 BRATHWAIT *Boulster Lect.* 216 Stoicall apathists who are insensible of passion. **1818** COLERIDGE *Lit. Rem.* I. 119 Writing in a remote village among apathists and ignorants.

apathistical (æpəˈθɪstɪkəl), *a.* ? *Obs. rare*$^{-1}$. [f. prec. + -ICAL.] Of the nature of an apathist; unemotional.

1795 W. SEWARD *Anecd.* V. 252 (T.) Fontenelle was of a good-humoured and apathistical disposition.

apathize (ˈæpəθaɪz), *v. rare.* [f. Gr. ἀπαθ-ής insensible + -IZE.] To render insensible.

1848 SIR J. Y. SIMPSON in *Lancet* July 41 The hand.. in liquid chloroform is usually somewhat more deeply apathized than the other hand.. in the vapour.

ˈapathized, *ppl. a. rare.* [f. prec. + -ED.] Rendered insensible, sunk in apathy.

1852 EMERSON in *Corr. Carlyle, etc.* II. 214, I very well understand all that you say about 'apathized moods.'

apathy (ˈæpəθɪ). [a. Fr. *apathie*, ad. L. *apathīa*, a. Gr. ἀπάθεια, n. of state f. ἀπαθής without feeling, f. ἀ priv. + παθε- (πάθος) suffering, passion.]

1. Freedom from, or insensibility to, suffering; hence, freedom from, or insensibility to, passion or feeling; passionless existence.

1603 HOLLAND *Plutarch's Mor.* 74 They.. do terme those joies, those promptitudes of the will.. by the name of *Eupathies*, i.[e.] good affections and not of *Apathies*, that is to say, Impassibilities. **1660** STANLEY *Hist. Philos.* (1701) 469/2 He, from his Apathy and the Tranquillity of his life, had the attribute of fortunate bestow'd on him. **1665** BOYLE *Occas. Refl.* III. x. (1675) 214 Because the Passions are (sometimes) Mutinous, to wish an Apathy. **1732** POPE *Ess. Man* II. 91 In lazy Apathy let Stoic's boast Their virtue fix'd. **1847** LEWES *Hist. Philos.* I. 360 Apathy was considered by the Stoics as the highest condition of Humanity.

2. Indolence of mind, indifference to what is calculated to move the feelings, or to excite interest or action.

a **1733** NORTH *Lives* II. 158 He wanted a good general apathy.. [i.e.] 1. as to himself, equanimity; 2. as to all others, indifference. *a* **1764** R. LLOYD *Poetry Prof.* Wks. 1774 I. 35 Forsake their apathy a while. **1820** LAMB *Imperf. Symp.*, *Ess.* (1876) III. 220, I am.. a bundle of prejudices.. the veriest thrall to sympathies, apathies, antipathies. **1855** PRESCOTT *Philip II*, I. II. vi. 202 A certain apathy or sluggishness in his nature which led him.. to leave events to take their own course.

3. *transf.* (of the markets, etc.)

1881 *Daily News* 17 Jan. 3/3 The piece market shows great apathy.

apatite (ˈæpətaɪt). *Min.* [mod. f. (by Werner 1786) Gr. ἀπάτη deceit + -ITE; in reference to the diverse and deceiving forms of the mineral.] A native crystallized phosphate of lime, varying in colour from white to green, blue, violet, brown; transparent, translucent, or opaque.

1803 *Edin. Rev.* III. 51 It is.. much better to talk.. of phosphate of lime, than of apatite. **1869** PHILLIPS *Vesuv.* x. 284 Apatite.. is found crystallized in ejected blocks and lava. **1879** RUTLEY *Stud. Rocks* x. 146 Under the microscope apatite appears in elongated hexagonal prisms.

†**aˈpause**, *v. Obs. rare*$^{-1}$. [f. A- *pref.* 11 + PAUSE *v.*] To cause to stop, to stop (any one).

1554 PHILPOT *Exam. & Writ.* 86 With this saying he [Bonner] was apaused.

apawl, obs. form of APPALL *v.*

apay (əˈpeɪ), *v. arch.* Forms: 3–4 **apaie**, 4–5 **apaye, apey**, 6 **appaie**, 5–7 **appay, apay**. [a. OFr. *apay-er, apai-er* (Pr. *apaiar, apagar*), f. late L. **adpācāre*, f. *ad* to, completely + *pācāre* to please, satisfy, *orig.* to pacify, f. *pāc-em* peace (cf. APPEASE and PAY). After 1500 often refashioned as *ap-pay*: see AP- *pref.*^{1} Since 1700, found only in pa. pple., as a poetic archaism: see APAID.]

1. To satisfy, content, please. *arch.*

a **1250** *Meid. Marg.* li, I sende him to þe, To turne þine herte ant apaie me. *c* **1374** CHAUCER *Troylus* V. 1249 She elleswhere hath now hire herte apeyde. *a* **1440** *Sir Degrev.* 574 Other ladyes wolde say, Myȝthe no womman the apay. *c* **1550** BALE *Sel. Wks.* (1849) 116 The priest of this household would be full well apayd both with you and with me. **1603** FLORIO *Montaigne* (1632) 292 To goe about to please and appay divine goodnesse. **1683** CHALKHILL *Thealma & Cl.* 76 Well appaid With what her greedy thoughts had tasted on. **1870** MORRIS *Earth. Par.* III. II. 32 Or all is nought.. Or of my tale shall ye be well apaid.

†**2.** To repay, requite. *Obs.*

1483 CAXTON *G. de la Tour* F j b, Thenne was the good man wel apayed by the falsnes of the old.. woman. **1596** SPENSER *F.Q.* V. v. 33 Eke with gratefull service me right well apay. **1603** FLORIO *Montaigne* II. iv. (1632) 200 The Gods.. reward and appay thee. **1631** QUARLES *Sampson* 290 E're he can appay His wrong with timely vengeance.

ape (eɪp), *sb.* Forms: 1 **apa**, 2– **ape**. *Pl.* 1 **apan**, 2–4 **apen**, 3– **apes**. [OE. *apa* m., *afe* f., cogn. w. LG. *ape*, Du. *aap*, OHG. *affo* m., *affe* f., MHG. *affe*, ON. *api* (Sw. *apa*). Prob. an adopted word in OTeut.; cf. OIr. *apa*, Wel. *epa*; Slav. *op-*, in Old Boh. *op*, Boh. *op-ec*, Slovak *op-itza*.]

1. An animal of the monkey tribe (*Simiadæ*); before the introduction of 'monkey' (16th c.), the generic name, and still (since 1700) sometimes so used poetically or rhetorically, or when their uncouth resemblance to men and mimicry of human action is the main idea (due to reaction of the vb. *ape* upon the sb. whence it was formed).

a **700** *Epinal Gloss.* 827 (Sweet *O.E.T.*) *Phitecus*, apa. *c* **1000** *Sax. Leechd.* I. 366 Wið apan bite oððe mannes, smyre mid fearres geallan. *c* **1300** *K. Alis.* 6464 Visage after martyn apen: Folke heo buth, ful eovel y-schapen! *c* **1350** *Will. Palerne* 2298 Wilde beris & apes. **1366** MAUNDEV. xxii. 239 Babewynes, apes, marmesettes, and othere dyverse bestes. *c* **1400** *Rom. Rose* 6839 Make I not wel tumble myn apes? **1535** COVERDALE *Isa.* xiii. 21 Estriches shal dwell there, and Apes [**1611** Satyres] shal daunse there. **1539** TAVERNER *Erasm. Prov.* 39 The fayrest of Apes is fowle. **1589** PUTTENHAM *Eng. Poesie* (Arb.) 211 Prouerbe: An ape vvilbe an ape, by kinde as they say, Though that ye clad him all in purple array. **1610** SHAKS. *Temp.* IV. i. 249 Apes With foreheads villanous low. **1611** COTGR. s.v. *Femme*, Euerie Ape thinkes her puppie the fairest. **1650** B. *Discollim.* 5 The Proverb, A guilty conscience is as afraid of a feather, as an Apes tayl of a whip. **1727** POPE *Dunciad* I. 282 Less human genius than God gives an ape. **1857** Bohn *Handbk. Prov.* 310 An Ape's an ape; a varlet's a varlet; Though they be clad in silk or scarlet. **1870** MORRIS *Earth. Par.* I. I. 377 Quick-chattering apes, that yet in mockery Of anxious men wrinkle their ugly brows.

2. a. *spec.* A member of the *Simiadæ*, having no tail nor cheek-pouches; including the gorilla, chimpanzee, orang-outan, and gibbons.

1699 TYSON (*title*) Ourang-Outang sive Homo Sylvestris; or the Anatomy of a Pigmy compared with a Monkey, an Ape, and a Man. **1764** WILLIAMS *Dict. Arts* s.v., The ape, properly so called, is without a tail. **1834** *Penny Cycl.* II. 144 We say that an *ape* is a monkey without a tail, and a *baboon* a monkey with a short tail, reserving the term *monkey* more particularly for those species which have very long tails; and though our early writers use these three words indiscriminately.. yet the significations here given have generally prevailed since the time of Ray, and are now exclusively adopted. **1859** DARWIN *Orig. Spec.* vii. 181 Why have not apes acquired the intellectual powers of man?

b. ***to play the ape*** (referring to the way in which these animals mimic human form and gestures): to imitate, *esp.* in an inferior or spurious manner, to counterfeit, mimic the reality.

1579 TOMSON *Calvin's Serm. Tim.* 343/1 He playeth the Ape, and counterfeteth what God hath ordeined for our saluation. **1648** *Pet. Eastern Ass.* 23 Themselves may.. play the Apes in Pulpits.

c. Used quasi-advb. in *to go ape* (*slang*, orig. *U.S.*), to go 'crazy'; to become excited, violent, sexually aggressive, etc.; to display strong enthusiasm or appreciation; also, to malfunction.

See *American Speech* (1961) XXXVI. 150 for an account of the phrase's development.

1955 *Amer. Speech* XXX. 117 [Air Force slang] *Go ape*; *go ape shit, v. phr.*, react in an irrational manner; go into a frenzy. **1962** *Datamation* Feb. 31/1 Here is a great chance to go ape, for if the formats of cards are manifold, those of paper tape are megafold. **1963** D. B. HUGHES *Expendable Man* (1964) i. 23, I go ape over Johnny Mathis. **1966** 'T. WELLS' *Matter of Love & Death* vi. 63 I'm just keeping busy. I've been going ape with nothing to do. **1974** *Sunday Sun* (Brisbane) 4 Aug. 28/5 The local Shire Council has gone ape over the song, Laidley Where The Green Grass Grows, and they're launching it at a gala licensed cabaret in the Shire Hall on August 23. **1985** *Sunday Times* 10 Mar. 56/6 Brian Phelan's play.. is about.. a secret government computer centre that's gone ape... Its minders appear to have launched into freelance crime.

3. Hence *fig.* One who 'plays the ape'; an imitator, a mimic; **a.** contemptuously or derisively.

c **1230** *Ancr. R.* 248 And lauhweð þe olde ape [the devil] lude to bismare. **1561** DAUS *Bullinger on Apoc.* (1573) 316 Antichrist, the Ape of our Lord Christ. **1592** GREENE in *Shaks. Cent. Pr.* 2 Let these Apes imitate your admired inventions. **1607** HIERON *Wks.* I. 360 The diuell is Gods ape, and seekes to counterfeit Him almost in euery thing. **1762** H. WALPOLE *Vertue's Anecd. Paint.* (1786) IV. 298 Every genius has his apes. **1855** H. ROGERS *Ess.* II. vii. 332 This spurious liberalism, which is but a ridiculous ape of charity.

†**b.** in a good or neutral sense. *Obs.*

1594 CAREW *Huarte's Exam. Wits* (1616) 51 The wise and discreet is the Ape of God. **1607** TOPSELL *Four-footed Beasts* (1673) 10 The Poets (with their apes, the painters, limmers, and carvers). **1611** SHAKS. *Cymb.* II. ii. 31 O sleepe, thou Ape of death, lie dull upon her! **1650** ASHMOLE *Arcanum* (ed. 3) 201 Philosophy, which is the Ape of Nature.

†**4.** *transf.* A fool. ***God's ape***: a natural born fool. ***to make any one his ape, to put an ape in his hood***, to befool or dupe him. *Obs.*

c **1330** *Arth. & Merl.* 814 Sche nere so michel ape That sche hir laid doun to slape At hir dore. *c* **1386** CHAUCER *Prol.* 706 He made the person and the peple his Apes. *c* **1386** —— *Prioresses Prol.* 6 The monk put in the mannes hood an ape And in his wyves eek, by seint Austyn. **1513** DOUGLAS *Æneis* IV. Prol. 21 Ȝour trew seruandis [bene] silly goddis apis. **1596** SPENSER *F.Q.* III. ix. 31 Thus was the ape By their faire handling put into Malbeccoes cape. **1611** SHAKS. *Cymb.* IV. ii. 194 Iollity for Apes, and greefe for Boyes. **1741** RICHARDSON *Pamela* (1824) I. 154 That she should instigate the titled ape her husband to write to me.

5. sea ape: the fish *Squalus Vulpes*, also called Sea Fox, and Thresher.

1607 TOPSELL *Four-footed Beasts* (1673) 375 As the Lion recovereth by eating an Ape of the Earth, so is the Dolphin cured by eating an Ape of the Sea. **1769** PENNANT *Brit. Zool.* III. 86 Sea-fox, *Synon.* Sea-ape. **1861** J. COUCH *Brit. Fishes* I. 37 Sea ape = Thresher.

6. ***to lead apes in hell***: the fancied consequence of dying an old maid. ***to say an ape's paternoster***: to chatter with cold.

1579 LYLY *Euphues* (Arb.) 87 Rather thou shouldest leade a lyfe to thine owne lyking in earthe, than..leade Apes in Hell. **1596** SHAKS. *Tam. Shrew* II. i. 34 She is your treasure ..I must..for your loue to her, leade Apes in Hell. **1605** *Lond. Prodigal* i. 2 'Tis an old proverb, and you know it well, That women dying maids lead apes in hell. **1611** COTGR., *Grelotter*, To shake, tremble..say an Apes Pater-noster. **1653** URQUHART *Rabelais* I. xi, He would flay the Fox, say the Apes Paternoster. **1723** MRS. CENTLIVRE *Bold Stroke* II. i, Poor girl: she must certainly lead Apes, as the saying is. **1830** GEN. P. THOMPSON *Exerc.* (1842) I. 198 Joining with other old women, in leading their apes in Tartarus.

†7. as *adj.* Foolish, silly. *adv.* Foolishly, sillily.

c **1370** WYCLIF *Wks.* (1879) 412 Many siche ape resouns han men herd aȝenus crist. **1509** BARCLAY *Ship of Fooles* (1570) 33 Some are ape dronke, full of laughter and of toyes, Some mery dronke.

8. *Comb.* and *Attrib.*, as ***ape-headed***, ***ape-like***, ***ape-mind***; **†ape-bearer**, **-carrier**, one who carried a monkey about for exhibition, a strolling buffoon; **†ape-fox**, ? the opossum; **†ape-keeper**, **-ward**, = ape-bearer; **†ape-leader**, an old maid, see 6; **†ape-ware**, counterfeit wares.

1647 WARD *Simple Cobl.* 29 Ape-headed pullets, which invent Antique foole-fangles. **1859** R. BURTON in *Jrnl. R.G.S.* XXIX. 314 The general aspect in old age..among the women, is hideously ape-like. **1859** MILL *Lib.* 106 Any other faculty than the apelike one of imitation. **1611** SHAKS. *Wint. T.* IV. iii. 101, I know this man well: he hath bene since an Ape-bearer. *a* **1613** OVERBURY *Charac.* O 7 (T.) There is nothing in the earth so pitiful; no, not an ape-carrier. **1630** B. JONSON *New Inn* V. i, Jugglers, and gipsies..colonies of beggars, tumblers, ape-carriers. **1594** BLUNDEVIL *Exerc.* V. (ed. 7) 570 Gesner calleth this Beast an Ape-Foxe, or a Fox-Ape. **1600** CORNWALLYES *Ess.* ii. (1632) Let Ape-keepers, and Players catch the eares of their Auditory. **1651** BROME *Jov. Crew* II. (1652) 372, I will rather hazard my being one of the Devil's Ape-leaders, then to marry while he is melancholly. **1362** LANGL. *P. Pl.* A. VI. 119 'No,' quaþ an Ape-ward 'for nout þat I knowe.' *c* **1230** *Ancr. R.* 248 Ne mei he buten scheawe þe uorð sumwhat of his apeware.

ape (eɪp), *v.* [f. prec. sb.]

1. To imitate, mimic: **a.** pretentiously, irrationally, or absurdly.

1632 MASSINGER *City Mad.* IV. iv, Why should you ape The fashions of court-ladies? **1713** ADDISON *Cato* I. ii, Curse on the Stripling! how he apes his Sire! **1751** JOHNSON *Rambl.* No. 179 ⁋3 When they assume the dignity of knowledge, or ape the sprightliness of wit. **1866** G. MACDONALD *Ann. Quiet Neighb.* x. (1878) 172 That foolish emulation which makes one class ape another from afar.

b. in a good or neutral sense. *rare.*

1634 HERBERT *Trav.* 15 The women imitate (or ape) the men. **1662** FULLER *Worthies* (1840) III. 124 Alabaster.. which apes ivory in the whiteness and smoothness thereof. **1663** SIR G. MACKENZIE *Relig. Stoic* xiii. (1685) 119 Art, which is man's offspring, doth ape nature. **1835** SIR J. ROSS *N.-W. Passage* xvi. 252 Aping the appearance of the animal.

2. ***to ape it***: to play the ape, mimic the reality.

a **1658** CLEVELAND *Def. Protector* 2 What's a Protector? He's a stately Thing, That Apes it in the Non-age of a King. **1672** JACOMB *Rom.* viii. (1868) 304 The devil who loves to ape it after God. **1683** tr. *Erasm. Mor. Encom.* 81 One apes it about in the streets, to court popularity.

†a'peace, *v. Obs. rare.* [var. of APPEASE, assimilated to sb. PEACE.] To make at peace, pacify.

1523 LD. BERNERS *Froiss.* (1842) II. 621 Than I answered them, smylyng, to apeace them. **1548** HALL *Edw. V* (R.) She would mitigate and apeace his mynde.

†a'peacement. *Obs.* rare^{-1}. [f. prec. + -MENT. Variant of APPEASEMENT.] Propitiation.

1581 MARBECK *Bk. of Notes* 700 The head which is gone before into heauen, in whom is apeacement for our sinnes.

a-peak (əˈpiːk), *adv.* (*a.*) *Naut.* Forms: 6–7 **a-pike**, 7– **a-peek**, 8– **a-peak.** [a. Fr. *à pic* vertically; in naval lang. 'le bâtiment est à pic sur son ancre' vertically over its anchor; f. *à* 'to, at, according to' + *pic* 'vertex, summit': see PEAK, PIKE.]

1. In a vertical position; vertical. **a.** 'A *ship* drawn directly over the anchor is ***apeek***; when the forestay and cable form a line, it is ***short stay apeek***; when in a line with the main stay, ***long stay apeek***. The anchor is *apeek* when the cable has been sufficiently hove in to bring the ship over it.' Adm. Smyth *Sailor's Word-bk.* 1867.

1596 SIR F. VERE *Comm.* 30 By reason of my riding with my Anchor a pike. **1627** SMITH *Seaman's Gram.* ix. 38 Is the Anchor a pike, that is, to heaue the Hawse of the ship right ouer the Anchor. **1670** DRYDEN *Tempest* I. i, Come, Bullies, chear up! heave lustily. The Anchor's a Peek. **1790** BEATSON *Nav. & Mil. Mem.* I. 172 The resolution, to order all their anchors to be heaved a-peak. **1812** MAR. EDGEWORTH *Manœuvring* iii, The anchor a-peak, and the sails ready for dropping.

b. *fig.*

1748 SMOLLETT *R. Random* (1812) I. 14 He's going, the land crabs will have him; his anchor's a-peak.

c. ***'yards apeek***: when they are topped, so as to resemble St. Andrew's cross; it is done as a token of mourning, or for convenience.' Adm. Smyth.

1692 in *Smith's Seaman's Gram.* xvi. 80 *To Ride a Peek*, is when the Yards are so ordered, that they seem to make the Figure of St. Andrews Cross.

d. ***oars apeak***: held vertically.

[**1628** LE GRYS tr. *Barclay's Argenis* 306 Setting their Oares on pike.] **1870** *Sund. at Home* 281 (Burial of Mr. Peabody) The 'Leyden'..steamed slowly..up the harbour, followed by the boats, the men with oars apeak.

apease, -eese, obs. forms of APPEASE.

apece, -cy: see ABC.

aped (eɪpt), *ppl. a.* [f. APE *v.* + -ED.] Imitated; counterfeit.

a **1711** KEN *Hymnotheo* Poet. Wks. 1721 III. 37 Himself he in ap'd Regal Robe attires.

apedom (ˈeɪpdəm). *rare.* [f. APE *sb.* + -DOM.] The estate or state of apes.

1853 DE QUINCEY *Wks.* XIV. ii. 85 [They] had not yet emerged from this early condition of apedom.

apehood (ˈeɪphʊd). [f. APE *sb.* + -HOOD.] The condition or nature of an ape.

1825 R. AYTON *Ess. & Sk. Char.* 89 A handful of nuts brought out, in a moment [discovers] the inalienable apehood of the monkey-players. **1839** CARLYLE *Chartism* iv. (1858) 18 He too may be ignorant; but he has not sunk from decent manhood to squalid apehood.

apeire, var. APPAIR *v. Obs.*, to impair.

apel-: see later sp. under APPEL-.

apel, obs. form of APPLE *sb.*

apeling (ˈeɪplɪŋ). *rare.* [f. APE *sb.* + -LING.] A diminutive or young ape.

1861 CDL. WISEMAN *Ess.* (1865) 27 Probably a gorilla points out man to his apelings as a very degenerate specimen of his descendants.

Apelles (əˈpɛliːz). The name of a distinguished Greek painter in the time of Alexander the Great; sometimes used connotatively for a master artist.

c **1630** DRUMM. OF HAWTH. *Wks.* 1711, 2/1 Gold-smith of all the stars, with silver bright Who moon enamels, Apelles of the flow'rs. **1711** SHAFTESB. *Charac.* (1737) I. 227 That none besides..an Apelles shou'd draw their picture.

†ape'luchier, *v. Obs.* rare^{-1}. [a. OFr. *apeluchier*, *espeluchier*, mod.Fr. *éplucher*, f. *es*:—L. *ex* out + *pelucher = Pr. *pelucar*, It. *piluccare*, according to Diez, deriv. vb. f. L. *pīlāre* to pull out hairs, f. *pīlus* hair: cf. PLUSH.] To pick faults, to carp.

1340 *Ayenb.* 253 Naȝt uor to apeluchier, ne zeche kendelich scele, huer he non ne heþ.

ape-man. *Anthropol.* One of a hypothetical genus of mammals supposed by Haeckel to have been intermediate in character and development between the apes and man. Cf. *missing link* (b) s.v. MISSING *ppl. a.* 4. Also in extended use (quot. 1914).

1879 tr. *Haeckel's Evol. Man* II. 182 The ape-men, or *Alali*, were therefore probably already in existence toward the close of the Tertiary Epoch, during the Pliocene Period. **1895** *Westm. Gaz.* 17 Dec. 8/2 Professor Virchow..held that Dubois's discoveries did not at all prove the existence of an antediluvian ape-man. **1914** E. R. BURROUGHS *Tarzan of Apes* (1917) xxvi. 240 The ape-man threw the warm carcass of Numa across his shoulders and took to the trees once more.

apen-: see later spelling APPEN-.

apen, apenion, obs. ff. OPEN, OPINION.

a'pent, var. form of APPEND v^1. *Obs.* To pertain.

a **1400** *Chester Pl.* (1847) 131 Our Lorde will us lere whereto it [the star in the East] will apente. *Ibid.* 189 Yf you wiste wherto it would apente. **1470** HARDING *Chron.* xxvi, To you, my lorde of Yorke, this dooeth appent.

apepsy (əˈpɛpsɪ). *Med.* [ad. mod.L. *apepsia* (often used instead), a. Gr. ἀπεψία indigestion, f. ἀ priv. + πέπτ-ειν to digest. Cf. mod.Fr. *apepsie*.] Lack of digestive power.

1678 PHILLIPS, *Apepsie*, incoction, crudity of the stomach. **1751** CHAMBERS *Cycl.*, *Apepsy*, *apepsia*. **1801** E. DARWIN *Zoon.* III. 202 Violent apepsy, as in low fevers, and total want of digestion. **1876** BARTHOLOW *Mat. Med.* (1879) 123 The condition known as apepsia.

aper-: see later spelling APPER-.

aper (ˈeɪpə(r)). rare^{-0}. [f. APE *v.* + -ER^1.] One who apes; 'a ridiculous imitator or mimick.' J.

‖aperçu (apɛrˈsy). [Fr., pa. pple. of *apercevoir* to perceive.] A summary exposition, a conspectus. Also, a revealing glimpse; an insight.

[**1821** HAZLITT *Table-T.* I. xv. 362 To give the modern reader *un petit aperçu* of the tone of literary conversation about five or six and twenty years ago.] **1828** DISRAELI *Voyage Capt. Popanilla* iv. 33 [He] flew off to an airy *aperçu* of the French Revolution. **1844** J. S. MILL in *Edin. Rev.* LXXIX. 22 Every one of the chapters we have cited is full of interesting *aperçus*. **1882** *St. James's Gaz.* 15 Feb., Who could read Mr. Green's book without finding in it much new knowledge and many luminous aperçus. **1882** *Pall Mall G.* 18 Nov. 21 Demonstrations or aperçus of considerable scientific value. **1957** *Times Lit. Suppl.* 27 Dec. 783/2 Almost always in the course of each essay there are *aperçus* of great penetration. **1963** *Med. Ævum* XXXII. 152 The notes..are reminiscent, in their expansive relevance and out-of-the-way *aperçus*, of the best nineteenth-century editing.

†a'pere, *v. Obs.* [a. OFr. *apere*, *apaire*, pres. sing. of *aparie-r* to make equal or similar, to liken:—late L. **ad-*, *ap-pariā-re*, f. *ad* to + *par-em* equal. Cf. APPARIATE.] *intr.* (for *refl.*) To be equal.

c **1440** LONELICH *Graal* II. 37 Thanne seide the peple.. that he to god aperede.

aperient (əˈpɪərɪənt), *a.* and *sb.* [ad. L. *aperient-em*, pr. pple. of *aperī-re* (orig. *āperī-re*) to open, f. *ā* = *ab* off, away + *par(i)-ēre* to get; cf. Eng. *undo*] **A.** *adj.* Opening the bowels; laxative. **B.** *sb.* [sc. medicine, article of diet.]

1626 BACON *Sylva* §961 (J.) They be of three intentions: refrigerant, corroborative, and aperient. **1674** GREW *Anat. Plants* iii. (1682) 257 Agrimony an Aperient. **1765** TUCKER *Lt. Nat.* II. 234 Air, exercise, proper regimen of diet, and aperients may relieve them. **1872** BAKER *Nile Trib.* i. 6 A small piece..renders the draught a strong aperient.

aperiodic (ˌeɪpɪərɪˈɒdɪk), *a.* [f. Gr. ἀ- priv. (A- *pref.* 14) + PERIODIC *a.*^{1}] Not periodic; without regular recurrence. In various techn. senses (see quots.); *spec.* of a galvanometer, without periodic vibrations, 'dead-beat'.

1879 *Encycl. Brit.* X. 50/2 An intermediate stage called the aperiodic state. **1884** KROHN tr. *Glaser de Cew's Magn.- & Dyn.-Electr. Mach.* 228 The commutator am-meter is an aperiodic galvanometer. **1894** W. L. DALLAS in *Indian Meteorol. Mem.* VI. 2 The annual periodic changes and the aperiodic changes [are] both very slight. **1930** *Engineering* 31 Jan. 129/3 Another new instrument shown was an aperiodic balance, in which air damping is provided in order to bring the beam to rest rapidly. **1943** *Gloss. Terms Telecomm.* (*B.S.I.*) 68 *Aperiodic aerial*, an aerial designed to operate over a substantial range of frequencies. **1952** E. HYAMS *Soil & Civilization* i. 7 The man's motions abrupt, aperiodic and angular.

aperispermic (əˌpɛrɪˈspɜːmɪk), *a. Bot.* [f. A- *pref.* 14 priv. + PERISPERMIC.] Having no albumen round the embryo of the seed; non-albuminous.

1878 MASTERS *Henfrey's Bot.* 302 Aperispermic seeds.

aperitif (əˈpɛrɪtiːf, ‖aperitif). Also **‖apéritif.** [F. *apéritif*:—L. *aperitīvus*, f. *aperīre* to open.] An alcoholic drink taken, before a meal, to stimulate the appetite.

1894 *Idler* Mar. 187 They..sipped their *aperitifs* tranquilly. **1905** *Daily Tel.* 22 Feb. 9/2 A teacup-full of whisky which was handed to him by the cook as an aperitif. **1929** *Graphic* 12 Jan. 54 A memento of Prince George's visit to Bermuda... He is having an after-the-bathe apéritif. **1959** *Listener* 30 July 191/1 Apéritif ports and sherrys can be served very lightly chilled, too.

fig. **1920** *Sat. Rev.* 21 Aug. 154/2 But the young artists.. mistook the apéritif for the dinner. **1937** *Burlington Mag.* June p. xxvi/1 A magnificent scene by Jacob van Ruisdael.. and a pair of huge game and fish compositions..are *apéritifs* for any Gargantua.

aperitive (əˈpɛrɪtɪv), *a.* Also 7 **apperitive**, 6–8 **aperative.** [variant of APERTIVE, after mod.Fr. *apéritif*, *-ive*, older Fr. *aperitif*, med.L. *aperitivus* and *aperitīvus*, It. *apertivo* and *aperitivo*.]

A. *adj.* **†1.** Tending to open. *Obs. rare.*

1685 BOYLE *Free Enq.* 381 Its [a key's] Power of opening a Door (which, perhaps, some School-Men would call its aperitive Faculty).

2. *Med.* Tending to open the bowels; aperient.

1582 HESTER *Phiorav. Secr.* I. xvi. 16 Warme and drie and aperatiue. **1603** FLORIO *Montaigne* II. xxxvii. (1632) 434 Aperitive things are good for a man thats troubled with the collike. **1853** SOYER *Pantroph.* 167 Smallage is diuretic and aperitive.

B. *sb.* [sc. medicine, article of diet.]

1671 SALMON *Syn. Med.* III. xvi. 361 Apperitives..open the mouths of the vessels. **1727** SWIFT *Gulliver* III. vi. 216 Administer to each of them aperitives. **1841** *Chamb. Jrnl.* X. 260 The other physicians..all insisted on the use of the strongest aperitives.

apern, obs. form of APRON.

a per se, apersee: see A (the letter) IV.

apert (əˈpɜːt), *a.* and *adv. arch.* Also 4–6 **appert,** and aphet. PERT. [a. OFr. *apert*:—L. *apert-um* open, pa. pple. of *aperī-re* to open: see APERIENT. In OFr. the word was to some extent confused with *aspert* = *espert*:—L. *expertus*, 'expert,' which seems to have affected some of the senses.]

A. *adj.*

1. Open, manifest, public, plain, unconcealed. (Opposed to *privy*.) *arch.* since *c* 1700.

1330 R. BRUNNE *Chron.* 29 Gaf Saynt Cutbert Londes & liþes, with chartir aperte. **1395** PURVEY *Remonstr.* (1851) 8 Glotonie, lecherie, and othere synnis prevy or apert. *c* **1400** *Rom. Rose* 6153 Religiouse folk ben fulle covert; Seculer folk ben more appert. **1483** CAXTON *G. de la Tour* D ij b, Appert or knowen myracles. **1600** HOLLAND *Livy* XXIV. xxv, In vaine he had attempted to be king by apert and open force [*palam atque aperte*]. **1681** GLANVILL *Sadducismus* I. (ed. 2) 99 The apert confession of the Nullibists. **1849** S. MAITLAND *Ess.* 392 Gardiner got many 'nips,' both 'privy' and apert, for his share in the book. **1879** WARD *Chaucer* i. 41 Our national life in this period.. in its 'apert,' if not in its 'privy' sides.. lacks the seriousness belonging to men and to generations.

†**b.** 'Open' in sound. *Obs.*

1668 WILKINS *Real Char.* III. xi. (R.) They [vowels] are therefore stiled apert or open letters.

†**2.** Manifest to the understanding, plain, evident.

1340 *Ayenb.* 203 Yef þe wordes byeþ uoule.. þet is apert tokne þet þe uoulhede.. byeþ ine þe herte. **1589** PUTTENHAM *Eng. Poesie* 238 Which had bene the directer speech and more apert. **1674** HICKMAN *Hist. Quinquart.* 7 There are in Zuinglius.. most apert sentences from which it is gathered that God is the Author of sin.

†**3.** Straightforward, direct; brisk, bold. (With *batayle aperte* cf. 'open battle.'). *Obs.*

c **1300** *K. Alis.* 2450 Ther ros batayle aperte; Ten hundrid weoren to dethe y-dight. **1375** BARBOUR *Bruce* x. 73 Thai.. full manfully Grete and apert defens can ma. *c* **1425** WYNTOUN *Cron.* VIII. xxxiii. 113 Wyth þe Wachis sturdily Made ane apert and stout mellé.

†**4.** Distinguished, clever, ready, expert. *Obs.*

a **1330** *Sire Degarre* 95 Ther nas non in al the Kynges londe, More apert man than was he. **1483** CAXTON *Gold. Leg.* 276/2 Sharp in assoyllyng questyons, ryght appert in confundyng heretykes.

†**5.** Outspoken, forward in manner, bold, insolent. (Survives in the aphetized PERT.) *Obs.*

1330 R. BRUNNE *Chron.* 289 Modred a fole aperte was slayn [for] licherie. *c* **1394** *P. Pl. Crede* 541 Wiþ proude wordes apert þat passeth his rule. *a* **1400** *Sir Perc.* 681 Come I to the, appert fole, I salle caste the in the pole. **1483** CAXTON *G. de la Tour* B ij, She was aperte, for she praid me two or thre tymes that I shold not leue. **1688** *Vox Cleri pro Rege* 3 Another stroak of his Rhetorick.. to the same purpose, but only with a more apert and forward explanation.

†**6.** *in apert* (OFr. *en apert*): openly, in public. *into apert*: to public view. *Obs.*

1375 BARBOUR *Bruce* XIX. 217 Mony a knycht and ek lady Mak in apert richt euill cher. **1382** WYCLIF *Mark* iv. 22 Nether ony thing is preuy, the whiche shal not come in to apert [**1388** opyn]. **1393** GOWER *Conf.* I. 182 Alle tho, that hadden be Or in appert or in prive Of counseil to the mariage. **1496** *Dives & Paup.* (W. de W.) I. lxii. 105/1 Two maner of dedes . oone pryuely and an other in aperte or openly.

†**B.** *adv.* Openly, manifestly, plainly, publicly.

a **1300** *Cursor M.* 6355 Þis meracle sagh þai all aperte. *c* **1400** *Apol. Loll.* 78 Oueral goþ symonie priualy or apert. *c* **1450** MYRC 1448 Tell hyt owte now a-pert. **1556** ABP. PARKER *Ps.* cxix. 131 Rayse up my mouth I did apert.

†**aperté.** *Obs. rare*$^{-1}$. [a. OFr. *aperté* military skill, f. *apert* expert: see prec.] The public manifestation of skill; display of prowess.

1470 HARDING *Chron.* cxcviii, Consyderyng well his knightly aperte.

†**aperte'ment,** *adv. Obs.* [a. OFr. *apertement* openly: see APERT.] Openly, publicly; manifestly.

c **1320** *Cast. Loue* 781 Bi-leeue is apertement Of alle vertues foundement. *a* **1400** *Leg. Rood* (1871) 182 To hem þow seydust apertment [*v.r.* a-pertement] 'Ne wepe ȝe not.'

†**a'pertion.** *Obs.* [ad. L. *apertiōn-em*, n. of action f. *aperīre* to open: see APERIENT.]

1. The action of opening.

1615 CROOKE *Body of Man* 379 Anastomosis or inoculation or apertion and opening of two vessels one into another. **1743** tr. *Heister's Surg.* 353 The Apertion of an Artery with a sharp Instrument.

2. An opening, an aperture.

1599 A. M. *Gabelhouer's Bk. Physic* 12/1 Make a little apertion in the one end of the Egge, and let the water runne therout. **1624** WOTTON *Archit.* in *Reliq.* (1672) 17 Apertions, under which term I do comprehend Doors, windows.. or other Conducts. **1684** tr. *Bonet's Merc. Compit.* I. 4 You may make the apertion as long and deep as the malady and your curiosity require.

3. Openness (in sound). Cf. APERT 1 b. *rare.*

1668 WILKINS *Real Char.* I. iv. §5. 17 The Vowels ought to haue something answerable in their Character unto the several kinds of Apertion which they haue in their sound.

apertive (ə'pɜːtɪv), *a.* ? *Obs.* [a. Fr. *apertif*, *-ive*:—late L. *apertīv-us*, f. *apert-* ppl. stem of *aperīre* to open: see -IVE.]

†**1.** Open, manifest. (So in Fr.) *Obs. rare.*

1681 BLOUNT *Glossogr.*, *Apertive*.. clear and manifest.

2. = APERIENT.

1605 TIMME *Quersit.* III. 181 Take of the rootes of eryngium.. and of the fiue rootes apertive. **1713** *Lond. & Countr. Brew.* I. (1742) 42 Hops, being endowed with discutient apertive Qualities.

a'pertly, *adv.* ? *Obs.* Forms: 3–4 **apertelyche**, 4 **-lyke, apeartlye**, 4–5 **apertelich(e, -teli, -tli, appert(e)ly**, 4–6 **apertely(e**, 5–6 **-art(e)ly**, 6 **apartlie**, 4–8 **apertly**. [f. APERT *a.* + -LY².]

1. Openly to the senses, publicly, plainly; without secrecy or concealment. (Opposed to *privily*.)

1297 R. GLOUC. 375 Me myȝte bere.. Tresour aboute & oþer god oueral apertelyche. *a* **1450** *Knt. de la Tour* 46 As he shewed unto this good lady apertely. *c* **1450** *Merlin* iv. 76 He hadde aperteliche the semblaunce of the Duke. **1577** HOLINSHED *Chron.* I. 73/1 Going about manie things both priuilie and apertlie. **1603** KNOLLES *Hist. Turks* (1621) 123 Giving aid both apertly and covertly unto the weaker. *a* **1734** NORTH *Examen* I. iii. ¶131 So long as no positive Charge is apertly made to the Prejudice of any one.

2. Manifestly (to the understanding), clearly, evidently, plainly.

c **1315** SHOREHAM 96 That other heste apertelyche Schewed mannes defaute. **1377** LANGL. *P. Pl.* B. III. 256 It is a permutacioun apertly, a peny-worth for an othre. **1481** CAXTON *Myrr.* I. v. 27 Otherwise may not be knowen appertly the certayn ne the incertayn. **1581** MARBECK *Bk. of Notes* 410 Paule spake simplie and apertlie. **1680** H. MORE *Apocal. Apoc.* 285 There is apertly mention made of the sixth and seventh Trumpet.

3. Straightforwardly, boldly; with distinction.

1375 BARBOUR *Bruce* x. 315 This gud Erll nocht-for-thi The Sege tuk full apertly. *Ibid.* XIV. 77 The Scottis men in that fechting Swa apertly and weille thame bar.

a'pertness. *arch.* [f. APERT *a.* + -NESS.]

1. The quality of being apert; openness; frankness.

1618 M. BARET *Horsemanship* I. 52 It will be very decerneable to the spectators; which apertnesse is nothing commendable in a Horseman. **1655** *Let.* in Hartlib. *Ref. Commonw. Bees* 33, I.. did conceive my apertnesse a candid Testimony of my intentions. *a* **1817** D'ISRAELI *Cur. Lit.* 482 This has arisen from a want of what Ashmole calls 'apertness.'

†**2.** Plainness of speech; freedom of utterance.

1604 WRIGHT *Passions of Mind* v. §4. 192 The reasons.. require great perspicuitie and apertnesse in deliuerie. **1669** HOLDER *Elem. Speech* (J.) The freedom or apertness and vigour of pronouncing.

apertometer (æpə'tɒmɪtə(r)). [f. L. *apert-us* open + -(O)-METER.] An appliance attached to a microscope for determining the angular aperture of object-glasses.

1880 *Nature* XXI. 433 Some remarks on the apertometer. **1881** *Athenæum* 26 Nov. 707/3 An Abbe apertometer of dense glass for measuring apertures up to 1·50 N.A.

apertural (ə'pɜːtjʊərəl), *a.* [f. L. *apertūra* + -AL¹.] Of the nature of, or pertaining to, an aperture.

1854 WOODWARD *Mollusca* (1856) 118 Mangelia.. apertural slit at the suture.

aperture ('æpətjʊə(r)). [ad. L. *apertūra*, f. *apert-* ppl. stem of *aperīre* to open: see -URE.]

†**1.** The process of opening. *Obs.*

1669 HOLDER *Elem. Speech* (J.) From an appulse to an aperture, is easier than from one appulse to another. **1686** GOAD *Celest. Bod.* I. vi. 21 The aperture and explication of the willing Flower. **1708** *Phil. Trans.* XXVI. 170 His Brother.. desired an Eminent Surgeon.. to open him; but as the Aperture was to be perform'd gratis, he put it off.

†**2.** The opening up of what is involved, intricate, restricted. *Obs. rare.*

1649 JER. TAYLOR *Gt. Exemp.* Add. v. §4 The apertures and permissions of marriage have such restraints of modesty and prudence, that, etc. **1660** —— *Worthy Commun.* Introd. 8 The aperture and dissolution of distinctions.

3. An opening, an open space between portions of solid matter; a gap, cleft, chasm, or hole; the mouth of the shell of a mollusc.

1665 GLANVILL *Sceps. Sci.* vi. 26 If memory be made by the easy motion of the Spirits through the open passages, images, without doubt, pass through the same apertures. **1696** WHISTON *Th. Earth* IV. (1722) 409 So much Water was run down.. as the Apertures could receive. **1794** SULLIVAN *View Nat.* II. 88 The internal structure.. may be compared to a spunge, though the apertures cannot in general be perceived. **1856** WOODWARD *Fossil Shells* 44 The thickening and contraction of the aperture in the univalves.

4. *Opt.* The space through which light passes in any optical instrument (though there is no material opening). Also *attrib.* ***aperture number, ratio*** (see quot. 1953).

1664 *Phil. Trans.* I. 19, I saw.. with one Aperture of my glass more than 40 or 50. **1751** CHAMBERS *Cycl.* s.v., The focal distances of the eye-glasses are to be proportional to the Apertures. **1879** LOCKYER *Elem. Astron.* vi. 218 The aperture of the object-glass, that is to say, its diameter. **1879** H. GRUBB in *Proc. R. Dubl. Soc.* 181 That roundness and relief that is admired so much in photographs taken with large aperture lenses. **1889** W. A. WATTS in *Year-bk. Photogr.* *1889* 91 The desirability of ascertaining the aperture ratio (f/n) of each stop employed is universally admitted. **1953** AMOS & BIRKINSHAW *Telev. Engin.* I. 166 The aperture number or aperture ratio, which is defined as the ratio of the focal length of the system to the diameter of the entrance pupil.

5. 'In some Writers of Geometry, the Inclination, or Leaning of one Right-line towards another, which meet in a point and make an Angle.' Phillips 1706.

So in CHAMBERS 1751, HUTTON 1796.

6. The opening in the sight of a rifle. Usu. *attrib.*, as ***aperture sight***.

a **1884** KNIGHT *Dict. Mech.* Suppl. 43/1 *Aperture-sight*, another name for the open bead-sight. **1913** A. G. FULTON *Notes on Rifle Shooting* 8 In choosing an aperture backsight, a pattern which is perfectly rigid throughout.. should be chosen... One can hardly be better than the latest No. 9c B.S.A. aperture sight. *Ibid.* 9 The size of aperture depends.. on the individual. **1915** F. H. LAWRENCE *Let.* 26 Apr. in *Home Lett. T. E. Lawrence* (1954) 708 If Pearson wants my rifle sell it him. The aperture back sight wants to be screwed down tight.

apery ('eɪpərɪ). [f. APE *sb.* + -RY, or APER + -Y. In sense treated partly like *mocker-y*, partly like *fine-ry*, partly like *rook-ery*.]

1. The practice of an aper; aping; pretentious or silly mimicry.

1616 HAYWARD *Sanct. Troubled Soule* II. §6 (1620) 133 An outward Apery of Religion. *c* **1700** *Gentlem. Instr.* (1732) 152 Hate.. Hypocrisy as Poison, and a base Complaisance as meer Apery. **1844** MARG. FULLER *Woman in 19th C.* (1862) 145 Women, dressed.. in apery, or as it looked, in mockery of European fashions.

2. *concr.* A pretentious imitation. *rare.*

1812 COLMAN *Two Parsons* xxxiv, His rooms were crowded with Etruscan aperies.

3. A silly or apish action or performance.

1851 CARLYLE *Sterling* III. iii. (1872) 195 The.. sickly superstitious aperies and impostures of the time. **1858** —— *Fredk. Gt.* I. III. xx. 265 A young Fritzchen's cradle, who.. will speak and do aperies one day.

4. A collection or colony of apes. *rare.*

1862 KINGSLEY *Water Bab.* in *Macm. Mag.* Nov. 8 More apish than all the apes of all aperies.

apese, obs. form of APPEASE *v.*

†**'apess.** *Obs.* [f. APE + -ESS; the OE. distinction, *apa* m., *ape* f., being lost.] A she-ape.

1623 J. WODROEPHE *Marrow Fr. Tong.* (1625) 256 The Ape loues his Apesse, and sweares she is the fairest of all beasts.

apet-: see later spelling APPET-.

apetaloid (ə'pɛtəlɔɪd), *a. Bot.* [f. as next + -OID.] Of apetalous form.

1870 BENTLEY *Bot.* 222 When there is but one whorl of floral envelopes.. the flower is then termed apetaloid.

apetalous (ə'pɛtələs), *a. Bot.* [f. mod.L. *apetal-us* (a. Gr. ἀπέταλ-ος, leafless, f. ἀ priv. + πέταλ-ον leaf) + -OUS.] Without petals.

1706 PHILLIPS, *Apetalous* flowers or plants are such as want the fine colour'd Leaves of Flowers, which they call Petals. **1749** MORTIMER in *Phil. Trans.* XLVI. 53 Trees and Shrubs having apetalous Flowers. **1870** HOOKER *Stud. Flora* 44 [Sweet Violet has] apetalous autumnal flowers, chiefly fertile.

a'petalousness. *rare*$^{-0}$. [f. prec. + -NESS.] The quality or state of being apetalous.

1731 in BAILEY.

apex ('eɪpɛks). *sb.*¹ Pl. **apices** ('eɪpɪsiːz, 'æp-), **apexes**. [a. L. *apex* peak, tip, the small rod at the top of the flamen's cap, perh. f. *ap-* to fit to (cf. *vertex*, f. *vertĕre* to turn); whence, the tip of anything.]

1. (*As in Latin.*) *rare.*

1603 B. JONSON *James I.'s Entert.* Wks. 1838, 532 Upon his head a hat of delicate wool, whose top ended in a cone, and was thence called apex. **1753** CHAMBERS *Cycl. Supp.*, The *Apex* is described as a stitched cap in form of a helmet, with the addition of a little stick fixed on the top. **1820** MAIR *Tyro's Dict.* 7 *Apicatus*, wearing an apex, tufted.

2. The tip of anything, the top or peak of a mountain, pyramid, or spire; the pointed end of anything pyramidal or spiral, as a shell or leaf.

1610 HEALEY *St. Aug., City of God* 77 Apex, is any thing.. added to the toppe, or highest part of a thing. **1637** HEYWOOD *Royal Ship* 2 In the very Apex and top thereof [Mt. Ararat], there is still to be discerned a blacke shadow. **1727** DE FOE, etc. *Tour Gt. Brit.* (1769) III. 319 The Precipices were surprisingly variegated with Apices, Prominences, etc. **1848** MRS. JAMESON *Sacr. & Leg. Art* (1850) 108 In the apex of the dome, is seen the Celestial Dove. **1853** C. BRONTË *Villette* xxix. (1876) 325 It formed the apex to a blooming pyramid. **1866** R. TATE *Brit. Mollusks* iii. 56 The shells.. have their apices eroded. **1864** T. MOORE *Brit. Ferns* 111 The apices of the fronds. **1873** H. SPENCER *Sociol.* iii. 49 Crystals.. modified by truncations of angles and apices. **1881** RAYMOND *Mining Gloss.*, *Apex*, in the U.S. Revenue Statutes, the end or edge of a vein nearest the surface.

3. *Geom.* The vertex of a triangle or cone.

1678 PHILLIPS, *Apex*, principally in a Geometrical signification, the top of a Conical figure, which ends and sharpens into a point. **1869** RAWLINSON *Anc. Hist.* 56 Memphis, not much above the apex of the Delta. **1879** *Cassell's Techn. Educ.* I. 68 The apex of this triangle.

4. *fig.* (Cf. *acme, climax.*)

1641 R. BROOKE *Nat. Eng. Episc.* 21 Now.. I am neere the Apex of this question. *a* **1643** W. CARTWRIGHT *To C'tess Carlile*, You who have gained the apex of your kind. **1868** M. PATTISON *Academ. Org.* §5. 124 Commencing with the rudiments of grammar and terminating in the apex of the Doctorate. **1883** A. BLAKE in *Harper's Mag.* 902/1 They have attained the apex of the comic.

5. The highest or culminating point of time. *rare.*

1677 HALE *Prim. Orig. Man.* 292 In the beginning, the first Apex of Time which began with the Being of Matter.

1864 HEAVYSEGE *Shaks. Tercent. Ode* 2 The apex of the years, The period's culmination.

6. *Bot.* †**a.** An early name for the ANTHER or summit of the stamen (*obs.*). **b.** The tip of a young plant-shoot, 'the growing point.'

1691 RAY *Creation* I. (1777) 104 The masculine or prolific seed contained in the chiues or apices of the stamina. **1751** CHAMBERS *Cycl.* s.v., On the tops of the stamina or chives, grow those little capsulæ or knobs, called Apices. **1862** DARWIN *Orchids* vi. 251 This apex consists of a thin flattened filament. [See also under ANTHER.]

‖7. A horn or projecting point on a Hebrew letter. (So Vulg. translates κεραία *Matt.* v. 18; Eng. 'tittle.')

a **1646** J. GREGORY *Posthuma* 193 There being no difference between *gimel* [ג] and *nun* [נ] but a small apex or excrescence.

†8. Hence *fig.* A tittle, a jot; the least portion of anything written or said. *Obs.*

1635 JACKSON *Creed* VIII. xxvii. Wks. VIII. 113 The words .. answer punctually and identically to every apex or tittle of St. Matthew's quotation. **1661** *Origen's Opin.* in *Phœnix* 1721 I. 77 To establish the Sense and Interpretation .. upon Tittles and Apices. **1680** S. MATHER *Iren.* 8 Every *Apex* of truth is precious, the least Jota thereof is not to be despised.

9. *Comb.*, as **apex-beat**, the impulse of the contraction of the heart.

1877 ROBERTS *Handbk. Med.* II. 7 In health the apex-beat is usually felt in the 5th left interspace.

'Apex, *sb.*[2] (*a.*) Also **APEX**. [Acronym, f. the initial letters of *A*dvance *P*urchase *Ex*cursion.] A system whereby airline tickets for scheduled flights may be bought at a reduced rate on certain conditions (usually including payment in advance and a specified interval between outward and return flights); a fare offered on these conditions. Freq. *attrib.* or as *adj.*

[**1970** *Aviation Week & Space Technol.* 15 June 24/3 Pan American would also add a new excursion fare, tentatively referred to as an 'advance purchase fare' .. at a lower rate than the standard excursion tariff.] **1971** *Time* 23 Aug. 53/3 The West Germans argued that .. APEX [advance-purchase excursion plan] would only add confusion to .. fares. **1974** *Aviation Week & Space Technol.* 28 Oct. 24/2 The Apex fare, if it is allowed to become effective Nov. 1, will be the lowest of all scheduled fares. **1976** *Holiday Which?* May 60 *APEX*, Advance Purchase Excursion Fare. Available on various routes, using scheduled flights. Book and pay at least two months in advance. *Ibid.*, Johannesburg .. £356 (Apex). **1980** *Times* 16 Feb. 11/8 Travel notes... Low season Super-Apex £282. **1985** *Washington Post* 18 Aug. E8/1 They fly nonstop from New York to Nice for an APEX fare of about £900 round-trip.

'Apex, *sb.*[3] Also **APEX**. [Acronym, f. the initial letters of *A*ssociation of *P*rofessional, *E*xecutive, *C*lerical and *C*omputer *S*taff, with substitution of *X* for *CCS* (ks).] A British trade union representing clerical and other non-manual workers.

1972 *Times* 28 Apr. 21/1 Mr Roy Grantham, general-secretary of the Association of Professional, Executive, Clerical and Computer Staff (Apex). **1972** *Times* 3 July 20/5 APEX is engaged in an active recruitment battle with Mr Clive Jenkins's Association of Scientific, Technical and Managerial Staffs. **1981** *Economist* 24 Jan. 69/1 The GMWU has also been having discussions with the electricians' union, the clerical union (Apex) and the shopworkers' union about a grand federation.

'apex, *v.* [f. APEX *sb.*[1]] *trans.* To form with an apex or pointed top; to raise to a point or tip.

1905 HOLMAN HUNT *Pre-Raph.* I. 87 Should the several parts of the composition be always apexed in pyramids? **1924** *Scribner's Mag.* Jan. 56/1 Phil apexed his fine even eyebrows in the direction of Mary.

apexed ('eɪpɪkst), *ppl. a.* [f. APEX *sb.*[1] + -ED.] Having an apex, pointed.

1869 BURGH in *Eng. Mech.* 9 Apr. 51/2 Two apexed angles.

apfelstrudel: see apple strudel, APPLE *sb.* B. II.

aph-, repr. Gr. ἀφ', phonetic variant of ἀπό 'off, away from,' used before an aspirated vowel.

aphæresis (ə'fɪərɪsɪs). Also **aphe-**. [a. L. *aphæresis*, a. Gr. ἀφαίρεσις a taking away, n. of action f. ἀφαιρέ-ειν, f. ἀφ' = ἀπό off, away + αἱρέ-ειν to take, snatch. The Latin grammarians gave it the transf. sense.]

1. *Gram.* The taking away or suppression of a letter or syllable at the beginning of a word.

1611 COTGR., *Aphairese*, the figure Aphæresis. **1789** MRS. PIOZZI *Fr. & It.* II. 24 The figure aphærisis [will] alter the appellation entirely. **1846** TREGELLES tr. *Gesenius Heb. Lex.* 2/2 In Hebrew, א without a vowel is very often rejected from the beginning of a word by aphæresis. **1864** WEBSTER *Aphæresis, Apheresis.*

†2. *Med. Obs.*

1753 CHAMBERS *Cycl. Supp.*, *Aphæresis* in medicine denotes a necessary taking away or removal of something that is noxious. In surgery, an operation whereby something superfluous is taken away. **1880** *Syd. Soc. Lex.*, *Aphæresis*, formerly used for large and injurious extraction of blood.

aphæretic (æfɪ'rɛtɪk), *a. rare.* [ad. Gr. ἀφαιρετικ-ός: see prec.] Of the nature of aphæresis.

aphakia (ə'feɪkɪə). *Path.* [mod.L., f. Gr. ἀ- priv. (A- *pref.* 14) + φακ-ός lentil + -IA[1].] Absence of the crystalline lens of the eye. Hence **a'phakic** *a.* and *sb.*

1864 W. D. MOORE tr. *F.C. Donders' On Anomalies of Accommodation & Refraction* ii. 84 Of the disturbances in the lenticular system the condition of total absence of the lens, which I have termed aphakia, comes almost exclusively under observation. **1874** DUNGLISON *Dict. Med. Sci.* 69/2 *Aphakia*, an anomalous state of refraction caused by the absence of the crystalline lens, as after operations for cataract. **1889** *Cent. Dict.*, Aphakic, adj. **1894** *Pop. Sci. Monthly* XLIV. 559 Dazzled and dazed the scientific mind is at present like the *aphakic*, suddenly brought to see, but not recognizing or knowing what he sees. **1964** S. DUKE-ELDER *Parsons' Dis. Eye* (ed. 14) viii. 92 The retinal image of the aphakic eye is about a quarter larger than the emmetropic retinal image.

a'phanesite. *Min.* [badly formed on Gr. ἀφανής non-apparent + -ITE.] A synonym of the mineral called by Dana CLINOCLASITE.

‖**Aphaniptera** (æfə'nɪptərə), *sb. pl. Zool.* [mod.L., f. Gr. ἀφαν-ής unseen + -πτερος winged, f. πτερόν wing.] A small order of insects, in which the wings exist only as rudimentary scales.

1835 KIRBY *Hab. & Inst. Anim.* II. xx. 317 The Aphaniptera [Flea, Chigoe] are apterous and parasitic.

aphanipterous (æfə'nɪptərəs), *a. Zool.* [f. prec. + -OUS.] Of or pertaining to the *Aphaniptera*.

aphanistic (æfə'nɪstɪk), *a. rare*[—0]. [ad. Gr. ἀφανιστικ-ός, f. ἀφανίζ-ειν to make invisible, f. ἀφαν-ής: see next.] Indistinct, not manifest.

aphanite, -yte ('æfənaɪt). *Min.* [mod. f. (by Haüy) Gr. ἀφαν-ής unmanifest + -ITE.] A compact dark-coloured hornblende rock, so uniform in texture that it shows no distinct grains (whence its name), and breaks with a smooth flint-like fracture; also called *Corneine*.

1862 DANA *Man. Geol.* 79 Aphanite consists mainly of hornblende with some feldspar .. It has been called hornrock. **1883** N. JOLY *Man bef. Metals* I. vii. 167 They contain weapons of unpolished aphanite, a species of greenstone.

aphanitic (æfə'nɪtɪk), *a. Min.* [f. prec. + -IC.] Of the nature of or containing aphanite.

1862 DANA *Man. Geol.* 79 An aphanitic slate.

aphanozygous (æfə'nɒzɪgəs), *a. Anthrop.* [mod. f. Gr. ἀφαν-ής unmanifest + ζυγ-όν (for ζύγωμα cheekbone) + -OUS.] Having the cheek-bones invisible when the skull is viewed from above.

1871 DAWKINS *Cave Hunt.* vi. 207 They are dolicho-cephalic, quite orthognathous, and wholly aphanozygous.

‖**aphasia** (ə'feɪzɪə). *Path.* [mod.L., a. Gr. ἀφασία, n. of quality f. ἄφατος speechless, f. ἀ priv. + φά-ναι to speak (cf. φάσ-ις speech).] Loss of speech, partial or total, or loss of power to understand written or spoken language, as a result of disorder of the cerebral speech centres.

1867 *Chamb. Jrnl.* XXXVIII. 85 A musician, the subject of aphasia .. who had lost the ability to read and write as well as to speak. **1878** A. HAMILTON *Nerv. Dis.* 72 Embarrassment of speech may vary from simple awkwardness of articulation to decided aphasia. **1890** W. JAMES *Princ. Psychol.* I. ii. 54 The condition in question is *word-deafness*, and the disease is *auditory aphasia*. **1907** *Practitioner* Oct. 544 Pierre Marie .. recognises three terms:—(1) Aphasia of Wernicke, in which intelligence is impaired, but speech possible. (2) Aphasia of Broca, in which intelligence is impaired, and no speech possible. (3) Anarthria. **1926** H. HEAD *Aphasia* I. I. vi. 91 Complete sensory aphasia invariably leads to some intellectual want of power to manipulate written speech.

aphasiac (ə'feɪzɪæk), *sb.* and *a.* [f. prec. + -AC; cf. *mania-c.*]

A. *sb.* One suffering from aphasia.

1868 OGLE in *Lancet* 21 Mar. 370/2 The testamentary capacity .. of aphasiacs without apoplexy or paralysis. **1929** W. J. LOCKE *Ancestor Jorico* i. 14 The ordinary aphasiac could be got at through his ears.

B. *adj.* = APHASIC *a.*; also *transf.* (*jocular*), incapable of 'speaking' or sounding. *rare.*

1892 STEVENSON & OSBOURNE *Wrecker* xxi. 326 The old familiar room, .. with .. the aphasiac piano. **1906** DORLAND *Med. Dict.* (ed. 4), *Aphasic, Aphasiac*, pertaining to or affected with aphasia.

aphasic (ə'fæzɪk), *a.* and *sb.* [f. APHASIA + -IC.]

A. *adj.* Suffering from aphasia, having lost the power of speech; of, characteristic of, or characterized by aphasia.

1867 *Chamb. Jrnl.* XXXVIII. 86 Most aphasic patients answer very well by signs. **1874** *Brit. Med. Jrnl.* 2 May 575/1 Hemiplegia is, as a rule, noticed at some stage of the progress of aphasic disease. **1880** BASTIAN *Brain* xxix. 649 He had regained the power of speaking to a considerable extent, and now .. he had become Amnesic rather than Aphasic. **1901** *Lancet* 26 Jan. 276 Slight aphasic symptoms. **1906** *Westm. Gaz.* 2 June 9/1 A curious form of aphasic amnesia.

B. *sb.* = APHASIAC (which is more analogical).

1867 *Chamb. Jrnl.* XXXVIII. 85 We must .. turn our attention to the writing of aphasics. **1869** HUNT in *Eng. Mech.* 7 May 147/1, I call him an aphasic in whom the signs of thought cannot manifest themselves.

aphelian (ə'fiːlɪən), *a. Astr. rare*[—1]. [f. next + -AN.] Of or pertaining to the aphelion; farthest from the sun.

1738 MACHIN in *Phil. Trans.* XL. 221 Putting the Aphelian Distance .. instead of the Perihelian Distance.

aphelion (ə'fiːlɪən). *Astr.* Pl. **aphelia.** [Græcized form of mod.L. *aphēlium*, f. Gr. ἀφ' = ἀπό off, from + ἥλιος sun; formed, by Kepler, after the *apogæum*, ἀπόγαιον, of the Ptolemaic astronomy (see *Prodr. dissert. cosmographicarum*, 1596, and *Epitome astronom. Copernic.* 1618). *Aphelium* was also the earlier form in Eng.; cf. PARHELION, Gr. παρήλιον. Fr. has *aphélie*, like *apogée.*]

1. That point of a planet's or comet's orbit at which it is farthest from the sun.

1656 tr. *Hobbes's Elem. Philos.* (1839) 443 The apogæum of the sun or the aphelium of the earth ought to be about the 28th degree of Cancer. **1676** HALLEY in Rigaud *Corr. Sci. Men* I. 237 The Aphelion, Eccentricities, and Proportions of the Orbs of the Primary Planets. **1794** SULLIVAN *View Nat.* II. 410 Of these distances, the least of all is called the perihelium, and the greatest the aphelium. **1837** WHEWELL *Hist. Induct. Sc.* (1857) II. 131 The aphelia of Mercury, Venus, the Earth, and Mars, slightly progress. **1880** WALLACE *Isl. Life* viii. 132 The effect is intensified by winter being there in aphelion.

2. *fig.*

1845 H. ROGERS *Ess.* I. iii. 137 The dark aphelion of the eccentric orbit in which the church of Christ had wandered. **1858** GEN. P. THOMPSON *Audi Alt.* II. lxxvi. 29 France, which is just now in what astronomers call the aphelion or furthest point of political cold.

apheliotropic (ə,fiːlɪəʊ'trɒpɪk), *a.* [f. Gr. ἀφ' = ἀπό from + ἥλιος sun + τροπικός belonging to turning: see -TROPIC.] Bending or turning away from the sun: said of leaves, and other parts of plants.

1880 DARWIN *Movem. Plants* 552 The sub-aërial roots observed by Wiesner were all apheliotropic. **1882** F. DARWIN in *Nature* 27 Apr. 600 The light, causing apheliotropic movement in the leaves.

a,phelio'tropically, *adv.* [f. prec. + -AL[1] + -LY[2].] In a direction away from the sun.

1880 DARWIN *Movem. Plants* 567 The tip, which, when laterally illuminated, causes the adjoining part of the root to bend apheliotropically.

apheliotropism (ə,fiːlɪ'ɒtrəpɪz(ə)m). [f. APHELIOTROP-IC + -ISM.] The habit (in plants) of bending away from the light.

1880 DARWIN *Movem. Plants* 5 It is much more convenient to confine the word heliotropism to bending towards the light, and to designate as apheliotropism bending from the light. **1880** F. DARWIN in *Nature* No. 582. 179 Hyponasty will of course be opposed by apheliotropism and geotropism.

‖**aphemia** (ə'fiːmɪə). [mod.L., f. Gr. ἀ priv. + φήμη voice, speech, fame; but Gr. ἄφημος, = 'not famed, unknown.'] Loss of power of articulation, as a result of cerebral affection; *spec.* a form of APHASIA, in which words are understood and conceived but cannot be uttered.

1864 *Jrnl. Ment. Sc.* X. 260 The seat of morbid change in aphemia. **1878** A. HAMILTON *Nerv. Dis.* 163 Broca [*c* 1861] denominated the condition 'aphemia.'

aphemic (ə'fɛmɪk), *a.* and *sb.* [f. prec. + -IC.] (One) suffering from aphemia.

1869 HUNT in *Eng. Mech.* 30 Apr. 125/2, I dissected an old aphemic subject, who, during his life, had only five words at his disposal .. M. Charcot had three aphemics whose cerebral lesions were exactly in the same spot.

aphengescope (ə'fɛndʒɪskəʊp). [mod.f. Gr. ἀφεγγή-ς without light (f. ἀ priv. + φέγγ-ος light) + -SCOPE.] A kind of magic lantern for exhibiting opaque objects, such as coins, photographs, etc.

1869 *Eng. Mech.* 12 Nov. 218/2 The construction and mode of working the aphengescope.

aphesis ('æfɪsɪs). [a. Gr. ἄφεσις a letting go, f. ἀφιέναι, f. ἀφ' off, away + ἱέναι to send, let go, suggested by the Editor in 1880.] The gradual and unintentional loss of a short unaccented vowel at the beginning of a word; as in *squire* for *esquire*, *down* for *adown*, *St. Loy* for *St. Eloy*, *limbeck* for *alimbeck*, *'tention!* for *attention!* It is a special form of the phonetic process called *Aphæresis*, for which, from its frequency in the history of the English language, a distinctive name is useful. Now also used in the sense of APHÆRESIS.

1880 J. A. H. MURRAY in *Trans. Philol. Soc.* 175 The Editor can think of nothing better than to call the phenomenon *Aphesis* .. and the resulting forms *Aphetic* forms. **1930** A. WESTERN in *Gram. Misc. Jespersen* 135, I do not quite see the difference between aphesis and aphæresis, but use the former term as the shorter and therefore more convenient of the two. **1932** W. L. GRAFF *Lang.* vi. 234 A loss at the beginning is called aphaeresis or aphesis .. *bishop*

< Lat. *episcopus*, *knife* and *write* in which *k* and *w* were formerly sounded.

‖**'apheta.** *Astrol.* [L., ad. Gr. ἀφέτης a letter-off; applied, according to Du Cange, to the Prætor, who gave the signal for starting in the chariot-races; hence *fig.* to the planet which starts a human being in his career.] The giver of life in a nativity.

1647 LILLY *Chr. Astrol.* clvi. 650 You may alwayes import a danger of death, when you find the Apheta come to the hostill Beams of the killing Planet. **1696** PHILLIPS, *Apheta*, otherwise called Hylech, the giver of Life. **1755** in JOHNSON. **1819** J. WILSON *Dict. Astrol.* 8 When..a number of planets are so situated that it seems doubtful which is the Apheta.

a'phetic, *a.*[1] and *sb. Astrol.* [f. prec. + -IC.] Of or pertaining to the apheta; life-giving; also *sb.*

1652 GAULE *Magastrom.* 141 Now they have inspected.. and found..all the apheticks safe and sound. **1819** J. WILSON *Dict. Astrol.* 7 According to Ptolemy, the Aphetic Places are five.

aphetic (ə'fɛtɪk), *a.*[2] [f. Gr. ἄφετ-ος (cf. σύνετος) vbl. adj. f. ἀφιέναι (see APHESIS) + -IC.] Pertaining to, or resulting from, aphesis.

1880 [see APHESIS]. **1884** *New Eng. Dict.* s.v. *A-*, Many words with *a-* in one or other of the preceding senses have *aphetic* forms with the *a-* lost, as *adown down*, *amid mid*. **1905** *Eng. Dial. Dict.*, *Tankerous*, an aphetic form of 'cantankerous'. **1959** *N. & Q.* CCIV. 434/2 *Serued*..may be merely an aphetic form of OF. *deservir*.

a'phetical, *a. Astrol.* [f. APHETIC *a.*[1] + -AL[1].]

1647 LILLY *Chr. Astrol.* civ. 529 If such a Planet be in an Apheticall place, he shall be Prorogator. **1819** J. WILSON *Dict. Astrol.* 7 That [planet] must be taken which is found in the strongest aphetical place.

aphetically (ə'fɛtɪkəlɪ), *adv.*[1] *Astrol.* [f. prec. + -LY[2].] In the manner or position of the apheta.

1819 J. WILSON *Dict. Astrol.* 8 If it be aphetically situated.

a'phetically, *adv.*[2] [f. APHETIC *a.*[2] + -AL[1] + -LY[2].] In an aphetic manner; by way of aphesis.

1884 *New Eng. Dict.* s.v. *Across*, *Across*..also aphetically *cross*. **1914** *Ibid.* s.v. *Spend*, The ME. *spende*..may also have been formed aphetically from OF. *despendre*.

aphetism ('æfɪtɪz(ə)m). [n. of result f. next: cf. *Latinism*.] An aphetized form of a word; a form, such as *squire*, *limn*, *peach*, resulting from the loss of the weak initial vowel.

aphetize ('æfɪtaɪz), *v.* [f. Gr. ἄφετ-ος (see APHETIC) + -IZE; cf. Gr. συνετίζειν.] To render aphetic, to shorten by aphesis.

1884 *New Eng. Dict.* s.v. *Acute*, In the sense of *sharp in business*, *shrewd*, it [*acute*] is familiarly aphetized..to *'cute*. **1900** B. A. P. VAN DAM *Shakespeare* ii. 23 The very frequent use of aphetised forms was specially characteristic of the negligent parlance of every-day life.

aphid ('eɪfɪd, 'æfɪd), anglicized form of APHIS (from the pl. *aphides*).

1884 BROWNING *Ferishtah's Fancies* xii. 117 The aphis feeds, nor finds his leaf Untenable, because..Lightning strikes sere a moss-patch close beside, Where certain other aphids live. **1925** R. W. G. KINGSTON in E. F. Norton *Fight for Everest* 285 Aphids were numerous at 15,000 feet.

aphidian (ə'fɪdɪən), *a.* and *sb. Zool.* [f. *aphid-* stem of mod.L. APHIS + -IAN.]

A. *adj.* Of or pertaining to aphides.

1855 OWEN *Invert. Anim.*, Phenomena analogous to those of Aphidian generation.

B. *sb.* An aphidian insect; one of the aphides.

aphidious (ə'fɪdɪəs), *a. rare*[−0]. [f. as prec. + -(I)OUS.] = APHIDIAN.

1853 in MAYNE *Exp. Lex.*

aphidiphagous (æfɪ'dɪfəgəs), *a. Zool.* [f. *aphid-* (see APHIS) + Gr. -φαγ-ος -eating + -OUS.] = APHIDIVOROUS.

1853 in MAYNE *Exp. Lex.*

aphidivorous (æfɪ'dɪvərəs), *a. Zool.* [f. as prec. + L. *-vor-us* -devouring + -OUS.] Devouring or feeding on aphides; like the common lady-bird.

1828 KIRBY & SPENCE *Entomol.* IV. xliv. 228 One of the aphidivorous flies. **1833** GRIFFITH *Cuvier* XV. 760 The larva of the syrphi, or aphidivorous worms.

aphidologist (æfɪ'dɒlədʒɪst). *rare*[−1]. [f. as prec. + -(O)LOGIST.] A student of the *Aphides*.

1876 BUCKTON *Brit. Aphides* (Ray Soc.) I. 40 Accepted as true by almost all aphidologists.

aphikoman, var. AFIKOMAN.

aphilanthropy (æfɪ'lænθrəpɪ). ? *Obs.* [f. Gr. ἀφιλάνθρωπ-ος not loving men: see A- *pref.* 14 and PHILANTHROPY.]

1. 'Want of love to mankind.' J.

2. *Med.* A morbid state of melancholy in which solitude is preferred to society; anthropophobia.

1753 CHAMBERS *Cycl. Supp.*, s.v.

‖**aphis** ('æfɪs). Pl. **aphides** ('æfɪdi:z). [mod.L. (Linnæus); of unknown etymology. A number of conjectures are offered in Buckton's *Monograph of Brit. Aphides*, the least improbable being that the plural is for Gr. ἀφειδεῖς pl. of ἀφειδής 'unsparing, lavishly bestowed' (? in reference to their prodigious rate of production, or to their voracity), and the sing. formed on it in imitation of *orchis*, *orchides*, *chrysalis*, *caryatis*, etc. The quantity of the *i* with Linnæus is unknown; it is now made short.]

1. A family of minute insects, also called *plant-lice*, which are very destructive to vegetation. They are prodigiously prolific, multiplying through the summer by parthenogenesis; they form the food of lady-birds, and are tended by ants for the honeydew which they yield, whence sometimes called *ant-cows*.

1771 RICHARDSON in *Phil. Trans.* LXI. 183 The Aphides are distinguished by Linnæus into more than thirty species. **1776** WITHERING *Bot. Arrangem.* (1796) II. 277 The honey dew is the excrement of a species of *Aphis*. **1793** WHITE *Selborne* (1853) 380 The people of Selborne were surprised by a shower of aphides. **1859** DARWIN *Orig. Spec.* viii. (1878) 207 An ant..began to play with its antennæ, on the abdomen first of one aphis and then of another. **1876** BUCKTON *Brit. Aphides* I. 80 Except for accidents, a single aphis in one year might produce more aphides than is represented by the weight of the population of China.

2. *Comb.* and *Attrib.*, as **aphis-blight, aphis-lion, aphis-sugar** (see quot.).

1882 *Birm. Weekly Post* 30 Dec. 1/6 Aphis blight is the consequence of an unhealthy state of the hop plant brought about by climatic conditions, as cold winds, white frosts, etc. ..which..weaken them and render them unable to grow away from the aphides. **1870** NICHOLSON *Zool.* (1880) 351 Fig. 185. Neuroptera: The Aphis-lion (*Chrysopa perla*), imago, larva, and eggs. **1842** *Penny Cycl.* XXIII. 225 Honey-dew, or aphis-sugar, and the honey of the bee are intermediate between animal and vegetable sugars.

aphlogistic (æflɒʊ'dʒɪstɪk), *a.* [f. Gr. ἀφλόγιστος uninflammable + -IC.] Without flame.

aphlogistic or ***flameless lamp***: a spirit-lamp invented by Sir H. Davy, having a coil of fine platinum wire wound loosely round the lower part of the wick, which continues in a state of ignition after the flame of the wick is extinguished, till all the spirit is consumed; used in mines which contain fire-damp.

1831 T. P. JONES *New Convers. Chem.* xxix. 297 The lamp is called the aphlogistic or flameless lamp. **1847** in CRAIG.

aphonia (ə'fəʊnɪə). See APHONY.

aphonic (ə'fɒnɪk), *a. rare.* [f. as next + -IC.] Having no sound or pronunciation, non-vocal.

1827 *Edin. Rev.* XLV. 533 These [hieroglyphics] he divides into Emphonic, Symphonic, and Aphonic. **1877** ROBERTS *Handbk. Med.* I. 353 Voice is completely lost, and cough becomes aphonic.

aphonous ('æfənəs), *a. rare*[−0]. [f. Gr. ἄφων-ος voiceless (see next) + -OUS.] Voiceless.

1852 ROGET *Thesaurus* 581 Aphonous, dumb, mute.

aphony ('æfənɪ). [ad. mod.L. *aphōnia* (oftener used unchanged), a. Gr. ἀφωνία, n. of quality f. ἄφων-ος voiceless, f. ἀ priv. + φωνή voice.] Inability to produce vocal sound; total loss of voice.

1684 tr. *Bonet's Merc. Compit.* XVI. 580, A most grievous Aphony. **1719** *Glossogr. Nova*, *Aphony*, want of voice. **1778** FOTHERGILL in *Phil. Trans.* LXIX. 5 A disease, somewhat similar to the above, though..not attended with the aphonia. **1878** A. HAMILTON *Nerv. Dis.* 162 Aphasia must not be confounded with aphonia.

aphorism ('æfərɪz(ə)m). Also 6 **afforysme**, 6–7 **aphorisme**, 7 **apor-**. [a. Fr. *aphorisme*, *afforisme*, ad. med.L. *aphorism-us*, *aforismus*, a. Gr. ἀφορισμός a distinction, a definition, f. ἀφορίζ-ειν; see APHORIZE. From the 'Aphorisms of Hippocrates,' transferred to other sententious statements of the principles of physical science, and at length to statements of principles generally.]

1. A 'definition' or concise statement of a principle in any science.

1528 PAYNELL *Salerne Regim.* B iv b, Galen saythe in the glose of this aphorisme, *qui crescunt*, etc. **1541** R. COPLAND *Guydon's Quest. Cyrurg.*, Of this vtylyte Arnolde of vylle maketh an afforysme. **1605** BACON *Adv. Learn.* I. v, Knowledge, while..in aphorisms and observations..is in growth. **1664** POWER *Exp. Philos.* III. 190 The old and uncomfortable Aphorism of our Hippocrates. **1879** *De Quatrefages' Hum. Spec.* 50 The aphorism..which was formulated by Linnæus in regard to plants.

2. Any principle or precept expressed in few words; a short pithy sentence containing a truth of general import; a maxim.

c **1590** MARLOWE *Faustus* i. 19 Is not thy common talk found aphorisms? **1642** HOWELL *For. Trav.* (Arb.) 37 'Tis an old Aphorisme *Oderunt omnes quem metuunt*. **1687** H. MORE *App. Antidote* (1712) 191 That sensible Aphorism of Solomon, Better is a living Dog than a dead Lion. **1750** JOHNSON *Rambl.* No. 68 ¶10 Oppression, according to Harrington's aphorism, will be felt by those that cannot see it. **1880** GOLDW. SMITH in *Atl. Month.* No. 268. 201 The suggestive aphorism, 'The want of belief is a defect that ought to be concealed when it cannot be overcome.'

†3. *abstractly*, The essence or pith. *Obs. rare.*

1594 J. KING *Jonah* (1864) 184 The aphorism and juice of the whole song.

†**'aphorism,** *v. Obs. rare*[−1]. [f. prec. sb.] To utter as an aphorism.

1627 E. F. *Hist. Edw. II.* (1680) 62 These passages discours'd and Aphorism'd at large in the House.

aphorismatic (,æfərɪz'mætɪk), *a.* [irreg. f. Gr. ἀφόρισμα, which was not used in the sense of its cognate ἀφορισμός.] = APHORISMIC or APHORISTIC.

1822 *Edin. Rev.* XXXVII. 136 Paley is rather dry and aphorismatic. **1846** O. GREGORY *Robt. Hall* I. 85 Opinions ..clothed in an aphorismatic terseness of language.

†**'aphorismer.** *Obs.* [f. APHORISM + -ER[1].] A dealer in aphorisms. (*contemptuous.*)

1641 MILTON *Reform.* II. (1851) 56 All the tribe of Aphorismers, and Politicasters.

aphorismic (æfɒ'rɪzmɪk), *a.* [f. as prec. + -IC.] Having the form of an aphorism or aphorisms.

1794 MATHIAS *Pursuits Lit.* (1798) 432 Said the Father of Physick in the depth of his aphorismick wisdom. **1833** COLERIDGE *Table T.* 264 The style of Junius is a sort of metre, the law of which is a balance of thesis and antithesis. When he gets out of this aphorismic metre....

apho'rismical, *a. rare.* = prec.

1880 *Edin. Rev.* Apr. 438 The 'Aphorismical Discovery' was known to the omnivorous Carte.

aphorisming ('æfə,rɪzmɪŋ), *ppl. a. rare.* [f. APHORISM *v.* + -ING[2].] Dealing in aphorisms.

1641 MILTON *Reform.* II. (1851) 33 Soyl'd and slubber'd with aphorisming pedantry. **1817** COLERIDGE *Biogr. Lit.* 138 Certain immethodical aphorisming Eclectics.

aphorist ('æfərɪst). [n. of agent f. APHORIZE, as if ad. Gr. *ἀφοριστής: see -IST.] One who writes or utters aphorisms.

1713 NELSON *Bp. Bull* 246 (T.) Justifying what he had written against the aphorist. **1864** *Daily Tel.* 20 Aug., Constitutional aphorists tell us that the King can do no wrong.

aphoristic (æfɒ'rɪstɪk), *a.* [ad. Gr. ἀφοριστικ-ός; cf. Fr. *aphoristique*: see prec. and -IC.] Of or pertaining to an aphorist; of the nature of an aphorism.

1753 CHAMBERS *Cycl. Supp.*, *Aphoristic* method has great advantages, as containing much matter in a small compass. **1824** D'ISRAELI *Cur. Lit.* (1866) 392/1 This vast body of aphoristic knowledge. **1859** MASSON *Milton* I. 323 To let loose his epigrammatic and aphoristic tongue.

†**apho'ristical,** *a.* = prec.

1681 in BLOUNT *Glossogr.* **1846** GEO. ELIOT tr. *Strauss's Life of Jesus* II. II. vi. §76. 102 The dictum accords with either context, and from its aphoristical conciseness would be likely to recur.

apho'ristically, *adv.* [f. prec. + -LY[2].] In an aphoristic manner; by way of aphorisms; pithily.

1655 MOUFFET & BENN. *Health's Impr.* (1746) 386 His own Words; which I have aphoristically set down in these Sentences following. **1773** JOHNSON in *Boswell* (1831) II. 274, I fancy mankind may come, in time, to write all aphoristically. **1873** *Brit. Q. Rev.* LVII. 178 Expressing aphoristically the truth that all our knowledge recedes into mystery.

aphorize ('æfəraɪz), *v. rare.* [ad. Gr. ἀφορίζειν 'to define,' in mid. voice 'to lay down determinate propositions,' f. ἀφ' = ἀπό off + ὁρίζ-ειν to set bounds, f. ὅρ-ος boundary. The English sense is taken from APHORISM.] To write or speak in aphorisms; to make terse general reflections.

1669 *Addr. Yng. Gentry Eng.* 55 Tacitus himself aphorizeth..in his short and poynant conclusion. **1824** COLERIDGE *Aids to Refl.* 17 This twofold act of circumscribing and detaching, when it is exerted by the mind on subjects of reflection and reason, is to aphorize, and the result an Aphorism. **1860** WINDSOR *Ethica* vii. 326 Aphorizing on the instability of human greatness.

aphorizer ('æfəraɪzə(r)). *rare*[−1]. [f. prec. + -ER[1].] One who aphorizes; an aphorist.

1851 HELPS *Friends in C.* 124 There, Mr. Aphoriser general, what do you say to that?

aphotic (ə'fəʊtɪk), *a.* [f. A- *pref.* 14 + PHOTIC *a.*] Not reached by sunlight (cf. PHOTIC *a.*).

1903 W. R. FISHER tr. *Schimper's Plant-Geogr.* III. v. i. 782 The *aphotic* or dark region, in which only non-assimilating organisms can exist. **1913** J. MURRAY *Ocean* vii. 137 The Aphotic or Deep-Sea Zone extends from the lower limit of the photic zone down to the bottom of the greatest 'deeps'. **1928** E. NEAVERSON *Stratigraph. Palaeontol.* iv. 97 Two general light-regions recognised by oceanographers are based on the distribution of plants: the *photic region*..and the *aphotic region*, where the light is insufficient for this process [*sc.* photosynthesis] to be carried on.

aphototropic (ə,fəʊtəʊ'trɒpɪk), *a. Bot.* [f. A- *pref.* 14 + PHOTOTROPIC *a.*] Bending or turning away from the light (cf. APHELIOTROPIC *a.*). So **apho'totropism.**

1903 *Nature* 9 July 237/2 At the moment of hatching, Convoluta is aphototropic. **1916** B. D. JACKSON *Gloss. Bot. Terms* (ed. 3) 28/2 *Aphototropism*, turning away from light.

aphrite ('æfraɪt). *Min.* [f. Gr. ἀφρ-ός foam + -ITE; = *foam-stone.*] A variety of carbonate of lime or calcite.
1868 DANA *Min.* 678 Aphrite, in its harder and more sparry variety is a foliated white pearly calcite, near argentine; in its softer kinds it approaches chalk, though lighter, pearly in lustre..and more or less scaly in structure.

aphrizite ('æfrɪzaɪt). *Min.* [mod. f. Gr. ἀφρίζειν to foam + -ITE.] 'Black tourmaline from Krageröe in Norway.' Dana.

aphrodisiac (æfrəʊ'dɪzɪæk), *a.* and *sb.* [ad. Gr. ἀφροδῑσιακ-ός venereal, f. ἀφροδίσι-ος; see below.]
A. *adj.* Venereal; having a venereal tendency.
1830 LINDLEY *Nat. Syst. Bot.* 103 The nut..is eatable and aphrodisiac. **1862** RAWLINSON *Anc. Mon.* I. vii. 175 Ishtar's aphrodisiac character.
B. *sb.*
1. A drug or preparation inducing venereal desire.
1719 *Glossogr. Nova, Aphrodisiacks,* things that excite Lust or Venery. **1874** M. COOKE *Fungi* 103 Truffles are no longer regarded as aphrodisiacs.
2. *fig.*
1873 J. MORLEY *Rousseau* I. vi. 198 Like some evil mental aphrodisiac. **1881** LD. LYTTON in *19th Cent.* Nov. 774 A sadly serious literature of sentimental aphrodisiacs! Faugh!

aphrodisiacal (ˌæfrəʊdɪ'zaɪəkəl), *a.* [f. prec. + -AL[1].] Of aphrodisiac character.
1719 *Glossogr. Nova, Aphrodisical,* belonging to Venus or Love. **1721** BAILEY, *Aphrodisiacal.* **1792** *Gentl. Mag.* Apr. 357 Indulging aphrodisiacal passion. **1869** J. DAVENPORT *Aphrodisiacs* iii. 111 An account of certain aphrodisiacal charms practised by women of his time. **1918** A. BENNETT *Pretty Lady* xxiii. 151 The rag-time music..bathed everyone at the supper tables in a mysterious aphrodisiacal fluid. **1959** *New Biol.* XXX. 47 Few Europeans are familiar with that great delicacy of Chinese cuisine, bird's nest soup (or its alleged aphrodisiacal properties).

aphrodisian (æfrəʊ'dɪzɪən), *a.* [f. Gr. ἀφροδίσι-ος, adj. f. Ἀφροδίτη the Grecian Venus + -AN.] Belonging to Venus, devoted to sensual love.
1860 C. READE *Cloister & Hearth* III. 151 The state nursery of those aphrodisian dames their favourites.

‖**Aphrodite** (æfrəʊ'daɪtiː), *sb.*[1] [Gr. Ἀφροδίτη 'foam-born,' the Grecian Venus. Formerly 'æfrəʊdaɪt.]
1. The Grecian Venus.
c **1658** CLEVELAND *Poems* 89 A medal where grim Mars, turn'd right, Proves a smiling Aphrodite. **1867** MISS BRADDON *Aur. Floyd* xvii. 155 He sprang from the mire of the streets, like some male Aphrodite rising from the mud.
2. *Zool.* A genus of marine worms with bristles of brilliant iridescent hues; also called *Sea-mouse.*
1857 WOOD *Com. Obj. Seashore* 99 The bristles of the aphrodite are..worthy of notice on account of their wonderful colouring. **1869** W. BAIRD in *Eng. Mech.* 30 Apr. 123/1 They differ from the Aphrodites, or sea-mice, in many respects.

aphrodite ('æfrəʊdaɪt), *sb.*[2] *Min.* [f. Gr. Ἀφροδίτη (see prec.), taken as a mineral name from its ending -ITE, in sense of *foam-stone, aphrite* being already occupied.] A soft opaque milk-white mineral, consisting mostly of bisilicate of magnesium, allied to Sepiolite or meerschaum.
1837–68 DANA *Min.* 457.

'aphronitre. ? *Obs.* [ad. L. *aphronitrum,* a. Gr. ἀφρόνιτρον, better ἀφρὸς νίτρου, *spuma nitri.*] 'Foam of nitre'; a name formerly applied to the sulphur salts of various alkalis and earths.
1398 TREVISA *Barth. De P.R.* XVI. lxix. (1495) 575 The fome of Nitrum hyghte *Affronitum.* **1601** HOLLAND *Pliny* (1634) II. 421 The Ægyptian Aphro-nitre or Salt-petre. **1751** CHAMBERS *Cycl.* s.v., Some modern naturalists rather take the antient Aphronitre to have been a native salt-petre.

aphrosiderite (æfrəʊ'sɪdəraɪt). *Min.* [mod. (1847) f. Gr. ἀφρό-ς foam + σίδηρ-ος iron + -ITE.] A soft ferruginous mineral of a dark olive-green colour, classed by Dana as a variety of Prochlorite.

‖**aphtha** ('æfθə). *Path.* [L. *aphtha* (in cl. L. always in pl. *aphthæ*), a. Gr. ἄφθα, mostly in pl. ἄφθαι; usually connected with ἅπτ-ειν to set on fire, inflame.] A name given to the infantile disease 'thrush,' and, in the plural, to the small white specks on the mouth and tongue which characterize it, and which also occasionally appear in adults of enfeebled condition.
1657 *Phys. Dict., Aptha,* certain ulcers bred in the uppermost part of the mouth. **1862** H. MACMILLAN in *Macm. Mag.* Oct. 465 Aphtha or thrush, is caused by the growth and development of a parasitic plant. **1879** KHORZ *Digest of Med.* 26 The lips and tongue are covered with aphthæ.

aphthitalite (æf'θɪtəlaɪt). *Min.* [mod. f. (1835) Gr. ἄφθιτ-ος undecaying + λίθος stone; so called because unalterable in the air (Dana).] A native sulphate of potash found upon lava at Vesuvius; also called Vesuvian Salt, Aphthalose, Arcanite, and Glaserite.

aphthong ('æfθɒŋ). [mod. ad. Gr. ἄφθογγ-ος voiceless, ἄφθογγον a consonant.] 'A letter which is not sounded in the pronunciation of a word; a mute.' Craig 1847.

aphthonite ('æfθənaɪt). *Min.* [mod. f. Gr. ἄφθονον-ος plentiful + -ITE.] A steel-gray ore of sulphide of antimony and copper, with traces of zinc and silver; 'resembling tetrahedrite, if not identical with it' (Dana). Corruptly *aftonite.*

aphthous ('æfθəs), *a.* *Path.* [ad. mod.L. *aphthōs-us* (Fr. *aphtheux*), f. APHTHA: see -OUS.] Of the nature of, or characterized by, aphtha.
1757 WHYTT in *Phil. Trans.* L. 572 Tongue..with a beginning aphthous crust on some parts of it. **1830** LINDLEY *Nat. Syst. Bot.* 7 Aphthous affections of the mouth. **1849–52** TODD *Cycl. Anat.* IV. 1155/1 An aphthous tongue.

aphyllous (ə'fɪləs), *a.* *Bot.* [f. mod.L. *aphyllus,* a. Gr. ἄφυλλ-ος leafless (f. ἀ not + φύλλον leaf) + -OUS.] Destitute of leaves, naturally leafless.
1830 LINDLEY *Nat. Syst. Bot.* 29 Cassytha is aphyllous and parasitical. **1836** TODD *Cycl. Anat. & Phys.* I. 132/2 Those plants that are aphyllous.

apiaceous (eɪpɪ'eɪʃəs), *a.* *Bot.* [f. mod.L. *Apiāce-æ,* f. *apium* celery: see -ACEOUS.] Of the N.O. *Apiaceæ* or *Umbelliferæ,* containing such plants as celery, anise, hemlock; umbelliferous.
1839 *Penny Cycl.* XIII. 6/1 The partial umbels of an apiaceous plant. **1853** in MAYNE *Exp. Lex.*

apian ('eɪpɪən), *a.* [ad. L. *apiān-us,* f. *apis* bee.] Of or belonging to bees.
1862 F. HALL *Hindu Philos. Syst.* 122 If a human soul.. were..born a bee, an apian body would be inadequate to contain it. **1880** G. ALLEN *Evol. at Large* 7 Abstract ideas are not likely to play a large part in apian consciousness.

apiarian (eɪpɪ'ɛərɪən), *a.* and *sb.* [f. L. *apiārium* bee-house, *apiāri-us* bee-keeper + -AN.]
A. *adj.* Pertaining to bee-hives or bee-keeping.
1801 *(title)* Transactions of the Western Apiarian Society. **1816** KIRBY & SPENCE *Entomol.* (1843) II. 168 These apiarian battles are often fought in defence of the property of the hive. **1871** *Athenæum* 27 May 658 All the apiarian works which were written.
B. *sb.* = APIARIST. *rare.*
1858 *Penny Cycl.* 2nd Supp. 680/2 The dust of the common puff-ball..used by Apiarians for stupefying bees.

apiarist ('eɪpɪərɪst). [f. L. *apiār-ium* or Eng. APIARY + -IST.] One who keeps an apiary; a bee-keeper, a bee-master.
1816 KIRBY & SPENCE *Entomol.* (1828) I. v. 164 Certain idlers called by apiarists corsair-bees. **1860** SAMUELSON *Honey Bee* i. 7 The Queen is fed..upon honey, or as it is called by apiarists, royal paste.

apiary ('eɪpɪərɪ). [ad. L. *apiāri-um* bee-house, f. *api-s* bee: see -ARY.] A place where bees are kept; a bee-house.
1654 EVELYN *Mem.* (1857) I. 307 Transparent apiaries, which he had built like castles and palaces. **1703** MAUNDRELL *Journ. Jerus.* (1721) 66 A smell of Honey and Wax, as strong as if one had been in an Apiary. **1836** MARRYAT *Midsh. Easy* vi. 18 He had pitched into a small apiary, and had upset two hives of bees.

apical ('æpɪkəl, 'eɪpɪ-), *a.* [f. L. *apic-em* (see APEX *sb.*[1]) + -AL[1].] **1.** Of or belonging to an apex; situated at the summit or tip.
1828 KIRBY & SPENCE *Entomol.* III. xxxv. 613 The proportion that the apical area bears to the rest of the wing. **1882** H. WARD in *Jrnl. Microsc. Sc.* Jan. 4 This germinal tube rapidly grows forwards, extending by apical growth.
2. *Phonetics.* Pertaining to articulation with, or sounds made by, the tip of the tongue. Hence as *sb.*, an apical sound.
1899 RIPPMANN *Elem. Phonet.* 71 The part of the tongue which helps to form the narrowing is the front rim. The front rim of the tongue: *apical* formation. **1902** E. W. SCRIPTURE *Elem. Experimental Phonet.* xxi. 296 An articulation of the extreme point [of the tongue] is often termed 'apical'. **1935** G. K. ZIPF *Psycho-Biol. of Lang.* (1936) iii. 78 The apical trill or 'rolled r' of Italian. **1964** E. PALMER tr. *Martinet's Elem. Gen. Linguistics* ii. 49 It [a consonant] is apical if it is pronounced with the tip of the tongue (apex) like the [t] of *touche. Ibid.* iii. 64 'Apicals' are always stops in French.

'apically, *adv.* [f. prec. + -LY[2].] At or towards the apex.
1870 ROLLESTON *Anim. Life* 258 Their pseudopodia.. anastomose apically.

a'picial, incorrectly formed variant of APICAL.
1836–37 TODD *Cycl. Anat. & Phys.* II. 621/1 The apicial part of the left ventricle. **1842** E. WILSON *Anat. Vade M.* 489 The short or apicial band.

apician (ə'pɪʃən), *a.* [f. *Apīci-us* name of a famous Roman epicure + -AN.] Of or pertaining to epicures or to luxurious diet.
1699 EVELYN *Acetaria* (1729) 115 A voluptuary Apician art. *Ibid.* 164 Apician Tables. **1834** *Penny Cycl.* II. 159/1 Certain cakes, honourably distinguished by the epithet *Apician.*

apicifixed ('æpɪsɪˌfɪkst, 'eɪpɪ-), *ppl. a.* *Bot.* [f. L. *apici fix-us* + -ED.] Fixed to the apex.
1878 MASTERS *Henfrey's Bot.* 121 In some cases the anther is pendulous from the apex; it is then sometimes called apicifixed. **1880** in *Syd. Soc. Lex.*

a'picilar, apicillar, *a. rare.* [ad. Fr. *apicilaire,* ad. L. **apicillāris,* f. **apicillus,* dim. of APEX *sb.*[1]] = APICULAR.
1880 *Syd. Soc. Lex., Apicilar dehiscence, Apicilar embryo.*

api'cillary, variant of prec.
1864 WEBSTER cites HENSLOW.

a pick a back, apickpack: see PIGGY-BACK.

apico- ('æpɪkəʊ, 'eɪ-), comb. form of APICAL *a.*, as in ***apico-basal, -dental, -palatal*** adjs., ***apico-alveolar*** adj. and sb.
1926 J. S. HUXLEY *Ess. Pop. Sci.* xviii. 256 In the frog's eggs at the onset of gastrulation there exist two main gradients—the apico-basal from animal to vegetative pole, ..and the dorso-ventral. **1958** *Archivum Linguisticum* X. 101 A direct change from apico-dental [θ] to labio-dental [f]. **1962** *Amer. Speech* XXXVII. 166 Under terminal contour before apico-alveolars. *Ibid.* 169 It is normally a lengthened monophthong in Ocracoke speech..except under a terminal contour before an apico-alveolar consonant. **1964** *Language* XL. 58, q, gq, and nq (voiceless, voiced, and nasal apicopalatal clicks).

apicular (ə'pɪkjʊlə(r)), *a.* *rare.* [f. mod.L. *apicul-us* (see next) + -AR.] Of or belonging to a little apex; situated at the tip.
1854 BALFOUR *Bot. Gloss., Apical,* or *Apicular,* at the apex; often applied to parts connected with the ovary.

apiculate (ə'pɪkjʊlət), *a.* [ad. mod.L. *apiculāt-us,* f. *apicul-us*: see below, and -ATE.] Having a minute apex or point; minutely tipped.
1830 LINDLEY *Nat. Syst. Bot.* 318 An apiculate tubercle at its base. **1852** DANA *Crust.* I. 223 Teeth tumid, apiculate.

apiculated (ə'pɪkjʊleɪtɪd), *ppl. a.* [f. prec. with ppl. ending -ED.] = prec.
1845 LINDLEY *Sch. Bot.* ix. (1858) 154/2 Leaves concave, ovate, apiculated. **1876** tr. *Schützenberger's Ferment.* 56 The apiculated ferment does not belong to the genus.

apicultural (eɪpɪ'kʌltjʊərəl, -tʃər-), *a.* [f. APICULTURE + -AL.] Of or pertaining to apiculture.
1884 J. PHIN *Dict. Pract. Apiculture* p. iii, In matters of general apicultural practice we have depended largely upon our own experience. **1914** KIPLING *Diversity of Creatures* (1917) 392 Apicultural exhibitions. **1961** *Bee Research Assoc. Handbk.* 7 'Bee World' is recognized as the leading international apicultural journal.

apiculture ('eɪpɪˌkʌltjʊə(r), -tʃə). [f. L. *api-s* bee + *-cultūra* tending.] Bee-keeping or -rearing.
1864 *Sat. Rev.* 10 Dec., 731/1 The practice of what, we perceive, it is high-polite to call 'apiculture.' **1882** *N.Y. Tribune* 16 Aug., Comb foundation is one of the great aids in apiculture.

apiculturist (eɪpɪ'kʌltjʊərɪst, -tʃər-). [f. APICULTURE + -IST.] One who practises apiculture, a bee-keeper.
1883 *(title)* The American Apiculturist. **1884** W. H. HARRIS *Honey-Bee* 271 Apiculturists, like agriculturists, are subject to many and great alternations of hope and fear.

‖**apiculus** (ə'pɪkjʊləs). [mod.L. dim. of APEX *sb.*[1]] A minute point or tip.
1863 BERKELEY *Brit. Mosses* iii. 24 The lid..is either.. with or without a central apiculus.

apiece (ə'piːs), *adv.* Forms: 4–6 **a pece,** 6 **apece, apesse,** 6–7 **a peece, a-peece, apeece,** 7 **a peice,** 6– **a piece, a-piece, apiece.** [orig. two words, *a piece,* as to reckon coins, pottery, cloth, etc., at so much *a piece*; but soon extended to objects of any collection, or individuals of a company; so that no consciousness of the connexion with *piece* is ordinarily retained.]
For each piece, article, thing, or (*colloq.*) person; each, for each, to each; severally, individually.
[**1465** *Mann. & Househ. Exp.* 476 The prise of a pece, vii.*s.* **1556** *Chr. Gr. Fr.* 47 A new qwyne of sylver, of xij[d] apece.] *c* **1430** *Bk. Curtasye* 376 Ffor cariage þe porter hors schall hyre, ffoure pens a pece. **1526** TINDALE *John* ii. 6 Six water-pottes of stone..contaynynge two or thre fyrkins a pece. [**1611** apiece]. **1595** SIR J. GILBERT *Let.* in *N. & Q.* Ser. III. V. 109 Too other greate shyppes..off 600 tones apesse. **1611** BIBLE *Luke* ix. 3 Neither haue two coates apeece. **1728** NEWTON *Chronol. Amended* i. 52 Kings reign, one with another, about eighteen or twenty years a-piece. **1836** CAR. FOX *Jrnls.* I. 18 She promised her and Leonora a Cashmere shawl apiece.

†**a-'pieces,** *advb. phr. Obs.* [A *prep.*[1] in, into + *pieces*: see PIECE *sb.*] In pieces, to pieces.
1560 J. HEYWOOD *Seneca's Thyestes* 22 Their limmes eche one apeeces let them go Disperste. **1662** H. MORE *Enthus. Triumph.* (1712) 38 And break a-pieces their lanthorns against the ground. **1678** CUDWORTH *Intell. Syst.* I. ii. 84 The whole structure..must needs fall a-pieces.
b. *fig.*
1653 SHIRLEY *Court Secr.* I. i, This jealousy will take my brains a-pieces! **1663** PEPYS *Diary* 6 Nov., The plot is

spoiled, and the whole committee broke, Mr. Montagu and the Duke of Buckingham fallen a-pieces.

†**api'factory.** *Obs. rare.* [f. L. *apis* bee + FACTORY.] An apiary kept for economic purposes.
1677 PLOT *Oxfordsh.* 182 William Tayler, though a Northamptonshire Man, has Apifactories in this County.

†**api'facture.** *Obs. rare.* [f. L. *api-s* bee + *factūra* making, production.] The work of bees.
1622 MALYNES *Anc. Law-Merch.* 231 Let vs somewhat digresse from Manufacture, to Apifacture.. for the increase of Hony and Waxe.. and let mans helpe succour this Apifacture. **1775** ASH, *Apifacture*, the curious work of bees.

apill, obs. form of APPLE *sb.*

a-pinch (ə'pɪnʃ), *advb. phr.* [A *prep.*[1] + PINCH *sb.*; cf. *a-gape*.] Pinching, so as to pinch.
1857 MRS. BROWNING *Aur. Leigh* 149 Has Dickens turned his hinge A-pinch upon the fingers of the great?

aping ('eɪpɪŋ), *vbl. sb.* [f. APE *v.* + -ING[1].] Imitation, simulation, mimicry.
1687 SETTLE *Refl. Dryden's Plays* Pref. 2 That Billingsgate Style, which is but Aping of him. **1875** SEARS *Serm. & Songs* 45 Wilfulness, which is but a poor aping of conscientiousness.

apiocrinite (æpɪ'ɒkrɪnaɪt). *Palæont.* [mod. f. Gr. ἄπι-ον pear + κρίν-ον lily + -ITE, after *encrinite*.] The 'pear-encrinite,' a stalked echinoderm of the Oolite, so called from its shape.
1830 LYELL *Princ. Geol.* (1875) II. III. xlviii. 580 A crinoid referable to the Apiocrinite type. **1851** RICHARDSON *Geol.* viii. 227 The stem in apiocrinites is cylindrical.

apioid ('eɪpɪɔɪd, 'æp-). *Geom.* [f. Gr. ἄπιον pear: see -OID.] **a.** A species of plane curve, being that one of a pair of Cartesian ovals which is within the other. **b.** A species of solid of revolution, being the form assumed by a rotating liquid when the velocity of rotation exceeds a certain amount. Hence **api'oidal** *a.*, pertaining to or having the form of an apioid.
1898 G. W. MYERS in *Astrophys. Jrnl.* VIII. 163 The distance of centers does not materially differ from the sum of the radii of the components [of the star U Pegasi], suggesting the probable existence of the 'apioidal' form of Poincaré. **1905** A. M. CLERKE *Mod. Cosmog.* vi. 104 An 'apioid', or pear-shaped body, replaces the antecedent ellipsoid.

apiol ('eɪpɪɒl). *Chem.* and *Med.* [f. L. *api-um* parsley + -OL.] A crystalline substance obtained by distilling parsley seeds with water; parsley-camphor. (Watts *Dict. Chem.* VIII. 118.)
1872 in THOMAS *Dis. Wom.* 577. **1875** H. WOOD *Therap.* (1879) 538 Apiol.. as a remedy in intermittent fever.

apiologist (eɪpɪ'ɒlədʒɪst). *rare*[−1]. [f. L. *api-s* bee + -(O)LOGIST.] A scientific student of bees.
18.. EMERSON in Sanborn *Thoreau* (1882) 251 What Thomas Fuller records of Butler the apiologist, 'that either he had told the bees things, or the bees had told him.'

†**apirsmart**, *a. Obs. Sc.* [Apparently a comp. of SMART, in its early sense of *sharp*; the first element is doubtfully referred to ON. *apr*, sharp (said of cold or fighting), and to Fr. *âpre*:—L. *asper-um* sharp, rough. G. Douglas uses it to translate L. *asper*.] Sharp-tempered, harsh.
1501 DOUGLAS *Pal. Honour* III. lxxiii, Hir wordis war sa apirsmart. **1513** —— *Æneis* I. v. 88 Apirsmert Juno.

apish ('eɪpɪʃ), *a.* [f. APE *sb.* + -ISH.]
1. Of the nature or appearance of an ape.
1570 LEVINS *Manip.* 144 Apish, *simialis.* **1851** RUSKIN *Stones of Ven.* (1874) I. App. 363 Two devilish apes or apish devils, I know not which.
2. Ape-like in manner; befitting an ape; fantastically foolish, affected, silly, trifling.
1532 MORE *Confut. Tindale* Wks. 358/2 Mad apishe iesting against the.. blessed sacrementes. **1579** TOMSON *Calvin's Serm. Tim.* 513/1 The Popish priests are appointed to play other apish toyes. **1711** ADDISON *Spect.* No. 35 ⁋7 Little Apish Tricks and Buffooneries. **1751** SMOLLETT *Per. Pic.* lxxxviii, He bowed with a thousand apish congees. **1826** SCOTT *Woodst.* xxiv, The apish gallantry of a finished fop.
3. Ape-like in imitation; unreasoningly imitative.
1579 TOMSON *Calvin's Serm. Tim.* 174/2 This was but an apishe following of that which God had appointed the fathers. **1621** SANDERSON *Serm.* Ad. Pop. iii. (1674) 178 We are but too apish, apt to be led much by examples. **1818** BYRON *Childe Har.* IV. lxxxix, Men bled In imitation of the things they fear'd, And fought and conquer'd, and the same course steer'd At apish distance.

'apishly, *adv.* [f. prec. + -LY[2].] In an apish manner; with silly or ridiculous imitation.
1581 MARBECK *Bk. of Notes* 644 The Bishop of Rome too apishly followeth Christ in many things. **1644** MILTON *Areop.* (Arb.) 40 So apishly romanizing that the word of command still was set downe in Latine. **1753** RICHARDSON *Grandison* (1781) I. xxxix. 297 The behaviour of my Lord to her.. is.. affectionate, but not apishly fond.

apishness ('eɪpɪʃnɪs). [f. as prec. + -NESS.] The quality of being apish; silly or ridiculous imitation, silliness of behaviour.
1533 MORE *Confut. Barnes* VIII. Wks. 1557, 736/1 Thys felowes folishe apishenesse, and al hys asseheded exclamacions. **1609** *Man in Moone* (1857) 81 The fantasticallity of each man's apparell, and apishnesse of gesture. *a* **1779** WARBURTON *Serm.* (T.) The apishness of foreign manners. **1868** GEO. ELIOT *Sp. Gypsy* I. 17 To please my lord, who gives the larger fee For that hard industry in apishness.

apism ('eɪpɪz(ə)m). [f. APE + -ISM.] The practice of aping.
1843 CARLYLE *Past & Pr.* (1858) 203 His Dilettantism, Dead-Sea Apism, crying out,'Down with him [*i.e.* Labour], he is dangerous.'

†**'apize**, *v. Obs. rare*[−1]. [? f. APE *sb.* + -IZE.] ? To ape, simulate.
1598 *Herring's Tale* (N.) Thus apizing in shape and hew the spiry fire, Like stying doth to his like element aspire.

apjohnite ('æpdʒɒnaɪt). *Min.* [named in 1847, from its first analyzer Apjohn (*Phil. Mag.* XII. 103; 1838).] Manganese alum; a double sulphate of potash and manganese, occurring as a mineral in fibrous or asbestiform masses, white, and with a silky lustre.

†**a'place**, *advb. phr. Obs.* [A *prep.*[1] in, into + PLACE *sb.*; cf. Fr. *en place*.] Into this place, in place.
1393 GOWER *Conf.* II. 152 To telle How such goddes come aplace. **1413** LYDG. *Pylgr. Sowle* IV. xx. (1483) 65 O gabryel whan that thou come a place and madest vnto me thy saluynge. **1637** GILLESPIE *Eng.-Pop. Cerem.* III. ii. 22 Things abused to Idolatry.. are farre better away then aplace.

aplacental (æplə'sɛntəl), *a. Zool. rare.* [f. A- *pref.* 14 + PLACENTAL.] Having no placenta.
1857 PAGE *Advd. Text-Bk. Geol.* (1876) 182 *Aplacental*, bringing forth immature young. 1. Monotremata, Ornithorhyncus, Echidna. 2. Marsupialia, Kangaroos, Opossums.

†**a'plake**, *v. Obs. rare.* [ad. Sp. *aplac-ar* (pret. *aplaqué*) to appease, f. *a*:—L. *ad* to + *plācāre* to calm. Perh. only as transl. Sp.] To calm, allay.
1578 T. N. tr. *Conq. W. India* 218 Cortez aplaked the yre of the priestes. *Ibid.* 264 They coulde not aplake the fire.

aplanat ('æplənæt). [a. G. *aplanat* (A. Steinheil, 1866); cf. APLANATIC *a.*] An aplanatic lens. Also *attrib.*
1890 *Anthony's Photogr. Bull.* III. 129 After Steinheil invented his applanat [*sic*], Dallmeyer copied the same and called it Rapid Rectilinear. **1895** J. A. HODGES *Photographic Lenses* viii. 44 Prior to 1866, when Steinheil introduced his rapid aplanat working at f/7, all doublet lenses required comparatively small apertures in order to obtain sufficient definition and flatness of field. **1901** *Brit. Jrnl. Photogr.* 1 Nov. 695/1 These aplanats consist of strong refracting flint glasses, whose quotient and colour diversion do not much differ. **1951** *Engineering* 9 Mar. 297/2 The two-mirror aplanat telescopes.

aplanatic (æplə'nætɪk), *a.* [f. Gr. ἀπλάνητ-ος free from error (f. ἀ priv. + πλανά-ειν to wander) + -IC.] Free from aberration; *spec.* applied to a compound lens which is free from spherical aberration or divergence of rays of light from the focus.
1794 G. ADAMS *Nat. & Exp. Phil.* II. xxii. 468 As.. [Blair] conceives that he has thus removed the aberration, he distinguishes his instrument by the term Aplanatic. **1867** J. HOGG *Microsc.* I. ii. 26 An 'aplanatic doublet' consisting of a double convex lens and a meniscus. **1869** TYNDALL *Light* §165 A spherical lens cannot be rendered aplanatic.

aplanatism (ə'plænətɪz(ə)m). *rare.* [f. as prec. + -ISM.] Freedom from spherical aberration.
1869 *Eng. Mech.* 2 Apr. 33 To certify to the perfect achromatism and aplanatism of their instruments.

aplanogamete ('æplənəugə,miːt). *Biol.* [f. Gr. ἀ- priv. (A- *pref.* 14) + πλάνος wandering (PLANO-[2]) + GAMETE.] A non-ciliated stationary gamete or conjugating cell, as distinguished from a PLANOGAMETE.
1886 [see GAMETE].

aplasia (ə'pleɪzɪə). [mod.L., f. Gr. ἀ- priv. (A- *pref.* 14) + πλάσις formation (πλάσσειν to form, mould): see -IA[1].] Congenital irregularity or absence of an organ or structure (see APLASTIC *a.*).
1885 in *N.E.D.* s.v. *Aplastic*, a. **1908** *Practitioner* Sept. 460 Aplasia of the muscularis of the last sections of the large gut. **1962** *Lancet* 6 Jan. 45/2 Aplasia of the gallbladder and of the appendix.

aplastic (ə'plæstɪk), *a.* [mod. f. Gr. ἄπλαστ-ος unshapen + -IC, after πλαστικός.] Characterized by, or tending to, irregularity or absence of organic structure (technically called APLASIA).
1839-47 TODD *Cycl. Anat. & Phys.* III. 754/1 Caco-plastic and aplastic deposits. **1875** H. WOOD *Therap.* (1879) 49 The blood was also rendered very aplastic. **1952** M. E. FLOREY *Clin. Applications Antibiotics* xxi. 567 In aplastic anaemia and leukaemia penicillin in large doses can usually control infection.

†**a'plat**, *advb. phr. Obs.* [A *prep.*[1] + PLAT (cf. *2 Kings* ix. 26).] Flat on the ground.
c **1330** *Arth. & Merlin* 9034 And Aroans with the swerd aflat That he threwe of his hors aplat.

†**a'play**, *advb. phr. Obs.* [A *prep.*[1]] In play.
1459 *Plumpton Corr.* Introd. 39 [He] said, halfe apley, Prey my brother to gett somwhat to my new chappell.

a-'plenty, aplenty, *adv.* or *pred. a.* orig. *U.S.* [f. A *prep.*[1] + PLENTY B.I. 2c.] In plenty; in abundance.
1830 J. F. COOPER *Water Witch* III. ii. 68 A sailor's blessing on you—fair winds and a plenty. **1841** [see PLENTY B.I. 2c]. **1876** 'MARK TWAIN' *Tom Sawyer* vi. 59 Sho, there's ticks a-plenty. **1910** MULFORD *Hopalong Cassidy* xi. 72 There's water a-plenty there. **1917** J. C. MCCORQUODALE *In Divers Moods* 30 And [I] dreamed wild dreams aplenty Of how I should Do what I could. **1945** *Scrutiny* XIII. 99 There is in passing ambiguity aplenty.

†**a'plight**, *advb. phr. Obs.* [A *prep.*[1] + OE. *pliht* danger, engagement, promise, pledge.] In faith, in truth, truly, certainly, surely. Often expletive, or in asseveration.
1297 R. GLOUC. 511 Hii smite out of hor castles iarmed wel apli3t. *c* **1306** *Pol. Songs* 218 He com yn at Newegate, y telle yt ou aplyht. *c* **1400** *Sowdone* 573 Fifteen thousande lefte in the feelde aplight. **1460** *Lybeaus Disc.* 45 Anoon without any dwellyng, Tell me thyn name aplyght.

†**a'plight**, *v. Obs. rare*[−1]. In 5 **a-plyht.** [f. A- *pref.* 1 + PLIGHT *v.*; cf. prec.] To plight or pledge one's word.
c **1450** LONELICH *Grail* xii. 78, I schal the telle, I the a-plyht.

aplite ('æplaɪt), var. HAPLITE.
1879 [see HAPLITE]. **1923** *Nature* CXII. 117/2 The well-known aplite from Meldon in Devonshire. **1965** G. J. WILLIAMS *Econ. Geol. N.Z.* xii. 181/2 Pegmatites, and possibly aplites, are also represented and several large quartz lodes.

‖**aplomb** (a'plɔ̃, ə'plɒm). [Fr. *aplomb* perpendicular position, steadfastness, assurance, f. the phr. *à plomb* 'according to the plummet.']
1. 'The perpendicular'; perpendicularity.
1872 C. KING *Sierra Nev.* iii. 69 We sprang on, never resting long enough to lose the aplomb. **1880** MRS. WHITNEY *Odd or Even* iii. 23 The girl jumped, with clean aplomb, from the wagon-wheel to the broad door-stone.
2. Assurance, confidence, self-possession, coolness.
1828 GEN. P. THOMPSON *Exerc.* (1842) IV. 548 They never present themselves with any aplomb; but always with some lurking recognition of the power of their adversaries. **1849** C. BRONTË *Shirley* xi. 162 Impatience of her chilly ceremony and annoyance at her want of aplomb.
3. *attrib.* quasi-*adj.* Self-possessed, confident.
1865 *Gayworthys* II. 29 Her ordinary aplomb fashion of speech.

aplotomy (ə'plɒtəmɪ). *Surg.* [mod. f. ἁπλό-ος simple + -τομη cutting, f. τέμν-ειν to cut.] Simple incision.
1852 in OGILVIE. **1880** in *Syd. Soc. Lex.*

†**a-pluck**, *advb. phr. Obs. rare.* [A *prep.*[1] + PLUCK *sb.*] With spirit; pluckily, heartily.
c **1560** *Thersites* in Hazl. *Dods.* I. 416 Darest thou try masteries with me a-pluck. **1570** *Marriage Wit & Sc.* IV. iii. *ibid.* II. 368 Arise, and dance with us a-pluck.

aplustre (ə'plʌstrɪː). [L. (pl. *aplustria*), ad. Gr. ἄφλαστον.] The curved and ornamented stern of an ancient Greek or Roman ship.
1705 ADDISON *Italy* 344 The one holds a Sword in her Hand to represent the Iliad,.. as the other has an *Aplustre* to represent the Odyssy, or Voyage of Ulysses. **1842** W. SMITH *Dict. Gk. & Rom. Antiq.* 58/2 A bird.. which perches on the aplustre of the ship Argo. **1880** WALLACE *Ben-Hur* 141 The aplustre of the galley. **1929** *Times* 1 Feb. 7/5 Their [Phoenicians'] earliest coins.. show a long rakish vessel with .. a handsome aplustre astern.

apneumatic (æpnjuː'mætɪk), *a. rare*[−1]. [f. Gr. ἀ priv. + πνευματικ-ός spiritual, f. πνευματ- (πνεῦμα) spirit.] Of or pertaining to the non-existence of soul or spirit; non-spiritual.
1864 BREVIOR *Two Worlds* 25 The apneumatic theory of Dr. Rogers.

‖**apnoea** (æp'niːə). *Path.* [mod.L., a. Gr. ἄπνοια, f. ἄπνο-ος breathless.] Suspension of breathing; cessation of respiration.
1719 *Glossogr. Nova*, *Apnœa*, want of breath; an entire suppression of breathing. **1881** MIVART *Cat* 221 Death by what is called apnœa.

apnœic (æp'niːɪk), *a. Path.* [f. APNŒA + -IC.] Characterized by or suffering from apnœa.
1883 *Science* I. 524/2 Rabbits in which the vagi are intact are made apnoeic by free artificial respiration. **1961** *Lancet* 9 Sept. 573/2 The patient suddenly became unresponsive and apnœic. **1963** *Ibid.* 5 Jan. 46/2 The anæsthetist accepts unconscious, apnœic patients.. as part of his everyday routine.

apo- *pref.*; repr. Gr. ἀπο- off, from, away; quite. **1.** In compounds already formed in Gr., or others analogous to them. **2.** In modern scientific words, not on Gr. analogies, with sense of 'standing off or away from each other, detached, separate,' as ***apo-carpous***.

apocalism (in Bailey) for APOCHYLISM.

apocalypse (əˈpɒkəlɪps). Forms: 3–7 **apocalips(e**, 4 **appocalyppce**, **-lipse**, 4–5 **apocolyps**, **-lips**, (5 **pocalyps**), 5–7 **apocalyps**, 6 **-lippis**, **appocalypse**, 6– **apocalypse**. [ad. L. *apocalypsis*, a. Gr. ἀποκάλυψις, n. of action f. ἀποκαλύπτειν to uncover, disclose, f. ἀπό off + καλύπτειν to cover.]

1. (With capital initial.) The 'revelation' of the future granted to St. John in the isle of Patmos. The book of the New Testament in which this is recorded.

[*c* **1175** *Lamb. Hom.* 81 Herof seid Seint Johan þe ewangeliste *in apocalipsi*.] *c* **1230** *Ancr. R.* 94 'Hit is a derne halewi,' seið sein Johan ewangeliste in þe Apocalipse. *c* **1400** *Rom. Rose* 7395 That sallow horse of hewe, That in the Apocalips is shewed. *a* **1440** *Sir Degrev.* 1437 The Pocalyps of Ion. **1581** WALKER in *Confer.* IV. (1584) Z iij b, The Laodicean Councill omitteth Lukes Gospel & the Apocalyps. **1667** MILTON *P.L.* IV. 2 That warning voice which he who saw Th' Apocalyps, heard cry in Heaven aloud. **1870** DISRAELI *Lothair* xliv. 230 The long-controverted point whether Rome in the great Apocalypse was signified by Babylon.

2. By extension: Any revelation or disclosure.

1382 WYCLIF *1 Cor.* xiv. 26 He hath techinge, he hath apocalips, or *reuelacioun*, he hath tunge. **1621** BURTON *Anat. Mel.* 677 (L.) Interpret apocalypses, and those hidden mysteries to private persons. **1704** SWIFT *T. Tub* i. (1750) 31 The Revelation or rather the Apocalypse of all State-arcana. **1831** CARLYLE *Sart. Res.* II. v, The new apocalypse of Nature unrolled to him.

apocalypst (əˈpɒkəlɪpst). *rare.* [irreg. formation = *apocalypt*, or *apocalyptist*.] A revealer of the unknown; an interpreter of the Apocalypse.

1829 GEN. P. THOMPSON *Exerc.* I. 114 So far the unknown apocalypst has chosen to carry his operations. **1863** THORNBURY *True as Steel* III. 148 Help to fill the madhouse as these pretended apocalypsts do.

apocalypt (əˈpɒkəlɪpt). *rare.* [ad. Gr. *ἀποκαλύπτης, n. of agent f. ἀποκαλύπτειν, see above; cf. κλέπτης, ἀλείπτης, &c.] = APOCALYPTIST.

1834 COLERIDGE *Lit. Rem.* III. 168 According to the belief of the Apocalypt, the line of the Emperors would cease in Titus.

apocalyptic (əˌpɒkəˈlɪptɪk), *a.* [ad. Gr. ἀποκαλυπτικός of the nature of revelation, f. ἀποκαλύπτειν: see APOCALYPSE and -IC.] **A.** *adj.*

1. Of or pertaining to the 'Revelation' of St. John. ***apocalyptic number***: see *Rev.* xiii. 18.

1663 J. SPENCER *Prodigies* 314 The Apocalyptick Angel which should pour out one of the Vials upon the Beast. *a* **1711** KEN *Edmund* Poet. Wks. 1721 II. 104 A Babylonian purple Robe he wore, Like that of the apocalyptick whore. **1859** MASSON *Milton* I. 481 Meade was at the head of the Apocalyptic commentators.

2. Of the nature of a revelation or disclosure; revelatory, prophetic.

1683 E. HOOKER *Pref. Pordage's Myst. Div.* 66 This veri waie of Apocalyptic Manifestation. **1859** MASSON *Brit. Novelists* iv. 289 Interpretative of all around and apocalyptic of all beyond, the vision of his beatified Beatrice. **1880** SWINBURNE *Stud. Shaks.* i. 4 The recognition of the apocalyptic fact that a workman can only be known by his work. **1950** *Economist* 14 Jan. 57/2 The apocalyptic promises of Communism can be met by the sober reality of rising standards of living. **1955** *Times* 18 July 7/5 It would be foolish, even dangerous to work oneself up into a frenzy of apocalyptic fervour.

†**3.** Of persons: Dealing with the Apocalypse or with prophetic revelations generally; apocalyptical.

1667 E. CHAMBERLAYNE *St. Gt. Brit.* I. Introd. 3 Without consulting our Astrologers or apocalyptic men. *c* **1690** SOUTH *Serm.* V. ii. (R.) That some apocalyptick ignoramus or other must presently..pick it out of some abused, martyred prophecy of Ezechiel.

B. *sb.* **1.** The writer or recorder of the Apocalypse, St. John the Divine; also = APOCALYPST.

1629 LIGHTFOOT *Misc.* 107 (T.) The divine apocalyptick, writing after Jerusalem was ruined. **1872** DE MORGAN *Budg. Paradoxes* 292 If the cyclometers and the apocalyptics would lay their heads together.

2. Apocalyptic teaching, philosophy, or literature.

1898 R. H. CHARLES in Hastings *Dict. Bible* I. 109/2 Prophecy and Apocalyptic..both claim to be a communication through the Divine Spirit of the character and will and purposes of God. **1940** *Scrutiny* IX. 286 A periodical which has previously discussed the problems of the relation between culture and the coming social-economic revolution mainly in terms of the crudest Marxian apocalyptic. **1957** *Oxf. Dict. Chr. Ch.* 67/2 In the NT, the element of Apocalyptic appears in various places.

aˌpocaˈlyptical, *a.* [f. as prec. + -AL[1].] Connected or dealing with the Apocalypse, or with prophetic revelations generally.

1633 HOWELL *Lett.* (1650) 200 Much symbolizing in spirit with our apocalypticall zelots. *a* **1638** MEDE *Apost. Lat. Times* 91 In his [St. John's] Apocalypticall vision. **1858** LONGF. *M. Standish* IV. 5 As out of the heavens, with apocalyptical splendours, Sank the city of God, in the vision of John the Apostle.

aˌpocaˈlyptically. *adv.* [f. prec. + -LY[2].]

1. After the manner, or by means, of revelation or of the Apocalypse.

1731 BAILEY, *Apocalyptically*, by way of revelation. **1830** COLERIDGE *Lect. Shaks.* II. 341 The date apocalyptically deduced..for the commencement of the Millennium.

2. *jestingly*, So as to reveal what should be concealed.

1845 *Bach. Albany* (1848) 296 The women soon reflected how apocalyptically they were arrayed.

apocalypticism (əˌpɒkəˈlɪptɪsɪz(ə)m). [f. APOCALYPTIC *a.* + -ISM.] An apocalyptic doctrine or belief, esp. one based on an expectation of the imminent end of the present world order.

1884 *Encycl. Brit.* XVII. 842/2 No one has dealt such deadly blows to Chiliasm and Christian apocalypticism as Origen. **1948** J. L. ADAMS tr. *Tillich's Protestant Era* ii. 23 Later apocalypticism emphasizes those miraculous elements, thus breaking through all limits of time and space. **1952** *Sc. Jrnl. Theol.* V. 120 Apocalypticism threatened to paralyse the life of the Church.

apocalyptism (əpɒkəˈlɪptɪz(ə)m). [f. APOCALYPT(IC *a.* + -ISM.] = prec.

1889 *Edin. Rev.* Jan. 77 The second book of Esdras represents a literary development of Hebrew Apocalyptism. **1915** W. R. INGE in F. J. Foakes-Jackson *Faith & War* v. 103 A belief, corresponding to the apocalyptism of the Jews, was widespread that the 'Kingdom of Saturn'..was immediately to appear. **1930** —— *Chr. Ethics* i. 19 Apocalyptism has left traces in almost all the books of the New Testament.

apocalyptist (əˌpɒkəˈlɪptɪst). [f. Gr. ἀποκαλύπτειν (see above) + -IST.] The writer of the Apocalypse. Also, the writer of any apocalyptic work; the writer of a commentary on the Apocalypse.

1835 *Fraser's Mag.* XI. 332/2 Does the apocalyptist represent the Angel of the Covenant with a Rainbow on his head? **1864** *Nation. Rev.* No. 36. 335 When we see the apocalyptist using favourite words and phrases foreign to the Evangelist. **1889** *Cent. Dict.*, *Apocalyptist*, an interpreter of the Apocalypse. **1922** W. R. INGE *Outspoken Ess.* (2nd Ser.) ii. 101 The idea of 'the Kingdom of God'..in the writings of the apocalyptists. **1957** *Oxf. Dict. Chr. Ch.* 67/1 The Apocalyptists were pre-eminently writers, directing their attention towards the end of things and to the destiny of the world in general.

apocarpous (æpəʊˈkɑːpəs), *a. Bot.* [mod. f. Gr. ἀπό off, away from + -καρπ-ος, comb. adj. f. καρπός fruit + -OUS.] Having the carpels distinct.

1830 LINDLEY *Nat. Syst. Bot.* Introd. 30 What I call apocarpous ovaria, or those of which the carpella are distinct. **1876** HARLEY *Mat. Med.* 767 Ranunculaceæ.. distinguished..by the apocarpous fruit.

‖**apocatastasis** (ˌæpəʊkəˈtæstəsɪs). *rare.* Also **apokatastasis**. [L., a. Gr. ἀποκατάστασις re-establishment, f. ἀπο-καθιστάναι to set up again.]

1. Restoration, re-establishment, renovation. *spec.* in *Theol.* (see quot. 1957).

1678 CUDWORTH *Intell. Syst.* 328 A Tradition.. concerning the Apocatastasis of the world..partly by Inundation and partly by Conflagration. **1867** R. E. WALLIS tr. *Delitzsch's Syst. Biblical Psychol.* vii. 552 No doctrine.. contradicts the Holy Scripture in a more unwarrantable manner than that of the so-called Apokatastasis. **1956** *Sc. Jrnl. Theol.* IX. 242 All of this is not to infer a doctrine of *apokatastasis*. **1957** *Oxf. Dict. Chr. Ch.* 67/2 *Apocatastasis*, the Greek name..for the doctrine that ultimately all free moral creatures—angels, men, and devils—will share in the grace of salvation.

2. *Path.* Return to a previous condition.

1753 CHAMBERS *Cycl. Supp.* s.v., We read of Apocatastasis or urine..of tumours, and other diseases. **1880** *Syd. Soc. Lex.*, *Apocatastasis*, The subsidence of a tumour, or the re-establishment of an exudation or secretion.

3. *Astr.* Return to the same apparent position, completion of period of revolution. (So in Gr.)

1822 T. TAYLOR *Apuleius* I. 33 *note*, The accurate apocatastasis (i.e. regression to the same sign) of the moon, and in a similar manner of the sun.

apocatastic (ˌæpəʊkəˈtæstɪk), *a. rare*[−1]. [ad. med.L. *apocatasticus*, ad. Gr. ἀποκαταστατικός; see prec.] Of or pertaining to an apocatastasis.

1822 T. TAYLOR *Apuleius* I. 33 *note*, If the apocatastic times compared with each other are primary.

apocathartic (ˌæpəʊkəˈθɑːtɪk), *a.* and *sb. Med.* [ad. Gr. ἀποκαθαρτικ-ός, f. ἀποκαθαίρ-ειν to purge; see -IC.] **A.** *adj.* Purging, aperient. **B.** *sb.* An aperient medicine.

1859 in HOOPER *Med. Dict.*

apocentre (ˈæpəʊsentə(r)). *Astr.* [f. APO- + CENTRE *sb.*] The point in the eccentric orbit of a body at which it is most distant from the body or point around which it moves.

1901 NEWCOMB *Stars* 160 In some cases there may be two pericentres and two apocentres to the apparent orbit. **1902** *Science* 7 Feb. 221 The apparently needless introduction of new terms in place of the familiar old ones, such as the logically inappropriate apocenter, pericenter, for apastron, periastron, in connection with double star orbits.

†**ˈapocha**. *Obs. rare*[−1]. [a. L. *apocha*, a. Gr. ἀποχή receipt, f. ἀπέχειν to have or receive in full, f. ἀπό from + ἔχειν to have.] An acquittance.

a **1670** HACKET *Abp. Williams* I. 25 (D.) If he had his apocha or quietance..he were free from all insequent demands.

apochromatic (ˌæpəʊkrəʊˈmætɪk), *a.* (*sb.*) [f. Gr. ἀπό from, after ACHROMATIC *a.*] Epithet of an improved form of achromatic lens invented by Abbe. Also as *sb.*, an apochromatic lens; in *Photogr.* further shortened to **ˈapochroˌmat**. So **apoˈchromatism**, apochromatic condition or quality.

1887 *Jrnl. R. Microsc. Soc.* 2nd Ser. VII. 23 In the new objectives..the elimination of these errors realizes an achromatism of higher order than has hitherto been attained. The objectives of this system may be therefore distinguished from achromatic lenses in the old sense of the word by the term apochromatism, and may be called apochromatic objectives. **1890** *Anthony's Photogr. Bull.* III. 318 The apochromatic objectives give absolutely the same photographic image as that seen upon the screen. *Ibid.* 319 In 1884, before the apochromatics were brought out. **1901** *Photogr. Jrnl.* 31 July 324 Remarkably perfect microscope objectives—the Abbe apochromats. **1939** W. CLARK *Photogr. by Infrared* xvi. 342 The 'apochromatic' lenses... Apochromats of low aperture are..sometimes used for photoengraving and colour photographic cameras.

†**aˈpochylism**. *Obs.*[−0] [ad. Gr. ἀποχύλισμα, f. ἀποχυλίζ-ειν to extract juice.] (See quot.)

[**1706** PHILLIPS, *Apochylisma*, any Juice boil'd and thicken'd with Honey or Sugar, into a kind of hard Consistence. It is otherwise call'd Rob, Robob, and Succago.] **1775** ASH, *Apochylism* [with similar definition].

†**ˈapoclasm**. *Obs.*[−0] [ad. Gr. ἀπόκλασμα fracture of an extremity, f. ἀποκλά-ειν to break off.]

1719 *Glossogr. Nova*, *Apoclasm*, the breaking off of any part of the Body. [Whence **1721** in BAILEY, &c.]

apocopate (əˈpɒkəpeɪt, -ət), *ppl. a.* [ad. mod.L. *apocopāt-us*, ppl. adj. f. APOCOPE.] Cut short by apocope. (Used *spec.* of words from which the last letter or syllable has disappeared.)

c **1850** *Pinnock's Heb. Catech.* 20 The apocopate future.. occurs only in the second and third person.

apocopate (əˈpɒkəpeɪt), *v.* [f. as prec.] To cut off (esp. the last letter or syllable of a word).

1851 S. JUDD *Margaret* II. i. (1871) 168 You apocopate that from the alphabet and Deacon Hadlock will apocopate you from the school.

aˈpocopated, *ppl. a.* [f. prec. + -ED.] = APOCOPATE *a.*

1846 TREGELLES *Gesenius' Heb. Lex.* s.v. *Gālāh*, *higlāh*, future apocopated, *wăyyĕgĕl*. **1876** E. PALMER in *Academy* 30 Sept. 332 The apocopated genitive in 'bliss.'

apocopation (əˌpɒkəʊˈpeɪʃən). [n. of action f. APOCOPATE *v.*: see -TION.] The action of apocopating: the state of being apocopated.

1727–51 CHAMBERS *Cycl.* s.v. *Apocope*, When the Apocopation is marked with a superior comma..the word is said to be *apostrophated*. **1873** F. HALL *Mod.Eng.* 187 We should have had..*alt*, *cit*, *plenipo*..if there had been as popular a demand for the apocopation of *altitudes*, *citizen*, *plenipotentiary*.

‖**apocope** (əˈpɒkəpiː). [L., a. Gr. ἀποκοπή a cutting off, f. ἀποκόπ-τ-ειν to cut off.] The cutting off or omission of the last letter or syllable of a word. Hence **apoˈcopic** *a.*

1591 PERCIVALL *Sp. Dict.* B ij a, Apocope..as for *vamos nos*, they say *vamonos*. **1711** J. GREENWOOD *Eng. Gram.* 196 Hence [from *mis*] comes the French Preposition *Mes*, and by an Apocope *Me*, as in *mecontent*. **1860** FARRAR *Orig. Lang.* viii. 175 Words and roots in a violent state of fusion and apocope.

apocrif, obs. form of APOCRYPHA.

apocrine (ˈæpəkrɪn), *a. Histol.* [f. APO- + Gr. κρίν-ειν to separate.] (See quot. 1961.)

1926 H. HOMMA in *Bull. Johns Hopkins Hosp.* XXXVIII. 365 (*title*) On apocrine sweat glands in white and Negro men and women. **1940** MACLEOD & MUENDE *Handbk. Path. Skin* xxiv. 252 Instead of opening on the surface of the skin like the small sweat-glands, the apocrine glands open into the hair-follicle between the funnel and the mouth of the sebaceous gland. **1955** *Sci. News Let.* 1 Oct. 213/2 The distinctive apocrine odor of the axilla (underarms). **1961** *Brit. Med. Dict.* 123/1 *Apocrine*. 1. A term descriptive of a gland cell which loses part of its protoplasmic substance when it is secreting. 2. Applied to sweat glands which differ from ordinary (eccrine) sweat glands in that they occur only in hairy regions.

apocrisiary (æpəʊˈkrɪzɪərɪ). Also **aˈpocrisary**. [ad. med.L. *apocrisiārius* delegate, deputy, f. Gr. ἀπόκρισι-ς answer: see -ARY.] A person appointed to give and receive answers; *spec.* a papal nuncio, or secretary.

1432–50 tr. *Higden* Rolls Ser. VI. 337 Pope Nichol..sente Arsenius his apocrisary. **1610** CARLETON *Jurisdict.* 131 The Pall was offered you by our Apocrisiaries, (that is Chaplanes). **1725** tr. *Dupin's Eccl. Hist. 17th C.* I. v. 109 Afterwards, they sent those who were to reside at Court, and to manage all Affairs which might come before them. Their Names were Apocrisiaries. **1744** LEWIS *Bp. Pecock* 124 The Pall was tendered to him by his [Paschal's] apocrisiaries.

apocrustic (æpəʊˈkrʌstɪk), *a.* and *sb. Med.* Also **apocroustic.** [ad. mod.L. *apocrūstic-us*, a. Gr. ἀποκρουστικός, f. ἀποκρού-ειν to beat off, repel.]

A. *adj.* 'Having power to repel,' astringent. **B.** *sb.* An astringent medicine.

1706 PHILLIPS, *Apocrousticks* are such Medicines as hinder the flowing of the Humours into any particular Part of the Body, and force back those that are beginning to flow thither. **1853** MAYNE *Exp. Lex., Apocrustic*, Having the power of repelling and astringing.

†**apocryph(e,** *a.* and *sb. Obs.* Also **apocrif(e.** [a. Fr. *apocryphe*, f. L. *apocrypha*: see next.] By-form of next.

A. *adj.* Of unestablished authenticity, apocryphal.

1548 COVERDALE *Erasm. Paraphr. Jude* 21 The boke of Enoch which is Apocryphe, that is to say, without autoritie.

B. *sb.* An apocryphal document.

c **1449** PECOCK *Repr.* iii. xii. 356 The contrarie parti is an apocrif. *Ibid.* 366 The seid epistle is an untrewe Apocrife.

Apocrypha (əˈpɒkrɪfə), *a.* and *sb.* Forms: 4–6 **apocripha,** (8 **apocryphy**), 6– **apocrypha.** [neut. pl. (sc. *scripta*) of late L. adj. *apocryphus*, a. Gr. ἀπόκρυφος hidden, *hence*, of unknown authorship, spurious, f. ἀποκρύπτ-ειν to hide away. Formerly used (in pl. *apocrypha*, sing. *apocryphum*) as adj. As sb., still properly treated as a plural, with singular of Gr. form *apocryphon*; but in common usage *apocrypha* is sing. with pl. *apocryphas.* In this sense *apocryphy* was also formerly in use. Cf. prec.]

†**A.** *adj.* Of unknown authorship; not authentic, spurious; uncanonical (see B); false. *Obs.*

1387 TREVISA *Higden* V. 105 The writynge is Apocripha whanne þe auctor þerof is unknowe. **1460** CAPGRAVE *Chron.* 7 'The Penauns of Adam' be cleped Apocriphum, whech is to sey, whanne the mater is in doute, or ellis whan men knowe not who mad the book. **1690** LOCKE *Government* II. I. xi. §143. 150 That..Kings enjoy'd their Crowns by Right descending to them from Adam, that we think not only Apocrypha, but also utterly impossible.

B. *sb.*

1. A writing or statement of doubtful authorship or authenticity; *spec.* those books included in the Septuagint and Vulgate versions of the Old Testament, which were not originally written in Hebrew and not counted genuine by the Jews, and which, at the Reformation, were excluded from the Sacred Canon by the Protestant party, as having no well-grounded claim to inspired authorship.

1539 BIBLE ('Great') *Apocrypha, Pref.*, The other [bookes] folowynge, which are called apocripha. **1587** GOLDING *De Mornay* xxx. 470 The Iewes account those bookes for Apocryphaes. **1597** HOOKER V. xx. (1841) i. 483 We hold not the apocrypha for sacred. **1704** *Lond. Gaz.* mmmmxxii/3 The Contents of each Chapter in the Bible, and Apocryphy. *c* **1735** POPE *Donne Sat.* iv. 286 What's now apocrypha, my wit, In time to come may pass for holy writ. **1834** *Penny Cycl.* II. 163/2 About 1826, it was decided that the Apocrypha should not be circulated by the British and Foreign Bible Society. **1881** W. R. SMITH *Old Test. in Jew. Ch.* v. 27 The presence of an apocryphon in a Christian MS.

b. *attrib.*

1590 J. GREENWOOD *Sland. Art.* B iv b, Theire Apochripha liturgye. **1666** BUNYAN *Grace Abound.* §65 Casting my eye upon the Apocrypha books, I found it in Ecclesiasticus.

2. [As in Gr.] Hidden things; secrets. *rare.*

1839 BAILEY *Festus* viii. (1848) 80 Every man's life has its apocrypha; Mine has, at least.

†**aˈpocrypha, apocryphy,** *v. Obs. rare.* [f. prec. sb.] To reckon as apocryphal or spurious.

1625 J. DAVIES *Paper Persec.* 80 (D.) The Bible ne'er was more Apocryphide Than by their bold excursions. **1661** H. BOLD *St. George's Day* 3 Works [as opposed to Faith] are Apocripha'd, as little worth.

apocryphal (əˈpɒkrɪfəl), *a.* and *sb.* [f. as prec. + -AL[1].] **A.** *adj.* Of doubtful authenticity; spurious, fictitious, false; fabulous, mythical.

a. *orig.* of a writing, statement, or story.

1590 J. GREENWOOD *Sland. Art* B ij b, We hold them..not only a babling, but apochriphall & Idolatrous. **1678** BUTLER *Hud.* III. i. 492 If but one word be true..In all th' apocryphal romance. **1868** FREEMAN *Norm. Conq.* II. App. 569 The tale has a somewhat apocryphal sound.

b. *spec.* Of or belonging to the Jewish and early Christian uncanonical literature.

1615 *Curry-C. for Coxe-C.* ii. 93 Peremptory..against the Canonizing of these Apogriphall bookes. **1711** ADDISON *Spect.* No. 28 ¶6 Our Apocryphal Heathen God [Bel]..in conjunction with the Dragon. **1865** LECKY *Ration.* (1878) I. 210 The apocryphal gospels..were for the most part of Gnostic origin.

c. *gen.* Unreal, counterfeit, sham, 'imitation.'

1610 B. JONSON *Alchemist* I. i, A whoreson, upstart, apocryphal captain. **1649** C. WALKER *Hist. Indep.* II. 226 This Agreement was..complained of in the apocryphal House of Commons. **1843** JERROLD *Punch's Lett.* xx. Wks. I. 473 He lived by putting off pencils, with apocryphal lead in them.

†**B.** *sb.* An apocryphal writing. *Obs. rare.*

1661 *Grand Debate* 13 Some Psalm or Scripture Hymn..instead of that Apocryphal [the Benedicite]. **1677** J. HANMER *View of Antiq.* 419 (T.) Nicephorus and Anastasius..did rank these epistles in the number of apocryphals.

apocryphalist (əˈpɒkrɪfəlɪst). *rare.* [f. prec. + -IST.] One who supports the inclusion of the Apocrypha in editions of the Bible.

1834 *Penny Cycl.* II. 163/2 The apocryphalists were finally defeated by the anti-apocryphalists.

aˈpocryphally, *adv. rare.* [f. as prec. + -LY[2].] In an apocryphal manner; fabulously, falsely.

1833 *Blackw. Mag.* XXXIV. 508 Samuel, 'tis said apocryphally, used to drink as a toast 'An insurrection in the West Indies and success to it!'

aˈpocryphalness. *rare.* [f. as prec. + -NESS.] The quality of being apocryphal.

1641 SMECTYMNUUS *Vind. Answ.* §13. 160 To prove not onely the Apocryphalnes, but the falsenesse of these susbscriptions. **1755** JOHNSON, *Apocryphalness*, Uncertainty, doubtfulness of credit.

†**aˈpocryphate,** *a.* and *sb. Obs.* Also 5 **ypocrafet,** 5–6 **appocrifate,** 6 **apocrafate.** [f. APOCRYPHA + -ATE[2]: cf. *literate*, etc.]

A. *adj.* Of apocryphal origin; of spurious creation or character.

1486 *Bk. St. Albans, Herald.* B ij b, Ther be ij dyuerse gentylmen made of gromys..that other is called in armys a gentill man appocrifate, that is to say made vpp and gouyn to him the name and the lyueroy of a gentylman. *Ibid.* A vj b, Ther is a gentylman ypocrafet. **1586** FERNE *Blaz. Gentrie* 56 Our bastardly and apochryphate poets. **1655** CARTER *Honor Rediv.* (1660) 22 It is but rude and false Honour, and is by Sir John Ferne termed apocryphate, and debarred of all priviledges of gentility.

B. *sb.* A spurious or sham gentleman.

1586 FERNE *Blaz. Gentrie* 92 Such Apocrafates, as be..crept into the honorable assemblyes of the Inns of Court.

†**apoˈcryphical,** *a. Obs. rare*[−1]. [f. Gr. ἀπόκρυφ-ος hidden, spurious + -ICAL.] = APOCRYPHAL.

1719 BP. BULL *Corrupt. Ch. Rome* (T.) Certain apocryphical and ridiculous stories.

†**aˈpocryphous,** *a. Obs. rare*[−1]. [f. as prec. + -OUS.] = APOCRYPHAL.

1677 GALE *Crt. Gentiles* III. 183 That apocryphous Author, *Wisd.* viii. 1, teacheth us that, etc.

apocynaceous (əˌpɒsɪˈneɪʃəs), *a. Bot.* [f. mod.L. *Apocynāceæ*: see next and -ACEOUS.] Of or belonging to the N.O. *Apocynaceæ*, or 'Dog-banes,' including the Periwinkles and Oleanders.

1883 *Knowl.* 7 Sept. 154/2 A new apocynaceous plant, which..yields abundant supplies of pure caoutchouc.

apocyneous (æpəʊˈsɪnɪəs), *a. Bot.* [f. mod.L. *Apocyne-æ* (f. *Apocynum* 'dog's-bane,' ad. Gr. ἀπόκυνον, f. ἀπό off + κυν- dog) + -OUS.] = prec.

1852 T. ROSS tr. *Humboldt's Trav.* II. xvi. 51 The first shoots of the apocyneous plants. **1854** HOOKER *Himal. Jrnls.* II. xxx. 334 A climbing apocyneous plant.

apod(e (ˈæpɒd, ˈæpəʊd), *a.* and *sb.* [f. Gr. ἄπους, ἀποδ- footless, f. ἀ priv. + πούς foot; after mod.L. *Apod-es, Apod-a*, applied to groups in Zoology.]

A. *adj.* Footless; = APODAL 1, 2.

1816 KIRBY & SPENCE *Entomol.* (1828) I. iv. 139 An apode larva. **1835** —— *Hab. & Inst. Anim.* II. xxii. 416 The Ophidians and Apod fishes evidently tend towards each other. **1874** LUBBOCK *Orig. Metam. Ins.* i. 16 The larvæ..of the Weevils..are apod.

B. *sb.* (usually *pl.* = mod.L. *Apodes, Apoda.*) Term applied to certain birds, fish, and reptiles, in which feet or ventral fins are either wholly absent or merely rudimentary.

1601 HOLLAND *Pliny* (1634) II. 383 The greater kind of Swallows or Martins called Apodes. **1836** *Blackw. Mag.* XXXIX. 306 In birds, reptiles and insects, there are some which have been falsely called apteroids, or apods; for they possess in concealment the members which their name declares them to want.

apodacrytic (ˌæpəʊdəˈkrɪtɪk), *a.* and *sb. Med.* [ad. Gr. ἀποδακρυτικ-ός f. ἀπο-δακρύ-ειν to weep much.] **A.** *adj.* Exciting tears. **B.** *sb.* Anything having this tendency.

1719 *Glossogr. Nova, Apodacrysticks.* **1853** MAYNE *Exp. Lex., Apodacrytic*..as onions, hellebore, etc.

apodal (ˈæpədəl), *a. Zool.* [f. APOD(E + -AL[1].]

1. Footless.

1802 G. SHAW *Zool.* III. 309 Apodal Lizard. **1836–39** TODD *Cycl. Anat. & Phys.* II. 862/1 The larvæ of these insects are generally apodal.

2. Of fish: Lacking the ventral fin.

1769 PENNANT *Zool.* III. 113 The eel is placed by Linnæus in the genus of Muræna, his first of the apodal fish. **1855** OWEN *Skel. & Teeth* 23 Wholly wanting..in the fishes called 'apodal.'

apodal (ˈæpədəl). [f. mod.L. *Apoda* (f. Gr. ἀποδ-, ἄπους footless) + -AL.] A batrachian belonging to the order Apoda, a group of the Cæcilians.

1856 *Encycl. Brit.* XII. 229/1 Sub-Order III.—Ribbon Apodals. **1902** *Ibid.* XXV. 383 To say nothing of the scales, present in many genera of Apodals and absent in all Caudates.

apodan (ˈæpədən) = APODAL *a.* (In mod. Dicts.)

apodemal (əˈpɒdɪməl),. *a. Zool. rare.* [f. APODEME + -AL[1].] Of or pertaining to an apodeme.

1877 HUXLEY *Anat. Inv. An.* vi. 309 The floor of the thoracic cavity is seen to be divided into a number of incomplete cells..by these apodemal partitions.

apodematal (æpəʊˈdɛmətəl), *a. Zool. rare.* [f. mod.L. *apodema, -at-* (see next) + -AL[1].] = prec.

1870 ROLLESTON *Anim. Life* 100 The muscles [of the crayfish] may be seen passing through the apodematal cells.

apodeme (ˈæpədiːm). *Zool.* [ad. mod.L. *apodema* (itself often used), f. Gr. ἀπό from + δέμας body, frame.] One of the peculiar processes on the exoskeleton of the thorax of *Arthropods*, which serve as attachment for muscles and other appendages.

1852 DANA *Crustac.* I. 49 No sella turcica or median apodeme. [**1880** HUXLEY *Cray-Fish* iii. 99 The front end..is fixed to a series of processes of the exoskeleton of the thorax called apodemata.]

apodiabolosis (ˌæpəʊdaɪəbəˈləʊsɪs). *rare.* [f. Gr. διάβολος devil, on the model of *apotheosis.*] Lowering to the rank of a devil; a making or treating as diabolical.

1827 HARE *Guesses* (1859) 162 The apotheosis of the Middle Ages, and the apodiabolosis of the Reformation and its effects. **1864** *Realm* 25 May 2 With one base imbecile smugness, which is the very apodiabolosis of Art.

apodictic, -deictic (æpəʊˈdɪktɪk, -ˈdaɪktɪk), *a.* [ad. L. *apodīctic-us*, a. Gr. ἀποδεικτικ-ός of the nature of demonstration; f. ἀποδεικ-νύναι to show off, demonstrate. (The analogical spelling is *-dict-.*)] Of clear demonstration; established on incontrovertible evidence. (By Kant applied to a proposition enouncing a necessary and hence *absolute* truth.)

1652 URQUHART *Jewel* Wks. 1834. 291 This apodictick course..to infer consequences from infallible maxims. **1816** COLERIDGE *Statesm. Man.* 358 In the heights of geometry..there exist truths of apodictic force in reason, which the mere understanding strives in vain to comprehend. **1877** CAIRD *Philos. Kant* II. iii. 242 With apodeictic certainty.

apoˈdictical, -ˈdeictical, *a. arch.* [f. prec. + -AL[1].] Of apodictic nature; absolutely demonstrable; of absolute certainty.

a **1638** MEDE *Rem. Apocal.* III. iii. 586 It follows not by Apodictical necessity, but it may perswade morally as a probability. **1677** HALE *Prim. Orig. Man.* To Reader 1 Arguments demonstrative, or at least little less than apodeictical. **1788** REID *Aristot. Log.* v. §1 When the premises are certain, and the conclusions drawn from them in due form, the syllogism is called apodictical. **1860** MANSEL *Prolegom. Log.* vii. 251 Judgments, according to Kant, are of three kinds, problematical, assertorial and apodeictical.

apoˈdictically, -ˈdeictically, *adv.* [f. prec. + -LY[2].] In an apodictic manner; by way of absolute demonstration.

1615 *Curry-C. for Coxe-C.* iii. 112 Had he deliuered his mind elsewhere positively, and apodectically. **1832–4** DE QUINCEY *Span. Nun* Wks. 1862 III. 20 There were no roasted potatoes in Spain at that date [1608], which can be apodeictically proved, because in Spain there were no potatoes at all, and very few in England.

‖**apodiˈoxis.** ? *Obs.* [L., a. Gr. ἀποδίωξις, n. of action f. ἀπο-διώκειν to drive away.] (See quot.)

1657 J. SMITH *Myst. Rhet.* 229 *Apodioxis*, a figure when any argument or objection is with indignation rejected as extreamly absurd. **1753** CHAMBERS *Cycl. Supp., Apodioxis*, in logic, the rejection of such things as do not necessarily belong to the question considered.

‖**apodixis, -deixis** (æpəʊˈdɪksɪs, -ˈdaɪksɪs). ? *Obs.* [L. *apodīxis*, a. Gr. ἀπόδειξις, f. ἀπο-δεικ-νύναι: see APODICTIC.] Demonstration, absolute proof.

a **1623** BUCK *Rich. III*, 60 (T.) If he had not afterwards given an apodixis in the battle, upon what platform he had projected and raised that hope. **1692** PITCAIRNE *Babell* 251 My second argument is..a compleat apodyxis Against this pray'r. **1755** in JOHNSON (*apodixis*); and in mod. Dicts.

‖**apodosis** (əˈpɒdəsɪs). *Rhet.* [L. *apodosis*, a. Gr. ἀπόδοσις, n. of action f. ἀποδιδόναι to give back.] The concluding clause of a sentence, as contrasted with the introductory clause or *protasis*; now usually restricted to the consequent clause in a conditional sentence, as 'If thine enemy hunger, *feed him.*'

a **1638** MEDE *Wks.* I. xxi. 77 Let us consider a little of the Protasis ['Even so hath the Lord ordained, that they which preach the Gospel'], whereof the words I have now read ['should live of the Gospel'] are the Apodosis. **1866** F. HARPER *Peace thro' Truth* 253 The word 'turned' [μεταβέβληκεν] must be understood of a physical change in the protasis; it must be therefore equally understood of a physical change in the apodosis.

apodous ('æpədəs), *a. Zool.* [f. Gr. ἀποδ-, see APOD(E + -OUS.] Footless, apod.

1816 KIRBY & SPENCE *Entomol.* II. xxi. 269 Apodous larvæ, or those that move without legs. **1836** TODD *Cycl. Anat. & Phys.* I. 166/2 A certain number of Annelida are completely apodous.

‖**apodyterium** (æpəʊdɪ'tɪərɪəm). [L., a. Gr. ἀποδυτήριον, f. ἀπο-δύ-ειν to put off, undress.] *orig.* The apartment in which clothes were deposited by those who were preparing for the bath or *palæstra*; hence *gen.* a dressing-room, a robing-room.

a **1695** WOOD *Life* (1848) 193 Conducted in his doctor's robes from the apodyterium into the convocation house. **1820** T. MITCHELL *Com. Aristoph.* I. Introd. 55 It was my lot to be sitting where you saw me, in the apodyterium.

apo-enzyme (ˌæpəʊ'ɛnzaɪm). *Chem.* [a. F. *apoenzyme*, f. APO- + ENZYME 2.] (See quot. 1961.)

[**1936** *Union Internat. de Chimie Compt. Rend.* 43 Le complexe total sera appelé *holoenzyme* et le résidu, après séparation de ses activateurs, sera appelé *apoenzyme*.] **1936** *Chem. Abstr.* 6397 A comprehensive treatise discussing.. character and action of coenzymes and apoenzymes. **1944** *Jrnl. Pharm. & Exp. Therap.* LXXXI. 246 This enzyme like substance appears to attack the apoenzyme or protein part of the oxidative enzyme system. **1950** [see CO-ENZYME]. **1961** *Brit. Med. Dict.* 123/2 *Apo-enzyme*, the protein carrier, or enzyme proper (e.g. carboxylase) which, with a co-enzyme (co-carboxylase), carries out an enzymic reaction.

apogæic, -gaic (æpəʊ'dʒiːɪk, -'geɪɪk), *a.* [f. Gr. ἀπόγαι-ος far from the earth (see APOGEE) + -IC.] = APOGEAN.

1839 LADY LYTTON *Cheveley* II. ix. 299 That when this enterprising and apogæic old lady had gone up so high.. she went still farther, even to the moon. **1880** P. GREG *Across Zodiac* I. ii. 44 The lunar angle.. confirmed the reading.. giving the same apogaic distance or elevation.

apogamy (ə'pɒgəmɪ). *Bot.* [f. Gr. ἀπό APO- + γάμος marriage (cf. GAMO-).] Absence of sexual reproduction; asexual reproduction, agamogenesis; *spec.* in ferns and other cryptogams, production of the perfect plant directly from a bud on the prothallus instead of by the usual sexual process. So **apogamic** (æpəʊ'gæmɪk), **apogamous** (ə'pɒgəməs) *adjs.*, characterized by or of the nature of apogamy; agamogenetic (*spec.* in the way described above); hence **a'pogamously** *adv.* (Cf. APOSPORY, etc.)

1878 VINES in *Jrnl. Bot.* VII. 360 A transition from an oophore to a sporophore without the intervention of sexual reproductive organs. Apogamy (De Bary). *Ibid.* 361 We may speak of this plant as being 'aposporous', using a word which is symmetrical with the term 'apogamous', applied by De Bary to those Ferns in whose life-history no process of sexual reproduction occurs. **1883** *Ann. Rep. Smithsonian Inst. 1881* 403 Forms where oogonia are found without male pollinodia.. considered as representing a distinct apogamous species. **1886** *Jrnl. R. Microsc. Soc.* 2nd Ser. VI. 298 The author could not detect any act of impregnation [in a parasite on the olive], and believes that reproduction is apogamic. **1886** VINES in *Encycl. Brit.* XX. 431/2 By the suppression either of the sexually produced spore or of the asexually produced spore; the former is an instance of apogamy, the latter of apospory. *Ibid.* 431/1 [Spores] formed.. without a sexual process—in a word, apogamously. **1921** *Ann. Bot.* XXXV. 184 We see.. in the true apogamy of other species, a further manifestation of the powers of heterosis.. ending in apomictical reproduction.

apogeal (æpəʊ'dʒiːəl), *a. Astr.* [f. L. *apogē-us*, a. Gr. ἀπόγαιος -γειος (see APOGÆIC, -GAIC *a.*) + -AL[1].] = APOGEAN.

1743 *Phil. Trans.* XLVIII. 166 The difference between the apogeal and perigeal diameters of the sun. **1797** *Encycl. Brit.* II. 584/1 Set the moon's apogeal wire to its place in the ecliptic for that time.

apogean (æpəʊ'dʒiːən), *a. Astr.* [f. as prec. + -AN.] **a.** Proceeding off from the earth or land. **b.** Of or pertaining to apogee.

a **1644** QUARLES *Sol. Recant.* ix. 49 Let not that rude, that Apogean storm Of flesh and blood dismay thee. **1812** WOODHOUSE *Astron.* xxxiii. 313 The apogean and perigean lunar distances. **1876** CHAMBERS *Astron.* 173 The Moon being more or less in an apogean position.

apogee ('æpəʊdʒiː). *Astr.* [a. Fr. *apogée* (in Cotgr. 1611), f. L. *apogæum*, a. Gr. ἀπόγαιον (also ἀπόγειον), adj. neut. 'away from the earth,' (f. ἀπό off, from + γάϊος, γεῖος of the earth, f. γαῖα, γῆ the earth), but used absol. by Ptolemy (sc. διάστημα distance) in the modern astronomic sense. Formerly used in Gr. or L. form *apogeon*, *-gæum*, *-geum*.]

1. The point in the orbit of the moon, or of any planet, at which it is at its greatest distance from the earth; also, the greatest distance of the sun from the earth when the latter is in *aphelion*. (A term of the Ptolemaic Astronomy, which viewed the earth as the centre of the universe; in modern astronomy strictly used in reference to the moon, and popularly said of the sun in reference to its apparent motion.)

1594 J. DAVIS *Seamans Secr.*, Her Slowe Motion is in the point of Auge or *apogeo*. **1656** tr. *Hobbes' Elem. Philos.* (1839) 443 The apogæum of the sun or the aphelium of the earth. **1727–51** CHAMBERS *Cycl.*, *Apogee* is a point in the heavens at the extreme of the line of the apsides. **1812** WOODHOUSE *Astron.* xix. 206 Apogee, if the Sun be supposed to revolve, Aphelion, if the Earth. **1868** LOCKYER *Heavens* (ed. 3) 130 The greatest distance of the Moon from the Earth is about 64¾ the equatorial radius of our globe. When the Moon is at this distance, it is said to be in apogee.

†**2.** The greatest altitude reached by the sun in his apparent course; his meridional altitude on the longest day. *Obs.*

1605 BACON *Adv. Learn.* (1640) 146 The *Apogée* or middle point; and *Perigée* or lowest point of heaven. **1646** SIR T. BROWNE *Pseud. Ep.* VI. v. (1686) 242 In the Apogeum or highest point it is not so hot under that Tropick.

3. Hence *fig.* **a.** The most distant or remote spot. **b.** The highest point, climax, culmination.

1600 FAIRFAX *Tasso* II. lxvii. 33 Thy Sunne is in his Apogæon placed, And when it moueth next, must needes descend. **1642** H. MORE *Song of Soul* II. III. II. xii, She [the Soul] doth ascend, Unto her circles ancient Apogie. **1670** EACHARD *Contempt Clergy* 54 Sometimes he withdraws himself into the apogæum of doubt, sorrow, and despair. **1858** MOTLEY *Dutch Rep.* VI. Introd. 33 The trade of the Netherlands.. had however by no means reached its apogee.

4. The point in the trajectory of a missile, rocket, or the like at which it is at its greatest distance from the earth.

1958 in *Aero-Space Terms.* **1961** *Flight* LXXX. 756/1 When the satellite reaches the 22,300 mile apogee of the trajectory.. the solid-propellant apogee motor will be used to inject the satellite into a circular, near-synchronous orbit. **1962** J. GLENN in *Into Orbit* 6 The apogee or highest point of the capsule's orbit was over eight times that altitude.

apogeotropic (ˌæpəʊdʒiːəʊ'trɒpɪk), *a. Bot.* [f. (by Darwin 1880) Gr. ἀπό from + γῆ (in comb. γεω-) earth + τροπικ-ός turning.] Bending or turning away from the ground. (Said of leaves and other parts of plants.)

1880 DARWIN *Movem. Plants* 189 When they [the rhizomes] were cultivated in water their tips turned upwards, and they became apogeotropic.

ˌ**apogeo'tropically**, *adv.* [f. prec. + -AL[1] + -LY[2].] In a direction away from the ground.

1880 F. DARWIN in *Nature* No. 582. 179 There is no reason why they should bend apogeotropically in one direction more than another.

apogeotropism (ˌæpəʊdʒiː'ɒtrəpɪz(ə)m). [f. as prec. + -ISM.] The tendency of leaves and other parts of plants to turn away from the earth.

1880 DARWIN *Movem. Plants* 5 Apogeotropism will mean bending in opposition to gravity or from the centre of the earth. **1881** *Academy* 12 Feb. 121 The motion produced by apogeotropism is sometimes remarkably straight.

apograph ('æpəʊgrɑːf, -æ-). [ad. (perh. through Fr. *apographe*) Gr. ἀπόγραφ-ον a copy, f. ἀπο-γράφ-ειν to write off, copy.] An exact copy or transcript.

1601 HOLLAND *Pliny* (1634) II. 546 The counterfeit taken from this table and made by it (which kind of pattern the Greekes call Apographon). **1656** BLOUNT *Glossogr.*, *Apograph*, a copy written out of another pattern; also an Inventory of ones goods. **1875** POSTE *Gaius* Pref. 8 An apograph or facsimile edition of the Veronese MS. **1878** GARLAND *Genesis* Pref. 8 Not from the original manuscripts, but from the apographs.

†**a'pographal**, *a. Obs. rare*[−1]. [f. prec. + -AL[1].] Of the nature of an apograph; copied.

1752 LEE *Diss. Theol.* I. 104 (L.) Parallel places—nowhere else extant but in these apocryphal or apographal pieces.

apohyal (æpəʊ'haɪəl). [f. APO- + HY(OID + -AL.] (*a*) *Ornith.*, the ceratobranchial bone. (*b*) *Ichth.*, the basihyal bone.

1860 in MAYNE *Expos. Lex.* Suppl. **1884** COUES *Key N. Amer. Birds* (ed. 2) 207 Ceratobranchials proper, commonly called apo-hyals.

‖**a'pointcee.** [a. Fr. *apointée* pa. pple.; cf. *appoint* (formerly *appoinct*) 'somme qui fait le solde d'un compte,' Littré.] The net amount.

1682 SCARLETT *Exch.* 20 Substract the Provision and Courtagie, and the Remainder is the Apoinctee (the Neat Sum).

†**a'point.** *Obs. rare.* [a. OFr. *apoint*, in Cotgr. *appoinct*.] Fitness, readiness.

c **1400** *Destr. Troy* II. 401 No filisofers.. Might approche to þat precious apoint of her wit.

apoious (ə'pɔɪəs), *a. rare.* [f. Gr. ἄποι-ος without quality + -OUS.] Having no active qualities; neutral; *e.g.* water, starch.

1880 in *Syd. Soc. Lex.*

†**a'poison, -oyson,** *v. Obs.* [a. OFr. *apoisone-r*, variant of *empoisoner*: see A- *pref.* 10.] To poison.

1297 R. GLOUC. 122 Þo luþer wommon.. apoysnede þe godeman, and to þe deþe hym broȝte. *c* **1400** *Chron. Eng.* 781 (Ritson *M.R.* II. 302) His stepmoder.. Him apoisonede that he was ded.

apojove ('æpəʊdʒəʊv). *Astr.* [(a. Fr. *apojove*), ad. mod.L. *apojovium*, f. Gr. ἀπό from + L. *Jov-* Jupiter; cf. *apogee*.] The point in the orbit of a satellite of the planet Jupiter at which it is at its greatest distance from the planet.

[**1761** DANTHORNE in *Phil. Trans.* LII. 106 The apojovium of the fourth satellite.. moves forward about 12° in 20 years.] **1867** E. DENISON *Astron. without Math.* 179 Each moon is less accelerated at apojove than perijove.

apokatastasis, var. APOCATASTASIS.

‖**apo koinou, apo-koinou** ('æpəʊ 'kɔɪnaʊ), *advb. phr. Gram.* [Gr. ἀπὸ κοινοῦ in common.] Applied to a construction consisting of two clauses which have a word or phrase in common (see quots.).

1892 KELLNER *Hist. Outl. Eng. Syntax* 62 The whole construction may be apprehended as a sentence *with one subject and two predicates*. This is the so-called construction ἀπὸ κοινοῦ. **1927** JESPERSEN *Mod.Eng. Gram.* III. vii. 133 Our constructions are often explained on the so-called *apokoinou* principle, according to which something is expressed only once instead of twice, but in such a way that the hearer connects it both with what precedes and with what follows. *Ibid.* 134 In the later language, too, we have many sentences with contact-clauses in which the *apo-koinou* explanation cannot be applied on account of the word-order, as the common element does not stand in the middle. **1963** VISSER *Hist. Syntax Eng. Lang.* I. i. 11 (*heading*) In apo koinou constructions. Utterances of the type 'I have an uncle is a myghty erle' consist of two syntactical units with one element in common (in this example 'an uncle') which functions as the subject in the second unit. *Ibid.*, The apo koinou construction with 'understood' subject already occurred in Old English, although instances are not frequent and mainly restricted to combinations the second part of which contained the verb 'hatan'.

†**apo'lactize,** *v. Obs.*[−0] [ad. L. *apolactīzā-re*, ad. Gr. ἀπο-λακτίζ-ειν to kick away.] 'To spurne with the heele.' Cockeram 1623.

apolar (ə'pəʊlə(r)), *a. Biol.* [f. A- *pref.* 14 priv. + POLAR.] Having no 'poles' or fibrous processes; sometimes applied to those nerve cells which have no 'polar' connexion with the nerve-fibres.

1859 TODD *Cycl. Anat. & Phys.* V. 436/2 The ganglionic corpuscles.. termed by Stannius apolar cells. **1880** BASTIAN *Brain* iii. 48 Many of the so-called apolar nerve-cells may be nothing more than imperfectly developed ganglion cells.

apolaustic (æpəʊ'lɔːstɪk), *a.* and *sb.* [ad. Gr. ἀπολαυστικ-ός, f. ἀπολαύ-ειν to enjoy.]

A. *adj.* Concerned with or wholly devoted to seeking enjoyment; self-indulgent.

1871 T. ARNOLD in *Wyclif's Wks.* III. 346 *note*, 'Rehetours' might mean lazy apolaustic fellows, idlers, supernumeraries. **1880** *Sat. Rev.* No. 1289. 63 The lordly, apolaustic, and haughty undergraduate.

B. *collect. sb.* A suggested synonym for ÆSTHETICS; the science of the pleasurable.

1836–7 SIR W. HAMILTON *Metaph.* vii. I. 124 Baumgarten .. first applied the term Æsthetic to the doctrine which we vaguely.. denominate the Philosophy of Taste, the Theory of the Fine Arts.. The term Apolaustic would have been a more appropriate designation.

apo'lausticism (-sɪz(ə)m). [f. APOLAUSTIC *a.* + -ISM.] Devotion to enjoyment.

1883 *Sat. Rev.* 15 Dec. 763 He combined the lessons of economy with apolausticism. **1894** 'X. L.' *Aut Diabolus aut Nihil* 6 He was indeed only fervent in his apolausticism.

†'**apolepsy.** *Path. Obs.* [ad. L. *apolēpsia*, ad. Gr. *ἀποληψία = ἀπόληψις, n. of action f. ἀπο-λαμβάν-ειν to take off, intercept, arrest.] (See quot.)

[**1706** PHILLIPS, *Apolepsia*.. among Physicians, a Stoppage in the Course of the Blood or Animal Spirits.] **1719** *Glossogr. Nova*, *Apolepsy*. [In mod. Dicts.]

apolitical (eɪpəʊ'lɪtɪkəl), *a.* [f. A- 14 + POLITICAL *a.*] Detached from, not interested in or concerned with, political issues or activities.

1952 M. MCCARTHY *Groves of Academe* (1953) iii. 49 You are not political. You are a-political. **1958** *Times Lit. Suppl.* 28 Nov. 689/4 By an apolitical attitude I meant the attitude of the heroes of *Hurry On Down* or *Lucky Jim*, for instance; the attitude which Mr. Priestley once described as one of 'opting out'. **1960** *Guardian* 12 Apr. 8/3 Comparatively a-political young people may be quite willing to join a Young Conservative club for the sake of its social activities.

†**A'pollinar,** *a. Obs.* [ad. L. *Apollināris* of Apollo.] = next.

1601 HOLLAND *Pliny* II. 541 The Apollinar games.

Apollinarian (əˌpɒlɪ'nɛərɪən), *a.* [f. L. *Apollināri-s* of Apollo; also a proper name + -AN.]

A. *adj.* **1.** Sacred to or in honour of Apollo.

1753 CHAMBERS *Cycl. Supp.* s.v., The *Apollinarian* games.

2. Of or pertaining to Apollinaris of Laodicea, a noted heretic of the 4th c., who held peculiar opinions on the Incarnation.

1659 PEARSON *Creed* (1864) 281 The Apollinarian heresy.

B. *sb.* An adherent of the opinions of Apollinaris.

1586 T. ROGERS 39 *Art.* (1607) 44 Some will have a quaternity of persons, not a Trinity.. So.. the Apollinarians did hold. **1852** SIR W. HAMILTON *Discuss.* 191 Collier.. was .. in his religious.. speculations.. an Apollinarian.

Apolli'narianism. The doctrine of the Apollinarians.

1877 P. SCHAFF *Creeds Gk. & Lat. Churches* II. iii. 63 The addition of a new Creed is justified by the subsequent Christological heresies (Apollinarianism, Nestorianism, and Eutychianism). **1921** *Contemp. Rev.* Nov. 623 The Dean of Carlisle warns theologians against the peril of Apollinarianism or Monotheism. **1946** E. L. MASCALL *Christ* i. 11 The heresies of Apollinarianism and Nestorianism.

Apollinaris (ɑpɒlɪ'nɛərɪs). Short for ***Apollinaris water***, an effervescent mineral water produced at Apollinarisburg near Bonn in Germany, and used as a beverage.

1875 R. BROWNING *Inn Album* i. 9 Dinner, Apollinaris,—what they please. **1878** *Fun* 26 Jan. (Hoppe), Sweet champagne and Apollinaris—Sham and Polly, as it is slangily called. **1897** FLANDRAU *Harvard Episodes* 335 Mrs. Lauriston brought some apollinaris from her table. **1914** J. JOYCE *Dubliners* 114 Weathers said he would take a small Irish and Apollinaris.

Apolli'narist. ? *Obs.* [ad. med.L. *Apollināristа*, f. *Apollinār-is*: see -IST] = APOLLINARIAN *sb.*

1640 BP. HALL *Chr. Moder.* 37/2 Makes Christ of meal, therefore not of the blessed Virgin, therefore an Apollinarist. **1702** tr. *Le Clerc's Prim. Fathers* 228 Apollinarists who believed that the Divinity of Christ was instead of a Soul to his Body. **1882** SCHAFF *Herzog's Encycl. Rel. Knowl.* 109.

Apolline (ə'pɒlaɪn, -lɪn), *a.* [ad. L. *Apollineus*, f. *Apollin-*, Apollo.] Pertaining to or resembling Apollo: = APOLLONIAN *a.* 1. So **Apollinic, -inian** (æpə'lɪnɪk, -'ɪnɪən) *adjs.* in same sense.

1605 P. ERONDELL *French Garden* x, It was called of the ancient heathen, the Apolline Stone. **1884** *Encycl. Brit.* XVII. 808/2 Apolline oracles, such as the Delphic. **1886** *Ibid.* XX. 360 Apollinic (Delphic) religion. **1923** J. M. MURRY *Pencillings* 220 Elderly spinsters made the fortune of a lady-novelist who..invariably represented one of their kind as the beloved of an ardent, Apolline youth. **1924** E. & C. PAUL tr. *Baudouin's Psycho-analysis & Aesthetics* vi. 255 Dionysian art is being converted into apollinian art. **1963** *Times* 19 Apr. 15/5 The most characteristic features of Apollo and the Apollinian movement.

Apollonian (æpə'ləʊnɪən), *a.* and *sb.* [f. L. *Apollōni-us*, a. Gr. ἀπολλώνι-ος of Apollo; also pr. name + -IAN]

A. *adj.* 1. Pertaining to, resembling, or having the characteristics of Apollo, the sun-god of the Greeks and Romans, the patron of music and poetry.

1663 GERBIER *Counsel* B vj a, To destroy the very foundation of it; partly on pretence that..the string of an Apollonian-like harp did not sound pleasing to their ears. *a* **1822** SHELLEY *Hymn to Merc.* lxiii, Every Apollonian limb Is clothed with speed, and might, and manliness.

2. Of Apollonius of Perga, a famous Greek geometer and investigator of conic sections.

1727-51 CHAMBERS *Cycl.* s.v. *Hyperbola*, The Apollonian Hyperbola is..the Hyperbola of the first kind; thus called in contradistinction to the hyperbolas of the higher kinds. **1798** ATWOOD in *Phil. Trans.* LXXXVIII. 208 The Apollonian or conic parabola.

B. *sb.* A worshipper or follower of Apollo; one having the characteristics of Apollo (opp. Dionysian).

1925 CHESTERTON *Everl. Man.* II. v. 274 There would still be intelligent Apollonians apparently worshipping the sun-god. **1936** G. B. SHAW *Millionairess* Pref. 120 The Teutons and Latins, the Apollonians and Dionysians.

Apollonic (æpə'lɒnɪk), *a. rare.* [f. Gr. ἀπολλώνι-ος (see prec.) + -IC.] Of or pertaining to Apollo.

1880 MAX MÜLLER *Select. Ess.* I. 456 One large web of Apollonic theology.

apo'llonicon. [f. as prec. after *harmonicon*, etc.] (See quot.)

1834 *Penny Cycl.* II. 165/2 *Apollonicon*, the name given to a chamber organ of vast power, supplied with both keys and barrels..first exhibited..in 1817. *a* **1849** H. COLERIDGE *Ess.* I. 305 Sing 'Songs of Reason' to the grinding of a steam apollonicon.

Apollonize (ə'pɒlənaɪz), *v. rare*$^{-1}$. [f. as prec. + -IZE.] To act the Apollo; to decide oracularly on the merits of music, poetry, etc.

1835 *Blackw. Mag.* XXXVIII. 599 The literary patient under this influenza..imagines himself authorized to Apollonize.

Apolloship (ə'pɒləʊʃɪp). *nonce-wd.* [f. APOLLO + -SHIP.] The position of Apollo; pre-eminence in poetry and prophecy.

1867 J. H. STIRLING in *Fortn. Rev.* Oct. 384 Predestinate to Apolloship, the godship of prophecy, the godship of song.

‖**Apollyon** (ə'pɒlɪən). [L., a. Gr. ἀπολλύων, pr. pple. of ἀπολλύ-ειν to destroy.] The destroyer, a name given to the Devil; whence **Apollyonist**, a subject or follower of Apollyon.

1382 WYCLIF *Rev.* ix. 11 The aungel of depnesse, to whom the name bi Ebru, Labadon, forsothe bi Greke, Appolion. *c* **1400** *Rowland & Ot.* 1209 Mahoun, And appolyne that he one levede. **1627** P. FLETCHER (*title*) The Locusts, or Apollyonists. [See Rev. ix. 3-11.] **1678** BUNYAN *Pilgr.* 93 He espied a foul Fiend coming over..to meet him: his name is *Apollyon*.

†**a'pologal,** *a. Obs. rare*$^{-1}$. [f. L. *apolog-us*, Gr. ἀπόλογ-ος, story + -AL[1].] Of the nature of an apologue or fable.

1652 URQUHART *Jewel* Wks. 1834, 292 Allegories of all sorts, whether apologal, affabulatory, parabolary, etc.

†**a'pologer.** *Obs.* [f. prec. + -ER[1].] One who tells apologues, a fabulist.

1621 BURTON *Anat. Mel.* III. ii. v. ii, A mouse (saith an Apologer) was brought up in a chest. **1653** WATERHOUSE *Apol. Learn.* 258 (L.) A sober apologer.

apologetic (ə,pɒlə'dʒɛtɪk), *a.* and *sb.* Also 7 apologetique, apollogetick. [a. Fr. *apologétique*, ad. L. *apologēticus*, a. Gr. ἀπολογητικός fit for defence, f. ἀπολογέ-εσθαι to speak in defence: see APOLOGY.] A. *adj.*

1. Of the nature of a defence; vindicatory.

1649 (*title*) An Apologetic Declaration of the conscientious Presbyterians of the Province of London. **1724** A. COLLINS *Gr. Chr. Relig.* 46 Many apologetick writings of the ancient Christians. **1875** *Encycl. Brit.* (ed. 9) s.v. *Apologetics*, Augustine's..*De Civitate Dei* is apologetic in so far as it endeavours to show that Christianity and the church are the only ark of safety.

2. Regretfully acknowledging or excusing fault or failure.

1855 MACAULAY *Hist. Eng.* IV. xviii. 170 Forced to speak in a subdued and apologetic tone. **1867** DICKENS *Lett.* (1880) II. 295 All manner of apologetic messages.

B. *sb.*

1. A formal apology for, or defence of, a person, doctrine, course of action, etc.

1605 BACON *Adv. Learn.* (1640) To Reader 1 The intended Apologetique..is not publish'd. *a* **1733** NORTH *Lives* I. 335 That all, which did not then please, must be attributed to the Lord Keeper and not to him. A stately apologetic! **1751** JORTIN *Eccl. Hist.* I. 239 Tertullian, in his Apologetic, inveighs..against the inconsistency and absurdity of this.

2. *pl.* or *collect. sing.* The defensive method of argument; often *spec.* The argumentative defence of Christianity.

a **1733** NORTH *Lives* (1826) II. 156 To drop these apologetics. **1834** *Penny Cycl.* II. 169/2 The science of apologetics..was unknown till the attacks of the adversaries of Christianity assumed a learned and scientific character. **1882** *Athenæum* 25 Nov. 700/1 The kind of book..most rational of all in the way of Christian apologetic.

a,polo'getical, *a.* [f. as prec. + -AL[1].]

1. = APOLOGETIC *a.* 1.

a **1600** HOOKER *Eccl. Pol.* VIII. 505 Writings apologetical of her royal authority. **1640** FULLER *Abel Rediv.*, *Bradford* (1867) I. 219 A long apologetical oration of his own innocency. **1859** JOWETT *Romans* II. 580 The former have a dogmatical, the latter an apologetical character.

2. = APOLOGETIC 2.

1634 R. H. *Salerne Regim.* Pref. 1, I thought fit to wave all Apologeticall expressions, of this Workes weakenesse. **1865** LECKY *Rational.* (1878) II. 88 Persecution became languid ..grew apologetical, timid, and evasive.

a,polo'getically, *adv.* [f. prec. + -LY[2].] In apologetic manner; by way of apology.

1649 C. WALKER *Hist. Indep.* II. 242 These Letters.. being Apologetically published for satisfaction of the Souldiery. **1836** CAR. FOX *Jrnls.* I. 23 Coleridge.. murmured apologetically 'I got that book cheap.'

‖**apologia** (æpə'ləʊdʒɪə). [L., see APOLOGY *sb.*] = APOLOGY *sb.* 1; esp. a written defence or justification of the opinions or conduct of a writer, speaker, etc.

The currency of the word is largely due to J. H. Newman's *Apologia pro Vita Sua*, 1864.

1784 J. NEWTON (*title*) Apologia. Four letters to a Minister of an independant Church: by a Minister of the Church of England. **1876** M. DAVIES *Unorth. Lond.* 356 A very manful..apologia was that with which Miss Miller favoured the large audience. **1883** *Sat. Rev.* 10 Nov. 613/1 The Duke [of Argyll] has put his own version of the story on record. This apologia is a pamphlet, entitled *Crofts and Farms in the Hebrides*. **1903** *Westm. Gaz.* 20 Jan. 8/2 They may be taken as his 'Apologia'—though not in any sense an apology—for the achievements of his official career. **1927** A. H. MCNEILE *Introd. N.T.* ii. 12 His [St. Mark's] Gospel is not an *apologia* to Jews but an *apologia* to the world of the truth of Christianity.

†**apo'logical,** *a. Obs.* [f. Gr. ἀπολογ-ία defence, or ἀπόλογ-ος fable + -ICAL.]

1. Of the nature of an apology or defence.

1607 *Sharpham's Fleire* Pref. A iij, I had of him..an Epistle or Apological præamble..directed vnto you. **1665** J. BROWN (*title*) An apologicall Relation of the particular Sufferings of the faithfull Ministers..of the Church.

2. Of the nature of an apologue, parable, or fable.

c **1633** T. ADAMS *Wks.* (1862) II. 166 (D.) To this silent objection Christ makes an apological answer.

†**a'pologism.** *Obs.*$^{-0}$ [ad. Gr. ἀπολογισμ-ός the rendering of an account, f. ἀπολογίζ-εσθαι; but referred in meaning to APOLOGIZE, APOLOGIST.] 'A defence or excuse, a speech or written answer made in justification of anyone.' Blount *Glossogr.* 1656.

apologist (ə'pɒlədʒɪst). [a. Fr. *apologiste*, f. Gr. ἀπολογία defence, after ἀνταγωνιστ-ής, σοφιστής, etc.: see APOLOGY and -IST.] One who apologizes for, or defends by argument; a professed literary champion.

1640 BP. HALL *Episc.* I. 12 The Apologist professeth for them, that they greatly desired to conserve the government of the Bishops. **1728** YOUNG *Love Fame* vi. (1757) 156 Thus pleads the devil's fair apologist. **1844** LD. BROUGHAM *Brit. Const.* xv. (1862) 233 Mr. Hume, the staunch apologist of.. all the Stuarts. **1868** GLADSTONE *Juv. Mundi* vii. (1870) 184 Never was the heathen creed..so sublimated, as when it perished under the blows of the Christian apologists.

apologize (ə'pɒlədʒaɪz), *v.* [APOLOGY + -IZE; cf. Gr. ἀπολογέ-εσθαι to speak in defence: ἀπολογίζεσθαι, to which the formation corresponds, is a deriv. of ἀπόλογος APOLOGUE.]

1. *intr.* To speak in, or serve as, justification, explanation, or palliation of a fault, failure, or anything that may cause dissatisfaction; to offer defensive arguments; to make excuses. Also in modern usage: To acknowledge and express regret for a fault without defence, by way of reparation to the feelings of the person affected. Const. *for*.

1597 DANIEL *Civ. Wars* IV. ii, Enforced to apologize With foreign states for two enormous things. **1656** H. MORE *Antid. Ath.* Pref. 12, I can justly apologize for my self that Necessity has no law. **1725** DE FOE *Voy. round World* (1840) 96 They had very little wine, which the governor apologised for. **1755** *Mem. P. Drake* Ded., Circumstances which might well have apologized for such a Conduct. **1860** *Cornh. Mag.* 243 We are wont in a sneaking, contemptible sort of way, to apologize for our holidays. **1878** SEELEY *Stein* III. 497 Stein, as usual, sins by over-emphatic expressions for which he later freely apologises.

†**2.** *trans.* (by omission of prep. *for*.) *Obs. rare.*

1733 SWIFT *Apol.* Wks. 1755 IV. I. 212 The doctor takes his hint from hence, T' apologise his late offence.

apologizer (ə'pɒlə,dʒaɪzə(r)). [f. prec. + -ER[1].] One who apologizes (in modern usage for a fault or offence; in early use = APOLOGIST).

1660 H. MORE *Myst. Godl.* III. ii. 61 Another sort of Apologizers for Heathenism. **1677** J. H[ANMER] *View of Antiq.* 239 (T.) His apologisers labour to free him.

a'pologizing, *vbl. sb.* [f. as prec. + -ING[1].] Defence, vindication, offering of an apology.

1611 (*title*) Anti-Coton..for the apologizing of the Jesuites Doctrine.

apologue ('æpəlɒg). Also 6-7 -logy, 7 -loge. [a. Fr. *apologue*, ad. L. *apologus*, a. Gr. ἀπόλογος account, story, fable, f. ἀπό off + λόγος speech.] An allegorical story intended to convey a useful lesson; a moral fable. (Applied more especially to a story in which the actors or speakers are taken from the brute creation or from inanimate nature.)

1552-5 LATIMER *Serm. & Rem.* (1845) 210 To teach the people in apologies, bringing in how one beast talketh with another. **1607** TOPSELL *Four-footed Beasts* 578 A pretty apology of a league that was made betwixt the wolves and the sheep. **1699** BENTLEY *Phal.* 496 Æsop a poor Slave could make Apologues at Samos. **1837-9** HALLAM *Hist. Lit.* (1847) II. 118 Employing the veil of apologue. **1879** FARRAR *Paul* I. 633 The apologue of the self-asserting members in *1 Cor.* xii. reminds us at once of the ingenious fable of Menenius Agrippa.

apology (ə'pɒlədʒɪ), *sb.* [(? a. Fr. *apologie*), ad. L. *apologia* (APOLOGIA), a. Gr. ἀπολογία defence, a speech in defence, f. ἀπό away, off + -λογία speaking.] Const. (*of* obs.) *for*.

1. The pleading off from a charge or imputation, whether expressed, implied, or only conceived as possible; defence of a person, or vindication of an institution, etc., from accusation or aspersion.

1533 MORE (*title*) Apologie of Syr Thomas More, Knyght; made by him, after he had geuen ouer the Office of Lord Chancellor of Englande. **1589** F. TRIGGE (*title*) An Apologie or Defence of our Dayes. **1650** BAXTER *Saints' Rest* I. v. (1662) 56 Now they shall both by Apology be maintained just. **1754** SHERLOCK *Disc.* (1759) I. iv. 165 And before the same great Court of Areopagites Paul made his Apology. **1796** BP. WATSON (*title*) An Apology for the Bible. **1850** J. H. NEWMAN *Difficult. Anglic.* 4 Apologies for various of the great doctrines of the faith.

2. Less formally: Justification, explanation, or excuse, of an incident or course of action.

1588 SHAKS. *L.L.L.* v. i. 142 His *enter* and *exit* shall bee strangling a Snake; and I will haue an Apologie for that purpose. **1725** DE FOE *Voy. round World* (1840) 249 The consequence of those measures will be the best apology for my conduct. **1824** DIBDIN *Libr. Comp.* 58, I make no apology to the readers for the subjoined extract. **1855** PRESCOTT *Philip II*, I. III. vi. 385 To furnish an apology for his close confinement, a story was got up of an attempt to escape.

3. An explanation offered to a person affected by one's action that no offence was intended, coupled with the expression of regret for any that may have been given; or, a frank acknowledgement of the offence with expression of regret for it, by way of reparation.

1594 SHAKS. *Rich. III*, III. vii. 104 My Lord, there needes no such Apologie. **1667** MILTON *P.L.* IX. 854 In her face excuse Came Prologue, and Apologie to prompt. **1692** RAY *Disc.* Pref. 14, I have in this Edition removed one Subject of Apology. **1754** CHATHAM *Lett.* iv. 21 If you are forced to desire further information..do it with proper apologies for the trouble you give. **1848** L. Hunt *Jar of Honey* x. 136 After many apologies for the liberty he was taking.

4. Something which, as it were, merely appears to apologize for the absence of what ought to have been there; a poor substitute.

1754 *Connoisseur* No. 25 Waistcoats edged with a narrow cord, which serves as an apology for lace. **1858** C. Mathews in *Life* (1879) I. 1, Gibbon, the historian, was said to have had no nose at all, only an apology for one. **1874** Forster *Dickens* 120 To swallow a hasty apology for a dinner.

¶ Obsolete form of APOLOGUE, q.v.

† **a'pology**, *v. Obs. rare.* [f. prec. sb.] To apologize.

1633 Heywood *Eng. Trav.* III. 55 Thus much let me for him Apoligie. ? **1671** J. Webster (in Webster) For which he can not well apology.

apomecometer (ˌæpəʊmiːˈkɒmɪtə(r)). [f. Gr. ἀπό away, off + μῆκ-ος length + μέτρ-ον measure.] An instrument for measuring the distance of objects.

1869 in *Eng. Mech.* 23 July 389/3 The only mistake which could occur in using the apomecometer would be in assuming a wrong level.

apomecometry (ˌæpəʊmiːˈkɒmɪtrɪ). [f. as prec. + Gr. -μετρία measuring.] The art or science of measuring the distances of objects.

1570 Dee *Math. Præf.* 16 To vnderstand [by geometry].. how farre, a thing seene (on land or water) is from the measurer..may be called Apomecometrie. [In Phillips, Bailey, and mod. Dicts.]

† **'apomel.** *Obs. rare.* [ad. Gr. ἀπόμελι.] 'A kind of decoction prepared of honey or an honeycomb mixed with vinegar, and boiled a short time.' Chambers *Cycl. Supp.* 1753.

[**1657** Tomlinson *Renou's Disp.* 529 Apomeli is made also after the like manner.] **1681** Blount *Glossogr.*, *Apomel.*

apomict (ˈæpəʊmɪkt). *Biol.* [Back-formation from next.] An organism produced or reproducing by apomixis. Also *attrib.*

1938 J. R. Carpenter *Ecol. Gloss.* 24 *Apomict population*, a parthenogenetically produced population. **1939** *Nature* 11 Feb. 252/2 Apomicts should receive distinct treatment. **1953** *Rep. 13th Internat. Hort. Congress 1952* I. 54 The *apomict* (abbreviated as *ap.*) is a plant reproducing by means of seed, the embryos of which are produced without fertilization.

apomictic (æpəʊˈmɪktɪk), *a. Biol.* Also **apo'mictical.** [f. APO- + Gr. μικτός mixed + -IC; see next.] Pertaining to or produced by apomixis; reproducing without sexual fusion. Hence **apo'mictically** *adv.*, by means of apomixis.

1913 *Amer. Naturalist* XLVII. 283 Parthenogenesis, the apomictic origin of a sporophyte from an egg. **1920** *Trans. Nat. Hist. Soc. Northumberland & Durham* V. 278 We have on the one hand the tetraploid *Pimpinellifoliae* microgenes pollinated normally, and on the other the tetraploid *Villosae* apomictical... It is a reasonable assumption to make that the apomictical roses are derived from the sexual types. **1921** *Ann. Bot.* XXXV. 183 Seedlings showing hybrid characters have originated from flowers, pollinated with foreign pollen, growing on the same bush as those castrated, and producing seed apomictically. **1939** *Nature* 4 Mar. 383/1 Embryos sometimes arise apomictically from unfertilized eggs. *Ibid.* 22 Apr. 684/1 Reproduction may be ..entirely non-sexual, apomictic.

apomixis (æpəʊˈmɪksɪs). *Biol.* [mod.L. (H. Winkler 1908, in *Progressus Rei Bot.* II. 303), f. APO- + Gr. μίξις mingling.] Reproduction of organisms without fertilization (see quot. 1932). (Opp. *amphimixis*; see AMPHI-.)

1913 *Amer. Naturalist* XLVII. 282 Winkler divides all reproductive phenomena into three divisions, namely: Amphimixis, Pseudomixis, and Apomixis. **1920** *Trans. Nat. Hist. Soc. Northumberland & Durham* V. 277 We are compelled to take up the view that in the *Rosae* apogamy, or whatever form of apomixis they present, is a phenomenon originating in hybridity. **1932** C. D. Darlington *Rec. Adv. Cytol.* xv. 416 Apomixis may be defined (following Winkler, 1908) as a system of reproduction having the external character of sexual reproduction but omitting one or both of its essential internal processes.

apomorphia (æpəʊˈmɔːfɪə). *Chem.* [f. Gr. ἀπό from + MORPHIA.] A white crystalline powder, $C_{17}H_{17}NO_2$, obtained by heating morphia with an excess of hydrochloric acid: also **apomorphine.**

1869 *Eng. Mech.* 1 Oct. 43/1 The physiological effects of apomorphia are very different from those of morphia. **1875** H. Wood *Therap.* (1879) 438 Dr. Gee was the first to announce that apomorphia is a certain and prompt emetic. **1888** *Brit. Med. Jrnl.* 14 Jan. 110/2 *(heading)* Poisoning by Nitre: Treatment with Apomorphine. **1891** *Daily News* 6 Oct. 2/7 One of the apomorphine tablets were missing. *Ibid.*, The deceased..had recourse to the apomorphine in order to produce vomiting. **1966** *Listener* 17 Mar. 401/2 The hero of William Burroughs's latest novel is apomorphine, a vaccine, prepared by boiling morphine in hydrochloric acid, whose function it is, through its action on the back brain, to regulate human metabolism and cure junk-addiction.

apon, obs. form of UPON.

aponeurography (ˌæpəʊnjʊˈrɒgrəfɪ). [f. APONEURO-SIS + -GRAPHY.] The description of aponeuroses.

1880 in *Syd. Soc. Lex.*

aponeurology (-ˈɒlədʒɪ). [f. as prec. + -LOGY; cf. mod.Fr. *aponeurologie.*] The scientific study of aponeuroses.

1859 in Worcester.

‖ **aponeurosis** (-ˈəʊsɪs). *Phys.* Pl. **-es.** [L., a. Gr. ἀπονεύρωσις, f. ἀπονευρό-ειν to change into a tendon, f. ἀπό off, away + νεῦρον sinew.] A white, shining, fibrous membrane, sometimes serving as the sheath of a muscle, sometimes forming the connexion between a muscle and a tendon.

1676 in *Phil. Trans.* XI. 769 The lower [muscle]..arises from the vertebræ of the loyns, and ends in the same aponeurosis. **1804** Abernethy *Surg. Observ.* 93, I removed the cyst from off the aponeurosis of the external oblique muscle. **1873** Mivart *Elem. Anat.* viii. 281 Muscles are.. separated from each other by membranes termed aponeuroses.

aponeurotic (-ˈɒtɪk), *a. Phys.* [ad. Fr. *aponeurotique*: see prec. and -IC.] Of, pertaining to, or consisting of, aponeuroses.

1751 Stack in *Phil. Trans.* XLVII. 327 An interior aponeurotic lamina. **1845** Todd & Bowman *Phys. Anat.* I. 71 Aponeurotic, tendinous expansions, [are]..very useful in protecting the walls of cavities.

aponeurotomy (-ˈɒtəmɪ). [f. APONEURO-SIS + Gr. -τομία cutting.] Dissection of the aponeuroses.

1859 in Worcester.

a-poop (əˈpuːp), *advb. phr.* [A *prep.*[1] + POOP *sb.*] On the poop, astern.

[**1597** J. Payne *Royal Exch.* 33 Steere at an ynch, or miss the haven, a fogg, at the entrans, storme and bellow on poope.] **1809** W. Irving *Knickerb.* II. ii. (1849) 88 She.. could get along very nearly as fast with the wind ahead, as a-poop.

† **a'poor,** *v. Obs. rare*$^{-1}$. In 4 apore. [a. OFr. *apovri-er, apauri-er* to impoverish.]

a **1400** *MS. Cantab* (Halliw.) To hem that were aporet in his londe.

apopemptic (æpəʊˈpɛmptɪk), *a.* and *sb. rare.* [ad. Gr. ἀποπεμπτικ-ός, f. ἀπο-πέμπ-ειν to send away.]

A. *adj.* Pertaining to dismissal; valedictory.

1753 Chambers *Cycl. Supp.* s.v., The antients had certain holy days, wherein they took leave of the gods with apopemptic songs. **1815** *Encycl. Brit.* II. 470 They dismissed them, following them to the altars with apopemptic hymns.

B. *sb.* A farewell hymn.

1753 Chambers *Cycl. Supp.*, *Apopemptic*..a hymn addressed to a stranger on his departure from a place to his own country.

apopetalous (æpəʊˈpɛtələs), *a. Bot.* [f. Gr. ἀπό away + πέταλ-ον petal + -OUS.] Having distinctly separate or free petals.

1875 Bennett & Dyer *Sachs' Bot.* 471 If the leaves of the perianth-whorl are not coherent, but free, this is expressed by the terms..*eleutherosepalous* or *aposepalous*, and *eleutheropetalous* or *apopetalous.*

‖ **apophasis** (əˈpɒfəsɪs). *Rhet.* [L., a. Gr. ἀπόφασις denial, f. ἀπο-φάναι to 'speak off,' deny.]

1657 J. Smith *Myst. Rhet.* 164 Apophasis..a kind of an Irony, whereby we deny that we say or doe that which we especially say or doe. **1753** Chambers *Cycl. Supp.*, *Apophasis*..whereby we really say or advise a thing under a feigned show of passing over, or dissuading it. [In mod. Dicts.]

apophatic (æpəʊˈfætɪk), *a. Theol.* [ad. Gr. ἀποφατικός negative (see G. W. H. Lampe *Patristic Greek Lexicon* s.v.).] Applied to knowledge of God obtained by way of negation. Hence **apo'phaticism**, an apophatic approach to knowledge of God.

1869 D. W. Simon tr. *Dorner's Doctrine of Person of Christ* Div. II. vol. I. 427 The distinction between the communicable and the incommunicable in God (in which, probably, we may trace the influence of the cataphatic and apophatic theology). **1938** G. Reavey tr. *Berdyaev's Solitude & Society* I. ii. 33 *Apophatic* knowledge..knowledge in the process of discarding all notions and determinations. **1956** V. White *God the Unknown* I. ii. 19 The Greeks called it *apophatic* theology—'denying' theology. St. Thomas calls it the *via remotionis* or the *via negativa*: the negative way of removing from our statements about God all that he is not. **1957** tr. *V. Lossky's Myst. Theol.* ii. 38 Apophaticism..is, above all, an attitude of mind which refuses to form concepts about God. **1961** H. Armstrong in I. T. Ramsey *Prosp. Metaphys.* vi. 104 Negative or apophatic theology.. certainly does not lead to complete ignorance.

† **ˌapophleg'matic,** *a.* and *sb. Med. Obs.* [mod. formation, not on Gr. analogies, with reference to ἀποφλεγματίζ-ειν (see below) and form of PHLEGMATIC.] **A.** *adj.* Promoting the removal of phlegm; expectorant. **B.** *sb.* (sc. agent.)

1727 Swift *Gulliver* III. vi. 216 Administer to each of them..apophlegmatics. **1731** Bailey, *Apophlegmatick Medicine*, medicines to be chewed that have the faculty to purge the head and brain of cold phlegmatick humours by the nose, mouth, etc. **1880** in *Syd. Soc. Lex.* as 'old term.'

† **ˌapophleg'matical.** *a. Med. Obs.* = prec.

1706 Phillips, *Apophlegmatical Medicines.*

† **apo'phlegmatism.** *Med. Obs.* [ad. Gr. ἀποφλεγματισμ-ός, f. ἀποφλεγματίζ-ειν: see below.]

1. The action of purging phlegm from the head.

1753 Chambers *Cycl. Supp.*, *Apophlegmatism* by the mouth is a kind of particular Salivation.

2. An apophlegmatic agent or treatment.

1615 Daniell *Queen's Arcad.* (1717) 184 Strange Speech ..Of Trochises, Opiats, Apophilegmatisms. **1684** tr. *Bonet's Merc. Compit.* I. 8 Cupping the head and blistering the neck [in Apoplexy] signify little if Apophlegmatisms will not do. **1755** in Johnson; and in mod. Dicts.

† **apophleg'matizant,** *a.* and *sb. Med. Obs.* [f. **apophlegmatize*, ad. Gr. ἀποφλεγματίζ-ειν to purge away phlegm + -ANT: cf. *anæsthesiant.* (Prob. there was mod.L. *apophlegmatizāre, -āntem.*)]

1718 Quincy is cited in Johnson. **1753** Chambers *Cycl. Supp.*, *Apophlegmatizants* are of two kinds, one administred by the way of the mouth..the other given by the nostrils.

† **apo'phlegmatizer.** *Med. Obs.* [f. **apophlegmatize* (see prec.) + -ER[1].] = APOPHLEGMATIC *sb.*

1671 Salmon *Syn. Med.* III. xvii. 377 Apophlegmatizers, are such as by chewing or gargling, draw down Phlegmatick excrements from the brain by the Pallet.

apophony (əˈpɒfənɪ). *Philol.* [ad. F. *apophonie*, f. APO- + Gr. φωνή sound.] Variation in vowel quality in the formation of grammatically related words, as in Eng. *give, gave*, G. *sprechen, sprach.* (Also called *ablaut* and *vowel gradation.*)

1883 I. Sydow *German Convers.-Gram.* 253 The Germans call this..Ablaut, that may be rendered by apophony. **1894** V. Henry *Compar. Gram. Eng. & Ger.* 358 Mod. German, though keeping the apophony, obscures it by borrowing the metaphony from the subjunctive.

† **a'pophoret.** *Obs.*$^{-0}$ [ad. L. *apophorētum*, a. Gr. ἀποφόρητον thing carried away, present, f. ἀποφέρ-ειν to bear away.] (See quot.)

1623 Cockeram, *Apopheret*, a new yeeres gift. **1676** Bullokar, *Apophoret*, a thing presented at some solemn time; as a New-years gift, or the like.

apophthegm, apothegm (ˈæpəθɛm). Forms: 6 **apothegma,** 6–8 **apo(ph)thegme,** 7 **apophthem,** 7– **apothegm,** 6– **apophthegm.** [ad. (perh. through med.L. **apothegma*) Gr. ἀπόφθεγμα something clearly spoken, a terse saying, f. ἀποφθέγγ-εσθαι to speak one's opinion clearly, f. ἀπό forth + φθέγγεσθαι to utter a sound, speak. The spelling *apothegm* was the more usual till preference was expressed in Johnson's Dict. for *apophthegm*, which is now more frequent in England. Webster adopts *apothegm*, which Worcester also thinks 'perhaps best supported by common usage.' Cf. Fr. *apophthegme*, Sp. *apothegma*, It. *apotegma.*] A terse, pointed saying, embodying an important truth in few words; a pithy or sententious maxim.

1553–87 Foxe *A. & M.* III. 145 *marg. note*, Another Apothegma of D. Taylor. **1572** Bossewell *Armorie* II. 106 b, His Apothegme or word, *Cor vnum, via una.* **1586** J. Hooker *Girald. Hist. Irel.* in *Holinsh.* II. 97/1 Graue and pithie apophthegmes. **1646** Sir T. Browne *Pseud. Ep.* 23 The Apothegmes, or reputed replyes of wisdome, whereof many are to be seen in Laertius. **1791** Boswell *Johnson* (1816) II. 360 Johnson suddenly uttered..an apophthegm, at which many will start: 'Patriotism is the last refuge of a scoundrel.' **1813** Knox & Jebb *Corr.* II. 170 The apothegms, and aculeated sayings of the ancients. **1832** Scott *Talism.* (1854) 359 Hearing his misery made..the ground of apothegms and proverbs. **1855** Milman *Lat. Chr.* (1864) IX. xiv. v. 204 The rare talent of compressing a mass of profound thought into an apophthegm. **1879** Farrar *Paul* I. 593 The admirable Hebrew apophthegm, Learn to say I do not know.

apophthegmatic, apothegm- (ˌæpəʊθɛgˈmætɪk), *a.* [ad. Gr. ἀποφθεγματικ-ός sententious: see prec. and -IC.] Of, pertaining to, or of the nature of, an apophthegm; addicted to the use of apophthegms; sententious, pithy.

1796 W. Taylor in *Month. Rev.* XX. 517 The utility of apophthegmatic instruction. **1840** Sir J. Stephen *Eccl. Biog.* II. 410 The apophthegmatic sententiousness of Burke.

ˌapophtheg'matical, apothegm-, *a.* [f. as prec. + -AL[1].] = prec.

1589 Nashe *Almond for Parrat* 15 b, Such a Chaos of common places no apothegmatical Lycosthenes euer conceited. **1603** Holland *Plutarch* 167 (R.) That apophthegmatical and powerful speech of theirs. **1837** Lytton *Athens* I. 393 The apothegmatical Hipparchus.

ˌapophtheg'matically, apothegm-, *adv. rare.* [f. prec. + -LY[2].] In an apophthegmatic manner; sententiously, pithily.

1630 J. Taylor (Water P.) *Wit & Mirth* Ded., Wks. II. 176 Quips, and Ierkes; Apothegmatically bundled vp and garbled. **1863** Thornbury *True as Steel* II. 133 'All quarrels,' said the Emperor apophthegmatically, 'have two sides.'

apophthegmatist, apothegm- (æpəʊˈθɛgmətɪst). [f. Gr. ἀποφθεγματ- (ἀπόφθεγμα) APOPHTHEGM + -IST.] A professed maker of apophthegms.

1727 POPE *Art Sinking* 115 A poet or orator would have no more to do but to send.. to the ironist for his sarcasms, to the apothegmatist for his sentences.

apophthegmatize, apothegm- (æpəʊˈθɛgmətaɪz), *v.* [f. as prec. + -IZE.] To write or speak in apophthegms. Hence **apophthegmatizing** *vbl. sb.* and *ppl. a.*

1785 PALEY *Philos.* I. Pref. (R.) This sententious apothegmatizing style. **1818** TODD, *Apothegmatize.*

apophyge (əˈpɒfɪdʒiː). *Arch.* [a. Gr. ἀποφυγή 'escape,' hence 'the curve with which the shaft escapes into the base or capital,' f. ἀπο-φεύγειν to flee away. In L. *apophygis*, mod.Fr. *apophyge*; hence better ˈæpəʊfɪdʒ.] The part of a column where it springs out of its base, or joins its capital, usually moulded into a concave sweep or cavetto.

1563 J. SHUTE *Archit.* C iij a, The second part [of the Capitall] deuide into 3 partes; 2 of those shalbe for Echinus ..the rest is lefte for the 3 Ringes which be called Apophiges, or Anuli. **1719** *Glossogr. Nova, Apophyge*..is that part of a column where it seems to fly out of its base.. and begins to shoot upwards. **1872** SHIPLEY *Gloss. Eccl. Terms* 411 The apophyge or curvature at the top and bottom of the shaft of a column.

apophyllite (əˈpɒfɪlaɪt, æpəʊˈfɪlaɪt). *Min.* [mod. f. Gr. ἀπό off + φύλλον leaf + -ITE; 'so named by Haüy, 1805, in allusion to its tendency to exfoliate under the blow-pipe' (Dana).] A zeolitic mineral, a hydrated silicate of lime and potash, with a trace of fluorine; occurring in glassy square prisms or octahedrons, or laminated masses, with a pearly lustre; widely distributed in nature, and produced artificially.

1810 *Edin. Rev.* XVII. 119 The sparry lustre which characterizes apophyllite. **1878** LAWRENCE *Cotta's Rocks Class.* 26 Apophyllite is found in the geodic cavities of volcanic rocks.

apophyllous (æpəʊˈfɪləs), *a. Bot. rare.* [f. as prec. + -OUS.] Having the sepals distinct.

1875 BENNETT & DYER *Sachs' Bot.* 471 Where there is only one perianth-whorl, and it is desired to state that] it consists of..free leaves, the terms *eleutherophyllous* or *apophyllous* may be used.

apophysary (əˈpɒfɪsərɪ), *a. Phys.* [ad. Fr. *apophysaire*: see below and -ARY.] = APOPHYSIAL.

1837 *Penny Cycl.* VIII. 502/2 The ethmoïd surface of the temporal bone..is..a portion of a hollow transverse cylinder, with an apophysary lamina [*une lame apophysaire*].

apophysate (əˈpɒfɪseɪt), *a. Bot. rare.* [f. APOPHYS-IS + -ATE².] (See quot.)

1863 BERKELEY *Brit. Mosses*, Gloss., *Apophysate*, furnished with an apophysis. **1880** in *Syd. Soc. Lex.*

apophysial (æpəʊˈfɪzɪəl), *a. rare.* Less correctly **apophysal**. [f. APOPHYSI-S + -AL¹.] Belonging to, or of the nature of, an apophysis.

1851 RICHARDSON *Geol.* viii. 232 The ventral valve [in Brachiopoda]..supports..the apophysal apparatus. **1880** *Syd. Soc. Lex., Apophysial point*, the tender point over a vertebral spinous process which is next to the place of exit of a painful spinal nerve.

‖**apophysis** (əˈpɒfɪsɪs). Pl. -es. Also 7–8 **apophyse**. [a. Gr. ἀπόφυσις off-shoot, f. ἀπό from + φύσις growth. Cf. Fr. *apophyse*, also used in English in 17–18th c.]

1. *Phys.* A natural protuberance or process, arising from, and forming a continuous part of, a bone; *esp.* one of the processes on the spinal vertebræ.

1611 COTGR., *Procés*..the Processe, Apophyse, or outstanding part of a bone. **1646** SIR T. BROWNE *Pseud. Ep.* 181 Such [fish] as have the Apophyses of their spine made laterally like a combe. **1753** *Phil. Trans.* XLVIII. 32 The rocky apophyse of the ear bone. **1847–9** TODD *Cycl. Anat. & Phys.* IV. 370/2 The paramastoid apophysis is dilated.

2. *Bot.* A dilatation of the base of the theca or spore-case in some mosses.

1794 MARTYN *Rousseau's Bot.* xxxii. 493 A kind of receptacle..called by Linnæus Apophysis, by Haller the Disk. **1863** BERKELEY *Brit. Mosses* iii. 22 In an early stage of growth..the apophysis belongs quite as much to the stem as the sporangium.

3. *Geol.* A branch from the main mass of an intrusive igneous rock.

1888 F. H. HATCH in J.J.H. Teall *Brit. Petrography* 424 *Apophysis*, a vein or branch from the main mass (boss or dyke) of an igneous rock. **1893** A. GEIKIE *Geol.* (ed. 3) IV. vii. 580 All over the world it is common for eruptive bosses of this rock to have a fringe of intrusive veins (*Apophyses*). **1925** B. N. ODELL in E. F. Norton *Fight for Everest* 293 Thoroughly metamorphosed and crystalline limestone resting on the schorl granite, which sent off apophyses into it.

apoplectic (æpəʊˈplɛktɪk), *a.* and *sb.* [ad. Fr. *apoplectique* (16th c. in Littré) or L. *apoplēcticus*, a. Gr. ἀποπληκτικός apoplectic, f. ἀπόπληκτος disabled by a stroke, f. ἀποπλήσσειν: see APOPLEXY and -IC.] **A.** *adj.*

1. Of, pertaining to, or causing, apoplexy.

1611 BEAUM. & FL. *Triumph. Hon.* i, An apoplectic fit I use to have, After my heats in war carelessly cool'd. **1762** GOLDSM. *Cit. World* xviii. (1837) 68 Choang fell lifeless in an apoplectic fit upon the floor. **1839** DICKENS *Nich. Nick.* xxxv. (C.D. ed.) 279 One of your stiff-starched apoplectic cravats. **1878** A. HAMILTON *Nerv. Dis.* 85 Certain elements of the apoplectic attack.

2. Suffering from, or showing symptoms of, apoplexy. Also *fig.*

1721 in BAILEY. **1743** tr. *Heister's Surg.* 354 The Operation has been twice performed by me on two apoplectic Patients. *c* **1812** MISS AUSTEN *Mansf. Pk.* (1851) 17 A short-necked, apoplectic sort of fellow. **1837** DICKENS *Pickw.* (1847) 216/1 A gentleman with an apoplectic countenance. **1863** KEMBLE *Res. Georgia* 61 The swollen, apoplectic-looking cotton bags.

†**3.** Of use against apoplexy; = ANTAPOPLECTIC.

1678 tr. *Charras' Royal Pharmac.* 214 This Balsom bears the Name of *Apoplectick* by reason it is a great Remedy against Apoplexies. **1704** ADDISON *Italy* (1766) 47 Apoplectic balsam. **1753** BAILEY, *Apoplectick*..good against the apoplexy. [Not in JOHNSON.]

B. *sb.* One liable to, or suffering from, apoplexy.

a **1670** HACKET *Abp. Williams* II. 134 (D.) So often we see there is life in an apoplectick, though he seem to be dead. **1725** BRADLEY *Fam. Dict.* s.v. *Lethargy*, Those who fall into it should be manag'd as pituitous Apoplecticks.

apoˈplectical, *a. arch.* [f. prec. + -AL¹.]

1. = APOPLECTIC 1.

1656 BLOUNT *Glossogr., Apoplectical*, pertaining to the apoplexy. **1668** *Lond. Gaz.* ccxxvii/2 Dangerously ill of an Apoplectical distemper. **1779** JOHNSON in *Boswell* (1816) III. 455 Mr. Thrale has been in extreme danger from an apoplectical disorder.

2. = APOPLECTIC 2.

1615 CROOKE *Body of Man* 500 Such men as dye Apoplecticall. **1739** BADDAM *Mem. R. Soc.* 140 The one, lame of the gout; the other, extremely appoplectical.

3. = APOPLECTIC 3.

1721 BAILEY, *Apoplectical*..good against Apoplexy. **1753** CHAMBERS *Cycl. Supp., Apoplectical medicines*, a name used by some for what we more properly call *antapoplectics*.

apoˈplectically, *adv.* [f. prec. + -LY².] In an apoplectic manner; with symptoms of apoplexy.

1881 MISS BRADDON *Asph.* I. 156 The Rector was sighing, somewhat apoplectically.

apoplectiform (æpəʊˈplɛktɪfɔːm), *a. Path.* [a. Fr. *apoplectiforme*: see APOPLECTIC and -FORM.] Having the form of apoplexy.

1876 BARTHOLOW *Mat. Med.* (1879) 545 The apoplectiform variety of acute cerebral congestion. **1878** A. HAMILTON *Nerv. Dis.* 6 The apoplectiform variety..is.. generally a slight cerebral hemorrhage.

ˈapoplex. *arch.* [ad. L. *apoplēxis*, a. Gr. ἀπόπληξις, variant of ἀποπληξ ία.] = APOPLEXY.

1533 ELYOT *Cast. Helth* (1541) 46 Immoderate sleep maketh yᵉ body apt unto palseis, apoplexis, falling siknes. **1605** B. JONSON *Volpone* I. iv. 36 How do's his apoplexe? **1690** LOCKE *Hum. Underst.* III. vi. (ed. 3) 246 An Apoplex [may] leave neither Sense, nor Understanding, no nor Life. **1790** COLERIDGE *Happiness* I. 34 Apoplex of heavy head That surely aims his dart of lead.

b. *fig.*

1688 DRYDEN *Brit. Rediv.* 239 And here the sons of God are petrified with woe; An apoplex of grief.

ˈapoplex, *v. arch.* [f. prec. sb.; chiefly in pa. pple.] To strike with apoplexy, paralyze, benumb.

1602 SHAKS. *Ham.* III. iv. 73 Sure, that sense Is apoplex'd. **1624** HEYWOOD *Gunaik.* III. 160 Finding her husband.. apoplext in all his limbes. *Ibid.* VIII. 403 To apoplex all the vitall spirits. **1813** BYRON *Let.* Wks. 1832 II. 269 If suddenly apoplexed, would he rest in his grave?

†**apoˈplexious**, *a. Obs. rare*⁻¹. [f. next + -OUS; cf. *acrimonious*.] Of apoplectic nature.

a **1734** ARBUTHNOT (in Ogilvie) Apoplexious and other congenerous diseases.

apoplexy (ˈæpəʊplɛksɪ). Forms: 4–7 **apoplexie** (4–5 poplexie, 6 poplesye), 7– **apoplexy**. [a. Fr. *apoplexie*, ad. L. *apoplēxia* (occas. used in Eng.), a. Gr. ἀποπληξία name of the same malady, f. ἀποπλήσσ-ειν to disable by a stroke, f. ἀπό off, (in comb.) completely + πλήσσ-ειν to strike.]

1. A malady, very sudden in its attack, which arrests more or less completely the powers of sense and motion; it is usually caused by an effusion of blood or serum in the brain, and preceded by giddiness, partial loss of muscular power, etc.

c **1386** CHAUCER *Nun Pr. T.* 21 Napoplexie [*v.r.* nepoplexie] ne shente nat hir heed. **1398** TREVISA *Barth. De P.R.* III. xv. (1495) 59 Apoplexia is a euyll that makith a man lese all maner feling. **1552** LYNDESAY *Monarche* IV. 5117 Sum ar dissoluit suddantlye Be Cattarue or be Poplesye. **1597** SHAKS. *2 Hen. IV*, I. ii. 126 This Apoplexie is (as I take it) a kind of Lethargie, a sleeping of the blood, a horson Tingling. **1748** THOMSON *Cast. Indol.* lxxvii. 692 Whilst Apoplexy cramm'd Intemperance knocks Down to the ground at once, as butcher felleth ox. **1861** HULME *Moquin-Tandon* I. ii. 11 Frequent apoplexies would be the result.

b. in *Falconry*.

1614 MARKHAM *Cheape Hvsb.* (1623) 163 The Apoplexie or falling euill in Hawkes. **1725** BRADLEY *Fam. Dict., Apoplexy*..a Disease that seizes the Heads of Hawks, commonly by reason of two much Grease and Store of Blood.

2. *transf.* or *fig.*

1589 *Pasquil's Return* B iij b, His disease is the very Apoplexie of the Donatistes. **1678** *Yng. Man's Call.* 52 Foolishness: it is the souls apoplexy, wherein all the noble faculties of the mind are cast into a dead sleep. **1866** MOTLEY *Dutch Rep.* VI. iii. 824 The country was without a centre. There was small chance of apoplexy where there was no head.

3. Also applied by some to the effusion of blood in other organs.

1853 MAYNE *Exp. Lex., Apoplexy cutaneous*, a singular term employed by certain French writers for a great and sudden determination of blood to the skin. **1880** *Syd. Soc. Lex., Apoplexy retinal*, effusion of blood in the retina from rupture of its vessels.

apoponax, obs. variant of OPOPANAX.

apopyle (ˈæpəʊpaɪl). *Zool.* [f. Gr. ἀπό APO- + πύλη gate.] An aperture by which an endodermal chamber in a sponge communicates with the central cavity or paragaster.

1887 W. J. SOLLAS in *Encycl. Brit.* XXII. 414/1 A comparatively large aperture, which we may term for distinction an apopyle. **1888** [see PARAGASTER].

apore. *Obs.*⁻⁰ [ad. Gr. ἄπορος: see next.] = APORIME.

apoˈretic, *a.* [a. Fr. *aporetique* (Cotgr.), ad. Gr. ἀπορητικ-ός, f. ἀπορέ-ειν to be at a loss, f. ἄπορ-ος impassable, f. ἀ priv. + πόρος passage.] Inclined to doubt, or to raise objections.

1605 Z. JONES *De Loyer's Specters* 51 Phirrhon was called the Aporrhetique or Sceptique. **1656** BLOUNT *Glossogr., Aporetique*, ever doubting, never certain in anything. **1935** A. C. BOUQUET tr. *Przywara's Polarity* iii. 104 In its 'aporetic' character the entire subsequent development of the true teaching of St. Thomas is displayed. **1949** *Mind* LVIII. 247 In the 'aporetic dialogues' [of Plato]..Essence never appears.

†**apoˈretical**, *a. Obs. rare.* [f. prec. + -AL¹.] Of aporetic nature; full of doubts and objections.

1667 H. MORE *Div. Dial.* IV. iii. (1713) 292 The greatest Wits of the World have been..Sceptical or Aporetical. *a* **1688** CUDWORTH *Immut. Mor.* (1731) 137 Chose rather an Aporetical and Obstetricious Method. [In mod. Dicts.]

‖**aporia** (əˈpɔərɪə, əˈpɒrɪə). [L., a. Gr. ἀπορία, n. of state f. ἄπορ-ος: see APORETIC.] **1.** *Rhet.* See quots.

1589 PUTTENHAM *Eng. Poesie* (Arb.) 234 Aporia, or the Doubtfull. [So] called..because oftentimes we will seeme to cast perils, and make doubt of things when by a plaine manner of speech wee might affirme or deny him. **1657** J. SMITH *Myst. Rhet.* 150 Aporia is a figure whereby the Speaker sheweth that he doubteth, either where to begin for the multitude of matters, or what to do or say in some strange or ambiguous thing. **1751** in CHAMBERS; and in mod. Dicts. [E.g. *Luke* xvi. 3.]

2. A perplexing difficulty.

[**1888** *Athenæum* 18 Aug. 219/3 No quibble was too sophistical, no ἀπορία too transparent, for him to think it worth examination.] **1893** W. CLARKE ROBINSON tr. *Ten Brink's Hist. Eng. Lit.* II. 80 The solution of many an *aporia*, as attempted by the idealistic thinker. **1902** *Daily Chron.* 12 Dec. 3/4 Mr. Kidd does not seem to us to surmount this *aporia* very successfully.

aporime. *Obs.*⁻⁰ [f. Gr. ἀ priv. + πόριμ-ον easy to be passed, accessible.] (See quot.)

1706 PHILLIPS, *Apore* or *Aporime* (in *Mathem.*), a Problem, which tho' it be not impossible yet is very difficult ..The Squaring of a Circle may be called an Apore. **1775** in ASH.

aporobranchian (ˌæpɒrəʊˈbræŋkɪən), *a.* and *sb. Zool.* [f. mod.L. *Aporobranchia* (f. Gr. ἀ priv. + πόρο-ς passage, pore + βράγχι-α gills) + -AN.] **A.** *adj.* Having no apparent respiratory tubes. **B.** *sb.* Arachnids or Spiders so distinguished, otherwise called *Podosomata*.

1835 KIRBY *Hab. & Inst. Anim.* II. xix. 282 These [parasites] from their having no apparent respiratory apparatus, he [Latreille] named Aporobranchians.

aporose (ˌæpɒˈrəʊs), *a. Zool.* [f. Gr. ἀ priv. + mod.L. *porōsus* POROUS, f. L. *porus*, a. Gr. πόρ-ος passage: see -OSE.] Not porous, imperforate; *spec.* applied to the corals of the sub-order *Aporosa*.

1865 DUNCAN in *Athenæum* No. 1979. 441/1 Species of Aporose Madreporaria. **1877** HUXLEY *Anat. Inv. An.* iii. 163 The simple aporose corals.

†**apoˈrrhœa.** *Obs.* [mod.L, a. Gr. ἀπόρροια, f. ἀπορρέ-ειν to flow off.] An emanation, effluvium.

1646 SIR T. BROWNE *Pseud. Ep.* 86 Amulets doe worke by Aporrhoias, or emanations from their bodies. **1681** GLANVILL *Saducismus* 23 Subtile streams and aporrhœa's of minute particles, which pass from one body to another. **1721** in BAILEY. **1880** in *Syd. Soc. Lex.*

a-port (əˈpɔət), *advb. phr.* [A *prep.*¹ + PORT.] On or towards the port side of the ship, or the left side when looking forward. *to put the helm a-port* (= 'to port the helm'): to move the rudder to the starboard side, making the ship turn to the right.

1627 SMITH *Seaman's Gram.* v. 24 The haling them is called the Topping the Lifts, as top a starboard, or top a port. **1630** J. TAYLOR (Water P.) *Wks.* III. 39/2 Making them both to beare vp, the one aport, and the other a starbord. **1795** NELSON in Nicolas *Disp.* II. 13 Braced up our after-yards, put the helm a-port, and stood after her again.

aport, var. APPORT *sb. Obs.*, bearing, carriage.

aposematic (æpəʊsiːˈmætɪk), *a. Zool.* [f. Gr. ἀπό APO- + σηματ-, σῆμα sign (cf. SEMATIC *a.*).] Applied to colours, markings, or other attributes serving to warn or alarm, and thus to repel the attacks of enemies. So **aposeme** (ˈæpəʊsiːm), an aposematic marking, etc.

1890 POULTON *Colours of Animals* xvii. 337 Pseudaposematic colours..deceptively resemble Aposematic colours. **1902** *Encycl. Brit.* XXVII. 147 We often see the combination of Cryptic and Sematic methods, the animal being concealed until disturbed, when it instantly assumes an Aposematic attitude. **1920** F. A. DIXEY in *Rep. Brit. Assoc. Advancem. Sci. 1919* 202 Adopting Professor Poulton's terminology, we may say that..one form may possess..the Aposemes belonging to two distinct models. *Ibid.* 204 The..most conspicuous of these common aposemes or danger-signals belong to the under surface. **1940** *Nature* 3 Aug. 144/2 Aposematic or warning colours [in animals].

aposepalous (æpəʊˈsɛpələs), *a. Bot.* [mod. f. Gr. ἀπό away from, off + SEPAL + -OUS.] Having free sepals.

1875 [See APOPETALOUS.]

‖**aposiopesis** (ˌæpəʊsaɪəʊˈpiːsɪs). [L., a. Gr. ἀποσιώπησις, n. of action f. ἀπο-σιωπά-ειν to keep silent.] A rhetorical artifice, in which the speaker comes to a sudden halt, as if unable or unwilling to proceed.

1578 TIMME *Calvin on Gen.* 146 A figure called Aposiopesis, after the which something not expressed is to be understood. **1618** *Hist. P. Warbeck* in *Harl. Misc.* (1793) 63 His communication was still seasoned with savoury parentheses and breakings off, or, if you will, aposiopesises. **1727** POPE *Art Sinking* 95 The Aposiopesis, an excellent figure for the ignorant, as 'what shall I say?' when one has nothing to say, or 'I can no more,' when one really can no more. **1853** DE QUINCEY *Wks.* XIV. v. 150 At this aposiopesis I looked inquiringly at the speaker.

aposiopetic (ˌæpəʊsaɪəʊˈpɛtɪk), *a. rare.* [f. prec. after Gr. σιωπητικός taciturn.] Of the nature of aposiopesis.

1652 URQUHART *Jewel* Wks. 1834, 292 Epanorthotick revocations and aposiopetick restraines. **1761** STERNE *Tr. Shandy* (1802) IV. xxvii. 126 That interjection of surprize.. with the apposiopestic [*sic*] break after it, marked thus Z——ds!——

apositic (æpəʊˈsɪtɪk), *a. Med.* [ad. Gr. ἀποσιτικός, f. ἀπόσιτος without appetite, f. ἀπό away from + σῖτος food.] Tending to diminish appetite; causing *apositia* or distaste for food.

1853 in MAYNE *Exp. Lex.*

†**aˈposity.** *Obs.*—⁰ [ad. Gr. ἀποσιτία aversion to food: see prec. *Apositia* is now used.]

1719 *Glossogr. Nova, Aposity*, a loathing of Meat.

apospory (əˈpɒspərɪ). *Bot.* [f. APO- + Gr. σπόρος seed + -Y³.] Absence or suppression of spores where they are normally produced, as in certain ferns, mosses, and other cryptogams in which the sexual organism (prothallus in ferns, etc., or perfect plant in mosses) is developed directly from the sporangium or from the leaf instead of from a spore. So **aˈposporous** *a.*, characterized by or of the nature of apospory; hence **aˈposporously** *adv.* (Cf. APOGAMY.)

1878 VINES in *Jrnl. Bot.* VII. 361 To indicate..that no spores are..produced..by the sporophore of *Chara*, we may speak of this plant as being 'aposporous'. **1884** *Jrnl. Linn. Soc., Bot.* XXI. 360 (*title*) On Apospory in Ferns. **1886** [see APOGAMY]. **1886** *Encycl. Brit.* XX. 431/2 In the aposporous Ferns and Mosses and in the Characeæ the oophore is developed as a bud from the sporophore. **1892** *Athenæum* 12 Nov. 667/3 Prothalli developed aposporously.

apost, variant of APPOST *v. Obs.*

†**apoˈstaile.** *Obs. rare.* [variant of APOSTOILE, OFr. *apostoile* and *apostelle*:—L. *apostoli-um.*] prop. *adj.* Apostolic; but in quot. treated (through imperfect translation) as quasi-*sb.* The apostolic see.

c **1380** ? WYCLIF *Rule St. Francis* xi. in *Wks.* (1880) 44 Þo to whom fro þe see of apostaile is licence grauntid. *c* **1400** *Prymer* in Maskell *Mon. Rit.* II. 103 That thou fouche saaf the lord of apostaile, [*ut dominum apostolicum..conservare digneris*]..we preien thee to heere us.

†**aˈpostasied,** *ppl. a. Obs. rare*—¹. [pa. pple. of *apostasy* vb. (not otherwise found), f. prec. or Fr. *apostasier* (15th c.).] Apostatized, apostate.

1393 GOWER *Conf.* III. 275 Lucifer..With al the route apostazied..that ben to him allied.

apostasy (əˈpɒstəsɪ). Also 6–9 **apostacy**. [(? a. Fr. *apostasie*), ad. L. *apostasia*, a. later Gr. ἀποστασία = ἀπόστασις 'standing off,' hence, desertion of one's faith, f. ἀπο-στα- to stand off, withdraw.]

1. Abandonment or renunciation of one's religious faith or moral allegiance.

c **1380** WYCLIF *De Dot. Eccl.* Wks. 1871 III. 438 Apostasye þat goiþ evene aȝen þe ordre of Crist. **1395** PURVEY *Remonstr.* (1851) 24 Apostasie, either goinge abak fro cristene feith. *a* **1520** *Myrr. Our Ladye* 194 They felle.. in apostasye by idolatry, from the worshypynge of very god. **1667** MILTON *P.L.* VII. 44 Raphael..had forewarned Adam by dire example to beware Apostasie. **1726** AYLIFFE *Parerg.* 85 The Canon Law defines Apostacy to be a rash and wilful Departure from that State of Faith, Obedience or Religion, which any Person has profess'd himself to hold in the Christian Church. **1852** MISS YONGE *Cameos* (1877) I. xxix. 246 The rest had the choice of death or apostacy. **1876** GREEN *Eng. People* ix. §6. 655 The most devoted loyalists began to murmur, when James demanded apostasy as a proof of their loyalty.

b. *R.C. Ch.* The action of quitting a religious order or renouncing vows without legal dispensation.

1532 MORE *Confut. Barnes* VIII. Wks. 1557, 793/2 That freres may..breake their vowes, & runne in apostasy. **1877** DOWDEN *Shaks. Prim.* vi. 64 To charge with error their original vows of seclusion and to justify their present apostasy.

2. By extension: The abandonment of principles or party generally.

1579 LYLY *Euphues* (Arb.) 47 Readier in the defence of it [wisdom] to haue made an Apologie, than any way to turne to Apostasie. **1660** *Trial Regic.* 36 To Doubt, or Hesitate, in a point of Allegiance, is direct Treason, and Apostasie. **1773** MRS. CHAPONE *Improv. Mind* I. 192 Your apostacy from every good principle. **1838** THIRLWALL *Greece* V. xl. 128 This however was not his last political apostasy.

†**aˈpostatate,** *ppl. a. Obs. rare.* [f. late L. *apostatāt-* ppl. stem of *apostatā-re*: see APOSTATE *v.*] Apostatized, apostate.

1536 *Pilgr. T.* 299 in *Thynne's Animadv.*, Thes that from christ be appostatat. **1629** H. BURTON *Babel no Bethel* 33 An apostatate Minister of the Church of England.

apostate (əˈpɒstət), *sb.* and *a.* Forms: 4– **apostate, 7 apostat**; also 4 **apostota**, 4–8 **-tata**, 5–6 **appostita, -tata.** [a. Fr. *apostate* and L. *apostata*, ad. Gr. ἀποστάτ-ης, n. of agent f. ἀποστα- (see APOSTASY). The L. *apostata* was by far the commoner form from 1350 to 1650, with pl. *apostata(e)s*.]

A. *sb.*

1. One who abjures or forsakes his religious faith, or abandons his moral allegiance; a pervert.

1340 *Ayenb.* 19 Þe heretike and þe apostate þet reneyeþ hire bileaue. *c* **1380** WYCLIF *Wycket* 1 Infideles papistes and apostates. *c* **1400** *Apol. Loll.* 93 To haue brokyn þe cristun feiþ..& to be paynims & apostatais. **1491** CAXTON *Vitas Patr.* (W. de W.) II. 309 a/1 Julyan thappostata. **1583** GOLDING *Calvin on Deut.* cc. 1246 For if we play yᵉ Papistes ..we shall be apostataes. **1622** MASSINGER *Virg. Mart.* III. i, In hopes to draw back this apostata..Unto her father's faith. **1667** MILTON *P.L.* VI. 100 High in the midst exalted as a God Th' Apostate in his Sun-bright Chariot sate. **1728** YOUNG *Love Fame* I. (1757) 80 Polite apostates from God's Grace to Wit. **1808** SCOTT *Marmion* II. iv, For inquisition stern and strict On two apostates from the faith.

b. *R.C. Ch.* A member of a religious order who renounces the same without legal dispensation.

c **1387** TREVISA *Higden* VII. iv. Rolls Ser. VII. 309 An apostata þat brekeþ his ordre þey fongeþ nevere aȝen. **1401** *Pol. Poems* II. 19 If you leave your habite a quarter of a yeare, ye should be holden apostataes. **1577** HOLINSHED *Chron.* III. 1239/1 One Rafe sometime a moonke of Glastenburie, and now become an apostata. **1855** MILMAN *Lat. Chr.* (1864) IX. XIV. i. 26 The renegade who pursued his private interests by sacrificing those of his order..stood alone a despised and hated apostate.

2. One who deserts his party, or forsakes his allegiance or troth; a turncoat, a renegade.

1362 LANGL. *P. Pl.* A. I. 102 He þat passeþ þat poynt is apostata in þe ordre. [**1393** Ys apostata of knyȝt-hod.] **1608** J. DAY *Hum. out Breath* (1881) 53 Should he proue Apostata, denie Loue which he first enforcd vs to profes. *a* **1687** PETTY *Pol. Arith.* iii. (1691) 58 Apostates, to their own Country, and Cause. **1769** *Junius Lett.* i. (1804) I. 5 We see him, from every honourable engagement to the public, an apostate by design. **1826** DISRAELI *Viv. Grey* VII. ii. 388 No one is petted so much as a political apostate, except, perhaps a religious one.

B. *adj.*

1. Unfaithful to religious principles or creed, or to moral allegiance; renegade, infidel; rebellious.

1382 WYCLIF *Ezek.* ii. 2 Folkis apostataas, that han broken her religioun. *c* **1486** *Bk. St. Albans Arms* Cj a, The maruellis deth of Julian thappostita Emproure. **1590** H. BARROW in J. Greenwood *Confer.* 6 All the parish..were generally apostate. **1592** NASHE *P. Peniless* 33 b, Those Apostata spirits that rebelled with Belzebub. **1667** MILTON *P.L.* I. 125 So spake th' Apostate Angel. **1758** JORTIN *Erasmus* I. 176 Eggs of heresy, which the apostata Fryer Luther had before laid. **1878** C. STANFORD *Symb. Christ* i. 7 The last witness left for God in the midst of an apostate land.

2. *gen.* Deserting principles or party; perverted.

1671 MARVELL *Corr.* 198 Wks. 1872 II. 394 The apostate patriots, who were bought off. **1712** STEELE *Spect.* No. 516 ¶7 Those apostate abilities of men.

†**aˈpostate,** *v. Obs.* [f. prec. sb.; or a. Fr. *apostate-r*, ad. late L. *apostatā-re* to apostatize, f. *apostata*: see prec.] = APOSTATIZE.

1553–87 FOXE *A. & M.* (1596) 267/2 Some marrieng wiues amongst them [the Saracens]..for hope of honor did apostat to their law. **1633** BP. HALL *Hard Texts* 340 But we are not of them which apostate from Christ. **1679** T. HARBY *Key Sacr. Script.* i. 5 Rome..partly Orthodox, but beginning to apostate in practice.

†**aˈpostated,** *ppl. a. Obs.* [f. prec. + -ED.] Fallen from religious faith; become apostate.

1642 SIR E. DERING *Sp. on Relig.* 163 A ninth is told that I am apostated. **1680** H. MORE *Apocal. Apoc.* 112 An emblem of the latter Apostated Times.

apostatic (æpəʊˈstætɪk), *a. rare.* [ad. med.L. *apostaticus*, a. Gr. ἀποστατικ-ός, f. ἀποστα- (see APOSTASY).] = APOSTATE *a.* 1.

1583 GOLDING *Calvin on Deut.* xxxviii. 228 The Apostatike or backeslyding Church of Rome. **1841** *Englishm. Mag.* 1 Oct. 114 Rome is opposed to our.. apostolic Church, as unholy, schismatical, and apostatic.

apoˈstatical, *a.* [f. as prec. + -AL¹.]

1. Of the nature of apostates or apostasy; heretical.

1532 MORE *Confut. Tindale* Wks. 1557, 723/1 Tindall, Luther..or some suche other apostaticall preachers. **1624** BEDELL *Lett.* xii. 159 To set aside the inquirie of Doctrine.. were..Apostaticall, rather then Apostolicall. **1726** AYLIFFE *Parerg.* 143 If a Pope was inthron'd without a Canonical Election of Cardinals..he was not to be deem'd Apostolical, but Apostatical. **1878** LECKY *Eng. in 18th C.* II. vi. 120 Their Church in respect to both [faith and doctrine] apostatical.

†**2.** Departing, withdrawing, retrograde. *Obs.*

1620 MELTON *Astrolog.* 53 That Saturne was Apostaticall and retrograde.

†**aˈpostating,** *vbl. sb. Obs.* [f. APOSTATE *v.* + -ING¹.] Apostatizing.

1660 HEXHAM *Dutch Dict.*, *Af-val*..a Revolting, an Apostating, a Backsliding.

†**aˈpostating,** *ppl. a. Obs.* [f. as prec. + -ING².] = APOSTATIZING *a.*

a **1656** BP. HALL *Occas. Medit.* 9 (R.) Perhaps some of these apostating stars have thought themselves true.

apostatism (əˈpɒstətɪz(ə)m). *rare.* [f. APOSTATIZE: see -ISM.] The practice of apostatizing.

1814 SIR R. WILSON *Pr. Diary* II. 308 If our arms do not prosper, we are damned for political apostatism.

apostatize (əˈpɒstətaɪz), *v.* [ad. late L. *apostatizā-re* for earlier *apostatāre*, f. *apostata*: see -IZE.]

1. To abandon or renounce one's religious faith or moral allegiance; to become an apostate.

1611 COTGR., *Apostasier*, to play th' Apostata, to Apostatize it. **1634–46** ROW *Hist. Kirk* (1842) 373 Who will not perjure themselves by apostatizing with perjured prelatts. **1754** EDWARDS *Freed. Will* II. xi. (ed. 4) 162 A very great part of the angels apostatised. **1849** MACAULAY *Hist. Eng.* II. 14 If ever he [Kirke] did apostatize, he was bound by a solemn promise..to turn Mussulman.

b. Const. *from* the original faith, *to* the new.

1552 LATIMER *Serm. & Rem.* (1845) 313 Many princes and supreme pontiffs..have been found to apostatise from the faith. **1676** I. MATHER *Philip's War* (1862) 108 A wretched English man that apostatized to the Heathen. **1839** *Blackw. Mag.* XLVI. 817 All China apostatized to the new faith.

2. *gen.* To abandon a principle, desert a party.

1648 CROMWELL *Lett.* liii. (Carl.) He apostatised from your cause and quarrel. **1722** WOLLASTON *Relig. Nat.* ix. 177 To cast off reason..apostatize from humanity, and recoil into the bestial life. **1851** DIXON *Penn.* xi. (1872) 89 Some of the courtiers were apostatising.

†**3.** *Med.* To become resolved into a purulent discharge. (Cf. medical Gr. ἀπόστασις suppurative inflammation.) *Obs. rare.*

1651 BIGGS *New Dispens.* ¶236 Whatsoever has once apostatized into..corruption in the body.

aˈpostatized, *ppl. a.* [f. prec. + -ED.] = APOSTATE *a.*

1629 H. BURTON *Babel no Bethel* 19 An Apostatized Church. **1827** *Q. Rev.* XXXVI. 7 An apostatised clergyman from the Established Church.

aˈpostatizing, *vbl. sb.* [f. as prec. + -ING¹.] Renunciation of faith or principles. Often *attrib.*

1659 HARDY *1 John* (1865) liv. 348 Too many such reeds may be seen everywhere in these apostatising days.

aˈpostatizing, *ppl. a.* [f. as prec. + -ING².] Abandoning faith or principles; faithless.

1652 BENLOWE *Theoph.* Pref. 18 Mockt by new false lights of apostatizing Hypocrisie. **1880** E. WHITE *Cert. in Relig.* 48 That Eye..which reclaimed the apostatizing Peter.

†**aˈpostatous,** *a. Obs. rare*—¹. [f. L. *apostata* APOSTATE + -OUS.] = APOSTATIC, APOSTATE *a.*

1588 CDL. ALLEN *Admon.* 55 The Apostatous and hereticall Emperours.

†**aˈpostatrice,** *sb.* and *a. Obs. rare*—¹. [a. OFr. *apostatrice*, ad. late L. *apostātrix* (Vulgate) fem. of *apostātor* one who apostatizes, f. *apostāre* for

apostatāre: see APOSTATE *v.*] A female apostate. (Here used as *adj.*)

1546 BALE *Eng. Votaries* II. (1550) 113 b, That chapel Apostatrice, as they than called it ful wisely.

† **'apostem(e, -tume, -thume,** *sb. Obs.* Forms: 4 **apostym,** 4–8 **-teme,** 7–8 **-tem;** 5–7 **-tume,** 6 **-tom,** 6–8 **-thume.** [a. OFr. *aposteme, apostume* (13th c. in Littré), ad. L. *apostēma*, a. Gr. ἀπόστημα separation, *spec.* separation of purulent matter into an abscess, f. ἀποστα-, ἀποστῆναι to stand off, withdraw (cf. *abs-cess*). Much distorted by false etymology; in OFr. made *apostume*, as if connected with L. *postumus*; also changed in 14th c. to *empostume*; whence an Eng. *impostume* found side by side with *apostem(e c* 1500, which, further corrupted to IMPOSTHUME (cf. *posthumous*), became in 18th c. the only form. Accented *apo'stem* in 14th c.; *a'postem* in 17th; *'apostem* by Johnson.]

1. A gathering of purulent matter in any part of the body; a large deep-seated abscess.

1340 HAMPOLE *Pr. Consc.* 2995 Som, for envy, sal haf in thair lyms, Als kylles and felouns and apostyms. **1474** CAXTON *Chesse* 100 To serche woundes and hurtes and to cutte apostumes. **1585** LLOYD *Treas. Health* T iv, Mulberies verye ripe.. breke wonderfully the apostoms. **1616** SURFL. & MARKH. *Countr. Farm* 729 The Linnet is troubled.. with hot apostemes, conuulsions, and gowts. The Finch is wont to haue impostumes. *a* **1631** DONNE *Poems* (1650) 238 A dangerous Apostem in thy brest. **1655** CULPEPPER *Riverius* VI. vii. 143 Others put a Wax Candle.. into the Œsophagus to break the Aposthume. **1714** *Phil. Trans.* XXIX. 75 If an Aposteme breaks out. **1751** CHAMBERS *Cycl.*, *Aposthume* or *Apostem*.. called also *abscess* and *imposthume*.

2. *fig.*

c **1380** WYCLIF *De Eccl.* vi. Wks. 1871 III. 353 Apostemes þat ben harmful in þe Chirche. **1577** HOLINSHED *Chron.* III. 1054/2 So is sedition.. the apostume of the realme, which when it breaketh inwardlie, putteth the state in great danger of recouerie. **1681** BAXTER *Answ. Dodwell* iv. §24. 40 This opens the Core of the Aposthume.

† **a'postemate, -umate,** *ppl. a.* and *sb. Obs.* [f. med.L. *apostēmāt-* ppl. stem of *apostēmā-ri* to break into an APOSTEM.]

A. *adj.* Formed into an 'apostem'; festering.

1540 RAYNALD *Birth Man.* (1564) 94 b, Yf by chaunce.. the mouth of the Matrix be exulcerate or apostumate. **1541** R. COPLAND *Guydon's Quest. Cyrurg.*, In a holowe apostumate and nyghe to a noble membre.

B. *sb.* [Cf. late L. *apostēmātia.*] = APOSTEM.

a **1627** MIDDLETON *Widow* IV. ii, Have you no convulsions, pricking aches, sir, Ruptures, or apostemates?

† **a'postemate, -umate,** *v. Obs.* [f. prec. ppl. adj., or on analogy of vbs. so formed. Cf. Fr. *apostumer* 16th c. in Littré.] (Mostly in pa. pple.)

1. *pass. trans.* To be affected with an 'apostem.'

1582 HESTER *Phiorav. Secr.* II. xix. 97 When [the wounde].. is neither cancrenated nor apostumated. **1615** CROOKE *Body of Man* 416 The heart ful of purulent matter; which deceiueth many vnskilfull people, who cry out that his heart was apostumated. **1671** SALMON *Syn. Med.* II. xlix. 320 Both sides are aposthumated.

2. *intr.* To form an 'apostem' or abscess; to fester.

1616 SURFL. & MARKH. *Countr. Farm* 171 The leaues of Sorrell.. cause to Apostumate the swellings of the eyes. **1684** tr. *Bonet's Merc. Compit.* XVIII. 641 A young Man.. bruised the back of his Hand: it inflamed and apostemated.

† **aposte'matic,** *a. Obs. rare*⁻¹. [mod. ad. Gr. ἀποστηματικός abscess-like.] Of, pertaining to, or resulting from, abscesses.

1666 G. HARVEY *Morb. Angl.* v. 55 An Apostematick Consumption generally oweth its production to an Apostem breaking within the body.

† **a,poste'mation,** etc. *Obs.* Forms: 6–8 **apostemation, -umation,** 7 **aposthemation, -humation.** [a. OFr. *apostemation, apostumacion* (Godef.), ad. med.L. *apostēmātiōn-em*, n. of action f. *apostēmāri* (see APOSTEMATE *a.*).]

1. The formation of an 'apostem' or abscess; the gathering of matter in a purulent tumour; festering.

1578 LYTE *Dodoens* 132 Motherworte.. layde upon woundes keepeth them both from inflammation and apostumation. **1607** TOPSELL *Serpents* (1653) 664 A vehement apostumation. **1671** SALMON *Syn. Med.* II. lv 337 Dislocations of the Shoulder.. with.. Aposthumation, are hard to Cure.

2. = APOSTEME.

1540 RAYNALD *Birth Man.* (1564) 79 b, Howe to.. clense suche Apostumations. **1764** MARTIN in *Phil. Trans.* LV. 41 An abscess or apostemation in the lungs.

apostematous (æpəʊ'stɛmətəs), *a. Path.* [f. L. *apostēmat-*, or Gr. ἀποστήματ- stem of ἀπόστημα (see APOSTEME) + -OUS.] Of the nature of an 'apostem'; characterized by abscesses.

1634 T. JOHNSON *Parey's Chirurg.* (1678) XIII. ii. 309 An Apostematous Ulcer is perceived by.. sight and handling. **1844** GRAHAM *Domest. Med.* 342 The apostematous species mostly attacks young persons of a high florid complexion.

† **a'posteme, -ume,** *v. Obs. rare.* [a. Fr. *apostume-r* (15th c. in Littré), f. *apostume*; see prec.] To form or break into an abscess.

1525 LD. BERNERS *Froiss.* II. cli. 417 He was in ieopardy of dethe, for his hed apostumed. **1530** PALSGR. 434/1, I apostume, as a sore dothe, *Japostume.*

† **a'postemed, -umed,** *ppl. a. Obs.* [f. prec. + -ED.] Formed into an abscess; festered. Also *fig.*

a **1626** BP. ANDREWES *Serm.* (1856) I. 161 To prick the swelling, and let out the apostumed matter of pride from a many of us. *c* **1700** *Gentl. Instruc.* (1732) 252 (D.) From this apostem'd member flows the corruption of atheism.

† **a'posteming, -uming,** *ppl. a. Obs.* [f. as prec. + -ING².] Forming an abscess; purulent.

1615 BP. HALL *Contempl.* IV. xi. (1833) 166 The inwardly apostuming tumours of pride.

‖ **a posteriori** (eɪ pɒ,stɛrɪ'ɔəraɪ, ɑː pɒ,stɛrɪ'ɔːrɪ), *advb.* (and *adj.*) *phr.* [L. *ā posteriōri* 'from what comes after' (as opposed to *ā priōri* 'from what is before').] **1.** A phrase used to characterize reasoning or arguing from effects to causes, from experience and not from axioms; empirical, inductive; inductively.

1624 FRANCIS WHITE *Replie to Fisher* sig. C4ᵛ, Your other argument.. is, *à posteriori*, from an example of the.. French King, Henry the fourth, to whom you wish his Maiestie to bee a parrallell. **1647** H. HAMMOND *Power of Keyes* sig. A3ᵛ, This, I conceive, is not by me magisterially dictated, but already demonstrated *à posteriori*, by the experience which the few last moneths have yeelded us. **1710** BERKELEY *Princ. Hum. Knowl.* §21, I think arguments *à posteriori* are unnecessary for confirming what has been.. sufficiently demonstrated *à priori.* **1834** *Penny Cycl.* II. 199/1 In common language, we reason *à priori* when we infer the existence of a God from the general difficulties in the supposition of the existence of what we then call the creation on any other hypothesis; but we reason *à posteriori* when we infer the same from marks of intelligent contrivance in this particular creation with which we are acquainted. **1836–7** SIR W. HAMILTON *Metaph.* xxi. (1870) II. 26 Knowledge *a posteriori* is a synonym for knowledge empirical, or from experience. **1873** H. SPENCER *Study Sociol.* vii. 174 Accounts of existing uncivilized races.. show us *à posteriori*, what we might infer with certainty *à priori.*

2. *Facetious.* From behind, on the back, on the buttocks. Cf. POSTERIOR B. 2.

1762 SMOLLETT *Launc. Greaves* ix. 200 One of them clapped a furze-bush under the tail of Gilbert, who, feeling himself thus stimulated *a posteriori*, kicked and plunged and capered. **1837** CARLYLE *Fr. Rev.* II. III. v. 182 Accelerated.. by smitings, twitchings,—spurnings, *a posteriori*, not to be named. **1861** *Temple Bar* Nov. 534 A golden cross sewn on *à posteriori.*

aposthume, -ation, etc.: see APOSTEME.

apostil, -ille (ə'pɒstɪl), *sb.* Also 7 **-style, -stle.** [a. Fr. *apostille*, of uncert. origin: see POSTIL.

Diez and Littré say from *à* to + *postille*; but Littré's first quotation suggests a connexion with OF. pa. pple. *apost*:—L. *apposit-um*, placed, added, annexed to. Fr. perhaps confused *l'apostille, la postille.*]

A marginal note, comment, or annotation.

1527 *State Papers Hen. VIII*, I. 225 Copies of the same, with suche apostillis.. in the mergentes, as in reding of them came unto my mynde. **1683** TEMPLE *Mem.* Wks. 1731 I. 423 The second Article they consented to, with an Apostyle of their own upon it. **1858** MOTLEY *Dutch Rep.* ii. 128 The world, in his [Philip's] opinion, was to move upon protocols and apostilles. **1860** —— *Netherl.* (1868) II. xvii. 303 He sat at his table, scrawling his apostilles.

apostil (ə'pɒstɪl), *v. rare.* [ad. Fr. *apostille-r*, f. *apostille*: see prec.] To annotate or write marginal notes to.

1637 CHARLES I in *3rd Rep. Hist. MSS.* (1872) 74/1 This copy.. being apostiled with his own hand. *a* **1670** HACKET *Abp. Williams* II. (1692) 156 He apostyles that article with his own hand.

apostle (ə'pɒs(ə)l). Forms: *α.* 1–4 **apostol,** 2–5 **apostel,** 4–6 **-till,** 4–5 **apostill(l,** 5 **-tyle, apostylle, -teyl,** 6 **apostyl, -tell.** *β.* 2– **apostle,** 4–5 **appostle.** *γ.* *Aphetic* 3–7 **postel, postle,** 4 **postyll,** 5 **postill(e.** [Two forms must be distinguished: *α.* OE. *apostol* (whence ME. *apostel, -yl*), ad. Romanic *apostol(o* or L. *apostol-us* (a. Gr. ἀπόστολ-ος a messenger, one sent forth, f. ἀπο-στέλλ-ειν to send away). *β.* the current *apostle* (found already *c*1225), a. OFr. (12th c.) *apostle* (13th c. *apostre*, mod. *apôtre*); with the mutescence of final *e*, the two were confused, and in 16th c. the OFr. spelling prevailed. The popular form in ME. was the aphetized *postel*, now obs.]

I. A person sent.

†**1. a.** (As in Gr.) One sent on an errand, a messenger. (A verbalism of translation.) *Obs.*

c **950** *Lindisf. Gosp.* John xiii. 16 Nis esne mara drihtne his ne æc apostol [*Ags. & Hatton*, ærendracca, arendrake] mara ðæm se sendes hine. *c* **1382** WYCLIF *ibid.*, Neither apostle is more than he that sente him. **1582** *Rhem.* ibid., Neither is an apostle [**1611** he that is sent] greater then he that sent him. —— *Phil.* ii. 25 Epaphroditus.. your Apostle [so WYCLIF and TINDALE; **1611** messenger].

b. Applied in N. T. to Jesus Christ.

c **1382** WYCLIF *Hebr.* iii. 1 Biholde ȝe the apostle and bischop of oure confessioun, Jhesu. **1611** *ibid.*, The Apostle and high Priest of our profession, Christ Jesus.

2. *spec.* (Now with capital initial.) The twelve witnesses whom Jesus Christ sent forth to preach his Gospel to the world; also the subsequently-commissioned Barnabas (Acts xiii. 2, xiv. 14), and Paul, the 'Apostle of the Gentiles.'

c **975** *Rushw. Gosp.* Matt. x. 2 þara twelf apostola noma sindun þas. *c* **1175** *Lamb. Hom.* 99 Crist ableow þana halȝa gast ofer þa apostlas. —— 93 Of þon apostlum. —— 117 þe apostel Paulus. —— 133 His halie word.. þurh ðere apostlene muðe. *c* **1230** *Ancr. R.* 8 Seint Iames.. þet was Godes apostle. **1340** HAMPOLE *Pr. Consc.* 4300 To God mare dere, þan ever war Cristes appostels here. *c* **1400** *Apol. Loll.* 39 Bi autorite of Peter & Poule, princis of postlis. **1549** COVERDALE *Erasm. Paraphr. Rom.* Argt., Some of them, whiche so accused Peter, were of thapostles them selfe. *a* **1658** CLEVELAND *Parliam.* xi, Because th' Apostles Creed is lame, Th' Assembly doth a better frame. *Te Deum*, The glorious company of the Apostles praise Thee.

3. a. One who in any way imitates, or may be said to resemble, the Apostles.

1377 LANGLAND *P. Pl.* B. VI. 151 Ne posteles, but þey preche conne, and haue powere of þe bisschop. *c* **1400** *Rom. Rose* 6273 If ther be wolves of sich hewe, Amonges these apostlis newe. **1533** MORE *Apol.* xxiv. Wks. 1557, 888/1 The new Paule, thys apostle Frith. **1659** BURTON *Diary* (1828) IV. 79 As if the King's booted apostles had been coming to plant the faith among them, by plundering the little that was left. **1751** CHAMBERS *Cycl.*, *Apostolici, Apostoli*, or *Apostles*, was a name assumed by two different sects of heretics, on account of their pretending to imitate the manners and practice of the apostles.

b. *esp.* The missionary who first plants Christianity in any region. (Also used of certain specially successful ministers of the Gospel.)

c **1425** WYNTOUN *Cron.* v. xiii. 74 Quhen conwertyd he had þat Land, Ðe Appostil þai cald hym of Ingland. **1844** MACLAINE *Mosheim's Eccl. Hist.* VIII. I. i. §4 Boniface has gained the title of the Apostle of Germany. **1883** *Echo* 1 Sept. 4/1 Dr. Macdonald, of Ferintosh.. familiarly called the 'Apostle of the North.'

c. The chief advocate of a new principle or system; the leader of a great reform; *e.g.* Father Mathew, the 'Apostle of Temperance.'

1810 T. JEFFERSON *Writ.* (1830) IV. 137 The first and chiefest apostle of the desolation of men and morals. **1870** BALDW. BROWN *Eccl. Truth* 233 M. Comte is distinctly an apostle of science. **1871** SMILES *Character* v. (1876) 154 Who has not heard of.. Miss Nightingale and Miss Garrett as apostles of hospital nursing?

d. (With capital initial.) A member of 'The Apostles', an exclusive society in the University of Cambridge, founded in 1820 as the Cambridge Conversazione Society, and numbering many subsequently pre-eminent literary and other figures. Freq. in *pl.*

1829 R. M. MILNES *Let.* 5 Dec. in T. W. Reid *Life Ld. Houghton* (1891) I. ii. 80 We have had some capital debates in our society called 'The Apostles'. **1830** A. H. HALLAM *Let.* 23 June in J. F. Maurice *Life F. D. Maurice* (1884) I. ix. 110 The effect which he [*sc.* F. D. Maurice] has produced on the minds of many at Cambridge by the single creation of that Society of the Apostles (for the spirit, though not the form, was created by him) is far greater than I can dare to calculate. **1887** R. FRY *Lett.* (1972) I. 115 As a great secret —I have been made an Apostle. **1902** A. LYALL *Tennyson* i. 7 Tennyson was numbered among the Apostles at Cambridge. **1914** V. WOOLF *Let.* Apr. (1976) II. 47 We've let it to Keynes for a reading party next week... I gather they are to be mostly Apostles. **1964** C. MACKENZIE *My Life & Times* III. vi. 236 At Cambridge he [*sc.* Desmond MacCarthy] had been the golden boy of the Apostles, as Hallam had been once upon a time and Rupert Brooke would be presently. **1967** M. HOLROYD *Lytton Strachey* I. v. 157 The Apostles differed from the usual undergraduate societies in the fact that members did not cease to belong once they had graduated or gone down. *Ibid.* 158 The Apostles had been—and still are—a 'secret' body. **1979** A. BOYLE *Climate of Treason* ii. 73 Another attachment between Burgess and Blunt was their common membership of the exclusive club of cultural élitists known as The Apostles.

†**4.** The Acts and Epistles of the Apostles. *Obs.*

a **1400** in *Rel. Ant.* II. 48 Hem that reversyng the aposteyl and seyden, 'do we yvel thingis that ther comyn gode thingis.' **1753** CHAMBERS *Cycl. Supp.*, *Apostle* is also used to denote the book of St. Paul's epistles, or the epistle which was taken out of them. **1794** PALEY *Evid.* I. ix. §3 (1817) 231 The Christian Scriptures were divided into two parts under the general titles of the Gospels and Apostles.

II. A message. [The non-ecclesiastical L. use of *apostolus*, found in the Pandects. Also in OF.]

†**5.** A letter dimissory: **a.** *pl.* in *Rom. Law*, A short statement of the case, sent up by a lower to a higher court, when an appeal is made. **b.** in *Eccl. Law* (see quot. 1753). *Obs.*

1726 AYLIFFE *Parerg.* 75 The Cause why it is appeal'd, and the Demand or Petition for Apostles. *Ibid.* 345 This is called a Dimissory Libel, or Letters Dimissory; and, in other Terms, by the Name of Apostles. **1753** CHAMBERS *Cycl. Supp.* [transl. Du Cange] *Apostle*.. a letter dimissory given by a bishop either to a clerk or a layman, when going into another diocese.

III. *Comb.* and *Attrib.*, as **apostle-bird** (also *apostle*), a name applied to various birds in Australia (see quots.); †**apostles' ointment**, a purifying ointment composed of twelve ingredients; †**apostles' salt**, an obsolete medicinal preparation; **apostle skull** (see quot.). Also ***apostle-like***; and APOSTLE SPOONS, q.v.

[1901 J. A. NORTH *Nests & Eggs of Birds* (Austral. Mus., Sydney, Spec. Catal. 1) I. 18 From their habit of associating in flocks, they are known nearly all over New South Wales, and the south-eastern portions of Queensland, as the 'Twelve Apostles', a name also shared in some parts with that of 'Happy Family' for *Pomatostomus Temporalis.*] **1934** WEBSTER, *Apostle bird*, the gray jumper. **1945** S. J. BAKER *Austral. Lang.* xii. 211 The Grey-crowned Babbler is known also as the *apostle-bird*. **1962** *New Scientist* 15 Mar. 606/1 They are members of the babbler or apostle-bird family (Timaliidae). **1964** A. LANDSBOROUGH THOMSON *New Dict. Birds* 442/2 The Apostlebird *Struthidea cinerea*..is..about 13 inches in length..of grey plumage..and has a short, stout bill. It gets its name from its habit of going about in parties of about twelve. The bird lives in the drier parts of eastern Australia. **1611** COTGR., *Apostolique*..apostlelike. **1720** GIBSON *Disp.* xv. (1734) 281 The Apostles Ointment.. to deterge and cleanse foul Sores. **1605** TIMME *Quersit.* viii. 34 The Apostles Salt..preserueth the sight to a very great age, clenseth the lunges from tough phleame, etc. **1866** LAING *Preh. Rem. Caithn.* 70 Very long and narrow skulls, known as 'Apostle skulls.'

apostlehood (ə'pɒs(ə)lhʊd). *arch.* [f. prec. + -HOOD.] The office or position of an apostle.

a **1000** *Poetry Codex Vercell.* 3300 (1843) ȝehalȝode fore þam heremæȝene þurh apostolhad. **1382** WYCLIF *Acts* i. 25 This mynisterie and apostilhed [**1388** apostlehed; TINDALE *et seqq.*, Apostleship]. *c* **1449** PECOCK *Repr.* III. iv. 295 Crist here clepid this ȝong man into apostilhode. **1483** *Cathol. Angl.*, An Apostyllehede; *apostolatus.*

apostleship (ə'pɒs(ə)lʃɪp). [f. APOSTLE + -SHIP.] The office or position of an apostle; proclamation of a religious system; leadership of a social reform.

1526 TINDALE *Acts.* i. 25 This ministracion and apostleshippe from the which Judas..fell. **1697** tr. *Dupin's Eccl. Hist.* II. 44 St. John..was called to the Apostleship when he was very young. **1843** MARRIOTTI *Italy Past & Pr.* (1848) I. 29 Italy was to assume the apostleship of civilisation and freedom. **1855** MILMAN *Lat. Chr.* (1864) II. IV. ii. 221 The Mahomedan apostleship of fire and sword.

Apostle spoons. Old-fashioned silver spoons, the handles of which end in figures of the Apostles. They were the usual present of sponsors at baptisms.

[**1531** *Rec. St. Mary at Hill* (1905) 47 Item, xiij spons with the postells.] **1614** B. JONSON *Barth. Fair* I. iii, Two Apostle spoons..and a cup to eate a cawdle in. **1630** MIDDLETON *Chaste Maid* III. ii, Two great 'postle spoons. **1796** PEGGE *Anonym.* (1809) 182 The Apostle-spoons..very common in the last century, but are seldom seen now. The set consists of a dozen, and each had the figure of an Apostle, with his proper ensign, at the top. **1857** RUSKIN *Pol. Econ. Art* 59 The old plate except a few apostle spoons..is sent to be melted down.

† **a'postly**, *a. Obs. rare.* [? f. APOSTLE + -LY[1]; OE. *apostolíc* (for *apostol-líc*)), ME. **apostelich*.]

c **880** K. ÆLFRED *Bæda* I. xxvi. (Bosw.) þæt apostolíce lif ðære frymþelican cyricean. *a* **1520** *Myrr. Our Ladye* 319, I byleue on holy comon and apostly chirche.

† **apo'stoile.** *Obs.* Forms: 3 apostolie, 4 apostoyle, -oile, 5 apostoyll. [a. OF. and AFr. *apostolie*, later Central Fr. *-oile*:—late L. **apostoli-us*; prop. adj. APOSTOLIC, but, like *apostolicus*, in med.L., used as title of the pope. 'Ipse summus pontifex vocetur *apostolicus*.' Du Cange.] The pope.

1205 LAY. 29614 Menen to Gregorie þan holi apostolie [**1250** pope]. **1330** R. BRUNNE *Chron.* 130 To Thomas þe kyng bisouht þe bishop to assoile, Bot Thomas wild nouht, bot þorgh grace of þe apostoile. *c* **1440** *Sir Gowther* 250, Y wyll to Rome to þe apostoyll.

apostolate (ə'pɒstəleɪt). [ad. L. *apostolātus*: see APOSTLE and -ATE[1].] **a.** The office or position of an apostle; leadership in a propaganda.

1642 SIR E. DERING *Sp. on Relig.* 132 To take Matthias from a Disciple into the lot and fellowship of an Apostolate. **1748** WESLEY *Wks.* 1872 XII. 102, I no otherwise assume the Apostolate of England (if you choose to use the phrase) than I assume the Apostolate of all Europe. **1839** *Blackw. Mag.* XLVI. 10 The zeal with which he discharged the apostolate of infidelity.

b. A society or sodality of persons having as their object the propagation of a method or rule of faith, life, or conduct.

1897 *Westm. Gaz.* 1 Oct. 4/2 The little settlement is an apostolate of mercy. **1905** *Tablet* 14 Oct. 607/2 The mere mention of that oxymoron the 'lay-apostolate' causes among Catholics of the elder generation a wise shaking of heads. **1911** *Catholic Encycl.* XII. 107 Ven. Vincent Mary Pallotti ..gave to his society the name of 'Catholic Apostolate', afterwards changed by Pius IX to the 'Pious Society of Missions'.

† **a'postoless.** *Obs.* Also 5-6 apostylesse, -tlesse, -telesse. [a. OFr. **apostlesse* (14th c. *apostresse*): see APOSTLE and -ESS; assimilated in Eng. to L. *apostolus, apostola.*] A female apostle.

c **1410** LOVE *Bonavent. Myrr.* lvii. (Gibbs MS.) 111 Mawde-leyne þe bylouede discyplesse and of þe apostoles apostolesse [*v.r.* apostelesse, -tlesse]. **1652** SPARKE *Prim. Devot.* (1663) 260 Mary Magdalen, *Apostolorum Apostola* (as Cajetan calleth her), she was the first preacher of the Resurrection, the Apostoless of the Apostles.

Apo'stolian. = APOSTOLIC *sb.* (heretic).

apostolic (æpə'stɒlɪk), *a.* and *sb.* Also 5-7 -ique, 6-7 -ike, 7 -ick. [a. Fr. *apostolique*, ad. L. *apostolicus*, a. Gr. ἀποστολικός, f. ἀπόστολος: see APOSTLE and -IC.] **A.** *adj.*

1. Of or belonging to the Apostles; contemporary with the Apostles, as the ***Apostolic Fathers***.

1549 *Nicene Creed* in *Bk. Com. Prayer*, One Catholick and Apostolike Church. **1635** PAGITT *Christianogr.* I. ii. (1636) 62 St. Matthew, and other Apostolike men. **1664** H. MORE *Myst. Iniq.* xvi. 58 Idolatry is as contrary to the Apostolick Doctrine, as any thing can be. **1818** BYRON *Childe Har.* IV. cx, And apostolic statues climb To crush the imperial urn. **1847** YEOWELL *Anc. Brit. Ch.* iii. 23 The British church was founded during the apostolic age.

2. Of the nature or character of the Apostles; befitting or suited to an apostle.

1549 COVERDALE *Erasm. Paraphr. 1 Cor.* xi. 7 Is it not an apostolique act to bring Corinthe..to Christes gospell? **1781** COWPER *Hope* 583 His apostolic charity. **1839** DE QUINCEY *Recoll. Lakes* Wks. II. 183 Illimitable, apostolic devotion to the service of the poor.

3. Of or pertaining to the pope as successor of St. Peter; papal.

1477 CAXTON *Dictes* 145 Defendour and directour of the siege apostolique. **1591** *Troub. Raigne K. John* (1611) 42, I Pandulph of Padua, Legate from the Apostolike See. **1844** LINGARD *Anglo-Sax. Ch.* (1858) II. xiv. 323 Made dependent on the Apostolic See alone.

4. Of, pertaining to, or characteristic of the Apostles (sense 3 d).

1832 J. SPEDDING *Let.* 4 May in H. Tennyson *Alfred Ld. Tennyson* (1897) I. 85 Only think of an 'Apostolic' dinner next Friday. **1900** H. SIDGWICK in A. & E. M. Sidgwick *Henry Sidgwick* (1906) ii. 35 It was rather a point of the apostolic mind to understand how much suggestion and instruction may be derived from what is in form a jest. **1906** R. FRY *Let.* 12 Apr. (1972) I. 261 He's [*sc.* Cresswell's] the most interesting mind here.., quite Cambridge mind, speculative and detached, in fact, almost Apostolic. **1979** L. EDEL *Bloomsbury* I. 54 There were vivid memories of Apostolic weekends and walking tours. **1986** *Nature* 13 Feb. 548/2 Several roots of Whitehead's later philosophy are to be found in his Apostolic comradeship.

B. *sb.* A heretical sect. (See quot.)

1580 FULKE *Retentive* 314 (T.) The apostolicks in their vow of continence. **1645** PAGITT *Heresiogr.* (1661) 36 Apostolicks, a kind of Anabaptists, because they would be like the Apostle, they wandred up and down the Countreys, without staves, shooes, money, or bags. **1751** [See APOSTLE 3].

apo'stolical, *a.* and *sb.* [a. OFr. *apostolical* (13th c.), f. as prec. + -AL[1].]

A. *adj.* **1.** Connected with or relating to the apostles, or to what is apostolic; conformable to, or derived from, apostolic manner, usage, or institution. ***apostolical succession*** (*Eccl.*), an uninterrupted transmission of spiritual authority through a succession of bishops from the apostles downward.

1577 tr. *Bullinger's Decades* Introd., A..preaching of the Euangelical and Apostolicall truth. **1616** R. C. *Times' Whistle* IV. 1595 Some think he was not Apostolicall, But alwaies in his heart papisticall. **1836** *Edin. Rev.* LXIII. 44 Their watch-word, Apostolical Succession. **1840** MACAULAY *Ranke's Hist., Ess.* II. 142 Hearers who sleep very composedly while the rector preaches on the apostolical succession.

2. Of the Apostolic See.

1546 LANGLEY *Pol. Verg. De Invent.* VIII. ii. 145/1 Suche thynges as belong to the Apostolicall penitencers Benet the XII. deuised first. **1864** BURTON *Scot Abr.* II. i. 101 The office of Apostolical Secretary under two successive pontiffs.

3. Formerly (and still sometimes) = APOSTOLIC.

1548 UDALL, etc. *Erasm. Par. Matt.* xiv. (R.) The Apostolycall men..shuld purpose nothyng vnto them whiche they had not receiued of Christ. *a* **1568** COVERDALE *Hope of Faithf.* xiv. Wks. II. 168 The article in the holy apostolical creed. **1704** NELSON *Fest. & Fasts* i. (1739) 19 The Apostolical Institution of the Lord's Day. **1751** JORTIN *Eccl. Hist.* I. 35 The authors called Apostolical, as Clemens, Hermas, Barnabas, Ignatius.

B. *sb.* One who maintains the doctrine of 'apostolical succession.'

1839 SARA COLERIDGE *Mem.* I. 223 On some points I think the apostolicals quite right, on others clearly unscriptural.

apo'stolically, *adv.* [f. prec. + -LY[2].] In apostolic manner; according to the practice of the Apostles, or to what is apostolic.

1641 SMECTYMNUUS *Vind. Answ.* § 13. 129 Apostolically or Evangelically employed in taking care of all the Churches. **1845** LD. CAMPBELL *Chancell.* (1857) VI. cxxiv. 83 A priest, apostolically ordained.

apo'stolicalness. ?*Obs.* [f. as prec. + -NESS.] The quality of being apostolical, apostolicity.

1664 H. MORE *Myst. Iniq.* 214 The number 144..signifies symbolically the Apostolicalness of that Company. **1680** —— *Apocal. Apoc.* 221 The pure Apostolicalness in this constitution of the church.

apostolicism (æpə'stɒlɪsɪz(ə)m). *rare.* [f. APOSTOLIC + -ISM; cf. *mysticism.*] Profession of, or claim to, apostolicity.

1864 MASSON in *Macm. Mag.* Oct. 474 Not kept apart from other Churches by any doctrine of exclusive apostolicism.

apostolicity (ə,pɒstə'lɪsɪtɪ). [a. Fr. *apostolicité*: see APOSTOLIC and -ITY.] The quality of being apostolic in character or origin.

1832 G. FABER (*title*) The Apostolicity of Trinitarianism. **1855** I. TAYLOR *Restor. Belief* (1856) 120 Good anchor-hold in the roadstead of apostolicity.

† **apo'stolicness.** *Obs. rare*[−1]. [f. APOSTOLIC + -NESS.] = APOSTOLICITY, APOSTOLICALNESS.

1632 BP. M. SMITH *Serm.* 236 You must leaue one of them, either Lordlinesse or Apostolickenesse, you may not vse both.

‖ **apo'stolicon.** *Obs. rare*[−1]. [neut. of Gr. ἀποστολικ-ός: see APOSTOLIC.] A reputed cure for all kinds of wounds. (Cf. APOSTLE III.)

? *c* **1600** *Pathw. Health* I. (N.) For to make a white treate called apostolicon, Take oyle olive, litarge of lead, etc.

† **apo'stolicship.** *Obs. rare*[−1]. [f. APOSTOLIC + -SHIP.] (Here used as a title for the Pope.)

c **1593** NASHE *Lent. Stuffe* 57 Some euill spirit of an heretique..which thus molesteth his Apostoliqueship.

apostolize (ə'pɒstəlaɪz) *v. rare.* [f. Gr. ἀπόστολ-ος APOSTLE + -IZE; cf. *evangelize.*] **a.** *trans.* To proclaim (a message). **b.** *intr.* To act as or like an apostle.

1652 BENLOWE *Theoph.* VII. lxxi, Which God t' apostolize did bring to passe By th' Holy Ghosts descent. **1787** BECKFORD *Italy* II. 9 Wesley, who came apostolising into Cornwall.

apostrophal (ə'pɒstrəfəl), *a.* ? *Obs. rare*[−1]. [f. APOSTROPHE[1] + -AL[1].] Of the nature of, or containing, an apostrophe.

1652 URQUHART *Jewel* Wks. 1834, 292, I could have used ..apostrophal and prosopopœial diversions.

† **a'postrophate**, *v. Obs. rare*[−1]. [f. med.L. *apostrophāt-*, ppl. stem of *apostrophā-re* to apostrophize.] To cut short, bring to a close. (Cf. APOSTROPHIZE 2.)

1622 MALYNES *Anc. Law-Merch.* 335 To apostrophate this discourse.

† **a,postro'phation.** *Obs. rare*[−1]. [n. of action f. med.L. *apostrophāt-*: see prec. and -TION.] The making of an apostrophe or direct personal address.

a **1529** SKELTON *Ware the Hauke* 30, I shall make you relacion, By waye of apostrofacion.

apostrophe[1] (ə'pɒstrəfiː). Also 8 **-phy**. [a. L. *apostrophe*, a. Gr. ἀποστροφή, n. of action f. ἀποστρέφ-ειν to turn away, f. ἀπό away + στρέφ-ειν to turn, στροφή a turning.]

1. *Rhet.* A figure of speech, by which a speaker or writer suddenly stops in his discourse, and turns to address pointedly some person or thing, either present or absent; an exclamatory address. (As explained by Quintilian, *apostrophe* was directed to a person *present*; modern use has extended it to the *absent* or *dead* (who are for the nonce supposed to be present); but it is by no means confined to these, as sometimes erroneously stated.)

1533 MORE *Apol.* vii. Wks. 1557, 859/1 With a fygure of apostrophe and turning his tale to God criyng out: O good Lorde. **1649** ROBERTS *Clavis Bibl.* 678 An Apostrophe, or affectionate Compellation of all that passe by to be sensibly touch't with her sorrows. **1794** GODWIN *Cal. Williams* 98 Themistocles..accosted him with that noble apostrophe, Strike but hear. **1830** COLERIDGE *Lect. Shaks.* II. 118 The apostrophe to light at the commencement of the third book [of *Paradise Lost*] is particularly beautiful. **1859** GEO. ELIOT *Ad. Bede* 30 Bursting out into wild accusing apostrophes to God and destiny.

2. *Bot.* The aggregation of protoplasm and chlorophyll-grains on the cell-walls adjacent to other cells, as opposed to *epistrophe* when they collect on the free cell-walls.

1875 BENNETT & DYER *Sachs' Bot.* 672 Apostrophe takes place under unfavourable external conditions.

apostrophe[2] (ə'pɒstrəfiː). Also 6-8 **-phus.** [a. Fr. *apostrophe*, ad. L. *apostrophus*, a. Gr. ἡ ἀπόστροφος, prop. adj. (sc. προσῳδία the accent) 'of turning away, or elision.' It ought to be of three syllables in Eng. as in French, but has been ignorantly confused with the prec. word.]

† **1.** The omission of one or more letters in a word. *Obs.*

1611 [See APOSTROPHIZE 2.] *c* **1620** A. HUME *Orthogr. Brit. Tong.* (1865) 23 Apostrophus is the ejecting of a letter or a syllab out of one word, or out betuene tuae. **1642** HOWELL *For. Trav.* (Arb.) 39 The freedom [of Spanish] from Apostrophes which are the knots of a Language.

2. The sign (') used to indicate the omission of a letter or letters, as in *o'er, thro', can't*; and as a sign of the modern English genitive or possessive case, as in *boy's, boys', men's, conscience', Moses'*.

In the latter case, it originally marked merely the omission of *e* in writing, as in *fox's, James's*, and was equally common in the nominative plural, esp. of proper names and foreign words (as *folio's = folioes*); it was gradually disused in the latter, and extended to all possessives, even where *e* had not

been previously written, as in *man's, children's, conscience' sake*. This was not yet established in 1725.
1588 SHAKS. *L.L.L.* IV. ii. 123 You finde not the apostraphas [? apostrophus], and so misse the accent. **1727** W. MATHER *Yng. Man's Comp.* 35 An Apostrophus (commonly, but not rightly called an Apostrophe) thus markt (') .. as *Th' appurtenances*. **1876** MASON *Eng. Gram.* 29 It is .. an unmeaning process to put the apostrophe after the [possessive] plural *s* (as *birds'*), because no vowel has been dropped there.

apostrophic (æpəʊ'strɒfɪk), *a.* [f. prec. + -IC, after Gr. στροφικός.]
1. Of, pertaining to, or addicted to the use of rhetorical apostrophe.
1820 BYRON in Moore *Life* 448 Mrs. Hemans is .. too stiltified and apostrophic. **1861** TULLOCH *Eng. Purit.* ii. 248 Passages of apostrophic grandeur.
2. Of or pertaining to the grammatical apostrophe.
1795 L. MURRAY *Gram.* II. iii. (R.) Sometimes when the singular terminates in *ss* the apostrophic *s* is not added. **1816** GILCHRIST *Phil. Etym.* 49 The genitive has the apostrophic'.

apostrophism (ə'pɒstrəfɪz(ə)m). *rare*$^{-1}$. [f. next: see -ISM.] The act of apostrophizing.
1866 *Morn. Star* 18 Dec. 6/2 The .. incoherent tearful apostrophism which the poor women could not suppress.

apostrophize (ə'pɒstrəfaɪz), *v.* [f. APOSTROPHE + -IZE.]
I. From APOSTROPHE[1].
1. *Rhet.* To address with or in an apostrophe.
1725 POPE *Odyss.* XIV. 41 *note*, Homer's manner of apostrophizing Eumæus. **1760** STERNE *Tr. Shandy* xxx. Wks. IX. 289 'Best of honest and gallant servants!'—but I have apostrophiz'd thee Trim, once before. **1825** SCOTT *Betrothed* ii, 'And what though thou, O scroll,' he said, apostrophizing the letter .. 'dost speak with the tongue of the stranger.'
b. *absol.* or *intr.*
1824 DIBDIN *Libr. Comp.* 228 Indeed, apostrophising and mystifying apart. **1865** *Pall Mall G.* 19 June 4 That additional half-hour of hesitation, repetition, and apostrophizing on his part.
II. From APOSTROPHE[2].
2. To omit one or more letters of a word; to mark with the sign (') the omission of letters.
1611 COTGR., *Apostropher* .. to apostrophise; to cut off (by an Apostrophe) the last vowell of a word. **1818** [See next.]

a'postrophized, *ppl. a.* [f. prec. + -ED.] **a.** Addressed in an apostrophe. **b.** Contracted by apostrophe.
1818 tr. *Matthiæ's Grk. Gram.* (1829) I. 49 The apostrophized word is often contracted into one with the following word [*e.g.*] διὸ .. more correctly written δι' ὅ.

apostume, -ation, etc.: see APOSTEME, etc.

†**apo'tactical**, *a. Obs. rare*$^{-1}$. [f. Gr. ἀπότακτ-ος, vbl. adj. f. ἀποτάσσειν to set apart, ἀποτάσσεσθαι (cf. *Luke* ix. 61) to say adieu to, renounce + -ICAL.] Renouncing, recreant.
1627 BP. HALL *No Peace with Rome* lvii. 661 Monsters of men .. apotacticall and apostaticall miscreants.

apotactite (æpəʊ'tæktaɪt). [a. med.L. *apotactīta*, ad. Gr. ἀποτακτίτης, f. ἀπότακτ-ος: see prec.] A member of an early Christian sect, who renounced all their possessions in imitation of what is recorded concerning the early church in Jerusalem.
1727–51 CHAMBERS *Cycl.*, *Apoctactitæ* .. affecting to follow the evangelical counsels of poverty. **1838** *Penny Cycl.* XII. 156/2 Called, from their habits of abstinence, Apotactites.

†**a'potelesm** (ə'pɒtɪlɛzm). *rare.* [ad. Gr. ἀποτέλεσμα n. of completed effect, f. ἀποτελέ-ειν to bring to an end, f. ἀπό off + τελέ-ειν to finish.]
1. (as in Gr.) The result, the sum and substance.
1636 *Raleigh's Tubus Hist.* Pref. B, In this succinct Recollection is contrived .. the *Apotelesma* and effect of infinite Volumes.
2. *Astrol.* The 'casting' of a horoscope.
1651 *Father Sarpi* (1676) 11 That the Horoscope .. of the Beast might be known .. Which being done and reduced into the form of a Figure or Apotelesm, etc. **1753** CHAMBERS *Cycl. Supp.* s.v., The answers of astrologers deduced from the consideration of the stars are particularly called Apotelesms.
3. *Med.* The result or termination of a disease.
1859 in WORCESTER.

apotelesmatic (apɒtɪlɛz'mætɪk), *a.* [ad. Gr. ἀποτελεσματικ-ός, f. ἀποτέλεσμα: see prec.] Of or pertaining to the casting of horoscopes.
1655–60 STANLEY *Hist. Philos.* (1701) 24/1 It consists of two parts; Meteorologick, which considers the Motions of the Stars; the other Apotelesmatick, which regards Divination. **1837** WHEWELL *Hist. Induct. Sc.* (1857) I. 229 This apotelesmatic or judicial astrology.

†**apotele'smatical**, *a. Obs. rare*$^{-1}$. = prec.
1753 CHAMBERS *Cycl. Supp.*, Apotelesmatical astronomy.

†**a'pothec.** *Obs.* Also 6 **oppatheke, -icke,** 7 **apothect(e.** [a. OFr. *apotheque, apoteque* shop, magazine; ad. L. *apothēca*, a. Gr. ἀποθήκη a store-house, f. ἀποτιθέ-ναι to lay away.] A shop, store-house, or magazine; *esp.* for drugs. Also *fig.*
1591 HORSEY *Trav.* (1857) 201 [He] comaunds the master of his oppathicke .. to prepare and atend for his solace and bathinge. One sent .. to the oppatheke for marigold and rose water. **1647** R. BARON *Cyprian Acad.* A ij b, In your lovely sex, as in the Apothecke or magasine of perfection. **1657** TOMLINSON *Renou's Disp.* 3 The Apothecary from the Apothectes or shop where his medicines are placed.

apothecal (ə'pɒθɪkəl), *a. rare*$^{-1}$. [f. prec. + -AL[1].] Of or pertaining to a shopman.
1872 M. COLLINS *Pr. Clarice* I. vii. 108, I laugh equally at bucolic menace and apothecal libel.

†**apothecariry.** *Obs. rare*$^{-1}$. [a. Fr. *apothicairerie*, f. *apothicaire*: see -RY.] A drug-store.
1748 *Phil. Trans.* XLV. 179 The apothecariry of the Army.

apothecary (ə'pɒθɪkərɪ). Forms: 4–6 **apotecary, -rie,** 4–7 **apothecarie,** 5 **apotiquare, -ry, apotecarye, -tycary, appotecary, appoticary,** 6 **-thecarie, apothicarie, -ticary,** 4– **apothecary.** *Aphet.* 4–5 **potecary(e, -carie,** 5 **-kary,** 5–6 **potycary(e,** 6 **-ticary, -rie,** 7 **pottecary, -icary,** 8 **pothecary.** [a. OFr. *apotecaire, apoticaire* (13th c. in Littré):—late L. *apothēcārius* store-keeper, f. *apothēca*: see APOTHEC and -ARY.]
†**1.** *orig.* One who kept a store or shop of non-perishable commodities, spices, drugs, comfits, preserves, etc.
(This passed at an early period into the next: in 1617 the Apothecaries' Company of London was separated from the Grocers'.)
2. *spec.* The earlier name for: One who prepared and sold drugs for medicinal purposes—the business now (since about 1800) conducted by a druggist or pharmaceutical chemist. From about 1700 apothecaries gradually took a place as general medical practitioners, and the modern apothecary holds this status legally, by examination and licence of the Apothecaries' Company; but in popular usage the term is archaic.
Apothecaries' Weight: that by which drugs are compounded.
1366 MAUNDEV. v. 51 The marchauntis and the apotecaries countrefeten it [bawme]. *c* **1386** CHAUCER *Prol.* 425 Ful redy hadde he hise apothecaries [*v.r.* -tecaryis, -caries, appot-] To send him drogges. **1466** *Mann. & Househ. Exp.* 369, I toke of .. the potekary, a lytel barel of water fore the sekenes. **1474** CAXTON *Chesse* 100 The pawn .. signefyeth the physicien, spicer, apotiquare. **1535** COVERDALE *Song Sol.* iii. 6 All maner spyces of the Apotecary. **1578** T. N. tr. *Conq. W. Ind.* 199 Manie Poticaries, who doe bring into the market, oyntments, sirops, waters, and other drugges. **1592** SHAKS. *Rom. & Jul.* V. iii. 119 O, true Appothecary: Thy drugs are quicke. **1635** N. CARPENTER *Geog. Delin.* II. iii. 53 Our Physicians and Apothecaries .. owe most of the medicinable drugges to India. **1709** POPE *Ess. Crit.* 108 Modern 'Pothecaries, taught the art By Doctor's bills to play the Doctor's part. **1765** BROWNRIGG in *Phil. Trans.* LV. 229 The Pouhon water .. was found to weigh twenty ounces, seven drachms, and fourteen grains, apothecaries weight. **1812** COMBE (Dr. Syntax) *Picturesque* VIII. 129 'Tis known that I took full enough, Of this Apothecary's stuff.
†**3.** [cf. OFr. *apotecarie, apotiquerie*, and late L. *apothēcāria*, the wares or shop of a drug-seller.] Drugs collectively: hence **a.** A store of drugs; **b.** Medical treatment by drugs. *Obs.*
1561 HOLLYBUSH *Hom. Apoth.* 4 b, Made in the Apothecarye. **1589** *Hawkins's 2nd Voy.* in Arb. *Garner* V. 131 They have for apothecary, herbs, trees, roots, and gums in great store. **1621** BURTON *Anat. Mel.* II. i. IV. iii, The ordinary is threefold .. Diet or Living, Apothecary, Chirurgery.
4. *attrib.* quasi-*adj.*
1562 in Heath *Grocers' Comp.* (1869) 97 Poticarie wares such as shall be pure and perfyt good. **1601** HOLLAND *Pliny* (1634) II. 176 To set vp Apothecary shops. **1615** LATHAM *Falconry* (1633) 79 She hath no phisicall medicines, nor Apothecary scowrings giuen her.

a'pothecaryship. *rare.* [f. as prec. + -SHIP.] The practice of an apothecary.
1611 COTGR., *Apothicairerie*, Apothicariship, the trade, or skill of Apothicaries.

apothecial (æpəʊ'θiːʃɪəl), *a.* [f. APOTHECIUM + -AL.] Of or pertaining to an apothecium.
1882 J. M. CROMBIE in *Encycl. Brit.* XIV. 559 Apothecial reactions for the most part take place either externally on the epithecium or internally on the hymenial gelatin.

‖**apothecium** (æpəʊ'θiːʃɪəm). *Bot.* Pl. **-a.** [mod.L., a. Gr. *ἀποθήκιον, dim. of ἀποθήκη: see APOTHEC.] The 'shield' or spore-case, containing the fructification in lichens.
1830 LINDLEY *Nat. Syst. Bot.* 331. **1861** H. MACMILLAN *Footn. Page Nat.* 72 *Apothecia* correspond with the flowers of the higher plants.

apothegm, -them, variants of APOPHTHEGM.

apothem ('æpəθɪm). [mod. f. Gr. ἀποτιθέ-ναι to set off, put aside, deposit, etc.; after θέμα, from the simple τιθέναι to place; cf. Fr. *apothème.*]
1. *Math.* In a regular polygon: The perpendicular dropped from the centre upon one of the sides. Cf. *off-set.* (In mod. Dicts.)
2. 'A term applied by Berzelius to the insoluble brown deposit which forms in vegetable extracts .. exposed to the air.' Watts *Dict. Chem.*

apotheose (ə'pɒθiːəʊz), *v. rare.* [f. APOTHEOSIS, like *metamorphose.*] = APOTHEOSIZE.
1671 F. PHILIPPS *Reg. Necess.* 269 He must be Apotheosed, or more than Mortality or mankind will permit, and so omnipresent. **1766** PORNY *Heraldry* vi. (1777) 209 Emperors, when they were Apotheosed or ranked among the Gods. **1869** *Echo* 31 Aug., Persons less gifted have not the power of apotheosing vice.

apotheosis (æpəʊ'θiːəsɪs, ə,pɒθiː'əʊsɪs). [a. L. *apotheōsis* (Tertull.), a. Gr. ἀποθέωσις, n. of action f. ἀποθεό-ειν to deify, f. ἀπό off, (in comb.) completely + θεό-ειν to make a god of, f. θεός god. The great majority of orthoepists, from Bailey and Johnson downward, give the first pronunciation, but the second is now more usual.]
1. The action of ranking, or fact of being ranked, among the gods; transformation into a god, deification; divine status.
[**1577** tr. *Bullinger's Decades* (1592) 759 Truely Aurelius Prudentius in his *Apotheosis* .. saith.] **1605** BACON *Adv. Learn.* I. 32 That which the Grecians call *Apotheosis* .. was the supreme honour, which a man could attribute unto man. **1677** HALE *Prim. Orig. Man.* II. ii. 137 The Apotheoses or Inaugurations of many of the Heathenish Deities. **1879** FARRAR *Paul* I. 664 The early Emperors rather discouraged .. this tendency to flatter them by a premature apotheosis.
2. By extension: The ascription of extraordinary, and as it were divine, power or virtue; glorification, exaltation; the canonization of saints.
[**1553–87** FOXE *A. & M.* I. 662/2 You .. affirm, that in this my Calendar, I make an αποθεωσιν, or Canonization of false Martyrs.] **1651** HOBBES *Govt. & Soc.* xviii. §14. 362 The canonization of Saints which the Heathen called Apotheosis. **1739** *Gentl. Mag.* (*title*) The Apotheosis of Milton. **1758** JORTIN *Erasmus* I. 305 He promises .. to send him the apotheosis of his friend Reuchlin. **1879** O'CONNOR *Beaconsfield* 73 The meeting developed into an apotheosis of the Marquis of Chandos.
3. The deification, glorification, or exaltation of a principle, practice, etc.; a deified ideal.
1651 BIGGS *New Disp.* ¶211 Because in the Apotheosis of phlebotomy they will have good bloud emitted. **1810** COLERIDGE *Friend* (1865) 143 The apotheosis of familiar abuses .. is the vilest of superstitions. **1846** PRESCOTT *Ferd. & Is.* I. Introd. 35 The apotheosis of chivalry, in the person of their apostle and patron, St. James. **1852** MRS. JAMESON *Leg. Madonna* (1857) 47 Here all is spotless grace, etherial delicacy .. the very apotheosis of womanhood.
4. In loose usage: Ascension to glory, departure or release from earthly life; resurrection.
1649 C. WALKER *Hist. Indep.* II. 111 His Majesties Speech upon the Scaffold, and His Death or Apotheosis. **1680** H. MORE *Apocal. Apoc.* Pref. 17 The most assured argument .. of the apotheosis of Christ. **1684** T. BURNET *Th. Earth* I. 326 The general apotheosis; when death and hell shall be swallowed up in victory. **1850** CARLYLE *Latter-d. Pamphl.* i. (1872) 25 Let us hope the Leave-alone principle has now got its apotheosis; and taken wing towards higher regions than ours. **1858** R. VAUGHAN *Ess. & Rev.* I. 8 The philosophical school of Alexandria had become extinct, and there was no apotheosis.

apotheosize (æpəʊ'θiːəsaɪz, ə'pɒθiːəʊ,saɪz), *v.* [f. prec. + -IZE.] To elevate to, or as if to, the rank of a god; to deify, glorify, exalt.
1760 STERNE *Tr. Shandy* II. 280, I have apostrophiz'd thee, Trim, once before—and could I apotheosize thee also, with good company, I would do it. **1834** EMERSON in *Athenæum* No. 2852. 796 It is a singular piece of good nature in you to apotheosize him. **1851** H. SPENCER *Soc. Stat.* xvi. §3 The rage for accumulation has apotheosized work.

apotheosized (see prec.), *ppl. a.* [f. prec. + -ED.] Deified, immortalized.
1827 LYTTON *Pelham* xvii. 81 O exalted among birds—apotheosised goose. **1876** H. SPENCER *Princ. Soc.* I. 431 There were apotheosized mortals too, among the Greek deities.

†**apo'theosy.** *Obs. rare*$^{-1}$. A variant of APOTHEOSIS (cf. *poesy*).
1600 TOURNEUR *Transf. Metam.* Ded., To thee I write my Apotheosie.

†**apo'therapy.** *Obs. rare*$^{-1}$. [a. Fr. *apothérapie*, ad. Gr. ἀποθεραπεία a being rubbed and anointed after exercise (Galen).] (See quot.)
1653 URQUHART *Rabelais* I. xxiv, By way of apotherapie (that is, a making the body healthful by exercise) did recreate themselves in botteling up of hay, etc.

‖**apothesis** (ə'pɒθɪsɪs). [L., a. Gr. ἀπόθεσις, n. of action f. ἀποτιθέναι to lay aside, deposit.]
1. (As in Gr.) The setting of a fractured or dislocated limb.

1811 in HOOPER *Med. Dict.*
2. *Arch.* = APOPHYGE.

apotome (ə'pɒtəmiː). Also **-tomy.** [a. Gr. ἀποτομή a cutting off, f. ἀπο-τέμν-ειν to cut off.] **1.** *Math.* The difference of two quantities, commensurable only in power (*i.e.* in their squares, cubes, etc.; see Euclid Bk. X); *e.g.* the difference between $\sqrt{2}$ and 1, which is the difference between the diagonal and side of a square.

1571 DIGGES *Geom. Pract.* IV. i. T iij b, $\sqrt{180}$ − 6.. deducted from 12, leueth this Apotome 18 − $\sqrt{180}$. **1656** BLOUNT *Glossogr.*, *Apotomy.* **1673** WALLIS in Rigaud *Corr. Sci. Men* II. 567 Of which binomial and apotome, the cubic roots are to be extracted. **1706** in PHILLIPS. **1796** HUTTON *Math. Dict.* s.v., The doctrine of apotomes, in lines, as delivered by Euclid in the tenth book.

2. *Mus.* (See quot.)

1696 in PHILLIPS. **1753** CHAMBERS *Cycl. Supp.*, Apotome, in music, is the difference of the tone major and Limma, expressed by $\frac{2187}{2048}$. **1806** CALCOTT *Mus. Gram.* II. iii. 112 This Semitone was termed by the Pythagoreans Apotome.

apotropaic (ˌæpəʊtrəʊ'peɪɪk), *a.* [f. Gr. ἀποτρόπαιος averting evil (f. ἀποτρέπειν to turn away, avert) + -IC.] Having or reputed to have the power of averting evil influence or ill luck. Hence **apotro'paically** *adv.*

1883 *Encycl. Brit.* XV. 570/1 The sacrifice of the 'October horse' in the Campus Martius.. had also a naturalistic and apotropaic character. **1904** W. M. RAMSAY in Hastings *Dict. Bible* V. 115/1 The.. employment of a bull's head on.. sarcophagi.. evidently.. had at first an apotropaic purpose. **1918** L. STRACHEY *Eminent Victorians* 230 The same doctrine led him [*sc.* Gordon].. to append, in brackets, the apotropaic initials D.V. after every statement in his letters implying futurity. **1945** *Proc. Prehist. Soc.* XI. 55 In the centre, an apotropaic ornament, a severed head between two volutes. **1956** W. H. AUDEN *Old Man's Road*, Apotropaically scowling, a tinker Shuffles past.

apotropous (ə'pɒtrəpəs), *a. Bot.* [f. Gr. ἀπότροπος turned away (f. ἀποτρέπειν to turn away) + -OUS.] (See quot.)

1880 GRAY *Bot. Text-bk.* 397 *Apotropous*, Applied to an erect or ascending ovule with its rhaphe next to the placental axis, and a hanging one has its rhaphe averse from it.

apoun, obs. form of UPON.

a-pout (ə'paʊt), *adv.* [f. A *prep.*[1] + POUT.] Pouting.

1886 J. ASHBY-STERRY *Lazy Minstrel* 150 Ah! sweet are those eloquent lips a-pout. **1893** F. THOMPSON *Poems* 74 (*The Poppy*) With mouth wide a-pout for a sultry kiss. **1922** JOYCE *Ulysses* 268 Richie cocked his lips apout.

apozem ('æpəzɪm). *Med. Obs.* or *arch.* Also 7 apozume, 7–8 **apozeme.** [a. Fr. *apozème*, ad. late L. *apozema*, a. Gr. ἀπόζεμα, n. of result f. ἀποζέ-ειν, f. ἀπό off, (in comb.) completely + ζέ-ειν to boil.] A decoction or infusion.

1603 B. JONSON *Sejanus* I. i, Physic.. More comforting Than all your opiates, juleps, apozems. **1626** BACON *Sylva* §65 Apozumes or preparing Broths. **1684** tr. *Bonet's Merc. Compit.* II. 43, I made use of an opening Apozeme for several days. **1753** SMOLLETT *Ct. Fathom* (1784) 19/2 [He] swallowed a whole dispensary of boluses, draughts, and apozems. **1880** M. B. EDWARDS *Forestalled* I. xiv, A remedy of his own, a decoction, an apozem, of wonderful narcotic power.

†**apo'zemical**, *a. Med. Obs.* [f. prec. + -ICAL.] Of the nature of an apozem.

1638 J. WHITAKER *Blood of Grape* 33 (T.) Wine that is dilute, may.. be adhibited in an apozemical form in fevers.

apozymase (ˌæpəʊ'zaɪmeɪs). *Chem.* [G. (Neuberg & Gottschalk 1925, in *Biochem. Zeitschr.* CLXI. 248), f. APO- + ZYMASE.] The residue of zymase after separation of cozymase.

1926 *Chem. Abstr.* 923 (*title*) Apozymase and cozymase: phosphorylation. **1930** J. B. S. HALDANE *Enzymes* 136 Zymase (yeast press-juice) can be separated into a colloidal, thermolabile fraction (apozymase), and a thermostable dialysable organic fraction (cozymase)... An amount of cozymase produces.. activation of a given apozymase. **1946** *Nature* 21 Dec. 900/2 In the inactivation of cozymase by apozymase.. the reaction velocity was little affected by variation in cozymase concentration.

appaid, later sp. of APAID *ppl. a.*

†**a'ppair, a'pair**, *v. Obs.* Forms: 4 **ampayr-i, anpayr-i, apayr-i, -eir-i,** 3–6 **apeyre,** 4–5 **apeire,** 4–6 **apayre,** 5 **apaire, -eyer, appeare, appere,** 5–6 **appayre, -peyre, -paire, -peir(e, -pare,** 6–7 **-air(e.** Also aphetic PAIR. [ad. OF. *empeire-r, ampeire-r* (mod. *empirer*), to worsen, f. *em-* = *en-* into + **peire-r*:—L. *pēiōrā-re* to make worse, f. *pēiōr-* worse: cf. Pr. *apejurar*. The prefix of the early *ampayre, anpayre*, was subseq. treated like the native *an-* before a consonant, and reduced to *a-*, which was in 15th c. erron. spelt *ap-* by form-assoc. with words like *ap-pear*: see AP- *pref*[1]. As early as 1300 *a-paire* was aphetized to *paire, peire.* Caxton restored the Fr. form *empeyr, empayr, empair*, which, early in 16th c., began to be refashioned after L. as IMPAIR, now the current form. *Ampayr, anpayr, apayr, appair, enpayre, empair, impair*, are thus variants of the same word.]

1. *trans.* To make worse, less valuable, weaker, or less; to injure, damage, weaken; to IMPAIR.

1297 R. GLOUC. 279 Destrude and apeyrede Cristendom. **1303** R. BRUNNE *Handl. Synne* 1517 Bakbyters.. apeyryn many mannys lyfe. **1340** *Ayenb.* 10 To ampayri his guode los. *Ibid.* 237 þe kueadnesse of þe ministre may anpayri þe oþre. *c* **1450** *Merlin* vii. 110 Haueth pite of cristen feith that it be not a-peired thourgh yow. **1528** MORE *Heresyes* III. Wks. 1557, 226/2 Sacramentes.. the goodnes whereof his noughtinesse can not appayre.. That sacred sacrifice.. can take none empayryng by the fylthe of his synne. **1561** T. N[ORTON] *Calvin's Inst.* I. xvii. (1634) 90 For fear of appairing his feeble health. **1643** PRYNNE *Power Parl.* II. 71 The ancient lawes.. be greatly appaired.

2. *intr.* (by omission of refl. pron.) To grow or become worse, less valuable, weaker, or less; to deteriorate, fall off, or decay.

1340 HAMPOLE *Pr. Consc.* 1475 Als þis lyfe es ay passand, Swa es þe worlde, ilk day, apayrand. *c* **1450** LONELICH *Grail* li. 300 This piers, that hurt was so sore, Every day gan apeyren more and more. **1496** *Dives & Paup.* (W. de W) VII. xxvi. 315/1 Yf the beste dye or appeyre, he that hyreth it shall stande to that losse. *a* **1509** HENRY VII in Ellis *Orig. Lett.* I. 21 I. 46 My syghte.. will appayre dayly. **1534** WHITTINTON *Tullyes Offices* III. (1540) 154 He that wetyngly sellyth wyne that is apayring. **1581** W. STAFFORD *Exam. Compl.* iii. (1876) 80 As the coyne appayred, so rose the prices of things.

†**a'ppaired**, *ppl. a. Obs.* [f. prec. + -ED.] Injured, impaired.

1475 SIR J. PASTON in *Lett.* 766 III. 145 The said manoir diffaced, hurt, and appeired. **1637** GILLESPIE *Eng.-Pop. Cerem.* III. viii. 193 Guilty of appaired [*læsa*] Majesty.

†**a'ppairer.** *Obs. rare.* [f. as prec. + -ER[1].] He who or that which impairs.

1382 WYCLIF *James* Prol., A falsere, and a distroȝere, *or apeirere*, of holi scripture. **1555** *Fardle Facions* II. iii. 123 That time might be founde an appairer of al thinges.

†**a'ppairing**, *vbl. sb. Obs.* [f. as prec. + -ING[1].] The action of injuriously affecting or impairing; weakening, deterioration, damage.

1388 WYCLIF *Phil.* iii. 7 Whiche thingis weren to me wynnyngis Y haue demed these apeyryngis for Crist. **1549** COVERDALE *Erasm. Par. Rom.* iii. 31 Thabolishement or thappayryng of the authoritie of the lawe. **1611** COTGR., *Diminution*, A diminution, appairing, lessening, impairing.

†**a'ppairment.** *Obs. rare.* For forms see APPAIR. [ad. OF. *ampeirement*, f. *ampeirer*: see APPAIR.] IMPAIRMENT, injury, damage.

1388 WYCLIF *Phil.* iii. 8 Alle thingis to be apeirement [*v.r.* peirement] for the cleer conscience of Jhesu Crist my Lord. **1413** LYDG. *Pylgr. Sowle* I. lv. 15 None appeyrement byfallyth it. *c* **1450** *Rel. Ant.* I. 109 Thou maist done awey the lettres without any apeyrement.

appal, appall (ə'pɔːl), *v.* Forms: 4–7 **a-pall(e, appalle,** 6 **a-pawl,** 7 **appaule,** 5–9 **appall,** 6–9 **appal.** *Inflected* **appalled, appalling.** [? a. OF. *apalir, apallir*, later *ap(p)alir*, to wax pale, be in consternation; languish, waste away; also *trans.* to make pale, etc. This derivation accounts satisfactorily for the *senses*, but presents difficulties as to the *forms*: the natural repr. of *apalir* would be *apale, appale*, actually found in 16th c., in the literal sense (see below); the earlier *appall*, which points, like *all, ball, fall*, etc. (with which it rhymes from the 14th c.), to an originally short *a*, may perhaps repr. the Fr. form *appall-ir*. But *appall* cannot be separated from the simple PALL *v.*, for the relations of which to PALE *v.* and *a.* see that word. Both on etymological and phonetic grounds, the better spelling is *appall*, as in the derivatives.]

I. *intr.*

†**1.** To wax pale or dim. *Obs.* Cf. APPALE 1.

1393 GOWER *Conf.* II. 107 Of thought, which in min herte falleth, Whan it is night min hede appalleth. *c* **1430** LYDG. *Min. Poems* 24 The night doth folowe, appallith all his chere, Whan Western wawis his stremys overclose.

†**2.** *fig.* To wax faint or feeble in any characteristic quality; to fade, fail, decay. *Obs.*

c **1315** SHOREHAM 91 Ther [in heaven].. none swetnesse appalleth. *c* **1430** LYDG. *Bochas* I. i. (1544) 2 b, Their youth by ful great displeasaunce Gan to appall. **1494** FABYAN V. lxxxiii. 61 The fayth of Criste began sore to apalle. **1596** SPENSER *F.Q.* IV. vi. 26 Therewith her wrathfull courage gan appall.

†**3.** To lose flavour, savour, or briskness; to become flat or stale, as fermented liquor when left exposed to the air. *Obs.* Cf. PALL *v.*

1528 MORE *Heresyes* III. Wks. 1557, 226/1 If the salt once apalle, the woorde muste nedes waxe vnsauery. **1530** PALSGR. 433/1, I appalle, as drinke dothe or wyne, whan it leseth his colour, or ale whan it hath stande longe. *Je appalys.* This wyne is appaled all redy. **1568** (ed. 2) NORTH *Diall Princes* (1619) 622/2 He found the wine wel watered before that it had stood a pawling long.

†**4.** To lose heart or resolution; become dismayed. *Obs.*

c **1450** *Vox Populi* 206 in Hazl. *E.P.P.* III. 275 Yf theise men appall, And lacke when you do call.

II. *trans.*

†**5.** To make pale, to cause to lose or change colour. *Obs. rare.* Cf. APPALE 4.

c **1386** CHAUCER *Sqrs. T.* 357 Hir liste nat apalled [*v.r.* appalled, appallid] for to be Ne on the morwe vnfeestlich for to se. **1583** STUBBES *Anat. Abuses* I. (1877) 95 [Adultery] appalleth the countenance, it dulleth the spirits.

†**6.** *fig.* To cause to fade or cease to flourish; to dim, weaken, enfeeble, impair. *Obs.*

c **1386** CHAUCER *Knts. T.* 2195 Whan his name apalled [*v.r.* appelled, -alled, apeyred] is for age. **1548** UDALL, etc. *Erasm. Paraphr. Luke* vi. 22 To appalle or derken your glorie. **1574** tr. *Marlorat's Apocalips* 26 Restored mee my strength whiche was appalled with feare. **1586** J. HOOKER *Girald. Hist. Irel.* in *Holinsh.* II. 134/2 How often he preuailed against the enimie, and appalled their courages. **1616** [See APPALLED.]

†**7.** To quell (anger, pride, etc.). *Obs. rare.*

1470 HARDING *Chron.* xxxvi, Wherfore the kyng his yre myght not apall. **1598** SYLVESTER *Du Bartas* I. vii. (1641) 62/1 God beats his Dears, from birth to buriall, To make them know him, and their pride appall.

8. To cause the heart of (anyone) to sink; to dismay, shock, discomfit, terrify.

1532 MORE *Confut. Tindale* Wks. 1557, 646/2 Then wyll thys poynt as sore appall Tindal in thys debate. **1603** KNOLLES *Hist. Turkes* 813 To appaule and discourage the minds.. of the mercinarie souldiors. **1605** SHAKS. *Macb.* III. iv. 59 A man.. that dare looke on that Which might appall the Diuell. **1768** BEATTIE *Minstrel* I. ii, Him, who ne'er listened to the voice of praise, The silence of neglect can ne'er appal. **1855** MILMAN *Lat. Chr.* (1864) V. IX. viii. 403 The calmness of the heretics in the fire amazed, almost appalled, their judges.

b. *absol.*

a **1631** DRAYTON *Tri. David* in Farr's *S.P.* (1848) 116 His brazen armour gaue a iarring sound.. which did like death apall. **1827** KEBLE *Chr. Y.* Trin. S., Thoughts that awe but not appal.

†**c.** *refl. Obs.*

1447 BOKENHAM *Lyvys of Seyntys* 165 But thus [Christ] seyd, Marye the not appalle.

†**a'ppal, appall**, *sb. Obs. rare.* [f. prec. vb.] The act of appalling; sudden shock to courage or self-possession; dismay.

1596 CHAPMAN *Iliad* XI. 32 Had engraven, full of extreme appall, An ugly Gorgon. **1616** —— *Batrachom.* (1858) 17 Cold appal The wretches put in rout past all returne.

Appalachian (æpə'leɪtʃɪən), *a.* and *sb.* Also 7 **Apalatæan, Apalatean,** 8– **Apalatchian, Apalachian. A.** *adj.* **1.** Designating or forming part of an extensive system of mountain ranges in the eastern United States, stretching from the northern border with Canada to Georgia.

[**1607** *Capt. Newport's Discoveries* in Alvord & Bidgood *First Explorations Trans-Allegheny Region* (1912) 28 Mountaynes Apalatsi.] **1672** W. TALBOT tr. *Lederer's Discoveries* in *Three Marches from Virginia* 2 The Apalatæan mountains.. are barren rocks. **1682** T. ASH *Carolina* 34 It's supposed.. that the Apalatean Mountains.. yields ore both of gold and silver. **1743** M. CATESBY *Nat. Hist. Carolina* I. p. v, The Apalatchian Mountains have their southern Beginning near the Bay of Mexico. **1820** W. IRVING *Sketch Bk.* I. 59 They are a dismembered branch of the great Appalachian family. **1853** W. G. SIMMS *Sword & Distaff* 47 The mountain rangers from that section of the Apalachian slopes. **1863** J. D. DANA *Man. Geol.* IV. vi. 724 The Appalachian chain varies much in directions southwest of New York. **1917** C. J. SHARP in Campbell & Sharp *Eng. Folk Songs S. Appalachians* p. iii, The Southern Appalachian Mountains of North America. **1951** W. FAULKNER *Requiem for Nun* III. i. 246 The long looping skeins of electric lines bringing electric power from the Appalachian mountains. **1985** *Washington Post* 12 Dec. (Maryland Weekly Suppl.) 1, Every August.., Jim Fazenbaker used to head for Western Maryland's rugged Appalachian foothills.

2. Of, pertaining to, or characteristic of these mountains, this region as a whole, or its inhabitants.

1763 tr. *Le Page du Pratz's Hist. Louisiana* II. i. 7 The Apalachean beans are so called because we received them from a nation of natives of that name. **1860** *Historical Mag.* (U.S.) Feb. 40/1 (*heading*) Specimen of the Appalachian language. **1878** R. J. HINTON *Hand-bk. Arizona* 54 A series of limestones, shales, sandstones, and conglomerates totally unlike that which has been established in the New York and Appalachian province. **1904** *Amer. Jrnl. Sci.* Feb. 150 The folding in the rocks of the area is of three types: minute crinkling, small unsymmetrical wavy folds, and broad Appalachian ones in which the adjustment appears to have taken place along the bedding. **1906** V. A. LEWIS *Rep. Dept. Archives & Hist., W. Virginia* 31 The Potomac Area, the South Appalachian Area, and the Ohio Valley Area. **1941** *Amer. Speech* Oct. 180 *Ned* for bacon or salt pork, *set his hoss*, a gambling stake, are variously Appalachian. **1964** MRS. L. B. JOHNSON *White House Diary* 24 Apr. (1970) 121 We arrived at the Tom Fletcher home, chosen to illustrate the human toll the declining mining industry has taken on these Appalachian families. **1974** *Florida FL Reporter* XIII. 34/3 So opponents of the *status quo* in the USA could similarly 'authorize' promoting Black or Appalachian English as *the* single national norm. **1979** *United States 1980/81* (Penguin Travel Guides) 581 Appalachian meat pie and beer-batter shrimp are other dinner items. **1985** *N.Y. Times* 21 Dec. 1. 52/4 A lovely rendition of the Appalachian folk song 'I Wonder as I Wander'.

3. ***Appalachian revolution*** [REVOLUTION *sb.* 6 c], the formation of the Appalachian Mountains in eastern N. America.

1856 J. D. DANA *Amer. Geol. Hist.* 16 The deposits, with small exceptions, were a single unbroken record, until this Appalachian revolution. **1915** PIRSSON & SCHUCHERT *Text-bk. Geol.* II. xli. 749 During the Appalachian Revolution much of eastern North America was again thrown into pronounced folds.

B. *sb.* **1.** *pl.* The Appalachian mountains.

1834 *Penny Cycl.* II. 178/2 The rivers which rise in the Appalachians, flow in long valleys between the chains. **1917** CAMPBELL & SHARP (*title*) English folk songs from the Southern Appalachians. **1954** LEFLER & NEWSOME *North Carolina* ii. 19 The third physical region of North Carolina embraces the mountains of the Southern Appalachians. **1974** *Encycl. Brit. Macropædia* I. 1016/1 The highest altitudes in the Appalachians are in the northern division.

2. A native or inhabitant of the Appalachian area.

1888 S. WALLACE *Land of Pueblos* 277 The Pimo Indians ..are dark brown, differing in complexion from the Appalachians east of the Rocky Mountains and the olive hues of the California tribes. **1973** *Black Panther* 8 Sept. 4/3 Most Black people in Appalachia live in worse conditions than White Appalachians.

†**appale, apale** (əˈpeɪl), *v. Obs.* [See APPAL, APPALL *v.*: Doubtful whether (1) a later adoption of Fr. *appalir*, (2) an assimilation of *appall* to PALE *a.*, or (3) an independent new formation on PALE *a.* or *v.*, after *appall* had lost its literal sense, and evident connexion with *pale*. The senses are, to a great extent, parallel to those of APPAL.]

1. *intr.* To become pale. Cf. APPAL 1.

1535 *Goodly Prymer* (1834) 202 Would not even shortly thy mirth abate, thy colour apale, thy flesh faint.

2. To wax faint or feeble. Cf. APPAL 2.

1583 STANYHURST *Aeneis* III. (Arb.) 71 My blud with terror apaling. **1598** *Tofte's Alba* Pref. (1880) 11 Like the Fire, whose heat doth soone appale.

3. To lose brightness or briskness; to become flat or stale, as liquor exposed to the air.

1530 [See quot. from PALSGR. under APPAL 3, which is spelt both *appalle* and *appale*.]

4. *trans.* To make pale, to dim. Cf. APPAL 5.

a **1500** *E.E. Misc.* (1859) 28 Now ame I dede, my colour is appalyde. **1541** R. COPLAND *Guydon's Quest. Cyrurg.*, They be applyed..to clense and appale ye lepry. **1686** GOAD *Celest. Bod.* II. ii. 162 The sullen Fog..apaling the brightness.

5. To cause to fade or wane, to weaken, enfeeble. Cf. APPAL 6.

1529 RASTELL *Pastyme* (1811) 114 Revived the fayth of Crist whiche was sore appalid. **1588** CHURCHYARD *Spark Friendsh.* in *Harl. Misc.* (Malh.) II. 116 Any thing..that may impeach hinder or appale the good name and credit of them. **1609** SIR E. HOBY *Let. to T.H.* 7 Whose learning is no whit appayled, nor courage daunted.

6. To make pale with fear, to dismay. Cf. APPAL 8.

1563 *Myrr. Mag.* Induct. xix, Dread and dolour erst did so appale. **1583** STANYHURST *Aeneis* I. (Arb.) 34 No.. trouping horsmen can apale the virago. **1602** SHAKS. *Ham.* II. ii. 590 Make mad the guilty, and apale the free. **1640** FULLER *Abel Rediv.* (1867) I. 157 'Twas not a prison could his heart apale.

†**a'ppalement.** *Obs. rare.* [f. prec. + -MENT. See also APPALMENT.] The action of dismaying; the state of dismay.

1579 FENTON *Guicciard.* XVII. 810 The Pope was growne into a maruellous discourage and appalement of mind. **1622** BACON *Hen. VII*, 35 The furious slaughter of them was a great discouragement and appalement to the rest.

†**a'ppaling,** *vbl. sb. Obs.* [f. as prec. + -ING[1].] The action of overwhelming with consternation or dismay; terrifying, dismaying.

1603 KNOLLES *Hist. Turks* (1638) 16 They raised a great.. outcry, to the great appaling of them that were fighting.

appalled (əˈpɔːld), *ppl. a.* [f. APPAL *v.* + -ED.]

†**1.** Made pale or faint; enfeebled. *Obs.*

1577 *St. Aug. Manuell* 33 To refresh my appalled sprights. **1616** SURFL. & MARKH. *Countr. Farm* 349 To set in strength againe their feebled and appalled force.

†**2.** Rendered flat or stale, as a fermented liquor. *Obs.*, but see PALLED.

1601 HOLLAND *Pliny* XXIII. i, If it be too weake and apalled, the way to revive it againe, is with Pepper. *Ibid.* (1634) I. 425 Wine..will lose the strength, and become apalled in extremitie of cold.

3. Bereft of courage or self-possession at the sudden recognition of something dreadful; dismayed; also *fig.*

1606 SHAKS. *Tr. & Cr.* IV. v. 4 Giue with thy Trumpet a loud note..that the appauled aire May pierce the head of the great Combatant. **1866** KINGSLEY *Herew.* xvii. 208 Hereward sat down, silent and appalled.

appalling (əˈpɔːlɪŋ), *ppl. a.* [f. APPAL *v.* + -ING[2].] **1.** Such as to overwhelm with consternation or dismay; dismaying, shocking.

1817 SHELLEY *Laon & Cythna* I. xi. p. 6 Within the sphere of that appalling fray. **1824** DIBDIN *Libr. Comp.* 592 Hogarth never depicted a more appalling subject. **1836** GEN. P. THOMPSON *Exerc.* (1842) IV. 159 The newspapers have reported two or three 'appalling accidents' already.

2. *colloq.* In weakened sense: distasteful, 'shocking'. Cf. DREADFUL *a.* 3.

1919 *Punch* 7 May 357 What appalling rot! **1935** *Discovery* Aug. 222/2 The work involved is truly appalling.

a'ppallingly, *adv.* [f. prec. + -LY[2].] **1.** In an appalling manner; terrifically, shockingly.

1825 *Examiner* 11 Apr. 235/1 The prisoner was appallingly altered. **1843** F. PAGET *Ward. Berkingh.* 72 Massillon himself has not stated the case more thrillingly and appallingly. **1864** *Realm* 13 Apr. 8 The arithmetical chances of a real accident become appallingly probable.

2. In weakened sense: exceedingly; very. *colloq.*

1937 in Partridge *Dict. Slang.* **1946** R. LEHMANN *Gipsy's Baby* 123 We got appallingly hungry working so late.

appalment (əˈpɔːlmənt). *rare.* [f. APPAL *v.* + -MENT.] The action of overwhelming with dismay; the state of dismay or consternation.

1611 COTGR., *Esbahissement*, a wondering..admiration, appallment, astonishment. **1815** BENTHAM *Springs of Action* Wks. I. 204/3 Transient emotions..2 Terror, 3 Appalment, 4 Consternation.

Appaloosa (æpəˈluːsə). Also (now mostly disused) **Apaloochy, Apalousey, Appaloosie, Appalucy.** [ad. *Opelousa*, place-name in Louisiana, or f. *Palouse* River, Idaho, U.S.A.: see *D.A.*] A breed of horse with white hair and dark patches of colour on the body, much used in former times by Indian tribes of western N. America.

[**1849** in *Amer. Speech* (1944) XIX. 69 Nach diesen kommt das sogenannte Kreolen-pferdchen, auch Opelousas poney genannt, ein ausgezeichnetes Damenpferd.] **1924** DAVIES *Skyline Trail* 49 They find death in a dramatic flare: Trying to ride the apaloochy mare. **1947** DEVOTO *Across Wide Missouri* 77 The Nez Perces had learned selective breeding..and had developed a distinctive stock called the Pelouse horse, the 'Appaloosa' of a later date. **1950** in *Amer. Speech* XXV. 310 By 1890 the name had become Apalousey, but today's accepted spelling is Appaloosa. **1963** *Times* 7 Mar. 6/6 Experts believe the Appaloosa to be the oldest breed of horse in the world... They belong to China.

‖**a'ppalto.** [It., f. *appaltáre* to let or farm out.] A monopoly.

1847 DISRAELI *Tancred* IV. iv. (1871) 272 We might..get an appalto of the silk.

appanage, variant spelling of APANAGE.

†**appa'rage,** *sb. Obs.* [a. OF. *aparage*, f. *aparer*, f. *à*:—L. *ad* to + *par* equal, peer. Cf. mod.F. *parage*.] Noble extraction, nobility, rank, quality.

1503 HAWES *Examp. Virtue* viii. 152 For she is comen of royall apparage. *Ibid.* xiii. 252 A gowne of syluer for grete aparage.

†**a'pparage,** *v. Obs. rare*$^{-1}$. [a. OF. *app-, aparagie-r* to make of equal rank, f. *aparage*; see prec. Cf. *disparage*.] *intr.* To be of equal rank (OF. *s'aparager*).

a **1450** *Knt. de la Tour* (1868) 20 No worldely plesaunce and worshipe may not apparage to goodnesse.

apparail, -ment, obs. form of APPAREL, etc.

†**a'pparament.** *Obs. rare*$^{-1}$. [ad.L. *apparāment-um*, n. of process f. *apparā-re*: see next and -MENT.] Array; military preparation, armament.

1460 CAPGRAVE *Chron.* 298 Alle his apparament with which he thoute to besege Caleys.

†**apparance.** *Obs. rare.* [a. OFr. *aparance*, f. *aparant*:—L. *adparānt-em*, pr. pple. of *ad-, apparā-re* to make ready for: see -ANCE.] Preparation.

1546 LANGLEY *Pol. Virg. De Invent.* II. v. 44 a, The sunne rising is the begynning of al affaires..the night is a time of counselling & apparaunce. **1594** HOOKER *Eccl. Pol.* v. (1793) II. 41 To go about the building of an house to the God of heaven with no other apparance, than if his end were to rear up a kitchen.

apparance, obs. f. APPEARANCE, APPARENCE.

apparancy, -ant, obs. ff. APPARENCY, -ENT.

‖**apparat** (æpəˈrɑːt). [Russ., a. Ger. *apparat* apparatus, instrument, f. L. *apparātus* APPARATUS.] The party machine of the Communist party in Russia, etc. Also *attrib.*

1950 A. KOESTLER *God that Failed* I. i. 46, I found Communist apparat-work much less efficient than its scared opponents presume. **1952** —— *Arrow in Blue* xxviii. 262 This is true not only of members of the 'Apparat' but of militant Communists in general. **1955** H. HODGKINSON *Doubletalk* 14 *Apparat*, the administrative apparatus, usually of State or Party; the 'Party machine'. **1960** *Encounter* Mar. 69/1 The dead-weight of a clumsy bureaucratic *Apparat* having been disposed of, a fresh team of leaders..succeeded in tackling the reconstruction of the intellectual formulation of Social Democratic policy [in E. Germany].

‖**apparatchik** (æpəˈrɑːtʃɪk). Pl. **apparatchiki, apparatchiks.** [Russ.] **1.** A member of the APPARAT; also, a Communist agent or spy.

1941 KOESTLER *Scum of Earth* 122 The dark silhouette of the 'Tchekist, the 'Aparat-chik', or G.P.U. agent had replaced the once bright and lively symbols of the struggle for a happier world. **1950** —— *God that Failed* I. i. 46 A full-fledged 'apparatchik' (the homely euphemism used in the Party for agents and spies). **1957** *Observer* 29 Dec. 6/7 As the year ended, the domination of Khrushchev and the ideologists and *apparachiki* of his machine seemed complete. **1960** *Encounter* Mar. 41/1 The *apparatchiks* of Stalinism. **1963** *Camb. Rev.* 16 Feb. 277/1 The party bureaucrat, or *apparatchik*, is distinguished from the ordinary party member by his professional attachment to the party, for as a rule he devotes himself exclusively to party activity.

2. *transf.* A member of a political party in any country, who is responsible for the execution of policy; a functionary of a public or private organization (in quot. 1969 used *attrib.* of machinery).

1969 *Listener* 10 July 34/3 Thus machine will make machine. These apparatchik units will be able to examine what design characteristics are necessary through the medium of the central mother device. **1973** *Daily Colonist* (Victoria, B.C.) 5 July 5/1 The United States was indeed being pushed in the direction of a police state. The pushers were not mere apparatchiks such as John Dean, but President Nixon and his closest associates. **1976** *New Society* 10 June 562 But the labour intensive character of the Post Office could be reduced with a more zealous drive to mechanize. This would involve big staff cuts and the corporation apparatchiks are in no position to insist on that. **1983** *Observer* 20 Feb. 7 The general secretary of the Labour Party..is a dry man, but not a grey apparatchik with a zeal for office work. **1985** *Sunday Times* 27 Jan. 38/5 The radio programmes were put together in the privacy of his own computer-equipped studio at home, away from the controlling influence of BBC apparatchiks.

†**'apparate.** *Obs. rare.* [ad. L. *apparāt-us* preparation; cf. Fr. *apparat*.] An anglicized form of APPARATUS. (Cf. *state, status*.)

?*c* **1600** *MS. Bodl.* 313 (Halliw.) The whole English apparate, and the English popular calculation tables. **1616** SHELDON *Rom. Miracles* cxiii. 271 Such apparate and order for publike sacrifices.

†**'apparated,** *ppl. a. Obs. rare*$^{-1}$. [f. L. *apparāt-us*, pa. pple. of *apparā-re* (see APPARATUS) + -ED. Of a vb. *apparate* (cf. *separate*), no instances have been found.] Prepared, equipped.

1663 WATERHOUSE *Comm. Fortescue* 528 A well apparated servant to attend them.

†**appa'ration.** *Obs. rare.* [ad. L. *apparātiōn-em*, n. of action f. *apparāre* to make ready: see APPARATUS.] Preparation, array.

1533 BELLENDENE *Livy* v. 414 Maid thare beddis..with maist apparacioun and magnificence that micht be devisit. **1657** TOMLINSON *Renou's Disp.* 561 The apparation of this Medicament.

apparator, -our, obs. forms of APPARITOR.

apparatoryes, prob. pl. of *apparator*; perh. of a synonymous *apparatory*.

a **1528** SKELTON *Image Hypocr.* 87 Deanes and sumners, Apparatoryes preste To ryde est and west.

apparatus (æpəˈreɪtəs). Pl. (rare) **-atus, -atuses.** [a. L. *apparātus*, n. of state f. *apparā-re*, *adparā-re* to make ready for, f. *ad* to + *parā-re* to make ready. Cf. the anglicized APPARATE.]

†**1.** The work of preparing; preparation, preparatory arrangement, array. *Obs.*

1638 *Penit. Conf.* ii. (1657) 10 An apparatus and necessary introduction thereunto. **1684** T. BURNET *Th. Earth* III. 16 How easie had it been for him, without this apparatus, to have told them, etc. **1722** WOLLASTON *Relig. Nat.* v. 112 The apprehension of but a vein to be opend is worse to some, than the apparatus to an execution is to others.

2. The things collectively in which this preparation consists, and by which its processes are maintained; equipments, material, mechanism, machinery; material appendages or arrangements.

a **1628** F. GREVILLE *Sidney* (1652) 15 Where humor takes away this pomp and apparatus from King, Crown, and Scepter. **1767** FORDYCE *Serm. Yng. Wom.* II. viii. 16 The gaudy apparatus of female vanity. **1796** BURKE *Regic. Peace* ii. Wks. VIII. 221 The greatest skill conducting the greatest military apparatus has been employed. **1818** BENTHAM *Ch. of Eng.* Introd. 50 Which of the two apparatus would your Graces..recommend? **1832** HT. MARTINEAU *Irel.* iii. 56 Workhouses, or any part of the apparatus of a legal charity.

3. *esp.* **a.** The mechanical requisites employed in scientific experiments or investigations.

1727–51 CHAMBERS *Cycl.* s.v., The furniture or apparatus of an air-pump, microscope, etc. **1758** *Elaboratory* 34 The apparatus for levigating testaceous, and other hard bodies. **1871** NAPHEYS *Prev. & Cure Dis.* II. iii. 673 The many apparatuses designed to apply electricity.

b. The organs or means by which natural processes are carried on.

1718 J. CHAMBERLAYNE *Relig. Philos.* I. vii. §4 That by all this Apparatus..the Voice might be thereby formed. **1736** BUTLER *Anal.* I. i. 30 The whole apparatus of vision. **1833** CHALMERS *Const. Man* (1835) I. iii. 146 That defensive apparatus wherewith the embryo seed of plants is guarded.

c. Materials for the critical study of a document. In full ***critical apparatus***: = next.

1727–51 CHAMBERS *Cycl.* s.v., Glossaries, comments &c. are also frequently called Apparatus's. **1794** GODWIN *Cal. Williams* 305 The apparatus of my etymological enquiries. **1868** *Jrnl. Philol.* I. No. 2. 66 His collation of the poem, with a description of the MS., a careful apparatus, and an interesting explanatory commentary. **1876** *Hermathena* II. 389 Professor W. Ramsay compiled his text very carefully, with apparently all the requisite data and critical apparatus. **1879** *Q. Rev.* Apr. 334 A thorough examination of the Old Testament by modern critical apparatus of research.

†**d.** 'Sometimes also used in chirurgery for the bandages, medicaments, and dressings of a part; or the several matters applied for the cure of a wound, ulcer, or the like.' Chambers *Cycl.* 1727–51.

1684 tr. *Bonet's Merc. Compit.* VIII. 278, I use all the Apparatus of Medicines to suppress [Hæmorrhage from Hæmorrhoids]. **1727-51** Chambers *Cycl.*, There is no judging of the quality of a hurt, till after taking off the first apparatus or covering.

4. = APPARAT; any (Communist) organization.
1935 tr. in S. & B. Webb *Soviet Communism* I. App. VII. 369 Resolution of the Central Executive Committee..to do away with the shortcomings of organisation in the work and structure of the apparatus of the Narkomsovkhos of the USSR. **1946** *N.Y. Times* 7 July 1/6 For the Soviet government 'apparatus', as the Russians use the word, is a political machine. **1949** *Manch. Guardian Weekly* 7 July 14/4 To get a common friend to join a Communist apparatus. **1950** *Time* 13 Feb. 13/2 He..had turned over the films to the Soviet spy apparatus. **1959** E. H. Carr *Socialism in One Country* II. xix. 199 The rising power of the secretariat led to the emergence of a new and prominent feature in the party and Soviet landscape—the 'apparatus' and the 'apparatus-man', the body of obscure and anonymous officials who were the cogs of the..party machine.

‖**apparatus criticus** (æpəˈreɪtəs ˈkrɪtɪkəs). [mod.L.: see APPARATUS and CRITICAL *a.*] A collection of palæographical and critical matter accompanying an edition of a text.
1865 Conington *Vergili Opera* I. p. x, The publication of Ribbeck's *apparatus criticus* has made a new recension necessary. **1867** *Athenæum* 8 June 758/1 In the notes are found all the various readings of MSS., as given by preceding editors, followed by the testimonies of ancient writers in support of them; the whole forming as complete a *criticus apparatus* as could be desired. **1887** *Classical Rev.* Mar. 17/1 The *apparatus criticus* is still simple and the new editor's personality is rarely obtruded on the reader. **1928** *Observer* 4 Mar. 7/3 The second half of the volume comprises the Geographical Text..with a complete *apparatus criticus*.

apparel (əˈpærəl), *v. arch.* Forms: 3-5 aparaile, 4-6 -ayle, 5 ap- *or* app-araill(e, -eyl(le, -aill(e, -yl, appairelle, 5-6 aparal(l, apparayl(e, -ayll(e, 5-7 -ail(e, -al(l, -ell, 6 aperayle, appareyll, -ayrayl, 6-7 -aral, -arrell, aparel(l, 5- apparel. *Aphet.* 4 parail, -ayl. Also 5 enparel. In inflexions -*l* is at present usually doubled before a vowel in G. Brit., left single in U.S. [a. OFr. *apareille-r*, *aparaille-r* (mod.Fr. *appareiller*), cogn. with Pr. *aparelhar*, Pg. *apparelhar*, Sp. *aparejar*, It. *apparecchiare*:—Romanic *adpariculāre to make equal or fit, f. *ad* to + *paricul-um (It. *parecchio*, Sp. *parejo*, Pr. *parelh*, Fr. *pareil*), dim. of L. *par* equal. The 15th c. spellings were almost endless, the typical being *apaˈrail*, passing with retracted accent to *aˈparel*. For *app-*, see AP- *pref.*¹.] Usually *trans.* or *refl.*

†**1.** *trans.* To make ready, or prepare (*for* a purpose); to fit out, get ready, put into proper order.
c **1250** *Kent. Serm.* in *O.E. Misc.* 26 Hi hedden aparailed here offrendes. *c* **1386** Chaucer *Melib.* ¶375 Ye oughte purveyen yow and apparaile [*v.r.* -aillen, -ayle, -el] yow in this caas with greet diligence. *a* **1450** *Knt. de la Tour* cii. 134 To aparaille mete and drinke for hym. **1541** R. Copland *Guydon's Quest. Cyrurg.*, The hert hath two eares..to let the ayre in and out that is appareylled for it fro yᵉ lunges. **1631** Markham *Way to Wealth* III. II. iv. (1668) 115 Aparel it [the wine] thus: take the whites only of ten Eggs, etc.

†**b.** *intr.* (for *refl.*). *Obs. rare.*
1523 Ld. Berners *Froiss.* I. ix. 8 In the meane tyme the quene aparailed for her needis and besynesse.

†**2.** To make preparations for (an event, work). *Obs.*
c **1314** *Guy Warw.* 22 Therl dede anon aparaile Gyes dobing. *c* **1385** Chaucer *L.G.W.* 2473 There he wolde hire weddynge aparayle [*v.r.* appayille, -eylle, -aille]. **1534** Ld. Berners *Gold. Bk. M. Aurel.* (1546) O iiij b, The Romaynes shulde apparell his triumphe..right glorious and rychly.

3. To furnish, or fit up with things necessary (a room, a ship, etc.). Also *fig. arch.*
1366 Maundev. xx. 217 Alle thinges, that men apparayle with ony Halle. **1480** Caxton *Chron. Eng.* ccxliii. 290 Ryal shippes that were ful wel arayd and enparelled and enarmed. **1502** *Ord. Crysten Men* (W. de W.) II. xvii, Martha was desyrous to lodge our lorde and his appostles, and to aparayle them. **1590** Swinburn *Testaments* 154 The cause wherewith the prohibition is saide to bee apparelled. **1605** Camden *Rem.* 46 The which Chappell..his executors did fully make, and apparail. *a* **1670** Hacket in Wallcot *Life* App. (1865) 159 Honest communication apparelleth the mind with good thoughts. **1863** Longf. *Wayside Inn, Mus. T.* xiv. 9 Never..owned a ship so well apparelled.

†**4.** To prepare, equip, or accoutre for fighting.
c **1325** *Cœur de L.* 4333 Ser Fouke gan hym apparayle With hys folk the toun to assayle. **1375** Barbour *Bruce* IX. 132 The Kingis men..thame apparalit Till defend, gif thai thame assalit. **1470-85** (ed. 1634) Malory *Arthur* (1816) II. 18 They apparalled them to joust Sir Gawaine. **1655** Fuller *Ch. Hist.* IV. 107 Apparelled..with his Bow and Quiver of Arrows. *a* **1672** Wood *Life* (1848) 85, I have apareled my solldiors..upon my creditt to the Marchant.

5. To array with proper clothing; to attire, dress. (Now the ordinary sense, but somewhat *arch.*, and hardly in spoken use.)
1362 Langl. *P. Pl.* A. II. 186 Apparayleden him as a prentis. **1393** —— C. III. 224 And paraileD hym lyke here prentys. **1494** Fabyan VII. ccxxxiii. 267 The Empresse..apparaylyd hyr & hir company in whyte clothynge. **1538** Starkey *England* 130 Be not appayraylyd in sylkys and veluettys. **1610** Healey *St. Aug. City of David* 833 Apparelling him with sot-like habites. **1611** Bible *Luke* vii. 25 They which are gorgeously apparelled. **1774** J. Bryant *Mythol.* II. 124 All the vestments..in which they used to apparel their Deities. **1838** Southey *Charlemain* xii, All apparell'd in costly array, Exulting they come to the palace of Aix.

†**b.** To invest (with an official robe). *Obs. rare.*
1576 Lambarde *Peramb. Kent* (1826) 73 To apparell Canterbury with the Archbishop of Londons Palle.

6. In many *fig.* senses: cf. to *clothe*. *arch.*
c **1374** Chaucer *Boeth.* I. ii. 8 þe fyrste somer sesoun þat ..apparaileþ þe erþe wiþ rosene floures. **1481** Caxton *Myrr.* III. viii. 147 [The sonne] apparaylleth the trees with leues. **1558** Bp. Watson *7 Sacram.* ii. 11 To be appareled and cladde with Christe and his rightwisnes. **1608** Tourneur *Reveng. Trag.* I. i, When thou wert appareld in thy flesh. **1635** A. Stafford *Fem. Glory* (1869) 44 She apparrell'd them [her thoughts] in a cleare, smooth calme of language. **1806** Wordsw. *Ode on Intim. Immort.* 4 When meadow, grove, and stream, To me did seem Apparelled in celestial light.

†**7.** To deck, adorn, embellish. *Obs.* exc. as 6.
1366 Maundev. xiv. 153 Clothes..apparayled with greet Perles. **1388** Wyclif *Luke* xxi. 5 The temple..was apparailid [**1382** ourned, Tindale garnissed, **1611** adorned] with gode stoonus. **1565** Calfhill *Answ. Treat. Crosse* (1846) 122 Ye apparel it with a few pearls of Scripture. **1741** T. Robinson *Gavelkind* ii. 29 To be apparelled with the Title of Gentry.

†**8.** *fig.* To dress up (speciously), to trick out. *Obs.*
1590 Shaks. *Com. Err.* III. ii. 12 Looke sweet, speake faire ..Apparell vice like vertues harbenger. **1615** T. Adams *Spir. Navig.* 55 They apparrell bloud-red murther..in the white robes of religion. **1636** B. Jonson *Discov.* (1692) 696 To apparel a Lye well, to give it a good dressing.

apparel (əˈpærəl), *sb.* Forms: 3-5 aparail, 4-5 ap- *or* app-araill(e, -ayll(e, 4-6 -ail(e, -ayl(e, -ale, -ell, 5 apareylle, -elle, appayraille, 5 apparall, 6 apperell, 5- apparel. *Aphet.* 5 pareylle, 6 -el, 7 parrell. [a. OFr. *aparail*, *apareil* (mod.Fr. *appareil*), f. vb. *apareiller*: see APPAREL *v.*]

†**1.** *abstr.* The work of fitly preparing for anything, preparation, array. *Obs.*
c **1430** Lydg. *Min. Poems* 40 Soone was dihte, Al that wedlok askethe..Al was redy to plesaunt apparailes. **1483** Caxton *Gold. Leg.* 246/4 That yere was halowed..with right grete appareylle of games. **1485** —— *Paris & V.* 14 The grete apparaylle of thys feste.

†**2.** *concr.* Things provided for any purpose, and employed in its performance; material, requisites, apparatus. *Obs.*
1330 R. Brunne *Chron.* 121 þe Londreis herd it telle, & ȝared þam fulle welle, With gode aparaile of alle þat þei mot gete. *c* **1430** Lydg. *Bochas* VII. ix (1554) 174 Rosted her chyld whan vitayle dyd fayle; She had of store, none other apparayle. **1477** Caxton *Dictes* 147 Socrates sayde That women ben thapparaylles to cacche men. **1631** Markham *Way to Wealth* III. II. iv. (1668) 115 Give it [the wine] aparel ..the Aparel is this: Take the yelks of ten Eggs, etc. **1725** tr. *Dupin's Eccl. Hist. 17th C.* I. v. 63 The Apparel of the Mass ..the Habits, the Vessels, and other Ornaments..made use of in the Celebration of it.

†**3.** The furniture and appendages of a house, fortress, gun, etc. *Obs.*
1375 Barbour *Bruce* XI. 118 Apparall of chalmyr and hall. *Ibid.* XVII. 293 Schot and othir apparale. *c* **1420** *Chron. Vilod.* 448 þis chapelle..wᵗ alle þe pareylle þᵗ longede þerto. **1503** *Act 19 Hen. VII*, iv.§3 To forfett the same Crosebowe with all the apparell therto belongyng. **1535** Coverdale *1 Kings* vii. 48 All the apperell [*Wyclif* & **1611** vessels] that belonged vnto the house of the Lorde.

4. The outfit or rigging of a ship. *arch.*
1330 R. Brunne *Chron.* 154 Fiue oþer galeis with alle þer apparaile. **1575-6** *Act 18 Eliz.* ix. §2 The said Shippes or Vessells with all theyr Apparell and Furnyture. **1709** *Lond. Gaz.* mmmmdlxxix/4 The Ship Margaret..her Tackle, Apparel and Furniture. **1819** Wordsw. *Waggoner* II. 161 Back to her place the ship he led; Wheeled her back in full apparel. **1882** *Charter-party*, What she [the vessel] can reasonably stow..over and above her Tackle, Apparel, Provisions, and Furniture.

5. Personal outfit or attire (†**a.** military; **b.** ordinary); clothing generally, raiment, dress. *arch.*
1330 R. Brunne *Chron.* 54 Fourscore armed Knyghtes, in suilk apparaille dight, þat so riche armes was neuer sene with sight. **1362** Langl. *P. Pl.* A. IX. 111 Was no pride on his apparail ne pouert noþer. *c* **1400** *Rom. Rose* 575 Semyde by hir apparayle She was not wont to gret travayle. *c* **1532** Ld. Berners *Huon* 609 One of her apareyles to put on hir. *a* **1547** Surrey *Aeneid* IV. 337 A shining parel..of Tirian purple. **1602** Shaks. *Ham.* I. iii. 72 Costly thy habit..rich, not gawdie: For the Apparell oft proclaimes the man. **1711** Steele *Spect.* No. 302 ¶12 Neglect of Apparel, even among the most intimate Friends, does insensibly lessen their Regards to each other. **1823** Lamb *Elia* II. xix. (1865) 368, I am ill at describing female apparel. **1883** *Newsp. Advt.*, Piece Goods, Apparel, etc. for Sale by Auction.

c. *fig.* 'Attire.' *arch.*
1610 E. Bolton in *Shaks. C. Praise* 91 Style (the apparell of matter). **1683** tr. *Erasm. Moriæ Enc.* 2 Nature forthwith changes her apparrel. **1711** Addison *Spect.* No. 74 ¶2 The rude Stile and evil Apparel of this antiquated Song. **1831** Carlyle *Sart. Res.* III. ix, The Thirty-Nine Articles themselves are articles of wearing-apparel (for the Religious Idea). **1881** N. T. (Revised) *1 Pet.* iii. 4 The incorruptible apparel of a meek and quiet spirit.

†**d.** as hunting term (see quot.). *Obs.*
1575 Turberv. *Venerie* 128 At his sides..a thinne kinde of redde fleshe which hunters call the apparel of an hart.

†**6.** Appearance, aspect. *Obs.*
1377 Langl. *P. Pl.* B. XIII. 278 As in apparaille and in porte proud amonges þe peple. **1481** Caxton *Myrr.* III. iv. 130 How moche the ferther she [the mone] is fro the sonne so moche the more we see of her apparayl. **1526** Tindale *Phil.* ii. 8 Was found in his aparell [Wyclif abite, **1611** fashion] as a man.

†**7.** Ornament, decoration, embellishment. *Obs.*
c **1340** *Gaw. & Gr. Knt.* 601 þe apparayl of þe payttrure ..acorded with þe arsounez. *c* **1350** *Will. Palerne* 3224 þat was perles a-parrayl. *c* **1400** *Rowland & Otuel* 413 Ane helme of riche entayle, Of precyouse stanes the appayrayle.

b. *esp.* Ornamental embroidery on certain ecclesiastical vestments. *revived.*
1485 *Churchw. Acc. St. Mary Hill* (1797) 112 To Thomas Pate browderer—for his workmanship upon it and the appareyle belonging thereto—10*d.* **1844** Pugin *Gloss. Eccl. Orn.* 5 The Albe..should be made..with apparells.. worked in silk and gold, embroidered with ornaments. **1849** Rock *Ch. of Fathers* I. v. 438 Apparels were..stitched on to the upper part of the amice, like a collar to it.

apparelled, -eled (əˈpærəld), *ppl. a.* [f. APPAREL *v.* + -ED.] Prepared, made ready, furnished (*obs.*); equipped, rigged; clothed, attired, dressed; decked, adorned; *spec.* embroidered (as ecclesiastical vestments).
1483 Caxton *Cato* F ij b, Paradyse whyche is euer apparaylled and redy for to receyue them that haue been stronge and vertuous in this worlde. **1598** Barret *Theor. Warres* II. i. 21 To go well apparelled and well armed. **1823** Lamb *Elia* I. viii. (1865) 67 In the goodly ornature of well-apparelled speech. **1849** Rock *Ch. of Fathers* I. v. 434 An appareled alb of linen.

apparelling, -eling (əˈpærəlɪŋ), *vbl. sb.* [f. APPAREL *v.* + -ING¹.]

1. The process of making ready or preparing, preparation (*obs.*); attiring, dressing, or adorning.
c **1315** Shoreham 53 An apparyllynge, Thet hys in holy cherche y-cleped wel The furste scherynge Of clerke. *c* **1386** Chaucer *Melib.* ¶376 The longe appareiling biforn the bataille maketh short victorie. **1540** J. Heywood *Four P's* in Hazl. *Dodsl.* I. 350 What causeth this: That women after their arising, Be so long in their apparelling? *a* **1649** Drumm. of Hawth. *Wks.* 161 The apparelling of truth.

2. *concr.* Dress, attire; rigging, equipment.
1567 Maplet *Gr. Forest* 27 The sadde blew coloured flower, as is Calcedonie, hath bene taken of some for black, onely for their most like kinde of appareiling. **1795** *Edinb. Advt.* 6 Jan 15/3 For sale: The Brigantine..with her float boats and appareling. **1858** De Quincey *Autobiog. Sk.* Wks. II. 53 Transformation; or, if we prefer a Grecian to a Roman apparelling..metamorphosis.

apparelment (əˈpærəlmənt). *rare.* [a. OFr. *apareillement*, n. of process f. *apareiller* to prepare: see APPAREL *v.* and -MENT.]

†**1.** The action of making ready, preparation. (Misunderstood by Cowel, Blount, etc.) *Obs.*
[**1378** *Act 2 Rich. II*, I. vi, Et les tiegnent longement a tiel force y feisantz mou des maners dappa[r]illementz de guerre. *transl.* And hold the same long with such Force, doing many Manner Apparelments of War.] **1607** Cowel *Interpr.* (1672) *Apparlement*, cometh of the French *Pareilment*, that is, *Similiter*..It signifies a resemblance or likelihood, as Apparlement of War, 2 R. 2 Stat. I. cap. 6.

2. *concr.* Equipment, outfit, array, garb, apparel.
c **1325** *E.E. Allit. P.* A. 1051 With alle þe apparaylmente vmbe pyȝte. *c* **1374** Chaucer *Boeth.* II. v. 49 Apparailled wiþ straunge apparaillementz. *c* **1440** *Morte Arth.* (Roxb.) 65 A full riche aparaylmente Off samytte grene. **1866** Conington *Æneid* x. 332 Mincius, whom Benacus breeds, In grey apparailment of reeds [*Velatus arundine glauca*].

†**aˈpparement.** *Obs. rare.* [a. OFr. *aparement*, f. *apare-r*:—L. *apparā-re* to prepare for, equip: Cf. APPARAMENT.] Equipment, outfit.
c **1325** *E.E. Allit. P.* B. 1270 Alle þe apparement þat pented to þe kyrke. *c* **1340** *Sir Gawayne* 106 (Halliw.) Pride with apparementis.

†**apparence, -ance.** *Obs.* Also aparence, -ance, -aunce. [a. OFr. *aparence*, *-ance*. The earlier form of the sb. answering to adj. *apparent*, which was subseq. refashioned as APPEARANCE, by assimilation to the vb. *appear*. *Apparence* survived, esp. in senses which connected it more closely with *apparent* than *appear*, till *c* 1686: cf. next.]

1. = APPEARANCE (which see for other quotations) in all its senses.
c **1384** Chaucer *H. of Fame* 265 Allis what harme doth apparence Whan hit is fals in existence. **1686** Goad *Celest. Bod.* I. iv. 11 Some Excess..but whether..as to Wind, or Drought, or Wet, they [comets] do not determine; that Determination belongeth to no one Apparence.

2. The position of being heir apparent; apparency.
c **1375** Wyclif *Serm.* cxxi. Wks. 1869 I. 402 ȝif a man be eire of þe blisse of hevene..apparaunce of þis heritage is more licli to trewe men. **1628** Coke *On Litt.* 35 b, It is in respect of the constant and perpetuall apparance that the son and heire apparent may endow his wife of his father's Land.

apparency (əˈpɛərənsɪ, əˈpær-). *arch.* or *Obs.* Also 5 apparancie, 6-7 -cy. [ad. L. *appārentia*, abst. n. f. *appārent-em*: see APPARENT and -ANCY, -ENCY. Cf. *transparency*. Strictly, it seems to have been at first formed on ME. *apparance*,

-*aunt* (see prec. and next) with the -*ie*, -*y* repr. L. -*ia*.]

†**1.** The quality, state, or fact of appearing or seeming; seemingness, semblance, appearance. *Obs.*

1393 GOWER *Conf.* I. 63 This double ypocrisie With his devoute apparancie A viser set upon his face. 1597 DANIEL *Civ. Wars* VII. lxi, Both sides did labour..to crown Their cause with the apparency of might. 1657 G. STARKEY *Helmont's Vind.* 8 Who not comparable to him in reality, would yet seem to excell him in apparency. 1684 tr. *Bonet's Merc. Compit.* XVIII. 644 Apparencies, which have informed me when the patient has been any way irregular.

2. The quality of being apparent to the senses; visibility, apparentness. *rare.*

1668 CULPEPPER & COLE *Barthol. Anat.* I. ix. 315 *Saphœda* (so cal'd because of its apparency more than other foot-Veins). 1810 COLERIDGE *Friend* (1818) III. 90 The non-apparency of either..being accounted for by the disproportion of our senses.

3. The quality of being apparent or evident to the mind; show of reason; apparentness.

1604 E. G. *D'Acosta's Hist. Ind.* I. xi. 36 Some..strive to proove, that the new-found world was knowne to the Ancients. And..wee cannot deny, but that there was some apparency. 1626 T. H. *Caussin's Holy Crt.* 123 Yet would you, that God should fauour your infidelity by extraordinary wayes. What apparancy is there for this?

4. The position of being heir apparent.

1741 T. ROBINSON *Gavelkind* II. ii. 183 Tho' he is Heir apparent at that Time, yet there is not that constant and perpetual Apparency. 1815 *Encycl. Brit.* XI. 655/2 The bare right of apparency founds the action against the life-renter.

apparent (ə'pɛərənt, ə'pær-), *a.* and *sb.* Forms: 4 **aparant**, 5–6 **apparaunt(e**, 5–7 **-ant(e**, (7 **appearant**), 5– **apparent**. *Aphet.* 5–6 **parent**. [a. OFr. *aparant*, *-ent*:—L. *appārēnt-em* (after which it has been subseq. refashioned), pr. pple. of *appārē-re* to come in sight: see APPEAR, and -ANT, -ENT. Apt to be confused with *aperand*, the north. pr. pple. of *apere*, APPEAR (see -AND¹), whence the mixed form *appearant*.]

A. *adj.* **1.** Meeting the eyes, showing itself; open to sight, visible, plainly seen. *arch.*

1393 GOWER *Conf.* III. 269 This merveile, which they sigh So apparaunt to-fore her eye. 1481 CAXTON *Myrr.* II. xxxi. 125 By cause that it [the mone] is next to therthe it semeth grettest and most apparaunt of alle the other [planetes]. *a* 1520 *Myrr. Our Ladye* 53 Whiche they dyd nat to the apparaunte syght of the worlde, but secretly. 1613 WITHERS *Abuses Stript* I. vii. (*Juvenil.* 1633) 51 An Owl-eyed buzzard that by day is blinde, And sees not things apparant. 1637 GILLESPIE *Eng.-Pop. Cerem.* III. ix. 199 Flee..from appearant destruction. *a* 1725 POPE *Odyss.* vi. 392 This heard Minerva, but forbore to fly (By Neptune awed) apparent from the sky. 1873 BLACK *Pr. Thule* xxv. 418 With a very apparent and hearty gratitude in his face.

†**2.** Conspicuous, prominent. *Obs.*

1541 R. COPLAND *Guydon's Quest. Cyrurg.*, The synewy cordes be made bare of the flesshe and apparentes. 1594 T. B. *La Primaud. Fr. Acad.* II. 129 That place is very fitte.. being high, eminent, and apparant. 1603 KNOLLES *Hist. Turkes* (1621) 830 In a place more apparant than the rest, sitting in great majestie.

3. Manifest to the understanding; evident, plain, clear, obvious; palpable.

c 1400 *Rom. Rose* 5 Some swevene..Which hardely that false ne ben, But afterward ben apparaunte. 1599 *Warn. Faire Wom.* II. 1569 Ile cleere my conscience And make the truth apparent to the world. 1618 DONNE *Serm.* cxliii. V. 556 The Broadest and apparantest outward Seal by which he testifies his love to Man. 1645 [See 6]. 1779 JOHNSON *L.P.*, *Gay* Wks. III. 214 The mind is repelled by useless and apparent falsehood. 1806 A. KNOX *Rem.* I. 24 The spirituality of our Lord's meaning..may be made more apparent.

4. In ***heir apparent*** (and its imitations): Manifest, evident, obvious; applied to one who will undoubtedly inherit, if he survive the present possessor, as opposed to an heir *presumptive*, who though at present the nearest in succession, is liable to have his hope intercepted by the birth of a nearer heir.

c 1375 WYCLIF *Wks.* 1869 I. 402 ȝif a man were ayre aparant of Englond. [1375 BARBOUR *Bruce* IV. 71 His son.. The eldest and apperande air. *c* 1475 *Rauf Coil.* 935 Scho is appeirand air To twa Douchereis.] 1490 CAXTON *Eneydos* xxix. 113 The mooste parent heyre of the lynage. 1574 tr. *Littleton's Tenures* 122 b, If tenant in the taile enfeoffe his heyre apparante. 1645 HOWELL *Lett.* vi. 21 The Heir apparant of the Crown of France. 1711 ADDISON *Spect.* No. 287 ¶6 Hopeful Heirs apparent to great Empires. 1841 MIALL *Nonconf.* I. 248 What will the premier apparent do when he comes into power?

†**5.** Likely so far as appearances go. *Obs.*

1523 LD. BERNERS *Froiss.* I. cclviii. 383 They knewe of no maner apparant reskewe comyng to them warde. 1524 WOLSEY in *State Papers* (1836) IV. 197 The high benefites ..apparant to ensue unto theym. 1594 SHAKS. *Rich. III*, II. ii. 130 As well the feare of harme, as harme apparant..ought to be preuented. 1654 FULLER *2 Serm.* 40 Utterly unable without his apparent ruine, to contest with the fore-said Duke. 1754 H. WALPOLE *Lett. H. Mann* 252 III. 61 The three apparent candidates are Fox, Pitt and Murray.

6. Appearing to the senses or mind, as distinct from (though not necessarily opposed to) what really *is*; seeming. Contrasted with *real*. (The commonest sense now, but treated as novel in 1645.)

1645 J. G[OODWIN] *Innoc. Tri.* 27 Not an *apparant*, but an *apparent* Schisme..for there is no realitie or truth, but onely an appearance or shew of a schisme. 1781 GIBBON *Decl. & F.* III. 57 His real merit, and apparent fidelity, had gained the confidence both of the prince and people. 1785 REID *Intell. Powers* 265 What Berkeley calls visible magnitude, was by Astronomers called apparent magnitude. 1831 BREWSTER *Optics* iii. 21 The difference between the real and apparent place of any point of an object. 1868 FREEMAN *Norm. Conq.* II. App. 618 The great apparent discrepancy between the two Chroniclers is merely apparent.

†**7.** quasi-*adv.* Evidently, manifestly. *Obs. rare.*

1565 JEWEL *Repl. Harding* 125 He auoucheth that thing for true, that the simplest..knoweth to be apparant false.

8. *Comb.* **apparent magnitude** [MAGNITUDE 3], the magnitude of a celestial body classified according to its apparent brightness, opp. *absolute magnitude*; **apparent (solar) time**: see quot. 1940.

1875 *Encycl. Brit.* II. 822/1 The gathering of stars of the leading orders of **apparent* magnitude in the galactic zone shows that stars of many orders of *real* size and brightness are there gathered together. 1902 [see *absolute magnitude*]. 1940 *Chambers's Techn. Dict.* 522/1 *Apparent magnitude* is the measure of the brightness on Pogson's logarithmic scale, in which each step of one whole magnitude represents a light ratio of 2·512, and this increases numerically with decreasing brightness. 1694 J. SMITH *Horolog. Disquisitions* 30 Now the Clock being still naturally inclined to lose, I therefore..set him again..so he is again too fast for the sun 3' 45" (which is the most I suffer him to differ from the *apparent Time). 1706, 1764, 1834 [see TIME *sb.* 27]. 1922 H. SPENCER JONES *Gen. Astr.* 48 If the sun is used as a reference body the time so determined is called apparent solar time. 1940 *Chambers's Techn. Dict.* 45/1 *Apparent solar time*, the hour angle, at any moment, of the *true*, or *apparent*, *sun* as distinguished from the *mean sun*... Sundials read apparent solar time. 1942 F. DEBENHAM *Astrographics* (ed. 2) 20 The shadow of the real sun will only give us the irregular real sun time (called *Apparent Time*), so we have to add or subtract the Equation of Time to get Mean Time.

†**B.** *sb.* [by ellipsis.] An heir-apparent. Also *fig.*

1393 GOWER *Conf.* I. 216 He that tho was apparant Upon the regne expectant. 1593 SHAKS. *3 Hen. VI*, II. ii. 64 Draw thy Sword in right..*Prince*, Ile draw it as Apparant to the Crowne. 1611 —— *Wint. T.* I. ii. 178 Next to thy selfe, and my young Rouer, he's Apparant to my heart. 1646 Row *Hist. Kirk* (1842) 389 My Lord of Lorn (appearand of Argyle).

†**a'pparent**, *v. Obs. rare.* [f. prec. adj.] To make apparent or manifest.

1577 HOLINSHED *Chron.* II. 36/2 It hath beene manifestlie apparented. 1602 FULBECKE *1st Pt. Parall.* 73 The qualitie of euery thing should be apparanted by termes of efficacie.

apparentation (apɛərən'teɪʃən, əpær-). [f. APPARENT(ED *ppl. a.* + -ATION; cf. F. *apparentage* alliance, connexion (by marriage).] The relation between an earlier society and a later one that is apparented to it.

1934 A. J. TOYNBEE *Study of Hist.* I. I. iv. 44 The 'affiliations' and 'apparentations' between one society and another resemble the relations between parent and child. 1939 *Ibid.* IV. 79 The society that passes away through incorporation into another society, and not through apparentation and dissolution, preserves..some continuity in its material fabric. 1946 R. G. COLLINGWOOD *Idea of Hist.* IV. i. 160 One of these categories is *affiliation* and its correlative *apparentation*.

apparented (ə'pɛərəntɪd), *ppl. a.* [ad. F. *apparenté* related, akin.] Of societies: related, as an earlier society to a later one that is derived from it.

1934 A. J. TOYNBEE *Study of Hist.* I. I. i. 52 Unidentified societies which may be 'apparented' or otherwise related to any of the societies which..our operations have brought to light. 1952 E. HYAMS *Soil & Civilization* pl. 111 (*caption*), Potato and maize, on the basis of which Incarial and apparented civilizations were built, are frequent ceramic motifs.

a'pparently, *adv.* [f. APPARENT *a.* + -LY².]

†**1.** Evidently or manifestly to the sight; visibly, openly. *Obs.*

a 1400 *Chester Pl.* I. 1 Pagentes set fourth apparently to all eyne. 1567 MAPLET *Gr. Forest* 16 In this stone is apparantly seene verie often the verie forme of a Tode. 1651 HOBBES *Govt. & Soc.* xvi. §11. 273 The Prophets..who saw not God apparently like unto Moyses.

2. Evidently or manifestly to the understanding; clearly, plainly.

1553 J. HEYWOOD *Play of Wether*, Our dedes declare us apparauntly. 1644 QUARLES *Boanerges & Barn.* (1881) 93 When thou knowest not apparently, judge charitably. 1770 *Junius Lett.* Pref. 21 Cutting off ears and noses..penalties so apparently shocking to humanity. 1853 H. ROGERS *Ecl. Faith* 138 The malady, which is but too apparent, is also as apparently without a remedy.

3. To external appearance; seemingly. (Distinguished from, though not necessarily opposed to, *really*.)

1566 KNOX *Hist. Ref.* Wks. 1846 I. 49 The Bischoppis.. hes had heirtofoir sick authoritie upoun thy subjectis, that appearandly thei war rather King, and thow the subject. 1646 Row *Hist. Kirk* (1842) Introd. 25, I left him appirandlie in a better case then I fand him. 1794 S. WILLIAMS *Hist. Vermont* 126 They found many frogs apparently inactive. 1871 TYNDALL *Fragm. Sc.* I. xxi. 493 A cannon-ball..would have its flight apparently arrested.

4. So far as it appears from the evidence; so far as one can judge; seemingly.

1846 J. RYLAND in *Foster's Life* (1846) II. 107 It has been remarked, and apparently with truth. 1877 LYTTEIL *Landm.* II. ii. 57 This early ecclesiastic has a church in Kintyre, and another apparently in Glen Sannocs, Arran.

a'pparentness. *rare.* [f. as prec. + -NESS.] The quality of being apparent or evident; obviousness.

1583 GOLDING *Calv. on Deut.* clxxxv. 1151 The apparantnes..was so great, that it needed not any great reason to conceive it. 1611 COTGR., *Eminence*, eminencie, excellencie, apparantnesse. 1731 BAILEY, *Apparentness*, plainness to be seen. [In mod. Dicts.]

†**a'ppariate**, *v. Obs. rare*⁻¹. [f. after F. *apparier*, with ending -ATE, as if f. L. **appariāre*, *-ātum* (Du Cange has med.L. *appariātio*), f. *ad* to + *par* equal.] To make equal, to match.

1652 URQUHART *Jewel* Wks. 198 To appariate the words of the universal language with the things of the universe.

†**a'pparish**, *v. Obs. rare.* [f. OFr. *apariss-* lengthened stem of *aparir* to appear: see next. *Apariss-* was a by-form of *aparaiss-*:—L. *appārēscĕre*, inceptive of *appārēre* to appear. Cf. *ēvānēscĕre*, *evaniss-*, *evanish*.] To appear.

1483 CAXTON *Gold. Leg.* 420/3 After..hir marterdom She apparysshed before Saynt Sebastyen.

†**a'pparissaunt, -yssaunt**, *ppl. a. Obs.* [a. OFr. *aparissant*, pr. pple. of *aparir*, by-form of *apareir*, *-oir*:—L. *appārēre* to APPEAR. OF. *aparir*, *apariss-* were assimilated to the L. type *-ire*, *-īscĕre*, while the normal *apareir*, *apareiss-* were:—L. *appārēre*, *appārēsc-ĕre*. Strictly *apparyshande* is northern pr. pple. of prec. vb. See -AND¹.] Appearing, apparent; evident.

1485 CAXTON *Chas. Gt.* 29 Of body he was moche ample & boystous of stature well apparysaunt. *c* 1490 —— *Bk. Divers Matters* (Halliw.) The moost fayrest and apparysshande comelynesse.

apparition (æpə'rɪʃən), *sb.* [a. Fr. *apparition* (15th c. in Litt.), ad. L. *appāritiōn-em*, n. of action f. *appārē-re* to APPEAR: see -TION. The senses are those of late L. and Fr. Cl. L. had only the sense 'attendance, service, servants,' f. a special sense of *appārēre* 'to appear at a summons, wait upon, attend': see APPARITOR, APARAUNT. (Etymologically, exactly = APPEARANCE, and having a parallel development of senses. But now almost restricted in common use to sense 9, and when used in other senses, having generally from this association some idea of *startling* or *unexpected* appearance.)]

1. The action of appearing or becoming visible. **a.** The supernatural appearance of invisible beings, etc.

c 1525–30 MORE *De Quat. Noviss.* Wks. 1557, 77/2 The apparicion of a very ghost. 1650 FULLER *Pisgah Sight* II. ix. 194 The first apparition God made to Abraham. 1703 MAUNDRELL *Journ. Jerus.* (1732) 105 That Apparition of the two Angels to the Apostles. 1725 tr. *Dupin's Eccl. Hist. 17th C.* I. v. 49 The History of many Apparitions of the Cross. 1814 SCOTT *Wav.* xiii. 56 Presbyterian divines put to the rout by a sudden apparition of the foul fiend.

b. Of a visitor; of a person, a comet, etc.

1652 GAULE *Magastrom.* 18 The apparition of this starre in Bethlehem. 1794 GODWIN *Cal. Williams* 2, I..contrived to satisfy my love of praise with an unfrequent apparition at their amusements. 1867 F. PARKMAN *Jesuits N. Amer.* v. (1875) 45 Amazed at the apparition of the white stranger.

c. Appearance in history or before the world.

1860 FARRAR *Orig. Lang.* x. 216 The apparition of the main races of humanity. 1865 M. ARNOLD *Ess. Crit.* 43 Jealous of the apparition of a new public body in the State.

2. *Astr.* The first appearance of a star or other celestial body after disappearance or occultation.

1556 RECORDE *Cast. Knowl.* 196 That owghte not to bee called proprelye rysynge of any Starre when it getteth oute of the Sonne beames, and maye shewe or shine..but it oughte rather to be called Apparition or appearynge. 1660 STANLEY *Hist. Philos.* 330/1 The apparition of the Dog-star is its rising together with the Sun. 1751 CHAMBERS *Cycl.*, *Apparition*, in astronomy..stands opposed to occultation. 1859 SIR J. HERSCHEL *Astron.* §567 (ed. 5) The intervals of these successive apparitions being 75 and 76 years.

†**3.** The manifestation of Christ; the Epiphany; the festival or season commemorating it. (*Apparitio* = *Epiphania* in Du Cange.) *Obs.*

1652 SPARKE *Prim. Devot.* (1663) 142 Epiphania..the day of Apparition or manifestation of Christ from above. 1681 WHARTON *Fasts & Fest.* Wks. 1683, 23 The Epiphany, or Apparition, or the Feast of Twelfthday after Christmass. 1703 MAUNDRELL *Journ. Jerus.* (1721) 72 The Chappel of the Apparition.

†**4.** Manifestation, demonstration, display.

1533 BELLENDENE *Livy* IV. (1822) 312 Commandit ane army to be rasit with na les apparicioun and magnificence than it wes afore. 1590 GREENE *Neuer too late* (1600) 11 No vaine-glorious shewes Of royall apparition for the eye. 1627 F. E. *Edw. II* (1680) 5 The melancholy apparitions of their parting.

5. *Astr.* The state or condition of being manifest to sight, or of being visible; *esp.* the visibility of a star, planet, or comet.

1601 HOLLAND *Pliny* (1634) I. 9 The Moone..shines the first day of her apparition, ¾ parts, and the foure and twentieth part of an hour. 1635 SWAN *Spec. Mundi* v. §2 (1643) 129 The Rain-bow is..the apparition of certain colours. **1666** *Phil. Trans.* I. 301 Representations of its Head and Train in each day of its apparition. **1833** SIR J. HERSCHEL *Astron.* i. 61 The circle of perpetual apparition, between which and the elevated pole the stars never set.

†**6.** A seeming to the eyes or mind, appearance, semblance. *Obs.*

1613 SHERLEY *Trav. Persia* 27 [Great] distinction between the effects of the world, and the workings of God.. permanency in the last, and no more but apparition in the other. **1650** WELDON *Court K. James* 41 There was an apparition of Southamptons being a Favourite to his Majesty. **1667** MILTON *P.L.* VIII. 293 A dream, Whose inward apparition gently moved My fancy.

†**7.** The form in which anything appears; aspect. *Obs.*

1610 GWILLIM *Heraldry* III. iii. (1660) 110 According to the divers apparitions of the Moon, hath she her divers denominations in Heraldry. **1632** BROME *North. Lasse* I. iv, A Devil in a most Gentlewoman-like apparition. **1660** BOYLE *New Exp. Phys.-Mech.* xxxvii. 307 By their whiteishness, to emulate in some measure the apparition of Light.

8. That which appears; an appearance, especially of a remarkable or unexpected kind; a phenomenon.

1481 CAXTON *Myrr.* III. ix. 151 Tholomeus, whiche knewe so many demonstraunces of apparicions and so moche loued astronomye. **1587** FLEMING *Contn. Holinshed* III. 356/2 To looke for some strange apparition or vision in the aire. **1667** MILTON *P.L.* XI. 211 The heavenly bands..on a hill made halt, A glorious apparition. **1776** GIBBON *Decl. & F.* I. xxi. 593 So strange an apparition excited his surprise and indignation. **1865** LIVINGSTONE *Zambesi* iii. 79 The steamer was such a terrible apparition to them.

9. *spec.* An immaterial appearance as of a real being; a spectre, phantom, or ghost. (The ordinary current sense.)

1601 SHAKS. *Jul. C.* IV. iii. 277, I thinke it is the weakenesse of mine eyes That shapes this monstrous Apparition. **1685** LUTTRELL *Brief Rel.* I. 338 A common report..of some apparition that walks at Whitehall. **1742** YOUNG *Nt. Th.* I. 120 The land of apparitions, empty shades! **1820** W. IRVING *Sketch Bk.* II. 348 The dominant spirit..is the apparition of a figure on horseback without a head.

b. *transf.* or *fig.*

a **1845** HOOD *Wint. Nosegay* ii, The very apparition of a plant. **1848** H. MILLER *First Impress.* xi. (1857) 178 The apparition of vanished states of things.

†**10.** A deceptive appearance counterfeiting reality; an illusion, a sham. *Obs.*

1610 HEALEY *St. Aug., City of God* 662 That which man can doe with true coullours, the Divell can do with apparitions. **1679** PENN *Addr. Prot.* Pref., Without which Religion is a Cypher..an Apparition at most: No solid or valid thing.

apparition, *v.* *rare*$^{-1}$.

1876 MRS. WHITNEY *Sights & Ins.* II. xvii. 468 Flowers that apparition themselves out of the unseen.

apparitional (æpəˈrɪʃənəl), *a.* [f. prec. + -AL[1].]

1. Of, or of the nature of, a phantom; spectral, immaterial, subjective.

1824 GALT *Rothelan* III. 173 Such apparitional coincidences are..not uncommon. **1866** LIDDON *Bampt. Lect.* i. (1875) 25 That Christ's body was real, not apparitional.

2. Belonging to the sphere of mere appearances or phenomena.

1899 A. C. LYALL *Asiatic Studies* Ser. II. 89 The Hindu in his conviction of the illusory nature of all phenomena..will not contest the authenticity, in an..apparitional sense, of historic religions.

apparitor (əˈpærɪtə(r)). Also 6-8 **appar(r)iter**, **-our**, **appar(r)ator**, **-our**, etc. See also aphet. PARITOR. [a. L. *appāritor* (Fr. *appariteur*) an attendant, public servant, lictor, n. of agent f. *appārēre*, in spec. sense 'to appear as an attendant, wait upon': see APPEAR.]

1. The servant or attendant of an officer or authority. **a.** *Rom. Ant.* A general name for the public servants of the Roman magistrates.

1533 BELLENDENE *Livy* II. (1822) 192 The consul..mon obey to all empire and change of tribunis, as he war bot ane serjand and apparatoure thareto. **1741** MIDDLETON *Cicero* I. iii. 155 Lictors, and Apparitors. **1781** GIBBON *Decl. & F.* II. 36 Six hundred apparitors, who would be styled at present either secretaries, or clerks, or ushers, or messengers. **1853** KINGSLEY *Hypatia* xvi, The apparitors of Orestes, who followed in his robes of office.

b. An officer of a civil court.

1593 NASHE *4 Lett. Confut.* 17, I sawe him make an Apparriter..eate his Citation waxe and all. **1671** F. PHILIPPS *Reg. Necess.* 174 Sheriffs Apparitors or their Bayliffs. **1771** FRANKLIN *Autobiog.* Wks. 1840 I. 7 One of the children stood at the door to give notice if he saw the apparitor coming. **1824-9** LANDOR *Imag. Conv.* II. 6 The judges will hear reason, when the wand of the Apparitor is tipped with gold.

c. An officer of an ecclesiastical court.

1528 TINDALE *Obed. Chr. Man* Wks. I. 238 The commissaries, and officials, with their somners and apparitors. **1641** MILTON *Animadv.* (1851) 230 With all the hell pestering rabble of Sumners and Apparitors. **1856** J. H. NEWMAN *Callista* 108 Seized by the apparitor, and hurried to the rack. **1875** FARRAR *Christ* II. lix. 344 The apparitors of the Jewish court.

d. '*Apparitor*, or *Apparitour*, or *Apparator*, a beadle in an university, who carries the mace before the masters, and the faculties.' Chambers *Cycl.* 1727. Also applied to other similar functionaries.

2. *gen.* A herald, pursuivant, usher. *lit.* and *fig.*

1561 T. N[ORTON] *Calvin's Inst.* II. 133 He [John the Baptist] onely executeth the office of an apparitor. **1582** T. BENTLEY *Mon. Matrons* III. 328 Yee holie spirits, the apparitors of the Lords Maiestie. **1625** PURCHAS *Pilgrims* II. 1268 Jubilees, whereof Crusado's were Forerunners and Apparitors. **1650** USSHER *Annals* VI. (1658) 614 But suspected all apparitours, cryers, praisers, and friends.

3. One who appears, an appearer. *rare.*

1843 CARLYLE *Past & Pr.* (1858) 211 The Higher Court.. in which..every Human Soul is an apparitor.

†**a'ppart**, *v.* *Obs. rare*$^{-1}$. [app. f. PART *v.* in imitation of *apportion*.] To portion out, assign.

1798 Root's *Law Rep.* I. 69 She has right to have apparted and set out to her, seven acres.

appase, obs. form of APACE.

†**a'ppassionate**, *ppl. a.* *Obs.* [ad. It. *appassionato* (cogn. w. OFr. *apassionné*, Sp. *apasionado*).] Influenced by passion of any kind, impassioned.

1580 SIDNEY *Arcad.* (1622) 477 The strangers vehement speech, or rather appassionate exclayming. **1609** DOULAND *Ornith. Microl.* 38 Musicke..reformeth appassionate minds.

†**a'ppassionate**, *v.* *Obs.* [see prec.] To rouse to passion; to impassion.

1589 PUTTENHAM *Eng. Poesie* (Arb.) 166 By your Hyperbole..seeking to inueigle and appassionate the minde. **1611** FLORIO, *Ammartellare*, to appassionat with ielousie or doubt till ones heart pant..*Appassionare*, to appassionate.

†**a'ppassionated**, *ppl. a.* *Obs.* [f. prec. + -ED.] = APPASSIONATE *a.*

1580 SIDNEY *Arcad.* (1622) 211 The seuen appassionated shepheards. **1631** *Celestina* x. 117 The appassionated begge remedy, the wounded craue healing.

†**a'ppast.** *Obs.* [a. Fr. *appast* (mod. *appât*) food, bait, f. *à* to + *past*:—L. *pāstus* food, f. *pāscĕre* to feed.] Food, bait.

1580 SIDNEY, etc. *Ps.* cxlviii, You vapors, sunnes appast. **1611** COTGR., *Appast*, An appast, a bait..also, a repast, or meale. **1633** H. COGAN *Pinto's Trav.* xxi. 74 Hungry Lizards ..allured by the appast of those formerly thrown overboard.

appatriation (æˌpeɪtrɪˈeɪʃən). *rare.* [n. of action f. L. *ad* to + *patria* native country: see -TION. Cf. *expatriation*, *affiliation*.] Assignment to a native country; attribution of national origin.

1857 L. HUNT in *Athenæum* 7 July 1883, 16/2 The Portuguese sonnets, the appatriation of which (what is the proper word?) I always grudged them.

‖**appaumé** (a'pome), *ppl. a.* *Her.* [Fr., f. *à* to + *paume*:—L. *palma*.] Having the hand opened out so as to display the palm.

1864 BOUTELL *Hist. Heraldry* xiii. 94 A sinister hand, couped at the wrist and appaumée.

appay, late sp. of APAY *v.*, to please, satisfy.

†**a'ppeach**, *v.* *Obs.* Forms: 4-6 **apeche**, 5-6 **appech(e**, **-eache**, 6 **apeach(e**, 5-7 **appeach**. See also aphet. PEACH. [Represents an earlier **anpeche* (see A- *pref.* 10, AN- *pref.* 4), Eng. or AFr. form of *enpeche-r*, OF. *empechier*, *empeechier*, cogn. with Pr. *empedegar*:—L. *impedicā-re* to catch by the feet, entangle, f. *im* in + *pedica* a chain or gin for the feet, a fetter, f. *ped-em* foot. *An-peche*, after phonetic reduction to *a-peche*, was popularly aphetized in 15th c. to *peche*, now PEACH *v.*; but also, in same century, erroneously refashioned as *ap-peche* (after words from OF. in *a-* = L. *ad-*: see AP- *pref.*[1]), which in the reformed spelling of *c* 1525 was written *appeach*. Meanwhile Caxton had reintroduced *enpeche*, *empeche* from contemporary Fr. *empescher*; which, latinized and respelt as IMPEACH, has since displaced *appeach*, and is the extant word.]

1. To hinder, impede, delay. (Fr. *empêcher*.)

c **1460** *Towneley Myst.* 10 How long wilt thou me appech With thy sermonyng. *Ibid.* 168 My fader lyst may none appeche.

2. To charge with crime, accuse, inform against, impeach (a person).

1401 *Pol. Poems* II. 46 Thou spekist proudely, apechyng oure prestes. **1580** BARET *Alv.* A 464 To appeach or bewray his felowes, *Conscios prodere.* **1593** SHAKS. *Rich. II*, V. ii. 79 Now by mine honor..I will appeach the Villaine. **1650** S. CLARKE *Eccl. Hist.* (1654) I. 18 Other men which are appeached..are not condemned till they are first convicted.

b. Const., *of* or *for* the offence, *to* or *unto* a judge.

c **1315** SHOREHAM 38 Betere hys ffor te apeched be Of more forȝefnesse Than wreche. **1414** BRAMPTON 7 *Penit. Ps.* xviii, 3yf God..Of no synne may the apeche. **1540** ELYOT *Image Govt.* (1556) 155 They apeached him unto the emperour. **1587** FLEMING *Contn. Holinshed* III. 356/1 Who also..appeached manie for stealing of horsses. **1649** MILTON *Eikon.* iv. (1851) 366 Twelve Cypher Bishops, who were immediately appeacht of Treason.

3. To bring a charge against, cast imputation upon, asperse (honour, character, etc).

1430 LYDG. *Chron. Troy* III. xxii, Shameful reporte your honour shall apeche. **1641** MILTON *Animadv.* (1851) 196 Whether this appeach not the judgement, and approbation of the Parliament. **1700** DRYDEN *Pal. & Arcite* I. 300 Nor dar'st thou, traitor, on the plain Appeach my honour.

4. To accuse, inform against (a crime, etc.).

1430 LYDG. *Chron. Troy* IV. xxv, My bloude your gylte hereafter shall apeche. **1548** HALL *Chron.* 459 To appeache and quenche this newe spronge conspiracy. **1658** ROWLAND *Mouffet's Theat. Ins.* 1051 Galen..hath proved it to be false, and appeacheth it for a lie.

5. *intr.* To give accusatory evidence; to 'peach.'

1601 SHAKS. *All's Well* I. iii. 197 Disclose the state of your affection, for your passions Haue to the full appeach'd.

†**a'ppeach**, *sb.* *Obs. rare*$^{-1}$. [f. prec. vb.] An impeachment or accusation.

1628 COKE *On Litt.* 123 b, Appeale..commeth of the French word Appeller, that signifieth to accuse or to appeach: An Appeach.

†**a'ppeacher.** *Obs.* [earlier *apechour*, a. AFr. *enpechour*, OFr. *empecheor*: see prec. vb. and -ER.] One who impeaches; an accuser or informer.

1440 *Promp. Parv.*, Apechowre, or apelowre, *Appellator.* **1548** COVERDALE *Erasm. Par. Rom.* v. 13 The lawe is not the authour of synne, but the..apeacher thereof. **1580** NORTH *Plutarch* (1676) 286 Common appeachers and accusers of the..chiefest Citizens. **1618** RALEIGH *Rem.* (1644) 116 The Angels would plead against you, and your own self..be your own most sharp appeacher.

†**a'ppeaching**, *vbl. sb.* *Obs.* [f. as prec. + -ING[1].] The action of impeaching; accusation.

1401 *Pol. Poems* II. 79 Paide tribute..for to fleen occasioun of aftirward apechinge. **1656** HOBBES *Six Less.* Wks. 1845 VII. 226 The appeaching of others.

†**a'ppeaching**, *ppl. a.* *Obs.* [f. as prec. + -ING[2].] Accusing, fault-finding.

1637 GILLESPIE *Eng.-Pop. Cerem.* B, Sibber to appeaching Hostility, then fraternall Charity.

†**a'ppeachment.** *Obs.* [see prec. and -MENT.] The action or instrument of accusation or impeachment; a criminal charge.

1450 SOMNER in *4 C. Eng. Lett.* 4 He was arreyned..upon the appechements and fonde gylty. **1599** BP. HALL *Sat.* Postscr., It is impossible so violent an appeachment should be quietly brooked. **1644** MILTON *Judgm. Bucer* (1851) 304 Perhaps we may obtain to get our Appeachment new drawn.

appeal (əˈpiːl), *v.* Forms: 4-6 **apele**, 5 **apeele**, 6 **apeal(e**, 5-6 **appel(e**, 6-7 **appeal(e**, 6- **appeal**. Also 5-7 **appell(e**, 6 **apell(e**. [a. OFr. *apele-r* to call:—L. *app-*, *adpellā-re* to accost, address, call upon, also in Law 'to appeal to, to impeach,' a secondary form of *adpell-ĕre* to drive to, direct (a ship) towards, land upon. Cf. the history of *aboard* and *accost*, both of which similarly passed from the sense of 'land upon,' to 'make up to, address, speak to.' For refashioning of prefix, see AP- *pref.*[1]; the change of *-e-* to *-ea-* was part of the spelling reform of 16th c.; *appell* was a latinized form.]

†**I.** *trans.* To appeal a person. *Obs.* or *Hist.*

†**1.** To call (one) to answer before a tribunal; in *Law*: To accuse of a crime which the accuser undertakes to prove. *spec.* **a.** To impeach *of* treason. **b.** To accuse an accomplice of treason or felony. **c.** To accuse of a heinous crime whereby the accuser has received personal injury or wrong, for which he demands reparation. (Const. *of*, *for*, the crime; *to* the tribunal.) All *Obs.* exc. as *Hist.*

1366 MAUNDEV. xii. 139 Straungeres..schulle thus appelen us & holden us for wykked Lyveres. **1450** SHIRLEY *Dethe of James I* (1818) 27, I appell you afor God..that ye bene the varay cause of the losse of my saule. **1464** J. PASTON in *Lett.* 486 II. 152 They were apelyd of othyr se[r]teyn poyntys of treson. **1523** LD. BERNERS *Froiss.* I. ccxlii. 357 If the prince were apeled to ye court of parlyament. **1548** UDALL, etc. *Erasm. Par. John* vii. 19 He did appele them of sinne-full transgression of the lawe. **1593** SHAKS. *Rich. II*, I. i. 9 If he appeale the Duke on ancient malice. *Ibid.* I. i. 27 To appeale each other of high treason. **1628** COKE *On Litt.* 287 b, To appeale a man is as much as to accuse him. **1643** PRYNNE *Power Parl.* II. 38, I..appeale you to the Tribunall of that high Judge above. **1649** SELDEN *Laws of Eng.* I. lxvii. (1739) 171 No Man shall be appealed by a Woman for the death of any but her own Husband. **1756** NUGENT *Montesquieu* (1758) II. 279 A man, who was appealed of a crime. **1768** [See APPROVEMENT[1] I.] **1809** TOMLINS *Law Dict.* s.v., If the wife kill her husband, the heir may appeal her of the death. **1839** KEIGHTLEY *Hist. Eng.* I. 307 They came before the king..and appealed of treason the Archbishop of York.

2. To call one to defend himself (as by wager of battle); to challenge. *arch.*

c **1400** *Rowland & Ot.* 343, I appelle hym for trouthe broken. **1470-85** (ed. 1634) MALORY *Pr. Arthur* (1816) I. 322 Sir Blamor de Ganis..hath appealed me to fight with him. *a* **1649** DRUMM. OF HAWTH. *Wks.* (1711) 224 Being appealed to a duel, he had killed his adversary.

†**3.** To invoke or claim as judge. (So in cl. L.) *Obs. rare.* See 6.

1382 WYCLIF *Acts* xxv. 12 Cesar I apele [Vulg. *Cæsarem appello*; *other MSS. and vers.* To Cesar] Thanne Festus.. answeride, Cesar thou hast apelid, To Cesar thou schalt go.

†**4.** To invoke or call to witness. *Obs. rare.* See 8.

1645 *Lib. Consc.* 19, I must appeal the consciences of those who now plead so much for liberty of conscience. **1649** MILTON *Eikon.* 89 He hath presum'd to appeale the.. testimony of God.

II. *intr.* Const. *to.*

5. a. To call to a higher judge or tribunal for deliverance from the adverse decision of a lower; to remove a case formally from an inferior to a higher court. Also *fig.* as in *proverbial phrase*, To appeal from Philip drunk to Philip sober.

c **1400** *Apol. Loll.* 22 He appellid stalliworþli fro þe court of Innocent þe ferþe, vn to þe barre of Crist. **1502** *Ord. Cryst. Men* (W. de W.) IV. iii. (1506) 169 From the courte of Iustice a man may apele and call un too the courte of mercy. **1651** HOBBES *Leviath.* I. xi. 50 They appeale from custome to reason. **1876** E. MELLOR *Priesth.* ii. 62 We appeal from the narrow officialism of the disciple, to the.. merciful benevolence of the Master.

b. with mention of one or both tribunals omitted; also *against* a decision.

1330 R. BRUNNE *Chron.* 100 S. Anselm þerfor appeld vnto þe courte of Rome. **1393** GOWER *Conf.* III. 192 Alisaundre .. a worthy knight.. Forjuged hath, and he appelleth. *c* **1425** WYNTOUN *Cron.* VIII. x. 25 Fra his Curt.. Ðis Makduff appellyd. **1538** STARKEY *England* 127 Appelyng to the Court of the Byschope of Canterbury. **1611** SHAKS. *Cymb.* v. iv. 91 Helpe (Iupiter) or we appeale, and from thy iustice flye. **1883** TREVELYAN *Sp. in Parl.* 25 Aug., The Revising Barrister's.. decisions have never been appealed against. **1883** *Times* 27 Aug. 10/2 As there was doubt on the point he[the Judge] gave him liberty to appeal.

c. ***to appeal to the country*** (sc. from parliament): to dissolve parliament after vote of the House of Commons adverse to the ministry, in order that the constituencies may express their mind on the question in electing the members of the new house.

6. a. To call upon a recognized authority to vindicate one's right or decide in one's favour in a dispute.

1393 GOWER *Conf.* III. 196 Unto thy dome, lorde, I appele, Beholde and deme my querele. **1586** JAMES VI. in Ellis *Orig. Lett.* I. 224 III. 19 Appealing to youre rypest judgement to discerne thereupon. **1711** ADDISON *Spect.* No. 122 ¶5 Mr. Touchy and he must appeal to him upon a Dispute that arose between them. **1878** SEELEY *Stein* III. 364 We find him appealed to.. in the constitutional dispute which had begun to rage.

b. *fig.* of decision by physical means.

1849 MACAULAY *Hist. Eng.* xxiii, They appealed to the sword.

c. *Cricket.* To call upon an umpire for his decision; to make an appeal (see APPEAL *sb.* 4 b).

1744 *Laws* [of Cricket] in *New Dict. Arts & Sci.* (1755) IV. 3460/1 [The umpires] are not to order any man out, unless appealed to by one of the players. **1830** M. R. MITFORD *Our Village* IV. 26 They.. finally appealed to the umpires as to the fairness of the play. **1897** K. S. RANJITSINHJI *Jubilee Bk. Cricket* vi. 254 When a catch at the wicket is appealed for, an umpire should.. take into consideration both sound and sight.

7. To call *to* a witness for corroboration; to call attention *to* some testimony as confirmation.

1414 BRAMPTON *7 Penit. Ps.* lxvi. 25 Forsake me noȝt.. And ȝyf thou do, I will apele To *Ne reminiscaris, Domine*! **1593** SHAKS. *2 Hen. VI*, II. i. 190 To Heauen I doe appeale, How I haue lou'd my King, and Common-weale. **1712** STEELE *Spect.* No. 555 ¶13, I appeal to the judicious observers for the truth of what I assert. **1850** MCCOSH *Div. Govt.* I. i. (1874) 8 For the proof of the existence of the conscience, we appeal.. to the consciousness.

8. To call for a favour of any kind; to make supplication, entreaty, or earnest request, *to* a person *for* a thing.

1540 CROMWELL in Ellis *Orig. Lett.* II. 142 II. 168, I appell to your Highnes for mercy. **1883** *Daily News* 3 Sept. 5/2 A letter from the Lord Mayor appealing to the public for subscriptions. *Mod.* I appeal to you to let me alone.

9. a. To address oneself, specially and in expectation of a sympathetic response, *to* some principle of conduct, mental faculty, or class of persons. Also, to be attractive or pleasing *to* (a person).

1794 SULLIVAN *View Nat.* I. 103 Imagination here needs not be appealed to. **1803** SIR J. MACKINTOSH *Def. Peltier* Wks. 1846 III. 268 To what interests does it appeal? What passions is it to rouse? **1835** *N. Amer. Rev.* Oct., An author who treats it [the subject of Dress], appeals.. to the young men and maidens. **1869** FREEMAN *Norm. Conq.* III. xiii. 296 He appealed to their sense of feudal honour. **1881** MRS. J. H. RIDDELL *Senior Partner* III. iii. 70 Mr. McCullagh, to whom Mr. Mostin's general assertion appealed with the force of experience. *a* **1885** *Mod.* Pictures appeal to the eye, arguments to the reason. **1898** SAINTSBURY *Short Hist. Eng. Lit.* VIII. iii. 524 Its poetical and romantic attractions.. appeal even to a person so little poetical as Hobbes. **1928** C. SINGER *From Magic to Science* i. 16 Such a point of view appealed greatly to the Middle Ages.

b. To 'make an appeal'; to be attractive.

1907 *Smart Set* Mar. 23/1 The speciousness of Betty's words appealed.

III. *trans.* with a thing as obj.

10. To remove to a higher tribunal.

1481 CAXTON *Reynard* (Arb.) 76, I apele this mater into the court to fore our lord the kyng. *c* **1590** MARLOWE *Faustus* 9 To patient judgments we appeal our plaud. **1828** WEBSTER *s.v.*, We say the cause was appealed before or after trial. **1870** LOWELL *Among my Bks.* I. (1873) 178 To appeal a case of taste to a court of final judicature. **1900** *Westm. Gaz.* 22 Aug. 2/2 Possibly the case will be appealed. **1932** E. WILSON *Devil take Hindmost* xvii. 192 The defense will appeal the case to the Supreme Court. **1963** *Publisher's Weekly* 2 Sept. 45/1 Curtis has announced that it will appeal the verdict.

appeal (əˈpiːl), *sb.* Forms: 3–5 apel, 4 apeel, 4–6 apele, 5 appelle, 5–6 appel(e, 6 apell, 6–7 appeale, 7 appeill, 6– appeal. *Aphet.* 4–5 pele. [a. OFr. *apel* (mod. *appel*), f. *apeler*: see APPEAL *v.*]

†**1.** A calling to account before a legal tribunal; in *Law*: A criminal charge or accusation, made by one who undertook under penalty to prove it; *spec.* **a.** Impeachment of treason or felony. **b.** 'The accusation of a felon, at common law, by one of his accomplices, which accomplice was then called an approver.' **c.** 'An accusation by a private subject against another for some heinous crime, demanding punishment on account of the particular injury suffered, rather than for the offence against the public' (Blackstone). Formerly a regular mode of criminal procedure. (All *Obs.* exc. *Hist.*)

1377 LANGL. *P. Pl.* B. XVII. 300 Þere þat partye pursueth · þe pele [**1393** apeel, appel] is so huge, þat þe kynge may do no mercy. **1471** SIR J. PASTON *Lett.* 676 III. 18 Iff they be [maryed], than the appelys wer abbatyd there by. **1528** PERKINS *Profit. Bk.* iii. §202 (1642) 91 The heire who is partie unto the death of his father shall not have an appeale thereof. **1593** SHAKS. *Rich. II*, IV. i. 79 Aumerle is guiltie of my true Appeale. **1691** BLOUNT *Law Dict.* s.v., Cognizance of Criminal Causes, is taken either.. upon Indictment or Appeal.. Accusation or Appeal is a lawful Declaration of another Mans crime (which, by Bracton, must be Felony at least) before a competent Judge, by one that sets his name to the Declaration, and undertakes to prove it, upon the penalty that may ensue of the contrary. **1809** TOMLINS *Law Dict.* s.v., It does not appear that the appeal of treason is taken away by this statute (*1 Hen.* 4. c. 14) or any other. **1863** COX *Inst. Eng. Govt.* II. v. 456 At the time when Blackstone wrote.. private subjects might prosecute others for heinous crimes by 'Appeal of felony.'

†**2.** A call to any one to defend his innocence or honour by arms; a challenge. *Obs.* exc. *Hist.*

c **1450** LONELICH *Grail* lii. 858 They.. founden kyng Marahans anon In the court to-forn kyng lucye, his apel there forto complye. **1598** FLORIO, *Appellagione*, an appeale, a challenge. *a* **1700** DRYDEN (J.), Nor shall the sacred character of king Be urged to shield me from thy bold appeal.

3. a. The transference of a case from an inferior to a higher court or tribunal, in the hope of reversing or modifying the decision of the former; *techn.* the application for such transference, *or* the transferred case. ***Court of Appeal***: a court occupied in rehearing cases previously tried in inferior courts. Also ***Court of Appeals*** (U.S.).

1297 R. GLOUC. 473 To the bissop fram ercedekne [h]is apel [he] solde make. **1393** GOWER *Conf.* III. 192 Fro thy wrath.. To thy pite stant min appele. **1561** T. N[ORTON] *Calvin's Inst.* IV. 22 The Synodes, from whom there might be no appelle but to a Generall Counsel. **1642** HOWELL *For. Trav.* (Arb.) 85 Appeales in som cases may be made to the Mufiti who is their chiefest Bishop. **1777** *Journals Cont. Congress* (1907) VIII. 607 The propriety of establishing a court of appeals. **1849** DICKENS *Let.* 2 Feb. in W. C. Macready *Diaries* (1912) II. 417 The indispensable necessity there is for a public and solemn Court of Appeal in all criminal cases. **1855** FERNANDO WOOD in X.D. MacLeod *Biogr.* (1856), There is.. a Court of Appeals, to which to apply against the subjection. **1880** MCCARTHY *Own Time* IV. liv. 161 The decision was that the appeal must be dismissed. **1883** TREVELYAN in *Times* 27 Aug. 6/3 The principles laid down by the Court of Appeal. **1883** [See APPEALABLE 1].

b. *transf.* as 'an appeal to the country.'

1799 COLERIDGE *Own Times* I. 180 By this appeal to the universal suffrage, the sovereignty of the people is admitted. **1844** BROUGHAM *Brit. Const.* i. (1862) 16 An appeal to the people by a dissolution is the resource of the Constitution.

4. a. The call to a recognized authority for sanction, or decision in one's favour, or to a witness for corroborative testimony. Cf. APPEAL *v.* 6, 7.

a **1626** BACON (J.), The casting up of the eyes and lifting up of the hands, is a kind of appeal to the Deity. **1782** PRIESTLEY *Matt. & Spirit* I. xi. 132 In all metaphysical subjects, there is a perpetual appeal made to consciousness. **1868** FREEMAN *Norm. Conq.* II. vii. 144 They saw no hope but in an appeal to arms.

b. *spec.* in *Cricket.* A call made to an umpire, by any player, for his decision on any point arising during a match, esp. whether a batsman is 'out' or not.

1844 F. W. LILLYWHITE *Hand-Bk. Cricket* 20 After the umpire has given you out, further appeal is useless. **1882** *Daily Tel.* 24 June (*cricket*) An appeal for a catch at the wicket was given in favour of Giffen. **1908** W. E. W. COLLINS *Country Cricketer's Diary* iv. 71 'How's that?' came the second appeal, as the wicket-keeper, ball in hand, pulled up a stump.

5. A call for help of any kind, or for a favour; an earnest request; an entreaty.

1859 TENNYSON *Vivien* 231 She lifted up A face of sad appeal. **1879** J. A. H. MURRAY (*title*) An Appeal to the English-speaking and English-reading public to read books and make extracts for the Philological Society's New English Dictionary. **1882** PAYN *For Cash* III. 4 An appeal to his nephew for forgiveness. **1883** *Times* 27 Aug. 5/2 Contributions received in answer to my last appeal.

6. a. Language specially addressed *to*, or adapted to exert influence *upon*, some particular principle of conduct, mental faculty, or class of persons.

1833 GEN. P. THOMPSON *Exerc.* II. 472 The appeal to humane and Christian feeling. **1853** MISS MITFORD in L'Estrange *Life* III. xiv. 254 Slavery.. must not be treated by appeals to the passions. **1876** J. PARKER *Paracl.* I. ii. 17 To the intellectual man, the Christian appeal is this: 'You have a spiritual consciousness.'

b. *fig.* Attractive influence or power; esp. in phr. ***to make an appeal (to)*** = APPEAL *v.* 9.

1916 H. WALPOLE *Dark Forest* II. i. 209 The appeal of her ignorance and strength and credulity—ah! she won our hearts simply whenever she pleased. **1920** ROSE MACAULAY *Potterism* I. i.§4 Mrs. Potter was rather sadly aware that she made no appeal to the twins. *Ibid.* I. iv. §1 His was the sort of beauty which.. makes so strong an appeal to the senses of the sex other than that of the possessor. **1925** W. DEEPING *Sorrell & Son* xxiii. §3 The enticements that might be expected to make an appeal to a very young man. *Ibid.* xxvii. §1 She was standing close to him,.. and Kit was conscious of the sudden shock of her appeal. **1926** *Grand Mag.* Aug. 587/2 The sport of manhunting had lost its appeal.

†**7.** A summons by bell-ringing, a PEAL. *Obs.*

1440 *Promp. Parv.*, A-peele of belle ryngynge [**1499** apele of bellis].

8. Special Comb. **appeal court** (also **appeals court**) = *Court of Appeal* s.v. APPEAL *sb.* 3; **appeal fund,** a fund established for money collected in response to a charitable appeal.

1872 *Rep. Sel. Comm. Appellate Jurisdiction* 62 in *Parl. Papers* VII. 193 Such cases as now go to the Exchequer Chamber from the Common Law Courts, and to the *Appeal Court in Chancery from the Equity Courts. **1907** *Parl. Deb.* 29 July 598 They would have list upon list occupying this new Appeal Court [*sc.* the Court of Criminal Appeal] day after day. **1972** *Times* 23 Feb. 27/5 (*heading*) Appeal Court reproved for ignoring precedent. **1985** *Financial Times* 29 Oct. 4/4 Yesterday, an appeals court ruled that the state-of-siege decree empowered President Alfonsin to order arrests. **1976** *Cumberland & Westmorland Herald* 4 Dec. 1/4 He said the *appeal fund at present stood at £248. **1985** *Guardian Weekly* 8/2 Some 200,000 NZ dollars flooded into the Greenpeace appeal fund.

appealable (əˈpiːləb(ə)l), *a.* [f. APPEAL *v.* + -ABLE.]

1. That can be appealed against, or carried for decision to a higher tribunal.

1622 HOWELL *Lett.* (1650) I. 86 To clip the power of the council of state.. by making it appealable to the council of Spain. **1783** W. MARTYN *Geog. Mag.* II. 80 The king's Revision Court to which all civil causes are appealable. **1883** *Law Times* LXXV. 181/1 On appeal, the Court had great doubt whether the order, being discretionary, was appealable.

2. That can be appealed *to*; responsive to appeal.

1846 RUSKIN *Mod. Paint.* V. IX. xii. §6 No impulses but those of the brute (says the modern political economist) are appealable to in the world.

appealant: see APPELLANT.

appealer (əˈpiːlə(r)). [f. as prec. + -ER[1].] One who makes an appeal; an appellant; *spec.* **a.** One who brings an accusation (see APPEAL *sb.* 1). **b.** One who carries his case to a higher court. (See also APPELLOR.)

1519 HORMAN *Vulg.* 225 Wolde to god the false apelers [*delatores*].. were openly shamed. **1649** SELDEN *Laws of Eng.* I. lxvii. (1739) 172 If the party appealed was acquitted, the appealer should not only render damages, but be imprisoned for a year. **1805** W. TAYLOR in *Ann. Rev.* III. 319 If the newest authorities.. do not satisfy the appealer.

appealing (əˈpiːlɪŋ), *vbl. sb.* [f. as prec. + -ING[1].] The action of accusing or impeaching (*obs.*), of transferring a case to a higher court, or of calling for aid, etc. (Mostly gerundial.) Also, the action of making an appeal; attractive influence or power.

1440 *Promp. Parv.*, Apeel or apelynge. **1600** *Quips vpon Quest.* Hj b, To you I appeale: to whom in my appealing, I craue forgiuenes, giuing this hard dealing. **1876** G. M. HOPKINS *Wr. Deutschland* (1918) st. 27 The appealing of the Passion is tenderer in prayer apart. **1889** *Times* 19 June 15/3 A moderate sum, if we consider.. the arbitrating, the judging, the appealing that are thrown in for this modest shilling.

aˈppealing, *ppl. a.* [f. as prec. + -ING[2].] That appeals; applying to a higher tribunal; suppliant, imploring. In mod. use, freq. merging into sense 'attractive'.

1598 FLORIO, *Appellatiuo*, appealing. **1725** tr. *Dupin's Eccl. Hist. 17th C.* I. II. vi. 56 He ordains, that.. one of the three appealing Priests should be put into his Place. **1813** SCOTT *Rokeby* v. viii, With somewhat of appealing look. **1891** HARDY *Tess* II. xxxvi. 234 Corporeal presence is sometimes less appealing than corporeal absence. **1898** *Daily News* 1 Mar. 6/1 Froment.. is.. the most appealing character in the book. **1922** JOYCE *Ulysses* 358 The old love was waiting.. with blue appealing eyes. **1932** E. BOWEN *To North* xx. 220 We find her a very dear person: there is something appealing about her.

aˈppealingly, *adv.* [f. prec. + -LY[2].] In an appealing manner; imploringly.

1847 LD. LINDSAY *Chr. Art* I. 128 Her hands are held forth appealingly towards the spectator. **1883** WOOLSON in *Harper's Mag.* Feb. 414/1, 'I have been a good wife to him ..,' she murmured, appealingly, piteously.

a'ppealingness. [f. prec. + -NESS.] The quality of being appealing.

1876 GEO. ELIOT *Dan. Der.* III. xxxv. 23 A certain appealingness in her behaviour towards him. **1880** MISS LAFFAN *Christy Carew* I. iv. 204 A gaze intense in its appealingness.

appear (ə'pɪə(r)), *v.* Forms: 3-6 **apere**, 4-5 **apeer(e**, 6-7 **apear(e**; 5 **appeere**, **-iere**, 5-6 **apper(e**, 6-7 **appeare**, 6 **appear**. [a. *aper-*, tonic stem (cf. pres. subj. *apere*,) of OFr. *apar-eir*, *-oir*:—L. *adp-*, *appārē-re* to appear, f. *ad* to + *pārē-re* to come in sight, come forth. Subseq. with prefix Latinized, *appere* (see AP- *pref.*[1]), and in the reformed spelling of 16th c. *appear* (which then rhymed with *bear*, *pear*, but now with *beer*, *peer*). An aphetic *'pear* occurs in 17th c. poetry, and is now dialectal.]

1. To come forth into view, as from a place or state of concealment, or from a distance; to become visible.

1375 BARBOUR *Bruce* I. 93 Quhat perell to ȝow mycht apper. **1382** WYCLIF *Gen.* i. 9 Gadrid be watris..in to o place, and apere the drie. **1473** WARKW. *Chron.* 5 There apperyde a blasynge sterre in the weste. **1596** SPENSER *F.Q.* v. iii. 7 So soone as morrow light Appear'd in heaven. **1642** H. MORE *Song of Soul* I. II. ii, They 'pear and then are hid. **1667** MARVELL *Corr.* 71 Wks. 1872-5 II. 212 The Dutch begin to appear again near Gravesend. **1712** POPE *Messiah* 30 Prepare the way! a God, a God appears. **1855** MACAULAY *Hist. Eng.* III. 678 The fleet..on the twenty-first appeared before the harbour.

2. *esp.* of angels, disembodied spirits, and visions.

c **1250** *Kent. Serm.* in *O.E. Misc.* 27 Aperede an ongel of heuene in here slepe. **1340** HAMPOLE *Pr. Consc.* 2280 God wil þus Suffer þe devel apere til us. **1382** WYCLIF *Matt.* xxvii. 53 And many bodies of seintes..apeeriden to manye. **1714** BYROM *Spect.* No. 587 ¶3 A Shape, like that in which we paint our Angels, appeared before me. **1862** TRENCH *Miracles* xxxiii. 455 Men do not *see* them [angels], but they *appear to* men.

3. To be in sight, be visible.

c **1360** *Deo Gratias* in *E.E.P.* (1862) 129 Nou appeereþ. non of þo. **1366** MAUNDEV. xvii. 180 This Sterre..that wee clepen the Lode Sterre, ne apperethe not to hem. *c* **1400** *Destr. Troy* v. 1642 To all the prouyns þe toures apperit. **1535** COVERDALE *2 Esdr.* xi. 13 The place therof appeared no more. *a* **1631** DONNE *Poems* (1650) 2 My face in thine eye, thine in mine appeares. **1734** tr. *Rollin's Anc. Hist.* (1827) II. II. §2. 1 Nothing appeared to the eye but a few pitiful cottages.

4. To present oneself formally before an authority or tribunal; to put in an appearance. *Hence*, to present oneself as legal representative of another; to act as counsel.

1330 R. BRUNNE *Chron.* 255 With right he leses his chance þorgh faut þat not apers. *c* **1425** WYNTOUN *Cron.* IX. Prol. 45 At a court I mon appeir, Fell accusationis þare til here. **1589** *Marprel. Protest.* (*title-page*) By open disputation to apear in the defence of his cause. **1712** STEELE *Spect.* No. 427 ¶2 Many..are known to have Ill-will to him for whom I [Cicero] appear. **1809** TOMLINS *Law Dict.* H vij/1 Attornies subscribing warrants to appear, are liable to attachment, upon non-appearance. **1849** MACAULAY *Hist. Eng.* II. 97 The Bishop of London was cited before the new tribunal. He appeared. **1883** *Times* 21 Aug. 10/1 Mr. —— appeared for the prosecution. Mr. —— appeared to defend.

5. To come before the public in any character or capacity; to display oneself on the stage of action or acting.

1607 SHAKS. *Coriol.* IV. iii. 35 Your noble Tullus Auffidius will appeare well in these Warres. **1711** ADDISON *Spect.* No. 1 ¶5, I appear on Sunday nights at St. James's Coffee House. **1883** *Athenæum* 15 Sept. 348/1 The Vokes family will appear..at the Prince of Wales's Theatre.

6. To come before the public in the character of an author by his works.

1713 *Guardian* No. 10 And so am forced..to appear in print. *c* **1735** POPE *Epil. Sat.* I. i, Not twice a twelvemonth you appear in print. **1881** GREEN *Short Hist.* vii. 419 Fifty dramatic poets..appeared in the fifty years which precede the closing of the theatres by the Puritans.

7. To come before the public as a book or other publication does; to be published, come out.

1711 ADDISON *Spect.* No. 10 ¶3 That where the Spectator appears, the other publick Prints will vanish. **1782** COWPER *Lett.* 18 Nov., I little thought when I was writing the history of John Gilpin, that he would appear in print. **1877** LYTTEIL *Landm.* III. i. 98 Several works on Arran..have already appeared.

8. To show itself or be plainly set forth in a document; to be shown, declared; to occur.

c **1531** *Pol. Rel. & L. Poems* (1866) 34 As more large apperyth in for-sayde autoryte. **1605** CAMDEN *Rem.* 5 As appeereth in an antient Roman Provinciall. **1735** POPE *Hor. Ep.* II. ii. 165 Mark where a bold expressive phrase appears. **1817** JAS. MILL *Brit. India* II. v. ii. 373 Enough does not appear to condemn any individual.

9. To be clear or evident to the understanding; to be plain, manifest.

c **1400** CHAUCER *Rom. Rose* 5511 Now apperith her folye. **1477** EARL RIVERS (Caxton) *Dictes* 12 Suche workes wol not be hidde, but at the last they wol appere. **1540** COVERDALE *Fruitf. Les.* ii. Wks. 1849 I. 316 Thus appeareth the power of his death. **1667** MILTON *P.L.* II. 257 Our greatness will appear Then most conspicuous. **1710** PRIDEAUX *Orig. Tithes* ii. 101, I am next to make appear that no such alteration is made by the change of country. **1756** BURKE *Vind. Nat. Soc.* Wks. I. 15 The more clearly their excellences must appear.

b. *impers.* It is clear or evident.

c **1374** CHAUCER *Boeth.* v. iv. 162 Þat it may apere þat þe prescience is signe of þis necessite. **1428** in Heath *Grocers' Comp.* (1869) 6 As it aperith pleynely be here aconte, as followyth. **1596** SHAKS. *Merch. V.* IV. i. 236 It doth appeare, you are a worthy Iudge. **1875** BRYCE *Holy Rom. Emp.* xii. 186 Nor does it appear that authority was ever exercised by any Emperor in Spain.

†**c.** To promise, be expected, be likely in due course (*to become something*). See APPARENT 5.

c **1425** WYNTOUN *Cron.* VIII. i. 95 That Madyn fayre That ..apperyd till have bene Be the lawch of Norway Quene. *Ibid.* IX. xvi. 4 Robert þe kelt..apperand þan For to be a Lord of mycht.

10. To be to the mind, or in one's opinion; to be taken as, to seem.

1388 WYCLIF *Isa.* lix. 15 And the Lord siȝ, and it apperide yuel in hise iȝen. **1603** SHAKS. *Meas. for M.* II. iii. 30 Where their vn-taught loue Must needs appear offence. **1651** HOBBES *Leviath.* I. xxvii. 153 They choose that which appeareth best for themselves. **1833** HT. MARTINEAU *Brooke Farm* i. 1 Strangers do not appear struck with it.

b. *impers.* It seems.

1603 SHAKS. *Meas. for M.* III. i. 72 *Page.* Hee's the man should fight with him.. *Shal.* It appeares so by his weapons. **1754** HUME *Hist. Eng.* (1803) I. 41 Solely, as it appears, for what you believe to be for our advantage. **1812** SIR H. DAVY *Chem. Philos.* 5 Theophrastus did not, it appears, adopt the sublime doctrines of his master.

11. To seem, as distinguished from *to be*; to be in outward show, or to the superficial observer.

1559 *Myrr. Mag., R. Tresilian* iv, And matters of most wrong, to haue appered most right. **1611** BIBLE *Matt.* vi. 16 That they may appeare vnto men to fast. **1667** MILTON *P.L.* II. 113 His Tongue..could make the worse appear The better reason. **1712** STEELE *Spect.* No. 445 ¶7, I am afraid of making them appear considerable by taking notice of them. **1860** TYNDALL *Glac.* II. §1. 223 Raindrops which descend vertically appear to meet us when we move swiftly.

†**a'ppear,** *sb. Obs. rare*$^{-1}$. [f. prec. sb.] The act of appearing, appearance.

a **1610** FLETCHER *Faithf. Sheph.* v. i, Dew, Which she on every little grass doth strew..against the Sun's appear.

†**a'ppearable,** *a. Obs. rare*$^{-1}$. [f. prec. vb. + -ABLE. Cf. 16th c. Fr. *aparable* clear.] Able to appear or be seen; visible.

1651 J. F[REAKE] *Agrippa's Occult. Phil.* 403 The other Demons are neither so appearable, nor invisible.

appearance (ə'pɪərəns). Forms: 4-5 **aparaunce**, 5 **apparens**, 5-6 **appearaunce**, 5-7 **-ance**, **-ence**, (6 **aparance**); 5 **apperans**, 5-6 **-aunce**, **-ance**, (**appeerance**), 6-7 **appearaunce**, 6- **-ance**. *Aphet.* 5 **perance**. [orig. a. OFr. *aparance*, *-ence* (later *apparence*):—L. *appārēntia*, abst. n. f. *appārēnt-em*, pr. pple. of *appārē-re* to APPEAR. Subseq. assimilated to the vb. *appere*, APPEAR, though *apparance*, *-ence*, were still used *c* 1685. Cf. APPARENCE, -ENCY, -ENT.]

1. The action of coming forward into view or becoming visible.

c **1400** *Epiph.* (Turnb. 1843) 119 They all thre Thys day were seyn by sothfast apparence. **1583** STANYHURST *Æneis* II. (Arb.) 68 Her woonted image..mad her..aparance. **1611** BIBLE *2 Macc.* xv. 27 Through the appearance of God, they were greatly cheered. **1794** S. WILLIAMS *Hist. Vermont* 115 The usual times of the appearance..and disappearance of these birds. **1869** FREEMAN *Norm. Conq.* III. xiv. 336 The appearance of the fleet was unlooked for.

2. The action of appearing formally at any proceedings; *esp.* formal presentation of oneself in a court to answer (or prosecute) a suit or charge; called *making* or *putting in* an appearance.

c **1400** *Beryn* 2623 Wherfor wee must..Such answers us purvey..Tomorow at our apparaunce. **1494** FABYAN VII. 351 To make summons, and distrayne for lacke of appearaunce. **1581** LAMBARDE *Eiren.* II. ii. (1588) 112 Although this recognusance doe not comprehend any time of apparence. **1660** INGELO *Bentiv. & Ur.* (1682) II. 164 The obedient Theoprepians made appearance at the time appointed. **1669** PENN *No Cross, etc.* vi. §10 The Souls of true Worshippers see God, make their Appearance before Him. **1809** TOMLINS *Law Dict.* H vij/1 Appearance in person and by attorney are very different. **1883** SPURGEON in *Chr. Herald* 24 Oct. 235/1 All men must put in a personal appearance at the Last Assize.

†**3.** *collect.* A company presenting themselves; a muster, attendance, gathering, a 'turn-out.' *Obs.*

1599 *Life Sir T. More* in C. Wordsworth *Eccl. Biog.* (1853) II. 140 There was a great appearance of the clergie to have the oath tendered. **1660** EVELYN *Mem.* (1857) I. 371 An innumerable appearance of gallants. **1704** *Lond. Gaz.* mmmdccccxciii/2 Her Grace..invited all the Ladies..of whom there was a very great Appearance. **1747** in *Col. Rec. Penn.* V. 153 So thin an appearance of the Representatives.

4. a. The action of coming before the world or the public in any character.

1671 MILTON *P.R.* II. 41 Will he now retire After appearance? **1711** ADDISON *Spect.* No. 1 ¶2 The gravity of my behaviour at my very first appearance in the world. **1711** *Ibid.* No. 13 ¶2 The Lion has changed his manner of acting ..since his first appearance. **1794** SULLIVAN *View Nat.* II, 'The first great event in history,' says Berosus, 'was the appearance of Oannes.' **1880** GROVE *Dict. Music* II. 263 [Mendelssohn's] first appearance before an English audience.

b. The coming out or publication of a book.

1882 PALGRAVE *Ess.* in *Spenser's Wks.* IV. 43 The appearance of his first book.

5. Occurrence so as to meet the eye in a document.

1868 FREEMAN *Norm. Conq.* II. App. 615 The single appearance of the word in Domesday is the earliest instance.

6. The action of appearing conspicuously; display, show, parade.

1591 RALEIGH *Last Fight Rev.* (Arb.) 15 The Spaniardes ..fill the world with their vaine glorious vaunts, making great apparance of victories. **1711** STEELE *Spect.* No. 4 ¶2, I gratify the vanity of all who pretend to make an Appearance. **1849** MACAULAY *Hist. Eng.* I. 294 Their fine horses, their rich housings..made a splendid appearance.

†**7.** Clear manifestation to the sight or understanding; disclosure, detection. *Obs. rare.*

1587 FLEMING *Contn. Holinshed* III. 325/2 His secret and guilefull behauiour made perfect appeerance of his wicked intent. **1608** CHAPMAN *Byron's Trag.* (N.) And with such apparence Have prov'd the parts of his ingratefull treasons. **1650** SHERWOOD, A plaine apparance of a crime, *Flagrance d'un delict.*

8. The action or state of appearing or seeming to be (to eyes or mind); semblance; looking like. ***to all appearance***: so far as appears to anyone.

c **1430** LYDG. *Chorle & Birde* (1818) 1 Emblemes..By resemblance of notable apparence With moralitees concludyng on prudence. **1539** BIBLE ('Great') *1 Thess.* v. 22 Abstayne from all euell appearaunce [**1611** all appearance of euill]. **1793** SMEATON *Edystone L.* §253 The weather..had remained to all appearance much the same. **1839** JAMES *Louis XIV*, I. 182 Disdaining the slightest appearance of coveting a sceptre.

†**9.** Semblance of truth or certainty; likelihood, probability; verisimilitude. *Obs.*

a **1533** FRITH *Answ. Fisher* (1829) 202 Neither yet can I imagine any way whereby they may have any appearance to escape. **1693** *Mem. Count Teckely* III. 8 These Discourses, wherein was observed something of appearance, were capable of seducing a world of Persons. **1793** SMEATON *Edystone L.* §333 As near the extremity..as they could with the appearance of safety be built.

†**10.** *subjectively*: Perception, idea, notion of what a thing appears to be. *Obs.* (Cf. 'to my seeming.')

a **1400** *Cov. Myst.* 271 This that shewyth as bred to your apparens, Is mad the very flesche and blod of me. **1607** TOPSELL *Four-f. Beasts* 509 Many times they leap a great distance and are supported without sinking to mans appearance. **1627** I. D. in *Hakewill's Apol.* (1630) 491 A place [*Rom.* viii.] which, as to your appearance, so to me, seemes, in truth, very pressing.

11. a. The state or form in which a person or thing appears; apparent form, look, aspect.

c **1385** CHAUCER *L.G.W.* 1372 Ladyis of thyn statly aparaunce [*v.r.* apparaunce, -ance]. **1398** TREVISA *Barth. De P.R.* III. xvii. (1495) 62 All the lynes..make appearaunce, shapen as a tope. *a* **1581** CAMPION *Hist. Irel.* v. (1633) 13 Pittyfull in apparance. **1607** SHAKS. *Coriol.* IV. v. 66 Thou hast a grim apparance, and thy Face Beares a Command in't. **1722** DE FOE *Plague* (1754) 9 Men..fitted out for travelling, as any one might perceive by their Appearance. **1872** RUSKIN *Eagle's Nest* §148 In drawing, represent the appearances of things, never what you know the things to be.

b. *pl.* The general aspect of circumstances or events; the 'look' of things.

1677 TEMPLE *Let.* Wks. 1731 II. 430 The Appearances were ill; but Campaigns did not always end as they began. *a* **1745** SWIFT (J.) Appearances were all so strong The world must think him in the wrong. **1814** SOUTHEY *Roderick* xiii, All appearances Denote alarm and vigilance. *Mod.* Appearances are all in your favour.

12. a. *esp.* as distinguished from *reality*: Outward look or show.

c **1384** CHAUCER *H. of Fame* 265 Allis what harme dothe Apparence Whan hit is fals in existence. **1413** LYDG. *Pylgr. Sowle* IV. xxx. (1483) 80 Ther must nedes be a difference by-twene trouthe and apparence. **1581** CAMPION in *Confer.* II. (1584) L, They were of vs in apparance, & in outward shewe. **1611** BIBLE *John* vii. 24 Iudge not according to the appearance. **1667** MILTON *P.L.* IX. 413 The Fiend Meer Serpent in appearance. **1790** PALEY *Hor. Paul.* I. 8 To preserve an appearance of consistency. **1871** BLACKIE 4 *Phases of Mor.* i. 8 But the truth behind the appearance was, etc.

b. ***to save*** or ***keep up appearances***: to maintain artificially the outward signs, so as to conceal the absence of the realities which they are assumed to represent; see also SAVE *v.* 12.

1711 STEELE *Spect.* No. 97 ¶2 It often happen'd that a Duel was fought to save Appearances to the World. **1760** C. CHURCHILL *Night* (ed. 3) 14 Keep up appearances, there lies the test, The world will give thee credit for the rest. **1761** CHURCHILL *Rosciad* Poems 1763 I. 15 Appearances to save his only care. **1836** [see KEEP *v.* 57 e]. **1861** *Sat. Rev.* 9 Mar. 244/1 Sacrificing real comfort to the desire of keeping up appearances.

†**13.** Illusive seeming or semblance; *concr.* an illusion. *Obs.*

c **1386** CHAUCER *Sqrs. T.* 212 An apparence ymaad by som Magyk. —— *Frankl. T.* 412 Diuerse apparences swiche as thise subtile tregetours pleye. *c* **1400** *Beryn* 2774 Perfite of nygramance And of the art of apparen[c]e.

14. a. *concr.* That which appears; an object meeting the view; *esp.* a natural occurrence presenting itself to observation; a phenomenon.

1666 *Phil. Trans.* I. 378 The Flux and Reflux of the Sea.. Dr. Wallis his Theory touching that Apparence. **1667** E. KING *ibid.* II. 426 White and clean appearances..all figur'd like the lesser sort of Birds Eggs. **1783** COWPER *Lett.* 13 June, I am..a great observer of natural appearances. **1879** LOCKYER *Elem. Astron.* i. iii. 18 A careful examination of the stars..reveals to us the most startling appearances.

b. That which appears without being material; a phantom or apparition.

c **1470** HENRY *Wallace* v. 206 Quhat perance he sawe thair. *a* **1500** *Lancelot* 364 So befell hyme that nycht to meit An aperans. **1597** SHAKS. *2 Hen. IV*, I. ii. 128 Whose well-labouring sword Had three times slaine th' appearance of the King. **1613** PURCHAS *Pilgr.* I. v. vi. 406 Other things are shadowes and apparances. **1722** DE FOE *Plague* 26 This appearance passed for as real a thing as the blazing star itself. **1831** CARLYLE *Sart. Res.* I. viii, What is this *Me*? A voice, a Motion, an Appearance.

15. Special Comb. **appearance money**, money paid to a (leading) sportsman or sportswoman for participating in an event (see quot. 1981).

1977 *Washington Post* 5 Nov. D7/3 While national advertising featured the unique concept of such a match, the loser's appearance money was never advertised. **1981** *Event* 9 Oct. 27/4 *Appearance money*, essentially a euphemism for expenses which are offered to technically 'amateur' athletes to lend their presence and thus status to a particular event.

appeare, var. APPAIR *v. Obs.*, to impair.

†**a'ppearency.** *Obs.* [var. APPARENCY, refashioned like APPEARANCE.] Appearance, phenomenon.

1646 SIR T. BROWNE *Pseud. Ep.* 346 Any other Meteor or celestiall appearency.

appearer (əˈpɪərə(r)). [f. APPEAR *v.* + -ER[1].]

1. One who or that which appears.

1608 SHAKS. *Per.* v. iii. 18 This is your wife. *Per.* Reverend appearer, no. **1646** SIR T. BROWNE *Pseud. Ep.* v. xxi. §2 Owles and Ravens are ominous appearers. **1880** BROWNING *Pietro of Abano* 6 The promptest of appearers.

2. *spec.* One who formally appears (in court, etc.).

1863 *Times* 21 Apr. 11/1 The other beforenamed appearers do solemnly and sincerely declare that, etc. **1880** *Law Rep., Appeal Cases* V. 129 Firstly, These appearers declared to give and bequeath, etc.

appearing (əˈpɪərɪŋ), *vbl. sb.* [f. APPEAR *v.* + -ING[1].] The action of coming in sight, appearance; the action of formally coming before a tribunal, etc.; an appearance.

c **1375** WYCLIF *Serm.* xlvii. Sel. Wks. 1869 I. 134 þe fourth apperynge was maad to two disciplis. *c* **1430** LYDG. *Bochas* II. xiii. (1554) 51 b, Dido tooke of Juno this oracle Other by apparing, or by aduision. **1526** TINDALE *Tit.* ii. 13 Lokinge for that..glorious apperenge of the myghty god. **1656** *Artif. Beauty* (1662) 200 Spots and appearings of leprosie. **1668** PEPYS *Diary* 24 Mar., Comes to me Mr. Shish, to desire my appearing for him. **1810** BENTHAM *Packing* (1821) 36 The 12 whose names stand first upon the appearing list will constitute the serving list.

a'ppearing, *ppl. a.* [f. APPEAR *v.* + -ING[1].]

1. Coming into sight, coming forth.

1597 SHAKS. *2 Hen. IV*, I. iii. 39 As in an early Spring We see th' appearing buds.

†**2. a.** Meeting the view, showing itself, visible. **b.** Specially apparent, conspicuous. *Obs.*

1549 *Compl. Scot.* xi. 90 Sen ye knau the apering dangeir of ȝour natif cuntre. **1598** FLORIO, *Larua*..a hobgoblin, a walking or appearing spirit. **1640** FULLER *Joseph's Coat* vi. (1867) 160 He was not so eminent, and appearing in piety. **1691** RAY *Creation* (1714) 78 There is no appearing Impellent but the external Air.

c. With defining word preceding, as *best-*, *fine-appearing*. U.S.

1839 W. D. WILLIAMSON in *Mass. Hist. Soc. Coll.* (1846) 3rd Ser. IX. 95 All these..rendered him the best appearing Indian ever seen in this quarter. **1879** HOWELLS *Lady of Aroostook* xviii. 215 'She is very fine-appearing,' said Lydia. Staniford smiled at the countrified phrase. **1897** *Outing* (U.S.) XXX. 352/1 First prize for best-appearing club at Long Branch.

†**3.** Evident to the mind, manifest. *Obs.*

1566 KNOX *Hist. Ref.* Wks. 1846 I. 457 It was verray appeiring, that..thair wes some treassoun. **1736** BUTLER *Anal.* II. vi. 321 Many appearing completions of prophecy.

†**4.** Seeming, apparent. *Obs.*

1656 EARL MONM. *Advt. fr. Parnass.* 69 A young Stoick, of appearing civil behaviour. **1667** MILTON *P.L.* IX. 354 By some fair appearing good surprized. **1754** HUME *Hist. Eng.* I. xiv. 343 The appearing union of all parties.

†**a'ppearingly**, *adv. Obs.* or *dial.* [f. prec. + -LY[2].] Apparently, seemingly.

1554 KNOX *Godly Letter* B ij, The uprore..in which, appearinglye, he coulde not haue escaped the death. **1656** R. ROBINSON *Christ all* 177 The branches and the vine are not united appearingly, but truly. [Still used in Scotland.]

appeasable (əˈpiːzəb(ə)l), *a.* [a. OFr. *apaisable*, f. *apaiser*: see APPEASE and -ABLE.] Capable of being appeased or pacified; placable.

1549 UDALL, etc. *Erasm. Par. Heb.* iv. 16 Let vs goe vnto hys seate, not hys terrible, but appesable seate. **1664** H. MORE *Myst. Iniq.* xii. 40 Considering how perfectly appeasable and propitious..God is through the only name and mediation of Jesus Christ. **1855** SINGLETON *Virgil* II. 215 Where, unctuous and appeaseable, The altar of Diana stands.

a'ppeasableness. *rare*[−0]. [f. prec. + -NESS.] The quality of being appeasable; 'reconcileableness.' J.

1731 in BAILEY.

appeasably (əˈpiːzəblɪ), *adv. rare*[−0]. [f. as prec. + -LY[2].] In an appeasable manner; placably.

appease (əˈpiːz), *v.* Forms: 4–5 **apese, -ayse**, 5 **-aise, -eise, -ees(e**, 5–6 **-ease**, (6 **apeace**); 5–6 **appese**, 5–7 **-aise**, 6 **-ayse, -ayze**, 5– **appease.** See aphet. PEASE. [a. OFr. *apese-r*, *apaisie-r*, *apeisie-r* (mod. *apaiser*) to bring to peace, f. *à* to + *pais, peis, pes* (mod. *paix*):—L. *pāc-em* peace. *Apaisier* was thus a later formation from the same elements as *apaier*:—L. *adpācāre* (see APAY), with a more literal sense. Already in 14th c. aphetized as *pese*. In 15th c. refashioned as *app-*, and in spelling reform of 16th c. written *appease*. A form APEACE, assimilated to *peace*, occurs in 16th c.]

1. a. To bring to peace, pacify, quiet, or settle (strife or disorder).

1330 R. BRUNNE *Chron.* 245 Sir Edward gos to Gascoyn forto apese. **1400** LD. GREY in Ellis *Orig. Lett.* II. i. I. 3 To apees the misgouernance and the riote. **1525** LD. BERNERS *Froiss.* II. lxi. 207 Praying hym to apease the matter with yᵉ kynge of Aragon. **1605** BACON *Adv. Learn.* I. vii. §26 [Julius Cæsar] could with one word appease a mutiny in his army. **1722** DE FOE *Mem. Cavaliers* (1840) 16 [She] appeased this tumult..by her prudence. **1872** YEATS *Growth Comm.* 154 To appease their continual feuds. **1920** W. S. CHURCHILL *Let.* 24 Mar. in *World Crisis: Aftermath* (1929) xvii. 378, I should be prepared to make peace with Soviet Russia on the best terms available to appease the general situation.

b. To bring to peace, calm, or quiet (persons at strife or in disorder). Also *fig. Obs.* exc. as in 4 b.

c **1380** *Sir Ferumb.* 3212 Betwene hem wente kyng Sortybron : & a-paysede hem. **1491** CAXTON *Vitas Patr.* (W. de W.) I. vii. 11 b/2 Moued by charyte..tacorde & appese them togider. **1582** N. T. (Rhem.) *Acts* xix. 35 When the Scribe had appeased the multitudes. **1603** KNOLLES *Hist. Turks* (1638) 53 Busied in appeasing..the disordred city. **1774** J. BRYANT *Mythol.* II. 317 To appease the troubled ocean.

2. a. To pacify, assuage, or allay (anger or displeasure). Also *fig.*

c **1374** CHAUCER *Boeth.* IV. vii. 148 Hercules..apaised[e] wiþ þat deeþ þe wraþþe of euander. *a* **1450** *Knt. de la Tour* 13 Forto apese the wrathe of God..thei fasted. **1534** LD. BERNERS *Gold. Bk. M. Aurel.* Ff viij, The iuste goddis neuer appease theyr yres agaynst vniuste men. **1697** DRYDEN *Virg. Past.* IX. 9 These two kids t'appease his angry mood, I bear. **1750** JOHNSON *Rambl.* No. 79 ⁋5 To appease enmity by blandishments and bribes. **1846** RUSKIN *Mod. Paint.* IV. v. vi. §9 By the mists..his [the sun's] implacable light is divided, and its separated fierceness appeased into the soft blue.

b. To pacify or propitiate (him who is angry).

c **1374** CHAUCER *Troylus* III. 22 Ye fers Mars apesyn of his yre. *c* **1450** *Merlin* xxvi. 501 Thus apeesed the Queen Sir Gawein. **1579** TOMSON *Calvin's Serm. Tim.* 187/2 Christe..hath once appeased God his father toward vs. **1667** MILTON *P.L.* x. 846 Hasten to appease The incensed Father, and the incensed Son. **1762** GOLDSM. *Cit. World* xlix, This well-timed compliment instantly appeased the angry fairy. **1849** MACAULAY *Hist. Eng.* II. 244 The king was silenced, but not appeased.

c. *Politics.* In derog. sense (cf. sense 2 a, quot. 1750), used esp. of the British Prime Minister's efforts from 1937 to 1939 to placate, and so stave off the threatened aggression of, the Axis powers: to engage in a policy of appeasement (see APPEASEMENT).

1939 *Ann. Reg. 1938* 104 So far were they from trying to 'appease' the Dictators that they might rather be described as 'facing up' to them. **1940** *War Illustr.* 16 Feb. 106/3 If at any time..there are signs of a renewed desire for appeasement, let the fate of the Polish people remind us of the power we wish to appease. **1940** *New Statesman* 21 Dec. 650/1 He took a different view of the Nazis, whom he thought we could successfully appease. **1940** *New Republic* 23 Dec. 852/2 While England is appeasing Franco in this strictly limited sense, Franco is certainly not appeasing world opinion.

3. To assuage, soothe, allay, or relieve: **a.** physical pain (*obs.*) or mental suffering.

c **1374** CHAUCER *Compl. Mars.* 10 Apeseth [*v.r.* appeseth, -ease, -eesiþe, -esith, apaysith] sumwhat of your sorowes smart. *c* **1420** *Pallad. on Husb.* IV. 448 In the wynter season Covert of stre thaire coldes must appeson. **1543** TRAHERON *Vigo's Chirurg.* II. iv. 19 To appayse the payne of all apostemes. **1706** ADDISON *Rosamond* III. iii, Fain would my tongue his griefs appease. **1828** HAWTHORNE *Fanshawe* v. (1879) 78, I pray you to appease your anxiety.

†**b.** the sufferer or part affected. *Obs.*

c **1374** CHAUCER *Troylus* III. 887 Berith hym this blew ring, For ther is nothing might..better his hert apese. **1413** LYDG. *Pylgr. Sowle* IV. i. (1483) 58 Solace..wherwith to appesen his herte. **1566** PAINTER *Pal. Pleas.* I. Pref. 11 The sicke [shall be] appaysed of griefe.

4. To pacify, by satisfying demands (*lit.* or *fig.*): **a.** complaints (*obs.*), cravings, appetites, prejudices.

1548 COVERDALE *Erasm. Par. 1 Cor.* xi. 25 To apease mennes bodyly thruste. **1596** SPENSER *F.Q.* I. iii. 29 Now then your plaint appease. **1783** JOHNSON *Lett.* 329 II. 330 To have no assistance..in resolving doubts, in appeasing scruples. **1863** BURTON *Bk. Hunter* 42 The savage who seeks but to appease the hunger of the moment.

b. the person who makes the demand or has the appetite. Const. *with.*

1561 T. N[ORTON] *Calvin's Inst.* Pref., He hymselfe was appeased with a cardinalls hatte. **1728** NEWTON *Chronol. Amended* ii. 223 Bacchus appeased him [Vulcan] with wine. **1833** HT. MARTINEAU *Berkeley* I. iii. 60 What did you do to appease these insolent fellows?

†**5.** *refl.* in prec. senses. *Obs.*

c **1386** CHAUCER *Melib.* ⁋895 Whan he is debonaire and meeke, and appesith [apeiseth, -aiseth] him lightly. **1485** CAXTON *Paris & V.* 47 She appeased hyr self. **1523** LD. BERNERS *Froiss.* I. vii. 6 Fayre suster appease your selfe.

†**6.** *intr.* in prec. senses. *Obs.*

c **1440** *Partonope* 3986 Hys hert somwat ganne apese. *c* **1500** *Colyn Blowbol's Test.* in Halliw. *Nug. P.* 2 Whan his angwyssh somwhat gan apese. **1523** LD. BERNERS *Froiss.* I. xcii. 114 The thirde day..the see apeased. **1561** T. N[ORTON] *Calvin's Inst.* I. 18 After the crueltie appeased.

†**a'ppease**, *sb. Obs. rare.* [f. prec. vb.] An appeasing, allaying; appeasement.

c **1330** *Arth. & Merl.* 2342 Tho thai were al at aise Ich went to his in apaise. **1667** WATERHOUSE *Fire Lond.* 59 The engines of raising water [were] so destroyed, that there was no suitable appease to it.

appeased (əˈpiːzd), *ppl. a.* [f. APPEASE *v.* + -ED.] Pacified, quieted, satisfied.

1532 MORE *Confut. Tindale* Wks. 1557, 414/1 They fele theyr passions appeased. **1870** RUSKIN *Lect. Art.* vii. 185 Lead the appeased river by alternate azure promontories.

appeaseless (əˈpiːzlɪs), *a. rare*[−1]. [f. APPEASE + -LESS. Cf. *ceaseless.*] Not able to be appeased; implacable, insatiable.

1864 *Morn. Star* 16 Apr., The appeaseless maw of the furnace.

appeasement (əˈpiːzmənt). For forms see APPEASE *v.* [a. OFr. *apaisement*, *apeisement*, n. of action f. *apaisier*: see APPEASE and -MENT.]

1. The action or process of appeasing; pacification, satisfaction.

1430 *Instruct. Ambass.* in Rymer's *Fœdera* (1710) X. 725 To peine hem to th' Appesement of these Werres. **1579** FENTON *Guicciard.* xv. (1599) 690 For appeasement of their ancient controuersies. **1678** CUDWORTH *Intell. Syst.* 223 They might possibly sacrifice thereunto..for its Appeasement and Mitigation. **1836–7** SIR W. HAMILTON *Metaph.* xlii. (1870) II. 433 It is..altogether different to feel hunger and thirst, as states of pain, and to desire or will their appeasement.

†**2.** The instrumentality or means of appeasing; propitiation. *Obs.*

1561 T. N[ORTON] *Calvin's Inst.* III. 245 Jesus Christ yᵉ righteous is the appeasement for our sinnes. **1678** CUDWORTH *Intell. Syst.* 295 To have found out Expiations for wicked Actions..and Appeasments of the Divine Displeasure.

3. The result of appeasing; the state of being appeased; pacification, satisfaction.

1586 WEBBE *Eng. Poetrie* (Arb.) 39 The Comedies .. alwayes ended to the ioy and appeasement of all parties. *a* **1627** HAYWARD *Edw. VI*, 54 They were reduced to some good appeasement. **1836** J. GILBERT *Chr. Atonem.* iii. (1852) 79 He has no pleasure in witnessing suffering..he cannot derive the least appeasement from it.

4. Freely used in political contexts in the 20th century, and since 1938 often used disparagingly with allusion to the attempts at conciliation by concession made by Mr. Neville Chamberlain, the British Prime Minister, before the outbreak of war with Germany in 1939; by extension, any such policy of pacification by concession to an enemy.

1919 *Gen. Smuts' Messages to Empire: Problem of Peace* 14 In our policy of European settlement the appeasement of Germany..becomes one of cardinal importance. **1920** W. S. CHURCHILL *Let.* 24 Mar. in *World Crisis: Aftermath* (1929) xvii. 378 Here again I counsel prudence and appeasement. Try to secure a really representative Turkish governing authority, and come to terms with it. **1929** J. M. KEYNES in *Nation & Athenæum* 9 Mar. 782/2 Apart from Russia, Mr. Churchill appears, in a degree to which public opinion has done much less than justice, as an ardent and persistent advocate of the policy of appeasement—appeasement in Germany, in Ireland, in Turkey. **1934** LD. LOTHIAN *Let.* in *Times* 4 May 15/5 A limitation of armaments by political appeasement. **1936** ANTHONY EDEN in *Hansard Commons* 5th Ser. CCCX. 1446, I assure the House that it is the appeasement of Europe as a whole that we have constantly before us. **1937** W. K. HANCOCK *Survey Brit. Commonw. Affairs* I. 262 Equality and Appeasement, 1926–1936. **1938** *Encycl. Brit. Bk. of Year 1938* 194/1 Economic appeasement must precede any world-wide political appeasement. **1938** *Times* 3 Oct. 13/2 The policy of international appeasement must of course be pressed forward... There must be appeasement not only of the strong but of the weak... With the policy of appeasement must go the policy of preparation —preparation not so much for war as against war. **1939** *Ann. Reg. 1938* 10 One of the new Foreign Minister's first steps was to extend to Germany the methods of appeasement—as the Prime Minister was fond of calling them—which were now being tried with Italy. **1939** *New Statesman* 29 July 165/1 First, provided that there is a Russian pact, proposals that now smell of appeasement in the most dangerous sense at once become proper and, indeed, the only possible policy. *transf.* **1940** *Mind* XLIX. 327 Thus objectivity or qualified spatio-temporality is the '*Lebensraum*' provided for the 'appeasement' of the finite *actus-potentia*. **1949** F. MACLEAN *Eastern Approaches* III. iv. 351 Clearly appeasement formed no part of her nature.

appeaser (əˈpiːzə(r)). Also 6 -oure. [a. AFr. *apaisour* (mod.Fr. *appaiseur*): see APPEASE *v.* and -ER.] **1.** One who, or that which, appeases; a pacifier or satisfier.

1533 MORE *Apol.* xii. Wks. 1557, 871/1 Thys appeasoure ..dothe in all these thynges the contrarye. **1611** COTGR., *Propitiateur*..a reconciler, pacifier, appeaser. **1869** *Eng. Mech.* 3 Sept. 522/3 Cold tea is certainly a thirst appeaser.

2. *Politics.* One who supports a policy of appeasement (see APPEASE *v.* 2 c, APPEASEMENT 4).

1940 *Economist* 12 Oct. 456/1 Obviously, the United States is not going to play the appeaser's game. **1940** in *Amer. Speech* (1941) XVI. 145 Wouldn't it be better to make our own country impregnable..? People who say so are being called 'fifth columnists' and 'appeasers'.

appeasing (əˈpiːzɪŋ), *vbl. sb.* [f. APPEASE *v.* + -ING^1.] (Now mostly gerundial.)

1. The action of pacifying or calming; pacification.

1525–30 MORE *De quat. Noviss.* Wks. 1557, 87/1 Thappeasyng of his minde that is so stricken. **1660** *Hist. Indep.* IV. 55 For the only appeasing whereof, most of the county forces..did speedily march.

†**2.** The means of bringing peace or pacification.

1561 T. N[ORTON] *Calvin's Inst.* II. 169 He first loued vs, and sent hys sonne to be the appeasing for our sinnes. **1624** BEDELL *Lett.* vii. 113 The same..words may be a thanksgiving for one, and an appeasing of God's wrath for another.

aˈppeasing, *ppl. a.* [f. as prec. + -ING^2] That appeases; pacifying, quieting, calming.

a **1650** CRASHAW *Sacr. Poems* (1858) 148 The airy shop of soul-appeasing sound. **1753** CHAMBERS *Cycl. Supp.*, *Appeasing Remedies*..are those which assuage the pain in a disease.

aˈppeasingly, *adv. rare*$^{-1}$. [f. prec. + -LY^2.] In an appeasing or pacifying manner; soothingly.

1859 GEO. MEREDITH *R. Feverel* II. viii. 144 'Wall!' said the farmer appeasingly, 'we all do at your age.'

†**aˈppeasive,** *a. Obs. rare*$^{-1}$. [f. APPEASE *v.* + -IVE: cf. *amusive*.] Tending to appease, pacificatory, propitiative.

1610 HEALEY *St. Aug., City of God* (1620) 125 Their appeasiue and sacrificial banquets, in the temples. **1611** COTGR., *Mitigatif*, Mitigatiue, lenitiue, appeasiue. (In mod. Dicts.)

†**aˈppeirant,** *ppl. a. Sc. Obs.* [old north. pr. pple. *apperand*, modified after *apparant*, *-ent*.] [See quot. under APPARENT.]

appellancy (əˈpɛlənsɪ). ? *Obs.*$^{-0}$. [f. next: see -NCY.] 'Appeal; capability of appeal.' Todd 1818.

appellant (əˈpɛlənt), *a.* and *sb.* Also 6–7 **appealant**. [a. Fr. *appellant*, pr. pple. (also used subst.) of *appeller*: see APPEAL *v.* and -ANT. Occas. conformed to *appeal* vb. in 16–17th c.]

A. *adj.*

1. *Law* and *gen.* Appealing: **a.** accusing, challenging; **b.** appealing to a higher tribunal against an unsatisfactory decision; **c.** asking or crying for assistance.

(In *Lords Appellants*, orig. *adj.*, but soon treated as *sb.*: cf. ACCOUNTANT.) See B 1.

1593 SHAKS. *Rich. II*, I. i. 34 Free from other misbegotten hate, Come I appealant to this Princely presence. **1700** R. BRADY *Cont. Hist. Eng.* Rich. II, Index C, Appellant Lords in Richard II's Reign. **1808** BENTHAM *Sc. Reform* 111 Power to the House of Lords..to decree payment..by any of the parties appellant. **1871** J. MACDUFF *Mem. Patmos* xi. 143 An appellant voice represented as rising loud before Him who sitteth on the throne.

2. *Law.* As regards appeals; appellate.

1818 HALLAM *Mid. Ages* (1841) I. v. 458 Their jurisdiction in private causes was merely appellant. **1827** —— *Const. Hist.* (1876) II. 200 The presbyterian tribunals were made subject to the appellant control of parliament.

B. *sb.*

1. One who 'appeals' another of treason or felony: see APPEAL *v.* 1. *Obs.* exc. *Hist.*

[**1387–8** *Rot. Parl.* III. 236 (xi. Rich. II.) Les ditz Duc & Countes Appellantz.] **1593** SHAKS. *Rich. II*, IV. i. 105 Lords Appealants, your differences shal all rest vnder gage. **1628** COKE *On Litt.* 287 b, Wrongs done to the Appellants themselves, as Robbery, Rape. **1691** BLOUNT *Law Dict.*, Appellant, Is he who hath committed some Felony..and now Appeals, that is, Accuses others who were complices. **1700** R. BRADY *Cont. Hist. Eng.* Rich. II, 371 C, The protestation of the Five Lords Appellants. **1809** TOMLINS *Law Dict.* H ib, If the appellant [in an Appeal of Death] does not prosecute his appeal, or if he release to the appellant, the appellee may be indicted. **1840** *Blackw. Mag.* XLVII. 279 A person was charged with having poisoned a man; the accuser, called the appellant, etc. **1875** GAIRDNER *Ho. York & Lanc.* ii, §7 ¶1 Three of the five 'lords appellants' of 1387.

†**b.** Hence, One who challenges another to single combat (*orig.* to prove upon his body the treason or felony of which he 'appealed' him). *Obs.*

1480 CAXTON *Chron. Eng.* VII. (1520) 143/2 A great batayll ..bytwene two squyers..Gloucestre that was the appellaunt and Arthur the defendaunt. **1593** SHAKS. *2 Hen. VI*, II. iii. 49 Ready are the Appellant and Defendant..to enter the lists. **1671** MILTON *Samson* 1220 Answer thy appellant..Who now defies thee thrice to single fight.

2. One who appeals to a higher court against the decision of a lower one; also, *gen.* One who appeals for vindication or corroboration.

1611 COTGR., *Bailler griefs en plaiderie*, an Appealant to alledge the wrongs..done vnto him by the sentence from which he hath appealed. **1726** AYLIFFE *Parerg.* 72 Pending the Appeal nothing can be attempted in Prejudice of the Appellant. **1826** SOUTHEY *Vind. Eccl. Ang.* 523 You called for such proofs... I am not the appellant in this controversy. **1846** LD. CAMPBELL *Chancellors* (1856) V. 490 To retain him as junior to prepare the appellant's case.

b. *Ch. Hist.* in *pl.* The Jansenists and others who appealed to a general council against the 'Unigenitus' bull issued by Pope Clement XI. against Quesnel's French translation of the New Testament.

1753 in CHAMBERS *Cycl. Supp.*

3. *gen.* One who appeals, who makes a request, entreaty, or specially pointed address.

1704 SWIFT *T. Tub* Ded., An humble and an earnest appellant for the laurel. **1853** C. BRONTË *Villette* viii. (1876) 67, I have seen her feelings appealed to, and I have smiled in half-pity, half-scorn at the appellants.

appellate (əˈpɛlət), *ppl. a.* and *sb.* [ad. L. *appellāt-us*, pa. pple. of *appellāre*: see APPEAL *v.*]

A. *adj.* †**1.** Appealed against. *Obs. rare.*

1726 AYLIFFE *Parerg.* (J.) The party appellate, or person against whom the appeal is lodged.

2. Appealed to; taking cognizance of appeals.

1768 BLACKSTONE *Comm.* I. 105 The earls of Derby, as lords of Man..exercising an appellate jurisdiction. **1790** BURKE *Fr. Rev.* 288 The judges, neither the original nor the appellate, are of his nomination. **1862** S. LUCAS *Secularia* 16 Provision against error or injustice..in the long series of appellate tribunals.

†**B.** *sb.* One who is appealed against. *Obs. rare.*

1726 AYLIFFE *Parerg.* 78 A wholesome Doctrine in Favour of Appellates, against rash Appellants.

appellate (ˈæpəleɪt), *v. rare.* [f. L. *appellāt-* ppl. stem of *appellā-re* to call: see APPEAL *v.*] To call, to designate.

1765 TUCKER *Lt. Nat.* I. 475 The vast Pacific Ocean, commonly..appellated (as the saying is) and annominated, the South-sea. **1834–43** SOUTHEY *Doctor* cxxxvi. (1849) I. 339 What some of our own writers..appellate an entire horse.

appellation (æpəˈleɪʃən). [a. Fr. *appellation* (13th c.), ad. L. *appellātion-em*, n. of action f. *appellāre*: see APPEAL *v.* and -TION.]

I. Appealing, appeal. [from OFr. *apeler*.] *Obs.*

†**1.** The action of appealing to a higher court or authority against the decision of an inferior one; the appeal so made; = APPEAL *sb.* 3. *Obs.*

1494 FABYAN vii. 479 In iugement vpon the appellacions before made by the erle of Armenak..agayne prynce Edwarde. **1538** STARKEY *England* 125 Another grete mysordur, in appellatyon of such as be callyd spiritual causys. **1547** *Homilies* I. ix. (1859) 92 The condemnation both of body and soul, without either appellation or hope of redemption. **1609** SKENE *Reg. Maj.* 65 In Ecclesiasticall causes appellation is admitted within fourtie dayes. **1669** HONYMAN *Surv. Naphtali* II. 105 Pauls appellation to Cæsar, Acts XXV. II. **1679** FILMER *Freeholder* 66 There might be Appellation made to the Kings Person.

†**b.** Ground of appeal, title, claim. *Obs. rare.*

1630 NAUNTON *Fragm. Reg.* (Arb.) 26 He could not find out any appellation to assume the Crown in his own Person.

†**2.** *gen.* The action or process of appealing or calling on; entreaty, or earnest address. *Obs.*

1587 M. GROVE *Pelops & Hipp.* (1878) 18 No god there was but him they had in appellation. **1589** *Hay any Work* 43 His appellation to the obedient cleargie. **1671** *True Non-Conf.* 399 Master Knox his reasoning..in his appellation and admonition to the commonalty.

II. Calling, designation. [from later Fr. *appeler*, or L. *appellāre*.]

3. The action of calling by a name; nomenclature.

1581 CAMPION in *Confer.* III. (1584) U iiij, Euery piece of bread is called bread..because it was bread by appellation. **1630** PRYNNE *Anti-Armin*, 126 If it be grace in truth, as well as in appellation. **1742** HUME *Ess.* (1817) I. 36 The government, which in common appellation receives the appellation of free. **1875** WHITNEY *Life Lang.* ii. 27 They must be carefully distinguished in appellation.

4. A designation, name, or title given: **a.** to a particular person or thing.

1447 BOKENHAM *Lyvys of Seyntys* 44 Anne is as myche to seyn as grace And worthyly thys appellacyoun To hyr pertenyth. **1610** *Histriom.* I. 136 *Seri.* Your appellations? *Post.* Your names he meanes. The man's learn'd. *a* **1674** CLARENDON *Hist. Reb.* I. i. 15 Stenny, an appellation he allways used of and towards the Duke. **1774** PRIESTLEY *Observ. Air* 178 By the common appellation of phlogisticated air. **1833–48** H. COLERIDGE *North. Worth.* (1852) I. 69 Which entitles him to the appellation of a prose Juvenal.

b. to a class: A descriptive or connotative name.

1581 MARBECK *Bk. of Notes* 665 Manes the Hereticke, whereof the Maniches haue their appellation. **1651** HOBBES *Govt. & Soc.* vii. §3. 112 If he..Rule well..they afford him the appellation of a King; if not, they count him a Tyrant. **1709** SWIFT *T. Tub.* iii. 50 These men seem..to have understood the appellation of critic in a liberal sense. **1841** BORROW *Zincali* I. vi. §1. 102 If not sorcerers, they have always done their best to merit that appellation.

appellational (æpəˈleɪʃənəl), *a. rare.* [f. prec. + -AL^1.] Of or pertaining to appellations.

1882 *Cornh. Mag.* Feb. 213 Those appellational oddities.

‖**appellation contrôlée** (apɛlasjɔ̃ kɔ̃trole). [Fr. (in full *appellation d'origine contrôlée*), lit. 'controlled name'.] In France: a description awarded to wine, guaranteeing that it was produced in the region specified in its name, using vines and production methods which satisfy the regulating body. Also applied to some foodstuffs.

1950 *Wine & Food* Autumn 167 One should note also the growing importance of the protected labels (*appellation controlée* [sic]) in Bordeaux. While the great châteaux generally ignore them, the lesser ones proudly place the proper *appellation controlée* on their labels. **1952** A. LICHINE *Wines of France* vii. 74 Wines from a region come under regulations whose stringency depends on the '*Appellation Contrôlée*' claimed by them. **1966** P. V. PRICE *France: Food & Wine Guide* 48 The most vaunted type of lamb..is known as *pré salé* (salty meadow) and has an *Appellation Contrôlée*. **1966** *Sunday Times* 27 Nov. 46/6 A first-class 'Appellation Contrôllée' wine must come from a single vineyard in a single year, and carry the names of grower and bottler. **1968** [see VIN 1]. **1985** *Financial Times* (Weekend Suppl.) 31 Aug. p. viii/8 It must always be borne in mind that the AOC system is primarily aimed at helping the producer rather than the consumer... A wine bearing an *appellation contrôlée* on its label is by no means necessarily good: it has simply satisfied the appropriate regulations.

appellative (əˈpɛlətɪv), *a.* and *sb.* [ad. L. *appellātīvus*, f. *appellāt-*: see APPEAL *v.* and -IVE.]

A. *adj.* Having the characteristic of naming.

1. Designating a class; *common* as opposed to *proper*.

1520 WHITTINTON *Vulg.* (1527) 4 b, If they be nownes appellatyue. **1590** SWINBURN *Testaments* 179 b, By names appellatiue..I vnderstand euerie name, which is common or maie comprehend diuers persons. **1755** JOHNSON *Pref. Dict.* Wks. IX. 203 As my design was a dictionary, common or appellative, I have omitted all words which have relation to proper names. **1882** J. ROBERTSON tr. *Müller's Heb. Synt.* 48 Words that have almost or entirely lost their appellative meaning, as *tehom*, 'abyss,' 'the deep.'

†**2.** Of the nature of an appellation, or descriptive name given to a thing or person. *Obs.*

1607 TOPSELL *Four-f. Beasts* 111 Many particular Dogs, and their names appellative.. as Scylax, Speude, Alke, Rome. **1654** GAYTON *Fest. Notes* IV. iii. 191 All Knights and doughty men gave to themselves some name appellative.

3. Of or pertaining to the giving of names.

1860 FARRAR *Orig. Lang.* iii. 64 The appellative faculty in the savage and in the infant.

B. *sb.*

1. A 'common' noun or name applicable to any one member of a whole class.

1591 PERCIVALL *Sp. Dict.*, Of the Substantiues some be proper, as *Vasco*, *Alonso*. Some common, called also appellatiues, as *Arbol*, a tree. **1612** BRINSLY *Lud. Lit.* 76 Your rules of Appellatiues, or Common Nownes. **1747** JOHNSON *Plan Dict.* Wks. 1787 IX. 171 Appellatives, or the names of species. **1854** DE QUINCEY in Page *Life* II. xviii. 86 Appellatives, words not expressing an individual but a class or species.

2. That which a thing or person is 'called'; an appellation, designation, or descriptive name.

1632 SANDERSON *12 Serm.* 140 The Philistims called their Kings by a peculiar appellatiue. *a* **1733** NORTH *Lives* III. 112 Whig and Tory..were the appellatives; but the mythology was seditious and loyal. **1814** SCOTT *Wav.* III. iv. 52 Wily Will justified his appellative. **1869** GLADSTONE *Juv. Mundi* ii. 31 The several appellatives by which Homer describes the army engaged in the siege of Troy.

aˈppellatived, *ppl. a. rare.* [f. prec. sb. + -ED^2.] Having an appellative.

1828 LYTTON *Disowned* I. xi. 66 Mr. De Warens, the nobly appellatived foot-boy, was laying the breakfast cloth.

aˈppellatively, *adv.* [f. prec. adj. + -LY^2.] In an appellative manner; as a common noun.

1613 PURCHAS *Pilgr.* I. I. vi. 29 In the *land of Nod*, which some take to be appellatively spoken, as if his misery had given name of *Moving* unto the place. **1662** FULLER *Worthies* II. 18 The Fallacy lieth in the Homonymy of Ware, here not taken for that Town so named, but appellatively for all vendible Commodities. **1875** WHITNEY *Life Lang.* x. 205 Whether the quality-denoting word shall be used attributively or appellatively.

aˈppellativeness. *rare*$^{-1}$. [f. as prec. + -NESS.] The quality of being appellative.

1662 FULLER *Worthies* III. 70 [To] reduce the proper names in the Genealogies to such an Appellativeness as should compose a continued sense.

†**aˈppellatory,** *a.* and *sb. Obs.* [ad. L. *appellātōri-us*, f. *appellātōr-*, n. of agent f. *appellāre*: see APPEAL and -ORY.]

A. *adj.* Pertaining to an appellant or an appeal.

1553–87 FOXE *A. & M.*, *Edw. VI*, 1207 (R.) He requireth that letters dimissories or appellatories might be given him. **1726** AYLIFFE *Parerg.* (L.) An appellatory libel ought to contain the name of the party appellant.

B. *sb.* [sc. letter.] *rare.*

1747 CARTE *Hist. Eng.* I. 607 The legates..gave them appellatories.

appellee (æpəˈliː, əˌpɛˈliː). *Law.* Also 7 **appealee**. [a. Fr. *appelé*, pa. pple. of *appeler* to APPEAL: see -EE.] One who is appealed against.

1. One who is accused of crime, informed against, or challenged to prove his innocence.

[**1387–8** *Rot. Parl.* III. 229 (xi. Rich. II) Qe touz les ditz Appellez seroient a dit Parliament, a respondre sur l'Appell.] **1531** *Dial. Laws Eng.* II. xlviii. (1638) 152 Though the appellee were neuer so great an offender. **1679** *Trial of Langhorn* 27 If the Approver be pardoned, by the Law the Appellee ought to be discharged. **1768** BLACKSTONE *Comm.* IV. 311 If the appellee be acquitted, he cannot be afterwards indicted for the same offence. **1851** SIR F. PALGRAVE *Norm. & Eng.* I. 240 The appellor and appellee dismounted, wielding club and staff.

†**2.** The defendant in a case carried to a higher court; now called the *respondent*. *Obs.*

1611 COTGR. s.v. *Anticipé appel*, A speciall Commission, procured by th' Appealee.

† **a'ppelling**, *ppl. a. Obs. rare.* [f. vb. *appell (ad. L. *appell-ĕre*, f. *ap-* = *ad-* to + *pellĕre* to drive) + -ING[2].] Driving, pushing, or forcing onwards.
1666 G. HARVEY *Morb. Angl.* x. 116 A glowing heat.. excited through the appelling purulent corrosive steams. **1693** *Phil. Trans.* XVII. 662 Stick there till other appelling Substances give them a farther Comminution.

appellor (əˈpɛ,lɔː(r), ,æpɛˈlɔː(r)). *Law.* Also 5-7 -our(e; *aphet.* pelour. [a. AFr. *apelour*:—OFr. *apeleor*:—L. *appellātōr-em*, n. of agent f. *appellā-re*: see APPEAL and -OR.] One who accuses of crime, demands proof of innocence by wager of battle, or informs against an accomplice. (See also APPEALER, APPELLANT.)
c **1400** *Harl. MS.* Rolls Ser. VII. 519 Gunnildas nory karf the fals pelours hamme. **1440** *Promp. Parv.*, Apechowre or apelowre, *Appellator.* **1660** R. COKE *Power & Subj.* 199 That thieves or appellors may confess their offences unto priests. **1768** BLACKSTONE *Comm.* IV. xxiii, If the appellee be acquitted, the appellor..shall suffer one year's imprisonment. **1809** TOMLINS *Law Dict.* H i b. **1851** [see APPELLEE].

appely, -ily, obs. forms of HAPLY.

appenage, obs. form of APANAGE.

† **a'ppend**, *v.*[1] *Obs.* Also 4 **apend, apent,** 5 **appent.** Aphetic 4-5 **pend, pent.** [a. OFr. *apendre* (3rd sing. *il apent*, whence ME. variant *apent*), to depend on, belong to, pertain:—L. *appendĕre* (in cl. L. only trans.) for *appendēre*, f. *ap-* = *ad-* to + *pendēre* to hang (intr.). Obsolete before 1500, and not connected (in Eng.) with APPEND *v.*[2]] *intr.* To belong *to* as a possession, natural accompaniment, or right; to pertain; to relate, to refer; to be suited or proper *to*. *Obs.*
c **1325** *E.E. Allit. P.* B. 1270 Alle þe apparement þat pented to þe kyrke. *c* **1340** *Gaw. & Gr. Knt.* 623 Quy þe pentangel apendeȝ to þat prynce noble. *c* **1386** CHAUCER *Pers. T.* ¶970 Holy orisoun..appendith specially to penitence. *a* **1400** *Chester Pl.* (1847) 131 Oure Lorde will us lere whereto it [the star in the East] will apente. *Ibid.* 189 Yf you wiste wherto it would apente. *c* **1400** *Towneley Myst.* 239 That [harnes] appentys unto me. **1470** HARDING *Chron.* xxvii, His wife..With all aray that to the werre apent [*v.r.* her wer apent]. *Ibid.* lvii, All bokes or ornamentes, Bellys, relyquys, that to [the church] appendes.

append (əˈpɛnd), *v.*[2] [a. (perh. through mod.Fr. *append-re*) L. *append-ĕre* to hang to. In form the same word as prec., re-adopted from L. or Fr. in the transitive sense of *appendĕre*, after the prec. vb. had been long obsolete.]
1. To hang on, to attach as a pendant.
1646 SIR T. BROWNE *Pseud. Ep.* II. v, If amulets do work by emanations from their bodies upon those parts wherunto they are appended. **1831** CARLYLE *Sart. Res.* II. iii, A Conquering Hero, to whom Fate has malignantly appended a tin-kettle of Ambition.
2. To attach, join on, annex, as an accessory either material or attributive.
1779-81 JOHNSON *L.P. Shenstone* Wks. IV. 214 Hales-Owen..in the division of the kingdom, was appended..to a distant county. **1835** J. HARRIS *Gt. Teacher* (1837) 382 One thing to which everything else desirable is appended. **1863** KEMBLE *Resid. Georgia* 34 The purposes for which hands and arms were appended to our bodies.
3. To add in writing by way of supplement or appendix.
1843 MILL *Logic* II. iii. §8 Some additional remarks..are appended. **1879** FARRAR *Paul* I. Pref. 9 To append notes to the more difficult expressions.

appendage (əˈpɛndɪdʒ). [f. prec. + -AGE: cf. *equipage*; also *apanage* (in 17th c. *appennage*), by which the sense was perhaps influenced.] That which is attached as if by being hung on; a subsidiary external adjunct, addition, or accompaniment, which does not form an essential part of that to which it is added, but is usually natural or appropriate to it. (Cf. APPENDIX.)
1. of things material. **a.** generally.
1713 DERHAM *Phys. Theol.* IV. xii. 214 Clothing, another necessary Appendage of Life. **1790** BEATSON *Nav. & Mil. Mem.* II. 30 An army, with all its necessary appendages. **1854** BREWSTER *More Worlds* iv. 76 The planet Saturn, encompassed with the extraordinary appendage of a ring.
esp. **b.** An addition to territory or property. Cf. APANAGE 3, APPENDANT B. 1.
1667 E. CHAMBERLAYNE *St. Gt. Brit.* I. I. iii. (1743) 15 Two of their [the Cinque-Ports'] appendages, Winchelsea and Rye, are in Sussex. **1796** MORSE *Amer. Geog.* I. 783 The other islands..should be regarded as appendages to Curassou. **1876** DIGBY *Real Prop.* i. §1. 7 Dwelling-houses and their appendages.
† **c.** An addition in writing; an APPENDIX. *Obs.*
1651 HOBBES *Govt. & Soc.* Ded., That Appendage which is added concerning the Regiment of God.
d. *Nat. Hist.* A subordinate or subsidiary organ.
1785 J. E. SMITH in *Leis. Hour* June 1883, 353/1 The angular appendage to the nose of the American bat. **1870** H. MACMILLAN *Bible Teach.* vii. 135 All the appendages borne on the stem—such as scales, leaves, bracts, flowers, and fruit. **1874** CARPENTER *Ment. Phys.* I. ii. §59 Antennae and other appendages used for feeling.
2. of things immaterial.
1649 JER. TAYLOR *Gt. Exemp.* xvii. §5 If the pious action have been formerly joined with anything..truly criminal.. I give cause..to think I approve of the old appendage. **1673** CAVE *Prim. Chr.* I. x. 327 Confirmation which ever was a constant appendage to Baptism. **1763** J. BROWN *Poetry & Mus.* §4. 40 The Dance..being only secondary, and merely an Appendage to the Song. **1848** MARIOTTI *Italy Past & Pr.* I. 8 Religion and gallantry soon made humanity an indispensable appendage of true valour.
3. *transf.* of persons.
1838 ELIZA COOK *Melaia* xxv, That rare appendage to a king, A friend that never played the slave. **1858** DORAN *Court Fools* 121 Such an official was not an uncommon appendage to legations.

appendaged (əˈpɛndɪdʒd), *ppl. a.* [f. prec. + -ED[2].] Furnished with, or having, an appendage.
1854 WOODWARD *Man. Mollusca* (1856) 134 *Litorinidæ*.. operculum-lobe appendaged. **1875** BROWNING *Inn Album* 36 This pretty cousin's place, Appendaged with your million, tempts my hand.

appendance, -ence (əˈpɛndəns). [a. Fr. *appendance*, f. *a(p)pendre*: see APPEND[1] and -ANCE.]
† **1.** A dependent possession, a dependency. *Obs.*
1523 LD. BERNERS *Froiss.* I. ccxii. 258 Townes, castels, landes..or theyr appurtenaunces and appendaunces, whatsoeuer they be. **1598** HAKLUYT *Voy.* I. 2 Many other Islands beyond Norway..are appendances of Scantia. **1662** FULLER *Worthies* III. 116 So numerous is the Church with its Appendences.
† **2.** An external or extraneous adjunct, addition, or concomitant; an appendage. *Obs.*
1561 T. N[ORTON] *Calvin's Inst.* IV. xviii. (1634) 712 The Masse taken in her most picked purenesse..without her appendances. **1615** CROOKE *Body of Man* 969 Some haue thought them onely Appendances of certaine rootes left in the iaw. **1677** HALE *Contempl.* II. 15 Even such a Tranquillity of mind..hath certain appendances to it, that abate that sincereness of Happiness.
3. *Law.* The fact of being appendant.
1832 AUSTIN *Jurispr.* (1879) II. l. 852 What is called appendance (if I may be permitted to coin an abstract name corresponding to the concrete appendant) is merely a species or modification of appurtenance. The distinction.. is merely, that, into common appendant there enters the notion of the feudal relation constituted by tenure.

† **a'ppendancy, -ency.** *Obs.* [strictly n. of quality f. APPENDANT (see -NCY), but also concr.]
1. The quality or state of being appendant.
1641 SPELMAN *De Sepult.* 176 (R.) Abraham..bought the whole field, and by right of appendency had the cave with it.
2. = APPENDANCE 2.
1615 CROOKE *Body of Man* 925 Their Perforations, Cauities, Bosomes, Appendancies, Prominences, and Processes. **1669** PENN *No Cross, etc.* I. v. §5 All Worldly Temples, and their ceremonious Appendencies.

appendant, -ent (əˈpɛndənt), *a.* and *sb.* [a. Fr. *appendant*, pr. pple. of *appendre*. Orig. belonging to APPEND *v.*[1], but subseq. influenced by APPEND *v.*[2]]
A. *adj.* Const. *to, on.*
1. *Law.* Attached or belonging to a possession or tenure as an additional but subsidiary right.
1523 FITZHERB. *Surv.* vi. (1539) 9 Those tenantes that haue commen appendaunt. **1649** SELDEN *Laws of Eng.* I. xxxi. (1739) 46 Liberties..granted by Kings as appendant to Manors. **1768** BLACKSTONE *Comm.* II. 33 Common appendant is a right, belonging to the owners or occupiers of arable land, to put commonable beasts upon the lord's waste. **1844** WILLIAMS *Real Prop. Law* (1877) 322 Incorporeal hereditaments which are appendant to such as are corporeal.
2. Of things material: Attached in a subordinate capacity or relation; annexed, adjunct.
1577 HOLINSHED *Chron.* II. 13/2 The Orchades are adjudged to be appendant to Ireland. **1664** POWER *Exp. Philos.* I. 66 The stomach and guts, and their appendent Vessels, the lacteal Veins. **1775** JOHNSON in *Boswell* li. (1847) 463 Trianon is a kind of retreat appendant to Versailles. **1836** *Blackw. Mag.* XXXIX. 462 That they are merely appendant on the great metropolis, and have no independent local character. **1865** *Sat. Rev.* 18 Feb. 85 The Encyclical with its appendant Syllabus.
† **b.** *transf.* of persons. *Obs.*
1599 MARSTON *Sc. Villanie* II. vii. 203 His faire appendant whore That lackies him. **1655** FULLER *Ch. Hist.* VII. 406 Chancellours, and Officialls, and other appendant limbs.
3. Attached by a relation of cause or purpose; pertinent, attendant, consequent.
1509 HAWES *Past. Pleas.* XVI. vii, Because phisyke is appendaunt Unto the body by helpe of medecyne. **1539** ELYOT in Ellis *Orig. Lett.* I. 142 II. 118 That office wherunto is as it were appendant losse of money and good name. **1692** SOUTH 12 *Serm.* (1697) I. 41 A pleasure, embased with no appendant sting. **1779** JOHNSON *L.P., Watts* Wks. IV. 187 He offered to remit the salary appendant to it. **1808** COLEBROOKE *Vedas* in *Asiat. Res.* VIII. 380, I have learnt.. the sciences appendant on holy writ. **1833** CHALMERS *Const. Man* (1835) I. ii. 127 The unavoidable pleasure appendant to the gratification of each of them.
4. *lit.* Hanging attached (*to*).
1576 THYNNE in *Animadv.* 115 Who further have appendante to that honour's cheyne, Don Jasons Flese of golde. **1662** FULLER *Worthies* (1840) II. 51 A rhyming epitaph is appendant on a pillar. **1664** POWER *Exp. Philos.* I. 22 With an Appendent Proboscis or Trunk. *a* **1711** KEN *Edmund* Poet. Wks. 1721 II. 347 Dire knotted whips, arm'd with appendent Lead. **1762** H. WALPOLE *Vertue's Anecd. Paint.* (1786) II. 282 To which was appendent a gold medal. **1874** RILEY *4th Rep. Com. Hist. MSS.* 449/2 The seal.. appendant by a silken cord.
b. 'Hanging' *with*; decorated *with* (hanging ornaments).
a **1797** H. WALPOLE *George II* (1847) III. i. 8 The right arm lined with fur, and appendent with many black ribands.
B. *sb.* [the adj. used *absol.*] *arch.*
1. *Law.* A lesser right or property attached by prescription to one more important.
1525 LD. BERNERS *Froiss.* II. vii. 16 The towne of Sluse, with the apendauntes and profytes of the see. **1628** COKE *On Litt.* 121 b, Appendant is any inheritance belonging to another that is superior or more worthy. **1809** TOMLINS *Law Dict.* I. H vij/2 Appendants are ever by prescription, and this makes a distinction between appendants and appurtenances.
2. A material addition of a subordinate nature; an adjunct, appendage; a dependency.
1587 FLEMING *Contn. Holinshed* III. 416/1 The said dukedome of Burgundie and the appendants. **1633** P. FLETCHER *Purple Isl.* II. *note*, The first [entrail-pipe]..is called 'blind;' at whose end is an appendant. **1692** RAY *Disc.* iii. (1732) 24 The Sea with all its Creeks, Bays, and Inlets and other Appendants.
b. *transf.* of persons.
1641 SMECTYMNUUS *Vind. Answ.* §13. 115 It is granted by our Remonstrant, and his appendant Scultetus. **1654** LESTRANGE *Charles I*, 167 All the Judges..with all the Officers and appendants of their Courts. **1814** MISS BURNEY *Wanderer* I. 395 An equal member of the community, not a poor..appendant to it.
3. A quality, property, principle, etc. naturally attached or logically resulting.
1587 GOLDING *De Mornay* xiv. (1617) 219 The doctrine of Gods prouidence, and the immortalitie of our soules are so linked together, that the one is as an appendant to the other. **1749** WESLEY *Wks.* 1872 X. 124 To satisfy, though but as an appendant to the satisfaction of Christ. **1824** COLERIDGE *Aids to Refl.* (1848) I. 198 The numerous corollaries or appendents.
4. An appendix; a pendant.
1570 T. NORTON *Nowel's Catech.* (1853) 202 A certain appendant of the Lord's Prayer. 'For thine is the kingdom,' etc. **1836** SOUTHEY *Cowper's Wks.* II. 96 To publish the Task and its appendants as a second [volume].

appendectomy (,æpɛnˈdɛktəmɪ). *Surg. U.S.* [f. APPEND(IX *sb.* + Gr. ἐκτομή cutting out.] = APPENDICECTOMY.
1894-5 D. MASON in *N. Orleans Med. & Surg. Jrnl.* XXII. 570 (*title*) Appendectomy. **1903** *N.Y. Med. Jrnl.* 4 July 5/2 The methods of appendectomy can be divided into two classes, those with a stump and those without a stump. **1961** J. HELLER *Catch-22* (1962) xxxiii. 347 A nude, ridiculous man with a blushing appendectomy scar appeared in the doorway.

appended (əˈpɛndɪd), *ppl. a.* [f. APPEND + -ED.] Hung on; added as supplementary, annexed.
1727-51 CHAMBERS *Cycl.*, *Appended Remedies*..are outwardly applied, by hanging about the neck. **1856** KANE *Arct. Expl.* I. xx. 249 The appended report of Dr. Hayes.

appendical (əˈpɛndɪkəl), *a.* [f. L. *appendic-em* APPENDIX + -AL[1].] **a.** Of the nature of an appendix.
1850 *Athenæum* 19 Jan. 80 A thing superfluous and appendical to the drama. **1866** —— No. 2095. 216/3 The appendical list of country professors.
b. Of or pertaining to the vermiform appendix. *rare.*
1909 *Practitioner* Nov. 646 A typical history of appendical perforation.

† **a'ppendicate**, *v. Obs. rare.* [f. as prec. + -ATE[3].] To add as an appendix; to append.
1677 HALE *P.O.M.* IV. i. 290 Explications..which..draw in question the Truth itself to which they are appendicated.

† **a,ppendi'cation.** *Obs. rare.* [n. of action f. prec.: see -TION.] Addition by way of appendix.
1677 HALE *Prim. Orig. Man.* 74 Some great and considerable parts..appendications unto the *Mundus aspectabilis.* *a* **1677** —— *Relig.* I. 9 Superadditions and Appendications to Christian Religion.

† **a'ppendice**, *v. Obs. rare.* [f. *appendice* sb.; see APPENDIX 4.] **a.** *trans.* To add as an appendix. **b.** *intr.* To form an appendix. Hence **appendicing** *ppl. a.*, appendant.
1661 MORGAN *Sph. Gent.* III. iii. 28 A double chain of gold ..the appendicing Jewel being within an oval a Lilly. **1702** C. MATHER *Magn. Chr.* III. Introd. §4, I have appendiced the life of a famous Thomas.

appendicectomy (ə,pɛndɪˈsɛktəmɪ). *Surg.* [f. L. *appendic-*, stem of APPENDIX *sb.* + Gr. ἐκτομή cutting out.] Excision of the vermiform appendix of the cæcum.
1894 T. MYLES in *Med. Press & Circular* LVIII. 637/2 (*title*) Appendicectomy, with notes of two cases. **1905** *Nursing Times* 23 Dec. 666/2 Appendicectomy: After Results... The late after-results of removal of the appendix.

appen'dicious, -itious, *a. rare.* [f. med.L. *appendicius, -itius.*] Of the nature of an appendix.
1656 BLOUNT *Glossogr.*, *Appenditious.*

appendicitis (əˌpɛndɪˈsaɪtɪs). *Path.* [mod.L., f. as APPENDICECTOMY + -ITIS.] Inflammation of the vermiform appendix of the cæcum.

1886 R. H. FITZ in *Amer. Jrnl. Med. Sci.* Oct. 323 As a circumscribed peritonitis is simply one event..in the history of inflammation of the appendix, it seems preferable to use the term appendicitis to express the primary condition. **1887** BUCK *Handbk. Med. Sci.* IV. 185/2 The symptoms of appendicitis, pure and simple, are probably very slight, and not easily recognizable. **1905** KELLY & HURDON *Verm. App.* 382 Some cases of appendicitis occasioned by influenza.

appendicle (aˈpɛndɪk(ə)l). [ad. (perh. through Fr.) L. *appendicula*, dim. of APPENDIX.] A small appendix or appendage.

1611 COTGR., Appendicule, An appendicle or little appendix. **1677** GALE *Crt. Gentiles* IV. ii. v, An appendicule or little appendix of a thing. **1853** MAYNE *Exp. Lex.*, *Appendicula*, A little appendage; an appendicle.

appendicular (æpənˈdɪkjʊlə(r)), *a.* [f. L. *appendicula* (see prec.) + -AR; cf. Fr. *appendiculaire*.] Belonging to, or of the nature of, an appendicle.

1651 WELDON *Crt. K. Charles* 196 A seale appendicular to an office erected by him. **1857** HENFREY *Elem. Bot.* §42 Leaves and their modifications, forming the lateral or appendicular organs. **1872** MIVART *Anat.* 25 The skeleton of the limbs..is called the Appendicular skeleton.

appendicularian (æpənˌdɪkjʊˈlɛərɪən), *a.* and *sb. Zool.* [f. mod.L. *Appendiculāria* (see prec.) + -AN.] **A.** *adj.* Pertaining to the *Appendicularia*, a family of minute ascidian molluscs, with long tail-appendages. **B.** *sb.* A member of this family.

1880 A. WILSON in *Gent. Mag.* CCXLVI. 43 The appendicularians..the existing representatives of the stock and ancestry which gave origin alike to the sea-squirt race and to the great vertebrate group itself.

appendiculate (æpənˈdɪkjʊlət), *a. Biol.* [f. L. *appendicula* (see above) + -ATE[2].] Furnished with small appendages; forming an appendicle.

1835 *Penny Cycl.* s.v. *Botany*, *Appendiculate*, having some kind of appendages. **1863** BERKELEY *Brit. Mosses* Gloss. 311 Appendiculate, fringed with little fragmentary bodies. **1870** ROLLESTON *Anim. Life* 138 External appendiculate organs such as locomotor setæ or gills.

appenˈdiculated, *ppl. a. rare.* = prec.

1752 SIR J. HILL *Hist. Anim.* 19 (JOD.) With a subulated tail appendiculated to each side. **1774** HUNTER in *Phil. Trans.* LXIV. 317. The pancreas..of the Gillaroo trout..is appendiculated.

aˈppending, *ppl. a.* [f. APPEND *v.*[1] + -ING[2].] = APPENDANT.

1527 ANDREW *Brunswyke's Distyll. Waters* A j, The appendyng gowtes of laxatyfe medycynes. **1624** HEYWOOD *Gunaik.* III. 137 The casualties appending on so harsh a journey. **1662** FULLER *Worthies* (1840) III. 461 Appending to this cathedral is the Chapter-house. **1774** JOHNSON *Journ. W. Isl.* Wks. 1787 X. 333 The parchment..is, with the seal appending, fastened to a ribband.

appendix (əˈpɛndɪks), *sb.* Pl. -ices (-ɪsiːz) and -ixes. [a. L. *appendix*. f. *appendĕre*: see APPEND. A sing. *appendice* after Fr. appears in 17th c.] That which is attached as if by being hung on; = APPENDAGE, but now of more restricted use.

1. a. Of things material: A subsidiary external adjunct, addition, or accompaniment; an additional possession, a dependency. *Obs.* in gen. sense exc. by transference from 2.

1592 GREENE *Upstart Courtier* in *Harl. Misc.* (Malh.) II. 230 If it be his pleasure to haue his appendices primde, or his mouchaches fostred. **1645** HOWELL *Lett.* i. 26 Normandy, once an Appendix of the Crown of England. **1665** J. SPENCER *Prophecies* 125 The Ark, the Shechinah, the heavenly fire, and the rest, were ceremonial appendices. **1710** SHAFTESB. *Charact.* VI. v. (1737) III. 379 Figures of Men..accidentally introduc'd, as Appendices, or Ornaments. **1880** tr. *Wurtz Atom. The.* 150 The bodies added as appendices have become the heads of their respective families.

†**b.** *transf.* of persons; cf. APPENDANT 2 b. *Obs.*

1596 SHAKS. *Tam. Shr.* IV. iv. 104 To bid the Priest be readie to come against you come with your appendix. **1692** E. WALKER *Epictetus* (1737) xxiii, My Children..are but the Appendixes of me.

2. An addition subjoined to a document or book, having some contributory value in connexion with the subject-matter of the work, but not essential to its completeness.

1549 LATIMER 7 *Serm. bef. Edw. VI* (Arb.) 46 The commentaries, contaynyng the solemnities of their religion wyth manye other appendixes. **1638** *Penit. Conf.* xii. (1657) 317 Towards the end whereof is an Appendix or Post-script. **1711** F. FULLER *Med. Gymn.* Pref., As I have related in the Appendix to this Treatise. **1880** *Athenæum* 23 Oct. 567 Two important Appendixes. **1881** *Academy* 18 June 457/2 His numerous appendices.

3. a. *Biol.* A small process or prolongation developed from the surface of any organ. *spec.*, short for *vermiform appendix* (of the cæcum): see VERMIFORM *a.* 3 a.

1615 CROOKE *Body of Man* 113 The appendix of the Mesenterie..of the nature of a ligament. **1658** SIR T. BROWNE *Gard. Cyrus* 526 The appendices or beards in the calicular leaves [of the rose]. **1863** OLIVER *Less. Bot.* (1873) 142 *Viola odorata*..two narrow dorsal appendices from the base of the connective of the two anterior anthers. **1886** [see APPENDICITIS]. **1902** *Scotsman* 2 July 7/3 This operation, removal of the appendix. **1905** KELLY & HURDON *Verm. App.* 2 The first recorded case of disease of the appendix is the classical one of Mestivier, reported in 1759. **1905** H. G. WELLS *Modern Utopia* App. 377, I had seen the ancestral cæcum shrink to that disease nest, the appendix of to-day.

†**b.** The sucker of a plant or tree. *Obs.*

1664 EVELYN *Sylva* (1679) 30 Both these sorts [of elms] are rais'd of Appendices, or Suckers.

†**4.** Of things immaterial: A subsidiary addition, accompaniment, or consequence; an accessory. *Obs.*

1542 BOORDE *Brev.* (1870) 103 The Apendex to all the premisses that foloweth. **1578** TIMME *Calvin on Gen.* 360 His promise was an addition, or an appendix of that principal point. **1621** BURTON *Anat. Mel.* I. ii. II. vi. (1651) 86 Idleness is an appendix to nobility. **1662** J. CHANDLER *Van Helmont's Oriatr.* 267 Therefore the will of a blessed Soul should be a burdensome appendice. **1699** BOYER *Fr. Dict.* (1759) s.v., Who look upon Idleness as an Appendix of their Greatness.

appendix (əˈpɛndɪks), *v. rare.* [f. prec. sb.] To add as an appendix. Hence **appendixed** *ppl. a.*

1755 MAGENS *Insurances* I. 456 The appendix'd Piece marked Letter B. **1772** GROSE *East Ind.* I. 211 The catalogue appendixed by Mr. Fraser to his history of Nadir Shah.

appennage, obs. form of APANAGE.

†**aˈppense**, *v. Obs. rare*[−1]. [a OFr. *a(p)pense-r* to append a seal, ad. L. **appensā-re*, frequentative of *appendĕ-re*.] To append (a seal).

1599 HAKLUYT *Voy.* II. I. 158 We haue caused..our seale thereunto to be appensed.

appense (əˈpɛns), *a. Bot. rare.* [f. L. *appens-us*, pa. pple. of *appendĕre* to APPEND.] (See quot.)

1829 LOUDON *Encycl. Plants* (1855) 409 Pimenta..ovules solitary, appense. *Ibid.* 1095 *Appense*, being hung up as a hat is upon a pin; an approach to pendulous.

†**aˈppension.** *Obs. rare.* [n. of action f. L. *append-ĕre*: see prec. and -ION[1]. Cf. Fr. *appension*.] The action or process of appending.

1646 J. G[REGORY] *Notes & Obs.* (1650) 56 And then hang'd the Earth upon the same Nothing. But of this manner of appension somewhat more is to be said. **1677** J. WEBSTER *Witchcr.* xiii. 267 The curing of diseases by.. amulets, appensions and transplantions.

†**aˈppentice.** *Obs. rare*[−1]. [a. Fr. *appentis*, OF. *apentis*, nom. of *apentif*. f. *apendre*, 3 sing. *apent* (see APPEND *v.*[1]), by form-assoc. w. adjs. in *-tis*, *-tif*:—L. *-tivus*, *-tivum*: cf. APPRENTICE. Hence aphetic PENTICE, corrupted to PENTHOUSE.] A lean-to building, a penthouse.

1616 SURFL. & MARKH. *Countr. Farm* 18 Ouer against the porch of the Barne, you shall make a place of a competent height, in manner of an Appentice, to set your Ploughes, etc.

†**apperˈceivant**, *ppl. a. Obs. rare*[−1]. [a. OFr. *apercevant*, pr. pple. of *aperceveir*: see next.] Discovering, cognizant.

c **1450** *Merlin* iv. 73 Ye be sone aperceyvaunte of hym.

apperˈceive, *v.* Forms: 4–5 **apar-**, **aper-**, 5 **appar**, **apper-**, **-ceive**, **-ceyve**, **-ceve**, **-seive**, 5–6 **apperceyve**, 6 **-ceave**, **-save**, 7 **apparceive**. [a. OFr. *aperceveir*, *aparcevoir* (tonic form *aperceive*), cogn. w. Sp. *apercebir*, Pg. *aperceber*:—late L. or early Rom. **appercipĕre* for **appercipĕre*, f. *ap-*, *ad-* to + *percipĕre* to PERCEIVE. For change to *app-* see AP- *pref.*[1]]

†**1.** To perceive, observe, recognize, notice, remark: **a.** *Obs.* with *simple obj.*

c **1300** *Vox & Wolf* 213 Ich the aperseiuede. *c* **1391** CHAUCER *Astrol.* II. §36. 44 Thanne shaltou aperceyve wel the Moevyng of a planete. *c* **1450** LONELICH *Grail* xxxviii. 309 Non man hym aparceyven myhte. **1494** FABYAN I. ii. 9 The which Temple, when Brute had apperceyued, anone he yode into it. **1549** CHALONER *Erasm. Moriæ Enc.* S iv b, Some devoute persones..did, without aperceivyng the difference, drinke lampe oyle in steede of wyne. **1614** W. BROWNE *Sheph. Pipe* I. 25 When apparceived had she this, she cry'd.

b. with *of*, *subord. cl.*, or *absol.*

c **1320** *Seuyn Sag.* (W.) 1433 The burgeis aparseiued of his wiue Fele nightes was gon him fram. **1491** CAXTON *Vitas Patr.* (W. de W.) I. viii. 13 a/2 The holy man aperceyuyd that the bestes were almost deed. **1588** A. KING *Canisius' Catech.* H vj, As ȝow may appersave be yis calculation.

2. *Psychol.* To be or become conscious of perceiving; to comprehend (something perceived) by a mental act which unites and assimilates the perception to a mass of ideas already possessed; to have apperception of: see APPERCEPTION.

1876 J. SULLY in *Mind* Jan. 41 Where two impressions are simultaneously apperceived, it is because they are such as can be brought under one complex impression as parts of the whole. **1892** —— *Human Mind* I. 163 The new presentative element is said..to be apperceived or assimilated by a pre-existing cluster of ideas or an ideal mass. **1894** *Academy* 7 July 6/2 A thousand people, observes Lange, may read Virgil; but every one will apperceive him differently.

Hence **apperˈceiving** *ppl. a.*; ***apperceiving mass*** [cf. J. F. Herbart's expression (1825) 'appercipirende Vorstellungsmasse'] = *apperception mass* (see next, 3 b, and cf. *apperceptive mass* and MASS *sb.*[2]); whence **apperˈceivingly** *adv.*

1890 [see APPERCEPTION, 3 b]. **1893** C. DE GARMO et al. tr. *Lange's Apperception* (1896) 101 When ideal norms are apperceivingly active in the field of knowledge..true culture is attained. **1890** W. JAMES *Princ. Psychol.* II. xix. 109 A child who hitherto has seen none but four-cornered tables apperceives a round one as a table; but by this the apperceiving mass ('table') is enriched. **1914** R. M. JONES *Spir. Reformers in 16th & 17th Cent.* xiii. 263 The representative of the old system..condemning a dawning movement which with his apperceiving material he could not understand.

†**apperˈceiving**, *vbl. sb. Obs.* [f. prec. + -ING[1].] The action of perceiving or noticing.

c **1386** CHAUCER *Sqrs. T.* 278 Ffor drede of Ialouse mennes aperceyuynges *c* **1400** *Rom. Rose* 6320 So sligh is the aperceyvyng That al to late cometh knowyng.

apperception (æpəˈsɛpʃən). *Metaph.* [ad. F. *aperception* (mod.L. *apperceptiōn-em*, Leibnitz), f. *apercevoir*: see APPERCEIVE and -TION.]

1. The mind's perception of itself as a conscious agent; self-consciousness.

1753 CHAMBERS *Cycl. Supp.*, *Adperception* in the Leibnitzian style, denotes the act whereby the mind becomes conscious to itself of a perception. **1763** REID *Inquiry* II. xv. (1785) 220 By apperception he understands that degree of perception, which reflects, as it were, upon itself: by which we are conscious of our own existence, and conscious of our own perceptions. **1877** CAIRD *Philos. Kant* v. 79 The monad that has consciousness of itself..that has not only perception, but apperception.

2. Mental perception, recognition.

1839 BAILEY *Festus* xix. (1848) 217 Meet apperception of the sum of things. **1857** MAURICE *Mor. & Met. Phil.* IV. viii. §65 The recognition or apperception of these truths by men.

3. a. *Psychol.* The action or fact of becoming conscious by subsequent reflection of a perception already experienced; any act or process by which the mind unites and assimilates a particular idea (esp. one newly presented) to a larger set or mass of ideas (already possessed), so as to comprehend it as part of the whole: see quots.

1876 J. SULLY in *Mind* Jan. 36 The entrance of a presentation into the internal field of view is termed a Perception; its entrance into the point of view an Apperception. **1887** J. DEWEY *Psychol.* 89 Apperception is the relating activity which combines the various sensuous elements presented to the mind at one time into a whole, and which unites these wholes, recurring at successive times, into a continuous mental life, thereby making psychical life intelligent. **1893** C. DE GARMO et al. tr. *Lange's Apperception* (1896) 28 Apperception is the subsumption of a notion, usually newly given and more or less individual, under a predicate which is more complete..and..usually older and more familiar. Apperception does not always follow perception immediately, for years sometimes intervene between the learning of a fact and its comprehension. **1923** H. G. BAYNES tr. *Jung's Psychol. Types* xi. 524 Apperception is a psychic process by which a new content is articulated to similar already-existing contents in such a way as to be understood, apprehended, or clear.

b. *attrib.*, as ***apperception mass***, ***process***, ***product***. (H. Steinthal (1871) used the expressions 'Massen Apperception' and 'Massen Apperceptions-Process'.)

1890 W. JAMES *Princ. Psychol.* II. xix. 109 An apperception-product arises: the knowledge of the perceived being as a horse. *Ibid.*, Apperception-processes can perfectly well occur in which the new observation transforms or enriches the apperceiving group of ideas. **1896** W. J. ECKOFF tr. *J. F. Herbart's ABC of Sense-Perception* 88 Conscience..we have seen to be a complex apperception mass aboriginally compounded of innumerable presentations. **1933** *Brit. Jrnl. Psychol.* July 24 Subjects having a marked perseveration of the ideas and 'apperception masses' previously stimulated would presumably be more likely..to overlook words wrongly spelt.

Hence **apperˈceptionism** *Psychol.*, the explanation and systematization of the process of apperception; **apperˈceptionist**, one who holds or affects the doctrine of apperceptionism; **apperceptioˈnistic** *a.*, of, pertaining to, or characterized by apperceptionism.

1903 H. MÜNSTERBERG *Harvard Psychol. Stud.* I. 644 Without returning to apperceptionism we can overcome the one-sidedness of associationism if full use is made of the means which the world of phenomena offers to theory. *Ibid.* 653 Apperceptionistic psychology. **1904** *Jrnl. Philos., Psychol. & Sci. Methods* 18 Aug. 466 (Cent. D. Suppl.), The idealist's view is that of the 'apperceptionists'.

apperceptive (æpəˈsɛptɪv), *a.* [f. prec., after PERCEPTIVE *a.*] Pertaining to or involving apperception; also = next; ***apperceptive mass*** = *apperception mass* (see prec.).

1884 E. MONTGOMERY in *Mind* July 381 It is after all nothing but our own apperceptive faculties, potentially idealised, that are made to serve for the consciousness of a universal subject. **1886** F. A. CASPARI tr. *P. Radestock's Habit & Education* 45 Blending or apperceptive synthesis, that is, a union of impressions following one another, in which the latter exist in the new conception produced by their union. **1891** G. F. STOUT in *Mind* XVI. 31 Apperceptive processes differ for the most part from those which result in the formation of a percept. *Ibid.* 37 An apperceptive system is, apart from fatigue, more prompt to apperceive the more recently it has been brought into play.

1892 *Monist* Jan. 306 Under normal conditions the necessary alternation of different apperceptive masses produces a corresponding variation in the conditions of belief. **1952** W. J. H. SPROTT *Social Psychol.* x. 211 All these psychological elements..form the 'apperceptive mass', which receives new material, and the matrix out of which changes emerge.

appercipient (æpə'sɪpɪənt), *a.* [f. as prec., after PERCIPIENT *a.*] Having or exercising the faculty of apperception.

1906 H. H. JOACHIM *Nature of Truth* iii. 93 Every judgement..is informed, conditioned, and to some extent constituted by the appercipient character of the mind which makes it. **1922** S. GREW *Art of Player-Piano* 161 Only the musician may be entirely appercipient as regards the subtle beauty of poetry.

†**a'pperil.** *Obs. rare.* [f. PERIL *sb.* See A- *pref.* 11.] Peril, risk.

1607 SHAKS. *Timon* I. ii. 32 Let me stay at thine apperill, Timon. **1632** B. JONSON *Magn. Lady* v. x, Faith, I will bail him, at mine own apperil.

appertain (æpə'teɪn), *v.* Forms: 4–5 **apertene, -teyn,** 5 **appertene, -artene, -urteyn(e,** 5–6 **appertein, -teyn(e, -teigne,** 6 **adpertene, apparteyne, -ertayne,** 6–7 **-taine,** 7 **-tane, -taigne, apertain,** 7– **appertain.** [a. OFr. *aparten-ir, aperten-ir*:—late L. *adpertinē-re*, f. *ad-* to, completely + *pertinēre* to belong to, f. *per* through + *tenēre* to hold. For change to *app-* see AP- *pref.*[1]]

1. *intr.* To belong as parts to the whole, or as members to a family or class, and hence, to the head of the family; to be related, akin *to*.

c **1450** *Merlin* xxi. 373 These other tweyne..aperteyne to the kynge loot..and be Erles sones. **1578** LYTE *Dodoens* VI. xlvii. 719 Of plummes..some apparteyne to the garden, and some are of a wilde kinde. **1611** BIBLE *Numb.* xvi. 32 All the men that appertained vnto Korah. **1794** SULLIVAN *View Nat.* I. 454 Disunited particles, which appear to have originally appertained to stones or rocks. **1843** MILL *Logic* Introd. (1868) 7 To this science appertain the great and much debated questions.

2. To belong as a possession *to*.

1416 LANGLEY in Ellis *Orig. Lett.* II. 18 I. 51 Withinne youre Churche..ther shulde be certein thyng that to yowe appertenenth. **1564** *Wills & Inv. N. Count.* (1835) 219 Dubbletts and all other rayments apperteynyng vnto me. **1667** E. CHAMBERLAYNE *St. Gt. Brit.* II. I. ii. (1743) 294 The Abbey of Deer..appertained to the Cistercian monks. **1790–1** Dallas' *Amer. Law Rep.* 71 Whether all property found in the city..should appertain to the United States. **1809** TOMLINS *Law Dict., Appurtenances*..things both corporeal and incorporeal appertaining to another thing.

3. To belong as a right or privilege *to*.

1483 CAXTON *Gold. Leg.* 155/4 This place apperteyneth to no man but to preestes. **1598** BARRET *Theor. Warres* II. i. 16 The punishment..appertaineth to the Campe-maister. **1651** HOBBES *Leviath.* IV. xliv. 350 Shall not all Judicature appertain to Christ? **1793** T. JEFFERSON *Writ.* (1859) IV. 34 The right of raising troops..appertaining exclusively to the nation itself. **1883** *Law Times* 20 Oct. 410/1 Until the present reign probate jurisdiction appertained solely to the Ecclesiastical Courts.

4. To belong naturally or by inherent fitness; to be suited, proper, appropriate *to*.

c **1386** CHAUCER *Pers. T.* ¶976 To fastyng appurteynen [*v.r.* -ertenen, -arteyneth, -artenen, partenyth] foure thinges. *c* **1470** *Hors, Shepe, & Ghoos* (1822) 5 Hardynesse ..apperteyneth to euery manly knyght. **1535** STEWART *Cron. Scotl.* II. 18 How he fure adpertenis nocht to me To tell. **1599** SHAKS. *Much Ado* IV. i. 210 Do all rites, That appertaine vnto a buriall. **1756** C. LUCAS *Ess. Waters* II. 13 That appellation seems more properly to appertain to the phlogiston. **1813** MISS AUSTEN *Pride & Prej.* x. 43 The degree of importance which is to appertain to this request.

5. To belong as an attribute, function, or affecting circumstance; to pertain, relate.

c **1391** CHAUCER *Astrol.* Prol. 1 A certein nombre of conclusions apertenyng to the same instrument. **1601** SHAKS. *Jul. C.* II. i. 282, I should know no Secrets That appertaine to you. **1850** DAUBENY *Atom. The.* vi. 168 The crystalline form of a body is not always determined by any unalterable property appertaining to its component atoms.

†**6.** *impers.* (chiefly in senses 3 and 4.) *Obs.*

c **1386** CHAUCER *Melib.* ¶15 It apperteyneth [*v.r.* aperteneth, -tyneth, -teigneþ, perteyneth] not to a wys man, to make such sorwe. **1477** EARL RIVERS (Caxton) *Dictes* 19 It apparteigneth to euery man..to seke science. **1605** BACON *Adv. Learn.* II. 23 Further than appertaineth to the degree of a creature. **1623** LISLE *Test. Antiq.* Pref., Unto whom it did first appertaine to exact of Priests..this profession.

†**b.** *absol.* *As appertains*: as is proper or due. *Obs.*

1524 WOLSEY *State Papers* (1836) IV. 89 To see theym conduyted in saufetye..as shall appertain. **1611** BIBLE *1 Esdr.* i. 12 They rosted the Passeouer with fire, as appertaineth.

†**7.** *trans.* (by omission of *to*.) To belong to, become, befit. *Obs. rare.*

a **1420** OCCLEVE *De Reg. Princ.* 4838 It appertenethe a kyng for to be A kyng in verray sothe. **1491** CAXTON *Vitas Patr.* (W. de W.) I. clxiv. 173a/2 It aperteynyth thy dygnytee, for to doo that this poore synfull woman askith. **1598** SYLVESTER *Du Bartas* 622 The Soule..longing to behold the place that appertains her, Doth loath the bodie. **1601** DOLMAN *Fr. Acad.* (1618) 657 Have attributed that to their nation which properly appertaineth not them.

†**apper'tainance.** A variant of APPURTENANCE assimilated to prec. vb.

1525 LD. BERNERS in *Froiss.* (1812) Pref. 14 The appertaynens of your realme. **1824–8** LANDOR *Imag. Conv.* Wks. 1846 I. xxxviii. 249 The noblest elevations of the human mind have in appertainance their sands and swamps. **1852** SIR. W. HAMILTON *Discuss.* 551 A Schoolhouse with appertainances.

apper'taining, *vbl. sb.* [f. prec. vb. + -ING[1].] The fact of belonging to; †*concr. pl.* Belongings, appurtenances (*obs.*).

a **1597** *Lover's Compl.* 115 His real habitude gave life and grace To appertainings and to ornament. [See APPERTAINMENT.]

apper'taining, *ppl. a.* [f. as prec. + -ING[2].] Pertaining, belonging, proper, appropriate (*to*).

c **1386** CHAUCER *Chan. Yem. Prol. & T.* 231 Many another thing, That is to oure craft appertenyng. **1592** SHAKS. *Rom. & Jul.* III. i. 66 The appertaining rage To such a greeting. **1883** *Daily News* 21 Sept 5/4, 108 guns, with the appertaining forces of pioneers and train.

†**apper'tainment.** *Obs. rare*[−1]. [f. as prec. + -MENT.] That which belongs to; appurtenance.

1606 SHAKS. *Tr. & Cr.* II. iii. 87 We lay by Our appertainments [*v.r.* appertainings], visiting of him.

appertinance, -ence, obs. ff. APPURTENANCE.

†**a'ppertinancy.** *Obs. rare*[−1]. [See APPERTENANCE and -ANCY; the regular spelling from L. would be *appertinency*.] The quality of being appertinent. *Also* = appurtenance.

1646 SIR T. BROWNE *Pseud. Ep.* Pref., Our sober enquiries in the doubtfull appertinancies of Arts.

appertinent (ə'pɜːtɪnənt), *a.* [a refashioning of *appurtenant* after L. *appertinēnt-em*.] Another form of APPURTENANT, used especially in the non-legal sense: Appertaining, properly belonging or relating.

1386–1819 [See APPURTENANT 2.]

†**appertise, -yse,** *sb. Obs.* [a. OFr. *appertise, -artise* (mod. *apertise*), f. *apert* open, manifest: see APERT 4.] Open display, proof, or evidence of dexterity, skill, or valour, *esp.* in arms.

1480 CAXTON *Ovid's Met.* XI. xxii, He was wyse, dyscrete, and ful of al appertyse. **1485** —— *Paris & V.* 10 None durst ..withstonde hys appertyse in armes. **1489** —— *Faytes of Armes* I. ix. 24 Grete appertyses of armes.

†**appertise, -yse,** *a. Obs. rare.* [a. OFr. *aperti*, pl. *-is*, 'skilful,' pa. pple. of *apertir* to render 'apert': see APERT 4, and prec. (Badly spelt with final *-e*.)] Skilful, adroit, of ready wit.

1483 CAXTON *G. de la Tour* M iij, The most appertyse and wyse fynd them self..by suche delynge mocked and blamed.

†**a'ppete,** *v. Obs.* [a. Fr. *appéte-r* (14th c. in Littré), ad. L. *appetĕre*, f. *ap-* = *ad-* to + *petĕre* to seek.] To seek after, desire, covet, long for.

c **1385** CHAUCER *L.G.W.* 1582 Matire appetith [*v.r.* apetitith, appetyteth] forme alwey. *c* **1530** RHODES *Bk. Nurture* in *Babees Bk.* 105 What sensuall concupiscence appeteth. **1538** BALE *Thre Lawes* 1018 Ambycyon, whose dyposycyon Is honour to appete. **1685** SIR G. MACKENZIE *Relig. Stoic* xiii. 117 Would never appete this separation.

appetence ('æpɪtəns). [a. Fr. *appétence* desire, ad. L. *appetentia*: see next.] The action of seeking for or longing after; appetite, desire.

1610 G. FLETCHER *Christ's Vict.* xxxix, Whatsoe'er might ..please the appetence, Here it was poured out in lavish affluence. **1765** TUCKER *Lt. Nat.* II. 256 An inward feeling, a moral sense, or appetence towards the thing apprehended. **1836** W. A. BUTLER in *Blackw. Mag.* XXXIX. 454 To love, and in the appetence of love To deem thyself beloved.

appetency ('æpɪtənsɪ). [ad. L. *appetentia*, n. of state f. *appetent-em*: see next and -ENCY.]

1. *strictly*, The state of longing for, desiring, craving; appetite, passion. But also used as = APPETENCE. Const. *of*, *for*, *after*.

1631 SANDERSON *21 Serm.* Ad. Aul. i. (1673) 13 God hath ingrafted in our Nature..an appetency of praise and glory. **1652** SPARKE *Prim. Devot.* (1663) 502 Vicious concupiscence and all brutish appetencies. **1824** D'ISRAELI *Cur. Lit.* (1866) 205 Fanaticism and robbery..will satiate their appetency for blood and plunder. **1881** MASSON in *Macm. Mag.* XLV. 74 An appetency after literary distinction.

2. Instinctive inclination or propensity.

1802 PALEY *Nat. Theol.* ix. (1827) 466 That the parts of animals may have been all formed by what is called appetency, *i.e.* endeavour, perpetuated, and imperceptibly working its effect, through an incalculable series of generations. **1826** KIRBY & SPENCE *Entomol.* (1828) III. xxxii. 348 There is no formative appetency in the animals themselves.

3. Of things inanimate: Natural tendency, affinity.

1627 G. WATTS *Bacon's Adv. Learn.* (1640) 147 Whoever shall..intentively observe the appetencies of matter. **1831** BREWSTER *Newton* (1855) I. xii. 323 The spherical form of the planets had been ascribed by Copernicus to the gravity or natural appetency of their parts. **1846** Knight's *Cur. Phys. Geog.* ad fin., The extraordinary appetency for oxygen of several of these bases.

4. *Metaph.* Suggested term including both desire and volition, as distinguished from cognition and feeling.

1836–7 SIR W. HAMILTON *Metaph.* xi. (1870) I. 186 The term appetency..comprehending both desires and volitions.

appetent ('æpɪtənt), *a.* [ad. L. *appetent-em*, pr. pple. of *appetĕre*: see APPETE and -ENT.]

1. Longing, eagerly desirous. Const. *after*, *of*.

c **1420** *Pallad. on Husb.* IV. 697 [Oxen] ever appetent metes to seek. **1646** SIR G. BUCK *Rich. III*, 60 (T.) Thirsty and appetent after glory and renown. **1861** HOOK *Lives Abps.* I. iv. 165 Eager to be instructed and appetent of knowledge.

2. *Metaph.* Connected with desire and volition.

1837 SIR W. HAMILTON *Metaph.* xli. (1877) II. 415 The mental modifications were divided into Gnostic or Cognitive, and Orectic or Appetent.

†'**appetently,** *adv. Obs. rare*[−1]. [f. prec. + -LY[2]: cf. APPETITELY.] Eagerly, with appetite.

a **1479** CAXTON *Maxims* in Blades *Caxton* 199 Go to thy mete appetently.

appetibility (,æpɪtɪ'bɪlɪtɪ). ? *Obs.* [f. L. *appetībil-is* desirable: see next and -BILITY. Cf. Fr. *appétibilité*.] The quality of being desirable; desirableness, attractiveness.

1604 T. WRIGHT *Passions of Mind* v. iv. 257 Goodnes..is the perfection or appetibilitie of every thing reall or apparant. **1656** HOBBES *Liberty, etc.* (1841) 309 To resist both the appetibility of objects, and the unruliness of passions. **1824** BARETTI *It. Dict.*, Appetibility, *qualità che rende desiderevole.*

appetible ('æpɪtɪb(ə)l), *a.* and *sb.* [ad. L. *appetībil-is* desirable, f. *appetĕre*: see APPETE and -BLE.] **A.** *adj.*

†**1.** Having appetite or affinity; attractive. *Obs.*

1471 RIPLEY *Comp. Alch.* in Ashm. (1652) 1, Kynd to kynde hath appetyble inclynacyon.

2. Worthy of being sought after, desirable.

1622 MABBE *Aleman's Guzman D' Alf.* II. 307 Such Graces are Appetible in their owne nature. **1660** STANLEY *Hist. Philos.* (1701) 259/2 The Appetible Object, which moveth the Appetite. **1847** *Blackw. Mag.* LXI. 589 The appetible fruit.

†**B.** *sb.* An object of desire. *Obs.*

a **1716** SOUTH *Serm.* IV. v. (R.) Sufficient to draw forth, and determine the actings of it [the will], unless there interpose some stronger appetible.

†'**appetibleness.** *Obs.* [f. prec. + -NESS.] 'Worthiness to be desired.' Bailey 1731; = APPETIBILITY.

†**appe'tisse, -'tyce,** *v. Obs. rare.* [a. Fr. *appetisser* (Cotgr.), 12th c. *apetisier*, mod. *apetisser* (on Romanic type **adpetitiāre*), f. *à* to + *petit* small.] To make small, diminish, lessen.

1474 CAXTON *Chesse* 91 All wordly thynges ben mortefyed and appetissed in olde men. **1484** —— *Ordre of Chyv.* 85 Thus shalle be..yre and Inpacyence and the other uyces appetyced and lassed.

appetite ('æpɪtaɪt), *sb.* Forms: 4–5 **apetyte,** 5 **-yght, appetit, -yt, appatyt,** 5–6 **apetite,** 6 **-ide, appetyd(e,** 4–6 **appetyte,** 4– **appetite.** [a. OFr. *apetit*, ad. L. *appetītus* desire toward, f. *appetĕre*: see APPETE.] Const. *for*; formerly *to*, *of*, and *inf.*

1. Bent of the mind toward the attainment of an object or purpose; desire, inclination, disposition.

1382 WYCLIF *Ezek.* xxi. 16 Whidir euere is the appetit, *or desier*, of thi face. **1494** FABYAN VII. ccxxii. 247 To staunche yᵉ apetyte of his couetyse mynde. **1528** MORE *Heresyes* IV. Wks. 273/1 Suche cruell appetyte..ascrybe they to the benygne nature of almyghtye God. **1621** BURTON *Anat. Mel.* I. ii. III. xi, These Concupiscible and Irascible Appetites..twining about the heart. **1756** BURKE *Vind. Nat. Soc.* Wks. I. 12 This society, founded in natural appetites.. I shall call natural society. *a* **1871** GROTE *Eth. Fragm.* v. (1876) 129 Obeying without reflection the appetite of the moment.

b. with the object of desire expressed.

c **1400** *Destr. Troy* XXII. 9104 Achilles hade appetite..The Citie for to se. **1549** LATIMER *7 Serm. bef. Edw. VI* (Arb.) 103 She dyd it not for appetite of vengeaunce. **1614** RALEIGH *Hist. World* II. IV. vi. §5. 239 Ptolomie had a great appetite ..to the Isle of Cyprus. **1775** SHERIDAN *Rivals* v. i, With such an appetite for consolation. **1875** HAMERTON *Intell. Life* II. i. 48 Gratification of an appetite for melody or colour.

2. *vaguely*, Inclination, preference, liking, fancy. *to* or *after one's appetite*: just as one pleases, so as to suit one's tastes. *arch.*

1490 CAXTON *Eneydos* xix. 71 That I myghte vse my lif to myn appetyte and..be at my fre wyll. **1526** SKELTON *Magnyf.* 1437 Syr, ye shall follow mine appetyte and intent. **1534** LD. BERNERS *Gold. Bk. M. Aurel.* (1546) Zij, This oratour spake after the appetite of them that bee in prosperitie. **1580** LYLY *Euphues* 248, I have an appetite it were best for me to take a nap. **1860** MOTLEY *Netherl.* (1868) I. v. 237 He will make a treaty according to the appetite and pleasure of his Highness.

3. *esp.* The determinate desire to satisfy the natural necessities, or fulfil the natural functions, of the body; one of those instinctive cravings which secure the preservation of the individual and the race.

1366 MAUNDEV. xix. 157 The folk..han but litille appetyt to mete. **1393** GOWER *Conf.* II. 102 Which ȝiveth great appetite To slepe. *c* **1425** WYNTOUN *Cron.* VIII. Prol. 3 Naturally As Woman and Man has appetyte. **1601** HOLLAND *Pliny* II. 443 Craifishes..in wine..moue appetite to the siege. **1711** ADDISON *Spect.* No. 120 ¶4 The most violent Appetites in all Creatures are Lust and Hunger. **1855** BAIN *Sens. & Intell.* II. iii. §1 (1864) 255, I am of opinion that Appetite, being a species or form of Volition, is ..a combination of instinct and education. **1876** MOZLEY *Univ. Serm.* vii. 147 We have those appetites so long as we remain in the flesh.

4. *spec.* Craving for food, hunger.

1303 R. BRUNNE *Handl. Synne* 7235 Sum of hem [chyldryn] wex ful tyte, þarfore ys more here appetyte. **1375** BARBOUR *Bruce* III. 541 Thai eyt It with full gud will, That soucht nane othir salss thar-till Bot appetyt. **1444** *Pol. Poems* II. 220 Whoo that is hungry, and hath no thyng but boonys To staunche his apetyght. **1509** FISHER *Wks.* 294 She restrayned her appetyte tyl one mele and tyl one Fysshe on the day. **1605** SHAKS. *Macb.* III. iv. 38 Now good digestion waite on Appetite, And health on both. *a* **1652** BROME *Demoiselle* Prol., 'Tis appetite makes dishes, 'tis not cooks. **1857** BUCKLE *Civiliz.* xi. 629 Men must have appetite before they will eat.

b. *transf.* or *fig.*

1605 BACON *Adv. Learn.* I. viii. §2 Learning doth minister to all the diseases of the mind..sometimes helping digestion, sometimes increasing appetite. **1825** *Bro. Jonathan* III. 286 The truth was too insipid for..your pampered appetite.

5. Capacity for food, feeling as regards food; relish.

c **1398** CHAUCER *Fortune* 55 Wikke appetyt comth ay before sykeness. **1542** BOORDE *Dyetary* ix. (1870) 252 Althoughe he haue eate ynoughe, whan he seth better meate come before hym, agaynst his appetyde he wyll eate. **1711** ADDISON *Spect.* No. 7 ¶2, I have seen a Man in Love..lose his appetite. **1830** HOR. SMITH *Tin Trump.* 30 Appetite—a relish bestowed upon the poorer classes, that they may like what they eat, while it is seldom enjoyed by the rich, because they may eat what they like.

†**6.** Of things: Natural tendency towards. *Obs.*

1626 BACON *Sylva* §293 In all Bodies, there is an Appetite of Union. **1667** BOYLE *Orig. Forms & Qual.*, Matter hath no appetite to these Accidents more then to any others.

7. The object of desire or longing. *arch.*

c **1386** CHAUCER *Knts. T.* 822 Hontyng..is his joye and his appetyt. *c* **1500** *Partenay* 2896 Ha! Melusine, my hertes Appetite. **1642** ROGERS *Naaman* To Reader §2 Adam was so created, that God was his appetite. **1798** WORDSW. *Lines Tintern Abb.* 81 The mountain, and the deep and gloomy wood..were then to me An appetite.

†**8.** Something used to create an appetite; a whet, a relish. (So in Fr.) *Obs.*

1693 EVELYN *De la Quint. Compl. Gard.* II. 191 English Cives [Chives], otherwise called Appetites. **1725** BRADLEY *Fam. Dict.* s.v. *Herring*, Red Herrings..salted and dried.. they cry in the Streets of Paris by the Name of Appetite.

†**'appetite**, *v. Obs.* [f. prec. sb. Cf. *to stomach.*]

1. To have an appetite for; to desire greatly, long for, seek after.

c **1385** CHAUCER *L.G.W.* 1582 As matier apetiteth forme alwey [*v.r.* appetith; see APPETE]. **1481** CAXTON *Myrr.* I. v. 17 Thise philosophres apetyted not these grete mangeries. **1502** *Ord. Cryst. Men* (W. de W.) I. vii. (1506) 53 It behoueth yt a creature resonable loue god and hym appetyte soueraynly. **1652** CULPEPPER *Eng. Phys.* (ed. Parkins 1809) 220 Such whose stomachs are so weak they cannot.. appetite it.

b. with *inf. phr.*

1484 CAXTON *Curial* 2 She appetyteth and desireth to haue that thyng whyche she hath not. **1531** ELYOT *Governor* 70 (T.) Appetiting by generation to bring forth his semblable.

2. To fulfil the desires of, satisfy.

1509 FISHER *Wks.* (1876) 251 Persons inordynately desyrous for to haue worldly pleasures..shall neuer be.. appetyted.

appetited ('æpɪtaɪtɪd), *ppl. a.* [f. APPETITE *sb.* + -ED².] Having an appetite. (Chiefly in *comb.*)

1829 ?JESSE *Jrnl. Nat.* 237 The hedge blackberry..for humbler-appetited natives. **1880** BLACKMORE *M. Anerley* I. xvi. 256 Seven fine-appetited children.

appetiteless ('æpɪtaɪtlɪs), *a.* [f. APPETITE *sb.* + -LESS.] Having no appetite; marked by want of appetite.

1853 SURTEES *Sponge's Sp. Tour* lx, Having finished a poor appetiteless breakfast. **1890** *Temple Bar* July 303 He sits appetiteless over his solitary breakfast.

†**'appetitely**, *adv. Obs. rare*⁻¹. [f. as APPETITED *ppl. a.* + -LY². See also APPETENTLY.] With an appetite.

a **1500** *Maxims* in *Babees Bk.* 359 Goo to thy mete apetitely, sit therat discretely.

appetition (æpɪ'tɪʃən). [ad. L. *appetītiōn-em*, n. of action f. *appetīt-*: see APPETITE *sb.* and -TION.] The direction of desire towards an object or purpose; longing for, craving, seeking after.

1603 HOLLAND *Plutarch* 917 (R.) Action requireth two things..the apprehension or imagination of that which is convenient..and the instinct or appetition driving unto the same. **1660** STANLEY *Hist. Philos.* (1701) 177/1 Philosophy ..being the appetition of Divine Knowledge. **1775** HARRIS *Philos. Arrangem.* (1841) 379 The cause of motion is appetition; of appetition, is privation. **1871** CALDERWOOD *Kant's Ethics* III. (ed. 3) 161 Appetition, when its inward ground of determination..depends upon the reason of the subject himself, is called *Will.*

†**appe'titious**, *a. Obs.* [f. prec.; cf. *ambition, ambitious.*] Belonging to, of the nature of, or suited to, appetite.

1653 GAUDEN *Hierasp.* 203 Filthy falsehoods..tempered ..with some mixtures of Scripture Texts..to make them more appetitious. **1668** H. MORE *Div. Dial.* III. xii. II. 396 An appetitious liking of Man's flesh.

appetitive ('æpɪtaɪtɪv, ə'pɛtɪtɪv), *a.* [a. Fr. *appétitif, -ive*, ad. L. **appetītīvus*, f. *appetīt-*: see APPETITE *sb.* and -IVE.]

1. Characterized by appetite or desire. *spec.* in *Biol.* (see quots.).

1577 tr. *Bullinger's Decades* (1592) 756 Since man, and also other liuing creatures haue an appetitiue or desiring soule. **1722** WOLLASTON *Relig. Nat.* ix. 173 He has not only a superior faculty of reason, but also an inferior appetitive faculty. **1878** GLADSTONE *Prim. Homer* 88 The appetitive part of humanity..adheres to the Olympian gods. **1951** W. H. THORPE in *Bull. Animal Behaviour* Mar. 37/1 Appetitive Behaviour = The variable introductory phase of an instinctive behaviour pattern or sequence. **1958** *New Biol.* XXVII. 74 Sometimes an animal moves over a large area before performing a specific action... This variable introductory activity in a behaviour sequence is called appetitive behaviour.

2. Giving an appetite; appetizing, attractive. *rare.*

1864 *Reader* 16 Jan. 75/2 These [family bills of fare]..are not at all times sufficiently appetitive to the eye.

†**appe'titual**, *a. Obs. rare*⁻¹. [f. L. *appetītu-s* APPETITE + -AL¹; cf. *spiritual.*] Of the nature of, or belonging to, appetite.

1616 R. C. *Times Whis.* i. 494 That's only good..whose visibility And appetitual sensibility Lies open to their sence.

appetize ('æpɪtaɪz), *v. rare*⁻⁰. [f. Fr. *appétissant* (14th c. in Littré), *appétiss-é* (Cotgr.), formally pples. of **appetissier* as if:—L. **appetītiāre*; in Eng. assimilated to vbs. in -IZE. In Fr. only the pples. are found; and in English the simple vb. is perhaps only colloquial.] To give (a person) appetite, to cause relish for food.

'appetized, *ppl. a.* [f. prec. + -ED.] Furnished with an appetite, made hungry.

1820 SCOTT *Monast.* Introd. Ep., Supper, for which I feel rather more appetized than usual. **1823** —— *St. Ronan's* xvii, A corpulent and well-appetized elderly gentleman.

appetizement ('æpɪtaɪzmənt). *rare.* [f. as prec. + -MENT.] Craving for food, hunger.

1826 SCOTT *Woodst.* (1829) 23 The appeteezement has been coming on for three days or four, and the meat has been scarce.

appetizer ('æpɪtaɪzə(r)). [f. as prec. + -ER¹.] Anything taken to create appetite or relish for food; a whet or stimulant to appetite.

1862 in D. Macdonald *Brit. Columb.* 308 The tiny cup full of a species of Chinese liquor, by way of an appetiser. **1877** WALLACE *Russia* x. 150 Pickled mushrooms..as an appetizer before dinner.

'appetizing, *ppl. a.* [f. as prec. + -ING².] Exciting a desire or longing, esp. for food; stimulating or whetting the appetite.

1653 URQUHART *Rabelais* II. xxxi, Which he ate up all, he found them so appetizing. **1733** CHEYNE *Eng. Malady* II. v. §3 (1734) 158 A Course of innocent, tho' neither palatable nor appetizing Medicines. **1856** LEVER *Martins Cro' M.* 264 A very appetising luncheon. **1865** *Reader* 9 Sept. 283/1 The title is appetising; the book has..outward promise.

appe'tizingly, *adv.* [f. prec. + -LY².] In an appetizing manner; so as to excite appetite.

1882 MISS BROWNE in *Girl's Own Paper* Mar. 294/2 It is not always cooked appetisingly.

†**a'ppinged**, *ppl. a. Obs.*⁻⁰ [f. L. *apping-ĕre* to paint upon (f. *pingĕre*), also, to join to (f. *pangĕre*) + -ED.] 'Joined or added to; also painted.' Blount *Glossogr.* 1656.

applanate ('æplənеɪt), *a. Bot.* [ad. mod.L. *applānātus*, pa. pple. of *applānāre*, f. *ap-* = *ad* to + late L. *plānāre* to level, f. *plānus* PLANE.] Of a flattened or horizontally expanded form.

1887 W. PHILLIPS *Brit. Discomycetes* 2 Pileus sessile and applanate. *Ibid.* 101 *Peziza depressa*..from its applanate growth. **1950** *Proc. Prehist. Soc.* XVI. 123 Macroscopically, the Flixton specimens showed the applanate, then ungulate, shape typical of the species.

applaud (ə'plɔːd), *v.* [ad. L. *applaud-ĕre*, f. *ap-*, = *ad-* to + *plaud-ĕre* to clap, esp. the hands. Cf. Fr. *applaudir*, earlier *aplaudir* (14th c. in Litt.), app. not the immed. source of the Eng., though the early Sc. instance, in sense 2 b, may be an adoption from Fr., in which *aplaudir à* was an early const.]

1. *intr.* (and phr. *applaud it*, obs.) To clap the hands in expression of approbation; *hence*, to express approval in any loud or lively manner.

1598 FLORIO, *Applaudere*..to applaude or clap hands for ioy. **1602** SHAKS. *Ham.* IV. v. 107 Caps, hands, and tongues, applaud it to the clouds. **1605** [see 3]. **1774** GOLDSM. *Retal.* 114 If dunces applauded, he paid them in kind. **1859** TENNYSON *Enid* 1806 There he kept the justice of the King So vigorously yet mildly, that all hearts Applauded. **1883** H. IRVING in *Daily News* 31 Oct. 5/6, I was surprised to hear the audience applaud loudly.

†**2.** To applaud *to*: **a.** To give approbation *to.*

1595 SPENSER *Epithal.* 144 The people standing all about ..doe thereto applaud. **1685** tr. *Gracian's Court. Manual* 101 Men applaud to themselves in those [qualities] they have, how vulgar and ordinary soever they be.

†**b.** To express agreement with, assent *to* a thing as worthy of praise. (The earliest sense found.) *Obs.*

1536 BELLENDENE *Cron. Scotl.* I. 11 Of thir Pichtis writis mony auld and recent authoris, to whom applaudis Cornelius Tacitus. **1635** PERSON *Varieties* I. x. 40 Unto that ..Horace applaudeth, while he saith *fortes creantur fortibus.*

3. *trans.* To express approval of, in any audible manner.

1596 SHAKS. *I Hen. IV*, I. iii. 302 Till fields, and blowes, and groues applaud our sport. **1605** —— *Macb.* v. iii. 54, I would applaud thee to the very Eccho, That should applaud again. **1769** ROBERTSON *Chas. V*, III. VIII. 121 With one voice all applauded, or feigned to applaud the undertaking. **1883** *Daily Tel.* 15 May 2/7 (*Cricket*) Peate was applauded on joining Wild.

4. To express approval of in any way; to approve of, praise.

1591 SHAKS. *Two Gent.* I. iii. 48 O that our Fathers would applaud our loues. **1651** HOBBES *Leviath.* II. xxv. 135 Those that have applauded the contrary opinion. **1769** BURKE *Pres. State Nat.* Wks. II. 15 Having highly applauded their conduct. **1802** MAR. EDGEWORTH *Moral T.* (1816) I. 226, I applaud him for standing forward in defence of his friend.

b. *refl.*

1631 PRESTON *Breastpl. Love* 186 Men are ready to applaud themselves in their knowledge. **1711** ADDISON *Spect.* No. 256 ¶2 They..applaud themselves for the Singularity of their Judgment. **1805** FOSTER *Ess.* IV. vi. 207 The heart applauds itself for feeling an irresistible captivation.

†**a'pplaud**, *sb. Obs.* [f. prec. vb.] Applauding; applause, plaudit.

1598 FLORIO, *Applauso*, applaude, applause. **1607** ROWLANDS *Famous Hist.* 3 To which all men yield a general applaud. **1636** T. SANFORD in *Ann. Dubrensia* (1877) 50 Why strive I to amplifie your pride With these Applauds?

applauded (ə'plɔːdɪd), *ppl. a.* [f. prec. vb. + -ED.] Greeted with applause, loudly approved.

1628 EARLE *Microcosm.* lviii, One that justifies..[no] opinion out of the applauded way. **1647** SIR G. BUCK in *Beaum. & Fl's. Wks.* Pref., Shakespeare, Chapman, and applauded Ben. **1777** HUME *Ess. & Treat.* I. 112 That.. eloquence..of which they [the ancients] have left us such applauded models.

applauder (ə'plɔːdə(r)). [f. as prec. + -ER¹.] One who applauds, approves, or loudly commends.

1612 WOODALL *Surg. Mate* Wks. 1653 Pref. 12 Their words seeming as Oracles to their own applauders. **1775** DE LOLME *Eng. Const.* II. xvii. (1784) 284 Surrounded by thousands of applauders and partisans. **1837** CARLYLE *Fr. Rev.* II. v. v. 309 Paragraph-writers, Placard-Journalists; 280 applauders at 3 shillings a day.

applauding (ə'plɔːdɪŋ), *vbl. sb.* [f. as prec. + -ING¹.] The loud expression of approval or commendation.

1615 HIERON *Wks.* I. 620 Specially inclined to the applauding of himselfe. **1865** HEAVYSEGE *Jephthah's Dau.* 8 Conquering Jephthah, filled With honour and applaudings.

a'pplauding, *ppl. a.* [f. as prec. + -ING².] Loudly expressing approval or commendation.

1607 SHAKS. *Timon* v. i. 200 These words..enter in our eares, like great Triumphers In their applauding gates. **1704** J. TRAPP *Abra-Mulé* I. i. 300 Throng'd with Multitudes Of the applauding soldiers. **1855** MACAULAY *Hist. Eng.* IV. 17 Amidst the applauding hums of the audience.

a'pplaudingly, *adv.* [f. prec. + -LY².] With applause or loud commendation.

1742 RICHARDSON *Pamela* IV. 76 Very chearfully and applaudingly gave her his Consent. **1839** LADY LYTTON *Cheveley* II. iii. 82 'She's right,' said Datchet applaudingly.

†**a'pplaudit.** *Obs. rare*⁻¹. [f. APPLAUD *v.* after *plaudit.*] A loud expression of approval or commendation.

1606 J. RAYNOLDS *Dolarny's Prim.* (1880) 56 Aiax had an applawdit for his rough plainenes.

†**a'pplaudity.** *Obs. rare*⁻¹. [irreg. f. APPLAUD; see *plaudity.*] Applause.

1623 COCKERAM *Eng. Dict.* II, *Clapping* of hands for ioy, Applause, Applaudity. **1627** R. BERNARD *Isle of Man* 196 They..make them preach at home very idly..though abroad, either for their hire, or applaudity more diligently.

applause (ə'plɔːz), *sb.* [ad. L. *applaus-us*, vbl. sb. f. *applaud-ĕre*: see APPLAUD *v.* Cf. It. *applauso*, and Sp. *aplauzo.*]

1. Approbation loudly expressed; acclamation.

[**1553-87** FOXE *A. & M.* III. 828 They should depart speaking last, *cum applausu populi*, with the rejoycing triumph of the people.] **1596** SHAKS. *Merch. V.* III. ii. 144 Hearing applause and vniuersall shout. **1623** BINGHAM *Xenophon* 81 The Souldiers hearing his words gaue an applause. **1725** POPE *Odyss.* VIII. 404 Loud applauses rend the vaulted sky. **1879** FROUDE *Cæsar* xiii. 175 Applause rang out from a hundred thousand throats.

2. Demonstrative approbation, marked approval or commendation.

1601 CORNWALLYES *Ess.* xii, Nothing goeth with full applause, that holdes not his perfection to the end. **1714** *Spect.* No. 610 ¶5 We should not be led away by the Censures and Applauses of Men. **1781** GIBBON *Decl. & F.* III. 17 The preacher understood the true value of popular applause. **1804** WELLINGTON in Gurw. *Desp.* III. 133 He has always conducted himself in such a manner as to gain my applause.

†3. Agreement or assent formally or publicly expressed. Cf. APPLAUD *v.* 2b. *Obs. rare.*

1612 BRINSLEY *Lud. Lit.* x. (1627) 153 The Latine of Tully being the purest, by the general applause of all the Learned.

†4. The object of applause. Cf. *aversion. Obs.*

1623 B. JONSON in *Shaksp. C. Praise* 148 The applause! delight! the wonder of our Stage.

†a'pplause, *v. Obs.* [by-form of APPLAUD, f. L. *applaus-* ppl. stem of *applaud-ĕre*, as in *erase* f. *ērās-*, *ērādĕre*, *diffuse* f. *diffūs-*, *diffundĕre*. Perh. the pple. *applaused* was first formed on L. *applausus*, and the vb. educed from it.] = APPLAUD *v.*

1602 WARNER *Alb. Eng.* IX. xlix. (1612) 226 Her sweete Presence, so applaus'd as in Sea-stormes a Calme. **1612–5** BP. HALL *Contemp.* XIX. (1628) 1286 That applaused consent of his [Ahab's] rabble of prophets. *a* **1634** CHAPMAN *Alphonsus*, Plays III. 222 With a general voice applaus'd his death.

a'pplauseful, *a.* ? *Obs. rare*$^{-1}$. [f. APPLAUSE *sb.* + -FUL.] Full of applause; applausive, laudatory.

1630 J. TAYLOR (Water P.) *Wks.* (N.) With applawsefull thankes they doe rejoyce.

a'pplausefully, *adv.* ? *Obs. rare*$^{-1}$. [f. prec. + -LY^{2}.] In a manner full of applause or praise.

1630 J. TAYLOR (Water P.) *Wks.* II. Aaib, As it is applawsefully written and commended to posterity in the Midsummer nights dreame.

†a'pplausible, *a. Obs. rare.* [f. L. *applaus-* ppl. stem of *applaud-ĕre* (see -BLE); prob. ad. med.L. **applausibilis*.] Worthy to be applauded; to be treated with applause.

1551 GARDINER *Explic. Cath. Faith* 1 (R.) Coniectures and argumentes applausible to idle wittes. **1605** *Sir T. Smith's Voy. Russia* (N.) His wise-seeming and applausible raigne. **1670** G. H. *Hist. Cardinals* III. iii. 326 The promotion of Cardinal Sirleto, who was otherwise an applausable man.

†a'pplausing, *ppl. a. Obs.* [f. APPLAUSE *v.* + -ING^{2}.] = APPLAUDING *ppl. a.*

1655 GURNALL *Chr. in Arm.* (1669) 19/1 This might.. occasion some self-applausing, rather than mercy-admiring thoughts in the Creature.

†a'pplausion. *Obs. rare.* [a. Fr. *applausion* (16th c. in Litt.), prob. ad. med.L. **applausiōn-em*, n. of action f. L. *applaus-*: see APPLAUSE *v.* and -ION^{1}.] Applauding, applause.

1576 WOOLTON *Chr. Manual* (1851) 46 Tickled with the vain applausion of the ignorant. **1589** PUTTENHAM *Eng. Poesie* (Arb.) 67 A Psalme of new applausions.

applausive (ə'plɔːsɪv), *a.* [f. L. *applaus-* ppl. stem of *applaud-ĕre* + -IVE, as if ad. L. **applausīv-us*.] Characterized by applause.

1. Loudly expressive of approbation.

1609 HEYWOOD *Bryt. Troy* XIV. xl, In the campe with much applausive ioy, Grim Pyrrhus is received. **1823** SCOTT *Quentin D.* iv, Laughter, more scornful than applausive. **1843** TENNYSON *Vis. Sin* 135 Greet her with applausive breath.

2. Expressive of approval; approbative.

1628 EARLE *Microcosm.* xlvi, He can listen to a foolish discourse with an applausive attention. **1660** STANLEY *Hist. Philos.* (1701) 85/1 If he sneezed himself before the enterprize, it was applausive. **1866** J. ROSE *Virg. Ecl. & Georg.* 103 Then let them [horses] learn their master's voice to know, And arch the neck to his applausive blow.

†3. Worthy of applause: agreeable, acceptable.

1605 CHAPMAN *All Fools* II, That same vayne of rayling became Now most applausive; your best poet is He that rails grossest. **1607** HEYWOOD *Wom. Kilde* 128 The pleasing taste of these applausive newes.

a'pplausively, *adv.* [f. prec. + -LY^{2}.] In an applausive manner; with applause or approbation.

1741 RICHARDSON *Pamela* (1824) I. 12 Having read it..to audiences where the tears were applausively eloquent. **1837** CARLYLE *Fr. Rev.* I. II. i. 43 She in all things will applausively second him.

apple (æp(ə)l), *sb.* Forms: 1 æppel, æpl, 2–7 appel, 2–4 eppel(e, epple, 3–4 appell, 3–5 appil(e, 4–5 -yl(le, -ulle, 4–6 -ul, 5 apille, -elle, 6 -ill, aple, 4– apple. Pl. 3– apples; 1 æp(p)la (*the fruit*), æpplas *of the eye*, 3–4 applen. [common Teut.: with OE. *æppel* cf. OFris. *appel*, OHG. *aphul*, *aphal*, *apfal*, mod.G. *apfel*, all masc.; ON. *epli* (for *apli*), OSw. *æpli*, (Goth. unkn. ?*apuls*, pl. *apuleis*, masc., or *apli*, pl. *aplja*, neut.); cf. Lith. *óbŭlas*, *-is*, Samogitian *abolis*, Lettish *ahbols*, OSl. *jabl'ko*, Russ. *jablo-ko*, Pol. *jabl-ko*; also Irish *abhal*, *ubhal*, Welsh *afal*. The relation of these to the Teutonic, and the origin of the word are unknown (see Grimm I. 532–3); nor does it seem certain whether the general or special meaning is the earlier.]

A. 1. a. The round firm fleshy fruit of a Rosaceous tree (*Pyrus Malus*) found wild, as the crab-apple, in Europe and the Caucasus, and cultivated in innumerable varieties all over the two temperate zones.

c **885** K. ÆLFRED *Gregory's Past.* xv. 94 Ða readan apla [*v.r.* appla, L. *poma granata*] onȝemang ðæm bellum. *c* **1175** *Lamb. Hom.* 25 He..beð al swa is an eppel iheowed. **1297** R. GLOUC. 283 Upe þe hexte bowe tueye applen he sey. **1398** TREVISA *Barth. De P.R.* VI. v. (1495) 192 Chyldren loue an apple more than golde. *c* **1449** PECOCK *Repr.* II. iv. 160 This tree..bringith forth soure Applis. **1533** ELYOT *Cast. Helth* II. vii. 21 Rough tasted appules are holsome where the stomake is weake. **1596** SHAKS. *Merch. V.* I. iii. 102 A goodly apple rotten at the heart. **1712** STEELE *Spect.* No. 509 ¶2 Venders of..apples, plumbs. **1813** SIR H. DAVY *Agric. Chem.* 255 Most of our best apples are supposed to have been introduced into Britain by a fruiterer of Henry the Eighth.

b. Common in proverbial expressions. Phr. *(as) sure as God made little apples*, and similar phrases.

1340 *Ayenb.* 205 A roted eppel amang þe holen, makeþ rotie þe yzounde. **1532** MORE *Confut. Tindale* Wks. 689/1 Let him take mine yie for an apple, if, etc. **1579** FULKE *Heskins's Parl.* 241 Your argument is as like, as an apple is like an oyster. **1596** SHAKS. *Tam. Shr.* I. i. 139 Faith (as you say) there's small choise in rotten apples. **1623** SANDERSON *Serm.* Wks. 1681 I. 95 Of a wavering and fickle mind; as we say of children; won with an apple, and lost with a nut. **1874** M. CLARKE *His Natural Life* (1875) III. xv. 261 I'll tie you up and give you fifty for yourself, as sure as God made little apples. **1912** MULFORD & CLAY *Buck Peters* xxii. 198 It's Buck as sure as little apples Kesicks. **1926** J. BLACK *You can't Win* (1927) ix. 121 Sure as God made little apples I'll see that you get ten days. **1942** M. LASSWELL *Suds in Eye* ix. 112 I'm gonna learn to read sure as God made little apples.

c. Short for APPLE-TREE.

a **1626** BACON (T.) Oaks and beeches last longer than apples and pears. **1785** [see PEAR *sb.* 2]. **1940** E. STEP *Wayside & Woodland Trees* 40 The Wild Apple has not the pyramidal form of the Wild Pear.

2. a. Any fruit, or similar vegetable production; especially such as in some respect resemble the apple, but, from the earliest period, used with the greatest latitude.

a **1000** *Sax. Leechd.* I. 64 Genim brembel-æppel. *c* **1000** ÆLFRIC *Numb.* xi. 5 Cucumeres þæt sind eorþæppla. **1398** TREVISA *Barth De P.R.* XVII. cviii. (1495) 670 Al manere apples that ben closyd in an harde skynne, rynde, other shale, ben callyd Nuces. **1555** R. EDEN *Decades N. Worlde* v, Venemous apples wherwith they poyson theyr arrowes. **1607** TOPSELL *Four-footed Beasts* (1673) 516 The fruit or Apples of Palm-trees. **1765** TUCKER *Lt. Nat.* 377 The fly injects her juices into the oak-leaf, to raise an apple for hatching her young. **1861** HULME *Moquin-Tandon* II. III. v. 153 Bedeguars, commonly called 'Soft apples.' This name is given to Galls which are covered with numerous close-set hairs or fibres.

b. *Bot.* Any fruit of the structure of the apple; 'an inferior fleshy many-celled fruit'; a pome.

1729 J. MARTYN *Lect. Bot.* 20 in Chambers *Cycl. Supp.*

3. Hence forming part of the name of a large number of fruits; as **apple Punic**, obs. name of the pomegranate; **apple of Sodom**, or *Dead Sea Fruit*, described by Josephus as of fair appearance externally, but dissolving, when grasped, into smoke and ashes; a 'traveller's tale' supposed by some to refer to the fruit of *Solanum Sodomeum* (allied to the tomato), by others to the *Calotropis procera*; *fig.* Any hollow disappointing specious thing.

c **1250** *Gen. & Ex.* 1129 Quane here apples ripe ben, fier-isles man mai ðor-inne sen. **1398** TREVISA *Barth. De P.R.* XIII. xiii, Ther [by the dead sea] groweþ most feyre applis.. and when þou takest, he fadeþ and falleþ in to ashes and smokeþ as þouȝe he were brennynge. **1601** HOLLAND *Pliny* (1634) I. 398 Hereof cometh the colour of Puniceus (*i.* a light red, or a bay) taking the name of the apple Punicke, or Pomegranat. **1634** RAINBOW *Labour* (1635) 6 Those apples of Sodom which dye betwixt the hand and the mouth. **1703** MAUNDRELL *Journ. Jerus.* (1721) 85 As for the Apples of Sodom..I neither saw nor heard of any. **1869** *Eng. Mech.* 24 Dec. 354/1 Mecca galls, Dead Sea apples, Sodom apples, or mad apples..are occasionally imported from Bussarah.

b. **apple of Adam** = ADAM'S APPLE; **apple of love** = LOVE APPLE.

¶ See also ALLIGATOR A., BALSAM A., CHERRY A., CUSTARD A., DEVIL'S A., EGG A., ELEPHANT A., JEW'S A., KANGAROO A., MAD A., MANDRAKE A., MAY A., MONKEY A., OAK A., OTAHEITE A., PERSIAN A., PINE A., PRAIRIE A., ROSE A., STAR A., THORN A.

4. 'The fruit of that forbidden tree, whose mortal taste brought death into the world, and all our woe' (Milton).

a **1000** CÆDMON *Gen.* 637 (Grein) Æppel unsælȝa, deáp-beámes ofet. *c* **1230** *Ancr. R.* 52 Eue biheold o þen uorbodene eppele. *a* **1300** *Cursor M.* 755 Adam brake goddis co-mandement of the appil. *a* **1450** *Knt. de la Tour* (1868) 59 The delite of the apille slow Eve. **1667** MILTON *P.L.* x. 487 Him by fraud I have seduc'd From his Creator..with an Apple. **1829** SOUTHEY *All for Love* II, The Apple had done but little for me, If Eve had not done the rest.

5. **apple of discord**: the golden apple inscribed 'For the fairest,' fabled to have been thrown by Eris, the personification of discord, into the assembly of the gods, and contended for by Juno, Minerva, and Venus; whence, any subject of disagreement and dissension.

[*c* **1400** *Destr. Troy* VI. 2434 Hit semit me..þat Venus the vertuus was verely þe fairest, And I duli..demyt hir the appull.] *a* **1649** DRUMM. OF HAWTH. *Irene* Wks. 1711, 173 Who throw the apple of dissension amongst your subjects. **1680** *Established Test* 10 The Apple of Contention between the Prince and the People. **1867** FREEMAN *Norm. Conq.* I. iv. 195 This great and wealthy church constantly formed an apple of discord.

6. Anything resembling an apple in form or colour; any smooth globular body of metal, glass, etc. ***golden apple***: the orb in the British Regalia.

a **1000** *Sal. & Sat.* 28 Irenum aplum. **1366** MAUNDEV. i. 8 He was wont to holden a round Appelle of Gold in his Hond. *c* **1430** LYDG. *Bochas* (1554) 220b, Ye mot forsake of gold your apple round, Scepter and swerde. **1559** MORWYNG *Evonym.* 207 To make the apple of the chieck ruddy. **1601** HOLLAND *Pliny* (1634) II. 598 A round bal or hollow apple of glasse. **1881** *N.Y. Art Interchange* 27 Oct. 93/1 Of double-faced Canton flannel, finished with fringe and floss apples.

7. a. **apple of the eye**: the pupil or circular aperture in the centre of the eye through which the dark retina is seen; so called, because it was supposed to be a globular solid body. Sometimes extended to the *iris* and *pupil*; or to the *eyeball*; but apparently only by misunderstanding.

c **885** K. ÆLFRED *Gregory's Past.* xi. 68 On ðæs siweniȝean eaȝum beoð ða æplas [*v.r.* æpplas] hale..Sio scearpnes bið ȝewierd ðæs æples [*v.r.* æpples]. *a* **1300** W. DE BIBLESW. in Wright *Voc.* 145 *La prunele*, the appel of the eye. **1483** *Cath. Angl.*, Appylle of ee, *pupilla*. **1586** T. B. *La Primaud. Fr. Acad* 145 We see our owne eies shine within the apples of our neighbours eies. **1600** CHAPMAN *Iliad* XIV. 409 The dart did undergore His eye-lid, by his eye's dear roots, & out the apple fell. **1601** HOLLAND *Pliny* XI. 37 None have their eyes all of one color, for the bal or apple in the midst is ordinarily of another color than the white about. **1753** CHAMBERS *Cycl. Supp.* s.v., He cut asunder the Apple of the eye in several animals. **1827** *Blackw. Mag.* XXII. 374/1 Dull people turn up..the apples of their eyes on beholding Prose by a Poet.

b. Used as a symbol of that which is cherished with the greatest regard.

c **885** K. ÆLFRED *Boeth.* xxxix. §10 Hí scilde swa ȝeorn-líce swá swá man dép ðone æpl on his eáȝan. *a* **1300** *E.E. Psalter* xvi. 8 Als appel of eghe yheme þou me. **1535** COVERDALE *Zech.* ii. 8 Who so toucheth you, shal touche the aple of his owne eye. **1816** SCOTT *Old M.* xx, Poor Richard was to me as an eldest son, the apple of my eye. **1930** R. CAMPBELL *Poems* 11 Live and die The apple, nay the onion, of his eye? **1941** F. GRUBER *Hungry Dog* (1950) x. 81 He may have been the apple of *your* eye, but to me he was only a cinder.

8. ***apple(s) and pears***: rhyming slang for 'stairs'; also (*ellipt.*) *apples*.

1857 'DUCANGE ANGLICUS' *Vulg. Tongue* 1, Apple and Pears, stairs. **1909** WARE *Passing Eng.* 9/1 Bill an' Jack's gone up apples. **1914** C. MACKENZIE *Sinister Street* II. IV. ix. 1100, I soon shoved him down the Apples-and-pears. **1962** J. G. BENNETT *Witness* xviii. 218 One of the removal men asked him if a sofa was to go 'up the apples'.

9. *(to be)* ***apples*** [rhyming slang for *apples and rice* (or *spice*), nice]: (to be) fine or satisfactory. *Austral.* and *N.Z. slang.*

1943 J. BINNING *Target Area* 140 If everything is running smoothly 'she's apples'. **1952** T. A. G. HUNGERFORD *Ridge & River* 44 How's it going, Wally? Everything apples? **1958** R. STOW *To Islands* iv. 92 She felt their faint movements of relief and surprise. 'Well,' said Dixon, 'that'd be a break. That'd be apples, that would.' **1963** R. H. MORRIESON *Scarecrow* (1964) xii. 133 Don't cry, Pru. Yuh go and see old Len Ramsbottom and betcha everything'll be apples. **1975** *Sydney Morning Herald* 24 June 6 No one reckons it's 'apples' in the battle for Bass.

B. *Comb.* and *Attrib.* I. General relations.

1. *obj.* with active pple., or *objective gen.* with n. of agent or action, as ***apple-bite***, ***-buyer***, ***-gathering***, ***-paring***, ***-quarterer***, ***-seller***, ***-stealing***.

a **1300** *Cursor M.* 795 Of þat ilk appel bitt þair suns tethe ar eggeid yitt. *c* **1500** *Cock Lorells Bote* 5 Andrewe of habyngedon apell-byer. **1870** MORRIS *Earthly Par.* II. III. 161 As in the apple-gathering tide. **1879** D. HILL *Bryant* 39 Huskings and apple-parings had not gone out of fashion. **1440** *Promp. Parv.*, Appulseller, *Pomilius*. **1865** *Athenæum* 28 Jan. 120/2 The well-known 'apple-stealing' capital in the south transept of Wells Cathedral.

2. a. *similative*, as ***apple-bright***, ***-green***, ***-smelling***, ***-yellow***; passing into *synthetic derivatives*, as ***apple-cheeked***, ***-faced***, ***-leaved***, ***-rotten***, ***-scented***, ***-shaped***.

1930 E. SITWELL *Coll. Poems* 90 Their *apple-bright and ruddy flesh. **1864** TENNYSON *Enoch Arden*, etc. 158 A bevy of Eroses *apple-cheek'd. **1921** W. DE LA MARE *Crossings* 86 A shy, fat, apple-cheeked child. **1837** DICKENS *Pickw.* II. xlii. 457 A little white-headed *apple-faced tipstaff. **1848** —— *Dombey* (C.D. ed.) 9 A plump, rosy-cheeked..apple-faced young woman. **1648** HEXHAM *Groot Woorden-Boeck*, *Appel-groen*, *Apple-greene. **1797** HEIDELOFF *Gallery of Fashion* Nov. in R. W. Chapman *Sense & Sensibility* (1933) 387 Hungarian robe of apple-green satin. **1812** SIR H. DAVY *Chem. Philos.* 426 Oxides of uranium give bright colours to glass..brown, apple green, or emerald green. **1917** D. H. LAWRENCE *Look! We have come Through!* 54 The dawn was apple-green. **1905** 'Q' *Shining Ferry* III. xxvi. 271 The schooner might be *apple-rotten. **1923** W. DE LA MARE *Riddle* 2 The cool *apple-scented pantry. **1880** BROWNING *Pan & Luna* 42 That *apple-shaped Head which its hair binds close into a ball. **1809** PEARSON *Phil. Trans.* XCIX. 331 The same *apple-smelling liquid. **1953** BANNERMAN *Birds Brit. Isles* I. 180 Young birds..are more grey-green, that colour replacing the brighter *apple-yellow of the adult.

b. **apple head**, a type of rounded skull found in certain small dogs; so ***apple-domed***, ***-headed*** adjs.

1883 W. G. STABLES *Our Friend the Dog* vii. 59 *Apple-headed*, the roundness of the top of the skull. **1922** R. LEIGHTON *Compl. Bk. of Dog* v. xx. 290 These small dogs usually have 'apple-heads'. **1948** C. L. B. HUBBARD *Dogs in*

Britain xix. 216 The head [of the Chihuahua] is well rounded and apple-domed. **1959** *Observer* 1 Feb. 11/3 'Apple' heads (that is a thick, domed skull with snipey fore-face)..are particularly deplored [in toy poodles].

3. *attrib.* **a.** simply, as ***apple-bloom, -blossom, -core, -flower, -graft, -harvest, -hoard, -juice, -legend, -seed, -stem, -time***; **b.** of purpose or use, as ***apple-loft, -orchard, -room, -stall***; **c.** of material (= made of or with apples), as ***apple-dumpling, -fritters, -ice, -jelly, -pap, pasty, -pudding, -tart, -toddy.***

1949 BLUNDEN *After Bombing* 50 As new *apple-bloom May be by hailstones ravaged. **1824** MISS MITFORD *Village* Ser. II. (1863) 244 Her *apple-blossom complexion. **1711** W. BYRD *Secret Diary* 18 Aug. (1941) 391 At dinner I ate some *apple dumpling. **1721** AMHERST *Terræ Fil.* 293 A regimen of bread and water; or, what is little better, of small beer and apple-dumplings. **1596** CHAPMAN *Iliad* III. 509 Fragrant *appleflowers. *c* **1460** RUSSELL *Bk. Nurt.* 502 *Appulle fruture is good hoot, but þe cold ye not towche. *a* **1691** BOYLE (J.) Twenty sorts of *apple-grafts upon the same old plant. **1861** GEN. P. THOMPSON *Audi Alt.* III. clxxviii. 214 Apples in *apple-harvest, and potatoes in potato time. *a* **1732** GAY *Wks.* 1745 I. 107 Now the squeez'd press foams with our *apple hoards. **1879** R. EDWARDS *Russ. at Home* I. 197 Frozen apples, like lumps of *apple-ice. **1727** BRADLEY *Fam. Dict.* s.v. *Apple*, Make an *Apple-Jelly..by extracting the Juice of the Rind and Cores. **1708** E. COOK *Sot-weed Factor* 19 There with good punch and *apple juice We spent our hours without abuse. **1766** CAVENDISH in *Phil. Trans.* LVI. 177 The air, discharged from apple-juice by fermentation. **1961** *Harrods Food News* 11/1 Canadian Apple Juice, natural. **1872** BLACK *Adv. Phaeton* xxviii. 382 The *apple legend of Tell. **1740** MRS. DELANY *Autobiog.* (1861) II. 120 Go see what's doing in the cheese-chamber and the *apple-loft. **1721** *New-Eng. Courant* 14–21 Aug. 2/2 There was a larger *Apple Orchard at that Place. **1807** VANCOUVER *Agric. Devon* (1813) 236 Very good apple-orchards. *a* **1625** FLETCHER *M. Thomas* III. i, Which will down easily without *applepap. **1728** E. SMITH *Compleat Housewife* (ed. 2) 108 *Apple-Pasties to Fry. **1880** MRS. PARR *Adam & Eve* 281 A couple of apple pasties. **1710** W. BYRD *Secret Diary* 24 Aug. (1941) 222, I ate some *apple pudding for dinner. **1807** HOME in *Phil. Trans.* XCVII. 143 A child..who..ate so large a quantity of apple-pudding that it died. **1699** J. LORD *Let.* 21 Feb. in *Mass. Hist. Soc. Coll.* (1861) 4th Ser. V. 306 *Apple-seeds, sown by us since we came, came up in January. **1930** T. S. ELIOT *Ash-Wed.* 19 Spitting from the mouth the withered apple-seed. **1907** YEATS *Deirdre* 10 Praise the blossoming *apple-stem. **1596** SHAKS. *Tam. Shr.* IV. iii. 89 A sleeue..caru'd like an *apple Tart. **1865** SWINBURNE *Chastelard* IV. i. 120 And now the flower, and deadly fruit will come With *apple-time in autumn. **1809** W. IRVING *Knickerb.* (1849) 239 Great roysters, much given to..*apple-toddy.

II. Special combinations.

apple-aphis, the insect (*Lachnus lanigerus*) which produces **apple-blight**, a cottony substance found on apple-trees; **apple-bee**, (*a*) *dial.* a wasp; (*b*) *U.S.* (see BEE *sb.*[1] 4); **apple-berry**, an Australian shrub and its fruit, of genus *Billardiera*; **apple-borer** *U.S.*, an insect attacking apple-trees; **apple-box, -gum**, names for species of *Eucalyptus*; **apple-brandy**, a spirit distilled from cider; **apple-bug**, a water-beetle of the family Gyrinidæ, which exudes a milky liquid having an odour of apples; **apple-butter** (see quot. 1860); **apple charlotte**: see CHARLOTTE; **apple-cheese**, compressed **apple-pomice**; **apple-corer**, an instrument for cutting out the core of apples; **apple-crook**, a crook for gathering apples from the trees, also *fig.*; **apple-dowdy** chiefly *U.S.*, a kind of apple-pie made in a deep dish (cf. PANDOWDY); **apple-drone, -drane**, *dial.* a wasp; **apple-eating** *a.*, used *fig.* for 'easily-tempted'; †**apple-fallow** *a.*, of the yellowish-red colour of apples, bay; **apple-fly** (see quot.); †**apple-garth**, an apple-garden or orchard; †**apple-gray** *a.* (ON. *apal-grár*), having the streaky colour of an apple; **apple-jack**, American name for apple-brandy, in east of England for an apple-turnover; †**apple-monger**, a dealer in apples, fruiterer; **apple-moss**, a genus of moss with apple-shaped capsules; **apple-moth**, *Tortrix pomana*; **apple-oil**, a synthetic chemical used to imitate the odour of apples in confectionery; **apple-pear**, probably the tankard-pear; **apple-peru** *U.S.*, the thorn-apple; **apple-plum**, one grafted on an apple stock; **apple-polishing** *vbl. sb.* (*U.S. slang*), currying favour; toadying; so **apple-polisher**, a toady; **apple-pomice**, the residue of apple-pulp after expressing the juice; **apple's queen**, Pomona; **apple-sauce** (see sense B. I. 3 c), (*a*) lit.; (*b*) *transf.* nonsense, absurdity; insincere flattery (*U.S. slang*); **apple-scoop**, an instrument made of bone or ivory used in eating apples; **apple-shell, -snail**, a family of Gasteropods, so named from their shape; **apple-slump** *U.S.* (see quot. 1872); **apple snow**: see SNOW *sb.*[1] 5 a; **apple strudel** [partial tr. of G. *apfelstrudel* (also used), f. *apfel* apple + *strudel* flaky pastry], a baked sweet consisting of a spiced mixture of apples rolled in flaky pastry; †**apple-water**, cider; **apple-wife, -woman**, a female who keeps a stall for sale of apples; **apple-worm**, the maggot bred in apples; **apple-wort**, any plant of the sub-order *Pomaceæ*; †**apple-yard** (= *apple garth*).

Also APPLE-JOHN, -MOSE, -PIE, -SQUIRE, -TREE, q.v.

1815 KIRBY & SPENCE *Entomol.* (1843) I. 23 The *apple aphis..has done such extensive injury to our orchards. **1808** *Monthly Mag.* XXVI. 421/2 **Apple-bee*, a wasp. C[ornwall]. **1912** C. MACKENZIE *Carnival* xxxix. 397 It was vain for Thomas to assure her that apple-bees did not sting without provocation. **1859** *Trans. Ill. Agric. Soc. 1857–8* III. 344 The most destructive of these..is that known as the *apple borer. **1890** *Melbourne Argus* 9 Aug. 4/6 An ironstone hill.. with *apple-box and ironbark dotted about. **1944** F. D. DAVISON in *Coast to Coast* 238 The creek made a horseshoe bend under its bower of apple-box-trees. *c* **1780** in *Maryland Hist. Mag.* (1907) II 256, [I] accepted 13 gals. of peach brandy in satisfaction of the damage... He cheated me with *apple brandy. **1809** W. IRVING *Knickerb.* (1861) 123 Flushed with victory and apple-brandy. **1832** J. P. KENNEDY *Swallow B.* I. xii. 129 The *apple-bugs (as school-boys call that glossy black insect which frequents the summer pools, and is distinguished for the perfume of the apple) danced in busy myriads over the surface of the still water. **1869** *Rep. U.S. Commissioner Agric. 1868* 80 The fifth family, gyrinidae, comprises those oval water-beetles usually known by the name of 'whirligigs' or apple-bugs. *c* **1774** CRÈVECŒUR *Sk. 18th-Cent. Amer.* (1925) 105 We often make *apple-butter. **1860** BARTLETT *Dict. Amer.*, *Apple Butter*, A sauce made of apples stewed down in cider. **1870** *Congress. Globe* Apr. 2685/1 Apple-butter is a substitute for butter; it is spread upon bread and eaten in like manner. **1706** J. PHILIPS *Cyder* II. 110 The *Apple-Cheese..will cherish and improve the Roots Of sickly Plants. **1796** MRS. GLASSE *Cookery* v. 71 Some carrot..cut round with an *apple-corer. **1382** WYCLIF *Pref. Epist.* vii. 70 The *appel croke drawinge tourmentis to synful men. **1923** W. NUTTING *Massachusetts* 241 Did ever a dish of *apple dowdy go to the spot like that? **1952** M. LASKI *Village* vii. 114 To make an apple-dowdy in the kitchen. **1620** MELTON *Astrol.* 53 Foolish, credulous, and *Appleeating women will believe them. *a* **1000** *Beowulf* 4336 Feower mearas ..*æppel-fealuwe. **1753** CHAMBERS *Cycl. Supp.*, **Apple Fly* ..a small green fly found sometimes within an Apple. **1483** *Cath. Angl.*, *Appelle garth, *pometum*. **1640** *King & North. Maid* 54 in Hazl. *E.P.P.* IV. 295 As though his eyes were *apple gray. **1847** LEICHHARDT *Jrnl.* viii. 264 Another Eucalyptus [*E. Stuartiana*]..with smooth upper trunk and cordate ovate leaves..; we called it the *Apple-gum. **1963** W. S. RAMSON in *Austral. Quart.* XXXV. Sept. 53 Some have been named after their supposed resemblance to the foliage or timber of European trees, like *apple gum*, [etc.]. **1816** 'OLD SCENE PAINTER' *Emigrant's Guide* 30 A partial distillation is also made from apples..called *Apple-Jack. **1865** *N.Y. Tribune* in *Morn. Star* 20 Apr., The genuine Virginia stimulant known as apple-jack, or apple whisky. **1932** E. WILSON *Devil take Hindmost* i. 1 The old cider mills are still barrelling applejack and hard cider. **1552** HULOET, *Applemonger, *Pomilius*. **1864** *Intell. Observ.* V. 263 The straight-leaved *Apple-moss grows on Alpine rocks. **1857** *Apple oil [see VALERIANATE]. **1867** BLOXAM *Chem.* 553 The valerianate of amyle, which has the flavour of apples,..is known as apple-oil. **1784** CUTLER in *Mem. Amer. Academy* (1785) I. 419 *Apple-peru..Common by the waysides. August. **1850** HAWTHORNE *Scarlet L.* (1851) i. 60 A grass-plot, much overgrown with burdock, pig-weed, apple-peru, and such unsightly vegetation. **1601** HOLLAND *Pliny* (1634) I. 437 They began to graffe plums vpon apple-tree stocks, and those brought forth plums named *Apple-plums. **1928** *Amer. Speech* III. 218 *Apple polisher. **1947** E. A. MCCOURT *Music at Close* 116 The apple-polishers in the front row laughed with forced heartiness. **1935** A. G. KENNEDY *Current Eng.* ii. 28 The college boy with his pet phrases such as **apple-polishing*, currying favor with a professor. **1664** EVELYN *Pomona* Advt. 95 Water, wherein a good Quantity of *Apple-pomice hath been boil'd. *a* **1649** DRUMM. OF HAWTH. *Wks.* 1711 6/2 Fair looketh Ceres with her yellow hair; And *apple's-queen, when rose-cheek'd she doth smile. **1739** E. SMITH *Compleat Housewife* (ed. 9) 104 Boil them as you do *Apple-sauce. **1824** MISS MITFORD *Village* (1863) II. 321 Names quite as inseparable as goose and apple-sauce. **1921** *Collier's* 1 Jan. 18/4 That's all apple sauce! **1924** WODEHOUSE *Bill the Conqueror* xii. 210 It sounds to me a good deal like apple sauce. Seems like there ain't no sense in it. **1926** *S.P.E. Tract* XXIV. 119 *Applesauce* (noun or interjection). One of the latest pieces of slang in this country [*sc.* U.S.A.]. It has two quite distinct meanings, (1) *nonsense!* and (2) *flattery*. It is commonly used as a term of jocular contempt in reply to effusive but unjustifiable flattery. 'He a great author? Apple-sauce!' **1934** J. O'HARA *Appt. in Samarra* (1935) ii. 45, 'I just didn't want to spoil your evening, that's all.' 'Applesauce,' said Irma. **1870** NICHOLSON *Zool.* (1880) 408 *Ampullaria canaliculata*. one of the *Apple shells. **1831** H. J. FINN *Amer. Comic Annual* 140 The pumpkin pies and *apple slump..were smoking on the table. **1872** SCHELE DE VERE *Americanisms* 415 *Apple-Slump* is..a favorite New England dish, consisting of apples and molasses baked within a bread-pie in an iron pot. **1884** E. E. HALE *Christmas in Narragansett* i. 11 Guessed that they had done justice to.. Polly's apple-slump. **1863** MRS. BEETON *Bk. Househ. Managem.* xxix. 703 **Apple Snow*,..10 good-sized apples, the whites of 10 eggs, the rind of 1 lemon, ½ lb. of pounded sugar. *a* **1887** Apple snow [see SNOW *sb.*[1] 5 a]. **1936** LUCAS & HUME *Au Petit Cordon Bleu* 148 *Apfelstrudel. **1963** *Punch* 2 Jan. 27 What I lose on the nursery slopes I gain on the apfelstrudel. **1923** HEMINGWAY *In our Time* (1926) xi. 164 We have some *apple strudel if you want it. **1935** M. LANE *Faith, Hope, No Charity* iv. 108 Ada's friend from the Jewish caterers..came round with a four-pound apple strudel. **1606** *Choice, Chance, etc.* (1881) 11 *Apple water, otherwise called Sider. **1599** NASHE *Lent. Stuff* (1871) 72 Pomona, the first *apple-wife. **1741** POPE & ARBUTHNOT *Mem. M. Scriblerus* vi. 46 Yonder are two *Apple-women scolding. **1840** GEN. P. THOMPSON *Exerc.* (1842) V. 330 If members of parliament had the spirit of apple-women. **1869** *Eng. Mech.* 23 July 393/2 The *apple-worm moth. **1847** LINDLEY *Veg. K.* (ed. 2) 559 *Appleworts are closely allied to Rose-worts. **1440** *Promp. Parv.*, *Appullyerde, *Pomerium*.

apple (æp(ə)l), *v. rare.* [f. prec. sb.; OE. had pa. pple. *æppled*.]

1. a. *trans.* and *intr.* To form or turn into apples; to bear apples, or similar fruit; to fruit.

a **1000** *Juliana* 688 Æpplede gold. **1601** HOLLAND *Pliny* (1634) II. 98 Either they floure, or they apple or els be ready to bring forth fruit.

b. *intr.* Of turnips: to swell into globular shape.

1712 J. MORTON *Nat. Hist. Northants.* ix. 483 Unless the Soil has some mixture of Sand the Turnips do not apple, as they call it: that is, do not bottom well. **1731** MILLER *Gard. Dict.* s.v. *Rapa*, If the Autumn should not prove very mild, [the Turnips] will not have time to Apple before Winter. **1796** MARSHALL *Gardening* (T.) The cabbage turnep is of two kinds; one apples above ground.

2. *intr.* To gather apples.

1799 A. YOUNG *Agric. Surv. Linc.*, The poor people supply themselves with very good fuel by gathering the fir-apples..*appleing*, as they call it.

†**a'pplease**, *v. Obs.* Forms: 5 **apleyse, applesse**, 6 **-eis, -ese.** [either ad. OFr. *aplaisir*, inf. (used only subst., cf. *plaisir*) cogn. w. Sp. *aplazer*, on type of L. **applacēre*, f. *ap-* = *ad-* to, completely + *placēre* to please; *or* an imitative formation like APARDON: see A- *pref.* 11.] To please, content, satisfy.

c **1450** *E.E. Misc.* (1855) 18 Yf hit do the apleyse. **1536** BELLENDENE *Cron. Scot.* (1821) I. Pref. 7 To do the thing that micht him best appleis. **1552** LYNDESAY *Papyngo* 132 Dame Ceres..Full Ioyfullie Iohane Vpponland applesit.

apple-cart. [APPLE B. 3 b.] **a.** *lit.* A cart for carrying apples. **b.** Phr. ***to upset the*** (or someone's) ***apple-cart***, humorously used for 'to cause an upset'; *esp.* to upset a person's plans, to ruin the undertaking. Also in similar expressions.

1788 J. BELKNAP in *Mass. Hist. Soc. Coll.* (1882) 5th Ser. III. 17 S. Adams had almost overset the apple-cart by *intruding* an amendment of his own fabrication on the morning of the day of ratification [of the Constitution]. **1796** GROSE *Dict. Vulgar Tongue* (ed. 3) s.v., Down with his apple-cart; knock or throw him down. **1834** CARRUTHERS *Kentuckian in N.Y.* I. 101 Smash my apple-cart, if there wasn't more crying..than I've seen at many an honest man's funeral. **1848** in Hodder *Life Shaftesbury* (1887) xvii. 396 If the Prince goes on like this, why he'll upset our apple-cart. **1871** G. P. R. PULMAN *Rustic Sketches* (ed. 3) Gloss. 77 'Don't upsit th' apple-cart.' That is—be careful you do not let fall anything carried. **1883** *Pall Mall Gaz.* 26 Oct., If the Control had done more it might have upset the apple-cart altogether. **1897** *Review of Rev.* Aug. 114 Somebody will lose patience, and then over will go the apple-cart. **1955** *Sci. Amer.* Aug. 68/2 Names such as ammoniated tincture of valerian can safely be revealed to the patient without upsetting the psychological applecart.

appled (æp(ə)ld), *ppl. a.* [f. APPLE *v.* + -ED.] Formed into or like an apple.

a **1000** *Elene* 1260 þeáh he in medohealle mæðmas þége æplede gold. **1873** BROWNING *Red Cotton Nt.-Cap* III. 145 One October morning, at first drop of appled gold.

'apple-john. Also **John-apple.** ['so called because it is ripe about S. John's Day.' Britten and Holl.] A kind of apple said to keep two years, and to be in perfection when shrivelled and withered.

1597 SHAKS. *2 Hen. IV.* II. iv. 5 A Dish of Apple-Iohns [see context]. **1623** MABBE *Aleman's Guzman D'Alf.* II. 310 Her face (like an old Apple-John) all shrivelled. **1708** J. PHILLIPS *Cyder* I. (N.) John-apple, whose wither'd rind, entrench'd By many a furrow, aptly represents Decrepid age. *c* **1811** W. IRVING in Warner *Life* (1882) 77 Poor Jemmy —he is but a withered little apple-john.

appleless ('æp(ə)llıs), *a.* Without apples.

1830 MISS MITFORD *Village* IV. (1863) 248 Taking care that none should go appleless in the midst of his fun.

†**apple-mose.** *Obs.* [f. APPLE *sb.* + OE. *mós* (cogn. w. OFris. *mós*, OHG. *môs, muos*) pap, pottage: cf. MHG. *epfelmuos*.] A dish made with the pulp of stewed apples and other ingredients.

c **1400** *Forme of Cury* 96 For to make Appulmos. *c* **1450** *Noble Bk. Cookry* (1882) 121 To mak an appillmose, tak appelles and sethe them and lett them kelle, then fret them throughe an heryn syff. **1552** HULOET, Apple moyse.

apple-pie. [APPLE B. 3 c.] A pie made with apples; *transf.* applied to the Willow-herb from the odour of the flowers and young shoots.

1590 GREENE *Arcadia* (1616) 67 Thy breath is like the steame of apple-pyes. **1741** RICHARDSON *Pamela* (1824) I. 163, I made shift to get down a bit of apple-pye, and a little custard. **1861** MRS. LANKESTER *Wild Fl.* 52 Willow-herb.. Applepie Plant.

apple-pie bed: a bed in which, as a practical joke, the sheets are so folded that a person cannot get his legs down; **apple-pie order**: complete, thorough order; also *ellipt.* [It has been suggested that this may be a corruption of '*Cap-a-pie order*,' but no instance of the latter phrase appears.]

1781 J. WOODFORDE *Diary* (1924) I. 302 Had but an indifferent night of Sleep, Mrs. Davie and Nancy made me up an Apple Pye Bed last night. **1840** *New Monthly Mag.* LVIII. 246 He..began to fancy that the bed was too small for him, when..little Oxtowne..told him..'it was only an apple-pie'. **1917** A. WAUGH *Loom of Youth* IV. vii. 308 His dormitory made him apple-pie beds.

1780 T. PASLEY *Private Sea Jrnls.* 12 May (1931) 87 Their Persons Clean and in apple-Pie order on Sundays. **1813** SCOTT in Lockhart *Life* IV. (1839) 131 The children's garden is in apple-pie order. **1835** MARRYAT *Jac. Faithf.* viii. 29 Put the craft a little into apple-pie order. **1898** W. RALEIGH *Let.* 13 Sept. (1926) I. 208 We had an artist in the back room..so I could not leave it as apple-pie as I should have liked. **1904** J. LONDON *Sea-Wolf* xi. 88 The boat-pullers and steerers have..put their boats in apple-pie order.

†**apple-squire.** *Obs.* A harlot's attendant; a pimp. Cf. APRON-SQUIRE.

c **1500** *Way to Spyttel Hous* 832 in Hazl. *E.P.P.* IV. 60 Applesquyers, entycers, and rauysshers. **1599** *Warn. Faire Wom.* II. 1158 Trusty Roger, her base apple-squire. **1738** *Poor Robin* (N.), Whores, pimps, panders, and apple-squires.

Appleton layer ('æp(ə)ltən 'leɪə(r)). *Physics.* [f. the name of Edward V. *Appleton* (1892–1965), British physicist + LAYER.] The upper, or F, stratum of the ionosphere above the Heaviside (or E) layer.

Appleton himself used the term 'F layer' for this stratum (*Proc. Internat. Scientific Radio Union*, Washington Meeting, 1927).

1932 *Techn. Tables & Gloss. (B.B.C.)* 44/1 *Appleton Layer*, an ionised layer of the upper atmosphere thought to exist above the *Kennelly-Heaviside* layer. It has been suggested that it is this layer which is responsible for the reflection of short waves which are attenuated but not reflected in their passage through the *Kennelly-Heaviside* layer. The height of the Appleton layer above the earth has been measured as approximately 230 kilometres. **1943** *Electronic Engin.* XV. 342 Presumably the Heaviside, Appleton..etc. layers in the upper atmosphere also give rise to harmonics of radio waves.

apple-tree. 1. A tree which bears apples.

a **1100** in Wright *Voc.* 79/2 *Malus*, æpeltre. *a* **1300** *Cursor M.* 1367 Pepins..quilk a þe appel tre he nam. **1447** *Lyvys of Seyntys* 54 b/2 He that..hys appyltre Eche day watryth. *c* **1525** SKELTON *Replyc.* 157 Suche apple tre, suche frute. **1805** SOUTHEY *Madoc in W.* XIV. Wks. V. 105 The crooked apple-trees, Grey with their fleecy moss and misseltoe.

2. In Australia applied to various indigenous trees, esp. to a species of Eucalyptus (= *apple-gum*: see APPLE *sb.* B. II), and to another myrtaceous tree, *Angophora subvelutina*.

1801 in *Hist. Rec. Australia* (1915) III. 414 The Timber at the back blue-gum and apple trees. **1820** J. OXLEY *Jrnl. Exped. N.S. Wales* 187 That species of eucalyptus which is vulgarly called the apple tree. **1885** MRS. C. PRAED *Head Station* I. iv. 60 A giant eucalyptus of the kind called 'appletree'. **1885** *Spons' Mechanics' Own Bk.* 127 Apple (Australian) (*Angophora subvelutina*). The so-called apple-tree of Queensland yields planks 20–30 in. in diameter.

†**a'ppliable,** *a.* [f. APPLY *v.* + -ABLE; earlier than the current APPLICABLE.]

†**1.** Ready to apply one's self or to hearken (*to*); docile, compliant, well-disposed. Cf. PLIABLE. *Obs.*

1499 *Plumpton Corr.* 134, I have advysed him so to doe, the which he is right glad and aplyable. **1532** MORE *Confut. Tindale* Wks. 698/2 With willing and applyable myndes. **1635** SHIRLEY *Lady of Pleas.* III. i, She has a very appliable nature. **1699** TEMPLE *Hist. Eng.* 583 Tho' constant to his Ends, yet appliable to Occasions.

2. Capable of being applied. (See APPLY 1–10.)

c **1555** HARPSFIELD *Divorce Hen. VIII.* (1878) 51 This case is not appliable against our case. **1586** WEBBE *Eng. Poetrie* (1870) 59 Dytties applyable to euery tune that may be sung or sayd. **1624** SANDERSON *Serm.* Ad. Mag. ii. (1674) 104 Conceive the words as..appliable to the Accuser. **1642** HOWELL *For. Trav.* (Arb.) 16 Like the Shoomakers Last, that may bee applyable to any foot. **1679** OATES *Serm. St. Mich. Wood-St.*, The purchase of Christ..should be appliable to man without any fraud or limitation. **1855** *Jrnl. R. Agric. Soc.* XVI. II. 563 A practical and appliable knowledge. **1874** *Contemp. Rev.* XXIV. 731 Abundance..of wealth..appliable to other purposes.

†**3.** Having relation, suitable, pertinent, applicable. *Obs.*

1555 *Fardle of Facions* II. xi. 239 [Mahomet] extolled him [Christe] to a more heigth then was appliable to the nature of man. *a* **1656** HALES *Gold. Rem.* (1688) 29 How this advice ..was appliable or how it fitted the question..belongs not to me to discuss. **1742** BAILEY, *Appliable*, that may be applied, has relation to, or, is conformable to.

†**a'ppliableness.** *Obs.* [f. prec. + -NESS.] The quality of being compliant or docile; readiness, willingness; pliableness.

1587 FLEMING *Contn. Holinshed* III. 402/2 Hir maiestie might perceiue the appliablenesse of those hir people. *a* **1631** DONNE *Select.* (1840) 76 The holy gentleness and appliableness, implied in that form of man [a minister of God].

†**app'liably,** *adv. Obs.* [f. as prec. + -LY².] So as to be applied; applicably, suitably.

c **1530** (*title*) The Dialogues of Creatures moralysed, applyably..to euery mery and iocund Mater. **1665** R. CARPENTER *Pragm. Jesuit* 27/2 An Ecliptick..bow'd appliably to all our purposes.

†**a'pplial.** *Obs. rare*⁻¹. [f. APPLY *v.* + -AL².] The action of applying, application.

1548 GESTE *Pr. Masse* 98 The appliall of Christes merytes unto us.

appliance (ə'plaɪəns). [f. APPLY *v.* + -ANCE.]

†**1.** Compliance, willing service; subservience.

1601 SHAKS. *All's Well* II. i. 116, I come to tender it, and my appliance With all bound humblenesse. **1603** —— *Meas. for M.* III. i. 89 Too noble, to conserue a life In base appliances.

2. The action of putting to, administering, using, putting into practice; application.

1561 T. N[ORTON] *Calvin's Inst.*, It remaineth that by applyance all the same [benefits] may come to us. **1608** SHAKS. *Per.* III. ii. 86 An Egyptian, had nine hours lien dead, By good appliance was recovered. **1831** CARLYLE *Sart. Res.* II. iii, The human soul..could be acted-on through the muscular integument by the appliance of birch-rods. **1851** LONGF. *Gold. Leg.* I. xx, Have you done this, by the appliance and aid of doctors? **1868** G. MACDONALD *Eng. Antiphon* xviii. 264 He becomes either a man of appliance, a man of science, a mystic, or a poet.

3. a. A thing applied as means to an end; apparatus.

1597 SHAKS. *2 Hen. IV*, III. i. 20 With all appliances and meanes to boote. **1613** —— *Hen. VIII*, I. i. 124 Aske God for Temp'rance; that's th' appliance onely which your disease requires. **1861** STANLEY *East. Ch.* ii. Introd. 60 All the appliances of antiquarian and artistic knowledge. **1876** FAWCETT *Pol. Econ.* II. viii. 231 To avail themselves of improved mechanical appliances.

b. *spec.* A fire-engine.

1899 *Daily News* 10 May 7/2 The driver..and one of the firemen on the 'manual' were injured, and the appliance sustained some damage. **1958** *Listener* 14 Aug. 247/3 The fire-engines ('appliances' to the Service) tore off into the night.

appliancy (ə'plaɪənsɪ). *rare*⁻¹. [f. as prec. + -ANCY.] The quality of accommodating one's self; adaptability, pliancy.

1836 I. TAYLOR *Phys. The. Another Life* (1857) 91 When the same mind comes to be lodged in a body that has more appliancy, and a higher finish.

†**a'ppliant,** *a. Obs.* [a. OFr. *apliant*, pr. pple. of *aplier*: see APPLY *v.* and -ANT.] Const. *to*.

1. Applying or inclining the mind; favourably inclined, docile, pliant; diligent.

1413 LYDGATE *Pylgr. Sowle* IV. xxx. (1483) 78 Theyr wylle was not aplyaunt to the counceyll of the..peple that they had to gouerne. **1509** HAWES *Past. Pleas.* XI. xxxvii, Hym that is ryght well applyaunt For to bere it. **1549** LATIMER 7 *Serm.* (Arb.) 24 Pharao..applyant unto the lustes of his owne herte. **1658** LENNARD *Charron's Wisdom* III. xxxvi. §3 That the soul may be alwaies..appliant unto reason.

2. Applicable, pertinent *to*. *rare*.

1548 GESTE *Pr. Masse* 99 Y^t [which] I have spoken..is..appliaunt to the latter portion of the sayde supper.

applicability (,æplɪkə'bɪlɪtɪ). [f. next: see -BILITY. Cf. mod.Fr. *applicabilité*.] The quality of being applicable; capability of being fitly applied; pertinence.

1653 H. MORE *Conject. Cabbal.* (1713) 110 There is a continued suitableness and applicability to the Text of Moses all along. **1818** HALLAM *Middle Ages* (1872) I. 480 The applicability of gunpowder to purposes of war. **1843** POE *Purl. Lett.* Wks. 1864 I. 274 If words derive any value from applicability. **1875** WHITNEY *Life Lang.* vii. 130 Multiplying the applicabilities, and so the usefulness, of its material.

applicable ('æplɪkəb(ə)l), *a.* [f. L. *applicā-re* to apply + -ABLE: cf. It. *applicabile* (Florio 1611) and mod.Fr. *applicable*. It has taken the place of the earlier APPLIABLE in all its senses.]

†**1.** Well-disposed, pliable; = APPLIABLE 1. *Obs.*

1563 *Homilies* II. ii. II. (1859) 208 Leo the third..having the king of the Francons..very applicable to his mind. *a* **1674** CLARENDON *Hist. Reb.* I. I. 6 The habit and temper of men's minds being..very applicable to the Publick ends.

2. Capable of being applied; having reference. (See APPLY *v.* 1–11.)

1660 R. COKE *Just. Vind.* 23 Art..as it is applicable to some material subject cannot be taught without experience. **1678** HOBBES *Decam. Phys.* viii. 97 Your Argument ought to be applicable to the weighing of Bodies in a pair of Scales. **1825** MᶜCULLOCH *Pol. Econ.* II. §2. 115 That portion of the produce of industry extrinsic to man, which may be made applicable to his support.

3. Fit or suitable for its purpose, appropriate.

1835 I. TAYLOR *Spir. Despot.* iv. 117 The applicable quality of the worship and polity which he consigned to his followers. **1851** *Art Jrnl. Catal. Gt. Exhib.* 76/2 The few water-leaves which adorn it..being applicable and unobtrusive.

'**applicableness.** *rare.* [f. prec. + -NESS.] The quality of being applicable; = APPLICABILITY.

1661 BOYLE *Style H. Script.* 251 A greater Familiarity with..the sense and the applicableness of Scripture. **1819** FOSTER *Evils Pop. Ignor.* 224 The soul..acquiring an unwonted applicableness of its faculties to thought.

applicably ('æplɪkəblɪ), *adv.* [f. as prec. + -LY².] In applicable manner; so as to be applied.

1755 in JOHNSON; and in mod. Dicts.

'**applicancy** ('æplɪkənsɪ). *rare.* [See next and -ANCY.] The state or quality of applying.

1859 in WORCESTER.

applicant ('æplɪkənt), *a.* and *sb.* [ad. L. *applicānt-em*, pr. pple. of *applicāre*: see APPLY *v.* and -ANT. Cf. mod.Fr. *appliquant*.]

A. *adj.* †**1.** Pliant, docile. *Obs. rare.*

2. Applying, making request. *rare.*

B. *sb.* One who applies or makes request.

c **1485** *Digby Myst.* (1882) II. 429 Mans mynd ys applicant, as I lyst to ordeyne. **1818** in TODD. **1821** *Min. Gen. Assembly Presb. Ch. U.S.A.* 23 Applicants from other denominations. **1836** H. TAYLOR *Statesm.* xxix. 218 To give it such a repulse as shall mortify and expose the party applicant. **1856** MERIVALE *Rom. Emp.* xxxii. III. 502 Doling gratuitous alms to every poor or lazy applicant.

applicate ('æplɪkeɪt, -ət), *ppl. a.* and *sb. rare.* [ad. L. *applicāt-us* closely adapted, pa. pple. of *applicāre* to APPLY.] **A.** *adj.*

†**1.** Closely adapted, suited, conformed. *Obs.*

1534 WHITTINTON *Tullyes Offices* I. (1540) 45 The agylite of the mynde is to be approbate and alowed, and [= if] such is applycate to nature.

†**2.** Inclined or directed towards. *Obs.*

1652 GAULE *Magastrom.* 87 Planets..applicate, refluent, &c. of the celestiall houses.

3. Put to practical use; applied, concrete.

1796 HUTTON *Math. Dict.* s.v., Applicate Number = concrete. **1838** I. TAYLOR *Home Educ.* 318 The applicate and the mixed sciences. **1855** —— *Restor. Belief* 6 The physical sciences both abstract and applicate.

B. *sb.* **1.** In Conic Sections: An ordinate.

1706 PHILLIPS, *Applicate*, a Right-line, otherwise called the *Ordinate* or *Semi-ordinate* in a Conick Section. **1796** in HUTTON *Math. Dict.*

2. An applied department; an application. See A 3.

1855 I. TAYLOR *Restor. B.* 99 Geometry and its applicates.

† '**applicate,** *v. Obs.* [f. L. *applicāt-* ppl. stem of *applicā-re* to APPLY. The pa. pple. was at first also *applicate*: cf. prec.] By-form of APPLY.

1531 ELYOT *Gov.* III. iii. (1557) 146 He wolde..folyshely applycat himselfe to the nature of creatures unreasonable. **1541** R. COPLAND *Guydon's Quest. Cyrurg.*, Howe ought the bolsters to be applicate? Somtyme they be layde to drye, somtyme they ought to be moysted. **1563** *Homilies* II. xv. I. (1859) 444 To applicate his merits unto thyself. **1659** PEARSON *Creed* (1839) 479 The act of faith is applicated to the object according to the nature of it.

application (æplɪ'keɪʃən). Also 5–7 **apply-**. [a. Fr. *application*, *-acion* (14th c.), ad. L. *applicātiōn-em*, n. of action f. *applicāre* to APPLY.] The action of applying; the thing applied. Cf. the senses of APPLY.

1. a. The action of putting a thing to another, of bringing into material or effective contact.

1632 SANDERSON *12 Serm.* 278 The fit applycation of the one to the other. **1683** RAY *Corr.* (1848) 131 By the application of a lighted candle. **1854** SCOFFERN in *Orr's Circ. Sc.* Chem. 333 The application of..heat to the bulb. **1879** THOMSON & TAIT *Nat. Phil.* I. I. §218 The place of application of a force.

b. *esp.* in *Geom.* (Cf. APPLY 1 b.)

1727–51 CHAMBERS *Cycl.*, *Application* also signifies the fitting or applying of one quantity to another, whose areas, but not figures, are the same.

2. The putting on or administration of a medicament; the remedial means so applied.

1601 SHAKS. *All's Well* I. ii. 74 The rest haue worne me out With seuerall applications. **1664** BUTLER *Hud.* II. iii. 287 Application Of Medicines to th' Imagination. **1727–51** CHAMBERS *Cycl.*, The application of a vesicatory to the neck. **1804** ABERNETHY *Surg. Observ.* 131, I began again to try some medicated applications. **1881** *Girls' Own P.* 4 June 571 Rheumatic pains..cured by the application..of spirits of camphor.

3. The bringing of any thing to bear practically upon or affect another. *spec.* in *Theol.* in reference to 'the redemption purchased by Christ.'

1647 *Assembly's Shorter Catech.* 2 The effectual application of it to us by his Holy Spirit. **1656** BRAMHALL *Replic.* ii. 99 The holy Eucharist is..an application of the all-sufficient propitiatory Sacrifice of the Crosse. **1751** CHAMBERS *Cycl.* s.v., It is by this application of the merits of Christ, that we are to be justified. **1859** MILL *Lbty.* ii. 53 A sufficient application of legal penalties.

4. a. The putting of any thing to a use or purpose; employment, specific use.

1538 STARKEY *England* 8 Wythout applycatyon of hyt to any use or profyt of other. **1737** WATERLAND *Eucharist* 124 They are..no more common Bread and Wine (at least not during this their sacred Application). **1794** SULLIVAN *View Nat.* II. 87 The application which is made of the loadstone to navigation. **1833** HT. MARTINEAU *Brooke F.* v. 68 The application of labour and capital.

b. The employment of a word to express an idea.

1788 REID *Act. Powers* i. ii. 517 Instances of the application of active verbs to things which we now believe not to be active.

5. a. The bringing of a law or theory, or of a general or figurative statement, to bear upon a particular case, or upon matters of practice generally; the practical lesson or 'moral' of a fable.

1493 *Petronylla* (Pynson) 129 Make of this mater an applicacion. **1605** B. JONSON *Volpone* Ded., Application is now growne a trade with many; and there are that professe to haue a key for the decyphering of euery thing. **1651** HOBBES *Leviath.* II. xxvi. 143 The application of the Law to the present case. **1736** BUTLER *Anal.* II. vii. 349 A fable or a parable, related without any application or moral. **1769** *Lett. Junius* i. 10 The facts..are too notorious to require an application. **1853** ROBERTSON *Serm.* Ser. III. xvi. 190 Christian applications which flow out of this exposition.

1882 A. MACFARLANE *Consanguin.* 2, I wish to present the method, and some applications.

b. The quality or capacity of being thus practically used; relevancy, valid reference.

1842 H. ROGERS *Introd. Burke's Wks.* 85 Matter which.. is of universal application. **1854** FARADAY *Exp. Res.* lv. 473 It has not that generality of application which can make it of any value. *Mod.* This has no application to present circumstances.

6. a. The action of applying one's self closely *to* a task; assiduous effort, attention, diligence.

1605 BACON *Adv. Learn.* II. xx. §12 The tenderness and want of application in some of the most ancient philosophers. **1693** *Mem. Count Teckely* III. 84 They had lately block'd up the Place with more Application than ever. **1717** POPE *Let. to Blount* Wks. 1737 VI. 58, I am obliged.. to give up my whole application to Homer. **1779** J. MOORE *View Soc.* II. 153 Some application to other studies. **1823** LAMB *Elia* II. xxiii, Application for ever so short a time kills me.

b. *ellipt.* The object of assiduous attention.

1734 tr. *Rollin's Anc. Hist.* IV. IX. 182 He made it his sole application to gain their affections.

†**7.** Self-adaptation, compliance, deference, obsequiousness. *Obs. rare.*

1605 BACON *Adv. Learn.* I. iii. §10 Not that I can tax or condemn the.. application of learned men to men in fortune. *Ibid.*, The like applications and stooping to points of necessity.

8. *Astr.* The action of approaching. ? *Obs.*

1594 J. DAVIS *Seamans Secr.* (1607) 6 The quantitie of the Moone's separation and application to and from the Sunne. **1647** LILLY *Chr. Astrol.* xix. 108 Application is when two Planets are drawing neere together. **1819** J. WILSON *Dict. Astrol.* 10 Application is stronger than Separation, either for good or evil.

9. The action of making an appeal (*obs.*), request, or petition *to* a person; the appeal or request so made.

1647 COTTRELL *Davila's Hist. Fr.* (1678) 8 With pride.. slighting the applications of strangers. **1680** BURNET *Rochester* (1692) 50 Frequent applications to God in prayer. *a* **1718** PENN *Life* Wks. 1726 I. 74, I have not chosen this Way of Application [by Letter]. **1808** WELLINGTON in Gurw. *Disp.* IV. 63 In answer to various applications which have been made to me. **1883** *Law Rep., Queen's B.* 592 An application was made on behalf of the prosecutor for a remand.

10. A kind of needlework; appliqué.

1861 SALA *Tw. round Clock* 191 Cobweb collars.. worked in Guipure, or crochet, or application.

11. a. *Comb.*: **application money**, the sum of money paid when applying for the allotment of shares; **application(s) program(me)**, (*a*) a space exploration programme with a particular application in view; (*b*) *Computing*, a program designed to carry out tasks or solve problems which are specific to a given use; cf. *system(s) program* s.v. SYSTEM III. 11 d; also **application(s) programmer**.

1900 *Westm. Gaz.* 12 Mar. 9/1 The lists may be closed earlier than Thursday.. to avoid the unnecessary locking up of *application money. **1907** *Ibid.* 9 Mar. 15/1 A special form of application is provided, under which the application money will have to be paid as in the case of new subscriptions. **1965** *Aviation Week & Space Technol.* 11 Oct. 69/1 Final review of proposed experiments for National Aeronautics and Space Administration's Apollo *Applications program is under way. **1966** *Electronics* 14 Nov. 73 The National Aeronautics and Space Administration, pushing ahead to get the Apollo Applications Program moving, will ask Congress for funds for initial hardware. **1969** D. LEFKOVITZ *File Structures for On-Line Syst.* i. 19 Some of these parts provide control information for routing the query, calling applications programs, and designating output terminals. **1970** O. DOPPING *Computers & Data Processing* xix. 305 The user's normal programmers are sometimes called problem programmers or application programmers. **1973** [see *system(s) program* s.v. SYSTEM III. 11 d]. **1980** C. S. FRENCH *Computer Sci.* xxx. 252 In many cases the user produces his own applications programs called user programs.

b. General attrib. and Comb. uses (*sing.* and *pl.*), esp. in *Computing*.

1965, etc. [see *applications program*, sense 11 a above]. **1967** *Technology Week* 20 Feb. 16/3 It would be composed primarily of *Apollo* Applications flights in Earth orbit and *Voyager*. **1970** *Sci. Amer.* May 103 Do you need printouts? Get the quiet printer that operates in an office or lab environment... You also get an extensive.. library of applications oriented programmes. **1973** *New Scientist* 10 May 327 Despite an increasing tendency to think in terms of applications satellites, the European Space Research Organisation is still maintaining a viable scientific programme. **1978** *Pract. Computing* July-Aug. 56/4 For instance, an operating system is not applications software since it does not produce usable end results. **1983** *Austral. Personal Computer* Aug. 146/3 The 16-bit version.. will offer colour, probably an extra application package.. and two 16-bit operating systems. **1985** *Personal Computer World* Feb. 124/4 Point-of-sale terminals in retail computer stores.. make and dispense disks of applications software in about one minute.

†**appli'cationer.** *Obs.* [f. prec. + -ER[1].] One who makes an application or appeal.

1710 *4 Lett. Friend in N. Brit.* iv. 28 Papists or Non-jurors, Applicationers, or Addressors. **1710** *Managers' Pro & Con* 77 Some Remedy.. against Applicationers and Occasional Abjurors.

applicative ('æplɪkeɪtɪv, -ətɪv), *a.* [f. L. *applicāt-* (see APPLICATE) + -IVE: cf. Fr. *applicatif.*] Having the attribute of application.

1. Characterized by being put into actual or effective contact with anything.

1680 MORDEN *Geog. Rect.* (1685) 280 All Measures.. are either Applicative or Receptive. The smallest Applicative Measure is a Barley corn. **1723** W. MATHER *Yng. Man's Comp.* (1727) 196 Applicative Measures, or Things measured outwardly. **1850** MRS. BROWNING *Poems* II. 289 We wring from our souls their applicative strength, And bend to the cord the strong bow of our ken.

2. Of or pertaining to putting into practice; practical.

1638 *Penit. Conf.* viii. (1657) 226 The Priest.. absolveth from sin, 1. applicative, 2. and dispositive. *a* **1703** BURKITT *On N.T.* Matt. xxvi. 75 The remembrance of Christ's words, was an applicative and feeling remembrance of them. **1862** in *Lond. Rev.* 23 Aug. 170 His genius is wholly applicative, for he invents nothing.

†**3.** Relative; practical as opposed to *formal*.

1668 H. MORE *Div. Dial.* i. §15 II. 64, I did not mean Succession in that proper and formal sense, but only a virtual, applicative or relative Succession.

'applicatively, *adv. rare*[−1]. [f. prec. + -LY[2].] By way of application; practically.

1668 H. MORE *Div. Dial.* i. §15 II. 62 [Not] properly and formally, but only virtually and applicatively.

applicator ('æplɪkeɪtə(r)). [a. L. **applicātor*, n. of agent f. *applicāre* to APPLY.] He who (*obs.*) or that which applies; *spec.* an instrument for medical application. Also *attrib.*

1659 GAUDEN *Tears of Ch.* 494 (D.) Such quacking applications and applicators as are no way apt for the work. **1876** BARTHOLOW *Mat. Med.* (1879) 217 The solid caustic may be quickly brushed over the mucous membrane, or a concentrated solution may be applied with a suitable 'applicator.' **1909** *Westm. Gaz.* 29 Jan. 1/2 Mr. Hartigan.. had invented a radium applicator. **1959** *Woman's Own* 20 June 52/1 (Advt.), The only home perm lotion in a tube with its own easy-to-use applicator-tip. **1962** *Listener* 10 May 831/3 This can be spread with a synthetic sponge applicator.

† **'applica,torily,** *adv. Obs.* [f. next + -LY[2].] By way of application; cf. APPLICATION 3.

1625 BP. MOUNTAGU *App. Cæsar* 194 (T.) Faith is.. said to justify.. instrumentally or applicatorily. **1658** BAXTER *Saving Faith* §5. 33 To be applicatorily my Saviour in particular.

applicatory ('æplɪkətərɪ), *a.* and *sb.* [f. L. *applicāt-* (see APPLICATE) + -ORY.]

A. *adj.*

1. Having the property of applying (a thing to effective or practical use).

c **1540** COVERDALE *Christ's Cross* v. Wks. II. 249 A sacrifice ..not only applicatory, but also propitiatory, because it applieth the propitiatory sacrifice of Christ. *a* **1631** DONNE *Select.* (1840) 190, I may perish without I have this applicatory faith. **1655** FULLER *Ch. Hist.* IX. 112 Revelations ..not explicatory or applicatory of Scripture. *a* **1703** BURKITT *On N.T., Rom.*, Pref., The applicatory or practical part of this epistle. **1853** LYNCH *Self-Impr.* vi. 152 Some other supplementary remark of an exhortative and applicatory kind.

†**2.** Proper to be applied, applicable.

1649 BLITH *Eng. Improv. Impr.* (1653) 33 The remedies being equally applicatory to both.

†**3.** Making application, appeal, or request. *Obs.*

1653 BAXTER *Chr. Concord* 4 We speak of Ministers Applicatory. **1673** MARVELL *Reh. Transp.* II. (1674) 233 Applicatory discourses.

†**B.** *sb.* A means of applying to practical use.

1660 JER. TAYLOR *Worthy Commun.* i. §4. 71 Faith is the inward applicatory. *a* **1667** —— *Serm.* III. ii. (R.) All these being practical.. need no other applicatory but a plain exhortation.

† **'applicature.** *Obs. rare*[−1]. [f. as prec. + -URE.] = APPLICATION 4 a.

1652 GAULE *Magastrom.* 59 Whether those principles.. true in astronomie be of a right applicature in astrologie?

applied (ə'plaɪd), *ppl. a.* [f. APPLY *v.* + -ED.]

†**1.** Folded. *Obs. rare.*

c **1500** *To serve a Lord* in *Babees Bk.* 367 The boteler.. shall brynge forthe clenly dressed and fayre applyed Tabill-clothis. *Ibid.* 372 A longe towaile applyed dowble.

2. Put to practical use; practical, as distinguished from *abstract* or *theoretical*.

1656 *Artif. Beauty* (1662) 216 In their applied sense or meaning. **1832** BABBAGE *Econ. Manuf.* xxxv. 379 The applied sciences. **1806** ABP. THOMSON *Laws of Th.* Introd. 5 Applied logic (as distinguished from pure). **1912** A. BRAZIL *New Girl at St. Chad's* x. 152 One of her boys has turned out so clever that he has been sent to the Technical School to study 'applied arts'. **1928** *Forestry* II. 133 It is probably far wiser for the applied scientist to credit insects with acumen than to attribute to them nothing but forced movements or tropisms. **1933** *Burlington Mag.* Apr. p. xvi/2 The second collection contains works of fine and applied art from a castle in Upper Hesse, Germany. **1936** *Discovery* Apr. 129/1 The study of practical psychology or applied psychology. **1958** *Year's Wk. Eng. Stud. 1956* 37/1 His book will reward study by all interested in what now tends to be called 'applied linguistics'.

3. *Dressmaking.* Laid on as appliqué.

1880 E. GLAISHER *Needlework* iv. 37 Velvet does not bear applied work well. **1882** CAULFEILD & SAWARD *Dict. Needlework* s.v. *Appliqué.* The various applied pieces are laid in position one at a time, and secured by being sewn down round their edges. **1901** *Westm. Gaz.* 25 July 3/2 A lace applied collar. **1910** *Ibid.* 29 Jan. 15/2 Applied velvet.

†**a'ppliedly,** *adv. Obs. rare*[−1]. [f. prec. + -LY[2].] By or in practical application.

1625 BP. MOUNTAGU *App. Cæsar* 267 (T.) Such acts as bee of themselves, or appliedly, acts of religion and piety.

applier (ə'plaɪə(r)). [f. APPLY *v.* + -ER[1].] He who, or that which, applies.

1565 CALFHILL *Answ. Treat. Cross* (1846) 200 Either the collector of this tale was a liar, or you a fond applier. **1607** HIERON *Wks.* I. 423 The immediate.. applyer of the new-birth vnto the conscience. **1705** STANHOPE *Paraphr.* III. 67 Such false Applyers and Censurers are too busy abroad. **1819** *Edin. Rev.* XXXII. 379 The.. first applier [of gas light]. **1865** OWEN in *Reader* 429/3 The applier of the term.

appliment, variant of APPLYMENT.

appling ('æplɪŋ), *vbl. sb.* [f. APPLE *v.* + -ING[1].] The process of forming an apple or similar growth.

1750 W. ELLIS *Mod. Husb.* I. ii. 104 Prevent their [seedling potatoes] appling or bottling. **1807** VANCOUVER *Agric. Devon* (1813) 197 The appleing of the potatoe keeps the mould in continual motion.

†**a'pplique, a'pplike,** *v. Obs.* [a. later Fr. *applique-r*, ad. L. *applicāre.*] By-form of APPLY *v.*

1483 CAXTON *Gold. Leg.* 430/3 He.. applykd on his waye and with ryght grete hoost arryued into egypte. **1558** WARDE *Alexis' Secr.* (1568) 8 b, Anye tender place of the bodye.. whereunto a man dare not applicque any strong or smartyng thyng.

‖**appliqué** (aplike), *sb.* [Fr., pa. pple. of *appliquer* (see prec.), used as sb.] Work applied to or laid on another material; *spec.* A trimming cut out in outline and laid on another surface. Also in metal work; and *fig.* Hence **appliquéd**.

1841 D'ISRAELI *Amen. Lit.* (1859) II. 198 Like all rapid in-layers, the appliqué did not fit to his [Voltaire's] work. **1880** *Birm. Weekly Post* 1/5 A new sort of work at the art schools ..is appliqué, on satin or velvet. **1881** *New York Art Interch.* 27 Oct. 93/1 Bands of contrasting materials are frequently appliquéd with fancy stitches. **1883** *Standard* 26 June 3/3 Appliqué, cut from cambric, and laid on net by means of point stitches.

applot (ə'plɒt), *v.* [f. PLOT, apparently after *lot, allot.*] To divide into plots or parts; to apportion.

1647 JER. TAYLOR *Dissuasive* I. i. §3 Rightly applotted according to every man's need. **1648** *Articles of Peace* xxvii. in *Milton's Wks.* 1738 I. 337 Power to applot, raise and levy Means with Indifferency and Equality. *a* **1687** PETTY *Pol. Arith.* v. 95 Might not the Taxes be equally applotted. **1882** G. O. TREVELYAN *Sp. in Parl.* 30 June, That any charge for additional constabulary shall be applotted rateably upon all rateable hereditaments.

applotment (ə'plɒtmənt). [f. APPLOT *v.* + -MENT.] Division into plots; apportionment.

1648 *Articles of Peace* xxvii, And for the Arrears of all former Applotments, Taxes, and other public Dues. **1697** *Phil. Trans.* XIX. 629 Their Surveys and Applotments of Lands, between Neighbour and Neighbour. **1736** CARTE *Ormonde* II. 61 To raise the money charged on them by way of applotment. **1882** HEALY *Sp. in Parl.* 30 June, Premises ..unoccupied at the date of any such applotment.

a'pplotting, *vbl. sb.* [f. as prec. + -ING[1].] = prec.

1648 *Articles of Peace* xxvii, The applotting, subdividing, and levying of the said Public Assessments.

†**a'pplumbature.** *Obs.*[−0] [ad. med.L. *applumbātūra*, f. *applumbā-re* to apply lead to, solder, f. *ad* to + *plumbum* lead.] 'A joining or soldering with lead.' Blount *Glossogr.* 1656.

apply (ə'plaɪ), *v.* Forms: 4–6 **aplie**, 5 **aplye**; 4–6 **applie**, 5–6 **applye**, 6– **apply**. [a. OFr. *aplie-r*:—L. *applicā-re*, f. *ap-* = *ad-* to + *plicā-re* to fold. Cf. APPLIQUE, a. later Fr. *appliquer.*]

I. To put a thing into practical contact with another.

1. a. *trans.* To bring into, or place in, more or less prolonged contact, or effective proximity; to put close *to*; *e.g.* to *apply* a light, heat, a foot-rule *to*. Formerly said of bringing together men or things generally; also of fastening or sticking.

1382 WYCLIF *1 Sam.* xiv. 38 Aplieth hidir [**1388** Brynge ȝe hidur] alle the corners of the puple. **1388** —— *Numb.* xvi. 5 He schal applie to hym hooli men. **1398** TREVISA *Barth. De P.R.* v. xxiii. (1495) 130 His [a frogges] tongue is aplied the mouth afore. **1530** PALSGR. 434/1, I applye one thyng to another, *Je applicque*. Applye them togyther, and than you shall se there is a great difference. **1635** AUSTIN *Med.* 177 Thomas applyed Christ to himselfe by touching. **1718** POPE *Iliad* I. 769 Each to his lips applied the nectar'd urn. **1854** SCOFFERN in *Orr's Circ. Sc.* Chem. 333 On applying heat to the retort. **1874** LUBBOCK *Orig. & Met. Insects* i. 18 The head is applied against the breast.

b. *esp.* in *Geom.* To bring lines or figures into contact extending over some space or area.

1660 BARROW *Euclid* I. Ax. viii, The parts of the one being applyed to the parts of the other. **1695** ALINGHAM *Geom. Epit.* 12 A right line is said to be applied in a Circle, when the ends thereof fall upon the circumference. **1862** TODHUNTER *Euclid* I. iv, If the triangle ABC be applied to DEF so that the point A may be on D.

c. *Dressmaking.* To lay on as appliqué; to trim or ornament with appliqué.

1880 E. Glaisher *Needlework* v. 49 The heraldic figures ..are applied in white cloth. **1882** Caulfeild & Saward *Dict. Needlework* 12/1 The foundation was generally muslin, and the net applied or let in. **1901** *Westm. Gaz.* 14 Mar. 4/2 Everything is applied with insertions or cut-out flowers and figures of lace.

†**2.** *intr.* **a.** To come into contact, join itself, attain *to*. **b.** To be in contact, fit closely, adhere, stick *to*. *Obs.*

c **1374** Chaucer *Boeth.* v. iv. 161 þe moeuynge of þe resoun of mankynde ne may nat moeuen to, þat is to sein, applien, or ioygnen, to þe simplicite of þe deuyne prescience. *c* **1430** Lydg. *Bochas* vii. v. (1554) 169 a, Euery vyce to other doth applye. **1530** Palsgr. 434/2, I applye or cleave..as glue dothe to a tree or thynges that be glued, *Je adhers.* **1693** Moulen in *Phil. Trans.* XVII. 624 This Sand did apply to the Magnet. **1793** Smeaton *Edystone L.* §121 The manner in which it [the building] was to apply to the rock.

3. *trans.* To place (a plaster, unguent, or the like) in effective contact with the body; *hence*, to administer a remedy of any kind.

1541 R. Copland *Guydon's Quest. Cyrurg.*, Wherfore are horse leaches applyed? **1579** Langham *Gard. Health* (1633) 459 Apply the iuyce to any wound. **1590** Shaks. *Mids. N.* iii. ii. 450 Ile apply [to] your eie gentle louer, remedy. **1747** in *Col. Rec. Penn.* V. 93 The most speedy Remedy, which.. is not in our Power to Apply. **1806–31** A. Knox *Rem.* (1844) I. 45 Such palliatives as it is fully in his..power to apply. *Mod.* Apply a mustard plaster to the chest.

4. *fig.* and *transf.* To administer *to*, to bring (a thing) to bear upon, in order to produce an effect.

1596 Spenser *F.Q.* ii. xii. 32 To Guyon..Their pleasaunt tunes they sweetly thus applyde. **1633** Bp. Hall *Hard Texts* 5, I..can only apply unto you the outward sign of baptism. **1646** Fuller *Wounded Consc.* (1841) 289 To apply comfort to him who is not..ready for it. **1817** Jas. Mill *Brit. India* II. v. v. 502 They applied coercion to the English resident.

5. To put *to* a special use or purpose; to devote, appropriate *to*.

c **1460** Lydg. in *Rel. Ant.* I. 157 The best morsell..Hole to thiself alway do not applye. *c* **1460** Fortescue *Abs. & Lim. Mon.* (1714) 44 Pondage and Tonnage..owght to be applyyd only to the kepyng of the See. **1667–8** Marvell *Corr.* 87 Wks. 1872–5 II. 234 The Poll money hath likewise been applyd to the use of the warre. **1793** Smeaton *Edystone L.* §146 Having procured a carpenter to be applied to that purpose. **1848** Mill *Pol. Econ.* v. v. §1 The act of directing industry to a particular employment is described by the phrase 'applying capital' to the employment.

6. To put to use; to employ, spend, dispose of.

1502 Arnold *Chron.* (1811) 276 Whether ony executor.. applye or appropir ony thing of the goodis of the deed man. **1534** Ld. Berners *Gold. Bk. M. Aurel.* (1546) C., [He] hadde applied the moste parte of his lyfe in warre. **1712** Steele *Spect.* No. 485 ⁋2 Knife or a pistol, if he finds stomach to apply them. **1832** Ht. Martineau *Life in Wilds* ii. 28 They know how to apply their labour.

7. To make use of (a word) in special reference *to*, or to describe or characterize (a thing).

1628 Coke *On Litt.* 121/2 *Regardant*..is..only applyed to a villeine. **1690** Locke *Hum. Und.* iii. x. (R.) He that applied the words..to ideas different to those to which the common use applies them. **1877** Lytteil *Landm.* i. i. 17 The word *fell* is applied to rocky heights, peaks, and cliffs.

8. To bring (a law, rule, test, principle, etc.) into contact with facts, to bring to bear practically, to put into practical operation. (Cf. to apply a foot-rule to a wall, a test to a mineral, a principle to actions.)

1586 Cogan *Haven Health* (1636) 293 These precepts.. must bee applyed particularly to every man's owne estate. **1754** Sherlock *Disc.* (1759) I. i. 35 The Difficulty is, how to apply this Rule. **1810** Coleridge *Friend* (1865) 125 The principles which our understandings are to apply. **1859** *Ecce Homo* iv. 29 By applying practical tests.

9. To give (to a general, theoretical, or figurative statement) a specific reference *to* a particular instance; to use it as relative or suitable *to*.

c **1375** Wyclif *Sel. Wks.* 1871 II. 394 Wordis..which semen best þus to be aplied. **1509** Fisher *Wks.* (1876) 289 Which dyalogue I wolde applye vnto this noble prynces. **1659** Pearson *Creed* (1839) 325 The apostle repeated the words of the Psalmist, and then applied them. **1749** Fielding *Tom Jones* (1836) II. xi. ix. 82 To apply all this to the Bœotian writers. **1767** Fordyce *Serm. Yng. Wom.* II. xi. 169, I leave you to apply the remark. **1853** Robertson *Serm.* Ser. iii. xvii. 218 Two ways in which this deep truth applies itself.

10. *intr.* To have a practical bearing upon, a valid or suitable reference *to*.

1790 Paley *Hor. Paul.* i. 3 This test applies to every supposition. **1851** Maurice *Proph. & Kings* 18 This observation applies to Saul's history. **1866** J. Martineau *Ess.* I. 95 It will apply no less to our own case.

†**11.** *trans.* To connect with attributively or causally, to refer, ascribe. *Obs.*

1393 Gower *Conf.* III. 121 Unto this signe [i.e. Virgo] is Augst applied. **1530** Palsgr. 434/2, I applye or assyne the cause of a mater to a persone, *Jattribue*: I applye the cause herof to the malyce of Saturne. **1709** Pope *Ess. Crit.* 396 Thus Wit, like Faith, by each man is apply'd To one small sect, and all are damn'd beside.

†**12.** To connect with by association of similarity, compare, liken. *Obs.*

1588 Mellis *Briefe Instr.* Biij, A marchant may be applied vnto Argus. **1661** Tatham *Lond. Tri.* in Heath *Grocers' Comp.* (1869) 482 My woes may aptly be apply'd to theirs That lost their king.

II. To bring oneself into close practical contact with a pursuit.

13. To give or devote (any faculty) assiduously *to* some pursuit, or *to do* something.

c **1450** *Pol. Rel. & L. Poems* (1866) 49 Of here beaute sumwhat too say I will applye my wittes all. **1530** Palsgr. 434/2, I applye or gyve my mynde to a thyng, *Je madonne.* **1535** Coverdale *Ps.* lxxxix. 12 That we maye applie oure hertes vnto wyssdome. **1673** Ray *Journ. Low Countr.* 200, I applyed my mind to consider..the physical reason of it. *c* **1746** Hervey *Medit.* (1818) 160 Apply your thoughts to religion. *Mod.* He does not apply his mind to his lessons.

14. *refl.* To set oneself closely *to* a task or *to do* something.

a **1400** *Cov. Myst.* 34, I wyl fforthwith applye me therto. **1477** Earl Rivers (Caxton) *Dictes* 9 Applying him self to do good dedis. **1594** J. Dickenson *Arisbas* (1878) 88 He and his accursed companions applied themselves wholly to myrth. **1631** Markham *Way to Wealth* i. i. ii. (1668) 19 [He] stubbornly applyes himself to disobey you. **1711** Addison *Spect.* No. 1 ⁋3, I applied myself..to my Studies. **1818** Scott *Hrt. Midl.* 188 She..applied herself to her sister's relief. **1874** Blackie *Self-Cult.* 70 He could apply himself.. to comprehend two such antipodal characters.

15. *intr.* in same sense: To attend assiduously (*to*).

c **1485** *Digby Myst.* iii. 1982 My londdes to gyddyn I must a-plye. **1605** Shaks. *Macb.* iii. ii. 30 Let your remembrance apply to Banquo. **1740** Chesterf. *Lett.* I. lix. 167 The more you apply, the easier you will find your learning. **1774** Hallifax *Anal. Rom. Law* (1795) Pref. 16 Those who apply to the study of the Common Law. **1817** W. Taylor in *Month. Rev.* LXXXIII. 492 He applied to English literature. **1848** C. Brontë *J. Eyre* (1857) 103, I found my pupil..disinclined to apply.

†**16.** *trans.* To devote one's energy to, to handle vigorously; to wield, practise. **a.** one's business, or any pursuit or activity. **b.** an implement or tool. *Obs.* and replaced by ply.

? **1495** *Plumpton Corr.* 123 That the poor man for dread dare not apply his busines. **1531** Elyot *Gov.* (1834) 111 Quintius..repaired again to his plough and applied it diligently. **1549** Latimer 7 *Serm. bef. Edw. VI* (Arb.) 53 The[y] applye the world harde. **1555** *Fardle of Facions* ii. i. 116 The mooste parte of the Sabeis apply husbandrye. **1577** Harrison *England* i. ii. i. 18 A notable spurre unto all..to applie their bookes. **1616** Surfl. & Markh. *Countr. Farm* 391 You shall apply him[the horse] at least three or foure times a day. **1662** Fuller *Worthies* (1840) III. 402 That he might the more effectually apply his private devotions. **1667** Milton *P.L.* iv. 264 The birds thir quire apply.

†**17.** To keep at (a person) *with* (something presented to his attention). *Obs.*; but see ply.

1559 *Myrr. Mag.*, *Dk. Suffolk* xxii. 1 [They] applyed the Parliament with billes. **1590** Swinburn *Testaments* 243 [If she] busily applie him with sweete and flattering speeches. **1594** Willobie in *Shaks. C. Praise* 10 Apply her still with dyvers thinges.

III. To bend, conform, or adapt *to*.

18. *trans.* To bend (the mind or oneself). *refl.* To comply, conform, be subservient *to*. *Obs.*

1413 Lydg. *Pylgr. Sowle* i. xxxvi. 40 As he wylle that shal be done, we shal applye vs fully withoute ayenseynge. **1509** Barclay *Ship of Fools* (1570) 18 Priamus his minde would not apply To the counsayle of Cassandra. **1533** *Anne Boleyn's Fort.* in Furnivall *MS. Ball.* I. 406 Wholy applyinge himselfe to the Kings humour. **1622** Heylin *Cosmogr.* iii. (1673) 8/1 Applying themselves unto the times, they were alwaies favourable to the strongest.

†**19.** *intr.* To comply, hearken, consent *to*. *Obs.*

c **1460** *Play Sacr.* 825 Onto our prayers thow hast applyed. **1494** Fabyan 4 The Scottes that neuer coude apply To kepe theyr Allegeaunce. *a* **1553** Udall *Roister D.* iv. v, To bee his wife I ne graunt nor apply. **1553–87** Foxe *A. & M.* (1596) 88/2 If she would applie to his request, she should be..set at libertie.

†**20.** *refl.* To adapt or suit oneself *to*, to suit. *Obs.*

1574 tr. *Marlorat's Apoc.* 3 God applieth himselfe not a little vnto our affections. **1605** Bacon *Adv. Learn.* i. iii. §7 They fail sometimes in applying themselves to particular persons.

†**21.** *intr.* (as in prec.) *Obs.*

c **1450** Lonelich *Grail* xxxiii. 296 Al manere of delicasye That to ony mannes wyt may applye. *Ibid.* xxvii. 141 Wenges that lyhtly wolde folde And aplyen to his flyht. **1598** Shaks. *Merry W.* ii. ii. 247 Would it apply well to the vehemency of your affection that I should, etc. **1605** Bacon *Adv. Learn.* ii. xxii. §3 The precedent state or disposition, unto which we do apply.

IV. To bend or direct a ship, one's course, oneself, one's words *to*. (Cf. L. *applicare* (*navem*), and accost, address.)

†**22.** *trans.* To bring (a ship) to land; to direct or steer (a ship, her course, one's course, etc). *Obs.*

1576 Sir T. Smith in Wright's *Lett. Q. Eliz.* (1838) II. 33 To whether haven I shall applie my ship. **1596** Spenser *F.Q.* v. iv. 21 To whom his course he hastily applide. **1613** W. Browne *Brit. Past.* i. i. (1772) I. 19 To a grove at hand her steps applide.

†**23.** *refl.* To direct oneself, make one's way (by ship or otherwise) *to*. *Obs.*

c **1450** Lonelich *Graal* II. 133 To theke contre he wolde don hem aplye. *a* **1618** Raleigh *Observ.* (1651) 45 Light things apply themselves upwards.

†**24.** *intr.* **a.** To land, arrive. **b.** To steer, proceed, betake oneself, go. *Obs.*

1382 Wyclif *1 Macc.* iii. 42 The oost appliede, *or londide*, at the coostis of hem. *c* **1450** Lonelich *Grail* xxi. 41 This schip to þe rocke gan aplye. **1545** *State Papers Hen. VIII*, I. 816 With the nexte fludde..we entend tapplye towardes Dover. **1662** R. Mathew *Unl. Alch.* §89. 146 A Woman taken sick of a violent Fever..presently applied to her Bed. **1677** Moxon *Mech. Exerc.* (1703) 99 [He] then lets it go again, so that it swiftly applies to its first position. **1759** Martin *Nat. Hist.* I. 17 In such prodigious shoals do the Pilchards apply to the Cornish Coasts. **1819** J. Wilson *Dict. Astrol.* 10 Planets preceding apply to those that follow.

†**25.** *trans.* To go to, visit. *Obs. rare.*

1596 Chapman *Iliad* xi. 61 (N.) He applied each place so fast.

†**26.** *trans.* To address or direct (words) to. *Obs.*

[Cf. **1596** in 4.] **1667** Milton *P.L.* x. 172 God at last To Satan, first in sin, his doom apply'd, Though in mysterious terms. *a* **1744** Pope (J.) Sacred vows and mystic song apply'd To grisly Pluto.

†**27.** *refl.* *to apply oneself*: in same sense as next. *Obs.*

1650 T. B. *Worcester's Apophth.* 22, I spied a young man ..I applyed myself to him. **1691** T. H[ale] *New Invent.* 53 Howard and Company further applyed themselves to..the Admiralty in their humble Memorial. **1711** Addison *Spect.* No. 117 ⁋3 An old Woman applied herself to me for my Charity. **1743** M. Tomlinson *Prot. Birthr.* 18 Apply ourselves to Persons of Learning and Integrity.

†**28.** *intr.* with *to*. **a.** To appeal to, address (*obs.*). **b.** To address oneself for information or aid, to have recourse, make application to. (Also *pass.* e.g. I have been applied to for a certificate.)

? *c* **1642** Rogers (J.) God knows every faculty and passion, and in what manner they can be most successfully applied to. *a* **1680** Butler *Rem.* (1759) II. 13 Those who apply to Men's Fancies and Humours. **1759** Robertson *Hist. Scotl.* I. ii. 121 The French king..applied to the parliament of Scotland. **1769** *Junius Lett.* xxxv. 163 He applied only to their honour, as gentlemen, for protection. **1774** J. Bryant *Mythol.* I. 48 His temples were applied to as oracular. **1793** Smeaton *Edystone L.* §262 On applying to the bridle..we found that the chain was dragging upon the rocks. **1802** Mar. Edgeworth *Moral T.* (1816) I. xii. 98 A friend..to whom she resolved to apply in her distress. **1849** Macaulay *Hist. Eng.* II. 81 Exiles, who had come..to apply for succour.

†**a'pply**, *sb. Obs.* [f. prec. vb.]

1. Ply, trim, state.

a **1600** *Sir Egeir* 43 (Jam.) They found him in a good apply Both hay and corn and bread him by.

2. Application.

1657 Colvil *Whigs Supplic.* (1751) 71 For the apply will be to Sharp. **1681** *Lond. Gaz.* mdcliv/3 We envy much their more early Apply.

applying (əˈplaɪɪŋ), *vbl. sb.* [f. apply *v.* + -ing[1].] Application. (But now mostly gerundial.)

1. A putting into practical contact, into practice, into relation with specific cases.

1538 Starkey *England* 171 In the applying of the ground to the plowgh. **1607** Hieron *Wks.* I. 451 Being, by the powerfull applying of the word, conuicted of sin. **1653** Gauden *Hierasp.* 95 Proportionable applyings of all orderly and prudential means for union.

2. Assiduous practice or attention; plying.

c **1380** Wyclif *Clerks Possess.* xxx. Wks. 1880, 134 To triste more in special preynge & applyinge of synful men. **1541** Hyrde *Vives' Instr. Chr. Wom.* (1592) Bvij, The applying of their worke is bosted of. **1612** Brinsley *Lud. Lit.* 302 Continuall applying brings learning, and the credit of a schoole.

†**a'pplyingly**, *adv. Obs. rare*[−1]. [f. *applying* pr. pple. + -ly[2].] With application; assiduously.

1648 Sanderson *21 Serm.* Ad. Aul. xvi. (1673) 236 Let us all..applyingly consider whether it can be reasonable.

applyke, var. applique, obs. by-form of apply *v.*

†**a'pplyment.** *Obs.* Also **appliment.** [f. apply *v.* + -ment; cf. *employment.*] = application, appliance.

1604 J. Webster *Induct. Marston's Malcont.* Wks. (1857) 326 They will wrest the doings of any man to their own base and malicious appliments. **1615** Latham *Falconry* (1633) 67 Without any medicine, scowring, or other inward appliments. **1633** T. Adams *Exp. 2 Pet.* ii. 2 An inconsiderate applyment of themselves to another's will.

‖**appoggiatura** (ap,poddʒaˈtuːra). *Mus.* [It., f. *appoggiare* to lean upon, rest. Cf. appui.] A grace-note or passing tone prefixed as a support to an essential note of a melody. Also *transf.* A prop, a point of support.

1753 Chambers *Cycl. Supp.*, *Appoggiatura* is commonly marked by a smaller kind of note. **1833** Coleridge *Table T.* 289 In the latter [Nonnus, Tryphiodorus]..All the *appoggiaturas* of time are lost. **1875** Ouseley *Harmony* xviii. 206 Accented auxiliary notes are usually called *appoggiaturas*, as they are supposed to be a kind of buttress or leaning support to the note before which they are placed.

appoint (əˈpɔɪnt), *v.* Forms: 4–6 **apoint(e, apoynt(e**, 4–7 **appoynt(e**, 5 **ap(p)unct, appoynct, apoinct**, 5– **appoint.** *Aphet.* 5–7 **point.** [a. OFr. *apointe-r*, *-ier*, f. *à point* to the point, into condition: see point. Sometimes refashioned after med.L. *appunctāre*, whence also some of the senses were taken. The chief senses were already developed in OF., and did not appear in logical order in Eng.]

I. To come, or bring matters, to a point; agree, arrange, settle.

†**1.** *intr.* (and *pass.*) usually with *inf.* or *subord. cl.*: To come to a point about a matter in discussion, to agree, settle, arrange definitely. *Obs.*

c **1374** CHAUCER *Troylus* III. 405 Apoyntedyn ful warly.. how ferre they wold procede. **1462** *Paston Lett.* 461 II. 115 Sir John Fastolff and your seid besecher comenauntyd and apoynted be writyng for the seid mater. **1488** *Act. Dom. Conc.* 93 (JAM.) It is apunctit and accordit. **1528** MORE *Heresyes* IV. Wks. 282/1 Theyr intent and purpose that they appoynt vpon. **1604** SIR W. COPE in *Shaks. C. Praise* 62 Thys ys apointed to be playd to Morowe night. **1660** *Hist. Indep.* IV. 50 They appointed to sell ten brace of Buckes.

b. To make an appointment. *arch.* (This and the two following senses were evidently influenced by the earlier II. 7.)

1509 HAWES *Past. Pleas.* XXIX, At xi. of the clocke, in the nyght.. They did appoynt for to fulfyll this worke. **1711** BUDGELL *Spect.* No. 77 ¶9 The very place where he had appointed to be. **1802** MAR. EDGEWORTH *Moral T.* (1816) I. 199 Gentlemen, who had appointed to meet him at.. Berlin.

2. *trans.* To fix by arrangement the time or place of (a meeting); to arrange. *arch.*

1588 SHAKS. *Tit. A.* IV. iv. 102 Appoint the meeting, Even at his father's house. **1633** HEYWOOD *Eng. Trav.* III. Wks. IV. 54 Heere all the Countrey Gentlemen Appoint A friendly meeting.

3. *trans.* To make an appointment for a meeting with (a person). (Cf. *disappoint*, to break an appointment with.)

1528 GARDINER in Pocock *Rec. Ref.* I. l. 99 Appointing us to the repair again the next day. **1601** MANNINGHAM in *Shaks. C. Praise* 45 Shee appointed him to come that night. **1728** GAY *Beggar's Op.* II. x, I appointed him at this hour. **1797** W. TAYLOR in *Month. Rev.* XXIII. 582 She then appoints him deceptiously in the bath house.

†**4.** *trans.* To bring to a point, settle, decide (a thing disputed). *Obs. rare.*

a **1619** DONNE *Biathan.* (1644) 79 Almost all the points controverted.. may be decided and appointed by it [this law].

†**5.** *refl.* and *pass.* To bring oneself to the point or resolution; to make up one's mind, resolve, determine. *Obs.*

c **1386** CHAUCER *Merch. T.* 351 He at the last appointed him on on. *Ibid.* 372 He was appoynted [*v.r.* apoynted, -ointed] ther he wold abyde. **1513** MORE *Rich. III*, Wks. 54/1 Yf you appoint your selfe to tary here. **1550** CROWLEY *Waie to Wealth* 273 Apointe thy selfe therfore to beare it.

6. *intr.* To determine, resolve, purpose. *arch.*

c **1440** *Generyd.* 2120 Of euery ward to make a capteyn Ffirst he appoynted in especiall. **1529** MORE *Comf. agst. Trib.* III. Wks. 1214/2 And appointe in his heart.. that.. he would rather dye than forsake yᵉ faith. **1611** BIBLE *2 Sam.* xvii. 14 The Lord had appointed to defeate the good counsell of Ahithophel. **1722** DE FOE *Hist. Plague* 11 To appoint to go away.

II. To determine authoritatively, prescribe, decree, ordain.

7. *trans.* To determine authoritatively, prescribe, fix (a time, *later* a place) for any act.

1393 GOWER *Conf.* III. 67 He wolde his time kepe As he, whiche hath his houre apointed. **1596** SHAKS. *1 Hen. IV*, I. ii. 190 We wil.. appoint them a place of meeting. **1625** BACON *Ess.* (Arb.) 576 Pointing days for pitched fields. **1722** DE FOE *Moll. Fl.* (1840) 317 The time appointed for execution.

8. To ordain authoritatively, prescribe, establish, fix: **a.** *that* it shall be; **b.** a thing.

1538 STARKEY *England* 53 Thus hyt was.. appoyntyd by wysdome and pollycy, that ever.. they schold be [so] gouernyd. **1611** BIBLE *Gen.* xxx. 28 And he said, Appoint me thy wages, and I will giue it. **1613** SHAKS. *Hen. VIII*, I. i. 74 Why.. tooke he vpon him.. t'appoint Who should attend on him? **1831** CARLYLE *Sart. Res.* II. x, Strangely.. it is appointed that Sound.. should be the most continuing of all things. **1850** MᶜCOSH *Div. Govt.* II. i. (1874) 139 The laws .. are appointed by God.

†**9.** To decree, assign, or grant, authoritatively or formally (a thing *to* a person). *Obs.*

1494 FABYAN I. iv. 11 He beset or apoynted to hym the Countre of Walys. **1540** *Househ. Ord.* 211 That there be one chamber appointed for two Masters of the household. **1601** SHAKS. *Jul. C.* IV. i. 30, I do appoint him store of Prouender. **1764** PRIESTLEY *Ess. Educ.* in *Lect. Hist.* 28 Let him appoint rewards to those who shall handle the subject in the most judicious manner.

10. *Law.* To declare, in exercise of an authority conferred for that purpose, the destination of specific property. Cf. APPOINTMENT 7.

1601 *Act 43 Eliz.* iv. §1 Uses and intents.. for whiche they were given, limited, assigned, or appointed. **1874** DAVIDSON *Concise Preced.* 310 A power to appoint to 'issue' includes all issue, however remote. **1883** *Daily News* 16 Nov. 2/1 He should not allow any power to the wife to appoint by will in favour of the husband.

11. To ordain, destine, devote (a person or thing) **a.** *to* or *for* a fate or purpose. *arch.*

1526 TINDALE *1 Thess.* v. 9 God hath not apoynted us unto wrath [so in **1611** and **1881** *Revised*]. **1605** ROWLANDS *Hell's Br. Loose* 47 To their deserued deaths they are appoynted. **1625** BACON *Ess.* (Arb.) 550 If you doe not point any of the lower roomes for a dining place of seruants. **1712** BUDGELL *Spect.* No. 404 ¶1 The Creator.. has appointed every thing to a certain Use.

b. *to do* or *suffer something. arch.*

1496 LD. BOTHWELL in Ellis *Orig. Lett.* I. 12 I. 23 He has na wach bot yᵉ kings, apoinctit to be about him. **1526** TINDALE *Acts* xxvii. 2 A ship.. apoynted to sayle by the costes off Asia. **1535** COVERDALE *Ps.* xliv. 22 As shepe apoynted to be slayne. **1615** CROOKE *Body of Man* 426 [They] do appoynt the Patient to lie long vpon his backe. **1722** DE FOE *Moll. Fl.* (1840) 310 Next day I was appointed to be tried. **1736** BUTLER *Anal.* II. 410 Assistance, which nature.. appoints them to afford.

12. To ordain or nominate a person **a.** *to* an office, or *to perform* functions.

1557 *Ord. Hospitalls* D v, The Clerke.. is appointed to many Recepts and Payments. **1711** ADDISON *Spect.* No. 50 ¶4 The Queen of the Country appointed two Men to attend us. **1859** MERIVALE *Rom. Emp.* (1865) IV. xxxii. 4 The Roman citizens appointed to all the higher magistracies.

b. with *complement*: (*for* obs.) *to be* an official.

1611 BIBLE *2 Sam.* vi. 21 To appoint me ruler ouer the people of the Lord. **1651** HOBBES *Leviath.* III. xl. 253 He appointed Joshua for the Generall of their Army. **1759** ROBERTSON *Hist. Scotl.* I. II. 117 Bonot was appointed governor of Orkney. **1839** KEIGHTLEY *Hist. Eng.*, Cranmer was appointed to be her confessor.

c. *simply.*

1526 TINDALE *Luke* x. 1 The Lorde apoynted other seventie also. **1667** MILTON *P.L.* VI. 808 Vengeance is his, or whose he sole appoints. *Mod.* Who appointed you, then?

13. To ordain, set up, nominate, establish (an officer; and in *Law* a trustee, guardian, etc.).

c **1460** FORTESCUE *Abs. & Lim. Mon.* (1714) 110 A cheffe Ruler.. chosyn and appointyd by the Kyng. **1529** *Petit.* §6 in Froude *Hist. Eng.* I. 194 The said prelates.. appointed.. apprysers, and other ministers for the approbation of Testaments. **1711** ADDISON *Spect.* No. 1 ¶9 We have appointed a Committee. **1768** BLACKSTONE *Comm.* I. 462 This he may do [choose his own guardian] unless one be appointed by the father. **1875** BRYCE *Holy Rom. Emp.* ix. 152 Henry deposed them all, and appointed their successor. **1883** F. POLLOCK *Land Laws* 61 The father was empowered to appoint persons of his own choice to be his children's guardians.

III. To put into proper state or condition. (Cf. APPOINT *sb.* 2, and Fr. *en bon point.*)

†**14.** *trans.* To put in suitable order or condition; to prepare, make ready. *Obs.* in gen. sense.

1393 GOWER *Conf.* II. 151 Yet shuld he nought apoint his herte With jelousy. **1540** HYRDE *Vives' Instr. Chr. Wom.* (1592) N viij, Appoint thy self, that thou maiest in such wise binde him unto thee with love. **1583** STANYHURST *Aeneis* II. (Arb.) 54 They brandish weapons sharp edgde, to slaghter apoincted [L. *neci parata*]. **1615** HEYWOOD *Four Prent.* I. Wks. II. 240 Prepare to meet them and appoint our powers.

15. *esp.* To equip completely, fit out, furnish; to accoutre. *Obs.* exc. in pa. pple.

1490 CAXTON *Eneydos* xv. 55 Thus appoynted she mounted on horsebacke. **1526** TINDALE *Luke* xvii. 8 Apoynt thy selfe and serve me. **1590** MARLOWE *Edw. II*, IV. ii, To see us there, appointed for our foes. **1660** INGELO *Bentiv. & Urania* II. (1682) 193 Their several Lodgings, which were as well appointed as such a season would permit. **1770** BURKE *Pres. Discont.* Wks. II. 288 The house of commons.. is miserably appointed for that service. **1823** SCOTT *Peveril* II. iv. 96 Thus appointed.. he was in readiness to depart.

IV. Isolated uses after Fr. and L.

†**16.** To put a stop or limit to. *Obs. rare.*

1534 LD. BERNERS *Gold. Bk. M. Aurel.* (1546) F f iv, Great is that couetyse, whiche the shame of the worlde doth not repreue.. nor reason appoynt.

†**17.** To point to or at, to point out. *Obs.*

a **1547** SURREY *Æneid* II. (920) A blazing sterne.. By a long tract appointing vs the way. **1554** PHILPOT *Exam. & Writ.* (1842) 113 He.. fetched Cyprian and appointed out these words in one of his Epistles. *a* **1556** CRANMER *Wks.* I. 10 As well as if you had appointed me with your finger.

†**18.** To assign or impute blame *to*; to stigmatize, arraign. *Obs. rare.*

a **1612** in *Harington's Nugæ Ant.* I. 48 (Halliw.) If anye of theise wants be in me, I beseeche your lordshipp appoint them to my extreme state. **1674** MILTON *Samson* 373 Appoint not heavenly disposition, father. Nothing of all these evils hath befallen me But justly.

a'ppoint, *sb.* [f. prec. vb.; cf. Fr. *appoint*, 'somme qui fait le solde d'un compte;' Littré.]

†**1.** Agreement, settlement. *Obs.*

1555 *Fardle Facions* I. v. 77 When thei are ones fallen at appoyncte, the bodye is delyuered. **1565** T. STAPLETON *Fortr. Faith* 50 Let bothe those truthes and these truthes be beleved, and we shall be at appoinct.

†**2.** Array, equipment. *Obs.*

1592 WYRLEY *Armorie* 62 Sir Charls Bloys doth aduance .. In best appoint that hath been seene in Fraunce.

3. Settlement ***per appoint*** (*Comm.*): Exact and independent settlement of a transaction, *i.e.* not by entering it in account, or by payments on account.

Mod. Each transaction will be settled per appoint.

appointable (əˈpɔɪntəb(ə)l), *a.* ? *Obs. rare.* [f. prec. vb. + -ABLE.] Capable of being, or proper to be, appointed.

1563 FOXE *A. & M.* 696/2 The externe rytes and ceremonies be.. appointeable by superioures powers.

‖**appointé** (apwɛ̃te), *a. Her.* [Fr., pa. pple. of *appointer.*]

1753 CHAMBERS *Cycl. Supp.*, *Appointee* is when two or more things are placed touching each other at the points or ends.

appointed (əˈpɔɪntɪd), *ppl. a.* [f. as APPOINTABLE *a.* + -ED.]

1. Fixed by agreement; settled beforehand.

1585 ABP. SANDYS *Serm.* (1841) 275 Peter had his appointed hours of prayer. **1611** BIBLE *Judg.* xx. 38 There was an appointed signe. **1704** ROWE *Ulysses* IV. i. 1496 At this appointed Hour I wait her here. **1850** E. WARBURTON *Reg. Hastings* III. 4 At length he reached the appointed bridge.

2. Fixed by authority; ordained.

1535 COVERDALE *Jer.* viii. 10 The Storke knoweth his apoynted tyme. **1611** BIBLE *Num.* ix. 2 Keepe the Passe-ouer at his appointed season. **1718** POPE *Iliad* III. 574 The appointed fine let Ilion justly pay. **1805** SOUTHEY *Madoc in Azt.* viii. Wks. V. 255 Her, who blessed among women, fed The Appointed at her breast. **1858** ROBERTSON *Serm.* Ser. III. v. 75 Apportion to each its appointed penance.

3. With qualifying adv. (*well*, *ill*, etc.): Provided with requisites, fitted out, equipped.

1535 COVERDALE *Jer.* vi. 22 Horses wel apointed to yᵉ battel. **1662** MORE *Antid. Ath.* III. xv. (1712) 135 Ill-favoured and ill appointed Monsters. **1787** J. BARLOW *Oration 4th July* 11 The bravest and best appointed armies. **1859** MERIVALE *Rom. Emp.* (1865) V. xl. 18 A well-appointed road.

appointee (əˌpɔɪnˈtiː). [f. APPOINT *v.* + -EE, after F. *appointé.*]

1. a. *gen.* One who is appointed or nominated to an office. **b.** in *Law*, One in whose favour a power of appointment is executed: see APPOINTMENT 7.

1768 *Circular Mass. Repr.* (Webster) The commission authorizes them to make appointments, and pay the appointees. **1768** BLACKSTONE *Comm.* II. xxxii, The ordinary of courts grants administration to such appointee of the crown. **1829** GEN. P. THOMPSON *Exerc.* (1842) I. 40 The people's king flew back to his throne without a sword being drawn for the foreign appointee.

†**2.** *Mil.* [*appointé* in Cotgr.]

1727-51 CHAMBERS *Cycl.*, *Appointee*, a foot-soldier in the French army, etc., who for his long service.. receives pay above private sentinels. **1753** —— *Cycl. Supp.*, These have been suppressed in France, except in the.. guards where forty *Appointees* are still retained to each company.

appointer (əˈpɔɪntə(r)). [f. as prec. + -ER¹.] One who arranges a settlement or agreement (*obs.*), who ordains, or nominates. (See also APPOINTOR.)

1523 LD. BERNERS *Froiss.* I. lxiii. 84 Foure sufficyent persons, to treat on some good way to acorde the parties.. These apoynters shuld mete in a lytell chapell. **1633** AMES *Fresh Suit* II. 210 Christ is the only teacher of his church, and appointer of all means whereby it should be taught. **1857** TOULM. SMITH *Parish* 132 The Chief Constable.. is the appointer of all county constables.

a'ppointing, *vbl. sb.* [f. as prec. + -ING¹.] The action of the vb. APPOINT; appointment.

1520 WINGFIELD in Ellis *Orig. Lett.* I. I. 173 For the appoincting of.. officers for the howse. **1529** MORE *Comf. agst. Trib.* II. Wks. 1199/2 In the shooting of this arowe of pryde, ther be diuers purposinges and apoyntinges. **1687** *Assur. Abbey Lands* 65 For want of appointing how particularly these Lands should be applyed.

a'ppointing, *ppl. a.* [f. as prec. + -ING².] That makes appointments.

1730 SWIFT *Panegyr. on Dean* Wks. 1755 IV. I. 142 Where appointing lovers rove.

appointive (əˈpɔɪntɪv), *a. U.S.* [f. APPOINT *v.* + -IVE, by form-assoc. with *inventive*, etc.]

1. Dependent on appointment; that is filled by appointment; holding one's place by appointment.

1881 TOURGEE in *N. Amer. Rev.* CXXXII. 314 Every appointive place in the Government except the cabinet. **1886** *N. Amer. Rev.* Aug. 203 Whether the entire judiciary should be appointive or elective. **1889** *Nation* (N.Y.) 4 July 1/1 Mr. Geer being an appointive officer of the Custom-house. **1914** T. C. SMITH *Wars Eng. & Amer.* iii. 54 The Quebec Act altered the government of the province by the creation of an appointive council.

2. 'Of or pertaining to appointment; appointing; as, the appointive power of the President' (*Cent. Dict.*).

appointment (əˈpɔɪntmənt). Also in 6 **appunctuament**; for other forms see APPOINT *v.* [a. OF. *apointement*: see APPOINT *v.* and -MENT. In 15-16th c. often assimilated to med.L. *appunctā-*, *appunctuā-mentum.*]

†**1.** A pointing out, indication. *Obs. rare.*

c **1425** WYNTOUN *Cron.* VIII. Prol. 12, I haf stablit myne entent Now to mak here apoyntment Qwhen þe succession lynealle Endit.

†**2.** The action of agreeing, or coming to an arrangement; an agreement, pact, contract. *Obs.*

a **1440** *Paston Lett.* 25 I. 39 Accordyng to poyntment that ye made. **1461** *Ibid.* 408 II. 35 Without agreement or apoyntement taken. **1526** *Acts James V* (1814) 310 (JAM.) Ratifijs and appreuis the contract and appunctuament made. **1631** QUARLES *Samson* in Farr's *S.P.* 128 The long stay Betwixt th' appointment and the mariage-day. **1745** DE FOE *Eng. Tradesm.* I. xix. 182 The ordinary appointment of people to meet either at place or time.

†**3.** *spec.* The act of capitulating, or coming to terms with an opponent; terms of capitulation. *Obs.*

1494 FABYAN VI. clxxxi. 179 Delyuered yᵉ cytie by appoyntement, that he with the people myght departe thens without bodely harme. **1521** ARNOLD *Chron.* (1811) Introd. 48 The Kynge.. lyed syege to the cyte of Torney, and wan it by poyntment. **1533** BELLENDENE *Livy* IV. 326 Sic appunctment as the victoure plesis to gif. **1603-5** SIR J. MELVIL *Mem.* (1735) 240 They would have taken any reasonable Appointment.

4. *spec.* An agreement or arrangement for a meeting; engagement, assignation. (Cf. quot. 1745 in 2.) Also *attrib.*, as ***appointment book.***

c **1530** J. HEYWOOD *Interlude* (1846) Introd. 40, I and ij or thre Of my frendes made an appoyntement.. That in a place we wolde sup together. **1583** STANYHURST *Aeneis* II. (Arb.) 67 With mee shee kept not apointment. **1598** SHAKS. *Merry W.* III. i. 92 For missing your meetings and appointments. **1745** DE FOE *Eng. Tradesm.* I. xix. 181 A promise or appointment for a further day. **1864** DICKENS *Mut. Fr.* I. viii. 65 Would you take a seat..while I look over our Appointment Book? **1879** READE *Drink*, I shall break an appointment. **1950** T. S. ELIOT *Cocktail Party* II. 91 The Nurse-Secretary enters, with Appointment Book.

†5. Resolution, purpose. *Obs.*

1529 MORE *Comf. agst. Trib.* II. Wks. 1199/2 The proude man himself hath no certain purpose or appointment. **1606** SHAKS. *Ant. & Cl.* IV. x. 8 Where their appointment we may best discover, And looke on their endeuor.

6. The action of ordaining or directing what is to be done; direction, decree, ordinance, dictation.

c **1440** *Generydes* 2100 These princes hadde vj thowsand knyghteȝ In ther poyntement. **1574** tr. *Marlorat's Apocalips* 15 All things are done and disposed by his determination and appoyntment. **1583** STANYHURST *Aeneis* I. (Arb.) 27 By Gods forwarned apointcement. **1651** *Father Sarpi* (1676) 96 Making one of his Writers read to him, or write at his appointment. **1736** BUTLER *Anal.* I. i. 19 According to a natural order or appointment. **1833** HT. MARTINEAU *Tale of Tyne* iv. 67 The wind also failed,..a more merciful appointment than if it had blown a great storm.

7. *Law.* The act of declaring the destination of any specific property, in exercise of an authority conferred for that purpose.

1601 *Act 43 Eliz.* iv. §1 Such giftes, limitacions, assignements, and appoyntments. **1768** BLACKSTONE *Comm.* II. 119 An appointment by tenant in tail of the lands entailed, to a charitable use. **1874** G. FARWELL *Powers* 2 The ordinary power of appointment among children in a marriage settlement where personalty is vested in trustees. **1876** DIGBY *Real Prop.* vii. §2. 326 Powers of appointment, that is, conferring on a person a power of disposing of an interest in lands quite irrespective of the fact whether or not he has any interest in the land himself.

8. The action of nominating to, or placing in, an office; the office so given. Esp. in phr. ***by appointment***, by or as by royal warrant.

1658-9 LD. LAMBERT in Burton *Diary* III. 333 By your appointment agree the Government. Then appoint officers. **1863** COX *Inst. Eng. Govt.* II. iii. 342 The appointment of incompetent judges. *Ibid.* These appointments are made by the ministers of the Crown. **1864** DICKENS *Mut. Fr.* I. v. 33 He..settled it with himself..that he was errand-goer by appointment to the house at the corner. **1868** GEO. ELIOT *F. Holt* 36 A poor baronet, hoping for an appointment. **1874** DAVIDSON *Concise Preced.* 477 Appointment of new trustees of a will. **1878** LECKY *Eng. in 18th C.* I. iii. 426 His appointment to the lucrative office of Joint Vice-Treasurer of Ireland. **1962** *Guardian* 2 Dec. 12/1 A list of Royal Warrant holders..shows that only two firms are now permitted to style themselves 'By Appointment to the late Queen Alexandra'.

9. Equipment, equipage, outfit, accoutrement, furniture, or any article thereof. Now usually *pl.*

1575 LANEHAM *Lett.* (1871) 48 Hiz honorz exquisit appointment of a beautifull garden. **1593** SHAKS. *Rich. II*, III. iii. 53 That from this Castles tatter'd Battlements Our faire Appointments may be well perus'd. **1658** EVELYN *Corr.* 8 Nov., To allow him [him son] an appointment so noble and considerable as does become his greatness. **1759-67** STERNE *Tr. Shandy* (1802) III. xxii. 335, I have not one appointment belonging to me which I set so much store by, as I do by these jack-boots. **1864** BOUTELL *Heraldry* xxiv. 402 Royal blazonry upon the appointments as well of his horse as of his own person.

†10. An allowance paid to anyone, especially to a public officer. *Obs.*

1715 BURNET *Own Time* an. 1674 (R.) He had the appointments of an ambassador. **1727-51** CHAMBERS *Cycl.* s.v., Appointments differ from wages, in that the latter are fixed and ordinary..whereas appointments are annual gratifications granted by brevet for a time uncertain, and are paid out of the privy purse. **1753** HANWAY *Trav.* (1762) II. I. ix. 51 The appointment of the stadt-holdership..is one hundred thousand guilders. **1761** SMOLLETT *Gil Blas* I. xvii. (1802) I. 109 His parents will turn thee away..perhaps even without paying thee thy appointments.

appointor (ə,pɔɪn'tɔːr). *Law.* [repr. actual or possible ME. and AFr. *appointour*:—OF. *apointeor*: see APPOINT and -OR.] The form of APPOINTER used in a specific legal sense: The person who exercises a power of appointment.

1882 JESSEL *Law Rep.* Ch. Div. XXI. 336 The parties to this deed intended that the appointor..should be the judge of the period at which the portions should vest.

†**a'ppoise**, *v. Obs. rare*$^{-1}$. [f. AP- *pref.*[1] + POISE *v.* See A- *pref.* 11. (Apparently unconnected with OFr. *apoiser*, *apeser* to weigh upon.)] To weigh or estimate by comparison.

a **1670** HACKET in Wolcott *Life* (1865) App. 173 We must believe without appoising the articles of our faith to the balance of reason.

†**a'ppopulate**, *v. Obs. rare*$^{-1}$. [f. AP- *pref.*[1] + POPULATE *v.* Cf. It. *appopolare*, *-ato* (Florio 1598).] To people, render populous.

1625 PURCHAS *Pilgrims* II. 1424 The principall cities of the Turkish Empire are much appopulated with them.

a'pport, *sb.* In 5-6 **aport**. [a. OF. *aport* action of bringing, what is brought, revenue (Cotgr.), f. *aporter*: see next, and AP- *pref.*[1]]

†1. Bearing, carriage, demeanour. *Obs.*

a **1423** JAMES I *King's Q.* II. xxxi, In hir was ȝouth, beautee, with humble aport. **1519** HORMAN *Vulg.* 19 b, The great Turke shall hastely abate his hye aport. **1606** B. BARNES *Offices* 18 This outward apport of their degrees and riches.

†2. *pl.* Things brought; offerings; revenues; aids. *Obs.*

1481 CAXTON *Myrr.* II. xviii. 106 Thyder [to helle] come all euylles and all the euyll apportes. **1530** in Rymer *Fœdera* (1710) XIV. 372 Pensions, Portions, Apportes, Rentes.

3. The production of material objects, supposedly by occult means, at a spiritualistic séance; also, an object so produced. Usu. in *pl.*

1894 A. LANG *Cock Lane* 53 Objects are brought from places many miles distant, and tossed on the table. These are technically termed *apports*. **1926** CONAN DOYLE *Hist. Spiritualism* I. xiv. 327 A number of fresh flowers and fruits, still wet, fell upon the table—a phenomenon of apports.

†**a'pport**, *v. Obs.* [a. F. *apporte-r*, f. OF. *aporter*:—L. *apportā-re*, f. *ap-* = *ad-* to + *portāre* to carry.]

1. *trans.* To bring, produce.

1590 R. BRUCE *Serm. Sacram.* M iij a (JAM.) Quhat the resurrection and glorification apports to the bodie. **1604** T. WRIGHT *Passions of Mind* v. §4. 185 The euil or great dammages it apporteth.

2. *intr.* To arrive *at.* [Cf. Fr. *apporter* 'to arriue or approach neere to the hauen or shore' Cotgr.]

1578 T. N. tr. *Conq. W. India* 33 We apported at Iamayca.

†**a'pportable**, *a. Obs.* [f. prec. + -ABLE.] Capable of being brought forward, or produced.

1604 T. WRIGHT *Pass. Mind* v. §4. 273 All the reasons apportable to render the thing amiable.

†**a'pporter.** *Obs. rare*$^{-1}$. [f. prec. vb. + -ER[1].] An introducer, bringer in.

1678 HALE *Hist. Plac. Coronæ* xx. (T.) This makes only the apporters themselves..traitors; not those who receive it at second hand.

apportion (ə'pɔəʃən), *v.* Also 6 **apporcion**, 7 **aportion**. [a. OF. *apportionner*, *-cionner*, f. *à* to + *portionner*, f. *portion* portion, share.]

1. To assign (*to* any one) as his proper portion or share; to allot.

1587 GOLDING *De Mornay* xv. 241 Euery certeine Soule must neede be apportioned and appointed to some one certeine body. **1660** JER. TAYLOR *Worthy Commun.* i. §11. 17 What reward God please to apportion to it. **1824-8** LANDOR *Imag. Conv.* (1846) 52 The first duty of a legislator is to apportion penalties. **1870** DISRAELI *Lothair* vii. 25 His guardians had apportioned to him an allowance..adequate to his position.

2. To assign in proper portions or shares; to divide and assign proportionally; to portion out, to share.

1574 tr. *Littleton's Tenures* 46 a, The rent service..shalbee apporcioned after the value of the land. **1703** COLLIER *Ess. Mor. Subj.* II. (1709) 111 The Matter in competition is often Indivisible. An Office, or a Mistress, can't be Apportion'd out like a Common. **1778** G. MORRIS in Sparks *Corr. Amer. Rev.* (1853) II. 131 A contribution..to be apportioned upon the inhabitants, according to their wealth. **1848** MILL *Pol. Econ.* III. xvi. §1 To apportion the expenses of production between the two.

3. To adjust according to due proportion or measure; to proportion. *arch.*

1615 CROOKE *Body of Man* 43 The number wee cannot better aportion, then from the nature and definition of a Principle. **1794** SULLIVAN *View Nat.* I. 245 This seems apportioned to animal wants. **1823** LAMB *Elia* I. xviii. (1865) 136 It was the measure for the birds to apportion their silver warblings by.

†**a'pportion**, *sb. Obs. rare*$^{-1}$. [f. prec. vb.] Division in just proportion.

1628 COKE *On Litt.* 148 a, Apportion signifieth a Diuision or partition of a Rent, common, etc.

apportionable (ə'pɔəʃənəb(ə)l), *a. rare.* [f. prec. vb. + -ABLE.] Liable to apportionment.

1628 COKE *On Litt.* 148 a, Such Rent services are apportionable by Common law.

†**a'pportionate**, *v. Obs.* [f. med.L. *apportiōnāt-* ppl. stem of *apportiōnā-re*, ad. AF. *apportioner*: see APPORTION *v.* Like other early words in *-ate*, occurs first as pa. pple.] = APPORTION *v.*

1523 FITZHERB. *Surv.* 23 The relefe shalbe apporcyonate accordyng to the same. **1531** ELYOT *Gov.* I. iii. (1544) 13 Possessions which they may apporcionate to theyr owne living. *a* **1670** HACKET *Abp. Williams* II. 75 By free apportionating them [*i.e.* fostering allowances] according to the duty and wisdom of the children.

†**a'pportionateness.** *Obs. rare.* [f. APPORTIONATE (pple.) + -NESS.] The quality of being proportionally adjusted.

1645 HAMMOND *View of Directory* Pref. The apportionateness of [the English liturgy] to the end to which it was designed. [So **1679** PULLER *Mod. Ch. Eng.* (1843) 28.]

a'pportioner. [f. APPORTION *v.* + -ER[1].] One who apportions.

1611 COTGR., *Borneur*, a limiter, bounder; apportioner. **1884** BROWNING *Ferishtah's Fancies* ix. 83 The apportioner of every lot of ground. **1893** *St. James' Budget* 23 June 6/3 The apportioners of the Chantrey Bequest. **1905** C. KERNAHAN *Visions* 259 The..dishonest Apportioner of life's good and evil.

apportionment (ə'pɔəʃənmənt). [f. as prec. + -MENT; also in med.L. *apportionamentum* and Fr. *apportionnement.*]

1. The action of distributing or allotting in proper proportion or suitable shares.

1628 COKE *On Litt.* 149 b, The apportionment shall not be according to the quantity of the land, but according to the quality. **1807** W. TAYLOR in *Ann. Rev.* V. 210 By a wiser apportionment of the custom and excise duties. **1852** GROTE *Greece* II. lxxviii. X. 316 For the apportionment of houses and lands among the citizens. **1861** MILL *Utilit.* v. 85 The proper apportionment of punishment to offences.

2. The state or fact of being thus distributed.

1681 NEVILE *Plato Rediv.* 52 Wherever this apportionment of Lands came to be changed. **1858** (27 Oct.) BRIGHT *Sp.* (1876) 287 When the apportionment of the Members to the Constituencies approximates to a just arrangement.

†**a'pposal.** *Obs.* Also 5 **opposayle, apposaylle, -yl,** 6 **-elle.** [f. APPOSE[1] + -AL[2].]

1. The process of apposing; interrogation, examination; a posing question, a puzzle.

c **1470** *Pol. Poems* II. 282 Pray theym all to take the to grace, In appoysaylle [*v.r.* apposaile]. *c* **1525** SKELTON *Garl. Laurel* 141 Madame, your apposelle is well inferrid.

2. Legal examination of accounts. (See APPOSER 2.)

1461-83 *Ord. R. Househ.* 61 To sette with the judges as audytoures..also at the accomptes in many apposylys. **1691** BLOUNT *Law Dict.*, *Apposal* of Sheriffs, is the charging them with Money received, upon their account in the Exchequer. **1809** in TOMLINS *Law. Dict.*

†**a'ppose**, *v.*[1] *Obs.* Forms: 4-5 **opose, apose,** 5-7 **appose.** [orig. a variant spelling of OPPOSE, ME. *oposen* and *aposen*, = OFr. *oposer* and *aposer* (both languages showing substitution of the more common atonic *ă-* for atonic *ŏ-*: even med.L. confounded *appositum* and *oppositum*), used in the common scholastic sense of L. *oppōnĕre* 'to argue against, bring forward objections or difficulties to be answered' (*oppōnere et respondēre*). In senses more obviously connected with the primary meaning of *oppōnĕre* and *opposition*, the form *oppose* was at length established; but in those in which this connexion was not apparent, and which might even be plausibly explained from *appōnĕre*, as if 'to put it to one,' *appose* early prevailed. Also aphetized in 15th c. to POSE, the mod. repr. For the artificial affiliation of *-pose* to L. *pōnĕre*, *positum*, see next.]

1. To confront with objections or hard questions; to examine, interrogate, question.

c **1315** SHOREHAM 145 Ʒef the faly throf to be aposed, Sey God nys nauȝt in ther wordle a-closed. **1387** TREVISA *Higden* (Rolls Ser.) IV. 291 Þe childe Jesus..sittynge and apposynge þe doctours. *a* **1400** *Cov. Myst.* (1841) 137 The Busschop xal your lyff appose. **1440** *Promp. Parv.*, Examyn, or apposyn (posyn, posen), *Examino.* **1553** *Short Catech. Edw. VI*, 495 Thus beginneth the Master to appose his Scholar..I thought it best to oppose thee by certain questions. **1558** BP. WATSON 7 *Sacram.* xxi. 130 The mynister should not be compelled to appose and examine the penitent. **1581** CAMPION in *Confer.* III. (1584) O ij, You come to appose mee, as if I were a scholer in the Grammar schoole. **1615** T. ADAMS *Two Sonnes* 65 Question against question: the Jewes appose Jesus, Jesus apposeth the Jewes.

2. *absol.* and *intr.*

c **1325** *E.E. Allit. P.* A. 901 Þaȝ I appose, I schulde not tempte þe wyt so wlonc. **1491** CAXTON *Vitas Patr.* (W. de W.) I. xciii. 127 b/1, I woll apose and dyspute wyth hym of some necessary thynges. **1551** T. WILSON *Logic* 61 The one aunswering and denying, and the other still apposing. **1581** CAMPION in *Confer.* III. (1584) U iij b, I would I might appose.

3. *spec.* To examine as to accounts, to audit. (Cf. APPOSER 2.)

1601 TATE *Househ. Ord. Ed. II*, §44 (1876) 26, A serjant naper..shal aunswere for it as often as he shal be apposed. **1738** *Hist. Crt. Exchequer* v. 96 The Sheriff was apposed anciently in open Court and now by the Cursitor Baron.

4. = OPPOSE, q.v.

appose (ə'pəʊz, emphatic ,æ'pəʊz), *v.*[2] [formed to represent L. *appōnĕre*, on the analogy of *compose*, *expose*, *suppose*, and the other assumed representatives of compounds of *pōnĕre*, formed on OFr. *poser*:—L. *pausāre*, after this vb. came, through form-assoc. with *positio*, *positum*, to be treated as the representative of L. *pōnĕre* (see PAUSE, POSE). In Fr. *apposer* is found as early as 13th c.]

1. To put or apply one thing *to* another, as a seal to a document; to put (food) before.

1593 J. CAREY *Let.* in Tytler *Hist. Scotl.* (1864) IV. 206 The king doth too much appose himself to the Papist faction. **1596** CHAPMAN *Iliad* IX. 95 Atrides..food sufficient Appos'd before them, and the peers appos'd their hands to it. **1614** RALEIGH *Hist. World* II. 228 Fire to heate whatsoever is apposed. **1662** EVELYN *Chalcog.* (1769) 43 One of the ancientest gravings..to which any mark is apposed. **1862** F. HALL *Hind. Philos. Syst.* 214 As the iron moves, when the precious stone..is apposed to it. **1868** BROWNING *Ring & Bk.* IV. 1495 The last seal publicly apposed to shame.

2. To place in apposition or juxtaposition; to range side by side.

c **1800** K. WHITE *Rem.* (1837) 391 Original conceptions luminously displayed and judiciously apposed. **1870** ROLLESTON *Anim. Life* Introd. 20 The boundaries of species ..may be closely apposed..along considerable lengths.

apposed (əˈpəʊzd), *ppl. a.* [f. APPOSE[2] + -ED.] Put or applied to; put in apposition.

1596 CHAPMAN *Iliad* II. 371 Kindled at Apposed fire. **1861** T. GRAHAM *Pract. Med.* 321 The apposed surfaces of the pericardium.

†**aˈpposer.** *Obs.* [f. APPOSE[1] + -ER[1].]

1. One who apposes; a questioner, examiner.

1551 T. WILSON *Logic* 61 The apposer must fight with the weapon of his wit. **1577-87** HARRISON *England* I. II. iii. 84 In those [Windsor, Wincester, Eaton, Westminster schools] ..the triall is made by certeine apposers yearelie appointed to examine them. **1759** BOYER *Fr. Dict.*, Apposer, *Examinateur*.

2. An Exchequer officer who examined or audited the sheriffs' accounts. (The office was abolished in 1833.)

1641 *Termes de la Ley* 165 Forrein Apposer is an Officer in the Exchequer, to whom all Sherifes and Baylifes doe repaire by him to be apposed of their greene waxe. **1738** *Hist. Crt. Exchequer* v. 108 A new Officer, before whom the Sheriff was to account on his Process, who is called the Foreign Apposer.

†**aˈpposing,** *vbl. sb. Obs.* [f. APPOSE[1] + -ING[1].] Questioning, examination.

1407 W. THORPE in Arb. *Garner* VI. 46, I should write mine Apposing and mine Answering. **1575** *Troub. ad. Com. Prayer* 139 An examination and apposinge off them. **1612** BRINSLY *Lud. Lit.* 74 Let the manner of the apposing be.. by short questions.

apposite (ˈæpəzɪt), *a.* [ad. L. *apposit-us*, pa. pple. of *app-*, *adpōnĕre*, f. *ad* to + *-pōnĕre* to place, put.]

†**1.** Put or applied to. *Obs. rare*$^{-0}$.

1656 in BLOUNT, **1706** in PHILLIPS, etc.

2. Well put or applied; appropriate, suitable (*to*).

1621 BURTON *Anat. Mel.* II. ii. II. (1651) 239 A most apposite remedy. **1634** HABINGTON *Castara* (1870) 15 Her language is not copious but appposit. **1709** SWIFT *T. of Tub* §3. 54 The types are so apposite. **1849** GROTE *Greece* II. lv. (1862) V. 31 Mastery of apposite and homely illustrations. **1869** GOULBOURN *Purs. Holiness* i. 6 The truth most apposite to the whole argument.

†**3.** Of persons: Ready with appropriate remarks, apt. *Obs.*

1699-1703 POMFRET *Poet. Wks.* (1833) 31 In all discourse she's apposite and gay. **1788** H. WALPOLE in *Reader* 7 Oct. 1865, 392/3 Qualified to talk on any subject; easy, agreeable, and apposite in their observations.

†**4.** *absol.* or as *sb.* That which is placed beside or in apposition. *Obs.*

1677 GALE *Crt. Gent.* II. IV. 516 The negation of it implies a contradiction in the Adject or an Opposite in an Apposite.

5. See OPPOSITE.

apposited (əˈpɒzɪtɪd), *ppl. a. rare.* [f. L. *apposit-us* (see prec.) + -ED.] Put or applied to.

1822 HAZLITT *Table-t.* II. x. 233 Sight, apposited with interest, can retain tolerably exact copies of sensations.

ˈappositely, *adv.* [f. APPOSITE + -LY[2].] In an apposite manner, appropriately, to the point.

1633 T. ADAMS *Exp. 2 Pet.* ii. 6 The pulpit can prove nothing so appositely..by Scripture. **1637** GILLESPIE *Eng.-Popish Cer.* IV. iii. 12 Thus spake the learned Friar very appositly. **1774** T. WARTON *Eng. Poetry* xx. III. 36 This fable appositely suggests a train of sensible and pointed observations. **1830** SIR J. HERSCHEL *Nat. Philos.* 54 They are not on that account less appositely cited as instances.

ˈappositeness. [f. as prec. + -NESS.] The quality of being apposite, aptness.

1664 H. MORE *Myst. Iniq.* 429 The appositeness of these four last Prophecies for the setting out the Merchandizing of the Church of Rome. **1816** KIRBY & SP. *Entom.* (1828) II. xxvii. 490 The appositeness of this question. **1873** HOLLAND *A. Bonnic.* xix. 288 There was a pathetic and poetic appositeness in these words to the facts of his expiring life.

apposition[1] (æpəʊˈzɪʃən). [a. OFr. *aposicion*, *apposition*, variant of *opposition*, in med.L. sense of *oppōnĕre*: see APPOSE *v.*[1]] A public disputation by scholars; a formal examination by question and answer; still applied to the 'Speech day' at St. Paul's School, London.

1659-60 PEPYS *Diary* 9 Jan., My brother John's speech, which he is to make the next apposition. **1864** *Press* 18 June 588 St. Paul's School..celebrated its annual Apposition on Wednesday.

apposition[2] (æpəʊˈzɪʃən). [ad. (perh. through mod.Fr. *apposition* 16th c.) L. *appositiōnem*, n. of action f. *appōnere* to put to: see APPOSITE.]

1. The action of putting or placing one thing *to* another; application.

1541 R. COPLAND *Guydon's Quest. Cyrurg.*, Yf after the fyrste apposycyon..it blede nat wel. **1559** MORWYNG *Evon.* 367 All suche thinges as..fomentacions, apposicions, embroches, etc. **1650** FULLER *Pisgah* IV. vi. 117 By apposition, or putting of sweet odours to the dead body. **1726** AYLIFFE *Parergon* 308 By the Apposition of a Publick Seal. **1875** POSTE *Gaius* II. 220 The apposition of the seals of seven attesting witnesses.

†**2.** That which is put to or added; an addition.

1610 GWILLIM *Heraldry* §1. i. (1660) 10 For distinction sake, to annex some apposition over and above their paternall Coat. **1655** FULLER *Ch. Hist.* II. 67 The Place is plainly written *Cern*, without any paragogical apposition.

3. The placing of things in close superficial contact; the putting of distinct things side by side in close proximity.

1660 STANLEY *Hist. Philos.* 64/2 The mistion of the Elements is by apposition. **1669** GALE *Crt. Gentiles* I. I. vi. 35 [The word] according to the various apposition of the leters, may signifie either a foot, or a river. **1830** LYELL *Princ. Geol.* (1875) I. II. xix. 488 These layers must have accumulated one on the other by lateral apposition. **1850** DAUBENY *Atom. The.* iv. 121 The result of the apposition of an assemblage of smaller crystals.

4. The fact or condition of being in close contact, juxtaposition, parallelism.

1606 G. CARLETON *Tithes Exam.* iv. 21 b, There is an apposition betweene things of the same kinde. *a* **1652** J. SMITH *Sel. Disc.* v. 160 A mere kind of apposition or contiguity of our natures with the divine. **1801** FUSELI *Lect. Art.* (1848) The true medium between dry apposition and exuberant contrast. **1824-8** LANDOR *Imag. Conv.* (1846) 159 He places strange and discordant ideas in close apposition. **1878** T. BRYANT *Pract. Surg.* I. 145 The cut surfaces and edges of the wounds are to be brought into apposition.

†**5.** *Rhet.* The addition of a parallel word or phrase by way of explanation or illustration of another. *Obs.*

1561 T. N[ORTON] *Calvin's Inst.* III. 187 Calling faith the worke of God, and geuing it that title for a name of addition, and calling it by figure of apposition Gods good pleasure. *a* **1638** MEDE *Wks.* I. xxiv. 93 It is an Apposition, or ἐξήγησις, the latter words declaring the meaning of the former; 'Peace on earth,' that is, 'Good will towards men.'

6. *Gram.* The placing of a word beside, or in syntactic parallelism with, another; *spec.* the addition of one substantive to another, or to a noun clause, as an attribute or complement; the position of the substantive so added.

c **1440** *Gesta Rom.* (1879) 416 Yonge childryn that gone to the scole haue in here Donete this question, how many thinges fallen to apposicion? **1591** PERCIVALL *Span. Dict.*, A Preposition..either in Composition, as, *Contrahecho*..or in Apposition, as, *En la casa.* **1657** J. SMITH *Myst. Rhet.* 191 Apposition is a figure..whereby one Noune Substantive is for Declaration and distinction sake added unto another in the same case. **1860** JOWETT *Ess. & Rev.* 398 In the failure of syntactical power..in various forms of apposition, especially that of the word to the sentence.

appositional (æpəʊˈzɪʃənəl), *a.* [f. prec. + -AL[1].] Of or belonging to apposition; appositive.

1841 LATHAM *Eng. Lang.* (1850) §559 The appositional construction is, in reality, a matter of concord. **1865** N. DALGLEISH *Gram. Anal.* 13 The appositional complement. **1879** G. MACLEAR in *Camb. Bible, Mark* i. 5 River of Jordan: *of* is here redundant and appositional.

appoˈsitionally, *adv. rare.* [f. prec. + -LY[2].] In apposition; appositively.

1882 ROBERTSON *Müller's Heb. Synt.* 60 [The words] could equally well stand appositionally in the absolute state after the word qualified.

appositive (əˈpɒzɪtɪv), *a.* [f. L. *apposit-* (see APPOSITE) + -IVE, as if ad. L. **appositiv-us*: cf. It. *appositivo* (Florio), mod.Fr. *appositif.*] Of, pertaining to, or standing in apposition. Also as *sb.*

1693 KNATCHBULL *Annot.* 42 The words in the parenthesis being only appositive to the words going immediately before. **1847** A. CROSBY *Grk. Gram.* §331 An appositive agrees in case with its subject. **1883** H. KENNEDY *Ten Brink's E.E. Lit.* 20 The separation of appositive words.

aˈppositively, *adv.* [f. prec. + -LY[2].] In appositive construction, in apposition.

1881 WHITNEY *Mixt. in Lang.* 23 Genitives of different kinds..those used more attributively and those used more appositively. **1883** H. KENNEDY *Ten Brink's E.E. Lit.* 19 Substantive expressions which..are put appositively beside the real designation.

†**aˈppositor.** *Obs.* [n. of agent (L. in form) f. APPOSE[1] (for *oppositor*).] = APPOSER.

1601 CORNWALLYES *Ess.* II. xxxv. (1631) 86 The overthrow of an Appositor is counted discourtesie.

†**aˈppost,** *v. Obs. rare.* [a. Fr. *apposte-r*, ad. It. *appostare*:—late L. **appositā-re*, f. *apposit-us* conveniently appointed, APPOSITE.] To place or arrange for a purpose. Hence, **apposted** *ppl. a.*

1611 COTGR., *Apposter*, to apposte, suborne, procure underhand. **1633** T. STAFFORD *Pac. Hib.* xiii. (1821) 608 They will thinke this Letter is aposted, and take this to be a finesse. **1611** COTGR., *Assassin*, an appoasted manslayer.

appraisable (əˈpreɪzəb(ə)l), *a.* [f. APPRAISE + -ABLE.] Capable of having the value fixed.

1864 SALA in *Daily Tel.* 24 Sept., But there they are, merchantable and appraiseable. **1868** M. PATTISON *Academ. Org.* §5. 202 He has no appraisable value.

appraisal (əˈpreɪzəl). [f. next + -AL[2].] The act of appraising. **a.** *lit.* The setting of a price. **b.** *fig.* Estimate of worth.

1817 COLERIDGE *Biogr. Lit.* 151 Criticism as employed in the appraisal of works [poems] more or less imperfect. **1838** DE QUINCEY (*title*) A Brief Appraisal of Greek Literature. **1863** B. TAYLOR *H. Thurston* I. 67 An inventory and appraisal of the live stock. **1876** M. ARNOLD *Lit. & Dogma* 222 Here are both inward appraisal and self-renouncement.

appraise (əˈpreɪz), *v.* [Of rather late appearance; f. PRAISE *v.*, previously, and, for some time, contemporaneously, used in same sense. Perh. formed on analogy of the synonymous PRIZE, APPRIZE: see the latter.]

1. To fix a price for, assign a money value to: *esp.* as an official valuer or appraiser.

[**1383** WYCLIF *Matt.* xxvii. 9 The pris of a man preysid, whom thei preysiden, of the sonys of Yrael. **1590** SWINBURNE *Testaments* 220 Others praise them among the moueables; but it were better to praise them seuerally.]

1535 in Wood's *Lett. Illustr. Ladies* (1852) II. 164 The stuff..was appraised by the appraisers. **1661** PEPYS *Diary* 2 Oct., All this morning at Pegg Kite's..appraising her goods that her mother has left. **1762** HUME *Hist. Eng.* (1806) IV. lxii. 665 The cartoons..were only appraised at three hundred pounds. **1878** BOSW. SMITH *Carthage* 151 They [mercenaries] transferred their services..to those who would appraise them more highly.

2. *transf.* To estimate the amount, quality, or excellence of. Also *refl.*

1841 MYERS *Cath. Th.* IV. §40. 385 Rightly to appraise the value of various truths. **1864** TENNYSON *En. Arden* 154 The feeble infant..Whom Enoch took, and handled all his limbs, Appraised his weight. **1869** ARBER *James I's Ess.* Introd. 4 The king's Sonnets and Poems..appraise themselves.

appraised (əˈpreɪzd), *ppl. a.* [f. prec. + -ED.] Estimated at a money value, fixed by valuation; having its worth calculated.

1864 D. WELLS *Our Strength, etc.* 17 A discrepancy between the real and appraised value of property. **1879** GEO. ELIOT *Theo. Such* v. 110 A carefully appraised end to serve.

appraisement (əˈpreɪzmənt). [f. as prec. + -MENT.]

1. The action of appraising or valuing; valuation by an official or authorized appraiser.

1642 *Ord. & Declar. Lords & Comm.* 20 Oct. 4 A true appraysement [shall be] made of the same. **1745** *Season. Adv. Protest.* 20 The Landlords are paid their Rents, and no Appraisements are heard of in twenty Years. **1867** LYD. CHILD *Rom. Repub.* vi. 68 The tedious details of Mr. Royal's liabilities, and the appraisement of his property.

2. A price fixed by appraising, estimated value.

1703 *Lond. Gaz.* mmmdccccclxxx/3 Bars of Silver..to be set up at 1*d.* 2*q.* per Ounce under the Appraisement. **1748** RICHARDSON *Clarissa* (1811) IV. ix. 52, I have consented to take the household linen at an appraisement. **1881** W. SPRINGER in *N. Amer. Rev.* CXXXII. 377 If the appraisement is exorbitant.

3. *transf.* Estimation of quality or worth generally.

a **1858** DE QUINCEY *Whiggism* Wks. VI. 45 Ground more important to Dr. Parr's reputation, and, at the same time, much more susceptible of a sincere latitude of appraisement. **1881** MRS. LINTON *My Love* III. 5 A lover's keen appraisement of the value of the thing he wants.

appraiser (əˈpreɪzə(r)). [f. as prec. + -ER[1].]

1. One who appraises: *spec.* a person appointed and sworn to estimate the value of property.

1529 *Petition* in Froude *Hist. Eng.* I. 194 There be limited and appointed so many judges, scribes, apparitors, summoners, appraysers. **1696** *Lond. Gaz.* mmmccxxxviii/3 Officers, who are to be Appraisers and Sellers of all moveable Goods. **1783** BURKE *Rep. Aff. India* Wks. 1842 II. 3 Having ordered the appraiser of the company's cloths..to be severely flogged. **1857** TOULM. SMITH *Parish* 130 The appraisers sworn to appraise goods sold under distress for rent.

2. *transf.* One who estimates quality or worth.

1801 MAR. EDGEWORTH *Belinda* I. vi. 111 Any fair appraiser of delicate distresses, would decide that I am.. more to be pitied than you are. **1824** COLERIDGE *Aids to Refl.* (1848) I. 149 You have appointed the many as your judges and appraisers.

appraising (əˈpreɪzɪŋ), *vbl. sb.* [f. as prec. + -ING[1].] The action of setting a price or value on.

1727-51 CHAMBERS *Cycl.*, *Appraising*, the act of rating, valuing or setting a price on goods by a person who is a competent judge, and is authorized thereto.

aˈppraising, *ppl. a.* [f. as prec. + -ING[2].] That appraises or estimates; valuing, estimating. Hence **appraisingly** *adv.*

1880 MISS BROUGHTON *Sec. Th.* II. II. vi. 25 Eying appraisingly, as to its capabilities, her robust yet delicate beauty.

appraisive (əˈpreɪzɪv), *a.* [f. APPRAISE *v.* + -IVE.] Of language, etc.: used in making, or of the type used in making, appraisals or valuations. Hence **aˈppraisively** *adv.*

1934 in WEBSTER. **1946** C. W. MORRIS *Signs, Lang. & Behav.* v. 129 The work itself does not, as fiction, appraisively signify. *Ibid.* 136 Poetry may serve as an example of discourse which is primarily appraisive-valuative. *Ibid.* 138 Appraisive-incitive discourse may be illustrated by the language of morality. *Ibid.* 140 'Criticism' (or 'evaluation') serves to illustrate appraisive-systemic discourse. **1956** J. WHATMOUGH *Lang.* vi. 88 The merely designative use of language has in each case become appraisive. **1967** NABOKOV *Speak, Memory* (ed. 2) ii. 40 Her grim father would..give the heaviest racket an appraisive shake.

†**ˈapprecate,** *v. Obs. rare.* [f. L. *apprecāt-* ppl. stem of *adp-*, *apprecā-ri*, to pray to, f. *ad* to + *precāri* to pray, f. *prec-em* prayer.] To pray for, invoke, devoutly wish, *to.*

1631 DONNE *Serm.* vii. 69 All that the Queen and Councell could wish and apprecate to the king. **1674** *Ch. & Crt. Rome* 13 Appreciating Destruction to those of his Family..who should attempt a departure to Popery.

†**appre'cation.** *Obs.* [n. of action f. prec.: see -TION.] The action of praying for or invoking a blessing on another; a devout wish.

1608 BP. HALL *Epist.* I. viii. Wks. 1634 I. 263 Not without desire and apprecation. **1618** HOWELL *Lett.* I. I. iii, With apprecation of as much happinesse to you at home, as I shall desire to accompany me abroad. *a* **1679** POOLE *Annot.* (1852) III. 275 The salutation.. common among the Jews.. was an apprecation of all blessing and happiness.

†**'apprecatory,** *a. Obs.* [f. L. *apprecāt-* (see APPRECATE) + -ORY.] Of the nature of praying for a blessing on any one; intercessory.

1633 T. ADAMS *Exp. 2 Pet.* iii. 18 [Glory] is either a praise, or a wish; gratulatory or apprecatory. **1649** BP. HALL *Cases Consc.* III. ix. (1654) 261 The (not so much apprecatory as declaratory) benedictions.

appreciable (ə'priːʃɪəb(ə)l), *a.* [f. L. *appretiā-re*, in later spelling *appreciā-re* + -BLE, as if ad. L. **appretiābilis*; cf. Fr. *appréciable*.]

1. Capable of being estimated, weighed, judged of, or recognized by the mind.

1818 COLEBROOKE *Obligations* I. 37 In the performance.. of which the party stipulating has an appreciable interest. **1875** WHITNEY *Life Lang.* ii. 9 There is hardly an appreciable element of Celtic in the French language.

2. Capable of being recognized by the senses, perceptible, sensible.

1820 FARADAY *Exp. Res.* xvi. 59 This specimen has all the appreciable characters of the best Bombay wootz. **1878** HUXLEY *Physiog.* 76 A very appreciable increase of weight.

appreciably (ə'priːʃɪəblɪ), *adv.* [f. prec. + -LY[2].] To an appreciable extent, so as to be appreciated.

1859 *Lit. Ch.-man.* V. 449 We speak.. with the cheerfulness of those who are appreciably succeeding. **1862** DANA *Man. Geol.* 653 The tidal waves.. become appreciably translation or propelling waves on soundings. **1871** B. STEWART *Heat* §13 The former will not be appreciably changed in temperature.

appreciant (ə'priːʃɪənt), *a. rare*[−1]. [a. mod.Fr. *appréciant*, pr. pple. of *apprécier*, ad. L. *appretiāre*: see next.] Appreciating, appreciative.

1829 SOUTHEY *Colloq.* Ded. Wks. III. 173 The man whom Henry, of desert Appreciant alway, chose for highest trust.

appreciate (ə'priːʃɪeɪt), *v.* Also 8–9 **appretiate.** [f. L. *appretiāt-* ppl. stem of *appretiā-re* to set a price to, appraise, f. *ap-*, *ad-*, to + *preti-um* price. Cf. Fr. *apprécier* (15th c. in Godef.). The literal sense of the Fr. is supplied by APPRAISE, APPRIZE. In Eng., as in Fr., the med.L. spelling *appreciāre* has been followed. Neither this verb nor any derivative is in Johnson; but see sense 3.]

1. *trans.* To make or form an estimate of worth, quality, or amount.

1769 BURKE *Pres. St. Nat.* Wks. II. 59 Let us calmly.. appreciate those dreadful and deformed gorgons and hydras. **1817** W. TAYLOR in *Month. Rev.* LXXXIII. 458 The extreme want of candour.. with which Priestley appretiated Hume. **1818** ACCUM *Chem. Tests* 496 The weight of the gold is to be appreciated. **1837** SIR W. HAMILTON *Metaph.* ii. (1877) I. 22 It was the bias of antiquity.. to appreciate all knowledge principally by the higher standard.

2. To estimate aright, to perceive the full force of.

1798 FERRIAR *Illustr. Sterne* iv. 124 The physiological reader only can appreciate the profound sagacity of this conclusion. **1842** ALISON *Hist. Eur.* lvii. §43 IX. 41 Napoleon.. instantly appreciating the magnitude of the danger. **1875** GRINDON *Life* xiii. 167 Until the truth of any thing.. be appreciated, its error, if any, cannot be detected.

b. *esp.* To be sensitive to, or sensible of, any delicate impression or distinction.

1833 BREWSTER *Nat. Magic* ii. 32 The retina has not appreciated the influence of the simple red rays. **1862** F. HALL *Hindu Philos. Syst.* 236 In like manner, a blind man is able to appreciate sound, touch, etc., but not colours. **1879** PRESCOTT *Sp. Telephone* 7 If the number of vibrations exceeds forty thousand per second, the ear becomes incapable of appreciating the sound.

3. To esteem adequately or highly; to recognize as valuable or excellent; to find worth or excellence in.

1655 [See APPRECIATING.] **1742** BAILEY, *Appretiate*, to set an high Price, Value, or Esteem upon anything. **1795** *Fragm. Pol. & Hist.* I. 230 Your labours will not be fully known and appreciated till the succeeding generation. **1858** GLADSTONE *Homer* I. 25 The mental culture necessary in order to appreciate Homer. **1858** HAWTHORNE *Fr. & It. Jrnls.* I. 171 It requires a finer taste than mine to appreciate him.

4. To raise in value; opposed to *depreciate*. (This and the following sense have been long in use in U.S.)

1779 P. WEBSTER *Pol. Ess.* (1791) 33 Any probable attempt to raise or appreciate the value of the money. **1880** R. MACKENZIE in *19th Cent.* 207 Rents have been unduly appreciated. **1881** H. H. GIBBS *Double Standard* Pref. 9 The resumption of specie payments in Gold, thus appreciating that metal.

5. *intr.* To rise in value.

1789–96 MORSE *Amer. Geog.* I. 323 A great demand for specie and bills, which occasioned the latter.. to appreciate. **1882** P. TIDMAN *Gold & Silv. Money* 85 Gold has been steadily appreciating in value.

a'ppreciated, *ppl. a.* [f. prec. + -ED.] **a.** Adequately valued. **b.** Enhanced in exchangeable value.

1881 H. H. GIBBS *Double Standard* 32 The more remediable evils of depreciated Silver, or appreciated Gold.

a'ppreciating, *ppl. a.* [f. APPRECIATE + -ING[2].] That appreciates or values.

1655 GURNALL *Chr. in Arm.* xi. §2 (1669) 273/1 Show what appreciating thoughts thou hast of that blissful state. *Mod.* Appreciating friends recommended its publication.

a'ppreciatingly, *adv.* [f. prec. + -LY[2].] In an appreciating manner; with appreciation.

1870 *Daily News* 7 May 5/5 Who love pictures warmly and appreciatingly for their own sake. **1881** SHAIRP in *Academy* 29 Jan. 74/1 The editor discourses, if not tenderly yet.. appreciatingly, of Cowper.

appreciation (əpriːʃɪ'eɪʃən). Also 7–9 **appretiation.** [Found once *c* 1400; then not till 17th c. Both in early and mod. use prob. a. Fr. *appréciation*, n. of action f. *apprécier*, ad. L. *appretiāre*: see APPRECIATE and -TION.]

1. The action of setting a money value upon; valuation, appraisement. *rare.*

1799 J. ROBERTSON *Agric. Perth* 83 To take the sheep-stock off the outgoing tenant's hands by appreciation of arbiters.

2. a. The action of estimating qualities or things; deliberate judgement.

1604 PLAYFERE *Serm. bef. Prince Hen.* 57 (L.) According to a man's appretiation, and according to his intention. **1864** G. MASSON in *N. & Q.* 411 He is.. very severe in his appreciation of Buchanan. **1880** MCCARTHY *Own Time* IV. lxvi. 500 Entirely mistaken in his appreciation of the condition of things.

b. An expression (in speech or writing) of one's estimate of something: often implying a favourable estimate (cf. 4).

1858 M. PATTISON *Essays* (1889) II. xix. 344 In the last page he has written, in his small and fine hand, a short appreciation of the book and its author. **1889** PATER (*title*) Appreciations, with an essay on style. **1907** J. A. HAMMERTON (*title*) Stevensoniana: an anecdotal life and appreciation of R. L. Stevenson.

3. Perception, recognition, intelligent notice; *esp.* perception of delicate impressions or distinctions.

c **1400** *Apol. Loll.* 52 Þis word for *notiþ* or *takiþ appreciacoun.* **1859** MILL *Liberty* iii. (1865) 33/1 The appreciation of means towards an acknowledged end. **1879** C. KING in *Cassell's Techn. Educ.* IV. 113/1 A much better appreciation of the intricacies of the country. *Mod.* Men differ greatly in their appreciation of varieties of vowel sound.

4. Adequate or high estimation, sympathetic recognition of excellence.

1650 FULLER *Pisgah Sight* II. xii. 259 Not the intrinsecall worth of their tears, but Gods gracious appretiation of the sincerity thereof. **1870** H. MACMILLAN *Bible Teach.* xii. 246 An eye and mind that have no appreciation of scenery.

5. Rise in exchangeable value; cf. APPRECIATE 4.

1789–96 MORSE *Amer. Geog.* I. 323 Considered rather as an appreciation of Gold and Silver than a depreciation of paper. **1883** GOSCHEN in *Times* 20 Feb. 7 A considerable appreciation in the value of gold.

appreciative (ə'priːʃɪətɪv), *a.* [f. L. *appretiāt-* ppl. stem of *appretiāre* + -IVE. Cf. mod.Fr. *appréciatif, -ive.*] Showing appreciation: having the quality of forming an adequate estimate, of recognizing the good points in an object, or of being sensitive to delicate impressions. Const. *of.*

a **1698** J. FRASER *Mem.* (1738) vii. 239 Tho' in my sensitive Faculty I find not these Impressions of Joy and Fear, yet do I find them in my estimative appretiative Faculty. **1850** LYNCH *Theoph. Trin.* v. 84 Kindly appreciative words. **1867** DICKENS *Lett.* (1880) II. 313 A very quiet audience.. appreciative but not demonstrative. **1879** CHURCH in *Cassell's Techn. Educ.* I. 247/1 The eye has become less appreciative of red, and more appreciative of the other colours. **1943** H. READ *Polit. of Unpolit.* xii. 134 Developing the creative and appreciative exercise of the aesthetic impulse in the child.

a'ppreciatively, *adv.* [f. prec. + -LY[2].] In an appreciative manner: with estimation of comparative value; discriminatingly; with sympathetic recognition of excellence.

1656 HOBBES *Liberty, etc.* (1841) 315 Yet appreciatively in the estimation of judgment, he accounts the offence of God a greater evil than any temporal loss. **1656** JEANES *Mixt. Schol. Div.* 13 Appretiatively, preferring him, and his will, before all other things. **1879** T. ESCOTT *Eng.* I. 166 Slowly, lovingly, and appreciatively acquired, not purchased ready-made.

a'ppreciativeness. [f. as prec. + -NESS.] The quality of being appreciative; the habit of recognizing excellence.

1862 *Fraser's Mag.* July 12 A liberality of judgment and an appreciativeness of taste. **1881** *Daily News* 7 Nov. 3/3 The thorough appreciativeness of the crowded audience.

appreciator (ə'priːʃɪeɪtə(r)). [n. of agent (on L. analogy) f. *appretiāre*: see APPRECIATE. Cf. mod.Fr. *appréciateur.*] One who appreciates or forms an adequate estimate.

1842 DE QUINCEY *Philos. Herodot.* Wks. IX. 208 A discovery for which there was no permanent appreciator. **1849** MILL *Ess.* (1859) II. 358 An incapable appreciator of the situation and its exigency.

appreciatorily (ə'priːʃɪəˌtərɪlɪ), *adv.* [f. next + -LY[2].] In an appreciatory manner; appreciatively.

appreciatory (ə'priːʃɪətərɪ), *a.* [f. APPRECIATOR: see -ORY.] Of or befitting an appreciator; appreciative.

1819 W. TAYLOR in *Month. Rev.* LXXXIX. 36 That appretiatory criticism which scrupulously weighs the evidence adduced. **1861** GEO. ELIOT *Silas M.* 68 Mr. Macey.. paused, in the expectation of some appreciatory reply.

appredicate (æ'prɛdɪkeɪt). [ad. mod.L. *appraedicātum* (= Gr. προσκατηγορούμενον): see AP- *pref.*[1] and PREDICATE.] An addition to the predicate: (see quot.)

1837–8 SIR W. HAMILTON *Logic* xiii. I. 228 By Aristotle, the predicate includes the *Copula*; and.. the latter has, by subsequent Greek logicians, been styled the *appredicate*.

apprefe, variant of APPROOF, *Obs.*, proof.

apprehend (æprɪ'hɛnd), *v.* [a. Fr. *appréhende-r* (15th c. in Godef.), ad. L. *app-*, *adprehend-ĕre* to lay hold of, seize, f. *ad* to + *prehend-ĕre* to seize. In the contracted form *apprend-ĕre*, the word survived in the Romance langs. in the fig. sense 'lay hold with the mind, comprehend, learn,' whence also later 'teach, inform': cf. Fr. *apprendre*, and Eng. APPRISE. Subsequently, the full *apprehend-ĕre* was taken into Fr. and Eng. in its orig. form and sense. APPREND is occas. in 16–17th c.]

I. Physical.

†**1.** To lay hold upon, seize, with hands, teeth, etc. Also said of fire, and *fig.* of trembling, fear, etc. *Obs.* or *arch.*

1572 BOSSEWELL *Armorie* III. 5 A great quakyng and tremblyng dyd apprehende hys hande. **1607** TOPSELL *Four-f. Beasts* 124 His dogs.. apprehending the garments of passengers. **1613** *Life William I.* in *Harl. Misc.* (1793) 28 A fire began.. which apprehending certain shops and warehouses, etc. *c* **1643** *Maximes Unf.* 8 Fury and affrightment apprehend the desperate. **1645** RUTHERFORD *Tryal & Tri. Faith* (1845) 63 A lame hand that cannot apprehend. **1843** E. JONES *Sensat. & Event* 122 While those two lips his brow did apprehend.

†**b.** *transf.* To seize upon, take down, in writing. *fig.* To seize upon (points of a subject). *Obs.*

1611 CORYAT *Crudities* 480, I apprehended it [an epitaph] with my pen while the Preacher was in his pulpit. **1615** T. ADAMS *Spir. Navig.* 24, I will only apprehend so much as may serve to exemplify this dangerous world.

2. To seize (a person) in name of law, to arrest.

1548 UDALL, etc. *Erasm. Par. John* vii. 1 (R.) To fynde sum occasion.. to attache and apprehende him. **1642** ROGERS *Naaman* 44 Paul.. going like a Pursivant.. to Damascus, to apprehend the Saints there. **1768** BLACKSTONE *Comm.* IV. 287 A justice of the peace cannot issue a warrant to apprehend a felon upon bare suspicion. **1855** MACAULAY *Hist. Eng.* III. 328 Troops had been sent to apprehend him.

†**3.** To seize upon for one's own, take possession of. Also *fig. Obs.*

1513 DOUGLAS *Æneis* XI. vii. 70 Ellis quhare.. to wend, Thayre dwelling place for ay to apprehend. **1611** BIBLE *Phil.* iii. 12 If that I may apprehend that for which also I am apprehended of Christ Iesus. **1652** NEEDHAM tr. *Selden's Mare Cl.* 21 That Vacancies are his who apprehend's them first by occupation.

†**4.** To seize or embrace (an offer or opportunity).

1586 T. B. *La Primaud. Fr. Acad.* 750 If we apprehend not that great grace and mercy of the Father offered to all. *a* **1619** DONNE *Biathan.* (1644) 126 If he apprehend not an opportunity to escape. **1633** BP. HALL *Hard Texts* 56 His faith, whereby he did firmely apprehend the.. aid of his eternal Father.

II. Mental.

†**5.** *gen.* To learn, gain practical acquaintance with. Also *absol.* (The earliest use in Eng.; cf. Fr. *apprendre.*) *Obs.*

1398 TREVISA *Barth. De P.R.* II. ii. (1495) 28 He holdeth in mynde.. without foryetynge, all that he apprehendyth. **1531** ELYOT *Governour* (1834) 215 Thereby they provoke many men to apprehend virtue. *a* **1680** BUTLER *Rem.* (1759) I. 204 Children.. Improve their nat'ral Talents without Care, And apprehend, before they are aware.

6. To become or be conscious by the senses of (any external impression).

1635 AUSTIN *Medit.* 60 When this Light shone in darkenesse, and our darkenesse, though it apprehended it, yet it comprehended it not. **1651** HOBBES *Leviath.* III. xxxiv. 212 That caused Agar supernaturally to apprehend a voice from heaven. **1855** BAIN *Sens. & Int.* III. i. §37 If I see.. two candle flames, I apprehend them as different objects.

†**7.** To feel emotionally, be sensible of, feel the force of. *Obs.*

1592 NASHE *P. Penilesse* 29 b, The.. soules of them that haue no power to apprehend such felicitie. **1605** B. JONSON *Volpone* II. i, Dead. Lord! how deeply, sir, you apprehend it. **1670** WALTON *Lives*, That [kindness] was so gratefully apprehended by M. Hooker.

8. To lay hold of with the intellect: **a.** to perceive the existence of, recognize, see.

1577 VAUTROULLIER *Luther's Ep. Gal.* 5 Who so doth not understand or apprehend this righteousness in afflictions and terrors of conscience. **1609** *C. Butler's Fem. Mon.* Ad Auth. 16 There is not half that worth in Mee Which I have apprehended in a Bee. **1743** J. MORRIS *Serm.* vii. 184 We shall apprehend reason to conclude, that.. they were not so very young. **1872** BROWNING *Fifine* lxxi. 7 Each man.. avails him of what worth He apprehends in you.

b. to catch the meaning or idea of; to understand.

1631 HEYWOOD *Lond. Jus Hon.* 279 As soone known as showne, and apprehended as read. **1755** B. MARTIN *Mag. Arts & Sc.* I. xiii. 87 This is all so plain, that I can't but apprehend it. **1849** MACAULAY *Hist. Eng.* I. 463 The nature of the long contest between the Stuarts and their parliaments, was indeed very imperfectly apprehended by foreign statesmen. **1871** C. DAVIES *Metric Syst.* II. 24 To apprehend distinctly the signification of a number, two things are necessary.

c. *absol.* or with *subord. cl.*

1599 SHAKS. *Much Ado* II. i. 84 Cousin, you apprehend passing shrewdly. **1660** STANLEY *Hist. Philos.* 46/1 Periander.. immediately apprehended that he advised him to put the most eminent in the City to death. **1712** STEELE *Spect.* No. 532 ¶2, I cannot apprehend where lyes the trifling in all this. **1785** REID *Intell. Powers* i. i, No one can explain by a Logical Definition what it is to think, to apprehend.

9. To understand (a thing *to be* so and so); to conceive, consider, view, take (it) as.

1639 FULLER *Holy War* IV. ix. (1840) 193 They apprehended it a great courtesy done unto them. **1736** WESLEY *Wks.* 1830 I. 100, I apprehended myself to be near death. **1858** GLADSTONE *Homer* III. 393 The eternal laws, such as the heroic age apprehended them.

b. *absol.* or with *subord. cl.*

1614 B. JONSON *Barth. Fair* I. iv. 8 If hee apprehend you flout him once, he will flie at you. **1775** J. LYON in Sparks *Corr. Amer. Rev.* (1853) I. 101, I apprehend that secrecy is as necessary now as ever it was. **1839** HALLAM *Hist. Lit.* IV. vi. §17 In general, I apprehend, the later French critics have given the preference to Racine.

10. To anticipate, look forward to, expect (*mostly* things adverse).

1603 SHAKS. *Meas. for M.* IV. ii. 149 A man that apprehends death no more dreadfully, but as a drunken sleepe. **1749** FIELDING *Tom Jones* (1836) I. III. iii. 100 A triumphant question, to which he had apprehended no answer. **1879** TOURGEE *Fool's Errand* ii. 11 Love had taught her with unerring accuracy to apprehend the evil which impended.

11. To anticipate with fear or dread; to be fearful concerning; to fear. **a.** with *obj.*

1606 SHAKS. *Tr. & Cr.* III. ii. 80 Oh let my Lady apprehend no feare. **1643** SIR T. BROWNE *Relig. Med.* I. §54 Which makes me much apprehend the ends of those honest Worthies. **1702** *Eng. Theophr.* 53 He apprehends every breath of air as much as if it were a Hurricane. **1832** HT. MARTINEAU *Hill & Valley* xiii. 125 No one.. could think.. that any further violence was to be apprehended.

b. with *subord. cl.* To be apprehensive, to fear.

1740–61 MRS. DELANY *Life & Corr.* (1861) III. 210, I don't apprehend that even the Bath could hurt her. **1868** HAWTHORNE *Our Old Home* (1879) 186, I sometimes apprehend that our institutions may perish.

appre'hended, *ppl. a.* [f. prec. + -ED.]

1. Taken hold of, seized; arrested.

1597 DANIEL *Civ. Wares* VI. lviii, Th' apprehended Duke.

2. Laid hold of by the mind, conceived.

1668 HOWE *Bless. Righteous* (1825) 129 Lord! whence is this apprehended inconsistency? **1880** CYPLES *Hum. Exp.* i. 17 The intellectually-apprehended Executive System.

3. Anticipated (with aversion), dreaded.

1742 RICHARDSON *Pamela* IV. 7 When the apprehended Time shall be over. **1825** SOUTHEY *Paraguay* iv. 29 On Monnema the apprehended ill Came first.

apprehender (æprɪ'hɛndə(r)). Also 7 -or. [f. as prec. + -ER[1].]

1. One who lays hold of or seizes; *esp.* one who seizes or arrests in the name of justice.

1608 CHAPMAN *Byrons Trag.* Plays II. 282 This short sword.. which if I haue time To show my apprehendor, he, etc. **1684** CHARNOCK *Attrib. God* (1834) II. 65 How would the.. number of malefactors be greater than that of apprehenders?

2. One who lays hold with the senses or mental faculties.

a **1619** DONNE *Biathan.* (1644) 84 All these proceed from the indisposition and distempred taste of the apprehendor. **1678** CUDWORTH *Intell. Syst.* I. v. 639 Truth is bigger than our minds, and we are.. rather apprehenders than comprehenders thereof. **1862** F. HALL *Hindu Philos. Syst.* 177 By 'beholder' is meant knower, or apprehender.

appre'hending, *vbl. sb.* [f. as prec. + -ING[1].] The action of the vb. APPREHEND; APPREHENSION, esp. in senses 3, 7, 12.

1398 TREVISA *Barth. De P.R.* III. ix, The vertu of apprehendynge [L. *apprehensiva potentia*], þat is maner knowynge, is departid a tweyne. **1553–87** FOXE *A. & M.* III. 321 Going from place to place, to avoid the peril of apprehending. **1581** SIDNEY *Astrophel* lxvi, Quick apprehending.. Of euerie image which may comfort show. **1855** MACAULAY *Hist. Eng.* III. 508 To issue a proclamation for the apprehending of Ludlow. **1880** CYPLES *Hum. Exp.* ii. 40 Experience includes the apprehending of a regulative order, &c.

appre'hending, *ppl. a.* [f. as prec. + -ING[2].] That apprehends; understanding, perceptive.

1656 RIDGLEY *Pract. Physic* 206 Imagination.. is an apprehending power. **1823** LAMB *Elia* Ser. II. xviii. (1865) 359 Newly-apprehending gratitude at second life bestowed.

appre'hendingly, *adv. rare.* [f. prec. + -LY[2].] By apprehending or laying hold.

1581 NOWELL & DAY in *Confer.* I. (1584) E iiij, Faith doeth iustifie apprehendingly, workes doe iustifie declaringly.

apprehensibility (æprɪˌhɛnsɪ'bɪlɪtɪ). [f. next: see -BILITY.] The quality of being apprehensible.

1827 DE QUINCEY *Lessing* Wks. XIII. 287 Clothed in a form of sensuous apprehensibility. **1875** WHITNEY *Life Lang.* i. 6 Simplicity and popular apprehensibility will be everywhere aimed at.

apprehensible (æprɪ'hɛnsɪb(ə)l), *a.* [ad. L. *apprehensibil-is* (Tertull.), f. *apprehens-* ppl. stem of *apprehend-ĕre*: see APPREHEND and -BLE. Cf. mod.Fr. *appréhensible.*] Capable of being apprehended or grasped by the senses or intellect; liable to be felt emotionally (*obs.*) Const. *by*, *to*.

a **1631** DONNE *Select.* (1840) 181 It is apprehensible by sense. **1632** SIR T. HAWKINS *Unhappy Prosp.* 95 Who wept not for himselfe; for an object so sad and apprehensible as this could not bend his gravity. *a* **1716** SOUTH *12 Serm.* (1717) IV. 318 Discoursing of the Nature.. of God in a language neither warrantable nor apprehensible. **1841** DE QUINCEY *Rhet.* (1860) 358 Apprehensible even to the uninstructed. **1855** MILMAN *Lat. Chr.* (1864) II. III. vii. 151 A world of invisible beings.. assuming forms, uttering tones, distilling odours, apprehensible by the soul of man.

appre'hensibly, *adv. rare.* [f. prec. + -LY[2].] In an apprehensible manner; so as to be apprehended or laid hold of.

1672 SIR T. BROWNE *Let. to Friend* vii. (1881) 131 The dead and deep part of the night, when Nox might be most apprehensibly said to be the daughter of Chaos. *Mod.* The two notions are not apprehensibly distinct.

apprehension (æprɪ'hɛnʃən). [ad. (? through Fr. *appréhension*, 15th c. in Littré) L. *apprehensiōn-em*, n. of action f. *apprehend-ĕre* to seize upon: see APPREHEND and -ION[1].] *gen.* The action of seizing upon, seizure, grasp. As in other adopted words, employed in the mental before the physical senses, for which native Eng. and OFr. words were in use.

I. Physical.

1. The action of laying hold of or seizing (physically); prehension, grasping. *rare.*

1646 SIR T. BROWNE *Pseud. Ep.* (J.) [A lobster's claw is] a part of apprehension whereby they seize upon their prey. **1835** SOUTHW. SMITH *Philos. Health* I. v. 262 The superior extremities [of the body] are organs of apprehension.

2. *Law.* The action of taking manual possession.

1832 AUSTIN *Jurispr.* (1879) II. lvi. 928 The absolute property *rei singulæ* cannot be acquired commonly without an apprehension or a taking possession of the thing by the acquirer. **1875** POSTE *Gaius* II. 203 Either constructive delivery (*traditio*) or apprehension (*perceptio*).

3. The seizure of a person, a ship, etc., in the name of justice or authority; arrest. Const. *subjective gen.* of the actor, *objective gen.* of the person arrested, the latter being more frequent: 'The king's apprehension of Pym,' 'Pym's apprehension by the king.'

1577 HARRISON *Eng.* I. II. iv. 103 If they be taken the third time and have not since their second apprehension applied themselves to labour. **1614** SIR R. DUDLEY in *Fortesc. Pap.* 6 Your answer tuiching his Majestys aprehension of the forcible vessell. **1881** *Chamb. Jrnl.* No. 916. 457 A warrant for his apprehension was obtained.

II. Mental.

†**4.** *gen.* The action of learning, the laying hold or acquirement of knowledge. *Obs.*

1398 TREVISA *Barth. De P.R.* V. vi. (1495) 111 Meane moeuynge of the eye is to be praysed, for it sygnefyeth easy apprehensyon. **1641** WILKINS *Math. Magick* I. i. 3 The ancient Philosophers esteemed it a great part of wisdome to conceale their learning from vulgar apprehension or use.

5. The action of laying hold of with the senses; conscious perception. *arch.*

1590 SHAKS. *Mids. N.* III. ii. 178 Dark night, that from the eye his function takes, The eare more quicke of apprehension makes. **1635** AUSTIN *Medit.* 9 She [the Virgin] had a corporall, as well as a mental apprehension of the Messenger. **1732** LAW *Serious Call* xi. 177 Invisible to his Eyes, being too glorious for the apprehension of flesh and blood.

†**6.** The action of 'feeling' anything emotionally; sensitiveness or sensibility to; sympathetic perception. *Obs. rare.*

1605 BACON *Adv. Learn.* I. iii. §6 [They] have not their thoughts established.. in the love and apprehension of duty. **1612** T. TAYLOR *Comm. Titus* i. 15 If men did consciously and in right apprehension of Gods goodnes blesse their meate. **1644** HEYLIN *Laud* I. 206 The Queen.. out of a deep apprehension of that lamentable accident, forthwith directed, etc.

7. The action of grasping with the intellect; the forming of an idea; conception; intellection.

1597 J. PAYNE *Royal Exch.* 25 Better.. ys a short and diligent readinge.. then to turn manie leaves with small regard and less apprehention. *a* **1680** GLANVILL (J.) Simple apprehension denotes no more than the soul's naked intellection of an object. **1751** JOHNSON *Rambl.* 177 ¶3 My quickness of apprehension, and celerity of reply. **1866** DK. ARGYLL *Reign of Law* ii. 110 A clear apprehension of this Abstract Idea was necessary to a right understanding. **1870** BOWEN *Logic* i. 28 Simple Apprehension corresponds very nearly to that sort of thinking which we now call Conception.

8. The apprehensive faculty; ability to understand; understanding.

1570 DEE *Math. Præf.* 4 So.. dull is our apprehension. **1607** DEKKER *Westw. Hoe* III. i, O the quick apprehension of women. **1636** HEYWOOD *Love's Mistr.* Pref., It was above my apprehension to conceive. **1851** HAWTHORNE *Snow Image* (1879) 214 How forcibly the lapse of time.. came home to my apprehension.

9. The product of grasping with the mind; a conception or idea; *also*, the abiding result of such conception; a view, notion, or opinion entertained upon any subject.

1579 TOMSON *Calvin's Serm. Tim.* 763/2 We haue no apprehension of yᵉ heauenly life, when we are thus tyed to this world. **1670** BAXTER *Cure Ch.-Div.* 19 Fix not too rashly upon your first apprehensions. **1758** JOHNSON *Idler* No. 10 ¶4 Which according to vulgar apprehension swept away his legs. **1774** REID *Aristot. Log.* ii. §1 The first part of logic treats of simple apprehensions and of terms. **1871** R. W. DALE *Ten Command.* Introd. 11 We must obey the moral law to have a true apprehension of it.

†**10.** The conception or idea expressed by a word; meaning, sense. *Obs. rare.*

1615 T. ADAMS *Leaven* 102 'The kingdom of Heaven'.. hath a diverse sense and apprehension in the Scriptures. **1646** SIR T. BROWNE *Pseud. Ep.* 15 Other wayes there are of deceit which consist not in false apprehension of words.

11. The representation to oneself of what is still future; anticipation; *chiefly* of things adverse.

1603 SHAKS. *Meas. for M.* III. i. 78 The sence of death is most in apprehension. **1693** OWEN *Holy Spirit* 12 Sorrow had filled their Hearts upon the Apprehension of his Departure. **1719** WATERLAND *Vind. Christ's Div.* Pref. A ij, The following Queries were drawn up.. when I had not the least apprehension of their appearing in print. **1853** KANE *Grinnell Exp.* xxxix. (1856) 358 Leaving us to the thaws of summer and the stormy winds of September before our imprisonment ceases. The apprehension has no mirth in it.

12. Fear as to what may happen; dread.

1648 SANDERSON *21 Serm.* Ad Aul. xvi. (1673) 227 The bare fears of such things and apprehensions of their approach. **1709** *Tatler* No. 108 ¶1, I.. looked about with some Apprehension.. for Fear any Foreigner should be present. **1825** T. JEFFERSON *Autobiog.* Wks. 1859 I. 67 Their representatives at Paris expressed apprehensions that France would interfere. **1836** MACGILLIVRAY *Humboldt's Trav.* xviii. 263 Not without apprehension of being bitten by serpents.

apprehensive (æprɪ'hɛnsɪv), *a.* [ad. med.L. *apprehensīv-us*, f. *apprehens-*, ppl. stem of *apprehendĕre*: see APPREHEND and -IVE. Cf. Fr. *appréhensif*, *-ive.*] Characterized by apprehension; habitually apprehending.

†**1.** In the habit of seizing, ready to seize or embrace (an offer or opportunity). *Obs.*

1620 SANDERSON *Serm.* Ad Pop. i. (1674) 136 So apprehensive of but an outward enforced semblance of contrition from the hands of an Hypocrite. *a* **1641** LD. STRAFFORD (O.) I shall be very apprehensive of any occasions wherein I may do any kind offices.

2. Pertaining to, or fitted for, the laying hold of sensuous or mental impressions.

1398 TREVISA *Barth. De P.R.* III. vi. (1495) 53 All the wyttes come of the vertue Racional and apprehensiue. **1589** PUTTENHAM *Eng. Poesie* (Arb.) 268 Illfauorednesse or disproportion to the partes apprehensiue, as.. when a sound is either too loude or too low. **1671** MILTON *Samson* 623 Thoughts, my tormentors, armed with deadly stings, Mangle my apprehensive tenderest parts. **1862** F. HALL *Hindu Philos. Syst.* 88 When the apprehensive faculties of the soul are in their full vigour.

3. Of mental faculties and their operations: Showing apprehension or grasp of a subject; intelligent, discerning, quick.

1621 BURTON *Anat. Mel.* I. ii. III. i, If the Imagination be very apprehensive, intent, and violent. **1785** COWPER *Task* VI. 612 In some [animals] are found Such teachable and apprehensive parts. **1863** MRS. C. CLARKE *Shaks. Char.* x. 258 The reasons he gives.. are neat, apprehensive, and witty. **1874** J. H. NEWMAN *Gerontius* 20 A sense so apprehensive and discriminant.

4. Of intelligent beings: In the habit or capable of grasping with the mind, perceptive; *hence*, quick to learn, intelligent, 'sharp.' Const. *of*.

1601 SHAKS. *Jul. C.* III. i. 67 And Men are Flesh and Blood, and apprehensiue. **1627** *Lisander & Cal.* IV. 63 Those who are apprehensive of love. **1636** HEYWOOD *Challenge* III. i, My daughter is an apt, and wittie lasse: I know her apprehensive, and well-brayn'd. **1670** MILTON *Hist. Eng.* II. (1851) 84 More fond of Miracles, than apprehensive of Truth. **1697** EVELYN *Numism.* ix. 295 Spaniels.. docile and apprehensive. **1868** BROWNING *Ring & Bk.* III. VIII. 1500 The lower phrase that suits the sense O' the limitedly apprehensive.

5. Having an apprehension or notion; understanding, realizing, conscious, sensible. Const. *of* or *subord. cl. arch.*

1611 SPEED *Hist. Gt. Brit.* IX. vii. 70 The King apprehensiue of his Lords, called his Lords. **1683** *Lond. Gaz.* mdcccxlix/2 We are deeply apprehensive of the Confluences of Blessings, which.. we enjoy. **1764** HARMER *Observ.* XI. iii. 104, I am apprehensive that this is an additional proof of the requisiteness of attending to the customs of the East when we would explain the Scriptures. **1843** J. H. NEWMAN *Miracles* 58 Miracles..wrought..by instruments but partially apprehensive that they are such.

6. Anticipative of something adverse; fearful of what may be about to happen. (Now the most usual sense.) **a.** *simply*.

1718 POPE *Iliad* XIII. 812 From death he flies, And turns around his apprehensive eyes. **1742** RICHARDSON *Pamela* III. 418, I am a sad weak, apprehensive Body; to be sure I am! **1837** CARLYLE *Fr. Rev.* III. v. vi. (1857) II. 311 Though physically of a timid apprehensive nature.

b. with *of*.

1633 T. ADAMS *Exp. 2 Pet.* ii. 22 Swine are naturally apprehensive of wind and weather, by an ingrafted knowledge; and run crying home before the storm. **1768** H. WALPOLE *Hist. Doubts* 107 Noah's niece, being apprehensive of the deluge, set out for Ireland. **1848** C. BRONTË *Jane Eyre* v. (1873) 37 Mortally apprehensive of some one coming in and kidnapping me.

c. with *subord. cl.*

1704 SWIFT *T. Tub* Apol., Wks. 1778 I. 202 Being apprehensive it might spoil the sale of the book. **1756** BURKE *Subl. & B.* Wks. I. 224, I am apprehensive that experience was not sufficiently consulted. **1802** *Gentl. Mag.* Mar. 282/1 He was apprehensive an operation would be necessary.

d. the source *from* which apprehensions come, or the object *for* whose safety they are entertained, may be expressed.

1665 BOYLE *Occas. Refl.* II. xv. (1675) 142 Why should I be more apprehensive for my Body than my Mind. **1791** BURKE *Nat. Assembly* Wks. VI. 41 More apprehensive from his servants..than from the hired blood-thirsty mob without. **1836** MACGILLIVRAY *Humboldt's Trav.* xvii. 220 They became apprehensive for the safety of their canoe.

†**7.** Capable of being apprehended, apprehensible; intelligible. *Obs. rare.*

1692 DRYDEN *St. Euremont's Ess.* 176 Who cannot suffer that things should be rendred apprehensive to Idle Persons, which he has learned amongst the Ancients with pains.

appre'hensively, *adv.* [f. prec. + -LY^{2}.] In an apprehensive manner; with apprehension.

†**1.** By laying hold. *Obs.*

1656 TRAPP *Exp. Rom.* iii. 29 Men are said to be justified ..apprehensively by faith.

2. With anticipation, esp. of danger; with fear as to what may be coming.

1753 RICHARDSON *Grandison* (1810) VI. xxxii. 236 What think you..made me write so apprehensively? **1828** SOUTHEY *To A. Cunningham* Wks. III. 315 The face Composed and apprehensively intent Upon the necessary operation About to be perform'd.

†**3.** So as to be apprehended, intelligibly. *Obs.*

1692 DRYDEN *St. Euremont's Ess.* 14 The Quality considered in it self, to speak apprehensively, was very savage.

appre'hensiveness. [f. as prec. + -NESS.]

1. Aptness to apprehend; intelligence, perceptiveness, discernment.

a **1639** *Reliq. Wotton.* 81 We shall often mark in it [the eye] a dulness, or apprehensiveness, even before the understanding. **1702** S. P[ARKER] *Tully's De Fin.* 144 The Winged World make frequent Discoveries of their Apprehensiveness and Memory. **1805** WORDSW. *Prel.* VIII. (1851) 190 Yet knowledge came..In fits of kindliest apprehensiveness, From all sides.

2. The habit of anticipating things adverse; fearfulness as to what may be coming.

1748 RICHARDSON *Clarissa* (1811) IV. 243 So much apprehensiveness that her fears are aforehand with her dangers. **1860** WINDSOR *Ethica* vii. 399 Nervous anxiety and ..exaggerated apprehensiveness.

†**a'pprend**, *v. Obs. rare.* [a. Fr. *append-re* or L. *append-ĕre*, contr. of *apprehend-ĕre*: see APPREHEND.] To seize; to lay hold of with the mind.

1567 DRANT *Horace Epist.* I. xi, Apprende with greatfull hande eche hower that god hath lente the here. **1642** H. MORE *Song of Soul* III. II. xxviii., The soul..Oretakes each outgone beam; apprends it by advertence.

†**a'pprension.** *Obs. rare*$^{-1}$. [contr. var. of APPREHENSION. Cf. next.]

1586 T. B. *La Primaud. Fr. Acad.* (1589) 182 Mad men, who have alwaies before their eies those Ideas and shapes which worke the apprension of their furie.

†**a'pprensive**, *a. Obs. rare*$^{-1}$. [contr. var. of APPREHENSIVE: cf. L. *apprensus* for *apprehensus*.]

1689 BURNET *Tracts* I. 63 Of the importance of which they are now very apprensive.

apprentice (ə'prɛntɪs), *sb.* and *a.* Forms: 4–5 **aprentys, apprentys**, 6 **apprentise**, 5– **apprentice**. [a. OF. *aprentis*, nom. of *aprentif*, f. *aprendre* to learn (see APPREHEND), 3rd sing. *aprent*, by form-assoc. with words in *-tis*, *-tif*:—L. *-tīvus*, *-tīvum*: see -IVE. (Mod.F. takes *apprentis* as pl. with sing. *apprenti*.) Cf. APPENTICE. The aphetic PRENTICE appears in Eng. as early as the full word, and was for several centuries the more usual form.]

A. *sb.* **1.** A learner of a craft; one who is bound by legal agreement to serve an employer in the exercise of some handicraft, art, trade, or profession, for a certain number of years, with a view to learn its details and duties, in which the employer is reciprocally bound to instruct him.

1362 LANGL. *P. Pl.* A. II. 190 Apparayleden him as a prentis. *Ibid.* III. 218 Alle kunne craftes men· craueþ Meede for heore prentys [**1393** for here aprentys]. **1551** T. WILSON *Logic* 26 To make servaunts and apprentices free. **1660** R. COKE *Power & Subj.* 5 His duller child he binds an apprentice to some trade. **1756** C. LUCAS *Ess. Waters* III. 299 A fact known to the apprentices of apothecaries. **1863** MARY HOWITT *F. Bremer's Greece* I. i. 11 Poor boys, of good families, will often take service as apprentices.

†**2.** A barrister-at-law of less than 16 years' standing. *Obs.* exc. *Hist.*

c **1375** WYCLIF *Wks.* 1869 I. 382 Boþe aprentis and avocatis. **1377** LANGL. *P. Pl.* B. XIX. 226 Prechoures & prestes & prentyces of lawe. **1628** COKE *On Litt.* 303 a, In ancient time the Serieants and Apprentices of Law did draw their owne pleadings. **1768** BLACKSTONE *Comm.* I. 23 Barristers (first stiled apprentices)..who answered to our bachelors. **1863** COX *Inst. Eng. Govt.* II. iii. 373 In the time of Edward IV apprentices were a class distinct from the serjeants.

3. By extension: One who is only learning the rudiments; an unskilled novice, a tyro.

1489 CAXTON *Faytes of Armes* I. xvi. 47 Noo prentiz..in puttyng his oost in fayre ordenance. **1639** FULLER *Holy War* IV. xxvii. (1840) 228 As yet they were apprentices to piracy. **1863** MRS. C. CLARKE *Shaks. Char.* xv. 377 A mere apprentice in treason.

B. *adj.* or *attrib.* [in quot. 1400, a. OFr. *aprentis* adj. 'ignorant, qui a besoin d'apprendre,' Godef.; in later quots., attrib. use of the Eng. sb.; cf. a *master builder*, a *master mind*.]

c **1400** *Rom. Rose* 687 These briddis, that nought unkunnyng Were of her craft, & apprentys [*v.r.* a prentise]. **1666** PEPYS *Diary* (1879) IV. 72 She was not a 'prentice girl, to ask leave every time she goes abroad. **1794** BURNS *Wks.* III. 284 Her prentice han' she tried on man, An' then she made the lasses, O. **1831** BREWSTER *Newton* (1855) II. xvi. 105 He tried his apprentice hand on an inferior institution.

apprentice (ə'prɛntɪs), *v.* Also in 7 -ize. [f. prec. sb.] To bind as an apprentice; to indenture.

1631 T. POWELL *Tom All Trades* 144 To be apprentized betimes. **1769** BURKE *Pres. St. Nat.* Wks. II. 109 When they are apprenticed, this provision will cease. **1882** BLADES *Caxton* 5 In 1438 Caxton was apprenticed to Robert Large.

†**a'pprenticeage.** *Obs.* Also -isage, -issage. [a. Fr. *apprentissage*: see APPRENTICE *sb.* and -AGE.] Apprenticeship; time wherein to learn or acquire experience. Often *fig.*

1592 BACON *Observ. Libel* (T.) To be utterly without apprentisage of war. **1621** DONNE *Serm.* cxvii. V. 73 Seven years apprenticeage which your occupations cost you. **1678** YOUNG *Serm. Whitehall* 29 Dec. 22 Christianity is our Profession, and Life is our Apprentisage.

apprenticed (ə'prɛntɪst), *ppl. a.* [f. APPRENTICE *v.* + -ED.] Bound as an apprentice; bound in covenanted service.

1639 FORD *Lady's Trial* I. i. (R.) Now appears the object Of my apprentic'd heart. **1732** POPE *Mor. Ess.* III. 267 Him portion'd maids, apprentic'd orphans, blest.

†**a'pprenticehood.** *Obs.* [f. APPRENTICE *sb.* + -HOOD.] = APPRENTICESHIP.

1377 LANGL. *P. Pl.* B. v. 256 And haue ymade many a knyȝte · bothe mercere & drapere, þat payed neuere for his prentishode. **1417** *York Girdlers Ord.*, Yat nan apprentice efter yᵉ tyme of apprenticehed wyrk any werk..prively. **1593** SHAKS. *Rich. II*, I. iii. 271 Must I not serve a long apprenticehood? **1619** J. HEATH *House Correct.* D iij b, Who in his apprenticehood, being brought up to the Art of Poleing, is now made free of the Shavers.

apprenticement (ə'prɛntɪsmənt). *rare.* [f. APPRENTICE *v.* + -MENT.] An apprenticing; apprenticeship.

1823 LAMB *Elia* (1860) 173 The premature apprenticements of these tender victims. **1848** *Blackw. Mag.* LXIV. 487 Seven centuries of painful apprenticement.

apprenticeship (ə'prɛntɪsʃɪp). Also 6–7 **apprentiship(pe.** [f. APPRENTICE *sb.* + -SHIP; superseding APPRENTICEHOOD.]

1. The position of an apprentice; service in the capacity of an apprentice; initiatory training, under legal agreement, in a trade, etc.; *esp.* in the phr. *to serve apprenticeship.*

1612 WOODALL *Surg. Mate* Wks. 1653 Pref. 18 Holding them in more base subjection then their masters ever did in their apprentiship. **1776** ADAM SMITH *W.N.* I. I. x. 106 During the continuance of the apprenticeship the whole labour of the apprentice belongs to the master. **1855** MACAULAY *Hist. Eng.* III. 625 Prince George..was serving his apprenticeship in the military art.

2. *transf.* or *fig.*

1592 GREENE *Disput.* 22 Such as onely ayme at your faire lookes, tye but their loues to an apprentishippe of beauty. **1638** BAKER *Balzac's Lett.* II. (1654) 46 On whose banks the Romans have performed the Apprentiships of their rare victories. **1862** MAX MÜLLER *Chips* (1880) I. v. 118 Men who have passed through a regular apprenticeship in Sanskrit grammar.

3. The period for which an apprentice is bound.

a **1667** COWLEY *Liberty* Wks. 1710 II. 677 This is but a short Apprenticeship, after which we are made free of a Royal Company. **1758** JOHNSON *Idler* No. 47 ¶2 Three months after the expiration of his apprenticeship. **1826** DISRAELI *Viv. Grey* v. x. 218 That long apprenticeship of sorrow.

4. *Hence*: A period of seven years.

1780 MRS. DELANY *Corr.* Ser. II. II. 506 Two apprenticeships have past since my dearest Mrs. Dewes celebrated her birth-day here. *a* **1845** HOOD *Sniffing a Birthd.* i, Three 'prenticeships have past away..Since I was bound to life.

a'pprenticing, *vbl. sb.* [f. APPRENTICE *v.* + -ING^{1}.] The action of binding as apprentice.

1870 *Daily News* 12 Dec., The apprenticing of parish boys.

apprentis, -age, obs. f. APPRENTICE, -AGE.

appress (æ'prɛs), *v.* [f. L. *appress-* ppl. stem of *apprimĕre*, f. *ap-* = *ad-* to + *premĕre* to press.] To press close to each other, or to a surface, *e.g.* leaves to the stem; = ADPRESS. Hence **appressed** *ppl. a.*

1791 E. DARWIN *Bot. Gard.* II. 25 *note*, During the night the upper..surfaces of the leaves are appressed together. **1845** LINDLEY *Sch. Bot.* vii. (1858) 126 Leaves..obtuse, appressed, convex. **1870** ROLLESTON *Anim. Life* 258 Has its lips so closely appressed as to make the aperture invisible.

appress, obs. form of OPPRESS.

appressorium (æprɛ'sɔərɪəm). *Bot.* Pl. -ia. [mod.L., f. L. *appress-*, ppl. stem of *apprimĕre*, f. *ad* AD- + *premĕre* to press: see -ORIUM.] The organ by which certain fungi attach themselves to their hosts.

1897 W. G. SMITH tr. *Tubeuf's Diseases Plants Cryptogr. Parasites* I. i. 10 The mycelium retains its hold by adhesion-discs or appressoria, and from certain parts of these a fine thread-like process is given off. **1902** *Encycl. Brit.* XXVIII. 555/1 Appressoria are also formed by some parasitic Fungi, as a minute flattening of the top of a very short branch..or the swollen end of any hypha which comes in contact with ..the host. **1937** GWYNNE-VAUGHAN & BARNES *Struct. & Devel. Fungi* (ed. 2) 187 An external disc or appressorium, from which,..the haustorium proper arises and pushes into the epidermal cell.

†**a'pprest**, *Obs.* [a. Fr. *appreste* (mod. *apprêt*), OFr. *apreste*, f. *aprester* to make ready, f. *à* to + *prest* (mod. *prêt*):—L. *præstus* ready.]

1. Preparation, provision.

1539 *State Papers Hen. VIII*, I. 594 There is no apprest of any ships in Spayne. **1570** HOLINSHED *Scot. Chron.* (1806) I. 408 The Christian princes..made their apprests for a new expedition.

2. Pecuniary provision; loan. (Cf. F. *prester*, *prêter*.)

1443 HENRY IV in Ellis *Orig. Lett.* III. 34 I. 80 Easing vs by wey of apprest of the summe of c. marks.

appretiate, less usual sp. of APPRECIATE.

†**a'ppreve**, *v. Obs.* or *dial.* [ad. OF. *a(p)-preuve*, tonic stem of *aprover* (sometimes even extended to inf. *appreuver*, Godef.); the northern and, esp., Sc. equivalent of APPROVE *v.*^{1} With *approbā-*, *apreuve*, *apreve*, cf. *afforā-*, *affeure*, *affeer*, and the north. *meve* for *move*. Now obs., exc. in later pa. pple. *approven* (on analogy of *weave*, *woven*, etc.), which is regarded merely as a Sc. variant of *approved*.] = APPROVE *v.*^{1}

c **1375** WYCLIF *Wks.* (1880) 388 Eny state aprevyd of God. *c* **1400** *Destr. Troy* XIX. 8055 Hit is a propertie apreuit. **1526** *Act Jas. V* (1814) 310 (JAM.) Ratifijs and appreuis the contract and appunctuament made. **1535** STEWART *Cron. Scotl.* II. 175 Richt mony..Apprevit weill that that counsall wes gude. **1676** W. ROW *Suppl. Blair's Autobiog.* xi. (1848) 291 After some smoothings of it, it was approven. **1823** CHALMERS *Serm.* I. 146 It is approven of as having about it the solemn and suitable Characteristics of Godliness.

†**a'pprinze.** *Obs. rare*$^{-1}$. [a. OF. *aprinse*, variant of *aprise*.] Enterprise; ? seizure.

1559 *Myrr. Mag., Dk. Suffolk* vi. 5 The apprinze of Pucel Jone, In which attempte my travayle was not smal.

†**a'pprisable**, *a. Obs. rare*$^{-1}$. [f. APPRIZE *v.*^{2} + -ABLE.] Capable of being apprized or appreciated; laudable, praiseworthy.

1536 BELLENDENE *Cron. Scotl.* II. 123 Otheris thocht nane of hir doingis apprisable, bot repugnant to the law of God.

†**a'pprise**, *sb. Obs.* Forms: 4 **apryse**, 4–5 **aprise**, **apprise**. [a. OF. *aprise*, *-ize*, 'thing learned'; subst. use of fem. sing. of *apris*, pa. pple. of *aprendre* to learn: see next. For *app-* see AP- *pref.*^{1}] That which is learned; lore, learning, instruction, information.

1303 R. BRUNNE *Handl. Synne* 3951 ȝyf þou euere.. Lettydyst any man for to lere Crafte..But fordeddyst hys aprise. **1393** GOWER *Conf.* II. 81 Thus cam in the first apprise Of bokes. *c* **1425** *Seven Sages* (P.) 128 To ordayne.. Or the childe ware sette aprise, Ware they myȝte a stude make.

apprise (ə'praɪz), *v.*^{1} Also apprize. [f. (in 17th c.) F. *apprendre* (OF. *aprendre*) to teach, inform (pa. pple. *appris*, *-ise*), on analogy of *comprise*, *surprise*, and Fr. *comprendre*, *surprendre*. *A(p)prendre*:—L. *adprendĕre*:—*adprehendĕre* 'lay hold of,' had passed from the sense of 'lay hold with the mind, learn,' to 'teach, inform': see APPREHEND. (The prec. sb. was obs. bef.

1500, and had nothing to do with the formation of this vb.)]

1. To impart knowledge or information to; give formal notice to; inform, acquaint.

1694 LD. DELAMER *Wks.* 41 Though the King of England may be never so well apprized in the use of them. **1741** RICHARDSON *Pamela* I. (1824) 52, I hope she has had the duty to apprise you of her intrigue with the young clergyman. **1801** MAR. EDGEWORTH *Angelina* iv. (1832) 61 Miss Hodges is above stairs—she shall be apprized directly. **1869** GLADSTONE *Juv. Mundi* xv. §1. 519 Telemachos apprises Menelaos that Ithaca is a goat-feeding island.

b. Hence in *pass.* To be informed or aware, to know.

1712 STEELE *Spect.* No. 518 ¶9 You must be extremely well apprised, that there is a very close correspondence. *a***1797** H. WALPOLE *George II* (1847) I. iv. 89 The little Princes, less apprized of his history..talked a good deal to him. **1819** SCOTT *Ivanhoe* I. vi. 88 The adjoining cell, as the reader is apprised, was occupied by Gurth.

c. *refl.* (= Fr. *s'apprendre.*)

*a***1719** ADDISON *Chr. Relig.* VI. i, The learned Pagans might apprise themselves from oral information.

2. To give formal notice of, notify, advise. *rare.*

1817 BYRON *Works* IV. 71 Morlands have not yet written to my bankers, apprising the payment of your balances.

apprize, -ise (əˈpraɪz), *v.*[2] *arch.* Forms: 5– apprise, 6– apprize. [a. OF. *aprise-r*, earlier *aprisier*, f. *à* to + *prisier*, *preisier* to price, prize, praise; or perh. directly on phrase *à pris*, as if *mettre à prix*. Retained in Sc. Law, and used occasionally by Eng. writers, but ordinarily represented in Eng. by APPRAISE, in its analysis the same word, but with a different history. Cf. also PRAISE and PRIZE.]

1. *Sc. Law.* To put a selling price upon, put up for sale at a set price, appraise.

1533 BELLENDENE *Livy* III. 226 Thay..apprisit and sauld all the gudis. **1682** *Lond. Gaz.* mdccxlvi/4 Very fine Spanish Cloth..Apprized from 10 to 16*s.* per Yard. **1754** ERSKINE *Princ. Sc. Law* (1809) 258 The sheriff was to apprise or tax the value of the lands.

2. To estimate the worth of, value, appreciate.

*a***1400** *Leg. Rood* (1871) 218 þe riche prince was þere aprised. **1401** *Pol. Poems* II. 113 Thou apprisist not the curse of seint Franceis. **1536** BELLENDENE *Cron. Scotl.* (1821) I. 16 This last opinioun wes maist apprisit. **1617** R. WILKINSON *Barw.-bridge* Ded., How highly your Highnes apprizeth peace. **1868** BROWNING *Ring & Bk.* VIII. 668 Whosoever at the proper worth Apprises worldly honour. **1877** *Daily News* 5 Nov. 5/2 Art among women was apprized ..on very much the same sort of principle.

†**a'pprized,** *pa. pple. Obs.* [pa. pple. of vb. *apprize*, not otherwise found, intensive of PRIZE *v.* 'to seize as a prize.' See A- *pref.* 11.] Seized, possessed as of a prize.

1521 WOLSEY in Strype *Eccl. Mem.* I. ii. 29 Divers ships have been rescued..whereof one, with certain Frenchmen apprized thereof, arrived here..this day.

†**apprizement, apprise-.** *Obs. rare*[—1]. [a. F. *apprisement*, OF. *aprisement*, n. of action f. *aprisier*: see APPRIZE *v.*[2] and -MENT.] The action of setting a value upon; appraisement.

1605 BACON *Sp. K. James* (T.) By law, they ought to make but one apprisement.

apprizer, -ser (əˈpraɪzə(r)). *arch.* [f. APPRIZE *v.*[2] + -ER[1].] One who appraises; *Sc. Law*, A creditor for whose behoof an appraisal is made.

1609 SKENE *Reg. Maj.* vii. 150 Apprysers of flesh..to appryse the flesh..alswell for the profite of the fleshers, as of the people. **1754** ERSKINE *Princ. Sc. Law* (1809) 257 The heritable rights belonging to the debtor were sold for payment of the debt due to the appriser. **1815** SCOTT *Guy M.* i, The apprizer (as the holder of a mortgage was then called) entered upon possession.

apprizing, -sing (əˈpraɪzɪŋ), *vbl. sb. arch.* [f. as prec. + -ING[1].] The action of attaching a value to; estimation of value, appraisement; appreciation.

*c***1449** PECOCK *Repr.* 26 The iust apprising of Holi Scripture. **1533** BELLENDENE *Livy* III. 294 That na werkis war done be thame war wourthy to have apprising. **1754** ERSKINE *Princ. Sc. Law* II. xi. (1809) 257 So that apprisings were, by their original constitution, proper sales of the debtor's lands, to any purchaser who offered.

appro., appro (ˈæprəʊ). Abbrev. of APPROBATION or APPROVAL, in the phrase ***on*** (or ***upon***) ***appro.*** Also *attrib.*

1874 HOTTEN *Slang Dict.* 74 Most of the extensive show of chains, watches, and trinkets in a shop window is obtained 'on appro', *i.e.*, 'on sale or return'. **1901** *Punch* 26 June 467/1 You ordered it 'upon appro'. **1906** *Daily Chron.* 20 June 6/6 We have..purchases on 'appro.'. **1908** *Westm. Gaz.* 10 Jan. 2/1 The goods on appro. we left to Lavinia's maid. **1910** *Ibid.* 10 Feb. 8/1 The head salesman..said it was not an 'appro' transaction. **1950** WODEHOUSE *Nothing Serious* 40 She took him on again—on appro., as it were. The idea was that if he proved himself steady and serious, those wedding-bells would ring out.

approach (əˈprəʊtʃ), *v.* Forms: 4 aprochi, 4–6 aproch(e, 5–7 approch(e, 7– approach. [a. OFr. *aprochie-r* (mod. *approcher*), cogn. w. OIt. *approcciāre*, Pr. *apropchar*, early Rom. **adpropjāre*:—late L. *adpropi-āre* (Vulgate), f. *ad* to + *propi-āre* to draw near, f. *propi-us* (Pr. *propi*, Fr. *proche*, for *propche*, *propj*) nigher, near, compar. of *prope* nigh. For *app-*, see AP- *pref.*[1] About 1600 the phonetic *oa* was introduced for *ō*.]

1. *intr.* To come nearer (relatively), or draw near (absolutely), in space. **a.** *simply.*

*c***1374** CHAUCER *Boeth.* I. i. 6 Sche sauȝ þese poetical muses aprochen aboute my bedde. *c***1400** *Destr. Troy* IV. 1276 þan pollux aprochet in hast. **1557** PHAËR *Æneid* VI. Q iv, Whom the Troyan duke had found, Approching nere. **1605** SHAKS. *Lear* II. ii. 170 Approach, thou Beacon to this vnder Globe, That by thy comfortable Beames I may Peruse this Letter. **1627** SPEED *Eng. Abridged* xxx. §8 A Spittle for Lazers, a disease then newly approched in this Land. **1795** SOUTHEY *Joan of Arc* I. 20 At his bidding Claude Approach'd. **1863** MRS. OLIPHANT *Sal. Ch.* xvii. 301 A footstep outside approaching softly.

b. with *to. arch.*

*c***1325** *E.E. Allit. P.* B. 1781 To þe palays pryncipal þay aproched. *c***1386** CHAUCER *Man of Lawes T.* 805 Hire ship approched to the londe. **1587** TURBERV. *Trag. T.* (1837) 152 The cruell wightes..Approched to the doore. **1611** BIBLE *2 Sam.* xi. 20 Wherefore approached ye so nigh unto the city? **1860** TYNDALL *Glaciers* I. §17 Masses sufficiently large approached near to the shore.

2. a. *trans.* To come near to.

*c***1305** *St. Lucy* 118 in *E.E.P.* (1862) 104 þat a þousend men scholde in mi side falle..and me aprochi noȝt. **1393** GOWER *Conf.* I. 282, I approche..The place, where my lady is. **1605** SHAKS. *Macb.* II. iii. 76 Approch the Chamber. **1847** YEOWELL *Anc. Brit. Ch.* iii. 28 When he came to Rome ..he evidently approached it from the East.

b. *fig.* with reference to a place in the field of conception. *intr.* and *trans.*

*a***1577** GASCOIGNE *Str. Passion* (R.) I thinke How ioyes approch, when sorrowes shrinke. **1777** PRIESTLEY *Matt. & Spir.* xx. (1782) I. 254 As we approach nearer the age of the schoolmen. **1867** MACFARREN *Harmony* ii. 35 And so approach the fundamental..harmonic school by the path of history.

3. *trans.* Said of lines or things in a line: To be so situated in space that the parts lie successively nearer to a given point or line (which a body moving along the line in question would therefore approach, in sense 2). rarely *intr.*

1598 FLORIO, *Approssimare*, to approch, to neighbour. **1712** ADDISON *Spect.* No. 477 ¶1 Trees rising one higher than another in proportion as they approach the centre. **1748** HARTLEY *Observ. Man* I. i. §1 ¶7 The Ventricles of the Brain approach towards each other. **1751** CHAMBERS *Cycl.*, *Asymptote*, a line which continually approaches nearer and nearer to another, yet will never meet therewith, tho' indefinitely prolonged. *Mod.* At this point the boundary approaches, but does not quite reach the river.

4. To come near to a person: *i.e.* into personal relations; into his presence or audience; or *fig.* within the range of his notice or attention. **a.** *intr.* with *to. arch.*

*c***1325** *E.E. Allit. P.* B. 7 Renkeȝ of relygioun þat.. aprochen to hys presens. *c***1400** *Destr. Troy* XIX. 7998 He approchet toþe prinse. **1611** BIBLE *Isa.* lviii. 2 They take delight in approching to God. **1794** MATHIAS *Pursuits Lit.* (1798) 381 To the Peers approach with awe.

b. *trans.* Also, *fig.* to make an overture or proposal to; to seek for an interview; to make advances to (a person) with a view to influencing his actions; to attempt to influence or bribe.

*c***1325** *E.E. Allit. P.* B. 147 So prest to aproche my presens. **1393** GOWER *Conf.* III. 288 He..goth to approche The kinges court and his presence. **1597** SHAKS. *2 Hen. IV*, v. v. 65 When thou dost heare I am, as I haue bin, Approach me. **1711** STEELE *Spect.* No. 118 ¶1, I cannot approach her without Awe. **1821** SCOTT *Kenilw.* xvii, The Earl was approached..by a person quaintly dressed. **1857** *Lawrence* (Kansas) *Republican* 30 July 2 An editor of this place had approached him..offering inducements to him to become an organ under it. **1893** *Congress. Rec.* Sept. 1874/1 Nearly every bit of everything that is said about public men being corrupted or approached is false. **1929** *Daily News* 10 Apr. 7/3 When the 'Daily News' approached the Admiralty on the subject an official said [etc.].

5. *euphem.* Of sexual relations. (*intr.* and *trans.*)

1611 BIBLE *Lev.* xviii. 6 None of you shall approche to any that is neere of kinne to him. **1798** COLEBROOKE *Digest Hind. Law* (1801) III. 196 If either brother..approach the wife, he is degraded.

†**6.** To embrace or take up with (a habit). *Obs.*

1574 HELLOWES *Gueuara's Epist.* (1577) 15 Shunne euil, and approch to do wel.

7. *intr.* Of time or events: To draw nigh.

*c***1374** CHAUCER *Troylus* v. 1 Aprochen gan the fatel destyne. **1393** LANGL. *P. Pl.* C. XVIII. 209 þe tyme aprocheþ faste. **1599** THYNNE *Animadv.* 51 When deathe approched. **1697** DRYDEN *Virg. Georg.* III. 195 When now the Nuptial time Approaches. *a***1732** GAY (J.) The hour of attack approaches.

8. To come near in quality, character, or state; to be nearly equal. **a.** *intr.* with *to.*

*c***1400** *Destr. Troy* II. 401 No filisofers..Might approche to þat precious apoint of her wit. **1538** STARKEY *England* 21 Man so dowyng neryst approchyth to the nature of God. **1756** BURKE *Vind. Nat. Soc.* Wks. I. 36 We judge..of them as they approach to, or recede from this standard. **1871** B. STEWART *Heat* §66 The coefficients of dilation..approach more nearly to equality.

b. *trans.*

*a***1698** TEMPLE (J.) He was an admirable poet, and thought even to have approached Homer. **1824** DIBDIN *Libr. Comp.* 187 That copy..more decidedly approached such a form.

1872 FREEMAN *Norm. Conq.* IV. xviii. 143 Vigorous youths fast approaching manhood.

9. *Mil.* To make 'approaches' to; to work forward towards, by means of entrenchments. See APPROACH *sb.* 9.

1598 BARRET *Theor. Warres* v. i. 127 To aproach neare vnto the walles, with trenches, or such like aprochings. *a***1674** CLARENDON *Hist. Reb.* (1703) II. VII. 228 The ground was very easy to Approach, and as inconvenient, and dangerous to Storm. **1861** SHEPPARD *Fall of Rome* vi. 339 The town..had to be approached in regular form.

10. *causal.* To bring near locally, to move or draw nearer; approximate. (Common in mod.Fr.) *arch.*

1541 R. COPLAND *Galyen's Terap.* 2 D j, Yf thou assay to approche them [the lips of an ulcer] by force. **1665** BOYLE *Occas. Refl.* I. vi. 87 All those changes..shall serve to approach him the faster to the blest mansion. **1795** T. JEFFERSON *Writ.* (1859) IV. 114, I..should have been tempted to approach myself to it. **1821** SCOTT *Kenilw.* x. (1853) 107 So saying, he approached to the fire a three-footed stool.

11. *fig.* To bring near in character, quality, rank.

*a***1649** DRUMM. OF HAWTH. *Wks.* 1711, 226 In matter, none approach him [Petrarch] to Sidney. **1850** MERIVALE *Rom. Emp.* (1865) II. xiii. 103 His object was..to approach the Gaulish provincials to Rome. **1863** LD. LYTTON *Ring of Amasis* I. 148 Forced these images into the foreground of Fancy, thus approaching them nearer to reality.

12. *Golf. intr.* To play the approach stroke.

1887 W. G. SIMPSON *Golf* viii. 140 When the player's ball is within less than a driver shot of the hole, approaching commences. **1898** '*House' on Sport* I (Advt.), Auchterlonie's special registered approaching cleek kept in stock. **1903** *Westm. Gaz.* 9 Jan. 2/1 Mr. Laidlay used to approach better than any other man I have ever seen play.

13. *Aeronaut.* Of an aircraft or pilot, to make an approach (see APPROACH *sb.* 13).

1927 *Aviation* XXII. 1080/2 Upon approaching an airdrome at night, the pilot is interested in the limits of the landing area. **1950** *Gloss. Aeronaut. Terms* (*B.S.I.*) I. 8 *Approach*, to manœuvre an aircraft into position relative to the landing area for flattening-out and alighting.

approach (əˈprəʊtʃ), *sb.* [f. prec. vb.; cf. mod.Fr. *approche*, 16th c. in Littré.]

1. The act of coming nearer (relatively), or of drawing near (absolutely), in space.

*c***1555** R. MORICE in Strype *Eccl. Mem.* III. I. xxviii. 233 The Bishop..entered into the University church..whose approach being honorable, Latymer..surceased from farther speaking. **1588** SHAKS. *L.L.L.* II. i. 81 Nauar had notice of your faire approach. **1696** WHISTON *Th. Earth* II. (1722) 180 The approach of a Comet to the Earth. **1736** BUTLER *Anal.* I. ii. 52 The destruction of our bodies..upon too near approaches to fire. **1859** GEO. ELIOT *A. Bede* 9 Casson's thoughts were diverted by the approach of the horseman.

†**2.** Nearer advance of an enemy; offensive or hostile movement. *Obs.*

1489 CAXTON *Faytes of Armes* I. xxv. 80 Or euer thou make eny approche vpon thin enemies. **1607** SHAKS. *Timon.* v. i. 167 So soone we shall driue backe Of Alcibiades th' approaches wild. **1652** NEEDHAM tr. *Selden's Mare Cl.* 229 Intercept the provision and supplies of their Enemies Shipping, and by diligent watchfulness discover their approaches.

3. a. *pl.* Movements towards the establishment of personal relations with one; advances.

1642 ROGERS *Naaman* 22 Thy timorous and weake approaches toward his grace. **1654** GAYTON *Fest. Notes* III. vi. 109 What Approaches, Smiles, Shrugs, Habits, are.. requirible from them! **1678** H. VAUGHAN *Thal. Rediv.* (1858) 234, I note their coarse and proud approaches, Their silks, perfumes, and glittering coaches. **1681** BAXTER *Apol. Nonconf. Min.* 4 Concessions and approaches. **1805** FOSTER *Ess.* I. ii. 24 Repel the approaches of sleep.

b. Advances made to a person for the purpose of improperly influencing his actions. *U.S.*

1893 *Congress. Rec.* Sept. 1874/1 The idea that..[Mr. Hooper] was subject to approach is ridiculous.

4. Power of approaching, access. *arch.*

1563 GRAFTON *Chron. Mary* an. 3 (R.) The French men had the more easie approche to the castell. *a***1626** BACON (J.) Honour hath in it..the approach to kings and principal persons. **1713** SWIFT *Caden. & Van.* Wks. 1755 III. II. 17 The learned met with free approach. **1726** GAY *Fables* I. xvi. 15 Rais'd again from low approach, She visits in the doctor's coach.

5. a. A means or way of approach; an access, passage, avenue. Also *fig.*

1633 G. HERBERT *Dulnesse* v. in *Temple* 108 Where are my lines then? my approaches? views? **1790** COWPER *Odyss.* VII. 109 Mastiffs in gold and silver lined the approach. **1878** F. WILLIAMS *Mid. Railw.* 344 In the station and its approaches some 60,000,000 of bricks..have been employed.

b. *fig.* A way of considering or handling something, esp. a problem.

1905 R. B. PERRY *Approach to Philos.* 1 (*heading*) Approach to the problem of philosophy. **1916** A. W. SHAW *Approach to Business Prob.* p. v To discover a classification molded on the living activities of business, to supply a uniform method of approach to business problems in whatever form they may arise, and to illustrate the application of this method to typical problems..these are the purposes of this book. **1937** R. LAMBERT (*title*) Approach to love. **1950** *Times* 5 May 4/3 The authorities have the matter under consideration, but their approach to the problem is coloured by their anxiety to help Britain to earn dollars by finding markets in Canada. **1969** *Mod. Lang. Rev.* LXIV. 876 The typological approach..does not preclude other methods of interpreting Milton's symbolism. **1986** *N.Y. Times* 7 May A10/4 We reaffirm the continued importance of the case-by-case approach to international debt problems.

6. A drawing near in time or circumstantial relation.

1593 SHAKS. *2 Hen. VI*, III. iii. 6 Where death's approach is seene so terrible. **1659** HAMMOND *On Ps.* Pref. 21 At their next approaches to that part of the office. **1704** POPE *Autumn* 97 Thus sung the shepherds till th' approach of night. **1878** SEELEY *Stein* III. 375 Signs of the approach of an intense reaction in Prussia.

7. A coming near in quality, or character; approximation.

1750 JOHNSON *Rambl.* No. 81 §1 Questions..discussed without any approach to decision. **1756** BURKE *Subl. & B.* I. 166 Some sort of approach towards infinity. **1869** FREEMAN *Norm. Conq.* III. xii. 204 A type of cities to which England..can present but feeble approaches. **1881** GUILLEMARD *Let.* in *Life Maxwell* xiii. (1882) 414, I never.. heard an approach to a murmur.

†**8.** A drawing near in reckoning; an approximation. *Obs.*

1672 PETTY *Pol. Anat.* (1691) 51 By the best Estimates and Approaches that I have been able to make..London is more healthful than Dublin by 3 in 32.

9. a. *Mil.* in *pl.* Entrenchments or other works whereby the besiegers draw closer to the besieged.

1633 T. STAFFORD *Pac. Hib.* xvi. (1821) 387 That..wee might the better make our neerer Approaches. **1710** *Lond. Gaz.* mmmmdclxxxvii/2 We have advanced our Approaches to the first Ditch. **1834** *Penny Cycl.* II. 195/2 These approaches sometimes consist of covering masses only, formed either with earth in bags, with fascines, stuffed gabions, wool-packs, or bales of cotton.

b. *fig.*

1847 TENNYSON *Princ.* III. 267 Oh if our end were less achievable By slow approaches. **1869** GOULBOURN *Purs. Holiness* vi. 52 Approaches must be thrown up by prayers and fastings.

10. *Hort.* The bringing of the branch of one tree close to that of another on which it is to be grafted, in the method called ablactation or inarching.

1658 EVELYN *Fr. Gard.* (1675) 87 Either inoculate or graff them by approach. **1727** BRADLEY *Fam. Dict.* s.v. *Grafting*, All Pear-trees may be grafted by Way of Escutcheon, Slit, Crown, or Approach. **1838** *Penny Cycl.* XI. 342/2 Inarching ..is sometimes called grafting by approach.

11. *Golf.* The play or stroke by which a player hits his ball on to the putting-green or approaches the hole; chiefly *attrib.*, as ***approach play, shot, stroke.***

1879 *Encycl. Brit.* X. 765/2 Having got within some moderate distance of it [*sc.* a hole], he proceeds to make his 'approach shot'. *Ibid.*, The 'approach' and the 'putting' are by far the most difficult..parts of the game. **1887** W. G. SIMPSON *Golf* viii. 155 There are four clubs used for ordinary approach work—the putter, the cleek, the iron, and the mashy. **1903** *Westm. Gaz.* 10 Mar. 2/3 Plenty of opportunities still will be afforded for approach strokes. *Ibid.*, Approach play is not to be considered in laying out a hole. **1919** WODEHOUSE *Damsel in Distress* i. 23 Does it [*sc.* love] make you slice your approach-shots? *Ibid.* xv. 173 His approach-putting has to be seen to be believed.

12. *Bridge.* Denoting a type of bidding (see quots.). Usu. *attrib.*, as ***approach bid, bidding; approach(-forcing) system***, etc.

1929 *Bridge World* Nov. 14/1 The Approach System at Auction, also introduced by the Culbertsons, practically revolutionized bidding methods. **1930** E. CULBERTSON *Contract Bridge Blue Book* vi. 89 Whenever a hand contains a biddable suit..the suit and not the no-trump should be preferred. (The Approach principle.) **1930** A. E. M. FOSTER *Contract Bridge for All* i. 7 You read of approach bids. *Ibid.* 11 The idea in approach bidding is..to decide on the final declaration after the reaction of partner and opponents has been discovered. **1931** J. H. REFORD *Contract up-to-date* i. 34 The system advocated in this book embodies..the approach-forcing system.

13. *Aeronaut.* The final stage in flight before landing; also, the air space through which the approach is made. Also *attrib.*

1930 *Airway Age* XI. 381/1 In addition to..green and white boundary and approach lights, each hangar is equipped with obstacle and flood lights. **1931** *Flight* 6 Feb. 121/2 An approach which ended in the aircraft reaching the after limits of the deck too low..resulted in the undercarriage being severely damaged. **1931** P. V. H. WEEMS *Air Navigation* ix. 129 Landing field approach lights are green lights in the boundary lighting circuit at the end of runways. **1933** *Bur. of Standards Jrnl. of Research* XI. 485 The compass bearing is followed until after hearing the signals from the approach marker beacon. **1940** *War Illustr.* 19 Jan. 620 With wheels and landing flaps lowered the pilot makes his approach. **1944** *Jrnl. R. Aeronaut. Soc.* XLVIII. 285 The best approach speed, flaps and undercarriage down, is about 95 m.p.h. **1948** *Daily Tel.* 23 June 4/6 Radar navigational and approach aids could be standardized by international companies. **1951** *Gloss. Aeronaut. Terms (B.S.I.)* III. 22 *Approach*, the air space over an approach area. **1958** *Times* 24 Oct. 5/3 (*caption*) Testing..the new precision approach radar (talk-down) equipment installed in the Approach control room at London Airport.

14. *attrib.*, as ***approach island*** (see ISLAND *sb.* 2 c), ***road*** (cf. ACCESS 7 a), ***span.***

1958 *Times* 24 June 5/5 A motor cycle..came into collision with the kerb of an approach island. **1833** LOUDON *Encycl. Archit.* 463 The approach-road to the house. **1962** *Listener* 7 June 989/1 The control of large motor-coaches on the very narrow approach-roads to the moor. **1924** *Times Trade & Engin. Suppl.* 29 Nov. 252/3 The bridge..will be carried on five main piers and built in four arch and two approach spans.

approachability (əˌprəʊtʃəˈbɪlɪtɪ). *rare.* [f. next: see -BILITY.] The quality of being approachable; accessibility.

1851 RUSKIN *Stones Ven.* I. xvi. §9 The approachability of the window..is the real point to be attended to.

approachable (əˈprəʊtʃəb(ə)l), *a.* [f. APPROACH *v.* + -ABLE; cf. mod.Fr. *approchable.*]

1. Capable of being approached; accessible.

1571 DIGGES *Pantom.* x. D ij a, Without shadowe..to take heighthes approchable. *a* **1797** H. WALPOLE *George II.* (1847) III. v. 125 The town was..approachable only by a narrow causeway. **1856** KANE *Arct. Exp.* I. v. 50 It was desirable that..it should be approachable by boats.

2. *fig.* in various uses of the vb.

1611 COTGR., *Abordable*, affable, abboordable, approachable. **1750** JOHNSON *Rambl.* No. 72 ¶11 He that regards the welfare of others should make his virtue approachable. **1828** CARLYLE *Goethe, Misc.* I. 174 This Truth..approachable by most, attainable by some small number.

aˈpproachableness. *rare.* [f. prec. + -NESS.] The quality of being approachable; accessibility.

1731 in BAILEY. **1876** J. PARKER *Paracl.* 47 There must be in that life [Christ's]..such simplicity and approachableness as shall qualify it for admission into society.

approacher (əˈprəʊtʃə(r)). *arch.* [f. as prec. + -ER[1].]

1. One who approaches or comes near.

1586 BRIGHT *Melanch.* vi. 28 Such [fishes] are.. approchers nigh the sand. **1607** SHAKS. *Timon* IV. iii. 216 Thou gau'st thine eares, (like Tapsters, that bad welcom) To Knaues, and all approachers. **1704** SWIFT *Batt. Bks.* (1711) 264 He furiously rush'd on against this new Approacher.

2. (See APPROACH *v.* 12).

1887 W. G. SIMPSON *Golf* viii. 146 Approachers of equal skill indulge in all the variations [of grip].

approaching (əˈprəʊtʃɪŋ), *vbl. sb.* [f. as prec. + -ING[1].] The action of coming or drawing near; *spec.* in *Mil., Hort.* and *Golf* = APPROACH *sb.* 9, 10, and 11.

c **1386** CHAUCER *Pers. T.* ¶800 Avoutrie, in Latine, is for to saye, approching of another mannes bedde. **1596** SHAKS. *Merch. V.* II. ix. 88 One that comes before To signifie th' approaching of his Lord. **1598** [See APPROACH *v.* 9.] *a* **1674** CLARENDON *Hist. Reb.* (1703) II. VII. 178 The Officers of Horse..were all for a Storm, and the Foot Officers for Approaching. **1887, 1898** [See APPROACH *v.* 12].

aˈpproaching, *ppl. a.* [f. as prec. + -ING[2].]

1. Drawing near, in space, time, or circumstance.

c **1450** *Court of Love* vii, Whan I was young, at eighteen yere of age..Approaching on ful sad and ripe corage. **1598** BARRET *Theor. Warres* Pref. 5 These approaching times. **1610** SHAKS. *Temp.* v. i. 80 The approching tide Will shortly fill the reasonable shore. **1855** MACAULAY *Hist. Eng.* III. 537 Preparations for the approaching campaign.

†**2.** Lying near, in proximity, neighbouring. *Obs.*

1533 BELLENDENE *Livy* IV. 317 Ane plebeane sall nocht have his hous approcheand to ane patriciane. **1598** FLORIO, *Approssimante*, approching, neighbouring.

3. Coming near in quality or character.

1874 BLACK *Pr. Thule* 35 Not that he fell in love with her at first sight, or anything even approaching to that.

4. *Bridge.* (See quots. and cf. APPROACH *sb.* 12).

1926 *Auction Bridge Mag.* Sept. 174/1 A call may be tentative, perhaps to be followed by a second one. In America they call this the approaching bid. **1927** M. C. WORK *Contract Bridge* (1928) v. 131 *Approaching bid*, one designed to guide partner toward the most advantageous declaration.

5. As *adv.* Almost, nearly (a specific number, amount, or proportion).

1951 *Sunday Times* 30 Dec. 4 The members of the Lithographic Printing Productivity Team have..received and accepted approaching one hundred invitations to speak to firms, union branches, and others interested. **1959** *Times* 2 Sept. 7/1 Approaching half the Lancashire cotton industry has applied to go out of business the easy way with financial compensation from the Government. **1971** *Soviet Weekly* 3 Apr. 5 Approaching a thousand people live comfortably in its 220 big flats. **1982** *Financial Times* (City of London Survey) p. ii/6 They believe that rents, now approaching £30 a sq ft, are likely to continue to increase this year.

approachless (əˈprəʊtʃlɪs), *a. poet.* [f. APPROACH *sb.* + -LESS.] Unapproachable; inaccessible.

1647 R. STAPYLTON *Juvenal* 243 Yet all the prophesie did well befit The approachlesse oracle. **1652** BENLOWES *Theoph.* VIII. x. 110 Archessence! Thou, self-full! self-Infinite! Residing in approachlesse Light. [In mod. Dicts.]

approachment (əˈprəʊtʃmənt). [a. Fr. *approchement*, n. of action f. *approcher*: see APPROACH *v.* and -MENT.]

†**1.** The action of approaching; approach. *Obs.*

1544 *Late Exp. Scotl.* in Arb. *Garner* I. 125 Upon the approachment of the men to their entries. **1607** TOPSELL *Four-footed Beasts* 372 Turning about and looking upon his pursuers, as if it were to dare their approchment. **1646** SIR T. BROWNE *Pseud. Ep.* (J.) Ice..will not concrete, but in the approachment [cf. APPROACH *sb.* 4] of the air.

2. Approach in character, affinity.

1830 LINDLEY *Nat. Syst. Bot.* 193 Beyond this resemblance in the fruit..I find nothing to confirm the approachment.

†**ˈapprobate,** *ppl. a. Obs.* [ad. L. *approbāt-us*, pa. pple. of *approbā-re* to assent to as good, f. *ap-* = *ad-* to + *probā-re* to try the goodness of, f. *prob-us* good.] Approved formally or expressly; particularly by some competent authority. (Used after formation of vb. APPROBATE as its pa. pple.)

c **1430** LYDG. *Bochas* VIII. xii. (1554) 183 b, That he in his estate By the Pope afore be approbate. **1547** BOORDE *Dyetary* xvi. (1870) 272 Galen, with other auncyent and approbat doctours. **1577** HOLINSHED *Chron.* III. 924/2 Decrees..which by long custome hath beene receiued and approbate.

approbate (ˈæprəbeɪt), *v.* [f. prec.]

1. To approve expressly or formally; to express approbation of, sanction authoritatively. Obs. in England since 17th c., but preserved in U.S., and often used as simply = *approve.*

1470 HARDING *Chron.* cvi, As Flores saieth, and hath it approbate. **1528** ROY *Satire* (Arb.) 91 Obedience and wilfull poverte Which allmyghty god doth approbate. **1557** BARCLAY *Jugurtha* (Paynell) 42 Whether they wold approbate and alowe the sayd composicion. **1623** COCKERAM, *Approbate*, to allow, to like. **1833** GEN. P. THOMPSON *Idioms of America* in *Exerc.* (1842) III. 470 There are many Americanisms which in the course of time will work their way into the language of England..The verbs 'approbate,' 'consider' (in the sense of 'believe'), and even 'guess,' are making their way gradually in their peculiar senses. **1849** in *Proc. Amer. Phil. Soc.* V. 52 A letter approbating the affair.

2. *Sc. Law.* To approve or assent to as valid. Chiefly in phr. ***to approbate and reprobate***: to take advantage of those portions of a deed which are in one's favour, while repudiating the rest. Also *transf.*

1836 *Blackw. Mag.* XXXIX. 662 You cannot approbate and reprobate the same instrument. **1836–7** SIR W. HAMILTON *Metaph.* xv. (1870) 280, I approbate the one, I reprobate the other. **1880** *Law Rep., Appeal* V. 325 He is in substance..approbating and reprobating, a course which is not allowed either in Scotch or English Law.

ˈapprobated, *ppl. a.* [f. prec. + -ED.] = APPROVED.

1547 BOORDE *Introd. Knowl.* (1870) 167 The ministracion of the vii sacraments and other approbated thynges.

approbation (æprəʊˈbeɪʃən). [a. Fr. *approbation*, ad. L. *approbātiōn-em*, n. of action f. *approbāre*: see prec.]

†**1.** The action of proving true; confirmation, attestation, proof. *Obs.*

1393 GOWER *Conf.* II. 86 With calcination Of verray approbation Do that there be fixation. **1533** MORE *Debell. Salem* Wks. 1006/1 And in approbacion of hys other saying, conclude and say thus much ferther. **1611** SHAKS. *Cymb.* I. iv. 134 Would I had put my Estate..on th' approbation of what I haue spoke. *a* **1718** PENN *Life* Wks. 1726 I. 152 So great an Approbation of their Impostures.

2. The action of formally or authoritatively declaring good or true; sanction.

1502 *Ord. Cryst. Men* (W. de W.) I. v. (1506) 48 Charyte, by some approbacyon, is ayenst yͤ fader. **1529** *Petition* in Froude *Hist. Eng.* I. 194 Summoners, appraysers, and other ministers for the approbation of Testaments. **1613** SHAKS. *Hen. VIII*, I. ii. 71 By learned approbation of the Iudges. **1713** *Lond. & Country Brew.* IV. (1742) 320 Dry their Malt according to the London Brewers Approbation. **1839** KEIGHTLEY *Hist. Eng.* II. 57 Received the royal approbation.

3. a. The action of expressing oneself pleased or satisfied with anything; or the mere feeling of such satisfaction; approval expressed or entertained.

1548 UDALL, etc. *Erasm. Par. Rom.* ii. 29 (R.) God.. whose approbation is perfite blisse and saluacion. **1652** NEEDHAM tr. *Selden's Mare Cl.* Ded., So rare a Jewel as this, which hath drawn..the Approbation of All. **1708** LD. SUNDERLAND in Ellis *Orig. Lett.* II. 401 IV. 252 They hope what steps they have made will meet with your approbation. **1711** BUDGELL *Spect.* No. 77 ¶5 Those Nods of Approbation which I never bestow unmerited. **1806** METCALFE in *Wellesley Disp.* 810 Something more than cold approbation is required to foster great minds—the approbation should be hearty. **1827** HARE *Guesses* Ser. II. (1873) 549 Approbation speaks of the thing or action.. Praise is always personal.

b. ***on approbation***: on approval (see APPROVAL b).

1880 L. HIGGIN *Handbk. Embroidery* 101 Designs on paper are not supplied under any circumstances nor can work be sent out on approbation. **1901** *Strand Mag.* XXI. June p. i/2 (Advt.), The London Shoe Co. Ltd. Goods sent on approbation. **1920** *Conquest* Jan. p. viii, Please send these books on Approbation.

†**4.** Probation, trial. *Obs.*

1603 SHAKS. *Meas. for M.* I. ii. 183 This day, my sister should the Cloyster enter, And there receiue her approbation. **1654** GODDARD in *Burton's Diary* Introd. (1828) I. 169 The ejecting of scandalous ministers..[and] the bringing in of them that have passed an approbation.

approbative (ˈæprəbeɪtɪv), *a. arch.* [a. Fr. *approbatif, -ive*, ad. L. *approbātīv-us*, f. *approbāt-*: see APPROBATE and -IVE.]

Characterized by approving; expressing approbation or approval.

1611 Cotgr., *Approbatif*, approbative, approving. **1643** Bramhall *Serpent-Salve* Wks. 1844 III. 391 There is a vast difference between..an approbative consent..and an active consent. **1678** Gale *Crt. Gentiles* III. 17 His [God's] approbative wil whereby he declares what he approves and what he disapproves. **1786** Tooke *Purley* (1798) I. 111 Get rid of that farrago of useless distinctions into..Effective, Approbative, Discretive. **1828** Webster cites Milner.

'appro,bativeness. [f. prec. + -ness.] The quality of being approbative; tendency to approve; in *Phrenol.* love of approbation.

1860 O. & L. Fowler *Self-Instruc. Phrenol.* iv. §12. 108 Approbativeness, Regard for character, appearances, etc., love of praise. **1860** *All Y. Round* No. 51. 21 A morbid habit of reserve, which my approbativeness often burst through.

approbator ('æprəbeɪtə(r)). ? *Obs. rare*⁻¹. [a. L. *approbātor*, n. of agent f. *approbāre*: see approbate and -or. Cf. mod.Fr. *approbateur*.] One who formally approves or sanctions; an approver.

1667 Evelyn *Mem.* III. 162 And so others may not think it dishonour to..accept them for judges and approbators.

approbatory ('æprə,beɪtərɪ, -ə,tərɪ), *a.* [ad. med.L. *approbātōri-us* (cf. L. *probātōri-us*), f. *approbātōr-em*: see prec. and -ory.] Of or belonging to one who approves; of the nature of or tending to approbation or sanction. (Orig. in phr. ***letter approbatory*** = L. *epistola probātōria*.)

1548 Hall *Chron. Hen. V*, an. 8 (R.) Letters approbatory and confirmacions of the peres of his realme. **1655** Gurnall *Chr. in Arm.* i. 181 God hath delivered in a sense this world to Satan, but not..by any approbatory act given him a Patent to vouch him his Vice-Roy. **1837** Carlyle *Fr. Rev.* III. vi. i. 214 Robespierre, at first approbatory, knew not at last what to think.

approbrious, obs. var. opprobrious.

†**appro'clivity**, *Obs. rare*⁻¹. [f. L. *ap-* = *ad-* to + *prōclīvitas* proclivity.] Proclivity, inclination, tendency towards.

1546 Langley *Pol. Verg. De Invent.* ii. i. 35 a, Procreation of issue, and approcliuitie to norishe the same.

approfound (æprəʊ'faʊnd), *v.* [ad. F. *approfondir*, f. *ap-* ad- + *profond* profound *a.*] *trans.* To go deeply into, to search the depths of (a subject of study). (A Gallicism.)

1885 R. G. White *Stud. Shakespeare* 35 Subtle theories as to Shakespeare's purpose in this play have been set forth by critics who engage in the task of approfounding him. **1897** *Sat. Rev.* 8 May 520 These seven pages of M. Mallarmé would take longer to approfound than all the back numbers of 'Cosmopolis' put together.

†**a'pprompt**, *v.*¹ *Obs. rare*⁻¹. [a. AFr. *aprompte-r*, *apromte-r*, for OFr. *enpromte-r* (mod. *emprunte-r*): see a- *pref.* 10.] To borrow.

1548 Hall *Chron.* 336 Repayment and redelyuery of the Summes of Money appromptcd and layde out.

†**a'pprompt**, *v.*² *Obs. rare*⁻¹. [f. L. *ap-* = *ad-* to + *prompt-us* ready, prompt. See a- *pref.* 11.] To make ready; to prompt, stimulate.

1605 Bacon *Adv. Learn.* ii. xiii. §9 Neither may these places serve only to apprompt our invention.

approof (ə'pru:f). *arch.* Also 5 appreffe, apref. [a. OFr. *aprove*, *-euve*, proof, trial, f. *aprove-r*:—L. *approbā-re*: see approbate and approve. Cf. the simple *proof*, a. OFr. *prove*, *preuve*.]

1. The act of proving; trial, experience, proof.

1436 *Pol. Poems* (1859) II. 167 Thys good kynge, be wytt of such appreffe, Kepte hys marchauntes..fro myscheffe. **1601** Shaks. *All's Well* ii. v. 3 A Souldier..and of verie valiant approofe. **1881** Swinburne *Mary Stuart* iv. i, Known By proof more potent than approof of law In all points guilty.

2. Sanction, approval, approbation.

1439 *E.E. Wills* (1882) 119 In witnessyng and very a-pref whereof.. I have put the seale of my Armes. **1603** Shaks. *Meas. for M.* ii. iv. 174 One and the selfesame tongue, Either of condemnation, or approofe. **1652** Gaule *Magastrom.* 114 Whether any sound orthodox Christian ever did write in the approof of judiciary and predicting astrologie? *a* **1850** Rossetti *Dante & Circle* i. (1874) 111 She bowed her mild approof And salutation to all men of worth.

approper, variant of appropre *v. Obs.*

†**a'pproperate**, *v. Obs.*⁻⁰ [f. L. *approperāt-* ppl. stem of *appr-*, *adproperā-re* to hasten, hurry.]

1623 Cockeram, *Approperate*, to make haste. **1755** Johnson, *Approperate*, to hasten, to set forward.

appropinquate (æprəʊ'pɪŋkweɪt), *v. arch.* [f. L. *appropinquāt-* ppl. stem of *appropinquā-re* to draw nigh to, f. *ap-* = *ad-* to + *propinquā-re*, f. *propinqu-us* neighbouring, f. *prope* nigh, near.]

1. *intr.* To come near *to*; to approach.

1623 in Cockeram. **1642** Bridge *Wound. Consc. Cured* v. 34 Neither herein..doe we appropinquate to the Popish doctrine. **1657** Tomlinson *Renou's Disp.* 145 Liquid and humid [herbs]..appropinquating to heat, are brought to their pristine state. **1873** Lytton *K. Chillingly* iv. v. (1875) 238 That party to which Mivers professed—not to belong—but to appropinquate.

†**2.** *trans.* To bring near or close. *Obs. rare.*

1646 J. Hall *Horæ Vac.* 115 'Tis great art..to appropinquate things remote.

appropinquation (,æprəʊpɪŋ'kweɪʃən). [ad.L. *appropinquātiōn-em*, f. *appropinquāre*: see prec.]

1. The action of coming near, approach.

1628 Donne *Serm.* xlviii. 476 He gave him a rapture..and in that an appropinquation, an approximation to Himselfe. **1636** Evelyn *Mem.* App. I. 423 At the appropinquation of the King..the Vice-Chancellor spoke a speech. **1670** Wallis in *Phil. Trans.* V. 2074 The Earth and Moon's Appropinquation and Elongation. **1842** De Morgan *Calculus* 412 The appropinquation of the straight lines.

2. The action of bringing into contiguity. *rare.*

1864 T. Trollope *Lindisf. Chase* II. 149 The ants too..evidently communicate intelligence..by the appropinquation of noses.

†**appro'pinque**, *v. Obs. rare*⁻¹. [f. L. *appropinqu-āre*: see prec. Cf. *advoke*, *advocate*.] To draw near to, approach.

1663 Butler *Hud.* i. iii. 590 The knotted bloud..With mortal Crisis doth portend My days to appropinque an end.

appropinquity (æprəʊ'pɪŋkwɪtɪ). *rare.* [f. as prec. after *propinquity*.] Nearness.

1646 J. Gregory *Notes & Obs.* xxxi. (1665) 133 An Appropinquity of Vision, that all things are open and naked unto his sight. **1848** Thackeray *Van. Fair* xiv, Six weeks—appropinquity—opportunity—had victimised him completely.

†**appro'portionate**, *v. Obs. rare*⁻¹. [f. L. *ap-* = *ad-* to + proportionate; cf. apportion *v.*] To render proportionate, to proportion.

1662 H. More *Antid. Ath.* (1712) 77 The extream lightness of her [a Bird's] furniture being approportionated to the thinness of that Element [Air].

†**a'ppropre, a'pproprie**, *v. Obs.* Forms: α. 4–5 apropre, 4–6 appropre, -yr, 6 appropir, 6–7 approper. Also β. 4 approprie, 4–5 -ye, *Pa. pple.* 4–7 appropried. [a. OFr. *aproprie-r*:—late L. *appr-*, *adpropriā-re* (*c* 450), f. *ad* to, with idea of 'rendering' + *propri-us* own. Two forms: one (from AFr.) suppressing *-i-*; the other, used chiefly in pa. pple., preserving *-i*, *-y*. Superseded in 17th c. by the Latinized equivalent appropriate.]

1. To assign as private property or possession *to*; to set apart for a special purpose; *spec.* in *Eccl.* to annex to a religious corporation.

α. **1340** *Ayenb.* 40 þe y-halȝede stedes þet byeþ apropred to guodes seruise. *Ibid.* 41 Ofhyaldeþ mid wrong..þe þinges þet byeþ apropred to holy cherche. *c* **1449** Pecock *Repr.* iii. xiv. 368 Whanne a parisch chirche is approprid to an abbey. **1496** *Dives & Paup.* (W. de W.) iv. vii. 170 a, The lyght of the sonne may not be..appropred to one place more than to an other.

β. **1398** Trevisa *Barth. De P.R.* xiv. xlvii. (1495) 484 That manere of felde that hyghte Campus is apropryed to noo man. **1587** Golding *De Mornay* xxi. (1617) 364 A Chapter appropried to the same purpose.

2. To assign or attribute as proper *to*.

α. **1384** Chaucer *Gentilesse* 18 His vertuous noblesse That is appropred [*v.r.* enpropred] unto no degree. *a* **1400** *Relig. Pieces fr. Thornt. MS.* 27 Godd þe ffadyre to whaym is appropyrede myghte. **1508** Fisher *Wks.* i. 205 But to lye longe and contynue in synne is appropred to the deuyll. **1614** Selden *Titles Hon.* 67 Astrologers approper certain starres to Kings only.

β. **1340** Hampole *Pr. Consc.* 8149 Þus salle endles lyfe appropryed be, Tylle þe saved bodyse. **1557** *Primer* (*Sarum*) Hij, God to whome it is appropried to be mercifull ever. **1614** Selden *Titles Hon.* 265 *Capitaneus* and *Valuasor* was also appropried to speciall Dignities beneath a Count.

3. To make one's own; to take possession of. (Orig. with *refl. pron.* etc., afterwards *absol.*)

α. **1366** Maundev. v. 35 Kyngdomes that he hath conquered and apropred to him be strengthe. *c* **1400** *Destr. Troy* xxx. 12193, I haue approprid to oure partis prouyns besyde. **1502** Arnold *Chron.* 276 Whether ony executor..appropir ony thing of the goodis of the deed man.

β. **1474** Caxton *Chesse* 77 To kepe them from appropryyng to them self that thyng that aperteyneth to the comyn.

†**a'ppropred, -ried**, *ppl. a. Obs.* [f. prec. + -ed.] Assigned as a property; set apart for a purpose; appropriate.

1393 Gower *Conf.* III. 99 Eche of hem his owne sete Appropred hath within a man. *c* **1449** Pecock *Repr.* iii. xiv. 369 In othere not approprid chirchis. **1503** Hawes *Examp. Virt.* i. 18 No thynge appropred to his prosperyte.

appropriable (ə'prəʊprɪəb(ə)l), *a.* [f. L. *appropriā-re* (see appropre) + -ble, as if ad. L. **appropriābilis*.] Capable of being appropriated; to be fitly attributed or applied.

1646 Sir T. Browne *Pseud. Ep.* 274 This conceit applyed unto..the beginning of the world, is more justly appropriable unto its end. **1662** Fuller *Worthies* i. 74 Consciencious people, allow that word [*create*] appropriable to God alone. **1824** Southey *Sir T. More* (1831) I. 136 Appropriable to other purposes.

†**a'ppropriament.** *Obs.* [f. L. *appropriā-re* (see prec.) + -ment; perh. after Fr. *appropriement* 'a fitting, conforming, accommodating' Cotgr.] What is proper or peculiar to one; a characteristic.

1633 Ford *Love's Sacr.* i. i, If you can neglect Your own appropriaments.

appropriate (ə'prəʊprɪət), *ppl. a.* and *sb.* [ad. L. *appropriāt-us* pa. pple. of *appropriā-re*: see appropre.]

A. *pple.* or *adj.*

1. Annexed or attached (*to*), as a possession or piece of property; appropriated. *spec.* in *Eccl.* Annexed as a benefice to a religious corporation.

1599 Sandys *Europ. Spec.* (1637) 145 The Parish Priests in Italy..have..certeine Farmes as Gleabland appropriate. **1652** Needham tr. *Selden's Mare Cl.* Pref., The Sea's now made appropriate, And yields to all the Laws of state. **1751** Chambers *Cycl.* s.v., There are computed to be in England 3845 churches appropriate and impropriate.

†**2.** Belonging to oneself; private; selfish. *Obs.*

1627 Feltham *Resolves* i. lxxxiii. Wks. 1677, 127 Policy..works ever for appropriate ends; Love euer takes a partner into the Benefit.

†**3.** Assigned to a particular person; special, individual. *Obs. rare.*

1796 Miss Burney *Camilla* viii. x, The end, therefore, of her deliberation was to show general gaiety, without appropriate favour.

4. Attached or belonging as an attribute, quality or right; peculiar to, own. **a.** *absol.*

1538 Starkey *England* ii. i. §25. 162 We notyd..in..the hede, an appropryat dysease, wych we callyd then a frencey. **1794** Sullivan *View Nat.* I. 174 That the sun darts out light and heat to the limits of its appropriate system. **1809** Coleridge *Friend* (1837) I. i. 9 To charm away..*Ennui*, is the chief and appropriate business of the poet.

b. with *to*.

1525 Tindale *Par. Wicked Mamm.* Wks. I. 50 The forgiveness of sins and justifying is appropriate unto faith only. **1651** Hobbes *Leviath.* ii. xxx. 177 Honour, appropriate to the Soveraign onely. **1812** Southey *Lett.* (1856) II. 307 *Coronet*..is [a word] appropriate to rank and heraldry.

5. Specially fitted or suitable, proper. Const. *to*, *for*.

1546 Phaër *Regim. Lyfe* Bj, Remedies..appropriat to every membre throughout the body. **1594** Plat *Sorts of Soyle* 56 Salts..most appropriate for the nature of mortar. **1661** Boyle *Style H. Script.* Wks. 1744 II. 101/2 The Bible's being appropriate..to make wise the simple. **1809** Coleridge *Friend* (1865) 29 Two mottos equally appropriate. **1869** Freeman *Norm. Conq.* III. xi. 47 Prayers and collects appropriate for the great solemnity.

†**B.** *sb.* [the adj. used *absol.*] A thing appropriated or appropriate; a property, attribute. *Obs.*

1618 Chapman *Hesiod* ii. 551 To prophane The Gods' Appropriates. **1642** Jer. Taylor *Episc.* (1647) 102 The appropriates of their office so ordain'd by the Apostles.

appropriate (ə'prəʊprɪeɪt), *v.* [f. prec. Has replaced the earlier approppre from Fr.]

†**1.** To make (a thing) the private property of any one, to make it over to him as his own; to set apart. *Obs.* exc. as in next.

1535 Coverdale *Mic.* iv. 13 Their goodes shalt thou appropriate vnto the Lorde. **1625** Williams in *Fortesc. Pap.* 209 My Lord, to whose grace I doe appropriat the worke. **1723** De Foe *Col. Jack* (1840) 332 Whatever the ladies of his family required..he would appropriate to them.

2. Const. *to oneself*: = next.

1583 Golding *Calvin on Deut.* xx. 118 Here hee appropriateth the title of God to himselfe saying 'The Lord my God.' **1651** Hobbes *Govt. & Soc.* Ded., The concupiscible part..desires to appropriate to it selfe the use of those things in which all others have a joynt interest. **1740** Anson *Voy.* i. iii. 32 Appropriating 'the whole ships provisions to themselves. **1876** E. Mellor *Priesth.* i. 15 The name 'priest-hood'..was never appropriated by apostles to themselves.

3. Hence *ellipt.* To take possession of for one's own, to take to oneself.

1635 Austin *Medit.* 181 Christ cannot bee so appropriated, or inclosed. **1784** Cowper *Task* v. 761 A liberty like his, who unimpeached Of usurpation..Appropriates nature as his Father's work. **1871** Tyndall *Fragm. Sci.* II. vi. 83 The bud appropriates those constituents..for which it has elective attraction.

4. *Eccl.* To annex (a benefice) to some religious corporation, as its property.

1528 Perkins *Profit. Bk.* xi. §811 (1642) 363 If a man bee bounden for to appropriate a Church at his owne costs. **1691** Blount *Law Dict.* s.v., Before the time of Richard the 2nd, it was lawful to appropriate the whole Fruits of a Benefice to an Abbey or Priory. **1809** Tomlins *Law Dict.* s.v. *Appropriation*, The monasteries..appropriated as many benefices as they could by any means obtain.

†**5.** To allot, annex, or attach a thing to another as an appendage. *Obs.*

1535 Coverdale *1 Esdr.* vi. 18 All the ornamentes that Nabuchadonosor..appropriated vnto his owne temple. **1667** E. Chamberlayne *St. Gt. Brit.* i. iii. x. (1743) 258 They have annexed and appropriated the Market Towns of England..to the respective Postages.

6. To devote, set apart, or assign to a special purpose or use. Const. *to*, *for*.

1605 Verstegan *Dec. Intell.* i. (1628) 10 Hauing apropriated their first day of the weeke to the peculiar adoration of the sun. **1674** Playford *Skill Mus.* i. x. 33 This Swifter Measure is appropriated or used in..Corants, etc. **1779** J. Moore *View Soc.* II. liv. 49 The front gallery..is appropriated to the court. **1868** M. Pattison *Academ. Org.* §2. 41 The revenue is appropriated to the payment of University officers. **1882** *Daily Tel.* 4 May, After appropriating £18,424 for the payment of interest on debentures.

7. To assign or attribute as properly pertaining *to*; to attribute specially or exclusively. *arch.*

1533 TINDALE *Supper of Lord* 30 His manhood..cannot have this glory only which is appropriated to the Godhead. **1675** BAXTER *Cath. Theol.* II. v. 104 Appropriating our Original Guilt to Adam's sin alone. **1801** STRUTT *Sports & Past.* Introd. 7 These amusements..were appropriated to the season of Lent. **1809** COLERIDGE *Friend* I. iv. (1867) 13 The word presumption I appropriate to the internal feeling.

8. To make, or select as, appropriate or suitable *to*; to suit. *arch.*

1594 T. B. *La Primaud. Fr. Acad.* II. 435 Albeit they [tools] be appropriated and fitted to the woorke that is wrought. **1635** PERSON *Varieties* Ded., Accustomed to appropriate the matter of their offerings..to the nature..of the Deity to whom they immolated; as to Mars a horse. **1686** PLOT *Staffordsh.* 340 The best methods of Cultivating, appropriating Seeds and manures, and cureing the diseases of land. **1802** PALEY *Nat. Theol.* iii. (1819) 41 The *membrana tympani*..is appropriated to the action of air. **1839** HALLAM *Hist. Lit.* III. III. vii. §12 The subject chosen is appropriated to the characteristic peculiarities of the poet.

†**9.** To make proper, to fashion suitably. (So Fr. *approprier.*) *Obs.*

1594 T. B. *La Primaud. Fr. Acad.* II. 79 That God hath so appropriated it [the eye], as to make such a goodly piece of woorke thereof.

a'ppropriated, *ppl. a.* [f. prec. + -ED; as pple. replacing the earlier APPROPRIATE, which remains as the adj.]

1. Made over or assigned to a special owner; set apart for a special purpose; specially limited.

1618 BOLTON *Florus* I. xvii. 51 The under-going of generall curses, for the generall good, which was now growne appropriated to his [Decius'] family. **1756** BURKE *Subl. & B.* Wks. I. 129 This species of relative pleasure I call Delight..The word is not commonly used in this appropriated signification. **1828** LD. GRENVILLE *Sinking Fund* 34 To place at the disposal of the community any portion of its now appropriated taxation.

†**2.** Specially suited; suitable, appropriate. *Obs.*

1641 FRENCH *Distill.* iii. (1651) 67 Ten or twenty drops..being taken in any appropriated Liquor. *a* **1733** NORTH *Lives* II. 327 Rich liveries of the appropriated colours. **1780** SIR J. REYNOLDS *Disc.* x. (1876) 9 When to correctness and perfect form is added..appropriated expression.

appropriately (əˈprəʊprɪətlɪ), *adv.* [f. APPROPRIATE *a.* + -LY[2].] In an appropriate manner.

†**1.** Peculiarly, specially, particularly. *Obs.*

1531 *Dial. Laws of Eng.* II. lv. (1638) 167 That is taken appropriately to be the Law of God, that is contained in scripture. *a* **1665** GOODWIN *Filled w. the Spirit* (1867) 345 When that worship which is appropriately due unto God is given unto any other.

2. In a manner properly suited; fittingly.

1795 SEWARD *Anecd.* I. 43 (JOD.) The praise that Robert Bembo so appropriately gives to this great painter. **1832** LANDER *Exp. Niger* III. xviii. 122 Dressed very appropriately in a handsome robe of silk.

a'ppropriateness. [f. as prec. + -NESS.]

†**1.** The state of being appropriated or devoted to some special purpose; special destination. *Obs.*

a **1638** MEDE *Wks.* I. ii. 9 (R.) Some state of singularity or appropriateness, whereby it is advanced above the common condition of things of the same order.

2. Special fitness, suitability, or applicability.

1731 in BAILEY. **1816** GILCHRIST *Philos. Etym.* 209 The appropriateness to my present purpose of the following quotation. **1871** EARLE *Philol. Eng. Tong.* §644 When the musical appropriateness of the word is the chief care.

appropriating (əˈprəʊprɪeɪtɪŋ), *vbl. sb.* [f. APPROPRIATE *v.* + -ING[1].] A making over to a special owner or purpose; a taking as one's own.

1611 COTGR., *Appropriance*, an appropriation, or appropriating. **1645** MILTON *Tetrach.* Wks. 1851, 230 The appropriating of that good which Nature at first made common. *a* **1711** KEN *Urania* Wks. 1721 IV. 476 The ecstatick Bliss..In the appropriating of Love immense.

a'ppropriating, *ppl. a.* [f. as prec. + -ING[2].] That assigns to a special owner or purpose.

1633 SANDERSON *21 Serm.* Ad. Aul. iii. (1673) 43 Appropriating and distinctive titles. **1702** LUTTRELL *Brief Rel.* V. 155 An appropriating clause added to the land tax. **1882** CORY *Eng. Hist.* II. 540 Resistance to the appropriating party.

appropriation (əˌprəʊprɪˈeɪʃən). [ad. L. *appropriātion-em*, n. of action f. *appropriā-re*: see APPROPRIATE and -TION.]

1. The making of a thing private property, whether another's or (as now commonly) one's own; taking as one's own or to one's own use; *concr.* the thing so appropriated or taken possession of.

1393 GOWER *Conf.* I. 240, I wolde..Of other mannes love iwis..Have made appropriation. **1651** BIGGS *New Disp.* ¶172 In dying men..there is an application of medicines, but not an appropriation. *a* **1711** KEN *Christoph.* Wks. 1721 I. 494 When God, my God, with confidence they call, Appropriation makes amends for all. **1825** MᶜCULLOCH *Pol. Econ.* III. §1. 252 To employ labour in the production or appropriation of a commodity. **1868** M. PATTISON *Academ. Org.* §1. 7 The rapacious appropriation of the abbey lands.

2. *Eccl.* The transference to a monastic house, or other corporation, of the tithes and endowments intended for the maintenance of religious ordinances in a parish; *concr.* the benefice or tithes so appropriated.

c **1370** WYCLIF *Agst. Beg. Friers* (1608) 14 This appropriation is made by false suggestion that such religious men han not enough for lifelode. **1528** PERKINS *Profit. Bk.* xi. §811 (1642) 363 If a man bee bounden for to appropriate a Church..and afterwards before the appropriation a pension is graunted out of the same. *a* **1641** SPELMAN *Tithes* 137 (R.) In old times, whilst these churches were in the clergy-hand, they were called appropriations. **1876** GREEN *Short Hist.* viii. 495 To meet it by buying up the appropriations of livings.

3. The assignment of anything to a special purpose; *concr.* the thing so assigned, *esp.* a sum of money set apart for any purpose. *Appropriation Bill*: a Bill in Parliament, allotting the revenue to the various purposes to which it is to be applied.

1789 *Const. U.S.* i. §9 No money shall be drawn from the treasury but in consequence of appropriations made by law. **1825** MᶜCULLOCH *Pol. Econ.* II. §2. 73 The consequent appropriation of particular individuals to particular employments. **1858** FONBLANQUE *How we are Gov.* vii. (L.) The resolutions in the Committee of Supply are embodied into what is called the Appropriation bill.

†**4.** Special attribution or application; specialization; *concr.* a special attribute. *Obs.*

1596 SHAKS. *Merch. V.* I. ii. 46 Hee makes it a great appropriation to his owne good parts, that he can shoo him [his horse] himselfe. **1657** W. COLES *Adam in Eden* Introd., A Table of the Appropriations shewing for what part every Plant is medicinable. **1690** LOCKE *Hum. Und.* III. iii. (1856) 219 The particular name that belongs to every one [thing], with its peculiar appropriation to that idea.

appropri'ationist. [f. prec. + -IST.] An adherent or supporter of appropriation; in *Hindu Philos.* One who holds that the soul is an appropriation of the being of Brahma.

1862 F. HALL *Hindu Philos. Syst.* 244 Those who hold the soul to be Brahma as appropriated to the internal organ,—the appropriationists.

appropriative (əˈprəʊprɪətɪv), *a.* [f. L. *appropriāt-* (see APPROPRIATE) + -IVE; as if ad. L. **appropriātīvus.*] Of appropriating character or tendency; pertaining or tending to appropriation.

1655 GOUGE *Comm. Hebr.* i. 8 This relative *thy* is discriminative and appropriative. **1825** MᶜCULLOCH *Pol. Econ.* II. §2. 95 To resort immediately to some species of appropriative industry. **1871** M. COLLINS *Mrq. & Merch.* I. 185 Mr. Mowbray was looking at the little girl with appropriative eyes.

a'ppropri,ativeness. [f. prec. + -NESS.] Appropriative quality; tendency to take as one's own.

1882 *East. Daily Press* 17 July 3 A rather amusing display of appropriativeness..when all day long the sweet stalls..were besieged by battalions of the common honey bee.

appropriator (əˈprəʊprɪeɪtə(r)). [a. L. **appropriātor*, n. of agent f. *appropriāre*: see -OR.]

1. One who appropriates or takes to his own use.

1840 DE QUINCEY *Mod. Superst.* Wks. III. 325 The appropriator of a treasure. **1858** MISS MULOCH *Th. ab. Wom.* 75 A dishonest appropriator of other people's property.

2. The religious house, or corporation, that owns the fees and endowments of a benefice.

1726 AYLIFFE *Parerg.* 86 These Appropriators, by reason of their Perpetuities, are accounted Owners of the Fee Simple. **1809** TOMLINS *Law Dict.* s.v. *Appropriation*, The appropriators..are perpetual parsons of the church.

†**approprietary.** *Obs. rare.* [f. APPROPRIATE, after PROPRIETARY, but with no corresponding derivation; L. *appropriāre* could only have given *appropriatory.*] = APPROPRIATOR 2.

1547 *Injunc. Edw. VI* in Cardwell *Document. Ann.* (1839) I. 9 The Charges..shall be ratably borne between the parson and approprietary and parishioners. *a* **1641** SPELMAN *Tithes* 141 (R.) The perpetual incumbent, which is the approprietary.

†**a'ppropring,** *vbl. sb. Obs.* [f. APPROPRE *v.* + -ING[1].] Appropriation.

c **1380** WYCLIF *De Eccl.* iv. Wks. 1871 III. 347 Þis styward chafferiþ wiþ approp ryng of chirchis.

approvable (əˈpruːvəb(ə)l), *a.* [f. APPROVE *v.*[1] + -ABLE.] Able to be approved; worthy or deserving of approval.

c **1449** PECOCK *Repr.* 540 That such Religioun be is alloweable and approvable of ech. **1579** FULKE *Ref. Rastel* 709 As they be approuable or disprouable by the saide old auncient and Catholike doctrine. **1617** F. MORYSON *Itin.* III. 32 Inordinate desire of Martyrdome is not approueable. **1753** RICHARDSON *Grandison* (1781) III. xv. 120 Fine qualities, but unhappily blended with others less approveable. **1835** I. TAYLOR *Spir. Despot.* i. 20 Measures..approvable to the quiet good sense..of the people. **1865** CARLYLE *Fredk. Gt.* III. IX. ii. 81 He is..approvable as a practical officer and soldier, by the strictest judge then living.

a'pprovableness. [f. prec. + -NESS.] Approvable quality; worthiness of approval.

c **1812** T. BROWN *Philos. Hum. Mind* lxxiii. (1838) 488/2 This irresistible approvableness..constitutes to us..the virtue of the action. **1833** WARDLAW *Chr. Ethics* iii. (1844) 95 The ground of its approvableness.

approval (əˈpruːvəl). [f. APPROVE *v.*[1] + -AL[2]. Rare bef. 1800; now generally used instead of next.] **a.** The action of approving; sanctioning approbation.

1690 TEMPLE *Her. Virtue* (J.) A censor of justice..without whose approval no capital sentences are to be executed. **1814** CARY *Dante, Parad.* XXIV. 57, I..in her looks Approval met. **1843** MILL *Logic* v. vii. §2 Mankind had stamped its approval upon certain actions.

b. *on approval*: phr. in commercial use denoting that goods sent to a customer are submitted for his examination only, without obligation to purchase (if they are returned undamaged). Also without prep. and *attrib.*

1870 *St. James's Mag.* IV. 598 They had evidently brought most of the things 'on approval'. **1877** *Design & Work* 15 Dec. 667/2 Watch... English lever..approval. *Ibid.* 22 Dec. 690/3 Sheets of stamps sent on approval. **1880** *Bazaar, Exchange & Mart* Suppl. 2 Jan. 1/1 Breech-loaders. Great Bargains... Approval. Deposit. *Ibid.* 5/2 Mulready envelope and 380 foreign stamps. Sent on approval. **1891** *Stamp Collecting* June 21 Is there no way of suppressing the Approval-sheet Swindler? **1902** *Connoisseur* Jan. (Advt.), Stamps... We are sending out Approval Sheets and Books. **1906** *Drapers' Record* 27 Oct. 190 These goods cannot be sent on approval.

approvance (əˈpruːvəns). *arch.* [a. OFr. *aprovance*, f. *aprover*: see APPROVE *v.*[1] and -ANCE.] = APPROOF; APPROVAL.

1592 WYRLEY *Armorie* 122 As valiant foes as welden sheild or targe..and of as good approuance. **1621** SANDERSON *Serm.* Ad. Pop. iv. (1674) 191 To find approvance in the sight of our God. **1728** THOMSON *Spring* 625 Should she seem..the least approvance to bestow. **1883** *Contemp. Rev.* Mar. 341 Silent approvance of the proceeding.

†**a'pprovant.** *Obs. rare.* [a. OFr. *aprovant*, pr. pple. of *aprover*: see APPROVE *v.*[1] and -ANT.] The party offering proof. Cf. APPROVER[1].

1577–87 HOLINSHED *Chron.* III. 1256/2 Sir William de Facknaham..on the one side approvant; and this sir John Sitsylt..on the other side defendant.

approve (əˈpruːv), *v.*[1] Forms: 4–7 **aprove**, 5–6 **approuve**, 6–7 **approove**, 5– **approve**. [a. OFr. *aprove-r* (now *approuver*):—L. *app-*, *adprobā-re* to make good, assent to as good, f. *ad* to + *probā-re* to try the goodness of, prove, f. *prob-us* good. Cf. APPREVE, a form repr. the tonic stem of the Fr. as in *appreuve*; and its pa. pple. APPROVEN. In some senses the word appears to represent Fr. *éprouver*, OFr. *esprover*, not otherwise found in English. See A- *pref.* 9.]

I. (= Fr. *approuver.*)

†**1.** To make good (a statement or position); to show to be true, prove, demonstrate. **a.** *simply. Obs.*

1382 WYCLIF *Mic.* vi. 9 Who shal aproue it? **1481** CAXTON *Myrr.* III. vi. 141 They had lerned to approue the daye and tyme whan suche thynges [eclipses] shold happe. **1571** DIGGES *Geom. Pract.* I. xx. F iij b, The rule..may two wayes be approued, geometrically and arithmetically. **1614** RALEIGH *Hist. World* II. v. iii. §15. 442 He had approued vnto the vulgar, the dignitie of his Science. **1639** FULLER *Holy War* v. x. (1840) 259 To approve the truth..thereof against some one who questioned. **1651** HOBBES *Leviath.* I. v, We demonstrate or approve our reckonings to other men.

†**b.** with *subord. cl. Obs.*

1340 HAMPOLE *Pr. Consc.* 4746 Yhit for certayn approves noght he þat þa fifteen days of takens sal be. **1483** CAXTON *Cato* E iiij b, I haue..approuyd that none may know the secretes of God. **1624** HEYWOOD *Gunaik.* II. 72 This aproves unto us, that order is a cheefe rule in memorie.

†**c.** with *complement. Obs.*

1587 FLEMING *Contn. Holinshed* III. 345/2 He was approoued guiltie at his arreignment. **1611** SHAKS. *Cymb.* v. v. 245 One thing..which must approue thee honest. **1644** *Vind. Treat. Monarchy* iv. 20, I..doubt not to approve it firme truth. **1676–7** MARVELL *Corr.* 290 Wks. 1872–5 II. 527 Mr. Onslow was approved not to have been culpable.

†**2.** To attest (a thing) with some authority, to corroborate, confirm. *Obs.*

c **1380** WYCLIF *Antick. & Meynee* (Todd) 137 Crist confermed his lawe and wiþ his deþ approved hit. **1596** SHAKS. *Merch. V.* III. ii. 79 What damned error, but some sober brow Will..approue it with a text? **1781** GIBBON *Decl. & F.* III. 183 The trembling emperor..solemnly approved the innocence and fidelity of their assassins.

b. with a thing as subject.

a **1674** CLARENDON *Hist. Reb.* III. Ded. 10 The success has approved this judgement. **1862** TRENCH *Mirac.* Introd. 98 The miracles proving the doctrines, and the doctrines approving the miracles.

3. To demonstrate practically or to the experience of others, display, exhibit, make proof of. Also *refl.*

1551 ROBINSON *More's Utop.* 151 They by quicke repentaunce approue the amendement of their liues. **1610** *Chester's Tri.* (1844) *Chester* 15 Such Olympian sports as shall approve Our best devotion. *c* **1630** RISDON *Surv. Devon* §56 Who..approved himself..valiantly at the taking of Strigonium. **1876** EMERSON *Ess.* Ser. II. iv. 104 Many opportunities to approve his stoutness and worth.

b. To display or exhibit to advantage. *rare.*

1849 RUSKIN *Sev. Lamps* iv. §42. 133 The sculpture is approved and set off by the colour.

4. with *compl.* To show or prove practically (a thing or person) to be (so and so).

1680 BUTLER *Rem.* (1759) IV. 4 Approv'd the most profound, and wise To solve Impossibilities. **1812** BYRON *Childe Har.* II. xxxv, 'Tis an old lesson; Time approves it true. **1865** PARKMAN *Champlain* i. (1875) 176 His account.. approves him a man of thought and observation.

b. *refl.* To prove or show oneself practically to be.

1559 ABP. HETHE in Strype *Ann. Ref.* I. App. vi. 11 All such as shall approve themselves not to be the obedient children of Chryst's churche. **1649** SELDEN *Laws of Eng.* II. xi. (1739) 58 Edward the Third approved himself not only King of England, but of himself. **1656** TWISLETON in Burton *Diary* (1828) I. 148 He was in Wales, and approved himself a very vile person. **1765** TUCKER *Lt. Nat.* II. 305 The latter..approved himself a neighbour by acting agreeably to that character. **1840** MACAULAY *Clive* 92 When he approved himself ripe for military command.

†**c.** *intr.* (refl. pron. omitted) To prove itself, prove, turn out to be. *Obs. rare.*

1587 FLEMING *Cont. Holinshed* III. 372/1 If he will say that it was but inuention, it will approue false.

5. To confirm authoritatively; to sanction. *Hence* the techn. term: **a.** in *Sc. Parl.* for confirming, or deciding in the affirmative, by a vote of the house; **b.** for confirming the sentence of a court-martial.

1413 LYDG. *Pylgr. Sowle* v. xiv. 82 þere may no thing be approvid, ne affermed, but if it be founde in the feith. **1480** *Bury Wills* (1850) 59, I..by this my present testament.. myne seyde mynde, wyll and entent..approue, ratifie, and conferme. **1590** SWINBURN *Testaments* 40 The lawe dooth not approoue such testamentes. *a* **1619** FOTHERBY *Atheom.* Pref. 13 The old may not be proued, because it is approued. **1726** in *Wodrow Corr.* (1843) III. 248 The vote was stated, Whether Approve the overture of the Committee, or Delay. **1816** C. JAMES *Mil. Dict.* (ed. 4) 141 The colonel or commanding officer approves the sentence of a regimental court-martial.

6. To pronounce to be good, commend. **a.** *trans.*

c **1380** WYCLIF *Pseudo-Freris* iv. Wks. (1879) 306 Non word of iames approueþ þise newe religions. **1447** BOKENHAM *Lyvys of Seyntys* (Roxb.) 31 Fully they approvyd al his entent. **1538** STARKEY *England* 81 Vayn ornamentys by corrupt jugement commynly approvyd. **1606** SHAKS. *Ant. & Cl.* v. ii. 149, I approue your Wisedom in the deede. **1709** POPE *Ess. Crit.* 391 Fools admire, but men of sense approve. **1803** WELLINGTON in *Wellesley Disp.* 313, I entirely approve that precaution. **1878** SEELEY *Stein* III. 522 Niebuhr..admired and approved the Revolution of 1688.

†**b.** with *inf. phr.* or *subord. cl. Obs.*

1475 CAXTON *Jason* 36 That thing that thou approuedest to seche aboue alle other. **1663** GERBIER *Counsel* A iv a, They will approve that Work men may have this little Book in their Pockets. **1667** MILTON *P.L.* IV. 880 Others who approve not to transgress By thy example.

c. *intr.* Const. (*on* obs.) *of.*

1658 R. FRANCK *North. Mem.* (1821) 9 Our modern assertors and predicators approve on it. **1658–9** GIBBONS in Burton *Diary* III. 557 Such as shall be named and approved on by this House. **1711** STEELE *Spect.* No. 2 ¶2 He has read all, but approves of very few. **1866** KINGSLEY *Herew.* x. 149 Would his grandfather approve of what he had done.

7. *trans.* To recommend oneself, one's qualities, actions, etc., as worthy of approval; to commend *to.*

1611 BIBLE *Pref.* 1 We doe seeke to approue our selues to euery ones conscience. **1657** CROMWELL in Burton *Diary* I. 415 Without integrity, without sincerity, without approving the heart to God. **1829** I. TAYLOR *Enthus.* ii. (1867) 49 If anticipations such as these approve themselves to reason.

II. [= mod.Fr. *éprouver.*]

†**8.** To put to the proof or test of experience; to try, test. *Obs.*

1380 [See APPROVED]. **1483** CAXTON *Cato* D iiij, This rule is gyuen to euery man and approued of euery man. **1532** HERVET *Xenoph. Treat. Househ.* (1768) 64 Men of olde antyquitie, approuinge it by experience. **1596** SHAKS. *1 Hen. IV*, IV. i. 9 Nay, taske me to my word: approue me Lord. **1770** LANGHORNE *Plutarch's Lives* (1879) I. 60/2 Neither fear nor rashness was likely to approve men so disposed.

†**9.** To find by experience, to experience. *Obs.*

1578 *Gorgious Gallery*, A Louer approuing his Lady unkinde. **1591** RALEIGH *Last Fight Rev.* 24 Vnto them a spectacle, and a resolution sildome approued, to see one ship turne toward so many enemies. **1651** HOBBES *Leviath.* II. xix. 101 He hath approved that government in himselfe.

a'pprove, a'pprow, *v.*[2] *Law.* Also 5 aproue, aprowe. [a. OFr. *aproe-r, approer, approuer, apprower* to profit, 'faire profiter, enricher' (Godefroi), f. *à* to + *pros*, obj. *prode, pro, prou, preu* (Pr., Sp., Pg. *pro*, It. *pro, prode*) 'advantage, profit,' a difficult word, pointing to an early Romanic subst. use of the prep. *pro* or *prod-* in *prod-est* (as if *prod est mihi*, it is a profit or advantage to me), perh. declined as **prod-is, prod-em.* Cf. the adj. use in It. *prode, pro*, Pr. *pros.* OFr. *proz, pros, prous, preus*, obj. *prode, prou, preu*, mod.Fr. *preux* good, worthy, valiant, i.e. *vir qui prod-est.* (Cf. also It. *prodezza*, Pr, Sp. *proeza*, OFr. *proesce*, Fr. *prouesse* prowess, and OFr. *prozom, prodom*, Fr. *prud' homme*; and see Diez, Littré, Brachet.) The mod.Eng. form ought to be *approw* (cf. *allow*), but through confusion of *u* and *v*, *approue* was erroneously printed in 17th c. Law-dicts. *approve*, as if a sense of the prec.]

lit. To make profit to oneself of (*e.g.* land), by increasing the value or rent. *esp.* Said of the lord of a manor enclosing or appropriating to his own advantage common land, as permitted by the Statute of Merton (20 Hen. III. c. iv.). Cf. IMPROVE.

[The Stat. of Merton exists only in Latin, but its phrase '*faciant commodum suum*' exactly translates OFr. *aproent*, and is rendered in Stat. Westminster '*appruare se possint de*'; other latinized adaptations of the Fr. were *approare, approvare*, and finally (in 17th c.) *approbare.*]

1483 *Cath. Angl.*, To approwe, *Approare, sicut domini se faciunt de vastis.* **1691** BLOUNT *Law Dict.* s.v., To approve Land is to make the best benefit of it by increasing the Rent. **1768** BLACKSTONE *Comm.* II. iii, This enclose, when justifiable, is called in law approving. **1818** HALLAM *Mid. Ages* (1872) III. 362 By the Statute of Merton..the lord is permitted to approve, that is to inclose the waste lands of his manor. **1865** TURNER in *Morn. Star* 29 Apr., Sir T. Wilson not only considered himself entitled to 'approve' portions of the [Hampstead] Heath, but also contemplated letting out the plots which he might 'approve' for building purposes.

approved (əˈpruːvd), *ppl. a.* [f. APPROVE *v.*[1] + -ED.]

1. a. Proved or established by experience, tried, tested.

c **1380** *Sir Ferumb.* 1409 A noble kny3t aproued. **1489** CAXTON *Faytes of Armes* I. xxiii. 71 The..mooste approued men of armes. **1563** T. GALE *Antidot.* Pref. 1 Diuers approued medicines. **1656** BRAMHALL *Replic.* iv. 177 Persons..of approued integrity. **1709** *Lond. Gaz.* mmmmccccxxi/3 The humble Address of the Bayliff, Steward, Approved-men, and Burgesses of..Andover. **1790** BURKE *Fr. Rev.* Wks. V. 64 The old approved mode. **1824** SCOTT *St. Ronan's* xx, The mortar and stone of the most approved builder.

†**b.** Proved, convicted. *Obs.*

1599 SHAKS. *Much Ado* IV. i. 45 To knit my soul to an approued wanton. **1635** SWAN *Spec. Mundi* i. §3 (1643) 11 Approved liars.

3. Pronounced good; justified, sanctioned, commended, esteemed.

1667 MILTON *P.L.* VI. 36 To stand approv'd in sight of God. **1690** LOCKE *Hum. Und.* III. v. (1695) 244 To have.. very good and approved Words in their Mouths. **1737** WHISTON *Josephus' Wars* I. i. §2 The most approved among them were put to death.

4. ***approved-of***: regarded with commendation.

1670 EACHARD *Contempt Clergy* 22 An approved-of cobler or tinker.

5. approved school, a place of training for boys or girls who have been found guilty of offences or exposed to moral danger.

1932 *Hansard Commons* CCLXI. 1179 The question of the approved schools, as they will in future be called—the schools which are known to the public at present as reformatory and industrial schools. **1933** *Act 23 Geo. V* c. 12 §107 (1), 'Approved school' means a school approved by the Secretary of State under section seventy-nine of this Act. **1938** *Times* 7 Dec. 10/3 The effect of the change of name from 'Reformatory' and 'Industrial' to 'Approved Schools' cannot be exaggerated. No youth is ashamed of having been in an approved school. **1956** A. WILSON *Anglo-Saxon Attitudes* II. i. 228 Larrie's an orphan, an institution boy who's been in a lot of trouble, he's had three convictions for petty thieving and he's been to an Approved School.

6. approved society, a Friendly Society (see FRIENDLY *a.* 8) legally empowered to administer benefits under the National Insurance Act of 1911 and subsequent Acts down to that of 1946.

1911 *Act 1 & 2 Geo. V* c. 55 §23 (1) Any society.. which complies with the requirements of this Act..may be approved by the Insurance Commissioners, and, if so approved, shall be an approved society for the purposes of this Part of this Act. **1952** *Oxf. Jun. Encycl.* X. 171/1 Under the 1911 National Health Act certain registered friendly societies, known as 'approved societies', were used by the Government as part of the health scheme to pay out as 'sick benefit' sums of money provided by the Government... But after the National Insurance Act of 1946 this use of friendly societies by the Government was discontinued.

approvedly (əˈpruːvɪdlɪ), *adv.* [f. prec. + -LY[2].] In an approved manner or degree.

1611 SPEED *Hist. Gt. Brit.* VIII. vii. (1632) 417 Bare himselfe most approuedly towards the vertuous. **1656** BP. HALL *Let. Apol.* (R.) Approvedly orthodox.

a'pprovedness. *rare.* [f. as prec. + -NESS.] The quality of being approved or pronounced good.

1874 SIDGWICK *Ethics* iii. 394 The..coincidence of rightness or approvedness and utility.

approvement[1] (əˈpruːvmənt). Also 6–7 approove-. [a. OFr. *aprovement*, later *approuvement* (Cotgr.), f. *aprove-r*: see APPROVE *v.*[1] and -MENT.]

1. The action of proving guilty, or convicting, by becoming 'approver.'

1768 BLACKSTONE *Comm.* IV. 324 Approvement..is when a person, indicted of treason or felony, and arraigned for the same, doth confess the fact before plea pleaded; and appeals or accuses others, his accomplices, of the same crime, in order to obtain his pardon. **1824** THESIGER *Trial Thurtell & Hunt* 161 The doctrine of approvement has been obsolete now for 150 years.

†**2.** Expression of sanction or satisfaction; approbation, approval. *Obs.*

1615 G. SANDYS *Trav.* 61 Without his approuement. *a* **1617** HIERON *Wks.* I. 27 The worst things haue had the greatest consent, and the fullest and most generall approouement. **1665** R. B. *Comm. Two Tales* 197 Their high Approvement of them induced..the Author to go on with the rest.

†**3.** That which is approved. *Obs.*

1673 PENN *Alex. Coppersmith* 22 The Meeting could not passe it as their Approvement.

a'pprovement[2]**, a'pprowment.** *Law.* Forms: 5 appro-, aprowe-, aprou-, 5–6 approwe-, approu(e), 7– approvement. [a. OFr. *aproement, aprouement, aprowement*, n. of process f. *aproer*: see APPROVE *v.*[2]]

1. The action of making one's profit of, making the best of (*e.g.* land); *hence*, the conversion to his own profit, by the lord of the manor, of waste or common land by enclosure and appropriation. Cf. IMPROVEMENT.

1475 *Bk. Noblesse* 64 Labouragis and approwementis of londes and pastures. **1482** *Paston Lett.* 863 III. 291 My lord is sette sore to approvement and husbondry. **1523** FITZHERB. *Surv.* 15 b, This newe aprouement maye fortune to encresce of rent or decrese. **1691** BLOUNT *Law Dict.*, *Approvement*..is more particularly used for the enclosing part of a Common by the Lord of the Mannor, leaving sufficient nevertheless for the Commoners. **1883** BAGGALLAY *Law Times Rep.* 595/1 The *onus probandi* is on the commoners, and not on the lords, as in the case of approvement.

†**2.** 'Also used for the profits of the lands themselves. Crompton *Jurisd.* 152.' Tomlins *Law Dict.* 1809. So in OFr. '*aprowement* profit, bénéfice.' Godefroy. *Obs.*

1489 *Plumpton Corr.* 88 Send me word what increse and aproment ye wyll give.

approven (əˈprəʊv(ə)n), *ppl. a. Sc.* [pa. pple. of APPREVE, after strong vbs. like *weave, woven*, etc.] = APPROVED.

1609 SKENE *Reg. Maj.* 37 Ane man, quha is ane approven theif (*bruted and commonlie suspected as ane theife*). **1637** GILLESPIE *Eng.-Pop. Cerem.* III. ii. 19, I fortify my proposition by approven examples. [See also APPREVE.]

approver[1] (əˈpruːvə(r)). [f. APPROVE *v.*[1] + -ER[1].]

1. One who proves or offers to prove (another) guilty; *hence*, an informer, an accuser. Now restricted to: One who confesses a felony and gives evidence against his accomplices in order to secure their conviction; one who turns king's (queen's) or state's evidence. [In this sense generally *provour* in AFr. (Britton) and ME.]

c **1400** *Apol. Loll.* 69 Oiþer he schal dampne þe prouar, or til he fauor þe accusar, þat mi3t not proue, schal iuge þe vngilty. **1533** MORE *Debell. Salem* Wks. 976/2 Some peraduenture became approuers when they were caste, and called for a coroner. **1581** LAMBARDE *Eiren.* III. ii. (1588) 344 A Prouour..must beginne with confession of his owne fault, before he may be permitted to burthen an other man. **1586** FERNE *Blaz. Gentrie* 315 He is the assailaunt, and is commonly called the approouer or maintainer. **1611** SPEED *Hist. Gt. Brit.* IX. xxiv. 851/2 Suffer neither the said prouer, nor defender to take any of their weapons. **1613** SIR H. FINCH *Law* (1636) 387 The Defendant confessing an enditement of felonie may accuse others, in which case wee call him an Approuer. **1679** *Trial Langhorn* 27 An Approver, while he is in that service, hath a Peny a day. **1855** MACAULAY *Hist. Eng.* IV. 670 The testimony of a crowd of approvers swearing for their necks.

†**2.** One who proves, tests, or tries. *Obs.*

1541 R. COPLAND *Guydon's Quest. Cyrurg.* Q ij, Whan that the approuers come..for to examyne them. **1691** WOOD *Ath. Oxon.* II. col. 444 [John Rowe] was appointed one of the Approvers of Ministers according to the Presbyterian way.

3. One who confirms, sanctions, pronounces good, or commends.

1548 UDAL, etc. *Erasm. Par. 2 Cor.* (R.) Jesus Christe is my witnes and approuer. **1611** SPEED *Hist. Gt. Brit.* IX. viii. (1632) 581 Not onely.. witnesses at the doing, but also approuers of the deed. **1790** BURKE *Fr. Rev.* Wks. V. 30 Among the approvers of certain proceedings in France. **1835** LYTTON *Rienzi* x. vii. 427 The loudest grumbler..now the loudest approver. **1864** *Q. Rev.* CXV. 196 Even the flesh of the conger has approvers in modern days.

†**a'pprover**[2]**, a'pprower.** *Obs.* Also 4–5 approwour, -ouour, -ouer. [a. AFr. *aprouour*, OFr. **aproeor*, f. *aproer*: see APPROVE *v.*[2] In med.L. *apruātor* and *approuātor*; corrupt mod.L. *approbātor.* Ought to be written *apprower.*] One who looks after the profit or interest of an employer; or who manages land for the owner; a steward or bailiff; an agent in any business.

[**1326** *Act 1* Edw. III, II. viii. (*Stat. Realm*, I. 256) Qils sount grevez par viscountes qi se fount nomer *approuours le Roi.* **1618** transl. in PULTON: That they be grieved by Sheriffes, naming themselues the King's approuers.] *c* **1386** CHAUCER *Friar's T.* 43 This false theef, this Somonour.. Hadde alwey bawdes redy to his honde..They weren his approwours [*v.r.* apprououris, aprouers, approwers] priuely; He toke hym self a greet profit therby. **1691** BLOUNT *Law Dict.* s.v., Bailiffs of Lords in their Franchises are called their Approvers. Approvers of the King are those that have the letting of the King's Demeans in small Mannors, to his best advantage. **1721** BAILEY, *Approvers* in the Marches of Wales, were such as had Licenses to buy and sell Cattle into those parts. **1758** *Month. Rev.* 464 Wardens or approvers.. Each in his county was almost usually the chief collector of the royal revenue.

approving (əˈpruːvɪŋ), *vbl. sb.* [f. APPROVE *v.*[1] + -ING[1].] The action of testing, proving; or confirming, sanctioning; approbation; probate.
1523-4 *Act 15 Hen. VIII*, v, Letters testimonials of their approuing and examination. **1580** HOLLYBAND *Treas. Fr. Tong.*, *Approbation*, approuing or auouching. **1591** *Durh. Wills* (1860) 198 For the execution and approving of his will. **1612** WOODALL *Surg. Mate* Ep. Ded., Your good likings and well approvings of my former works. **1653** MILTON *Hirelings* Wks. 1851, 356 Far..from the approving of Tithes.

approving (əˈpruːvɪŋ), *ppl. a.* [f. as prec. + -ING[2].] That gives approval.
1702 ROWE *Tamerlane* I. i. 18 Approving Heav'n Still crown'd the Righteous Warrior with Success. **1855** MACAULAY *Hist. Eng.* IV. 498 An approving vote was obtained.

aˈpprovingly, *adv.* [f. prec. + -LY[2].] In an approving manner; so as to imply approval.
1837 CARLYLE *Fr. Rev.* v. ii. II. 285 His two brothers.. who look down on him approvingly. **1882** J. HAWTHORNE *Fortune's Fool* I. xii, Nodding her head approvingly.

†**aˈpproximant**, *a.* *Obs.* *rare*$^{-1}$. [ad. L. *approximānt-em* pr. pple. of *approximā-re*: see next.] Approaching closely, resembling.
1641 SIR E. DERING *Sp. on Relig.* 21 June, Whereby our times might be approximant, and conformant to the Apostolicall..Church.

approximate (əˈprɒksɪmət), *ppl. a.* and *sb.* [ad. L. *approximāt-us* pa. pple. of *approximā-re* (Tertull.) to draw near to, f. *ap-* = *ad-* to + *proximā-re*, f. *proxim-us* very near, next.]
A. *adj.*
1. Very near, in position or in character; closely situated; nearly resembling.
1646 SIR T. BROWNE *Pseud. Ep.* 159 Holding some community with our selves, and containing approximate disposition unto animation. **1859** DARWIN *Orig. Spec.* xii. (1876) 318 The above-named three approximate faunas of Eastern and Western America.
2. *Phys. Sc.* Set very close together.
1839 JOHNSTON in *Proc. Berw. Nat. Club* I. vii. 198 Towards the base of the arm..they soon become approximate. **1870** HOOKER *Stud. Flora* 411 Carex.. spikelets 2-6, short, ovoid, approximate.
3. *ellipt.* Nearly approaching to accuracy; fairly or reasonably correct.
1816 BURROWES *Encycl.* s.v. *Arithmetic*, Approximate decimals. **1831** BREWSTER *Optics* viii. 77 We may..obtain the approximate indices of refraction. **1853** H. ROGERS *Ecl. Faith* 123 There is an approximate uniformity.
B. *sb.* An approximate result or quantity. *rare.*
1784 WARING in *Phil. Trans.* LXXIV. 407 In finding approximates to the roots of given equations. **1816** BURROWES *Encycl.* s.v. *Arithmetic*, Examples of the arithmetic of approximates.

approximate (əˈprɒksɪmeɪt), *v.* [f. prec., or on analogy of vbs. so formed.]
1. *trans.* To bring close or near, to cause to approach or be near (*to*). Rarely, and chiefly in scientific language, of physical motion (as of molecules), but common in other relations: see 2.
1660 BARROW *Serm.*, *Bounty to Poor*, Goodness.. approximates the angels to God. **1765** JOHNSON *Pref. Shaks.* Wks. IX. 245 Shakespeare approximates the remote, and familiarizes the wonderful. **1790** BURKE *Fr. Rev.* 137 Whenever man is put over men..he should as nearly as possible be approximated to his perfection. **1806** W. TAYLOR in *Ann. Rev.* IV. 773 The comb..with which the weaver approximates the threads of shoot. **1830** LINDLEY *Nat. Syst. Bot.* 80 Of very uncertain affinity: its fruit approximates it to *Bixineæ*. **1842** W. GROVE *Corr. Phys. Forces* 37 Percussion..by approximating their particles, makes them specifically more dense. **1855** MILMAN *Lat. Chr.* IV. VII. vi. 168 Everything which approximated the human Saviour to the heart.
2. *intr.* To come near or close (*to*). Rarely (in scientific language) of physical motion, but often of the convergence of lines or surfaces, and of the position resulting from such convergence; commonly used of conceptions to which ideas of space are transferred, and of approach to similarity, identity, or accuracy, in any respect.
1789-96 MORSE *Amer. Geog.* II. 497 Their morality approximated to that of Christianity. **1835** SIR J. ROSS *N.-W. Pass.* xxiii. 238 The shores gradually approximate. **1835** GEN. P. THOMPSON *Exerc.* (1842) III. 237 Some who believe themselves to approximate to statesmen. **1848** HARDY in *Proc. Berw. Nat. Club* II. vi. 336 Those on the third segment closely approximate. **1853** LYNCH *Self-Impr.* vi. 147 But approximate to a judgement we often must. *c* **1854** STANLEY *Sinai & Pal.* iv. (1858) 209 A narrower valley, almost approximating to the character of a ravine. **1857** SIR J. STEPHEN *Lect. Hist. Fr.* xvii. II. 154 All we can expect..is to approximate to the true solution.
3. *trans.* (by omission of the prep.) To come close to, approach closely. Used like prec.
1789-96 MORSE *Amer. Geog.* I. 34 As the telescope approximates perfection. **1793** RENNEL in *Phil. Trans.* LXXXIII. 190 Having no time keeper on board, we..can only approximate our longitude. **1794** SULLIVAN *View Nat.* I. 100 But, we may yet approximate..a certainty that is demonstrative. **1848** W. GROVE *Contrib. Sc.* 348 Olefiant gas, which closely approximates air. **1883** *Pall Mall G.* 17 July 4/2 Rentals approximating £4,000 per annum.

aˈpproximated, *ppl. a.* [f. prec. vb. + -ED.] Brought close; nearly reached; approximate.
1789 MORGAN in *Phil. Trans.* LXXIX. 50 The approximated values of the three joint lives. **1846** RUSKIN *Mod. Paint.* v. xx. §23 IV. 368 An approximated perfection. **1847** HARDY in *Proc. Berw. N.C.* II. 237 Intermediate coxæ approximated.

approximately (əˈprɒksɪmətlɪ), *adv.* [f. APPROXIMATE *a.* + -LY.] In an approximate manner, nearly; *ellipt.* with near approach to accuracy.
1845 CARLYLE *Cromwell* (1871) I. 39 When he went.. cannot be known except approximately by years. **1870** HOWSON *Metaph. Paul* ii. 42 And they will only be approximately intelligible to us.

approximating (əˈprɒksɪmeɪtɪŋ), *ppl. a.* [f. APPROXIMATE *v.* + -ING[2].] That approximates or brings near.
1774 GOLDSM. *Nat. Hist.* I. 12 Attraction: a sort of approximating influence, which all bodies..are found to possess. **1783** COWPER *Corr.* (1824) I. 293 The approximating powers of the telescope.

approximation (əˌprɒksɪˈmeɪʃən). [n. of action f. L. *approximā-re*: see APPROXIMATE and -TION.]
1. The action of bringing or coming near in place, time, or any conception to which ideas of space apply; approach; the state of being near, proximity. *lit.* and *fig.*
1646 SIR T. BROWNE *Pseud. Ep.* 283 Unto that position it had been in a middle point, and that of ascent, or approximation. **1664** POWER *Exp. Philos.* III. 188 The World's decay and approximation to its period. **1794** SULLIVAN *View Nat.* II. 417 The approximation of the comet..near to our earth. **1849** MISS MULOCH *Ogilvies* xxxvi. (1875) 273 Striving..to bring the young man in closer approximation to her chair. **1870** H. MACMILLAN *Bible Teach.* xvi. 315 It is in diatoms and confervæ..that the vegetable kingdom makes an approximation to the animal.
†**b.** *spec.* in *Med.* Communication of a disease by contact; **c.** in *Hort.* = APPROACH *sb.* 11. *Obs.*
1678 PHILLIPS, *Approximation*..in Natural Magick..see *Transplantation*. **1753** CHAMBERS *Cycl. Supp.*, *Approximation*..transplanting a disease into some other subject, whether animate or vegetable, by bringing it in immediate contact with the patient. **1765** TUCKER *Lt. Nat.* II. 111 Grafting by approximation.
2. The action of approaching in feeling or personal relations; advance towards union in sentiment or interests.
1824 SOUTHEY *Sir T. More* (1831) I. 233 An approximation of feeling among those whom opinions have divided. **1850** MERIVALE *Rom. Emp.* (1865) II. xii. 38 The renewed approximation of Pompeius to the party from which he had been so long estranged.
3. A coming or getting near to identity in quantity, quality, or degree; an approach to a correct estimate or conception of anything. *concr.* The result of such a process.
1660 H. MORE *Myst. Godl.* v. xvi. 199 The nearer approximation of the Root of 666 to 26 then to 25. **1672** JACOMB *Comm. Rom.* viii. (1868) 56 The excellency of persons..to be measured by their..approximation to that which is most excellent. **1748** HARTLEY *Observ. Man.* I. iii. §2 ¶87 The true Root, or such an Approximation as is practically equivalent. **1854** SIR G. NICHOLLS *Eng. Poor Law* I. 13 An approximation to the principle of a Poor Law. **1868** GLADSTONE *Juv. Mundi* v. (1870) 143, I take them as very rough approximations to the truth. **1868** PEARD *Waterfarm.* vi. 73 How an approximation to the cost of construction may be obtained.
4. *Math.* A process of solving problems, wherein a continual approach is made to the exact quantity.
1695 WALLIS in *Phil. Trans.* XIX. 2 Mr. Newton's Method of Approximation for the Extracting of Roots. **1838-9** HALLAM *Hist. Lit.* II. II. viii. §5 He devised a method of solving equations by approximation.

approximative (əˈprɒksɪmətɪv), *a.* [f. L. *approximāt-* (see APPROXIMATE *a.*) + -IVE: cf. F. *approximatif.*] Of approximate character; nearly approaching, but not reaching, absolute accuracy.
1830 SIR J. HERSCHEL *Nat. Philos.* 213 A first or approximative verification. **1878** FOSTER *Phys.* I. i. §2 An approximative knowledge of the nature of coagulation.

aˈpproxiˌmatively, *adv.* [f. prec. + -LY[2].] In an approximative manner; approximately.
1836 TODD *Cycl. Anat. & Phys.* I. 123/2 Calculated approximatively according to their masses. **1866** HUXLEY *Preh. Rem. Caithn.* 111 The per-centages given must be regarded merely as approximatively correct.

aˈpproxiˌmativeness. *rare.* [f. as prec. + -NESS.] The quality of being approximative.
1879 GEO. ELIOT *Theo. Such* xvii. 301 A slovenly approximativeness and self-defeating inaccuracy.

approximator (əˈprɒksɪmeɪtə(r)). *rare.* [f. L. *approximāt-* (see APPROXIMATE *a.*) + -OR.] One who approximates or approaches.
1858 CDL. WISEMAN *4 Last Popes* 346 Canonico Baini, the closest approximator, in modern times, to Palestrina.

‖**appui** (apɥi, əpˈwiː), *sb.* [F. *appui*, *appuy* (Cotgr. 1611), f. vb. *appuyer*: see next. Now treated as Fr., though formerly naturalized.]
†1. Support, stay, prop. *Obs.* in gen. sense.
a **1573** *Lett. Lethington* in Keith *Hist.* (1734) 233 (JAM.) What appuy, or of whom shall she have, being forsaken of her own and old friends? **1601** HOLLAND *Pliny* I. 538 If a Vine be to climbe Trees that are of any great height, there would be stayes and appuies set to it.
2. *Mil.* Defensive support. *point of appui* (Fr. *point d'appui*): see quot. Also *fig.*
1809 WELLINGTON in Gurw. *Disp.* V. 44 Give an appui to my left flank. **1830** GEN. P. THOMPSON *Exerc.* (1842) I. 266 Was the object to provide a point of appui for the spirit of change? **1832** *Prop. Reg. Instr. Cavalry* III. 46 Point of Formation or Appui—Any fixed object or marker upon which a body of troops is directed to commence its formation into line.
3. *Horsemanship.* (See quot.)
1727-51 CHAMBERS *Cycl.*, *Appui*, in the manage..is the reciprocal effort between the horse's mouth and the bridle-hand; or the sense of the action of the bridle on the hand of the horseman. **1816** C. JAMES *Mil. Dict.* 19 Horses for the army ought to have a full appui, or firm stay upon the hand.

appui, appuy, *v.* [a. F. *appuye-r*, OF. *apuye-r*, *apouie-r*, *apoie-r* (= It. *appoggiare*):—late L. *appodiā-re* to lean upon, f. *ap-* = *ad-* to + *podium* a support, a. Gr. πόδιον base, f. πούς (ποδ-) foot.] To prop or stay; *spec.* in *Mil.* to post (troops) near some point which affords support.
1656 BLOUNT *Glossogr.*, *Appuyed*, stayed, propped..also, rested, or leaned upon. **1813** SIR R. WILSON *Diary* I. 361 The enemy have their right appuied upon these mountains. *Ibid.* I. 451 The allied main army..will be appuyed so as to succour or receive succour from both flanks.

appulse (əˈpʌls). [ad. L. *appuls-us*, n. of completed action f. *appuls-* ppl. stem of *appellĕre*, f. *ap-* = *ad-* to + *pellĕre* to drive. Some pronounce ˈæpʌls; cf. *ˈimpulse, reˈpulse.*]
1. A driving or energetic motion toward or against a place. †*spec.* The running of a ship towards any point (*obs.*).
a **1626** BACON *Phys. Ess.* (R.) The hours differ according to the appulse of the water to the shores. **1673** GREW *Anat. Roots* II. §28 The continual appulse of fresh sap. **1675** BAXTER *Cath. Theol.* I. III. 16 Light..operateth by appulse upon the eye. **1774** J. BRYANT *Mythol.* II. 412 The history of Deucalion, and of the appulse of the Ark. **1854** OWEN in *Orr's Circ. Sc. Org. Nat.* I. 265 The grinding surface of the crown receives the appulse of the opposing tooth.
b. *fig.*
1642 H. MORE *Song of Soul* II. I. II. xiii, Or 'fore some storm, when their [*i.e.* birds'] quick sprights be stird With nearer strong appulse. **1763** SHENSTONE *Elegies* xvi. 11 Foe to the dull appulse of vulgar joy.
2. *Astr.* The arrival of a star or planet at the meridian or other point; the coming into conjunction of two heavenly bodies.
1668 T. SMITH *Voy. Constant.* in *Misc. Cur.* (1708) III. 58 The fixed Stars, and the appulse of the Moon to them. **1760** *Chron.* in *Ann. Reg.* 65/1 A comet..made a near appulse to the star in Orion's right knee. **1834** U.K.S. *Nat. Philos.*, *Astron.* i. 13/1 Each star is found to have precisely the same interval between its successive appearances on, or as they are also termed, appulses to, the meridian.

†**aˈppulsion.** *Obs.* *rare*$^{-1}$. [n. of action f. L. *appuls-*: see prec. and -ION[1].] A driving against.
1615 CROOKE *Body of Man* 485 To breake the vehement appulsion, or rushing in of cold ayre.

appulsive (əˈpʌlsɪv), *a.* *rare*$^{-0}$. [f. as prec. + -IVE.] Characterized by driving against; impinging.
1846 in SMART.

aˈppulsively, *adv.* *rare*$^{-0}$. [f. prec. + -LY[2].] In an appulsive manner; with forcible contact.
1859 in WORCESTER.

appunct, -uament, obs. ff. APPOINT, -MENT.

†**aˈppunctuation.** *Obs.* *rare*$^{-1}$. [f. med.L. *appunctuāt-* ppl. stem of *appunctuā-re* to settle, define, f. L. *ad* to + *punctum* POINT, after F. *appointer*: see APPOINT.] The action of defining or fixing; determination.
1765 TUCKER *Lt. Nat.* I. 330 Concerning the stationing of substances, the appunctuation of time, and perpetual order of succession.

†**aˈppurchase**, *v.* *Obs.* *rare*$^{-1}$. [f. A- *pref.* 11 + PURCHASE *v.*] To purchase, gain, win.
c **1565** R. LINDSAY *Hist. Scot.* (1728) 53 The king's good mind and favour towards him which he appurchased to him by his moyen.

†**aˈppurpose**, *v.* *Obs.* *rare*$^{-1}$. [f. A- *pref.* 11 + PURPOSE *v.*: cf. *apardon.*] To purpose.
1569 GRINDAL *To Privy Council* Wks. 1843, 318 [I] was appurposed now..to deal with more of them to like effect.

appurtenance (əˈpɜːtɪnəns). Forms: 4-5 **apurtena(u)nce, -tynaunce, aportenance, -anse,** 6 **apertinaunce**; 4-6 **appur-, apper-,** 5 **appar-, apportenaunce, -tenanse,** 6 **appertaynens, appar-,** 6-9 **apper-,** 7-9 **appurtenance.** *Aphet.* 4-5 **portin-, porten-, purtenaunce.** [a. AF. *apurtenance* (12th c. in Littré), OF. *aper-* and, regularly, *apartenance* (cf. Pr. *apartenensa*, It. *appartenenza*):—late L. *appertinēntia*, f. *appertinēre*: see APPERTAIN and -ANCE. The second vowel has varied, as *a, e, o, u*, but the last is now the accepted spelling. For instances assimilated to *appertain*, see APPERTAINANCE. Formerly often used unchanged in the plural.]

1. *Law* and *gen.* A thing that belongs to another, a 'belonging'; a minor property, right, or privilege, belonging to another more important, and passing in possession with it; an appendage.

1377 LANGL. *P. Pl.* B. II. 103 To haue and to holde · and here eyres after, A dwellyng with þe deuel..Wiþ al þe purtenaunces [**1393** portinaunce] of purgatorie. **1418** *E.E. Wills* (1882) 28, I bequethe to..my wyf my Maner of Staverton with the appurtenaunces. **1490** CAXTON *Eneydos* lxv. 165 The cyte of Lawrence wyth the appartenaunces. **1557** *K. Arthur* VI. xi, I wolde that he receyued it as his ryght and appertenaunce. **1691** BLOUNT *L.D.*, *Appertinances* are things both Corporeal, belonging to another thing, as to the more principal; as Hamlets to a chief Mannor..and Incorporeal, as Liberties, and Services of Tenants. **1875** STUBBS *Const. Hist.* II. xiv. 94 The county of Chester, with valuable appurtenances, was transferred to Simon.

2. A thing which naturally and fitly forms a subordinate part of, or belongs to, a whole system; a contributory adjunct, an accessory.

1377 LANGL. *P. Pl.* B. xv. 184 Pryde with al þe appurtenaunce [*v.r.* appurtenaunces, purtenaunce; **1393** portinaunce]. **1570** DEE *Math. Præf.* 36 This, with all other Cases..and appertenances, this Arte demonstrateth. **1602** SHAKS. *Ham.* II. ii. 388 The appurtenance of Welcome is Fashion and Ceremony. **1722** WOLLASTON *Relig. Nat.* ix. 192 The soul would not appear to them as a faculty of the body, or kind of appurtenance to it. **1835** WILLIS *Pencillings* I. i. 10 A personification of the cholera, with skeleton armour and bloodshot eyes, and other horrible appurtenances of a walking pestilence.

3. *esp.* in *pl.* The mechanical accessories employed in any function or complex scheme; apparatus, gear. Also *fig.*

c **1386** CHAUCER *Pers. T.* ¶719 Now cometh hasardrie with his appertenaunce [*v.r.* apurtenaunces, -tynaunces, -tenance, -ortenancis, appurtenaunce] as tables and rafles. **1598** BARRET *Theor. Warres* V. I. 125 The Counterfortes, and the other appertenances of the Bulwarke. **1605** BACON *Adv. Learn.* II. §10 (1873) 80 Astrolabes..provided as appurtenances to astronomy. **1644** MILTON *Areop.* (Arb.) 66 The Pope, with his appertinences the Prelats. **1764** REID *Inquiry* vi. §1 The structure of the eye, and of all its appurtenances. **1840** J. M. WILSON *T. of Borders* (1851) XIX. 253 The wine, the plate, the servants in livery, and all the appurtenances of a great establishment.

4. The fact or state of appertaining.

1846 LANDOR *Exam. Shaks.* Wks. II. 276 (*archaic*) Swans and herons have something in their very names announcing them of knightly appertenance. **1875** WHITNEY *Life Lang.* v. 94 The word is a token of the most indefinite appurtenance.

† **a'ppurtenanced**, *ppl. a. Obs.* [f. prec. + -ED².] Furnished with, as an appurtenance.

1602 CAREW *Cornwall* 132 b, Amongst other commodities, it is appurtenanced with a walk.

appurtenant (ə'pɜːtɪnənt), *a.* and *sb.* Forms: 4-5 ap- *or* app-urtenaunt(e, apertinent, -ynent, -enent, 4-6 ap- *or* app-ertenaunt(e, -ant, 5-9 appertinent, -eynent, 6- appurtenant. [a. OF. *apartenant, -ertenant,* (pr. pple. of *apartenir*):—L. *appertinēnt-em*: see APPURTENANCE and -ANT. In sense 2 often refashioned after L. as *appertinent*.]

A. *adj.*

1. Belonging as a property or legal right (*to*); *spec.* in *Law*, constituting a property or right subsidiary to one which is more important.

c **1386** CHAUCER *Monkes T.* 325 Many a fair citee Apertenaunt unto the magesté Of Rome. **1393** GOWER *Conf.* III. 265 She by wey of covenaunt To his service apurtenaunt Was hole. **1598** KITCHIN *Courts Leet* (1675) 186 Common Appurtenant is for all manner of Beasts. **1654** USSHER *Annals* VI. (1658) 399 Two Cities of Thracia.. appurtenant to the Chersonese of Thracia. **1818** HALLAM *Mid. Ages* I. ii. 205 Villeins, appurtenant to the soil of the master. **1876** DIGBY *Real Prop.* iii. ii. §18. 155 Rights.. appurtenant, or rights which are exercised over tenement B (called the *praedium serviens*) by the successive owners of tenement A (*praedium dominans*) as and being such owners.

2. Appertaining as if by right (*to*); proper, suited, or appropriate to; relating, pertinent.

c **1386** CHAUCER *Clerkes T.* 954 Euery thing, That to the feste was apertinent. **1413** LYDG. *Pylgr. Sowle* IV. xxxvi. (1483) 84 More apperteynent to worshyp of a worthy knyght than a traylyng gowne. **1577** HARRISON *Eng.* I. II. vi. 144 White meats..are now reputed as food appertinent onelie to the inferiour sort. **1661** HICKERINGILL *Jamaica* 91 The most promising designs..promoted with all the appertinent utensills, that policy can contrive. **1793** SMEATON *Edystone L.* §100 (*note*) Appurtenant to the subject. **1819** COLERIDGE *Lett.* Sept. (1836) Those temptations..most appertinent to our particular calling.

B. *sb.* A thing appertaining; a 'belonging.'

1483 CAXTON *Gold. Leg.* 276/3 The same towne with alle thappertonentes. **1599** SHAKS. *Hen. V*, II. ii. 87 To furnish him with all appertinents Belonging to his Honour. **1649** SELDEN *Laws of Eng.* I. xli. (1739) 65 She passed therefore as an appurtenant to her Husband. **1824** COLERIDGE *Aids to Refl.* (1848) I. 240 The mysterious appurtenants and symbols of Redemption.

† **appur'vey**, *v. Obs. rare*⁻¹. [a. OF. *apourvei-r*, f. *à* to + *pourveir*:—L. *prōvidēre* to provide: see PURVEY.] To provide with what is necessary.

1375 BARBOUR *Bruce* IX. 424 He held..a gret menȝe, Swa that he mycht be appurvait To defend, gif he war assayit.

Apra ('æprə). **A.P.R.A., APRA.** [a. Sp., acronym f. the initial letters of *Alianza Popular Revolucionaria Americana* American Popular Revolutionary Alliance.] The name of a Peruvian reform movement and political party founded in 1924.

1935 *Foreign Affairs* XIII. 236 The American Popular Revolutionary Alliance, commonly known as APRA. **1957** *Encycl. Brit.* XI. 282/2 The Apra party is perhaps chiefly important for making politically conscious for the first time the Peruvian Indians who..comprise nearly half the country's population. *Ibid.* XVII. 623 Apra was outlawed in 1933 as an international organization akin to communism... In 1945,..President Prado..lifted the ban on Apra. **1963** *Times* 7 June 13/7 The chief role in the education of the Indian in the facts of modern life has been played by Dr. Haya de la Torre and the party he founded in 1924, the Alianza Popular Revolucionaria Americana (A.P.R.A.). **1970** D. GOLDRICH et al. in I. L. Horowitz *Masses in Lat. Amer.* v. 190 The opposition majority congressional coalition (composed of APRA, Peru's erstwhile radical reform party, and the personalist party of former dictator General Odría). **1979** *Penguin Dict. 20th Cent. Hist.* (1982) 300 Although Apra had a parliamentary majority from 1945 to 1948 it was unable to carry out any fundamental reforms. **1983** *Financial Times* 15 Nov. 5/1 The victors were the left-of-centre Apra party which swept the board in the majority of districts outside Lima.

Hence **A'prismo** = APRA above; **A'prista**, a member of Apra; also *attrib.* or as *adj.*

1935 *Foreign Affairs* XIII. 236 *Aprismo* just missed being swept into power. **1937** *Republics S. Amer.* (R. Inst. Internat. Affairs) vi. 165 Aprismo is potentially an international movement, but in practice it has come to mean the Aprista Party of Peru. From 1925 onwards cells had been formed both in Paris and Latin American countries where Apristas were in exile. **1953** H. KANTOR (*title*) The ideology and program of the Aprista movement. **1965** J. L. PAYNE *Labor & Politics in Peru* I. ii 42 In essence, the Aprista movement was one of reform. **1974** *Encycl. Brit. Macropædia* XIV. 136/1 The military, fearing an alliance between the conservatives and the Apristas.., stepped in and seized the government. **1983** *N.Y. Times* 20 Nov. 75/3 The Apristas, who were moderate leftists, had been harshly repressed by the dictatorships.

apraxia (ə'præksɪə). *Path.* [mod.L., ad. Ger. *apraxie* (H. Steinthal *Einleit. in d. Psychologie* (1871) 458), a. Gr. ἀπραξία inaction.] Inability to perform purposeful movements; loss of ability to 'do'.

1888 M. A. STARR in *Med. Record* XXXIV. 497 (*title*) Apraxia and Aphasia; their varieties, and the methods..for their detection. **1922** R. S. WOODWORTH *Psychology* iii. 57 Injury to the 'super-motor centers' causes loss of skilled movement, and produces the condition of 'apraxia', in which the subject, though knowing what he wants to do, and though still able to move his limbs, simply cannot get the combination for the skilled act that he has in mind. **1961** *Lancet* 12 Aug. 363/2 The nature of the fundamental deficits underlying constructional apraxia..has not been elucidated.

‖**après coup** (aprɛ ku), *advb. phr.* [Fr., lit. 'after stroke'.] As an afterthought; after the event.

1871 GEO. ELIOT *Let.* 27 Feb. (1955) V. 136 These letters, which must speak better for him than the finest eloquence après coup. **1887** *Athenæum* 18 June 796/3 The name has probably been affixed to the book *après coup*, so to speak, and to allure the unwary reader. **1890** W. JAMES *Princ. Psychol.* II. xxviii. 630 Our abstract and general discoveries usually come to us as lucky fancies; and it is only *après coup* that we find that they correspond to some reality.

‖**après-ski** (aprɛ ski). [Fr.] The time when skiing is over for the day; = *after-ski* (AFTER- I. 1). Freq. *attrib.*, of clothes worn, entertainment, etc., at such a time.

1954 R. MARTIN *Your Ski Holiday* iv. 35 The 'après-ski' outfit..is based on the outdoor version. *Ibid.* viii. 62 There is always a queue of Britons to read it [*sc.* an English newspaper], during the hours of 'après-ski'. **1959** *Guardian* 27 Nov. 8/4 The allurement, for après-ski, of a fluffy wool cuddle-skirt. **1961** *Sunday Express* 1 Jan. 11/1 The ski-suit above..[is] for the indoor après-ski party.

† **apressly**, *adv. Obs. rare*⁻¹. Variant of EXPRESSLY: cf. ONF. *apresseement* (= *expressément*, Godef.), and see A- *pref.* 9.

c **1450** LONELICH *Grail* xxviii. 5 It to vs scheweth apressly, The declarenge of this holy storye.

apricate ('æprɪkeɪt), *v. rare.* [f. L. *aprīcāt-* ppl. stem of *aprīcā-ri* to bask in the sun, f. *aprīcus* exposed (to the sun).]

1. *intr.* To bask in the sun.

a **1691** ? in BOYLE; see TODD. *a* **1697** AUBREY in Halliwell s.v. *Toms-of-Bedlam*, His lordship was wont to recreate himself in this place, to apricate and contemplate. **1704** RAY *Let. to Aubrey* II. 159 (T.) Cesar, I think, said that 'verbum insolens tanquam scopulum fugiendum est.' I'll name you one or two, to *Apricate, suscepted, vesicate.*

2. *trans.* To expose to sunlight. Also *transf.*

1851 DE QUINCEY *Wks.* XIII. 16 To apricate and refresh old gouty systems and old traditions. *a* **1858** —— *Autobiog. Sk.* vi. Wks. II. 337 Not sunning, but mooning himself—apricating himself in the occasional moonbeams.

aprication (æprɪ'keɪʃən). [ad. L. *aprīcātiōn-em*, f. *aprīcāt-*: see prec.] Basking in the sun.

1623 COCKERAM, *Aprication*, a beaking in the Sunne.

a'price. *Obs. rare*⁻¹. [f. *aprise*, APPRIZE *v.*] Value, price.

c **1460** *Play Sacr.* 185 Orengis a[nd] apples of grete apryce.

apricide ('æprɪsaɪd). *nonce-wd.* [f. L. *apr-um* wild boar + -CIDE.] Slaughter of a boar.

1864 *Weekly Scotsm.* 10 Dec. 4 Instances..in which monarchs rewarded brilliant apricide with knighthood and acres.

† **a'pricity.** *Obs.*⁻⁰ [ad. L. *aprīcitāt-em*, n. of quality f. *aprīc-us*: see APRICATE and -TY.] 'The warmeness of the Sunne in Winter.' Cockeram 1623.

† **a'prick**, *v. Obs. rare*⁻¹. [f. A- *pref.* 1 + PRICK *v.*] To prick, spur on.

1297 R. GLOUC. 553 Sir Edward bed Sir Simon, þat he him ȝeue, To aprikie stedes wiþoute toun, leue.

aprick (ə'prɪk), *adv.* or *pred. a. poet.* [f. A *prep.*¹ + PRICK *v.*] Erect, pricked or pricking up.

1856 MRS. BROWNING *Aurora Leigh* VI. 237 Watching gnats a-prick upon a pond. **1898** O. SEAMAN *In Cap & Bells* 15 (*At the sign of the cock*) Amazon spurs aprick at heel. **1903** *Academy* 21 Feb. 186/2 The earth was quick with green a-prick.

apricot ('eɪprɪkɒt). Forms: α. 6 abrecok, -cox, aprecox, 6-7 -cok, abrecock(e, aprickok(e, 6-8 -cock, 7 aprecock. β. 6-8 abricot(e, 6 abbrycot, 7 abricoct, 6-7 apricote, 7 aprecott, 6- apricot. [orig. ad. Pg. *albricoque* or Sp. *albaricoque*, but subseq. assimilated to the cognate F. *abricot* (*t* mute). Cf. also It. *albercocca, albicocca*, OSp. *albarcoque*, a. Sp. Arab. *al-borcoq(ue* (P. de Alcala) for Arab. *al-burqūq, -birqūq*, i.e. *al* the + *birqūq*, ad. Gr. πραικόκιον (Dioscorides, *c* 100; later Gr. πρεκόκκια and βερικόκκια pl.), prob. ad. L. *præcoquum*, variant of *præcox*, pl. *præcocia*, 'early-ripe, ripe in summer,' an epithet and, in later writers, appellation of this fruit, orig. called *prūnum* or *mālum Armeniacum*. Thus Pallad. (*c* 350): 'armenia vel præcoqua.' The change in Eng. from *abr-* to *apr-* was perhaps due to false etymol.; Minsheu 1617 explained the name, quasi, 'in *aprīco coctus*' ripened in a sunny place: cf. the spelling *abricoct*.]

1. a. A stone-fruit allied to the plum, of an orange colour, roundish-oval shape, and delicious flavour.

1551 TURNER *Herbal* II. 48 Abrecockes..are less than the other peches. **1578** LYTE *Dodoens* VI. xl. 709 There be two kindes of peaches..The other kindes are soner ripe, wherefore they be called abrecox or aprecox. **1580** HOLLYBAND *Treas. Fr. Tong., Abricot*, a fruit called Apricot. **1593** SHAKS. *Rich. II*, III. iv. 29 Yond dangling Apricocks. **1601** HOLLAND *Pliny* I. 436 Abricocts are ready to be eaten in Summer. **1736** BAILEY *Housh. Dict.* s.v., To make Marmalade of Apricocks. **1870** MORRIS *Earthly Par.* I. II. 559 And apricots hung on the wall.

b. *transf.* The pinkish yellow colour of an apricot. Also *Comb.*, as ***apricot-coloured, -tinted*** adjs.

1906 *Daily Chron.* 19 Apr. 6/1 'Juliet', a large apricot-tinted rose. **1907** GALSWORTHY *Country House* II. ii. 119 The moon, tinted apricot and figured like a coin, hung above the cedar-trees. **1907** *Westm. Gaz.* 24 June 3/1 A portrait of a little girl in an apricot-coloured frock and pink ribbons. **1923** *Daily Mail* 28 Feb. 1 The newest Paris shades of Coral, Lilac,..Apricot. **1933** D. PARKER *After such Pleasures* (1934) 12 Her apricot satin chaise-longue.

2. The tree which bears this fruit (*Prūnus Armeniaca*); said to have been introduced into Greece from Armenia, and now cultivated in almost all temperate and sub-tropical climates.

1573-80 TUSSER *Husb.* xxxiv, Of trees or fruites to be set or remooued: 1. Apple-trees..2. Apricockes. **1718** J. CHAMBERLAYNE *Relig. Philos.* II. xxiii. §32 If an Abricot be grafted upon a Plumb. **1861** DELAMER *Kitchen Gard.* 144 In England..in a few favoured southern localities, standard apricots are a possibility.

3. *attrib.*, as in ***apricot-ale, -apple, -tree.***

apricot sickness *S. Afr.* [lit. tr. Afrikaans *Appelkoossiekte*, so named because it often appears at the beginning of summer when apricots ripen], a form of dysentery, said to be caused by a bacillus.

1551 TURNER *Herbal* II. 48 Of the Abrecok Tre. **1617** J. RIDER *Dict.*, An abricot apple, *Malum armenium.* **1657** AUSTEN *Fruit Trees* I. 51 Aprecok buds. **1712** STEELE *Spect.* No. 454 §4, I landed with Ten Sail of Apricock Boats. **1713** *Lond. & Countr. Brew.* III. (1743) 193 To make an Ale that will taste like Apricot-Ale. **1748** ANSON *Voy.* II. 118 Plumb, apricock, and peach stones. **1859** LANG *Wand. India* 303 Encamped beneath a clump of apricot and walnut trees. **1945** *Cape Times* 27 Jan. 11/3 Apricot sickness is most troublesome when the entire gastro-intestinal tract is affected; that is to say, when there is vomiting as well as diarrhoea.

April ('eɪprɪl). Forms: α. 3-4 averil, 4-5 averel, -ylle, avyryle. β. 4-5 aprille, -yll, apprile, -ille, 5 apryle, -el, 6 -elle, -ill, 7- April. [a. OF. *avrill* (11th c. in Littré), cogn. w. Sp. Pr. *abril*, It. *aprile*:—L. *aprīlis* (sc. *mensis*). Soon refashioned after L. with initial *apr-*: at first accented *a'pril(e*, as still in many of the dialects. *Averil* long remained in Sc.]

1. a. The fourth month of the year.

[**1140** *O.E. Chron.* (Laud MS.) þat was xiii k'Ap'l.] **1297** R. Glouc. 506 In the monthe of Aueril. **1377** Langl. *P. Pl.* B. xiii. 269 In a drye apprile [*v.r.* auerel]. **1386** Chaucer *C.T.* Prol. 1 Aprille [*v.r.* Apprille, Auerylle] with hise schoures swote. **1440** *Promp. Parv.*, Apryle monythe [*v.r.* Aprel]. *c* **1450** Lonelich *Grail* xli. 215 þe mone schon .. Al so bryght as in Averylle. **1555** *Chron. Gr. Friars* (1852) 95 The vij. day of Aprelle. **1712** Steele *Spect.* No. 432 ¶12 The Present I received the second of April. **1864** Tennyson *Tithonus* 60 Half-opening buds of April.

b. *attrib.* quasi-*adj.*, as in ***April day***, ***green***, ***sky***.

1579 Spenser *Sheph. Cal.* Apr. 7 Like April shoure, so stremes the trickling teares. **1591** Shaks. *Two Gent.* i. iii. 85 The vncertaine glory of an Aprill day. **1833** Tennyson *Poems* 45 Tremulous eyes, like April skies. **1850** Mrs. Browning *Poems* II. 292 A garden April-green. **1870** Morris *Earthly Par.* I. i. 307 When April-tide was melting into May. **1912** W. de la Mare *Listeners* 42 Under the April-grey calm waste of the skies. **1917** T. S. Eliot *Prufrock* 20 These April sunsets, that somehow recall My buried life. **1940** Blunden *Poems 1930–1940* 252 Bright-tressed, ready-smiling, April-eyed. **1953** E. Sitwell *Gardens & Astronomers* 37 Upon your wood-wild April-soft long hair.

2. *fig.* **a.** In reference to the position of April as the first month of Spring. **b.** In reference to the changeable weather, the sudden showers and sunshine of the month. Also *attrib.*

1596 B. Griffin *Fidessa* (1876) 35 The Aprill of my time, The sweet of youth. **1606** Shaks. *Ant. & Cl.* iii. ii. 43 The Aprill's in her eyes, it is Loue's spring. **1713** C'tess Winchelsea *Misc. Poems* 261 But April-drops our Tears, Which swiftly passing, all grows fair. **1835** Lytton *Rienzi* ix. ii. 375 The bloom, the flush, the April of the heart, was gone. **1844** Welby *Poems* (1867) 22 She's like myself An April-hearted thing. **1850** Tennyson *In Mem.* xl, And hopes and light regrets that come Make April of her tender eyes.

3. *Comb.*, as †**April-esquire**, ? a new-made squire; **April-fool**, one who is sent on a bootless errand, or otherwise sportively imposed upon, on the first of April; hence ***April-fool-day***: now commonly ***April Fool's Day***; also ***April-fool*** v., ***April-fooling*** vbl. sb.; †**April-gentleman**, a newly-married husband; **April-gowk** (i.e. *cuckoo*), northern equivalent of *April-fool*.

1592 Greene *Upst. Courtier* in *Harl. Misc.* (Malh.) II. 247 Two pert april esquires; the one had a murrey cloth gowne on. **1687** Congreve *Old Bachel.* i. iv, That's one of Love's April-fools, is always upon some errand that's to no purpose. *c* **1830** Gen. P. Thompson *Exerc.* (1842) IV. 518 It will be difficult to make April-fools of a whole people that can read and write. **1832** Carlyle in *Fraser's Mag.* V. 260 Let the foolish April-fool-day pass by. **1863** H. A. London in *Amer. Speech* (1951) XXVI. 181/1, [I] April fooled some fellows. **1903** *Encycl. Brit.* XXXV. 45/2 April Fool's Day. **1919** E. H. Jones *Road to En-dor* (ed. 2, 1920) xviii. 185 We set out .. in true April-fooling spirit. *Ibid.* 186 The old British custom of April-fooling. **1592** Greene *Upst. Courtier* (1871) 1 That time when the cuckold's chorister began to bewray April Gentlemen with his never changed notes. **1777** Brand *Pop. Antiq.* 400 We in the North call Persons who are thus deceived, April-Gowks.

Aprilesque (eɪprɪ'lɛsk), *a.* [f. prec. + -esque: cf. *picturesque*.] April-like.

1880 *Echo* 11 Dec. 2/6 Quite an Aprilesque balm in the air.

Aprilian (eɪ'prɪlɪən), *a.* [f. April + -ian.] Of or characteristic of April.

1902 *Daily Chron.* 24 Mar. 8/1 Rain of a spitefully Aprilian character. **1904** Bliss Carman *Songs Northern Garden* (1905) 10 Fear not the mighty instinct, The great Aprilian Creed; The House of Spring is open And furnished for thy need.

†**'aprine**, *a. Obs. rare.* [ad. L. *aprīn-us*, f. *aper* wild boar: see -ine.] Of or pertaining to wild swine.

1519 Horman *Vulg.* 110 Swyne wode for loue .. let passe from them a poyson called aprine.

‖**a priori** (eɪpraɪ'ɔəraɪ), *advb.* (and *adj.*) *phr.* [L. *ā* from, *priōri* what is before: cf. *a posteriori*.]

1. A phrase used to characterize reasoning or arguing from causes to effects, from abstract notions to their conditions or consequences, from propositions or assumed axioms (and not from experience); deductive; deductively.

1710 [See a posteriori 1]. **1771** Smeaton in *Phil. Trans.* LXI. 210 Nor can we *a priori* determine the value of any new instrument. **1834** [See a posteriori 1]. **1862** McCosh *Supernat.* ii. i. §2. 132 Reason commands us, in matters of experience, to be guided by observational evidence, and not by *à priori* principles.

2. Hence *loosely*: Previous to any special examination, presumptively, in accordance with one's previous knowledge or prepossessions.

1834 *Penny Cycl.* II. 199/1 When a sentence begins with '*à priori* we should think, etc. etc.' [it] in most cases will be found to mean nothing more than an expression of the leaning which the speaker found his mind inclined to, when he had only heard the proposition, and before he had investigated it. **1882** Farrar *Early Chr.* I. 85 This, however, can have only been an *à priori* conjecture, and there is no evidence which can be adduced in its support.

3. By some metaphysicians used for: Prior to experience; innate in the mind.

1841 Sir W. Hamilton in *Reid's Wks.* 762/1 The term *a priori*, by the influence of Kant and his school, is now very generally employed to characterise those elements of knowledge which are not obtained *a posteriori*,—are not evolved out of experience as facticious generalizations; but which, as native to, are potentially in, the mind antecedent to the act of experience.

apriorism (eɪprɪ'ɔərɪz(ə)m). [f. prec. + -ism, after mod.F. *apriorisme*.] Employment of *a priori* reasoning; *concr.* an *a priori* idea, or principle. Also, the philosophical doctrine of *a priori* or innate ideas (see a priori 3). So **apri'orist**, one who holds this doctrine; also *loosely*, one given to *a priori* reasoning; also *attrib.* or as *adj.*; hence **aprio'ristic** *a.*, pertaining to apriorism or apriorists.

1873 Lewes *Probl. Life & Mind* Ser. i. I. 412 This will be disputed by the *à priorists*. **1874** Watson & Evans tr. *Van Oosterzee's Christian Dogmatics* I. 141 No authority .. must .. be conceded to such an aprioristic criticism. *Ibid.* II. 596 However little .. inclined to an abstract a-priorism. **1883** in *Chicago Advance* 13 Sept., Apriorisms as ultimate grounds of knowledge. **1889** *Athenæum* 2 Feb. 152/3 The problem of external perception has a unique character among the controversies that divide the empiricists and the apriorists. **1889** G. B. Shaw *Fabian Ess. Socialism* 177 The apriorist notion that among free competitors wealth must go to the industrious. **1891** *Monist* I. 635 Empiricism is wrong because it can at best show the temporal succession of two phenomena, and apriorism is wrong because *a priori* knowledge lies in the subject alone and not in the object. **1914** Teixeira de Mattos tr. *Maeterlinck's Unknown Guest* iii. 42 The 'apriorists', who hold that the idea of time is innate. **1930** *Philosophy* V. 449 This Experimental Empiricism or Operational Apriorism is obviously attractive. **1934** T. S. Eliot *Eliz. Essays* 173 His statement is too *apriorist* to be quite trustworthy. **1958** *Times Lit. Suppl.* 17 Jan. 25/4 The vast advances of science .. have set up strong, though often unformulated, resistances against aprioristic ethics or philosophies.

apriority (eɪprɪ'ɒrɪtɪ). [f. as prec. + -ity, after *priority*.]

1. The quality of being original and underived from experience; innateness in the mind.

1854 Tulk tr. *Chalybaus' Hist. Philos.* ii. 29 The same Kantian criterion of a-priority. **1870** C. Peirce *Notation Log. Rel.* 51 The question concerning the apriority of space. **1879** Lewes *Stud. Psychol.* 176 His forms are pure abstractions, and he declines to predicate anything of them except their à-priority and universality.

2. Deductiveness; practice of *à priori* reasoning.

1879 *Athenæum* 12 July 44/2 The sublime apriority of Prof. Fawcett descends to such concrete matters as Indian Exchequer Bills.

†**'aprique**, *a. Obs. rare*$^{-1}$. Also 7 **aprike**. [ad. L. *aprīc-us* exposed (to the sun).] Sunny.

1656 Blount *Glossogr.*, *Aprique*, warmed with the Sun, or that loves to be in the Sunshine, Sunny. **1657** Tomlinson *Renou's Disp.* 287 The pale .. santal-tree fruticates best in aprike places.

aprise, earlier f. apprise *sb. Obs.*, learning.

†**a'prise.** *Obs.* [a. OF. *aprise* for *anprise* = *en-*, *em-prise*, from *emprendre* to take in hand, undertake: see emprise, the ordinary form.] Emprise; enterprise, undertaking, achievement.

c **1320** *Seuyn Sages* (W.) 1941 Ac ȝif thou leuest hire lesing, Than the falle a werse aprise. *c* **1450** Lonelich *Grail* xxx. 520 For ȝif thou do, thou lesist thin aprise. *Ibid.* lii. 558 Sche merveilled he spak of so gret aprys.

aproctous (ə'prɒktəs), *a. Phys.* [mod.f. Gr. ἀ priv. + πρωκτ-ός anus + -ous.] Having no anus.

1870 Rolleston *Anim. Life* Introd. 33 No vertebrate animal is aproctous.

apron ('eɪprən, 'eɪpən), *sb.* Forms: 4 **naperonn**, 5 **naprun(e**, **-onne**, **napperone**, 5–6 **napron**, 6 **aprone**, **-eren**, **-arne**, **ap(p)urn**, 6–7 **aperne**, 5– **apron**. [a. OF. *naperon* (mod.F. *napperon*), dim. of *nape*, *nappe*, table-cloth:—L. *mappa* table-napkin. The change of L. *m* to F. *n* is also seen in *matta*, *natte*, *mespilum*, *nèfle*; the med.L. instances of *napa*, *nappa* for *mappa* are prob. f. French. In Eng., initial *n* has been lost by corruption of *a napron* to *an apron*. See a *adj.*[2]]

1. a. An article of dress, originally of linen, but now also of stuff, leather, or other material, worn in front of the body, to protect the clothes from dirt or injury, or simply as a covering.

1307 in Whitaker's *Craven* in Beck *Drapers' Dict.* s.v., Pro linen tela ad naperonns. *c* **1400** *Beryn* Prol. 33 With hir napron feir .. She wypid sofft hir eyen. **1440** *Promp. Parv.*, Naprun (or barmclothe), *Limas*. **1466** *Paston Lett.* 549 II. 268 For ii. napronnes .. x*d.* **1461–83** *Ord. Roy. Househ.* 36 Lynnen clothe for aprons. *Ibid.* 52 Naprons of the grete spycery. **1535** Coverdale *Gen.* iii. 7 They .. sowed fygge leaues together, and made them apurns [**1611** aprons; Wyclif brechis]. **1542** *Richmond. Wills* (1853) 27 Nappery ware, as kyrcherys, appurnys, blankytts. **1569** *Wills & Inv. N.C.* (1835) 305 A Napron of worsted. **1598** Stow *Survay* xii. (1603) 103 Bill men in Almaine Riuets, and Apernes of Mayle. **1601** Shaks. *Jul. C.* i i. 7 Where is thy Leather Apron, and thy Rule? **1750** H. Walpole *Corr.* 221 II. 370 He would not be waited on by drawers in brown frocks and blue aprons. **1822** Scott *Nigel* iii, A green apron, and a red petticoat.

2. a. A similar garment worn as part of a distinctive official dress, as by bishops, deans, Freemasons, etc.

1704 *Lond. Gaz.* mmmmxxix/4 Had a black Silk Hood on, a painted Linen Apron. **1859** Helps *Friends in C.* Ser. ii. I. i. 50 Never be a bishop, nor even wear the lesser apron of a dean.

b. ***green apron***: a lay preacher (contemptuous).

1654 Warren *Unbelievers* 145 It more befits a Green-apron-Preacher, than such a Gamaliel. **1705** Hickeringill *Priestcr.* i. (1721) 21 Unbeneficed Noncons (that live by Alms, and no Paternoster no Penny, say the Green Aprons). [**1765** Tucker *Lt. Nat.* II. 451 The gifted priestess among the Quakers is known by her green apron.]

3. Anything which resembles an apron in shape or function, *esp.* the leather covering for the legs in a gig or other open carriage.

1790 *Pennsylv. Packet* 22 Apr. 2/1 A new Sulkey, with a top and apron. **1835** Dickens in *Evening Chron.* 21 July 1/3 Cabs, with trunks and band-boxes between the drivers' legs and outside the apron. **1875** B. Taylor *Faust* i. iii. II. 50 The merest apron of leaf and bough. **1879** Sala in *Daily Tel.* 9 June, A movement of his hinder heels in the direction of the cab-apron. **1883** *Punch* 10 Nov. 226 Strapped and buckled within a leather apron [of a bath-chair].

4. Also in many technical uses: **a.** At the bottom of a sluice or entrance to a dock: A platform placed so as to intercept the fall of water, and prevent the washing away of the bottom. **b.** in *Gunnery*, A square piece of lead laid over the touch-hole. **c.** in *Ship-building* (see quot. 1850). **d.** in *Plumbing*, A strip of lead which conducts the drip of a wall into a gutter. **e.** in *Electr.* (see quot. 1869). **f.** in *Mech.* The piece that holds the cutting tool in a planing machine.

1633 T. James *Voyage* 75 The Aprons of our Gunnes. **1711** W. Sutherland *Ship Builder's Asst.* 25 Raising the Stem and false Stem (or Apron) together. **1719** *Glossogr. Nova*, *Apron* is a piece of Lead which laps over or covers the Touch-hole of a great Gun. **1721** Perry *Daggenh. Breach* 24 The fixing of the Apron of the Sluice to the depth as before observ'd. **1842** Loudon *Encycl. Farm.* §935 The aprons [of lead] round the chimney-stalks. *c* **1850** *Rudim. Nav.* (Weale) 92 *Apron*, a kind of false or inner stem, fayed on the aftside of the stem, from the head down to the dead-wood, in order to strengthen it. **1862** F. Griffiths *Artill. Man.* 230 The 2nd captain .. attends the apron. **1867** F. Francis *Angling* iv. (1880) 140 Under the apron of Hampton Court weir. **1867** Smyth *Sailor's Word-bk.*, *Apron of a dock*, the platform rising where the gates are closed, and on which the sill is fastened down. **1869** *Eng. Mech.* 24 Dec. 346/1 The electricity .. developed on the glass by the friction of the rubbers, is carried over by a kind of sheath, technically called the *apron*.

g. An endless belt or band for conveying material of any kind, or a receptacle on such a belt. Also ***apron-conveyor***.

1835 Ure *Philos. Manuf.* iii. 155 His business is to weigh the wool, and spread it in definite quantities on a travelling apron, which feeds the first pair of rollers. *a* **1875** Knight *Dict. Mech.* I. 126/1 *Apron*, a board or leather which conducts material over an opening, as, the grain in a separator, the ore in a buddle or frame, etc. **1909** *Cent. Dict.* Suppl. s.v. *Conveyer*, An apron-conveyer consists of endless chains upon which wood or metal slats are placed close together, forming a continuous traveling platform.

h. A protective covering (on a bank, etc.) against the action of a river or the sea.

a **1884** Knight *Dict. Mech.* Suppl., *Apron*, a protecting surface of logs and brush .. to protect or to form revetment for river sides.

i. *Geol.* An outspread alluvial deposit, esp. one at the extremity of a glacier or the mouth of a river.

1889 N. S. Shaler in *U.S. Geol. Survey 9th Ann. Rep.* 548 In front of the kames normally comes the moranial apron... Traces of this frontal apron exist along the southern shore of Cape Ann. **1955** *Sci. Amer.* Mar. 82/2 The rivers of the continents have been building aprons into the sea with their wash of silt, clay, sand and gravel.

j. *Theatr.* (See quot. 1903.) Also ***apron stage***.

1903 A. B. Walkley *Dramatic Criticism* 108 The 'apron' is the technical name for the stage-area in front of the curtain. In the Elizabethan theatre it jutted right out among the public, who surrounded it on three sides. This 'apron' slowly shrank .. till at last in our day it has altogether disappeared. **1933** P. Godfrey *Back-Stage* i. 20 Turns are being played on the half-stage or upon the apron. **1950** G. B. Shaw in *New Statesman* 6 May 511/2 The Elizabethan stage .. with .. an apron stage projecting into the auditorium.

k. A defence against hostile aircraft consisting of a series of wires suspended from a cable to which captive balloons are attached.

1917, etc. Balloon apron [see balloon *sb.*[1] 10c]. **1919** C. C. Turner *Struggle in Air 1914–18* ix. 134 Then the 'apron' was devised, to aircraft a sufficiently dangerous and invisible obstruction which caused raiders to maintain a certain minimum altitude.

l. *Mil.* (See quot. 1918.) Also, a strip of barbed-wire entanglements.

1918 E. S. Farrow *Dict. Mil. Terms*, *Apron*, in fortification, that portion of the superior slope of a parapet or the interior slope of a pit designed to protect the slopes against blast. **1926** F. M. Ford *Man could Stand Up* ii. i. 77 There was their own apron—a perfect village!—of wire over which he looked.

m. A flat, usually paved, surface in front of a building, hangar, etc., *esp.* an area on an aerodrome prepared for the easy handling, (un)loading, etc., of aircraft on the ground.

1925 *March's Thesaurus Dict.* App. 110/1 Apron, an open working surface in front of a hangar. **1933** *Jrnl. R. Aeronaut. Soc.* XXXVII. 6 Where the concrete or asphalt apron in front of the buildings meets the aerodrome. **1954** C. ARMSTRONG *Better to eat You* iii. 24 Opposite a three-car garage there was a wide paved apron. *Ibid.* vi. 63 He..ran across..the parking apron. **1955** *Daily Tel.* 28 Jan. 6/5 The waving base is on the 'airside' as distinct from the 'landside' of the building, and thus gives a clear view of the aircraft leaving the 'terminal apron'.

n. A wooden platform trailed aft by the mother ship of a flying boat as a landing platform or for smoothing rough water. (Now disused.)

1933 *Discovery* Dec. 366/1 To make the call for refuelling the *Westfalen* is equipped with an apron which can be let out over the stern and trailed slightly below the surface of the water. The seaplanes will thus have a fairly smooth area of water on which they can alight if the sea is rough. **1941** *Flight* 24 Apr. 294/1 These ships made use of 'aprons' trailed in the water aft of the vessel... The advantage of the apron was that it reduced to a few minutes the time which the flying boat had to spend on the open sea.

o. *Photogr.* (See quot. 1940.)

1935 *News Chron. Amat. Photogr.* v. 89 Next tuck the film end underneath the flexible apron so that the clip is holding both the apron and the end of the film. **1940** F. J. MORTIMER *Wall's Dict. Photogr.* (ed. 15) *Apron*, band of celluloid or other material used to separate successive turns of film when rolled up for development in a tank.

5. a. 'The caul of a hog.' Halliw. ***apron of a roast goose or duck***: the skin covering the belly, which is cut to get at the stuffing.

1755 in JOHNSON. **1855** MRS. RUNDELL *Dom. Cookery* Introd. 50 Cut off the apron in the circular line *a, b, c.*

b. (See quot. 1876.)

1855 *Fraser's Mag.* LI. 267 These [crabs] were lying apron upwards on the ground. **1876** *Field & Forest* II. 73 This mass is very conspicuous even in the rapidly swimming crab, and causes the abdominal flap (called apron by fishermen) to be opened almost to its fullest extent.

c. = TABLIER 3. Also called ***Hottentot apron, pudendal apron***.

1909 in *Cent. Dict.* Suppl. **1956** WINICK *Dict. Anthropol.* (1957) 33 There is some controversy as to whether the Hottentot apron is a genetic trait or an intentional deformation.

6. *Comb.* and *Attrib.*, as **apron-cloth** (see sense 3); **apron husband**, one that meddles with his wife's business; **apron-lining**, the cover of the *apron-piece*; †**apron-man**, a mechanic; an 'aproner'; **apron-piece**, a small piece of timber supporting the joists under the landing-place in a stair; †**apron-rogue**, a workman, mechanic; **apron-squire** = APPLE-SQUIRE; **apron wall** *Build.* (see quot. 1934). Also ***apron-like***; and APRON-STRING, q.v.

1857 D. H. STROTHER *Virginia Illustr.* ii. 139 The *apron-cloth was drawn up over their legs and with a..crack of the whip they started into the storm. **1611** MIDDLETON & DEKKER *Roar. Girl* Wks. 1873, 177, I cannot abide these *aperne husbands: such cotqueanes. **1859** TODD *Cycl. Anat. & Phys.* V. 326/2 The..*apron-like fold that covers the greater part of the intestinal canal. **1607** SHAKS. *Cor.* IV. vi. 96 You haue made good worke, You and your *Apron men. **1658** CLEVELAND *Rustic Ramp.* Wks. 1687, 429 Apron-men and Plough-joggers. **1859** J. GWILT *Encycl. Archit.* (ed. 4) 894 **Apron*, or *Pitching Piece*, an horizontal piece of timber, in wooden double-flighted stairs, for supporting the carriage pieces or rough strings and joistings in the half spaces or landings. The apron pieces should be firmly wedged into the wall. **1663** KILLEGREW *Parson's Wed.* in Dodsley (1780) XI. 382 *Apron-rogues with horn hands. **1593** NASHE *Christ's Teares* 83 b, They will..play the Brokers, Baudes, *Apron-squires, Pandars, or any thing. **1934** WEBSTER, **Apron wall*, that portion of the enclosing wall of a building between a window-head or lintel of one story and the sill of the window in the story above or, sometimes, only that portion between the floor line and the window sill of the same story. **1952** *Archit. Rev.* CXI. 262 A new system of wall construction (which can be briefly described as 3-ply apron walls formed in-situ).

apron (ˈeɪprən), *v.* [f. prec. sb.] To cover with, or as with, an apron.

1865 DICKENS *Mut. Fr.* III. iv. 289, I mean to apron it and towel it. **1880** BLACKMORE *M. Anerley* III. xvi. 230 The..bramble aproned the yellow dugs of shale with brown.

aproned (ˈeɪprənd), *ppl. a.* [f. prec. + -ED[2].] Having an apron (freq. in *comb.*); formerly used for: Of the working class, mechanic.

1628 FELTHAM *Resolves* xx. (1635) 73 Hee prodigals a Mine of Excellencie, that lavishes a terse Oration to an Apron'd Auditory. **1640** BP. HALL *Chr. Moder.* 33/1 A separatist, a blue-aproned man, that never knew any better school than his shop-board. **1868** GEO. ELIOT *Sp. Gypsy* 173 Leather-aproned smiths. *a* **1916** H. JAMES *Ivory Tower* (1917) III. i. 152 Only to collapse again like aproned puppets on removal of pressure from the squeak. **1922** JOYCE *Ulysses* 121 He walked on.., passing an old man, bowed, spectacled, aproned.

†**apro'neer.** *Obs.* [f. as prec. + -EER[1].] One who wears an apron; a shopman or mechanic. (Used contemptuously of the Parliamentary party during the Civil Wars: cf. APRON *sb.* 2 b.)

1659 GAUDEN *Tears of Ch.* 238 (D.) Some prating Sequestrator, or some surly Aproneer. **1690** D'URFEY *Collin's Walk* III. (D.) Every sturdy aproneer Arm'd with battoon did straight appear.

†**'aproner.** *Obs.* In 7 aperner. [f. as prec. + -ER[1].] One who wears an apron; a barman, waiter.

1611 CHAPMAN *May Day* Plays 1873 II. 376 We haue no wine here me thinks, where's this Aperner? *Drawer.* Here Sir.

apronful (ˈeɪprənfʊl). [f. as prec. + -FUL.] The quantity that can be held in an apron.

1865 *Pall Mall G.* 15 Aug. 10/1 The goodwife when she appears with her apronful of barley. **1868** MISS BRADDON *Dead Sea Fr.* II. x. 240 An apronful of flowers.

apronless (ˈeɪprənlɪs), *a.* Without an apron.

1865 DICKENS *Mut. Fr.* III. iv. 27 Bibless and apronless.

'apron-string. The string with which an apron is tied on. ***apron-string hold*** or ***tenure***: tenure of property in virtue of one's wife, or during her life-time only. ***tied to the apron-strings*** (of a mother, wife, etc.): unduly controlled by her, wholly under her influence. Also *transf.* Also **apron-string** *v. trans. rare.*

1542 UDALL *Erasm. Apophth.* 118 As wise as a gooce, or as wise as her mothers aperen string. **1647** WARD *Simp. Cobler* 67 Apron-string tenure is very weak. **1678** RAY *Prov.* (ed. 2) 226 To hold by the *Apron-strings. i.e.* in right of his wife. **1698** J. FRYER *New Acc. E. India & Persia* III. iii. 115 They ..would subjugate us, as they do all others that are harness'd witte the Apron-strings of Trade. **1750** ELLIS *Mod. Husb.* VI. ii. 118 [A man] being possessed of a house and large orchard by apron-string-hold, felled almost all his fruit trees, because he every day expected the death of his sick wife. **1804** MRS. BARBAULD *Richardson* I. 160 All her fortune in her own power—a very apron-string tenure. **1825** *Eng. Life* I. 165 A man of your inches ought to be above making such an apron-string booby of yourself. **1848** A. BRONTË *Wildfell Hall* I. iii. 44 Even at *his* age, he ought not to be always tied to his mother's apron string. **1849** MACAULAY *Hist. Eng.* II. 649 He could not submit to be tied to the apron strings even of the best of wives. **1912** A. S. M. HUTCHINSON *Happy Warrior* IV. ii. 196 That he should submit to be thus chained, thus apron-stringed! **1960** *Times* 26 Apr. 16/2 The drama..points insistently, in the last two acts, away from Rimsky-Korsakov's apron-strings.

apropos (æprəˈpəʊ, ‖aprɔpo), *adv.*, *a.*, *sb.* Also ‖**à propos.** [F. *à propos* (used in Fr. as adv., adj., and sb.), f. *à* to + *propos* purpose, plan, f. L. *prōpositum*, pa. pple. of *prōpōnĕre* to set forth, propose.] Const. *to*, *of*.

A. *adv.*

1. To the propose; fitly, opportunely.

1668 DRYDEN *Ess. Dram. Poesy*, The French..use them with better judgment, and more àpropos. **1708** ADDISON in Dk. Manch. *Crt. Eliz. to Anne* II. 315 Stanhope and Earl arrived very àpropos. **1714** MANDEVILLE *Fab. Bees* (1733) II. 187 Men of prodigious reading..who judge ill, and seldom say any thing à propos.

2. With regard *to*, in respect *of*, as suggested by. (Fr. *à propos de.*) *absol.* (as introductory to an incidental observation or question): By the way.

1761 SMOLLETT *Gil Blas* IX. i. (1802) III. 44 But a-propos! Hast thou seen the girl? **1840** HOOD *Up Rhine* 166 *Apropos* to which last, you will find enclosed, etc. **1883** BLACK *Shand. Bells* xxxiii, Suddenly, and *à propos* of nothing, asking him how it was possible for a man to have three godmothers.

B. *adj.* To the point or purpose; having direct reference to the matter in hand; pertinent, opportune, 'happy.'

1691 T. H[ALE] *New Invent.* 44 It is certainly..*a propos* what he had said before in that Page. **1730** SOUTHALL *Bugs* 20 The thought was à propos. *c* **1735** POPE *Hor. Epist.* II. ii. 154 A tale extremely apropos. **1826** DISRAELI *Viv. Grey* III. vii. 117 Is there not a passage in Spix apropos to this?

C. *sb.* An opportune or pertinent occurence (*obs.*); pertinency.

1783 *Europ. Mag.* III. 246 A greater apropos than this happened from mere accident. **1860** *Edinb. Rev.* No. 225. 96 Few men..have described what they have seen with more apropos.

D. Phr. ***à propos de bottes*** [Fr., lit. = 'with regard to boots'], without serious motive, without rhyme or reason.

1757 CHESTERFIELD *Let.* 23 Sept. (1774) II. 378 *A propos de bottes*, for I am told he always wears his; was his Royal Highness very gracious to you, or not? **1845** *Q. Rev.* LXXVI. 533 The first introduces that prince—very much àpropos de bottes—for the purpose of denying that he had any party. **1925** A. HUXLEY *Those Barren Leaves* I. i. 9 She would remember an ancient floater—just like that, *à propos de bottes.* **1934** 'G. ORWELL' *Burm. Days* (1935) xviii. 225 This was *àpropos de bottes*, but the subject needed no introduction.

aprosexia (æprəʊˈsɛksɪə). *Med.* [mod.L., a. Du. *aprosexia* (Guye 1887, in *Nederl. Tijdschr. v. Geneesk.* XXIII. 381), a. Gr. ἀπροσεξία, f. ἀ- priv. (A- 14) + προσέχειν to turn (the attention): see -IA[1].] Abnormal inability to concentrate one's attention.

1889 A. A. G. GUYE in *Brit. Med. Jrnl.* 28 Sept. 709/2 (*title*) On aprosexia, being the inability to fix the attention and other allied troubles in the cerebral functions caused by nasal disorders. *Ibid.* 710/1 What I call aprosexia is the inability to fix the attention on any definite more or less abstract subject. **1894** W. JAMES in *Psychol. Rev.* 528 His *aprosexia* is complete, and he is incapable of interest in anything whatever. **1901** BALDWIN *Dict. Philos. & Psychol.* I. 88/1 Aprosexia is also used in a more general sense for the inability to fix the attention; when due to neurasthenia, it would be neurasthenic aprosexia; when due to nasal obstruction, nasal aprosexia. **1948** *Brit. Jrnl. Psychol.* Dec. 119 The abnormalities of attention are classified as 'aprosexia', 'hyperprosexia', and 'paraprosexia'.

aprosopia (æprəʊˈsəʊpɪə). *Teratology.* [mod.L., f. Gr. ἀ- priv. (A- 14) + πρόσωπ-ον face + -IA[1].] Absence or imperfect development of the face.

1842 in R. DUNGLISON *Dict. Med. Sci.* (ed. 3) 61/2. **1922** JOYCE *Ulysses* 403 Aprosopia due to a congestion.

aprotic (eɪˈprəʊtɪk), *a. Chem.* [ad. G. *aprotisch* (J. N. Brönsted 1930, in *Zeitschr. f. angew. Chem.* XLIII. 232/1): see A- 14, PROTON, -IC.] Of a liquid, esp. a solvent: having little or no tendency to accept or donate protons; neither protogenic nor protophilic.

1931 *Chem. Rev.* VIII. 194 A solvent of opposite or aprotic character is represented by benzene, which neither gives up nor takes up protons to any considerable extent. **1940** [see PROTOGENIC *a.*[2]]. **1965** PHILLIPS & WILLIAMS *Inorg. Chem.* I. xv. 556 In 'aprotic' solvents the acid-base concept may be extended to regard those substances which generate the solvent cation (e.g. NO^+ in NOCl..) as 'Lewis' acids, and those which generate the solvent anion (e.g. Cl^- in NOCl..) as 'Lewis' bases. **1973** [see PROTIC *a.*]. **1983** *Chemical Week* 25 May 37/1 The aprotic solvents are expensive and the purification equipment that is necessary to recover them entails a considerable capital investment.

aps, OE. and dial. form of ASP, ASPEN.

apse (æps). Pl. **apses** (ˈæpsɪz). [ad. L. *apsis*: cf. *basis, base, axis, axe*, etc. See APSIS.]

1. *Arch.* A semi-circular or polygonal recess, arched or dome-roofed, in a building, *esp.* at the end of the choir, aisles, or nave of a church. Cf. APSIS 3.

1846 in PARKER *Concise Gloss. Arch.* **1849** FREEMAN *Archit.* 155 The altar was placed at the end of the nave, on the chord of the apse. **1876** M. DAVIES *Unorth. Lond.* 329 Behind this, occupying the apse, was an organ.

2. *Astr.* = APSIS 2.

1822 IMISON *Sci. & Art* II. 427 The two points in a planet's orbit..furthest and nearest to the body round which it moves, are called the apses, or apsides. **1879** LOCKYER *Elem. Astron.* ix. xlix. 307 The apses, or extremities of the major axis—the aphelion or perihelion points.

†**'apsid.** *Obs.* Also 7 abside. [a. It. *absíde*; or Fr. *abside* in Arch., *apside* in Astron., differentiated adaptations of L. *absīd-em* or *apsīd-em*, nom. *absis* or *apsis*, also *absīda.*] = APSE, APSIS.

1670 LASSELS *Voy. Italy* II. 103 The picture of our Saviour in the very Tribuno, or Abside [of St. John Lateran]. **1743** *Phil. Trans.* XLII. 346 A Body approaches from the higher Apsid toward the Centre.

apsidal (ˈæpsɪdəl), *a.* [f. L. *apsīd-em* + -AL[1].]

1. *Astr.* Of or belonging to the apsides.

1859 in WORCESTER. **1860** *All Y. Round* No. 52. 43 The name of apsidal line given to the major axis of the orbit.

2. *Arch.* Of the form or nature of an apse.

1846 HOOK *Ch. Dict.* 56 The apsidal termination of the chancel is still common. **1876** M. DAVIES *Unorth. Lond.* 254 Behind the choir there are seven apsidal and two rectangular chapels.

apsidiole (æpˈsɪdɪəʊl). *Archit.* Also **absidiole.** [ad. F. *absidiole* a small apse.] A small or secondary apse.

1889 in *Cent. Dict.* **1905** F. BOND *Goth. Arch.* (1906) ix. 170 The semicircular apses and absiodoles [*sic*] of Romanesque become polygonal in Gothic. **1951** *Archit. Rev.* CX. 338/3 The ambulatory with an apsidiole half buried in the ground enabling pilgrims to see the relics in the crypt.

apsie: see ABC.

‖**apsis** (ˈæpsɪs). Pl. **apsides** (æpˈsaɪdiːz, commonly in Eng. ˈæpsɪdiːz). Also 6–9 **absis.** [L. *apsis, absis* (pl. *aps-, absīdes*), a. Gr. ἀψίς, ἁψίς a fastening, the felloe of a wheel, *hence* a wheel, arch, vault, f. ἅπ-τ-ειν to join, fasten. It would be well to restrict *apsis* to the astronomical sense, leaving APSE in the architectural.]

†**1.** Circumference, circuit; orbit of a planet. *Obs.*

1601 HOLLAND *Pliny* I. 10 [The planets] seeme to moue more slowly when they goe their highest circuit..because the lines which are drawne from the top of the Absis, must needs grow narrow and neere together about the centre, as the spokes in cart wheeles. **1603** —— *Plutarch's Mor.* 1312 The Absis or rundle of the Sistrum. **1706** PHILLIPS, *Absis*.. the Ring or Compass of a Wheel.

2. *Astr.* One of the two points in the elliptic orbit of a planetary body, at which it is respectively at its greatest and least distance from the body about which it revolves; the aphelion or perihelion of a planet, the apogee or perigee of the moon. *Line of apsides*: the straight line joining these two points.

1658 PHILLIPS, *Absis*, when the Planets moving to their highest or lowest places, are at a stay; the *high Absis*, being call'd the *Apogæum*, and the *low Absis*, the *Perigæum*. **1681** SIR G. WHARTON *Mut. Empires* Wks. 129 The Change of the Absides of the Planets. **1750** *Phil. Trans.* XLVII. xi. 64 A given motion of the apsis, retrograde or direct. **1862** H. SPENCER *First Princ.* II. x. §83 The revolution of the line of apsides, which in course of time moves round the heavens.

3. *Arch.* = APSE I.

1706 PHILLIPS, *Absis* or *Apsis*, the bowed or arched Roof of a House, Room, or Oven. **1845** FORD *Handbk. Spain* vi. 509 One noble nave with a semicircular absis. **1852** MRS. JAMESON *Leg. Madonna* (1857) 6 The figure in the apsis of St. John Lateran.

b. Also, since these had their place in an apse or apsis, used for: (*a*) The bishop's seat or throne in ancient churches. (*b*) A reliquary.

apsychical (æp'saɪkɪkəl), *a. rare.* [f. Gr. ἀ priv. + ψῡχικ-ός (f. ψῡχή mind, spirit) + -AL¹.]

1. Unspiritual.

1678 J. J[ONES] *Brit. Ch.* 495 Rivers cannot ascend higher than their springs, nor an absychitical [*sic*] religion, higher than the body.

2. Not connected with or controlled by the mind.

1878 FOSTER *Phys.* II. ii. §6. 292 Apsychical nervous centres.

† **'apsychy.** *Obs.*—⁰ [ad. Gr. ἀψῡχία, abst. n. f. ἄψυχος lifeless, spiritless: see prec.] 'A swooning or fainting away.' Bailey 1731.

apt (æpt), *a.* [ad. L. *apt-us* fitted, suited, appropriate, pa. pple. of *ap-ĕre to fasten, attach.] Const. *to*, *for*, or *inf.*

1. Fitted (materially), fitting. *rare.*

1791 COWPER *Iliad* III. 393 His brother's corslet..apt to his own shape and size.

2. Suited, fitted, adapted (*to* (obs.) or *for* a purpose); having the requisite qualifications; fit.

a. of things. *arch.*

1398 TREVISA *Barth. De P.R.* XVII. clvii. (1495) 707 Stoble is apt to many dyuerse vses. **1432–50** tr. *Higden* Rolls Ser. I. 163 Thei toke places apte to make cites. **1526** TINDALE *N.T.* Addr., To make it more apte for the weake stomakes. **1625** BACON *Ess.* (Arb.) 471 States..apt to be the Foundations of Great Monarchies. **1677** MOXON *Mech. Exerc.* (1703) 181 The Workman chuses such sizes as are aptest for his Work. **1858** CARLYLE *Fredk. Gt.* I. II. ii. 54 Tracts of Preussen are ..frugiferous, apt for the plough.

b. of persons: Fit, prepared, ready. *arch.*

1474 CAXTON *Chesse* 27 Whiche of hem..was most apte for to sende to gouerne and juge the contre of spayn. **1526** TINDALE *Luke* ix. 62 No man that..loketh backe is apte to the kyngdom of God. **1601** SHAKS. *Jul. C.* III. i. 160 Liue a thousand yeeres, I shall not finde my selfe so apt to dye. *a* **1700** MRS. HUTCHINSON *Mem. Hutchinson* 22 He was apt for any bodily exercise. **1870** MORRIS *Earthly Par.* I. I. 20 Tall was he, slim, made apt for feats of war.

3. a. *ellipt.* Suited to its purpose; suitable, becoming, appropriate.

1563 *Myrr. Mag., Blacksmith* xix, The Plowman fyrst his land doth dresse and torne And makes it apte. **1597** MORLEY *Introd. Mus.* Annot., [Musicke is] a disposition of proportionable soundes deuided by apt distances. **1630** DEKKER *Honest Wh.* II. Wks. 1873 II. 99 Pray the good woman take some apter time. **1710** STEELE *Tatler* No. 8 ⁋ 1 Recommending the apt Use of a Theatre as the most agreeable..Method of making a..moral Gentry. **1807** WORDSW. *Resol. & Indep.* xvi, To give me human strength, by apt admonishment.

b. *esp.* of language: Suitable or appropriate to express ideas; apposite, expressive.

1590 SHAKS. *Mids. N.* V. i. 65 In all the play There is not one word apt. **1688** LD. DELAMER *Wks.* 20 Apt words and quaint Phrases are very good adornments of Speech. **1865** MILL *Liberty* v. 57/1 What in the apt language of Bentham is called pre-appointed evidence.

c. of thoughts, remarks, etc. Appropriate to the occasion, apposite.

1844 DISRAELI *Coningsby* v. vii. 216 The prompt reply or the apt retort. **1849** W. IRVING *Mahom. & Succ.* xiv. (1853) 63 The smoke was an apt thought, and saved his camp from being sacked. **1877** SPARROW *Serm.* xxi. 284 The apt reply of the little Sunday-school scholar, who, when asked what eternity was, replied, 'The life-time of God.'

4. Having a habitual tendency or predisposition (*to* do something).

1570 LEVINS *Manip.* (1867) 28 Apte, *aptus, idoneus*..is also the signe of verballes in *-bilis*, and participials in *-dus*: Apt to be taught, *docilis*; Apt to be red, *legibilis*.

a. of things: Calculated, likely; habitually liable, ready.

1528 MORE *Heresyes* IV. Wks. 248/2 Yet be such workes.. apte to corrupt and infect the reder. **1678** BUTLER *Hud.* III. i. 1048 For fat is wondrous apt to burn. **1784** COWPER *Lett.* Feb. 29 Wks. 1876, 161 Nothing is so apt to betray us into absurdity as too great a dread of it. **1868** FREEMAN *Norm. Conq.* II. vii. 12 Any kind of taxation is apt to be looked on as a grievance.

b. of persons: Customarily disposed, given, inclined, prone.

c **1550** *Lusty Juv.* in Hazl. *Dods.* II. 53 That I may be apt thy holy precepts to fulfil. **1592** SHAKS. *Rom. & Jul.* III. i. 34 So apt to quarell. **1718** POPE *Iliad* XXIV. 530 For apt is youth to err. **1771** FRANKLIN *Autobiog.* Wks. 1840 I. 85, I perceive I am apt to speak in the singular number. **1857** RUSKIN *Pol. Econ. Art* 26 We are apt to act too immediately on our impulses.

c. Inclined, disposed (in a single instance).

1677 R. CARY *Palæol. Chron.* II. II. I. iv. 195, I am apt to think, that..Vashti is meant. **1706** HEARNE *Rem. & Collect.* (1885) I. 297, I am apt to think he has not consulted Books enough upon this occasion. **1899** E. E. HALE *Lowell* 126, I am apt to think that this modest man was the first person.. to recognize [etc.].

5. Susceptible to impressions; ready to learn; intelligent, quick-witted, prompt. Mod. const. *at*.

1535 COVERDALE *Ecclus.* xxxvii. 22 Some man is apte and well instructe in many thinges. **1601** SHAKS. *Jul. C.* v. iii. 68 O hatefull error..Why do'st thou shew to the apt thoughts of men The things that are not. **1660** PEPYS *Diary* 28 Aug., Beginning to teach my wife some scale in musique, and found her apt beyond imagination. **1719** DE FOE *Crusoe* (1858) 220 He was the aptest scholar that ever was. **1832** HT. MARTINEAU *Life in Wilds* vi. 77 Men..are..apt at devising ways of easing their toils.

¶ quasi-*adv.*, as in ***apt-deceiving***, ***-divided***.

1597 DANIEL *Civ. Wars* I. lxx, Intestine strife..The apt-divided state entangle would. *Ibid.* (1717) 213 Such apt-deceiving Clemency And seeming Order.

† **apt,** *sb. Obs. rare.* [f. prec.] Natural tendency.

c **1400** *Test. Love* III. (1560) 301 b/1 They have as well divers aptes, and divers manner usings, and thilke aptes mowen in will been cleaped affections.

† **apt,** *v. Obs.* [f. prec. adj.: cf. *fit*, to *fit*.]

1. To make fit, adapt (*to*), prepare suitably (*for*).

1575 LANEHAM *Lett.* (1871) 35 A song wel apted too a melodious noiz. **1582** STANYHURST *Æneid* (Arb.) 38 In mydst of chaumber thee roume for bancket is apted. **1601** B. JONSON *Poetaster* I. i, He shall follow and observe what I will apt him to. **1672** DK. BUCKHM. *Rehearsal* II. v, Composing this Air, and apting it for the business.

b. *refl.*

1540 RAYNALD *Birth Man.* I. x. (1634) 37 The matter.. inclining and apting it selfe..to the..nature of the vessels. **1633** MASSINGER *New Way, etc.* III. ii, Apt thyself To the noble state I labour to advance thee.

2. *intr.* (for *refl.*) To suit, be suitable or fitting.

1602 WARNER *Alb. Eng.* IX. xliv. (1612) 212 Here occasion apteth that we catalogue a while. *Ibid.* Epit., Out of which I..have gleaned not a little apting to this our abridged Historie.

3. *trans.* To incline, dispose *to*.

a **1625** FLETCHER *Love's Pilgr.* II. iii. (T.) They are things ignorant, And therefore apted to that disposition Of doting fondness. **1641** DENHAM *Sophy* II. (1667) 19 The king is melancholy, Apted for any ill impressions.

† **'aptable,** *a. Obs.*—⁰ [f. APT *v.* + -ABLE.] That may be fitted or adapted.

1611 COTGR., *Accommodable*, Fittable, aptable, appliable.

† **'aptate,** *v. Obs.*—⁰ [f. L. *aptāt-* ppl. stem of *aptā-re* to fit, adapt, f. *aptus*: see APT *a.*]

1678 PHILLIPS, *Aptate*, to fit and prepare a thing properly to a designed end: as for example to *aptate* a Planet..is..to fortifie the Planet in Position of House, and dignities to the greatest advantage. [So in BAILEY.]

apteral ('æptərəl), *a. rare.* [f. Gr. ἄπτερ-ος wingless (f. ἀ priv. + πτερ-όν wing) + -AL¹.]

1. Wingless; in *Zool.* = APTEROUS.

1833 *Elgin Marb.* II. 60 Marbles from the Temple of apteral Victory.

2. *Arch.* Having no columns along the sides.

1834 *Penny Cycl.* II. 199/2 Our modern churches which have porticoes..are..generally, illustrations of the apteral arrangement.

'apteran, *a.* and *sb. Zool.* [f. as prec. + -AN.]

A. *adj.* Wingless. **B.** *sb.* A wingless insect; one of the *Aptera*.

1852 in BRANDE.

‖**apterium** (æp'tɪərɪəm). *Ornith.* Pl. -ia. [mod.L. (Nitzsch 1833), f. Gr. ἀ- priv. (A- 14) + πτερόν feather.] Each of the featherless spaces on the skin of a bird intervening between the feathered tracts or *pterylæ*.

1867 W. S. DALLAS tr. *Nitzsch's Pterylography* 16 To these feathered bands I give the name of Feather-tracts or Contour-feather-tracts (*pterylæ*, Federn-fluren), and to the naked bands, or those which are not beset with contour-feathers, that of featherless spaces (*apteria*, Federn-raine). **1894** [see PTERYLA].

apteroid ('æptərɔɪd). *Zool. rare.* [f. as APTERAN *a.* and *sb.* + -OID.] A bird having the wings merely rudimentary (as the emu).

1836 [See APOD.]

apterous ('æptərəs), *a.* [f. as prec. + -OUS.]

1. *Zool.* Wingless; *esp.* belonging to the *Aptera*, a sub-order of Insects including lice and spring-tails.

1775 WHITE *Selborne* lxv. (1865) 272 These apterous insects. **1786** LIGHTFOOT *Brit. Shells* in *Phil. Trans.* LXXVI. 169 The body of the single specimen which had wings was..narrower than the apterous ones. **1880** BASTIAN *Brain* 61 Blind insects are all apterous.

2. *Bot.* Of seeds, leaf-stalks, etc.: Having no membranous expansions; opposed to *alate*.

1830 LINDLEY *Nat. Syst. Bot.* 45 [The Mangosteen Tribe have] seeds..always apterous.

apterygial (æptə'rɪdʒɪəl), *a. Ichthyol.* [f. Gr. ἀ- priv. (A- 14) + PTERYG- + -(I)AL.] Destitute of fins, finless.

1902 *Nature* 25 Sept. 526 We may distinguish the Cyclostomes as apterygial and epicraniate.

apteryx ('æptərɪks). *Ornith.* [f. Gr. ἀ priv. + πτέρυξ wing: cf. ἀπτέρυγος wingless.] A New Zealand bird, about the size of a goose, with merely rudimentary wings and no tail, called by the natives Kiwi.

1813 G. SHAW *Natur. Misc.* XXIV. 1058 The Southern Apteryx. **1854** OWEN in *Orr's Circ. Sc.* I. 221 Birds devoid of the power of flight, such as the ostrich and apteryx.

Aptian ('æptɪən), *a.* (*sb.*) *Geol.* [f. place-name *Apt* (Vaucluse, France) + -IAN.] Epithet of a division of the Lower Cretaceous formation in France and Belgium; belonging to or found in this, as a fossil.

1864 J. D. DANA *Man. Geol.* (ed. 2) III. iii. 480 The subdivisions of the Cretaceous are variously named in different parts of Europe. *Lower Cretaceous.*—Superior Neocomian of D'Orbigny (the Wealden being the inferior); also his Aptian. *Ibid.* 776/2 Aptian group. **1885** A. GEIKIE *Geol.* (ed. 2) 831 In northern France the Aptian stage is chiefly clay. **1921** *Brit. Mus. Return* 151 Aptian fossils from Whale's Head.

aptitude ('æptɪtju:d). [a. F. *aptitude* (16th c. in Littré), ad. med.L. *aptitūdo*, n. of quality f. L. *aptus*: see APT *a.* and -TUDE. Cf. also ATTITUDE.]

1. The quality of being fit for a purpose or position, or suited to general requirements; fitness, suitableness, appropriateness.

1643 MILTON *Divorce* I. iv. (1847) 128/2 That sociable and helpful aptitude..between man and woman. **1654** WARREN *Unbelievers* 62 They lose their aptitude for heaven. **1749** *Power Pros. Numb.* 19 For the Sake of Aptitude of Expression. **1809** PINKNEY *Trav. France* 144 Its aptitude for the residence of a foreigner. **1851** HELPS *Comp. Solitude* xi. (1874) 188 In any comparison so frequently used there must be some aptitude.

2. Natural tendency, propensity, or disposition.

1633 EARL MANCH. *Al Mondo* (1636) 90 Nor hath [the bodie] aptitude in it selfe to reanimation. *a* **1704** LOCKE (J.) He that is about children should study their nature and aptitudes. **1859** OWEN *Class. Mamm.* 34 The aptitude of the Cheiroptera..to fall like Reptiles into a state of true torpidity.

3. a. Natural capacity, endowment, or ability; talent *for* any pursuit.

1789–96 MORSE *Amer. Geog.* I. 257 A remarkable aptitude for mechanical inventions. **1855** BAIN *Senses & Intell.* II. i. §23 Our estimate of time is one of the earliest of our mental aptitudes. **1879** CALDERWOOD *Mind & Br.* ix. 263 There is a physical acquisition, resulting in physical aptitudes.

b. *transf.* of countries: Capability, qualification.

1775 BURKE *Concil. Amer.* Wks. III. 123 If ever there was a country qualified to produce wealth, it is India..America has none of these aptitudes. **1878** BOSW. SMITH *Carthage* 47 The colonising and commercial aptitudes of Tyre.

c. *esp.* Natural capacity to learn or understand; intelligence, quick-wittedness, readiness.

1548 UDALL *Erasm. Par.* Pref. 14 Thy state of knowledge and aptitude or capacitie. **1838** DICKENS *Nich. Nick.* xxv. 205 The general idea..he had acquired with great aptitude.

4. *Comb.*, as **aptitude test** orig. *U.S.*, a test designed to determine a person's capacity in any given skill or field of knowledge.

1923 *Amer. Inst. Criminal Law Jrnl.* XIV. 376 An aptitude test for policemen. **1926** *Sci. Amer.* Feb. 93/3 The aptitude test simply consists in making telegraph signals..and then testing the memory of the men. **1952** M. MCCARTHY *Groves of Academe* (1953) iv. 53 By the use of aptitude tests, psychological questionnaires, even blood-sampling and cranial measurements, he hoped to discover a method of gauging student-potential.

† **apti'tudinal,** *a. Obs.*—⁰ [f. med.L. *aptitūdin-em* (see prec.) + -AL¹.] Relating to aptitude.

a **1700** WORCESTER cites BAXTER.

† **apti'tudinally,** *adv. Obs. rare*⁻¹. [f. prec. + -LY².] In a manner which shows aptitude.

c **1600** *Timon* IV. iii. (1842) 67 A man may hange himselfe ..either aptitudinally and catachrestically, or perpendicularly and inhæsiuely.

aptly ('æptlɪ), *adv.* [f. APT *a.* + -LY².]

1. 'With just connection or correspondence' (J.); with exact adjustment, well-fittingly.

1597 MORLEY *Introd. Mus.* 86 See what points will aptliest agree with the nature of it. **1712** BLACKMORE *Creation* (J.) What makes them aptly to the limbs adhere? **1794** SULLIVAN *View Nat.* II. 205 A thing that consists of a multitude of pieces, aptly joined. **1870** BRYANT *Homer* I. IX. 289, I broke my aptly-jointed chamber doors.

2. So as to suit a purpose or meet general requirements; fitly, suitably; appropriately.

1548 UDALL *Erasm. Par.* Pref. 19 A thyng aptlye geuen. **1651** HOBBES *Leviath.* II. xxix. 173 We may compare this Distemper very aptly to an Ague. **1795** T. TAYLOR *Apuleius* (1822) 338 The senses..being aptly formed, by nature, to the perception of sensibles. **1818** BYRON *Childe Har.* IV. vii, A form which aptly seems Such as I sought for.

b. *esp.* of language: Appositely, expressively, to the point.

c **1525** SKELTON *Speke Parrot* 46 To lerne all language, and it to spake aptely. **1661** BRAMHALL *Just Vind.* ii. 7 Such a passionate heat is aptly stiled..a paroxisme. *a* **1849** POE *Raven*, Reply so aptly spoken.

3. With ready susceptibility, with quick intelligence; readily.

1579 LYLY *Euphues* (Arb.) 136 He shall..bee able aptly to conceiue, and readily to vtter any thing. **1601** SHAKS. *Twel. N.* III. iv. 212, I know his youth will aptly receiue it. **1805** SOUTHEY *Madoc in Azt.* xiii. Wks. V. 288 Aptly she learnt, what willingly he taught.

aptness (ˈæptnɪs). [f. as prec. + -NESS.]

1. Fitness for a purpose; suitableness, appropriateness.

1538 STARKEY *England* 5 Your aptenes..no man doth dowte. **1702** ADDISON *Medals* ii. 134 The aptness of such a posture to represent an extreme affliction. **1844** KINGLAKE *Eothen* xi. (1878) 151 The universal aptness of a religious system.

2. Habitual tendency or predisposition; inclination, propensity, proneness: **a.** of persons.

1548 UDALL, etc. *Erasm. Par. Rom.* ii. 14 (R.) A forwardnes to sinne and a certaine aptnes therunto. **1767** FORDYCE *Serm. Yng. Wom.* II. viii. 22 That aptness..to be affrighted at trifling accidents.

b. of things.

1627 SMITH *Seaman's Gram.* x. 51 Aptnesse and disposition to putrifie. **1794** HERSCHEL in *Phil. Trans.* LXXXV. 64 The heat of any situation depends upon the aptness of the medium to yield to the impression of the solar rays.

3. Ready susceptibility, quickness of apprehension; capacity, proficiency, aptitude.

1598 YONG *Diana* 155 The aptnes and actiuitie of the iolly Shepherdes. **1612** BRINSLEY *Pos. Parts* (1669) Introd. 2 A Scholar of any aptness. **1742** RICHARDSON *Pamela* IV. 317 Tricks, of which the Aptness or Docility of their Natures makes them capable. **1830** ORME *Baxter* 19 A measure of aptness to teach and persuade men.

aptote (ˈæptəʊt). *Gram.* [ad. L. *aptōt-um*, a. Gr. ἄπτωτ-ον, f. ἀ priv. + πτωτός falling, cogn. w. πτῶσις case, f. πίπτ-ειν (stem πετ-) to fall.] A noun that has no distinction of cases; an indeclinable noun. Also *fig.*

1589 *Pappe w. Hatchet* C iii, We are all *Aptots*, in all cases alike. **1612** BRINSLEY *Pos. Parts* (1669) 100 Aptotes..have no several case, but are alike in all cases. **1769** PARKHURST *Gr. Lex.* (1822) 28 Aptotes..have but one case ending for every case.

aptotic (æpˈtɒtɪk), *a.* [f. prec. + -IC, after Gr. πτωτικός.] Uninflected. Applied to languages which have no grammatical inflexions.

[Not in CRAIG 1847.] **1849–52** TODD *Cycl. Anat. & Phys.* IV. 1346/1 The Aptotic type, of which the Chinese is an example. **1858** [See ANAPTOTIC].

‖**aptychus** (ˈæptɪkəs). *Palæont.* Pl. **aptychi**. [mod.L., f. Gr. ἀ- priv. (A- 14) + πτυχή fold, layer.] A calcareous plate or pair of plates found in the terminal chamber of some ammonites.

1877 HUXLEY *Anat. Inv. Anim.* 536 The *Aptychi*..occupy the middle of the posterior wall or terminal chamber of the Ammonite, and have their bases towards its mouth. **1893** H. WOODS *Palæont., Invert.* vii. 176 In the last chamber of some *Ammonites* and a few other genera, a pair of calcareous or horny plates, known as the *Aptychus*, are occasionally found.

Apulian (əˈpjuːlɪən), *a.* and *sb.* [f. L. *Apulia, Appulia* + -AN.] **A.** *adj.* Of or pertaining to the ancient province or the modern geographical district of Apulia in southern Italy, or its inhabitants. **B.** *sb.* An inhabitant of Apulia.

1607 TOPSELL *Four-f. Beasts* 187 There was such another charme or incantation among the Apuleians. *Ibid.* 625 All Christendome yealdeth praise and price vnto it next after the Apulian and Tarentinian wooll. **1709** S. DUNSTER tr. *Horace's Sat.* II. i. p. 127 Or rather, with intent, to keep the Lucanians and Apulians in awe. **1757** J. DYER *Fleece* II. 102 They..swell their fleeces, equal to the worth Of cloath'd Apulian. **1820** SHELLEY *Cenci* III. i. p. 45 That lonely rock, Petrella, in the Apulian Appennines. **1889** *Cent. Dict.*, *Apulian pottery*, a name given to the Italo-Greek pottery found in Apulia and southeastern Italy generally, especially to the vases with red figures on a lustrous black ground, some of the most important examples of which are from this region. **1932** *Times Lit. Suppl.* 21 Jan. 37/2 The Apulian officials and organizers spreading throughout Frederick's Italian territories. **1955** S. RUNCIMAN *Eastern Schism* ii. 38 In 1020 an Apulian called Melo raised a revolt in southern Italy against Byzantium.

apulmonic (æpʌlˈmɒnɪk), *a. rare.* [f. A- *pref.* 14 + PULMONIC.] Having no lungs.

1874 RITCHIE *Creation* iii. 42 Innumerable races of living apulmonic creatures.

†**a'pyke**, *v. Obs. rare.* [f. A- *pref.* 1 intensive + PIKE *v.* Cf. Chaucer *Prol. C.T.* 367 'Ful freshe and newe hir gere ypiked was.'] To adorn.

c **1325** *E.E. Allit. P.* B. 1479 Þe pyleres apyked þat praysed hit mony. *Ibid.* 1637, I schal Apyke þe in porpre cloþe.

apyretic (æpɪˈrɛtɪk), *a. Path.* [mod. f. Gr. ἀπύρετ-ος without fever (ἀ priv. + πυρετ-ός fever) + -IC; cf. Fr. *apyrétique.*] Free from fever.

1842 F. BLACK *Homœop.* iii. 38 A general apyretic eruption a little analogous to scarlatina. **1853** MAYNE *Exp. Lex.*, *Apyretic*..applied to the days of an intermission in ague; also to local diseases which do not induce febrile excitement.

apyrexial (æpɪˈrɛksɪəl), *a. Path. rare.* [f. mod.L. *apyrexia* (see next) + -AL[1].] = prec.

1878 KINGZETT *Anim. Chem.* xxii. 437 The subsequent apyrexial periods [of relapsing fever].

apyrexy (ˈæpɪrɛksɪ). *Path.* [ad. mod.L. *apyrexia* (also used), a. Gr. ἀπυρεξία, f. ἀ priv. + πυρέσσειν to be feverish. Cf. F. *apyrexie.*] The period of intermission in a fever.

1656 BLOUNT *Glossogr.*, *Apyrexie*, the remitting of a Fever, or the shaking in the course of an ague. **1742** BAILEY *Apyrexy.* **1876** tr. *Wagner's Gen. Path.* 16 The normal interval in a febrile disease is denominated Apyrexia.

apyrous (əˈpaɪərəs, ˈæpɪrəs), *a.* [f. Gr. ἄπυρ-ος without fire, unsmelted (f. ἀ priv. + πυρ- fire) + -OUS. Cf. Fr. *apyre.*] Not altered by exposure to fire.

1782 WEDGWOOD in *Phil. Trans.* LXXII. 309 A clay sufficiently apyrous or unvitrescible. **1802** BOURNON *ibid.* XCII. 323 Haüy..gives it the name of apyrous felspar.

aqu-, earlier spelling of ACQU-, q.v.

‖**aqua**[1] (ˈækwə, ˈeɪkwə). The Latin word for *water*, used in many descriptive names in Pharmacy and Chemistry, with sense of: Liquid, solution. See esp. AQUA FORTIS, MIRABILIS, REGIA, VITÆ.

1398 TREVISA *Barth. De P.R.* XVII. cxxxvi. (1495) 692 Of grene rose *aqua rosacea* is made by sethyng.

aqua[2] (ˈækwə). [Abbrev. of AQUAMARINE.] A light greenish blue colour.

1936 *New Yorker* 8 Feb. 56 (Advt.), Gold, navy, grey, rustic, blue, rose, aqua. **1959** *Woman's Own* 23 May 52/3 She admired the plate which was aqua.

aqua- (ˈækwə). L. *aqua* 'water' used as a combining form or quasi-*adj.*, esp. in expressions referring to aquatic entertainment; **aquacade** (ˈækwəkeɪd) *U.S.* [-CADE], an elaborate display of aquatic events and turns.

1887 *Gentl. Mag.* June 549 When the 'Théâtre Nautique' first opened its doors the bill presented..a three act aqua-drama of Chinese life, entitled 'Kao-Kang'. **1930** *Birmingham Post* 28 Feb. 8 A daring new aquatic sport introduced at Winter Haven, Florida, U.S.A.—riding in an 'aqua-glider' fitted with an aeroplane wing and attached to a speed boat. **1935** A. P. HERBERT *What a Word!* v. 164 Every week some new thing is flung into the news..Cinema, vitamin..—and, I regret to say, television and aquadrome—here are only a few. **1936** *London Transport, Country Walks*, 1st Ser., A big lake set with wooded eyots, the Aquadrome is really an old ballast pit. **1937** *Daily Progress* (Charlotteville, Va.) 16 Nov. 6/5 Billy Rose, the little man who creates big shows, is pictured with Eleanor Holm Jarrett, his star of the Cleveland aquacade. **1949** R. GRAVES *Seven Days in New Crete* xx. 248 Several naked girls slipped into the pool and swam languidly around like a Hollywood aquacade. **1952** GRANVILLE *Dict. Theatr. Terms* 17 *Aqua show*..Aquatic turns are performed in tanks on the stage or in suitable settings according to the size of the theatre. **1961** *Daily Mail* 12 Sept. 13/2 Mr. B. is running an 'aqua-camp'. .. He has bought a 16 ft. cabin cruiser..for use by the campers, who bring canoes and diving equipment.

aquabib (ˈeɪkwəbɪb). [f. L. *aqua* water + *bibĕre* to drink.] A water-drinker.

1731 BAILEY, *Aquabibe*, a water drinker. **1883** *Pall Mall G.* 5 Feb. 11/2 Our worthy friend ['Water-drinker'] might be known henceforth as an 'aquabibist,' or, if he prefers three syllables, 'aquabib.'

'aqua,culture, occas. var. AQUICULTURE. Also, = HYDROPONICS.

1887 *Athenæum* 21 May 667/1. **1929** W. F. GERICKE in *Amer. Jrnl. Bot.* XVI. 862 (*title*) Aquaculture. A means of crop-production..growth of plants in water. **1962** *Daily Tel.* 4 Apr. 12/3 The systematic exploitation of the sea—marine husbandry or aqua-culture.

aquaduct, obs. form of AQUEDUCT.

†**aquæ-'oleous**, *a. Obs. rare*[−1]. [f. L. *aqua* + -OLEOUS, f. *oleum* oil.] Containing or consisting of both water and oil (as new milk).

1674 GREW *Anat. Plants* III. iv. §13 The Aquæ-oleous Liquors of Plants.

†**aqu-a'erial**, *a. Obs.* [f. as prec. + AERIAL.] Of water and air, or of the air contained in water.

1672 *Phil. Trans.* VII. 4070 Conjecture..that Amber is a bituminous fluid substance, hardned by the operations of the aqu-aerial particles upon it.

aquafer, var. AQUIFER.

‖**aquafortis** (ˌeɪkwəˈfɔːtɪs). [L.; = strong water.]

1. The early scientific, and still the popular, name of the Nitric Acid of commerce (dilute HNO_3), a powerful solvent and corrosive.

1601 WEEVER *Mirr. Martyrs* Dj, For inke strong aqua-fortis. **1626** BACON *Sylva* §789 Dissolve the Iron in the Aqua-Fortis. **1762** H. WALPOLE *Vertue's Anecd. Paint.* (1786) IV. 178 Lord Lovat..etched in aquafortis by William Hogarth. **1878** HUXLEY *Physiogr.* vi. 86 Nitric acid, the substance known commonly as aquafortis.

†**2.** Also used of other powerful solvents. *Obs.*

1607 TOPSELL *Four-footed Beasts* 308 Wash all his tail with aqua fortis, or strong water, made in this sort: take of green copperas, of allum, of each, one pound,—of white copperas a quartern. **1875** URE *Dict. Arts* I. 202 Aquafortis did not always mean nitric acid.

3. *fig.*

1611 MIDDLETON & DEK. *Roar. Girl* Wks. 1873 III. 156 Mony is that *Aqua fortis*, that eates into many a maidenhead. **1670** EACHARD *Contempt Clergy* 55 The blotts and blurrs of our sins must be taken out by the aqua-fortis of our tears. **1873** SYMONDS *Grk. Poets* viii. 256 The sceptical aqua-fortis of his age is as strong in Aristophanes as in Euripides.

aquafortist (ˌeɪkwəˈfɔːtɪst). [f. prec. after words in -IST.] One who makes etchings or engravings by means of aquafortis.

1880 *Mag. Art* Dec. 77 As an aquafortist he was worthy to rank with Rembrandt.

†**'aquage**. *Obs.*[−0]. [ad. L. *aquagium* aqueduct, f. *aqua* + *agĕre* to lead, bring.] = AQUEDUCT.

1706 PHILLIPS, *Aquagium*, (in old Records) an Aquage, or Water course. **1731** in BAILEY.

†**a'quake**, *v. Obs.* [f. A- *pref.* 1 intensive + QUAKE *v.*] To quake, tremble.

1303 R. BRUNNE *Handl. Synne* 7839 ȝyf he hadde slept, hym nedede awake, ȝyf he were wakyng, he shulde a-quake. *c* **1330** *Kyng of Tars* 434 Hire flesch i-wis was al aquaked For drede.

aquake (əˈkweɪk), *adv.* or *pred. a. poet.* [f. A *prep.*[1] + QUAKE *v.*] In a quaking condition; quaking.

1875 MORRIS *Æneids* III. 616 My mates aquake with dread. **1883** MEREDITH *Poems of Joy of Earth* 54 The valley aquake with the tread Of an iron-resounding hoof.

aqualung (ˈækwəlʌŋ). [f. AQUA- + LUNG.] A portable diving apparatus consisting of containers of compressed air strapped on the back which feed air automatically through a valve and mouthpiece to the diver as he requires it. Also *attrib.* Hence **'aqualunger** (-ŋ-), a user of the aqualung; **'aqualung** *v. intr.*, to use this equipment; **'aqualunging** *vbl. sb.*

1950 *Sci. News Let.* 11 Nov. 306/3 The underwater photographer is equipped with an 'Aqualung', an automatic compressed air, self-contained diving unit. **1952** J. Y. COUSTEAU in *Nat. Geogr. Mag.* Oct. 434 Moving in a dense element, Aqualungers must learn to be languid. **1953** COUSTEAU & DUMAS *Silent World* i. 1 In June 1943..a new and promising device..an automatic compressed-air diving lung conceived by Émile Gagnan and myself... No children ever opened a Christmas present with more excitement than we did when we unpacked the first 'aqualung'. *Ibid.* 96 (*caption*) Auguste Piccard, inventor of the Bathyscaphe, the undersea dirigible, tries aqualunging at Dakar. **1959** *Elizabethan* June 21/1 Fishermen are still bringing up old cannon and bits of bronze from the great galleons of the Spanish Armada, some awaiting excavation by aqualung divers. **1961** I. FLEMING *Thunderball* xviii. 199 You oughtn't to aqualung by yourself.

aquamanile (ˌækwəməˈnaɪliː, -ˈiːliː). Also **aquæmanale**. [late L., ad. (rare) L. *aquaemanālis* basin for washing the hands, f. *aquae* (gen. sing. of *aqua* water) + *mānāle* ewer.] **a.** A water vessel or ewer, freq. made in the form of an animal or bird, etc. **b.** *Eccl.* A basin used for washing the hands at the celebration of Mass.

1875 S. CHEETHAM in Smith & Cheetham *Dict. Chr. Antiquities* I. 134/1 *Aquamanile*, the bason used for the washing of the hands of the celebrant in the liturgy. The aquamanile with the urceus are the bason and ewer of the sacred ceremony. **1889** *Cent. Dict.*, Aquæmanale. **1910** R. FRY in *Burlington Mag.* Aug. 289/2 A late Sassanid aquamanile in the form of a bird. **1911** *Encycl. Brit.* XV. 544/2 In the 13th and 14th centuries a special type of metal ewer takes the form of animals, men on horseback, &c.; these are generally known as aquamaniles. **1939** *Oxoniensia* IV. 113 Sherd from a cylindrical cup, or perhaps from the body of an aquamanile, T. $\frac{3}{16}$ in. **1956** *Daily Tel.* 5 Dec. 8/3 A bronze equestrian aquamanile..was used as a water vessel for church purposes. The water pours out from the aperture in the horse's forehead. **1957** MANKOWITZ & HAGGAR *Conc. Encycl. Eng. Pott. & Porc.* 8/1 *Aquamanile*, a ewer for handwashing in medieval times, usually in the form of a mounted figure or animal. **1962** *Victoria & Albert Mus. Internat. Art Treasures Exhib.* 74/2 A Dinanderie Aquamanile, of circular turret form,..supported on three human legs and feet.

aquamarine (ˌeɪkwəməˈriːn). [ad. L. *aqua marīna* sea-water (from its colour); the earlier equivalent was AIGUE MARINE from Fr., also written *ag-, aque-marine.*]

1. A bluish-green variety of beryl.

[**1598** STOW *Surv.* (ed. Strype 1754) I. I. xx. 121/2 One entire Stone of a sea-water green colour, known by the name of the Agmarine.] **1727–51** CHAMBERS *Cycl.*, *Aqua Marina, Aque Marine.* **1802** BOURNON *Corundum* in *Phil. Trans.* XCII. 318 Of a fine bluish green, like the aqua marine.

2. Hence as *adj.* and *sb.* Bluish-green (colour); sea-colour(ed.

1846 RUSKIN *Mod. Paint.* I. II. v. i. §10 Its general hue of aquamarine green. **1862** MISS BRADDON *Lady Audley* i. 11 The wet aquamarine upon the palette.

‖,**aqua mi'rabilis**. *Obs.* [L.] 'The wonderful water, prepared of cloves, galangals, cubebs, mace, cardomums, nutmegs, ginger, and spirit of wine, digested twenty-four hours, then distilled.' J.

1741 *Compl. Fam.-Piece* I. i. 24 Take..Plague-water and Aqua Mirabilis. **1818** SCOTT *Hrt. Midl.* viii, Gin ye take a morning's draught, let it be aqua mirabilis.

aquanaut (ˈækwənɔːt). [f. AQUA- + Gr. ναυτικός, f. ναύτης sailor, ναῦς ship; cf. ASTRONAUT.] An underwater 'explorer' or swimmer.

1881 W. D. HAY *300 Years Hence* vii. 132 The small apparatus fixed to the back of every aquatic helmet, and..

called in the early days 'the aquanaut's lungs'. **1964** *Discovery* Oct. 9/3 The experiences of these 'Aquanauts' vividly underlined the need for new underwater tools. **1965** *Observer* 28 Mar. 13/1 'Thermal protection'..is..a serious problem for 'aquanauts'. **1966** *Daily Tel.* 31 Oct. 9/8 Each 'aquanaut'..has small measured weights sewn into the arms and legs of his special diving suit.

aquaplane (ˈækwəpleɪn). orig. *U.S.* [f. AQUA- + PLANE *sb.*^{3}] A board which rides on the surface of the water when towed with its rider by a speedboat. Hence *v. intr.*, to ride standing on such a board. Hence also **ˈaquaplaner**, a rider of an aquaplane; **ˈaquaplaning** *vbl. sb.*, the sport of riding an aquaplane; also [cf. PLANE *v.*^{2}], 'gliding' or skidding out of control on water (quots. 1961, 1963).

1914 *Outing* (U.S.) May 143/2 The wonderful sensation of shooting through the air and skimming the surface of the water may be enjoyed..by the use of the waterboard or aquaplane. *Ibid.* 147/2 With these cautions strictly heeded, the sport of aquaplaning at once becomes as thoroughly safe as it is wonderfully exciting. **1915** *Harper's Weekly* 9 Oct. 347/1 When the aquaplane made its first public appearance two years ago, the machine was a long, narrow board which could be used, without guide ropes, behind boats whose speed did not exceed 15 miles an hour. It was about 12 feet long, a foot or so wide, and was marked to show where to stand at various speeds. **1928** *Daily Express* 14 July 4/5 There will be..a women's aquaplane race and various other 'speedbug' activities. *Ibid.* 24 Aug. 15/2 Lady Cunard..is often to be seen admiring the prowess of aqua-planers or shooting out to the islands in a rapid motor-boat. **1941** F. E. BAUME *I lived these Years* viii. 183 Lady Catherine Manley ..aquaplaned behind a launch from Boulogne to Folkestone. **1961** *Aeroplane* CI. 34/1 The phenomenon of 'aqua-planing', in which an aircraft can ride down a wet runway supported on a film of water with the effectiveness of the wheel brakes reduced virtually to zero. **1963** *Guardian* 18 Dec. 3/5 The phenomenon known as 'aqua-planing', when a car tyre leaves the surface of a wet road... There is a speed at which the tyre can no longer disperse the water, so that it 'aquaplanes'.

† **ˈaquapoise.** *Obs. rare*$^{-1}$. [f. L. *aqua* water + POISE; cf. *equipoise*.] A balance for weighing a substance in water.

1688 I. CLAYTON in *Phil. Trans.* XVII. 794, I could not trie any thing as to their specifick Gravity, having neither Aquapoise, nor those other Glasses I had contrived.

aquapuncture (ˈeɪkwəˈpʌŋktjʊə(r)). *Med.* [f. L. *aquā* with water + PUNCTURE.] Puncture of the skin by means of a fine jet of water from a forcepump; used to give relief in neuralgia, lumbago, etc.

1876 BARTHOLOW *Mat. Med.* (1879) 542 The method of aquapuncture consists in the introduction of water subcutaneously.

‖**aqua regia** (ˌeɪkwəˈriːdʒɪə). Also **aqua regis.** [L.; = royal water.] A mixture of nitric and hydrochloric acids, so called because it can dissolve the 'noble' metals, gold and platinum.

1610 B. JONSON *Alch.* II. v, What's cohobation? 'Tis the pouring on Your *aqua regis*, and then drawing him off. **1641** FRENCH *Distill.* iii. (1651) 70 *Aqua regia*, or *Stygia*..will dissolve Gold. **1869** ROSCOE *Elem. Chem.* 275 Gold trichloride, obtained when gold is dissolved in aqua regia.

‖**aquarelle** (ækwəˈrɛl). [Fr., ad. It. *acquerella* water-colour, dim. of *acqua*:—L. *aqua* water.] A kind of painting or illuminating with Chinese ink, and very thin, transparent water-colours; used to represent flowers, small landscapes, etc. Also, the design so produced.

1869 *Eng. Mech.* 2 July 340/3 Aniline colours are utilised for the colouring of..aquarelles, photographs, etc.

aquarellist (ækwəˈrɛlɪst). [f. prec. + -IST.] An artist in aquarelle.

1882 *St. James's Gaz.* 17 Feb. 6 A real desire to portray the true aspects of nature—a desire too often wanting to Italian aquarellists.

aˈquarial, *a. rare.* [f. as next + -AL^{1}.] = next.

1864 *Leis. Hr.* 542/1 Boston Aquarial Gardens.

aquarian (əˈkwɛərɪən), *a.* and *sb.* [f. L. *aquārius* pertaining to water (in pl. masc. *Aquārii* name of a heretical sect) + -AN; senses A 2 and B 1, 3 normally take a capital initial.]

A. *adj.* **1.** Of, or pertaining to, an aquarium. *rare.*

1865 *Intell. Observ.* No. 46. 260 Aquarian principles.

2. *Astrol.* Of or pertaining to the sign of Aquarius; characteristic of a person born under this sign.

1940 [see AQUARIUS 3]. *a* **1963** L. MACNEICE *Astrol.* (1964) iii. 101 The American film actor James Dean (1931–55). Astrologers would label his sensitive good looks as typically Aquarian—and Aquarius was Dean's Sun-sign. **1970** *Americana Ann.* 482 The pretext..was an outdoor music festival advertised as 'three days of peace and music' and subtitled 'An Aquarian Exposition', in reference to the newly dawning Age of Aquarius on the astrology charts. **1979** N. MAILER *Executioner's Song* (1980) II. iv. 552 He was there to represent free and open dealing... His responsibility was to be very Aquarian and even report things about himself and his feelings that might seem strange.

B. *sb.* **1.** One of a sect of Christians in the primitive church, who used water instead of wine in the Lord's Supper.

1586 T. ROGERS 39 *Art.* (1607) 296 The Aquarians..for wine..gave water unto the people. **1751** in CHAMBERS *Cycl.*

2. One who keeps an aquarium.

1857 *Nation. Mag.* I. 352 An aquarian in trouble.

3. *Astrol.* = AQUARIUS 2.

1911 I. M. PAGAN *From Pioneer to Poet* xi. 169 Developed Aquarians, generally speaking, are too tranquil in temperament, too gentle and kindly in disposition, to outrage the feelings of their families. **1945** AUDEN *Coll. Poetry* 68 Though a staunch Aquarian, Graciously accept the Verbal celebrations Of a doubtful fish. **1984** *Observer* 11 Mar. 12/7 The switchback rhythm of life at the Soviet top is reflected in the forecast for Aquarians.

aquarist (ˈækwərɪst, *U.S.* əˈkwɛərɪst). Also formerly **aˈquariist** (*U.S.*). [f. AQUAR(IUM + -IST.] One who keeps an aquarium.

1893 *Funk's Stand. Dict.*, *Aquariist*, the manager or keeper of an aquarium. **1920** WEBSTER, Aquariist or aquarist. **1924** (*title*) The Amateur Aquarist. **1958** *Times Lit. Suppl.* 10 Jan. 23/5 The object of this book is to enable the aquarist to identify most of the tropical fishes available for culture in this country.

aquarium (əˈkwɛərɪəm). Pl. **-iums, -ia.** [L., neut. sing. of *aquārius* (see AQUARIAN *a.* and *sb.*); cf. cl. L. *aquārium* a watering-place for cattle.] An artificial pond or tank (the latter usually with glass sides), in which aquatic plants and animals are kept alive for purposes of observation and study. Also, in recent usage, a place of public entertainment, in which such aquariums are exhibited. Also *attrib.* and *Comb.*

[**1853** *Athenæum* 28 May, The new Fish house..has received the somewhat curious title of the 'Marine Vivarium.' **1853** *Guide Zool. Gard.*, Aquatic Vivarium.] **1854** GOSSE (*title*) The Aquarium; an Unveiling of the Wonders of the Deep Sea. **1855** KINGSLEY *Glaucus* 154 A prawn or two, and a few minute star-fish will make your aquarium complete. **1869** *Eng. Mech.* 14 May 179/3, I have had aquariums made of other materials. **1875** *Encycl. Brit.* II. 217/2 An impetus to the popular aquarium movement. **1880** DISRAELI *Endym.* xx. 86 There were no Alhambras then..no casinos, no music-halls, no aquaria, no promenade concerts. **1900** E. GLYN *Visits of Eliz.* 27 A regular aquarium specimen of turbot sat on its dish opposite him. **1931** A. HUXLEY *Cicadas* 44 Oh, how aquarium-still, how brooding-warm This paradise! **1941** BLUNDEN *T. Hardy* ix. 201, I must lay by *A Pair of Blue Eyes* as one of the works of Hardy which have at best aquarium value.

‖**Aquarius** (əˈkwɛərɪəs). *Astr.* Also 5–7 **Aquary.** [L. = water-carrier, subst. use of *aquārius* adj.: see above.] **1.** One of the zodiacal constellations, giving its name to the eleventh sign of the zodiac, which the sun enters on the 21st of Jan.

1398 TREVISA *Barth. De P.R.* VIII. x. (1495) 314 The sygne Aquarius is the butlere of goddes and yeuyth them a water potte. *c* **1400** *Epiph.* (Turnb. 1843) 102 When in Aquarye Phebus schad hys lyght. **1686** GOAD *Celest. Bod.* II. i. 141 In Aquary you see the ☌ brings Rain. **1870** PROCTOR *Other Worlds* xii. 287 The Water-can of Aquarius.

2. *Astrol.* A person born under the sign of Aquarius. Also *attrib.* or as *adj.*

1894 E. KIRK *Influence of Zodiac upon Human Life* xiii. 98 Aquarius people are remarkable spiritual healers. **1958** [see CAPRICORN 1 c]. **1979** D. & A. EDMANDS *Child Signs* II. 135 Your Aquarius child may not give a fig about who's at the top of the heap. *Ibid.* 136 Your Aquarius may embarrass you. **1985** *N.Y. Times Mag.* 10 Mar. VI. 82/4 'That has to do,' she says, 'with growing up freely, and being an Aquarius.'

3. *Age of Aquarius*, an astrological age characterized by world freedom and brotherhood, which is said to have begun during the 1960s; also used as a symbol of freedom or permissiveness.

[**1940** R. GLEADOW *Astrol. in Everyday Life* I. xi. 144 The future is always associated in astrological circles with the so-called 'Aquarian Age'. **1961** J. B. PRIESTLEY *Saturn over Water* xix. 282 We are moving now, for we're at the end of an age, from Pisces to Aquarius, from the Fish to the Water.] **1967** RAGNI & 'RADO' *Aquarius* (1968) (*song*) 3 This is the dawning of the age of Aquarius. **1970** *Time* 6 July 6 Evangelist Billy Graham..fingered his collar-length silver-blond curls and gave his blessing to the Age of Aquarius. **1976** N. THORNBURG *Cutter & Bone* ii. 52 Cutter moved on without a backward look, slipping easily into the mid-sixties, that golden age of cant, of bare feet and acid and Aquarius. **1985** *Christian Science Monitor* 26 Aug. 21/2 Beattie's six books..have been greeted as graceful if facile bulletins about the survivors of the Age of Aquarius.

a-quarter (əˈkwɔːtə(r)), *advb. phr. Naut.* [A *prep.*^{1} + QUARTER *sb.*] On the quarter, *i.e.* 45° abaft the beam.

1849 *Blackw. Mag.* LXV. 333, I felt the ship bring her wind a-quarter.

aquatic (əˈkwætɪk), *a.* and *sb.* Also 5 **aquatyque,** 7 **-ique.** [a. F. *aquatique*, ad. L. *aquāticus* watery, living in water, f. *aqua* water: see -ATIC.]

A. *adj.*

† **1.** Of or pertaining to water as a substance; watery, rainy. *Obs.*

1490 CAXTON *Eneydos* xxiv. 91 The grete poundes and ryuers, alle thynges aquatyque. **1686** GOAD *Celest. Bod.* II. vi. 289 We are troubled with Aquatique Signs.

2. Of or pertaining to water as a habitat or resort; *esp.* **a.** of plants and animals: Living or growing in or near water.

1642 HOWELL *For. Trav.* (Arb.) 67 Jonas..was shut up in the body of that great (aquatique) beast. **1794** SULLIVAN *View Nat.* I. 200 The smaller seeds of terrestrial and aquatic plants. **1833** HT. MARTINEAU *Charmed Sea* i. 10 Aquatic birds on the opposite margin. **1867** F. FRANCIS *Angling* vi. (1880) 204 Many spiders..lead an aquatic existence.

b. Pertaining to pastime in or upon the water.

1866 *Reader* 17 Mar. 277/3 The aspirant after aquatic fame. *Mod.* Aquatic sports.

B. *sb.*

1. An aquatic plant or animal (*arch.*); a person given to aquatic pastimes.

? *c* **1600** in Scott *Antiq.* xxx. *Motto*, He tilted with a sword-fish—Marry, Sir, Th' aquatic had the best. **1669** WORLIDGE *Syst. Agric.* (1681) 272 Osiers, Willows, and other Aquaticks. **1815** LD. CAMPBELL *Let.* in *Life* I. 313 Continue a determined aquatic [*i.e.* bather]. **1859** F. PAGET *Curate Cumberw.* 70, A cartload of aquatics for her own pond. **1866** *Reader* 17 Mar. 277/2 With the applause of the thousands.. ringing in his ears, the exultant aquatic, etc.

2. A water-drinker. *rare*$^{-1}$.

a **1790** FRANKLIN *Autobiog.*, That the 'American aquatic,' as they used to call me, was stronger than those who drank porter.

3. *pl.* Pastimes conducted in or upon the water.

1865 *Daily Tel.* 12 July 9/4 Aquatics—Amateur Championship of the Thames. **1866** *Chamb. Jrnl.* 31 Jan. 10/1 Come..and take an oar. Papa has gone wild on aquatics.

† **aˈquatical,** *a. Obs.* [f. as prec. + -AL^{1}.] Of aquatic nature; having to do with water.

1603 HOLLAND *Plutarch* 692 (R.) Animals..terrestrial, aquaticall, volatile, and cœlestial. **1603** SIR C. HEYDON *Jud. Astrol.* v. 146 Aquaticall Instruments, houre-glasses, dyals. **1695** CONGREVE *Love for Love* II. v, Fiery Trigons and Aquatical Trigons.

aˈquatically, *adv. rare.* [f. prec. + -LY^{2}.] In an aquatic manner; in the direction of aquatics.

1882 *Daily News* 12 June 3/2 Those of their party who were aquatically disposed.

aquatile (ˈækwətɪl, -aɪl), *a.* and *sb. arch.* [ad. L. *aquātilis* aquatic, f. *aqua* water: see -ATILE.]

A. *adj.* Living in water; = AQUATIC *a.* 2.

1622 SIR R. HAWKINS *Voy. S. Sea* (1847) 119 Part terrestryall and part aquatile as the mare-maid. **1727–51** CHAMBERS *Cycl.* s.v. *Aquatic*, The antient Romans had also their aquatic or aquatile gods. **1865** F. LOCKER *Select.* 145 His deity was aquatile, A rough and tough old Crocodile.

B. *sb.* An aquatic animal or plant; = AQUATIC *sb.* 1.

1638 WILKINS *Disc. New World* I. (1684) 174 Observations concerning the Nature of Aquatils. **1706** *Phil. Trans.* XXV. 2314 Fishes and other Aquatiles. **1731** BAILEY, *Aquatiles*, such plants as grow in water.

aquatint (ˈækwəˌtɪnt), **aqua-tinta** (ˌækwəˈtɪntə), *sb.* [a. F. *aqua-tinte*, and It. *acqua tinta*:—L. *aqua tincta* dyed water (*tingĕre* to dye).] A method of etching on copper, by the use of a resinous solution and nitric acid, which produces effects resembling those of Indian-ink or water-colour drawing; also, the design so produced.

1782 W. GILPIN *Observ. Wye* (1800) Introd. 8 The process of working in aquatint. **1862** THORNBURY *Turner* I. 88 To publish a fine series of aquatints.

b. *attrib.* quasi-*adj.*

1782 W. GILPIN *Observ. Wye* (1792) Introd. 8 The aqua-tinta mode of multiplying drawings. **1879** SPON *Workshop Rec.* 162 Aqua-tinta engraving..is recognised by its similarity to Indian ink or sepia drawing.

ˈaquatint, *v.* [f. prec.] To etch in aquatint.

1819 REES *Cycl.* II. s.v. *Aquatint*, This method of aqua-tinting. **1882** *Athenæum* 9 Sept. 343/1 C. Turner mezzo-tinted many 'Libers,' but he aquatinted none.

aquatintan (ækwəˈtɪntən), *a. rare*$^{-1}$. [f. AQUATINT *sb.* + -AN.] In aquatint.

1855 W. BOYD *Oakw. Old* 1, Aquatintan Etchings.

aquatinted (ˈækwəˌtɪntɪd), *ppl. a.* [f. AQUATINT *v.* + -ED^{1}.] Etched in, or as in, aquatint.

1880 HARDY *Trumpet-Major* II. xxviii. 271 The rain decreased, and the lovers went on..aqua-tinted by the weak moon and mist. **1931** BLUNDEN *Votive Tablets* 186 External nature, aquatinted with remarkable sense of solitude. **1958** *Observer* 10 Aug. 11/3 A strangely aquatinted telerecording.

aquatinter (ækwəˈtɪntə(r)). [f. AQUATINT *v.* + -ER^{1}.] One who etches in aquatint.

1834 *Penny Cycl.* II. 203 Modern aquatinters.

† **aˈquation.** *Obs. rare*$^{-1}$. [ad. L. *aquātiōn-em* watering, rain, n. of action f. *aquā-ri* to bring water.] Watering; getting of water.

1623 COCKERAM, *Aquation*, abundance of raine. **1695** E. GIBSON *Camden's Brit.* in Symonds *Rec. Rocks* vi. 198 Commodiously situated for aquation by reason of the nearness of the river Teme.

aquavalent (əˈkwævələnt). *Chem.* [f. L. *aqua* water + *valēnt-em* pr. pple. of *valēre* to be strong, to equal; cf. *equivalent*.] The molecular proportion between an anhydrous salt and the water of its cryohydrate, *i.e.* the number of

molecules of water with which one molecule of the salt unites.
1881 in WATTS *Dict. Chem.* VIII. 1005.

aquavit (ækwə'vi:t). Also **akvavit** (akva'vi:t). [ad. Norw., Sw., Da. *akvavit* AQUA-VITÆ.] A colourless or yellowish alcoholic spirit distilled from potatoes or other starch-containing plants; the 'schnapps' of Scandinavia.
1890 T. BENNETT *Handbk. Travellers in Norway* (ed. 26) 36 Those who suffer from *cardialgy* (heartburn) and indigestion are recommended to take the Norwegian 'Akvavit'—a kind of brandy flavoured with carraway seeds, which must be drunk without being mixed with water. **1896** *Wine List* (*T. W Stapleton & Co.*) Dec., Aquavit (Norwegian)—54/-. **1920** G. SAINTSBURY *Notes on Cellar-Book* viii. 130 The Norwegian 'Aquavit', which used to flow so freely. **1936** *New Yorker* 7 Mar. 74/4 A Swedish Aquavit which is remarkably soft and smooth. **1964** *Punch* 15 Jan. 92/2 Fortified by a full potion of akvavit.

‖**aqua-vitæ** (,eɪkwə'vaɪti:). Also 5–7 **aqua-vite**, 7–8 **aqua-vita**. [L.; = water of life; cf. F. *eau de vie*, Ir. *uisge bheatha*, '*usquebaugh*.']
1. A term of the alchemists applied to ardent spirits or unrectified alcohol; sometimes applied, in commerce, to ardent spirits of the first distillation.
1471 RIPLEY *Comp. Alch.* in Ashm. 1652, 115 With Aquavite ofttimes, both wash and drie. **1586** BRIGHT *Melanch.* xxii. 126 From the lyes of wine is distilled a strong and burning aqua vitæ. **1674** PETTY *Disc. bef. R. Soc.* 95 A Lamplike Vessel of common Aquavitæ. **1762** H. WALPOLE *Vertue's Anecd. Paint.* (1786) II. 207 He cleansed them with aqua-vitae alone.
2. *Hence, pop.* Any form in which ardent spirits have been drunk, as brandy, whisky, etc.
1547 BOORDE *Dietary* x. 258 To speake of.. aqua vite or of Ipocras. **1552** *Chron. Gr. Friars* (1852) 74 A woman.. that made aqwavyte. **1678** BUTLER *Hud.* III. III. 298 Restor'd the fainting High and Mighty With Brandy-Wine and Aqua-vitae. **1785** BURNS *Earnest Cry* iii, That curst restriction On Aquavitæ. **1818** SCOTT *Rob Roy* xviii, A tass of brandy or aqua vitæ.
3. *fig.*; or in the literal L. meaning.
c **1600** J. DAVIES in Farr's *S.P.* I. 254 Couer this Aqua vitæ with your wings From touch of infidels and Jewes.
4. *Comb.* and *Attrib.*
1601 *Sherley's Trav. Persia* (1863) 46 A crue of aqua-vitæ-bellyed fellowes. **1634** HOWELL *Lett.* (1650) II. 76 Sacks and canaries.. us'd to be drunk in aquavita measures. **1749** H. WALPOLE *Corr.* (1837) I. 143 Was glad to hear the aqua vitæ man crying a dram.

aquaynt, obs. f. ACQUAINT.

†**a'queath**, *v. Obs.* 1–3. For forms see QUEATH. [OE. *acweðan*, f. A- *pref.* 1 + *cweðan* to say: see QUEATH, and cf. BEQUEATH.] To speak out; to resound, re-echo.
a **1000** *Cædmon's Gen.* (Gr.) 639 Word acwæþ wuldres aldor. **1205** LAY. 27717 þer wes wunderlic grure: þa welcnen aqueðen.

aqueduct ('ækwɪdʌkt). Also 6–8 **aquæ-**, **aquaduct**. [ad. L. *aquæductus*, *aquæ ductus*, *ductus aquæ*, conveyance of water, f. *duc-ĕre* to lead, bring. Cf. F. *aquéduc*.]
1. An artificial channel for the conveyance of water from place to place; a conduit; *esp.* an elevated structure of masonry used for this purpose.
1538 LELAND *Itin.* IV. 77 At the place of the midle meeting of these Streets, is an Aquæduct. **1621** BURTON *Anat. Mel.* II. ii. I. i, That Segouian Aqueduct in Spaine.. vpon three rowes of pillars, one aboue another, convaying sweet water to euery house. **1647** R. STAPYLTON *Juvenal* 51 The charge of aquaducts or publike conduits. **1858** HAWTHORNE *Fr. & It. Jrnls.* II. 219 The Claudian aqueduct ..looks like a long procession, striding across the Campagna.
b. *transf.* or *fig.*
1646 J. HALL *Horæ Vac.* 32 Preaching is the Christall aquaeduct that conveighs the water of Life to us. **1857** H. REED *Brit. Poets* iii. 94 The poets were apt to fill their urns chiefly from the classical aqueducts of antiquity. **1875** GRINDON *Life* vi, Looking at the clouds merely as aqueducts.
2. The similar structure by which a canal is carried over a river, etc. (Also called *aqueduct-bridge*.)
1791 NEWTE *Tour Eng. & Sc.* 296 One of the most remarkable curiosities upon this magnificent canal is the aqueduct bridge of Cesse. **1842** WHITTOCK *Bk. Trades* 204 'Aqueducts' are frequently employed on a canal for the purpose of carrying it over rivers.
3. *Phys.* Name given to several small canals, chiefly in the head of mammals.
1709 BLAIR in *Phil. Trans.* XXVII. 108 The boney part of the Aqueduct. **1718** —— *ibid.* XXX. 890 The Aqueduct['s] ..Use is to receive the superfluous Moisture from the *Cavitas Tympani*. **1881** MIVART *Cat* 66 The facial nerve.. traversing in its way a canal termed the Aqueduct of Fallopius.

aqueighte, aqueiȝte, pa. t. of AQUETCH *v. Obs.*

aqueint, pa. t. and pple. of AQUENCH *v. Obs.*

†**aqueity.** *nonce-wd.* [f. as if from L. **aqueus* (see AQUEOUS) watery + -ITY.] The essential principle of water; watery quality.
1610 B. JONSON *Alch.* II. v, The Aqueitie, Terreitie, and Sulphureitie Shall runne together againe.

†**a'quell**, *v. Obs.* 1–4. For forms see QUELL *v.* [OE. *acwęllan*, f. A- *pref.* 1 intensive + *cwęllan* to kill, QUELL: cogn. with OHG. *arquelljan*, *archwellan*.] To slay, destroy, put an end to.
c **950** *Lindisf. Gosp.* John vii. 25 Ahne ðes is ðone soecað to a-cuellane? *c* **1175** *Lamb. Hom.* 207 His pine on rode and his deað acwellen mine sunnen. *a* **1250** *Owl & Night.* 1370 þar-mide beoþ men a-cwalde. *a* **1300** *Floriz & Bl.* 725 Quaþ blauncheflur, 'aquel þu me, And let floriz aliue be.' *c* **1330** *Arth. & Merl.* 400 Hou Fortiger hir king aqueld.

†**a'quench**, *v. Obs.* For forms see QUENCH *v.* [OE. *acwęncan*, f. A- *pref.* 1 intensive + *cwęncan* to QUENCH. Orig. trans., but afterwards used as intr.]
1. To quench, extinguish, put out (fire, light, life).
c **1000** *Ags. Gosp.* Matt. xxv. 8 Ure leoht-fatu synt acwencte. *c* **1175** *Lamb. Hom.* 135 Weter acwencheð fur. *c* **1230** *Ancr. R.* 124 Lutel fur was ter þer of, þet a puf acweinte. **1393** LANGL. *P. Pl.* C. XXI. 394 Aquykye · þat was aqueynt þorw synne. **1482** WARKW. *Chron.* 22 It wulde seme aquenched oute; and sodenly it brent fervently ageyne.
2. *intr.* To go out, become extinguished.
c **1230** *Ancr. R.* 426 þe Holi Gostes fur acwencheð, hwon þe brondes.. beoð i-sundred. *c* **1305** *St. Dunstan* 6 in *E.E.P.* (1862) Here liȝt aqueinte oueral. **1485** CAXTON *Trevisa's Higden* III. xxxv. (1527) 132 The fyre of the sacrefyce acquenched.
3. *trans.* To quench, satisfy, appease (appetite).
c **1300** *Vox & Wolf* 13 in Hazl. *E.P.P.* I. 51 He thohute his hounger aquenche.. mid mete. **1393** GOWER *Conf.* III. 10 Me thinketh My thurst shall never be acqueint.
4. *fig.* To extinguish, put an end to.
c **1175** *Lamb. Hom.* 135 Alswa weter acwencheð fur, alswa elmes dede acwencheð sunne. *c* **1305** *St. Katherine* 78 in *E.E.P.* (1862) On of oure knaues miȝte hire resouns sone aquenche. **1485** CAXTON *Trevisa's Higden* VII. xxxvii. (1527) 306 With his mylde lyuing and holy bedes he aqueynt many trybulacyons of holy chyrche. **1578** *Louer's Plight* in *Gorgious Gallery*, The colde that should acquench the heat.
b. (with personal obj. by inverted construction.)
c **1480** *Childe of Bristowe* 476 in *E.P.P.* (1864) 128 To aqueynche me of mykel care.

aqueo- (,eɪkwi:əʊ), comb. f. AQUEOUS; as in **aqueo-glacial** *a. Geol.*, formed or acted upon by glacial ice or water; **aqueo-igneous**, *a.* of, pertaining to, or resulting from the joint action of heat and water.
1892 W. M. DAVIS in *Proc. Boston Soc. Nat. Hist.* XXV. 321 Aqueo-glacial gravels are as inconspicuous as deposits of till.. but they are seen in the Catskill trench. **1880** J. D. DANA *Man. Geol.* (ed. 3) IV. v. 744 The view that the fusion of lavas is due to the combined action of moisture and heat, or is *aqueo-igneous*, was early presented by Scrope. **1920** *Discovery* Apr. 110/1 The earth's surface was originally in a state of aqueo-igneous fusion. **1879** LE CONTE *Elem. Geol.* §3. 93 Aqueo-igneously fused matter. **1727** DESAGULIERS in *Phil. Trans.* XXXIV. 272 An Aqueo-mercurial Gage.

aqueous ('eɪkwi:əs), *a.* [f. as if from L. **aqueus* (cf. *terreus* f. *terra*) + -OUS. Cf. Fr. *aqueux* (ad. L. *aquōsus*), 16th c. in Littré.]
1. a. Of, or of the nature of, water; watery; diluted with water.
1646 SIR T. BROWNE *Pseud. Ep.* 336 The phlegme or aqueous evaporation. **1667** BOYLE in *Phil. Trans.* II. 608 To freeze an Aqueous body. **1794** SULLIVAN *View Nat.* I. 120 The aggregation of aqueous particles in the air, forming the drops of rain. **1860** MAURY *Phys. Geog. Sea* iv. §228 Aqueous vapour is very much lighter than atmospheric air. **1871** TYNDALL *Fragm. Sc.* I. iv. 115 Aqueous hydrochloric acid.
b. ***aqueous humour*** of the eye.
1643 HERLE *Answ. Ferne* 2 It sees every thing coloured, as the distemper of the aqueous humour.. gives it tincture. **1879** HARLAN *Eyesight* ii. 20 The aqueous humor is nearly pure water, and is contained in the space between the cornea and lens.
2. Connected with, or relating to, water.
1731 BAILEY, *Aqueous Ducts*.. whereby the aqueous humour is supposed to be conveyed into the inside of the membranes which inclose that liquor. **1860** MAURY *Phys. Geog. Sea* ii. §96 The aqueous equilibrium of the planet would thereby be disturbed.
3. *Geol.* Of or pertaining to water as an agent; produced by the action of water.
1802 PLAYFAIR *Illustr. Hutton. The.* 320 The general system of aqueous deposition. **1833** LYELL *Elem. Geol.* i. (1874) 3 The 'aqueous' rocks, sometimes called the sedimentary.
4. as *sb.* Short for *aqueous humour*: see 1 b.
1879 *St. George's Hospital Rep.* IX. 481 During one week she had the aqueous tapped daily.

'**aqueously**, *adv. rare.* [f. prec. + -LY².] In, or by means of, water.
1857 *Nation. Mag.* I. 141 The passage of electricity through an insulated wire aqueously submerged.

'**aqueousness.** *rare*⁻⁰. [f. as prec. + -NESS.] Wateriness.
1731 in BAILEY; and in mod. Dicts.

†**aquerne.** *Obs.* [OE. *ácweorna*, later *ácwern*, cogn. w. OHG. and mod.G. *eichhorn*, LG. *êker-ken*, MDu. *êncoren*, Du. *eekhoren*, *eikhoren*, *inkhoren*, ON. *íkorni*. Of unknown origin; in OE. and some other langs. the first syllable is identified with *oak*.] A squirrel.
a **800** *Oldest Eng. Gl.* (Sw.) *Epinal* 911, aqueorna; *Erfurt*, aquorna; *Leiden* 236, acurna; *Cotton* 1811, aqueorna. *c* **1000** ÆLFRIC *Gl.* (Wr. 22/2) *Scirra, aquilinus, sciurus*, acwern. *c* **1200** *Moral Ode* 363 Ne aquerne ne metheschele [*v.r.* ocquerne ne martres cheole] ne beuer ne sabeline.

†**a'quetch**, *v. Obs.* 1–4. Pa. t. **acwehte**, **aqueighte.** [OE. *acwęcc(e)-an*, f. A- *pref.* 1 + *cwęccan*: see QUETCH *v.* Orig. trans., but afterw. used as intr.] To move quickly, shake, vibrate.
a **1000** *Byrhtnoth* (Gr.) 310 Æsc acwehte. *c* **1300** *K. Alis.* 5257 þe wode aqveiȝte so hi sunge. *c* **1330** *Arth. & Merl.* 3260 The strop to-bent, the hors aqueight.

aqueynt, obs. f. ACQUAINT, and var. of AQUEINT.

†**a'quick**, *v. Obs.* Forms: 1–3 **acwic-ian**, 2–4 **aquik-ien.** [OE. *acwician*, f. A- *pref.* 1 + *cwician* to QUICKEN; cogn. with OS. *aquicôn*, OHG. *arquicchan*, mod.G. *erquicken*.]
1. *trans.* To quicken, give life to, vivify, excite.
a **1000** *Ags. Ps.* cxix. 159 On ðinre mild-heortnesse me scealt acwician. *c* **1220** *Ureisun* in *Lamb. Hom.* 189 þurh his wunende grace þet acwikeð me. **1340** *Ayenb.* 203 Be zuych blest [of voule wordes].. is ofte aquyked þet uer of lecherie. **1393** LANGL. *Pl. Pl.* C. XXI. 394 Aquyte and aquykye · þat was aqueynt þorw synne.
2. *intr.* To revive, come to life again.
c **885** K. ÆLFRED *Bæda* v. vi. (Bosw.) Ðá acwicode ic. *c* **1175** *Lamb. Hom.* 81 Me mei blauwen, and he [the spark] wule aquikien. **1220** *Hali Meid.* 17 Ne acwikeð neauer meidenhad after þat wunde.

aquiculture ('eɪkwɪ,kʌltjʊə(r), -tʃə(r)). *erron.* aque-. [mod. f. L. *aqui-* (see AQUIFORM) + *cultūra* tending.] Culture of the natural produce of water; fish-breeding as a branch of industry. Cf. AQUACULTURE.
1578 LYTE *Dodoens* 166 This floure is now called in Latine *Aquilegia*, or *Aquileia*. **1599** A. M. *Gabelhouer's Bk. Physic* 203/1 Boyle Aquilege, and redde Nettles. **1867** *Even. Stand.* 13 July 3 The fish, aquiculture, and boat exhibition. **1868** PEARD *Water-farming* i. 2 Aqueculture actually existed in China centuries before luxury gave it birth in civilised Rome. **1947** *Endeavour* VI. 7 Aquiculture, or the cultivation of aquatic life, has been conducted on a very limited scale compared with agriculture.

aquiesce, -esse, obs. f. ACQUIESCE.

aquiet, var. ACQUIET *v. Obs.* to quiet.
1529 MORE *Comf. Trib.* II. Wks. 1186/1 To aquyet hys mynde.

aquifer ('ækwɪfə(r)). *Geol.* Also **aquafer** (irreg. form). [f. L. *aqui-*, combining form of *aqua* water + *-fer* bearing (f. *ferre* to bear).] A water-bearing or aquiferous stratum.
1901 *Science* 22 Nov. 794/1 The artesian system shows four or five aquifers, or water-bearing strata, more or less completely separated from one another. **1939** *Nature* 12 Aug. 274/2 The limestones are important aquifers for artesian and subartesian water. **1962** *Engineering* 9 Mar. 332 The whole system of aquifer storage can be likened to a U-gauge with one open limb and a short closed limb. **1966** *Listener* 1 Sept. 309/2 There are only two methods of [water] storage: in surface reservoirs and in the aquifers from which we pump a part of our supplies.

aquiferous (ə'kwɪfərəs), *a.* [f. L. *aqui-* (see next) + -FEROUS.] Conveying or yielding water.
1836 TODD *Cycl. Anat. & Phys.* I. 43/2 The aquiferous canals of the ciliograda. **1858** LEWES *Sea-side Stud.* 108 The Eolis has.. a system of aquiferous pores.

aquiform ('eɪkwɪfɔ:m), *a. erron.* **aqueform.** [f. L. *aqui-*, comb. f. *aqua* water (as in *aquigenus*, *aquilegus*) + -FORM.] Of watery form, liquid.
1835 KIRBY *Hab. & Inst. Anim.* (1852) II. 160 All the requisite materials, whether gaseous, aqueform, or solid.

'**aquilated**, *ppl. a. Her.* [f. med.L. *aquilāt-us* (f. *aquila* eagle) + -ED.] (See quot.)
1678 HOLME *Armory* I. v. §90 Others term such a cross.. aquilated, if [adorned] with Eagles heads.

†**a'quile**, *v. Obs. rare.* [Deriv. and meaning unknown. Dr. Morris suggests: To demand, ask, or obtain?]
c **1325** *E.E. Allit. P.* A. 960 Of þe lombe I haue þe aquylde For a syȝt þer of þurȝ gret fauor. (Cf. l. 689.)

aquilegia (ækwɪ'li:dʒ(ɪ)ə). *Bot.* Also 6 **aquilege** [ad. med.L. *aquilēja*, *aquilēgia*.] A plant of the genus of this name consisting of several species of ranunculaceous plants, the flowers of which are pentamerous with spurred petals; = COLUMBINE *sb.*² 1.
The genus-name *Aquilegia* is in Lyte 1578, Gerarde 1597, etc.
[**1578** LYTE *Dodoens* 166 This floure is now called in Latine *Aquilegia*, or *Aquileia*.] **1599** A. M. *Gabelhouer's Bk. Physic* 203/1 Boyle Aquilege, and redde Nettles. **1871** W. ROBINSON *Hardy Flowers* I. ix. 31 The larger type of alpine and herbaceous plants, beginning with such as the Aquilegias, and rising to the finer Phloxes. **1920** *Chambers's Jrnl.* May 326/2 Old-world flowers.. as delphinium and

antirrhinum and aquilegia. **1931** H. H. THOMAS *Amateur's Week-end Gard. Book* 100 The Columbine or Aquilegia is one of the most delightful of early summer flowers. **1934** G. A. PHILLIPS *Aristocrats of Flower Border* viii. 109 Aquilegias are mid-border plants.

†**aquiliferous** (ækwɪ'lɪfərəs), *a. Obs.*$^{-0}$. [f. L. *aquilifer* 'eagle-bearer,' + -OUS.] 'That bears the Picture of an Eagle in his Ensign; such was the Roman Standard-bearer.' Blount *Glossogr.* 1656.

aquiline ('ækwɪlɪn, aɪn), *a.* [ad. L. *aquilīnus*, f. *aquila* eagle: see -INE. Cf. F. *aquilin*, 16th c.]

1. Of or belonging to an eagle.

1656 in BLOUNT *Glossogr.* **1835** KIRBY *Hab. & Inst. Anim.* II. xvii. 155 The aquiline tribes, soaring in the air beyond human ken.

2. Eagle-like; *esp.* of the nose or features: Curved like an eagle's beak, hooked.

1646 SIR T. BROWNE *Pseud. Ep.* 130 Whence the Epithite Grypus for an hooked or Aquiline nose. **1742** YOUNG *Nt. Th.* IX. 967 When mortals lived Of stronger wing, of aquiline ascent. **1783** COWPER *Task* III. 192 Terribly arch'd, and aquiline his nose. **1791** BURKE *App. Old Whigs* Wks. VI. 263 A penetrating aquiline eye. **1855** TENNYSON *Maud* I. II. 10 The least little delicate aquiline curve in a sensitive nose.

†**aquilon.** *Obs.* [a. OF. *aquilon* (13th c. in Littré), ad. L. *aquilōn-em* (*aquilo*).] The north or north-north-east wind.

c **1325** *E.E. Allit. P.* C. 133 Eurus and aquiloun.. Blowes boþe at my bode. *c* **1374** CHAUCER *Boeth.* I. vi. 25 þe felnesse of þe wynde þat hyȝt aquilon. **1549** *Compl. Scot.* vi. 62 The thrid collateral vynd is callit aquilon.. The vulgaris callis it northest. **1606** SHAKS. *Tr. & Cr.* IV. v. 9 Blow.. till thy sphered Bias cheeke Out-swell the collicke of puft Aquilon. [In mod. Dicts.]

aquite, aquyte, obs. forms of ACQUIT *v.*

a-quiver (ə'kwɪvə(r)), *advb. phr.* [A- *prep.*[1] + QUIVER.] In a quiver, trembling.

1883 *Harper's Mag.* Feb. 428/2 All aquiver with the fun.

aquose (ə'kwəʊs), *a. rare.* [ad. L. *aquōsus*: see -OSE.] Watery, abounding in water.

1727-51 CHAMBERS *Cycl.*, *Aquose Ducts*.. whereby the aqueous humour of the eye is supposed to be conveyed into the inside of the membranes which inclose that liquor. **1813** W. TAYLOR *Eng. Synon.* (1856) 284 The land has been so well drained that, though aquose, it is no longer wet.

aquosity (ə'kwɒsɪtɪ). [ad. med.L. *aquōsitāt-em*, n. of quality f. *aquōsus*: see prec. and -ITY.]

1. Moist or watery quality, wateriness.

1528 PAYNELL *Salerne Reg.* P iij b, Of moche aquosite and humidite. **1650** tr. *Bacon's Hist. Life & Death* 38 To weare next the Body, Garments that have in them, some Vnctuosity, or Oleosity, not Aquosity. **1868** HUXLEY *Phys. Basis Life* 140 What better philosophical status has 'vitality' than aquosity?

†**2.** *concr.* Moisture, humour. *Obs.*

1528 PAYNELL *Salerne Reg.* Q iij, Ventosites and aquosites engendred of peres. **1601** HOLLAND *Pliny* II. 51 [Purslane is].. good for the aquosities gathered within the body. **1720** W. GIBSON *Dispens.* §16 (1734) 301 Boil to the consumption of the aquosity, that is, till the watry parts are evaporated.

aquoy, variant of ACOY *adv.*

c **1600** *Songs Lond. Prent.* (1841) 44 And looking all aquoy, Quoth she, What shall I have to do With any prentice boy?

aqw-: See ACQU-.

aqwere, obs. f. ACQUIRE.

ar (ɑː(r)). Name of the letter R.

c **1460** *Pol. Poem* in *Archæol.* XXIX. 331 There was an N and thre arres to-gydre. *c* **1470** *Pol. Rel. & L. Poems* 2 Iij ares for iij Richardes. **1802** MAR. EDGEWORTH *Moral T.* (1816) I. 252 The letter *r*, in this word, was made differently from all the *ars* in the rest of the inscription.

ar, obs. f. ARE (see BE *v.*), and EAR *v.* to plough.

ar, var. AIR *adv.* early; var. HER *pron.* her, their; obs. form of ARR, ERE, OR, OAR, ORE.

†**ar-,** *pref.*[1] The original WGer. form of the prefix, which in OE. was reduced as a proclitic to *a-* (exc. in *ar-æ̆fnan*); OHG. *ar-*, *er-*, *ir-*, mod.G. *er-*. See A- *pref.* 1 and Æ- *pref.* Cf. ARISE.

ar-, *pref.*[2], assimilated form of L. *ad-* used before *r-*, as in *adrogantia*, *arrogantia*, arrogance. Reduced in OF. to *a-*, which in 14th c. was often re-spelt *ar-* after L., and so usually in Eng. from 15th c.; hence most words from OF. in *ar-* are now written *arr-*, e.g. *arrange*, *array*, *arrive*. In 16th c. this spelling was erroneously extended to words with *a-* from other sources: as *a(r)raise*, *a(r)reach*, *a(r)rear*. See AD- 2.

-ar, *suff.*[1] **1.** of *adjs.* repr. L. *ār-em* (*-ār-is*, *-ār-e*, stem *-āri*) 'of the kind of, belonging to,' cogn. w. *-ālem*, and used where *l* preceded, as in *ālār-*, *stellār-*, *lūnār-*, *regulār-*, *similār-*, *līneār-* or *līneāl-*; hence always with diminutives in *-ul-*, *-ell-*, as *globulār-*, *orbiculār-*. See -AL[1]. The regular OF. descendant of *-ārem* was *-er*, later *-ier*, as *singulārem*, *populārem*, *sanglier*, *peuplier*; so *familier*, *régulier*; but later words of literary formation took *-aire* as *angulaire*, *militaire*. In Eng. those adopted from OF. had orig. *-er*, but were afterwards assimilated to L. with *-ar*, e.g. L. *scholār-em*, OF. *escolier*, AFr. *escoler*, ME. *scoler*, now *scholar*. Many words with this suffix have been adapted from L. or F., or formed on L., in modern times; but some of these, through mod.F. use of *-aire* for both *-āris* and *-ārius*, take -ARY; e.g. *military*.

2. of *sbs.* In L. the neuter of adjs. in *-āris*, gave sbs. in *-āre*, *-ar*, meaning 'thing pertaining to,' some of which have come into Eng., through F., as *alter*, *coler*, *piler*, now *altar*, *collar*, *pillar*, or directly from L., as *exemplar* (cogn. w. *sampler* through OF.).

-ar, *suff.*[2], occas. repr. of L. *-ārius*, *-ārium* (ordinarily repr. by -ER, -ARY). Generally, a refashioning of an earlier *-er* from OF. *-ier*, after the prec., as *bursar*, ME. *burser*, F. *boursier*, med.L. *bursārius*; *medlar*, ME. *medler*, OF. *meslier*, L. **mespilārius*; *mortar*, ME. *morter*, OF. *mortier*, L. *mortārium*; or after the mod.F. in *-aire*, as *vicar*, ME. also *viker* and *vicary*, F. *vicaire*, L. *vicārius*. To the F. forms in *-aire* are due the Sc. *notar*, *ordinar*, *testamentar*, etc. See -ARY[2].

-ar, *suff.*[3], casual variant of -ER, -OR, suffix of agent, and -ER suffix of comparative. Very common in north. dial., as *syngar* singer, *forebear* predecessor, *soutar* sutor; *hear* higher. And in modern Eng. in *beggar*, *liar*, *pedlar*. Probably imitating the refashioned *scholar*, *vicar*, *pillar* for earlier *scoler*, *viker*, *piler*: see -AR[1], and -AR[2], above.

Arab ('ærəb), *sb.* and *a.* [a. F. *Arabe*, ad. L. adj. *Arab-em* (nom. *Arabs*), a. Gr. Ἄραψ, Ἀραβ-.]

A. *sb.* **1.** One of the Semitic race inhabiting Saudi Arabia and neighbouring countries.

1634 T. HERBERT *Trav.* 324 (T.) The vulgar Arabs. **1851** RUSKIN *Stones Ven.* (1874) I. App. 360 Neither an Arab nor Byzantine ever jests in his architecture. **1893** F. ADAMS *New Egypt* 65 All, or nearly all, retain a sense of their superiority to the 'Arabs' (under this term, which is quite inaccurate, of course, except in so far as it alludes to the speech, it is usual to include all the Egyptians). **1902** [see ETHNIC *sb.* 2]. **1936** *Discovery* June 172/2 In Africa the term 'Arab' is commonly applied to any people professing Islam, however much Negro, Hamitic, or other foreign blood may run in their veins.

2. An Arab horse (prized for pure breed and fleetness).

a **1666** EVELYN *Diary* 25 Oct. an. 1644 (1955) II. 195 A stable of incomparable Horses of all Countries, Arabs, Turks, Barbs, [etc.]. **1844** DISRAELI *Coningsby* III. iii. 274 'A fine Arab, the finest in the world!' said the Duke, who was very fond of horses. **1880** G. A. MACKAY *21 Days in India* 114 Next morning sees the entire party.. mounted on Arabs.

3. (Orig. ***Arab of the city, city Arab, street Arab.***) A homeless little wanderer; a child of the street.

1848 GUTHRIE *Plea for Ragged Sch.*, The Arab of the City .. The City Arab. **1848** LD. SHAFTESB. *Sp. in Parl.* 6 June, City Arabs.. are like tribes of lawless freebooters, bound by no obligations, and utterly ignorant or utterly regardless of social duties. **1872** CALVERLEY *Fly-Leaves* (title) The Arab. **1883** *Pall Mall G.* 27 Oct. 5 The hero and heroine began life as street Arabs of Glasgow.

B. *adj.* **1.** Of or pertaining to Arabia or the Arabs.

1816 SHELLEY *Alastor* 129 An Arab maiden brought his food. **1855** TENNYSON *Maud* I. xvi. 15 The delicate Arab arch of her feet.

2. Special collocation. **Arab League,** an association of Arab nations formed in Cairo on 22 March 1945 in order to consolidate political and other relationships between member states.

1945 *Facts on File* 21–27 Mar. 93/2 Delegates of six Arab states today signed the final draft of the constitution of an *Arab League, Cairo reports. **1958** *Listener* 21 Aug. 256/1 The Sudan protested to the Arab League. **1985** *N.Y. Times* 27 Nov. A9/2 King Hassan said that Mr. Peres had asked to be invited to Morocco to talk with the King, who is chairman of the 21-nation Arab League.

‖**araba** (ə'rɑːbə). Also **aroba.** [a. Arab. and Pers. *arābah*, a wheeled carriage.] A wheeled carriage used in the East.

1845 THACKERAY *Cornh. to Cairo* (1872) 620 Dragged about in little queer arobas, or painted carriages. **1882** MRS. PITMAN *Mission Life Greece & Pal.* 359 Hauling stone in creaking arabas drawn by bullocks.

araban ('ærəbæn). *Chem.* [a. G. *araban*, f. ARAB(IC *a.* + -AN.] = ARABIN.

1892 *Jrnl. Soc. Chem. Industry* XI. 931/1 The Pentosans (Wood-Gum, Xylan, and Araban) of Lignified Fibre. **1938** *Thorpe's Dict. Appl. Chem.* II. 287/1 The pentoses do not occur as such in plants, but in the form of condensation products of high molecular weight, termed 'pentosans' (araban or xylan). **1943** *Ibid.* VI. 155/2 Araban.. yields arabinose, galactose and glycuronic acid on hydrolysis.

Arabdom ('ærəbdəm). [f. ARAB *sb.* + -DOM.] Arabs collectively; the state or condition of being an Arab.

1949 *International Affairs* 475 The fate of Arabdom. **1957** *Listener* 24 Oct. 663/1 Distinguished Englishmen who were drawn to Arabdom by a kind of elective affinity. *Ibid.*, Jordan east of the river was somehow different from all Arabdom. **1958** [see ARABISM 2].

arabesque (ærə'bɛsk), *a.* and *sb.* Also 8 **arabesk.** [a. F. *arabesque* Arabian; cf. It. *rabesco* (Florio 1611), and earlier REBESK.]

A. *adj.* **1.** Arabian, Arabic.

1842 *Encycl. Brit.* II. 693/1 The inglorious obscurity in which the Arabesque doctors have in general slumbered.

2. *esp.* Arabian or Moorish in ornamental design; carved or painted in arabesque (see B 2).

[**1611** COTGR., *Arabesque*, Rebeske worke; a small, and curious flourishing.] **1656** BLOUNT *Glossogr.*, *Arabesque*, Rebesk work; branched work in painting or in Tapestry. **1779** H. SWINBURNE *Trav. Spain* xxxi. (T.) Armorial ensigns.. interwoven with the arabesque foliage. **1849** FREEMAN *Archit.* 282 A sort of arabesque pattern with festoons of fruit and flowers.

3. *fig.* Strangely mixed, fantastic.

1848 DICKENS *Dombey* (C.D. ed.) 105 Surrounded by this arabesque work of his musing fancy. **1863** MRS. CLARKE *Shaks. Char.* xvi. 411 Launcelot is a sort of 'arabesque' character.

B. *sb.* [the adj. used *absol.*]

†**1.** The vulgar Arabic language. *Obs.*

1770 W. GUTHRIE *Geogr.*, *Egypt* (T.) The Arabick, or Arabesque, as it is called, is still the current language. **1796** MORSE *Amer. Geog.* II. 580 The vulgar language.. is the Arabesk, or corrupt Arabian.

2. A species of mural or surface decoration in colour or low relief, composed in flowing lines of branches, leaves, and scroll-work fancifully intertwined. Also *fig.*

As used in Moorish and Arabic decorative art (from which, almost exclusively, it was known in the Middle Ages), representations of living creatures were excluded; but in the arabesques of Raphael, founded on the ancient Græco-Roman work of this kind, and in those of Renascence decoration, human and animal figures, both natural and grotesque, as well as vases, armour, and objects of art, are freely introduced; to this the term is now usually applied, the other being distinguished as Moorish Arabesque, or Moresque.

1786 tr. *Beckford's Vathek* (1868) 66 Could.. paint upon vellum the most elegant arabesques that fancy could devise. **1827** CARLYLE *Misc.* (1857) I. 14 His manner of writing is —a wild complicated Arabesque. **1844** DISRAELI *Coningsby* I. iii. 16 A vestibule, painted in arabesque. **1868** *Chambers's Encycl.* I. 344 The arabesques with which Raphael adorned the galleries of the Vatican, and which he is said to have imitated from those which he had been instrumental in discovering in the baths of Titus, are at once the most famous and the most beautiful which the modern world has produced. **1880** LONGF. *My Cathedr.* 5 Not Art but Nature .. carved this graceful arabesque of vines.

3. The figure described by the leading lines of the composition, in a drawing or painting.

1883 W. ARMSTRONG in *Eng. Illus. Mag.* 155/1 The same qualities, but with more freedom and a finer arabesque.

4. *Ballet.* A pose in which the dancer stands on one foot with one arm extended in front and the other arm and leg extended behind.

1830 R. BARTON tr. *C. Blasis' Code of Terpsichore* II. v. 74 Nothing can be more agreeable to the eye than those charming positions which we call *arabesques*, and which we have derived from antique basso relievos, from a few fragments of Greek paintings, and from the paintings in fresco at the Vatican, executed after the beautiful designs of Raphael. **1911** J. E. C. FLITCH *Mod. Dancing* iii. 42 One of her [*sc.* Marie Taglioni's] most wonderful attitudes was an *arabesque* which gave her the appearance of actually flying. **1928** A. L. HASKELL *Some Stud. in Ballet* 151 Everything in it depends on line, absolute precision of movement and the purity of the arabesque.

5. *Mus.* (See quot. 1879.) Also *transf.*

1864 *Cramer, Beale & Wood's New Eds. Piano Forte Works* Misc. Ser., No. 4 (*title*) Arabesques, by R. Schumann. **1879** *Grove's Dict. Mus.* I. 80/2 *Arabesque*..(1) The title has been given.. by Schumann to one of his pianoforte pieces.., which is written in a form bearing some analogy to that of the rondo, and it has been since occasionally used by other writers for the piano. (2) The word 'Arabesque' is sometimes used by writers on music to express the ornamentation of a theme. **1924** A. D. SEDGWICK *Little French Girl* III. vii, Listening to a blackbird that fluted golden arabesques.

ara'besque, *v.* [f. ARABESQUE *sb.*] *trans.* To ornament in arabesque. Hence **ara'besquing** *ppl. a.*

1858 HAWTHORNE *Fr. & It. Jrnls.* I. 264 A small room.. arabesqued in rich designs by Raphael. **1861** SALA in *Temple Bar* I. 306 The same embroideress who arabesqued the hems of her under-skirts pinked the shrouds. **1867** H. LATHAM *Black & White* 21 A cell in which a weaver had arabesqued the walls. **1877** J. HAWTHORNE *Garth* IX. lxviii, The skylight was arabesqued with frost. **1908** SAINTSBURY in *Camb. Hist. Eng. Lit.* II. 191 A sort of vignetting or arabesquing fringe and atmosphere of exaggeration and fantasy.

ara'besquely, *adv. rare.* [f. ARABESQUE *a.* + -LY[2].] In the style of the Arabs, or of arabesques.

1845 HIRST *Poems* 66 The Arabesquely-shapen barks of Carthaginian lands.

A'rabia. The country so named; *fig.* Spices.
1711 POPE *Rape Lock* I. 134 All Arabia breathes from yonder box.

Arabian (əˈreɪbɪən), *a.* and *sb.* [f. prec. + -AN.]
A. *adj.* Belonging to Arabia. ***Arabian bird***: the phœnix, *fig.* a unique specimen. ***Arabian horse*** = ARAB *sb.* 2. ***Arabian nights***: fabulous stories.
1606 SHAKS. *Ant. & Cl.* III. ii. 12 Oh Anthony, oh thou Arabian Bird! **1737** S. BERINGTON *Mem. G. di Lucca* 47 The Arabian Horses are the best in the World, tho' not very large. **1771** SHERIDAN *Aristænetus* XII. vii, Her kisses, like Arabian gales, The scent of musky flowers impart. **1807** 'CERVANTES HOGG' *Rising Sun* III. xvi. 166 The prince,.. mounted on an Arabian horse as fleet as the wind, followed with the utmost eagerness. **1808** SYD. SMITH *Plymley's Lett.* Wks. 1859 II. 180/2 To cram him with Arabian-night stories about the Catholics.

B. *sb.* a. A native of Arabia; also, one of a sect that arose in Arabia in the 3rd century, holding that the soul died with the body, and rose again with it at the resurrection.
c **1391** [see ARABIC]. **1526** TINDALE *Acts* ii. 11 Grekes and Arabians. **1670** G. H. *Hist. Cardinals* I. II. 52 [The] Arabians..were in a short time suppress'd by the industry of St. Origen.

b. = *Arabian horse*.
1770 H. BROOKE *Fool of Qual.* V. 299 Her six spotted Arabians. **1792** A. YOUNG *Trav. in France* 16 There are all kinds of horses, but chiefly Arabian, Turkish and English. Three years ago four Arabians were imported. **1824** M. R. MITFORD *Our Village* I. 101 That gay, gallant boy, on the gallant white Arabian. **1966** R. STOUT *Death of Doxy* (1967) ix. 94 She liked horses and had four Arabians.

A'rabianize, *v.* [f. ARABIAN *a.* + -IZE.] *trans.* To make Arabian, give an Arabian character to; to assimilate to the Arabian language.
1893 F. ADAMS *New Egypt* 9 The fiercely protracted effort of Islam to Arabianise Egypt.

Arabic (ˈærəbɪk), *a.* Forms: 4 **Arabik,** 5 **-yke, -yque,** 6–8 **-ick(e,** 7 **-ique,** 8 **-eck(e,** 8– **Arabic.** [a. OF. *Arabic* (13th c. in Litt.), ad. L. *Arabicus.*]
1. Of or pertaining to Arabia or its language. ***arabic numerals***: the figures 1, 2, 3, 4, etc.
c **1650** WORTHINGTON *Epist. Hartlib* vii. (T.) His Arabick translation of Grotius. **1727–51** CHAMBERS *Cycl.*, The *Arabic* characters stand contradistinguished to the Roman. **1858** LONGF. *M. Standish* I. 9 Its mystical Arabic sentence.
2. *esp.* in ***gum arabic***, which is exuded by certain species of Acacia, and ***arabic acid***, obtained from it.
[*a* **1500** in *Rel. Ant.* I. 163 Put thereto iij ounces of gumme of Arabyke. **1590** GREENE *Mourn. Garm.* (1616) 9 The Arabick-tree, that yeelds no gumme but in the darke night.] **1616** SURFL. & MARKH. *Countr. Farm* 19 a, Adding thereto ..Gum-arabecke, and Tragacanth. **1866** *Treas. Bot.* 5/1 Gum arabic is an exudation from various species of acacia.
3. *absol.* The language of the Arabs.
c **1391** CHAUCER *Astrol.* 2 To arabiens in arabik. **1485** CAXTON *Chas. Gt.* 206 A cyte called Salancadys, in arabyque. **1611** BIBLE *Pref.* 5 John Bishop of Siuil [is reported] to haue turned them [the Scriptures] into Arabicke. **1871** EARLE *Philol. Eng. Tong.* §353 Those English (or rather European) nouns..derived from Arabic, as *alchemy, alcohol, alcove*, etc.

arabica (əˈræbɪkə). Used *ellipt.* for the tree *Coffea arabica* (see COFFEE 3) or for coffee obtained from this tree. Also *attrib.*
1922 W. H. UKERS *All about Coffee* xx. 201 Strong, chilly winds and intensely hot sunlight are foes of coffee trees, especially of the *arabica* variety. *Ibid.* 215 Of this area, 110,903 acres were planted with *robusta*, 15,314 acres with *arabica*. **1959** *Times* 22 Sept. 11/6 The Southern Cameroons, where crops of both *arabica* and *robusta* are grown. **1964** *Economist* 28 Mar. 1198/1 The high standards of cultivation required for Arabica coffee.

†**A'rabical,** *a. Obs.* [f. ARABIC *a.* + -AL[1].] = ARABIC *a.*
1548 HALL *Chron.* (1809) 46 This Prince was almost the Arabicall Phenix. **1612–20** SHELTON *Quix.* II. II. i. (T.) Written in Arabical characters.

†**A'rabically,** *adv. Obs. rare.* [f. prec. + -LY[2].] According to Arabic usage; in Arabic.
1634 T. HERBERT *Trav.* 139 Bagdat..signifies arabically a garden.

†**A'rabican,** *a. Obs. rare.* [f. ARABIC + -AN; cf. OF. *arabican(t* (Godefroy).] = ARABIC.
1607 TOPSELL *Four-f. Beasts* 569 The Arabican Writers.

Arabicism (əˈræbɪsɪz(ə)m). *rare.* [f. ARABIC + -ISM; cf. *anglicism.*] An Arabic idiom or peculiarity of language.
1827 SOUTHEY in *Q. Rev.* XXXV. 188 Hebraisms, and Arabicisms, which might send the best scholar to his Lexicons.

Arabicize (əˈræbɪsaɪz), *v.* [f. as prec. + -IZE; cf. *anglicize.*] To make like Arabic; to conform to Arabic usage. Hence **arabicized** *ppl. a.*
1872 BEAMES *Aryan Lang. India* I. 96 Superseded by Hindi in its Arabicised form of Urdu.

arability (ærəˈbɪlɪtɪ). [f. ARABLE *a.*: see -BILITY.] Capability of being used as arable land.
1879 *Athenæum* 28 June 817/2 The term [*sc.* hide] being.. variable according to the arability..of the land. **1963** *Spectator* 22 Feb. 224 The arability of its [Venezuela's] *llanos*.

arabin (ˈærəbɪn). *Chem.* [f. ARAB-IC + -IN.] The pure soluble principle in gum arabic and similar substances. **arabi'nose**, the sugar derived from arabin. Hence **ara'binic, arabi'nosic** *a.*
1840 PEREIRA *Mat. Med.* II. 1150 Soluble Gum or Arabin. **1854** BALFOUR *Bot.* 29 Arabine, soluble in cold water, constituting the chief ingredient of gum-arabic.

‖**arabis** (ˈærəbɪs). *Bot.* [med.L. *Arabis*, so named prob. from growing on sandy or stony places.] A genus of cruciferous plants, species of which are grown on rock-work, and as border-flowers in early spring; a plant of the genus.
[**1578** LYTE *Dodoens* 629 This herbe [candy Thlaspi] is called..in Latine *Arabis* and *Draba*.] **1706** PHILLIPS, *Arabis*, a sort of Water-cress call'd candy Thlaspy. **1794** MARTYN *Rousseau's Bot.* xxiii. 324 Arabis has four glands, within the leaflets of the calyx. **1870** W. ROBINSON *Alpine Flowers* I. 48 The dwarf green Iberises,..Arabises, [etc.]. **1876** RHODA BROUGHTON *Joan* v, Milk-white arabis haunted by the drowsy booming bees. **1905** *Westm. Gaz.* 10 June 16/1 The white blossoms of the double arabis.

'Arabism. [mod. f. ARAB + -ISM; cf. F. *arabisme.*] 1. = ARABICISM.
1614 SELDEN *Titles Hon.* 98 Hee stiles himself *Amir*..In Arabisme [*amîr*]. **1751** CHAMBERS *Cycl.* s.v., So zealous a partizan of Arabisms. **1898** SAYCE *Early Israel* iii. 109 Hebrew had retained a few 'Arabisms', a few traces of its ancient contact with Arabic-speaking tribes. **1958** *Archivum Linguisticum* X. 26 The Arabism *bellota*, absent from Portuguese.
2. The state or condition of being an Arab; the influence of Arab culture. Also, Arab nationalism, sympathy with Arab movements of self-assertion.
1874 DRAPER *Hist. Conflict Relig. & Sci.* iii. 99 Arabism, which had done so much for the intellectual advancement of the world, came to an end when the Turks and the Berbers attained to power. **1952** *Middle East Jrnl.* VI. 473/2 Arabism, now the creed of a large number of people, is not the only political philosophy in vogue in the Arab world. **1958** *Times* 16 July 11/6 '*Aruba*, 'arabism' or 'arabdom', the word which is on the lips of every politician and the pen of every journalist, means the fact of being an Arab. The positive elements of arabism are not so much racial as a sense of common history, and, much more potent, the existence of a common language.

Arabist (ˈærəbɪst). [f. as prec. + -IST; cf. F. *arabiste.*] A professed student of the language, or follower of the medical system, of the Arabs.
1753 CHAMBERS *Cycl. Supp.* s.v., Severinus gives all the surgeons in the thirteenth century the title Arabists. **1847** CRAIG, *Arabist*, one skilled in Arabian literature.

Arabize (ˈærəbaɪz), *v.* [f. ARAB + -IZE.] *trans.* To make Arab; to give an Arab or Arabic character to. Hence **'Arabized** (-aɪzd), **'Arabizing** *ppl. adjs.*, **Arabi'zation.**
1883 CUST *Mod. Lang. Africa* I. viii. 83 The Arabizing process [in Africa] has taken place in various ways. **1884** *Science* 12 Dec. 531/1 These Arabs of the Sudan are not true Arabs, but to a great extent merely Arabized negroes. **1898** SAYCE *Early Israel* iii. 114 The dialect of Edom agreed with Hebrew in those Arabising peculiarities. **1920** *19th Cent.* Aug. 229 The civil administration of the country should be Arabised to a greater extent. **1931** C. G. SELIGMAN in W. Rose *Outl. Mod. Knowl.* 466 The prestige of the dominant religion..accounts for such arabisation as has taken place. **1937** *Times* 20 Oct. 15/6 They [*sc.* the Arab leaders] regard ..the Zionist Jew, who..refuses to be Arabized, as an obstacle to that unity.

arable (ˈærəb(ə)l), *a.* [ad. (perh. through F. *arable*, 15th c. in Littré) L. *arābilis*, f. *arā-re* to plough. Preceded in use by a word *erable* (also in 16th c. *errable, earable, aerable*), referred to the cogn. Eng. vb. *ere*, EAR, of which *arable* was perh. at first intended as a correction after L. In 17th c. the two existed side by side (Coke uses both), but in the 18th *earable* became obs. exc. in dialects.] Capable of being ploughed, fit for tillage; opposed to *pasture-* or *wood-land*.
1577 TUSSER *Jan. Husb.* liii, Land arable. **1628** COKE *On Litt.* 53 b, If the tenant conuert arable land into wood. [*Ibid.* 85 b, Errable land.] **1725** POPE *Odyss.* xx. 356 Unnumber'd acres arable and green. **1866** ROGERS *Agric. & Prices* I. ii. 15 Half the arable estate, as a rule, lay in fallow.
b. *absol.* quasi-*sb.* Arable land.
1576 LAMBARDE *Peramb. Kent* (1826) 3 Consisting indifferently of arable, pasture, meadow, and woodland. **1697** DRYDEN *Virg. Georg.* II. 321 Tis good for Arable, a Glebe that asks Tough Teams of Oxen. **1883** HARDY in *Longm. Mag.* July 258 A group of these honest fellows in the arable.

Araby (ˈærəbɪ), *a.* and *sb.* [a. OF. *arabi, arrabi*, Arabian, an Arab, Arab horse.]
A. *adj.* Arabian, Arabic. *arch.* and *poet.*
1502 ARNOLD *Chron.* 158 Arabye language. **1547** BOORDE *Brev. Health* Pref., Many obscure termes..some and fewe beynge Araby wordes.
B. *sb.*
†1. A native of Arabia; an Arab. *Obs.*
1398 TREVISA *Barth. De P.R.* XIII. xxii. (1495) 455 The Arabees dwelle there. **1525** LD. BERNERS *Froiss.* II. ccxxxiii. 725 Great puyssaunce of men of warre, of turkes, arabyes, tartaryes. **1587** D. FENNER *Def. Ministers* F iiij, Why you call vs..scoffing Hammonites, conspiring Arabies.
†2. An Arab horse. *Obs.*
c **1175** *Lamb. Hom.* 5 He mihte ridan..on riche stede and palefrai and mule and arabisȝ. *c* **1440** *Morte Arth.* 2288 Elfaydes, and Arrabys, and olifauntez noble.
3. [a. F. *Arabie.*] The country of Arabia.
1297 R. GLOUC. 397 He an kniȝtes heued of Arabye of smot. **1622** MASS. & DEKK. *Virg. Mart.* IV. iii, The Power I serve Laughs at your happy Araby. **1792** D. LLOYD *Voy. Life* IV. 77 Spicy gales from fragrant Araby.

†**a'race,** *v. Obs.* Forms: 4–6 **arace,** 5 **aras(e,** 6 *Sc.* **arraise.** [a. AF. *arace-r*, OF. *aracier*, Norman dial. f. *arachier*: see ARACHE. *Arace* was much the commoner in ME.] To pull up by the roots; to tear up or away, pull or snatch away; to tear.
c **1315** SHOREHAM 95 That he hyt wolde arace. *c* **1386** CHAUCER *Clerkes T.* 1047 Whan sche gan hem tembrace.. The children from her arm they gonne arace [*v.r.* race, rase]. **1413** LYDG. *Pylgr. Sowle* III. iv. (1483) 52 These hokes to renten and a racid two caitifs. *c* **1425** WYNTOUN *Cron.* VII. xxxv. 127 And wyth gret strynth owt can aras Þe Trownsown, þat þare stekand was. *a* **1440** *Morte Arth.* 4099 ȝif any renke theme arase, reschowe theme sone. **1530** PALSGR. 435/2, I arace, I pull a thyng by violence from one, *Je arrache.*

arace, var. ARASE *v. Obs.* to raze, erase.

araceous (əˈreɪʃəs), *a. Bot.* [f. mod.L. *Araceæ*, f. *arum*, a. Gr. ἄρον the cuckoo-pint: see -ACEOUS.] Belonging to the N.O. *Araceæ*, of which one species, the Cuckoo-pint or Wake-robin (*Arum maculatum*), is native to Britain.

arach: see ORACH.

†**a'rache,** *v. Obs.* Forms: 4–6 **arache, arrache,** 6 **arasshe.** [combines (as does mod.F. *arracher*) two OF. vbs. (1) *arachier*:—L. **abrādīcā-re*; (2) *érachier, esrachier*:—L. *exrādīcā-re*; f. *ab* away, *ex* out + *rādīc-em* root.] = ARACE *v.*
c **1315** SHOREHAM 156 Hye weren..ouȝt of hare loȝ arached For hare senne. **1483** CAXTON *G. de la Tour* M viij b, I tooke and arrached oute of his bely his herte. **1490** —— *Eneydos* iv. 24 To arache or plucke up a gretter tree. *c* **1530** LD. BERNERS *Arth. Lyt. Bryt.* (1814) 214 She..arasshed clene of his helme.

arachidic, *a.*: see ARACHIS.

arachidonic (ə,rækɪˈdɒnɪk), *a. Chem.* [f. ARACHID(IC *a.* + -ONIC.] ***arachidonic acid***: an unsaturated fatty acid found in animal fats.
1913 J. LEWKOWITSCH *Chem. Technol. of Oils* I. iii. 211 Arachidonic Acid, $C_{20}H_{32}O_2$. The existence of an acid of this composition is inferred from the formation of octo-bromo-arachidic acid...As Hartley has not named this acid the author suggests the term *arachidonic acid*. **1924** L. G. WESSON in *Jrnl. Biol. Chem.* LX. 183 Arachidonic acid, so named by Lewkowitsch, is the tetra unsaturated, normal, aliphatic C_{20} acid, which is present in brain tissue. **1964** J. A. LOVERN in H. Barnes *Oceanogr. & Marine Biol.* II. 187 The mammal can convert linoleic acid..into the essential arachidonic acid (eicosa-5,8,11,14-tetraenoic acid), without which it cannot survive.

arachin (ˈærəkɪn). [f. ARACH(IS + -IN[1].] A globulin found in arachis oil, groundnuts, etc.
1905 G. M. GOULD *Dict. New Med. Terms* 88/2 *Arachin*, $C_{20}H_{40}O_2$, a glycerid of arachic acid. It occurs as the chief constituent of Rambutan tallow obtained from the seeds of *Nephelium lappaceum*. **1913** J. LEWKOWITSCH *Chem. Technol. of Oils* I. i. 27 *Triarachin, Arachin*, $C_3H_5(O.C_{20}H_{39}O)_3$, (prepared by *Berthelot* from diarachin and arachidic acid) is..soluble... Arachin occurs in arachis oil, and in smaller quantities in rape oil and butter fat. **1946** *Nature* 5 Oct. 475/1 Hitherto..it has merely been possible to convert globular proteins, such as casein, arachin and egg albumin, into the fibrous form.

‖**'arachis.** *Bot.* [mod.L., ad. Gr. ἄραχος, ἄρακος, or ἀρακίς, some leguminous weed.] A genus of leguminous plants, one of which is cultivated in warm countries, and known as the ground nut. Hence **arachis oil**, peanut oil. **arachidic** as in ***arachidic acid*** ($C_{20}\,H_{40}\,O_2$), obtained from the oil of the ground nut.
1853 MAYNE *Expos. Lex.* 80/2 Arachis. **1866** W. ODLING *Lect. Anim. Chem.* 31 Monatomic Fatty Acid Series.. $C_{20}H_{40}O_2$ Arachidic. **1875** GAMGEE tr. *Hermann's Physiol.* 13 The series of the fatty acids at present known includes.. arachidic acid. **1876** *Encycl. Brit.* IV. 151/2 In some Leguminosæ, as Arachis, Cathartocarpus Fistula, and the Tamarind, the fruit must be considered a legume, although it does not dehisce. **1889** *Cent. Dict.* s.v., *Arachis-oil*, the oil expressed from the seeds of *Arachis hypogæa*, the fine limpid nut-oil of commerce. **1900** SADTLER *Handbk. Industr. Org. Chem.* (ed. 3) 50 Arachis oil (peanut oil, erdnuss oil)...The best qualities..are used for table oil and the inferior grades for soap-making. **1916** *Chambers's Jrnl.* May 313/1 The arachis nut (popularly known as the 'monkey nut').

arachnean (æræk'niːən), *a. rare.* [f. Gr. ἀραχναῖ-ος, f. ἀράχνη a spider or its web + -AN.] Resembling a spider's web, gossamer.
1854 BADHAM *Halieut.* 539 Hebes in arachnean robes.

arachnid (əˈræknɪd). *Zool.* [mod. f. Gr. ἀράχνη spider + -ID; cf. F. *arachnide.*] A member of the *Arachnida*. ‖**A'rachnida**, *sb. pl.* [mod.L.], a class of the *Arthropoda*, comprising spiders, scorpions, and mites; closely allied to Insects and Crustacea, but distinguished by the possession of eight legs, the absence of wings and antennæ, and by breathing by means of tracheal tubes or pulmonary sacs. **a'rachnidan,** *a.* of or belonging to the *Arachnida*; *sb.* an arachnid. **arachnidean, -ian,** *a.* and *sb.* = prec. **arach'nidial,** *a.* [f. next] of or pertaining to the *arachnidium.* ‖**arachnidium** (ærræk'nɪdɪəm) [mod.L.], the apparatus by which the spider produces its web. **a'rachnidous,** *a.* of the nature of the *Arachnida*.

1869 HUXLEY *Classif. Anim.* 77 A Crustacean, an *Arachnid, a Myriapod, or an Insect. **1881** GEIKIE in *Nature* No. 627. 3 There can be little doubt that it [scorpion] is the most ancient type of Arachnid. **1834** *Penny Cycl.* II. 232/1 The greater number of the *arachnida are carnivorous. **1881** MIVART *Cat* 511 The *arachnidan external parasite is a sort of itch insect. **1828** KIRBY & SPENCE *Entomol.* III. xxviii. 51 No genuine insect or *Arachnidan has yet been found to inhabit the ocean. **1865** in *Morn. Star* 7 Nov., All the rails in front of my residence had their busy group of *arachnidean workers. **1854** BUSHNAN in *Orr's Circ. Sc.* Org. Nat. I. 77 The Pulmonary *Arachnidians, of which the true spiders and the scorpion are examples. **1877** HUXLEY *Anat. Inv. An.* vii. 381 The six prominent *arachnidial mammillæ. *Ibid.* vii. 380 One of the most characteristic organs..is the *arachnidium, or apparatus by which the fine silky threads which constitute the web are produced. **1875** *Encyc. Brit.* (ed. 9) II. 273 The higher, at least, of the *arachnidous orders.

arachnitis: see ARACHNOIDITIS.

arachnoid (ə'ræknɔɪd), *a.* and *sb.* [ad. mod.L. *arachnoīdes*, a. Gr. ἀραχνο-ειδής cobweb-like: see -OID.] **A.** *adj.*

1. *Bot.* Covered with or formed of long, delicate, cobweb-like hairs or fibres.

1857 BERKELEY *Cryptog. Bot.* §401 An arachnoid or woven veil attached to the edge, and sometimes entirely covering the gills. **1874** M. COOKE *Fungi* 91 Arachnoid threads.

2. *Phys.* Of or pertaining to the arachnoid. (See B.)

1789 *Loiterer* 26 Sept. No. 35, p. 9 The dura and the pia Mater, and the arachnoid coat, entirely consisted of the Wings of Moths. **1836–39** TODD *Cycl. Anat. & Phys.* II. 278/1 The chamber is lined by the arachnoid membrane. **1872** HUXLEY *Phys.* xi. 249 It secretes..the arachnoid fluid.

3. *Ent.* Resembling the *Arachnida*.

1852 DANA *Crust.* I. 14 The Arachnoid type, as in Nymphon.

B. *sb.* The delicate serous membrane or membranous sac lining the *dura mater*, and enveloping the brain and spinal cord.

[**1751** CHAMBERS *Cycl.*, *Arachnoides*..a fine, thin, transparent membrane..supposed to invest the whole substance of the brain, medulla oblongata, and spinal marrow.] **1839–47** TODD *Cycl. Anat. & Phys.* III. 638/1 The arachnoid covers the superior surface of the cerebellum.

arachnoidal (æræk'nɔɪdəl), *a.* [f. prec. + -AL[1].] Of the nature of, or pertaining to, the arachnoid. **arachnoideal, -ean, -eous,** *a.* unnecessary variants of ARACHNOID, -AL.

1855 RAMSBOTHAM *Obstet. Med.* 64 An extremely delicate arachnoidal membrane. **1874** JONES & SIEV. *Pathol. Anat.* 235 Arachnoidal effusion..speedily proves fatal. **1842** E. WILSON *Anat. Vade M.* 373 The arachnoid is attached to the pia mater of the brain by a loose cellular tissue, the subarachnoidean. **1851** CRABB, *Arachnoideous* in *Bot.* **1877** BURNETT *Ear* 89 The arachnoideal sac of the brain.

arachnoi'ditis. *Path.* [f. ARACHNOID + -ITIS.] Inflammation of the arachnoid membrane. Also in less correct form **arach'nitis.**

1827 J. FORBES tr. *Laennec's Dis. Chest* (ed. 2) I. i. 71, I have witnessed the supervention of peritonitis, severe dysentery, and arachnitis, to fluxes suppressed by the use of hot wine and spices. **1857** DUNGLISON *Dict. Med. Sci.* (ed. 15), *Arachnitis*, more properly *Arachnoiditis*. **1910** *Practitioner* July 48 Sometimes the effusion is localised and secondary to atrophy of the convolutions, and sometimes it may be general and due to serous arachnoiditis (Meningitis serosa externa). **1961** *Lancet* 22 July 178/1 Spinal arachnoiditis, and weakness in the legs were noted.

arachnological (əˌræknəʊ'lɒdʒɪkəl), *a.* Of, or pertaining to, arachnology. **arachnologist** (æræk'nɒlədʒɪst), a student of, or proficient in, arachnology. **arachnology** (-'ɒlədʒɪ) [f. Gr. ἀράχνη spider + -(O)LOGY.], the department of Zoology relating to spiders or the *Arachnida* generally.

1861 BLACKWALL *Spiders* I. Pref. 5 Arachnological science. **1816** KIRBY & SPENCE *Entomol.* (1843) II. 277 The English Arachnologists—may I coin this term? **1880** *Nature* XXI. 273 Mr. Pickard-Cambridge's reputation as an arachnologist. **1861** BLACKWALL *Spiders* I. Introd. 5 Dr. Lister, and the earlier systematic writers on arachnology.

arack(e, obs. variant of ARRACK.

arad ('ɛərəd). *Bot.* [f. AR-UM + -AD.] An araceous plant, as the Wake Robin.

1853 LINDLEY *Veg. K.* 127 The hooded spathe of the order of Arads.

aræometer, areo- (ɛərɪ:'ɒmɪtə(r)). [mod. f. Gr. ἀραιός thin + μέτρον measure: see -METER. App. through F. *aréomètre*: whence the prevalent spelling, as if from AREA, or AREO-, of Mars.] An instrument, consisting of a graduated glass tube terminating in a loaded bulb, for measuring the specific gravity of fluids; a hydrometer. Hence: **aræometric** (əˌri:əʊ'metrɪk), *a.* [see -IC], of or pertaining to aræometry. **aræo'metrical** *a.* = prec. **aræometry** (ɛərɪ:'ɒmɪtrɪ). [Gr. -μετρία measurement], the art or science of estimating the specific gravity of fluids by means of an aræometer.

1706 PHILLIPS, *Areometer.* **1730** DESAGULIERS in *Phil. Trans.* XXXVI. 277 The Hydrometer, by some called Areometer. **1731** BAILEY, *Aræometer.* **1751** CHAMBERS *Cycl.*, The Aræometer or waterpoise is usually made of glass. **1876** URE *Dict. Arts* I. 207 The areometer of Baumé is used in France. **1871** B. STEWART *Heat* §54 The areometric method, or that of weighing a solid in the liquid. **1847** CRAIG, *Areometrical.* **1778** *Phil. Trans.* LXVIII. 419 An Essay on Pyrometry and Areometry. **1819** *Rees' Cycl.* II. s.v. *Aremometer*, Invented by Wolfius in 1708, and first published in his 'Areometry.'

aræostyle (ə'ri:əʊstaɪl), *a.* and *sb. Arch.* Also 6–9 areo-. [ad. L. *aræostylos*, a. Gr. ἀραιόστυλος, f. ἀραιός rare, few + στῦλος pillar; cf. F. *aréostyle*.]

A. *adj.* Of columned buildings: Having the distance between the columns equal to four or more diameters of the column. **B.** *sb.* A building, or style of building, in which the columns are so arranged.

[**1563** SHUTE *Archit.* E iiij b, This first being Areostylos.. the distaunce betwene the 2 pillors to be 4, 5, or 6 Diameters.] **1706** PHILLIPS, *Areostyle.* **1876** GWILT *Archit.*, *Aræostyle*, one of the five proportions used by the ancients for regulating the intercolumniation..in porticoes and colonnades.

aræosystyle (əˌri:əʊ'sɪstaɪl), *a.* and *sb. Arch.* [a. F. *aréosystyle* (Perrault 1673), f. Gr. ἀραιός rare, few + σύστυλος (Vitruvius) with columns close together: see SYSTYLE.] (See quot. and cf. prec.)

1834 *Penny Cycl.* II. 233 *Aræosystyle*..an alternately very wide and very narrow intercolumniation, or, what is familiarly called coupled columns. **1876** GWILT *Archit.* Gloss., *Aræosystyle*..in the principal façade of the Louvre ..in the west front of St. Paul's.

†**aræ'otic,** *a.* and *sb. Med. Obs.* [ad. late L. *aræōticus*, a. Gr. ἀραιωτικός, f. ἀραιό-ειν to make thin: see -IC.] **A.** *adj.* Tending to make thin or reduce the fluids or humours of the body. **B.** *sb.* [sc. medicine.]

1634 T. JOHNSON *Parey's Chirurg.* XXVI. xi. (1678) 636 The Aræotick [Medicins], which we may call weak Resolvers. **1815** *Encycl. Brit.* (ed. 5) II. 531 Aræotics.. rarefy the humours, and render them easy to be carried off by the pores.

araft, araȝt, araht, pa. t. of AREACH *v. Obs.*

arage, obs. f. ORACH: see also AVERAGE *sb.*

†**a'rage,** *v. Obs.* [a. OF. *arage-r, aragier*, f. *à* to + *rage*.] To enrage. Hence **araged** *pa. pple.* enraged, furious, mad.

1470–85 MALORY *Arthur* (1816) I. 367 He was nyghe hand araged oute of his wyt. **1480** CAXTON *Ovid's Met.* x. vii, Am I araged and mad? ? **1568** G. FERRERS *Winn. Calais* in Arb. *Garner* IV. 180 Not induring this sight any longer, as a man araged, he ran among his men.

Aragonese (ærəgə'ni:z), *a.* and *sb.* Also 9 Arragonese. [ad. Sp. *aragonés*, f. *Aragón* name of a region and former kingdom of north-eastern Spain; see -ESE.] **A.** *adj.* Of or pertaining to Aragon, or its inhabitants, or their speech. **B.** *sb.* An inhabitant of Aragon; the dialect of Spanish spoken in Aragon.

1513 R. FOX *Let.* 16 May (1929) 63 The treuxe..is.. proclamed bothe in Spaigne and France bytwyxt the Frenche and Aragonesse Kyngis. **1823** C. BUTLER *Contin. Lives Saints* App. p. xvi, Charles was acknowledged by his Arragonese subjects. **1823** T. ROSS tr. *Bouterwek's Hist. Span. Lit.* I. 7 The geographical boundaries, which.. separated the Portuguese from the Castilians, and the latter from the Arragonese. **1843** BORROW *Bible in Spain* I. xiii. 266, I went to the secretary, whose name was Oliban, an Aragonese... 'Then His Excellency cannot give you permission,' said the Aragonese secretary. **1932** W. L. GRAFF *Lang. & Langs.* x. 377 Spanish group, with the Castilian, Andalusian, Aragonese..dialects. **1939** S. DE MADARIAGA *Columbus* xxv. 309 The future Catalina..let her Aragonese lover know of the mines.

aragonite, arr- ('ærəgənaɪt). *Min.* [named by Haüy, 1800, from *Aragon* or *Arragon*, a province of Spain, where first found + -ITE.] A carbonate of lime, crystallizing in orthorhombic prisms and many derived forms, whence several varieties are distinguished.

1803 BOURNON *Carbonate of Lime* in *Phil. Trans.* XCIII. 332 Their specific gravity is nearly the same. The Abbé Haüy states that of the Arragonite at 2946. **1837** DANA *Min.*, Aragonite. **1863** WATTS *Dict. Chem.* I. 358 Carbonate of calcium, in its two forms of calc spar (rhombohedral) and arragonite (rhombic or right prismatic) exhibits one of the most striking examples of dimorphism.

aragonspath, aragon spar, = prec.

‖**araguato.** [see ALOUATTE.] The 'howling monkey.'

1852 T. ROSS *Humboldt's Trav.* I. viii. 278 The plaintive howling of araguatoes.

Arahat: see ARHAT.

arai(e, araign(e, obs. ff. ARRAY, ARRAIGN.

‖**araignée** (areɲe). *Mil.* [Fr.; = spider's web.] The arrangement of a military mine, when some obstacle necessitates the construction of branching galleries.

1706 in PHILLIPS.

†**a'rail,** *v. Obs. rare*[−1]. [f. A- *pref.* 1 (or 2) + RAIL *v.*] To fasten to rails, tie up.

c **1380** WYCLIF *Wks.* (1869) I. 100 þe þridde traveile herof [in þis vyneȝerde] were to araile þes growynge vynes.

†**arain.** *Obs.* exc. *dial.* Forms: 4 arayne, iran, -ain, -eyn(e, irany, yreyn(e, 5 aranye, aranee, arein, erayne, -ane, -eyne, erany(e; *dial.* 7 arain, 9 arran, arrand. [a. OF. *araigne* (*aragne, iragne, iraigne*), cogn. w. Pr. *aranha, eranha*:—L. *arānea*.] A spider.

a **1300** *E.E. Psalter* xxxviii. 12 And to skulke als irain þou made saule his. **1388** WYCLIF *Isa.* lix. 5 Thei han..maden webbis of an yreyn. **1398** TREVISA *Barth. De P.R.* XIX. lv. (1495) 896 The hony sholde be corrupte that is in the combes and Araynes sholde be gendrid. **1440** *Promp. Parv.* 14 Aranye or erayne, *Aranea. Ibid.* 140 Eranye or spider. **1460** CAPGRAVE *Chron.* 297 A thing withoute soule wers than a tode or a ereyne. *c* **1460** *Bk. Quintess.* I. 2 By generacioun of flies, and areins. **1674** RAY *N. Countr. Words* 2 An *Arain*: a Spider..used only for the larger kind of Spiders. *Nottinghamshire.* **1849** C. BRONTË *Shirley* v. 45 'You never heard of Bruce, perhaps?' 'And th' arrand?'

araine, obs. form of ARRAIGN *v.*[2]

†**a'raise,** *v. Obs.* Forms: 4–5 arayse, areise, 4–6 areyse, 5 arrays, -reise, -reyse, 6 -raise, arais, 5–8 araise. [f. A- *pref.* 1 + RAISE *v.*; cf. the pair *rise, arise*. Cf. also AREAR: *rear* and *raise* being the cogn. forms from OE. and ON.]

1. To raise, lift up, elevate. *lit.* and *fig.*

1303 R. BRUNNE *Handl. Synne* 7650 Swych men areysen baner Aȝens holy chirches power. *c* **1450** *Merlin* 57 [He] areised his brother's tombe moche hier than eny of the tother. **1489** CAXTON *Faytes of Armes* I. xxvii. 85 They that.. arreyse hem self in to arrogaunce. **1557** *Prayer after Sacr.* in *Primer*, Continual remembraunce of thy blessed passion, so that..when I am falling it may araise me.

2. To raise from the dead. (Cf. *arise*.)

a **1300** *Cursor M.* (Trin. MS.) 14363 þis tiþing ras þat laȝar þus areysed [*v.r.* vpraised, resusced] was. *c* **1500** *Wyse Chylde & Adrian* (W. de W.) (1860) 25 Laȝar the broder of marye magdaleyne..the which god areysed. **1601** SHAKS. *All's Well* II. i. 79 A medicine..whose simple touch Is powerfull to arayse King Peppin.

3. To bring into activity, to excite, arouse.

c **1374** CHAUCER *Boeth.* IV. ii. 118 Ire þat araiseþ in hem þe floodes of troublynges. *Ibid.* V. vi. 178 Areise þi corage to ryȝtful hoopes. **1494** FABYAN V. cxiv. 88 To appease certeygne rebellions there arreysyd.

4. To raise or levy (money, troops, etc.).

c **1386** CHAUCER *Pers. T.* ¶493 To areysen wrongful custumes and taillages. **1471** *Arrivall Edw. IV* (1838) 23 They would gather and arrays up the powere of Devonshire and Cornewaile. **1548** HALL *Chron.* 112 (Halliw.) They.. arreised a greate power of xiii. m. and came to the passage.

5. To raise (a siege, or the besiegers).

c **1450** *Merlin* xiv. 202 He hadde not peple in his reame sufficient to a-reyse hem fro the sege, ne to chase hem oute of his reame. *c* **1530** LD. BERNERS *Arth. Lyt. Bryt.* (1814) 498 We are riding in purpose to areyse youre syege.

6. To take off (cf. Fr. *enlever*).

c **1460** RUSSELL *Bk. Nurture* 418 in *Babees Bk.* 129 Areyse þe whynges furst.

7. ? To make up. *rare.*

a **1440** *Morte Arth.* 1677 He has araysede his accownte, and redde alle his rolleȝ, ffor he wylle gyfe a rekenyng.

†**a'raised,** *ppl. a. Obs.* [f. prec. + -ED.] Raised, exalted, elevated.

c **1340** HAMPOLE *Pr. Treat.* 12 Thurghe þe joye of araysede thoghte.

araison, obs. form of AREASON.

arak, var. ARECA, and obs. f. ARRACK.

Arakanese (ærəkə'ni:z), *a.* and *sb.* Also 9 Ar(r)acanese. [f. *Arakan* (see def.) + -ESE.] **A.** *adj.* Of or pertaining to Arakan, a district on the west coast of Burma, or its inhabitants. **B.** *sb.* **1.** An inhabitant of Arakan. **2.** The Burmese dialect spoken by the people of Arakan.

1820 A. JUDSON *Diary* 20 Feb. in F. Wayland *Mem. A. Judson* (1853) I. 211 Arracanese, who speak a language similar to the Burman. *Ibid.* 26 Feb. 213 Collect the Arracanese converts. **1882** in E. FORCHHAMMER *Notes Lang. & Dial. Burma* (1884) 6 The Burmese-Chin language-family comprises the Arakanese, Tavoy (?), Burmese, Chin. **1910** *Encycl. Brit.* II. 315/2 The Arakanese are of Burmese origin..and they have a dialect and customs of their own. **1934** 'G. ORWELL' *Burmese Days* i. 2 One of those vivid Arakanese longyis..which the Burmese wear on informal occasions.

a-rake (ə'reɪk), *advb. phr.* [A *prep.*[1] + RAKE.] On the rake; inclined from the perpendicular.

1883 *Pall Mall G.* 5 Nov. 2/1 These crossing masts a-rake.

aralia (əˈreɪlɪə). [mod.L., of uncertain origin.] A genus of trees, shrubs, and herbs, the type of the family *Araliaceæ*; also, a plant of this genus.
1756 P. BROWNE *Civ. & Nat. Hist. Jamaica* II. II. 189 Aralia.. The *Galapee*, or Angelica Tree. **1829** J. C. LOUDON *Encycl. Plants* 230 *Aralia*. Aralia. *Araliaceæ* . **1897** [see GINSENG 2]. **1908** *Westm. Gaz.* 25 Nov. 5/1 A tall aralia growing in a corner of the well-lighted entrance-hall of the hotel. **1914** *Chambers's Jrnl.* Mar. 154/1 The fertilisers may be given in weak doses to foliage plants such as aralias. **1942** L. BENNETT (*Jamaica*) *Dial. Verses* 25, I was gwine to sen' pure orellia bush, As yuh wanted so-soh greens. **1953** *West Indian Med. Jrnl.* II. 237 Aralia guilfoylei.. Aralia. The leaves are used in Jamaica to prepare tea for colds. It is common in gardens as a hedge plant and is not indigenous.

araliaceous (əreɪlɪˈeɪʃəs), *a. Bot.* [f. mod.L. *Araliaceæ*, f. *Aralia*, the typical genus: see -ACEOUS.] Belonging to the family *Araliaceæ*, comprising various herbs, shrubs, and trees, including the ivy.
1866 BRANDE & COX *Dict. Sci. & Art* II. 780/1 *Panax*, a name applied to some plants of the Araliaceous order. **1884** *Spectator* 24 May 685 Virtues.. attributed to the araliaceous plant Jinseng.

Aramæan (ærəˈmiːən), *a.* and *sb.* [f. L. *Aramæ-us*, Gr. Ἀραμ αἶ-ος, pertaining to Aram or Syria.] **A.** *adj.* Belonging to the country or language of Aram; Syrian, Syriac. **B.** *sb.* A native of Aram.
1834 *Penny Cycl.* II. 239/2 The numerous Aramæan colonies. **1864** *Nat. Rev.* No. 36. 336 How could he [the Apostle John in writing the Apocalypse] fall back into the Aramæan colouring? **1878** *N. Amer. Rev.* CXXVII. 523 The Aramæans also.. have the form *mata*.

Aramaic (ærəˈmeɪɪk), *a.* [f. as prec.: see -IC.] Of Aram; *spec.* applied to the northern branch of the Semitic family of languages, including Syriac and Chaldee. Often used *absol.* sc. language.
1834 *Penny Cycl.* II. 239/2 Translations of the Old Testament into the East-Aramaic language. **1882** FARRAR *Early Chr.* I. 207 Even if the Jews of the Dispersion understood Aramaic, the Gentiles did not.

Aramaicism (ærəˈmeɪɪsɪz(ə)m). [f. ARAMAIC + -ISM.] An Aramaic idiom; = ARAMAISM.
1898 BLASS *Philology of the Gospels* xi. 194 In the [first twelve chapters of the Acts] Aramaicisms abound.

Aramaism (ærəˈmeɪɪz(ə)m). [f. ARAMAIC *a.* + -ISM.] An Aramaic idiom or peculiarity of language.
1849 CURETON *Corpus Ignat.* 288 The Aramaisms in which these Epistles abound.

Aramaize (ærəˈmeɪaɪz), *v.* [f. as ARAMAICISM + -IZE.] *trans.* To render Aramaic, imbue with Aramaisms.
1868 LIGHTFOOT *Ep. to Philippians* 147/2 In Aramaised Greek.

† **ˈAramite, Araˈmitic,** obsolete equivalents of ARAMÆAN, ARAMAIC.
1642 ROGERS *Naaman* 7 Naaman a stranger and Heathen Aramite. **1678** CUDWORTH *Intell. Syst.* 283 Balaam the Aramitick Sorcerer.

Aran (ˈærən), *a.* Of, pertaining to, or characteristic of the Aran Islands, off the west coast of Ireland; *spec.* designating a type of patterned knitwear. So **ˈAraner**, a native or inhabitant of the Aran Islands.
1902 *Irish Rosary* Jan. 21/2 The Araners of to-day.. are deeply religious. **1919** W. B. YEATS *Two Plays for Dancers* 2 He seems an Aran fisher. *Ibid.* 3 Until an Aran coracle puts in at Muckanish. **1962** *Times* 1 Jan. 13/1 A great deal of 'Aran knitwear' is now sold that never saw the three limestone islands. **1963** *Guardian* 30 Oct. 6/5 Aran patterns, fisherman's ribs, cables, and lace stitches.

aran, pa. t. of ARINE *v. Obs.*, to touch.

Aranda (əˈrændə), *sb.* and *a.* Also **Aranta, Arunta,** † **Aralta.** [Native name.] **A.** *sb.* **1.** An aboriginal people of central Australia; a member of this people. **2.** The language of this people. **B.** *adj.* Pertaining to this people or their language.
1891 W. H. WILLSHIRE *Aborigines of Central Australia* iv. 16 The 'Aralta' draw peculiar designs on flat upright rocks. **1896** W. B. SPENCER *Horn Sci. Exped. Central Australia* I. I. 39 These natives belong to the Arunta tribe, which occupies a large tract of land stretching from the Macumba Creek in the south to about seventy miles north of Alice Springs. **1910** *Encycl. Brit.* I. 947/1 The Aruntas.. believe that local spirits of trees.. enter women as they pass by their haunts. **1927** SPENCER & GILLEN (*title*) The Arunta: a study of a Stone Age people. **1951** R. FIRTH *Elem. Soc. Organiz.* i. 3 The Aranda of Central Australia practise sub-incision. **1956** J. WHATMOUGH *Lang.* ii. 33 Aranda in Australia, which has practically no formally distinctive 'parts of speech'. **1959** S. H. COURTIER *Death in Dream Time* iii. 29 The Aranda tribes and.. their language, ways, customs, ceremonies and myths.

† **a-ranˈdoun,** *advb. phr. Obs.* [a. F. *à randon*: see RANDOM.] Violently, headlong, at full speed.
c **1380** *Sir Ferumb.* 824 Þe Sarsynȝ gun prykie a-raundoun.

araneidal (ærəˈniːɪdəl), *a. Zool.* = ARANEIDAN *a.* So **araˈneidiform** *a.* = ARANEIFORM *a.*
1826 KIRBY & SPENCE *Entomol.* III. xxx. 171 The *Corydalina*.. is Chilopodiform, but with a tendency to the Araneidiform Type. **1895** *Naturalist* Jan. 29 The Araneidal Fauna of the northern counties of England.

araneidan (ærəˈniːɪdən), *a.* and *sb. Zool.* [f. mod.L. *Arāneida* the typical family of ARACHNIDA, f. L. *arānea* spider: see -ID, -AN.] **A.** *adj.* Of or belonging to the *Araneida* or spiders. **B.** *sb.* A spider. Also **araneiform** (ærəˈniːɪfɔːrm), *a.* (cf. F. *aranéiforme*), having the shape of a spider.
1835 KIRBY *Hab. & Inst. Anim.* II. xix. 283 No animals fall more universally under observation than the Araneidans or spiders. **1847** *Araneiform*: CRAIG cites KIRBY.

araneology (əreɪnɪˈɒlədʒɪ). [f. L. *arānea* spider + -(O)LOGY.] The department of zoology relating to spiders. Hence **aˌraneoˈlogical** *a.*, belonging to araneology; **araneˈologist**, one versed in araneology.
1798 *Monthly Mag.* Jan. 53/2 Araneology... The Araneological Calendar. **1875** *Encycl. Brit.* II. 296/1 An eminent araneologist. **1880** *Jrnl. Linn. Soc.* XV. 152 Indebted to the last-named araneologist. **1884** *Science* 4 July 24/1 Facts.. new to the field of American araneology.

araneose (əˌreɪnɪˈəʊs), *a.* [ad. L. *arāneōs-us* full of, or like, cobwebs, f. *arānea* spider: see -OSE.] 'Like spider-web; same as *Arachnoid*.' Gray *Bot. Text-bk.* 1880.

aˈraneous, *a.* [same deriv.] = ARACHNOID.
1656 BLOUNT *Glossogr.*, *Araneous* (*araneosus*), ful of spiders webs. **1693** *Phil. Trans.* XVII. 621 Its leaves break with araneous filaments. **1696** PHILIPS, Araneous Tunicle, the Tunicle that surrounds the Crystalline Humor. **1713** DERHAM *Phys.-Theol.* IV. ii. 102 Its [the eye's] curious Araneous Membrane. **1880** in *Syd. Soc. Lex.*

† **aˈrang.** *Obs. rare*⁻¹. [a. OF. *arenge* (15th c. in Littré), cogn. w. Sp. *arenga*, It. *aringa*.] Early form of HARANGUE *sb.*
c **1475** *Ratis Raving* 243 To tell the al how mycht befall, To lang arang men wald it call.

‖ **arango** (əˈræŋgəʊ). Pl. **-oes.** 'A species of beads made of rough carnelian.. formerly imported from Bombay for re-exportation to Africa.' McCulloch *Dict. Comm.* 1844.
1715 *Lond. Gaz.* mmmmmcccxiv/3 Arangoas, Ostridge Feathers, Beads.

† **a-ˈrank,** *advb. phr. Obs.* [A *prep.*[1] + RANK.] In a rank or row.
c **1300** *St. Brand.* 273 Sette hem a-doun A-renk, and wosche here fet alle. *c* **1380** *Sir Ferumb.* 4588 Wyþ ys hol host al and some, þe brigge þay toke a-rank. **1570** *Galfrido & Bern.* i. (Halliw.) The pretty dames.. Do go so sagely on the way By two and two a-ranke.

aranye, variant of ARAIN, *Obs.*, spider.

Arapaima (ærəˈpaɪmə). [South American native name.] A genus of fishes of the family Osteoglossidæ, remarkable for their size; (with small initial) a fish of this genus.
1840 R. H. SCHOMBURGK *Brit. Guiana* 39 The Arapaima or Pirarucu (*Sudis Gigas*), and.. the Lau-lau, are from ten to twelve feet long. **1896** LYDEKKER *Roy. Nat. Hist.* V. 478 The true arapaima (*Arapaima gigas*) of the larger rivers of Brazil and the Guianas.. occupies the proud position of being the largest fresh-water bony fish. **1908** C. F. HOLDER *Big Game at Sea* xix. 288 The *arapaima*.. the game fish of South American waters—a monster that attained a length of twelve feet and a weight of twelve hundred pounds. **1955** *Times* 11 May 20/1 Capture of an arapaima fish at Karanamloo, Rupununi.

† **a-ˈrape,** *advb. phr. Obs.* [A *prep.*[1] + ME. *rape* haste.] In haste, hastily.
c **1300** *K. Alis.* 4239 Over theo table he leop arape.

araphoˈrostic, araˈphostic, *a.* [Apparently bad formations on Gr. ἄρραφος unsewed, f. ἀ priv. + ῥάπτ-ειν to sew.] Unsewed, seamless.
1828 LYTTON *Pelham* xxxiii. 85 You are as impervious as an araphorostic shoe. **1833** *Blackw. Mag.* XXXIV. 674 A few years ago.. araphostic sandals were worn by every body.

araponga (ærəˈpɒŋgə). Also **arapunga.** [F., f. Pg.] The campanero or bell-bird of South America.
The name *arapunga*/*araponga* was established in R. P. Lesson's *Traité d'Ornithologie* (1831).
1824 H. E. LLOYD tr. *Spix & Martius' Trav. in Brazil* I. II. ii. 247 Above all these strange voices, the metallic tones of the uraponga sound from the tops of the highest trees, resembling the strokes of the hammer on the anvil, which.. according to the position of the songster, fill the wanderer with astonishment. **1881** *Imp. Dict.*, Arapunga. **1910** *Encycl. Brit.* IV. 443/2 Species having strident voices and peculiar unmusical calls, like.. the *araponga* (*Chasmorhynchus nudicollis*). **1951** J. C. FENNESSY *Sonnet in Bottle* III. ii. 62 An araponga, a tall bird with a screeching note.

aras, obs. north. form of AROSE: see ARISE.

aras(e, obs. form of ARRAS, ARACE.

† **aˈrase,** *v. Obs.* Forms: 6 **arace, arrace, arrase.** [a. OF. *arase-r* to raze, level with the ground, demolish, f. phr. *à ras*, as if 'mettre *à ras* de terre,' f. *ras* level:—L. *rās-us*, f. *rād-ĕre* to shave, scrape smooth. Cf. ERASE. In form confused with ARACE.] To raze, level with the ground, lay low. Also (? erroneously) To erase, obliterate. Hence **arasing, arracyng,** *vbl. sb.*, levelling with the ground, demolition.
1523 *State Papers Hen. VIII*, IV. 46 The goodly valiaunt exployt.. at Gedworth, with the arracyng and destruccion of the same. **1530** PALSGR. 435/2, I arace, I scrape out a worde or a blotte.. *Je efface.* **1532** MORE *Confut. Tindale* Wks. 355/2 So that the remembraunce of theire pestylent errours were araced out of englishe mennes heartes. **1553** *Let.* in *Harrington's Nugæ Ant.* 175 Sickness whearewith your Lordshipp hath oftentimes bene arrased. [**1721** BAILEY, *Arace*, to deface.]

† **aˈrate,** *v. Obs. rare.* [Etymol. uncertain: see RATE *v.*] To rate, rebuke, reprove.
1377 LANGL. *P. Pl.* B. XI. 98 To arate dedly synne. **1393** —— C. VI. 11 Thus reson me aratede.

aration (əˈreɪʃən). *arch. rare.* [ad. L. *arātiōn-em*, n. of action f. *arāt-* ppl. stem of *arāre* to plough: see -TION.] Ploughing; tillage.
1663 COWLEY *Agric.* Wks. 1710 II. 710 First, Aration.. Secondly, Pasturage. **1813** VANCOUVER *Agric. Devon* 13 Of sufficient depth for the purposes of aration.

arational (ˈeɪræʃənəl), *a.* (and *sb.*) [f. A- 14 + RATIONAL *a.*] That does not purport to be rational; not governed by the laws of reason, non-rational. Also *ellipt.* as *sb.*
1935 *Mind* XLIV. 265 Absolute justice though a necessary concept, is indefinable: it is an 'a-rational ideal', and thus beyond the scope of science which is reason applied to facts of experience. **1955** *Bull. Atomic Sci.* May 193/2 The gradual transition of humanity from this 'arational' behavior to the more 'rational' of our times. **1970** E. DE BONO *Lateral Thinking* xx. 226 PO may be used to produce arrangements of information that are unreasonable but they are not really unreasonable because lateral thinking functions in a different way from vertical thinking. Lateral thinking is not irrational but arational. **1972** *Science* 16 June 1209/3 The irrational, or, better yet, the arational, will not disappear from the human situation. **1982** *Times Lit. Suppl.* 23 Apr. 465/5 There is an equally obvious mystique: a set of arational (but not necessarily irrational) attitudes that are inculcated by gossip and habit and movies.

† **ˈaratory,** *a. Obs.*⁻⁰ [ad. L. *arātōri-us*, f. *arāt-* (see ARATION): cf. F. *aratoire*.] 'Belonging to tillage.' Bailey 1731; 'contributing to tillage.' Johnson; and in mod. Dicts.

† **ˈaratrate,** *v. Obs.*⁻⁰ [f. L. *arātrāt-* ppl. stem of *arātrā-re* to plough over again.] 'To til or plough, to stir or ear ground.' Blount *Gl.* 1656.

† **ˈarature.** *Obs.*⁻⁰ [ad. med.L. *arātūra*.] 'Ploughing, tillage.' Bailey 1731.

Araucanian (ærɔːˈkeɪnɪən), *sb.* and *a.* [f. Sp. *Araucanía*, the name of a region of southern Chile + -AN: cf. Sp. *araucano*.] **A.** *sb.* **1.** A member of the Mapuche Indian people of central Chile and Argentina.
[**1703** A. & J. Churchill in *Coll. Voy.* (1704) III. v. xxii. 150/2 This Declaration reach'd the Ears of the *Araucanos*, and there assembled at *Arauco* Sixteen Caciques, and many other Captains, to Treat about what was best for them to do.] **1809** R. ALSOP tr. *J. I. Molina's Geogr., Nat. & Civil Hist. Chili* II. II. i. 53 The Araucanians.. derive their appellation.. from the province of Arauco. **1828** *Kaleidoscope* 8 July 2/1 The interpreter.. an Araucanian by birth. **1875** *Encycl. Brit.* I. 701/1 The Araucanians.. occupy about 200 miles of the sea-coast, between the 37th and 39th parallels. **1959** *Chambers's Encycl.* XIV. 223/1 The native Araucanians.. defeated and killed him [*sc.* Pedro de Valdivia] at Tucapel on 1 Jan. 1554. **1977** *Word* 1972 XXVIII. 245 Lenz observed that in the seventeenth century Araucanians had difficulty pronouncing the /dr/ group of Chilean Spanish.
2. (Any of) a group of languages spoken by the Araucanian Indians (see quot. 1977).
1809 R. ALSOP tr. *J. I. Molina's Geogr., Nat. & Civil Hist. Chili* II. 331 The original language of Chili, generally called the Araucanian, is denominated by the natives *Chili dugu*, the Chilian tongue. **1911** *Encycl. Brit.* I. 811/2 Araucanian, Pampas. **1970** *Chicago Linguistics Soc.* VI. 57 (*heading*) Mayan affinities with Araucanian. **1977** C. F. & F. M. VOEGELIN *Classification & Index World's Lang.* 287 According to the *Penutian* hypothesis, Araucanian and the *Chipayan* family of languages are members of the [Penutian] phylum... In the classification by Greenberg.. Araucanian and *Chipayan* are placed in the *Andean Equatorial* phylum.
B. *adj.* Of or pertaining to the Araucanians or their language.
1809 R. ALSOP tr. *J. I. Molina's Geogr., Nat. & Civil Hist. Chili* II. II. i. 54 Those Spaniards, who had left the army in the Netherlands to serve in Chili, gave to this country the name of Araucanian Flanders, or the Invincible State. **1828** *Kaleidoscope* 22 July 23/3 The Adjutant, Talmayancu, was an Araucanian Indian. **1902** *Encycl. Brit.* XXXI. 675/1 The language of Chile is Spanish, pronounced.. with the sounds of the Araucanian language substituted. **1921** *Chambers's Jrnl.* June 382/1 Their having learned a thing or two from the Araucanian medicine-women. **1933** L. BLOOMFIELD *Language* iv. 73 In South America, we note.. the *Araucanian* [family] in Chile, and *Kechuan*, the language of the Inca civilization. **1957** *Publ. Amer. Dial. Soc.* 1956 XXVI. 24 Those influences which were really Araucanian were

limited to the lowest classes or to Indian bilinguals. **1985** MANELIS KLEIN & STARK *S. Amer. Indian Lang.* xviii. 713 An analysis of a traditional Araucanian tale.

araucaria (ærɔːˈkɛərɪə). [f. *Arauco* name of a province, whence the *Araucanos* Indians, and the territory of *Araucania*, south of Chili.] A genus of lofty coniferous trees, native to the southern hemisphere, one species of which (*A. imbricata*, familiarly termed 'puzzle-monkey' or 'monkey-puzzler'), with the branches in regular whorls, and closely-imbricated stiff sharp-pointed leaves, has been, since about 1830, cultivated as an ornamental tree in Britain.

1833 *Penny Cycl.* II. 249 Araucaria, in Botany, is the name of a singular genus of gigantic firs. *A. imbricata*.. is expected to be naturalised in this country, as some individuals now exist as far north as London. **1870** H. MACMILLAN *Bible Teach.* iv. 73 The formal educated look of the tree in the Araucarias that cover the wild slopes of the Chilian Andes.

arauˈcarian, *a.* and *sb.* [f. prec. + -AN.] **A.** *adj.* Of or belonging to the genus Araucaria. **B.** *sb.* A species of this or some closely allied genus.

1854 H. MILLER *Test. Rocks* iii. (1857) 135 The youth of the earth.. was a youth of dusk and tangled forests, of huge pines and stately Araucarians. **1862** DANA *Man. Geol.* 334 The Araucarian pines.

araught, pa. pple. of AREACH and ARECCHE *v.* *Obs.*

araw(e, obs. form of AROW *adv.*

Arawak (ˈærəwæk, -ɑːk), *sb.* and *a.* Also †**Arrowauk**, †**Arowack** and variants. **A.** *sb.* **1.** A group of Indian peoples in South America; a member of one of these peoples. **2.** The language of these peoples. **B.** *adj.* Of or pertaining to the Arawaks or their language. Hence **Araˈwakan** *a.* and *sb.*

1769 E. BANCROFT *Nat. Hist. Guiana* iii. 253 The Arrowauks.. are a friendly, hospitable people. *Ibid.* 304 An Indian.. of the Arrowauk tribe. **1851** R. G. LATHAM *Ethnol. Brit. Colonies* vi. 259 The Arawaks are our nearest neighbours, and, consequently, the most Europeanized. **1868** W. H. BRETT *Indian Tribes of Guiana* vi. 117 These names respectively signify in Arawâk, 'the resorts of the Ituri', [etc.]. **1910** *Encycl. Brit.* II. 322/2 The Arawaks have given their name to a linguistic stock of South America, the Arawakan, which includes many once powerful tribes. The Arawakans were once numerous. **1932** W. L. GRAFF *Lang. & Langs.* xi. 431 Arawakan continued to be used only by the females and Carib by the males. **1937** R. H. LOWIE *Hist. Ethnol. Theory* viii. 89 The discovery of unsuspected Arawak and Carib tribes in the interior of Brazil. **1965** *Canad. Jrnl. Linguistics* Spring 101 Arawakan and other Caribbean area groups.

†**a-ˈray,** *advb. phr. Obs.* [A *prep.*[1] + RAY (= rank, order).] In row, in rank, in order.

c **1450** HENRYSON *Mor. Fables* 11 In stubble array throw gerse and corne.. priuily could they creepe. **1583** T. WATSON *Poems* (Arb.) 119 In chaines of roases linked all araye.

aray(e, arayn, obs. forms of ARRAY, ARRAIGN.

†**aˈrayne,** *v. Obs. rare.* [a. OF. *aresner*, *areiner*, *arainer*, f. *à* to + *resne*, mod. *rêne*; see REIN.] To draw by the bridle, to rein, stop.

a **1400** *MS.* in *Chester Plays* II. 215 Thou arte risen us to wayle, And arayne us from woo. **1470–85** MALORY *Arthur* I. 156 (Halliw.) Thenne he alyghte doune, and arayned his hors on the brydel.

arays, obs. form of ARRAS.

arb (ɑːb). Colloq. abbrev. of ARBITRAGEUR.

1983 *Securities Week* 28 Feb. 2 As with most tender offers, large amounts of the target stock accumulated in the hands of arbitrageurs. Paine Webber only solicited stock from arbs. **1984** *Sunday Tel.* 25 Mar. 19/3 For a start you often have to make use of the 'arbs', very useful gentlemen indeed in a bid battle. **1985** *Observer* 23 June 29/1 'Arbs' are professional dealers who take principal positions in the shares of companies which are the subject of a takeover bid and gamble on the terms being increased. **1986** *Daily Tel.* 19 Nov. 16/4 He has intervened in several British bid battles.., but only as a genuine 'arb'; taking a position after the bid, and betting on being able to sell out higher up.

arbage, obs. form of HERBAGE.

ˈarbalest, -balist, -blast. *Obs.* exc. *Hist.* Forms: *α.* 2–3 arblast(e, 4 arblest(e, 4, 9 arbelast(e, 5, 8 arbalust(e, (7–8 arbalet), 7–9 arbalist, 9 -est. *β.* 4–5 alblast, 5 alablast(e, awblast, ablast(e. *γ.* 4 are-, arwe-, 5 arowblast, (7 arobalist). [a. AFr. *_arb(e)leste_, *_arb(e)laste_, OF. *arbaleste* (also *arbeleste*, *arbaste*, *arblatt*, mod. *arbalète*), cogn. w. Pr. *arbalesta*, *albaresta*:—L. *arcuballista*, f. *arcus* bow + *ballista* military engine for throwing missiles, q.v. The forms in *γ* are due to pop. assoc. with *arrow*; *arbalet* in 17–18th c. is after mod.F. As the word survives only in military antiquities, it has no standard modern spelling. See also ARCUBALIST.]

1. A cross-bow, consisting of a steel bow fitted to a wooden shaft, furnished with special mechanism for drawing and letting slip the bowstring, and used for the discharge of arrows, bolts, stones, etc.

a **1100** *O.E. Chron.* (MS. D) an. 1079 Mid anan arblaste of scoten. **1297** R. GLOUC. 377 Myd bowe & arblaste. *c* **1300** *Alisaunder* 268 With atling of areblast. *c* **1325** *Cœur de L.* 2524 Wente alsoo faste As quarrel dos off the arweblast. *c* **1330** *Arth. & Merl.* 313 With arwe and bowe and alblast. *c* **1380** *Sir Ferumb.* 3312 Arbelastes y-mad of tre. *c* **1400** *Le Bone Florence* 861 They sende.. quarels wyth alablaste. **1440** *Promp. Parv.*, Ablaste (**1499** Alblast), *Balista*. *c* **1450** in Wright *Voc.* 196, *Hec balista*, ane awblast. *c* **1475** *Ibid.* 264 *Balista*, a arowblaste. **1480** CAXTON *Chron. Eng.* xxviii. 23 He bent an arblast. **1483** —— *Gold. Leg.* 314/4 A quarel.. shotte out of Arbalaste. **1622** HEYLYN *Cosmogr.* I. (1682) 178 Richard the First was slain by a shot from an Arbalist. **1672** MARVELL *Reh. Transp.* I. 60 One might shoot with the Arbalet. **1693** W. ROBERTSON *Phraseol. Gen.* 120 An Arbalist, or rather Arobalist. **1795** SOUTHEY *Joan of Arc* VIII, From the arbalast the fire-tipt dart Shot lightning through the sky. **1825** SCOTT *Talism.* xii, Unbend thy arblast, and come into the moonlight. **1840** BROWNING *Sordello* IV. 362 Arbalist, manganel, and catapult. **1879** GREEN *Read. Eng. Hist.* xiii. 60 Six newly-headed shafts for the deadly arbalest.

2. = ARBALESTER. (Cf. med.L. *arbalista* = *ballistarius*, Du Cange; the ending *-ista* commonly indicating a personal agent.)

c **1450** *Merlin* vii. 113 Viij *ml.* knyghtes, with-outen seriantz and arblastis. **1844** LINGARD *Anglo-Sax. Ch.* (1858) I. App. 365 Odo, the arbalist.

3. A mathematical instrument, called also a *Jacob's staff*, formerly used to take the altitude of stars. (So in Fr.)

1816 in C. JAMES *Mil. Dict.* s.v. *Arbalet.*

ˈarbalester, -balister, -blaster. *Obs.* exc. *Hist.* Forms: 4–5 alblaster(e, 4–7 arblaster(e, 5 awblaster, allblawster, 5–7 arbalaster, 5–9 arbalester, 9 arbalister, -estier. Also 5 arowblaster. [a. AFr. *alblaster*, *arblaster*, OF. *arbalestier*, *arbelestier*:—L. *arcuballistāri-us* one who used an *arcuballista*; mixed with other OF. synonyms, as *arbalestre*:—L. *_arcuballistor_, and *arbalestre*, accus. *arbalesteor*:— L. *arcuballistātor*, *-ōrem* (med.L. *arbalistātor*); and phonetically or etymologically corrupted as in ARBALEST.] A soldier armed with an arbalest, a cross-bowman.

1330 R. BRUNNE *Chron.* 205 Þat sauh an alblastere, a quarelle lete he flie. **1388** WYCLIF *2 Sam.* viii. 18 Forsothe Bananye.. was ouer.. archeris and arblasteris [**1382** alblasters; *v.r.* arowblasters]. *c* **1425** WYNTOUN *Cron.* IX. vi. 20 Foure hundyre Awblasteris. **1430** LYDG. *Chron. Troy* II. xxi, Their Arbalasters.. and their best archers. *c* **1440** *Morte Arth.* 2426 All-blawsters at Arthure egerly schottes. **1480** CAXTON *Chron. Eng.* VII. (1520) 82/2 The arbalesters smote hym with a quarel. **1611** SPEED *Hist. Gt. Brit.* IX. vii. 67 An Arbalaster.. standing vpon the wall. **1643** PRYNNE *Doom Coward.* 4 Men of Armes and Arblasters. **1848** in *Chron. Crusaders* (Bohn) 322 An arbalester.. to stretch the arbalest. **1861** G. MUSGRAVE *By-roads* 288 The said arbalestier corps comprehending the greater part of the French nobility. **1866** KINGSLEY *Herew.* vii. 131 The archers and arbalisters amused themselves with shooting.

†**ˈarbalestre, -ter, -blaster.** *Obs.* Forms: 3–5 alblastre, 5 awblaster, ablauster, arbalestre, -ter, arbelater, 5–7 arblaster, 6 alablaster, aublestere, arblestre, arbalaster. [a. AFr. *alblastre*, *albrastre*, OF. *arbalestre* (also *arbelestre*, *arblastre*, *arbastre*):—L. *arcuballistra*, var. of *arcuballista*: see ARBALEST. In Fr. partly, in Eng. greatly, confused in form with prec.]

1. = ARBALEST.

1387 TREVISA *Higden* Rolls Ser. I. 297 Þe men.. vseþ balles and alblastres [L. *arcubalistis*]. *c* **1400** *Rom. Rose* 4196 Of arblasters grete plente were. *c* **1480** *Robt. Devyll* 42 With arbelaters they shot many a quarrell. **1485** CAXTON *Chas. Gt.* 104 A quarel out of an arbalestre. **1548** HALL *Chron.* 143 The shot of the Alablasters and Crosse-bowes.

2. The missile shot from the arbalest.

c **1300** *K. Alis.* 1211 With alblastres and with stones They slowe men. *c* **1400** *Destr. Troy* XIV. 5707 Of arowes & awblasters þe aire wex thicke. **1494** FABYAN VII. ccxxxv. 271 Many an arblaster & stone was shot & caste.

arbaˈlestrier, alblastrer. *Obs.* exc. *Hist.* [a. AFr. *_alblastrer_, *_arblastrer_, OF. *arbalestrier* (mod.F. *arbalêtrier*):—L. *arcuballistrāri-us*, f. *arcuballistra* var. of *arcuballista*: see ARBALEST. In Fr. this form outlived *arbalestier*, but was less common in Eng.] = ARBALESTER.

c **1300** *K. Alis.* 2613 Bowe-men, and alblastreris. **1483** *Cath. Angl*, An Alablasterer, *arblastator*. **1860** READE *Cloister & H.* xxiv. (D.) The arbalestrier's face.. was.. gay and quiet. **1874** AINSWORTH *Merry Eng.* II. II. x. 118 Lined with archers, arbalestriers, and piquiers.

arbalestry (ˈɑːbəlɛstrɪ). Also 5 alblastrye. [f. ARBALESTER: see -RY. Cf. OF. *arbalesterie*, *-rerie*.] The art or practice of shooting with an arbalest.

a **1423** JAMES I *King's Q.* v. v, There sawe I.. the elk for alblastrye. **1860** *Sat. Rev.* 6 Oct. 431/1 [He] enjoined that his subjects should.. practise only archery and arbalest[r]y.

arbe, arbolist, obs. ff. HERB, HERBALIST.

arbeale, -bell, obs. spellings of ABELE.

arber, obs. form of ARBOUR.

†**ˈarber, ˈerber.** *Obs.* or *arch.* [a. F. *herbière* in Cotgr. 'the weason or wind-pipe of a bird; and the throat-boll, throat-pipe, or gullet of a beast'; cf. also *herberie* in Cotgr., and *herbier* in Littré.] The wind-pipe or weasand; sometimes extended to the whole 'pluck' of an animal. ***to make the erber*** (hunting phrase): to take out the 'pluck,' the first stage in disembowelling.

(Wrongly explained by Sir W. Scott in Notes to *Sir Tristram*, p. 268: cf. the whole context of the first three quotations, in which the operation is described.)

c **1320** *Sir Tristr.* I. xlv, The erber diȝt he ȝare. *c* **1340** *Gaw. & Gr. Knt.* 1330 Syþen þay slyt þe slot, sesed þe erber. **1486** *Bk. St. Albans, Hunting* F iij, Begynne fyrst to make the Erbere. *c* **1600** *Wyll Burke's Test.* in Halliw. *Lit. 16th C.* 54 Take the skine that is abought the herte, and that is called the erber. **1635** B. JONSON *Sad Sheph.* I. ii, When the arbor's made—Pull'd down, and paunch turn'd out. **1727** BRADLEY *Fam. Dict.* s.v. *Hart*, Cutting of the Throat downwards, making the Arber, that so the Ordure may break forth.

arbery(e, variant of ARBORY. *Obs.*

arbiter (ˈɑːbɪtə(r)). Also 6–7 -or, -our. [a. L. *arbiter* (? f. *ar-* = *ad-* to + *bētĕre*, *bītĕre*, to go, 'one who goes to see,' *hence*, who looks into or examines) a judge in equity, a supreme ruler. Cf. ARBITRATOR, ARBITRER. *Arbiter* was the orig. L. word, still extant in F. as *arbitre*; *arbitrātor* was a later L. n. of agent from *arbitrāri* to act as arbiter; of this the OF. descendant was *arbitreor*, *-our*, by the side of which *arbitrateur*, *-our*, was also adopted as a technical term by the jurists. In Eng., *arbitrour* seems to have been the earliest, then *arbitratour*, and in 16th c. *arbiter* from L., though *arbitre* may well have existed in ME. (The 16th c. spelling *arbitour*, *-or*, was, as in *ancestor*, merely imitative of words properly in *-our*.)]

1. *gen.* One whose opinion or decision is authoritative in a matter of debate; a judge.

1502 ARNOLD *Chron.* (1811) 160 Abdalazys.. most iust arbiter and juge of trouth. **1601** HOLLAND *Pliny* II. 151 As a deputed judge or arbiter delegat to determin of mans health, and the preseruation thereof. **1790** COWPER *Odyss.* VIII. 314 Nine arbiters appointed to intend The whole arrangement of the public games. **1824** DIBDIN *Libr. Comp.* 520 The late Mr. Fox (no mean arbiter in literary taste).

2. a. *spec.* One who is chosen by the two parties in a dispute to arrange or decide the difference between them; an arbitrator, an umpire. (See note to ARBITRATOR 1.)

1549 HOOPER *Ten Commandm.* x. Wks. 1843–52, 348 To solicitate the same by honest arbiters and godly friends. **1609** SKENE *Reg. Maj.* 20 Ane Judge haueand ane ordinar jurisdiction, may nocht be ane Arbitour. **1754** ERSKINE *Princ. Sc. Law* (1809) 492 The power of arbiters is wholly derived from the consent of parties. **1852** GLADSTONE *Gleanings* IV. xiv. 150 Beyond the Atlantic.. things civil and things spiritual move in their separate spheres, without any need for an arbiter between them. **1873** DIXON *Two Queens* I. IV. i. 179 Appointed arbiter of the dispute.

b. *transf.* or *fig.*

a **1568** COVERDALE *Hope of Faithf.* xii. (1574) 83 Christ.. the arbiter and mediator betwene God and men. **1580** SIDNEY *Arcadia*, The sun [at the equinox].. indifferent arbiter between the night and the day. **1667** MILTON *P.L.* IX. 50 Twilight.. short Arbiter 'Twixt Day and Night.

3. One who has power to decide or ordain according to his own absolute pleasure; one who has a matter under his sole control. Also *fig.*

1628 LE GRYS tr. *Barclay's Argenis* 286 Thou sittest as it were the arbiter of the fortune of thy neighbour Kings. **1652** NEEDHAM *Selden's Mare Cl.* 19 Absolute Lord or Arbiter of the whole world. **1785** REID *Int. Powers* I. i. §11 Use.. which is the arbiter of language. **1814** BYRON *To Napoleon*, The arbiter of others' fate, A suppliant for his own. **1874** MOTLEY *Barneveld* I. i. 61 The proud.. position of arbiter of Europe.

4. ‖***arbiter elegantiarum, elegantiæ*** [L., lit. 'judge of elegance': Petronius Arbiter was the *elegantiæ arbiter* of Nero's court (Tacitus *Ann.* xvi. 18)], a judge of matters of taste, an authority on etiquette.

1818 LADY MORGAN *Fl. Macarthy* II. iii. 175 He looked *up* to Lord Frederick Eversham, as the *arbiter elegantiarum* of that system. **1841** CRAIK & MACFARLANE *Pict. Hist. Eng. Geo. III* I. 651/1 Derrick.. succeeded Nash as *arbiter elegantiarum* at Bath. **1933** BALMER & WYLIE *When Worlds Collide* v. 49 A connoisseur of life and living—an *arbiter elegantiae*. **1957** R. N. CAREW HUNT *Guide Communist Jargon* xxi. 76 Zhdanov was appointed Stalin's *arbiter elegantiarum* in the late 'forties.

ˈarbitrable, *a.* [f. L. *arbitrā-ri* to judge, decide + -BLE.] Subject to the decision of an arbiter, arbitrator, or other constituted authority; discretionary.

1531 *Dial. Laws Eng.* II. viii. (1638) 73 Damages be arbitrable, and not certaine no more then trespasse is. **1581** LAMBARDE *Eiren.* IV. ii. (1588) 380 The place of holding them [sessions] is arbitrable, and at the pleasure of the Justices themselves. **1649** BP. HALL *Cases Consc.* i. (1654) 4 The value of moneys.. is arbitrable according to the soveraigne authority. *c* **1650** in Somers *Tracts* I. 504 Fines of such Copy-holds of Inheritance are arbitrable upon every Descent and Alienation. **1706** PHILLIPS *Arbitrable*, that may be put to, or decided by Arbitration. [So in BAILEY.] **1896** *Columbus* (O.) *Even. Dispatch* 18 July 1/4 Secretary Olney points out in support of his amendments that they make all disputes prima facie, arbitrable. **1915** T. ROOSEVELT

America & World War xi. 237 They would not be made arbitrable, any more than an individual's right to life and limb is made arbitrable.

arbitrage ('ɑːbɪtrɪdʒ), *sb.* [a. F. *arbitrage*, f. *arbitrer*: see ARBITRE *v.* and -AGE.]

1. Exercise of the functions of an arbitrator; decision by arbitration; the process of arbitration. *arch.*

1480 CAXTON *Ovid's Met.* XI. ii, Parys sayd, I shall thynke and trewly determyne this arbytrage. **1682** LUTTRELL *Brief Rel.* I. 172 He will referr the differences between him and the King of Spain to the arbitrage of the King of England. **1839** JAMES *Louis XIV*, III. 364 Commissioners acting under the arbitrage of the Queen of Spain.

2. Exercise of individual judgement, authoritative decision or determination. *arch.*

1601 FULBECKE *1st Pt. Parallel* 39 Respite must bee giuen by the arbitrage of the Iudge. **1691** T. H[ALE] *New Invent.* 92 Not by the arbitrage of private Patentees..but by the Public Conservators. **1818** BENTHAM *Ch. Eng.* 212 According to the arbitrage of the same ever excellent Judge.

3. *Comm.* The traffic in Bills of Exchange drawn on sundry places, and bought or sold in sight of the daily quotations of rates in the several markets, each operation being based in theory on the calculation known as ARBITRATION of Exchange, q.v. Also, the similar traffic in Stocks, so as to take advantage of the difference of price at which the same stock may be quoted at the same time in the exchange markets of distant places. [In this sense adopted from mod.F., and usually pronounced (ˈɑːbitrɑːʒ).]

1875 *Encycl. Brit.* II. 311/2 The great Government loans are..the natural subject-matter of arbitrage. **1881** *Daily News* 27 Apr. 6 Foreign arbitrage brokers. **1882** *Pall Mall G.* 24 June 1 He cannot..tell what the outcome of the unfathomable arbitrage business will be.

arbitrage ('ɑːbɪtrɑːʒ), *v.* [f. the sb.] *intr.* To engage in arbitrage (see ARBITRAGE 3). Hence **'arbitraging** *vbl. sb.*

1900 S. A. NELSON *ABC of Wall Street* 126 *Arbitraging*, trading in two markets in order to profit by the difference in prices. **1923** J. M. KEYNES *Tract on Monetary Reform* iii. 129 The surcharge representing the profit of a bank for arbitraging between spot and forward transactions may much exceed the moderate figure indicated above. **1953** *Economist* 16 May 461/1 Possible for authorized banks in these countries to arbitrage between the six currencies concerned.

arbitrageur (ɑːbɪtrɑːˈʒɜːr). *Comm.* Also in anglicized form **'arbitrager.** [Fr.] (See quot. 1875.)

1870 O. HAUPT *London Arbitrageur* p. iv, To furnish the experienced *arbitrageur* with a number of valuable hints. **1875** *Encycl. Brit.* II. 311/1 Arbitrage properly known as such, is the business of an arbitrageur, who is almost always a member of a Stock Exchange or 'Bourse', and his arbitrations..are..in Government and other stocks and shares. **1923** J. M. KEYNES *Tract on Monetary Reform* iii. 128 If in these conditions the purchasers of forward dollars, other than arbitragers, exceed sellers of forward dollars, then this excess of demand for forward dollars can be met by arbitragers. **1948** G. CROWTHER *Outl. Money* (ed. 2) vii. 219 These rates are all in equilibrium, there are no divergences out of which an arbitrageur can make a profit.

arbitragist ('ɑːbɪtrɪˌdʒɪst). *Comm.* [a. F. *arbitragiste*, f. *arbitrage*: see prec. in sense 3, and -IST.] One who transacts arbitrage business.

1881 *Times* 9 July The exchange will be rather regulated by the operations of arbitragists.

arbitral ('ɑːbɪtrəl), *a.* [a. F. *arbitral*, ad. late L. *arbitrālis*, f. *arbiter*: see -AL[1]. Chiefly in *Sc. Law.*]

1. Of or pertaining to arbiters or arbitration.

1609 SKENE *Reg. Maj.* vii. Argt., In qvhat place or at qvat time ane decreit arbitrall sould be given. **1612** MONIPENNIE *Abr. Chron.* in *Misc. Scot.* I. 20 Elected as judge arbitrall to discerne upon certain high controversies. **1799** J. ROBERTSON *Agric. Perth* 40 Their decisions are of the nature of a decreet arbitral. **1871** *Daily News* 22 Apr. 6 To concede power to the arbitral jury to reduce all rents. **1911** *Amer. Year Book 1910* 103 The most significant event of the past year in the development of international arbitration has been the virtual establishment..of the New Court of Arbitral Justice.

2. Subject to the exercise of will.

1662 CHANDLER *Van Helmont's Oriatr.* 119 Not as free contingencies, or arbitral, and much lesse as necessary ones.

arbitrament, -ement (ɑːˈbɪtrəmənt). Forms: 5–9 **arbitre-**, 5–8 **arbitri-**, 6–7 **arbiter-**, 7 **arbitter-**, 6– **arbitrament.** [a. OF. *arbitrement*, f. *arbitre-r*: see ARBITRE *v.* and -MENT; latinized as *arbitrament*, a form rare before *c* 1830, and disapproved by Johnson, but now the more usual. Du Cange has *arbitrāmentum* in med.L.]

†**1.** The right or capacity to decide for oneself; freedom of the will, free choice, pleasure. *Obs.*

c **1400** *Test. Loue* III. (R.) Euery man hath free arbitrement to choose good or yuel to perform. **1548** GESTE *Pr. Masse* 136 If we moughte order Christes supper after our arbitrement. **1667** MILTON *P.L.* VIII. 641 To stand or fall Free in thine own Arbitrement it lies. **1810** COLERIDGE *Friend* I. xv. (1867) 65 The oldness of my topics, evil and good, necessity and arbitrement.

2. The power to decide for others; absolute decision, direction, or control. *Obs.* (exc. as it approaches 3 b.)

1534 LD. BERNERS *Gold. Bk. M. Aurel.* (1546) E vj, I committe to your charge and arbitrement, that thing. **1594** HOOKER *Eccl. Pol.* III. (1617) 119 Some things belonging vnto externall Discipline and Ceremonies, are in the power and arbitrement of the Church. **1622** MALYNES *Anc. Law-Merch.* 168 But of late yeares all is left to the arbitrement of the Admiralls, to consider the finder or taker with some portion for his trauells, charges, and danger. *a* **1734** NORTH *Exam.* III. vii. ¶36. 529 The Affairs of the Crown were.. lapsing into the total Arbitriment of the Commons. **1842** ALISON *Hist. Eur.* XIV. xcv. §46. 121 The arbitrament of the affairs of Europe. **1856** RUSKIN *Mod. Paint.* III. IV. iii. §16 Subduing all his powers, impulses, and imaginations, to the arbitrement of a merciless justice.

3. The deciding of a dispute by an authority to whom the conflicting parties agree to refer their claims in order to their equitable settlement.

1549 COVERDALE *Erasm. Par. 1 Cor.* Argt. 2 To finishe it among themselves, by the arbitremente of any suche, as they thought mete. [*Rom.* Argt. 'arbitrament.'] *c* **1613** ROWLANDS *More Knaues Yet* 39 An arbiterment, To make all friends. **1622** MALYNES *Anc. Law-Merch.* 447 By way of Arbitrement, when both parties doe make choice of honest man to end their causes. **1831** BREWSTER *Newton* I. iv. 87 In the arbitraments of science it has always been a difficult task to adjust the rival claims of competitors. **1876** BANCROFT *Hist. U.S.* I. ix. 293 The controversy had required the arbitrament of the elders.

b. *fig.* and *transf.*

1599 SHAKS. *Hen. V*, IV. i. 168 The arbitrement of Swords. **1751** SMOLLETT *Per. Pic.* (1779) I. xxv. 230 Impossible to bring the cause to mortal arbitrement at that time. **1863** KIRK *Chas. the Bold* I. 211 Appeal to the slow arbitrament of Time. **1870** GLADSTONE *Glean.* IV. xxix. 219 An immediate resort to the arbitrament of war.

4. The sentence pronounced by an arbitrator, or by one deciding authoritatively; decision; sentence accepted as authoritative.

1424 *Paston Lett.* No. 4 I. 14 Wolde have holde and performyd the sayd ordinaunce, arbitrement, and award. **1576** ABP. GRINDAL *Fruitf. Dial.* (1843) 61 But will you stand to St. Augustine's arbitrement in the matter? **1642** BRIDGE *Wound. Consc. Cured* v. 37 To renounce their arbitrement and sentence. **1848** LYTTON *Harold* v. 324, I will not abide by the arbitrement of a pope. **1872** RUSKIN *Eagle's Nest* §182 Neither stone, flower, beast, nor man can understand any single reason of the arbitrement.

†**5.** Settlement or arrangement of a dispute; compromise, friendly agreement. *Obs.*

1549 OLDE *Erasm. Par. 1 Tim.* i. 5 He whiche shoulde make the arbitrement of concorde bytwene God and menne. **1625** BACON *Unity Relig., Ess.* (Arb.) 427 As if they would make an Arbitrement, betweene God and Man.

arbitrarily ('ɑːbɪtrərɪlɪ), *adv.* [f. ARBITRARY + -LY[2].] In an arbitrary manner, at will; **a.** merely at will, without sufficient reason, capriciously; **b.** unconstitutionally, despotically.

a **1626** DAVIES *Quest. Impositions* 131 This power of laying on arbitrarily new impositions. **1656** HOBBES *Six Less.* Wks. 1845 VII. 394 The point F is not to be taken arbitrarily. **1754** EDWARDS *Freed. Will* IV. §2 (ed. 4) 279 The meaning that they arbitrarily affix to a word. **1769** *Junius Lett.* xxxv, Their rights have been arbitrarily invaded by the present House of Commons. **1849** MACAULAY *Hist. Eng.* II. 126 The Bishop of Dunkeld..was arbitrarily ejected from his see. **1882** A. MACFARLANE *Consanguin.* 1 The arbitrarily chosen names of substances.

'arbitrariness. [f. as prec. + -NESS.] The quality of being arbitrary or uncontrolled in the exercise of will; **a.** capriciousness; **b.** despotism.

1643 HERLE *Answ. Ferne* 16 He may..governe with the Arbitrarinesse of a Father. **1657** CROMWELL *Sp.* 21 Apr. (Carl.) The horridest Arbitrariness that ever was exercised in the world. **1750** CARTE *Hist. Eng.* II. 843 The Arbitrariness of his prosecutions, and the severity of his punishments. **1754** EDWARDS *Freed. Will* IV. §7 (1762) 235 Senseless Arbitrariness, determining and acting without Reason, Design, or End. **1846** RUSKIN *Mod. Paint.* I. II. v. i. §12 There is, however, a strange arbitrariness about this elongation of reflection. **1853** BANCROFT *Hist. U.S.* (1876) V. lxvii. 291 The country was outraged by the arbitrariness of the military occupation.

†**arbi'trarious,** *a. Obs.* [f. L. *arbitrāri-us* (see ARBITRARY) + -OUS.] = ARBITRARY.

1642 H. MORE *Song Soul* (1647) 156/2 Whether..an arbitrarious or naturall efflux. **1692** RAY *Disc.* III. viii. (1732) 394 If the Dissolution of the World be effected by supernatural..means, the signs of it must be arbitrarious. **1806–31** A. KNOX *Rem.* (1844) I. 53 How are the two Churches one..except in the arbitrarious..position of the articles of Union?

†**arbi'trariously,** *adv. Obs.* [f. prec. + -LY[2].] = ARBITRARILY.

1662 MORE *Antid. Ath.* I. vii. (1712) 20 Under a pretence that [the soul] does arbitrariously and fortuitously compose the several impresses she receives from without. **1678** CUDWORTH *Intell. Syst.* I. v. 653 To which nothing can be arbitrariously added, nor nothing detracted from.

†**arbi'trariousness.** *Obs.* [f. as prec. + -NESS.] = ARBITRARINESS.

1808 KNOX & JEBB *Corr.* I. 462 The notion of positive [divine] institutions seems closely connected with a preconceived arbitrariousness in the Divine nature.

arbitrary ('ɑːbɪtrərɪ), *a.* and *sb.* [ad. L. *arbitrāri-us*, f. *arbiter* (perh. after F. *arbitraire*, 15th c.): see -ARY.]

A. *adj.* †**1.** To be decided by one's liking; dependent upon will or pleasure; at the discretion or option of any one. *Obs.* in general use.

1574 WHITGIFT *Def. Answ.* ii. Wks. 1851 I. 227 The same things were arbitrary, and might have been otherwise. **1628** BP. HALL *Right. Mammon* 727 It is not left arbitrary to you that you may doe good if you will. **1673** *Lady's Call.* I. §5, ¶64 As if they thought it a very arbitrary matter whether they come or no. **1768** BLACKSTONE *Comm.* II. 26 He might give them to what priests he pleased; which were called arbitrary consecrations of tithes.

2. *Law.* Relating to, or dependent on, the discretion of an arbiter, arbitrator, or other legally-recognized authority; discretionary, not fixed.

1581 LAMBARDE *Eiren.* IV. xv. 572 Judgements.. arbitrarie, or referred to discretion. **1693** WHARTON *Spec. Burnet's Err.* 67 (T.) Impropriated livings, which have now no settled endowment and are therefore called not vicarages, but perpetual or sometimes arbitrary curacies. **1704** *Lond. Gaz.* mmmmlxxxiii/4 A Mannor..with Quit Rents and Fines Arbitrary. **1880** MUIRHEAD *Gaius* IV. §163 If the defender have demanded a reference to an arbiter, he obtains what is called an arbitrary formula. **1882** SCRIVEN *Copyholds* (ed. 6) 155 An admission fine is *primâ facie* uncertain, or in legal phraseology *arbitrary*. But the fines on admission to copyholds of inheritance, even if arbitrary, must be reasonable.

3. Derived from mere opinion or preference; not based on the nature of things; *hence*, capricious, uncertain, varying.

1646 SIR T. BROWNE *Pseud. Ep.* 170 From succeeding spectators they received arbitrary appellations. **1753** JOHNSON *Advent.* No. 111 ¶6 Our estimation of birth is arbitrary and capricious. **1865** TYLOR *Early Hist. Man.* iii. 35, I do not believe there is a really arbitrary sign among them. **1865** R. W. DALE *Jew. Temple* xiii. (1877) 143 Their whole scheme of interpretation is purely arbitrary.

4. Unrestrained in the exercise of will; of uncontrolled power or authority, absolute; *hence*, despotic, tyrannical.

1642 in Rushw. *Hist. Coll.* III. (1692) I. 763 Acts of Will and Tyranny, which make up an Arbitrary Government. **1718** POPE *Iliad* I. 236 Rule thy own realms with arbitrary sway. **1832** HT. MARTINEAU *Demerara* i. 5 No tyrant, no arbitrary disposer of the fortunes of his inferiors. **1862** HOOK *Lives Abps.* II. ii. 159 The conduct of the Archbishop appears to have been arbitrary and harsh.

5. *Printing.* ***arbitrary character***: a character used to supplement the letters and accents which constitute an ordinary fount of type.

1829 [see CHARACTER *sb.* 3 a]. **1890** (*title*) Clarendon Press Inventory of Accents, Arbitrary Characters, &c. compiled April 1890. **1900** H. HART *Notes Century Typogr.* 139, I thought it unnecessary to 'set' the matrices for all the arbitrary characters.

B. as *sb.* (sc. number, term, etc.)

1879 THOMSON & TAIT *Nat. Phil.* I. I. §343 f, The complete solution of the differential equations..written as follows, to show its arbitraries explicitly. **1928** *Periodical* 15 Feb. 17 The variety of type used, the many languages involved, and the multiplication of 'arbitraries' have demanded technical knowledge and minute accuracy to an extent probably unequalled in any other work.

arbitrate ('ɑːbɪtreɪt), *v.* [f. L. *arbitrāt-* ppl. stem of *arbitrā-ri* to examine, give judgement, f. *arbiter*: see ARBITER and -ATE. Cf. earlier ARBITRE, through Fr.]

1. *gen.* (*intr.* or with *subord. cl.*) To give an authoritative decision, to decide. *Obs.* or *arch.*

1590 SWINBURN *Testaments* 41 He did arbitrate and awarde, that..the cooke should bee recompensed. **1641** MILTON *Ch. Govt.* vi. (1851) 124 Let all impartial men arbitrate what goodly inference these two maine reasons.. have. **1692** SOUTH *12 Serm.* (1697) I. 18 The mind..with an universal Superintendence, arbitrates..upon them all.

2. *trans.* To give an authoritative decision with regard to, decide, determine. *arch.*

1605 SHAKS. *Macb.* V. iv. 20 But certaine issue strokes must arbitrate. **1631** J. TAYLOR (Water P.) *Fortune's Wheele* 13 Now swordes, not wordes, doe kingdoms arbitrate. *a* **1677** BARROW *Serm.* (1716) I. 6 Things must be compared to and arbitrated by her standard. **1785** COWPER *Task* II. 600 The sycophant That waits to dress us, arbitrates their date. **1872** TENNYSON *Last Tourn.* 104 But thou, Sir Lancelot, sitting in my place Enchair'd to-morrow, arbitrate the field.

b. To judge of. (J.)

1637 MILTON *Comus* 411 An equal poise of hope and fear Does arbitrate the event.

3. *intr.* To act as formal arbitrator or umpire, to mediate (*in* a dispute, *between* contending parties).

1619 SANDERSON *Serms.* Ad. Cler. i. (1674) 2 The blessed Apostle..taketh upon him to arbitrate and to mediate in the business. **1806** WELLINGTON in *Wellesley Disp.* (1877) App. 97 Offers to arbitrate in the Mahratta claims. **1849** MACAULAY *Hist. Eng.* II. 3 He must relinquish all thought of arbitrating between contending nations.

4. *trans.* To settle by, or submit to, arbitration.

1592 SHAKS. *Rom. & Jul.* IV. i. 63 Twixt my extreames and me, this bloody knife Shall play the vmpeere, arbitrating that, Which, etc. **1647** DIGGS *Unlawf. Taking Arms* iv. 153 Let them arbitrate the differences. **1803** *Wellesley Disp.* (1877) 300 To arbitrate..the terms of accommodation between Scindiah and Holkar. **1861** (Dec. 4) BRIGHT *America, Sp.* (1876) 98 Government may discuss this matter, they may arbitrate it.

ˈarbitrated, *ppl. a.* [f. prec. + -ED.] Settled by arbitration; *spec.* in *Comm.* Determined or conducted by 'Arbitration of Exchange.'

1611 COTGR., *Arbitré, Arbitrated, stickled..compounded, agreed.* **1811** P. KELLY *Univ. Cambist* (1821) II. 107 When the actual or direct price is found to differ from the arbitrated price, advantage may be made by drawing or remitting indirectly. **1852** MᶜCULLOCH *Dict. Comm.* 581 The arbitrated price between London and Madrid. **1868** ROGERS *Pol. Econ.* xv. (ed. 3) 209 The third city then may intervene, and the difference between Paris and London may be settled by this indirect, or..arbitrated exchange.

ˈarbitrating, *vbl. sb.* [f. as prec. + -ING¹.] Arbitration. (Mostly gerundial.)

1643 NETHERSOLE *Proj. Peace* (1648) 21 The arbitrating of such..points to be referred to some one.

arbitration (ɑːbɪˈtreɪʃən). [a. OF. *arbitracion, -tion,* ad. L. *arbitrātiōn-em,* n. of action f. *arbitrāt-*: see ARBITRATE and -TION.]

†**1.** A deciding according to one's will or pleasure; uncontrolled or absolute decision. *Obs.*

c **1386** CHAUCER *Melib.* ⁋787 That a man..putte hym al outrely in the arbitracion and Iuggement..of hise enemys. *c* **1400** *Apol. Loll.* 63 He demiþ after þe lawe, & doþ no þing aftur his oune arbitracoun. **1651** HOBBES *Govt. & Soc.* VII. §4. 113 The arbitration of War, and Peace.

2. The settlement of a dispute or question at issue by one to whom the conflicting parties agree to refer their claims in order to obtain an equitable decision.

1634 BRERETON *Trav.* (1844) 8 To mediate in a friendly manner in a way of arbitration. *a* **1716** BLACKALL *Wks.* 1723 I. 109 To put their Differences to the Arbitration of some of their Brethren. **1840** MACAULAY *Clive* 45 To submit the points in dispute to the arbitration of Meer Jaffier.

b. *attrib.*, as in ***arbitration bond, rate,*** etc.

1768 BLACKSTONE *Comm.* III. i, Arbitration-bond..a bond entered into by two or more parties to abide by the decision of an arbitrator. **1878** F. WILLIAMS *Midl. Rail.* 212 Running powers over the line at arbitration rates.

3. ***Arbitration of Exchange*** (cf. F. *arbitrage* in same sense): The determination of the rate of exchange to be obtained between two countries or currencies, when the operation is conducted through a third or several intermediate ones, in order to ascertain the most advantageous method of drawing or remitting bills.

1811 P. KELLY *Univ. Cambist* (1821) II. 108 In the foregoing questions, the profit or loss is ascertained on an operation already completed: but in arbitration it is ascertained beforehand, and the different results are compared in order to determine the most advantageous mode of proceeding. **1844** *Pract. Arith.* (*Sc. Schoolbk. Assoc.*) Arbitration of Exchange is, when the rates of exchange between three or more places are given, to find a proportionate rate between the first and last. **1852** MᶜCULLOCH *Dict. Comm.* 581 In compound arbitration, or when more than 3 places are concerned. **1866** CRUMP *Banking* vii. 146 A circuitous mode of payment..called the 'arbitration of exchanges.'

arbiˈtrational, *a.* [See -AL.] Pertaining to, involving, or effected by arbitration.

a **1889** A. HAYWARD *Ethics of Peace* (Cent. D.), Arbitrational settlement of the Alabama claims. **1939** *Mind* XLVIII. 161 Doing nothing to enforce a standard of behaviour but merely giving arbitrational decisions between conflicting parties.

arbitrationist (ɑːbɪˈtreɪʃənɪst). [f. ARBITRATION + -IST.] One who is in favour of arbitration.

1884 *Pall Mall Gaz.* 24 June 3/1 Fine doctrine this for the arbitrationists! **1902** *Q. Rev.* Oct. 667 As an arbitrationist, he has been a hero with the emotional Radicals.

arbitrative (ˈɑːbɪtreɪtɪv), *a.* [f. ARBITRATE *v.* + -IVE.] Having power to arbitrate; done by arbitration.

1831 WADDINGTON *Hist. Church* I. II. xiii. 221 The arbitrative authority of the Primitive Bishops was tolerated ..by the Pagan Emperors. **1875** R. J. HINTON *Eng. Radical Leaders* 117 He urged arbitrative tribunals as one of the better modes of treatment.

arbitrator (ˈɑːbɪtreɪtə(r)). [a. OF. *arbitratour, -eur,* 13th c., ad. L. *arbitrātōr-em,* n. of agent f. *arbitrā-ri*: see ARBITER and ARBITRER.]

1. One who is chosen by the opposite parties in a dispute to arrange or decide the difference between them; an arbiter.

It is often the practice to appoint two or more *arbitrators,* with an *umpire,* chosen usually by them, as final referee. *Arbitrator* is now the legal term, *arbiter* remaining as a literary word.

1424 *Paston Lett.* 4. I. 14 The seyd arbitrement and ordinaunce of the seyd arbitratores. **1598** KITCHIN *Courts Leet* (1675) 182 One juror was chosen arbitrator for one party. **1609** SKENE *Reg. Maj.* 21 Ane ordinar Judge may be ane Arbitratour, or amicabill compositor [cf. ARBITER 2]. **1809** TOMLINS *Law Dict.* s.v. *Award,* The arbitrator has a jurisdiction over the costs of the action. **1866** MOTLEY *Dutch Rep.* VI. i. 793 In case of their inability to agree, they were to appoint arbitrators.

†**2.** Hence *fig.* of that which brings about a definite issue. *Obs.*

1591 SHAKS. *1 Hen. VI,* II. v. 28 The Arbitrator of Despaires, Iust Death, kinde Vmpire of men's miseries. **1606** —— *Tr. & Cr.* IV. iii. 225 That old common Arbitrator, Time, Will one day end it.

3. One who decides or ordains according to his own absolute pleasure; a supreme ordainer; = ARBITER 3.

1579 FENTON *Guicciard.* I. (1599) 22 The only arbitrator and oracle of all Italy. **1675** CROWNE *Androm.* V. 44 Who made thee arbitratour of his fate? **1737** WHISTON *Joseph. Wars* I. x. §9 God is the arbitrator of success in war. **1877** MRS. OLIPHANT *Makers of Flor.* i. 10 The Church as the grand arbitrator of all national concerns.

ˈarbiˌtratorship. [f. prec. + -SHIP.] The position or function of an arbitrator.

1667 *Lond. Gaz.* ccxiv/1 The Arbitratorship between the two Crowns of Spain and France. **1882** H. BROWNSON in *O. Brownson's Wks.* I. 22 The popes..exercised often an arbitratorship in disputes between sovereign and sovereign.

arbitratrix (ɑːbɪˈtreɪtrɪks). [a. L. *arbitrātrix* (in Tertull.), fem. of *arbitrātor*: see -TRIX.] A female arbitrator, an arbitress.

1577 HOLINSHED *Descr. Brit.* xxii. 122 Arbitratrix betweene hir naturall love to the one, and matrimoniall dutie to the other. **1648** JOS. BEAUMONT *Psyche* xix. 168 (D.) Her prerogative alone Who Arbitratrix sits of Heav'n and Hell. **1809** TOMLINS *Law Dict.* s.v. *Award,* An unmarried woman may be an arbitratrix.

arbitre, *sb.*: see ARBITRY.

†**ˈarbitre,** *v. Obs. rare.* [a. F. *arbitre-r*:—L. *arbitrā-ri*: see ARBITRATE.] Earlier equivalent of ARBITRATE.

1494 FABYAN V. cxxvii. 108 For this were chosen. xii. noble men of Fraunce to arbytre & deme betwene the fader and the sone. **1548** HALL *Chron. Hen. VI,* an. 4 (R.) All that shal be declared, ordained, and arbitred by the forsaide Archebishop.

arbitrement, earlier form of ARBITRAMENT.

†**ˈarbitrer, -or.** *Obs.* Also 4–6 -our. [a. AFr. *arbitrour,* OF. *arbitreor, -eour*:—late L. *arbitrātōr-em*: see ARBITRATOR and ARBITER.] Earlier equivalent of ARBITRATOR.

1382 WYCLIF *1 Esdr.* viii. 23 Ordeine domesmen and arbitrouris [**1611** justices]. **1393** LANGLAND *P. Pl.* C. VII. 382 þe betere þyng, by arbitrours [*v.r.* arbytours] · sholde bote þe werse. *c* **1440** *Promp. Parv.* 14 Arbitrowre, *arbiter.* **1479** J. PASTON *Lett.* 841 III. 257 It was other wyse a-poynted befor the arbytrorys. **1560** DAUS *Sleidane's Comm.* 129 b, Arbitrers, who..should determine the case. **1641** *Termes de la Ley* 26 Arbitrors. **1814** SOUTHEY *Roderick* XXI. 413 The arbitrer of her own destiny.

arbitress (ˈɑːbɪtrɪs). [a. OF. *arbitresse,* fem. of *arbitre*: see -ESS.] A female arbiter.

1. One who settles disputes, a mediatress.

1340 *Ayenb.* 154 A trewe arbitres betuene þe goste and þe ulesse. *c* **1630** DRUMM. OF HAWTH. *James I.* Wks. (1711) 11 Had France but shown herself an indifferent arbitress of the blows between Scotland and England. **1748** RICHARDSON *Clarissa* (1811) II. xlix. 368 The arbitress of the quarrels of unruly spirits. **1835** I. TAYLOR *Spir. Despot.* vii. 308 The Church is sovereign arbitress of controversy.

2. A female who has absolute control or disposal.

1594 DANIEL *Cleopatra* (1717) 278 O fearful frowning Nemesis..That art the World's great Arbitress. **1667** MILTON *P.L.* I. 784 While over head the Moon Sits Arbitress. **1796** BURKE *Regic. Peace* Wks. 1842 II. 293 To make England..the arbitress of Europe. **1826** DISRAELI *Viv. Grey* VII. ii. 393 The arbitress of fashion is one who is allowed to be singular, in order that she may suppress singularity.

arbitriment, obs. form of ARBITRAMENT.

arbitror, -our, earlier forms of ARBITRER.

†**arbitry.** *Obs.* Forms: 4–6 **arbitre,** 5 **arbytre, -try,** 5–7 **arbetrie,** 6–7 **arbitrie,** 7 **-ry.** [Two words: 1. *Arbitre* (*e* mute), a. OF. *arbitre*:—L. *arbitrium* judgement, will; 2. *Arbitrie, -y,* later ad. L. *arbitri-um* (cf. *ministry*). In 15th c. the spelling *arbitre* might represent either, as in *cite, citie, city.* OF. had also a rare *arbitrie.*]

1. Power to choose or act; own will or pleasure; arbitrary will.

c **1374** CHAUCER *Boeth.* V. iii. 156 To distroien..þe fredome of oure arbitre · þat is to seyn of oure fre wille. **1483** CAXTON *Cato* E v, His free wylle and lyberalle arbytre for to doo hit or not. **1537** *Instit. Chr. Man* B vj b, At his owne godly wyl, arbitre and dispensation. **1649** SELDEN *Laws of Eng.* I. xxii. (1739) 40 Their rule..was made not by the arbitry of the General, but by Parliament.

2. Arbitration.

1535 STEWART *Cron. Scot.* III. 132 Thair richtis bayth on arbetrie wes done. **1582–8** *Hist. James VI.* (1804) 89 To putt thair mater in arbitrie. **1609** SKENE *Reg. Maj.* 20 Arbitrie is ane lawfull deid of persons contendand.

3. Decision, sentence, award.

1375 BARBOUR *Bruce* I. 75 He suld that arbytre disclar. *c* **1615** CHAPMAN *Odyss.* XI. 738 Though arbitry Of all a court of war pronounc'd it mine.

arblast, -er, variants of ARBALEST, -ER, -RE.

†**arbolare,** *v. Obs. rare*⁻¹. [a. Sp. *arbolar* 'to make a stand as pikemen' (Minsheu 1623), f. *arbol*:—L. *arbor* tree.] (See quot.)

1598 BARRET *Theor. Warres* III. i. 36 How to arbolare or aduance his pike, that is; to reare his pike vpright against his right shoulder, and, etc.

arbolist, obs. f. HERBALIST and ARBORIST.

arbor¹ (ˈɑːbə(r)). *Mech.* Also 7 arber, 8 arbre. [a. F. *arbre* tree, also axis or principal piece of a wheel or machine; subseq. assimilated to L. *arbor.*] **a.** The main support or beam of a machine (*e.g.* of a crane or windmill); **b.** The axle or spindle on which a wheel revolves, esp. in clocks and watches. (Cf. *axle-tree.*) ***arbor-chuck***: (see quot.)

1659 LEAK *Water-works* 28 To the Arber of the said Pinion there shall be a Wheel having 32 Teeth. **1727–51** CHAMBERS *Cycl.* s.v. *Crane,* The modern crane consists of several members..the principal whereof is a strong perpendicular beam, or arbor. **1759** PULLEIN in *Phil. Trans.* LI. 27 Two wheels..fixed upon one common arbre. **1847** CRAIG *Arbor-chuck*..a chuck, consisting merely of a spindle, generally made of metal, projecting from the mandril of the lathe, used in turning and polishing rings, hollow cylinders, etc. **1857** DENISON *Clocks & Locks* 4 The prolonged arbor of the centre wheel.

‖**arbor**² (ˈɑːbɔː(r)). The Latin word for 'tree,' used as part of various names in *Bot., Chem.,* etc.; as in *Bot.* **arbor Judæ,** the Judas tree (*Cercis siliquastrum*); in *Chem.* **arbor Dianæ,** the arborescent or tree-like appearance formed upon the introduction of mercury into a solution of nitrate of silver; **arbor Saturni,** the similar precipitate formed when a piece of zinc is put into a solution of acetate of lead; ARBOR VITÆ, q.v.

1669 WORLIDGE *Syst. Agric.* (1681) 100 As Arbor-Judæ, Laburnum, etc. **1741** *Compl. Fam.-Piece* II. iii. 362 Transplant the Arbor Judæ.

arbor, variant spelling of ARBOUR.

arboraceous (ɑːbəˈreɪʃəs), *a.* [f. prec. + -ACEOUS.] Of tree-like or wooded character.

1848 H. MILLER *First Impress.* ix. (1857) 139 A sequestered arboraceous lane. **1875** SCHMIDT *Desc. & Darw.* 78 Palms and arboraceous plants.

†**ˈarborage.** *Obs. rare*⁻¹. [f. ARBOUR + -AGE.] A work or structure of arbours.

1697 *World in Moon* (N.) The scene, an arborage of palms and laurels, consisting of nine arches.

arboral (ˈɑːbərəl), *a.* [f. L. *arbor* + -AL¹.] Pertaining to, or of the nature of, trees; = ARBOREAL 1.

1657 TOMLINSON *Renou's Disp.* 150 All suaveolent flowers whether herbal..or arbustal, or arboral. **1867** *Athenæum* 26 Oct. 541/3 This tree..has..very little arboral character.

arborary (ˈɑːbərərɪ), *a. rare.* [ad. L. *arborāri-us,* f. *arbor* tree: see -ARY.] = prec.

1656 in BLOUNT *Glossogr.* **1881** ELWES tr. *Pinto's Africa* I. iii. 54 The soil is granitic, and the arborary vegetation luxuriant.

†**arboˈrator.** *Obs. rare.* [a. L. *arborātor* (Pliny), n. of agent f. **arborā-re* to cultivate trees.] One who attends to the culture of trees.

1664 EVELYN *Sylva* 78 Our ingenious Arborator [would] frequently incorporate..the Arms and Branches of some young and flexible Trees which grow in consort.

Arbor Day (ˈɑːbə deɪ). orig. *U.S.* [L. *arbor* tree. Cf. ARBOR².] A day set apart by law, orig. in the state of Nebraska, afterwards observed throughout the U.S. and adopted in Australia, Canada, and New Zealand, to be yearly observed for the planting of trees.

1872 in *Encycl. Brit.* (1902) XXXI. 112/2 Resolved that Wednesday, the 10th day of April 1872, be..set apart..for tree-planting in the state of Nebraska, and the State Board of Agriculture hereby name it Arbor Day. **1888** *Daily Inter-Ocean* 14 Mar. (Farmer), Governor Oglesby has designated April 13 as Arbor Day in Illinois. **1892** *Congress. Rec.* June 5404/2 In every quarter of the country 'arbor days' are days named by law, and also by custom, for planting forest trees to make lumber for the generations yet to come. **1902** *Encycl. Brit.* XXXII. 731/2 In order to encourage tree-planting [in S. Australia], a yearly school holiday devoted to this purpose, and known as Arbor Day, was established in 1886. **1967** *N.Z. Listener* 28 July, In New Zealand..Arbor Day is celebrated on the first Wednesday in August.

arboreal (ɑːˈbɔərɪəl), *a.* [f. L. *arbore-us* (f. *arbor* tree) + -AL¹.]

1. Pertaining to, or of the nature of, trees.

a **1667** COWLEY *Of Plants* 201 Young colonies of Trees thou dost replace I' th' empty realms of our arboreal race. **1870** H. MACMILLAN *Bible Teach.* iv. 68 Where the pine forms the sole arboreal vegetation.

2. Connected with, haunting, or inhabiting trees.

1834–43 SOUTHEY *Doctor* ccxv. (D.) A vivid feeling connected with his arboreal existence. **1865** WOOD *Homes without Hands* xii. 246 Arboreal ants, which make their nests among the branches.

arborean (ɑːˈbɔərɪən), *a.* [see -AN.] = prec.

1837 HOWITT *Rur. Life* VI. viii, An aerial, arborean lodge.

arboreous (ɑːˈbɔərɪəs), *a.* [f. as prec. + -OUS.]

1. Abounding in trees, wooded.

1664 EVELYN *Sylva* (1776) 604 Those arboreous amenities and plantation of woods. **1854** H. MILLER *Sch. & Schm.* (1858) 166 That arboreous condition of our country.

2. = ARBOREAL.

1646 SIR T. BROWNE *Pseud. Ep.* 98 They surely speake probably who make it [*i.e.* misseltoe] an arboreous excrescence. **1753** CHAMBERS *Cycl. Supp.* s.v., The Arboreous bird, by which he means, the barnacle. **1833** *Blackw. Mag.* XXXIV. 280 Their [Cigalas'] arboreous disposition.

3. = ARBORESCENT.

1753 CHAMBERS *Cycl. Supp.* s.v., An Arboreous cloud..a cloudy meteor resembling the appearance of a tree. **1772** FORSTER in *Phil. Trans.* LXII. 58 The plant..is arboreous, with small leaves. **1845** LINDLEY *Sch. Bot.* vi. (1858) 76 Leaflets ovate. Stem arboreous.

arboresce (ɑːbəˈrɛs), *v. rare.* [ad. L. *arborēscĕre* to grow into a tree, f. *arbor* tree.] To assume the appearance of a tree; to branch like a tree.

1804 CARLISLE in *Phil. Trans.* XCV. 6 The arteries arboresce copiously upon the reticular coat.

arborescence (ɑːbəˈrɛsəns). [f. next: see -NCE.] Tree-like growth or formation. Also *fig.*

1856 R. VAUGHAN *Mystics* (1860) I. 98 The mazy arborescence of his verbiage. **1883** W. GIBSON in *Harper's Mag.*, Jan. 192 'Mid stony arborescence submarine.

arborescent (ɑːbəˈrɛsənt), *a.* [ad. L. *arborēscent-em*, pr. pple. of *arborēsc-ĕre*: see ARBORESCE and -ENT.]

1. Tree-like in growth; approaching the size of a tree, or having a woody stem.

1675 GREW *Anat. Trunks* i. §32 Examples of Trees or Arborescent Plants. **1845** DARWIN *Voy. Nat.* xi. 244 An arborescent grass, very like a bamboo. **1859** TENNENT *Ceylon* II. IX. vii. 553 Coco-nut palms and arborescent mimosas.

2. Tree-like in general appearance, or in the arrangement of parts; branching like a tree.

1679 *Phil. Collect.* XII. 6 A Clift all interwoven with Arborescent Marchasites. **1766** PENNANT *Brit. Zool.* VI. 67 (JOD.) Asterias arborescent with five rays. **1775** ELLIS in *Phil. Trans.* LXVI. 17 The arborescent figures of the Cornish native copper. **1881** MIVART *Cat* 233 An arborescent network of veins.

b. in *Arch.* (See quot.)

1849 FREEMAN *Archit.* 260 Not growing out of their support as in the arborescent Gothic. **1851** RUSKIN *Stones Ven.* I. xxi. §27 All good ornamentation is thus arborescent, as it were, one class of it branching out of another and sustained by it.

c. *fig.* Manifoldly branching.

1867 E. BURR *Ecce Cœlum* vi. 167 God whose unity is arborescent with endless varieties of beauty and power.

arboˈrescently, *adv.* [f. prec. + -LY².] In arborescent manner; like a tree or its ramification.

1847–9 TODD *Cycl. Anat. & Phys.* IV. 342/1 The caniculi [are] distributed arborescently.

arboresque (ɑːbəˈrɛsk), *a. rare.* [f. ARBOR + -ESQUE.] Artistically tree-like.

1861 *Eng. Home* 167 These beautiful modellings and arboresque chasings.

arboret¹ (ˈɑːbərɛt). *arch.* [f. L. *arbor* tree + -ET¹: cf. It. *alboretto, alberetto*, Fr. *arbret.*] A little tree, a shrub.

1596 SPENSER *F.Q.* II. vi. 12 No arborett with painted blossomes drest. **1667** MILTON *P.L.* IX. 435 Among thick-wov'n Arborets and Flours. **1805** SOUTHEY *Madoc in Azt.* x, The kingdom o'er all trees and arborets.

†**ˈarboret**². *Obs.* [ad. L. *arborēt-um*, see next: cf. It. *alboreto*, Florio; or a dim. of *arbor*, ARBOUR.] A grove, shrubbery; arbour.

1604 EDMONDS *Observ. Cæsars Comm.* 24 Pleasant places for the refreshing of wearied spirits, gardens, groues, walkes, riuers, and arborets. **1612** DRAYTON *Polyolb.* xix. (1748) 333 Dainty summer bowers and arborets.

‖**arboretum** (ɑːbɔəˈriːtəm). Pl. **-a.** [L. *arborētum* a place grown with trees, f. *arbor* tree.] A place devoted to the cultivation and exhibition of rare trees; a botanical tree-garden.

1838 LOUDON *Arboretum et Frut. Brit.*, Collecting trees from a distance..to assemble them in one plantation or arboretum. **1869** *Black's Guide to Devon* 168 Amid the mazes of its Arboretum, its glorious pinery, etc.

arborical (ɑːˈbɒrɪkəl), *a. rare.* [f. L. *arbor* tree + -ICAL. (Not on L. anal.)] = ARBORAL, ARBOREAL 1.

c **1650** HOWELL *Lett.* IV. xxiii, The whole bulk of that Arborical Discourse. **1696** BROOKHOUSE *Temple Op.* 54 That the Arborical Reign may be Establish'd [*Isa.* lv. 13]. **1861** CLAR. BROMLEY *Wom. Wand.* 4 A sugar plantation..did not make so pleasing an impression as other new arborical acquaintances.

arboricidal (ˌɑːbɒrɪˈsaɪdəl), *a.* [f. L. *arbor* tree + -CID(E 2 + -AL.] Given to cutting down trees; tree-felling.

1866 BLACKMORE *Cradock Nowell* xii, Condemnation of this arboricidal age. **1877** E. H. YATES *Celebrities at Home* I. 50 The arboricidal tastes of the Master of Hawarden.

arboricide (ɑːˈbɔərɪsaɪd). [See prec.] The wanton destruction of trees.

1899 H. G. GRAHAM *Social Life of Scotl. 18th Cent.* I. v. 199 This crime of arboricide was distressingly frequent. **1930** *London Mercury* Mar. 386 The charge of arboricide Mr. Lansbury was able to meet completely.

arboricole (ɑːˈbɒrɪkəʊl), *a. rare.* [a. F. *arboricole*, f. L. *arbor* tree + *-cola* inhabiting.] Inhabiting or haunting trees.

1874 COUES *Birds N.-W.* 323 [Burrowing Owls]..constitute a notable exception to the general rule of arboricole habits in this family.

arboricultural (ˌɑːbərɪˈkʌltjʊərəl), *a.* [f. next + -AL¹.] Pertaining to arboriculture.

1828 STEUART *Planter's Guide* 355 A proposal for the establishment of an Arboricultural Society in Scotland..would be universally approved. **1871** M. COLLINS *Mrq. & Merch.* I. 6 Looking after matters agricultural, arboricultural, ornithological. **1882** *Pall Mall G.* 10 Aug. 5/2 Attractive to the arboricultural mind.

arboriculture (ˈɑːbərɪˌkʌltjʊə(r)). [f. L. *arbor* tree + *cultūra* tending.] The cultivation of trees and shrubs for use or ornament.

1828 STEUART *Planter's Guide* i. 5 Arboriculture..will at length share the same distinction. **1834** LOUDON (*title*) Encyclopædia of Gardening, comprising..Horticulture, Floriculture, Arboriculture. **1870** A. ADAMS *Nile Valley* 117 The asperities of climate [in Malta] might be very much modified by arboriculture.

arboriculturist (-ˈkʌltjʊərɪst). [f. prec. + -IST.] One who practises arboriculture.

1825 in Lockhart *Scott* (1839) VII. 394 Sir W. is..a most zealous agriculturist and arboriculturist especially. **1865** LIVINGSTONE *Zambesi* xii. 259 The Batoka, the only arboriculturists in the country, rear native fruit trees.

arborification (ɑːˌbɔərɪfɪˈkeɪʃən). [f. L. *arbor* tree + -FICATION.] A tree-like or branching formation.

1809 J. GRAHAM in *Philos. Mag.* XXXIII. 192 No description..can convey any idea either of the beauty or curiosity of these several icy arborifications. **1936** C. S. LEWIS *Alleg. Love* vii. 304 The shield of Arthur is borrowed from the shield of Atlant,..Fradubio's arborification from Astulph's.

arboriform (ˈɑːbərɪfɔːm, ɑːˈbɒrɪ-), *a.* [f. L. *arbor* tree + -(I)FORM.] = ARBORESCENT 2.

1848 DANA *Zooph.* 276 Arboriform in shape.

arborist (ˈɑːbərɪst). [In 16th c. a. F. *arboriste*, now refashioned as *herboriste*: see Littré, and cf. ARBOUR. In later use f. L. *arbor* tree + -IST; so in mod.F.; *arbolist* was after Sp. *arbol* tree.]

†**a.** A keeper of a 'herber,' a herbalist (*obs.*). **b.** A scientific student or cultivator of trees.

1578 LYTE *Dodoens* 13 Some Arboristes do call it [Anthyllis] Glaudiola. **1645** HOWELL *Dodona's Grove* 11 The Mulberry, which the Arbolists observe to be long in begetting..his buds. **1648** W. LAWSON *Orch. & Gard.* III. i. (1668) 2 Most of our great Arborists plant Apricocks, Cherries, and Peaches by a wall. **1755** in JOHNSON. **1883** R. HUTCHISON *Trans. Highl. & Agric. Soc.* XV. 35 The intelligent arborist.

arborization (ˌɑːbəraɪˈzeɪʃən). [n. of action f. next: see -TION.] The production of a tree-like appearance. **a.** *Min.* and *Chem.* A tree-like formation in the aggregation of crystals, as in dendritic silver ore, or in the markings of agates, etc. **b.** *Anat.* A tree-like appearance produced by the distension or injection of capillary vessels.

1794 SULLIVAN *View Nat.* I. 448 Agates that present arborisations. **1800** HENRY *Epit. Chem.* (1808) 223 A beautiful arborization of reduced silver. **1878** A. HAMILTON *Nerv. Dis.* 77 The internal surface of the dura mater was furrowed by capillary arborization.

arborize (ˈɑːbəraɪz), *v.* [f. L. *arbor* tree + -IZE: cf. F. *arborisé.*] **a.** *trans.* To make tree-like, to give the appearance of a tree. Perhaps only in ppl. adj. **b.** *intr.* To make tree-like formations.

1847 CRAIG, *Arborized*, Applied to agates which have the ramified appearance of plants, due to the infiltration of water charged with metallic oxides. **1907** *Practitioner* June 860 Some of the fibres from the posterior nerve-root pass directly into the posterior grey cornu, and arborise around cells at its base.

arborous (ˈɑːbərəs), *a.* [f. L. *arbor* tree + -OUS.] Of, belonging to, or consisting of trees.

1667 MILTON *P.L.* v. 137 From under shadie arborous roof. **1796** COLERIDGE *To G. Coleridge*, Old boughs, That hang above us in an arborous roof. **1881** *Athenæum* 25 June 854 The floral and arborous forms.

†**arbor vine** (J.), **arbor** (? *arbour*) **wind.** *Obs.* name of the Sarsaparilla.

1551 TURNER *Herbal* II. 141 The smoth smilax..may be called in English Arbor winde..Thys doth also wind it self aboute trees. [Cf. 1745 ARBUSTIVE.]

arborvirus (ɑːbəˈvaɪərəs). Also **arbovirus.** [f. AR(THROPOD + BOR(NE *ppl. a.* + VIRUS.] A virus borne and transmitted by an arthropod. Also *attrib.*

1957 *Trans. N.Y. Acad. Sci.* XIX. 219 All known Arbor viruses are pathogenic for Swiss mice. **1959** C. E. GORDON SMITH in *Brit. Med. Bull.* XV. 235/1 'Arborvirus'..is a convenient abbreviation but must not be thought of as having Linnean rank. **1962** *Times* 26 June 3/1 (Advt.), The immunochemistry of viruses, especially those of the pox-virus and arborvirus groups. **1965** C. ANDREWES *Common Cold* ix. 77 The virus families..are:..(vi) Arboviruses.

‖**arbor vitæ** (ˌɑːbɔː ˈvaɪtiː). [L.; = tree of life.]

1. *Bot.* Popular name of several evergreen shrubs of the genus *Thuja*, N.O. *Coniferæ*.

1664 EVELYN *Silva* (1812) II. 40 This tree [Thuya] by some called Arbor Vitæ..is of a hardy green all the winter. **1860** RUSKIN *Mod. Paint.* V. VI. ix. §2 In some ambiguous trees (as the *arbor vitæ*) there is no proper stem to the outer leaves.

2. *Phys.* The arborescent appearance of a longitudinal section of the cerebellum.

1800 CARLISLE in *Phil. Trans.* XCI. 142 The intermixture of the cortical and medullary substances form the appearance called Arbor vitæ. **1880** in *Syd. Soc. Lex.*

†**ˈarbory**, *sb. Obs.* [See the separate senses.]

1. Growth of trees or shrubs; timber, wood, coppice. [a. OF. *arboirie*, 'pousse d'arbres' Godef.]

1366 MAUNDEV. xxiv. 256 In that Contree is but Lytille Arberye. *c* **1440** *Morte Arth.* 3245 Enhorilde with arborye and alkyns trees.

2. = ARBOUR. [An assimilation of that to words in -ORY, or -RY. Cf. also It. *arborata* 'an arbor or bowre of boughs or trees' (Florio 1598), of which the Fr. equivalent would be *arborée.*]

1600 HAKLUYT *Voy.* (1810) III. 335 Their houses are made of round poles..as is used in many arbories in our gardens. **1695** KENNETT *Par. Antiq.* ix. 610 Sheds or Arbories, made up with branches and boughs of trees.

3. A place where trees are cultivated; an orchard. [App. f. L. *arbor* after words like *rectory, armory.*]

1792 D. LLOYD *Voy. Life* 96 Yon celestial arbory, where fruits Ambrosial blush unfading tints.

†**ˈarbory**, *a. Obs. rare*⁻¹. [ad. L. *arborius*, variant of *arboreus.*] = ARBOREAL.

1572 BOSSEWELL *Armorie* II. 118 b, He beareth Azure, iij. Gees arborie Dargent. [Cf. ANATIFEROUS.]

arbour, -or (ˈɑːbə(r)). Forms: see under the separate senses. [This word has undergone great change of form and signification. Orig. (*h*)*erber*, a. AF. (*h*)*erber*, OF. (*h*)*erbier*, a place covered with grass or herbage, a garden of herbs:—L. *herbārium* a collection of herbs, f. *herba* grass, herb: see -ARIUM. *Erber* became *arber* by a change that was frequent with *-er* before a cons. (cf. *harb, arb, yarb*, obs. or dial. forms of *herb* itself; also *arber, harbour, carve, starve, farm*, etc., and the spoken forms of *clerk, sergeant, Derby, Hertford, Cherwell*); and *arber* was in 16th c. written *arbour, -or*, in accordance with the common scribal interchange of *-er, -our, -or* (cf. *arbiter, -our, sailer, -our, -or*).

These phonetic and graphic changes were facilitated by the change of sense, as the word ceased to be associated with *herb*; the final acceptance of *arbour, arbor*, was probably aided by the natural tendency to connect it with L. *arbor* tree, or It. *arborata* bower. Hence, from *c* 1550, there was a tendency to distinguish *herbour* and *arbour*, restricting the latter to senses 3, 5. LEVINS *Manip.* (1570) has 'An Arboure, *arboretum*; an Herboure, *viretum, herbaretum*'; also, 'Harboure, *hospitium.*' This last word has also been supposed by some to have influenced the form of *arbour*; but of this there is no trace. Occasional instances of confusion between *arbour* and *harbour* are merely the mistakes of individuals.]

†**1.** A plot of ground covered with grass or turf; a garden lawn, or 'green.' Forms: 4–5 **erber(e, herber(e.** *Obs.*

c **1325** *E.E. Allit. P.* A. 9 Allas! I leste hyr in on erbere, þurȝ gresse to grounde hit fro me yot. *Ibid.* A. 38, I entred in þat erber grene..57, I felle vpon þat floury flaȝt. *c* **1380** *Sir Ferumb.* 1773 Faste þar-by was he, Sittynge on a grene erber. *c* **1400** *Rowland & Ot.* 994 Greses broghte þat fre, þat godd sett in his awenn herbere. *a* **1460** *Medulla Gram.*, *Viretum, locus pascualis virens*, a gres-ȝerd, or an herber.

†**2.** A garden of herbs or flowers; a flower-garden; a flower-bed. Forms: 3–5 **erber(e,** 3–6 **herber(e,** 5 **eerbir, erbare,** 6 **herbour.** *Obs.*

c **1300** *K. Alis.* 331 Herbes he tok in an herber, And stamped heom in a morter. **1330** R. BRUNNE *Chron.* 280 Pride in pes es nettille in herbere, þe rose is myghtles, þer nettille spredis ouer fer. *c* **1430** *Hymns to Virg.* (1867) 6 Marie þat art flour of alle, As roose in eerbir so reed! *c* **1435** *Torr. Portugal* 1968 Uppon the low..An erber wrought with mannus hond, With herbis that were good. *c* **1482** CAXTON *Vocab. Eng. & Fr.* in *Promp. Parv.* 141 Richer the carter shall lede dong on my land whan it shall be ered, and on my herber [F. *courtil* = cottage garden] whan it shall be doluen. **1500** *Ortus Vocab.* in *Promp. Parv.* 141 *Herbarium*, an herber, *vbi crescunt herbe, vel vbi habundant*, or a gardyn. **1548** HALL *Chron. Hen. VIII.* an. 14 in *P.P.* 141 A quadrant stage where on was an herber full of roses, lyllies, and all other flowers curiously wrought. **1578** LYTE *Dodoens* 656 She threw herself into a bed or herbour of prickley Roses.

†**3.** A garden of fruit-trees, an orchard. [Cf. *orchard*:—OE. *wyrt-ȝeard*, i.e. herb-yard, and F. *verger*:—L. *viridārium*, i.e. a 'green.' Orchards were usually formed on grass.] Forms: 4–6 **erber(e, herber(e,** 5 **erbor(e,** 6 **arbre, arber, arbour.**

1377 LANGL. *P. Pl.* B. XVI. 15 Þat frute..groweth in a gardyne, þat god made hymseluen..Herte hatte þe herber [*v.r.* erber] þat it in groweth. *a* **1400** *Thom. Erceldoune* (1875) 177 Scho lede hym intill a faire herbere [*v.r.* erbore] Whare frute was growand gret plentee; Pere and appill, both ryppe þay were, The date, and als the damasee, etc. **1413** LYDG. *Pylgr. Sowle* (1859) 63 He saw syttynge vnder an ympe [=

sapling] in an herber, a wonder fayre damosel. ? *c* **1475** *Sqr. lowe Degre* 28 In the garden, as i wene, Was an arber fayre and grene, And in the arber was a tre. **1580** BARET *Alv.* A 520 An arbour, *Arboretum, Vne parc d'arbres, bocage.*

†**4.** Trees or shrubs, such as the vine, trained on framework or trellis-work; espaliers. Forms: 5 **erber,** 6 **herber, -or, -our,** 6–7 **harbour, arbour.**

1428 in Heath *Grocers' Comp.* (1869) 6 For costages of the gardyne 4*s.* 8*d.* and..for making of the Erber, carvyng newe railing off alle the vynes and gardyne £8 8*s.* 7*d.* **1554** *Acc. Edw. VI.* in *Trevelyan Papers* II. 15 Sir John Wulfe.. deviser of the Kinges herbors & plantes of grafts. **1563** HYLL *Arte Garden.* (1593) 13 The herbers either straight running vp, or else vaulted or close ouer the head, like to the vine herbers now a daies made. **1648** GAGE *West Ind.* xviii. (1655) 113 Excellent grapes..not planted like vine-yards, but growing up in harbours.

5. A bower or shady retreat, of which the sides and roof are formed by trees and shrubs closely planted or intertwined, or of lattice-work covered with climbing shrubs and plants, as ivy, vine, etc. Forms: 4–6 **erber(e, herber(e,** 5 **herbier, erbor, arbre,** 5–6 **arber,** 6 **herbor, harber, herbour, arboure** (all *obs.*), 6– **arbour, arbor.**

(The original characteristic of the 'arbour' seems to have been the floor and 'benches' of herbage; in the modern idea (since 16th c. at least) the leafy covering is the prominent feature.)

c **1350** *Will. Palerne* 1768 In þe gardyn to pleie, To bi-hold þe estres & þe herberes so faire. *c* **1385** CHAUCER *L.G.W.* 203 A litel herber[*Bodley MS.* erber] that I have, That benched was on turves fressh ygrave. *c* **1400** *Flower & Leaf* 64 And shapin was this herber, rofe and all, As is a pretty parlour. [See the full description of this *herber*, with its close-shaven turf, thick hedge, etc.] **1460** *Pol. Rel. & L. Poems* (1866) 56 In an herbier made ful plesantly Thei restid them. **1528** MORE *Heresyes* II. Wks. 177/2 We walked into a gardine. And..sitting in an arber beganne to go forth in our matter. [Cf. 247/1 Sitting down in an herber.] **1549** THOMAS *Hist. Italie* 6 Vnder the fresshe herbers, hedges and boowes.. they triumph in as muche pleasure as maie be imagined. **1575** LANEHAM *Let.* (1871) 2 A goodlie Chase..beautified with manie delectabl, fresh and vmbragioous Boow[r]z, Arberz, Seatz, and walks. **1580** LYLY *Euphues* (Arb.) 361 Sitting in an herbor. **1563** HYLL *Arte Garden.* (1593) 161 You may make a couer ouer them like to an harbour. **1597** MORLEY *Introd. Music* 70 Go and sit in yonder shadie Arbor. **1598** FLORIO, *Arborata*, an arbor or bowre of boughs or trees. **1684** BUNYAN *Pilgr.* II. 183 An Arbor, warm, and promising much Refreshing to the Pilgrims; for it was finely wrought above-head, beautified with Greens. **1817** COLERIDGE *Sib. Leaves* (1862) 224 Those hollies of themselves a shape As of an arbour took, A close, round arbour. **1823** J. THACHER *Jrnl. Amer. Revol.* 244 We erected a large arbor, with the boughs of trees. **1850** LAYARD *Nineveh* viii. 178 Upon carpets spread under an arbour, formed by a wide-spreading vine. **1873** BROWNING *Red Cott. N.-Cap* 251 Pulled down earthward, pegged and picketed, By topiary contrivance, till the tree Became an arbour.

†**b.** A shaded or covered alley or walk. *Obs.*

1573 *Richmond. Wills & Inv.* (1853) 234, I geve my soule unto Almightie God, and my bodye to be buried within ye arbour on the north side off the church of Richmonde. **1580** BARET *Alv.* A 521 An open galerie, arbour or walke, *Paradromis. Ibid.* A 523 A worke made of trees, bushes, bryers, or hearbes, with places to sitte and walke in for pleasure, as they now make arboures, *Topiarium.* **1590** GREENE *Arcadia* (1616) 17 The mountaine tops shall be thy morning walke, and the shadie Vallies thy euenings Arbour. **1667** MILTON *P.L.* IV. 626 Yon flourie Arbors, yonder Allies green, Our walks at noon, with branches overgrown. **1712** BUDGELL *Spect.* No. 425 ¶1 A Wilderness parted into Variety of Allies and Arbours.

6. *Comb.*, as *arbour-maker*, *-wise.*

1647 HAWARD *Crown Rev.* 27 Arbor-maker, and planter of Trees. **1548** HALL *Chron. Hen. VIII.* an. 12 (1809) 611 On the Mountaigne [artificial] was a place Harber wise, where the Herauldes were. *a* **1687** GOOKIN *Mass. Hist. Coll.* I. 149 Wigwams, built with small poles fixed in the ground, bent and fastened together with barks of trees, oval or arbour-wise on the top.

arboured ('ɑːbəd), *ppl. a.* [f. prec. + -ED².] **a.** Placed in or as in an arbour, arched over as by an arbour; embowered. **b.** Furnished with arbours.

1598 SYLVESTER *Du Bartas, Captaines* 343 Whose horrid clifts below are hollowèd And with two Forrests arbour'd over head. **1610** G. FLETCHER *Christ's Vict.* II. xlv, All the room about was arboured. **1859** TENNENT *Ceylon* II. VII. ii. 123 Arboured in the shades of these luxuriant groves, nestle the white cottages of the natives.

arbre, obs. form of ARBOR.

arbuscle ('ɑːbʌs(ə)l). [ad. L. *arbuscula*, dim. of *arbor, arbos* tree; also, a tuft of feathers.]

a. A dwarf tree; a shrub of tree-like growth. **b.** A tuft of feathery cilia.

1657 in *Phys. Dict.* **1831** MACGILLIVRAY tr. *Richard's Bot.* 49 Arbuscles, when they are branched at their base and carry buds, e.g. the Hasel and Lilac. **1860** *Encycl. Brit.* XXI. 996/1 Medusidæ..their rims ornamented with fringes, furbelows, and arbuscles of such delicacy.

arbuscular (ɑː'bʌskjʊlə(r)), *a.* [f. L. *arbuscula* + -AR.] Of or pertaining to arbuscles; tufted.

1847 in CRAIG. **1860** *Encycl. Brit.* XXI. 983/2 Arbuscular tentacula.

†**ar'bust,** *sb. Obs. rare*⁻¹. [a. F. *arbuste*, ad. L. *arbust-um* a plantation, in *pl.* trees, boughs; in med.L. = *arbuscula*; f. *arbos, arbor* tree.] A dwarf tree, a shrub.

1658 EVELYN *Fr. Gard.* (1675) 39 Arbusts, and all shrubs.

†**ar'bust,** *v. Obs. rare*⁻¹. [a. F. *arbuste-r*, ad. L. *arbustā-re.*] To plant with trees; hence, **arbusted** *ppl. a.*

1623 in COCKERAM. **1647** R. BARON *Cyprian Acad.* 54 What pleasures poets fame of after death, In the Elizean arbusted grooves.

†**ar'bustal,** *a. Obs. rare*⁻¹. [f. L. *arbust-um* (see ARBUST) + -AL¹.] Of or pertaining to shrubs.

1657 [See ARBORAL].

†**ar'bustive,** *a. Obs.* [a. F. *arbustif, -ive* (Cotgr.), ad. L. *arbustīvus* planted with trees: see -IVE.] **a.** 'Of or belonging to shrubs or young trees, shrubby.' Blount *Glossogr.* 1656. **b.** Trained or bound to a tree.

1745 tr. *Columella's Bk. Trees* iv, This kind of vines we call arbustive or arbour-vines.

arbute ('ɑːbjuːt). *arch.* or *poet.* Also 6–7 **arbut.** [ad. L. *arbutus.*] = ARBUTUS. Also *attrib.*

1551 TURNER *Herbal* (1568) 41 The fruite of the arbut tree. **1697** DRYDEN *Virg. Georg.* II. 96 The thin-leav'd Arbute Hazle Graffs receives. **1846** LONGF. *To a Child* iii, In falling, clutched the wild arbute. **1866** CONINGTON *Æneid* XI. 368 Weave..Of oaken branch and arbute spray A funeral bier.

arbutean (ɑː'bjuːtiːən), *a. rare*⁻¹. [f. L. *arbute-us* + -AN.] Of arbutus; made of arbutus wood.

a **1706** EVELYN *Virgil* (T.) Arbutean harrows.

‖**arbutus.** [L. *arbutus* or *arbitus.*]

1. ('ɑːbjuːtəs). A genus of evergreen shrubs and trees (N.O. *Ericaceæ*). The name belonged originally, and is still usually applied, to the species *Arbutus Unedo*, or Strawberry Tree, a native of the south of Europe, long established in the south-west of Ireland, and commonly cultivated for ornamental purposes.

1551 TURNER *Herbal* (1568) 41 *Arbutus* may be called in englishe *strawberry tree.* **1672** PETTY *Pol. Anat.* 374 That part of Kerry..where the arbutus groweth in great quantity. **1752** MRS. DELANY *Autobiog.* III. 121 The arbutus bears fruit and flowers at the same time. **1877** MRS. H. KING *Ugo Bassi* VI, Brushwood of myrtle, heath, and arbutus, With here and there a solitary pine.

2. *U.S.* (ɑː'bjuːtəs). Applied to a North American ericaceous plant, *Epigæa repens*, called also *trailing arbutus*, *ground laurel*, and MAYFLOWER, and prized as a harbinger of spring.

1785 H. MARSHALL *Arbustrum Amer.* 42 *Epigæa repens.* Trailing arbutus. This grows naturally upon northern hills, or mountains, with trailing shrubby stalks. **1869** J. G. FULLER *Uncle John's Flower Gatherers* 14 It comes forth with softly perfumed garments, and we call it Trailing Arbutus. **1888** WHITTIER *Writ.* II. 35 The trailing arbutus, or mayflower, grows abundantly in the vicinity of Plymouth, and was the first flower that greeted the Pilgrims after their fearful winter.

arbytall, obs. form of ORBITAL.

arbyter, -tress, obs. forms of ARBITER, etc.

arc (ɑːk), *sb.* Forms: 4–7 **ark(e,** 6 **arcke,** 6– **arc.** [a. OF. *arc*:—L. *arcum* (nom. *arcus*) bow, arch, curve.]

1. a. Part of the circumference of a circle or other curve.

1570 BILLINGSLEY *Euclid* III. Introd., Right lines subtended to arkes in circles. **1750** *Phil. Trans.* XLVII. 64 Any arc described by the revolving body. **1871** C. DAVIES *Metric Syst.* I. 18 The French Government..measured a degree of the arc of a meridian on the earth's surface.

b. *transf.* or *fig.*

1643 MILTON *Divorce* vi. (1851) 33 One of the highest arks that human contemplation circling upwards, can make. **1805** SOUTHEY *Madoc in Azt.* VII, The Britons shrunk Beyond its arc of motion. **1871** TYNDALL *Fragm. Sc.* II. vii. 97 The circle of human nature, then, is not complete without the arc of the emotions.

2. *spec.* in *Astr.* The part of a circle which a heavenly body appears to pass through above (*diurnal arc*) or below (*nocturnal arc*) the horizon. The earliest use in Eng. Also *fig.*

c **1386** CHAUCER *Merch. T.* 551 Parfourmed hath the sonne his ark diourne. *c* **1391** —— *Astrol.* II. vii, Tak ther thin ark of the day. The remenant of the bordure vnder the Orisonte is the ark of the nyht. *c* **1430** LYDG. *Bochas* I. xx. (1554) 39 a, As faire as Phebus shineth in his arke. *c* **1590** MARLOWE *2nd Pt. Tamburl.* III. ii, The stars fix'd in the Southern arc. **1787** BONNYCASTLE *Astron.* 428 Nocturnal arc is that space of the heavens which the sun apparently describes from the time of his setting to the time of his rising. **1878** GEO. ELIOT *Coll. Breakf.* 572 Say, the small arc of Being we call man Is near its mergence.

3. A band or belt contained between parallel curves; anything presenting this form optically or superficially, e.g. the rainbow (F. *arc-en-ciel*), the brass arc of a quadrant on which the degrees are marked off, etc.

1642 H. MORE *Song of Soul* II. I. III. xx, The higher causes of that coloured Ark. **1768** WALES in *Phil. Trans.* LX. 120 The quadrant..we found much tarnished, especially the arc. **1831** BREWSTER *Newton* (1855) I. vii. 161 He describes the arcs and circles of colours.

†**4.** An arch. (Cf. Fr. *arc de triomphe.*) *Obs.*

1563 SHUTE *Archit.* E iij a, The arke triumphant of Seuerus. **1671** MILTON *P.R.* IV. 37 Statues and Trophees, and Triumphal Arcs. **1731** POPE *Mor. Ess.* II. 30 Turn arcs of triumph to a garden-gate.

5. *Electr.* The luminous bridge formed between two carbon poles, when they are separated by a small air space, and a powerful current of electricity is sent through them. Often *attrib.*

1821 SIR H. DAVY in *Phil. Trans.* 427 The poles were connected by charcoal so as to make an arc, or column of electrical light. **1894** *Phil. Trans. R. Soc.* A. CLXXXV. 983 The photographic arc spectrum of electrolytic iron. **1900** *Jrnl. Soc. Arts* XLVIII. 820/1 The multiple arc furnace.. has lately become much used, because it enables the area of arc heating to be greatly extended. **1935** *Discovery* Sept. 260/2 The appearance in the arc-spectrum of the 'raies ultimes' of copper at λ 3274 and λ 3248 completed the identification of the pigment. **1940** *Chambers's Techn. Dict.* 47/1 *Arc furnace*, an electric furnace in which the heat is produced by means of an electric arc between carbon electrodes, or between a carbon electrode and the furnace charge. *Ibid.* 47/2 *Arc spectrum*, a spectrum originating in the non-ionised atoms of an element; usually capable of being excited by the application of a comparatively low stimulus, such as the electric arc. **1946** *Nature* 2 Nov. 631/1 Faulty power lines which are maintained in operation through the use of arc-suppression coils. **1956** *Ibid.* 28 Jan. 157/2 Resistance-type (calrod) heaters embedded in the cast-copper charge oven and arc-chamber support block.

6. *transf.* in *Phys.* Circuit, round.

1855 H. SPENCER *Psychol.* (1872) I. I. ii. 42 The nervous arc..consists of the afferent nerve..the ganglion corpuscle to which its central extremity runs, and the efferent nerve thence issuing.

arc (ɑːk), *v.* Inflected **arced, arcing** (with *c* pronounced k). [f. ARC *sb.*] **1.** *intr.* To form an electric arc. So **'arcing** *vbl. sb.*

1893 *Westm. Gaz.* 20 June 6/3 In 'arcing' or jumping from one conductor to another the current damaged the [gas] pipes. **1905** *Daily Chron.* 19 Apr. 6/5 The contact or arcing between the telephone cables and the conductor rail. **1908** *Installation News* II. 19/2 The fuse is provided with a phosphor bronze arcing tongue. **1910** *Ibid.* IV. 63/1 Fires.. due to the melting of soft compo gas-pipe, by arcing. **1943** *Gloss. Terms Electr. Engineering* (*B.S.I.*) 59 *Arcing contacts*, contacts which open after and close before the main contacts to protect the latter from injury by an arc.

2. To move or fly in an arc.

1954 J. CHRISTOPHER *22nd Cent.* 116 Bouncing round in three complete circuits before arcing down to land. **1961** *Guardian* 4 May 4/2 The rocket arc-ed majestically into the cloudless sky.

arc, obs. form of ARK.

‖**arcabucero** (arkabu'θero). [Sp.] = HARQUEBUSIER.

1858 LONGF. *Miles Stand.* I. 28 Fired point-blank at my heart by a Spanish arcabucero.

arcabuzier, obs. form of HARQUEBUSIER.

arcade (ɑː'keɪd), *sb.* [a. Fr. *arcade* 'an arch or half a circle' Cotgr., ? ad. It. *arcata* 'an arch of a bridge, a bending' Florio, med.L. *arcāta* an arch, f. L. *arc-us*, It. *arc-o* bow, arch: see -ADE.]

†**1.** A vaulted place, open at one or both sides; an arched opening or recess in a wall. *Obs.*

[**1644** EVELYN *Diary (in Italy)* 8 Nov., In the arcado.. stand 24 statues of great price.] **1762** H. WALPOLE *Vertue's Anecd. Paint.* (1786) I. 187 The application of loggias, arcades, terrasses and flights of steps, at different stages of a building. **1782** WARTON *Hist. Kiddington* 6 On the opposite side is a small arcade or receptacle for holy water. **1823** NICHOLSON *Pract. Build.* 580 *Arcade*, an aperture in a wall with an arched head; also, a range of apertures with arched heads. [See 3.]

2. 'A continued arch' (J.); a passage arched over; a walk formed by a succession of arches having a common axis, and supported on columns or shafts. Also applied to an avenue similarly arched over by trees or shrubs; and extended to any covered avenue, esp. one with rows of shops or stalls on one or both sides.

1731 POPE *Mor. Ess.* II. 35 Shall call the winds thro' long Arcades to roar. **1815** WORDSW. *Wh. Doe* IV. 45 And shades Of trellis-work in long arcades. **1829** T. ALLEN *Antiq. Lond.* IV. 302 A passage, with a range of shops on each side, called Burlington Arcade, which..is one of the most fashionable promenades. **1849** RUSKIN *Sev. Lamps* ii. §15 Pictured landscapes at the extremities of alleys and arcades. **1862** THACKERAY *Four Georges* iii. 142 A garden, with trim lawns, green arcades and vistas of classic statues.

3. *Arch.* A series of arches on the same plane: 'a series of arches, either open or closed with masonry, supported by columns or piers.' Parker *Gloss. Arch.* 'In mediæval architecture, an ornamental dressing to a wall, consisting of colonnettes supporting moulded arches.' Gwilt. (= F. *arcature.*)

1795–1807 J. CARTER *Anc. Archit. Eng.* I. 20 Arcade on the third story of the keep of Rochester castle..In the third story the wall is cut through by four magnificent arches. **1823** [See 1]. **1830** R. STUART, *Dict. Arch., Arcade*, a series of apertures or recesses with arched ceilings or soffets. The use of this word is very vague and indefinite. **1849** RUSKIN *Sev. Lamps* v. §12 In the uppermost arcade..the arches, the same in number as those below, are narrower than any of the façade. **1861** PARKER *Goth. Archit.* (1874) I. iii. 67 The small Arcades..are frequently used as decorations of the walls.

4. Special Comb. **arcade game**, a (mechanical or electronic) game of a type orig. popularized in amusement arcades.

[**1977** *Washington Post* 10 June (District Weekly) 10/1 Since Gunchers is located on Georgetown's night life strip, we weren't sure that the atmosphere would be suitable for children, but its pin ball machines and penny arcade games presented party possibilities.] **1978** *Washington Post* 21 July (Weekend Suppl.) 7/3 Another ten cents will animate any number of 50-year-old arcade games of shooting, hitting or shaking. **1983** *Listener* 20 Oct. 37/4 Laser Vision's interactive feature has been snapped up by the cut-throat arcade games industry in the USA. **1984** *Personal Software* Winter 44/1 The adventures of Pat the Postman is a twenty screen arcade game for the 48K ZX Spectrum.

arcade (ɑː'keɪd), *v.* [f. prec. sb.] To furnish with, or form into, an arcade. Hence **arcaded** *ppl. a.*

1805 W. TAYLOR in *Ann. Rev.* III. 61 A long arcaded court. **1860** *All Y. Round* No. 46. 457 In Stamboul, as in London, a bazaar means an arcaded covered walk. **1861** A. B. HOPE *Eng. Cathedr. 19th C.* vi. 221 That expanse [of wall] may be arcaded, and if the arcading-shafts are of coloured materials, so much the better.

‖**Arcades ambo** ('ɑːkədiːz 'æmbəʊ). [L. phr. (Virgil *Ecl.* VII. 4), lit. 'both Arcadians', i.e. both pastoral poets or musicians.] Two persons of the same tastes, profession, or character (often derogatory).

1821 BYRON *Juan* IV. xciii. p. 117 Each pull'd different ways with many an oath, 'Arcades ambo', *id est*—black-guards both. **1882** T. MOZLEY *Remin.* lxxxiii. II. 92 [Denison and Neate] were *Arcades ambo.* They could talk and chaff about anything... They were both good scholars, rather above the Oxford run. **1888** RIDER HAGGARD *Colonel Quaritch* xvii, 'Well, I'm a lawyer too, and a pretty sharp one —*arcades ambo*,' said Johnnie with a coarse laugh.

Arcadian (ɑː'keɪdɪən), *a.*[1] and *sb.* [f. L. *Arcadi-us* (f. Gr. Ἀρκαδία a mountainous district in the Peloponnesus, taken as the ideal region of rural contentment) + -AN.] **A.** *adj.* Belonging to Arcadia; ideally rural or rustic. **B.** *sb.* An ideal rustic.

1590 T. WATSON *Melib.* 49 Let Arcadians altogether sing a woefull song. **1667** MILTON *P.L.* XI. 132 Charm'd with Arcadian pipe. **1759** GOLDSM. *Polite Learn.* iv, The wits even of Rome are united into a rural group of nymphs and swains under the appellation of modern Arcadians. **1829** SOUTHEY *Ol. Newman* VI. Wks. X. 317 Peopling some Arcadian solitude With human angels.

ar'cadian, *a.*[2] [f. ARCADE + -IAN.] Of, pertaining to, or furnished with arcades.

1870 DISRAELI *Lothair* lxix. 369 An arcadian square flooded with light. **1880** *Daily News* 17 Apr. 2/3 Scheme for extending Arcadian London.

ar'cadianism. [f. ARCADIAN *a.*[1] + -ISM.] Ideally simple rusticity, pastoral simplicity.

1824 D'ISRAELI *Cur. Lit.* (1866) 412/1 That Shenstone not only 'affected that arcadianism.' **1859** MASSON *Brit. Novelists* iv. 216 A spirit of lyrical pathos, and of poetical Arcadianism.

ar'cadianly, *adv.* [f. as prec. + -LY[2].] In accordance with Arcadian manners or ideas.

1882 FROUDE *Carlyle* II. vii. 152 If Arcadianly given, he might fancy the yellow buttercups were asphodel.

arcading (ɑː'keɪdɪŋ), *vbl. sb.* [f. ARCADE *v.* + -ING[1].] *concr.* Architectural ornament consisting of arcades (see ARCADE *sb.* 3).

1849 FREEMAN *Archit.* 190 Towers..enriched with arcading. **1861** A. B. HOPE *Eng. Cathedr. 19th C.* vi. 221 The back spaces of the arcading may be diapered in relief, tinted or stencilled.

arcado, obs. form of ARCADE: see -ADO.

Arcady ('ɑːkədɪ). *poet.* [ad. L. *Arcadia*: see ARCADIAN.]

1590 T. WATSON *Melib.* 363 Diana matchlesse Queene of Arcadie. **1850** TENNYSON *In Mem.* xxiii. 24 To many a flute of Arcady.

arcanal (ɑː'keɪnəl), *a.* [f. L. *arcān-us* (see next) + -AL[1].] Of arcane character; mysterious, dim.

c **1828** SOUTHEY *Life & Corr.* (1850) V. 366 Sunk in arcanal ages and in night.

arcane (ɑː'keɪn), *a.* Also 6 **archane**. [ad. L. *arcānus*, f. *arcē-re* to shut up, *arca* chest; cf. F. *arcane*.] Hidden, concealed, secret.

1547 BOORDE *Brev. Health* Pref. 2 The eximiouse and Archane science of physicke. **1595** *Locrine* v. iv. 187 Have I bewrayed thy arcane secrecy? **1678** CUDWORTH *Intell. Syst.* Pref., To Reveal the Arcane Mysteries of Atheism. **1876** E. GOSSE in *Academy* 9 Dec. 557 Walking in the arcane world of wonder.

arcanist (ɑː'keɪnɪst). [f. ARCAN(UM + -IST.] Used *spec.* of a person who has knowledge of a secret process of manufacture, esp. of the manufacture of porcelain.

1905 R. L. HOBSON *Catal. Coll. Eng. Porc. Brit. Mus.* p. xv, The royal houses vied with each other in securing the services of the arcanists from Meissen. **1939** *Burlington Mag.* Oct. 172/2 The death of the arcanist and manager.. brought to an end..the first period of the [porcelain] factory. **1959** *Times* 10 Oct. 9/3 We also had our wandering arcanists.

arcanite, synonym of APHTHITALITE.

†**ar'canna, ar'canne.** *Obs.* [a. F. *arcanne* 'rudle, red chaulke, red oaker,' Cotgr., prob. ad. **arcanna*, variant of It. *alcanna* or Sp. *alcana*: see ALCANNA, ALKANET.] A kind of red chalk used by carpenters for marking timber.

1753 CHAMBERS *Cycl. Supp.* **1880** *Syd. Soc. Lex.*, *Arcanne*, a synonym of red ochre.

‖**arcanum** (ɑː'keɪnəm). Usually in pl. **arcana** (ɑː'keɪnə). [L., neut. of adj. *arcānus* (see ARCANE) used subst. In 17–18th c. the pl. form *arcana* was occas. treated as sing. with pl. *arcanas*.]

1. A hidden thing; a mystery, a profound secret.

1599 SANDYS *Europ. Spec.* (1632) 238 The Arcana of those their ineffable crossings and convertings. **1626** D'EWES in Ellis *Orig. Lett.* I. 322 III. 218 Because..the anointing of his naked shoulders, armes, hands, and head, were arcana. **1646** J. HALL *Horæ Vac.* 19 It is an arcanum of his Empire to conceale from us the date of our dayes. **1772** WATSON in *Phil. Trans.* LXIII. 14 Having..revealed the principal arcana in the manufacture of isinglass. **1864** BURTON *Scot. Abr.* I. iii. 133 The mysterious arcana of political intrigue.

2. One of the supposed great secrets of nature which the alchemists aimed at discovering; *hence*, a marvellous remedy, an elixir.

1646 SIR T. BROWNE *Pseud. Ep.* 135 The Philosophers stone, potable gold, or any of those Arcana's. **1689** MOYLE *Sea Chyrurg.* II. xxi. 76 The Quintessenses of Cloves and Colocynthis are great arcanums as to the Tooth-ach. **1796** BURKE *Regic. Peace* iii. Wks. VIII. 343 The infallible arcanum for that purpose. **1821** SCOTT *Kenilw.* xxii. (1853) 222 The pursuit of the grand arcanum.

‖**arc-boutant** (ˌarbu'tɑ̃). *Arch.* [Fr.] An arched or 'flying' buttress, 'whose object is to counteract the thrust of the main vault of the edifice' (Gwilt).

1731 in BAILEY. **1767** DUCAREL *Anglo-Norm. Antiq.* 27 The walls of this Church are cased on the outside by thirty-two arc-boutants or buttresses. **1823** RUTTER *Fonthill* 9 The ceiling is divided..by a broad arc-boutant in the middle.

†**'arceate**, *v. Obs. rare*$^{-1}$. [improper f. L. *arcēre* to keep off + -ATE[3].] To keep off, prevent.

1657 TOMLINSON *Renou's Disp.* 511 It arceates putretude.

arce-bishop, -deacon, obs. ff. ARCH-.

arcel, arcenal, obs. ff. ARCHIL, ARSENAL.

†**arceter, -tour, arcister.** *Obs.*$^{-0}$ [app. f. med.L. *arcista* for *artista* (cf. OF. *arcien*, *artien*), with Eng. ending *-er*, as if *artist-er*, *arcister*, *arceter*: cf. *barrist-er*, and *ancestor*, *ancetor*.] One skilled in the arts; a master of arts who has passed on to the study of philosophy.

1440 *Promp. Parv.*, Arceter, or he þat lernethe or techethe arte, *artista*. *c* **1460** *Gloss.* in Wright's *Voc.* 262 *Hic dioleticus* [*dialecticus*], *hic arcista* [*artista*], a arcister. **1530** PALSGR. 195/1 Arcetour, *arcien*.

arch (ɑːtʃ), *sb.* Also 4–6 **arche**. [a. OF. *arche*:—L. *arca* chest, coffer; also, through some confusion, used in OF. for *arc*:—L. *arc-um* bow (see ARC *sb.*).]

I. = L. *arcus*.

†**1.** Any part of a curve; = ARC *sb.* 1, 2. *Obs.*

c **1391** CHAUCER *Astrol.* II. vii. 27 The arch of the day.. from the sonne arisyng til hit go to reste. **1551** RECORDE *Pathw. Knowl.* I. Def., The compassed line..is called an arche lyne, or a bowe lyne. *Ibid.* I. iv, Draw an arch of a circle. **1646** SIR T. BROWNE *Pseud. Ep.* 62 An Arch of the Horizon. **1677** HALES *Prim. Orig. Man.* I. vi. 119 The convex Superficies of the highest Arch of being. **1790** WILDBORE in *Phil. Trans.* LXXX. 544 The arch-line of this sector. **1831** BREWSTER *Optics* x. 93 The arch of vibration was more rapidly diminished in the sun's light.

2. A curved structure of firm material, either capable of bearing weight or merely ornamental.

1387 TREVISA *Higden* I. 215 An arche of marbel..þe arche of Augustus Cesar his victories. *c* **1425** WYNTOUN *Cron.* VIII. xxiii. 25 Ane Arche of fayre werk and of fyne. **1551** RECORDE *Pathw. Knowl.* I. x, The arche of a brydge or of a house or window. *a* **1637** B. JONSON *To Sir E. Sackville* (R.) 'Tis the last keystone That makes the arch. **1751** J. BROWN *Shaftesb. Charac.* 74 The very key-stone of this visionary arch, which he hath..thrown over the depths of error. **1818** BYRON *Ch. Har.* IV. xcii., For *this* the conqueror rears The arch of triumph!

3. a. *transf.* Anything having the form of the curves or structures, described in the prec. 1 and 2.

c **1590** GREENE *Fr. Bacon* ix. 125 The circled arches of thy brows. **1676** MOXON *Print Lett.* 7 The Arches upon the feet of Letter A is the Footing of that Letter. **1702** ADDISON *Medals* ii. 112 His head is encompassed with..an arch of glory. **1854** OWEN in *Orr's Circ. Sc.* I. 168 The neural arch is formed by a pair of bones, called 'neurapophyses'. **1881** RAYMOND *Mining Gloss.*, *Arch*..1. A portion of a lode left standing when the rest is extracted. 2. The roof of a reverberatory furnace.

b. *esp.* The rainbow.

1610 SHAKS. *Temp.* IV. i. 71 The Queene o'th Skie, Whose watry Arch, and messenger, am I. **1728** THOMSON *Spring* 215 Behold th' amusive arch before him fly. **1851** RUSKIN *Stones Ven.* I. x. 123 God's arch, the arch of the rainbow.

4. a. Curvature in the shape of an arch.

1855 TENNYSON *Maud* I. xvi, The delicate Arab arch of her feet. **1880** C. & F. DARWIN *Movem. Plants* 89 The fact of so many organs..being all arched whilst they break through the ground, shows..the importance of the arch to seedling plants.

b. *Anat.* One of the arches formed by the tarsal and metatarsal bones of the foot; ***fallen arch***, one that has flattened. Also *attrib.*, as ***arch support***, a device worn in the shoe to provide support for the arch of the foot.

1858 G. M. HUMPHRY *Treat. Human Skeleton* 492 The plantar arch. The foot is..made in the shape of an arch. The summit of the arch is at the top of the astragalus. The hinder limb of the arch is formed..by the os calcis; and the anterior limb is formed by the other tarsal and the metatarsal bones. *Ibid.* 495 The arch yields..at the joint between the astragalus and the navicular bone, the person becomes 'flat-footed'. *Ibid.*, The well-formed foot presents other arches besides the one chief plantar arch which we have been considering. **1875** *St. George's Hosp. Rep.* VII. 211 Cases in which the tarsal arch has given way, but has not been obliterated. **1939** M. L. SPRING RICE *Working-Class Wives* v. 109 She has had varicose veins..for which the doctor has advised elastic stockings and arch supports. **1945** B. MACDONALD *Egg & I* (1947) i. 16 She toed out and had trouble with her arches.

5. An arched roof, a vault; *fig.* the heavens.

1606 SHAKS. *Tr. & Cr.* III. iii. 120 Who, like an arch, reuerb'rate The voyce againe. **1611** —— *Cymb.* I. vi. 33 Hath Nature giuen them eyes To see this vaulted Arch? **1738** GLOVER *Leonidas* I. 149 The arch of heav'n resounded. **1813** SCOTT *Trierm.* III. xvii, While the deep arch with sullen roar Return'd their surly jar.

6. Court of Arches, or briefly *Arches*: the ecclesiastical court of appeal for the province of Canterbury, formerly held at the church of St. Mary-le-Bow (or 'of the Arches'), so named from the arches that supported its steeple.

1297 R. GLOUC. 415 Seyn Mary chyrche ofþe arches. **1393** LANGL. *P. Pl.* C. III. 61 Vokettus of þe Arches. **1553–87** FOXE *A. & M.* III. 140 Cited to appear in the Arches at Bow Church. **1768** BLACKSTONE *Comm.* III. 64 The court of arches..whereof the judge is called the dean of the arches. **1863** COX *Inst. Eng. Govt.* II. xi. 569.

7. Chiefly *pl.* Collectors' name for certain species of moths: see quots.

1766 M. HARRIS *Aurelian* 64 *Red Arches.* This Moth is generally taken by beating the boughs of the oak..the latter end of June. **1832** J. RENNIE *Butterfl. & Moths* 169 The Rufous Arch (*S*[*emasia*] *rufana*, Stephens). **1869** E. NEWMAN *Brit. Moths* 407 The Gray Arches (*Aplecta nebulosa*)... The costal margin of the fore wings is very slightly arched, the margin very slightly scalloped. *Ibid.* 408 The Silvery Arches (*Aplecta tincta*)... The fore wings are slightly arched beyond the middle of the costal margin. **1921** *Conquest* Sept. 496/2 The Dark Arches (*Xylophasia monoglypha*).

II. (= L. *arca*, OF. *airche, arche.*) Archives.

1600 HOLLAND *Livy* IX. xlvi. 349 The civile law..was laid up..in their Arches [*penetralibus*]. **1651** W. G. *Cowel's Inst.* 179 Enrolled in the Arches and Treasuries of the Court.

III. *Attrib.* and *Comb.*, **arch-board**, 'the part of the stern over the counter, immediately under the knuckles of the stern-timbers' (Adm. Smyth); **arch-brick, arch-stone**, a wedge-shaped brick or stone used in the construction of arches; **arch-brow**, an arched brow; **arch-buttress** = ARC-BOUTANT; **arch-head**, a curved head or terminal piece; **arch-roof**, a vaulted roof; **archways** = ARCHWISE; **arch-work**, structure consisting of arches. Also ***arch-like***, ***-moulding***, ***-order***; and ARCHWAY, -WISE, q.v.

1883 J. KELLY in *Harper's Mag.* Aug. 449/2 A fan-tail over-hang, which ends in a moulded arch-board. **1742** RICHARDSON *Pamela* IV. 241 Your Ladyship's fine Arch-Brow. **1760** FITZGERALD in *Phil. Trans.* LI. 827 The arch-head of the lever. **1879** G. SCOTT *Lect. Archit.* I. 127 The arch mouldings are filled with the most exquisite foliage. *Ibid.* 284 The tracery of a window is always viewed as an arch-order. **1594** T. B. *La Primaud. Fr. Acad.* II. 150 A Vault or arch-roofe set vpon three pillers. **1828** HUTTON *Course Math.* II. 138 The voussoirs or arch-stones..have their faces always perpendicular to the respective points of the curve upon which they stand. **1799** J. ROBERTSON *Agric. Perth* 272 The sods..should be laid down archways. **1610** HOLLAND *Camden's Brit.* I. 333 A verie goodly stone bridge of arch-worke. **1742** YOUNG *Nt. Th.* VII. 1234 An archlike strong foundation.

arch (ɑːtʃ), *v.*[1] [a. OF. *arche-r* (13th c.); cf. mod.F. *arquer*.]

1. To furnish with an arch or vault.

c **1400** *Destr. Troy* v. 1577 By the sydes..the strete was archet full abilly. **1463** *Bury Wills* (1850) 37 That the Rysbygate [be]..archyd and enbatelyd. **1530** PALSGR. 435/2, I arche a buyldyng with arches, *Je arche.* **1646** SIR T. BROWNE *Pseud. Ep.* 72 Dinocrates began to Arche the Temple..with Load stone. **1695** BLACKMORE *Pr. Arth.* IV. 84 And Arch'd the Chambers of the Vaulted Sky. **1881** *Daily News* 28 Sept. 5/4 The gateway..was arched with black.

2. To form into an arch or vault, to curve. **a.** *trans.* and *refl.*

1625 BACON *Gardens, Ess.* (Arb.) 561 Fine Deuices, of Arching Water without Spilling. **1713** *Guardian* No. 10 ¶3 He may arch his eyebrows. **1858** KINGSLEY *Lett.* I. 21 It arched itself into one vast dome of red-hot iron. **1875** BUCKLAND *Log-Bk.* 77 Arched like the back of a frightened Cat.

b. *absol.* and *intr.*

1732 POPE *Ess. Man* III. 102 Build on the wave, or arch beneath the sand. **1818** KEATS *Endym.* III. 221 His snow-white brows went arching up. **1875** B. TAYLOR *Faust* xvi. I. 157 Arches not there the sky above us?

3. with *over.* (In prec. senses and const.)

1626 BACON *Sylva* §202 The sound..archeth over the wall. **1692** BENTLEY *Boyle Lect.* iii. 98 Arched over with an exterior Crust of Earth. **1797** W. TAYLOR in *Monthly Rev.* XXII. 282 Hope arches her glistering rainbow over every scene of storm. **1849** ROBERTSON *Serm.* Ser. I. xv. (1866) 256 Because the Infinite above is arching over the soul.

†**4.** (esp. with *together*.) To put together like the stones of an arch, so that all mutually support each other. ***to arch up***: to support on the same principle. *Obs.*

1581 [see ARCHED]. **1649** SELDEN *Laws of Eng.* I. xliii. (1739) 70 The Saxon Commonwealth was a building.. arched together both for Peace and War. **1655** FULLER *Ch. Hist.* IX. 227 Mutually arching up one another. **1662** —— *Worthies* (1840) III. 173 How the statesmen in that age were arched together in affinity.

5. *trans.* To overarch; to span.

1795 SOUTHEY *Joan of Arc* II. 21 The vine that arch'd His evening seat. **1860** TYNDALL *Glac.* II. §4. 249 The blue blocks that arch the source of the Arveiron.

arch (ɑːtʃ), *v.*[2] [Back-formation f. ARCHER, ARCHERY.] *intr.* To practise archery. So **'arching** *vbl. sb.* and *ppl. a.*

1648 A. ROSS *Myst. Poet.* (ed. 2) viii. 179 Apollo's Musick, and skill in arching, were more pleasing to him. **1871** W. CORY *Let.* 25 Aug. in *Extr. Lett. & Jrnls.* (1897) 275 We arch —we don't often hit the target..but we know how to bend a bow. **1950** C. FRY *Venus Obs.* 39 All the arching duchesses.

arch (ɑːtʃ), *a.* [ARCH- *pref.* used as a separate word: see next.]

A. *adj.* **1.** Chief, principal, prime, pre-eminent. (Now rarely used without the hyphen.)

1547 *Life Abp. Canterb.* Pref. D viij b, The fauour off any thoughe neuer so arch a Prelate. **1594** SHAKS. *Rich. III*, IV. iii. 2 The most arch deed of pittious massacre. **1613** —— *Hen. VIII*, III. ii. 102 An Heretique, an Arch-one. **1647** WARD *Simp. Cobler* 88 We cannot helpe it though we can, which is the Arch infirmity in all morality. **1649** PRYNNE *Vind. Lib. Eng.* 45 And proclaim them the Archest Impostors under Heaven. **1678** [See 2]. **1834** LYTTON *Pompeii* (1877) 231 Thou mayest have need of thy archest magic to protect thyself.

2. [Arising from prec. sense, in connexion with *wag*, *knave*, *rogue*, hence with *fellow*, *face*, *look*, *reply*, etc.] Clever, cunning, crafty, roguish, waggish. Now usually of women and children, and esp. of their facial expression: Slily saucy, pleasantly mischievous.

1662 MORE *Antid. Ath.* I. viii. (1712) 151 That arch wag ..ridiculed that solid argument. **1678** BUNYAN *Pilgr.* II. 147 *Greath.* Above all that Christian met.. By-ends was the arch one. *Hon.* By-ends; What was he? *Greath.* A very arch Fellow, a downright Hypocrite. **1710** *Tatler* No. 193 ¶1 So arch a leer. **1775** WESLEY *Wks.* (1872) IV. 41 Some arch boys gave him such a mouthful of dirt. **1810** CRABBE *Borough* xv, Arch was her look and she had pleasant ways. **1872** BLACK *Adv. Phaeton* xxiii. 324 Her arch ways, and her frank bearing. **1877** M. ARNOLD *Poems* I. 27 The archest chin Mockery ever ambush'd in.

†**b.** Const. *at*, *upon*. *Obs.*

1670 EACHARD *Contempt Clergy*, Lads that are arch knaves at the nominative case. **1712** STEELE *Spect.* No. 432 ¶5 A Templar, who was very arch upon Parsons. **1741** RICHARDSON *Pamela* (1824) I. 135 'Sir Simon..you are very arch upon us.'

†**B.** *absol.* quasi-*sb.* A chief (one). *Obs.*

1605 HEYWOOD *If you know not* Wks. (1874) 239 Poole that Arch, for truth and honesty. **1605** SHAKS. *Lear* II. i. 61 The Noble Duke my Master, My worthy Arch and Patron.

arch, Sc. var. ARGH *a.* *Obs.* timid, pusillanimous.

arch- (ɑːtʃ; exc. in archangel), *prefix*: repr. Gr. ἀρχι-, ἀρχ'-, comb. form of ἀρχ-ός chief (cogn. w. ἄρχ-ειν to begin, take the lead), as in ἀρχι-διάκονος chief-minister, ἀρχι-επίσκοπος chief-bishop, ἀρχ-άγγελος chief-angel. Hence in later L. *archidiāconus*, *archiepiscopus*, *archangelus*; in OF. *arce-archediacne*, *arce-archevesque*, *arc-archangele*. (In L. the *ch* was treated as *c*; hence, in Romanic, it remained = *k* in *archangelus*; in other words, it became in It. *arce-*, *arci-*, Pr., Sp., Pg. *arce*, OF. *arce-*, later *arche-*; whence G. *erz-*, Du. *aarts-*.)

In OE. at first translated by *héah-* high (*héah-diacon*, *héah-biscop*, *héah-ęngel*, etc.), but also at length adopted from L. as *arce-*, *ærce-*, *ęrce-* (? orig. *arci-*), in *ęrce-diacon*, *ęrce-biscop*, *ęrce-stól* arch-see, *ęrce-hád* archiepiscopal dignity. The OE. *ęrce-*, *arce-*, became in ME. *erche-*, *arche-*, the latter coinciding with OF. *arche-*, whence also *archangel* was added. From these, in later times, *arch-* became a living formative, prefixable to any name of office. The same happened in med.L. and most mod. langs.; hence many of the Eng. examples, e.g. *archduke*, are adaptations of foreign titles. Since the 16th c., *arch-* has been freely prefixed to names of agents and appellatives (like *arci-* in Ital., and *archi-* in French, as *archifou*, *archipédant*); in a few instances also to appellations of things, and occasionally even to adjectives. Finally, from its faculty of being prefixed to any appellative, *arch* has gradually come to be a separate adjective; see prec. word. (In modern literary words from Gr., the prefix is, in Eng., as in all the Romance langs., ARCHI- q.v.) In pronunciation, the compounds of *arch-* have two accents, either of which may be the stronger, according to emphasis, as in *right hand*. But established compounds, as *archangel*, *-bishop*, *-deacon*, *-duke*, tend to have the main stress on *arch-*, especially when they are prefixed to a name, as, the *'Archduke 'Charles*, *'Archbishop 'Cranmer*. As a prefix the usual sense is 'chief, principal, high, leading, prime,' occasionally 'first in time, original, initial,' but in modern use it is chiefly prefixed intensively to words of bad or odious sense, as in *arch-traitor*, *arch-enemy*, *arch-rogue*.

1. a. In titles of office, rank, or dignity: meaning, 'Chief, principal, -in-chief; superior, master-; one who occupies a position or rank above those who bear the simple title'; as ARCHBISHOP, ARCHDEACON, ARCHDUKE; **arch-beadle, -brahmin, -chaplain, -druid, -eunuch** (Gr. ἀρχιευνοῦχος), **-gunner** (*obs.*), **-ma'girist** (Gr. ἀρχι-μάγειρος) chief cook, **-mime** (= ARCHIMIME), **-minister, -phylarch** chief magistrate of the tribe, **-satrap, -visitor**; especially in many titles of offices in the Holy Roman or German empire, as **arch-butler, -chamberlain, -chancellor, -count, -cupbearer; arch-dapifer**, chief sewer, whose office it was to carry on horseback the first meal to the newly-crowned emperor, whence **archdapifership; arch-earl, -marshal, -sewer, -steward, -treasurer**,

b. In appellations formed after these, and applied in a similar sense, as **arch-apostle** chief apostle, or chief of the apostles; **arch-chief, -corsair, -dæmon, -emperor, -engineer, -genethliac** (Gr. γενεθλιακός) chief caster of nativities, **-governor, -magician, -patriarch, -pontiff, -primate, -prince, -publican, -regent, -ruler, -sacrificator, -sacrificer, -shepherd, -vestryman, -workmaster**.

a. 1693 *Apol. Clergy Scot.* 20 *Arch-Bedle to the Kirk. **1727-51** CHAMBERS *Cycl.* s.v., The elector of Brandenbourg is *arch-chamberlain of the empire. **1842** ALISON *Hist. Eur.* XIII. lxxxix. §6. 185 Talleyrand in his capacity of *arch-chancellor of the empire. **1614** SELDEN *Titles Hon.* 243 *Arch-Chaplains constituted, in those elder times in the Court for Ecclesiastical matters. **1753** CHAMBERS *Cycl. Supp.*, **Arch-Count*, a title antiently given to the Earl of Flanders. **1690** *Lond. Gaz.* mmdxxxiii/3 The Elector of Bavaria, as *Arch-dapifer, rid in his Robes to the Kitchin. **1661** MORGAN *Sph. Gentry* IV. vi. 82 The *archdapifirship with all the prerogatives thereof. **1747** CARTE *Hist. Eng.* I. 32 The *Arch-Druid's mansion house. **1839** KEIGHTLEY *Hist. Eng.* I. 2 Presided over by an *arch-druid. **1599** A. M. tr. *Gabelhouer's Bk. Physic* 338/1 The *Archearle Fredericke. **1727-51** CHAMBERS *Cycl.* s.v., The *archeunuch was one of the principal officers in Constantinople. **1664** *Floddan Field* VIII. 72 Th' *archgunner on th' 'English part. **1814** *Sch. Good Living* 26 Cadmus, *archmagirist to the king of Sidon. *a* **1634** CHAPMAN *Alphonsus* Plays 1873 III. 206 Augustus Duke of Saxon, *Arch Marshall to the Emperor. **1678** MARVELL *Corr.* 361 Wks. 1875 II. 631 One Mr. Welch is their *arch-minister. **1683** BURNET tr. *More's Utopia* 76 Another Magistrate..called..the *Arch-philarch. **1847** LD. LINDSAY *Chr. Art.* I. Introd. 55 The *archsatrap Satan. **1622** HEYLIN *Cosmogr.* II. (1682) 103 The Office of Archidapifer, or *Arch-Sewer. **1643** PRYNNE *Power Parl.* App. 156 The king verily hath his great Master or *Arch-Steward. **1661** MORGAN *Sph. Gentry* IV. vi. 82 The Count Palatine was created..*Arch Treasurer of the Empire. *a* **1672** WOOD *Life* (1848) 41 By the favour of the Warden Sir N. Brent the *Arch-visitor.

b. 1726 J. TRAPP *Popery* I. (T.) The highest titles would have been given to St. Petre, such as *arch-apostle. **1590** BARROW & GREENW. in *Confer.* 43 Christ being..*Arch-cheif, high Bishop of Bishopps. **1728** MORGAN *Algiers* II. iv. 288, I bid this *Arch-Corsair a final Adieu. **1849** SIR J. STEPHEN *Eccl. Biog.* (1850) I. 365 Indolence, self-will, and selfishness..*archdæmons of the cloister. **1816** SOUTHEY in *Q. Rev.* XVI. 230 Grand Monarque, Emperor, or *Arch-emperor, if it liked him better. **1835** BROWNING *Paracels.* II. 32 The dupes of this Old *arch-genethliac. **1567** JEWEL *Def. Apol.* (1611) 420 Yee *Archgouerners of Christs Church. **1553-87** FOXE *A. & M.* 88/2 The magicians and *archmagicians. **1579** FULKE *Heskins's Parl.* Title-p., *Archpatriarches of the Popish Synagogue. **1790** BURKE *Fr. Rev.* 16 This *archpontiff of the rights of men. **1583** STUBBES *Anat. Abuses* 17 At the command of their superintendent, or *arch-primate. **1649** BP. HALL *Cases Consc.* vii. (1654) 47 The *Arch-publican Zacheus. ?**1650** *Don Bellianis* 107 *Arch-ruler over so many territories. **1818** BENTHAM *Ch. Eng.* 361 The Noble Reformer, in the character of *Arch-Sacrificator. **1656** TRAPP *Comm. Matt.* ii. 6 Christ is the *arch-Shepherd, that feeds his people daily. **1859** HELPS *Friends in C.* Ser. II. I. i. 23 The *arch-vestryman, who objects to every thing proposed by everybody. **1630** J. TAYLOR (Water P.) *Superb. Flag.* Wks. I. 28/1 Then did the *Archworkmaster of this All Create this Massie Vniversall Ball.

2. In descriptive appellations: meaning, 'One pre-eminent as, who performs the action or possesses the quality before others; greatest, chief, leading'; as ***arch-antiquary, -artist, -builder, -consoler, -critic, -defender, -diplomatist, -divine, -dogmatist, -exorcist, -friend, -host, -jockey, -leader, -lexicographer, -mystagogue, -philosopher, -player, -politician, -prophet, -protestant, -puritan, -representative, -saint, -semipelagian, -urger, -wag, -wench, -worker***.

In modern use especially with terms of odium or execration: meaning, 'Extreme, out-and-out, worst of, ringleader of'; as ***arch-agitator, -botcher, -boutefeu*** (= incendiary), ***-buffoon, -charlatan, -cheater, -conspirator, -corrupter, -cosener, -criminal, -deceiver, -depredator, -despot, -devil, -dissembler, -disturber, -dolt, -felon, -fool, -gomeril, -humbug, -hypocrite, -informer, -knave, -liar, -metaphysician, -mistress, -plotter, -plunderer, -pretender, -rationalist, -robber, -rogue, -scandalmonger, -sceptic, -scoundrel, -seducer, -snake, -spy, -tempter, -turncoat, -traitor, -tyrant, -vagabond***. Many of these are used with a specific reference to the Devil.

1840 GEN. P. THOMPSON *Exerc.* (1842) V. 158 Thanking the '*Arch-Agitator' [O'Connell]. **1611** SPEED *Hist. Gt. Brit.* v. iii. 12 Proued by our *arch-Antiquary in his famous work. **1640** SANDERSON *21 Serm.* Ad. Aul. xii. (1673) 176 The great *Arch-architect, the builder and maker of all things. **1579** J. STUBBES *Gaping Gulf* B vij b, That Romish *archbaalam. *a* **1635** CORBET *To Ghost R. Wisdome* (T.) *Archbotcher of a psalm or prayer. **1685** EVELYN *Diary* (1827) III. 164 The *arch-boutefeu Ferguson, Matthews, were not yet found. **1577** HOLINSHED *Chron.* II. 26/2 The *archbrochers of their brethrens bloud. *c* **1600** HOOKER *Eccl. Pol.* VII. 441 The very blessed Apostle..giveth unto himself the title of an *arch-builder [*1 Cor.* iii. 10]. **1853** TRENCH *Proverbs* 141 Men fancy they can cheat the *arch-cheater. **1548** HALL *Chron. Hen. IV.* an. 1 (1809) 24 Hector Boece, the Scottish *Arche-chronocler. **1859** HELPS *Friends in C.* Ser. II. I. 8 Change is the *arch-consoler. **1594** *Merry Knack* I. in Hazl. *Dodsl.* VI. 528 When I came to the Exchange, I espied..An *arch-cosener. **1938** R. G. COLLINGWOOD *Princ. Art* v. 85 Hair-raising fiction concerned with *arch-criminals, gunmen, and sinister foreigners. ?**1626** tr. *Boccalina* 187 (T.) Promoted..to be the *archcritick of the sacred muses. **1849** MACAULAY *Hist. Eng.* II. 520 A new crime of the *archdeceiver. **1616** R. C. *Times' Whis.* v. 2111 Drunkennesse hath got an *arch-defender. **1818** BENTHAM *Ch. Eng.* 349 Wealth thus devoured by the *arch-depredator. **1649** S. CLARK *Lives Fathers* (1654) 245 Luther ..called the Zinglians, *Archdevils. **1869** FREEMAN *Norm. Conq.* III. xii. 116 The King of France then, is the *arch-disturber. **1551** ROBINSON tr. *More's Utopia* (1869) 39 Thies wysefooles and verye *archedoltes. **1612-5** BP. HALL *Contempl.* III. i. 61 They accuse him for an *archexorcist, for the worst kinde of magician. **1667** MILTON *P.L.* IV. 179 Which when th' arch-fellon saw, Due entrance he disdained. **1866** CARLYLE *Remin.* (1881) I. 132 Robert Owen, the then incipient *arch-gomeril. **1826** SOUTHEY *Lett.* (1856) IV. 40 The 'Life of an *Arch-humbug.' **1685** BAXTER *Paraphr. Matt.* xxvii. 6 Thus *Arch-hypocrites make conscience of Ceremony, and make no conscience of Perjury. **1761** STERNE *Tr. Shandy* (1802) IV. xx. 93 As if the *arch-jockey of jockeys had got behind me. **1866** *Spectator* 6 Jan., Calling you or your friend 'an *arch-knave.' **1827** HARE *Guesses* I. (1873) 82 Vice is the greatest of all Jacobins, the *arch-leveler. **1905** W. JAMES *Let.* 24 Aug. (1920) II. 232 When you write your treatise against philosophy, you will be classed as the *arch-metaphysician. **1930** R. CAMPBELL *Poems* 18 Your muse..*Arch-mistress of the slowly crawling theme. *a* **1711** KEN *Poet. Wks.* 1721 IV. 76 A Legion led, With the *Arch-Murderer at Head. **1856** R. VAUGHAN *Mystics* (1860) I. 231 Following Dionysius, that *arch-mystagogue. **1610** HEALEY *St. Aug., City of God* 254 One old *arch-plaier plaid the Mimike. **1625** tr. *Camden's Hist. Eliz.* III. (1688) 344 The *Arch-plotter..of this Treason. **1665** BOYLE *Occas. Refl.* IV. xiii. (1675) 250 The Old Serpent himself, that *Arch-politician. **1677** GILPIN *Dæmonol. Sac.* (1867) 169 Arch-heretics have been *arch-pretenders to sanctity. *a* **1910** W. JAMES *Some Probl. Philos.* (1911) ii. 35 Plato, the *arch-rationalist, explained the details of nature by their participation in 'ideas'. **1873** J. MORLEY *Rousseau* I. ix. 309 Voltaire was the *Arch-representative of all these elements. *a* **1650** MAY *Satyr. Puppy* 46 Some *Arch-Rogue..hath done her wrong. **1920** D. H. LAWRENCE *Let.* 4 Jan. (1962) I. 606 She is staying with an *arch-scandalmonger. **1936** *Mind* XLV. 336 Their specific intellectual relationship to the *arch-sceptic himself [*sc.* Hume]. **1896** *Westm. Gaz.* 21 May 2/1 There is no knowing how many gullible young women this *arch-scoundrel might not have married and fleeced. **1674** HICKMAN *Hist. Quinquart.* (ed. 2) 38 Forged by Faustus that *Arch-Semipelagian. **1881** G. M. HOPKINS *Sermons & Dev. Wr.* (1959) 199 So that if the Devil is symbolised as a snake he must be an *archsnake and a dragon. **1630** WADSWORTH *Sp. Pilgr.* viii. 89, I was an *Arch-spye against their State. **1916** JOYCE *Portr. Artist Young Man* iii. 135 Eve yielded to the wiles of the *arch tempter. **1654** GATAKER *Disc. Apol.* 64 As did that *Arch-turncoat of Spalata. **1862** MERIVALE *Rom. Emp.* (1865) VII. lv. 2 This *arch-tyrant.. most detestable of the Cæsarean family. **1656** tr. *B. Valentine's Twelve Keyes* 6 That *arch-wench Venus. **1877** E. CONDER *Bas. Faith* iv. 189 The materials with which Reason, the *arch-worker, toils to construct her fabric.

3. As prec., with sense of, 'First in time, original'; as ***arch-father*** (1541), ***-founder, -god, -messenger, -plagiary***. Mostly *archaic*.

1541 COVERDALE *Old Faith* v. Wks. 1844 I. 29 [Cain] the *archfather of all murderers. **1641** MILTON *Ch. Govt.* ii. (1851) 106 Him whom they fain to be the *archfounder of Prelaty, S. Peter. **1846** GROTE *Greece* (1869) I. 12 Homer knows nothing of Uranus, in the sense of an *arch-God, anterior to Kronos. **1835** LYTTON *Rienzi* VII. vi. 334 The *arch-messenger to smooth the way and prepare the welcome. **1659** GELL *Amendm. Bible* 787 Adam the *arch-plagiary, who hath brought us all into bondage.

4. Of things: with sense of **a.** 'Chief, principal, main, prime'; as ***arch-beacon, -city, -fire, -heart, -machine, -piece, -pillar*** (1553), ***-practice, -synagogue*** (all *Obs.* or *archaic*); ***arch-infamy, -mediocrity, -mock, -mockery, -sin*** (1598), etc. **b.** 'Primitive, original'; as †***arch-christendom, arch-essence, -form***. *Spec.* **arch-house**, archducal house (of Austria); †**arch-pall**, archiepiscopal pall; †**arch-sea**, archipelago; **arch-see**, archiepiscopal see.

1602 CAREW *Cornwall* (1723) 138b, The top of the Cornish *Archbeacon Hainborough. *c* **1630** RISDON *Surv. Devon.* §314 Their order..was..utterly abolished in *Arch-christendom. **1633** FLETCHER *Purple Isl.* II. xliv, That *arch-city of this government. **1652** BENLOWES *Theoph.* VIII. x, *Archessence! Thou, self full! self infinite! Residing in approachlesse light. **1654** GODDARD in *Burton's Diary* (1828) I. 171 A piece of that *archfire, that hath been in this your time. **1873** MA. BLIND *Strauss's Old Faith* li. 208 The two *arch-forms of organic life. **1685** tr. *Gracian's Courtier's Man.* 122 The Heart of Alexander was an *Arch-heart, seeing a whole world lodged easily in a corner of it. **1834** BANCROFT *Hist. U.S.* VI. Index 497 Decadence of the *arch-house. **1871** BROWNING *Pr. Hohenstiel* 1529 That lie of lies, *arch-infamy. **1861** EMERSON *Cond. Life* i. 14 Man is the *arch-machine. **1844** DISRAELI *Coningsby* I. II. i. 155 The *Arch-Mediocrity who presided, rather than ruled, over this Cabinet of Mediocrities. **1604** SHAKS. *Oth.* IV. i. 71 O, 'tis the spight of hell, the Fiend's *Arch-mock. **1826** E. IRVING *Babylon* II. VI. 85 Its *arch-mockery, and master-piece of wickedness. **1866** *Jrnl. Sacr. Lit.* No. 19. 187 Little less than an *arch-mystery. **1848** PETRIE tr. *O.E. Chron.* (1853) 79 [He] went to Rome after his *arch-pall. **1630** NAUNTON *Fragm. Reg.* (Arb.) 38 Sir Nicholas Bacon, An *arch-piece of Wit and Wisdom. **1553–87** FOXE *A. & M.* 209/1 *Archpillers of all papistrie. **1586** BRIGHT *Melanch.* xxxv. 193 That *archpiller of faith and assurance in Christ Jesus our hope. **1628** EARLE *Microcosm.* liii. 115 It may be an *Arch-practice of State. **1613** ZOUCHE *Dove* 25 The *Arch-Sea rowling from th' unruly North. **1612** DRAYTON *Polyolb.* xxiv. (1748) 360 Next these *arch-sees of ours now London place doth take. **1865** *Morn. Star* 16 Feb., The *arch see of Canterbury. **1598** J. DICKENSON *Arisbas* (1878) 55 The Seede of all mischiefe, that *Arch-sinne usurie. **1655** FULLER *Ch. Hist.* III. vi. §33 They had their *Arch-Synagogue at the North corner of the Old-Jury.

5. Adjectives: as †**arch-chemic**, chief in alchemy; †**arch-noble**, noble in a superior degree.

1667 MILTON *P.L.* III. 609 Th' *Arch-chimic Sun so farr from us remote. **1761** SMOLLETT *Gil Blas* III. ix. I. 301 The ladies of the stage are not only noble, but *arch-noble.

'arch,abbey. [ARCH- 4.] The head abbey of a Benedictine congregation. So **'archabbot**, also called *abbot-general*.

1881 B. WELDON *Engl. Congreg. St. Benedict* p. ix, The Arch-Abbey of Monte Cassino. **1889** *Cent. Dict.*, Archabbot. **1897** BEDE CAMM *Benedictine Martyr* iv. 82 In the Order of St. Benedict..a confederacy of Abbeys and Priories,..united together under one President (sometimes called Abbot-General or Arch-Abbot). **1912** *Cath. Encycl.* XV. 648/2 The location where St. Vincent Archabbey, College, and Seminary stand to-day. **1923** SETON *Memories of Many Years* 264 We had dinner at different tables, in the gallery. Arch-Abbot Krug..presided at the principal one.

Archæan (ɑː'kiːən), *a. Geol.* [f. Gr. ἀρχαῖ-ος ancient + -AN.] Of or pertaining to crystalline rocks of Pre-Cambrian age (see quots.). Also *ellipt.* as *sb.*

1872 DANA in *Amer. Jrnl. Sci.* Apr. 253, I propose to use for the Azoic era and its rocks the general term *Archæan*. **1881** C. FISH in *Pop. Sc. Monthly* XIX. 25 The granitic or Laurentian is of archæan origin. **1882** *Pall Mall G.* 13 Nov. 5/1 The still problematic archæan schists. **1903** GEIKIE *Textbk. Geol.* (ed. 4) II. VI. i. 861 Pre-Cambrian, also called Archæan. **1944** A. HOLMES *Princ. Physical Geol.* vii. 104 The term Archæan refers to the oldest Pre-Cambrian crystalline rocks of a given region. **1944** RASTALL in *Geol. Mag.* LXXXI. 159 There is now a marked tendency in international geology to draw a clear distinction between the ancient highly metamorphic continental blocks and the overlying..sedimentary but unfossiliferous groups. These may be conveniently called the Archaean and Algonkian respectively.

archæbacterium (ɑːkɪbæk'tɪərɪəm). *Bacteriol.* Also **archæobacterium** (*rare*) and with capital initial. Pl. **-bacteria.** [f. ARCHÆO- + BACTERIUM.] Any of a diverse group of micro-organisms similar to ordinary bacteria in size and simplicity of structure, but radically different in their molecular organization.

1977 WOESE & FOX in *Proc. Nat. Acad. Sci.* LXXIV. 5089/1 There exists a third kingdom which, to date, is represented solely by the methanogenic bacteria, a relatively unknown class of anaerobes that possess a unique metabolism based on the reduction of carbon dioxide to methane... The apparent antiquity of the methanogenic prototype plus the fact that it seems well suited to the type of environment presumed to exist on earth 3–4 billion years ago lead us tentatively to name this urkingdom the archaebacteria. **1978** *Jrnl. Molecular Evol.* XI. 246 The archaebacteria include anaerobes, aerobes, autotrophs, heterotrophs, thermophiles, acidophiles, and even photosynthetics... They can be rods, cocci, sarcinae, and spirilla. **1981** *Nature* 1/8 Jan. 95/2 The archaebacteria are a group of prokaryotes which seem as distinct from the true bacteria (eubacteria) as they are from eukaryotes. **1983** *Ibid.* 2 June 381/3 The new bacteria, like other extreme thermophiles, are probably archaebacteria, organisms which, with a long separate evolution from the more cosmopolitan eubacteria, have membranes based on a different design—long-chain ether lipids that span from one surface to the other. **1984** HOLT & KRIEG *Bergey's Man. Systemat. Bacteriol.* (ed. 9) I. 32/1 The *Archaeobacteria*.. comprise the methanogens, halobacteria and thermoacidophiles. *Ibid.* 32/2 The *Archaeobacteria* are distinguished by a number of specialized characters from the rest of the procaryotes ('Eubacteria' has had too many meanings in the past to be a useful term)... But these distinctions are not suitable to kingdom status. **1986** *Nature* 20 Mar. 220/2 The division of the archaebacteria into two branches, methanogens plus halophiles and sulphur-dependent archaebacteria, had been recognized.

Hence **archæbac'terial** *a.*

1978 *Jrnl. Molecular Evol.* XI. 247 (*heading*) The archaebacterial cell wall. **1981** STACKEBRANDT & WOESE in M. J. Carlile et al. *Molecular & Cellular Aspects Microbial Evol.* 20 Archaebacterial lipids are not of the usual ester-linked, straight-chain variety found in true bacteria and eukaryotes. **1981** *Sci. Amer.* June 103/1 In the course of the ribosomal-RNA studies another unexpected archaebacterial property emerged, one that was to provide the first clue to the significance of the differences between archaebacteria and true bacteria. **1982** *Naturwissenschaften* LXIX. 203/2 The increasing evidence for a specific relation between archaebacteria and the eukaryotic cytoplasm could be interpreted to mean that the latter has an archaebacterial origin.

archæo- (ˌɑːkiːəʊ-), ad. Gr. ἀρχαιο- comb. form of ἀρχαῖος ancient, primitive (f. ἀρχή beginning). Formerly, and still occas., spelt *archaio-*. In compounds and derivatives, as ARCHÆOLOGY; also: **archæo-ge'ology**, the geology of ancient periods of the earth's history. **archæo'lithic** *a.* [λίθος stone], of or pertaining to the most ancient stone implements used by prehistoric man. **archæo'stomatous** *a.* [στόμα mouth], having the primitive orifice of invagination of the wall of the embryo persistent as a mouth. **archæo'zoic** *a.* [ζωή life], pertaining to the era of the earliest living beings on our planet.

1877 SHIELDS *Final Philos.* 143 Archæo-geology..has ventured still further backward through the past organic epochs. **1865** LUBBOCK *Preh. Times* 60 The period of the drift, which I have proposed to call the archæolithic period. **1877** HUXLEY *Anat. Inv. An.* xii. 684 The limits within which the archæostomatous condition prevails. **1872** DANA *Corals* App. I. 373 The era..styled the Archeozoic.

archæoastronomy (ˌɑːkiːəʊə'strɒnəmɪ). [f. ARCHÆO- + ASTRONOMY.] The study of astronomy as it was practised in prehistoric times or is represented by archæological remains.

1971 *Listener* 28 Jan. 120/2 This is Professor Thom's second book on archaeoastronomy, the study of astronomical practices in ancient times (Gerald Hawkins's term 'astro-archaeology', 'star archaeology', is misleading and could well be dropped). **1975** A. F. AVENI *Archaeoastron. in Pre-Columbian Amer.* p. xiii, The first large-scale meeting of scholars interested in Pre-Columbian Archaeoastronomy, here defined as the study of the extent of the astronomical knowledge and practice of the ancient people of Mesoamerica. **1977** *Sci. Amer.* May 15/2 Eddy has also done research in infrared astronomy, the history of astronomy, and archaeoastronomy (particularly the astronomical alignment of Indian medicine wheels in the U.S. and Canada). **1981** *New Scientist* 18 June 752/1 Gerry Hawkins in his book *Stonehenge Decoded*..broke spectacularly into the news in the mid-1960s and first brought archaeoastronomy (or astroarchaeology, as it was then called) into the public eye.

Hence **ˌarchæoa'stronomer**; **ˌarchæo-astro'nomical** *a.*

1975 J. E. REYMAN in A. F. Aveni *Archaeoastron. in Pre-Columbian Amer.* x. 205 During the past several years, I have had occasion to read or hear approximately one hundred reports relating to archaeoastronomical research. **1978** *Nature* 7 Sept. 75/1 For some time now there has been a clear need for a book which presents the findings of the 'archaeoastronomers'—and this means mainly Professor Alexander Thom and his family—on the British prehistoric standing stone sites to the informed general public. **1978** *New Scientist* 22 June 825 Nineteen basalt pillars at a megalithic site in northwestern Kenya are aligned towards the 300 BC rising directions of seven star formations of significance in the Cushitic calendar still used in the area today. This is the first archaeoastronomical site in sub-Saharan Africa and implies that a prehistoric calendar based on astronomical observations was in use in eastern Africa 2300 years ago. **1983** *Sci. Amer.* June 66/2 These ranged from attributing the drawings to the work of extraterrestrials marking their desert spaceports to the claim by archaeoastronomers that the drawings provided sight lines for the observation of celestial phenomena.

archæocyte ('ɑːkiːəsaɪt). *Zool.* Also **archeocyte.** [f. ARCHÆO- + -CYTE.] A wandering amœboid cell, esp. in a sponge: see quots.

1887 W. J. SOLLAS in *Encycl. Brit.* XXII. 419/2 Amœboid wandering cells or *archæocytes* are scattered through the matrix of the collenchyme. **1900** E. A. MINCHIN in E. R. Lankester *Treat. Zool.* II. iii. 58 The archaeocytes may be considered from two points of view: first, as wandering cells, or *amoebocytes*; secondly, as reproductive cells, or *tokocytes*. **1951** E. N. WILLMER in G. Bourne *Cytology* (ed. 2) xi. 463 Two archeocytes are seen at the posterior end.

archæographical (ˌɑːkiːəʊ'græfɪkəl), *a.* [f. next + -ICAL.] Of or connected with archæography.

1877 WALLACE *Russia* xxix. 466 Works published by the Imperial Archæographical Commission.

archæography (ɑːkiː'ɒgrəfɪ). [f. ARCHÆO- + Gr. -γραφια (see -GRAPHY), after Gr. ἀρχαιογράφος writing of antiquities.] Systematic description of antiquities.

1804 *Month. Mag.* XVIII. 289 The best lexicon of archeography. **1836** HERMANN *Pol. Antiq. Greece* 1 History is learnt from them..and the name archæography has consequently been proposed for the science which treats of them.

archæologer (ɑːkiː'ɒlədʒə(r)). [f. Gr. ἀρχαιολόγ-ος (see below) + -ER[1].] One who cultivates archæology.

1851 TORRENS in *Jrnl. Asiat. Soc. Bengal* 14 Modern archaiologers.

archæologian (ˌɑːkiːəʊ'ləʊdʒɪən). [f. as ARCHÆOLOGY + -AN; cf. *theologian*.] An archæologist.

1849 FREEMAN *Archit.* 3 All who call themselves archæologians. **1859** *Edin. Rev.* No. 223. 49 The patient and minute research..of the archæologian.

archæologic (ˌɑːkiːəʊ'lɒdʒɪk), *a.* [ad. Gr. ἀρχαιολογικός: see ARCHÆOLOGY and -IC. Cf. F. *archéologique*.] Of or pertaining to archæology; archæological.

1731 BAILEY, *Archialogick*. **1806** W. TAYLOR in *Ann. Rev.* IV. 562 Higher interests than those of archæologic curiosity. **1872** M. COLLINS *Pr. Clarice* I. x. 161 Said by archæologic authorities to be two centuries older.

ˌarchæo'logical, *a.* [f. as prec. + -AL[1].] Belonging to, having reference to, or dealing with archæology. Also *absol.* quasi-*sb.*

1782 (*title*) An Archæological Epistle to the Reverend and Worshipful Jeremiah Milles, D.D., President of the Society of Antiquaries. **1832** *Athenæum* No. 242. 383 Archæological studies are too little pursued among us. **1865** *Pall Mall G.* 25 Aug. 9/2 The archæologicals at Durham. **1871** TYLOR *Prim. Culture* I. 19 Archæological inference from the remains of pre-historic tribes.

ˌarchæo'logically, *adv.* [f. prec. + -LY[2].] In an archæological manner, from an archæological point of view.

1790 *Gentl. Mag.* LX. II. 291 The hook on which he is so archæologically suspended. **1871** *Athenæum* 29 July 150 Archæologically considered, the place has no great attractions.

archæologist (ɑːkiː'ɒlədʒɪst). [f. ARCHÆOLOGY: see -IST.] A professed student of archæology.

1824 DIBDIN *Libr. Comp.* 330 English historical archæologists. **1880** DAWKINS *Early Man* i. 2 The archæologists have raised the study of antiquities to the rank of a science.

archæologize (ɑːkiː'ɒlədʒaɪz), *v.* [f. ARCHÆOLOG(Y + -IZE.] **1.** *trans.* To treat or explain archæologically. *rare.*

1884 LYTTON in *19th Cent.* Dec. 886 The attempt to archæologise the Shakespearean drama is one of the stupidest pedantries of this age of prigs.

2. *intr.* To study or practise archæology; to play the archæologist. Hence **archæ'ologizing** *vbl. sb.*

1885 *Harper's Mag.* Mar. 654/1 To archæologize in that delightful air..is one good way of enjoying existence. **1914** T. E. LAWRENCE *Let.* 28 Feb. (1938) 165 He forbade Newcombe to map, and me to photograph or archaeologise. I photographed what I could, I archaeologised everywhere. **1954** G. BOAS in *Essays & Studies* VII. 35 Besides archæologizing round Oxford he practised revolver shooting for fun. **1958** E. L. MASCALL *Recov. Unity* vi. 134 Avoiding both the archaeologising which would make the Church's liturgical life irrelevant..and also the modernism.

archæologue ('ɑːkiːəlɒg). *arch.* Also **archæolog.** [ad. F. *archéologue* archæologist, f. Gr. ἀρχαιολόγος telling of ancient times (cf. ARCHÆOLOGY).] An archæologist or antiquarian.

1839 WISEMAN in *Dublin Rev.* Jan. 23 The learned Cav. Borghesi..consulted in his retreat by the first archeologues of Germany, for his extraordinary sagacity in antiquarian difficulties. **1863** DICKENS *Let.* 29 July (1880) II. 205 If you were coming to the archæologs at Rochester. **1876** *Nation* 7 Dec. 342/2 Even an American archæologue or art-student might have preferred to keep all the Cesnola discoveries together in one museum.

archæology (ɑːkiː'ɒlədʒɪ). Also 6–9 **archai-.** [ad. Gr. ἀρχαιολογία, f. ἀρχαῖο-ς (see ARCHÆO-) + -λογία discourse: see -LOGY.]

1. Ancient history generally; systematic description or study of antiquities.

1607 BP. HALL *Holy Observ.* (1879) 196 Sozomen..[wrote] all the archaiology of the Jewes till Sauls gouernment. **1669** GALE *Crt. Gentiles* I. III. vi. 69 The Grecians were ignorant of the account of true Archeologie or Antiquitie. **1731** BAILEY, *Archialogy*. **1803** *Archæologia* XIV. 211 The contents of the Archaiology of Wales are derived from..old manuscripts. **1869** LECKY *Europ. Morals* I. iii. 481 The Decian persecution is remarkable in Christian archæology.

2. *spec.* The scientific study of the remains and monuments of the prehistoric period.

1837 WHEWELL *Hist. Induct. Sc.* XVIII. v. §1 Theoretical geology..has a strong resemblance..to philosophical archæology. **1851** D. WILSON *Preh. Ann.* (1863) I. i. 27 The closing epoch of geology is that in which archæology has its beginning. **1871** TYLOR *Prim. Culture* I. 38 Archæology displays old structures and buried relics of the remote past.

archæomagnetism (ˌɑːkiːəʊ'mægnətɪz(ə)m). *Archæol.* [f. ARCHÆO- + MAGNETISM.] (The study and interpretation of) the remanent magnetism of archæological remains, esp. for dating purposes. Cf. PALÆOMAGNETISM.

1958 COOK & BELSHÉ in *Antiquity* XXXII. 167 (*heading*) Archaeomagnetism: a preliminary report on Britain. **1959** *Times* 7 May 11/4 Archaeomagnetism is based on the principle that many clays and stones, if heated beyond a certain point.. tend to get a fixed magnetism in the direction of the earth's magnetic north at the time they cooled after firing. The earth's magnetic field varies with time in direction, so that the remanent magnetization of a piece of fired clay or stone should be characteristic of some particular time in the earth's history at that place. **1962** *Archaeometry* V. 17 At present the magnitude of the scatter of remanent directions in samples from the same structure is a serious obstacle to attaining the quarter of the century originally hoped for as the dating span obtainable from archaeomagnetism. **1980** *Times* 18 Aug. 14/7 The hearths within the buildings are also being measured for their archaeomagnetism.

Hence ˌ**archæomag'netic** *a.*, of or pertaining to archaeomagnetism.

1962 *Archaeometry* V. 4 (*heading*) Magnetic dating: some archaeomagnetic measurements in Britain.. **1970** *Science* 3 Apr. 111 A series of archeomagnetic measurements have been carried out on archeologic materials from Arizona and Mexico. **1972** *Oxf. Univ. Gaz.* CII. Suppl. 2. 11 Dating by archaeomagnetic and thermoluminescent methods. **1979** *Rescue News* Dec. 5/6 The dating of Medieval pottery.. is being tackled by selective kiln excavations where archaeomagnetic dates can be obtained. **1981** *Archaeometry* XXIII. 23 (*heading*) Archaeomagnetic determination of past geomagnetic intensity using ancient ceramics.

archæometry (ɑːkiːˈɒmɪtrɪ). [f. ARCHÆO- + -METRY.] The application of modern scientific and technical methods to the interpretation of archæological remains.

1958 (*title*) Archaeometry. **1961** M. J. AITKEN *Physics & Archæol.* p.v, *Archæometry*, measurements made on archæological material. **1975** *Nature* 20 Mar. p.xiv (Advt.), The book contains much of interest for the general scientific reader as well as for people with a specific interest in archaeometry. **1977** *Sci. News* 26 Mar. 198 The new UC experiments confirm that the timber came from a tree that was chopped down around A.D. 700, UCLA archaeologist Rainer Berger reported last week at a symposium on archaeometry. **1977** *Oxford Times* (City ed.) 13 May 11 The subject of archaeometry—a term coined by our first archaeological associate, Prof. C. F. C. Hawkes—is now well established throughout the world.

Hence **archæo'metric** *a.*, of or pertaining to archaeometry; **archæ'ometrist**, a person involved in archaeometry.

1972 *Nature* 31 Mar. 225/1 The magnetic charts now being prepared from these data may be used as an archaeometric standard with which to date other remains from this part of the world. **1974** *Jrnl. Field Archaeol.* I. 224/2 Archaeometrists may not be able to analyze large numbers of finds on demand. **1982** H. P. SCHWARCZ in Ivanovich & Harmon *Uranium Series Disequilibrium* xii. 305 This would cause at least a partial resetting of radiometric dates; therefore, the archaeometrist must always be on guard. **1984** *Jrnl. Field Archaeol.* XI. 341/1 A repository of archaeometric research collections.. has been established at the Conservation Analytical Laboratory of the Smithsonian Institution.

‖**archæopteryx** (ɑːkiːˈɒptərɪks). *Palæont.* [f. ARCHÆO- + πτέρυξ wing, bird.] The oldest known fossil bird, having a long vertebrate tail.

1859 DARWIN *Orig. Spec.* xi. (1878) 302 The wide interval between birds and reptiles.. partially bridged over.. by the ostrich and extinct Archeopteryx. **1879** LE CONTE *Elem. Geol.* 436 The only bird bones found in the Jurassic are those of the Archæopteryx.

archæus, var. f. ARCHEUS.

archaic (ɑːˈkeɪɪk), *a.* [ad. Gr. ἀρχαϊκός, old-fashioned, f. ἀρχαῖος ancient: see -IC. Cf. F. *archaïque*.] **a.** Marked by the characteristics of an earlier period; old-fashioned, primitive, antiquated. *spec.* in *Archæol.*, designating an early or formative period of artistic style or culture.

1846 ELLIS *Elgin Marb.* I. 111 A later specimen of the archaic period of bas-relief. **1875** LUBBOCK *Orig. Civiliz.* i. 2 A social condition ruder and more archaic than any which history records. **1879** GLADSTONE *Gleanings* II. vii. 345 A population.. of archaic covenanting puritans. **1902** E. A. W. BUDGE *Hist. Egypt* II. i. 1 With the ending of the IIIrd Dynasty we close our chapter on the archaic period of Egyptian civilization. **1928** H. C. DAWSON *Age of Gods* xiii. 289 The decline of the Archaic Culture and the invasions of the warrior peoples at the beginning of the second millennium. **1961** S. LLOYD *Art Anc. Near East* ii. 64 The first two Egyptian dynasties are usually referred to as the 'Archaic period'.

b. *esp.* of language: Belonging to an earlier period, no longer in common use, though still retained either by individuals, or generally, for special purposes, poetical, liturgical, etc. Thus the pronunciation *obleege* is archaic in the first case; the pronoun *thou* in the second.

1832 (*title*) Boucher's Glossary of Archaic and Provincial Words. **1876** M. DAVIES *Unorth. Lond.* 286 An archaic form of diction.

ar'chaical, *a. rare.* [f. prec. + -AL¹.] Of or relating to what is archaic; also used as = ARCHAIC.

a **1804** BOUCHER *Gloss.* Introd. 63/2 A collection of archaical [*i.e.* archaic] words. **1845** *Proc. Amer. Phil. Soc.* IV. 187 Occupied in archaical investigations.

ar'chaically, *adv.* [f. prec. + -LY².] In archaic style; in regard to archaism.

1883 *Athenæum* 4 Aug. 133/3 Individual examples, which are.. archaically true only in part.

archaicism (ɑːˈkeɪɪsɪz(ə)m). [f. ARCHAIC + -ISM; cf. *romanticism*.] Ancient style or quality.

1864 *Daily Tel.* 1 Dec., It has rather the air of imitative, not of authentic, archaicism. **1883** *Q. Rev.* July 191 Remnants of archaicism.

archaicist (ɑːˈkeɪɪsɪst). [f. ARCHAIC *a.* + -IST.] = ARCHAIST b.

1896 M. BEERBOHM *Works* 20 The kilt is now confined entirely to certain of the soldiery and to a small cult of Scotch Archaïcists. **1957** H. READ *Tenth Muse* iii. 32 Gauguin, far from being a modernist of his time, was a traditionalist and even an archaicist.

archaism (ˈɑːkeɪɪz(ə)m). [ad. Gr. ἀρχαϊσμός, f. ἀρχαΐζ-ειν to copy the ancients in language, etc., f. ἀρχαῖος ancient: see -ISM. Cf. F. *archaïsme*.]

1. The retention or imitation of what is old or obsolete; the employment in language, art, etc., of the characteristics of an earlier period; archaic style.

[**1612** BRINSLEY *Pos. Parts* (1669) 13 This is called Archaismus, in imitation of the ancient kind of speaking.] **1643** SLATYER *Psalms* A v, Very neare it [the authorized version] saving where by the archaisme.. occasioned to recede. **1783** LEMON *Eng. Etym.* (JOD.) Archaism, a fondness for antient customs, antiquated phrases, obsolete words, etc. **1839** HALLAM *Hist. Lit.* III. III. vii. §33 A slight tinge of archaism was thought by Bacon and Raleigh congenial to an elevated style.

2. An archaic word or expression. Also, an archaic feature in script.

a **1748** WATTS (J.), I shall never use archaisms, as Milton. *a* **1804** BOUCHER *Gloss.* Introd. 20/1 *Erciscere*.. used once by Cicero, but.. avowedly as an archaism. **1864** PUSEY *Daniel* 310 The Pentateuch has marks of greater antiquity, having archaisms which the book of Joshua has not. **1954** N. DENHOLM-YOUNG *Handwr. Engl. & Wales* 42 A sufficient number of archaisms survived into the thirteenth and fourteenth centuries... The most obvious of such features are (i) the retention of majuscule R. **1960** N. R. KER *Eng. MSS. Cent. after Norman Conquest* 22 He might have some difficulty in interpreting two archaisms of the script, the special *ra* and *rt* ligatures.

archaist (ˈɑːkeɪɪst). [f. ARCHA-ISM + -IST.] **a.** One who studies what is archaic; an antiquary. **b.** One who employs archaism, who makes use of archaic methods or language in art or literature.

1851 MRS. BROWNING *Casa Guidi W.* 1, Archaists mumbling dry bones up the land. **1867** *Athenæum* 812/2 A revivalist or affected archaist.

archaistic (ɑːkeɪˈɪstɪk), *a.* [f. prec. + -IC.] Of or pertaining to an archaist; imitatively archaic; affectedly antique.

1850 LEITCH *Müller's Anc. Art* §86 The features harsh and archaistic. **1881** SAYCE in *Academy* 20 Aug. 143 It [language of Homer] is archaistic rather than archaic. **1882** *Q. Rev.* Oct. 381 Archaistic works.. like the so-called Queen Anne furniture in our days.

archaistically (ɑːkeɪˈɪstɪkəlɪ), *adv.* [f. ARCHAISTIC *a.*: see -ICALLY.] In an archaistic way; as an archaism.

1891 S. R. DRIVER *Introd. Lit. O.T.* vi. 327 'Ephraim' must in this case be used emblematically or archaistically. **1965** W. S. ALLEN *Vox Latina* ii. 60 An early disyllabic form .. is sometimes preserved or archaistically revived in Plautus.

archaize (ˈɑːkeɪaɪz), *v.* [ad. Gr. ἀρχαΐζ-ειν: see ARCHAISM.] To imitate the archaic; to render archaistic. Hence **'archaizer**, one who uses archaisms, an archaist; **'archaizing** *vbl. sb.* and *ppl. a.*

1850 LEITCH *Müller's Anc. Art.* §310 The painting of marble in the antique and archaizing style. **1880** WALDSTEIN *Pythag. Rhegion* 20 Those who merely look for archaising. **1881** MAHAFFY in *Athenæum* 2 July 14/3 An archaizing hand of the ninth century. **1882** *Encycl. Brit.* XIV. 332 It may be remembered that Varro was himself something of an archaizer. **1906** *Academy* 1 Dec. 543/1 Poets in uncritical times do not archaise. **1921** GLOVER *Jesus in Exper. Men* viii. 134 The rather fabulous 'Age of Faith' is not for us, however much we archaize. **1933** *Burlington Mag.* Dec. 287/1 The artist obviously has consciously archaized it. **1939** A. J. TOYNBEE *Stud. Hist.* VI. v. 67 Modern Ottoman Turkish—as it was until the other day, when the archaizers took it in hand.

†**'archal**, *a. Obs. rare*⁻¹. [f. ARCH *sb.* + -AL¹.] Of the nature of arches, constructed with arches.

1602 SEGAR *Honor Mil. & Civ.* IV. v. 216 Their crownes are both floreall and Archall.

archane, obs. form of ARCANE *a.*

archangel¹ (ˈɑːkˈeɪndʒəl: see ARCH-). Forms: 2– archangel, 4–5 -ell(e, 3 arc, 5–6 ark-awngell, -angel. [a. OF. *archangel*, *-ele*, *-le*, or perh. ad. L. *archangel-us*, a. Gr. ἀρχάγγελος (see ARCH- and ANGEL *sb.*): the OE. translation *héah-ęngel* survived to 1200. On account of the following *a*, the prefix in this word remained hard (*arc-*, *ark-*) in all the Rom. langs.: Gothic had *arkaggilus*; in Eng., early spellings occur with *arc-*, *ark-*. No satisfactory explanation known of the transferred senses.]

1. An angel of the highest rank. Also *fig.*

[*a* **1000** ÆLFRIC *Gl.* (Wr.) 41/2 *Archangelus* heah encgel. *a* **1000** *Blickl. Hom.* 147 Micahel se heahengel. *c* **1200** ORMIN 13512 Hehenngell Gabriæl.] *c* **1175** *Lamb. Hom.* 41 Mihhal þe archangel. *c* **1230** *Juliana* 48 Englene ifere ant arcanglene freond. *c* **1320** *Cast. Love* (Halliw.) 1575 Ne non so bryȝht archangelle. *c* **1440** *Gesta Rom.* I. xliii. 143 To whom Gode sent the archangell Gabrielle. **1528** PERKINS *Profit. Bk.* ix. §601 The feast of S. Michael the Ark-angell. **1794** SOUTHEY *Botany Bay Ecl.* iv. Wks. II. 88 The Archangel's trump at the last hour. **1853** KINGSLEY *Hypatia* vi. (1879) 71 Fanatical archangel that she [Hypatia] is.

2. *Herb.* Herbalists' name: **a.** of several species of Dead-Nettle and allied plants (*Lamium*, *Galeopsis*, *Galeobdolon*, *Stachys*); **b.** formerly of the Black Stinking Horehound (*Ballota nigra*).

[*c* **1000** ÆLFRIC *Gloss.*, *Archangelica*, blindnetle. **1440** *Promp. Parv.*, Deffe nettylle, *Archangelus*.] **1551** TURNER *Herbal* II. 7 The iuice of rede archangell scatter[s] away.. cancres. **1578** LYTE *Dodoens* 257 Called.. in English blacke Horehounde.. and of some blacke Archangell. **1607** TOPSELL *Four-f. Beasts* 145 Against the bitings of dogs.. the leaves of black horehound, or archangel. **1657** S. PURCHAS *Pol. Flying Ins.* I. xv. 94 Archangel, both with the white and yellow flowers. **1727** BRADLEY *Fam. Dict.* s.v. *Bee*, Rub the Place with.. Wormwood, Archangel, or other noisome Herbs. **1882** *Cornh. Mag.* Jan. 32 Our English archangels and a few others are yellow.

c. A book-name for *Archangelica officinalis* and allied plants, as *Angelica sylvestris* (wild archangel): = ANGELICA 1.

1855 A. PRATT *Flower. Pl.* III. 54 *Angelica sylvestris* (Wild Archangel). **1884** W. MILLER *Dict. Names Plants*, Archangel, *Archangelica officinalis*.

†**3.** ? A titmouse. (Cf. F. *mesange*.) *Obs.*

c **1400** *Rom. Rose* 915 With fynche, with lark, and with archaungelle.

4. A kind of fancy pigeon.

1867 TEGETMEYER *Pigeons* xx. 168 Archangels are prolific.

Archangel² (ˈɑːkeɪndʒəl). Name of a district of European Russia and its chief town, used *attrib.* in ***Archangel mat***, a bast mat used by horticulturists as a protective covering for plants, garden frames, etc.

1854 *F. & A. Dickson's* (of Chester) *Catal.*, Mats, large Archangel. **1909** *Daily Chron.* 9 Mar. 7/5 The plants being covered.. with what are known as Archangel mats. **1954** A. G. L. HELLYER *Encycl. Garden Work* 15/1 Archangel mats.. were much used in gardens for covering frames or tender plants in winter. Nowadays they are seldom seen.

archangelic (ɑːkænˈdʒɛlɪk), *a.* [ad. late L. *archangelic-us*, a. Gr. ἀρχαγγελικ-ός: see ARCHANGEL¹ and -IC.] Of or pertaining to archangels; of the nature of an archangel.

1667 MILTON *P.L.* XI. 126 Th' archangelic host prepared For swift descent. *a* **1711** KEN *Hymnotheo* Wks. 1721 III. 18 You.. To guard yourself have Arch-angelick might. *a* **1859** DE QUINCEY *Dr. Parr*, Such a vision is placed by the archangelic comforter before Adam.

archan'gelical, *a.* [f. as prec. + -AL¹.] = prec.

1652 URQUHART *Jewel* Wks. 1834, 278 The arch-angelical inchantment of fifteen double angels. **1678** CUDWORTH *Intell. Syst.* 565 Angelical, and Arch-Angelical Orders.

archangelship (ɑːkˈeɪndʒəlʃɪp). [f. ARCHANGEL¹ + -SHIP.] State or position of an archangel.

1856 MASSON *Ess.* 70 In the days of my archangelship.

archar, obs. form of ARCHER.

archard (Chambers *Cycl. Supp.*), erron. f. ACHAR.

archarde (*Promp. Parv.*), ? for *accharne*, ACORN.

archbalister, obs. form of ARCUBALISTER.

archbishop (ˈɑːtʃˈbɪʃəp: see ARCH-). Forms of pref.: 1 ærce-, erce-, 1–5 arce-, 2–4 erche-, 3 ærche, 2–6 arche-, 4 erch-, erse-, arz-, 4–5 ers-, 5 ars-, 4– arch-. See forms of BISHOP. [ad. L. *archiepiscop-um* in its Romanic form **arcebiscobo*; or perhaps rather a substitution of the prefix of this for *héah* in the earlier OE. equivalent *héah-biscop* 'high-bishop.' The southern form in ME. was *erche-*:—OE. *ęrce-*; *erse-*, *ers-*, *ars-*, *arz-*, were northern.] The chief bishop; the highest dignitary in an episcopal church, superintending the bishops of his province; a metropolitan.

c **885** K. ÆLFRED *Gregory's Past.* Pref. 6 Æt Pleȝmunde minum ærcebiscepe. **994** *O. E. Chron.*, Her forðferde Siȝeric arcebiscop. *a* **1067** *Charter* in *Cod. Dip.* IV. 208 Eadweard cyng gret Stigand ercebiscop. *c* **1175** *Cotton Hom.* 237 Archebiscopes, and biscopes, prestes. **1205** LAY. 24459 þe ærchebiscop of Lundene. **1297** R. GLOUC. 367 Erchebyssop of Euerwyk. *c* **1325** *Metr. Hom.* 86 Sa sorful was this erz-bischop. *c* **1330** R. BRUNNE *Chron.* 73 Elred þe archbisshop of ȝork. *c* **1386** CHAUCER *Friar's T.* 202 As to therchebisschop [*v.r.* þe erchbisshope] seynt Dunstan. *c* **1405** *Lay Folks' Mass-Bk.* 64 For al ercebischops. *c* **1450** *Nominale* in Wright *Voc.* 209 *Hic archyepiscopus*, an ersbychope. **1480** CAXTON *Chron. Engl.* 258 Metropolitanes and archebisshoppes. **1613** SHAKS. *Hen. VIII*, III. ii. 74 We shall see him For it, an Arch-byshop. **1782** PRIESTLEY *Corrupt. Chr.* II. x. 237 The term Arch-bishop was first used by Athanasius. **1884** *St. James's Gaz.* 4 Feb. 6/2 Planned nearly thirty years ago by the Philological Society at the suggestion of Archbishop Trench.

b. Used to translate Latin *Pontifex maximus*.

1600 HOLLAND *Livy* XXVIII. xxxviii. 697 d, P. Licinius Crassus the Archbishop.

Hence deriv. [see -ESS, -HOOD, -LING, -LY[1], -SHIP]:— **arch'bishopess** (*nonce-wd.*), the wife of an archbishop. **arch'bishophood, arch'bishopship**, the rank or position of an archbishop. **arch'bishopling**, a little archbishop. **arch'bishoply** *a.*, of or pertaining to an archbishop.

1781 H. WALPOLE *Lett. C'tess Ossory* II. 72 She set me down to whist with..the Archbishopess of Canterbury. *c* **1449** PECOCK *Repr.* IV. ii. 426 Bischophode and archi-bischophode. **1845** CARLYLE *Cromwell* (1871) I. 255 There was little good to be got of his Archbishophood. **1851** SIR F. PALGRAVE *Norm. & Eng.* II. 191 The archbishopling, 'Hugo Parvulus.' **1862** *All Y. Round* 10 May 204 The disgrace of having his archbishoply orders countermanded. **1556** *Chron. Grey Friars* (1852) 96 Desgradyd of hys leggatsheppe and of hys archebyshoppecheppe.

arch'bishop, *v.* [f. prec.] *trans.* To make or call archbishop. In phr. *to archbishop it*: to act as archbishop.

1692 WASHINGTON tr. *Milton's Def. Pop.* viii. (1851) 191 [They] pretended to Archbishop it by Divine Providence. **1836** *Blackw. Mag.* XXXVI. 301 To archbishop him was by right; for he was already arch-hypocrite..and arch-rogue.

archbishopric (ɑːtʃˈbɪʃəprɪk). [see -RIC; cf. *bishopric.*] **a.** The see or jurisdiction, **b.** the rank or office, of an archbishop.

994 *O. E. Chron.*, Feng Ælfric..to ðam arcebiscoprice. **1297** R. GLOUC. 417 þe kyng..þulke erchebyssopryche Of Canterbury adde in hys hond. *c* **1425** WYNTOUN *Cron.* VII. viii. 55 Ðat had þe Archebyschapryk Of Yhork. **1613** SHAKS. *Hen. VIII*, II. i. 164 For not bestowing on him..The Arch-bishopricke of Toledo. **1796** MORSE *Amer. Un. Geog.* II. 442 Cagliari has an university, an archbishopric. **1849** MACAULAY *Hist. Eng.* II. 438 The archbishopric [of Cologne] became vacant.

arch-butler, -chamberlain, etc.: see ARCH- 1.

arch-buttress: see ARCH *sb.* III.

†**'arch-'chanter.** *Obs.* exc. *Hist.* [ad. med.L. *archicantor* (also in Eng. use), f. ARCHI- + L. *cantor* singer, chanter.] A choir-leader, precentor.

1387 TREVISA *Higden* (Rolls Ser.) VI. 133 Iohn þe arche-chaunter. **1577** HOLINSHED *Chron.* I. 123/2 Archchanter of S. Peter's church at Rome. **1682** N. O. *Boileau's Le Lutrin* IV. 31 Drown'd in sweet Sleep th' Arch-chanter roll'd at ease. **1751** CHAMBERS *Cycl.*, *Arch-chantor.* **1844** LINGARD *Anglo-Sax. Ch.* (1858) I. vii. 278 Arch-cantor of St. Peter's.

,archconfra'ternity. *R.C. Ch.* [ARCH- 1.] 'A confraternity empowered to aggregate or affiliate other confraternities of the same nature, and to impart to them its indulgences and privileges' (*Cath. Encycl.*).

1636 R. MASON (*title*) A Manuell of the Arch-Confraternitie of the Cord of the Passion. **1661** BLOUNT *Glossogr.* (ed. 2) s.v. *Rosary*, Such Romanists who are of the Arch-confraternity of the Rosary, instituted by St. Dominick. **1844** *Dublin Rev.* Mar. 11 The wonderful blessings, which have followed in the train of this religious association, have induced his present Holiness to..raise it to the title of an arch-confraternity. **1910** GASQUET *Order of Visitation* II. 57 The Archconfraternity of the Guard of Honour of the Sacred Heart.

arch-dapifer, etc.: see ARCH- 1.

archdeacon (ˈɑːtʃˈdiːkən: see ARCH-). Forms of pref.: 1–5 arce-, 1–4 erce-, 4 ers-, erse-, erres-, erche-, 4–5 archi-, 5 ars-, 5–7 arche-, 4- arch-. See forms of DEACON. [OE. *arce-*, *ęrce-diacon*, ad. L. *archidiācon-us* (*c* 420 Jerome), a. Gr. ἀρχιδιάκονος; see ARCHI- 1 and DEACON. Cf. OF. *arc(h)ediacne* 12th c., later *archediacre.*]

The chief deacon; *orig.* the chief of the attendants on a bishop, who, through the scope of his duties in relation to the services of the church and the administration of charity, gradually acquired a rank above the priests and next in importance to the bishop. In *Eng. Ch.* the archdeacon is appointed by, and gives assistance to, the bishop, superintending the rural deans, and holding the lowest ecclesiastical court, with the power of spiritual censure.

c **1000** ÆLFRIC *Gl.* (Z.) 299 *Archidiaconus*, ercediacon [*v.r.* arce-]. **1297** R. GLOUC. 468 Ercedekne of Kanterbury Sein Tomas tho was. *c* **1386** CHAUCER *Freres T.* 2 An erchedeken, a man of gret degrè. *c* **1449** PECOCK *Repr.* I. xviii. 102 Noo bischop or archideken. **1577** HARRISON *Eng.* I. II. i. 17 Which archdeacons are termed in law the bishops eies. **1704** NELSON *Fest. & Fasts* II. iii. (1739) 474 Where the Bishops had many Deacons, one among them had the Title of Arch-Deacon. **1881** HATCH *Bampton Lect.* ii. 53 [The] archdeacon ..was conceived to be, in an especial sense, the bishop's assistant in ecclesiastical administration.

Hence the derivatives [see -ATE, -ESS, -SHIP]:— **arch'deaconate** (L. *archidiāconātus*), the position of archdeacon; archidiaconate. **arch'deaconess**, the wife of an archdeacon. **arch'deaconship**, the office of archdeacon.

1882 SCHAFF *Herzog's Encycl. Rel. Knowl.* 128 The archdeaconates were generally held by the provost of the cathedral and the canons. **1861** *Wheat & Tares* 50 'Excellent,' cried the Archdeaconess. **1591** PERCIVALL *Sp. Dict.*, *Arcedianadgo*, an archedeaconship, *Archidiaconatus.* **1755** JOHNSON, *Archdeaconship.*

archdeaconry (ɑːtʃˈdiːkənrɪ). [f. prec. + -RY.] **a.** The jurisdiction, or district under the ecclesiastical control, of an archdeacon. **b.** The rank or office of an archdeacon. **c.** The residence of an archdeacon.

1555 BONNER in Foxe *A. & M.* III. 151 The best learned in every deanary of their Archdeaconry. **1590** SWINBURN *Testaments* 65 Emolumentes..belonging to anie Arch-deaconrie. **1779** SWINBURNE *Trav. Spain* iv. (T.) The arch-deaconry, once the palace of the prætor. **1847** YEOWELL *Anc. Brit. Ch.* xi. 121 Isle of Anglesey..now an arch-deaconry of the diocese of Bangor. **1872** R. ANDERSON *Missions Am. Board* III. xvii. 287 Elevated..to an arch-deaconry..under the 'Great Church' at Constantinople.

†**'arch'dean.** *Obs.* exc. *Hist.* [f. ARCH- + DEAN.] The chief or superior of the deans. Used by Sc. writers for ARCHDEACON.

c **1425** WYNTOUN *Cron.* VII. ix. 174 Ðe Archdene of Yhork ..Wes þe toþir. **1535** STEWART *Cron. Scot.* II. 340 Ane vther archidene callit Deueintius. **1634–46** ROW *Hist. Kirk* (1842) 46 Certaine names, such as Archbishop, Bishop, Archdean, Dean..savouring of the Romish hierarchie.

†**arch'deanery.** *Hist.* [f. prec. + -ERY; cf. *deanery.*] The jurisdiction, rank, or office of an archdean; Sc. for *archdeaconry.*

1828 TYTLER *Hist. Scot.* (1864) I. 293 Leisure which he [Barbour] spared from the duties of his archdeanery.

†**archdi'acre.** *Obs. rare*⁻¹. [a. OF. 13th c. *archediacre*:—12th c. *archediacne*:—L. *archidiāconus.*] = ARCHDEACON.

c **1450** *Chaucer's Dream* 2138 Archbishop, and archdiacre.

archdiocese (ˈɑːtʃˈdaɪəsiːs). [f. ARCH- 4 + DIOCESE.] The see or jurisdiction of an archbishop.

1844 LINGARD *Anglo-Sax. Ch.* (1858) II. xiii. 265 Within the arch-diocese [of York]. **1869** H. E. MANNING in *Echo* 6 Apr., Permission that collections may be made in this archdiocese.

archducal (ɑːtʃˈdjuːkəl), *a.* Also 7 archi-. [a. F. *archiducal*: see ARCHDUKE and -AL[1].] Of or pertaining to an archduke.

1665 MANLEY *Grotius's Low-C. Wars* 573 He shew'd himself publikely in his Archiducal Habit. *a* **1770** W. GUTHRIE (T.) Armorial bearings of the archducal family. **1861** *Sat. Rev.* 14 Sept. 270 His Imperial, Royal, Archducal, and Apostolic Majesty [of Austria].

†**archducate.** *Obs.* [ad. med.L. *archidūcāt-us*: see ARCHDUKE and -ATE[3].] The rank or dignity of an archduke.

1586 FERNE *Blaz. Gentrie* 137 Another dignity..called an Archeducate, whereof I find but one.

archduchess (ˈɑːtʃˈdʌtʃɪs). [ad. F. *arche-*, *archiduchesse*; see ARCH- 1 and DUCHESS.] The wife of an archduke; or *spec.* a daughter of the Emperor of Austria.

1618 *Barneveld's Apol.* E iiij, The Arch-Dutchesse of Arschot. **1708** *Lond. Gaz.* mmmmccccxxxii/6 The two young Arch-Dutchesses, Daughters to the present Emperor. **1837** CARLYLE *Fr. Rev.* III. I. viii. 81 The Austrian Archduchess will herself see real artillery fired.

archduchy (ˈɑːtʃˈdʌtʃɪ). [ad. earlier F. *archeduché*:—L. **archidūcātus*: see ARCH- 4 and DUCHY.] The territory subject to an archduke.

1680 MORDEN *Geogr. Rect.* (1685) 122 The only Arch-Dutchy in Europe is Austria. **1837** *Penny Cycl.* IX. 446/1 The Provinces of the Ens constitute the archduchy of Austria.

archduke (ˈɑːtʃˈdjuːk, ˈɑːtʃˌdjuːk: see ARCH-). [a. OF. *archeduc*, now *archiduc*:—Merovingian L. *archidūc-em*, *c* 750: see ARCH- 1 and DUKE.]

The chief duke: *formerly* title of the rulers of Austrasia, Lorraine, Brabant, and Austria, being assumed by those of Austria in 1359; *now* titular dignity of sons of the Emperor of Austria.

1530 PALSGR. 195/1 Archeduke, *archeduc.* **1602** CAREW *Cornwall* (J.) Philip, archduke of Austria..was weather-driven into Weymouth. **1800** COLERIDGE *Own Times* II. 353 Attempts are made at Vienna, to reconcile the Archduke and Suwarrow.

archdukedom (ɑːtʃˈdjuːkdəm). [f. prec. + -DOM.] = ARCHDUCHY.

1530 PALSGR. 195/1 Archedukedome, *archeduché.* **1579** J. STUBBES *Gaping Gulf* C vij, Moe countyes then king Phillip had archdukedomes. *a* **1770** W. GUTHRIE (T.) Austria is but an archdukedom.

†**arche.** *Obs.* [a. OF. *arche*:—L. *arca*: cf. ARK. It is possible that the OE. *arc*, *arce* may itself have become *arch* in some dialects, but the use of this form down to the 16th c. is clearly from Fr.]

1. Noah's ark; = ARK 3.

1205 LAY. 26 Noe & Sem, Japhet & Cham and heore four wiues þe mid heom weren on archen. *c* **1230** *Ancr. R.* 334 Eihte i þen arche. *c* **1250** *Gen. & Ex.* 580 Ðan noe was in to ðe arche cumen. *a* **1300** *Cursor M.* 1843 On þe streme þat arche can ride. **1393** LANGL. *P. Pl.* C. XII. 247 For *archa noe* ..Ys no more to mene Bote holy churche.

2. The ark of the covenant; = ARK 2. Also *transf.*

c **1450** LONELICH *Grail* xvi. 290 To kepen this holy arch [of the Grail] in this manere. **1483** CAXTON *Gold. Leg.* 422/4 The arche of the testamente of god. **1532** MORE *Confut. Tindale* Wks. 420/2 They abhorred not in the arche the ymages of the angels.

arche, obs. form of ARCH *sb.*

†**ar'cheal,** *a. Obs. rare.* [f. ARCHE-US + -AL[1].] Of or pertaining to the archeus.

1727–51 CHAMBERS *Cycl.* s.v. *Archeus*, When this [the archeus] is corrupted, it produces..archeal diseases.

archebiosis (ɑːkɪbaɪˈəʊsɪs). *Biol.* [mod.L., f. Gr. ἀρχή beginning + βίος life + -OSIS (cf. βίωσις way of life).] H. C. Bastian's term for 'spontaneous generation'; = ABIOGENESIS.

1872 BASTIAN *Beginnings of Life* I. v. 232. **1872** DARWIN *Let.* 28 Aug. in F. Darwin *Life & Lett.* (1887) III. 169, I should like to live to see Archebiosis proved true. **1874** FISKE *Cosmic Philos.* I. II. viii. 430 Archebiosis, or the origination of living matter in accordance with natural laws, must have occurred at some epoch of the past.

arched (ɑːtʃt, -tʃɪd), *ppl. a.* [f. ARCH *v.*[1] + -ED.]

1. Furnished with, formed into, or consisting of, an arch or arches.

1598 SHAKS. *Merry W.* III. iii. 59 The right arched-beauty of the brow. **1665** MANLEY *Grotius's Low-C. Wars* 361 It hath an Arched Bridg. **1686** PLOT *Staffordsh.* 358 A sort of arched-Bricks..bent round to fit the Eyes of their Cole-pits. **1718** POPE *Iliad* VI. 305 Raised on arch'd columns of stupendous frame. **1827** KEBLE *Chr. Year* Trin. Sun., As travellers..Lose in arched glades their tangled sight.

†**2.** Joined in mutual support; cf. ARCH *v.*[1] 4. *Obs.*

1581 LYLY *Euphues* (1636) D ij, Arched bands of amity.

†**archegay** (ˈɑːtʃɪgaːɪ). *Obs.* exc. *Hist.* [a. F. *archegaie*, *archigaie*, variant of *arcigaye*, also *azegaye*, *azagaye*, ad. Pg. and Sp. *azagaya*, a. Arab. *az-zaghāyah*, i.e. *al* the + *zaghāyah*, Berber name of a javelin or dart: now called in Eng. (from Pg.) *assagai*, *assegai*. (Erroneously made two syllables by W. Morris.)]

An iron-pointed wooden dart; an assagai.

1523 LD. BERNERS *Froiss.* I. ccxxxvii. 340 With speares, iauelyns, archegayes, and swerdes. *Ibid.* ccxli. 355 They of Granade..fought ferseley with their bowes and archegayes. **1858** MORRIS *Harpdon's End* 76 Bows, archgays, lances.

archegonial (ɑːkɪˈgəʊnɪəl), *a. Bot.* [f. next + -AL[1].] Of or pertaining to the archegonium.

1865 HOWLETT in *Intell. Observ.* No. 37. 35 At the bottom of the archegonial shaft. **1880** in *Syd. Soc. Lex.*

‖**archegonium** (ɑːkɪˈgəʊnɪəm). *Bot.* Pl. -a. [mod.L., dim. of Gr. ἀρχέγονος founder of a race, f. ἀρχε- = ἀρχι- (see ARCHI-) + γόνος race. Rarely archegon.] The female organ in Cryptogams, corresponding to the pistil in flowering plants.

1854 BALFOUR in *Encycl. Brit.* V. 156/1 The pistillidium or archegonium contains a germ-cell..which produces a germinating body. **1863** BERKELEY *Brit. Mosses* iii. 19 The archegon..is flask-shaped. **1872** OLIVER *Elem. Bot.* II. 288.

archelogy (ɑːˈkɛlədʒɪ). [ad. mod.L. *archelogia*, f. Gr. ἀρχή beginning: see -LOGY.] The scientific study of principles.

[**1633** G. HARVEY (*title*) Archelogia Philosophica Nova.] **1856** FLEMING *Vocab. Philos.* (1858) 44 Archelogy..treats of principles, and should not be confounded with Archæology.

†**'archemaster.** *Obs.* [f. next, after *master.*] A supreme master; one who has supreme skill.

1570 DEE *Math. Pref.* 39 The Emperour Augustus (in whose daies our Heauenly Archemaster was borne). *Ibid.* 48 The Archemaster steppeth in, and leadeth forth on, the Experiences.

†**'archemastry.** *Obs.* Also archi-, arch-. [? f. ARCHI- + MASTERY; but perh. confused with, or originally a corruption of, *alchemistry*: cf. ARCHYMIST.] Supreme skill; mastery of applied science, or applied mathematics.

1477 NORTON *Ord. Alch.* (Ashm. 1652) i. 13 Mastrye full merveylous and Archimastrye Is the tincture of holi Alkimi. **1570** DEE *Math. Pref.* A iij, Now end I with Archemastrie.. This Arte, teacheth to bryng to actuall experience sensible, all worthy conclusions by all the Artes Mathematicall purposed, and by true Naturall Philosophie concluded: and both addeth to them a farder scope, in the termes of the same Artes, and also by hys propre Method, and in peculiar termes, procedeth, with helpe of the foresayd Artes, to the performance of complet Experiences, which of no particular Art are hable (formally) to be challenged. **1594** J. DAVIS *Seaman's Secr.* Ep. Ded., Thomas Digges Esquire..the great Master of Archmastrie.

'arch-'enemy. [ARCH- 2.] **1.** A chief enemy.

1550 COVERDALE *Spir. Perle* xxix. (1588) 299 He is the deadly Archenemy of God, and of all mankind. **1615** CROOKE *Body of Man* 346 Vacuity that Arch-enemy of Nature. **1851** HAWTHORNE *Twice-told T.* I. i. 17 Edward Randolph, our arch-enemy.

2. *spec.* The arch-fiend Satan. (Cf. quot. 1550 in 1.)

1850 MRS. JAMESON *Sacr. & Leg. Art* 430 The persecutions of the arch-enemy.

archenteron (ɑːˈkɛntərɒn). *Zool.* [mod.L., f. Gr. ἀρχή beginning + ἔντερον intestine.] The primitive intestinal or alimentary cavity of a gastrula. (Cf. METENTERON, PERIENTERON.) Hence **archenteric** (-ɛnˈtɛrɪk) *a.*, pertaining to the archenteron.

1877 [see METENTERON]. **1881** E. R. LANKESTER in *Encycl. Brit.* XII. 548/2 The archenteron or primitive digestive space. *Ibid.*, The closure or shutting off of the axial from the periaxial portion of the archenteric space. **1962** D. NICHOLS *Echinoderms* x. 120 An inpushing at one end forms the beginning of the larval gut, or *archenteron*.

archeocyte, var. ARCHÆOCYTE.

archer (ˈɑːtʃə(r)). Forms: 4 **archeer, archar,** 4–5 **archere, archier,** 4– **archer.** [a. AFr. *archer*, OF. *archier*:— L. *arcāri-um*, f. *arcus* bow.]

1. One who shoots with bow and arrows, *esp.* one who uses them in war; a bowman. Also *fig.*

1297 R. GLOUC. 199 Archers and vot men. **1375** BARBOUR *Bruce* IX. 151 Thair archaris furth to thame thai send. *c* **1465** *Chevy Chase* 103 Of xv C archars of ynglonde went a-way but vij^x^ & thre. **1477** EARL RIVERS (Caxton) *Dictes* 89 An archier to faile of the butte is no wonder. **1594** SHAKS. *Rich. III*, v. iii. 339 Draw, Archers, draw your Arrowes to the head. **1599** —— *Much Ado* II. i. 401 If wee can doe this, Cupid is no longer an Archer. **1670** COTTON *Espernon* I. II. 53 The Payment of the Grand Provost, and his Archers. **1808** SCOTT *Marm.* v. xvii, But Nottingham has archers good, And Yorkshire men are stern of mood.

b. *attrib.*, as in *archer-craft, -god, -queen, -rank.*

1814 SCOTT *Ld. Isles* VI. xxiii, They rush'd among the archer-ranks. **1870** MORRIS *Earthly Par.* I. I. 73 Little could avail Their archer craft. **1870** BRYANT *Homer* I. I. 2 Apollo, archer-god.

†**2.** An arrow. (Perh. by confusion: cf. *arbalester.*)

c **1400** *Rom. Rose* 4191 Springolds, gonnes, bowes, and archers. **1470–85** (ed. 1634) MALORY *Pr. Arth.* (1816) I. 91 One of them, with a bow and archer, smote sir Gawaine.

†**3.** Old name of the bishop in chess. *Obs.*

1656 F. BEALE *Chesse-play* 2 A Bishop, or Archer, who is commonly figured with his head cloven.

4. The ninth zodiacal constellation, *Sagittarius.*

1594 BLUNDEVIL *Exerc.* III. I. xxiv. 329 Sagittarius, that is to say, the Archer.. hath his head towards the North. **1742** YOUNG *Nt. Th.* v. 1022 Near heav'n's archer, in the zodiac, hung. **1868** LOCKYER *Heavens* (ed. 3) 328 Then partly in the Milky Way, the Archer.

5. *Ichthyol.* A fish (*Toxotes jaculator* Cuvier), found in Java and Sumatra, which has the power of shooting a drop of water at insects that rest near.

1834 *Penny Cycl.* II. 272/2 The drop seldom fails to hit the mark and precipitate the insect into the water, where it is, of course, within reach of the archer. **1847** *Nat. Encycl.* II. 14/2 The archer.. is of a yellowish colour, marked in the back with five brown spots.

†**6. water archer**: obs. name of the Arrowhead (*Sagittaria sagittifolia*).

1617 MINSHEU *Ductor* 493 Water Archer, or Arrowhead.. because it is good to pull out arrows. **1783** AINSWORTH *Lat. Dict.* (ed. Morell), Water archer, *Sagittaria*.

archeress (ˈɑːtʃərɪs). [f. prec. + -ESS.] A female archer.

1646 FANSHAWE *Pastor Fido* 143 (T.) To thee I recommend it, O archeress eternal! **1791** COWPER *Iliad* XXI. 560 But thus the consort of the Thund'rer.. reproved the Archeress of heaven. **1876** GEO. ELIOT *Dan. Der.* I. x. 73 Miss Arrowpoint was one of the best archeresses.

archership (ˈɑːtʃəʃɪp). Skill as an archer.

1791 COWPER *Odyss.* VIII. 275 Him, angry to be call'd To proof of archership, Apollo slew.

archery (ˈɑːtʃərɪ). [a. OF. *archerie*, f. *archier.*]

1. The practice or art of shooting with bow and arrow; skill as an archer. Also *fig.*

a **1400** *Cov. Myst.* 44 Myht nevyr man fynde My pere of archerye. *c* **1425** WYNTOUN *Cron.* IX. xxvii. 309 Gud yomen for Archery. **1588** SHAKS. *Tit. A.* IV. iii. 2 Sir Boy let me see your Archerie. **1812** BYRON *Ch. Har.* I. lxxii, Doomed to die .. by Love's sad archery. **1859** J. LANG *Wand. India* 25 An Archery meeting or a pic-nic.

2. *collect.* An archer's weapons; bows, arrows, etc.

1440 *Promp. Parv.*, Archerye, *Sagittaria, arcus.* **1828** SCOTT *F.M. Perth* III. 77 [Their bows] as well as their arrows, were.. far inferior to the archery of merry England. **1882** *Pall Mall G.* 3 July 8/2 An archery manufacturer.

3. *collect.* A company or corps of archers.

c **1465** *Chevy Chase* (Percy Fol.) 85 He rod uppon a corsiare Throughe a hondrith archery. **1814** SCOTT *Ld. Isles* VI. xxii, Signal for England's archery To halt and bend their bows.

†**4.** A feudal service; (see quot.) *Obs.*

1691 BLOUNT *Law Dict.*, *Archery* was a Service of keeping a Bow for the Use of the Lord, to defend his Castle [*per Serjeantiam Archeriæ*, Coke *On Litt.* 107 a.]

arches (ˈɑːtʃɪz). [Cf. *arch-sea*, ARCH- 4.] 'A common term among seamen for the Archipelago.' Smyth *Sailor's Word-bk.* 1867.

1626 SIR T. ROE *Negotiations* 512 An island called Augusto near Paros, in the Arches. **1725** DE FOE *Voy. round World* (1840) 93 The sea of Borneo and the upper part of the Indian Arches. **1812** SIR R. WILSON *Pr. Diary* I. 69 Entering the Archipelago, or, according to the sailor phrase, the Arches.

arches-court: see ARCH *sb.* 2.

archespore, archispore (ˈɑːkɪspɔə(r)). *Bot.* and *Zool.* Also **archesporium.** [ad. mod.L. *archesporium* (K. Goebel 1880, in *Bot. Zeitg.* XXXVIII. 546), f. Gr. ἀρχε-, ἀρχι- ARCHI- + SPORE.] A protoplasmic body from which spores or similar reproductive bodies are developed. Hence **archeˈsporial** *a.*, pertaining to or of the nature of an archespore.

1882 VINES tr. *Sachs's Bot.* 403 By repeated divisions the archesporial cell produces the spore-mother-cells. **1901** G. N. CALKINS *Protozoa* v. 151 The entire organism takes part in the formation of archispores (or sporoblasts), each archispore gives rise to spores, and each spore to sporozoites. **1902** OLIVER tr. *Kerner's Nat. Hist. Plants* II. 95 Within [the anther], large cells.. form what is known as the *archesporium*. *Ibid.* 96 The archesporial cells divide, giving rise to the pollen-mother-cells.

†ˈ**archet.** *Obs. rare*^−1^. [a. F. *archet*, dim. of *arc*: see ARC *sb.*] The bow of a violin.

1627 G. WATTS *Bacon's Adv. Learn.* (1640) 107 The Archet, or musicall Bow of the mind.

archetypal (ɑːˈkɛtɪpəl, ˈɑːkɪtaɪpəl), *a.* [f. L. *archetypum* ARCHETYPE + -AL^1^.

(In Platonic philosophy, *archetypal* is applied to ideas or forms of natural objects, held to have been present in the divine mind prior to creation, and still to exist, as cognizable by intellect, independently of the reality or *ectypal* form.)]

1. Of the nature of, or constituting, an archetype; of or pertaining to an archetype; primitive, original.

1642 H. MORE *Song of Soul* Notes 146/1 The Archetypal seal, which we call the intellectuall world, is the very word of God, the Archetypall Paradigme. *a* **1711** KEN *Hymnotheo* Wks. 1721 III. 383 Our great, our sole, Archetypal High Priest. **1848** H. ROGERS *Essays* I. vi. 287 Plato's 'archetypal ideas' correspond to our 'general notions' as expressed by 'general terms,' and *something more*; that is, he believed in their real existence.. external to any and to all minds. **1869** FARRAR *Fam. Speech* ii. 41 Reconstruct extinct and archetypal forms of language.

2. *spec.* In the psychology of C. G. Jung: of, pertaining to, concerned with, or constituting an archetype (see ARCHETYPE 2 c). Freely used in *Literary Criticism*, esp. of motifs which recur in mythologies, fairy tales, etc., e.g. the Great Mother, the Wise Man, the Enchanted Prince, and by extension of any pervasive symbolic representation.

1923 H. G. BAYNES tr. *Jung's Psychol. Types* 277 The latent primordial image of the goddess, which is in fact the archetypal soul-image. **1926** W. MCDOUGALL *Outl. Abnormal Psychol.* 203 Jung would regard all the main features of this dream as instances of archetypal thinking thrown up from 'the Collective Unconscious'. **1934** M. BODKIN (*title*) Archetypal Patterns in Poetry. **1945** KOESTLER *Yogi & Commissar* III. i. 122 Jung showed that certain archaic or archetypal images and beliefs are the collective property of our race. **1948** H. READ *Art Now* (ed. 4) v. 110 If we can accept the hypothesis of the collective unconscious as formulated by Jung, it is even possible that an artist like Picasso is able to reveal those archetypal images which are its characteristic content. **1950** *Brit. Jrnl. Psychol.* June 236 Archetypal images and motives are particularly prevalent in decisive phases of life. **1957** N. FRYE *Anat. of Crit.* ii. 99 Archetypal criticism is primarily concerned with literature as a social fact.

archetypally (see prec.), *adv.* [f. prec. + -LY^2^.] In the archetype; originally.

1854 OWEN in *Orr's Circ. Sc.* Org. Nat. I. 260 Coalescence of parts primarily and archetypally distinct.

archetype (ˈɑːkɪtaɪp). Also 7–8 **archi-**, 7–9 **arch-.** [ad. L. *archetypum*, a. Gr. ἀρχέτυπον, f. ἀρχε- = ἀρχι- first + τύπος impress, stamp, type.]

1. The original pattern or model from which copies are made; a prototype.

[**1599** THYNNE *Animadv.* 42 The originall or fyrste archetypum of any thinge.] **1605** BACON *Adv. Learn.* I. 27 Let vs seeke the dignitie of knowledge in the Arch-tipe or first plat-forme, which is in the attributes and acts of God. **1690** LOCKE *Hum. Underst.* II. xxx. (1695) 205 By real Ideas, I mean such as have a Foundation in Nature; such as have a Conformity.. with their Archetypes. **1795** MASON *Ch. Music* i. 54 There was little if any Music printed.. that could serve as an Architype. **1849** MACAULAY *Hist. Eng.* I. 17 The House of Commons, the archetype of all the representative assemblies which now meet. **1875** SCRIVENER *Lect. Gk. Test.* 9 These [manuscripts] were made the archetypes of a host of others.

2. *spec.* **a.** in *Minting*. A coin of standard weight, by which others are adjusted. ? *Obs.*

b. in *Compar. Anat.* An assumed ideal pattern of the fundamental structure of each great division of organized beings, of which the various species are considered as modifications.

1849 MURCHISON *Siluria* xx. 477 Approaching to the vertebrated archetype. **1854** OWEN in *Orr's Circ. Sc.* Org. Nat. I. 169 The archetype vertebrate skeleton.

c. In the psychology of C. G. Jung: a pervasive idea, image, or symbol that forms part of the collective unconscious. For the use of the term in *Literary Criticism* see ARCHETYPAL *a.* 2.

1919 JUNG in *Brit. Jrnl. Psychol.* X. 22 A factor determining the uniformity and regularity of our apprehension.. I term the archetype, the primordial image. **1923** H. G. BAYNES tr. *Jung's Psychol. Types* 475 Since earliest times, the inborn manner of *acting* has been called *instinct*, and for this manner of psychic apprehension of the object I have proposed the term *archetype*... This term embraces the same idea as is contained in 'primordial image'... The archetype is a symbolical formula, which always begins to function whenever there are no conscious ideas present. *Ibid.* 507 These archetypes, whose innermost nature is inaccessible to experience, represent the precipitate of psychic functioning of the whole ancestral line. **1957** N. FRYE *Anat. of Crit.* ii. 99, I mean by an archetype a symbol which connects one poem with another. **1962** A. M. DRY *Psychol. of Jung* iv. 92 For the most part it is the archetypes, not the instincts, with which Jung is concerned.

archeˈtypical, *a.* [f. prec. after Gr. ἀρχετυπικῶς; see -ICAL.] = ARCHETYPAL^1^. Also *absol.* Hence **archetypiˈcality**, archetypical character.

1737 B. MARTIN *Bibliotheca Techn.* x. 200 Perfect or Adequate Ideas represent their archetypical objects, compleatly and perfectly. **1738** WARBURTON *Div. Legat.* VI. v, The final archietypical Sacrifice of the Son of God was figured in the command to offer Isaac. **1868** D. W. SIMON tr. *Dorner's Hist. Person Christ* (Div. 2) III. 203 Supposing the only thing necessary to redemption to be a consciousness of the idea of the archetypical. *Ibid.* 204 A productivity of His archetypicality lies in His royal plenipotence and deed. **1949** *Commentary* VIII. 41/1 [Joel Chandler] Harris, the archetypical Southerner, sought the Negro's love, and pretended he had received it.

archetypist (ˈɑːkɪtaɪpɪst). [f. as prec. + -IST.] One who studies early typography.

1881 *Athenæum* 6 Aug. 175/3 [He], like many other archetypists, subsequently found that 1468 was an impossible date.

†**arˈchetypous,** *a. Obs. rare*^−1^. [f. as prec. + -OUS.] = ARCHETYPAL^1^.

1683 E. HOOKER *Pref. Pordage's Myst. Div.* 67 The veri Archetypous Globe of all Globes.

‖**archeus** (ɑːˈkiːəs). *Obs.* exc. *Hist.* [mod.L., *archæus* (Basil Valentine), f. Gr. ἀρχαῖος original.]

1. The immaterial principle supposed by the Paracelsians to produce and preside over the activities of the animal and vegetable economy; vital force. (It was held that the chief *archeus* was situated in the stomach, and that subordinate *archei* regulated the action of other organs.)

1641 FRENCH *Distill.* vi. (1651) 175 The Archæus, the servant of nature. **1651** BIGGS *New Dispens.* 183 ¶247 The Archeus doth daily dispence.. so much bloud to the parts, as may serve for their nutrition. **1797** PEARSON in *Phil. Trans.* LXXXVIII. 16 The archeus, or vital power, of the bladder. **1848** HOOPER *Med. Dict.* (ed. 8) 164 The chief Archeus kept watch at the cardiac orifice of the stomach.

2. (See quot.) Also *attrib.*

1706 PHILLIPS, *Archeus*.. Also, the highest, most exalted and invisible Spirit that can be separated from mixt Bodies. **1798** in *Phil. Trans.* LXXXVIII. 16 When the archeus spirit of urine meets with a volatile earthy spirit.

arch-fiend (ˈɑːtʃˈfiːnd). [ARCH- 2.] A chief or leader of fiends; Satan.

1667 MILTON *P.L.* I. 209 So stretcht out huge in length the Arch-fiend lay. *a* **1711** KEN *Poet. Wks.* 1721 I. 115 Each of the curst Arch-fiends their Legions led. **1796** SOUTHEY *To Penates* Wks. II. 279 Shrinks like the Arch-Fiend at Ithuriel's spear. **1872** H. MACMILLAN *True Vine* vii. 295 A fallen spirit, an archangel become an archfiend.

arch-flamen (ˈɑːtʃˈfleɪmɛn). [ad. med.L. *archiflāmen* = *archiepiscopus*; see ARCHI- and FLAMEN.] A chief flamen or priest; an archbishop. Hence **archflamenship**.

c **1425** WYNTOUN *Cron.* v. viii. 41 Þe Archebyschopys callyt þan wes Arche flamynes. **1576** LAMBARDE *Peramb. Kent* (1826) 71 King Lucius.. changed the Archflamines of London, York, and Caerleon, into so many Archbishops. *c* **1640** HOWELL *Dodona's Grove* 204 (L.) Melissanus, who now sways the great archflamenship. **1656** TRAPP *Comm. John* ix. 22 That archflamen of Rome, the pope. **1823** LAMB *Elia* I. xiii, Bishop Valentine! thou venerable Arch-flamen of Hymen.

arch-foe (ˈɑːtʃˈfəʊ). [ARCH- 2.] Arch-enemy; *spec.* the Devil.

1615 HEYWOOD *Four Prent.* I. Wks. 1874 II. 224 Oh that I could see.. My Arch-foe. **1667** MILTON *P.L.* VI. 259 The arch foe subdu'd, Or Captive drag'd in Chains. **1800** COLERIDGE *Piccolom.* I. xii, The arch-foe of his Emperor.

ˈ**arch-ˈheretic.** [ARCH- 1, 2.] A chief heretic; a first heretic; a founder or leader of heresy. **arch-heresy**, fundamental or extreme heresy.

1528 MORE *Heresyes* IV. Wks. 260/1 The archeheritiques themselfe, well declare the holynesse of their doctrine by theyr own liuing. **1579** FULKE *Ref. Rastel* 743 The Pope, the Archheretique of the world. **1659** PEARSON *Creed* (1839) 228 Simon Magus, the arch-heretic, first began. **1858** FROUDE *Hist. Eng.* IV. xviii. 40 The arch-heretic Henry of England. **1668** BUTLER *Char. of Time-Server*, He accounts it.. arch-heresy to approve of anything.. that is laid by.

arch-house: see ARCH- 4.

archi- (ˌɑːkɪ-), *pref.*, a. L. *archi-*, Gr. ἀρχι-: see ARCH-. This form of the prefix is retained in words taken in modern times from Gr. or L., directly or through mod.Fr., and in compounds formed on the model of these. Hence it is sometimes found in the adjectives, etc. belonging to substantives, which, from their earlier introduction, have themselves the form *arch-*, as *archdeacon*, *archidiaconal*, *archbishop*, *archiepiscopal*. Some words have both forms, as *archi-presbyter*, *arch-presbyter*.

1. = ARCH-; chief, principal, first in authority or order. **a.** in *sbs.*, as ‖**archidi'dascalus** [latinized f. Gr. ἀρχι-διδάσκαλος], head-master of a school; whence **archidida'scalian, -ine,** *a.*, of a headmaster; †**archigu'bernacy** [L. *archigubernus* chief pilot], office of governor-in-chief; **archi-master**, see ARCHEMASTER; **archi-ty'pographer** [mod.L. *architypographus* in Laudian Statutes], chief printer, superintendent of printing office. So †*archibellows* (nonce-wd.), *archi-table*. **b.** in *adjs.*, as ARCHIDIACONAL, ARCHIEPISCOPAL, etc.; also *archi-heretical*, *-prelatical*, *-supreme*, *-symbolical*.

1599 JAMES I *Basil. Doron* (1682) 69 Buchanan's or Knoxe's Chronicles..these *archibellouses of rebellion. **1811** PARR *Wks.* 1828 VII. 440 The long exercise of petty *Archididascalian authority. **1881** *Athenæum* 15 Jan. 93/2 Beneath the clerical and *archididascaline roof. **1844** SIR J. STEPHEN *Eccl. Biogr.* (1850) II. 367 The responsible office of **Archididascalus*. **1865** STAUNTON *Gt. Sch. Eng.* Westm. ii. 133 Two masters styled respectively *Archididascalus and Hypodidascalus. **1665** *Surv. Aff. Netherl.* 231 They did that at the Sea by an *Archigubernacy, or chief Governour and Admiral. **1721** BAILEY, **Archiheretical*, false in the highest and most dangerous degree. **1637** BASTWICK *Ld. Bishops* i. A iiij, *Archiprelaticall Iurisdiction is grounded upon Canon and Positive Law. **1813** G. EDWARDS *Meas. True Policy* 63 Arranged under the Supreme Administrative, as *archi-supreme. **1660** JER. TAYLOR *Worthy Commun.* i. §21 The Divinest and *Archisymbolical feast. **1842** MRS. GORE *Fascin.* 48 The pedigree to be deposited upon the *architable of the king. *a* **1672** WOOD *Life* (1848) 172*n.*, Dr. F..would not suffer him to execute the place of *architypographer.

2. In *Biol.* and *Anthrop.*, meaning 'archetypal' or 'primitive': as **archi'nephron**, the primitive kidney, whence **archi'nephric** *a.*; **archipte'rygium**, the primitive fin or wing, whence **archipte'rygian** *a.* Also **archi'lithic**, **archi'zoic**: see ARCHÆO-.

1880 HUXLEY *Cray-Fish* iv. 211 The primitive alimentary apparatus or archenteron. **1878** BELL *Gegenbauer's Anat.* 603 The most anterior end of the archinephric duct. **1878** GREEN *Coal* iv. 146 The archipterygian type is not plainly visible in such a limb. **1879** tr. *Haeckel's Evol. Man* II. xv. 9 The Primordial, Archizoic, or Archilithic Epoch.

archiater (ɑːkɪ'eɪtə(r)). [a. F. *archiatre*, ad. L. *archiātrus*, Gr. ἀρχίατρος, f. ἀρχι- chief + ἰατρός physician.] The chief physician, *esp.* the one appointed to attend a monarch.

1634 T. HERBERT *Trav.* 233 (T.) The advice and help of archiater, the king's doctor. **1879** J. GRANT in *Cassell's Techn. Educ.* IV. 96/1 The title of Archiater, or Dean to the College of Physicians.

Archibald ('ɑːtʃɪbɔːld). *slang.* [f. the proper name.] = ARCHIE.

1915 *Sphere* 20 Mar. 304/1 They laugh at the 'Archibalds' which fling destruction at them whenever they come within range. **1916** H. G. WELLS *Mr. Britling* II. iv. 334 Our anti-aircraft guns were having a go at it. Then, as suddenly, Archibald stopped. **1917** G. B. SHAW in *New Republic* 6 Jan. 271/2 He must have been flying at a speed of nearly a hundred miles an hour, perhaps 12,000 feet up (to avoid Archibalds). **1917** G. S. GORDON *Let.* 12 Mar. (1943) 72 Our Archibalds are peppering a Boche aeroplane.

archibenthal (ɑːkɪ'bɛnθəl), *a.* [f. mod.L. *archibenthos*, f. ARCHI- + Gr. βένθος depth + -AL[1].] Belonging to or inhabiting the **archi'benthos**, or depths of the primitive (palæozoic) ocean.

1904 *Science* 7 Oct. 463 The archibenthal species..have a greater range than those restricted to..the shallow waters of the coast. **1912** J. MURRAY & HJORT *Depths of the Ocean* viii. 459 The archibenthal area (that is to say, the steep continental slopes).

archiblast ('ɑːkɪblæst). *Embryol.* [f. ARCHI- + -BLAST.] The formative yolk in an ovum, which constitutes the germ; also applied to the epiblast. (In both uses distinguished from PARABLAST 2, q.v.) Hence **archi'blastic** *a.*

1876 tr. *Wagner's Gen. Pathol.* 462 The archiblast embraces all tissues. **1876** [see PARABLAST 2]. **1885** W. STIRLING tr. *Landois' Human Physiol.* II. 1128 He calls these structures parablastic, in opposition to the archiblastic, which belong to the three layers of the embryo.

†**'archical**, *a.* *Obs.* [f. Gr. ἀρχικός, f. ἀρχή beginning, rule + -AL[1].]

1. Of the nature of rule; governmental.

1651 HOBBES *Leviath.* (1839) 569 Nor hath [the power of the Pope] anything of archical, nor cratical, but only of didactical. **1692** HALLYWELL *Mor. Virtue* 48 (T.) That principality and archical rule..over all our corporeal passions.

2. Of the nature of a first principle; primordial.

1678 CUDWORTH *Intell. Syst.* 73 They are no Archical things..they have not the Nature of a Principle in them.

archicerebrum (ɑːkɪ'sɛrɪbrəm). *Zool.* [mod.L., f. ARCHI- 2 + CEREBRUM.] The primitive brain of an insect or other arthropod.

1881 [see *syncerebrum*, s.v. SYN-]. **1882** *Athenæum* 14 Jan. 60/2 In Apus the two pairs of antennæ are not supplied by nerves from the archi-cerebrum.

archichoke, obs. form of ARTICHOKE.

archidapifer: see ARCH- 1.

archideclyne, erron. form of ARCHITRICLINE.

archidene, obs. variant of ARCHDEAN.

archidiaconal (ˌɑːkɪdaɪ'ækənəl), *a.* [f. L. *archidiācon-us* archdeacon + -AL[1].] Of, pertaining to, or holding the position of, an archdeacon.

1651 *Reliq. Wotton.* 328 (T.) I can exercise an archidiaconal authority. **1674** MARVELL *Reh. Transp.* II. 156 The Flattery of Archidiaconal Preachers. **1849** MACAULAY *Hist. Eng.* II. 91 The Archidiaconal Courts..were revived.

archidi'aconate. *rare*$^{-0}$. [ad. med.L. *archidiācōnāt-us*: see prec. and -ATE.] The office or order of archdeacons.

‖**archi'doxis.** *Obs.* [mod.L., f. Gr. ἀρχι- ARCHI- + δόξις opinion.] The title of a work of Paracelsus; a collection of philosophical secrets.

1643 SIR T. BROWNE *Relig. Med.* (1682) 45 Having perused the Archidoxes, and read the secret Sympathies of things. **1665** GLANVILL *Sceps. Sci.* xxv. 156 A full prospect of the whole Archidoxis of Nature's secrets.

archiducal, obs. variant of ARCHDUCAL.

Archie ('ɑːtʃɪ). *slang.* [abbrev. of ARCHIBALD: see quot. 1922.] An anti-aircraft gun, orig. applied to those used by the Germans in the war of 1914–18. Hence **Archie** *v. trans.*, to fire at with an anti-aircraft gun.

Occas. used in the war of 1939–45 (see ACK-ACK).

1915 H. ROSHER *Let.* 19 June in *In R.N.A.S.* (1916) 116 There are some beastly Archies..which come unpleasantly near first shot. **1917** 'CONTACT' *Airman's Outings* vi. 159 Only somebody who has been Archied from Pluspres can realise what it means to fly right over the stronghold at four thousand feet. **1918** 'WINGS' *Over German Lines* 30 The German gunners..are putting up a barrage of 'Archie' shells. **1920** *Blackw. Mag.* Dec. 757/1 So soon as they crossed the lines, they were heavily 'archied'. **1922** RALEIGH *War in Air* I. 343 The anti-aircraft guns got their name of 'Archies' from a light-hearted British pilot, who when he was fired at in the air quoted a popular music-hall refrain—'Archibald, certainly not!' **1939** *News Review* 30 Nov. 14/3 On each occasion fighters and heavy 'Archie' barrages drove the Nazis off. **1940** N. MONKS *Squadrons Up!* i. 29 Fly over the 'archie' (anti-aircraft) batteries.

archiemander, erron. f. ARCHIMANDRITE.

archiepiscopacy (ˌɑːkɪɪ'pɪskəpəsɪ). [f. late L. *archiepiscop-us*, a. Gr. ἀρχι-επίσκοπος (Athanasius *c* 320) archbishop + -ACY.] **a.** The system of church government by archbishops. **b.** = ARCHIEPISCOPATE. Also, an archbishop, archiepiscopal persons collectively or individually.

1642 SIR E. DERING *Sp. on Relig.* xvi. 83 Away with Archi-episcopacy both roote and branch. **1662** J. BARGRAVE *Pope Alex. VII* (1867) 63 Those many difficulties he met with in his archiepiscopacy. **1678** GODOLPHIN *Repert. Canon.* 4 Touching the Original of Episcopacy and Archiepiscopacy in Britain. **1848** ULLATHORNE in B. Ward *Seq. Cath. Emanc.* (1915) II. xxvii. 220 The leading impression appeared to be that your Lordship wished the Archiepiscopacy, and sought for it. **1892** J. A. FARRER *Books Condemned* iv. 98 Dering appears only really to have aimed at the abolition of Laud's archiepiscopacy. **1901** M. BEERBOHM *Variety of Things* (1928) 207 Royalty had opened it. Archiepiscopacy had blessed it.

archiepiscopal (-skəpəl), *a.* [f. as prec. + -AL[1].] Of, pertaining to, or of the nature of, an archbishop. Hence **archie'piscopalship** *sb.*

1611 SPEED *Hist. Gt. Brit.* VIII. iii. 385 His Archiepiscopall and sacred calling. **1776** GIBBON *Decl. & F.* I. xxi. 594 He refused to fill the vacancy of the archiepiscopal throne. **1869** FREEMAN *Norm. Conq.* III. xiii. 310 Either the young king or his successive archiepiscopal advisers. **1606** WHETENHALL *Disc. Abuses Ch.* 120 Cardinalship, Patriarkship, Archiepiscopalship, & briefly that whole Episcopall degree.

ˌarchieˌpisco'pality. [f. prec. + -ITY.] Archiepiscopal character.

1655 FULLER *Ch. Hist.* II. 106 The best Pillar of Lichfield Church, to support the Archiepiscopality thereof.

archie'piscopally, *adv.* [f. ARCHIEPISCOPAL *a.* + -LY[2].] In an archiepiscopal way; in the manner of an archbishop.

1839 *Fraser's Mag.* XX. 122 So fond is Mr. Philip of episcopacy, that at page 248 he archiepiscopally consecrates John Bunyan, 'Bishop Bunyan'. **1884** TENNYSON *Becket* III. iii, *Herbert.* And how did Roger of York comport himself? *Walter Map.* As magnificently and archiepiscopally as our Thomas would have done. **1886** F. C. PHILIPS *Jack & Three Jills* II. x. 174 His demeanour was archiepiscopally grave.

archiepiscopate (-skəpeɪt). [f. as ARCHIEPISCOPAL *a.* + -ATE[3].] An archbishop's tenure of office; also = ARCHBISHOPRIC.

1792 *Gentl. Mag.* Apr. 332 Will shed the most refulgent splendour on the archiepiscopate of Dr. Moore. **1855** MILMAN *Lat. Chr.* (1864) V. IX. vii. 371 Venice..had never become..the seat of an archiepiscopate.

†**ˌarchie'piscopy.** *Obs. rare.* [f. as prec. + -Y[3].] = ARCHIEPISCOPACY.

1642 SIR E. DERING *Sp. on Relig.* 143 Archiepiscopie! why, who ever voted that to be divine?

archigony (ɑː'kɪgənɪ). *Biol.* [f. Gr. ἀρχι- (see ARCHI- 2) + -γονία begetting.] A proposed equivalent of ABIOGENESIS: cf. *archebiosis*.

1876 tr. *Haeckel's Hist. Creat.* I. 183 We shall have to consider Spontaneous Generation, or Archigony.

†**ar'chigrapher.** *Obs.*$^{-0}$. [f. late L. *archigraph-us* + -ER[1].] 'The Chief Secretary or principal Clerk.' Blount *Glossogr.* 1656.

archil ('ɑːtʃɪl, 'ɑːkɪl). Forms: 6 archall, 7 -al, 8 -el, arcel(l, 8–9 archil. [a corruption of the more correct ORCHIL, in 15th c. *orchell*, a. OF. *orchel*, *orcheil* (late *orseil*), ad. It. *orcello*, earlier *oricello*, or OSp. *orchillo*. In mod.L. *roccella*, mod.Sp. *archilla*, F. *orseille*. Origin uncertain: see below.]

A name given to various species of lichens, also called Orchil and Orchilla-weed (*Roccella tinctoria*, etc.), which yield a violet dye, and the chemical test substance litmus. Also: The colouring-matter prepared from these and other lichens.

1483 *Act 1 Rich. III*, viii. §3 Diers usen to dye..with Orchell and Corke. **1551** TURNER *Herbal* I. Pj b, Of Orchall, otherwyse called corck..This is called in London archall, and the dyers vse it to dy withall. **1678** PHILLIPS, *Archal*, otherwise called Derbishire Liverwort, because it groweth upon the Freestones of the Mountain Peak. **1727** THRELKELD *Synop. Stirp. Hibern.*, Sold by the name of Archel in this city. **1758** *Phil. Trans.* I. 673 A red dye.. preferable to the cork, or arcel. **1791** HAMILTON *Berthollet's Dyeing* Introd. 11 A kind of archil. **1860** PIESSE *Chem. Wond.* 146 This archil yields a beautiful blue pigment, known..by the name of litmus. **1863** WATTS *Dict. Chem.* (1872) I. 355 A variety of archil manufactured in Glasgow..is much esteemed, and sold by the name of *cudbear*.

[Erroneously derived by Littré from the name of its discoverer or introducer into Italy, Federigo *Rucellai* or *Oricellari*, *c* 1300. For the *Oricellari*, afterwards vulgò *Ruccellari* or *Rucellai*, took their surname from the *oricello*: cf. GAMURRINI *Istoria genealogica delle famiglie nobili della Toscana* (1668) I. 274, *Giornale de' letterati d' Italia* (1722) XXXIII, art. 6, and MANNI *De Florentinis inventis* (1731). According to the second of these, Federigo, on noticing the properties of the plant in the Levant, 'intesi chiamarsi *Respio* in quella parte, *Orciglio* in Ispagna.' Whether the original was *Oricello* or *Orciglio*, a derivation from *rocca* rock, founded on mod.L. *roccella*, is out of the question.]

Archilochian (ɑːkɪ'ləʊkɪən), *a.* [f. L. *Archilochī-us* (f. Gr. Ἀρχίλοχος) + -AN.] Pertaining to, or derived from, Archilochus, an early Greek satiric poet, the alleged originator of iambic metre.

1751 CHAMBERS *Cycl.*, It is usual to mix iambic verses of six feet, abating a syllable, with Archilochian verses. **1849** GROTE *Greece* II. lxvii. VI. 34 The Iambic or Archilochian vein.

†**ar'chiloquy.** *Obs.* [f. ARCHI- + L. *-loquium* speech.] 'The first part or beginning of a speech.' Blount *Glossogr.* 1656.

archimage ('ɑːkɪmeɪdʒ). [f. ARCHI- + L. *magus*, It. *mago*, F. *mage* (ad. Gr. Μάγος Magian), magician, enchanter. Formerly also in L. form *archimagus* and quasi-It. *archimago*.] A chief magician or enchanter, a great wizard. (Used by Spenser in the *Faëry Queene* as the name of his personification of hypocrisy).

1553–87 FOXE *A. & M.* (1596) 88/2 The archimagus espieng his time, compleineth unto the king. **1596** SPENSER *F.Q.* II. i. Argt., Guyon, by Archimage abusd, The Redcrosse knight awaytes. *Ibid.* 21 So had false Archimago her disguysd. **1678** CUDWORTH *Intell. Syst.* 267 An archimago or grand magician. **1801** W. TAYLOR in Robberds *Mem.* I. 383 Shall we not see the Mackintoshes archimages of Hindostan? **1817** SCOTT *Rob Roy* (1855) 91 Dismiss from your company the false archimage, Dissimulation.

archimandrite (ɑːkɪ'mændraɪt). [ad. med.L. *archimandrīta*, ad. late Gr. ἀρχιμανδρίτης, f. ἀρχι- (see ARCHI-) + μάνδρα an enclosed space, a monastery.] In *Grk. Ch.* The superior of a monastery or convent, corresponding to the *abbot* in the Western Church. Occasionally also used of a superintendent of several monasteries, corresponding to the Western *superior abbot* or *provincial father*.

1591 HORSEY *Trav.* (1857) 174 The principall priors, abbetts, archiemanders. **1656** in BLOUNT *Glossogr.* **1776** GIBBON *Decl. & F.* xlvii. (1782–8) IV. 564 Eutyches was the abbot, or archimandrite, or superior of three hundred monks. **1879** *Mem. Cath. & Cr. Tait* 487 The Archbishop of Syra and Tenos was there, and his two Archimandrites.

Archimedean (ɑːkɪˈmiːdɪən, -miːˈdiːən), *a.* Also -ian. [f. L. *Archimēde-us* (f. next) + -AN.] Of, pertaining to, or invented by Archimedes.

Archimedean drill (see quot. 1940); *Archimedean Screw* or *Archimedes' Screw*: an instrument for raising water, formed by winding a tube into the form of a screw around a long cylinder.

1813 G. EDWARDS *Meas. True Policy* 29 An archimedean lever and fulcrum, able to sway..the World. **1829** U. K. S. *Nat. Philos.* I. ii. 8 The principle of the Archimedian Screw is occasionally adopted in the wheel-form. **1889** in *Cent. Dict.* **1914** *Lancet* 4 July 35/2, I have found the all-metal archimedean drill..much more satisfactory than other mechanical drills for making the screw-holes in plating fractures. **1940** *Chambers's Techn. Dict.* 48/2 *Archimedean drill*, a drill in which to-and-fro axial movement of a nut on a helix causes an alternating rotary motion of the bit.

Archimedes (ɑːkɪˈmiːdiːz). Also anglicized Archimede (ˈɑːkɪmiːd). [Gr. proper name.] A philosopher of Syracuse, celebrated for his discoveries in applied mathematics and mechanics, and for his statement, that with a lever long enough and a point to stand upon he could move the world. (Here used connotatively.)

c **1630** DRUMM. OF HAWTH. *Wks.* (1711) 34/2 Those numbers which no Archimede can tell. **1711** SHAFTESB. *Charac.* (1737) II. 190 They are all Archimedes's in their way; and can make a world upon easier terms than he offer'd to move one.

archimime (ˈɑːkɪˌmaɪm). Also arch-. [ad. L. *archimimus*, a. Gr. ἀρχίμῖμος: see ARCHI- and MIME.] A chief buffoon, or jester; the chief mimic, who in Roman funeral processions imitated the gait and gestures of the deceased.

1658 SIR T. BROWNE *Hydriot.* iv. 59 The Archimime or Jester attending the Funerall train. **1751** CHAMBERS *Cycl.*, *Archimimes*..imitated the manners, gestures, and speech, both of persons living, and those who were dead. **1824** D'ISRAELI *Cur. Lit.* (1866) 434/1 The arch-mime who followed the body of the Emperor Vespasian at his funeral.

†**archiˈmimic.** *Obs. rare*$^{-0}$. = prec.

1656 in BLOUNT *Glossogr.*, *Archimimick.*

archine, variant of ARSHEEN.

arching (ˈɑːtʃɪŋ), *vbl. sb.* [f. ARCH *v.*[1] + -ING[1].] The action of the vb. ARCH; *concr.* structure consisting of arches; arched curve.

1598 STOW *Surv.* (1633) 398/1 The Arching begunne on the East side the Steeple. *a* **1821** KEATS *Sleep & Poetry* 238 The very archings of her eyelids.

arching (ˈɑːtʃɪŋ), *ppl. a.* [f. ARCH *v.*[1] + -ING[2].] Forming an arch, having a convex curve.

1677 MOXON *Mech. Exerc.* (1703) 66 Ground more or less Arching. **1810** SCOTT *Lady of L.* v. xviii, The steed obeyed, With arching neck. **1842** TENNYSON *Margaret* v, The arching limes are tall.

archipallium (ɑːkɪˈpælɪəm). *Anat.* [mod.L., f. ARCHI- 2 + PALLIUM.] A portion of the brain of earlier development than the neopallium, comprising the olfactory area of the cerebral cortex. Hence **archiˈpallial** *a.*, of or pertaining to the archipallium.

[**1904** L. EDINGER *Vorlesungen Nerv. Zentralorgane* (ed. 7) I. xvii. 288.] **1908** H. E. SANTEE *Anat. Brain & Spinal Cord* (ed. 4) iii. 98 Rhinencephalon (archipallium). **1921** TILNEY & RILEY *Form & Functions Central Nervous System* xxxvi. 657 The mammalian rhinencephalon..consists of a primordial (sometimes called peripheral) and an archipallial (often referred to as central) portion. **1933** *Proc. Nat. Acad. Sci.* XIX. 7 This cortex..consisting of one thin layer of cells which are arranged in three chief sheets or areas—medially the archipallium (hippocampal cortex), laterally the palaeopallium..and between these the dorsal or 'general' cortex.

†**archiˈpel.** *Obs. rare.* [a. F. *archipel*, earlier *archipelague*; see below.] = ARCHIPELAGO.

1596 T. DANETT *De Commines' Hist.* (1614) 223 Diuers goodly Iles in the sea called Archipell..(*marg.*) This Archipell is *Mare Ægeum.*

archipelagian (ˌɑːkɪpɪˈleɪdʒ(ɪ)ən). [f. as next + -IAN.] Of, or pertaining to, an archipelago.

1881 H. NICHOLSON *Sword to Share* iv. 23 This archipelagian kingdom.

archipelagic (-ˈlædʒɪk), *a.* [f. next + -IC.] = prec.

1841 *Blackw. Mag.* XLIX. 484 The archipelagic neighbourhoods of Kent Road, etc.

archipelago (ɑːkɪˈpɛləgəʊ). Pl. -os, -oes. Also 6 archpelago, 6–7 archipelagus, 7 -pelage. [ad. It. *arcipelago*, f. *arci-* chief, principal (ARCH- 4) + *pélago* deep, abyss, gulf, pool; cogn. w. Sp. *piélago*, Pg. *pego*, Pr. *peleg*:—L. *pelagus* (very common in med.L.), a. Gr. πέλαγος sea. In most of the langs. the word had at first the prefix in the native form: OSp. *arcipielago*, OPg. *arcepelago*, ME. *archpelago*, *arch-sea*. All exc. It. have now *archi-*. Cf. also ARCHES.

No such word occurs in ancient or mediæval Gr.; Ἀρχιπέλαγος in mod. Gr. Dicts. is introduced from western langs. *Arcipelago* occurs in a Treaty of 30th June 1268, between the Venetians and the emperor Michael Palaeologus: 'Item, quod pertinet ad insulas de Arcipelago'; it is used also by Villani *c* 1345. It was evidently a true Italian compound like *arciduca*, *arcipoltrone*, *arcifelice*, suggested probably by the med.L. name of the Ægean Sea, *Egeopelagus* (Venetian state-papers of 1419 have still *Ducatus Egeopelagi*), repr. Gr. αἰγαιοπέλαγος, αἰγαῖον πέλαγος, and alluding to the vast difference in size between this and the lagoons, pools, or ponds, to which *pelago* was popularly applied. That it was a corruption or perversion of *Egeopelago* itself is less probable.]

1. The Ægean Sea, between Greece and Asia Minor.

1502 ARNOLD *Chron.* (1811) 143 Many other iles within the archpelago, that is the gulf be-twix Grese and Turkye. **1684** *Lond. Gaz.* mdccccxci/2 Cruised..with a Squadron of 14 or 15 Men of War in the Archipelago. **1847** GROTE *Greece* II. i. (1862) II. 4 The line [of Eubœan hills] is further prolonged by a series of islands in the Archipelago.

Hence (as this is studded with many isles):

2. Any sea, or sheet of water, in which there are numerous islands; and *transf.* a group of islands.

[**1529** PARMENTIER in Jal *Gloss. Nautique*, Et me faisois près de l'Archypelague d'auprès de Calicut.] **1600** HAKLUYT *Voy.* (1810) III, These broken lands and Islands being very many in number, do seeme to make there an Archipelagus. **1633** H. COGAN *Pinto's Voy.* x. (1663) 32 The Seas of China, Sunda, Banda, and the Molucques..that great Archipelage. **1830** LYELL *Princ. Geol.* I. 122 The numerous archipelagos of the polar ocean. **1845** DARWIN *Voy. Nat.* xviii. (1873) 417 Within the archipelagoes. **1857** B. TAYLOR *North. Trav.* xx. 206 A Skärgaard—archipelago, or 'garden of rocks,' as it is picturesquely termed in Norsk.

fig. **1862** MERIVALE *Rom. Emp.* (1865) VII. lx. 260 The continent was an archipelago of insulated communities.

archipelagoed (ɑːkɪˈpɛləgəʊd), *pa. pple.* Interspersed (*with*...) like an archipelago.

1880 'MARK TWAIN' *Tramp Abroad* xlix, Gravy, archipelagoed with mushrooms. **1906** W. D. HOWELLS *Delightful Eng. Towns* 91 The tender blue sky, thickly archipelagoed with whity-brown clouds.

archiphoneme (ˌɑːkɪˈfəʊniːm). *Linguistics.* [ad. F. *archiphonème* (R. Jakobson 1929, in *Trav. Cercle Ling. de Prague* II. 8), f. ARCHI- + PHONEME.] A phonological unit comprising the totality of distinguishable features common to two or more phonemes. Hence **archiphoˈnemic** *a.*

1937 A. TANAKADATE in *Mélanges de Linguistique offerts à J. van Ginneken* 360 Taguti finds in films of the Japanese sonants wave elements corresponding to their surds, which are their archiphonemes. **1952** A. COHEN *Phonemes of English* ii. 35 In the phenomenon known as neutralization of opposition he [*sc.* Troubetzkoy] works with the notion of archiphoneme which is: 'die Gesamtheit der distinktiven Eigenschaften, die zwei Phonemen gemeinsam sind.' **1956** *Archivum Linguisticum* VIII. 115 The suspension of phonematic opposition which is often called 'archiphonemic'. **1964** E. PALMER tr. *A. Martinet's Elem. Gen. Linguistics* iii. 69 If the phoneme is defined as the sum of the relevant features, the archiphoneme is the sum of the relevant features common to two or more phonemes which alone present them all.

archipresbyteral (ˌɑːkɪprɛzˈbɪtərəl), *a.* [f. med.L. *archipresbyter* archpresbyter + -AL[1].] Of or pertaining to an archpresbyter.

1844 DANSEY *Horæ Dec. Rur.* I. iv. i. 261 Archipresbyteral supervisorship over the manners..of the clergy.

archipresbyterate (ˌɑːkɪprɛzˈbɪtərət). [ad. med.L. *archipresbyterātus.*] The office of archpriest; the order of archpriests; the term of office of an archpriest.

1915 J. H. POLLEN in *Month* Nov. 495 Mary..thought..that Persons had made the Pope erect the Archipresbyterate in England. **1921** T. J. CAMPBELL *Jesuits 1534–1921* v. 153 It is clear that the Jesuits are not responsible for the establishment of an archipresbyterate instead of an episcopate to rule England. **1936** *Downside Rev.* LIV. 504 A letter written in the interregnum between the Archipresbyterates of Birkhead and William Harrison.

archispore: see ARCHESPORE.

†**archiˈsynagogue.** *Obs.* Also 6 archsynagogue. [ad. L. *archisynagōgus*, a. Gr. ἀρχισυνάγωγος (in N.T.); also in OF. *archisynagogue.*] The ruler of a synagogue.

1582 N. T. (Rhem.) *Mark* v. 22 And there commeth one of the Archsynagogs, named Iairus. **1660** STILLINGFLEET *Irenicum* (1662) II. vi. §6. 245 The Jews..retained their Archisynagogues still. **1753** in CHAMBERS *Cycl. Suppl.*

architect (ˈɑːkɪtɛkt), *sb.* [? a. F. *architecte* or It. *architetto*, ad. L. *architectus*, f. Gr. ἀρχιτέκτων, f. ἀρχι- (see ARCHI-) + τέκτων builder, craftsman. Several of the derivatives are formed as if on L. *tect-us* from *tegĕre*; e.g. *architective*, *-tor*, *-ture.*]

1. A master-builder. *spec.* A skilled professor of the art of building, whose business it is to prepare the plans of edifices, and exercise a general superintendence over the course of their erection. (Cf. ARCHITECTURE 1.) ***naval architect***: one who takes the same part in the construction of ships.

1563 SHUTE *Archit.* A ij b, John Shute painter and Architecte. **1667** MILTON *P.L.* I. 732 The work some praise And some the Architect. **1758** JOHNSON *Idler* No. 30 ¶ 5 One pulls down his house and calls architects about him. **1815** SCOTT *Ld. Isles* IV. x, Temples deck'd By skill of earthly architect. **1854** RUSKIN *Lect. Archit.* Add. 113 No person who is not a great sculptor or painter *can* be an *architect*. If he is not a sculptor or painter, he can only be a *builder*.

b. *loosely*, A builder.

1665–9 BOYLE *Occas. Refl.* IV. xiii. (1675) 249 Babel, whose scattered architects have indeed made themselves a name.

2. One who designs and frames any complex structure; *esp.* the Creator; one who arranges elementary materials on a comprehensive plan.

1659 *Parl. Speech* 2 The grand Architect would never have so framed it. **1788** REID *Act. Powers* I. vi. 526 Plato made the causes of things to be matter, ideas, and an efficient architect. **1817** CHALMERS *Astron. Disc.* i. (1852) 21 The great Architect of nature. **1846** GROTE *Greece* II. xxi. 209 The inference that Peisistratus was the first architect of the Iliad and Odyssey.

3. One who so plans, devises, contrives, or constructs, as to achieve a desired result (especially when the result may be viewed figuratively as an edifice); a builder-up.

1588 SHAKS. *Tit. A.* V. iii. 122 Chiefe Architect and plotter of these woes. **1607** TOPSELL *Four-f. Beasts* 526 Most strange belly-gods and architects of gluttony. **1649** MILTON *Eikon.* xxi, The architects of their own happiness. **1873** BURTON *Hist. Scot.* I. ix. 298 The Architect of his own fortunes.

b. *transf.* of things.

1835 LYTTON *Rienzi* VIII. iii. 365, Gold is the Architect of Power! **1871** J. MACDUFF *Mem. Patmos* xviii. 251 The deeds done to-day will be the architects of our bliss or woe.

ˈarchitect, *v.* [f. the sb.] To design (a building). Also *transf.* and *fig.* Hence **ˈarchitected** *ppl. a.*, designed by an architect; **ˈarchitecting** *vbl. sb.* and *ppl. a.*

1818 KEATS *Let.* 23 July (1931) I. 219 This was architected thus By the great Oceanus. [But see ARCHITECTURE *v.*] **1890** *Harper's Mag.* Apr. 809/2 We would not give being the author of one of Mr. Aldrich's beautiful sonnets to be the author of many 'Wyndham Towers', however skilfully architected. **1912** ROSE MACAULAY *Views & Vag.* viii. 153, I have no sort of interest in the architecting or building trades. **1913** RALEIGH *Some Authors* (1923) 3 He has come out of the prison-house of theological system, nobly and grimly architected. **1923** *Public Opinion* 29 June 622/3 A..vague notion that a building ought to be architected.

†**ˈarchitectist.** *Obs.* [f. ARCHITECT *sb.* + -IST.] = ARCHITECT *sb.*

1650 BAYLY *Herba Parietis* 3 There were many buildings..yearly children of a right architectist.

architective (ˈɑːkɪtɛktɪv), *a.* [f. as prec. + -IVE. See ARCHITECT *sb.*] Pertaining to architecture; fitted for or characterized by construction.

1611 COTGR., *Architectonique*, architective. **1713** DERHAM *Phys.-Theol.* IV. xiii. 237 How could the Bodies of many of them..be furnished with architective Materials? **1883** TRUMAN in *Chicago Advance* 15 Mar., Agitation is architective as well as destructive.

†**ˌarchitecˈtonially,** *adv.* *Obs.* [cf. Gr. ἀρχιτεκτονία architecture.] Architecturally.

1679 EVELYN *Silva* 134 (not in *ed.* 1664) Columns and pilasters architectonially shaped.

architectonic (ˌɑːkɪtɛkˈtɒnɪk), *a.* and *sb.* [ad. L. *architectonic-us*, a. Gr. ἀρχιτεκτονικός, f. ἀρχιτέκτων: see ARCHITECT *sb.* and -IC. Cf. F. *architectonique* (14th c. in Littré).]

A. *adj.*

1. Of or pertaining to architecture; suited or serviceable for the construction of buildings.

1645 EVELYN *Mem.* (1857) I. 219 Incrusted with marbles and other architectonic ornaments. **1774** G. WHITE *Selborne* xx. (1843) 235 With what different degrees of architectonic skill Providence has endowed birds. **1850** LEITCH *Müller's Anc. Art* §17 There are musical and architectonic, but no plastic instincts. **1859** GULLICK & TIMBS *Paint.* 188 To harmonize with the architectonic requirements. **1931** E. WENHAM *Domestic Silver* ii. 8 The various ornamental bands such as the egg and tongue, the ovolo, acanthus leaves and other foliation,..were all of architectonic origin. **1936** *Burlington Mag.* Apr. 191/1 The general effect produced by Boulle is somewhat plastic and architectonic.

2. Of or pertaining to construction; constructive.

1678 CUDWORTH *Intell. Syst.* I. iv. xxiii. 406 The Demiurgus, or Architectonick Framer of the whole world. **1846** GROTE *Greece* I. xxi. II. 191 The architectonic functions ascribed by Wolf to Peisistratus..in reference to the Homeric poems.

3. Having the function of superintendence and control, *i.e.* having the relation that an architect bears to the artificers employed on the building; directive, controlling. (So used in Gr. by Aristotle.)

1678 *Hist. Indulg.* in G. Hickes *Spir. Popery* 74 Architectonick and Magisterial Power of making Laws. **1873** SYMONDS *Grk. Poets* iii. 82 Aristotle so regarded one of their most important aphorisms on architectonic supremacy of justice.

4. *esp.* in *Metaph.* Pertaining to the systematization of knowledge.

1801 W. TAYLOR in *Month. Mag.* XII. 422 These days of architectonic metaphysicians. **1837** WHEWELL *Hist. Induct. Sc.* III. xv. viii. §1. 227 Classification is the architectonic science, to which Crystallography and the Doctrine of External Characters are subordinate. **1877** CAIRD *Philos. Kant* II. xvi. 575 The architectonic impulse of reason, which seeks to refer all science to one principle.

B. *sb.* **architectonic(s** [F. *l'architectonique*]: the science **a.** of architecture; **b.** *Metaph.* of the systematic arrangement of knowledge.

1660 H. MORE *Myst. Godl.* III. vi. 72 The Invention of Letters, of Musick, of Architectonicks. **1838** SIR W. HAMILTON *Log.* App. (1866) II. 230 That [science] which treats of those conditions of knowledge which lie in the nature, not of thought itself, but of that which we think about..has been called..Architectonic, in so far as it treats of the method of building up our observations into system. **1850** LEITCH *Müller's Anc. Art* §42 A style of architectonics ..which aimed at magnificence.

ˌarchitecˈtonical, *a.* [f. as prec. + -AL[1].]

1. = ARCHITECTONIC 1, 2. ? *Obs.*

1608 TOPSELL *Serpents* 643 [Bees] build their combes with such an architectonical prudence. **1611** CORYAT *Crudities* 453 A very faire architectonical Machine made of wainscot. **1678** CUDWORTH *Intell. Syst.* 417 The Divine Mind being.. Architectonical of the World.

2. = ARCHITECTONIC 3, 4. Also as *sb.*

1595 J. KING *Serm. Queen's Day* Wks. (1864) 327 His art ..is architectonical..and commander of all other functions. *a* **1619** FOTHERBY *Atheom.* II. i. §8. 186 Ministeriall Arts.. subiected vnto others, as to their Architectonicals. **1640** BP. REYNOLDS *Passions* xxxvi, That supreme and architectonical power in man's little world, his will. **1857** MAURICE *Mor. & Met. Phil.* III. ii. §50. 66 Homage to theology as the primary architectonical science.

ˌarchitecˈtonically, *adv.* [f. prec. + -LY[2].] In relation to architectonics; with architectural fitness.

1850 LEITCH *Müller's Anc. Art* §286 The simple fitness.. with which the manifold purposes and aspects of life were architectonically satisfied. **1883** *Times* 29 May, The dome of St. Peter at Rome..lit up architectonically.

†**ˈarchitector.** *Obs.* Also 5-7 -our, 6-7 -ur(e, 7 -er. [a. F. *architecteur*, and med.L. *architector*, It. *architettore*, due to form-assoc. with L. agent-nouns in *-tor*: see ARCHITECT *sb.*]

1. = ARCHITECT *sb.* 1.

1563 SHUTE *Archit.* B j b, One Calimachus, an excellent Architectur. **1637** HEYWOOD *Royal Ship* 16 A long boate, or Galley, of which one Argus was the Architector. **1656** EARL MONM. *Advt. fr. Parnass.* 7 That so famous an Architecter should mispend his time. **1660** BLOOME *Archit.* B iij, This Pillar, which the most excellent Architecture, Marcus Vitruvius, used. **1702** *Lond. Gaz.* mmmdccclxxvii/4 Revised by some of the best Architectors.

2. *transf.* and *fig.* Cf. ARCHITECT *sb.* 2, 3.

1612 WOODALL *Surg. Mate* Wks. 1653 Pref. 1 God, the Architector of the world. **1660** *Plea Monarchy* in *Harl. Misc.* I. 15 Our architectors of a commonwealth.

3. One who has chief control; a superintendent.

1461-83 *Ord. R. Househ.* 42 The office of Iewell-house hath an architectour, called..keeper of the king's Iewelles.

architectress (ˈɑːkɪtɛktrɪs). [f. prec. + -ESS: cf. *director, directress.*] A female architect.

1601 CORNWALLYES *Ess.* II. xxxviii, This Architectresse shewes the first ground of Policy. **1651** *Reliq. Wotton.* (1672) 139 If Nature herself (the first Architectress) had.. windowed your breast. **1860** H. MARRYAT *Resid. Jutland* I. v. 62 Queen Thyre Danebod, architectress of the Danevirke.

architectural (ɑːkɪˈtɛktjʊərəl), *a.* [f. ARCHITECTURE + -AL[1].] Of, relating to, or according to, architecture. *spec.* Of furniture or other household objects: resembling architecture in style or ornament. Also *transf.* and *fig.* Cf. ARCHITECTURE *sb.* 5.

1762-94 J. STUART *Antiq. Athens* (R.) No fragment of sculpture or architectural ornaments was to be found there. **1841** SPALDING *Italy & Isl.* I. 31 The architectural monuments of the Romans. **1868** GEO. ELIOT *F. Holt* 11 A folio volume of architectural engravings. **1876** C. M. YONGE *Womankind* xxx. 268 Architectural furniture..seems to me simply fitted for puppets. **1941** AUDEN *New Year Let.* 14 Repair the antique silence the insects broke In an architectural passion. **1959** D. COOKE *Lang. Mus.* i. 2 Medieval music was largely architectural in conception. **1960** H. HAYWARD *Antique Coll.* 17/2 *Architectural clock*, a clock in which the hood, in long-case, and the top in mantel clocks, is in the style of a classical pediment.

architecturalist (-ˌɪst). [f. as next + -IST.] A professed student of, or connoisseur in, architecture.

1861 A. B. HOPE *Eng. Cathedr. 19th C.* viii. 278, I have also been arguing as an architecturalist.

architecturalization (-aɪˈzeɪʃən). [n. of action f. next: see -ATION.] Adaptation to the purposes of architecture.

1879 G. SCOTT *Lect. Archit.* I. 103 A very valuable element in the architecturalisation of foliage.

architecturalize (-ˌaɪz), *v.* [f. ARCHITECTURAL + -IZE.] To adapt to architectural purposes or design.

1879 G. SCOTT *Lect. Archit.* II. 139 To architecturalise the arched opening.

archiˈtecturally, *adv.* [f. as prec. + -LY[2].] In an architectural manner; as regards architecture.

1843 *Penny Mag.* 409 The east end..is treated architecturally. **1876** MISS BRADDON *J. Haggard's Dau.* I. 29 Architecturally Mr. Haggard's dwelling-place had no claim to be admired.

architecture (ˈɑːkɪtɛktjʊə(r)), *sb.* [a. F. *architecture* (? or It. *architettura*), ad. L. *architectūra*, f. *architect-us*: see ARCHITECT *sb.* and -URE.]

1. The art or science of building or constructing edifices of any kind for human use. Regarded in this wide application, *architecture* is divided into *civil, ecclesiastical, naval, military*, which deal respectively with houses and other buildings (such as bridges) of ordinary utility, churches, ships, fortification. But *architecture* is sometimes regarded solely as a fine art, and then has the narrower meaning explained in quots. 1849, 1879 below.

1563 SHUTE (*title*) The first and chief Grounds of Architecture vsed in all the auncient and famous monyments. **1581** W. STAFFORD *Exam. Compl.* i. (1876) 24 Architecture, that is to say, the scyence of building. **1756** BURKE *Subl. & B.* Wks. I. 292 The management of light is a matter of importance in architecture. **1800** J. CHARNOCK (*title*) History of Marine Architecture. **1849** RUSKIN *Sev. Lamps* i. §1. 7 Architecture is the art which so disposes and adorns the edifices raised by man..that the sight of them contributes to his mental health, power, and pleasure. **1879** G. SCOTT *Lect. Archit.* II. 292 Architecture, as distinguished from mere building, is the decoration of construction.

2. The action or process of building. *arch.*

1646 SIR T. BROWNE *Pseud. Ep.* 381 [If] the great Cities Anchiale and Tarsus were built..both in one day.. Certainely, it was the greatest Architecture of one day, since that great one of sixe. **1736** BUTLER *Anal.* I. i. 36 Carriages and leavers and scaffolds are [necessary] in architecture.

3. *concr.* Architectural work; structure, building.

1611 TOURNEUR *Ath. Trag.* v. i, On these two pillars stood the stately frame And architecture of my loftie house. **1759** JOHNSON *Rasselas* xxix. (1787) 85 The ruins of their architecture are the schools of modern builders. **1864** BURTON *Scot Abr.* I. v. 291 Architecture, especially if it be of stone.

4. The special method or 'style' in accordance with which the details of the structure and ornamentation of a building are arranged.

1703 MAUNDRELL *Journ. Jerus.* (1732) 135 The adjectitious Buildings are of no mean Architecture. **1853** RUSKIN *Stones Ven.* II. vi, Many other architectures besides Gothic. **1883** RIDEING in *Harper's Mag.* July 180/1 The Queen Anne architecture of the day.

5. *transf.* or *fig.* Construction or structure generally; both *abst.* and *concr.*

c **1590** MARLOWE *1st Pt. Tamburl.* II. vii, The wondrous architecture of the world. **1607** TOPSELL *Serpents* 627 Hieroglyphical Emblems..made ready and squared for the architecture of this discourse. **1794** SULLIVAN *View Nat.* II. 391 Millions of opaque globes..constitute the moving order of its architecture. **1875** GRINDON *Life* xxvi. 337 In beautiful and ingenious architecture, the birds, the bees, and the wasps, have been competitors. **1907** F. R. SABIN in Morris & McMurrich *Human Anat.* (ed. 4) v. 490 (*heading*) The Architecture of the Heart. **1936** *Discovery* Nov. 363/1 The architecture of molecules. **1959** D. COOKE *Lang. Mus.* i. 1 We speak of the 'architecture' of a symphony, and call architecture, in its turn, 'frozen music'. **1962** 'C. E. MAINE' *Darkest of Nights* ii. 32 He's our protein chemistry expert and he knows a great deal about the architecture of the Hueste virus.

6. *Computing.* The conceptual structure and overall logical organization of a computer or computer-based system from the point of view of its use or design; a particular realization of this.

1962 F. BROOKS in W. Buchholz in *Planning Computer Syst.* ii. 5 Computer architecture, like other architecture, is the art of determining the needs of the user..and then designing to meet those needs as effectively as possible. **1964** *IBM Jrnl. Res. & Devel.* VIII. 87 (*heading*) Architecture of the IBM System/360. *Ibid.*, The term *architecture* is used here to describe the attributes of a system as seen by the programmer, i.e., the conceptual structure and functional behavior, as distinct from the organization of the data flow and controls, the logical design, and the physical implementation. **1967** H. HELLERMAN *Digital Computer Syst. Princ.* viii. 328 A most important factor in machine architecture is the recognition of the increasingly important role of the high-level languages as the principal medium of user-system interaction. **1975** *Sci. Amer.* May 35/1 One architecture may emphasize facility of arithmetic operations and another may stress convenience of input and output operations. **1979** KRAFT & TOY *Mini/Microcomputer Hardware Design* iii. 121 In the most widely used minicomputer architecture, the CPU communicates with main memory over a high-speed store bus; all program-controlled operations involving external devices are required to take place over a separate I/O bus. **1981** I. FLORES *Data Base Archit.* i. 22 All three data base architectures have implementations which compete on the marketplace. **1984** *Freetime* Autumn 51/2 (Advt.), Fast, powerful 32-bit architecture: allows windowing..and multi-tasking. **1985** *Which Computer?* Apr. 20 (Advt.), Because of its multi-processor architecture, its performance doesn't deteriorate as more users are added.

ˈarchitecture, *v. rare.* [f. prec. sb.] To design as architect.

a **1821** KEATS *Fingal's Cave* (D.) This was architectur'd thus By the great Oceanus. **1893** *Strand Mag.* VI. 268/1 The house..was architectured by John Belcher from plans by its owner. **1939** AUDEN & ISHERWOOD *Journey to War* 120 The slope has been architectured into terraces.

architecture, variant of ARCHITECTOR. *Obs.*

†**archiˈtemple.** *Obs. rare.* [? ad. med.L. **architemplum*, or F. **archi-temple* (see ARCHI- and ARCH-). It could hardly be an English compound.] A chief temple.

1297 R. GLOUC. 74 And þre architemples..London, and Euerwik, and in Glomorgan on. *Ibid.* þe erchbishopricks as þe þre architemples were.

architrave (ˈɑːkɪtreɪv). *Arch.* [? a. F. *architrave* (*ch* soft), or It. *arco-, architrave*, f. ARCHI- + *trave*:—L. *trabem* (nom. *trabs*) beam.]

1. The lowest division of the entablature, consisting of the main beam that rests immediately upon the abacus on the capital of a column; the epistyle.

1563 SHUTE *Archit.* C i b, Vpon the Capitall shalbe layde or set Epistilium, named also Trabes, called in oure English tonge the Architraue. **1667** MILTON *P.L.* I. 710 Doric pillars overlaid With Golden Architrave. **1677** PLOT *Oxfordsh.* 339 Stone-Heng is made up of three circles..the stones of each circle joyned with Architraves. **1789** SMYTH tr. *Aldrich's Archit.* (1818) 102 The inscription is seen both in the frieze and architrave. **1856** BRYANT *Forest Hymn* 2 Ere man learned To hew the shaft, and lay the architrave.

2. Collective name for the various parts (lintel, jambs, and their mouldings) that surround a doorway or window. Also *attrib.*

1663 GERBIER *Counsel* 76 Architrave doore-cases. **1725** POPE *Odyss.* XXI. 46 Folding gates..With pomp of various architrave o'erlay'd. **1847** BARHAM *Ingol. Leg.* (1877) 85 With a shell-pattern'd architrave over the door.

3. Ornamental moulding round the exterior of an arch. Also *attrib.*

1849 FREEMAN *Archit.* 152 The arches too are channeled with architrave mouldings.

ˈarchitraved, *ppl. a.* [f. prec. + -ED[2].] Furnished with an architrave.

1664 EVELYN *Archit.* (R.) Arched or plainly architrav'd buildings in form of cloysters and galleries. **1791** COWPER *Odyss.* VII. 108 The lintels silver, architraved with gold.

†**architricline.** *Obs.* [a. F. *architriclin*, also in OF. *archedeclin*, ad. L. *architriclīnus*, a. Gr. ἀρχιτρίκλῖνος (in N.T.), f. ἀρχι- chief + τρίκλῖνος the triple couch of a banquet-room.] The president or 'ruler' of a feast. (Taken in mediæval legend as proper name of a rich lord.)

c **1250** *Kent. Serm.* in *O.E. Misc.* 29 Bereth to Architriclin, þat was se þet ferst was i-serued. **1382** WYCLIF *John* ii. 8 Bere ȝe to [**1388** the] architriclyn.. And as [**1388** the] architriclyn tastide the water. *c* **1430** LYDG. *Min. Poems* 13 (Halliw.) The watyr of Archideclyne, Wiche be meracle were turned into wyne. **1493** *Festyvall* (W. de W.) (1515) 111 At yͤ feest of Archytryclyne.

†**ˈarchiture.** *Obs.* [? contr. f.] ARCHITECTURE.

1594 *Zepheria* xvii. in Arb. *Garner* V. 73 The gold ceiling of thy brow's rich frame Designs the proud pomp of thy face's architure.

archival (ˈɑːkɪvəl, ɑːˈkaɪvəl), *a.* [f. next + -AL[1].] Of or pertaining to archives.

1847 in CRAIG. **1903** *Daily Chron.* 5 Mar. 3/2 His photographs and his archival researches. **1962** *Unesco Bull. for Libraries* XVI. 9 Archival material is usually recorded for preference on roll microfilm.

archive (ˈɑːkaɪv, -kɪv). Mostly in *pl.* [a. F. *archif, archive*, ad. late L. *archīum, archīvum*, a. Gr. ἀρχεῖον magisterial residence, public office, f. ἀρχή government.]

1. A place in which public records or other important historic documents are kept. Now only in *pl.*

1645 HOWELL *Lett.* VI. 5 Lubeck, wher the Archifs of their ancient Records is still. **1667** E. CHAMBERLAYNE *St. Gt. Brit.* I. III. x. (1743) 217 The Tower of London is likewise ..the Great Archive where are conserved all the ancient records. **1777** SIR W. JONES *Poems & Ess.* Pref. 13 Preserved in the archives of the Royal Society. **1775** BP. LOWTH *Let. Warburton* 43 Laid up in the same Archive. **1866** FELTON *Anc. & Mod. Greece* II. xi. 209 That authenticated copies.. should be deposited in the public archives.

2. A historical record or document so preserved. Now chiefly in *pl.*

1638 *Penit. Conf.* xii. (1657) 319 Constitutions..found amongst the Archives at Bennet College. **1683** DRYDEN *Plutarch* 63 He had travell'd over Greece to peruse the archives of every city. **1795** LD. AUCKLAND in *Corr.* (1862) III. 284 Lord St. Helens was obliged to burn all our Hague archives. **1823** LAMB *Elia* (1860) 15 Some rotten archive, rummaged out of some seldom-explored press. **1863** MARY HOWITT *F. Bremer's Greece* I. i. 19 These inscriptions constitute a portion of the archives of ancient Athens.

3. *transf.* or *fig.* in both prec. senses.

1603 HOLLAND *Plutarch's Mor.* 140 These curious meddlers..make of their memorie a most unpleasant Archive or Register. **1830** LYELL *Princ. Geol.* (1875) II. III. xxxv. 268 Those periods of the past, of which they [geologists] were studying the archives. **1865** CARLYLE *Fredk. Gt.* XI. ii. IV. 38 So expert was he, and a living archive in that business. **1878** SEELEY *Stein* III. 421 The Universities, archives of all the errors of the age.

4. *attrib.* and *Comb.*

1937 *Discovery* Oct. 323/1 The promotion of archive science. **1959** *Chambers's Encycl.* I. 570/1 Archive keeping is essential for a civilized community.

archive (ˈɑːkaɪv), *v.* [f. the sb.] *trans.* To place or store in an archive; in *Computing*, to transfer to a store containing infrequently used files, or to a lower level in the hierarchy of memories, esp. from disc to tape.

1934 in WEBSTER. **1950** *Times* 3 Mar. 5/7 The Government's clandestine censors are not content merely to open letters, copy the contents, and then reforward them; they either archive or destroy the letter. **1979** *Nature* 29 Nov. 538/3 Before being archived, data will also be examined by an Advisory Committee. **1982** *Amer. Speech* LVII. 163 All..files will be archived at the University of Wisconsin after the project is complete. **1985** *Computerworld Focus* 19 June 22/4 Finished plans would be transmitted to a DNC host computer where they would be archived and managed.

Hence **'archiving** *vbl. sb.*

1978 *Nature* 23 Nov. 328/1 Most of these data..should be provided by satellites within the next few years but their processing and archiving will require considerable additional effort. **1981** [see *electronic mailbox* s.v. ELECTRONIC *a.* 3]. **1982** *Papers Dict. Soc. N. Amer. 1979* 142 The conversion programming which is at the heart of a dictionary archiving project with a single central data format, is expensive and difficult. **1982** *What's New in Computing* Nov. 53/2 An electronic mail package which features..recorded delivery of messages, archiving, delayed purging, [etc.]. **1983** *Computerworld* 15 Aug. 54/3 The Archive Restore System..manages the archiving of CMS files in VM environments.

archived ('ɑːkaɪvd), (*ppl.*) *a.* [f. ARCHIVE *sb.*, ARCHIVE *v.* + -ED[2],[1].] Situated in archives, preserved as archives.

1886 M. F. TUPPER *My Life* vii. 84, I have just found among my old archived papers, faded by nearly six decades of antiquity, a treatise which I wrote at nineteen. **1979** M. SPARK *Territorial Rights* xii. 166 Then he pressed a button and spoke into a flat instrument beside his blotter, 'Please bring me archived cards Leaver.'

archivist ('ɑːkɪvɪst). [f. ARCHIVE + -IST; perh. directly after med.L. and It. (in Florio 1611) *archivista*, or F. *archiviste.*] A keeper of archives.

1753 CHAMBERS *Cycl. Supp.*, Under the emperors the Archivist was an officer of great dignity. **1813** W. TAYLOR in *Month. Mag.* XXXV. 214 Moses had the command over these archives. He was their archivist. **1879** O. W. HOLMES *Motley* xiv. 91 Under the editorship of the archivist-general of Holland.

archivolt ('ɑːkɪvəʊlt). *Arch.* Also 8 **-vault.** [ad. It. *archivolto, arcovolta* (or F. *archivolte*, with *ch* soft), f. *arco*:—L. *arcus* arch + *volta* VAULT, arch, *volto* arched. *Archivoltum* is found in med.L.] The under curve or inner contour of an arch, from impost to impost; the band of mouldings which ornaments this curve.

1731 in BAILEY. **1761** J. KIRBY *Perspect. Archit.* 11 Archivaults always fall upon the impost. **1823** NICHOLSON *Pract. Builder* 311 When they [architraves] traverse the curve of an arch, they are called archivolts. **1862** RAWLINSON *Five Gt. Mon.* I. vi. 360 Spanned by an arch above, the archivolte being covered with enamelled bricks.

archlet ('ɑːtʃlɪt). [f. ARCH *sb.* + -LET.] A little arch.

1862 H. MARRYAT *Year Swed.* II. 433 A fine brick church ..with archlets gored in white.

archlute ('ɑːtʃljuːt). [ad. F. *archiluth*, It. *arciliuto*: see ARCH- and LUTE.] (See quot.)

1727-51 CHAMBERS *Cycl.*, *Arcileuto, Archilute*, a long, and large lute, having its bass strings lengthened after the manner of a theorbo, and each row doubled either with a little octave or a unison. It is used by the Italians for playing a thorough bass. **1834** *Penny Cycl.* II. 285.

archly ('ɑːtʃlɪ), *adv.* [f. ARCH *a.* + -LY[2].] In an arch manner; cleverly, waggishly; with good-humoured slyness or sauciness.

1662 MORE *Antid. Ath.* I. viii. (1712) 147 Not wittily or archly feign'd, to amuse withal. **1732** MRS. DELANY *Autobiog.* (1861) I. 394 [He] played his part very archly; he is a comical spark. **1858** LONGF. *M. Standish* III. 153 Archly the maiden smiled. **1863** KINGLAKE *Crimea* III. i. 81 He archly resolved to have the meaning..expanded into plain French.

archmarshal: see ARCH- 1.

archmastrie, variant of ARCHEMASTRY, *Obs.*

archness ('ɑːtʃnɪs). [f. ARCH *a.* + -NESS.] The quality of being arch; cleverness, waggishness; good-humoured slyness, pleasantry.

1709 *Answ. Sacheverell* 10 He brought this Archness down the Pulpit Stairs with him. **1753** RICHARDSON *Grandison* (1781) I. i. 6 With a provoking archness in her looks. **1870** EMERSON *Soc. & Solit.* xi. 242 The wise Socrates treats this matter with a certain archness.

archoke, obs. form of ARTICHOKE.

archology (ɑː'kɒlədʒɪ). [f. Gr. ἀρχ-ή beginning, origin; government + -(O)LOGY.] **a.** Doctrine of the origin of things. **b.** Science of government.

1825 COLERIDGE *Rem.* (1836) II. 339 In contra-distinction from the Hebrew archology on the one side, and from the Phœnician on the other. **1877** *Sat. Rev.* 27 Oct. 530 (D.) That which Mr. Blakeslee, with a somewhat clumsy pedantry, calls archology, meaning the science of government.

†'**archon**[1]. [a. OF. *arçon, archon*, dim. of *arc* bow, arch; cf. ARSON[1] and ARCHET.] A fiddlebow; ? a plectrum.

1480 CAXTON *Ovid's Met.* x. iv, He [Phebus] held his archon in hys ryght hande And hys Lyre in hys lyfte honde.

archon[2] ('ɑːkən). [a. Gr. ἄρχων ruler, magistrate, pr. pple. of ἄρχ-ειν to rule.]

1. The chief magistrate, and, after the time of Solon, one of the nine chief magistrates of the Athenian republic.

1659 PEARSON *Creed* (1839) 104 Their annual archon [ἐπώνυμος], whose name they used in their distinction of years. **1754** *Phil. Trans.* XLVIII. 473 Solon..must have been about 52 the year that he was archon. **1874** MAHAFFY *Soc. Life Greece* xii. 361 The chief archon had charge of heiresses and orphans. The king archon tried cases of impiety.

2. A ruler or president generally.

1735-8 BOLINGBROKE *Parties* viii. (T.) We might establish a doge, a lord Archon, a Regent. **1857** LIVINGSTONE *Trav.* xiv. 256 The ancient physicians thought we all possessed an archon, or presiding spirit. **1862** DANA *Man. Geol.* 573 Man ..stands alone, the Archon of Mammals.

3. A power subordinate to the Deity, held by some of the Gnostics to have made the world.

1751 CHAMBERS *Cycl.* s.v. *Archontici*, Certain subordinate powers called *archontes* or angels. **1868** tr. *Hippolytus' Ref. Heresies* VII. xiii, The great Archon..possesses an empire with limits extending as far as the firmament.

archonship ('ɑːkənʃɪp). [f. prec. + -SHIP.] The office, or tenure of office, of an archon.

1699 BENTLEY *Phal.* 271 The year of Solon's Archonship. **1866** FELTON *Anc. & Mod. Greece* II. v. 80 The archonship and the higher offices of state were open only to the first class.

archontate ('ɑːkənteɪt). [ad. L. **archontātus* (cf. F. *archontat*), f. Gr. ἀρχοντ- stem of ἄρχων; see prec. and -ATE[1].] An archon's tenure of office.

1762 GIBBON *Misc. Wks.* (1814) V. 272 All our dates in olympiads or archontats. **1847** GROTE *Greece* II. xi. III. 125 The period immediately preceding the Archontate of Solon.

archontic (ɑː'kɒntɪk), *a.* and *sb.* [ad. med.L. *archonticus*, Gr. ἀρχοντικός, f. ἄρχων: see prec.]

A. *adj.* Of or pertaining to an archon.

1865 GROTE *Plato* I. ix. 311 The archontic office.

B. *sb.* One of a sect of Gnostic heretics in the 2nd century, who held that the world was created by *archontes* (ἄρχοντες). See ARCHON 3.

1586 T. ROGERS *39 Art.* (1607) 202 The Symbonia of the Archontics. **1675** COLVIL *Whigs Supplic.* (1751) 142 Some [turn] Archontics, some Aetians. **1751** CHAMBERS *Cycl.*

archosaur ('ɑːkəsɔː(r)). *Palæont.* and *Zool.* [Back-formation f. next.] An archosaurian reptile (living or extinct).

1933 A. S. ROMER *Vertebr. Paleont.* viii. 163 The archosaurs are unique in that they tended toward a bipedal gait, the animal running semi-erect on its hind legs. **1962** *New Scientist* 5 July 34 The remains of small archosaurs, probably representative of the primitive stock from which the dinosaurs originated. **1979** *Nature* 17 May 234/1 We recently began a study of the otic region in archosaurs and birds, in search of advanced, homologous features, which would give definitive support to one theory or the other. **1981** J. Z. YOUNG *Life of Vertebrates* (ed.3) xiv. 312/2 The archosaurs were the dominant land animals of the late Mesozoic, and they include the dinosaurs and pterosaurs. **1983** *New Scientist* 7 Apr. 12/2 The thecodontians were the first of the archosaurs.

archosaurian (ɑːkəʊ'sɔːrɪən), *a.* and *sb.* *Palæont.* and *Zool.* [f. mod.L. *Archosauria* (see def.), f. Gr. ἀρχός chief + SAURIA *sb. pl.*: see -IAN.] **A.** *adj.* Belonging to or characteristic of the subclass Archosauria of reptiles, which includes crocodilians and extinct groups like dinosaurs and pterosaurs.

1888 R. LYDEKKER *Catal. Fossil Reptilia Brit. Mus.* I. 1 (*heading*) Archosaurian branch [of Class Reptilia]. **1933** A. S. ROMER *Vertebr. Paleont.* viii. 163 The archosaurian bipedal pose. **1977** A. HALLAM *Planet Earth* 270 The commonest skull type is diapsid, present not only in lizards and snakes but also in the great group of archosaurian reptiles—the dinosaurs and their ancestors the thecodonts, their relatives the crocodiles and pterosaurs, and their descendants, the birds. **1979** *Sci. Amer.* Oct. 129/1 Of all the archosaurian reptiles only the crocodilians survived, apparently little affected by whatever proved fatal to many other animals.

B. *sb.* = ARCHOSAUR.

1909 in *Cent. Dict.* Suppl. **1962** PARKER & HASWELL *Text-bk. Zool.* (ed. 7) II. 498 The archosaurians form an assembly of reptiles which differ widely from the lepidosaurian Eosuchia, Rhynchocephalia, and Squamata.

arch-pall: see ARCH- 4.

'arch-'papist. [f. ARCH- 2.] A chief, leading, or extreme, papist. Hence **arch-papistical** *a.*

1554 KNOX *Faythf. Admon.* E vj b, Thou..art become an open archpapist agayne. **1636** PRYNNE *Unbish. Tim. & Titus* (1661) 114 Peresius the Spaniard and an Archpapist. **1574** *Life Abp. Canterb.* Pref. E v b, That Archpastorall or Archpapisticall staffe.

'arch-'pastor. [f. ARCH- 1, after Gr. ἀρχιποίμην.] A chief or first pastor (of souls). Hence **arch-pastoral** *a.*

1574 *Life Abp. Canterb.* Pref. C vj b, That princely Arch-pastor and pastorall Archprince..Peter. [See also prec. word.] *a* **1600** HOOKER *Eccl. Pol.* VII. 440 Christ's prerogative to be named an arch-pastor simply.

'arch-'pirate. [f. ARCH- 1, after L. *archipīrāta*, ad. Gr. ἀρχιπειρατής.] A chief pirate; a pirate captain. Also *transf.* of literary piracy.

1489 CAXTON *Faytes Armes* II. ix. 107 An archepyrate, that is to say a grete thef of the see. **1567** JEWEL *Def. Apol.* (1611) 382 The Pope..called him Arch-pirate, Arch-heretike, and Apostata. **1577** HOLINSHED *Chron.* I. 58/1 One of the mates slew the archpirat or capteine rover as I may call him. **1610** HOLLAND *Camden's Brit.* I. 144 Hasting, a Norman Arch-pirate. *a* **1797** H. WALPOLE *George II* (1847) I. xii. 395 A sea-captain..gave the first claims to kings and archpirates over an unknown tract of country. **1828** SOUTHEY *To A. Cunningham*, The Arch-Pirate Galignani hath prefix'd, A spurious portrait to a faithless life.

'arch-'poet. [f. ARCH- 1, after med.L. *archipoēta.*] **a.** Chief or first poet. **b.** A poet-laureate (*obs.*)

1610 HOLLAND *Camden's Brit.* I. 186 Henrie of Aurenches, Archpoet to King Henrie the Third. **1648** HERRICK *Hesper.* (1844) II. 150 After the rare arch-poet died, The sock grew loathsome. **1714** IRONSIDE *Orig. Canto of Spencer* (ed. 2) Pref. 5 England's Arch-Poet Spencer. *a* **1744** POPE *Poet Laureat* (T.) The title of 'archipoeta,' or arch-poet, in the style of those days: in ours, poet laureat. *a* **1754** FIELDING *Pleas. Town* Wks. I. 208 The election of an arch-poet, or, as others call him, a poet-laureate to the goddess of Nonsense.

'arch-'prelate. [f. ARCH- 1.] Chief prelate; archbishop. Hence **archprelatic, -ical.** *a.*

1594 HOOKER *Eccl. Pol.* V. (1617) 271 S. Basil..an Arch-prelate in the house of God. **1640** BASTWICK *Ld. Bishops* viii. H ij b, Doe not Archprelates take place of Dukes, and Prelats of Lords? **1648** MILTON *Observ. Art. Peace* Wks. 1851, 564 The late King himself, with Strafford, and that Arch-Prelat of Canterbury. **1851** HAWTHORNE *Twice-told T.* II. xvi. 241 If this king and this arch-prelate have their will. **1651** CLEVELAND *On Abp. York* 14 A general Metropolitan, An Arch-Prelatique Presbyterian. **1882** PAXT. HOOD *Cromwell* 232 Laud..that ridiculous old archprelatical absurdity.

archpresbyter (ɑːtʃ'prɛzbɪtə(r)). Also **archi-.** [ad. L. *archipresbyter*, ad. Gr. ἀρχιπρεσβύτερος: see ARCHI- and PRESBYTER.] = ARCHPRIEST.

1562 in Strype *Ann. Ref.* I. xxvii. 320 One grave and discrete priest, to be Archipresbyter, or *decanus ruralis.* **1610** FIELD *Church* v. 509 That the archdeacon and archpresbyter..shall reforme the lighter and smaller things. **1861** PERRY *Hist. Ch. Eng.* I. iv. 157 The arch-presbyter, Blackwell, who had been thus disgraced by the Pope. **1882** *Boston (U.S.) Evg. Transcr.* 18 Jan. 1/5 The dignity of archipresbyter of St. Peter's [at Rome].

†**,arch'presbytery.** *nonce-wd.* [f. ARCH- 4 + PRESBYTERY: see prec.] 'The absolute dominion of presbytery.' T.; full-blown presbyterianism.

1649 MILTON *Eikon.* xiii. Wks. 1851, 444 Not Presbytery but Arch-Presbytery, Classical, Provincial, and Diocesan Presbytery, claiming to it self a Lordly power.

archpriest ('ɑːtʃ'priːst). [a. F. *archeprestre* (mod. *archiprêtre*):—L. *archipresbyter* (see prec.).] A chief priest; *spec.* in early times, as still in the Italian Church, a kind of vicar to the bishop, acting also as dean of the cathedral; *later*, a rural dean. *Also*, the title of the superior of the Roman Catholic clergy in England from 1598 to 1623.

1485 CAXTON *Chas. Gt.* 31 Another whyche named hym self Dauyd archeprest. **1577** HARRISON *Eng.* I. II. i. 15 Our deanerie churches..now called mother churches and their incumbents archpreests. **1710** *Lond. Gaz.* mmmmdccxvi/1 The Cardinal Marescotti is chosen Arch-Priest of St. Peter's Church. **1854** *N. & Q.* Ser. I. IX. 185/2 The Rectory of Haccombe..gives to its incumbent for the time being the dignity of Arch-priest of the diocese [of Exeter].

b. *transf.* or *fig.*

a **1797** H. WALPOLE *Mem. Geo. III* (1845) III. vii. 193 Whitfield their archpriest..preaching his funeral sermon. **1866** *Daily Tel.* 26 Jan. 4/6 The archpriest of agitation, O'Connell.

Hence **arch'priesthood, arch'priestship** (*obs.*), the position or office of an arch-priest.

1560 DAUS *Sleidane's Comm.* 336 b, Whiche do vtterly contemne..archepreistship. **1670** MILTON *Hist. Eng.* II. Wks. 1851. 45 Contending sometimes about the archpriesthood. **1691** WOOD *Ath. Oxon.* I./512 Libels against the Archpriestship. **1881** *Athenæum* 27 Aug. 268/1 The archpriesthood of the collegiate church of Sta. Maria Maggiore.

'arch-'rebel. [ARCH- 1, 2.] Chief rebel, leader of rebellion. Hence **arch-rebellious** *a.*

1583 LD. BURLEIGH *Exec. Treason* (1675) 33 An end due to such an Arch-rebel. **1611** SPEED *Hist. Gt. Brit.* IX. ix. 102 The Arch-rebellious Earle of Leicester. **1648** MILTON *Observ. Art. Peace* Wks. 1847, 263/2 Dillon..and other arch-rebels. **1765** TUCKER *Lt. Nat.* I. 508 The arch rebel.. would pinch me to nothing with a gripe of his iron claw. **1853** TALFOURD *Castil.* v. iv, The brother of the arch-rebel's wife?

arch-sea, arch-see: see ARCH- 4.

arch-thief ('ɑːtʃ'θiːf). [ARCH- 2, 3.] A first or chief thief; a chief of thieves or (formerly) robbers; *spec.* Prometheus.

1652 *News, Lowe-Countr.* 1 That the Arch-Theef's stolen Fire Did, first, the Thing, call'd Man, inspire. **1693** W. ROBERTSON *Phraseol. Gen.* 1082 An Arch-thief or robber. *a* **1805** in Nicolas *Disp. Nelson* III. 417 That horde of thieves who went to Egypt with that arch-thief, Buonaparte.

'arch-'traitor. [ARCH- 2.] Chief traitor; *spec.* Satan, Judas Iscariot.
1539 in Froude *Hist. Eng.* III. xv. 354 The cankered and venomous serpent Paul, Bishop of Rome, and the archtraitor Reginald Pole. **1630** J. TAYLOR (Water P.) *Wks.* I. 49/2 Archtraitours against the Maiesty of Heauen. **1751** WATTS *Improv. Mind* (1801) 356 Satan the arch-traitor. **1867** FREEMAN *Norm. Conq.* (1876) I. App. 719 Was he the great-nephew of the arch-traitor Eadric?

'arch-'villain. [ARCH- 2; cf. med.L. *archivillānus*.] Chief villain, begetter or ringleader of villainy. Hence **arch-villainy**.
1603 SHAKS. *Meas. for M.* v. i. 57 Euen so may Angelo.. Be an arch-villaine. **1623** MASSINGER *Dk. Milan*, Thou art a villain! All attributes of archvillains made into one, Cannot express thee. *a* **1625** FLETCHER *Woman's Prize* III. iv, All their arch-villanies, and all their doubles. **1814** SOUTHEY *Roderick* VIII. Wks. IX. 75 Then did the Arch-villain urge the Moor at once To cut off future peril.

archway ('ɑːtʃweɪ). [f. ARCH *sb.* + WAY.]
1. An arched or vaulted passage.
1802 in *Penny Mag.* (1832) I. 257 Under the denomination of the 'Thames Archway Company.' **1856** KANE *Arct. Exp.* II. xxi. 207 A great archway or tunnel poured out a dashing stream.
2. The arched entrance to a castle, etc.
1808 SCOTT *Marm.* VI. xiv, Lord Marmion.. Like arrow through the archway sprung. **1868** Q. VICTORIA *Life in Highl.* 22 Part of the old castle and the archway remains.

'archwayed, *ppl. a.* [f. prec. + -ED².] Furnished with an archway.
1864 in WEBSTER.

†**'archwife.** *Obs.* [f. ARCH- 2 + WIFE.] 'A wife of a superior order' (Tyrwhitt); a strong or masterful wife, a virago ('Mannweib' Mätzner).
c **1386** CHAUCER *Clerk's T.* 1139 Ye archiwyuis [*v.r.* Arche wiffes], stondeth at defense, Syn ye be stronge. *c* **1430** *Pol., Rel. & L. Poems* (1866) 46 But archwyfes, eger in ther violence, Ferse as a tigre for to make affray.

archwise ('ɑːtʃwaɪz), *adv.* [f. ARCH *sb.* + WISE.] In the form of an arc, arch, or vault.
1577 B. GOOGE *Heresbach's Husb.* (1586) 175 b, [Bees] frame their houses archwise within the hives. **1610** GUILLIM *Heraldrie* II. v. 49 In ancient roles I find the Bend drawne somewhat archwise. **1747** CHALKLEY *Wks.* (1766) 93 A large Caue.. formed archwise.

archy ('ɑːtʃɪ), *a.* ? *Obs. rare*⁻¹. [f. ARCH *sb.* + -Y¹.] Arched, arching.
1633 *Parthen. Sacra* Proem A v b, Black and archy brows.

archychock(e, obs. form of ARTICHOKE.

archymist, obs. f. ALCHEMIST; cf. F. *arquemie*.
1620 MELTON *Astrolog.* 18 All these Gold-engendring Chymists, are Archymists.

arcifinious (ɑːsɪ'fɪnɪəs), *a. rare.* [f. L. *arcifīni-us* (f. *arc-* (*arx*) defence, or *arcēre* to ward + *fīnis* boundary) + -OUS.] Having a frontier which forms a natural defence. (The exact sense of the word in Latin is disputed.)
1859 in WORCESTER. **1884** TWISS *Law of Nations* II. 215 A title to Territory by reason of contiguity, in the case of Arcifinious States, so called according to Varro because their territory admits of boundaries fit to keep the enemy out (*fines arcendis hostibus idoneos*), in other words, of States whose territory admits of practical limits, such as rivers and mountains, is a reciprocal title.

arciform ('ɑːsɪfɔːm), *a.* [mod. f. L. *arc-us* bow + -(I)FORM; cf. F. *arciforme*.] Bent like a bow, bow-shaped; *spec.* applied to nerve-fibres passing from the brain to the spinal cord through the medulla oblongata.
1839 TODD *Cycl. Anat.* III. 681/1 The arciform fibres.

arcinall, obs. form of ARSENAL.

arcister, var. of ARCETER. *Obs.*

†**ar'citenent,** *a. Obs.*⁻⁰ [ad. L. *arcitenēnt-em*, f. *arc-us* bow + *tenēnt-em*, pr. pple. of *tenē-re* to hold.] 'Which bears or shoots with a bow.' Blount *Glossogr.* 1656.

arc-lamp. [See ARC 5.] A lamp in which the light is produced by an electric arc. Also *attrib.*
1882 J. GORDON *Electr. Lighting* 62 In arc lamps.. the resistance which converts the current into heat, is that of the heated air between the ends of two carbon rods. **1906** *Daily Chron.* 30 Nov. 7/3 The arc-lamp standards were torn up and twisted like straw. **1911** *Encycl. Brit.* XVI. 659/2 F. P. É. Carré in France in 1876 began to manufacture arc lamp carbons of high quality from coke, lampblack and syrup. **1932** C. MORGAN *Fountain* i. 10 A steep bank already equipped with arc-lamps, sentry boxes and barbed wire.

arc-light. [ARC 5.] = prec. So **arc-lighting.**
1880 *Wesleyan-Methodist Mag.* Dec. 951/2 Electric lighting by incandescence was just as simple as arc lighting was difficult. **1881** *Cassell's Family Mag.* Aug. 571/2 The arc lights, in which the electricity leaps across a gap of air from the point of one carbon rod to another. **1897** *Daily News* 29 Apr. 3/5 Repairs of the arc-lighting mains. **1933** C. DAY LEWIS *Magnetic Mountain* 34 Switch on the arc-lights.

‖**arco** ('ɑːkəʊ). *Mus.* [It.] The bow; used as a direction in string music when the bow is to be resumed after a *pizzicato* passage. Hence as *adj.* and *adv.*, (played) with the bow.
1740 GRASSINEAU *Mus. Dict.* 6 *Arco*, a bow or fiddle stick. *Stromenti d'Arco*, instruments played with a bow. **1806** T. BUSBY *Dict. Mus.* (ed. 2), *Arco*.. is frequently used in violin music, in opposition to the term *pizzicato*, to denote that the bow is again to be used, instead of applying the fingers to the strings. **1931** G. JACOB *Orch. Technique* ii. 17 Note the effect of the *pizzicato* chord.. and that the directions 'arco, unis.', have not been omitted from the 1st violin part on its re-entrance. **1955** L. FEATHER *Encycl. Jazz* (1956) 65 Present day bassists have a legitimate technique and sound in both pizzicato and arco (bow) work. **1958** J. ALDAM in P. Gammond *Duke Ellington* III. 207 His technique, *arco* or *pizzicato*, is impressive.

arcograph ('ɑːkəʊgrɑːf, -æ-). [f. L. *arcus* bow, arc + -GRAPH.] An appliance for drawing an arc of a circle without using a central point; a cyclograph.
1822 in *Trans. Soc. Arts* XXXIX.

arcosolium (ɑːkəʊ'səʊlɪəm). Pl. **-ia.** [med.L., f. *arcus* bow, arch + *solium* seat, sarcophagus.] An arched cell or niche, vaulted in semi-circular form, serving as a tomb in the Roman catacombs.
1876 [see *table-tomb*, TABLE *sb.* 22]. **1905** *19th Cent.* Nov. 785 Both the 'table-tomb' and the 'arcosolium' are as a rule confined to those many crypts.. which opened out of the various galleries.

arct, var. ART *v.*¹ *Obs.* to cramp, constrain.

†**arct,** *a. Obs.*⁻⁰ [a. AF. *arct* (Lyttelton), ad. L. *ar(c)tus*.] Narrow, confined, tight.
1540 [See ARCTLY].

Arctalian (ɑːk'teɪlɪən), *a. Zoogeography.* [f. mod.L. *Arctalia* (f. Gr. ἄρκτος: cf. ARCTIC + ἅλς sea) + -AN.] Belonging to or designating the marine region called *Arctalia*, comprising the seas of the northern hemisphere as far south as the isocryme of 44° Fahr.
1885 T. GILL in *Proc. Biol. Soc. Washington 1882–4* II. 33 A primary combination of the marine faunas is most natural under the categories of Tropicalian, Arctalian, and Notalian. *Ibid.* 33 The Arctalian realm.. for the sake of definition, might be confined to the seas of the northern hemisphere, limited southward by the course of floating ice .. but.. the isocryme of 44° seems to be a more natural approximate limit.

arctation (ɑːk'teɪʃən). *Med.* [n. of action f. L. *arctā-re*, prop. *artā-re*: see ART *v.*¹, and cf. ARTATION.] The action of drawing close together; compression, constriction.
1656 in BLOUNT *Glossogr.* **1877** ERICHSEN *Surgery* II. III. xlii. 4 Arctation, or even complete occlusion, of the artery.

Arctic ('ɑːktɪk), *a.* and *sb.* Forms: 4 **artik,** 6 **-tyke, -tike, arctike,** 6–7 **artic, -tique,** 6–8 **-tick(e, arctick(e,** 7– **arctic.** [a. OF. *artique*, ad. L. *articus, arctic-us*, a. Gr. ἀρκτικ-ός of the Bear, northern, f. ἄρκτος bear, the constellation *Ursa Major*. Refashioned after L. since 17th c.]
A. *adj.*
1. a. Of or pertaining to the north pole, or north polar regions; northern. *Arctic Pole*: the north pole of the heavens or earth.
c **1391** CHAUCER *Astrol.* II. xxii. 31 The heyhte of owre pool Artik fro owre north Orisonte. **1549** *Compl. Scot.* 48 The pole artic, boreal, or septemtrional. **1621** BURTON *Anat. Mel.* II. ii. III. (1651) 241 Whether the sea be open and navigable by the Pole artick. **1706** J. PHILLIPS *Cyder* 11, Did not the arctick tract spontaneous yield A cheering purple berry. **1772–84** COOK *Voy.* (1790) VI. 2125 We observed several fulmars, and arctic gulls. **1835** SIR J. ROSS *N.-W. Pass.* vi. 85 To know what an arctic night can be. **1856** KANE (*title*) Arctic Exploration.
b. *Arctic Circle* of the heavens (*obs.*): the small circle of the sphere, parallel to the celestial equator, which touches the horizon of any latitude, and, being entirely above it, bounds all those stars which never set; opposed to the *Antarctic Circle*, which, being similarly entirely below the horizon, bounds the stars which in any latitude never rise. (The modern *arctic circle* of the heavens, rarely used, corresponds to the) *Arctic Circle* of the earth: the fixed parallel of 66° 32′ North, which separates the North Temperate and North Frigid Zones.
1556 RECORDE *Cast. Knowl.* 27 The Arctike circle is the greattest of all those circles whiche do alwaies appear, and toucheth the Horizonte in one onely pointe.. All the starres that bee within this circle nother rise nother sette. **1622** HEYLIN *Cosmogr.* Introd. (1674) 19/2 The Artick Circle.. passeth through Norway, Muscovy, Tartary, etc. **1622** PEACHAM *Compl. Gent.* vii. (1634) 61 The Arcticke Circle, anciently accounted the Horizon of Greece. **1775** BURKE *Sp. Conc. Amer.* Wks. III. 45 Whilst we are looking for them beneath the arctick circle. **1834** *Penny Cycl.* II. 289/2 Every different latitude had a different arctic circle; and in the latitude in which astronomy was first cultivated, the great bear just swept the sea, and did not set, whence the boundary circle obtained its name.
c. In Special Combs., as *Arctic fox*, a small fox of the arctic regions (*Vulpes lagopus*); *A. hare*, the polar hare; *A. hysteria* (see quot. 1924); *A. (sea) smoke* (SMOKE *sb.* 3 b): see quots.; *A. stone age*, an early Stone Age culture of Scandinavia; *A. willow*, a low shrub (*Salix arctica*) with pale foliage.
1772 *Phil. Trans. R. Soc.* LXII. 370 Arctic Fox,.. *Canis Lagopus*, Linn. Severn River. A most beautiful specimen in its snowy winter furr. **1840** C. H. SMITH *Nat. Hist. Dogs* II. 237 The Arctic fox is smaller than the common, measuring only one foot eleven inches. **1863** Arctic fox [see BLUE *a.* 12]. **1910** *Encycl. Brit.* V. 371/2 The Arctic fox.. of which there is a blue and a white phase, has the tail very full and bushy. **1842** *Trans. Lit. & Hist. Soc. Quebec* IV. 133 The animals frequenting this country, are.. the Arctic Hare, a variety of a very large size, [etc.]. **1910** *Encycl. Brit.* XII. 546/1 The other land mammals, the polar bear, the polar fox, the Arctic hare.. are perfectly circumpolar forms. **1924** S. NOVAKOVSY in *Ecology* V. 113 Travellers passing through the snowy deserts of extreme northeastern Siberia have more than once come across a nervous disorder, now most commonly known as Arctic Hysteria. **1940** BAUGHMAN *Aviation Dict.* 30/1 Arctic smoke. **1941** *Jrnl. R. Aeronaut. Soc.* XLV. 79 Fogs are sometimes observed when cold air streams over a water surface the temperature of which is very much higher than the air temperature. These fogs are known as Steam Fogs or Arctic Sea Smoke. **1945** R. W. MUDGE *Meteorol. for Pilots* vi. 106 Land and river steam fog, at times known as *arctic sea smoke* or *convection fog*, is the result of cold air flowing over a much warmer water surface. [**1909** A. W. BRØGGER in *Videnskabs-Selskabets Skrifter II, Hist.-filos. Klasse* (*title*) Den arktiske stenalder i Norge.] **1926** R. A. SMITH *Guide Antiq. Stone Age* (*Brit. Mus.*) (ed. 3) 159 The Arctic Stone Age.. is represented by slate lance- and arrow-heads, celts .. and pottery [etc.]. **1937** E. V. GORDON tr. *Shetelig & Falk's Scand. Archaeol.* vi. 73 A conspicuous and attractive feature of the Arctic stone age in the north of Scandinavia is a distinctive naturalistic art.. in rock-carvings and rock-paintings in Norway and Sweden. **1911** *Encycl. Brit.* XIX. 833/1 A carpet of mosses allows the arctic willow (*Salix polaris*) to develop.
2. *fig.* in reference to extremeness or cold.
1670 EACHARD *Contempt Clergy* 54 Heathens and unbelievers.. are all artick and antartick reprobates. **1821** W. HAVERGAL in *Life* (1882) 31 The diocese is still in an Arctic sea, notwithstanding it has had a fine sun in its bishop for several years. **1877** E. CONDER *Bas. Faith* iii. 99 Truths within the arctic circle of doubt.
3. Applied by Blytt to the earliest of the successive periods of vegetation in Scandinavia after the glacial period.
1876 A. BLYTT *Immigr. Norwegian Flora* 67 We must presume that the arctic flora was here before all the others; that the subarctic came next; that the subboreal and the subatlantic.. came later than the boreal and the atlantic. *Ibid.*, Arctic plants should be found on the present shores which were submerged during the arctic time.
B. *sb.* [the adj. used *absol.*] **1.** The north pole, or north polar regions; the arctic circle. Also *fig.*
1569 J. SANFORD *Agrippa's Van. Artes* 14 b, They.. that affirme the frosen Sea to be under the Arcticke. **1647** WARD *Simp. Cobler* (1843) 22 Beyond the Artique of my comprehension. [See also ANTARCTIC C.] **1678** JORDAN *Tri. Lond.* in Heath *Grocers' Comp.* (1869) 535 Th' antartick and artick we visit by turn, In one we are frozen, in t'other we burn.
2. *pl.* Thick waterproof over-shoes for winter wear; in full **arctic boots.** *U.S.*
1867 *Daily Territorial Enterprise* (Virginia, Nev.) 1 Mar. 1/1 The 'arctic' boots are taking the place of rubber over-shoes,.. and are more serviceable. **1878** 'MARK TWAIN' in *Atlantic Monthly* XLI. 327 He shook the snow of his native city from his arctics. **1883** M. ARNOLD *Lett.* (1895) II. 279, I have bought a pair of *arctics*, the lined waterproof boots which everybody here [in Boston] wears in winter.

arctician (ɑːk'tɪʃən). [f. prec. + -IAN; cf. *tactician*.] One skilled in the navigation, history, etc. of the arctic regions; an arctic explorer.
1881 tr. *Nordenskiöld's Voy. Vega* II. xx. 451 The distinguished Secretary of the Geographical Society and famous Arctician and geographical writer.

arcticize ('ɑːktɪsaɪz), *v.* [f. as prec. + -IZE; cf. *acclimatize*.] To make arctic; to accustom to arctic conditions. Hence **arcticized** *ppl. a.*
1853 KANE *Grinnell Exp.* xxx. (1856) 261 If you are a good Arcticized subject.

arctitude ('ɑːktɪtjuːd). [ad. med.L. *arctitūdo*, n. of state, f. L. *ar(c)tus*: see ARCT.] Tightness, narrowness, straitness; cf. ARCTATION.
[**1811** HOOPER *Med. Dict.*, *Arctitudo*.] **1828** in WEBSTER.

†**'arctly,** *adv. Obs. rare*⁻¹. [f. ARCT *a.* + -LY².] Closely, tightly.
1540 RAYNALD *Birth Man* I. iv. (1634) 24 They be the more arctly and straightly affixed or fastened vnto himselfe.

arctogæal (ɑːktəʊ'dʒiːəl, -'giːəl), *a.* [f. mod.L. *Arctogæa* (f. Gr. ἄρκτο-ς northern, arctic + γαῖα earth) + -AL¹.] Of or belonging to the *Arctogæa* or arctic regions of the earth.
1870 HUXLEY in *Q. Jrnl. Geol. S.* Addr. 55 In the widespread arctogæal province.. The existing fauna of Eastern Arctogæa.

Arctoid ('ɑːktɔɪd), *a.* (*sb.*) *Zool.* Also **arctoid.** [f. mod.L. *Arctoidea* neut. pl., f. Gr. ἄρκτος bear (see ARCTIC *a.*): see -OID.] Resembling a bear; *spec.* belonging to, or having the characters of, the division *Arctoidea* of Carnivora, comprising the bears and allied animals; as *sb.*, an animal of this division. Also **Arc'toidean** *a.*
1869 W. H. FLOWER in *Proc. Zool. Soc.* 14 Jan. 24 The reproductive organs [of the dogs] belong neither to the Arctoid nor to the Æluroid type. *Ibid.* 30 An arboreal, prehensile-tailed, omnivorous, Procyonine Arctoid. **1885**

Athenæum 3 Jan. 20/3 The view that the Pinnipedia were evolved from some arctoid, probably ursine, form of land Carnivora. *Ibid.* 2 May 570/1 The arctoidean carnivorous mammals. **1923** *Glasgow Herald* 27 Mar. 6/2 The polecat.. has nothing to do with any cat... It is Arctoid, not Feline.

‖**Arcturus** (ɑːˈkˈtjʊərəs). *Astr.* Also 4 **arthurus, arturis; arture, ariture, arctour.** [L. *arctūrus*, a. Gr. ἀρκτοῦρος, f. ἄρκτος the Bear + οὖρος guardian, ward (from its situation at the tail of the Bear); the forms *arture*, etc. were from Fr.] The brightest star in the constellation Bootes; formerly, also, the whole constellation, and sometimes the Great Bear itself.

c **1374** CHAUCER *Boeth.* IV. v. 132 þe sterres of arctour. **1382** WYCLIF *Amos* v. 8 Arture and Orion. **1398** TREVISA *Barth. De P.R.* VIII. xxiii. (1495) 334 Arthurus is a signe made of vij sterres.. but properly Arthurus is a sterre sette behynde the tayle of the sygne that hyght Vrsa maior. **1611** BIBLE *Job* xxxviii. 32 Canst thou guide Arcturus with his sons? **1704** POPE *Windsor For.* 119 When moist Arcturus clouds the sky.

arcual (ˈɑːkjuːəl), *a.* [f. L. *arcu-s* bow, arc + -AL[1].] Of, pertaining to, or of the nature of an arc; arcuate.

1642 H. MORE *Song of Soul* II. III. III. xxxviii, An arrow.. its circular course hath bended Toward the East, and in proportion due That arcuall Eastern motion did pursue. **1876** CHAMBERS *Astron.* 627 The arcual value corresponding to each.

arcuate (ˈɑːkjuːət), *a.* [ad. L. *arcuāt-us* pa. pple. of *arcuā-re* to curve like a bow, f. *arcus* bow.] Curved like a bow, arc-shaped, arched. (Chiefly in scientific use.)

1626 BACON *Sylva* §224 Sounds that move in Oblique and Arcuate Lines. **1766** PENNANT *Zool.* (1768) I. 181 The bill is short, weak and a little arcuate. **1875** BLAKE *Zool.* 30 Horns have a tendency to become arcuate in the Goat.

arcuate (ˈɑːkjuːeɪt), *v. rare*[−0]. [f. prec.: see -ATE[3].] To curve like a bow.

1678 in PHILLIPS.

ˈarcuated, *a.* [f. prec. + -ED.] **a.** = ARCUATE *ppl. a.* **b.** *spec.* in *Arch.* Characterized by arches.

1766 PENNANT *Zool.* IV. 80 A very thick, coarse, opaque shell.. bending inward on one side, or arcuated. **1860** MUIR *Pagan or Chr.* 21 The leap from Trabeated to Arcuated Structure. **1877** HUXLEY *Anat. Inv. An.* vi. 318 A transverse, slightly arcuated cardiac plate. **1879** G. SCOTT *Lect. Archit.* I. 18 Arcuated architecture was perfected by the Mediaeval builders.

arcuately (ˈɑːkjuːətlɪ), *adv.* [f. ARCUATE *a.* + -LY[2].] In arcuate manner; in form of an arch.

1850 DANA *Geol.* I. 713 Reniform, thin, arcuately flexed.

†**ˈarcuatile**, *a. Obs.*[−0] [ad. late L. *arcuātilis.*] 'Bowed or bent.' Bailey 1731.

arcuation (ɑːkjuːˈeɪʃən). [ad. late L. *arcuātiōn-em*, n. of action f. *arcuā-re*: see ARCUATE *a.* and -TION. Cf. F. *arcuation.*]

1. A curving into the shape of an arch; incurvation.

1696 PHILLIPS, *Arcuation*, the bending of the bones. **1751** CHAMBERS *Cycl.*, *Arcuation* is used, by some writers in surgery, for an incurvation of the bones. **1880** in *Syd. Soc. Lex.*

2. *Hort.* A method of raising trees, by bending down twigs and pegging them into the ground, so that they take new root independent of the parent stock. ? *Obs.*

1727–51 in CHAMBERS *Cycl.*

3. The use of the arch in building; arched work.

1856 E. DENISON *Ch. Build.* ii. 66 The principles of arcuation. **1879** G. SCOTT *Lect. Archit.* I. 19 Arcuation plastered over to look like trabeation.

†**ˈarcuature.** *Obs.*[−0] [ad. L. **arcuātūra*, f. as prec.: see -URE.] 'The bowing or bending of an Arch.' Bailey 1731.

arcubalist (ˈɑːkjuːbəlɪst). [ad. L. *arcu-ballista*: see ARBALEST.] = ARBALEST.

[**1605** CAMDEN *Rem.* (1657) 205 The arcubalista or arbalist was first shewed to the French by our King Richard.] **1774** T. WARTON *Eng. Poetry* I. 158 (T.) The shot of an arcubalist.

arcubalister (ɑːkjuːˈbælɪstə(r)). Also 6 **archb-**. [ad. L. *arcuballistārius*: see prec.] = ARBALESTER.

1577 HOLINSHED *Chron.* II. 156 Four hundred archbalisters, that is, the best of them that bare crossebowes. **1577** —— *Chron. Scot.* 130 (Halliw.) He set first archers and arcubalisters. **1605** CAMDEN *Rem.* 202 He was espied by a very good Arcubalister. **1813** HOGG *Queen's Wake* 120 The arcubalister has thrown His threatening, thirsty arrows down!

arcubos, -use, obs. forms of HARQUEBUS.

arcular (ˈɑːkjʊlə(r)), *a.* [? f. L. *arcus* bow; cf. *circular.*] ? Of the form of an arc.

1797 A. CUMMING *Com. Board Agric.* II. 366 But the dishing (or oblique position of the spokes) is by no means peculiar to conical wheels, and is equally applicable to cylindrical: and the advantages arising from this arcular construction of the wheel, etc.

arcus senilis (ˈɑːkəs siːˈnaɪlɪs). *Path.* [L., lit. 'senile bow'.] A narrow opaque band encircling the cornea, common in old age.

1795 J. WARE *Remarks Ophthalmy* (ed. 3) App. 25 In elderly persons an opacity.. appears round the whole circumference of the Cornea... This change in the structure of the Cornea has been described by authors under the name of Gerontoxon, vel Arcus Senilis. *Ibid.*, After the Arcus Senilis had been some time formed, a slight Ophthalmy ensued. **1920** A. E. W. MASON *Summons* i. 8 The pupils of his pale eyes were ringed with so pronounced an *arcus senilis* that they commanded the attention like a disfigurement. **1942** *Lancet* 5 Sept. 287/2 Arcus senilis and arteriosclerosis both arise in elderly people.. but.. it is safe to say that the possession of an arcus senilis does not mean its owner has vascular disease.

arc welding: see ARC *sb.* 5 and ELECTRIC *a.* 2 b. Hence ***arc welder***.

1890 *Sci. Amer.* Suppl. XXX. 12271 (*caption*) Coffin's Arc Welding Machine. *Ibid.* 12272/1 Mr. Coffin even proposes to make a very minute arc welder for jewelers' use. **1923** *Jrnl. Inst. Electr. Engineers* LXI. 253/1 Arc welding was originally tried for repair work. **1926** *Gloss. Terms Electr. Engin.* (*B.S.I.*) I. 212 *Arc Welding*, the welding of metals by means of heat generated by passing a current between the metals and an electrode of carbon or other material.

ard (ɑːd). *Archæol.* [a. Norw., ad. ON *arðr* plough: cf. ARDER and EAR *v.*[1]] A primitive light plough, which scratched the surface of the land rather than turning furrows.

1931 *Acta Archaeologica* II. 131 The balk-enclosed fields were cultivated by means of a plough without the mould-board, a primitive plough of the type which in Nordic languages is called ard, arl or ahl. **1936** *Ibid.* VII. 244/1 In the Bronze Age the soil was cultivated with the *ard*, as is evidenced by the rock carvings in Bohuslän. **1946** PRIEBSCH & COLLINSON *German Lang.* (ed. 2) I. i. 16 They cleared the woods.. and then tilled the ground with a wheel-less *ard*-plough. **1950** *Oxoniensia* XV. 9 On the Berkshire Downs, the use of a light plough or 'ard' is implied by the deliberate avoidance of the clay soils which we have noted. **1960** *Antiquity* XXXIV. 144 The Donnerupland ard was found in 1944 and is dated to the middle of the 1st millennium B.C. **1974** J. BULMAN tr. *Glob's Mound People* vi. 148 The earth was treated with a plough of the kind known as an ard that does not turn the soil over as the plough does, but cuts broad furrows in it. **1978** *Rescue News* Dec. 4/2 We are fortunate to have found a set of plough-marks, made by a single-share ard plough, preserved on a patch of clay.

ard, -en, obs. forms of HARD, -EN.

-ard, *suffix*, a. OF. *-ard, -art*, a. German *-hart, -hard*, 'hardy,' often forming part of personal names as OHG. *Regin-hart* Raynard, *Ebur-hart* Everard; also in MHG. and Dutch a formative of common nouns, generally pejorative, whence adopted in the Rom. langs. Used in Fr. as masculine formative, intensive, augmentative, and often pejorative, cf. *bastard, couard, canard, mallard, mouchard, vieillard.* It appeared in ME. in words from OFr., as *bastard, coward, mallard, wizard*, also in names of things, as *placard, standard* (flag); and became at length a living formative of English derivatives, as in *buzzard, drunkard, laggard, sluggard*, with sense of 'one who does to excess, or who does what is discreditable.' In some words it has taken the place of an earlier *-ar, -er* of the simple agent, as in *bragger, braggar, braggard, stander, standard* (tree). In some it is now written -ART, as *braggart*; in *cockade*, orig. *cockard*, corrupted to -ADE.

†**ardagh, ardawe.** *Obs.* [Seems to repr. an ON. **ar-dagi* 'ploughing-day,' ploughing, f. *erja* to plough (cf. *bardagi* 'battle day,' battle, f. *berja*; cogn. w. MHG. *artac, ertac* (also used as a measure of land). For the abst. sense, cf. also MHG. *irretac* error, etc.] Ploughing, the quantity of land that may be ploughed in a day (or other space of time).

c **1400** *Destr. Troy* I. 175 Ayre vp þe erþe on ardagh wise. **1483** *Cath. Angl.*, A Days ardawe (*v.r.* Dayserth), *juger.*

‖**ardass.** ? *Obs.* [a. F. *ardasse*, f. Pers. *ardan* raw silk.] A very fine sort of Persian silk. Hence **ardassine**, a fabric from this silk.

1701 *Lond. Gaz.* mmmdccl/4 A Parcel of Raw Stitchling Ardas Silk. **1721** C. KING *Brit. Merch.* I. 297 Silk Raw. Ardass, Sherbassee, etc. *Ibid.* 298 Ardasses, 19 Pieces.

‖**ardeb** (ˈɑːdɪb). [Arab. *irdab, urdab.*] An Egyptian dry measure of $5\frac{1}{8}$ bushels (185 litres).

1861 SALA *Tw. round Clock* 142 Ardebs of beans and pulse from Egypt.

‖**ardelio, -on.** *Obs.* [a. L. *ardelio*, f. *ardēre* to burn, be eager or zealous. Cf. F. *ardélion.*] A busybody, meddler; 'one that hath an oare in others boates' (Florio).

1621 BURTON *Anat. Mel.* I. ii. IV. vii, Striving to get that which we had better be without, ardelios, busybodies as we are. **1653** URQUHART *Rabelais* III. xx, What is it that this Polypragmonetick Ardelione.. doth aim at?

ardency (ˈɑːdənsɪ). [f. next: see -ENCY.]

1. Intensity of heat, burning quality.

1634 T. HERBERT *Trav.* (1677) 27 (T.) How much heat any one receives externally from the ardency of the sun. **1881** W. RUSSELL *Sailor's Sweeth.* II. iv. 231 Folds of red heat, which lifted and sank by their own fierce ardency.

2. *fig.* Warmth of feeling or desire; intense eagerness, zeal, fervency, ardour.

1549 LATIMER *Serm. Edw. VI*, iii. (Arb.) 93 With a great ardency of spirit, he pierced Gods ear. **1655** GOUGE *Comm. Hebr.* v. 7 'Crying'.. implieth.. ardency in prayer. **1830** SIR J. HERSCHEL *Stud. Nat. Philos.* 7 An unbounded spirit of enquiry, and ardency of expectation.

ardent (ˈɑːdənt), *a.* Forms: 4–6 **ardaunt**, 5 **hardaunt, ardant,** 5– **ardent.** [a. OF. *ardant*:—L. *ardĕntem*, pr. pple. of *ardēre* to burn, subseq. assimilated to L.: see -ANT.]

1. Burning, on fire, red-hot; fiery, hot, parching.

c **1440** *Morte Arth.* 193 Sewes.. Ownd of azure alle over and ardant þem semyde. **1481** CAXTON *Myrr.* II. xviii. 107 Fyre so ouer moche ardaunt hote. **1514** BARCLAY *Cyt. & Uplandyshm.* (1847) Introd. 36 Though thou shouldest perishe for very ardent thirst. **1601** HOLLAND *Pliny* II. 160 Ardent feuers. **1794** SULLIVAN *View Nat.* II. 118 Receptacles of molten ore, and ardent liquids within the cavities of mountains. **1882** *Nature* XXVI. 504 The sun was not very ardent.

2. Inflammable, combustible. *Obs.* exc. in the phr. ***ardent spirits***, in which the meaning of *ardent* is now usually referred to their fiery taste: cf. L. *ardentis Falerni pocula.*

1471 RIPLEY *Comp. Alch.* in Ashm. 1652, 190 Waters corrosyve and waters ardent [*i.e.* acids and spirits]. **1674** PETTY *Disc. bef. R. Soc.* 93 The Spirituosity of Liquors, or in what proportions several Liquors contein more or less of inflameable or ardent parts. **1684** T. BURNET *Th. Earth* II. 63 Inflammable salts, coal and other fossiles that are ardent. **1833** BREWSTER *Nat. Magic* iv. 79 Spirits of wine, or any ardent spirit.

†**3.** That burns like vitriol; corrosive. *Obs.*

1799 G. SMITH *Laboratory* II. 437 An Ardent Water to engrave Steel deeply.. Take a sponge, dipt into ardent water.

4. Glowing or gleaming like fire; flaming, fierce.

1603 HOLLAND *Plutarch* (1657) 117 Fixing his eyes fast upon a fiery and ardent mirror. **1718** POPE *Iliad* III. 525 From rank to rank she darts her ardent eyes. **1827** HOOD *Mids. Fairies* 3 Fish, Quenching their ardent scales in watry gloom.

5. *fig.* Glowing with passion, animated by keen desire; intensely eager, zealous, fervent, fervid: **a.** of persons and their faculties; *transf.* of ships.

c **1374** CHAUCER *Boeth.* IV. iii. 121 ȝif he [be] ardaunt in auarice. **1483** CAXTON *Gold. Leg.* 288/2 He was the more ardaunt to martirdome. **1538** STARKEY *England* 144 Yf we desyre wyth pure affecte and ardent mynd. **1539** TONSTALL *Serm. Palm Sund.* (1823) 51 He was of all the apostels moste ardent in fayth. **1777** WATSON *Philip II* (1793) II. XIV. 221 Ardent to behold him, after an absence of several years. **1848** MARIOTTI *Italy* II. i. 20 Many an ardent patriot. **1867** SMYTH *Sailor's Word-Bk.*, *Ardent*, said of a vessel when she gripes or comes to the wind quickly.

b. of emotions and their expression.

c **1374** CHAUCER *Boeth.* III. xii. 106 þe most ardaunt loue of hys wiif. **1485** CAXTON *Chas. Gt.* 1 Their grete strength and ryght ardaunt courage. **1651** HOBBES *Leviath.* III. xxxii. 196 He finds an ardent desire to speak. **1742** YOUNG *Nt. Th.* VIII. 721 Pray'r ardent opens Heav'n. **1849** MACAULAY *Hist. Eng.* I. 174 His zeal for Episcopacy.. was now more ardent than ever.

ˈardently, *adv.* [f. prec. + -LY[2].] In an ardent manner; with great eagerness or keen desire; passionately, earnestly, zealously.

1340 *Ayenb.* 51 þet me etþ and dryngþ.. oþer out of mesure, oþer to ardentliche. **1474** CAXTON *Chesse* 10 Whom a man louyd so ardantly. **1607** TOPSELL *Four-f. Beasts* 454 Panthers, ardently thirsting. **1786** BURKE *Art. W. Hastings* Wks. 1842 II. 215 That the rajah would ardently catch at the objects presented to his ambition. **1816** SCOTT *Black Dw.* ii. 13 Ardently attached to this sport.

ˈardentness. *rare*[−0]. [f. as prec. + -NESS.] The quality of being ardent; ardour, ardency.

1632 in SHERWOOD. **1721** in BAILEY, etc.

†**ˈarder.** *Obs.* Forms: 6–7 **arder**, 7 **ardor, -our, -ure.** [Prob. a ON. *arðr* plough, prob. ad. L. *aratrum*; cf. also Gael. *arad* plough, and *ardar* plough, *ardur* ploughman, in *West Cornwall Gloss.* Cf. ARDAGH.]

1. Ploughing; *esp.* the fallowing, or ploughing up vacant land some time before the seed is put in.

1581–2 *Invent.* in *Best Farm. Bks.* (1856) 172 For tyllinge of barlye land, one arder. **1616** SURFL. & MARKH. *Countr. Farm* 534 In one arder or two you shall make your ground as cleare of weeds as possible. **1688** M. ROBINSON *Treat. Faith* 117 Who can expect to reap much from a single ardour, or once ploughing? [**1793–1813** *Agric. Surv. Durh.* 68 What is here called four aders, viz. wheat, clover, oats, and fallow.]

2. The state of being ploughed up.

1524 *MS. Leases Dean & Ch. York* i, [The lessee to] leve the arable land in gud ardure and tilht.

3. Land ploughed up and left fallow, fallow land.

1641 BEST *Farm. Bks.* (1856) 132 To sowe olde ardure. **1668** *Invent.* in *Best Farm. Bks.* (1856) 176 The winter corne sowne on the grounde and the arders, 45*l.*

ardi, -liche, obs. forms of HARDY, HARDILY.

ardour, ardor (ˈɑːdə(r)). Forms: 4–7 **ardure**, 5 **ardeur**, 7– **ardour, -or**. [a. OF. and AF. *ardour*, earlier OF. *ardor*, *-ur*, mod. *ardeur*:—L. *ardōr-em* heat, f. *ardē-re* to burn. The spelling *ardor*, assimilated to L., has been in use since 16th c.]

1. Fierce or burning heat; *concr.* fire, flame.

c **1645** HOWELL *Lett.* I. xxix. 41 That grand Universal-fire ..may by its violent ardor vitrifie and turn to one lump of Crystal, the whole Body of the Earth. **1670** COTTON *Espernon* II. VIII. 409 To qualifie the excessive ardours of the Sun. **1755** B. MARTIN *Mag. Arts & Sc.* 103 A Degree of Ardour equal to that at the Comet. **1814** CARY *Dante* 80 Within these ardours are the spirits, each Swath'd in confining fire.

†**2.** *poet.* An effulgent spirit. (Cf. *Heb.* i. 7.) *Obs.*

1667 MILTON *P.L.* v. 249 The wingéd Saint..from among Thousand Celestial ardors..up springing light.

3. *fig.* Heat of passion or desire, vehemence, ardent desire; warmth of emotion, zeal, fervour, eagerness, enthusiasm. Const. *for*. (The earliest sense in Eng.: formerly used of evil passions, but now only of generous or noble impulses.)

c **1386** CHAUCER *Pers. T.* ¶84 The wicked enchaufing or ardure [*v.r.* ordure, ordour] of this sinne. **1483** CAXTON *Gold. Leg.* 240/4 The Ardeur and brennyng of lecherye. **1602** SHAKS. *Ham.* III. iv. 86 When the compulsiue Ardure giues the charge. **1644** MILTON *Educ.* (1738) 137 Infusing into their young breasts such an ingenious and noble ardour. **1678** MARVELL *Growth Popery* Wks. 1875 IV. 313 This dispute was raised to a greater ardure and contention than ever. **1756** BURKE *Vind. Nat. Soc.* Wks. I. 14 And feel such refreshing airs of liberty, as daily raise our ardour for more. **1769** ROBERTSON *Chas. V*, III. IX. 139 Hurried on by a martial ardor. **1819** J. Q. ADAMS in C. Davies *Metr. Syst.* III. 131 Inquiries..pursued with ardor and perseverance. **1847** J. WILSON *Recr. Chr. North* (1857) II. 9 The bright ardours of boyhood.

Ardri (ˈɑːdrɪ). *Anglo-Irish.* Also **-righ**. [f. Ir. *árd-* chief- + *ríog* king.] A head king. Hence **ˈArdriship**.

1881 *Imp. Dict.*, Ardrigh, Ardriagh. **1889** *Athenæum* 17 Aug. 215/2 The usurpation of the ardrigh-ship by Brian Boru. **1896** *Westm. Gaz.* 29 Dec. 3/1 To make the Ardriship (or head kingship) a reality. **1922** *Edin. Rev.* Apr. 243 Ireland will now welcome any native Government strong enough..to give her peace, whether Free State, or Republic, or an Ard-ri chosen from one of her royal races to rule once more from the hill of Tara.

†**arˈduity.** *Obs. rare.* [cogn. w. F. *arduité*, It. *arduità*, ad. L. *arduitāt-em*, f. *arduus*: see next and -ITY.] Steepness, arduousness, difficulty.

1623 in COCKERAM. **1653** WATERHOUSE *Apol. Learn.* 95 (L.), I hope the arduity will not be unconquerable. **1755** in J.

arduous (ˈɑːdjuːəs), *a.* Also 6 **harduos**. [f. L. *ardu-us* high, steep, difficult + -OUS.]

1. Lofty, high, steep, difficult to climb; also *fig.*

1709 POPE *Ess. Crit.* 95 Those arduous paths they trod. **1713** STEELE *Guard.* No. 20 ¶1 To forgive is the most arduous pitch human nature can arrive at. **1831** MACAULAY *Boswell, Ess.* (1854) I. 174/2 Knowledge at which Sir I. Newton arrived through arduous and circuitous paths.

2. Hard to accomplish or achieve; requiring strong effort; difficult, laborious, severe.

1538 STARKEY *England* 27 A mater..of grete dyffycullty and harduos. **1718** POPE *Iliad* XIV. 523 An arduous battle rose around the dead. **1775** HARRIS *Philos. Arrangem.* (1841) 259 A task too arduous for unassisted philosophy. **1849** MACAULAY *Hist. Eng.* I. 206 Such an enterprise would be in the highest degree arduous and hazardous.

3. By transference to the activity required for the task: Strenuous, energetic, laborious.

1753 [See ARDUOUSLY]. **1860** TYNDALL *Glac.* I. §22. 160 Less than two good ones [guides]..an arduous climber ought not to have. **1873** BURTON *Hist. Scot.* VI. lxxiii. 376 Montrose made arduous efforts to reconstruct his army.

ˈarduously, *adv.* [f. prec. + -LY².] In an arduous manner, with difficulty, laboriously, strenuously.

1753 MISS COLLIER *Art Torment.* 188 Arduously endeavouring to shew that these our precepts, etc. **1858** FROUDE *Hist. Eng.* IV. xviii. 55 The work of fusion was accomplished at last, though painfully and arduously.

ˈarduousness. [f. as prec. + -NESS.] The quality of being arduous; difficulty.

1731 in BAILEY. **1748** RICHARDSON *Clarissa* (1811) V. xxii. 248 The arduousness of the case. **1859** MERIVALE *Rom. Emp.* xlii. V. 13 The arduousness of the task of governing it.

ardure, obs. form of ARDER and ARDOUR.

ˈardurous, *a. poet. rare.* [? for *ardorous*: cf. *amorous*.] Full of ardour, ardent.

a **1770** CHATTERTON *Poems* (1777) 25 And glowe ardurous onn the Castle steeres. **1775** T. BARLOW *Let.* in F. Burney *Early Diary* (1889) II. 63 Stop, oh ardurous Pen, and presume not. **1814** CARY *Dante's Par.* x. 248 Lo! further on, Where flames th' ardurous spirit of Isidore. **1918** P. MAUBYN *Wartime Ballad* 20 She felt ardurous in her breast The rising fires of love.

†**are,** *sb.*¹ *Obs.* [Common Teut.: OE. *ár*, *áre*, cogn. w. ON. *eir*, OFris. *ére*, OS. and OHG. *êra*, MHG. *ére*, mod.G. *ehre*:—OTeut. **aizā*. In 13th c. the long *á* in due course became *ō*, exc. in the north; hence the ME. form ORE, q.v.]

1. Honour, reverence.

c **950** *Lindisf. Gosp.* John iv. 44 Witȝa on his œðle uoršcip *vel* aare [*Rushw.* are] ne hæfis. **1205** LAY. 31957 Þa ȝet he dude mare: to Peteres are [**1250** Peter his are].

2. Grace, clemency. See ORE *sb.*¹

c **1200** *Moral Ode* 127 Wenne deð is attere dure wel late he biddeþ are. *c* **1200** ORMIN 1041 Propitiari, þatt maȝȝ onn Ennglissh nemmned ben Millcenn & shæwenn are. *c* **1320** *Sir Tristr.* II. xciii, Swete Ysoude, thin are!

†**are, a re** (ˈɑːreː), *sb.*² *Mus. Obs.* [*A*, one of the notes of the gamut + *re*, the second note of each hexachord.] In Guido Aretino's arrangement of the musical scale, the name of the note A in those hexachords (the 1st, 4th, and 7th), in which it coincided with the second lowest note, sung to the syllable *re*. In the collective gamut, A *re* was, distinctively, A of the *first* hexachord (*i.e.* the note A on the lowest or first space of the modern bass staff), the lowest note but one of Guido's whole scale; A of the octave, which was *la* of the 2nd hexachord, and *mi* of the 3rd, as well as *re* of the 4th, being distinguished as A *la-mi-re*. (See Grove, *Dict. Mus.* I. 734.) Cf. GAMUT.

c **1450** *Burlesque* in *Rel. Ant.* I. 83 Every clarke..seythe that are gothe befor bemy. **1596** SHAKS. *Tam. Shr.* III. i. 74 Are to plead Hortensio's passion. **1705** T. SALMON in *Phil. Trans.* XXV. 2080 An Octave, from Are to Alamire. **1760** [See ALAMIRE].

‖**are** (ar), *sb.*³ [Fr., ad. L. *ārea*.] The unit of superficial measurement in the French metric system; a square of which the side measures ten metres, equal to 119·6 sq. yards.

1819 J. Q. ADAMS in C. Davies *Metr. Syst.* 147.

†**are,** *v.*¹ *Obs.* [OE. *árian*: see ARE *sb.*¹] To show grace or clemency to, respect, spare.

c **1000** ÆLFRIC *Josh.* ix. 21 Ac árodon heora life. *c* **1200** ORMIN 5704 And Drihhtin..Shall arenn himm. *Ibid.* 1462 Swa þatt tu mihht wel arenn himm þatt iss ȝæn þe forrgilltedd.

are (ɑː(r), ə(r), (ə)(r), (r)), *v.*² Pl. pres. Ind. of BE. One of the remaining parts of the orig. substantive vb.: cf. AM.

are, var. AIR *adv. north.* Before, earlier.

c **1320** *Song* in *Rel. Ant.* I. 292 Of ef fa ut [*printed* u3] and e la mi, ne coud y nevere are.

are, obs. f. EAR, ERE, HEIR, HER, OAR, THEIR.

area (ˈɛərɪə). Pl. **areas**, *rarely* **areæ**. [a. L. *ārea* a vacant piece of level ground in a town.]

1. A vacant piece of ground, a level space not built over or otherwise occupied; a clear or open space within a building, such as the unseated part of a church, the arena of an amphitheatre, etc.

1538 LELAND *Itin.* IV. 60 In the west Part of this Street is a large Area invironed with meetly good Buildinges. **1651** *Wotton. Reliq.* 45 (R.) A floor or area of goodly length. **1726** CAVALLIER *Mem.* I. 107 The Gun-powder being..spread over Floors and Areas made for that purpose. **1740** CIBBER *Apol.* (1756) I. 301 The area or platform of the old stage. **1762** HUME *Hist. Eng.* (1806) IV. lii. 88 That the communion table should be removed from the middle of the area. **1869** LUBBOCK *Preh. Times* viii. 273 With a level area at the summit. **1884** *Daily News* 10 Mar. 4/2 (*Theat. Advt.*) Comfortable area seats at sixpence.

2. a. An enclosed court, *spec.* a sunken court, shut off from the pavement by railings, and approached by a flight of steps, which gives access to the basement of dwelling-houses. ***dry area***: a covered channel round the external walls of a building to prevent damp.

1649 JER. TAYLOR *Gt. Exemp.* II. Add. xi. 24 The Temple was the area and court of Religion. **1694** *Lond. Gaz.* mmmxii/4 The Dining-Room Floor..hath..a pleasant Airy 30 foot long. **1712** STEELE *Spect.* No. 454 ¶6 One of the Windows which opened to the Area below. **1810** WELLINGTON in Gurw. *Disp.* VI. 9 To go, like gentlemen, out of the hall door..and not out of the back door, or by the area. **1839** DICKENS *O. Twist* (1850) 45/2 Pulling the caps from the heads of small boys and tossing them down areas.

b. Often *attrib.*, as in ***area-bell, -door, -gate, -head, -railing, -step***, etc. **area-sneak**: a thief who steals into kitchens through area-gates left open; so ***area-sneaking, -sneak v.***; **area-way** = AREA 2; also *U.S.*, an area serving as a passage-way.

1836 DICKENS *Sketches* v. (1850) 16/2 [I] rang the area-bell. **1864** DICKENS *Mut. Fr.* I. v. 34 A piece of fat black water-pipe which trailed itself over the area-door. **1913** C. MACKENZIE *Sinister St.* I. I. iv. 62 The area door slammed. **1841** DICKENS *Barn. Rudge* xxxv, Area-gates is left open. **1917** T. S. ELIOT *Prufrock* 31, I am aware of the damp souls of housemaids Sprouting despondently at area gates. **1841** DICKENS *Barn. Rudge* viii, To retail at the area-head above pennyworths of broth. **1836** —— in *Bell's Life in London* 17 Jan. 1/1 The hungry wayfarer..plods wearily by the area railings. **1838** DICKENS *Nich. Nick.* vi. (C. D. ed.) 42 With spears in their hands like lacquered area railings. **1946** R. CAMPBELL *Talking Bronco* 18 Like a cane That's rattled down an area-railing. **1812** J. H. VAUX *Flash Dict.*, *Area sneak*, or *Area slum*, the practice of slipping unperceived down the areas of private houses, and robbing the lower apartments of plate or other articles. **1839** DICKENS *Nickleby* lix, Why wasn't I a thief, swindler, housebreaker, area-sneak? **1861** MAYHEW *Lond. Labour* Extra vol. (1862) 311/2 Most of the lodgers were out prowling over the various districts of the metropolis, some picking pockets, others area-sneaking. **1869** *Eng. Mech.* 14 May 181/1 Would infallibly become pickpockets or area-sneaks. **1906** *Daily Chron.* 14 May 6/3 To prevent burglary and area-sneaking. **1834** DICKENS *Sk. Boz* (1836) I. 147 The area and the area-steps..were..clean and bright. **1899** M. P. BREEN *Thirty Years N.Y. Politics* 731 Surplus rain..made its way into area-ways. **1907** *Chicago Even. Post* 4 May 3 The building is connected with the main hospital by a covered areaway. **1931** D. RUNYON *Guys & Dolls* (1932) iii. 56 Then Louie gets the back door open and takes it on the lam through an areaway.

3. The amount of surface contained within given limits; superficial extent. (Formerly used also of cubic content.) ***area of planetary motion***: the space contained by any arc of the orbit and the two radii which intercept it.

1570 BILLINGSLEY *Euclid* I. iv, The area of a triangle, is that space, which is contayned within the sydes of a triangle. **1635** N. CARPENTER *Geogr. Del.* I. viii. 201 The Areæ or spaces comprehended of Solide figures. **1685** BOYLE *Free Enq.* 312 So the Bigness or Area of the Pupil varies. **1710** STEELE *Tatler* No. 179 ¶6 The Area of my Green-House is a Hundred Paces long, Fifty broad. **1727–51** CHAMBERS *Cycl.* s.v., A line, or radius, drawn from the centre of the sun to the centre of the planet, always sweeps or describes elliptic Areas proportional to the times. **1831** BREWSTER *Optics* v. 46 Increasing the size of the lens or the area of its surface. —— *Newton* (1855) II. xiv. 11 Newton regarded the areas of curves as generated by drawing the ordinate into the abscissa. **1833** SIR J. HERSCHEL *Astron.* v. 201 The equable description of areas by the earth about the sun.

4. a. A particular extent of surface, *esp.* of the earth's surface; a space, region, tract. Also in many specific uses: (i) with adjs., as ***depressed, derestricted area***, etc.; (ii) with sbs., as ***defence, sterling area***, etc.: see under the first elements. Also *attrib.* and *Comb.*, as ***area board*** (BOARD *sb.* 8 b); **area bombardment, bombing**, the bombing of an extended area rather than of a strictly limited target; similarly ***area shoot*** (see quot. 1925).

1845 DARWIN *Voy. Nat.* xx. (1852) 480 The East Indian archipelago..is in most parts an area of elevation. **1854** LATHAM in *Lect. Educ. R. Instit.* 95 The area over which a language is spoken. **1879** GEORGE *Progr. & Pov.* II. ii. 107 There are still in India great areas uncultivated. **1920** *Act 10 & 11 Geo. V.* c. 50. §7 Where a district is co-extensive with an area, the district committee shall perform the functions of the area board as well as of the district committee. **1925** FRASER & GIBBONS *Soldier & Sailor Words* 8 *An area shoot*, a widespread bombardment over a whole district to make it untenable by the enemy. **1941** *Western Evening Herald* (Plymouth) 11 June 3/4 The city is divided into areas, each under the control of an area commander. **1942** *Aeronautics* Oct. 33/3 Area bombing was probably the correct type of bombing to adopt against the German ships in Brest. **1944** *Hansard Lords* 5th Ser. CXXX. 739 Do the Government understand the full force of what area bombardment is doing and is destroying now? *Ibid.* 741 The first outstanding raid of area bombing was..in the spring of 1942. **1962** *BBC Handbk.* 37 There are regional and area news bulletins..and other events which are carried locally. *Ibid.* 70 Most VHF transmitters cover an area smaller than a BBC region and can be used for what is called area broadcasting.

b. *Biol.* A limited part of the surface of any organism, distinguished by colour, texture, etc., from that which surrounds it.

1851 RICHARDSON *Geol.* viii. 232 The part which is bent against the ventral valve is called the area. **1857** BERKELEY *Crypt. Bot.* §395 Anastomosing so as to form little areæ. **1880** *Syd. Soc. Lex.* s.v., The germinative area..an opaque spot in which the embryo appears.

5. *fig.* Of extent conceived by the mind: Surface (*obs.*); scope, range, extent.

1627 G. WATTS *Bacon's Adv. Learn.* (1640) Pref. 29 The minds of men are after such strange waies besieged, that for to admit the true beams of things, a sincere and polisht Area is wanting. **1852** D. MITCHELL *Dream Life* 163 The whole area of life. **1872** LIDDON *Elem. Relig.* i. 26 The exact area and import of these truths. **1955** D. DAVIE *Articulate Energy* vii. 87 The images serve to indicate roughly the area of experience that the poet is dealing with. **1957** G. FABER *Jowett* v. 85 The feeling which dictated his unequivocal choice of words..was strongly rooted in a still hateful area of memory.

†**6.** A bed or border in a garden. (So in L.) *Obs.*

1658 SIR T. BROWNE *Gard. Cyrus* i. 95 The area or decussated plot might be a perfect square. **1669** J. ROSE *Eng. Viney. Vind.* (1675) 25 That when the ridges come to be levell'd, the top of your sets may be even with the area.

7. A bald place on the head; a disease of the hair which causes it to fall off and leave bald patches. (So in L.)

1706 in PHILLIPS. **1727–51** CHAMBERS *Cycl.*, *Area* is a general kind of depilation. **1880** in *Syd. Soc. Lex.*

8. Special Comb. **area code** *N. Amer.*, a dialling code identifying an area or region within a national telephone system, and used in conjunction with a local number.

[**1951** *Pop. Mechanics* Nov. 130/2 Each area..has been given a three-digit number. These are the national-area codes you will someday dial before spinning out the local number you want in a distant city.] **1961** *N.Y. Times* 1 June 37/8 On Oct. 1, customers calling the city from the suburban counties will first dial the New York *area code, 212, then the local number. **1965** 'E. MCBAIN' *He who Hesitates* ii. 42 He sat in the booth..and dialled the area code for Carey, and then the number, Carey 7-3341, and waited while the phone rang on the other end. **1985** *N.Y. Times* 14 Dec. 13/2 By dialling 1, 0, a three-digit access code and the area code and number, a caller can use any of eight different long distance companies and have the charge for the call tacked onto the telephone bill.

† **a'reach**, *v. Obs.* For forms see REACH *v.* [OE. *arǽcan*, f. A- *pref.* 1 + *rǽcan* to REACH; cogn. with OHG. *arreichôn*, mod.G. *erreichen*. Cf. ARECCHE, with which this vb. was occas. confused.]

1. *trans.* To reach, get at; *esp.* to get at with a weapon, to strike.
1014 *O.E. Chron.* (Laud MS.) Sloh eall þet man cynn þæt man arǽcan mihte. *c* **1230** *Ancr. R.* 166 Þe halewen makeden of al þe worlde ase ane stol..uorto arechen þe heouene. *a* **1330** *Sir Otuel* 1312 Otuwel, for wraþþe, a non Arei3te him on þe cheke bon. **1393** GOWER *Conf.* II. 140 The flood in such condicion Avaleth, that his drinke arecche He may nought. *c* **1460** *Lybeaus Disc.* 1129 For wham Lybeaus arafte, After hys ferste drawghte He slep for evermare. **1475** CAXTON *Jason* 30 b, For whom he arecheth shall neuer after see fayr daye. **1513** DOUGLAS *Æneis* II. x. (ix) 42 With grundin lance..Almaist he haid him tuichit and arrekit.

2. *fig.* To get into possession of, obtain.
1393 GOWER *Conf.* I. 150 For ofte shall a woman have Thing, whiche a man may nought areche. **1596** SPENSER *F.Q.* II. x. 34 Till his ambitious sonnes vnto them twaine Arraught the rule.

3. *trans.* To reach (a thing to a person); to hand, deliver.
c **1000** ÆLFRIC *Gram.* xxviii. §5 Arǽce me ða bóc. **1205** LAY. 10539 He..wapnen him arǽhte [**1250** arahte]. *a* **1300** *Floriz & Bl.* 812 To Daris..Twenti pund he ara3te. **1388** WYCLIF *John* xiii. 26 To whom Y schal areche a sop of breed. **1530** PALSGR. 435/2, I areche a thing to one touchyng or handlyng of it, *Jattayns.*

4. *intr.* To reach, stretch, extend (*to*).
c **1225** *St. Marherete* (1866) 12 As þah ha sehe..þe deore rode areachen to þe heouene. **1382** WYCLIF *Gen.* xlix. 13 Zabulon..arechynge [**1388** schal stretche] vnto Sidon. **1398** TREVISA *Barth. De P.R.* VIII. xvi. (1495) 324 Noo thynge..growyth but the sonne beme aretche therto. **1506** GUYLFORDE *Pylgr.* 55 They do areche ferre in lengthe. **1513** DOUGLAS *Æneis* III. x. 44 And hedis semand to the heuin areik.

5. Hence in various fig. senses: To reach or attain in thought, imagine; to be sufficient or able.
c **1220** *Ureisun* in *Cott. Hom.* 193 Ne mei non heorte..arechen..Hu muchel god ðu 3eirkest wið-inne paradise. *c* **1230** *Ancr. R.* 166 Hwo se wule bi3iten hire & areachen þerto [*i.e.* to heaven]. **1398** TREVISA *Barth. De P.R.* v. xvii, Þe tonge my3te not areche to speke. **1399** *Rich. Redeles* IV. 12 Ne alle the prophete of þe lond..My3te not areche..To paie þe pore peple. **1541** *State Papers Hen. VIII*, I. 671 As farre as our poure wyttes can arreche.

aread, arede, areed (ə'riːd), *v. arch.* Forms: 1 arédan, arǽdan, 2–3 areden, 3–9 arede, 6 areede, 6–7 arreed, 7–9 areed, 6–9 aread. *Pa. t.* 1 arǽdde, 4 arad(de, 6–9 ared. *Pa. pple.* 1 arǽded, aræd, 6–9 ared, (9 areded). [OE. *arédan*, WSax. *arǽdan*, f. A- *pref.* 1 out + *rédan*: see READ. Cogn. w. OHG. *irrâtan*, mod.G. *errathen*, to guess, divine; orig. a strong vb., but already in OE. with weak inflexion: pa. t. *arǽdde*. Although *aread* is a derivative of READ, yet having been more or less archaic for 300 years, it is found in modern writers in various ME. spellings: the regular conjugation is *a'read, a'red, a'red.*]

I. Regular senses.

† **1.** *trans.* To determine by counsel; to decree.
c **885** K. ÆLFRED *Bæda* IV. v. (Bosw.) Ðá dómas ðá ðe fram fæderum arǽdde and 3esette wǽron. *Ibid.* II. xvii, [He] sende 3ewrit, on þam he 3esette and arǽdde.

† **2.** To declare by supernatural counsel, oracularly; to divine, augur, soothsay, prophesy. *Obs.*
c **1000** *Ags. Gosp.* Luke xxii. 64 Arǽd, hwylc ys se ðe þe slóh. *c* **1175** *Lamb. Hom.* 121 Hehten hine aredan hwa hit wereþet hine smite. **1393** GOWER *Conf.* II. 158 He feigneth him to conne arede Of thing which afterward shuld falle. **1526** TINDALE *Luke* xxii. 64 Arede who it is that smoote the? **1587** GOLDING *De Mornay* xxii. (1617) 368 Fauna whom the good huswiues call Fatua of Fate, that is to say, Destinie, because shee was wont to areede their fortunes. **1600** HOLLAND *Livy* I. xxxvi. 27 b, Come on Sir Soothsayer areed, and tell me by the flight of your birds, whether that may possiblie be done, which I now conceive in my mind.

† **3.** In a more general sense: To declare, make known, utter, tell (things unknown to others). *Obs.*
c **885** K. ÆLFRED *Boeth.* xxiii, Ðá se Wisdom þis spell aræd hæfde. *c* **1300** *K. Alis.* 5115 No man ne couthe areden The nombre bot the heuene kyng. **1613** W. BROWNE *Brit. Past.* I. iii. (1772) I. 87 Sad swaine areade, What cause so great effects of grief hath wrought? **1622** WITHER in Farr's *S.P.* (1848) 216 Areed Of whom thou learn'dst to make such songs as these. **1642** H. MORE *Song of Soul* I. II. lxv, Aread then Psittaco what sights these be.

4. To divine, guess, conjecture (things unknown to oneself). *arch.*
c **1374** CHAUCER *Troylus* II. 1456 What it is, I leye I kanne arede. **1532** MORE *Confut. Tindale* Wks. 525/1 To geasse & arede vpon his dark ridles..which of these two eleccions he meaneth. **1796** SOUTHEY *Joan of Arc* Wks. VII. 34 Rightly he ared the Maid's intent. **1847** BARHAM *Ingol. Leg.* (1877) 373 Areed my counsel aright.

5. To divine the meaning of (obscure words), interpret (a dream), solve (a riddle or enigma). *arch.*
a **1000** *Cædmon's Daniel* (Gr.) 734 Ne mihton arǽdan men engles ǽrend-béc. *c* **1315** SHOREHAM 24 Hy that aredeth thyse redeles. *a* **1300** *Cursor M.* 4474, I shal arede wel þi sweuene. **1393** GOWER *Conf.* I. 25 The sweven..That Daniel anone arad. **1483** CAXTON *G. de la Tour* G ij b, They my3t not arede a certayne deuynal. *a* **1535** MORE *Wks.* 552 (R.) Arede my riddle, what is that? **1654** GATAKER *Disc. Apol.* 28 We have need of some Oedipus, to aread us his riddles. **1870** MORRIS *Earthly Par.* II. III. 348 So is thy dream areded.

† **6.** To interpret or solve (written symbols); to READ. *Obs.*
c **885** K. ÆLFRED *Gregory's Past.* Pref. 7 Ðeah moni3e cuðon Englisc 3ewrit arǽdan. *c* **1340** *Alisaunder* 573 Let write euery worde..that more folke myght hit arede.

b. *intr.*
1205 LAY. 22719 Her mon mai arede [**1250** reade] of Arðure.

II. Later archaistic senses, formed on READ.

7. *trans.* To counsel, advise.
1559 *Myrr. Mag., James I*, xviii, I arede therfore all people to be wise. **1596** SPENSER *F.Q.* Introd., Me..the sacred Muse areeds. **1643** MILTON *Divorce* (1851) Introd. 5 Let me arreed him, not to be the foreman of any mis-judg'd opinion.

b. *intr.* or *absol.*
1599 BP. HALL *Sat.* VI. i. 69 Let him that hath nought, feare nought, I areed. **1763** CHURCHILL *Poems* I. 114 What cant be cur'd, So Donald right areeds, must be endur'd.

8. To decide, decree advisedly, adjudge. *arch.*
1593 R. HARVEY *Philad.* 1 We may best areede who is most credible. **1596** SPENSER *F.Q.* v. iii. 35 Thereby Sir Artegall did plaine areed That unto him the horse belong'd. **1863** LD. LYTTON *Ring of Amasis* I. 288 The king areads the monarchy to him that shall read the riddle of the ring.

† **a'read**, *sb. Obs.* Also in 6 arreede. [f. prec. vb. after *rede, reed* sb.] Advice, counsel.
1590 LODGE *Euphues' Gold. Leg.* in Halliw. *Shaks.* VI. 22 Follow mine arreede. **1601** *Earl Huntington* I. iii. in Hazl. *Dodsl.* VIII. 116 Thus by my areed you shall provide.

areadde, var. of AREDDE *v. Obs.*

† **a'readily**, *adv. Obs.* [f. AREADY + -LY[2].] Readily, easily, suitably.
c **1350** *Will. Palerne* 5025 All þe men vpon mold · ne mi3t it descriue A-redili to þe ri3tes. *Ibid.* 5230 Held a-redili to ri3t · þe riche & þe pore.

† **a'readiness.** *Obs.* Also 5 aredynes, 6–7 aredines(se, 7 arredi-. [f. next + -NESS.] Readiness, preparedness.
a **1500** HEN. VII in Ellis *Orig. Lett.* I. ii. I. 20 In aredynes to resiste her malice. **1548** *Procl.* in Strype *Eccl. Mem.* II. I. xii. 97 To have in ful areadiness..two good and hable horses. **1620** EARL HERTF. in *Fortesc. Papers* 141 My arredinesse to serve your Majesties most vertuous daughter.

† **a'ready**, *a. Obs.* Forms: 3 aredi, 4–5 aredy. [f. READY: the prefix perhaps a variant of *3e-, i-*, in the common ME. *3e-redi, i-redi, y-redy*: see A- *pref.* 6.] Ready, prepared; in readiness.
1250 LAY. 7978 Þilke nihtes a-redi were his cnihtes. **1340** *Ayenb.* 121 Þe pine of helle þet is eche daye aredy. **1480** CAXTON *Chron. Eng.* ccvi. 187 Al tho men were a redy.

† **a'ready**, *v. Obs.* Forms: 5 arredye, 5–6 aredy(e, -ie. [f. prec.] To make ready.
1470 *Reb. in Linc.* 6 He wolde arredye hym self to com. **1534** LD. BERNERS *Gold. Bk. M. Aurel.* (1546) K k b, They haue aredyed the mylle.

areal ('ɛəriːəl), *a.* [ad. L. *āreālis*, f. *ārea*: see AREA and -AL[1].] Of, pertaining to, or of the nature of, an area.
1676 COLLINS in Rigaud *Corr. Sci. Men* II. 402 His calculus of the areal ordinate. **1881** *Hist. Coll. Stafford.* II. 89 The areal Hundred.

areality (ɛəriː'ælɪtɪ). [f. prec. + -ITY; cf. *neutrality*.] Condition in respect of area.
1881 *Standard* 6 July 5/8 The areality of the population of London is ·0197 acres..to each person.

† **a'rear**, *v. Obs.* Forms: 1–2 arǽr-an, 2 arer-en, 3 arær-en, 3 areri, 2–6 arere, 3–6 areare, 5 areyre, 5–6 arrere, 6–7 ereare, arreare. [OE. *arǽran*, f. A- *pref.* 1 up, out + *rǽran* to REAR. In 15–17th c. the *r* was corruptly doubled: see AR- *pref.*[2] The OE. *arǽran*, cogn. with Goth. *urraisjan*, was the causal of ARISE. The parallel form from ON. was ARAISE.]

1. To raise, erect, build, rear (an edifice, etc.).
a **800** *Runic Stone* in *Yorksh. Arch. Jrnl.* (1883) XXIX. 81 Igilsuiþ arǽrde æfter Berhtsuiþe becun. *c* **1000** *Ags. Gosp.* John ii. 19 A-rærst þu hit on þrym da3on? **1250** LAY. 26222 And radde 3am bitwine: ane castel a-reare. *c* **1380** *Sir Ferumb.* 2914 Þe Galwys arered an hye. **1494** FABYAN *Chron.* II. xlvii. 31 He arreryd a fayre and stronge gate. **1571** DIGGES *Pantom.* Biv, How Perpendiculares vppon any straight line are exeared. **1627** SPEED *Eng. Abridged* ii.§10 [They] arreared a Crosse vpon Stanemore.

2. *fig.* To set up, establish (an institution, etc.).
? *a* **800** *O.E. Chron.* an. 718 Sio Cuþburh þæt liif æt Winburnan arærode. *a* **1000** *Andreas* 1647 And æ godes riht arǽred. *c* **1175** *Lamb. Hom.* 93 Efter þissere bisnunge weren arerede munechene lif. *c* **1375** WYCLIF *Serm.* xlv. Sel. Wks. I. 129 Goddis lawe quenchid and Anticristes arerid. *a* **1400** *Octouian* 21 Crystendom how they gonne arere.

3. To lift up, to raise (in local position).
c **1175** *Cott. Hom.* 205 Þet arerde [*printed* aredde] al moncun up, þet was adun a-fallen. *c* **1230** *Ancr. R.* 252 Hwon he ualleð he naueð hwo him areare. **1382** WYCLIF *Ex.* xiv. 16 Thow forsothe arere [**1388** reise] thin 3erde. **1398** TREVISA *Barth. De P.R.* III. i, He 3af to men visagis arerid towarde þe sterris. *c* **1440** *Gesta Rom.* 255 He arerid vp the childe with his owne hondis. **1566** DRANT *Wailings Jer.* K vj b, Let us arreare our handes..to God. **1621** BURTON *Anat. Mel.* II. ii. VI. ii, Things down must not be dejected, but ereared.

b. To raise (an animal) on its hind legs.
1622 PEACHAM *Compl. Gent.* III. (1634) 157 Rampant is said when the Lion is arreared up in the Scotcheon.

4. *fig.* in various senses: To raise in rank, honourable position, or estimation, mental or moral condition, etc.; to exalt.
c **885** K. ÆLFRED *Gregory's Past.* xi. 67 Hie ne ma3on hiera 3eðohtes staðol uparæran. *c* **1175** *Lamb. Hom.* 115 Ðes kingges rihtwisnes arereð his kine setle. **1340** *Ayenb.* 85 Uirtue areref þane man an he3. **1382** WYCLIF *Isa.* iii. 16 Arered ben the do3tris of Sion. **1398** TREVISA *Barth. De P.R.* III. i. (1495) 48 The spyryte is areryd vp to the contemplacion of god. **1577** HELLOWES *Gueuara's Epist.* 27 There was no man areared to honor, but he that deserued it. **1621** BURTON *Anat. Mel.* III. iv. I. ii, A spiritual wing to ereare us.

5. To raise (a shout).
c **1380** *Sir Ferumb.* 3020 Þe Sara3yns sone þat cry arereþ. *c* **1425** *Seven Sages* (P.) 497 Bot I hadde areryd cry.

6. To raise from the dead, raise to life or health.
c **1000** *Ags. Gosp.* John vi. 54 And ic hine arære on þam ytemestan dæ3e. *c* **1175** *Cott. Hom.* 211 Of soule deaðe arer me. **1393** GOWER *Conf.* III. 38 That any dede man were arered. *c* **1450** LONELICH *Grail* xxxvi. 58 Of his siknesse he did him arere. *a* **1520** *Myrr. Our Ladye* 123 The bodyes of them shal be arered to endelesse ioye.

7. To start (a wild animal from its lair). *rare.*
a **1400** *Cov. Myst.* 215 The hare fro the fforme we xal arere.

8. To rouse into activity, arouse, excite, stir up.
c **1230** *Ancr. R.* 426 He is euer umbe to arearen sume wreððe. *c* **1340** *Alex. & Dind.* 92 Whan þe winde..þe wawus arereth. *a* **1400** *Cov. Myst.* 132 More slawndyr we to [= two] xal arere. **1577** HOLINSHED *Chron.* I. 112/1 He arreareth battell against the Northumbers. **1603** JAMES I in Fuller *Ch. Hist.* x. i. V. 277 Lest..a desperate presumption be arreared by inferring the necessary certainty of persisting in grace. **1607** TOPSELL *Serpents* 641 They arrear deadly war against strangers.

9. To raise (a person, agent) in hostility *against*.
c **1175** *Lamb. Hom.* 113 He arereð his mod mid modinesse on3ein God. *c* **1430** *Life St. Kath.* (Gibbs MS.) 100 Ihesu crist shal arere a3enst the an aduersary. **1611** SPEED *Hist. Gt. Brit.* VI. liii. (1632) 184 In Spain against him was arreared Maximus.

10. To raise, levy (troops).
1366 MAUNDEV. v. 38 He may arrere mo than 50000 [men]. **1494** FABYAN VI. ccxi. 226 A fayre Company, that he had areyred in Oxenfordeshyre. **1579** FENTON *Guicciard.* v. (1599) 205 To areare a sufficient strength to oppresse the conspirators.

11. To raise, levy (taxes, etc.).
c **1340** *Alisaunder* 360 Þei þat raunson with right arere ne might. **1480** CAXTON *Chron. Eng.* cxcix. 179 He lete arere a tallyage of al the goodes of Englond. **1529** RASTELL *Pastyme* (1811) 132 He areryd grete sommys of money. **1609** HEYWOOD *Bryt. Troy* XVII. lxxxiii, And arrear'd a tax of the Tenth Penny.

12. *refl.* To rise, get up.
c **1220** *Leg. St. Kath.* 1114 Aras, & arearde him self fram deaðe. **1340** *Ayenb.* 179 Arereþe and do þi wyl. *c* **1380** *Sir Ferumb.* 210 Sone he arerd him after þan.

13. *intr.* **a.** To arise, happen, occur. **b.** To rear, as a horse does.
1205 LAY. 22966 3if on uolke feondscipe arereð..bitweone twon monnen. *c* **1330** *Kyng of Tars* 250 Ar eny more serwe arere. *c* **1430** *Syr Generides* 5924 The sted arerud and fel bakward.

a-rear (ə'rɪə(r)), *advb. phr.* [A *prep.*[1] + REAR *sb.*; cf. ARREAR *adv.* from Fr.] In the rear.
1849 CARLYLE *Irish Journ.* 94 Wind is arear of us. **1865** *Fredk. Gt.* XIII. x. V. 104 The Saxons dragged heavily arear.

arear(e, obs. form of ARREAR.

† **a'rearer.** *Obs. rare*[−1]. [f. AREAR *v.* + -ER[1].] One who rears, raises up, or arouses.
1382 WYCLIF *Judith* xiv. 9 That not of the arereris [*v.r.* rereres; Vulg. *ab excitantibus*]..Olofernes shulde waken.

† **a'rearing**, *vbl. sb.* [f. as prec. + -ING[1].] The action of raising, lifting up, or elevation.
1382 WYCLIF *Lev.* vii. 34 The litil brest forsothe of areryng [COVERDALE, Wauebrest]. **1398** TREVISA *Barth. De P.R.* VIII. xi. (1495) 317 The vij planetes..now ben in exaltacion and arerynge.

† **a'reason**, *v. Obs.* Also 3 aresun, 4–5 areson(ne, 5 araison, 6 arraison. [a. OFr. *ares-, areis-, araisone-r*, mod.F. *arraisonner*, levelled form of earlier *araisnier* (1 sing. pres. *araisone*):—late L. *adratiōnāre*, f. *ad* to + *ratiōnāre* to discourse, f. *ratiōn-em*: see REASON.] By-form of ARRAIGN *v.*; to address words and esp. questions to; to question, examine, call to account.
c **1250** *Kent. Serm.* in *O.E. Misc.* 35 Þo aresunede ure lord þe paens..vre-fore hi hedden i-be so longe idel. **1340** HAMPOLE *Pr. Consc.* 2460 And be aresoned, als right es Of alle his mysdedys. **1470** HARDING *Chron.* clxxxviij, Walworth..Areasoned hym then of his greate lewdenesse. **1475** CAXTON *Jason* 41 b, And spack not one worde but if he were demanded or araisoned. **1594** CAREW *Tasso* (1881) 100 He..Arraisons him with this besmoothing art.

†**areason**, *sb. Obs. rare*⁻¹. In 3 areisun. [f. prec.] Examination, interrogation.
a **1300** *Floriz & Bl.* 248 þe porter is culuart and felun, He wule him sette areisun. [? or *a reisun*]

†**a'reasoner**. *Obs. rare.* In 5 aresonere. [f. AREASON *v.* + -ER¹: cf. OF. *araisneor* and ARRAIGNER.] One who addresses or questions.
1483 *Cath. Angl.*, Aresonere, *Alloquitor, concionator.*

†**a'reast, a'reasted**, *ppl. a. Obs.* [pa. pple. of REAST *v.*: see A- *pref.* 6.] Reasty, rancid. **areastiness**, reastiness, rancidity.
1440 *Promp. Parv.* 14 A-reste, or resty, as flesche [*v.r.* areestyd, areest or reestyd], *Rancidus*.. A-restenesse of flesshe, *Rancor*.

†**'areatour**. *Obs.*⁻⁰ [f. L. *ārea* threshing-floor: see -ATOR.] 'A thresher, or he that makes clean the floor.' Blount *Glossogr.* 1656.

areawe, obs. form of AROW *adv.*; var. ARUE *v.*

areca ('ærɪkə). Forms: 6 **archa, arreca,** 7 **arrequa, arecca,** 8 **areka,** 9 **areeka,** 7– **areca;** also 7 **areque, arek,** 8 **areek,** 9 **arak.** [a. Pg. *areca*, ad. Malayálam *áḍekka*, = Canarese *áḍike*, Tamil *áḍaikāy*, f. *aḍai* denoting close arrangement of the cluster + *kāy* nut, fruit (Bp. Caldwell). The accent is on the first syllable in all the languages.]
Name of the tree and fruit of a genus of palms, of which one species (*A. Catechu*) bears nuts of the size of a nutmeg, which the natives roll up with a little lime in the leaves of the betel, and chew, thereby tingeing their teeth and saliva red.
[**1510** VARTHEMA *Trav.* transl. J. W. Jones (1863) 144 The tree of the said coffolo is called Arecha.] **1599** HAKLUYT *Voy.* II. 223 Great quantie of Archa.. which fruit they eat.. with the leaf of an Herbe which they call Bettell. *Ibid.* II. I. 262 Cocos, figges, arrecaes, and other fruits. **1615** tr. *De Montfart's Surv. E. Indies* 39 The fruit.. called Areque. **1625** PURCHAS *Pilgrims* II. 1157 This Arrequa.. maketh men almost drunke. **1702** W. J. *Le Bruyn's Voy. Levant* (1737) II. lxvii. 101 The Areek is a fruit which grows in thick bunches. **1808** PARSONS *Trav. Asia* xii. 259 Arak nuts, wrapped in beetle leaf. **1871** MATEER *Travancore* 56 The thick, leather-like leaf sheath of the areca palm tree.

†**a'recche**, *v. Obs.* 1–3. Forms: 1 **arecc(e)an,** 2–3 **arecche, (areche).** *Pa. t.* **arehte, aræhte.** *Pa. pple.* **araht, arouȝt.** The mod. spelling would be *aretch.* [OE. *aręcc(e)an*, f. A- *pref.* 1 + *ręcc(e)an*: see RECCHE. Cf. OHG. *arrechen, arrechan.* (Very early confused with AREACH, as was the simple *recche* with *reach.*)]
1. To explain, expound, declare the meaning of.
c **885** K. ÆLFRED *Gregory's Past* Pref. 7 Swæ ic hie andȝitfullicost areccean meahte. *c* **975** *Rushw. Gosp.* Matt. xiii. 36 Arecce us þa ȝelicnisse. *c* **1000** *Ags. G.*, Aræce us. *c* **1160** *Hatton G.*, Areche us. **1205** LAY. 28097 Sweuen mid sorȝen arecchen. *c* **1300** *MS. Bodl.* No. 652. 5 (Halliw.) Josep here sweuen sone haueth arouȝt. **1393** GOWER *Conf.* II. 188 Crist wroughte first and after taught, So that the dede his word araught.
2. To utter, speak.
c **1400** *Beryn* 3735 Vnneth he myȝt areche O word, for pure anguyssh.

areche, obs. form of AREACH *v.*, and ORACH.

arect, later corrupt var. ARET *v. Obs.*

†**a'redde**, *v. Obs.* Forms: 1 **ahredd-an,** 2 **aredd-e(n,** 3 **arædde, arudde, areadde.** *Pa. t.* 1 **ahredde,** 2–4 **aredde.** *Pa. pple.* 1 **ahreded,** 2–4 **ared.** [f. A- *pref.* 1 out, away + OE. *hreddan*, RID. Cogn. w. OHG. *arrettan, irretjan*, mod.G. *erretten.* Obs. before the simple vb. became *rid.*] To set free, liberate, deliver, rid.
c **885** K. ÆLFRED *Oros.* I. v. þe he hí æt hungre ahredde. *c* **1175** *Lamb. Hom.* 87 God heom aredde wið heore ifan. **1205** LAY. 12612 þat heo arædde þis lond. *c* **1230** *St. Marhar.* 6 Arude.. mi sawle of sweordes egge. *c* **1230** *Ancr. R.* 170 He aredde of deaðe al hire uolc. *c* **1330** *Florice & Bl.* 712 This ring schal ared me.

arede, areed, var. forms of AREAD *v.*

aredy, -ness, var. forms of AREADY, -INESS.

a-reek (ə'ri:k), *advb. phr.* [A *prep.*¹ + REEK.] Reeking.
1706 SWIFT *To Peterborough* Wks. 1755 IV. I. 1 A messenger comes all a-reek, Mordanto at Madrid to seek.

†**are'fact**, *v. Obs.* [f. L. *ārefact-* ppl. stem of *ārefacĕre*: see AREFY.] To dry up, wither. Cited only in ppl. adjs. **arefacted, arefacting.**
1599 A. M. *Gabelhouer's Bk. Physic* 212/1 Invngate therwith the arefacted membre. *Ibid.* 211/2 Therwith cover the arefactinge membre.

arefaction (ærɪ'fækʃən). ? *Obs.* [n. of action f. *ārefacĕre*: see next and -TION.] The action or process of drying; dried condition.
1576 T. NEWTON *Lemnie's Touchst. Complex.* (1633) 112 But if coldnesse be joyned with moystnesse.. use arefaction. *a* **1626** BACON *New Atl.* (1627) 28 The restoring of Man's Body from Arefaction. **1677** HALE *Prim. Orig. Man.* 302 The separation of the Water, and the arefaction of the Earth. **1870** SMITH *Syn. & Antonyms*, Madefaction.. *Ant.* Exsiccation, Drying, Arefaction.

areful, earlier f. OREFUL *a. Obs.* merciful.

arefy ('ærɪfaɪ), *v.* ? *Obs.* [irregular ad. L. *ārefacĕre*, f. *ārēre* to dry + *facĕre* to make. Cf. *satisfy*, and see -FY.] *trans.* and *intr.* To dry up, parch, wither. Hence the ppl. adjs. **arefied, arefying.**
1542 BOORDE *Dyetary* viii. (1870) 247 For fyre doth aryfye.. a mannes blode. **1599** A. M. *Gabelhouer's Bk. Physic* 209/1 Vnguent for the arefyinge Ioynctes. *Ibid.*, Annoyncte therwith the arefyede Ioyncte. **1626** BACON *Sylva* §320 That heat which is in lime and ashes.. doth neither liquefy nor arefy. **1657** TOMLINSON *Renou's Disp.* 586 The powders will soon arefie.

aregh, areȝ, aref, arehwe: see ARGH *a.* and *v.*

areiȝt, pa. t. of AREACH *v. Obs.* to reach.

areik, areke, obs. forms of AREACH *v.*

†**areim-en**, *v. Obs. rare.* [Deriv. unknown. (Not = OE. *arǽman.*)] To set at large, liberate.
c **1230** *Ancr. R.* 124 Ponewes uorte acwiten & areimen him mide. *Ibid.* 126 Raunsun þet we schulen areimen us mide.

arein, variant of ARAIN: see also ARAYNE *v.*

areise, obs. form of ARAISE *v.*

areisun, variant of AREASON *sb. Obs.* question.

arek, areka, obs. forms of ARECA.

areli, obs. form of EARLY.

arem(e, var. of ARM *a. Obs.* poor, wretched.

aren, obs. 3rd. pl. of ARE *v.*²; inf. of ARE *v.*¹

arena (ə'ri:nə). Pl. **arenas.** [a. L. *arēna*, prop. *harēna*, sand, the sand-strewn place of combat in an amphitheatre, etc.]
1. The central part of an amphitheatre, in which the combats or spectacular displays take place, and which was originally strewn with sand to absorb the blood of the wounded and slain. Used also, by extension, of the whole amphitheatre.
1627 HAKEWILL *Apol.* (1630) 396 The *Arena*, the place below in which their games were exhibited. **1776** GIBBON *Decl. & F.* I. 352 The arena, or stage, was strewed with the finest sand. **1812** BYRON *Ch. Har.* I. lxviii, The thronged arena shakes with shouts for more. **1879** FROUDE *Cæsar* vi. 55 Exhibiting a hundred lions in the arena matched against Numidian archers.
2. *fig.* A scene or sphere of conflict; a battle-field.
1814 BYRON *Lara* II. ix, But dragg'd again upon the arena, stood A leader not unequal to the feud. **1817** CHALMERS *Astron. Disc.* ii. (1852) 50 The arena on which the modern philosophy has won all her victories. *c* **1854** STANLEY *Sinai & Pal.* ix. 329 It would naturally become the arena of war. **1863** H. ROGERS *J. Howe* vii. 181 Howe seldom entered the arena of controversy.
3. Any sphere of public or energetic action.
1798 MALTHUS *Popul.* (1878) 330 A large arena for the employment of an increasing capital. **1857** H. REED *Lect. Brit. Poets* iv. 127 Rushing into the arena of authorship.
4. *Med.* 'Gravel bred in a Human Body.' Phillips 1706. 'Sand or gravel deposited from the urine.' *Syd. Soc. Lex.* 1880.
5. Applied *attrib.* to a style of play production in which the stage is so positioned in the auditorium that it is surrounded by the audience, who thus, as in the Greek *theatron*, see the players 'in the round'.
This style was introduced in November 1932 by Glenn Hughes, director of the Washington School of Drama. His first productions were known as 'Penthouse' from the place of their performance; the word *arena* came later as the technique was adopted elsewhere in America and abroad.
1944 N. FELTON in *National Theatre Conference Bull.* (U.S.) VI. 17 (*title*) Arena Theatre. Method for Producing a Play. **1948** *Theatre Arts* June—July 58 Called variously central staging, theatre-in-the-round, or arena theatre, the new form has suddenly made any large unencumbered room a possible stage. **1949** *Here & Now* (N.Z.) Oct. 14/2 From the point of view of a touring company the advantages of an arena production are fairly obvious. **1955** *Times* 11 May 7/2 The auditorium.. is in the shape of a semi-circle, but may be changed into a circle for what is called the 'arena stage', when the movable sides of the proscenium opening are taken away and the curve of the cyclorama is extended to make a wall behind three additional rows of seats on the stage itself.

arenaceo- (ærɪ'neɪʃi:əʊ), comb. f. L. *arēnāceus* (see next); = sandy, mixed with sand, as in **arenaceo-argillaceous**, of the nature of sandy clay.
1850 DANA *Geol.* viii. 438 Arenaceo-argillaceous deposits. **1881** DARWIN *Veg. Mould* 275 Arenaceo-calcareous loam.

arenaceous (ærɪ'neɪʃəs), *a.* [f. L. *arēnāce-us*, f. *ārēna* sand: see -ACEOUS.] Having the appearance or consistency of sand; sandy; largely composed of sand or quartz grains.
1646 SIR T. BROWNE *Pseud. Ep.* 203 Fishes.. whose egge or spawne is arenaceous and friable. **1749** *Phil. Trans.* XLVI. 144 A hard or stony arenaceous greyish substance. **1833** LYELL *Princ. Geol.* III. 39 A limestone.. becomes more arenaceous, until it finally passes into sand or sandstone. **1854** H. MILLER *Sch. & Schm.* ii. (1857) 22 A soft arenaceous mud.
b. *fig.*
1870 LOWELL *Among my Bks.* Ser. II. 239 There is an arenaceous quality in the style which makes progress wearisome.

‖**arenaria** (ærɪ'nɛərɪə). [L., fem. of *arēnārius*: see next.] The Sandwort; a genus of small herbs (N.O. *Caryophyllaceæ*) allied to chickweed.
a **1806** MRS. C. SMITH *Flora's Horol.* ix, Among the loose and arid sands The humble arenaria creeps. **1881** *Garden* 313 Other Arenarias in cultivation.

arenarious (ærɪ'nɛərɪəs), *a.* ? *Obs.* [f. L. *arēnāri-us*, f. *arēna* sand: see -ARIOUS.] = ARENACEOUS.
1758 PLATT in *Phil. Trans.* L. 527 This stratum.. being arenarious, and too soft for their use. [In mod. Dicts.]

†**'arenary**, *a. Obs.*⁻⁰ [ad. L. *arēnārius.*] 'Of or belonging to sand or gravel.' Bailey 1731.

†**'arenate**, *v. Obs.*⁻⁰ [f. L. *arēnāt-us* sanded: see ARENA and -ATE³.] (See quot.)
1623 COCKERAM *Dict.* II, To *Ruffe-cast*, Arenate. **1656** BLOUNT *Glossogr.*, *Arenated*, mixed with sand, sandy.

arenation (ærɪ'neɪʃən). *Med.* ? *Obs.* [ad. L. *arēnātiōn-em* a sanding: cf. F. *arénation.*] Application of hot sand to the body as a remedy.
1717 BERKELEY in Fraser *Life* (1871) 587 Arenation is good against leprosy. **1751** CHAMBERS *Cycl.*, *Arenation*.. a kind of dry bath, in which the patient only sits with his feet on hot sand.

arenavirus (ə'ri:nəvaɪərəs). *Microbiol.* Also **areno-.** [f. L. *arēnōsus* sandy (see quot. 1970) + -O + VIRUS; *arena-* by alteration (see quot. 1971).] Any of a group of animal viruses consisting of enveloped single-stranded RNA, of which many are carried by various rodents and some cause disease in man, including Lassa fever and lymphocytic choriomeningitis.
1970 W. P. ROWE et al. in *Jrnl. Virol.* V. 651/1 The name 'arenoviruses'... This name was chosen to reflect the characteristic fine granules seen in the virion in ultrathin sections. **1971** *Proc. Soc. Exper. Biol. & Med.* CXXXVI. 637/1 Arenavirus was approved as the group name by the International Committee on Nomenclature of Viruses (personal communication). Arenovirus was suppressed because it might be confused with adenovirus, particularly in oral communication. **1978** *Brit. Med. Jrnl.* 4 Mar. 529/2 Arenaviruses have rodents or bats as their natural hosts and reservoirs. **1978** *Nature* 17 Aug. 724/3 Important groups of animal viruses (arenoviruses, bunyaviruses, most insect viruses) are not mentioned. **1983** *Oxf. Textbk. Med.* I. v. 116/1 Like other arenaviruses, Lassa produces a persistent tolerated infection in its rodent reservoir host with no ill effects in *Mastomys natalensis* and without any immune response.

arend, obs. form of ERRAND.

arendalite (ə'rɛndəlaɪt). *Min.* [mod. f. (1800) *Arendal* in Norway + -ITE.] A synonym of EPIDOTE, retained by Dana for one of its varieties.
1868 DANA *Min.* 282 The Arendal Epidote (Arendalite) is mostly in dark green crystals.

arendator: see ARR-.

arenicolite (ærɪ'nɪkəlaɪt). [f. mod.L. *arēnicol-a* sand-worm, lob-worm (f. *arēna* sand + *-cola* inhabiting) + -ITE.] A worm-hole made originally in sand, and preserved in a sandstone rock.
1864 in WEBSTER.

arenicolous (-ələs), *a.* [f. as prec. + -OUS.] Inhabiting sand.
1851–9 OWEN in *Man. Sc. Enq.* 381 Arenicolous mollusks.

Arenig (ə'reɪnɪg). The name of a mountain in Merionethshire, Wales, applied *attrib.*, esp. to a series of rocks of the Lower Ordovician age. Hence **Are'nigian** *a.*, of or pertaining to this series.
1854 A. SEDGWICK in *Phil. Mag.* VIII. 362 Festiniog group (Middle Cambrian).. Arenig slates and porphyries, &c. **1865** LYELL *Elem. Geol.* xxvii. 564 This Arenig group may therefore be conveniently regarded as the base of the great Silurian system. **1879** *Encycl. Brit.* X. 331/2 *Arenig or Stiper Stone Group.* These rocks consist of dark slates, shales, flags, and bands of sandstone. **1929** EVANS & STUBBLEFIELD *Handbk. Geol. Gt. Brit.* iii. 59 The lowest part of the Ordovician has been also called the Arenig or Arenigian Series.

arenilitic (ə,rɛnɪ'lɪtɪk), *a.* [f. ***arenilite** (f. L. *arēna* sand + Gr. λίθος stone) + -IC.] Of or pertaining to sandstone.
1799 KIRWAN *Geol. Ess.* 305.

arenose (,ærɪ'nəʊs), *a.* [ad. L. *arēnōsus*, f. *arēna* sand: see -OSE.] Sandy.
1731 in BAILEY. **1848** DANA *Zooph.* 194 Lateral surfaces arenose.

arenosity (ærɪˈnɒsɪtɪ). *rare*$^{-1}$. [n. of quality f. prec.: see -ITY.] Sandiness; granulousness.
1687 H. MORE *App. Antid.* (1712) 219 The solute Arenosity (as I may so speak) of Air and Fire.

arenoso- (ærɪˌnəʊsəʊ), comb. f. L. *arēnōsus*, Eng. *arenose*; as in **arenoso-denticulate**, covered with small notches like grains of sand.
1848 DANA *Zooph.* 344 Lamellæ.. very minutely arenoso-denticulate.

†**ˈarenous**, *a.* *Obs.* [ad. L. *arēnōsus*: see above. Cf. Fr. *aréneux*: see -OUS.] Sandy, gritty.
1664 EVELYN *Silva* (1776) 425 The water.. arenous and gravelly. 1759 tr. *Duhamel's Husb.* I. viii. (1762) 24 Arenous and sandy earth.. wants ligature.

arenovirus, var. ARENAVIRUS.

†**ˈarent**, *a.* *Obs.* *rare*$^{-1}$. [ad. L. *ārentem*, pr. pple. of *ārēre*.] Drying up, withering.
1607 TOPSELL *Four-f. Beasts* 377 Ardent, arent, burning.

arent, -ation, var. of ARRENT, -ATION, *Obs.*

aren't (ˈɑːnt), colloq. form of *are not* and *am not* (chiefly in standard interrogative use: *aren't I?* = 'am not I?'). Cf. AN'T.
1794 Ar'n't [see BE *v.* A. I 1-3 ¶]. 1810 [see UNDECENT *a.* 3]. 1848 MRS. GASKELL *Mary Barton* I. xiii. 233 Come! Mary, ar'n't you ready? 1872 [see SKILLIGALEE 1]. 1907 LADY GROVE *Social Fetich* 38 If 'ain't I?' is objected to, surely 'aren't I?' is very much worse. 1916 JOYCE *Portrait of Artist* (1969) ii. 71 And they're a very rich order, aren't they, Simon? 1925 F. SCOTT FITZGERALD *Great Gatsby* vii. 143 Aren't we going to let any one smoke a cigarette first? 1934 DYLAN THOMAS *Let.* 2 May (1966) 117 The first thing I would do.. would be to peep, with a nasty aren't-I-a-lad expression, into the pages. 1946 K. TENNANT *Lost Haven* (1947) ii. 44 'Oh, Christ!' Kelly moaned. ' Aren't I telling you I aren't deserting you?' 1955 *Sci. Amer.* Aug. 78/3 Comic strips and some other contemporary literature (literachoor) recognize the prevalence of these forms in speech by spelling them that way: aintcha, arentcha, betcha, etc. 1977 *Private Eye* 15 Apr. 14/1 Aren'tcha sick to death of the cold weather?? 1982 *N.Y. Times* 9 June B1/6 But these young men aren't fighting for mere real estate.

†**aˈrenulous**, *a.* *Obs.* *rare*$^{-1}$. [f. L. *arēnula*, dim. of *arēna*.] Like grains of sand.
1664 POWER *Exp. Philos.* I. 73 Those arenulous Atoms.

areo-, f. Gr. Ἄρεος of Ares or Mars; *esp.* in astronomical terms relating to the planet Mars; as **areocentric** (ˌæriːəʊˈsɛntrɪk), *a.*, having Mars as centre. **areˈographer**, one who describes the appearance of Mars. **areoˈgraphic** *a.*, pertaining to areography. **areˈography**, description of the physical features of Mars. **areˈology**, scientific investigation of the substance of Mars.
1877 D. GILL in *Mem. R. A. S.* XLVI. 94 The areocentric angle between the Earth and the Sun. 1878 NEWCOMB *Pop. Astron.* 566 Hourly motion in areocentric longitude. 1880 *Nature* XXI. 213 The local indistinctness and confusion that so often puzzle the areographer. 1870 PROCTOR *Other Worlds* ix. 93 The Martial geography—or perhaps I ought rather to say areography. 1881 —— *Poetry Astron.* viii. 288 Compare.. geology with areology.

‖**areola** (əˈriːələ). Pl. areolæ. [L., dim. of *ārea*.] A very small area.

1. One of the small spaces marked out on a surface by intersecting lines, such as those between the veins of a leaf or the nervures of an insect's wing.
1664 POWER *Exp. Philos.* I. 49 Pentagonal and hexagonal areola's [on Corn Poppy seeds]. 1830 LINDLEY *Nat. Syst. Bot.* 313 A cluster of sporule-like areolæ of cellular tissue.

2. One of the interstices in the tissue of any organized substance.
1848 QUAIN *Elem. Anat.* (1882) II. 107 The cell spaces in the calcified matrix [of bone].. being termed the primary areolæ. 1874 VAN BUREN *Dis. Urin. Org.* 2 The areolæ of this tissue become distended with blood.

3. A circular spot; a coloured circle such as that around the human nipple, and that which surrounds the vesicles or pustules in eruptive diseases.
1706 PHILLIPS, *Areola Papillaris*, the Circle about a Nipple. 1852 W. GROVE *Contrib. Sc.* 365 Surrounded by a dusky and ill-defined areola. 1877 ROBERTS *Handbk. Med.* I. 164 A faint red areola appears.

4. *Biol.* **a.** A slightly depressed spot on any surface. **b.** The cell-nucleus of a plant.
1862 DARWIN *Orchids* v. 206 With a faint areola or nucleus visible. 1872 NICHOLSON *Palæont.* 105 A round or oval smooth and excavated space which is termed the areola.

areolar (əˈriːələ(r)), *a.* [f. prec. + -AR.]

1. Consisting of areolæ, full of interstices; *spec.* in *areolar* (or *connective*) *tissue*: the mixture of fibrous and elastic tissue, which underlies the skin, and connects and supports the organs in other parts of the body.
1818 W. LAWRENCE *Nat. Hist. Man* II. ii. (1848) 185 The areolar tissue of the cutis. 1859 CARPENTER *Anim. Phys.* i. (1872) 39 This Areolar tissue is diffused through almost the whole fabric of the adult animal.

2. Of or pertaining to a small area. Cf. AREA 3.
1879 NEWCOMB & HOLDEN *Astron.* 126 This area is called the areolar velocity of the planet.

areolate (əˈriːəleɪt, ˈɛəriːəʊleɪt), *ppl. a.* [f. L. *āreola* + -ATE^{2}.] Marked by areolæ; divided into small distinct spaces by intersecting lines.
1847 LINDLEY *Elem. Bot.* Gloss., The skin of a plant is areolate. 1852 DANA *Crust.* I. 33 Cancridæ, having an areolate carapax.

areolated (əˈriːəleɪtɪd, ˈɛəriːəʊ-), *ppl. a.* [f. prec. + -ED.] Marked by, or consisting of, areolæ.
1802 G. SHAW *Zool.* III. 50 Areolated Tortoise. 1829 LOUDON *Encycl. Plants* (1841) 925 Frond tubular.. with a striated areolated surface. 1836 TODD *Cycl. Anat. & Phys.* I. 509/2 A soft, areolated, and elastic substance.

areolation (ˌɛərɪəʊˈleɪʃən). [f. as prec. + -TION.] Division into areolæ.
1830 LINDLEY *Nat. Syst. Bot.* 171 Striking resemblance in the areolations of the seeds. 1852 DANA *Crust.* I. 155 The antero-lateral region has imperfectly the usual areolation.

areole (ˈɛəriːəʊl). [a. F. *aréole*.] = AREOLA.
1856 in WEBSTER. 1870 HOOKER *Stud. Flora* 188 Knapweed.. Fruit compressed, basal areole oblique. 1878 NEWCOMB *Pop. Astron.* II. i. 117 A bright star.. surrounded by a blue or violet areole.

areolet (əˈriːəlɛt, ˈɛəriːəʊ-). [f. AREOLA, AREOLE + -ET^{1}.] A small areola, a very small area or space.
1828 KIRBY & SP. *Entomol.* xlvii. IV. 381 Wings.. reticulated with numerous areolets. 1852 DANA *Crust.* I. 29 The areolets of the frontal region.

areometer, variant form of ARÆOMETER.

areˈopagist. [see -IST.] Rare variant of next.
1859 in WORCESTER.

Areopagite (æriːˈɒpəgaɪt). [ad. L. *arēopagītes*, a. Gr. ἀρεοπαγίτης: see AREOPAGUS and -ITE.] A member of the court of Areopagus.
1382 WYCLIF *Acts* xvii. 34 Dionyse Ariopagite, *or greet man of comun scole.* 1430 LYDG. *Chron. Troy* I. v, Dyonysyous Whiche.. Was called in scholes Ariopagyte. 1616 HOLYDAY *Juvenal* 180 As secret as the Athenian court of the Areopagites. 1807 ROBINSON *Archæol. Græca* I. xiv. 62 After they had once become Areopagites.

areopaˈgitic, *a.* and *sb.* [ad. L. *Arēopagīticus*, a. Gr. Ἀρεοπαγῖτικός, f. Ἀρεοπαγίτης: see prec. and -IC.] **A.** *adj.* Of or pertaining to the Areopagus or its court. **B.** *sb.* A speech imitating the oration of Isocrates addressed to the court of Areopagus.
[1644 MILTON *Areopagitica*.] 1649 J. H. *Motion to Parl.* 28 And degenerate into some Satyre or Pasquill, rather then an Areopagitick. 1856 GROTE *Greece* II. xcv. XII. 406 The other citizens included in the areopagitic report.

areopaˈgitical, *a.* [f. prec. + -AL^{1}.] Of Areopagitic nature or character; also = prec.
1594 T. B. *La Primaud. Fr. Acad.* 583 The areopagiticall lords in Athens. 1846 HT. MARTINEAU *Hist. Peace* I. II. v. 400 To keep within reasonable bounds that predominating areopagitical spirit.

‖**Areopagus** (æriːˈɒpəgəs). [L., a. Gr. Ἄρειος πάγος the hill of Ares, or Mars' hill.] A hill at Athens where the highest judicial court of the city held its sittings; *hence* used for the court itself, and *transf.* of any important tribunal.
1642 SIR E. DERING *Sp. on Relig.* xvi. 86 Who hath descended into this Areopagus [of polemics]? *a* 1670 HACKET *Scrinia Reserata* (1693) II. §159. 169 And therefore, my H. Lordships, here I have fixt my Areopagus, and dernier Resort, being not like to make any further Appeal. 1900 *Daily News* 28 Apr. 5/3 A permanent areopagus has been created, with fixed arbitrators, secretaries, &c. 1919 tr. *Von Tirpitz's Mem.* I. xvi. 249 The European 'areopagus' (as Bethmann called it), proposed by Grey, ought not to have been refused. 1920 *Q. Rev.* Apr. 475 The Commission of Reparations, whose duty it should be to become a.. Rhadamanthine Areopagus.

†**areˈopagy.** *Obs.* [f. L. *Areopag-us* + -Y.] A conclave, a secret tribunal.
1646 SIR T. BROWNE *Pseud. Ep.* 39 It was not in the power of earth, or Areopagy of hell to work them from it. 1682 —— *Chr. Mor.* 101 Conscience.. sits in the areopagy and dark tribunal of our hearts.

areophane, a common spelling of AEROPHANE.
1851 *Times* 1 Apr. 10/6 Areophane crape.

areostyle, -systyle, areotic: see ARÆ-.

†**areotecˈtonics.** *Obs.*$^{-0}$ [f. AREO- + Gr. τεκτονική building: cf. *architectonics*.] (See quot.)
1706 PHILLIPS, *Areotectonicks*, that part of Military Architecture or Fortification, which shews how to attack safely, and to encounter an enemy at the best Advantage.

areowe, var. of ARUE *v.* *Obs.* to pity, grieve.

†**aˈrep(pe**, *v.* *Obs.* [f. A- *pref.* 1 + OE. *hreppan* to touch.] To reach, lay hold of, seize.
1205 LAY. 26034 þa nolde Arður on slepen nawiht hine areppen [1250 arecche]. *c* 1230 *Ancr. R.* 128 Draweð al into hore holes þet heo muwen arepen & arechen.

arere, var. AREAR *v.* *Obs.*; earlier f. ARREAR.

[**arerisement** [AFr. f. *ariere*], 'action of putting behind, or at a disadvantage, drawback, injury'; inserted in Blount and later Dicts. as Eng.]

ares, -esse, -este, obs. forms of ARRAS.

†**areˈscation.** *Obs.* *rare*$^{-1}$. [? improp. f. L. *āresc-ĕre* to grow dry.] ? A drying up.
1627 FELTHAM *Resolves* I. xli. Wks. 67 A World, which hath in itself Convulsions, Arescations, Enlargements, Erections.

†**aˈrese**, *v.* *Obs.* *rare.* [OE. *ahrisian, ahrysian*, f. A- *pref.* 1 + *hrisian* to shake: see RESE *v.*] *trans.* and *intr.* To shake violently.
c 885 K. ÆLFRED *Gregory's Past.* lxiv. 461 Ac hudeniȝe ærest hine selfne.. & ahrisiȝe siððan oðre. *c* 1000 *Ags. Ps.* xxviii. 6 Drihten ahrysode þa westan eorþan. *c* 1320 *Seuyn Sages* (W) 915 The tusches in the tre he smit; The tre aresede as hit wold falle.

areson, -ere, variants of AREASON, -ER, *Obs.*

arest, obs. form of ARREST, and of ERST.

†**aˈret, aˈrett(e**, *v.* *Obs.* 4-7; also 5-7 **arret(te**, 5 **arect**, 5-6 **arrect**. [a. OF. *arete-r, aretter*, f. *à* to + *reter* (Pr. and OSp. *reptar*):—L. *reputā-re* to count, reckon: see REPUTE. After 1400 erroneously latinized (in England) as *arrectāre*, as if connected with *rectum*, whence the common 15-16th c. spelling *arect, arrect*.]

1. *trans.* To reckon, count; also with *compl.*
c 1386 CHAUCER *Prol.* 726, I praie you.. That ye ne arette [*v.r.* ret(te] it nat my vilanie. 1388 WYCLIF *Luke* xxii. 37 He is arettid [1382 demyd] with wickid men. *c* 1400 *Apol. Loll.* 26 We arettid Him as smitun of God& lafte. *c* 1430 LYDG. *Bochas* II. Prol., They arect it fortunes variaunce. 1470-85 MALORY *Arthur* (1634) Prol., In hym.. myght wel be aretted grete folye.

2. *trans.* To reckon to the credit or debit of a person; **a.** in a good or neutral sense: To impute, ascribe, attribute *to*.
c 1340 HAMPOLE *Prose Tr.* 31 Arett all thi gude dedis sothefastely to Hyme. *c* 1380 WYCLIF *Pater Noster* Sel. Wks. III. 107 It was aretted to him into riȝtwysnesse. *c* 1430 *Life St. Kath.* (1884) 47 Godhed ys not to be aretted to suche thynges þat are sette vnder þe disposicion of God. 1496 *Dives & Paup.* (W. de W.) I. xxi. 57/1 All the goodnesse sholde be arected to the fader & to the moder, & not to god. 1549 CHALONER *Erasm. Moriæ Enc.* F ij b, It is arrected for a great praise and charitable kyndnesse unto theim.

b. chiefly, in a bad sense: To lay to the charge of, impute as a fault *to*, charge *upon*.
1388 WYCLIF *1 Chron.* xxi. 3 This thing, that schal be arettid in to synne to Israel. *c* 1386 CHAUCER *Pars. T.* ⁋506 He that aretteth vpon god, or blameth god, of thyng of which he is hym self gilty. 1430 LYDG. *Chron. Troy* I. vi, Lest men thy death arected unto me. 1477 CAXTON *Dictes* 147 Yf they fynde ony faulte tarette it to Socrates and not to me. 1574 tr. *Littleton's Tenures* 122 b, No follye maye bee areted to him beeynge within age. 1602 SPEGHT *Chaucer's Wks.* 3, I rather aret it to the negligence and rape of Adam Scriuener, that I may speake as Chaucer doth.

3. To charge, accuse, or indict a person (*of*). [So commonly in OF.]
1375 BARBOUR *Bruce* XIX. 20 Schir dauid the brechyne Wes of this deid arettit syne. 1641 *Termes de la Ley* 27 Arretted is hee that is convented before any Judge, and charged with a Crime. [So in BLOUNT *Law Dict.* 1691.]

b. *intr.* To allege. (*pseudo-archaic.*)
a 1643 W. CARTWRIGHT *Ordinary* in Dodsl. *O.P.* (1780) X. 236, I do arret thou shalt acquainted bin With nymphs and fauns and hamadryades.

¶ To commit a charge to, entrust, deliver. (A false use of Spenser's, due to misunderstanding the obs. ***arrett to the charge of*** in 2 b; imitated by others.)
1596 SPENSER *F.Q.* II. viii. 8 The charge, which God doth unto me arrett, Of his deare safety I to thee commend. 1625 GIL *Sacr. Philos.* ii. 133 When God had created man, and arretted the charge of him and his posteritie to the Angels.

aretaics (ærɪˈteɪɪks), *sb. pl.* [f. Gr. ἀρετή virtue; cf. *spondaic*.] (See quot.)
1865 J. GROTE *Moral Ideas* i. (1876) 1 [In] Moral Philosophy there are two sciences.. the science of virtue, Aretaics.. the science of happiness, Eudæmonics.

†**areˈtaloger.** *Obs.*$^{-0}$ [f. L. *aretālog-us*, a. Gr. ἀρεταλόγος + -ER^{1}.] (See quot.)
1623 COCKERAM *Aretalogon* [sic], a vaunter of his owne vertues. 1656 BLOUNT *Glossogr.*, *Aretaloger*, one that braggs or boasts of vertue in himself, a talking fellow, a lyer.

aretalogy (ærɪˈtælədʒɪ). [ad. Gr. ἀρεταλογία, f. ἀρετή excellence, wondrous deed, miracle: see -LOGY.] A narrative of the miracles performed by a god or semi-divine hero. So **aretalogical** (ærɪtəˈlɒdʒɪkəl) *a.*
1887 W. CORY *Lett. & Jrnls.* (1897) 525 The aretalogical succession is that traced back to the Scipio and Regulus of Cicero, Livy, and Horace. 1912 J. S. PHILLIMORE tr. *Philostr. Apollon.* I. p. xiii, A life, or rather an edifying *Aretalogy*, of Pythagoras. 1925 W. R. HALLIDAY *Pagan Background* vi. 185 The aretalogy, which narrates the miraculous acts of some thaumaturge.

aretch, obs. f. ORACH (*Atriplex*); var. AREACH *v.*

‖**arête** (arɛːt). [Fr.:—OF. *areste*:—L. *arista* ear of corn, fish-bone or spine, hence, in Fr., ridge, sharp edge. Cf. ARRIS.] A sharp ascending ridge or 'edge' of a mountain. The local name in

French Switzerland, whence it has become a technical term with mountain-climbers.

1862 *Lond. Rev.* 23 Aug. 164 The Weisshorn..is formed of three great ridges, like the edges of a bayonet, culminating in a beautiful pyramidal point. Two of the arêtes are probably impracticable. **1865** *Sat. Rev.* 29 July 141/2 Three ridges or arêtes of precipitous rock.

† **'arethede, arthede.** *Obs. rare.* [f. *ar(e*, OE. *ǽr* before (cf. AIR *adv.* and ERE) + THEDE, OE. *þéod* people.] The people of former times; antiquity.

a **1440** *Sir Isumbras* 6 Elders that by-fore us were That lyffede in arethede. *a* **1440** *Sir Degrev.* 7 That levede on arthede.

Aretine, var. ARRETINE *a.*

† **are'tology.** *Obs.*$^{-0}$ [f. Gr. ἀρετ-ή virtue + -(O)LOGY.] 'That part of moral philosophy that treats of virtue.' Bailey 1731.

areu, obs. variant of ARGH *a.* cowardly.

arew(e, obs. f. ARGH, ARROW, AROW, and ARUE.

† **'areward.** *Obs. rare*$^{-1}$. ? Before, formerly.

c **1325** *E.E. Allit. P.* B. 208 He [Lucifer] vndkyndely as a karle kydde areward.

areyn(e, obs. form of ARRAIGN.

arf, dial. form of ARGH *a.* timid, loath.

'arf, arf (ɑːf). Slang corruption of HALF *sb.*, *a.* or *adv.*

1854 *Punch* XXVI. 82/1 *First Polite Native.* Who's 'im, Bill? *Second ditto.* A stranger! *First ditto.* 'Eave 'arf a brick at 'im. **1889** FARMER *Americanisms* 201/2 The rough's traditional 'arf brick. **1903** SHAW *Man & Superman* II. 70 Here! Mister! arf a mo! steady on! **1915** 'BARTIMEUS' *Tall Ship* 69 Not 'arf. **1934** T. S. ELIOT *Rock* I. 12 'Arf a mo', 'arf a mo'. It's lucky for you two as you've got someone what's done a bit o' lookin' into things to keep you in line.

arfeð, variant of ARVEÐ *a. Obs.* difficult.

† **'arfname.** *Obs.* [f. OE. *ęrfe, ięrfe*, ON. *arfr* (cf. OFris. *erf*, OHG. and Goth. *arbi*) inheritance + OE. **numa* taker, f. *niman* to take. With OE. *ięrfe, yrfe-numa* cf. Goth. *arbi-numja*, OHG. *arbinomo*, OFris. *erfnoma, erfnama*: the ON. cognate, the probable source of Ormin's *arrfname*, is not found.] Inheritor, heir.

c **1000** *Ags. Gosp.* Matt. xxi. 38 Ðes ys yrfenuma. *c* **1160** *Hatton G.* ibid., Ðes ys se earfedneme. *c* **1200** ORMIN 17744 Arrfname off heffness riche.

arfvedsonite (ɑː'vɛdsənaɪt). *Min.* [f. *Arfwedson* a man's name + -ITE.] A ferruginous variety of hornblende, occurring in black crystals in Greenland and Norway; also called *soda-hornblende*.

1837–68 DANA *Min.* 243.

† **'arga.** *Chem. Obs.* [f. L. *argilla*: see ARGIL.] The name proposed by Dr. Black (*c* 1790) for the earth *alumina*. Cf. ARGIL.

argabushe, obs. variant of HARQUEBUS.

argaile, argal, obs. and var. form of ARGOL.

'argal, *conj. adv.* Perversion of L. *ergo* 'therefore'; hence *subst.* a clumsy piece of reasoning.

1602 SHAKS. *Ham.* v. i. 21 He drownes not himselfe. Argal, he..shortens not his owne life. **1861** *Times* 23 Aug., Mr. Buckle's argument [is] as absurd an *argal* as ever was invented by philosopher or gravedigger. **1871** J. MORLEY *Crit. Misc.* 152 And, as we should not be beaten if we did not deserve it, argal, suffering is a merited punishment.

argal ('ɑːgəl), *sb.* Short form of ARGALI.

1904 R. G. THWAITES *Jrnls. Lewis & Clark Exped.* I. 169 The Rocky Mountain sheep or argal (*Ovis montana*). **1928** CHILDE *Most Anc. East* ii. 44 The third variety of Old World sheep, the argal, lives to the east of the urial.

‖ **argala** ('ɑːgələ). *Ornith.* Better **ar'geelah.** [Hind. *hargīlā.*] The adjutant-bird (*Ciconia Argala*), a gigantic species of stork inhabiting India.

c **1754** IVES *Voy. India* (1773) 183 An extraordinary species of birds, called by the natives *Argill* or *Hargill.* **1798** PENNANT *Hindostan* II. 156 The Argali or Adjutant. **1808** *Orient. Field Sports* I. 99 That cumbrous bird the argeelah. **1838** *Penny Cycl.* XII. 170 The African Marabou is less in size than the Indian Argala. **1847** CARPENTER *Zool.* §449 The Adjutant Stork or Argala of India.

‖ **argali** ('ɑːgəlɪ). *Zool.* [Mongol and Tungusian.] The wild or rock sheep of Asia.

a **1779** COOK *Voy.* (1790) VI. 2185 The wild mountain sheep, or argali. **1847** CARPENTER *Zool.* §274 The Argali, or wild Sheep of Siberia..supposed to be the original stock of the domestic Sheep.

‖ **argan.** *Bot.* [a. Arab. *arjān*, in Barbary pronounced *argān.*] An evergreen tree (N.O. *Sapotaceæ*), found in Morocco, furnishing a very hard, heavy wood, and an oil from its seeds.

1809 J. JACKSON *Morocco* 123 The argan tree is the favourite resort of this bird. **1875** URE *Dict. Arts, Argan-oil*, expressed from the kernels of the *Argania Sideroxylon.*

argand ('ɑːgænd). [from the inventor's name.] **1.** Applied to a lamp invented by Aimé Argand about 1782, with a cylindrical wick, which allows a current of air to pass to both inner and outer surfaces of the flame, thus securing more perfect combustion and brighter light; also to a ring-shaped gas burner constructed on the same principle.

1790 ROY in *Phil. Trans.* LXXX. 162 A simple Argand's burner. **1805** SIR H. DAVY *ibid.* XCV. 158 Exposed to the heat of an Argand lamp. **1832** BABBAGE *Econ. Manuf.* xxiv. 237 An argand burner, whether used for consuming oil or gas. **1859** M. SCOTT *Tom Cringle* ii 39 A large argand with a brilliant reflector. **1869** *Daily News* 18 June, None of the fish-tails seem to be as economical for common gas as the argands.

2. Surname of Jean Robert *Argand*, a French mathematician (1768–1822), applied to a diagram used for the graphical representation of a complex number.

1908 J. H. JEANS *Math. Theory Electr. & Magnet.* viii. 258 The representation of a complex quantity in a plane in this way is known as an Argand diagram. **1959** G. & R. C. JAMES *Math. Dict.* 20/1 *Argand diagram*, two perpendicular axes on one of which real numbers are represented and on the other pure imaginaries, thus providing a frame of reference for graphing complex numbers.

argel ('ɑːdʒəl). *Med.* [ad. Arab. *ḥarjil* (Sharaf *Dict. Med.*).] The leaves of the African asclepiadaceous plant *Solenostemma argel*, formerly used to adulterate senna; also, the plant itself.

1803 *Phil. Mag.* XV. 58 The plant arguel, called senna of Mecca, placed in the class of the cynanchum by C. Nectoux, who has given an ample description of it. **1818** A. T. THOMSON *Lond. Disp.* (ed. 2) 93 The leaf of argel is an inch or 14 lines long, while that of senna never exceeds nine lines. **1874** GARROD & BAXTER *Mat. Med.* 242 This addition to senna is important, as the argel is supposed to gripe and nauseate. **1920** H. G. GREENISH *Mat. Med.* (ed. 3) 34 Argel leaves, *Solenostemma Argel*, Hayne;..formerly regularly mixed with the senna but now of rare occurrence.

‖ **argema** ('ɑːgɪmə). *Med.* Also **argemon.** [L., a. Gr. ἄργεμα, -μον, f. ἀργ-ός white: cf. ALBUGO.] A small white ulcer or speck on the margin of the cornea.

1661 LOVELL *Hist. Anim. & Min.* 83 It helps bleare eyes ..also it helps the argema. **1753** CHAMBERS *Cycl. Supp.*, *Argemon*, or *Argema*..an ulcer about the iris of the eye. **1880** in *Syd. Soc. Lex.*

argent ('ɑːdʒənt), *sb.* and *a.* [a. F. *argent*, ad. L. *argentum* white money, silver.]

A. *sb.* **1.** The metal silver. *arch.* or *poet.* ***spume of argent*** (L. *argenti spuma*): litharge of silver.

[*c* **1485** *E.E. Misc.* (1855) 3 The flore schold be of argentum, Clene sylver alle and sume.] *c* **1530** LD. BERNERS *Arth. Lyt. Bryt.* (1814) 252 It semed well to be of argent; that is to say, syluer. **1589** FLEMING *Virg. Georg.* III. 51 They doo mingle therwithall The spume of argent. **1790** COWPER *Iliad* II. 55 His argent-studded sword. **1851** LONGF. *Gold. Leg.* I. lxvii, Clouds of gold and argent. [See also C.]

† **2.** Silver coin; hence *gen.* money, cash. *Obs.*

c **1500** *Partenay* 1119 Euery day had ther money and argent. **1583** STUBBES *Anat. Abus.* I. 52 Whether they haue Argente, to mayntaine this geare. **1630** J. TAYLOR (Water P.) *To Hon. O'Toole* Wks. II. 18/2 Some hound-like senting sergeant..tires him out for argeant. **1742** BAILEY, *Argent*, Silver or Coin.

3. *Her.* The silver of a coat of arms; the silver or white colour in armorial bearings.

1562 LEIGH *Armorie* (1597) 4 Called Siluer, and blased by the name of Argent. **1628** EARLE *Microcosm.* lxviii. 146 Whole fields of gold and silver, or and argent. **1751** CHAMBERS *Cycl.*, *Argent* is expressed, in engraving, by the parts being left plain, without any strokes from the graver.

B. *adj.* Of, or resembling, silver; silvery white.

c **1590** MARLOWE *Massac. Paris* I. vi, The argent crosses in your burgonets. **1600** FAIRFAX *Tasso* XIV. (R.) The azure skie, With argent beames of siluer morning spred. **1850** H. COLERIDGE *Poems* II. 161 In the full brightness of the argent moon.

b. *esp.* in *Her.* Cf. A 3.

1591 HARINGTON *Ariosto's Orl. Fur.* XXXVI. xxviii, The argent Eagle that he bare. **1681** JORDAN *London's Joy* in Heath *Grocers' Comp.* (1869) 541 He bears a Target Azure with a Saltier argent. **1814** SOUTHEY *Roderick* XVIII, Within that argent field Thou saw'st the rampant Lion.

C. *Comb.*, as ***argent-clear, -horned, -lidded***; † ***argent-content*** (F. ***argent comptant***), ready money; ARGENT-VIVE, q.v.

1842 LONGF. *Sp. Stud.* II. x. viii, Thou moon that shinest Argent-clear above! **1649** LOVELACE *Poems* 151 The Argent-horned Moone. **1830** TENNYSON *Arab. Nts.* 135 Serene with argent-lidded eyes. **1536** BELLENDENE *Cron. Scot.* XIII. v. (JAM.) Ane hundredth thousand poundis..the tane half to be payit with argent content.

argentaffin (ɑː'dʒɛntəfɪn), *a. Histol.* Also †-**ine.** [ad. F. *argentaffine* (P. Masson 1914, in *Compt. Rend.* CLVIII. 60), f. L. *argent-um* silver + *affin-is* akin, after *chromaffine* CHROMAFFIN *a.*] Pertaining to or possessing the property of being readily stained black by ammoniacal silver in the absence of a reducing agent; chiefly *spec.* designating numerous isolated endocrine cells in the gastro-intestinal epithelium which contain cytoplasmic granules with this property.

1925 *Bull. Johns Hopkins Hosp.* XXXVII. 135/1 'Argentaffine' or silver-staining granules are always demonstrable in these cells. *Ibid.*, The argentaffine cells may proliferate. **1926** *Jrnl. Path. & Bacteriol.* XXIX. 137 The specialised argentaffin cells of the crypts of Lieberkühn. **1947** DAWSON & MOYER in *Anat. Rec.* XCVII. 328 These cells are demonstrable by the Bodian protargol method (even without reduction or gold toning)..but are not chromaffin positive and are not impregnated by the Masson-Hamperl technique. Accordingly they are referred to as argentophile rather than argentaffin. **1948** *Ibid.* C. 324 Maturation of the argentaffin granules. **1964** *Jrnl. Anat.* XCVIII. 499 The number of argentaffin cells..and of argentaffin granules in a particular cell, can be expected to vary depending on the functional state of the cells. **1965** LEE & KNOWLES *Animal Hormones* ix. 125 Tumours of the argentaffin tissue in man occur and large quantities of 5-HT are released leading to high blood pressure in the blood vessels of the lungs. **1969** *Anat. Anzeiger* CXXV. 18 In type 'c' some of the granules in the cell are argyrophile as well as argentaffin. **1976** *Path. Ann.* XI. 201 The evolution of our concepts regarding the neoplasms arising from the family of endocrine (or neuroendocrine) cells, variously called Kultschitzky's, enterochromaffin, argentaffin, argyrophil, and basal cells, is a good example of the way ideas in pathology slowly germinate over decades.

Hence **ˌargenta'ffinity**, the property of being argentaffin; **ˌargentaffi'noma** [-OMA], a tumour (occurring chiefly in the appendix) whose tissue stains like argentaffin cells, from which it is thought to develop.

1934 O. T. BAILEY in *Arch. Path.* XVIII. 843 Because of the presence of the specific silver granules in the cytoplasm of these neoplastic cells, the term 'argentaffinoma' seems more descriptive than 'carcinoid'. **1961** WEBSTER, Argentaffinity. **1961** R. D. BAKER *Essent. Path.* xvi. 401 The tumor cells are argyrophylic [*sic*], with silver-staining granules in the cytoplasm, and are called argentaffinomas. **1969** *Anat. Anzeiger* CXXV. 18 The property of argentaffinity or of argyrophilia rests not in these cells as such but in the individual granules that lie in their cytoplasm. **1976** EDINGTON & GILLES *Path. in Tropics* (ed. 2) 541 The tumours called 'carcinoids' or argentaffinomas arise from these cells. **1982** *Amer. Jrnl. Surg. Path.* VI. 131/1 Rectal carcinoids and normal rectal mucosa were compared for the presence of argentaffinity and argyrophilia. **1984** TIGHE & DAVIES *Pathology* (ed. 4) xvi. 149 Neoplasms of the small intestine are rare and include argentaffinoma.

argental (ɑː'dʒɛntəl), *a.* [a. F. *argental* (Haüy): see ARGENT *sb.* and *a.* and -AL^{1}.] Of silver; as in ***argental mercury***, the *amalgam* of Dana.

1816 CLEAVELAND *Min.* 444. **1819** *Pantolog.*, *Argental Mercury*, a native amalgam of silver..It received its present appellation from C. Haüy.

argentan ('ɑːdʒəntæn). [a. F. *argentan*, f. L. *argent-um.*] An alloy of nickel, copper, and zinc; nickel silver, German silver.

1857 CHAMBERS *Inform. People* I. 373 Argentane or German silver. **1863** WATTS *Dict. Chem.* I. 356 Argentan.

† **'argentane.** *Chem. Obs.* [f. L. *argent-um* + -ANE 2 a.] Davy's name for argentic chloride.

1812 SIR H. DAVY *Chem. Philos.* 444 The compound.. argentane, has been long known by the name of hornsilver.

† **argen'tanginy.** *Obs.*$^{-0}$ [ad. F. *argentangine* (Cotgr.), ad. mod.L. *argentangina*, f. *argent-um* silver, money + *angina* quinsy, after Gr. ἀργυράγχη (used in reference to Demosthenes).] 'The silver squincy, when one for money faigns himself sick and not to speak.' Blount *Glossogr.* 1656.

1623 COCKERAM, *Argentageny*, the siluer sickenesse.

† **'argentary.** *Obs. rare*$^{-1}$. [ad. L. *argentāri-us*, f. *argent-um*: see ARGENT and -ARY.] A worker in silver, a silver-smith.

1382 WYCLIF *Acts* xix. 24 Demetrie by name, argentarie [Vulg. *argentarius*], makinge siluerene housis to Dian.

argentate ('ɑːdʒənteɪt), *sb. Chem.* [f. L. *argent-um* silver + -ATE^{4}.] A combination of a base with argentic oxide, as in *Argentate of Ammonia*, or 'fulminating silver.'

1880 in *Syd. Soc. Lex.*

'argentate, *a.* [ad. L. *argentātus* silvered: cf. F. *argenté.*] 'Silvery, or shining white with a tinge of gray.' Gray *Bot. Text-Bk.* 1880.

argentation (ɑːdʒən'teɪʃən). *rare*$^{-0}$. [n. of action f. L. *argentāt-*: see prec. and -ATION. Cf. F. *argentation* (Littré *Supp.*).] The action of silvering or coating with silver.

1731 in BAILEY; whence in JOHNSON, etc.

argenteous (ɑː'dʒɛntɪəs), *a.* [f. L. *argente-us* silvery + -OUS: see ARGENT and -EOUS.] Silvery.

1881 J. BAKER in *Jrnl. Lin. Soc.* XVIII. 267 A much smaller species, not at all argenteous. **1883** *Chamb. Jrnl.* 301 A diminutive, argenteous, truncated cone.

† **'argenter.** *Obs. rare*$^{-1}$. [a. OF. *argentier*:—L. *argentārius* a money-changer, f. *argent-um*: see ARGENT and -ER.] A money-changer, banker.

1483 CAXTON *Gold. Leg.* 125/1 Ledde hym to y^{e} market & solde hym to an argenter.

argentic (ɑːˈdʒɛntɪk), *a. Chem.* [f. L. *argent-um* silver + -IC.] Containing silver in chemical composition. Applied to compounds in which silver combines as a monad, as ***argentic chloride***, AgCl, occurring native as horn-silver; ***argentic nitrate***, $AgNO_3$, lunar caustic.

1868 WATTS *Dict. Chem.* V. 300 The use of argentic iodide in photography.

argentiferous (ɑːdʒənˈtɪfərəs), *a.* [f. as prec. + -(I)FEROUS: cf. F. *argentifère*.] Yielding or producing silver.

1801 HITCHINS in *Phil. Trans.* XCI. 163 The argentiferous crosslode. **1849** GROTE *Greece* II. xxxiv. IV. 369 Auriferous and argentiferous mountains.

argentify (ɑːˈdʒɛntɪfaɪ), *v.* [f. as prec. + -FY.] To turn into silver. **argenˈtific** *a.*, producing silver.

1687 *Turkish Spy* IV. xx. 354 Mercury..aurifies the very Seed of Gold, and argentifies that of Silver. **1671** J. WEBSTER *Metallog.* xxix. 365 The agent..is a seed of an aurifick or argentifick nature.

†**ˈargentil.** *Herb. Obs.* [ad. med.L. *argentilla*, dim. of *argentum*.] The plant Parsley-piert.

1597 GERARD *Herbal* Supp. Ffff iij, Argentill is Percepier. **1753** CHAMBERS *Cycl. Supp.*, *Argentil*, an old English name for the plant called *Percipier Anglorum*.

argentine (ˈɑːdʒəntaɪn), *a.* and *sb.* [a. F. *argentin*, ad. L. *argentinus* of silver.] **A.** *adj.*

1. Of, made of, or containing silver.

1537 W. HOLME *Fall Reb.* 40 An antick deaurate with letters argentine. **1791** PEARSON in *Phil. Trans.* LXXXI. 353 Argentine spicula were seen in the larger grains. **1849** MRS. SOMERVILLE *Connex. Phys. Sc.* xxiv. 224 The property of blackening argentine salts.

2. Silvery.

1578 LYTE *Dodoens* 526 Argentine, or Siluer Thistel. **1608** SHAKS. *Per.* V. i. 251 Celestial Dian, goddess argentine. **1841** HOR. SMITH *Moneyed Man* I. iii. 46 The meanest sounds that pampered mine ear have been argentine. **1859** W. GREGORY *Egypt* II. 35 The argentine raiment which the moon..had thrown over Karnak.

B. *sb.*

1. Silver, or a material simulating it: **a.** ? Wrought silver, silver filagree. **b.** Imitation silver, electroplate. **c.** The silvery lamellæ on the scales of fish, used in the manufacture of artificial pearls.

1577 HOLINSHED *Chron.* III. 857/1 Images of sore and terrible countenances, all armed in curious worke of argentine. **1839–47** TODD *Cycl. Anat. & Phys.* III. 972/1 The material which gives this metallic lustre to the scales of Fishes, known in commerce under the name of 'Argentine.' **1847** *Bachel. Albany* (1854) 115 The argentine and albata did their best to look silvery.

2. *Zool.* A genus of small fishes, of the family *Salmonidæ*, with very silvery scales: see 1 c. Also applied by Pennant to the *Scopelus Pennanti* or *Humboldtii*, now called the Pearlside.

1769 PENNANT *Brit. Zool.* III. 432. **1854** BADHAM *Halieut.* 285 Shoals of argentine are consumed annually in this commerce.

†**3.** *Herb.* The Silver-weed (*Potentilla anserina*), Gerard, 1597; Withering. ***Argentine Thistle***, the Cotton Thistle (*Onopordium Acanthium*) Lyte, 1578.

4. *Min.* Slate-spar (Humble *Dict. Geol.*).

1794 KIRWAN. **1868** DANA *Min.* 678 Argentine..a pearly lamellar calcite..colour white, grayish, yellowish, or reddish.

Argentine (ˈɑːdʒəntaɪn), *a.*[2] and *sb.*[2] [ad. Sp. *Argentina*: see def.]

A. *adj.* Of or belonging to Argentina, the federal republic (*República* or *Confederación Argentina*) which occupies the greater part of the southern end of South America, and is named from the Rio de la Plata (Sp. *plata* silver).

1830 *Ann. Reg. 1829* xii. 243/1 As to the confederation which formed the Argentine republic,..the different provinces had their armies in the field, and were fighting equally bitterly against each other. **1875** *Encycl. Brit.* II. 488/2 Along the Argentine slopes of the Andes. **1891** T. CHILD *Spanish-Amer. Republics* 280 The Argentine love of showy novelties. **1917** G. RÖSS *Argentina & Uruguay* 46 According to Argentine Law, all children born on Argentine soil are *ipso facto* Argentines. **1920** *Cornhill Mag.* Sept. 334 No two Argentine horses are of the same mind for more than a few seconds at a time.

b. ***Argentine ant***, a small brown South American ant, *Iridomyrmex humilis*, which has been introduced into and become a household and orchard pest in parts of the United States, South Africa, and elsewhere.

1908 C. W. WOODWORTH in *California Agric. Exper. Station Circular* No. 38, p. 1 (*title*) The Argentine Ant in California. **1948** F. WIGHTMAN *Wind is Free* (1949) vii. 105 Like the Argentine ant in South Africa, the white ant appeared suddenly on the island and now is attacking everything.

B. *sb.* **1.** A native or inhabitant of Argentina. Also, a horse or pony of a breed peculiar to Argentina.

1829 *Ann. Reg. 1828* Chron. 432/1 An intrepid chief, with a handful of Argentines, has recovered our old possessions. **1860** *Chambers's Encycl.* I. 388/2 The Banda Oriental has been a bone of contention between the Brazilians and the Argentines. **1891** T. CHILD *Spanish-Amer. Republics* 275 In all that concerns civilization, the Argentines look up to the French. **1893** C. E. AKERS *Argentine Sketches* 42 In very rare cases is an Argentine found doing anything that requires severe physical exertion. **1901** KIPLING *Five Nations* (1903) 163 Atop of a sore-backed Argentine.

2. ***the Argentine***, Argentina.

1891 T. CHILD *Spanish-Amer. Republics* 276 In the Argentine and in Uruguay. *Ibid.* 279 The auctioneer..is a great personage in the Argentine.

Hence **Argentinian** (ɑːdʒənˈtɪnɪən) *a.*, belonging to the Argentine; also *sb.* = **Argentino** (ɑːdʒɛnˈtiːnəʊ), a native of the Argentine.

1918 C. B. JORDAN tr. *V. Blasco Ibáñez's Four Horsemen of the Apocalypse* (1919) I. i, I am an Argentinian citizen. *Ibid.*, She was speaking alone to the Argentinian. **1920** *Cornhill Mag.* Sept. 335 The work of the Texans was neat and expeditious, that of the Argentiños clumsy and slow.

argentite (ˈɑːdʒəntaɪt). *Min.* [f. L. *argent-um* silver + -ITE.] Silver-glance or argyrose, a native sulphide found in veins traversing granite, etc.

1837–68 DANA *Min.* 39 Malleable like ordinary argentite.

argento- (ɑːˈdʒɛntəʊ), comb. form of L. *argentum* silver; = 'Having silver as a constituent.'

1837–68 DANA *Min.* 39 Argentopyrite..a pseudomorph consisting of the minerals argentite, marcasite, pyrrhotite, pyrargyrite. **1868** WATTS *Dict. Chem.* V. 305 Argento-cuprous Sulphide..Argentiferous Copper-glance.

argentocracy (ɑːdʒənˈtɒkrəsɪ). *nonce-wd.* [f. prec. + -CRACY: cf. *plutocracy*.] The rule or paramount influence of money.

1868 *Pall Mall G.* 23 May 11 The disease of argentocracy.

argentometer (-ˈɒmɪtə(r)). [f. as prec. + -METER.] An instrument for determining the strength of silver solutions.

1879 SPON *Workshop Rec.* 250 To use the argentometer.

argentous (ɑːˈdʒɛntəs), *a. Chem.* [f. L. *argent-um* silver + -OUS.] Containing silver in composition; applied to compounds containing silver in twice the proportion of that in those called argentic, as ***argentous chloride***, Ag_2Cl; ***argentous oxide***, Ag_4O, suboxide or hemioxide of silver.

1869 ROSCOE *Elem. Chem.* 273 A small quantity of argentous chloride.

argentry (ˈɑːdʒəntrɪ). [ad. F. *argenterie*; cf. L. *argentāria* (sc. *vasa*, etc) silver vessels, plate, etc.: see ARGENT and -RY.] Silver plate, wrought silver. *Obs.* exc. *fig.*

1622 HOWELL *Lett.* I. II. xvii, Pawning his own argentry and Jewels. **1641** —— *ibid.* (1753) 124 Costly Bowls of frosted Argentry. **1852** D. MOIR *Bower of Peace* Wks. I. 61 The round moon's calm argentry.

†**argenture.** *Obs. rare.* [a. F. *argenture*, f. *argenter* to silver.] ? A silvering amalgam.

1576 BAKER *Gesner's Jewel Health* 142 b, Of these two make an argenture.

†**ˌargent-ˈvive.** *Obs.* [a. F. *argent vif*:—L. *argentum vivum* (Pliny).] Quicksilver, mercury.

1453 in Heath *Grocers' Comp.* (1869) 422 Argent Vyff, ye bolyon..iiijd. **1610** B. JONSON *Alch.* II. i, The Bulls our fornace..our argent-viue, the Dragon. **1662** CHANDLER *Van Helmont's Oriatr.* 84 Argent-vive or Quick-silver.

†**argh,** *a. Obs.* exc. *dial.* Forms: 1 **arg** (WS. **earg, earȝ, earh**), 2–3 **erȝ, arȝ,** 3 **ærh, arh, eærȝh, eruh, erew, areu, arewe, areȝ,** 3–5 **arwe,** 4– 5 **argh,** 5 **arwhe, arow(e.** *Sc.* 6– **arch,** 9 **argh, ergh, erf, arrow;** *north Eng.* 7– **arf.** [com. Teut.; cogn. w. ON. *argr* (Sw. and Da. *arg*), OHG. *ark*, mod.G., Du. *arg*, OFris. *arg*, *ergh*:—OTeut. **arg-oz*.]

1. Cowardly, pusillanimous, timid, fearful. (Still in north. dial.)

c **885** K. ÆLFRED *Bæda* I. xii. (Bosw.) Se earȝa féðe Brytta. **1205** LAY. 4336 þu eart swa eærȝh cniht. *c* **1230** *Wohunge* in *Cott. Hom.* 277 Arh ich was meself and wah. *c* **1230** *Ancr. R.* 288 He, kene þet was ær eruh. **1297** R. GLOUC. 457 His hert arwe as an hare. *c* **1400** *Destr. Troy* VI. 2540 If Elinus be argh, & ournes for ferde. **1440** *Promp. Parv.* 14/2 Arwe, or ferefulle (**1499** arwhe, arowe, or ferdfull), *Timidus pavidus*. *a* **1450** *York Myst.*, *Barbers* L viij b, So am I arow to do þat dede. **1483** *Cath. Angl.*, Arghe, *pusillanimis*. **1535** STEWART *Cron. Scot.* II. 621 King Duncane so arch ane man wes he. **1691** RAY *N. Countr. Words*, *Arf*, afraid. *a* **1800** R. JAMIESON *Pop. Ball.* I. 233 Fearful will it be to me, I'm erch, or a' be o'er. **1808** JAMIESON *Sc. Dict.*, *Arch, argh, ergh, erf.* **1875** ROBINSON *Whitby Gloss.* (E.D.S.), *Arf* or *arfish*, afraid, reluctant: 'I felt arfish i' t' dark.'

2. Inert, sluggish, lazy, slow, loath, reluctant. (Still in north. dial.)

a **1000** *Gnom. Vers.* (Gr.) 188 Ful oft mon wearnum tihð earȝne. *c* **1200** *Moral Ode* 16 Erȝe [*v.r.* erewe, arȝe, ærwe] we beoð to donne god. **1513** DOUGLAS *Æneis* XI. vii. 119 The pepil haill grantis that thai wayt..bot thai ar arch to schaw. **1813** D. ANDERSON *Poems* 116 (JAM.) An' rouges o' Jews, they are nae arrow Wi' tricks fu' sly. **1877** *Holderness Gl.* (E.D.S.), *Arf*, *Arfish*, unwilling, indisposed, disinclined: 'He's nobbut varry arfish te begin.'

†**3.** Vile, base, good-for-nothing. (So in Ger.) *Obs.*

c **950** *Lindisf. Gosp.* Matt. xii. 39 Cneorisse yflo & árȝ becon soecas.

†**4.** as *sb.* ? Wretch, betrayer, enemy. *Obs.*

a **1275** *Prov. Alfred* 228 in *O.E. Misc.* 117 Gif þu hauist sorwe, ne say þu hit þin areȝe [*v.r.* arewe, erewe].

†**argh(e,** *v. Obs.* exc. *dial.* Forms: 1 **arȝian, earȝian,** 2 **erȝian,** 3–4 **arȝe(n,** 4–5 **argh(e.** *Sc.* 8–9 **ergh.** [f. prec.]

1. To be disheartened, timid, fearful, loath; to hesitate from timidity. (Still in Sc.)

c **1175** *Lamb. Hom.* 13 þet eower heorte erȝian swiðe and eower feond strongian. *c* **1325** *E.E. Allit. P.* B. 713 þenne arȝed Abraham, & alle his mod chaunged. *c* **1400** *Destr. Troy* V. 1976 Antenor arghet with austerne wordes. **1728** RAMSAY *Gentle Sheph.* III. iii, Dear Jenny, I wad speak..and yet I ergh.

†**2.** *impers.*, ***me arghes***: I am afraid. *Obs.*

c **1340** *Alex.* (Stevenson) 19 Me arȝes of my selfe, I am alle in aunter.

†**3.** *trans.* To daunt, frighten. *Obs.*

c **1325** *E.E. Allit. P.* B. 572 In þe anger of his ire þat arȝed monye. **1393** LANGL. *P. Pl.* C. IV. 237 Ac þow þy-self..Hast arwed meny hardy men · that hadden wil to fyghte. *c* **1400** *Sir Perc.* 69 That arghede alle that ther ware, Bothe the lesse and the mare.

arghan (ˈɑːgæn). [Etym. unknown.] The fibre of a South American plant, later cultivated in Malaya, which can be spun into a strong fine yarn. Also *attrib.*

1922 *Conquest* Oct. 485 Arghan, the new British textile. **1924** J. S. M. WARD *Textile Fibres* 52–3. **1927** *Chambers's Jrnl.* 236 The Arghan plant is Sir Henry [Wickham's] second gift to the Inde.

†**ˈarghhood.** *Obs.* In 3–4 **arhhede.** [f. ARGH *a.* + -HOOD.] Cowardice, pusillanimity.

c **1350** in *O.E. Misc.* 74 Prude and modynesse, Ne arhhede ne sorynesse.

†**ˈarghly,** *adv. Obs.* [f. ARGH *a.* + -LY[2].] Timidly, cowardly; also (in OE.) basely.

c **1000** ÆLFRIC *Gen.* xx. 4 Abimeleh andwirde earhlice. **1086** *O.E. Chron.* (Laud MS.) And hine earhlice ofsloȝon. *c* **1400** *Destr. Troy* v. 1831 Antenor arghly auntride of ship.

†**ˈarghness.** *Obs.* [f. ARGH *a.* + -NESS.] Cowardice, pusillanimity, timidity.

1340 *Ayenb.* 31 þe oþer is arȝnesse, þet is tyene of herte. *c* **1400** *Destr. Troy* VI. 2203, I ournand in elde with arghnes in hert. **1483** *Cath. Angl.*, Arghnes, *pusillanimitas*.

†**ˈarghship.** *Obs.* In 3 **ærhscipe.** [f. ARGH *a.* + -SHIP.] = prec.

1205 LAY. 12411 Heo sulf mid ærhscipe arnden to heolde.

†**arghth.** *Obs.* In 3 **ærhðe, arhþe, areȝthe.** [f. ARGH *sb.* + -TH[1].] = prec.

1205 LAY. 23520 Arður ærhðe bi-deled [**1250** arhþe]. *a* **1250** *Owl & Night.* 404 He vor areȝthe hit ne for-lete.

Argie (ˈɑːdʒɪ), colloq. abbrev. of ARGENTINIAN *a.* and *sb.*, ARGENTINE *a.*[2] and *sb.*[2] Freq. in the context of the Anglo-Argentinian conflict over sovereignty of the Falkland Islands (1982).

1982 *Daily Tel.* 6 Apr. 30/6 We yelled at the Argies. **1982** *Private Eye* 21 May 3/1 It is my proud privilege to loan the ship to the British Government for use in our heroic crusade against the Argie hordes. **1983** *Washington Post* 22 June A23/5 Mrs. Thatcher's 'lesson' for them..does not have to do with..the Argie-bashing affair. **1986** *Financial Times* 2 Apr. 19/7 The programme rages at the Arts Council, Fergie, the 'Tory propaganda machine in White City'..and zapping Argies (*still?*). **1986** *Sunday Tel.* 9 Nov. 18/3 Small boys still play at Argies and Commandos.

argil (ˈɑːdʒɪl). [a. F. *argille* (mod. *argile*), ad. L. *argilla* (formerly in Eng. use), a. Gr. ἄργιλλος, f. ἀργής white, shining.] Clay, *esp.* potter's clay. Also proposed as a name for alumina when the nature of that base was first discovered.

1530 PALSGR. 195/1 Argile a kynde of erthe, *Argille*. **1599** A. M. *Gabelhouer's Bk. Physic* 318/2 Hard baked Argille or loame. **1675** EVELYN *Terra* (1729) 20, I do not reckon Loam among the clays, though it seem to be but a succulent kind of Argilla. **1778** WOULFE in *Phil. Trans.* LXIX. 20 The blue argilla from Paris. **1792** *Ibid.* LXXXII. 34 Argil precipitated from alum by an alkali. **1859** R. BURTON *Africa* in *Jrnl. R.G.S.* XXIX. 158 Soil..yellow with argile. **1879** SPON *Workshop Rec.* 42 Argillaceous clay or alumina clay..is called argil.

argillaceo- (ɑːdʒɪˈleɪʃɪəʊ), comb. f. next; in ***argillaceo-calcareous***.

1845 DARWIN *Voy. Nat.* vi. (1873) 106 It consists of a crumbling argillaceo-calcareous rock.

argillaceous (ɑːdʒɪˈleɪʃəs), *a.* [f. L. *argillāce-us* + -OUS: see -ACEOUS.] Of the nature of clay; largely composed of clay; clayey.

1731 in BAILEY. **1781** DILLON *Trav. Spain* 253 A mixture of argillaceous, or calcareous earth. **1794** SULLIVAN *View Nat.* I. 486 The argillaceous hills of Tuscany. **1841** TRIMMER *Pract. Geol.* 88 The argillaceous odour given out by minerals containing alumina.

argilliferous (ɑːdʒɪˈlɪfərəs), *a.* [f. L. *argill-a* clay + -(I)FEROUS: cf. F. *argilifère*.] Yielding or abounding in clay.

c **1800** KIRWAN is cited in WEBSTER.

argillite (ˈɑːdʒɪlaɪt). *Min.* [f. as prec. + -ITE.] Argillaceous schist, clay slate. **argiˈllitic** *a.*, of or containing argillite. Craig, 1847.

1795 MILLS in *Phil. Trans.* LXXXVI. 39 Bare rocks..a variety of argillite. **1850** DANA *Geol.* xiii. 564 The rock somewhat resembles an argillite.

argillo- (ɑːˈdʒɪləʊ), comb. f. ARGILLOUS, as in **argillo-calcareous** *a.*, calcareous with an admixture of clay; **argillo-calcite**, a clayey limestone.

1802 HOWARD in *Phil. Trans.* XCII. 173 The Professor considers the stone..argillo-ferruginous. **1823** J. BADCOCK *Dom. Amusem.* 183 Card-paper, covered with an argillo-calcareous mixture.

argillose (ˌɑːdʒɪˈləʊs), *a.* ? *Obs.* [ad. L. *argillōsus* clayey: see ARGIL and -OSE.] = next.

c **1420** *Pallad. on Husb.* II. 148 Lande argillose, and not clay by it selve. **1731** BAILEY, *Argillose*, full of white clay.

argillous (ɑːˈdʒɪləs), *a. rare.* [a. OF. *argillus*, *-os*, *-ous* (mod. *argileux*):—L. *argillōsum*: see prec. and -OUS.] Clayey, argillaceous.

c **1420** *Pallad. on Husb.* IV. 496 With stones myxt it stont in argillous Lande. **1646** SIR T. BROWNE *Pseud. Epid.* 321 The sand and argillous earth at the bottome. **1882** ELWES tr. *Capello's Benguella* I. iv. 104 This argillous silicious soil.

†**argin(e.** *Obs. rare.* [a. It. *argine*, according to Diez:—pop. L. **arger-em* for **adger-em*, *agger-em*, a mound.] An embankment or rampart in front of a fort.

1589 IVE *Fortif.* 3 The Fort..must also haue..an argine or banke to empeache the approach. *c* **1590** MARLOWE *2nd Pt. Tamburl.* III. ii, High argins..To keep the bulwark-fronts from battery.

arginase (ˈɑːdʒɪneɪz, -s). *Chem.* [G. (Kossel and Dakin 1904, in *Z. Physiol. Chem.* XLI. 322): see next and -ASE.] An enzyme capable of hydrolysing arginine into ornithine and urea.

1904 *Nature* 16 June 160/2 The enzyme has been named 'arginase', and is the first representative of the class of urea-forming enzymes capable of being isolated and of acting outside the body. **1931** *Lancet* 9 May 1021/2 Eldbacher and Merz have recently shown that 'all malignant mammalian and human tumours..are distinguished from normal tissue by their arginase content'. **1953** *New Biol.* XV. 90 The enzyme arginase..is present in large amounts in all the body tissues [of the dogfish] except blood and brain.

arginine (ˈɑːdʒɪnaɪn, -iːn, -ɪn). *Chem.* Also -in. [G. *arginin* (E. Schulze and E. Steiger 1886, in *Chem. Berichte* XIX. 1177), of uncertain derivation.] An amino-acid, $C_5H_{13}N_4COOH$, present in many animal proteins and certain vegetable tissues.

1886 *Jrnl. Chem. Soc.* L. 725 The nitrate of the base, to which the authors give the name of *arginine*.., crystallises out on cooling in groups of slender needles. **1919** *Nature* 20 Nov. 322/2 The importance of the diamino-acids lysin, histidin, and arginin must be recognised. Their presence has been shown to be necessary for growth. **1930** *Biochem. Jrnl.* XXIV. 1181 In the case of tumour tissue there is experimental evidence that arginine induces an increase in the rate of growth. **1949** *New Biol.* VII. 77 The basic proteins..are relatively rich in the amino-acid arginine.

Argive (ˈɑːgaɪv), *a.* and *sb.* [ad. L. *Argīvus* (Gr. Ἀργεῖος) pertaining to Argos.]

A. *adj.* Of or belonging to the ancient city of Argos or the territory of Argolis. Hence used in Homer and later classical writers as = Grecian, Greek.

1598 CHAPMAN *Iliad* I. Argt., Apollos Priest to th' Argiue Fleete doth bring Gifts for his daughter. *Ibid.* 2 Till in my Royall Argiue court, her bewties strow my bed. **1676** HOBBES *Iliad* I. 1 The two Atrides..Who of the Argive Army were the best. **1858** BIRCH *Anc. Pottery* II. 107 The Lacedæmonian, Teian, Chian, and Argive cups were also esteemed. **1875** MORRIS *Æneids* II. 254 And now the Argive host comes forth. **1925** G. MURRAY *Eumenides* 15 Myself, mine Argive people, and my home Shall without war be hers.

B. *sb.* A native of Argos or of Argolis; *gen.* a Greek.

c **1530** T. ELYOT tr. *Plutarch's Educ. Children* sig. Eᵛ, Polynyces the yonger brother, hauynge in his ayde the Argyues. **1579** S. GOSSON *School of Abuse* fol. 7ᵛ, The Lacedæmonians instructed by Tyrtæus verse, The Argiues by the melody of Telefilla. **1676** HOBBES *Iliad* XVII. 267 Just so Patroclus body tugged they, Trojans to Troy, and Argives to the Fleet. **1716** POPE *Iliad* VIII. 436 Long since had Hector stain'd these Fields with Gore, Stretch'd by some Argive on his native Shore. **1875** MORRIS *Æneids* I. 40 And Pallas, might not she Burn up the Argive fleet and sink the Argives in the sea..? **1922** FOAKES-JACKSON & LAKE *Beginnings Chr.* II. 12 The ivory or other material.. supplied by the Elians, Athenians, or Argives.

†ˈ**argle**, *v. Obs.* exc. *dial.*; also in the reduplicated **argle-bargle**, **argol bargol**. [prob. a popular perversion of *argue*, or confusion of that word with *haggle*.]

1. *trans.* To argue obstinately, dispute about.

1589 *Hay any Work* (1844) 11, I will neuer stand argling the matter any more. **1827** D. MOIR *Mansie Wauch* 78 Me and the minister were just argle-bargling some few words on the doctrine of the Camel and the Eye of the Needle.

2. *intr.* To bandy words, dispute, wrangle.

1823 GALT *Entail* I. vii. 53 'Weel, weel,' said the Laird, 'dinna let us argol bargol about it.' **1827** J. WILSON *Noct. Ambr.* Wks. 1855 I. 336 But I hate a' argling and hargle-bargling. **1861** RAMSAY *Reminisc.* Ser. II. 99 And all argle-bargling, as if at the end of a fair.

ˈ**argle-ˈbargle**, *sb.* [f. *argle-bargle* vb.: see ARGLE *v.*] Disputatious argument, bandying of words, wrangling.

1872 A. J. CUPPLES *Tappy's Chicks* 252 During these days of 'argle bargle', as our smith's wife called it. *a* **1881** CARLYLE in W. A. Knight *Retrospects* (1904) 15, I have for a long time given up the argle-bargle of metaphysics. **1927** *Observer* 11 Dec. 15/2 Can they..stand up to a good and sufficient argle-bargle that lasts for the best part of three hours?

So ˈ**argy-ˈbargy** (**argue-bargue**) *v. intr.* and *sb.* (orig. *Sc.*).

1887 *Jamieson's Sc. Dict.* Suppl. s.v. *Argewe*, The terms *argie-bargie*, *argie*, and *bargie*, are applied to such contentions. **1888** BARRIE *Auld Licht Idylls* 35 I'se nae time to argy-bargy wi' ye. **1905** H. G. WELLS *Kipps* I. ii, An occasional argey-bargey that sprang up between Carshot and Buggins at dinner. **1906** W. DE MORGAN *Joseph Vance* xxiii, He argue-bargues with you like a winkle that won't come out of its shell. **1922** *Blackw. Mag.* July 65/1 Do not argy-bargy with such scoundrels. **1948** J. B. PRIESTLEY *Linden Tree* II. i, 'Avin' a proper argy-bargy in 'ere, aren't you? Losing your tempers too.

argol¹ (ˈɑːgəl). Forms: 4–5 **argoyle, -oile, -oille,** 6 **-uyll, -ell, -oll,** 6–7 **-all,** 7 **-aile,** 9 **argal,** 7– **argol.** [Origin unknown: found also as *argoil* in Anglo-French 1250–1300 in *Liber Albus* I. 225, 231]. The tartar deposited from wines completely fermented, and adhering to the sides of the casks as a hard crust; crude bitartrate of potassium, which, when purified, becomes *cream of tartar*.

[*c* **1260** *Liber Albus* I. 231 Des avoirs qe veignent doutre meer: ciere, argoil, quivere, estein.] *c* **1386** CHAUCER *Chan. Yem. Prol. & T.* 260 Of tartre, alym, glas, berm, wort, and argoyle [*v.r.* -oile, -oille]. **1540** RAYNALD *Birth Man.* IV. vi. (1634) 202 Wine lees dryed..which the Goldsmiths do call Arguyll. **1610** B. JONSON *Alch.* I. iii, You have arsnike, Vitriol, saltartre, argaile. **1611** COTGR., *Tartre*: Tartar or Argall, the lees or dregs that sticke to the sides of wine-vessells. **1714** MANDEVILLE *Fab. Bees* (1725) I. 412 Argol we might have from the Rhine. **1834** *Penny Cycl.* II. 309/2 Nearly 1000 tons of argol are annually imported into this kingdom. It comes to us from almost all wine-producing countries. **1863** WATTS *Dict. Chem.* I. 356 Argal or Argol. **1875** URE *Dict. Arts* III. 970 There are two sorts of argol known in commerce, the white and the red; the former, which is of a pale pinkish colour, is the crust let fall by white wines; the latter is a dark red from red wines.

¶ Erroneously for ARCHIL, ORCHIL, q.v.

1758 *Phil. Trans.* L. 668 Another of the..useful plants of this division is the orchel, or argol, as it is commonly called. **1776** WITHERING *Bot. Arrangem.* (1796) I. 372 One [lichen] brought from the Canary Islands, viz. the Orchel or Argol.

‖**argol**², **-al** (ˈɑːgəl). [Mongol.] Dried cow-dung used as fuel in Tartary.

1856 HAZLITT *Huc's Trav.* 35 Alas! how should we make a fire, when we have no argols? **1883** *Athenæum* 10 Nov. 605/3 In summer, when the dried argals fail as fuel.

†ˈ**argolet, -oulet.** *Obs.* [a. F. *argoulet.*] A light-armed horse-soldier; *orig.* a mounted bowman.

c **1580** PEELE *Batt. Alcazar* Wks. II. 95 Pisano, take a cornet of our horse, As many argolets. **1687** *Spon's Hist. Geneva* 133 Troops of Argoulets or light Horsemen.

†ˌ**argoleˈtier.** *Obs.* Also 6 **argletier,** 7 **arguliteer.** [f. prec., after *chevalier*, etc.] = prec.

1579 DIGGES *Stratiot.* 109 Light Horsemen, Argoletiers and such like. **1588** *Let.* in *Harl. Misc.* (Malh.) II. 75 Such other [horsemen] as are termed Carbines or Argletiers. **1642** *Orders* ibid. V. 252 The which arguliteers shall stand you in as great stead, as horse of better account. **1800** BAILEY, *Argoletiers*, light armed horsemen.

†**arˈgology.** *Obs.*—⁰ [ad. Gr. ἀργολογία, f. ἀργός idle.] 'Idle or vaine speaking.' Cockeram 1623.

argon (ˈɑːgɒn). *Chem.* [mod.L., f. Gr. ἀργόν, neuter of ἀργός idle, inactive, f. ἀ- priv. + ἔργον work.] A colourless odourless gas occurring in very small quantity (less than 1 per cent.) in the air, used in 'gas-filled' electric light bulbs, etc. Discovered in 1894 and named from its chemical inertness. Symbol Ar, atomic number 18, atomic weight 39·944.

1894 *Daily News* 28 Dec. 3/2. **1895** LD. RAYLEIGH & W. RAMSAY in *Phil. Trans.* CLXXXVI. A. 187 Argon, a New Constituent of the Atmosphere. *Ibid.* 234 The gas deserves the name 'argon', for it is a most astonishingly indifferent body, inasmuch as it is unattacked by elements of very opposite character. **1913** *Bloxam's Chem.* (ed. 10) 293. **1958** *Engineering* 7 Feb. 187/1 It is necessary to melt titanium either in the presence of a suitable inert gas, such as argon, or else in a vacuum.

Argonaut (ˈɑːgənɔːt). [ad. L. *Argonauta*, ad. Gr. Ἀργοναύτης a sailor in the ship Argo.]

1. a. One of the legendary heroes who accompanied Jason in the Argo in his quest of the Golden Fleece.

1596 SPENSER *F.Q.* IV. i. 23 The dreadfull discord, which did drive The noble Argonauts to outrage fell. **1846** GROTE *Greece* I. xiii. (1869) I. 231 The Argonauts again owed their safety to the stratagem of Medea.

b. *transf.* Also with small initial.

1807 W. IRVING *Salmagundi* 20 Mar. 109 A celebrated Roman knight..who..became a great favourite of prince Madoc, and accompanied that famous Argonaut in the voyage which ended in the discovery of this continent. **1893** K. A. SANBORN *S. California* 1 The *fin-de-siècle* Argonaut, in Pullman train, flees the cold and grip.

c. An adventurer who went to California in search of gold soon after its discovery there in 1848. *U.S. Obs.* exc. *Hist.*

1848 in C. C. Cutler *Greyhounds of the Sea* (1930) xiv. 134 The ship will be commanded by a man of experience, and if the adventurers of the *Trescott* do not bring home their full share of the golden fleece, we have overestimated the qualities of the Argonautes. **1948** P. JOHNSTON *Lost & Living Cities of California Gold Rush* 28/1 How those argonauts who first beheld this contorted country must have labored to penetrate it with pack mules and ox-drawn wagons!

2. Name of a genus of cephalopod molluscs of the octopod type, *esp.* of the species which, from the delicacy and whiteness of its shell, is also known as the 'paper nautilus,' and was formerly believed to sail on the surface of the sea.

1835 KIRBY *Hab. & Inst. Anim.* I. x. 306 The Argonaut, or paper nautilus. **1847** CARPENTER *Zool.* §891 By the action of the arms, the Argonaut can swim backwards in the same manner as other Octopi.

Argonautic (ɑːgəʊˈnɔːtɪk), *a.* and *sb.* [ad. L. *Argonauticus*: see prec. and -IC.] **A.** *adj.* Of or pertaining to the Argonauts. **B.** *sb.* **a.** An Argonaut. **b.** A poem concerning the Argonauts.

1583 WATSON *Poems* (Arb.) 133 The Argonauticks of Apollonius. **1614** SELDEN *Titles Hon.* 42 When the Argonautiques came to Chiron's Den. **1794** SULLIVAN *View Nat.* II. 443 Newton supposed the Zodiac to relate to the Argonautic expedition. **1846** GROTE *Greece* I. xiii. (1869) I. 248 The Argonautic legend.

†**argoˈsine.** *Obs. rare.* [In the two forms *Argosie*, *Argosine*, prob. ad. It. *Raguseo*, *Ragusino*, Ragusan: for initial *Arg-* cf. next.] ? A Ragusan.

1559 *Contn. Fabyan* VII. 709 An argosie came from the batilment of the same churche, vpon a cable. **1565** STOW *Summarye* (ed. 1) 208 b, an Argosie. **1580** —— *Chron.* 1036 an Argosine. **1587** FLEMING *Contn. Holinsh.* III. 979/2 (quoting Stow) an Argosine. **1590** STOW *Summarie* 539 an Argosine. **1645** HOWE, ed. *Stowe's Annals* 594/1 a man of the nation of Arragosa. [*a* **1650** LE NEVE *Appendix* to *Leland's Collectanea* (ed. 2) IV. 320 A Man, a Stranger, being a Native of Arragon.]

argosy (ˈɑːgəsɪ). Forms: 6 **ragusye, arguze,** 6–7 **argose,** 7 (**rhaguse, ragosie,**) **argosea, argosey, argozee,** 6–9 **argosie,** 7– **argosy.** [App. ad. It. *Ragusea*, pl. *Ragusee*, i.e. *una* (nave *or* caracca) *Ragusea*, a Ragusan (vessel or carack), best repr. by the earliest form *ragusye*; the transposition in *argosea*, *arguze*, *argozee*, etc., is no doubt connected with the fact that Ragusa (in Venetian, *Ragusi*) itself appears in 16th c. English as *Aragouse*, *Arragouese*, *Arragosa*. Cf. also the prec. word, in which *Argosine* seems to represent It. *Ragusino*, synonym of *Raguseo*.

That argosies were reputed to take their name from Ragusa, is stated by several writers of 17th c.; and the derivation is made inductively certain by investigations made for us by Mr. A. J. Evans, showing the extent of Ragusan trade with England, and the familiarity of Englishmen with the *Ragusee* or large and richly-freighted merchant ships of Ragusa, 'Argosies with portly saile, Like Signiors and rich Burgers on the flood [which] ouer-peere the pettie Traffiquers That curtsie to them, do them reuerence, As they flye by them with their wouen wings.' (SHAKS. *Merch. V.* I. i. 9.) No reference to the ship Argo is traceable in the early use of the word.]

[*a* **1500** PALLADIUS FUSCUS (of Padua) *De Situ oræ Illyricæ* 1, Nulla Europæ pars adeo abdita est..ut in ea Ragusinos non invenias negotiantes. **1517** SIR R. TORKINGTON *Pilgrimage* (1884) 16 The most strong and myȝghty towne called *Aragouse*. **1518** *Diario di Marco Samudo* (Feb.) Una (nave) Ragusea presa per esso corsaro.

Hist. and *poet.* A merchant-vessel of the largest size and burden; esp. those of Ragusa and Venice.

1577 DEE *Mem. Perf. Art Navig.* 9 Ragusyes, Hulks, Caruailes, and other forrein rich laden ships. **1587** FLEMING *Contn. Holinsh.* III. 313/2 A great argosie..hauing streamers and flags verie warlike, with two boats at either sterne. **1590** GREENE *Wks.* (Gros.) VII. 224 All the Argoses, Gallyes, Galeons, and Pataches in Venice. **1596** SHAKS. *Tam. Shr.* II. 376, etc. **1600** HAKLUYT *Voy.* (1810) III. 373 The greatest shippes of France, yea, the Arguzes of Venice may enter in there. **1608** CHAPMAN *Byron's Conspir.*, A full-saild Argosea. **1627** N. BURLEY in Smith *Seaman's Gram.* A ij, The Argozees first the Illyrians made. **1638** L. ROBERTS *Map of Commerce* 237 Rhagusa..from hence was the original of those great ships here built, and in old times vulgarly called Argoses properly Rhaguses. **1668** RYCAUT *Ottoman Emp.* (1675) xiv. 119 It is said that those vast Caracks called Argosies, which are so much famed for the vastness of their burthen and Bulk, were corruptly so denominated from Ragosies, and from the name of this city. **1841–6** LONGF. *Belfr. Bruges* xii, Venetian merchants with deep-laden argosies.

b. *transf.* or *fig.*

1621 DONNE *Serm.* lxx. (1640) 716 If St. Paul, so great an Argosie, held no more but *Christum Crucifixum*, what can thy Pinnace hold? **1801** T. JEFFERSON *Writ.* (1830) III. 454 The tough sides of our Argosie have been thoroughly tried. **1873** HIGGINSON *Oldport Days* i. 16 Wagons of sea-weed just from the beach..each weed an argosy.

†**'argot**[1]. *Obs.* Also argo. [a. F. *argot* 'the Spurre of a Cocke.. the heele or talon of a hog' (Cotgr.), mod. *ergot*; origin unknown. Cf. ERGOT.]

a. The spur of a cock; the similarly-situated excrescence on the feet of other animals. **b.** A spur left in pruning a tree.

c **1400** *MS. Maystre of Game* (Halliw.) More gret argos then hath an hynde. **1693** EVELYN *De la Quint. Compl. Gard.* II. 38 Argot.. the Old Extremity of a Branch which has been formerly shorten'd at some distance from the Eye. **1708** *Phil. Trans.* XXVI. 79 *Plectronites*, the Argot, or Cockspur Ichthyodont.

‖**argot**[2] (argo). [Fr. Of unknown origin.] The jargon, slang, or peculiar phraseology of a class, *orig.* that of thieves and rogues.

1860 FARRAR *Orig. Lang.* vi. 134 Leaves an uninviting argot in the place of warm and glowing speech. **1869** —— *Fam. Speech* ii. (1873) 78 The argots of nearly every nation.

argotic (ɑː'gɒtɪk), *a.* [ad. F. *argotique*: see prec. and -IC.] Of the nature of slang.

1863 quoted in *Sat. Rev.* 149 Argotic locutions.

arguable ('ɑːgjuːəb(ə)l), *a.* [f. ARGUE *v.* + -ABLE.] Capable of being argued, open to argument.

1611 COTGR., *Plaidoyable*, pleadable, arguable. **1860** BAGEHOT *Hist. Unref. Parl.* 13 The Jacobites.. claimed the Crown, not on arguable considerations of policy. **1883** *Law Times* 22 Sept. 356/1 It was a very arguable point whether this Act applied to.. Cape Colony.

arguably ('ɑːgjuːəblɪ), *adv.* [f. ARGUABLE *a.* + -LY[2].] As may be shown by argument or made a matter of argument.

1890 *Sat. Rev.* 22 Feb. 216/2 His policy, if sometimes arguably mistaken, was almost always a.. generous policy. **1920** *Q. Rev.* Apr. 404 The zeal for order and moral righteousness is arguably more purely Jewish in its origin than [etc.]. **1959** *Times* 18 Dec. 5/5 Mozart's sinfonia concertante for violin and viola, arguably the greatest of his concertos.

argue ('ɑːgjuː), *v.* 4–; also 4 arguwe, 5 argwe, 6 argoue, argew. [a. OF. *argue-r*:—L. *argūtāre*, freq. of *argu-ĕre* to make clear, prove, assert, accuse, blame; of which latter Fr. *arguer* and Eng. *argue* are now taken as the equivalents.]

I. To bring evidence, convict, prove, indicate.

†**1.** To make good an accusation against, prove wrong or guilty, convict. Const. *of Obs.*

c **1400** *Apol. Loll.* 31 þat þe prest be miȝti to.. argu hem þat aȝen seyn þe feiþ. **1576** WOOLTON *Chr. Manual* (1851) 8 [They] dissent from themselves, and with their life argue their tongue of untruth. **1582** N. T. (Rhem.) *John* viii. 46 Which of you shal argue me of sinne. **1660** STANLEY *Hist. Philos.* (1701) 171/2 He, not to argue him of Perjury, affirmed, etc.

†**2.** *trans.* To accuse, impeach, arraign, find fault with, call in question. Const. *of. Obs.*

c **1425** WYNTOUN *Cron.* VII. vi. 79 And argwyd hym rycht scharply. **1513** DOUGLAS *Æneis* XIII. vi. 173 Not ȝou, nor ȝit the kyng.. Will I argew of this maneir offens. **1643** SIR T. BROWNE *Relig. Med.* 127 Nor would we argue the definitive sentence of God. **1692** RAY *Disc.* II. v. (1732) 213 Erroneously argues Hubert Thomas.. of a mistake.

3. To prove or evince; to afford good ground for inferring, show weighty reasons for supposing; to betoken, indicate. (Passing from *prove* in early use to *evidence* or *imply* in modern use.) **a.** a person or thing *to be* so-and-so.

1494 FABYAN VI. clxxxiv. 182 But that proueth nat or argueth hym to be the firste. **1593** SHAKS. *3 Hen. VI*, II. ii. 25 Which argued thee a most vnlouing Father. **1667** MILTON *P.L.* IV. 831 Not to know mee argues your selves unknown. **1703** MAUNDRELL *Journ. Jerus.* (1732) App. 8 Which seem to argue it to be ancient. **1877** L. MORRIS *Epic Hades* I. 55 The gems Which argued her a Queen.

b. *that* it is.

1585 ABP. SANDYS *Serm.* (1841) 178 That we are delivered.. argueth that we once were in their hands. **1639** FULLER *Holy War* IV. xxvi. (1647) 214 The speedy withering of their religion argueth it wanted root. **1690** LOCKE *Hum. Und.* II. xxi. §54 Contrary choices that Men make in the World, do not argue that they do not all pursue Good.

c. with *simple object*.

1538 STARKEY *England* 74 Thys rudeness and barrennes of the ground arguth.. neclygent idulnes. **1593** SHAKS. *2 Hen. VI*, III. iii. 30 So bad a death, argues a monstrous life. **1642** FULLER *Holy & Prof. St.* II. iv. 60 Such purulent spittle argues exulcerated lungs. **1702** *Eng. Theophrast.* 181 Imitation argues esteem, a desire of equality argues envy. **1879** MACLEAR *Celts* xi. 181 Nor.. did the use of this material argue poverty.

II. To bring reasons, to reason, dispute.

4. *intr.* To bring forward reasons concerning a matter in debate; to make statements or adduce facts for the purpose of establishing or refuting a proposition; to discuss; to reason.

1303 R. BRUNNE *Handl. Synne* 6436 He [the executor] argueþ vpon þys skylle And byt þe dede answere þartylle. **1393** LANGL. *P. Pl.* C. XII. 122 Aristotle and oþere to arguen ich tauhte. **1413** LYDG. *Pylgr. Sowle* II. lxiv. (1859) 59 Now arguest thou folyly; for thy reson is more to my purpos than it is to thyne. **1525** LD. BERNERS *Froiss.* II. xxvi. 76 He argued in himselfe, and was full of malencoly. **1665** GLANVILL *Sceps. Sci.* 54 His philosophy and faculty of arguing. **1855** KINGSLEY *Lett.* (1878) I. 442 He would argue by the hour, but never for arguing sake.

b. *Hence*, To reason in opposition, raise objections, contend, dispute.

1393 LANGL. *P. Pl.* C. XVII. 115 Quath Actyf þo al angryliche · and argueyinge as hit were, 'What is pouerte pacient?' **1605** BACON *Adv. Learn.* I. ii. §1 More ready to argue than to obey. **1713** STEELE *Guard.* No. 17 ¶7 The virgin argued no longer. **1861** GEO. ELIOT *Silas M.* 63 'Confound it, sir, don't stay arguing, but go and order my horse.'

c. Const., *with* (in general sense), *against* (in direct opposition to the position of), an opponent; *for* or *against* a proposition; *about* (*of* obs.) a matter under discussion.

c **1374** CHAUCER *Troylus* II. 645 She gan in her herte argue Of this matere. *c* **1430** *Babees Bk.* 11 Argue not aȝen þat. **1477** EARL RIVERS (Caxton) *Dictes* 139 Better.. to holde his peas than to contrarye and argue with a foole. **1535** COVERDALE *Job* xxxvi. 4 The knowledge wherwithall I argue agaynst the. **1667** MILTON *P.L.* II. 562 Of good and evil much they argu'd then. **1710** LADY MONTAGUE *Lett.* lxvii. 111, I am not.. arguing for an equality of the two sexes. **1711** STEELE *Spect.* No. 118 ¶3 I'd give ten Pounds to hear her argue with my Friend.. about Trade. **1756** BURKE *Vind. Nat. Soc.* Wks. I. 13 They argue against a fair discussion of popular prejudices. **1795** SOUTHEY *Maid of Orl.* III. 33 And argue thence of kingdoms overthrown, And desolated nations. **1847** [see 8].

5. *trans.* To bring forward the reasons for or against (a proposition, etc.); to discuss the pros and cons of; to treat by reasoning, examine controversially.

1494 FABYAN V. xcix. 72 The sayd causes warre well and sufficiently argued. **1613** SHAKS. *Hen. VIII*, II. i. 168 Wee are too open heere to argue this. **1725** DE FOE *Voy. round World* (1840) 27, I laid it all before them again, arguing every part of it.. clearly. **1732** BERKELEY *Alciphr.* V. §34 If our tenets are absurd, we allow them to be freely argued. **1883** MRQ. SALISBURY *Sp. in Parl.* 17 July, I do not see that it is my business to argue the legal considerations adverted to.

6. With *subord. cl.* To maintain, by adducing reasons, the proposition or opinion *that*.

1548 GESTE *Pr. Masse* 90 In consideration wherof he argueth, yf Christ shuld be often offered, nedes must he oft suffer. **1574** tr. *Littleton's Tenures* 101 a, Peradventure some will argue.. yt he shall have no writ. **1711** *Spect.* No. 2 ¶3 He will often argue that if this Part of our Trade were well cultivated, we should gain. **1847** YEOWELL *Anc. Brit. Ch.* iii. 24 He is arguing with the Jews, that the Messiah.. was already come.

7. *trans.* To bring forward as a reason (for or against), to use as an argument. *arch.*

1626 SHIRLEY *Brothers* III. i, What can she argue to thy birth or person? **1722** DE FOE *Hist. Plague* (1754) 11 He told me the same thing, which I argued for my staying.. was the strongest Repulse to my Pretensions.

8. ***to argue*** (a thing) ***away***, ***off***, etc.: to get rid of by argument.

1713 *Guardian* No. 60 Which.. have clearly argued that animal out of the creation. **1719** YOUNG *Revenge* I. i, We call on wit to argue it away. **1865** D'A. THOMPSON *Odds and Ends*, Men.. would argue a dog's tail off.

9. ***to argue*** (a person) ***into*** or ***out of***: to persuade him by argument into, or out of, a course of action, an opinion or intention.

1685 CONGREVE *Old Bachel.* Ded. (J.) A sort of poetical logick.. to argue you into a protection of this play. *Mod.* He was argued out of his opposition.

‖**arguendo** (ɑːgjuː'ɛndəʊ), *adv. Law.* [Med.L., abl. of *arguendum*, gerund of *arguĕre* argue (Cl. Lat. make clear, assert).] In the course of the argument. Also loosely, for argument's sake.

1817 *Rep. Supreme Court U.S.* XV. App. I. 17 *Per* Sir W Scott, *arguendo*, in Smart v. Wolff. **1850** *Ibid.* XLIX. 174 Even assuming *arguendo*, that such administration was necessary,.. in that event her administrator would have recovered. **1911** G. S. BOWER *Law Actionable Misrepresentation* xi. 284 Very frequently, indeed, as will be noticed on reference to the language used *arguendo* in the authorities, 'laches' and 'delay'.. serve to indicate a consciousness on the part of the advocate that he cannot support a case of affirmation or waiver. **1940** E. POUND *Cantos* lxvii. 151 The single dictum of a counsel at bar uttered *arguendo*, As an ornament to his discourse, not pertinent to his argument. **1973** *N.Y. Law Jrnl.* 23 July 3/3 Assuming, arguendo, that such activities are not unconstitutional. **1983** *Fortune* 7 Mar. 47/2 We will assume, arguendo, that American business and American workers are being hurt by the MTA deal.

arguer ('ɑːgjuːə(r)). [f. ARGUE + -ER[1]; cf. OF. *argueur*.] One who argues, adduces reasons, or engages in discussion; a disputant, a reasoner.

1377 LANGL. *P. Pl.* B. x. 116 Augustyne to suche argueres · he telleþ hem þis teme. **1649** FULLER *Just Man's Fun.* 21 The third sort of people, are the Arguers or Disputers. **1763** JOHNSON in *Boswell* (1831) I. 454, I was a great arguer for the advantages of poverty. **1836** HOR. SMITH *Tin Trump.* (1876) 269 Personality and invective are not only proofs of a bad argument but of a bad arguer.

argufier ('ɑːgjuːˌfaɪə(r)). [f. ARGUFY *v.*] One who argufies or is given to arguing.

1805 FESSENDEN *Democr. Unveiled* vi. 203 His honour might have pass'd.. For quite a decent country Squire, And no bad Jury — argufier. **1871** JOWETT *Plato* III. 494 We know that they are tremendous argufiers, and are able to impart their own skill to others. **1880** W. CLARK RUSSELL *Sailor's Sweetheart* i, I have noticed that your people who are pretty well agreed are always the fiercest argufiers.

argufy ('ɑːgjuːfaɪ), *v. colloq.* [An illiterate formation on ARGUE. Cf. *speechify*.] A colloquial and dialectal equivalent of ARGUE, usually with the idea of pertinacious or petty argument.

1. *intr.* To prove or be evidence of something; *hence*, to be of importance, consequence, or use; to signify. Cf. ARGUE 3.

1751 SMOLLETT *Per. Pic.* (1779) III. lxxviii. 44 'Howsomever, that don't argufy in reverence of his being in a hurry.' *c* **1800** C. DIBDIN *Poor Jack* iii, What argufies sniv'ling and piping your eye?

2. To argue, dispute, wrangle.

1800 MAR. EDGEWORTH *Will* ii. (1832) 104, 'I can't stand argufying here about charity.' **1865** *Sat. Rev.* 12 Aug. 197/2 People who are always argufying are the.. worst of bores.

3. *trans.* To worry with argumentation. Cf. ARGUE 9.

1771 SMOLLETT *Humph. Cl.* 797 'Would you go for to offer for to arguefy me out of my senses?' **1876** BLACK *Madcap V.* vii. 64, 'I am thwarted, crushed, argufied at every turn.'

arguing ('ɑːgjuːɪŋ), *vbl. sb.* [f. ARGUE + -ING[1].] **a.** Accusation, fault-finding (*obs.*). **b.** Argumentation, argument.

c **1385** CHAUCER *L.G.W.* 475 Sche answerde lat be thyn arguynge. **1598** SYLVESTER *Du Bartas Job Tri.* I. 911 List you now vnto my Arguing. **1611** BIBLE *Habb.* ii. 1 When I am reproved [*marg.* upon my reproofe or arguing]. *c* **1705** BERKELEY in Fraser *Life* (1871) 487 From Locke's arguings it can't be proved that, etc. **1839** CARLYLE *Chartism* v. 141 However obscure the arguings.

†**ar'guitive**, *a. Obs. rare*$^{-0}$. [f. L. *arguit-* ppl. stem of *argu-ĕre* + -IVE, as if ad. L. **arguitīvus*.] Characterized by argument. Hence †**arguitively** *adv.*, in a way that proceeds by argument.

a **1665** J. GOODWIN *Filled w. the Spirit* (1867) 389 The new truths.. are arguitively or consequentially contained or comprehended in them [the old ones].

arguliteer, var. ARGOLETIER, *Obs.*

argument ('ɑːgjuːmənt). [a. F. *argument* (13th c.), ad. L. *argūment-um*, f. *arguĕre* (or refashioning, after this, of OF. *arguement*, f. *arguer*): see ARGUE. For use of the L. form, see 3 c.]

1. Proof, evidence, manifestation, token. (Passing from *clear proof* in early, to *proof presumptive* in later usage; cf. ARGUE 3.) *arch.*

1382 WYCLIF *Acts* i. 3 To which and he ȝaf hym silf a lyue.. in manye argumentis, *or prouyngis.* **1447** BOKENHAM *Lyvys of Seyntys* 53, I wante the argumentes of a man. **1599** SHAKS. *Much Ado* II. iii. 242 It is no addition to her witte, nor no great argument of her folly. **1678** *Trans. Crt. Spain* 91 Flight is not then an argument of a bad Conscience. **1728** T. SHERIDAN *Persius* (1739) 20 *note*, Beating the Desk and biting of Nails were Arguments of taking Pains. **1759** MARTIN *Nat. Hist.* I. 251 To remove the two Giants.. would be a greater Argument of Taste than fixing them up.

2. *Astr.* and *Math.* The angle, arc, or other mathematical quantity, from which another required quantity may be deduced, or on which its calculation depends.

c **1386** CHAUCER *Frankl. T.* 549 Hise othere geeris, As been his centris and hise Argumentz. *c* **1391** —— *Astrol.* xliv. 54 To knowe the mene mote and the argumentis of any planete. **1796** HUTTON *Math. Dict.* I. 141/2 Annual argument of the moon's apogee.. is the distance of the sun's place from the place of the moon's apogee. **1879** THOMSON & TAIT *Nat. Phil.* I. I. §54 An arc of the circle referred to.. is the Argument of the harmonic motion.

3. a. A statement or fact advanced for the purpose of influencing the mind; a reason urged in support of a proposition; *spec.* in *Logic*, the middle term in a syllogism. Also *fig.*

c **1386** CHAUCER *Frankl. T.* 158 Clerkes wol seyn as hem leste By Argumentz that al is for the beste. **1475** CAXTON *Jason* 88 Why replye not ye to this argument. **1535** COVERDALE *Job* xxiii. 3 To pleate my cause before him, and to fyll my mouth with argumentes. **1664** H. MORE *Myst. Iniq.* 338 But that the Beast that was, and is not, is not the Devil, we shall now evince by other arguments. **1724** WATTS *Logic* III. ii. §7 The middle term.. is often called the Argument, because the force of the syllogisms depends upon it. *c* **1790** REID *Let.* in *Wks.* I. 81/2 It is a good argument *ad hominem*, against the scheme of Necessity held by Hume. **1852** MISS YONGE *Cameos* (1877) II. i. 5 Well provided with golden arguments. **1865** MOZLEY *Mirac.* viii. 187 Anything is an argument which naturally and legitimately produces an effect upon our minds, and tends to make us think one way rather than another.

b. Const. (*to* obs.), *for*, a conclusion; hence (of later origin) *against* the contrary.

c **1374** CHAUCER *Troylus* I. 466 Argumentis to this conclusion, That she on hym wold have compassion. **1643** BURROUGHES *Hosea* i. (1652) 7 It is a great argument to obedience to know it is the word of the Lord that is spoken. **1863** COX *Inst. Eng. Govt.* II. iii. 349 The arguments for and against the preservation of trial by jury.

c. In certain phrases borrowed from the formal terminology of the schools, the L. *argumentum* is in current use, esp. in ***argumentum ad hominem***. ***argumentum e*** (or ***ex***) ***silentio***, an argument from silence: used of a conclusion based on lack of contrary evidence.

1690 LOCKE *Hum. Und.* IV. xvii. (1695) 391 To press a Man with Consequences drawn from his own Principles, or Concessions.. is already known under the Name of *Argumentum ad Hominem.* [Cf. quot. 1790 in 3 a.] **1934** TOYNBEE *Stud. Hist.* II. 274 This *argumentum ex silentio* does not, of course, go very far. **1939** L. H. GRAY *Foundations of Lang.* iv. 99 We perceive that the absence of a common designation in the Indo-European period for a given concept or thing by no means necessarily implies the non-existence of that concept or thing at that period. The *argumentum e silentio* is notoriously fragile. **1962** *Listener* 6 Sept. 364/2 Doesn't Dr. Needham.. give the Chinese the benefit of a doubt, sometimes, with an *argumentum e silentio*?

4. A connected series of statements or reasons intended to establish a position (and, *hence*, to refute the opposite); a process of reasoning; argumentation.

1393 GOWER *Conf.* III. 139 To trete upon this jugement Made eche of hem his argument. *c* **1440** *Gesta Rom.* I. lxvii. 248 Therfore lat vs fle the wordle.. and by good argument we shulle haue the kyngdome of Heuene. **1577** HOLINSHED *Chron.* II. 16/2 Truly this argument hangeth togither by verie strange gimbols. **1660** BARROW *Euclid* I. xvi, By the like argument is the angle *ICH* = *ABH*. *a* **1704** T. BROWN *Table T.* Wks. 1730 I. 140 You're out in your argument. **1877** LYTTEIL *Landm.* I. iv. 35 To recapitulate the successive steps of the argument.

5. a. Statement of the reasons for and against a proposition; discussion of a question; debate.

1494 FABYAN VII. ccxxviii. 257 Than ye stryfe.. was brought in argument before the pope. **1588** SHAKS. *L.L.L.* III. i. 105 How did this argument begin? **1671** MILTON *Samson* 903 In argument with men a woman ever Goes by the worse. **1711** SHAFTESB. *Charac.* II. iv. (1714) II. 305 So intent in upholding their own side of the argument. **1883** J. GILMOUR *Among Mongols* xvii. 207 The greater part of [such difficulties] are advanced merely for the sake of argument.

†**b.** *transf.* Subject of contention, or debate. *Obs.*

1595 SHAKS. *Hen. V*, III. i. 21 And sheath'd their Swords, for lack of argument. **1614** RALEIGH *Hist. World* II. 472 Much argument of quarrel ministred betweene them and the Townesmen.

†**6.** Subject-matter of discussion or discourse in speech or writing; theme, subject. *Obs.* or *arch.*

1570 ASCHAM *Scholem.* Pref. 21 How to write in this kinde of argument. **1596** SHAKS. *1 Hen. IV*, II. ii. 100 It would be argument for a Weeke. *Ibid.* II. iv. 310 And the argument shall be, thy runing away. *a* **1674** CLARENDON *Hist. Reb.* II. VII. 205 He grew the Argument of all Tongues, every Man enquiring who, and what He was. **1791** STORMONT *Monody Pr. Wales* i, Should woo the British muse.. To strains of bitter argument. **1834** DISRAELI *Rev. Epick* III. vii, The throbbing deed Shall make thy name a household argument Familiar with their voices.

7. The summary or abstract of the subject-matter of a book; a syllabus; *fig.* the contents.

1535 *Goodly Primer* (1848) 290 The argument into the xxivth psalm. In this psalm David singeth all things to be the Lord's; etc. **1607** SHAKS. *Timon* II. ii. 187 If I would.. try the argument of hearts, by borrowing. **1728** POPE *Dunc.* I, Argument to Book the First. **1824** J. JOHNSON *Typogr.* I. 165 Orations, which with the argument.. take up nineteen leaves.

†**'argument,** *v.* *Obs.* [a. F. *argumente-r*, ad. L. *argūmentā-ri* to conduct an argument, f. *argūment-um*: see prec.]

1. *intr.* To adduce arguments, argue, reason.

c **1320** *Seuyn Sages* (W.) 195 The fifte yer, he gan argument Of the sterre, and of the firmament. *c* **1374** CHAUCER *Troylus* I. 377 Thus argumentyd he. **1607** TOPSELL *Four-f. Beasts* 153 Thus they argument for the horns of Elephants. **1637** GILLESPIE *Eng.-Pop. Cer.* II. ix. 42 We argument also from the Scandall of them.

2. To give evidence, furnish proof, *that*.

1558 KENNEDY *Compend. Treat.* in *Misc. Wodr. Soc.* (1844) 114 Albeit that it apperteneth to the Apostolis.. it argumentis not that utheris etc.

3. To furnish with arguments or syllabuses. *rare.*

1611 H. BROUGHTON *Req. Agreement* 52 He [Homer] caused both workes to be argumented by 24 verses.

4. *trans.* To make the subject of argument or debate.

1746 DA COSTA in *Phil. Trans.* XLIV. 406 As for the regular Figure of the Belemnites being excepted against, I believe few Fossilists will argument that.

†**argu'mentable,** *a.* *Obs.* [ad. L. *argūmentābilis*, f. *argūmentāri*: see prec. and -ABLE.] Admitting of argument; that may be argued; *also* argumentative.

1588 FRAUNCE *Lawiers Log.* II. ix. 101 b, Disputation is an argumentable discussion of a doubtfull proposition. **1622** CALLIS *Stat. Sewers* (1824) 187, I thought that an argumentable point.

argumental (ɑːgjuːˈmɛntəl), *a.* ? *Obs.* [ad. L. *argūmentāl-is*, f. *argūment-um*: see ARGUMENT *sb.*] Of, pertaining to, or characterized by, argument; argumentative.

1595 MARKHAM *Sir R. Grinuile* (Arb.) 49 (D.) With instances and argumentall sawes. *a* **1744** POPE (J.) Oppress'd with argumental tyranny. **1774** *Westm. Mag.* II. 283 The most vociferous and argumental coxcomb existing.

†**argu'mentate,** *v.* *Obs.* *rare*$^{-1}$. [f. L. *argūmentāt-*, ppl. stem of *argūmentāri*.] By-form of ARGUMENT *v.*

1586 SIDNEY *Wanst. Play* (1674) 622 (D.) 'Nunc are you to argumentate of the qualifying of their estate first.'

argumentation (ˌɑːgjuːmənˈteɪʃən). [a. F. *argumentation, -acion* (14th c. in Littré), ad. L. *argūmentātiōn-em* f. *argūmentāri*: see ARGUMENT *v.*]

1. The action or operation of inferring a conclusion from propositions premised; methodical employment or presentation of arguments; logical or formal reasoning.

1491 CAXTON *Vitas Patr.* (W. de W.) II. 293 b, That whiche he commaundeth not; thou sekest it by argumentacyon. **1551** T. WILSON *Logic* 3 Logike.. doth plainly and nakedly set foorth.. the summe of things, by the way of argumentation. **1692** BENTLEY *Boyle Lect.* i. 2 [They] preclude any argumentation from the Revealed Word of God. **1750** JOHNSON *Rambl.* No. 156 ¶2 The evidence obscured by inaccurate argumentation. **1816** SCOTT *Antiq.* xxix, The eloquence and argumentation of the bar.

2. Interchange of argument, discussion, debate.

1538 STARKEY *England* 149 We wyl not.. consume the tyme in argumentatyon. **1676** CLARENDON *Surv. Leviath.* 286 But what argumentation can a man hold with him. **1712** STEELE *Spect.* No. 429 ¶10 Conscious that he is too much given to Argumentation. **1836** H. TAYLOR *Statesm.* xxii. 154 Inevitably drawn into protracted argumentation.

3. A sequence or chain of arguments, a process of reasoning; = ARGUMENT 4.

1548 GESTE *Pr. Masse* 106 What a misfashioned argumentation is this. **1656** COWLEY *Pind. Odes* 29 *note*, For when their argumentation is broken, they are forced to save themselves by flight, that is, by evasions. **1694** CANNE *Necess. Separ.* (1849) 265 Who have their syllogisms and argumentations not in mood and figure, but in their heels. **1877** S. OWEN in *Wellesley Desp.* Introd. 23 His solemn warnings.. his ingenious argumentations.

argumentative (ɑːgjuːˈmɛntətɪv), *a.* [a. F. *argumentatif, -ive*, f. L. *argūmentāt-* (see ARGUMENTATE) + -IVE, as if ad. L. **argūmentātīvus*.]

†**1.** Of the nature of an argument (*for*); of weight as evidence (*of*). *Obs.*

1642 SIR E. DERING *Sp. on Relig.* 35 Even this is argumentative for us. **1661** *Refl. Oathes of Suprem. & Alleg.* 41 Their silence in this point.. is surely very argumentative. **1691** RAY *Creation* (1714) 113 If Pliny, a heathen, could make this fertility of wheat argumentative of the bounty of God to Man.

2. Of, pertaining to, or characterized by argument; controversial; logical.

1647 MAY *Hist. Parl.* I. ix. 115 To vent their opinions in argumentative way. **1828** MACAULAY *Hallam, Ess.* (1851) I. 52 Hallam [gives us] a critical and argumentative history. **1861** STANLEY *East. Ch.* vii. (1869) 245 The close argumentative style of his writings.

3. Given or addicted to argumentation; capable or fond of arguing.

1667 DRYDEN *Ind. Emp.* Pref. (1668) 16 It is not out of any design to play the Argumentative Poet. **1781** GIBBON *Decl. & F.* xxxiii. II. 257 He possessed a strong, capacious, argumentative mind. **1861** GEO. ELIOT *Silas M.* 4 The argumentative Mr. Macey.. shook his head.

argu'mentatively, *adv.* [f. prec. + -LY².] In an argumentative manner, in respect to argument.

a **1660** HAMMOND *Wks.* II. 28 (R.) It is argumentatively weak and unconcluding. **1695** *Lond. Gaz.* mmmxcv/4 The Mystery of Curing.. Explained and Proved, Argumentatively and practically. **1876** MISS BRADDON *Haggard's Dau.* III. 218, 'I don't call it honouring the Sabbath to sit down to a worse dinner than on a work-a-day,' Jim remarked argumentatively.

argu'mentativeness. [f. as prec. + -NESS.] The quality of being argumentative.

1731 in BAILEY. **1831** CARLYLE *Sart. Res.* II. iii, A state of windy argumentativeness. **1882** *Daily News* 8 Mar. 2/1 Public business in the House of Commons was delayed by unprecedented argumentativeness at private business time.

argumentator (ˌɑːgjuːmənˈteɪtə(r)). [a. L. *argūmentātor*, n. of agent f. *argūmentāri*: see ARGUMENT *v.* Cf. F. *argumentateur*.] One who conducts an argument; a reasoner.

1635 PERSON *Varieties* I. 38 Thus it standeth then with these Argumentators. **1678** CUDWORTH *Intell. Syst.* 836 Our Atheistick Argumentator yet further urges. **1827** *Gentl. Mag.* XCVII. II. 53 Mr. M'Nicoll is a profound argumentator.

†**argu'mentive,** *a.* *Obs.* *rare*$^{-1}$. [irreg. f. *argument-* + -IVE.] = ARGUMENTATIVE.

1668 DRYDEN *Ess. Dram. Poesy*, Quickness of repartees in argumentive scenes receives an ornament from verse.

†**'argumenˌtize,** *v.* *Obs.* [f. ARGUMENT *sb.* + -IZE.] To conduct an argument; to argue. Hence also **argumentizer, argumentizing.**

a **1641** FINETT *Philoxenis* (1656) 8 If one would argumentize thereupon. **1680** MANNYNGHAM *Disc.* 34 (T.) The unmixed and argumentizing philosophy. **1684** BRADY *Introd. O.E. Hist.* 241 (L.) This argumentizer should.. have cited this proclamation. **1691** WOOD *Ath. Oxon.* III/200 The true way of argumentizing.

†**argumen'tose,** *a.* *Obs.*$^{-0}$ [ad. L. *argumentōsus*] 'Full of argument, reason, matter or proof; pithy, full of wit or skill.' Bailey 1731.

‖**argumentum:** see ARGUMENT.

Argus (ˈɑːgəs). [L., a. Gr. Ἄργός.]

1. A mythological person fabled to have had a hundred eyes. *Hence*, a very vigilant person, a watcher or guardian.

1387 TREVISA *Descr. Brit.* (Caxton) 37 They ben in araye tormentours in wynnyngis argi. **1557** *Myrr. Mag.*, *Induct.* xvii, With more then Argus' eyes. **1580** TUSSER *Husb.* xlix, If cheeses in dairie haue Argusses eies. **1741** RICHARDSON *Pamela* (1824) I. 65, I hope still, Argus, to be too hard for thee. **1855** MILMAN *Lat. Chr.* (1864) IX. XIV. x. 349 The Argus-eyes of the still ubiquitous clergy.

[After the death of Argus, his eyes were transferred by Hera to the tail of the peacock.]

1596 SPENSER *F.Q.* I. iv. 17 Fayre pecocks.. full of Argus eyes their tayles dispredden wide.

2. A genus of pheasants, natives of Asia, of which one species (*A. giganteus*) is as large as a turkey.

1768 *Gentl. Mag.* XXXVIII. 521 The argus.. is the largest species of pheasant yet known. **1829** GRIFFITH, etc. *Cuvier* VIII. 237 The argus was brought for the first time to Batavia from Malacca in 1780. **1834** *Malte-Brun's Univ. Geog.* III. 431 The coo-ow, or Argos pheasant, is remarked for its uncommon beauty.

3. A name for certain butterflies of the genus *Polyommatus*, with many eye-like spots on the wings.

1827 JERMYN *Butterfly Coll. Vade Mecum* 146/7 Brown Argus; Scotch Argus.

4. *Comb.* or *Attrib.*, as **argus-eyed, -like** *a.*, extremely watchful or sharp-sighted; **argus-queller,** a title of the god Mercury; **argus-shell,** name of a species of porcelain-shell; **argus-snake** (see quot.).

1603 FLORIO *Montaigne* (1634) 305 No humane judgement is so.. Argos-eied, but sometimes shal fall a sleep. **1861** MOTLEY *Dutch Rep.* Pref. 3 Argus-eyed Venetian envoys. **1663** GERBIER *Counsel* Gija, All Creatures, from the Mole to the most Argus-like above ground. **1870** BRYANT *Homer* II. XVI. 122 The mighty Argus-queller saw the maid. **1750** SIR J. HILL *Hist. Anim.* 152 (JOD.) The argus shell, the oblong oculated porcellana. **1802** G. SHAW *Zool.* III. 439 The Argus Snake.. is beautifully marked from head to tail by numerous transverse rows of round ocellated red spots.

†**argu'tation.** *Obs.* [ad. L. *argūtātiōn-em*, n. of action f. *argūtāre, -āri*, freq. of *arguĕre*: see ARGUE.] Cavilling, cavil, quibble.

1641 *Ans. Vind. Smectym.* Pref. 8 It is not the force of their argutation, that could move me one foot forward. *a* **1656** BP. HALL *Myst. Godl.* viii, Their devilish and frivolous argutations. **1681** GLANVILL *Saducismus* I. 150 That which this Objection further urges.. is.. a very unlearned and unskilful argutation.

argute (ɑːˈgjuːt), *a.* [ad. L. *argūt-us* clear, sharp, keen, pa. pple of *arguĕre*: see ARGUE.]

†**1.** Of taste: Sharp. *Obs. rare.*

c **1420** *Pallad. on Husb.* IV. 572 [Figs] of savor pure Argute ynough.

2. Of sounds: Shrill.

1719 in *Glossogr. Nova.* *a* **1864** LANDOR *To Barry Cornw.*, A rich but too argute guitar.

3. Of persons, faculties, actions, etc.: Quick, sharp, keen, subtle, shrewd, *esp.* in small matters.

1577 [See next]. **1644** BULWER *Chiron.* 112 With that argute and vehement action, his eyes were almost dazled. **1676** *Phil. Trans.* XI. 554 Curious and argute Historians. **1818** *Q. Rev.* XVIII. 234 Argute emendations of texts. **1875** BROWNING *Aristoph. Apol.* 90 Thou, the argute and tricksy.

ar'gutely, *adv.* [f. prec. + -LY².] In an argute manner; sharply, shrewdly.

1577 HANMER *Anc. Eccl. Hist.* (1619) 277 Such Aristotle hath so argutely and subtilly written. **1762** STERNE *Tr. Shandy* xxxi. V. 241 'You are wrong,' said my father argutely.

ar'guteness. [f. as prec. + -NESS.] Mental sharpness, shrewdness, or cunning; *also*, shrillness.

1653 H. MORE *Conject. Cabbal.* (1713) 133 But what an insipid and unsatisfactory Arguteness there is in such Conceptions. **1683** DRYDEN *Life Plutarch* 118 This [writer] tickles you by starts with his arguteness. **1822** HAZLITT *Men & Mann.* II. i. (1869) 16 A certain arguteness of voice.

†**ar'gutious,** *a.* *Obs.*$^{-0}$ [f. L. *argūtus* ARGUTE + -IOUS; cf. *cautious*.] 'Subtile, witty, of deep-reach, full of words.' Blount *Glossogr.* 1656.

argy-bargy, etc.: see under ARGLE-BARGLE.

argyll, argyle (ɑːˈgaɪl). [f. proper name.] A vessel of silver or metal, like a small coffee-pot, in which to serve up gravy, so as to keep it hot.

1797 M. UNDERWOOD *Treat. Dis. Children* III. 74 The pot is formed in the shape of an Argyle, or gravy-pot. **1822** KITCHINER *Cook's Oracle* 338 We have in the English kitchen, our 'argyll' for gravy. **1922** *Weekly Dispatch* 31 Dec. 6 Especially quaint were the argyles, in which there was a receptacle for hot water so that the gravy might not be cooled down by the use of a cold ladle. **1931** E. WENHAM *Domestic Silver* v. 67 When, in the eighteenth century, it became fashionable to carve the joint on the table, a now almost forgotten gravy-holder, known as an argyle, was popular.

Argyll Robertson (ɑːˈgaɪl ˈrɒbətsən). The name of a Scottish physician (1837–1909) applied *attrib.* to a pupil of the eye which fails to contract in response to light, but contracts on accommodation to near distance.

1881 J. H. JACKSON in *Trans. Ophthalmol. Soc. 1880* I. 149 The common condition described is what is called the Argyll Robertson pupil; the pupil does not act to light and does act during accommodation. **1908** *Practitioner* Jan. 11 The existence of a sluggish reaction to light, or the Argyll-Robertson pupil inactive to light while active to accommodation, would be certain evidence in favour of general paralysis. **1911** *Encycl. Brit.* XVI. 855/2 In 1869 Argyll Robertson discovered that the eye-pupil [in cases of locomotor ataxia] is inactive to light but acts upon accommodation in the great majority of cases. This most important sign is named the 'Argyll Robertson pupil'.

argyr-, argyro- ('ɑːdʒɪr-, -rəʊ-), repr. Gr. ἀργυρο- comb. form of ἄργυρ-ος silver. In numerous technical words, as: **argy'ranthemous** (Craig 1847), **argy'ranthous** (*Syd. Soc. Lex.* 1880), *a. Bot.* [Gr. ἄνθος, ἀνθεμίς flower], having silvery white flowers. **argy'raspid** [L. *argyraspid-es*, Gr. ἀργυράσπιδες], in *pl.* the silver-shielded; a corps of the Macedonian army. ‖**ar'gyria**, *Med.*, affection of the system by the action of silver; silver-poisoning. **argyric** (ɑː'dʒɪrɪk), *a. Chem.* [Gr. ἀργυρικός], of silver; = ARGENTIC. **'argyrite, argy'rose**, *Min.*, synonyms of ARGENTITE (Dana). **argyro'cephalous**, *a.* [Gr. κεφαλή head], having a silvery or shining white head (Craig 1847). **argyro'ceratite**, *Min.* [CERATITE = horn stone, f. Gr. κέρατ- horn], synonym of CERARGYRITE (Dana). **argyro'phyllous**, *a.* [Gr. φύλλον leaf], silvery-leaved (Gray *Bot. Text-bk.* 1880). **argyrythrose**, *Min.* [Gr. ἐρυθρός red], Ruby Silver, Antimonial Red Silver, PYRARGYRITE (Dana).

1599 *Broughton's Lett.* v. 18 As the *Argyraspides* answered some forward youths..so say I. **1801** FUSELI *Lect. Art* ii. (1848) 404 The Argyraspids and the Macedonian phalanx. **1875** H. WOOD *Therap.* (1879) 48 Convulsions and paralysis are present in acute argyria, or silver-poisoning. *Ibid.* 52 Chronic .argyria, or discoloration of the skin by silver. **1880** *Syd. Soc Lex., Argyric salts*, silver salts.

argyrodite (ɑː'dʒɪrəʊdaɪt). *Min.* [ad. Ger. *argyrodit* (A. Weisbach 1886, in *N. Jahrb. f. Mineralogie* II. 67), f. Gr. ἀργυρώδης rich in silver (ἄργυρος silver): see -ITE[1].] A mineral (Ag_8GeS_6) containing silver, sulphur, and germanium.

1886 *Athenæum* 13 Mar. 364/2 Prof. Clemens Winkler.. describes a new element—to which he has given the name of 'Germanium'—in a mineral named Argyrodite. **1910** *Encycl. Brit.* II. 488/2 Argyrodite..is a silver sulpho-germanate..and crystallizes in the cubic system. **1959** *Times Rev. Industry* Sept. 24/2 Ores like argyrodite, containing silver and germanium sulphides,..are not mined in appreciable quantities.

argyrol ('ɑːdʒɪrɒl). *Pharmacy.* [Proprietary term, f. Gr. ἄργυρος silver + -OL.] Vitellin of silver, a dark brown powder of which the aqueous solution is used as a local antiseptic.

1908 *Offic. Gaz. U.S. Pat. Off.* Apr. 1423/1 Barnes & Hille..Argyrol. Description of Goods—Antiseptics. **1910** *Practitioner* Mar. 397 The ducts..should be swabbed out on each of these days with a solution of argyrol. **1956** *Blakiston's New Gould Med. Dict.* 106/1 *Argyrol*, proprietary preparation somewhat similar to mild silver protein; used as a nonirritating antiseptic in infections of the mucous membranes. **1960** *Times Lit. Suppl.* 28 Oct. 698/4 Argyrol is an antiseptic drug used in treating infections of the eye and throat.

arh, variant of ARGH *a.*

arh-: see ARRH-.

Arhat, Arahat ('ɑːhæt, 'ærəhæt). Also with small initial letter. [a. Skr. *arhat* adj., deserving. *Arahat* is the Pali form.] A Buddhist saint of the highest rank. Hence **'Ar(a)hat-ship**, the state of an Arhat.

[**1850** R. S. HARDY *Eastern Monachism* xxii. 282 To say that any one has 'seen nirwána', is to say that he has become a rahat... There are some persons who obtain the rahatship instantaneously.] **1870** F. M. MÜLLER tr. *Buddha's Dhammapada* in *Buddhagosha's Parables* p. cix, 'Arhat', the venerable, the perfect, who has reached the highest stage that can be reached, and from which Nirvâna is perceived. *Ibid.* p. lxxxi, Ridding themselves of lust by the wisdom which Arhat-ship confers. **1877** T. W. R. DAVIDS *Buddhism* 84 The Buddhist Arahats or saints. **1882** *Encycl. Brit.* XIV. 226/1 The central point of primitive Buddhism was the doctrine of 'Arahatship'. **1912** H. G. RAWLINSON *Bactria* vii. 111 The Siamese tradition of Menander's attainment to Arhatship. **1956** TOYNBEE *Hist. Approach Relig.* vi. 84 The arhat, as the Hinayanian philosopher is called in the Buddhist terminology.

‖**aria** ('ɑːrɪə). *Mus.* [It.: see AIR *sb.*[1]] = AIR *sb.*[1] 19.

1742 in BAILEY. **1862** *Macm. Mag.* Oct. 501 The oyster wench, with her prolonged musical aria of 'Wh' all o' caller ou?' **1876** tr. *Blaserna's Sound* ix. 178 The aria..represents in music almost that which the column represents in architecture.

Arian ('ɛərɪən), *a.* and *sb.* Also 6–7 arr-. [ad. L. *ariān-us*, f. *Arius Arīus*, Gr. Ἄρῐος Ἀρεῖος, prop. name; see below.]

A. *adj.* Of, pertaining to, or adhering to the doctrine of, Arius, a presbyter of Alexandria in the 4th c., who denied that Jesus Christ was *consubstantial*, or of the same essence or substance with God. His opinions were embraced by large sections of Christendom, and the dissensions by which the church was rent lasted for nearly a century.

1642 ROGERS *Naaman* 552 All the world is become Arrian. **1726** J. TRAPP *Popery* I. (T.) The Arian heresy was suppressed. **1861** STANLEY *East. Ch.* ii. 71 Our first Teutonic version of the Scriptures was by an Arian missionary, Ulfilas.

B. *sb.* An adherent of the doctrines of Arius.

1532 MORE *Confut. Tindale* Wks. 502/2 The counsailes against the Arrians of old. **1673** MILTON *True Relig.* Wks. 1851, 410 The Arian and Socinian are charg'd to dispute against the Trinity. **1740–61** MRS. DELANY *Life & Corr.* (1861) III. 213 A very absurd, bad book, and written by an Arian. **1876** FREEMAN *Gen. Sketch* v. §6 Chlodwig..became a Christian, and not only a Christian but a Catholic, which greatly favoured his conquests, as all the other Teutonic kings were Arians.

Arian ('ɛərɪən), *sb.*[2] and *a.*[2] *Astrol.* [f. ARIES: see -(I)AN.] **A.** *sb.* One born under the zodiacal sign of Aries. **B.** *adj.* Of or pertaining to this sign; characteristic of a person born under the sign of Aries.

1917 H. T. WAITE *Compend. Natal Astrol.* 38 It takes an Arian to deceive an Arian, as they are extremely perceptive and intuitive. *Ibid.* 39 The Arian nature is to create the *idea*. **1976** *Star* (Sheffield) 29 Nov. (Women's Mag.) 4/3 Arians always appreciate toiletries. **1980** S. GEDDES *Art of Astrol.* ii. 27 Aries is of the *fire* triplicity and the *cardinal* quadruplicity. This already tells us quite a lot about the personality of the Arian native. *Ibid.*, Since the nature of fire is to be *enthusiastic*, *energetic* and *positive* and the cardinal quality to be *active*, the birth chart which shows a strong Arian influence will represent a person who is all of these things.

Arian, -ize, *Ethnol.* See ARYAN.

-arian ('ɛərɪən) *suffix*, based on L. *-ārius* -ARY[1] with the addition of -AN, used to form adjs. or corresponding sbs. The earliest formations of a general character are *disciplinarian* (sb.) of the late 16th century, *agrarian*, *antiquarian* (sb.), *corpuscularian*, *proletarian*, and *veterinarian* (sb.) of the 17th century; of the numeral adjs. *quinquagenarian* (1569) and *septuagenarian* (1715) are the earliest recorded. The commonest use of the suffix is in terms denoting religious or moral tenets, as *Millenarian*, *Predestinarian*, *sectarian*, *Sublapsarian*, *Supralapsarian*, *Trinitarian*, *Unitarian* of the 17th century, *Tractarian* (1824), on the analogy of which were formed *humanitarian*, *necessitarian*, *utilitarian*, the jocular *anythingarian* and *nothingarian* of the 18th century, and the nonce-word *strictarian* (after *sectarian*).

1838 SOUTHEY *Devil's Walk* in *Poet. Wks.* III. 94 My Utilitarians, My all sorts of -inians And all sorts of -arians My all sorts of -ists. **1867** F. H. LUDLOW *Little Brother* 125 I believe there are strictarians who think it too gay.

Arianism ('ɛərɪənɪz(ə)m). [f. ARIAN + -ISM. Cf. Fr. *arianisme*.] The Arian doctrine or heresy.

a **1600** HOOKER *Eccl. Pol.* VII. 373 The church of Alexandria in Egypt, where Arrianisme begun. **1781** GIBBON *Decl. & F.* III. 20 The opinions of Arianism might satisfy a cold and speculative mind. **1839** KEIGHTLEY *Hist. Eng.* II. 84 A Dutchman named Van Parr was burnt for Arianism.

†**aria'nistical**, *a. Obs.* [f. med.L. *ariānist-a* + -ICAL.] Partaking of, or leaning to, Arianism.

1791 *Life J. Lackington* xxix. (D.) A member of the arianistical dipping community.

Arianize ('ɛərɪə,naɪz), *v.* [f. ARIAN + -IZE; cf. Fr. *arianiser* 17th c.] **a.** *intr.* To follow the doctrines of Arius. **b.** *trans.* To convert to Arianism.

1605 BELL *Motives Rom. Faith* Ded. 1 If Tertullian.. erred montanizing..if Eusebius arrianizing. **1803** SOUTHEY *Lett.* (1856) I. 226 Ulphilas who was bishop of the Visigoths ..converted and Arianised them. **1845** J. H. NEWMAN *Ess. Develop.* 14 St. Justin arianizes.

'Aria,nizer. [f. prec. + -ER[1].] One who holds the doctrines of, or who converts others to, Arianism.

a **1680** CHARNOCK *Attrib. God* (1834) II. 273 Others.. only assert his Divine authority..For which interpretation Maldonat calls Calvin an arianizer. **1842** J. H. NEWMAN *Ch. of Fathers* 148 Eudoxius, the Arianizer of the Gothic tribes.

'Aria,nizing, *ppl. a.* [f. as prec. + -ING[2].] Professing, favouring, or teaching Arianism.

?*c* **1760** WORTHINGTON *Misc.* 89 (T.) The downfal of the Arianizing Vandals. **1845** J. H. NEWMAN *Ess. Develop.* 13 The arianizing tone of Eusebius.

ariboflavinosis (ə,raɪbəʊfleɪvɪ'nəʊsɪs). *Path.* [mod.L., f. A- 14 + RIBOFLAVIN: see -OSIS.] Deficiency of riboflavin; the condition resulting from such a deficiency.

1939 J. W. ODEN et al. in *Public Health Rep.* (U.S.) LIV. 792 The ease with which these cases were found..leads us to believe that ariboflavinosis is, in all probability, a common dietary-deficiency disease in the southern United States. **1942** *Ann. Reg. 1941* 344 Important advances in vitamin research included..descriptions..of symptoms of human ariboflavinosis.

aricine ('ærɪsaɪn). *Chem.* [f. *Arica*, name of a sea-port in Peru + -INE.] An alkaloid.

1847 in CRAIG. **1872** WATTS *Dict. Chem.* I. 357 Aricine is extracted from the cinchona bark in the same manner as quinine.

aricite ('ærɪsaɪt). *Min.* [f. L. *Aricia*, a town of Latium, now La Riccia + -ITE.] Synonym of GISMONDITE (Dana).

arid ('ærɪd), *a.* [ad. L. *ārid-us*, f. *ārē-re* to be dry, parched with heat. Perh. directly from F. *aride*, 15th c. refashioning of OF. *are, arre.*]

1. Dry, without moisture, parched, withered.

†**a.** of substances: Dry; anhydrous. *Obs.*

1652 L. S. *People's Lbty.* ix. 17 Aride and liquide fruicts. **1742** SHENSTONE *Schoolmistr.* 106 Lavender..in arid bundles bound. **1803** *Phil. Trans.* XCIII. 14 Arid white salt ..*Arid*, may be appropriated to express the state of being devoid of combined water.

†**b.** *Med.* of the skin. *Obs.*

1704 SWIFT *Batt. Bks.* (1711) 248 Her Body grew white and arid. **1727** ARBUTHNOT & POPE (J.) My complexion is become adust, and my body arid.

c. of the ground or climate. *Hence*, barren, bare.

1656 BLOUNT *Glossogr.*, *Arid*, dry, barren, withered, unfruitful. **1730** THOMSON *Autumn* 147 Without him summer were an arid waste. **1849** DICKENS *Barn. Rudge* (1866) I. lviii. 265 The dry, arid look of the dusty square. **1872** BAKER *Nile Tribut.* Pref. 7 Arid sands and burning deserts.

2. *fig.* Dry, uninteresting, barren, jejune.

1827–39 DE QUINCEY *Murder* Wks. IV. 26 An old arid and adust metaphysician. **1846** LYTTON *Lucretia* (1853) 167 Ardworth grappled with his arid studies. **1863** GEO. ELIOT *Romola* lxxi, Arid of all good.

†**'aridate**, *v. Obs.*[−0] [f. L. *ārid-us* + -ATE[3]: cf. *invalid-ate*.] To make dry, parch, wither.

1656 in BLOUNT *Glossogr.*

a-ridge (ə'rɪdʒ), *advb. phr. rare*[−1]. [A *prep.*[1] + RIDGE.] In a ridge; in ridge-like position.

1862 LOWELL *Biglow P.* Ser. II. 41 To set your back aridge.

aridify (ə'rɪdɪfaɪ), *v.* [f. ARID *a.* + -IFY.] *trans.* To make arid. Hence **a'ridified** *ppl. a.*

1920 *Glasgow Herald* 5 Mar. 8 As in Charles Darwin's case, prolonged and continuous absorption in hard thinking may aridify the emotions and destroy the appreciation of genuine poetry. **1930** W. DE LA MARE *Desert Islands* 149 Definitions aridify arguments. **1937** —— in *Proc. Brit. Acad. 1936* XXI. 249 Only a puritan aridified by a sense of duty could finally condemn it [*sc.* rhyme].

aridity (ə'rɪdɪtɪ). [ad. L. *āriditas*, f. *ārid-us*: see ARID and -ITY. Cf. Fr. *aridité*.] Arid state or quality, parched or withered condition, lack of moisture, dryness, barrenness; *spec.* in early medical use, of the state of the body.

1599 A. M. *Gabelhouer's Bk. Physic* 209/1 The Consumptione, or aridítye of the Ioynctes. **1731** ARBUTHNOT *Aliments* (J.) Salt taken in great quantities will reduce an animal body to the great extremity of aridity. **1796** MORSE *Amer. Geog.* II. 601 They [winds] are of..extreme heat and aridity. **1835** THIRLWALL *Greece* I. iii. 65 The natural aridity of a part of the Argive soil.

2. *fig.* Dryness, lack of interest; 'in the theological sense a kind of insensibility in devotion, contrary to unction or tenderness.' J.

1692 DRYDEN *St. Eurem. Ess.* 347 That sad State which is called Aridity and Dryness in Monasteries. **1765** TUCKER *Lt. Nat.* II. 36 We hear them complain of frequent coolness, aridities, and desertions. **1865** LECKY *Ration.* (1878) I. 342 The excessive aridity of scholasticism. **1882** G. CHRYSTAL in *Nature* XXVI. 217 The aridities of modern English mathematical text-books.

aridly ('ærɪdlɪ), *adv.* [f. ARID *a.* + -LY[2].] In an arid manner; with aridity.

1883 R. BROUGHTON *Belinda* II. III. iv. 228 'I think,' he says aridly, 'that..we had better keep to the subject in hand.' **1906** HARDY *Dynasts* II. II. vi. 201 Were I as coarse a wife As I am limned in English caricature..You could not speak more aridly.

'aridness. [f. ARID + -NESS.] Dryness, aridity.

1731 in BAILEY. **1856** *Scottish Rev.* IV. 295 Amid the aridness of the desert.

†**ariel**[1]. *Obs.* A word transferred by Wyclif from the Vulgate (after Ἀριήλ of the LXX, *ărīēl* of the Heb.), rendered by Coverdale and version of 1611 'altar.'

(Gesenius would here translate 'fire-hearth of God,' after Arab. *ari*; elsewhere in O.T. the same word occurs as a man's name, and appellation of Jerusalem, where it is taken as = 'lion of God.') *Ariel* in T. Heywood and Milton is the name of an angel, in Shakspere of 'an Ayrie spirit'; in *Astron.* of one of the satellites of Uranus.

1382 WYCLIF *Ezek.* xliii. 15, 16 Forsothe the ylk ariel *or* auter [**1388** thilke ariel, *that is the hiȝere part of the auter*], of foure cubitis, and fro ariel [**1388** the auter] vn to above, foure corners.

ariel[2] ('ɛərɪəl). [a. *Arab. aryil* (var. of *ayyil* stag), applied in Syria to the Gazelle (Dozy).] A species or variety of the Gazelle found in Western Asia and Africa.

[**1828** HEMPRICH & EHR. *Symb. Phys.*, *Antilope arabica*: Arabis vocatus *ghazale*. In Syria eidem, uti videtur passim nomen *ghazal*, passim vero nomen *ariel* seu *aiel* dederunt, quod Cervo Elapho competit.] **1832** *Penny Cycl.* II. 83 The Ariel Antelope so called by the Arabs on account of its light, elegant, and graceful form. **1872** BAKER *Nile Tribut.* iv. 59 A herd of about fifty ariels.

ariere, obs. form of ARREAR, ARRIÈRE.

Aries (ˈɛərɪiːz, ˈɛəriːz). Also 4–5 **ariete**. [L.; = ram.] **1.** The ram; one of the zodiacal constellations, which the sun enters on the 21st of March.

c **1374** CHAUCER *Troylus* IV. 1593 Or Phebus suster.. The Lion passe, out of this Ariete. *c* **1386** —— *Sqrs. T.* 43 In Aries the colerik, hoote signe. *c* **1430** LYDG. *Min. Poems* 243 Tyme makithe his resoort, In gerysshe Marche toward the ariete. **1670** EACHARD *Cont. Clergy* Pref., Born when the sun is in aries. **1812** WOODHOUSE *Astron.* viii. 53 At the vernal equinox the first point of Aries and the Sun are on the meridian together.

2. *Astrol.* A person born under the sign of Aries. Freq. *attrib.* or as *adj.*

1894 E. KIRK *Influence of Zodiac upon Human Life* viii. 41 It is almost impossible to hide anything from an Aries individual who has recognised his or her power of intuition. **1936** 'J. TEY' *Shilling for Candles* xix. 206 Lydia had several times told him that he was 'typically, oh but typically, Aries'. **1965** C. P. TOBEY *On Astrol.* viii. 61 Scorpio must be a part of something, while Aries must lead or go it alone. **1986** P. MYERS *Deadly Cadenza* ii. 33 He was an Aries looking for a soulmate born under the right star.

ˈarietate, *v. rare*$^{-0}$. [f. L. *arietāt-* ppl. stem of *arietāre*, f. *ariēs*, *ariet-* ram.] To butt like a ram.

1731 in BAILEY; and in mod. Dicts.

arietation (ˌærɪ-, ˌɛərɪˈteɪʃən). *arch.* [ad. L. *arietātiōnem*, n. of action f. *arietāre*: see prec.] **1.** The action of butting like a ram; *hence*, the striking with a battering-ram or similar instrument.

1625 BACON *Ess.* (Arb.) 575 The Strength of the Percussion; wherein likewise Ordnance doe exceed all Arietations. **1639** FULLER *Holy War* IV. xxiv. (1840) 222 Before Ordinance was found out, ships were both gunnes and bullets themselves, and furiously ranne one against another. They began with this arietation.

2. *transf.* and *fig.* Battering, concussion, clashing.

1625 JACKSON *Creed* v. xiii. Wks. IV. 100 Examining the certainty of truth.. by a kind of arietation, a trial which floating conceits.. cannot abide. **1665** GLANVILL *Sceps. Sci.* vii. 36 Such tumultuary motions, cross thwartings, and arietations of other particles. **1797** TAYLOR in *Month. Rev.* XXIV. 534 Props of our old constitution against the arietations of democracy.

†**ˈarietine**, *a. Obs.*$^{-0}$ [ad. L. *arietīn-us*, f. *ariēs*.] 'Of or like a Ram.' Blount *Glossogr.* 1656.

‖**arietta** (ɑːrɪˈettə, æ-). *Mus.* [It.; dim. of ARIA.] A short air.

1742 in BAILEY. **1771** SMOLLETT *Humph. Cl.*, An *arietta* of her own composing. **1880** HULLAH in Grove *Dict. Mus.*, *Arietta*.. a short air, generally of sprightly character, and having no second part.

‖**ariette** (ɑrɪˈɛt). *Mus.* [Fr., ad. It. *arietta*.]

1818 MISS FERRIAR *Marriage* xxxv, She warbled a sprightly French ariette. **1883** A. DOBSON *Fielding* v. 143 The Gallic sportsman sings the following ariette.

aright (əˈraɪt), *adv.*, orig. *phr.* Forms: 1–3 **ariht**, 0 **riȝt**, 3–4 **ariȝt**, **aryȝt**, 4 **ariȝht(e**, **aryht**, 4–6 **aryght**, 4– **aright**. [f. A *prep.*[1] + RIGHT *sb.*, OE. *riht*.]

1. In a right way or manner; rightly, justly, correctly, properly.

c **970** *Laws of Edgar* Canon 67 (Bosw.) Ȝif man hit ariht asméap. *c* **1175** *Lamb. Hom.* 89 Ȝif we hit arihṭ haldeð. *c* **1260** *Fall & Passion* 72 in *E.E.P.* (1862) 14 Ȝosep of arimathie: þat louid ihsu wel ariȝt. *c* **1386** CHAUCER *Frankl. Prol.* 22 Ther he might leren gentillesse aright [*v.r.* aryht]. **1398** TREVISA *Barth. De P.R.* XVIII. xii. (1495) 771 Euyll kynges that rulyth theym not a ryght. **1535** COVERDALE *Ps.* lxxvii. 8 A generacion that set not their herte aright. **1627** P. FLETCHER *Locusts* II. xxv, Few step aright, but most goe with the croud. **1742** YOUNG *Nt. Th.* I. 59 If heard aright, It is the knell of my departed hours. **1860** TYNDALL *Glac.* II. §29. 398 If I understand aright, this is the main argument.

†**2.** Straight, straightway. *Obs.* (Cf. RIGHTS.)

c **1250** *Gen. & Ex.* 1299 Abraham was buxum o riȝt, Hise weie he tok sone bi niȝt. **1297** R. GLOUC. 218 Ther were duntes aryȝt, and suerdes wel ydraw. *c* **1460** *How a Marchande, etc.* 237 in Hazl. *E.P.P.* 207 They on-dedyn the mouth aryght, There they sawe a ryalle syght.

3. Right: **a.** Exactly, just (*arch.*). †**b.** Directly, straight, in a straight line (*obs.*).

c **1386** CHAUCER *Prol.* 267 His eyghen twynkeled in his heed aright, As don the sterres. **1571** DIGGES *Geom. Pract.* I. xviii. F b, Vntill the second marke offer it selfe aright betweene the extreeme part of your length and sight. **1611** SPEED *Hist. Gt. Brit.* IX. xix. (1632) 936 He neuer after could indure to looke aright on King Richard. **1850** MRS. BROWNING *Dram. Exile, Poems* I. 89 Is it true besides—Aright true?

†**4.** Right, on the square: cf. A-WRY. *Obs.*

1571 DIGGES *Pantom.* I. B iij b, If all the sides be equall, and no angle aright, then is it called Rombus.

5. On the right (hand). *arch. rare.*

1795 SOUTHEY *Joan of Arc* VI. 308 Aright, aleft, The affrighted foemen scatter from his spear.

†**aˈright**, *v. Obs.* [f. A- *pref.* 1 or 2 + RIGHT *v.* Cf. Ger. *anrichten*, *einrichten*, *zurichten*.] To make right, to put to rights; to arrange or treat properly. Occas. *ironically*.

c **1420** *Chron. Vilod.* 279 All wrongus to a ryȝt. *c* **1435** *Torr. Portugal* 1366 Such gestenyng he aright, That there he dwellid alle nyȝt. *a* **1500** *Sir Gowghter* 129 in Utterson *E.P.* I. 166 She bad him here pappe, And he ariȝhte here soo, He tare the oon side of here brest.

†**aˈright-half**, *phr. Obs.* [See A *prep.*[1], and HALF.] On the right side.

1340 *Ayenb.* 38 And nimeþ aryȝthalf and alefthalf þet no þing ne may ham ascapie. *Ibid.* 23 Þes boȝ him spret.. ariȝthalf and alefthalf.

aˈrightly, *adv.* [A mixture of ARIGHT and RIGHTLY.] Aright, rightly.

1588 A. KING *Canisius' Catech.* 18 Quhatsoeuer thing [is] profitable in this life to man, is arychtlie desyrit, and askit at god. **1622** PEACHAM *Compl. Gentl.* i. 1 If we consider arightly the Frame of the whole Vniverse. **1844** *Blackw. Mag.* LVI. 743 If seen arightly by the spiritual eye.

†**aˈrights**, *adv. Obs.* [A mixture of ARIGHT and RIGHTS, earlier *rihtes*, advb. gen.]

1596 SPENSER *F.Q.* V. x. 4 When they had seene and heard her doome a-rights Against Duessa.

ariht, obs. form of ARIGHT.

aril (ˈærɪl). *Bot.* [ad. mod.L. arillus (also in use; cf. mod.F. *arille*), f. med.L. *arilli*, Sp. *arillos*, raisins.] See quot.

1794 MARTYN *Rousseau's Bot.* xvi. 208 Two seeds covered with an aril or detached coat. **1857** HENFREY *Elem. Bot.* §297 The mace of the nutmeg is an arillus, adhering both to the hilum and micropyle. **1870** HOOKER *Stud. Flora* 14 A sac-like fleshy aril. **1880** GRAY *Bot. Text-bk.* viii. 308 The true arillus is an accessory seed-covering, more or less incomplete, formed between the time of fertilization and the ripening of the seed, by a growth from the apex of the funiculus, at or just below the hilum.

Hence the derivatives: **arillary** (ˈærɪlərɪ), *a.* of or pertaining to the aril. **arillate** (ˈærɪleɪt), **ˈarillated**, **ˈarilled**, *ppl. a.*, furnished or covered with an aril. **aˈrilliform** *a.*, having the form of an aril (A. Gray, 1880). **ˈarillode**, a false aril, which originates from the micropyle or rhaphe.

1880 *Syd. Soc. Lex.*, The arillary tunic. **1830** LINDLEY *Nat. Syst. Bot.* 148 Arillate seeds. **1870** HOOKER *Stud. Flora* 13 *Nymphæaceæ*.. seeds naked or arillate. **1876** HARLEY *Mat. Med.* 379 Seeds many, arilled. **1854** BALFOUR *Bot.* 262 A false or micropylar aril, or sometimes Arillode. **1857** HENFREY *Elem. Bot.* §297 Recent authors distinguish the true arillus.. from the arillode, which originates at or near the micropyle.

Arimasp (ˈærɪmæsp). [ad. L. *Arimaspī* pl., Gr. Ἀριμασποί, said to mean in Scythian 'one-eyed'.] One of the Arimaspi, a mythical race of one-eyed men in northern Europe, occupied in endeavouring to wrest gold from the griffins (γρῦπες) who guarded it. They are sometimes figured on Greek vases, fighting with griffins. Also *attrib.* or as *adj.*

1579 [see GRYPH(E 1]. **1600** tr. *de Torquemada's Sp. Mandeuile* 11 b, The Arimaspes, being a people with one eie. **1872** C. W. KING *Antique Gems & Rings* Index 472 Arimasp and Gryphon. **1889** *Cent. Dict.* s.v., Figures of Arimasps occur sometimes in Greek art, represented in Oriental dress and fighting griffins. **1905** H. B. WALTERS *Anc. Pottery* II. 148 In one instance an Arimasp woman is seen shooting at a Gryphon of curious type. **1913** E. H. MINNS *Scythians & Greeks* iv. 56 An Arimasp such as we find on the calathos from the Great Bliznitsa.

Arimaspian (ærɪˈmæspɪən). [f. L. *Arimaspī* (see prec.) + -IAN.] = prec.

1667 MILTON *P.L.* II. 945 As when a Gryfon through the Wilderness.. Pursues the Arimaspian, who by stelth Had from his wakeful custody purloind The guarded Gold. **1774** J. BRYANT *Anc. Mythol.* I. 380 This may have been one reason.. why the Cyclopians and Arimaspians are represented with one eye. **1827** *Blackw. Mag.* XXI. 780/1 Mermaid or salamander.. miser or arimaspian. **1913** E. H. MINNS *Scythians & Greeks* v. 113 The representations of Arimaspians and griffins in art. *Ibid.* xi. 391 The centre group, in which there are two griffins to one Arimaspian.

†**aˈrime**, *v. Obs.* [OE. *ariman*, f. A- *pref.* 1 + *riman* to count: see RIME.] To count, enumerate.

c **885** K. ÆLFRED *Gregory's Past.* xvi. 99 He arimde ða dioȝolnesse ðæs ðriddan hefones. **1205** LAY. 25392 Þa lette þe kaisere arimen al þene here. *Ibid.* 28937 Þis ferde wes isomned and his folc arimed.

†**aˈrine**, *v. Obs.* Forms: 1 **ahrín-an**, 2–3 **arine(n**. *Pa. t.* 1 **ahran**, 2–3 **aran**, 3 **arinede**. [OE. *ahrínan*, f. A- *pref.* 1 + *hrínan* to touch: see RINE. Rarer in OE. than *æthrínan*, ATRINE.] To touch.

c **1000** *Ags. Gosp.* Luke xi. 46 Ȝe ne ahrinað ða séamas mid eowrum anum fingre. [*Hatton G.*, æthrinað.] *c* **1220** *Ureisun* in *Cott. Hom.* 197 Ne þole þu þene unwine þet he me arine. *c* **1220** *St. Marhar.* 20 Ant com þe culure ant aran hire. *c* **1230** *Ancr. R.* 408 Al þet he arinede þere-mide.

a-ˈring, *advb. phr. rare*$^{-1}$. [A *prep.*[1] and RING *sb.*] In circumference.

c **1633** T. ADAMS *Wks.* 1861 I. 369 (D.) Two orchards of the king's, whereof the greater was twenty days a-ring.

†**ˈariolate**, *v. Obs. rare*$^{-1}$. [f. L. *ariolāt-*, properly *hariolāt-* ppl. stem of *hariolāri*, f. *hariolus* soothsayer. (The etymological *h-* was seldom written in med.L., and has hardly ever been used by English writers.)] To divine, foretell from omens.

1652 GAULE *Magastrom.* 259 All to vaticinate and ariolate his Persian victory.

†**ariolater, -or.** *Obs.* Also **har-**. [f. prec. + -ER[1]; or after L. agent-nouns in -ATOR; cf. ARIOLER.] A diviner or soothsayer.

1652 GAULE *Magastrom.* 300 Ariopharnes.. gave judgement.. better than all the ariolaters. **1657** PIERCE *Div. Philanthr.* Ded. 10 You are not either a Lord or a Lady, as the shrewd Hariolator doth seem to think.

†**arioˈlation.** *Obs.* [ad. L. (*h*)*ariolātiōn-em*, n. of action f. (*h*)*ariolāt-*: see ARIOLATE and -ATION.] Soothsaying, divination.

1646 SIR T. BROWNE *Pseud. Ep.* I. iii. 11 Deluding their apprehensions, with Ariolation, South-saying, and such oblique Idolatries. **1652** GAULE *Magastrom.* 193 Vaticination.. ariolation, praesagition. [In mod. Dicts.]

†**ˈariole.** *Obs.* [a. OF. *ariole*, *har-*, ad. L. (*h*)*ariolus*.] A soothsayer, diviner.

1398 TREVISA *Barth. De P.R.* 126 Aryoles, nygromancers brought theym to the auctors of their god. **1525** LD. BERNERS *Froiss.* II. ccxx. [ccxvi.] 680 His phisycions, and arioles.. said surely howe the kynge was poysoned or bewytched.

†**ˈarioler.** *Obs. rare.* [f. OF. *ariole* (see prec.) + -ER; cf. *astronom-er*, etc.] = prec.

c **1400** *Apol. Loll.* 92 Ne be þer not found in þe þat.. askiþ ariolers, nor dremis, ne chitering of briddis. *Ibid.*, Bow þu not to þer wicchis, ne axe no þing of þer ariolers.

†**ˈariolist.** *Obs. rare.* [f. L. (*h*)*ariol-us* + -IST.] = prec.

1652 GAULE *Magastrom.* 352 At the accusation of an ariolist or Pythian vaticinator.

ariose (ˌɑːrɪˈəʊs, æ-), *a. Mus.* [ad. It. *arioso*: see next.] Characterized by melody, song-like.

1742 BAILEY, *Ariose*, *Arioso*, signifies the Movement or Time of a common Air, Song or Tune. **1845** E. HOLMES *Mozart* 209 A style of instrumental music at once light and ariose.

‖**arioso** (ɑːrɪˈəʊsəʊ, æ-), *a.*, *adv.*, *sb. Mus.* [It.; = airy, f. *aria* air.] Ariose, melodious. Used of instrumental music, it describes a sustained, vocal style; of vocal music 'it would seem to mean that kind of air which, partaking both of the character of air and recitative, requires rather to be *said* than *sung*' (Hullah in Grove *Dict. Mus.* 1879). Hence used *advb.* as a musical direction, and *subst.* of a piece of music of this description.

1742 [see prec.] **1787** BURNS *Wks.* III. 91 In arioso trills and graces. **1879** HOPKINS in Grove *Dict. Mus.* I. 23 A solo .. of an arioso character. **1879** HULLAH *ibid.* I. 83/1 Mendelssohn's 'But the Lord is mindful'.. [is] marked 'Arioso.'

a-riot (əˈraɪət), *advb. phr.* [A *prep.*[1] + RIOT.] In riot, riotously, running riot.

1851 MARY HOWITT *Sk. Nat. Hist.* (ed. 7) 14 Till the Parrots, all a-riot, Chattered too to keep you quiet. **1881** *Cornh. Mag.* Mar. 310 The rose-trees.. have gone wandering a-riot into country hedges.

-arious, *comp. suffix*, forming adjs.; **1.** f. L. *-ārius*, *-a*, *-um* 'connected with, pertaining to' + -OUS (as if ad. L. *-āriōsus*; cf. *cariōsus*, carious). The reg. Eng. repr. of *-ārius* is -ARY[1]; but the compound suffix is of occasional use, as in *cibarious*, *gregarious*, *temerarious*, *vicarious*, and as a by-form in *arbitrarious*, *contrarious*, etc. (*Hilarious*, f. L. *hilari-s* + *-ous*, seems to owe its form to association with this suffix.)

a-ripple (əˈrɪp(ə)l), *advb. phr.* [A *prep.*[1] + RIPPLE.] In a ripple, rippling.

1855 BROWNING *Men & Wom.*, *Cleon* II. 186 The muscles all a-ripple on his back.

aris, arish: see ARR-.

†**arisard.** *Obs.* Also **arisad**, **airisad**, **-sard**. An ancient female costume; 'a long robe or tunic girdled round the waist.'

See PLANCHÉ *Brit. Costume* (1834) 344, (1847) 441 and *Cycl. Costume* (1876) 11.

arise (əˈraɪz), *v.* Forms: *Inf.* 1 **ar-**, **arís-an**, 2–4 **aris-en**, 3– **arise**, 4–5 **aryse**. *Pa. t.* 5– **arose**; also 1–4 **ar-**, **arás**, 3–5 **aros**, 4–5 **aroos**, 5 **aroose**, 7 occas. **aris** (əˈrɪz). *Pa. pple.* 1– **arisen** (əˈrɪz(ə)n); also 4 **arisè**, **arysè**, 6–8 **arose**. [f. A- *pref.* 1 up, out, away + RISE; = to 'rise up,' intensive of *rise*; cf. L. *exorīri*. An OTeut. comp.; in Goth. *us-*, *ur- reisan*, OHG. *ur-*, *ar-*, *ir-rîsan*, OS. *arîsan*. Northumbrian preserved *ar-rísan*, *ar-rás*, etc. Obs. 3rd sing. pres. *arist* = *ariseth*. The pa. t. *aris* in 17th c, was formed on pa. pple.: cf. obs. *writ*, and extant *bit*; the pa. pple. *arose* was assimilated to pa. t.: cf. *abode*, *shone*. Now almost superseded in ordinary language by the simple RISE, in all senses, exc. those in branch III, of which 17–18 are the ordinary prose uses of the word. Still used poetically in senses 1–9; 10–13 seem entirely obs.]

I. To get up from sitting, lying, repose.

1. To get up from sitting or kneeling, to stand up. *arch.*: see RISE.

c **1000** ÆLFRIC *Gen.* xviii. 16 Ða arison ða þri weras. **1205** LAY. 30841 Þat folc..arisen from heore seten. *c* **1230** *Ancr. R.* 34 Ariseð þeonne & biginneð þesne antefne. **1297** R. GLOUC. 369 Þys hey men..Knely to God..Ac be hii aryse, & abbeþ yturnd fram þe wened her wombe, Wolues dede hii nymeþ vorþ. *c* **1450** LONELICH *Grail* xxxv. 93 A-rys and go with me. **1593** SHAKS. *3 Hen. VI*, II. ii. 61 Edward Plantagenet, arise a Knight. **1611** BIBLE *John* xiv. 31 Arise, let us go hence. **1779** J. MOORE *View Soc.* II. liv. 49 All the audience..immediately arise, and remain in a standing posture till their sovereign sit down. **1808** SCOTT *Marm.* VI. xii, I dub thee knight. Arise, Sir Ralph, De Wilton's heir.

† Hence in *transf.* and *fig.* senses; as **a.** Of a court: To suspend sittings for the time, to adjourn. **b.** Of a thing: To erect itself on end (as hair). *Obs.*

c **1385** CHAUCER *L.G.W.* 831 And pale he wex, therwith his heer [*v.r.* herte; see 7] aroos [*v.r.* a-ros, roos]. *a* **1649** WINTHROP *Hist. New Eng.* (1853) II. 279 The court being about to arise he desired leave for a little speach.

†**2.** To get up from a fall. Also *transf.* and *fig.*

c **885** K. ÆLFRED *Gregory's Past.* lviii. 443 He swa micle stranglicor arise swa he hefiglicor afeoll. *c* **1175** *Lamb. Hom.* 49 Þa þe liggeð inne swilc sunne and ne þencheð noht for to arisen. **1205** LAY. 9427 Þus Portcheestre to-ræs and nauere seoððen aras. **1340** *Ayenb.* 50 Huanne þe kempe heþ his uelaȝe yueld..wel onneaþe he arist. *c* **1386** CHAUCER *Pars. T.* ¶999 As ofte as he falleth he may arise [*v.r.* arrise, aryse] agayn by penitence. **1605** SHAKS. *Lear* I. iv. 99 Come sir, arise, away! **1667** MILTON *P.L.* I. 330 Awake, arise, or be for ever fall'n.

3. To get up from sleep or rest. *arch.*: see RISE.

c **950** *Lindisf. Gosp.* Matt. ii. 20 Arris and onfoh ðone cnæht. *c* **1000** ÆLFRIC *Gen.* xxviii. 18 On morȝen he aras. *c* **1175** *Lamb. Hom.* 39 Ne beo eow noht lað to arisene er dei. *c* **1300** *K. Alis.* 5760 Kyng Alisaunder amorowe arist. **1340** *Ayenb.* 52 Þet uolk þet..late guoþ to bedde and ariseþ late. *c* **1450** LONELICH *Grail* xvi. 29 Erly on the morwe, whanne þe kyng aros. **1535** COVERDALE *Prov.* vi. 9 Whan wilt thou aryse out of thy slepe? **1604** SHAKS. *Oth.* I. i. 89 Arise, arise, Awake the snorting Cittizens with the Bell. **1762** GOLDSM. *Beau Nash* 232 Nash generally arose early in the morning. **1820** KEATS *St. Agnes* xxxix, Arise, arise! the morning is at hand.

4. Of the sun, moon, and stars: To come above the horizon. Also *transf.* of the day, morning. Now *arch.* and *poet.*: see RISE.

c **975** *Rushw. Gosp.* Mark iv. 6 Ða aras sunne. *c* **1220** *Hali Meid.* 11 Meidenhad is te steorre þat beo ha eanes..igan adun..neauer eft ne ariseð ha. *c* **1350** *Will. Palerne* 2744 Whan the mone aros. *c* **1391** CHAUCER *Astrol.* I. §21. 12 Thilke sterres..arisen rather than the degree of hire longitude. **1480** CAXTON *Chron. Eng.* ccxliv. 298 The morne aroos, the day gan spryng. **1592** SHAKS. *Rom. & Jul.* II. ii. 4 Arise faire Sun and kill the enuious Moone. **1667** MILTON *P.L.* v. 170 While day arises, that sweet hour of Prime. **1820** BYRON *Mar. Fal.* I. ii. 570 At what hour arises the moon? *a* **1842** TENNYSON *Miller's Dau.* 205 Many suns arise and set.

5. To rise from the dead, return to life from the grave. Now *poetic*: see RISE.

c **950** *Lindisf. Gosp.* Matt. xxvii. 52 Moniga lichoma halga wæra ða ðe slepdon arison. —— xiv. 2 Ðis is Johannes Baptista ðe arras from deadum. *c* **1175** *Lamb. Hom.* 143 Þenne sculen..alle dede arisen. *c* **1260** *Signs bef. Judgm.* 53 in *E.E.P.* (1862) 9 Þan þe dede up sal arise up har biriles forto sitte. **1380** WYCLIF *De Eccles.* ii. Sel. Wks. 1871 III. 340 Þe þridde day oure God aroos from deþ to lyf. **1537** *Exp. Creed* in *Formul. Faith* (1856) 60 Even like as our Saviour Jesu Christ..did arise from death to life. **1611** BIBLE *Matt.* xxvii. 52 Many bodies of the saints which slept arose. **1712** STEELE *Spect.* No. 356 ¶9 The Temple rends, the Rocks burst, the Dead Arise. **1859** TENNYSON *Enid* 1505 Till yonder man upon the bier arise.

6. To rise from inaction, from the peaceful, quiet, or ordinary course of life; *esp.* to rise in hostility or rebellion (*against*). Now *poetic*: see RISE.

c **825** *Vesp. Ps.* iii. 7 Aris dryhten, halne me doa. *c* **950** *Lindisf. Gosp.* Matt. x. 21 Wið arisas suna in áldrum. *c* **1440** *Arthur* 208 How darst þow..Aȝenst the Emperour þus aryse. *c* **1460** FORTESCUE *Abs. & Lim. Mon.* (1714) 96 Nothyng may make his People to arise, but..lacke of Justyce. **1480** CAXTON *Chron. Eng.* ccxxxix. 264 The comunes arisen vp in dyuerse partyes of the reame and dyden moch harme. **1535** COVERDALE *Ps.* ix. 12 Aryse o Lorde God, lift vp thine honde. **1604** SHAKS. *Oth.* III. iii. 447 Arise, blacke vengeance, from the hollow hell. *a* **1703** T. COOKE *Tales, Prop. etc.* (1729) 211 Had no Genius arose against the Tyranny of Custom.

7. To rise in violence or agitation, as the sea, the wind; to boil up as a fermenting fluid, the blood; so of the heart, wrath, etc. Now *poet.*: see RISE.

c **950** *Lindisf. Gosp.* John vi. 18 Ðe sæ ofstod *vel* aras. *a* **1300** *K. Horn* 868 Horn him gan to agrise, And his blod arise. **1340** *Ayenb.* 47 Alleþe þinges, huerby þet uless him arist. *c* **1385** CHAUCER *L.G.W.* 831 Pale he wex therwith his herte [*v.r.* heer; see 1 b] a-ros. **1393** GOWER *Conf.* I. 20 A tonne, whan his lie arist, To-breketh. **1526** TINDALE *John* vi. 18 The see arose [WYCLIF, rose vp] with a greate winde that blew. [So all subseq. vers.] **1611** BIBLE *2 Sam.* xi. 20 If so be that the kings wrath arise. —— *Ps.* lxxxix. 9 When the waues thereof arise, thou stillest them. **1847** TENNYSON *Princess* i. 96 A wind arose and rush'd upon the South.

8. *transf.* Of sounds: To come up aloud, or so as to be audible, to be heard aloud. *arch.*

a **1300** *Cursor M.* 2840 Strange cry in þe toun a-ras. *c* **1330** *Arth. & Merl.* 7409 In euerich lond arist song. *c* **1350** *Will. Palerne* 3270 Þe cry rudli aros þat reuþe it was to hure. **1393** GOWER *Conf.* I. 267 Through all the world the fame arose. **1611** BIBLE *Acts* xxiii. 9 And there arose a great cry. **1859** TENNYSON *Enid* 1812 And in their halls arose The cry of children.

II. To ascend, go or come higher.

9. To go up, come up, ascend on high, mount. Now only *poet.*: see RISE.

a **1000** *Elene* (Gr.) 803 Of þære stówe steám up arás. *c* **1374** CHAUCER *Boeth.* IV. vi. 143 Þe lyȝte fyre arist into heyȝte. *c* **1450** *Merlin* xiv. 207 The duste arose with the wynde. **1594** WILLOBIE in *Shaks. C. Praise* 9 From whence these flames aryse. **1596** SPENSER *F.Q.* I. x. 4 Dame Cælia..as thought From heav'n to come, or thether to arise. **1676** HOBBES *Iliad* XXIII. 763 And on his steps trod ere the dust aris. **1704** POPE *Winter* 46 Nor morning odours from the flow'rs arise. **1820** KEATS *Hyperion* I. 258 A mist arose, as from a scummy marsh.

†**10.** To rise with its summit (as a tree), or surface (as water); to grow taller, or higher, to swell up. *Obs.*: see RISE.

c **1225** *St. Marherete* (1866) 18 Te hude..barst on to bleinen þet hit aras up oueral. **1393** GOWER *Conf.* II. 169 Her womb, which of childe aros. **1398** TREVISA *Barth. De P.R.* XVIII. lxxxviii. (1495) 838 The place brennyth soo that bleynes aryseth there. *c* **1425** *Seven Sages* (P.) 204 The flore ne may nouȝt aryse. **1652** FRENCH *Yorksh. Spa* ii. 15 In a close glass it [water] ariseth onely *ad evitandum vacuum.* **1664** POWER *Exp. Philos.* II. 105 [It] makes a lesser quantity of Quicksilver arise in the Tube.

†**11.** To rise in rank or eminence. *Obs.*: see RISE.

1340 *Ayenb.* 24 Þe ilke þet is zuo heȝe arise ine prosperite. **1534** MORE *Comf. agst. Trib.* III. Wks. 1252/2 Some by handy crafte..some by other kynde of liuing, arise & come forward in yᵉ world. **1664** POWER *Exp. Philos.* I. 59 In these minute Animals their nutritive Liquor never arises to the perfection of bloud. *a* **1733** NORTH *Lives* I. 81 Good fortune ..in his circuit practice, which made him arise in it faster than young men have commonly done. **1756** J. WARTON *Ess. Pope* (1782) I. iv. 229 Obstacles, which might prevent his arising to that height, which the figure of his nativity promised.

†**12.** To rise in price or amount. *Obs.*: see RISE.

1340 *Ayenb.* 35 Uor to do arise þet gauel. **1643** CARYL *Sacr. Covt.* 11 They perceived the charge to arise so high. **1714** SWIFT *Corr.* II. 515 Stocks arose three per cent. upon it in the city.

†**b.** To amount *to*. *Obs.*

1594 BLUNDEVIL *Exerc.* I. xxvii. 72 If the Summe..do arise to the Summe of 60, or exceed the Number of 60. **1649** ROBERTS *Clavis Bibl.* Introd. iii. 56 The whole time..will arise to 591 y[ears] in all. **1679** PENN *Addr. Prot.* I. §4 (1692) 20 They would arise to Three Times more Money.

†**13.** To come up to a point in a scale, attain to, reach. *Obs.*: see RISE.

1611 COTGR. s.v. *Doublement*, The price..which he that arises vnto, most commonly carries the thing. **1798** MALTHUS *Popul.* (1817) II. 2 The number arising annually to the age of puberty.

III. To spring up, come above ground, into the world, into existence.

14. To spring forth, as a river, from its source. *Obs.*: see RISE. Also *transf.* To take its rise, originate. (Still in use.)

c **950** *Lindisf. Gosp.* Luke viii. 7 Ongelíc arison ðornas. **1398** TREVISA *Barth. De P.R.* XIII. viii. (1495) 444 The ryuer Doryx arysyth a lytyll fro the heed of Eufrates. **1548** UDALL, etc. *Erasm. Par. Luke* ii, To haue the talke of his birth..to aryse and beginne of suche reporters. **1645** PAGITT *Heresiogr.* (1662) 87 A third sort of Brownists did arise from one Mr. Wilkinson. **1875** GRINDON *Life* xxv. 319 Simple and original forms, from which they [carnations, etc.] have arisen under the stimulus of culture. **1879** TIMBS in *Cassell's Techn. Educ.* IV. 250/2 The lymphatics..absorb lymph from the organs in which they arise.

15. To be born, come into the world of life or action.

c **950** *Lindisf. Gosp.* Matt. xxiv. 11 Monigo lease wítgo arisað. **1205** LAY. 1248 Þer scal of þine cunne kine-bearn arisen. **1535** COVERDALE *Deut.* xxxiv. 10 There arose [WYCLIF, there roos] no prophet more in Israel like vnto Moses. **1646** SIR T. BROWNE *Pseud. Ep.* 274 There was.. never any Autochthon, or man arising from the earth but Adam. **1763** J. BROWN *Poetry & Mus.* xii. 198 After many Centuries had passed in Darkness, Guido arose. **1875** BRYCE *Holy Rom. Emp.* xv. 241 In the fourteenth century there arose in Italy the first great masters of painting and song. *Mod.* A false prophet calling himself the Mahdi has arisen in the Soudan.

16. Of things: To spring up, usually with some reference to the literal sense of *rise*, as if: To be raised, built. Mostly *poet.* or *rhet.*

a **1000** *Riddles* (Grein) iv. 20 Aríseþ dún ofer dýpe. **1704** POPE *Windsor For.* 26 And 'midst the desart fruitful fields arise. **1859** TENNYSON *Vivien* 525 So long, that mountains have arisen since With cities on their flanks. **1864** —— *Aylmer's F.* 147 Beyond her lodges..arose the labourers' homes.

17. Of circumstances viewed as results: To spring, originate, or result *from* (*of* obs.).

1205 LAY. 9383 Nu þu iherest of wuche gomen aras þer þe to-nome. **1393** LANGL. *P. Pl.* C. XIII. 230 So of rychesse vpon richesse · arisen al vices. **1393** GOWER *Conf.* I. 240 Therof might arise a sclaunder. **1599** SHAKS. *Hen. V*, IV. vii. 186 Some sodaine mischiefe may arise of it. **1605** BACON *Adv. Learn.* II. v. §2 Out of which several inquiries there do arise three knowledges. **1651** HOBBES *Leviath.* II. xxv. 131 Arising from the Imperative manner of speaking. **1661** LOVELL *Hist. Anim. & Min.* 219 Whence arised the old proverb, as sound as a Roche. **1793** SMEATON *Edystone L.* §131 Comfort arose from the reflection. **1837** J. H. NEWMAN *Par. Serm.* I. xviii. 266 This..arises from ignorance of religion itself.

18. Of matters generally: To spring up, come into existence or notice, 'come up,' present itself. ***arising out of***: used, with loose construction, to introduce a circumstance, action, proposal, etc., arising out of an event, statement, etc.

a **1000** *Guthlac* (Grein) 10 Sindon costinga..monige arisene. *c* **1230** *Ancr. R.* 234 In þe muchele anguise aros þe muchele mede. *c* **1400** *Rom. Rose* 7543 And on the folke ariseth blame. **1513** DOUGLAS *Æneid* v. iv. 43 Heir first guid hope arrais to the twa last. **1526** TINDALE *Mark* iv. 17 As trouble and persecucion aryseth for the wordes sake. [So CRANM., *Geneva*, **1611**; WYCLIF, riseth.] **1590** SHAKS. *Com. Err.* v. i. 388 Thereupon these errors are arose. **1704** SWIFT *Batt. Bks.* (1711) 228 If a new Species of controversial Books had not arose of late years. **1833** I. TAYLOR *Fanat.* x. 433 Noticing as it arises, whatever fairly bears upon the question. **1849** MACAULAY *Hist. Eng.* II. 145 All questions which arose in the Privy Council. **1922** JOYCE *Ulysses* 310 Arising out of the question of my honourable friend,..may I ask [etc.]? **1928** *Daily News* 8 Dec. 9/3 Arising out of the Goddard case, [a man] was summoned..for threatening.. an ex-Constable.

b. With more of the literal sense. (Hence often *rise*. Cf. 7, 9.)

1708 POPE *St. Cecilia* 24 If in the breast tumultuous joys arise. **1711** ADDISON *Spect.* No. 166 ¶3 Those Thoughts which arise and disappear in the Mind of Man. **1790** BURKE *Fr. Rev.* 11, I beg leave to throw out my thoughts, and express my feelings, just as they arise in my mind. **1857** MAURICE *Epist. St. John* iv. 55 Then arises in our minds a terrible sense of shame.

†a'rise, *sb. Obs. rare.* [f. prec. vb.; cf. RISE, and earlier ARIST.] Arising, rising.

1590 GREENE *Neuer too late* (1600) 61 Brighter then the sunnes arise. **1646** SIR T. BROWNE *Pseud. Ep.* 286 To beginne harvest at the arise of the Pleiades. *c* **1665** H. WOOLRICH *Sheph. Israel to Bps.* (title page) The arise of the Beast, False Prophet, and Anti-Christ.

†a'riser. *Obs. rare*⁻¹. [f. prec. vb. + -ER¹.] One who arises, a riser.

1382 WYCLIF *Pref. Epist.* vii. 72 Dauid..precheth Crist with the harp, and in the ten cordid sawtri arereth vp the ariser fro helle.

arising (əˈraɪzɪŋ), *vbl. sb.* [f. ARISE *v.* + -ING¹.]

1. The action of the vb. ARISE in various senses; now chiefly *Obs.* or *arch.*, and supplied by RISING; as **a.** Rising from a seat, from bed, from the dead; rising of the sun.

1340 *Ayenb.* 14 Þe tuelfte article is to leue þe general arizinge of bodye. *c* **1386** CHAUCER *Frankl. T.* 559 And kneu the arisyng of his moone wel. *c* **1430** *Life St. Kath.* (1884) 113 Wher of dounfallyng foleweth so glorious arysynge. **1540** *Four P.P.* in Hazl. *Dods.* I. 350 What causeth this: That women after their arising Be so long in their apparelling? **1548** UDALL, etc. *Prol. Luke* (R.) His arisyng from death to life. **1646** SIR T. BROWNE *Pseud. Ep.* 285 Unto the arising of the Dog-star.

b. Excited rising, insurrection.

1340 *Ayenb.* 9 Naȝt dyadlich zenne, ase byeþ manie arizinges of ulesse. **1591** PERCIVALL *Sp. Dict.*, *Levantamiento*, arising, rising, rebelling.

c. Springing up, origination.

1340 *Ayenb.* 147 Ne non arizinge of wreþe. **1603** KNOLLES *Hist. Turks* (1638) 96 The arising of new troubles.

2. *pl.* In concrete use: applied to materials that 'arise' as secondary or waste products of an operation (see quots.). Spec. in naval use: the remains of consumable stores.

1923 'BARTIMEUS' *Seaways* ix. 131 'Arisings' are an important item of Naval store accounts. They represent what is left over. For instance, the 'arisings' of a candle is a puddle of wax, which is the property of the State. **1955** *Metal Age* Feb. 2 (Advt.), Cobalt..Tungsten, Vanadium. Buyers of stocks and continuous arisings. **1957** *Times* 20 Nov. 4/3 The London board..invited tenders for their 'arisings of scrap metal' over the ensuing 12 months. **1958** *Optima* Mar. 40/2 The final waste from the separation process consists of mixed fission products with a specific activity of up to 800 curies per gram... These arisings.. must be stored without possibility of escape for many decades.

a'rising, *ppl. a.* [f. ARISE *v.* + -ING².] = RISING.

1605 *Verstegan's Dec. Intell.* Pref. Verses, Phebus bright arising rays. *a* **1749** CHALKLEY *Wks.* (1766) 474 The present arising Generation. **1814** SCOTT *Ld. of Isles* III. xii, The sun's arising gleam.

†a'risness. *Obs. rare*⁻¹. [f. *arisè, arisen* (see ARISE *v.*) + -NESS.] Rising, resurrection.

a **1300** *Creed* in *Reliq. Ant.* I. 282 Forȝiufenesse of sinnen, arysnesse of flesse, and eche lif.

†'arist. *Obs.* Forms: 1 ǽríst, -est, érist, -est, 1–3 ærist, 2–3 arist(e. [OE. *ǽríst* (cogn. w. Goth. *us-rists*), vbl. sb. of *arísan* to ARISE; f. *Æ- pref.*, accented form of A- *pref.* 1 + **ríst* rising, f. *rís-an* + -T, as in *migh-t*, *gif-t*, etc.]

1. Rising, rise from a seat or from bed; sunrise.

c **825** *Vesp. Ps.* cxxxviii. 2 Ðu oncneowe ȝesetenisse mine & ereste mine. *a* **1000** *Ags. Ps.* ibid., Ðú mín setl swylce oncnéowe and mínne ǽríst æfter ȝecyþdest. *c* **1391** CHAUCER *Astrol.* II. §12. 23 At the sonne ariste. **1393** GOWER *Conf.* II. 45 And that was er the sonne arist.

2. Rising from the dead, resurrection.

c **885** K. ÆLFRED *Greg. Past.* xlvii. 363 Deadra monna æerestes [*v.r.* æristes]. *c* **950** *Lindisf. Gosp.* John xi. 24 Eft arisæð in erist. 25 Ic am erest and lif [*Rushw.* erist]. *c* **1000** *Ags. G.*, ærist. *c* **1160** *Hatton G.*, arist. *c* **1200** *Trin. Coll. Hom.* 97 Þis dai is cleped..aristes dai for þat þe he þis dai aras of deaðe. *c* **1230** *Ancr. R.* 250 Efter his ariste. *c* **1250** in *O.E. Misc.* 54 Vre louerdes aryste.

‖**arista** (ə'rɪstə). Pl. -æ. [L.] The awn or beard (in L. also the whole ear) of grain and grasses; *hence* used of similar bristle-like processes, as the fibrils which fringe the convex edge of a fish's gills, etc.

1691 RAY *Creation* (1701) 81 The Aristæ or radii of a fish's gills. **1875** HOUGHTON *Sk. Brit. Ins.* 112 The basal joints of the arista.

Aristarch ('ærɪstɑːk). [ad. L. *Aristarchus*, a. Gr. Ἀρίσταρχος, name of a severe Greek critic of the Homeric poetry, who rejected many lines of it as spurious; hence used connotatively.] A severe critic. **Ari'starchian** *a.*, severely critical.

1621 MOLLE *Camerar. Liv. Lib.* Pref., Learned and judicious Aristarchs. **1751** J. BROWN *Shaftesb. Charact.* 364 Who..hath chastised the noble writer somewhat roughly, and Aristarchus-like. **1820** SCOTT *Abbot* Introd. (1831) 5 Even the aristarch Johnson allowed that, etc. **1853** F. HALL in *Leslie's Misc.* II. 169 Grave aristarchs vouchsafed to accept it as matter of creed, rather than of criticism.

[**Aristarchy.** Erroneous alteration of *Aristarchi* 'severe critics' (= Gr. Ἀρίσταρχοι: see ARISTARCH) in some later edd. of the works cited below. Hence in WEBSTER (1828-32) and some later Dicts. (with erroneous definition).

a **1612** HARINGTON *Brief View Ch. Eng.* in Park *Nugæ Antiquæ* (1804) II. 207 (from autograph copy) Some of the *Aristarchi* [ed. 1653 p. 153 Aristarchy] and sowr censurers of theise dayes. **1656** EARL MONM. tr. *Boccalini's Advts. fr. Parnassus.* II. v. 205 The onely *Aristarchi* [ed. 1674 Aristarchy] of the world [*orig.* gli Arristarchi del Mondo].]

aristate (ə'rɪsteɪt), *ppl. a.* [ad. L. *aristāt-us*, f. *arista*.] Furnished with aristæ; awned, bearded.

1838 in LOUDON *Encycl. Plants.* **1870** HOOKER *Stud. Flora* 189 *Centaurea calcitrapa*..lobes recurved, aristate.

ariste, aryste, obs. forms of ARRAS.

†**ari'stiferous,** *a. Obs.*$^{-0}$ [f. L. *aristifer* (f. *arista* + *-fer* bearing) + -OUS.] 'Bearing ears of corn.' Bailey 1731.

†**ari'stippus.** *Obs.* [Name of a Greek philosopher, luxurious in his living.] A cant name for canary wine.

a **1627** MIDDLETON *Wks.* II. 422 (Halliw.) Rich Aristippus, sparkling sherry. **1703** DE FOE *True Born Eng.*, The Sages..Praise Epicurus rather than Lysander, And Aristippus more than Alexander.

aristo (ə'rɪstəʊ). *colloq.* [Fr., shortened form of *aristocrate*.] An aristocrat.

1864 M. J. HIGGINS *Ess.* (1875) 172 In 1795, the aged Honorius died..in consequence of the..imprisonment to which he had been subjected as an *aristo*. **1888** LD. R. GOWER *Rec. & Remin.* (1903) 425 Charles Villiers..said how snubbed Dizzy used to be in old days by the aristos whom he got to serve him in his later life. *Ibid.* 133 Now that aristo-Liberals vote often with Conservatives. **1958** *Times Lit. Suppl.* 13 Jan. 325/3 Did Jacobins think about nothing but Liberty,..aristos about nothing but adultery?

aristo- ('ærɪstəʊ), comb. f. Gr. ἄριστος best; as in **aristo-monarchy**, government by the best; **aristo-democratical**, having a democratic constitution limited by aristocratic elements.

1660 R. COKE *Justice Vind.* 20 It must be either Aristo-Monarchy or Demo-Monarchy, in plain English the Government of one man alone, or the People-government of one alone. **1801** W. COXE *Trav. Switz.* I. Introd. 21 The aristo-democratical cantons.

aristocracy (ærɪ'stɒkrəsɪ). Also 6-7 -cratie, -y. [ad. L. *aristocratia*, Gr. ἀριστοκρατία, f. ἄριστος best + -κρατία rule. Cf. F. *aristocracie* (14th c.).] In earlier usage generally contrasted with *monarchy*; since the French Revolution, with *democracy*.

1. In the literal sense of the Gr.: The government of a state by its best citizens. Also *fig.*

[**1531** ELYOT *Gov.* (1875) 9 In the Greke tunge called Aristocratia..in englisshe, the rule of men of beste disposicion.] **1561** T. N[ORTON] *Calvin's Inst.* Table, Aristocracy [is] the government of the best choisest men. *c* **1651** HOBBES *Rhetoric* (1840) 435 Aristocracy is that, wherein the highest magistrate is chosen out of those that have had the best education. **1781** GIBBON *Decl. & F.* xlv. (1846) IV. 257 A perfect aristocracy of reason and virtue. **1850** CARLYLE *Latter-d. Pamph.* iii. 41 The attainment of a truer and truer Aristocracy, or Government again by the Best.

†**2.** *concr.* A ruling body of the best citizens.

1605 B. JONSON *Foxe* III. iii, If the Senate Right not my quest in this; I will protest 'hem, To all the world, no *aristocracy*.

3. That form of government in which the chief power lies in the hands of those who are most distinguished by birth or fortune; political supremacy of a privileged order; oligarchy.

1577 tr. *Bullinger's Decades* (1592) 169 The Aristocracie is the superior power of a few Peeres. **1623** MASSINGER *Bondman* I. iii, To change the aristocracy of Corinth Into an absolute monarchy. **1701** BP. LLOYD *Marg. Readg. to Gen.* xxxvi. 39 After his death was an aristocracy. **1876** BANCROFT *Hist. U.S.* VI. l. 378 Despotisms, monarchies, and aristocracies must conform to them.

b. A state having this form of government.

1603 HOLLAND *Plutarch's Mor.* 72 Those States which be called Aristocraties..governed by a Senate or Counsel of the greatest men. **1751** CHAMBERS *Cycl.* s.v., The republic of Venice is an aristocracy. **1865** *Pall Mall G.* 29 Sept. 1/2 If by an aristocracy we mean..a country in which distinguished birth, inherited wealth, and education, are the chief titles to political power.

4. *concr.* A ruling body of nobles, an oligarchy.

1611 CORYAT *Crudities* 390, I cannot informe thee of their aristocratie [of Venice]. **1660** R. COKE *Power & Subj.* 55 Aristocracy is when a company of men met in Councel, ascribe to themselves whatsoever power is due to any rightful monarch..Such were the Roman Senate, and Ephori of Lacedæmon. **1719** STEELE *To Earl Oxford* 322 The aristocracy over these dominions.

This passes gradually into:

5. The class to which such a ruling body belongs, a patrician order; the collective body of those who form a privileged class with regard to the government of their country; the nobles. The term is popularly extended to include all those who by birth or fortune occupy a position distinctly above the rest of the community, and is also used *fig.* of those who are superior in other respects.

1651 HOBBES *Leviath.* II. xix. 98 Aristocracie..an Assembly of certain persons nominated, or otherwise distinguished from the rest. **1776** ADAM SMITH *W.N.* II. v. iii. 547 No oppressive aristocracy has ever prevailed in the colonies. **1795** in *Trans. Philol. Soc.* (1858) 52 [The Attorney-General in Horne Tooke's trial says] To the rich was given the name *aristocracy*. **1838** HALLAM *Hist. Lit.* II. II. iv. §52 The distinguishing characteristic of an aristocracy is the enjoyment of privileges which are not communicable to other citizens simply by anything they can themselves do to obtain them. **1843** F. PAGET *Ward. Berking.* 74 A test of what our Aristocracy do in proportion to their means. **1845** DISRAELI *Sybil* (1863) 88 There is no longer in fact an aristocracy in England, for the superiority of the animal man is an essential quality of aristocracy. **1861** MILL *Utilit.* (1864) 95 So it will be..with the aristocracies of colour, race, and sex. **1866** ROGERS *Agric. & Prices* Introd., Our aristocracy and gentry date, on the whole, from the days of Henry the Eighth. **1881** SEELEY in *Macm. Mag.* XLV. 47/1 From the democracy of readers..appeal must be made to the aristocracy of students, to those who make a business of knowledge.

6. = ARISTOCRATICISM.

1822 BYRON in Moore *Lett.* 558 My aristocracy which is very fierce makes him a favourite of mine.

aristocrat ('ærɪstəʊ,kræt, ə'rɪstəkræt). [a. F. *aristocrate* (not on Gr. analogies), f. *aristocrat-ie*, *-ique*. A popular formation of the French Revolution.]

A member of an aristocracy; *strictly*, one of a ruling oligarchy; *hence*, one of a patrician order, a noble; *occasionally*, one who favours an aristocratic form of government (opposed to *democrat*).

1789 BELSHAM *Ess.* II. xl. 473 The genuine spirit of the haughty *aristocrate*. **1790** W. TAYLOR *Let. fr. Paris* in Robberds *Mem.* I. 69 All Paris is still in a ferment..These handbills and pamphlets..all tend to accuse the aristocrats of little or great treasons. **1792** A. YOUNG *Trav. France* 225 Their excellencies, the *aristocrats* of Venice. **1793** BURKE *Corr.* (1844) IV. 151 The royalists of France, or as they are (perhaps as properly) called, the aristocrats. **1794** COLERIDGE in *Own Times* III. 968 In came that fierce Aristocrat, Our pursy woollen-draper. **1840** GEN. P. THOMPSON *Exerc.* (1842) V. 408 The aristocrat-made law. **1849** GROTE *Greece* II. xlvii. VI. 26 So violent and pointed did the scission of aristocrats and democrats become.

b. *fig.*

1883 G. ALLEN in *Knowledge* 3 Aug. 65/2 The honey-loving aristocrats of the insect world.

c. *attrib.* quasi-*adj.*

1873 TROLLOPE *Australia* I. 475 The class of which I am now speaking is an aristocrat class.

†**aristo'cratian,** *a. Obs. rare*$^{-1}$. [f. L. *aristocratia* + -AN.] Aristocratic.

1609 tr. *Sir T. Smith's Commonw. Eng.* I. vii. 7 Generall Councels made strife with him, to make the Popes power either Aristocratian, or at the least *legitimum regnum*.

aristocratic (,ærɪstəʊ'krætɪk), *a.* [a. F. *aristocratique*, ad. Gr. ἀριστοκρατικ-ός: see ARISTOCRACY and -IC.]

1. Of or pertaining to an aristocracy; attached to or favouring aristocracy.

1602 WARNER *Alb. Eng.* x. lvii. (1612) 250 Aristocratick gouernment nor Democratick pleas'd. **1791** BURKE *Let. Nat. Assemb.* Wks. VI. 37 To destroy these aristocratick prejudices. **1868** G. DUFF *Polit. Surv.* 35 The so-called aristocratic party, the landlords.

2. Befitting an aristocrat; grand, stylish.

1845 DISRAELI *Sybil* (1863) 89 The principal tradesmen..deemed it more 'aristocratic'; using a favourite and hackneyed epithet, which only expressed their own servility. **1876** MISS BRADDON *J. Haggard's Dau.* II. 65 Rooms so much..more aristocratic than those in which she had lived.

,aristo'cratical, *a.* (and *sb.*) [f. as prec. + -AL^1.]

A. *adj.* **1.** Of or pertaining to the rule of an aristocracy; oligarchical.

1589 *Hay any Work* (1844) 48 Such is the civill governement..Aristocraticall in the higher house of Parliament. **1660** R. COKE *Justice Vind.* 19 Where was there ever any such dissention..as in Democratical and Aristocratical States? **1756** BURKE *Vind. Nat. Soc.* Wks. 1842 I. 15 The monarchick, and aristocratical, and popular, partisans. **1874** MAHAFFY *Soc. Life Greece* v. 136 The aristocratical complexion of Athenian life.

2. Of or belonging to the higher classes.

a **1733** NORTH *Lives* I. 201 There were bickerings against this power..in a manner aristocratical. **1791** T. PAINE *Rights M.* 26 Accustomed to kiss the aristocratical hand. **1849** MACAULAY *Hist. Eng.* I. 356 No aristocratical mansion is to be found in that once aristocratical quarter. **1861** GEN. P. THOMPSON *Audi Alt.* III. cl. 144 Needy aristocratical families.

B. as *sb.* A partisan of aristocracy.

1651 HOBBES *Leviath.* II. xxii, Patricians, and plebians..aristocraticals and democraticals.

,aristo'cratically, *adv.* [f. prec. + -LY^2.]

1. In an aristocratic manner; by means of, or with a leaning towards, an aristocracy.

1594 T. B. *La Primaud. Fr. Acad.* 561 If a citie be assembled..aristocraticallie under certain chiefe lords. **1624** BEDELL *Lett.* x. 127 Geneva was..gouerned Aristocratically. **1869** SEELEY *Ess. & Lect.* i. 14 Augustus was in all things aristocratically disposed.

2. As befits an aristocrat; grandly, stylishly.

1837 GEN. P. THOMPSON *Exerc.* (1842) IV. 262 Every aristocratically dressed man you meet.

,aristo'craticalness. [f. as prec. + -NESS.] Aristocratical quality; aristocratic style.

1731 in BAILEY. **1880** EARL DESART *M. O'Connor* III. 97 Fall in love with his face, his figure, and his aristocraticalness.

aristocraticism (,ærɪstəʊ'krætɪsɪz(ə)m). [f. ARISTOCRATIC + -ISM.] Adherence to aristocratic principles or customs.

1860 *Sat. Rev.* No. 252. 251/1 Our aristocraticism, our religion, our social restrictions he cannot abide.

,aristo'craticness. = ARISTOCRATICALNESS.

1877 FURNIVALL *Leopold Shaks.* Introd. 68 So had Bertram [to be emptied] of his silly aristocraticness.

aristocratism ('ærɪstəʊ,krætɪz(ə)m, ,ærɪ'stɒkrətɪz(ə)m). [f. ARISTOCRAT + -ISM.] The principles or practices of aristocrats; haughty exclusiveness.

1792 ROMILLY *To Durant* 10 Sept. (R.), Accused of being aristocrats, though their only aristocratism consists in their wishing to defend a constitution which all France has sworn to maintain. **1837** CARLYLE *Fr. Rev.* III. I. ii. 12 Aristocratism rolls in its carriage. **1878** P. BAYNE *Purit. Rev.* vi. 217 The spirit of religious caste, of spiritual aristocratism, had reappeared.

aristocratize, *v.* [f. as prec. + -IZE: cf. F. *aristocratiser*.] **a.** *trans.* To make or render aristocratic. **b.** *intr.* To lean towards or favour aristocracy. Hence **aristocratizing** *ppl. a.*

1799 W. TAYLOR in Robberds *Mem.* I. 297 His opinions are sensibly aristocratized. **1841** *Blackw. Mag.* L. 151 A petty aristocratizing princedom like Weimar.

aristocraty, -ie, obs. forms of ARISTOCRACY.

‖**Aristolochia** (,ærɪstəʊ'ləʊkɪə). *Bot.* Formerly also in 5-6 **aristologia**; and in Eng. form in 6 **aristology**, 6-7 **aristoloch, -loche**, 6-8 **aristolochy**. [a. med.L. *aristologia* (also Sp. and It.), and of F. *aristoloche*, 16th c. *aristolochie*, ad. L. *aristolochīa*, a. Gr. ἀριστολόχεια, -ία, f. ἀριστόλοχος well-born (from its repute in promoting childbirth).] A genus of shrubs, of which one species, *A. Clēmatītis*, the Common Birthwort, is found in Britain as an old escape from cultivation.

1398 TREVISA *Barth. De P.R.* XVII. xiv. (1495) 612 Aristologia is a full medycynall herbe though it be bytter. **1541** R. COPLAND *Guydon's Quest. Cyrurg.*, With the rote of Arystologie, or of Affodylles. **1551** TURNER *Herbal* (1568) 43 The seconde kynd of aristolochia. **1578** LYTE *Dodoens* 312 Sarrasines herbe or Astroloche..Long Aristoloche, Rounde Aristoloche. *Ibid.* 314 The long and rounde Aristolochias growe plentifully in Spayne..called in English Aristologia and of some Byrthwort. **1572** MASCAL *Govt. Cattle* (1627) 128 Of nettle seed, of Aristolochy, of ech 2 drams. **1585** LLOYD *Treas. Health* D iii, Aristologye caryed upon a man cureth hym. **1601** HOLLAND *Pliny* II. 226 All the sort of these Aristolochies yeeld an aromaticall odour. **1607** TOPSELL *Four-f. Beasts* 269 Aristoloch, otherwise called round Hartwort. —— *Serpents* 775 Long Aristolochie or Hartwort. **1725** BRADLEY *Fam. Dict.*, *Aristolochy*..is proper to bring away Women's After-burden in their Lying-in. **1854** BADHAM *Halieut.* 21 Pliny records that all aristolochias yield an aromatic smell.

aristological (,ærɪstəʊ'lɒdʒɪkəl), *a.* [f. as next + -ICAL.] Of or pertaining to aristology.

1873 M. COLLINS *Sq. Silchester's* I. xv. 192 Inhibited..from aristological observations, or he would here describe a good Devonshire dinner.

aristologist (ærɪ'stɒlədʒɪst). [f. next + -IST.] One skilled in aristology.

1835 T. WALKER *Original* No. 13, I call the art of dining Aristology, and those who study it, Aristologists. **1864** (*title*) Cookery for the Many. By an Australian Aristologist.

ari'stology. [f. Gr. ἄριστο-ν breakfast, luncheon + -λογία discourse: see -LOGY.] The art or 'science' of dining.

1835 [see prec.] **1879** M. COLLINS *Pen Sketches* I. 235 The Romans..defied all the rules of aristology by their abominable excesses.

Aristophanic (,ærɪstəʊ'fænɪk), *a.* and *sb.* [ad. L. *Aristophanicus*, Gr. Ἀριστοφανικός.]

A. *adj.* Of or pertaining to Aristophanes, the Athenian comic dramatist, or his plays; used by, occurring in, resembling that of, or characteristic of Aristophanes.

1827 CARLYLE *Germ. Rom.* II. 6 He had laughed with his whole heart, in a true Aristophanic vein. **1827** P. W. BUCKHAM *Theatre of Greeks* (ed. 2) 109 The expressions which the Aristophanic Euripides employs in assailing Æschylus. **1835** T. MITCHELL *Acharn. of Aristoph.* 148 The word λαῶν occurs in the Aristophanic writings. **1873** SYMONDS *Gk. Poets* viii. 245 If we are to seek for an approximation to Aristophanic humour, we shall find it perhaps in Rabelais.

B. *sb.* A logaœdic tripody beginning with a dactyl (–◡◡|–◡|–◡̄); a first Pherecratic.

1874 J. M. MARSHALL *Horati Op.* I. p. xxxiv, Sapphic (the greater). Alternately an Aristophanic and a greater Sapphic.

Aristotelean (,ærɪstɒtɪ'liːən), **Aristotelian** (,ærɪstəʊ'tiːlɪən), *a.* and *sb.* [The former is f. L. *Aristotelē-us*, Gr. Ἀριστοτέλει-ος + -AN; the latter, f. L. *Aristotelēs*, Gr. Ἀριστοτέλης + -IAN (cf. *Christian*), is more common]. A. *adj.* Of or pertaining to Aristotle, the famous Greek philosopher, or to his system. B. *sb.* One who follows, or is skilled in, the philosophy of Aristotle. Hence **Aristo'telianism**, the philosophic system or any doctrine of Aristotle. Similarly: **Aristotelic** (,ærɪstəʊ'telɪk), *a.* [Gr. Ἀριστοτελικ-ός] and † **Aristo'telical** *a.* = Aristotelian. **Ari'stotelism** and † **Aristo'telity** (*rare*⁻¹) = Aristotelianism. **Ari'stotelize** *v.*, to lean towards or teach the system of Aristotle.

1607 TOPSELL *Serpents* 653 What sense I should give to that *Aristotelean Proverb. **1684** T. BURNET *Th. Earth* III. 15 Those of the Jews that were *Aristoteleans. **1840** CARLYLE *Heroes* (1858) 249 School-divinity, *Aristotelean logic. **1581** CHARKE in *Confer.* IV. (1584) Cc ij b, Hermogenes..saying as an *Aristotelian Philosopher, yᵗ God made al things of *materia prima*. **1634** M. SANDYS *Essays* 210 (T.) The *Aristotelians were of opinion, that superfluity of riches might cause a tumult in a commonwealth. **1724** WATTS *Logic* I. vi. §9 *Aristotelian fooleries and scholastic subtilties. **1870** LOWELL *Among my Bks.* I. (1873) 171 We respect in Goethe the *Aristotelian poet. **1727–51** CHAMBERS *Cycl.*, *Aristotelianism, the reigning system of many ages. **1610** HEALEY *Vives on St. Aug. City of God* (1620) 417 Hee [Saint Thomas] is too *Aristotelique. **1836–7** SIR W. HAMILTON *Metaph.* vii. (1859) I. 116 The *Aristotelic philosophy was..during the middle ages, the one exclusive philosophy in Europe. **1678** CUDWORTH *Intell. Syst.* 53 The whole *Aristotelical System of Philosophy. **1845** J. H. NEWMAN *Ess. Developm.* 451 The theology of St. Thomas..is built on that very *Aristotelism which the early Fathers denounce as the source of all misbelief. **1651** HOBBES *Leviath.* IV. xlvi. 370 That study is not properly Philosophy, but *Aristotelity. **1842** SIR W. HAMILTON in *Reid's Wks.* II. 765/2 The *Aristotelizing commentary of Proclus.

Aristotle's Lantern: see LANTERN *sb.* 6 b.

aristulate (ə'rɪstjʊleɪt), *ppl. a. Bot.* [f. mod.L. *aristula*, dim. of *arista* + -ATE².] 'Bearing a diminutive awn.' Gray.

Arita (ə'riːtə). The name of a town on the island of Kyushu, south-west of Japan, used *attrib.* to designate a variety of porcelain made in the neighbourhood since the early seventeenth century, or an object made of this porcelain, usually characterized by an asymmetric style of decoration, commonly either cobalt blue and white underglaze or polychrome enamel.

[**1876** W. E. GRIFFIS *Mikado's Empire* 616 Of the two platforms in the Japanese section, one was devoted to porcelain of Arita and Karatsŭ, in Hizen.] **1878** [see IMARI]. **1880** A. W. FRANKS *Jap. Pott.* 90 (*heading*) Arita ware. **1881** C. C. HARRISON *Woman's Handiwork* III. 233 An Arita bowl, gorgeous with stippled red, at $5. **1925** tr. *Hannover's Pott. & Porc.* II. III. ii. 210 This early Arita porcelain also seems to have been blue-and-white. **1954** H. GARNER *Oriental Blue & White* xi. 62 The square bottle and the ewer have border designs which are typical of the Arita wares, both blue and white and polychrome. **1965** S. JENYNS *Jap. Porcelain* iii. 89 The decoration of the earliest blue and white Arita pieces is primitive; the most common decoration is a sketchy foliage scroll. **1970** *Oxf. Compan. Art* 610 By *c.* 1650 the Dutch were already trading in Arita blue-and-white.

arithmancy ('ærɪθ,mænsɪ). [contracted for ARITHMOMANCY, but earlier.] Divination by numbers.

1577 HOLINSHED *Descr. Brit.* ix. 28/2 An old kind of arithmancie, fathered on Pythagoras, yet never invented by him. **1878** J. GRAY *China* II. xvii. 25 Other systems of telling fortunes are in vogue, as for instance..arithmancy.

arith'mantical, *a.* [f. prec.: see -MANCY.] Of or pertaining to arithmancy.

1569 J. SANFORD *Agrippa's Van. Artes* 62 That Alphabetarie, and Arithmantical diuinitie.

arithmetic (ə'rɪθmɪtɪk), *sb.*¹ Forms: 3 arsmetike, 4 -metique, 4–5 -metyk, ars metrik(e, 4–6 arsmetrik(e, 5 -metryk(e, -metrique, -matryk, arce metrik, 6 arsmetrycke, arsemetricke; 5 arismetrik; 6 arithmetryk, -metricke, -metike, -metique, 6–7 arithmatick(e, -matique, -meticke, 6–8 -metick, 7 -metic. [orig. a. OF. *arismetique*, ad. Pr. and late L. *arismetica*, for L. *arithmētica*, a. Gr. ἡ ἀριθμητική (sc. τέχνη) the art of counting, f. ἀριθμέ-ειν to number, count, reckon, f. ἀριθμός number. Erroneously referred in ME. to L. *ars metrica* 'art of measure,' and made into *arsmetrike*, the common form from 14th to 16th c., which was gradually corrected, through *arismetrik* in Caxton, *arithmetricke* in Sir T. More, to *arithmetyke* in Recorde 1543. In 16th c. it was also sometimes conformed in ending to *mathematick*, and to *geometry*: see ARSMETRY.]

1. The science of numbers; the art of computation by figures.

c **1250** *Gen. & Ex.* 792 Egipte clerkes..hem lerede, witterlike, Astronomiȝe and arsmetike. *c* **1305** *St. Edmund E.E.P.* (1862) 77 Arsmetrike is a lore: þat of figours al is. *c* **1386** CHAUCER *Knts. T.* 1040 That geometry or arsmetrike can [*v.r.* Ars Metrik(e, arsmetrik, arce metrik]. *c* **1400** *Cov. Myst.* 189 Also of augrym and of asmatryk. **1477** EARL RIVERS (Caxton) *Dictes* 103 Arismetrik & astrologie. **1494** FABYAN VII. 604 The .vii. artes or scyences lyberall.. grammer, logyke, rethoryke, musyke, arsmetryke, gemetry, and astronomye. **1528** MORE *Heresyes* I. Wks. 111/1 Arithmetricke meete for marchauntes. **1530** RASTELL *Purgat.* II. xix, Methematycall scyens as geometrye, arithmetryk. **1543** RECORDE *Gr. Arts* 6 Bothe names are corruptly writen: Arsmetrike for Arithmetyke, as the Grekes call it, and Awgrym for Algorisme, as Arabyans sounde it. **1589** *Pasquil's Ret.* B iij, [It] multiplies..by Arithmaticke, it makes a thousand of one. **1596** NASHE *Saffron Walden* 52 These roguish Arsmetrique gibbets or flesh-hookes, and cyphers or round oos. **1669** GALE *Crt. Gentiles* I. I. ii. 16 Arithmetic..is supposed to have been first invented by the Phenicians. **1750** HARRIS *Hermes* (1841) 202 Arithmetic is excellent for the gauging of liquors. **1850** CARLYLE *Latter-d. Pamphl.* vi. (1872) 200 Is Arithmetic,—a thing more fixed by the Eternal, than the laws of justice.

2. Arithmetical knowledge, computation, reckoning.

1607 SHAKS. *Cor.* III. i. 245 But now 'tis oddes beyond Arithmetick. **1712** ADDISON *Spect.* No. 549 ¶1 Such innumerable articles, that I want arithmetic to cast them up. **1807** WORDSW. *Sonn. Liberty* I. xxiv, What if our numbers barely could defy The arithmetic of babes.

3. A treatise on computation.

1623 J. JOHNSON (*title*) Arithmetick. **1711** ADDISON *Spect.* No. 92, §5, I would advise all young wives to make themselves Mistresses of Wingate's arithmetick.

arith'metic, *a.* and *sb.*² 7 arithmetick. [a. F. *arithmétique*, or ad. L. *arithmēticus*: see next.]

A. *adj.* **a.** = ARITHMETICAL.

arithmetic mean, progression: = *arithmetical mean*, etc., s.v. ARITHMETICAL *a.* (and *sb.*). ***arithmetic shift***: a shift (SHIFT *sb.* 14 g) which makes provision for retaining a sign bit and allows for the possible loss of digits by truncation or overflow.

1673 MORLAND (*title*) Description and Use of two Arithmetic Instruments. **1767** HORSLEY in *Phil. Trans.* LVII. 399 The semi-circle being a mean arithmetic between AC and ABC. **1866** W. ODLING *Lect. Animal Chem.* 151 The proportional number of bromine is intermediate between those of chlorine and iodine, and..approximates very closely to the true arithmetic mean. **1886** G. CHRYSTAL *Algebra* I. xx. 466 An Arithmetic Series, or an Arithmetic Progression, as it is often called, is a series in which each term exceeds the preceding by a fixed quantity, called the common difference. **1901** BEMAN & SMITH tr. *K. Fink's Brief Hist. Mathematics* 96 Among the Italians of the thirteenth and fourteenth centuries..the course of an arithmetic operation was expressed entirely in words. **1951** *Proc. IRE* Mar. 272/1 *Arithmetic element*, that part of a computer which performs arithmetic operations. **1954** T. W. CHAUNDY et al. *Printing of Mathematics* 64 In changing practice some mathematical terms have shortened. Thus we say 'convergence' rather than 'convergency'; 'algebraic', 'geometric' generally replace 'algebraical', 'geometrical', and even 'arithmétic' (so accented), can be an adjective as in 'arithmetic mean'. **1960** *Communications Assoc. Computing Machinery* III. 301/2 Delimiters..<operator> ::= <arithmetic operator>|<relational operator>|<logical operator>|<sequential operator>. **1963** *KDF9 Programming Man.* (Eng. Electric Leo Computers Ltd.) 108 Arithmetic shifts are designed to deal with *numbers* only. **1965** C. M. SPRINGER et al. *Advanced Methods & Models* iii. 69 Any sequence of *n* numbers in which each term differs from the preceding term by a constant amount is called an arithmetic progression. **1972** M. KLINE *Math. Thought* iii. 32 If *p* and *q* are two numbers..the harmonic mean *H*..is the reciprocal of the arithmetic mean of 1/*p* and 1/*q*. **1980** C. S. FRENCH *Computer Sci.* xxiv. 174 Arithmetic shifts ie moving bits in registers either left or right in order to multiply or divide. **1984** *Which Micro?* Dec. 31/2 Full range of arithmetic and relational operators.

b. ***arithmetic*** (***and logic*** or ***logical***) ***unit***: a unit in a computer which carries out arithmetical and logical operations; abbrev. ALU (A III. 1).

1946 J. P. ECKERT in *Theory & Techniques Design Electronic Digital Computers* (Univ. Penn.) (1947) I. x. 16 When successively adding several numbers, it is possible to hold the sum in the arithmetic unit. **1962** *Automatic Data Processing Gloss.* (U.S. Bureau of Budget) 2/2 *ALU*, Arithmetic and Logical Unit. **1969** P. B. JORDAIN *Condensed Computer Encycl.* 32 The arithmetic unit performs the bulk of the internal processing commands of a computer. **1977** *Sci. Amer.* Sept. 88/2 The arithmetic and logic unit (ALU), as its name implies, contains devices such as adders for arithmetic and logic operations on data received over the bus. **1984** I. R. WHITWORTH *16-bit Microprocessors* i. 2 An 8-bit arithmetic-and-logic unit (ALU) operates upon arguments held in programmer-accessible registers or accumulators.

† **B.** *sb.* [Cf. It. *arithmetico.*] An arithmetician. *Obs.*

1652 GAULE *Magastrom.* 178 The cabalistical rabbins, the Greek arithmeticks.

arithmetical (ærɪθ'mɛtɪkəl), *a.* (and *sb.*) [f. L. *arithmētic-us*, a. Gr. ἀριθμητικ-ός numeric (see ARITHMETIC *sb.*¹) + -AL¹.]

A. *adj.* Of, pertaining to, or connected with, arithmetic; according to the rules of arithmetic. ***arithmetical mean, progression, proportion***: see quot.

1543 RECORDE *Gr. Arts* (1646) 299 The reasons of works Arithmeticall. **1594** BLUNDEVIL *Exerc.* I. xiii. 39 Arithmeticall Progression..is that which proceedeth by like difference of quantity, as thus; 3, 5, 7, 9, 11, 13. **1660** R. COKE *Justice Vind.* 23 As 3. 4. 5. 6. are in Arithmetical proportion, for they increase equally; and 3. added to 6. is equal to 4. added to 5. **1798** HUTTON *Course Math.* (1810) I. 114 To find an Arithmetical Mean..Add the two given extremes or terms together, and take half their sum. **1855** MACAULAY *Hist. Eng.* IV. xix. 327 In the face of arithmetical demonstration.

B. as *sb.* A number in an arithmetical progression.

1798 HUTTON *Course Math.* (1827) I. 123 The sum of the extremes is equal to double the mean, which is the property of arithmeticals.

arith'metically, *adv.* [f. prec. + -LY².] In arithmetical manner, according to arithmetic; by numerical calculation. ***arithmetically proportional***: standing in arithmetical proportion.

[**1477** NORTON *Ord. Alch.* in Ashm. 1652, v. 60 Joyne them together also Arithmetically.] **1571** DIGGES *Geom. Pract.* II. xxiv. P iij, Arithmetically to attayne the quantitie of this longer portion, ye shall thus worke. **1656** tr. *Hobbes' Elem. Philos.* (1839) 147 Four magnitudes arithmetically proportional. **1865** CARLYLE *Fredk. Gt.* VI. xv. vii. 33 The regiments are..complete, arithmetically and otherwise.

arithmetician (ə,rɪθmɪ'tɪʃən, ,ærɪθ-). Also 6 -trician, 7 -titian. [a. F. *arithméticien* (15th c. in Littré), f. L. *arithmētica*: see ARITHMETIC *sb.*¹ and -ICIAN.] One who works out arithmetical problems; a proficient in the science of numbers.

1557 RECORDE *Whetstone* Lij, To proue the cunnyng of a braggyng Arithmetician. **1571** DIGGES *Geom. Pract.* IV. xxii. Dd ij b, The skilfull Arithmetrician. **1608** T. JAMES *Apol. Wickliffe* 74 You may know them to bee cunning Arithmetitians. **1792** A. YOUNG *Trav. France* 464 Useful data for political arithmeticians. **1869** LUBBOCK *Preh. Times* xiv. 502 They are such bad arithmeticians that the enumeration of ten is a labour..with many of them.

arithmeticize (ærɪθ'mɛtɪsaɪz), *v. rare.* [f. L. *arithmētic-us* + -IZE.] To treat arithmetically.

1878 T. SINCLAIR *Mount* 241 Let men reverence poetry; and..they will not set themselves to arithmeticise it.

arithmetization (ə,rɪθmɪtaɪ'zeɪʃən). [f. ARITHMETIZE *v.* + -ATION.] The action, or the result, of arithmetizing, in various senses.

1902 *Encycl. Brit.* XXVIII. 544 The Theory of Functions of Real Variables..has been remodelled in the process of complete arithmetization. **1903** B. RUSSELL *Princ. Math.* xxxii. 259 What is called the arithmetization of mathematics has shown that all the problems presented..are already present in pure arithmetic. *a* **1910** W. JAMES *Some Probl. Philos.* (1911) xi. 173 The 'new infinite' and the 'number-continuum' are outgrowths of a general attempt to accomplish what has been called the 'arithmetization' (ἀριθμός meaning number) of all quantity. **1935** *Mind* XLIV. 501 An arithmetisation of syntax, based upon the method of Gödel, in which numbers are assigned to simple signs.

a'rithmetize, *v.* [f. ARITHMET-IC + -IZE.]

† **1.** To work sums in arithmetic, to cipher. *Obs.*

a **1658** CLEVELAND *Publ. Faith* 33 But now the Cub can count, arithmatize.

2. *Math.* **a.** To reduce (any other part of mathematics) to arithmetic, by defining mathematical entities and operations in terms of the natural numbers and their properties. Hence *gen.*, to express in a numerical form.

1892 H. B. FINE in *Bull. N.Y. Math. Soc.* I. 175 It is not merely that the purely arithmetical problems growing out of algebra were attractive to him [*sc.* Kronecker]—he 'arithmetized' algebra itself. **1937** *Mind* XLVI. 311 A time in which there is genuine change or process can scarcely be 'arithmetised' or 'logicised' in its full meaning. **1948** BRODIE & COLEMAN tr. *L. Chwistek's Limits of Sci.* p. xxx, Weierstrass and Kronecker..maintained that..it is logically possible to arithmetize all portions of mathematics. **1951** *Ess. in Criticism* I. 5 There has been a strong tendency in modern times to *arithmetize* criticism.

b. To apply the metamathematical method invented by Kurt Gödel of assigning a special number to each part of an utterance in order to formulate mathematical proofs about its properties.

1937 A. SMEATON tr. *R. Carnap's Logical Syntax Lang.* §19. 57 The definitions and sentences of syntax arithmetized in this way do not differ fundamentally from the other definitions and sentences of arithmetic. **1940** *Mind* XLIX. 240 The method of arithmetising axiom systems, used to such effect in Gödel's work, is fully explained.

Hence **a'rithmetizing** *vbl. sb.*, the action of the verb.

1896 *Bull. Amer. Math. Soc.* II. 243 The arithmetizing of mathematics began originally..by ousting space intuition. **1919** B. RUSSELL *Introd. Math. Philos.* i. 4 Pythagoras..was the discoverer of the most serious obstacle in the way of what is called the 'arithmetising' of mathematics.

a'rithmic. *rare.* [f. Gr. ἀριθμ-ός number + -IC.] The principle of numbers; arithmetic.

1879 E. ARNOLD *Lt. Asia* v. 132 The fixed arithmic of the universe, Which meteth good for good and ill for ill. *Ibid.* VI. 167 By sure arithmic.

arith'mocracy. *nonce-wd.* [f. Gr. ἀριθμό-ς number + -κρατία rule: see -CRACY.] A form of government in which the power is vested in the simply numerical majority.

1850 KINGSLEY *Alt. Locke* Pref. (1879) 116 A 'democracy' of mere numbers is no democracy, but a mere brute 'arithmocracy.'

arithmo'cratic, *a. nonce-wd.* [f. as prec. after Gr. adjs. in -κρατικός: cf. *aristocratic*.] Of the nature of an arithmocracy.

1850 KINGSLEY *Alt. Locke* Pref. (1879) 100 American Democracy, being merely arithmocratic.

arithmogram (ə'rɪθməʊgræm). [f. Gr. ἀριθμό-ς number + γράμμα a thing written: see -GRAM.] A number expressed by the letters of a word, name, or phrase, e.g. the number 666 made up by the Greek letters of the word λατεῖνος (for λατῖνος).

1869 LD. STRANGFORD *Select.* II. 301 My efforts to work it [Dr. Cumming's name] out honestly as an arithmogram.

arithmography (ærɪθ'mɒgrəfɪ). [f. as prec. + -γραφία writing: see -GRAPHY. Cf. Fr. *arithmographie*.] Representation of a number by letters.

1869 LD. STRANGFORD *Select.* II. 301 Who has successfully solved a great problem in theology and arithmography.

arithmological (ə,rɪθməʊ'lɒdʒɪkəl). [f. as prec. + Gr. -λογικός discoursing of + -AL[1].] Pertaining to the scientific treatment of numbers.

1882 *Nature* XXVII. 193 The arithmological papers are numerous.

arith'mology. ? *Obs.* [f. as prec. + Gr. -λογία: see -LOGY. Cf. Fr. *arithmologie*.] A treatise on numbers, or statement bearing upon them.

1572 L. LLOYD *Pilgr. Princes* (1607) 104b, A few Arithmologies which Salomon the wise, and Jhesus the sonne of Syrach..have amongst their chiefe writinges noted.

arithmomancy (ə'rɪθməʊ,mænsɪ). [ad. mod.L. *arithmomantīa*, f. Gr. ἀριθμός number + -μαντεία divination. Cf. Fr. *arithmomancie*.] Divination by numbers; arithmancy.

1621 BURTON *Anat. Mel.* II. ii. IV, Fulks Arithmomantia and the rest of those curious games. **1660** STANLEY *Hist. Philos.* 384/2 Upon the near affinity which Pythagoras..conceived to be betwixt the gods and numbers, he collected a kind of Arithmomanty.

arithmomania (ə,rɪθməʊ'meɪnɪə). *Psychiatry.* [f. Gr. ἀριθμό-ς number + MANIA. Cf. Fr. *arithmomanie*.] A compulsive desire to count objects and make calculations. So **arithmo'maniac**, one who suffers from arithmomania.

1890 W. S. COLMAN in *Lancet* 5 July 14/2 In France cases have been described as 'arithmomaniacs', epileptics who are usually of weak intellect and occupy themselves habitually with simple arithmetical calculations. **1892** D. H. TUKE *Dict. Psychol. Med.* 678 He eventually experienced the like trouble in regard to..the number of articles (books, dishes, &c.) falling under his observation (*arithmomania*). **1895** tr. *M. Nordau's Degeneration* III. i. 242 Erotomania (love madness), arithmomania (madness of numbers), oniomania (madness for buying), etc. **1924** J. RIVIERE et al. tr. *Freud's Coll. Papers* I. vii. 132 Obsession of arithmomania. A woman became obliged to count the boards in the floor, the steps in the staircase. **1934** S. BECKETT *More Pricks* iv. 89 The voice of the arithmomaniac was heard.

arithmometer (ærɪθ'mɒmɪtə(r)). [a. F. *arithmomètre*, f. as ARITHMOMANCY + Gr. -μέτρον: see -METER.] An instrument for working out arithmetical problems.

1876 in *S. Kens. Sci. Catal.* **1879** THOMSON & TAIT *Nat. Phil.* I. I. §401 Calculating Machines.. up to the Arithmometer of Thomas of Colmar [in 1862].

†**'aritude.** *Obs.* [ad. L. *āritūdo*, f. *ārēre* to be dry.] = ARIDITY.

1656 in BLOUNT *Glossogr.*

arity ('ærɪtɪ). *Math.* [f. -ARY[1] (in BINARY, TERNARY *adjs.*, etc.) + -ITY.] The number of elements by virtue of which something is unary, binary, etc.

1968 *Fundamenta Mathematicae* LXII. 191 E. Marczewski introduced..the order of enlargeability and the arity or the order of reducibility of abstract algebras. **1973** *Colloquium Mathematicum* XXVII. 175 (*heading*) On the arity of idempotent reduct of abelian groups. **1974** *Encycl. Brit. Macropædia* I. 554/2 With each member ω of Ω an integer $n(\omega)$ is associated, to indicate the arity of the resulting operation. **1979** *Proc. IEEE Computer Soc. Conf. Pattern Recognition & Image Processing* 202/1 Any heuristic for problem solving..is based on the recognition of a unary relation (subset) or a relation of higher arity on the set of states of the problem. **1983** *Jrnl. Symbolic Logic* XLVIII. 1231 (*heading*) Point-arity—the new cardinality index for ideals.

-arium, *suffix* of sbs., a. L. *-ārium* 'thing connected with or employed in, place for,' orig. neuter of adjs. in *-ārius*. Of this the regular adapted form in Eng. is *-ary*: see -ARY[1], but the unchanged L. form is used with a few terms of classical and ecclesiastical antiquities, or of learned use, as *caldarium, frigidarium, sacrarium, honorarium, herbarium*, the last of which, being in general use, has probably popularized the use of *vivarium* and *aquarium*.

arive, obs. form of ARRIVE.

arizonite (ærɪ'zəʊnaɪt). *Min.* [f. *Arizona*, a state of U.S.A. + -ITE[1].] A titanate of iron found in Arizona.

1909 C. PALMER in *Amer. Jrnl. Sci.* XXVIII. 355 The crystallographic determinations strengthen the view that this titanate of iron cannot be assigned to any known species, but is entirely new. I propose to name it *Arizonite*. **1947** H. B. GRAVES *Mineral Key* 136 *Arizonite*. Hardness, 5.5.. Color, steel gray.

ark (ɑːk), *sb.* Forms: 1–4 arc, 1–2 earc, 1 ærc, erc, erk, ark, 2 eark, 3 (*Orm.*) arrke, 3–7 ark(e, 7 arcke, 4– ark. [Common Teutonic: with OE. *arc* (*earc, ærc, erc, erk*), acc. *arce*, cf. OFris. *erke*, OHG. *archa*, mod.G. *arche*, ON. *örk* (gen. *arkar*), Sw., Da. *ark*, Goth. and OTeut. *arka*, prob. a. L. *arca* chest, box, coffer; whence OF. *arche*, also adopted in senses 2, 3, alongside of the native word: see ARCHE.]

1. A chest, box, coffer, close basket, or similar receptacle; *esp.* **a.** in *north. dial.* a large wooden bin or hutch for storing meal, bread, fruit, etc.

a **1000** *Riddles* (Gr.) lxii. 2 Oft mec fæste bileác freolícu meowle ides on earce. *c* **1200** ORMIN 18823 þatt arrke þatt iss wrohht off tre. **1330** R. BRUNNE *Chron.* 136 To þe ordre of Cisteans he gaf two þousand mark..to lay vp in arke. **1535** COVERDALE *Ex.* ii. 3 She toke an Arke of redes [WYCLIF, a ionket of resshen; **1388** a leep of segge *or* seggis]. **1611** *Ibid.*, An arke of bul-rushes. **1648** HERRICK *Hesper.* Wks. (Gros.) II. 9 They With Wicker Arks did come To kiss and beare away The richer Couslips home. **1845** PETRIE *Eccl. Archit. Irel.* 203 The relics of St. Ronan..were put into an ark or shrine.

a. *c* **1450** HENRYSON *Mor. Fables* 8 The cheese in Arke, and meill in Kist. **1557** *Lanc. Wills* I. (1857) 72 Ij gret arke standinge in the nursarie. **1724** RAMSAY *Tea-T. Misc.* (1733) II. 181 My bairn has tocher of her awin, An ark, an ambry, and a ladle. **1870** MORRIS *Earthly Par.* III. IV. 42 And from the ark at last did take Meal forth for porridge and for cake.

b. *fig.* 'Casket, treasury.'

c **1200** ORMIN 8971 Ure laffdiȝ Marȝe..leȝȝde itt all..Inn hire þohhtess arrke.

2. *spec.* in *Jew. Hist.* The wooden coffer containing the tables of the law, kept in the Holiest Place of the Tabernacle. Also called ***Ark of the Covenant, Ark of Testimony.*** See also ARCHE.

c **825** *Vesp. Ps.* cxxxi. 8 Ðu & erc ȝehalȝunge ðinre. *c* **1000** *Ags. Ps.* ibid., þu earce eart eall-haliȝra. *a* **1300** *E.E. Psalter* ibid., þou, and arke of þi halinesse. **1382** WYCLIF *1 Sam.* vi. 11 Thei putten the arke of God upon the wayn. **1667** MILTON *P.L.* XII. 251 Therein An Ark, and in the Ark his Testimony. **1853** MAURICE *Proph. & Kings* i. 4 The ark, the symbol of the people's unity, was captured by the Philistines.

b. *fig.*, as in phrases, ***to touch*** or ***lay hands on the ark***: to interfere with, treat irreverently, what is held to be sacred; (in reference to *2 Sam.* vi. 6.)

1641 MILTON *Ch. Govt.* i. (1851) 100 The living arke of the holy Ghost. **1842** H. ROGERS *Introd. Burke's Wks.* 83 Laying irreverent hands on the ark of the constitution. **1868** M. PATTISON *Academ. Org.* §1. 7 The House of Commons only touched the ark of our property with half a heart.

3. The large covered floating vessel in which Noah was saved at the Deluge; hence *fig.* a place of refuge. (In 13–14th c. commonly ARCHE.)

c **950** *Lindisf. Gosp.* Matt. xxiv. 38 Inneode in ærce Noë [*Rushw.* arkæ, *Ags. & Hatt.* earce]. *c* **1175** *Cott. Hom.* 225 Werc [*MS.* wrec] þe nu an arc. *c* **1200** ORMIN 14542 Drihhtin badd Noe gan till & wirrkenn himm an arrke. **1382** WYCLIF *Gen.* vi. 14 Make to thee an ark [*v.r.* schip] of planed trees. **1600** SHAKS. *A.Y.L.* v. iv. 36 There is sure another flood toward, and these couples are comming to the Arke. **1679** *Establ. Test.* 46 No safety..out of the Ark of their Church. **1807** CRABBE *Par. Reg.* III. 876 How spake the Serpent, and where stopped the Ark. **1863** (3 Feb.) BRIGHT *America, Sp.* (1876) 116 The United States has been..an ark of refuge to the people of Europe.

4. *transf.* A ship, boat, or similar floating vessel; *spec.* in U.S., a large flat-bottomed boat formerly used on rivers for the transport of produce.

1475 CAXTON *Jason* 67b, That thou go into pyrre for to make an arke. **1640** YORKE *Union Hon., Battels* 64 Skilfull navigators, whereof the Admirall in the Arke royall was chiefe. *a* **1813** A. WILSON *Foresters* Poet. Wks. 244 Huge loaded arks rush down the boiling tide. **1822** J. FLINT *Lett. fr. Amer.* 125 The beach is lined with keel boats, large arks for carrying produce, family boats. **1823** BYRON *Island* I. viii, Commits him to his fragile ark.

†**5.** An enclosure for catching or confining fish. *Obs.* [So *arche* in Ger. dialects; and cf. G. and F. *arche* a coffer-dam.]

1883 *Athenæum* 2 June 695/3 That Edinburgh had an eel-ark of its own at the east end of the North Loch.

6. *Comb.* and *Attrib.*, as ***ark-born, ark-ship.*** Also †**ark-wold**, the wooden sides or beams of the ark; **ark-full**, an assemblage as numerous and diverse as that which Noah's ark contained; **ark-net**, a kind of fish-trap (cf. *eel-ark* in 5); **ark-shell**, a species of bivalve mollusc.

1774 J. BRYANT *Mythol.* II. 435 (JOD.) The ark-born deity, Dionusus. **1613** *Decree* in *Law Rep.* Com. Pl. V. 714 To place ark-nets and other engines in the said river. **1854** WOODWARD *Man. Mollusca* II. 268 The Ark-shells of the Palæozoic and Secondary strata. **1851** FORBES in *Art. Jrnl. Illus. Cat.* Veg. W., An ark-full of living animals. **1853** LYNCH *Self-Improv.* ii. 43 Christianity..is the ark-ship, the ark of safety. *c* **1250** *Gen. & Ex.* 576 Quan he [Noah] dede him in ðe arche-wold.

†**ark,** *v. Obs.* [f. prec.] To shut up in an ark. Hence **arked** *ppl. a.*

1586 WARNER *Alb. Eng.* I. i, Arked Noah, and seauen with him. *a* **1644** QUARLES *Judgem. & Mercy* (1881) I. 128 Ark it up like Israel's manna. **1652** BENLOWES *Theoph.* v. 63 From flood of Tears may an Arkt Dove try..to descry That land unknown to Nature, Vast Eternitie.

ark, obs. form of ARC *sb.*, ARCH.

Arkansas ('ɑːkənsɔː, also (outside U.S.) ɑː'kænzəs). [Name of a state of U.S.A.]

1. A fine-grain variety of novaculite found in Arkansas, U.S.A. Also, a whetstone made of this. In full ***Arkansas hone, stone*** (see quots.).

1869 G. A. ROGERS in *Eng. Mechanic* 22 Oct. 125 A sharp-edged Arkansas can be rubbed on the outside. **1875** *Carpentry & Join.* 34 We often find it a good plan to rub down a tool on a bit of Arkansas of coarse quality. **1885** *Spon's Mechanic's Own Bk.* 242 Oilstones.—These are of several kinds, the best known being the Charnley Forest, Turkey, Arkansas, and Washita brands. **1889** *Cent. Dict.* s.v. *stone*, *Arkansas stone*, a fine-grain whetstone found in Arkansas, and used to sharpen surgical and dental instruments. **1910** *Encycl. Brit.* XIII. 653/1 Of Arkansas stones there are two varieties... The finer kind, known as Arkansas hone, is obtained in small pieces at the hot springs.

2. ***Arkansas toothpick***: see TOOTHPICK 4.

arkansite. *Min.* A variety of BROOKITE.

arkawngell, obs. form of ARCHANGEL[1].

arkite ('ɑːkaɪt), *a.* and *sb.* [f. ARK + -ITE.]

A. *adj.* Of or pertaining to Noah's ark. **B.** *sb.* An inmate of the ark.

1774 J. BRYANT *Mythol.* II. 329 A repository, where the Arkite rites and history were preserved. **1804** *Edin. Rev.* III. 429 The Arkites, a dignified and appropriate name for the family of Noah. **1867** M. ARNOLD *Celtic Lit.* 32 Bryant..found in Greek mythology what he called an arkite idolatry, pointing to Noah's deluge and the ark.

arkless ('ɑːklɪs), *a.* [f. ARK *sb.* + -LESS.]

1819 BYRON *Proph. Dante* I. 24 The arkless dove.

arkose (ɑː'kəʊs). *Geol.* A sandstone containing grains of felspar and quartz, found in the Vosges.

1839 MURCHISON *Silur. Syst.* I. xxix. 375 The 'arkose' of central France. **1879** RUTLEY *Stud. Rocks* xiv. 280 Amongst the carboniferous and triassic rocks of some countries a sandstone occurs to which the name Arkose is given.

arksutite ('ɑːksuːtaɪt). *Min.* [f. (1866) *Arksut* fiord in Greenland, where found + -ITE.] A white, vitreous fluoride of lime, soda, and alumina.

1868 DANA *Min.* 128.

arle (ɑːl), *v. north.* [f. ARLES. Cf. Fr. *arrher*.] To give earnest-money to or for.

1609 SKENE (JAM.) All gudes, quhilkis ar forestalled, coft, or arled be forestallers. **1663** BLAIR *Autobiog.* iv. (1848) 66, I arled you with a sixpence which yet you have.

arled, *ppl. a. Obs.* [Mätzner suggests for *arred*.] ? Speckled.

c **1250** *Gen. & Ex.* 1724 Sep or got, hafwed, arled, or grei.

arles (ɑːlz). *north. dial.* Also 3–7 erles. [Apparently a. OF. **erle*, **arle*:—L. **arrhula* dim. of ARRHA. Cf. also OF. *erres, arres*, mod. *arrhes*:—L. *arrha*. Historically a plural, but sometimes used as sing.; the formal sing. *arle* is hardly in use.]

1. Money given in confirmation of a bargain; *esp.* that given, when a servant is hired, in confirmation of the engagement; earnest-money.

1540 *Act Jas. V.* (JAM.) Gif ony maner of persoun gefis arlis or money on ony maner of fische. **1652** *MS. Grassman's Bk. at Durham* (Raine), Spent when we hired the hird, 1s. Given him in arles, 6d. **1674** *Ch. Accts. Bedlington Northld.*, Given the smith in arles for the bell, 1s. **1691** BLOUNT *Law Dict.*, *Argentum Dei*..Money given in Earnest of a Bargain: In Lincolnshire called Erles, or Arles. **1816** SCOTT *Old Mort.* xxiii. 166 Ye gae me nae arles, indeed.

2. *fig.* An earnest, a foretaste.

c **1220** *Hali Meid.* 7 As on erles of þe eche mede þat schal cume þ[e]rafter. *c* **1425** WYNTOUN *Cron.* VIII. xxvii. 21 (JAM.) This was bot erlys for to tell Of infortune, that eftyr fell. **1513** DOUGLAS *Æneis* XI. Prol. 160 Wyth grace in erlis of glore.

3. arles-penny is used in the prec. senses.

1590 BRUCE *Serm. Sacram.* S ij a/2 (JAM.) The heart gets a taist of the swetnes..quhilk taist is the only arlis-penny of that full and perfite joy. **1794** BURNS *My Tocher's, etc.* Wks. IV. 309 Your proffer o' luve's an airle-penny.

arlice, -liche, -ly, obs. forms of EARLY.

† **'arling.** *Obs.* [OE. *eorðling* 'agricola,' f. *eorðe* earth. Cf. 'clod-bird,' and 'fallow-smiter.'] A species of bird; the Wheatear.

c **1000** ÆLFRIC *Gloss.* in Wright *Voc.* 29/2 *Tanticus*, ærðling. *Ibid.* 281/1 *Cucuzata*, irþling..*Birbiccariolus*, irþling. *a* **1100** *Ibid.* 63/1 *Birbicaliolus*, eorðling. **1544** TURNER *Avium Hist.* 44 *Κυανός*, *Cæruleo*, a clotburd, a smatche, an arlyng, a steinchek. **1580** BARET *Alv.* A 544 Arling, a byrde that appeareth not in winter: a clotbyrde: a smatch. **1655** MOUFFET & BENN. *Health's Impr.* (1746) 185 The..Arling is as big almost as a Thrush, feeding chiefly upon Cherries. **1753** CHAMBERS *Cycl. Supp.*, *Arlyng*..a name by which the common œnanthe is called.

arlotrie, obs. form of HARLOTRY.

arloup, obs. form of ORLOP (deck).

arm (ɑːm), *sb.*[1] Forms: 1- **arm**, 1-3 (WS.) **earm**, 2-3 **erm**, (**eorm**), 3 **ærm**, (*Orm.*) **arrm**, **arum**, 4-7 **arme**. [Common Teutonic: cf. OS. *arm*, OFris. *arm*, *erm*, OHG. *aram*, *arm*, ON. *armr*, Goth. *arms*:—OTeut. **armoz*, cogn. w. L. *armus* shoulder; cf. Gr. *ἀρμός* joint, Skr. *īrmas*, f. Aryan root *ar-* to fit, join.]

I. The limb.

1. a. The upper limb of the human body, from the shoulder to the hand; the part from the elbow to the hand being the *fore-arm*.

c **950** *Lindisf. Gosp.* Luke ii. 28 He onfeng him on armum his. **1123** *O.E. Chron.* (Laud MS.) Se kyng..alehte hine betwux his earmes. *c* **1200** ORMIN 7616 [He] himm toc bitwenenn armmess. **1205** LAY. 28035 þat mi riht ærm to-brac. *Ibid.* 2233 He heo mid armen i-nom. *c* **1220** *Ureisun* in *Cott. Hom.* 213 Mi leofmonnes luft erm halt up min heaued. *a* **1300** *Havelok* 2408 Smot him þoru þe riht arum. **1377** LANGL. *P. Pl.* B. XIV. 241 Hondes and armes of a longe lengthe. **1489** CAXTON *Faytes of Armes* I. ix, Heue vp his armes for to smyte edgelyng. **1611** SHAKS. *Cymb.* II. iv. 101 She stript it from her Arme. **1785** COWPER *Task* IV. 222 The basket dangling on her arm. **1802** PALEY *Nat. Theol.* viii. (1827) 455 The fore-arm..consists of two bones lying alongside each other, but touching only towards the ends.

b. as a measure of length.

1572 BOSSEWELL *Armorie* II. 86 Popiniayes..exceedinge in lengthe an arme and an halfe.

2. *phr.* **a.** ***arm-in-arm*** (improperly *arm-and-arm*): said of two persons, when one interlinks his arm with the other's, that they may walk close together; hence *fig.* in close communion. Also *attrib.* (So humorously ***arm-in-armly***.) ***to give*** or ***offer one's arm*** (***to***): to allow *or* invite a person to walk arm-in-arm with one, or lean on one's arm. ***to take the arm*** is to accept this invitation. ***a child, baby***, or ***infant in arms***: one that cannot yet walk, and has to be carried. ***with open arms***: with eager welcome. † ***his arms!*** an obsolete oath.

c **1374** CHAUCER *Troylus* II. 1067 They wenten arme in arme yfere Into the gardyn. *a* **1553** UDALL *Roister D.* II. i, Then, his armes and woundes! I woulde not haue slacked for ten thousand poundes. *Ibid.* III. iii, Armes! what dost thou? **1591** HARINGTON *Ariosto's Orl. Fur.* XLVI. xxxv, Don Leon arm in arm Rogero led. *a* **1600** HOOKER *Serm.* i. III. 590 Continually to walk arm in arm with angels. **1735** POPE *Prol. Sat.* 142 With open arm receiv'd one Poet more. **1743** H. WALPOLE *Lett. to H. Mann* 67 I. 246 A clerk who had observed them go out together so arm-in-armly. **1781** COWPER *Charity* 314 Philosophy..Walks arm in arm with Nature all his way. **1819** KEATS *Let.* 24 Sept. (1958) II. 215 A child in a[r]ms was passing by his chair toward the mother, in the nurses a[r]ms. **1837** CARLYLE *Fr. Rev.* II. II. IV. iii. 10 A thickset Individual..arm-and-arm with some servant. **1848** THACKERAY *Van. Fair* lxvii. 618 You are no more fit to live in the world than a baby in arms. **1862** *Sat. Rev.* 633 Brummel..replied, 'I did my best for the young man; I gave him my arm down St. James' Street.' *a* **1885** *Mod.* She took the proffered arm. Children in arms free. **1937** E. GARNETT *Family from One End St.* viii. 146 All the children went half price, the younger ones, with luck, 'in arms'. **1958** G. BARKER *Two Plays* 65 Why, even a Kelk'd be kissing itself This arm-in-arm evening. **1978** *N.Y. Times* 30 Mar. B3/1 Arm-in-arm couples.

b. ***at arm's end*** (obs.), ***at arm's length***: as far out or away from one as one can reach with the arm; *hence*, away from close contact or familiarity, at a distance; *spec.* in *Law*, without fiduciary relations, as those of trustee or solicitor to a client; *(at) arm's length*: *Comm.*, designating a sale or transaction in which neither party controls the other. ***to work at arm's length***: awkwardly or disadvantageously. ***within arm*** (or ***arm's***) ***reach***: so as to be reached by a movement of the arm only. ***to make a long arm*** (colloq.): to reach out the arm a long way after something; see also LONG *a.*[1] 1 c. ***as long as one's arm***: colloq. for 'very long'.

1580 SIDNEY *Arcadia* (J.) Such a one as can keep him at arms end, need never wish for a better companion. *a* **1652** BROME *Crt. Beggar* I. i, A man May come within his armereach of his money In the Exchequer. **1655** GURNALL *Chr. in Arm.* xiv. (1669) 108/1 The Moabites could not give Israel the fall at arms-length. **1669** PENN *No Cross* xiii. §18 Live loose to the World, have it at Arm's-End. *a* **1704** T. BROWN *Praise Pov.* Wks. 1730 I. 96 No Penelopes..to keep importunate suitors at arms-end. **1714** SWIFT *Pres. State Aff.* Wks. 1755 II. I. 220 To stand at arm's length with her majesty. **1846** J. F. COOPER *Redskins* (1888) xii. 198 Leases as long as my arm, I calcerlate? **1856** KANE *Arct. Exp.* II. vii. 79 Wood..piled within arm-reach. **1857** H. MELVILLE *Confidence-Man* vi. 39 A fellow with a face as long as my arm. **1858** LD. ST. LEONARDS *Handy-bk. Prop. Law* VI. 35 Unless there is perfect fair-dealing, and the dealing is, as it is termed, at arm's-length, it would not be allowed to stand. **1860** TROLLOPE *Framley P.* (1861) II. i. 9 God be with the good old days when I could..make a long arm for a hot potato whenever the exigencies of my plate required it. **1879** T. LEWIN *Trusts* (ed. 7) 441 The parties must be put so much at arm's length that they stand in the adverse relations of vendor and purchaser. **1884** *Daily News* 26 Jan. 6/2 Monkeys..making long arms..for stray beans or sweetmeats. **1938** M. ALLINGHAM *Fashion in Shrouds* xx. 370 Jock has a record as long as your arm. **1961** WEBSTER, *Arm's length*, the condition or fact that the parties to a transaction or negotiation are independent and that one does not dominate the other (sale at arm's length) (arm's length bargaining). **1962** *Taxation of Short-Term Gains* (Cmnd. 1710) 9 Where an asset changes hands as a result of a bargain which is not at arm's length (i.e. generally speaking, at an artificial price) it is normally deemed to pass for its then market value. **1962** *Economist* 8 Dec. 1040/1 Some [companies]..are..'arm's length buyers' of imported crude wherever—and as cheap as—they can get it.

c. Slang phr. ***under the arm***: inferior, poor, bad.

1937 in PARTRIDGE *Dict. Slang* 17/1. **1958** F. NORMAN *Bang to Rights* 31, I read no matter how bad the book and some are right under the arm, stand on me. **1963** *New Statesman* 18 Oct. 537/1 All that's under the arm (i.e. no good).

3. *fig.* **a.** Might, power, authority. ***secular arm***: the authority of a secular or temporal, as distinguished from an ecclesiastical, tribunal.

c **950** *Lindisf. Gosp.* John xii. 18 Arm drihtnes huæm is ædeaued [*Rushw.* eorm]. **1382** WYCLIF *ibid.*, To whom is the arm of the Lord schewid? **1535** COVERDALE *Ezra* iv. 23 And forbad them with the arme and auctorite. **1611** BIBLE *Ezek.* xxx. 21, I haue broken the arme of Pharaoh. **1782** PRIESTLEY *Corrupt. Chr.* II. IX. 145 The relapsed [are] delivered to the secular arm. **1831** BREWSTER *Newton* (1855) II. xviii. 186 No period of his life can be named when his intellectual arm was shortened.

b. That on which one relies for support or assistance; a prop, support, stay. ***right arm***: main stay, chief executive agent.

1382 WYCLIF *Jer.* xvii. 5 Cursid the man that trostith in man, and putteth flesh his arm. **1535** COVERDALE *ibid.*, That taketh flesh for his arme. **1859** TENNYSON *Guinev.* 426 Sir Lancelot, my right arm, The mightiest of my knights.

c. in fig. expressions that attribute *arms* (in various relations) to things that have none.

1597 J. PAYNE *Royal Exch.* 7 He reserved neither legg nor arme of that lyvinge to hym self. ? *a* **1700** *Sir Patrick Spens*, I saw the new moon, late yestreen, Wi' the auld moon in her arm. **1850** TENNYSON *In Mem.* xxi. 18 Science reaches forth her arms To feel from world to world. **1866** B. TAYLOR *Mariners* 290 Cradled in the arms of the tide.

4. a. The fore limb of an animal: said, popularly, of apes, bears, and other animals that rise on their hind legs; in scientific use, of any of the mammalia.

1607 TOPSELL *Four-f. Beasts* (1658) 3 Apes..have..their breasts and armes like men, but rougher. **1781** SMELLIE *Buffon's Nat. Hist.* (1785) V. 14 The bear..has fleshy legs and arms. **1847** CARPENTER *Zool.* §90 The arm and the thigh each present, among all the Mammalia, but one bone. *Ibid.* §330 In Birds..the conformation of the arm and fore-arm differs little from that of the same parts in man.

b. *Falconry.* The leg of a hawk from the thigh to the foot.

1575 TURBERV. *Falconrie* 8 This Eagle Royall..hath not hir armes or feete in any condition couered with plume as the Vulture hath. **1678-1706** in PHILLIPS and in mod. Dicts. under ARM(s *sb.*[2]

c. The flexible limbs or other appendages of invertebrate animals; as the locomotive and prehensile organs of cuttle-fish, the tentacula of the hydroid polypes, the rays of star-fish, etc.

1822 BURROWES *Cycl.* IX. 786/2 the Cuttle-Fish..besides eight arms has two tentacula longer than the arms. **1867** CARPENTER *Zool.* §1043 In the Hydra, the arms vary in number, being usually from six to ten. *Ibid.* §1044 When in search of prey, the Hydra permits its arms to float loosely through the water. **1870** NICHOLSON *Zool.* xix. (1880) 201 The body [of Star-Fishes]..consists of a central..'disc' surrounded by five or more lobes or 'arms.'

5. The part of dress covering an arm; a sleeve.

a **1797** H. WALPOLE *George II.* (1847) III. i. 8 The right arm lined with fur. **1831** CARLYLE *Sart. Res.* III. vi, The Coatarm is stretched out.

II. Things resembling arms.

6. A narrower portion or part of anything projecting from the main body.

a. In *arm of the sea*, of ancient use, and quite *transferred*. **b.** Also of the land (*obs.*), a mountain (*fig.*).

c **885** K. ÆLFRED *Oros.* I. i. §28 On oþre healfe þæs sæs earmes is Ibernia. **1538** LELAND *Itin.* VII. 143 The Marsch Land..runnyng ynto a Poynt standeth as an Arme, Foreland, or Nesse. **1598** HAKLUYT *Voy.* I. 65 The Great sea, out of which the arme of S. George proceedeth. **1724** DE FOE, etc. *Tour Gt. Brit.* (1769) III. 60 That Arm of the Sea which is now called the Humber. *c* **1854** STANLEY *Sinai & Pal.* Introd. (1858) 53 The arms of the mountain closing us in.

c. of a machine, or other object.

1833 BREWSTER *Nat. Magic* v. 110 On a projecting arm..I fixed a broad collar. **1881** GREENER *Gun* 18 The powder-chamber or arm of the bombard is of much smaller diameter.

7. One of the branches into which a main trunk divides. † **a.** *spec.* of a vine. *Obs.* **b.** *fig.* A main branch or limb of any tree (usually with something of personification).

1398 TREVISA *Barth. De P.R.* XVII. cxvi, 'Palmes' is propirly a bowe oþer a spray of a vine, and..sprygeþ oute in newe armes. **1580** LYLY *Euphues* (Arb.) 473 They that feare theyr Vines will make too sharpe wine, must not cutte the armes. **1579** SPENSER *Sheph. Cal.* Feb. 104 A goodly Oake..With armes full strong. **1611** COTGR., *Avantin*, the arme, or braunch of a vine. **1697** DRYDEN *Virg. Georg.* III. 514 Some ancient Oak, whose Arms extend In ample Breadth. **1863** LONGF. *Falc. Federigo* 5 A huge vine..with its arms outspread.

c. of a river, a nerve, or the like.

1330 R. BRUNNE *Chron.* 67 His flete alle pleyn In an arme of Ouse vnder Ricalle lay. **1601** HOLLAND *Pliny* I. 118 The great riuer Tanais, which runneth into Mœotis with two armes or branches. **1846** GROTE *Greece* XX. II. 490 The Pelusian arm of the Nile. **1870** ROLLESTON *Anim. Life* 132 An azygos nerve trunk..which..has two lateral arms.

8. One of two lateral (and generally horizontal) parts, which answer to each other, like the two arms of the body.

a. *Naut.* (*a*) The parts of an anchor, at right angles to its shank, which bear the flukes that grip the bottom. (*b*) The parts of the yard extending on either side of the mast; see YARD-ARM. (*c*) 'The extremity of the bibbs which support the tressel trees' (Smyth *Sailor's Word-bk.* 1867).

1665 PEPYS *Diary* 18 Sept., The yard-arms sticking in the very rocks. **1706** PHILLIPS, *Arm of an Anchor*, that part of it to which the Flook is set.

b. of machines; as of a balance. In a lever: The part or length from the fulcrum to the point of application of the power or weight respectively. (In levers of the *second* and *third* kind, the ***power arm*** and ***weight arm*** are both on the same side.)

1659 LEAK *Water-wks.* 17 The said Levers shalbe also fitted to two arms or branches. **1727-51** CHAMBERS *Cycl.* s.v. *Crane*, The middle and extremity of this [beam] are again sustained by arms from the middle of the arbor. **1866** NEWTH *Nat. Phil.* (1873) 34 It is convenient to describe the perpendiculars drawn from the fulcrum to the directions of the power and the weight as the power's arm and the weight's arm respectively.

9. One of the two rails or projecting supports at the sides of a chair, sofa, etc., on which the arms of one who is using it may rest. See ARM-CHAIR.

1633 [See ARM-CHAIR]. **1859** TENNYSON *Elaine* 437 Two dragons gilded, sloping down to make Arms for his chair. **1882** J. HAWTHORNE *Fort. Fool* xiv, The chairs and sofas having curved and arabesqued backs, legs, and arms.

III. *Comb.* and *Attrib.*, as ***arm-badge***, ***-eddre*** (= vein), ***-glove***, ***-linked***, ***-sweep***, ***-twister***, ***-wrist***. Also **arm-band**, a band worn round the arm; **arm-bone**, the bone of the arm, the *humerus*; † **arm-circle**, **arm-coil**, a bracelet, an armlet; **arm-cylinder**, a cylindrical ornament worn on the arm; † **arm-gaunt** *a.*, (meaning not certainly known) ? with gaunt limbs; † **arm-great** *a.*, as large round as an arm; **arm-guard**, (*a*) in *Boxing*, defence with the arm; (*b*) a protective covering for the arm; † **arm labour**, manual labour; **arm-lock**, a close hold by the arm in wrestling and judo; also *v. trans.* (*nonce-wd.*); **arm-piece**, armour to protect the arm; **arm-rest**, a device constructed for the arm to rest upon; **arm-ring**, an ornamental ring worn on the arm; an armlet; † **arm-slasher**, one who cuts his arm to get blood with which to drink his mistress' health; † **arm-strong** *a.*, strong of arm; **arm-twisting** (orig. *U.S.*), (persuasion by) the use of moral pressure, force, or threats of physical violence (cf. TWIST *v.* 9e); **arm-wrestling** = *wrist-wrestling* s.v. WRIST 5 d; also **arm-wrestle** *v. intr.*, to engage in arm-wrestling. See *arm's-end*, *-length*, *arm-reach*, under 2 b. Also ARM-CHAIR, -HOLE, -PIT, ARMFUL, ARMLESS, q.v.

1931 A. P. HERBERT *Derby Day* III, The policeman's helmet and *arm-badge are on the table as he is off duty. **1797** B. HAWKINS *Let.* 26 Nov. (1916) 253 The goods he wants are..3 pair *arm bands, 3 pair wrist bands. **1846** T. L. MCKENNEY *Memoirs* I. 178, I opened a box and took out a pair of silver arm-bands. **1906** *Yorks. N. & Q.* III. 101/1 A fragment of a jet arm-band was found on the same horizon. **1922** D. H. LOW tr. *Ballads of Marko Kraljević* 135 On his feet two fetters, On his arms two armbands. **1952** *Manch. Guardian Weekly* 21 Feb. 5/1 After them came the Sheffield's officers, in white uniforms with black armbands. *a* **1639** ABP. SPOTISWOOD *Ch. & St. Scotl.* (1677) 5 The *Arm-bone, three Fingers, and as many Toes of St. Andrew. **1851** RICHARDSON *Geol.* viii. 308 In the anterior extremities we find an arm-bone. **1382** WYCLIF *Ecclus.* xxi. 24 As an *arm-cercle in the riȝt arm. **1866** LIVINGSTONE *Jrnl.* iii. (1873) 68 *Arm-coils of thick brass wire. **1937** *Antiquity* XI. 114 The axes, dagger, and *arm-cylinder of the Danish hoard. **1957** CHILDE *Dawn Europ. Civ.* (ed. 6) v. 69 From Asia came an arm-cylinder of twisted silver wire (like a gold one from Troy II) found in a grave on Levkas. c 1230 *Ancr. R.* 258 Hwon heo beoð ileten blod on one *erm eddre. 1606 SHAKS. *Ant. & Cl.* I. v. 48 Did mount an *Arme-gaunt Steede. 1816 SCOTT *Old Mort.* xi, Mounted upon his arm-gaunt charger. 1740 C'TESS HARTFORD *Corr.* (1806) II. 127 Black velvet *arm-gloves. c 1386 CHAUCER *Knts. T.* 1290 A wreth of gold *arm-gret. c 1420 *Pallad. on Husb.* III. 412 An *arme greet withi bough. 1889 MICHELL *Boxing* 148–9 Figure ix, Left *arm guard. *Ibid.* 156 Right arm guard. 1899 *Daily News* 20 June 3/5 Two massive gold arm-guards, set with..diamonds. 1677 YARRANTON *Engl. Improv.* 185 Will draw more Wire in one day, than six men can..by *arm labour. 1839 BAILEY *Festus* vi. (1848) 53 A shadow not thine own *armlinked with mine. 1905 A. M. BINSTEAD *Mop Fair* vi. 102 Whose simple faith in all mankind has been mercilessly *arm-locked and thrown clear off the mat. 1905 F. R. TOOMBS *How to Wrestle* (1906) 61 (*caption*) The Near Leg Hold and Arm Lock. 1956 K. TOMIKI *Judo* 127 Kansetsu-waza..*ude-hishiji* (armlock) and *ude-garami* (entangled armlock). 1844 MARG. FULLER *Wom. in 19th C.* (1862) 86 A golden helmet and *arm-pieces. 1889 *Cent. Dict.*, *Arm-rest. 1898 SLOANE *Stand. Elect. Dict.* App., *Arm rest*, a device for lessening the fatigue of holding a telephone receiver to the ear. 1908 *Daily Chron.* 12 Mar. 5/6 The deceased's head was..over the mouth of the barrel, which was leaning against the arm-rest. 1962 *Which?* (Suppl.) July 91/2 This measurement excludes the permanent centre armrest in the two sports cars. 1903 W. B. YEATS *In Seven Woods* 49 I'll give you gifts, but I'll have something too An *armring or the like. 1933 E. E. EVANS-PRITCHARD *Ess. Social Anthrop.* (1962) vii. 143 Azande.. made a pact by drinking water from a gourd which contained an iron arm-ring. 1611 COTGR., *Taille-bras*, A hackster, *arme-slasher. c 1000 ÆLFRIC *Gloss.* in Wright 43 *Torosus*, *earm-strang. 1589 GREENE *Menaphon* (Arb.) 56 Alcides, the arme-strong darling of the doubled night. 1856 MRS. BROWNING *Poems* II. 276 Like a fly..By queen Juno brushed aside, a Full white *arm-sweep, from the edge. 1938 *New Statesman* 8 Jan. 58/2 A great *arm-twister, and the sort of man who ought never to have been born. 1967 K. GILES *Death in Diamonds* ix. 164 A brute and a bully, an arm-twister and a threatener. 1957 *Newsweek* 30 Dec. 31/3 *Arm twisting is used to induce 'wavering elements, petty bourgeois, and the non-productive' to sign 'voluntary petitions' for rural service. 1963 W. H. MISSILDINE *Your Inner Child of Past* xi. 106 We are so accustomed to overly coercive attitudes that arm-twisting, demanding commercials on television and anxiety-arousing articles in the press seem right to us. 1984 *Listener* 23 Aug. 9/1 Diplomatic pressure..would be accompanied by the selective use of South African economic and military arm-twisting. 1971 J. WAMBAUGH *New Centurions* xii. 209 When he got to the latticework he peered through and saw two young men, long sideburned twins with chain belts, *arm wrestling on a swaying table with a burning candle at each side of the table to scorch the back of the loser's hand. 1973 [see *wrist-wrestling* s.v. WRIST 5 d]. 1978 *Globe & Mail* (Toronto) 14 Aug. 5/1 The muscled gladiators who prevailed..will represent Canada on Sept. 16 at Worlds of Fun Amusement Park in Kansas City, at the World Professional Armwrestling Association championships. 1986 P. BOOTH *Palm Beach* ii. 39, I remember the time when your ol' man and your granpappy set to arm wrestling on the bar. 1656 HEYLIN *Two Journ.* 42 Hands and *arme-wrists free from scabs.

arm, *sb.*[2] Commonly in *pl.* **arms** (ɑːmz). Forms: 3–7 **armes** (5 **-is**, **-ys**), 6– **arms**, 8– **arm**. [a. F. *armes*, Pr. *armas*:—L. *arma* (no sing.) 'arms, fittings, tackle, gear'; from root *ar-* to fit, join. The sing. *arm* is late and rarely used.]

I. *pl.* Defensive and offensive outfit for war, things used in fighting.

1. Defensive covering or appendages for the body; armour, mail. Now only *poet.*

1340 *Ayenb.* 165 Þe cloþinge ne makeþ naȝt þane monek, ne þe armes þane knyȝt. 1382 WYCLIF *Eph.* vi. 11 Clothe ȝou with the armer [*v.r.* armes] of God. c 1400 *Sowdone Bab.* 188 Armed in Stele In armes goode and profitable. 1593 SHAKS. *Rich. II*, III. ii. 114 Clap their female ioints In stiffe vnwieldie Armes. 1718 POPE *Iliad* II. 200 Once more refulgent shine in brazen arms. 1872 TENNYSON *Gareth* 908 These arm'd him in blue arms.

2. a. Instruments of offence used in war; weapons. ***fire-arms***: those for which gunpowder is used, such as guns and pistols, as opposed to *swords*, *spears*, or *bows*. ***small-arms***: those not requiring carriages, as opposed to *artillery*. ***stand of arms***: a complete set for one soldier.

a 1300 *K. Horn* 516 Þin armes he haþ and scheld To fiȝte wiþ upon þe feld. 1382 WYCLIF *John* xviii. 3 He cam with lanternis, and brondis, and armys. 1484 CAXTON *Ordre Chyv.* viii. 61 b, He ought not to trust in his armes, ne in his strengthe. 1650 T. B. *Worcester's Apophth.* 97 They were come to search his house for Armes. 1710 *Lond. Gaz.* mmmmdccviii/2 The remaining 12,500 Arms not already contracted for. *Ibid.* mmmmdccii/2 Powder, small Ball, and small Arms. 1777 MARION in *Harper's Mag.* Sept. (1883) 546/1 To parade with their side arms. 1794 TRUSLER *Eng. Synon.* I. 37 By *arms*, we understand those instruments of offence generally made use of in war; such as firearms, swords, etc. By *weapons*, we more particularly mean instruments of other kinds (exclusive of fire-arms), made use of as offensive on special occasions. 1870 *Instr. Musketry* 7 Each lesson in cleaning arms..to occupy half an hour.

b. *sing.* A particular species of weapon; (cf. *a wine*, *a sugar*, *an ash*).

1861 SIR W. FAIRBAIRN *Addr. Brit. Assoc.*, A rifled small arm and gun which have never been surpassed. 1877 *World* No. 178. 11 An extraordinarily well-balanced arm, and highly effective.

3. ***man of arms***, later ***man-at-arms***: **a.** one practised in war, a warrior, soldier; **b.** a fully-armed knight. ***man-in-arms***: an armed man.

1393 GOWER *Conf.* III. 2 He is a noble man of armes. 1489 CAXTON *Faytes of A.* I. xi, The proprietes that men of armes ought to haue. c 1590 MARLOWE *2nd Pt. Tamburl.* III. i, I have a hundred thousand men-in-arms. 1593 SHAKS. *3 Hen. VI*, v. iv. 42 And make him, naked, foyle a man at Armes. 1598 BARRET *Theor. Warres* v. ii. 141 The Man at Armes is armed complete. *Ibid.*, Men at Armes are commonly men of title and qualitie. 1611 BIBLE *Transl. Pref.* 2 For the loue that he bare unto peace..iudged to be no man at armes. 1670 COTTON *Espernon* III. xi. 580 Worth the pains, or notice of men of Arms. 1855 KINGSLEY *Heroes* iv. 57 The men-at-arms drew their swords and rushed on him.

4. In many phrases. **a.** ***to arms!*** (formerly [OFr.] ***as armes! at arms!***): take to your arms, be ready for fight! **b.** ***in arms***: armed, furnished with weapons, sword in hand, prepared to fight; as ***to rise in arms*** (of a number); ***up in arms***, in active readiness to fight, actively engaged in struggle or rebellion; also *fig.* **c.** ***to take up arms***: to arm oneself, rise in hostility defensive or offensive, to draw the sword; also *fig.* ***to bear arms***: to serve as a soldier, do military service, fight. ***to turn one's arms against***: to make war upon, attack. ***to lay down arms***: to surrender, cease hostilities, give up the struggle.

a. 1330 R. BRUNNE *Chron.* 162 Richard, 'has armes!' did crie. c 1380 *Sir Ferumb.* 2933 'Asarmes!' þanne cride Rolond, 'asarmes, euerechon!' c 1450 *Merlin* xxii. 406 And ronne to armes moo than xxvii squyers. c 1450 LONELICH *Grail* xiii. 231 Anon, 'As Armez,' they gonnen to crie. 1470–85 MALORY *Arthur* I. xi. (1634) 22 'Lords, at arms! for here be your enemies at your hand.' 1711 POPE *Rape Lock* v. 37 'To arms! to arms!' the fierce Virago cries. 1842 MACAULAY *Horatius* xx, To arms! To arms! Sir Consul.

b. 1503 HAWES *Examp. Virtue* vii. 97 Whan in armes..He all his ennemyes dyd abiecte. 1588 SHAKS. *L.L.L.* v. ii. 636 Heere comes Hector in Armes. 1593 —— *2 Hen. VI*, IV. i. 93 Hating thee, and rising vp in armes. 1611 BIBLE *1 Macc.* xii. 27 Ionathan commaunded his men..to be in armes. 1704 SWIFT *T. Tub* Apol., All the men of wit..were immediately up in Arms. 1810 SCOTT *Lady of L.* III. xiv, In arms the huts and hamlets rise. 1868 *Digby's Voy. Medit.* Pref. 32 As soon as the facts came to the knowledge of the Admiralty.. Buckingham's Secretary was up in arms.

c. 1297 R. GLOUC. 63 Alle þat armes bere Aȝen þe king. c 1590 MARLOWE *Massac. Paris* III. i, The Guise hath taken arms against the King. 1602 SHAKS. *Ham.* III. i. 59 To take Armes against a Sea of troubles. 1769 ROBERTSON *Charles V*, V. III. 329 Obliged to take arms in self-defence. *Ibid.* V. IV. 410 He turned his arms against Naples. 1795 SEWELL *Hist. Quakers* I. Pref. 7 For bearing arms and resisting the wicked by fighting. 1831 BREWSTER *Newton* (1855) II. xiv. 2 Newton took up arms in his own cause. 1848 ST. JOHN *Fr. Rev.* 245 Lay down your arms. 1872 YEATS *Growth Comm.* 180 Albuquerque turned his arms towards Ormuz.

5. Also in the mod. phrases: ***under arms*** (of troops); bearing arms; standing or marching arms in hand, in battle array; so, ***to lie upon their arms. stand to your arms!*** i.e. in order of battle with arms presented. For the various military words of command, ***Order arms***, ***Port arms***, ***Present arms***, ***Shoulder arms***, ***Slope arms***, ***Trail arms***, etc., see the respective verbs.

1697 DRYDEN *Virg. Georg.* III. 537 Thus, under heavy Arms, the Youth of Rome Their long laborious Marches overcome. 1710 *Lond. Gaz.* mmmmdccxv/2 Obliged to halt and lye all Night on their Arms. 1777 ROBERTSON *Hist. Amer.* (1783) II. 265 In a moment the troops were under arms. 1847 GLEIG *Waterloo* 275 The Anglo-Belgian army lay on its arms in the field which its valour had won. *Ibid.* 108 No cry of 'Stand to your arms!' or other notices expressive of danger near at hand. a 1850 ROSSETTI *Dante & Circ.* (1874) I. 8 The whole city got under arms.

II. Elliptical senses. (Only *pl.* exc. in 9.)

6. The exercise or employment of arms; fighting, war, active hostilites. †***to bid arms*** (obs.): to offer battle. ***to carry arms***: to wage war. ***to appeal to arms***: see APPEAL *v.* 6 b.

c 1374 CHAUCER *Anel. & Arc.* 1 Fiers god of armes Mars the rede. c 1590 MARLOWE *2nd Pt. Tamburl.* II. ii, An hundred Kings, by scores, will bid him arms. 1662 DRYDEN *Astræa Red.* 4 Worser far Than arms, a sullen interval of war. 1711 STEELE *Spect.* No. 2 ¶3 It is a barbarous Way to extend Dominion by Arms. 1720 OZELL *Vertot's Rom. Rep.* I. IV. 236 Her Arms were carried abroad. 1780 HARRIS *Philol. Enq.* (1841) 478 Success in arms. 1790 BEATSON *Nav. & Mil. Mem.* I. 4 A cessation of arms having been agreed on. 1847 GLEIG *Waterloo* 297 There shall be a suspension of Arms.

7. The practice or profession of arms, service as a soldier, the military profession.

c 1450 LONELICH *Grail* lii. 1077 Whanne to harmes that he cam, He wax a worthy chevalrows man. 1475 CAXTON *Jason* 78 b, He accorded..and putte hym anone to armes. 1489 —— *Faytes of Armes* I. i, The right honorable offyce of armes & of chyualrye. 1591 SHAKS. *1 Hen. VI*, II. i. 43 Since first I follow'd Armes. 1596 SPENSER *F.Q.* I. iv. 1 Young knight, what euer that dost armes professe. 1814 SCOTT *Wav.* vi, To take up the profession of arms.

8. a. Deeds or feats of arms. Now only *poet.*; *deeds*, *feats*, etc. being expressed in prose.

c 1384 CHAUCER *H. Fame* 144, I wol now synge yif I kan The Armes and also the man That first cam of Troy Contree. 1485 CAXTON *Paris & V.* (1868) 35 [They] made grete chyualryes & dyd grete armes. 1697 DRYDEN *Æneid* I. 1, Arms and the man I sing, who, forced by fate, etc. [1711 ADDISON *Spect.* No. 309 ¶13 Contentions at the Race, and in Feats of Arms.]

b. *phr.* ***a passage of*** (or ***at***) ***arms***: an exchange of blows by armed opponents, an encounter; also *fig.* a controversial bout. ***an assault of*** (or ***at***) ***arms***: an attack made upon each other by two fencers, etc., as an exercise or trial of skill; and, in a wider sense, a display of hand-to-hand military exercises. See PASSAGE, ASSAULT.

1824 TREVELYAN in *Macaulay's Life* I. iii. 136 His connection with the Review was that passage of arms. 1857 HUGHES *Tom Brown* II. v. (1876) 269 An account of his passage-at-arms with the only one of his school-fellows whom he ever had to encounter in this manner.

9. *sing.* and *pl.* **a.** Each kind of troops of which an army is composed: the infantry, cavalry, artillery, and engineers; originally, the two first. ***of all arms***: of every description of troops. (So in Fr.) Also used of other branches of the armed forces, esp. the air force (often called ***the fourth arm***). See FLEET *sb.*[1] 1 d.

1798 CRAIG in *Wellesley, Desp.* (1877) 605 Abounding in cavalry, and acting in a country the most favourable to that arm. 1829 SOUTHEY *Inscr.* xxx. Wks. III. 142 Nor force of either arm of war, nor art of skilled artillerist. 1842 ALISON *Hist. Eur.* X. lxvi. §69. 182 The supposition that the English had no heavy artillery..The English general had already secured that vital arm. 1847 GLEIG *Waterloo* 101 They numbered about 12,000 of all arms. 1879 in *Cassell's Techn. Educ.* III. 267 The three so-called 'arms' of the service; the infantry, the cavalry, and the artillery. 1908 H. G. WELLS *War in Air* iv. 106 The Emperor..placed him in control of the new aeronautic arm of the German forces. 1914 *Engineering* 4 Sept. 312/2 Aircraft in Warfare: the Dawn of the Fourth Arm. By F. W. Lanchester. 1916 [see AERONAUTICAL *a.*]. 1917 [see AIR *sb.*[1] B. III. 3]. 1919 [see *aerial arm*]. 1940 *Ann. Reg. 1939* 62 This was the first occasion on which the Civil Defence Forces had been recognized as a Fourth Arm.

b. *transf.* and *fig.* A branch of an organization, movement, company, etc., not necessarily or usually military. (Freq. with defining word.)

1952 C. I. GLICKSBERG in *Amer. Lit. Crit.* 50 The failure of the so-called Marxist critics to take the aesthetic properties of literature into account, thus making literature serve utilitarian and ulterior ends as an arm of propaganda. 1968 *Time* 17 May 66 The Institute for Defense Analyses, a civilian research arm of the Government. 1976 *Survey* Summer–Autumn 303 The Mau Mau movement had hardly any external diplomatic arm. 1985 *Oxford Times* 20 Dec. 9/5 It is primarily a training unit, not a fund-raising arm of the Spastics Society.

III. Transf. and fig. senses. (Usually *pl.*)

10. in *Law.* (See quot.)

1641 *Termes de la Ley* 51 Arms, in the understanding of the Law, is extended to any thing that a man, in his anger or fury, takes into his hand to cast at, or strike another. [So in BLOUNT, TOMLINS, etc.]

11. Instruments of defence or offence possessed by animals; the ARMATURE or ARMOUR of plants.

1711 ADDISON *Spect.* No. 121 ¶3 That great Variety of Arms with which Nature has differently fortified the Bodies of..Animals, such as Claws, Hoofs, and Horns.

12. a. *fig.* (from 2) of things immaterial.

c 1230 *Ancr. R.* 60 Eien beoð..te ereste armes of lecheries pricches. 1340 *Ayenb.* 170 Þe armes of penonce, huerby he may ouercome his y-uo. 1616 BRENT *Counc. Trent* (1629) 756 Which would bee as much as to put Armes into the hands of the heretikes. 1646 SIR T. BROWNE *Pseud. Ep.* I. iii. (1686) 7 Unable to wield the intellectual arms of reason. 1872 FREEMAN *Norm. Conq.* IV. xvii. 90 And had himself fought, perhaps with temporal, certainly with spiritual arms.

b. *sing.*

1762 GIBBON *Misc. Wks.* (1814) V. 259 He employed every arm both of argument and pleasantry.

†**c.** (from 1) *collect.* as *sing.* 'Armour.' *Obs.*

1646 H. LAWRENCE *Comm. & Warre w. Angels* 141 An armes fitted on purpose.

13. (*sing.*) Protection, guard. [Perh. from ARM *v.*[1]]

c 1374 CHAUCER *Troylus* II. 1601 For I woll have no wite To bring in prease, that myht done him harme, Or him diseasen, for my better arme.

IV. Heraldic Arms.

14. a. Heraldic insignia or devices, borne originally on the shields of fully armed knights or barons, to distinguish them in battle (hence properly called ARMORIAL bearings), which subsequently became hereditary, and are the property of their families. Also the similar ensigns of countries, corporations, trading companies, etc.

1330 R. BRUNNE *Chron.* 8 Þe lond lese þe armes, changed is þe scheld. c 1384 CHAUCER *H. Fame* 1331 Al these armes that ther weren That they thus on her cote beren. 1489 CAXTON *Faytes of Armes* IV. xv. 274 The lordes in a bataylle myght be known by his armes. a 1553 UDALL *Roister D.* III. iv, By the armes of Caleys, it is none of myne. 1587 FLEMING *Contn. Holinshed* III. 369/2 The heralds of armes dooing him such honour. 1589 *Pappe w. Hatchet* Biij, His armes shalbe set on his hearse. 1601 CORNWALLYES *Ess.* xxv, They can find Titles as fast as Heralds devise Armes. 1611 GUILLIM *Heraldry* I. iii. 2 Armes are tokens or resemblances signifying some act or quality of the bearer. 1655 FULLER *Ch. Hist.* II. iv. §40 I. 313 The ancient Armes were assigned to Oxford about this time. 1787 PORNY *Heraldry* 243 Three lions passant gardant..the Royal Arms of England. 1794 TRUSLER *Eng. Synon.* II. 31 Heraldry is the science of arms. 1864 BOUTELL *Hist. Heraldry* xiv. 136 The lawful holder of Arms has in them a true estate in fee.

b. *collective* as *sing.*

c 1590 MARLOWE *Edw. II*, II. ii. 1035 What is thine arms? 1607 TOPSELL *Four-f. Beasts* 68 This the reason why the Romans gave such an arms.

15. Hence the phrases, ***in arms with***: quartered with. † ***to give arms*** (obs.): to show or exhibit armorial bearings. Also *to bear arms*; *to grant* or *assign arms*. *coat of arms*: (see ARMOUR *sb.* 10.) *College of Arms*: the Heralds' College, by which armorial bearings are granted. *King at Arms*: a Chief Herald.

1466 *Test. Ebor.* (1855) II. 278 With all my doghtirs in armes with thair husbandis apon my right syde, and with all my sones and thair wifes in armes apon my left side. *c* **1590** MARLOWE *2nd Pt. Tamburl.* III. v, Now you are a King, you must give arms. **1599** GREENE *George a Gr.* (1861) 259 We are gentlemen. *Geo.* Why, sir, So may I, sir, although I give no arms. **1642** BP. MOUNTAGU *Acts & Mon.* 489 Advanced to the Title of a Lord or Baron; permitted to beare Arms. **1647** R. STAPYLTON *Juvenal* 250 *note*, A coate of Armes cut in a pretious Sardonix stone. *a* **1649** DRUMM. OF HAWTH. *Hist. Jas. V*, Wks. 81 Lyon king of arms is directed to him, to acquaint him with their proceedings. **1671** F. PHILLIPS *Reg. Necess.* 468 Mr. William Dugdale, Norroy King at Armes. **1808** SCOTT *Marm.* IV. vii, Sir David Lindesay of the Mount, Lord Lion king-at-arms.

V. *Comb.* and *Attrib.* in sense I, as *arms-bearing*, *arm-chest*, *arms-control*, *-dump* (DUMP *sb.*[4] 1 c), *arm-rack*, *arms-smuggler*, *-store*, *town*; in sense IV, as *arms-painter*; **arms race**, competition between unfriendly nations or other groups in the accumulation and development of weapons.

1639 FULLER *Holy War* V. xix. (1840) 274 Employ all their arms-bearing people in their martial service. **1678** BUTLER *Hud.* III. i. 142 Upon their sharing In any prosperous arms-bearing. **1823** BYRON *Island* II. xx, As when the arm-chest held its brighter trust. **1961** *Economist* 14 Jan. 109/2 Their preferred term, 'arms control', embraces not only disarmament by controlled agreement but also such measures as the banning of nuclear tests. **1939** 'N. BLAKE' *Smiler with Knife* xi. 168 She knew there was an arms-dump beneath Major Keston's house. **1827** *Gentl. Mag.* XCVII. II. 51 One Lilly an armes-painter and pedigree maker. **1936** *Hansard Commons* 5th Ser. CCCIX. 1842 This House cannot agree to a policy which in fact seeks security in national armaments alone and intensifies the ruinous arms race between the nations, inevitably leading to war. **1937** *Daily Express* 20 Apr. 2/7 Arms Race Worry... All were worried at the armament race. **1938** AUDEN & ISHERWOOD *On Frontier* II. ii. 78 The arms race is good for another five years at least. **1964** *Ann. Reg. 1963* 138 In a speech of 10 June.. Mr. Kennedy called for a halt to the arms race. **1844** *Regul. & Ord. Army* 337 To prevent the arm-racks being damaged. **1937** KOESTLER *Spanish Test.* 24 A spy or an arms smuggler or a foreign agent. **1899** *Westm. Gaz.* 3 Mar. 5/1 A number of artillerymen were removing a quantity of ammunition from one arms-store to another. **1944** *Ourselves in Wartime* 95 The attack on Coventry was the forerunner of similar attempts to smash the arms towns.

†**arm**, *a.* *Obs.* Forms: 1–3 **arm(e**, **earm**, 2 **erm(e**, 3 **ærm**, **areme**. [Common Teutonic: cogn. w. OS. *arm*, OFris. *erm*, *arm*, OHG. *aram* (mod.G. *arm*), Goth. *arms*, ON. *armr*.]

1. Poor, needy.

c **1000** *Ags. Gosp.* Mark xii. 42 Þa com án earm wuduwe. *c* **1200** *Moral Ode* 227 Edi men and arme. **1205** LAY. 23941 Auere ælche ærmen [**1250** neod-fol] mon, þe æð scal iwurðen.

2. Miserable, wretched.

1104 *O.E. Chron.* (Laud MS.) Eall þis wæs..þas arme leode mid to treȝienne. *c* **1175** *Lamb. Hom.* 27 Drieð his erme saule in eche pine. **1205** LAY. 14893 Alre kinge si he ærmest. *a* **1250** *Owl & Night.* 1160 Both sori and areme.

arm (ɑːm), *v.*[1] [a. F. *arme-r*:—L. *armā-re*, f. *arma*: see ARM *sb.*[2]]

1. *lit.* To furnish with arms defensive or offensive. In early use, *chiefly*, To cover (a man or horse) with armour or mail; *now*, To provide (a man, garrison, stronghold, ship, etc.) with weapons.

1205 LAY. 15313 [He] lette ærmi his cnihtes. **1250** *Ibid.* 8655 Ac armede his cnihtes. *c* **1330** *Arth. & Merl.* 5937 On hors y-armed and well atired. *c* **1400** *Destr. Troy* VII. 3197 Þai armyt hom at all peces, abill to werre. *c* **1420** *Avow. Arth.* xxiv, Quen thou art armut in thi gere, Take thi schild and thi spere. **1611** BIBLE *Gen.* xiv. 14 He armed [COVERDALE, harnessed] his trained seruants. **1716** *Lond. Gaz.* mmmmmccccxc/2 Stores for Rigging and Arming another Man of War. **1771** *Junius Lett.* lix. 308 The only case in which the king can have a right to arm his subjects in general. **1847** GLEIG *Waterloo* 280 To arm the whole population of the country, and fight to the last extremity.

b. in *Falconry*, etc.

1575 TURBERVILLE *Falconrie* 161 When he hath armed or cased the hearons tronke with a cane or reed. **1801** STRUTT *Sports & Past.* III. vii. 250 The arming their [fighting cocks'] heels with sharp points of steel is a cruelty.

†c. *to arm out* (a ship): to fit out with arms. (Also *intr.* for *refl.*: see 4.) *Obs.*

1670 MARVELL *Corr.* 152 Wks. 1875 II. 334 That he must ..arme out fifty great ships the next Spring. **1687** *Lond. Gaz.* mmccc/5 Three Gallies..and several low Boats that arm out in the Summer.

2. Hence, in many transferred and fig. uses; as: *to arm* (a person) a. with requisite tools or appliances for any work; b. with qualities, attributes, offensive or defensive.

1340 *Ayenb.* 180 Þet hauberk of penonce huermide God armeþ his newe knyȝt. *a* **1586** SIDNEY *Sonn.* in Arb. *Garner* II. 170 Armed with beauty. **1611** SHAKS. *Cymb.* I. vi. 19 Arme me, Audacitie, from head to foote! **1647** WARD *Simp. Cobler* 52 To arme your minde with patience of proofe. **1711** STEELE *Spect.* No. 113 ¶4 She will arm herself with her real Charms, and strike you with Admiration. **1860** TYNDALL *Glac.* I. §12. 88 Each of us was..armed with his own axe.

c. (an animal) with natural organs of offence or defence.

1607 TOPSELL *Four-f. Beasts* 30 Being armed with teeth on both sides, like a saw. **1664** POWER *Exp. Philos.* I. 2 Nature having armed him [the Flea] thus Cap-a-pe. **1711** ADDISON *Spect.* No. 121 ¶2 A Creature so armed for Battle and Assault as the Lion. **1815** KIRBY & SP. *Entomol.* (1843) I. 336 Three or four similar but smaller aculei arm the head.

d. (a thing) with appendages requisite or effective, or with any preparation fitting it for work.

1534 LD. BERNERS *Gold. Bk. M. Aurel.* (1546) K k b, They haue aredyed the mylle, and armed it with stones of encreace. **1653** WALTON *Angler* 110 First you must arm your hook. **1689** MOYLE *Sea Chyrurg.* II. v. 40 Dip your Dorcells ..squeeze them, then arm them with your Restringent. **1761** STERNE *Tr. Shandy* III. xvi. 71 The points of my forceps have not been sufficiently arm'd. **1787** T. BEST *Angling* 13 For setting on the hook, or more scientifically speaking, arming it, use strong but small silk.

e. To prepare (for resistance, action, etc.).

1590 SHAKS. *Mids. N.* I. i. 117 Arme your selfe To fit your fancies to your Fathers Will. **1601** —— *All's Well* I. ii. 11 He hath arm'd our answer, and Florence is deni'de before he comes. [See ARMED 2.]

3. *refl.* (in prec. senses.)

c **1300** *Beket* 2230 This lithere Kniȝtes, armeden hem eft sone. *c* **1386** CHAUCER *Sec. Nonnes T.* 385 Armith you in armur of brightnes. **1489** CAXTON *Faytes of Armes* III. xxii, Neuermore shulde arme hym self aienst the King of France. *a* **1602** PERKINS *Cases Consc.* (1611) 291 To arme our selues with patience.

†b. Of a horse. (see quot.) *Obs.*

c **1580** BLUNDEVIL in *Lit. Times* (1863) 14 Mar., He [the horse]..will arm hymselfe and run away. **1611** in COTGR. **1751** CHAMBERS *Cycl.* s.v., A horse is said to arm himself, when he presses down his head, and bends his neck, so as to rest the branches of the bridle upon his brisket.

4. *intr.* for *refl.* To arm oneself, take up arms.

c **1400** *Sowdone Bab.* 491 Arise vp..And armes anone, every wight. **1599** SHAKS. *Hen. V*, II. iv. 49 Princes, looke you strongly arme to meet him. **1605** —— *Macb.* V. v. 46 Arme, arme, and out. **1779** BURKE *Corr.* (1844) II. 303 It certainly cannot be right to arm in support of a faction, though it is most laudable to arm in favour of our country. **1852** TENNYSON *Penny-wise* in *Morn. Chron.* 24 Jan., Is this a time to cry for peace, When we should shriek for rifles? Arm, arm, arm!

†b. To set traps. *Obs.*

1574 HELLOWES *Gueuara's Epist.* 19 The pastime..of Arthabanus king of Hircans was to arme for rats. **1591** PERCIVALL *Sp. Dict.*, *Armar*, to arme, prepare, set a snare.

c. *to arm against*: to take defensive or precautionary measures against.

1727 SWIFT *What passed in Lond.* Wks. 1755 III. I. 187 A pestilential malignancy in the air..which might be armed against by proper and timely medicines.

5. *trans.* To plate (*with* anything) for strength; to furnish with any protective covering.

1398 TREVISA *Barth. De P.R.* V. lix. (1495) 175 The grystill..armyth the endes of the bones. **1627** SMITH *Seaman's Gram.* xiv. 67 To Arme a shot..for fear of bursting the Peece, which is to binde a little Okum in a little Canuasse at the end of each Pike. **1692** *Ibid.* II. xxxi. 150 The Cases..must be Armed about with strong Twine. **1697** DRYDEN *Virg. Georg.* I. 220 First Ceres..arm'd with Iron Shares the crooked Plough. **1854** WOODWARD *Man. Mollusca* (1856) 29 The gizzard is armed with numerous small plates.

6. To furnish (a magnet) with an armature.

1664 [see ARMED *ppl. a.*[1]]. **1727–51** CHAMBERS *Cycl.* s.v., The best way to arm a loadstone. **1832** U.K.S. *Nat. Phil.*, *Magnet.* v. §214 For this purpose it should be armed, as it is called; that is, an armature of iron should be applied to both its poles. **1837** WHEWELL *Hist. Induct. Sc.* XII. i, The increased energy which magnets acquire by being armed.

7. *Her.* See ARMED: also *fig.*

1590 TARLETON *Newes out of Purg.* 76 He armes the asse with a marvellous paire of long and large Ears. The emblason, etc.

†8. *Cookery*, To dress, garnish, season *with*. *Obs.*

c **1440** *Anc. Cookery* in *Househ. Ord.* (1790) 439 Craunes and Herns shall be armed with larde.

arm (ɑːm), *v.*[2] [f. ARM *sb.*[1]]

†1. To take in one's arms. *Obs. rare.*

1611 SHAKS. *Cymb.* IV. ii. 400 Come, Arme him.

2. To give one's arm to, conduct by walking arm-in-arm with. See ARM *sb.*[1] 2.

c **1612** *Two Noble Kinsm.* V. iii. 135 Arm your prize: I know you will not lose her. **1675** WYCHERLEY *Plain Dealer* II. (1735) 51 To arm her to her lawyer's Chambers. **1871** *Daily News* 11 Feb., Assiduously arming along the crowded street this shambling half-blind old woman.

3. To put one's arm round.

1863 W. LANCASTER *Præter.* 59 The princess arm'd his neck.

†4. *intr.* To project like an arm. *Obs.*

1538 LELAND *Itin.* VII. 143 The Marsch Land beginneth to nesse and arme yn to the Se.

armada (ɑːˈmɑːdə, formerly ɑːˈmeɪdə). Also 6–7 **armado**, 7 **armatho**, **armade**, 7–8 **armata**. [a. Sp. *armada*, cogn. w. Eng. ARMY (used in same sense), F. *armée*, It. *armata*:—L. *armāta*, pa. pple. of *armā-re* to ARM, used in Rom. langs. as sb. = 'armed force, army, navy, fleet.' At first used in erroneous form *armado*; also in the adapted form *armade* (see -ADO and -ADE), and It. form *armata*.]

1. A fleet of ships of war.

†α. in forms *armado*, *armade*. *Obs.*

1533 M. KYNG in Ellis *Orig. Lett.* II. 108 II. 46 The Turks Armado was before Coron. **1590** SHAKS. *Com. Err.* III. ii. 140 Spaine..sent whole Armadoes of Carrects to be ballast at her nose. **1604** EDMONDS *Observ. Cæsar's Comm.* 56 Such huge armades, as appeareth by the sea fight with the maritimate cities of Gallia. **1697** DAMPIER *Voy.* (1729) I. 27 When the Armado lyeth at Portabell.

†β. in form *armada*.

1599 HAKLUYT *Voy.* II. 217 These ships be..guarded with the Armada of the Portugals. **1606** HOLLAND *Sueton.* Annot. 11 The sumptuous Armada of Antonie and Cleopatra was defaited. **1809** J. BARLOW *Columb.* VII. 547 The matcht armadas still the fight maintain. **1815** SCOTT *Ld. Isles* V. xiii, South and by west the armada bore.

†γ. in form *armata*. *Obs.*

1683 T. SMITH *Observ. Constant.* in *Misc. Cur.* (1708) III. 46 He puts to Sea with his Armata of Gallies. **1697** *Phil. Trans.* XIX. 661 The great Defeat given the Turkish Armata..by the Venetians. **1753** CHAMBERS *Cycl. Supp.*, *Armada* or *Armata*.

2. *spec.* The 'Invincible Armada' sent by Philip II of Spain against England in 1588.

1588 D. ARCHDEACON *Of the Armie* 14 The forces of the Spaniards, this their great Armado. **1603** *Eng. Mourn. Garm.* in *Harl. Misc.* (1793) 205 The Spaniards, having their armatho ready. **1641** MILTON *Reform.* II. (1851) 69 The proud Ship-wracks of the Spanish Armado. **1860** MACAULAY (*title*), The Armada. **1864** BURTON *Scot Abr.* I. iv. 187 Within eighteen months after the death of Mary, the Armada was in the Channel.

†3. A single large war-vessel. *Obs.*

1586 *Lanc. Lieuten.* II. 177 Viij armadoes or greate shippes. **1662** FULLER *Worthies* III. 84 He sunk and took nine Spanish ships, whereof one was an Armada of 600 Tunn.

4. An armament generally.

1728 MORGAN *Algiers* I. iv. 153 The mighty Armadas set on Foot by the Saracen Khalifas. **1837** LYTTON *Athens* II. 121 Nor was the naval unworthy of the land armada.

‖**armaˈdilla**. *Obs.* Also -illo. [Sp., dim. of *armada*; like that erroneously with *-o*.] a. A small fleet of ships of war. b. A small war-vessel.

1697 DAMPIER *Voy.* (1729) I. 30 In company of 11 Armadilloes, which are small Vessels of War. **1753** CHAMBERS *Cycl. Supp.*, *Armadilla*, in the Spanish America, denotes a squadron of men of war, to the number of six or eight.

armadillo (ɑːməˈdɪləʊ). Also 6–8 **armadillio**, 7 **-ilio**, **-ile**, 7–8 **-illa**. [a. Sp. *armadillo*, dim. of *armado* one armed:—L. *armātus*, pa. pple. of *armar*:—L. *armāre* to ARM. The spellings *-illio*, *-ilio*, represented the Sp. pronunciation; *armadile* was perh. from Fr. As a 16th c. word, the plural is historically in *-oes*, but *-os* is now usual.]

1. Name of several species of burrowing animals (order *Edentata*), peculiar to South America; specially distinguished by the bony armour in which their whole body is encased, and by the habit of rolling themselves, when captured, into an impregnable ball, sheltered by this armour.

1577 FRAMPTON *Joyf. Newes* II. 73 b, He is called the Armadillo, that is to saie a beaste armed. **1594** BLUNDEVIL *Exerc.* V. xii. 555 The beast Armadillio is found in the Realme of Mexcio. *a* **1618** RALEIGH *Apol.* 37 Tortoyses, Armadiles. **1764** WATSON *Armadilla* in *Phil. Trans.* LIV. 57 Called by naturalists the American Armadilla. **1781** SMELLIE *Buffon's Nat. Hist.* (1785) V. 362 The armadillos, instead of hair, are covered..with a solid crust. **1834** SIR C. BELL *Hand* 51 Ant-eaters, armadilloes and sloths have this bone [the clavicle]. **1868** WOOD *Homes without Hands* i. 42 All the Armadillos..are mighty burrowers.

2. *transf.* A genus of small terrestrial Crustacea (order *Isopoda*), allied to the wood-louse; so called after the preceding, because they have the power of rolling themselves into a ball, so as to expose nothing but the plates of the back.

1847 CARPENTER *Zool.* §799. **1859** WOOD *Com. Obj. Countr.* iv. 65 Formerly the armadillo was used in medicine, being swallowed as a pill in its rolled up state.

armado, obs. variant of ARMADA.

Armageddon (ɑːməˈgɛdən). [See Rev. xvi. 16 (A.V.)] The place of the last decisive battle at the Day of Judgement; hence used allusively for any 'final' conflict on a great scale. Also *attrib.*

1811 SHELLEY *Let.* 12 Jan. (1964) I. 45 Do we not now see Superstition decaying..except where Faber..and several others of the Armageddon-Heroes maintain their posts. **1886** SUFFOLK & CRAVEN *Racing* 247 As long as we have racing we shall have betting—that ceaseless war between layers and backers will still be waged... At present we see no sign of a final Armageddon. **1896** KIPLING *England's Answer* in *Poems* (1919) I. 237 In the day of Armageddon, or the last great fight of all. **1910** *Encycl. Brit.* II. 561/1 From the application of the word Armageddon to the great battle of the End of Time comes the use of the phrase 'an Armageddon' to express any great slaughter or final conflict. **1917** F. M. FORD *Let.* 5 Jan. (1965) 83, I am sure you could not have done a better 'bit' during Armageddon. **1928** W. DEEPING *Old Pybus* ii. §2 Mr. Pybus had been able to speak of the war as Armageddon without cribbing an obvious bleat from the popular press.

Armagnac (ɑːˈmænjæk). A superior brandy made in the district of France formerly called Armagnac (department of Gers).

1850 A. K. JOHNSTON *Dict. Geogr.* 539/2 Gers, a dep. in the S.W. of France... Wine is produced..and a good deal of it is converted into Armagnac brandy. **1910** *Encycl. Brit.* XI. 904/2 The remainder [of the wine produced in the department of Gers] is chiefly manufactured into brandy, known by the name of Armagnac, second only to Cognac in reputation. **1920** SAINTSBURY *Notes on Cellar-bk.* 119 You may drink Armagnac after Burgundy now and they won't quarrel.

armalcolite (ɑːˈmælkəʊlaɪt). *Min.* [f. the names of the three U.S. astronauts Neil *Arm*strong, Edwin *Al*drin, and Michael *Col*lins who brought the sample from the moon + -ITE[1].] An orthorhombic titanate of magnesium and iron, $(Mg,Fe^{2+})Ti_2O_5$, first discovered in lunar rocks.

1970 A. T. ANDERSON et al. in *Proc. Apollo 11 Lunar Sci. Conf.* I. 55 Armalcolite ($Fe_{0.5}Mg_{0.5}Ti_2O_5$), a new magnesium-rich opaque oxide related to the pseudobrookite series, was discovered independently by six research groups in their examination of different samples of the lunar material collected from Mare Tranquillitatis. *Ibid.* 56 Armalcolite is opaque, gray and distinctly pleochroic. **1973** *Times* 28 Sept. 7/5 Moon samples of armalcolite..were first analysed in the United States in 1969. Armalcolite has been since found in great abundance on the Moon's surface by the Apollo 17 astronauts. **1975** *Physics & Chem. of Earth* IX. 305 The first terrestrial occurrence of armalcolite..is reported from DuToitspan [in South Africa]. **1978** PASACHOFF & KUTNER *University Astron.* xiv. 398 (*caption*) A crystal of armalcolite..examined under a polarization microscope.

ArmaLite (ˈɑːməlaɪt). orig. *U.S.* Also **Armalite, armalite.** [f. ARM *sb.*[2] + *-a-* + *-lite* (alteration of LIGHT *a.*[1]).] A proprietary name (in the U.S.) for a type of small-bore weapon. Freq. as ***Armalite rifle.***

1958 *Official Gaz.* (U.S. Patent Office) 4 Mar. TM5/1 ArmaLite. For small bore weapons comprising pistols, rifles, and carbines. **1966** *Courier-Mail* (Brisbane) 17 Sept. 11/2 The US armalite rifle is to go on..issue to all Australian Army battalions and training units. *Ibid.*, Armalite ammunition. **1978** K. WARNER *Pract. Bk. Guns* ix. 99/1 There are those who can convince themselves that such items as the Armalite AR-180 in 223 are utility guns. **1980** *Washington Post* 28 June B1/6 The weapon believed used in both shootings was a Colt AR15 rifle, Colt AR15 carbine or Armalite AR180 rifle. **1985** *Economist* 27 Apr. 34 In 1982 Sinn Fein..decided to fight through the ballot box as well as with its Armalite rifles.

armament (ˈɑːməmənt). [ad. L. *armāmentum* (in cl. L. only in pl.), f. *armāre* to ARM: see -MENT. Prob. after F. *armement* (16th c. in Littré).]

1. A force military or (more usually) naval, equipped for war. Also *fig.*

1699 LUTTRELL *Brief Rel.* IV. 506 To..make a report of what sea armaments are making there. **1718** POPE *Iliad* XX. 153 To guard his life..We, the great armament of heaven came down. **1831** CARLYLE *Sart. Res.* III. v, That boundless Armament of Mechanisers and Unbelievers threatening to strip us bare. **1866** KINGSLEY *Herew.* xvii. 207 William's whole armament had crossed the channel.

2. Military equipments, munitions of war: *spec.* the great guns on board a man-of-war.

1721 BAILEY, *Armament*, a Store-house for Arms; also the Arms and Provisions of a Navy. **1740** JOHNSON *Drake* Wks. IV. 456 To view the ship, with the warlike armaments. **1877** *Echo* 25 Oct. 1/5 Their armament will consist of 12 guns.

3. *gen.* Equipment or apparatus for resistance or action of any kind.

1870 LOWELL *Among my Bks.* Ser. I. (1873) 91 How far above all modern armament is his prophylactic against his insubstantial fellow-lodger. [**1880** N. KERR in *Med. Temp. Jrnl.* July 153 Ergot and other obstetric *armamenta.*]

4. The process of equipping for purposes of war.

1813 SOUTHEY *Nelson* ii. (1854) 71 During the armament which was made upon occasion of the dispute concerning Nootka Sound. **1868** H. F. BOURNE *Eng. Seamen* II. 13 With the armament of the navy, Hawkins had not much to do.

5. *attrib.*

1914 W. RALEIGH *Let.* 5 Dec. (1926) II. 407 One has to think of public gains, the private gains being not very obvious except to..armament syndicates. **1919** G. B. SHAW *Peace Conference Hints* vii. 107 Hegemonies are impossible, and attempts at them certain to end in armament races and finally in war. **1936** *Hansard Commons* 5th Ser. CCCIX. 1851 They were engaged in the same armaments race, piling up more and more armaments.

armamentarium (ˌɑːməmɛnˈtɛərɪəm). [L., lit. 'arsenal, armoury'; see ARMAMENTARY.] The equipment of medicines, instruments, and appliances used by a medical man. Also *transf.* and *fig.*

1874 ROOSA *Dis. Ear* 171 The ordinary armamentarium of the surgeon. **1906** V. HORSLEY in S. Paget *Life* (1919) 236 A whole armamentarium of drugs. **1935** *Nature* 7 Sept. 385/1 The pituitary body provides the brain with an armamentarium of hormones, which are secreted in several ways.

†**armaˈmentary.** *Obs. rare.* [ad. L. *armāmentārium* arsenal, f. *armāmentum*: see ARMAMENT and -ARY.] An armoury, an arsenal; *transf.* (in L. form) a case of (surgical) apparatus.

1731 in BAILEY. **1753** CHAMBERS *Cycl. Supp.* s.v. *Armourer*, There were fifteen Armamentaries, or repositories of arms, in the eastern empire.

arman (ˈɑːmən). ? *Obs.* [Fr.] 'A confection for restoring appetite in horses.' J.

1639 in T. DE GREY *Compl. Horsem.* 66. **1706** PHILLIPS, *Arman*, a Confection for Horses, made of Honey of Roses, Crums of White Bread, Powder of Nutmegs and Cinnamon, etc.

arˈmarian. [f. med.L. *armāri-us* = *custos bibliothēcæ* Du Cange (f. med.L. *armāria*: see ARMARY) + -AN.] See quot. (App. never used in Eng.)

1849 *Chamb. Jrnl.* No. 276, 239 *Armarian*, an officer in the monastic libraries who had charge of the books to prevent them from being injured by insects, and especially to look after bindings. He had also to keep a correct catalogue.

†**arˈmariol.** *Obs.* [ad. L. *armāriolum*, dim. of *armārium* a storehouse, closet. The forms *almariol, armoriol*, follow med.L. spellings. Cf. AMBRY.] A little closet or cabinet.

1807 J. T. SMITH *Antiq. Westm.* 204, 12 March [26 Edw. III]..a certain almariole in the vestry for keeping the vestments in. *Ibid.* A certain armoriol within the king's chapel.

†**ˈarmary, -ie.** *Obs.* [ad. L. *armārium* 'place for arms or tools (*arma*), chest, closet, ambry,' used in med.L. (also in form *armaria* after It. and Fr.) esp. for 'bookcase, library.'] For the history of the word, see its extant representative, AMBRY. The latinized *armary* is used by Wyclif for 'library,' and occas. in 16th c. as = ARMOURY.

1382 WYCLIF *Ezra* iv. 15 Thou shalt find write in armaries. **1538** LELAND *Itin.* IV. 54 [The] White Tour, wherein is now the Kinges Armary. [**1731** BAILEY, *Armary*, a tower.]

‖**arˈmata.** It. form of ARMADA, freq. in 17th c.

armature (ˈɑːmətjʊə(r)). [ad. L. *armātūra* armour (perh. through 15-16th c. Fr. *armature*), f. *armāt-* ppl. stem of *armāre* to ARM: see -URE. The same L. word coming down through OF. *armeure*, is now ARMOUR *sb.*]

1. Arms, armour, military accoutrement; *esp.* defensive armour.

1669 GALE *Crt. Gentiles* I. ii. v. 65 Mars was the first who furnished armature. **1699** *Phil. Trans.* XXI. 165 Swords, Daggers, or the like sort of Armiture. **1830** GEN. P. THOMPSON *Exerc.* (1842) I. 340 Take for example the armature of the Infantry..Pay, clothing, food..and armature with the common musquet. **1850** BLACKIE *Æschylus* II. 243 Massy armature of shields.

2. *fig.* esp. in Theol. lang. [Cf. Vulg. *Eph.* vi. 11 *Induite armaturam Dei*; Wyclif 'armure,' Tindale 'armoure.'] (The earliest use in Eng.)

1542 BECON *Pathw. Prayer* (1843) 144 Prayer is truly called a..heavenly armature. **1682** SIR T. BROWNE *Chr. Mor.* (1756) 34 Not the armour of Achilles, but the Armature of St. Paul. **1865** BUSHNELL *Vicar. Sacr.* III. iii. (1868) 269 That armature of strength upon his feeling that enables him to inflict pain without shrinking.

†**3.** Armed troops. (So in Lat.) *Obs.*

1609 HOLLAND *Amm. Marcell.* XIV. xi. 26 Captaine of the Armature [*Armaturarum Tribunus*]. **1765** TUCKER *Lt. Nat.* I. 474 We mean no attacks either upon your battalion or light armature.

4. The art of protecting with armour, or with defensive materials.

1611 GUILLIM *Heraldrie* IV. viii. 207 For by Armature we vnderstand not onely those things which appertaine to Military profession, but also those defensiue Sciences of Masonry and Carpentry and Metall works. **1721** BAILEY, *Armature*, Armour; also Skill in Arms.

5. *transf.* Protective or defensive covering of animals or plants; *occas.* apparatus of attack.

1662 MORE *Antid. Ath.* II. viii. (1712) 64 His [a horse's] Hoofs are made so fit for..that round armature of Iron. **1713** DERHAM *Phys.-Theol.* IV. xii. 221 Some with Scales, some with Shells, and some with firm and stout Armature. **1816** KEITH *Phys. Bot.* II. 76 Armature..to defend the plant against the attack of animals. **1861** HULME *Moquin-Tandon* II. vii. iv. 353 Having its mouth provided with a corneous armature. **1874** WOOD *Nat. Hist.* 631 Destroying them with the terrible armature called the tooth-ribbon.

6. a. *Magnetism.* A piece of soft iron placed in contact with the poles of a magnet, which preserves and increases the magnetic power; or any arrangement which produces the same result. †**b.** *Electr.* The coatings of tinfoil on the inside and outside of a Leyden jar (*obs.*; in Fr.).

1752 JOHNSON *Rambl.* No. 199 ¶13 The efficacy of the magnet..depends much upon its armature. **1871** tr. *Schellen's Spectrum Anal.* §11. 33 And the magnet, becoming weaker, lets loose the armature.

7. a. *Arch.* 'Iron bars or framing employed in the consolidation of a building.' Parker *Conc. Gloss. Arch.* 1846. (So in Fr.)

b. A framework of wire, wood, etc., round which a sculptor builds a clay or plaster model.

1903 E. LANTERI *Modelling* II. 137 (*caption*) Armature in Twisted Copper Wire. **1947** J. C. RICH *Materials & Methods of Sculpture* ii. 29 Armatures constructed of flexible metal wire, pipe or tubing are very often employed as artificial 'skeletons' or supporting structures over which the 'flesh' or clay is formed and shaped. *Ibid.* 35 There are several types of armatures available commercially for use as supports in modeling heads, busts, and figures.

8. a. *Electr.* [from 6 a.] A core of laminated iron wound round by coils of insulated copper wire in which an electrical current is generated when it rotates in a magnetic field (as in a dynamo), or which, when a current is passed through the wire, provides the motive power (in a motor). Also applied to the moving member in any electromagnetic device, as a relay, electric bell, etc.

1835 W. STURGEON in *London & Edin. Phil. Mag.* Sept. 233, I produce electric shocks..by revolving coils of wire (having an iron axis or armature) in front of the poles of a horse-shoe magnet. **1902** *Encycl. Brit.* XXVII. 575/1 Since these inductors are very commonly mounted on an iron structure, which may be likened to the keeper or 'armature' of a magnet rotating between its poles, the term 'armature' has been extended to cover not only the iron core, but also the wires on it, and is often applied to the copper conductors themselves even when there is no iron core. **1922** GLAZEBROOK *Dict. Appl. Physics* II. 198/1 Alternators are made in almost all cases with the armature stationary, and the field revolving. **1931** *Boys' Mag.* XLV. 157/1 The aerial wires are connected to opposite sides of the buzzer interrupter, one to the fixed contact and the other to the pillar carrying the vibrating armature.

b. *attrib.* and *Comb.*

1884 F. KROHN tr. *Glaser de Cew's Magn.- & Dyn.-Electric Mach.* 34 The armature-bobbins revolve as near the magnetic poles as possible. *Ibid.* 247 The employment of only half as many inducing magnets as of armature magnets. **1902** J. BLACK *Illustr. Carp. & Build. Techn. Man.* II. vii. 79 The winding of the armature conductors inside insulating tubes. **1902** *Encycl. Brit.* XXVII. 580/1 The separate small sections of the armature winding. **1908** *Daily Chron.* 24 Aug. 9/6 Armature winder wanted. **1910** *Encycl. Brit.* VIII. 768/1 The iron armature core must be laminated. **1934** *B.B.C. Year-Bk.* 172 An alarm..operates in the event of the occurrence of a leakage between either armature winding and the armature iron.

armazine, variant of ARMOZEEN.

ˌarm-ˈchair, armchair Also 7-8 armed-chair. [f. ARM *sb.*[1], ARMED *ppl. a.*[2]] A chair with arms: see ARM *sb.*[1] 9. **b.** *attrib.*, in the home; hence domesticated, comfortable; often applied to persons who confine themselves or are addicted to home-made views or criticism of matters in which they take no active part, or of which they have no first-hand knowledge, as ***armchair critic, politician, travel(ler).***

1633 H. COGAN *Pinto's Voy.* lvi. 218 Born in Pallaquins or Arm-chairs. **1693** *Lond. Gaz.* mmdcccxlv/2 The Commissioners went to the two Armed Chairs placed for them. **1795-9** SOUTHEY *Sonn.* xv. Wks. II. 97 Seated in thy great arm'd chair. *c* **1840** ELIZA COOK, I love it, I love it, and who shall dare To chide me for loving that old arm-chair? **1858** *Househ. Words* 10 July 82/1 Gentler heads and hands have been at work there since, or that county would not rejoice in its line of 'arm-chair cobs'. **1878** BROWNING *Poets of Croisic* xcvii, Arm-chair moodiness. **1886** *Times Register Events 1885* cxxxii, Mr. Chamberlain..met the expostulations..of his moderate allies with sneers at..'the arm-chair politicians'. **1895** W. JAMES *Let.* 12 Oct. in R. B. Perry *Tht. & Char. W.J.* (1935) II. 9 As an arm-chair professor, I frankly admit my great inferiority as a laboratory-teacher and investigator. **1896** W. H. S. AUBREY *Stock Exch. Investm.* i. 5 The arm-chair critic of politics, war, literature, or finance. **1902** *Lond. Q. Rev.* Jan. 70 Even to the armchair traveller the perusal of this Handbook would..suffice to attest the reality of the transformation of the..province. **1914** *Eng. Rev.* Sept. 259 Arm-chair strategists. **1914** E. A. POWELL *Fighting in Flanders* vi. 133 After..the arm-chair historians have settled down to the task of writing a connected account of the campaign. **1935** *Economist* 19 Jan. 128/1 The book is perhaps a little too encyclopaedic for armchair reading, but it will be very valuable as..a source of reference. **1936** *Discovery* Aug. 259/2 Armchair travel becomes easier and more pleasant every day. **1952** C. DAY LEWIS tr. *Virgil's Aeneid* XI. 246 We don't want big talk from an armchair critic.

arme, obs. spelling of ARM, ARMY, HARM.

armed (ɑːmd, ˈɑːmɪd), *ppl. a.*[1] [f. ARM *v.*[1]]

1. *lit.* Furnished with arms or armour; fully equipped for war. In *intensive phr.* 'Armed to the teeth.' In ***armed demonstration, neutrality***, it refers to the persons or power making the demonstration or remaining neutral. ***armed camp***, used of any territory regarded as fully armed ready for war.

1297 R. GLOUC. 386 Þe knyȝtes wel yarmed wende hem out anon. **1375** BARBOUR *Bruce* XI. 96 Armyt clenly at fut and hand. *c* **1425** *Seven Sages* (P.) 1417 Armyd men by nyght thareȝede. **1596** SPENSER *F.Q.* I. ii. 12 A faithlesse Sarazin, all armde to point. **1695** *Anc. Const. Eng.* 37 Who had the armed Force of the Nation on his side. **1695** *Lond. Gaz.* mmmcii/3 Half Galleys and other Armed Boats. **1776** GIBBON *Decl. & F.* I. 323 The caprice of an armed multitude. **1790** BEATSON *Nav. & Mil. Mem.* I. 329 An armed ship of ten guns. **1849** COBDEN *Speeches* 12 Is there any reason why we should be armed to the teeth. **1864** BRAMWELL in *Morn. Star* 12 Jan., By 'armed,' I suppose it would be meant ordinarily that she had cannon, but if she had a fighting crew, muskets, pistols, powder, shot, cutlasses, and boarding appliances, she might be well said to be equipped for warlike purposes, though not armed.

1861 M. B. CHESNUT *Diary* 15 Aug. (1949) 111 This appalling picture of New York as an *armed camp. **1898** *Daily News* 6 Oct. 5/7 The armed camp, which we call the continent. **1876** GREEN *Short Hist.* iii. §7. 150 *An armed demonstration drove them in flight over sea. 1780 J. Adams *Let.* 2 May in F. Wharton *Revol. Diplom. Corr.* (1889) III. 646 The invitation of the Empress of Russia to accede to an *armed neutrality. c1803 Foster *Corr.* 42 (1846) I. 242 Social decorum is a kind of armed neutrality. 1827 [see neutrality 1]. 1906 W. James *Coll. Ess. & Rev.* (1920) 462 Pragmatism, according to Papini, is thus only a collection of attitudes and methods, and its chief characteristic is its armed neutrality in the midst of doctrines.

2. *transf.* and *fig.* **a.** Of persons: Furnished, fortified, provided, ready.

c1585 Pilkington *Wks.* (1841) 444 A man forewarned is half armed. 1588 Shaks. *L.L.L.* i. i. 22 If you are arm'd to doe, as sworne to do. 1737 Pope *Hor. Epist.* i. i. 94 He's armed without that's innocent within. 1831 Carlyle *Sart. Res.* i. ix, A Defender of Property.. armed with the terrors of the law.

b. Of animals: Furnished with horns, teeth, etc., or protected by natural mail.

1596 Shaks. *1 Hen. IV*, iii. ii. 102 The Lyons armed Iawes. 1605 —— *Macb.* iii. iv. 101 The arm'd Rhinoceros, or th' Hircan Tiger. 1803 G. Shaw *Zool.* IV. 373 Armed Chætodon.. Native of the Indian seas. 1859 Owen *Classif. Mamm.* 76 Formidably armed jaws.

c. Of plants: Furnished with thorns, prickles, etc.

1875 Buckland *Log-Bk.* 45 A seed literally armed with formidable claws.

d. Of things: Furnished, plated, cased, tipped, with anything that gives strength or efficiency, or fits for a purpose. ***armed eye***: one provided with a magnifying glass.

1598 Barret *Theor. Warres* i. i. 4 The strength of the Battaile is the armed Pike. 1599 Shaks. *Hen. V*, iv. vii. 83 Wounded steeds.. Yerke out their armed heeles at their dead masters. 1711 Pope *Rape Lock* ii. 120 Tho' stiff with hoops, and armed with ribs of whale. 1816 Coleridge *Lay Serm.* 319 The fixed stars, which appear of the same size to the naked as to the armed eye. 1853 De Quincey *Sp. Mil. Nun* §6. 12 With her armed finger (ay, by the way, I forgot the thimble). 1858 J. Mansfield in *Merc. Mar. Mag.* V. 20 The armed lead would have shown him that.. he was deviating from his.. course. 1878 Huxley *Physiogr.* xvi. 261 The lead is armed, that is to say, the bottom of the weight.. is covered with tallow.

3. Of a magnet: Furnished with an armature.

1664 Power *Exp. Philos.* iii. 176 We took a very good arm'd Loadstone. 1730 Savery in *Phil. Trans.* XXXVI. 309 That an armed Loadstone can lift more. 1831 Brewster *Optics* x. 93 An armed natural loadstone.

4. Adorned with heraldic devices; blazoned.

c1394 *P. Pl. Crede* 183 Tombes.. Of armede alabaustre.

5. *Her.* Having the claws or talons painted of a different tincture from that of adjoining parts. *Also*, represented with claws, teeth, horns, etc.

1572 Bossewell *Armorie* ii. 44 A Lyon Passante, Gules, armed, and langued d'Azure. 1661 Morgan *Sph. Gentry* i. v. 59 Membred doth signify the legs, and Armed doth imploy the Bill and Claws. 1663 Butler *Hud.* i. ii. 259 Armed, as Heraulds cant, and langued, Or, as the Vulgar say, sharp fanged. 1763 *Brit. Mag.* IV. 238 An eagle.. sable, armed and membered, or. 1866 Cussans *Gram. Heraldry* 29 A lion is armed of its teeth and claws, and 'langued' of its tongue.

armed, *ppl. a.*[2] [f. arm *sb.*[1] + -ed[2].] Having arms; fitted with arms. (Chiefly in *comb.*, as *long-armed*; and in *armed-chair*: see arm-chair.)

a1625 Beaum. & Fl. (in Webster) Her shoulders broad and long, armed long and round. 1791 Cowper *Iliad* v. 896 Juno the white-arm'd. 1878 Gurney *Crystallog.* 27 An equal-armed cross.

armee, obs. spelling of army.

armelin, var. ermelin, *Obs.*: see ermine.

Ar'meniac, *a.* [ad. L. *Armeniacus*, Gr. Ἀρμενιακός: see next and -ac.] Armenian. In *bole armeniac*, corrupted to *bole ammoniac*: see next, and cf. ammoniac.

1533 Elyot *Cast. Helth* (1541) 87 Base redde, lyke to bole armenac. 1683 Pettus *Fleta Min.* ii. 6, I find these words of kin.. viz. Amoniack, Armenick, and Armoniack. 1853, 1934 [see Anatolic *a.*].

Armenian (ɑːˈmiːnɪən), *a.* and *sb.* [f. L. *Armenia*, Gr. Ἀρμενία, a country east of Asia Minor.]

A. *adj.* Of or pertaining to Armenia or the Armenians. ***Armenian bole***: a pale red-coloured earth from Armenia, used medicinally, and in the composition of tooth-powders. ***Armenian stone***: a blue carbonate of copper, formerly administered as an aperient and as a remedy for epilepsy.

[1621 Burton *Anat. Mel.* ii. iv. i. iv, Lapis Lazuli and Armenus because they purge.] 1727-51 Chambers *Cycl.*, Armenian bole is.. prescribed internally against diarrhœas. 1867 Lady Herbert *Cradle L.* iii. 97 The great Armenian Convent at Venice.

B. *sb.* **a.** A native of Armenia. **b.** An adherent of the Armenian Church, one of the oriental christian communities.

1598 Greenwey *Tacitus Ann.* xiii. viii, The Armenians being doubtfull, and faithfull to neither side. 1875 Scrivener *Text New Test.* 106 The Armenians of the orthodox faith.

c. The Indo-European language of Armenia.

1718 [see Turkish *sb.* 1]. 1817 Byron *Let.* 2 Jan. (1846) 336/1 Padre Paschal, with some little help from me.. is also proceeding in a MS. Grammar for the *English* acquisition of Armenian, which will be printed also. 1847 E. Riggs (*title*) A vocabulary of words used in modern Armenian. 1910 *Encycl. Brit.* II. 571/2 Armenian lost its genders long before the year A.D. 400.

Armeno-, used as comb. form of *Armenia* or *Armenian* (L. *Armenius*, Gr. Ἀρμένιος).

1898 P. Geddes in *Ethical World* 12 Mar. 167/1 The Turcophobes and Turcophiles, the Hellenophobes and Hellenophiles, Armenophobes and Armenophiles of recent journalism. 1898 *Daily News* 25 Aug. 4/7 The Armenophile movement in England. 1905 *Westm. Gaz.* 15 Nov. 2/1 The Armenophobia of Russian officialdom.

Armenoid (ˈɑːmənɔɪd), *a.* [G. *armenoïd* (F. von Luschan 1892, in *Archiv f. Anthrop.* (*Correspondenz-Bl.*) Oct. 98/2); cf. Armenian and -oid.] Of or pertaining to a type of the Alpine race of ancient western Asia. Also *absol.* and as *sb.*

1899 A. H. Keane *Man, Past & Present* xii. 457 Armenoid, akin to von Luschan's pre-Semitic of Asia Minor. *Ibid.* xiii. 514 E. Chantre constitutes in Western Asia an Armenoid group. 1911 F. von Luschan in *Jrnl. R. Anthrop. Inst.* XLI. 244 When I first upheld in 1892, in my paper on the anthropological position of the Jews, the homogeneous character of these groups, I called them 'Armenoids'. 1934 F. Stark *Valleys of Assassins* ii. 193 This is an Armenoid type of head, with marked flattening of the occiput. 1935 Huxley & Haddon *We Europeans* iv. 122 The so-called 'Jewish' nose is really Armenoid. *Ibid.* vi. 178 The Armenoid.. type is widely distributed in the near East. This ethnic type is of medium stature, stocky and fleshy.

†**ar'mental**, *a. Obs.*[−0] [ad. L. *armentāl-is*, f. *arment-um* herd of cattle.] 'Of or belonging to a drove or herd.' Bailey 1731.

†**armen'tose**, *a. Obs.*[−0] [ad. L. *armentōsus*: see armental and -ose.] 'Full of great cattle, abounding with herds or beasts.' Bailey 1731.

armer (ˈɑːmə(r)). [f. arm *v.*[1] + -er[1]. Cf. OF. *armeor*, *-eur*.] One who arms.

1611 Cotgr., *Armateur*, An Armer, a provider of armes or weapons.

armer, -er, -y, obs. ff. armour *sb.*, -er, -y, armory.

armesine, obs. form of armozeen.

armet (ˈɑːmɪt). [a. F. *armet*, also in OF. *armette*, dim. of *arme*.] A kind of helmet introduced about the middle of the 15th century, in place of the basinet. It consisted of a globular iron cap, spreading out with a large hollowed projection over the back of the neck, and protected in front by the visor, beaver, and gorget. (Boutell.)

1507 *Justes May & June* 87 in Hazl. *E.P.P.* II. 124 They spared not cors, armyt, nor yet vambrace. 1577 Holinshed *Chron.* III. 853/1 Foure headpieces called armites. 1795 Southey *Joan of Arc* Wks. IX. 279 Smote on his neck, his neck Unfenced, for he in haste aroused had cast An armet on.

armet, obs. form of hermit.

armeure, armey(e, obs. ff. armour *sb.*, army.

armful (ˈɑːmfʊl). [f. arm *sb.*[1] + -ful.] As much as can be held in both arms (or in one); *hence*, a large quantity, a 'heap.'

1579 J. Stubbes *Gaping Gulf* C vij, By armefuls lading [money] out of the exchequer. c1613 Rowlands *More Knaues* 28, I like a handfull of old loue and true, Better then these whole armefuls of your new. c1720 Mrs. Centlivre *Wonder* i. i, Thou shalt have an armful of flesh and blood. 1824 Galt *Rothelan* I. i. xiii. 123 Followed by the nurse with an armful of apparel.

arm-gaunt, -great: see arm *sb.*[1] III.

'arm-,hole. [f. arm *sb.*[1]]

1. An arm-pit. *arch.* or *Obs.*

1391 Chaucer *Astrol.* i. §21. 13 Gemini [hath] thyn arm-holes and thin armes. 1535 Coverdale *Jer.* xxxviii. 12 Put these ragges and cloutes vnder thine arme holes. 1621 Burton *Anat. Mel.* ii. ii. iv. (1651) 268 [They] will wade up to the Armholes. 1696 Bp. Patrick *Comm. Exod.* xxix, The Girdle.. about him under the Arm-holes.

fig. 1865 *Cornh. Mag.* 38 Mr. Ruskin has been rightly praised for applying such a bold yet true metaphor as 'arm-holes' to those pits which are scooped under the branches at the point where they leave the tree.

2. The similar cavity in other animals, *e.g.* behind the fore-legs of a horse. *arch.* or *Obs.*

1607 Topsell *Four-f. Beasts* 309 The horse.. will be very hollow in the brisket towards the arme-holes. 1615 Crooke *Body of Man* 76 Where it toucheth the arme-holes, it becommeth in dogs and Apes very fleshy.

3. The hole in a garment through which the arm is put.

1775 in Ash. 1835 Miss Kemble *Rec. Later Life* I. 38 Tight waistbands, tight armholes and tight bodices. 1865 Trollope *Belton Est.* v. 57 With his thumbs fixed into the armholes of his waistcoat.

armie, obs. form of army.

armied (ˈɑːmɪd), *a. rare*[−1]. [f. army *sb.*] Forming an army, army-like.

1839 Bailey *Festus* xxxiii. (1848) 358, I hear the armied torrent of their wings, Hitherward streaming.

†**ar'miferous**, *a.* [f. L. *armifer* bearing arms, warlike + -ous.] Bearing arms or weapons.

1656 in Blount *Glossogr.*

armiger (ˈɑːmɪdʒə(r)). [a. L. *armiger* bearing arms, an armour-bearer; in med.L. a squire.] An esquire; *orig.* one who attended a knight to bear his shield, etc.; in later usage, one entitled to bear heraldic arms.

[1598 Shaks. *Merry W.* i. i. 10 A Gentleman borne.. who writes himselfe *Armigero*.] 1762 H. Walpole *Vertue's Anecd. Paint.* (1786) V. 111 Carew Reynell, armiger. c1840 De Quincey *Autobiog. Sk.* ii. Wks. II. 92 Entitled to proclaim himself an Armiger; which is the newest.. mode of saying that one is privileged to bear arms in a sense intelligible only to the Heralds' College. 1869 Blackmore *Lorna Doone* xiii. 74 He.. could buy up half the county armigers.

ar'migeral, *a. nonce-wd.* [f. prec. + -al[1].] Of the character of a squire; of squires.

1806 Syd. Smith *Mem. & Lett.* (1855) II. 21 In armigeral, priestly, and swine-feeding society. 1821 —— *Wks.* 1859 I. 324/2 A live armigeral spring gun would distinguish an accidental trespasser from a real poacher.

armigerous (ɑːˈmɪdʒərəs), *a.* [f. L. *armiger* + -ous.] Entitled to bear (heraldic) arms.

1731 in Bailey. a1858 De Quincey *Bentley* Wks. VII. 45 They belonged to the armigerous part of the population, and were entitled to write themselves Esquire.

armil (ˈɑːmɪl). Also 5-6 armille, -ylle, 7-8 -ill. [partly a. OF. *armille*:—L. *armilla*; partly a more recent adaptation of *armilla*.]

1. A bracelet; = armilla 1.

1480 Caxton *Ovid's Met.* xiv. xiv, The Armilles hangyng on their lyfte sides. 1483 —— *Gold. Leg.* 68/4 The dyademe fro his heed and the armylle fro hys arme.

2. One of the insignia of royalty, put on at the coronation. Cf. armilla 2.

1485 *Coron. Hen. VII* in *Rutl. Papers* 18 The king.. shall take armyll of the Cardinall.. and it is to wete that armyll is made in maner of a stole wovyn with gold and set with stones. 1761 *Brit. Mag.* II. 503 His majesty was then invested with the armill, the purple robe or imperial pall, and orb. 1847 Maskell *Mon. Rit.* III. 28. 1849 Rock *Ch. of Fathers* I. v. 436 The armil, or bracelet, was looked upon by the Anglo-Saxons as one among the badges of royalty.

3. = armilla 4.

1837 Whewell *Hist. Induct. Sc.* I. iii. iv. §3 Eratosthenes is said to have obtained, from the munificence of Ptolemy Euergetes, two Armils or instruments compounded of circles, which were placed in the portico at Alexandria. 1876 Mrs. Whitney *Sights & Ins.* II. xiv. 441 A marble gnomon and two bronze armils.. for noting the lines of light.

†**4. armil sphere** = armillary sphere. *Obs.*

1556 Recorde *Cast. Knowl.* 54 Rather.. an Armylle or Ringe sphere, then absolutely a sphere. 1611 Guillim *Heraldry* iii. ii. 85 Whether.. a Solide or Armill sphere.

‖**armilla** (ɑːˈmɪlə). [L.; = bracelet, hoop; f. *armus* shoulder.]

1. A bracelet; now esp. in *Archæology*.

1706 Phillips, *Armilla*, a Bracelet or Jewel worn on the Arm or Wrist. 1721 in Bailey. 1791-1824 D'Israeli *Cur. Lit.* (1866) 293/1 They had on their left arm, an armilla, an iron ring. 1834 *Penny Cycl.* II. 364 The wearing of the Armilla, or bracelet, is of very high antiquity. 1851 D. Wilson *Preh. Ann.* (1863) I. iii. 81 An armilla or ring of cannal coal. 1872 Wright *Uricon.* vii. 284 Bronze armillæ.. of large dimensions.

2. 'One of the Coronation Garments.' Bailey 1721.

3. 'An Iron-Ring, Hoop, or Brace, in which the Gudgeons of a Wheel move.' Phillips 1706.

4. An ancient astronomical instrument, consisting of a circular hoop fixed in the plane of the equator (*Equinoctial Armilla*), sometimes crossed at right angles by another fixed in the plane of the meridian (*Solstitial Armilla*). The shadows cast on the concave surfaces of these indicated the recurrence of the equinoxes and solstices.

1797 *Encycl. Brit.* II. 419/1 Those armillas or spheres, which Hipparchus and Ptolemy.. employed. 1810 Vince *Astron.* xxiv. 273 The armilla, or hoop representing the ecliptic. 1834 U.K.S. *Hist. Astron.* vi. 32/1 The construction of the astrolabium.. was rather more complicated than that of the solstitial or equatorial armillæ.

†**5.** A ring or aureola. *Obs.*

1737 G. Smith *Cur. Relat.* I. iv. 550 Incircled with an Armilla or Ring of Light.

†**6.** The annular ligament of the wrist. (Perhaps not in Eng.) *Obs.*

[1672 Barbetti *Chirurg.* v. i, Armilla membranosa manus.] 1721 in Bailey, etc.

†**ar'millar**, *a.* and *sb. Obs.* [see next.] **A.** *adj.* 'Of or like a hoop or ring.' Bailey 1731. **B.** *sb.* armillary circle or sphere.

1603 Sir C. Heydon *Jud. Astrol.* iv. 143, I haue taken the right ascentions of certaine fixed starres.. by another faire Armillare.

armillary (ˈɑːmɪlərɪ, ɑːˈmɪlərɪ), *a.* and *sb.* [mod. f. L. *armilla*; cf. Fr. *armillaire*. Bailey and Chambers cite a mod.L. *armillāris*. See -ary.]

A. *adj.* Of or pertaining to bracelets or hoops. ***armillary sphere***: a skeleton celestial globe or sphere, consisting merely of metal rings or

hoops representing the equator, ecliptic, tropics, arctic and antarctic circles, and colures, revolving on an axis, within a wooden horizon.
1664 POWER *Exp. Philos.* III. 169 All the Circles of the Armillary Sphære. **1703** J. HARRIS *Descr. Globes* (J.) That sphere is called an armillary sphere, because it appears in the form of several circular rings. **1797** *Encycl. Brit.* II. 420/2 An armillary astrolabe, like that which had been used by Hipparchus and Ptolemy. **1816** KIRBY & SP. *Entomol.* (1843) II. 297 Never had any armillary sphere so many zones. **1856** MRS. BROWNING *Aur. Leigh* VIII. 56 Her quadrant and armillary dials.
B. *sb.* = ARMILLA 4.
1841 BREWSTER *Martyrs Sc.* II. ii. (1856) 123 Equatorial armillaries.

ˈ**armillated**, *a. rare*$^{-0}$. [f. L. *armillāt-us* + -ED.] 'Wearing bracelets.' Cockeram 1623; whence in Bailey, Johnson, and mod. Dicts.

† **armillet, armilet.** *Obs.* [a. OF. *armillet*, dim. of *armille.*] A small bracelet.
1656 BLOUNT *Glossogr.*, *Armilet* [1681 *Armillet*].

armine, obs. form of ERMINE.

† ˈ**arming**, *sb.* Also 1–2 earming, 2–3 erming, 7 armine; the identity of the last is doubtful. [OE.; f. *earm*, ARM *a.*, poor: see -ING.] A poor or miserable creature. Rarely *attrib.*
c **1000** ÆLFRIC *Hom.* (Sweet *Reader* 80) ʒe sind earmingas ʒewordene. *c* **1175** *Lamb. Hom.* 41 To pinen þer wiðinnen þa earming saulen. *c* **1200** *Trin. Coll. Hom.* 61 Makede him.. erming þer he was er king. **1605** *Lond. Prodigal* 122 O here God, so young an armine! *Flo.* Armine, sweetheart, I know not what you mean by that, but I am almost a beggar.

arming (ˈɑːmɪŋ), *vbl. sb.* [f. ARM *v.*^{1} + -ING^1.]
1. The action or process of furnishing (oneself or others) with arms or armour; †*concr.* arms, armour (*obs.*).
1375 BARBOUR *Bruce* VII. 218 Na war the armyng that he had, He had beyn ded. *c* **1386** CHAUCER *Sir Thopas* 136 For to telle tales Anoon in myn armynge. *c* **1450** LONELICH *Grail* xiv. 240 Ne non point of al his armeng. **1598** BARRET *Theor. Warres* IV. i. 120 His arming is the proper arming of a Captaine. **1626** MARKHAM *Souldiers Gram.* II. 13 His office extendeth.. to the well arming, ordering and disposing of bodies. **1849** MACAULAY *Hist. Eng.* xii, The arming was now universal.
†**b.** *esp.* quasi-*adj.* in attrib. uses: = Forming part of arms or armour, used in military accoutrement; as in ***arming-dagger, -gauntlet, -girdle, -nail, -sword, -tusk***; **arming-points**, ends of strong twine used to fasten together the plates of mail at the joints of the arms and legs. *Obs.*
1472 SIR J. PASTON in *Lett.* 692 III. 40 And I gaffe hym a ffayr armyng sworde. **1481–90** *Howard Househ. Bks.* 385 For ijc. off armyngnayle of on sorte, ijd. *a* **1500** *Agincourt* 74 in Hazl. *E.P.P.* II. 96 Speres and bylles.. And armynge dagers. **1577** HARRISON *Engl.* I. ii. xxiv. 359 An arming girdle, harnessed with pure gold. **1598** FLORIO, *Balteo*, a belt, a sword or arming girdle. **1603** KNOLLES *Hist. Turkes* (1638) 274 With their lances and arming swords. **1611** COTGR., *Brasselet*.. an arming gantlet, that reaches up almost to the elbow. **1697** DRYDEN *Virg. Georg.* III. 398 The bristled Boar.. New grinds his arming Tusks. **1860** FAIRHOLT *Costume* 543 [Palettes] are secured to the plate beneath by arming points.
2. Any apparatus or structure intended for defensive or protective covering; *spec.* those of a ship.
1466 *Mann. & Househ. Exp.* 347 For the lynenge of the toppe armynge.. xxd. **1587** FLEMING *Contn. Holinshed* III. 543/1 Thereupon also the arming might be set much more firmlie than upon anie other mould. **1627** SMITH *Seaman's Gram.* xiii. 59 His.. top armings.. is a long red cloth. **1751** CHAMBERS *Cycl.*, *Armings*.. red clothes, hung about the outsides of the ship's upper works, fore and aft. **1867** SMYTH *Sailor's Word-bk.*, *Top-armings*, hammocks stowed inside the rigging for the protection of riflemen.
3. The equipment or completion of anything with that which gives it strength or efficiency, or fits it for a purpose. *concr.* The completing part thus furnished. In various *spec.* uses, as: the tallow at the bottom of a sounding-lead; the armature of a magnet. Often *attrib.*
1552 HULOET, Armynge coarde of a nette, *Plaga.* **1581** STUDLEY *Seneca's Trag., Hippol.* 56 b, Some with the arming coarde by pensell paynted red.. shall make the Beastes adred. **1598** BARRET *Theor. Warres* IV. iv. 113 Neither that anie Pike do want his head, cheekes, or arming. **1601** SHAKS. *All's Well* IV. iii. 72 To the full arming of the veritie. **1653** WALTON *Angler* 150 Carrying your arming wyer along his back. **1731** GRAY in *Phil. Trans.* XXXVII. 32 A small key hung by one of its [a loadstone's] arming Irons. **1775** DALRYMPLE *ibid.* LXVIII. 396 There was the mark of rock on the arming of the lead. **1855** WHICHCORD in *Archæol. Jrnl.* X. 48 The lines of the lead-work, or arming, which held the glass. **1867** F. FRANCIS *Angling* iv. (1880) 118 A bait thus put on.. shows enough arming.. to hook any fish. **1875** BEDFORD *Sailor's Pocket Bk.* v. 153 The necessary tallow for arming.
4. The action of furnishing with heraldic devices; †*concr.* heraldic arms (*obs.*). *Attrib.*, as in **arming-press**, a bookbinder's machine used in stamping and lettering the covers of books.
1598 MARSTON *Pigmalion's Im.* i. 140 Oh golden Ierkin! Royall arming coate! **1611** BEAUM. & FL. *Knt. Pestle* I. 51, I must bespeak my Shield and arming Pestle. **1627** DRAYTON *Agincourt etc.* 14 Or by the difference of their Armings knowne, Or by their Colours. **1875** URE *Dict. Arts* I. 422 The upper bed of an arming press.

ˈ**arming**, *vbl. sb.*^{2} [f. ARM *v.*^{2} + -ING^1.] Carrying in arms; *attrib.* for carrying in arms. Cf. *walking-stick, drinking water.*
a **1658** FORD, etc. *Witch Edmonton* v. i, If you can translate yourself into a lady's arming puppy, there you might lick sweet lips.

arming (ˈɑːmɪŋ), *ppl. a.* [f. ARM *v.*^{1} + -ING^2.] That arms; that furnishes armour or defence.
1673 PENN *Chr. Quaker* iv. 530 That Light.. is a Searching, Expelling, Powerful and Arming Light, against Darkness.

Arminian (ɑːˈmɪnɪən), *a.* and *sb.* [f. *Arminius*, Latinized form of the surname Harmensen.]
A. *adj.* Of, belonging to, or following the doctrine of, James Arminius or Harmensen, a Dutch Protestant theologian, who put forth views opposed to those of Calvin, especially on predestination. Arminius died in 1609; in 1618–19 his doctrines were condemned by the synod of Dort; but they spread rapidly, and were embraced, in whole or part, by large sections of the Reformed Churches.
1618 tr. *Barneveld's Apol.* H, The point in question is not concerning the Arminian Religion, but Romish Poperie. **1674** HICKMAN *Hist. Quinquart.* 133 Before Bishop Laud ruled.. those who embraced the Opinions since called Arminian, were indeed out of the way to preferment. **1853** MARSDEN *Early Puritans* 99 The Calvinistic and Arminian controversy.
B. *sb.* An adherent of the doctrine of Arminius.
1618 tr. *Barneveld's Apol.* D, Winbergen is principall of the Perfectists, and you of the Arminians. **1673** MILTON *True Relig.* 7 The Arminian.. is condemn'd for setting up free will against free grace. *c* **1760** WESLEY *Wks.* 1872 X. 360 The Arminians believe, it [predestination] is conditional; the Calvinists, that it is absolute. **1834** *Penny Cycl.* II. 365 The Wesleyan Methodists call themselves Arminians, and their Magazine appeared formerly under the title of the *Arminian Magazine.*

† **Arˈminianish**, *a. Obs. rare.* = ARMINIAN.
a **1700** in Somers *Tracts* V. 17 They have.. suffered to be printed all arminianish, popish, vain books.

Arˈminianism. [f. ARMINIAN + -ISM.] Arminian doctrines, or adherence to them.
1618 tr. *Barneveld's Apol.* Ded. A iij, Already wholy bent to Arminianisme. **1627** *Let. fr. Jesuit* in Rushw. *Hist. Coll.* (1659) I. 475 That Soveraign Drug Arminianism, which we hope will purge the Protestants from their Heresie. **1674** HICKMAN *Hist. Quinquart.* 227 He.. confirmed himself in his debauchedness, by his Arminianism. **1822** SYD. SMITH *Wks.* 1867 II. 5 The Articles of Religion are older than Arminianism, *eo nomine.*

Arˈminianize, *v.* [f. ARMINIAN + -IZE.] **a.** *trans.* To make Arminian. **b.** *intr.* To teach Arminianism. **Arminianized, -izing,** *ppl. a.* **Arminianizer**, one who teaches or promotes Arminianism.
1637 GILLESPIE *Eng. Pop. Cerem.* Ep. A iij b, Many.. who are either Popish and Arminianized.. or silly ignorants. **1674** HICKMAN *Hist. Quinquart.* 185 Some of our Arminianizing English Writers. **1692** *Christ Exalted* §106 Antisozzo leans on the contrary side, and Arminianizeth. **1698** *Ibid.* Ded. A iij, This will not go down with Arminianizers. **1698** CLARK *Script. Justif.* Introd. B, I have no Arminianizing Principles or Design.

arˈmipotence. *rare*$^{-0}$. [ad. L. *armipotentia*, n. of quality f. *armipotent-em*: see next.] 'Puissance at arms.' Bailey 1731.

armipotent (ɑːˈmɪpətənt), *a.* [ad. L. *armipotent-em*, f. *arma* arms + *potens, -tentem* powerful.] Mighty in arms: originally an epithet of Mars.
c **1386** CHAUCER *Knts. T.* 1124 Ther stood the tempul of Marz armypotent. **1513** DOUGLAS *Æneis* VI. xiv. 83 And of Achillis armypotent ofspring. **1600** FAIRFAX *Tasso* III. lxx, Our God the Lord Armipotent. *a* **1717** PARNELL *Poet. Wks.* (1833) 46 'Twas thus the' armipotent advised the gods. **1827** HARE *Guesses* Ser. I. (1873) 86 So ought England.. to plant.. English manliness, English freedom.. wherever the simple natives bow to her armipotent sceptre.

arˈmisonant, *a. rare*$^{-0}$. [f. L. *arma* arms + *sonānt-em* sounding; cf. next.] 'Rustling with armour.' Ash 1775.

arˈmisonous, *a. rare*$^{-0}$. [f. L. *armison-us* (f. *arma* arms + *sonus* -sounding) + -OUS.] 'Sounding or rustling with arms or armour.' Bailey 1731.

armistice (ˈɑːmɪstɪs). [ad. mod.L. *armistitium*, f. L. *arma* arms + *-stitium* stopping, f. *sistĕre, -stitum*, to stop, as in *interstitium, jūstitium, sōlstitium.* Cf. also F. *armistice*: see quot. 1688.]
[**1664** GOULDMAN *Dict.*, *Armistitium*.. a cessation from arms for a time, a short truce. **1688** MIEGE *Fr. Dict.*, *Armistice* [marked † as 'not current in any style']. **1699** *Treaty of Carlowitz* in RYCAUT *Hist. Turks* III. 572 Duret armistitium hocce.]
1. A cessation from arms; a short truce.
1707 in *Gloss. Angl. Nova.* **1727–51** in CHAMBERS *Cycl.*, *Armistitium.* *a* **1733** NORTH *Exam.* III. vi. ¶64 Much of which Time was Armistice or Cessation, when all the Parties, instead of fighting, fell to intriguing. **1813** WELLINGTON in Gurw. *Disp.* X. 443, I do not think that the Russians and Prussians can agree to the armistice without submitting entirely.
2. *fig.* A cessation from hostile proceedings.
1814 L. M. HAWKINS *Rosanne* II. xxxv. 131 There was an armistice between father and daughter. **1841** BREWSTER *Martyrs Sc.* v. (1856) 68 The leader of the philosophic band had broken the most solemn armistice with the Inquisition.
3. Armistice Day, the day, 11 Nov. 1918, on which the armistice was concluded which brought the war of 1914–18 to an end; also, any anniversary of that day. Combined, since the war of 1939–45, with Remembrance Day.
1919 *Times* 7 Nov. 12/1 The Armistice-day service at St. Paul's Cathedral will be the office of Holy Communion. *Ibid.* 12 Nov. 15/1 The first anniversary of Armistice Day was celebrated throughout the Empire yesterday. **1946** *Times* 8 Oct. 4/6 There will be general cooperation in the observance of Remembrance Day as there has been in previous years in the observance of Armistice Day. *Ibid.* 8 Nov. 2/1 Remembrance Day.. takes the place in the calendar that till 1938 was filled by Armistice Day; but instead of November 11 it will be the previous Sunday, except when November 11 or 12 is a Sunday.

armit, -age, obs. forms of HERMIT, -AGE.

ˈ**armless**, *a.*^{1} [f. ARM *sb.*^{1} + -LESS.] Without arm or branch.
c **1386** CHAUCER *Monkes T.* 213 And saugh an hond armles, that wroot ful fast. **1596** R. L[INCHE] *Diella* (1877) 74 The crazen tops of armelesse Trees. **1859** LEWES *Phys. Com. Life* II. xii. 382 Progenitors of armless and legless babies.

armless (ˈɑːmlɪs), *a.*^{2} [f. ARM *sb.*^{2} + -LESS.] Without weapons of offence or defence, unarmed.
a **1619** BEAUM. & FL. *Q. of Corinth* IV. iii. (T.) Integrity thus armless seeks her foes. **1661** MORGAN *Sph. Gentry* I. vi. 87 We shall find them all armed but the armless Hind. **1870** SPURGEON *Treas. David* Ps. xxxvii. 17 Toothless malice, armless malevolence!

armlet (ˈɑːmlɪt). [f. ARM *sb.*^{1} + -LET. Cf. OFr. *bracelet* in first three senses.]
1. An ornament or band worn round the arm. (Sometimes distinguished from *bracelet*, which is worn only at the wrist.)
1535 COVERDALE *Ecclus.* xxi. 21 Lernynge is vnto a wyse man.. like an armlett vpon his right arme. **1648** HERRICK *Hesper.* I. 23 Working.. Of soft and dainty maiden-haire, A curious Armelet. **1859** TENNYSON *Elaine* 1177 An armlet for the roundest arm on earth. **1879** MACLEAR *Celts* ii. 13 They wear.. bracelets and armlets.
2. A small inlet of the sea or branch of a river.
1538 LELAND *Itin.* II. 31, I markid diverse armelettes breking out of the 2 Streames. **1577** HOLINSHED *Descr. Brit.* xii. 55/1 The water separateth it selfe into two armelets. **1864** VAMBERY *Trav. Centr. Asia* 149 In the main stream it was well enough, but in the armlets at the side we settled every ten paces on the sand.
3. A piece of armour for the arm.
1706 in PHILLIPS.

† ˈ**armlich**, *a. Obs.* Forms: 1 earmlíc, 2 ermlic, 3 ærm-, armlich. [f. ARM *a.* + *-lich*:—OE. *-líc*: see -LY^1.] Miserable, pitiable.
a **1000** *Boeth. Metr.* xix. 28 Ðæt is earmlícost ealra þinga. *c* **1175** *Lamb. Hom.* 115 þenne bið hit ermlic, ʒif he bið unrihtwis. **1205** LAY. 593 His broþer wes in armliche benden. *Ibid.* 20756 He andswarede wið ærmliche stefene.

† ˈ**armliche**, *adv. Obs.* Forms: 1 earmlíce, 2 erm-, 3 armliche. [f. ARM *a.* + *-liche*:—OE. *-líce*: see -LY^2.] Miserably.
c **885** K. ÆLFRED *Bæda* v. xiii. (Bosw.) He wæs earmlice beswicen. *c* **1175** *Lamb. Hom.* 17 He wes ipinet ermliche to deðe. *c* **1230** *Ancr. R.* 328 Hu eruedliche [*v.r.* armliche] he ariseð þet under wune of sunne haueð ileien longe.

‖ **armoire** (armwar). [a. Fr. *armoire*, refashioned from OFr. *aumoire*, found by the side of *aumaire, almaire*, earlier *arˈmarie*, ad. L. *armārium*: see AMBRY.] A cupboard; an ambry.
1571 *Wills & Inv. N. Count.* (1835) 361 Ij owld chystes ijs. vjd... ij armoires jl. **1823** RUTTER *Fonthill* 51 Articles of virtu which fill the open armoires. **1836** MARRYAT *Midsh. Easy* xxxii, Loading the landing-place with armoires and chests of drawers.

armoirie, obs. form of ARMORY.

armoisin, obs. form of ARMOZEEN.

armomancy (ˈɑːməʊˌmænsɪ). [ad. med.L. *armomantia*, f. *armus* shoulder; see -MANCY.] 'Divination by the shoulders of beasts.' Blount *Glossogr.* 1656.

armoniac, obs. form of AMMONIAC.

armonical, -nize, -ny, obs. forms of HARM-.

armor(e, armorer, obs. form of ARMOUR *sb.*, -ER.

† **armorace.** *Herb. Obs.* [a. OF. *armoracee*, ad. L. *armoracea, -ia.*] Horse-radish.
c **1420** *Pallad. on Husb.* IV. 169 Now holyhocke is sowe and armorace Or arborace that wilde raves are.

armorial (ɑːˈmɔərɪəl), *a.* and *sb.* [f. ARMORY + -AL[1]. Cf. mod.Fr. *armorial.*]

A. *adj.* **1.** Pertaining to heraldic arms.

1576 THYNNE *Burghley's Crest* 295 An olde armoriall booke. **1683** *Brit. Spec.* 179 The Soveraign Ensigns Armorial of the King of Great Britain. **1803** SOUTHEY *Sel. Lett.* (1856) I. 224, I often found my armorial vocabulary scant. **1857** BUCKLE *Civilis.* I. ix. 562 In the twelfth century armorial bearings were invented.

2. Of porcelain, etc., bearing heraldic arms.

1907 F. A. CRISP (*title*) Armorial China. A Catalogue of Chinese Porcelain with Coats of Arms in the Possession of Frederick Arthur Crisp. **1925** A. TUDOR-CRAIG *Armorial Porc. 18th Cent.* iii. 10 Errors in many of the coats of arms on armorial china. **1933** *Burlington Mag.* June p. xvii/1 The fine display at the recent British Antique Dealers' exhibition of armorial porcelain.

B. *sb.* A book containing coats of arms.

1753 CHAMBERS *Cycl. Supp.* s.v., In this sense we meet with the French Armorial, the Spanish Armorial. *c* **1800** (*title*) An Armorial of the Extinct and Dormant Peerage of England.

armorially (ɑːˈmɔərɪəlɪ), *adv.* [f. ARMORIAL *a.* + -LY[2].] In an armorial manner; in a way that pertains to arms or armour.

1861 *Temple Bar* Aug. 134 With big iron boots encasing their legs armorially. **1887** *N. & Q.* 7th Ser. IV. 54/2 Armorially speaking, I find no trace of Cornish Gunns in Burke's 'General Armory'.

‖**Armorica** (ɑːˈmɒrɪkə). [L.] Name of the north-western part of Gaul, now called Bretagne or Brittany. **Arˈmoric** *a.*, of Armorica or its people, *absol.* its language.

c **1386** CHAUCER *Frankl. T.* 1 In *Armorike that cleped is Bretaigne. **1753** CHAMBERS *Cycl. Supp.* s.v., The name *Armorica was antiently given to all the northern and western coast of Gaul. **1667** MILTON *P.L.* I. 581 Begirt with British and *Armoric Knights. **1753** CHAMBERS *Cycl. Supp.*, The *Armoric is a dialect of the Welch.

Armorican (ɑːˈmɒrɪkən), *a.* [f. ARMORICA + -AN.] **1.** = *Armoric* s.v. ARMORICA; also as *sb.*, an inhabitant of Armorica.

1480 CAXTON *Chron. Eng.* xlix. 33, I will that this lond *Armorican be callyd lytel britayn. *c* **1645** HOWELL *Lett.* (1650) II. 78 The *Armoricans or the inhabitants of Britany. **1875** WHITNEY *Life Lang.* x. 183 The *Armorican..so nearly allied to the Cornish.

2. *Geol.* Of or pertaining to mountain-building movements which occurred towards the end of the Palæozoic era, or the mountains then formed, traceable from southern Ireland across southern Britain and Brittany to central France. Hence **Arˈmoricanoid** *a.*, resembling such a movement.

1906 H. B. C. SOLLAS tr. *Suess's Face of Earth* II. 93 This is the great pre-Permian range of western Europe. The traces of its interior and presumably most elevated zone lie in Brittany and the Vendée; for this reason we give these fragments the general name of the *Armorican chain.* **1913** C. LAPWORTH *Birmingham Country* 43 E.W... is suggestive of the..'Armorican Movement' of Northern France and the southern part of the British Isles; but to avoid all implications whatsoever of geological *age*, this trend in the Midlands can only be safely referred to as *Armoricanoid.* **1960** L. D. STAMP *Britain's Struct.* (ed. 5) xii. 123 The Carboniferous Period was brought to a close by the great Armorican earth movements. *Ibid.* 124 The Armorican mountains and valleys determined the main pattern of the geography which was destined to persist throughout the Mesozoic.

armoried (ˈɑːmərɪd), *ppl. a.* [f. ARMORY + -ED[2].] Decked with armorial bearings or escutcheons.

1866 *Pall Mall G.* 23 Oct. 9 Its plumed and armouried hearse.

armoriol, var. ARMARIOL, *Obs.*, a little cabinet.

armorist (ˈɑːmərɪst). [f. ARMORY + -IST; cf. F. *armoriste.*] One who is skilled in heraldry, or in blazoning coats of arms.

1586 FERNE *Blaz. Gentrie* Ded., The professed Armorists. **1602** SEGAR *Mil. & Civ. Honour* Ded., A subiect proper to Armorists, and men of my profession. **1868** CUSSANS *Handbk. Her.* ii. 47 Thus it is commonly written by English Armorists.

armory[1] (ˈɑːmərɪ). Forms: 5 (Caxton) **armoirie**, **-oyrye**, 5–6 **-orye**, **-orie**, 6 **-ery**, 5– **armory**, 6– **armoury**. [a. OF. *armoierie*, *armoirie*, f. *armoier*, or *armoieor*, *-oyeur*, a blazoner, f. *armoier*, *-oyer*, to blazon = It. *armeggiāre*, a Romanic vb. f. *arma* arms. See also ARMOURY.]

1. The science of blazoning arms, heraldry.

1489 CAXTON *Faytes of Armes* IV. xvii, Of the armoirie.. White that men calle in armoyrye siluer..Blak that men calle in armoyrie sable. **1586** J. HOOKER *Girald. Irel.* ii. in *Holinsh.* II. 152 In histories and armories. **1611** GUILLIM *Heraldry* I. i. 5 Armory is an Art rightly prescribing the true knowledge and use of Armes. **1651** J. C. *Poems* 9 Mettal on Mettal is ill Armorie. **1662** J. BARGRAVE *Pope Alex. VII* (1867) 128 The king learned armory, geography, and history. **1868** CUSSANS *Handbk. Her.* i. 21 Anterior to the period in which a system of Armory was established.

2. Armorial bearings, 'arms'. *arch.*

a **1500** *Agincourt* 120 in Hazl. *E.P.P.* II. 98 Full well broydered with armory gaye. **1589** PUTTENHAM *Eng. Poesie* 224 The Lion being her owne noble armory. **1611** SPEED *Hist. Gt. Brit.* IX. xi. (1632) 672 Knights, Esquiers, and men of Armories. **1628** COKE *On Litt.* 7 b, He first quartered the French Armories with the English in his great Seale. **1868** MORRIS *Earthly Par.* II. 167 Some great man's badge of war, or armoury.

†**3.** Ensigns of war; 'colours.' *Obs.*

1523 LD. BERNERS *Froiss.* I. clx. 194 Great nobles of fayre harnesse and riche armory of baners and penons. *Ibid.* ccxxxvii. 338 The baners and penons, and yᵉ noble armery.

†**ˈarmory**[2]. *Obs.* [A refashioned form of AMBRY after F. *armoire.*] A cupboard or ambry.

1602 WARNER *Alb. Eng.* XII. lxix. (1612) 290 In yonder chamber Hath Mandeuil his closet, and no common Armorie.

armory, variant of ARMOURY.

†**armosie.** *Obs.* [ad. Fr. *armoise*, synonym of *armoisin.*] ARMOZEEN.

1578 *Invent.* (1815) 219 (JAM.) Ane lang lows gowne of blak armosie taffetie.

armour (ˈɑːmə(r)), *sb.* Forms: 3–6, (9) **armure**, 4–5 **armur**, 4– **armour**; also 4 **aarmour**, **aarmer**, 4– 5 **armer**, **armowr(e**, 4–6 **-oure**, 4–9 **armor**, 5 **armeure**, **-ewr(e**, **-ore**, 5–6 **armeur**. [a. OF. *armeüre* (13th c. *armure*):—L. *armātūra* ARMATURE. The current spelling in *-our* is not etymological, the termination being the same as in *vest-ure.*]

1. *collect. sing.* Defensive covering worn by one who is fighting; mail. Cf. ARM *sb.*[2] 1.

1297 R. GLOUC. 397 He & hys armure were þoru out hot. **1393** LANGL. *P. Pl.* C. II. 155 May non Armure hit lette. *c* **1485** *Digby Myst.* (1882) I. 352 Harneysed in armour of plate and maile. *c* **1500** *Lancelot* 824 Aȝaine his strok resistit non armour. **1667** MILTON *P.L.* VI. 209 Arms on Armour clashing. **1718** POPE *Iliad* III. 407 Beside each chief his azure armour lay. **1880** DISRAELI *Endym.* lix, Prince Florestan, in a suit of blue damascened armour.

†**2.** (with a *pl.*) A suit of mail. *Obs.* (Cf. 7.)

1375 BARBOUR *Bruce* XI. 76 Wapnys and armowris purvayit thai. **1483** CAXTON *Gold. Leg.* 278/1 He had.. armours ynowe for to garnysshe with seuen thousand men. **1569** *Tract in Grocers' Comp.* (1869) 75 Rich and costly armours, guilt and engrauen. **1635** BRERETON *Trav.* 140 Furnished with about sixty or seventy armours for horse. **1681** *Trial S. Colledge* 38 Did he discourse anything to you about Arms..Yes, he did, I had an Armour from him. **1751** CHAMBERS *Cycl.* s.v., A compleat Armor antiently consisted of a casque or helm, a gorget, cuirasse, gantlets, tasses, brassets, cuisses, and covers for the legs.

†**3. a.** *collect. sing.* with *pl.* Military equipment or accoutrement, both offensive and defensive, in the widest sense; the whole apparatus of war. *Obs.* exc. in *Law.*

a **1300** *Becket* 955 Other armure nadde he none, for holi churche to fiȝte. **1388** WYCLIF *1 Sam.* xx. 40 Jonathas ȝaf hise armeris to the child. **1460** CAPGRAVE *Chron.* 195 This herd the Kyng, and stuffid the Toure with vitaile and armoure. **1489** CAXTON *Faytes of Armes* II. xxxv. 151 With the same armewres they deffended and kepte theyre cyte. **1618** BOLTON *Florus* (1636) 319 The armours of the vanquisht were not consumed with fire. **1759** DUMARESQUE in *Phil. Trans.* LI. 485 Their armour for war is a bow and arrows. **1809** TOMLINS *Law Dict.* s.v., Nor go armed, in affray of the peace, on pain to forfeit their armour.

†**b.** in obs. phrases in which *arms* is the usual word; cf. ARM *sb.*[2] 4.

1563 *Homilies* II. xxi. I. (1859) 559 Subjects who..take armour wickedly..to break the publique peace. **1570** HOLINSHED *Scot. Chron.* (1806) I. 73 The people..were up in armour against the King. *Ibid.* 102 Rising up in armour against him. **1577** —— *Chron.* I. 85/1 Caused the trumpet to sound to armor. **1577** HANMER *Anc. Eccl. Hist.* (1619) 41 The Jewes beganne..to take up Armour against the Romans.

†**4.** The exercise or employment of arms; warfare, fighting, active hostilities. Cf. ARM *sb.*[2] 6. *Obs.*

1387 TREVISA *Higden* Rolls Ser. II. 275 Nynus bare out armour [*arma foris extulit.*] *Ibid.* IV. 41 þe Romaynes hadde imeoved noon armour wiþoute Italy. **1526** BP. CLERK *To Wolsey* in *MS. Cott. Calig.* D ix. 104 For a suspention off armeur. **1589** WARNER *Alb. Eng.* VI. xxxii. (1612) 159 She armour still pursu'd. **1602** *Ibid.* Epit., Insurrections, and ciuill-armor.

5. *fig.* from prec. senses; but now only from 1.

1340 *Ayenb.* 203 þet is þe armure þet þe dyeuel dret mest. **1382** WYCLIF *Rom.* vi. 13 Neither ȝyue ȝe ȝoure membris aarmours [TINDALE & **1611** instruments, *Genev.* weapons] of wickidnesse to synne. *Ibid.* xiii. 12 Be we clothid with the armeris of liȝt. **1526** TINDALE *ibid.*, Let vs put on the Armoure of lyght. [So subseq. vers.] **1597** J. PAYNE *Royal Exch.* 37 Put on the whole armor of God. **1667** MILTON *P.L.* XII. 491 And also arme With spiritual Armour. **1711** STEELE *Spect.* No. 114 ¶7 Putting on unnecessary Armour against improbable Blows of Fortune. **1822** BYRON *Werner* I. i, Suspicion is a heavy armour.

6. *transf.* in *Naut.* **a.** = ARMING *vbl. sb.* 2 (*obs.*). **b.** The steel or other metallic protective sheathing of a warship, military fortification, vehicle, or aircraft.

1466 *Mann. & Househ. Exp.* 351 Blanket for sheldes for toppe armore of the kervelle xiiijd. **1855** W. M. GWIN (D.A.E.) (*title*) Report [of] the Committee on Naval Affairs, who were instructed to inquire into the expediency of using submarine armors in the United States navy. **1861** in *Offic. Rec. Union & Confed. Navies* (U.S.) 1st Ser. IV. 222 (D.A.E.), This addition would nearly treble the strength of the armor. **1870** in *Eng. Mech.* 7 Jan. 396/2 A belt of armour ..to protect broadside guns. **1883** *Times* 27 Aug. 3/5 Three balls penetrated the armour of the Bayard.

c. Armoured vehicles collectively.

1944 *Return to Attack* (Army Board, N.Z.) 18/1 Effective enemy 88-millimetre guns, which moved with the tanks, had done much damage to our armour. **1945** *News Chron.* 18 Apr. 1/5 British armour..has pushed to within 25 miles of Hamburg.

7. A diver's water-tight suit; (cf. 2.)

1822 BURROWES *Cycl.* IV. 175/1 In the year 1617 Francis Kessler gave a description of his water-armour, intended also for diving. **1869** *Eng. Mech.* 1 Oct. 39/1 The best armours now in use are those made of rubber and canvas.. The use of this bell has been superseded by the submarine armour.

8. *Nat. Hist.* Protective or defensive covering of animals or plants; *abst.* protection, defence (*obs.*).

1605 BACON *Adv. Learn.* II. vii. §7 The firmness of hides is for the armour of the body against extremities of heat or cold. **1647** COWLEY *Mistr.*, *Request* vi, Piercing the armour of their [*i.e.* Fishes] Scales. **1814** W. TAYLOR in *Month. Mag.* XXXVIII. 148 Thy burnish'd armure speck with glossier jet. **1854** OWEN in *Orr's Circ. Sc.* Org. Nat. I. 165 In these colossal armadillos the trunk-armour was in one immovable piece.

†**9.** *Magnetism.* = ARMATURE 6 a. *Obs.*

1730 SAVERY in *Phil. Trans.* XXXVI. 333 Touched on the soft Armour of a Magnet. **1751** CHAMBERS *Cycl.*, The usual armour of a loadstone.

10. Heraldic insignia or devices. ***coat armour*** = 'coat of arms,' originally a vest of silk or other rich material embroidered in colours, worn over the armour of a knight, to distinguish him in the lists or on the field of battle. Cf. ARM *sb.*[2] 14.

c **1340** *Gaw. & Gr. Knt.* 585 With ryche cote armure. *c* **1384** CHAUCER *H. Fame* 1326 Euery man..Had on him throwen a vesture Whiche that men clepyn a cote armure Enbrowded wonderly ryche. **1393** LANGL. *P. Pl.* C. XXI. 12 þese aren cristes armes, Hus colours and hus cote-armure. **1548** HALL *Chron.* 87 To colouren or hiden in any maner tho [? the] armures. **1628** COKE *On Litt.* 18 b, If a Nobleman haue his coat armor and Pennions with his armes. **1679–88** *Secr. Serv. Moneys Chas. II* (1851) 43 For a suite of silk armour 31 *li.* **1683** LUTTRELL *Brief Rel.* I. 264 A pair of pistolls, and an armour made of silk.

¶ For ARMER or ARMOURER.

1550 CROWLEY *Epigr.* 426, He turneth no manne To profite or gayne Except it be the surgian, or the armore. **1629** *S'hertogenbosh* 38 We brought also in the Towne many armours, and a Serjeant of theirs.

11. *Comb.* and *Attrib.*, as ***armour-joint***, ***-work***; **armour-fish** (see quot.); **armour glass**, toughened glass (cf. ARMOUR-PLATE[1] 2); **armour-piercing** *a.*, (of a shell, bomb, gun, etc.) designed to pierce the armour-plating of ships, tanks, etc.; **armour-proof** *a.*, as impenetrable as armour, or ? proof against weapons; **armour-shelf**, a wide shelf extending below the waterline of an armoured ship, supporting the edge of the armour plating; **armour-wise** *adv.*, in the manner of armour. Also ARMOUR-BEARER, -CLAD, -PLATE, q.v.

1748 *Phil. Trans.* XLV. 170 *Cataphractus Americanus*, the Armour-Fish..less than a Foot in length, and four Inches broad. **1932** *Jrnl. Soc. Glass Technol.* XVI. 478 Armour Glass..similar to that made by Messrs. Pilkington Bros. in this country. **1878** BROWNING *Two Poets Croisic* cvii, Stabbed..through the armour-joints! **1897** *Daily News* 19 July 9/5 Their 12-inch armour-piercing shot. **1922** *Encycl. Brit.* XXX. 122/1 Armour-piercing projectiles for maximum penetration. **1940** R. W. B. CLARKE *Britain's Blockade* 17 Armour plate of high resistance power and armour-piercing bombs of great penetrating power. **1664** H. MORE *Myst. Iniq.* Apol. 561 They that believe all things alike..shall be armour-proof. **1868** E. J. REED *Shipbuilding in Iron & Steel* xx. 460 The armour shelf having been completed for a portion of the length amidships, the working of the skin-plating behind armour and of the longitudinal girders is commenced. **1890** W. J. GORDON *Foundry* 35 The next, in frame up to her armour-shelf, is an iron-clad of 10,000 tons, building for Her Majesty's Navy. **1875** BROWNING *Aristoph. Apol.* 240 That which himself went wearing armour-wise. **1664** POWER *Exp. Philos.* I. 2 [The Flea's] head, body, and limbs also, be all of blackish armourwork.

armour (ˈɑːmə(r)), *v.* [f. prec. sb.] To put armour on; to furnish with a defensive or protective covering.

c **1450** LONELICH *Grail* xiii. 242 Eualach comanded anon His men to armure thame euerichon. **1864** *Daily Tel.* 22 June, The Kearsage had been armoured during the night with her chain-cables. **1870** *Eng. Mech.* 11 Mar. 625/3 Cables for submarine use may be afterwards armoured.. with wires. **1883** SPURGEON *Purit. Gard.* 175 Our glorious Leader would never have armed and armoured all his followers.

ˈarmour-ˌbearer. One who carried a warrior's armour or weapons; a squire.

1611 BIBLE *1 Sam.* xiv. 14 That first slaughter which Jonathan and his armour-bearer made [WYCLIF, squyer; COVERDALE, wapen bearer]. **1772** PENNANT *Tours Scotl.* (1774) 296 Each chieftain had his armour-bearer. **1870** BRYANT *Homer* I. x. 305 Meriones, the armor-bearer of Idomeneus.

ˈarmour-ˌclad, *ppl. a.* Clad in, or protected by, armour. *Ellipt.* as *sb.* A vessel of war protected by a sheathing of iron or steel. Cf. *ironclad.* Also *transf.*

1862 *Cassell's Illustr. Fam. Paper* 11 Jan. 104/2 The armour-clad vessels of the South. **1863** [see IRONCLAD *a.* 1 *note*]. **1869** in *Eng. Mech.* 1 Oct. 32/2 Like an armour-clad war steamer. **1881** *Edin. Rev.* Jan. 35 There was an active demand for armour-clads. **1901** *Westm. Gaz.* 11 Apr. 10/2

Miolania, a large armour-clad aquatic tortoise. **1903** LYDEKKER *Mostly Mammals* 308 Armour-clad whales. **1930** *Engineering* 25 Apr. 557/1 The struggle between cubicle and armour-clad [switch] gear is still going on.

armoured ('ɑːməd), *ppl. a.* [f. ARMOUR *v.*]

1. Clad in armour; also *transf.*

1601 CHESTER *Love's Mart.* lxxvii, The Brytaines went not proudly armoured. **1872** TENNYSON *Last Tourn.* 170 One knight..armour'd all in forest-green. **1876** *Daily News* 30 Sept. 3/2 Lusty fish, armoured in red and gold.

2. a. *esp.* of war-vessels; cf. ARMOUR-CLAD. Also, of military vehicles, aircraft, etc., and of forces supplied with armoured vehicles or warfare carried on by their use.

1862 *Guardian* 16 Apr. 366/2 Fighting armoured gunboats 'down' stream. **1869** SIR E. REED *Iron-Clad Ships* Introd. 12 Our armoured frigates. **1900** J. RALPH *Towards Pretoria* vii. 115 The destruction of a British armoured train. **1911** *Sci. Amer.* 22 Apr. 410/3 Armoured cars in the Mexican Revolution... An ordinary box car..is sheathed inside with quarter-inch steel plates. **1914** *Illustr. War News* 21 Oct. 16/1 Armoured aeroplanes carrying machine-guns. *Ibid.* 28 Oct. 32 An armoured car outside the Headquarters Hotel at Ostend. **1944** *Return to Attack* (Army Board, N.Z.) 15/1 His bogged transport and armoured fighting vehicles were vulnerable to air attack. **1945** *News Chron.* 18 Apr. 1/5 The advance of the 7th Armoured Division and the 4th Armoured Brigade..was cut in two places. **1947** R. W. COOPER *Nuremberg Trial* viii. 166 General Guderian, Germany's foremost expert on armoured warfare.

b. Of cables, hoses or the like: encased in armouring.

1898 E. J. HOUSTON *Dict. Electr. Words* (ed. 4) 67/1 *Cable, Armored*, an electric cable provided, in addition to its insulating coating, with a protective coating or sheathing, generally made of metal tubing or wire. **1930** *Engineering* 7 Mar. 324/3 The suction pipe of the pump is an armoured hose. **1967** *Gloss. Mining Terms* (*B.S.I.*) VIII. 5 *Armoured flexible conveyor*, a heavy duty chain conveyer designed to carry a coalcutter or power loader on the framework and capable of being continually snaked forward, section by section, as the face advances.

3. Of glass: toughened. (Cf. ARMOUR-PLATE 2.)

1935 *Economist* 7 Dec. 1140/2 Laminated or sandwich glass [and]..toughened or armoured glass..are termed safety glass..used for [car] windows and windscreens. **1949** *Archit. Rev.* CV. 181 An armoured glass table the length of the wall below the window provides a large working space.

armourer ('ɑːmərə(r)). Forms: 4–5 **armurer**, 5 **-erer**, 5–9 **-orer**, 7– **-ourer**. [a. AFr. *armurer*, OF. *-urier*, *-eurier*, f. *armeüre* ARMOUR *sb.*: see -ER[1].]

1. A maker of armour; in mod. use, a manufacturer of arms.

*c***1400** *Destr. Troy* v. 1588 Armurers & Arowsmythis. *c***1450** *Pol. Rel. & L. Poems* 19 Yff hit stoode that no wer ware, loste were the craffte of Armoreres. **1598** STOW *Surv.* (ed. Strype 1754) II. v. xii. 296/1 The society or company of the Armourers. *a***1744** POPE (J.) When arm'rers temper in the ford The keen-edg'd pole-ax. **1825** T. JEFFERSON *Autobiog.* Wks. 1859 I. 98 Such weapons as they could find in armorers' shops. **1859** TENNYSON *Enid* 283 At this the armourer..Came forward with the helmet yet in hand.

2. One who equipped men-at-arms in their mail. Also *fig. Obs.* exc. *Hist.*

*c***1386** CHAUCER *Knts. T.* 1649 Faste the Armurers also With fyle and hamer prikynge to and fro. **1599** SHAKS. *Hen. V*, IV. Cho. 12 The Armourers accomplishing the Knights. **1606** —— *Ant. & Cl.* IV. iv. 7 Thou art The Armourer of my heart. **1605** CAMDEN *Rem.* 190 His armorer put on his backe-peece before, and his breast-plate behinde.

3. An official who has charge of the arms of a ship, regiment, etc.

1753 in CHAMBERS *Cycl. Supp.* **1758** J. BLAKE *Mar. Syst.* 23 Armourers and sail-makers shall be entered..among the crews. **1835** SIR J. ROSS *N.-W. Passage* iii. 53 The engineers and armourers were still employed on the engine. **1844** *Regul. & Ord. Army* 148 The Serjeant-Armourer is responsible that the Portable Forge and Chest of Tools be kept in a serviceable state.

¶ By confusion for *armure*, ARMOUR *sb.*

*c***1374** CHAUCER *Boeth.* II. vi. 51 Ne blode yshed by egre hate ne hadet nat deied ȝit armurers.

armouried: see ARMORIED.

armouring ('ɑːmərɪŋ), *vbl. sb.* [f. ARMOUR *v.* + -ING[1].] An external covering, usually of steel wire or bands, to give protection to electric cables or the like.

1924 in S. R. ROGET *Dict. Electr. Terms* 11/2. **1930** *Engineering* 14 Feb. 223/2 The cables are clamped in cone clamps for securing the sheath or armouring. **1940** *Chambers's Techn. Dict.* 51/2 Armouring causes eddy current loss in single-core cables.

armourless ('ɑːməlɪs), *a.* [f. ARMOUR *sb.* + -LESS.] Without armour, defenceless.

1398 TREVISA *Barth. De P.R.* XVIII. xxx. (1495) 792 The harte chaungyth his hornes..and thenne he is armourles. ?**1650** *Don Bellianis* 93 Seeing him armourless.

'armour-,plate. 1. One of the metal pieces or plates forming the material of defensive armour; *esp.* one of the plates of iron or steel with which the sides of vessels of war are covered. Hence **armour-plated** *ppl. a.*; also *fig.*, insensitive to attack; callous. **armour-plating** *vbl. sb.* (used *concr.* for 'armour-plates').

1860 J. CLARE in *Evening Standard* 30 Oct. 3/5, I am the originator of placing timber between..the internal metal and fastening and the external armour-plating. **1863** A. WYNTER *Subtle Brains* xxii. 235 The Admiralty have lately taken to manufacture their own armour-plates. **1863** *Illustr. London News* 13 June 658/1 The frames of armour-plated ships. **1894** *Cassell's Fam. Mag.* Dec. 69/2 Hard armour-plated gambling. **1864** TENNENT *Story of Guns* 227 Supposed to be an insuperable obstacle to the use of Armour-plating. **1869** SIR E. REED *Iron-Clad Ships* i. 6 A main-deck battery armour-plated. **1874** BOUTELL *Arms & Arm.* x. 187 We add inch to inch in the thickness of our armour-plates. **1906** *Westm. Gaz.* 17 July 10/1 His armour-plated indifference. **1908** H. G. WELLS *War in Air* i. 11 Some confusion of ideas about armour plates. **1909** *Ibid.* 13 Aug. 3/1 His incisive humour, which got between the joints of his armour-plated victims. **1940** [see *armour-piercing adj.*].

2. The trade name of a kind of toughened plate glass; = *armour(ed) glass.*

1931 in *Trade Marks Jrnl.* 25 Nov. 1560/1. **1932** *Jrnl. Soc. Glass Technol.* XVI. 78 Now comes a further development, namely, the glass described by Messrs. Pilkington Bros. as 'Armour plate' or 'toughened glass'. **1933** *Ibid.* XVII. 149 'Armourplate' is the trade name given to plate glass which..has acquired a degree of strength far in excess of that with which the original plate glass was endowed, and the property, if broken, of shattering into small and comparatively harmless fragments. **1941** *Archit. Rev.* LXXXIX. 97 The balustrade is formed of 'armour-plate' glass.

armoury, -ory ('ɑːmərɪ). Forms: 4 **armurie**, 5–6 **armery**, **armorye**, **-orie**, **-ary**, 6– **armory**, **armoury**. [Perh. orig. a. OF. *armoierie*, *armoirie*. But from the earliest period treated as a derivative of ARMOUR *sb.*, and spelt like it *armurie*, *armery*, *armory*, *armoury*. With senses 3–5, cf. also OF. *armeurerie*, now *armurerie*, the office or store of the *armeurier*, arsenal (in which sense Godefroy has also *armoirie*). By some, in 16th c., referred to L. *armārium* (see AMBRY), and spelt *armary*. As *armour* was, in 16th c., often written *armor*, the spelling *armory* was common down to the present century. Cf. ARMORY.]

1. Armour collectively. *arch.*

1330 R. BRUNNE 194 If I may be auaile of hors or amurie. **1400** GRIFFITH in Ellis *Orig. Lett.* II. 2. I. 6, I boȝt armery..and horses, and other araement. **1577** HARRISON *England* II. v. 115 Armorie meet for their defense and service. **1596** SPENSER *F.Q.* I. i. 27 That armory, Wherein ye have great glory wonne this day. **1667** MILTON *P.L.* IV. 553 Celestial Armourie, Shields, Helmes, and Speares. **1783** COWPER *Task* v. 139 The armory of Winter. **1802** WORDSW. *Sonn. Liberty* I. xvi, In our halls is hung Armoury of the invincible Knights of old.

†2. An armed force. *Obs.*

*c***1400** *Syr Tryam.* 49 The kyng bad ordeygne hys armoryes, Knyghtys, squyers, and palfrays, Alle redy for to goo. *c***1532** LD. BERNERS *Huon* 523 That with an armeri al ye haue passed, & taken castels.

3. A place where arms are kept, an arsenal.

1538 LELAND *Itin.* IV. 54 A great large Tour caullid White Tour: wherin is now the Kinges Armary. **1588** SHAKS. *Tit. A.* IV. ii. 11 The goodliest weapons of his armorie. **1611** BIBLE *Song Sol.* iv. 4 The tower of Dauid builded for an armorie. **1671** MILTON *Samson* 1281 Their armories and magazines contemns. **1711** *Vind. Sacheverell* 8 Like one of the Figures in the Queens-Armory in the Tower. **1796** MORSE *Amer. Geog.* I. 678 The public buildings are, an exchange..armoury, poor house. **1820** W. IRVING *Sketch Bk.* I. 171 The armoury..a gothic hall furnished with weapons of various kinds and ages.

4. *fig.* (Cf. also ARMORY[2].)

1615 HIERON *Wks.* I. 618 The diuels storehouse and his armory of tentations. **1689** SELDEN *Table T.* 9 A Book of Apothegms is an armoury of thought. **1817** COLERIDGE *Biog. Lit.* II. 31 Language is the armoury of the human mind; and at once contains the trophies of its past and the weapons of its future conquests. **1877** L. MORRIS *Epic Hades* I. 31 The subtle wiles a woman draws From the armoury of hate.

5. The workshop of an armourer; a place where arms are manufactured (U.S.).

1841 in WEBSTER. **1859** in WORCESTER. **1860** BARTLETT s.v., The Springfield Armory.

6. The craft of the armourer.

1718 POPE *Iliad* VII. 270 The work of Tychius, who..in all arts of armoury excell'd.

armoyrye, obs. form of ARMORY.

armozeen (ɑːmə'ziːn). Also 6–7 **armesine**, 7 **armoisin**, **armazine**. [a. F. *armoisin*, *-ine*, OF. *armesin* taffata. (Of uncertain origin: see Littré.)] A stout plain silk, usually black, used for clerical gowns and for mourning scarves.

1599 HAKLUYT *Voy.* II. I. 222 Ueluets, Damasks, and Sattens, Armesine of Portugall. **1667** E. CHAMBERLAYNE *St. Gt. Brit.* I. I. vii. (1743) 39 We yearly imported from France..Taffaties, Stuffs, Armoisins. **1733** MRS. DELANY *Autobiog.* (1861) I. 431 Lady Dysart's clothes were pink armazine trimmed with silver. **1763** *Advt.* in *Brit. Chron.* (in *Draper's Dict.*) Tabbies, Ducaps, black Armozeens, Rasdumores.

'arm,pit. [f. ARM *sb.*[1]]

1. The hollow under the arm where it is jointed to the trunk.

*a***1400** *Metr. Voc.* in Wright *Voc.* 179 *Acella*, arme-pytt. **1528** PAYNELL *Salerne Regim.* Rj, Under y[e] arme pittis, and in the groynes. *a***1656** BP. HALL *Rem. Wks.* 130 We are unwilling to put the rags under our arme-pits. **1855** MACAULAY *Hist. Eng.* III. 630 The English infantry struggled through the river, up to their armpits in water.

2. The corresponding cavity in other animals. Cf. ARM-HOLE. *arch.* or *Obs.*

1601 HOLLAND *Pliny* II. 347 The Elephant alone hath twaine vnder his shoulders or legs before..lying hidden as it were within the arm-pits.

†3. *fig.* The axil of a plant. *Obs.*

1601 HOLLAND *Pliny* II. 123 Vnder the wings or arm-pits (as it were) of the leaues.

4. *fig.* Used (esp. in the formula ***the armpit of the nation***, etc.) to designate a place or part considered disgusting or contemptible; a place that 'stinks'. *colloq.* (chiefly *U.S.*).

[**1965**: see PIT *sb.*[1] 9a]. **1968–70** *Current Slang* (Univ. S. Dakota) III–IV. 3 *Armpit of the nation, n.* Las Cruces.—New Mexico State. **1973** *N.Y. Times* 19 Aug. 15 She is an amateur,..with no real notion of who might be out there in the armpit of America, grunting at what she says. **1978** J. WAMBAUGH *Black Marble* iv. 40 77th Street Station..was the armpit of detective duty. **1986** *Washington Post* 14 Jan. B3/2 Your alma mater is still the armpit of the universe.

arm's-end, -length, -reach: see ARM *sb.*[1] 2 b.

†armth(e. *Obs.* [variant of ERMTH(E, OE. *ęrmþ(u*, OTeut. **armiþâ*, f. ARM *a.* poor + -TH[1]. Prop. with umlaut, but occas. found without it, as OE. *earmþu*, ME. *ærmðe*, *armðe*: cf. *warmth.*] Poverty, wretchedness, misery.

*c***885** K. ÆLFRED *Boeth.* xxxviii. 2 ȝif þá earmþa ealle sóðe sint. **1205** LAY. 20438 þa wes Ænglene lond mid ærmþe of-fulled. *c***1220** *Hali Meid.* 37 þeos & oðre armðen þat of wedlac awakeneð. *a***1275** *Prov. Alfred* 523 in *O.E. Misc.* 133 Wer hachte is hid, þer is armþe inoch.

armure, -rer, -rie, obs. ff. ARMOUR *sb.*, -RER, -RY.

armure ('ɑːmjʊə(r)). [Fr.] A woollen or silk fabric, or a mixture of the two, with a twilled or ribbed surface.

1880 in WEBSTER Suppl. **1882** CAULFEILD & SAWARD *Dict. Needlework*, *Armure*, this is a silk textile; plain, striped, ribbed, or with a small design. Sometimes it is made of wool and silk. There is also Satin Armure and Armure Bosphore. **1894** *Daily News* 20 Jan. 5/7 Rich cream-coloured silk of the sort known as 'armure'. **1923** G. G. DENNY *Fabrics* I. 16 *Armure*..so called because the fabric has a small ridgy or pebbly pattern which suggests chain armor.

army ('ɑːmɪ). Forms: 4–5 **armee**, 5 **armeye**, 5–6 **arme**, **armye**, 6 **armey**, 6–7 **armie**, 6– **army**. [a. F. *armée*, cogn. with Sp., Pg., Pr. *armada*, It. *armata*, subst. use of pa. pple. of L. *armāre*, to arm, *lit.* 'act of arming, armament, armed force.' The concrete sense is late in Fr. and Eng., and occurs first in reference to a *naval* force; cf. ARMADA.]

I. Literal senses.

†1. An armed expedition by sea or land. *Obs.*

*c***1386** CHAUCER *Prol.* 59 In the grete See At many a noble Armee [*v.r.* arme, armeye] hadde he be. **1489** CAXTON *Faytes of Armes* II. xxxviii. 160 They that by the see wol goo, be it in armee or to som other adoo. **1502** ARNOLD *Chron.* (1811) Introd. 37 This yere[21 Edw. IV] y[e] kinge made a gret Army into Scotland. **1525** LD. BERNERS *Froiss.* II. xvii. 33 They gette the duke of Burgoyne in great desyre to make an armye into Englande.

2. *gen.* An armed force (by sea or land); an assemblage of men for belligerent purposes; a host. *Obs.* exc. when qualified, as in *a land-army*.

*c***1460** FORTESCUE *Abs. & Lim. Mon.* (1714) 52 If ther come a sodein Armye upon this Lond, by See or by Land. **1556** *Chron. Grey Friars* (1852) 25 The kynge went to Callys with a grete armé agaynst France. **1603** KNOLLES *Hist. Turkes* (1621) 1314 He sent a navall armie towards the mouth of the river Danowe. **1751** CHAMBERS *Cycl.* s.v., A naval or sea Army is a number of ships of war, equipped and manned with sailors and marines, under the command of an admiral. **1865** F. PALEY *Æschylus* 113 He gave the instant order to his land-army and rushed away.

3. *specifically*:

†a. A naval armament, an armada, a fleet. *Obs.*

1545 (June 24) LISLE *Disp.* in *State Papers* (1830) I. 791 The rest of tharmye comyng out of Thames..sholde be in the Downes. **1588** D. ARCHDEACON (*title*) A true Discourse of the Armie [*i.e.* 'Spanish Armada']..assembled in the hauen of Lisbon. **1652** NEEDHAM tr. *Selden's Mare Cl.* 270 The King commanded that 21000*l.* should bee paid to his Armie; (For so that Fleet is called every where in English Saxon) which rode at Grenewich. **1751–86** [see 2].

b. A land force; a body of men armed for war, and organized in divisions and regiments each under its officer, the whole body being under the direction of a commander-in-chief or general. (The common use.)

Standing army, an army of professional soldiers kept permanently on foot, as distinguished from one raised on a special occasion and again disbanded, as were the English armies before the 17th century.

1557–8 *Act* 4 & 5 *Mary* iii. §5 During the tyme that any Armye or nombre of Men being under a Leiutenaunte, shalbee assembled and continue together. **1579** GOSSON *Sch. Abuse* (Arb.) 16 Caligula lying in Fraunce with a greate armie of fighting menne. **1605** BACON *Adv. Learn.* II. xvii. §8 Prejudicial..to the proceeding of an army to go about to besiege every little fort or hold. **1762** KAMES *Elem. Crit.* (1833) 487 A number of men under the same military command, are termed an army. **1831** CARLYLE *Sart. Res.* III. iv, After the invention of fire-arms and standing-armies.

4. ***the Army***: the whole of the regular troops or land forces of a state; the military service. (This use came gradually in with the formation of a standing army; its growth may be traced in the

title 'The Army,' applied to the parliamentary forces c1647, to the forces of James II in 1687, and to those of William III, when it seems to have been fully established.)

[**1647** (*title*) Two Letters of his Excellencie Sir Thomas Fairfax.. Published at the instant desire of the Army. ? **1686** JAMES II in *Royal Tracts* (1692) 13 Let no man take exception that there are some Officers in the Army not qualified according to the late Tests.] **1698–9** *Act 11 William III*, viii, An Act..to..determine the Debts due to the Army, Navy, and for Transport-Service. **1712** STEELE *Spect.* No. 544 ¶4 Such Gentlemen as have served their Country in the Army. **1714** *Ibid.* No. 566 ¶4 A Man who goes into the Army a Coxcomb will come out of it a sort of Publick Nuisance. **1860** HT. MARTINEAU *Biog. Sk.* (1876) 204 Entering the army at the age of thirteen. *Mod.* The eldest son is in the Army, the second at the Bar. *Toast*, The Army, Navy, and Volunteers.

II. Figurative and transferred senses.

5. *transf.* A vast assemblage, resembling an army in number; a 'host,' a multitude: **a.** of men.

c **1500** *Virgilius* in Thoms *E.E. Rom.* 22 He raysed a great armey of people. **1525** LD. BERNERS *Froiss.* II. ccxxvii. Argt., Of the great armye[*Heading*, assemble] that was made in the citye of Reynes. **1535** COVERDALE *2 Kings* v. 15 He [Naaman] turned agayne..with all his armye. **1611** BIBLE *Ezek.* xxxvii. 10 They liued, and stood vp vpon their feet, an exceeding great armie. *Mod.* A whole army of waiters was engaged for the banquet.

b. *fig.* of things. *arch.*

1596 SPENSER *F.Q.* v. v. 34 Armies of lovely lookes and speeches wise. **1628** COKE *On Litt.* Pref., You shall meet with a whole Army of words. **1675** TRAHERNE *Chr. Ethics* ii. 16 When we can cheerfully look on an army of misfortunes. **1751** WATTS *Improv. Mind* (1801) 377 The army of my sins rises up before me.

6. (*fig.* from 3.) A marshalled host.

1593 SHAKS. *Rich. II*, III. iii. 87 Mustring..on our behalfe, Armies of Pestilence. **1611** BIBLE *Joel* ii. 25 The caterpiller, and the palmer worme, my great armie. **1845** WHATELY *Let.* in *Life* (1866) II. 77 It is time that these two armies [the two opposed parties in the House of Commons] should as soon as possible be disbanded. **1857** LIVINGSTONE *Trav.* v. 104 An army of locusts.

7. (*fig.* or *transf.* from 2, 3, 4.) A body of men organized for a purpose, or viewed as striving for the advancement of a cause. Hence assumed by such organizations as the ***Salvation Army***, the ***Blue Ribbon Army***.

1543 *Te Deum* in *Primer*, The noble armye of Martyrs do prayse the. **1712** ADDISON *Spect.* No. 465 ¶1 Latimer, one of the glorious Army of Martyrs. **1855** KINGSLEY *Glaucus* (1878) 1 The ignoble army of idlers. **1878** *Christian* 16 May (*heading*), Gospel-Temperance in Hoxton. A 'Blue Ribbon Army.' *Ibid.*, Hard-working men who have only recently joined the 'Blue Ribbon Army.' **1879** *Chr. World* 23 May 330/4 The band of people calling themselves 'The Salvation Army.' **1883** W. BOOTH in *Whitaker's Almanac* 439/1 The Salvation Army was commenced as a Christian Mission in 1865..In the course of 1878..the name 'Salvation Army' was taken.

III. *Comb.* and *Attrib.* (chiefly from sense 4): as ***army-council***, ***-man***; also **army ant**, a popular name for certain predatory ants (esp. of the genera *Dorylus* and *Eciton*) which move about in swarms (also called *driver ants*, *visiting ants*, etc.); **army-broker**, **-clothier**, **-contractor**, **-furnisher**, who carry on their respective businesses on behalf of, or in connexion with, the Army; **army co-operation**, co-operation of the air force with the army; freq. *attrib.*; **army-corps**, a main division of an army in the field; †**army-debenture**, a security for money lent on behalf of the Army; **army-list**, an official list of all the commissioned officers of the Army; **Army Service Corps** (in 1918 renamed *Royal Army Service Corps*), that part of the army establishment which is concerned with commissariat and transport; previously called the Commissariat Staff Corps; abbrev. (R.)A.S.C.; **army-worm** *U.S.* the larva of any of various destructive moths.

1874 T. BELT *Naturalist in Nicaragua* ii. 17 Ecitons, or Foraging Ants... In Nicaragua they are generally called 'Army Ants'. **1961** P. GRAY *Encycl. Biol. Sciences* 41/1 Ant colonies may contain..several millions, as in the African *Anomma* army ants. **1858** GEN. P. THOMPSON *Audi Alt.* I. lxiv. 247 Being in the position of what was called an army-broker. **1855** MACAULAY *Hist. Eng.* IV. 547 He had become an army clothier. **1817** COLERIDGE *Biogr. Lit.* 242 Whose father had made a large fortune..as an army-contractor. **1935** C. G. BURGE *Compl. Bk. Aviation* 532/2 Co-operation with the army is performed by army co-operation aircraft. **1940** E. C. SHEPHERD *Britain's Air Power* 26 They are called Army Co-operation aeroplanes and they work invariably with and for the Army. **1868** GLADSTONE *Juv. Mundi* xi. (1870) 431 The members of the Army-council contend freely in argument with Agamemnon. **1702** *Lond. Gaz.* mmmdccccxxxviii/4 Lost..a Pocket-Book, wherein there was two Army-Debentures. **1870** *Pall Mall G.* 19 Oct. 11 Accompanied by an army-furnisher. **1814** SCOTT *Wav.* lxi, This good lady had the whole army-list by heart. **1857** MRS. GASKELL *Let.* 5 June (1966) 451 Will you send me an *East Indian* Army-List, if there is such a thing? **1935** G. GREENE *Basement Room* 152 He would look up his record in the old Army Lists when he got home. **1674** HICKMAN *Hist. Quinquart.* 133 Many of those Army-men..gloried..in trampling all Law and Right under foot. **1871** *Hansard* CCVI. 961 The Army Service Corps is divided into three branches—supply, transport, and stores, with officers and men attached. **1900** S. L. NORRIS *S. Afr. War* iii. 57 To Cape Town there went from England..two companies A.S.C. **1916** 'BOYD CABLE' *Action Front* 124 Army Service Corps supply points. **1930** J. FORTESCUE (*title*) The Royal Army Service Corps. A History of Transport and Supply in the British Army. **1819** D. THOMAS *Travels Western Country* 155 The *army worm*..has ravaged the meadows. **1852** *Let.* in De Bow *S. & W. States* I. 171 They..lay millions of eggs..and thus they increase until they deserve the name of army worm. **1865** *Pall Mall G.* No. 192. 6/1 Seriously injured by the army-worm. **1961** R. SOUTH *Moths Brit. Isles* (ed. 4) 1st Ser. 205 The White speck or American Wainscot (*Leucania Unipuncta*)..is known in America..as the 'Army Worm'.

armyll(e, **armyte**, obs. f. ARMIL, HERMIT.

arn, obs. f. EARN *v.*, and (*Ayenb.*) ERNE, eagle.

arn, obs. form of *ran*, pa. t. of RUN.

arn(e, early form of ARE *v.*: see BE.

†**arn(e.** *Obs.* or *dial.* [perh. = *alrn*, *allern*, OE. *ælren*: see ALDERN.] The alder tree.

1791 NEWTE *Tour Eng. & Scot.* 415 The aller or arne..is also found in marshy places. c **1830** *Trans. Highl. Soc.* Ser. II. II. 216 (JAM.) An infusion of arn or alder-bark.

arnatto, variant of ANATTA.

Arnaut (ɑːˈnaʊt). Also **Arnaout**, etc. [See ALBANIAN *a.*[2] and *sb.*[2]] An Albanian, *spec.* one serving in the Turkish army. Also *attrib.*

1717 LADY M. W. MONTAGU *Let.* 1 Apr. (1965) I. 319 The Arnounts..are natives of Arnountlick, the Ancient Macedonia,..being the best militia in the Turkish Empire. **1802** C. JAMES *Mil. Dict.*, *Arnauts*, Turkish light cavalry. **1833** *Penny Cycl.* I. 258/1 The population of Albania has always been of a warlike character... At present, under the denomination of Arnauts, they rank among the flower of the Ottoman army. **1863** PATON *Hist. Egypt. Revol.* II. xxiii. 256 Instances occurred of Arnaut soldiers getting richly dressed prostitutes, adorned with jewels, into their houses. **1910** *Encycl. Brit.* IX. 107/1 The Arnaut (or Albanian) soldiers in the service of Khosrev tumultuously demanded their pay. **1922** D. H. LOW tr. *Ballads of Marko Kraljević* 129 A wild Arnaut woman bore me.

arnd, **arnede**, obs. forms of ERRAND.

arndern: see UNDERN, and cf. ANDERS-MEAT.

arneis, **-eys**, obs. forms of HARNESS.

†**ˈarnement.** *Obs.* [? corruption or phonetic change of OF. *arrement*:—L. *ātrāment-um* ink, f. *ātr-um* black.] Ink, or materials with which it is made.

c **1300** *K. Alis.* 6418 Blak is heore visage..Eyghnen they haveth so arnement. c **1320** *Seuyn Sages* (W.) 2776 He let him make a garnement, Ase blak as ani arnement. **1496** *Bk. St. Albans* C. vij, Fille the hooll with a powdre of arnement Ibrente. **1586** LUPTON *Thous. Notable Things* (1675) 197 Take Arnement, Hony, and the white of Eggs.

†**arne-morwe.** *Obs.* [OE. *ǽrne morȝen*, accus. of *ǽr morȝen*.] Early morn.

c **950** *Lindisf. Gosp.* John xviii. 28 Uæs untudlice ar morȝen. c **1330** *Arth. & Merl.* 4797 Fram arnemorwe to the midday.

arnest, obs. form of EARNEST.

arnica (ˈɑːnɪkə). [mod.L. of unknown origin.] **1.** A genus of Composite plants, of which the species *A. montana* or Mountain Tobacco, a native of Central Europe, has valuable medicinal properties.

1753 CHAMBERS *Cycl. Supp.*, *Arnica*..a species of doronicum, with plantane leaves. **1881** *Blackw. Mag.* Apr. 486 Golden arnica, autumnal cyclamen, blue cornflowers.

2. A medicine prepared from the plant, *esp.* in the form of a tincture.

1788 *Edin. New Dispens.* (1791) 133/1 Arnica..has been of late recommended as a very powerful antispasmodic. **1864** BROWNING *Sludge* 1479 Stiffish cock-tail, taken in time, Is better for a bruise than arnica.

Hence **arnicin** (ˈɑːnɪsɪn). *Chem.*, a yellow, non-crystallizable, bitter substance, the active principle of arnica. **arnicine** (-aɪn), an alkaloid found in the same plant.

1847 *Nat. Encycl.* II. 150/2 An acrid bitter principle.. called Arnicine. **1869** WATTS *Dict. Chem.* VI. 192 According to Bastick, arnica flowers contain a non-volatile bitter alkaloid, arnicine. **1876** HARLEY *Mat. Med.* 537 The root is rich in arnicin.

Arnoldian (ɑːˈnəʊldɪən), *a.* and *sb.* [f. Thomas *Arnold* (1795–1842), Headmaster of Rugby School, or his son Matthew *Arnold* (1822–88), poet and critic, + -IAN.] **A.** *adj.* Belonging to or characteristic of either Thomas Arnold or his son Matthew Arnold. **B.** *sb.* An admirer or follower of either Arnold.

1888 MRS. H. WARD *R. Elsmere* I. I. v. 112 The 'earnestness' of an Arnoldian Rugby. **1902** *Daily Chron.* 24 Dec. 3/6 The Arnoldian tradition had almost died out... When it was announced that the new Headmastership was to be given to the Liberal Principal of Kneller Hall, everybody was gratified, even the boys, and the old school resumed its Arnoldian glory. **1904** *Ibid.* 19 Mar. 3/1 In only one respect is it likely to disappoint Arnoldians seriously. **1953** *Essays in Criticism* III. 2 It was in that conviction.. that its founders gave this journal its Arnoldian title. **1957** *Times Lit. Suppl.* 1 Nov. 658/4 The reference will produce the refutation of some possible charge of want of Arnoldian seriousness. **1966** *Punch* 5 Jan. 31/2 Dennis..sees in him.. something Arnoldian and headmasterly.

ˈArnoldism. [f. as prec. + -ISM.] Doctrine, theory, or practice formed after the precepts and example of either Thomas Arnold or his son Matthew.

c **1845** T. KEBLE in G. Battiscombe *John Keble* (1963) xiii. 253 Mr. Ward seems to me so strongly tinctured with Arnoldism that it shows itself in all his writings, that particular delight..which T. A. had in speaking provokingly of people and things whom one respected. **1858** J. CAIRNS *Let.* 20 May in A. R. MacEwen *Life & Lett.* (1895) xvi. 433 It is Arnoldism in its aphelion, and I fear will not come back to the sun. **1888** GLADSTONE *Let.* in *Westm. Gaz.* (1910) 2 Apr. 1/3 [Mrs. Humphry Ward]..is a fruit, I think, of what must be called Arnoldism. **1892** *Nation* 28 Apr. 322/2 The predilections we have indicated and the slavish Arnoldism of the essays, except when dealing with the Hebrews, disable the writer in the higher field [of criticism]. **1934** R. CAMPBELL *Broken Record* vii. 153 Like Arnoldism-of-Rugby Russellism has this in common with it —that it presupposes the child to be a villain and that only a super-amount of 'treatment' can save him.

Arnoldist (ˈɑːnəldɪst). *Ch. Hist.* Also **Arnaldist**. A follower of Arnold (or Arnaldus) of Brescia, a reformer of the 12th century.

1669 PENN *No Cross, etc.* xx. §18 They [the Waldenses] had many other names, as Arnoldists, Esperonists. **1882** SCHAFF *Herzog's Encycl. Rel. Knowl.* I. 150.

arnotto, variant of ANATTA.

ar'n't, contr. for *are not*; cf. AIN'T, AN'T.

a **1845** HOOD *To Mrs. Fry* xvii, O come and teach our children—that ar'n't ours—That heaven's straight pathway is a narrow way.

arnut, obs. form of EARTH-NUT.

a-roar (əˈrɔə(r)), *advb. phr.* Also **arore**. [A *prep.*[1] + ROAR *sb.*] In a roar, roaring.

1461 MARG. PASTON in *P. Lett.* II. 65 The byll that Howard hathe mad a yens yow and odyr hathe set the pepyll in thys contre a rore. **1836** *Blackw. Mag.* XXXIX. 842 Hail! day of storms! with thy woods a-roar like rivers, and thy rivers a-roar like seas!

†**a-ˈroast**, *ppl. a.* *Obs.* In 4 **a-rost(e.** [= *i-rost*: see A *particle* and ROAST *v.* (Stratmann takes *roast* here as sb. and *a* as prep.)] Roasted.

c **1300** *Pol. Songs* 151 Thenne mot ych habbe hennen a-rost. *Ibid.* 237 The deuel huem afretye, Rau other a-roste.

arob, **aroba**, **arobe**, obs. variants of ARROBA.

aroba, var. ARABA.

arobalist, erron. form. of ARBALEST.

aroid (ˈɛərɔɪd). *Bot.* [f. ARUM + -OID. The N.O. *Araceæ* is also called *Aroideæ*.] A plant allied to the Arum or Wake-robin; an arad. **aˈroideous** *a.*, allied to Arum.

1830 LINDLEY *Nat. Syst. Bot.* 252 The eatable Aroideous plants, Orchises, Yams. **1860** *Let.* in *Athenæum* 29 June (1861) 863 Festoons of aroideous plants. **1876** H. EVERSHED in *Macm. Mag.* XXXIV. 53 The moist and heated air covers the..trunks of trees with a drapery of aroids.

aroint, **aroynt** (əˈrɔɪnt). [Origin unknown. Used by Shakspere, whence by some modern writers.]

1. In ***aroint thee!*** (? verb in the imperative, or interjection) meaning apparently: Avaunt! Begone!

1605 SHAKS. *Macb.* I. iii. 6 Aroynt thee, Witch, the rumpefed Ronyon cryes. **1605** —— *Lear* III. iv. 129 He met the Night-Mare..Bid her a-light, and her troth-plight, And, aroynt thee, Witch, aroynt thee. **1816** SCOTT *Antiq.* vi, Aroint thee, witch! wouldst thou poison my guests with thy infernal decoctions. [Also in *Quentin D.* (1823) II. xix. 364.] **1831** HEIDIGER *Didoniad* IX. 248 Aroynt, thou lingering, long-drawn mortal Strife.

2. Used by Mr. and Mrs. Browning as a vb.: To drive away with an execration.

1850 MRS. BROWNING *To Flush* xviii, Whiskered cats arointed flee. **1878** BROWNING *Two Poets Croisic* 156 That Humbug, whom thy soul aroints. **1880** —— *Dram. Idyls*, *Pietro* 22 Aroint the churl who prophesies.

[The origin of Shakspere's *aroynt* has been the subject of numerous conjectures, none of which can be said to have even a *prima facie* probability. (Cf. also ARUNT.) The following passages are usually cited as pointing to the same word:

RAY *North C. Wds.* (1691) has: *Ryntye*, by your leave, stand handsomely. As '*Rynt you, witch*, quoth Bessie Locket to her mother'; Proverb. *Cheshire.* THORESBY *Lett. to Ray* 1703 (Yorksh. Words) has: '*Ryndta*, used to cows to make them give way, and stand in their stalls or booyses.'

In parts of Cheshire (and ? Lancashire) *ou* (aʊ) is pronounced *ī*, *ȳ* (aɪ)—i.e. (aʊ) has been umlauted to (aʏ), and delabialized to (aɪ); elsewhere it is reduced to (aə), (a(ə)), or (aː)—so that *round* becomes *rȳnd*. *Rynd-ta!* is thus merely a local pronunciation of 'round thee, = move round, move about!' The local nature, the meaning, and form of the phrase, seem all opposed to its identity with Shakspere's *aroynt*.]

arolla (əˈrɒlə). [ad. F. *arolle.*] Name given in French Switzerland to the *Pinus cembra.*

1881 MISS BRADDON *Asph.* III. 196 Where huge arollas of a thousand years' growth spread their black branches against the snow-line.

aroma (əˈrəʊmə). Forms: 3–7 **aromat,** (*pl.* 3–4 **-az,** = *-atz*), 4–7 **aromate,** 8– **aroma.** [a. OF. *aromat* (now *aromate*), ad. L. *arōmata*, pl. of *arōma*, a. Gr. ἄρωμα. In mod. times altered back to L. and Gr. form; occas. even with pl. *a'romata*, though *a'romas* is usual.]

†**1.** Spice; usually in *pl.* spices. *Obs.*

c **1220** *Leg. Kath.* 2225 Wið smirles of aromaz. *c* **1230** *Ancr. R.* 376 þeos þreo Maries bouhten swote smellinde aromaz uorto smurien mide ure Louerd. *a* **1300** *Cursor M.* 21299 þe foerth sauurs als aromat. **1494** FABYAN I. iii. 10 With dyuers Aromats & spyces of moste swettest odour. **1637** NABBES *Microcosm.* in Dodsl. *O.P.* IX. 240 And breathes perfumes, no Persian aromats Can imitate. **1686** W. HARRIS *Lemery's Chym.* I. xvii. 408 You may make use of other Aromates or Spices. **1753** CHAMBERS *Cycl. Supp.*, *Aroma* is, by some authors, particularly applied to denote myrrh.

2. The distinctive fragrance exhaled from a spice, plant, etc.; *gen.* an agreeable odour, a sweet smell.

1814 *Edin. Rev.* XXIII. 116 The more odorous plants.. whose aroma we may wish to retain. **1873** E. SMITH *Foods* 23 The nutritive qualities of the lean meat are there, except the aromas, which may have escaped under the influence of heat.

b. An aromatic essence or oil.

1830 COLERIDGE *Lect. Shaks.* II. 203 Its [a plant's] balsams, gums, resins, aromata.. are.. mere excretions from the vegetable.

3. *fig.* A subtle pervasive quality or charm.

1851 CARLYLE *Sterling* I. ii. (1872) 11 The delicate aroma of his nature. **1861** TROLLOPE *T. All Countr.* viii. 281 The language of the people has not the pure Parisian aroma.

aromal (əˈrəʊməl), *a.* [f. AROMA + -AL.] Of or pertaining to, concerned with, or involving, aroma or aromas.

1848 *Tait's Mag.* XV. 704 Man, being in a proper state, *presto*, the aromal spherical bath will start forth and do its work. *Ibid.*, That the earth clogs the sun, in default of aromal discharges. *Ibid.*, Still, though dead, she has her use, that of 'mummy, or aromal loadstone'. **1851** WHITTIER *My Summer with Dr. Singletary* ii, in *Writ.* (1889) V. 206 Nature's healing ministrations came to me through all my senses. I felt the medicinal virtues of her sights, and sounds, and aromal breezes. **1888** A. S. WILSON *Lyric of Hopeless Love* §l. p. 168 Love is.. an aromal fire That sweeps the spirit to dismiss All but its own desire.

†**aroma-olent**, *a.* *Obs. rare*⁻¹. [L. *olēnt-em* smelling.] Fragrant.

1657 TOMLINSON *Renou's Disp.* 337 Aromatic seeds, odorate, acrimonious and Aromaolent.

†**a'romatary.** *Obs. rare*⁻¹. [ad. L. *arōmatāri-us*, f. *arōma*: see -ARY.] A dealer in spices, a perfumer.

1657 TOMLINSON *Renou's Disp.* 484 Which Aromataries sometimes use in dividing their powders.

aromatic (ærəʊˈmætɪk), *a.* and *sb.* Also 4–8 **-yk, -yque, -icke.** [a. F. *aromatique* (14th c.), ad. L. *arōmatic-us*, a. Gr. ἀρωματικός: see AROMA.]

A. *adj.*

1. Having the fragrant smell, and warm, slightly pungent, taste, of spice; yielding aroma; spicy, fragrant, sweet-smelling.

1366 MAUNDEV. xvi. 174 Ensense and other aromatyk thinges of noble smelle. **1486** CAXTON *Curial* 6 The grete and delycious wynes aromatyques that he dranke. **1542** BOORDE *Dyetary* iv. (1870) 239 Herbes of aromatyck and redolent sauours. **1664** H. MORE *Myst. Iniq.* 469 Whose dead Bodies were embalmed with Aromatick odours. **1712** tr. *Pomet's Hist. Drugs* I. 150 Of a very agreeable Smell, and a biting Aromatick Taste. **1732** POPE *Ess. Man* I. 200 Die of a rose in aromatic pain. **1845** DARWIN *Voy. Nat.* ii. (1879) 31 The leaves of the camphor, pepper, cinnamon, and clove trees were delightfully aromatic.

2. *Chem.* Epithet of an extensive group of organic compounds, consisting of benzene and its homologues (i.e. hydrocarbons of the formula $C_n H_{2n-6}$, with the alcohols, acids, and bases derived from them). In mod. use, pertaining to or designating a compound with one or more planar conjugated rings of the form typified by the benzene molecule; ***aromatic sextet***, a group of six pi-electrons in the ring of an aromatic molecule regarded as responsible for its aromaticity.

Called *aromatique* by Kekulé in 1865 (*Bull. de la Soc. Chim. de Paris*), on account of the peculiar and fragrant odours possessed by some of them, especially by certain derivatives of benzene, such as benzoic acid, bitter almond oil, &c.

[**1814** SIR H. DAVY *Agric. Chem.* 146 Woods that contain aromatic oils are remarked for their indestructibility.] **1869** WATTS *Dict. Chem.* VI. 193 The aromatic compounds form a group running parallel, as it were, with the fatty bodies, and like the latter including hydrocarbons, alcohols, acids, amines, etc. *Ibid.* 206 Several monatomic aromatic acids exist as natural products. Thus benzoic acid exists ready formed in gum benzoin. **1879** *Jrnl. Chem. Soc.* XXXVI. 633 By this synthesis, the aromatic nature of phloroglucinol is definitely established. **1909** C. A. KEANE *Mod. Org. Chem.* vii. 119 Ethylene forms both aromatic and aliphatic hydrocarbons. **1925** ARMIT & ROBINSON in *Jrnl. Chem. Soc.* CXXVII. 1605 Six electrons are able to form a group which resists disruption, and may be called the aromatic sextet. **1955** *Chem. Rev.* LV. 10 One of the most important developments in organic chemistry in recent years has been the attention devoted to what may be described collectively as 'non-benzenoid aromatic compounds'. [*Note*] This term is taken here to refer to carbocyclic compounds only and is not meant to include heterocycles. **1964** J. W. LINNETT *Electronic Struct. Molecules* vi. 89 The benzene molecule is too complicated for a complete theoretical treatment of all the thirty valence-shell electrons. Consequently attention has always been focused on the six electrons which, in the molecular orbital terminology, form the π-system. This is the group which has also been called the aromatic sextet. **1972** *Sci. Amer.* Aug. 32 (*caption*) Whether a given system is aromatic, nonaromatic or antiaromatic depends on how many of its electrons are 'delocalized'. **1986** *Pure & Applied Chem.* LVIII. 197 There is generally a decrease in the stability of aromatic compounds as the number of heteroatoms increases.

B. *sb.* A substance or plant emitting a spicy odour; a fragrant drug; a spice.

1494 FABYAN VI. clxv. 160 Enoynted with ryche and precyous bawmys, and other oyntmentis, and aromatykes. *a* **1680** BUTLER *Rem.* (1759) I. 111 It keeps our Spice, and Aromatics sweet. **1748** ANSON *Voy.* II. i. 117 The trees.. are most of them aromaticks. **1821** COMBE (Dr. Syntax) *Wife* I. 278 While Ma'am the Aromatics blended, To gain the scent which she intended.

aro'matical, *a.* ? *Obs.* [f. prec. + -AL¹.] = prec.

1578 LYTE *Dodoens* 284 The seede whereof is of a very pleasant and Aromaticall sauour. **1656** TRAPP *Comm. Matt.* xiii. 52 Like aromatical trees that sweat out their sovereign oils. **1732** ARBUTHNOT *Rules Diet* 260 The Juices of pungent and aromatical Fruits. [**1809** PARKINS *Culpepper's Eng. Physician Enlarged* 303 Of an aromatical taste.]

aro'matically, *adv.* [f. prec. + -LY².] With aromatic odour or taste; spicily.

1657 W. COLES *Adam in Eden* 148 The smell thereof is somewhat aromatically sweet.

aro'maticalness. ? *Obs.* [f. as prec. + -NESS.] The quality of being aromatic; spiciness.

1731 in BAILEY.

aromaticity (ˌærəməˈtɪsɪtɪ). *Chem.* [f. AROMATIC *a.* + -ITY.] The property of being aromatic (sense 2); aromatic character.

1932 *Recueil des Travaux Chim. des Pays-Bas* LI. 1054 The best definition of aromaticity is probably one which is concerned with general properties. **1955** *Chem. Rev.* LV. 10 Molecular orbital theory.. has been used.. to predict that aromaticity will be shown only by those rings having (4*n* + 2) π-electrons. **1965** PHILLIPS & WILLIAMS *Inorg. Chem.* I. xvii. 627 All the phosphonitrilic chlorides show comparable aromaticity. **1983** *New Scientist* 28 July 266/1 The concept of delocalisation is used by chemists to explain the increased stability (known as aromaticity) of molecules like benzene. **1986** *Pure & Applied Chem.* LVIII. 197 The concept of aromaticity has been one of the most useful generalizations in heterocyclic chemistry, just as in carbocyclic chemistry.

aro'maticness. [f. AROMATIC + -NESS.] = AROMATICALNESS.

1731 in BAILEY. **1803** W. TAYLOR in *Month. Mag.* XV. 324 The original or concrete idea of sensation, in which roundness, blueness, bitterness, aromaticness consists.

†**a'romatiˌzate**, *ppl. a.* *Obs.* [ad. L. *arōmatīzāt-us*, f. *arōmatīzāre*: see below.] = AROMATIZED.

1576 BAKER *Gesner's Jewell of Health* 78 Let all be.. aromatizate with the powder of three Saunders.

†**a'romatiˌzate**, *v.* [f. prec.] To aromatize.

1576 BAKER *Gesner's Jewell of Health* 99 a, This water of Lyfe is only aromatizated with the Levaunt spyces. **1610** BARROUGH *Physick* VII. x. (1639) 398 Make an Apozema.. and aromatizate it with.. Cinamon.

aromatization (əˌrəʊmətaɪˈzeɪʃən). [ad. med.L. *arōmatīzātiōn-em*, f. *arōmatīzā-re*: see next. Also in mod.Fr.] **1.** The action or process of rendering aromatic; aromatic flavouring.

1603 HOLLAND *Plutarch's Mor.* (1657) 604 They.. give it a tincture and aromatization with saffron. **1612** WOODALL *Surg. Mate* Wks. 1653, 268 Aromatization.. whereby medicaments are made more suaveolent and odoriferous. **1753** CHAMBERS *Cycl. Supp.*, *Aromatisation*.. the art of mixing aromatic, or spicy, matters, as cinnamon, mace.. with some drug.

2. *Chem.* Conversion into an aromatic compound.

1936 *Chem. Abstr.* XXX. 6713 (*heading*) Aromatization of some cyclopentane homologs. **1940** *Industr. & Engin. Chem.* Apr. 529/1 The well-known dehydrogenation of cyclohexanes to the corresponding aromatics (Zelinsky) is often referred to as aromatization. **1979** *Experientia* XXXV. 273/2 There is increasing support for the hypothesis that testosterone aromatization to estradiol is an important step in androgen-induced aggression in male mice. **1985** *Oil & Gas Jrnl.* 21 Oct. 67/2 Reactions which make up the composite reaction referred to as 'catalytic cracking'.. are: ..isomerization, aromatization, [etc.].

aromatize (əˈrəʊmətaɪz), *v.* [a. F. *aromatise-r* (12th c.), ad. L. *arōmatīzāre*, ad. Gr. ἀρωματίζ-ειν to spice, f. ἀρωματ- AROMA.] **1.** To render aromatic or fragrant; to impart a spicy flavour to; to season with spice. Also *fig.*

1480 CAXTON *Ovid's Met.* XIV. xi, Whyche Venus aromatysed wᵗ oynement dyvyne. **1582** HESTER *Phiorav. Secr.* III. v. 11 Aromatise it with two caretes of Muske. **1646** SIR T. BROWNE *Pseud. Ep.* 204 Unto converted Jews.. no man imputeth this unsavoury odor; as though Aromatized by their conversion.. they smelt no longer then they savoured of the Jew. **1685** *Reflect. Baxter* 17 This Spirit Aromatizes the Doctors whole Interpretation of the Apocalypse. **1798** W. TAYLOR in Robberds *Mem.* I. 216 Attempting with otr of roses to aromatize the fumes of tobacco. **1830** LINDLEY *Nat. Syst. Bot.* 27 Europeans employ them to aromatise certain liquors.

2. *Chem.* To convert into an aromatic compound or structure.

1936 *Chem. Abstr.* XXX. 6714 An isoparaffin which is then aromatized. **1941** *Jrnl. Amer. Chem. Soc.* LXIII. 520/2 [Various catalysts] do not aromatize 2,2,4-trimethylpentane at 475°. **1979** *Nature* 17 May 239/1 Androgen is capable of being aromatized to oestrogen in neural tissues of neonatal rats in both *in vitro* and *in vivo* conditions. **1985** *Oil & Gas Jrnl.* 5 Aug. 96/1 For both of these catalysts, it appears that the H_2 transfer capabilities are strong enough to move H_2 rapidly and sufficiently out of one ring to aromatize it.

a'romatized, *ppl. a.* [f. prec. + -ED.] Rendered aromatic or fragrant; spiced.

1661 LOVELL *Hist. Anim. & Min.* Introd., The body.. boiled with wine, with aromatized broth, is commended against the leprosy. **1884** *Pall Mall G.* 16 Feb. 4/2 Each bather gargles mouth and throat with cold aromatized water.

a'romatizer. [f. as prec. + -ER¹.] He who or that which aromatizes.

1699 EVELYN *Acetaria* 148 Other Strewings and Aromatizers which may likewise be admitted to enrich our Sallet.

a'romatizing, *vbl. sb.* [f. as prec. + -ING¹.] = AROMATIZATION.

1606 HOLLAND *Sueton.* Annot. 30 The artificiall besprinkling and aromatizing of banqueting rowmes. **1975** *Nature* 24 July 260/1 Fat from normal breast tissue and that from subjects with cancer seems to have identical aromatising ability. **1980** JOHNSON & EVERITT *Essential Reproduction* ii. 32 Local aromatizing activity.

a'romatizing, *ppl. a.* *Chem.* [f. as prec. + -ING².] Causing or promoting aromatization.

1941 *Jrnl. Amer. Chem. Soc.* LXIII. 520/1 Further work is in progress on the determination of isomerization properties of aromatizing catalysts at higher temperatures. **1974** *Nature* 15 Nov. 260/1 Aromatising enzymes are absent in the cortex. **1979** *Sci. Amer.* Aug. 162/1 [They] have identified aromatizing enzymes in the brain of turtles and snakes.

†**a'romatous**, *a.* *Obs. rare*⁻¹. [f. L. *arōmata* or F. *aromat*, as if ad. L. **arōmatōsus* or F. **aromateux.*] = AROMATIC.

1483 CAXTON *Gold. Leg.* 34/3 The encence which is brent ..is aromatous or wel smellyng.

aron, obs. form of ARE *v.*, and of ARUM.

a-rood, 'on (the) cross': see A *prep.*¹ and ROOD.

1340 *Ayenb.* 64 þe gyewes, þet hine dede a-rode.

†**a-'room**, *adv.* *Obs.* Forms: 3–4 **aroum(e,** 5 **a-rowme, arombe,** 6 **a-room.** [orig. *on rúm, on rúme*, to or at a space or distance: see A *prep.*¹ and ROOM.] To or at a distance; apart, aside, off.

c **1250** *Gen. & Ex.* 4000 He bad balaac stonden ðor-bi, And ȝede onrum. *c* **1300** *K. Alis.* 1637 Aroum anon he drow. *c* **1384** CHAUCER *H. Fame* 540, I a roume was in the field. *c* **1449** PECOCK *Repr.* II. xx. 271 Forto haue it arombe. *c* **1530** *Hickscorner* in Hazl. *Dodsl.* I. 154 Aware, fellows, and stand a-room.

†**a'room**, *v.* *Obs.* [f. prec.] To extend, prolong.

c **1440** *Morte Arth.* 340 ȝif yis journee sulde halde, or be aroumede forthyre.

a-'root, *advb. phr.* [A *prep.*¹ + ROOT.] On root; *hence*, rooted, firm.

c **1374** CHAUCER *Troylus* II. 1329 So rulith her her hertis gost withynne, That thogh she bende, yet she stont a-rote [*v.r.* on rote].

aroph. [According to Scott *Suppl. to Chambers*, a contr. for *aroma philosophorum* philosophers' spice.] Name given to various medicinal preparations of Paracelsus and the Paracelsians, said to be efficacious against the stone, quartan ague, etc.

1657 G. STARKEY *Helmont's Vind.* 327 Thus is made the most noble Aroph of Helmont out of Satyrion. **1753** CHAMBERS *Cycl. Supp.*, *Aroph* was a preparation of saffron and rye-bread, digested with spirits of wine.

aror, obs. form of ERROR.

arore, obs. form of A-ROAR.

arose (əˈrəʊz), pa. t. of ARISE.

aroughcun, early form of RACOON.

1624 CAPT. SMITH *Virginia* II. 27 A beast they call Aroughcun, much like a badger, but vseth to liue on trees as Squirrels doe.

arought, pa. pple. of ARECCHE *v.* *Obs.* to explain.

around (əˈraʊnd), *adv.* and *prep.* [f. A- *pref.* 2 + ROUND; cf. *across.* Rare bef. 1600; not in Shakspere, nor Bible 1611; twice in Milton *Poet. Wks.*]

A. *adv.* (Often strengthened by *all.*)

†1. In the round, in circumference; in a round, in a circle. *Obs.*

c **1300** *K. Alis.* 6603 They [*i.e.* the eggs] beon more feor aroun. **1330** R. BRUNNE *Chron.* 368 Non was set at non ende, But alle a round, for alle were hende. **1579** SPENSER *Sheph. Cal.* June 60 The fountaine, where they sat arounde. **1596** —— *F.Q.* I. i. 18 [The dragon]..Wrapping up her wrethed sterne arownd.

2. On or along the circuit or surface (of a circular or globular body).

1596 SPENSER *F.Q.* I. x. 54 Whose head full hie [is] Adorn'd with fruitful olives all around. **1697** DRYDEN *Virg. Georg.* III. 658 And hissing, rowls his glaring Eyes around. **1699** —— *Flower & Leaf* 229 All their heads around With chaplets green of cerrial-oak were crowned. **1794** SULLIVAN *View Nat.* I. 67 A shell, which stretches quite around, and envelopes the whole globe.

3. *gen.* On every side, in every direction.

c **1320** *Sir Beves* 1373 [The sense is here doubtful] God, that made this world aronde, The saue, sire king Brademond. **1709** POPE *Spring* 100 While op'ning blooms diffuse their sweets around. **1820** KEATS *St. Agnes* xl, For there were sleeping dragons all around. **1861** BUCKLE *Civilis.* II. vi. 601 The signs of the time are all around.

4. In U.S.: = ROUND. Perhaps orig. *U.K.* (cf. quot. 1816). Now coming back into British use under U.S. influence.

1816 JANE AUSTEN *Emma* I. x. 187 Emma..was beginning to think how she might draw back a little more, when they both looked around, and she was obliged to join them. **1883** *Harper's Mag.* Feb. 446/1 The apples and nuts are just enough to go around. **1883** J. KELLY in *Ibid.* Aug. 453/1 It is not the best all-around boat. **1936** WODEHOUSE *Laughing Gas* xxvi. 269 'I want to know why you haven't tied him up.' .. 'We was aiming to get around to it later.' **1952** *Manch. Guardian Weekly* 9 Oct. 7/3 They tended to get rubbed out before he got around to it.

5. In U.S.: = ABOUT. **a.** Here and there with no fixed direction; all about, at random; as in 'to travel around,' 'to fool around.' **b.** Somewhere near; as in 'to stand around.' For ***shop, sleep around***, see the verbs.

1776 A. R. ROBBINS *Jrnl.* (1850) 6 Exercised and walked around with the officers in A.M. **1834** *Congressional Globe* 6 Feb. 492 In looking around, the President had a right to select an officer who would honestly..discharge his duty. **1848** BARTLETT *Dict. Amer.* 170 *To hang around*, to loiter about. **1869** S. BOWLES *Our New West* viii. 170 We generally 'boarded around'. **1870** in Schele de Vere *Americanisms* (1872) 435 She..is witty,..and must be pleasant to have around. **1883** *N.Y. World* in *Glasg. Week. Her.* 9 June 8/3 It can be kicked, rolled around, or hammered. **1926** J. BLACK *You can't Win* iii. 16 When a new boy showed up, I was the one to show him around. **1927** E. WALLACE *Hand of Power* xliv. 215, I shall be just eating around. **1948** GORE VIDAL *City & Pillar* (1949) II. ix. 195 Well, I'll see you around, Cy. **1965** J. FLEMING *Nothing is Number* II. v. 87 She hasn't been seen since the beginning of last term... All I know is that she hasn't been around.

c. Going about; astir; out of bed. *U.S.*

1849 N. KINGSLEY *Diary* (1914) 58 Our Captain is out around to day as it is so pleasant. **1884** *Lisbon* (Dakota) *Star* 18 July, He is now able to be around, but has not yet fully recovered. **1887** F. FRANCIS Jr. *Saddle & Mocassin* 61 Mr. Maroney ain't long gone to bed... I guess he'll be around at midday. **1908** S. E. WHITE *Riverman* xvi. 142, I wasn't here until nine o'clock. I thought, of course, you'd be around.

d. Phr. ***to have been around***: to have gained much experience in the world. *colloq.* (orig. *U.S.*).

1927 HEMINGWAY *Fiesta* vii. 72 We've all been around. I dare say Jake here has seen as much as you have. **1938** 'G. GRAHAM' *Swiss Sonata* vi. 229 You do have a very unnerving effect on me sometimes, although I'm four years older and I've been around, as Ted would say.

B. *prep.*

1. On or along the circuit: **a.** of position.

1399 *Rich. Redeless* III. 264 Rewlers of rewmes around all þe erthe. **1629** MILTON *Nativity* iv, Nor war or battle's sound Was heard the world around. **1807** CRABBE *Par. Reg.* I. 41 Around the walls are heroes, lovers, kings.

b. of motion: So as to encircle, or make the circuit of.

a **1700** DRYDEN (J.) A lambent flame arose, which gently spread Around his brows. **1855** KINGSLEY *Westw. Ho* (1879) 501 They would follow Sir Amyas Leigh around the world. **1869** *Eng. Mech.* 2 Apr. 27/2 Passing the tape..around each of the..pulleys.

2. So as to surround, encompass, or envelop; surrounding, enveloping; about.

1816 J. WILSON *City of Plague* I. i. 147 My mother put her arms around my neck. **1817** WOLFE *Burial Sir J. Moore* iii, With his martial cloak around him.

3. a. On all sides of, in all directions from.

1667 MILTON *P.L.* II. 900 They around the flag Of each his faction..Swarm populous. **1711** STEELE *Spect.* No. 118 ¶1 The Prospects around me. **1860** TYNDALL *Glac.* I. §11. 84 The air around and above us was..clear. **1882** PEBODY *Eng. Journalism* xxi. 158 The woods that lie around a Flintshire castle.

b. *fig.*

1818 HALLAM *Mid. Ages* (1841) I. 496 To pour the radiance of unclouded reason around the last struggles of dissolution. **1877** LYTTEIL *Landm.* III. vii. 134 Around the Stone of the bedesman's cell quite a romance has been woven.

4. a. In U.S.: Hither and thither over, at random through, about; as in 'to travel around the country.'

b. Of time, amount, etc.: about, sometime near. *U.S.*

1888 *N.Y. Mercury* (Farmer), Presuming he was born around three o'clock in the afternoon, he is under Leo and the Sun. **1920** *Daily Tel.* 3 Apr. 10/6 (N.Y. Lett.), S. Motor Company shares, which usually sell around $100 each. **1931** W. G. MCADOO *Crowded Years* x. 158 The convention adjourned around four o'clock.

arousable (əˈraʊzəb(ə)l), *a.* [f. AROUSE *v.* + -ABLE.] That can be aroused.

1890 W. JAMES *Princ. Psychol.* II. xix. 122 The particular process which currents from the sense-organs arouse would seem under normal circumstances to be arousable in no other way. **1894** *Blackw. Mag.* July 36 The Tuaregs are a wild people of a kind easily arousable to religious fanaticism.

arousal (əˈraʊzəl). [f. next + -AL².] The action of arousing, or fact of being aroused.

[Not in CRAIG 1847. Webster cites HARE.] **1854** tr. *Lamartine's Celebr. Char.* II. 122 The sudden arousal of the Dauphin by her voice. **1865** *Gayworthys* II. 22 Listening to the sounds of arousal about the country side.

arouse (əˈraʊz), *v.* [f. A- *pref.* 11 + ROUSE, after such pairs as *rise, arise, wake, awake.*]

1. To raise or stir up (a person) from sleep or inactivity; to awaken.

1593 SHAKS. *2 Hen. VI*, IV. i. 3 Loud houling Wolues arouse the Jades That dragge the Tragicke melancholy night. **1791** COWPER *Iliad* x. 36 Grasping his spear, forth issu'd to arouse His brother. **1860** TYNDALL *Glac.* I. §11. 80 [I] fell asleep. My friend, however, soon aroused me.

2. To stir up into activity, excite (principles of action, emotions, etc.).

[**1602** SHAKS. *Ham.* II. ii. 510 A roused Vengeance sets him new a-worke.] **1728** THOMSON *Spring* 1002 But absent, what fantastick woes arous'd Rage in each thought. **1859** MERIVALE *Rom. Emp.* xlv. V. 225 No suspicion was aroused. **1863** KEMBLE *Resid. Georgia* 20 It arouses the killing propensity in me.

3. *intr.* (for *refl.*) To wake up, bestir oneself.

1822 W. HAVERGAL in *Life* (1882) 33 The parish began to arouse and visitors to inquire.

arouse (əˈraʊz), *sb. rare.* [f. prec. vb.] An act of arousing, an alarum.

1881 CHR. ROSSETTI *Pageant, etc.* 7, I blow an arouse Through the world's wide house To quicken the torpid earth.

arouse, -owze, var. ARROUSE *v. Obs.* to water.

arouser (əˈraʊzə(r)). [f. as prec. + -ER¹.] One who arouses.

1869 MRS. WHITNEY *Hitherto* ix. 98 She sprang from her bed, and followed her arouser.

arousing (əˈraʊzɪŋ), *ppl. a.* [f. AROUSE *v.* + -ING².] Rousing, stirring, exciting.

1841 MYERS *Cath. Th.* III. §48 Arousing as a trumpet-call.

†**aˈrout**, *v. Obs.* [A doubtful word, the reading and sense being uncertain in both quotations. The first may read *arounted*, see ARUNT, or *a-routed* from *rout*; the second reads *route* in all the early MSS. If *arout* existed, it might represent OF. *arouter* to start (one) on his way, send away, f. *à* to + *route*.]

1399 *Rich. Redeless* III. 221 But, arouutyd ffor his ray, and rebuked ofte, He had leue of þe lord..to go or he drank. **1721** *Chaucer's Man of Lawes T.* (ed. Urry) 442 In all that lond no Cristin durst arout [*Six-text*, no Cristen dorste route].

arove, obs. pa. t. of ARRIVE *v.*

a-row (əˈrəʊ), *adv.* Forms: 3 areawe, 3–5 arewe, 4 arawe, 4–6 arowe, a-row(e, a-rew(e, 5 o rowe, 6–7 arew, 6–9 a-row, arow. [A *prep.*¹ + ROW *sb.*]

1. Of place: In a row, rank, or line.

a **1300** *Floriz & Bl.* 298 Alle þilke þat clene maidenes beo Schulle sute arewe under þat treo. *c* **1380** *Sir Ferumb.* 4605 An hep of frenschemen þat leye arawe. **1580** SIDNEY *Arcadia* (1622) 83 Till home they walk arowe. **1600** CHAPMAN *Iliad* VI. 259 Twelve lodgings of like stone, like height, were likewise built arew. **1737** POPE *Imit. Hor. Epist.* I. vii. 77 A little House with trees a-row. **1858** LONGF. *Ropewalk* i, That building..with its windows all a-row.

†**2.** Of time or order: In succession, one after another, successively. *Obs.*

c **1230** *Ancr. R.* 198 Her beoð nu areawe itold þe seouen heaued sunnen. **1387** TREVISA *Higden* Rolls Ser. I. 79 Prouinces and londes þe whiche I schal descriue and rekene al arewe [*per ordinem*]. *c* **1420** *Chron. Vilod.* 603 Thre nyȝtes arowe he seyȝe þe same syȝt. *c* **1430** *Freemasonry* 348 For to be stwardus alle o rowe, Weke after weke. **1553–87** FOXE *A. & M.* III. 552 Christ demanded of Peter..three times a-row, *Petre, amas me?* **1598** SYLVESTER *Du Bartas* II. iv. IV. Argt., Jehu's line likewise Shallum supplants. King-killing Treacheries Succeed a-row.

arow, obs. f. ARROW; var. of ARGH *a. Obs.* timid.

arowblast, -er, obs. forms of ARBALEST, -ER.

arpeggiated (ɑːˈpɛdʒɪeɪtɪd), *ppl. a. Mus.* [f. ARPEGGIO + -ATE² + -ED.] Of a chord or series of chords: played or sung in arpeggio.

1901 *Westm. Gaz.* 31 May 2/1 Arpeggiated accompaniments of a rather old-fashioned type. **1922** S. GREW *Art of Player-Piano* 96 The initial note preceded by an arpeggiated chord. **1924** P. A. SCHOLES *1st Bk. Gramophone Record* 21 A melody..smoother in motion, and hence well contrasted with the preceding, arpeggiated, theme.

arpeggiation (ɑːpɛdʒɪˈeɪʃən). *Mus.* [f. ARPEGGIO + -ATION.] Playing or singing in arpeggio.

1889 in *Cent. Dict.*

‖**arpeggio** (‖arˈpeddʒeo, ɑːˈpɛdʒɪəʊ). [It., f. *arpeggiare* to play upon the harp, f. *arpa* harp.] The employment of the notes of a chord in rapid succession instead of simultaneously; a chord thus played or sung.

1742 in BAILEY. **1786** J. C. WALKER *Irish Bards* 17 (T.) A racaraide, or rhapsodist, who occasionally sustained his voice with arpeggios swept over the strings of the harp. **1868** GEO. ELIOT *Sp. Gipsy* I. 39 Juan..touched his lute With soft arpeggio. **1879** F. TAYLOR in Grove *Dict. Mus.* I. 87/2 The downward arpeggio..is but rarely employed in modern music.

arˈpeggio, *v.* [f. prec.; cf. It. *arpeggiare*, F. *arpéger*] To play or sing (a chord) as an arpeggio.

1864 tr. *Spohr's Autobiog.* I. 2, I arpeggiod the chord to her.

‖**arpeggione** (‖arpedˈdʒone, ɑːpɛdʒ(ɪ)ˈəʊniː). [G., f. It. *arpeggio.*] A stringed musical instrument of the early 19th century (see quots.).

1879 GROVE *Dict. Mus.* I. 89/1 *Arpeggione*, or Guitar Violoncello, a stringed instrument, played with a bow, which was invented by G. Staufer, of Vienna, in 1823. **1959** *Chambers's Encycl.* XIV. 328/1 The arpeggione, now completely forgotten, derives some importance from the fact that no less a composer than Franz Schubert wrote a sonata for arpeggione and pianoforte.

‖**arpent** (see below). Also 7 **arpen, -ine** (*erron.* **arpentier**). [a. F. *arpent* (= Pr. *arpen, aripin*):—L. *arepennis* (Columella), *arapennis* (Isidore) = *semijugerum* 'half an acre,' according to Columella a Gallic word. See Littré. Formerly quite naturalized as ˈɑːpənt, ˈɑːpɪn; now again treated as French: arpɑ̃.] An obsolete French measure of land, containing a hundred square perches, and varying with the different values of the perch from about an acre and a quarter to about five-sixths of an acre.

1580 HOLLYBAND *Treas. Fr. Tong.*, *Demi arpent*, halfe an arpent, that is, nine hundreth foote of grounde. **1601** HOLLAND *Pliny* I. 550 An Acre or Arpen of ground, called in Latine Iugerum. **1622** MALYNES *Anc. Law-Merch.* 51 The partition of Lands by Measures, Acres, Arpentiers, Bunderen. **1623** J. WEBSTER *Devil's Law-Case* III. iii. in Hazl. *Dodsl.* III. 74 If he be master Of poor ten arpines of land. **1727** BRADLEY *Fam. Dict.* s.v. *Corn*, As many Pounds of Salt-petre..as you have Arpents of Land to sow. **1869** PARKMAN *Discov. Gt. West* i. (1875) 7 La Salle had..assigned to each settler half an arpent, or about a third of an acre.

[**arpentator.** Latinized form of F. *arpenteur*, in Spelman (1664), whence in some mod. Dicts.]

‖**arpenteur** (arpɑ̃ˈtœːr). [F. agent-noun f. *arpent.*] A measurer of land; a land-surveyor.

1792 A. YOUNG *Trav. France* 149 Mons. Arthaud, the arpenteur..answered my enquiries satisfactorily.

arpsicord, arpy: see HARP-.

arquated, obs. variant of ARCUATED, after Fr. *arquer*: in Worcester 1859.

arquebus, and derivatives: see HARQUEBUS.

arquerite (ˈɑːkwəraɪt). *Min.* [f. (1842) *Arqueros*, mines in Chili, where found + -ITE.] A native amalgam of silver.

arquifoux, variant of ALQUIFOU.

†**arr**, *sb. Obs.* exc. in *north. dial.* Also 3–5 **erre** (a nerre), 4–6 **arre**, 5 **ar**. [a. ON. *örr, ör*; cf. Da. *ar.*] A wound, scar. Only in northern writers, and still common dialectally.

a **1300** *E.E. Psalter* xxxvii. 6 Stanke and roten mine erres ere ma. **1340** HAMPOLE *Pr. Consc.* 5600 þe erres of his [Christes] wondes sal speke. **1388** WYCLIF *Lev.* xxii. 22 If it hath a scar [*v.r.* arre]. *c* **1450** *Gloss.* in Wright *Voc.* 209 *Hec cicatrix*, a nerre. **1564** *MS. Depos. Eccl. Crt. Yrk.*, Hayth not any arre or arres of his legg or legges. **1655** W. RAWMARSH *MS. Depos. Yrk. Castle*, A young man with pock arrs in his face. **1691** RAY *N. Countr. Words*, An *Arr*; A Skar. *Pock-arrs*, the Marks made by the Small Pox. This is a general Word, common both to North and South. **1863** ATKINSON *Whitby Gloss.* s.v., 'I'll gie thee an arr to carry to thy grave,' ..An arr on the conscience, is the inward impression of having done wrong.

†**arr**, *v.*¹ *Obs.* [Origin uncertain: Mätzner compares LG. *arren* to vex, f. *arre* anger = OE. *erre, ierre, eorre.* Cf. next.] To anger, vex, worry.

[**1382** WYCLIF *Deut.* xxxii. 16 Thei eggiden him in alyen goddis, and in abomynaciouns to wraththe arreden [*v.r.* arereden, rereden; Vulg. *concitaverunt*]. *a* **1400** *Cov. Myst.* 306 The Jewys xal crye for joy with a gret voys, and arryn hym, and pullyn of his clothis. **1651** N. BACON *Hist. Disc.* xiv. 216 He arred both the Clergy and Laity.

†**arr**, *v.*² *Obs.* [A word imitating the sound; whence also R is called by Persius *littera canina*. In some modern dialects *narr*, and *nurr*.] To snarl as a dog.

1483 CAXTON *G. de la Tour* C ij b, Eche arred at other lyke houndes. **1600** NASHE *Summer's Last Will* in Hazl. *Dodsl.* VIII. 44 They arre and bark at night against the moon. **1603**

Holland *Plutarch's Mor.* 726 (R.) A dog is..fell and quarrelsome, given to arre.

arra, variant of ARRAH and ARRHA.

arrable, obs. form of HORRIBLE.

‖**Arracacha** (ærəˈkɑːtʃə). *Bot.* [native Indian name.] A genus of umbelliferous plants, with tuberous roots, found in the north of South America, of which one species (*A. esculenta*) is a staple article of food with the inhabitants.

1823 *Agric. & Bot.* in *Ann. Reg.* 304/2 Several excellent roots of the famous Arracacha. **1832** *Veg. Subst. Food* 169 Arracacha..is cultivated..for its root, which is farinaceous, and easy of digestion.

arrace, obs. form of ARRAS; var. ARASE *v. Obs.*

arrach, obs. form of ORACH (*Atriplex*).

arrache, var. ARACHE *v. Obs.* to pluck out.

†**a'rrachement.** *Obs. rare*$^{-1}$. [a. F. *arrachement*, f *arracher*: see ARACHE.] That which is torn or broken off; a fragment.

1638 Sanderson *21 Serm.* Ad. Aul. vii. (1673) 99 These precious Souls of ours, the very exhalations and arrachements (if I may so speak) of the breath of God.

arrack (əˈræk, ˈærək). Forms: 7 **arak, aracke,** 7–9 **arack,** 9 **arrac,** 7– **arrack.** *Aphet.* 7– **rack.** [Ultimately Arab., ʿ*araq* sweat, juice, esp. in ʿ*araq at-tamr* 'the (fermented) juice of the date,' whence extended to all sorts of fermented beverages. The word has been adopted in all Mohammedan countries; the Pg. *araca, araque*, Sp. *arac*, Fr. *arack*, and Eng. *arrack*, are taken from Indian vernaculars, with the Indian sense. See also RACK.]

A name applied in Eastern countries to any spirituous liquor of native manufacture; especially, that distilled from the fermented sap of the coco-palm, or from rice and sugar, fermented with the coco-nut juice.

[**1516** Barbosa *Trav.* transl. Ld. Stanley (Hakl.) 59 They bring cocoa-nuts, huraca (which is something to drink).] **1602–5** E. Scot *Java* in Purchas (1625) I. 173 Kept a victualing house, and brewed Aracke. **1694** T. R. in *Phil. Trans.* XVIII. 277 A sort of Jaundise, contracted by the frequent drinking of Arak or Rack. **1697** Dampier *Voy.* (1729) I. 293 Arack is distill'd also from Rice, and other things. **1782** J. Trumbull *M'Fingal* iv, And well invok'd with punch of arrack, Hold converse sweet in tent or barrack. **1834** *Penny Cycl.* II. 233/1 Arack or Arrac. **1859** Tennent *Ceylon* II. 127 Toddy drawers..ascending the (coco-nut) trees in quest of the sap drawn from the spathes of the unopened flowers to be distilled into arrack.

b. *attrib.*

1602–5 E. Scot *Java* in Purchas I. 184 Drave them into a Racke-house. **1748** Smollett *Rod. Rand.* (1812) I. 102 The arrack punch with which he treated them. **1808** *Orient. Field Sports* I. 88 The bad effects of these arrack shops.

arrage: see AVERAGE *sb.*

arraged, arragonite: see ARA-.

arrah (ˈærə), *int.* [Irish. (Farquhar was of Irish birth.)] An expletive expressing emotion or excitement, common in Anglo-Irish speech.

1705 Farquhar *Twin Rivals* III. ii, Arah, you Fool, ish it not the saam ting? **1707** —— *Beaux Strat.* v. ii, Arra Honeys, a clear Caase. **1753** Smollett *Ct. Fathom* (1784) 119 Upon which he bade me turn out. 'Arra, for what?' said I. **1820** Combe (Dr. Syntax) *Consol.* II. 157 Arrah, my Dears, it does confound me.

arrai, -ment, obs. forms of ARRAY, -MENT.

arraign (əˈreɪn), *v.*[1] Forms: 4 **arayne,** 4–5 **areyne, ar(r)ene,** 5 **arenȝi, arreyne,** 5–6 **arreygne, -aynge,** 6–7 **arrain(e, -eign,** 7 **araigne, arraigne,** 6– **arraign.** *Aphet.* 5–6 **reyne, reygne.** [a. AF. *araine-r, areine-r, arene-r*, OF. *arais-, areis-, aresnier*:—L. *adratiōnāre*, f. *ad* to + *ratiōnāre* to reason, talk reasonably, talk, f. *ratiōn-em* reason, reasoning, discourse. The later F. *araisonner* was adopted in Eng. as AREASON.]

†**1.** *trans.* To call (a person) to account, or to answer for himself; to interrogate, examine. *Obs.*

c **1325** *E.E. Allit. P.* C. 191 Arayned hym [Jonah] ful runyschly what raysoun he hade..to slepe so faste. *c* **1360** *Mercy* 85 in *E.E.P.* (1862) 121 Þeose are þe werkes of Merci, Of whuche crist wol vs areyne. **1387** Trevisa *Higden* Rolls Ser. IV. 303 Augustus areyned [*interrogavit*] hym and seide. **1447** Bokenham *Lyvys of Seyntys* 15 He hyr thus areynyd wyth a pale faas.

2. *esp.* To call upon one to answer for himself on a criminal charge; to indict before a tribunal. Hence *gen.* To accuse, charge with fault.

a **1400** *Leg. Rood* 147 To a-rene Wrecches þat wrappe þi chylde. **1450** Somner in 4 *C. Eng. Lett.* 4 He was arreyned upon the appechements and fonde gylty. *c* **1450** Henryson *Mor. Fa.* 42 The Sheepe againe before the Wolfe arenȝied. **1528** More *Heresyes* III. Wks. 212/2 Y^{t} were arreygned for a felonye. **1542** Brinklow *Complaynt* v. (1874) 18 The day whan ye shal be reygned at the iudgement seate of God. **1611** Shaks. *Wint. T.* III. ii. 14 Thou art here accused and arraigned of High Treason. **1722** De Foe *Moll Fl.* (1840) 310, I was carried down to the Sessions house, where I was arraigned. **1754** Richardson *Grandison* IV. xxiv. 177 Lady Olivia is grieved..and arraigns herself and her wicked passion. **1876** Freeman *Norm. Conq.* IV. xviii. 129 For that crime he was arraigned..before the King and his Witan.

3. To accuse of some fault or imperfection, impeach, call in question, find fault with (actions, measures, statements, opinions).

1672 Dryden *Conq. Granada* I. i, Judge-like thou sit'st, to praise or to arraign The flying Skirmish of the darted Cane. **1772** *Junius Lett.* Pref. 10 They arraign the goodness of Providence. **1776** Gibbon *Decl. & F.* I. xxiv. 681 He boldly arraigned the abuses of public and private life. **1820** Byron *Mar. Fal.* v. i. 269 You do not then..arraign our equity?

b. *absol.*

1746 Smollett *Reproof* 202 And let me still the sentiment disdain Of him, who never speaks but to arraign.

†**4.** To try, judge. *Obs. rare.*

1623 Heming & Cond. in *Shaks. C. Praise* 145 Though you be a Magistrate of wit, and sit on the Stage..to arraigne Playes dailie.

†**5.** To sentence, condemn. *Obs. rare.*

1658 J. Rowland *Mouffet's Theat. Ins.* 1102 When they finde they are arraigned to die.

†**a'rraign,** *v.*[2] *Law. Obs.* Also 6–7 **araine, arraine.** [a. late AFr. *arraigner, arainer*, the latter originating in a mis-spelling of *aramer*, OF. *aramier*, also *aramir*, cogn. w. Pr. *aramir*, OCat. *aremir* (Diez) :—late L. *adhramīre* (*adrh-, adchr-, ˈadcr-*) in Salic and Longobard Laws; f. *ad* to + **hramīre* (in Pr. *ramir*), according to Grimm and Diez ad. Goth. *hramjan*, whence *ushramjan* to crucify, perh. to hang up. In England, the AFr. *aramer* was re-latinized as *arramāre* (in Bracton, *Fleta*).

The Goth. *hramjan* is prob. cogn. w. Gr. κρεμα- 'hang.' The literal sense in which it was taken into late L. is unknown: Müllenhoff (in Waitz, *Alte Recht der sal. Franken*, 277) shows that it probably named some sensible, perhaps symbolical, action, which was afterwards disused and forgotten, while the technical phrases containing the word remained: see *adramire sacramentum, testimonia, testes, vadium, bellum, arramare assisam*, in Ducange. The true origin of *arraign* in this sense was pointed out by Spelman (s.v. *Adrhamire*), but as he unfortunately failed to see that it was a distinct word from the prec., and took *aramer* as the source of both, his successors rejected his truth along with his error, and in all Dictionaries this word now erroneously stands as a sense of the prec.]

To appeal to, claim, demand; in phr. ***arraine*** (i.e. *arrame*) ***an assize.***

[*c* **1275** Bracton IV. i. 15 Et arramavit assisam novæ disseysinæ. *c* **1290** Britton III. vi. 13 Si ambedeus eynt arramé assise de mort de auncestre vers une estraunge persone. **1481** Littleton §442 Si home seit disseisi, et il arraine un assise envers le disseisour.] **1528** Perkins *Profit. Bk.* v. §377 If his disseisor arraign an assise against him. **1574** tr. *Littleton Tenures* 78 a, The lessee arraineth an assise of Novel disseisin of ye land againste the lessour. **1628** Coke *On Litt.* 262 b, To arraigne the Assise is to cause the Tenant to be called, to make the plaint, and to set the cause in such order as the Tenant may bee enforced to answer thereunto; and is deriued of the French word *Arraigner*. **1641** *Termes de la Ley* 26 Arraine is to put a thing in order, or in his place: As hee is said to arraine an Assise of Novel Disseisin. **1714** Fortescue-Aland in *Fortescue's Abs. & Lim. Mon.* 126. **1809** Tomlins *Law Dict.* s.v. *Arraign.*

arraign (əˈreɪn), *sb.* [f. ARRAIGN *v.*[1]] Arraignment, indictment.

1638 Heywood *Rape Lucr.* 187 The freest Citizens without attaint, Arraigne, or judgement, we to exile doome. **1849** Macaulay *Hist. Eng.* v. I. 645 The clerk of the arraigns stood up in great disorder.

arraigner (əˈreɪnə(r)). [f. as prec. + -ER[1]; cf. OF. *araisneor*.] One who arraigns, accuses, or finds fault.

1860 *Sat. Rev.* X. 183/1 A subject on which the doctor can challenge his arraigners without fear. **1876** Bancroft *Hist. U.S.* IV. xxviii. 32 Imperfect compliance..would open a fair field to the arraigners of America.

a'rraigning, *vbl. sb.* [f. as prec. + -ING[1].] The action of the verb ARRAIGN; arraignment.

c **1530** More *Debell. Salem* Wks. 976/2 Neither at the endeighting nor at hys arreighning. **1670** *Tryal Rudyard, etc.* in *Phœnix* 1721 I. 352 The manner of that Bench's Arraigning and Condemning. **1851** Carlyle *Sterling* vii, Those mean repinings, miserable arraignings and questionings of the Eternal Power.

arraignment (əˈreɪnmənt). Also 6 **arrain-, arreign(e-,** 7 **araygn-.** [a. OF. *araisnement*, f. *araisnier*: see ARRAIGN *v.* and -MENT.]

1. The act of arraigning or fact of being arraigned; accusation before a tribunal, indictment, charge.

1548 Coverdale *Erasm. Par. Phil.* i. 12 Y^{e} emprisonment, fetters, arraignementes, and my other calamities. **1586** Thynne in *Animadv.* Pref. 74 The books of the law..(where his arreignement is liberallie set downe). **1635** Chapman & Shirley *Chabot* IV. i, But away, Judges; and pursue the arraignment Of this polluted Chancellor. **1722** De Foe *Moll Fl.* (1840) 310 At the arraignment I pleaded not guilty. **1864** Ainsworth *Tower Lond.* 152 The different peers appointed to hear the arraignment of the prisoners.

2. A charging with, or formal imputation of, faults; accusation, hostile criticism.

1595 Mosse (*title*) Arreignment and Conviction of Userie, its Iniquities and Unlawfulness. **1722** in Keble *Bp. T. Wilson* xvi. (1863) 502 One Article whereof was an arraignment of their proceedings in the case of Mr. Bridson's suspension. **1810** Scott *Lady of L.* v. vi, Wrothful at such arraignment foul, Dark lowered the clansman's sable scowl.

arraiment, obs. form of ARRAYMENT.

arraise, -ays, var. ARAISE *v. Obs.* to raise.

arraise, Sc. var. ARACE *v. Obs.* to snatch away.

arraison, var. AREASON *v. Obs.* to question.

arrand, obs. f. ERRAND, ARRANT; dial. f. ARAIN.

arrange (əˈreɪndʒ), *v.* Forms: 4–6 **arayngé,** 5–6 **ar(r)enge,** 8– **arrange.** [a. OF. *arangie-r, arengier*, f. *à* to + *rangier, rengier*, f. *rang, reng*, RANK. A rare word until modern times; not in Bible 1611, Shakspere, Milton's poetry, or Pope.]

1. a. *trans.* To draw up in ranks or in line of battle.

1375 Barbour *Bruce* XII. 36 He saw hym swa araynge [? = arraying] his men on raw. **1489** Caxton *Faytes of Armes* I. i. 2 Who gauest manere & ordre to arenge batailles. **1523** Ld. Berners *Froiss.* cccxxv. (R.) There he arraynged his men in the stretes. **1596** Spenser *F.Q.* I. vi. 38 To see two knights ..arraung'd in battell new. **1830** Gen. P. Thompson *Exerc.* (1842) I. 226 The marvel is, that the well-informed part of the middle classes..does not arrange itself on the side of the reformers. **1843** Carlyle *Past & Pr.* (1858) 93 Arranged in supreme regimental order.

b. *intr.* (for *refl.*).

1523 Ld. Berners *Froiss.* I. ccxv. 269 The residewe (who were worste harneysed), arenged alonge on the hylle syde.

2. a. *trans.* To put (the parts of a thing) into proper or requisite order; to adjust.

1802 Paley *Nat. Theol.* ii.§2 A mechanism previously arranged. **1837** Disraeli *Venetia* I. xvi, Squire Mountmeadow then, arranging his countenance, announced that the bench was prepared. **1868** Geo. Eliot *F. Holt* 11 His soft white hair was carefully parted and arranged.

b. *refl.* To put oneself in order; prepare oneself.

1865 Carlyle *Fredk. Gt.* VII. xviii. vii. 212 Friedrich.. hastens to arrange himself for the new contingencies.

3. *Mus.* To adapt (a composition) for instruments or voices for which it was not originally written. Also *intr.*

1808 *Monthly Pantheon* I. 85/1 An immense expense..the reward of the composer, who selected and arranged the music. **1831** F. Reynolds *Playwright's Adv.* iv. 64 A musician, who, by teaching, arranging, and composing, acquired an income of above one thousand pounds 'per annum'. *a* **1838** (*title*) A Selection of National Airs Arranged for the Harp or Pianoforte by Mrs. Gibson. **1849** *Athenæum* 20 Oct. 1067 Even though the composers 'arranged' be Haydn, Mozart, etc. **1879** C. Parry in Grove *Dict. Mus.* I. 95/1 Brahms has arranged..his piano string quintett as a 'Sonata' for four hands on two pianos.

4. a. *trans.* To place (things) in some order, dispose.

1791 Boswell *Johnson* x. (1848) 81 The greengrocers and fruiterers were beginning to arrange their hampers. **1815** Wordsw. *Poet. Wks.* I. Pref. 16 Poems, apparently miscellaneous, may with propriety be arranged..with reference to the powers of mind predominant in the production of them. **1853** Soyer *Pantroph.* 390 Lettuces, olives, pomegranates, Damascus plums, tastefully arranged on silver dishes. **1869** Freeman *Norm. Conq.* (1876) III. xii. 215 The parts in the two dramas were differently arranged.

b. *intr.* (= *refl.*) To get into order, fall into place.

1805 Scott *Last Minstr.* VI. xviii, Forms..Cloudy and indistinct..Till, slow arranging, and defined, they seem To form a lordly and a lofty room.

5. *trans.* To settle (relations between parties, conflicting claims, matters in dispute, differences); to adjust.

1837 Macready *Remin.* II. 82, I sent the authors out of the room to arrange the matter. **1867** Froude *Short Stud.* (1872) I. 24 The relations between himself and his dependants will have to be arranged on other principles. **1878** Seeley *Stein* III. 498 The quarrel, partly by the interference of the Crown Prince, was arranged.

6. *intr.* (= To arrange matters): To come to an agreement or understanding as to mutual relations, claims, matters in dispute.

1796 Burke *Regic. Peace* Wks. VIII. 90 We cannot arrange with our enemy in the present conjuncture. **1831** B'ness Bunsen in Hare *Life* I. ix. 359 He then went on to Copenhagen to arrange with his father.

7. *trans.* To settle the order, manner, and circumstantial relations of (a thing to be done); to plan beforehand.

1786 Burke *Art. W. Hastings* III. Wks. XI. 432 That the acts done should be arranged with the Rajah. **1837** Harris *Gt. Teacher* 340 Every step he took was calculated and arranged. **1849** Macaulay *Hist. Eng.* ii. I. 267 The details of a butchery were frequently discussed, if not definitely arranged.

8. *intr.* (*simply*, or with *inf.* or *subord. cl.*) To come to, or make, a settlement with other persons as to a matter to be done, so that all concerned in it shall do their part.

1849 Macaulay *Hist. Eng.* II. 369 For Halifax had arranged that 21 temporal peers..should be ready. **1858** Hawthorne *Fr. & It. Jrnls.* (1872) I. 26 To arrange about my passport. **1860** Tyndall *Glac.* I. §17. 121, I had arranged to meet Ramsay this morning. **1869** A. Morris *Open Secr.* ii. 186 God knew that we should deserve and require suffering, and arranged accordingly. *Mod.* They have arranged for a concert on Monday week.

arrangeable (ə'reɪndʒəb(ə)l), *a.* [f. ARRANGE *v.* + -ABLE.] That can be arranged.

a **1832** BENTHAM *Deontol.* (1834) I. I. vii. 88 Sanctions are arrangeable according to their nature, or according to their sources. **1858** CARLYLE *Fredk. Gt.* I. v. iii. 565 Let these be as in the Treaty of Utrecht; arrangeable in the lump.

arranged (ə'reɪndʒd), *ppl. a.* [f. ARRANGE *v.* + -ED.] **a.** Drawn up in ranks. **b.** Put in order; disposed.

1489 CAXTON *Faytes of Armes* I. xii. 32 They shal lette eche othre..in arrenged batailles. **1840** CARLYLE *Heroes* (1858) 303 How ill many arranged forces of society fulfil their work. **1879** O'CONNOR *Beaconsfield* 231 Abject, though artistically arranged, flattery.

c. ***arranged marriage*** (also ***match***), a marriage the partners to which are chosen by others, usu. their parents.

1878 H. JAMES *Europeans* II. v. 211 With these arranged marriages there is often the deuce to pay. **1937** E. SNOW *Red Star over China* VI. iii. 230 Marriage regulations included interesting provisions against..the custom of 'arranged matches'. **1960** N. EPTON *Love & English* VI. v. 355 The 'arranged' marriage often took more account of a prospective suitor's fortune than of his qualities. **1985** P. CAPLAN *Class & Gender in India* iii. 42 Without..help, the marriage may founder, thus providing..another dire example to romantic young people that 'arranged marriages are best'.

arrangement (ə'reɪndʒmənt). [a. F. *arrangement* (Cotgr. 1611), f. *arranger*: see -MENT.]

1. The action of arranging or disposing in order.

1727–51 CHAMBERS *Cycl.*, *Arrangement*, or rangement, the disposition of the parts of a whole, in a certain order. **1816** MISS AUSTEN *Emma* II. xiii. 366 There was time only for the quickest arrangement of mind; she must be collected and calm. **1870** JEVONS *Elem. Logic* xxxii. 278 In large libraries ..such modes of arrangement are adopted.

2. Arranged condition, orderly disposition, order.

a **1743** CHEYNE (J.) There is a proper arrangement in the parts of elastick bodies. **1742** YOUNG *Nt. Th.* IX. 1108 Arrangement neat and chastest order reign. **1771** FOOT *Penseroso* I. 49 O'er the dark arrangements of the globe December throws his solemn glooms.

3. Style or mode in which things are arranged.

1785–91 T. WARTON *Notes on Milton's Min. Poems* (T.) In my new arrangement, I ought to have placed this piece under the Translations. **1822** DE QUINCEY *Conf.* (1862) 97 The clouds passed slowly through several arrangements. **1871** TYNDALL *Fragm. Sc.* I. xxi. 491 To every act of consciousness belongs a determinate molecular arrangement of the brain.

4. *concr.* A structure or combination of things arranged in a particular way or for any purpose; hence loosely, like *affair*, *concern*, *production*.

1800 HERSCHEL in *Phil. Trans.* XC. 491 An arrangement of twelve bricks, placed on a stand. **1871** B. STEWART *Heat* §165 Such an arrangement is called a thermopile. **1881** MISS BRADDON *Asph.* II. 46 That lace arrangement which you call a cap.

5. *Mus.* The adaptation of a composition for voices or instruments for which it was not originally written; *concr.* a piece so adapted.

1849 *Athenæum* 20 Oct. 1067 It was disheartening, too, to find the appendix..crammed with arrangements. **1879** C. PARRY in Grove *Dict. Mus.* I. 93/1 Arrangements of pianoforte works for full orchestra.

6. A settlement of mutual relations or claims between parties; an adjustment of disputed or debatable matters; a settlement by agreement.

1855 MACAULAY *Hist. Eng.* xi. (1858) III. 12 It was impossible to make an arrangement that would please everybody. **1860** MASSEY *Hist. Eng.* xxvii. III. 153 But personal prejudices again interposed to prevent an arrangement so desirable.

b. *euphem.* An affair of gallantry, an amour.

1751 CHESTERF. *Lett.* 227 (1792) III. 26 *Un arrangement*, which is, in plain English, a gallantry. *Ibid.* 240 III. 99 Bragging of..such an arrangement will equally discredit you among men and women.

7. Disposition of measures for the accomplishment of a purpose; preparations for successful performance.

1786 BURKE *Art. W. Hastings* III. Wks. XI. 432 Arrangements with the Rajah..for the better government and management of his Zemindary. **1837** MACREADY *Remin.* II. 82 With the latter I made arrangements about ballet, &c. **1855** THACKERAY *Newcomes* xxvi. 251 His own arrangements were made in another quarter. **1855** MACAULAY *Hist. Eng.* xxii. IV. 713 Donelagh made the arrangements for the flight.

arranger (ə'reɪndʒə(r)). [f. ARRANGE *v.* + -ER[1].] One who arranges.

1780 BURKE *Refl. Exec.* Wks. IX. 273 None of..the directors and arrangers have been convicted. **1826** MISS MITFORD *Village* Ser. II. (1863) 400 The arranger of the flowers in their vases. **1879** C. PARRY in Grove *Dict. Mus.* I. 92/2 Arrangement..of a gavotte of Gluck's..as much marked by the personality of the arranger as that of the composer.

† **a'rranges**, *sb. pl. Obs.* [? f. F. *arranger*; there is no such sb. in Fr., and Bailey did not know the vb. as Eng.] 'Ranges or arrangements, ranks.' Bailey 1731.

a'rranging, *vbl. sb.* [f. ARRANGE *v.* + -ING[1].] The action of placing in order, settling relations or details.

1818 W. HAVERGAL in *Life* (1882) 19 The arranging and planning it has much straitened me for time.

a'rranging, *ppl. a.* [f. ARRANGE *v.* + -ING[2].] Of a debtor: that makes an arrangement with his creditors.

1920 *Act 10 & 11 Geo. V.* c. 30 §26 In the distribution of the property of a bankrupt or arranging debtor.

arrant ('ærənt), *a.* Also 6 **arraunt**, 6–7 **-and(e.** [A variant of ERRANT, 'wandering, vagrant, vagabond,' which from its frequent use in such expressions as *arrant thief*, became an intensive, 'thorough, notorious, downright,' especially, from its original associations, with opprobrious names. For the vowel-change cf. *arrand* = *errand*, *Harry* = *Herry*, *Henry*, FAR = earlier *fer*, etc.]

†**1.** Wandering, itinerant, vagrant; esp. in **knight arrant**, **bailiff arrant**; in which the etymological ERRANT is now alone used.

[*c* **1400** *Circumcis.* (Turnb. 1843) 97 To bryng the lost schepe ageyn..That was errawnt, ydyl, and in vayne.] **1550** CROWLEY *Epigr.* (1872) 12 *Title*, Of Baylife Arrantes. **1557** *K. Arthur* (Copland) VII. x, With that knyght wyll I juste, for I see that he is a knyght arraunt. **1602** WARNER *Alb. Eng.* IX. xlvi. 217 Arrant Preachers, humming out a common-place or two. **1647** HOWARD *Crown Rev.* 18 Bayliffe arrant. Fee.—4*l.* 11*s.* 3*d.* [**1691** BLOUNT *Law Dict.*, *Bailiffs Errant* are those whom the Sheriff appoints to go up and down the County to serve Writs, etc.]

2. In **thief errant**, **arrant thief** [= robber]: *orig.* an outlawed robber roving about the country, a freebooter, bandit, highwayman; *hence*, a public, notorious, professed robber, a 'common thief,' an undisguised, manifest, out-and-out thief.

c **1386** CHAUCER *Manc. T.* 120 An outlawe or a thef erraunt. [See the whole passage.] **1553** BALE *Vocacyon* in *Harl. Misc.* (Malh.) I. 362 The most errande thefe and mercilesse murtherer. **1563** GRAFTON *Chron. Hen. IV*, an. 1 (R.) There is not so ranke a traytor, nor so arrant a thefe. **1637** POCKLINGTON *Sund. no Sabb.* 13 The arrantest Pharisee theefe in Jerusalem. *a* **1744** SWIFT *Wks.* 1841 II. 79 Every servant an arrant thief as to victuals and drink. **1822** W. IRVING *Braceb. Hall* xxvii. 247 Who, like errant thieves, could not hold up their heads in an honest house.

3. Hence: Notorious, manifest, downright, thorough-paced, unmitigated. Extended from *thief* to *traitor*, *knave*, *rebel*, *coward*, *usurer*; after 1575 widely used as an opprobrious intensive, with *fool*, *dunce*, *ass*, *idiot*, *hypocrite*, *Pharisee*, *Papist*, *Puritan*, *infidel*, *atheist*, *blasphemer*, and so on through the whole vocabulary of abuse.

1393 LANGL. *P. Pl.* C. VII. 307 An erraunt vsurer. **1494** FABYAN v. lxxx. 58 Beyng a errant Traytoure. **1538** TUNSTALL in Strype *Eccl. Mem.* I. I. xliv. 338 Reginald Pole, comen of a noble blood, and thereby the more errant traitor. **1553** *Procl.* ibid. III. App. vi. 10 The most arrande traytour Syr John Dudley. *c* **1588** GREENE *Fr. Bacon* v. 26 Why, thou arrant dunce, shall I never make thee a good scholar? **1596** DRAYTON *Legends* i. 112 Which she to Sots and arrant Ideots threw. **1602** SHAKS. *Ham.* I. v. 124 Hee's an arrant knaue. **1621** BURTON *Anat. Mel.* II. iii. II. (1651) 316 A nobleman therefore in some likelihood..is..a proud fool, an arrant asse. **1660** H. MORE *Myst. Godl.* v. xiii. 168 Either an arrant Infidel or horrid Blasphemer. **1679** MANSELL *Narr. Popish Plot* Addr., Who may prove good tools, though errant Fools. **1719** DE FOE *Crusoe* 482 They are errant cowards. **1749** FIELDING *Tom Jones* XIV. iii. (1840) 205 The arrantest villain that ever walked upon two legs. **1824** W. IRVING *T. Trav.* II. 34 As arrant a crew of scapegraces as ever were collected together. **1837** HOWITT *Rur. Life* II. v. (1862) 141 The inhabitants of solitary houses are often most arrant cowards.

b. *transf.* of things, i.e. opprobrious deeds and qualities, theft, presumption, lie, device, etc.

1639 FULLER *Holy War* v. xxx. (1840) 301 It were arrant presumption for flesh to prescribe God his way. **1692** BENTLEY *Boyle Lect.* i. 9 They cover the most arrant Atheism under the mask and shadow of a Deity. **1753** RICHARDSON *Grandison* (1781) IV. xxxiv. 241, I am afraid I have written arrant nonsense. **1776** PENNANT *Tour Scot.* II. 327 This hill, till about the year 995, was an errant desert.. and uninhabitable. **1858** BUCKLE *Civilis.* (1869) III. v. 480 Little better than arrant trifling.

4. Without opprobrious force: Thorough, downright, genuine, complete, 'regular.'

1570 LEVINS *Manip.* 25 Arrant, *grandis, magnus.* **1575** TURBERV. *Venerie* 193 Good and arrant Terriers..to make the foxe or Badgerd start the soner. **1664** EVELYN *Sylva* 95 He that shall behold its grain..will never scruple to pronounce it arrant wood. **1704** ROWE *Ulysses* Epil. 15 They Like arrant Huswives, rise by Break of Day. **1820** W. IRVING *Sketch Bk.* II. 59 A tight brisk little man, with the air of an arrant old bachelor.

†**5.** With the opprobrious force transferred to the adj.: Thoroughly bad, good for nothing, rascally.

1581 B. RICHE *Farewell* (1846) 25 Her beautie had so entangled her arrant hoste. **1592** G. HARVEY *Pierce's Superer.* 6 So forward to accuse, debase, revile..as the arrantest fellow in a Country? **1676** WYCHERLEY *Plain-Dealer* III. i, Mine's as arrant a Widow-Mother, to her poor Child, as any's in England. **1708** POPE *Lett.* Wks. 1736 V. 61 You are not so arrant a critic of the modern Poets as..to damn them without a hearing. **1761** SMOLLETT *Gil Blas* VII. iii, It was easy to see through all his piety that he was an arrant author at the bottom.

b. as *pred.*

1641 MILTON *Animadv. Def. Smectymn.* ii, The authority of some synodal canons which are now arrant to us.

6. as *sb.* A person of no reputation, a good-for-nothing.

1605 BRETON *Be not angry* 8 Her good-man who should be sent of errands, while she were with her arrants.

'arrantly, *adv.* [f. prec. + -LY[2].] Thoroughly (in a bad sense), notoriously, 'abominably.'

a **1600** *John Bon* 81 in Hazl. *E.P.P.* IV. 10 Ye sing so arantly well, ye make me fal a slepe. *c* **1660** LESTRANGE (J.) Funeral tears are as arrantly hired out as mourning clokes. **1834** SIR H. TAYLOR *Artevelde* II. v. iii, That is a heavy falling-off, my friends, And arrantly ill-timed.

arras ('ærəs). Forms: 5–6 **aras**, **ares**, 6 **arays**, **arase**, **aresse**, **arres**, (**aryste**, **-iste**), 6–7 **arasse**, 7 **arrace**, 4–9 **arras**. [a. *Arras*, name of a town in Artois famed for its manufacture of the fabric.]

1. A rich tapestry fabric, in which figures and scenes are woven in colours. Also ***cloth of arras***.

[**1397** *Will of John of Gaunt* in Nichols *Royal Wills* 156 Draps d'Arras.] *c* **1400** *Epiph.* (Turnb. 1843) 114 Or was ther arras abowt hur hede bownd? **1531** ELYOT *Gov.* III. ii. (1557) 144 With riche arasse or tapestrye. **1536** BELLENDENE *Cron. Scotl.* (1821) II. 56 Claithis of arres, and tapestreis. **1596** *Unton Invent.* 7 One olde cover-lett of Ariste. *a* **1626** BACON *Maxims Com. Law* xxv. (1636) 92 My suit of Arras with the story of the Nativity and Passion. **1790** COWPER *Odyss.* x. 14 Stateliest couches, with rich arras spread. **1816** BYRON *Siege Cor.* xxi, Like the figures on arras, that gloomily glare. **1823** LINGARD *Hist. Eng.* VI. 69 The walls hung with cloth of arras.

2. A hanging screen of this material formerly placed round the walls of household apartments, often at such a distance from them as to allow of people being concealed in the space between.

1598 SHAKS. *Merry W.* III. iii. 97 She shall not see me, I will ensconce mee behinde the Arras. **1678** R. LESTRANGE *Seneca's Mor.* (1702) 203 The Rusling of a Rat behind the Arras. **1823** SCOTT *Quentin D.* x, His guide..vanished through a side-door behind the arras. **1876** GREEN *Eng. People* vii. §8. 446 She called for a sword..and thrust it from time to time through the arras.

3. *fig.* or *transf.* from prec. senses. (See also next.)

c **1630** DRUMM. OF HAWTH. *Irene* Wks. 1711, 170 When ye enter into the cabinets of your own hearts, and there, for finest arras and pourtraits, find millions of Christians.. disfigured, massacred, butcher'd. **1856** KANE *Arct. Exp.* I. xiv. 153 Fires, buffalo-robes, and an arras of investing sailcloth, were unavailing to bring up the mean temperature to the freezing-point.

4. *attrib.*, as ***arras cloth***, ***hangings***, ***weaver work***.

1485 *Inv.* in *Ripon Ch. Acts* 366 Coopertorium lecti, de areswerke. **1542** UDALL *Erasm. Apophth.* (1564) 13 Aresse hanginges, and the other delices of riche men. **1565** GOLDING *Ovid's Met.* VI. (1593) 131 And with an arras weaver's combe of box she fiercely smit Arachne. **1575** CHURCHYARD *Chippes* (1817) 185 My houses..Stuft with rich things, and arras clothes inow. **1643** HERLE *Answ. Ferne* 3 Clemens Alexandrinus called his..bookes of Divinity.. pictured tapistry or Arras-work. **1776** GIBBON *Decl. & F.* I. 278 Linen from Egypt and Arras cloth from Gaul? **1831** CARLYLE *Sart. Res.* II. iii. 71 Our dim arras-picture of these University years. **1852** D. MOIR *Tombless Man* v. Wks. II. 365 From the panelings, in mouldy shreds, Hung what was arras loom-work.

arrased ('ærəst), *ppl. a.* [f. prec. + -ED[2].] Furnished or covered with arras.

1600 CHAPMAN *Iliad* v. 199 Eleven fair chariots.. Curtain'd and arrass'd under foot. **1881** ROSSETTI *Ball. & Sonn.* 131 The shadows cast on the arras'd wall.

arrasene (ærə'siːn). [f. ARRAS.] An embroidery material of wool and silk which is stitched into a fabric in the same way as crewels.

1881 *Girls' Own P.* 29 Jan. 288/1 Arrasene work is not the same as crewel; the material is a kind of woollen chenille. **1881** *N.Y. Art Interch.* 27 Oct. 90/1 Silver-gray satin sheeting, with border of vine leaves, worked in claret-colored arrasene.

‖**arrastre** (a'rastre, -æ-). [Sp., f. *arrastrar* to trail along the ground, f. L. *rastrum* harrow.] An apparatus for grinding and mixing ores by the action of a heavy stone dragged round on a circular bed.

1881 RAYMOND *Mining Gloss* s.v., The arrastre is chiefly used for ores containing free gold, and amalgamation is combined with the grinding. (Sometimes incorrectly written *arraster*, *arrastra*, or *raster*.) **1883** *Standard* 20 Jan. 1/5 The whole of it has been treated, partly by means of arrastras.

arras-wise, erron. f. *arris-wise*: see ARRIS.

arraught (Spenser), pa. t. of AREACH *v. Obs.*

array (ə'reɪ), *v.* Forms: 3–7 **aray(e**, 4–6 **araie**, (5 **araȝe-n**, **arey**), 5–7 **arraie**, **arraye**, 6– **array**. [a. AF. *araye-r*, *araie-r*, = OF. *areyer*, *-eier*, early OF. *areer* (1st pers. sing. *arei*), later *a(r)royer*, cogn. w. Sp. *arrear*, Pg. *arreiar*, Pr. *aredar*, It. and early Rom. *arrēdāre*, f. *a*, *ad* to + **rēdo* (OF. *rei*, *rai*, *roi*), 'preparation, order,' ad. LG. *rêde* (OFris. *rêde*, *rêd*, OE. *rǣde*, *ȝerǣde*), Goth. *garaid-s*, ready, prepared; cf. *garaidjan* to make ready, *garaideins* preparation, order. *Arrēdāre, areer*, was thus 'to make ready, put into order.']

I. Of order of position.

1. To set or place in order of readiness, to marshall. *esp.* To draw up prepared for battle, and in obs. phr. ***to array a battle***. **a.** *lit.* To raise in arms. See ARRAY *sb.* 3.

c **1325** *E.E. Allit. P.* B. 1442 Þe iueles out of Ierusalem.. Bi þe syde of þe sale were semely arayed. *c* **1350** *Will. Palerne* 3560 To þe feld he went..his batailes to araie. **1375** BARBOUR *Bruce* III. 233 Hannyball his mekill mycht Aganys thaim arayit was. **1382** WYCLIF *Isa.* liv. 11, I shal araie bi order thi stones. *c* **1400** *Destr. Troy* xv. 6105 The secund batell..þe soueran araiet. **1576** LAMBARDE *Peramb. Kent* (1826) 245 This place is of it selfe very fit..to array an host of men upon. **1855** MACAULAY *Hist. Eng.* xviii. IV. 226 A force of thirteen thousand fighting men were arrayed in Hyde Park. **1879** O'FLANAGHAN *Munst. Circ.* 197 They could persecute any rebel with fire and sword; and for this purpose might array any of the queen's loyal subjects.

b. *fig.* esp. in *phr.* To array *against*.

1823 BYRON *Island* III. x, All round them seem'd array'd Against them. **1849** MACAULAY *Hist. Eng.* II. 375 On the other side were arrayed almost all the eminent forensic talents of the age. **1857** BUCKLE *Civilis.* vii. 341 To induce nearly the whole of the clergy to array themselves against Science. **1871** FARRAR *Witn. Hist.* ii. 56 These doubts will be arrayed before their minds.

2. *Law.* To array a panel, a jury. Cf. ARRAY *sb.* 7.

1591 LAMBARDE *Archeion* (1635) 207 Arraying of Pannels. **1641** *Termes de la Ley* 26 Aray is the taking or ordering of a Jury..from whence cometh the Verbe to array a pannell. **1768** BLACKSTONE *Comm.* III. xxiii. 359 If he [the sheriff] arrays the panel..under the direction of either party, this is good cause of challenge to the array. **1863** [see ARRAY *sb.* 7].

II. Of order of condition.

†**3.** To order, arrange, put or keep in order. *Obs.*

c **1440** *Morte Arth.* 509 He askes hyme..How he arayes þe rewme and rewlys þe pople.

III. Of orderly equipment, dress.

†**4.** To put in order for a purpose; to make (a thing) ready, prepare. *Obs.*

c **1325** *E.E. Allit. P.* A. 718 To suche is heuen-ryche arayed. **1382** WYCLIF *Isa.* lviii. 5 Sac and asken to araȝen [**1388** make redi]. **1388** —— *Acts* xxiii. 30 The Aspies that thei arayden [**1382** maden redy] for hym. **1393** GOWER *Conf.* II. 254 The bathes weren than araied. **1483** CAXTON *Gold. Leg.* 26/2 Thou arayest us lord to the, and thou arayest the to us. **1485** —— *Chas. Gt.* 209 Amende and araye theyr harnoys.

†**b.** *refl.* To prepare oneself, make ready. *Obs.*

c **1320** R. BRUNNE *Medit.* 990 And arayde hem faste þen for to gone. **1377** LANGL. *P. Pl.* B. v. 11 Resoun gan arrayen hym alle þe reume to preche. **1398** TREVISA *Barth. De P.R.* II. x. (1495) 38 We sholde..araye vs to receyue thynges that euerlastyth. *c* **1440** *Gesta Rom.* 322 The stiward perceivid þe Emperour in chambir, and araiyng him to bed.

†**c.** *intr.* To make preparations. *Obs. rare.*

1387 TREVISA *Higden* Rolls Ser. IV. 281 While Herode arayeþ for þe children deeþ..[*de nece puerorum disponeret*].

†**5.** To make ready (food). **a.** To prepare, 'dress.' **b.** To serve up in proper fashion. *Obs.*

1366 MAUNDEV. xix. 214 Arraye for me, to morwe, a gode Dyner. **1393** GOWER *Conf.* III. 23 The coke, which shal his mete array. *c* **1440** *Gesta Rom.* 149 The Coke, whan he had araied the hert. **1508–13** W. DE WORDE *Bk. Keruynge* in *Babees Bk.* 277 Yf the capons be soden, araye hym in the maner aforesayd.

†**6.** To fit (any one) out with needful preparations, to equip *with* (a force, etc.). *Obs.*

1393 GOWER *Conf.* III. 288 He was with worthy compaignie Arraied. *c* **1400** *Destr. Troy* IV. 1143 He will aray hym full rad with a route noble.

†**7.** To furnish (a house, etc.). *Obs.*

1366 MAUNDEV. v. 48 The prestes arrayen her Awtere honestly. *c* **1386** CHAUCER *Frankl. T.* 459 So wel arrayed hous as ther was oon. **1387** TREVISA *Higden* Rolls Ser. I. 217 The Capitol was arrayed with hiȝe walles i-heled with glas and with gold. *c* **1400** *Destr. Troy* III. 750 An Inner chamber, þat was rially arayed with a riche bede. *c* **1450** LONELICH *Grail* xx. 68 A large hostel for twenty men..he gan areyen.

8. To furnish the person with raiment (= arrayment), to attire, dress; *now*, to dress up with display. **a.** *trans.*

1297 R. GLOUC. 36 Tho kyng Leir arayed was. *c* **1340** HAMPOLE *Prose Tr.* 27 To wirchipe his heuede and his face, and aray it faire and curyusly. *c* **1450** *Merlin* xiv. 225 The kynge made his doughter to aray hem in riche robes. **1523** FITZHERB. *Husb.* 49 Take vp thy chyldren and aray them. **1535** COVERDALE *Isa.* xxii. 21 Araye him with thy cote, and gyrde him with thy gyrdle. **1611** BIBLE *Gen.* xli. 42 Pharaoh ..arayed him in vestures of fine linnen. **1755** YOUNG *Centaur* i. Wks. 1757 IV. 110 As the Jews arrayed our blessed Lord in a purple robe, to mock him.

b. *refl.* To dress; *now*, to dress oneself up.

a **1300** *Cursor M.* 3365 Scho hir arayed in better wede. ? *c* **1475** *Squyr Lowe Degre* 305 There he araied him in scarlet reed. **1603** SHAKS. *Meas. for M.* III. ii. 26, I drinke, I eate, array my selfe, and liue. **1802** MAR. EDGEWORTH *Moral T.* I. x. 80 A plaid, in which Miss McEvoy had arrayed herself.

c. *intr.* (= *refl*).

1718 POPE *Iliad* III. 409 The beauteous warrior now arrays for fight, In gilded arms.

d. To put on (dress, armour, etc.).

1611 COTGR. s.v. *Sot*, The robes that women doe array, their priuate fooleries bewray. **1809** CAMPBELL *Gert. Wyom.* III. xx, As he the sword and plume in haste array'd.

9. *transf.* and *fig.* **a.** To 'clothe,' 'attire.'

1388 WYCLIF *1 Tim.* ii. 9 Wymmen..with schamefastnesse & sobrenesse araiynge hem silf. **1477** EARL RIVERS (Caxton) *Dictes* 68 Arraye you withe iustice. **1786** W. GILPIN *Tour Lakes*, A mountain..arraying itself in the majesty of darkness. **1846** KEBLE *Lyra Innoc.* (1873) 154 In fear and love thy heart array.

b. To adorn, deck, set off.

1652 BENLOWES *Theoph.* XII. lvii, Pearld dew arraies As yet the virgin-meads. **1697** DRYDEN *Virg. Eclog.* v. 91 The Purple Spring Arrays the various Ground. **1823** BYRON *Island* IV. vii, She..thus array'd the grot with torchlight.

†**10.** *ironically*, **a.** To 'dress,' giving a dressing to, drub, thrash; discomfit, rout. Cf. DERAY. *Obs.*

c **1380** *Sir Ferumb.* 417 A man heȝ of mod: Sarasynȝ to yule [= ill] arraye. *c* **1400** *Beryn* 603 We wolde aray hym so That he [ne] shuld have legge ne foot, to-morow on to go. **1481** *Reynard* (1844) 85, I am so sore arayed, and sore hurte. *c* **1530** LD. BERNERS *Arth. Lyt. Bryt.* (1814) 131 A! syr..thus hath arayed me two armed knightes.

†**b.** To put into a (sore) plight, trouble, afflict.

a **1500** *Lancelot* 3270 Remembir the, how yhow haith ben araid..With love. **1509** HAWES *Past. Pleas.* xviii. xxxix, Hath love suche myght for to aray you so In so short a space? **1548** UDALL, etc. *Erasm. Par., Luke* xiii. 11 Araied with a disease both incurable and peiteous to see. *a* **1600** *Passion of Cryste* 419 in Hazl. *E.P.P.* III. 17 Vyce..Whiche hathe hym so Encombered and arayed.

†**c.** To disfigure, dirty, befoul, defile. *Obs.*

1530 PALSGR. 435/2, I araye or fyle with myer. *Jemboue. Ibid.* 436/1 You have arrayed your gowne agaynst the wall. **1530** *Calisto & Melib.* in Hazl. *Dodsl.* I. 78 Indeed age hath arrayed thee! That thou art she, now can scant be espied. **1575** *Gamm. Gurton's Needle* I. ii, See, so cham arrayed with dabbling in the dirt.

array (əˈreɪ), *sb.* Forms: 4 **arai**, 4–6 **aray(e**, **araie**, (5 **arey**), 5–6 **arraie**, **arraye**, 5– **array**. *Aphet.* **ray**. [a. AFr. *arai* = OF. *arei* (later *aroi*, *arroi*), = Pr. *arrei*, It. *arredo*, f. *areer*: see prec. (The final diphthong imitates the accented forms of the vb. and the primitive sb. *rei*.)]

I. Order of position.

1. a. Arrangement in line or ranks, *esp.* martial order. Phrases: ***in battle array***, ***out of array*** (obs.).

c **1350** *Will. Palerne* 1597 Þe bolder ouȝt we be, þei ben out of araie. **1475** CAXTON *Jason* 29 b, The king of Sklauonye helde his men in araye. **1535** COVERDALE *Joel* ii. 7 Euery man in his goinge shal kepe his araie. **1584** POWEL *Lloyd's Cambria* 108 He followed apase and brake their Arraie. **1570–87** HOLINSHED *Scot. Chron.* (1806) I. 44 They found them out of araie in following the chase. **1599** GREENE *Alphonsus* (1861) 242 Place thy men-at-arms In battle 'ray. **1667** MILTON *P.L.* II. 887 With Horse and Chariots rankt in loose array. **1693** *Mem. Count Teckely* IV. 31 Their Infantry was drawn up in Battel-array in the Plain beyond. **1776** GIBBON *Decl. & F.* i. (1782) I. 16 Wedged together in the closest array. **1814** SCOTT *Ld. Isles* VI. xxxi, The boldest broke array. **1839** JAMES *Louis XIV*, III. 411 A young officer ..drew his little force up in array.

b. *fig.*

1393 LANGL. *P. Pl.* C. VI. 158 Boþe monkes and chanouns Han ride out of a-ray. **1611** BIBLE *Job* vi. 4 The terrors of God doe set themselues in array against mee. **1757** YOUNG *Last Day* III. 239 All Heav'n's terrors in array surround the ball. **1859** HELPS *Friends in C.* I. 77 When all Europe was distinctly marked off into Protestant and Catholic, you might bring these two great sections face to face in hostile array.

†**2.** A disposition of men in martial order, a display of military force. *Obs.*

c **1350** *Will. Palerne* 1597 Al þat real aray reken schold men neuer. *c* **1380** *Sir Ferumb.* 2423 Of þat host to be-holde þe huge aray. *c* **1461** EARL OXFORD in *Paston Lett.* 390 II. 12 If Howard purposith hym to make any aray at oure manor of Wynche. **1553** Q. MARY in Strype *Eccl. Mem.* III. App. i. 3 And that ye stir not in a forcible array.

3. The calling forth of a military force, the arming of the militia; *esp.* in Hist. phrase, ***Commission of Array***.

1640–4 CHAS. I *Let.* in Rushw. *Hist. Coll.* III. (1692) I. 657 In ancient time the Militia of the Kingdom was ever disposed of by the Commissions of Array. **1647** MAY *Hist. Parl.* II. vi. 115 The time of these contentions between the Ordinance of the Militia and Commission of Array. **1809** TOMLINS *Law Dict.* s.v. *Militia*, The form of the commission of array was settled in parliament *anno* 5 Hen. 4. **1844** LD. BROUGHAM *Brit. Const.* xiii. (1862) 181 The public servants who had charge of the musters and arrays. **1875** STUBBS *Const. Hist.* I. xiv. 135 Wales was to furnish infantry raised by the new plan of commissions of array

4. *concr.* A host in array; a military force. *Hist.* The militia of a county or city.

1643 [ANGIER] *Lanc. Vall. Achor* 15 The Array, with some three hundred armed men..possessed themselves of Blackburne. **1821** SCOTT *Kenilw.* xv, Instructions to have a part of the array of the county ready. **1842** MACAULAY *Horatius* i, And bade his messengers ride forth..To summon his array. **1849** —— *Hist. Eng.* i. I. 150 The whole array of the city of London was under arms.

†**5.** Order, orderly sequence. *Obs. rare.*

1598 HAKLUYT *Voy.* I. 17 To the ende that I may proceed in some maner of array, I will first shewe, etc.

6. a. A series of things exhibited or displayed in line or order; an imposing series.

1814 BYRON *Corsair* III. i, Their long array of sapphire and of gold. **1843** PRESCOTT *Mexico* III. iii. (1864) 148 Displaying a formidable array of teeth. **1846** GROTE *Greece* II. iv. (1883) II. 300 An array of powerful Doric cities. **1856** KANE *Arct. Exp.* I. v. 47 On the right we have an array of cliffs. **1875** BRYCE *Holy Rom. Emp.* xvi. 285 A long array of Transalpine chivalry. **1883** J. BROWNING in *Knowledge* 24 Aug. 113/2 Something more than an array of figures.

b. *Math.* An arrangement of quantities or symbols in rows and columns; = MATRIX *sb.* 6.

1880 R. F. SCOTT *Theory of Determinants* i. 2 These when written one under the other in rows form a rectangular array... In the theory of determinants we have frequently to deal with several such arrays. **1902** *Encycl. Brit.* XXV. 277/2 The square array being termed the *matrix* of the determinant. **1908** G. H. HARDY *Pure Math.* 301 Arrange all the possible products of pairs u_m v_n in the form of a doubly infinite array

$u_0\ v_0\ u_1\ v_0\ u_2\ v_0 \ldots$
$u_0\ v_1\ u_1\ v_1\ u_2\ v_1 \ldots$
$u_0\ v_2\ u_1\ v_2\ u_2\ v_2 \ldots$

1943 MARGENAU & MURPHY *Math. Physics & Chem.* x. 288 A collection of real or complex quantities is called an array if it can be displayed in an orderly table of rows and columns.

c. In *Statistics*, an arrangement of correlated phenomena or data.

1896 K. PEARSON in *Phil. Trans. R. Soc.* A. CLXXXVII. 260 Let A and B be two correlated organs (variables or measurable characteristics) in the same or different individuals, and let the sub-group of organs B, corresponding to a sub-group of A.., be extracted. Let the first of these sub-groups be termed an *array*, and the second a *type*. **1938** L. J. HOLMAN *Simplified Statistics* iii. 24 This arrangement, whether of men or any other items in order of size or other value, is called by statisticians an array. **1957** KENDALL & BUCKLAND *Dict. Statist. Terms* 11 *Array*,.. More usually, the term denotes some special arrangement of the observations, *e.g.* in order of magnitude.

d. *Computing.* A set of memory locations or data items in which each member is identified by a common identifier together with one or more subscripts (according to the number of dimensions of the array), so that the set can be treated as a linear series.

1957 *Proc. Western Joint Computer Conf.* 192/2 This compilation involves..the generation of (symbolic) tags for those arithmetic instructions which refer to subscripted variables (variables which denote arrays) which in combination with the indexing instructions..will refer correctly to the individual members of those arrays. **1961** *Communications Assoc. Computing Machinery* IV. 60/1 One of the more challenging features of ALGOL 60 is the possibility of allowing the dimensions of an array to be defined by variables which take on their values only dynamically, so that no fixed amount of storage in the computer can be reserved by the compiler at compilation time. **1971** P. I. HASKEL in R. A. Wisbey *Computer in Lit. & Ling. Res.* 166 All collocating words within the span of plus and minus four are placed into an array (a particular kind of data object in SNOBOL4) with the appropriate keyword. **1973** [see SUBSCRIPT *sb.* 2 b]. **1984** J. SCRIVEN *Working Electron* iii. 62 Lines 1270–1290 read the character definition from the normal character set for each letter and load them into array Z(X). **1984** *Personal Software* Winter 21/1 The workhouse of the program is the array A(x, y).

7. *Law.* The order of impanelling a jury; the panel.

1579 FULKE *Heskins's Parl.* 389 The last couple..make vp a ful Iewrie..but we may lawfully chalenge the aray. **1628** COKE *On Litt.* 156 a, The Jurors names are ranked in the pannel one vnder another, which order or ranking the Jurie is called the array. **1863** COX *Inst. Eng. Govt.* II. iii. 353 Challenge to the array is an exception to the whole panel, on account of partiality or some default in the..officer who arrayed the panel. **1865** *Daily Tel.* 2 Dec. 5/6 The officer to whom the array was entrusted being a Catholic.

II. Order of condition or state.

8. a. A condition of special preparation, or which has been attained by special preparation; the state of being specially fitted out, as for war, festivities, solemnities. Now only *poet.*

c **1330** R. BRUNNE *Chron.* 110 Þe barons on gode aray, at London mad þei feste. *c* **1386** CHAUCER *Clerkes T.* 206 Al the paleys put was in array. *c* **1440** *Morte Arth.* 74 One ryalle araye he helde his rounde table. **1447** BOKENHAM *Lyvys of Seyntys* 34 The fyrst day of this solenne aray. **1484** RICH. III in Ellis *Orig. Lett.* Ser. II. 54 I. 106 To be redy in their moost defensible arraye. **1702** POPE *Jan. & May* 308 The pomp, the pageantry, the proud array. **1816** SCOTT *Old Mort.* ii, To be partakers of the array and the sports which took place. *c* **1840** ALFORD *Poems*, Stand up before your God In beautiful array.

b. ***in evil array***: in a bad condition, badly.

c **1400** *Ywaine & Gaw.* 2969 Thair clothes war reven on evil arai.

c. (Combining 6 and 8.)

1851 D. MITCHELL *Fresh Glean.* 60 Flowers and fruits in pretty array stretch down the French table-d'hôte. **1858** LONGF. *M. Standish* I. 8 Glittering weapons of warfare, Hanging in shining array along the walls of the chamber.

†**9.** Arrangement, order, or position of matters; a plight, a case; a (pretty) state of affairs! *Obs.*

c **1386** CHAUCER *Wife's T.* 46 Thow stondest yet..in such array, That of thy lyf hastow no sewerté. *c* **1420** *Pallad. on Husb.* I. 320 But uppon clay If thou wilt bilde an other is the array. **1470–85** (ed. 1634) MALORY *Arthur* (1816) II. 399 'Aha! what array is this?' said sir Launcelot. *a* **1529** SKELTON *El. Rummyng* 163 Some have no mony—For theyr ale to pay; That is a shrewd array. **1568** *Jacob & Esau* v. v. in Hazl. *Dodsl.* II. 252 Where are we now become? marry sir, here is array!

†**10.** The work of special preparation. *Obs.*

c **1460** *Towneley Myst.*, *Coliphiz.* 192 How myght that be trew? it toke more aray; The masons I knewe that hewed it, I say. **1660** STANLEY *Hist. Philos.* (1701) 99/2 The *Phrygians* is Euripides new Play. But Socrates gave it the best Array.

11. a. Outfit, attire, dress. Now only *poet.*

a **1300** *Cursor M.* 3364 In better aray hir forto dyht. *c* **1386** CHAUCER *Prol.* 330 He rode but homely in a medlee cote..Of his array tell I no lenger tale. *c* **1410** *Sir Cleges* 255 In pore clothyng was he tho, And in sympull araye. *a* **1450** *Knt. de la Tour* (1868) 29 Be not the furst to take new shappes and gises of array of women. **1451** *Test. Ebor.* (1855) II. 156 All my kerchieffs and array that longes to my hede. **1535** COVERDALE *Rev.* iii. 5 Clothed in whyte araye. **1596** SHAKS. *Tam. Shr.* III. i. 325 We will haue rings, and things, and fine array. **1699** DRYDEN *Flower & Leaf* 35 Dressing, by the Moon, in loose Array. **1768** BEATTIE *Minstrel* I. iii, Though homely in array. **1810** SCOTT *Lady of L.* II. xxxvi, Such array As best might suit the watery way.

b. *fig.* and *transf.*

c **1500** *Lancelot* 675 Wp goith the sone in to his fresh aray. **1591** SHAKS. *1 Hen. VI*, I. iii. 55 Thou Wolfe in Sheepes array! **1592** —— *Rom. & Jul.* III. iii. 142 Happinesse Courts thee in her best array. **1877** BRYANT *May Evening* xii, Earth renews Her beautiful array.

12. An assembly of directional radio aerials. See AERIAL *a.* 6 b, BEAM *sb.*^{1} 24.

1919 G. A. CAMPBELL *Coll. Papers* (1937) 280 Antenna Arrays. **1929** *Bell Syst. Techn. Jrnl.* VIII. 309 Comparisons of calculated and observed directional diagrams of.. wave-antenna arrays are.. discussed. **1930** [see AERIAL *a.* 6 b]. **1938** *P.O. Electr. Engin. Jrnl.* XXXI. 94/1 Array type antennæ.. are usually employed for ultra-short wave links. .. Arrays consisting of up to 24 half-wave elements.. may be erected. **1940** [see ANTENNA 5 b]. **1965** *New Scientist* 16 Sept. 676 A laser beam can correlate signals received by an extremely complex radar array.

III. 13. Special Combs.: **array processing**, the computer processing of arrays (sense 6 d); so **array processor**, a computer specially designed for processing arrays; *spec.* a specialized computer which does this, usu. by parallel processing, for a mainframe or host computer.

1960 L. J. SPIEKER (*title*) Seismometer *array and data processing system. (Texas Instr. Final Rep., Phase I.) **1964** *Bull. Seismol. Soc. Amer.* LIV. 278 Applications of array-processing techniques to seismic recordings of earthquakes and blasts have been few. **1980** *Economist* 21 June 97/2 Different supercomputers take different approaches to problem-solving. At the moment, there are two basic approaches: the pipeline approach and the array-processing technique. **1964** E. W. MOORE (*title*) Effect of changing multiple *array processor output filter band width. (United Electrodynamics Rep.) **1975** *Aviation Week & Space Technol.* 7 July 40 Package containing a spread-spectrum modem.., an adaptive antenna array processor, [etc.]. **1977** *Sci. Amer.* Sept. 224/2 Machines such as this one are called array processors or single-instruction-stream, multiple-data-stream machines. **1983** W. S. DAVIS *Operating Systems* (ed. 2) xviii. 425 Once defined, the arrays will be passed to an array processor, where the rules of linear algebra will be applied.

arrayal (əˈreɪəl). [f. ARRAY *sb.* + -AL^2.] The process of arraying; muster of a force; array.

1818 H. MURRAY *Disc. & Trav. Africa* II. 36 Here he held his Arrayal or Camp. **1849** *Mem. Kirkaldy of Grange* xxix. 342 The arrayal of the different divisions beneath their several standards. **1864** NEALE *Seaton. Poems* 50 The treasures hid in dread arrayal there.

arrayed (əˈreɪd), *pa. pple.* [f. ARRAY *v.* + -ED.] Put into array or order, attired, dressed.

c **1386** CHAUCER *Frankl. T.* 459 So wel arraied hous.. Aurilius in his lif saw never non. **1525** LD. BERNERS *Froiss.* II. cxxiv. [cxx.] 353 Poore people, rude and yvell arayed. **1664** *Floddan Field* VII. 71 The Admiral did plainly aspect, The Scots aray'd in battles four. **1864** BOUTELL *Hist. Heraldry* (ed. 3) xxi. §2. 359 Three lady's heads, issuant, arrayed and veiled.

arrayer (əˈreɪə(r)). In 4 arraiour, 7 arreyer. [a. OF. *araieor, areeor*, f. *areer* to ARRAY.]

1. *gen.* One who arrays.

c **1370** WYCLIF *Prelates* xxxiv. Wks. 1879, 100 Arraiouris of sathanas batailis.

2. *spec.* in *Hist.* (= *Commissioner of Array*).

1617 J. RIDER, *Arreyers*, vide Muster masters. **1706** PHILLIPS, *Arrayers*, or *Commissioners of Array*, certain Officers, whose Business is to take care of the Soldiers Armour, and to see them duly accoutred. **1875** STUBBS *Const. Hist.* II. xvii. 543 To array men-at-arms, and to pay them and convey them to Scotland.. at the cost of the commons, arrayers and conveyers.

arraying (əˈreɪɪŋ), *vbl. sb.* [f. ARRAY *v.* + -ING^1.] Putting or setting in array, dressing or decking; also (*arch.*), dress, attire.

c **1340** HAMPOLE *Prose Tr.* 28 All þe payntynge and þe arraynge þat þou haue made aboute his heuede. **1398** TREVISA *Barth. De P.R.* x. iii. (1495) 374 Eche element hath his arayenge and ornament. *c* **1400** *Apol. Loll.* 99 ȝor feet to be shod in arayng of þe gospel of pees. **1850** MRS. BROWNING *Poems* II. 32 Who prefers at her bridal a brown rosary To a worldly arraying.

arrayment (əˈreɪmənt). For forms see ARRAY *v.* [a. AFr. *araiement* = OF. *areement*, f. *areer* to ARRAY: see -MENT.] Outfit, accoutrement; attire, dress; RAIMENT. Also, the act or fact of arraying or being arrayed.

1400 GRIFFITH AP GR. in Ellis *Orig. Lett.* II. 2. I. 6 Boȝt armery at all pees, and horses, and other araement. **1462** *Test. Ebor.* (1855) II. 256, I wille that my wife have ij of the best beddes and al hir arayment hole. **1475** *Bk. Noblesse* 80 Escheweng alle costius arraiementis of clothing. **1520** *State Papers Hen. VIII*, II. 43 Souldeours can not live on 4^d a day, and reserve any thyng to by theyme arrayment withall. **1606** J. RAYNOLDS *Dolarnys Prim.* (1880) 62 The Aspen trees.. In like arraiment, then were neatly seene. **1708** J. CHAMBERLAYNE *State Gt. Brit.* II. III. vi, Solemn apparel, or manner of arrayments for members of Parliament. **1875** MORRIS *Æneids* II. 450 Other some.. The other doorways of the place in close arrayment hedge. *Ibid.* XII. 442 Then in arrayment close Antheus and Mnesthus rush to war. **1892** *Guardian* 11 May 706/2 Whose light arrayment is a mist of green. **1907** *Daily Chron.* 8 Nov. 4/6 The same arrayment of civic dignitaries in scarlet and fur.

arrays, variant of ARAISE *v. Obs.*

arre, obs. form of AR (the letter), ARROW, ERE, ERR.

†**aˈrrear**, *adv. Obs.* Forms: 4–6 arere, 6 arear(e, arreir, 6–7 arreare, 6–8 arrere, 7–8 arrear. [a. OF. *arere, ariere* (mod.F. *arrière*), Pr. *a(r)reire*:—Merovingian L. *ad retro*, f. *ad* to, *retro* backward.]

1. Of direction: Backward, to the rear, behind, into the background.

1393 LANGL. *P. Pl.* C. VII. 405 Thanne gan he go.. Som tyme asyde · and som tyme a-rere. *c* **1450** HENRYSON *Test. Creseide* 196 All earthly ioy and mirth I set arere. **1591** SPENSER *Virgils Gnat* 468 She.. Obseru'd th' appointed way .. Ne euer did her eysight turne arere.

2. Of position: In the rear, behind; in the background. Cf. A-REAR.

1393 GOWER *Conf.* I. 315 Shall no man knowe by his chere, Which is avaunt, ne whiche arere. *c* **1449** PECOCK *Repr.* I. xvi. 90 Grees goon on out of gree and prechingis rennen arere. **1509** BARCLAY *Ship of Fooles* (1570) 208 When a simple seruaunt must needes stande arere. **1600** FAIRFAX *Tasso* II. xl, To leaue with speed Atlanta swift arreare.

3. Of action: *to do, put arrear*: to rout. *to run arrear*: to fall into confusion or disorder.

1330 R. BRUNNE *Chron.* 241 Þe Walsch com þam ageyn, did our men alle arere. **1529** LYNDESAY *Complaynt* 122 Than did my purpose ryn arreir. **1530** —— *Papyngo* 567 The court of Rome, that tyme, rane all aureir.

4. Of time: **a.** Behindhand, behind date, overdue. (Replaced by *in arrear*.)

1477 NORTON *Ord. Alch.* in Ashm. 1652 ii. 30 He with haste shall bringe his warke arreare. **1552** HULOET, Arrere to be with accompt or reckenynge, *Reliquor*. **1648** *Petit. East. Ass.* 25 To order Collectors.. to distrain for what is Arrear. **1768** BLACKSTONE *Comm.* II. 42 In case they be behind, or arrere, at the day appointed, the lord may distrein.

b. Behind us in time, past and gone.

1587 TURBERVILLE, Not with such friendly face.. As earst thou hadst: those louely lookes and blincks are all arreare.

5. In various combinations in which the simple REAR is now used; as **arrear-admiral, arrear-supper**; where it also varies with the mod.F. form *arrière*. Also **arrear-ban(d**: see ARRIÈRE-BAN; ARREAR-GUARD, -WARD, q.v.

1600 HOLLAND *Livy* XXXVII. xxix. 961 Eudamus the arriere-admirall [*qui cogebat agmen*].. made head with his owne ship against the very admirall of the enemies.

arrear (əˈrɪə(r)), *sb.* Forms: 4 ariere, 7 arrier, arrere, arreare, 7– arrear. [The prec. adv. used absolutely: 'that which is behind.' At first only in the phr. *in arrear*, which was perhaps rather a compound adverb, like F. *en arrière, en avant* (answering to ARREAR *adv.* in senses 2–4), but led the way to truly substantive uses, in which the *pl. arrears* is now common.]

I. *in arrear.*

†**1.** In time past. *Obs.*

1340 *Ayenb.* 165 Ase habbeþ ydo ine ariere and þe filozofe payen and þe holy Cristene man.

†**2.** In the hinder place or position: see REAR.

1642 HOWELL *For. Trav.* (Arb.) 33 Mind and Tongue go commonly together (and the first comes sometimes in the arreare).

3. Backward, behindhand as to state or condition. *in arrear of*: behind.

1845 FORD *Handbk. Spain* i. 59 The arts of medicine and surgery are somewhat in arrear in Spain. **1859** REEVE *Brittany* 238 The science of natural history [was] in arrear of the arts.

4. a. Behind in the discharge of duties or liabilities; in indebtedness, in debt. Cf. ARREARAGE.

1621 JAMES I in Ellis *Orig. Lett.* I. 300 III. 169 If he once runne in arreare, he will ever goe bakkwarde. **1676** CLARENDON *Surv. Leviath.* 297 Who in truth are in too great an arrear to him. **1678** R. LESTRANGE *Seneca's Mor.* (1702) 72 But when I have paid that, I am still in Arrier. **1713** STEELE *Englishm.* Pref. 6 The World is in Arrear to your Virtue. **1806–31** A. KNOX *Rem.* (1844) I. 70, I am two or three letters in arrear to different persons.

b. *in arrears*: (with same meaning.)

1620 NAUNTON in *Fortesc. Papers* 140 The arreares they ar in for them. **1700** A. CHARLETT in *Pepys' Diary* VI. 228, I am very much in arrears to you for a thousand civilities. **1718** *Free-thinker* No. 93. 264, I am run deeply in Arrears to my Correspondents. **1810** HUTTON *Course Math.* I. 260 When an annuity is forborn for some years, or the payments not made for that time, the annuity is said to be in Arrears.

II. Without *in.*

5. The hinder part of anything, especially of a train or procession; the rear. *arch.*

a **1627** HAYWARD *Edward VI* (1630) 18 Lastly followed the Arrier wherein were betweene 3 and 4000 foote. **1661** HEYLIN *Hist. Ref.* (1674) II. 83 (D.) The Duke of Suffolk and Sir John Cheek.. shutting up the arrear. **1869** DIXON *Tower* in *Casquet of Lit.* (1877) IV. 132/1 A vessel firing guns in front, and a long arrear of craft behind.

†**6. a.** A portion held back; a deduction. *Obs.*

1768 SIMES *Mil. Medley*, s.v., Arriers, is a deduction made from the officers according to their full pay.

†**b.** *fig.* Something held in reserve; a sequel. *Obs.*

1659 HAMMOND *On Ps.* i. 3 Though there were never an arrear behinde of eternal hell. **1676** BATES *Immort. Soul*, There remains in another world a dreadful arrear of misery.

7. a. That wherein one has fallen behind. A duty or liability overdue and still remaining undischarged, *esp.* a debt remaining unpaid.

1658 *Whole Duty Man* xiv. §24. 116 When Josiah had destroyed idolatry.. yet there was an old arrear of Manasseh his grandfather. *a* **1733** NORTH *Lives* I. 435 Nothing sat heavier on his spirits than a great arrear of business. **1796** BURKE *Let. Noble Ld.* Wks. VIII. 4 Having so faithfully and so fully acquitted towards me whatever arrear of debt was left undischarged. **1840** DICKENS *Lett.* (1880) I. 32 To you .. I owe a long arrear of thanks.

b. in *plural.* Outstanding liabilities, amounts, or balances; moneys due; debts. Also used as a *sing. U.S.*

1648 *Petit. East. Ass.* 24 To pay the late Arrears of the Army. **1655** FULLER *Ch. Hist.* II. I. 134 The Profits and long-detained Arreres of the Popes *Patrimoniolum*. *a* **1711** KEN *Poet. Wks.* 1721 IV. 11 The Blood of dying God alone, can for my vast Arrears atone. **1833** MARRYAT *P. Simple* (1863) 189 To obtain my arrears of pay, and some prize-money which I find due. **1868** PATTISON *Academ. Org.* §1. 22 The arrears of two centuries require to be cleared off. **1902** *Rep. Librarian Congress* 30 They constitute a large arrears, which should be dealt with speedily.

†**aˈrrear**, *v. Obs.* Forms: 4–6 arere, 6 aryere, 7 arrear. [a. OF. *arere-r*, later *arierer, arrierer*, to put back, draw back, f. *arrière*. Cf. *avant, avancer, aval, avaler*.]

1. *trans.* To keep back, allow to fall behind.

c **1525** SKELTON *Vox Pop. Vox Dei* 494 Except the fermour wyll aryere The rent hyere by a hole yeare. **1635** J. SLACKE in Hearne's *Langtoft's Chron.* (1810) 393 To pay unto me such Pentions as were arreared.

2. *intr.* To draw back, fall back, retreat, recede. (*Arere!* may be imperative of the vb., or the adv. used interjectionally, like *Back!*)

c **1340** *Gaw. & Gr. Knt.* 1902 And he schunt for þe scharp, & schulde haf arered. **1399** *Rich. Redeless* III. 110 A-rere now to Richard, and reste here a while. *c* **1400** *Beryn* 1972 Somtyme thowe wolt auaunte, and som tyme [wolt] arere. **1509** BARCLAY *Ship of Fooles* (1570) ¶¶ iij, Ye London galantes arere, ye shall not enter.

arrear(e, later corrupt form of AREAR *v.*

arrearage (əˈrɪərɪdʒ). Forms: 3–7 arer-, 4 arrir-, 4–7 arrer-, 5 (arrage), 6 arear-, 7 arrier-, arrere-, arreer-, (arreage), 5– arrearage. See aphet. REARAGE. [a. OF. *arerage*, f. *arere* behind, mod. *arrérage*; cf. *avant-age*, ADVANTAGE.]

†**1.** The state or condition of being behind, or *in arrear*, with the payment of what is due; indebtedness, debt. *Obs.*

1330 R. BRUNNE *Chron.* 319 Now salle I wite þe taile, & put þe in þe Arerage. **1340** HAMPOLE *Pr. Consc.* 5913 Many in arrirage mon falle, And til perpetuele prison gang. *c* **1386** CHAUCER *Prol.* 604 Ther couthe noman bringe him in arrerage [*v.r.* a-rerage]. **1540** ELYOT *Image Govt.* (1556) 79 Yf any were found in arrerage, he shuld.. paye.. four tymes as muche as the arrerage amounted to. **1608** *2nd Pt. Def. Reasons Refus. Subscr.* 238 For his daily borrowing of him, is likely to run into that arrerage that he will not easely gett out of his debt. *a* **1637** B. JONSON *Epigr.* I. (1692) 283 Th'art in arrearage grown Some hundred Quarrels.

†**b.** with pl. *in arrearages*: in arrears. *Obs.*

1393 LANGL. *P. Pl.* C. XII. 297 So deepe in arerages. **1525** LD. BERNERS *Froiss.* II. lxi. [lxiv.] 205 [He was] in his det in a grete some of money, longe renne in arrerages. **1605** *Lond. Prodigal* I. ii. 230 The rogue puts me in 'rearages for orient pearl. **1642** ROGERS *Naaman* 614 Play most unfaithfull parts .. and thus run into arrearedges.

2. *gen.* Backwardness, state of being in arrear.

1576 LAMBARDE *Peramb. Kent* (1826) 298 Charging him with great arrearage of account. **1841** MISS KEMBLE *Rec. Later Life* II. 159 When such an arrearage took place, the fittest thing to do was to answer first those received first. **1883** A. HARDY *But yet a Wom.* 103 Practitioners who make up their arrearage in science by.. wide experience.

3. *concr.* That which is in arrear; an amount overdue, an outstanding or unpaid sum or balance.

1466 *Paston Lett.* 557 II. 289, Xxli., which I will be gathered of the arrerage of my lyvelode. **1483** *Cath. Angl.*, An Arrerage [*v.r.* Arreage], *erreragia*. *a* **1500** *Reg. Civ. Ebor.* 366 a, The arrerage of the said fee ferme. **1617** BACON in *Fortesc. Papers* 23 To continewe the payment of the anuetye .. and allso to pay the arrerage thereof. **1790** COWPER *Odyss.* XXI. 18 Demanding payment of arrearage due. **1870** *Daily News* 21 Sept., The employers had no funds.. and a large arrearage of wages accumulated.

b. Something still in reserve.

1594 DRAYTON *Idea* 36 My Joyes arrerage leades me to my losse. **1854** DE QUINCEY in Page *Life* (1877) II. xviii. 84 Which.. leaves even to the thief a conscious arrearage of nobility and possible redemption.

4. *pl.* Items overdue, outstanding amounts, arrears; *esp.* moneys overdue; debts; = ARREAR 7.

c **1315** SHOREHAM, 96 Nere the milse and merci of God self .. That wolle the arerages forȝeve. **1453** *Test. Ebor.* II. 191 All þarrages.. to me dewe at my dethe. **1483** ARNOLD *Chron.* (1811) 271 First, the areragis of the last acompter. **1611** SHAKS. *Cymb.* II. iv. 13 He'le grant the Tribute, send th' Arrerages. **1637** *Reliq. Wotton.* (1672) 54 Such Arrearages as shall appear due unto me. **1691** BLOUNT *Law Dict.*, *Arrearages*, the Remain of an Accompt, or a Sum of Money remaining in the Hands of an Accomptant. It is sometimes used more generally for any Money unpaid at a due Time. **1850** W. IRVING *Granada* 24 A formal demand for the payment of arrearages.

†a'rrearance. *Obs.* [a. OF. *arrierance*, f. *arrierer*, earlier *arerer*, *arerer*, to put behind: see ARREAR *v.* and -ANCE.] An arrear.

1731 BAILEY, *Arrearances, Arrears*, are the remainders of any rents or monies unpaid at the due time.

†arrear-guard: *Obs.*, see ARRIÈRE-GUARD.

†a'rrear-ward. *Obs.* Forms: 6 **arrier-**, 7 **arere-**, **arrere-ward.** [f. ARREAR *adv.* + WARD: see prec. There may have been an early *arere-ward*, as well as *rere-ward* (cf. ONFr. *arere-*, *rere-warde*), but existing evidence shows only *rere-ward* in 13th c., *rere-*, *arrere-garde* int. by Caxton in 15th c., and *arrere-ward* in end of 16th.] = prec.

1589 *Late Voy. Sp. & Port.* (1881) 75 The Battaile and the arrierward stood in Armes al the night. **1600** HOLLAND *Livy* 863 (R.) The second legion which was in the arrereward. **1664** S. CLARKE *Tamerlane* 3 The Prince of Thanais..led the Arereward.

arreca, obs. form of ARECA.

arrect, later corrupt f. ARET *v.* *Obs.* to impute.

†a'rrect, *v.* *Obs.* Also 6 **arecte.** [f. L. *arrect-* ppl. stem of *arrig-ĕre* to raise up, incite, f. *ar-* = *ad-* to + *-rigĕre* = *regĕre* to straighten.]

1. To set upright.

1530 PALSGR. 436/1, I arecte, I adresse up or set up a thyng, *Je metz sus..je metz debout*, or *je metz a point.* This banner is nowe arrected. **1534** WHITTINTON *Tullyes Off.* I. 6 Whiche dylygence doth arrecte hertes and maketh them more encouraged to playe the men.

2. To direct upwards, raise, lift up.

a **1529** SKELTON *Poems* 9 (T.) Arrectynge my sight towarde the zodiake. **1556** ABP. PARKER *Psalter* cviii, Yea Psalmes to thee I wyll arrect, Among all folke of euery sect.

3. To set right, direct.

1530 PALSGR. 436/2, I arecte..*Jadresse.* Be nat afrayde. If thou be out of the waye, thou shalte be arrected.

arrect (ə'rɛkt), *ppl. a.* and *sb.* [ad. L. *arrect-us*: see prec.]

A. *adj.* Set upright, pricked up (as the ears of a beast); having the faculties directed towards; *fig.* intent, attentive, on the alert.

1646 J. G[REGORY] *Notes & Obs.* (1650) 142 His eares are said to bee arrect and intent only to those [prayers] that are made in this place. *c* **1794** AKENSIDE *Pleas. Imag.* I. 269 Eager for the event, Around the Beldame all arrect they hang. **1846** T. AIRD in *Blackw. Mag.* LX. 279 The rabbit.. pauses a moment—with its form and ears arrect to listen.

†B. *sb.* Proposed term for 'upright stratum.' *Obs.*

1811 PINKERTON *Petralogy* I. 213.

†a'rrectary. *Obs. rare*$^{-1}$. [ad. L. *arrectārius*, f. *arrect-us*: see prec. and -ARY. Used subst. in L.] An upright post or beam.

c **1620** BP. HALL *Serm. Gal.* ii. 20 (R.) The arrectary or beam of his cross.

arredie, -ye, var. AREADY *v.* *Obs.* to make ready.

arrend, obs. form of ERRAND.

arrendation: see ARRENTATION.

‖arrendator (ærən'deɪtɔː(r)). [med.L., f. *arrendāre* = *arrentāre*, f. F. *arenter*, *arr-*: see ARRENT.] One who rents or farms at a yearly rent.

arrenotokous (ærɪ'nɒtəkəs), *a.* [mod. f. Gr. ἀρρενοτόκ-ος (f. ἄρρην male + -τόκος begetting) + -OUS.] (See quot.) **arre'notoky**, 'that form of parthenogenesis in which the unimpregnated females produce only males' (*Syd. Soc. Lex.* 1880).

1877 HUXLEY *Anat. Inv. An.* vii. 446 The terms arrenotokous and thelytokous have been proposed by Leuckart and Von Siebold to denote those parthenogenetic females which produce male and female young respectively.

arrent (ə'rɛnt), *v.* [a. F. *arrenter* (14th c. in Littré), also in OF. *arentir*, f. *à* to + *rente* RENT. Cf. med.L. *arrentāre*, common in Eng. charters and law-books (f. the Fr.).] To let out or farm at a rent; *spec.* to allow the enclosure of forest lands 'with a low hedge, and small ditch' under a yearly rent. Hence **arrenting** *vbl. sb.*

1598 MANWOOD *Lawes Forest* ix. §3 (1615) 70 Which must be entred of record at the time of the arrenting thereof. **1755** CARTE *Hist. Eng.* IV. 22 Upon pretence that no [lands] can be assarted, but what have been formerly arrented.

arrentable (ə'rɛntəb(ə)l), *a.* [f. prec. + -ABLE.] That may be arrented; chargeable at a (yearly) rent.

1598 MANWOOD *Lawes Forest* x. §2 (1615) 75 The building of any new house..within a Forest, is a Purpresture.. arrentable for the tolleration or suffering of that to stand.

arrentation (ærən'teɪʃən). Also 6 **arrend-**, 7 **arent-.** [(ad. med.L. *arrentātiōn-em*), n. of action f. *arrentāre*: see ARRENT. Other forms of the med.L., after F. *rendre*, It. *rendere*, were *arrendāre*, *-ātio.*] The action, or privilege, of arrenting.

[**1306** *Ord. Forestæ, Act 34 Edw. I*, v, Quod haye et fossata facta medio tempore prosternantur et penitus commoveantur et adnichilentur, saluis arentacionibus nostris quas secundum assisam foreste volumus remanere. *Transl.* in Pulton: That the hedges and diches..shall be wholly cast downe, remoued, and avoided: saving our Arrentations which we will have remaine according to the assise of the Forest.] *c* **1525** SKELTON *Image Hypocr.* II. 390 He robbeth all nations With his..Arrendations. **1738** *Hist. Crt. Exchequer* v. 87 The Profit of the County was likewise increased by Arentations of Assarts.

†a'rreption. *Obs. rare.* [n. of action f. L. *arrept-* ppl. stem of *arripĕre* to snatch away, carry off, f. *ar-* = *ad-* to + *-ripĕre* = *rapĕre* to seize.] A carrying off, sudden removal.

1612–5 BP. HALL *Contempl.* XIX. (1628) 1295 This arreption was sudden, yet Elisha sees both the charet, and the horses. **1633** EARL MANCH. *Al Mondo* 196 This is a kinde of Arreption to heaven: when a man abstracts himselfe from earth, and by Contemplation grows into acquaintance with God.

†arrep'titious, *a.* *Obs.* [f. L. *arreptīci-us*, f. *arreptus*: see prec. and -ITIOUS.]

1. Liable to raptures, ecstatic, frantic, mad.

a **1641** BP. MOUNTAGU *Acts & Mon.* 201 Such arreptitious ones fashion to themselves rivers, mountaines, beasts, monsters..which proceed meerly from disturbance of the brain. *c* **1645** HOWELL *Lett.* (1650) I. 475 Odd arrepititious frantic extravagancies. **1656** BLOUNT *Glossogr., Arreptitious*, caught or tormented by a devil.

2. Characterized by having been hastily seized or caught up; hasty, hurried.

1653 MANTON *Exp. James* ii. 19 Assent now is nothing so much as it was then, especially when it is trivial and arreptitious, rather than deliberate.

¶ Also referred by Blount to L. *arrēpĕre*, 'to creep to,' and defined 'he that steals or creeps in privily' (cf. *surreptitious*); whence in Bailey, etc.

arrere, obs. f. ARREAR: see also AREAR *v.* *Obs.*

arrest (ə'rɛst), *v.* Forms: 4 **areiste**, 4–6 **arest(e**, 6 **areest**, (*Sc.* **arreist**), 5– **arrest.** *Aphet.* 6–7 **rest.** [a. OF. *areste-r* intr. and trans., = Pr. *a(r)restar*, It. *arrestare*:—late L. *adrestāre*, f. *ad* to, at + *restāre* to remain, stop, f. *re-* back + *stāre* to stand. Orig. intr. in Rom. langs., but in OFr. also trans. long before its adoption in Eng.]

I. *intr.* To stop, stay, remain, rest.

†1. To stop, come to a stand, halt. *Obs.*

c **1325** *E.E. Allit. P.* B. 766 Þenne arest þe renk & raȝt no fyrre. **1483** CAXTON *Gold. Leg.* 130/1 Without arestyng for to helpe them.

†2. To stay, remain, continue, rest. *Obs.*

c **1325** *E.E. Allit. P.* C. 144 Durst nowhere for roȝ arest at þe bothem. **1393** GOWER *Conf.* I. 164 A wilde beast, In whom no reson might areste. **1538** LELAND *Itin.* VI. 40 A white Starre..whiche to every mans sighte did lighte and arrest apon the Standard of Albry.

†3. To rest, repose (in confidence). *Obs.*

1523 LD. BERNERS *Froiss.* I. ccxlii. 358 One submyssion, wheron the kyng and his counsayle arested moost.

†4. To rest or dwell *upon* (a subject). (Cf. 8) *Obs.*

a **1619** DONNE *Biathan.* (1644) 182 We must arrest awhile vpon the nature, and degrees, and effects of charity.

5. *Med.* To suffer cardiac arrest.

1982 *Brit. Med. Jrnl.* 13 Nov. 1373/1 She might arrest postoperatively. **1985** *Verbatim* Winter 3/2 The patient never dies, though he may arrest (short for 'suffer cardiac arrest').

II. *trans.* (and *refl.*) To cause to stop, detain.

6. To cause to stop; to stop the course of: **a.** a person or animal. *Obs.* in literal sense since 1600, but still used in reference to a course of action, where it passes into 15 b.

1375 BARBOUR *Bruce* XVI. 281 His host all than arestit he. *c* **1386** CHAUCER *Prol.* 829 Oure ost bigan his hors areste. *c* **1450** LONELICH *Grail* xli. 8 As they wenten, mochel folk they fownde that hem arested. **1523** LD. BERNERS *Froiss.* I. ccclxxiv. 620, I arest you all, so that ye shall nat departe this day. *a* **1540** *Christis Kirk of Gr.* vi, Steven cam steppand in with stendis, Na rynk mycht him arreist. **1668** SHADWELL *Sullen Lovers* I. i. Wks. 1720 I. 19 As I was coming..Sir Positive At-all, that fool..arrests me with his impertinence. **1781** GIBBON *Decl. & F.* III. lvi. 365 In the pursuit of greatness he was never arrested by the scruples of justice. **1803** G. ROSE *Diaries* (1860) II. 26 Mr. Pitt's resuming office would arrest Buonaparte in his..career. **1862** STANLEY *Jew. Ch.* (1877) I. xiii. 252 The five Danite warriors, as they pass by..are arrested by the sound of a well-known voice.

b. a thing; usually a stream or train of things in motion or progress.

1375 BARBOUR *Bruce* XII. 7 He gert arest all his battale. *c* **1374** CHAUCER *Boeth.* I. vi. 29 Þe fletyng streme..is arestid and resisted ofte tyme by þe encountrynge of a stoon. **1470–85** (1634) MALORY *Arthur* (1816) I. 158 That all the navy of the land should be arrested. **1635** QUARLES *Emblems* III. xiii. (1718) 177 Forbear t' arrest My thriftless day too soon. **1650** FULLER *Pisgah Sight* II. x. 211 Where Joshua's prayer arrested the moon to stand still. **1794** SULLIVAN *View Nat.* I. 332 The mountains..attract, and as it were arrest, the vapours and the rain that float in the atmosphere. **1796** MORSE *Amer. Geog.* I. 133 Many springs..in winter are arrested by the frost. **1869** PHILLIPS *Vesuv.* vii. 195 These deep cavities have often arrested the lava-currents. **1871** MACDUFF *Mem. Patmos* vii. 91 Has He arrested the axe, and revoked the sentence? **1876** GEO. ELIOT *Dan. Der.* III. xxiii. 197 Her tears were arrested. **1879** LOCKYER *Elem. Astron.* ix. xlviii. 293 The cannon-ball will in time be arrested by the resistance of the air.

c. motion, course, pace; growth, decay, etc.

c **1374** CHAUCER *Boeth.* II. i. 32 Enforcest þou þe to aresten or wiþstanden þe swyftnesse..of hir tournyng. **1699** DRYDEN *Theod. & Hon.* 181 My Dogs with better speed Arrest her Flight. **1877** E. CONDER *Bas. Faith* Pref. 12 The pace..too rapid to be thus led or arrested. **1879** CARPENTER *Mental Phys.* I. ii. §54 Its progress is arrested.

d. in Law, *to arrest judgement*: to stay proceedings after a verdict, on the ground of error.

1768 BLACKSTONE *Comm.* III. 395 If judgment is not by some of these means arrested. **1871** ARCHBOLD *Crim. Plead.* (ed. 17) 170 If the judgment be arrested, all the proceedings are set aside, and judgment of acquittal is given.

†7. *refl.* To stop, stand still. (Cf. 1.) *Obs.* (Fr. *s'arrêter*.)

a **1470** TIPTOFT *Cæsar's Comm.* iv. (1530) 4 They marveylyd greatly and arested themself.

†8. *refl.* To rest oneself, remain, tarry. (Cf. 2.) *Obs.*

1543 GRAFTON *Cont. Harding's Chron.* 531 He and his compaignie, after their laboures, arested thaim for the space of iii. dayes. **1563** —— *Chron. Rich. I*, an. 8 (R.) When he had arested him a little while, he then roade..to Notingham.

†9. *trans.* and *refl.* To keep our minds, ourselves, resting or fixed upon the consideration of a subject.

1502 *Ord. Crysten Men* (W. de W.) I. vii, And who soo hym wyll areest in this medytacyon he there shall fynde, etc. **1626** AILESBURY *Passion-serm.* 9 Let us arest our selves awhile upon his foretold passions. *a* **1667** JER. TAYLOR (in Webster) We may arrest our thoughts upon the divine mercies.

III. *trans.* To stop and lay hold of.

10. *gen.* To catch, capture, seize, lay hold upon. *Obs.* exc. as fig. use of next.

1481 CAXTON *Myrrour* II. v. 70 Bestes..whiche..haue so grete vngles or clawes that areste alle that they can holde. **1509** HAWES *Joyf. Med.* 13 Dethe by his course naturall Hathe him arested. **1596** SPENSER *F.Q.* I. iv. 44 Whenas Morpheus had with leaden mace Arrested all that courtly company. **1718** POPE *Iliad* XV. 527 The pointed death arrests him from behind. **1791** COWPER *Iliad*, Well skilled..to rouse and with unerring aim arrest All savage kinds that haunt the mountain wilds. *a* **1883** RUSKIN in *Royal Acad. Catal.* 12 We cannot arrest sunsets nor carve mountains.

11. *esp.* To capture, seize, lay hold upon, or apprehend by legal authority; 'to restrain a man of his liberty, obliging him to be obedient to the law.'

1375 BARBOUR *Bruce* I. 174 He was arestyt syne and tane. **1393** GOWER *Conf.* III. 268 Tho bad the king men shulde areste His body. *a* **1400** *Chester Pl.* 182 The Kinge hase commaunded me All suche for to areiste. **1460** CAPGRAVE *Chron.* 264 The kyng..ded his officeres arestin..the Duke of Gloucetir. **1514** BARCLAY *Cyt. & Uplondyshm.* 23 Some 'rest men gyltles & caste them in pryson. **1589** *Hay any Work* 40 The Wardens..rested him with a Purciuant. **1613** SHAKS. *Hen. VIII*, I. i. 201, I Arrest thee of High Treason. **1745** DE FOE *Eng. Tradesm.* I. xxix. 293 Sends an officer.. and arrests him for the money. **1839** KEIGHTLEY *Hist. Eng.* II. 27 It was deemed advisable to arrest the Holy Maid of Kent.

12. *transf.* To seize (property) by legal warrant. (Now only in Scotch and Admiralty Law.)

1598 SHAKS. *Merry W.* V. v. 119 Twenty pounds of money, which must be paid..His horses are arrested for it. **1599** GREENE *George a Gr.* (1861) 263 George will arrest his pledge unto the pound. **1609** SKENE *Reg. Maj.* 61 His gudes may be arreisted. **1638** COTTON *Tower Rec.* 15 He arrested all the Tinne in South-hampton, and sold it to his owne present use. **1861** RILEY tr. *Liber Albus* 39 All his goods, lands, and tenements shall be arrested for all expenses. **1869** *Law Rep., Adm. & Eccl.* II. 363 The Roecliff was arrested in a cause of collision. **1881** MAUDE & POLLOCK *Merch. Ship.* (ed. 4) I. 619 In this form of action [*in rem*] the ship, and, if necessary, the freight, may be arrested.

13. *fig.* To take as security.

1588 SHAKS. *L.L.L.* II. i. 160 We arrest your word. **1603** —— *Meas. for M.* II. iv. 134.

†14. To fix, bind, pledge, engage. *Obs.*

1489 CAXTON *Faytes of Armes* IV. vii. 246 Two knyghtes had arrested themself for to fight one ayenst that other. **1509** HAWES *Past. Pleas.* XVI. xxiii, Thy beaute therto dyd me sure arest.

15. a. *trans.* To catch and fix (the sight, hearing, attention, mind, etc.).

1814 BYRON *Corsair* III. i, The gleaming turret..and yon solitary palm arrest the eye. **1873** GEO. ELIOT *Middlem.* xliii, Her mind was evidently arrested by some sudden thought. **1878** BOSW. SMITH *Carthage* 185 Their attention was arrested by the rapid progress of Hasdrubal.

b. To catch and fix the attention of (a person). This passes into 6 a, since it may result in a literal stopping of action or motion.

1835 MACREADY *Remin.* I. 456 [I was] arrested and held by the interest of the story. **1866** GEO. ELIOT *F. Holt* (1868) 13 Years had over-laid it with another likeness which would have arrested her. **1876** MOZLEY *Univ. Serm.* ii. 29 Language which is altogether tremendous; it arrests us, it astonishes us.

¶ *catachr.* To wrest.

1593 BILSON *Govt. Christes Ch.*, Not to suffer the sacred scriptures to be so violently arrested. **1656** MILTON *Lett. State* Wks. 1738 II. 227 In great danger of having them arrested out of his hands by Force and Violence.

arrest (ə'rɛst), *sb.*[1] Forms: 4–5 **areste, areest**, 4–7 **arest**, 5 **arreste**, 5– **arrest.** *Aphet.* 6–7 **rest(e.**

[a. OF. *areste* stoppage, delay, and *arest* act of arresting.]

I. Senses pertaining to the intransitive vb.

†1. The act of standing still, halting, or stopping; stoppage, stop, halt, delay. *Obs.* ***without arrest***: cf. *without abode* (Chaucer, Lydgate, and Sc. poets).

1375 BARBOUR *Bruce* VIII. 356 The folk fled.. For-outen arest. *Ibid.* XVII. 844 For southren men vald that he maid Arest thar. *c* **1385** CHAUCER *L.G.W.* 1929 Withoute areste [*v.r.* arest, arreste, areest].. He wolde him ete. **1430** LYDG. *Chron. Troy.* I. ix, To whom Castor withouten more areste Hath.. gyue a mortall wounde. *c* **1500** *Lancelot* 3307 Non abaid he makith, nor arest. **1513** DOUGLAS *Æneis* IV. v. 119 Mercuir, but arest, Drest to obey his gret faderis behest. **1598** FLORIO, *Posate*, arests which a horse doth make in advancing his forepart.

†2. Remaining, abiding, continuance. *Obs.*

c **1386** CHAUCER *Sompn. T.* (Wright) [342] An irous man is lik a frentik best In which ther is of wisdom noon arrest.

†3. Abiding-place, abode, mansion. *Obs.*

a **1400** *Coventry Myst.* (Shaks. Soc. 1841) 91 Welcome, Joachym, onto myn areste, Bothe Anne thi wyff and Mary clere. *c* **1400** *Epiph.* (Turnb. 1843) 158 A mey hym harburd yn hur hall.. And held that hend yn hur arest.

†4. ***in arrest***: in rest, as a lance. ***at arrest***: at attention. *Obs.*

c **1400** *Rom. Rose* 7563 Thou here watchest at the gate, With spere in thine arest alweye. *c* **1440** *Morte Arth.* 548 That they be redye in araye, and at areste foundyne. **1481** CAXTON *Tulle of Old Age* ix. 8 (R.) He mowntyng upon his courser, and his spere in his arrest, spurrid on his horse.

II. From the transitive vb.

5. a. The act of stopping anything in its course; a stop put to anything, stoppage, stay, check.

c **1400** *Test. Love* II. (1560) 285 b/2 Mallice.. slily to bridle, and with a good bitte of areste to withdraw. **1523** LD. BERNERS *Froiss.* I. cccxcviii. 689 Certayne arest of this warre. **1625** BACON *Empire, Ess.* (Arb.) 297 That they must have some Checke or Arrest in their Fortunes. **1649** JER. TAYLOR *Gt. Exemp.* II. ii. 155 Words are the arrest of the desires, and keep the spirit fixt. **1665** GLANVILL *Sceps. Sci.* 49 An arrest of all ingenious and practical indeavour. **1835** KIRBY *Hab. & Inst. Anim.* II. xvii. 150 These [bristles] as well as the scales.. are.. points of arrest, in each wing. **1879** TIMBS in *Cassell's Techn. Educ.* IV. 119/2 A partial arrest of the vital processes.

b. *Med.* A sudden, sometimes temporary, cessation of function of an organ or system, *spec.* the heart. Cf. *cardiac arrest* s.v. CARDIAC *a.* I.

1883 *Jrnl. Physiol.* IV. 35 Calcium oxide.. or calcium chloride, added to saline solution, prevent the weakening and arrest of the ventricle which occurs with saline solution alone. **1904** *Amer. Jrnl. Physiol.* XI. 372 Certain conclusions can be drawn with regard to the arrest of the heart caused by this reagent. **1939** *Lancet* 4 Nov. 970/1 Houssay and Hug.. found that respiration and even reflexes might return after arrest of the circulation for 5 min. **1944** R. C. ADAMS *Intravenous Anesthesia* xxv. 471 Respiratory arrest was usually followed by a rise in blood pressure. **1950**, etc. [see *cardiac arrest* s.v. CARDIAC *a.* I]. **1962** J. H. BURN *Drugs, Med. & Man* ix. 99 It was realized that arrest of the patient's respiration might sometimes assist the surgeon. **1977** *Lancet* 11 June 1224/1, 385 arrests happened in casualty, with 49 survivors. **1982** *Macmillan Guide Family Health* 388/1 When coronary heart disease is not to blame, the cause of the arrest is sometimes a disorder of rhythm known as ventricular fibrillation.

6. In Law, ***arrest of judgement***: a stay of proceedings, after a verdict for the plaintiff or the Crown, on the ground of manifest error therein.

1660 *Trial Regicides* 94, I may do it in Arrest of Judgment. **1768** BLACKSTONE *Comm.* III. 393 Whatever is alleged in arrest of judgment must be such matter, as would upon demurrer have been sufficient to overturn the action or plea. **1772** *Junius Lett.* Pref. 14 If the paper be not criminal.. he may move the court in arrest of judgment. **1841** BREWSTER *Martyrs Sc.* v. (1856) 79 Galileo might have pleaded them with success in arrest of judgement.

7. The act of seizing or laying hold of; seizure. *lit.* and *fig.*

c **1386** CHAUCER *Nonne Pr. T.* 80, I saugh a beest, Was lik an hound, and wold have maad arrest Upon my body, and wold han had me deed. **1622** HEYLIN *Cosmogr.* I. (1682) 183 Aquitain and the rest of the English Provinces were seized on by the French.. But notwithstanding this arrest, the English still continued their pretentions to it. **1823** LAMB *Elia* Ser. I. xviii. (1865) 135 The first arrests of sleep.

8. *spec.* 'The apprehending or restraining of one's person, in order to be forthcoming to answer an alleged or suspected crime.' Blackstone.

1440 *Promp. Parv.*, A-reste, or a-restynge, *Arestacio.* **1576** LAMBARDE *Peramb. Kent* (1862) 179 To make arrest of all such as.. provoked to the Pope. **1590** GREENE *Neuer too late* (1600) 56 His creditours threatned him with an arrest. **1619** DALTON *Countr. Just.* cxviii. (1630) 335 An arrest.. may be called the beginning of imprisonment. **1876** GREEN *Short Hist.* vii. (1877) 348 The Duke of Norfolk had been charged with the minister's arrest. **1880** MUIRHEAD *Gaius* IV. §21 The latter was not allowed to resist the arrest or defend himself in person.

9. a. The condition resulting from being arrested; custody, imprisonment, durance.

c **1386** CHAUCER *Knts. T.* 452 [Man] dwelleth eek in prisoun and arreste. **1647** COWLEY *Mistress* Wks. 1710 I. 152 Now I suffer an Arrest. **1820** BYRON *Mar. Fal.* I. ii. 212 The Forty hath decreed a month's arrest.

b. ***under (an) arrest***: under legal restraint, in the hands of the law, arrested.

c **1386** CHAUCER *Merch. T.* 38 In libertee and vnder noon arreest. *c* **1500** *Lancelot* 912 [He] stood under hir arest. **1603** SHAKS. *Meas. for M.* I. ii. 135 If I could speake so wisely vnder an arrest, I would send for certaine of my Creditors. **1710** STEELE *Tatler* No. 105 ¶2 Poor Will was under an Arrest, and desired the Assistance of all.. or he must go to Gaol. **1836** MARRYAT *Midsh. Easy* xii. 39 Sir, consider yourself under an arrest. **1860** FROUDE *Hist. Eng.* VI. 60 Lord Russell was soon after placed under arrest.

10. *fig.*

c **1430** *Hymns to Virg.* (1867) 71 Godis seruauntis in areest haþ þee take. **1633** EARL MANCH. *Al Mondo* (1636) 95 The arest of death shall not alwayes keepe him that lyes downe in peace. **1642** ROGERS *Naaman* 18 Paul being under the arrest of God's might and power, lay for dead. **1677** GILPIN *Dæmonol. Sacra* (1867) 268 Satan claps an arrest upon him of a far greater debt than God chargeth upon him. **1873** tr. *Van Oosterzee's Chr. Dogm.* lxxviii. 430 Guilt is the conscious arrest of our life under the Divine law.

11. *transf.* Of a ship.

1848 ARNOULD *Law Mar. Insur.* III. ii. (1866) II. 706 Arrest is a temporary detention of ship, etc. with a view to ultimately releasing it, or repaying its value.

12. The act of arresting (the attention).

1876 GEO. ELIOT *Dan. Der.* I. xvii. 341 This strong arrest of his attention made him cease singing.

†13. A judgement, decree, order, or sentence; *prop.* of a French supreme court of law; also *transf.* and *fig. Obs.*, and replaced by *arrêt* from mod.Fr.

1509 HAWES *Past. Pleas.* 203, I obeyed his rest; there was no remedy. [**1553-87** FOXE *A. & M.* (1596) 7/2 By the Arestum of the Councell of Paris anno 1463.] **1599** SANDYS *Europ. Spec.* (1632) 130 To dispense with God's Law in this world, and to alter his arrests and judgements in the other. **1600** HOLLAND *Livy* XLII. ix. 1120 That the arest [*senatus consultum*] devised against him might be reversed. **1602** SHAKS. *Ham.* II. ii. 67 He sends out Arrests On Fortinbras, which he (in breife) obeyes. **1699** *Lond. Gaz.* mmmdxxxii/3 An Arrest will shortly be published for raising to 13 Livers the old Lewis d'Or and the Spanish Pistols. **1721** C. KING *Brit. Merch.* I. 231 By an Arrest of Council in France.. the strict execution of that edict is enjoin'd.

a'rrest, *sb.*[2] ? *Obs.* [a. F. *areste* (14–16th c. *arreste*):—L. *arista*: see ARÊTE.] (See quot.; both senses occur in mod.Fr.)

1639 T. DE GREY *Compl. Horsem.* 81 Rat-tayles.. which now we doe call the Arraistes. **1731** BAILEY, *Arrests*, mangey tumours upon the sinews of the hinder-legs of a horse between the ham and the pastern. **1742** —— *Arrests*, the small Bones of a Fish. **1753** CHAMBERS *Cycl. Supp.*, *Arrests* or *Arrets*, among farriers.. called also *Rat-tails.* The name is taken from the resemblance they bear to the *Arretes*, or backbones of fishes.

arrestable (əˈrɛstəb(ə)l), *a.* [a. OF. *a(r)restable*, f. *a(r)rester*: see ARREST *v.* and -ABLE.] a. Liable to be arrested.

1555 *Fardle Facions* I. v. 71 The body was not arrestable. **1837** CARLYLE *Fr. Rev.* IV. vi. III. 266 Explaining withal who the Arrestable and suspect specially are. **1883** *Autobiog. Sir A. Alison* II. xvii. 248 The wages were only arrestable.

b. *transf.* In *Law*, applied to an offence which renders the offender liable to summary arrest.

1965 *7th Rep. Criminal Law Revision Comm.* 24 in *Parl. Papers 1964–65* XVIII. 865 The powers of summary arrest conferred by the following subsections shall apply to offences for which the sentence is fixed by law or for which a person may under or by virtue of any enactment be sentenced for a term of five years, and to attempts to commit any such offence; and in this Act (including any amendment made by this Act in any other enactment) 'arrestable offence' means any such offence or attempt. **1977** C. BRANDRETH *Parking Law* 10 The only parking offence which of itself is arrestable is 'wilful obstruction'. **1984** *Times* 4 Dec. 9/4 Although the defendant had undoubtedly committed an offence of failing to give full particulars, that was not an arrestable offence.

†**a'rrestance.** *Obs.* In 5 arestaunce. [a. OF. *arestance*, f. *a(r)rester*: see ARREST *v.* and -ANCE.] Action of remaining or staying; sojourn.

1475 CAXTON *Jason* 33 b, To lyue and dye for you in your seruice in whiche I toke arestaunce.

arrestation (ærɛˈsteɪʃən). [a. F. *arrestation*, n. of action f. *arrester*: see ARREST *v.* and -ATION.] The action of arresting; arrest. a. Stopping.

1793 T. JEFFERSON *Writ.* (1859) IV. 72 This necessary arrestation of the proceedings. **1881** TYNDALL in *Nature* XXIV. 467 The arrestation of infusorial life.

b. Apprehension by legal authority. (More or less a Gallicism.)

1792 HEL. WILLIAMS *Lett. on France* I. i. (JOD.) The arrestation of the English resident in France was decreed by the National Convention. **1803** *Hist. Europe* in *Ann. Reg.* 70/2 The arrestation of Colonel Despard.. at an obscure public house in Lambeth. **1823** BENTHAM *Not Paul* 96 That visit of Paul to Jerusalem, by which his arrestation and.. confinement were produced. **1835** REEVE *De Tocquev. Democr. in Amer.* I. v. 131 The arrestation of criminals.

arrested (əˈrɛstɪd), *ppl. a.* [f. ARREST *v.* + -ED.] Stopped, put a stop to, checked, stayed; seized by legal warrant. ***arrested development***: development stopped at some stage of its progress.

1611 COTGR., *Arresté*, stayed, stopped, arrested. **1859** HUXLEY *Oceanic Hydroz.*, The Hydrozoa are [not] in any sense 'arrested developments' of higher organisms. **1871** DARWIN *Desc. Man* I. iv. I. 121 Arrested development differs from arrested growth, as parts in the former state still continue to grow, whilst still retaining their early condition.

arrestee (əˌrɛˈstiː). [f. ARREST *v.* + -EE.] *Sc. Law.* The person in whose hands the movables of another, or a debt due to another, are arrested by the creditor of the latter. See ARRESTMENT.

1847 *Nat. Encycl.* II. 167/1 The person who uses it [arrestment] is called the arrestor; he in whose hands it is used is called the arrestee.

arrester (əˈrɛstə(r)). [f. ARREST *v.* + -ER[1].]

1. a. He who or that which arrests, stops, or checks. b. He who arrests by legal authority.

1440 *Promp. Parv.*, A-rester, or a-tacher, or a catcherel, or a catchepolle. **1628** EARLE *Microcosm.* lxxv. 155 Satan.. is at most but an Arrester, and Hell a dungeon. **1879** PRESCOTT *Sp. Telephone* 28 A lightning arrester is provided in each box for the protection of the apparatus. **1880** MUIRHEAD *Gaius* IV. §21 He was carried home by the arrester and put in chains.

c. (Also *arrestor.*) A device in chimneys, etc., as an electrical precipitator, for preventing smoke or fire; also ***spark-arrester***. Cf. also LIGHTNING *sb.* 3 e.

1838, 1879 [see SPARK *sb.*[1] 7]. **1881** *Times* 17 Feb. 11/4 The alleged negligence of the defendants in having a defective spark arrester on the engine. **1922** W. SCHLICH *Man. Forestry* (ed. 4) I. 190 Measures necessary to prevent forest fires must be taken, such as.. the provision of efficient spark arresters. **1950** *Hansard Commons* CCCCLXXVIII. 271/1 The British Electricity Authority are in process of.. installing what are known as [smoke] arresters.

d. A contrivance for bringing to rest aircraft alighting on an aircraft carrier; usu. *attrib.*, as ***arrester gear, hook, wire***. See also ARRESTING *ppl. a.* b.

1926 *Flight* XVIII. 696/2 It is in connection with deck landing that the arrester gear is most likely to be of service. **1927** V. W. PAGÉ *Mod. Aircraft* (1928) xvii. 714 (*heading*) Catapults and Airplane Arresters. **1937** *Aeroplane* 9 June 691/2 About the same time our Fleet Air Arm gave up arrester-wires and took to trusting to wheel-brakes on bare decks. **1940** *Flight* 15 Feb. 147/1 A deck arrester hook is fitted. **1954** P. K. KEMP *Fleet Air Arm* vii. 92 A more satisfactory type of arrester gear was eventually fitted ['Courageous' and 'Glorious'] consisting of transverse wires on the after part of the deck which were picked up by a trailing hook on the aircraft.

2. *Sc. Law.* One who under legal authority arrests a debt or property in the hands of another. (In this sense now more formally spelt ARRESTOR.)

1754 ERSKINE *Princ. Sc. Law* (1809) 358 Where a poinding was forcibly stopped by the possessor of the goods, on pretence that they had been already arrested in his hands by another, it was considered as completed in a question with the prior arrester. **1847** (See ARRESTEE.)

arresting (əˈrɛstɪŋ), *vbl. sb.* [f. ARREST *v.* + -ING[1].] The action of stopping or checking; of seizing or apprehending by legal authority.

1424 *Act Jas. I* (1597) §7 Gif sik persones takis ony skaith in the arreisting of them. *c* **1440** *Promp. Parv.* 14/1 A-reste or a-restynge, *arestacio.* **1628** EARLE *Microcosm.* lxix. 148 If they escape arresting. **1630** J. TAYLOR (Water P.) *Wks.* II. 131/2 Writs, Warrants, and Attachments, Arestings. **1849** RUSKIN *Sev. Lamps* iv. §34. 125 It is but the arresting upon the stone-work of a stem or two of the living flowers.

a'rresting, *ppl. a.* [f. as prec. + -ING[2].] a. That arrests; that takes hold of the attention; striking.

1792 S. ROGERS *Pleas. Memory* II. 104 He, whose arresting hand divinely wrought Each bold conception. **1843** J. H. NEWMAN *Mirac.* 152 This most solemn and arresting occurrence. **1883** R. NOEL in *Contemp. Rev.* Nov. 714 One of Browning's most.. arresting poems.

b. *Aeronaut.* That stops or checks aircraft. Cf. ARRESTER 1 d.

1936 M. W. BURGESS *Warships To-day* ii. 48 A touch on the arresting wires.. and slowly the aeroplane comes to rest. **1951** *Gloss. Aeronaut. Terms* (*B.S.I.*) III. 25 *Arresting gear*, a device, usually installed in aircraft carriers, for bringing an aircraft to rest.

a'rrestingly, *adv.* [f. prec. + -LY[2].] In a manner that arrests attention; strikingly.

1883 F. HALL in *Amer. Jrnl. Philol.* III. No. 12 Professor Newman's English is arrestingly eccentric.

arrestive (əˈrɛstɪv), *a.* [f. ARREST *v.* + -IVE; cf. OF. *arrestif, -ive.*]

1. Having as its attribute or tendency to arrest.

1834 T. COWAN *Art of Poetic Painting* 3 Strength in expression.. and arrestive power in all forms of discourse and composition, consist.. in the employment of descriptive and illustrative Imagery. **1850** McCOSH *Div. Govt.* (1862) 407 Partaking of the nature of the arrestive and instigative [are].. emotions of astonishment, surprise and wonder. **1878** STANFORD *Symb. Christ* iii. 64 A startling and arrestive sight.

2. *Gram.* Applied to conjunctions such as *but.*

1863 BAIN *Eng. Gram.* 65 The second class of Co-ordinating Conjunctions are the *Adversative*.. This class is subdivided into three species.. The Arrestive, represented by 'but,' 'but then,' 'still,' 'yet,' 'only,' 'nevertheless,' 'however.' Phrases: 'for all that,' 'at the same time.'

arrestment (əˈrɛstmənt). [a. OF. *arestement* (later *arrêtement*): see ARREST *v.* and -MENT.]

1. The action of stopping, staying, or checking.

1836-9 TODD *Cycl. Anat. & Phys.* II. 612/1 An arrestment of the movements of the muscles. **1845** *Vest. Creat.* 276 An arrestment of this principle at a particular early point. **1875** DARWIN *Insectiv. Plants* ix. 201 Any such arrestment of movement.

b. *concr.* The material result of such stoppage or check.

1872 H. MACMILLAN *True Vine* vii. 316 Just as fruit is the arrestment and metamorphosis of the branch, so are thorns an arrestment and blight in the formation of branches.

2. The action of apprehending a person by legal authority; arrest, apprehension. (Chiefly Scotch.) Formerly *fig.* forcible or authoritative seizure.

1474 *Act 7 Jas. III* (1597) §52 Arreistmentes be Crowners or Serjandes. **1601** CHESTER *Love's Martyr* XXIII. (1878) 86 To deaths arestment he began to yeeld. **1645** RUTHERFORD *Tryal & Tri. Faith* (1845) 101 Loosed from the arrestment of vanity. **1791** NEWTE *Tour Eng. & Scot.* 375 Judgment in a civil case..upon which execution and personal arrestment can proceed in fourteen days. **1883** *Blackw. Mag.* June 800 Rothesay's arrestment and custody.

3. Seizure of property by authority of law; attachment. *Esp.* in *Sc. Law*, 'A process by which a creditor may attach money or moveable property, which a third party holds for behoof of his debtor.' Craig.

1581 *Act 7 Jas. VI* (1597) §117 Quhen Arreistmentes ar maid to mak the gudes furthcummand. **1754** ERSKINE *Princ. Sc. Law* (1809) 17 Action cannot be brought against him till his effects be first attached by an arrestment *jurisdictionis fundandæ causa.* **1824** SCOTT *Redgaunt.* xiii, 'Ye have omitted to speak a word of the arrestments.' **1864** *Daily Tel.* 16 Aug., The peculiarities of Scotch common law.. Arrestment to found jurisdiction is one of them. It was derived from the Roman law, and is still existent..by force of custom in London..under the name of 'foreign attachment.'

†**arre'stographer.** *Obs.* [f. F. *arrestographe* (= mod.F. *arrêtiste*) + -ER[1].]

1753 CHAMBERS *Cycl. Supp.*, *Arrestographer* is applied by some French writers to those who have published collections of Arrets.

arrestor (ə'rɛˌstɔːr), *Law*: see ARRESTER 2.

‖**arrêt** (a'rɛː, ə'rɛt). [F.:—OF. *arest*, f. *arester*, now *arrêter*: see ARREST.] An authoritative sentence or decision, *prop.* of the King or Parliament of France; a decree. = ARREST *sb.* 13.

c **1650** CLARENDON in *Evelyn's Mem.* (1819) II. 201 Your arrett is not yet dispatched. **1787** BONNYCASTLE *Astron.* vi. 100 The following arret was pronounced against him, by seven cardinals. **1820** SCOTT *Ivanhoe*, Expert..in all matters concerning the arrets of love. **1841** SIR J. STEPHEN *Eccl. Biog.* (1850) I. 510 Parliamentary *arrêts* flew thick and fast through the troubled air.

Arretine ('ærɪtaɪn), *a.* Also **Aretine.** [ad. L. *Ar(r)etinus*, f. *Ar(r)etium* Arretium (see def.): see -INE[1].] Of or pertaining to Arretium (modern Arezzo), an ancient city of central Italy; *spec.* designating fine red pottery made at Arretium and elsewhere from *c.* 100 B.C. until the Flavian period; = TERRA SIGILLATA.

1782 J. ELPHINSTON tr. *Martial* p. 426 (*title*) Aretine (or Aretian) Ware. **1858** S. BIRCH *Hist. Anc. Pottery* II. 342 The two collections of Aretine vases at Arezzo. *Ibid.* 343 Patina of Aretine Ware. **1863** W. CHAFFERS *Marks on Pottery* 12 The pattern round the top of the Aretine vases is evidently the *ovolo*, or egg and arrow decoration. **1880** *Encycl. Brit.* XIII. 496/2 Intrusions which may be called Emilian have also been noted..in the district where the Arno and the Tiber take their rise (Aretine dialects). **1954** *Proc. Prehist. Soc.* XX. 8 The Arretine stamps found at Silchester include a number..which do not figure in the extensive series from Camulodunum.

arreyne, obs. form of ARRAIGN.

arreyse, var. ARAISE *v. Obs.* to raise.

‖**arrha** ('ærə). Pl. **-æ.** Also 6 **arra.** [L. *arr(h)a*, also *arr(h)abo*, a. Gr. ἀρραβών. See Liddell and Scott. Cf. ARLES.] Earnest-money, a part of the purchase-money given to ratify a contract; *fig.* a pledge.

1573 ANDERSON *Hymn Bened.* 4 b (T.) By his spirite..we have..our arra and earnest penny of his assured covenant. **1754** ERSKINE *Princ. Sc. Law* (1809) 308 Arrhæ, or earnest, is sometimes given by the buyer, as an evidence that the contract is perfected.

arrhal ('ærəl), *a.* [ad. L. *arr(h)ālis*: see prec. and -AL[1].] Of the nature of earnest-money; given as a pledge.

1873 JEFFERSON *Brides & Brid.* I. i. 7 In the case of a wealthy bridegroom these arrhal gifts were several.

arrhaphostic: see ARA-.

Arrhenius (ə'riːnɪəs, -'reɪn-). *Chem.* The name of S. A. *Arrhenius* (1859–1927), Swedish physical chemist, used *attrib.* with reference to the description of the rates of chemical reactions by the ***Arrhenius equation***, $k = A \exp(-E/RT)$, where k is the rate constant of a reaction, A is a constant, E is the activation energy, R is the gas constant, and T is the temperature. [Propounded by Arrhenius in *Zeitschr. f. physik. Chem.* (1889) IV. 226.]

1924 F. O. RICE in H. S. Taylor *Physical Chem.* II. xiv. 901 We cannot derive the empirical Arrhenius equation by postulating that the water is present in two forms. **1948** GLASSTONE *Textbk. Physical Chem.* (ed. 2) xiii. 1088 The Arrhenius equation is widely applicable not only to homogeneous gas reactions, but also to reactions in solution and to heterogeneous processes. **1967** MARGERISON & EAST *Introd. Polymer Chem.* iv. 207 For the simple three-reaction polymerization scheme.., the effect of temperature on the various parameters can be predicted by replacing the rate constants by the appropriate Arrhenius expressions. **1978** P. W. ATKINS *Physical Chem.* xxvi. 852 The rates of chemical reactions..depend very strongly on the temperature, and many follow the Arrhenius rate law. **1979** *Nature* 26 July 326/2 The latency between depolarisation of the fibre and the onset of the rise in intracellular free Ca^{2+} is proportional to the reciprocal temperature, but..on an Arrhenius plot this relationship shows a change in slope at a temperature which depends upon the Ca^{2+} concentration in the bathing solution.

arrhizal (ə'raɪzəl), *a. Bot.* Also **arh-.** [f. Gr. ἀ priv. + ῥίζα root.] Destitute of root; rootless.

1880 in GRAY *Bot. Text-bk.*

a'rrhizous, *a. Bot.* [Cf. Fr. *arrhize.*] = prec.

1880 in *Syd. Soc. Lex.*

arrhythmia (ə'rɪθmɪə). *Path.* [mod.L., f. Gr. ἀρρυθμία: see ARRHYTHMY.] Want of rhythm or regularity; *spec.* of the pulse.

1888 F. P. FOSTER *Illustr. Med. Dict.* I. 392/1 *Arrhythmia*, lack of rhythm. **1907** *Practitioner* LXXIX. 492 Note the cardiac arrhythmia. *Ibid.* 694 Various types of arrhythmia of the heart's action. **1961** *Lancet* 22 July 185/1 The sixth patient had complained only of occasional arrhythmia. **1966** *Ibid.* 24 Dec. 1389/1 Propranolol..has been used in the treatment of cardiac arrhythmias.

arrhythmic (ə'rɪθmɪk), *a.* Also **arh-.** [f. A- *pref.* 14 + RHYTHMIC; cf. ARRHYTHMOUS and Gr. ῥυθμικός.] Not rhythmic, without rhythm or regularity; *spec.* in *Path.* of the pulse.

1853 *Fraser's Mag.* XLVIII. 465/1 The fitting rhythm will never be found, the subject itself being arhythmic. **1880** in *Syd. Soc. Lex.* **1928** G. COOKE *Theory of Music* v. 53 There is nothing so wearisome as listening to music which is arhythmic. **1963** R. P. DALES *Annelids* vi. 130 Only arhythmic activity can be observed if the ganglia of the intact part of the cord are subsequently touched.

a'rrhythmical, *a.* [f. prec. + -AL[1].] = prec.

1881 PALGRAVE *Vis. Engl.* Pref. 12 The irregular, arrhythmical lyric seems..to want this essential purity, this severity, of metre.

a'rrhythmically, *adv.* [f. prec. + -LY[2].] Without rhythm.

1880 *Lyra Eccles.* II. 22 The *Pater Noster*, the *Preface*, the *Exultat*, and the like..may be sung arrhythmically.

arrhythmous (ə'rɪθməs), *a.* Also **arh-.** [f. Gr. ἀρρυθμ-ος (f. ἀ priv. + ῥυθμός measure) + -OUS.] = ARRHYTHMIC.

1853 in MAYNE.

arrhythmy ('ærɪθmɪ). [ad. Gr. ἀρρυθμία, n. of quality f. ἄρρυθμος.] Want of rhythm or measure.

1844 BECK & FELTON *Munk's Grk. & Rom. Metres* i, The variety of the rhythm is interrupted, and instead of eurhythmy, arrhythmy is produced. **1859** in WORCESTER.

arriage: see AVERAGE.

Arrian, -ism, etc., obs ff. ARIAN, -ISM, etc.

[**a'rrid**, error for *avoid*, to empty.

1586 BRIGHT *Melanch.*, A mill driven by the winde..for.. arriding of rivers of water out of drowned fens.]

arride (ə'raɪd), *v.* [ad. L. *arrīdē-re* (or It. *arridere*) to smile upon, to be pleasing to, f. *ar-* = *ad-* to, at + *rīdē-re* to laugh, smile.]

†**1.** To smile at, laugh at, scorn. *Obs.*

1612 DEKKER *If not good* Wks. 1873 III. 294 If your Grace Arride the toyes they bragd of. **1628** tr. *Owen's Epigrams* (N.) What means arrided Rider's book, thus stil'd A library? **1656** BLOUNT *Gloss.*, *Arride*, to smile or look pleasantly upon.

2. To please, gratify, delight. *arch.*

1599 B. JONSON *Ev. Man out of Hum.* II. i, *Fas.* 'Fore Heavens, his humour arrides me exceedingly. *Car.* Arrides you? *Fas.* I, pleases me. **1671** SHADWELL *Humourists* III. Wks. 1720 I. 170 It arrides me extreamly, to think how he will be bobb'd. *a* **1757** CIBBER in *New Hist. Eng. Stage* (1882) I. 240 A new opera..which infinitely arrided both sexes and pleased the town. **1823** LAMB *Elia* II. xvii. (1865) 344 That conceit arrided us most..and still tickles our midriff to remember. **1862** *Temple Bar* IV. 468 The malt consumer is mightily consoled and arrided by the notion. **1884** BROWNING *Ferishtah* x. 87 That verse of thine..much arrides myself. **1905** *Academy* 7 Oct. 1027/1 That which would have the most arrided *Elia* is the note on the poet's description of Hell. **1937** KIPLING *Something of Myself* iv. 92 My normal output seemed to have the gift of *ariding per se* the very people I most disliked.

†**a'rrident**, *a. Obs. rare.* [ad. L. *arrīdēnt-em*, pr. pple. of *arrīdēre*: see prec. and -ENT.] Smiling; pleasant, gratifying.

1616 T. ADAMS *Pract. Wks.* (1861) I. 504 A pleasing murderer, that with arrident applauses tickles a man to death. **1630** R. H. in *J. Taylor's* (Water P.) *Wks.* A v b/1 Thine Amphitritean Muse growes more arrident, and Phœbus Tripos stoopes to Neptunes trident.

arridge, dial. form of ARRIS.

‖**arrière** (a'rjɛr). Modern French form of ARREAR (OF. *arere*), used in combinations, partly modern French, partly refashionings of Anglo-Fr. or earlier English equivalents in *arrere*, *arrear*.

arriere-band [cf. also ARRIÈRE-BAN], a rear-division of an army; **arriere-fee or -fief** [Fr. in 13th c. (Littré)], a fief held from a mesne-lord who is himself a vassal, a sub-fief; **arriere-supper** (also REAR-SUPPER), a late supper; one served up in the bed-room; †**arriere-tenant**, the tenant of a mesne-lord, a sub-tenant; **arriere-vassal** [Fr.], the vassal of a vassal, the holder of an arriere-fief.

1882 W. WHITMAN in *Academy* 18 Nov. 358/3 An inferr'd arrière of such storms, such wrecks. **1824** WIFFEN *Tasso's Jerus. Del.* XI. v, The reverend pair Bring up their arriere bands. **1523** LD. BERNERS *Froiss.* I. cccxi. 474 All his landes, and arere fees in Gascoyne. **1727–51** CHAMBERS *Cycl.*, *Arriere-fees* commenced at the time when counts and dukes rendering their governments hereditary in their families, distributed to their officers certain parts of the royal domains which they found in their provinces. **1818** HALLAM *Mid. Ages* (1841) I. ii. 142 The Châtelains belonged to the order of Vavassors, as they held only arriere fiefs. **1577** HOLINSHED *Chron. Scot.* 208/1 Diuers delicate dishes, and sundry sorts of drinke for theyr arere supper or collation. **1727–51** CHAMBERS *Cycl.*, *Arriere-tenant* or *Vassal.*

‖**arrière-ban** ('ærɪə-'bæn, arjɛr-'bɑ̃). Also 6 **arere-, rere-band,** 7 **arrear-band, arrière-van,** 7–8 **arrier-ban.** [a. F. *arrière-ban*, OF. *ariere-ban* (12th c.), for **ari-ban, hari-ban*, f. OHG. *hari, heri*, army, host + *ban* edict, proclamation, order under penalty; in Merov. Lat. *hari-, heri-, here-bannum*, elsewhere also *ari-, are-bannum*: see Du Cange. The first element was early perverted by pop. etymol. to *ariere*, *arrière*, and the word variously misunderstood in accordance with this (see Cotgr. 1611), the prevailing fancy being that it meant the summoning of the *arrière-vassals*, or holders of *arrière-fiefs*, as distinct from the great feudatories supposed to be summoned by the *ban.* Hence the later use of *ban et arrière-ban* in conjunction. In English further perverted to *arrear-band*, *rear-band*, and *arrear-van.*]

Properly, The order of a (Frankish or French) king summoning his vassals to the military service due by holders of fiefs; the whole body of vassals thus summoned or liable to be summoned; the whole body of tenants by military tenure; the noblesse. Also applied to similar bodies, *e.g.* that of Poland. *Corruptly*: see above.

1523 LD. BERNERS *Froiss.* I. ccccxviii. 732 He hadde with hym out of the towne a ten thousande men in harnes for the arerebande [Fr. *dix mille hommes pour l'arrière-ban*]. *Ibid.* ccccxvi. 727, I wyle go to Gaunt, to fetche ye rerebande [*l'arrière-ban*]. **1591** UNTON *Corr.* (1847) 54 He hath sente abroade to assemble his van and arriere van. **1671** CROWNE *Juliana* I. 8 The Ban and the Arrierban are met arm'd in the field to choose a king [of Poland]. **1684** *Scanderbeg Rediv.* iv. 70 The King having summoned the Arrier Ban (that is, a General Convention of all the Nobless throughout his Dominions) to appear in their Arms. **1690** LUTTRELL *Brief Rel.* II. 106 The arrear-band is raised all along the coasts. **1748** THOMSON *Cast. Indol.* II. xxx, Thus Vice the standard rear'd; her arrier-ban Corruption called. **1858** MORRIS *Def. Guinevere*, When the arriere-ban goes through the land Six basnets under my pennon stand. **1864** KIRK *Chas. Bold* I. vi. 283 Coming with ban and arrière ban to his sovereign's relief.

‖**arrière-guard,** †**a'rrear-guard.** Forms: 5 **arryere-,** 6 **arere-, arrier-, areare-gard(e,** 7 **arrere-,** 7–8 **arrear-,** 7–9 **arrière-guard.** [a. 15th c. Fr. *arrière-guarde*; in 16–17th c. quite conformed to the Eng. spelling of *arrear* and *guard*; but by mod. writers again spelt partly as French. Also, from the first, aphetized as *ryere-*, *rere-*, REAR-GUARD, which is now the current form. OFr. had *arere-guarde* and *rere-guarde* (both in *Chanson de Roland*). Cf. ARREAR-WARD: *ward* was the native Eng., and *warde* the North. F. form of the Teut. word which became in Central Fr. *guarde*, *garde*.] = REAR-GUARD.

1489 CAXTON *Faytes of Armes* I. xxiii. 72 Wythout noon other forwarde nor arryeregarde. **1523** LD. BERNERS *Froiss.* I. xcviii. 119 The constable of Fraunce made the areregarde. **1542** *Harl. Misc.* (Malh.) I. 237 In the arriergarde or hinder warde was the Italyans and the Rhodyans. **1579** FENTON *Guicciard.* XIII. (1599) 605 From the auaungard he became the areareg ard. **1601** HOLLAND *Pliny* I. 194 The eldest of them leadeth the vaward..the next to him in age commeth behind with the conduct of the arrereguard. **1687** *Lond. Gaz.* mmcclxvii/2 The Arrear-Guard was Commanded by the Elector of Bavaria. **1721** BAILEY, *Arriere Guard.* **1824** CAMPBELL *Theodric* Wks. 1837. 43 Our arrière-guard had check'd the Gallic van.

‖**arrière-pensée** (arjɛrpɑ̃se). [Fr., = 'behind-thought'.] A concealed thought or intention.

1824 LADY MORGAN *Salvator Rosa* I. vi. 300 Such drear and fearful aspects of nature, mingled with such views of society, concealed an '*arrière pensée*'. **1884** *Eng. Illustr. Mag.* Dec. 246 He knew that I had guessed his *arrière-pensée.* **1900** H. B. FORMAN *Compl. Wks. Keats* I. 106 The meaning [of 'rest'] here is probably merely inactivity, without the recuperative *arrière-pensée.*

‖**arriero** (ari'ero). [Sp.] A muleteer.
1826 HEAD *Rough Notes Pampas* 165 A mulish-looking sort of man who used to terrify all the arrieros and peons who passed. **1832** W. IRVING *Alhambra* I. 14 The most valuable part of our luggage had been forwarded by the arrieros. **1845** [see MULETEER]. **1923** *Blackw. Mag.* Sept. 339/2 We were probably reckoned as rather less than the *arriero* who owned two lean donkeys.

[**arriont** in Wright's Chaucer *Monk's Tale* 210; the MSS. of the Six-text edition all read *appetite*.]

arris ('ærɪs). Also 8 **ariss, arriss,** 9 **aris,** *dial.* **arridge.** [Corruption of F. *areste* (mod. *arête*) used in same sense: see ARÊTE.]

1. The sharp edge formed by the angular contact of two plane or curved surfaces; *e.g.* the edges of a prism, or the raised edges that separate the flutings in a Doric column.
1677 PLOT *Oxfordsh.* 75 Burford-stone.. carries by much a finer Arris than that at Heddington. **1793** SMEATON *Edystone L.* §11 It can by no means be brought to an Arriss or sharp corner. **1855** *Whitby Gloss., Arridges*, the edges of a piece of squared stone or wood. **1879** G. SCOTT *Lect. Archit.* I. 150 A wonderfully studious grouping of the hollows, rounds, and arrises. **1884** F. BRITTEN *Watch & Clockm. Handb.* 50 The chamfering tool with which the aris is removed.

2. *Comb.* and *Attrib.*, as *arris-rail*; **arris-cut** (see quot.); **arris-fillet**, 'a slight piece of timber of a triangular section, used in raising the slates against chimney-shafts, or against a wall that cuts obliquely across the roof' (Gwilt); **arris-gutter**, a V-shaped wooden gutter fixed to the eaves of a building; **arris-piece** (see quot.); **arris-ways, -wise** *adv.*, so as to present a sharp edge, diagonally, ridge-wise.
c **1850** *Rudim. Nav.* 123 *Arris-cut*, this term is applied when the edges of planks are cut to an under bevelling to fay one on another, as the berthing or sides of the well, so that no ballast may get in at the joints. **1867** SMYTH *Sailor's Word-bk., Aris pieces*, those parts of a made mast which are under the hoops. **1833** LOUDON *Encycl. Archit.* 438 The calf-pens to be parted off with oak posts and arris rails (rails presenting two surfaces to the eye, which two surfaces unite in forming an edge or arris between them). **1883** in *N. Middl. Chron.* 6 Jan. 8/1 Nine feet Yellow Arris Rails. **1962** *Listener* 23 Aug. 299/3 Even if you cannot treat all the timber [of the fence] in this way, you may at least be able to treat the ends of the arris rails. **1963** *Gloss. Terms Timber (B.S.I.)* 48 *Arris rail*, a rail, mainly used in fencing, formed by cutting a square section across its diagonal. **1677** MOXON *Mech. Exerc.* (1703) 240 An excellent Pavement and pleasing to the Eye, especially when laid Arris ways. **1796** *Gentl. Mag.* LXVI. 17 Part of an old monument formed ariss-ways.

arrish, arish ('ærɪʃ). Also 6–7 **ersh.** [Dialectal variant of EDDISH. (Cf. OE. *ersc-hen* = *edischen* quail.) The retracted *r* and *d* of s.w. dialects are scarcely separable.] (See quot.)
1597 GERARD *Herbal* (1633) 1018 The wheat ershes about Mapledurham. **1674** RAY *S. & E. Countr. Wds.* 65, *Ersh*, the same that Edish. *Sussex.* **1813** VANCOUVER *Agric. Devon* 152 The wheat arish, or stubbles, are in these cases found less to abound with coarse grass, and other unprofitable rubbish. **1851** *N. & Q.* Ser. I. III. 252/1 In Devon a cornfield which has been cut and cleared, is called an 'arrish.' **1856** CAPERN *Poems* 72 To bid the skylark o'er the arrish roam.

arrision (ə'rɪʒən). *rare*$^{-0}$. [ad. L. *arrīsiōn-em*, n. of action f. *arrīdēre*: see ARRIDE.] The action of smiling upon or at.
1656 in BLOUNT *Glossogr.*

†**arrivage.** *Obs.* [a. OF. *arivage* act of landing, landing-place:—late L. *arribāticum* for **adrīpāticum*, f. *adrīpāre*: see ARRIVE *v.* and -AGE. Orig. accented *arrīvage.*]

1. The act of coming to shore or into port; landing, arrival.
c **1384** CHAUCER *H. Fame* 223 And previly toke arryvage In the contree of Cartage. **1413** LYDGATE *Pylgr. Sowle* II. xli. 46 Here is the porte of syker arryuage. **1611** SPEED *Hist. Gt. Brit.* VIII. vii. §29 At his arriuage from Sea. **1627** —— *Eng. abridged* iii. §5 Creeks and Hauens for Ships arriuage.

2. A landing-place.
c **1450** *Merlin* iii. 56 When they be come from their a-rivage, than go be-twene hem and the aryvage. **1542** *Lam. & Piteous Treat.* in *Harl. Misc.* (1745) IV. 512 Our Enemyes ..went downe to our Arryuage, to Thenteñt to kyll theim, whom the Tempest had spared.

3. That which happens to or befalls one. Cf. ARRIVE 9 c.
1603 HOLLAND *Plutarch's Mor.* 516 Man's life is even a short passage, Paine upon paine is his arrivage: And then comes death that spareth none.

arrival (ə'raɪvəl). Forms: 4 **aryvayle, arrivaile,** 5 **ariuaill, -vall, arryuayll, aryvell,** 6–7 **arrivall,** 7– **arrival.** [a. AF. *arrivaille* landing, f. *arriver*: see ARRIVE *v.* and -AL[2].]

1. The act of coming to shore, landing in a country, disembarkation. (Now merged in sense 3.)
c **1384** CHAUCER *H. Fame* 451 Tho saugh I grave [= pictured] al the aryvayle That Eneas had in Itayle. *c* **1400** *Destr. Troy* XIV. (title) Stronge fight at þe Ariuaill. **1494** FABYAN I. i. 7 Ye Geauntes that Brute founde in this Ile at his arryuayll. **1610** HOLLAND *Camden's Brit.* 259 That the Normans might have..more secure arrivall in England. **1702** C. MATHER *Magn. Christi* I. iv. (1852) 70 They set apart the sixth day of August, after their arrival, for fasting and prayer.

†**2.** A landing-place; = ARRIVAGE 2. *Obs. rare.*
1495 *Act 11 Hen. VII*, v, The Portys Havens Ryvers Crekis and aryvell of Shippis..be..hurte and dekaied.

3. *gen.* The act of coming to the end of a journey, to a destination, or to some definite place; appearance upon the scene. (For const. see ARRIVE *v.* 5.) Also *attrib.*, esp. in connection with the place (platform) or time at which a train arrives at a station, or an aeroplane at an airport.
1518 WOLSEY in Strype *Eccl. Mem.* I. i. 21 Your arrival to that reame. **1593** SHAKS. *Rich. II*, I. iii. 8 Demand of yonder Champion The cause of his arriuall heere in Armes. **1616** FORDE *Serm.* 77 The time of her arrival into this countrey. **1711** ADDISON *Spect.* No. 123 ¶5 The Morning after his Arrival at the House. **1720** T. BOSTON *Hum. Nature* (1812) 326 Their arrival in the regions of bliss. **1838** F. W. SIMMS *Public Wks. Gt. Brit.* 2 On the opposite side an arrival stage or platform is erected. **1879** BARTLETT *Egypt to Pal.* xxvi. 517 The Natives..on our arrival, civilly gave way for us. **1886** *Encycl. Brit.* XX. 235/2 The two general arrival platforms, one on each side of the cab road, are 721 feet long by 12½ wide. **1897** *Westm. Gaz.* 31 Dec. 3/3 It is the arrival time, the departure being timed several minutes later. **1903** *Ibid.* 25 Mar. 6/3 A new wide roadway for carriages..will be used by arrival passengers. **1967** P. LORAINE *W.I.L. One to Curtis* xii. 216 He..told the taxi-driver to take him straight past the main entrance and deposit him at the Arrival department. **1968** *Listener* 20 June 806/1 Gate Number 9 at Heathrow's arrival lounge.

4. *transf.* of things. ***for arrival***: (a cargo) to be delivered when the ship arrives. '*arrival*' is also techn. used to describe such a cargo.
1712 ADDISON *Spect.* No. 452 ¶2 Our Time lies heavy on our Hands till the Arrival of a fresh mail. **1860** TYNDALL *Glac.* I. §12. 90 To await the arrival of the money. **1882** *Daily Tel.* 4 May (*Markets*), But for arrival a steamer cargo ..was sold at 7*s.* 3*d.* **1882** *Manch. Guard.* 10 Mar., The brokerage on 'arrivals' should be reduced.

5. The coming to a position, state of mind, stage of development, etc. Cf. ARRIVE *v.* 7, 8.
Mod. There was long debate, but no arrival at any agreement.

6. One that arrives or has arrived.
1847 TENNYSON *Princess* II. 82 To-day the Lady Psyche will harangue The fresh arrivals. *Mod.* The new arrival is a little daughter.

†**a'rrivance.** *Obs.* or *dial.* [f. ARRIVE *v.* + -ANCE: cf. *contrivance.*] The act or fact of arriving, arrival; *concr.* people arriving, arrivals: in which sense the 1st folio of Shakspere has **arrivancie**(= y).
1604 SHAKS. *Oth.* II. i. 42 (Qo. 1) For euery Minute is expectancie Of more Arriuance [**1623** *Folio*, arriuancie]. **1646** SIR T. BROWNE *Pseud. Ep.* III. ix. (R.) Its sudden arrivance into growth and Maturity. **1879** MISS JACKSON *Shropsh. Wd.-bk.* 12, 'I spec' they'n be wantin' yo', Betty, to 'elp 'em a bit at the owd Maister's; I sid an arrivance theer'.'

arrive (ə'raɪv), *v.* Forms: 3–7 **arive,** 3–6 **aryve,** (4 **ariffe**), 5–6 **arryve,** (6 **arriff**), 5– **arrive.** [a. OF. *arive-r*, cogn. with Pr. *arivar, aribar*, It. *arrivare*, Sp., Pg. *arribar*, OIt., late L. *arribāre*:—*arripāre, adripāre*, f. *ad* to + *rīpa* shore; = *ad rīpam appellĕre*; cf. mod.It. *arripare* in orig. sense. With the subseq. widening of sense (which took place before the word was adopted in Eng.), cf. the use of *to land.* In 14–15th c. occas. aphetized to *rive*; and inflected after strong vbs., with pa. t. *arove* (*rove, arofe*), pa. pple. *ariven* (*aryven*).]

I. Of reaching by water.

†**1.** *trans.* To bring (a ship, its crew or passengers) to shore or into port; to land (a ship, etc.).
[The first two quotations may belong to 2.]
1205 LAY. 16063 Nu beoð of Brutaine beornes arived..i þis lond at Tottenæs [**1250** at Dertemuþ in Totenas]. *c* **1300** *Beket* 1854 Hou Seint Thomas the holi man at Sandwych aryved was. *c* **1374** CHAUCER *Boeth.* IV. iii. 122 Þe wynde aryueþ þe sayles of vlixes..and hys wandryng shippes by þe see in to þe isle þere as Circe..dwelleþ. **1624** CHAPMAN *Homer's Hymn Apollo* 684 And made the sea-trod ship arrive them near The grapeful Crissa. **1650** W. BROUGH *Sacr. Princ.* (1659) 486 Some points of wind..may as soon Overturn, as Arrive the ship. **1664** *Floddan Field* III. 28 Had promis'd plight..His Fleet in merry ray to arive.

2. a. *intr.* (through *refl.*) To come to shore or into port; to land. (Said of a ship, its crew, or passengers: till about 1550 the only prevalent sense.) Now merged in 5.
1297 R. GLOUC. 371 Þat folc of Denemarch..myd þre hondered ssypuolmen..aryuede in þe Norþ contreye. **1375** BARBOUR *Bruce* IV. 559 We may thair ariffe in-to saufte. **1387** TREVISA *Higden* Rolls Ser. VII. 87/1 Þe navy of Danes rove up at Sandwyche [*Sandwicum appulit*]. **1393** GOWER *Conf.* III. 288 Till that he arriveth Sauf in the porte of Antioche. *c* **1450** LONELICH *Grail* xxxii. 57 Tweyn schepis to þat yl a-ryved there. **1470** HARDING *Chron.* xlii, His nauye greate.. In Thamis aroue. **1538** STARKEY *England* 57 The schype arryvyth at the haven purposyd. **1611** BIBLE *Luke* viii. 26 They arriued at the countrey of the Gadarenes. **1790** BEATSON *Nav. & Mil. Mem.* I. 57 The fleet..with the troops and stores, were arrived at Jamaica. **1874** *Marine Insur. Policy*, Until the said Ship..shall be arrived at ——.

b. Of things: To be brought by ship. ***sold to arrive***: (a cargo) sold for delivery on arrival in port.
1755 MAGENS *Insurances*, The goods are arrived and brought a-shore safe. **1861** *Du Chaillu's Equat. Afr.* ii. 13 Shipments of slaves sold 'to arrive,' but which do not come to hand.

3. *trans.* (by omission of prep.) To come to, land at, reach (a shore, port, etc.). *arch.* See 6.
1587 M. GROVE *Pelops & Hipp.* (1878) 96 Nowe we arriue the hauen. **1601** SHAKS. *Jul. C.* I. ii. 110 Ere we could arriue the Point propos'd. **1630** WADSWORTH *Sp. Pilgr.* i. 5 Through a Million of dangers we arriued the Spanish coasts. **1667** MILTON *P.L.* II. 409 Ere he arrive The happy Ile.

II. Of reaching generally.

†**4. a.** *trans.* To bring, to convey; to 'land' a person in any situation. *Obs.*
1489 CAXTON *Faytes of Armes* II. xxiii. 136 Habillementes for to conueie and arrive the thynges that ben nedefull. **1607** CHAPMAN *Bussy D'Ambois* Plays 1873 II. 82 And belief must arrive him on huge riches. **1667** WATERHOUSE *Fire Lond.* 95 These remisnesses..arrive men at woe.

b. *refl.* in sense of next.
1480 CAXTON *Chron. Eng.* ccxxii. 216 Tho toke they the mortimer as he arryued hym at the toures dore.

5. a. *intr.* To come to the end of a journey, to a destination, or to some definite place; to come upon the scene, make one's appearance.
c **1384** CHAUCER *H. Fame* 1047 Both he and y As nygh the place arryved were As men may casten with a spere. *a* **1400** *Sir Degrev.* 59 The eorlle hadd i-revayd, And in hys ȝerd lyȝthus. **1596** SPENSER *F.Q.* v. iv. 6 When Artegall arriving happily Did stay awhile their greedy bickerment. **1611** SHAKS. *Wint. T.* I. ii. 422 A sauour, that may strike the dullest Nosthrill Where I arriue. **1831** CARLYLE *Sart. Res.* III. ix, New labourers will arrive; new Bridges will be built. **1866** GEO. ELIOT *F. Holt* (1868) 22 Before Harold could actually arrive.

b. Const. *at, in, upon* (*into, to*, obs.).
c **1325** *E.E. Allit. P.* A. 447 Alle þat may ther-inne [in þe kyndom of god] aryue. *c* **1435** *Torr. Portugal* Fragm. 1 In a forest she is aryven. **1518** SIR A. BROWNE in Strype *Eccl. Mem.* I. App. xiv. 32 By foor your Grace cowd wel arriff at Amyas. **1539** CROMWELL *ibid.* I App. civ. 272 Yesterday arrived to me hither Your Majesties servants. **1539** TONSTALL *Serm. Palme Sund.* (1823) 14 Into what howse or place so euer ye shall arriue. *a* **1586** SIDNEY (J.) We arrived upon the verge of his estate. **1661** BARROW *Serm.* i. I. 2 He shall in good time arriue to his designed journey's end. **1855** MACAULAY *Hist. Eng.* xi. III. 39 There was no outbreak till the regiment arrived at Ipswich. *Mod.* Two policemen at length arrived upon the scene.

c. Of things: To be brought or conveyed. (Now only of things material.)
1651 HOBBES *Leviath.* II. xxvii. 155 The Law cannot arrive time enough to his assistance. **1667** DRYDEN *Ess. Dram. Poesy* Wks. 1725 I. 46 Let the rest arrive to the Audience by narration. **1709** *Tatler* No. 5 ¶3 Letters..immediately after arrived from the court of Madrid. **1860** TYNDALL *Glac.* I. §11. 71 The ladder now arrived, and we crossed the crevasse.

6. *trans.* (by omission of prep.) To come to, reach. *arch.*
1647 H. MORE *Song of Soul* III. App. xxxiii, Humours did arrive His knobby head. **1647** R. STAPYLTON *Juvenal* 191 Till the crime Arrive the people, and the prince's eare. *a* **1823** SHELLEY *Eurip. Cyclops* 668 While I ask and hear Whence coming they arrive the Ætnean hill. **1850** TENNYSON *In Mem.* lxxxiv, Arrive at last the blessed goal.

III. Of reaching a position, state, or time.

7. To come to a position or state of mind, or reach an object, as the result of continuous effort; to attain, gain, achieve, compass. **a.** *intr.* with (*to* obs.) *at.*
1393 GOWER *Conf.* III. 202 Leoncius Was to thempire of Rome arrived. **1607** SHAKS. *Timon* IV. iii. 512 Many so arriue at second Masters, Vpon their first Lords necke. **1642** HOWELL (*title*), Instructions for Forreine Travell. Shewing by what cours..one may..arrive to the practical knowledge of the Languages. **1671** SIR C. LYTTELTON in *Hatton Corr.* (1878) 72 If he arrives at any employment of that nature. **1737** WATERLAND *Eucharist* 80 They affect to contemn, what they cannot arrive to. **1850** McCOSH *Div. Govt.* (1874) III. i. 290 We arrive at a knowledge of a law of nature by the generalization of the facts presented to the senses. **1862** H. SPENCER *First Princ.* I. iv. §22 The same conclusion is thus arrived at.

†**b.** with *inf.* *Obs.*
1673 DRYDEN *Marr. A-la-Mode* I. i, You have learn'd the advantages of Play, and can arrive to live upon't. **1719** SWIFT *To Yng. Clergyman* Wks. 1755 II. II. 2 If such gentlemen arrive to be great scholars.

c. *trans.* Only *poet.* See 6.
1649 G. DANIEL *Trinarch., Hen. V*, cxlvii, And by what waies Hee may arrive his End.

8. a. *intr.* To come to a certain stage of development, by natural growth, lapse of time, etc.; to reach, attain. Const. (*to* obs.) *at.*
1599 SHAKS. *Hen. V*, III. Cho. 21 Eyther past, or not arriu'd to pyth and puissance. **1634** EVELYN *Diary* (1827) I. 10 Being arriv'd to her 20 yeare of age. **1711** ADDISON *Spect.* No. 123 ¶4 They were each of them arrived at Years of Discretion. **1747** GOULD *Eng. Ants* 49 When the Worms arrive to their Period of Transmutation. **1850** LYNCH *Theo. Trin.* ix. 162 We and the world have arrived at our present, and shall arrive at our future.

b. Of time and temporal states: To come, so as to be present.
1748 SMOLLETT *Rod. Rand.* v. (1804) I. 20 At length the hour arrived. **1847** BUSHNELL *Chr. Nurture* II. v. (1861) 318 As the knowledge of his nobler, unseen Fatherhood arrives. **1849** MACAULAY *Hist. Eng.* II. 31 The time had arrived.

9. a. To come about, come to pass, occur, happen, as an event. *Obs.* (exc. where it has somewhat of the temporal sense of 8, as 'come about in course of time.')
1633 H. COGAN *Pinto's Voy.* lxxv. 305, I will speak no further of him, but will deliver that which arrived in other

Countries. **1651** HOBBES *Leviath.* I. xii. 52 Causes of all things that have arrived hitherto, or shall arrive hereafter. **1713** ADDISON *Cato* III. iv. 6 That whate'er arrive, My friends and fellow-soldiers may be safe. **1817** JAS. MILL *Brit. India* II. v. v. 501 Under whose management such misfortunes had arrived. **1862** TRENCH *Mirac.* xvii. 278 This was precisely what they had long hoped would arrive.

†**b.** Const. *to*, rarely *at*. *Obs.*

a **1677** BARROW *Serm.* I. i. (R.) No considerable damage can arrive to us. **1713** *Guardian* No. 1 ¶5 All sorrows which can arrive at me. **1749** FIELDING *Tom Jones* XV. vi. (1840) 221/2 Any such event may arrive to a woman.

†**c.** *trans.* To happen to, befall. *Obs.*

1655 EVELYN *Mem.* (1857) III. 65 The calamity which lately arrived you. **1659** MILTON *Civ. Power* Wks. 1847. 418/2 Let him also forbear force..lest a worse woe arrive him.

10. Of a person: to be successful, establish one's position or reputation. [After F. *arriver.*]

1889 E. C. DOWSON *Let.* 3 Feb. (1967) 32 Imagine a man of low origin, extremely strong, cynical & determined to 'arrive'. **1893** F. ADAMS *New Egypt* 197 He is a younger man, and has, in the large sense of the word, only arrived comparatively recently. **1914**[see ARRIVISTE]. **1936** *English Studies* XVIII. 53 The book was Herrick's greatest success. .. With *Together* Herrick arrived.

†**a'rrive**, *sb. Obs.* [f. prec. vb. (In the early instance prob. an error for *armé*, which is the prevalent reading.)] Landing; arrival.

c **1386** CHAUCER *Prol.* 60 (Harl. MS.) At manye a nobil ariue [*Cambr. MS.* aryue, *others* arme, -ee, -eye] hadde he be. **1538** STARKEY *England* 57 The haven or place of hys arryve. **1615** CHAPMAN *Odyss.* II. 379 His wife should little joy in his arrive. **1646** SIR T. BROWNE *Pseud. Ep.* 275 At his arrive at Babylon, he would enquire of the antiquity of their Records.

arrived, *ppl. a.* Also **arrivéd**. [ad. F. *arrivé.*] That has reached a position of success or distinction. Also *absol.*

1896 *Godey's Mag.* Feb. 133/2 On the outskirts of the Monceau quarter, which is peopled with 'arrived' artists. **1899** *Westm. Gaz.* 3 July 3/1 Had Elizabeth come of that arrivéd race. **1907** *Daily Chron.* 4 Nov. 3/3 Mrs. Atherton is one of the arrived. **1960** *20th Cent.* Nov. 437 The arrived poets of the post-war generation.

arriver (ə'raɪvə(r)). [f. ARRIVE *v.* + -ER[1].] One who arrives.

1623 WHITBOURNE *Newfoundland* 19 The first arriuers into an Harbour. **1860** *Cornh. Mag.* 88 Conveyed high gratification to the arriver who was thus greeted.

arriving (ə'raɪvɪŋ), *vbl. sb.* [f. as prec. + -ING[1].] Reaching the shore, landing; arrival.

1375 BARBOUR *Bruce* v. 122 Richt in the first begynnyng, Newly at his ariwyng. **1542** *Lam. & Piteous Treat.* in *Harl. Misc.* (Malh.) I. 234 After the arryuynge of the sayde shippes. **1611** COTGR., *Arrivement*, an arriving.

‖**arriviste** (arivist). [Fr., f. *arriver* to arrive + *-iste* -IST.] One who is bent on 'arriving', *i.e.* on making a good position for himself in the world; a pushing or ambitious person, a self-seeker. So as *adj.* Hence **arrivisme**, the attitude or behaviour of an *arriviste*. Also occas. in anglicized form **a'rrivist**, **a'rrivism**.

1901 GABRIELLE GISSING *Let.* 12 July in R. A. Gettmann *Geo. Gissing & H. G. Wells* (1961) 189 What we call an '*arriviste*', such as Lashmar. **1908** W. RALEIGH *Let.* 10 June (1926) II. 331 Haldane is *arriviste* and worldly—not in the least perceptive. **1914** *National Rev.* Dec. 479 The latter are still arrivistes who have so far failed to arrive. **1925** *Contemp. Rev.* Aug. 174 He [*sc.* Canning] was an *arriviste*—an *arriviste* naked and unashamed. **1934** C. LAMBERT *Music Ho!* ii. 84 Both Stravinsky and Chirico stand a little outside the more unscrupulous and arriviste work of their disciples. **1936** 'C. BRAHMS' *Footnotes to Ballet* ii. 51 But 'arrivist' though the theme might be, it still found time for..the dancing cadenza. **1936** M. FRANKLIN *All that Swagger* xxi. 199 Arrivism was his creed. **1944** A. L. ROWSE *Eng. Spirit* xii. 92 Its *arrivisme* can be exaggerated: people did not rise, under Elizabeth, from the bottom of the social scale.

‖**arroba** (ə'rəʊbə). Forms: 6–8 **aroba**, 7–8 **arobe**, 9 **arob**, 7– **arroba**. [Sp., ad. Arab. *ar-rubʿ* 'the quarter,' the weight being a quarter of the Spanish quintal.

(Since the introduction of the French metrical system in 1859, the *arroba* has had no official existence in Spain.)]

1. A weight, used in Spain, Portugal, and Spanish America, of the standard value of 25 Spanish or 25·36 English pounds, but varying locally between 25 and 36 pounds.

1598 W. PHILLIP *Linschoten's Trav. India* (1864) 163 An Aroba which is 32 pound. **1691** *Lond. Gaz.* mmdccxxiv/1 Five Arobes of fine Gold, each Arobe weighing 25 Pounds. **1708** —— mmmmccccIxxxvii/2 It brings 10,000 Arobas of Gold, each Aroba is 32 pound weight. **1853** T. ROSS *Humboldt's Trav.* III. xxxi. 258 The price of sugar at the Havannah is always by the arroba of 25 Spanish pounds. *Ibid.* xxxii. 405 An arob of gold.

2. A Spanish liquid measure, varying in different places, and according to the liquid, from 2·6 to 3·6 gallons.

[**1623** in MINSHEU.] **1633** T. STAFFORD *Pac. Hib.* xxvi. (1821) 469 And sixe hundred Arrobas of Oyle.

†**a'rrode**, *v. Obs.*—[0] [ad. L. *arrōd-ĕre.*] To gnaw or nibble at.

1731 in BAILEY.

arrogance ('ærəgəns). [a. F. *arrogance* (12th c. in Littré), ad. L. *arrogāntia*: see ARROGANT and -ANCE.] The taking of too much upon oneself as one's right; the assertion of unwarrantable claims in respect of one's own importance; undue assumption of dignity, authority, or knowledge; aggressive conceit, presumption, or haughtiness.

1303 R. BRUNNE *Handl. Synne* 3120 þys ys pryde and arrogaunce Vnwrþyly þe to auaunce. **1340** *Ayenb.* 21 þe þridde boȝ of prede is arrogance..þanne þe man wenþ more of him-zelue þanne he ssolde. *c* **1420** *Pallad. on Husb.* I. 213 War arrogaunce in takyng thing in hande. *c* **1500** *Lancelot* 1694 Be not pensyve, nore proud in arrogans. **1613** SHAKS. *Hen. VIII*, III. ii. 278 My Lords, Can ye endure to heare this Arrogance? **1781** GIBBON *Decl. & F.* II. xxxi. 184 Their arrogance was soon humbled by misfortune. **1858** DORAN *Crt. Fools* 63 When things went well with him, his arrogance was insufferable.

arrogancy ('ærəgənsɪ). [ad. L. *arrogāntia*: see prec. and -ANCY.]

1. The quality or state of being arrogant.

1529 MORE *Supplic. Soules* Wks. 290/1 Proude arrogancie vnder yᵉ name of supplicacion. **1538** STARKEY *England* 112 A certayne arrogancy, wherby..every Jake wold be a gentylman. **1611** BIBLE *Prov.* viii. 13 Pride and arrogancie, and the euill way..doe I hate. **1718** J. CHAMBERLAYNE *Relig. Philos.* (1730) Pref. 19 Some Men are apt to advance such their Notions with great Arrogancy. **1856** F. PAGET *Owlet Owlst.* 5 And I don't wish to be arrogant myself, while preaching against arrogancy.

†**2.** A piece of arrogance; an arrogant act or assumption. *Obs.*

1581 NOWELL & DAY in *Confer.* I. (1584) F b, Yet were it an intollerable arrogancie for vs to say, We fed thee when thou wast hungry. **1649** MILTON *Tenure of Kings* 10 The titles of Sovran Lord, naturall Lord, and the like, are either arrogancies, or flatteries.

arrogant ('ærəgənt), *a.* and *sb.* [a. F. *arrogant* (14th c.), ad. L. *arrogāntem* assuming, overbearing, insolent, pr. pple. of *arrogāre*: see ARROGATE and -ANT.] **A.** *adj.* Making or implying unwarrantable claims to dignity, authority, or knowledge; aggressively conceited or haughty, presumptuous, overbearing. (Used of men, their actions, manner, etc.)

c **1386** CHAUCER *Pers. T.* ¶322 Arrogaunt, is he that thinketh that he hath thilke bountees in him, that he hath not. **1538** STARKEY *England* 18 Some..juge al vyce and vertue only to consiste in the opinyon of man, wych ys arrogant blyndnes. *a* **1587** R. GLOVER in Foxe *A. & M.* III. 354 Master Chancellor here noted me to be arrogant, because I would not give place to my Bishop. **1796** BURKE *Let. Noble Ld.* Wks. VIII. 72 It would be a most arrogant presumption in me to assume to myself the glory of what belongs to his majesty. **1872** DARWIN *Emotions* xi. 264 The arrogant man looks down on others, and with lowered eyelids hardly condescends to see them.

†**B.** as *sb.* A proud, haughty person. *Obs.*

1489 CAXTON *Faytes of Armes* I. i. 4 To repress the arrogaunts. **1668** HOWE *Bless. Righteous* Wks. 1834. 230/2 Proud arrogants formed, by necessity and misery, into humble supplicants.

'**arrogantly**, *adv.* [f. prec. + -LY[2].] In an arrogant manner, with haughty assumption.

1538 LELAND *Itin.* I. Pref. 19 That counte, as the Grekes did ful arrogantly, al other Nations to be barbarus and on-letterid. **1656** HARDY *Serm. 1 John* Introd. (1868) 8 Who arrogantly affect to blazon their own names and titles. **1835** LYTTON *Rienzi* I. iv. 27 Knowest thou him whom thou addressest thus arrogantly?

'**arrogantness.** *rare.* [f. as prec. + -NESS.] = ARROGANCY.

1553–87 FOXE in Maitland *Reform.* 501 The bishop [Bonner] and his chaplains laughed and said, Jesu, Jesu, what a stubbornness and arrogantness is this! [In mod. Dicts.]

arrogate ('ærəʊgeɪt), *v.* [f. L. *arrogāt-* ppl. stem of *adr-*, *arrogā-re* to ask or claim for oneself, to adopt one whose consent may legally be asked, f. *ad-* to + *rogāre* to ask. Modern writers on Roman Law have appropriated the form ADROGATE to the specific legal sense.]

1. *Rom. L.* To adopt as a child. (See ADROGATE.)

1649 JER. TAYLOR *Gt. Exemp.* III. §15. 89 He did arrogate John..into Maries kindred.

†**b.** *transf.* To adopt (that which is proper to another). *Obs.*

? *c* **1530** *Epit. Barnes Wks.* 371 (R.) The Byshops..doe arrogate vnto themselues some thyng of the Phariseis pride.

2. To claim and assume as a right that to which one is not entitled; to lay claim to and appropriate (a privilege, advantage, etc.) without just reason or through self-conceit, insolence, or haughtiness. **a.** with *to* and *refl. pron.*

1537 LATIMER *Serm.* (1844) 43 How much soever we arrogate these holy titles unto us. **1671** MILTON *P.R.* IV. 315 To themselves all glory arrogate, to God give none. **1777** WATSON *Philip II* (1793) II. XIII. II. 154 The Spaniards.. had arrogated to themselves every important branch of the administration. **1844** BROUGHAM *Brit. Const.* ix. §2 (1862) 120 They arrogated to themselves the right of approving or rejecting all that was done.

b. with *simple obj.* only.

1593 BILSON *Govt. Christ's Ch.* 18 Yet may they not arrogate any parte of Christes honour. **1667** MILTON *P.L.* XII. 26 Will arrogate Dominion undeserv'd Over his brethren. **1702** ROWE *Tamerlane* I. ii. 575 And arrogate a Praise that is not ours. **1858** DORAN *Crt. Fools* 92 The liberty arrogated by the professor of wit.

3. To lay claim, without reason or through self-conceit, to the possession of (some excellence); to assert without foundation that one has; to assume. **a.** with *to* and *refl. pron.*

1563 *Homilies* II. xvi. II. (1859) 461 Whether all men doe justly arrogate to themselves the Holy Ghost, or no? *a* **1638** MEDE *Wks.* IV. xii. 757 Nor do I arrogate so much ability to myself. **1789** BELSHAM *Ess.* II. xl. 501 They arrogate..all wisdom, knowledge, and even honesty, to themselves. **1872** BLACK *Adv. Phaeton* xxix. 384 She arrogated to herself a certain importance.

b. with *simple obj.* only.

1598 BARCKLEY *Felic. Man* Ded., One that arrogateth superioritie over all. **1660** STANLEY *Hist. Philos.* (1701) 428/2 Thus Pythagoras might arrogate the soul of Euphorbus. **1768** *Phil. Trans.* LVIII. 149, I can arrogate no merit in the discovery. **1848** H. ROGERS *Ess.* I. vi. 321 Arrogating the exclusive possession of wisdom.

†**c.** with *inf.* or *absol.* *Obs.*

1628 WITHER *Brit. Rememb.* v. 203 Doe falsly arrogate to be inspired. **1648** C. WALKER *Relat. & Obs.* I. 29 They arrogate to be the peculiar people of God. **1648** MILTON *Tenure of Kings* 13 Surely no Christian Prince would arrogate so unreasonably above human condition.

4. To lay similar claim to (something) on behalf of another; to ascribe or attribute *to*, or demand for, without just reason.

1605 TIMME *Quersit.* I. vi. 24 We deny that those inset and naturall qualities..are to be arrogated to hotte, moist, and drie. **1810** COLERIDGE *Friend* I. iv. (1867) 12 To antiquity we arrogate many things, to ourselves nothing. **1863** COX *Inst. Eng. Govt.* I. viii. 111 An attempt was made..to arrogate to the Crown the privilege of issuing writs.

'**arrogated**, *ppl. a.* [f. prec. + -ED.] Claimed unduly or pretentiously. (See also ADROGATED.)

1831 CARLYLE *Sart. Res.* III. v, The universally-arrogated virtue..of these days..Independence.

arrogating ('ærəʊgeɪtɪŋ), *vbl. sb.* [f. as prec. + -ING[1].] Undue assumption; the advancing of unwarrantable or pretentious claims. (See also ADROGATING.)

1574 CARTWRIGHT *Full Declar.* 182 Only the Arrogatinge off the name off Bishopp vnto him selffe was tollerable. **1653** GAUDEN *Hierasp.* 238 No more doth the Evangelicall Ministry and Sacraments cease, by reason of any Papall arrogatings. **1871** MACDUFF *Mem. Patmos* i. 10 No arrogating of title or assumption of Apostolic dignity.

'**arrogating**, *ppl. a.* [f. as prec. + -ING[2].] Unduly assuming, pretentious, overbearing.

1602 DEKKER *Satirom.* Wks. 1873 I. 195 The one a light voluptuous Reueler, The other, a strange arrogating puffe. **1823** SCOTT *Quentin D.* xix, The arrogating manner in which the Bohemian had promised to back his suit.

'**arro,gatingly**, *adv.* [f. prec. + -LY[2].] With undue assumption, pretentiously.

1652 GAULE *Magastrom.* 109 Such learning..as may make the artists so arrogatingly suppose themselves learned above all others.

arrogation (ærəʊ'geɪʃən). [ad. L. *arrogātiōnem*, n. of action f. *arrogā-re*: see ARROGATE and -ATION. Cf. OF. *arrogacion* (Godefroy).]

1. = ADROGATION. (So usually spelt in this sense.)

1590 SWINBURN *Testaments* 162 For of adoption, arrogation, or any other meanes to make children lawfull, except marriage, wee haue no vse here in England. **1880** MUIRHEAD *Gaius* IV. §77 If a *paterfamilias*..gives himself to you in arrogation.

2. The action of claiming and assuming without just reason; unwarrantable assumption.

1594 J. KING *Jonah* (1864) 64 Nor [was] the publican as he, in arrogation of justice. **1653** MANTON *Expos. James* iii. 1 Censuring..is an arrogation of mastership over others. **1664** H. MORE *Myst. Iniq.* 412 It seem'd so high an Arrogation, that he rent his clothes and said he had spoken blasphemie. **1839** J. ROGERS *Antipopopr.* I. iii. II. 76 Flattering to the power and arrogation of the priesthood.

†'**arrogative**, *a. Obs. rare*—[1]. [f. L. *arrogāt-* ppl. stem of *arrogā-re* + -IVE, as if ad. L. **arrogātīvus*; cf. OF. *arrogatif.*] Wont to arrogate.

1647 H. MORE *Poems* 371 *note*, The more spiritual arrogative life of the soul, that subtill ascribing that to ourselves that is Gods.

arrogator ('ærəʊgeɪtə(r)). [a. L. *arrogātor*, n. of agent f. *arrogāt-*: see prec. and -ATOR.]

1. One who adrogates. (See ADROGATOR.)

2. One who advances pretentious claims.

1652 GAULE *Magastrom.* 376 Against all Merlinicall arrogators, prorogators, derogators.

arrondell: see HIRONDELLE.

‖**arrondi** (arɔ̃di), *ppl. a. Her.* [Fr., pa. pple. of *arrondir* to make round.] Rounded: applied to parts of a coat of arms, represented (by shading) as having a rounded surface.

1727–51 in CHAMBERS *Cycl.*

‖**arrondissement** (arɔ̃dismɑ̃). [Fr., f. *arrondiss-* lengthened stem of *arrondir*: see prec. and -MENT.]

1. The action of rounding off an outline. *rare.*

1815 SCOTT *Paul's Lett.* (1839) 171 Arrondissements.. under sanction of which cities and..kingdoms have been passed from one government to another.

2. An administrative sub-division of the departments of France, comprising a number of communes.

1807 PINKERTON *Mod. Geog.* (1811) 121 The electoral colleges of the *arondissements* or districts. **1863** KINGLAKE *Crimea* (1876) I. xiv. 259 The Deputies assembled at the Mayoralty of the 10th arrondissement.

†**a'rrosed,** *ppl. a. Obs.*⁻⁰ [f. L. *arrōs-us*, pa. pple. of *arrōd-ĕre* (see ARRODE) + -ED.] 'Gnawed or pilled.' Bailey 1731.

arrosie, obs. form of HERESY.

†**a'rrosion.** *Obs. rare*⁻¹. [n. of action f. L. *arrōs-*: see prec. and -ION¹.] The action of gnawing.

1644 BULWER *Chirol.* 160 This arrosion of the nailes..the property of men inraged with choler.

†**a'rround,** *v. Obs.* [f. AR- *pref.*¹ + ROUND. Cf. Fr. *arrond-ir.*] To flow round, encompass.

1625 SIR T. HAWKINS *Horace Odes* (1638) I. vii, Moystned with gliding brooke which it arrounds. **1652** HOLYDAY *Horace Odes* I. xxxi, The grounds Which silent Liris with soft streames arrounds.

arrour(e, obsolete form of ERROR.

†**a'rrouse,** *v. Obs.* 5–7; also 5 **arrowse, -ze, arouse,** 5–6 **arowse,** 7 **-ze.** [a. F. *arrouse-r* (Palsgr.), OF. *arouser, aroser* (12th c.), mod. *arroser* (Pr. *arrosar, -zar*), according to Brachet:—L. *adrōrā-re*, f. *ad* to + *rōs, rōr-* dew.] To bedew, sprinkle, moisten, water. (Common from Caxton to 1630.)

1480 CAXTON *Ovid's Met.* XIII. v, Some she embraced, kyssed, and arowsyd with teeris. **1491** —— *Vitas Patr.* (W. de W.) I. vii. 11 a/1 The ryuer of Nyle..watred and aroused the regyons of Egypte. **1558** WARDE *Alexis' Secr.* (1568) 20 a, Ye shall take likewise of the sayd greene herbes arowsed wyth vinaigre. **1612** *Two Noble Kins.* v. iv. 103 The blisful dew of heaven does arrose [*Qo.* arowze] you. **1635** PERSON *Varieties* IV. 198 The sea..doth continually arrouse or water the sulphureous vaine.

†**a'rrousement.** *Obs. rare*⁻¹. In 5 **aro-.** [a. OF. *arousement, arosement* (mod. arr-), f. *arouser*: see prec. and -MENT.] Sprinkling, bedewment, watering.

1483 CAXTON *Gold. Leg.* 34/2 Thyse arousemens or sprynggyng of blood were made with the sprynele of humylyte.

arrow (ˈærəʊ), *sb.* Forms: 1 **earh,** 1–5 **arwe, arewe,** 3 **earewe, harewe,** 4 **aro, aru, arw, arraw, aruwe,** 4–6 **arow(e,** 6–7 **arrowe,** 6–9 **arrow.** *Pl.* **-s;** 1 **-an,** 2–3 **-en,** 3–7 **-es.** [OE. had two cognate forms, *earh* for *arh*:—OTeut. *arhwo-* neuter, and *arwe* for *arhwe*:—**arhwôn* weak fem.; akin to ON. *ör, örvar*:—**arhwâ* str. fem., and Goth. *arhwazna* from *arhw* (cf. *hlaiwasna* 'grave,' from *hlaiw*); prob. 'the thing belonging to the bow,' *arhw* being cognate with L. *arqu-us, arc-us*, bow. (Cf. OHG. *fingiri*:—**fingrio-* the thing belonging to the finger, ring, f. *fingar.*) A rare word in OE. the ordinary terms being *strǽl*, and *flá, flán*, of which the former disappeared after 1200, the latter occurred in Scotch after 1500. But *arrow* was the ordinary prose word after 1000.]

I. A missile.

1. a. A slender pointed missile shot from a bow, usually feathered and barbed. Sometimes also applied to the *bolts*, or *quarrels*, with thickened heads, discharged from the cross-bow.

a **835** *Egbert's Penit. Laws* IV. §28 Gif hwylc man mid arwan deor ofsceóte. *a* **1000** *Andreas* (Gr.) 1333 Earh áttre gemæl. **1083** *O.E. Chron.*, On þære rode sticodon on mæ nige arewan. **1205** LAY. 2476 On arwe him com to heorte. *c* **1230** *Ancr. R.* 98 (MS. C) þach hit reine arewen, ich habe a nede erende. **1297** R. GLOUC. 48 Myd arwen & myd quareles so muche folke..me slow. *a* **1300** *Cursor M.* 10036 þe berbikans..wel tas kepe to þat castell, For aro [*v.r.* arw], scott, and for quarel. *c* **1386** CHAUCER *Prol.* 104 A sheef of pocock arwes brighte and kene. *c* **1530** R. HILLES *Commonpl. Bk.* (1858) 140 (*Proverb*) Thys arrow comyth never owt of thyn ownne bow. **1598** BARRET *Theor. Warres* I. i. 3 A vollie of musket..goeth with more terrour..then doth your vollie of arrowes. **1611** BIBLE *1 Sam.* xx. 20, I will shoot three arrowes..as though I shot at a marke. **1782** COWPER *Gilpin* xxxix, Like an arrow swift he flew Shot by an archer strong. **1855** LONGF. *Hiaw.* III. 165 From an oak-bough made the arrows, Tipped with flint, and winged with feathers.

b. *fig.*

c **1230** *Ancr. R.* 60 Erest heo scheot þe earewen of þe liht eien. *c* **1386** CHAUCER *Clerkes T.* 1147 The arwes of thy crabbed eloquence. *c* **1440** *Gesta Rom.* 335 Thou shalt smyte hym with the arowe of penaunce. **1596** BP. BARLOW *Three Serm.* ii. 59 By the Arrowes of Famine, he meaneth the Canker and Palmer wormes. **1602** SHAKS. *Ham.* III. i. 58 The Slings and Arrowes of outragious Fortune. **1678** BUTLER *Hud.* III. i. 941 Love's arrows are but shot at rovers, Tho' all they hit they turn to lovers. **1751** JOHNSON *Rambl.* No. 144 ¶3 A mark to the arrows of lurking calumny. **1854** B. TAYLOR *Hassan* 291 *Poems of Orient* (1866) 101 Slain by the arrows of her beauteous eyes. **1862** GOULBURN *Pers. Relig.* IV. xii. 355 The arrow of conviction rankling in their conscience.

c. With qualifications: **broad arrow**: see III. below. **elf-arrow**: see ARROW-HEAD 1 b. **fire-arrow**: one which carried some burning substance so as to set fire to thatch, sails, etc. **musket-arrow**: one fired from a musket or other fire-arm.

1721 BAILEY, *Elf-arrows*, Flint-stones sharpened and jagged like Arrow-heads, used in War by the ancient Britons. **1753** CHAMBERS *Cycl. Supp.*, *Elf-arrows*, a name given by the people of Scotland, to certain stone weapons which they find, and which had been in use before tools and weapons of iron were used there. **1692** in *Smith's Seaman's Gram.* II. xxxi. 137 To make Darts or Fire-Arrows. **1819** *Pantologia* s.v. *Arrow*, Fire-Arrows were first used in war by the Persians under Xerxes. **1603** SIR C. HEYDON *Jud. Astrol.* xi. 254 He taketh his words to be musket arrowes..and his breath gunpowder.

d. *Darts slang.* A dart (sense 1 d).

1946 *Dart* (Feltham) 16 Mar. 3/1 The team with the first throw has an advantage of three arrows. **1961** PARTRIDGE *Dict. Slang* Suppl. 982/2 *Arrow, in good*, in good form: dart-players' s[lang]. **1976** *Morecambe Guardian* 7 Dec. 9/1 Best individual scores: B. Lilly (Royal) 180 in three arrows; B. Norris (Smugglers) 180 in three arrows. **1981** R. LEWIS *Seek for Justice* iii. 94 Freddy's arrows kept hitting the wire.

2. in *Surveying*, Straight sticks shod with iron (originally real arrows), or iron pins, used to stick in the ground at the end of each chain.

[**1571** DIGGES *Pantom.* F b, Whatsoeuer you mete the space G E withall, whether it be halberd, bill, arrow or staffe.] **1753** CHAMBERS *Cycl. Supp.* s.v. *Surveying*, He ought likewise to have ten arrows, or small strait sticks, near two feet long, shod with iron ferrils..The leader sticks one of the ten arrows in the ground at the far end of the chain. **1883** *Mod. Price List*, Arrows, made from No. 11 Steel Wire, the set of ten Arrows..*2s. 6d.*

3. A representation or figure of the missile: **a.** *gen.* Any arrow-shaped index, pin, or ornament.

Mod. The spire is surmounted by an arrow. She wore a silver arrow in her hair, etc.

b. in *Cartography*, A mark like an arrow, or arrow-head, used to point out the course or direction of a river, road, railway, etc.

1834 *Penny Cycl.* II. 156/1 The direction of the earth's motion represented by the arrow. **1882** EVERETT *Deschanel's Nat. Phil.* 6 If the directions of all three arrows are reversed, the forces will still be in equilibrium.

4. *Astr.* A small constellation of the Northern Hemisphere, *Sagitta.*

1727–51 in CHAMBERS *Cycl.* **1868** LOCKYER *Heavens* 328 The Fox, the Arrow, the Dolphin..contain no remarkable star.

II. Things resembling an arrow.

†**5.** *fig.* The penis. *Obs.*

1382 WYCLIF *Ecclus.* xxvi. 15 (see margin). So later vers.

†**6.** *Geom.* The *sagitta*, or versed sine of an arc.

1594 BLUNDEVIL *Exerc.* II. 10 Sinus versus..is also called in Latine *Sagitta*; in English a Shaft or Arrow, for the Demonstrative figure thereof..is not unlike to the string of a bow ready bent, having a Shaft in the middest thereof. **1751** in CHAMBERS *Cycl.*

7. The leading shoot of a plant or tree.

†**a.** The main young shoot of a vine or other tree, or, that which in pruning is left to run up and form the main stem. (Perh. only transl. L. *sagitta.*) *Obs.*

1580 BARET *Alv.* A 568 Arrow, the longest twigge that is left in the vine when it is cut. **1745** tr. *Columella* III. xvii, Rustics call the utmost or last part of the shoot the Arrow.

b. The flowering stem of the sugar-cane.

1779 *Phil. Trans.* LXIX. 278 All canes have not arrows, and the coming out of an arrow depends on the season, and not on the age of the cane. **1833** M. SCOTT *Tom Cringle* xix. (1859) 533 The cane-fields then in arrow. **1870** KINGSLEY in *Gd. Words* 1 June 382/1 More handsome still..when the 'arrow,' as the flower is called, spreads over the cane-piece a purple haze.

8. in *Fortification* (see quot.).

1816 C. JAMES *Mil. Dict.* (ed. 4) 247 *Arrow* is a work placed at the salient angle of the glacis, and consists of two parapets, each above 40 fathoms long; this work has a communication with the covert-way, of about 24 or 28 feet broad, called *caponnière*, with a ditch before it of about 5 or 6 fathom, and a traverse at the entrance, of 3 fathom thick, and a passage of 6 or 8 feet round it. [Cf. ARROW-HEADED 1.]

III. **broad arrow.**

9. *lit.* One having a *broad arrow-head* (see ARROW-HEAD), used for cleaving.

1377 LANGL. *P. Pl.* B. xx. 116 (Wright) He bar a bowe in his hand, and manye brode arewes. **1440** *Promp. Parv.*, Brood arowe (*v.r.* brodarwe), *Catapulta*. *c* **1490** *Adam Bel* 613 in Ritson *Anc. P. Poetry* 28, I myselfe with a brode arow Shall cleue the apple in two. **1530** PALSGR. 201/2 Broode arrowe, *rallion*. **1611** COTGR., *Rallion*, an arrow with a forked or barbed head; a broad arrow.

10. a. For *broad arrow-head*: The arrow-head-shaped mark, used by the British Board of Ordnance, and placed upon government stores. In *Her.* = PHEON, which is properly a broad-arrow with the inner edge of the barbs indented.

1551 *Grant of arms to John Cooke* (20 Feb. 6 Edw. VI), Brode arrowes. **1687** *Charter of James II to Tower of Lond.*, Upon all which Boundary houses, His Majesty's Mark, the Broad Arrow, by his late Majesty's special command, have been set up. **1698** *Act 9 & 10 Will. III*, xli, Or any other Stores [marked] with the Broad Arrow. **1823** SCOTT *Quentin D.* vi, The same rude resemblance..which certain talismanic scratches, well known to our revenue officers, bear to a *broad arrow*. **1839–44** TUPPER *Prov. Phil.* (1862) 128 The broad arrow of the Great King, carved on all the stores of his Arsenal. **1865** *Times* 13 Feb., If the broad arrow be found on any stores in Confederate hands, it will be found that they were condemned and sold, or that the mark is forged.

b. The figure of an arrow-head having the point upwards, with which the clothes of convicts were formerly marked. Also *allusively*. Hence **broad-arrowed** *a.*, marked with this.

1859 'OLINÉ KEESE' (*title*) The Broad Arrow, being passages from the history of Maida Gwynnham, a lifer. **1886** P. ROBINSON *Valley Teetotum Trees* 50 The tiny double puncture which is the viper's broad-arrow of death. **1896** *Daily News* 29 July 7/4 Dr. Jameson..was..garbed in the prison shoes and broad-arrowed suit. **1901** *Daily Chron.* 17 June 5/6 His broad-arrow trousers. **1914** *N. & Q.* 11th Ser. IX. 482/2 The Prison Commissioners..wrote..that..the broad arrow..has been used in Convict Prisons and Hulks for more than 80 years, and was also used in Australia. **1934** J. A. LEE *Childr. of Poor* i. 21, I can..see that shuffling parade of men in broad-arrowed moleskins.

IV. **11.** *caustic arrow* (Surg.): see quot. 1890.

1879 *St. George's Hosp. Rep.* IX. 384 A tumour around the anus was removed by the insertion of caustic arrows. **1890** BILLINGS *Med. Dict.*, *Caustic arrows*,..small, pointed cylinders or cones made of chloride-of-zinc paste or other caustics, intended for introduction into the substance of morbid growths.

V. Combinations.

1. General relations: **a.** objective, as ***arrow-bearing, -maker, -straightener***; **b.** instrumental, as ***arrow-smitten***; **c.** parasynthetic, as ***arrow-leaved, -pointed, -shaped***; **d.** attributive, as ***arrow-flight, -line, -point, -range, -wound.***

1818 SCOTT *Hrt. Midl.* lii, Woggarwolfe's arrow-bearing page. **1808** —— *Marm.* VI. xxvi, Fell England's arrow-flight like rain. **1812** WITHERING *Bot. Arrangement* (ed. 5) III. 972 Arrow-leaved Splachnum. **1880** GRAY *Bot. Text-bk.* 397 The Arrow-leaved Polygonum. **1902** BELLOC *Path to Rome* 246 My undeviating arrow-line to Rome. **1952** J. FISHER *Fulmar* vii. 148 Fulmars were seen..prospecting by a direct arrow-line. **1681** CHETHAM *Angler's Vade-m.* i. §4 (1689) 4 Let the Arrow-maker divide this with a Saw. **1751** CHAMBERS *Cycl.*, *Arrow-makers* are called fletchers. **1855** LONGF. *Hiaw.* x. 83 At the doorway of his wigwam Sat the ancient arrow-maker. **1775** ADAIR *Amer. Ind.* 425 One of those flint arrow-points. **1766** *Complete Farmer* s.v. *spinage*, The prickly spinage with arrow-pointed leaves. **1926** M. LEINSTER *Dew on Leaf* I. vi. 75 Arrow-pointed specks of birds in flight. **1853** KINGSLEY *Hypatia* xxi. (1879) 262 Out of arrow-range! Slip the dogs, Syphax! **1765** J. LEE *Introd. Bot.* (ed. 2) 473 *Sagittatum folium*, an Arrow-shaped Leaf. **1909** *Cent. Dict.* Suppl., Arrow-straightener. **1919** H. G. WELLS *Outl. Hist.* x. 59/1 Certain of their implements are said to be 'arrow-straighteners' by distinguished authorities. **1935** *Discovery* July 207/2 Eskimo carvings in ivory—human figures,..arrow-straighteners, toggles, [etc.]. **1870** BRYANT *Homer* I. VIII. 262 An arrow-wound or gash of spear, Given as he leaps on board.

2. Special combinations: **arrow-case,** a quiver, also *fig.*; **arrow-finger,** the fore-finger; †**arrow-girdle,** a girdle in which arrows were carried; **arrow-leaf** *U.S.*, = ARROW-HEAD 4; **arrowless** *a.*, without arrows; **arrow-like** *a.* and *adv.*, like an arrow; **arrow-loop, arrow-slit,** a narrow loop-hole or slit for shooting through; **arrow-plant** (see quot.); **arrow-proof** *a.*, proof against arrows; **arrow-shot,** the shooting of an arrow; also, the distance to which an arrow is shot, a bow-shot; **arrow-smith,** a maker of iron arrow-heads; **arrow-snake,** or *javelin-snake*, a species of snake (*Acontias jaculus*) so called from the spring with which it darts forward; **arrow-stitch,** the triangular set of stitches with which the ends of whalebone in stays are sometimes secured; **arrow-stone** (*obs.* or *dial.*), a belemnite; **arrow-weed,** (*a*) = ARROW-HEAD 4; (*b*) a western American composite shrub, *Pluchea sericea*; **arrow-wise** *adv.*, after the manner of an arrow; **arrow-worm,** any worm of the class Chætognatha of small transparent marine worms.

1388 WYCLIF *Ecclus.* xxvi. 15 And schal opene the *arowe caas aȝens eche arowe. **1513** DOUGLAS *Æneis* I. VIII. 13 On hir schuldir the arrow caice bare sche. **1578** *Lanc. Wills* (1857) II. 60 An arrowe case of strawe with locke and kay. **1875** MAINE *Hist. Inst.* ix. 256 You must call the forefinger the '*arrow'-finger. **1382** WYCLIF *Ezek.* xxvii. 11 Pigmeis.. hangiden her *arew girdlis [**1388** arowe casis] in thi wallis. **1880** *Harper's Mag.* June 70 The frog pond with lush growth of *arrow leaves and pickerel weed. **1931** CLUTE *Common Names Plants* 22 The starchy tubers of the arrow-leaf (*Sagittaria latifolia*). **1881** G. STABLES in *Boy's Own P.* 8 Oct. 22 Plunging *arrow-like into the watery ravines. **1840** BROWNING *Sordello* v. 429 She..thrid somehow, by some glimpse of *arrow-loop, The turnings to the galleries below. **1779** T. FORREST *Voy. N. Guinea* 156 On cutting an *arrow-plant (a species of pine), I found fresh water drop from it. **1831** *Tatler* 1 Nov. 417/2 Our author and his party..were obliged to provide themselves with arms and with *arrow-proof dresses. **1906** *Daily Chron.* 13 Nov. 6/4 The horsemen ..upon horses dressed in thick arrow-proof coats. **1513** DOUGLAS *Æneis* XI. xii. 27 Wythin ane *arrow schot on athir syde. **1653** HOLCROFT *Procopius* III. 79 Attending the cure of his Wound without Arrow-shot. **1852** MISS YONGE *Cameos* I. Introd. 1 Tyrrell's arrow-shot. **1851** MELVILLE *Moby Dick* III. xvi. 117 From their *arrow-slit in the skull, the priests perceived me. **1870** F. Wilson *Ch. Lindisf.* 92 The lower storey lighted only by an arrow-slit. **1878** Smiles *Robt. Dick* iv. 31 Perforated here and there with arrow-slits. *c* **1400** *Destr. Troy* v. 1588 Armurers and *Arowsmythis. **1618** Pulton *Coll. Stat.* 7 Hen. IV, vii, Because the arrow smithes doe make many faultie heads for arrowes and quarrels. **1611** Bible *Gen.* xlix. 17 Dan shall be a serpent by the way, an adder [*marg.* *arrowsnake] in the path. **1833** *Penny Cycl.* I. 88/2 The Hebrew denomination *Kippoz* [*Isa.* xxxiv. 15]..which the learned Bochart..has shown to refer more properly to the *acontias* or *anguis jaculus*, the arrow or dart-snake of the Greeks and Romans. **1846** J. W. Abert in Emory *Mil. Reconn.* 434 Some brackish pools..bordered with the..*arrow weed (*sagittaria sagittifolia*). **1876** *Field & Forest* II. 55 These Mexican jumping seeds,..are derived from a plant called arrow weed, or *Yerba de flecha*, and *Colliguaja* by the Mexicans. **1889** *Cent. Dict.*, *Arrow-worm. **1952** J. Fisher *Fulmar* xviii. 428 The arrow-worm *Sagitta*..was found..in fulmars in Spitsbergen.

arrow (ˈærəʊ), *v. rare.* [f. prec. sb.]

1. *intr.* To shoot arrows.

1865 Sir K. James *Tasso* II. xx. lxv, While she arrowed.

2. To shoot into blossom (said of the sugar-cane).

18.. *Simmonds Colon. Mag.* (in Hoppe), The West-Indian planter must prevent his sugar-cane from arrowing.

†**3.** *trans.* To pierce, wound (? confused with *harrow*). *Obs.*

1627 Feltham *Resolves* I. ii. (1647) 6 By a noble not-caring, arrow the intenders bosome, who will ever fret most, when he finds his designes most frustrate.

4. *intr.* To move swiftly through space, like an arrow in its flight; to dart. Also *to arrow one's way*.

1827 *Blackw. Mag.* XXII. 446 About an hour ago did we ..see that identical salmon..arrowing up the Tay. **1866** Whyte Melville *Cerise* xliv, Streams..where the otter lurked and vanished, where the noble salmon himself came arrowing up triumphant from the sea. **1905** W. Holman Hunt *Pre-Raphaelitism* I. 71 Here the kingfisher arrowed his way. **1927** *Chambers's Jrnl.* 4/1 She [*sc.* a filly] arrowed over her hurdles like the 'class' young lady that she was. **1936** R. Lehmann *Weather* (1951) I. v. 72 A figure..came arrowing down the last flight in one straight skim.

5. *trans.* To send forth like an arrow. *poet.*

1892 Tennyson *Death Œnone* [etc.] 39 Shadow-maker, shadow-slayer, arrowing light from clime to clime.

arrow, vulgar corruption of *e'er a*, *ever a*.

1749 Fielding *Tom Jones* v. viii. (D.), 'I don't believe there is arrow a servant in the house.' **1771** Smollett *Humph. Cl.* I. 126 (D.), 'I now carries my head higher than arrow private gentlewoman of Vales.'

arrow, north. form of argh *a. Obs.* cowardly.

arrowed (ˈærəʊd), *a. poet.* [f. arrow *sb.* + -ed.]

a. Made into an arrow. **b.** Furnished or provided with arrows. **c.** Pierced with arrows. **d.** Wearing the broad arrow.

1652 Benlowes *Theoph.* I. lxv, Sol..shoots delight through Nature with each arrow'd ray. **1821** Joanna Baillie *Met. Leg.*, *Wallace* lii, The arrow'd sportsman strays at will. **1908** E. M. Sneyd-Kynnersley *H.M.I.* xxv. 296 The visitor to Continental picture galleries catches sight of S. Sebastian—'arrowed, but unharrowed'. **1930** R. Campbell *Adamastor* 70 Arrowed like convicts.

ˈ**arrow-grass.** **1.** English name of the endogenous genus *Triglŏchin*, containing humble marsh plants with grass-like leaves. [Referring, like the Gr. name, to the '3-barbed' appearance of the burst capsule.]

1792–1807 Sir J. E. Smith *Eng. Bot.* VI. 366 All cattle will eat the marsh Arrow-grass. **1801** Withering *Bot. Arrangem.* (ed. 4) II. 352 *Triglochin Palustre*, Arrow-headed grass. Marsh Arrow-grass. The pointed valves of the capsule opening at the bottom, give it the appearance of the head of an arrow. **1882** *Pall Mall G.* 8 June 4/1 Overgrown by thick-leaved salt-marsh plants..glass-wort and arrow-grass.

2. A Brazilian grass of the same genus as the Pampas Grass. [Cf. arrow *sb.* 7 b.]

1863 Bates *Nat. on Amazons* vii. 168 Large tracts of arrow-grass (*Gynerium Saccharoides*), which bears elegant plumes of flowers like those of the reed, and grows to a height of twenty feet.

ˈ**arrow-head.** **1.** The head or pointed part of an arrow, made separately and of different material from the shaft.

1483 *Cath. Angl.*, Arowhede, *barbellum, catella.* **1545** Ascham *Toxoph.* (Arb.) 135 Two maner of arrowe heades.. was vsed in olde tyme. The one..hauyng two poyntes or barbes, lookyng backewarde to the stele and the fethers, which surely we call in Englishe a *brode arrowe head* or a *swalowe tayle*. The other..hauing .ii. poyntes stretchyng forwarde, and this Englysh men do call a *forke-head*. The Parthyans vsed brode Arrowe heades..Our Englyshe heades be better in war than eyther *forked heades* or *brode arrowe heades*. **1618** Pulton *Coll. Stat.* 7 Hen. IV, vii, Arrow-heads shall be well boiled, brased, and hardened. **1870** Bryant *Homer* iv. I. 110 He forced the string to meet His breast, the arrow-head to meet the bow.

b. *esp.* Those of flint, jade, or similar substances, found among the relics of prehistoric times.

1661 Sir R. Gordon in Burton *Hist. Scotl.* I. 136 *note*, Hos vulgus patrio sermone *elf arrow-heads* vocant. **1753** Chambers *Cycl. Supp.* s.v. *Elf Arrows*, Very small arrow-heads made out of a talky fissile stone are found in Virginia and Barbadoes. **1769** Pennant *Tour Scot.* 115 (Jam.) *Elf-shots*, i.e. the stone arrow-heads of the old inhabitants of this island, are supposed to be weapons shot by Fairies at cattle. **1851** D. Wilson *Preh. Ann.* I. vi. 181 Arrow-heads, are for the most part made of flint. **1855** Longf. *Hiaw.* iv. 263 Made his arrow-heads of sandstone, Arrow-heads of chalcedony.

2. broad arrow-head. **a.** *prop.* a kind of arrow-head: see quot. 1545 in 1 a. **b.** *transf.* = *broad-arrow*: see arrow *sb.* 10. **c.** *fig.* Any mark or impression resembling these.

1865 Dickens *Mut. Fr.* i, At every stationary boat or barge that split the current into a broad-arrow-head.

3. in *Cartography*, etc. = arrow 3 b.

1836 Yarrell *Brit. Fishes* II. 297 In the vignette the arrow heads indicate the direction of the currents. **1870** Todhunter *Mech. for Beg.* 3 Sometimes an arrow head is used in a figure to indicate [the direction in] which the force tends.

4. *Bot.* English name of the endogenous genus of plants, *Sagittaria*, of which the common European species, *S. sagittifolia* (found from Virginia to China and Japan), has floating leaves shaped like an arrow-head.

1597 Gerard *Herbal* 337 *Sagittaria* may be called in English the water Archer, or Arrow heade. **1611** Cotgr., *Sagette*..the Ditch-weed called Arrow-head. **1809** Crabbe *Tales* 37 The Fen itself has a dark and saline herbage; there are rushes and Arrow-heads. **1883** Howells in *Harper's Mag.* Dec. 70/2 The cat-tails and arrow-heads in the 'ma'sh' at Ponkwasset.

5. *attrib.* or *adj.*; = arrow-headed 2.

1875 Emerson *Lett. & Soc. Aims* i. 24 'Tis easier to.. decipher the arrowhead character, than to interpret these familiar sights. **1877** Dawson *Orig. World* i. 24 The arrow-head writing, afterwards used by the Assyrians.

Comb., as **arrow-head-maker**.

1598 Stow *Surv.* (ed. Strype 1754) II. v. xiii. 304/2 Besides these two trades belonging to Archers there were also two more, Stringers and Arrow head makers. **1647** Haward *Crown Rev.* 26 Arrow-head-maker: Fee..6*l.* 1*s.* 8*d.*

ˈ**arrow-ˌheaded**, *a.* [f. prec. + -ed.]

1. *gen.* Having the shape of an arrow-head.

1876 Bancroft *Hist. U.S.* V. xiv. 490 At Princeton, where Donop had thrown up arrow-headed earthworks.

2. *spec.* = Cuneiform; applied to the characters of the ancient inscriptions of Nineveh, Babylon, Persepolis, etc.

1816 T. Maurice *Ruins Bab.* 158 The name of *arrow-headed*, bestowed upon these characters by himself [Dr. Hager]. **1829** J. Kenrick in *Philos. Mag.* May 321 A stroke which, when elaborately made, resembles the head of an arrow; when less carefully cut or impressed, a wedge or a nail; and hence the inscriptions have been called *arrow-headed, nailheaded*, or *cuneiform*. **1847** *Q. Rev.* No. 158. 416 These cuneiform or arrow-headed characters are so called from one of the elements of which they consist, a straight line, slightly divided at the top like the notch of an arrow, and ending in a point, so as to represent a kind of wedge; the other element is an angle.

†ˈ**arrow-ˌheader.** *Obs.* A maker, or fitter on, of arrow-heads.

c **1510** *Cocke Lorelle's Bote* 10 Arowe heders, maltemen, and corne mongers.

ˈ**arrowlet.** [f. arrow + -let dim. suff.] A little arrow; *fig.* applied to the stalked and plumose seeds of the Dandelion and allied plants.

1872 Tennyson *Gareth* 1002 The flower That blows a globe of after arrowlets.

arrowre, obs. form of error.

ˈ**arrow-root.** [From use made of the fleshy tubers to absorb poison from wounds, especially those of poisoned arrows: see the quotations from Sir Hans Sloane, infra.]

1. *Bot.* A plant; originally *Maranta arundinacea*, an endogenous herb with fleshy tuberous rhizomes, native to some, and cultivated in other, of the West Indian Isles; extended to other species of Maranta yielding similar products.

1696 Sloane *Catal. Plant. Jamaica* 122 Canna Indica radice alba alexipharmaca. L'herbe aux flèches, *Du Tertre* p. 90, *Rochef.* p. 130. ? An 'yerva que con el sumo de su rayz remedia la ponsonna de las mansanillas ponsonnosas,' *Lop. de Gomara*, cap. 71, *hist. gen...* Cyperus longus inodorus quartus, seu radix contra venenatas sagittas, *C.B. pin.* p. 14? ..*Indian arrow root.* **1725** —— *Voy. Madeira* I. xvi. 253–4 Indian Arrow-root [Account of its introduction]. **1788–9** Howard *Cycl.* I. 224 Indian Arrow-root is the same with the *maranta*. It is esteemed a sovereign remedy against the bite of wasps, and the poison of the manchineel tree. **1858** R. Hogg *Veg. K.* 786 *Maranta arundinacea*, Arrow-root, is a native of the West Indies.

2. *Comm.* A pure nutritious starch, prepared from the tubers of *Maranta*; the name has been given commercially to starches prepared from many other plants, but since the passing of the Adulteration Act, none of these may legally be sold in Great Britain as 'arrow-root.'

1811 *Lond. Dispens.* 402 Sago, salep, tapioca, arrowroot.. are only different modifications of starch. **1822** *Ibid.* 541 *note*, Arrowroot is the pith of the *Maranta arundinacea*. **1866** *Treas. Bot.* 720 Other descriptions of Arrow-root are furnished by plants belonging to the following genera: *Arum, Canna, Curcuma, Jatropha, Tacca. Ibid.* 93 'English Arrow-root' is the starch obtained from the tubers of the potato. [See also arum.]

3. The food prepared from this starch.

1848 Thackeray *Van. Fair* xxxix, They smooth pillows, and make arrowroot: they get up of nights.

4. *attrib.*

1861 Sala *Tw. round Clock* 192 The refreshment counter, where they sell the arrow-root cakes.

arrow-wood. An American name for species of *Viburnum* (*V. dentatum, pubescens*, etc.) from the long straight stems of which the American Indians make the shafts of their arrows. Also applied to other shrubs having straight tough shoots, as *Euonymus, Pluchea sericea*, etc.

1709 Lawson *New Voy. Carolina* 100 Arrow-wood, growing on the banks, is used, by the Indians, for arrows and gun-sticks. **1717** J. Petiver *Petiveriana* III. 221 Arrow-wood. Used by the Indians for Arrows and Gun-sticks. **1819** McMurtrie *Sk. Louisville* 217 *Euonymus carolinensis*, Indian Arrow Wood. **1848** in Bartlett *Dict. Amer.* **1850** *New Eng. Farmer* II. 60 The first [dogwood]..is the Arrowwood. **1866** in *Treas. Bot.*

arrowy (ˈærəʊɪ), *a.* [f. arrow + -y.]

1. Consisting of, or abounding in, arrows.

1671 Milton *P.R.* iii. 324 Sharp sleet of arrowy showers. **1791** E. Darwin *Bot. Gard.* I. 11 The arrowy throne of rising Moon. **1810** W. Taylor in *Month. Mag.* XXIX. 210 On the helmet rings the arrowy hail. **1864** Ld. Derby *Iliad* I. 60 On man the last, Was poured the arrowy storm.

2. Like an arrow: **a.** in shape or appearance.

1637 Heywood *Dialogues* 301 And thrild their arrowie Javelins after him. **1852** T. Ross *Humboldt's Trav.* II. xxiv. 486 The arrowy branches of the palm-trees. **1877** A. B. Edwards *Up Nile* vi. 151 Clustered cupolas and arrowy minarets.

b. in swift or darting motion; swift as an arrow.

1816 Byron *Ch. Har.* iii. lxxi, By the blue rushing of the arrowy Rhone. **1837** Howitt *Rur. Life* iii. i. (1862) 260 Flew along with arrowy swiftness. **1855** Longf. *Hiawatha* xx. 72 Homeward shoots the arrowy swallow.

c. in action, effect, etc.; darting, piercing, keen.

1785 Cowper *Task* vi. 782 The lambent homage of his arrowy tongue. *a* **1822** Shelley in *Casquet Lit.* (1877) IV. 363/1 Violets..dart their arrowy odour through the brain. **1824** Miss Mitford *Village* Ser. I. (1863) 63 Rain that comes chilling and arrowy like hail in January. **1861** W. Collier *Hist. Eng. Lit.* ix. 234 Sharp arrowy wit. **1868** Geo. Eliot *F. Holt* 59 Arrowy words, each one hitting its mark.

‖**arroyo** (əˈrɔɪəʊ). Also *erron.* **arroya.** [Sp.:—OSp. *arrogio*, med.L. *arrogium*, found as early as 775 (Diez); origin uncertain.] A rivulet or stream; *hence*, the bed of a stream, a gully. (*in U.S.*)

[**1807** *Deb. Congress* 1st Sess. I. App. 571/1 The country east of the Sabine to the Arroyo Hondo.] **1845** Frémont *Exped. Rocky Mts.* 252 We discovered..groves of oak trees on a dry arroyo. **1846** Sage *Scenes Rocky Mts.* xix, The banks of this *arroyo* are very steep and high. **1850** B. Taylor *Eldorado* v. (1862) 49 The deep gullies or arroyos with which it is seamed. **1872** C. King *Sierra Nev.* vi. 119 At brief intervals, were sharp, narrow arroyos.

ˈ**Arry** (ˈærɪ). [The common Christian name *Harry* vulgarly pronounced without the aspirate.] Used humorously for: A low-bred fellow (who 'drops his *h*'s') of lively temper and manners. Hence ˈ**Arryish** *a.*, vulgarly jovial.

1874 *Punch's Almanac*, 'Arry on 'Orseback. **1881** *Sat. Rev.* No. 1318. 148 The local 'Arry has torn down the famous tapestries of the great hall. **1880** W. Wallace in *Academy* 28 Feb. 156/1 He has a fair stock of somewhat 'Arryish animal spirits, but no real humour.

arsadine: see arsedine.

arsanilic (ɑːsəˈnɪlɪk), *a. Chem.* [f. ars(enic + anilic *a.*; cf. G. *arsanilsäure* (Ehrlich and Bertheim 1907, in *Chem. Zentralbl.* II. 898).] Of or derived from arsenic acid and aniline, esp. *arsanilic acid*, $C_6H_8O_3NAs$ (= $NH_2.C_6H_4.AsO(OH)_2$), a compound used in the preparation of arsenicals.

1907 *Chem. Abstr.* 2715 The 'arsenic anilide' is really *p-aminophenylarsinic acid* or *arsanilic acid*, as the author [*sc.* Ehrlich & Bertheim] terms his compound. **1937** *Thorpe's Dict. Appl. Chem.* I. 486/2, *p-Arsanilic acid*..was first obtained by Béchamp by heating a mixture of aniline and arsenic acid at 190°–200° with stirring. **1959** *Times* (Agric. Suppl.) 7 Dec. p. vii/1, Arsanilic acid..used both as the free acid and as the sodium salt..to improve feathering and pigmentation [in poultry].

arse, *sb. Obs.* in polite use. Forms: 1 **ærs, ears,** 1–7 **ars,** 4–5 **ers(e, eeres, arce,** 4–9 **arse.** [common Teut.: cf. OHG., ON., Da., Sw. *ars*, OFris. *ers*, G. *arsch*, OTeut. *ars-oz, cogn. w. Gr. ὄρρος, *ὄρσος.]

1. a. The fundament, buttocks, posteriors, or rump of an animal.

c **1000** Ælfric *Gloss.* in Wright 44/2 *Nates*, ears-lyre. **1377** Langl. *P. Pl.* B. v. 175 Baleised on þe bare ers [*v.r.* ars], and no breche bitwene. **1398** Trevisa *Barth. De P.R.* vii. liv. (1495) 267 Emoroides ben fuyue veynes whyche stretche out atte the eeres. **1480** Caxton *Chron. Eng.* ccxxvi. 233 They lete hange fox tailles..to hele and hyde her arses. **1547** Boorde *Brev. Health* xxv. 15 b, The 25th chapitre dothe shewe of a mannes ars. **1663** Butler *Hud.* I. iii. 964 Then mounted both upon their Horses, But with their Faces to the Arses. **1704** Swift *Batt. Books* (1711) 235 Do you think I have nothing else to do but to mend and repair after your Arse? [i.e. behind you, in your rear.]

b. in phr. *heavy arse*: a lazy fellow, a lie-a-bed. *to hang the arse*: to hold back, be reluctant or tardy. ***arse upwards***: in good luck. ***arse over tip*** (or ***tit***), head over heels; also *fig.*

1530 PALSGR. 436/2 What up, heavy arse, cannest thou nat aryse. *c* **1600** *Timon* I. v. (1842) 20 This man this daye rose with his arse upwards; To daye a fidler, and at night a noble. **1611** COTGR., *Fesse-cul*, A Pedanticall whip-arse. **1633** MASSINGER *Guardian* v. iv, Nay, No hanging an arse. **1663** BUTLER *Hud.* I. i. 456 Could he stir To active trot one side of's Horse The other would not hang an arse. **1922** JOYCE *Ulysses* 461 Arse over tip. Hundred shillings to five. **1932** W. S. MAUGHAM *Narrow Corner* xi. 73 I'm pretty nimble on me feet, but I nearly come arse over tip two or three times. **1968** A. DIMENT *Gt. Spy Race* x. 184, I scrambled down a sharp bank.. almost going arse over tit when my foot caught in a branch. **1972** *Observer* 24 Sept. 37/3 An alternative system which.. turns Marx arse over tip. **1974** P. TINNISWOOD *Except you're Bird* xi. 69 He'll have me out of the job as soon as look at me. It'll be an arse over tit job in double quick time.

2. *transf.* or *fig.* The bottom; the lower or hinder end; the fag end, tail.

c **1400** *Rom. Rose* 7580 Thou shalt for this sinne dwelle Right in the divels arse of helle. **1556** *Chron. Grey Friars* (1852) 73 Whyppyd.. at the carttes arse.. for vacobondes. **1622** MASS. & DEKK. *Virg. Mart.* II. i. Wks. IV. 37 The arse, as it were, or fag end of the world. **1750** W. ELLIS *Mod. Husb.* V. i. 11 [Lay the sheaves] in a sloping posture, close together, with their arses outward. **1880** [see *arse-end*, sense 3 below].

3. *Comb.* and *Attrib.*, as ***arse-end***; also spec. ***arse-end Charlie*** (see quot. 1942); ***arse-hole***, ***-tharme***, ***-therl***, ***-winning***, ***-wisp***; **arse-board** (still *dial.*), the tail board of a cart; **arse-gut**, the rectum, also *fig.*; **arse-licking** *vbl. sb.* and *ppl. a.*, toadying; **arse-long** (cf. *side-long*); **arse-push**, a heavy backward fall; **arse-ropes**, intestines. Also ARSEFOOT, ARSELING, ARSESMART, ARSEWARD, q.v.

1880 R. HOLLAND in *O. Farming Words* 2 In Cheshire the stalk-end of a potato [is called] the 'arse-end of a 'tater.' **1942** R. HILLARY *Last Enemy* 132, I was shot down acting as Arse-end Charlie to a Squadron of Hurricanes. Arse-end Charlie is the man who weaves backwards and forwards above and behind the Squadron to protect them from attack from the rear. **1958** P. SCOTT *Mark of Warrior* I. 52 We *are* out of date. We get the arse-end of any new equipment that's going. **1599** A. M. *Gabelhouer's Bk. Physic* 139/2 For the comminge out of the Arsegutte. **1668** R. LESTRANGE *Vis. Quevedo* (1708) 55 The very Arse-Gut, the Drain and Sink of Monarchies. *a* **1400** in Wright *Voc.* 183 Arce-hoole, *podex*. **1930** E. POUND *XXX Cantos* xiv. 61 Faces smeared on their rumps... Addressing crowds through their arse-holes. **1948** *Landfall* II. 178 It's absolute comfort from arse-hole to breakfast-table. **1950** DYLAN THOMAS *Let.* 17 July (1966) 350 This arsehole of the universe.. this.. fond sad Wales. **1912** D. H. LAWRENCE in F. Lawrence *Memoirs* (1961) 189 [Written in D. H. L.'s hand over a flattering letter] Arse-licking. **1958** P. SCOTT *Mark of Warrior* I. 30, I can't go up and say Were you my brother's C.O.?.. it'd look like arse-licking. **1960** F. RAPHAEL *Limits of Love* I. ix. 116 The new fighting Yid still squeals like the old arse-licking kind. **1540** RAYNALD *Byrth Man.* (1564) 54 When it [the fœtus] proceedeth.. sidelong, arselong, or backlong. **1611** COTGR., *Culant*, giuing an arse-posse vnto. **1660** HOWELL, *Arsepush*. **1382** WYCLIF *1 Sam.* v. 9 The arsroppis of hem goynge out stonken. *c* **1450** in Wright *Voc.* 186/2 *Cirbus*, hars-tharme. *c* **1000** ÆLFRIC *ibid.* 44/2 *Anus* vel *verpus*, ears þerl. **1393** LANGL. *P. Pl.* C. VII. 306 An hore of hure ers-wynninge · may hardiloker tythe. **1440** *Promp. Parv.*, Arswyspe, *Maniperium*, *anitergium*.

arse, *v.* [f. sb.] (Cf. *to elbow*.) ***to arse about***, ***around***, to 'mess around', fool about. (Cf. ASS *v.* 2.) *slang.*

1664 COTTON *Scarron.* 9 Arsing about. **1922** JOYCE *Ulysses* 307 Arsing around from one pub to another. **1944** 'N. SHUTE' *Pastoral* ii. 22 Up in London you arse around and go to the local. **1947** N. STREATFEILD *Grass in Piccadilly* 148 Mrs. Dill would understand. She would never arse about yattering all over the place. **1960** A. WESKER *I'm Talking about Jerusalem* 1, Don't arse around Ronnie, the men want their tea.

Arsechieles tables, i.e. *Arzachel's*: see ALMANAC, *note* 1.

c **1391** CHAUCER *Astrol.* II. §45.

arsed, *ppl. a.* Now *slang* (chiefly *coarse*). Also (-)assed. [f. ARSE *sb.* + -ED².] Having an arse. (Chiefly in *comb.*) Usu. as a terminal element: ***half-arsed***, ***smart-arsed***, etc. (see first word).

c **1000** ÆLFRIC *Gloss.* in Wright 45/2 *Tergosus*, earsode. **1562** J. HEYWOOD *Prov. & Epigr.* (1867) 16 To beg a breeche of a bare arst man. **1611** COTGR., *Cul-pelé*, bauld-arst. **1770** P. LUCKOMBE *Conc. Hist. Printing* 495 *Bottle-arsed*.., when letter is wider at the bottom than the top. **1938** *Amer. Speech* XIII. 270 The sides of hand-cast letters were frequently not parallel, and consequently they drove in or out of a form. Such letters were called bottle arsed letters. **1956** B. HOLIDAY *Lady sings Blues* (1973) vii. 65 All alone in a room upstairs,.. cuddling a big-assed bottle of champagne. **1963** R. I MCDAVID *Mencken's Amer. Lang* 756 The Navy name for a lady marine, *i.e.*, Broad-assed marine.

ˈarsedine. Also **arsowde, assidue, asidew, orsedew, orsidue, orsade, orsady, assady, -dyn, -den, orsden, arsadine.** [Etymology, and correct form unknown: see also ORSIDUE.] A gold-coloured alloy of copper and zinc, rolled into very thin leaf, and used to ornament toys, etc.; 'Dutch gold,' 'Mannheim gold.'

1472-8 *Accts.* in T. Sharp's *Dissertation* 193 For assady and redde wax.. Item for assadyn, silver papur and gold papur.. Item for assaden for the harnes. **1481-90** *Howard Househ. Bks.* (1844) 339 For ij. lb. of arsowde.. iiijs. **1550-1600** *Customs Duties* Add. MS. B.M. 25097 Orsedew, the dosen pounds xiis. iiijd. **1596** NASHE *Saffron Walden* 49 As day-light [is] beyond candle-light, or tinsell or leafe-gold aboue arsedine. **1599** —— *Lent. Stuffe* in *Harl. Misc.* VI. 172 A London vintner's signe.. fringed with theaming arsadine. **1614** B. JONSON *Barth. Fair* II. ii, Puft vp with the pride of your.. Arsedine. **1730** *Gent's Hist. York* Advt. in Hone *Every-d. Bk.* 26 Sept. 632 Assidue or horse-gold. **1816** *Ibid.*, Importer of bronze powder, Dutch metal, and orsedew. **1826** *Ibid.* 631 Garlands.. rustling with asidew.

†**ˈarsefoot.** *Ornith. Obs.* [f. ARSE *sb.* + FOOT; on account of its feet being placed so far back.] A bird; identified by Willoughby with the Great and Little Dabchick, species of the Grebe; by Goldsmith with the Penguin.

1598 FLORIO, *Giuero*.. a bird called a diuer, a didapper, or arsefoote. **1678** RAY *Willughby's Ornith.* 339 The Greater Loon or Arsfoot, *Colymbus major. Ibid.* 340 The Didapper, or Dipper, or Dobchick, or small Doucker, Loon, or Arsfoot: *Colymbus sive Podicipes minor.* **1774** GOLDSMITH *Nat. Hist.* (1862) II. VII. vii. 217 Our sailors.. give these birds [penguins] the very homely, but expressive, name of arse-feet.

†**ˈarseling(s**, *adv. Obs.* or *dial.* [f. ARSE *sb.* + -LING(s; cf. *backling(s*.] Backwards.

c **1000** *Ags. Ps.* xxxiv. 5 Syn hi ȝecyrde on earsling. **1768** ROSS *Helenore* 43 (JAM.) Then Lindy to stand up began to try; But—he fell arselins back.

arsemetrick, obs. form of ARITHMETIC.

arsen- (ˈɑːsən), short for ARSENIC, used

1. in *Comb.*: esp. in names of combinations of arsenic with organic radicals, as in *Arsendimethyl* (= cacodyl, $As_2 (CH_3)_4$).

2. in derivatives, in which it varies with *arseni-* (ɑːˈsiːnɪ); as **ˈarsenate** or **arˈseniate** [see -ATE⁴], a salt of arsenic acid, e.g. *sodium arsenate*, *arseniate of nickel* or nickel bloom. **ˈarsenetted** *ppl. a.*, combined chemically with arsenic, arseniuretted. **arˈseniate** *a. rare*, mixed or treated with arsenic. **arˈseniated** *ppl. a.* = arseniate, and (*obs.*) arsenetted. **ˈarsenide** [see -IDE], a primary combination of arsenic with another element, (as hydrogen, a metal,) or an organic radical. **ˈarsenite**, *Chem.* [see -ITE], a salt of arsenious acid, as *arsenite of silver*, *of lead*, etc.; *Min.* synonym of ARSENOLITE.

1800 HENRY *Epit. Chem.* (1808) 255 With alkalies, earths, and oxides, it constitutes a class of salts called *arsenates. **1863** WATTS *Dict. Chem.* I. 379 The *arsenates of the alkali metals are soluble in water. **1875** URE *Dict. Arts* I. 215 An acid *arsenate of soda is now used in calico-printing. **1796** HATCHETT in *Phil. Trans.* LXXXVI. 317 If *arseniate of ammoniac is distilled, gas is produced. **1876** HARLEY *Mat. Med.* 214 *Arseniate of Iron. **1863** WATTS *Dict. Chem.* I. 372 *Arsenetted hydrogen is a colourless gas.. Small animals are instantly killed by it. **1851-9** OWEN in *Adm. Man. Sc. Enq.* 377 The inside.. brushed with *arseniate soap [and] stuffed with cotton. **1808** SIR H. DAVY in *Phil. Trans.* XCVIII. 367 Potassium separates arsenic from *arseniated hydrogene. **1846** *Blackw. Mag.* LX. 65 Volley of Russian candles, and the flames of an *arseniated Hougomont. **1863** WATTS *Dict. Chem.* (1872) I. 370 Many metallic *arsenides occur in natural minerals, e.g. copper-nickel Ni_2As_2. *Ibid.* 397 *Arsenides of ethyl. **1876** HARLEY *Mat. Med.* 287 Arsenic is most extensively diffused in combination with other metals, as in the *arsenides of iron, nickel, copper, cobalt. **1800** HENRY *Epit. Chem.* (1808) 254 Oxide of arsenic.. has therefore been called arsenous acid, and its compounds *arsenites. **1865** *Pall Mall G.* 19 Sept. 11/1 Sweetmeats.. rendered terrible with *arsenite of copper. **187.** THORPE *Inorg. Chem.* I. 392 Copper *arsenite, or Scheele's Green is employed as a pigment. A copper aceto- *arsenite, known as Schweinfurth, or imperial green, is also largely used. *Ibid.* 391 Arsenious oxide.. constitutes the mineral known as *arsenite. [See also ARSENOLITE.]

arsenal (ˈɑːsɪnəl). Forms: 6 **archy-, archinale,** 6-7 **ars-, arzenale,** 6-7 **arcenal,** 7 **-all, -el, arci-, arsi-, arsenall,** 6- **arsenal.** [a. It. *arze- arsenale*, Sp. Pg. F. *arsenal*, earlier forms of which are It. *arzenà* (Dante), *arzanà* (still in use), 16-17th c. F. *arsena*, *arsenac* (see Littré), all in the current sense; cf. It. and Sp. *darsena*, Sicilian *tirzanà* (Diez), Pg. *taracena*, *tercena*, F. *darse*, *darsine*, 'a dock'; also Sp. *atarazána*, *atarazanál*, 'arsenal, factory, wine-cellar, etc.' The original is the Arab. *dār aççināʕah*, workshop, factory (i.e. *dār* house, place of, *al* the, *çināʕah*, art, mechanical industry, f. *çanaʕa* to make, fabricate), which is directly represented by the Romance *darsena*, *taracena*; *atarazana* is prob. a Sp. Arab. form with article *al-*, *ad-* prefixed; *arsena* is either (as Diez thinks) from *darsena*, with *d* dropped (perh. by assoc. with *de*, *d'*, preposition, cf. *dante*, ANTE *sb.*¹), or (as Defrémery and others hold) from *aç-çināʕah* alone. See Dozy, and Devic in Littré's *Supp.* The final *-ale*, *-al* was added in It. or Sp. The wider sense of the Arabic is retained in Sp.; the other languages have narrowed it to *dock* and *armoury*. The earliest forms in Eng. were from It., but the existing one is that common to Fr., Sp. and Pg.]

1. A dock possessing naval stores, materials, and all appliances for the reception, construction, and repair of ships; a dockyard. *Obs.* exc. *Hist.*

1506 GUYLFORDE *Pilgr.* (1851) 7 At the Archynale there be closed within.. an .C. galyes. **1549** THOMAS *Hist. Italy* (1561) 74 b, The Arsenale [at Venice] in myne eye excedeth all the rest: For there they haue well neere two hundred galeys. **1580** NORTH *Plutarch* (1676) 372 Set up an arsenal or store-house to build gallies in. **1601** HOLLAND *Pliny* I. 175 Making the Arsenall at Athens, able to receiue 1000 ships. **1611** CORYAT *Crudities* 216, I was at the Arsenall which is so called *quasi ars naualis*, because there is exercised the Art of making tackling and all other necessary things for shipping. **1693** URQUHART *Rabelais* III. lii, Carricks, Ships.. and other vessels of his Thalassian arsenal. **1838** ARNOLD *Hist. Rome* (1846) I. xxi. 461 Building ships, and arsenals to receive and fit them out properly.

2. A public establishment for the manufacture and storage, or for the storage alone, of weapons and ammunition of all kinds, for the military and naval forces of the country.

1579 FENTON *Guicciard.* VIII. (1599) 317 A fire kindled.. in their storre house called the Arzenale.. where was their saltpeter. **1625** BACON *Ess.* (Arb.) 473 Stored Arcenalls and Armouries. **1660** HOWELL *Let. Ital. Prov.* in *Dict.*, The whole Arsenal of Venice is not able to arm a Coward. **1676** BULLOKAR, *Arcenel*, an Armoury, Storehouse of Armour or Artillery. **1727** CHAMBERS *Cycl.* s.v., The Arsenal at Paris is that where the cannon or great guns are cast. **1781** GIBBON *Decl. & F.* II. 53 Offensive weapons of all sorts, and military engines, which were deposited in the arsenals. **1811** D. LYSONS *Environs Lond.* I. 594 The gun-wharf at Woolwich .. is now called the Arsenal, or Royal Arsenal. This Arsenal is the grand depôt of the ordnance belonging to the navy. **1876** J. THORNE *Environs Lond.* II. 742/1 The Royal Arsenal [Woolwich] stretches for a mile along the Thames E. of the Dockyard. It is the only arsenal in the kingdom; the smaller establishments at the other dockyards are called gun-wharfs, and receive their supplies from Woolwich.

b. *fig.*

1598 SYLVESTER *Du Bartas* I. (1633) 24 Of changefull chances common Arcenal. **1604** T. WRIGHT *Passions Mind* v. §4. 185 Their arcinall or storehouse of persuasiue prouission. **1643** FEATLY *Pref. Newman's Concord.* 1 Scripture is.. the spirituall arsenall of munition. **1857** H. REED *Lect. Brit. Poets* ix. 300 Weapons from the arsenal of poetic satire.

arsenate, -etted, -iate, etc.: see ARSEN-.

arsenic (ˈɑːsnɪk), *sb.*¹ Forms: 4-5 **arsnek, arsenyk, arcenyk, arsynek,** 6 **arsenik, arsnecke,** 6-8 **arsenick(e,** 7 **arsnic, -nike,** 7-8 **arsnick,** 7- **arsenic**; also in Lat. form. [a. OF. *arsenic* (14th c. in Littré), ad. L. *arsenicum* (*arrenicum*), a. Gr. ἀρσενικόν (ἀρρενικόν) 'yellow orpiment,' subst. use of ἀρρενικός adj. 'masculine, male.']

1. Name of one of the chemical elements, and of some of its compounds, which are violent poisons.

†**a.** *orig.* A bright yellow mineral (hence also distinguished as ***yellow arsenic***), found native, and as a product of art, properly called ORPIMENT (*auri pigmentum* of the Romans, ἀρσενικόν of the Greeks), which is chemically the trisulphide of arsenic (As_2S_3), and is used as a pigment under the name of King's Yellow.

c **1386** CHAUCER *Chan. Yem. Prol. & T.* 245 Arsnek [*v.r.* arsenyk(e, arcenyk, arsynek], sal armoniak, and brimstoon. **1398** TREVISA *Barth. De P.R.* XIX. xxx. (1495) 878 Arsenicum hyghte Auripigmentum for the colour of golde and is gaderyd in Pontus. **1567** MAPLET *Gr. Forest* 10 The stone Arsenick.. which also they call the golden earth. **1601** HOLLAND *Pliny* II. 521 As for Arsenicke.. that which is best of this kind, resembleth burnished gold in colour. **1634** R. H. *Salerne Regim.* 158 Auripigmentum which some Arsenicke call.

†**b.** *Formerly*, sometimes extended to the *disulphide* (As_2S_2), a native mineral and product of art, commonly known as REALGAR, or *ruby sulphur*, formerly also as *red orpiment*, and ***red arsenic*** (the σανδαράκη, *sandaraca* of the Greeks and Romans).

1591 PERCIVALL *Sp. Dict.*, *Rejalgar*, poison, arsenicke, or ratsebane. **1599** THYNNE *Animadv.* 36 This Resalgar is that whiche by some is called Ratisbane, a kynde of poysone named Arsenicke. **1751** CHAMBERS *Cycl.* s.v., There are divers kinds of Arsenic. *Orpiment* is called *native* or *yellow* arsenic.. *Red arsenick* is a preparation of the white or crystalline Arsenic.

c. in pop. use: A white mineral substance, native (as ARSENOLITE) and manufactured, originally distinguished as ***white arsenic***, which is chemically the trioxide of arsenic (As_2O_3). ***flowers of arsenic***: the same substance sublimed.

1605 TIMME *Quersit.* I. vii. 26 White sublimate and arsnic .. foster and hide most burning and deadly fire. **1672** DAVENANT *Wits* (1673) 193 Arsnick my Girl to strengthen thy Aunts Broth. **1675** *News fr. Ring-Cross* 3 Another time putting white Arsenick into her broth. **1727-51** CHAMBERS *Cycl.* s.v., Arsenic is made by sublimation from cobalt. **1788-9** HOWARD *Encycl.* s.v., White arsenic, or arsenic strictly so called.. is a most violent poison to all animals. **1813** SIR H. DAVY *Agric. Chem.* ii. (1814) 49 Arsenic may be procured by heating the powder of common white arsenic of the shops strongly in a Florence flask with oil. **1863** WATTS *Dict. Chem.* I. 374 The Tyrolese peasants are said to swallow arsenic in considerable quantities. **1877** ROSCOE, etc. *Chem.* (1881) I. 516 White arsenic or the trioxide is first distinctly spoken of by Geber, who states that he obtained it by roasting the sulphide of arsenic.

d. *Chem.* and *Min.* The element: a very brittle semi-metallic substance, of steel-grey lustrous colour, crystallizing in rhombohedrons, and volatilizing without fusion, with an odour of garlic. It forms a link between the metals, and non-metallic bodies: see ANTIMONY. Symbol As.

native arsenic: the above element occurring as a mineral. ***antimonial a.***: a native alloy of arsenic with antimony.

1812 SIR H. DAVY *Chem. Philos.* 453 A metal sublimes, and condenses in the upper part of the vessel, which is arsenic. **1837–68** DANA *Min.* 18 Native arsenic commonly occurs in veins in crystalline rocks and the older schists. **1863** WATTS *Dict. Chem.* I. 360 Native arsenic forms botryoidal, kidney-shaped, spherical and conchoidal masses. **1869** ROSCOE *Elem. Chem.* 163 Arsenic closely resembles phosphorus in its chemical properties. **1879** *Academy* 27 Dec. 467 Arsenic is definitely regarded as a non-metal.

e. *fig.* Poison.

1598 SYLVESTER *Du Bartas* 69 Neither in Golden Platters doth he lick For sweet ambrosia deadly arsenick. *c* **1630** DRUMM. OF HAWTH. *Wks.* 1711, 33 Since hell disgorg'd her baneful arsenick.

2. *attrib.* = Of arsenic, arsenical; *esp.* in *Chem.* in systematic names of compounds, as ***arsenic trihydride*** = trihydride of arsenic, ***pentoxide, disulphide***. **arsenic bloom**, arsenic trioxide in native crystals, arising from the oxidation of elementary arsenic. **arsenic glass**, the same in a vitreous mass obtained from the powder by re-sublimation.

1656 EVELYN *Mem.* (1857) I. 333 Deprived of their sulphur and arsenic malignity. **1799** G. SMITH *Laboratory* I. 218 Add eight or ten ounces of arsenic glass. **1860** ROSCOE (*title*) On the alleged practice of Arsenic eating in Styria. **1881** —— *Chem.* I. 528 The reasons which the arsenic-eaters give for the practice. *Ibid.*, An antidote against arsenic poisoning.

‖ **'arsenic**, *sb.*[2] *Herb. Obs.* Arsesmart.

1552 HULOET, Arsenicke herbe, *Artonicum.* **1570** LEVINS *Manip.*, Arnsnick, herb, *artonicum.* **1585** *Nomenclator* 126 Water-pepper or arsenicke: some call it kill-ridge or culerage.

arsenic (ɑːˈsɛnɪk), *a. Chem.* [f. ARSENIC *sb.*[1], the ending being identified with -IC in *nitric, phosphoric.*] Of or belonging to arsenic; in *Chem.* applied to compounds in which arsenic combines as a pentad. ***arsenic anhydride*** = arsenic pentoxide.

1801 CHENEVIX in *Phil. Trans.* XCI. 219 It was found to contain arsenic acid. **1876** HARLEY *Mat. Med.* 295 Arsenic Anhydride is the highest state of oxydation of the metal. **1881** ROSCOE &c., *Chem.* I. 530 The salts of arsenic acid, or the arsenates, are isomorphous with the phosphates.

'arsenic, *v. rare.* [f. the sb.; cf. *to physic.*] To mix or dose with arsenic; to arsenicate.

1844 TUPPER *Heart* iv. 34 How is it no housekeeper has arsenic[k]ed my soup?

arsenic- (ɑːˈsɛnɪk-), in derivation; as in **arˈsenicane** [see -ANE 2 a], Davy's systematic name for arsenious chloride. **arˈsenicate** *v.*, to mix or treat with arsenic. **arˈsenicated** *ppl. a.*, mixed or treated with arsenic; combined chemically with arsenic, arsenetted. **arˈsenicism**, disease produced by arsenic, also called *arseˈniasis*; arsenic-poisoning. **arˈsenicite**, *Min.*, a synonym of PHARMACOLITE. **arˈsenicized** *ppl. a.*, treated or impregnated with arsenic. **arsenicophagy** (-ˈkɒfədʒɪ), *Med.*, the eating of arsenic, as practised by the peasants of Styria and the Tyrol (*Syd. Soc. Lex.* 1880).

1812 SIR H. DAVY *Chem. Philos.* 455 The only compound of chlorine and arsenic known..which may be called *arsenicane. **1794** G. ADAMS *Nat. & Exp. Phil.* I. xi. 450 *Arsenicated zinc. **1823** FARADAY *Exp. Res.* (1859) 130 The arsenicated hydrogen gas retains its aeriform state. **1864** *Athenæum* No. 1928, 465/1 Arsenicated sweetmeats. **1883** *Daily News* 31 July 5/3 Wholesale poisoning by means of arsenicated wheat. **1875** H. WOOD *Therap.* (1879) 377 Characteristic phenomena of chronic *arsenicism. **1875** *Civ. Serv. Rev.* 3 July 425/2 No insect or worm will attack *arsenicized paper.

arsenical (ɑːˈsɛnɪkəl), *a.* and *sb.* [f. L. *arsenicum* + -AL[1].] **A.** *adj.* Of, of the nature of, or containing arsenic; pertaining to or effected by arsenic.

In many names of minerals into which arsenic enters, as *arsenical iron, nickel, pyrites.*

1605 TIMME *Quersit.* I. xiii. 60 They..worke venemous and mortal effects, and that by reason of the arsenical mercury. **1671** in *Phil. Trans.* VI. 2210 The Nature and Causes of the Plague..deducing the Pestilential venom from the Air infected and corrupted chiefly by Arsenical Exhalations. **1791** HAMILTON *Berthollet's Dyeing* I. I. I. v. 80 Phosphoric and arsenical acids. **1812** SIR H. DAVY *Chem. Philos.* 412 The ore known by the name of arsenical cobalt. **1859** [see ARSENIURET]. **1863** W. BALDWIN *African Hunting* 410 Having no arsenical soap, [I] was unable to preserve the skin. **1881** ROSCOE, &c., *Chem.* I. 541 The..employment of arsenical wall-papers..is much to be deprecated, still more is the employment of the insoluble arsenical green for colouring light cotton fabrics.

B. *sb.* A substance containing arsenic.

1909 in *Cent. Dict.* Suppl. **1943** [see ATOXYL]. **1949** H. W. FLOREY et al. *Antibiotics* II. xxxvi. 1199 It seems clear that doses of arsenicals and penicillin..were effective in experimental animals when combined. **1955** *Sci. News Let.* 16 July 40/2 Many of the itch remedies used today..such as ..arsenicals, may depend for their results on a partial blocking of the..itch enzymes.

arsenide, -ite: see ARSEN-.

arsenio- (ɑːˈsiːnɪəʊ), comb. form of next, as in **arˈsenio-ˈsulphide, -ˈsulphuret**, *Chem.*, a compound of arsenious sulphide with a metallic sulphide; an arseno-sulphide. **arˈsenio-ˈsiderite**, *Min.* [σίδηρος iron], a fibrous mineral of yellowish-brown and somewhat golden colour, containing arsenic acid, sesquioxide of iron, and lime (Dana).

arsenious (ɑːˈsiːnɪəs), *a. Chem.* [f. ARSEN(IC) + -IOUS.] Of the nature of, or containing, arsenic. In *Chem.* applied to those compounds in which arsenic combines as a triad, as ***arsenious oxide*** or (less correctly) ***acid***, common white arsenic.

1818 ACCUM *Chem. Tests* 145 Two or three grains of arsenious acid. **1873** FOWNES *Chem.* 481 Arsenious iodide. **1879** G. GLADSTONE in *Cassell's Techn. Educ.* IV. 272/1 Arsenious acid, the ordinary form in which arsenic is employed.

arseniuret (ɑːˈsɛnjʊərɪt). *Chem.* [See -URET; cf. *sulphuret.*] A primary combination of arsenic with another element; for which, in recent chemical nomenclature, ARSENIDE is generally used. Hence **arˈseniuretted** *a.*, combined with arsenic, chiefly in ***arseniuretted hydrogen*** (= arsenic trihydride, AsH_3), for which Watts uses ARSENETTED (cf. *sulphur-etted*).

1834 E. TURNER *Elem. Chem.* (ed. 5) 569 The products are water and arseniuret of copper. **1812** SIR H. DAVY *Chem. Philos.* 456 Arseniuretted hydrogene gas..has an extremely fetid smell. **1854** SCOFFERN in *Orr's Circ. Sc.* Chem. 478 Gaseous arseniuret of hydrogen—or *arseniuretted* hydrogen. **1859** CARPENTER *Anim. Phys.* vi. (1872) 292 Arsenical poisoning..from the inhalation of a small quantity of arseniuretted hydrogen.

arseno- (ˈɑːsənəʊ), combining form of ARSENIC, or ARSENOUS, in compounds and derivatives; as

a. in *Chem.* **arseno-sulphide**, a combination of arsenous or arsenious sulphide with a metallic sulphide; ***arseno-benzene***, etc.

b. in *Min.* **ˌarsenoˈcrocite**, synonym of ARSENIOSIDERITE. **arˈsenolite** [Gr. λίθος stone: see -LITE], Dana's name for white arsenic as a native mineral. †**arseˈnomelan**, obs. synonym of Sartorite and Dufrenoysite, two native arsenio-sulphides of lead. **ˌarsenoˈpyrite** [Gr. πυρίτης firestone: see PYRITE], native arsenio-sulphide of iron, a mineral of metallic lustre, and silvery-gray colour, called also Mispickel (Dana). In *Brit. Mus. Catal.*, a synonym of Dufrenoysite.

1881 RAYMOND *Mining Gloss.*, *Arsenic ores*: mispickel (arsenopyrite, arsenical pyrites, arseno-sulphide of iron). **1854** DANA *Min.* (1880) 184 As the name *arsenite* is used in chemistry for compounds of arsenous acid, the author in 1854 changed it to *arsenolite.* **1875** URE *Dict. Arts* s.v., White Arsenic or Arsenious Acid (*Arsenolite*) occurs either in minute radiating capillary crystals and crusts investing other substances, or in a stalactitic or botryoidal form.

arsenous (ˈɑːsənəs), *a. Chem.* and *Min.* [f. ARSEN- + -OUS.] A synonym of ARSENIOUS.

1800 HENRY *Epit. Chem.* (1808) 376, I use the term *arsenic*, instead of the more proper *arsenous acid*..because.. more generally understood. **1868** DANA *Min.* 184 Arsenous acid.

arsesmart (ˈɑːsmɑːt). *Bot.* Forms: 6 **arssmart, -mert, arsse-smart, arsmert,** 7 **asmart,** 6–9 **arsmart, arsesmart.** [See quot. 1617.] A name of the plant Water-pepper (*Polygonum Hydropiper*); also applied by some to the allied species *P. Persicaria*, called by Gerard 'Dead Arsemart.'

1551 TURNER *Herbal* 133 Arssmert groweth..in watery places. **1572** MASCALL *Govt. Cattle* (1627) 190 If your saddle doe chafe your horse, take an hearbe called Arsmart, in Latine *Parcicaria*, stampe it, and lay it to. **1578** LYTE *Dodoens* 632 Arsesmart..is lyke to water Pepper..but it is neither hoat nor sharpe. **1617** MINSHEU *Ductor* 544 *Arsmart* ..because if it touch the taile or other bare skinne, it maketh it smart, as often it doth, being laid into the bed greene to kill fleas. **1639** T. DE GREY *Compl. Horsem.* 83 Take the leaves of Arsmart. **1747** WESLEY *Princ. Physic* (1765) 78 Drink..of Decoction of Arsesmart. **1784** TWAMLEY *Dairying* 113 Arsmart, or lakeweed, is a bitter plant. **1878** BRITTEN & HOLL. *Plant-n.*, *Arsesmart.*

†**arseward**, *adv.* and *a. Obs.* or *dial.* Also 5–6 **ars-**. [f. ARSE *sb.* + -WARD.]

A. *adv.* Backward, in a contrary direction; *fig.* contrariwise; perversely.

1401 *Pol. Poems* II. 64 If ȝe taken as ȝe usen arseworde this gospel. **1553** BALE *Gardener's Vera Obed.* Pref. H ij, Whence he can neuer escape except he com out arsewarde. **1565** GOLDING *Ovid's Met.* VII. (1593) 164 Cerberus..dragging arsward still. **1616** FLETCHER *Knt. Malta* IV. ii, Hang arse-ward. **1877** E. PEACOCK *Linc. Gloss.*, *Arserd*, backward. 'Go arserds, cousin Edward, go arserds.'

B. *adj.* Backward, contrary; perverse.

c **1500** *Almanak for 1386* (1812) 12 A crab es an arsword best. **1579** TOMSON *Calvin's Serm. Tim.* 127/1 How arseward a thing it is for euerie man to be giuen to his owne profite. **1686** G. STUART *Joco-Ser. Disc.* 30 Sae take some pity on your love And do not still so arseward prove.

†**'arsewardly**, *adv. Obs.* [See -LY[2].] = prec.

1530 PALSGR. 829/2 All arsewardly, all frowardly, *tout a rebours.* **1579** TOMSON *Calvin's Serm. Tim.* 8/2 Behold how arswardly we goe alwayes when we pray to God.

‖ **arsheen** (ɑːˈʃiːn). Also 8–9 **arshine, archine.** [Russ.] A measure of length used in Russia and Turkey.

1734 *Treaty* in Magens *Insurances* II. 592 English Cloth.. two Copyks in Rixdollars for each Archine. **1783** MARTYN *Geog. Mag.* II. 40 The arshine or Russian ell, equal to twenty-eight and one-tenth inches English. **1819** J. Q. ADAMS in C. Davies *Metric Syst.* (1871) III. 185 Suwarrow ..said to his troops, 'A soldier's step is an arsheen.' **1828** WEBSTER, *Arshine.* **1881** *Nature* XXV. 88 The new system ..of weights and measures..in Turkey..The archine..is exactly equal to the French metre.

arsine[1] (ˈɑːsaɪn, now usu. ɑːˈsiːn). *Chem.* [f. ARS(ENIC) + -INE, here used to form a term analogous to *am-ine.*] A compound having the structure of ammonia or an amine, with arsenic instead of nitrogen; i.e. *arseniuretted hydrogen* (AsH_3), and any derivative bearing the same relation to it that the amines do to ammonia (NH_3); as ***trimethyl arsine*** $(CH_3)_3As$. Hence **arsinic** (ɑːˈsɪnɪk), *a.*, as in *dimethylarsinic acid.*

1876 *Encycl. Brit.* V. 541/1 Arsine and stibine..are formed whenever hydrogen is evolved in presence of an arsenic or antimony compound. **1910** *Ibid.* II. 652/1 Arsenic *trihydride* (arsine or arseniuretted hydrogen), AsH_3, is formed by decomposing zinc arsenide with dilute sulphuric acid. *Ibid.*, The arsines and arsine chlorides are liquids of overpowering smell, and..exert an extremely irritating action on the mucous membrane. **1922** F. W. ASTON *Isotopes* vi. 77 The gases phosphine PH_3 and arsine AsH_3 were used in the experiments on these elements.

arsine[2] (ɑːˈsiːn), var. ARSHEEN.

1932 B. KINCEAD tr. *M. Ilin's What Time is It?* 107 The meter counted out the versts, sagens, and arsines.

arsinoïtherium (ˌɑːsɪnəʊɪˈθɪərɪəm). *Palæont.* [mod.L., f. Gr. Ἀρσινόη, an ancient Egyptian city of the Fayum, so named, after his second wife Arsinoë II, by Ptolemy II Philadelphus (308–246 B.C.), who developed it as the metropolis of that region + θηρίον, dim. of θήρ wild beast: cf. THERIO-.] An animal of an extinct genus of mammals, as large as the rhinoceros, with two large and two small horns.

1902 H. J. L. BEADNELL *Prel. Note Arsinoitherium Zitteli* 3 Discovery of Eocene mammalian and reptilian remains made last year by the Geological Survey of Egypt... The most important of these is a large, heavily built, ungulate, about the size of a rhinoceros, and for which the writer proposes the generic name *Arsinoitherium*, from Queen Arsinoe, after whom the Fayum was called in Ptolemic times. **1904** *Daily Chron.* 4 Jan. 9/1 The four-horned arsinöitherium. **1930** *Discovery* Nov. 386/2 The arsinöitherium, a huge beast the size of a rhinoceros, was among the most fantastic mammals which have ever existed.

‖ **arsis** (ˈɑːsɪs). [L., a. Gr. ἄρσις lifting, raising, f. αἴρειν to lift. There has been much dispute as to the exact meaning of this word. In Greek, according to Liddell and Scott, it was 'the raising of the foot in beating time'; but it is uncertain whether this concurred with the syllables which had greatest or least force; and 'perhaps the original meaning was the raising of the voice to a higher pitch' (A. J. Ellis). Latin writers explain it as the raising of the voice (to greater force) on the first syllable of a metrical foot.]

1. (The following quots. illustrate the various opinions of writers.)

1398 TREVISA *Barth. De P.R.* XIX. cxxxi. (1495) 941 Arsis is rerynge of voys and is the begynnyng of songe. Thesis is settynge and is the ende. **1749** *Numbers in Poet. Comp.* 22 The following Iambicks move *per Arsin et Thesin*, and are measured by the Hand first up and then down, because they begin with a short Quantity.

ar. th. ar. th. ar. th. ar. th.
When all | thy Mer|cies, O | my God.

1795 MASON *Ch. Mus.* iv. 258 What the writers on Verbal Pronunciation mean by acute and grave sounds, or what they technically term Arsis and Thesis. **1819** *Pantolog.* s.v., Thesis implies the emphatic or accentuated part of the bar; and arsis the weak, or unaccented part. **1876** STAINER & BARRETT *Dict. Mus. Terms* s.v., Forasmuch as the confusion among musicians in using these terms [*arsis, thesis, ictus*] has resulted from the disagreement of scholars as to their proper application, it is much to be hoped that they will be allowed to sink into disuse.

2. In modern acceptation: The strong syllable in English metre (or classical metre as read by Englishmen), the strong note in barred music; thus identical with the modern meaning of L. *ictus.* (A.J.E.)

1834 *Penny Cycl.* II. 406/2 The dactylic arsis, or the arsis followed by two depressions. **1876** KENNEDY *Pub. Sch. Lat. Gram.* §259 In Dactylic and Trochaic verse the arsis is on the first part of each foot; *lítora, árma.* In Anapæstic and Iambic on the last: *patulǽ, canó.*

‖**3.** In Mus. ***per arsin***: By descent of voice or sound from higher to lower pitch. ? *Obs.*

1706 in PHILLIPS. **1751** CHAMBERS *Cycl.* s.v., Fugha per arsin et thesin. **1879** OUSELEY in Grove *Dict. Mus.* I. 95/1 When applied to the voice, a subject, counterpart, or fugue, is said to be 'per thesin,' when the notes ascend from grave to acute; 'per arsin' when they descend from acute to grave. A fugue 'per arsin et thesin' is the same thing as a fugue 'by inversion.'

arsk(e, obs. f. ASK *sb.* water-newt; and of HARSH.

arsmart, variant spelling of ARSESMART.

arsmetik, -tric, -trik, obs. ff. ARITHMETIC.

†**'arsmetry.** *Obs.* A corruption of *arsmetrick* ARITHMETIC, by form-assoc. with *geometry*.

1594 GREENE *Look. Glass* (1861) 132 Have I taught you arsmetry.

†**'arson**[1]. *Obs.* Forms: 4–5 arsoun, 5 -oune, -own, -un, 6–7 arzon, 5–7 arson. [a. OF. *arçun, arzon* (also *archon*), cogn. with Sp. *arzon*, It. *arcione*:—late L. *arciōn-em*, f. *arcus* bow. Cf. ARCHON *sb.*[1]]

1. A saddle-bow; a name given to two curved pieces of wood or metal, one of which was fixed to the front of the saddle, and another behind, to give the rider greater security in his seat.

c **1325** *Cœur de L.* 5539 Both hys arsouns weren off yren. *a* **1400** *Octouian* 1040 Two bole-axys.. In hys former arsun were y-honge. *c* **1450** LONELICH *Grail* xiv. 293 His body he toclaf.. Evene to his sadelis arsown. **1557** *K. Arthur* (Copland) VI. vii, The arson of his sadel brake, and so he flewe ouer his hors tayle. **1598** STOW *Surv.* (ed. Strype 1754) II. v. xiv. 318/1 All his Arzons, i.e. Saddle bows that he makes. **1623** MABBE *Aleman's Guzman d'Alf.* 68 A Petronell hanging at the arson of his saddle.

2. Occas. used for: A saddle.

c **1300** *K. Alis.* 4251 And leop himseolf in the arsoun. *c* **1460** *Lybeaus Disc.* 1613 Unnethe that he myghte sytte Upryght yn hys arsoun.

arson[2] ('ɑːsən). [a. OF. *arson, -oun, -un*:—late L. *arsiōn-em*, n. of action f. *ars-* ppl. stem of *ardēre* to burn. First used as Eng. by Hale.] The act of wilfully and maliciously setting fire to another man's house, ship, forest, or similar property; or to one's own, when insured, with intent to defraud the insurers.

[**1275** 1 *Stat. Westm.* (3 *Edw. I*) xv, Ceux qui sont pris pur arsoun feloniousement fait. *Transl.* 1618: Such as be taken for house burning feloniously done. **1583** STAUNDFORDE *Plees del Coron* 36 a, Arsons de measons felonisement faits est felony per le comen ley. **1640** COKE *3rd Pt. Inst.* xv, Indictment of burning. *a* **1680** HALE quotes the prec. as 'Indictment of arson.']

a **1680** HALE *Pleas of Crown* 566 The felony of arson or wilful burning of houses. **1768** BLACKSTONE *Comm.* IV. 220 Arson.. is the malicious and wilful burning of the house or outhouses of another man. **1831** CARLYLE *Sart. Res.* II. vi, Stampings, smitings, breakages of furniture, if not arson itself. **1856** MOTLEY *Dutch Rep.* (1861) I. 24 Murder, larceny, arson, rape.. were commuted for a definite price.

arsonist ('ɑːsənɪst). [f. prec. + -IST.] One who commits arson.

1864 R. BURTON *Dahome* II. 305 Those whose houses were first seen in flames were not proved to be the real arsonists. **1958** M. PUGH *Wilderness of Monkeys* xii. 149 A born arsonist should never try to be a fireman. **1962** *Economist* 3 Nov. 452/2 They attacked Unip as a party of thugs, arsonists and intimidators.

'arsonite. *rare*[−1]. [f. as prec. + -ITE.] = prec.

1859 G. MEREDITH *R. Feverel* I. xiii. 195 The man was.. a very extraordinary Arsonite.. It was a thing unknown in the annals of rick-burning.

arsonium (ɑː'səʊnɪəm). *Chem.* [f. ARS-ENIC + termination of AMMONIUM.] A name applied (chiefly in combination) to a univalent organic arsenic radical, analogous in composition to ammonium and phosphonium, as *tetramethyl-arsonium* $As(CH_3)_4$. Hence **arsonic** (ɑː'sɒnɪk), *a.*, pertaining to arsonium; applied to a group of acids, analogous to the phosphonic acids (Fownes).

arsoun(e, -un, variants of ARSON[1], *Obs.*

arsphenamine (ɑːs'fɛnəmaɪn, -iːn). [f. ARS(ENIC + PHEN- + AMINE.] A synthetic compound of arsenic, $C_{12}H_{12}O_2N_2As_22HCl$, used in the treatment of spirillic diseases, as syphilis and yaws. Cf. SALVARSAN.

1917 *Jrnl. Amer. Med. Assoc.* LXIX. 1989/2 The Federal Trade Commission has entered orders for licenses to three firms to manufacture and sell arsphenamine, the product heretofore known under the trade name of salvarsan, patent rights to which have been held by German subjects. **1935** *Lancet* 13 July 74/2 A sensitivity to the arsphenamines may develop gradually. **1944** *Ibid.* 11 Mar. 336/2 A similar process may be at work in bone-marrow dyscrasias following arsphenamine therapy. **1950** G. M. FINDLAY *Recent Adv. Chemotherapy* (ed. 3) I. i. 8 The first of these arseno-benzene derivatives, arsphenamine.. contained both amino- and hydroxy-groups in the benzene nucleus.

arst, obs. form of ERST *adv.*

†**'ars-table.** *Obs.* [App. a perversion of ASTROLABE, after L. *ars* art, and TABLE.] = ASTROLABE.

c **1300** *K. Alis.* 287 His ars-table he tok out sone. Theo cours he tok of sonne and mone. *Ibid.* 309 He lokud in his ars-table. *Ibid.* 336.

'arsy-'versy, *adv.* and *a.* *Obs.* in polite use. Also **arse-, arsie-versie, arsee-versee, arsy-varsy,** etc. [f. ARSE *sb.* + L. *versus*, pa. pple. of *vertĕre* to turn, assimilated to reduplicated compounds like *hurly-burly*, etc.]

A. *adv.* Backside foremost, upside-down, contrariwise; perversely, preposterously.

1539 TAVERNER *Erasm. Prov.* (1552) 62 Ye set the cart before the horse.. cleane contrarily and arsy versy as they say. **1577** HOLINSHED *Chron.* II. 26/2 The estate of that flourishing towne was turned arsie versie, topside the otherwaie. **1683** E. HOOKER *Pref. Pordage's Myst. Div.* 24 As if everi man went the wrong waie to work; All Arsi-varsi. **1721** BAILEY, *Arsy-versy*. **1855** *Whitby Gloss.*, *Arsy-varsy*, head over heels, vice-versa. **1881** DUFFIELD *Don Quixote* II. 360 You do not go enchanted, but only with your head turned arsie varsie. **1957** S. BECKETT *All that Fall* 29 Like Dante's damned, with their faces arsy-versy.

B. *adj.* Contrary, perverse, preposterous.

1659 BROME *Eng. Moor* III. ii, It is the Arsivarsiest Aufe that ever crept into the world. **1692** DUNTON *Postboy Robb'd* (1706) 173 Go to, let us not enter Rome, that is, not into a Discourse of Arsey-versey Love.

art (ɑːt), *sb.* 3-. Also 3–4 **ars, arz,** 4–7 **arte.** *Sc.* 6–7 **airt.** [a. OF. *art*:—L. *artem*, prob. f. *ar-* to fit. The OF. nom. sing. *ars*:—L. *ars*, and pl. *ars*: —L. *artes*, were also in early Eng. use, but without distinction of case.]

I. Skill; its display or application. Sing. *art* (abstractly); no plural.

1. *gen.* Skill in doing anything as the result of knowledge and practice.

c **1225** *St. Margarete* 194 Telle me of ȝoure art.. Whi werrie ȝe cristene men. **1340** HAMPOLE *Pr. Consc.* 7434 Couth never telle, bi clergy, ne arte.. þe thowsand parte. **1539** TAVERNER *Erasm. Prov.* (1552) 23 Arte or cunninge euerye countrey nourysheth. Yt is to saye, cunnynge men, & such as haue anye facultie or science, whether so euer they goo, shall lacke no lyuynge. **1611** BIBLE *Acts* xvii. 29 Golde, or siluer, or stone grauen by arte, and mans deuice. **1663** BUTLER *Hud.* I. i. 87 Else when with greatest art he spoke, You'd think he talk'd like other folk. **1718** POPE *Iliad* III. 285 The copious accents fall with easy art. **1849** MACAULAY *Hist. Eng.* II. 129 The potato, a root which can be cultivated with scarcely any art.

2. a. Human skill as an agent, human workmanship. Opposed to *nature*.

c **1386** CHAUCER *Sqrs. T.* 189 Nature ne Art ne koude hym nat amende. **1573** G. HARVEY *Common-pl. Bk.* (1884) 87 Nature herself is changeable.. and arte, after a sorte her ape, conformith herself to the like mutabilitye. **1592** SHAKS. *Rom. & Jul.* II. iv. 94 Romeo: now art thou what thou art, by Art as well as by Nature. **1643** SIR T. BROWNE *Relig. Med.* I. §16 Now nature is not at variance with art, nor art with nature: they being both the servants of his providence. Art is the perfecttion of Nature.. Nature hath made one World, and Art another. In briefe, all things are artificiall, for Nature is the Art of God. **1699** DRYDEN *Cock & Fox* 452 Art may err, but nature cannot miss. **1742** COLLINS *Ode to Pity* 23 Youth's soft notes unspoil'd by art. **1839** LONGF. *Hyperion* III. v. (1865) 165 Nature is a revelation of God; Art, a revelation of man.. Art pre-exists in Nature, and Nature is reproduced in Art.

†**b.** Artifice, artificial expedient. (Cf. 12.) *Obs.*

1667 OLDENBURG in *Phil Trans.* II. 415 That some of the Natives there can stay under Water half an hour without any art.

3. The learning of the schools; see 7. †**a.** *spec.* The *trivium*, or one of its subjects, grammar, logic, rhetoric; dialectics. *Obs.*

c **1305** *St. Edmund* 220 in *E.E.P.* (1862) 77 Of art he radde six ȝer: contynuelliche ynourȝ, & siþþe for beo more profound: to arsmetrike he drouȝ. **1330** R. BRUNNE *Chron.* 336 (R.) Of arte he had the maistrie. *c* **1430** *Freemasonry* 567 Gramer forsothe ys the rote.. But art passeth yn hys degre, As the fryte does the rote of the tre. **1573** G. HARVEY *Common-pl. Bk.* (1884) 76 It makith no matter howe a man wrytith untoe his frends.. Præceptes of arte and stile and decorum.. ar to be reservid for an other place.

b. *gen.* Scholarship, learning, science. *arch.*

1588 SHAKS. *L.L.L.* IV. ii. 113 Where all those pleasures liue, that Art would comprehend. **1675** R. BARCLAY *Apol. Quakers* ii. §15. 64 A Mathematician can infallibly know, by the Rules of Art, that the three Angles of a right Triangle, are equal to two right Angles. **1709** POPE *Ess. Crit.* 61 So vast is art, so narrow human wit. *c* **1840** LONGF. *Psalm of Life*, Art is long, and time is fleeting.

c. ***words*** or ***terms of art***: words peculiar to, or having a peculiar use in, a particular art or pursuit; technical terms.

1628 COKE *On Litt.* Pref., The Termes and Words of Art. **1701** SWIFT *Cont. Nobles*, etc. Wks. 1755 II. I. 22 By which he brought many of them, as the term of art was then, to Philippize. **1754** EDWARDS *Freed. Will* I. §3. 15 If we use the Words, as Terms of Art, in another sense. **1807** MORRIS & KENDRICK (*title*) Explanation of the Terms of Art in Anatomy. **1816** SCOTT *Antiq.* (1852) 256 A few thumping blustering terms of art.

†**4.** *spec.* Skill in applying the principles of a special science; technical or professional skill. *Obs.*

c **1300** *K. Alis.* 737 Thyn erbes failith and thyn art! **1393** LANGL. *P. Pl.* C. XVIII. 96 Astronomyens al day · in here art faillen. **1605** SHAKS. *Macb.* IV. i. 101 Tell me, if your Art Can tell so much. **1656** H. PHILLIPS *Purch. Patt.* (1676) 31 Without sufficient knowledge in point of art. **1677** MOXON *Mech. Exerc.* (1703) 253 Work, in which they have taken a great deal of pains, and used a great deal of Art.

5. The application of skill to subjects of taste, as poetry, music, dancing, the drama, oratory, literary composition, and the like; *esp.* in mod. use: Skill displaying itself in perfection of workmanship, perfection of execution as an object in itself. Phr. ***art for art's sake***. Hence in many allusive phrases (see quots.).

1620 J. TAYLOR in *Shaks. C. Praise* 133 Spencer and Shakespeare did in art excell. **1675** TRAHERNE *Chr. Ethics* iii. 25 Art.. more frequently appears in fiddling and dancing, then in noble deeds. **1711** SHAFTESB. *Charac.* (1737) I. 244 Remarking what this mighty Genius and Judg of Art declares concerning tragedy. [**1836** V. COUSIN *Cours de Philosophie 1818* 224 Il faut de la religion pour la religion, de la morale pour la morale, comme de l'art pour l'art.] **1840** H. ROGERS *Ess.* II. v. 259 It is just such art as this that we ask of the preacher.. that he shall take diligent heed to do what he has to do as well as he can. **1867** MILL *Inaug. Add. St. Andrews* 46 If I were to define Art, I should be inclined to call it the endeavour after perfection in execution. **1872** SWINBURNE *Ess. & Stud.* (1875) 41 The well-known formula of art for art's sake.. has, like other doctrines, a true side to it, and an untrue. **1879** M. ARNOLD *Guide Eng. Lit.* in *Mixed Ess.* 193 We mean by art, not merely an aim to please, but also a law of pure and flawless workmanship. **1920** B. RUSSELL *Pract. & Theory Bolshevism* iv. 48 There it stands, this old art, the purest monument to the nullity of the art-for-art's-sake doctrine. **1925** A. HUXLEY *Those Barren Leaves* II. i. 86, I was not an art-for-arter. **1928** —— *Point Counter Point* xvi. 291 We're frankly missionaries, not an art for art concern. **1937** 'G. ORWELL' *Road to Wigan Pier* xii. 243 Our leading writers, who a dozen years ago were art for art's saking for all they were worth.. are now taking a definite political standpoint. **1942** *Burlington Mag.* May 115/1 The first exponents of 'art for art' did not, as do their descendants, uphold the claims of the senses abstractly and in isolation. **1948** J. W. ALDRIDGE in *Penguin New Writing* XXXV. 115 *Ulysses* represents the extreme of the art-for-art's-sake doctrine. **1950** E. C. PETTET in *Essays & Studies* III. 45 The advocate of the 'practical' Shakespeare, allied on this occasion with the art-for-art's-saker, says [etc.].

6. The application of skill to the arts of imitation and design, *painting, engraving, sculpture, architecture*; the cultivation of these in its principles, practice, and results; the skilful production of the beautiful in visible forms.

This is the most usual modern sense of *art*, when used without any qualification. It does not occur in any English Dictionary before 1880, and seems to have been chiefly used by painters and writers on painting, until the present century.

1668 J. E[VELYN] (*title*) An Idea of the Perfection of Painting demonstrated from the Principles of Art. *a* **1700** DRYDEN *To Kneller*, From hence the rudiments of art began, A coal or chalk first imitated man. *c* **1777** J. BARRY in Cunningham *Brit. Painters* II. 96 A solid manly taste for real art, in place of our contemptible passion for daubing. **1801** FUSELI *Lect. Art* i. 8 Greek Art had her infancy. **1834** *Prospectus of Edin. Art Union*, It is proposed to form an Association for the purchase of works of art. **1848** MRS. JAMESON (*title*) Sacred and Legendary Art. **1856** RUSKIN *Mod. Paint.* III. IV. iii. §12 *note*, High art differs from low art in possessing an excess of beauty in addition to its truth, not in possessing excess of beauty inconsistent with truth. **1869** GLADSTONE *Juv. Mundi* xv. §2. 520 By the term Art, I understand the production of beauty in material forms palpable; whether associated with industrial purposes or not. **1876** HUMPHREY *Coin Coll. Man.* i. 4 The coins of Greece and Rome form in themselves a complete history of Art.

II. Anything wherein skill may be attained or displayed. Sing. *an art*; pl. *arts*.

7. a. chiefly in *pl.* Certain branches of learning which are of the nature of intellectual instruments or apparatus for more advanced studies, or for the work of life; their main principles having been already investigated and established, they are in the position of subjects requiring only to be acquired and practised. Applied in the Middle Ages to 'the *trivium* and *quadrivium*, a course of seven sciences, introduced in the sixth century... the trivium contained *grammar, logic*, and *rhetoric*; the quadrivium *arithmetic, geometry, music*, and *astronomy*' (Hallam); called also the *free* or *liberal* arts. Hence the 'faculty' of arts, and arts 'curriculum,' embracing the portions of these, with subsequent additions and alterations, still studied at the Universities, and the degrees of 'Bachelor' and 'Master of Arts' conferred upon students who attain to a prescribed standard of proficiency in these branches of knowledge, or, as it is called, 'graduate in arts.'

c **1300** *K. Alis.* 665 The sevethen maister taught his pars, And the wit of the seoven ars. *c* **1305** *St. Kath.* 4 in *E.E.P.* (1862) 90 þere nas non of þe soue artz þat heo gret clerk of nas. *c* **1320** *Seuyn Sages* (W.) 182 And eke alle the seven ars. **1377** LANGL. *P. Pl.* B. x. 150 He hath wedded a wyf.. Is sybbe to þe seuene artz. *c* **1400** *Destr. Troy* IV. 1497 Cassandra.. enfourmet was faire of þe fre artis. *c* **1425** WYNTOUN *Cron.* VIII. iv. 9 Mayster of Art. **1503** HAWES *Examp. Virtue* vii. 103, I am grounde of the artes seuen. **1557** *N. T.* (Genev.) *Epist.* iiij, They.. beat their wittes night and daie in the artes liberall or other sciences. **1579** FULKE *Refut. Rastel* 751 He being a Master in all the seuen liberall Arts, is not so ignorant in grammer. **1594** CAREW *Huarte's Exam. Wits* (1616) 7 Moreouer, mans life is very short, and the arts long and toilsome. **1608** SHAKS. *Per.* II. iii. 82 My education been in arts and arms. **1795** GIBBON

Autobiog. 29 How many [professors] are stationed to the three faculties, and how many are left for the liberal arts? **1794** REID *Acc. Univ. Glasgow* Wks. II, 723/1 Four [Faculties]..Theology, Canon Law, Civil Law, and the Arts... The Arts, under which was comprehended logic, physics, and morals, were considered as a necessary introduction to the learned professions. *Ibid.* 724/1 In some universities, Masters of Arts are called Doctors of Philosophy. *Ibid.* 725/2 The dean conferred the degree of Bachelor of Arts. **1868** M. PATTISON *Academ. Org.* §5. 191 The first seven years..were employed on studies, which varying in their nature in various periods of the university history went under the common name of 'Arts.'

attrib. **1912** W. OWEN *Let.* 12 June (1967) 141, I definitely abandon the *thought* of Divinity Training *till* at least an Arts Degree is won. **1946** *Universities Quarterly* I. 52 The Arts faculties ought to include sufficient knowledge of general science to provide a general appreciation of science and the scientific method as applied to the problems of daily life. **1960** *Guardian* 20 Apr. 8/3 It should be possible to make scientists literate and arts men 'numerate'. **1967** J. PHILIP et al. *Best of Granta* 104 *Granta's* characteristic role in the 'sixties has been as an avant-garde arts magazine.

†**b.** *sing.* Any one of the above-mentioned subjects.

c **1300** *K. Alis.* 72 Barounes..That this ars [astrology] wel undurstode..Wis in this ars, and malicious. *c* **1450** *Merlin* v. 86 An arte that is cleped astronomye.

8. A practical application of any science; a body or system of rules serving to facilitate the carrying out of certain principles. In this sense often contrasted with *science.*

1489 CAXTON *Faytes of Armes* I. i. 2 Emonge thother noble artes and sciences. *c* **1538** STARKEY *England* II. i. 160 Scholes in euery Arte, syence and craft. **1588** FRAUNCE *Lawiers Log.* I. i. 1 b, An art is a methodicall disposition of true and coherent preceptes, for the more easie perceiving and better remembring of the same. **1599** SHAKS. *Hen. V*, I. i. 51 So that the Arte and Practique part of Life must be the Mistresse to this Theorique. **1724** WATTS *Logic* II. ii. §9 This is the most remarkable distinction between an art and a science, viz. the one refers chiefly to practice, the other to speculation. **1825** BENTHAM *Ration. Reward* 204 Correspondent..to every art, there is at least one branch of science; correspondent to every branch of science, there is at least one branch of art. **1852** MCCULLOCH *Dict. Comm.* 449 Agriculture is little known as a science in any part of America, and but imperfectly understood as an art. **1870** JEVONS *Elem. Logic* i. 7 A science teaches us to know and an art to do.

9. a. *esp.* An industrial pursuit or employment of a skilled nature; a craft, business, profession.

1393 GOWER *Conf.* III. 142 Artificers Whiche vsen craftes and mestiers, Whose art is cleped mechanique. **1557** SEAGER *Sch. Vertue* in *Babees Bk.* 353 Ye seruauntes, applie your busines and arte. **1660** STANLEY *Hist. Philos.* 165 Arts of three kinds. The first diggeth out Metals, and fells Wood. **1705** ADDISON *Italy* 6 The Fisher-men can't employ their Art with so much success in so troubled a Sea. **1745** DE FOE *Eng. Tradesm.* I. i. 8 To be taught the art and mystery which his master engages to learn him. **1851** D. WILSON *Preh. Ann.* (1863) I. II. ii. 358 Aboriginal learners slowly acquiring the new art.

b. A guild, or company of craftsmen. Cf. Florio: '*Arte*..a whole company of any trade in any city or corporation town.'

1832 SISMONDI *Ital. Rep.* viii. 184 These men, belonging to the woollen art. **1872** YEATS *Growth Comm.* 107 The industry of the free republic was controlled by guilds or arts.

10. A pursuit or occupation in which skill is directed towards the gratification of taste or production of what is beautiful. Hence *the Arts*: (specifically) = the fine arts; see next sense. (Cf. 5, 6.)

1597 [see 11 b]. **1769** SIR J. REYNOLDS *Disc.* i. Wks. 1870 I. 306 There is a general desire among our Nobility to be distinguished as lovers and judges of the Arts. **1778** —— *ibid.* vii. I. 426 All arts having the same general end, which is to please. **1827** *Continental Advent.* li. III. 243 The true Italian feeling for the Arts. **1842** PARKER *Baptistery* Pref. xii, The sister Art that speaks in stone. **1884** *Punch* 3 May 210/2 You will speak only of music, extolling this Art above all others.

11. In prec. senses, but particularized:—

a. by an adjective, as *magic art* (or the *black art*), *military art*, the *healing art*, *industrial*, *mechanical*, *useful arts*: those in which the hands and body are more concerned than the mind. *fine arts*: those in which the mind and imagination are chiefly concerned.

1393 GOWER III. 80 Thexperience Of art magique. **1611** BIBLE *Wisd.* xvii. 7 The illusions of arte Magicke. **1667** MOXON *Mech. Exerc.* (1703) 1 Smithing is an Art-Manual. **1697** DRYDEN *Virg. Georg.* IV. 178 My song to flowery Gardens might extend, To teach the Vegetable Arts. **1711** ADDISON *Spect.* No. 5 ¶4 How an Amazon should be versed in the Black Art. **1734** tr. *Rollin's Rom. Hist.* (1827) III. 96 A treatise..upon the art military. **1767** FORDYCE *Serm. Yng. Wom.* I. vi. 250 They..wanted instruction in the principles of the Fine Arts. **1785** REID *Int. Powers* VI. vi, The fine arts are very properly called the arts of taste. **1854** RUSKIN *Two Paths* ii, Fine art is that in which the hand, the head, and the heart of man go together. **1884** GLADSTONE *Sp. in Parl.* 28 Apr., The Reform Bill of 1866 was defeated by obstruction, though at that period the art of obstruction was not so much of a fine art as it was now. *Mod.* A professor of the healing art.

b. by a genitive or genitive phrase, as 'the painter's art,' 'the art of painting.'

1509 HAWES *Past. Pleas.* 189 Set with magykes arte. **1560** BIBLE (Genev.) *2 Chron.* xvi. 14 Spices made by the arte [WYCLIF, TINDALE, craft] of the Apoticarie. **1611** *Ibid.*, Apothecaries arte. **1597** MORLEY *Introd. Mus.* 181 The arte of dauncing being come to that perfection. **1691** T. H[ALE] *New Invent.* 29 The art of making gold. **1774** T. JEFFERSON *Autobiog.* Wks. 1859 I. App. 141 The whole art of government consists in the art of being honest. **1821** JOANNA BAILLIE *Met. Leg., Wallace* lxiii. 6 The soldier's dext'rous art. **1849** MACAULAY *Hist. Eng.* I. 301 The rapid improvement, both of the art of war and of the art of navigation. **1875** FORTNUM *Maiolica* iii. 34 To have encouraged the potter's art.

12. An acquired faculty of any kind; a power of doing anything wherein skill is attainable by study and practice; a knack.

1637 RUTHERFORD *Lett.* 120 (1862) I. 299, I thought the guiding of grace had been no art. I thought it w[d] come of will. **1781** COWPER *Convers.* 4 Conversation..may be esteemed a gift, and not an art. **1849** MACAULAY *Hist. Eng.* II. 201 The art of saying things well is useless to a man who has nothing to say. **1876** HAMERTON *Intell. Life* III. iii. 91 The delicate art of verbal selection.

III. Skilful, crafty, or artful conduct.

13. Studied conduct or action, especially such as seeks to attain its ends by artificial, indirect, or covert means; address; cunning, artfulness.

c **1600** SHAKS. *Sonn.* 139 Use power with power and slay me not by art..What need'st thou wound with cunning when thy might Is more, etc. **1738** POPE *Epil. Sat.* i. 32 Smile without Art, and win without a Bribe. *a* **1762** LADY MONTAGUE *Lett.* lxxiv. 122, I am incapable of art. **1801** MAR. EDGEWORTH *Belinda* I. xvi. 300 Her art and falsehood operated against her own views.

14. An artifice, contrivance, stratagem, wile, trick, cunning device. Chiefly in *pl.*

1597 SHAKS. *Lover's Compl.* 295 His passion, but an art of craft, Even there resolved my reason into tears. **1625** BACON *Simul., Ess.* (Arb.) 506 Attributing Arts or Policy to Augustus, and Dissimulation to Tiberius. **1681** DRYDEN *Abs. & Achit.* I. 402 The next successor..My Arts have made obnoxious to the State. **1712** STEELE *Spect.* No. 510 ¶4 All the little arts imaginable are used to soften a man's heart. **1769** ROBERTSON *Chas. V*, V. I. 172 All the arts of address and policy. **1813** MISS AUSTEN *Pride & Prej.* (1833) 34 The arts which ladies sometimes condescend to employ for captivation. **1849** MACAULAY *Hist. Eng.* I. 536 No art was spared which could draw Monmouth from retreat.

IV. Phrases.

15. *art-of-memory*: an old game at cards. (Described in the *Compleat Gamester* (1709) 101.)

1674 COTTON *Compl. Gamester* (1680) 99 This Art of Memory is a sport at which men may play for money, but it is most commonly the way to play the drunkard.

16. art and part (*Sc. Law* and *gen.*): **a.** orig. in such expressions as *to be concerned in* (*either*) *by art or part*, either by *art* in contriving it, or by the *part* taken in actually executing it; whence, *to have* art or (and) part in: to have a share in, either by contrivance or participation; **b.** (corruptly) *to be* art or part in (*be* for *have*, or perh. for 'to be *of* art or part in'): to be concerned either in the contrivance or the execution of; *to be* art *and* part in: to be accessary both by contrivance and participation, often used loosely, as a mere jingling phrase for 'accessary, participating, sharing' (the sense of *art* being merged in that of *part*).

a. *c* **1425** WYNTOUN *Cron.* VII. ix. 539 All þa Ðat (oþir) be art or part or swike Gert bryn..þis erle Patryke. **1582–8** *Hist. James VI* (1804) 60 Thame that has bein foirfaltit for airt and pairt of the slauchter. **1609** SKENE *Rej. Maj.* 118 Thou thy selfe full airt had, and parte in harming and skaithing of me. *a* **1670** HACKET *Abp. Williams* II. 86 (D.) The old man which is corrupt (Eph. iv. 22), who had art and part, as the Scottish indictment runs, in all our Bishop's persecutions. **1767** H. BROOKE *Fool of Qual.* i. 6 (D.) He had neither art nor part in this frightful discomfiture. **1864** *Spectator* 529 He has no further art or part in the matter.

b. **1515** *Acts Jas. V.* (1597) §2 He salbe halden airt & partaker of his evill deedis. **1536** BELLENDENE *Cron. Scot.* XII. viii. (JAM.) Gif evir I wes othir art or part of Alarudis slauchter. **1691** BLOUNT *Law Dict., Art and Part* is a Term used in Scotland and the North of England. When one is charged with a Crime they say, He was *Art and Part* in committing the same..He was both a contriver, and acted his Part in it. **1753** *Stewart's Trial* 283 Find unanimously, the pannel James Stewart guilty, art and part, of the murder of Colin Campbell. *c* **1876** *Nat. Encycl.* I. 105 The law of Scotland makes no distinction between the accessory to any crime (called *art and part*) and the principal. **1878** TENNYSON *Q. Mary* III. iv, You are art and part with us In purging heresy.

17. arts and crafts: the arts of decorative design and handicraft; *spec.* work done by or under the auspices of the Arts and Crafts Exhibition Society, founded in London in 1888, or similar later work; also *attrib.* Hence (*colloq.*) **art-and-crafty, arts-and-craftsy** *adjs.*, pertaining to or characteristic of the arts and crafts or of the 'arts and crafts' movement, esp. its more pretentious side. Cf. ARTY-AND-CRAFTY *a.*

1888 *Times* 29 Sept. 6/1 The Arts and Crafts Exhibition at the New Gallery..may best be described as an exhibition with a purpose. **1894** *Studio* 48/1 The impression..on the mind of a person who had previously had little experience of collective 'Arts and Crafts' may not be without practical value. **1899** J. W. MACKAIL *Life W. Morris* II. xviii. 200 The newly-formed association was at first known by the name of the Combined Arts. The name of the Arts and Crafts was the invention of Mr. Cobden-Sanderson. He was also..responsible for another of the new departures made in the first Arts and Crafts Exhibition. **1902** [see ARTY-AND-CRAFTY *a.*]. **1909** *Westm. Gaz.* 24 Dec. 2/2 An art and crafty tea-table. **1939** O. LANCASTER *Homes Sweet Homes* 44 The fervent mediaevalism..found its final expression in the Arts-and-Crafts movement. **1943** G. GREENE *Min. Fear* I. i. 8 Short blunt fingers prickly with big art-and-crafty rings. **1957** R. CAMPBELL *Portugal* vi. 202 The arts-and-craftsy, self-conscious supervision, patronage, and spurious jollity given to morris dancing..in England.

V. 18. *Comb.* chiefly *attrib.* from sense 6, as ***art-activity***, ***-appreciation***, ***-collecting*** vbl. sb., ***-collection***, ***-collector***, ***-connoisseur***, ***-correspondent***, ***-critic*** (hence ***art-critical*** adj., ***-critically*** adv., ***-criticism***), ***-dealer***, ***-furniture***, ***-instinct***, ***-lover*** (hence ***-loving*** ppl. a.), ***-magazine***, ***-manufacture***, ***-monger***, ***-product***, ***-sale***, ***-school***, ***-student***, ***-style***, ***-teacher***, ***-teaching*** vbl. sb., ***world***; or *instrumental*, as ***art-spun***, etc. Also **art centre** (see CENTRE *sb.* 6 a); **art director**, one who is responsible for the décor, properties, scene-painting, etc., in a theatre or in cinematographic films; **art editor**, one who is responsible for the illustrations or the section devoted to the arts in a book, magazine, etc.; hence ***art-edit*** v. trans. (*rare*); **art-educate** v. trans., to educate in the arts of design; **art-form** [cf. G. *kunstform*], (*a*) an established form taken by a work of art, e.g. a dialogue, novel, sonata, sonnet, triptych, madrigal; (*b*) a theme or motif constituting a traditional subject of works of art, e.g. the Madonna and Child; (*c*) a medium of artistic expression; **art gallery** [GALLERY *sb.* 6], a building or portion of a building devoted to the exhibition of works of art; formerly also ***art museum***; **art history** [cf. G. *kunstgeschichte*], the history of art, esp. as an academic study; hence ***art-historian***, ***art-historical*** adj.; **art object**, an object of artistic value; = OBJET D'ART; **art paper**, paper coated on one or both sides with china clay or the like to give a smooth surface; coated paper (see COATED *ppl. a.* 3); **Arts Council**: in full ***Arts Council of Great Britain***, an organization established by Royal Charter in 1946 to promote and support (esp. financially) the development and appreciation of the arts in Britain; **art square**, a patterned square of carpet woven in a single piece; **art-union**, a union of persons for the purpose of promoting art (in sense 6), chiefly by purchasing the works of artists, and distributing them among their members, which is usually done by lottery; in Australia and New Zealand, a lottery with cash prizes.

1923 D. H. LAWRENCE *Stud. Classic Amer. Lit.* vi. 93 The rhythm of American art-activity is dual. **1896** *Peterson Mag.* VI. 225/2 Art-appreciation, like art-creation, is a slow evolution. **1937** *Burlington Mag.* June 310/1 General hints on art-appreciation for the ordinary public. **1908** A. BENNETT *Buried Alive* vii. 176 London, the acknowledged art-centre of the world. **1967** *Listener* 20 July 76/2 One of those exclusive civic centres or art centres in the South Kensington or South Bank tradition. **1902** *Encycl. Brit.* XXV. 683/2 They acted as a most healthy stimulus to art collecting. *Ibid.*, The first really important art collection to come under the hammer. **1936** *Burlington Mag.* July 46/2 The Veronese art-collector Bendetto Maffei. **1904** W. JAMES *Let.* 30 June (1920) II. 206 The bulk of 'Modern Painters' and the other artistic writings..have made us take him [*sc.* Ruskin] primarily as an art-connoisseur and critic. **1882** WILDE *Let.* 19 Feb. (1962) 96, I would undertake to be your art-correspondent for London and Paris—two articles a month. **1865** ROSSETTI *Let.* 15 Nov. (1965) II. 580 The Art-critic's original *dicta*. **1866** *Argosy* (Midsummer) 61, I should certainly have liked to consult our great modern art-critic before making so daring a statement. **1879** HIBBS in *Cassell's Techn. Educ.* IV. 263/2 As desirous of improving the style of their work as any art-critic could possibly wish them to be. **1944** H. TREECE *Herbert Read* 53 Read has always been more artist than art critic. **1936** *Burlington Mag.* June 303/1 Extensive art-historical and art-critical work. **1880** SWINBURNE *Let.* 17 May (1960) IV. 143 A sample of the 'first manner' (to speak art-critically) of the poem. **1867** *Fine Arts Q. Rev.* II. 174 We must recognize an immense advance in the tone and character of art-criticism, especially in..leading journals. **1891** WILDE *Intentions* 258 It is only in art-criticism, and through it, that we can apprehend the Platonic theory of ideas. **1935** *Burlington Mag.* Nov. 202/1 The merciless scrutiny of modern art-criticism. **1934** A. WOOLLCOTT *While Rome Burns* 11 The young art-dealer was not precisely what would have been called pro-Ally. **1933** *Archit. Rev.* LXXIII. 127 The newest and most satisfactory examples of decoration in the world of the movie art-director. **1933** P. GODFREY *Back-Stage* xiii. 160 The first art director to do so. **1923** T. E. LAWRENCE *Let.* 13 Dec. (1938) 443 Hogarth will literary-edit the proofs for me: & Kennington art-edit the blocks. **1877** *Harper's Mag.* Dec. 53/2 The day editor [puts]..news relating to art in the hands of the art editor. **1941** *Oxoniensia* VI. 93 The art-editors of the Commission are not entirely aware why a good photograph is good, or a bad one not good. **1880** POYNTER *Lect. Art* I. 16 It has never been thought worth while to art-educate the workman. **1868** G. M. HOPKINS *Notebks.* (1937) 97 An intellectual attraction for very sharp and pure dialectic or, in other matter, hard and telling art-forms. **1887** *Magazine of Art* 135/2 Some such accidental juxtaposition of decorative bird-woman and galleys..suggested the *art-form* or myth of Odysseus and the Sirens. **1894** *World* 21 Feb. 23/1 This type of musical farce is not an elevating or intellectual art-form. **1928** H. READ *Phases of Eng. Poetry* i. 11 Anglo-Saxon poetry is already a highly developed art-form. **1929** H. G. WELLS *King who was King* i. 8 (*heading*) The Film, the Art Form of the Future. **1952** D. TALBOT RICE *Eng. Art 871–1100* v. 132 Before the crosses were finally eclipsed as an art-form, a very wide repertory of different types of decoration was to appear on their shafts and heads. **1870** *Athenæum* 21 May 681 Little more than a pretty piece of art-furniture. [**1845** DISRAELI *Sybil* III. v. i. 14 Something of the splendour or the rarities of the metropolis; its public buildings, museums, and galleries of art. **1860** *Birmingham Council Proc.* 15 May 195 The scheme ..should comprise a central Reference Library.., a Museum and Gallery of Art. **1863** *Ibid.* 5 May 198 The Fine Art Gallery now being erected in connection with the Central Free Library.] **1865** *Ibid.* 28 Nov. 37 An offer..to deposit in the Art Gallery several valuable pictures belonging to the Society. **1885** M. DAVITT *Prison Diary* II. xxiv. 46 Every public library in all towns of say 5000 inhabitants should have in connection with it a museum and an art gallery. **1946** *Ann. Reg. 1945* 333 This year of victory saw the gradual resumption of their normal functions by most of our public art galleries and museums. **1890** WILDE *Critic as Artist* in *Wks.* (1948) 958 The Greeks..wrote essays on art, and produced their art-historians. **1907** *Daily Chron.* 5 June 6/4 In its way the most thorough piece of art-historian work that was ever produced. **1957** *Times Lit. Suppl.* 27 Dec. 790/1 The writer is an archaeologist and historian of art, not an 'art-historian', so those interested in this unfamiliar aspect of Greek art are better referred not to the text but to the plates. **1933** R. FRY *Art History as Acad. Study* 11 The whole tendency of their [*sc.* the Germans'] art-historical studies has been to regard works of art almost entirely from a chronological point of view..without reference to their aesthetic significance. **1874** *Temple Bar* XLII. 204 Incidentally may here be mentioned, though not strictly within the limits of art history, the wonderful power which was exercised this year by a portrait of the period. **1876** *Mind* I. 477 Hasty inductions drawn from a narrow area of art-history are erected into general principles. **1927** R. H. WILENSKY *Mod. Movement in Art* I. 51 The genius is so rare in art history. **1891** WILDE *Pict. Dorian Gray* iv, She has not merely art, consummate art-instinct, in her, but she has personality also. **1857** RUSKIN *Pol. Econ. Art* 30 A certain quantity of Art-intellect is born annually in every nation. **1862** THORNBURY *Turner* I. 13 The very starting-point of the boy's art life. **1876** GLADSTONE *Relig. Th.* in *Contemp. Rev.* June 23 The splendid and elaborate art-life of the people. **1874** *Daily Tel.* 4 May 5/6 This is..what artists and art-lovers will thank him for. **1861** TROLLOPE *Tales of all Countries* Ser. II (1863) 52 The haunts in Rome which are best loved by art-loving strangers. **1934** *Burlington Mag.* Oct. 146/2 The English might have a reputable art magazine. **1928** A. HUXLEY *Point Counter Point* v. 71, I envy you art-mongers your success. **1856** *Art-Jrnl.* 2nd Ser. II. 93/1 If the money spent in the Art-museums of France was taken into consideration, it would be found that the assistance..was on a..liberal scale. **1857** *Ibid.* 239/1 As a national Art-museum it [*sc.* the South Kensington Museum]..is a success. **1904** *Westm. Gaz.* 20 Oct. 1/2 Everyone..remarked how very flat the picture market has been, compared with that of'art objects'. **1913** T. E. LAWRENCE *Let.* 16 Oct. (1954) 269 Arab glass..is the rarest art object in the world. **1962** W. NOWOTTNY *Lang. Poets Use* vi. 137 Different ways of looking at a house..as an art-object. **1905** *Jrnl. Soc. Chem. Industry* XXIV. 771/2 The unpleasantness and fatigue caused by the reflection of light from the surface of high-glazed art papers. **1958** *Times Lit. Suppl.* 3 Oct. 567/4 To print both illustrations and text on coated paper (that is, so-called art paper). **1904** W. JAMES in *Atlantic Monthly* July 102/2 All his [*sc.* Spencer's] dealings with the art-products of mankind. **1882** W. F. POOLE *Index Period. Lit.* (ed. 3) 64/1 Art and Art Sales in England, in the 18th Century. **1902** *Encycl. Brit.* XXV. 684/1 The greatest art sale in the annals of Great Britain. **1866** *Once a Week* 3 Feb. 134/1 The Universities do not teach art, the Art-schools do not teach anything else. **1935** *Discovery* Jan. 17/2 Groups drawn from art schools. **1945** *Times* 13 June 2/4 The Government have decided that..the Council for the Encouragement of Music and the Arts is to continue after the war under a new name. The new body will be known as the Arts Council of Great Britain. **1951** *Oxf. Compan. Theatre* 36/1 The defined purposes of the Arts Council..are 'to develop a greater knowledge, understanding and practice of the Fine Arts, to increase their accessibility to the public and to improve their standard of execution'. **1957** *Times Lit. Suppl.* 1 Nov. 652/3 The Hallé's experience with an Arts Council grant. **1967** *New Charter of Incorporation of Arts Council of Gt. Britain* 7 Feb., The objects for which the Council are established..(*a*) to develop and improve the knowledge, understanding and practice of the arts; (*b*) to increase the accessibility of the arts. **1984** *Listener* 26 Apr. 3/3 When the Arts Council came to launch its new initiative towards the regions, those funds were inviolate. **1902** *Encycl. Brit.* XXVI. 605/1 The products of these two processes are well known under the trade-names of 'Parquet Carpets' and 'Art Squares'. **1849** *Art-Jrnl.* XI. 107/3 In ordinary times there resides at Paris a numerous body of artists and Art-students **1934** R. BENEDICT *Patterns Cult.* (1935) iii. 48 What has happened in the great art-styles happens also in cultures as a whole. **1872** RUSKIN *Eagle's Nest* i. §3 The least part of the work of any sound art-teacher must be his talking. **1857** —— *Pol. Econ. Art* ii. 101 The most singular concentration of art-teaching and art-treasure. **1857** *Ibid.* i. 41 The picture which most truly deserves the name of an art-treasure. **1837** (*title*) Art Union of Scotland. **1839** DICKENS *Let.* 18 Feb. (1965) I. 509 All good fortune to the Art Union. **1849** *Sydney Morning Herald* 27 Nov. 1/4 The undersigned guarantees the..sums of £50 and £40 to the Painters of the 1st and 2nd Prizes, in his Art Union. **1851** ROSSETTI *Let.* 30 Aug. (1965) I. 103 A Notice about an Art-Union print. **1868** CHAMBERS *Encycl.* I. 446 Scotland preceded England in the establishment of Art Unions. **1931** *Dominion* (Wellington) 26 Dec. 13/7 Here we have art unions freely sanctioned..for every conceivable object from sports of every kind to first aid. **1948** D. BALLANTYNE *Cunninghams* 148 But it would be a long, long time before she got a new dress—unless her ship came home and she won an art union. **1966** *Courier-Mail* (Brisbane) 5 May 3/11 A Scottish couple..yesterday won first prize in a Queensland consultation, the Scarborough art union. **1880** POYNTER *Lect. Art* I. 16 The Art-workmen who have studied in our schools of design. **1890** *Atlantic Monthly* Dec. 753/1 January and February, 1890, saw the culmination of a new movement in the art world of Paris.

19. a. Designed to produce an artistic effect, as ***art furniture, needlework, pottery,*** etc.

1868 *Building News* 25 Dec. 869/3 (*heading*) Messrs. Walford and Donkin's art furniture. **1870** Art-furniture [see sense 18]. **1879** M. E. BRADDON *Vixen* I. xvii. 327 Your last piece of art needlework. **1880** L. HIGGIN *Handbk. Embroidery* 98 The School was founded in 1872... It was first established, under the title of School of Art-Needlework, in Sloane Street; but in 1875 was removed to the present premises in the Exhibition Road. **1881** C. C. HARRISON *Woman's Handiwork* 47 Canton flannel,..a soft downy fabric,..comes in all the 'art' shades. **1885** C. M. YONGE *Two Sides of Shield* I. v. 75 'Don't you love art needlework?' 'Maude Sefton has been working Goosey Goosey Gander on a toilet-cover.' **1887** G. B. SHAW *Don Giovanni Explains* in *Wks.* (1932) VI. 99 Some exquisitely fine fabric in an 'art shade' of Indian red. **1887** *Trade Marks Jrnl.* 9 Feb., 'Liberty' Art Fabrics. **1893** YONGE & COLERIDGE *Strolling Players* x. 77 What she called 'an art-frock' in Liberty silk. **1894** MRS. H. WARD *Marcella* I. vii. 61 Marcella wore 'art serges' and velveteens. **1895** *British Warehouseman* Feb. 17/2 Chintzes, Art Blinds, Window Hollands,..Art Serges. *Ibid.* 38/2 A new..shade-card, comprising all the newest art tints. **1897** *Daily News* 23 Mar. 7/1 Great art-pottery establishments..are busy in the preparation of vases and other articles. **1900** J. K. JEROME *Three Men on Bummel* viii. 171 A yard or so of art muslin. **1930** W. S. MAUGHAM *Cakes & Ale* xii. 151 Curtains of art serge and a bilious green.

b. [cf. G. *kunstlied, -musik.*] Produced by an artist, composed with conscious artistry: said of poetry and music, opp. to *popular* or *folk*, as ***art ballad, music, song.***

1890 A. B. BACH (*title*) The Art Ballad. Loewe and Schubert. *Ibid.* 19 Schubert was the creator of the art song, Loewe the creator of the art ballad. **1934** WEBSTER, Art music. **1940** [see ARTIFY *v.*]. **1950** M. J. C. HODGART *Ballads* iii. 49 Ballad music, like other folk music, sounds strange to anyone familiar only with 'art' music. *Ibid.* 57 Folksong is at variance with modern 'art' song, in which the practice is to make the musical stresses correspond to the speech-stresses. **1959** L. BERNSTEIN *Joy of Music* (1960) 172 The songs of these shows are closer to art songs than they are to Tin Pan Alley.

c. Applied *spec.* to a theatre, cinema, etc., specializing in consciously artistic productions, opp. to *commercial, popular*, etc.; hence ***art film.***

1929 S. CHENEY *Theatre* xxiii. 520 Georg Fuchs of the Munich Art Theatre. **1932** W. ROTHENSTEIN *Men & Memories* II. xix. 154 Rumours of Craig's success at the Moscow Art Theatre reached London. **1933** P. GODFREY *Back-stage* xiii. 160 The studio or art theatre exists..to prevent dramatic art from being wiped out by the commercially minded. **1944** L. MACNEICE *Columbus* 15 The radio play..is competing with the Soviet art-cinema rather than with Hollywood. **1959** *Encounter* XIII. 52 The most the art-house circuit can do is $600,000. **1960** *Guardian* 15 Dec. 6/3 French art film makers..spin romantic webs around works of art. **1962** *Listener* 8 Mar. 448/2 Films as sheer entertainment..are slowly being ousted by these art-films. **1967** *Guardian* 5 Aug. 7/8 The Latin Quarter is rich in art cinemas.

VI. ‖**art** (ar), the French equivalent, occurring in certain phrases used in English contexts, as:

a. art autre [lit. 'other art'] = TACHISM(E.

1959 *Vogue* June 115 *Art autre* makes painting a truly visual art. **1963** *Times* 17 May 18/4 Official taste remains complacently becalmed at action-painting and *art autre*.

b. art brut [lit. 'raw art'], primitive or unsophisticated art.

1955 A. C. RITCHIE *New Decade* 21 Jean Dubuffet.. intensified interest in *l'Art brut*, the work of prisoners, mediums, the insane and other non-professionals. **1960** *Times* 10 Oct. 7/2 A certain aestheticism, under the obligatory roughnesses of *art brut*, is discernible.

c. art deco [abbrev. of *art décoratif*, lit. 'decorative art' (from the name of the exhibition *L'Exposition Internationale des Arts Décoratifs et Industriels Modernes* held in Paris in 1925)] (often with capital initials), the name applied subsequently to a style of interior design (furniture, textiles, ceramics, etc.) popular in the 1920s and 1930s, characterized by geometrical shapes and harsh colours.

1966 *Times* 2 Nov. 15/1 Earlier this year the Musée des Arts Decoratifs in Paris staged a fascinating exhibition.. which highlighted the style now known by connoisseurs as Art Deco. **1968** B. HILLIER *Art Deco* 13 Art Deco can be held to cover the Ballet Russe fripperies of Erté as well as the 'architectural nudism' of Le Corbusier. **1972** T. MENTEN *Art Deco Style* Introd., Art Deco..might best be characterized as an attempt to unite arts with industry, embracing the machine age and repudiating the old antithesis of 'fine' and 'industrial' art. **1979** E. H. GOMBRICH *Sense of Order* v. 118 Where *Art Nouveau* relished the sinuous line, *Art Deco* went in for angularity. **1983** Y. BRUNHAMMER (*title*) The art deco style. **1985** *Daily Tel.* 23 Jan. 16/2 Our former consulate [in Shanghai]..is now a.. travel agency. However, a rather splendid art-deco house has been found as a replacement.

d. art mobilier [lit. 'portable art'], a term applied to prehistoric decorated or carved objects.

1946 *Proc. Prehist. Soc.* XII. 153 Engraved plaques of clay-slate from the Bann diatomite indicate..that the *art mobilier* of the Iberian Peninsula has, to some extent, its counterpart in Ireland also. **1959** J. D. CLARK *Prehist. S. Afr.* x. 259 The famous *art mobilier* which is found together with the implements and other occupation material.

e. art moderne, modern art.

1934 D. PARKER *After Such Pleasures* 97 There was no tallying the gifts of Charvet handkerchiefs, *art moderne* ash-trays, etc. **1937** L. BROMFIELD *Rains Came* I. xxiii. 115 Atrocious bits of *art moderne*.

f. art nouveau (ar nuvo) [lit. 'new art'] (often with capital initials), a style of art developed in the last decade of the 19th century, characterized by the free use of ornament based on organic or foliate forms and by its flowing (i.e. non-geometrical) lines and curves. (Called 'Jugendstil' in Germany.)

[**1899** *Studio* XVII. 44 Jewellery..executed at Mr. Bing's establishment 'l'Art Nouveau'.] **1901** *Times* 15 July 12/5 It is much to be regretted that the authorities of South Kensington have introduced into the Museum specimens of the work styled, 'L'Art nouveau'. **1908** G. B. SHAW *Lett. to G. Barker* (1956) 137 A model cemetery with Art Nouveau tombstones. **1909** J. THORP *Æsthetic Conversion* (*Heal & Son*) 10 The *art nouveau*, with its meandering tulips and inconsequent squirms and dots. **1928** J. BUCHAN *Runagates Club* 103 A new plate of gun-metal and oxidised silver, lettered in the best style of *art nouveau*. **1939** O. LANCASTER *Homes Sweet Homes* 54 A recurrent passion for tortuous curves and sinuous lines..which..finds expression in..the flamboyant Gothic of the later Middle Ages, mid-eighteenth century rococo and, most deplorably, in *Art Nouveau*. **1939** A. THIRKELL *Before Lunch* iv, An oxidized silver stand representing the Three Graces in Art Nouveau style.

† **'art**, *v.*[1] *Obs.* Forms: 4–7 **art(e**, 6 **arct.** [prob. direct ad. L. *artā-re* to draw close, contract, f. *artus* confined; Godefroy, however, has OF. pa. pple. *arcté*. In Eng. also occas. assimilated to mediæval L. forms *arctus, arctāre.*]

1. To confine, cramp, restrict, limit, in local position or in action.

1382 WYCLIF *Judg.* i. 34 Amorre artide [**1388** maad streit] the sones of Dan in the hil. *c* **1410** LOVE *Bonavent. Mirr.* xliii. 93 So is he constreyned and arted þat he may noȝt meue. **1496** *Dives & Paup.* (W. de W.) I. xviii. 522 God is ..free in his doynge, and not arted by the planetes.

2. To constrain (a person) *to do* something.

c **1375** BARBOUR *Troy-bk.* II. 3031 A lettir That arted him sone to retorne. *c* **1450** *Crt. of Love* 46 Love arted me to do my observaunce To his estate. **1530** PALSGR. 437/1, I arte, I constrayne..I maye be so arcted that I shall be fayne to do it. **1553** FOXE *A. & M.* (1563) 790/2 Not arcting him to prove euery and singuler thinges..of the premisses.

3. ? To press, urge, insist on.

c **1374** CHAUCER *Troylus* I. 388 What for to speke, and what to holden inne, And what to arten.

4. *pa. pple.* Closely allied. *rare.*

1583 STANYHURST *Æneis* I. (Arb.) 28 No doubt, a Goddesse, too Phœbus sister, or arcted Too Nymphs in Kynred.

art, *v.*[2] [f. ART *sb.*]

† **1.** *Obs.* To instruct in arts, or in any particular art.

1660 STANLEY *Hist. Philos.* 118/2 Agesilaus sent his Sons to be educated at Sparta, to learn and art them..how to obey and command.

† **2.** *Obs.* To make artificial, to artificialize. *rare.*

1627 FELTHAM *Resolves* I. lxiii. Wks. 1677, 97 The nature that is arted with the subtilties of time and practice.

† **3.** *Obs.* To obtain or gain by art. *rare.*

1602 WARNER *Alb. Eng.* XIII. lxxvii. (1612) 319 Skill ..(whereby they arted men's good will).

† **4.** *Obs.* phr. *to art it*: to use art or artifice.

1637 H. SYDENHAM *Serm.* 152 Hee that can art it hansomely in ways of dissimulation. **1655** GURNALL *Chr. in Arm.* xxvi. §2 (1669) 324/2 When they have Arted it most in packing their sins, to hide them from the Worlds eye.

5. ***to art up***: to make arty; to decorate in an arty fashion. *colloq.*

1929 *Amer. Mag.* Jan. 126/3 The knowledge that spinning wheels are perfectly good antique stuff..had been impinged upon..by the desire to art up and decorate indiscriminately. *Ibid.* 127/2 The general arting up they have done, with regard to cottages, tea rooms, gift shops..must have had its effect. **1940** A. THIRKELL *Cheerfulness* vi. 104 The necks.. wanted arting up a bit, as the frocks were so very plain in cut. **1959** *Motif* 3 Sept. 16/1 Attempts to art up the superstructure, to trick it out with forms that have no reasonable development.

art (ɑːt, ət, (ə)t), *v.*[3] 2nd sing. pres. ind. of BE. One of the remaining parts of the orig. substantive vb.; cf. AM.

art, obs. f. AIRT *sb.*, *north. dial.* direction.

a **1400** *Cursor M.* (Trin. MS.) 2268 Þere were alle þe speches part Of dyuerse londes to dyuerse art.

artailȝeryt, artalȝeit: see ARTILLERIED, ARTILLIED.

† **ar'tailye**, *Obs. Sc.* Also 5–6 **artailȝe**, 6 **-ȝee, artalȝe, -allie, -aillie.** [Form not satisfactorily explained; the termination suggests F. *artillé*, pa. pple.] Scotch form of ARTILLERY.

c **1470** HENRY *Wallace* VII. 994 The Sotheron men maid gret defens that tid, With artailye, that felloune was to bid. **1548** *Compl. Scot.* 41 Gunnaris cum heir, and stand by ȝour artailȝee. **1552** LYNDESAY *Papyngo* 947 Nor cum within the schote of thare artailȝe. **1565** R. LINDESAY *Cron.* (1814) 310 (Jam.) Artallie, pouder, and bullettis. *Ibid.* 326 They heard the artaillie schott on both sides.

† **ar'tation.** *Obs. Sc.* [ad. L. *artātiōn-em*, f. *artāre* to compress.] Pressure, urging, instigation.

1528 *Acts Jas. V* (1814) 327 (JAM.) To geif thame artatioune to invaid his hieness. **1536** BELLENDENE *Cron.* XII. iii. (JAM.) His wyfe impacient of lang tary..gaif hym gret artation to persew the thrid weird.

artcher, obs. form of ARCHER.

1553 *Four Supplic.* 100 Shepeherdes be but yll artchers.

† **'arted**, *ppl. a.* [f. ART *v.*² and *sb.* + -ED.]

1. Versed in any art, or in artifice; skilled, trained.

1627 FELTHAM *Resolves* I. xii. Wks. 1677. 18 Throughly arted in navigation. *Ibid.* I. lxxxviii, To sing or play like an arted musician. **1646** GAULE *Cases Consc.* 33 Either the Arted or the Pacted Witch.

2. Made artificial, artificialized.

1638 *Albino & Bellama* (N.) In her which arted lookes does ware, Men looke for natures steps, and cannot trace her.

3. Made by art or artifice, artificial.

1652 GAULE *Magastrom* 5 Was she instructed by an arted speculation or by a divine revelation? **1655** H. VAUGHAN *Silex Scint.* I. (1858) 49 And sweeter aires streame from a grone, Than any arted string.

artefac. = ARTEFACT *sb.* and *a.* (Disused.)

1906 CHAMBERLIN & SALISBURY *Geol.* III. 502 Following European precedent, the earlier students classed the rougher artefacs as paleolithic... The better fashioned artefacs were classed as neolithic. **1911** *Encycl. Brit.* XXI. 836/1 The difficulty of employing *artefacs* of stone as chronological indicators.

artefact ('ɑːtɪfækt), *sb.* and *a.* Also **arti-**. [f. L. *arte*, abl. of *ars* art + *factum*, neut. pa. pple. of *facere* to make. (Cf. Sp., Pg. *artefacto*, It. *artefatto*, adj. and sb.)] **A.** *sb.* Anything made by human art and workmanship; an artificial product. In *Archæol.* applied to the rude products of aboriginal workmanship as distinguished from natural remains.

1821 COLERIDGE in *Blackw. Mag.* X. 256 The conception of all these, as realized in one and the same artéfact, may be fairly entitled, the Ideal of an Ink-stand. *a* **1834** COLERIDGE *Lit. Rem.* III. 347 A lump of sugar of lead lies among other artefacts on the shelf of a collector. **1884** G. S. HALL *Diestemey's Teaching Hist.* 8 School artifacts, mistaken for perplexities inherent in the subject itself. **1890** D. G. BRINTON *Races & Peoples* ii. 75 This is shown..by the presence of artefacts and shells from the Pacific in old graves on the Atlantic coast. **1922** *Class. Q.* XVI. 24 The shadows seem to be real till their originals are exposed as the paltry artefacts they are. **1925** *Times Lit. Suppl.* 13 Aug. 529/1 The distribution of artifacts. **1927** G. MURRAY *Class. Tradition* 243 Poetry..is an 'artifact'—I mean, it is a thing made.

b. In technical and medical use, a product or effect that is not present in the natural state (of an organism, etc.) but occurs during or as a result of investigation or is brought about by some extraneous agency.

1908 *Practitioner* LXXXI. 383, I must quote a case of dermatitis artefacta, which was hardly hysterical... The alternatives for diagnosis..were (1) Some local pyodermic infection. (2) A trophic lesion (?). (3) An 'artefact'. **1940** *Chambers's Techn. Dict.* 52/2 *Artefact* (Zoology), any apparent structure which does not represent part of the actual specimen, but is due to faulty preparation. **1943** *Electronic Engin.* XVI. 189/3 The reverse kick [on the cathode-ray oscilloscope]..was not to be expected on theoretical grounds... This artefact is probably unimportant. **1946** *Brit. Jrnl. Psychol.* Sept. 22 The recognition of artefacts, such as those due to circulatory or respiratory changes..comes with experience. **1947** *Electronic Engin.* XIX. 82/2 An amplifier which will be free from the annoying 'artefacts' which are so often due to self-generated input stage noise. **1961** *Brit. Med. Dict.* 138/2 *Artefact.* In histology, a misleading appearance in a preparation caused by some form of contamination, or by physical or chemical changes induced by manipulation or the reagents employed in making the preparation. In electro-encephalography, any wave that has its origin elsewhere than in the brain. In dermatology, a self-induced lesion.

c. *transf.*

1934 TOYNBEE *Stud. Hist.* III. III. 156 It is a mere accident..that the material tools which Man has made for himself should have a greater capacity to survive..than Man's psychic artif[a]cts. **1949** *Foreign Affairs* XXVII. 384 The police power of a government cannot be a pure political artifact.

B. *adj.* Made by human art and workmanship. *rare.*

1909 J. A. STEWART *Plato's Doctr. Ideas* 179 The rêverie-image of an object natural or artefact.

artefactual (ɑːtɪ'fæktjuːəl), *a.* Also **arti-**. [f. ARTEFACT *sb.* + *-ual*, as in *factual*, etc.: see -AL¹.] **1. a.** *Archæol.* That consists of or pertains to an artefact or artefacts.

1950 *Antiquity* XXIV. 193 Much of the interest of the catalogue of Jarmo materials lies in the non-artifactual materials. **1956** *Ibid* XXX. 224 In western Asia, we can now show that the village, as an architectural (artifactual) manifestation, is the hall-mark of the appearance of the second phase. **1963** KWANG-CHIH CHANG *Archaeol. Anc. China* 1 The study of bygone cultures and civilizations by means of their artifactual remains has never ceased to be a part of the historical method. **1979** P. L. BROWN *Megaliths & Masterminds* 88 The strongest artefactual evidence of Mediterranean trade lay in the finding of the so-called faience beads. **1983-84** *Rescue News* Winter 4/3 The artefactual database is being enlarged.

b. *gen.* Of or pertaining to man-made or manufactured objects.

1960 M. SCRIVEN in S. Hook *Dimensions of Mind* xiii. 119 If we define 'machine' as an inanimate artifactual device, we cannot go on to ask whether machines might one day be conscious. **1966** T. LEARY *Politics of Ecstasy* xi. 170 I'll teach them how to live as an animal and as a creature of nature.. before I will force artifactual symbols..on their 2-billion-year-old cellular machineries. **1979** *Amer. Speech 1978* LIII. 268 The basis for sound symbolism, provided we allow properly for regional and artifactual differences in environments, is presumably a human universal. **1979** *Encounter* Oct. 59/2 Other artifactual fields of endeavour have in the past been made to play this false role of an all-seeing mirror to man, notably clothes, ornaments and sculpture. **1981** B. A. FARRELL *Standing of Psychoanal.* iv. 62 The material also contains a manufactured, or artefactual component.

2. Of a scientific observation or phenomenon: of the nature of an artefact; arising from the method of procedure; spurious, artificial.

1962 D. G. COGAN in A. Pirie *Lens Metabolism Rel. Cataract* 293 When the lens substance does survive the sectioning and mounting, artefactual clefts and vacuoles are regularly present. **1972** *Jrnl. Social Psychol.* LXXXVIII. 304 Eye contact results in the latter study could be regarded as artifactual. **1973** *Nature* 21/28 Dec. 511/1 Extreme care must be taken when using spatial filtering methods to improve the quality of very noisy images, or an artefactual structure defined by the spatial filter may be generated in the reconstructed image. **1977** *Lancet* 2 July 34/2 The rare finding of a low plasma-total-CO_2 ('bicarbonate') with no obvious reason should immediately lead the chemical pathologist to exclude artefactual causes such as a small or old blood specimen.

Hence **arte'factually** *adv.*, by artefactual means, as a result of the occurrence of an artefact (sense b); artificially.

1962 D. G. COGAN in A. Pirie *Lens Metabolism Rel. Cataract* i. Plate 3 (*caption*) The epithelium is artefactually separated from superficial fibres in the upper right hand corner. **1971** *Jrnl. Gen. Psychol.* Jan. 158 Quite artifactually, therefore, the 'recognition' score for X was elevated. **1976** *Path. Ann.* XI. 213 (*caption*) In this thymic carcinoid, a ball with necrotic calcified center has artefactually detached from the stroma. **1977** *Lancet* 1 Jan. 46/2 Large doses of toxic compounds administered as antagonists may themselves artifactually diminish fluid production by damaging the test animal.

arteir, variant of *artere*, by-form of ARTERY.

artel (ɑː'tɛl). [Russ. *artél'*.] In Russia, an association of craftsmen or other workers for work in common. Also *attrib.* in ***artelman*** [partial tr. of Russ. *artél'shchik*].

1884 J. RAE *Contemp. Socialism* vii. 280 The *artel* or labourers' association and the commune. **1892** *Daily News* 22 Jan. 5/2 The only other kind of trade organization existing in the Empire is known as the 'Artel', and is peculiar to Russia. **1895** *Chambers's Jrnl.* 9 Nov. 705/2 The authority of an artelman is unlimited. **1900** L. MAUDE tr. *Tolstoy's Resurrection* 226 We are all masons, and belong to the same *artel.* **1921** S. GRAHAM *Europe—Whither Bound?* vi. 89 An *artel* of Rostof engineers. **1955** H. HODGKINSON *Doubletalk* 27 A brigade, or *artel*, chosen without regard for family connections, undertake particular functions—ploughing, reaping, processing, milking, etc.—as and where required.

arteller, var. ARTILLER, *Obs.*, maker of bows.

artellere, artelrie, obs. forms of ARTILLERY.

† **artemage.** *Obs. rare*⁻¹. [a. OF. *artimage*, f. *art* art + *magie* magic.] Magic art: see ART *sb.* 11 a.

1393 GOWER *Conf.* III. 67 And through the craft of artemage Of wexe he forged an ymage.

‖ **Artemisia** (ɑːtɪ'mɪzɪə). [L., a. Gr. ἀρτεμισία, f. Ἄρτεμις the goddess Diana.] A genus of plants (N.O. *Compositæ*), distinguished by a peculiarly bitter or aromatic taste, including the Common Wormwood, Mugwort, and Southernwood.

1398 TREVISA *Barth. De P.R.* XVII. xvi. (1495) 613 Artemisia is callyd moder of herbes and was somtyme halowed..to the goddesse that hyghte Arthemis. **1753** CHAMBERS *Cycl. Supp.*, *Artemisia*, a medicinal herb of great efficacy as an uterine. **1866** *Treas. Bot.* 95/1 The *Artemisias* abound in the arid soil of the Tartarian Steppes.

† **'arter.** *Obs.* [a. OF. *artre*, mod. *artison*; cf. *artiron* in Cotgr.] A wood-worm. (Cf. ART-WORM.)

1622 R. HAWKINS *Voy. S. Sea* (1847) 119 A certain worm called *broma* by the Spaniards and by us *arters*..eat it so full of holes that all the water soaked out.

arter, dial. or vulgar pronunciation of AFTER.

arter(e, early form of ARTERY, from F. *artère*.

† **ar'teriac**, *a.* and *sb.* *Obs.* [ad. L. *artēriacus*, Gr. ἀρτηριακός, also subst. *artēriacē*, ἡ ἀρτηριακή, f. ἀρτηρία: see ARTERY and -AC.] **A.** *adj.* Of or pertaining to the windpipe. **B.** *sb.* A remedy for disease of the windpipe.

1661 LOVELL *Hist. Anim. & Min.* 359 The vice of the voice and speech..are cured..by arteriacks. **1699** in *Phil. Trans.* XXI. 402 An Arteriac..(to smooth the Trachea, and promote Expectoration). **1859** in WORCESTER.

arteriacal (ɑːtə'raɪəkəl), *a.* [f. as prec. + -AL¹.] = ARTERIAL. (In mod. Dicts.)

arterial (ɑː'tɪərɪəl), *a.* [a. F. *artérial* (16th c.), mod. *artériel*: see ARTERY and -AL¹.]

1. Of, belonging to, or of the nature of, an artery. ***arterial vein*** (obs.): the pulmonary artery.

1541 R. COPLAND *Guydon's Quest. Cyrurg.*, One parte called veyne arteryall goth to nourysshe the lunges. **1594** CAREW *Huarte's Exam. Wits* vi. (1616) 87 The naturall heat that is in the vitall spirits, and the arteriall bloud run forthwith to the head. **1680** BUTLER *Rem.* (1759) I. 405 Examines the arterial Pulsation of its left Foreleg. **1743** tr. *Heister's Surg.* 292 Diminished Resistance in the arterial coats. **1872** HUXLEY *Phys.* iv. 75 The scarlet blood is commonly known as arterial.

2. Resembling an artery in having a main channel of communication with many branches. ***arterial drainage***: a system of drains ramifying like an artery (objection has been taken to this term on the ground that the flow through such a system of drains is in the opposite direction to that of the arterial system of the body, and really identical with the current in the veins). Applied esp. to main roads or lines of transport or communication. Also as *sb.*, an arterial road.

1831 CARLYLE *Sart. Res.* III. vii, Venous-arterial circulation of Letters. **1841** G. DEANE (*title*) A plea for an Arterial Drainage. **1865** *Chr. Misc. & Family Visitor* Ser. II. XI. 154/1 The termini of the different trunk or arterial railways. **1867** *Morn. Star* 12 Mar., The Great Southern and Western Railway..a great arterial line. **1898** *Daily News* 17 Nov. 4/4 He urged that wide arterial improvements of the streets were needed. **1920** *Act 10 & 11 Geo. V* c. 57 §2 Land required for or in connection with the construction of any arterial road. **1932** H. NICOLSON *Public Faces* xii. 310 Jane Campbell..sped along the Kent arterial.

arterialization (ɑːˌtɪərɪəlaɪ'zeɪʃən). [n. of action f. next; cf. F. *artérialisation.*] The action or process of arterializing.

1836 TODD *Cycl. Anat. & Phys.* I. 260/2 The arterialization of the blood. **1872** HUXLEY *Phys.* iv. 76 The arterialization of blood in the lungs seems to be a very mixed process, partly physical, and yet to a certain extent chemical.

ar'terialize, *v.* [f. ARTERIAL + -IZE; cf. F. *artérialiser.*]

1. To convert venous into arterial (blood) by exposure to oxygen in the lungs. Hence **arterialized** *ppl. a.*

1833 ROGET in Tweedie's *Cycl. Pract. Med.* I. 178/2 The arterialized blood. **1858** H. GRAY *Anat.* 630 The blood, arterialized by its passage through the lungs, is returned to the left side of the heart by the pulmonary veins.

2. To furnish with an arterial system. Also *transf.*

1881 PALGRAVE *Vis. Eng.* 2 Her hand With network milepaths binding plain and hill, Arterialized the land.

arterio- (ɑː'tɪərɪəʊ) [a. Gr. ἀρτηριο-.] Comb. form of *artery*, *arterial*; as in ***arterio-capillary***, etc.

1836-39 TODD *Cycl. Anat. & Phys.* II. 772/1 The left side of the heart..is in the hibernating animal..only arterio-contractile.

arteriogram (ɑː'tɪərɪəʊgræm). [f. ARTERIO- + -GRAM.] † **1.** = SPHYGMOGRAM. *Obs.*

1885 STIRLING tr. *Landois's Text-bk. Human Physiol.* I. II. §67. 134 In every pulse-curve—sphygmogram or arteriogram—we can distinguish the ascending part of the curve.

2. A picture obtained by arteriography (sense b).

1929 *Amer. Jrnl. Roent.* XXII. 80 New technique of arterial encephalography... Cases are described in which the arteriograms were of more or less diagnostic value. **1944** *Lancet* 26 Aug., The third arteriogram in the series..shows the outline of the popliteal artery.

arteriography (ɑːˌtɪərɪ'ɒgrəfɪ). [f. ARTERIO- + Gr. -γραφία: see -GRAPHY.] † **a.** Systematic description of the arteries; = SPHYGMOGRAPHY. *Obs.*

1842 DUNGLISON *Dict. Med. Sci.* (ed. 3) 70/2 *Arteriography*, a description of the arteries. **1859** in WORCESTER.

b. Examination of the arteries by means of radiology after injection of a radio-opaque material. Hence **arterio'graphic** *a.*, of or pertaining to arteriography.

1929 D. M. GREIG *Edin. Med. Jrnl.* XXXVI. 632 Arteriography in the living subject. The injection of arteries by..shadow-casting material and subsequent radiography ..on the living subject is recent and as yet restricted to few operators..Moniz, Pinto and Lima, who have carried out seventy cerebral arteriographies without..untoward symptom. **1944** *Lancet* 26 Aug. 271/1 It was necessary to determine the exact size, shape and anatomical location of the sac. Arteriography is the only certain method of deciding this preoperatively. **1955** *Gloss. Terms Radiology* (*B.S.I.*) 56 *Arteriography*, the radiological examination of arteries following direct injection of a contrast medium. **1962** *Lancet* 8 Dec. 1225/1 Based on arteriographic criteria, 7 (45%) of the 15 arterial clots were lysed after approximately 60 hours' intensive therapy.

arteriolar (ɑːtɪərɪ'əʊlə(r)), *a.* [f. ARTERIOL(E + -AR¹.] Of, belonging to, or of the nature of, an arteriole.

1941 in DORLAND *Med. Dict.* **1961** *Lancet* 9 Sept. 573/2 Examination of the fundi showed bilateral retinal arteriolar narrowing.

arteriole (ɑː'tɪərɪəʊl). [ad. mod.L. *artēriola*, dim. of *artēria* ARTERY; cf. F. *artériole.*] A minute or ultimate artery.

1839-47 TODD *Cycl. Anat. & Phys.* III. 989/2 The branchial artery..giving off arterioles to the branchial laminæ. **1878** *Smithsonian Rep.* 424 The arterioles of the muscles.

arteriology (ɑːˌtɪərɪˈɒlədʒɪ). [f. ARTERIO- + Gr. -λογία: see -LOGY.] Scientific study of, or a treatise upon, the arteries.
1859 in WORCESTER.

arteriosclerosis (ɑːˌtɪərɪəʊsklɪəˈrəʊsɪs). *Path.* [f. ARTERIO- + SCLEROSIS.] Abnormal thickening and hardening of the walls of the arteries, occurring chiefly in old age.
1886 D. MACALISTER tr. *Ziegler's Text-bk. Path. Anat. & Pathogenesis* II. 21 Gull and Sutton were the first to call special attention to the arterial changes associated with contracted kidney... However..they did not sufficiently distinguish between primary arteriosclerosis and the secondary form. **1901** *Practitioner* Mar. 315 The patient may be handicapped in his struggle with the fever by arterio-sclerosis. **1948** tr. *A. Brodal's Neurol. Anat.* 409 Among conditions which in some cases have benefited from sympathetic denervation may be mentioned..arterio-sclerosis.

Hence **arˌterioscleˈrotic** *a.*, of, pertaining to, or affected by arteriosclerosis; as *sb.*, an arteriosclerotic person.
1886 D. MACALISTER tr. *Ziegler's Text-Bk. Path. Anat. & Pathogenesis* II. 20 The affection..is best described by the term arteriosclerotic atrophy. The renal arteries and their branches in aged persons are very frequently the seat of sclerotic changes. **1907** W. JAMES *Let.* 2 Jan. in R. B. Perry *Tht. & Char. W. J.* (1935) II. 452 All is well with the James family—all but an increase of my arterio sclerotic symptoms in the last six months. **1909** *Practitioner* Nov. 616 The arterio-sclerotic kidney. **1961** *Lancet* 5 Aug. 306/2 Arteriosclerotic brain disease. *Ibid.* 26 Aug. 492/2 A short bruit can be related to kinking and lengthening of the iliac arteries in arteriosclerotics.

†**arˌteriˈose**, *a.* *Obs. rare*⁻¹. [f. L. *artēri-a* ARTERY + -OSE.] = ARTERIAL.
1661 LOVELL *Hist. Anim. & Min.* 321 Vessels arteriose.

arteriotomy (ɑːˌtɪərɪˈɒtəmɪ). [ad. L. *artēriotomia*, Gr. ἀρτηριοτομία, f. ἀρτηριο- (see above) + -τομία cutting; cf. ANATOMY.] The operation of cutting into or opening an artery, esp. for the purpose of blood-letting. Also, that part of anatomy which treats of the dissection of arteries. **arteriˈotomist**, one who practises arteriotomy.
1634 T. JOHNSON tr. *Parey's Chirurg.* XVII. lix. (1678) 411 Arteritomy, is the opening of an artery. **1683** *Phil. Trans.* XIII. 224 Arteriotomy formerly used for the Gout. **1876** BARTHOLOW *Mat. Med.* (1879) 546 When bloodletting is indicated in intracranial maladies, venesection or arteriotomy is to be preferred. **1684** tr. *Bonet's Merc. Compit.* VIII. 274 There lived at Padua an experienced Arteriotomist.

arterious (ɑːˈtɪərɪəs), *a.* *arch.* [f. L. *artēri-a* + -OUS.] = ARTERIAL.
1634 T. JOHNSON tr. *Parey's Chirurg.* IX. iv. (1678) 217 Large effusion of..arterious blood. [**1656** BLOUNT *Glossogr.*, *Arterious*, full of arteries.] **1713** CHESELDEN *Anat.* III. xv. (1726) 246 The cut orifices of the arterious and venous vessels. **1819** REES *Encycl.* s.v., If any arterious trunk were accidentally compressed.

arteriovenous (ɑːˌtɪərɪəʊˈviːnəs), *a.* [f. ARTERIO- + VENOUS *a.*] Of, pertaining to, or affecting an artery and a vein.
1880 *Syd. Soc. Lex.*, *Arteriovenous murmur*..where there is a communication between a large artery and a vein. **1890** BILLINGS *Med. Dict.* I. 109/1 *Arterio-venous aneurism*, an aneurism opening into a vein. **1946** *Lancet* 20 July 85/2 The signs of an arteriovenous fistula were found in his right femoral region. **1961** *Ibid.* 29 July 250/1 Systolic or continuous murmurs can be heard in the upper abdomen in patients with..arteriovenous shunts.

‖**arteritis** (ɑːtəˈraɪtɪs). *Path.* [f. as ARTERIOUS *a.* + -ITIS.] Inflammation of an artery.
1836 TODD *Cycl. Anat. & Phys.* I. 226/2 An example of acute arteritis. **1878** T. BRYANT *Pract. Surg.* I. 37 The gradual closure of a vessel from local arteritis.

†**ˈarterizing**, *vbl. sb.* *Obs. rare*⁻¹. [as if from a vb. *arterize*, from *artery*.] The conveyance of the vital spirits. See ARTERY 2.
1600 TOURNEUR *Transf. Met.* v, Their infernall smell With [? will] all thy arterizing strength expell, And make thy heart an agonizing hell.

artery (ˈɑːtərɪ), *sb.* Forms: α. 4–6 **arterie**, 6– **artery**; also β. 6 **arter(e**, 6–7 **arture**, **artier**, 7 **arteir**, **-ir**, **-ire**. [ad. L. *artēria*, a. Gr. ἀρτηρία, prob. f. αἴρ-ειν to raise, lift up (cf. AORTA), but referred by some of the ancients to ἀήρ 'air,' in accordance with their idea of arterial functions: see below. The parallel forms β. from F. *artère* were common in 16–17th c.]

†**1.** The trachea or windpipe. (Called in L. *arteria aspera*, from the rough surface presented by its cartilaginous rings.) *Obs.*
1547 BOORDE *Brev. Health* ccxxvi. 77 The longes, the midryffe, the arter trache, the Epigloote. **1594** T. B. *La Primaud. Fr. Acad.* II. 93 That pipe which is called the rough artery or wind-pipe. **1607** TOPSELL *Four-f. Beasts* 522 The artery of his voice is pressed, and so he cannot cry aloud. **1626** BACON *Sylva* §199 [The Lungs] expelleth the air: which through the Artire, throat and mouth, maketh the voice. **1661** LOVELL *Hist. Anim. & Min.* Introd., In respect of the..rough arterie, serpents are like birds.

2. a. One of the membranous, elastic, pulsating tubes, forming part of the system of vessels by which the blood is conveyed from the heart to all parts of the body.
Among the ancients, the arteries, as they do not contain any blood after death, were popularly regarded as air-ducts, ramifying from the trachea; see prec. sense. Mediæval writers supposed them to contain an ethereal fluid quite distinct from that in the veins, called 'spiritual blood' or 'vital spirits' (cf. ANIMAL SPIRITS), an error which, after Harvey's discovery of the circulation of the blood, only gradually died out.
1398 TREVISA *Barth. De P.R.* v. lxi. (1495) 177 A veyne callid Arteria..to bere and brynge kindely heete from the herte to al the membres..The other arterie of the herte is more than the fyrste. **1533** ELYOT *Cast. Helth* 12 Spirit vitall procedeth from the harte, and by the arteries or pulses is sente into all the body. **1541** R. COPLAND *Guydon's Quest. Cyrurg.*, The vaynes bereth the nourysshyng blode, and the arteres the spyrytual blode..For the veynes brede of the lyuer, and the arteres of the hert. **1621** BURTON *Anat. Mel.* I. i. II. iii. 16 Arteries are long and hollow, with a double skin to convey the vital spirits. **1706** PHILLIPS, *Arteries*, in which the most thin and hottest part of the Blood, together with the Vital Spirits, pass thro' the Body. [Similarly in BAILEY 1742]. *c* **1718** QUINCY (J.) The coats of the veins seem only to be continuations of the capillary arteries. **1872** BAKER *Nile Tribut.* viii. 118 The arteries being divided, the animal would quickly bleed to death.

b. *attrib.*
1519 HORMAN *Vulg.* 27 b, The arter strynge is the condyte of the lyfe sprite. **1528** PAYNELL *Salerne Regim.* 2 B i, Veyne bludde ruddye and obscure: and arterie bludde ruddye and clere. **1836** TODD *Cycl. Anat.& Phys.* I. 228/1 A forceps, not unlike the common artery-forceps.

3. *fig.*
1590 GREENE *Mourn. Garm.* (1616) Pref. 5 To see the vanity of youth, so anatomised, that you may see euery veine, muscle and arterie. **1835** LYTTON *Rienzi* v. vi. 264 The awful curse of the papal excommunication..seemed to freeze up all the arteries of life.

4. a. *transf.* A main channel in a ramifying system of communication.
1850 GLISAN *Jrnl. Army Life* (1874) 27 Those great arteries of commerce—the railroads. **1860** MAURY *Phys. Geog. Sea* v. §270 These streams are the great arteries of inland commerce. **1924** GALSWORTHY *White Monkey* III. vii. 258 But along the main artery at the end the traffic streamed and rattled.

b. A major river in a river-system. *U.S.*
1805 JEFFERSON in E. O. Rowland *Life W. Dunbar* (1930) 177 We shall delineate with correctness the great arteries of this great country. **1827** J. F. COOPER *Prairie* xxiv, The mighty arteries of the Missouri and Mississippi.

†**5.** A ligament. *Obs.*
1621 QUARLES *Esther* (1717) 96 The strongest Arteries that knit and tie The members of a mixed Monarchy. **1658** A. FOX tr. *Wurtz' Surg.* II. xv. 120 The bones in the Joynt ..are covered with Arteries, which are weaker than bones.

artery (ˈɑːtərɪ), *v.* [f. prec. sb.] To furnish with, or as if with, arteries.
1856 BOKER *L. de Guzman* III. i, A kingdom veined and arteried with plots. **1878** A. CAMERON in *N. Amer. Rev.* CXXVI. 491 Great rivers that arteried every state.

artesian (ɑːˈtiːʒən), *a.* [ad. F. *artésien*, f. OF. *Arteis*, now *Artois*, name of an old province of France.] Pertaining to Artois, or resembling the wells made there in the 18th cent., in which a perpendicular boring into a synclinal fold or basin of the strata produces a constant supply of water rising spontaneously to the surface of the ground. By extension applied to water obtainable by artesian boring.
1830 LYELL *Princ. Geol.* (1875) II. III. xlviii. 578 Artesian borings at Calcutta. **1860** TRISTRAM *Gt. Sahara* xvii. 287 Here, in every village, centuries before the principle of the artesian well was acknowledged in Europe, the Rouar'a have been in the habit of boring simple artesian wells. **1878** HUXLEY *Physiogr.* 33 The fountains in Trafalgar Square are fed with water from an Artesian well. **1893** *Pop. Sci. Monthly* XLII. 607 In the West many people discredit the possibility of artesian water in many favorable localities, because of the absence of consolidated strata. **1897** *Westm. Gaz.* 21 Apr. 8/2 A very large part of the interior of Western Australia is wholly unfitted for the purposes of human habitation. Its appearance may ultimately be changed by the discovery of artesian water.

artetik, obs. f. ARTHRITIC; cf. OF. *artetique*.

Artex (ˈɑːrtɛks). A proprietary name for: (*a*) a kind of distemper used in the manufacture of paint; (*b*) a textured paint applied, esp. in decorative patterns, to walls and ceilings. Hence **ˈArtex** *v. trans.*, to paint or decorate with Artex paint; **ˈArtexing** *vbl. sb.*, treatment with Artex.
1952 *Trade Marks Jrnl.* 7 May 391/1 '*Artex*', use claimed from..1945... Distemper in powder form for use in the manufacture of water plastic paint. Artex Products (Decorations) Limited, Worthing Road, Rustington, Sussex; Manufacturers. **1976** *Eastern Even. News* (Norwich) 27 Aug., (Advt.), The property has a double garage, Artex ceilings, wood finish doors..sun blinds. **1976** *Southern Even. Echo* (Southampton) 2 Nov. (Advts. Suppl.) 8/6 A 12 × 12 ceiling Artexed for £9. Money back if not satisfied. **1976** *Liverpool Echo* 22 Nov. 13/6 (Advt.), Artexing and plastering. **1984** *Trade Marks Jrnl.* 1 Aug. 1936/2 *Artex Ax*... Paints and decorative texturable coatings (in the nature of paint). Artex Limited, Artex Avenue, Newhaven, East Sussex BN9 9DD; Manufacturers. **1987** *Brentwood Gaz. & Mid-Essex Recorder* 17 Apr. 60 (Advt.), Artex textural applications. A short course..in the application of textured coatings to wall and ceiling surfaces.

artful (ˈɑːtfʊl), *a.* [f. ART *sb.* + -FUL.]

I. Of persons or agents.

†**1.** Versed in the (liberal) arts; learned, wise.
1613 HEYWOOD *Braz. Age* II. ii. Wks. III. 213 A beauteous Lady, art-full wise. **1681** JORDAN *Lond. Joy* in Heath *Grocers' Comp.* (1869) 544 A piece worthy of an artful man's Examination.

2. Having practical, operative, or constructive skill; dexterous, clever. *arch.*
1697 DRYDEN *Life Virgil* (R.) Too artful a writer to set down events in exact historical order. **1710** SHAFTESB. *Charac.* III. i. (1737) II. 385 Subtile Threds spun from their artful Mouths! **1718** POPE *Iliad* XIV. 204 Her artful hands the radiant tresses tied.

3. Skilful in adapting means to ends, so as to secure the accomplishment of a purpose, adroit; passing gradually into: Skilful in taking an unfair advantage; using stratagem, wily; cunning, crafty, deceitful.
1739 T. SHERIDAN *Persius* i. 23 Horace was more artful, and in a merry Way touched upon his Friends' Faults without putting them out of Humour. **1760** MITCHELL in Ellis *Orig. Lett.* II. 480 IV. 419 Make use of the artful pen of Voltaire to draw secrets from the King of Prussia. **1797** BEWICK *Brit. Birds* I. 73 Made use of by artful and designing men. **1857** Bohn's *Handbk. Prov.* 67 An artful fellow is the devil in a doublet.

II. Of things, actions, etc.

4. Displaying or characterized by technical skill; performed or executed in accordance with the rules of art; artistic. *arch.*
1615 *Latham's Falconry* Pref. Verses, To..force her to your voice and luring fall, Is strangely artfull. **1637** MILTON *Comus* 494 Thyrsis! whose artful strains have oft delayed The huddling brook. **1718** J. CHAMBERLAYNE *Relig. Philos.* I. vi. §8 So artful a Machine as every Man is. **1799** G. SMITH *Laboratory* I. 41 It would not be deemed an artful performance to fire one cartouch after another.

5. Produced by art, as opposed to what is natural; artificial, imitative, unreal.
1706 ADDISON *Rosamond* II. i, In yon cool grotto's artful night. **1779** J. MOORE *View Soc. Fr.* viii. (1789) I. 55 The artful distresses of a romance. **1857** EMERSON *Poems* 114 Smite the chords..That they may render back Artful thunder.

6. Skilfully adapted for the accomplishment of a purpose; ingenious, clever; passing gradually into: Cunning, crafty, deceitful.
1705 STANHOPE *Paraphr.* I. 217 Artful Reasonings, and most moving Eloquence. **1712** STEELE *Spect.* No. 400 ⁋2 Artful Conformity to the Modesty of a Woman's Manners. **1843** MILL *Logic* II. iv. §4 The marks, by an artful combination of which men have been able to discover and prove all that is proved in geometry. **1865** DICKENS *Mut. Fr.* xv, This is a very artful dodge.

ˈartfully, *adv.* [f. prec. + -LY².]

1. In an artful manner, with skill or art.
1613 MIDDLETON *Tri. Truth* in Heath *Grocers' Comp.* (1869) 453 Hence is Artfully derived the onely difference betweene Prodigality and Bounty. **1711** STEELE *Spect.* No. 33 ⁋10 Colours artfully spread upon Canvas may entertain the eye. **1835** LYTTON *Rienzi* III. ii. 167 Brightly polished and artfully flexile armour.

2. Cunningly, craftily, by underhand means.
1744 H. WALPOLE *Lett. H. Mann* 100 (1834) I. 337 The French fled shamefully, that was I suppose designedly and artfully. **1849** MACAULAY *Hist. Eng.* II. 63 In these fatal follies the King was artfully encouraged.

ˈartfulness. [f. as prec. + -NESS.] The quality of being artful; skill, dexterity; craftiness.
a **1743** CHEYNE (J.) Consider with how much artfulness his bulk and situation is contrived. **1874** BLACK *Pr. Thule* 19 The artfulness with which he reaches some little result.

arthen, obsolete form of EARTHEN.

arthralgia (ɑːˈθrældʒ(ɪ)ə). *Path.* [mod.L., f. Gr. ἄρθρον joint + ἄλγος pain.] Pain in a joint. Hence **arˈthralgic** *a.*
1848 DUNGLISON *Dict. Med. Sci.* (ed. 7), *Arthralgia*, arthrodynia, gout. **1878** E. S. WOOD tr. *von Ziemssen's Cycl. Pract. Med.* XVII. 566 An attack of colic or arthralgia [in lead-poisoning]. **1890** BILLINGS *Med. Dict.*, *Arthralgic*.., pertaining to arthralgia.

arthritic (ɑːˈθrɪtɪk), *a.* and *sb.* Forms: 4–5 **artetyke**, **-ik**, 6 **arthetyke**, **-ycke**, 7–8 **arthritick**, 8– **arthritic**. [orig. a. OF. *artetique*, corrupt ad. L. *arthriticus*, a. Gr. ἀρθρῑτικός, f. ἄρθρον joint. Gradually altered back to the L. and Gr. form.]

A. *adj.*

1. Of or pertaining to diseased joints; *spec.* gouty.
1366 MAUNDEV. xxxi. 315 Gowtes artetykes, that me distreynen. **1543** TRAHERON *Vigo's Chirurg.* II. iv. 19 Good for goutes arthetyke of the fete. **1651** BIGGS *New Dispens.* ⁋256 The sciatica, and Arthritick pains. **1785** COWPER *Task* I. 105 Pangs arthritic that infest the toe Of libertine excess.

2. Causing gout. *rare.*
1713 *Lond. & Countr. Brewer* I. (1742) 67 Adulterated, tartarous, arthritic Wines.

†**3.** Good against gout or affections of the joints.
1684 tr. *Bonet's Merc. Compit.* v. 145 Remedies..made of capital and arthritik simples. **1752** CHAMBERS *Cycl.* s.v. *Water*, Arthritic Waters are waters good against the gout.

B. *sb.* †**a.** Affection of the joints, gout (*obs.*). **b.** A person subject to the gout.
[**1398** TREVISA *Barth. De P.R.* VII. lvi. (1495) 270 Arthetica is an ache and euyl in the fyngres and toes.] **1486**

Bk. St. Albans, Hawking C iiij b, A medecine for an hauke that has the artetik. **1801** E. DARWIN *Zoon.* IV. 215 Seized with the gout in a degree that none but arthritics .. can easily conceiue.

ar'thritical, *a.* and *sb.* ? *Obs.* [f. prec. + -AL[1].]

A. *adj.* **1.** = ARTHRITIC.

1528 PAYNELL *Salerne Regim.* R iij b, Vexynge with artetical grefes. **1656** RIDGLEY *Pract. Physic* 18 One man will be Arthritical, another not. **1791** NEWTE *Tour Eng. & Sc.* 189 The sovereign alleviation of rheumatic and arthritical pain.

†**2.** Of the nature of a joint, articular. *Obs. rare.*

1646 SIR T. BROWNE *Pseud. Ep.* 104 Though some want bones, and all extended articulations, yet have they arthriticall analogies.

†**B.** as *sb.* A remedy for affections of the joints.

1671 SALMON *Syn. Med.* III. xv. 359 Arthriticals are such Medicines as are appropriated to the Ioynts.

‖**arthritis** (ɑːˈθraɪtɪs). *Path.* [L., a. Gr. ἀρθρῖτις, f. ἄρθρον joint: see -ITIS.] General term for inflammation of the joints; *spec.* gout.

1544 PHAËR *Regim. Lyfe* (1546) L iij, Paine of the jointes .. is generally called arthritis. **1753** CHAMBERS, *Supp.* s.v. *Gout*, A light arthritis is very often called a fit of the rheumatism. **1847–9** TODD *Cycl. Anat. & Phys.* IV. 577/2 Chronic arthritis of the shoulder.

arthritism (ˈɑːθrɪtɪz(ə)m). [irreg. f. prec. + -ISM.]

1882 D. DUCKWORTH *Barthol. Hosp. Rep.* XVIII. 363 Arthritism .. the peculiar disposition .. whereby affections of the joints are liable to occur, and these especially of rheumatic or gouty nature.

arthro-, comb. form of Gr. ἄρθρον joint, as in: **arthrodesis** (ɑːθrɒˈdiːsɪs) *Surg.* [*ad. G. arthrodese* (E. Albert 1878, *Lehrb. d. Chirurgie* (1883) II. 505), f. Gr. δέσις binding together (δέειν to bind)], an operation to produce ankylosis. **arthrodynic** (ɑːθrəʊˈdɪnɪk), *a. Path.* [Gr. ὀδύνη pain], of or pertaining to *Arthrodynia*, i.e. pain in the joints, chronic rheumatism. **arthrography** (ɑːˈθrɒgrəfɪ) [see -GRAPHY], (*a*) systematic description of the joints; (*b*) examination of the joints by radiography. **ar'thrometer** [see -METER], an instrument (patented in 1919 by W. W. P. Falconer) for measuring the movement-range of joints; hence **ar'thrometry**, the science or study of such measurements; **arthro'metrical** *a.*, of or pertaining to arthrometry. **ar'thropathy** [see -PATHY], painful affection of the joints. **'arthroplasty** [see -PLASTY], the construction of an artificial joint; hence **arthro'plastic** *a.* ‖**arthrosia** (ɑːˈθrəʊzɪə), [mod.L.] = ARTHRITIS (Mayne *Exp. Lex.* 1853). **ar'throsis** [L., a. Gr. ἄρθρωσις], articulation, connexion by a joint. **arthrostome** (ˈɑːθrəʊstəʊm), *Zool.* [Gr. στόμα mouth], name given by L. Agassiz to the mouth of the *Arthropoda*. **arthrotomy** (ɑːˈθrɒtəmɪ) *Surg.* [see -TOMY; cf. Fr. *arthrotomie*], incision of a joint. **arthrozoic** (ɑːθrəʊˈzəʊɪk), *a. Zool.* [Gr. ζωικός of an animal], applied by Huxley to his sixth series of the *Metazoa*, containing the *Arthropoda*, *Nematoscolices*, etc.

1901 *Amer. Jrnl. Med. Sci.* CXXII. 597 *Arthrodesis.* This operation is performed with the aim of establishing a firm right angular ankylosis at the ankle-joint, thus allowing the patient to dispense with apparatus. **1903** TUBBY & JONES *Surgery of Paralyses* I. iii. 89 Complete paralysis of the muscles around the ankle-joint calls invariably for arthrodesis. **1952** M. E. FLOREY *Clin. Appl. Antibiotics* I. vii. 212 An operation for arthrodesis of the knee. **1849** SMART, *Arthrodynic.* **1857** DUNGLISON *Dict. Med. Sci.* 96/2 *Arthrography*, a description of the joints. **1937** *Lancet* 8 May 1119/1 Arthrography also explains the unsatisfactory clinical results sometimes obtained in cases where the radiographic report on the reduction [of a dislocation] has been encouraging. **1949** G. CLAESSEN *Diagnostic Radiol.* ii. 71 The semilunar cartilages of the knee joint do not show on the straight X-ray film except when calcified, but can be demonstrated after the injection of a contrast solution into the joint. This is known as arthrography. **1918** *Lancet* 9 Nov. 632/2 The illustration depicts a new device for measuring the angles of movements of joints... This 'arthrometer' is simple in construction and easily adjusted to the limbs. **1918** W. W. FALCONER (*title*) Arthrometry or the Measurement of the Movements of Joints. *Ibid.* 27 In connection with joint-movement mensuration I have .. prepared a complete series of 'Arthrometrical Charts'. **1878** A. HAMILTON *Nerv. Dis.* 279 During life the evidences of such arthropathies are sometimes numerous. **1913** DORLAND *Med. Dict.* (ed. 7), Arthroplastic. **1918** *Reveille* Aug. 67 There were very few stiff joints in which arthroplastic operations were urgently needed. **1890** BILLINGS *Med. Dict.*, Arthroplasty. **1962** *Lancet* 19 May 1036/1 In the Ullevål series, 16 patients had a primary arthroplasty with Thompson's prosthesis. **1634** T. JOHNSON tr. *Parey's Chirurg.* VI. xlii. (1678) 165 All the bones are composed after two sorts .. by Arthrosis, an Articulation or joynt, and by Symphysis. **1874** ROOSA *Dis. Ear* 202 The joint between the processus lenticularis of the incus and the head of the stapes is an arthrosis. **1888** F. P. FOSTER *Med. Dict.* I. 438/1 Arthrotomy. **1907** *Practitioner* Apr. 575 Robin .. reiterated his condemnation of arthrotomy, except in the case of suppuration supervening in the articulation. **1961** *Lancet* 30 Sept. 745/1 In the infected hips .. early arthrotomy should be undertaken. **1877** HUXLEY *Inv. An.* xii. 680 The lowest known term of the Arthrozoic Series is a Nematoid worm.

‖**arthrodia** (ɑːˈθrəʊdɪə). *Phys.* [mod.L., a. Gr. ἀρθρωδία, f. ἀρθρώδης well-articulated.] A kind of articulation in which the surfaces of the bones are either plane, or but slightly convex and concave respectively; *e.g.* the shoulder-joint. **ar'throdial** *a.*, of, pertaining to, or characterized by, arthrodia. **arthrodic** (aˈθrɒdɪk), *a.*, = prec.

1634 T. JOHNSON tr. *Parey's Chirurg.* VI. xlii. (1678) 165 Arthrodia is when a lightly engraven cavity admits a small and short head. **1842** E. WILSON *Anat. Vade M.* 92 Arthrodia is the movable joint in which the extent of motion is slight and limited. **1836** TODD *Cycl. Anat. & Phys.* I. 256 Arthrodial joints are generally provided with ligaments.

arthrology (ɑːˈθrɒlədʒɪ). [f. Gr. ἄρθρο-ν joint + -λογία discourse, speech.]

1. A scientific treatise on the joints.

1859 in WORCESTER.

†**2.** Finger speech for the deaf and dumb. *Obs.*

1644 BULWER *Chiron.* 99 Order an Alphabet upon the joynts of their Fingers, which Artifice of Arthrologie obtained a privy force.

‖**Arthropoda** (ɑːˈθrɒpədə), *sb. pl. Zool.* Also *sing.* **arthropod.** [mod.L., f. Gr. ἄρθρον joint + πούς (ποδ-) foot. The singular, Eng. in form, is *arthropod* (ˈɑːθrəpɒd); also pl. *-pods.*] Animals with jointed feet; a name for the more highly organized *Annulosa* or *Articulata*, comprising Insects, Spiders, Crustacea, and Myriapoda, having segmented bodies to which hollow jointed appendages (antennæ, wings, legs) are articulated in pairs. **arthropod-borne** *a.*, of a pathogenic organism carried by an arthropod.Cf. ARBORVIRUS. Hence **ar'thropodal** *a.*, of or belonging to the *Arthropoda*. **ar'thropodous** *a.* = prec.

1870 ROLLESTON *Anim. Life* Introd. 105 Accordingly, as the respiration is aquatic or aerial, the Arthropoda are divisible into two great groups. *Ibid.* 107 The Crustacea, the earliest representatives of the Arthropodal type. **1877** HUXLEY *Anat. Inv. An.* vii. 390 In these Arthropods, the body is divided into many segments, the most anterior of which takes on the characters of a distinct head. *Ibid.* xii. 679 Its nervous system is .. Arthropodal. **1882** G. ALLEN *Col. Flowers* ii. 24 Bees and butterflies, the aristocrats of the arthropodous world. **1922** *Encycl. Brit.* XXXI. 896/1 Such arthropoda .. being specific 'nurses' or intermediary hosts of the parasite actually causing the disease, are known as 'carriers' or 'vectors'. **1924** *Glasgow Herald* 27 Sept. 4/2 A crowd of joint-footed Arthropod animals .. that grip firmly with their claws. **1956** *Nature* 25 Feb. 367/2 A comprehensive .. study of acute febrile illnesses .. was undertaken to .. determine the part that arthropod-borne viruses might play in their causation. **1962** *Lancet* 29 Dec. 1363/2 One suggestion is that this may be a virus tumour dependent on some arthropod vector. **1968** *Times* 14 Nov. 8/8 Insects belong to the large group of animals known as arthropods.

arthrosia, arthrostome: see ARTHRO-.

Arthurian (ɑːˈθjʊərɪən), *a.* and *sb.* [See -IAN.]

A. *adj.* Of or pertaining to the legendary British king Arthur, his court, and his knights; also, resembling these or the romances in which they figure.

1853 J. H. BURTON *Hist. Scot. 1689–1748* I. 174 If any reality could be extracted from the Arthurian histories. **1869** STUART-GLENNIE *Arthurian Localities* 5 The Arthurian Cycle. **1875** A. W. WARD *Eng. Dram. Lit.* I. 121 The Arthurian legend. *Ibid.*, The Arthurian cycle of legend. **1899** A. NUTT *Celtic & Mediæval Romance* 14 The later works of the Charlemagne cycle are in detail, tone and spirit often as 'Arthurian' as any purely Breton romance. Huon and Ogier are Arthurian heroes who have strayed by accident to the Court of Charlemagne. **1942** *Burlington Mag.* Feb. 45/1 William Morris and his ideal of the Arthurian unity of the four countries.

B. *sb.* A follower of King Arthur, a knight of the Round Table; one who studies the Arthurian legend.

1907 J. W. H. ATKINS in *Camb. Hist. Eng. Lit.* I. xiv. 312 The noble Arthurian [*sc.* Gawain] .. grants the life of the defiant Golagros. **1957** G. ASHE *King Arthur's Avalon* vi. 221 Giraldus .. was no gullible Arthurian. **1966** *English Studies* XLVII. 145 Many Arthurians .. will feel that the Celtic elements in Geoffrey have been somewhat neglected.

Arthurianism (ɑːˈθjʊərɪənɪz(ə)m). [f. prec. + -ISM.] A form of doctrine, theory, or practice based upon the actions and beliefs of the legendary King Arthur.

1908 A. NOYES *Wm. Morris* ii. 22 One true Church of Arthurianism. **1932** *Times Lit. Suppl.* 21 July 521/2 The Arthurianism of the sixteenth century comes to little more than a topic for pageantry.

†**Arthur's hufe.** *Obs. rare*[−1]. [lit. *Arthur's haunt*; from med.L. use of *Arcturus* as = *Arturus* Arthur.] The star Arcturus or constellation Boötes.

1513 DOUGLAS *Æneis* III. viii. 21 Euery sterne .. That in the stil heuin moue cours we se, Arthuris huyfe, and Hyades betaiknand rane.

artiad (ˈɑːtɪæd). *Chem.* [f. Gr. ἄρτι-ος even + -AD 1 a.] A chemical element or radical with *even* degrees of quantivalency or atomicity, *e.g.* a dyad, tetrad, or hexad, in opposition to *perissads*, which include monads, triads, and pentads.

1870 WATTS *Dict. Chem.* VI. 238 The elements may be divided in this respect into two classes, one of *odd*, the other of *even* equivalence, the former distinguished as *perissads*, the latter as *artiads*.

artic, colloq. abbrev. of *articulated lorry* (*vehicle*, etc.); see ARTICULATED *ppl. a.* 2 b.

1951, **1958** [see ARTICULATED *ppl. a.* 2 b]. **1970** G. F. NEWMAN *Sir, you Bastard* i. 26 Tiny turnings where he would have lots of fun manœuvring a forty-foot artic. **1977** 'D. RUTHERFORD' *Return Load* i. 12 To see a woman at the wheel of a big artic was surprising. **1985** *Sunday Times* 24 Feb. 7/3 He found artics couldn't carry the load of 60 ton containers needed for economical operation.

artic, -ik(e, obs. forms of ARCTIC.

artichoke (ˈɑːtɪtʃəʊk). Forms: 6 **archecokk, archichoke, archychock(e, artochock(e, -choke, hortichock, artichok, -chault, -chowe, artechock, -choke, archoke, artychough,** 6–7 **harti-, artichock(e,** 6–8 **-chau(x,** 7 **artichoake, -chou(x, -choach, hartichoak(e, -choke, hartechooke,** 7–8 **artichoak,** 6– **artichoke.** [ad. north. It. *articiocco, arciciocco*, for *arcicioffo* (all in Florio), perverted forms of **alcarcioffo*, mod.It. *carciofo*, *-offo* (Florio has pl. '*carcioffi, carciocchi, carcioffoli*, hartichokes'), ad. or cogn. w. OSp. *alcarchofa* (mod. *alcachofa*, Pg. *alcachofra*), a. Sp. Arab. *al-kharshōfa* (P. de Alcala) = Arab. *al-kharshūf* (Bocthor and others; but Freytag gives the word with *ḥ*, as *ḥarshaf*).

The phonetic genealogy seems to be: Sp. Arab. *alkharshōf*(*a*, OSp. *alcarchofa*, (? OIt. *alcarcioffo*), North It. *arcicioffo, arciciocco* (whence Eng. *archychock*), *articiocco*, Eng. *artichock*. Like other words of foreign origin, much influenced in its forms by popular etymology. Association with native words, *arci-* arch-, chief, *cioffo* horse-collar, *ciocco* stump, must have caused the North It. changes; in Fr. the terminal *-chau* was variously assimilated to *chou* cabbage, *chaud* warm, *hault, haut* high, as *artichau, -chou, -chaud, -chault, -chaut*; the It. and Fr. forms were latinized in the 16th c. as *articoccus, -coctus, -cactus*, all with plausible though delusory etymologies, *cactus* being actually the ancient Latin name of the Cardoon; in Eng., explanations of the name were found in its *choking* the *garden* or the *heart* (*horti-, harty-chocks*), or having a 'chock' or 'choke' in its *heart*. Hence also the change from *-chock* to *-choak, -choke*. As to alleged Arabic *ardi-shaukī*, see Skeat.]

1. A composite plant (*Cynara Scolymus*), allied to the thistles, originally from Barbary and the south of Europe, widely cultivated in kitchen-gardens; its eatable parts are the fleshy bases of the involucral leaves or scales of the gigantic thistle-like flower, and its receptacle or 'bottom,' when freed from the bristles and seed-down or 'choke.'

(According to De Candolle the Artichoke is only a cultivated variety of the Cardoon *C. Cardunculus*, and occurs nowhere truly wild. It was brought to Florence from Naples in 1466. For its introduction to England, see quot. 1599.)

1531 *MS. Acc. Bk.* in *N. & Q.* 2 Feb. (1884) 85/2 Bringing Archecokks to the Kings Grace. **1542** BOORDE *Dyetary* xx. 280 There is nothing vsed to be eaten of Artochockes but the hed of them. **1548** TURNER *Names of Herbes*, *Carduus* should be wylde Archichoke, and *Cinara* shoulde be the gardin Archichoke. **1551** —— *Herbal* 87 Archy-chock. **1552** HULOET, Thystle called archoke or cowe thistle, *Scolymus*. *Ibid.*, Artochokes herbe, *Cynara*. **1555** *Fardle Facions* I. iii. 37 Gardein Thistles (whiche we calle Hortichockes). **1563** HYLL *Arte Garden.* 101 The Artichocke groweth like in the heade unto the Pine apple. **1577** B. GOOGE *Heresbach's Husb.* (1586) 63 a, The Hartichoch .. is a kind of Thistell, by the diligence of the Gardner brought to be a good Garden hearbe. **1578** LYTE *Dodoens* lxi. 522 Of Artechokes. **1589** *Shuttlew. Stewards' Acc.* (1856) I. 53 A mayed w[ch] broughte artychoughs, iiij *d.* **1598** B. JONSON *Ev. Man in Hum.* iv. ii, Like a yong artichocke, that alwayes carries pepper and salt, in it selfe. **1599** HAKLUYT *Voy.* II. 165 In time of memory things haue bene brought in that were not here before, as .. the Artichowe in time of Henry the eight. **1599** *Mirr. Policie* 71 [He] did not yet forget the niggardlinesse, but parted Lettice and Artichaux in two. **1601** HOLLAND *Pliny* II. 78, I haue spoken somewhat of Thistles and Artichoux. **1634** *Althorp MS.* 24 For 14 dozen of hartichoakes £02 16s. 00d. **1655** MOUFFET & BENN. *Health's Impr.* (1746) 312 Artichokes grew sometimes only in the Isle of Sicily; and since my remembrance, they were so dainty in England, that usually they were sold for Crowns a-piece. **1688** *Lond. Gaz.* mmccccxxxiv/4 Right Dutch Artichoaks .. for Six Shillings and eight Pence the Hundred. **1725** BRADLEY *Fam. Dict.* s.v. *Sallet*, Artichaux, hot and dry. **1727** SWIFT *Past. Dial.* Wks. 1755 IV. I. 78 The dean .. shall .. steal my artichoaks no more. **1832** *Veg. Subst. Food* 281 Nowhere does the artichoke arrive at greater perfection than in the Orkney Islands.

b. *fig.*

c **1600** J. DAY *Begg. Bednall Gr.* III. ii. (1881) 60 Let him alone you cross-legg'd hartichoak. **1870** E. STRACHEY in *Daily News* 26 Nov., They have eaten, leaf by leaf, a whole artichoke of treaties, taking the September Convention for the last mouthful.

2. Jerusalem Artichoke: a species of Sunflower (*Helianthus tuberosus*), a native of tropical America, cultivated in Europe, having edible tuberous roots, somewhat resembling the Artichoke proper in flavour.

'The name of Jerusalem Artichoke is considered to be a corruption of the Italian *Girasóle Articiocco* or Sunflower Artichoke, under which name it is said to have been distributed from the Farnese garden at Rome, soon after its introduction to Europe in 1617.' W. B. Booth in *Treas. Bot.* **1620** VENNER *Via Recta* vii. 134 Artichocks of *Ierusalem*, is a roote vsually eaten with butter, vinegar, and pepper. **1641** R. BROOKE *Nat. Eng. Episc.* I. iv. 16 Error being like the *Jerusalem-Artichoake*; plant it where you will, it overrunnes the ground and choakes the Heart. **1741** *Compl. Fam.-Piece* II. iii. 358 Set Potatoes, and Jerusalem Artichoaks. **1861** R. PEACOCK *Gryll Grange* i, From this *girasol* we have made Jerusalem, and from the Jerusalem artichoke we make Palestine soup.

article ('ɑːtɪk(ə)l), *sb.* Also 4-7 **articul(e, 5 artycul, artykele, -kle, artikil,** 5-6 **artycle.** [a. F. *article*, ad. L. *articul-us* (which lives on in F. as *orteil*), dim. of *artus* joint, f. *ar-* to join; cf. ARM, ART.]

I. Literally.

†1. A joint connecting two parts of the body. *Obs.*

1541 R. COPLAND *Galyen's Terap.* 2 G ij, Woundes of the artycles are Cacoethes and wycked. **1607** TOPSELL *Foure-f. Beasts* 745 Their legges are without Articles. **1643** J. STEER tr. *Exp. Chyr.* iv. 11 The Nerves and Articuls. **1693** W. ROBERTSON *Phraseol. Gen.* 139 An Article, or joynt, of the body or bones thereof.

II. Of time.

2. a. A nick of time which joins two successive periods, a juncture, a moment; the very moment, the critical point or moment.

1398 TREVISA *Barth. De P.R.* II. xx. (1495) 47 They ben not suffysaunt to the artycle of temptacyon. **1502** *Ord. Crysten Men* (W. de W.) I. ii. (1506) 9 Conferme the holy baptem in the artycle of necessyte. **1634** HABINGTON *Castara* 44 And each article of time Her pure thoughts to heaven flie. **1665-6** *Phil. Trans.* I. 348 Very thick Exhalations..in the Article of the Setting of the Sun. **1709** *Let.* in W. Peek *Axholme* (1815) 207 Pulled him out, just in the article of time that the roof fill in. **1722** WOLLASTON *Relig. Nat.* v. 99 An infirm building, just in the article of falling.

b. esp. in ***article of death.***

?*a* **1475** *Craft of Deyng* 37 (1870) Thai that are in the artykle of ded has vþer temptations. **1483** CAXTON *Cato* F vj b, Euery man ought to haue good hope whan he is in the article of deth. **1512** *MS. Reg. Test. Ebor.* VIII. 101 b, Seyng the articlys of deth comyng apon me. **1635** EVELYN *Diary* (1827) I. 11 To the very article of her departure. **1782** BP. NEWTON *Wks.* II. 706 In the article of death he commended his soul to God. **1861** MAINE *Anc. Law* vi. (1876) 207 Roman citizens originally made their Wills only in the article of death.

III. The separate members or portions of anything written. [*Articulus* in L. was extended from the joint, to the parts jointed on, limbs, members, 'joints' of a finger, etc.; whence *transf.* to the component parts of discourses, writings, actions.]

3. The separate clauses or statements of the Apostles' Creed; the separate items of any summary of faith; the thirty-nine statements to which those who take orders in the Church of England subscribe.

c **1230** *Ancr. R.* 262 Þe articles, þet beoð, ase þauh me seide, þe liðes of ure bileaue. **1340** *Ayenb.* 11 Þe tuelf Articles of þe Cristene Byleve. *a* **1400** *Relig. Pieces fr. Thornt. MS.* (1867) 27 Þe twelue artycles of þe trouthe. *a* **1420** OCCLEVE *De Reg. Princ.* 384 In alle the articles of the feithe I beleeve as holy writte seithe. **1599** *Broughton's Lett.* xi. 38 This article *He descended into Hell*, is but an explication of the former *He dyed and was buried*. *a* **1654** SELDEN *Table-T.* (R.) A minister should preach according to the articles of religion established in the church where he is. **1692** LOCKE *Toleration* i, Articles of Faith (as they are called)..cannot be imposed on any Church by the Law of the Land. **1719** SWIFT *To Yng. Clergym.* Wks. 1755 II. II. 17 That you are any where directed in the canons or articles to attempt explaining the mysteries. **1855** MILMAN *Lat. Chr.* (1864) II. IV. i. 172 The six great articles in the faith of Islam. **1862** BROUGHAM *Brit. Const.* xvii. 272 *note*, The Church is not even synonymous with the clergy..according to the definition in the Thirty-nine Articles. **1865** BUSHNELL *Vicar. Sacr.* Introd. (1868) 31 Will some one undertake to give us Othello by dogmatic article?

4. a. A separate clause or provision of a statute; an enactment, or act. [Common in med. (English) L., as in the *Articuli Cleri*, *Articuli Coronæ*.]

[**1315** *Act 9 Edw. II, Articuli Cleri*, made at Lincolne.] **1523** FITZHERB. *Surv.* j, This statute..wherin is contayned many and dyuers chapiters and artycles. **1547** *Act 1 Edw. VI*, xii, The statute made for the abolishment of diuersity of opinions, in certaine articles concerning Christiane Religion commonly called the vi articles. **1637** *Decree Star Chamb.* viii. in *Milton's Areop.* (Arb.) 13 Books, Ballads..printed contrary to this Article. **1711** C. M. *Let. to Curat* 5 The Famous act of the six articles in the Year, 1539.

b. *Sc. Hist.* **Lords of the Articles**: a standing committee of the Scottish Parliament, who drafted and prepared the measures submitted to the House.

1483 *Act 13 Jas. III* (1597) §95 The Lordes of the Articles thinkis expedient, etc. **1827** HALLAM *Const. Hist.* (1876) III. xvii. 308 From the reign of James IV the lords of articles are regularly named in the records of every parliament. *a* **1862** BUCKLE *Civilis.* (1869) III. ii. 71 The Lords of the Articles whose business it was to digest the measures to be brought before Parliament.

c. the Articles of War: regulations made for the government of the military and naval forces of Great Britain and the United States.

1716 *Lond. Gaz.* mmmmmccccxlvi/10 All having had the Articles of War read to them. **1748** in Beatson *Nav. & Mil. Mem.* (1790) I. 385 The Court unanimously agree, that Rear-Admiral Knowles falls under part of the fourteenth article of war. **1844** *Regul. & Ord. Army* 141 The Articles of War are to be read once in every Three Months to the Officers and Men. **1863** COX *Inst. Eng. Govt.* II. ii. 322 The Mutiny Act proceeds to authorize the Crown to make articles of war.

5. Each of the distinct charges, or counts, of an accusation or indictment; in *pl.* an indictment drawn up in articles.

1413 LYDG. *Pylgr. Sowle* I. xiv. 11, I shold..answere to these artycles of myn accusement. **1553-87** FOXE *A. & M.* III. 140 And charge him with what articles they lusted. **1593** SHAKS. *Rich. II*, IV. i. 243 My Lord dispatch, reade o're these Articles. **1605** BACON *Adv. Learn.* I. ii. §1 Anytus..laid it as an article of charge..against him, that, etc. **1649** SELDEN *Laws of Eng.* II. iii. (1739) 20 A trick of a new kind of Trial..by suggestions upon Articles exhibited against any man before the Council-Table. **1734** tr. *Rollin's Anc. Hist.* (1827) VIII. XIX. §9. 254 To have any articles to lay to his charge. **1864** BURTON *Scot Abr.* I. i. 17 Certain articles presented against this archbishop.

6. Each of the distinct heads or points of an agreement or treaty; hence **a.** in *pl.* a formal agreement. ***articles of apprenticeship***: terms of agreement between an apprentice and his employer. ***articles of association***: rules, conditions, etc., upon which a commercial agreement is founded.

1399 *Rich. Redeless* IV. 43 To reherse þe articlis and graunte all her askynge. **1475** *Bk. Noblesse* 14 The articulis of the pease finalle made between both kingis. **1494** FABYAN VI. clxxxix. 192 Amonges other artycles that he bounde theym vnto. **1614** B. JONSON *Barth. Fair* Introd., I am sent out to you here, with a scrivener, and certain articles drawn out in haste between our author and you. **1732** LEDIARD *Sethos* II. x. 479 To settle the articles of marriage with him. **1735** POPE *Donne Sat.* II. 94 Indentures, Cov'nants, Articles they draw. **1749** FIELDING *Tom Jones* (1775) III. 200 Articles of separation were soon drawn up, and signed between the parties. **1813** WELLINGTON in Gurw. *Disp.* XI. 94, I have just received the articles of capitulation of the Castle of San Sebastian. **1837** MACREADY in *Rem.* II. 80 Construction of the actors' articles of agreement.

b. *sing.* (in same sense). *arch.*

1741-3 WESLEY *Jrnl.* (1749) 79 On Monday an Article was drawn, wherein he agreed to put me in possession on Thursday. **1786** T. JEFFERSON *Writ.* (1859) II. 18 To prepare an article defining the extent of the powers over commerce.

c. *pl.* Terms, conditions. *arch.* Cf. ARTICLE *v.* 5.

1650 T. B. *Worcester's Apoph.* 101 You are all offered large Articles for your selves. **1659** D'OYLY in Burton *Diary* (1828) IV. 420 He may sue his articles. **1685** *Lond. Gaz.* mmlxxv/2 Caschaw has surrendred upon Articles. **1727** ARBUTHNOT *John Bull* (1755) 51 The matter was concluded, and Peg taken into the house upon certain articles. **1761** SMOLLETT *Gil Blas* v. i. (1802) II. 123 An actress enters into articles with a rich gallant.

†**d.** in horse-racing. ***Clerk of the Articles*** = clerk of the course. *Obs.*

1697 *Lond. Gaz.* mmmcccxxiii/4 Any Person may enter his Horse with the Clerk of the Articles till the 29th Instant. **1706** *Ibid.* mmmmccxix/4 To be governed by the Articles of the Race.

†**7.** A clause in a will; a legacy. *Obs.*

1480 *Bury Wills* (1850) 57 Wyllyng the seid will in eueri article to take pleyn effecte. *Ibid.* 60 Contrarie to the entent of this myn articule and laste will. **1761** SMOLLETT *Gil Blas* II. ii, Besides her residue under the will, she had some snug little articles.

8. *gen.* A paragraph, section, or distinct item of any document.

c **1430** *Freemasonry* 87 The furste artycul of thys gemetry. **1505** *Instruc. Hen. VII to Ambassadors* in *Facsim. Nat. MSS.* I. 66 Item, to note welle hir ies, &c.—As to thys articule, the ies of the saide Quyne be of colore browne. **1555** *Fardle Facions* App. 349 The ten articles of the lawe, whiche we commenly calle the .x. commandementes. **1675** BAXTER *Cath. Theol.* II. I. 124 This belongeth to the next Article though here you anticipate it. **1732** ARBUTHNOT *Rules of Diet* 261 All the Substances mentioned in the foregoing Article. **1734** tr. *Rollin's Anc. Hist.* xx. (1827) IX. 1 This 20th book contains 3 articles. *Mod.* Every Main word in this Dictionary is treated in a separate article.

9. A literary composition forming materially part of a journal, magazine, encyclopædia, or other collection, but treating a specific topic distinctly and independently. (Here the idea of a section or part of the book, is quite subordinated to that of the independent character of the 'article.' It is one of the articles *in* the paper, as distinguished from the articles *of* this Dictionary.)

1712 ADDISON *Spect.* No. 452 ¶5 They read the Advertisements with the same curiosity as the Articles of publick News. **1749** FIELDING *Tom Jones* VIII. i, The home articles of a newspaper. **1822** MISS MITFORD in L'Estrange *Life* II. vii. 151 Charles Lamb's articles, signed 'Elia.' **1850** THACKERAY *Pendennis* xxx. (1863) 257 Warrington..pointed to one of the leading articles in that Journal. *c* **1870** KINGLAKE *Crimea* I. (ed. 4) Advt. 13 The book..became the subject—not merely of reviews, but also—of what they call 'articles.'

IV. A separate thing (immaterial or material).

†**10. a.** A particular piece of business, a matter, business, or concern; a subject. ***of great article***: of great moment, of importance. *Obs.*

1430 *Paston Lett.* 14. I. 30 Ye are Vicar general in Inggelond of the worthy Prelate..and have hys power in many grete articles. **1602** SHAKS. *Ham.* v. ii. 122, I take him to be a soul of great article. **1712** STEELE *Spect.* No. 428 ¶1 In his Way to Wealth, which is the great Article of Life. **1748** RICHARDSON *Clarissa* (1811) I. xxxix. 288 To say, there was no article so proper for parents to govern in, as this of marriage. **1767** FORDYCE *Serm. Yng. Wom.* I. vi. 252 Permit me, before I dismiss this article, to offer a hint. **1786** T. JEFFERSON *Writ.* (1859) I. 549 Gardening..is the article in which it surpasses all the earth. **1793** SMEATON *Edystone L.* Introd. 2 In this article Josephus might be mistaken.

b. followed by *of*: The matter of, the particular item of, that which comes under the head of. (Said also of things material.) ***in the article of***: under the head of, so far as concerns, in regard to.

1598 SHAKS. *Merry W.* II. i. 53 Thou shouldst not alter the article of thy Gentry. **1711** ADDISON *Spect.* No. 119 ¶2 A very great Revolution that has happen'd in this Article of Good-breeding. **1788** PRIESTLEY *Lect. Hist.* v. li. 389 The very article of making and managing the ships themselves employs a great number of hands. **1805** S. BOURNE in Rose *Diaries* (1860) II. 206 He thinks himself..better, particularly in the article of sleep. **1874** F. HALL in *N. Amer. Rev.* CXIX. 321 As he views matters, we have been steadily going down hill, in the article of our mother-tongue.

†**11.** An item in an account, list, etc. *Obs.*

1722 DE FOE *Hist. Plague* (1754) 8 The Bills rise high, the Articles of the Fever, Spotted-Fever, and Teeth, began to swell. *Ibid.* (1756) 112 This was really a dismal Article. **1774** MRS. CHAPONE *Improv. Mind* II. 63 A considerable article in expence is saved by it.

12. One of the distinct parts or portions of any subject, action, or proceeding (although the latter is not *formally* divided into items); a piece, a distinct detail, a particular.

1741 MIDDLETON *Cicero* II. XI. 569 An uniformity of character in every article of his conduct. **1760** STERNE *Tr. Shandy* 209, I have an article of news to tell you. **1785** COWPER *Tirocin.* 241 If he there be tamed, Or in one article of vice reclaimed. **1817** JAS. MILL *Brit. India* II. v. ii. 374 An important article of the duty of the Supreme Council. **1875** GRINDON *Life* xviii. 227 To encourage love of work is the first article of sensible education.

13. ***an article of***: a material thing forming part of, or coming under the head of, any class.

1823 RUTTER *Fonthill* 50 That superb article of modern luxury. **1827** DE QUINCEY *Lessing* Wks. XIII. 292 The dress ..is brought before us article by article. **1840** MACREADY *Remin.* II. 160 Called at several shops and priced various articles of furniture. **1866** G. MACDONALD *Ann. Q. Neighb.* xi. (1878) 215 By the time books..come to be loved as articles of furniture.

14. a. *elliptically* (= article of trade, commerce, food, clothing, use, property): A commodity; a piece of goods or property, a chattel, a thing material.

1796 GROSE *Dict. Vulg. Tongue* (ed. 3), *Articles*, breeches: coat, waistcoat, and articles. **1804** J. GRAHAME *Sabbath* (1839) 17/2 The immediate consequence would be (to speak in mercantile phrase) a fall in the price of the article. **1819** BYRON *Juan* I. cxliii, Stockings, slippers, brushes, combs.. With other articles of ladies fair. **1824** DIBDIN *Libr. Comp.* 421 His folio..is yet a 'crack-article' with the knowing. **1829** CARLYLE *Misc.* (1857) I. 269 A superior demand for the article of dramas. **1833** HT. MARTINEAU *Fr. Wines & Pol.* v. 81 If this happened with every article..there would be an end of the cheapness. **1852** MCCULLOCH *Taxation* II. ix. 332 A taxed article, such as soap. **1856** F. PAGET *Owlet of Owlst.* 97 Lady Selina was just the article he wished for. **1859** LEWES *Phys. Com. Life* I. ii. 102 If..the purpose of food be to sustain the organism, that article which sustains it longest ..must be most nutritive of all. **1883** *Law Rep., Q. Bench* XI. 590 The prosecutor's house was feloniously broken into ..and several articles were stolen. *Mod. Shopkeeper*: 'The next article, Ma'am?'

b. Applied to a person: often derog. Formerly, in the U.S., used of a slave considered as an 'article' of merchandise. *slang.*

1811 *Lexicon Balatronicum. Article*, a wench. A prime article. A handsome girl. She's a prime article (*Whip slang*), she's a devilish good piece, a hell of a *goer*. **1837** H. MARTINEAU *Society* II. 325 The creditors..answered that these young ladies [his 'quadroon' nieces] were 'a first-rate article'. **1844** DICKENS *Mart. Chuz.* xxvi. 320 You're a nice article, to turn sulky on first coming home! **1852** STOWE *Uncle Tom* i, There's an article now! You might make your fortune on that ar gal in Orleans, any day. **1857** TROLLOPE *Three Clerks* III. ii. 41 She's the very article for such a man as Peppermint. **1863** L. M. ALCOTT *Hospital Sketches* v. 80 Here was a genuine article—no, not the genuine article at all, we must go to Africa for that—but the sort of creatures generations of slavery have made them. **1928** E. SUTTON tr. *A. Londres's Road to Buenos Ayres* iii. 20 Some 'articles' are ..women from seventeen to twenty years old. **1957** M. K. JOSEPH *I'll Soldier No More* (1958) 15 Listen, you sloppy article, who was on guard from twelve to two last night?

c. Colloq. euphemism for chamber-pot.

1922 JOYCE *Ulysses* 715 Pitcher and night article (on the floor, separate). **1932** *Statesman* (Calcutta) 24 July, A madman..crowned his amusement this morning by bringing an article which he..sat on. **1958** J. CANNAN *And be a Villain* iii. 62 How could he be so rude, she asked, when he said 'pot' instead of 'bedroom article'.

d. With defining word: applied to something judged to be authentic of its kind, not an imitation or counterfeit, esp. (***the***) ***genuine article***. Cf. *the real thing* (REAL *a.*[2] 4 c).

1863 [see sense b]. **1864** C. M. YONGE *Trial* II. iv. 82, I should think so! Genuine article—no mistake. **1913** A. BENNETT *Regent* I. vi. 161 Mr. Rollo Wrissell belonged to one of the seven great families which once governed.. England... Edward Henry breathed to himself, 'This is the genuine article.' **1919** D. Ashford *Young Visiters* (1951) v. 34 His mother was a decent family called Hyssops of the Glen so you see he is not so bad and desireus of being the correct article. **1922** Joyce *Ulysses* 643 Education (the genuine article).

V. In *Arithmetic.*

†**15.** The number 10; each of the *tens*, or round numbers between units (or digits) and hundreds.

1398 Trevisa *Barth. De P.R.* xix. cxxiii. 923 (1495) Eche symple nombre byneth ten is Digitus and ten is the fyrst Articulus, and the nexte is twenty. **1543** Recorde *Gr. Arts* (1640) 219 This is true both of Digits and Articles. **1594** Blundevil *Exerc.* i. i. 2 Article is any number ending in a Cypher, as 10 is one Article, 20 is two Articles. **1751** Chambers *Cycl., Article*, in arithmetic, signifies the number 10, or any number justly divisible into ten parts.

VI. In *Grammar.*

16. A name for the adjectives *the* (Definite Article) and *a, an* (Indefinite Article), and their equivalents in other languages, sometimes considered to form a distinct Part of Speech.

In this sense representing the L. *articulus*, a term used in Latin as early as the time of Quintilian as a transl. of the Gr. ἄρθρον, to denote the Gr. ὁ, ἡ, τό = *the*. The inclusion of *a* and its equivalents belongs to the grammar of the modern languages. Palsgrave (1530) makes two articles in Fr., *ung* and *le*, but he does not seem to know the terms *Definite* and *Indefinite*—which were possibly taken (in a new sense) from the language of the ancient Stoic grammarians who (using ἄρθρα to denote the pronouns) distinguished between ἄρθρα ὡρισμένα or *Definite articles*, and ἄρθρα ἀοριστώδη or *Indefinite articles*; the former being with them our personal pronouns, the latter the other pronouns and demonstratives including the art. ὁ, ἡ, τό = *the*. The exact sense in which ἄρθρον was first used in grammar is uncertain. (I. Bywater.)

1530 Palsgr. Introd. 14 Besydes the viii partes of speche commen betwene them and the latines.. they have also a nynth part of reason whiche I call article, borrowyng the name of the Grekes. **1532** More *Confut. Tindale* Wks. 450/2 This worde, *that* , putteth Tyndall for the article, *the*. *a* **1637** B. Jonson *Eng. Gram.* Wks. 1859. 778 We add a ninth [part of speech], which is the *article*: and that is two-fold; Finite.. *the*; Infinite.. *a*. **1711** J. Greenwood *Eng. Gram.* 62 There are two *articles, a* and *the*. These are really Nouns Adjective, and are used almost after the same Manner as other Adjectives. Therefore I have not made the Article (as some have done) a distinct Part of Speech. **1867** *N. & Q.* Ser. iii. XI. 52/1 Sir William Davenant contrived to write a poem 'the London Vacation' almost without the use of Articles.

article ('ɑːtɪk(ə)l), *v.* 5–6 **articule, artycule, -cle.** [f. prec.]

†**1.** *trans.* To formulate in articles, particularize, specify; with *clause*, To state *that*. *Obs.*

c **1450** *Paper Roll* in *3rd Rep. R. Com. Hist. MSS.* 279/1 The seid duke articled that after that he was come oute of prisone into England.. he went to Caleys. **1494** Fabyan vii. 567 It shuld haue ben set out and articuled, euery act therof. *a* **1581** Campion *Hist. Irel.* ii. x. (1633) 135 Lay your heads together, and article the points. **1592** Warner *Alb. Eng.* viii. xli, And daerst thou Minion, quoth the Queene, thus article to me That thou wert Non-plus.

2. To set forth (offences) in articles *against* (a person).

1494 Fabyan *Rich. II*, an. 1388 (R.) These iniuryes and many moo.. were artyculed agayne hym in .xxxviii. sundry artycles. **1650** Jer. Taylor *Holy Living* (1727) 92 All his errors and follies were articled against him. *a* **1700** *Mem. Col. Hutchinson* (1848) 211 They would article against him whatever they could accuse him of. **1883** *Law Rep., Probate* VIII. 196 The offences articled against him were committed whilst he was incumbent of St. Alban's, Holborn.

3. *absol.* To bring charges, make specific accusations *against.* (Also with *compound passive.*)

1530 Palsgr. 437/1 He hath artycled agaynst you other wyse than you wene of. **1611** Speed *Hist. Gt. Brit.* ix. xxii. 56 The Lords.. began forthwith to enuy and article against the Protector. **1648** Prynne *Plea for Lords* 41 They were.. articled against, at the command of the *the Lords.* **1655** Gurnall *Chr. in Arm.* i. §3 (1669) 62/1 He is a bold man sure that dare find fault with God, and article against Heaven. **1697** *Snake in Grass* 254 John Story, Wilkinson, etc. were.. Articl'd against for so much as allowing Liberty of Conscience to any Quaker to Pay Tythes.

4. *trans.* To indict, charge with specific offences.

a **1604** Hanmer *Chron. Irel.* 167 Articling, accusing, and disgracing one another. **1868** *Times* 30 Apr. 12/6 The defendant.. had been articled for an ecclesiastical offence.

†**5.** To arrange by treaty, or stipulations.

a. *trans. Obs.*

1447-8 Shillingford *Lett.* (1871) 97 After the manner and fourme that the saide Mayer and Commenalte have articled. **1580** North *Plutarch* (1676) 124 In which parly it was articled, that the Romans should pay a thousand pound weight of gold. **1600** Holland *Livy* 1014 (R.) Antiochus himselfe, with whom Scipio had articled peace and alliance. **1682** Evats *Grotius' War & Peace* 93 It was.. Articled between the Kings.. that the Egyptians should not come into that Sea with any long Ship.

†**b.** *intr.* or with *subord. clause* or *inf. Obs.*

1526 Wolsey in Strype *Eccl. Mem.* I. v. 65 The King of England articled to make war upon the Emperors. **1627** May *Lucan* iv. 260 Whilest we are articling Basely about thy safety. **1705** J. Logan in *Pa. Hist. Soc. Mem.* X. 55 The only secure way will be to article positively. **1762** H. Walpole *Vertue's Anecd. Paint.* (1786) I. 51 Another indenture of 1338.. articles, that the workman should have six-pence a foot for white glass.

†**c.** const. *with* (a person). *Obs.*

1611 Beaum. & Fl. *Philaster* iv. 33 He Articles with the gods. **1639** W. Cartwright *Royall Slave* v. iii, Must we be articled with by our women? **1645** Symonds *Diary* (1859) 278 The governour for his owne security had articled with the enemy. *a* **1705** Howe *Self-ded.* Wks. 1810 I. 480 God is pleased to article with dust and ashes. **1764** Wesley *Wks.* (1872) XII. 243, I will article with them to do so.

†**d.** const. *for* (a thing). *Obs.*

1656 Bramhall *Replic.* ii. 94 They articled for the free exercise of the Greek Religion. **1770** Langhorne *Plutarch's Lives* (1879) I. 491/1 Pausanias wanted a truce, that he might article for the dead.

6. *trans.* To bind by articles of apprenticeship.

1820 W. Irving *Sketch Bk.* II. 161 Their brother too, who had been articled to an attorney.

7. To furnish with articles (of faith). *rare.*

1826 E. Irving *Babylon* II. viii. 265 And the doctrines by which our fathers articled the Church, are become unapproachably high.

articled ('ɑːtɪk(ə)ld), *ppl. a.* [f. prec. + -ed.]

1. Formulated or set forth in articles.

1577 Holinshed *Chron.* I. 66/1 The confession of faith articuled in the Nicene councell. **1611** Cotgr., *Articulé*, articulated, articled; set downe in, reduced unto, articles.

2. Bound under articles of apprenticeship.

1837 Howitt *Rur. Life* vi. x. (1862) 506 A youth articled to an attorney. **1840-1** Dickens *Old C. Shop* II. xviii, My articled pupil. **1860** Smiles *Self Help* iii. 57 Austen Layard, originally an articled clerk in the office of a London solicitor.

3. Provided with articles (of faith).

1868 *Spectator* 10 Oct., Our elaborately articled Anglican system must be largely simplified.

articler ('ɑːtɪklə(r)). [f. as prec. + -er¹.] One who draws up articles or charges.

1625 Bp. Mountagu *App. Caesar.* 321 Those idle Articlers.. that in their Informations\ have carried themselves so magisterially.

articul(e, obs. form of article.

articulable (ɑːˈtɪkjʊləb(ə)l), *a.* [f. articul(ate *v.* + -able.] That can be articulated. Also *absol.*

1833 *Fraser's Mag.* VII. 706 Word-worshipping even the articulable clothing wherein the clear and ethereal harmony of Goethe is invested. **1897** W. James *Let.* 28 Apr. (1920) II. 58 Life and mysticism exceed the articulable, and if there is a *One*.. it must remain only mystically expressed. **1916** F. von Hügel *German Soul* 92 How impossible in practice is the maintenance of international obligations of any articulable kind.

articulacy (ɑːˈtɪkjʊləsɪ). [f. articul(ate *a.* + -acy.] The quality or state of being articulate; articulateness.

1934 in Webster. **1943** E. M. Almedingen *Frossia* ix. 313 She was angry, and anger denied her articulacy. **1960** J. B. Broadbent *Some Graver Subject* ii. 70 Satan's mobility, his articulacy, and muscularity.. make him the most vital character in *Paradise Lost.*

articular (ɑːˈtɪkjʊlə(r)), *a.* Also 5 -uler. [ad. L. *articulār-is*, f. *articulus* article; see -ar.]

1. Of, or pertaining to, the joints (of the body).

1432-50 tr. *Higden* (Rolls Ser.) IV. 117 An infirmite articuler. **1582** Hester *Phiorav. Secr.* i. xv. 15 Most commonly thei [swellynges] come in the articular parts. **1620** Venner *Via Recta* iv. 75 Troubled with rheumes, and articular griefes. **1836** Todd *Cycl. Anat. & Phys.* I. 247/2 Articular cartilage. **1861** *Sat. Rev.* XI. 430/2 In gouty joints, and the articular surfaces of bones and cartilages.

2. *Gram.* Of the nature of an article (*sb.* 16); having an article preposed.

1750 Harris *Hermes* ii. v. (Jod.) The definitives are either articular or pronominal. **1906** Moulton *Gram. N.T. Greek* I. 70 There is a very marked increase in the use of the articular nominative in address. **1926** Plater & White *Gram. Vulgate* 40 The Gerund with *in* is frequently used to render the Greek Articular Infinitive with preposition.

†**ar'ticularly**, *adv. Obs.* [f. prec. + -ly².] Article by article, in separate heads or divisions.

1474 in *Househ. Ord.* (1790) 27 Theise Statutes and Ordynaunces hereafter artycuelry ensueinge. **1555** in Strype *Eccl. Mem.* III. App. xlvii. 143 For other causes articularly and specially. **1622** Malynes *Anc. Law-Merch.* 282 To answer *gradatim* and articularly as followeth. **1744** Lewis *Bp. Pecock* 253 Articularly subscribed with their own names.

ar'ticulary, *a.* [ad. F. *articulaire*, or L. *articulāri-us* = *articulāris.*] = articular 1.

1880 Gunther *Fishes* 47 Linked.. by an articulary process.

‖**Articulata** (ɑːˌtɪkjʊˈleɪtə), *sb. pl. Zool.* [L., pl. neuter (sc. *animalia*) of *articulātus* jointed.] Cuvier's name for his third great subdivision or sub-kingdom of animals, embracing invertebrate animals with an external skeleton, having the body and limbs composed of segments jointed together, as Insects, Crustacea, Centipedes, and Worms. (Cf. Annuloida, Annulosa, Arthropoda.)

1834 *Penny Cycl.* II. 417 *Articulata*, or *Articulated Animals*, are so called because the different portions of their body are composed of moveable pieces articulated to each other. **1855** H. Spencer *Psychol.* (1872) I. iii. viii. 359 The crabs.. stand at the head of the sub-kingdom Articulata.

articulate (ɑːˈtɪkjʊlət), *a.* and *sb.* [ad. L. *articulāt-us* jointed: see article and -ate.]

A. *adj.* **I.** Jointed, having joints.

1. Jointed on, united by a joint.

1610 Healey *St. Aug. City of God* 526 Our articulate members.. our hands, or feete. **1870** Hooker *Stud. Flora* 467 Stipes not articulate with the rootstock.

2. Jointed, composed of segments united by joints; *e.g.* the vertebral column, some sea-weeds.

1607 Topsell *Four-f. Beasts* 231 Body straight, and articulate. **1869** Mrs. Somerville *Molec. Sc.* ii. ii. 180 Ceraminacea.. are filiform articulate plants with the nucleus naked.

b. *Zool.* Of the type of the Articulata.

1855 H. Spencer *Psychol.* (1872) I. i. ii. 16 The Articulate types, composed of segments bearing limbs. **1876** tr. *Haeckel's Hist. Creat.* I. iii. 52 The Articulate animals are characterized by their ventral nerve-chord.

†**3.** Of or pertaining to the joints. *Obs. rare.*

1638 T. Whitaker *Blood of Grape* 75 (T.) The causes internal of these articulate pains move upon one hinge of Hippocrates.

4. Distinctly jointed or marked; having the parts distinctly recognizable.

1664 H. More *Myst. Iniq.* Apol. 503 The outward Lineaments thus perfect and articulate in this Glorious Body. **1824** W. Irving *T. Trav.* II. 254 A miserable horse, whose ribs were as articulate as the bars of a gridiron.

5. Of things immaterial, in same sense.

1664 H. More *Myst. Iniq.* 223 These Apocalyptick Visions.. are made so as to seem very trim and express, very complete and articulate in the very outward Cortex. **1858** Carlyle *Fredk. Gt.* I. ii. i. 53 Added to the firm land of articulate History. **1877** Mrs. Oliphant *Mak. Flor.* Introd. 14 The most articulate and important period of Florentine history.

6. Of sound: Divided into distinct parts (words and syllables) having each a definite meaning; as opposed to such inarticulate sounds as a long musical note, a groan, shriek, or the sounds produced by animals. Also *fig.* speaking plainly or intelligibly.

1586 T. B. *La Primaud. Fr. Acad.* (1589) 120 Speech is made by aire, beaten and framed with articulate and distinct sound. **1642** R. Carpenter *Experience* i. viii. 28 Not in articulate and plaine speech, but in grones. **1667** Milton *P.L.* ix. 557 Beasts.. Created mute to all articulat sound. **1726** De Foe *Hist. Devil* ii. x. (1840) 325 Who talk.. with articulate plain voices, as if men. **1840** Carlyle *Heroes* (1858) 270 Truly, it is a great thing for a Nation that it get an articulate voice. **1875** H. E. Manning *Mission H. Ghost* ix. 244 Secret whispers of sorrow.. which may never be uttered in articulate and audible words.

b. ***articulate-speaking***: using articulate speech, speaking articulately, and thus, intelligibly.

1829 Carlyle *Misc.* (1857) I. 271 Language of articulate-speaking men. **1834** —— *Past & Pr.* (1858) 266 Articulate-speaking functionaries.

7. Hence transferred to hearing, and other sensations, and to thought and intelligence: Distinct.

1626 D'Ewes in Ellis *Orig. Lett.* i. 322 III. 217 The Byshopp saied in my articulate hearing. **1662** H. More *Antid. Ath.* iii. vi. (1712) 100 To clear up this dim and cloudy discovery of Spirits, into more distinct and articulate Apparitions. **1829** I. Taylor *Enthus.* v. (1867) 101 An articulate warning is presented. **1831** Carlyle *Misc.* III. 4 The mere upper surface [of our Thinking] that we shape into articulate Thoughts. **1855** Bain *Senses & Int.* ii. ii. §10 (1864) 187 The discriminative or articulate character of the sense of touch.

II. Articled; consisting of or treated in articles.

†**8.** Formulated in articles; *e.g.* a system of doctrine, a set of regulations, an agreement. *Obs.*

1579 J. Stubbes *Gaping Gulf* B j b, [Did not] make any precedent pact or articulat condition aforehand with the Idolaters. **1586** T. Rogers *39 Art.* (1607) 175 Neither tie we the Church so strictly to the signs articulate. **1622** Bacon *Hist. Hen. VII*, Wks. 1860. 475 His instructions were ever extreme, curious, and articulate.

†**9.** Charged or specified in articles. *Obs.*

1569 Hawkins in Arb. *Garner* V. 231 The articulate Sir William Garrard, Knight.. and others joined with them in Society. *Ibid.* 240 The Ship articulate, called the Swallow, was of the adventure. **1726** Ayliffe *Parerg.* 66 If the defendant does not believe the Sum Articulate.

†**10.** Consisting of tens. See article *sb.* 15. *Obs.*

1646 Sir T. Browne *Pseud. Ep.* 186 They accounted their digits and articulate numbers unto an hundred. *Ibid.* 280 Using the full and articulate number, [we] doe write the Translation of Seventy; whereas.. the precise number was Seventy two.

B. *sb. Zool.* An articulate animal, one of the Articulata.

1874 Wood *Nat. Hist.* 1 The Articulates, or jointed animals, form an enormously large division. **1878** O. W. Holmes *Motley* 152 Annalists will pile up facts for ever like so many articulates or mollusks or radiates.

articulate (ɑːˈtɪkjʊleɪt), *v.* [f. prec. or on analogy of vbs. so formed. At first *articulate* was used as its pa. pple. The chronological order of the senses is not the logical, branch II being earlier than I.]

I. To joint. (Later sense in English.)

1. *trans.* To joint, to attach by a joint. (Mostly in *pass.*)

1616 Surfl. & Markh. *Countr. Farme* 473 The mouth.. which is articulated or close ioined with the shanke. *Mod.* The point at which the limb is articulated to the trunk.

2. To joint together, connect by joints, into a series; to mark with apparent joints. (Mostly *pass.*)

1644 [See ARTICULATED *ppl. a.* 2 a.] **1872** MIVART *Anat.* 24 The most movable joints are those in which the adjacent bones are articulated on the principle either of a pivot, or of a hinge. **1873** BURTON *Hist. Scot.* I. ii. 71 They are not articulated into lines of hills. **1879** J. YOUNG *Ceramic Art* 40 A cylindrical Japanese vase in Sutton's Collection is reticulated, or articulated.

3. *intr.* (for *refl.*) To form a joint (*with*); to unite with by a joint.

1832 LYELL *Princ. Geol.* II. 15 The human head does not articulate in the centre of gravity. **1847** ANSTED *Anc. World* viii. 168 These latter bones again also articulate with the breast-bone. **1872** HUXLEY *Phys.* vii. 171 The hollow of the cup articulates with a spheroidal surface furnished by the humerus.

4. *trans.* To divide (vocal sound) into distinct parts (words and syllables) each representing a notion or relation.

1594 T. B. *La Primaud. Fr. Acad.* II. 87 This instrument fashioneth the voyce, & causeth it to yeeld a sound, & so prepareth it for the tongue, that it may be articulated and framed into speech by yᵉ same. **1615** CROOKE *Body of Man* 715 First to articulate the voyce. **1810** COLERIDGE *Friend* I. xiii. (1867) 57 He amuses himself with articulating the pulses of the air. **1817** —— *Biog. Lit.* I. 291 Air articulated into nonsense.

5. To pronounce distinctly; to utter, give utterance to; to express in words.

1691 RAY *Creation* (J.) The muscles of the tongue [of apes] which do most serve to articulate a word. **1772** PORTEUS *Civ. Negro States* (R.) The moment they are capable of articulating their words. **1826** DISRAELI *Viv. Grey* II. v. 41 That lady..began to articulate a horrible patois. **1839** CARLYLE *Chartism* i. (1858) 5 To interpret and articulate the dumb deep want of the people! **1847** BUSHNELL *Chr. Nurture* II. ii. (1861) 256 Wrongs which never get articulated.

6. *intr.* To utter words; to speak distinctly; *often*, to pronounce.

1642 MILTON *Apol. Smect.* (1851) 292 Measure a just cadence, and scan without articulating. **1670** COTTON *Espernon* I. IV. 190 He had..so great a weakness in his tongue that he could not articulate. **1788** V. KNOX *Winter Even.* III. IX. iii. 234 The capricious modes of dressing, articulating and moving. **1849** MACAULAY *Hist. Eng.* II. 356 His agitation was so great that he could not articulate.

II. To article. (The earlier sense in English.)

7. *trans.* To formulate in an article or articles; to set forth in articles, particularize, specify. ? *Obs.*

1562 FOXE *A. & M.* I. 308/1 Thought good to articulate the foresaid objections..in writing. **1589** NASHE *Almond for Parrat* 18b, If I articulate all the examples of their absurdeties that I could. **1625** BP. MOUNTAGU *App. Cæsar.* 51 Can you find this..so prescribed in our Church? or articulated unto our Teachers?

†**8.** *trans.* and *intr.* To charge, bring a charge *against*. *Obs.*

1553–87 FOXE *A. & M.* III. 356 It was articulate against him that..he did hold, etc. **1590** *Articles* in Fuller *Ch. Hist.* IX. vii. § 27 V. 142 We do object and articulate against him, that he..hath forsaken, etc. **1603** DRAYTON *Barons Wars* II. lxiv, Gainst whom, at Pomfret, they articulate.

†**9.** *trans.* To arrange by articles or conditions.

1602 FULBECKE *Pandects* 42 Articulating peace with the Albanes. **1676** BULLOKAR, *Articulate*, to set down articles or conditions of agreement.

†**10.** *intr.* To come to terms; to capitulate. *Obs.*

1597 DANIEL *Civ. Wares* v. xx, How to articulate with yielding Wightes. **1605** CAMDEN *Rem.* 212 The Inhabitants were willing to articulate, and to yeelde themselves to the Duke of Burgundie. **1607** SHAKS. *Cor.* I. ix. 76 Send vs to Rome The best, with whom we may articulate, For their owne good, and ours. **1643** PRYNNE *Power Parl.* III. 57 Those three gods..have thus Articulated, lest upon their intrenching on one anothers jurisdiction, they might make Warre among themselves.

articulated (ɑːˈtɪkjʊleɪtɪd), *ppl. a.* [f. prec. + -ED.]

1. *pple.* Jointed; connected by a joint. Also *fig.*

1616 [See ARTICULATE *v.* I.] **1666** J. SMITH *Old Age* 59 (T.) The scapula..is articulated to the humerus. **1802** PALEY *Nat. Theol.* viii. (1827) 458 A ridged bone, articulated at both ends to rigid bases. **1857** HENFREY *Elem. Bot.* §197 The base of the filament..is usually articulated to the receptacle. **1870** ROLLESTON *Anim. Life* 1 An ossicle articulated to its apex. **1886** A. WEIR *Hist. Basis Mod. Europe* iii. 122 The pettifogging lawyers who swarmed around the minutely articulated social structure.

2. a. Jointed, having segments united by joints; sensibly jointed; marked with apparent joints.

1644 BULWER *Chirol.* 157 The articulated Fingers. **1706** *Art of Paint.* (1744) 201 The hands and feet rather plump than sensibly articulated. **1747** GOULD *Eng. Ants* 5 The Antennæ of Ants are what Virtuosi call articulated. **1815** BAKEWELL *Introd. Geol.* 132 The columns at Fairhead are not articulated like those at the Giant's Causeway. **1851** *Gentl. Mag.* CXXII. I. 128 We next arrive at articulated figures. The Statue of Jupiter Ammon nodded. **1950** *Gloss. Aeronaut. Terms (B.S.I.)* I. 44 *Articulated blade*, a blade connected to the rotor head by one or more hinges or pivots. **1958** *Daily Mail* 19 Aug. 4/8 It should be fairly easy to devise some sort of articulated joint [in the steering column of a car] which would cause the column to fold up in a crash.

b. Of a road vehicle: consisting of elements joined in a flexible arrangement, as ***articulated lorry***. Abbrev. *artic* (slang). Also, of a locomotive, train, bus, etc., one fitted with a bogie or bogies, or other mechanical device making for flexibility.

1923 *Sci. Amer.* Jan. 12/3 Attention has been drawn to the articulated train, in which the abutting ends of the passenger cars are carried upon a common truck. **1930** *Engineering* 30 May 715/3 (*heading*) Articulated Steam Rail Coaches for the Egyptian State Railways. **1932** *Statutory Rules & Orders 1931* 1158 'Articulated vehicle' means a heavy motor car.. with a trailer drawn thereby. **1936** *Discovery* Nov. 356/2 High-speed articulated trains of three coaches. **1951** *Landfall* V. 106 Running those two big artics and that big car. **1958** *Times* 12 Apr. 7/6 Joe had a brand-new articulated truck, or artic (where the driving cab is separately joined to the lorry).

3. *spec.* in *Zool.* Formed like the ARTICULATA.

1836 TODD *Cycl. Anat. & Phys.* I. 750/1 The body of these animals [the Crustacea] is articulated. **1860** SAMUELSON *Honey Bee* ii. 11 An articulated animal; that is an animal..composed of a number of articulations or rings.

4. Made into articulate sound; = ARTICULATE 6, 7.

a **1704** LOCKE (J.) They would..not deceive themselves with a little articulated air. *a* **1711** KEN *Psyche* Poet. Wks. 1721 IV. 172 To speak..My sorrow in articulated Tear. **1824** COLERIDGE *Aids Refl.* (1848) I. 327 The same words may be repeated; but in each second of time the articulated air hath passed away. **1853** ROBERTSON *Serm.* Ser. IV. iii. (1876) 25 Speak, if your heart prompts, in articulated words. **1867** O. W. HOLMES *Guard. Angel* xii. 205 Which had hardly risen into the region of inwardly articulated thought.

5. Made distinct.

1855 BRIMLEY *Ess.* 23 Its luxuriant pictorial richness.. more articulated by fine drawing.

6. Formulated, set forth in, or reduced to articles.

1553–87 FOXE *A. & M.* II. 534 Every point and circumstance articulated against them. **1591** HORSEY *Trav.* (1857) 208 To declare and deliver [them] to his nunciat.. articulated in the cittie of Musko. **1848** HAMPDEN *Bampton Lect.* 100 A minutely articulated system of Theology. **1880** E. WHITE *Cert. Relig.* 23 They know nothing of an articulated creed which may be blindly assented to by young and old.

arˈticulately, *adv.* [f. ARTICULATE *a.* + -LY².] In an articulate manner.

1. By joints.

1728 EARBERY tr. *Burnet's State of Dead* I. 193 [Our Body] is formed of several parts of Matter articulately jointed and coagmented together.

2. With articulate voice, with words and syllables distinctly heard.

1531 ELYOT *Gov.* I. v. (R.) Englishe..cleane, polite, perfectly and articulately pronounced. **1637** GILLESPIE *Eng. Pop. Cerem.* III. ii. 16 To speake audibly and articulatly. **1656** tr. *Hobbes's Elem. Philos.* (1839) 494 The voice from the pulpit will not be heard so articulately as it would be, if there were no vaulting. **1824** SCOTT *St. Ronan's* v, Sir Bingo.. swore louder and more articulately than ever he was known to utter any previous sounds.

3. Distinctly, definitely, in sense or manner.

1660 JER. TAYLOR *Duct. Dubit.* II. iii. §20 Christians that ..do all of them explicitly and articulately long after the glories of an eternal love. **1865** CARLYLE *Fredk. Gt.* V. XIV. v. 217 It is the first time her Hungarian Majesty steps articulately forward with such extraordinary Claim of Damages.

4. In the form of distinct articles, article by article, specifically.

1620 BP. SNOWDEN in *Fortesc. Papers* 124 A more full declaracion of the matter is articulately expressed in the note. **1655** FULLER *Ch. Hist.* IX. 116, I had articulatly set down in writing our points. **1794** PALEY *Evid.* II. vi. (1817) 127 A detail of examples, distinctly and articulately proposed. **1845** LD. CAMPBELL *Chancellors* (1857) III. lv. 111 He then goes over the different charges articulately.

arˈticulateness. [f. as prec. + -NESS.] The quality of being articulate, distinctness.

1731 in BAILEY. **1843** J. H. NEWMAN *Miracles* 209 The articulateness, nay, the educated accent of these Confessors is especially insisted on.

articulating (ɑːˈtɪkjʊleɪtɪŋ), *vbl. sb.* [f. ARTICULATE *v.* + -ING¹.]

1. The action of uniting or joining together.

1865 DICKENS *Mut. Fr.* I. vii, You've no idea how small you'd come out, if I had the articulating of you.

2. Distinct sounding or utterance.

1609 DOULAND *Ornithop. Microl.* 2 Those Instruments which are commanded, either with the touching of the fingers, or articulating of the Keyes. *Ibid.* 89 No expressing of words, no articulating of syllables.

†**3.** The making of stipulations; stipulating. *Obs.*

1649 SELDEN *Laws of Eng.* II. vi. (1739) 38 The Clergy took this Articulating of the Commons in snuff.

arˈticulating, *ppl. a.* [f. as prec. + -ING².] That articulates; that forms a joint with something.

1808 BRODIE in *Phil. Trans.* XCVIII. 306 Half of the articulating surface for receiving the tarsus. **1835** SOUTHW. SMITH *Philos. Health* I. v. 212 Strong projections of bone, termed articulating processes.

articulation (ɑːˌtɪkjʊˈleɪʃən). [a. F. *articulation* (16th c. in Littré), ad. L. *articulātiōn-em*, n. of action f. *articulāre* to joint.]

1. The action or process of jointing; the state of being jointed; mode of jointing or junction.

1597 LOWE *Art Chyrurg.* (1634) 360 Bones..joyned together..by Articulation. **1706** *Art of Painting* (1744) 201 Expressing exactly the articulation of the members. **1873** BURTON *Hist. Scot.* I. i. 2 A long process of growth and articulation. **1881** MIVART *Cat* 65 Serves for the articulation of the lower jaw. **1881** G. MILNER *Country Pleas.* xxxv. 197 The wonderful structure and articulation of the branches.

b. *concr.* A jointed structure or series.

1873 BURTON *Hist. Scot.* I. iii. 82 An articulation of mountains.

2. A joint. **a.** In the animal body: The structure or mechanism whereby two bones, or two parts of the invertebrate skeleton, are connected, whether stiffly, or in such a way that one moves in or on the other.

1615 CROOKE *Body of Man* 913 Almost euery articulation is cursted ouer with a gristle to make the motion more easie. **1743** tr. *Heister's Surg.* 106 Fractures near the Articulations. **1835** KIRBY *Hab. & Inst. Anim.* I. vi. 205 To form a kind of ball and socket articulation. **1835** SOUTHW. SMITH *Philos. Health* I. v. 198 The union of the bones of the cranium affords an example of an immoveable articulation.

b. In plants. The place at which a deciduous member, as a leaf, separates from the plant; *also*, the knots or joints in the stems of grasses, canes, etc.

1658 SIR T. BROWNE *Gard. Cyrus* II. 540 In the parts of plants which are not ordained for motion, we do not expect correspondent Articulations. **1742** BAILEY, *Articulation* (among *Herbalists*), the Jointure or Knots that are in stalks or roots. **1830** LINDLEY *Nat. Syst. Bot.* 223 The petiole almost always having an articulation.

3. One of the segments of a jointed body; the part contained between two joints, in a limb, the stem of a grass, etc.

1664 H. MORE *Myst. Iniq.* iv. 10 The distinct Limbs and articulations thereof. **1833** LYELL *Elem. Geol.* xix. (1874) 330 The numerous 'articulations' once composing the stem, arms and body of the encrinite were scattered at random. **1860** SAMUELSON *Honey Bee* ii. 17 Distinctly divided into what appear to be perfect rings or articulations.

†**4.** Bending by flexible joints. *Obs. rare.*

1541 R. COPLAND *Guydon's Quest. Cyrurg.*, Without these [muscles] it is nat possyble to make artyculacyon or mouyng.

†**5.** (See quot.) *Obs. rare.*

1681 tr. *Willis' Rem. Med. Wks.*, *Articulation*, a shooting of spriggs from the joynts.

6. The utterance of the distinct elements of speech; articulate voice.

1615 CROOKE *Body of Man* 629 The Tongue..is the very organ of Articulation. **1626** BACON *Sylva* §194 Overgreat distance confoundeth the articulation of sounds. **1773** MONBODDO *Lang.* (1774) I. I. xv. 184 Articulation is not natural to man. **1881** WHITNEY *Proc. Amer. Philol. Assoc.* 22 Articulation is virtually syllabication,—a breaking of the stream of utterance into joints, by the intervention of closer utterances or consonants..between the opener utterances or vowels.

7. Utterance; speech.

a **1711** KEN *Anodynes* Poet. Wks. 1721 III. 418 My Spirit intercepts my Cries, E're they t'articulation rise. **1855** SINGLETON *Virgil* I. 311 And to my jaws articulation clave.

8. An articulate sound or utterance.

1764 REID *Inquiry* iv. §2 The articulations of the voice seem to be of all signs the most proper for artificial language. **1855** H. SPENCER *Psychol.* (1872) I. II. ii. 173 Sequent notes, or articulations, cling together with tenacity.

b. *esp.* A consonant.

1849 A. M. BELL *Princ. Elocut.* 39 All actions of the vocal organs which partially or wholly obstruct or which compress the breath or voice, are called articulations. **1878** —— *ibid.*, The oral actions here denominated 'articulations' have been more commonly called 'consonants.'

9. Articulate quality, distinctness. *rare.*

c **1785** COWPER *Needl. Alarm* 68 The looks and gestures of their griefs and fears Have all articulation in his ears. *a* **1834** COLERIDGE (in Webster), That definiteness and articulation of imagery.

articuˈlationist. [f. prec. + -IST.] One who teaches deaf-mutes to utter articulate sounds.

1882 R. STORRS in *N. Y. Indep.* 20 Apr., Articulationists of any considerable experience [know] how impossible it is by this method..to educate much the larger portion of those commonly called deaf-mutes.

articulative (ɑːˈtɪkjʊlətɪv), *a.* [f. ARTICULAT(E *v.* + -IVE.] Of or pertaining to articulation.

1849 A. M. BELL *Princ. Speech* II. ii. 155 The analogy between the articulative actions of R and S is generally of much service in leading the tongue to the position for the latter element. **1877** W. R. ALGER *Life E. Forrest* I. 68 The ponderous gutturality and sweetness of articulative energy.

articulator (ɑːˈtɪkjʊleɪtə(r)). [n. of action (on L. analogies) f. L. *articulā-re* to joint: see -OR.]

1. One who articulates or pronounces words.

1777 BOSWELL *Johnson* (1831) IV. 8 An elderly housekeeper, a most distinct articulator, showed us the house.

2. *techn.* One who articulates bones, and mounts skeletons.

1865 DICKENS *Mut. Fr.* I. vii, Articulator of human bones. **1883** *Nature* 5 Apr. (*Advt.*) Articulator.—Wanted, a Person skilled in the Preparation and Mounting of Skeletons.

3. An apparatus used in prosthetic dentistry to obtain correct articulation of the teeth.

1851 *Amer. Jrnl. Dental Sci.* Jan. 181 Cut a V shaped groove down the back of the cast, and oil it well, so that the articulator will not stick to it; then mix some plaster and drop it into the impression... The articulator should be about half an inch thick. **1953** *Faber Med. Dict.* 47/2 *Articulator*, instrument for supporting the casts of the jaws while arranging artificial teeth on the plates. **1963** G. F. KANTOROWICZ et al. *Inlays, Crowns & Bridges* vii. 74 A model of all teeth of the opposing jaw will allow assessment of the occlusion without the use of an articulator.

4. A movable vocal organ (as the tongue). (See quot. 1942.)

1942 BLOCH & TRAGER *Outl. Ling. Anal.* 13 The vocal organs are conveniently divided into two kinds: *articulators*, organs which can be moved more or less freely and can thus be made to assume a variety of positions; and *points of articulation*, fixed points or areas lying above the articulators, which these may touch or approach. **1943** K. L. PIKE *Phonetics* vii. 120 At the time in the production of some sound when any moveable part of the vocal apparatus causes any *stricture*.. it becomes an *articulator* unless it is a closure performing the function of an initiator. **1946** J. MURRAY in *Q. Jrnl. Speech* XXXII. 203/1 The second interpretation of 'explosive' pertains exclusively to plosions which characterize the syllabic thrust following closures of the glottis, or the articulators *and* glottis.

articulatory (ɑːˈtɪkjʊlətərɪ), *a.* [f. prec. + -Y: see -ORY.] Of or pertaining to vocal articulation. Sometimes used as = ARTICULARY.

1818 A. COOPER *Surg. Ess.* I. 41 The articulatory cartilage of the ball of the bone. **1860** H. SPENCER *Illust. Progr.* (1864) 202 Certain of the articulatory and vocal muscles. **1890** W. JAMES *Princ. Psychol.* II. xviii. 64 In persons whose auditory imagination is weak, the articulatory image seems to constitute the whole material for verbal thought. **1935** G. K. ZIPF *Psycho-Biology of Lang.* (1936) v. 230 Conceptual words relate our speech to our experience, articulatory words relate our conceptual words to one another. **1953** C. E. BAZELL *Linguistic Form* iv. 46 Some plausible articulatory-acoustic interpretation can be given of the distributional phoneme. **1955** H. A. GLEASON *Introd. Descriptive Linguistics* xiv. 187 Articulatory phonetics.. is concerned with the study of sounds usable in speech in terms of the mechanisms of their production by the human vocal apparatus. **1964** B. HONIKMAN in D. Abercrombie et al. *Daniel Jones* 73 By articulatory setting is meant the disposition of the parts of the speech mechanism and their composite action. **1964** R. H. ROBINS *Gen. Linguistics* iii. 84 It [*sc.* phonetics] can be studied primarily as the activity of the speaker in terms of the articulatory organs and processes involved; this is called articulatory phonetics.

Hence **articuˈlatorily** *adv.*, in relation to any matter of vocal articulation.

1952 A. COHEN *Phonemes of English* ii. 23 Two sounds of a language, related either acoustically or articulatorily, which never appear in the same phonetic context, are.. variants of one single phoneme.

arˈticulite. *Min.* [f. L. *articul-us* joint + -ITE.] A name given by some to Flexible Sandstone or *Itacolumite*.

articuˈlose, *a. rare.* [ad. L. *articulōsus.*] 'Full of joints.' Bailey 1731.

†**arˈticulous,** *a. Obs. rare.* = prec.

1684 tr. *Bonet's Merc. Compit.* XVIII 662 A Bullet.. by compressing a Nervous or Articulous Body.. causes great pain.

‖**arˈticulus.** The Latin word for *joint*, sometimes used in scientific language. Pl. **articuli.**

1877 HUXLEY *Inv. An.* ix. 583 New articuli are continually added to that end of the stem which lies nearest the calyx.

artifact: see ARTEFACT.

artifactual, etc.: varr. ARTEFACTUAL, etc.

‖**artifex** (ˈɑːtɪfɛks). [L., f. *arti-* art + *-fex, -ficem* maker, f. *fac-ĕre* to make.] Artificer.

1657 S. PURCHAS *Pol. Flying-Ins.* I. i. 2 The great artifex of nature. **1678** CUDWORTH *Intell. Syst.* I. iv. xxxii. 486 The Artifex of all things.

artifice (ˈɑːtɪfɪs). [a. F. *artifice*, ad. L. *artificium*, f. as prec. + *-ficium* making.]

†**1.** The action of an artificer, the making of anything by art, construction, workmanship. *Obs.*

1534 LD. BERNERS *Gold. Bk. M. Aurel.* xlii. (R.) As ye see a thing made by artifice perishe. **1646** SIR T. BROWNE *Pseud. Ep.* 312 Though they abounded in Milk, they had not the Artifice of Cheese. *Ibid.* v. v. (1686) 195 Adam immediately issued from the Artifice of God. *a* **1682** —— *Tracts* 4 The early artifice in Brass and Iron under Tubal-Cain.

†**b.** *esp.* Mechanic art, artificer's work. *Obs.*

1667 MILTON *P.L.* IX. 39 The skill of Artifice or Office mean.

†**2.** The product of art, work of art. *Obs.*

a **1652** J. SMITH *Sel. Disc.* iii. 52 God himself, the architect and mover of this divine artifice. *a* **1688** CUDWORTH *Immut. Morality* IV. ii. §13 (1731) 175 The Material Universe, which is the Artifice of God, the Artifice of the best Mechanist.

†**b.** An artificial substance; a composition. *Obs.*

1677 MOXON *Mech. Exerc.* (1703) 243, I find two kinds of Artifices used by the Antients, both of which is compounded of Lime and Hogs-grease.

†**3.** Mode or style of workmanship, artistic fashion. *Obs.*

1597 MORLEY *Introd. Mus.* 145 If you marke the artifice of the composition. **1663** CHARLETON *Chorea Gigant.* 25 As for the Artifice, or manner of Workmanship. **1730** A. GORDON *Maffei's Amphit.* 51 The indifferent Artifice shewn in those two last mentioned Coins. **1756** BURKE *Subl. & B.* III. §7 (1808) 228 Examine.. into the artifice of the contrivance.

†**4.** Constructive skill, ingenuity. *Obs.*

1646 SIR T. BROWNE *Pseud. Ep.* VI. v. (R.) Such as illustrate the artifice of its maker. **1695** BERNARD *Voy. fr. Aleppo* in *Misc. Cur.* (1708) III. 92 Carved with the greatest Artifice and Curiosity. **1777** HUME *Ess. & Treat.* I. 190 Does it not counterwork the artifice of nature?

5. Human skill as opposed to what is natural.

1857 H. REED *Lect. Brit. Poets* x. II. 24 Restoring nature, where it had been displaced by artifice.

6. Skill in designing and employing expedients; address, cunning, trickery.

1618 SIR H. MAY in *Fortesc. Papers* 47 Without any temporary ar[tifice] sincere and cordiall. **1628** DIGBY *Voy. Medit.* 55 Had it not bin by artifice they could neuer haue taken them. **1745** DE FOE *Eng. Tradesm.* I. xx. 189 All the artifice and sleight of hand they were masters of. **1790** PALEY *Hor. Paul.* I. 2 The consequence of meditation, artifice, and design.

7. An ingenious expedient, a manœuvre, stratagem, device, contrivance, trick. (The ordinary sense now.)

1656 COWLEY *Pind. Odes* Wks. 1710 I. 192 It now an Artifice does grow, Wrongs and Outrages to do, Lest men should think we owe. **1660** STANLEY *Hist. Philos.* (1701) 276/2 He condemned Rhetorick, as being used rather as an Artifice, than an Art. **1769** *Junius Lett.* xvi. 68 To practise these dishonest artifices. **1865** MILL *Repr. Govt.* 2/1 If they can be deluded by the artifices used to cheat them out of it.

†**arˈtifice,** *v. nonce-wd.* [App. f. ARTIFICE-R. Cf. *artificing*.] To frame or make by art.

1653 BROME *Damoiselle* v. i, And your whole gracefull Presence shall attract, (Beyond affection) admiration: As Ile artifice you.

artificer (ɑːˈtɪfɪsə(r)). Also 5 **artyficer, -fycer.** [App. AF. or ME. formation on ARTIFICE; cf. *officer*. *Artificier* in Fr. seems quite modern; it is not in Cotgr.; OF. had *artificien*. Med.L. *artificiārius*, in Du Cange from Rymer, seems formed upon the English or AF. word.]

1. One who makes by art or skill; *esp.* one who follows an industrial handicraft, a craftsman.

1393 GOWER *Conf.* III. 142 Artificers, Whiche usen craftes and mestiers Whose art is cleped mechanique. *c* **1460** RUSSELL *Bk. Nurture* 1037 in *Babees Bk.* 187 Worshipfulle merchaundes and riche artyficeris. **1592** NASHE *P. Penilesse* C, A base artificer, that hath no reuenues to boast on. **1659** MILTON *Hirelings* Wks. 1851. 386 From the Magistrate himself to the meanest Artificer. **1728** DE FOE *Syst. Magick* I. i. 11 Tubal Cain the first artificer, a true natural mechanic. **1809** KENDALL *Trav.* I. xxiii. 227 The inhabitants are principally artificers, as nailers, joiners and cartwrights.

2. a. *Mil.* A soldier mechanic attached to the ordnance, artillery, and engineer service, to be employed in the construction and repair of military materials.

1758 S. M. HAMILTON *Lett. to Washington* (1899) II. 321 The 2d. Company of Artificers of the 2d. Regiment. **1804** NELSON in Nicolas *Disp.* V. 508 The conduct of all the artificers on the late Hindostan's accident, was very meritorious. **1861** *U.S. Army Regulations* 520 Every volunteer non-commissioned officer,.. and artificer, who enters the service.

b. A mechanic in the Royal Navy. Also *attrib.* and *Comb.*

1884 *Encycl. Brit.* XVII. 294/1 The engine-room artificers, leading stoker, and stokers are under his [*sc.* the engineer's] immediate control. **1899** [see TIFFY]. **1902** *Monthly Rev.* Aug. 92 The Admiralty have conferred the charge of machinery in small vessels on fifty-six artificer-engineers. **1957** *H.M. Royal Forces Navy Openings for Boys* (*H.M.S.O.*) (ed. 2) 22 Aircraft Artificers. An apprentice in this branch is trained to undertake the most difficult maintenance and repair work on Naval aircraft. *Ibid.* 27 Radio electrical artificers.. deal with wireless and radar equipment.

†**3. a.** *gen.* Constructor, maker, manufacturer. *Obs.*

1638 WOTTON in *Four C. Eng. Lett.* 53 Intimating unto me (how modestly soever) the true artificer. **1699** BENTLEY *Phal.* 109 Called Thericlean, from their shape, whatsoever Artificer made them. **1751** JOHNSON *Rambl.* No. 145 ⁋8 The manufacturers of literature.. like other artificers.

b. ***Artificer of the Universe***: the Creator.

1659 PEARSON *Creed* (1839) 27 The great Artificer of the world. **1814** WORDSW. *Excursion* IV. 551 By the great Artificer endued With no inferior power.

4. *transf.* Contriver, inventor, deviser. (Cf. ARCHITECT *sb.*)

1605 BACON *Adv. Learn.* II. xxiii. §16 There is no such artificer of dissimulation. **1667** MILTON *P.L.* IV. 121 Artificer of fraud.. the first That practised falshood under saintly shew. **1728** YOUNG *Love of Fame* VI. (1757) 143 Wisdom, the sole artificer of bliss. **1860** PUSEY *Min. Proph.* 433 That artificers of death by their own art should perish.

†**5.** One who practises any 'art,' or applied science; a savant. (Cf. ARTIST.) *Obs.*

1635 N. CARPENTER *Geog. Delin.* I. xi. 242 Oftentimes in the Artificer there wants diligence in obseruing the right houre and moment of the Eclipse.

†**6.** An artful or wily person; a trickster. *Obs.*

1598 B. JONSON *Ev. Man in Hum.* III. v. 20 Who would have thought thou hadst been such an artificer? **1614** RALEIGH *Hist. World* IV. iii. §5. 492 Antipater.. a subtle artificer, well understanding their aptness to division, refused. **1621** BURTON *Anat. Mel.* II. i. IV. i. (1651) 226 Mountebanks, Quacksalvers, Empericks.. these base and illiterate Artificers.

artificership (ɑːˈtɪfɪsəʃɪp). [See -SHIP.] The quality of an artificer; workmanship.

artificery (ɑːˈtɪfɪsərɪ). *rare.* [f. ARTIFICER + -Y.] Artificer's work; workmanship.

1858 *Scot. Rev.* VI. 246 A 'Paradise Lost,' or a Pope's 'Iliad,' with their elaborate invention and splendid artificery.

artificial (ɑːtɪˈfɪʃəl), *a.* (and *sb.*) Also 5 **artyficiall, -fyciall, -fycyall, artificialle, -fyciall, -ficyall,** 5–7 **artificiall.** [a. F. *artificiel* (14th c. in Littré), ad. L. *artificiāl-is*, f. *artificium*: see ARTIFICE and -AL[1].]

A. *adj.* **I.** Opposed to *natural*.

1. Made by or resulting from art or artifice; contrived, compassed, or brought about by constructive skill, and not spontaneously; not natural. **a.** Artificial in result, as well as in process.

c **1382** WYCLIF *Matt.* Add. Prol., Not as bi naturel order, bot bi artificial ordre. **1430** LYDG. *Chron. Troy* III. xxviii, Bawme naturall That ran through pipes artyfyciall. **1563** HYLL *Arte Garden.* (1593) 154 In my litle treatise of Naturall and artificial conclusions. **1690** LOCKE *Hum. Und.*, An artificial thing being a production of Man, which the Artificer designed. **1753** HOGARTH *Anal. Beauty* 3 The elegant and beautiful in artificial, as well as natural forms. **1756** BURKE *Vind. Nat. Soc.* Wks. 1842 I. 19 A state of artificial society. **1825** McCULLOCH *Pol. Econ.* II. §5. 193 To give an artificial stimulus to population. **1837** HOWITT *Rur. Life* (1862) I. vii. 73 A garden.. is an artificial thing.. though formed from the materials of nature.

b. Of natural products or results artificially produced, e.g. ***artificial light***. (In contrast to the next, these are *real*, though artificial.)

1593 SHAKS. *3 Hen. VI*, III. ii. 184, I can.. wet my Cheekes with artificiall Teares. **1648** C. WALKER *Relat. & Obs.* I. 45 Many suspected his death was artificiall. *a* **1661** FULLER *Worthies* (1662) 191 Darknesse.. made artificial Lights to appear with the more Solemnity. **1828** F. WATKINS *Electro-Magnetism* 10 Sir H. Davy.. was enabled to produce the most intense artificial light ever seen. **1834** GEN. P. THOMPSON *Exerc.* (1842) III. 75 Those very men have seen their wives and children perish with artificial hunger. **1860** TYNDALL *Glac.* II. §24. 353 Harrison's.. machine for the production of artificial ice. **1879** HARLAN *Eyesight* vi. 71 Use the stronger glasses in artificial light only, and the old pair in daytime.

c. *spec.* (*a*) In *Physics*, applied to the disintegration of an element or particle (under bombardment, etc.), to radioactivity that is induced (as opposed to that which occurs naturally), to isotopes produced in this way, and to the radioactivity of such isotopes; (*b*) popularly applied to objects, real or imaginary, put into orbit by man, e.g. ***artificial moon, planet, satellite***.

1920 RUTHERFORD in *Proc. R. Soc.* A. XCVII. 398 The isotope of mass 3 arises in the artificial disintegration of lighter atoms like oxygen and nitrogen. **1926** R. W. LAWSON tr. *Hevesy & Paneth's Man. Radioactivity* xxvii. 228 Recent years have seen the initiation of the artificial disintegration of the elements, an achievement first successful in the case of nitrogen, and carried out by Rutherford in 1919. **1934** JOLIOT & CURIE in *Nature* 10 Feb. 201 (*heading*) Artificial production of a new kind of radio-element. *Ibid.* 202/1 These experiments give the first chemical proof of artificial transmutation. **1938** R. W. LAWSON tr *Hevesy & Paneth's Man. Radioactivity* (ed. 2) vii. 73 Neutrons disrupt the silicon nucleus and call forth an artificial radioactivity. *Ibid.* x. 123 It is possible to produce a number of artificial radio-elements in a variety of ways.

1880 P. GREG *Across Zodiac* I. iii. 51 The weeks I spent in the solitude of this artificial planet.. [in] a voyage through space. **1946** H. HARPER *Dawn Space Age* 68 Pirquet has worked out plans for an artificial island, or rather an 'artificial moon',.. stationed out in space.. as a permanent fuelling-point for space-craft setting out on interplanetary voyages. **1963** *Listener* 14 Feb. 287/1 Mariner has now entered a permanent orbit round the Sun, and has joined the increasing company of dwarf 'artificial planets'.

2. Made by art in imitation of, or as substitute for, what is natural or real. (These are not *real*.)

1577 HARRISON *England* III. ix. 80 If the colour hold.. the stone is thought to be naturall and good: but if it alter.. then it is not sound, but rather an artificiall [peece of] practise. **1611** ROWLAND *Four Knaves* 22 An artificiall flie of silk. **1655** MRQ. WORC. *Cent. Inv.* xlvi, How to make an artificial Bird to fly. **1684** *Lond. Gaz.* mdccclxx/4 Art of Drawing and Cleansing natural and setting in Artificial Teeth. **1736** BUTLER *Anal.* I. i. 31 It can walk by the help of an artificial leg. **1753** SMOLLETT *Ct. Fathom* (1784) 122/2 A knot of artificial flowers. **1867** F. FRANCIS *Angling* vi. (1880) 190 A list of artificial flies.

3. a. Merely made up; factitious; *hence*, feigned, fictitious. (Cf. 1593 in 1 b.)

c **1650** COWLEY *To his Majesty* Wks. 1710 II. 577 The Artificial Joy's drown'd by the Natural. **1678** BUTLER *Hud.* III. i. 730 Washes As artificial as their faces. **1719** YOUNG *Revenge* II. i, To elaborate An artificial happiness from pains. **1758** JOHNSON *Idler* No. 21 ⁋8 Endeavour to kindle in myself an artificial impatience. **1865** LECKY *Rational.* (1878) I. 319 Religion.. became an artificial thing of relics and ceremonies.

b. *spec.* in *Contract Bridge* (see quots.).

1930 E. CULBERTSON *Contract Bridge Blue Bk.* xx. 267 'Strength showing' optional or artificial bids.. are a polite warning to the enemy not to fall into the trap. **1950** J. CULBERTSON *Contract Bridge for Beginners* (rev. ed.) xv. 162 'Artificial' bidding. When the partner bids, for example, five hearts to show that he has two aces, his bid has nothing whatsoever to do with the hearts in his hand. **1961** *Listener* 28 Sept. 485/2 South's One Diamond was artificial.

4. Not natural in manners, affected.

1598 BARCKLEY *Felic. Man* (1631) 327 Artificiall apes, counterfeiting a formall kinde of strangers civilitie. **1679** STILLINGFL. *Serm. Whitehall* 7 Mar. 15 Hence the most artificial men have found it necessary to put on a guise of simplicity and plainness. **1823** LAMB *Elia* Ser. II. vi. (1865) 271 What if it is the nature of some men to be highly artificial? **1849** ROBERTSON *Serm.* Ser. I. ii. (1866) 20 Some will have become frivolous and artificial.

5. In various phrases, opposed to *natural*. ***artificial aid***, an aid (e.g. crampons, pitons) used in climbing; hence ***artificial climbing***, climbing with the assistance of such aids; †***artificial day*** (obs.), the period during which the sun is above the horizon; ***artificial fertilizer, manure***, a chemical fertilizer or manure; ***artificial globe***, a globe having a map of the world delineated on its surface, and revolving on an axis within rings representing the horizon and meridian; ***artificial grasses***, such as do not grow spontaneously in the locality, but are sown; ***artificial horizon***, a level reflecting surface, such as that of a fluid at rest, or a mirror laid horizontally on the earth's surface, used in taking altitudes; also, a gyroscopic instrument used in an aircraft to indicate the attitude of the aircraft in relation to the horizon; ***artificial insemination***, injection of semen into the uterus (of an animal) by other than the natural means (abbrev. *A.I.*); so *A.I.D.*, *A.I.H.*, artificial insemination (of a woman) with a donor's, the husband's, semen (see also DONOR d); ***artificial intelligence***, (the study of) the capacity of machines to simulate intelligent human behaviour; abbrev. *AI* s.v. A III; ***artificial kidney***, an apparatus that performs the functions of a human kidney in place of a diseased or injured organ; ***artificial language***, an invented language, esp. one designed for international use; ***artificial lines***, lines on a sector representing the logarithmic sines and tangents; ***artificial lung***, an apparatus which supplements the supply of oxygen available to the lungs or induces respiration; cf. *iron lung*; ***artificial numbers***, logarithms; ***artificial respiration***, a manual or mechanical procedure designed to restore the natural function of breathing when this has been suspended; ***artificial rubber***, a manufactured plastic substance resembling rubber; ***artificial silk***, see SILK; ***artificial sunlight***, a name given to light radiated from an ultra-violet ray lamp; see also SUN-RAY; ***artificial system*** or ***classification*** (in *Nat. Hist.*), a system which does not seek to embrace all natural affinities, but chiefly to serve as a key to the identification of species; ***artificial year*** (= *civil* year), the period from one new year's day to another (now 365 or 366 even days), as distinguished from the actual time taken by the earth in its annual revolution.

1934 E. R. BLANCHET in S. Spencer *Mountaineering* v. 107 *Artificial Aids.*—On rocks these are met with more and more frequently. The rope is no longer used merely for safety but also as a means of climbing and may be looked upon as an artificial aid. **1956** C. EVANS *On Climbing* iii. 53 'Artificial' climbing, on sections otherwise unclimbable, is the province of the advanced climber. *c* **1386** CHAUCER *Man of Lawes Prol.* 2 The brighte sonne The arke of his artificial day hath i-ronne The fourthe part. *c* **1391** —— *Astrol.* II. §7 To knowe the arch of the day, that some folk kallen the day artificial. **1432–50** tr. *Higden* (1865) I. 377 The clergy ..ȝiffenge attendaunce to preier and to abstinence by the day artificialle, spendenge the nyȝhtes in surfettes and in ryette. **1631** R. BYFIELD *Doctr. Sabb.* 142 To take the fourth commandement to bee understood of an artificiall day and not of a naturall. **1907** *Roy. Soc. S. Australia Trans. Index 1877–1900* 37 Artificial fertilizers. **1936** *Economist* 11 Jan. 71/2 The increase in imports is mainly due to larger imports of..artificial fertilisers. **1943** J. S. HUXLEY *TVA* 116 The artificial fertilizer industry. **1635** N. CARPENTER *Geog. Delin.* I. vii. 161 The artificiall Globe is an expression or imitation of the Spheare of the Earth. **1866** ROGERS *Agric. & Prices* I. ii. 17 In the absence of artificial grasses, natural meadow was exceedingly valuable. **1801** C. GOULD *Brit. Patent* 2559 Artificial horizon, to be attached to and used with the quadrant or sextant for taking altitudes on land or water. **1833** SIR J. HERSCHEL *Astron.* ii. 91 The reflecting surface of a fluid so used for the determination of the altitudes of objects is called an artificial horizon. **1912** *Engineering* 1 Mar. 285/3 The artificial horizon..brought out..as an attachment to sextants especially suitable for observations from balloons. **1920** *Flight* XII. 1258/1 In common with all artificial horizons when used in aircraft, however, the level is subject to error due to the acceleration of the machine acting on the bubble. **1897** *Proc. R. Soc.* LXI. 52 (*heading*) The Artificial Insemination of Mammals. **1923** in M. Box *Trial M. Stopes* (1967) 105, I am referring to that paragraph about artificial insemination of women with seed taken from other men. **1936** *Discovery* Oct. 328/2 We might..by 'artificial insemination' produce a race containing as many 'Lenins or Darwins' as we pleased. **1945** *Brit. Med. Jrnl.* 13 Jan. 40/1 We ourselves have used, and in certain respects developed, the technique of artificial insemination (A.I.) during the past five years. *Ibid.* 40/2 (*heading*) Male sterility and Other Indications for Artificial Insemination with Donated Semen (A.I.D.). *Ibid.* 43/1 In a recent series of 30 successive cases A.I.H. was carried out because of low invasive power of the semen. **1947** *Lancet* 19 Apr. 527/2 The signed statement of consent, usually obtained by the doctor from both the husband and wife before insemination with donor's semen (A.I.D.) is performed, is likely to be worthless legally. **1947** G. L. RUSSELL in *Artificial Human Insemination* vii. 56 A.I.D. involves adultery, whatever the motives, circumstances, or consequences. **1949** 'G. ORWELL' *Nineteen Eighty-Four* I. 68 All children were to be begotten by artificial insemination (*artsem*, it was called in Newspeak). **1959** *Observer* 25 Jan. 11/3 Intended originally for the small farmer, A.I. has proved of increasing interest also to the larger farmer and the pedigree breeder. **1956** M. L. MINSKY *Heuristic Aspects Artificial Intelligence Probl.* (M.I.T. Lincoln Lab. Group Rep. 34–55) IV. 4 In the random decisions desired in the domain of artificial intelligence, I am confident that the 'precision' required of pseudo-random sequences will be very much less than for mathematical or numerical purposes. **1970** O. DOPPING *Computers & Data Processing* xi. 173 Research on pattern recognition is carried out in various areas, for instance, in connection with 'learning machines' and 'artificial intelligence'. **1973** *Sci. News* 4 Aug. 76/1 Mathematicians and engineers..have combined a computer, a television camera and a mechanical arm into a system with enough artificial intelligence to recognize blocks of various sizes, colors and shapes. **1980** *Times* 18 Feb. (Computer Suppl.) p. viii/8 Now revived by government and private capital, British interest in robotics and artificial intelligence is nevertheless still feeding off the impetus from overseas work. **1985** *Personal Computer World* Feb. 164/1 The..almost *clichéd* applications being knowledge-based systems and artificial intelligence programs. **1913** *Brit. Med. Jrnl.* 16 Aug. 387/1 Salicylic acid injected into a vein was excreted in some cases more rapidly by this artificial kidney than by the normal excretory channels. **1914** *Jrnl. Pharmacol. & Exper. Therapeutics* Jan. 276 The apparatus constitutes what has been called an artificial kidney in the sense that it allows the escape of the diffusible constituents of the blood. **1961** *Lancet* 2 Sept. 553/2 Representatives of several artificial-kidney units.. expressed the opinion that clotting in the artificial kidney was commoner when machines of large surface-area were used. **1864** F. M. MÜLLER *Lect. Sci. Language* 2 ser. ii. 61 An artificial language might be much more perfect, more regular, more easy to learn, than any of the spoken tongues of man. **1865** F. W. FARRAR *Chapters on Lang.* iii. 37 All attempts to frame an artificial language have been a failure. **1919** G. WILLIS *Philos. of Speech* iv. 63 An artificial language, such as Esperanto, can never acquire any literary value, although it may possibly provide a useful vehicle of scientific or philosophic thought. **1870** *Century Mag.* Nov. 29/2 This result is obtained by means of an *artificial lung*... The diver carries this apparatus on his back. **1947** *Sci. Digest* Sept. 74 (*caption*) Oxygenated blood; external artificial lung. **1843** Artificial manure [see MINERAL *a.* 4]. **1882** *Encycl. Brit.* XIV. 568/1 The artificial manures which he [*sc.* Justus Liebig] introduced contained the essential mineral substances. **1922** A. HUXLEY *Mortal Coils* 31 His land was farmed in the best modern way—silos and artificial manures and continuous cropping and all that. **1852** *New Orleans Med. & Surg. Jrnl.* IX. 209 One thing that saved the child's life—the Artificial Respiration. **1854** W. MARCET in *Med. Times & Gaz.* 22 Apr. 401 An account of a new instrument for performing artificial respiration. **1922** *Man. Seamanship* (*H.M.S.O.*) I. 371 To effect artificial respiration put yourself astride or on one side of the patient's body, in a kneeling position, facing his head. **1911** C. CHRISTY *African Rubber Ind.* xvii. 232 There are hundreds of materials called rubber substitutes..but these are not artificial rubbers. **1930** *Engineering* 18 Apr. 525/2 Artificial rubber gave no spot diagram. **1942** *Electronic Engin.* Mar. 668/2 Polyethylene and polyisobutylene (artificial rubber) are almost as good. **1927** *Lancet* 29 Oct. 947/2 London clinic for artificial sunlight treatment. **1928** *Daily Express* 27 June 3/6 The Committee on Artificial Sunlight in Industrial Hygiene. **1704** HEARNE *Ductor Hist.* (1714) I. 3 The Artificial or Civil Year now used, was invented by the Emperor Julius Cæsar.

†**II.** Displaying special art or skill. (All *Obs.*)

†**6.** Displaying much skill; **a.** of things: Skilfully made or contrived. *Obs.*

1490 CAXTON *Eneydos* ii. 14 To destroye soo artyfycyall a werke. **1494** FABYAN VI. clvi. 145 An horologe or a clocke.. of a wonder artyfyciall makyng. **1578** T. N. tr. *Conq. W. India* 55 Things made of feathers verie curious, straunge, and artificiall. **1655** MRQ. WORC. *Cent. Inv.* lxxxviii, A Brazen or Stone-head..so artificial and natural, that..it will presently open its mouth, and resolve the question. **1678** CUDWORTH *Intell. Syst.* I. v. 875 A most artificial Contrivance of Nature..to hinder the regurgitation of the Fæces. **1738** J. KEILL *Anim. Econ.* Pref. 10 The artificial and elegant structure of the eye.

†**b.** of persons: Skilled in constructive art, skilful. *Obs.*

1541 BARNES *Wks.* (1573) 342/2 A conning and an artificyall grauer. **1600** HAKLUYT *Voy.* (1810) III. 553 They are very artificiall in making of images. **1682** NORRIS *Hierocles* 2 God who was the most artificial framer of the Universe.

†**7.** Displaying education or training; scholarly.

1618 LATHAM *2nd Bk. Falconry* (1633) 38 His Hawke hath hardly beene taught one good qualitie or artificiall condition. *a* **1619** DONNE *Biathan.* (1644) 23 Scholastique and artificiall men use this way of instructing. **1628** COKE *On Litt.* 62 a, Not..understood of euerie unlearned mans reason, but of artificiall and legal reason.

†**8.** Displaying technical skill; workmanlike.

1656 H. PHILLIPS *Purch. Patt.* (1676) 23 The best and most artificial way to make these Tables, is to find certain numbers in continual proportion decreasing.

†**9.** Displaying artifice; artful, cunning, deceitful. (Said of men and their actions.) *Obs.*

1548 UDALL, etc. *Erasm. Par.* Mark vi. (R.) [They] would for the..setting forthe of themselfes make vnto the people an artificial oracion or sermon. **1649** MILTON *Eikon.* Wks. 1738 I. 376 This is the artificialest piece of finesse to perswade Men to be Slaves, that the wit of Court could have invented. **1656** W. MONTAGUE *Accompl. Wom.* 105 Excessive praises which artificiall men offer. **1702** *Eng. Theophr.* 91 The great ones have a Trick as artificial to excuse themselves.

†**III.** Of or pertaining to art. (All *Obs.*)

†**10.** According to the rules of art.

1528 PAYNELL *Salerne Reg.* P b, It is not artificial to eate them [peas] in the huskes (for the nature of that within and the huskes) disagree. **1609** DOULAND *Ornithop. Microl.* 39 Rests..are of equall value with the Notes, and are measured with artificiall Silence. **1753** CHAMBERS *Cycl. Supp.*, *Artificial music*, that which is according to the rules of art; or executed by instruments invented by art.

†**11.** Pertaining to practical art; technical. *Obs.*

1660 STANLEY *Hist. Philos.*, Speech is of five kinds. Artificial, used by Tradesmen in their several Professions. **1739** CHESTERF. *Lett.* 49 I. 150 Technical..from the Greek word τέχνη, which signifies Art, and τεχνικός, which signifies Artificial. **1809** CHRISTIAN in *Blackstone's Comm.* II. 381 He knew their artificial import and signification.

B. as *sb.* [the adj. used *absol.* in *pl.*] **a.** Artificial things; products of art. *spec.* artificial manure.

1611 GUILLIM *Heraldry* IV. xiii. 222 Such Artificials as are in vse amongst men of Militarie Profession. **1652** GAULE *Magastrom.* 69 Animalls, vegetables, inanimates, minerall s, artificialls, etc. **1743** *Lond. & Countr. Brewer* II. i. (ed. 2) 87 Malt, like many other Artificials, is most genuine, when it is nearest to its Original Nature. **1860** in THIRSK & IMRAY *Suff. Farming 19th Cent.* (1958) 57 Artificial consumed. **1927** W. DEEPING *Doomsday* xix. §2 Plenty of stock..saved you from having to spend too much on artificials.

b. An artificial flower.

1840 H. COCKTON *Valentine Vox* xxvi. 196 A bouquet of variegated artificials on one side. **1848** MRS. GASKELL *Mary Barton* I. i. 8 Esther, I see what you'll end at with your artificials, and your fly-away veils.

c. An artificial bait.

1949 A. WANLESS *Fly Fisherman's Alphabet* 53 There are not so many flies which trout feed on and the artificials are definite imitations of them. **1959** *Times* 7 Feb. 9/3 There have been many instances of perch and chub being caught on..spun artificials.

arti'ficialism. [f. prec. + -ISM.] An artificial principle, or practice.

1869 MRS. WOOD *Rol. Yorke* III. 156 Made up of artificialisms—for nothing seemed real about him but his ill-temper.

artificiality (ˌɑːtɪfɪʃɪˈælɪtɪ). [f. as prec. + -ITY; cf. *reality*.]

1. The quality or state of being artificial; artificial character or condition.

a **1763** SHENSTONE *Ess.* 105 Trees in hedges partake of their artificiality. **1845** R. CHAMBERS *Vest. Creat.* 251 It would imply a curious artificiality of arrangement in the creative design. **1879** WARD *Chaucer* 23 The artificiality and extravagance of the costumes of these times.

2. with *pl.* An artificial thing or characteristic.

1848 MILLER *First Impr.* ix. (1857) 153 His artificialities had perished, like the artificialities of another kind of the poets his contemporaries. **1851** SIR F. PALGRAVE *Norm. & Eng.* I. 11 Book antiquarianisms and æsthetic artificialities. **1875** WHITNEY *Life Lang.* xv. 312 It is not an artificiality.

artificialize (ɑːtɪˈfɪʃəlaɪz), *v.* [f. as prec. + -IZE.] To make or render artificial. Hence **artificialized** *ppl. a.*, **artificializing** *vbl. sb.*

1684 T. R. *Amazem. Fut. Ages* 39 Every one having an artificialized natural Morion of his head. **1801** W. TAYLOR in *Month. Mag.* XI. 290 The British school of gardening naturalizes art; the French artificializes nature. **1848** MILL *Pol. Econ.* II. xiii. §1 It has artificialized large portions of mankind. **1855** KINGSLEY *Glaucus* (1878) 53 Athletic exercises are..becoming more and more artificialized and expensive. **1883** D. WHEELER *By-Ways of Lit.* i. 22 Fine dressing and artificializing of the person.

artificially (ɑːtɪˈfɪʃəlɪ), *adv.* [f. as prec. + -LY².]

1. By art as distinguished from the operation of nature. **a.** By artificial process. **b.** In an artificial, factitious, or designed way; with deliberate design to produce a contemplated result.

a. **1541** R. COPLAND *Guydon's Quest. Cyrurg.*, Cauterysacyon..is an operacyon made wᵗ fyre artyfycyally in yᵉ body. **1664** POWER *Exp. Philos.* I. 35, I have artificially frozen all the said Liquor into a mass of Ice. **1794** SULLIVAN *View Nat.* I. 368 The experiment of artificially congealing wetted snow. **1873** WILLIAMSON *Chem.* §227 Alcohol can be built up artificially from its elements.

b. **1586** T. ROGERS *39 Art.* (1607) 93 A great learned man ..(to whose acquaintance I was artificially brought). **1670** in Somers *Tracts* I. 17 This Fear was artificially put into them, as I could easily perceive. **1867** FREEMAN *Norm. Conq.* I. ii. 48 Mercia has every appearance of having been artificially mapped out. **1875** WHITNEY *Life Lang.* ii. 16 Reflectively and artificially called by its inventor magenta.

2. In accordance with the rules of art, *hence* technically, artistically, in workmanlike manner; with much art, skilfully, ingeniously, cleverly. *arch.* or *Obs.* but still used in legal phraseology in the primary sense.

1528 ROY *Satire*, A saynt. Even soche a one as paynters do paynt On walles and bordes artificially. **1543** RECORDE *Gr. Arts* (1646) 193 You have answered the question very artificially; and truly I commend you. **1609** HOLLAND *Amm. Marcell.* xxx. i. 380 Stringed..instruments, fingered right artificially. **1612** BRINSLEY *Lud. Lit.* viii. (1627) 105 To doe it artificially by Rule. **1612** W. MARTYN *Youth's Instruc.* 20 An artificially carued picture. **1691** RAY *Creation* I. (1704) 170 How wisely and artificially their Members are formed. **1740** JOHNSON *Drake* Wks. IV. 446 Baskets plaited so artificially that they held water. **1817** JAS. MILL *Brit. India* I. II. viii. 356, *note*, So artificially done, that they seemed natural. **1876** J. BLACKBURN in *Law Rep.* Exch. Div. I. 161 The instrument is not in all respects artificially drawn.

b. (With something of the next sense): With skill directed to hide or deceive.

1708 J. CHAMBERLAYNE *St. Gt. Brit.* II. III. vi. (1743) 416 Plaids..which they manage so artificially, as to supply the defect of drawers and breeches. **1715** BURNET *Own Time* (1766) I. 13 A cupboard that was very artificially hid. **1761** SMOLLETT *Gil Blas* v. i. (1802) II. 164 A little red beard of horse-hair, which he fixed so artificially to his ears, that one would have sworn it was the natural produce of his chin.

†**3.** With or by artifice; craftily, cunningly, cleverly. (Generally in bad sense.) *Obs.*

1573 G. HARVEY *Common-pl. Bk.* (1884) 31 So openly favur and incurrage the on, and so artificially and cunningly over-whart the other. **1622** BACON *Hist. Hen. VII*, Wks. 1860. 312 Having..given artificially, for serving his own turn, some hopes..to marry Anne. **1679** STILLINGFL. *Serm. Whitehall* 7 Mar. 46 It doth mischief secretly, spitefully and artificially. **1715** BURNET *Own Time* I. 205 Sharp dissembled so artificially. **1736** BUTLER *Anal.* I. iii. 81 Justice is often artificially eluded.

arti'ficialness. [f. as prec. + -NESS.]

1. The quality of being artificial, as opposed to naturalness.

1594 CAREW *Huarte's Exam. Wits* (1616) 195 This artificialnesse grew to such force, as it was converted into nature. **1791** NEWTE *Tour Eng. & Sc.* 327 The snug artificialness of the city. **1851** RUSKIN *Mod. Paint.* I. Pref. 24 The sense of artificialness, the absence of all appearance of reality.

†**2.** The quality of being skilfully made or contrived; artificial contrivance. *Obs.*

1611 COTGR., *Maistrise*..cunning, skill, artificiallnesse. **1667** H. MORE *Div. Dial.* III. xxiv. (1713) 236 Admiring the largeness and artificialness of their Vessels. **1678** CUDWORTH *Intell. Syst.* 111 The unguided Motion of Matter, without any Plastick Artificialness or Methodicalness.

ar'tificing, *vbl. sb. rare*⁻¹. [App. f. ARTIFIC-ER.] Execution of artificers' work.

1866 HOWELLS *Venet. Life* 300 Full of beautiful workmanship in every branch of artificing.

†**arti'ficious,** *a. Obs.* Also 6 **artyfyciouse.** [a. F. *artificieux*:—L. *artificiōs-us*, f. *artificium*: see ARTIFICE and -OUS.]

1. Displaying art or constructive skill.

1530 PALSGR. 305/2 Artyfyciouse, full of great crafte and workemanshyp, *artificieux*. **1603** HOLLAND *Plutarch's Mor.* 174 The most proper artificious and workemanlike instruments. **1659** HAMMOND *On Ps.* cxxxix. 6-12 The closest and most artificious recess.

2. Factitious, affected.

1655 JENNINGS *Elise* 59 The artificious disdain, the affected scorn of this damosel.

3. Cunning, artful.

1655 JENNINGS *Elise* 58 That makes known to the artificious Amazon what she knew already. **1679** OATES *Myst. Iniq.* 4 As Subtil and Artificious a Device, as ever yet the World brought forth.

†**arti'ficiously,** *adv. Obs.* Also 7 **-osely.** [f. prec. + -LY².] Artificially; with constructive skill; by art as opposed to nature; artfully, cunningly.

1662 J. BARGRAVE *Pope Alex. VII* (1867) 137 Made of porcupine quills very artificiously. **1677** GALE *Crt. Gentiles* II. III. 100 Artificiosely to circumvent some one. **1681** WHARTON *Soul of World* Wks. 1683. 647 Oyl Artificiously Extracted from Gold.

artify ('ɑːtɪfaɪ), *v. colloq.* [f. ART *sb.* + -IFY.] To bring art into; to make 'arty'. Hence **'artifying** *vbl. sb.*

1903 *Brighton Herald* 27 Oct. 11/4 Man's work..is 'to artify the world, and to be ever spiritualizing it towards the beauty of holiness'. **1940** *Scrutiny* VIII. 398, I am not in favour of a rapprochement between art-music and commerce because..the artifying of 'low' music has been demonstrably almost wholly bad. **1940** J. BETJEMAN in *Archit. Rev.* LXXXVIII. 162 Certain inn signboards are the people's idea of art, where the brewer has not arty-fied them or destroyed them for some wretched trade-mark. **1962** *Times* 28 Nov. 13/4 What can happen when an attempt is made to 'artify' folk elements.

†**ar'tigrapher.** *Obs. rare*⁻¹. [f. med.L. *artigraphus*, f. *arti-* art + Gr. -γραφ-ος writing, writer (see Du Cange) + -ER.] The writer of an *Ars*, esp. of an *Ars Grammatica*; a grammarian.

1753 CHAMBERS *Cycl. Supp.* s.v. *Artist*, From the same origin come also the words *Artistic*, and *Artigrapher*, found in some writers of those ages.

†**'artilize,** *v. Obs.* [ad. F. *artialiser.*] To make artificial. Cf. ARTIZE.

a **1744** BOLINGBROKE *To Pope* (T.) Says Montaigne, I would naturalise art, instead of artilising nature. **1778** *Phil. Surv. S. Ireland* 169 But, let us naturalize art, instead of artilising nature.

†**ar'tiller,** *sb. Obs.* [a. OF. *artiller, -ier, arteiller*, cogn. w. Sp. *artillero*, It. *artigliero*, L. type **articulārius*, also in OF. *articulier* (a Lat. Fr. Gloss. in Godef. has '*Artifex*, articulier, ouvrier'); cf. OF. *artill(i)er* to fortify, provide with engines of war:—L. **articulāre*; apparently f. late L. *articula* or *articulum* (Du Cange), dim. of *ars, artem* art. Cf. *engine* from *ingenium*. But some would connect these words with *articulus* joint.] A maker of artillery; *spec.* a bowyer.

c **1360** in *Househ. Ord.* (1790) 4 Artifficers and workmen —Artellers 6. **1483** *Act 1 Rich. III.* xi. §1 The said inhabitaunts Artillers myght competently lyve upon suche stuff as they than bought of Bowestaves at xl *s.* the C.

artilleried (ɑː'tɪlərɪd), *ppl. a.* Also 6 *Sc.* **artailyeryt.** [f. ARTILLERY + -ED².] Provided with artillery.

1513-75 *Diurn. Occurr.* (1833) 46 Quha thairefter past in England, and left..the toun weill artailyeryt.

artillerist (ɑː'tɪlərɪst). [f. ARTILLERY + -IST.]

1. One who studies the principles of gunnery.

1778 PRINGLE *Gunnery* 17 A treatise was published by one of our own artillerists. **1871** TYNDALL *Fragm. Sc.* I. x. 308 A widely spread opinion among artillerists.

2. A gunner, an artilleryman.

1781 G. CLINTON in Sparks *Corr. Amer. Rev.* (1853) III. 230 The want of some artillerists and field-artillery..was an evident disadvantage. **1870** *Daily News* 2 Dec., We lost one gun, whose artillerists and horses were all killed.

artillery (ɑː'tɪlərɪ), *sb.* Forms: 4 **artel-, artilrie,** 5 **artellerye, artilȝery, artylery, -lrye, artailȝierie,** 5-6 **artyllerye, artillary, -arie, -ari,** 6 **artelere, artellere, artilerie, artylary, -llary, -lerey,** 6-7 **artillerie,** 6- **artillery.** See also ARTAILLIE, ARTRY. [a. OFr. *artillerie, arteillerie*, cogn. w. It. *arti-, arteglieria*, Sp. *artillaria*, Pg. *arti-, artelharia*, Pr. *artilharia*: see ARTILLER and -ERY.]

†**1.** Warlike munitions, implements of war; ammunition in the wide sense. *Obs.*

c **1386** CHAUCER *Melib.* ¶367, I shal warnestoore myn hous with toures swiche as han Castelles and othere manere edifices and Armure and Artelries [*v.r.* artelleryes] by whiche thynges I may my persone and myn hous.. deffenden. **1481** *Act 11 Jas. III* (1597) §82 Victualles, men and artailȝierie. **1485** CAXTON *Chas. Gt.* (1880) 162 Anone the artylleryes were assembled. **1550-63** MACHYN *Diary* (1848) 191 All maner of artelere as drumes, flutes, trumpetes, gones, mores pykes, halbardes. **1582** *Lanc. Wills* (1857) I. 132, I geave..all maner of artyllerye or harneysse, as jack, salett, whyte harnesse. **1625** tr. *Gonsalvius' Span. Inquis.*, A cunning huntsman with all his furniture, hauing his artillery about him, his snares, grinnes, heyes, dogges, &c. **1794** S. WILLIAMS *Hist. Vermont* 177 A club made of hard wood, a stake hardened in the fire, a lance armed with a flint or a bone, a bow and an arrow constituted the whole artillery of an Indian war.

2. Engines for discharging missiles. **a.** Formerly including catapults, slings, arbalests, bows, etc.

1476 SIR J. PASTON in *Lett.* 776 III. 162 All hys ordynaunce and artylrye. **1489** CAXTON *Faytes of Armes* I. xii. 31 Artyllerye of al maner shot. **1545** ASCHAM *Toxoph.* (Arb.) 65 Artillarie now a dayes is taken for ii thinges: Gunnes and Bowes. **1601** HOLLAND *Pliny* I. 199 Brakes, slings and other engins of artillery. **1611** BIBLE *1 Sam.* xx. 40 Ionathan gaue his artillery [WYCLIF, aarmis; COVERDALE, wapens] vnto his ladde, and said vnto him, Goe, cary them to the citie. **1703** MAUNDRELL *Journ. Jerus.* (1721) 126 Amongst the Artillery was an old Roman Balista. **1874** BOUTELL *Arms & Arm.* xi. 213 Ancient artillery..could never have led the way to the introduction of modern artillery. They have really nothing in common.

b. Now: Large guns, cannon, ordnance.

c **1533** LD. BERNERS *Huon* 315 To take the way towardes Coleyne with al his artylerey and caryage. **1560** WHITEHORNE *Ord. Souldiours* (1588) 34 The toucheholes of artillerie to be nailed vp. **1595** SHAKS. *John* II. i. 403 Turne thou the mouth of thy Artillerie..against these sawcie walles. **1597** DANIEL *Civ. Wares* VI. xxvi, Artillerie, th' infernall instrument, New brought from hell to scourge mortalitie With hideous roaring, and astonishment. **1598** FLORIO *Serpentina*..a kind of ordinance, bumbard or artillerie. **1703** MAUNDRELL *Journ. Jerus.* (1732) 19 Port-holes for Artillery, instead of windows. **1803** LAKE in *Wellesley Disp.* (1877) 395 The enemy opposed to us a tremendous fire from a numerous artillery. **1806** A. DUNCAN *Nelson's Fun.* A large park of flying artillery. **1815** WELLINGTON in Knight *Crown Hist. Eng.* lix. 803 Napoleon ..mixed cavalry with his infantry, and supported both with an enormous quantity of artillery.

†**3.** Missiles discharged in war, shot, ammunition.

1563 GOLDING *Cæsar* (1565) 249 From whence wyth an engine artillery might have bene shotte among the thyckest of hys ennemyes. **1575** BANISTER *Chyrurg.* II. (1585) 270 Search with a probe, which way the pellet is gone, (this obserue in the drawing out of all artillerie). **1630** WESTCOTE *Devon.* 43 Hurling flints and pebbles and other such like artillery. **1867** PEARSON *Hist. Eng.* I. 23 The war-ships.. poured in their artillery on the British flank.

4. The science and practice of using artillery; †**a.** *formerly*, Archery. *Obs.*

1545 ASCHAM *Toxoph.* (Arb.) 21 That fletcher is an enemy to archers and artillery. **1550-3** *Four Supplic.* (1871) 100 It is a great decay to artyllary: for shepeherdes be but yll artchers. **1801** STRUTT *Sports & Past.* II. i. 51 Overseers of the science of artillery, by which was meant long-bows, cross-bows, and hand-guns.

b. Gunnery. (Craig 1847, and mod. Dicts.)

†**c.** (see quot.) *Obs.*

1727-51 CHAMBERS *Cycl.*, *Artillery* is also used for what we otherwise called *pyrotechnia*, or the art of fire-works, with the instruments and apparatus belonging thereto.

5. That branch of an army which manages the cannons in war; one of the 'arms of the service.'

1786 BEATSON *Pol. Index* II. 138 The Master General of the Ordnance..is Colonel in Chief of the Royal Regiment of Artillery. **1849** MACAULAY *Hist. Eng.* I. iii. 305 There was no regiment of artillery, no brigade of sappers and miners. **1866** *Standard* 2 Nov. 5/6 To transform the heavy cavalry into horse artillery. *Mod.* In the British Army, the 'Royal Regiment of Artillery' consists of two brigades of Horse Artillery, four of Field Artillery, and eleven of Garrison Artillery, each brigade consisting of from 8 to 20 or more batteries.

6. *fig.* (with reference to 1, 2, 3.)

1599 *Warn. Faire Wom.* I. 314 Repulse loves false Artillery. *a* **1667** COWLEY *Lover's Chron.* viii, And th' artillery of her eye. **1714** MANDEVILLE *Fab. Bees* (1733) II. 126 She has all the artillery of our sex to fear. **1764** REID *Inquiry* v. vii, And laughs at the artillery of the logician. **1809** SYD. SMITH *Wks.* (1859) I. 163/1 With his whole heavy artillery of argument and quotation. **1870** L'ESTRANGE *Miss Mitford* I. v. 157 Not proof against the artillery of puns.

7. Thunder and lightning. Only *poet.*

1596 SHAKS. *Tam. Shr.* I. ii. 205 Haue I not heard great Ordnance in the field? And heauen's Artillerie thunder in the skies? **1695** WOODWARD *Nat. Hist. Earth* II. (1723) 103 The whole Artillery of the Sky. **1718** POPE *Iliad* XII. 331 As when high Jove his sharp artillery forms.

8. *Comb.* and *Attrib.* (Chiefly in senses 2 b and 5), as ***artillery-brigade, -company, -founder, -officer, -practice.*** **artillery-boat,** a boat carrying artillery, a gun-boat; **artillery-company,** a company of archers (*obs.*), or of artillery in sense 5; **artillery-driver,** one who drives the horses that draw field-guns; †**artillery-garden,** an archery-ground; **artillery-harness** for horses that draw field-guns; **artillery-park,** the place in which the artillery is encamped, or in which during a seige it is collected; **artillery-train,** a number of pieces of ordnance mounted on carriages and fitted out with all appurtenances for marching; **artillery wheel,** a heavily-built dished wheel used on gun-carriages; a similar wheel on motor vehicles.

1876 BANCROFT *Hist. U.S.* V. ix. 428 The 'Carleton,' accompanied by the *artillery-boats. **1681** *Lond. Gaz.* mdcxxvii. 7 The President, Vice-President, Treasurer, Court of Assistants, and the rest of the *Artillery-Company of London. **1784-5** *Ann. Reg.* 64/1 This fraternity is to this day called the artillery-company, which is a French term signifying archery. **1844** MACREADY *Remin.* II. 242 A neat little fort with an artillery company commands the passage. **1832** GEN. P. THOMPSON *Exerc.* (1842) II. 275 Increasing the corps of *artillery-drivers with men expert in the vocation. **1877** *Daily News* 25 Oct. 5/5 Incessant *artillery firing is being carried on on both sides. **1728** MORGAN *Algiers* II. iv. 275 The Basha's *Artillery-founder, cast for them a huge iron mace. **1593** NASHE *Christes Teares* (1613) 39 Heauen..shall bee made an *Artillery-house of Haile-stones. **1855** W. SARGENT *Braddock's Exp.* 203 Four *artillery-officers were left with Dunbar. **1768** SIMES *Mil. Medley*, *Artillery-Park is a place appointed in the rear of both lines of the army for encamping the artillery. **1871** TYNDALL *Fragm. Sc.* I. 17 In *artillery practice the heat generated is usually concentrated upon the front of the bolt. [**1902** RHYS JENKINS *Motor Cars* 210 The wheels [of the Daimler cars] are of wood, artillery pattern, fitted with pneumatic tyres.] **1902** *Car* 15 Oct. 252/2 The Lanchester car was not strong enough to have *artillery wheels, and so was fitted with wire suspension wheels. **1904** A. B. F. YOUNG *Complete Motorist* 203 The wheels [of the Baby Peugeot car] are of the artillery type. **1642** BRIDGE *Serm. Norfolk Volunteers* 7 The heart of man is the *Artillery-yard, where all the thoughts of courage train continually.

ar'tillerying, *vbl. sb. nonce-wd.* The firing of artillery.

1837 CARLYLE *Fr. Rev.* III. v. vi. II. 311 With artillerying and *ça-ira-ing*, it shall be done.

artilleryman (ɑː'tɪlərɪmən). One whose military duty it is to serve a gun; one who belongs to the regiment of artillery.

1635 W. BARRIFF (*title*) Military Discipline: Or, The Yong Artillery Man. **1703** *Lond. Gaz.* mmmdcccxxxv/2 Four Companies of Artillery-men. **1855** RUSSELL *The War* II. xv, The artillerymen of our allies suddenly ceased, in order to let their guns cool.

ar'tilleryship. [See -SHIP.] The skilful management of cannon; artillery practice.

1762 STERNE *Tr. Shandy* V. xx. 84 In this stroke of artilleryship. *Mod.* The fine artilleryship of the English corps.

†**ar'tillied,** *ppl. a. Obs.* Also 6 **artalȝeit.** [f. F. *artillé (arteillé)*, pa. pple. of *artill(i)er* to provide with engines of war (see ARTILLER) + -ED.] Armed or provided with artillery.

1530 LYNDESAY *Papyngo* 929 Thay bene so artalȝeit, Thay purpose to defend thame with thair gounnis. **1565** R. LINDSAY 124 (JAM.) He was so well artillied and manned.

†**arti'llour.** *Obs.* [a. OF. *artilleur* (in med.L. *artillātōr-em*), f. *artill(i)er* vb.: see prec.] Engineer; officer in charge of military engines.

1483 CAXTON *Gold. Leg.* 294/3 Thartilloure that was mayster of the tormentys had gyuen a token to them.

†**arti-'natural,** *a. Obs.* 'Of or pertaining to nature imitated by art.' Bailey 1731.

artiness: see ARTY *a.*

†**'arting,** *vbl. sb. Obs.* [f. ART *v.*² + -ING¹.] Employment of art or artifice.

a **1619** FOTHERBY *Atheom.* I. xii. §2. 125 Without any arting, or fained palliation.

artiodactyl(e (,ɑːtɪəʊ'dæktɪl), *a.* and *sb. Zool.* [f. Gr. ἄρτιο-ς even in number + δάκτυλος finger, toe.] **A.** *adj.* Having an even number of toes. **B.** *sb.* An ungulate animal of this kind.

1849-52 TODD *Cycl. Anat. & Phys.* IV. 932/1 Artiodactyle ungulata. **1879** LE CONTE *Elem. Geol.* 508 The Artiodactyls always have their toes in pairs; there may be only two toes, as in Anoplothere and in Ruminants; or four as in the Hog and the Hippopotamus.

artique, artire, obs. f. ARCTIC, ARTERY.

artisan (ɑːtɪ'zæn). Also 7 **artisane, -zen,** 8 **-sant,** 6- **artizan.** [a. F. *artisan*, according to Diez ad. It. *artigiano*:—late L. **artītiānus*, f. *artītus*, pa. pple. of *artī-re* to instruct in arts. Cf. *partisan*.]

A. †1. One who practises or cultivates an art; an artist. *Obs.*

*c*1590 Marlowe *Faustus* i. 53 O what a world of profit and delight.. Is promis'd to the studious artizan. 1601 Holland *Pliny* II. 535 But Parrhasius hath deceiued Zeuxis, a professed artisane. 1621 Ainsworth *Annot. Pentat.* Ex. vii. 11 Devillish Arts and Artizens, such as God's law condemneth. 1795 Mason *Ch. Music* iii. 208 When a natural faculty is..advanced into an Art..its Artisans are ever ready to apply their exertions to it.

2. One who is employed in any of the industrial arts; a mechanic, handicraftsman, artificer.

1538 Starkey *England* 159 Few artysanys of gud occupatyon. 1611 Cotgr. s.v. *Doigt*, The Germans..are better Artisans then Artists, better at handy-crafts then at head-craft. 1713 *Phil. Trans.* XXVIII. 225 The Artisants here have wonderful Skill. 1751 Johnson *Rambl.* No. 145 ¶1 The meanest artisan..contributes more to the accommodation of life, than the profound scholar. 1849 Macaulay *Hist. Eng.* I. 420 We pass from the weavers of cloth to a different class of artisans.

3. *transf.* or *fig.*

1599 Harsnet *Agst. Darell* 21 Jesuites and Popish Artizans [*printed* Anti-]. 1623 Mabbe *Aleman's Guzman D'Alf.* II. 346 That Supreme Artizan that painted to the Life both heaven and Earth.

B. *attrib.* quasi-*adj.* (It is adj. in Fr.)

1859 Mill *Liberty* iv. (1865) 52/1 Opinions similar in principle..prevail widely among the artizan class.

arti'sanship. [See -SHIP.] The work and activity of an artisan or of artisans collectively.

1827 Carlyle *Germ. Romance* IV. 14 Intellectual artisanship..is less desirable than intellectual manhood. 1831 Chalmers in *Fraser's Mag.* III. 60 The toils of busy artisanship. 1832 Carlyle *Crit. & Misc. Ess.* (1840) IV. 102 Work out thy Artisanship in the spirit of an Artist! 1844 *N. Brit. Rev.* I. 139 Its [*sc.* the Byzantine Empire's] artisanship and commerce. 1907 W. de Morgan *Alice-for-Short* xiv, The sudden substitution of inspiration for mere artisanship.

artist ('ɑːtɪst), *sb.* and *a.* Also 6 **artiste.** [a. F. *artiste*, a. It. *artista*:—late L. *artista*, f. *ars* ART: see -IST.] A. *sb.* One who practises or is skilled in any art.

I. One skilled in the 'liberal' or learned arts.

†1. One who is master of the liberal arts (see ART *sb.* 7); a Master of Arts, learned man, philosopher. *Obs.*

1592 Chettle *Kind-Harts Dr.* (1841) 7 Idiots that think themselues artists because they can English an obligation. 1606 Shaks. *Tr. & Cr.* I. iii. 24 The Wise and Foole, the Artist and vn-read. 1653 Urquhart *Rabelais* II. x, He held dispute against all the Regents or Fellows of Colledges, Artists or Masters of Arts. 1680 T. Lawson (*title*) A Mite in the Treasury; being a Word to Artists, especially the Heptatechnists, or Professors of the Seuen Liberal Sciences. 1753 Chambers *Cycl. Supp.*, Artist, in an academical sense, denotes a philosopher or proficient in the faculty of arts.

†2. *gen.* One who pursues some practical science; a scientific man, man of science, savant. *Obs.*

1667 Milton *P.L.* I. 288 The Moon, whose Orb Through Optic Glass the Tuscan Artist views. 1686 [see 3 b].

†3. *specifically*: †a. A professor of the healing art; a medical practitioner, physician, surgeon.

1592 Chettle *Kind-Harts Dr.* (1841) 21 They must be artistes that are able to..resist the disease, by prouiding remedies. 1601 Shaks. *All's Well* II. iii. 10 Relinquisht of the Artists..both of Galen and Paracelsus. 1671 Salmon *Syn. Med.* III. lxxx. 695 Let the Artist grasp the Fracture with both his hands. 1761 Smollett *Gil Blas* III. vii, Luckily my wounds were not mortal, and I fell into the hands of a skilful artist.

†b. A professor of magic arts or occult sciences; an astrologer or alchemist; *later*, a chemist. *Obs.*

*c*1605 Rowley *Birth Merl.* IV. i, The artists..That seek the secrets of futurity. 1641 French *Distill.* vi. (1651) 175 In vain do Artists endeavour the reduction of metalls into their first matter. 1649 tr. *Du Ryer's Alcoran* 413 The knauery and wickedness of the Artists, the foolishness of credulous people, who suffer themselues to be deluded by them. 1686 W. Harris tr. *Lemery's Chym.* I. xvii. (ed. 3) 401 Volatile salts do rise from them which would very much incommode the Artist if he should hold his nose over it.

II. One skilled in the useful arts.

†4. *gen.* One who follows any pursuit or employment in which skill or proficiency is attainable by study or practice; *hence* a. A skilled performer, a proficient, a connoisseur. b. A practical man, as opposed to a *theorist*. *Obs.*

1594 Carew *Huarte's Exam. Wits* xiv. (1596) 253 From which two extreams a king ought to be farther distant, than any other artist. 1600 Chapman *Iliad* XXIII. 289 To make discharge of a design To please an artist. 1653 Walton *Angler* 125, I will give you more directions concerning fishing; for I would fain make you an Artist. 1721 Perry *Daggenh. Breach* 68 In all the questions..I had answer'd them like an Artist, and like a Workman. 1723 De Foe *Col. Jack* (1840) 190 The mate was an excellent sea artist, and an experienced sailor. 1793 Smeaton *Edystone L.* §76 A body of theoretic Men only..There might be many of that denomination; yet there were also many real artists in this body.

†5. a. A follower of a manual art; an artificer, mechanic, craftsman, artisan. *Obs.* exc. as in 6.

1633 G. Herbert *Priesth.* iii. in *Temple* 155 Fitted by the fire and trade Of skilfull artists. 1718 Pope *Iliad* XVIII. 479 Then from his anvil the lame artist rose. 1762 Goldsm. *Cit. World* lxv, A poor cobler sat in his stall..By this time my shoe was mended; and satisfying the poor artist for his trouble, etc. 1815 Southey *Roderick* XII. 78 Greek artists in the imperial city forged That splendid armour.

†b. *transf.* or *fig.* *Obs.*

1660 Stanley *Hist. Philos.* 157/2 A swarm of Bees, Artists of Hymettian Honey.

6. In this sense now influenced by 7 and applied to: One who practices a manual art in which there is much room for display of taste; one who makes his craft a 'fine art.' Cf. ARTISTE.

1849 Curzon *Visits Monast.* 316 We had a famous pilau, made by my artist [*i.e.* cook]. 1863 *Sat. Rev.* 138 The definition of Ary Scheffer..sinks into nothing in contact with such phrases as photographic artist, artist in hair, artist in wax flowers, and the like. 1883 *Pall Mall G.* 12 May (*Supp.*) Artists from the National Training School of Cookery will show the public..how fish ought to be cooked.

III. One who pursues an art which has as its aim to please.

7. a. *gen.* One who cultivates one of the fine arts, in which the object is mainly to gratify the æsthetic emotions by perfection of execution, whether in creation or representation.

It formerly included all who cultivated any of the *arts* presided over by the *Muses*, i.e. history, poetry, comedy, tragedy, music, dancing, astronomy; hence the application to actors, musicians, dancers, and perhaps Milton's 'artist' = *astronomer* in 2.

1581 Sidney *Def. Poesie* (Arb.) 52 The other Artists, & especially the Historian, affirming many things, can.. hardly escape from many lyes. But the Poet..neuer affirmeth..but euen for his entry, calleth the sweete Muses to inspire into him a good inuention. 1853 Maurice *Proph. & Kings* xx. 345 A man should be an artist to write a biography as much as to write a romance. 1855 H. Reed *Lect. Eng. Lit.* iii. (1878) 109 The true poet is always a true artist and words are the instruments of his art. 1876 Gladstone *Homer. Synch.* 190 [Homer] was too skilled an artist to bring freely upon the stage any figure which could vie with the subject of his song.

b. *fig.*

*c*1842 Tennyson *Memory* v, Well hast thou done, great artist, Memory.

8. *specifically*: †a. One skilled in music. *Obs.* exc. as in 7: see ARTISTE.

1590 *Plain Perc.* 21 Argues a bad eare, & a bungling Artist. 1674 Playford *Skill of Mus.* I. v. 19 If an Instrument be sounded by another who is an Artist. 1712 Addison *Spect.* No. 405 ¶1 That excellent Artist..having shewn us the Italian Musick in its Perfection.

b. One skilled in dramatic art; *hence* extended to any public performer: see ARTISTE.

1714 *Spect.* No. 570 ¶1 You may often see an Artist in the Streets gain a Circle of Admirers by carrying a long Pole upon his Chin. 1849 Macaulay *Hist. Eng.* I. 102 All who live by amusing the leisure of others, from the painter and the comic poet, down to the ropedancer and the Merry Andrew. For these artists well knew that, etc. 1853 C. Brontë *Villette* xxiii. (1876) 250 He told me his opinion of ..the actress: he judged her as a woman, not an artist.

c. Now *especially*: One who practises the arts of design; one who seeks to express the beautiful in visible form. In this sense sometimes taken to include sculptors, engravers, and architects; but popularly, and in the most usual current acceptation of the word, restricted to: One who cultivates the art of painting as a profession.

1747 J. Spence (*title*) Polymetis: an Enquiry concerning the agreement between the works of the Roman Poets and the Remains of the Ancient Artists. 1762 H. Walpole (*title*) Anecdotes of Painting in England, with some Account of the principal Artists. 1802 Mar. Edgeworth *Moral T.* (1816) 209 The artist, who shall produce..the most beautiful vase of china. 1821 Craig *Drawing, etc.* i. 24 Aristides..was the first artist who found a way to express the passions of the mind in the countenances of his figures. 1859 Geo. Eliot *A. Bede* 86 She's a perfect Hebe; and if I were an artist, I would paint her.

IV. One who practises artifice.

†9. One who practises artifice, stratagem, or cunning contrivance; a schemer, contriver. *Obs.*

1649 Bp. Hall *Cases Consc.* III. ii. (1654) 181 The Devill is a most skilfull Artist. *a*1677 Barrow *Serm. on Contentm.*, Those slippery, wily, artists, who can veer any whither with any wind. 1723 De Foe *Col. Jack* (1840) 51 The young artist that has done this roguery. 1813 Scott *Rokeby* VI. xxxii, A lifetime's arts, in vain essay'd, Are bursting on their artist's head!

10. Usu. preceded by a defining word: a person, 'chap', 'fellow'; also, one devoted to or unusually proficient in something (reprehensible). *U.S.*, *Austral.*, and *N.Z. slang.*

1890 Farmer *Slang* I. 75/1 *Artist* (American thieves'), an adroit rogue; a skilful gamester. 1919 Downing *Digger Dial.* 9 One-star artist—a second lieutenant. 1932 Runyon in Wentworth & Flexner *Dict. Amer. Slang* (1960) 468/2 Chiv artist. 1934 *Bulletin* (Sydney) 22 Aug. 49/2 Syd.. classified him as a species of booze-artist. 1940 *Ibid.* 3 Jan. 35/4 Dingbatting to a one-pip artist may be a bit more free and easy. 1941 Baker *Dict. Austral. Slang* 6 *Artist*, a fellow, a bloke. An expert, a specialist; also one who indulges in excesses, e.g., 'bilge a.', 'booze a.', 'bull a.'. 1949 D. M. Davin *Roads from Home* iii. 49 A real artist for the booze, isn't he?

11. *attrib.* and *Comb.*

1894 G. B. Shaw *Music in London 1890-4* (1931) III. 177, I still call for the artist-craftsman to give us once more a flute that is a flute, and a trumpet that is a trumpet. 1902 *Westm. Gaz.* 27 June 2/3 The artist-author has studied his subjects from every point of view. 1908 *Athenæum* 25 July 108/2 The monotonous laments of the artist-hero Tikipu. 1929 S. Cheney *Theatre* xxiii. 517 The development of artist-directors stimulated interest in the search for 'form' as an attribute of stage art. 1939 O. Lancaster *Homes Sweet Homes* 62 An 'artist designed' table of unstained oak. 1959 Halas & Manvell *Technique Film Animation* 13 A few individual artist-producers who have managed to combine a characteristic style of work with adequate business organization.

B. *adj.* [a. F. *artiste* adj. (in Montaigne), or attrib. use of sb.] Artistic, skilful.

1603 Florio *Montaigne* (1632) 62 The most artist productions. 1713 *Lond. & Countr. Brewer* I. (1742) Pref., I have here also divulged the Nostrum of the Artist Brewer.

artistdom ('ɑːtɪstdəm). [f. prec. + -DOM.] The class or estate of artists.

1861 *Sat. Rev.* 20 Apr. 421/1 An equestrian statue which has so captivated the judgment of all artistdom. *Ibid.* 20 July 67 Crushed down in the struggles of authorship and artistdom.

artiste (ar'tiːst). [Fr.: see ARTIST; a re-introduction of the Fr. word in consequence of the modern tendency to restrict *artist* to those engaged in the fine arts, and especially painting.] A public performer who appeals to the æsthetic faculties, as a professional singer, dancer, etc.; also, one who makes a 'fine art' of his employment, as an artistic cook, hairdresser, etc. = ARTIST 6, 8 a, b.

1823 *Drama, or Pocket Theatr. Mag.* IV. 355 He [*sc.* Charles Vestris] is clearly the least distinguished *artiste* of the whole race of Vestris. 1832 *Athenæum* No. 237. 307 The German *artistes* who did such ample justice to the choruses of the Freischütz. 1833 Macready *Remin.* I. 372 Went to Drury Lane to see Malibran—what an artiste! 1843 Prescott *Mexico* IV. i. (1864) 206 The Aztec artistes..had penetrated deep into the mysteries of culinary science. 1871 R. H. Horne in *Gentl. Mag.* Sept. 473 At his house were met artists and *artistes* of various kinds, all 'on their promotion' and students in literature, poetry, and science. 1909 Wodehouse *Swoop* II. viii. 101 They stood talking and blocking the gangway, as etiquette demands that a successful artiste shall. 1955 *Times* 19 Aug. 4/1 The artistes —they lose their *e* on notice boards inside the reception office—..were absent today.

artistess ('ɑːtɪstɪs). *nonce-wd.* [f. ARTIST + -ESS.] A female artist.

1773 H. Walpole *Lett. C'tess Ossory* I. 52 The artistess has brought over a group.

artistic (ɑː'tɪstɪk), *a.* [ad. F. *artistique*: see ARTIST and -IC.]

1. Of, pertaining to, or befitting an artist.

1753 in Chambers *Cycl. Supp.* s.v. *Artist.* 1836 Macready *Remin.* II. 51 All is chance and raw and wild, not artistic-like. 1855 Brimley *Ess.* 53 So as to satisfy the artistic sense of completeness.

2. Of or pertaining to art.

1854 Ruskin *Two Paths* ii. (1859) 69 Entirely wholesome artistic influence. 1867 *Good Cheer* 50 Another pleasure in his house is its artistic treasures.

ar'tistical, *a.* [f. prec. + -AL[1].]

1. Belonging to, or connected with, artists or art.

1801 W. Taylor in Robberds *Mem.* I. 389 An object of artistical imitation. 1857 Ruskin *Pol. Econ. Art* 31 There is another thing notable about this artistical gold.

2. = ARTISTIC.

1853 Thackeray *Eng. Humourists* vi. 284, I suppose Sterne had this artistical sensibility. 1857 Ruskin *Pol. Econ. Art* i. (1868) 31 In the greatest artists, their proper artistical faculty is united with every other.

†3. Produced by art, cleverly contrived. *rare.*

1849 Stovel *Canne's Necess.* Introd. 75 This Dr. Burgess wished to hide by artistical distinctions.

ar'tistically, *adv.* [f. prec. + -LY[2].] In an artistic manner, tastefully; from an artistic point of view.

1836 *Athenæum* No. 439. 224 A peculiar style of architecture with which they were neither artistically nor habitually conversant. 1865 Miss Braddon *Sir Jasper* I. i. 5 Artistically regarded, the Hermitage was perfection. 1879 C. Dresser in *Cassell's Techn. Educ.* II. 120/2 If you use paper for walls, use it artistically.

artist-like, *a.* and *adv.* [f. ARTIST + LIKE.]

A. *adj.* Befitting an artist, artistic.

1711 Shaftesbury *Char.* (1737) II. 407 A superiour art, or something artist-like which guided their hand. 1784 Reynolds *Disc.* xii. (1876) 52 The true method of forming an artist-like mind. 1837 Whewell *Hist. Induct. Sc.* XVII. ii. §1 We have no designs that are more artist-like.

B. *adv.* In the manner of an artist; artistically.

1837 Macready *Remin.* II. 90 Acted Leontes artist-like but not..very effectively. *c*1842 Tennyson *Memory* v, Artist-like Ever retiring thou dost gaze On the prime labour of thine early days.

artistly ('ɑːtɪstlɪ), *adv. rare.* [f. ARTIST + -LY[2].] Artistically, artist-like.

1754 J. Cleland *Let.* 31 July in *Garrick's Private Corr.* (1831) I. 56 The plots of two excellent plays..being wove artistly into one. 1811 Simond *Jrnl. of Tour in Gt. Brit.* 8 June (1815) II. 219 Tables, sofas, and chairs, were artistly *derangés* about the fire-places. **1839** LD. BROUGHAM *Statesm. Geo. III, Canning* 159 Mr. Canning's declamation entertained his hearers, so artistly was it executed.

artistry ('ɑːtɪstrɪ). [f. ARTIST + -RY; cf. *chemistry*.]

1. The pursuit or occupation of an artist.

1873 BROWNING *Red Cott. N.-Cap* 138 Artistry being battle with the age It lives in! **1878** —— *Poets of Croisic* clii, All fume and fret Of artistry.

2. Artistic characteristics; artistic ability.

1868 BROWNING *Ring & Bk.* I. 29 Prime nature with an added artistry. **1880** *Academy* 13 Mar. 197 He fully recognises Sir Christopher Wren's artistry.

† **'artize,** *v. Obs. rare.* [f. ART *sb.* + -IZE.] **a.** *intr.* To exercise an art. **b.** *trans.* To artificialize.

1598 FLORIO, *Arteggiare*, to artize, to liue by an arte. **1603** —— *Montaigne* III. v. (1632) 491, I would naturalize arte, as much as they artize Nature. [Fr. *artialisent*, cf. ARTILIZE.]

artless ('ɑːtlɪs), *a.* [f. ART *sb.* + -LESS.]

1. Devoid of art or skill: **a.** Unpractised, inexperienced, unskilful; unskilled, ignorant.

1589 NASHE *Anat. Absurd.* 40 The artlesse tongue of a tedious dolt. **1628** WITHER *Brit. Rememb.* VII. 1184 Such artlesse riders, that they cannot sit them. **1747** JOHNSON *Plan Eng. Dict.* Wks. IX. 165 The work in which I engaged is generally considered..as the proper toil of artless industry. **1847** LD. LINDSAY *Chr. Art* I. 124 The artless artists seem to have worked on, from arch to arch..without a thought..of economising their space.

b. Devoid of the fine or liberal arts; having no desire for or endeavour after artistic effect; uncultured.

1599 MARSTON *Sco. Villanie* II. Proem 192 Seeking conceits to sute these Artlesse times. **1636** BALLARD in *Ann. Dubrensia* (1877) 35 The rugged Poem of an Art-lesse Muse. **1774** J. BRYANT *Mythol.* I. 46 The most dry and artless historians are in general the most authentic. **1860** RUSKIN *Mod. Paint.* V. IX. ii. 216 A shadowy life—artless, joyless, loveless. No devices in that darkness of the grave.

2. a. Constructed without art or skill, rude, clumsy. **b.** Designed without art, inartistic, crude.

1695 WOODWARD *Nat. Hist. Earth* III. i. (1723) 166 That there is any thing incommodious and Artless..in the Globe. **1774** JOHNSON *West. Isl.* Wks. X. 373 Brogues, a kind of artless shoes. **1782** WARTON *Hist. Kiddington* (T.) Assemblages of artless and massy pillars. **1878** LUBBOCK *Preh. Times* v. 141 They enclose an artless stone vault.

3. Free from art (as opposed to nature); unartificial, natural, simple.

1672 DRYDEN in *Shaks. C. Praise* 348 Such Artless beauty lies in Shakespears wit. **1752** MRS. LENNOX *Fem. Quix.* I. I. ii. 8 Curls, which had so much the appearance of being artless, that all but her maid..imagined they were so. **1754** SHERLOCK *Disc.* (1759) I. iv. 169 The Doctrines of the Gospel were artless and plain. **1852** MRS. JAMESON *Leg. Madonna* 152 The same artless grace, the same dramatic grouping.

4. Simple-minded, sincere, guileless, ingenuous.

1714 BUDGELL *Spect.* No. 605 ¶9 Imitation is a kind of artless Flattery. **1766** WESLEY *Wks.* (1872) III. 247 The artless people drank in every word. **1822** W. IRVING *Braceb. Hall* v. 43 The delightful blushing consciousness of an artless girl. **1868** STANLEY *Westm. Ab.* i. 34 His artless piety and simple goodness.

'artlessly, *adv.* [f. prec. + -LY².]

1. Without art or skill.

1625 PURCHAS *Pilgrims* II. 1186 A crucifix painted on a linen cloth..yet artlessly wrought.

2. In an artless manner; without artifice; with frank simplicity, guilelessly.

1713 POPE *To Addison* 14 Dec. (J.) Nature and truth, though never so low or vulgar, are yet pleasing when openly and artlessly represented. **1853** C. BRONTË *Villette* xxix. 333 He liked that too—admired it artlessly, like a child.

'artlessness. [f. as prec. + -NESS.] The quality of being artless; freedom from artificiality, frank simplicity, guilelessness.

1741 RICHARDSON *Pamela* II. 331 Such a noble Simplicity in thy Story, such an honest Artlessness in thy Mind. **1879** B. TAYLOR *Germ. Lit.* 126 The attractive quaintness and artlessness of the old dialect.

artlet ('ɑːtlɪt). *rare.* [f. ART *sb.* + -LET.] A minor art.

1861 R. BURTON *City of Saints* 514 Music, dancing, drawing and other artlets, which go by the name of accomplishments.

art-like, *a.* and *adv.* [f. ART + LIKE.]

A. *adj.* **a.** In accordance with art; of the nature of art. **b.** Resembling or having the appearance of art.

1651 tr. *Bacon's Life & Death* 2 Now we think to adde some [rules] which shall be more Art-like. **1875** WHITNEY *Life Lang.* xiv. 289 A highly art-like, almost artistic, song.

B. *adv.* According to the rules of art.

1630 J. TAYLOR (Water P.) *Wks.* I. 9 Though the Method and the Phrase be plaine, Not artlike writ.

† **'artly,** *a. Obs. rare*⁻¹. [f. ART *sb.* + -LY¹; cf. *lovely*.] Characterized by art, skilful, ingenious.

1614 CHAPMAN *Odyss.* IX. 212 The description of all these countries..their artly and pleasing relation.

† **'artly,** *adv. Obs.* [f. ART *sb.* + -LY².] With art or skill; skilfully, dexterously.

1576 BAKER *Gesner's Jewell of Health* 34b, That the Dystillation may be the artlyer perfourmed. **1594** PLAT *Jewell-ho.* III. 14 You must artly moist the interlining of your letter. **1662** R. MATHEW *Unl. Alch.* §89. 157 Fit it unto the top of thy Funnel artly.

artocarpad (ɑːtəʊ'kɑːpəd). [f. mod.L. *artocarpus* bread-fruit tree (f. Gr. ἄρτο-ς bread + καρπός fruit) + -AD 1 d.] A tree belonging to the *Artocarpaceæ*, *Artocarpeæ*, or Bread-fruit group. **arto'carpeous, arto'carpous** *a.*, of or pertaining to this group.

1834 *Penny Cycl.* II. 421 Like all other Artocarpeous plants, this exudes..a viscid milky juice. **1846** LINDLEY *Veg. K.* 270 The old Urticaceous order should be..regarded as an Alliance, of which the Artocarpads form one of the Orders.

† **ar'tolater.** *Obs. rare*⁻¹. [f. next; cf. *idolater*.] A worshipper of bread.

1626 L. OWEN *Spec. Jesuit.* (1629) 10 Dare you (Artolaters) adore a peece of Bread, for the liuing God?

† **ar'tolatry.** *Obs.* [ad. Gr. ἀρτολατρεία, f. ἄρτο-ς bread + λατρεία worship.] The worship of bread.

[**1610** BP. HALL *Apol. Brownists* 88 That Popish ἀρτολατρεία.] **1626** L. OWEN *Spec. Jesuit.* (1629) 17 Their Idolatry, or if you will, Artolatry. **1658** J. ROBINSON *Eudoxa* v. 142 Who fear to approach too near to the Artolatry..dare not seem to worship the bread, by kneeling before it.

artophagous (ɑː'tɒfəgəs), *a. rare.* [f. Gr. ἀρτοφάγ-ος bread-eating + -OUS.] Bread-eating.

1816 GIFFORD in *B. Jonson's Wks.* 1875 V. 164 *note*, This artophagous propensity of the tailors.

artotype ('ɑːtəʊtaɪp). [irreg. f. ART *sb.* + -O + -TYPE.] In full ***artotype process***, the collotype process. Hence, the print or impression produced by this process.

1879 *Photogr. News* 9 May 222/1 In America..the introduction of a method of photo-collographic printing, named *Artotype*..[has] given a sudden impetus to..this mode of mechanical printing. *Ibid.* 222/2 The 'Artotype' process owes its invention to Europe. It is..the most recent ..form of collographic printing patented by Herr Obernetter. **1893** *Catal. Orig. & Early Editions of English Writers from Langland to Wither* (Grolier Club) p. xi, List of facsimiles. *Artotypes.* **1961** T. LANDAU *Encycl. Librarianship* (ed. 2) 26/1 *Artotype*, a photo-engraved illustration made by one of the gelatine processes.

artotyrite (ɑːtəʊ'taɪraɪt). *Eccl. Hist.* [ad. med.L. *artotȳrīta*, f. Gr. ἀρτό-τῡρος bread and cheese: see -ITE.] One of a sect who celebrated the Eucharist with bread and cheese.

1586 T. ROGERS *39 Art.* (1607) 295 Some, by adding thereto: so added was unto the bread cheese by the Artotarites. **1837** *Penny Cycl.* VII. 415/1 Followers of Montanus, who were called Artotyrites.

artou, artow, obs. contr. of *art thou*.

c **1386** CHAUCER *Frankl. T.* 362 O blisful artow now.

† **'artry(e.** *Obs.* Contracted form of ARTILLERY.

1447 in Nichols *Royal Wills* (1780) 288 All myn armery and all my artry. *Ibid.* 284 Armery and attry. *c* **1450** *Merlin* vii. 115 Garnysshe thy forteresses of euery Citee, and euery castell, with vitayle, and men, and stuff of other artrye.

† **'artship.** *Obs.* [f. ART *sb.* + -SHIP.] ? Artistic workmanship.

1598 SYLVESTER *Du Bartas* 306 Contempling th'Artship richly rare, Which gilds the ceeling of this globe so fair.

'arts-man. *arch.* [f. *art's*, genitive of ART *sb.* + MAN; cf. the earlier *craftsman*, later *sportsman*.]

† **1.** A craftsman, workman, artificer. *Obs.*

1551 RECORDE *Pathw. Knowl.* Pref., The artes man contemned, the woorke vnrewarded. **1600** CHAPMAN *Iliad* XVI. 446 A pine, New fell'd by arts-men on the hills. **1726** *Nat. Hist. Irel.* 76 And open the mouth thereof [of the furnace], or the timpas as the artsmen call it.

† **2.** One skilled in the liberal arts, a scholar. *Obs.*

1605 BACON *Adv. Learn.* II. xiii. §2 The pith of all sciences, which maketh the artsman differ from the inexpert, is in the middle propositions.

† **3.** One who practises the fine arts; an artist. *Obs.*

1633 FORD *Love's Sacr.* II. ii, Observe with what singularity the artsman hath strove to set forth each limb in exquisitest proportion.

4. One who cultivates a practical science.

1858 J. BROWN *Locke & Syd.* 62 [Sydenham] was what Plato would have called an artsman as distinguished from a doctor of abstract science.

'arts-,master, art-master. [f. as prec. + MASTER.]

1. (Now *art-master*.) A teacher of art, or of an art or craft. (Cf. *music-master*.)

1589 NASHE in *Greene's Menaphon* Ded. (Arb.) 5 Their idiot art-masters that intrude themselves..as the alcumists of eloquence. **1652** *Zeal Examined* Add. §3. 32 Herein is that old Serpent his Arts Master. **1740** *Prov. for Poor* 23 Apprenticed under proper Arts-masters. **1910** *Encycl. Brit.* II. 703/1 The Society of Art Masters..is an association of teachers of art schools.

† **2.** One who is master of an art or craft; a master craftsman, a chief artificer. *Obs.*

1623 DRUMM. OF HAWTH. *Cypress Grove* Wks. 124 What the Arts-master of this universe is in governing this universe, thou art in the body. **1624** HEYWOOD *Gunaik.* IV. 168 Daedalus, a great Arts-master..devised..a wodden cow.

artsy ('ɑːtsɪ), *a. colloq.* [f. *arts (and crafts)* + -Y¹.] **artsy-(and-)craftsy** *a.*: = *arty-(and-)crafty* (see ARTY-AND-CRAFTY *a.* and ART *sb.* 17); **artsy-fartsy** *a.*, pretentiously artistic.

1902 *Temple Bar* CXXVI. 63 The furniture is of the *Artsy-Craftsy order. **1942** COWARD *Blithe Spirit* II. iii. 85 It's no use trying to defend Ruth's taste to me—it's thoroughly artsy craftsy. **1942** J. B. PRIESTLEY *Blackout* iii. 27 That kind of woman frequently opened just that kind of artsy-craftsy shop. **1971** *Frendz* 21 May 2/2 *Artsy-fartsy. If they can call prophesy Art, we can call anything we bloody well please Art. **1984** A. F. LOEWENSTEIN *This Place* 31 This new one, Sonya, an artsy-fartsy feminist, the one thing their little staff had lacked until now.

† **'artuate,** *v. Obs.*⁻⁰. [f. L. pple. *artuātus* torn limb from limb, f. *artus* limb.] 'To divide by joints, to quarter, to dismember.' Bailey 1731.

art-union: see ART *sb.* V.

† **artu'ose,** *a. Obs.*⁻⁰. [f. L. *artus* limb.] 'Strong made, well jointed or limbed.' Bailey 1731.

arture, obs. form of ARTERY.

Arture, -turis, obs. forms of ARCTURUS.

art work. [f. ART *sb.* + WORK *sb.*] **1.** A work of art (see WORK *sb.* 14). Cf. G. *Kunstwerk*. Also, = ART *sb.* 6.

1877 RUSKIN *St. Mark's Rest* II. v. 60 The entire body of her noble art-work belongs to this time. **1889** G. B. SHAW *How to become Mus. Critic* (1960) 168 They have a right..to the most careful and earnest representation of any art work which appeals seriously to them. **1896** —— *Ibid.* 249 [Wagner's music-drama] The mightiest art work our century has produced. **1903** A. BENNETT *Truth about Author* iv. 57 They dreamed of great art-works, lovely compositions, impassioned song. **1941** L. MACNEICE *Poetry of Yeats* i. 7 Even before the artist has started his art-work proper he is..reacting emotionally to his subject. **1953** S. SPENDER *Creative Elem.* iii. 64 The statue first serves as an outside object, an art-work.

2. The illustrative or decorative material in printed matter, as distinct from the text.

1926 C. MORLEY *Thunder on Left* ix. 112 He spoke of the Elevated Railroad's limited appropriation for promotion.. asked what was her usual price for art work. **1959** 'S. RANSOME' *I'll Die* ix. 102 She stopped at a certain illustration... You said, 'I see you're admiring my art work.'

† **'art-worm.** *Obs. rare.* [f. F. *artre* + WORM.] = ARTER.

1623 WHITBOURNE *Newfoundland* 41 Art-wormes, wherewith ships..are sometimes much spoyled.

arty ('ɑːtɪ), *a. colloq.* [f. ART *sb.* + -Y¹.] **1.** A jocular epithet for furniture, decoration, etc., of artistic pretensions; also applied to persons who wish to be regarded as artistic in taste, dress, etc.

1901 *Academy* 16 Mar. 221 The *Kensington* is its title; it is broad in the page, handsomely printed, and decidedly *Arty*. **1910** *Daily Chron.* 5 Apr. 9/5 The house filled with badly made 'arty', not artistic, furniture. **1921** GALSWORTHY *Six Short Plays* 129 Pretty?..Arty? **1925** *Sat. Rev.* 7 Nov. 534/1, I do not like the long, rather 'arty' window on the front. **1927** *Daily Express* 30 Apr. 8/2 Artists and 'arty' persons—between the two there is a great gulf fixed. **1939** 'G. ORWELL' *Coming Up* IV. v. 260 They were arty-looking houses, another of those sham-Tudor colonies.

2. *arty-farty* adj. = *artsy-fartsy* adj. s.v. ARTSY *a.*

1967 P. TAMONY *Americanisms* (typescript) No. 17. 2 Under constant care and tutelage,..and entertained by specious arty-farty subjects labeled 'creative'. **1979** S. BRETT *Comedian Dies* v. 51 Television..was different then. Less sophisticated. Less bloody cameras... Now it's all arty-farty. **1982** BARR & YORK *Official Sloane Ranger Handbk.* 24/1 In dress, one wants to look tidy, reassuring and appropriate (Sloane), not visual and arty-farty. **1982** M. KINGTON *Miles & Miles* 61 The North is..trying to impose their bluff..values on our arty-farty-Dartington, southern way of life. **1985** S. LOWRY *Young Fogey Handbk.* vii. 58 They were elegantly photographed against suitable arty-farty and esoteric backgrounds.

Hence **'artiness.**

1901 *Academy* 12 Oct. 337 The infected age of artiness. **1907** *Daily Chron.* 17 Apr. 6/6 To go somewhat beyond the 'artiness' of the day. **1928** *Observer* 22 July 9/2 The same unambitious artiness recurs page after page.

arty ('ɑːtɪ), slang abbrev. of ARTILLERY *sb.*

1942 *Gen* 15 June 50/2 Their arty drove us off. He hit, exploded and burned. **1944** L. GLASSOP *We were the Rats* III. xxvii. 154 Hundreds of Jerries..moved their arty up to within rifle range of our forward posts.

arty-and-crafty ('ɑːtɪənd'krɑːftɪ, -æ-), *a. colloq.* Also (commonly) **'arty-'crafty.** [f. *arts and crafts* + -Y¹.] Characteristic of the work done by or under the auspices of the 'arts and crafts' movement (see ART *sb.* 17); jocularly applied to furniture, etc., of specially artistic style but not conspicuously useful or comfortable; also used of their makers; thus, pretentiously or quaintly artistic. Also *absol.* Hence **'arty-'crafty** *sb.*, an 'arty-crafty' person; **arty-(and-)craftiness,**

'arty-crafty' quality or characteristics. (Cf. *art-and-crafty*, etc., s.v. ART *sb.* 17.)

1902 *Daily Chron.* 28 July 3/4 Canon Barnett..spoke of a coming Exhibition of Arts and Crafts, which, if not too 'Arty-and-Crafty', should be excellent. **1920** A. HUXLEY *Limbo* 30, I liked..the way you went for the Arty-Crafties. **1925** —— *Along Road* III. 200 What I may call 'arty-craftiness' or 'peasantry' is a Tolstoyan derivation from the quaint. **1925** *Sat. Rev.* 7 Nov. 524/1 The 'arty and crafty' furniture that is uncomfortable in use,..the model house in which no man can be at ease. **1927** *Observer* 18 Sept. 15/4 Country lore gathered chiefly from the works of arty-and-crafty peasants from Belsize Park. **1930** E. WALLACE *Lady of Ascot* xiii. 136 What on earth can you find in Wolverhampton that can appeal to your arty-crafty mind? **1932** S. GIBBONS *Cold Comfort Farm* v. 71 She will only go and keep a tea-room in Brighton and go all arty-and-crafty about the feet and waist. **1932** *Daily Express* 30 June 5/5 Provided the 'bun' is not placed low on the nape of the neck, suggesting a mixture of 'arty-crafty' and demure. **1937** 'G. ORWELL' *Road to Wigan Pier* xii. 232 Deliberately to revert to primitive methods..would be a piece of dilettantism, of pretty-pretty arty and craftiness. **1945** L. A. G. STRONG *Tongue in Your Head* 47 The 'poetry voice' removes it from the sphere of art..to the arty-crafty sphere. **1962** *John O'London's* 29 Nov. 508/3 The general public, as distinct from the arty-crafties.

artyllary, -ery, etc., obs. ff. ARTILLERY.

aru, obs. form of ARROW.

†**a'rue**, *v. Obs.* For forms see RUE *v.* [:—OE. *ofhreowan*: see OF- *pref.* and RUE *v.*]

1. *intr.* To be sorry, to feel regret, compassion, or pity. Const. in OE. with genitive, represented in later times by *of*.

c **1000** ÆLFRIC *Hom.* (Sweet *Reader* 102) Se mæssepréost ðæs mannes ofhréow. *c* **1302** *Pol. Songs* 188 The commun of Bruges ful sore con arewe. *a* **1400** *E. E. Misc.* (1855) 3 Of thy ruthe I wold a-ruwe.

2. *trans.* (i.e. with simple object repr. orig. genitive). To be sorry for, regret, rue; to have compassion on, pity.

c **1220** *Leg. St. Kath.* 1379 Þe deore Drihtin areaw us. *c* **1300** *Harrow. Hell* 29 Jhesu Christ arew hem sore. *c* **1430** *Freemasonry* 338 That poynt thou schal never arewe.

3. *impers.* It grieves, vexes, troubles (one).

a **1230** *Juliana* 35 Me areoweð þi sar. *c* **1320** *Pol. Songs* 240 Ʒet hym shulde arewen Of the arrerage. *c* **1430** *Freemasonry* 90 Hyt shal hym never thenne arewe.

‖**arum** ('ɛərəm). *Bot.* Pl. **-s.** Also 6–8 **aron**; cf. AARON². [L., a. Gr. ἄρον (also formerly in Eng. use).] A genus of endogenous plants (N.O. *Araceæ*), the inflorescence of which consists of a large spathe, enclosing a fleshy spike or spadix bearing on its lower part the unisexual flowers succeeded by bright-coloured berries; one species, the Wake-robin, Cuckoo-pint, or Lords and Ladies (*A. Maculatum*), is a native of Britain.

1551 TURNER *Herbal* I. 44 Of aron or cockow pynt. **1607** TOPSELL *Four-f. Beasts* (1615) 30 The old Bears..do eat the hearb Arum, commonly called in English Wake-robbin or Calves-foot. **1769** SIR J. HILL *Fam. Herbal* (1812) 13 Aron ..is an excellent medicine in palsies. **1834** MARY HOWITT *Spring* in *Sk. Nat. Hist.* (1851) 83 Here too the spotted Arum green, A hooded mystery, is seen. **1866** MASTERS in *Treas. Bot.* 97/1 The common Arum of the hedges..From the tubers of this plant, in the Isle of Portland, a starch called Portland Arrowroot was formerly extensively prepared.

b. *attrib.* Esp. in **arum lily** (*Richardia æthiopica*): an arad with a pure white spathe and brilliant yellow spadix, a favourite ornamental flower in drawing-rooms.

1599 A. M. *Gabelhouer's Bk. Physic* 183/2 Take Aron roote. **1821** CLARE *Village Minstr.* I. 98 When April first Unclos'd the arum-leaves. **1856** MISS MULOCH *J. Halifax* 230 Gathering for her a magnificent arum lily.

arun, early form of ARE *v.*²: see BE.

arunde, obs. form of ERRAND.

Arundel ('ærəndəl). The name of the *Arundel* Society (1848–97) for promoting artistic knowledge, named in memory of Thomas Howard, 2nd earl of Arundel (1586–1646), used *attrib.* to designate prints, engravings, etc., issued by this Society.

1872 MRS. D. A. GODDARD (*title*) The Arundel Society pictures. **1879** C. M. YONGE *Magnum Bonum* xxxv. 529 He found Esther telling her little sister..histories of Arundel Society engravings. **1914** C. MACKENZIE *Sinister St.* II. IV. iv. 949 Corridors hung with Arundel prints and faded photographs of cathedrals. **1937** A. THIRKELL *Summer Half* ii. 60 An Arundel print of the Martyrdom of St Ursula.

arundell, obs. form of HIRONDELLE.

arundiferous (ærʌn'dɪfərəs), *a. rare*⁻⁰. [f. L. *arundifer*: see next and -OUS.] Producing reeds, reedy.

1656 in BLOUNT *Glossogr.*

arundinaceous (əˌrʌndɪ'neɪʃəs), *a.* [f. L. *arundināceus*, f. *arundo*, *harundo* a reed: see -ACEOUS.] Reed-like, reedy.

1657 in *Phys. Dict.* **1693** *Phil. Trans.* XVII. 686 Beesha, whose leaves are arundinaceous. **1791** tr. *Chaptal's Chem.* III. 15 Plants..such as the gramineous and arundinaceous.

arun'dineous, *a. rare.* [f. L. *arundineus*: see prec. and -EOUS.] Reedy.

1657 TOMLINSON *Renou's Disp.* 721 Wilde Bryony.. delighting in arundineous and watry places.

aˌrundi'nose, *a.* [ad. L. *arundinōsus*, f. *arundo*: see -OSE.] 'Full of or abounding with reeds.' Bailey 1731.

a'rundinous, *a.* = prec.

1775 in ASH.

†**a'runt**, *v. Obs.* [Etymol. unknown.] To rail at, revile, scold, rate; or ? to drive away. (If the latter is the sense, cf. Shakspere's AROINT.)

1399 *Rich. Redeless* III. 221 ? Arounted [MS. has Arouutyd] ffor his ray [= array, *dress*] and rebuked ofte. **1496** *Dives & Paup.* (W. de W.) VII. iv. 280 Make the plesaunt in speche to the congregacyon of poore folke..and yelde thy dette & answere peasable thynges & mekenesse, not to arunt them ne rebuke them ne chyde them.

Arunta, var. ARANDA.

aruspex, and derivatives: see more etymological spelling under HAR-.

aruwe, obs. form of ARROW.

†**'arval, -el, -ill.** *Obs.* exc. *dial.* Also 5–6 **arvell**, 7 **arvall.** [App. adopted from Norse: cf. Da. *arveöl*, ON. *erfi-öl* (Vigfusson), OSw. *arföl* (Ihre), f. *arf*, *arv*, ON. *arfr* (OE. *erfe*) inheritance + *öl* ale, a banquet: see ALE 3. Cf. also ON. *erfi* a wake, a funeral feast = *erfi-öl*.] A funeral feast.

1459 *MS. Reg. Test. Ebor.* IV. 249 b, [John Alanson leaues an ox] 'ad distrib. inter propinquos et amicos meos, scilicet ad meum arvell.' **1588** *Wills & Inv. Durh.* (1860) 181/2 That secke..which was drouncke at the arvell. **1623** *MS. Richmond Wills* Carthorpe, Her arvall, or funerall dinner. **1702** THORESBY *Diary* I. 362 The following arvill, or treat, of cold posset, stewed prunes, cake, and cheese, prepared for the company. **1860** MRS. GASKELL *C. Brontë* 17 The old custom of 'arvills,' or funeral feasts. **1880** *Yorksh. Archæol. Jrnl.* XXII. 290 The arval was held at the little village inn.

2. *attrib.*, as in ***arval-bread, -dinner***, etc.

1567 *MS. Durham Registry*, For his arvell supper. **1691** RAY *N. Countr. Words* 139 Arvel-Bread, *Silicernium.* **1778–80** W. HUTCHINSON *Northbld.* II. 20 in *Brand's Pop. Antiq.* (Hazl.) II. 193 On the decease of any person possessed of valuable effects, the friends and neighbours of the Family are invited to dinner on the Day of Interment, which is called the Arthel or Arvel-dinner. **1807** DOUCE *Illust. Shaks.* II. 203 (JAM.) In the North this feast is called an *arval* or *arvil-supper*; and the loaves that are sometimes distributed among the poor, *arval-bread*. **1875** *Whitby Gloss.*, *Averill-breead*, funeral loaves, spiced with cinnamon, nutmeg, sugar, and raisins.

3. ? Arval-bread.

1568 *Wills & Inv. N.C.* (1835) 294 A boxe of arvell xviij*d.* —Hony ijs.

arval ('ɑːvəl), *a.* [ad. L. *arvālis*, f. *arv-um* arable land: see -AL¹.] Of or belonging to ploughed land; esp. in ***Arval Brethren*** (= L. *Frātres Arvāles*), a college of twelve priests in Ancient Rome, who offered sacrifice to the field-Lares to secure the fertility of the soil.

1656 in BLOUNT *Glossogr.* **1854** KEIGHTLEY *Mythol. Greece & It.* (ed. 3) 461 The hymn of the Arval Brethren.

†**'arveth**, *a. Obs.* Forms: 1 **earfeðe, -oðe**, 2 **erfeð, ærveð**, 2–3 **erveð, arveð**, 3 (*Orm.*) **arrfeþþ, earfð.** [OE. *earfeðe*, *earfoðe*, cogn. w. ON. *erfiðr*; cf. OE. *earfeðe* sb. n., cogn. w. ON. *erfiði*, *erviði*, OS. *arbêdi* n., *arbêd* f., OFris. *arbeid*, OHG. *arabeit*, mod.G. *arbeit* labour, toil, Goth. *arbaiþs*.] Difficult, hard.

c **885** K. ÆLFRED *Boeth.* xxxix. §4 Spræce..ða earfoþestan to ʒereccenne. *c* **1000** ÆLFRIC *Man. Astron.* 19 Ne nære na ælmihtiʒ, ʒyf him æniʒ ʒefadung earfoðe wære. *c* **1175** *Cott. Hom.* 231 His folc was swiðe ærfeð-telle. *c* **1200** *Trin. Coll. Hom.* 185 Þat fiht was and is arueð to þolien. *c* **1200** ORMIN 17334 Forrþi wass himm full arrfeþþ ʒet To sen whatt gate he mihhte Ben borenn efft off Haliʒ Gast. *c* **1220** *Leg. St. Kath.* 999 Earfð to don. *c* **1230** *Ancr. R.* 254 An honful ʒerden beoð erueð forte breken.

†**'arvethlich**, *a. Obs.* [OE. *earfoðlíc*, f. *earfoðe* sb.: see prec. and -LY¹.] = prec.

c **1000** ÆLFRIC *Deut.* i. 17 Gif eow æniʒ þing þince earfoþlice, secʒað hit me. *c* **1200** *Trin. Coll. Hom.* 127 Þo com þe fader his speche and witeʒede þe childes arueðliche herbiwist. [Also on p. 125.]

†**'arvethliche**, *adv. Obs.* [OE. *earfoðlíce*: see ARVETH and -LY².] With difficulty or trouble, hardly.

c **1000** *Ags. Gosp.* Matt. xix. 23 Earfoðlíce se weleʒa gæð on Godes rice. *c* **1160** *Hatton G.* ibid., Ærfedlice. *c* **1200** *Trin. Coll. Hom.* 131 Ðe wunderliche..her-one arueðliche wunede. *c* **1230** *Ancr. R.* 328 Hu eruedliche he ariseð þet under wune of sunne haueð ileien longe.

†**'arvethness.** [OE. *earfoðnysse*: see ARVETH and -NESS.] Difficulty, trouble.

c **1000** ÆLFRIC *Man. Astron.* 19 God..ealle þing ʒediht buton earfoðnysse. *c* **1175** *Lamb. Hom.* 105 Þider we sculen hihʒen of þissere erfeðnesse. *c* **1175** *Cott. Hom.* 223 Þu scealt mid ærfeðnesse þe metes tylian.

ARVN, Arvin ('ɑːvɪn). Chiefly *U.S.* [f. the initials.] The Army of the Republic of (South) Vietnam; a member of this army.

1966 *Army* Oct. 112/2 Aggressive leadership on the part of the ARVN command resulted in heavy casualties for the Viet Cong. **1967** *Economist* 12 Aug. 571/1 An Australian officer expressed a common opinion: 'ARVN are good Buddhists—they shoot high'. **1969** *Guardian Weekly* 29 May 5, I was watching..the sort of war the Americans wage in Vietnam, and the kind of fighting for which they have generally helped to train the Arvins. **1970** *New Scientist* 17 Dec. 501/1 The strengthening of Arvin is an essential component of the Vietnamisation programme. **1983** *N.Y. Times Mag.* 13 Feb. 50/3 The war was turned over to the South Vietnamese Army—ARVN—which was given new training and improved weapons.

arvo ('ɑːvəʊ). *Austral. slang.* [repr. voiced pronunc. of *af-* of *afternoon* + -O².] Afternoon.

1933 *Bulletin* (Sydney) 6 Dec. 42/1 Alone on the bench this Sunday arvo. **1952** J. CLEARY *Sundowners* iii. 154 That how you spend your Sunday arvos, Rupe? **1957** 'N. CULOTTA' *They're a Weird Mob* (1958) iii. 34 I'll try an' drop back this arvo.

arvyst, obs. form of HARVEST.

arwe, obs. form of ARGH and ARROW.

†**ar'worthly**, *adv. Obs.* In 1–2 **arwurþlice.** [OE. *árwurþlíce*, adv. from *árwurþlíc*, deriv. of *árwurþ* venerable, f. *ár* honour + *wurþ* worth.] Honourably, reverently.

c **1000** ÆLFRIC *Gen.* xlv. 4 Þa grete hiʒ arwurþlice. *c* **1175** *Cott. Hom.* 229 Þa tweʒen ʒelefde men him arwrðlice [*printed* awr-] bebyriddon.

arwygyll, obs. derivative form of EARWIG; cf. OE. *eárwicʒa* and mod. Suffolk dial. *arrawiggle*, and see WIGGLE *v.*

1440 *Promp. Parv.* 15 Arwygyll worme, *aurealle.*

ary, *v. Obs.* [Cf. EAR *v.*] ? To plough.

1641 BEST *Farm. Bks.* (1856) 76 After Christmasse, when men shoulde beginne to fallowe and ary.

-ary¹, *suffix* of adjs. and sbs., ad. L. *-āri-us*, *-āri-um.* The regular phonetic repr. of these in OF. was *-air*, but most of the words that actually lived on into OF. had *-ier* (app. by confusion with words in *-iārium* or *-erium*, of which *-ier* was the regular repr.), in AFr. *-er*, instances of which still remain in Eng. *primer*, *danger*, *antiphoner*, and names of trades and offices, like *carpenter*, *usher* (Fr. *huissier*, L. *ostiārius*), while others, as *bursar*, *calendar*, *mortar*, *vicar*, have recently been refashioned with *-ar* after Latin. But in words of later learned adaptation in Fr., *-ārius*, *-um* were represented by *-aire*; in AFr. and ME. *-arie*, later *-arye*, now *-ary*, as L. *contrārius*, Fr. *contraire*, Eng. *contrarie*, *contrarye*, now *contrary*; and this is the regular form in which L. words in *-ārius*, *-arium*, or their Fr. representatives in *-aire* are now adapted in Eng., and on which new analogical formations are modelled. More than 300 such exist in the language, comprising:—

A. *adjs.* repr. (or on analogy of) L. *-ārius* 'connected with, pertaining to'; as *arbitrary*, *contrary*, *elementary*, *honorary*, *mercenary*, *necessary*, *primary*, *secondary*, *tertiary*, *voluntary*.

B. *sbs.* **1.** repr. (or on analogy of) L. *-ārius* 'a man (or male) belonging to or engaged in'; as *actuary*, *adversary*, *antiquary*, *apothecary*, *commentary* (liber), *February*, *January* (mensis), *lapidary*, *secretary*.

2. repr. (or on analogy of) L. *-ārium* 'a thing connected with or employed in, a place for'; as *aviary*, *breviary*, *diary*, *dictionary*, *formulary*, *glossary*, *granary*, *ovary*, *piscary*, *reliquary*, *salary*, *sanctuary*, *vocabulary*. See also -ARIUM.

3. repr. L. (often mediæval) *-āria* (Fr. *-aire*, *-arie*), forming fem. sbs. with same sense; as *Calvary*, *fritillary*.

-ary², *suffix* of adjs.; occasional ad. L. *-ār-is* (stem *-āri*) 'of the kind of, belonging to.' Of this the regular repr. in mod. Eng. is -AR¹, q.v. But even in Latin several of these words had forms both in *-āris* and *-ārius*; and in later Fr. words of literary introduction, both these L. endings are levelled under *-aire*, e.g. L. *contrārius*, *militāris*, Fr. *contraire*, *militaire*. Hence, as Fr. *-aire* from *-ārius* gives *-ary* in Eng., Fr. *-aire* from *-āris* has occasionally also been adapted as *-ary* instead of the more regular *-ar*; e.g. *capillary*, *exemplary*, *maxillary*, *military*, *salutary*.

ary-, shortened form of ARYTENO-.

1879 *St. George's Hosp. Rep.* IX. 162 The right aryepiglottidean fold. **1897** *Trans. Amer. Pediatric Soc.* IX. 180 A union of the aryepiglottic folds. **1931** G. O. RUSSELL *Speech & Voice* III. xvi. 176 The aryepiglottal..muscle. **1964** J. C. CATFORD in D. Abercrombie et al. *Daniel Jones* 34 Contraction of the ary-epiglottic folds.

Aryan, Arian ('ɛərɪən, 'ɑːrɪən), *a.* and *sb.* [f. Sanskrit *ārya*, in the later language 'noble, of good family,' but apparently in earlier use a national name 'comprising the worshippers of the gods of the Brahmans' (Max Müller); cf. Zend *airya* 'venerable,' also a national name, and Old Persian (Achæmenian) *ariya* national name (applied to himself by Darius Hystaspes); whence probably Gr. Ἀρεία, Ἀρία, L. *Aria*, *Aria*, and *Ariāna*, the eastern part of ancient Persia, and Pehlevi and mod.Pers. *Irân* 'Persia.' As a transl. of L. *Ariānus* 'of Aria or Ariana,' *Arian* has long been in English use: *Aryan* is of recent introduction in Comparative Philology, and is also by many written *Arian*, on the ground that *āria* was the original word, as shown by the Vedic language, *ārya* being only the later Sanskrit form; the spelling *Aryan* has the advantage of distinguishing the word from ARIAN in *Eccl. Hist.*

1601 HOLLAND *Pliny* I. 131 The region of the Arianes, all scorched and senged with the parching heate of the Sunne. **1794** SIR W. JONES tr. *Ordin. Menu* x. §45 All those tribes of men, who sprang from the mouth, the arm, the thigh, and the foot of Brahmá, but who became outcasts by having neglected their duties, are called *Dasyus*, or *plunderers*, whether they speak the language of the *Mlechch'has* or that of *Aryas*.]

A. *adj.* **1. a.** Applied by some to the great division or family of languages, which includes Sanskrit, Zend, Persian, Greek, Latin, Celtic, Teutonic, and Slavonic, with their modern representatives; also called *Indo-European*, *Indo-Germanic*, and sometimes *Japhetic*; by others restricted to the Asiatic portion of these. *absol.*, the original Aryan or Arian language.

The restricted use rests on the ground that only the ancient Indian and Iranian members of the family are known on historical evidence to have called themselves *Aria*, *Arya* or *Ariya*; the wider application rests partly on the inference that the name probably belonged in pre-historic times to the whole family, while this still constituted an ethnic and linguistic unity; and partly on the ground that even if it did not, it is now the most convenient and least misleading name for the primitive type of speech from which all the languages above-mentioned have sprung, inasmuch as *Indo-Germanic* is too narrow, and *Indo-European* too wide, for the facts, while *Japhetic* introduces speculations of which science has no cognizance. A frequent use of the word, in which all agree, is to distinguish the *Aryan* from the *non-Aryan* languages of India, the former being 'Aryan' whether the term is used in the restricted or the wider sense.

1839 *Penny Cycl.* XIII. 309/1 The Medo-Persic, or Arian branch; at the head of which stands the Zend. **1847** PRITCHARD *Rep. Brit. Assoc.* 241 The Indo-European, sometimes termed Indo-German, and, by late writers, Arian or Iranian languages. **1878** CUST *Mod. Langs. E. Indies* 49 That all the other Aryan Vernaculars are variants of Hindi, caused by the influence of non-Aryan communities. **1882** SWEET in *Trans. Phil. Soc.* 109 Parent Arian had already developed a perfectly definite word-order. *Ibid.* 111 The original Arian (not 'Aryan') forms.

b. *spec.* Of or pertaining to the ancient Aryan people.

The idea current in the 19th cent. of an Aryan race corresponding to a definite Aryan language was taken up by nationalistic historical and romantic writers. It was given especial currency by de Gobineau, who linked it with the theory of the essential inferiority of certain races. The term 'Aryan race' was later revived and used for purposes of political propaganda in Nazi Germany (see 2).

1851 [see CELT[1] 2]. [**1855** M. A. DE GOBINEAU *Essai sur l'inégalité des races humaines* IV. 350 La race germanique était pourvue de toute l'énergie de la variété ariane. Il le fallait pour qu'elle pût remplir le rôle auquel elle était appelée.] **1858** WHITNEY *Orient. Stud.* II. 5 The Aryan tribes—for that is the name they gave themselves. **1872** FREEMAN *Gen. Sketch* i. §2 History in the highest and truest sense is the history of the Aryan natives of Europe. **1911** J. LEES tr. *H. S. Chamberlain's Foundations 19th Cent.* I. iv. 266 Anthropologists, ethnographers and even historians, theologians, philologists and legal authorities find the idea 'Aryan' more and more indispensable... Though it were proved that there never was an Aryan race in the past, yet we desire that in the future there may be one. **1916** MADISON GRANT *Passing of Great Race* (1917) v. 62 The name 'Aryan race' must also be frankly discarded as a term of racial significance. **1939** J. S. HUXLEY *'Race' in Europe* 24 Biologically it is almost as illegitimate to speak of a 'Jewish race' as of an 'Aryan race'.

2. Under the Nazi régime (1933–45) applied to the inhabitants of Germany of non-Jewish extraction.

1932 L. GOLDING *Let. to Hitler* 25 What you and many of your followers imagine is the Arian manner. **1933** W. NORMAN BROWN (*title*) The Swastika, a Study of the Nazi Claims of its Aryan Origin. **1934** *Ann. Reg. 1933* II. 170 Germany... During April the so-called Aryan Decrees were introduced. **1940** *War Illustr.* 5 Jan. 574/1 The Founder of the Christian faith, he [*sc.* Rosenberg] asserts, was of 'Aryan' not Jewish descent. **1943** *Ann. Reg. 1942* 183 The town.. was cleared of its 'Aryan' population and made a centre, or rather a concentration camp, for all Jews.

B. *sb.* **1.** A member of the Aryan family; one belonging to, or descended from, the ancient people who spoke the parent Aryan language.

1851 *Edin. Rev.* 328 Times when neither Greece nor India were peopled by Arians. **1861** MAX MÜLLER *Sc. Lang.* (1873) I. vi. 273 The state of civilisation attained by the Aryans before they left their common home. **1870** EMERSON *Soc. & Solit.* vii. 137 The days are ever divine as to the first Aryans. **1878** CUST *Mod. Langs. E. Indies* 13 The Aryans advanced down the basins of the Indus and the Ganges. **1882** SWEET *Trans. Phil. Soc.* 114 The primitive Arians.

2. *spec.* under the Nazi régime (cf. sense A. 2).

1933 tr. *Hitler's Mein Kampf* in *Times* 25 July 15/6 The exact opposite of the Aryan is the Jew. **1933** *Education* 1 Sept. 170/2 The basic idea of the new law is that non-Aryans, that is to say mainly Jews, shall be admitted to Universities and to the higher and middle schools only in accordance with their ratio of the total population of Germany. **1940** *War Illustr.* 16 Feb. 107 Pitiable in the extreme is the plight of the Jews in Poland under Nazi rule. .. On their backs they must wear a triangle of yellow cloth to show that their faith is abominable to the Nazi, and they must walk in the gutter, for the pavement is for Aryans only.

Aryanism ('ɛərɪənɪz(ə)m). [f. ARYAN + -ISM.] **a.** Aryan principles or method of administration; belief in the historical existence of an Aryan race. **b.** A theory asserting the cultural and racial superiority of those of 'Aryan' descent. (Cf. ARYAN A. 1 b, 2.)

1888 S. C. B. PITMAN tr. *Renan's Hist. Israel* I. i. 7 Strict monogamy was the law of primitive Aryanism. **1905** *Harmsworth Encycl.* I. 403/1 The advocacy of the opposite theory is termed Aryanism—that Europe owes its culture and civilization to the Aryan, a tall, blond dolichocephalic race represented by the modern Germans, Scandinavians, and English. **1934** *Times Educ. Suppl.* 6 Jan. i/2 The brutalities of the new régime.. and the solemn absurdities of 'Aryanism' shocked outside nations.

Aryanization (ˌɛərɪənaɪ'zeɪʃən). [f. ARYANIZE *v.* + -ATION.] The act of Aryanizing or fact of being Aryanized.

1889 I. TAYLOR *Aryans* iv. §2. 212 The Aryanization of Europe doubtless resembled that of India. **1904** *Athenæum* 24 Dec. 871/3 This Aryanization of inferior races.

b. *spec.* Of the Nazi régime (cf. ARYANIZE *v.* b).

1939 *Sun* (Baltimore) 16 Feb. 1/4 A decree was issued today supplementing the December 5, 1938, order for the 'Aryanization' of German economic life, and providing for the payment of seventy per cent. of the 'Aryanization' profits to the German treasury. **1941** *Manchester Guardian Weekly* 31 Jan. 82 In the provinces young Nazis have invented their own technique of 'Aryanisation'... They make raids on Jewish families and demand contributions, with the threat that refusal to comply will mean the concentration camp.

Aryanize ('ɛərɪənaɪz, 'ɑːrɪən-), *v.* [f. ARYAN, ARIAN *a.* and *sb.* + -IZE.] **a.** To make characteristically Aryan. Hence **Aryanized** *ppl. a.*, made Aryan in language though not of Aryan race, as is the case with some East Indian tribes or peoples.

1858 WHITNEY *Orient. Stud.* II. 7 Thus all India.. was thoroughly Aryanized. **1880** K. JOHNSTON *Lond. Geog.* 313 To the aryanised groups belong the Bengali and the Assamese.

b. Under the Nazi régime, to make 'Aryan', to confer 'Aryan' status upon (a 'non-Aryan', e.g. a Jew); also, to dispossess a 'non-Aryan' of property, civil rights, etc.

1935 L. L. SNYDER *From Bismarck to Hitler* viii. 81 Only in their outer forms will Japan and other 'bearers of civilization' remain Asiatic; inwardly they will become Aryanized. **1939** B. R. EPSTEIN tr. *M. L. Berges's Cold Pogrom* 215 A half Jew might become 'Aryanized' if he had been a soldier. **1941** *Manchester Guardian Weekly* 31 Jan. 82 Plundering of Jewish property goes on, and the majority of Jewish shops in Prague have already become 'Aryanised'. **1952** KOESTLER *Arrow in Blue* 253 Though the Ullsteins were Jews, they tried to Aryanize the firm by degrees.

aryballos (ærɪ'bæləs). *Greek Antiq.* [ad. Gr. ἀρύβαλλος bag, purse, oil-flask.] A flask with a globular body and narrow neck used as a container for oil or unguent.

1848 G. DENNIS *Cities & Cemeteries Etruria* p. xcix, Ointment and perfume vases... The *aryballos* receives its name from its resemblance to a purse. **1858** S. BIRCH *Hist. Anc. Pott.* II. II. ix, The *aryballos* was a vase always described as like a purse... It.. was carried with the strigil to the bath. **1882** J. F. MOLLOY *It is no Wonder* II. x. 296 An aryballos, signed by Xenophantus, and magnificently ornamented by a wonderful crowd of figures in relief. **1935** RICHTER & MILNE *Shapes & Names Ath. Vases* 16 *Aryballos.* Oil bottle with narrow neck, commonly used by athletes at the bath. **1946** *Antiquity* XX. 53 The second, a flat-bottomed aryballos is an early middle Corinthian piece.

aryȝt, aryht, aryse, obs. ff. ARIGHT, ARISE.

aryl ('ærɪl, also commonly 'æraɪl). *Chem.* [ad. G. *arryl* (D. Vorländer 1899, in *Jrnl. Prakt. Chemie* LIX. 247), now *aryl*, f. AR(OMATIC + -YL.] A general term for an organic radical derived from an aromatic hydrocarbon by the removal of one hydrogen atom. So **ary'lation**, the introduction of an aryl group into a substance.

1906 M'GOWAN & SUDBOROUGH tr. *A. Bernthsen's Textbk. Org. Chem.* xxi. 365 The purely aliphatic alkyl radicals are termed alphyl groups, and the aromatic, aryl. **1918** J. C. CAIN *Manuf. Intermed. Prod. for Dyes* 4 Arylation is usually effected by means of the corresponding amine. **1955** BROWN & DEY *India's Mineral Wealth* (ed. 3) x. 391 Some of the more stable silicone esters, the aryl and higher alkyl silicates, are said to show promise as liquid media for heat-exchange and hydraulic systems. **1958** *Oxf. Univ. Gaz.* 23 Apr. 881 A quantitative study of the arylation of naphthalene by free radical reactions. **1959** *Times* 17 Mar. 4/3 Alkyl aryl sulphonates.

aryole, variant of ARIOLE, *Obs.*, a soothsayer.

aryste, var. ARIST, *Obs.*, arising; obs. f. ARRAS.

aryteno- (ærɪ'tiːnəʊ), comb. form of next.

1849–52 TODD *Cycl. Anat. & Phys.* IV. 1495/2 The aryteno-epiglottic portion of the vocal tube. **1881** MIVART *Cat* 229 The aryteno-epiglottidean folds.

arytenoid (ærɪ'tiːnɔɪd), *a.* and *sb. Phys.* Also **arytænoid**. [ad. mod.L. *arytænoīdes*, ad. Gr. ἀρυταινο-ειδής, f. ἀρύταινα funnel, pitcher + -ειδής -shaped.]

A. *adj.* Funnel-shaped, pitcher-shaped: applied *spec.* to two pyramidal cartilages of the larynx which regulate the action of the vocal chords, and to parts connected with them.

1727–51 CHAMBERS *Cycl.*, The arytænoideus [muscle] has its head in one arytænoid cartilage, and its tail in the other. **1836** TODD *Cycl. Anat. & Phys.* I. 345/2 The arytenoid bones. **1872** HUXLEY *Phys.* vii. 180 Perched side by side upon the upper edge of the back part of the cricoid cartilage are.. the arytenoid cartilages.

B. *sb.* [sc. cartilage, muscle.]

[**1691** RAY *Creation* II. (1701) 339 The cartilages called *Arytenoides*.] **1849–52** TODD *Cycl. Anat. & Phys.* IV. 1493/2 Arytenoids locked to each other.. by a cartilage.

arytenoidal (ˌærɪtiː'nɔɪdəl), *a. Phys.* [f. prec. + -AL[1].] Belonging to the arytenoid cartilages, etc.

1872 COHEN *Dis. Throat* 50 These arytenoidal movements can be beautifully demonstrated by means of the laryngoscope.

as (æz, əz), *adv.* (*conj.*, and *rel. pron.*) Forms: 1–3 **allswá, al-swá**, (WS. 1–2 **ealswá**). *North.* 2–6 **alswa (alsua)**, 4–5 **alsa, alse**, 4–7 **als**, 4– **as**. *Midl.* 3–4 **alswo, alsuo**, 3–6 **also**, 4–6 **alse, als**, 3– **as**, (4–5 **os**). *South.* 2–3 **alse**, 2–4 **ase**, 2– **as**. [A worn-down form of *all-so*, OE. *all-swá* 'wholly so, quite so, just so,' which in its simple demonstrative use remains dissyllabic (see ALSO), but as a relative and antecedent has been phonetically weakened through *alswá*, *alsa*, *alse*, *als*, *as*, and *alswá*, *alswo*, *also*, *alse*, *ase*, *as*, to (æz). This phonetic weakening, in each of its successive stages, began with the relative sense, whence it extended to the other senses: even the weak demonstrative was reduced in north. dial. to *als*, but remains *also* in standard Eng. The correlation in 'the colour is *as* bright *as* gold,' where the first *as* is demonstrative or antecedent, and the second relative, 'in *that* degree bright, in *which* degree gold (is bright),' was originally expressed by *so—so*, OE. 'swá beorht swá gold'; but the antecedent or principal form was also strengthened by *all*, '*all swá* beorht swá gold'; constructions which long survived in the south, as 'sō briht sō (se) gold,' and 'al sō (alse) briht sō (se) gold.' The prefixed *all*, though originally emphatic (= *altogether*, *quite*, *even*), soon lost its force, and *al-swá*, *al-so* came to imply no more than the simple *swá*, *sō*. Hence, by 1200 (in the north) *alswa* had begun to appear in the subordinate clause likewise, '*alswa* brihht *alswa* gold,' a construction soon generally adopted, though almost always with the relative in a phonetically weaker form than the antecedent, e.g. '*alswa* briht *alse* gold, *also* briht *alse* gold, *alse* briȝt *ase* gold, *als* bricht *as* gold,' but finally with both correlatives worn down, '*as* bright *as* gold.' *Alse*, *ase*, *as* was even substituted as the relative, when the original *swá*, *so* remained as the antecedent, whence the mod. 'not *so* bright *as* gold,' OE. ná *swá* beorht *swá* gold, 13th c. southern Eng. 'nowht *so* briht *sŏ* (*se*) gold,' and 'nowht *so* briht *alse* (*ase*) gold.'

With the wearing down of *al-so* to *as*, cf. mod.Ger. *also*, *als*, in '*also* bald *als* er kam' = ME. '*all-so* sone *als* he com,' mod. '*as* soon *as* he came.'

With many common adjectives and adverbs *as* (*als*, etc.) was formerly written in combination, especially in idiomatic constructions, e.g. *asmuch*, *aswell*, *asfaste*, *assoon*, *astite*; relics of this survive in *forasmuch*, *inasmuch*, *whereas*.]

The uses of *as* are here considered, A. in the main sentence, B. in the subordinate sentence, C. in phrases. At the end of B. are some phraseological combinations originating in ellipsis.

A. In a main sentence, as Antecedent or Demonstrative Adverb.

†**I.** With *so* in the relative clause. *Obs.*

As (*alswa*, *also*, *alse*, *als*, *ase*)... *so* (*swa*, *so*, *se*).

†**1.** Of quantity or degree: In that degree, to such extent... (in or to which)... *Obs.*

a **1000** ÆLFRIC *Hom.* in Thorpe *Anal.* 61 Seo beorhtnys is ealswá eald swá þæt fýr. *c* **1175** *Lamb. Hom.* 157 Alse raðe se he walde. **1205** LAY. 9968 Al swa longe swa þe woreld stondeð. *c* **1300** *K. Alis.* 395 Al so ofte so he wolde. *c* **1380** *Sir Ferumb.* 2329 Ase loude so he..miȝte: to ys men criede he there. **1393** LANGL. *P. Pl.* C. VIII. 232 A court as cleer so þe sonne. **1450** MYRC 394 Þenne schale þe husbonde als blyue Teche & preche so hys wyue. **1532** *Dice Play* (1850) 13 Not always as well so I would wish.

†**2.** Of quality or manner: In that way, in such wise...(in which)... *Obs.*

c **1175** *Lamb. Hom.* 25 Al swa he doð swa þe swica. *Ibid.* 159 Alswa se þe sunne drach up þene deu. *c* **1200** ORMIN *Ded.* 281 And all all swa se Godes Lamb..mihhte.

II. With *as* also in the relative clause: *As* (*alswa, also, alsa, alse, als, ase, as*)...*as* (*alswa*, etc.).

3. Of quantity: In that degree; to that extent ...(in *or* to which)... Expressing the *Comparative of Equality*: *as* good *as* gold; *as* wise *as* fair; *as* strong *as* ever; *as* soon *as* you can; and in innumerable proverbial similes, *as* black *as* jet, *as* brave *as* a lion, etc.

c **1175** *Cott. Hom.* 239 Alse lange alse ȝé lefede &..alse longe as ic lefie. *c* **1220** *Hali Meid.* 5 Syon [is] ase muchel on englische leodene ase heh sihðe. *a* **1300** *Cursor M.* 823 Als fast als þai had don þat sinne. *Ibid.* 7526 Þar he stod als still os stake. *c* **1314** *Guy Warw.* 87 Also litel als he may. *c* **1325** *E.E. Allit. P.* B. 984 Al-so salt as ani se. *c* **1325** *Cœur de L.* 2524 Alsoo faste As quarrel off the arweblast. **1377** LANGL. *P. Pl.* B. IV. 195 Als longe as owre lyf lasteth. *c* **1386** CHAUCER *Prol.* 287 Al so lene was his hors as is a rake. *c* **1420** *Amadace* xli, Als gay Als any erliche mon. *c* **1425** WYNTOUN *Cron.* VIII. 165 Alsa frely as before. **1485** CAXTON *Paris & V.* (1868) 63 Also sick as she was. **1530** *Sarum Man.* in Maskell *Mon. Rit.* II. 295 Alse often as thei be..required. **1583** STUBBES *Anat. Abus.* II. 10 As round as a ball. **1588** A. KING *Canisius' Catech.* 111 Als far as apperteins to yᵉ office. **1608** ARMIN *Nest Ninn.* 11 He was as dead as a doore nayle. **1701** W. WOTTON *Hist. Rome* Alex. iii. 504 He was as covetous as cruel. **1711** STEELE *Spect.* No. 155 ¶5 As busy as possible. **1849** MACAULAY *Hist. Eng.* I. 275 He used it, as far as he dared. **1879** BLACK *Macleod of D.* xxvi, He was as mad as a hatter about her.

†**4.** Of quality: In that very way, in such wise ...(in which)... *Obs.*

c **1175** *Lamb. Hom.* 153 He his sunnen undeð..alswa alse he heom haueð idon. *c* **1230** *Ancr. R.* 36 And eft biginneð.. also, ase er. **1340** *Ayenb.* 137 Alsuo ase þe zoþe milde hereþ þe oþre..alsuo he blameþ him zelve.

III. With relative clause wanting.

5. In qualifications of degree (cf. 3) the relative clause may be elliptically absent, especially where it expresses: **a.** 'as that or those just mentioned.' Here, *as* in the principal sentence may be rendered by *equally*.

c **1386** CHAUCER *Knts. T.* 339 And he loved him as tendurly agayn. *c* **1400** *Destr. Troy* IX. 4125 Kyng Sapmon ..With als-mony abill shippes auntrid hym seluyn. **1509** BARCLAY *Shyp of Folys* (1874) II. 81 Thoughe he be good, yet other ar als bad. **1551** TURNER *Herbal* (1568) 119 Galene sayeth that clinopodium is hote and dry in the thyrde degre, but our clinopodium is not al so hote. **1711** STEELE *Spect.* No. 113 ¶4 Chance has..thrown me very often in her way, and she as often has directed a Discourse to me. *Mod.* 'Come forward.' 'Thank you! I hear quite as well where I am.'

b. 'as not,' 'as the opposite course,' 'as anything else'; e.g. in ***as lief, as soon*** (as not). ***as good, as well***: See C. phrases.

1775 SHERIDAN *Rivals* v. iii, I'd as lieve let it alone.

c. 'as can be imagined,' 'as may be,' 'as possible,' cf. L. *quam* in *quam maximum*, etc. Esp. in AS-FAST, AS SOON, AS-TITE, ALSWITHE, q.v.

B. In a subordinate sentence, as a Relative or Conjunctive Adverb, introducing a clause which expresses I. II. the *mode* (manner and degree), whence also III. the *time, place*, IV. *reason*, V. *purpose, result*, of the principal sentence; passing into VI. a relative pronoun, a relative particle, VII. a merely subordinating conjunction, and VIII. a limiting or restrictive particle.

I. Of quantity or degree. (Preceded by *adjective* or *adverb*.)

1. a. With antecedent *as* (*alswa, alswo, also, alse, als*, etc.):...in which degree, to what extent. Expressing with antecedent *as*, the *Comparative of Equality*.

[See A. II. 3, all the quotations for which also illustrate this.]

b. Expressing a comparison with a hypothetical fact or state expressed by the subjunctive: As if, as though. (Cf. 9.) *arch.*

1366 MAUNDEV., As wel as thei had ben of the same Contree. **1399** LANGL. *Rich. Redeless* III. 46 Thanne cometh þer a congioun..As not of his nolle as he þe nest made. *c* **1590** MARLOWE *Jew Malta* I. i. 59 Will serve as well as I were present there. **1795** SOUTHEY *Joan of Arc* v. 325 As certain of success As he had made a league with Victory.

2. With antecedent *so* (*swa, swo*) in the same sense as 1.

a. *esp.* in negative sentences.

c **1220** *Ureisun* in *Cott. Hom.* 187 Hwi ne fele ich þe in mi breostes swo swote ase þu art. **1366** MAUNDEV. ix. 107 The cytee is not now so gret, as it was wont to be. **1595** SHAKS. *John* v. v. 21 The day shall not be vp so soone as I. **1818** SCOTT *Rob Roy*, You have never so much as answered me. **1849** MACAULAY *Hist.* I. i. 10 No country suffered so much ..as England.

b. in certain affirmative sentences. (See SO *adv.* 21.)

c **1460** *Towneley Myst.* 37 A child so lufand as thou art. **1594** SHAKS. *Rich. III*, II. i. 83 Looke I so pale, Lord Dorset, as the rest? **1605** —— *Macb.* I. ii. 43 So well thy words become thee, as thy wounds. **1690** LOCKE *Hum. Und.*, I shall be pardoned for calling it by so harsh a name as madness. **1742** RICHARDSON *Pamela* III. 82 To think I should act so barbarously as I did. **18..** MACAULAY *Essays* IV. 146 In a world so full of temptation as this. *a* **1850** LONGF. So long as you are innocent fear nothing. **1855** TENNYSON *Maud* I. xix. ii, When did a morning shine So rich in atonement as this?

3. With antecedent *as* (*so*) suppressed:

a. Giving emphasis or absoluteness to the attribute or qualification.

c **1200** *Trin. Coll. Hom.*, Fair alse mone, icoren alse sune. **1382** WYCLIF *Song Sol.* vi. 10 Faire as the moone, chosen as the sunne, ferful as of tentes sheltrun ordeyned. **1590** SHAKS. *Mids. N.* I. i. 144 Momentarie as a sound: Swift as a shadow, short as any dreame, Briefe as the lightening. **1596** SPENSER *F.Q.* I. iii. 5 Soone as the royall virgin he did spy. **1667** MILTON *P.L.* v. 138 Soon as they forth were come. **1742** RICHARDSON *Pamela* III. 241 My good Lady..made me proud as proud can be. **1835** CRABBE *Par. Reg.* I. 288 His favourite Lucy should be rich as fair. *Mod.* Quick as thought, Roger seized the oar.

b. *esp.* In parenthetical clauses forming an extension of the subject or predicate, the antecedent (*so, as*) formerly present is now omitted, and the relative has acquired somewhat of a concessive force = Though, however.

1297 R. GLOUC. 47 To brynge vs, so fre as we beþ, in to fyl seruage. *c* **1300** in Wright *Pop. Sc.* 137 And ȝut as gret as urthe and as lute as heo is, Ther nis bote, etc. **1393** LANGL. *P. Pl.* C. XIV. 185 So wis as þow art holde..so wide as þow regnest. **1622** HEYLIN *Cosmogr.* III. (1673) 114/1 As Pet. Ramas (as great a Clerk as he was)..hath most vainly told us. **1641** EVELYN *Mem.* (1857) I. 37, I took leave of.. Antwerp, as late as it was, embarking for Brussels. **1727** SWIFT *Wond. Wonders* Wks. 1755 II. II. 52 The world, as censorious as it is, hath been so kind, etc. **1742** RICHARDSON *Pamela* III. 45 Bad as his Actions were..would there not have been, etc.? **1835** CRABBE *Par. Reg.* I. 534 Fair as she is, I would my widow take.

†**4.** After the comparative degree = Than. *Obs.* exc. in dialects. (Cf. Ger. *so...als, besser als*, L. *tam...quam, plus quam*.)

1460 *Paston Lett.* 363 I. 534, I hadde never more neede.. as I have at this tyme. **1513** DOUGLAS *Æneis* II. xii. (xi.) 110 Quhat mair hard mischance..Apperit to me as that? **1523** LD. BERNERS *Froiss.* I. ccii. 238 They coude do no better.. as to make to their capitayne sir Eustace Damlreticourt. **1568** *Marr. Wit & Wisd.* (1846) 27, I had rather haue your rome as your componie. **1653** URQUHART *Rabelais* II. xxxii. (D.), I..never made better cheer in my life as then. **1824** SCOTT *St. Ronan's* ii. (D.), I rather like him as otherwise.

II. Of quality or manner. (Preceded by a *verb*.)

* *With antecedent expressed.*

†**5.** With antecedent *as* (*alswa, alsa, also, alse, als*, etc.):...in which way, in the way that. *Obs.*

[See A. II. 4, the quotations for which also illustrate this.]

6. With antecedent *so* (*swa, swo*), or an equivalent phrase containing *such, same*:...in the manner that...*arch.* (*So* is now usually omitted: see 8.)

See *so...as*...of result, infra V.

1205 LAY. 6753 And swa he þer agon ase þe oðer hæfde idon. **1393** GOWER *Conf.* III. 117 So as I shall rehercen The tides of the yere diversen. **1580** LYLY *Euphues* (1636) Hiv, God will so blesse you, as..your hearts can wish. **1611** BIBLE *Gen.* xviii. 5 So doe, as thou hast said. *Mod.* The committee was not so constituted as he had expected.

7. With the clauses transposed for emphasis; *as...so*: **a.** In what manner...(in that manner); in the way that...

1382 WYCLIF *Ps.* cii. 15 As the flour of the feld so he shal floure out. *c* **1420** *Liber Cocorum* 38 As I tolde byfore, so have þou cele. **1611** BIBLE *Isa.* xxiv. 2 It shall be as with the people, so with the priest, as with the seruant, so with his master, etc. **1614** R. TAILOR *Hog hath lost Pearl* in Dodsl. *O.P.* (1780) VI. 400 As she brews so let her bake. **1697** DRYDEN *Virg. Georg.* IV. 49 As the Cold Congeals into a Lump the liquid Gold; So 'tis again dissolv'd by Summer's Heat. **1860** TRENCH *Serm. Westm. Ab.* xi. 117 As our speech is, so we are.

b. In proportion or degree as...

1541 ELYOT *Image Govt.* 8 As they excelled in abhominacion, so preferred he theim.

c. Even as, just as; both...and, equally... and. Lat. *cum...tum. arch.*

1602 FULBECKE *Pandectes* 69 A thing as ancient, so necessarie. **1607** *Schol. Disc. agst. Antichr.* I. i. 28 Shee hath as bewayld, so also renounced her former countrey. **1635** NAUNTON *Fragm. Reg.* 200 in *Phœnix* (1707) I, As he was a great soldier, so was he of suitable magnanimity. **1713** DERHAM *Phys. Theol.* IV. x. (1752) 173 As they are the most pernicious of birds so are they the most rare. **1837** SIR W. HAMILTON *Metaph.* xxviii. (1870) II. 173 As some philosophers have denied to vision all perception of extension..so others have equally refused this perception to touch.

** *With antecedent not expressed.*

8. = with antecedent *so* omitted: **a.** ...in the manner or way that... ***as you were!*** (in Drill): 'Return to the position in which you were before!' (also *transf. colloq.*). ***as it stands***: taken or considered as it now is.

c **1175** *Lamb. Hom.* 17 Heore uuel..þu aȝest to.. wiðstewen ȝif þu miht al swa hit is nu laȝe a londe. *c* **1250** *Gen. & Ex.* 2212 Iosepes men ðor quiles deden Al-so Iosep hem adde beden. *a* **1300** *Havelok* 306 Shal it nouht ben als sho thenkes, Hope maketh fol man ofte blenkes. **1377** LANGL. *P. Pl.* B. Prol. 120 To tilie and trauaile as trewe lyf askeþ. **1535** COVERDALE *Ezra* vi. 9 There shalbe geuen them daylie as is acordinge. **1611** BIBLE *John* xv. 12 That ye love one another, as I have loved you. **1625** MARKHAM *Souldier's Accid.* 21 To reduce any of these words of direction to the same order or station in which the Souldier stood before.. you shall say..As you were. **1626** B. JONSON *Staple of Newes* in *Wks.* (1938) VI. 358 When my Muster-Master..cries, Faces about to the right hand, the left, Now, as you were. **1680** RADCLIFFE in *Rochester's Poems* 133 And be Godly a while ho, and then as you were. **1802** MAR. EDGEWORTH *Moral T.* (1816) I. xiii. 103 An Englishman..thought he might insult Scotchmen as he pleased. **1832** CARLYLE *Remin.* (1881) I. 15 Let me write my books as he built his houses. **1864** HOTTEN *Slang Dict.* 68 'As you were', a military phrase in drilling; used in a Slang sense to one who is going on too fast in his assertions, and wants recalling to moderation. **1865** —— *Fredk. Gt.* VI. (1873) 29 General amicable As-you-were between Austria and Bavaria. **1871** J. W. T. *Questions & Answers on Company Drill* 28 The men [are] frequently to be brought back to the 'ready' by the command 'as you were'. **1882** *Times* 5 July 11 The oath, as it stands, is and ought to be a religious test. **1925** FRASER & GIBBONS *Soldier & Sailor Words* 11 *As you were*: The ordinary military word of command, used colloquially by way of acknowledging a mistake in anything said, e.g., 'I saw Smith—as you were—I mean Brown.' **1935** *Man. of Ceremonial* (*War Office*) ii. 14 Numbers 1 and 4 of the front rank will then prove. On the command 'As you were', they will drop their arms to the side.

b. To the same extent as, in so far as; in proportion as; according as; just as, even as.

c **1225** *St. Marherete* (1866) 13 þat eiðer of oðeres, as of his ahne, beo trusti. **1596** SHAKS. *1 Hen. IV*, III. iii. 165 As thou art but man I dare, but, as thou art a Prince, I feare thee. **1670** R. COKE *Disc. Trade* 32 Since the Rents of Land are valuable, as the Trade of the place is. **1710** BERKELEY *Princ. Hum. Knowl.* I. §1 Which, as they are pleasing or disagreeable, excite the passions of love, hatred, etc. **1751** JOHNSON *Rambl.* No. 165 ¶3 Our state may indeed be more or less imbittered, as our duration may be more or less contracted. **1837** SIR W. HAMILTON *Metaph.* xxxviii. (1870) II. 374 It is blasphemy to say that God only is as we are able to think Him to be.

c. In the phrases ***according(-ly) as, in proportion as***, and the like.

[See instances under ACCORDING, etc.]

d. In antithetical or parallel clauses, introducing a known circumstance with which a hypothesis is contrasted, or beside which a new circumstance is placed:...as on the other hand; even as; whereas; whilst.

1523 LD. BERNERS *Froiss.* I. clxxvi. 213 If kyng Johan had ben in Fraunce, as he was in Englande [*i.e.* instead of being, as was the fact, in England], he durst not haue done as he dyd. **1602** SHAKS. *Ham.* v. ii. 347 Had I but time, (as this fell sergeant, death, Is strick'd in his Arrest). **1715** BURNET *Own Time* II. 2 The King's own religion was suspected, as his brother's was declared. **1848** THACKERAY *Bk. Snobs* (1869) xvi. 71 It has its prejudices, to be sure, as which of us has not? *Mod.* If I had been present, as I was not, I should have asked an explanation.

e. ***as also*** introduces an additional circumstance: Also in the same way, and likewise, and...as well.

1793 SMEATON *Edystone L.* §252 To carry her a rope to the landing-place, as also one to the..rocks on each side.

9. a. Introducing a supposition, expressed by the subjunctive mood: As if, as though. *arch.* (Cf. 1 b.)

1135 *O.E. Chron.*, Uuard þe sunne suilc als it uuare thre niht ald mone. *a* **1250** *Owl & Night.* 146 To-svolle..Also ho hadde one frogge i-svolȝe. *a* **1300** *Havelok* 508 Starinde als he were wod. **1413** LYDG. *Pylgr. Sowle* II. xlv. 51 Somme hadden longe hoked clawes, lyke as they had ben lyons. **1593** SHAKS. *2 Hen. VI*, I. i. 103 Vndoing all, as all had never bin. **1671** MILTON *P.R.* IV. 447, I heard the wrack As earth and sky would mingle. **1681** DRYDEN *Abs. & Achit.* 848 It looks as Heav'n our Ruin had design'd. **1800** COLERIDGE *Wallenstein* I. v, He looks as he had seen a ghost.

b. *If* and *though* are now commonly expressed.

a **1300** *Cursor M.* 7690 Als þof his wiperwin he war. **1523** FITZHERB. *Surv.* xi. (1539) 17 As and a lorde haue a manour. **1579** SPENSER *Sheph. Cal.* Jan. 18 As if my yeare were wast, and woxen old. **1795** SOUTHEY *Joan of Arc* I. 381 Wks. I. 14 As though by some divinity possess'd. **1867** CARLYLE *Remin.* (1881) II. 18, I was banished solitary as if to the bottom of a cave.

c. *esp.* in ***as it were***: as if it were so, if one might so put it, in some sort: a parenthetic phrase used to indicate that a word or statement is perhaps not formally exact though practically right.

c **1386** CHAUCER *Nonne Pr. T.* 26 She was as it were a maner deye. **1399** LANGL. *P. Pl.* C. IX. 22 Ich wolde a-saye som tyme for solas, as hit were. **1531** ELYOT *Gov.* (1834) 211 It draweth a man as it were by violence. **1579** E. K. in *Spenser's Sheph. Cal.* Mar. 11 *Gloss.*, The messenger, and as it were, the forerunner of springe. **1692** E. WALKER *Epictetus' Mor.* (1737) xxii, You're as it were the Actor of a Play. **1711** STEELE *Spect.* No. 32 ¶1 She has thought fit, as it were, to mock herself. **1881** BUCHANAN *God & Man* I. 124 She took him at once, as it were, into her confidence.

10. a. With the subordinate clause abbreviated: In the same way as, as if, as it were.

c **1000** *Ags. Gosp.* Matt. xxvi. 55 Eall-swá to þeófe ȝe synð cumene. **1382** WYCLIF *ibid.* 25 As to a theef ȝee han gon out. **1596** SPENSER *F.Q.* I. i. 1 His angry steede did chide his foming bitt, As much disdayning to the curbe to yield. **1611** BIBLE *Heb.* xii. 7 God dealeth with you as with sonnes. **1663** GERBIER *Counsel* C ij b, The Horse..is as to seek. **1763** J. BROWN *Poetry & Mus.* §6. 97 One of them (as wounded) fell down. **1817** BYRON *Manfred* I. ii. 15, I..Behold the tall pines dwindled as to shrubs. *a* **1821** KEATS *To England*, To sit upon an Alp as on a throne. **1859** TENNYSON *Enid* 210 His ..hand Caught at the hilt, as to abolish him.

†**b.** With numbers = About, as it were, Gr. ὡς, ὡσεί, OE. *swylce*, Goth. *swe*. *Obs.*

1382 WYCLIF *John* vi. 19 Whanne þei hadden rowid as fyue and twenty furlongis or þritty. **1523** LD. BERNERS *Froiss.* I. xliv. 59 They were a great nombre as a xl. M. men.

11. With subordinate clause reduced to its subject or object: **a.** After the manner of, in the likeness of, the same as, like.

c **1200** *Trin. Coll. Hom.* 109 Ure helende aros alse sunne. *c* **1220** *Leg. St. Kath.* 1361 Þe Keiser kaste his heaued as wod mon. *c* **1400** *Destr. Troy* I. 178 Alse sede in þe season sowe it on þe erthe. **1590** SPENSER *F.Q.* I. i. 29 And often knockt his brest, as one that did repent. **1611** BIBLE *Gen.* iii. 5 Yee shall bee as Gods, knowing good and euill. **1849** MACAULAY *Hist. Eng.* II. 559 To the.. ignorant populace the law of nations and the risk of bringing on their country the just vengeance of all Europe were as nothing. **1876** GREEN *Short Hist.* x. §4 (1881) 800 Spain rose as one man against the stranger.

b. In the character, capacity, or *rôle* of. *spec.* in theatrical use.

1523 LD. BERNERS *Froiss.* I. v. 4 Her sonne, who was as the next heire male. **1742** MIDDLETON *Cicero* I. IV. 303 Assisted by Pompey as augur. **1810** SCOTT *Lady of L.* III. vii, He as truth received What of his birth the crowd believed. **1837** SIR W. HAMILTON *Metaph.* xxvi. (1870) II. 139 The fact is assumed as an hypothesis; the hypothesis explained as a fact. **1846** RUSKIN *Mod. Paint.* (1851) I. I. I. i. 6 The lesson which men receive as individuals, they do not learn as nations. **1847** *Semi-Wkly. News* (Fredericksburg, Va.) 7 Oct. 1/4 His robust health.. gave him great advantage where unusual muscular strength is necessary, as Damon, Matamor, the Gladiator, etc. **1875** HIGGINSON *Hist. U.S.* xvi. 151 This design was afterwards used as a flag. **1954** *Times* 18 Oct. 2/3 *Toad of Toad Hall*, with Mr. Leo McKern as the irrepressible Toad. *Ibid.* 2/4 Mr. Victor Mature.. as an ambitious officer of low birth,.. Miss Jean Simmons as an honest serving wench.

c. Introducing a complemental nominative or objective after such verbs as *seem, appear, pass, rank; view, regard, represent, treat, acknowledge, know, consider, accept*, etc.: see these words.

1607 SHAKS. *Cor.* v. vi. 145 Regarded As the most Noble Coarse. **1711** ADDISON *Spect.* No. 9 ¶1 He was saluted as a Brother. *c* **1740** FIELDING *Ess. Convers.* ad init., Man is generally represented as an animal formed for.. society. **1742** RICHARDSON *Pamela* III. 76 Might have imputed to me as Arrogance, or Revenge. **1802** SCOTT *Minstr. Sc. Bord.* I. 8 He whom all civilized nations now acknowledge as the Father of Poetry. **1837** MACAULAY *Bacon, Ess.* (1854) I. 346/1 In what we consider as his weakness. **1876** GREEN *Short Hist.* x. §4 (1881) 787 Who still looked on themselves as mere settlers.. and who regarded the name of 'Irishman' as an insult.

12. as who: **a.** Like one who, as if one. *arch.*

1551-6 ROBINSON tr. *More's Utopia* 35 As who should sai it were a very daungerous matter. *a* **1586** *Answ. Cartwright* 9 Walke before me, and be thou vpright, and I will make my couenant betweene me and thee. As who say, one condition .. of the couenant is our vpright and good profession. **1606** HOLLAND *Sueton.* Annot. 14 His courteous cariage and affabilitie: as who was readie to accept of petitions and requests. **1848** DICKENS *Dombey* 212 The Manager inclined his head, and showed his teeth, as who should say.. Is that the case?

†**b.** As being he who. So, *as which*, etc. *Obs.*

1574 tr. *Marlorats Apocalips* 9 So consequently before Christ, as who sitteth by God the father. **1583** GOLDING *Calvin on Deut.* cxcvi. 1219 Let vs call vppon him, as which is the chiefe sacrifice that hee requireth at our handes.

Ibid. vi. 31 A verie notable point, as whereof wee may gather verie good and profitable doctrine.

13. Introducing a clause not dependent on the predicate of the principal sentence, but referring elliptically to some other word or part, or parenthetically to the statement itself contemplated in regard to its truth, authority, universality, etc. **as a rule**: to state the general rule disregarding exceptions; generally, in the great majority of cases. **as usual**: as is or was usually the case.

c **1175** *Lamb. Hom.* 17 Al swa ic er seide, ȝif eni mon touward criste isuneȝede, etc. *c* **1230** *Ancr. R.* 166 Nu, as ich sigge, þis deorewurðe healewi iðisse bruchele uetles, etc. *c* **1400** *Apol. Loll.* 27 He doþ ai þo þingis þat plesun God, os Himself seiþ. **1413** LYDG. *Pylgr. Sowle* I. xxiv. 29 His skryp and burdon, whiche, as he seyth, he ne left neuer. **1711** ADDISON *Spect.* No. 5 ¶3 This project, as I have since heard, is postponed 'till the Summer Season. **1711** STEELE *ibid.* No. 104 ¶3 The Model.. was, as I take it, first imported from France. **1754** HUME *Hist. Eng.* (1812) I. viii. 409 This war was, as usual, no less feeble in its operations, than.. frivolous in its cause and object. **1882** JESSOPP in *19th Cent.* Nov. 735 The masses in towns are, as a rule, destitute of faith in the unseen.

14. Introducing a clause used to attest a statement or to adjure any one by his faith, hopes, or fears: In such a manner as befits the prayer, wish (*obs.*), anticipation, belief, profession that...

c **1386** CHAUCER *Sqrs. T.* 461 If it lay in my might, I wold amenden it.. Als wisly help me grete God of kynde. *c* **1435** *Torr. Portugal* 1446 Sir Torent said, 'as God me spede, We wille firste se that ffede.' *Ibid.* 2504 Damyselle, also muste I the [= as may I prosper!], Sylver and assure beryth he. **1593** SHAKS. *Rich. II*, III. iii. 119 This sweares he, as he is a Prince, is iust, And as I am a Gentleman, I credit him. **1795** SOUTHEY *Joan of Arc* I. 422 Wks. I. 15 Think well of this; As you are human, as you hope to live In peace. **1849** MACAULAY *Hist. Eng.* II. 78 Admonished to speak with reverence of their oppressor.. as they would answer it at their peril.

†**15.** In exclamatory sentences or clauses: The manner in which..., in what manner, how. *Obs.* exc. in dialects; replaced by *how*.

c **1230** *Ancr. R.* 62 Louerd Crist, ase men wolden steken veste euerich þurl. **1566** KNOX *Hist. Ref.* Wks. 1846 I. 103 Which, as it was keapt, the ishew will witnesse. **1816** SCOTT *Antiq.* xxvi, 'But see as our gudemither's hands and lips are ganging.'

III. Of time and place.

16. a. At or during the time that; when, while; at any time that, whenever. Introducing a contemporaneous event or action. (*As when* rarely takes the place of simple *as*.)

c **1220** *Ureisun* in *Lamb. Hom.* 189 He strahte forþ his riht earm ase [he] stode o rode. **1297** R. GLOUC. 283 As þys kyng Edgar an honteþ ywend was, Alone he com fram ys men. *c* **1380** WYCLIF *Wycket* 8 The material bread that he had in hys handes as when he sayde (*Hoc est corpus meum*). **1483** CAXTON *G. de la Tour* F iiij, But as his wrath is gone she may wel shewe to hym y^t, etc. **1596** SPENSER *F.Q.* I. i. 29 And all the way he prayed as he went. **1697** DRYDEN *Virg. Georg.* III. 529 They wander, grazing as they go. **1742** RICHARDSON *Pamela* III. 88 One Day, as she and I sat together. *Mod.* The thought occurred to me as I was watching the procession.

b. as and when: whensoever (introducing a future event or action whose occurrence or frequency remains in doubt). Cf. *if and when* s.v. IF *conj.* 8c. Also *ellipt.* (in *colloq.* use) with loss of relative force: when possible, eventually.

1945 J. CORBETT *Death—by Appointment* xvii. 186, I gave her the key; told her that she could use the house as and when she wanted to. **1958** *Publisher's end-note* in J. N. CHANCE *Affair with Rich Girl* 191 If you are a subscriber to a circulating library you may like to be advised of our new books as and when published. **1965** *Listener* 17 June 892/1 They confirmed the existing main roads as future main traffic arteries to be widened 'as and when'. **1977** *Private Eye* 13 May 17/3 Perhaps as and when and if the Arabs do a deal on Bates.., someone, somewhere, will ask for an explanation. **1977** *Custom Car* Nov. 30/2 We hope to be half-inching a J72 in the near future, so more on that as and when. **1979** *Listener* 23 Aug. 243/3 The correct procedure, as and when we win our case, is then to apply for a writ of mandamus. **1986** J. HIBBS *Country Bus* vii. 95 Its responsibilities will be the undefined functions of leadership as and when there may be a call for them.

17. At the place that, in which, where. *Obs.* exc. as in last quotation, where it passes into sense 16a.

1297 R. GLOUC. 555 Bituene Seint Oswalde's ȝat, and þe Norþ ȝat iwis, Is a long wal inou, as þe abbode's orchard is. *c* **1305** *St. Andrew* 16 in *E.E.P.* (1862) 98 Wende to patras To þe cite.. as seint andreu was. *c* **1420** *Chron. Vilod.* 390 Þen went þey þederward as þis tresere lay. [**1711** STEELE *Spect.* No. 2 ¶2 He has his Periwig powdered at the Barber's as you go into the Rose. [*Cf.* It is right in front of you as you cross London Bridge.]]

IV. Of reason.

18. a. In conformity with, or in consideration of, the fact that; it being the case that; inasmuch as; since.

a **1400** *Cov. Myst.* 281 Lete me fro this deth fle, As I dede nevyr no trespace. **1664** BUTLER *Hud.* II. ii. 202 As no Peer is bound to swear.. it follows.. t'affirm it is no perj'ry. **1766** GOLDSM. *Vic. W.* i, My eldest son.. was bred at Oxford, as I intended him for one of the learned professions. *Mod.* As you are not ready, we must go without you. He may have one, as he is a friend.

b. Also with participial clause.

1631 WEEVER *Anc. Fun. Mon.* 794 He was enforced to returne, as destitute of those further succours. **1677** MOXON *Mech. Exerc.* (1703) 203 The whole Work will be spoiled, as being smaller than the proposed Diameter. **1699** BENTLEY *Phal.* Introd. 24 [He] is not handsom: as having a flat Nose.

V. Of result, actual or intended.

* *With antecedent*, so, such, that *in the principal sentence*.

†**19.** With finite verb. *Obs.* and replaced by *that*. **a. so...as**: in such manner, to such a degree...that.

c **1460** FORTESCUE *Abs. & Lim. Mon.* (1714) 93 The Commons.. be so poer, as they may not gyve any thyng of their own Goods. **1599** HAKLUYT *Voy.* II. II. 141 This so amazed our men.. as they forsooke their Commanders, and left them. **1622** SPARROW *Rationale* (1661) 245 A thing so plain as it needs no proof. **1742** MIDDLETON *Cicero* II. VII. 207, I despised you.. so as nothing could be prouder. **1777** ROBERTSON *Hist. Amer.* I. 203 His largest vessel was so clumsy and unfit for service, as constrained him to bear away for Hispaniola.

†**b. such...as**: of that kind...that. *Obs.*

1475 CAXTON *Jason* 23 The raynes of his horse faylled.. in suche wise as he tumbled, the hede under. *c* **1555** HARPSFIELD *Divorce Hen. VIII* (1878) 178 Such.. calamity .. as since Christ his birth it never suffered the like. **1628** FELTHAM *Resolves* I. x. Wks. 1677, 14 He that longs for Heaven with such impatience, as he will kill himself. **1671** MILTON *Samson* 350, I gained a son, And such a son as all men hailed me happy.

c. The transition from the earlier *as* to *that*, was effected by the intermediate *as that*. *arch.*

1599 GREENE *Alphonsus* (1861) 245 Hath god Mars such force.. As that he can. *a* **1687** PETTY *Pol. Arith.* Pref. (1691) A iij, The Price of Food so reasonable, as that Men refuse to have it cheaper. **1795** tr. *Mercier's Fragm. Pol. & Hist.* I. 31 The power.. placed in the hands of a chief, in such a way as that the principle of unity in the government will be appreciated. *a* **1866** J. GROTE *Exam. Util. Philos.* 362 In such a manner as that the thought of Him is, etc.

20. With infinitive of result or purpose. (Still in use.) Formerly *that* also occurred as antecedent instead of *such*: cf. 24.

c **1590** MARLOWE *Faustus* xiii. 13 Do us that favour, as to let us see that peerless dame. **1662** H. MORE *Antid. Ath.* I. xi. (1712) 35 To bear themselves so as.. to cause an Arbitrarious Ablegation of the Spirits. **1711** ADDISON *Spect.* No. 1 ¶2, I am not so vain as to think. **1818** SCOTT *Hrt. Midl.* xxxvi. (1878) 345 Announced in a voice so loud, as to make all.. aware of the important communication. *Mod.* He so acquitted himself as to please everybody. Be so good as to come.

** *With antecedent* so *wanting, or conjoined with* as *in the subordinate clause*.

†**21. a.** With finite verb: With the result or purpose that. *Obs.* and replaced by *so that*.

a **1300** *Cursor M.* 586 Adam was made of manes elde, Als he might him seluen welde. **1574** tr. *Littleton's Tenures* 21 b, So as hee that holdeth by escuage, holdeth by homage. *c* **1590** MARLOWE *Faustus* x. 31 The bright shining of whose glorious acts Lightens the world with his reflecting beams, As.. It grieves my soul I never saw the man. **1628** HOBBES *Thucydides* (1822) 120 He miscarried by unskilfulness so as the loss can no way be ascribed to cowardice. **1797** DOWNING *Disord. Horned Cattle* 118 The joints will bend so as the clees or horny part.. can be inclosed in the hand.

†**b.** The transition from *so as* to *so that* gave the intervening *so as that*. *arch.*

1772-84 COOK *Voy.* (1790) III. 795 [They] had never been sufficiently examined, so as that an accurate judgement might be formed of their coasts.

22. With infinitive of result or purpose.

Mod. Put on your gloves, so as to be ready.

VI. Introducing an attributive clause; after the antecedents *such, same*, or their equivalents.

23. a. The adjective *such* (OE. *swylc, swęlc*, Goth. *swâ-leik*) contains the adv. *swá, so*, and may be analyzed as 'so-constituted': like *so*, therefore, it is followed by *as*: see above, 19 b. **b.** *Same* was in OE. an adv. followed by *swá*. Hence, after *such* and *same, as* comes, through ellipsis, to act as a relative pronoun = That, who, which.

But *same as* usually expresses identity of kind, *same that* absolute identity, except in contracted sentences where *same as* is alone found: cf. 'he uses the same books *as* you do,' 'he uses the same books *that* you do,' 'he uses the same books *as* you,' 'you and he use the same books.'

c **1175** *Lamb. Hom.* 83 Ho nimeð al swuch hou [*i.e.* hue] alse ho þer on uint. *c* **1250** *Gen. & Ex.* 4108 Alswilc als hem bihu[f]lik bee. **1340** HAMPOLE *Pr. Consc.* 835 Þan sal he on þe same wys hethen wende.. right als he cam. **1548** *Compl. Scot.* 38 That samyn sound as thay beystis hed blauen. **1549** COVERDALE *Erasm. Par. Rom.* ix, Suche as growe out of kynde. **1611** BIBLE *Transl. Pref.* 2 Such a one as was the glory of the land of Israel. **1711** STEELE *Spect.* No. 118 ¶3 Such a Passion as I have had is never well cured. **1718** HICKES & NELSON *Life Kettlewell* App. 57 This is about the same Number as was now. **1789** G. WHITE *Selborne* xvii. (1853) 72 Such a severe stroke.. as put out one eye. **1832** CARLYLE *Remin.* (1881) I. 8 Never shall we again hear such speech as that was. **1879** LUBBOCK *Sci. Lect.* ii. 31 Bees like the same odours as we do.

†**24. a.** The antecedent *such* is also replaced by *that, those*, or entirely omitted, leaving *as* an ordinary *relative pronoun* = That, who, which. Cf. Norse use of *som*. *Obs.* in standard English, but common *dial.* in England and the United States.

c **1305** *St. Edmund* 225 in *E.E.P.* (1862) 77 Drauȝtes as me draweþ in poudre. **1366** MAUNDEV. v. 36 The firste Soudan was Zarocon.. as was fadre to Sahaladyn. **1475** *Bk. Noblesse* 32 Tho as were present. **1525** LD. BERNERS *Froiss.* II. Pref., The ymages as they used in olde tyme to erecte in worshyp. **1592** SHAKS. *Rom. & Jul.* II. i. 36 That kind of Fruite As Maides call Medlers. **1603** HOLLAND *Plutarch's Mor.* 222 To those as have no children. **1645** FULLER *Good Th. in Bad T.* (1841) 32 It is false that the marigold follows the sun, whereas the sun follows the marigold, as made the day before him. **1747** GOULD *Eng. Ants* 70 That prodigious Size as we see in many Places. *c* **1852** *Lamplighter* (1854) 91 It's he as lives in the great stone house.

†**b.** Extended to *as that*. *Obs.* Cf. *as which*, 12 b.

1663 MARVELL *Corr.* Wks. 1872-5 II. 140 If they had any thing as that remained on their part.

¶ *As* (after *such* or *that*), frequently represents not merely the simple relative, but the relative with its governing preposition; and then approaches the adverbial use in 6.

1693 *Mem. Count Teckely* I. 16 A City of that importance as [= of which] Cassovia was. **1711** STEELE *Spect.* No. 11 ¶5 She should be clothed in such Silks as his Wastecoat was made of.

25. a. In parenthetic clauses, affirming, explaining, or commenting on a word in the principal sentence. In parenthetic affirmations, e.g. 'fool as I am,' *that* is more common than *as*.

c **1550** *Jacke Jugeler* (1820) 24 Like a fole as I am and a drunken knave. **1577** *St. Aug. Manuell* 93 O hard and cursed case as it was. **1605** SHAKS. *Lear* III. vii. 33 Vnmercifull Lady, as you are, I'me none. **1607** —— *Temp.* I. ii. 346, I haue vs'd thee (Filth as thou art) with humane care. **1714** ADDISON *Spect.* No. 568 ¶1 He designs his chasm, as you call it, for an Hole to creep out at. **1835** LYTTON *Rienzi* xii, Crouch! wild beast as thou art!

b. *As* frequently refers to the whole statement contemplated as a fact: = A thing or fact which.

1552 T. BARNABE in Ellis *Orig. Lett.* Ser. II. II. 202 Yff so be y^t that we shoulde warre with them (as God defende). **1802** M. EDGEWORTH *Moral Tales* I. xiii. 103 (1816) He was an Englishman, as they perceived by his accent.

26. Introducing instances in exemplification or illustration of a general designation: Like and including, such as, of the kind of; for instance, for example.

Apparently an elliptical use of 23, 24; thus, 'a beast of prey, as the lion or tiger' = 'a beast of prey, *such* as the lion or tiger *is*,' where *as* is a relative pronoun, though in the elliptical sentence, it sinks into a conjunction.

1340 HAMPOLE *Pr. Consc.* 700 Many yuels, angers, and mescheefes Oft comes til man..Als feuyr, dropsy, and Iaunys. *c* **1380** WYCLIF *Prelates* iii. Wks. 1880. 60 A prelat, as an abott or a priour. *c* **1420** *Pallad. on Husb.* 42 Beestes that shal plowe, As hors and ox. *c* **1530** RHODES *Bk. Nurture* in *Babees Bk.* 68 And if your Mayster will haue any conceites after dinner, as appels, Nuts, or creame. **1705** ADDISON *Italy* 2, I pluck'd aboue Five different Sorts..as Wild-Time, Lauender, etc.

27. From its relative or conjunctive force, *as* was added (rarely prefixed) to the demonstrative adverbs *there, then, thither, thence, after*, to make them conjunctive; it was used for some time with the interrogatives *where, when, whither, whence*, after they were substituted for the demonstratives. *When as* is found in modern poets as an archaism; the others are *Obs.* Cf. *when that, after that*; and see WHEREAS, in which the local sense is now lost.

1297 R. GLOUC. 369 þere as þe batayle was, an abbey he let rere. **1366** MAUNDEV. x. 118 The colveres retournen aȝen where as thei ben norissht. *c* **1386** CHAUCER *Merch. T.* 138 Wel may the sike man wayle and wepe, Ther as ther is no wyf the hous to kepe. **1470–85** (1634) MALORY *Arthur* (1816) I. 80 Anon, after as Balin was dead, Merlin took his sword. **1483** CAXTON *G. de la Tour* F ij, Thou..shalt not go ..there as it pleseth me not. **1523** LD. BERNERS *Froiss.* I. lvii. 78 Can ye lede vs ther as they be? *Ibid.* ccxciv. 437 Retourned into Fraunce, thyder as they thought to haue some aduantage. *c* **1532** —— *Huon* 438 Let the shyppe go whether as it wyll tyll it come to the porte where as thou shalte aryue. **1538** BALE *Thre Lawes* 4 Where as is no lawe, can no good order be. *c* **1590** MARLOWE *Jew Malta* v. ii, What boots it thee..to be the Governor, When as thy life shall be at their Command? **1660** STANLEY *Hist. Philos.* (1701) 269/2 The year following..when as Philo..accused Sophocles for having done contrary to Law. **1808** SCOTT *Marm.* I. xxviii, When as the Palmer came in hall, Nor lord nor knight was there more tall.

VII. Introducing dependent sentences or clauses.

28. Introducing a noun sentence, after *say, know, think*, etc. Sometimes expanded into *as that*. *Obs.* and replaced by *that*; but still common in southern dialect speech, where often expanded to *as how*. (Connected with IV: cf. *that* in 'the man *that* is coming,' 'he says *that* he is coming.')

1483 CAXTON *G. de la Tour* F iiij b, I saye not as ye shalle be pryuely and alone one by other. **1578** TIMME *Calvin on Gen.* 331 It seemeth to be a very absurd reason that he giveth, as that the children of Abram could not be saved. **1689** *Tryal Bps.* 55 Do you know My Lord Bishop of St. Asaph's handwriting? Not as I know of. **1712** STEELE *Spect.* No. 508 ¶6 That the Fop..should say, as he would rather have such-a-one without a Groat, than me with the Indies. **1748** RICHARDSON *Clarissa* (1811) IV. 259 Pray let her know as that I will present her..my Lancashire Seat. **1771** SMOLLETT *Humph. Cl.* I. 274, I believe as how your man deals with the devil. **1833** MARRYAT *P. Simple* xiii. (Hoppe) Seeing as how the captain had been hauling him over the coals. **1856** MRS. STOWE *Dred* xi. 100, I don't know as you'll like the appearance of our place.

†**29.** Formerly used to introduce an imperative sentence. *Obs.*

c **1374** CHAUCER *Tr. & Cr.* v. 522 'For love of God,' full pitously he seide, 'as go we seene the paleis of Creseide.' *c* **1386** —— *Miller's T.* 590 That hoote kultour in the chymenee here, As lene it me: I haue ther-with to doone.

†**30.** Introducing contracted interrogative sentences: *as how?* (arch.) *as why?* (illiterate.)

1579 TOMSON *Calvin's Serm. Tim.* 16/1 We shall see sometime how heretikes come to turne the groundes of our faith wholy vpside downe. As how? If any denie that Iesus Christ is God euerlasting, etc. **1636** HEALEY *Epictetus' Man.* xxxi. 39 But I have yet no meanes to benefit my countrey! As how man? you cannot builde it a schoole, an Exchange, or a Bathe: what's all that to the purpose? **1742** FIELDING *J. Andrews* III. xii. (Mätz.) If he could be ruined alone, she should be very willing for it; for because, as why,..he deserved it. **1801** SOUTHEY *Thalaba* IV. xv. Wks. IV. 145 He might awe the Elements, and make Myriads of Spirits serve him!..But as how? By a league with Hell, a covenant that binds The soul to utter death!

31. Formerly prefixed to an infinitive clause, made the occasion of introducing a statement, where a participle (or gerund) is now used: *e.g.* 'Speaking of volcanos, I have seen Etna in full eruption.'

c **1374** CHAUCER *Troylus* v. 974 But as to speke of love..I hadde a lorde to whom I wedded was.

VIII. Prefixed to prepositions and adverbs.

32. The original sense is perhaps seen in such expressions as, ***as regards, as respects, as concerns***, i.e. 'so far as it concerns,' 'in the degree, manner, or case in which it concerns.' Cf. L. *quod attinet ad.*

1840 MACAULAY *Ranke, Ess.* (1854) II. 543/1 As respects natural religion..it is not easy to see, etc. **1867** *Gd. Words* Mar. 160 As regards the virtues that make it possible to live the life of a civilised social being. **1872** F. HALL *False Philol.* 50 Nor is he more fortunate as relates to pronunciation.

33. a. With prepositions, *as* has the general sense of *as far as, so far as*, and thus restricts or specially defines the reference of the preposition; e.g. ***as against, as between. as anent, as concerning, as for, as to, as touching*** (Fr. *quant à*), have all the sense of 'as it regards, so far as it concerns, with respect or reference to.' In ***as in, as by, as after***, and other obsolete combinations, *as* was almost pleonastic. See these prepositions severally.

a **1300** *Cursor M.* 6880, I shal ȝou shewe wiþouten les As anentis þis moyses. *c* **1375** WYCLIF *Antecrist* 117 He shal be lyoun as to violence; as a lyoun in his chouche as to trecherie. *c* **1386** CHAUCER *Melibeus* ¶ 189 And as touching thy frendes, thou schalt considere which of hem beth most faithful. *c* **1449** PECOCK *Repr.* IV. vi. 455 Her blamyng..muste needis be had as for vniust and vntrewe. **1535** COVERDALE *2 Macc.* xi. 20 As concernynge other thinges..I haue committed them to youre messaungers. **1611** BIBLE *1 Cor.* viii. 1 As touching things offered unto idols, we know. **1748** HARTLEY *Observ. Man.* I. i. §1 ¶5 As to myself, I am not satisfied. **1857** HELPS *Friends in C.* Ser. I. I. 18 My only doubt was as to the mode. **1856** T. HOOK *Gilb. Gurney* i, [He] was questioned as to what efforts he had made to rescue his companion. **1876** GLADSTONE in *Contemp. Rev.* June 6 The rights of laymen as against priests..depend..upon his judgment. *Mod.* As for you, Sir, your father shall hear of this.

†**b.** After *as for*, a pronoun was formerly omitted.

1525 LD. BERNERS *Froiss.* II. ccxlvi.[ccxlii.] 756 As for these townes wyll neuer tourne frenche, for they can nat lyue in their daunger. **1533** UDALL *Roister D.* iv. iii. (Arb.) 62 Let him keepe him there still..As for his labour hither he shall spende in wast. **1586** COGAN *Haven Health* (1636) 206 As for herbs and fruits, especially raw, at all times are to be refused.

c. ***as from***, in formal dating: from, after. Also, (orig. *U.S.*), ***as of***: (*a*) at the present time; (*b*) from this moment, from now.

1916 *Ann. Reg. 1915* 50 The British Government declared war against Bulgaria as from 10 P.M. on October 15 and the French Government as from 6 A.M. on October 16. **1918** *Act 8 Geo. V*, c. 5 §1 (1), The foregoing provision shall..have effect as from a date to be specified in the Order. **1943** *Oxfordshire County Council Quart. Meeting* 10 Feb., In these circumstances your Sub-Committee recommend that..the temporary addition to the basic salary of the Coroner for the Northern District be reduced from £70 to £45 as from the 1st of April, 1943.

1900 'MARK TWAIN' *Let.* 26 Jan. in *Howells Lett.* (1960) II. 716 Various samples & side-lights which bring the [human] race down to date, & expose it as of yesterday. **1955** D. W. MAURER in *Publ. Amer. Dialect Soc.* XXIV. 9 For as of 1955 well over one half of the crimes against property in the United States were committed by youths under twenty-five. **1956** A. H. COMPTON *Atomic Quest* 311 As of now there is no international authority whose strength comes near to being sufficient. **1957** D. KARP *Leave me Alone* vi. 96 I'm resigning from the committee as of now. **1968** *Punch* 18 Sept. 387/2 How would the papers celebrate the return of hot, topical, as-of-now photographs? **1970** *New Society* 5 Feb. 223/1 As of the end of 1973 women 'would become entitled to receive treatment..which ensured orderly progress towards equal treatment'. **1977** J. WAINWRIGHT *Do Nothin'* x. 176 As of now you have another job. **1986** *Oxf. Mag.* v. 6/1 As of last term, Oxford has a new centre for the performing arts.

34. With adverbs and advb. phrases. **a.** Of time: ***as then, as now, as to-day, as three years ago***, where *as* has a restrictive force. Still common dialectally: but literary English retains only ***as yet*** = up to this time, hitherto.

1297 R. GLOUC. 346 þo hys lyf was ney ydo, As in þe ȝer of hys kynedom tuenty & tuo. *c* **1386** CHAUCER *Frankl. T.* 249, I ne haue as now no leyser moore to seye. *c* **1400** *Ywaine & Gaw.* 153 Als this time sex yer, I rade allane. **1483** CAXTON *G. de la Tour* F iiij b, As yet they kepe and hold that custome. **1523** LD. BERNERS *Froiss.* I. cccxiii. 480, I vnderstode so as then. **1551** ASCHAM *Let.* Wks. 1865 I. II. 288 The prince of Spain, which as to-morrow should have gone into Italy. **1583** GOLDING *Calvin on Deut.* ii. 9 An immortalitie which is hidde from vs as now. **1618** BOLTON *Florus* (1636) 163 A province untoucht in a manner, and new to us as till then. **1651** *Reliq. Wotton.* 77 Who was then as yet in possession of the king's heart. **1653** HOLCROFT *Procopius* I. 15 He could not get John punished as then. **1760** MRS. DELANY *Autobiog.* (1861) III. 608 To carry us off to Longleat as last Thursday. **1849** MACAULAY *Hist. Eng.* II. 497 Things as yet looked not unfavourably for James.

b. Of place: ***as here, as there, as in that place.***

c **1220** *Leg. St. Kath.* 3 Constantin & Maxence weren on a time, as in Keiseres stude, hehest in Rome. *c* **1435** *Torr. of Portugal* 2086 Ffor Jhesu love thy sonne hym make, As in the stede of me. *c* **1449** PECOCK *Repr.* I. vii. 35 Thei diden not ellis as there for the vertues but this. *Ibid.* I. iv. 21 [He] groundith not as in that tho gouernauncis. *c* **1532** LD. BERNERS *Huon* clvi. 602 Let hym go and marry her, for as here he hath no thynge to do.

C. Phrases. (See A. III.)

1. ***as much*** (besides its ordinary use with and without *as*) has the sense of: The same; what practically amounts to that, all that, so phr. ***I thought as much.***

1386 CHAUCER *Frankl. T.* 290 This is as much to sayn as it was night. **1587** GOLDING *De Mornay* viii. 98 Is it not asmuch to say, as that the example of the Arke had imboldened them to venture vpon the Sea? **1593** SHAKES. *2 Hen. VI* II. i. 15 *Glost.* My Lord, 'tis but a base ignoble minde, That mounts no higher then a Bird can sore. *Card.* I thought as much, hee would be aboue the Clouds. **1615** BEDWELL tr. *Moham. Imp.* II. §65, I have heard as much, and all thou hast said is true. **1778** F. BURNEY *Evelina* I. xxiv. 150 'Only see, here's Miss!' cried the brother. 'Well, I declare I thought as much!' **1873** BLACK *Pr. Thule* xxi. 341 The old woman apparently anticipated as much.

2. ***as well*** (beside its obvious analytical import) has the senses: **a.** (with following *as*) Just as much...as; equally...with; no less... than; in the same way...as; both...and; like; in addition to, besides. **b.** (*ellipt.*) Just as much, equally, no less; also, too. **c.** (*absol.*) As well as not, as well as anything else; *hence* put deferentially for 'better,' in which sense ***as good*** is also less correctly used. ***as good as*** has also **d.** the sense of: As much (*or* as little as), what amounts in worth or practical effect to, practically.

a, b. 1483 CAXTON *G. de la Tour* E j, [Ye] haue as wel for to pay as she hath. **1484** *Churchw. Acc. Wigtoft* (Nichols 1797) 77 Of dyvers persones, alsowell of men as of women of the said towne. **1513–75** *Diurn. Occurr.* (1833) 81 Charging all our soueranes liegis, alsweill to burgh as to land. **1596** SPENSER *State Irel.* 50 They spoile aswell the subject as the enemy. **1718** *Free-thinker* No. 12. 80 They will conclude him to be a Weak Man, as well as a Bad Subject. **1853** TRENCH *Proverbs* 123 We have a right to assume this to be a voice of God as well.

c. 1523 LD. BERNERS *Froiss.* I. 754 We were as good to go towardes Flaunders as to Bologne. **1593** BILSON *Govt. Christ's Ch.* 311 Your Elders were as good spare their paines. **1768** STERNE *Sent. Journ.* (1778) II. 46 As I am at Versailles ..I might as well take a view of the town. **1773** GOLDSM. *Stoops to Conq.* II. i, You had as good not make me, I tell you. **1820** BYRON *Mar. Fal.* IV. ii. 5 It had been As well had there been time.

d. 1526 TINDALE *Heb.* xi. 12 Of one which was as good as deed. **1837** CARLYLE *Fr. Rev.* (1872) II. VI. vi. 244 Some men have heart, and some have as good as none.

3. ***as new***: of a commodity, second-hand (or shop-soiled), but offered for sale in a condition allegedly as good as new; also *attrib.* or as *adj.*, not yet soiled or impaired by use.

1925 J. A. HOLDEN *Bookman's Gloss.* 14 *As new*, a catalogue description of a volume or set approaching the condition of newness. **1956** *Bookman's Conc. Dict.* 23/2 *As new*, books in almost new condition, sometimes known as shop soiled, listed in catalogues. **1972** J. BELFRAGE in G. W. Turner *Good Austral. Eng.* vi. 115 Second-hand car dealers who..beg you to take as-new late models off their hands at absurdly low prices. **1976** *Conservation News* Sept./Oct. 8/2 We..asked whether they would pay more for the furniture if we could supply in an 'as new' condition. **1985** *N.Y. Times Mag.* 3 Mar. 22/2 *Fine* means 'virtually as new', just as a book was when taken off the press... Out of every 2,000 used books, maybe as many as 10 would be *as new.*

‖**as** (æs), *sb.* Also 7 **asse, aas.** [L.] A Roman copper coin, originally weighing twelve ounces, but reduced after the first Punic war to two ounces, during the second Punic war to one, and by the *Lex Papiria* (B.C. 191) to half an ounce.

1601 HOLLAND *Pliny* II. 463 This new brasen Asse..was stamped with a two faced Ianus. **1697** *Phil. Trans.* XIX. 517 A bit of Magnet of about the weight of an Aas. **1838** ARNOLD *Hist. Rome* I. 84 The As having been at first a full pound in weight.

†**as**, *pers. pron. Obs.* [Phonetic variant of *es, is, hes, his*: see HIS *pron.*[2]]

1. Her, it. **2.** Them.

c **1315** *Bodl. MS., Laud Misc.* 108 lf. 1 b, Ho so wole is soule sauui, He as mot alling for-leose, And who so leost is soule he as sauez, Nou maij ech man cheose. *Ibid.* lf. 3 For ȝwan heo iseoth swuch pine & wo, Heore joye and blis is wel þe more, ȝwane heo as habbuth for go.

as, occas. obs. var. of *has, hast*: see HAVE.

c **1250** *Gen. & Ex.* 1760 Qui as ðu min godes stolen?

as, obs. form of ACE *sb.*, ASS *sb.*, and ASH.

as, variant of ASK *sb. Obs.* request.

as-, *prefix*[1], assimilated form of L. *ad-* 'to, at,' used before *s-*, as in *as-sentīre, as-signāre*. Reduced in OF. to *a-*, and so originally adopted in Eng., as in *asent* (*acent*), *asygne*; but subseq. again spelt *as-* after L., as in *assent, assign*. While this restoration was taking place, *as-* was erroneously extended to several words in *a-* (before *s-*) from various sources, as *a(s)s-aumple*:—L. *exemplum*, *a(s)soil*:—L. *absolvere*. Most of these are obsolete, or have been changed back to *a-*, or further altered.

as-, *prefix*[2], AngloFr. and Eng. variant of OF. *es-*:—L. *ex-* 'out,' as in *as-cape, a(s)s-aumple, as-sart, a(s)s-ay, as-chew, as-soin, as-tonish*. In some words this form is still retained; in others it has been altered back to OF. *es-*, as in *escape, essay, eschew*, or L. *ex-*, as in *example*; in others the *a-* has been lost by aphesis, as in *scape, sample.*

†**a'sad**, *ppl. a. Obs.* [f. A- *pref.* 1 or 6 + OE. *sadian*: see SAD; cf. MHG. *ersaten*, mod.G. *ersätten.*] Satisfied, sated; *hence*, tired.

c **1306** *Pol. Songs* 212 Selde wes he glad That never nes asad Of nythe and of onde. *c* **1320** *Maximon* in *Rel. Ant.* I. 122, I dude as hue me bad, Of me hue is asad.

‖**asafœtida** (æsəˈfɛtɪdə). Forms: 4–9 **asa-**, 6–9 **assafetida, assafœtida**, 7– **asafœtida**; also 5 **asafetyday**, 6 **azafedida, assi-**, 7 **assefœtida, assaffetteda.** [med.L.: *asa*, latinized form of Pers. *azā* mastic + *fœtida*, fem. of *fœtidus* ill-smelling, stinking.] A concreted resinous gum, with a strong alliaceous odour, procured in Central Asia from the *Narthex asafœtida* and allied umbelliferous plants; used in medicine as an antispasmodic, and as a flavouring in made dishes.

1398 TREVISA *Barth. De P.R.* XIX. xl. (1495) 884 Some stynkynge thynges ben put in medycynes, as.. Brymstoon and Asafetida. *a* **1500** *MS. Sloan* No. 4. 83 in *N. & Q.* III. VI. 4/2 Take ij penyworth of Asafetyday. **1502** ARNOLD *Chron.* (1811) 234 Azafedida at xvid. **1598** E. GILPIN *Skial.* (1878) 27 Thow'lt doome them to th' Apotheta, To wrap Sope in, and Assifœtida. **1692** RAY *Disc.* iv. (1721) 52 A Lump of Asafœtida. **1762** GOLDSM. *Cit. World* xcvii, I am for sauce strong with assafœtida, or fuming with garlic. **1849** MACREADY *Remin.* II. 321 A bottle of asafœtida.. splashed my own dress, smelling of course most horribly.

b. The plant that produces this gum.

1607 TOPSELL *Four-f. Beasts* 419 The herb called Assafœtida. **1862** BELLEW *Afghan.* 270 The assafœtida.. grows wild on the sandy and gravelly plains that form the western portion of Afghanistan.

asaȝt, obs. form of ASSAULT.

asah, pa. t. of ASYE *v. Obs.* to sink down.

asaie, asaile, asale, obs. ff. ASSAY, ASSAIL.

†**a'sake,** *v. Obs. rare.* Pa. t. asoke. [f. A- *pref.* 1 + OE. *sacan* to charge, accuse, contend with (see SAKE *v.*), or more probably for earlier ATSAKE, q.v.] To deny, refuse, renounce.

1250 LAY. 6100 Bote þat Dense men his riht asoken [**1205** dunrih at-soken]. *a* **1300** *K. Horn* 65 Bute hi here laȝe asoke.

a-sale (ə'seɪl), *advb. phr.* [A *prep.*[1] + SALE.] On sale, for sale.

1553 BALE tr. *Gardiner's Obed.* G ij, He setteth them asale ..in an open place. **1577** HELLOWES *Gueuara's Epist.* 280 The first that set Physick asale.

‖**asarabacca** (ˌæsərə'bækə). *Herb.* Also 7 assaraback, assarabecca. [f. L. *asarum*, a. Gr. ἄσαρον name of the same plant + *bacca* berry.] The plant *Asarum Europæum*, sometimes called Hazelwort, used formerly as a purgative and emetic, and still as an ingredient of cephalic snuff.

1551 TURNER *Herbal* I. (1568) 48 Of Follfoote or Asarabacca. **1607** TOPSELL *Four-f. Beasts* 189 Goats.. love ..assaraback. **1621** BURTON *Anat. Mel.* II. iv. II. i, [Laurel] and asarabecca.. are two known vomits. **1741** *Compl. Fam.-Piece* I. i. 9 Such Things as cause Sneezing, as.. the Leaves of Assarabacca powder'd. **1866** *Treas. Bot.* 98 Asarabacca.. is said to be found wild in Westmoreland.

asarin ('æsərɪn). *Chem.* [f. L. *asar-um* (see prec.) + -IN.] A crystallizable, aromatic, camphorlike substance obtained from the root of asarabacca; also called *Camphor of Asarum*, and **asarone** ('æsərəʊn).

1834 *Penny Cycl.* II. 435/1 A camphor-like principle.. called asarin. **1863** WATTS *Dict. Chem.* I. 414 Asarin or Asarone.. Nitric acid converts asarone into oxalic acid.

asarmes! as armes! *Obs.* = 'To arms!' See ARM *sb.*[2] 4 a.

asault, asaut, asawte, earlier ff. ASSAULT.

†**a'saumple.** *Obs.* [a. OF. *assample*, var. *essample* (mod. *exemple*): see A- *pref.* 9.] = EXAMPLE.

c **1230** *Ancr. R.* 284 þenc of þis asaumple.

asay(e, asayl, earlier forms of ASSAY, ASSAIL.

asbest, archaic form of ASBESTOS.

asbestic (æz'bɛstɪk), *a.* [f. Gr. ἄσβεστ-ος (see below) + -IC.] Of the nature of asbestos.

1845 FORD *Handbk. Spain* II. 801 But an asbestic antiquarian may hire horses.. and ride across.

asbestiform (æz'bɛstɪfɔːm), *a.* [f. L. *asbestus* (see below) + -(I)FORM.] Having the form or appearance of asbestos.

1799 KIRWAN *Geol. Ess.* 205 Asbestiform steatite. **1804** *Edin. Rev.* III. 307 To divide it [actinolite] into the asbestiform, the common, and the glassy. **1866** KING & ROWNEY in *Q. Jrnl. Geol. Soc.* XXII. I. 187 *note*, Aragonite occurs.. asbestiform, as satin spar.

asbestine (æz'bɛstɪn), *a.* Also 7 -in. [ad. L. *asbestinus*, a. Gr. ἀσβέστινος, sb. f. ἄσβεστος: see -INE.] Of, pertaining to, or having the properties of, asbestos; not liable to take fire, incombustible.

1627 FELTHAM *Resolves* II. lvii. (1677) 278 A good man like an Asbestine Garment.. when foul, is clensed by burning. **1665** *Phil. Trans.* I. 116 An Asbestin Paper, that shall last perpetually. **1836-9** TODD *Cycl. Anat. & Phys.* II. 38/2 With a fine silky or asbestine lustre.

b. *fig.*

1828 LANDOR *Imag. Conv.* (1846) I. 204 The asbestine quality of my mind. **1855** BAILEY *Mystic, etc.* 134 They, their asbestine expurgation passed.. Thrice recreate, shall rise.

†**as'bestinite.** *Min. Obs.* A variety of amphibole.

1796 KIRWAN *Min.* I. 165 Asbestinite.. Lustre, silky.

asbestoid (æz'bɛstɔɪd), *a.* and *sb.* [f. Gr. ἄσβεστ-ος + -OID.] **A.** *adj.* Resembling asbestos. **B.** *sb. Min.* A fibrous variety of iron-manganese amphibole, also called Byssolite.

1796 KIRWAN *Min.* I. 166 Common Asbestoid. Colour, olive or leek green. *Ibid.* 167 Metalliform Asbestoid. Colour, grey.

asbe'stoidal, *a.* [f. prec. + -AL[1].] = prec. adj.

1852 T. ROSS tr. *Humboldt's Trav.* I. ii. 101 The fibres of the pumice-stone of the Peak are.. asbestoidal, like fibrous glass-gall.

asbestos (æz'bɛstəs, -ɒs). Forms: α. 4-8 **asbeston, abeston,** 4-5 **abiston,** 4-7 **albeston(e;** β. 6 **absistos,** 7 **asphestus,** 7-9 **asbestos, asbestus;** γ. 8 **abestos, -istos;** δ. 7 **abbest,** 7- **asbest.** [The mod. form is a. L. *asbestos* (mod.L. *asbestus*), a. Gr. ἄσβεστος, prop. adj. 'inextinguishable, unquenchable,' f. ἀ not + σβεστ-ός, f. σβεν-νύ-ναι to quench. OF. had also, adopted from L., *asbestos*, later *abestos*, whence an Eng. form *abestos*; but the common OF. form was a. L. acc. *asbeston*, phonetically changed to *abeston*, and (by confusion with *albus* white) *albeston*; hence the earlier Eng. forms *asbeston, abeston, abiston, albeston*, and (by assimilation to *stone*) *albestone*. Mod.Fr. is *asbeste*, formerly also *abeste*, whence Eng. *abest, abbest, asbest*. The current form is *asbestos*; *as'best*, *'asbest* remain in poetry.]

As a sb. *asbestos* was applied by Dioscorides to *quicklime* ('unslaked'). Erroneously applied by Pliny to an incombustible fibre, which he believed to be vegetable, but which was really the *amiantos* of the Greeks. Since the identification of this, *asbestos* has been a more popular synonymn for *amiantus* or *amiant*.

†**1.** 'The unquenchable stone'; a fabulous stone, the heat of which, when once kindled, was alleged to be unquenchable. (A distorted reference to the phenomena observed in pouring cold water on quick lime.) *Obs.*

1387 TREVISA *Higden* (Rolls Ser.) 187 Asbeston þat wil neuere quenche, be it ones i-tend. **1398** —— *Barth. De P.R.* XVI. xi. (1495) 558 Of albestone.. was made a candyll sticke on whiche was a lantern so brennynge that it myght not be quenched wyth tempeste nother with reyne. **1567** MAPLET *Gr. Forest* 2 Albeston is a stone of Archadie. *Ibid.* 2 b, The precious stone Absistos.. being once heate, keepeth hote seauen whole dayes. **1610** GWILLIM *Heraldry* IV. ix. (1660) 307 A certain Kind of Stone that is found in Arcadia.. called Asphestus. **1627** H. BURTON *Bait. Pope's Bull* 63 The stone Asbestos.. once inflamed, cannot be quenched againe. **1750** *Leonardus's Mirr. Stones* 70 Abeston or Abestus.. from its being inextinguishable.

†**2.** An alleged kind of incombustible flax. *Obs.*

(An erroneous notion of the mineral substance in 3.)

a **1661** HOLYDAY *Juvenal* 207 A sheet made of a kind of flax, call'd asbestinum, and asbeston.. of that nature, that it is not consum'd, but only cleans'd, by the fire. **1734** tr. *Rollin's Anc. Hist.*, Pliny gives the first place to the asbeston, the incombustible flax.

3. A mineral of fibrous texture, capable of being woven into an incombustible fabric; AMIANT or AMIANTUS. In *Min.* applied more widely than *Amiantus*, to all fibrous varieties of Hornblende or Amphibole, and of Pyroxene; *Amiantus* being specifically the finest Hornblende Asbestos, distinguished by its long silky fibres, usually pearly white.

1607 TOPSELL *Serpents* 749 This kinde of web rather cometh of a kinde of flax that Pliny writeth of, or rather of the Amiantus-stone, called the Asbest, which.. being cast into a fire, seems to be forthwith all in a flame, but being taken out again, it shineth the more gloriously. **1609** HEYWOOD *Bryt. Troy* I. lxviii, An abbest stone into the bole was brayed. **1667** *Phil. Trans.* II. 486 Of Asbestus, that can be drawn and spun. **1783** WEDGEWOOD *ibid.* LXXIII. 286 Filaments.. of asbestos, which suffer no change in a moderate red heat. *c* **1815** SOUTHEY *Yng. Dragon* I. Wks. VI. 263 With amianth he lined the nest, And incombustible asbest. **1878** T. BRYANT *Pract. Surg.* I. 130 Nitric acid applied on lint or asbestos. **1879** RUTLEY *Stud. Rocks* x. 131 Asbestus or amianthus is a fibrous variety of pyroxene, occurring in white silky fibres.

4. *fig.*

1831 CARLYLE *Misc.* (1857) II. 337 Woe to him whose Edifice is not built of true Asbest. **1835** GRESWELL *Exp. Parables* V. II. 414 Religion's holy lamp: Unspent to burn, with sacred asbest fed.

5. *attrib.* (lit. and fig.) and *Comb.*: **asbestos cement,** a mixture of asbestos and cement moulded into sheets, pipes, etc., and used as a building and insulating material; **asbestos cloth,** a cloth woven from asbestos fibres; **asbestos curtain,** (in a theatre) a safety curtain made of asbestos and other fire-proof material.

1599 GREENE *Alphonsus* (1861) 232 My mind is like to the asbeston-stone. **1762** G. GORDON *Let.* 21 June in *N. & Q.* (1906) 10th Ser. V. 208/1 Manner of making asbestos paper. *c* **1795** SOUTHEY *Love Eleg.* ii. Wks. II. 123 Fly, Salamanders, on Asbestos' wings, To wanton in my Delia's fiery glance. **1857** R. HUNT *Guide Mus. Pract. Geol.* 242 Asbestus [ed. 2, **1859**, asbestos] cloth.. may be exposed to the fire without being consumed. **1861** SALA *Tw. round Clock* 83 Asbestos stoves, gas cooking ranges. **1890** R. H. JONES *Asbestos* viii. 140 Asbestos cement is also very largely used for covering boilers, steam-pipes, hot-blast furnaces, and stills. *Ibid.* ix. 153 M. Henry Irving.. laid special stress on the necessity of shutting off the stage from the auditorium by means of an asbestos curtain. **1920** *Blackw. Mag.* Mar. 336/2 The great asbestos-lagged exhaust from the oil-engines. **1933** *Archit. Rev.* LXXIV. facing p. 47 (*caption*) The variety of colour in the different plywood, plaster board and asbestos cement coverings placed on the steel pavilions. **1944** *Coast to Coast 1943* 165 The walls were asbestos-lined. **1964** N. FREELING *Double-Barrel* iii. 99 She .. moved the asbestos mats.. and clanked the lid back on the pot.

asbestosis (æzbɛ'stəʊsɪs). *Path.* [mod.L., f. ASBESTOS + -OSIS.] A disease of the lungs caused by inhaling particles of asbestos. Also ***pulmonary asbestosis.***

1927 W. E. COOKE in *Brit. Med. Jrnl.* 3 Dec. 1024/1 (*title*) Pulmonary Asbestosis. *Ibid.* 1027/2 From what I have seen clinically of pulmonary asbestosis it resembles silicosis of the lungs in the marked shortness of breath on slight exertion. **1930** *Lancet* 1 Mar. 445/2 Although asbestos and asbestos products have been used in industry for a long time, it is only during the last few years that pulmonary asbestosis has been recognised as a serious industrial disease.

asbestous (æz'bɛstəs), *a.* [f. L. *asbest-us* (see ASBESTOS) + -OUS.] Asbestiform, asbestine.

1868 CHAMBERS *Encycl.* s.v., Minerals which resemble Asbestus in their fibrous character are.. called asbestous.

asbolan, asbolite ('æzbəʊlæn, -aɪt). *Min.* [f. Gr. ἀσβόλ-η soot: see -AN[2] 2, -ITE.] A variety of wad containing oxide of cobalt; also called *Earthy Cobalt.*

1837-68 DANA *Min.* 181. **1881** *Nature* XXV. 45 The earthy cobalt ore (asbolite).

asboline ('æzbəʊlaɪn). *Chem.* [f. as prec. + -INE[4].] An acrid volatile oil obtained from soot.

1863 WATTS *Dict. Chem.* I. 416 Asboline dissolves in nitric acid, yielding picric and oxalic acids.

ascan ('æskən), *a. Bot.* [f. mod.L. *ascus*, Gr. ἀσκός, bag.] Of or belonging to an *ascus*.

1876 tr. *Wagner's Pathol.* 87 Basidian and ascan spores.

ascan, obs. pl. form of ASH *sb.*[1].

ascance(s, -anche, -aunce, obs. ff. ASKANCE.

†**a'scape,** *v. Obs.* Also askape. [The common form of ESCAPE in ME., found down to 1523, due to phonetic levelling of proclitic *ĕ-* and *ă-*: see A- *pref.* 9. AFr. itself had occas. *ascaper* for *escaper*. Already in 13th c. it was aphetized to SCAPE, in common use in all ages, and still a poetic form, though now written as a conscious contraction *'scape* for *e)scape*. Cf. also ACHAPE, ATSCAPE, OFSCAPE, ASCHAPE.] = Escape.

1250 LAY. 1611 And vnneþe ascapede. **1330** R. BRUNNE *Chron.* 23 Non of þe Danes askaped. **1523** LD. BERNERS *Froiss.* I. xxii. 31 Ther ascaped neuer a person.

ascariasis (ˌæskə'raɪəsɪs). *Path.* [f. Gr. ἀσκαρίς intestinal worm + -ASIS.] Infestation, esp. of the gastro-intestinal canal, with *Ascaris lumbricoides*; the disease resulting from this infestation.

1888 in F. P. FOSTER *Med. Dict.* I. 448/2. **1904** *Brit. Med. Jrnl.* 29 Oct. 1170/2 (*title*) A case of ascariasis with 'enteric' temperatures. **1923** *Nature* 19 May 683/2 An epidemic of ascariasis on a skunk-farm.

‖**Ascarides** (ə'skærɪdiːz), *sb. pl. Zool.* [mod.L., a. Gr. ἀσκαρίδες, pl. of ἀσκαρίς. An anglicized sing. *ascarid* has occas. been used.] A genus of intestinal worms; thread-worms.

1398 TREVISA *Barth. De P.R.* VII. xlix. (1495) 262 Wormes that ben nourisshed and fedde in the nether grete bowelles hyghte Ascarides. **1655** CULPEPPER *Riverius* X. ix. 307 Ascarides, or little Worms like smal thrids. **1693** URQUHART *Rabelais* III. xxii, The ascarids and the lumbricks. **1785** BURKE *Nabob of Arcot's Debts* Wks. IV. 282 The whole brood of creeping ascarides.. which.. eat up the bowels of India. **1875** B. RICHARDSON *Dis. Mod. Life* 31 Those small wire-like worms called ascarides in the lower part of the alimentary canal.

ascaridol(e (ə'skærɪdɒl). *Chem.* [f. *ascarid* (see prec.) + -OL 3.] A terpene peroxide, $C_{10}H_{16}O_2$, the active principle of chenopodium oil, used in the treatment of hook-worm disease.

1908 *Schimmel & Co. Semi-Ann. Rep.* Apr. 114 The body, which we will call ascaridol on account of its pronounced action against ascarides, absorbs.. 2 atoms bromine. **1911** *Jrnl. Amer. Chem. Soc.* XXXIII. 1405 Schimmel & Co., in 1908, reported an extensive investigation of the oil... They separated a liquid substance, designated by them 'ascaridol'. .. Ascaridole afforded on analysis the formula $C_{10}H_{16}O_2$. **1947** *Lancet* 7 June 799/1 Ascaridole has undoubtedly been responsible for occasional fatalities, but.. none of the intestinal anthelmintics is free from such a risk.

ascaris ('æskərɪs). *Zool.* [mod.L (Linnæus, 1758), ad. Gr. ἀσκαρίς intestinal worm: see ASCARIDES.] The sing. of ASCARIDES; a parasitic nematode worm belonging to the genus so called.

1797 GMELIN tr. *Linnaeus' Syst. Nat. Hist.* XIII. 486 Intestinal Worms.. within other animals. Ascaris—Body round, tapering each way; head with three vesicles. **1807** MORRIS & KENDRICK *Edin. Med. Dict.* s.v. *Ascaris*, The body of the ascaris is cylindrical, filiform, and tapers at both ends. **1927** HALDANE & HUXLEY *Animal Biol.* ii. 59 The number of chromosomes is always the same for a given race of animals or plants.. in the Mexican salamander 28; in Ascaris 4. **1962** *Lancet* 29 Dec. 1360/2 Only 17% were found to be free from intestinal parasites, of which trichuris (in 72%) and ascaris (23%) were common.

asce-, words so beginning in OE. were regularly spelt ASCHE- in ME. and ASHE- (rarely ASKE-) in mod.E.: see the later spellings.

ascease, Obs. form of ASSESS.

† **a'scence**. *Obs.* [a. OF. *ascense*:—late L. *ascensa*, sb. formed on fem. sing. of *ascensus*, pa. pple. of *ascendĕre* to ASCEND; analogous to sbs. in *-āta*, *-ada*, F. *-ée*. Cf. *defence*.] Earlier equivalent of ASCENT, ASCENSION.

c **1450** HENRYSON *Mor. Fables* 86 Then may the storme on no way make ascence. **1481** EARL WORC. *Tulle on Friendship* (Caxton) A iv/3 To whom shold we deme that a liter ascence was graunted..than unto Scipio? **1578** *Psalm* li. in *Scot. Poems 16th c.* (1801) II. 114 This isope is humilitie Right law intill ascence.

ascend (ə'sɛnd), *v.* Also 4–5 **assende**, 4–6 **ascende**, 7 **adsend**. *Pa. pple.* 6 **ascend**. [ad. L. *ascend-ĕre*, *adscend-ĕre*, f. *ad-* to + *-scendĕre* = *scandĕre* to climb. The perfect tenses were sometimes conjugated with *be*.]

I. Literal senses.

1. *intr.* (occas. emphasized by a redundant *up*) To go or come up, originally by a gradual motion, to a relatively higher position; **a.** of voluntary agents: To climb up, travel up, walk up; to soar, mount.

1382 WYCLIF *1 Sam.* i. 22 Helchana stiede up..for to offre to the Lord..his vowe. And Anna assendide not. —— *2 Macc.* ii. 4 The hill in whiche Moyses ascendide. *c* **1440** *Gesta Rom.* II. xx. 339 Lette downe now the corde to me, that I may assende. **1526** TINDALE *John* vi. 62 Yf ye shall se the sonne of man ascende vp where he was before. **1601** SHAKS. *Jul. C.* III. ii. 21 The Noble Brutus is ascended: Silence. **1667** MILTON *P.L.* v. 198 Ye Birds, That singing up to Heaven gate ascend. **1782** PRIESTLEY *Nat. & Rev. Relig.* II. 5 Apollonius is..said to have ascended into heaven. **1864** TENNYSON *En. Ard.* 181 He..Ascending tired, heavily slept till morn.

b. of inanimate things: To rise, be raised, move to a higher level.

1514 BARCLAY *Cyt. & Uplondyshman* 44 When he would eate, the apples do ascende. **1605** BACON *Adv. Learn.* I. iv. §12 Water will not ascend higher than the level of the first springhead from whence it descendeth. **1665–6** *Phil. Trans.* I. 184 Subterraneal Steams..adscending into the Air. **1795** SOUTHEY *Joan of Arc* v. 42 Ascending slow..the curling smoke Melts in the impurpled air. **1859** TENNYSON *Enid* 1540 A cloud..With the dawn ascending.

c. of sounds: To rise in the air, or so as to be heard aloud.

1667 MILTON *P.L.* I. 496 The noise Of riot ascends above their loftiest Towrs. **1728** DE FOE *Syst. Magic* I. iii. 81 Voice always ascends, the vibration moving most naturally upwards. **1864** SKEAT *Uhland's Poems* 187 A roar of shouts ascends.

2. Of planetary bodies, signs of the zodiac, etc.: **a.** *spec.* To come above the horizon. **b.** *gen.* To move towards the zenith.

c **1391** CHAUCER *Astrol.* II. §3 To knowe..the degree of any signe that assendith on the est Orisonte. *Ibid.* II. §40 Iuppiter ascendit with 14 degrees of pisces. **1477** EARL RIVERS (Caxton) *Dictes* 10 Whan the planetes..ascended and whan they discended. **1557** SURREY *Æneid* IV. (R.) To morne, as soon as Titan shall ascend. **1594** BLUNDEVIL *Exerc.* III. I. xxxii. 342 Those Signes that do ascend rightly, do descend obliquely. **1695** CONGREVE *Love for Love* II. i, I was born, Sir, when the Crab was ascending. **1735** POPE *Mor. Ess.* II. 254 All mild ascends the Moon's more sober light. **1819** J. WILSON *Dict. Astrol.* 297 Less of the equator ascends with northern signs.

3. To rise by process of growth or construction; to be raised or reared, to erect itself. Only *poet.* Cf. ARISE *v.* 16.

1667 MILTON *P.L.* I. 722 Th' ascending pile Stood fixt her stately highth. **1731** POPE *Mor. Ess.* IV. 198 Bid Temples, worthier of the God, ascend. **1765** GOLDSM. *Trav.* 105 Far to the right, where Apennine ascends. **1809** J. BARLOW *Columbiad* I. 325 Exalt your heads ye oaks, ye pines ascend.

4. To slope upwards, lie along an ascending slope.

1832 BRANNON *Guide I. Wight* (1853) 96 This pretty village..is situated about a mile west of the town, ascending a hill. *Mod.* The path ascends by the Red Tarn.

5. *trans.* To go up by degrees to a relatively higher position upon; to walk up, climb, mount; *hence*, to go up to the top of, reach the summit of. ***to ascend*** a river: to go along it towards its source.

c **1400** *Epiph.* (Turnb. 1843) 103 Wherefor of sort the hyll thei ben ascendyd. **1513** DOUGLAS *Æneis* I. vii. 2 Quhill ascend ar thai The hill. **1718** LADY MONTAGUE *Lett.* II. lii. 72 We began to ascend mount Cenis. **1776** GIBBON *Decl. & F.* xiii, Their galleys ascended the river. **1860** TYNDALL *Glac.* I. §2. 17 Next day I ascended the valley of Hasli. **1851** DIXON *Will. Penn* xvii. 144 Ascending the Delaware.

6. To go up into or get up on (a place or object at a higher level); to mount. *Obs.* exc. *poet.*, and in the phrase, now hardly more than *fig.*, 'To ascend the throne,' the earliest cited instance of which shows the transition to this sense from the prec.

1593 SHAKS. *Rich. II*, v. i. 56 Thou Ladder wherewithall The mounting Bullingbroke ascends my Throne. **1598** —— *Merry W.* III. iii. 173 Ascend my Chambers. **1616** R. C. *Times' Whis.* III. 1017 When as thou wilt thy stately horse ascend. **1658** ROWLAND *Mouffet's Theat. Ins.* 932 When the male ascends the female. **1667** MILTON *P.L.* VI. 710 Ascend my Chariot. **1771** *Junius Lett.* xlix. 255 The moment he ascended the throne. **1861** HOOK *Lives Abps.* I. vii. 374 Edwy was permitted to ascend the throne.

II. Transferred and figurative senses.

7. *intr.* To proceed from the inferior to the superior; to rise in thought, degree of characteristic quality, social station, etc.

1549 *Compl. Scotl.* i. 20 Childir..incressis quhil thai be ascendit to the perfyit stryntht of men. **1646** SIR T. BROWNE *Pseud. Ep.* II. i. 53 Painted glasse of a sanguine red will not ascend in powder above a murrey. **1667** MILTON *P.L.* v. 512 In contemplation of created things By steps we may ascend to God. **1751** JORTIN *Serm.* (1771) VI. iv. 67 A rash desire to ascend to a rank—for which God's providence has not designed us. **1850** MCCOSH *Div. Govt.* I. ii. (1874) 27 We shall ascend..beyond laws to a lawgiver.

8. Of or in respect of sounds: To rise in pitch.

1597 MORLEY *Introd. Mus.* 81 Vnpossible to ascende..in continuall deduction without a discord. **1674** PLAYFORD *Skill of Mus.* III. 5 If the Bass shall ascend.

9. To go back in time (i.e. up the 'stream of time'), or in order of genealogical succession.

1574 tr. *Littleton's Tenures* 2 b, Inheritance may lineally descend, but not lyneally ascend. *a* **1800** COWPER tr. *Grk. Verses on Pedigree*, [They] from age to age Ascending, triumph their illustrious race. **1875** MAINE *Hist. Inst.* xi. 311 The eldest male of the eldest ascending line, the father, grandfather.

† **10.** *intr.* Of winds, etc.: To 'rise.' *Obs. rare.*

1715 POPE *Iliad* IV. 478 As when the winds, ascending by degrees, First move the whitening surface of the seas.

† **11.** *causal.* To raise in estimation, exalt. *Obs.*

1628 FELTHAM *Resolves* (1677) 33 They set him almost on the throne of a Deity; ascend him to an unmovedness.

ascendable (ə'sɛndəb(ə)l), *a. rare.* [f. prec. + -ABLE; cf. ASCENDIBLE.] That may be ascended.

1755 in JOHNSON. **1882** MAYNE REID in *N.Y. Tribune* 24 May, The highest ascendable point of the trunk.

ascendance, -ence (ə'sɛndəns). [f. ASCENDANT: see -ANCE.] *prop.* The action of ascending; but used as = ASCENDANCY.

1742 FIELDING *Jos. Andrews* ix. (L.) If fear had too much ascendance on the mind. **1824** BYRON *Juan* XVI. lxxvi, Common soldiers..Have..ascendance O'er the irregulars. **1830** HEIDIGER *Didoniad* III. 90 An advocate for Anglican ascendence.

ascendancy, -ency (ə'sɛndənsɪ). [f. ASCENDANT: see -ANCY.] The state or quality of being in the ascendant; paramount influence, dominant control, domination, sway. Const. *over.*

(Of 40 authors examined, *-ancy* occurred in 4 18th c. and 15 19th c. writers, including Watts, Lyell, Arnold, Dickens, Mill, Lecky, Seeley, Earle, Trollope; *-ency* in 2 18th c. and 14 19th c. writers, including Burke, Hallam, Lingard, Thirlwall, Alison, Macaulay, Froude, Freeman; *both* occurred in editions of 5 writers.)

1712 POLESWORTH *Hist. John Bull* in Arbuthnot *Misc. Wks.* 1751 II. xxii. 93 She had no small Ascendancy over John. *c* **1796** BURKE *Let. R. Burke* Wks. IX. 425 The poor word, *ascendency*..is now employed to cover to the world the most rigid, and perhaps not the most wise, of all plans of policy. In plain old English, as they apply it, it signifies 'pride and dominion' on the one part of the relation, and on the other, 'subserviency and contempt'—and it signifies nothing else. **1838–43** ARNOLD *Hist. Rome* III. xliii. 132 Overpowered by the ascendancy of Hannibal's character. **1849** MACAULAY *Hist. Eng.* I. 548 That he would not patiently submit to the ascendency of France.

ascendant, -ent (ə'sɛndənt), *a.* and *sb.* Also 4 **ass-**. [a. OF. *ascendant*, ad. L. *ascendent-em*, pr. pple. of *ascendĕre*: see ASCEND and -ANT. The astrological use is the earliest in Eng., and the sb. was adopted before the adj.

In the spelling, *-ant* is the prevalent, and in senses B 3–8 almost the only form; but *-ent* was formerly prevalent in senses A, and B 1, 2.]

A. *adj.*

1. *gen.* Rising; moving or tending upwards.

1591 GREENE *Maidens Dr.* liv, As thus ascendant fair Astræa flew. **1605** BACON *Adv. L.* II. vii. §1 A double scale or ladder, ascendent and descendent. **1829** SOUTHEY *Yng. Dragon* IV. Wks. VI. 279 Distended like a ball..The body mounts ascendant. **1851** RUSKIN *Stones Ven.* I. xxvii. §15 Rooted and ascendant strength like that of foliage.

b. *spec.* in *Phys.* and *Bot.* = ASCENDING *ppl. a.* 3.

1611 COTGR., *Artere sousclaviere*, Th' ascendent branch of the great arterie. **1753** CHAMBERS *Cycl. Supp.* s.v. *Stalk*, In the branched stalk, if the branches rise erect, it is expressed by ascendant.

2. = ASCENDING *ppl. a.* 5. ? *Obs.*

c **1555** HARPSFIELD *Divorce Hen. VIII* (1878) 269 The Levitt. prohibition doth not exceed the second degree..in the line ascendent or descendent.

3. *Astr.* **a.** in gen. sense: Rising towards the zenith. **b.** *spec.* in *Astrol.* Just above the eastern horizon: see B 1.

1594 BLUNDEVIL *Exerc.* III. I. xi. 296 Ascendent are those [signs] that rise from the South towards our Zenith. **1646** SIR T. BROWNE *Pseud. Ep.* 227 The Starres of Andromeda ..are about that time ascendent. **1735** POPE *Mor. Ess.* II. 285 Ascendant Phœbus watch'd that hour with care. **1860** R. VAUGHAN *Mystics* II. VIII. iv. 54 That of which ascendant Venus is the pure patroness—Rapturous Love.

4. *fig.* Superior; predominant.

? **1634** M. SANDYS *Essays* 150 (T.) Thus I pass from the descendent to the ascendent duty. **1806** A. KNOX *Rem.* I. 31 To quicken, exalt, and make ascendant all that is rational and noble in us. **1850** GROTE *Greece* II. lv. VII. 53 An ascendent position in public life.

B. *sb.* [the adj. used *absol.*]

I. In senses belonging to, or derived from, astrology.

1. *Astrol.* The point of the ecliptic, or degree of the zodiac, which at any moment (esp. *e.g.* at the birth of a child) is just rising above the eastern horizon; the horoscope. ***the house of the ascendant*** includes 5 degrees of the zodiac above this point and 25 below it. ***the lord of the ascendant***: any planet within the house of the ascendant. (The ascendant and its lord were supposed to exercise a special influence upon the life of a child then born.)

c **1386** CHAUCER *Wife's Prol.* 613 Min ascendent was Taur, and Mars therinne (cf. *Man of Lawes T.* 204). **1391** —— *Astrol.* II. §4 The assendent, & eke the lord of the assendent, may be shapen for to be fortunat or infortunat, as thus, a fortunat assendent clepen they whan þat no wykkid planete, as Saturne or Mars, or elles the tail of the dragoun, is in þe hows of the assendent. **1587** GOLDING *De Mornay* xxxiii. 533 They say that Jesus in his natiuitie, had for his ascendent, the signe of Virgo. **1643** SIR T. BROWNE *Relig. Med.* 179 At my Nativity my Ascendant was the earthly sign of Scorpio. **1837** WHEWELL *Hist. Induct. Sc.* (1857) I. 229 The most important part of the sky in the astrologer's consideration, was that sign of the Zodiac which rose at the moment of the child's birth; this was, properly speaking, the horoscope, the ascendant, or the first house.

2. *fig.* (with distinct reference to astrological use.)

1654 COKAINE *Loredano's Dianea* Author's Ep., Covetous his Labours should visit the Light under such an Ascendant of Felicity. **1824** W. IRVING *T. Trav.* I. 192 Here he was lord of the ascendant..the dominant genius. **1867** FREEMAN *Norm. Conq.* (1876) I. vi. 500 The star of Harold was fairly in the ascendant.

3. *gen.* Superiority, supremacy; = ASCENDANCY.

1596 DRAYTON *Legends* IV. 399 To my ascendant hasting then to clime. *c* **1630** DRUMM. OF HAWTH. *Wks.* (1711) 46/1 Who in wit's ascendant far Did years and sex transcend. **1702** *Eng. Theophr.* 359 The ascendant is a certain unaccountable force of superiority that springs from the Nature, and not the artifice nor affectation of him that has it. **1769** ROBERTSON *Chas. V*, III. VIII. 114 That ascendant which he had acquired in all the councils of the commonwealth. **1863** KINGLAKE *Crimea* (1877) I. iv. 67 A deterioration..which shook the ascendant of his better nature.

b. Const. *over* (*of*, *upon*, obs.).

1672 MARVELL *Reh. Transp.* I. 302 Having gained this Ascendent upon him. **1684** LUTTRELL *Brief Rel.* I. 316 Haveing gott the ascendant of him. **1752** CHESTERF. *Lett.* 277 III. 269 Strong minds have undoubtedly an ascendant over weak ones. **1839** KEIGHTLEY *Hist. Eng.* II. 81 Giving their spiritual guides an entire ascendant over them.

c. in the ascendant: supreme, dominant. (Sometimes erroneously: Rising, ascending.)

a **1698** TEMPLE (J.) Sciences that were then in their highest ascendant. **1844** DISRAELI *Coningsby* IV. v. 129 The hopes of the Conservative party were again in the ascendant. **1869** SEELEY *Ess. & Lect.* iv. 111 When..demure conventionalism and sentimentalism are in the ascendant.

4. One who favours a policy of (national or ecclesiastical) ascendancy. ? *Obs. rare.*

1795 BURKE *2nd Let. Langrishe* Wks. IX. 416 There is not a single particular in the Francis-street declamations, which has not..been taught by the jealous ascendants.

II. In general senses.

† **5.** An upward slope, an acclivity, a rise; a flight of steps. Also *fig. Obs.*

1548 HALL *Chron. Hen. VIII*, an. 31 (R.), The ascendant of the hyll. *a* **1619** FOTHERBY *Atheom.* II. i. §4 And climbe vp vnto God..by an Ascendent, consisting of fiue steppes. **1641** MILTON *Ch. Govt.* Wks. 1738 I. 53 A Lordly Ascendant..from Primate to Patriarch, and so to Pope.

† **6.** One who ascends or goes up. *Obs.*

1593 NASHE *Christes Teares* (1613) 31 Pryde can endure no Superiours, no equals, no ascendants. **1701** SEDLEY *Tyr. Crete* II. i, That like the ascendants To the altar, by degrees, I thus approach you.

† **7.** That which rises above its surroundings; a summit or peak; *spec.* in *Typogr.* = ASCENDER.

1650 VAUGHAN *Silex Scint.* 182 The mount whose white ascendants may Be in conjunction with true light. **1676** MOXON *Print Lett.* 6 All the Capitals are Ascendents, so called because they stand higher than the Head-line of the Short.

8. One who precedes in genealogical succession; an ancestor; a relative in the ascending line, whether lineal, as *father*, *mother*, or collateral, as *uncle*, *great-uncle*.

1604 E. G. *D'Acosta's Hist. Indies* VI. xviii. 469 Such as committed incest with ascendants or descendants in direct line were likewise punished with death. **1726** AYLIFFE *Parerg.* 32 Ascendants and Collaterals even to the tenth Degree. **1861** MAINE *Anc. Law* v. (1876) 133 Their highest living ascendant, the father, grandfather, or great-grandfather.

ascended (ə'sɛndɪd), *ppl. a.* [f. ASCEND + -ED.] That has risen or gone up.

1861 TRENCH *Sev. Ch. Asia* 26 The great ascended Bishop of the Church.

ascendental (æsɛn'dɛntəl), *a. rare.* [f. ASCENDENT + -AL[1]; cf. *transcendental*.] Of the nature of ascent; ascending.

1858 *Scot. Rev.* VI. 32 Impossible, by the ascendental method, to reach the conception of God.

ascender (ə'sɛndə(r)). [f. ASCEND *v.* + -ER[1].]

a. He who or that which ascends.

1623 BINGHAM *Xenophon* 63 Another Hill..that the night before, was by the first ascenders won from the enemies Guards. **1880** R. HOPE in *B. Googe's Pop. Kingd.* iv. 53 *marg.*, Birds are eaten, on Ascension Day, as ascenders.

b. *spec.* in *Typogr.* (see quot.)

1867 MACKELLAR *Amer. Printer* 48 Ascenders, all the capital letters, and the *b, d, f, h, i, j, k, l, t,* so called because they ascend to the top of the body of the types. A colloquial phrase for Ascending Letters.

c. In *Printing* and *Palæography*, an ascending stroke; a stroke which extends above the body of a letter.

1934 in WEBSTER. **1938** A. H. SMITH in *London Mediæval Stud.* I. 204 After *neah* there is a long ascender which may be part of *h* or *l* or *b*. **1955** C. E. WRIGHT *Bald's Leechbook* 24 The hook at the top of the ascender of *b*.

ascendible (ə'sɛndıb(ə)l), *a. rare*[−0]. [ad. L. *ascendibilis*: see ASCEND and -IBLE.] = ASCENDABLE.

1864 in WEBSTER.

ascending (ə'sɛndıŋ), *vbl. sb.* [f. ASCEND *v.* + -ING[1].] The action of the verb ASCEND; ascent, ascension. *attrib.* in ***ascending latitude***: the latitude of a planet when ascending or going northward. ***ascending node***: the point in a planet's orbit where it crosses the ecliptic in ascending.

1482 *Monk of Evesham* (1869) 108 Ther was no taryng yn her ascendyng. *a* **1619** FOTHERBY *Atheom.* II. viii. §5 The highest ascending of our contemplation. **1846** KEBLE *Lyra Innoc.* (1873) 20 Touch Me not till Mine ascending.

a'scending, *ppl. a.* [f. as prec. + -ING[2].]

1. Rising, mounting up.

1667 [see ASCEND *v.* 3]. **1715** POPE *Iliad* XVI. 436 Dark o'er the fields th' ascending vapour flies. **1878** HUXLEY *Physiogr.* 41 The uppermost portion of the ascending current.

b. *spec.* in *Typogr.*

1676 MOXON *Print Lett.* 6 The Top-line is the line that bounds the top of the Ascending Letters. **1867** [see ASCENDER.]

2. Sloping upwards; acclivitous.

1616 SURFL. & MARKH. *Countr. Farm* 5 Want of Water in high and ascending places. **1697** DRYDEN *Virg. Georg.* II. 754 Bak'd in the Sun-shine of ascending Fields. **1881** *Daily News* 31 Aug. 2/2 A handsome building..backed by ascending woods.

3. Directed upwards: applied *spec.* in *Phys.* to structures that pass, or serve as a passage, from a lower to a higher part of the body; in *Bot.* **a.** to a procumbent stem which gradually curves to an erect position; **b.** to ovules attached a little above the base of the ovary, and pointing obliquely upwards; **c.** *fig.* to development of higher forms from lower, as of petals from sepals, carpels from stamens, etc.

a **1713** CHESELDEN in Derham's *Phys.-Theol.* (1752) IV. vii. 157 The blood..brought to the heart by the ascending cava. **1854** BALFOUR *Bot.* 47 The stem is the ascending portion of the axis. **1859** TODD *Cycl. Anat. & Phys.* V. 365/2 The ascending colon lies on the right kidney. **1861** MISS PRATT *Flower. Pl.* I. 3 An ascending stem..on first emerging from the root, is horizontal, and then becomes erect. **1870** HOOKER *Stud. Flora* 113 *Dryas*..ovule 1, ascending.

4. In various transf. or fig. uses; cf. ASCEND *v.* 7, 8.

1762 KAMES *Elem. Crit.* iv. (1833) 114 An increasing series of numbers..is commonly called an ascending series. **1869** OUSELEY *Counterpoint* xiii. 72 The diminished fifth..should be prepared by a sixth, with an ascending bass.

5. Going backwards in order of genealogical succession; of or pertaining to ancestors.

1703 J. QUICK *Ser. Inquiry* 12 In the Right Line ascending and descending, there are as many Degrees as there be Generations and Persons. **1757** BURKE *Abridgm. Eng. Hist.* Wks. X. 334 The ascending collateral branch was much regarded amongst the ancient Germans. **1875** [see ASCEND *v.* 9.]

a'scendingly, *adv.* [f. prec. + -LY[2].] With ascending or upward motion.

1880 *World* 16 June, The ghost..glides ascendingly across the stage. **1882** PROCTOR in *Knowledge* II. 176 The constellation at those hours is moving ascendingly.

†**a'scensial,** *a. Obs. rare*[−1]. [irreg. f. ASCENCE + -AL[1].] Ascensional, upward.

1503 HAWES *Examp. Virtue* xii. 237 By this tyme phebus had begon His ascencyall cours.

ascension (ə'sɛnʃən). Also 4–6 **assencion, -sioun,** etc., 6–7 **ascention.** [ad. L. *ascensiōn-em*, n. of action f. *ascens-* ppl. stem of *ascendĕre*: see ASCEND and -ION[1]. Largely replaced by ASCENT, exc. in the specific senses 2, 3, which were also the earliest in English.]

1. *gen.* The action of ascending, upward movement.

1596 CHAPMAN *Iliad* I. 475 And then the ever-living gods mounted Olympus, Jove First in ascension. **1660** BOYLE *New Exper. Phys.-Mech.* xxiv. 193 In their ascension they kept an almost equal distance from each other. *a* **1711** KEN *Serm.* Wks. 1838, 131 Kept the fire always burning, always in ascension, always aspiring towards heaven. **1864** R. CHAMBERS *Bk. Days* II. 346 To attempt an ascension in such an unwieldy machine. **1881** RAYMOND *Mining Gloss.*, *Ascension-theory*, the theory that the matter filling fissure-veins was introduced in solution from below.

2. *spec.* The ascent of Jesus Christ to heaven on the fortieth day after His resurrection. Occas. used for *Ascension-day*. (The earliest use in Eng.)

c **1315** SHOREHAM 126 Fram Crystes resurreccioun, Wat cometh hys ascencion, At fourty daȝen ende. *c* **1425** WYNTOUN *Cron.* v. ii. 103 Eftyr þe Resurrectyowne of Cryst, and his Ascensyowne. **1539** TONSTALL *Serm. Palme Sund.* (1823) 17 The aungelles of heuen at his ascention gloryfied in hym the nature of man. **1667** MILTON *P.L.* x. 185 And with ascention bright, Captivity led captive. **1782** PRIESTLEY *Corrupt. Chr.* II. VIII. 134 Ascension was observed about the time of Austin.

b. ***Ascension-day***: the day on which this event took place, and on which it is annually commemorated; Holy Thursday.

1366 MAUNDEV. viii. 96 Fro that mount steighe oure Lord Iesu Crist to hevene, upon Ascenciounday. **1595** SHAKS. *John* IV. ii. 151 Ere the next Ascension day at noone. **1808** SCOTT *Marm.* II. xiii, This, on Ascension-day each year.. Must Herbert, Bruce, and Percy hear.

3. *Astr.* The rising of a celestial body; formerly, also, the increasing elevation of the sun in the heavens between the vernal equinox and summer solstice. ***right ascension*** of the sun or a star: the degree of the equinoctial or celestial equator, reckoned from the first point in Aries, which rises with it in a right sphere, or which comes with it to the meridian; the arc of the equator intercepted between this degree and the first point of Aries; celestial longitude. ***oblique ascension*** of a star: the arc of the equator intercepted between the first point of Aries and that point of the equator which rises with the sun or star in an oblique sphere.

c **1386** CHAUCER *Nonne Pr. T.* 35 He knew ech ascencion of equinoxial. **1556** RECORDE *Cast. Knowl.* 197 Ascension astronomicall is the certaine limitation of som pointe of the equinoctiall circle, which riseth iustelye with any starre. **1599** THYNNE *Animadv.* 62 The sonne was not farre from the middle of his ascentione. **1646** SIR T. BROWNE *Pseud. Ep.* 224 The cosmicall ascension of a starre we terme that, when it ariseth together with the Sun. **1796** HUTTON *Math. Dict.* I. 148 When the sun has north declination, the right ascension is greater than the oblique. **1874** MOSELEY *Astron.* ix. 43 Knowing the right ascension and declination of a star, we know its exact position in the great sphere of the heavens.

†**4.** *Alch.* Distillation, evaporation. Hence *concr.* that which arises as if from distillation, a fume.

c **1386** CHAUCER *Chan. Yem. Prol. & T.* 225 Ne eek oure spirites ascencioun. **1594** PLAT *Jewell Ho., Chim. Concl.* 6 In this rectifying by ascension you shall lose a great part of their tincture. **1610** B. JONSON *Alch.* II. iii, Two Of our inferiour workes are at fixation, A third is in ascension. **1646** SIR T. BROWNE *Pseud. Ep.* (J.) Conceiving the brain doth only suffer from vaporous ascensions from the stomach. **1817** COLERIDGE *Biog. Lit.* I. v. 102 Successive particles.. distilled, or filtrated by ascension.

†**5.** *fig.* Rise from the inferior to the superior; rise or advancement in thought or feeling, in station, dignity, or estimation; ascent. *Obs.*

1617 WITHER *Fidelia* in *Juven.* (1633) 483 And to what height Towre in my new ascension to delight? **1627** FELTHAM *Resolves* I. xxxiii. Wks. 1677, 56 To some, there is not a greater vexation, than to be advised by an Inferior. Directions are unwelcome, that come to us by ascensions. **1670** WALTON *Hooker* 39 This bishop's ascension to this place of dignity and cares. **1681** *Let.* in *Harl. Misc.* (1793) 467 To facilitate his ascension to the throne.

†**6.** A going back in the order of genealogical succession; reversion to an ancestor; ascent. *Obs.*

1574 tr. *Littleton's Tenures* 2 b, Hee commeth unto the lande by collaterall discent and not by lineall ascension. **1628** COKE *On Litt.* 11 a, Lineall ascention in the right line is prohibited.

7. Way of ascending, upward slope, ascent. *arch.*

1447 BOKENHAM *Lyvys of Seyntys* 59 Grees of marbyl.. Be whiche to the temple was the ascencyon. **1816** SOUTHEY *Poet's Pilgr.* I. viii. Wks. X. 59 Round and round The spiral steps in long ascension wound.

ascensional (ə'sɛnʃənəl), *a.* [f. prec. + -AL[1].]

1. Of or belonging to ascension. ***ascensional difference*** in *Astr.*: the difference between the right and oblique ascension of the sun or a star.

1594 BLUNDEVIL *Exerc.* III. I. xxxiv. 347 The ascentionall difference being knowne, all the oblique ascentions and descentions of the starres are easily knowne by the Tables of Directions. **1796** HUTTON *Math. Dict.* I. 148 The sun's Ascensional Difference, converted into time, shews how much he rises before or after 6 o'clock. **1834** U. K. S. *Nat. Phil.* III. *Hist. Astron.* ii. 12/1 The ascensional difference (that is, the arc measuring the increase of the day at any place).

2. a. Of or belonging to ascent; tending upwards.

1753 CHAMBERS *Cycl. Supp.* App. s.v. *Force*, Huygens [held] that bodies constantly preserve their ascensional force, that is, the product of their mass by the height to which their center of gravity can ascend. **1860** TYNDALL *Glac.* I. §20. 137 The current, however, continued ascensional. **1880** *Colliery Guard.* 5 Nov., The diffusion of gases in mines, and its relation to ascensional ventilation.

b. ***ascensional screw***: a helical propeller that gives a lifting motion to an airship or flying-machine.

1901 *Westm. Gaz.* 15 Aug. 6/1 With my ascensional screws..I am indifferent to wind, because I can rise and descend in search of a suitable belt of air. **1903** *Daily Chron.* 27 Sept. 7/4 A new flying machine... It is the invention of Mr. H. A. Chubb, and it rises by means of ascensional screws or helices.

a'scensionist. [f. as prec. + -IST.] One who makes ascents.

1863 *Fraser's Mag.* LXVIII. 668 The last lady-ascensionist who has scaled the white shoulders of Mont Blanc. **1882** *Daily Tel.* 25 Apr. (Advt.) Ethardo, the greatest ascensionist living.

Ascensiontide (ə'sɛnʃəntaıd). [f. ASCENSION 2 + TIDE *sb.* 6.] The period of ten days from Ascension Day to Whitsun Eve. Also *attrib.*

1871 (*title*) Ascensiontide. Thoughts on the Ascension Day Collect. **1898** *Westm. Gaz.* 19 May 10/3 The Ascensiontide feast. **1900** D. C. TOVEY *Lett. T. Gray* I. 90 These three spent the festival of Ascensiontide 1741, in Venice together.

ascensive (ə'sɛnsıv), *a.* [f. L. *ascens-* (see ASCENSION) + -IVE, as if ad. L. **ascensīvus*.]

1. Characterized by upward movement or tendency; rising, advancing, progressive.

1646 SIR T. BROWNE *Pseud. Ep.* IV. xiii. 227 Though the Sunne be then ascensive. **1806** W. TAYLOR in *Ann. Rev.* IV. 67 The ascensive benevolence which aspires to domineer. **1863** LYELL *Antiq. Man* xxiv. 480 In Man, the brain presents an ascensive step in development.

2. *Gram.* Increasing the force, augmentative, intensive.

1857 ELLICOTT *Comm. Phil.* iv. 12 *Καί* appears as ascensive, 'even.' **1870** MOULTON tr. *Winer's N.T. Gram.* III. liii. 555 Sometimes its [*καί's*] ascensive force..is very easily recognised—see 1 Cor. vii. 21.

ascent (ə'sɛnt). Also 7 **assent.** [(Not in Fr.) f. ASCEND *v.*, on the analogy of *descent* (see quot. 1628 in 3), a. F. *descente*, itself an imitative formation on *descendre*, after etymological forms like *vente, attente*, f. *vendre, attendre*: L. *vendita* gave F. *vente*, but L. *ascensa* gave F. *ascense*, Eng. ASCENCE.]

1. *gen.* The act of ascending, mounting, or soaring up; upward movement, rise.

1614 OVERBURY *A Wife, etc.* (1638) 301 The first degree of his ascent. **1667** MILTON *P.L.* x. 224 To him with swift ascent he up return'd. **1751** CHAMBERS *Cycl.* s.v., Ascent of Fluids is particularly understood of their rising above their own level. **1864** R. CHAMBERS *Bk. Days* II. 347 He had effected an ascent [in a balloon] at Edinburgh.

b. *fig.* Rise in thought, estimation, characteristic quality, social station, etc.; advancement.

1607 SHAKS. *Cor.* II. ii. 28 His assent is not by such easie degrees. **1744** HARRIS *Three Treat.* III. II. (1765) 225 What higher Combinations..subsist, we know not. Their Gradation and Ascent 'tis impossible we should discover. **1790** GIBBON *Misc. Wks.* (1814) III. 512 His ascent to one of the most eminent dignities of the republic. **1856** RUSKIN *Mod. Paint.* IV. v. xx. §23. 368 French and English art in precipitate decline, Italian in steady ascent.

2. *esp.* The act of climbing or travelling up; the going up a mountain, stairs, a river, etc.

1753 CHAMBERS *Cycl. Supp.* s.v. *Mountain*, Called the *needle Mountain*..being supposed impracticable to the ascent of any one. **1844** DICKENS *Lett.* (1880) I. 127 We began the ascent of the Simplon that same night. **1850** P. CUNNINGHAM *Handbk. Lond.* 384 The rest of the ascent is a dirty and somewhat fatiguing task.

b. *fig.*

1644 MILTON *Educ.* (1738) 136 The right path of a virtuous and noble education; laborious indeed at the first ascent. **1879** TENNYSON *Lover's T.* 29 To both there came The joy of life in steepness overcome, And victories of ascent.

3. A going back in time or in order of genealogical succession; †*concr.* a single step back in genealogy (*obs.*).

1628 COKE *On Litt.* 11 a, Hee commeth to the land by collateral discent and not by lineall ascent [*Littleton*, par collateral discent, et nemy par lineall ascention; *tr.* 1574 discent..ascension]. **1654** GAYTON *Fest. Notes* II. v. 57 Shee could scarce run two ascents without the help of a Town or Parish, where her grandfather was found. **1877** LYTTEIL *Landm.* IV. ii. 191 So does our ascent into the Past discover a beauty..till then unperceived.

4. Method or way of ascending.

1600 HOLLAND *Livy* 995 (R.) Dangerous places, steepe and hard of ascent. **1712** PARNELL *Spect.* No. 460 ⁋3 A Hill, green, flowery, and of an easy ascent. **1850** P. CUNNINGHAM *Handbk. Lond.* 384 The ascent to the ball is by 616 steps.

5. *concr.* A way by which one may ascend; upward slope, acclivity; a flight of steps.

1611 BIBLE *1 Kings* x. 5 His ascent by which hee went vp vnto the house of the Lord. **1667** MILTON *P.L.* v. 545 Winding with one ascent Accessible from Earth. **1727** BRADLEY *Fam. Dict.* s.v. *Garden*, A gentle Ascent or a Plain are healthy Expositions. **1762** H. WALPOLE *Vertue's Anecd. Paint.* (1786) II. 56 The ascent of steps from the hall. *c* **1854** STANLEY *Sinai & Pal.* iii. 190 Up that long ascent He came.

†**6.** A rising ground, an eminence. *Obs.*

1663 *Flagellum* or *O. Cromwell* (1672) 181 There was an Ascent raised where a Chair and Canopy of State was set.

a **1742** BENTLEY (J.) Diversified with depressed valleys and swelling ascents.

¶ For ASCENDANT.

?*c* **1400** CHAUCER *Wife's Prol.* (Harl. MS.) 613 Myn ascent was Taur, and Mars therinne. **1686** W. DE BRITAINE *Hum. Prud.* §20 Jupiter is Lord of that Ascent.

ascent, obs. form of ASSENT.

†**a'scentive**, *a. Obs.* [irreg. f. prec. + -IVE.] = ASCENSIVE.

1627 FELTHAM *Resolves* II. viii. Wks. 1677, 175 The thorny and ascentive path of Virtue. —— *Lusoria* ix. (1677) 10 So shall we..by this love Grow still ascentive.

ascertain (æsə'teɪn), *v.* Forms: 5 **acertein**, 5–6 **-teyne, -tayne, -tain(e**, 6 **-tene, accertaine**; 5 **assartayne**, 5–6 **assertayne**, 6 **asartayne, assertene, -teine**, 6–7 **-tain(e**; 5–6 **ascertayn(e**, 6 **-teyne, -taine**, 6– **ascertain**; also 5 **adcerteyne**, 6 **-taine**. [a. OF. *acertaine-* tonic stem of *acertene-r* (late AF. *asser-*, *ascer-*), f. *à* to + *certain*, CERTAIN. In Eng. assimilated to *certain*; pronounced (ə'sɜːtən) as late as 1650; the prefix *as-* for *ac-* began with the spelling *as-sertayne*, and is of course etymologically erroneous.]

I. To make subjectively certain: i.e. a person certain of a fact, or a thing certain to the mind.

†**1.** *trans.* To make (a person) certain, sure, or confident; to certify, assure; passing in looser usage into: To inform, apprise, tell. **a.** *simply. Obs.*

1465 *Paston Lett.* 531 II. 244 As I was credebly assartaynyed by a yeman. **1544** BALE *Sir J. Oldcastell* in *Harl. Misc.* (Malh.) I. 285 He was thoroughly assertained in his conscience for that conflyct of fayth. **1548** PHAËR *Æneid* III. (R.) Anchises I ascertaine then, and him declare the caas. **1602** CAREW *Cornwall* 126 a, Seeking by a fore-conjecture to bee ascertained. **1676** BULLOKAR, *Ascertain*, to assure, to certifie.

†**b.** Const. with *of*. *Obs.*

c **1400** *Floure & Leaf* 568 For now I am acertained throughly Of every thing I desired to know. **1490** CAXTON *Eneydos* xv. 61 Whan he was adcerteyned of the dooynge of dydo and of Eneas. **1528** MORE *Heresyes* I. Wks. 161/1 Now is y[e] church well acertened of goddes pleasure therin. **1649** G. DANIEL *Trinarch., Hen. V*, clxii, The French (ascertain'd of a Victory) Are but vnsattisfied. **1789** G. MORRIS in Sparks *Life* (1832) II. 3, I wish to be ascertained of the..intentions of the Court.

¶ Const. confused with 3 or 6.

1658 USSHER *Annals* 739 Mariamne had ascertained to Herod by oath of her chastity.

†**c.** with *subord. cl. Obs.*

1450 Q. MARGARET in *Four C. Eng. Lett.* 8 And how ye thinke to be disposed..ye will acertein us by the bearer. **1548** CRANMER *Catech.* 213 b, To asserten vs, that we are y[e] lyvely members of God's trew churche. **1550** BALE *Image both Ch.* I j b, These..assertayned me that he was the lyon of the trybe of Juda. **1684** BUNYAN *Pilgr.* II. 19 But how shall I be ascertained that I also shall be entertained? **1763–5** CHURCHILL *Candidate* Poems II. 30 Who may perhaps, in some ten years or more, Be ascertained that Two and Two make four.

†**2.** *refl.* To make oneself certain or confident; to gain trustworthy information. *Obs.*

1601 R. J[OHNSON] *The Worlde* Ded., Ascertaining my selfe, that the honorable vertues..have setled so good an impression. **1684** CHARNOCK *Attrib. God* (1834) I. 2 He could not so ascertain himself by convincing arguments. **1731** MEDLEY *Kolben's Cape G.H.* I. 92 Before I could ascertain myself of the religious institutions of the Hottentots.

3. *trans.* To make (a thing) certain to the mind; to render certain what or which it is. *arch.*

1494 FABYAN clxxvii. (R.) Whereof the tyme is nat duely ascertayned. *a* **1600** HOOKER (J.) The divine law..ascertaineth the truth. **1625** GIL *Sacr. Philos.* ii. 183 Postellus to ascertaine this matier to the understanding, brings these reasons. **1750** HARRIS *Hermes* (1841) 185 If the essence of an article be to define and ascertain. **1794** GODWIN *Cal. Williams* 266 The intelligence that was brought me by no means ascertained the greatness of the danger. **1850** SIR J. STEPHEN *Eccl. Biog.* I. 154 The crypt which then ascertained the spot where the Apostle..had won the crown of martyrdom.

†**b.** with *subord. cl. Obs.*

1736 BUTLER *Anal.* II. vii. 359 In order to ascertain and distinguish from all others, who is the object of our worship. **1787** BP. HORNE *Olla Podr.* xiii, But who shall exactly ascertain to us what superstition is? **1823** SCOTT *Peveril* III. vi. 101 Initial letters..which seemed to ascertain that it was addressed to himself.

†**4.** To make certain to us the existence of, establish as a certainty. *Obs.*

1791 BOSWELL *Johnson* (1816) I. 19 Which ascertains a defect that many of his friends knew he had, though I never perceived it.

†**b.** with *inf. phr.* To establish, prove (a thing to be so and so). *Obs.*

1670 G. H. *Hist. Cardinals* II. ii. 154 These reasons..do ascertain him to be Pope. **1791** BOSWELL *Johnson* (1831) I. 111 [This] would ascertain it not to be the production of Johnson. **1810** BOOTHROYD *Biblia Hebr.* II. 49 The use of this word clearly ascertains it to be a participle.

5. To find out or learn for a certainty by experiment, examination, or investigation; to make sure of, get to know. (The only current use.)

1794 SULLIVAN *View Nat.* I. 138 Those particular properties of bodies which are ascertained by the assistance of heat. *c* **1854** STANLEY *Sinai & Pal.* (1858) Pref. 16 It is important to ascertain the real facts. **1861** GEO. ELIOT *Silas M.* 9 Legal measures for ascertaining the culprit.

b. with *inf.* or *subord. cl.*

c **1803** FOX *James II* (1808) 23 Whether he would have acted upon this determination, his death..prevents us now from ascertaining. **1822** SOUTHEY in *Q. Rev.* XXVII. 2 The day is ascertained to have been Good Friday. **1849** MACAULAY *Hist. Eng.* I. 433 The Duke of York..ascertained that the city was perfectly quiet. **1880** tr. *Daudet's Fromont & Risler* II. iv. 76 He arose softly to ascertain who were these singular thieves.

II. To make (a thing) objectively certain, to fix.

†**6.** To make (a thing) sure (*to* a person); to render certain the possession of, ensure, secure. *Obs.*

1563 MAN *Musculus' Common-pl.* 287 a, Joynctly linked together, to assertayne the equalitie of Godhed to eche of them. **1681** BAXTER *Acc. Sherlock* iii. 175 They seem to ascertain salvation to the baptized. **1751** JOHNSON *Rambl.* No. 134 ⁋10 No diligence can ascertain success. **1823** SCOTT *St. Ronan's* iii, The squire's influence..ascertained him the support of the whole class of bucks.

†**7.** To make (a person) sure (*to* a thing); to bring or deliver certainly, destine or doom *to*. *Obs.*

1649 JER. TAYLOR *Gt. Exemp.* vii. §13 Would ascertain us into a possession of all the promises. **1658** *Whole Duty Man* x. §9 (1684) 81 Whomsoever thou..hast done thy part to ascertain to those endless flames. **1667** *Decay Chr. Piety* x. §1. 311 She..is ascertained to sink under all the methods of ruine.

†**8.** To make (a thing) certain, definite, or precise, by determining exactly its limits, extent, amount, position, etc.; to decide, fix, settle, limit. *Obs.*

1494 [see ASCERTAINED]. **1668** TEMPLE in *Four C. Eng. Lett.* 125 The proportions of money..being ascertained in the treaty. **1711** SHAFTESB. *Charac.* (1737) I. 17 To suppress by violence the natural Passion of Enthusiasm or to endeavour to ascertain it. **1727** SWIFT *Let. Eng. Tongue* Wks. 1755 II. I. 182 Some effectual method for correcting, enlarging, and ascertaining our language. **1789** *Const. U.S.* i. §6 A compensation for their services, to be ascertained by law.

†**9.** To make certain the existence or occurrence of; to reduce to a certainty. *Obs.*

1628 FELTHAM *Resolves* I. lxxi. Wks. 1677, 108 Evils, that are but probable, they ascertain.

†**a'scertain**, *a. Obs.*—[0] [a. OF. *acertain*, f. as prec.] Certain, sure.

1475 [see ASCERTAINLY].

ascertainable (æsə'teɪnəb(ə)l), *a.* [f. prec. vb. + -ABLE.] That may be ascertained.

†**1.** Capable of being fixed, settled, or decided.

1783 BLAIR *Rhetoric* (1801) I. 29 Ascertainable by no standard, but wholly dependent on changing fancy.

2. Capable of being discovered or learned by experiment, examination, or investigation.

1805 W. SAUNDERS *Min. Waters* 155 The water..does not actually deposit any other substance in any ascertainable quantity. **1859** RUSKIN *Two Paths* App. i. 257 Not a matter of opinion at all, but a matter of ascertainable fact. **1874** FARRAR *Christ* I. iii. 30 The exact year..is not ascertainable with any certainty from Scripture.

ascer'tainableness. [f. prec. + -NESS.] The quality of being ascertainable.

1868 P. CLAYDON in *Fortn. Rev.* May 505 The demarcating line..on the sharpness and ascertainableness of which Independency so essentially depends.

ascer'tainably, *adv.* [f. as prec. + -LY[2].] In an ascertainable manner; recognizably.

1863 KINGLAKE *Crimea* I. 335 His notions..of what was plausible and what was ascertainably false. **1872** LIDDON *Elem. Relig.* i. 25 To despair of knowledge only when knowledge is ascertainably out of reach.

ascertained (æsə'teɪnd), *ppl. a.* [f. ASCERTAIN *v.* + -ED.] †**a.** Determined, fixed (*obs.*). **b.** Discovered by investigation, known.

1494 FABYAN II. xxxiii. 26 So y[t] no tyme asserteyned, is to her deputed or set. **1858** SEARS *Athan.* xviii. 160 Professor Faraday considers it an ascertained fact.

ascertainer (æsə'teɪnə(r)). [f. as prec. + -ER[1].] One who ascertains.

1611 COTGR., *Certificateur*, a certifier, ascertainer, assurer. **1691** T. H[ALE] *Acc. New Invent.* 33 Our latest Ascertainers here of the time of its celebration.

ascer'taining. *vbl. sb.* [f. as prec. + -ING[1].] †Assurance, confirmation (*obs.*). (Now gerundial: see ASCERTAIN *v.* 5.)

1685 BAXTER *Paraphr. N.T.* Acts i. 9 The sight of Christ's Ascension must needs be..an ascertaining of the Apostles Faith. **1835** MACREADY *Remin.* I. 472 On ascertaining the time.

†**a'scertainly**, *adv. Obs. rare*—[1]. [f. ASCERTAIN *a.* + -LY[2].] Certainly, surely, assuredly.

1475 CAXTON *Jason* 12 She was so wreton by loue in his herte so ascertainly that he coude neuer kepe him fro thinking on her.

ascertainment (æsə'teɪnmənt). [f. ASCERTAIN *v.* + -MENT; cf. OF. *acertenement.*] The process or result of ascertaining.

1. Reduction to certainty; exact determination, limitation, settlement. *arch.*

1657 (21 Apr.) CROMWELL *Sp.* (1871) V. 37 That a period might be put, and some ascertainment made, and a time fixed. **1780** BURKE *Sp. Econ. Ref.* Wks. 1842 I. 255 For the ascertainment and security of tenant and other rights. **1848** ARNOULD *Law Mar. Insur.* (1866) I. I. i. 13 Essential to the very notion of an indemnity is the ascertainment of the perils insured against.

2. Determination as the result of investigation; finding out, discovery.

1799 SIR J. MACKINTOSH *Bacon & Locke* (1846) I. 329 Such facts bound our researches..and the ascertainment of them is the utmost possible attainment of Science. **1843** MILL *Logic* III. i. §2 The ascertainment of these angular distances. **1863** HUXLEY *Man's Place Nat.* ii. 57 The question of questions for mankind..is the ascertainment of the place which Man occupies in nature.

acescent, -ency, erron. var. ACESCENT, -ENCY.

ascesis (ə'siːsɪs). Also **askesis** (æ'skiːsɪs). [ad. Gr. ἄσκησις exercise, training, f. ἀσκεῖν to exercise.] The practice of self-discipline.

1873 PATER *Renaissance* p. xii, The charm of *ascesis*, of the austere and serious girding of the loins in youth. **1880** —— *Greek Studies* (1895) 267 The sanity of soul and body..the perfecting of both by reasonable exercise or *ascêsis*. **1890** E. JOHNSON *Rise Christendom* 107 In the conduct of life they establish a strict ascesis..as a means of a closer communion with the Divine. **1924** J. KELMAN *Prophets of Yesterday* i. 24 The Greek idea of *askesis* was but the habit of the athlete. **1944** AUDEN *For Time Being* (1945) 84 The vision That plain men can predict through an Ascesis of their senses.

ascetic (ə'sɛtɪk), *a.* and *sb.* [ad. Gr. ἀσκητικός adj., f. ἀσκητής a monk or hermit, f. ἀσκέ-ειν to exercise: see -IC.] **A.** *adj.*

1. Of or pertaining to the Ascetics, or to the exercise of extremely rigorous self-discipline; severely abstinent, austere.

1646 SIR T. BROWNE *Pseud. Ep.* viii. 126 This ascetic rule, which held that a saint was disgraced by the very society which his mild Master sought and loved. **1682** —— *Chr. Morals* (1756) 97 The old Ascetick christians found a paradise in a desert. **1757** BURKE *Abridgm. Eng. Hist.* Wks. X. 276 A monastery which had acquired great renown for..the severity of its ascetick discipline. **1850** TENNYSON *In Mem.* cix, High nature amorous of the good, But touch'd with no ascetic gloom.

2. = ASCETICAL 1.

1822 BURROWES *Cycl.*, *Ascetic*, the title of certain books on devout exercises. **1868** PATTISON *Academ. Org.* §5. 122 The knowledge to be cultivated is not ascetic divinity.

B. *sb.*

1. *Eccl. Hist.* (Freq. with cap. initial.) One of those who in the early church retired into solitude, to exercise themselves in meditation and prayer, and in the practice of rigorous self-discipline by celibacy, fasting, and toil.

1673 CAVE *Prim. Chr.* III. ii. 253 One of the primitive Asceticks. **1776** GIBBON *Decl. & F.* xxxvii. (R.) The Ascetics, who obeyed and abused the rigid precepts of the gospel. **1861** A. B. HOPE *Eng. Cathedr. 19th C.* v. 165 The deserts of the Thebaïd had been peopled by troops of sturdy and gaunt but God-fearing ascetics.

2. *gen.* One who is extremely rigorous in the practice of self-denial, whether by seclusion or by abstinence from creature comforts.

1660 JER. TAYLOR *Ductor Dubit.* II. iii. 8. §4 The primitive Christians were generally such ascetics in this instance of fasting. **1862** STANLEY *Jewish Ch.* (1877) I. i. 17 He is not an ascetic..but full of the affections and interests of family and household.

3. *pl.* An ascetical treatise.

1751 CHAMBERS *Cycl.* s.v., Books of spiritual exercises. As the ascetics, or devout treatises of St. Basil.

a'scetical, *a.* [f. prec. + -AL[1].]

1. Pertaining to, or treating of, the spiritual exercises by which perfection and virtue may be attained, as in *Ascetical Theology*.

a **1617** BAYNE *On Eph.* (1866) 331 Hence it is that ascetical sermons..are not in that request. **1697** tr. *Dupin's Eccl. Hist.* II. 145 The Ascetical Books attributed to St. Basil. **1884** ADDIS & ARNOLD *Cath. Dict.* s.v., St. Francis of Sales and St. Alphonsus Liguori may be mentioned as modern saints whose ascetical works are most esteemed.

2. = ASCETIC 1.

1836 HOR. SMITH *Tin Trump.* (1876) 161 Our English puritans with their ascetical bigotry.

a'scetically, *adv.* [f. prec. + -LY[2].] After the manner of an ascetic.

c **1800** MISS KNIGHT *Autobiog.* I. 82 The Duke of Parma used frequently to clothe himself in a friar's robe, and live ascetically. **1842** J. H. NEWMAN *Ch. of Fathers* 367 Nor live ascetically for the sake of them.

asceticism (ə'sɛtɪsɪz(ə)m). [f. ASCETIC + -ISM.] The principles or practice of the Ascetics; rigorous self-discipline, severe abstinence, austerity.

1646 SIR T. BROWNE *Pseud. Ep.* VIII. (1845) 126 Doomed to a life of celibacy by the asceticism which had corrupted the simplicity of Christianity. **1859** MILL *Liberty* ii. 89 In its horror of sensuality, it made an idol of asceticism.

ascetism (ə'sɛtɪz(ə)m). [f. Gr. ἀσκητής (see ASCETIC) + -ISM.] = ASCETICISM.

1850 W. HOWITT *Year-bk. of Country* iv. 106 Lent, with all its ascetism and abstinence, and gloom, is over. **1870** *Contemp. Rev.* XIII. 391 The melodramatic ascetism upon which such great store was then set. **1889** *Macm. Mag.* Jan. 236/1 There is certainly not a tinge in Shakespeare of sympathy with Catholic ascetism.

asch-, regular ME. spelling of OE. *asc-*, mod.E. ASH-, q.v. for words that survived into the modern period.

asch(e, obs. form of ASH and ASK *v.*

ascham ('æskəm). [named from Roger Ascham, author of *Toxophilus.*] A sort of cupboard or case to contain bows and other implements of archery.
1860 H. D. *Archer's Guide* 28 The best place [for keeping a bow] is a closet, or a wooden case made for the purpose, fixed up in a hall, and called an *Ascham.*

a-schamyed, obs. form of ASHAMED.

† **a'schape**, *v. Obs.* [A variant, due to phonetic levelling of proclitic *ĕ-* and *ă-* (see A- *pref.* 9), of *eschape*, a by-form of ESCAPE, imitating middle Fr. spelling *eschaper* (mod. *échapper*). Chiefly but not exclusively northern. Aphetized in 15th c. to *schape, shape*, which, as well as the full form, became obs. bef. 1500.] = ESCAPE.
c **1314** *Guy Warw.* 95 We ben aschaped unnethe. *c* **1460** *Bk. Quintessence* 1 þe teerme..þat noman may a-schape.

a-schepon: see ASHAPE *v.*

ascher, obs. variant of ESCHAR, a scar, a burn.

† **a'schewele**, *v. Obs. rare*⁻¹. [f. A- *pref.* 1 + **schewel*, SHEWEL, a scarecrow, used in Sidney's *Arcadia*, and still dial. Cf. OHG. *ir-sciuhen*, MHG. *erschiuhen*, mod.G. *erscheuen* to be frightened.] To scare, frighten away.
a **1250** *Owl & Night.* 1614 Heo hongeth me on heore hahe, Thar ich aschewele pie an crowe.

aschore, var. ASHORE *advb. phr. Obs.* a-straddle.

† **a'schrench**, *v. Obs.* [OE. *ascrencan*, f. A- *pref.* 1 + *screncan*: see SCHRENCH.] To deceive.
c **885** K. ÆLFRED *Gregory's Past.* xliii. 316 Ne eft sio ðræsting ðæs lichoman ðæt mod ne ascrence mid upahæfennesse. *c* **1300** *K. Alis.* 4819 Hy were asshreynt in her crook. *c* **1315** SHOREHAM 17 Ac eche othren aschrencheth. *c* **1320** *Seuyn Sages* (W.) 1485 A! dame, he saide, ich was asschreint, Ich wende thou haddest ben adreint.

aschrie, variant of ASCRY *v. Obs.*

aschyn, obs. form of ASHEN.

ascian, -en, obs. forms of ASK *v.*

Ascians ('æʃıənz), *sb. pl.* [f. med.L. *Ascii* ('æʃıaı), also used in Eng. (a. Gr. ἄσκιοι, f. ἀ priv. + σκιά shadow) + -AN.] Inhabitants of the torrid zone, who twice a year have the sun directly overhead at noon, and then cast no shadows.
1635 CARPENTER *Geog. Delin.* I. x. 226 These men haue the Sunne twice euery yeere in their Zenith, and then they make no shaddowes at all, and therefore they are called Ascij, or without shaddowes. **1709** MANDEY *Syst. Math.* (1729) 584 *Ascii*, are those which have no Meridian Shadow. **1847** CRAIG, *Ascians.*

ascidian (ə'sıdıən), *a.* and *sb. Zool.* [f. mod.L. *Ascidia* (see ASCIDIUM) + -AN.] **A.** *adj.* Of or pertaining to the Ascidia (or Ascidiæ), a group of animals belonging to the tunicate Mollusca, considered by evolutionists to constitute a link in the development of the Vertebrata. **B.** *sb.* A member of this group. ‖**ascidiarium** (ə,sıdı'ɛərıəm) [see -ARIUM], the aggregate mass of organisms in compound ascidians. **a'scidioid** *a.*, resembling the Ascidia. **ascidiozooid** (ə,sıdıəʊ'zəʊɔıd), one of the organisms forming an ascidiarium.
1856 WOODWARD *Man. Mollusca* III. 332 The relation between the ascidian test and mantle is that of the epidermis and the *cutis vera.* **1835** KIRBY *Hab. & Inst. Anim.* I. vi. 192 The Tunicaries or Ascidians as some call them. **1874** HELPS *Soc. Press.* ix. 136 If he started as a gelatinous ascidian, how he has got on in the world! **1878** *N. Amer. Rev.* CXXVII. 58 Our ascidian forefathers. **1877** HUXLEY *Anat. Inv. An.* x. 610 In the compound or social Tunicata many ascidiozooids ..are united by a common test into an ascidiarium. **1880** *Syd. Soc. Lex.* s.v. *Ascidia*, The tunicate or ascidioid Division of the Mollusca.

ascidiate (ə'sıdıeıt), *a.* (Craig 1847), and **ascidiform** (ə'sıdıfɔːm), *a.* (Webster 1864). [f. next + -ATE, -FORM.] Shaped like an ascidium.

‖**Ascidium** (ə'sıdıəm). Pl. **-a**. [mod.L., ad. Gr. ἀσκίδιον, dim. of ἀσκός leather bag, wine-skin.]
1. *Zool.* (Also *Ascidia*, pl. *-æ.*) A genus of tunicate molluscs, having the enveloping tunic elastic and leathery: see ASCIDIAN.
1766 PENNANT *Zool.* IV. 48 (JOD.) Ascidia, taken off Scarborough. **1856** GOSSE *Marine Zool.* II. 30 The Ascidiæ usually adhere to stones and old shells. **1878** BELL *Gegenbauer's Comp. Anat.* 391 In many Ascidia a new individual buds from the body of the adult animal.
2. *Bot.* A pitcher-shaped leafy appendage.
1830 LINDLEY *Nat. Syst. Bot.* 81 The presence of Ascidia, or pitchers among its leaves, resembling those of Nepenthes.

asciferous (ə'sıfərəs), *a.* [f. mod.L. ASCUS: see -FEROUS.] = ASCIGEROUS.
1882 *Encycl. Brit.* XIV. 557 There is a parallelism between the fructification of lichens and the asciferous section of fungi.

ascigerous (ə'sıdʒərəs), *a. Bot.* [f. mod.L. *ascus* + -(I)GEROUS producing.] Bearing or producing asci (see ASCUS).
1829 LOUDON *Encycl. Plants* (1841) 982 An ascigerous somewhat deliquescent nucleus. **1857** BERKELEY *Cryptog. Bot.* §235 This mode of fructification is called ascigerous.

ASCII ('æskı). *Computing.* [Acronym, f. the initial letters of *A*merican *S*tandard *C*ode for *I*nformation *I*nterchange.] A standard seven-bit character code by which information is stored and transmitted in a computer or a data transmission system.
1963 *Mag. Standards* (Amer. Standards Assoc.) Aug. 236/1 The American Standard Code for Information Exchange (ASCII), X3.4—1963, has been designed to serve this purpose. *Ibid.* 239/2 The ASCII provides the basic standard on which to base plans for automatic information processing systems. **1967** D. H. HAMSHER *Communication Syst. Engin. Handbk.* II. 18 Through the use of the shift and control keys in conjunction with the other keys, all 128 code combinations of ASCII can be generated. **1978** *Personal Computer World* Dec. 20/2 ASCII (American Standard Code for Information Interchange) is a code that was originally devised for serial communications to supersede Morse code. Its advantage over Morse code is that all its characters are of fixed length (seven bits) while the Morse code is..variable. **1983** *Daily Tel.* 22 Aug. 6/5 The national electronic mail service, Telecom Gold, accepts only the basic ASCII character fount.

ascill, variant of EISELL, *Obs.*, vinegar.

ascismus, for *ascisinus*: see ASSASSIN.

ascitan (ə'saıtən, 'æsıtən). *Eccl. Hist.* [f. med.L. *Ascītæ*, a. Gr. Ἀσκῖται, f. ἀσκός wine-skin: see -ITE, -AN.] A member of a heretical sect in the second century, who used to dance round an inflated wine-skin, in reference to *Matt.* ix. 17.
1727-51 in CHAMBERS *Cycl.* s.v. *Ascitæ.*

† **a'scite**, earlier f. ACCITE *v. Obs.*, to cite, summon. (The spelling was as in *ascertain*: *a-cite, assite, ascite*, subsequently assimilated to L. *accitāre.*)
1552-5 LATIMER *Serm. & Rem.* (1845) 289 He was ascited before certain bishops. *a* **1617** HIERON *Wks.* I. 27 At the last day all..shall be ascited to appeare.

‖**ascites** (ə'saıtiːz). *Path.* Also 4-5 **aschytes**. [L., a. Gr. ἀσκίτης (sc. ὕδρωψ dropsy), f. ἀσκός bag.] A collection of serous fluid in the peritoneal cavity; dropsy of the abdomen.
1398 TREVISA *Barth. De P.R.* VII. lii. (1495) 266 One manere dropesye hyghte Aschytes, for yf the wombes ben smyten they sowne as a flackette, other a botell. **1657** *Phys. Dict.*, Ascites is a swelling of the belly caused of a serous matter. **1748** SMOLLETT *Rod. Rand.* xxvii. (1804) 183 Loaded with a monstrous ascites or dropsy. **1839** in TODD *Cycl. Anat.*

ascitic (ə'sıtık), *a. Path.* [f. prec. + -IC.] Of, pertaining to, or affected with ascites.
1684 tr. *Bonet's Merc. Compit.* viii. 298 A Boy..ascitick with an Anasarca. **1880** DRYSDALE in *Med. Temp. Jrnl.* Oct. 6 Abundant ascitic effusion.

a'scitical, *a.* ? *Obs.* [f. prec. + -AL¹.] = prec.
1676 R. WISEMAN *Surg.* (J.) Either anasarcous or ascitical. **1694** in *Phil. Trans.* XVIII. 21 Some thought..she was Ascitical. **1749** *Ibid.* XLVI. 207 Died..under Ascitical and icterical Symptoms.

ascititious (æsı'tıʃəs), *a.* [f. L. *ascīt-* = *adscīt-* ppl. stem of *adscīsc-ĕre* (see ADSCITITIOUS) + -ITIOUS, as if f. L. **ascitīcius.*] = ADSCITITIOUS (which is now more common).
1628 PRYNNE *Love Lockes* 17 It is a very wicked thing, to attire the head, with dead and ascititious Haire. **1829** SCOTT *Demonol.* viii. 264 Those ascititious particles..being loosened at his vanishing, and so offending the nostrils.

Asclepiad¹ (əsk'liːpıæd). [ad. L. *Asclēpiadēus*, a. Gr. Ἀσκληπιάδειος, adj. f. Ἀσκληπιάδης name of a Greek poet.] In Greek and Latin prosody: A verse, invented by Asclepiades, consisting of a spondee, two (or three) choriambi, and an iambus. Also *attrib.* Hence the adjs.: † **a,sclepi'adic** (also used *subst.*), † **a,sclepi'adical, a,sclepia'dean.**
1656 in BLOUNT *Glossogr.* **1876** KENNEDY *Pub. Sch. Lat. Gram.* §265 Of the Asclepiad..Horace employed five systems. *Ibid.* A stanza composed of three lesser Asclepiad verses. **1546** LANGLEY *Pol. Verg. De Invent.* I. viii. 17a, Meters..hath their name, eyther..of the inuentour as Æsclepiadicall. **1580** SIDNEY *Arcadia* (1622) 229 Singing these verses called Asclepiadikes. **1652** MARBURY *Comm. Habakkuk* (1865) 156 Verses, heroic, iambic, asclepiadic [*printed* -idiac]. **1706** PHILLIPS, *Asclepiadean.* **1860** SCHMITZ *Lat. Gram.* 306 The second Asclepiadean metre.

a'sclepiad². *Bot.* [f. next + -AD.] A plant belonging to the order *Asclepiadaceæ*: see next.

a,sclepia'daceous *a.*, of or belonging to this order. **a,sclepia'deous** *a.*, of the genus *Asclepias.*
1859 DARWIN *Orig. Spec.* xiv. (1878) 375 Orchids and asclepiads having pollen-masses with viscid discs. **1872** OLIVER *Elem. Bot.* II. 208 The pollen of Asclepiads is held together by a secretion of the anther-cell. **1880** BURBIDGE *Gard. Sun* App. 342 A singular new asclepiadaceous genus.

‖**Asclepias** (əsk'liːpıæs). *Bot.* [mod.L., a. Gr. ἀσκληπιάς, f. Ἀσκληπιός Æsculapius.] A genus of plants, giving its name to a N.O., including the Milkweed, Swallow-wort, and some others, chiefly natives of the east coast of North America.
1578 LYTE *Dodoens* 317 We may call it in English *Asclepias, Vincetoxicum*, and Swallowurt. **1706** PHILLIPS, *Asclepias*..Swallow-wort or Silken Cicely. **1872** OLIVER *Elem. Bot.* II. 208 The exotic Asclepias Family, including the beautiful Hoyas and Stephanotis of our stoves. **1872** BAKER *Nile Tribut.* ii. 22 Cutting firewood from the asclepias.

asco- (,æskəʊ), comb. form of ASCUS, used in many scientific terms of Cryptogamic Botany, as: **ascocarp** ('æskəʊkɑːp) [Gr. καρπός fruit], the fruit body of an ascomycetous fungus. **ascogenous** (ə'skɒdʒınəs), *a.* [Gr. γενής producing + -OUS], that produces asci. **ascogonium** (-'gəʊnıəm) [cf. *archegonium*], the spirally-coiled organ from which the asci (see ASCUS) are produced. **ascomycetal** (-mı'siːtəl), **ascomy'cetous** *a.*, of or belonging to the *Ascomycetes*, or fungi, such as the yeast-plant and truffles, in which spores are formed asexually in the interior of asci. **ascophore** ('æskəʊfɔə(r)), an ascophorous hypha or filament. **ascophorous** (ə'skɒfərəs), *a.* [Gr. -φορος bearing], producing asci. **ascospore** ('æskəʊspɔə(r)), a spore developed in an ascus.
1887 GARNSEY & BALFOUR tr. *De Bary's Compar. Morphol. Fungi* 492/1 *Ascocarp*, in Ascomycetes: sporocarp producing asci and ascospores; its three kinds are apothecium or discocarp, perithecium or pyrenocarp, and cleistocarp. **1907** W. R. FISHER *Schlich's Man. Forestry* IV. III. ii. 465 Black spermagonia subsequently appear before winter, but their spores do not germinate, as ascocarps do not develop till the second year after infection. **1910** *Encycl. Brit.* XI. 340/2 The other divisions of the Ascomycetes..do not bear the asci free on the mycelium but enclosed in definite fruit bodies or ascocarps. **1940** *Chambers's Techn. Dict.* 54/2 *Ascocarp*, the fructification of the *Ascomycetes*, containing asci and ascospores; it may be a cleistocarp, an apothecium, or a perithecium. **1882** VINES *Sachs's Bot.* 239 The ascogenous filaments and the asci which proceed from them. **1959** *Chambers's Encycl.* VI. 118/1 The male and female nuclei do not fuse in the ascogonium but become associated in pairs and pass into the ascogenous hyphae. **1875** BENNETT & DYER *Sachs' Bot.* 257 The female organ, called by De Bary the Ascogonium. *Ibid.* 258 The Asci..owe their origin to the fertilised ascogonium. **1884** *Athenæum* 26 Jan. 124/1 Structurally it [Sphæria pocula] is hymenomycetal and not ascomycetal. **1867** J. HOGG *Microsc.* II. i. 304 Peziza belongs to the Ascomycetous fungi. **1877** BENNETT tr. *Thomé's Text-bk. Bot.* 282 The filaments which bear the asci (*ascophores*). **1857** BERKELEY *Cryptog. Bot.* §62 There is not a single instance amongst Algæ, of ascophorous fruit. **1875** BENNETT & DYER *Sachs' Bot.* 240 The Ascospores..arise by free cell-formation in the protoplasm of the..Ascus.

† **a-'scoff**, *advb. phr. Obs.* In 3 **a-skof**. [A *prep.*¹ + SCOFF.] In scorn, mockingly.
c **1300** *K. Alis.* 874, 41 Alisaundre lokid a-skof, As he no gef nought therof.

† **a'scoliasm.** *Obs.*⁻⁰ [f. Gr. ἀσκωλιάζ-ειν to hop on greased wine-skins (ἀσκοί) at the Ἀσκώλια or second day of the rural Dionysia.] 'A kind of Play, call'd, *Fox to thy Hole*, in which Boys hopping on one Leg, beat one another with Gloves or pieces of Leather.' Phillips 1706.
1753 CHAMBERS *Cycl. Supp.*, *Ascoliasm.*

† **a'scomfit**, *v. Obs. rare*⁻¹. [a. OF. *esconfire*, pa. pple. *esconfit*, f. *es* out of + *confire* to preserve:—L. *conficĕre*; cf. *discomfit*: see AS- *pref.*² The aphetic SCOMFIT is usual.] To discomfit, rout.
c **1450** LONELICH *Grail* xiv. 126 [He] beheeld His meyne as-scomfited in the feld.

Ascomycetes (,æskəʊmaı'siːtiːz). *Bot.* [mod.L., f. ASCO- + Gr. μυκητ-, μύκης mushroom.] A class of fungi (see ASCOMYCETOUS *a.*); in *sing.* **ascomycete** (,æskəʊ'maısiːt, -maı'siːt), a fungus belonging to this class.
1857 M. J. BERKELEY *Introd. Cryptogamic Bot.* 269 Fungales..*Ascomycetes.*—Asci formed from the fertile cells of an hymenium. *Ibid.* 270 *Ascomycetes, Berk.*.. The essential character of this important division consists in the development of definite or indefinite sporidia within certain of the external cells of the hymenium called asci. **1875** *Q. Jrnl. Microsc. Sci.* XV. 144 Reess..terms the mother-cells *asci*, the daughter-cells *ascospores*, and the *Saccharomyces* an *Ascomycete* in the broadest sense of the term. **1922** H. GWYNNE-VAUGHAN *Fungi* ii. 34 The Ascomycetes include over 15,000 species, all of which, excepting only the yeasts, possess a well-developed mycelium of richly-branded and septate hyphae. **1935** *Ann. Reg. 1934* 55 Fungal sexuality received much attention and it looks as if some ascomycetes may have one and others two nuclear fusions. **1953** J. RAMSBOTTOM *Mushr. & Toadst.* iii. 18 Ascomycetes, which

include cup-fungi, morels, ergot, candlesnuff fungus, and yeasts.

asconce, obs. form of ASKANCE.

ascorbic (əˈskɔːbɪk), *a. Chem.* [f. A- 14 + SCORB(UT)IC *a.*] ***ascorbic acid***, vitamin C, the anti-scorbutic vitamin.

1933 SZENT-GYÖRGYI & HAWORTH in *Nature* 7 Jan. 24/2 'Hexuronic Acid' (Ascorbic Acid)... We wish to ascribe the name ascorbic acid to the crystalline substance $C_6H_8O_6$. **1935** *Nature* 14 Sept. 439/1 Vitamin C (ascorbic acid)..is found..to accelerate the growth and increase the length of the shoots of germinating wheat.

†**a-ˈscorn**, *advb. phr. Obs.* [A *prep.*[1] + SCORN.] In scorn or mockery.

c **1485** *Digby Myst.* (1882) III. 1419 She wyll nat kysse þe on skorn. *Boy.* A skorn, no, no, I fynd it hernest!

†**aˈscorn**, *v. Obs. rare*[−1]. [a. OF. *escorne-r* to insult, affront: see AS- *pref.*[2]; or f. SCORN *v.* with A *particle* of pa. pple.] To insult, affront.

1553–87 FOXE *A. & M.* (1596) 309/2 Heereat prince Edward being ascorned, lifted up himselfe, and gaue him such a blow, that, etc.

Ascot (ˈæskət). Name of a village near Windsor in Berkshire, used *ellipt.* for a fashionable race-meeting held at Ascot Heath in June; freq. *attrib.*, applied esp. to hats, dresses, etc., designed for or suitable for wearing in the Royal Enclosure at Ascot. ***Ascot tie*** (see quot. 1957); also, *U.S.*, simply ***Ascot***.

[**1711** *London Gaz.* 12–16 July *Advertisements.* Her Majesty's Plate of 100 Guineas will be run for round the new Heat on Ascott Common near Windsor, on Tuesday the 7th of August next, by any Horse, Mare or Gelding, being no more than six Years old.] **1814** *Sporting Mag.* June 128/2 The visit to Ascot of the Prince Regent, Emperor of Russia, and King of Prussia, with the other illustrious Foreigners.. during the late Meeting, was too distinguished an honour paid to an English race-course, to be unnoticed in our pages. **1824** *Ibid.* June 131/1 Although the weather was not propitious, Ascot races never went off with more eclat. *Ibid.* 132/2 It would be well for himself and his subjects if there were more Ascots than one in the year. **1828** *Ibid.* June 202/2 Ascot still remains a pattern to all race courses throughout the kingdom. *Ibid.* 205/1 The Ascot Cup, value 100 sovs. **1867** 'OUIDA' *Under Two Flags* I. ii. 29 Cottage for Ascot week, yachting with the R.V.Y. Club. **1899** R. WHITEING *No. 5 John St.* xiv. 148 Sinclair is trying to form a party.. to run over to the Grand Prix... 'What about Ascot?' cries a protesting voice. **1907** B. M. CROKER *Company's Servant* xxix. 300 Ladies in Ascot frocks, and men with field glasses. **1908** 'O. HENRY' *Gentle Grafter* in *Wks.* (1928) 218 He had on a white flannel suit..and a pink ascot tie. **1912** C. MACKENZIE *Carnival* xxxiv. 352 His Ascot tie of red satin. **1957** M. B. PICKEN *Fashion Dict.* 10/1 *Ascot.* 1. Broad neckscarf, usually double. Tied so that ends come horizontally on each side of knot, then cross diagonally. Worn by men and fastened with scarf-pin. 2. Double scarf that is informally looped under the chin. Worn by men and women. **1959** *Listener* 19 Feb. 344/1 He loyally goes through the motions, military and social (Bank Picquet, Tower Guard, débutantes balls, Ascot, Lord's), that are required of him. **1967** *Guardian* 24 June 12/8 The flowery, floppy Ascot hat.

ascoye, ascoyne: see ASKOY, ASKOYNE.

ascribable (əˈskraɪbəb(ə)l), *a.* Also 7 ascriveable. [f. next + -ABLE.] That may be ascribed, attributed, or reckoned to the account of; attributable.

1671 *True Non-Conf.* 296 The gesture of adoration to be thereto only ascriveable. **1678** R. BARCLAY *Apol. Quakers* iv. §v. 106 The Iniquity and Sin here appears..Ascribable to the Parents. **1863** COX *Inst. Eng. Govt.* I. vii. 89 The only benefit ascribable to a second house is its acting as a remedy against precipitation.

ascribe (əˈskraɪb), *v.* Forms: 4–7 **ascrive**, 5 **ascryve, asscribe**, 6 **ascrybe**, 6–7 **adscribe** 6– **ascribe**. [a. OF. *ascriv-* stem of *ascrire*, cogn. w. It. *ascrivere*: —L. *ascr-*, *adscrīb-ĕre*, f. *ad-* to + *scrīb-ĕre* to write. In 16th c. altered to *ascribe* after L., though *ascrive* was occasionally used till late in the 17th. The historical appearance of the senses in Eng. does not correspond with the logical development in Latin.]

I. To write into; to add to a writing, register, list, etc.

†**1.** *trans.* To annex or add in writing, to subscribe: **a.** to subjoin (one's name); **b.** to subjoin one's name to (a document). *Obs.*

1603 B. JONSON *Sejanus* v. v. 4 Beare it [an Edict] to my fellow Consul to adscribe. **1649** NETHERSOLE *Self-Cond.* 3 The ascribing of my name would..have substracted from.. the weight of those discourses.

†**2.** To inscribe, dedicate *to.* (So in OFr.) *Obs.*

1554 PHILPOT *Exam. & Writ.* (1842) 328 Unto those [Princes] also the sentences and arguments ought to be ascribed. **1563** SHUTE *Archit.* Cij b, The secound pillor called Dorica, being ascribed to Hercules.

†**3.** To enroll, register, reckon in a class. *Obs.*

1532 MORE *Confut. Tindale* Wks. 376/1 Ascribed..into the noumber of his elect and peculier chosen people. *c* **1540** tr. *Pol. Verg.* (1846) I. 174 She died, and was ascribed emonge the sainctes. **1628** HOBBES *Thucydides* (1822) 18 Desiring you to ascribe them to the number of your confederates. **1680** AUBREY in Bliss *Lett. Emin. Pers.* (1813) II. 632 He would long since have been ascribed a member there.

†**4.** To appoint (*to* a vacancy). (So in OFr.) *Obs.*

1624 HEYWOOD *Gunaik.* VI. 272 One of the Priests of the foresaid number dyed, neyther..was any agreed upon or thought fit to be ascribed into his place.

II. To enter into an account, to reckon, count.

5. *trans.* To enter (a thing) *to* in an account, to set it to the credit of; to assign, attribute, impute, refer as due or owing *to.*

1382 WYCLIF *2 Sam.* xii. 28 Lest..to my name the victorie be ascrived. **1494** FABYAN VI. ccxvi. 235 The which dede he ascribed chefely vnto Harolde. **1528** MORE *Heresyes* IV. Wks. 286/2 Al which miracles al those blessed saintes do ascribe vnto the worke of god. **1651** HOBBES *Leviath* I. viii. 37 The same Græcians did often ascribe madnesse to the operation of the Eumenides. **1711** ADDISON *Spect.* No. 321 ¶6 This speech is..the finest that is ascribed to Satan in the whole Poem. **1746** JOHNSON *Plan Dict.* Wks. IX. 185 We usually *ascribe* good; but *impute* evil. **1833** HT. MARTINEAU *Berkeley* I. viii. 159 Others ascribed the whole disaster to the use of small notes. **1879** LOCKYER *Elem. Astron.* v. xxxiii. 193 The invention of clocks is variously ascribed to the sixth and ninth centuries.

†**b.** *ellipt.* (*intr.*) To give or attribute credit *to.*

1603 SIR C. HEYDON *Jud. Astrol.* ii. 56 Some..againe did as greatly admire, and ascribe vnto it. **1667** *Decay Chr. Piety* xvii. §15. 357 Many are apt to ascribe too unlimitedly to the force of a good meaning.

6. To reckon or count *to*, as a property or characteristic (*rarely* as a material possession); to consider or allege as belonging *to*, to claim for.

c **1400** *Apol. Loll.* 110 þei chalang not þis only þat is ascriuid, but þei tak a vey all þingis fro alle men. **1528** PAYNELL *Salerne Regim.* Q iv, The forsayde vtilites..be ascriued to prunes of Armeny. **1652** NEEDHAM tr. *Selden's Mare Cl.* 448 This sea also is ascribed by som to the King of Great Britain. **1667** *Phil. Trans.* II. 492 The use, which he adscribes to the Brain. **1880** G. P. MORRIS *Poems* 163 Ascribing with the true and just All 'holiness unto the Lord.' **1877** LYTTEIL *Landm.* II. ii. 93 The conclusion which ascribes to the lands of Trahour the site of an ancient Church.

†**7.** To reckon, reckon up, count. *Obs.*

1432–50 tr. *Higden* (1865) 37 þe Romanes..ascribede theire yeres from the begynnenge of theire cite y-made. **1601** HOLLAND *Pliny* II. 586 Sotacus ascribeth and setteth downe fiue sundry kinds of the load-stone.

†**8.** with *compl.* To reckon, consider as. *refl.* To reckon oneself, claim, pretend *to be.* (So in OFr.) *Obs.*

1535 STEWART *Cron. Scot.* II. 504 Ane lord thair wes than in Northumberland..Ascryvand him to be of Danis blude. **1580** NORTH *Plutarch* 181 (R.) Hereupon the Athenians do ascribe that day for a most unfortunate day.

¶? *catachr.* for DESCRIBE. But cf. 5.

1509 BARCLAY *Ship of Fooles* (1570) 217 Suche a wise man as Virgil doth ascribe.

ascribing (əˈskraɪbɪŋ), *vbl. sb.* [f. prec. + -ING[1].] The action of the verb ASCRIBE; addition in writing (*obs.*), assignment, attribution.

1649 [see ASCRIBE *v.* 1]. **1833** MACREADY *Remin.* I. 404 The ascribing all the misery of the sufferers to destiny.

ascrie, variant of ASCRY *v.* and *sb. Obs.*

†**aˈscript**, *ppl. a. Obs.* [ad. L. *ascrīptus*, pa. pple. of *ascrībĕre*: see ASCRIBE. Cf. also ADSCRIPT.] Enrolled, registered; appointed.

a **1564** BECON *Art. Chr. Relig.* (1844) 436 Make unto us this oblation ascript, reasonable, acceptable. **1610** HEALEY *St. Aug. City of God* (1620) 290 Tully calleth..those that merit heauen Gods ascript.

ascription (əˈskrɪpʃən). [ad. L. *ascrīptiōn-em*, n. of action f. *ascrīb-ere* to ASCRIBE: see -ION[1]. Cf. also ADSCRIPTION.]

†**1.** The action of adding in writing, subscription. *Obs.*

1597 MORLEY *Introd. Mus.* Annot., All diminution is signified either..by a number set to the signe, or else by ascription of the Canon.

2. Enrolment, inclusion in a class. *rare.*

1851 SIR F. PALGRAVE *Norm. & Eng.* I. 8 The ascription of the ancient Gaulish families into the Senatorial rank.

3. The action of setting to the credit of; attribution of origin or authorship.

a **1619** FOTHERBY *Atheom.* Pref. 4 Ascribing all his writing vnto Gods inward commanding..Which is indeed, a very true ascription. **1794** PALEY *Evid.* I. ix. § 5 (1817) 165 If the ascription of the Gospels to their respective authors had been conjectural. **1861** MAINE *Anc. Law* (1874) 1 The theoretical ascription of English law to immemorial unwritten tradition.

4. a. The action of ascribing, attributing, imputing, or declaring that something belongs to a person or thing; *concr.* the declaration thus made.

1600 CHAPMAN *Iliad* XIV. Comm., Which ascription our Spond takes to be given in scorn. **1845–6** TRENCH *Huls. Lect.* Ser. II. viii. 275 With thankful ascriptions of praise to ..God. **1877** HUXLEY *Anat. Inv. An.* xii. 661 The ascription of a spermatozoal nature to the striæ..is not warranted.

b. *spec.* The formula used by a preacher at the end of a sermon in which he ascribes praise to God ('Now to God the Father..be ascribed all praise..').

1899 DEARMER *Parson's Handbk.* 201 It has become customary to conclude the sermon with an ascription.

ascriptitious (æskrɪpˈtɪʃəs), *a. rare.* [f. L. *ascrīptīci-us* (see ASCRIPT and -ITIOUS) + -OUS. Cf. also ADSCRIPTITIOUS.]

†**1.** Appended to a list, additional. *Obs.*

a **1658** FARINGDON *Serm.* 82 (T.) An ascriptitious and supernumerary god.

2. Merely ascribed or attributed to. (Cf. *fictitious.*)

1652 GAULE *Magastrom.* 252 The spurious, fictitious, and ascriptitious books of Adam.

3. 'Registered, enrolled.' Bailey 1721.

ascriptive (əˈskrɪptɪv), *a. rare.* In 7 ads-. [ad. L. *ascr-*, *adscrīptīvus*: see ASCRIPT and -IVE.] Attributable, ascribable.

1650 CHARLETON *Paradoxes* Prol. 15 Sanation of Wounds ..is not rightly adscriptive to the single power of Nature.

†**aˈscry**, *v. Obs.* Forms: 4 **asscrie, aschrie, aschriȝe**, 4–5 **ascrie, ascrye**, 4–6 **ascry**, 5 **askerye, askrye**, 6 **asskrie, askry.** *Aphet.* 5 SCRY, q.v. [a. OF. *escrie-r* (mod. *écrier*), f. *es*:—L. *ex* out + *crier* to CRY. The Anglo-Fr. was prob. *ascrier* (see AS- *pref.*[2]), as ESCRY does not appear in Eng. before the time of Caxton, who introduced it from continental French. Aphetized in 15th c. to SCRY.]

1. *trans.* To call forth or out; to call upon.

c **1325** *E.E. Allit. P.* C. 195 þenne ascryed þay hym skete, & asked ful loude, What þe deuel hatȝ þou don? *c* **1350** *Will. Palerne* 3827 Wiȝtli he hem a-schriȝed, And cumfort hem craftli with his kinde speche. *c* **1450** LONELICH *Grail* xlix. 225 Thanne Iosephe gan hem ascrien anon, Ha! ȝe cursed peple everychon!

b. *esp.* To attack with outcry, call to fight, provoke, challenge.

1330 R. BRUNNE *Chron.* 217 Edward was hardie, þe Londres gan he ascrie. *c* **1350** *Will. Palerne* 3895 And stoutli him aschried, Bad him ȝepli him ȝeld or ȝerne he schul deie. **1480** CAXTON *Chron. of Eng.* ccxxiv. 227 The Englyssh mynstrelles blewe her..pypes and hydously ascryed the scottes. **1523** LD. BERNERS *Froiss.* I. lvii. 78 Assone as the Almayns sawe them, they ascryed them, and ran in fiersly among them.

2. *intr.* To cry out, shout, exclaim.

1352 MINOT *Poems* (1795) iii. 14 He herd ascry, That king Edward was nere tharby. **1393** GOWER *Conf.* III. 59 They ascriden also blive. *a* **1528** SKELTON *Ph. Sparowe* 903 Openly to askry, And to make an outcri Against odyous Enui.

3. *trans.* = DESCRY: to cry out upon on discovering; *hence* to espy, discover; to proclaim, denounce, publish, inform upon.

c **1400** *Ywaine & Gaw.* 3406 Thar he held him prevely, So that none sold him ascry. **1523** LD. BERNERS *Froiss.* I. cxcv. 232 The watchmen sayd, by likelyhode ther be some theuys ..commyng to steale this towne; let vs ascry them, and wake the men of the cytie. **1530** PALSGR. 437/2, I askry, as foreriders of an armye do their enemyes whan they make reporte where they have sene them, *Je descouures.* **1548** HALL *Chron.* 531 When the French men perceived that thei were asskried thei sodeinly returned. **1559** *Myrr. Mag., Clifford* i. 4, I thinke it best that men their crimes ascried.

†**aˈscry**, *sb. Obs.* Forms: 4–5 **ascry**, 4 **asscry, askrye**, 5–6 **ascrye, askrie**, 7 **ascrie.** [f. ASCRY *v.* Cf. the variant ESCRY and aphetic SCRY. In many places it is impossible to tell whether we ought to read *ascrye* or *a scrye*: cf. quotations 1532 and 1548.] Crying out, outcry, clamour, shout, exclamation.

c **1325** *E.E. Allit P.* B. 838 As a scowte wach scarred, so þe asscry rysed. **1393** GOWER *Conf.* II. 386 And all at ones set askry In hem. *c* **1532** LD. BERNERS *Huon* 652 They cryed out and made a scrye. **1548** HALL *Chron.* 532 The Britaynes made an askrie and sette their Beacons on fire. **1600** HOLLAND *Livy* IV. xxii. 154 Made an ascrie [*clamorem*] that the towne was taken.

ascue, obs. form of ASKEW.

‖**ascus** (ˈæskəs). *Bot.* Pl. -i. [mod.L., a. Gr. ἀσκός bag, sac.] A membranous tubular cell, *esp.* the swollen sac-like cell at the end of the branches of the hyphæ in certain fungi and lichens, in which the reproductive sporules or sporidia develop.

1830 LINDLEY *Nat. Syst. Bot.* 332 These cases (*thecæ*) are ..contained in other membranous cases (*asci*). **1875** BENNETT & DYER *Sachs' Bot.* 240 With the development and escape of the spores the ascus disappears.

ascuse, obs. var. EXCUSE: see AS- *pref.*[2]

Asdic (ˈæzdɪk). [f. the initials of *A*llied *s*ubmarine *d*etection *i*nvestigation *c*ommittee.] An echo-sounding device for the detection of submarines. Cf. SONAR.

1939 *War Illustr.* 29 Dec. 538/2 Asdic..mentioned by Mr. Churchill in one of his speeches..[is] a type of secret apparatus now used by the Navy. **1940** *Nature* 3 Aug. 171/1 On May 21, Dr. R. W. Boyle received the Flavelle Medal of the Society..in recognition of his researches, particularly on the development of 'Asdics' and his work on ultrasonics. **1943** *Penguin New Writing* XVIII. 27 Taff is an Asdic rating. They work with headphones and they pick up echoes underwater and can get the bearing and distance of the echo and often they can tell if it's a sub or not. **1952** J. V. NOEL *Naval Terms* 13 *Asdic*, British echo-ranging sound gear, equivalent to our [*sc.* American] Sonar. **1958** *Spectator* 8 Aug. 196/2 ASDIC, the device which sends out pulses of sound through the sea and records the echo where these are reflected back from a submarine.

ase, obs. form of ACE *sb.*, AS; var. ASEE *v. Obs.*

-ase, *Chem.*, a suffix taken from the ending of DIASTASE, and used in naming enzymes, as *lactase*, *maltase*, *pectase*, etc.

a-sea (ə'siː), *advb. phr.* [A *prep.*[1] + SEA.] On the sea, at sea; to the sea.
1858 BUSHNELL *Serm. New Life* 212 You are no more afloat or a-sea. **1878** J. MILLER *Songs Italy* 119 We stood looking a-sea.

aseal, var. ASSEAL *v. Obs.* to seal.

†**a'sear, a'sere**, *v. Obs.* [OE. *asearian*, f. A- *pref.* 1 + *searian*: see SERE *v.*] To dry up, wither.
c **1000** *MS.* in *Sax. Leechd.* III. 355 Treowa he deþ færlice blowan, & eft raþe asearian. *c* **1320** *Seuyn Sages* (W.) 606 That olde tre..asered.

†**a'search**, *v. Obs.* In 4 aserche. [a. AF. *asserchie-r*, OF. *acerchie-r*, f. *à* to + *cerchier* to seek; or ? var. of OF. *encerchier*: see A- *pref.* 10 and ENSEARCH *v.*] *trans.* and *intr.* To search, examine, investigate; inquire.
1382 WYCLIF *Gen.* xliv. 12 The which aserchinge..fonde the coppe in the sak of Beniamyn. —— *1 Kings* xx. 6 Thei shulen aserchen thin hows. —— *2 Sam.* xi. 3 David sente, and aserchede [**1388** enqueride], what was the womman.

aseclist, var. of ASSECLIST, *Obs.* follower.

†**a'see**, *v. Obs.* [A variant of *isee*, *ysee*: see A- *pref.* 6. But in the pa. pple., the *a-* may be A *particle*: in quot. 1250 it may be = *have.*] To see.
c **1250** *Gen. & Ex.* 2720 Ðat non egipcien..it wist, ne sulde a sen. *c* **1300** *K. Alis.* 847 Who me loveth now worth asene! *c* **1430** *Hymns to Virg.* (1867) 120 Vndyr erthe I-hydd they wold be Thatt Ihesu cryst scholl nott hem Ase. *a* **1500** *Rel. Ant.* I. 109 Thou maist done awey the lettres that hit schal nothyng beene a-sene.

†**a'seek**, *v. Obs.* For forms see SEEK. [OE. *asēc(e)an*, f. A- *pref.* 1 + *sēcan* to SEEK.] To seek for, search after.
c **1000** *Ags. Ps.* cxix. 95 Wyllað me laðe lifes asecean. **1205** LAY. 27866 Arður asechen lette, alle þa riche, Kinges and eorles. **1413** LYDG. *Pylgr. Sowle* I. xii. 9 He hath long tyme asoȝt the cyte of heuenly Jerusalem.

aseel, var. ASSEAL *v. Obs.* to seal.

aseeth, var. ASSETH, *Obs.*, satisfaction.

a-seethe (ə'siːð), *advb. phr.* [A *prep.*[1] + SEETHE.] Seething.
1879 DOWDEN *Southey* ii. 30 Young brains a-seethe with revolution and romanticism.

asege, var. ASSIEGE *v. Obs.* to besiege.

aseh, pa. t. of ASYE *v. Obs.* to sink down.

asein, obs. form of ASSIGN *v.*

aseingde, aseint, pa. t. of ASENCH *v. Obs.*

aseismic (ə'saɪzmɪk, eɪ-), *a.* [f. A- 14 + SEISMIC *a.*] Resistant to the destructive effects of earthquakes.
1884 *Nature* 24 Jan. 290 A house that my experience suggests as being aseismic. **1908** C. G. KNOTT *Physics of Earthquake Phenomena* iv. 50 D. and T. Stevenson, the well-known lighthouse engineers, made the method the foundation principle of their 'aseismic joint'. **1939** *Archit. Rev.* LXXXV. 223 A third structural problem was introduced by the necessity of aseismic design.

a-seity (ˌeɪ'siːɪtɪ, ə'siːɪtɪ). *Metaph.* [f. L. *ā* from, *se* oneself + -ITY; cf. F. *aséité.*] Underived or independent existence.
1691 NORRIS *Ideal & Int. World* I. (1701) 7 The Natural World..for any self Stability, Aseity, or Essential Immutability of its own, may again cease to be. *c* **1700** *Gentl. Instruc.* (1732) 425 (D.) By what mysterious light have you discovered that aseity is entail'd on matter? **1824** COLERIDGE *Aids to Refl.* (1848) I. 270 The obscure and abysmal subject of the divine A-seity.

aselar, Obs. form of ASHLAR *sb.*

asele, var. ASSEAL *v. Obs.*; obs. f. HAZEL.

asell, early variant of EISELL, *Obs.*, vinegar.

aselline (ə'sɛlaɪn), *a. rare.* [f. L. *asell-us* a little ass + -INE.] Of or pertaining to a little ass, or to the two stars in Cancer called *Aselli*.
1855 BAILEY *Mystic*, Between The Aselline starlets and the Manger dim.

asemoche, obs. form of AS MUCH.

asen(e: see ASEE *v.*

†**a'sench**, *v. Obs.* Forms of *pa. t.* 3 **asenchte, aseingde, aseint, asencte,** 4 **asenkte.** [f. A- *pref.* 1 + SENCH, OE. *sęncan*, causal of *sincan* to SINK. Cf. *adrench*, *adrink*, and see ASINK.] To cause to sink; to submerge, drown.
1205 LAY. 25627 Ure scipen he aseingde, þat folc he al adrente [**1250** Oure folk he aseint]. *a* **1230** *Juliana* 33 Þu.. asenchtest hare uan. **1297** R. GLOUC. 489 That water suththe heye aros, & muche is lond asencte. **1340** *Ayenb.* 49 And azenkte vif cities in to helle.

†**a'send**, *v. Obs.* [OE. *asęndan*, f. A- *pref.* 1 + *sęndan* to send.] To send forth.
c **1000** *Ags. Gosp., Matt.* xx. 2 He asende hiȝ on hys winȝeard. *c* **1175** *Lamb. Hom.* 91 Þat he walde his gast asenden ofer mennesc flesc.

asende, var. ASHEND *v. Obs.* to disgrace, ruin.

asepsis (ə'sɛpsɪs). *Med.* [f. A- 14 + SEPSIS.] Absence of micro-organisms likely to cause infection; methods or treatment that, by the use of sterilized instruments, etc., are aimed at preventing septic infection.
1892 F. J. THORNBURY in *N.Y. Med. Jrnl.* LVI. 741/1 Asepsis permanent and reliable..may be accomplished in a simple manner by sterilizing the dressings by heat applied..in the form of steam. **1900** *Daily News* 7 May 3/2 The conditions as regards asepsis were by no means ideal. **1919** W. T. GRENFELL *Labrador Doctor* (1920) iv. 70 Removing a leg at the thigh..without any attempt at or idea of asepsis. **1964** M. HYNES *Med. Bacteriol.* (ed. 8) iii. 26 The foundation of modern surgery is asepsis—the creation and preservation of a bacterium-free environment.

aseptic (ə'sɛptɪk), *a.* and *sb.* [f. A- *pref.* 14 + Gr. σηπτικός putrefying; cf. Gr. ἄσηπτος, and see ANTISEPTIC.] **A.** *adj.* Not liable to putrefy, non-putrescent. **B.** *sb.* [sc. substance.]
1859 in WORCESTER. **1883** J. BISHOP in Quain *Dict. Med.* 59 Putrid ulcers..may certainly be rendered aseptic by suitable means. **1883** *Standard* 20 Oct. 3/7 A perfectly aseptic drink. **1884** *Pall Mall G.* 12 Jan. 2 Is made from the finest water and has passed through processes which render it a perfect aseptic.

aseptically (ə'sɛptɪkəlɪ), *adv.* [f. ASEPTIC *a.*: see -ICALLY.] So as to be free from sepsis. Also *transf.*
1901 *Jrnl. Path. & Bacteriol.* VII. 260 All apparatus was ..carefully sterilised, and the operation wounds healed aseptically. **1940** *Mind* XLIX. 385 Every philosophical question answers itself if asked *aseptically* and fully enough.

asepticism (ə'sɛptɪsɪz(ə)m). [f. ASEPTIC *a.* and *sb.* + -ISM.] Aseptic or antiseptic treatment.
1880 MACCORMAC *Antisept. Surg.* 54 The very ligature is part of asepticism.

asepticize (ə'sɛptɪsaɪz), *v.* [f. ASEPTIC *a.* + -IZE.] *trans.* To render aseptic, sterilize.
1892 *N.Y. Med. Jrnl.* LVI. 755/1 A new combination sterilizer for asepticising simultaneously water, instruments, and dressings. *Ibid.* 755/2 The dressings, after having been asepticized, are removed. **1907** *Practitioner* June 803 Bottles and forceps were asepticised by being dipped in carbolic lotion.

aser, obs. f. ACIER steel.
1430 LYDG. *Chron. Troy* III. xxii, No uyser To save his face but only an aser.

aser, aserre, obs. forms of AZURE.

asere, var. ASEAR *v. Obs.* to dry up.

aserve, var. ASSERVE *v. Obs.* to serve, deserve.

†**a'set**, *v. Obs.* [OE. *asęttan*, f. A- *pref.* 1 + *sęttan* to SET.]
1. To set up, place; to appoint; to set out, array.
c **885** K. ÆLFRED *Oros.* VI. xv, And het ænne weall..asettan from sǽ oþ sǽ. *c* **975** *Rushw. Gosp.* Matt. iii. 10 Þenu is soþlice axe wyrtruma treowes aseted [*Ags. & Hatt.* asett]. *c* **1175** *Lamb. Hom.* 115 On a-sette tidan. **1340** *Ayenb.* 140 Hy hise agrayþeþ and azet mid alle hire ournemens.
2. ? To set upon, beset.
1413 LYDG. *Pylgr. Sowle* I. xv. 12 Myn enemy sore asettyth me.

aseth(e, aseyth, var. ASSETH, *Obs.* satisfaction.

a-seven: in seven: see A *prep.*[1] 6.
1297 R. GLOUC. 405 Her ost hii delde aseuene.

asexual (ə'sɛksjuːəl), *a. Biol.* [f. A- *pref.* 14 + SEXUAL.] **a.** Not sexual, without sex. In *Bot.* formerly applied to cryptogams; cf. *agamic*.
1830 LINDLEY *Nat. Syst. Bot.* Introd. 19 Asexual plants are flowerless. **1858** LEWES *Sea-side Stud.* 289 Reproducing themselves by sexual and asexual methods.
b. In general contexts: without sexuality.
1896 L. ECKENSTEIN *Woman under Monasticism* ix. 307 The high estimation of virgin purity..was advocated by the leaders of thought..and..the asexual existence..was extolled as virtue in itself. **1903** *Daily Mail* 10 Sept. 2/7 All doctors will tell you that, athletic or not, women are more asexual than men. **1928** D. H. LAWRENCE *Let.* ? 17 Aug. (1962) 1077, I feel I've shot it [*sc.* the book] like a bomb against all their false sex and hypocrisy—as my Florentine doctor said, against all their asexual sexuality.

asexuality (əˌsɛksjuː'ælɪtɪ). *Biol.* [f. prec. + -ITY.] Asexual condition, absence of sex.
1877 *Academy* 17 Mar. 232 In so highly-organised plants ..total asexuality would be an anomaly.

asexualization (əˌsɛksjuːəlaɪ'zeɪʃən, -lɪ'zeɪʃən). *Surg.* [f. A- 14 + SEXUALIZ(E *v.* + -ATION.] The action or process of sterilizing, or rendering sexually impotent, an animal or human being.
1895 E. STUVER in *Ohio Med. Jrnl.* VI. 193 (*title*) Asexualization for the limitation of disease, and the prevention and punishment of crime. **1909** *Boston Med. & Surg. Jrnl.* 21 Oct. 584/2 (*title*) Asexualization as a Remedial Measure in the Relief of Certain Forms of Mental, Moral and Physical Degeneration. **1961** *Brit. Med. Dict.* 144/1 *Asexualization*, the process of sterilization..in the male by castration or vasectomy; in the female by removal of ovaries or ligation of the uterine tubes.

a'sexually, *adv. Biol.* [f. ASEXUAL *a.* + -LY[2].] Without sexual agency.
1862 HUXLEY *Lect. Wrkg. Men* 86 They take place asexually. **1879** tr. *Haeckel's Evol. Man* I. viii. 185 These Primæval Animals reproduce themselves..asexually by division, the formation of buds, spores, germ-cells.

asey, obs. f. ASSAY.

†**as'fast, as fast**, *adv. phr.* Besides its obvious import (see AS A 3, 5, and FAST), this combination had formerly the sense of: As fast as might be, very quickly, straightway, immediately (Fr. *aussitôt*). Cf. ASSOON, ASTITE.
c **1374** CHAUCER *Troylus* v. 1641 And such a case betide, and that as fast, That Troilus well understood that she N'as nat so kind as that her ought to be. **1440** *Promp. Parv.*, Asfaste, or a-noon [**1499** asfast, or anone] *Statim, confestim, protinus, mox.*

ash (æʃ), *sb.*[1] Forms: 1–2 **æsc**, (3 **asse**, 4 **aychs**,) 4–5 **assch(e, asch(e**, 4–6 **assh(e**, 4–7 **ashe**, (5 **aish, esche**, 6 **ach**,) 6– **ash.** [Common Teut.: OE. *æsc* is cogn. with ON. *askr*, OHG. *ask*, MHG. *asch*, mod.G. *esche*, OTeut. **ask-oz.*]
1. a. A well-known forest tree, indigenous to Europe, Western Asia, and North Africa, and noted in Teutonic literature from the earliest times; having silver-grey bark, graceful pinnate foliage, a peculiar winged seed or samara called the 'ash-key,' and very tough close-grained wood valuable for implements.
b. The tribe of trees *Fraxineæ*, N.O. *Oleaceæ*, including the common ash (*Fraxinus excelsior*) with several American species, and the manna or flowering ashes (*Ornus Europæa* and *rotundifolia*).
c **700** *Epinal Gloss.* 416 Fraxinus, aesc. **935** *Chart. Æthelstan* in *Cod. Dipl.* V. 221 On ðæne ealdan æsc. *a* **1300** W. DE BIBLESW. in Wright *Voc.* 171 *De frene*, of asse. *c* **1305** *St. Kenelm* 171 in *E.E.P.* (1862) 52 A gret asch..stent in þulke place. *c* **1380** *Sir Ferumb.* 5248 Þe Emperour him liȝt a-doun anon, Vnder an Aychs. *c* **1386** CHAUCER *Knts. T.* 2064 Wilw, elm, plane, assh. **1440** *Promp. Parv.*, Esche, *fraxinus.* **1504** *Plumpton Corr.* 188 The okes are sold..& the aches. **1596** SPENSER *F.Q.* I. i. 9 The warlike beech; the ash for nothing ill. **1769** SIR J. HILL *Fam. Herbal* (1812) 16 The Manna Ash is a lower tree than the common ash. **1847** BLACKWELL *Malet's North. Antiq.* 413 (tr. *Edda*) The ash Yggdrasill..is the greatest and best of all trees. Its branches spread over the whole world, and even reach above heaven. **1866** JOHNS in *Treas. Bot.* 506 Several American species of ash resemble the European ash in general appearance and qualities. **1872** OLIVER *Elem. Bot.* II. 207 The wood of the Ash is very tough and elastic, and valued by cart- and wheelwrights.
2. The wood or timber of the ash-tree.
c **1380** WYCLIF *Sel. Wks.* (1871) III. 500 An ymage..of oke or of asshe. *c* **1450** *Merlin* xxii. 390 A grete growe spere of aish. **1823** P. NICHOLSON *Pract. Builder* 260 Ash is a species of wood very common in Britain. [See also 5.]
†**3.** The ashen shaft of a spear; a spear. *Obs.*
a **1000** *Beowulf* 3548 Æscum and ecȝum. **1607** SHAKS. *Cor.* IV. v. 114 That body, where against My grained Ash an hundred times hath broke. **1700** DRYDEN *Pal. & Arcite* III. 513 The tourney is allowed but one career Of the tough ash, with the sharp-grinded spear.
4. ground ash, a. An ash sapling. **b.** Applied locally to various umbelliferous herbs with pinnate leaves, esp. the ASHWEED or bishopweed, and wild angelica (Britten and Holl.) **mountain ash**, synonym of the rowan-tree or quickbeam (*Pyrus Aucuparia*); formerly also occas. of the aspen (*Populus tremula*), called also **quaking ash. wild ash**, identified by the herbalists sometimes with the mountain ash, sometimes with the *Ornus* of the continent.
1552 HULOET, Ashe called a wylde ashe with greate leaues, *Ornus.* **1562** TURNER *Herbal* II. 71 a, Wild ashe trees grow in the rooky or craggi mountaynes. **1578** LYTE *Dodoens* 748 Pliny and Columella calleth it *Ornus*, and *Fraxinus, syluestris* ..In English, Quickebeame, feelde Ashe, wild Ashe, and white Ashe. **1794** MARTYN *Rousseau's Bot.* xxi. 291 Mountain Ash and the Service..have pinnate or winged leaves like the Ash. **1814** WORDSW. *Excurs.* VII. 709 The Mountain Ash..lifts her head Decked with autumnal berries.
5. *Comb.* (chiefly *attrib.*), as *ash-bud*, *-plank*, *-spear*, *-staff*, *-tree*, *-wood*; and in many OE. compounds, in sense 3, as *æsc-here* a company armed with spears, *æsc-pleȝa* 'spear-play,' war, *æsc-róf* 'spear-famed,' noble. Also **ash-fly, ash-grub**, a fly and grub found on the ash-tree and used by anglers; **ash-key**, the winged two-celled seed or samara of the ash-tree; **ash-leaf**, an early potato with leaves resembling those of the ash.
a **1000** *Judith* 217 (Bosw.) Æt ðam æscplegan. *Ibid.* 337 Eorlas æscrófe. **1398** TREVISA *Barth. De P.R.* XVII. lxii.

(1495) 639 Yf a serpent be sette bytwene a fyre and asshe leuys: he woll fle in to the fire. **1440** *Promp. Parv.*, Asche tre, *Fraxinus.* *c* **1589** *Plaine Perc.* (1860) 3 With a quarter Ashe staffe on my shoulder. **1805** Scott *Last Minstr.* III. vi, The tough ash-spear, so stout and true. **1842** Tennyson *Gardener's Dau.* 28 More black than ashbuds in the front of March. **1879** *Cassell's Techn. Educ.* IV. 130/1 The timbers .. commonly in use in our carriage factories are English ash-plank.

1787 T. Best *Angling* (ed. 2) 24 Oak-fly, Ash fly, or Wood-cock fly, found on the body of an Oak or Ash. *Ibid.* 19 Bark-worm, or Ash-grub. **1676** Cotton *Angler* II. 353 The Ash-grub .. is plump, milkwhite .. with a red head. **1440** *Promp. Parv.*, Esch key, *Clava in fractinus.* **1562** Turner *Herbal* II. 6 a, Called in Inglishe ashe keyes because they hang in bunches after the manner of keyes. **1795** Barker in *Phil. Trans.* LXXXV. 412 The hedge fruits were in great abundance, excepting ash-keys. **1843** G. Darling in *Proc. Berw. Nat. Club* II. 77 The delicate early ash-leaved kidney. **1845** *Morn. Chron.* 22 Nov. 5/2 The Wimborne kidneys .. are not springing like the ash-leafs.

ash (æʃ), *sb.*[2] commonly in *pl.* **ashes** ('æʃɪz). Forms: *Sing.* 1 **asce**, 1–3 **axe**, 2–3 **aske**, 4 **esche**, **esssse**, **aische**, **asch**, 4–6 **ashe**, 4– **ash** (*north.* 3–6 **asse**; *Sc.* 6 **as**, **alse**, 6– **ass**). *Pl.* α. 1 **ascan**, **axsan**, 2 **æscan**, 2–6 **axan**, **-en**, 3 **acxen**, **axin**, 3–4 **asken**, 3–5 **asshen**, 4 **aishen**, 4–5 **aisshen**, **-chin**, **aschen**, **-yn**, 6 **axsen** (9 *dial.* **axen**, **-an**). β. 3 (*Orm.*) **asskess**, 3–5 **askes**, 4 **axses**, **axes**, **assches**, **aschis**, 4–5 **askys**, **-is**, 4–6 **asshes**, 5 **aisshes**, **aysshes**, **aischis**, 6 (*Sc.* **asses**, **-is**), 5– **ashes**. [Common Teut.: OE. *asce*, *axe* is cogn. w. ON. *aska*, Da. *aske*, OHG. *asgâ*, *ascâ*, MHG. *asche*, Goth. *azgo*, OTeut. **azgôn*. The northern *aske* was prob. the Norse word; thence also *asse*, like Sc. *buss* for *busk*.]

1. The powdery residue, composed chiefly of earthy or mineral particles, left after the combustion of any substance. **a.** *plural.*

α. *c* **1000** *Ags. Ps.* ci. 10 Ic anlic ætt æscean hlafe. *c* **1000** *Sax. Leechd.* I. 334 Heortes hornes axan. *c* **1230** *Ancr. R.* 214 þe ȝiscare .. lið euer iðen asken. *c* **1386** Chaucer *Sqrs. T.* 247 It was Wonder to maken of fern Asshen [*v.r.* aschyn, aisshen, aschen] glas. **1483** Caxton *Gold. Leg.* 224/2 A loof baken under asshen. **1578** Lyte *Dodoens* 271 [Dill] made into axsen. **1597** Gerard *Herbal* II. cxlvii. (1633) 429 The axen or ashes. **1863** W. Barnes *Poem in Dorset Dial.* in *Sat. Rev.* 124 The fleäme's red peaks, till axan white Did quench em.

β. **1200** Ormin 1001 Tatt lac wass brennd And turrnedd all till asskess. *c* **1325** *E.E. Allit. P.* B. 626 Vnder askeȝ ful hote. **1366** Maundev. xxviii. 289 Undir the assches there offe. **1413** Lydg. *Pylgr. Sowle* II. lviii. 56 Hit brenneth in to asshes. **1513** Douglas *Æneis* II. xi. (x.) 52 Fillit with assis reid. **1562** J. Heywood *Prov. & Epigr.* (1867) 22, I proud, and thou proud, who shall beare thashes out. **1697** Dryden *Virg. Georg.* I. 118 Sprinkle sordid Ashes all around. **1716–8** Lady Montague *Lett.* II. xliii. 14 The hot ashes commonly set the house on fire. **1806** Coleridge *Christabel*, The brands were dying, Amid their own white ashes lying.

b. *collective sing.*

1250 Lay. 25989 Al bi-walewed in axe. **1297** R. Glouc. 536 Hii sende Al the brut aske withoute. *a* **1300** *E.E. Psalter* ci. 10 Aske as bred I et. *a* **1300** *Havelok* 2840 Sket was [he] on þe asse leyd .. And brend til asken. **1382** Wyclif *Amos* ii. 1 He brente the bonys of the Kyng of Ydume vn to ash. *c* **1450** Henryson *Mor. Fables* 5 Scraping among the Ashe. **1535** Stewart *Cron. Scot.* (1858) I. 7 Also thair principall toun, Brynt it in as. **1548** *Compl. Scot.* 21 Brynt in puldir ande asse. **1818** Scott *Bride Lamm.* xi, 'What would ye collect out of the sute and the ass?' **1868** Sill *Hermitage* v. 6 A charring ember, smouldering into ash.

c. *simple sing.* (Now chiefly in scientific lang.)

c **1385** Chaucer *L.G.W.* 2649 Ded wex hire hew & lyk an asch to sene. **1799** W. Taylor in Robberds *Mem.* I. 287 Burn my last letter to an irrecollectable ash. **1864** Swinburne *Atalanta* 2074 My heart is within me As an ash in the fire. **1868** Dana *Mineral.* 747 Hircite .. after complete combustion leaves an ash.

d. ***ash*(*es*) *of roses***: a greyish-pink colour.

1872 *Young Englishwoman* Nov. 599/1 *Marmotte*, a dark ashes-of-roses shade. **1893** *Daily News* 17 May 3/4 The soft greyish pink known as 'ashes of roses'. **1901** Kipling *Five Nations* (1903) 113 Opal and ash-of-roses, Cinnamon, umber, and dun. **1927** *Daily Express* 14 Mar. 5 Pomegranate, mulberry red, mushroom, and ashes of roses, a colour that looks like blue ash with a touch of flame, are among the fashion reds.

2. ***volcanic ash***: the similar powdery matter ejected from volcanos. ***black ash***: a mixture of carbonate of soda and sulphide of calcium formed in the process of manufacturing soda from salt. (For other special products of similar nature, see BONE-ASH, COPPER-ASH, PEARLASH, POTASH.)

(In this sense now *collect. sing.* ***ashes*** = kinds of ash.)

1667 Badily *Phil. Trans. Abr.* I. 140 (*title*) A Shower of Ashes in the Archipelago. **1727–52** Chambers *Cycl.* s.v. *Potashes*, Fern also makes excellent pot-ashes. **1807** Pinkerton *Mod. Geog.* (1811) 627 With furious volcanic shocks .. The ashes were borne to the distance of 150 miles. **1863** Watts *Dict. Chem.* I. 420 Volcanic ash .. appears to be composed of fragments of lava, slag, mica, felspar, magnetic iron ore, augite, pumice, olivine, etc. **1868** Watts *Dict. Chem.* (1877) V. 326 Black Ash or Ball Soda. **1878** A. Ramsay *Phys. Geog.* i. 22 By the study of modern volcanic ashes, it is .. not difficult to distinguish those of ancient date.

3. *transf.* or *fig.* Ruins, remains. ***to lay in ashes***: to burn to the ground, destroy utterly.

1513 Douglas *Æneis* II. viii. (vii.) 122 O ȝe cauld assis of Troy. **1647** Cowley *Mistr.*, *Given Heart* iv, Then shall Love keep the ashes .. Of both our broken Hearts. **1711** Addison *Spect.* No. 163 ¶7 Whole Kingdoms laid in Ashes. **1877** Bryant *Ruins Italica*, The envy of earth's cities once wert thou—A weary solitude and ashes now! **1879** Froude *Cæsar* xii. 159 Where the ashes of the Sertorian rebellion were still smouldering.

4. a. From the ancient custom of burning the bodies of the dead: That which remains of a human body after cremation or (by *transf.*) total decomposition; hence *poet.* for 'mortal remains, buried corpse.'

c **1275** *Sinners Beware* in *O.E. Misc.* 78 þe wurmes hine ifyndeþ, To axe heo hyne gryndeþ. *c* **1350** *Will. Palerne* 4368 Sche shal be brent .. & þe aschis of hire body, etc. **1387** Trevisa *Higden* (Rolls Ser.) VII. 5 þe holy axes of seint Wilfrede þe bisshop. **1460** in *Pol. Rel. & L. Poems* (1866) 128 Ther be .. þe askes of Iohne þe baptyste. **1528** More *Heresyes* I. Wks. 110/1 And of yᵉ ashes of one heritique springeth up manye. **1683** E. Hooker *Pref. Pordage's Myst. Div.* 31 Rake not up the Ashes of the Dead. **1751** Gray *Elegy* xxiii, E'en in our ashes live their wonted fires. **1842** Macaulay *Horatius* xxvii, Facing fearful odds For the ashes of his fathers And the temples of his Gods. **1852** Tennyson *Wellington* ix, The mortal disappears; Ashes to ashes, dust to dust.

b. ***the ashes***: in *Cricket*, a term originating in a mock obituary notice published in the *Sporting Times* 2 Sept. 1882, after the sensational victory of Australia at the Oval on Aug. 29 of that year, announcing the cremation of the dead body of English Cricket and the taking of the ashes to Australia; hence, the losing or winning of the rubber in the series of test matches played periodically between the chosen representatives of English and Australian cricket is frequently described as the loss, or the recovery (if previously lost) or retaining (if previously held) of the ashes.

[**1882** *Sporting Times* 2 Sept., In Affectionate Remembrance of English Cricket Which died at the Oval on 29th August, 1882. Deeply lamented by a large circle of sorrowing friends and acquaintances. R.I.P. N.B.—The body will be cremated and the ashes taken to Australia.] **1903** Warner in *Westm. Gaz.* 8 Dec. 2/1 If we fail to bring home 'the ashes' it will certainly not be for want of trying. **1921** *Glasgow Herald* 21 Jan. 8 We must accept the transference of the 'Ashes' philosophically.

5. Dust of the ground. (Hence used to express man's mortal constitution.)

c **950** *Lindisf. Gosp.* Matt. x. 14 Sceaccas ða asca of fotum. *c* **1230** *Ancr. R.* 214 Euerich eorðlich eihte nis buten eorðe & asken. *c* **1315** Shoreham 107 Thench thou nart bote esche. **1340** *Ayenb.* 137 Huet am ich bote esssse and spearken. **1382** Wyclif *Mal.* iv. 3 Thei shuln be ashe vndir the soole of ȝoure feet. **1535** Coverdale *ibid.*, They shalbe like the asshes vnder the soles of your fete. [So in **1611**.] **1548** *Compl. Scot.* xvii. 152 Al men ar eird ande alse. **1588** A. King *Canisius' Catech.* 130 Quhairfoir than art thow proude, thow earthe and assis? **1738** Wesley *Hymn 'Eternal Power'* iii, Lord, what shall Earth and Ashes do? We would adore our Maker too.

6. a. (Used, in reference to the colour of wood ashes, to express excessive pallor of the countenance.) Hence the phrase ***pale as ashes***, and ***ashes*** used poet. for 'death-like paleness.'

c **1374** Chaucer *Anel. & Arc.* 173 Other coloure thanne Asshen hath she noone. **1678** Butler *Hud.* III. i. 1063 Turn'd pale as ashes or a clout. **1711** Addison *Spect.* No. 12 ¶3 Ghosts as pale as Ashes. **1814** Byron *Lara* I. xxviii, The lip of ashes, and the cheek of flame. **1879** Tennyson *Lover's T.* 91 And I .. saw his face Fire, and dead ashes, and all fire again, Thrice in a second.

b. Ash-colour.

1876 *Field & Forest* II. 41 Admitting that *tephrocotis* 'has the least ash on the head', how can this fact be attributed to climatological influences?

7. (From the employment of ashes among Eastern nations in token of mourning, used in many phrases symbolizing the expression of grief or repentance.)

c **950** *Lindisf. Gosp.* Matt. xi. 21 In asca .. hreownisse dydon [*Rushw.* ascan]. *c* **1000** *Ags. G.* ibid., On axan. *c* **1160** *Hatton G.*, On æscan. *c* **1375** Wyclif *Serm.* ccxviii. Sel. Wks. (1871) II. 187 Do penaunce in aishen and hayre. **1597** Shaks. *2 Hen. IV*, I. ii, Repents .. not in ashes, and sackecloath, but in new Silke, and old sacke. **1611** Bible *Jonah* iii. 6 Couered him with sackcloth, & sate in ashes. **1859** Mill *Liberty* ii. 52 A deplorable error and misfortune, for which humanity should mourn in sackcloth and ashes.

8. *Comb.* **a.** In a similative relation, as ***ash-brown***, ***-grey***, ***-looking***, ***-white***; passing into parasynthetic compounds, as **ash-bellied**, having a belly the colour of ashes; **ash-colour** (used attrib.), **ash-coloured**, of the colour of ashes, whitish- or brownish-grey. Also, in instrumental relation, ***ash-smeared***.

1811 Shaw *Zool.* VIII. 214 Ash-bellied Creeper. **1921** *Glasgow Herald* 25 June 5/7 The spotted fly-catchers .. are ash-brown above with a central dark line on the head feathers. **1959** *Times* 8 Sept. 12/7 On the log wall was an ashbrown felt. **1580** Sidney *Arcadia* (1622) 382 A faire smocke, wrought all in flames of ash-colour silke and gold. **1766** Pennant *Zool.* II. 438 The forehead is a reddish ash-colour. **1611** Cotgr., *Cendré* .. ash-coloured. **1656** *Roxb. Bal.* (1883) IV. 490 A Wench with an ash-coloured face. **1882** M. Arnold *Sel. Poems* 125 The sweet blue eyes—the soft, ash-colour'd hair. **1889** Yeats *Wanderings of Oisin* 125 An ash-grey feather. **1904** W. de la Mare *Henry Brocken* 88 The cadent wail of the ash-grey birds. **1797** Bewick *Brit. Birds* (1847) I. 65 Minute specklings of white, ash-grey, and brown. **1853** Kane *Grinnell Exp.* xlvii. (1856) 438 Ash-looking silt from the ground-up gneisses. **1901** Kipling *Kim* i. 4 Then there were holy men, ash-smeared *faquirs* by their brick shrines. **1927** D. H. Lawrence *Mornings in Mexico* 160 Some of these ash-smeared men held armfuls of snakes. **1873** Miss Broughton *Nancy* III. 113 His face growing even more ash-white than it was before.

b. Special combinations (chiefly *attrib.*): **ash-barrel** (chiefly *U.S.*), a barrel for holding ashes; also occas. ***ashes barrel***; **ash-bed**, a thick layer of ash; **ash-bin**, a receptacle for ashes and household refuse; **ash-blond(e** *a.*, applied to hair of a light blond colour; as *sb.*, the colour itself; a person with hair of this colour; **ash-blue**, a chemical product of copper and lime-water; **ash-box**, a receptacle for ashes, (*a*) a pan beneath a fire-grate, (*b*) a dust-bin; **ash-cake**, one baked on or under hot ashes; **ash-can** (chiefly *U.S.*) = *ash-bin*; also *fig.*; in *U.S. Services' slang*, a depth charge; †**ashes-cloth**, a cloth to carry ashes in; †**ashes-dodding**, the strewing of the head with ashes on Ash-Wednesday; **ash-drawer**, (*a*) obs. name of the tourmaline, from its electric properties; (*b*) a drawer for ashes beneath a fire-grate; **ash-fire**, a low fire of ash and cinders used in chemical operations; **ash-furnace**, a furnace used in glass-making; **ash-grate**, a grate that fits over the ash-hole; **ash-heap**, a heap of ashes; *also*, a collection of ashes and household refuse; hence, ***ash-heap-cake*** (= *ash-cake*); **ash-hoist**, a hoist for removing ashes from the ash-pit of an engine house, the stokehold of a vessel, etc.; **ash-hole**, a hole beneath a fire-place or furnace into which the ashes fall; *also*, a hole in which ashes and household refuse are thrown away; **ash-hopper** *U.S.*, a lye cask, resembling a hopper in a mill; **ash-leach**, a hopper or tub in which wood-ashes are placed that the alkaline salts may be dissolved from them; **ash-like** *a.*, resembling ashes; **ash-man**, one who covers himself with, or lives in the, ashes; a collector and remover of ashes; **ash-oven** (= *ash-furnace*); **ash-pan**, a utensil (fitted beneath a grate) in which the ashes are collected and removed; †*also* = *ash-hole*; also, earlier term for *ash-tray*; **ash-pit** (= *ash-hole*); **ash-receiver** *U.S.*, an ash-tray; **ash-riddling**, the northern custom of riddling ashes on the hearth on St. Mark's Eve as a method of divination; **ash-shoot**, a shaft through which the ashes are shot, or are raised from the stokehold to the deck of a ship; †**ash-stone** (= *ash-drawer*); **ash-tray**, a small bowl or other receptacle for tobacco-ash; **ash-tub** (= *ash-bin*). Also ASH-WEDNESDAY, ASKEBATHE, ASKEFISE, q.v.

1846 D. Corcoran *Pickings from Portfolio* 61 They were .. knocking over the *ashes barrels, shying stones at the lamps. **1870** 'F. Fern' *Ginger-Snaps* 55 Garbage-heaps and ash-barrels before the door of poverty. **1905** Kipling *Actions & Reactions* (1909) 6 That wilderness which is reached from an ash-barrel of a station called Charing Cross. **1947** E. H. Paul *Linden on Saugus Branch* 136 The Protestant deacons .. did not fail to note .. the empty bottles in the ash barrels. **1849** Murchison *Siluria* iv. 77 Felspathic agglomerates and *Ash-beds. **1883** *Pall Mall G.* 29 Dec. 10 There were no *ashbins. **1903** *Daily Chron.* 9 Mar. 3/1 My hair is a beautiful *ash-blonde. **1926** *Bulletin & Scots Pictorial* 29 June 10/3 A mass of ash-blond hair was braided and coiled around her head. **1947** E. Hyams *Wm. Medium* x. 197 They were ash-blondes, with heavenly skins and large blue eyes. **1833** Loudon *Encycl. Archit.* §605 The bottoms of these chambers should have an *ash-box fitted into them. **1847** *Rep. Comm. Patents 1846* (*U.S.*) 261 The chamber of combustion and its grate and ash-box. **1899** W. C. Morrow *Bohemian Paris* 103 The rows of heaped *ash-cans that lined the way. **1919** *World's Work* Oct. 604/2 The depth charge looked like the innocent domestic ash can, and that was the name by which it soon became popularly known. **1920** *Chambers's Jrnl.* Mar. 151/2 One of them upsets the ash can. **1944** Auden *For Time Being* (1945) 71 In a wet vacancy among the ash cans. **1959** G. Jenkins *Twist of Sand* iv. 68 'I give it five minutes before the ash-cans come.' .. Waiting for a depth-charge attack is probably as bad as the attack itself. **1461–83** *Ord. R. Househ.* 85 They shalle have *aysshes clothes .. to fetche aysshes in from every mannes chambres. *a* **1564** Becon *Humble Supplic.* Wks. (1844) 231 Bread-worshipping, *ashes-dodding, fire and tapers-hallowing. **1802** *Edin. Rev.* III. 307 *Ashdrawer as the English name for a tourmaline. **1833** Loudon *Encycl. Archit.* §599 With the fire-places near the hearth, with front bars beveled inwards, and with an ash-drawer, the fender may be made very low. **1920** *Chambers's Jrnl.* Apr. 264/2 An ash-drawer is arranged under the grate with the hot chamber below it. **1833** Loudon *Encycl. Archit.* §605 The *ash-grate, being taken out, and its contents thrown in the dusthole, might be replaced, and the chamber again filled with coals. **1837** *Mag. Domestic Econ.* III. 111 There should be an ash-grate and pit made under the fire-place, that the ashes may drop through the ash-grate into the pit, and leave the cinders over it. *c* **1650** Herrick *Wks.* I. 176 (Halliw.) *Ash-heapes, in the which ye use Husbands and wives by streakes to chuse. **1839** Stonehouse *Axholme* 47 Monday, ash-heap cake, with butter in a hole in the middle. *c* **1870** J. Murphy *Comm. Lev.* x. 19 The sin-sacrifice .. was to be burnt on the ash-heap. **1920** *Blackw. Mag.* Sept. 303/2 The noise of the *ash-hoist greeted his ear. **1641** French *Distill.* iii. (1651) 84 The *Ash-hole .. must be as wide as the Furnace. **1818** Miss Ferriar *Marriage* xxviii, I saw you .. throw all the good dreaming-bread into the ash-hole. **1871** Lowell *Study Wind.* in *Casquet Lit.* (1877) I. 394/1 The ash-hole of the glass-furnace. **1809** *Trans. Amer. Philos. Soc.* VI. 240

'Cubic salts'..thrown upon the *ash-hoppers..are supposed to assist in precipitating the lime. **1885** 'C. E. CRADDOCK' *Prophet Gt. Smoky Mts.* i. 18 Some fifteen or twenty hounds that suddenly materialized from the ash-hopper. **1611** COTGR., *Cendré*, ashy, *ash-like. **1625** PURCHAS *Pilgrims* II. 1478 Dervises..sleeping at night in the warme ashes, with which they besmeare their bodies. These *Ashmen suffer not the Rasor to come upon their heads. **1873** ALDRICH *Marj. Daw* 142 He has fought the ashman's boy, the grocer's boy [etc.]. **1959** E. FENWICK *Long Way Down* iii. 22 The ashman's visits: depressing, but routine. **1568** BIBLE *1 Kings* vii. 50 The *ashpannes [*other vers.* censers] of pure golde. **1727** BRADLEY *Fam. Dict.* s.v. *Chimney*, The Ash-pan..must be dug in the Hearth, of a convenient Depth. **1857** E. FITZGERALD *Let.* 3 Oct. (1889) I. 265 The last Cheroot he had tried lay three quarters smoked in its little China ash-pan. **1883** *Army & Navy Co-op. Soc. Catal.*, Ash Pans in brass, steel, and Berlin Black. **1898** G. B. SHAW *Mrs. Warren's Profession* IV. p. 216 A double writing-table..with a cigar box, ash pans. **1797** *Encycl. Brit.* (ed. 3) s.v. *Furnace*, The ashes drop down into a cavity..called the **ash-pit*. **1859** PARKES *Pract. Hygiene* ix. (ed. 3) 313 Proximity of ashpits..causing contamination of the air. **1930** D. PARKER *Laments for Living* 62 The *ash-receivers, of Japanese manufacture, were in the form of grotesque heads..given..mouths stretched into great gapes, into which those who had the heart for it might flick their ashes. **1825** BROCKETT *North Country Words* s.v. *Ass*, **Ass-riddlin*, the riddling or sifting of the ashes on the hearth, on the eve of St. Mark. The superstitious notion is, that, should any of the family die within the year, the shoe will be impressed on the ashes. **1893** K. SIMPSON *Jeanie* 240 Ash-riddling is an old custom which I like to keep up. **1889** *Cent. Dict.*, *Ash-shoot. **1898** KIPLING *Fleet in Being* 5, I heard Swinburne laying down the law to his juniors by the ash-shoot. **1920** *Blackw. Mag.* Sept. 303/2 He..watched the fireman unhook his first bucket of ashes from the hoist and carry them to the ash-shoot. **1759** WILSON in *Phil. Trans.* LI. 308 Experiments made upon the Tourmalin, or *Ashstone. **1887** KIPLING *Plain Tales fr. Hills* (1890) 116 He had tipped a bagful of his powder into the big silver *ash-tray. **1926** M. SUTHERLAND *One o' the Herd* v, A lacquered Chinese table with..a box of cigarettes and an ashtray upon it. **1620** QUARLES *Feast Wormes* 40 Though thou chuse an *Ash-tub for thy bed.

†**ash**, *sb.*³ Corruption of ACHE *sb.*², as in *sweet ash*: hare's parsley (*Anthriscus sylvestris*); and †*ash of Jerusalem* (obs.): prob. dyer's woad (*Isatis tinctoria*).

1548 TURNER *Names of Herbs* 40 Wyld wad is called in Englishe ashe of Hierusalem.

ash (æʃ), *sb.*⁴ Also 1, 9– **æsc**, 9 **asc.** [OE *æsc*: see ASH *sb.*¹] The name of the Old English runic letter ᚫ, corresponding to *æ* in the alphabetic writing of Old English, to which letter the name is also applied by modern scholars; named, like other runes, from the word of which it was the initial.

a **1000** *Runic Poem* (1915) 22 Æsc biþ oferheah, eldum dyre. *a* **1000** in C. Williamson *O.E. Riddles of Exeter Bk.* (1977) 95 Se torhta Æsc, an an linan. **1840** *Archaeologia* XXVIII. 338 (Fig.), Æsc. **1883** I. TAYLOR *Alphabet* II. viii. 219 The rune *asc*..derived from *epsilon*, denoting *a*. **1915** B. DICKINS *Runic & Heroic Poems* 4 To the original 24 letters the English eventually added six, *æsc, ac, yr, ear, calc, gar*, if not a seventh *ior*. **1942** E. V. K. DOBBIE *Anglo-Saxon Minor Poems* 159 The rune for *æsc*, 'ash'..[was] used for the sound *æ* after the early Anglo-Saxon sound change *a* > *æ*. **1955** QUIRK & WRENN *Old Eng. Gram.* i. 8 Æ is called 'ash', the OE word *æsc* 'ash' being the name of the corresponding runic letter. **1964** T. PYLES *Orig. & Devel. Eng. Lang.* ii. 29 The *æ* was called *æsc* 'ash', the name of the runic symbol which represented the same sound, though it in no way resembled the Latin-English digraph. **1985** R. W. BURCHFIELD *Eng. Lang.* ii. 7 The runes..were..powerful, symbolically representing simple concepts, in that each character was also a word: thus *ash*..meant 'ash-tree; a ship made from the ash'.

ash (æʃ), *v.*¹ *dial.* [f. ASH *sb.*¹] To flog with an ash-stick. Cf. *to birch*.

1877 in *Holderness Gloss.* (E.D.S.) 57/1, s.v. *Esh*. **1940** F. KITCHEN *Brother to Ox* i. 4 'Ashing a lad's behind' was the recognized form of punishment.

ash (æʃ), *v.*² [f. ASH *sb.*²] To sprinkle or strew with ashes.

c **1645** HOWELL *Lett.* IV. v, They ashe and powder their pericraniums. **1874** *Daily News* 30 Dec. 3/6 The trotting track..was very slippery, and had to be ashed.

ash, obs. form of ASK *v.*

†**a'shake**, *v. Obs.* [OE. *asceacan*. f. A- *pref.* 1 + *sceacan* to SHAKE.] To shake off; *fig.* to dispel; in *pass.* to be gone, depart.

c **975** *Rushw. Gosp.* Matt. x. 14 Ascakeð dust of fotum eowrum. *c* **1000** *Ags. G.*, Asceacað. *c* **1000** ÆLFRIC *Gen.* xxxi. 22 Iacob wæs asceacen. **1205** LAY. 19154 Ar þe dai weore al asceken Wes þe castel biȝeten.

a-shake (ə'ʃeɪk), *advb. phr.* [A *prep.*¹ + SHAKE.] 'On the shake,' shaking.

1856 MRS. BROWNING *Aur. Leigh* v. (1857) 190 Like wild swans hid in lilies all ashake. **1869** BLACKMORE *Lorna Doone* iii. (ed. 12) 18, I felt his lips and teeth ashake.

ashame (ə'ʃeɪm), *v.* Forms: 1 **asc(e)amian**, 3 **ascam-en**, 4–6 **aschame**, 6 **asshame**, (*Sc.* **eschame**), 4– **ashame**. [f. A- *pref.* 1 + OE. *sc(e)amian* to SHAME. Cf. MHG. *erschamen*, mod.G. *erschämen*.]

†**1.** *intr.* To feel shame, to be ashamed. (In quot. 1305 *aschame* may be imperative, or perh. sb. formed on the verb.) *Obs.*; but see next word.

c **1000** *Ps.* lxviii. 8 (Bosw.) Ná ascamien on me. *c* **1305** *E.E. Poems* (1862) 69 Hi suede & cride on hem aschame. **1533** BELLENDENE *Livy* II. (1822) 177 Thay eschamit that thair ennemies suld departe..unpunist. **1566** KNOX *Hist. Ref.* Wks. 1846 I. 397 Sche eschame nott to sett out ane Proclamatioun, in this forme.

2. *trans.* To put to shame, to make ashamed.

1591 P. ADAMSON in De Foe *Hist. Ch. Scot.* Add. 51 Neither is there any Thing that more ashameth me. **1603** KNOLLES *Hist. Turks* (1621) 814 The Graund master with this answere doth..ashame them. **1826** E. IRVING *Babylon* II. VIII. 291 He raiseth up..the foolish to ashame the wise.

ashamed (ə'ʃeɪmd), *pred. a.* [pa. pple. of prec., in OE. *asceamod*; probably also combining OE. *ȝesceamod*, ME. *yschamed*. Cf. Ger. *erschämt*.]

1. Affected with shame; abashed or put to confusion by a consciousness of guilt or error; disconcerted by a recognition that one's actions or circumstances are in any way not to one's credit.

a **1000** *Crist* (Grein) 1299 Hí ascamode swíciaþ on swíman. *a* **1300** *Cursor M.* 636 Naked were þei boþe tweyn, Ashamed were þei not certeyn. *c* **1400** *Rowland & Ot.* 289 þe Duke Naymes asschamede was, þe blode stert up in his face. *c* **1500** *Pol. Rel. & L. Poems* (1866) 31 Loue that servaunte as thy childe that sone is ashamyde. **1611** BIBLE *Jer.* xvii. 13 All that forsake thee shall be ashamed. **1711** ADDISON *Spect.* No. 292 ¶9 In Milton, the Devil is never described ashamed but once.

2. Const. **a.** *of* (*on, for*, obs.) the cause of shame. *For* a person: vicariously on his account.

1250 LAY. 29608 And weren ascam[ed] sore for þan owreaste deade. **1388** WYCLIF *Ezek.* xxxvi. 32 Be ȝe aschamed on ȝoure weies. **1513** DOUGLAS *Æneis* XII. Prol. 285 Eschamyt of hyr chance. **1673** CAVE *Prim. Chr.* I. i. 10 The honester and severer Romans were ashamed on't. **1752** JOHNSON *Rambl.* No. 192 ¶11, I began to be ashamed of sitting idle. *a* **1762** LADY MONTAGUE *Lett.* xlv. 157, I am ashamed for her who wrote them. **1825** *Bro. Jonathan* I. 378 Are you ashamed already of..sorrow and contrition?

b. with *subord. cl.*

1303 R. BRUNNE *Handl. Synne* 6570 To make hym be ashamede þat he shulde be so defamede. **1601** SHAKS. *Jul. C.* II. ii. 106, I am ashamed I did yeeld to them. **1859** TENNYSON *Enid* 577 Ashamed am I that I should tell it thee.

c. with *inf. phr.*

1647 COWLEY *Mistr., Discovery* i, Why should she asham'd or angry be, To be belov'd by Me? **1711** STEELE *Spect.* No. 302 ¶11, I am ashamed to be caught in this Pickle. **1855** TENNYSON *Maud* I. xiii. 25 Ashamed to be seen. *Mod.* I was ashamed to see it.

3. With *inf. phr.*: **a.** Reluctant through fear of shame *to*. **b.** With a negative: Prevented or deterred by fear of shame from.

1382 WYCLIF *Luke* xvi. 3, I am aschamyd to begge. **1414** BRAMPTON *Penit. Ps.* xli. 16 He, that was sumtyme my frende, Is noȝt aschamed me to assayle. *a* **1593** H. SMITH *Serm.* (1637) 396 We are ashamed of sinne and yet not ashamed to sinne. **1711** ADDISON *Spect.* No. 271 ¶4 He would have made us ashamed to show our Heads. **1849** MACAULAY *Hist. Eng.* II. 96 He was not ashamed to answer that he could not live out of the royal smile.

4. rarely *attrib. arch.*

c **1746** HERVEY *Medit.* (1818) 77 To hide their ashamed heads in the bottom of the ocean. **1872** DARWIN *Emotions* xiii. 322 An ashamed person can hardly endure to meet the gaze of those present.

ashamedly (ə'ʃeɪmɪdlɪ), *adv. rare*⁻⁰. [f. prec. + -LY².] With shame.

a **1600** HULOET is cited by TODD.

a'shamedness (ə'ʃeɪmdnɪs, -ɪdnɪs). [f. as prec. + -NESS.] The state of being ashamed.

c **1630** JACKSON *Creed* IV. II. iv. Wks. III. 258 May deny Christ or manifest their ashamedness of his gospel. **1880** MRS. WHITNEY *Odd or Even* xx. 206 She was ashamed of her ashamedness.

a'shaming, *ppl. a.* [f. ASHAME *v.* + -ING².] Putting to shame, making ashamed.

1819 CRABBE *T. of Hall* XI. 1043 Displeased, displeasing, discontented, blamed; Both, and with cause, ashaming and ashamed.

Ashanti (ə'ʃæntɪ). Also 8 **Assanti**, etc., 9– (*now rare*) **Ashantee**. [Native name.] One of the Akan peoples of West Africa; a member of this people. Also, their language. Hence **A'shantian** *a.*

1705 tr. *Bosman's Descr. Coast of Guinea* vi. 76 The Plunder after this Victory took up the Asiantines fifteen days time... This messenger of ours, who is now in the Asiantean Camp. **1721** J. ATKINS in *New Coll. Voyages & Travels* (1745) II. III. iv. 454/1 It seems, the Santîs, or Assantîs..had lately..driven them from their Habitations. **1824** J. DUPUIS *Jrnl. Residence in Ashantee* i. 21 A party of Ashantees ..suddenly approached. **1831** H. I. RICKETT (*title*) Narrative of the Ashantee War. **1873** J. MARSHALL *Let.* 9 Nov. in W. R. Brownlow *Memoir J.M.* (1890) ii. 19 His party had fired on some Ashantis two days before. **1874** J. G. CHRISTALLER et al. (*title*) A Dictionary, English, Tshi-Asàntè-Akra. **1875** —— *Gram. Tshi* p. xv, As a common name of the 'Asante and Fante Language' we have put down the name Tshi. **1880** G. A. SALA *Amer. Revisited* (1882) I. xvi. 227 [The features] of his companion were of almost brutish Ashantian or Dahomian ruggedness. **1880** J. MARSHALL *Let.* 9 Nov. in W. R. Brownlow *Memoir J.M.* (1890) iii. 51 Since the Ashanti War, communication is becoming more constant..with the interior. **1962** *Listener* 25 Jan. 156/1 There should be no reference to Fantis, Ashantis, Ewes, Gas, Dagombas, 'strangers', and so forth, but we should all call ourselves Ghanaians.

†**a'shape**, *v. Obs.* [OE. *asceppan*, f. A- *pref.* 1 + *sceppan*, to SHAPE. In the later quot., *a-* may be *ȝe-*.] To create, prepare, make, appoint.

a **1000** *Cædmon's Ex.* 381 (Gr.) Him god naman niwan asceóp. *c* **1325** *E.E. Allit. P.* B. 1076 Watȝ..no schroude hous so schene as a-schepon þare.

ash-cake. *U.S.* [ASH *sb.*² 8 b.] A cake baked in or under the ashes of a fire.

1809 HORRY & MARION *Life F. Marion* 47 A rasher of fat bacon from the coals, with a good stout lump of an ash cake. **1844** *Congress. Globe* App. 631/3 At this dinner, a large ash-cake was baked containing about three bushels of corn meal. **1888** 'C. E. CRADDOCK' *Keedon Bluffs* 25 Her father..deftly constructed an ash-cake.

ashe, obs. form of ASH, and of ASK *v.*

a-shelf (ə'ʃɛlf), *advb. phr.* [A *prep.*¹ + SHELF.] On a shelf or ledge of rocks. Also *fig.*

1587 HARMAR *Beza's Serm.* 231 (T.) That we jut not any more and run ashelf on such idolatry.

ashen ('æʃən), *a.*¹; also 4 (**esscen**), **aisshen**, 5–6 **asshen**, 6 **aschyn**. [f. ASH *sb.*¹ + -EN.]

1. Of or pertaining to an ash-tree. (Cf. ASPEN.)

1562 TURNER *Herbal* II. 6 b, The iuice..of ashen leaues..is good to make fatte men leane. *c* **1595** NORDEN *Spec. Brit.* Cornw. (1728) 34 *Penwith* signifieth the head of ashen trees. **1675** HOBBES *Homer* 188 A goodly ashen tree. **1741** *Compl. Fam. Piece* i. iii. 217 Put the Ashen Keys into the Pickle. **1850** TENNYSON *In Mem.* cxv, By ashen roots the violets blow.

2. Made of the wood of the ash.

a **1300** *Cursor M.* 5614 An esscen [? rescen] kyst sco did be wroght. *c* **1450** *Merlin* vii. 117 Arthur..griped a grete aisshen spere. *c* **1525** SKELTON *Vox Pop. Vox Dei* 253 in Hazl. *E.P.P.* III. 277 Thay that of latt did supe Owtt of an aschyn cuppe. **1815** SCOTT *Ld. Isles* IV. ix, Each his ashen bow unbent.

ashen ('æʃən), *a.*² [f. ASH *sb.*² + -EN.]

1. Of ashes. Also *fig.*

1850 MRS. BROWNING *Poems* I. 349 Wait soul, until thine ashen garments fall! **1879** TOURGEE *Fool's Errand* xlvi. 350 A Sodom-like fruitage of ashen words. **1882** *Pall Mall G.* 25 Oct. 2/2 The effects of the ashen shower were not instantaneous.

2. Ash-coloured, whitish-grey, deadly pale.

1808 SCOTT *Marm.* VI. xiv, The flush of rage O'ercame the ashen hue of age. **1875** LONGF. *Summer Day by Sea*, Yon little cloud of ashen gray and gold.

†**a'shend**, *v. Obs.* [f. A- *pref.* 1 + SHEND, OE. *scęndan*.] To confound, ruin, disgrace; to reproach, curse.

1250 LAY. 18067 þou letest vs alle asende [**1205** scenden]. **1297** R. GLOUC. 263 Hii adde alle ybe assend, ȝif þe niȝt nadde ybe. *c* **1300** *Beket* 458 He wold al that lond with thulke worth aschende. *Ibid.* 2383 Vyllokere than eni theof that folc him ther aschende.

Asherah (a'ʃiːra). Pl. **Asherahs**, **Asherim** (-rɪm). [Heb. *Ashērāh*.] A wooden post, pillar, or trunk of a tree used as the symbol of the goddess Ashera, occurring near the altar in Canaanitish high places devoted to the worship of Baal. Also the goddess herself, associated with Baal in Syrian, Phœnician, and Hebrew heathen worship. (Cf. GROVE 2 a.)

1863 G. GROVE in W. Smith *Dict. Bible* I. 120/2 Asherah is the name of the image or symbol of the goddess. This symbol seems in all cases to have been of wood, and the most probable etymology of the term (..*to be straight*..) indicates that it was formed of the straight stem of a tree, whether living or set up for the purpose. **1884** *Bible* (R.V.) Exod. xxxiv. 13 Ye shall cut down their Asherim. *Note.* Probably the wooden symbols of a goddess Asherah. *Ibid.*, Deut. xvi. 21 Thou shalt not plant thee an Asherah of any kind of tree beside the altar of the Lord thy God. **1886** CONDER *Syrian Stone-Lore* v. 189 The 'hangings for the grove', or robe for the Asherah—the sacred tree erected even in the Jerusalem Temple in Josiah's time. **1912** H. F. HAMILTON *People of God* I. II. iv. 55 Poles, which served as substitutes for trees, called *asherim*. **1925** W. EWING *J. E. H. Thomson* xviii. 259 The altars, the pillars, and *Asherahs* were not destroyed.

ashery ('æʃərɪ). [f. ASH *sb.*² + -ERY.] **a.** A place where potash or pearlash is manufactured. **b.** An ash-pit.

1831 A. SHERBURNE *Memoirs* viii. 185, I much wished to set up an ashery. **1837** *Fraser's Mag.* XVI. 690 Manufactories for reducing common ashes into pots and pearls are sometimes erected on a pretty large scale; in such cases, the individual to whom the 'ashery' belongs buys up all the ashes in the district. **1859** in WORCESTER. **1884** L. F. & R. L. ALLEN *New Amer. Farm Bk.* 62 Spent lye of the asheries, is the liquid which remains after the combination of the lye and grease in manufacturing soap.

ashet ('æʃɪt). *north. dial.* Also 6 **assett**. [a. F. *assiette*.] A dish or large flat plate.

1552 in Peacock *Eng. Ch. Furniture* (1866) 219 Item an Assett of Syluer. **1827** J. WILSON *Noct. Ambr.* Wks. 1855 I. 180 A board of oysters, or ashet o' rizzered haddies. **1866** *Leeds Mercury* 31 Mar., They then place it upon an ashet turned upside down.

†'**ashied**, *ppl. a. Obs. rare*⁻¹. [f. ASHY *a.* + -ED.] Made ashy or ash-coloured.

1613 HEYWOOD *Marr. Triumph* (N.) Old Winter..still doth goe In a rug gowne, ashied with flakes of snow.

a-shimmer (ə'ʃɪmə(r)), *adv. phr.* [A *prep.*¹ + SHIMMER.] Shimmering.

1926 *Chambers's Jrnl.* June 340/1 The marsh around them a-shimmer with heat. **1930** R. CAMPBELL *Adamastor* 80 His myriad spectacles a-shimmer Confront the lighted halls.

a-shine (ə'ʃaɪn), *adv. phr.* [A *prep.*¹ + SHINE.] Shining.

1840 BROWNING *Sordello* II. 288 The great morass..a-shine, Thick-steaming, all alive. **1849** C. BRONTË *Shirley* iii. 27 His hard features..all agrin and ashine with glee.

'ashing, *vbl. sb.* [f. ASH *v.*² + -ING¹.] **1.** Sprinkling or strewing with ashes.

1842 J. BUEL *Farmer's Companion* (ed. 3) 206 Draining improves the quality of the herbage, and marling, liming, or ashing increases the quantity.

2. Reducing to ashes, *spec.* for the purpose of analysis.

1937 HACKH & GRANT *Chem. Dict.* (1938) 88/2 *Ashing*, the process of burning organic matter, especially during analysis. **1946** *Nature* 20 July 96/1 Appreciable losses occur during ashing, owing to the volatility of inorganic components and adsorption to the surface of the ashing vessel. *Ibid.* 28 Dec. 946/2 Even low-temperature ashing of filter samples may alter the crystal structure.

a-'shipboard, *adv. phr.* On board ship.

1598 SYLVESTER *Du Bartas* II. ii. Argt. (1643) 113 Noah prepares the Ark..His exercise a-ship-board. **1680** *Trial Earl Castlemaine* in Howell *St. Trials* (1816) VII. 1074, I went a shipboard in April. **1870** MORRIS *Earthly Par.* I. II. 471 At point to go a-shipboard.

a-shiver (ə'ʃɪvə(r)), *adv. phr.* [A *prep.*¹ + SHIVER.] In a shiver, quivering.

1840 BROWNING *Sordello* III. 345 Branches..a-shiver soon With coloured buds. **1864** *Spectator* 538 Upon thy mantle all thy bees ashiver Shall twinkle in the sun.

Ashkenazim (æʃkɪ'nɑːzɪm), *sb. pl.* [mod.Heb., f. *Ashkenaz*, the name of a son of Gomer (Gen. x. 3, 1 Chron. i. 6), son of Japheth, son of Noah, typifying a race of people identified with the Ascanians of Phrygia, and, in medieval times, with the Germans.] Jews of middle and northern Europe as distinguished from Sephardim or Jews of Spain and Portugal. Hence **Ashke'nazic** *a.*, of or belonging to the Ashkenazim.

1839 R. M. MCCHEYNE *Let.* 23 July in *Familiar Lett.* (1848) 109 One of the Ashkenazim..invited us secretly to his house. **1842** BONAR & MCCHEYNE *Narr. Mission Jews in 1839* iv. 330 There are no rabbies properly speaking among the Ashkenazim. **1892** ZANGWILL *Childr. Ghetto* I. 4 All the Ashkenazic tribes lived very much like a happy family. *Ibid.* 38 Spanish Jews look down on the later imported Ashkenazim, embracing both Poles and Dutchmen in their impartial contempt. **1914** *East & West* XII. 154 The true Zionists are mostly Ashkenazim Jews from all Europe.

ashlar ('æʃlə(r)), *sb.* Forms: 4 **achiler**, 4–5 **as(s)cheler(e**, 5–7 **asheler**, 6 **aselar**, **aislar**, **achler**, 7 **axler**, **asler**, 8 **astler**, 9 **aisler** (*Sc.* 7 **eslar**, **islare**, 8 **estler**, 9 **ezlar**), 6– **ashler**, 9 **ashlar**. [a. OF. *aiseler*, *aisselier*, *esselier*:—L. *axillāris*, f. *axilla*, dim. of L. *axis*, *assis*, 'axle,' also 'board, plank' (cf. Fr. *ais*, It. *asse*). *Aisselle* retained in OF. both senses; in mod.F. they seem to be shared between *aisseau* (= OF. *aissel*) and *aisselle*. OF. *aiseler*, *aisselier* had senses pertaining to both; in Eng., senses 1–5 seem to arise out of the meaning 'board, plank,' 6 to be that which fills up the *axilla*, *aisselle*, 'arm-pit' or angle.]

1. A square hewn stone for building purposes or for pavement (? so called as resembling in appearance, or serving the same purpose as, a wooden beam); also used as a missile in defending fortresses. (Cf. Pr. *cairo* = *lapis quadratus*, in latter sense.)

1370 *Lay-Folks Mass-Bk.* App. iv. 364 Foul þei fond..As blac as pich was I-spred Vppon þe Aschelers euene. *a* **1450** *MS. Cott. Calig.* A ii. 117 That kyllede of þe Cristen, and kepten þe walles With arowes, and arblaste, and asschelers manye. *c* **1450** *Mann. & Househ. Exp.* 438 Every asheler is xij. ynche thykke and xviij. ynches longe. *c* **1530** LD. DACRES in *Archæol.* XVII. 203 Achlers redie hewen..that nighhand will fynyshe the said four towrs being bulwarks. **1552** ABP. HAMILTON *Catech.* 5 a (JAM.) A mason can nocht hew ane euin aislair without directioun of his rewill. **1611** COTGR., *Attendants*, ashlers, binding stones. **1870** F. WILSON *Ch. Lindisf.* 84 Alternated with courses of cream-coloured ashlars.

b. *collectively.*

1611 CORYAT *Crudities* 175 Pavier 'ex quadrato lapide' which we call Ashler in Somersetshire. **1677** PLOT *Oxfordsh.* 75 The Free-stone..if cut into oblong, or other sorts of squares, of a lesser bulk, they then call it Ashler. **1793** SMEATON *Edystone L.* §91 *note*, [*Ashler*] a term used by masons for stones prepared in the square for building with regular courses. **1854** H. MILLER *Sch. & Schm.* xiii. 269 It was a hard, compact, dark-coloured stone..and made excellent corner-stones and ashlar.

c. In this sense often *ashlar-stone*.

1536 BELLENDENE *Cron. Scot.* (1821) I. 82 The pavement hes bene of aselar stanis. **1600** HOLLAND *Livy* VI. iv. 219 The Capitoll was also built of squared ashler stone [*saxo quadrato*]. *a* **1758** RAMSAY *Poems* (1800) I. 60 (JAM.) Houses biggit a' with estler stane. **1837** CARLYLE *Fr. Rev.* (1872) I. v. vii. 173 Ashlar stones of the Bastille continue thundering through the dusk.

2. (Also *ashlar-work*): Masonry constructed of square hewn stones; opposed to *rubble-work*.

1398 *Indent. Dormitory Durh.* in Willis *Archit. Nomencl.* (1849) 25 Exterius de puro lapide vocato *achiler* plane inscisso, interius vero de fracto lapide vocato *roghwall*. **1426** AUDELAY *Poems* 78 Blak blood he se e-spred Apon the aschelere even. **1606** BIRNIE *Blame Kirkburial* xv, The Lords islare-work, the which is our edification. **1663** in Spalding *Troub. Chas. I* (1829) 13 The stately crown bigged of curious eslar work. **1818** SCOTT *Hrt. Midl.* vii, As well argue to the ashler-work and iron stanchels of the Tolbooth.

3. Similar masonry, usually in thin slabs, used as a facing to rubble or brick wall.

1823 P. NICHOLSON *Pract. Build.* 328 By ashlar is also meant the facing of squared stones on the front of a building. **1879** in *Cassells Techn. Educ.* I. 97 Ashlar work is a sort of facing to a wall built by one of the other methods or of bricks.

4. (See quot.) ? *only a loose use of* 1 b.

[Cf. **1677** in 1 b.] **1721** BAILEY, *Ashlar*, Freestone as it comes out of the Quarry. **1823** P. NICHOLSON *Pract. Build.* 328 Ashlar, a term applied to common or free-stones, as they come out of the quarry.

5. *attrib.*

1681 COTTON *Wond. Peake* (ed. 4) 79 A level axler floor. **1841** *Penny Cycl.* XX. 34/2 Aisler causeway. **1851** TURNER *Dom. Archit.* II. ii. 28 The masonry is rubble, with ashlar buttresses and quoins. **1879** E. BARTHOLOMEW in *Cassell's Techn. Educ.* I. 314/2 The ashler causeway consists of hammer-dressed granite stones.

6. *ashlar-rafter*, *-piece* = ASHLARING.

1846 PARKER *Conc. Gloss. Archit.* (1875) 227 Ashlar pieces are fixed to every one of the rafters in most mediæval roofs. **1876** GWILT *Archit.* §2052 f, The nearly upright stud or ashlar rafter.

ashlar ('æʃlə(r)), *v.* Also **ashler**. [f. ASHLAR *sb.*] *trans.* To face with ashlar; cf. ASHLAR *sb.* 3.

1836 *Mirror of Lit.* XXVIII. 147/1 It has been generally done by 'ashlering' them..with thin blocks or slabs of the same stone. **1895** HARDY *Jude the Obscure* v. vii, Sometimes setting the parapet of a town-hall, sometimes ashlaring an hotel at Sandbourne.

ashlared ('æʃləd), *ppl. a.* [f. ASHLAR *sb.* + -ED².] Covered with ashlar; cf. ASHLAR *sb.* 3.

1882 HARDY *Laodicean* III. xi, The ashlared face of inner wall which confronted him.

ashlaring ('æʃlərɪŋ), *vbl. sb.* Also **ashlering**. [f. ASHLAR *sb.* + -ING¹.]

1. 'In carpentry, **a.** the short upright quartering fixed in garrets about two feet six inches or three feet high from the floor, being between the rafters and the floor, in order to cut off the acute angle formed by the rafters. **b.** The upright quarterings seen in some open timber roofs between the inner wall plate and the rafters, is also so called.' Gwilt 1842.

1731 in BAILEY. **1940** *Chambers's Techn. Dict.* 54/2 *Ashlering*, the vertical timbers or quarterings, 2½ to 3 feet long, fixed in attics between floor-joists and rafters as supports for a partition wall, to cut off the sharp angle under the lower end of the rafter.

2. Ashlar masonry.

1757 SMEATON *Effects of Lightning* in *Phil. Trans.* L. 201 The whole ashlering..was torn off from the inner wall. **1823** P. NICHOLSON *Pract. Build.* 310 Ashlaring is a term used by masons to designate the plain stone work of the front of a building. **1858** *Skyring's Builders' Prices* 91 To ashlering take plain work to face, bed, and joint. **1876** GWILT *Archit.* §2284 a, Faced with Portland stone ashlaring.

ashling ('æʃlɪŋ). [f. ASH *sb.*¹ + -LING.] A young ash-tree, an ash sapling.

1883 A. BALFOUR in G. Hay *Round O* 23 Where the verdant ashlings spread a hallowed gloom.

ashore (ə'ʃɔə(r)), *adv.* [f. A *prep.*¹ + SHORE.]

1. Of motion: To, or on to, the shore; to land.

1586 T. B. *La Primaud. Fr. Acad.* (1589) 341 The first sort may easilie cast anchor, come a shore, and save themselves. **1697** COLLIER *Ess. Mor. Subj.* II. (1709) 31 Thrown a-Shoar when the Vessel is wreck'd. **1777** ROBERTSON *Hist. Amer.* (1783) II. 256 The ships were drawn ashore. **1876** BLACK *Madcap V.* viii. 75 'I must be getting ashore now.'

2. Of position: On shore, on the land.

1631 HEYWOOD *Maid of West* II. III. Wks. 1874 II. 375, I am come to sea, And left my heart ashore. **1713** STEELE *Englishm.* No. 21. 137 He behaves himself ashore as if he were still on board. **1823** MAR. GRAHAM *Resid. Chile* 115, I have now been two hours ashore.

†**a-'shore,** *adv. phr. Obs.* [A *prep.*¹ + SHORE = prop, support.] Shore-wise, a-straddle.

c **1460** RUSSELL *Bk. Nurture* in *Babees Bk.* 136 Ne settynge youre leggis a shore. ?*c* **1475** *Hunt. Hare* 257 The dogges wer so starke Thei stode aschore when thei schuld barke.

a-shosshe, variant of ASWASH *adv. Obs.*

ash-plant. [ASH *sb.*¹] A sapling of the ash tree, used as a walking-stick, whip, goad, etc.

1850 'H. HIEOVER' *Pract. Horsemanship* 180 Sit tight, and lay your ash plant well into his ears. **1852** MUNDY *Our Antipodes* III. i. 26 He..trudges away..supported by his son on one hand and an ash-plant in the other. **1918** P. MACGILL *Glenmornan* vi. 140 He hit a bullock near him with his ash-plant. **1935** S. SPENDER *Destructive Element* 82 Stephen..is only recognizable at all by being made inseparable from his ashplant.

Hence as *v.*, to flog with an ash-plant (cf. ASH *v.*¹).

1923 G. B. SHAW *Doctors' Delusions* (1932) 346 Nothing will persuade me that any boy..really likes being kicked and ashplanted into doing the drudgery of a professional footballer.

ashram ('ɑːʃrəm). [ad. Skr. *āśrama* hermitage, f. *ā* near to, towards + *śrama* exertion, earnest endeavour.] In India, a place of religious retreat, sanctuary, or hermitage. Hence **'ashramite**, an occupant of an ashram.

1917 W. W. PEARSON *Shantiniketan* 17 There was a farewell ceremony according to the ancient Hindu custom when a guest leaves an ashram for the outer world. *Ibid.* 47 An ashram, or religious retreat, where those in search of peace might have an opportunity for quiet and meditation. **1926** *Contemp. Rev.* Nov. 616 The traditional ashram is built of wattle and mud, and its roofs are of leaves. **1933** *Daily Express* 31 July 1/1 Gandhi has decided to vacate his ashram (seminary) at Sabarmati and start the mysterious 'fresh sacred mission' on Tuesday. This will begin with a march of thirty-two of the ashramites. **1959** *Times* 10 July 7/7 The buildings in the *ashrams* at Tiruppatur and Tenkasi are so strikingly Dravidian in effect that they could almost be mistaken for Hindu temples.

†**a'shun,** *v. Obs.* Forms: 1 **ascuni-an**, 4 **aschonne**. [OE. *ascunian*, f. A- *pref.* 1 + *scunian* to SHUN.] To shun, avoid, escape from.

1000 *Cnut's Sec. Laws* §7 (Bosw.) He mot þyllic ascunian. **1399** LANGL. *Rich. Redeless* II. 185 þey myȝte not aschonne þe sorow þey had serued.

†**a'shunch,** *v. Obs. rare*⁻¹. [f. A- *pref.* 1 + SCHUNCH, OE. *scuncan*.] To terrify, frighten.

c **1300** in Wright *Lyric P.* 38 Ne mey hit me ashunche.

Ash-'Wednesday. [f. ASH *sb.*² + WEDNESDAY.] The first day of Lent; so called from the custom in the Roman Catholic Church of sprinkling ashes on the heads of penitents on that day.

1297 R. GLOUC. 542 An Ax wednesdai..To Gloucetre he wende. **1387** TREVISA *Higden* (Rolls Ser.) VI. 429 In an Aschewednesday. **1539** *Bk. Cerem.* in Strype *Eccl. Mem.* I. App. cix. 291 The giving of ashes upon Ashwednesday, with these words, 'Remember, man, that thou art ashes and to ashes thou shalt return.' **1834** *Penny Cycl.* II. 454/2 Pope Gregory the Great introduced the sprinkling of ashes.. which gave it the name of Ash-Wednesday.

ashweed ('æʃwiːd). *Herb.* Also 6 **aish-**, 7 **aysh-**, 9 **ach-**, **ashe-**. [f. ASH *sb.*¹ + WEED.] The Goutweed (*Ægopodium Podagraria*).

1578 LYTE *Dodoens* 300 The seconde Imperatoria, or wylde Masterwort..is now called *Herba Gerardi*..In Englishe some call it Aishweede. **1617** MINSHEU, Ayshweede..or Goutworte. **1861** MISS PRATT *Flower. Pl.* III. 27 Common Gout-weed, or Bishop's weed..was called ..Asheweed.

ashy ('æʃɪ), *a.* Also 4–6 **asshy**, 5 **asky**, 6–7 **ashie**, **assie**, 7 **ashey**. [f. ASH *sb.*² + -Y¹.]

1. Consisting of ashes.

1483 *Cath. Angl.* 16 Asky, *cinerulentus*, *cinereus*. **1591** SPENSER *Ruins of Rome* 1 Whose ashie cinders lie Vnder deep ruins. **1671** MILTON *Samson* 1703 Like that self-begott'n bird..From out her ashie womb now teem'd, Revives, reflourishes. **1718** POPE *Iliad* XXIII. 312 And deep subsides the ashy heap below. **1869** PHILLIPS *Vesuv.* ii. 35 One continuous ashy shower.

2. Covered or sprinkled with ashes.

c **1386** CHAUCER *Knts. T.* 2025 With flotery berd, and ruggy asshy heeres. **1852** DICKENS *Bleak Ho.* iv, She slumbered before the ashy grate.

3. Ash-coloured, ashen, deadly pale.

1541 R. COPLAND *Quest. Cyrurg.* Rj, Whyte vryne, thynne, and asshy. **1597** LOWE *Art Chyrurg.* (1634) 116 The sore is..pale, sandy or assie coloured. **1633** FORD *Love's Sacr.* IV. i, The ashey paleness of my cheek Is scarletted in ruddy flakes of wrath. **1830** T. HAMILTON *Cyr. Thornton* (1845) 17 The ashy cheek, and hollow eye of my mother.

b. quasi-*adv.* in comb., as *ashy-blond*, *-green*, *-pale*.

1592 SHAKS. *Ven. & Ad.* 76 He low'rs and frets, 'Twixt crimson shame and anger, ashy-pale! **1865** CARLYLE *Fredk. Gt.* IV. II. ii. 38 Eyebrows..you can see are ashy-blond.

Asian ('eɪʃ(ɪ)ən), *a.* and *sb.* [ad. L. *Asiānus*, a. Gr. *Ἀσιāνός*, f. *Ἀσία*.]

1. = ASIATIC.

a. *arch.*

a **1563** BALE *Sel. Wks.* (1849) 293 Laodicea, a notable city of the Asians. **1607** TOPSELL *Four-f. Beasts* 75 African Camels are much more worth then the Asian. **1684** tr. *Corn. Nepos* 159 The Asians were much stronger in horse. **1864** NEALE *Seaton. Poems* 76 To upraise Their Asian flag on Europe's western shores.

b. In recent official use superseding *Asiatic* because of the alleged depreciatory implication of the latter term.

1930 *Kenya Legislative Council Debates* 4 Apr. 69 The first thing I notice about the motion is the word 'Asian'. I have tried to look it up, but I can find no dictionary which gives it—it is usually 'Asiatic'. **1930** *Official Gaz.* (*Kenya*) 9 Dec. 2825 (*heading*) Asian Clerical Staff Confirmation Examination. **1953** *Times Lit. Suppl.* 6 Feb., *Asian Review.* Volume XLIX, Number 177. January, 1953... After 68 years of existence the widely circulated quarterly hitherto known as the *Asiatic Review* makes a slight but important change of designation. The reason is to be found in the sensitiveness of the cultured classes of Asia about nomenclature... The term 'Asiatic' has come to be regarded with disfavour by those to whom it applied, and they feel entitled to be brought into line with usage in regard to Europeans, Americans and Australians. **1953** *Encounter* Oct. 74/1 Through European schools on Asian soil, and by study in Europe and America, young Asians entered the cultural world of the 20th century.

2. ***Asian 'flu***, the popular name of a kind of influenza caused by a virus first identified in Hong Kong in 1957. Also ***Asian influenza.***
1957 *Economist* 31 Aug. 670/2 The type of virus officially called A/Singapore/1/57, and popularly known as..Asian flu. **1958** *Punch* 1 Jan. 68/3 Three days later..all of us, including the cat, were struck down with Asian flu. **1958** *Listener* 19 June 1000/2 When Asian influenza strikes the population, we no longer appeal on our knees for help.

Asianic (eɪʃɪˈænɪk), *a.* [f. Asian *a.* + -ic.]
1. Of or pertaining to Asia Minor.
1883 I. Taylor *Alphabet* II. 116 A syllabic writing,.. which prevailed throughout the whole of Asia Minor, and which has been designated by Professor Sayce as the Asianic syllabary. **1927** W. Ramsay (title) Asianic Elements in Greek Civilisation. **1928** C. Dawson *Age of Gods* xiii. 289 The bulk of the population belonged to the native Asianic stock.
2. Pertaining to or characterized by the florid and inflated literary style characteristic of the Asiatic Greeks in the three centuries preceding the Christian era.
1920 *Q. Rev.* July 42 His elaborate Asianic style.

Asianize (ˈeɪʃ(ɪ)ənaɪz), *v.* [f. Asian *a.* + -ize.] *trans.* To make Asian in character, habits, customs, etc. Hence **ˈAsianized** *ppl. a.* So **ˌAsianiˈzation**, the process of becoming Asian.
1893 F. Adams *New Egypt* 50 Europe has indeed annexed this outpost of Asianised Africa [Cairo]. **1921** *19th Cent.* May 884 A humanity asianised in sentiment. *Ibid.* 888 The Arab and Hindu..who have undergone asianisation in the continent of their adoption.

asiarch (ˈeɪʃɪɑːk). [ad. L. *Asiarcha*, ad. Gr. Ἀσιάρχης, f. Ἀσία + -αρχης ruler.] The director of religious rites and public games in Asia Minor under the Romans. (Cf. *Acts* xix. 31.)
1753 Chambers *Cycl. Supp.* s.v., 'Tis disputed to what Asia..the Asiarchs were allotted; whether to Asia Minor, or the Proconsular Asia. **1866** Neale *Seq. & Hymns* 150 Slightly projected the Asiarch's throne.

Asiatic (eɪʃɪˈætɪk), *a.* and *sb.* [ad. L. *Asiāticus*, a. Gr. Ἀσιᾱτικός, f. Ἀσία: see -atic.] **A.** *adj.* Of or pertaining to Asia or its inhabitants; formerly used to describe a florid and imaginative literary style. ***Asiatic cholera*** (see cholera 3). **B.** *sb.* A native of Asia. †**ˈAsiatall**, †**Asiˈatical** *a.*, = Asiatic. **Asiˈatically** *adv.*, in Asiatic manner, in accordance with Asiatic customs. †**Asiˈatican** *a.* and *sb.*, = Asiatic. **Asiˈaticism**, imitation of Asiatic usage, an Asiatic phrase. **Asiˈaticize**, improperly **ˈAsiatize** *v.*, to make Asiatic, to conform to Asiatic customs.
1631 Massinger *Beleeve as you list* I. ii, Theis *Asiaticq marchants, whom you looke on With such contempt. **1752** Chambers *Cycl.* s.v. *Style*, The antients made a notable distinction of styles, into Laconic, and *Asiatic. **1831** T. W. Chevalier (*title*) On *Asiatic Cholera. **1832** *Deb. Congress* 30 June 3833/1 A deliverance from the impending judgment ..of the Asiatic cholera. **1865** M. Arnold *Ess. Crit.* ii. 62 It is *Asiatic prose, as the Ancient Critics would have said; prose somewhat barbarously rich and overloaded. **1634** T. Herbert *Trav.* 330 (T.) Such are the fanatick dogmata of the Alcoran, credited by most *Asiaticks. **1834** *Penny Cycl.* I. 473 These Greeks have long ago been changed into *Asiatics. **1615** tr. *De Montfart's Surv. E. Indies* 10 A true *asiatall Magnificence. *a* **1619** Fotherby *Atheom.* I. iv. §5. 26 His luxurious and *Asiaticall Oration vnto King Hezechiah. **1836** Landor in *Athenæum* No. 441. 254 Speaking by metaphor and *asiatically. **1869** Mrq. Salisbury in *Echo* 12 Mar., If we are to govern Asiatics well, we must govern them *Asiatically. **1594** Carew *Huarte's Exam. Wits* (1616) 200 The *Asiaticans..bare themselues verie couragiously. **1637** Gillespie *Eng.-Pop. Cerem.* I. ix. 32 The *Asiatican Doctors. **1774** T. Warton *Eng. Poetry* (1840) I. Diss. i. 24 Nor is this fantastic imagery the only mark of *Asiaticism, which appears in the Runic odes. **1882** *Van. Fair* 28 Oct. 250 The lay Parsee is, to use an expressive *Asiaticism, his belly-god. **1847** Grote *Greece* II. xxxiii. IV. 332 Half-*asiatised Hellenism. **1856** —— *ibid.* II. xciv. XII. 359 He was tending to *asiatize Macedonia. *Ibid.* 324 These *Asiatising marriages.

aside (əˈsaɪd), *adv.*, *prep.*, *adj.*, *sb.* Forms: 4 on syd, 5–6 on syde, on side; 4–6 a-syde, a syde, asyde, 5 acyde, 6 assyde, 5– aside. [orig. a phrase, *on side*: see a *prep.*[1] (Used in U.S. in various expressions where *apart* is used in England.)]
A. *adv.* **I.** Of motion.
1. To one side; out of the way, away.
c **1380** *Sir Ferumb.* 2297 Þe coupes of gold were treden a-syde: al with mannis fet. *a* **1450** *York Myst., Capmakers* O vj, This stone..remove and sette on syde. **1596** Shaks. *Merch. V*, II. viii. 1 Draw aside the curtaines. **1694** Luttrell *Brief Rel.* III. 292 The agent..is gone aside, and hath carried with him 2000*l.* in money belonging to the troop. **1790** Burke *Fr. Rev.* 245 To evade and slip aside from difficulty. **1810** Scott *Lady of L.* v. xv, Whose brazen studs and tough bull hide Had death so often dash'd aside.
2. Away from the general throng or main body, into seclusion or privacy, apart.
c **1450** Lonelich *Grail* lii. 925 Kyng Orkaws took he asyde. **1602** Shaks. *Ham.* v. i. 240 But soft, aside; heere comes the King. **1697** Dryden *Virg. Georg.* III. 249 When she has calved, then set the Dam aside. **1866** Geo. Eliot *F. Holt* xlvii. 407 One gentleman drew another aside to speak in an under-tone about Scotch bullocks.
3. Away from one's person; off, down.
1569 Spenser *F.Q.* I. iii. 4 Her fillet she vndight, And laid her stole aside. **1611** Bible *Hebr.* xii. 1 Let us lay aside every weight. **1697** Dryden *Virg. Georg.* III. 664 A Snake..has cast his Slough aside. **1859** Tennyson *Enid* 1443 Each.. cast his lance aside And doffed his helm.
4. Away from consideration or employment, out of thought or use; esp. in *to lay* or *set aside*: (fig.) to put away, give up, dismiss, reject.
c **1440** *Partonope* 5039 Hereth yt and than ley hyt asyde. **1535** Coverdale *Amos* ii. 4 He hath cast asyde the lawe of the Lorde. **1598** Shaks. *Merry W.* II. ii. 110 Setting the attraction of my good parts aside. **1607** —— *Cor.* I. iii. 75 Come, lay aside your stitchery. **1798** Ferriar *Illustr. Sterne* iii. 56 He often laid aside decorum. **1876** Green *Short Hist.* i. §5 (1882) 45 He set aside all dreams of the recovery of the West-Saxon overlordship. *Ibid.* vi. §4. 298 To fling aside traditional dogmas.
5. *Law.* **to set aside** (a verdict, judgement, etc.): to declare it of no authority; to quash.
1844 Ld. Brougham *Brit. Const.* (1862) App. iii. 428 Whose decisions it could set aside for error in law. **1883** Sir J. Mathew in *Law Rep. Queen's B.* XI. 591 A rule was subsequently obtained..to set that non-suit aside.
II. Of direction.
6. Towards one side, off from the direct line.
1398 Trevisa *Barth. De P.R.* VIII. xxx. (1495) 342 A lyghte beme is broke or shufte asyde. **1535** Coverdale *2 Sam.* vi. 6 For the oxen wente out asyde. **1611** Bible *Ps.* xiv. 3 They are all gone aside, they are together become filthy. **1815** Byron *Parisina* xiv, As bowstrings, when relax'd by rain, The erring arrow launch aside.
7. Sidewise, obliquely.
c **1369** Chaucer *Bk. Duchesse* 558 With that he loked on me asyde, As who sayth nay, that wol not be. **1440** *Promp. Parv.* 6 Acyde, *oblique*. *c* **1505** Dunbar *Golden Terge* xxv. 9 On syde scho lukat with a fremit fare. **1711** Pope *Rape Lock* IV. 33 Practis'd to lisp, and hang the head aside. **1775** Johnson in *Boswell* li. (1848) 463/1 We saw the Queen mount..Brown habit: rode aside.
III. Of position.
†**8.** On one side, away, off. *Obs.*
1375 Barbour *Bruce* VII. 111 Thai saw on syde thre men cumand. **1610** Holland *Camden's Brit.* (1637) 681 (D.) The twentieth legion..abode at Chester, scarce sixe miles aside from hence.
9. Apart from the general company; in privacy. *to speak aside*, i.e. apart, so as to be inaudible to the general company. Used as a stage direction in plays, to indicate that certain words are to be spoken out of the hearing of other characters on the stage.
c **1400** *Beryn* 619 The Pardonere stood a-syde. **1535** Coverdale *1 Chron.* xiii. 1 He was yet kepte asyde because of Saul. **1596** Shaks. *Tam. Shr.* v. i. 63 Let's stand aside, and see the end of this controuersie. **1801** M. Edgeworth *Belinda* II. xiv. 72 'You won't blow us to Clary,' added he *aside* to her ladyship. **1814** Scott *Ld. Isles* II. vii, Then lords and ladies spake aside.
10. a. = apart 5. (? Only in *U.S.*)
1860 Marsh *Eng. Lang.* 640 Leaving the question of competency aside. **1871** —— *Words & Uses* 21 But, pronouns..and 'auxiliary' verbs aside, it [Chaucer's English] is a mixture, etc.
b. aside from (= Brit. 'apart from'): (*a*) Besides, in addition to; without reckoning or including. *U.S.* (*b*) Except for. *U.S.*
1818 Ticknor in *Life, Lett., & Jrnls.* (1876) I. 206 Aside from this, the mere show is more magnificent than can be seen at any other court in Europe. **1847** L. Collins *Kentucky* 507 The college..possesses revenues, aside from tuition, sufficient to maintain the faculty. **1865** Grant White *Mem. Shaks.* 31 But, aside from question of the kind of training. **1905** *Forum* Apr. 598 The city, aside from being a great industrial..centre, enjoys..a high moral record.
1861 in *Maryland Hist. Mag.* (1910) V. 303 Aside from the upheavals made by our engineers,..I don't think I have ever seen a more dreary region. **1902** H. E. Bourne *Teaching Hist. & Civics* 303 Aside from the wars in Europe..the history of the colonies..is uneventful. **1931** H. F. Pringle *Theodore Roosevelt* I. iii. 35 Aside from boxing, Roosevelt's ..activities at Harvard are of slight importance.
11. By the side, alongside (*obs.*). *aside of*: by the side of, alongside of. *arch.* and *dial.*
1375 Barbour *Bruce* VII. 60 He ran on fut [*v.r.* syd, side] alwayis hym by. **1630** Wadsworth *Sp. Pilgr.* iv. 33 A shippe ..which tooke his course aside of vs. **1808** Scott *Marm.* III. iii, Brown ale..From ancient vessels ranged aside. **1856** Kane *Arctic Exp.* II. i. 24 We..are mere carpet-knights aside of these indomitable savages.
12. ? On each side. *rare.*
1859 Tennyson *Elaine* 47 A crown Of diamonds, one in front, and four aside.
IV. *Comb.* †**aside half**, †**aside-hand**, †**aside slips**, on or to one side.
1398 Trevisa *Barth. De P.R.* v. xxxv. (1495) 148 The lounge..byclippyth asyde halfe the substaunce of the herte. **1471** *Arriv. Edw. IV* (1838) 18 Turned asyde-hand, and went to Bristowe. **1577** Holinshed *Chron.* III. 312 He incamped somewhat aside slips of them.
B. *prep.* [by omission of *of*.]
1. At the side of, beside. (Still in *Sc.*)
1615 Chapman *Odyss.* VII. 215 And in the ashes sat, Aside the fire. **1743** Wesley *Wks.* (1872) XIII. 175 The shop that was aside the house. **1807** Tannahill *Poems* 153 Since, Maggie, I am in aside ye.
†**2.** Past, beyond. *Obs.*
1592 Shaks. *Rom. & Jul.* III. iii. 26 The kind Prince, Taking thy part, hath rusht aside the Law. **1663** *Flagellum or O. Cromwell* (1672) 22 Which resolution he had taken up before..and was put aside it, by the amplitude of that Fortune.
C. *adj.* [The adv. used *attrib.*]
1882 J. Hawthorne *Fort. Fool* I. xl, 'It's extraordinary'.. observed Sinclair, in an aside tone. [*U.S.*]
D. *sb.* [the adv. used *absol.*; cf. A 9.]
1. Words spoken aside or in an undertone, so as to be inaudible to some person present; words spoken by an actor, which the other performers, on the stage are supposed not to hear.
1727–51 Chambers *Cycl.* s.v., An Aside, *seorsim*, is something which an actor speaks apart, or, as it were, to himself. **1834** Macaulay *Chatham, Ess.* (1854) I. 293/2 Every tone from the impassioned cry to the thrilling aside. *a* **1845** Hood (*title of verses*) Domestic Asides.
2. An indirect effort, a side effort.
1877 A. Cave *Doctr. Atonement*, The asides of many writers possess a more lasting..influence than their deliberate and darling labours. **1882** *Times* 23 Jan. 3 The solar energy is there directed not towards the earth, but at a right angle..and we can hardly wonder if she does not respond to these solar asides.

¶ **aside, a-side,** formerly written for *a side*.

†**aˈsidely**, *adv. Obs. rare*[—1]. [f. aside *adv.* + -ly[2].] Indirectly.
c **1375** Wyclif *Serm.* xci. Sel. Wks. 1869 I. 324 Goddis wille is filled asideli by punishinge.

aˈsiden, *adv. Obs.* or *dial.* In 5–6 **asyden.** [variant of aside; cf. *besiden*: the *-en* may be the orig. dative.] Sidewise, obliquely, aslant. *Comb.* **asiden-hand(s**, = *aside-hand*; see aside A. IV.
1440 *Promp. Parv.* 6 A-cydenandys; or a-slet, or a-slonte (*v.r.* acydnande, acydenam), *Oblique* vel *a latere*. **1471** *Arriv. Edw. IV.* (1838) 18 He took nat his ground so even in the front..butt somewhate a-syden hande. **1502** Arnold *Chron.* (1811) 169 Se that the cuttyng be euin ouer thwarte the stok and a syden. *c* **1691** Ray *Proverbs* (1768) 51 All asiding as hogs fighting. [**1879** Miss Jackson *Shropsh. Word-bk.* 13 'Yo' hanna put yore shawl on straight, the cornels bin all asiden.']

aˈsideness. [f. aside *a.* + -ness.] The state of being aside; apartness, isolation.
1880 Mrs. Whitney *Odd or Even* xxi. 214 Lifted off the busy planet and set in some asideness. [*U.S.*]

†**aˈsides**, *adv. Obs.* In 4 **on-sydez, asydis, asidis.** [variant of aside after advb. genitives in *-s*; chiefly northern; cf. *abouts, besides*.] = aside.
c **1325** *E.E. Allit. P.* C. 218 Her sayl watz hem aslypped on-sydez. **1382** Wyclif *Matt.* xvii. 1 Ledde hem asydis in to an hiȝ hill. —— *Mark* vii. 33 Takynge him asydis fro the cumpanye.
b. *Comb.* **asides-half, asides-hand,** aside.
1382 Wyclif *Gal.* ii. 2 A sydis hond, *or by hemsilf*, to hem that weren seyn for to be sumwhat. —— *Mark* iv. 34 On sidis hond. —— *Acts* xxiii. 19 The tribune takinge his hond, wente with him a sydis half [*v.r.* asidis].

asidew: see arsedine.

asie: see asye *v. Obs.* to sink down.

asier, obsolete form of azure.

as if, *phr. Philos.* [Cf. as 9 b; often used to represent G. *als ob* (freq. in Kant and taken up by Vaihinger as a key expression).] Introducing a supposition, or way of conceiving some entity or situation, that is not to be taken literally, but yields some insight or convenience in metaphysics. Also *absol.* and *attrib.* Hence **as-ˈifness.**
1892 J. Royce *Spirit Mod. Philos.* iv. 113 You *act as if God were* your..visible companion, as if the moral law..were spoken in your ear..., as if the unsearchable God..were as familiar to you as your daily walk... This is to do what Kant calls postulating God's existence. **1900** —— *World & Indiv.* I. v. 206 This *as if*, or *as it were*, becomes to some thinkers, a sort of ultimate category. **1921** Hannay & Collingwood tr. *Ruggiero's Mod. Philos.* ii. 61 A champion has now arisen in Vaihinger to erect the 'as if' into a philosophical method! **1924** C. K. Ogden tr. H. Vaihinger (*title*) The Philosophy of 'As If'. **1937** G. W. Allport *Personality* (1938) xi. 289 There is no real objection to this 'as if' epistemology provided it is applied equally to all the data of psychology. **1937** *Mind* XLVI. 114 The 'as-if' concepts, like 'wave', 'corpuscle', etc., which we borrow from macroscopic perception in order to interpret the nature of phenomena too small to be perceived in their own right. **1940** H. H. Price *Hume's Theory of Ext. World* v. 154 There are different degrees of as-ifness. This is acknowledged in ordinary speech, where we find such phrases as 'to some extent as if', 'rather as if', 'very much as if', 'exactly as if'.

asigmatic (eɪsɪgˈmætɪk), *a.* [f. a- 14 + sigmatic *a.*] Not sigmatic, formed without sigma.
1893 F. W. Walker in *Classical Rev.* July 292/1 The one so called asigmatic tense that is not digammated is generally admitted to have dropped a sigma. **1967** *Language* XLIII. 628 An asigmatic aorist of *khéō*.

asigne, asingne, obsolete form of assign.

asile, var. form of asyle; cf. F. *asile*.

asilid (ˈæsɪlɪd), *a. Ent.* [ad. mod.L. *Asilidæ*, f. *asīlus*: see next and -id[3].] Belonging to the Asilidæ, a family of dipterous insects comprising the hornet-flies.
1904 *Athenæum* 24 Dec. 881/1 [Prof. E. B. Poulton] exhibited a photograph..showing the Xylocopid model and its Asilid mimic. **1951** Colyer & Hammond *Flies Brit. Isles* viii. 118 There is some evidence for the view that the instantaneous collapse of Asilid attack is due to the injection of poison. **1961** *New Scientist* 8 June 589/3 When feeding

the [blind] flies are also exposed to predatory wasps, asilid flies and dragon flies.

asilus (əˈsaɪləs). *Ent.* [L. *asīlus* gadfly.] A member of a genus of flies belonging to the order Diptera, family Asilidæ; a hornet-fly, hawk-fly, or robber-fly.

1752 J. HILL *Hist. Anim.* 32 The great, smooth, black, and red Indian Asilus. **1866** BLACKMORE *Cradock Nowell* xxv, They discuss the asilus and the oestrum.

a-simmer (əˈsɪmə(r)), *advb. phr.* [A *prep.*¹ + SIMMER.] On the simmer, simmering.

1849 J. WILSON in *Blackw. Mag.* LXV. 767 The furnace at a red heat, pots and pans a-simmer.

†**ˈasinal**, *a. Obs. rare*⁻¹. [ad. L. *asinālis*, f. *asinus* ass: see -AL¹.] = ASININE.

1566 ADLINGTON *Apuleius* To Reader, From their asinall fourme to their humaine and perfect shape.

†**ˈasinary**, *a. Obs.*⁻⁰ [ad. L. *asinārius*, f. *asinus* ass: see -ARY.] = prec.

1731 in BAILEY.

†**asine.** *Obs. rare.* [a. F. *asine* (still used dial.), ad. L. *asina.*] A she-ass. (In Bellendene perh. of common gender, OF. *asne.*)

1536 BELLENDENE *Cron. Scot.* (1821) I. 51 Thair hors ar litill mair than asinis. **1584** ARCHD. DOUGLAS (in *Sat. Rev.* 27 Nov. 1858, 539/2) Desired to borrow his asine for the use of her milk.

†**asiˈnego.** *Obs.* or *dial.* Also 7 asinico. [a. Sp. *asnico*, dim. of *asno* ass.]

1. A little ass.

1634 T. HERBERT *Trav.* 127 (T.) We jogged leisurely on upon our mules and asinegoes. **1685** R. BURTON *Eng. Empire in Amer.* xxii. (1730) 207 Their Horses, Cows, Hoggs, and Asinego's that they brought from Spain.

2. A 'donkey,' fool, dolt.

1606 SHAKS. *Tr. & Cr.* II. i. 49 An Asinico may tutor thee; Thou scuruy valiant Asse. **1714** MILBOURNE *Traitor's Rew.* Pref., These asinegoes are like those miserable comforters Job's friends. [**1880** in *West Cornw. Gloss.*]

asinine (ˈæsɪnaɪn), *a.* Also 7–8 ass-. [ad. L. *asininus*, f. *asinus* ass: see -INE¹.]

1. Of or pertaining to asses.

1624 BOLTON *Nero* 246 Her fiue hundred female asses.. her asinine dayrie. **1641** MILTON *Educ.* Wks. 1738 I. 137 That asinine feast of sowthistles. **1873** LONGF. *Monk Casal Magg.* 157 Since monkish flesh and asinine are one.

2. Having the qualities by which the ass is characterized; obstinate, stupid, doltish.

c **1610** CHAPMAN *Iliad*, To Reader 225 Your asinine souls, Proud of their burdens, feel not how they gall. **1781** COWPER *Convers.* 209 'Tis the most asinine employ on earth, To hear them tell of parentage and birth. **1859** HELPS *Friends in C.* Ser. II. I. ii. 153 And I.. should be asinine enough to go.

asininity (æsɪˈnɪnɪtɪ). [f. prec. + -ITY.] Asinine quality; stupidity.

1831 *Fraser's Mag.* Aug., Ears beyond the usual dimensions of asin[in]ity asinine. **1860** J. KENNEDY *Quodlibet* vi. 88 Meek, even to a degree of asininity, in his demeanor.

†**aˈsink**, *v. Obs.* [f. A- *pref.* 1 + SINK, OE. *sincan*. Cf. Ger. *ersinken*.] To sink down.

c **1275** MAPES *Body & Soul* 469 Into the aller deoppeste pit.. Heom self asonken in ther mit. *c* **1315** SHOREHAM 136 Hou fareth hy that hy nasynketh?

asiphonate (əˈsaɪfəneɪt), *a.* and *sb. Zool.* [f. A- *pref.* 14 + SIPHONATE.] **A.** *adj.* Having no respiratory siphon. **B.** *sb.* An acephalous mollusc so characterized.

1859 OWEN *Classif. Mamm.* 61 Holostomatous and asiphonate Gastropods. **1879** LE CONTE *Elem. Geol.* 304 Lamellibranchs are divided into Siphonates and Asiphonates.

-asis, *suff.*, L. -*āsis*, Gr. -ᾱσις, forming names of diseases, really nouns of state or process from verbs in -*άειν*; as from φθείρ louse, φθειρά-ειν to be lousy, φθειρίᾱσις *phthīˈriăsis*; so *elephantiasis, psoriasis*, and many modern words, more or less analogical, as *allantiasis, arseniasis*, etc.

asise, obsolete form of ASSIZE *sb.*

†**aˈsit**, *v. Obs.* [In sense 1 f. A- *pref.* 1 + *sittan* to SIT; cf. Ger. *ersitzen*: in sense 2 prob. for ATSIT, q.v.]

1. *intr.* To sit, settle; remain sitting.

a **1000** *Elene* (Grein) 998 Secᵹas, mid siᵹecwén, aseten hæfdon, on Créca land. **1205** LAY. 26353 Þa while þa þeos eorles þreo seiden heore erende, aset [**1250** sat] þe kaisere.

2. *trans.* To sit against; to withstand.

c **1330** *Arth. & Merl.* 8150 Non his dent asit might. *a* **1400** *Octouian* 1665 No man ne myghte with strengthe asytte Hys swordes draught.

asith, variant of ASSYTH, *Obs.*, satisfaction.

‖**asitia** (əˈsɪʃ(ɪ)ə). *Path.* [mod.L., a. Gr. ἀσιτία, f. ἄσιτος, f. ἀ priv. + σῖτος corn, food.] 'Loathing of food.' Mayne *Exp. Lex.* 1853. 'More correctly a want of food.' *Syd Soc. Lex.* 1881.

asiwe, variant of ASUE *v. Obs.*, to follow.

ask (ɑːsk, æ-), *v.* Forms: *α.* 1 ásci-an, ácsi-, áhsi-, áxi-, áhxi-, áhxsi-, áxsi-an, -ᵹan, -ᵹean, æcsian; 2–3 axien, acsien, 3 æxi, axi, 4 acsi, acsy, oxi, oxy, oxsi, oksi, 3–5 axen, (5 axse, exe,) 4–6 axe, ax, (6-*dial.* ax). Also *β.* 2 esci-, eski-en, 3 easki, (*Orm.*) asskenn, 3–5 ask-en, 3–7 aske, (5 haske, ascke, axke,) 4– ask. Also *γ.* 3–4 esch(e, esse, 3–5 asch(e, 5 ashe, 5–6 asshe, (*north.* asse, *pa. t.* ast). [Common Teut.: OE. *ácsian* was cogn. w. OFris. *âskia*, OS. *êscôn, êscan*, OHG. *eiscôn*, MHG. *eischen*, Ger. *heischen*, OTeut. **aiskôjan*: cf. Skr. *ish* to seek, *ichchhā* wish. The original long *á* gave regularly the ME. (Kentish) *ōxi*; but elsewhere was shortened before the two consonants, giving ME. *a*, and, in some dialects, *e*. The result of these vowel changes, and of the OE. metathesis *asc-, acs-*, was that ME. had the types *ōx, ax, ex, ask, esk, ash, esh, ass, ess.* The true representative of the orig. *áscian* was the s.w. and w.midl. *ash, esh*, also written *esse* (cf. *æsce* ASH, *wæsc(e)an* WASH), now quite lost. *Acsian, axian*, survived in *ax*, down to nearly 1600 the regular literary form, and still used everywhere in midl. and south. dialects, though supplanted in standard English by *ask*, originally the northern form. Already in 15th c. the latter was reduced dialectally to *asse*, pa. t. *ast*, still current dialectally.]

General senses: I. To call for; II. To call for an answer; III. To call for a thing desired, to make a request; IV. Pregnant and special uses; V. *fig.* as predicated of things.

†**I. 1.** *trans.* To call for, call upon (a person or thing personified) to come. *Obs.*

a **1000** *Beowulf* 2417 He for wlenco wean ahsode. *a* **1000** *Cædmon's Gen.* (Gr.) 2453 [Hi] common corþrum miclum cuman acsian. **1205** LAY. 19967 He lette axien anan Men þat cuðen hæuwen stan.

II. To call upon any one for information, or an answer; to question, inquire.

* *trans. With the thing asked as object*:

To call for an answer to (a question or inquiry).

2. without mention of the person asked:

a. with the thing asked as an object sentence or clause (in indirect, or, less commonly, direct oration).

c **1000** *Ags. Ps.* xiv. [2] Ic ahsiᵹe, Hwa þær eardað? *a* **1038** *Charter of Eanwene* in *Cod. Dipl.* IV. 54 Ðá ácsode ðe biscеop hwá sceólde andswerian for his mōdor. *c* **1200** ORMIN Te33 shollden.. asskenn what he wære. *a* **1300** *Cursor M.* 7887 He askes, quat was þat leuedi? *c* **1305** *St. Crist.* 149 in *E.E.P.* (1862) 63 Þis gode man.. eschte what hi wolde. *c* **1386** CHAUCER *Wife's Prol.* 21, I axe, why the fyfte man Was nought housbond to the Samaritan? *c* **1420** *Avow. Arth.* xxiv, Gauan asshes, 'Is hit soe?' **1455** E. CLERE in *Four C. Eng. Lett.* 5 He askid what the Princes name was. **1549** COVERDALE *Erasm. Par. Rom.* Prol., He axeth not whether good workes are to be done or not. **1597** SHAKS. *2 Hen. IV.* III. ii. 71 May I aske, how my Lady his Wife doth? **1711** STEELE *Spect.* No. 454 ¶6 To ask what I wanted. *Mod.* Ask who it is. He asks if you are ready. I merely ask, 'Is it true?'

b. with the question expressed by a sb. or pronoun: To ask a *question, this, something.* **to ask** (a horse) **the question**: to call upon him for a special effort.

c **1320** R. BRUNNE *Medit.* 430 Some axen questyons to do hym wrong. **1387** TREVISA *Higden* (1865) I. 67 Þre questiouns beeþ i-axed. **1803** PEGGE *Anecd. Eng. Lang.* 114 A true born Londoner, Sir, of either sex, always axes question, axes pardon, and at quadrille axes leave. **1850** TENNYSON *In Mem.* xiv, And ask a thousand things of home. **1894** H. CUSTANCE *Riding Recoll.* vi. 88 Until the last ten strides, when I really asked 'King Lud' the question.

c. with the question indicated by its subject or object: To ask the *way*, the *price*, a *name*, an *age*, etc.

1382 WYCLIF *Gen.* xxxii. 29 Wherto askist [*v.r.* axist] thou my name? *c* **1420** *Chron. Vilod.* 689 Ryse up.. and þe way asshe, To Wyltone. **1502** ARNOLD *Chron.* (1811) 208 To answere him that axith the lawe of the Lorde. **1549** LATIMER *7 Serm. bef. Edw. VI.* (Arb.) 27 The other axed ye price, he sayed: xx. nobles. **1597** SHAKS. *2 Hen. IV.* I. i. 39 He ask'd the way to Chester. **1842** TENNYSON *Dream Fair Wom.* 93 Ask thou not my name.

3. with the person asked introduced by a preposition:

†**a.** *at* a person. *Obs.* exc. *dial.*

1297 R. GLOUC. 16 Heo aschede at Corineus, how heo so hardi were. *c* **1325** *E.E. Allit. P.* B. 924 Als Abraham.. hit at himself asked. **1535** COVERDALE *Ecclus.* xxi. 17 It is axed at the mouth of the wyse. **1753** *Stewart's Trial* 197 To ask any question at Allan Breck about the murder, which he now related to them. **1843** BETHUNE *Scot. Peasant's Fireside* 47 'Why do you ask that question at me?'

†**b.** *to* a person. (Cf. Fr. *demander à.*) *Obs.*

c **1314** *Guy Warw.* 27 Than axed anon Sir Gii To the barouns that oned him bi. **1483** CAXTON *G. de la Tour* D vij b, Asking to her why she had trespaced his commaundments. **1663** GERBIER *Counsel* 13 Asking to passengers what weather it was without doores.

c. *of* a person.

1366 MAUNDEV. v. 61, I asked of the monkes.. how this be-felle. *c* **1380** *Sir Ferumb.* 1124 Þe Amyral of hym axeth.. wat tydynge þay had y-broȝt. *c* **1450** *Merlin* ii. 36 Axe of hem whi that that toure fill. **1562** TURNER *Herbal* II. 51 a, The sherif axed diligently of them.. what they had done. **1667** MILTON *P.L.* II. 957 [One] of whom to ask Which way the neerest coast of darkness lyes. *c* **1735** POPE *Hor. Epist.* II. ii. 211, I ask these sober questions of my heart. *Mod.* A farmer of whom I asked the way.

** *trans. With the person asked as object*:

To call upon (a person) for information or an answer; to put a question to, to question.

4. with personal obj. only: To ask a person.

a. *simply.*

c **1000** *Ags. Gosp.* Mark xii. 28 Hine ne dorste nan mann ahsian. *Ibid.* John ix. 21–23 Ahxsiað hine sylfne [*v.r.* acsiað, ahxiað, *Lindisf.* ᵹefraiᵹnas, *Rushw.* ᵹefræᵹnas]. *a* **1300** *Cursor M.* 1001 Syn þou askis me.. I wille þe telle. **1382** WYCLIF *Job* xii. 7 Aske the bestis, and thei shul teche thee. **1535** COVERDALE *Job* xii. 7 Axe the catell, & they shal enfourme the. **1591** SHAKS. *Two Gent.* II. v. 36 Aske my dogge. **1611** BIBLE *1 Cor.* xiv. 35 Let them aske their husbands at home. **1732** POPE *Ess. Man* II. 205 Ask your own heart; and nothing is so plain. **1842** TENNYSON *Dora* 142 I ask'd him, and he said, He could not ever rue his marrying me.

b. with the question introduced by 'saying,' etc.

c **1000** *Ags. Gosp.* John i. 19 Hi axsodon hine [*Hatton* axeden hym] and þus cwæðen, Hwæt eart þu? —— Matt. xii. 10 Hi ahsude[n] hyne, þus cweðende, etc. **1388** WYCLIF *Luke* xxiii. 3 Pilat axide hym, and seide, Art thou Kyng of Jewis. **1611** BIBLE *John* ix. 19 They asked them, saying, Is this your son?

c. ***I ask you***, exclamatory phr. indicating disgust or asseveration.

1855 DICKENS *Dorrit* I. ii. 12 'Now, I ask you,' said Mr. Meagles... 'I ask you simply, as between man and man, .. DID you ever hear of such damned nonsense as putting Pet in quarantine?' **1898** G. B. SHAW *Arms & Man* III in *Plays Pleasant & Unpl.* II. 73 Now, I ask you, would a woman who took the affair seriously have sent me this? **1902** CONRAD *Youth* 44 Now, I ask you, can anybody stand this kind of thing? **1932** *Punch* 18 May 536, I ask you—not a taxi in sight! **1937** C. DAY LEWIS *Starting Point* I. iii. 41 'My God, look at these people! Just look at them—I ask you,' he exclaimed.

d. colloq. phr. ***if you ask me***: in my opinion.

[**1856** DICKENS *Dorrit* II. ix. 394 And if you ask me for my advice, it is that you set off tomorrow.] **1910** GALSWORTHY *Justice* II, If you ask me, I don't think he was quite compos when he did it. **1930** J. B. PRIESTLEY *Angel Pavement* ii. 65 Girls *are* a bit silly, if you ask me, and it's a good job for the men they are. **1932** *Punch* 14 Dec. 654/2 If you ask me, a little of that sort of thing would brighten up the trade wonderfully.

5. with the thing asked as a second object: To ask a person a question.

a. with the question as an object sentence or clause.

c **1000** *Ags. Gosp.* John xxi. 12 Nan þæra.. ne dorste hine axian hwæt he wære. *c* **1175** *Lamb. Hom.* 25 Þe preost me walde eskien.. hwa me scriue. *Ibid.* 35 Esca hine hwet he habbe biᵹeten. *a* **1230** *Juliana* 257 He easkeð ham, ȝef ham biluueð to heren him. *c* **1275** *Passion of Our Lord* 567 in *O.E. Misc.* 53 Vre louerd hire gon axi, For hwi and for hwan wepestu? *a* **1300** *Cursor M.* 1125 Aske his fader quere he be. *c* **1314** *Guy Warw.* 98 He gan oxy what it might be, He hem oxed what it were. *c* **1420** *Chron. Vilod.* 939 And how he was .. he dude hym asshe. **1584** *Three Ladies Lond.* I. in Hazl. *Dodsl.* VI. 296 My lady axes you, when will you take possession of your house. **1601** SHAKS. *All's Well* II. ii. 38 Aske mee if I am a Courtier. **1711** ADDISON *Spect.* No. 10 ¶5, I have heard them asking the first man they have met with whether there was any news stirring. **1849** DICKENS *Dav. Copp.* xxi. (C.D. ed.) 181, I.. asked him what o'clock it was.

b. with the question expressed by a sb. or pronoun: *a question, this, something.*

c **1000** *Ags. Gosp.* Matt. xxii. 46 Ne man ne dorste hyne nan þing mare axiᵹean [*Rushw.* ᵹeasciᵹan; *Hatton* axien]. *c* **1315** SHOREHAM 136 Ich acsy the a questioun. *c* **1386** CHAUCER *Knts. T.* 489 Now lovyeres axe I this question. **1598** SHAKS. *Merry W.* IV. i. 16 Aske him some questions in his Accidence. **1611** BIBLE *Jer.* xxxviii. 14, I will aske thee a thing; hide nothing from me. **1773** GOLDSM. *Stoops to Conq.* III. 111 Ask me no questions and I'll tell you no fibs. *Mod.* Which of them asked you that?

c. with the question asked indicated by its subject or object: To ask a person the *way*, the *time*, his *name*, *age*, etc.

1593 SHAKS. *Rich. II.* I. iii. 9 Aske him his name. **1605** —— *Lear* v. iii. 117 Aske him his purposes, why he appeares Vpon this Call o' th' Trumpet. **1709** POPE *Ess. Crit.* 436 Ask them the cause. *Mod.* She asked me the reason.

d. colloq. phr. ***ask me another***: I do not know (the answer to your question). Also ***ask me, ask me a harder***, etc.

1910 A. BENNETT *Clayhanger* III. ii. 344 'Why's he wearing his best clothes?' Clara demanded... 'Ask me another!' said Edwin. **1912** A. BRAZIL *New Girl at St. Chad's* ix. 139 'Then who was it?' Honor shook her head. 'Ask me a harder!' she said briefly. **1915** MRS. H. WARD *Eltham House* xii. 212 'Tell me about Madge Whitton. There are all sorts of rumours..' ..Lewson shrugged his shoulders—'Ask me another, Duchess.' **1928** E. WALLACE *Gunner* ii. 24, I hope you are wearing warm undies. Why are undies indelicate and sable coats ladylike? Ask me. It's one of the mysteries. **1933** I. COMPTON-BURNETT *More Women* xiii. 202 'Devoted?' said Josephine, raising her brows. 'Ask me another. I am not in a position to give you an account of their feelings.'

6. with the matter introduced by a preposition: **a.** To ask a person *of* (arch.), *about*, in OE. *be, ymb* (= about), a matter. **b.** (To ask one *after* or *for* a person: see 7.)

c **885** K. ÆLFRED *Boeth.* xxxix. §4 Þæt is þæt ic þé ær ymb acsade.. Ðisse spræce ðe ðu me æfter ascast. *c* **1000** *Ags. Gosp.* Luke ix. 45 Hi ne dorston hine be þam worde ahsian.

c **1220** *Hali Meid.* 9 Aske þes cwenes . . of hare liflade. *a* **1300** *Cursor M.* 1294 He asked him of his errand. *c* **1300** *Beket* 2 And eschte him of Engelonde: and of the manere there. **1475** CAXTON *Jason* 40b, Thauncient man axid one of the marronners of this matere. **1597** SHAKS. *2 Hen. IV.* II. iv. 389 Knocking at the Tauernes, And asking every one for Sir John Falstaffe. **1601** —— *All's Well* IV. III. 317 Why do's he aske him of me? **1842** TENNYSON *Edw. Morris* 23 Once I ask'd him of his early life. *Mod.* Did you ask them about the books?

*** *intr. With no object expressed*:

To inquire, make inquiries.

7. To ask (*of* obs.) *about* (in OE. *be*, *ymb* = about). To ask *after* a thing missing, a person absent, his welfare, etc. To ask *for* a person; to ask to see; formerly (and still in *dial.*) = to ask *after*.

c **885** K. ÆLFRED *Boeth.* xxxix. §4 Se ðe ymb þæt ascian wile. *c* **1000** ÆLFRIC *Deut.* iv. 32 Ahsiað be ealdum dagum ða wæron ær þonne ȝe. *c* **1230** *Ancr. R.* 172 Axinde efter tiðinges. *a* **1250** *Owl & Night.* 711 Wi axestu of craftes mine. **1377** LANGL. *P. Pl.* B. v. 542, I seygh neuere palmere . . Axen after hym. **1588** SHAKS. *L.L.L.* III. i. 168 And Rosaline, they call her, aske for her. **1671** MILTON *Sams.* 40 Ask for this great deliverer now, and find him Eyeless in Gaza. **1849** DICKENS *Dav. Copp.* xx. (C.D. ed.) 178 That shows the advantage of asking, don't it. **1866** G. MACDONALD *Ann. Q. Neighb.* xxx. (1878) 524 To ask after their health when he met them. *Mod.* Did any one ask for me, while I was out? When you reach that point, ask again.

†**8.** To ask *of* or *at* a person *of* a matter, i.e. *from* a person *about* a matter. *Obs.*

1393 LANGL. *P. Pl.* C. XXI. 127 Ayþer axed of oþer · of þis grete wonder. *c* **1440** *Generydes* 309 He asckid of Medeyn Of his ffader. **1600** FAIRFAX *Tasso* VIII. liii. 152 To spie at whom to aske we gazed round. **1611** BIBLE *1 Sam.* xxviii. 16 Wherefore then doest thou aske of me?

III. To make request for a thing desired.

* *trans. With the thing asked as object*:

To make request for.

9. *simply.* To ask a thing. (Now more familiarly *to ask for*: see 16.)

c **1250** *Gen. & Ex.* 1668 Aske it wið skil and ðu salt ħauen. **1340** *Ayenb.* 114 Jesu Crist ous tekþ zuo to oxi uoryeuenesse. *Ibid.* 209 Verst oxseþ Godes riche. **1370** *Lay-Folks Mass-Bk.* App. iv. 510 Let him not · his offryng asch. *c* **1374** CHAUCER *Troylus* v. 594, I naxe in guerdon but a boone. *c* **1420** *Avow. Arth.* iv, Thenne the kyng asshet a chekkere. *c* **1460** *Towneley Myst. Coliphiz.* 200 That is it that I ast. **1509** HAWES *Conv. Swearers* 26 Come nowe to me and axe forgyuenes. **1570** *Play Wit & Sc.* (1848) 10, I axe no more. **1593** SHAKS. *3 Hen. VI.* II. vi. 69 Clifford, aske mercy. **1644** MILTON *Areop.* (Arb.) 76 Asking licence to do so worthy a deed. **1711** STEELE *Spect.* No. 6 ¶2 The beggar disabled himself in his Right Leg, and asks Alms all Day. **1837** DICKENS *Pickwick* xxvii, Ask a blessing, Mr. Stiggins. **1859** TENNYSON *Vivien* 155 Ask your boon, for boon I owe you.

b. ***to ask a price***: to ask so much as the price, to state the price.

1857 Bohn's *Handbk. Prov.* 323 Ask but enough, and you may lower the price as you list. **1864** TENNYSON *Brook* 142 How he sent the bailiff to the farm To learn the price, and what the price he ask'd. *Mod.* What do you ask for this? How much did he ask?

10. To ask a thing (*to* obs., *at* obs. or dial.) *of*, *from* a person.

1340 *Ayenb.* 110 Huet may þe zone betere acsy to his uader þanne bread? *c* **1450** *Compl. Lover's Life* lxix, That to my foo . . Mot axe grace, mercy, and pite. *c* **1460** FORTESCUE *Abs. & Lim. Mon.* (1714) 134 Such as axen of the Kyng, Offices. **1583** GOLDING *Calvin on Deut.* cviii. 661 A charmer . . that asketh counsell at spirites. **1647** CHAS. I. *Let.* in *Antiquary* I. 97 To aske leave of ye two houses to make a journey. **1796** BURNS *Let.* in *Wks.* (Globe) 563, I am ashamed to ask another favour of you. **1830** tr. *Aristoph. Acharnians* 43 The request of the bride, which she earnestly asks at me! *Mod.* He asked a larger sum from me.

11. To ask *to do*, or *be done to*.

c **1374** CHAUCER *Boeth.* III. i. 63 I . . axe gretely to heeren tho remedyes. **1477** EARL RIVERS (Caxton) *Dictes* 1, I had delyte & axed to rede some good historye. **1647** SPRIGG *Ang. Rediv.* III. iii. (1854) 149, I humbly ask to have this place slighted. **1833** I. TAYLOR *Fanat.* vii. 221 The country . . seemed to ask to be seized upon by men worthy to enjoy it.

** *trans. With the person asked as object*:

To make a request to.

12. To ask a person a thing. *Obs.*, or *arch.* in 'I ask you pardon, leave.'

1297 R. GLOUC. 16 He nolde no mon asche leue. *Ibid.* 196 Hii esseþ vs truage. *a* **1300** *Cursor M.* 3868 Jacob askid him his lemman. *c* **1308** *Pol. Songs* 200 What hast i-do, That thou me so oxist pes? *c* **1450** LONELICH *Grail* xxxvi. 493 Forto axen hem consaille. **1538** BALE *God's Promises* in Dodsl. *O.P.* (1780) I. 11 Good Lorde I axe the mercy. **1671** MILTON *P.R.* IV. 551 To stand upright Will ask thee skill. **1749** FIELDING *Tom Jones* xvi. vii. (1840) 238/2, I ask Mr. Blifil pardon.

b. with the second object wanting.

a **1564** BECON *Gen. Pref. Wks.* (1843) 22 Christ saith: 'Give to every one that axeth thee.'

13. To ask a person *to do* a thing.

a **1300** *Cursor M.* 3141 Nou es he askid . . Til gode to make of sacrifise. *c* **1400** *Destr. Troy* I. (*title*) How King Pelleus Exit Iason to get þe ffles of golde. **1860** TYNDALL *Glac.* I. §22. 152, I asked him to accompany me. **1872** BLACK *Adv. Phaeton* xxv. 350 He does not ask me to pay his bills.

14. To ask a person (*of* obs.) *for* a thing.

c **1386** CHAUCER *Pers. T.* (Wr.) ¶918 A man that . . cometh for to axe him of mercy [*Other MSS.* aske mercy]. **1483** CAXTON *Gold. Leg.* 24/3 For this first they ought to axe echeone other. **1590** SHAKS. *Com. Err.* II. i. 61 He ask'd me for a hundred markes in gold. **1600** —— *A.Y.L.* IV. i. 138, I might aske you for your Commission. **1735** POPE *Prol. Sat.* 50 You know his Grace, I want a Patron; ask him for a Place. **1810** SCOTT *Lady of L.* v. vii, Ask we this savage hill we tread For fatten'd steer or household bread? *Prov.* Ask a kite for a feather, and she'll say, she has but just enough to fly with.

*** *intr. With no object*: To make request.

15. *simply.* To ask.

c **1380** WYCLIF *Sel. Wks.* (1871) III. 328 He is redy to ȝeve him if he ax worþily. *c* **1400** *Rom. Rose* 5243 Man that worthy is of name, To axen often hath gret shame. **1535** COVERDALE *Matt.* vi. 7 Axe & it shalbe giuen you. **1535** STEWART *Cron. Scot.* II. 402 Ask and haue. **1611** BIBLE *Matt.* vi. 7 Aske [WYCLIF, axe ȝe] and it shalbe giuen you. *Mod.* It is rather those who ask loudest, than those who need most, that secure attention.

16. To ask (*after* obs.) *for* a thing.

c **1200** *Trin. Coll. Hom.* 81 Iuel mennish . . acseð after fortocne of heuene. **1377** LANGL. *P. Pl.* B. VI. 298 Al hunger eet in hast and axed after more. **1611** BIBLE *Micah* vii. 3 The iudge asketh for a reward. **1795** SOUTHEY *Joan of Arc* II. 246 Could hear a famish'd woman ask for food, And feel no pity. **1865** DICKENS *Mut. Fr.* II. vii. 202 I'll cut back and ask for leave.

b. phr. ***to ask for trouble*** (or the like), also (as slang or colloq. substitute) ***to ask for it***, to act in such a way as to bring trouble upon oneself, to give provocation.

1902 *Captain* VII. 549/2 The fly-away contingent were what is spoken of as 'asking for' bent spines and injured hearts. **1909** E. P. OPPENHEIM *Jeanne of Marshes* II. xiv. 274 'Whatever happens to him,' Forrest said, 'he's asking for it.' **1909** *Westm. Gaz.* 16 Sept. 12/2 There are vainglorious players in this world who, to use a vulgarism, 'ask for it', and deserve it when they get it. **1915** *Times Red Cross Story Book* 71 Certainly we were 'asking for it', as my . . offspring did not fail to remark. **1916** 'BOYD CABLE' *Action Front* 165 Silly fools. . . What do they want to hoist that huge Red Cross flag up there for, where any airman can see it? Fairly asking for it, I call it. **1925** E. F. NORTON *Fight for Everest, 1924* 343 It is asking for trouble to give out any money except the daily ration allowance. **1946** 'M. INNES' *From London Far* I. v. 42 'The damned scoundrels!' . . The girl was philosophical. 'I asked for it, all right.' **1960** H. PINTER *Room* 1, I don't know how they live down there. It's asking for trouble.

IV. Pregnant senses and special uses.

†**17.** To inquire into, examine, investigate. *Obs.*

c **1000** *Ags. Ps.* x. 5 His bræwas . . ahsað manna bearn. Se ylca Drihten ahsað rihtwíse and unrihtwíse. *c* **1175** *Lamb. Hom.* 35 Oðer he heo hafð i-escad oðer hafð ifunden on boke. **1382** WYCLIF *Ecclus.* xi. 7 Beforn that thou aske, ne blame thou any man. *Ibid. Ps.* x. 5 The eyelidis of hym asken[**1611** trie] the sones of men. The Lord asketh the riȝtwis man, and the vnpitous. **1612** *Arraignm. John Selman* 14 Sir Francis Bacon . . proceeded to judgment and asking on the prisoner, thus . . hee spake.

†**18.** To prosecute, exact from, oppress. *Obs.*

1388 WYCLIF *Isaiah* lviii. 3 Lo! ȝoure wille is foundun in the dai of ȝoure fastyng, and ye axen alle ȝoure dettouris.

19. To ask as by right, call for, demand.

1393 GOWER *Conf.* I. 36 They axen alle jugement Ayein the man. *c* **1430** *Syr Generides* 4795 His hors he ashed . . his wey he nam. *a* **1440** *Sir Degrev.* 393 He axit justes of were And prays the of answere. *c* **1460** *Townely Myst.* 58 To worshyp me as I wylle asse. **1509** BARCLAY *Shyp of Folys* (1874) I. 141 Nought . . to asshe agaynst right. **1544** BALE *Sir J. Oldcastell* in *Harl. Misc.* (Malh.) I. 258 God will axe no more of a Christen beleuer . . but only to obey the preceptes of that moost blessed lawe. **1580** BARET *Alv.* A 594 To aske agayne that is ones owne, or in a maner due to him, *Reposco.*

b. *esp.* in ***to ask an account***.

a **1450** *Knt. de la Tour* xxxix. 59 Of the which God wille axse hem accompte. **1523** LD. BERNERS *Froiss.* I. ccclxxxiii. 645 They wolde aske accomptes of the Chancellour of Englande to knowe where all the good was become that he had leuyed through the realme. **1559** *Myrr. Mag., Dk. Glouc.* xxi. 5 To axe a reckening of the Realmes reuenue.

20. To make proclamation of a thing in church or other public place, calling upon any who have claims or objections to put them forward. Formerly of things found, stray cattle, etc.; still used of marriages about to be contracted (***to ask the banns***); in popular phrase the parties are said to be 'asked in church.'

(The recognized expression is now to *publish the banns*; but *ask* is the historical word.) See BANN.

1450 MYRC 203 Aske the banns thre halydawes. **1523** FITZHERB. *Surv.* 28b, They ought to aske them [stray cattle] thre sondayes in thre or four next parysshe churches and also crye them thre tymes in thre the nexte market townes. **1596** SHAKS. *Tam. Shr.* II. i. 181 The day When I shal aske the banes, and when be married. **1606** *Wily Beguiled* in Hazl. *Dodsl.* IX. 304 We must be asked in church next Sunday. **1662** FULLER *Worthies* Westm. (1811) II. 105 (D.) His head was ask'd, but never married to the English Crown. **1841** ORDERSON *Creoleana* ii. 14 The fair sex . . preferring to be 'asked in church.'

21. a. *ellipt.* To ask (one) to come, to invite.

Mod. We ought to ask him to dinner. Why were you not at the ball? Because I was not asked.

b. *colloq.*, with adverbs: ***to ask back***, to reciprocate an invitation; ***to ask down***, to invite (someone) to come and stay in the country; ***to ask out***, to invite to something, esp. to an entertainment.

1834 DICKENS in *Monthly Mag.* Feb. 152 If I see him . . tomorrow, perhaps I'll ask him down. **1864** H. C. ADAMS *White Brunswickers* x. 167 Billy moved heaven and earth to get asked out on the same days. **1887** KIPLING *Plain Tales fr. Hills* (1890) 199 Now and again he was asked out to dinner. **1888** MCCARTHY & PRAED *Ladies' Gallery* I. xii. 289, I was asked out in a kind of way. **1922** 'R. CROMPTON' *More William* xiv. 231 But if he asks you to his you must ask him back. **1934** H. G. WELLS *Exper. Autobiogr.* II. viii. 532 People, often strange people, were beginning to ask us out.

22. ***to ask away***: to do away with by asking.

1649 MILTON *Eikon.* Wks. 1738 I. 112 His Prayer is so ambitious of Prerogative, that it dares ask away the Prerogative of Christ himself.

V. *fig.* Predicated of things.

23. To need, require, demand, call for (by its condition).

1340 *Ayenb.* 54 Be þan þet hare zennes okseþ. **1387** TREVISA *Descr. Brit.* (Caxton) 36 Whan tyme and place axeth. *c* **1400** *Destr. Troy* xv. 7067 He þat tas not his tyme, when þe tyde askes. *c* **1430** *Hymns to Virg.* (1867) 61 Quod conscience, þat axiþ coost. **1596** SHAKS. *Tam. Shr.* II. i. 15 Signior Baptista, my businesse asketh haste. **1598** BARRET *Theor. Warres* I. i. 7 These three matters handled would aske a great volume. **1615** MARKHAM *Eng. Housw.* (1660) 81 The Veal will aske a double quantity of Suet. **1623** SANDERSON *Serm.* Ad Mag. i. (1674) 89 It will ask some time, yea, and cunning too, to find it out. **1697** DRYDEN *Virg. Georg.* III. 478 Goats of equal Profit are . . and ask an equal Care. **1780** COWPER *Table T.* 559 To give a Milton birth ask'd ages more. **1880** CYPLES *Hum. Exp.* vi. 133 Limit of time asked for a sensation.

†**24.** To invite, provoke. *Obs.*

c **1485** *Digby Myst.* (1882) IV. 91 Such crabyysh wordes do aske a blow. **1605** CAMDEN *Rem.* (1637) 303 One ill word asketh another. One good turne asketh another.

†**25.** To seek, direct itself toward (lit. trans. of L. *petere*). *Obs. rare.*

1432-50 tr. *Higden* (1865) I. 63 The Redde see . . is departede in to ij. armes, of whom the arme Persicalle . . dothe aske the northe.

ask, *sb.*[1] Forms: 1 **æsce**, 3 **axe**, (?) **as**. [OE. *ǽsce*, f. *ásc̣ian* (see prec.); cf. ODu. *esch*. *As* is prob. = *ash* or *ask*: see the vb.] Asking, inquiry; thing asked, request.

a **1000** *Laws of Athelstan* §5 (Thorpe I. 230) Hæfdon ealle ða ǽscean. **1205** LAY. 1053 Eouer axe ich eou leue. *a* **1230** *Juliana* 16 He failed of his as. **1781** T. TWINING *Let.* 8 Dec. in *Recreat. & Stud.* (1882) 108, I am not so unreasonable as to desire you to . . answer all my asks. **1886** 'CAVENDISH' *Whist* 127 When your three comes down in the next round, it is not an ask for trumps.

ask ('ɑːsk, æ-), *sb.*[2] Also 4 **arske**, 4–6 **aske**, 5 **awsk**. [Apparently worn down from OE. *áðexe* newt (= OS. *egithassa*, OHG. *egidehsa*, MHG. *egedehse*, mod.G. *eidechse*), the phonetic contraction being paralleled by the Ger. dial. *edechs*, *egdes*, *eges*, *eckes*, given by Grimm III. 83; but no intermediate forms between *áðexe* and *aske*, such as *áðesce*, *aðsce*, or *aðxe*, *axe*, have been found.]

A newt or eft; the common name in Scotland, and in the north and north-east of England as far as Morecambe Bay and Lincolnshire. Sometimes applied also to the lizard; always classed among venomous animals, an idea encouraged by a general confusion of *ask* with *asp*. See also ASKER[2].

In the following Glossaries of the Eng. Dial. Soc., Cumberland, Swaledale, Mid Yorkshire, Whitby (*Ask* or *Aisk*: *Fleeing-ask*, the dragon-fly: cf. *Flying Adder*, *Flying Dragon*), Manley and Corringham (Lincolnsh.)

c **1325** *Metr. Hom.* 141 Snakes and nederes thar he fand, And gret blac tades . . And arskes and other wormes felle. *c* **1425** WYNTOUN *Cron.* I. xiii. 55 Nakyn best of venym . . as aske or eddyre, tade, or pade. *c* **1450** HENRYSON (JAM.) Cum with me in hy, Edderis, askis, and wormis meit for to be. **1501** DOUGLAS *Pal. Hon.* I. xxv, The water stank, the feild was odious Quhair dragouns, lessertis, askis, edders, swatterit. **1611** FLORIO, *Magrasio*, an Eft, a Nute, an Aske. **1840** J. M. WILSON *T. of Borders* (1851) XX. 31 He can lurk in the green moss like the yellow-wamed ask. **1876** SMILES *Scotch Nat.* ii. (ed. 4) 44 He looked at the beast. It was not an eel. It was very like an ask.

askable ('ɑːskəb(ə)l, æ-), *a.* [f. ASK *v.* + -ABLE.] Fit or proper to be asked.

c **1650** *T. Cromwell* in Percy's *Bal. & Rom.* I. 129 For if your boon be askeable, soone granted it shall be.

askance (ə'skæns), *adv.* Forms: 6 **a scanche**, **a scance**, **ascaunce**, 6–7 **asconce**, **ascance**, 6–8 **askaunce**, 7 **askauns**, **ascaunse**, 6– **askance**. [Etymology unknown. Wedgwood suggests It. *a schiancio* 'bias, slanting, sloping or slopingly, aslope, across, overthwart' (Baretti), where *schiancio* is = OFr. *esclanc*, *esclenc*, gauche, left hand. Skeat compares It. *scanso* f. *scansare*, expl. by Florio, among other meanings, as 'to go a slope, or a sconce, or a skew, to go sidelin.' Koch suggests a formation on ON. *á ská*: see ASKEW. Diefenbach compares Jutlandish *ad-skands*, West Fris. *skân*, *schean*, which he connects with Du. *schuin*, *schuins*: see ASKOYNE.

(There is a whole group of words of more or less obscure origin in *ask-*, containing *askance*, *askant*, *askew*, *askie*, *askile*, *askoye*, *askoyne*, (with which cf. *asklent*, *aslant*, *asquint*,) which are more or less closely connected in sense, and seem to have influenced one another in form. They appear mostly in the 16th or end of the 15th c., and none of them can be certainly traced up to OE.; though they can nearly all be paralleled by words in various languages, evidence is wanting as to their actual origin and their relations to one another.)]

1. a. Sidewise, obliquely, askew, asquint; with a side glance.

1530 PALSGR. 831/1 A scanche, *De travers, en lorgnant.* *a* **1541** WYATT *Meane & Sure Est.* 52 For, as she lookt a scance, Under a stole she spied two stemyng eyes. **1667** MILTON *P.L.* x. 668 He bid his Angels turne ascance The

Poles of Earth. **1768** BEATTIE *Minstr.* I. xxxv, They meet, they dart away, they wheel askance. **1848** MRS. JAMESON *Sacr. & Leg. Art* (1850) 154 Judas is at once distinguished, looking askance with a wicked sneer on his face.

b. With a side or indirect meaning.

1876 SWINBURNE *Erechtheus* 337 Journeying to the bright God's shrine Who speaks askance and darkling.

2. In the fig. phrases **to look, eye, view askance**, the idea expressed has varied considerably, different writers using them to indicate disdain, envy, jealousy, and suspicion. The last of these is now the prevalent idea, and ***to look at, eye, view askance*** = to look at with mistrust.

1579 SPENSER *Sheph. Cal.* Mar. 21 That scornefully lookes askaunce. **1596** SHAKS. *Tam. Shr.* II. i. 249 Thou canst not frowne, thou canst not looke a sconce. **1598** B. JONSON *Ev. Man. in Hum.* IV. ii, Nay, Boy, never look askance at me for the matter. **1602** *Life T. Cromwell* IV. ii, Yet look'd askance when as they saw me poor. **1667** MILTON *P.L.* IV. 504 The Devil..with jealous leer maligne Ey'd them askance. **1750** GRAY *Let.* in *Poems* (1775) 215 Whom meaner beauties eye askance, And vainly ape her art of killing. **1790** BURKE *Fr. Rev.* 155 It is envy and malignity.. that makes some look askance at the distinctions..set apart for virtue. **1824** W. IRVING *T. Trav.* I. 57 Eyeing the enemy askance from under their broad hats. **1875** GLADSTONE *Glean.* VI. xxiv. 120 Both rather abounded in self-confidence, and were viewed askance by authority. **1875** WHITNEY *Life Lang.* v. 97 Words..which come to be looked askance at and avoided.

3. elliptical, quasi-*adj.* Turned sidewise, sidelong.

1593 NASHE *Christes Teares* (1613) 48 Thy sight is no way ..impayred, by casting away one askance-regard on any. **1667** MILTON *P.L.* VI. 149 Whom the grand foe, with scornful eye askance, Thus answerd. **1824** GALT *Rothelan* II. IV. viii. 168 The fiend of night..retires with an askance and lurid eye. **1914** T. HARDY *Satires of Circ.* 32 Down there they are dubious and askance. **1938** E. BOWEN *Death of Heart* I. iii. 56 'Well, what, Matchett?' Anna said touchily. 'Young people like to wear what is usual.' Anna had been askance. *Ibid.* I. iv. 76 Looking at all this in here with a wild askance shrinking eye.

†**a'skance**, *v. Obs.* [f. prec.] To turn aside.

1593 SHAKS. *Lucr.* 637 That from their own misdeeds askance their eyes!

†**a'skance(s**, *conj. adv. Obs.* Also 4–5 **ascauns(e, ascance, ascaunce, ascaunces, askaunse, as skaunce, asscaunce,** 6 **ascanses, askaunces.** [Etym. unknown; the word was orig. of 3 syllables, and *ascaunces* was perh. the orig. form. See Skeat *Chaucer's Man of Law's T.*, etc., Glossary; also *Notes and Queries*, 4th ser. XI. 251, where its use is shown to correspond to that of Du. *kwantwijs*, ODu. *quantsuys*, *quansis*.]

1. As though, as if. (? On the pretence.)

c **1386** CHAUCER *Sompn. T.* 37 And wroot the names.. Ascaunce [*v.r.* ascance, askaunse] that he wolde for hem preye. *c* **1400** *Beryn* 1797 They walkid to and fro..as skaunce they knewe nauȝte. *c* **1420** *Pallad. on Husb.* VI. 39 And even the erthe above ascaunce her noon is. *c* **1430** LYDG. *Bochas* IV. xiv. 114 a, A sprite of feined pacience.. Ascaunce she had been in vertue strong. **1580** SIDNEY *Arcadia* (1622) 162 Keeping a countenance ascanses she vnderstood him not.

2. *ellipt.* As if saying, as much as to say.

c **1374** CHAUCER *Troylus* I. 292 Sche lete falle Hire loke a lite aside, in swich manere, Ascaunces, 'What! may I nat stonden here?' [Boccaccio: *quasi dicesse, E no ci si puo star?*]. **1572** GASCOIGNE *Flowers* Wks. 1587, 101 Therewith he raysed his heavy head alight, Askaunces, Ha! in deede and thinkst thou so.

askant (əˈskænt), *adv.* Forms: 7 **ascant, a-skaunt,** 7–9 **askaunt,** 8– **askant.** [apparently a later variant of ASKANCE q.v., with termination assimilated to ASQUINT or ASLANT.]

1. = ASKANCE 1.

1695 BLACKMORE *Pr. Arth.* II. 461 Man's Soul, by this rude Shock from 's Center driv'n, Stands so a-skaunt. **1795** SOUTHEY *Joan of Arc* x. 98 Whether this public zeal hath look'd askaunt To private ends. **1873** DIXON *Two Queens* I. I. v. 36 His mouth was big; his left eye turned askant.

2. = ASKANCE 2.

1633 P. FLETCHER *Purple Isl.* XII. lxxx, On which if Envie might but glance ascant, Her eyes would swell and burst. **1761** *Brit. Mag.* II. 133 All parties concur in looking askant upon turn-coats. **1880** MRS. PARR *Adam & Eve* II. 149 They looked askant on innovation and hated change.

3. = ASKANCE 3.

1791 COWPER *Iliad* XI. 657 With an eye askant, Watchful retreated.

¶ In the following passage from Shakspere, in which it appears as a prep., the folios read *aslant.*

1602 SHAKS. *Ham.* (Qq.) IV. vii. 167 There is a willow grows ascaunt the brook.

†**a'skanted,** *ppl. a. Obs. rare*$^{-1}$. In 7 **eskanted.** [f. prec. + -ED.] Turned askant.

1576 T. N[EWTON] *Lemnie's Touchst. Complex.* (1633) 221 With eyes sullen, sterne, terrible, glancing aside and eskanted.

†**'Askapart.** *Obs.* Forms: 4 **ascopard(e,** 5 **-parte,** 6–7 **ascapart(e, -upart,** 8 **askapart.** Name of a race of hardy warriors living in or near Arabia; also of a giant said to have been defeated by Sir Bevis of Southampton.

c **1320** *Sir Beues* 2341 A geaunt With a lotheliche semlaunt ..thrette fete long..Me name, a sede, is Ascopard. **1366** MAUNDEV. vi. 63 Arrabyenes, that Men clepen Bedoynes and Ascopardes. *c* **1400** *Sowdone Bab.* 2648 Ethiopis, Indens and Ascopartes, That bene boolde and hardy to fight. *c* **1550** *Syr Beuys* K ij, Beuis with a bolde herte..assayled Ascaparte. **1612** DRAYTON *Polyolb.* ii. 694 (N.) Sir Bevis ..(Goliah like) great Ascupart inforc'd To serve him for a slave. **1735** POPE *Donne Sat.* IV. 276 Each man an Askapart, of strength to toss For Quoits, both Temple-bar and Charing-Cross.

askape, var. of ASCAPE, obs. form of ESCAPE.

askar, obs. form of ESCHAR, a scab.

Askar (ˈæskə(r)). [Arabic, *'askar* army.] A native Moroccan infantryman. Also as *pl.*

[**1902** *Encycl. Brit.* XXX. 840/1 The infantry (Askária) are mostly rough, ill-trained levies.] **1918** FARROW *Dict. Mil. Terms, Askar*, in the Moroccan army, a native infantryman or foot soldier. **1925** *Blackw. Mag.* Nov. 619/1 An askar of the Riffi army. *Ibid.* 619/2 At our approach, bearded askar come to the salute.

Askari (æˈskɑːrɪ, ˈæskəriː), *sb. pl.* Also **-is.** [Arabic *'askarī* soldier.] Native soldiers of East Africa. Also as *sing.*

1889 LD. LUGARD *Diaries* (1959) I. 53, I have now 4 Headmen, 10 Askari, 96 porters..and 9 Persians. **1906** *Macm. Mag.* Oct. 929 Before him stood a..native, who acted as interpreter and clerk of the court, and a dozen *askari* whose onerous duty it was to preserve order. **1910** ROOSEVELT *African Game Trails* i. 18 The askaris were uniformed, each in a red fez, a blue blouse, and white knickerbockers. **1927** *Chambers's Jrnl.* 694/2 An askari or native constable took it in turns with two others to guard the market.

aske, obs. form of ASH *sb.*²

†**'askebathe.** *Obs.* [f. *aske*, ASH *sb.*² + BATHE.] One who sits among the ashes; = ASKEFISE.

c **1230** *Ancr. R.* 214 þe ȝiscare is þes feondes askebaðie, & lið euer iðen asken, & fareð abuten asken. *a* **1500** *Medulla Gram., Ciniflo*, a aske bathe, seu qui sedet in cineribus.

asked (ɑːskt, æ-), *ppl. a.* [pa. pple. of ASK *v.*] Mentioned as a request. Also ***asked-for.***

1900 *Westm. Gaz.* 5 Feb. 2/2 The asked-for area. **1901** *Ibid.* 9 July 4/3 The asked price. **1936** [see ASKING *ppl. a.* b].

†**'askefise.** *Obs.* [App. of Norse origin, though not recorded by Vigfússon; Sw. *askefis* (Grimm), (cf. Ger. *aschenfister*, Du. *aschevijster*) f. *aske* ashes + ON. and Sw. *físa*, Da. *fise*, to blow, to pass wind; cf. ON. *físi-belgr* small bellows.] One who blows the ashes or fire; a term of reproach among northern nations for an unwarlike fellow who stayed at home in the chimney-corner.

c **1400** *Promp. Parv.* 15 Askysye, Askefise, askefyse, *ciniflo. a* **1500** *Medulla Gram., Ciniflo*, an askfist, or iren heter. [*Other MSS.* A fyre blowere, an yryn hetere, an askefyce.. An aske fyse or irne eter.] **1500** *Ortus Voc.* (W. de W.) *Ciniflo, qui flat in cinere*, aske fyste, a fyre blawer or a yrne hotter.

askeletal (eɪˈskɛlɪtəl), *a.* [f. A- 14 + SKELETAL *a.*] Having no skeleton.

1904 J. MCCABE tr. *Haeckel's Wonders of Life* x. 288 The askeletal vermalia.

asken, obs. pl. form of ASH *sb.*²

asker¹ (ˈɑːskə(r), æ-). Also **askere, axere,** etc: see ASK *v.* [f. ASK *v.* + -ER¹.] One who asks.

1. A questioner, inquirer.

1388 WYCLIF *Ezek.* xiv. 10 Bi the wickidnesse of the axere, so the wickidnesse of the prophete shal be. *c* **1400** *Apol. Loll.* 69 After þe wickydnes of þe ascar schal be þe wichidnes of þe prophet. **1519** HORMAN *Vulg.* 22 The answers..were euer darke and deceyued the axer. **1645** MILTON *Tetrach.* Wks. (1851) 229 The trope of indignation, fittest account for such askers. **1749** BP. LAVINGTON *Enthus.* (1754) II. 155 Curious Beholders and Askers of impertinent Questions. **1886** J. J. WRIGHT *Little Asker* viii. 187 For every boy and girl..is only a little asker, made of such mind and spirit as can live, and learn. **1925** CHESTERTON *Everlasting Man* I. viii. 183 The sages had degenerated..into hired rhetoricians or askers of riddles.

2. One who asks favours, gifts, etc.; a suppliant; one who asks alms, a professional beggar.

c **1400** *Rom. Rose* 6676 Many a man That yeveth his good for..he Wolde of the asker delyvered be. **1569** J. SANFORD *Agrippa's Van. Artes* 91 So many presumptuouse monie askers. *a* **1631** DONNE *Ess. Divin.* (1651) 145 Love an Asker better than a Giver. **1858** LD. ST. LEONARDS *Handy bk. Prop. Law* xxv. 189 Each asking of leave is an admission that, at the time, the asker had no right. **1883** R. BURTON & CAMERON *Gold Coast* I. iii. 60 They beg with a good grace, and not with a curse or an insult like the European 'asker' when refused.

†**3.** A prosecutor, plaintiff; an exactor, oppressor. *Obs.*

c **1375** *Eng. Guilds* 361 And þat commune law hym be y-entred, þe axere and þe defendaunt. *Ibid.* 362 Of plee of dette..ȝif þat þe axkere bryngeþ skore oþer wryt. **1382** WYCLIF *Job* iii. 18 Thei herden not the vois of the askere [**1611** oppressour]. **1483** *Cath. Angl.*, An Asker wrangwysly, *exactor.*

'asker². Also 7 **ascar.** [f. ASK *sb.*² with suffix of uncertain origin; also altered to *askerd, ascard, askal, asgal, asgil.*] Common name of the newt in the west midland counties of England.

In the following Dialect Glossaries: Craven (*Asker, Askard*), Mid Yorksh. (*Ask, aisk*, or *askerd*), Lancash., Shropsh. (*Asker, askal, asgal*), West Worcester (*Asgill*), Dorset (Phil. Soc. Trans. 1864, 41).

1674 RAY *N. Countr. Wds., Asker*; a Newt, or Eft. **1677** J. WEBSTER *Witchcr.* xii. 242 Strange vomitings up of Frogs, lizards, askers and the like..attributed to witchcraft. **1686** PLOT *Staffordsh.* 252 It differs in colour from all the Newts or Ascars that ever I saw. **1755** JOHNSON, *Asker* a water newt. **1761** STERNE *Tr. Shandy* (1802) IV. xxvii. 126 A Newt or an Asker, or some such detested reptile.

asker, obs. form of ESCHAR, a scab.

askerye, variant of ASCRY *v. Obs.*

askesis, var. ASCESIS.

askew (əˈskjuː), *adv., a.,* (*sb.*) Forms: 6–7 **askewe,** 6 **a-skiew, a scew, ascue,** 7–8 **askue.** [Etymology uncertain; see the simple SKEW *v.* or *a.*, upon which this may have been formed with A *prep.*¹ Its relation to ASKOYE, which preceded it somewhat in the same sense, is uncertain. It corresponds also in sense to ON. *á ská*, and in form to Da. *skjæv*:—ON. *skeif* oblique, wry, skew, Ger. *schief*, LG. *scheew*, Du. *scheef.* Neither *askew* nor *skew* appears before 16th c. See note to ASKANCE.]

A. *adv.* **1.** Obliquely, to one side, off the straight, awry. Also *fig.* cross, untowardly, frowardly, unfavourably.

1573 TWYNE *Cont. Phaër's Æneid* XII. KK iv b, To dread that lucke shall light ascue. **1587** GOLDING *De Mornay*, The Zodiacke goes a-skiew. **1655** GURNALL *Chr. in Armour* I. 112 The Serpent goes a skue..winding and wreathing its body. **1695** BLACKMORE *Pr. Arth.* I. 266 And wrench'd the Poles some Leagues yet more askew. **1855** DICKENS *Lit. Dorrit* (C.D. ed.) 309 Lattice-blinds all hanging askew.

2. esp. in phr. ***to look askew***: i.e. sidelong, out at the corners of one's eyes, not straight in the face.

1579 E. K. in *Spenser's Sheph. Cal.* Mar. *Gloss.*, Ascaunce, askewe or asquint. **1599** B. JONSON *Ev. Man out of Hum.* v. I Let her fleer, and look a scew, and hide her Teeth with her Fan. *a* **1791** WESLEY *Wks.* (1830) XIII. 486 Your looks (in speaking) should be direct, neither severe nor askew. **1821** SCOTT *Kenilw.* x, The boy looking askew at him with his sharp gray eyes.

b. *fig.* To look as if pretending not to see, to look with contempt or disdain; to reflect ***upon.***

1580 LYLY *Euphues* (Arb.) 426 He beganne to look askew vppon Camilla. **1636** HEYWOOD *Challenge* II. i. Wks. 1874 V. 22 All I meete..look askue, and point, and laugh at mee. **1661** PEPYS *Diary* I. 25 Aug., My Lady Button and her daughter to look something askew upon my wife, because my wife..is not solicitous for their acquaintance. **1721** STRYPE *Eccl. Mem.* I. xxiii. 167 For some expressions..that looked askew upon the King's supremacy..he was laid in hold. **1840** BARHAM *Ingol. Leg.* 396 But Nelly Cook askew did look.

B. *adj.* Oblique, made or standing awry; skew.

[**1570** LEVINS *Manip.* 95 A Skewe, *limus.*] **1859** TURNER *Dom. Archit.* III. iv. 162 A room over the street, which rests on an askew arch. **1862** SMILES *Engineers* III 233 Bridges of masonry..several of them askew bridges. **1871** DARWIN *Desc. Man* II. xv. 165 In time the tail becomes quite askew.

†**C.** *sb.* A sidelong glance. *Obs.*

1655 HEYWOOD *Fort. by Land, &c.* II. i. Wks. 1874 VI. 383 Her face, the trick of her eye, her leer, her blink, her askue.

askewese, obs. form of EXCUSE.

†**a-'skie,** *adv. Obs.* [? f. A *prep.*¹ + *skey*, variant of *shey*, SHY: '*schey* or *skey* as horse' (*Promp. Parv.*): cf. also SKEIGH and ASKOYE.] ? Shyly; off at a tangent like a shying horse.

1393 GOWER *Conf.* II. 50 All sodeinly She passeth as it were a skie All clene out of this ladies sight.

†**a'skile,** *adv. Obs.* [See note to ASKANCE. Cf. Du. *scheel* squinting, *scheel zien* to squint.]

1599 BP. HALL *Sat.* v. ii. 135 What tho the scornefull waiter looks askile?

asking (ˈɑːskɪŋ, æ-), *vbl. sb.* Forms: 1 **ásc-, ácsung,** 3 **ax-, escunge, ascing,** 4–5 **ask-, axyng(e,** 4–6 **askinge,** 5– **asking**: other variants of the root as in ASK. [f. ASK *v.*: see -ING¹.]

1. The action of putting a question, interrogation, inquiry.

c **885** K. ÆLFRED *Boeth.* xxxix. §4 Hit is þeaw þære spræce and þære ácsunge. —— *Boeth. Metr.* xxii. 41 Mid ascunga. *c* **1230** *Ancr. R.* 338 Of þe axunge mei uallen vuel. *c* **1225** *St. Marherete* (1866) 16 Stew þe, steorue, ant stille beo þin escunge. *c* **1380** WYCLIF *Wicket* 15 The puttynge awaye of fylthenes of the fleshe, and the axynge of good conscience. [Cf. *1 Pet.* iii. 21 (*revised*) interrogation.] **1794** BURNS *Let.* in *Wks.* (Globe) 549 Do not miss asking for him.

†**2.** An inquiry, a question. *Obs.*

c **1325** *Metr. Hom.* 35 Quen Crist thair asking herd, Ful mildely he thaim ansuerd. *c* **1410** tr. *Bonaventura's Myrrour* (Pynson) viii. D j, Our lady..answereth sadly and shortly to theyr askynges.

3. The action of requesting a favour, gift, etc.; praying, begging.

c **1200** *Trin. Coll. Hom.* 11 After clepenge and ascinge. **1340** *Ayenb.* 198 He deþ bet þet yefþ wyþoute aksinge. **1613**

SHAKS. *Hen. VIII.* II. i. 4 Bestowing on him, at his asking, The Archbishopricke of Toledo. **1828** SCOTT *F. M. Perth* I. 34 A lass that may be had for the asking.

4. A petition, prayer, a supplication. *arch.*

c **1300** *Cursor M.* 3301 þine asking Es noght bot a litell thing. **1388** WYCLIF *Bar.* ii. 14 Lord here thou oure axyngis and our preyeris. **1482** *Monk of Evesham* (Arb.) 101 He neuer denyed hem her petycyons and askynges. **1513** DOUGLAS *Æneis* IX. iii. 53 Grant this ane axing quhilk I the requeyr. **1607** SHAKS. *Cor.* I. vi. 65 Yet dare I neuer Deny your asking. **1860** TENNYSON *Tithonus* 16 Then didst thou grant mine asking with a smile.

†**5.** A price asked, a demand. *Obs.*

1615 T. ADAMS *White Devil* 59 He makes his owne price, for they give him his asking. **1637** SANDERSON *21 Serm.* Ad Aul. v. (1673) 71 Naboth shall have his own asking.

†**6. a.** An appeal; a calling for justice, or to the law. **b.** Oppression, exaction. *Obs.*

1413 LYDG. *Pylgr. Sowle* I. viii. 6 In euery ryghtwys court ..admytted to maken his compleynt, and purpoos his askynge. **1480** CAXTON *Chron. Eng.* cxxxiv. 114 He did grete destruction to holy chirche thurugh wrongful taking and axyngs.

7. The publication of banns of marriage. *fam.*

1727-51 CHAMBERS *Cycl.* s.v. *Banns*, The publication of banns (popularly called asking in the church). **1824** BYRON *Juan* XVI. lxxxviii, At the third asking of the bans He started. **1865** B. BRIERLEY *Irkdale* II. 187 The 'askings' had been called over three consecutive Sundays.

8. ***asking price*** (***rate***), the price (or rate) asked for or set by the seller. Cf. ASK *v.* 9 b.

1755 MRS. C. CHARKE *Life* 151, I flew..to all the Brokers in Town, to buy my Houshold Furniture, gave the asking Price for every thing I bought. **1852** *Harper's Mag.* V. 534/1 The merchants..have two prices—an 'asking price' and a 'taking price'. **1924** *Times Trade & Engin. Suppl.* 29 Nov. 242/4 This is higher than recent f.o.b. sales for this autumn's delivery, but about £2 a standard lower than the 'asking' prices at the commencement. **1930** *Economist* 10 May 1051/1 The asking rate on 90-day bankers' bills has been cut to $2\frac{7}{8}$ per cent.

'asking, *ppl. a.* [f. ASK *v.* + -ING[2].] **a.** That asks; inquiring, begging, suppliant.

1735 POPE *Prol. Sat.* 412 Explore the thought, explain the asking eye. *c* **1750** SHENSTONE *Elegy* xx. 70 Shall, vainly suppliant, spread his asking hand. **1795** SOUTHEY *Joan of Arc* II. 187 The asking eye of hunger. **1813** BYRON *Corsair* III. xvi, With many an asking smile, and wondering stare.

b. ***asking bid*** (see quot. 1936).

1936 E. CULBERTSON *Contr. Bridge* 15 *Asking Bid*, an artificial bid requesting specific information in the asked suit. **1959** REESE & DORMER *Bridge Player's Dict.* 16 Asking-bids are a conventional way of locating controls for slam purposes.

'askingly, *adv.* [f. prec. + -LY[2].] In an asking manner; inquiringly, with entreaty.

1794 COLERIDGE *Young Ass*, How askingly its footsteps hither bend, It seems to say, 'And have I then one friend?'

askis, -ys, obs. plural form of ASH *sb.*[2]

a'sklent, a'sclent, *adv.* [Cf. *sclender, sclate* = *slender, slate*.] Scotch form of ASLANT.

1584 J. CARMICHAEL *Let.* in *Misc. Wodr. Soc.* (1844) 443 They..hes bene farther careit asklent then reason can warrand. **1657** COLVIL *Whigs Supplic.* (1751) 61 They always took the bog a-sclent [= they fled]. **1792** BURNS *Duncan Gray* i, Maggie coost her head fu' high, Look'd asklent and unco skeigh.

†**askoy'e, a'skoyne,** *adv. Obs.* Also 6 ascoye. [Actual origin uncertain: *skoyne* seems to be identical with Du. *schuin* sidewise, oblique; cf. *schuinte* slope. But see ASQUINT and ASKEW, with which in sense this word is closely allied, and note to ASKANCE.] Sidewise, askew, with sidelong glance, askance. (Always with *look*.)

1430 LYDG. *Chron. Troy* I. v, To him he spake With chere askoyne vnto the messengere. *Ibid.* II. xii, With loke askoye, and tourned vp the whyte Of hye desdayne. *c* **1430** —— *Bochas* VI. i. (1554) 143 b, Loking ascoyne, as she had had disdeyne. **1550** CROWLEY *Epigr.* 43 There wanton lokes, and lyftynge vp of eyes, And their lokinge ascoye in most wanton wise. **1552** HULOET, Glaye or loke a skoye, *Transuertere hirquos.*

askrie, askry, variants of ASCRY *v. Obs.*

askue, askuse, obs. forms of ASKEW, EXCUSE.

aslake (ə'sleɪk), *v. Obs.* or *arch.* [OE. *aslacian, asleacian*, f. A- *pref.* 1 + *slacian, sleacian*: see SLAKE *v.*]

†**1.** *intr.* To become slack; to become feeble, grow less; to diminish, abate. *Obs.*

c **1000** ÆLFRIC *Hom.* I. 610 Gif we asleaciað fram gódum weorcum. *c* **1386** CHAUCER *Milleres T.* 367 The water schal aslake and gon away. *c* **1430** LYDG. *Min. Poems* (1840) 231 Whan ȝe be heyest ȝe mowe aslake. *c* **1430** *Syr Generides* 6770 The winde beganne som dele a-slake. *c* **1430** *Hymns to Virg.* (1867) 80 Whanne oure bewte schal aslake. **1587** TURBERV. *Trag. T.* 34 My woes which never would aslake.

2. To become less hot, to grow cool. *arch. rare.*

1810 SOUTHEY *Kehama* XI. 11 Wks. VIII. 93 Last they cast it [the steel] to aslake, In the penal icy lake.

†**3.** *trans.* To slacken. *Obs. rare.*

1340 *Ayenb.* 253 Ne aslaky naȝt to moche þane bridel.

4. To mitigate, alleviate, assuage; to lessen, abate, diminish. *arch.*

c **1314** *Guy Warw.* 213 Til that mi sorwe aslaked be. **1493** *Petronylla* 154 That he of mercy oure sekenesse list aslake. **1599** SANDYS *Europ. Spec.* (1632) 195 These flames of controversies might bee extinguished or aslaked. **1652** SPARKE *Prim. Devot.* Ch. Milit., Aslake your grief. **1825** SOUTHEY *Paraguay* I. 14 Waits for the prey..its hunger to aslake.

†**b.** To appease (a person). *Obs. rare.*

1596 SPENSER *F.Q.* I. iii. 36 When mourning altars..The black infernall furies doen aslake.

aslant (ə'slɑːnt, -æ-), *adv.* and *prep.* Forms: 3-5 **o-slant(e, 3-4 on-slent, on-slont, aslante, 5 a-slent, 8 aslaunt, 6- aslant.** [f. ON (see A *prep.*[1]) + SLANT.] **A.** *adv.*

1. On the slant, in a slanting or sloping direction, obliquely.

a **1300** *Cursor M.* 6200 O-slant [*v.r.* on-slent, on-slont] fra þar þai ware. **1398** TREVISA *Barth. De P.R.* XVII. clxxvii. (1495) 718 In vynes the kyttynge shall be aslante. *c* **1440** *Morte Arth.* 2254 O-slante doune fro þe slote he slyttes. *c* **1440** *Promp. Parv.* 6 A-cyde..a-slet, or a-slonte, *Oblique.* **1677** MOXON *Mech. Exerc.* (1703) 208 You must not hold the Blade..parallel to the Pikes, but aslant. **1781** COWPER *Truth* 239 Blown all aslant, a driving, dashing rain. **1878** R. JEFFERIES *Gamekeeper at H.* 113 The shot, if it comes aslant, will glance off.

2. elliptically, quasi-*adj.* Slanting, oblique.

1790 COWPER *Odyss.* IX. 435 He..fell resupine With his huge neck aslant. **1814** SOUTHEY *Roderick* III. Wks. IX. 21 And with ray aslant..illumed the branchless pines.

3. *Comb.* **aslantwise**: aslant.

1852 HAWTHORNE *Blithed. Rom.* II. xiv. 253 The moon.. shone aslantwise over the river.

B. *prep.* Across in a slanting direction, athwart.

1602 SHAKS. *Ham.* IV. vii. 167 There is a Willow growes aslant a Brooke. **1677** MOXON *Mech. Exerc.* (1703) 204 The edge of the Chissel..lying aslant the Work. **1854** H. MILLER *Sch. & Schm.* (1858) 438 It sailed aslant our line of buoys. **1877** PAGE *De Quincey* II. xix. 176 To run somewhat aslant the ordinary conventionalities of life.

†**a'slay,** *v. Obs.* Forms: *Inf.* 1 asleán, 3 aslan, aslæn. *Pa. t.* 1-4 aslóh, 3-4 aslouȝ, -ough, -oȝe, -owe. *Pa. pple.* 1 aslaȝen, aslæȝen, asleȝen, 3 aslæȝe(n, aslaȝe(n, 3-4 aslawe. [OE. *asleán*, f. A- *pref.* 1 + *sleán* (for *sleahan, slahan*) to SLAY; cf. OHG. *arslahan*, MHG. *erslahen*, mod.G. *erschlagen*; prob. also for OE. *ofsleán*: see A- *pref.* 3.]

1. To strike off, strike. (Only in OE.)

c **950** *Lindisf. Gosp.* Matt. xxvi. 51 Asloȝ earo his. *c* **1160** *Hatton G.*, Asloh of anes þas sacerda ealdres þeowa eare.

2. To slay, kill. (? = OE. *ofsleán*.)

1205 LAY. 22576 Scullen þi lond wasten and þire leoden aslan. *Ibid.* 22271 He wold..þat londfolc aslæn. *a* **1300** *K. Horn* 897 Aslaȝen beþ mine heirs. *c* **1305** *Judas* 94 in *E.E.P.* (1862) 109 þe schrewe..his fader aslouȝ. *c* **1315** SHOREHAM 120 Ha nolde nauȝt he were aslawe.

asleep (ə'sliːp), *adv.* and *pred. a.* Forms: 2 **an slep, 3 on slæpe, o slæpe, 3-5 on slepe, 4 on slope, 5-7 (occas. in 9) on sleep(e; 3 aslæpe, 3-6 aslepe, 4 aslape, 4-7 asleepe, 5 asslepe, 6- asleep.** [f. A *prep.*[1] 11 + SLEEP. In OE. *on slǽpe* occurs = in sleep; see *Andreas* 851.]

1. In a state of sleep, sleeping.

1154 *O.E. Chron.* an. 1132 He lai an slep [? and slept] in scip. *c* **1200** ORMIN 8352 Fand himm þanne o slæpe. **1205** LAY. 1159 Heo weren on slæpe [**1250** a-slepe]. **1297** R. GLOUC. 547 Some abedde aslepe. *c* **1350** *Will. Palerne* 1995 My lady lis ȝit a-slape. *c* **1550** CHEKE *Matt.* ix. 24 This maid is not dead but on sleep. **1611** BIBLE *Matt.* viii. 24 But he was asleepe. **1855** BAIN *Senses & Int.* I. ii. §18 No voluntary movement is sustained when we are asleep.

b. *fig.* In a state of sloth, inactivity, or quiescence; at rest; dormant, inactive, idle.

1590 SWINBURN *Testaments* 280 The legacie not to be asleepe..but to be quite dead and extinguished. **1596** SHAKS. *1 Hen. IV*, IV. iii. 22 Their pride and mettall is asleepe. **1677** YARRANTON *England's Impr.* 63 The greatest part of the Iron-works are asleep. **1775** HARRIS *Philos. Arrangem.* (1841) 375 When sense and appetite are asleep. **1819** BYRON *Juan* I. cxlv, During this inquisition Julia's tongue Was not asleep.

2. Into a state of sleep; esp. in the phrases ***to fall, lull, lay*** (***bring*** obs.) ***asleep.***

a **1300** *Cursor M.* 7428 þe king he sal gar fall o-slepe. *c* **1450** *Merlin* xii. 181 A-noon after she fill on slepe. **1588** SHAKS. *Tit. A.* II. iii. 29 A Nurses Song Of Lullabie, to bring her Babe asleepe. *c* **1640** MILTON *L'Allegro* 116 By whispering winds soon lull'd asleep. **1879** TENNYSON *Lover's T.* 16 They fall asleep Into delicious dreams.

b. *fig.* Into a state of inactivity or quiescence.

1545 *Compline* in *Primer*, That we in sin fall not on sleepe. **1608** HIERON *Wks.* I. 706 Lulled a sleep in the common security of the times. **1659** BURTON *Diary* (1828) IV. 348 The sense of the House was, that he should not speak..Mr. Jenkinson moved the same, and so it fell asleep. **1777** WATSON *Philip II* (1793) I. VIII. 292 Their apprehensions were laid asleep. **1871** M. COLLINS *Mrq. & Merch.* III. ii. 64 Don't fall asleep about this affair.

3. *fig.* In (or into) the sleep of death; dead.

1297 R. GLOUC. 279 Kyng Edred nou aslepe in oure Louerd is. **1526** TINDALE *1 Cor.* xv. 18 They which are fallen a slepe in Christ. **1611** BIBLE *Acts* xiii. 36 David..fell on sleepe and was laide vnto his fathers. **1875** B. TAYLOR *Faust* I. xx. 175 Thy mother's soul That fell asleep to long, long torment.

4. *transf.* Of the limbs: In (or into) a state of numbness caused by continued pressure; benumbed, numb. Formerly also = Stunned.

1398 TREVISA *Barth. De P.R.* III. xxi. (1495) 68 Whan a lymme is a slepe. **1547** BOORDE *Brev. Health* §336 Stounynge of a membre of a man..He wyll saye 'my legge or myne armes is a slepe.' **1626** BACON *Sylva* §735 Leaning long upon any part maketh it numme, and, as we call it, asleepe. **1767** BROOKE *Fool of Qual.* (1859) I. 82 (D.) She.. gave Susy such a douse on the side of the head as left her fast asleep for an hour and upward. **1879** CARPENTER *Mental Phys.* I. ii. §41 Numbness, or diminution of Sensibility ..(the hand or foot being 'asleep').

5. *Naut.* 'The sail filled with wind just enough for swelling or bellying out,—as contrasted with its flapping.' Smyth *Sailor's Word-bk.* 1867.

A.S.L.E.F., ASLEF, Aslef ('æslɛf). Formerly also A.S.L.E. & F. [Acronym, f. the initials.] The Associated Society of Locomotive Engineers and Firemen, a British trade union; nowadays, the trade union to which train drivers belong.

1914 [see *N.U.R.* s.v. N. II. 1]. **1943** *Times* 3 Feb. 2/3 (*heading*) A.S.L.E.F. officers see Mr. Bevin. **1976** in R. Crossman *Diaries* II. 519 On December 3rd ASLEF did call for a work to rule but it was settled after a few days. **1983** *Financial Times* 12 Oct. 10 Gomba clinched the deal.. despite a last-minute attempt by a trade union consortium, headed by Mr Ray Buckton, leader of the train drivers' union Aslef, to make a counter-bid.

aslent, obs. form of ASLANT.

†**a'slept,** *ppl. a.* Also 3-4 asleped, -id. [Exact formation uncertain; perh. for *onsleped*, OE. *onslǽped*, pa. pple. of *onslǽpan* to sleep on, fall asleep. Cf. also *ahungered, athirst*.] Overcome with sleep.

a **1300** *Floriz & Bl.* 582 Heo is asleped suiþe. **1382** WYCLIF *Habb.* ii. 16 Drynke thou and be aslept. **1388** —— *Judith* xiii. 4 Holofernes lai in the bed, aslepid with ful myche drunkenesse.

†**a-'slet,** *advb. phr. Obs.* [? error for *aslent*.]

c **1440** *Promp. Parv.* 6 Acyde..aslet. *Ibid.* 15 Aslet ..*oblique.*

Aslib ('æzlɪb). Also **ASLIB, A.S.L.I.B.** [f. the initials.] The Association of Special Libraries and Information Bureaux, an organization set up in 1926 to facilitate the co-ordination of information, etc. Also *attrib.*

1926 *Assoc. Spec. Libr. & Inform. Bur.* (*Prospectus*) 2 History of the Development of A.S.L.I.B... On March 29th, 1926, a meeting was held at the Institution of Mechanical Engineers at which the new Association was formally inaugurated. **1928** (*title*) The Aslib Directory. **1937** *Discovery* June 192/2 It is obtainable by 'Aslib' members. **1945** *Lancet* 29 Dec. 856/1 The ASLIB Microfilm Service. **1951** *Engineering* 27 Apr. 503/3 Aslib..move into new premises.

†**a'slide,** *v. Obs.* [OE. *aslídan*, f. A- *pref.* 1 + *slídan* to SLIDE.] To slide, slip away.

c **1000** *Ags. Ps.* xciii. 17 þæt min sylfes fót..asliden wære. CHAUCER (Urry) 110 Let soche folie out of your herte aslide.

†**a'slip,** *v. Obs.* Forms: 3 asluppe (y), 4 aslyppe. [f. A- *pref.* 1 + SLIP. Cf. OE. *aslúpan*; also MHG. *entslüpfen, entslipfen*, Du. *ontslippen*.] To slip away, escape. (With *dat.* of person.)

[*a* **1000** *Cædmon's Gen.* (Grein) 2796 Lǽt ðé aslúpan sorȝe of breóstum.] *c* **1300** in Wright *Lyric P.* x. 38 Thah he me slowe, ne myht i him asluppe. *c* **1325** *E.E. Allit. P.* C. 218 Her sayl watz hem aslypped on-sydez.

aslogh, -oȝ, -oh, -owe, pa. t. of ASLAY *v. Obs.*

aslont(e, obs. form of ASLANT.

aslope (ə'sləʊp), *a.* and *adv.* [Evidence is wanting to show the exact history of this, and its relation to SLOPE; prob. it is later form of OE. *aslopen*, pa. pple. of *aslúpan*, lit. 'slipped away' (cf. *awake, acale* = OE. *awacen, acalen*); but it may be f. the simple *slope* adj. (itself apparently = OE. *slopen* 'slipped') with A- *pref.* 2. See SLOPE *a.*

Difficulty attaches to either derivation, as well as to that of *slope* itself, from the want of instances of *slopen, aslopen*, or the verbs to which they belonged, between the OE. period and the 15th c.; the second has the additional difficulty that, so far as evidence goes, *slope* appeared still later than *aslope*, and may have been an aphetic form. *Slope* vb. and sb. are comparatively recent derivatives of *slope* adj. In the absence of evidence, it is impossible to say whether *aslope* is primarily an adverb, like *alive, afloat*, or a participial adjective which only follows its sb., like *awake, athirst*, since these two classes of words run together in use.]

In a position or direction between vertical and horizontal, *i.e.* that of a body slipping or falling away; as *adj.* Inclined, slanting, sloping; as *adv.* On the incline, aslant, obliquely, crosswise, athwart. (The advb. use is the commoner.) Also *fig.*

[Cf. *c* **1230** *Ancr. R.* 148 Al min hope were etslopen.] *c* **1400** *Rom. Rose* 4464 Beguiled..For trust that they have set in hope, Which fell hem afterward a slope. [Cf. **1553-87** FOXE *A. & M.* III. 762 You hope and you hope: but your hope shall be slope.] **1482** CAXTON *Chron. Eng.* ccxliv. 298 That the stake myght be pyght in the erth a slope. **1543** GRAFTON *Cont. Harding's Chron.* 502 That poynt should be ..handled, not euen fully playne and dyrectlye, but touched a slope craftely. **1575** TURBERV. *Falconrie* 277 You must cut it off with a sharpe penknife aslope. **1597** DOULAND *Lyrics* in Arb. *Garner* IV. 44 Since Fortune still directs my hap aslope. **1599** *Warn. Faire Wom.* II. 600 My hope is aslope, and my joy is laide to sleepe. **1626** BACON *Sylva* §713 The Haire that lyeth asloape must needs rise. **1667** MILTON *P.L.*

x. 1053 On mee the Curse aslope Glanc'd on the ground. **1727** SWIFT *City Shower* Wks. 1755 III. II. 38 While the first drizzling show'r is borne aslope. *a* **1732** GAY *Poems* (1745) I. 151 Where porters hogsheads roll from carts aslope. *a* **1845** HOOD *Captain's Cow* iii, Against the mast he leans a-slope. **1860** RUSKIN *Mod. Paint.* V. VIII. ii. §4 The steps.. are now all aslope and broken.

†**a'slopen**, *pa. pple. Obs.* [prob. a regular descendant of OE. *aslápen*, pa. pple. of *aslápan* W.Sax. for *aslǽpan* to be sleepy, fall asleep; perh. a modern form after *spoken*, etc.] Fallen asleep.

1604 MIDDLETON *Blurt* II. ii, Good night; we are all aslopen. **1690** D'URFEY *Collin's Walk* i. 25 And rouze up Collin, half aslopen.

†**a-'slout**, *advb. phr. Obs.* [Derivation unknown. ? erroneously for *aslont*.] Aslant, obliquely.

c **1440** *Promp. Parv.* 6 Acyde, or a-slowte, *oblique*. *c* **1460** RUSSELL *Bk. Nurture* in *Babees Bk.* (1868) 155 The salt lamprey, goben hit a slout vij. pecis y assigne.

a-slug (ə'slʌg), *advb. phr.* [A *prep.*[1] + SLUG.] Sluggishly, slowly.

a **1619** FOTHERBY *Atheom.* II. xii. §2 (1622) 338 He.. That comes aslugg against the streame.

†**asma'tographer.** *Obs.*—[0] [f. Gr. ἀσματογράφ-ος (f. ᾆσμα, -ματ- song, lyric + -γράφος writing, writer) + -ER[1].] 'They who sell or make Songs, or Lessons for any Instruments.' Blount *Glossogr.* 1656. 'A composer of songs.' Ash 1775. **asma'tography**, 'the composition of songs.' Bailey.

†**a'smay**, *v. Obs.* [Intermediate form between ESMAY and AMAY; badly written *assmay*.] To dismay.

c **1420** *Chron. Vilod.* 735 All assmayed þey setton hem downe. *Ibid.* 381 Stode alle assmayhed as stylle as stone.

a-smear (əs'mɪə(r)), *advb. phr.* [A *prep.*[1] + SMEAR.] Smeared.

1861 DICKENS *Gt. Exp.* II. 6 All asmear with filth and fat.

†**a'smell**, *v. Obs. rare*—[1]. [f. A- *pref.* 1 + SMELL *v.*] To smell out, scent.

c **1320** *Seuyn Sages* 891 The bor hem gan ful sone asmelle.

a-smoke (ə'sməʊk), *advb. phr.* or *pred. a.* [f. A *prep.*[1] + SMOKE.] Smoking.

1827 *Blackw. Mag.* XXII. 554 Cottages all a-smoke. **1875** MORRIS *Æneids* VIII. 106 With yet warm blood the altars were a-smoke. **1904** B'NESS VON HUTTEN *Pam* 190 Its chimneys were all asmoke.

Asmonean, var. HASMONEAN.

a-smoulder (ə'sməʊldə(r)), *advb. phr.* [A *prep.*[1] + SMOULDER.] Smouldering.

1880 SWINBURNE *Gard. Cymodoce* 303 So blackens a brand.. asmoulder awhile from the fire.

asmuch, common way of writing *as much*, in 15–16th c. For specific sense see AS C. 1.

†**a'snese**, *v. Obs.* 1 asnǽs-an, 3 a(l)snesien. [OE. *asnǽsan*, f. A- *pref.* 1 (or perhaps 4: see AND- *pref.*) + *snǽsan* to strike with a spear.] To impale, gore, stab.

c **880** *Ælfred's Pol. Laws* §36 (Bosw.) ȝif beforan eáȝum asnǽse [*v.r.* asnáse]. *c* **1230** *Ancr. R.* 200 þene horn þet he asneseð mide alle þeo þet ha areacheð. *Ibid.* 212 þe deoflen schulen.. mid helle sweordes alsnesien ham.

‖**a'snillio.** *Obs.* [a. Sp. *asnillo*, dim. of *asno* ass; cf. ASINEGO.] A little ass.

1625 PURCHAS *Pilgrims* II. 1415 Horses and Asnillios.

a-snort (ə'snɔːt), *advb. phr.* [A *prep.*[1] + SNORT.] Snorting.

1850 MRS. BROWNING *Poems* II. 474 A sculptured porpoise, gills a-snort And vibrant tail.

a-soak (ə'səʊk), *advb. phr.* [A *prep.*[1] + SOAK.] Soaking. Also *fig.*

1609 C. BUTLER *Fem. Mon.* (1634) 161 Asoak in milk-warm fair water. **1636** FEATLY *Clavis Myst.* iv. 52 Laying our hearts asoake in teares. *a* **1746** HOLDSWORTH *On Virgil* (1768) 50 (JOD.) Seed which they lay asoak.

asocial (eɪ'səʊʃəl), *a.* [f. A- 14 + SOCIAL *a.*] Not social; antagonistic to society or social order; (*colloq.*) inconsiderate of or hostile to other people. Cf. ANTISOCIAL *a.*

1883 MAUDSLEY *Body & Will* III. i. 241 New products of an asocial or antisocial kind are formed in the retrograde metamorphosis of the human kind. **1920** W. H. R. RIVERS *Instinct & the Unconscious* xix. 156 Some channel which leads in an asocial or antisocial direction. **1932** *Daily Express* 20 Sept. 9/4 One cannot foresee to what end their asocial behaviour or maladjustments will ultimately lead. **1952** M. MCCARTHY *Groves of Academe* (1953) ii. 17 This ugly, a-social man, at home and suddenly garrulous in their midst.

Hence as *sb.*, an asocial person. *rare.*

1945 KOESTLER *Yogi & Commissar* III. iv. 249 Most asocials have some such sort of jealously-guarded private philosophy. **1961** R. KEE *Refugee World* iv. 41 A proportion of 'a-socials' there—people who *wouldn't* live anywhere else rather than couldn't.

asocie, var. ASSOCIE *v. Obs.* to associate.

†**a'soft, a'soften**, *v. Obs.* [f. A- *pref.* 1 + SOFT *v.*, SOFTEN.] To make soft, soften, mitigate.

c **1430** LYDG. *Min. Poems* (1840) 64 His olde gyltis bothe to a soft and swage. —— *Chron. Troy* III. xxvii, Whose herte might asoften nor aswage Nother prayer nor lamantacion.

asoght, asoȝt, pa. t. of ASEEK *v. Obs.* to seek for.

asoil(e, asoin(e, etc.: see ASS-.

asoke, pa. t. of ASAKE *v. Obs.*

asomatous (ə'səʊmətəs), *a.* [f. L. *asōmat-us*, a. Gr. ἀσώματ-ος (f. ἀ priv. + σῶμα, -ματ- body) + -OUS.] Unembodied, incorporeal.

1731 in BAILEY. **1864** R. BURTON *Dahome* II. 136 A belief so abstract as Monotheism, asomatous and non-local.

asonder, -ri, obs. forms of ASUNDER.

asone, variant of ASSOIN *v. Obs.*

asonken, pa. pple. of ASINK *v. Obs.* to sink.

asosshe, variant of ASWASH *adv. Obs.*

asottie, asotted, var. ASSOT, ASSOTTED.

asound, variant of A-SWOUND = A-SWOON.

asour, obs. form of AZURE.

a-south (ə'saʊθ), *advb. phr.* [see A *prep.*[1]] In the south.

1809 J. BARLOW *Columb.* I. 571 Asouth.. Relenting airs with boreal blasts contend.

asoyle, obs. form of ASSOIL *v.*

asp[1] (ɑːsp, æ-). Forms: 1 æspæ, æspe, æps, 1–6 espe, 4–7 aspe, 6 esp, 6– asp. [Common Teut.: with OE. *æspæ, æspe*, cf. OHG. *aspâ*, mod.G. *espe*, OTeut. **aspôn*, weak fem. With OE. *æps* = *æsp*, cf. ON. *ösp* (= *aspu*), OTeut. **aspâ*, strong fem. See also ASPEN.]

1. A tree of the poplar family (*Populus tremula*), with greyish bark and spreading branches, the leaves of which are specially liable to the tremulous motion that characterizes all the poplars. Sometimes loosely used of other poplars.

c **700** *Epinal Gloss.* 1006 *Tremulus* aespae, *Erfurt* espe ..*Corpus* 2048 aespe. *c* **1000** ÆLFRIC *Gloss.* (Zup.) 312 *Abies*, æps. *c* **1000** *Gloss.* in Earle *Plant-n.* 21 *Tremulos*, æspe. *c* **1385** CHAUCER *L.G.W.* 2645 And quok as dooth the leefe of aspe [*v.r.* espe, aspis, aspes] grene. **1578** LYTE *Dodoens* 749 The Popler is of three sortes.. white.. blacke, and the thirde is called Aspe. **1626** BACON *New Atl.* (1650) 27 An Ivy somewhat whiter then ours, like the leafe of a Silver Aspe. **1794** MARTYN *Rousseau's Bot.* xxix. 457 Trembling Poplar, or Asp, has leaves.. smooth on both sides. **1848** G. RUXTON in *Blackw. Mag.* LXIII. 713 Cherry and quaking asp.. belted the little brook.

b. *attrib.*

a **1000** *Sax. Leechd.* II. 332 Nim æps-rinde. **1548** TURNER *Names of Herbes* 64 Populus is of two kyndes, the fyrste.. whyte Popler or white Esptree. The seconde.. an Asp tree, or a blacke popler. **1616** SURFLET & MARKH. *Countr. Farm* 660 The white Poplar, otherwise called the Aspe tree. **1755** B. STILLINGFL. *Cal. Flora* in *Misc. Tracts* (1762) 261 Dec. 23 Asp flower buds begin to open.

2. The wood of this tree.

1551 TURNER *Herbal* (1568) 66 Flechers make prykke shaftes of byrche because it is heuier than espe is. **1801** STRUTT *Sports & Past.* II. i. 54 He commends sound ash for military arrows, and preferred it to asp.

asp[2] (ɑːsp, æ-). *Zool.* [ad. L. *aspis*, a. Gr. ἀσπίς. The L. form was also formerly in use, and was occas. treated as Eng. with pl. *aspisses*. Cf. OF. *aspe*, and see also ASPIC[1], ASPIDE.]

1. A small, venomous, hooded serpent, found in Egypt and Libya; the *Naja Haje*.

1340 *Ayenb.* 257 An eddre þet is yhote ine latin aspis. **1382** WYCLIF *Rom.* iii. 13 The venym of eddris, *that ben clepid aspis*, vndur her lippis. **1481** CAXTON *Myrr.* II. vi. 78 A beest named Aspis that may not be.. taken but by charmyng. **1526** TINDALE *Rom.* iii. 13 The poyson of Aspes. **1593** NASHE *Christes Teares* (1613) 148 At thy breasts (as at Cleopatras) Aspisses shal be put out to nurse. **1627** MAY *Lucan* IX. 806 Rose the sleep-causing Aspe with swelling head. **1781** COWPER *Truth* 159 Of temper as envenomed as an asp. **1869** RUSKIN *Queen of Air* §68 There is more poison in an ill-kept drain.. than in the deadliest asp of Nile.

2. Also applied to a species of Viper (*Vipera Aspis*) found in various parts of Europe, and used *poet.* of any venomous serpent.

1712 SWIFT *Sid Hamet* Wks. 1755 III. II. 71 Till metamorphosed by his grasp, It grew an all-devouring asp. **1818** BYRON *Ch. Har.* IV. clx, The enormous asp Enforces pang on pang, and stifles gasp on gasp. **1861** HULME tr. *Moquin-Tandon* II. v. i. 248 The Common Viper or Asp is a serpent to be carefully avoided.

3. *Comb.* and *Attrib.*, as in **aspworm** (*obs.*) = asp.

1587 GOLDING *De Mornay* xii. (1617) 191 We know the Aspworme by his stinging of vs. **1876** BIRCH *Rede Lect. Egypt* 39 Invested with the asp diadem of the crown.

asp[3]. See ASS *sb.*[1] 4.

‖**Aspalathus** (ə'spæləθəs). [L., a. Gr. ἀσπάλαθος. Formerly also in Eng. form '*aspalath*.] A genus of African shrubs (N.O. *Leguminosæ*); the fragrant wood of some of its species.

(What plant is referred to in the earlier quotations is not certainly known. LYTE (p. 346) gives *Aspalathum* as a L. name of Galangall, and (p. 685) *Aspalathus* as identified by some with the 'Acatia of Pontus.' Johnson gives as his first definition, 'A plant called the rose of Jerusalem, or our lady's rose.')

1601 HOLLAND *Pliny* I. 376 Aspalathus: a white thornie shrub.. beareth a floure resembling a rose. The root of it is in request for the making of sweet perfumes. **1611** BIBLE *Ecclus.* xxiv. 15 A sweete smell like cinamon, and aspalathus [COVERDALE, balme]. **1727–51** CHAMBERS *Cycl.*, *Aspalath*, *Aspalathum*, the wood of a foreign tree.. otherwise called *lignum Rhodium*, or *rosewood*.

‖**Aspalax** ('æspəlæks). *Zool.* [L., a. Gr. ἀσπάλαξ, more usually σπάλαξ, mole.] A genus of Rodentia, somewhat resembling the common mole.

1860 GOSSE *Romance Nat. Hist.* 76 The aspalax, or mole of eastern Europe.. habitually lives under ground.

aspalt, aspaltoun, obs. ff. ASPHALT, -UM.

asparagine (ə'spærədʒaɪn). *Chem.* [f. ASPARAGUS + -INE chem. suffix.] A nitrogenized crystallizable compound contained in asparagus, and many other vegetables. It is primary malic diamide $C_4H_4O_3(NH_2)_2$.

1813 SIR H. DAVY *Agric. Chem.* iii. (1814) 118 Asparagin. **1873** WILLIAMSON *Chem.* §301 Asparagine behaves as the malic amide. By prolonged contact with hot water it is converted into ammonic malamate.

asparaginous (æspə'rædʒɪnəs), *a.* [f. prec. + -OUS.] Allied to or resembling asparagus.

1832 *Veg. Subst. Food* 275 Asparaginous plants.. always belong to luxurious rather than to economic management.

asparagolite, asparagus-stone: see next 2.

asparagus (ə'spærəgəs). Forms: α. 1, 6 (med.L.) sparagi. β. 6–8 sperage, 7 sperach, sparage, asparage. γ. 6– asparagus. δ. 7 sparagus, 7–8 spargras, 7–9 sparrowgrass. [L., a. Gr. ἀσπάραγος, properly ἀσφάραγος, of doubtful origin. In med.L. often *sparagus, sparagi* (OIt. *sparagi, sparaci*), found in Eng. *c* 1000. Thence also mod.It. *sparagio*, G. *spargen*, MF. *esperage*, and Eng. *sperage*, the common name in 16th and early 17th c., occas., from etymological notions, made *sperach* (after *smallache, smallage*, etc.: see ACHE *sb.*[2]), or *sparage*. About 1600 the influence of herbalists and horticultural writers made *asparagus* familiar, and this in the aphetic form '*sparagus* at length displaced *sperage*, but was itself by popular etymol. corrupted before 1650 to *sparagrass, sparrow-grass*, which remained the polite name during the 18th c. Botanists still wrote *asparagus*, but according to Walker *Pron. Dict.* 1791, '*Sparrow-grass* is so general that *asparagus* has an air of stiffness and pedantry.' During the present century *asparagus* has returned into literary and polite use, leaving *sparrow-grass* to the illiterate; though 'grass' still occurs in cookery books.]

1. A plant (*Asparagus officinalis*, N.O. *Liliaceæ*) cultivated for the sake of its vernal shoots, which form a well-known delicacy of the table. *Bot.* The genus which contains this among many other species.

α. *c* **1000** *Sax. Leechd.* I. 188 Genim þysse wyrte wyrtruman þe man sparagi agrestis.. nemneð. **1555** *Fardle Facions* I. iii. 37 Ther be sene also Sparagi, of no lesse notable bigguenesse.

β. **1548** TURNER *Names of Herbes* (1881) 17 *Asparagus*.. of the poticaries *sparagus*, in Englishe *Sperage*, in Duche *Spargen*, in French *Esperage*. **1572** BOSSEWELL *Armorie* III. 19 Some reporte.. that of Rammes hornes buried, or hidde in the grounde, is broughte forthe an Herbe, called Asparagus, in Englishe, Sperage. **1580** HOLLYBAND *Treas. Fr. Tong.*, *Des asperges*, Sparage. **1601** HOLLAND *Pliny* II. 27 There is a middle sort of these Sperages, not so ciuill and gentle as the Asparagi of the garden. **1606** —— *Sueton.* 77 Quicker.. than Sparages can be sodden. **1615** G. SANDYS *Trav.* 300 Next Nesis stands with Sperage stored. **1669** DIGBY *Closet Open.* (1677) 220 Chop some of the Asparages among it. That hath served for Sparages. **1711** GREENWOOD *Eng. Gram.* 190 *Sperage* which the Vulgar wrest to *Sparagrass* or *Sparrowgrass* from *Asparagus* or *Sparagus*.

γ. **1548** TURNER [see in β]. **1551** —— *Herbal* (1568) 51 Sperage is called in Latin Asparagus. **1597** GERARD *Herbal* II. ccccl vii. 1112 Called.. likewise Asparagus after the Latine name. **1632** MASSINGER *City Mad.* III. i, The gardens Where we traffic for asparagus. **1640** BROME *Sparagus Gard.* II. ii. 136 Have you this Spring eaten any Asparagus yet? **1732** ARBUTHNOT *Rules of Diet* 270 Aromatick and balsamick as Saffron, Asparagus, Nutmeg. **1855** W. WHITE *Walk to Land's End* xi. 232 Around you grow the wild asparagus.. and samphire.

δ. **1611** COTGR., *Asperges pierreus*, Stone Sparage, wild Sparagus. **1618** HOLYDAY *Juvenal* 221 To gather sperage, or, as it is brokenly called from the Latin's, sparagus. **1640** BROME *Sparagus Gard.* II. ii. 137, I will have Sparagus every meale all the yeare long. **1649** BLITHE *Eng. Improver Impr.* (1652) 237 [The Hop plant] comes up with severall sprouts like Sparrowgrass. **1667** PEPYS *Diary* (1879) IV. 307 Brought with me from Fenchurch Street, a hundred of Sparrowgrass. **1668** *Ibid.* 22 Apr., Over to the 'sparagus garden. **1706** PHILLIPS, *Asparagus*, a Plant call'd Sparrow-grass by the Common People. **1710** STEELE *Tatler* No. 150 ¶6 A Dish of Chickens and Sparagrass. **1725** BRADLEY *Fam. Dict.* s.v. *Sparagrass*, Sparagrass may be soon had. **1734** GIBSON *Dispens.* III. iii. 131 Sparrow-grass. **1738** SWIFT *Wks.* 1755 IV. I. 276 Ripe 'sparagrass, Fit for lad or lass. **1785** COWPER *Lett.*, In May we shall have 'sparagus. **1801** SOUTHEY in C. Southey *Life* II. 154 Sparagrass (it ought to be spelt so) and artichokes, good with plain butter. *a* **1845** HOOD *Town & Country* iv, Grass..That makes no hay—called sparrow-grass By folks of vulgar tongue!

2. *Attrib.* and *Comb.*, as ***asparagus-bed***, also *transf.* (sometimes *ellipt.*), an anti-tank obstacle (*slang*); ***asparagus-garden***, ***-tip***, ***-tongs***, etc. **asparagus-bean** *U.S.*, a tropical American bean (*Dolichos sesquipedalis*); **asparagus-beetle**, a small beetle (*Crioceris Asparagi*) that feeds upon the foliage of the asparagus; **asparagus pea**, the Goa bean; **asparagus stone** (*Min.*), a yellowish-green variety of apatite.

1856 COZZENS *Sparrowgr. Papers* vii. 85 The asparagus bean, a sort of long-winded esculent, inclined to be prolific in strings. **1733** ELLIS *Chiltern & Vale Farming* xxxv. 257, I remember..the case of an Asparagus Bed. **1761** FITZGERALD in *Phil. Trans.* LII. 73 Apple-trees, planted in asparagus beds. **1939** *War Illustr.* 16 Dec. 426 Anti-tank 'asparagus', which consists of railway lines set in concrete at an angle of 45 degrees pointing towards the enemy lines and in some cases with high-explosive caps. **1943** HUNT & PRINGLE *Service Slang* 12 *Asparagus bed*, a form of anti-tank obstacle, designed to slow up the A[rmoured] F[ighting] V[ehicle] while it comes under fire. **1815** KIRBY & SP. *Entomol.* (1843) I. 158 The asparagus beetle and its larvæ feed upon the foliage after the heads branch out. **1618** HOLYDAY *Juvenal* 77 Thy patrone's fish, Deck'd round with sperage-buds. **1642** *Declar. Lords & Com.* 19 May 45 Hee should be with them that night at the Sparragus Garden at Supper. **1859** A. VAN BUREN *Sojourn in South* 155 The Asparagus Pea, with a small round pod that grows from a foot to three in length, makes a choice dish at table. **1958** *Times* 1 Feb. 9/6 An oddity among the peas is the so-called 'asparagus pea', which makes a spreading plant and produces flanged, rectangular pods. **1816** CLEAVELAND *Min.* 132 Asparagus stone..in consequence of its so frequently exhibiting an asparagus green color. **1932** H. SIMPSON *Boomerang* x. 264, I remember particularly asparagus-tips rolled up in brown-bread. **1965** J. WAINWRIGHT *Death in Sleeping City* I. 44 The appetising meal of braised cutlets, chipped potatoes and asparagus tips. **1851** *Art Jrnl. Catal. Gt. Exhib.* 142/1 The Asparagus tongs..an elegant appendage to the dinner-table.

aspa'ramic, a'sparamide = ASPARTIC, ASPARAGINE.

†a'spare, *v. Obs. rare.* [f. A- *pref.* 1 + SPARE *v.*, OE. *sparian*; cf. MHG. *ersparn*, mod.G. *ersparen*.] To spare, afford.

1377 LANGL. *P. Pl.* B. xv. 136 He was a nygarde þat no good myȝte aspare [*v.r.* spare, asspare]. **1393** *Ibid.* C. xi. 84 He..helpeth herteliche alle men of þat he may aspare.

†aspare, *a.* or *adv. Obs. rare*[−1]. [f. SPARE, apparently on form-analogy of *wake awake*, *live alive*, or of *ado*, or *aswim*.] To spare, at liberty.

1653 BAXTER *Saint's Rest* IV. vii.§1 Those that have more time aspare from worldly necessaries.

a-sparkle (ə'spɑːk(ə)l), *advb. phr.* [A *prep.*[1] + SPARKLE.] Sparkling.

1840 BROWNING *Sordello* IV. 381 With every point a-sparkle.

aspartame (ə'spɑːteɪm). [f. ASPART(IC *a.* + *-ame*, of uncertain origin.] A derivative of phenylalanine that contains the radical of aspartic acid and is used as a low-calorie artificial sweetener; 3-amino-*N*-(α-methoxycarbonyl phenethyl)succinamic acid, $C_{14}H_{18}N_2O_5$.

1973 *Chemistry* Feb. 5/1 One possibility is aspartylphenylalanine methyl ester, expected to be marketed under the name Aspartame. **1974** *Daily Colonist* (Victoria, B.C.) 28 July 3/5 The sweetener, called aspartame, contains the same number of calories as sugar but is 180 times sweeter. **1974** *Nature* 16 Aug. 529 Aspartame loses its sweetness on prolonged cooking. **1983** *Daily Tel.* 6 Oct. 6/3 Aspartame..is being sold under the trade names Canderel for a tea and coffee sweetener, and as Nutrasweet for the wholesale product available to food manufacturers. **1984** *Which?* Aug. 355/2 Aspartame is said to leave less of an aftertaste than saccharin, but our own taste tests were inconclusive.

aspartic (ə'spɑːtɪk), *a. Chem.* [Formed arbitrarily, with regard mainly to euphony, on *asparagus*.] Of or pertaining to asparagine; esp. in ***aspartic acid***, $C_4H_7NO_4$, produced by the action of alkalis or acids on asparagine. **'aspartate**, a combination of aspartic acid with a base.

1836 BRANDE *Man. Chem.* (ed. 4) 1042 When asparagin is long boiled with hydrated oxide of lead, magnesia, or other bases, it is resolved into ammonia, and into a new acid, called the aspartic acid. **1847** in CRAIG. **1863** WATTS *Chem. Dict.* I. 424 Aspartic acid is monobasic..The aspartates of the alkali-metals are soluble, and taste like broth.

a'spasiolite. *Min.* A variety of IOLITE or FAHLUNITE.

1850 DAUBENY *Atom. The.* vi. 179 The relation of form subsisting between..cordierite and aspasiolite.

a-spatial (ə'speɪʃəl), *a. rare.* [f. A- *pref.* 14 + SPATIAL.] Free from space, spaceless.

1870 D. SIMON tr. Dorner's *Pers. Christ* II. II. 273 Humanity is taken up into this a-spatial sphere.

aspeciall, -cyall, obs. forms of ESPECIAL.

aspect ('æspɛkt), *sb.* Also 4-6 **aspecte**, (6 espect). [ad. L. *aspect-us* (or AFr. *aspect* 15th c. in Littré), n. of action f. *a-*, *ad-spic-ĕre* to look at, f. *ad* to + *spec-ĕre* to look. Accented *a'spect* by Shakspere, Milton, Swift, and occas. by modern poets, but *'aspect* already in Tourneur 1609. The astrological sense was apparently the earliest, and often coloured the others.]

I. The action of looking at.

†1. a. The action of looking at anything; beholding, contemplation; gaze, view. *Obs.*

1398 TREVISA *Barth. De P.R.* III. vi. (1495) 53 The soule hath two manere aspectes . for he beholdyth the ouer thynges..and..the nether thinges. **1594** HOOKER *Eccl. Pol.* III. (1617) 73 That which we haue by plaine aspect and intuitive beholding. **1614** B. RICH *Honest. Age* (1844) 12 You good and gracious women..let mee intreat your fauourable aspect. **1626** BACON *Sylva* §924 The tradition.. that the basilisk killeth by aspect. **1712** STEELE *Spect.* No. 539 ¶1 The downcast Eye, and the Recovery into a sudden full Aspect. **1810** COLERIDGE *Friend* I. xiv. (1867) 62 The plain aspect or intuitive beholding of truth in its eternal and immutable Source [cf. quot. 1594].

b. A look, a glance. Also *fig.*

1590 SHAKS. *Com. Err.* II. ii. 113 Some other Mistresse hath thy sweet aspects. **1644** MILTON *Jus Pop.* 17 Borrowing resplendence like the Moon from the Suns aspect. **1711** STEELE No. 87 ¶8 To receive kind Aspects from those little Thrones. **1858** O. W. HOLMES *Aut. Breakf. T.* xi. 109 Meeting the cold aspect of Duty.

†2. Mental looking, sight; consideration, regard, respect. *Obs.*

1393 GOWER *Conf.* I. 143 In thin aspect ben alle aliche The pouer man and eke the riche. **1517** H. WATSON *Shyppe of Fooles* Argt., Hauynge aspecte vnto the capacyte of my tendre yeres. *c* **1525** SKELTON *Bk. Three Fooles*, O foole, haue aspecte vnto that whiche thou commyttest! **1643** DENHAM *Cooper's Hill* Ep. Ded., Those latter parts..have not yet received your Majesties favourable Aspect. **1673** *Lady's Call.* II. ii. §23. 73 Whatever duty is perform'd to Man with aspect on God, he owns as to himself.

†3. A looking for anything, expectation. *Obs.*

1587 FORMAN *Diary* 18. §3, I was discharged..contrary to the aspecte of all men.

II. Way of looking, as to position or direction.

4. *Astrol.* The relative positions of the heavenly bodies as they appear to an observer on the earth's surface at a given time. (*prop.*, The way in which the planets, from their relative positions, look upon each other, but *pop.* transferred to their joint look upon the earth.)

See quot. 1594. *Conjunction* and *opposition*, the former especially, were often not reckoned *aspects*.

c **1386** CHAUCER *Knts. T.* 229 Som wikke aspect or disposicion Of Saturne. *c* **1391** —— *Astrol.* I. iv. 19 Conforted with frendly aspectys of planetes. **1398** TREVISA *Barth. De P.R.* VIII. ix. (1495) 309 Coniunccion and apposicion ben..somtyme..callyd aspectes by misusynge and chaungynge of that name aspect. **1552** LYNDESAY *Papyngo* 133 The bad aspect of Saturne wes appesit. **1594** BLUNDEVIL *Exerc.* VII. x. 662 The Characters of which aspects are these heere following: ☌ ☍ △ □ ✶; Whereof the first signifieth a Conjunction, the second an opposition, the third a trine aspect, the fourth a quadrant aspect, and the fift a sextile aspect. **1597** BACON *Coulers Good & Evill* vii, The Sunne..is good by aspect, but euill by coniunction. **1606** SHAKS. *Tr. & Cr.* I. iii. 92 Corrects the ill Aspects of Planets euill. **1609** TOURNEUR *Fun. Poeme* 343 Partes, bodies, figures, aspects, distances. **1649** JER. TAYLOR *Gt. Exemp.* III. xiv. 24 Sisera fought when their was an evill aspect or malignant influence of heaven upon him. **1667** MILTON *P.L.* x. 658 Thir planetarie motions and aspects In Sextile, Square, and Trine, and Opposite. **1681** WHARTON *Planet. Aspects* Wks. (1683) 90 Kepler defines an aspect..an Angle made in the Earth by the Luminous Beams of two Planets, of strength to stir up the vertue of all sublunary things. **1713** SWIFT *On Partridge* Wks. 1755 III. II. 81 He Mars could join To Venus in aspect malign. **1819** J. WILSON *Dict. Astrol.* 100 Many authors deny the conjunction to be an aspect, because the stars do not behold each other, but their influence is on the Earth, which they behold with a conjunct aspect.

5. a. A looking in a given direction; the facing or fronting of anything, as a house, a window, or a steep or sloping surface, in any direction; exposure.

1667 MILTON *P.L.* IV. 541 The setting Sun..with right aspect Against the eastern Gate of Paradise. *a* **1745** SWIFT (J.) A strong wall, faced to the south aspect with brick. **1849** MRS. SOMERVILLE *Connex. Phys. Sc.* xxvi. 291 Aspect..has also a great influence [on line of perpetual snow]. **1864** KERR *Gentl. House* 88 The aspect of a room is the relation of its windows to sunshine and weather.

b. ***aspect ratio***, (*a*) *Aeronaut.*, the ratio of the span to the mean chord of an aerofoil; also, the ratio of the square of the span to the total area of the aerofoil; (*b*) of a television or cinematographic picture: the ratio of the width to the height.

1907 F. W. LANCHESTER *Aerodynamics* vi. 208 The normal pressure is a *continuous function* of the aspect ratio of the plane. **1910** R. W. A. BREWER *Art of Aviation* xvii. 232 Aspect ratio is the ratio of the length of span to that of chord. **1930** *Flight* 21 Feb. 234/1 As regards the aero-dynamic efficiency of the Do.X, the aspect ratio (if one may be so old-fashioned as to use this expression) is low. **1936** *Electronics* June 28/1 The formula used is $f = \frac{1}{2}$(no. lines) × aspect ratio × (no. pictures per second), where the aspect (width to height) ratio is 4/3. **1957** AMOS & BIRKINSHAW *Television Engin.* I. i. 29 For a given number of lines and aspect ratio the bandwidth occupied by the components of the video signal is directly proportional to the picture frequency.

6. The side or surface which fronts or is turned towards any given direction.

1849 JOHNSTON in *Proc. Berw. Nat. Club* II. vii. 372 Legs ..armed with short bristles..on the inner aspect. **1854** SCOFFERN in *Orr's Circ. Sc.* Chem. 218 The lower aspect of the cover..becomes vitreously electrified. **1881** G. BUSK in *Jrnl. Microsc. Sc.* Jan. 4 On the dorsal aspect the zoœcia present a still greater peculiarity.

7. The direction in which a thing has respect or practical bearing; bearing *upon*, reference *to*.

1509 HAWES *Past. Pleas.* x. iii, Gyvyng them place after the aspect. **1657** CROMWELL *Sp.* 20 Apr., Divers things.. which I hope have a public aspect. **1660** WATERHOUSE *Arms & Arm.* 4 Things that have no direct aspect on peace. **1710** PRIDEAUX *Orig. Tithes* ii. 35 It had a general aspect to all Mankind. **1836** J. GILBERT *Chr. Atonem.* vi. (1852) 167 The aspect of atonement is obviously towards creatures; working effects on them, not on God.

†8. The point from which one looks; a point of sight or of view. *Obs. rare.*

1660 JER. TAYLOR *Worthy Commun.* i. §15. 91 The beholders..as they stand in several aspects and distances, some see red and others..nothing but green.

9. a. One of the ways in which things may be looked at or contemplated, or in which they present themselves to the mind; a phase.

1824 DIBDIN *Libr. Comp.* 247 Their rarity and intrinsic worth render them acceptable under any aspect. **1870** BOWEN *Logic* viii. 188 Merely two aspects of one and the same thought.

b. *Gram.* In Russian and other Slavonic languages, a verbal category of which the function is to express action or being in respect of its inception, duration, or completion, etc.; by extension applied to such forms in other languages.

The earlier term in Slavonic grammars was 'branch'.

1853 C. P. REIFF *Eng.-Russ. Gram.* I. 86 The aspects have not all the same number of tenses; the imperfect aspect is used in all the three tenses; the perfect is employed in the preterit and future, while the iterative is met with only in the preterit. **1884** J. NESTOR-SCHNURMANN *Russ. Man.* 97 The variations in form of the same action are expressed by what is called in Russian branches or aspects..of a verb... There are four branches, viz.: the Indefinite, the Perfect, the Semelfactive.., and the Iterative... A Fifth Aspect might be added, viz.: the Inchoative. **1921** E. SAPIR *Lang.* v. 114 Aspect is expressed in English by all kinds of idiomatic turns. **1924** JESPERSEN *Philos. Gram* xx. 286 It is generally assumed that our Aryan languages had at first no real forms in their verbs for tense-distinctions, but denoted various aspects, perfective, imperfective, punctual, durative, inceptive, or others.

III. Appearance.

10. The look which one wears; expression of countenance; countenance, face.

c **1590** MARLOWE *1st Pt. Tamburl.* I. ii, Thy martial face and stout aspéct. **1596** SHAKS. *Merch. V.* I. i. 54 Of such vineger aspect, That they'll not show their teeth in way of smile. **1667** MILTON *P.L.* VIII. 336 But soon his cleer aspect Returned. **1794** S. WILLIAMS *Hist. Vermont* 152 Much time was spent to give his countenance the aspect he aimed at. **1817** BYRON *Manfred* III. iv. 76 Ah! he unveils his aspect: on his brow The thunder-scars are graven. *a* **1850** ROSSETTI *Dante & Circ.* I. (1874) 231 And for that thine aspèct gives sign thereof.

11. The appearance presented by an object to the eye; look.

1594 GREENE *Look. Glasse* (1861) 118 And thou bright Venus for thy clear aspéct. **1690-1** LADY R. RUSSELL *Lett.* 119 II. 84 Spots..with such an aspect, that the doctor thought it the small-pox. **1738** C. WESLEY *Psalms* (1765) III. No. 104 The Moon's inconstant aspect. **1781** J. MOORE *View Soc. It.* (1790) I. i. 5 The venerable aspect of the Churches. **1876** GREEN *Short Hist.* i. §2. 10 The physical aspect of the country.

12. The appearance presented by circumstances, etc., to the mind.

a **1704** LOCKE (J.) Shewing..their various aspects and probabilities. **1705-6** PENN in *Pa. Hist. Soc. Mem.* X. 102 Matters seem to look of a better aspect. **1883** J. GILMOUR *Among Mongols* xviii. 210 The superficial aspects of Buddhism.

†13. *concr.* A thing seen, a sight; an appearance.

c **1600** J. DAVIES in Farr *S.P.* (1845) I. 250 To view perspicuously this sad aspect. **1722** DE FOE *Plague* (1754) 30 That he saw such Aspects..I never believ'd.

14. *Ecology.* The characteristic seasonal appearance or constitution of a plant community.

1905 F. E. CLEMENTS *Research Meth. Ecology* iv. 296 The seasonal changes of a formation, which are called aspects, are indicated by changes in composition or structure, which ordinarily correspond to the three seasons, spring, summer, and autumn. **1916** —— *Plant Succession* vii. 132 In boreal and alpine regions the number of aspects is often but two, vernal and æstival, and the societies correspond. **1926** TANSLEY & CHIPP *Stud. Vegetation* ii. 17 The word 'aspect' is used as a technical term for the seasonal phases of vegetation. Thus we speak of the *prevernal*, *vernal*, *æstival*, *autumnal* and *hiemal* aspects of British vegetation. Societies dominated by species vegetating at particular seasons are often called *aspect societies*. **1952** P. W. RICHARDS *Tropical Rain Forest* viii. 191 The Tropical Rain forest..has no marked seasonal 'aspects' and no 'resting' period.

15. In *Signalling*: an indication given by means of a light (see quot. 1936).

1926 D. R. LAMB *Modern Railway Operation* xiii. 152 The colour light signal is now generally adopted in connection with power installations. The type which has so far found favour in Great Britain is that giving three aspects, green, orange and red, signifying, respectively, 'all right', 'caution' and 'danger'. **1936** *Gloss. Terms Railway Signalling (B.S.I.)* 47 *Signal aspects*, a term used to describe light indications of signals as opposed to indications given by semaphore arms.

† **a'spect**, *v. Obs.* [ad. L. *aspect-āre* freq. of *aspic-ĕre*: see prec. Cf. *respect*, *suspect*.]

1. To look for, expect. [Perhaps from OF. *especter* = *expecter*; cf. ASPECT *sb.* 3.]

1548 HALL *Chron.* 409 Frendes, which daily did aspect and tarie for his commyng. **1584** HUDSON *Du Bartas' Judith* IV. 316 Then may we well aspect Great good of her.

2. To look at, behold, face; to survey, watch.

1610 GWILLIM *Heraldry* VI. v. (1660) 397 As if they were worn by two persons aspecting, or beholding each other. **1625** DARCIE *Hist. Q. Eliz.* Ep. Ded., Those which aspect the beames of the Sunne..thinke a long time after they behold still a Sunne before their eyes. **1682** G. D. *Season. Caution fr. N. to S.* 4 When I look back for to aspect These Days. *a* **1698** TEMPLE *Heroic Virt.*, *Lucan* (R.) Those people whom The northern pole aspects.

3. Of a planet: To look upon, or be situated towards, another, in one of the 'Aspects.'

1586 LUPTON *Thous. Notable Things* (1675) 32 Jupiter.. being evil aspected of an infortunate Planet. **1652** GAULE *Magastrom.* 264 Venus in termes, and in the house of Saturne..Mars aspecting. **1671** SALMON *Syn. Med.* II. xv. 183 If the Moon upon a Critical day be well aspected of good Planets, it goes well with the Sick.

4. To look on with favour, to countenance. *rare.*

1663 *Flagellum, O. Cromwell* (1672) 144 What opinion Cromwel best aspected.

5. *intr.* To look; to have an aspect or bearing.

1635 PERSON *Varieties* II. 69 The countrey over which it [the comet] blazeth, or to which it aspecteth. **1651** N. BACON *Cont. Hist. Disc.* iii. 32 The influence of Society.. principally aspected upon some pleas belonging to the Crown.

aspectable, *a.* now *rare.* Also 7 -ible. [ad. L. *aspectābil-is*, f. *aspectāre*: see ASPECT *sb.* and -ABLE. Accented ('æspɛktəb(ə)l) by Mr. and Mrs. Browning; the analogical pronunciation is *a'spectable*.]

1. Capable of being seen, visible.

1614 RALEIGH *Hist. World* I. I. iv, God was the sole cause of this aspectable and perceivable universal. **1612** T. TAYLOR *Comm. Titus* i. 8 (1619) 162 In this aspectible world. **1699** EVELYN *Acetaria* (1729) 117 The most useful and admirable of all the aspectable Works of God. **1850** MRS. BROWNING *Soul's Trav.* 130 The ocean-grandeur, which Is aspectable from the place.

2. Fit to be beheld, fair to look upon.

1731 BAILEY, *Aspectable*, worthy to be look'd upon. **1868** BROWNING *Ring & Bk.* I. II. 203 Via Vittoria, the aspectable street Where he lived mainly.

† **a'spectabund**, *a. Obs. rare*[−1]. [f. L. *aspectā-re* (see ASPECT *v.*), after L. *lacrimābundus*, *osculābundus*, etc.] Expressive in face.

1708 J. DOWNES *Rosc. Angl.* 51 On the Stage, he's very Aspectabund, wearing a Farce in his Face.

aspectant (ə'spɛktənt), *a. Her.* [ad. L. *aspectānt-em*, pr. pple. of *aspectāre*: see -ANT[1].] Looking at, facing (each other); cf. ASPECT *v.* 2.

'aspected, *ppl. a.* [f. ASPECT *v.* or *sb.* + -ED.]

† **1.** *pple.* (*a'spected*). Looked at. *Obs.*

1627 FELTHAM *Resolves* II. lvi. (1677) 275 Noysom vapors centred on the eye..are taken by the eye of the aspected, and through it strike the very heart.

† **2.** *pple.* or *adj.* Looked at by a planet; (in *comb.*) subject to a particular aspect of the planets. *Obs.*

1603 DRAYTON *Heroic. Ep.* v. 17 That blessed Night, that mild-aspected Howre. **1635** SWAN *Spec. Mund.* iv. §3 (1643) 75 When they [planetes] are aptly and conveniently placed and aspected. **1686** GOAD *Celest. Bod.* II. i. 150 The ☽ aspected with the Sun.

3. *adj.* Having an aspect. (Usually in *comb.*)

1599 B. JONSON *Cynthia's Rev.* II. i, A labyrinthean face, now angularly, now circularly, every way aspected. **1727** BRADLEY *Fam. Dict.* s.v. *Exposition*, A South-aspected Wall. **1737** MILLER *Gard. Dict.* s.v. *Conyza*, An east-aspected border.

† **a'spectful**, *a. Obs.* [f. ASPECT *sb.* + -FUL.] Having favourable aspect, benignant.

1611 W. FENTON *Panegyr. Verses* in *Coryat's Crudeties*, Faire starre..which on us do'st shine With beauteous lustre and aspectfull cheare.

† **a'spection**. *Obs.* [ad. L. *aspectiōn-em*, n. of action f. *aspic-ĕre*: see ASPECT *sb.* (*Aspection* also occurred in OF.)] The action of looking at, beholding, viewing, watching.

1646 SIR T. BROWNE *Pseud. Ep.* 120 That this destruction should be the effect of the first beholder, or depend upon priority of aspection. **1652** GAULE *Magastrom.* 66 To alter the aspect, or the aspection.

† **a'spector**. *Obs. rare*[−1]. [a. L. *aspector*, n. of agent f. *aspicĕre*: see ASPECT *sb.*] Beholder.

a **1618** J. DAVIES *Extasie* (D.) Lyons, Dragons, Panthers, and the like That in th' aspectors harts doe terror strike.

a'spectual, *a.* [f. L. *aspectu-s* ASPECT *sb.* + -AL[1]: cf. *eventual.*] † **1.** Pertaining to aspects. *Obs. rare*[−1].

1652 in Ashmole *Theat. Chem.* vi. 100 The vertue of the Eight sphere..With her Signes and Figures and parts aspectuall.

2. *Gram.* Of or pertaining to an aspect or aspects (see ASPECT *sb.* 9 b).

1950 in WEBSTER Addenda. **1959** R. QUIRK in *Teaching of English* i. 33 We can even make suggestions about a kind of aspectual meaning with this verb by reason of the analogy of our frequentative series of English verbs like *sparkle*, *gabble*, *wriggle*. **1963** J. LYONS *Structural Semantics* vi. 117 The aspectual schemes set out..for the 'action'—'event'—'state' verbs.

aspen ('ɑːspən, æ-), *a.* and *sb.* Forms: ? 1 **æspen**, 4- **aspen**, 6-8 **aspine**, 7-9 **aspin**. [f. ASP[1] + -EN; cf. *ashen*. In *aspen leaf* we might suppose a survival of the OE. gen. *æspan*: see the first quot.; cf. MHG. *espenlaub*; the later subst. use evidently arose from taking *aspen* in such constructions as a sb. used attributively; later instances of the adj. may be really attrib. uses of the factitious sb.]

A. *adj.*

1. Of or belonging to the asp: see ASP[1].

[Cf. *c* **1000** *Sax. Leechd.* II. 116 Genim æspan rind.] *c* **1386** CHAUCER *Sompn. Prol.* 3 Lyk an aspen leef he quok for ire. **1588** SHAKS. *Tit. A.* II. iv. 45 Oh had the monster seene those Lilly hands, Tremble like Aspen leaues vpon a Lute. **1632** G. FLETCHER *Christ's Tri.* 66 Perch't on an aspin sprig. **1829** SOUTHEY *All for Love* vi. Wks. VII. 188 Like an aspen leaf he trembled.

2. *fig.* Tremulous, quivering; quaking, timorous.

a **1420** OCCLEVE *A de B* xvii, With aspen herte I praye hem abyde. **1596** CHAPMAN *Iliad* VIII. 405 Possess'd with aspen fear. *c* **1630** DRUMM. OF HAWTH. *Wks.* (1711) 7/1 And, as their aspin stalks those fingers bind [? band]..I wish'd to be a hyacinth in her hand. **1757** H. WALPOLE *Lett. H. Mann* 296 III. 191 Has the aspen Duke of Newcastle lived thus? **1820** KEATS *Hyperion* I. 94 His beard Shook horrid with such aspen malady.

3. *esp.* in reference to a woman's tongue.

1532 MORE *Confut. Barnes* VIII. Wks. 769/1 For if they [women] myghte be suffred to begin ones in the congregacion to fal in disputing, those aspen leaues of theirs would neuer leaue waggyng. **1597** T. HOWELL *Poems* (1879) 150 In womens mindes: are diuers winds, which stur their Aspin tunge, to prate and chat.

B. *sb.* = ASP[1].

1596 SPENSER *F.Q.* I. i. 8 The aspine good for staves. **1703** *Art's Improv.* I. 33 The whitest Wood..is fitest for this purpose; as Aspen, Abel, Sycamore. *a* **1717** PARNELL *Poet. Wks.* (1833) 51 Thy aspins quiver in a breathing breeze. **1870** MORRIS *Earthly Par.* I. II. 454 Above our heads rustle the aspens grey.

b. in similative relations; as ***aspen-like***, ***-weak***.

1863 GEO. ELIOT *Romola* lxii, A momentary aspen-like touch. **1879** J. TODHUNTER *Alcestis* 116 And leaves me weak, O, aspen weak.

† **a'spend**, *v. Obs. rare.* Forms: 1 **aspendan**, 3 **aspene-n**. [OE. *aspendan*, f. A- *pref.* 1 + *spendan* to SPEND.] To spend, expend.

c **885** K. ÆLFRED *Oros.* I. i. §22 Hys ʒestréon béoð þus eall aspended. *c* **1175** *Lamb. Hom.* 123 þet wit and þene wisdom ..aspenen we hit on godes willan.

† **'asper, 'aspre**, *a. Obs.* [a. OF. *aspre* (mod. *âpre*):—L. *asper* rough, harsh.]

1. Rough, rugged.

1491 CAXTON *Vitas Patr.* (W. de W.) I. xxxiii. 28 a/1 The wayes were soo aspre..that..they that shoed with gode and stronge shoes were cutte and broken. **1538** STARKEY *England* 134 The passage..through rough and asper montaynys. **1681** tr. *Willis' Rem. Med. Wks.*, Asper artery, the wind-pipe.

2. Harsh to the senses, in sound or taste.

1626 BACON *Sylva* §173 All Base Notes, or very Treble Notes, give an Asper sound. **1639** T. DE GREY *Compl. Horseman* 174 The medicines..when once they begin to grow stale, become sharp and asper.

3. Harsh to the feelings; bitter, cruel, severe.

c **1374** CHAUCER *Troylus* IV. 798 And in hire aspre pleynte, thus she seyde. **1483** CAXTON *Gold. Leg.* 122/2 Thise aspre tormentes and cruell doubte. **1578** *Oliver of Castille* vi. (T.) What dure and aspre strokes I have seen them give.

4. Of persons: Harsh, severe, stern.

c **1374** CHAUCER *Boeth.* II. i. 32 þou..makest fortune wroþe and aspere by þin inpacience. **1565** CALFHILL *Answ. Treat. Cross* (1846) 51, I am more aspre in my writing than ..modesty requireth. **1630** WESTCOTE *Devon.* 44 His melancholie..asper nature, by which he centureth other men.

5. Hardy, warlike; mettled, fierce, savage.

c **1374** CHAUCER *Anel. & Arc.* 23 The aspre folke of Cithe. **1475** CAXTON *Jason* 6 b, He fought none but..the most aspre. **1503** *Shepherd's Kal.* (1656) xlii, Naturally a man is ..avaricious as a dog, and aspre as the Hart.

‖ **asper** ('æspə(r)), *sb.*[1] *Gr. Gram.* [L. *asper* (sc. *spiritus*): see prec.] The rough breathing; the sign (ʽ) placed above an initial vowel, or over ρ, equivalent in power to a Roman *h*; thus ὧς = *hōs*, ῥάβδος = *rhabdos*.

asper ('æspə(r)), *sb.*[2] [a. Fr. *aspre*, or ad. It. *aspero*, ad. Byzantine Gr. ἄσπρον lit. 'white-money,' f. ἄσπρος, -ον white (said to be ad. L. *asper* rough: see Littré).] A small silver Turkish coin, of which 120 are reckoned equal to the piastre; now only a 'money of account.'

1589 T. SANDERS in Arb. *Garner* II. 20 Five Aspers.. which are but two-pence English. **1622** FLETCHER *Sp. Curate* III. iii, One..That would run on men's errands for an asper. **1781** GIBBON *Decl. & F.* III. lxviii. 733 His poverty was alleviated by a pension of 50,000 aspers. **1819** SCOTT *Ivanhoe* XV. II. 269, 'I relieve not with one asper those who beg for alms upon the highway.'

asperate ('æspərət), *ppl. a.* [ad. L. *asperātus*, pa. pple. of *asperāre* to roughen, f. *asper* rough.] Roughened, rough.

1623 in COCKERAM. **1848** DANA *Zooph.* 235 Lamellae alternate, asperate, truncate.

¶ See also ASPIRATE.

asperate ('æspəreɪt), *v.* [f. prec.] To make rough or uneven in surface, rugged or harsh in sound, manner, etc.

1656 in BLOUNT *Glossogr.* **1676** *Phil. Trans.* XI. 644 How to..sweeten or asperate a style according as the nature of the subject requireth. *a* **1691** BOYLE *Wks.* I. 683 (R.) The level surface of water being by agitation asperated with.. bubbles. **1858** POLSON *Law & Lawyers* 137 No opposition [could] asperate his voice.

'asperated, *ppl. a.* [f. prec. + -ED.] Roughened; made harsh.

1676 BOYLE in *Phil. Trans.* XI. 806 This Liquor..was far enough from being smooth, being variously asperated by many flaky particles. **1835** L. HUNT *Lond. Jrnl.* No. 73. 274 A very different F from ours—a sharper and more asperated consonant [? confused with *aspirated*].

asperation (æspə'reɪʃən). *rare*[−0]. [n. of action f. ASPERATE *v.*: see -ATION.] A making rough.

1721 in BAILEY.

aspere-hawk: see SPARROW-HAWK.

asperge (ə'spɜːdʒ), *v.* [(a. F. *asperge-r*) ad. L. *asperg-ĕre*, f. *a-* = *ad-* to, at + *spargĕre* to sprinkle.]

1. To sprinkle, besprinkle.

1547 BOORDE *Brev. Health* xlii. 21 b, A cockrel or a pullet ..rosted, and with butter and veneger asperged. **1637** GILLESPIE *Eng. Pop. Cer.* III. i. 5 He who entering into a Church doth not asperge himselfe. **1875** H. KINGSLEY *No. Seventeen* II. xvii. 205 Being asperged with holy water by a priest.

† **2.** = ASPERSE. (Bailey 1721.) *Obs.*

a'sperge, *sb.* [f. prec., or next.] **a.** A sprinkling of holy water (*obs.*). **b.** An aspergillum.

1579 TOMSON *Calvin's Serm. Tim.* 428/1 What are all their asperges of holie water that the Papistes vse? **1848** MRS. JAMESON *Sacr. & Leg. Art* (1850) 226 The pot of holy water, the asperge in her hand.

asperges (ə'spɜːdʒiːz). [a. L. *aspergēs*, 2nd pers. sing. fut. ind. of *aspergĕre* (see ASPERGE *v.*), from the words *Asperges me, Domine, hyssopo et mundabor*, with which the priest begins mass. Cf. F. *aspergès*.] = prec.

1553–87 FOXE *A. & M.* I. 658/2 With a little asperges of the Popes holy water. **1674** *Du Moulin's Papal Tyr.* 36 A petty Clark carrying holy water with an Asperges. **1884** ADDIS & ARNOLD *Cath. Dict.*, *Asperges*, a name given to the sprinkling of the altar, clergy, and people with holy water at the beginning of High Mass by the celebrant.

aspergill ('æspədʒɪl). Anglicized form of ASPERGILLUM.

1864 WEBSTER, *Aspergill.* **1899** *Blackw. Mag.* Aug. 157/2 It is the alliance of the sword and the aspergill. **1922** JOYCE *Ulysses* 333 Eyes on a dish, wax candles, aspergills, unicorns.

aspergillic (æspə'dʒɪlɪk), *a.* [f. ASPERGILL(US + -IC.] ***aspergillic acid***, an acid derived from *Aspergillus flavus* and used as an antibiotic.

1943 E. C. WHITE & J. G. HILL in *Jrnl. Bacteriol.* XLV. 433 The present paper presents details of the isolation of an active crystalline substance from liquid cultures of our strain of *Aspergillus flavus*... We propose to call our substance 'aspergillic acid'. **1949** FLOREY et al. *Antibiotics* I. vii. 315 Aspergillic acid ($C_{12}H_{20}O_2N_2$)..crystallizes in pale yellow rods. *Ibid.* 318 Sanders..found that aspergillic acid ..inhibited the growth of nearly all of a large number of fungi pathogenic to man.

aspergilliform (æspə'dʒɪlɪfɔːm), *a.* [f. ASPERGILLUM + -(I)FORM.] Shaped like an aspergillum, as are the stigmas of some grasses.

1847 in CRAIG.

aspergillin (æspə'dʒɪlɪn). *Biol.* [ad. F. *aspergilline* (G. Linossier 1891, in *Comptes Rendus* CXII. 489), f. ASPERGILL(US + -IN[1].]

1. A black pigment found in the spores of various species of *Aspergillus*.

1891 *Jrnl. Chem. Soc.* LX. 751 The spores of *Aspergillus niger*, when treated with very dilute ammonia, yield a dark-coloured solution from which a slight excess of hydrochloric acid throws down *aspergillin* as a black, bulky, flocculent precipitate. **1949** FLOREY et al. *Antibiotics* I. vii. 348 Since the name 'aspergillin' was originally proposed by Linossier (1891) for the black water-insoluble pigment of the spores of *A[spergillus] niger*, it would appear desirable to avoid applying it to other substances.

2. A name given to various antibiotic substances obtained from different species of *Aspergillus*.

1943 *Jrnl. Pharmacol.* LXXVIII. 164 In an abstract of this paper..our antibacterial substance is referred to as *aspergillin*. Due to the possible confusion with White's aspergillic acid..we thought it advisable to change the name of our antibacterial substance to *flavicin*. **1944** N. F. STANLEY in *Austral. Jrnl. Sci.* VI. 151/2 (*title*) Aspergillin, a Stable Antibacterial Substance of High Potency Produced by a Species of Aspergillus... Aspergillin is more soluble in organic solvents than in water.

aspergillosis (æspədʒɪˈləʊsɪs). *Path.* [mod.L., ad. F. *aspergillose* (A. Lucet 1896, in *Bull. Soc. Cent. Méd. Vét.* XIV. 593), f. ASPERGILL(US + -OSIS.] Infection with the fungus *Aspergillus*, most often found in the respiratory organs of birds and mammals including man.

[**1897** A. LUCET in *Vet. Jrnl.* XLV. 227 Some of which [*sc.* subjects] even (for instance, the birds), in a good many cases contract *spontaneous Aspergillose*.] **1898** *Med. Chron.* IX. 390 The basis of the following investigation was a case of aspergillosis observed by the author in March, 1896. **1902** *Encycl. Brit.* XXXI. 534/2 Aspergillosis, or pigeon-breeders' disease, is the result of the infection with the Aspergillus fumigatus. **1955** GAIGER & DAVIES *Vet. Path. & Bacteriol.* xxi. 414 *Aspergillosis*,..popularly known as brooder pneumonia. **1965** *Economist* 20 Feb. 780/2 He [*sc.* a penguin]..was found to have contracted the disease known as aspergillosis. Aspergillosis is a fungus which spreads through the lungs and is not unknown in humans.

‖**aspergillum** (æspəˈdʒɪləm). [f. L. *aspergĕre* + *-illum* dim. suffix: cf. *vexillum*, f. *vehĕre*.] *R.C. Ch.* A kind of brush used to sprinkle holy water: see ASPERGES.

1649 G. DANIEL *Trinarch., Rich. II*, xcix, Fitt for the Aspergillum of this Preist. **1868** *Perthsh. Jrnl.* 18 June, After the foundation-stone had been sprinkled with water from the aspergillum.

‖**Asperˈgillus.** *Biol.* A genus of microscopic fungi resembling the holy-water sprinkler in appearance, growing on decayed organic matter.

1847 *Nat. Encycl.* III. 988 *Aspergillus glaucus* is the blue mould which forms on cheese, bread, etc. **1861** H. MACMILLAN *Footn. Page Nat.* 235 There is the white or blue mould, forming the genus Aspergillus, from the resemblance of its fructification to the brush used for sprinkling holy water. **1883** TYNDALL in *Pall Mall G.* 30 Oct. 2/1 Supposing the aspergillus to be a human parasite.

asperging (əˈspɜːdʒɪŋ), *vbl. sb.* [f. ASPERGE *v.* + -ING[1].] The action of sprinkling (with holy water). Also *attrib.*

1865 TYLOR *Early Hist. Mankind* ix. 258 The priest stands with an asperging-brush in his hand, with which he sprinkles them with holy water.

‖**aspergoire.** *Obs. rare*$^{-1}$. [OF. *aspergoir*, *-geoir* (Godefroy); the mod.F. word is *aspersoir*.] An aspergillum.

1772 T. WARTON *Sir T. Pope* 129 (T.) An holy-water stop and aspergoire of silver parcel-gilt.

asperifoliate, -ous (ˌæspərɪˈfəʊlɪət, -lɪəs), *a. Bot.* [f. mod.L. *asperifoli-us* (f. *asper* rough + *foli-um* leaf) + -ATE, -OUS.] Having rough leaves; formerly applied specifically to the *Boragineæ*.

1686 *Phil. Trans.* XVI. 286 Asperifolious Herbs, whose Flowers are..reflected at the end like a Scorpions tail. **1753** CHAMBERS *Cycl. Supp.*, *Asperifolious* or *Asperifoliate* Plants, according to Mr. Ray, make a distinct genus.

asperity (əˈspɛrɪtɪ). Forms: 3-5 **asprete**, 6 **asperite, -tie**, 6- **-ty**. [a. OF. *asprete* (mod. *âpreté*):—L. *asperitātem*, f. *asper* rough: see -TY. Subseq. assimilated to the L. word.]

1. Unevenness of surface, roughness, ruggedness; *concr.* in *pl.* sharp, rough, or rugged excrescences.

1491 CAXTON *Vitas Patr.* (W. de W.) I. xxxvii. 50 a/1, Fewe people wente for to see him, for the grete asprete or sharp-nesse of the place. **1578** LYTE *Dodoens* 246 Iuyce of Mynte..taketh away the asperitie, and roughnesse of the tongue. **1662** H. MORE *Antid. Ath.* II. xii. (1712) 84 To view the Asperities of the Moon through a Dioptrick-glass. **1743** tr. *Heister's Surg.* 396 If any splinters or Asperities of Bones present themselves. **1830** LINDLEY *Nat. Syst. Bot.* 25 Almost all Delimaceæ have the leaves covered with asperities.

2. Roughness of savour, tartness, acridity, acrimony. *arch.*

1620 VENNER *Via Recta* v. 87 Very good for the asperity and siccity of the stomacke. **1667** *Phil. Trans.* II. 512 Esteeming the Mass of blood by reason of its asperity..unfit for nutrition. **1747** BERKELEY *Siris* §86 (T.) The asperity of tartarous salts.

3. Harshness of sound, grating quality. *arch.*

1664 H. MORE *Myst. Iniq.* 239 The shrilness and asperity of the noise they make. **1750** JOHNSON *Rambl.* No. 88 ¶12 Our language, of which the chief defect is ruggedness and asperity. **1774** J. BRYANT *Mythol.* I. 167 A place in Egypt, which he could not specify on account of its asperity.

4. Of literary style: Ruggedness, lack of polish, inelegance. *arch.*

1779 JOHNSON *Cowley* Wks. II. 66 Avoids with very little care either meanness or asperity. —— *Philips* ibid. II. 293 Those asperities that are venerable in the Paradise Lost are contemptible in the Blenheim.

5. *fig.* Harshness to the feelings, rigour, severity; *hence*, hardship, difficulty. (The earliest sense; *arch.* exc. in **b.** Bitter coldness, rigour, bleakness.)

c **1230** *Ancr. R.* 354 Vilte and asprete..scheome and pine ..beoð þe two leddre stalen þet beoð upriht to þe heouene. *a* **1535** MORE *Wks.* 1218 (R.) To..minysh the vygour and asperite of the paynes. **1659** HARDY *Serm. 1 John* xlix. (1865) 318/1 This oil [of gladness]..mitigateth the asperity of affliction. **1750** JOHNSON *Rambl.* No. 80 ¶4 The nakedness and asperity of the wintry world. **1866** *Daily Tel.* 16 Jan. 7/5 The great asperity of the climate in winter.

6. Harshness or sharpness of temper, esp. when displayed in tone or manner; crabbedness, bitterness, acrimony; in *pl.* harsh, embittered feelings.

1664 H. MORE *Myst. Iniq.* Apol. 554 Animosities, and asperities of mind about toys and trifles. **1757** JOHNSON *Rambl.* No. 176 ¶8 Quickness of resentment and asperity of reply. **1838** DICKENS *Nich. Nick.* iii. (C.D. ed.) 13 Demanded with much asperity what she meant.

†**ˈasperly,** *adv. Obs.* [f. ASPER *a.* + -LY[2].] Roughly, harshly; fiercely, bitterly.

c **1314** *Guy Warw.* 84 Ther he defended him asperliche. *c* **1325** *E.E. Allit. P.* C. 373 Heter hayreȝ..þat asperly bited. **1490** CAXTON *Eneydos* xv. 57 Tormented ryght asperly with ..grete heyle stones. **1531** ELYOT *Gov.* III. iv. (1557) 155 Warred most asprely agaynst the Romains.

aspermia (əˈspɜːmɪə, eɪ-). [mod.L., f. A- 14 + Gr. σπέρμα seed: see -IA[1].] The lack of, or inability to ejaculate, semen; absence of spermatozoa from the semen as ejaculated. Hence **aˈspermic** *a.*, of or pertaining to aspermia, lacking sperm.

1853 DUNGLISON *Dict. Med. Sci.* (ed. 12) 110/1 Aspermia. **1925** *Glasgow Herald* 5 Dec. 4 An egg-cell which normally requires to be fertilised by a sperm-cell may be launched on a voyage of aspermic development. **1946** *Nature* 23 Nov. 729/2 The groups [of semen samples] cover a very wide range from complete aspermia to slight oligospermia. **1956** *Ibid.* 28 Jan. 190/1 (*heading*) Zinc in aspermic human semen.

aspermous (əˈspɜːməs), *a. Bot.* and *Phys.* [f. Gr. ἄσπερμ-ος (f. ἀ priv. + σπέρμα, -ματ- seed) + -OUS.] Without seed. **aspermatous** (-mətəs), *a.* = ASPERMOUS *a.* **aˈspermatism**, lack of seed, impotence.

1853 all in MAYNE.

†**aˈspern(e,** *v. Obs. rare*$^{-1}$. [ad. L. *āspernāri*, f. *ā* = *ab* away from + *spernā-ri* to despise.] To despise, spurn.

1513 MORE *Rich. III* (1641) 403 It was prudent policie not to asperne and disdaine the little small power. [Also quoted in HALL *Chron.* 412.]

†**ˈaspernate,** *v. Obs.*$^{-0}$ [f. *āspernāt-* ppl. stem of *āspernā-ri*: see prec.] 'To contemn, reject, set light by, or abhor.' Blount *Glossogr.* 1656.

†**asperˈnation.** *Obs.*$^{-0}$ [ad. L. *āspernātiōn-em*, n. of action f. *āspernāri*: see prec.] 'A despising.' Bailey 1731. 'Neglect, disregard.' Johnson.

†**ˈasperness.** *Obs. rare*$^{-1}$. [f. ASPER *a.* + -NESS.] Sharpness, bitterness, severity.

c **1374** CHAUCER *Boeth.* IV. iv. 127 Tourmentid by asprenesse of peyne.

aˈsperolite. *Min.* [f. L. *asper* rough + Gr. λίθος: see -LITE.] A variety of CHRYSOCOLLA.

ˈasperous, *a.* [f. L. *asper* (see ASPER) + -OUS. Cf. *glabrous*, *dexterous*, etc.]

1. Rough, rugged. (Now only in technical use.)

1547 BOORDE *Brev. Health* ccclviii. 115 [Cough] doth come..of a reume distyllynge to the asperous arture. **1678** RYCAUT *Grk. Ch.* 243 (T.) They [cells of hermits] are all built in the rocks, and have a craggy and asperous ascent to them. **1752** LISLE *Husb.* 12 Arenous and sandy earths.. consist of sharp and asperous angles. **1880** GRAY *Bot. Textbk.* 397 *Asperous*, rough to the touch.

†**2.** Harsh to the senses; rough-tasted. *Obs.*

1670 BEALE in *Phil. Trans.* V. 1156 The asperous, and yet appeasing Particles in some Liquors.

†**3.** Harsh to the feelings; bitter, cruel, severe.

1556 ABP. PARKER *Psalter* xxxviii, Thy irefull dartes be asperous. **1606** WARNER *Alb. Eng.* ci. 398 A long and asperous Warre. **1653** A. WILSON *James I*, 125 The asperous edge of Opinion might be taken off.

†**4.** Fierce, savage; cf. ASPER *a.* 5. *Obs.*

1650 T. BAYLY *Herba Parietis* 78 The asperous vermine sets all the venemous nailes..into his trembling flesh.

†**ˈasperously,** *adv. Obs. rare*$^{-1}$. [f. prec. + -LY[2].] Roughly, harshly, severely, painfully.

1547 BOORDE *Brev. Health* cccxxvii. 106 Spasmos..doth drawe the synewes very straight, and asperouslye in the feete and legges.

asperse (əˈspɜːs), *v.* Also 7 **asperce**. [f. L. *aspers-* ppl. stem of *asperg-ĕre*: see ASPERGE. Cf. *aspersé* in Cotgr.] Always *trans.*

1. To besprinkle, bespatter (a person or thing) *with*.

1490 CAXTON *Eneydos* xxiv. 90 She dide asperse the place with the waters. **1607** TOPSELL *Four-f. Beasts* 174 There are Foxes aspersed over with black spots. **1659** LESTRANGE *Alliance Div. Off.* viii. (1846) 368 The child is thrice to be aspersed with water on the face. **1843** THACKERAY *Irish Sk.-Bk.* (1863) 157 The people, as they entered, aspersed themselves with all their might.

2. To sprinkle, scatter (liquid, dust, etc.).

1607 TOPSELL *Four-f. Beasts* (1658) 6 With some golden hair aspersed among the residue. **1815** SOUTHEY *Roderick* xxv. 487 Blood, which hung on every hair, Aspersed like dew-drops.

†**3.** To sprinkle in as an ingredient, intermingle.

1548 UDALL, etc. *Erasm. Par.* Pref. 6 Except he had in the moste desired birthe of the same, aspersed the deathe of your mooste dere Mother: we should by our immoderate felicitee have tempted and provoked hym to take you bothe from vs. **1607** TOPSELL *Four-f. Beasts* 65 Making a plaister thereof with Barley meal and a little Brimstone aspersed.

4. To bespatter (a person, his character, etc.) *with* damaging reports, false and injurious charges or imputations. In 17th c.: Injuriously and falsely to charge *with*.

1611 SPEED *Hist. Gt. Brit.* IX. viii. 40 Monkish humours haue aspersed other such men with bitter reproaches. **1662** J. BARGRAVE *Pope Alex. VII* (1867) 53 He is unjustly aspersed with pride. **1790** PALEY *Hor. Paul.* Rom. i. 10 The calumnies with which the Jews had aspersed him. **1817** JAS. MILL *Brit. India* III. i. 27 The criminations with which the leaders..appeared desirous of aspersing one another.

†**b.** *with* flattery or praise. *Obs. rare.*

1702 ROWE *Ambit. Step-Moth.* (ed. 2) Ded., Men of your Lordship's Figure and Station..ought [not] to be aspers'd with such Pieces of Flattery while living.

5. To spread false and injurious charges against; to detract from, slander, calumniate, traduce, defame, vilify: **a.** a person.

1647 SANDERSON *21 Serm.* Ad Aul. (1673) 216 Aspersing those that are otherwise minded than themselves. **1660** STANLEY *Hist. Philos.* 170/2 Xenophon asperseth him, that he went thither to share in the Sicilian Luxury. **1771** *Junius Lett.* xliv. 240 A libel tending to asperse or vilify the house of Commons. **1828** SCOTT *F.M. Perth* xiii, There were foul tongues to asperse a Douglas.

b. character, reputation, honour, etc.

1651 W.G. tr. *Cowel's Inst.* 215 He asperceth the credit and reputation of another by approbrious words. **1868** GEO. ELIOT *F. Holt* 49 Has any one been aspersing your husband's character?

†**6.** To sprinkle, cast (a damaging imputation or false charge) *upon*. *Obs. rare.*

1630 BRATHWAIT *Eng. Gentl.* (1641) 7 He can asperse no greater imputation on Gentry. **1635** —— *Arcad. Pr.* 243 Nor asperse upon the republike so foule a stain.

aspersed (əˈspɜːst), *ppl. a.* [f. prec. + -ED.]

1. Besprinkled; *spec.* in *Her.* strewed or powdered with a number of small charges, such as *fleur-de-lis*.

1882 CUSSANS *Handbook of Heraldry* 130.

2. Calumniated, slandered, defamed.

1655 LESTRANGE *Chas. I*, 181 The Archbishop of Canterbury stands aspersed in common fame. **1771** J. FLETCHER *Checks* Wks. 1795 II. 96 Mr. Wesley owed it to.. his own aspersed character. **1860** MOTLEY *Netherl.* (1868) I. v. 272 To vindicate his aspersed integrity.

asperser, -or (əˈspɜːsə(r)). [f. prec. + -ER[1], or (on L. analogies) -OR.]

1. One who asperses; a defamer or calumniator.

1702 *Schedule Review'd* 26 An Asperser of the Honourable House. **1738-9** MRS. DELANY *Autobiog.* (1861) II. 39 The aspersors of her husband's chastity. **1835** LYTTON *Rienzi* I. iii, Confronting the last asperser of the Colonna.

2. An aspergillum.

1882 *Times* 18 Apr. 5 Taking the asperser he made the sign of the cross with it on his own forehead.

aspersing (əˈspɜːsɪŋ), *vbl. sb.* [f. as prec. + -ING[1].] Aspersion. (Now mostly gerundial.)

1702 LUTTRELL *Brief Rel.* V. 139 The aspersing of the last house of commons..with receiving French money.

aˈspersing, *ppl. a.* [f. as prec. + -ING[2].] That asperses, slanders, or calumniates.

1674 HICKMAN *Hist. Quinquart* 104 What shall be done to thee thou aspersing Pen?

aspersion (əˈspɜːʃən). Also 7 **aspertion**. [ad. L. *aspersiōn-em*, n. of action f. *aspers-*: see ASPERSE and -ION[1].]

1. The action of besprinkling (a person or thing), or of sprinkling or scattering (liquid, dust, etc.).

1553-87 FOXE *A. & M.* I. 497/1 By the aspersion of the bloud of Jesus Christ. **1699** BURNET *39 Articles* xx. (1700) 193 Aspersion may answer the true end of Baptism. **1782** PRIESTLEY *Corrupt. Chr.* II. VIII. 109 They make many aspersions of holy water. **1846** MASKELL *Mon. Rit.* I. 209 St. Peter..baptized five thousand on one day; but this must have been by aspersion.

2. That which is sprinkled; a shower or spray.

1610 SHAKS. *Temp.* IV. i. 18 No sweet aspersion shall the heauens let fall To make this contract grow. **1845** *Blackw. Mag.* LVII. 584 An aspersion of cold water was dashed..in the impassioned faces of the pair.

†**3.** The sprinkling in of an ingredient. *Obs.*

1605 BACON *Adv. Learn.* I. 29 There is to bee found besides the Theologicall sence, much aspersion of Philosophie. *Ibid.* II. 79 Divinity Morality and Policy, with great aspersion of all other artes. *a* **1656** HALES *Golden Rem.* (1688) 34 Without any Aspersion of Severity.

†**4.** Bespatterment with what soils; soil, stain. *Obs.*

1614 T. ADAMS in Spurgeon *Treas. Dav.* Ps. vi. 6 (1870) I. 70 Whatsoever aspersion the sin of the day has brought upon us.

5. The action of casting damaging imputations, false and injurious charges, or unjust insinuations; calumniation, defamation.

1633 G. HERBERT *Charms & Knots* in *Temple* 89 Who by aspersions throw a stone At th head of others, hit their own. **1781** COWPER *Friendship* xvii, Aspersion is the babbler's trade, To listen is to lend him aid. **1873** GOULBURN *Pers. Relig.* IV. xi. 347 Imperious aspersion of God.

6. A damaging report; a charge that tarnishes the reputation; a calumny, slander, false insinuation. Esp. in the phr. ***to cast aspersions upon.***

1596 SPENSER *State Irel.* Pref. 2 Which may seeme to lay ..any particular aspersion upon some families. **1662** FULLER *Worthies* (1840) III. 120 As false is the aspersion of his being a great usurer. **1692** JAMES II, *Royal Tracts* * * G iv, Malicious Aspertions. **1749** FIELDING *Tom Jones* (1775) II. 209, I defy all the world to cast a just aspersion on my character. **1859** GEO. ELIOT *A. Bede* 53 Vindicating myself from the aspersions.

†**a'spersionating,** *ppl. a. Obs. rare*⁻¹. [f. as pres. pple. of a vb. *aspersionate*, f. prec. Cf. *proportionate*.] = ASPERSING *ppl. a.*

1635 BARRIFFE *Mil. Discip.* lxx. (1643) 188 Private and frosty nips from aspersionating tongues.

aspersive (ə'spɜːsɪv), *a.* ? *Obs.* [f. L. *aspers-* (see ASPERSE) + -IVE, as if ad. L. **aspersivus*.] Tending or calculated to asperse, defamatory.

1642 SIR E. DERING *Sp. on Relig.* xiv. 43 Passages..very aspersive to our Religion.

a'spersively, *adv.* ? *Obs.* [f. prec. + -LY².] In an aspersive manner; by way of aspersion.

1653 *Sir F. Drake Revived* (R.) Envious and injurious detractions, which the ignorant may aspersively cast thereon.

‖**aspersoir** (aspɛrswar). [Fr., f. L. *aspers-*: see ASPERSE and -OIR.] An aspergillum.

1851 MISS STRICKLAND *Queens Scot.* I. 4 The Archbishop of Canterbury had presented his goddaughter with a beautiful gold aspersoir. **1872** CUTTS *Scenes Mid. Ages* 219 The holy water-pot and aspersoir.

aspersor, variant form of ASPERSER.

‖**aspersorium** (æspɜː'sɔərɪəm). [med.L., f. L. *aspers-*: see -ORIUM.] A vessel for holding the holy water used for ceremonial sprinkling.

1861 C. READE *Cloister & H.* IV. 46 Our holy water is Pagan..See here is a Pagan aspersorium. **1880** *Edin. Rev.* Apr. 458 The aged bishop..after offering the aspersorium led Rinuccini to the high altar.

aspersory (ə'spɜːsərɪ), *a. rare*⁻⁰. [f. L. *aspers-* (see ASPERSE) + -ORY, as if ad. L. **aspersōrius*.] = ASPERSIVE.

1848 in WEBSTER.

aspersory (ə'spɜːsərɪ), *sb.* [Alteration of ASPERSORIUM.] A holy-water sprinkler; an aspersorium or aspergillum.

1881 F. E. WARREN *Liturgy Celtic Ch.* 116 It rather resembles an aspersory than a pastoral staff. **1897** *Pall Mall Mag.* Mar. 367 A holy-water stoup with an aspersory stood at the feet [of a corpse].

†**a'spert,** *a. Obs. rare*⁻¹. [a. OF. *aspert*, var. of *apert*, prob. mixed with *espert*: see APERT, EXPERT.] Apt, able, ready, clever.

1423 JAMES I, *King's Quair* v. xix, Though thy begynning hath bene retrograde, Be froward opposyt quhare till aspert, Now sall thai turn, and luke[n] on the dert.

†**'aspertee.** *Obs. rare*⁻¹. [a. Fr. *aspreté*: see ASPERITY.] Rigour, violence, force.

1660 BOND *Scutum Reg.* 234 Seeing that the King could not be reformed by Sute of Law, that ought to be done by aspertee that is by force.

†**a'spew,** *v. Obs. rare.* [OE. *aspíwan*, f. A- *pref.* 1 + *spíwan* to SPEW.] To spew out, vomit.

c **1200** *Trin. Coll. Hom.* 199 Þe nedre..hire atter aspeweð.

asphalt ('æsfælt, -fɔːlt, æs'fælt). Forms: 4 **aspaltoun, aspalt,** 6 **aspallto,** 7 **asphalta,** 7–8 **asphaltos, -us,** 8– **asphaltum, asphalt;** also 9 **asphalte.** [Has been used in many forms: α. in ME. a. OF. **aspaltoun*, **aspalt* (It. *aspalto*, Pr. *asfalto*), ad. late L. *asphalton, -tum*, a. Gr. ἄσφαλτον, var. of ἄσφαλτος, a word of foreign origin; β. from 17th c. in the Gr. and L. forms *asphaltos, -us, -um*, the last established in scientific use; γ. in recent times, a. mod.Fr. *asphalte*. Bailey, Johnson, and Todd knew only *asphaltos, -um*; Craig, 1847, has *as'phalt*, but since asphalt pavement became familiar, *'asphalt* has become usual.]

1. A bituminous substance, found in many parts of the world, a smooth, hard, brittle, black or brownish-black resinous mineral, consisting of a mixture of different hydrocarbons; called also *mineral pitch, Jews' pitch*, and in the O.T. '*slime*.'

c **1325** *E.E. Allit. P.* B. 1038 Þe spumande aspaltoun þat spyserez sellen. **1366** MAUNDEV. ix. 100 It castethe out of the Watre a thing that men clepen Aspalt. **1398** TREVISA *Barth. De P.R.* XVI. xix. (1495) 559 *Asphaltis* glewe of Iudea is erthe of blacke colour and is heuy and stinkynge. **1560** WHITEHORNE *Ord. Souldiours* (1573) 46 b, For every porcion of such thinges, [taking] five of aspallto. **1653** H. COGAN *Diod. Sic.* 77 The infinite quantity of Asphalta or Bytumen which grows there [Babylon]. **1657** TOMLINSON *Renou's Disp.* 674 Asphaltos, or dense Bitumen. **1667** MILTON *P.L.* I. 729 Blazing Cressets fed With Naphtha and Asphaltus. **1714** *Fr. Bk. of Rates* 89 Asphaltum per 100 weight. **1751** CHAMBERS *Cycl.*, *Asphaltos* or *Asphaltum*. **1796** MORSE *Amer. Geog.* I. 727 Amber and asphaltum, or bitumen of Judea. **1799** KIRWAN *Geol. Ess.* 326 A whole lake of asphalt is said to exist in the Isle of Trinidad. **1870** YEATS *Nat. Hist. Comm.* 370 Bitumen, or Asphalte, is an inspissated mineral oil.

b. *attrib.*

1752 FOOTE *Taste* I. i, The salutary application of the Asphaltum-pot. **1872** F. POPE *Telegraph* i. 19 Coat the zincs with asphaltum varnish.

2. A composition made by mixing bitumen, pitch, and sand, or manufactured from natural bituminous limestones, used to pave streets and walks, to line cisterns, etc. Mostly *attrib.*

1847 *Nat. Encycl.* II. 267/1 The Seyssel asphalte introduced into this country by Mr. Claridge..in 1837. **1860** DICKENS *Uncomm. Trav.* (C.D. ed.) iv. 18 Asphalt pavements substituted for wooden floors. **1864** BROWNING *App. Failure* 36 Some arch, where twelve such slept abreast, Unless the plain asphalte seemed best. **1881** GRANT WHITE *England* ii. 29 An asphaltum path.

b. ***artificial asphaltum***: a mixture of the thick pitchy residue of coal-tar with sand, chalk, or lime, used for the same purposes as the preceding.

1875 URE *Dict. Arts* I. 258.

3. *Comb.* **asphalt-like** *a.*

1837–68 DANA *Min.* 751 Solid asphalt-like substances soluble in ether and not in alcohol.

asphalt (æs'fælt), *v.* [f. prec.] To cover or lay with asphalt.

1872 *City Press* 6 Apr. (*Comm. Council*) A most opportune time for asphalting the thoroughfare. **1884** RIDEING in *Harper's Mag.* Mar. 526/2 The streets are..asphalted.

asphalted (æs'fæltɪd), *ppl. a.* [f. prec. + -ED.] Covered or laid with asphalt.

1845 *Penny Cycl.* Supp. I. 146 Asphalted tiles, set in Roman cement, should be first applied as a covering to the wall. **1882** *Pop. Sci. Monthly* XXII. 192 In London there are about nine miles of asphalted streets.

asphaltene (ˌæsfæl'tiːn). *Chem.* [a. mod.F. *asphaltène*, f. ASPHALT + -ENE.] A black solid substance, burning like a resin, supposed to be the solid constituent of asphalt. It is an oxygenated hydro-carbon.

1837–68 DANA *Min.* 751 A black, lustrous, asphalt-like solid, his asphaltene. **1872** WATTS *Dict. Chem.* I. 426 Asphaltene may be formed by the oxidation of petrolene.

asphalter (æs'fæltə(r)). [f. ASPHALT *v.* + -ER¹.] One who lays down asphalt.

1880 *Daily News* 20 March 5/4 Find the main approach to the Park in the hands of paviors and asphalters.

asphaltic (æs'fæltɪk), *a.* [f. ASPHALT-OS + -IC.] Of the nature of, or containing, asphalt. ***Asphaltic Lake, Pool, Lake Asphaltites***: the Dead Sea.

1643 SIR T. BROWNE *Relig. Med.* I. §19 There was an asphaltick and Bituminous nature in that Lake before the fire of Gomorrah. **1658** USSHER *Annals* 754 Horsemen which should conduct him to the Asphaltick Lake. **1667** MILTON *P.L.* I. 411 Eleale to th' Asphaltic Pool. **1809** J. BARLOW *Columb.* VII. 512 Flaming Phlegethon's asphaltic streams. **1875** URE *Dict. Arts* I. 258 *Asphaltic Mastic*..is composed of nearly pure carbonate of lime, and about 9 or 10 per cent. of bitumen.

as'phaltite, *a.* [ad. Gr. ἀσφαλτίτης bituminous, f. ἄσφαλτος.] Bituminous, asphaltic.

1822 BURROWES *Cycl.* I. 798 The Asphaltite Lake.

as'phaltos, -us, -um, forms of ASPHALT.

aspheric (əs'fɛrɪk, eɪ-), *a.* [f. A- 14 + SPHERIC *a.*] Not spherical. Hence **asphe'ricity,** want of sphericity.

1923 W. R. RAYTON in *Jrnl. Optical Soc. Amer.* VII. 197 Osculating paraboloids are, in general, much closer approximations to the required aspheric surfaces than are the osculating spherical surfaces. **1932** HARDY & PERRIN *Princ. Optics* xvi. 347 Any surface having other than a plane or spherical form is said to be *aspheric*... Aspheric surfaces are used to reduce the spherical aberration. **1944** *Jrnl. Optical Soc. Amer.* May 279/2 The asphericity of its plates is about four times greater than the asphericity of a parabolic mirror of the same diameter. **1948** *Electronic Engin.* XX. 314 An aspheric plastic objective lens..focuses infra-red radiation from a distant beacon on to the photo-cathode.

aspherical (əs'fɛrɪkəl, eɪ-), *a.* [f. A- 14 + SPHERICAL *a.*] = prec.

1922 A. H. LEVY tr. *M. von Rohr's Eyes & Spectacles* ii. 75 We consider an aspherical surface [of a lens] to be formed by adding material to a spherical surface. **1923** GLAZEBROOK *Dict. Appl. Physics* IV. 160/1 *Aspherical lens*, a type of spectacle lens designed to correct the aberration introduced when the eye looks towards the edge of the lens instead of to the centre.

aspheterism (æs'fɛtərɪzm). [f. Gr. ἀ priv. + σφέτερ-ος one's own, after Gr. σφετρισμός appropriation.] The doctrine that there ought to be no private property; communism.

1794 SOUTHEY in C. Southey *Life* I. 221 We preached Pantisocracy and Asphete[r]ism everywhere. **1880** DOWDEN *Southey* 36 Coleridge, to silence objectors, would publish a quarto volume on Pantisocracy and Aspheterism.

as'pheterize, *v. rare.* [f. as prec. after SPHETERIZE, Gr. σφετερίζειν.] To practise aspheterism.

1794 COLERIDGE in *Southey's Life* I. 227 The preponderating utility of our aspheterising in Wales.

asphodel ('æsfəʊdɪl). *Bot.* Also 6–7 **asphodill.** [ad. L. *asphodil-us, asphodel-us*, a. Gr. ἀσφόδελ-ος, of unkn. origin. The earlier form (ad. med.L. *affodillus*) was AFFODIL, q.v., whence DAFFODIL.]

1. A genus of liliaceous plants with very handsome flowers, mostly natives of the south of Europe. The White Asphodel or King's Spear covers large tracts of land in Apulia, where its leaves afford good nourishment to sheep. From the genus the order has sometimes been called *Asphodeleæ*.

[**1578** LYTE *Dodoens* 649 This herbe is called in Greke ἀσφόδελος; in shops *Affodilus*..in English also Affodyl and Daffodyll.] **1597** GERARD *Herbal* 85 To shew vnto you the sundry sorts of asphodils..Dioscorides maketh mention but of one asphodill: but Plinie setteth downe two. **1601** HOLLAND *Pliny* II. 128 Asphodel hath a property to chase away mice and rats. **1611** COTGR., *Asphodile* [Fr.], The Daffadill, Affodill, or Asphodill flower; also the root or bulbes thereof. **1712** tr. *Pomet's Hist. Drugs* I. 39 The Root is like the Asphodel, and yields..Salt and Oil. **1859** RAWLINSON *Herodotus* IV. cxc. III. 169 Dwellings..made of the stems of the asphodel, and of rushes, wattled together. **1877** MRS. KING *Discip.*, *Ugo Bassi* I. 51 The moonlight spires Of asphodel rose out of glossy tufts In straight white armies.

b. By the poets made an immortal flower, and said to cover the Elysian meads. (Cf. Homer *Odyss.* XI. 539 Ἀσφοδελὸς λειμών.)

1634 MILTON *Comus* 838 To embathe In nectared lavers strewed with asphodel. **1658** SIR T. BROWNE *Hydriot.* 37 The dead are made to eat Asphodels about the Elysian meadows. **1713** POPE *St. Cecilia's Day* 74 Happy souls who dwell In yellow meads of asphodel Or amaranthine bowers. *a* **1842** TENNYSON *Lotos-Eaters* 170 Others in Elysian valleys dwell, Resting weary limbs at last on beds of asphodel. **1858** LONGF. *Poems* 90 He who wore the crown of asphodels, Descending, at my door began to knock.

c. *attrib.* (sometimes = 'Elysian.')

1831 CARLYLE *Sart. Res.* I. xi, Is that a real Elysian brightness..Is it of a truth leading us into beatific Asphodel meadows? **1847** LONGF. *Ev.* II. iv. 149 Hereafter crown us with asphodel flowers. **1857** RUSKIN *Pol. Econ. Art* 37 In their race thro' the asphodel meadows of their youth.

2. With qualifications, popularly applied to several other plants:

a. Bog, English, or Lancashire Asphodel (*Narthecium Ossifragum*), common on moorlands in Britain. †**b.** Bulbous Asphodel, a species of Ornithogalum or 'Star of Bethlehem' (*O. pyrenaicum*). *Obs.* **c.** False Asphodel, in America, a species of Tofieldia. **d.** Scotch Asphodel (*Tofieldia palustris*), a British subalpine plant.

1599 GERARD *Cat.*, *Asphodelus Lancastriensis*, Lancashire Asphodill. *A. bulbosus*, Bulbous Asphodill. **1834** MARY HOWITT *Flower-Less.* in *Sk. Nat. Hist.* (1851) 195 The English asphodel: In the turfy bogs ye found it. **1863** BARING GOULD *Iceland* 190 In swampy spots clustered the white heads of the mountain asphodel.

asphodelian (æsfəʊ'diːlɪən), *a.* [f. L. *asphodel-us* (see prec.) + -IAN.] Of asphodel; Elysian.

1854 KEIGHTLEY *Mythol. Gr. & It.* 410 The asphodelian mead.

‖**asphyxia** (æs'fɪksɪə). [mod.L., a. Gr. ἀσφυξία, f. ἀ priv. + σφύξις pulse (whence also *asphyxis* has occas. been used). See also ASPHYXY.]

1. *lit.* Stoppage of the pulse.

1706 PHILLIPS, *Asphyxia*, a Cessation of the Pulse throughout the whole Body; which is the highest degree of Swooning and next to Death. **1731** BAILEY, *Asphyxia*, a Deficiency or Privation of the Pulse in some Cases, where it stops for a Time. **1864** WEBSTER, *Asphyxia*..applied also to the collapsed state in cholera, with want of pulse.

2. The condition of suspended animation produced by a deficiency of oxygen in the blood; suffocation. Also *fig.*

[It indicates a curious infelicity of etymology that the pulse in asphyxiated animals continues to beat long after all signs of respiratory action have ceased. *Syd. Soc. Lex.* 1881.]

1778 T. BRAND (*title*) The Cure of Asphyxis or apparent death by Drowning. **1836** TODD *Cycl. Anat. & Phys.* 259/1 Asphyxia may be produced by section of the spinal cord. **1858** O. W. HOLMES *Aut. Breakf. T.* xii. 120 Lingering asphyxia of soul. **1872** HUXLEY *Phys.* iv. 98 When a man is strangled, drowned, or choked..what is called asphyxia comes on.

as'phyxial, *a.* [f. prec. + -AL¹.] Of, pertaining to, or characterized by asphyxia.

1836 TODD *Cycl. Anat. & Phys.* I. 802/2 Asphyxial disorders. **1867** *Pall Mall G.* No. 813, 1001/1 The asphyxial stage of cholera.

asphyxiant (æsˈfɪksɪənt), *a.* and *sb.* [f. ASPHYXIA + -ANT.] A. *adj.* Causing asphyxia. B. *sb.* Any chemical substance that causes asphyxia.

1854 *Englishwoman in Russia* 302 Long-range guns and asphyxiant balls. **1888** *Chambers's Encycl.* I. 501 The term asphyxiants is applied to any gases having a suffocating.. effect on the human system. **1921** *19th Cent.* July 34 If in the Great War we had refused to use asphyxiant gas.

asphyxiate (æsˈfɪksɪeɪt), *v.* [f. as ASPHYXIAL *a.* + -ATE[3].] To affect with asphyxia, to suffocate.

1836 TODD *Cycl. Anat. & Phys.* I. 261/1 A rabbit was asphyxiated by tying the trachea. **1866** *Ch. & State Rev.* 23 Mar. 177/1 The atmosphere of indifferentism, on the contrary, half asphyxiates the very believer.

asˈphyxiated, *ppl. a.* [f. prec. + -ED.] Affected with asphyxia, suffocated.

1836 TODD *Cycl. Anat. & Phys.* I. 260/2 The carotid arteries of an asphyxiated animal. **1870** H. MACMILLAN *Bible Teach.* xiii. 257 This blue air by which the spirit lives, without which it becomes asphyxiated.

asˈphyxiating, *vbl. sb.* [f. as prec. + -ING[1].] Asphyxiation, suffocation.

1872 HUXLEY *Phys.* iv. 98 This asphyxiating process.

asˈphyxiating, *ppl. a.* [f. as prec. + -ING[2].] Causing asphyxia, suffocating. Also *fig.*

1859 F. PAGET *Curate Cumberw.* 166 Of all asphyxiating miseries it is the worst. **1861** *Sat. Rev.* 20 July 63 The stiff dinner, or the asphyxiating drum.

asphyxiation (æsˌfɪksɪˈeɪʃən). [n. of action f. ASPHYXIATE: see -ATION.] The action of producing asphyxia or condition of being asphyxiated; suffocation.

1866 HOWELLS *Venet. Life* xix. 312 The purple verge of asphyxiation. **1883** *Standard* 19 Mar. 5/2 Abandoned to garotting by night and asphyxiation by day.

asphyxiator (æsˈfɪksɪeɪtə(r)). [n. of agent f. as prec.: see -ATOR.] An asphyxiating agent; an apparatus for extinguishing fire by the agency of carbonic acid gas, etc.

1882 *Standard* 31 Oct. 5/3 Portable fire engines or asphyxiators on every car.

asphyxy (æsˈfɪksɪ). [ad. F. *asphyxie*, ad. L. *asphyxia.*] = ASPHYXIA.

1784 *(title)* Gardane's Catechism concerning the apparent Deaths, called Asphyxies [transl. from Fr.]. **1837** BEDDOES *Let.* in *Poems* Introd. 103 About to awake from her asphyxy of a hundred years. **1882** G. MACDONALD *Weighed & Want.* II. xv. 192 His letters.. absorbed her atmosphere, and after each followed a period of mental asphyxy.

asˈphyxy, *v.* [f. prec. Cf. Fr. *asphyxier.*] To asphyxiate. (Chiefly in pa. pple.)

1843 CARLYLE *Past & Pr.* (1858) 96 If said soul be asphyxied. **1881** TYNDALL *Float. Matt. Air* App. 334 Asphyxied by the defect of oxygen.

aspic[1] (ˈæspɪk). Forms: 6 **aspycke**, 6–7 **aspicke**, **aspike**, 7 **aspick**, 7– **aspic**. [a. F. *aspic* asp, a. Pr. *aspic*, unexplained derivative of L. *aspid-em*, nom. *aspis*: see ASP[2].]

1. By-form of ASP[2], used chiefly in poetry.

1530 PALSGR. 195/1 Aspycke sarpent, *aspicq*. **1606** SHAKS. *Ant. & Cl.* v. ii. 354 This is an Aspickes traile. **1611** FLORIO *Aspide* [It.], an aspike or aspe. **1649** JER. TAYLOR *Gt. Exemp.* I. iv. 42 A little child should boldly put his finger in the cavern of an Aspick. **1713** ADDISON *Cato* III. v, Why did I 'scape th'invenom'd Aspic's rage. **1830** TENNYSON *Dream Fair Wom.* xl, Shewing the aspic's bite.

b. *attrib.*

1742 C. OWEN *Serpents* 61 The Aspick Poison, which throws Persons into a pleasant Sleep, in which they die. **1807** LAMB *Let.* ix, Breath.. like distillations of aspic poison.

c. *fig.*

1649 G. DANIEL *Trinarch. Hen. V*, 237 Stung with the Aspicke of invadeing feare. *a* **1797** H. WALPOLE *Mem. Geo. III* (1845) I. xviii. 261 Lord Bute.. there first learned what an aspic was lodged near his bosom.

2. *transf.* 'A piece of ordnance which carries a 12 pound shot. The piece itself weighs 4250 pounds.' C. James *Mil. Dict.* 1816. (Perh. only Fr.)

aspic[2] (ˈæspɪk). [a. Fr. *aspic* (in *huile d' aspic* vulgar form of *huile de spic*) for *spic*, ad. It. *spigo* the Great Lavender, orig. Spikenard, = OF. *espic*:—L. *spīcus* (in med.L.) Spikenard, collateral form of *spīca* spike.] The Great Lavender or Spike (*Lavandula Spica*), a plant from which a volatile aromatic oil is obtained.

1604 E. G. tr. *D'Acosta's Hist. Indies* IV. xxix. 288 Oyle Of Aspicke, which the Physitians and Painters vse much, the one for plasters, the other to vernish their pictures. **1751** CHAMBERS *Cycl.* s.v. *Oil*, Oil of aspic or spike. **1819** REES *Encycl.* III, *Aspic*.. grows in plenty in Languedoc.

aspic[3] (ˈæspɪk). Also 8 **aspique**. [a. F. *aspic*. Littré suggests its derivation from *aspic* asp, because it is 'froid comme un aspic,' a proverbial phrase in Fr.] A savoury meat jelly, composed of and containing meat, fish, game, hard-boiled eggs, etc. Also *attrib.* in *aspic-jelly*.

1789 MRS. PIOZZI *France & It.* I. 47 Cased in Chrystal like our aspiques. **1848** THACKERAY *Van. Fair* lxii. (1866) 526 Died.. of an aspic of plovers' eggs. **1870** DISRAELI *Lothair* xxi. 89 He extracted a couple of fat little birds from their bed of aspic jelly.

†**ˈaspide.** *Obs.* Also 4 **aspidis**, 5 **aspyde**. [ad. L. *aspidem*, acc. of *aspis*: see ASP[2]. Cf. OF. *aspide.*] By-form of ASP[2].

c **1000** *Ags. Ps.* xci. 13 Þu ofer aspide [Vulg. *supra aspidem*] miht eaðe gangan. *a* **1300** *E.E. Psalter* ibid., Oure aspide and basilisk saltou ga. **1393** GOWER *Conf.* I. 57 A serpent, which that aspidis is cleped. **1483** CAXTON *Gold. Leg.* 221/2 And did doo be put to her.. two aspydes. **1601** HOLLAND *Pliny* II. 356 As for the aspides.. whomsoever they have stung, they die vpon it with a kind of deadly sleepinesse.

aspidelite (əˈspɪdəlaɪt). *Min.* [? f. Gr. ἀσπιδη- shield + -LITE.] A variety of TITANITE found at Arendal in Norway. (Dana.)

aspidistra (æspɪˈdɪstrə). [mod.L., f. Gr. ἀσπιδ-, ἀσπίς shield + *-istra*, after *tupistra.*] A plant of the genus so called, belonging to the family Liliaceæ and native to China and Japan; frequently grown as a pot-plant, and often regarded as a symbol of dull middle-class respectability.

1822 *Bot. Register* 628 *Aspidistra lurida.* Dingy-flowered Aspidistra. **1852** G. W. JOHNSON *Cott. Gard. Dict.* s.v., The mushroom-shaped stigma by which Aspidistræ are characterised. **1920** 'O. DOUGLAS' *Penny Plain* iii, An aspidistra in a pot completed the table decorations. **1925** W. DEEPING *Sorrell & Son* IV. i, Carrying out the aspidistras and washing them in the yard. **1936** 'G. ORWELL' *(title)* Keep the aspidistra flying.

¶ Illiterate forms were formerly frequent.

1895 *Daily News* 4 Dec. 6/7 The broad leaves of the aspidestria. **1899** *Westm. Gaz.*, They are just moderate-sized palms, ferns, and aspidestra.

Hence **aspiˈdistral** *a.*, of or pertaining to an aspidistra; abounding in aspidistras. Also *transf.*

1936 'G. ORWELL' *Keep Aspidistra Flying* iii. 73 He was a made man—or, by Smilesian, aspidistral standards, *un*made. *Ibid.* viii. 198 Why chew leathery beef in the aspidistral dining-room when he had ten quid in pocket? *Ibid.* x. 270 Flaxman's wife had forgiven him, and he was back at Peckham, in aspidistral bliss. **1939** R. CAMPBELL *Flowering Rifle* I. 13 The weed of Life that grows where air is hot With 'Meetings' for its aspidistral pot.

aspie, -ier, obs. forms of ESPY, -IER: see ASPY.

†**aˈspill,** *v. Obs.* [f. A- *pref.* 1 + SPILL *v.*:—OE. *spillan.*]

1. To spill, waste, render useless.

c **1230** *Ancr. R.* 148 Þeo þet forleoseð & aspilleð al hore god þuruh wilnunge of hereword. *a* **1250** *Owl & Night.* 348 So thu miȝt thine song aspille.

2. To destroy, kill.

c **1175** *Lamb. Hom.* 13 Eower burh heo forbernað and ehte aspillað. *c* **1275** *Orison* in *O.E. Misc.* 140 Ne may nouhtþe feond his saule aspille. *c* **1305** *St. Kenelm* in *E.E.P.* (1862) 50 Mid þis Askebert heo spac: þat child forto aspille.

aspin, obs. form of ASPEN.

Aspinall (ˈæspɪnəl), *v. trans.* To paint (articles of household furniture, esp. when old and shabby) with Aspinall's Enamel Paint. Hence **ˈAspinalling** *vbl. sb.*

1889 *Jrnl. Educ.* 1 Aug. 388/1 Three low wicker chairs 'Aspinalled' in dark green. **1891** M. E. MANN *Winter's Tale* II. I. xi. 25 The.. stool, which Erica herself had aspinalled in a spare hour. **1891** *(title)* Guide to Aspinalling. By A Lady. **1908** A. BENNETT *Buried Alive* vii. 165 What a smell of paint!.. You surely haven't been aspinalling that bath-room chair?

†**ˈaspine,** *a. Obs. rare*$^{-1}$. [irreg. f. ASP[2] + -INE. (Cf. *serpent-ine.*)] Of or pertaining to an asp; snaky.

1644 QUARLES *Sheph. Orac.* viii, Could thy passion lend No sleighter subject, for thy breath to spend Her aspine venome at.

aspirant (əˈspaɪərənt, *occas.* ˈæspɪrənt), *a.* and *sb.* [a. F. *aspirant* and ad. L. *aspīrāntem*, pr. pple. of *aspirer*, *aspīrāre*: see ASPIRE *v.* and -ANT.]

A. *adj.* = ASPIRING.

1. Striving for a higher position, seeking distinction.

1814 SOUTHEY *Lett.* (1856) II. 373, I receive plenty of letters from poets aspirant. **1850** MRS. BROWNING *Poems* I. 343 To muse upon eternity's constraint Round our aspirant souls.

2. Mounting up, ascending.

1845 MOZLEY *Blanco White, Ess.* (1878) II. 134 Nature is retracing her aspirant steps. **1865** SWINBURNE *Dolores* 249 With flame all round him aspirant Stood flushed.. the tyrant.

B. *sb.* One who aspires; one who, with steady purpose, seeks advancement to high position, or the acquirement of some privilege or advantage.

1751 WARBURTON *Pope's Wks., Dunciad* IV. 517 (JOD.) Each aspirant.. had proved his qualification and claim. **1823** BYRON *Juan* xiv. 57 Perhaps she wished an aspirant profounder, But whatsoe'er she wished, she acted right. **1849** MACAULAY *Hist. Eng.* I. 253 The way to greatness was left clear to a new set of aspirants.

b. Const. *to*, *after*, *for*.

1738 WARBURTON *Div. Legat.* I. 138 The Aspirant to the Mysteries. **1835** BROWNING *Paracelsus* II. 45 Degrade me.. To an aspirant after fame, not truth! **1863** KINGLAKE *Crimea* (1876) I. xiv. 218 A calculating and practical aspirant to Empire. **1879** B. TAYLOR *Germ. Lit.* 179 Aspirants for poetic honors.

aspirate (ˈæspɪrət), *ppl. a.* and *sb.* [ad. L. *aspīrātus*, pa. pple. of *aspīrāre*: see ASPIRE *v.* and -ATE[2]. Cf. Fr. *aspiré.*]

A. *ppl. adj.* = ASPIRATED.

? **1669** HOLDER (J.) They are not aspirate, i.e. with such an aspiration as *h*. **1751** CHAMBERS *Cycl.*, The *Spiritus* of the Greeks, our *h* aspirate. **1879** WHITNEY *Skr. Gram.* 13 Consonants—Aspirate Mutes.

B. *sb.*

1. A consonantal sound in which the action of the breath is prominently marked; one which is followed by or blended with the sound of H.

(Modern phonologists generally apply the term to a consonantal diphthong consisting of a mute or stop followed by 'the slipping-out of an audible bit of *flatus* or aspiration, between the breach of mute-closure and the following sound' (Whitney), which is believed to be the character of the Sanskrit 'aspirates,' and to have been the *original* value of the Gr. χ,θ,φ. But the term is also applied in Gr. grammar to the current *fricative* value of these letters; and in the Roman alphabet generally to any modification of sound indicated by the addition of *h*; e.g. to the Celtic *bh*, *mh* (= *v*, and nasalized *v*); in Hebrew it has been given to the gutturals, and in other languages it has been used with similar vagueness).

1727–51 CHAMBERS *Cycl.* s.v., Some.. write the aspirates, or letters aspirated. *Ibid.* The eastern languages which do not express the vowels, do yet express the Aspirates. **1859** MRS. SCHIMMELPENNINCK *Princ. Beauty* III. iii. §31 Gutturals, and rough aspirates, and strongly marked consonants are the most sudden and forcible inflections. **1879** WHITNEY *Skr. Gram.* 13 That the aspirates, all of them, are real mutes or contact sounds, and not fricatives (like European *th*, *ph*, *ch*, etc.) is beyond question.

2. The simple sound of the letter H, or its equivalent the πνεῦμα δασύ, or *spiritus asper* (ʽ) of Greek grammar. *Esp.* applied to the initial *h*- so often 'dropped,' or improperly inserted, by the uneducated in England.

1725 POPE *Pref. Homer*, The feebler Æolic which often rejects its aspirate or takes off its accent. **1872** GEO. ELIOT *Middlem.* xxxv. (1873) 196 A Middlemarch mercer of polite manners and superfluous aspirates. **1877** *Punch* 18 Aug. 65 Our old Cockney friend, 'Arry, who is weak in aspirates.

¶ Some writers have altered this word to *asperate*, after the *spiritus asper* of the Latin grammarians, an ingenious but unfounded conceit.

aspirate (ˈæspɪreɪt), *v.* [f. L. *aspīrāt-* ppl. stem of *aspīrāre*: see prec. Cf. F. *aspirer.*]

1. *trans.* To pronounce with a breathing; to add an audible effect of the breath to any sound; to prefix H to a vowel, or add H or its supposed equivalent to a consonant sound. Also *absol.*

a **1700** DRYDEN (J.) Our *w* and *h* aspirate. **1706** PHILLIPS, *Aspirate*, to pronounce with an Aspiration. **1801** MAR. EDGEWORTH *Irish Bulls* xi. (1832) 226 Londoners [are] always aspirating where they should not, and never aspirating where they should. **1877** LYTTEIL *Landm.* I. iv. 33 The Celts have aspirated the letter *m* in *gumi*.

2. *trans.* To draw out a gas or vapour from a vessel; cf. ASPIRATOR a, b.

1880 *Nature* XXI. 437 He proposes to aspirate the vapours of the chambers.

aspirated (ˈæspɪreɪtɪd), *ppl. a.* Pronounced with a breathing; having the sound of H prefixed, added, or blended.

1668 WILKINS *Real Char.* 14, 26 Consonants, to which they add 20 other aspirated Syllables. **1864** MAX MÜLLER *Sc. Lang.* II. iii. 146 Aspirated checks.

aspirating (ˈæspɪreɪtɪŋ), *ppl. a.* [f. ASPIRATE *v.* + -ING[2].] That operates by aspiration or suction.

a **1884** KNIGHT *Dict. Mech.* Suppl. 51/2 *Aspirating Filter*, one in which the action is expedited by the withdrawal of air from beneath the filtering material. *Ibid.*, *Aspirating Winnowing Machine*, one which draws air through the grain instead of blowing it. **1895** *Catal. Surg. Instruments* (Arnold & Sons), Aspirating Syringe, Aspirating Guarded Needle. **1902** *Times* 25 Sept. 3/4 The operation was performed with an aspirating needle.

aspiration (æspɪˈreɪʃən). Also 6 **adsp-**. [ad. L. *aspīrātiōn-em*, n. of action f. *aspīrāre*: see ASPIRE and -ATION.]

I. From ASPIRE.

†**1.** The action of breathing into; inspiration.

a **1535** MORE *Wks.* 357 (R.) Without the adspiracion and helpe of whose especiall grace no laboure of man can profite. *c* **1534** tr. *Pol. Verg. Eng. Hist.* (1846) I. 169 Which thinge [he].. sayde not withoute the aspiration and assent of the Hollie Spirit.

2. The action of breathing or drawing one's breath; a breath, sigh. *techn.* The drawing in of air in, or as in, breathing.

1607 TOPSELL *Serpents* 746 Corrupt inflamation taking away freedom or easinesse of aspiration. **1659** LEAK *Waterwks.* 7 One.. of those Syphons containes so much Air that it cannot be drawn forth by aspiration. **1775** SHERIDAN *Rivals* II. i. (1883) 93 There is.. not an aspiration of the breeze, but hints some cause. **1823** F. COOPER *Pioneer* xxv. (1869) 110/2 She sighed with an aspiration so low that it was scarcely audible. **1869** *Eng. Mech.* 31 Dec. 379/2 Valves of aspiration.. send the air into the body of the apparatus.

†**3.** That which is breathed out, an exhalation.

1635 SWAN *Spec. Mundi* vi. §2 (1643) 196 An hot and drie aspiration exhaled out of the earth.

4. The action of aspiring; steadfast desire or longing for something above one.

1606 SHAKS. *Tr. & Cr.* IV. v. 16 That spirit of his In aspiration lifts him from the earth. *a* **1748** WATTS (J.) A soul inspired with the warmest aspirations after celestial beatitude. **1862** TROLLOPE *Orley Farm* xlvii. 340 Assured that he need regard no woman as too high for his aspirations. **1866** ALGER *Solit. Nat. & Man* III. 120 Aspiration is a pure upward desire for excellence.

II. From ASPIRATE.

5. The action of aspirating: see ASPIRATE *v.*

1398 TREVISA *Barth. De P.R.* XVIII. lxxxv. (1495) 835 This name Pigargus hath none aspiracion . . and so it shall not be wryten wyth . h . but some men wryte Phigargus: and done amys. **1546** LANGLEY *Pol. Verg. De Invent.* I. vi. 13 b, H is no letter but a signe of aspiracion. **1646** SIR T. BROWNE *Pseud. Ep.* 130 The addition of an h, or aspiration of the letter π. **1845** O'DONOVAN *Irish Gram.* 39 Aspiration . . of the Celtic . . may be defined as the changing of the radical sounds of the consonants from being stops of the breath to a sibilance, or from a stronger to a weaker sibilance.

6. An aspirated sound or letter; the letter H or its equivalent; the breathings (‘) and (’) in Greek; = ASPIRATE *sb.*

c **1550** GRAFTON *Briteyn* (R.) Pritannia in Greke, with a circumflexed aspiracion, doth signifie metalles. **1605** J. DOVE *Confut. Ath.* 61 The letter ה *He*, which is but an aspiration. **1645** FULLER *Good Th. in Bad T.* (1841) 62 What is no substantial letter but a bare aspiration. **1673** HICKERINGILL *Greg. Father Greyb.* 292 Of less standing in the University, than Greek accents and aspirations. **1824** J. JOHNSON *Typogr.* II. 282 The Greek vowels admit of two aspirations, viz. spiritus asper [‘] and spiritus lenis [’].

7. The action or process of drawing in, out, or through by suction; *esp.* the drawing out (of fluids, gases, etc.) by means of an aspirator.

1842 *Civil Engin. & Archit. Jrnl.* V. 203/2 The fluid was absorbed throughout all the pores of the [felled] tree, by a process which is termed 'aspiration'. **1879** *Encycl. Brit.* IX. 344/2 Apparatus, in which the principle of aspiration, or drawing currents of air through the grain, is now extensively employed. **1881** *Trans. Obstetr. Soc. Lond.* XXII. 57 Aspiration was frequently resorted to, with the view of arresting the growth of the fœtus. **1950** *Engineering* CLXIX. 31/1 'Aspiration', or separation by means of ascending air currents, is much used in [flour] milling.

attrib. **1902** C. N. & A. M. WILLIAMSON *Lightning Conductor* 18 The 'aspiration pipe' . . had worked loose.

¶ Written *asperation*: see ASPIRATE *sb.* ¶.

1581 MARBECK *Bk. of Notes* 558 The letter of Asperation being altered out of his place.

aspirational (ˌæspɪˈreɪʃənəl), *a.* [f. ASPIRATION + -AL.] Belonging to or characterized by aspiration.

1887 H. R. HAWEIS *Christ & Christianity* I. iii. 83 Its sense of mystery feeble, and consequently its lift and aspirational power almost *nil*. **1916** A. M. RIHBANY *Syrian Christ* (1919) II. ii. 66 As pious in his imprecations and curses as he is in his aspirational prayer. **1967** *Listener* 30 Nov. 731/2 Everybody banging away at that final aspirational aria.

aspirator (ˈæspɪreɪtə(r)). [n. of agent f. (on L. analogies) L. *aspīrāre*: see ASPIRE *v.* and -ATOR. Cf. F. *aspirateur.*] He who or that which aspirates, breathes, or blows upon; *spec.* **a.** an apparatus for drawing a stream of air or gas through a tube; **b.** an instrument for evacuating pus from abscesses by means of an exhausted receiver; **c.** a kind of winnowing or fanning machine.

1863 WATTS *Dict. Chem.* I. 427 Mohr's aspirator has the form of an ordinary gasometer. **1878** T. BRYANT *Pract. Surg.* 20, I have drawn off the pus from a chronic abscess with the aspirator. **1883** E. INGERSOLL in *Harper's Mag.* June 76/1 The wheat . . falls into an aspirator on the seventh floor.

aspiratory (əˈspaɪərətərɪ), *a. rare*⁻⁰. [f. prec., as if ad. L. **aspīrātōrius*: see -ORY.] Of or pertaining to aspiration.

1864 in WEBSTER.

aspire (əˈspaɪə(r)), *v.* Forms: 5–6 **aspyre**, 6–7 **aspier**, 6– **aspire**. [(? a. F. *aspire-r*), ad. L. *asp-, adspīrā-re* to breathe upon, seek to reach, f. *ad* to, at + *spīrā-re* to breathe. The OF. *aspirer* is prob. partly for *enspirer*, ad. L. *inspīrāre*: see A- *pref.* 10.]

I. To breathe into or forth.

†**1.** *trans.* To breathe (breath or spiritual influence) *to* or *into*; to inspire. *Obs.*

1532 MORE *Confut. Tindale* Wks. 507/1 Though god . . aspired them his grace therein. **1533** —— *Apol.* xlix. Wks. 927/2 To spreade his beames vpon vs, and aspire hys breth into vs. **1633** P. FLETCHER *Purple Isl.* I. lix, Thereto may he his grace and gentle heat aspire.

†**2.** *intr.* To breathe forth, exhale. *Obs. rare.*

c **1750** SHENSTONE *Wks.* (1764) I. 290 In what lonely vale Of balmy med'cine's various field, aspires The blest refrigerent?

II. To breathe desire towards. (Cf. ANHELE.)

3. *intr.* To have a fixed desire, longing, or ambition for something at present above one; to seek to attain, to pant, long. **a.** with *to.*

c **1460** FORTESCUE *Abs. & Lim. Mon.* (1714) 59 Mannys Corage is so noble that naturally he aspyreth to hye thyngs and to be exaltyd. **1558** KNOX *First Blast* (Arb.) 20 Woman oght to be repressed . . if she aspire to any dominion. **1651** HOBBES *Leviath.* I. IV. 15 Any man that aspires to true knowledge. **1781** GIBBON *Decl. & F.* III. 225 The Barbarian still aspired to the rank of master-general of the armies of the West. **1839** KEIGHTLEY *Hist. Eng.* II. 52 Is it not possible that Pole secretly aspired to the hand of the princess Mary?

b. with *after, at; for*, obs.

1606 G. W[OODCOCKE] *Hist. Justine* 31 b, Which citty . . began to aspire at the whole Empire of Greece. **1649** LOVELACE *Poems* (1659) 22 [Thou] Aspiredst for the everlasting Crowne. **1675** TRAHERNE *Chr. Ethics* xvi. 246 We are able to desire, and aspire after . . the very throne of God. **1788** V. KNOX *Winter Even.* I. II. viii. 165 He who aspires at the character of a good man. **1794** SULLIVAN *View Nat.* II. 399 To aspire after a more perfect knowledge of his nature. **1869** F. NEWMAN *Misc.* 310 He does not lead the learner to aspire at any thing higher.

c. with *inf.*

c **1460** [See 3 a.] **1591** SHAKS. *Two Gent.* III. i. 153 Wilt thou aspire to guide the heauenly Car? **1605** BACON *Adv. Learn.* II. xxii. §15 Aspiring to be like God in power. **1879** FROUDE *Cæsar* xviii, Milo was aspiring to be made consul.

d. *absol.*

1592 WARNER *Alb. Eng.* VII. xxxvii. (1612) 185 To aspire is lawfull, if betwixt a Meane it stand. **1764** GOLDSM. *Trav.* 363 Ye powers of truth, that bid my soul aspire. **1877** E. CONDER *Bas. Faith* ix. 383 Man aspires. An immense instinct in his nature points upward, like a spire of flame.

†**4.** *trans.* To have an ardent desire for, to pant or long for, to be ambitious of, aim at. *Obs.*

1596 SPENSER *F.Q.* V. ix. 41 How for to depryve Mercilla of her crowne, by her aspyred. **1623** COCKERAM *Dict.* III. s.v. *Cleopatra*, He aspired the Empire. **1652** BROME *Jov. Crew* I. 362 But I aspire no merits, nor popular thanks. **1816** SOUTHEY *Lay of Laureate* Proem. 20 And Love aspired with Faith a heavenward flight.

III. To rise, mount up. (Influenced in use by various meanings of SPIRE *sb.* and *v.*)

5. *intr.* To rise up, as an exhalation, or as smoke or fire; hence *gen.* to mount up, taper up, tower, ascend, rise high, become tall.

1591 SPENSER *Ruins of Time* 408 Pyramides, to heauen aspired. **1598** SHAKS. *Merry Wives* V. v. 101 Whose flames aspire, As thoughts do blow them higher and higher. **1676** WORLIDGE *Cider* (1691) 44 The Tree is more apt to aspire than any other Apple-tree. **1697** DRYDEN *Virg. Georg.* III. 824 Tisiphone . . every Moment rises to the Sight: Aspiring to the Skies. **1738** JOHNSON *London* 208 Orgilio sees the golden pile aspire. *c* **1855** LD. HOUGHTON *Burial Gr. Scutari*, Above the domes of loftiest mosques, These pinnacles of death aspire.

6. *fig.* (with some sense of 3 combined.)

1585 ABP. SANDYS *Serm.* (1841) 146 To whose works man's thoughts aspire not. **1610** HOLLAND *Camden's Brit.* I. 301 It aspireth to the very top of ostentation. **1768** BEATTIE *Minstr.* I. vii, Let thy heaven-taught soul to heaven aspire. **1832** WORDSW. *Poems of Imag.* xli, Mount from the earth; aspire! aspire!

†**7.** To grow up *to* (the age of). *Obs. rare.*

1576 LAMBARDE *Peramb. Kent* (1826) 508 The Gardein . . shall keepe his [lands], untill the warde aspire to foureteene. **1596** SPENSER *F.Q.* I. vi. 23 To ryper yeares he gan aspire.

†**8.** *trans.* To mount up to, soar to, reach, attain. Also *fig. Obs.*

1581 A. ANDERSON *Serm. Paules Crosse* 89 The vigor . . should valiantly aspyre the top of smallest twigges. *c* **1585** *Faire Em* I. 68 And to aspire the bliss That hangs on quick achievement of my love, Thyself and I will travel in disguise. **1592** SHAKS. *Rom. & Jul.* III. i. 122 That gallant spirit hath aspir'd the clouds. **1596** CHAPMAN *Iliad* x. 309 Forth went they . . and presently aspir'd The guardless Thracian regiment fast bound with sleep, and tir'd.

¶ = EXPIRE. (Cf. OF. *espirer*, and see A- *pref.* 9.)

1574 HELLOWES *Gueuara's Epist.* (1577) 60 Christe aspiring uppon the Crosse.

†**a'spire.** *Obs.* [f. prec. vb.] Aspiration.

1562 J. NORTON in Farr's *S.P.* (1845) II. 459 Heau'd vp, hurl'd downe, dismay'd, or in aspire. **1643** SIR T. BROWNE *Relig. Med.* 76 Whose earthly fumes choak my devout aspires. **1667** H. MORE *Div. Dial.* iii. §28 (1713) 249 Thy serious Aspires . . after the true Knowledge of thy Maker.

†**a'spired,** *ppl. a. Obs.* [f. ASPIRE *v.* + -ED.] Having raised itself, elevated, lofty.

1599 BP. HALL *Sat., Def. Envie* 35 Those bays, and that aspired thought, In carelesse rage, she sets at worse than nought. **1627** SPEED *Eng. Abridged*, King Henry the 8 . . laid their aspired tops at his own feete.

†**a'spirement.** *Obs. rare.* [a. OF. *aspirement*, f. *aspirer*: see ASPIRE *v.* and -MENT.]

1. Breathing, breath.

1393 GOWER *Conf.* III. 93 Air . . Of whose kinde his aspirementes Taketh every livissh creature.

2. Aspiring, aspiration, steadfast upward desire.

1607 BREWER *Lingua* III. vi. in Hazl. *Dodsl.* IX. 399 By which aspirement she her wings displays, And herself thither, whence she came, upraise. *a* **1679** T. GOODWIN *Wks.* 1863 VII. 483 And not Christ only, but God also, is the object of our aspirement.

aspirer (əˈspaɪərə(r)). [f. ASPIRE *v.* + -ER¹.] One who aspires.

1584 *Copie of Letter* 46 A troden path of al aspirers. **1597** DANIEL *Civ. Wares* II. xv, Th' aspirer once attaind unto the top, Cuts off those meanes by which himselfe got up. **1674** BURNET *Royal Martyr, Serm.* (1710) 30 To satisfie the pretensions of all these lofty Aspirers. **1847** *Eclec. Rev.* XXVI. 210 The dreamy, irresolute aspirer.

aspirin (ˈæspɪrɪn). *Chem.* [G. (C. Witthauer 1899, in *Die Heilkunde* Apr.), shortened form of *A*cetylirte *Spir*säure (i.e. acetylated spiræic acid) + -IN¹.] A white crystalline compound, acetylsalicylic acid, used esp. as an analgesic and antipyretic; with *an* and *pl.*, a dose of this in tablet form. Also *attrib.*

1899 *Jrnl. Chem. Soc.* LXXVI. II. 605 Physiological Action of Aspirin (Acetylsalicylic Acid). **1901** *Ibid.* LXXX. II. 408 Aspirin (*o*-acetoxybenzoic acid) does not increase the flow of urine, but somewhat raises the total output of solids. **1922** *Blackw. Mag.* Apr. 460/1 He was always at hand with tea and brandy and aspirin. **1923** MRS. A. SIDGWICK *Nonego-by* xxix. 243, I think that frontal neuralgia is worse. You can give me an aspirin if you like. **1924** *Blackw. Mag.* June 801/2 Aspirin tablets. **1937** 'G. ORWELL' *Road to Wigan Pier* xii. 224 Every aspirin-eater in the outer suburbs. **1954** *Numbers* July 4 Flash of wet overcoats; artificial neon-lit expressions. Aspirin age. World gone sour. **1960** [see ANYTHING I b].

fig. **1930** *Time & Tide* 30 Aug. 1085/1 This aspirin remedy could continue only so long as the price of wheat and wool was high. **1957** M. SWAN *Brit. Guiana* I. i. 21 The living standards would eventually improve without the necessity for this aspirin from the Government.

aspiring (əˈspaɪərɪŋ), *vbl. sb.* [f. as ASPIRER + -ING¹.]

1. Aspiration, steadfast upward desire, longing.

1584 *Copie of Letter* 46 Neither is this arte of aspiring new or straunge. **1633** P. FLETCHER *Purple Isl.* VI. v, To lackey one of these is all my prides aspiring. **1783** W. F. MARTYN *Geog. Mag.* II. 55 Frozen regions . . might naturally be supposed to damp the aspirings of genius. **1821** SOUTHEY *Vis. Judgem.* xi. Wks. X. 238 Here were the gallant youths of high heroic aspiring.

†**2.** The upward tapering of a spire, etc. *Obs. rare.*

1634 SIR T. HERBERT *Trav.* 211 (T.) Nor are those so fastidious in pyramidical aspirings, nor curious in architecture . . as in many lesser towns.

a'spiring, *ppl. a.* [f. as prec. + -ING².]

1. Ardently desirous of advancement or distinction; of lofty aim, ambitious.

1577 tr. *Bullinger's Decades* (1592) 154 We which are not of that aspiring mind. **1679** *Establ. Test.* 5 Having little left of all their aspiring Graspings after Empire. **1756** BURKE *Vind. Nat. Soc.* Wks. 1842 I. 12 Even virtue is dangerous, as an aspiring quality, that claims an esteem . . independent of the countenance of the court. **1849** MACAULAY *Hist. Eng.* I. 408 Two able and aspiring prelates.

2. Rising, tapering upward, soaring.

c **1565** T. ROBINSON *Mary Mag.* 416 Beheld th' asp[i]ringe tower of vaine delight. **1669** WORLIDGE *Syst. Agric.* (1681) 135 It is usual to select aspiring Trees. **1718** POPE *Iliad* XII. 368 To sure destruction dooms the aspiring wall. **1810** SOUTHEY *Kehama* XIX. v, Wks. VIII. 160 Upward, to reach its head, For myriad years the aspiring Brama soar'd.

b. *fig.* (with some sense of 1 combined.)

1579 SPENSER *Sheph. Cal.* Oct. 84 Then make thee winges of thine aspyring wit. **1665–9** BOYLE *Occas. Refl.* (1675) 48 The devout Reflector cannot take an occasion of an aspiring Meditation; as in a hopeful morning the humble Lark can.

a'spiringly, *adv.* [f. prec. + -LY².] In an aspiring manner; ambitiously.

1627 G. WATTS tr. *Bacon's Adv. Learn.* Pref. (1640) 17 We may not be too aspiringly wise. **1863** MRS. C. CLARKE *Shaks. Char.* xix. 481 Aufidius is aspiringly self-seeking.

a'spiringness. [f. as prec. + -NESS.] Aspiring quality, ambitiousness.

1859 in WORCESTER. *a* **1866** J. GROTE *Exam. Util. Phil.* vi. 112 The aspiringness or upward tendency of human nature.

aspish (ˈɑːspɪʃ, æ-), *a.* [f. ASP² + -ISH.] Of or pertaining to asps; snaky.

1608 TOPSELL *Serpents* 632 Wicked gain . . Which Lybian deaths and aspish wares have brought into our lands. **1630** J. TAYLOR (Water P.) *Water Cormor.* Wks. III. 6/2 With Aspish poyson poysoning men.

asplenium, *Bot.*: see SPLEENWORT.

asport (æˈspɔət), *v.* [ad. L. *asportā-re*, f. *as-* = *abs-* = *ab-* away + *portā-re* to carry.] To carry away, remove feloniously.

1621 MOLLE *Camerar. Liv. Libr.* Pref., [Which] he used to asport and make his owne. **1882** *Blackw. Mag.* Nov. 622 Imagery asported not appropriated, seized but unassimilated.

asportation (æspɔːˈteɪʃən). [ad. L. *asportātiōn-em*, n. of action f. *asportāre*: see prec. and -ATION.] The action of carrying off; in *Law*, felonious removal of property (see quot. 1768).

1502 ARNOLD *Chron.* (1811) 175 Suche asportacion or awey-berynge. **1654** *Addr.* in *Sibbes' Heavenly Conf.* Wks. 1863 VI. 416 She dreams of a bodily asportation . . of Christ. **1768** BLACKSTONE *Comm.* IV. 231 A bare removal from the place in which he found the goods, though the thief does not quite make off with them, is a sufficient asportation. **1889** F. W. MAITLAND *Coll. Papers* (1911) II. 173 The imaginary defendant is charged . . with the asportation of all that is asportable. **1890** *Harper's Mag.* Oct. 702/1 If the silver . . could be deposited . . in bars too heavy for asportation.

†**a'sposit,** *ppl. a. Sc. Obs.* [by some confusion for *disposit*, DISPOSED.] In phr. *ill asposit*: **a.** evil-disposed; **b.** indisposed, ill.

1535 STEWART *Cron. Scot.* II. 541 Thair is in this kinrik ȝe ken, Rycht mony ill . . asposit men. *Ibid.* III. 215 Quhilk in his bed richt evill asposit la.

a-spout (əˈspaʊt), *advb. phr.* [A *prep.*¹ + SPOUT *v.*] On the spout, spouting.

1870 *Daily News* 17 May, [It] has its fountains aspout.

a-sprawl (əˈsprɔːl), *advb. phr.* [A *prep.*[1] + SPRAWL.] In a sprawling posture, sprawling.

1878 R. JEFFERIES *Gamekeeper at H.* 157 He throws himself all a-sprawl upon the ground. **1880** —— *Gt. Estate* 73 Dropping a-sprawl.

aspray, obs. form of OSPREY.

a-spread (əˈsprɛd), *advb. phr.* [A *prep.*[1] + SPREAD *v.*] Spread out, spread abroad.

1879 BROWNING *Ned Bratts* 162 His brown hair burst a-spread. **1881** *Academy* 3 Sept. 184/1 She threw up both hands, with the thumbs and fingers all aspread.

asprete, obs. form of ASPERITY.

†**a'spring**, *v. Obs.* For forms see SPRING *v.* [OE. *aspringan*, f. A- *pref.* 1 + *springan* to SPRING.]

1. To spring up, leap.

c **1315** SHOREHAM 120 Ine joye he gan to asprynge.

2. To spring forth, spread abroad.

c **1000** ÆLFRIC *Gen.* vii. 11 þa asprungon ealle wyllspringas. **1175** *Cott. Hom.* 227 þa asprang þis ȝedwéld ofer all middenard.

3. To spring into existence, originate, arise.

c **1000** ÆLFRIC *Hom.* (Sweet 83) Ða asprungon ȝedwolmenn on Godes ȝelaþunge. *c* **1175** *Cott. Hom.* 227 Of þan asprang þet eberisce folc. *c* **1485** *Digby Myst.* III. 1173 þis kenred is a-sprongyn late. Loo, mastyrs, of swyche a stokke he cam.

a-sprout (əˈspraʊt), *advb. phr.* [A *prep.*[1] + SPROUT *v.*] In a sprouting condition, sprouting.

1880 BROWNING *Dram. Idyls, Doctor* 79 Nip these foolish fronds of hope a-sprout.

†**a'spy**, *sb. Obs.* [a. AF. **aspie* = OF. *espie* SPY. The prevalent spelling of both sb. and vb. in early ME.; in 15th c. *espy*, after Fr., came into common use.] = SPY *sb.*

1297 R. GLOUC. 557 Hii adde gode aspies, hou hii hom þo bere. **1380** *Sir Ferumb.* 5232 To þe Amerel þe aspye aȝen is went. **1382** WYCLIF *Prov.* xi. 6 Wicked men in ther aspies shal be take. **1467** MARG. PASTON *Lett.* 576 II. 308 He.. sendyth dayly aspies to understand what felesshepe kepe the place.

†**a'spy**, *v. Obs.* [a. AF. **aspie-r* = OF. *espier*, mod. *épier*, to ESPY: see prec.] = ESPY *v.*

c **1230** *Ancr. R.* 196 Iðe wildernesse heo aspieden us to slean. *c* **1420** *Pallad. on Husb.*, Where the swarmes dwell is crafte to aspie. **1536** BELLENDENE *Cron. Scot.* II. 102 He was aspyit makand derision.

aspying, -ly, etc.: see ESPYING, -LY.

aspylede (Shoreham): see SPILE *v.*

a-square (əˈskwɛə(r)), *advb. phr.* [perh. A *prep.*[1] + SQUARE.] On the square; aloof, at a safe distance.

c **1400** *Beryn* 586 Hym had been better to have goon more a-sware. *Ibid.* 596 That herd the pardoner wele, and held him better a square. *Ibid.* 643 The Pardonere.. held him [right] a square, by þat othir syde.

a-squat (əˈskwɒt), *advb. phr.* [A *prep.*[1] + SQUAT.] In a squatting posture, squatting.

1748 RICHARDSON *Clarissa* (1811) I. xvi. 101 There was the odious Solmes sitting asquat between my mother and my sister. *c* **1784** *Rolliad* Ded. (1799) 18 Where wisdom sits a-squat in starch disguise. **1863** BROWNING *Sordello* I. Wks. III. 273 Crawl in then hag, and crouch asquat.

asquint (əˈskwɪnt), *adv.* (and *a.*) Forms: 3– asquint, 4 a squynte, 5 asquynt, 7 a squint. [Of uncertain origin; apparently f. A *prep.*[1] and a word corresponding to Du. *schuinte* 'slope, slant,' of the independent use of which no instances survive; the later *squint* adv. and adj. being an aphetic form of *asquint*, and *squint* vb. and sb. still later derivatives of this. Evidence is wanting to determine whether the original word was actually adopted from Dutch, or was a cognate word, unrecorded in OE.; the total absence of any related words in OE. (or ON.) makes the latter improbable.]

A. *adv.*

I. With *look* or a synonymous verb.

* Of voluntary turning of the eyes.

1. (To look) to one side instead of straight forward; obliquely, out at the corners of the eyes.

c **1230** *Ancr. R.* 212 Auh winckeð oðere half, & biholdeð o luft & asquint. **1594** BLUNDEVIL *Exerc.* v. 560 Looking somewhat asquint. **1611** DEKKER *Roar. Girle* Wks. 1873 III. 200 Didst neuer see an archer.. looke a squint when he drew his bow? **1679** EVERARD *Pop. Plot* 11 Who looking on me a-squint, went down the Privy Stairs. **1822** HAZLITT *Table T.* I. x. 217 He does not survey the objects of nature as they are in themselves, but lookes asquint at them.

b. *transf.* of things.

1642 FULLER *Holy & Prof. State* III. vii. 168 Let not the front look asquint on a stranger, but accost him right at his entrance. **1657** B. I. *Heroic Educ.* in *N. & Q.* 19 June 1880, 492 Sweden is a country on which the sun does not look asquint.

c. *fig.* of mental vision.

1601 CORNWALLYES *Ess.* II. xxviii, To look a squint, our hand looking one way and our heart another. **1639** SALTMARSH *Pract. Policie* 81 Be not too fixt nor intent upon what is before you.. but looke asquint into your considerations and about you.

2. With reference to various mental attitudes, of which averted, oblique, sidelong, or furtive glances are the outward expression: *arch.* (To look)

a. with distrust, suspicion; jealously, askance.

1413 LYDG. *Pylgr. Sowle* II. xiv. 51 Thou somtyme ar this mettist with enuye, that loked asquynt. **1670** COTTON *Espernon* II. VI. 252 The envy of many of the greatest men.. who had long look'd a squint upon the Duke's Prosperity. **1729** SAVAGE *Wanderer* III. 229 Envy asquint the future wonder eyes.

b. with unfairness, with prejudice or partiality.

1605 B. JONSON *Volp.* Ded., Men will impartially, and not asquint, look toward the Office and Function of a Poet. **1655** GURNALL *Chr. in Arm.* I. 376 O Sirs, do we think that Christ's love looks asquint? doth he pray for one child more than another?

c. with an eye drawn aside by interest.

1627 SANDERSON *Serm.* I. 270 His heart even then hankered after the wages of unrighteousness when he looked asquint upon Balaaks liberal offer. **1678** *Trial Coleman* in Howell *St. Trials* (1816) VII. 12 He had a little too much eye to the reward; he looked too much a-squint upon the matter of money.

d. with furtive or stolen glances.

1725 POPE *Odyss.* XIX. 82 In ambush here to lurk by night, Into the woman-state asquint to pry. **1845** CARLYLE *Cromwell* (1871) III. 228 Peering asquint into the Holy of Holies.

†**3.** To cast a passing glance; *fig.* to make incidental reference. *Obs.*

a **1638** MEDE *Apost. Later Times* (1641) 33 [Nothing] may so much as look asquint upon any other object, or behold any other face but the face of God alone. **1650** BULWER *Anthropomet.* xxii. 250 Others.. have lookt asquint upon the Body of Woman.

†**b.** *fig.* To glance unfavourably or adversely; to reflect unfavourably *upon*. *Obs.*

1658 OSBORN *Adv. to Son* (1673) 239 Uncharitable Censures.. against any judgement looking a squint upon theirs.

** Of habitual obliquity of vision.

4. *esp.* (To look) obliquely through defect in the eyes, to have the axes of the eyes not coincident, so that they look in different directions; to squint.

1398 TREVISA *Barth. De P.R.* VI. iv. (1495) 191 A place that is to bryghte.. ofte makyth chyldren to loke a squynte. **1540** RAYNALD *Birth Man* III. iii. (1634) 185 Of Goggle-eyes, or looking a-squint. **1657** COLVIL *Whigs Supplic.* (1751) 20 His other eye look'd so asquint, That it was hard to ward his dint. **1675** HOBBES *Homer* 21 Lame of one leg he was; and looked asquint. **1763** CHURCHILL *Rosciad* Poems (1769) I. 20 Doth a man stutter, look a-squint, or halt? *a* **1849** POE *Loss of Breath* Wks. 1864 IV. 305 The looking asquint—the showing my teeth.

b. *fig.* and *transf.* of things.

c **1744** SWIFT *Wks.* 1841 II. 73 Rather than suffer his learning to look asquint as it does, and make so frightful a figure from the press. **1881** BLACKIE *Lay Serm.* i. 31 The beer-toper.. finding the moon looking somewhat asquint, the houses all nodding.

c. *fig.* of mental vision: (To look) awry, so as to miss seeing or see distortedly.

1616 W. FORDE *Serm.* 35 If old, wee looke a squint, and see not death before our eyes. **1643** SIR T. BROWNE *Relig. Med.* 7 Those vulgar heads that look asquint on the face of Truth.

II. With other verbs. *rare.*

5. Off to one side; obliquely. ? *Obs.*

1645 MILTON *Tetrach.* Wks. 1851, 203 Whether is common sense flown asquint. **1651** CLEVELAND *Rupert.* 13 Could I thus write asquint, then Sir long since You had been sung a Great and Glorious Prince.

B. quasi-*adj.* (Only in pred. or after the sb. *eye.*)

1643 *Answ. W. Bridges' Observ. War* 1 As if every eye were asquint. *c* **1661** *Argyle's Last Will* in *Harl. Misc.* (1746) VIII. 29/1 His Eyes very much a-squint, so that he was nicknamed, in Scotland, *Gleed Argyle*. *a* **1764** R. LLOYD *Prog. Envy* Wks. 1774 I. 139 A ghastly grin and eyes asquint. **1876** EMERSON *Ess.* Ser. I. iv. 126 The eye is muddy and sometimes asquint.

a-squirm (əˈskwɜːm), *advb. phr.* [A *prep.*[1] + SQUIRM *v.*] On the squirm, squirming, writhing or wriggling. (*U.S.*)

1866 HOWELLS *Venet. Life* 257 Gigantic eels writhing everywhere set the soul asquirm.

Asquithian (æˈskwɪθɪən), *a.* and *sb.* [f. the name of H. H. *Asquith* (afterwards Earl of Oxford and Asquith), prime minister of Great Britain 1908–16 + -IAN.] **A.** *adj.* Pertaining to, resembling, or supporting Asquith as leader of the Liberal party or, later, as leader of a group of the divided party. **B.** *sb.* A supporter of Asquith.

1910 *Spectator* 2 Apr. 530/1 The Asquithian Peers will, we venture to say, prove the most intractable of 'backwoodsmen'. **1928** *Daily Express* 24 Apr. 3/3 Montague .. belonged to the central Asquithian group in the Cabinet, .. and as an Asquithian he preferred to support McKenna rather than Lloyd George. **1928** H. FYFE *Brit. Liberal Party* viii. 229 Liberals were still at loggerheads. Asquithians and Lloyd Georgians fought against each other. **1960** *Spectator* 14 Oct. 553 An old-fashioned Asquithian Liberal.

ass (æs), *sb.*[1] Forms: 1–2 assa, 2–8 asse, 3– ass (3–5 as, 3 has, 4–5 a nasse). Pl. 4– asses: 1 assan, 2–4 assen, 3–4 asse (*southern*). [OE. *assa* m. has no exact analogue in the cognate langs. OE. had also *ęsol*, app. for *ęsel*, *ęsil*, the common Teut. form, = OS. and OHG. *esil* (mod.G. *esel*, Du. *ezel*), Goth. *asilus*, like the Celtic and Slav. names (OIrish *asal*, Lith. *asilas*, OSlav. *osl*:—**osilu-*) evidently ad. L. *asinus*. From the Celtic was the Old Northumbrian *asal*, *assal*, *assald*, the only form in Lindisf. Gospels (occurs 10 times). Of the latter, *assa* was perh. a diminutive, formed like the dim. proper names *Ceadda*, *Ælla*, *Offa*, etc., which at length displaced the earlier *ęsol*. *Assa* had also fem. *assen*, on the type of *fyxen*, *wylfen*, *ælfen*, which did not survive into ME., where *he-asse*, *she-asse*, occur already in Wyclif. *Jack ass*, *Jenny-ass* are modern familiar appellations.

The reputed OE. fem. *asse* seems to be an error founded on *assan folan* in which *ass* is no more fem. than are *lion*, *tiger*, in *lion's whelp*, *tiger's cub*. The ON. *asna* f., *asni* m. appear to be independent late adaptations of L. *asina*, *asinus*, not actually connected with the OE. The Celtic, Teut., and Slavonic can hardly have been independent adoptions of the L.: the Slav. was apparently taken through Teutonic: was the latter through Celtic? The Ass had no original Aryan name: L. *asinus*, Gr. ὄνος (? = ὄσνος), were prob. of Semitic origin: cf. Heb. *āthōn*, she-ass.]

1. a. A well-known quadruped of the horse kind, distinguished from the horse by its smaller size, long ears, tuft at end of tail, and black stripe across the shoulders. Found wild in western and southwestern Asia, where it has been used from the earliest ages as a beast of burden, and whence, in later times, it appears to have been introduced as a domestic animal into Europe.

(In familiar use, the name *ass* is now to a great extent superseded by *donkey* (in Scotland *cuddie*); but *ass* is always used in the language of Scripture, Natural History, proverb, and fable; also, in ordinary use, in Ireland.)

c **1000** ÆLFRIC *Numb.* xxii. 23 Se assa ȝeseah ðone engel. *c* **1000** *Ags. Gosp.* Matt. xxi. 2 Sona finde ȝyt ane assene ȝetiȝȝede, and hyre folan mid hyre. —— John xii. 15 Uppan assan folan sittende. *c* **1175** *Lamb. Hom.* 3 Heo nomen þe asse and here colt. **1297** R. GLOUC. 404 Hii ete Her hors.. and hassen ar hii lete. *c* **1325** *Cœur de L.* 6453 Fyftene hundryd asse Bar wyn and oyle. *a* **1300** *Cursor M.* 3152 þe child he kest a-pon an ass. *Ibid.* 6156 Sheepe ne cow ox ne as. *a* **1300** *E.E. Psalter* civ. 11 Wilde asses in þar þrist sal abide. **1382** WYCLIF *Gen.* xlv. 23 Ten hee assis.. and as feele she assis [**1388** Ten male assis.. and so many femal assis]. *c* **1386** CHAUCER *Wife's Prol.* 285 Assen, oxen, and houndes. *c* **1400** *Apol. Loll.* 97 þe oxe knowiþ his weldar, and þe as þe crib of his lord. **1601** SHAKS. *Jul. C.* IV. i. 21 He shall but beare them, as the Asse beares Gold. **1617** F. MORYSON *Itin.* III. I. iii. 49 A Traveller to Rome must have the backe of an Asse, the belly of a Hogge, and a conscience as broad as the Kings highway. **1620** VENNER *Via Recta* v. 87 Asses milke appertaineth rather vnto physicke then vnto meat. **1739** T. SHERIDAN *Persius* i. 23 As the World goes, who has not Asses Ears? **1760** WESLEY *Wks.* (1872) III. 9 Procuring a fresh horse, about the size of a jackass, I rode on. **1782** COWPER *Gilpin* li, While he spoke, a braying ass Did sing most loud and clear.

b. *fig.* 'Beast of burden.'

1614 RALEIGH *Hist. World* II. v. iii. §1. 359 He.. makes himself.. an Asse; and thereby teacheth others, either how to ride, or driue him. **1635** PAGITT *Christianogr.* 237 This Kingdome.. usually stiled the popes Asse, which hee rode at his pleasure, til she was able to beare him no longer.

c. The ass has, since the time of the Greeks, figured in fables and proverbs as the type of clumsiness, ignorance, and stupidity; hence many phrases and proverbial expressions. (Chiefly since 1500; the early references to the animal being mostly Scriptural, with no depreciatory associations.)

c **1200** ORMIN 3714 Mannkinn.. skillæs swa summ asse. *c* **1400** *Apol. Loll.* 57 Wan an vndiscret is maad bischop in þe kirk, þan is an hornid asse born þer in. **1590** NASHE *Anat. Absurd.* E j b, That which thou knowest not peraduenture thy Asse can tell thee. **1599** THYNNE *Animadv.* (1875) 5 Wrangle for one asses shadow, or to seke a knott in a rushe. **1607** TOPSELL *Four-f. Beasts* 21 A dull Scholar not apt to learn, is bid to sell an Asse to signifie his blockishness. **1611** COTGR. s.v. *Asne*, As angrie as an Asse with a squib in his breech. **1620** SHELTON *Quix.* III. xxviii. 201 Well, well, the Honey is not for the Ass's mouth. *Ibid.* xxxv. 254 An Ass laden with Gold will go lightly up hill. **1622** MIDDLETON & ROWLEY *Old Law* III. i, Asses have ears as well as pitchers. **1653** URQUHART *Rabelais* I. xi, He.. would act the Asses part to get some bran. **1711** ADDISON *Spect.* No. 13 ¶4 The ill-natured world might call him the Ass in the Lion's Skin. **1868** FREEMAN *Norm. Conq.* II. viii. 277 An unlettered king is a crowned ass.

d. *to make an ass of*: to treat as an ass, stultify. *to make an ass of oneself*: to behave absurdly, stultify oneself.

1590 SHAKS. *Mids. N.* III. i. 124 This is to make an asse of me, to fright me, if they could. **1865** TROLLOPE *Belton Est.* xx. 241 Don't make such an ass of yourself as to suppose that, etc. **1866** *Fraser's Mag.* 284/1 They could not be deprived of the common right of Englishmen to make asses of themselves if they liked it.

e. *Asses' Bridge* or *Pons Asinorum*: a humorous name now given to the fifth proposition of the first book of Euclid's Elements.

c **1780** *Epigram*, If this be rightly called the bridge of asses, He's not the fool that sticks, but he that passes. **1860** *All Y. Round* 560 He never crossed the ass's bridge.

2. Hence *transf.* as a term of reproach: An ignorant fellow, a perverse fool, a conceited dolt. Now disused in polite literature and speech.

1578 LYTE *Dodoens* 348 Landleapers, roges, and ignorant asses. **1598** SHAKS. *Merry W.* I. i. 176, I am not altogether an asse. **1621** BURTON *Anat. Mel.* II. iii. II. (1651) 316 A nobleman..a proud fool, an arrant asse. **1717** POPE *Let. Hon. R. Digby* Wks. 1737 VI. 73 They think our Doctors asses to them. **1828** SCOTT *F.M. Perth* I. 39, I am but an ass in the trick of bringing about such discourse. **1843** LEVER *J. Hinton* iv. (1878) 25 Lord Dudley de Vere, the most confounded puppy, and the emptiest ass.

3. *Astr.* The ***Two Asses***: the stars γ and δ of the constellation Cancer, on either side of the nebula *Præsepe* (the *Crib*).

1556 RECORDE *Cast. Knowl.* 266 Other two starres are called the Asses whiche seeme to stande at the Crybbe. **1607** TOPSELL *Four-f. Beasts* 17 The two Asses, placed there as some say, by Bacchus.

4. *Paper Manuf.* (The relationship of the form *asp*, also used, is unexplained.) A donkey-rest (see DONKEY 3 b).

a **1875** KNIGHT *Dict. Mech.* I. 170/2 *Ass*, a post in the bridge of a pulp-vat to lay the mold upon while the water drains from it. Used in the hand-made paper work. **1927** *World's Paper Trade Rev.* 24 June 2002/2 *Ass*, the wooden strut against which the vatman places the mould for a moment to drain, shaped like a bow. **1947** D. HUNTER *Papermaking* (ed. 2) vi. 178 The coucher placed the mould ..against the inclined drainage-horn, or 'asp', which allowed the surplus water to drain back into the vat. *Ibid.* xv. 437 The coucher..leans the mould against the asp or horn at the proper angle.

5. *Comb.* **a.** General relations: (*a*) appositive, as ***ass beast***; (*b*) possessive genitive, as ***ass bone, ear, flesh, hoof, stall*** (where *ass's* would now be usual), ***ass colour***; (*c*) objective genitive, as ***ass-driver, -keeper***; (*d*) attrib. as ***ass argument*** (*i.e.* asinine); (*e*) parasynthetic deriv. as ***ass-coloured, ass-eared***.

c **1375** WYCLIF *Serm.* xcviii, Sel. Wks. 1869 I. 345 þanne mai we telle scorne by sich *asse argumentis. *a* **1300** *Cursor M.* 14963 þar sal yee find an *asse beist. *Ibid.* 7171 Hefand an *assban. **1607** TOPSELL *Four-f. Beasts* 356 This Beast..is of a Mouse or *Ass colour. **1658** ROWLAND *Mouffet's Theat. Ins.* 1048 A little creature with many feet, *Asse-coloured. **1564** BAULDWIN *Mor. Phil.* (Palfr.) i. (1595) 19 Till they perceived captaines of armies to be *asse-drivers. **1672** DAVENANT *Law agst. Lovers* (1673) 309 Have her *Ass-ears in publick bor'd, as Love's Known Slave. **1629** SYMMER *Spir. Posie* To Reader A iij b, Some *asse-ear'd Midas will misconstrue these words. **1831** CARLYLE *Misc.* (1857) II. 224 Not overloaded with *Ass-eared giants. **1822** T. MITCHELL *Aristophanes* I. 190 *Ass-flesh, as food, is far preferable to beef and even to veal. **1601** HOLLAND *Pliny* II. 338 To strew vpon them the ashes of an *asse-hoofe. **1591** PERCIVALL *Sp. Dict.*, *Asnero*, an *Asse keeper. *c* **1400** *Epiph.* (Turnb. 1843) 140 Lyyng in a *nasse stall, *Invenerunt puerum.*

b. Special combinations: **ass-back**, like *horseback*, in later times humorously; **ass-cart**, a cart drawn by an ass; **ass-colt** or **-foal**, the young of an ass; **ass-herd**, a keeper of asses; **ass-like** *a.*, like an ass, asinine; **ass-man**, a driver or letter out of asses; **assmanship, asswomanship**, humorously after *horse manship*; **ass-mare**, a she-ass; **ass-mill**, one driven by an ass; **ass-parsley**, obs. name of some umbelliferous plant; **ass-ship**, condition or quality of an ass; humorously after *lordship*; **ass-woman**, female of ass-man. Also ASS-HEAD, -HEADED q.v.

1377 LANGL. *P. Pl.* XVIII. 11 Barfote on an *asse bakke. **1766** SMOLLETT *Trav.* 42 The way of riding most used in this place is on *assback. **1800** SOUTHEY in C. Southey *Life* II. 109 Edith and myself on *ass-back. **1821** *Blackw. Mag.* Apr. 412/2 They met the country people coming in—some in horse-carts, others in *ass-carts. **1902** YEATS *Where there is Nothing* (1903) II, A little kennel of straw under the ass-cart. **1587** GOLDING *De Mornay* xxx. 481 Tying his *Assecolt [COVERDALE, asses colte] to the vyne, and the foale of his sheeasse to the hedge. *a* **1617** HIERON *Wks.* II. 166 In his birth he is but like a wild *asse-colt. **1595** HUNNIS *Life Joseph* 72 He shall bind his *Asse fole fast vnto the pleasant vine. *c* **1450** *Gloss.* in Wright *Voc.* 213 *Hic asinarius*, a *nashard. **1652** GAULE *Magastrom.* 351 Quoth the *asse-herd, the lot means another, and not me. **1567** DRANT *Horace Epist.* I. xiii. E iij, Least thou *asslyke unloden the with greater note of cryme. **1581** SIDNEY *Def. Poesie* (Arb.) 59 They would make an *Ass-like braying against Poesie. **1770** G. WHITE *Selborne* xxviii. 79 The head was about twenty inches long, and *ass-like. *a* **1500** *MS. Bodl.* 565 (Halliw.) And ye most ȝeve yowre *asman curtesy a grot other a grosset of Venyse. **1859** *N. & Q.* Ser. II. VIII. 17 Of ..this *assman, as he was called, I have an anciently engraved copper-plate card. **1882** *Punch* 24 June, They witch the world with noble *assmanship. **1598** BARCKLEY *Felic. Man* II. (1603) 88 Who rode..uppon a silly *asse-mare. **1591** PERCIVALL *Sp. Dict.*, *Atahona*, an *Asse mill. **1611** COTGR., *Cicutaire*, mock Chervill, wild Chervill, great Chervill, *Asse Perseley. **1610** HEALEY *St. Aug., City of God* 694 Yet had he his humane reason still, as Apuleus had in his *asse-ship. **1729** T. COOKE *Tales, Prop. &c.* 87 Ended thus his *Assship's Reign. **1728** *Daily Post* 7 July, The famous Stoke Newington *Ass-woman dares me to fight her for the 10 pounds. **1800** SOUTHEY *Lett.* (1856) I. 119 Edith has made a great proficiency in *asswomanship.

ass, *sb.*[2] Now chiefly *U.S.* [vulgar and dial. sp. and pronunc. of ARSE.]

1. a. = ARSE *sb.* 1 a.

(Webster 1961 'often considered vulgar'.)

1860 H. STUART *Seaman's Catech.* 37 The ass of the block is known by the scoring being deeper in that part to receive the splice. [Cf. **1721** BAILEY, *Arse*, (among sailors) the Arse of a Block or Pulley, through which any Rope runs, is the lower end of it.] **1930** J. DOS PASSOS *42nd Parallel* I. 100 My ass to habeas corpus. **1934** J. O'HARA *Appointment in Samarra* (U.S. ed., 1953) iv. 119 You give me a pain in the ass. **1949** 'N. BLAKE' *Head of Traveller* ii. 37 Put it to rights in two shakes of a cat's ass, you would. **1959** W. GOLDING *Free Fall* iv. 96 You sit on your fat ass in your 'ouse all the week. **1967** *Observer* 8 Oct. 31/2 All our trousers are designed to fit round the ass and not sag at the crutch.

b. Sexual gratification. Also, a woman or women, regarded as an object affording this.

1942, etc. [see *piece of ass* s.v. PIECE *sb.* 3 d]. **1960** J. UPDIKE *Rabbit, Run* (1961) 163 Then he comes back from the Army and all he cares about is chasing ass. **1970** R. D. ABRAHAMS *Positively Black* ii. 47 When we got upstairs I threw her on the floor I was anxious to get some ass off that frantic whore. **1976** N. THORNBURG *Cutter & Bone* i. 14 It made him almost wish he was sixteen again,..embarking on that long road of teenage ass. **1986** P. BOOTH *Palm Beach* iii. 77 Word is there's more ass up in the North End on the weekends than Heinz has varieties.

2. ***one's ass***: one's self or person. Usu. with *get* and an advb. (phr.), as a synonym for 'go'. Freq. as second element in contemptuous expressions, as *poor-*, *punk-*, *sad-ass* (see under first element). See also JIVE-ASS, SMART-ARSE, -ASS *a.* and *sb.*

1958 G. LEA *Somewhere there's Music* xxi. 180 If I knew it'd kill my ass, I'd follow. **1968** W. LABOV et al. in A. Dundes *Mother Wit* (1973) 337 Don't worry while they got your ass up there Breakin' up rocks like a grizzly bear. **1972** *Language* XLVIII. 914 Get your ass in here, Harry! The party's started! **1975** *Toronto Star* 27 Sept. B5/4, I protested at being told to 'get your ass home'. **1978** J. CARROLL *Mortal Friends* I. ii. 19 'Collins'll be off in America,' he bellowed, 'giving speeches while kids at football get their asses shot!'

3. Phrases. **a.** ***to kiss*** (a person's) ***ass***: see KISS *v.* 6 l; also ***to lick*** (a person's) ***ass*** in the same sense.

1973 C. MULLARD *Black Britain* II. iv. 44 We were treated like filth, not good enough to lick their asses. **1975** *Maclean's Mag.* Feb. 40/3 The guys who are returning to work are rookies. They're in there ass-licking. But when we get back, if they want to lick asses, they'll be licking our asses.

b. Used casually in various phrases as an intensifier, esp. to indicate strength of feeling, action, etc.: ***to work*** (***run***, etc.) ***one's ass off***; ***to chew ass***, to reprimand severely; ***to tear ass***, to move fast, to hurry.

1946 T. BELL *There comes Time* ix. 57 Here's a smart apple like you working your ass off for a lousy forty bucks a week. **1946** *Amer. Speech* XXI. 198 *Chew ass*, reprimand severely. **1949** H. ROBBINS *Dream Merchants* vii. 199 'Come on, kid,' he said. 'Let's break their asses!' And then he was running zig-zag across the field. **1954** *Amer. Speech* XXIX. 103 *Tear ass*, to drive fast or recklessly. **1958** J. BARTH *End of Road* (1962) xi. 196 I've run my ass off today getting it set up. **1970** R. D. ABRAHAMS *Positively Black* iii. 67 So John packed up his bags and tore ass the next day. **1973** *Black Panther* 17 Nov. 7/4 Maybe if he saw it, some pig might..get his ass chewed. **1976** *National Observer* (U.S.) 20 Mar. 11/2 You work your ass off for years so the kid can get a college education. **1984** *Melody Maker* 6 Oct. 13/2 You want to.. retire to your bedroom and practise your ass off for a year till you become competent enough to try it.

c. ***up your ass***: an exclamation of contemptuous rejection (often used *imp.*). Similarly in various descriptive phrases (see quots.). Cf. STICK *v.*[1] 18 d and UP *adv.*[2] 3 b.

1965 N. MAILER *Amer. Dream* i. 15 'Ain't you got any consideration?' he asked. 'Up your ass, friend.' **1970** R. D. ABRAHAMS *Positively Black* ii. 26 I'd 'a told that white motherfucker to fly up his own ass! **1971** A. HAILEY *Wheels* ii. 28 You can stuff a surrender flag up your ass and wave goodbye to any discipline around this place from this day on.

4. Special Combinations. **asshole**, (*a*) = *arse-hole* s.v. ARSE *sb.* 3; (*b*) someone or something foolish or contemptible; an uncompromising term of abuse; also *attrib.*; **ass-kissing** *ppl. a.* and *vbl. sb.*, toadying, flattering; hence [as back-formation] **ass-kiss** *v. trans.*, to flatter, truckle to; **ass-kisser**, one who does this; **ass-licker**, a toady; hence [as back-formation] **ass-lick** *v. intr.*

1935 DYLAN THOMAS *Let.* July (1966) 159 The best socialists suck all they can from the jaundiced *ass-hole of an anti-socialist state. **1948** *Amer. Speech* XXIII. 319 *Ass hole buddy*, comrade-in-arms. **1962** J. BALDWIN *Another Country* I. ii. 111 Of course, he's an asshole too. **1977** J. D. MACDONALD *Condominium* xxiv. 208 'What did you call me?' McGinnity demanded. Branhammer studied him and said distinctly, 'I called you an ass hole, you ass hole! I don't trust one of you overeducated ass holes sitting there in a goddam row.' **1981** R. SCHOENSTEIN et al. *I-Hate-Preppies Handbk.* 20 Two distinct kinds of Nerds are indigenous to America today: the asshole with a high IQ and the asshole with a low one. **1974** A. LURIE *War between Tates* xii. 195 It is bad enough to hear Jeffrey..call his teacher an '*ass-kissing idiot'. **1977** *Rolling Stone* 16 June 6/4 Glossy fringe publishing, T-shirt peddling and political ass kissing. **1978** S. BRILL *Teamsters* i. 28 He had to watch the ass-kissers court Fitzsimmons. **1984** S. BELLOW *Him with his Foot in his Mouth* 128 If it could have been done by ass-kissing his patrons and patronesses, B. B. would have dried away a good many tears. **1939** H. MILLER *Tropic of Capricorn* 18 Besides, I wasn't a good *ass-licker. **1970** R. LOWELL *Notebk.* 218 Not ass-licking for medals on the peacock lawn.

ass, *v. nonce-wd.* [f. ASS *sb.*[1]; but for sense 2, cf. ARSE *v.*]

1. *trans.* To call ass. **2.** *intr.* To act the ass. Now freq. in (orig. schoolboys') *slang*: to fool *about*.

1592 G. HARVEY *Pierces Superer.* 57 He..bourdeth, girdeth, asseth the excellentest writers of whatsoever note that tickle not his wanton sense. **1647** WARD *Simp. Cobler* (1843) 52 To keep their Kings from devillizing and themselves from Assing. **1899** KIPLING *Stalky* vii. 196 Don't mind learnin' my drill, but I'm not goin' to ass about the country with a toy Snider. **1932** A. J. WORRALL *Eng. Idioms for Foreign Students* 1 Those boys are not working; they are just assing about. *Ibid.*, Don't ass about with that valve, you'll break it.

assady: see ARSEDINE.

assafœtida, variant of ASAFŒTIDA.

assagai, assegai (ˈæsəgaɪ), *sb.* Forms: 6 **azagaia**, 7 **assagaie**, 8 **hassagay, -guay**, 9 **assagai, -gay, assegai, -gay**; also 7–8 **zagaie, zagaye**. [a. F. *azagaye* (Cotgr.), or Pg. *azagaia*, Sp. *azagaya*, a. Arab. *az-zaghāyah*, i.e. *az-* = *al-* the, *zaghāyah* native Berber word, adopted in Arabic, and thence in Sp. and Pg.; adopted from the Portuguese in Africa by the English and French. The proper spelling is *assagai*, but *assegai* was universal in the newspapers in 1879. Formerly also ZAGAIE, as still in Fr.; and in ME. ARCHEGAYE, q.v.]

A kind of slender spear or lance of hard wood, usually pointed with iron, used in battle. Originally, the native name of a Berber weapon adopted by the Moors; but extended by the Portuguese to the light javelins of African savages generally, and most commonly applied by Englishmen to the missile weapons of the South African tribes.

1625 PURCHAS *Pilgrims* II 969 They of Myna or the Golden Coast, their armes are Pikes, or Assagaies, Bowes, and Arrowes. **1773** MASSON in *Phil. Trans.* LXVI. 296 They were all armed with hassaguays. **1776** *Ibid.* 295 Being all armed with hassagays, they often throw twenty or thirty.. at once. **1789** BELSHAM *Ess.* I. 489 *note*, Their zagaye, or half-pike, is very well forged. **1811** SCOTT *Roderick* Concl. xv, Sharper than Polish pike or assagay. **1834** PRINGLE *Afr. Sk.* xii. 365 The Bushmen retain the ancient arms of the Hottentot race..a light javelin or assagai. **1859** R. BURTON in *Jrnl. R.G.S.* XXIX. 136 The spears and assegais. **1879** LD. STRAT. DE REDCLIFFE in *Times* 29 Mar., They shake the dreaded assegai.

b. *attrib.* **assagai tree, wood**, a large South African tree (*Curtisia faginea*, N.O. *Cornaceæ*).

1866 *Treas. Bot.* 363 The natives employ it to form shafts for their javelins or Assagays: hence the common name Assagay Tree. **1879** *Times* 5 Apr., No less than thirty-seven assegai wounds. **1880** 'SILVER & CO.' *S. Africa* (ed. 3) 127 In these kloofs grow..the Assegay wood.

'assagai, asse-, *v.* [f. prec.] To pierce with an assagai.

1836 *Editor Grahamstown Jrnl.'s Nar.* 185 (Pettman), When only a few yards from the village..he was assegaied. **1863** W. C. BALDWIN *Afr. Hunting* iii. 71 A Kaffir who had threatened to assagai one of Walmsley's Kaffirs. **1879** T. LUCAS *Zulus & Brit. Front.* xiii. 275 Killing six Fingoes and assegaing a colonist. **1880** MISS COLENSO *Zulu War* 413 They were nearly all assegaied.

‖**assai** (assaːˈi), *adv. Mus.* [It. = enough, very; cogn. with Fr. *assez*:—L. *ad satis* = *ad* to, up to, *satis* enough.] A direction equivalent to 'very,' as in *adagio assai* = very slow.

assaie, -er, -or, obs. forms of ASSAY, etc.

assaige, variant of ASSIEGE *v. Obs.* to besiege.

assail (əˈseɪl), *v.*[1] Forms: 3 **assailȝe, asale**, 3–4 **asayle**, 3–5 **asaile**, 4 **a-sayle, a-saile**, 4–5 **assaille, -aylle, -ale**, 4–7 **assaile, -ayle**, 5 **assaylle, asayl**, 6– **assail**; (*Sc.* 4–5 **assalȝe**, 4–6 **assailȝe, -ȝie**). *Aphet.* 4 **saile**, 4–5 **sayle**. [a. OFr. *asalir, asaillir* (mod. *assaillir*):—late pop. L. *adsalīre* (in Salic Law), f. *ad* to, at + *salīre* to leap, spring, an analytical form substituted for its cl. L. equivalent *ad-, as-silīre*. In 14–15th c. often aphetized to *sail(e*; in the full form refashioned with *ass-*, in Fr. and Eng., in 15th c. Certain uses seem to have been influenced by contact with the vb. ASSAY 'to try, tempt': see senses 9–13 below.] To leap upon or at, esp. with hostile intent; hence in most of its senses exactly synonymous with *attack*.

†**1.** *lit.* To leap upon, 'mount.' (So F. *assaillir*.)

1387 TREVISA *Higden* Rolls Ser. III. 179 He hadde mynde of þe mare þat he had assailed [*equæ suppositæ*].

2. To make a violent hostile attack upon by physical means, to assault (a person, stronghold, etc.).

c **1230** *Ancr. R.* 62 Hwile þat me mit quarreaus wiðuten asaileð þene castel. **1297** R. GLOUC. 394 Hii bygonne..þen toun asayl. *a* **1300** *Havelok* 1861 þe laddes..Him asayleden wit grete dintes. *c* **1314** *Guy Warw.* 1435 Than came Saddok prykande The dewke Segwyn saylande. **1375** BARBOUR *Bruce* III. 151 Wes nane..That durst assailȝe him mar in fycht. *c* **1450** LONELICH *Grail* xii. 359 That ȝate assailled ne myhte not ben. **1513** DOUGLAS *Æneis* IX. ii. 17 Gif thai assailȝeit wer..be hard fortoun of weyr. **1671** MILTON *Samson* 1165 No worthy match For valour to assail. **1713** STEELE *Englishm.* No. 12. 77 It is for the Vulgar to assail one another like brute Beasts. **1876** GREEN *Short Hist.* i. §2. 15 This district was assailed at once from the north and from the south.

3. To attack (institutions, customs, opinions, etc.) with hostile action or influence.

1564 BAULDWIN *Mor. Phil.* (Palfr.) vii. §2 They that be evill..beare..armour offensive to assayle the good manners of others. **1634** MILTON *Comus* 589 Virtue may be assail'd, but never hurt. **1844** BROUGHAM *Brit. Const.* xvii. (1862) 252 Choosing to assail the religion of the people before he had destroyed their liberty.

4. To attack with hostile, opprobrious, or bitter words; to speak or write directly against.

1593 SHAKS. *3 Hen. VI*, I. i. 65 Here in the Parliament Let vs assayle the Family of Yorke. *a* **1744** POPE *On Duke of Buckhm's. Verses* 3 Let crowds of Critics now my verse assail. **1855** PRESCOTT *Philip II*, I. II. vii. 222 Assailing the fallen minister with libels and caricatures.

5. To attack with reasoning or argument; to address with the object of prevailing upon, persuading, convincing, or controverting.

c **1440** *Morte Arth.* (Roxb.) 86 The kynge the messyngere thus dyd assayle: 'It were pite to sette warre vs bytwene.' **1602** SHAKS. *Ham.* I. i. 31 Let vs once againe assaile your eares That are so fortified against our story. **1695** BLACKMORE *Pr. Arth.* I. 43 Nor did his Arts in vain weak man assail. **1791** T. JEFFERSON *Writ.* (1859) III. 232 They would assail us on the subject of the treaty. **1833** HT. MARTINEAU *Manch. Strike* x. 114 She assailed her husband on the subject of taking work.

6. To approach (anything arduous or difficult) with the intention of mastering it.

a **1680** BUTLER *Rem.* (1759) V. 3 The lofty Tube, the Scale With which they Heav'n itself assail, Was mounted full against the Moon. **1725** POPE *Odyss.* XIX. 508 The thorny wilds the woodmen fierce assail. **1860** TYNDALL *Glac.* I. §25. 182 Assailing the rocks at their base, and climbing them to the cabin.

7. Of things: To come roughly against, so as to batter, injure, or hurt; to dash against, encounter.

1667 MILTON *P.L.* x. 417 And [Chaos] with rebounding surge the barrs assaild, That scorn'd his indignation. *a* **1800** COWPER *Watching with God* ii, No rude noise mine ears assailing. **1860** TYNDALL *Glac.* I. §3. 31 We were assailed by a violent hailstorm.

8. *fig.* Of states physical, emotional, or mental: To come upon with tendency to master or overcome; to invade, attack.

1340 HAMPOLE *Pr. Consc.* 2330 When þe ded assaylles a man. **1377** LANGL. *P. Pl.* B. II. 96 Til slepe hem assaille. *c* **1430** *Syr Generides* 1694 Ther had he rest but small, So loue assaled him ouerall. **1595** SHAKS. *John* v. vii. 9 That fell poison which assayleth him. **1697** DRYDEN *Æneid* III. (R.) New pangs of mortal fear our minds assail. **1807** CRABBE *Par. Reg.* II. 136 Compassion first assailed her gentle heart. **1837** NEWMAN *Par. Serm.* I. xix. 291 When doubt and unbelief assail us.

†**9.** To attack with temptations; to tempt, try.

c **1220** *Hali Meid.* 47 þu ne schalt beon icrunet bute þu beo assailȝet. **1340** *Ayenb.* 249 He [the devil] asaylede þane uerste man be þe mouþe. **1483** CAXTON *G. de la Tour* F iij b, Grete and euylle temptacions shall befight and assaylle yow. *a* **1564** BECON *New Catech.* Wks. (1844) 190 But doth God assail sinners only with this temptation of adversity?

†**10.** To address with offers of love, to woo. *Obs.*

c **1600** SHAKS. *Sonn.* xli, Beauteous thou art, therefore to be assail'd. **1601** —— *Twel. N.* I. iii. 60 Accost, is, front her, boord her, woe her, assayle her. **1611** —— *Cymb.* II. iii. 44, I haue assayl'd her with Musickes.

11. *absol.* quasi-*intr.* in prec. senses. (With quot. 1440 cf. OF. 'pour assaillir aux trois portes.' Littré.)

1297 R. GLOUC. 395 As noble men, hii asaylede euere vaste. **1375** BARBOUR *Bruce* IX. 31 Gif thai assalȝe, we mon defend. **1440** *Partonope* 6579 Thre to hym sayled of the rowte And held on his helme. **1594** SHAKS. *Lucr.* 63 When shame assail'd, the red should fence the white. **1779** J. NEWTON *Olney Hymns* vii, Though troubles assail, and dangers affright.

†**12.** To make trial of, venture on, ASSAY. *Obs.*

1393 GOWER *Conf.* I. 247 The souldan hath the feld assailed. *a* **1440** *Sir Degrev.* 1075 Ther was non so hardy That durst asayl the cry. **1595** MARKHAM *Sir R. Grinuile* xcviii, None darring to assayle a second fight.

†**13.** *intr.* **a.** with *inf.* To attempt, endeavour, ASSAY. *Obs.*

1393 GOWER *Conf.* III. 45 With nigromaunce he wolde assaile To make his incantacion. **1592** tr. *Junius' Comm. Rev.* xx. 1 Satan assayled to invade the Christian Church. **1606** G. W[OODCOCKE] *Hist. Justine* 122 b, Hee assailed to steale home into his kingdome.

†**b.** with *subord. cl.* To try, put to the test. *Obs.*

1536 BELLENDENE *Cron. Scotl.* (1821) I. 20 Delite ye ony further to assailye, gif ony band may be kepit with unfaithful pepill?

†**a'ssail**, *v.*[2] *Obs.* [f. *as-* for A- *pref.* 11 + SAIL *v.*] To sail. (But possibly an absol. use of ASSAIL *v.*[1] 12 'to venture.')

c **1384** CHAUCER *H. Fame* I. 434 (Bodley& Fairfax MSS.) Thoo sawgh I grave [= pictured] how that to Itayle Daun Eneas is goo for to assayle [*Caxt.* saylle, *Thynne* sayle]. **1482** WARKW. *Chron.* 26 And rode into Scottlande, and frome thens into Fraunce assailed.

assail (ə'seɪl), *sb. arch.* Forms: 4 **assale**, 5 **assall**, 6 **assailȝe**, 7 **assaile**, 6– **assail**. [orig. prob. a. OF. *assaille*. f. *assaillir* to ASSAIL; in later use referred to the Eng. vb.] Assault, attack.

1375 BARBOUR *Bruce* IX. 350 The toun wes hard to ta Vith oppyn assale. **1552** LYNDESAY *Monarche* 3980 Duryng the tyme of this assailȝe. **1603** P. HOLLAND *Plutarch's Mor.* 1269 Cities forced by assaile. **1768** B. THORNTON *Batt. Whigs* iii. 4 Rous'd from his torpor joins in fierce assail. **1813** J. HOGG *Queen's Wake* 261 As oft recoiled from flank assail.

assailable (ə'seɪləb(ə)l), *a.* [f. ASSAIL *v.*[1] + -ABLE]

1. Capable of being assailed; open to assault.

1605 SHAKS. *Macb.* III. ii. 39 There's comfort yet; they are assaileable. **1673** *Ladies Call.* I. ii. §4 To fortifie that so assailable part [the ear]. **1860** TYNDALL *Glac.* I. §20 We.. wound round the ledges, seeking the assailable points.

2. Open to hostile criticism.

1833 I. TAYLOR *Fanat.* viii. 320 *note*, Had his orthodoxy been assailable. **1883** *Law Times* 15 Dec. 116/2 Driven to admit that the adverse decision of the court is assailable.

†**a'ssailableness.** [f. prec. + -NESS.] The quality of being assailable; openness to attack.

1870 D. SIMON *Dorner's Pers. Christ* II. II. 241 They demonstrated..the assailableness of the Lutheran view.

assailant (ə'seɪlənt), *a.* and *sb.* Also 6–7 **assaylant**, **-aunt**. [a. F. *assaillant*. pr. pple. (also used subst.) of *assaillir*: see ASSAIL *v.* and -ANT.]

A. *adj.* Assailing, attacking, actively hostile. *arch.*

1592 WYRLEY *Armorie* 138 Assailant conqueror, this brave English king. **1671** MILTON *Samson* 1693 And as an ev'ning Dragon came, Assailant on the perched roosts. **1855** H. REED *Lect. Eng. Lit.* viii. (1878) 258 Such offensive, assailant unbelief as Gibbon's and Hume's.

B. *sb.*

1. He who, or that which, assails or attacks.

c **1532** LD. BERNERS *Huon* (1883) 339 Y[e] assaylauntes were fayne parforce to recule backe. **1600** SHAKS. *A.Y.L.* I. iii. 116 So shall we passe along, And neuer stir assailants. **1665** MANLEY *Grotius' Low-C. Wars* 487 They threw down Stones upon the Assaylants heads. **1777** JOHNSON *Pope* Wks. IV. 90 His most frequent assailant was the headach. **1839** KEIGHTLEY *Hist. Eng.* I. 341 His guards rescued him and slew all the assailants.

†**b.** *spec.* One who challenged another to wager of battle; one who accepted the defiance of a champion to combat in the lists. *Obs.*

1586 FERNE *Blaz. Gentrie* 315 Because he is the assailaunt ..it lyeth in his choyce, to take eyther a ciuill or martiall tryall. **1611** COTGR. s.v. *Preux*, The first time he presents himselfe, as an assailant, in the Lists. **1627** *Lisander & Cal.* IX. 180 Spurring against the assailants, and the assailants against them.

2. A hostile critic, controversial opponent.

1665 GLANVILL *Sceps. Sci.* Introd. 1 My Assailant takes the Liberty to recede from my Style. *a* **1764** R. LLOYD *Poet. Wks.* 1774 II. 150 Rome's fierce assailant. **1843** MILL *Logic* III. ix. 6 The assailants of the syllogism had also anticipated Dr. Whewell.

assailer (ə'seɪlə(r)). Forms: 4–6 **assailyeour**, **-ȝeour**, **-your**, 5 **assailour**, 6 **assayler**, 7– **assailer**. [a. OF. *assailleor*, *-eur*, n. of agent f. *assaillir*: see ASSAIL *v.* and -ER.] One who assails, an assailant.

1375 BARBOUR *Bruce* II. 541 Quhar the assailyeours [*v.r.* assailyours, -ȝeis] all Entryt and dystroyit the tour. **1475** *Bk. Noblesse* (1860) 5 They bring assailours uppon this lande. **1580** SIDNEY *Arcadia* (1622) 181 Palladius so pursued our assaylers. **1672** JACOMB *Comm. Rom.* viii. (1868) 117 If the town..yields upon the first summons, it is a sign that the assailers are very strong. **1877** MRS. OLIPHANT *Mak. Flor.* vi. 155 A besieging king or other potent assailer.

assailing (ə'seɪlɪŋ), *vbl. sb.* [f. ASSAIL *v.* + -ING[1].] The action of attacking, assault.

1340 *Ayenb.* 117 Wy ne moȝe naȝt..þolye þe asaylinges of þe dyeule. *c* **1425** WYNTOUN *Cron.* VIII. xxvi. 333 Wyth stout and manlyk assaylyng. **1598** BARRET *Theor. Warres* v. ii. 131 By a long and gallant assailing, it fall at last into the enemies hands. **1630** NAUNTON *Fragm. Reg.* (Arb.) 36 Why she should then admit him to private discourse..considering the condition of all assailings..was a piece of reach and hazard beyond my apprehension. **1815** LAMB *Life & Lett.* x. (1840) 96 Jove..tottering with the giant assailings.

a'ssailing, *ppl. a.* [f. as prec. + -ING[2].] That assails; attacking, assaulting.

1592 WYRLEY *Armorie* 41 We warely batteled..Th' assayling tempter. **1592** SHAKS. *Rom. & Jul.* I. i. 219 Nor bid [*v.r.* bide] th' incounter of assailing eyes. **1795** SOUTHEY *Joan of Arc* VIII. 195 Glacidas his eye Cast on the assailing host.

assailment (ə'seɪlmənt). [a. OF. *assaillement*: see ASSAIL *v.* and -MENT.]

1. The action of assailing; an assault, attack.

1592 WYRLEY *Armorie* 141 These three..cheefest praise at this assailment had. **1614** R. TAILOR *Hog hath lost Pearl* in Dodsl. *O.P.* (1780) VI. 412 Tortur'd by the weak assailments Of earth-sprung griefs. **1836** *For. Q. Rev.* XVII. 406 The progress of his constant couple through their various assailments.

2. Power or faculty of assailing.

1812 T. JEFFERSON *Writ.* (1859) IV. 182 They may strengthen Canada..beyond the assailment of our lax and divided powers.

†**a'ssale.** *Obs. rare*[−1]. In 6 **assayle**. [f. A- *pref.* 11 + SALE; or perh. for *a sale*.] Sale.

1566 DRANT *Horace Sat.* I. ii. A viij b, He..doth make assayle Of landes, and lordshippe wyde.

assalt, obs. form of ASSAULT.

†**assalve**, *v. Obs. rare*[−1]. [f. A- *pref.* 11 + SALVE *v.*] To salve.

1570 *Galf. & Bern.* (Halliw.), I seeke for to assalve my sore.

Assam (æ'sæm). The name of a state in north-eastern India, used *attrib.* or *absol.* to designate any of several varieties of tea grown there.

1842 *Penny Cycl.* XXIV. 285/1 The Assam tea-plant.. has lately attracted..much attention. **1878** E. MONEY *Cultiv. & Manuf. Tea* (ed. 3) 182 The sterner sex preferring Assam unmixed, while the working classes of both sexes are unanimous in favour of the unadulterated Indian article. **1887** *Rep. Col. Sect. Colonial & Indian Exhib. 1886* vi. 151 The tea known in commerce as 'Assam' is grown in that portion of the Province of Assam which lies in the valley of the Brahmapootra. **1892** [see PEKOE *v.*] *c* **1938** *Fortnum & Mason Price List* 6 Blend of choice Assam, Dooars, Ceylon and Darjeeling. **1974** *Encycl. Brit. Macropædia* XVIII. 17/1 The weight of 2,000 freshly plucked China bush shoots may be one pound..; the same number of Assam shoots may weigh two pounds. **1986** *Financial Times* 23 Apr. I. 36/1 Assams were generally strong with selected lines 'substantially dearer'.

assamar ('æsəmɑː(r)). *Chem.* [mod. f. L. *assus* roast + *amār-us* bitter.] 'Name given by Reichenbach to the peculiar bitter substance produced when gum, sugar, starch, gluten, meat, bread, etc. are roasted in the air till they turn brown.' Watts *Dict. Chem.* 1863.

Assamese (æsə'miːz), *a.* and *sb.* [f. the name of the Indian State *Assam* + -ESE.] **A.** *adj.* Of or pertaining to Assam or its inhabitants. **B.** *sb.* **1.** A native of Assam. **2.** The language of Assam.

1826 J. CONDER *Mod. Traveller* XI. 245 The Assamese came out of their hiding-places. *Ibid.* 246 The poverty of their native soil, and the fertility of the plains of Assam, induced the Sing-fos to settle in the plains, which they cultivated by means of Assamese captives. **1836** *Jrnl. Asiatic Soc.* V. 195 A great deal of opium is grown by the Miris, which they barter for grain with the Assamese. **1837** *Ibid.* VI. 18 Their [*sc.* the priests'] vernacular and common dialect, as well as that of the people, is *Assámese*. **1875** *Encycl. Brit.* II. 718/1 Aurangzeb..despatched a considerable force for the..invasion of the Assamese territory. *Ibid.* 721/1 The vernacular Assamese possesses a close affinity to Bengali. **1961** *Times* 18 May 12/4 The hill leaders were firmly opposed to Assamese as the official language of the state.

assapanick. *Zool.* (See quot.)

1706 PHILLIPS, *Assapanick*, a flying Squirrel, a little creature, peculiar to Virginia and Maryland. **1791** SMELLIE *Buffon's Nat. Hist.* V. 308 Called Assapanick by the Virginian Indians, and flying squirrel by the English.

assart (ə'sɑːt), *v. Law.* Also 6–7 **assert**. [a. AF. *assarter*, *-ier*, *-ir* (Britton), OF. *essarter*:—late L. *exsartāre*, *exartāre* (in Burgundian Laws), f. *ex* out + **sartāre*, freq. of *sar(r)īre*, ppl. stem *sarrīt-*, *sarīt-*, *sart-* (in derivatives, *sartio*, *sartūra*, etc.) to hoe, weed. There was an Eng. Law L. *assartāre*, f. AFr.] To grub up trees and bushes from forest-land, so as to make it arable. Also *absol.*

[**1276** *Act 4 Edw. I*, i. §4 De parcis et dominicis boscis quæ dominus ad voluntatem suam poterit assartare et excolere. (For transl. see 1876.)] **1523** FITZHERB. *Surv.* 4 b, Demeyne woode..whiche at the lordes wyll may be asserted and plucked vp. **1598** MANWOOD *Lawes Forest* ix. §1. (1615) 67/1 Whereas woods or thickets or any other land is assarted, that land cannot grow againe to become couerts. **1723** ASHMOLE *Antiq. Berks.* II. 425 The King granted to him..Power to assart his Lands. **1837** HOWITT *Rur. Life* v. i. (1862) 362 That none shall assart in the forest without being taken before the verderer. **1876** DIGBY *Real Prop.* iv. §1. 180 Parks and demesne woods which the lord may assart and improve at his pleasure.

assart (ə'sɑːt), *sb. Law.* [a. AF. *assart*, OF. *essart*:—late L. *exartum* = **exsartum*, pa. pple. (sc. *arvum* land) of **exsar(r)īre*, f. *ex* out + *sar(r)īre* to hoe, weed: see prec. The sb. might also have been formed in Fr. directly on the vb. (cf. *regarder*, *regard*), whence probably sense 2 arose. See also ESSART, after Fr., used by modern historians.]

1. A piece of forest land converted into arable by grubbing up the trees and brushwood; a clearing in a forest.

1628 COKE *On Litt.* 10 a, If an assart bee granted by the King. **1738** *Hist. Crt. Excheq.* v. 87 The Profit of the County was likewise increased by Arentations of Assarts. **1766** BARRINGTON *Anc. Stat.* (1796) 36 *note*, Assarts are places where the wood has been grubbed up.

2. The action of grubbing up the trees and bushes in a forest, so as to turn it into arable land.

1598 MANWOOD *Lawes Forest* ix. §1. (1615) 67/1 An Assart, is the plucking up of those woods by the rootes that are thickets or couerts of the Forest, to make the same a plaine or arrable land. *a* **1625** COPE in Gutch *Coll. Cur.* I. 123 Lately revived by your Majesty's Commission of Assarts. **1880** J. WILLIAMS *Rights of Common* 231 No person having lands within a forest could plough up any part of his lands which had not been ploughed up before, and to do so was considered a grievous offence and was called an assart.

3. *attrib.*

1670 [see next]. **1863** WISE *New Forest* iv. 43 James I. granted no less than twenty assart lands.

†**a'ssartment.** *Law. Obs.* [f. ASSART *v.* + -MENT.] = ASSART *sb.*

1670 BLOUNT *Law Dict.*, Assart-Rents, Were Rents paid to the Crown, for Forest Lands assarted. Assartments seems to be used in the same sence.

'assary. [ad. Gr. ἀσσάριον, or L. *assārius* = *as*: see AS *sb.*] A Roman copper coin, translated by 'farthing' in *Matt.* x. 29. (Commonly used in L. or Gr. form.)

1727 MATHER *Yng. Man's Comp.* 242 An *Assary*, or *Farthing*, Half-penny Farthing. **1872** O. W. HOLMES *Poet Breakf. T.* iii. 93, I have no change, says he, but this assarion of Diocletian.

assassin (ə'sæsɪn). Also 7 **assassine, -asin(e, -acine.** [a. F. *assassin*, or ad. It. *assassino*: cf. also Pr. *assassin*, Pg. *assassino*, Sp. *asesino*, med.L. *assassīnus* (OF. forms were *assacin, asescin, asisim, hasisin, hassissin, haussasin*, etc.; med.L. (pl.) *assessini, ascisini*, etc.), ad. Arab. *ḥashshāshīn* and *ḥashīshiyyīn*, pl. of *ḥashshāsh* and *ḥashīshiyy*, lit. 'a hashish-eater, one addicted to hashish,' both forms being applied in Arabic to the Ismā'īli sectarians, who used to intoxicate themselves with hashish or hemp, when preparing to dispatch some king or public man. The OF. variants, (pl.) *assacis, hassisis, haississis*, med.L. *assasi, haussasi*, med.Gr. χασίσιοι, point to the Arabic singular, but the form finally established in the European languages arises from the Arab. plural, as in *Bedouin*; cf. also It. *cherubino, serafino*, F. and earlier Eng. *cherubin, seraphin* (sing.). Naturally the plural was first in use, in the historical sense, and occurred in Eng. in the Lat. or It. form before *assassin* was naturalized: the latter was still accented '*assassin* by Oldham in 1679.]

1. *lit.* A hashish-eater. *Hist.* (in *pl.*) Certain Moslem fanatics in the time of the Crusades, who were sent forth by their sheikh, the 'Old Man of the Mountains,' to murder the Christian leaders.

[*c* **1237** R. WENDOVER *Flores Hist.* (1841) II. II. 246 Hos tam Saraceni quam Christiani Assisinos appellant.] **1603** KNOLLES *Hist. Turks* (1638) 120 This messenger..was..one of the Assasines, a company of most desperat and dangerous men among the Mahometans. **1611** SPEED *Hist. Gt. Brit.* IX. x. 5 That bloudy Sect of Sarazens, called Assassini, who, without feare of torments, vndertake..the murther of any eminent Prince, impugning their irreligion. *c* **1860** J. WOLFF, The assassins, who are otherwise called the People of the Man of the Mountain, before they attacked an enemy, would intoxicate themselves with a powder made of hemp-leaves, out of which they prepared an inebriating electuary, called *hashish*.

2. Hence: One who undertakes to put another to death by treacherous violence. The term retains so much of its original application as to be used chiefly of the murderer of a public personage, who is generally hired or devoted to the deed, and aims purely at the death of his victim.

[*a* **1259** M. PARIS *Angl. Hist. Maj.* (1589) 459 Qui tandem confessus est, se missum illuc, vt Regem more assessinorum occideret, à VVillielmo de Marisco.] **1531** *Dial. Laws Eng.* II. xli. (1638) 133 Hee is an Ascisinus [*printed* Ascismus] that will slay men for money at the instance of every man that will move him to it, and such a man may lawfully be slaine..by every private person. **1621** BURTON *Anat. Mel.* I. iii. I. iii, Men of all others fit to be assassins. **1679** OLDHAM *Sat. Jesuits* (1686) 7 Think on that matchless Assassin, whose name We with just pride can make our happy claim. **1702** ROWE *Tamerlane* III. i. 1330 When bold Assassines take thy Name upon 'em. **1778** WOLCOTT (P. Pindar) *To Reviewers* Wks. 1812 I. 5 That stabbed like brave assassins in the dark. **1855** MACAULAY *Hist. Eng.* IV. xxi. 668 Barclay's assassins were hunted like wolves by the whole population.

3. *fig.* or *transf.*

1736 THOMSON *Liberty* v. 385 The hir'd assassins of the Commonweal. **1824** DIBDIN *Libr. Comp.* 744 Lord Byron was the assassin of his own fame.

4. *attrib.* and in *comb.*, as ***assassin-like***; **assassin bug**, a predaceous insect of the family Reduviidæ.

1895 J. H. & A. B. COMSTOCK *Man. Stud. Insects* xiv. 137 Family Reduviidæ..There are many bugs which destroy their fellows, but the members of this family are so pre-eminently predaceous that we call them the Assassin-bugs. **1937** *Discovery* Dec. 368/2 A..cheerful brute occurs in North America, where it is known as the 'big bed bug' and the assassin bug. **1667** MILTON *P.L.* XI. 219 Who, to surprize One man, Assassin-like, had levied Warr, Warr unproclam'd. *a* **1846** B. R. HAYDON *Autobiogr.* (1927) vii. 104 On this principle I have acted in not making the assassins so assassin-like as perhaps they were. **1847** DISRAELI *Tancred* IV. ix. (1871) 305 He caught in his hand the assassin spear.

†**a'ssassin(e,** *v. Obs.* [a. F. *assassine-r* (16th c.), f. *assassin*: see prec.] To assassinate.

1670 MILTON *Hist. Eng.* Wks. 1738 II. 60 Cuichelm..sent privily Eumerus a hir'd Sword-man to assassin him. **1680** *Spir. Popery* 67 Mr. Mitchel..when he attempted to Assassin the Lord Primate. **1788** COWPER *Mrs. Throckm. Bullfinch* i, Assassin'd by a thief.

b. *fig.*

1647 WHARTON *Irel. War* Wks. 1683, 263 Attempt to Assassine the Honour of a whole Nation with his Invectives. **1675** HOWE *Living Temp.* Wks. 1834, 42/1 To assassine his own intellectual faculty.

†**a'ssassinacy.** *Obs.* [f. ASSASSINATE: cf. *conspiracy, confederacy*; see -ACY.] Assassination.

1611 G. H. *Anti-Coton* 48 To see the Iesuites..the (very) morning after this abhominable assassinacie, looking with a smiling and presumptuous countenance. *a* **1660** HAMMOND *Wks.* I. 470 (R.) This spiritual assassinacy..most satanically designed on souls.

†**a'ssassinant.** *Obs.* [a. F. *assassinant*, pr. pple. of *assassiner*: see above.] An assassin.

1655 GURNALL *Chr. in Arm.* xxvii. §1. (1669) 326/1 Some Assassinants (intending to stab a Prince).

†**a'ssassinate,** *sb. Obs.* Also 7 **assassinat, -asinate, -acinate.** [In sense 1, app. a. F. *assassinat* (16th c.), ad. med.L. *assassīnātus* (13th c. in Du Cange), f. med.L. (and It.) *assassīnāre* to assassinate. Of its use in sense 2, = ASSASSIN, no explanation appears; we may suspect some original misapprehension of the word, or perh. application of the analogy of *homicide, parricide*, etc.]

1. Murder, or an assault with intent to murder, by treacherous violence; assassination.

1602 S. PATERICKE tr. *Gentillet's Agst. Machiavell* 228 All murders, massacres, and assassinates, are alwaies found done to a good end. **1636** FEATLY *Clavis Myst.* v. 54 The bloudy assacinate of the Earl of Gowrie. **1671** *True Non-Conf.* 406 There can be no proper assassinat, without an intervening price. **1755** CARTE *Hist. Eng.* IV. 195 Following him to Portsmouth..he committed the assassinate on his person.

b. *fig.*

1672 MARVELL *Reh. Transp.* I. 187 Who commit these Assassinats upon the reputation of deserving persons.

2. = ASSASSIN 2.

1600 HOLLAND *Livy* II. xiii. 40 Nothing had saved him but the mistake of the Assassinate. **1621** BURTON *Anat. Mel.* I. ii. IV. vi. 159 Poverty alone makes men theeves, rebels, murderers, traitors, assacinates. **1676** W. ROW *Suppl. Blair's Autobiog.* xii. (1848) 519 Search out the villain, the assassinate. **1737** G. SMITH *Cur. Relat.* I. iii. 483 To raise the Number of Assassinates to three Hundred; then to fall upon the Magistrates.

b. *fig.* = ASSASSIN 3.

a **1659** CLEVELAND *Gen. Poems* (1677) 60 Scribling Assassinate!..Cub of the Blatant Beast. **1695** *Whether Parl. dissolved by Death Pr. Orange* 6 Those Miscreants, and Assassinates of their Country.

assassinate (ə'sæsɪneɪt), *v.* [f. *assassīnāt-* ppl. stem of med.L. *assassīnāre* = It. *assassinare*, F. *assassiner*, f. the sb.: see ASSASSIN and -ATE.]

1. a. *trans.* To kill by treacherous violence.

1618 BOLTON *Florus* IV. ii. 292 Brutus and Cassius..conspired to assassinate him. **1775** HARRIS *Philos. Arrangem.* (1841) 339 Cæsar, when he was assassinated, fell at the feet of Pompey's statue. **1813** SOUTHEY *Nelson* iii. 65 He was assassinated by some wretches set on..by Genoa.

b. *absol.*

1678 BUTLER *Hud.* III. II. 1022 To defend was to invade, And to assassinate to aid. **1803** MACKINTOSH *Def. Peltier* Wks. 1846 III. 274 The most learned incitement to assassinate that ever was addressed to such ignorant ruffians.

†**2.** *trans.* To endeavour to kill by treacherous violence; to attack by an assassin. *Obs.*

1683 *Apol. Prot. France* vi. 77 William of Orange was twice Assassinated, and lost his Life the Second time. **1706** DE FOE *Jure Div.* I. 19 Charles the Ninth carress'd the Admiral Coligni..Visited him when he had been Wounded, and Assassinated.

3. *fig.* To destroy or wound by treachery; to 'stab' reputation, etc. (Cf. MURDER *v.* 2.)

1626 MASSINGER *Rom. Actor* II. i, Sufficient For thee that dost assassinate my soul. **1683** DRYDEN *Dk. Guise* v. (R.) Your rhimes assassinate our fame. **1850** WHIPPLE *Ess. & Rev.* I. 378 After his death they tried to assassinate his name. **1920** WODEHOUSE *Damsel in Distress* ix. 115 The same feeling which a composer with an over-sensitive ear would suffer on hearing his pet opus assassinated by a school-girl. **1962** *Guardian* 15 Nov. 3/1 Helping the Prime Minister in his political battle to assassinate Mr. George Brown.

a'ssassinating, *ppl. a.* [f. ASSASSINATE *v.* + -ING[2].] That assassinates, murdering.

1682 *Lond. Gaz.* No. 1736/3 That Assassinating association. **1797** HOLCROFT tr. *Stolberg's Trav.* xci. (ed. 2) IV. 201 The assassinating sword of the Romans.

assassination (əˌsæsɪ'neɪʃən). [n. of action f. ASSASSINATE (or its L. or F. original): see -TION. Fr. has *assassinat.*] The action of assassinating; the taking the life of any one by treacherous violence, esp. by a hired emissary, or one who has taken upon him to execute the deed.

1605 SHAKS. *Macb.* I. vii. 2 If th' Assassination Could trammell vp the Consequence, and catch With his surcease, Successe. *a* **1674** CLARENDON *Hist. Reb.* I. I. 22 The Duke finished his course, by a wicked Assassination. **1855** MACAULAY *Hist. Eng.* IV. xxi. 660 The English regard assassination..with a loathing peculiar to themselves.

b. *fig.* Cf. 'killing.'

1800 FOSTER in *Life & Corr.* (1846) I. 136 Company is assembled for the assassination of time.

assassinative (ə'sæsɪneɪtɪv), *a. rare.* [f. ASSASSINATE *v.* + -IVE.] Disposed to assassinate, murderously inclined.

1845 CARLYLE *Cromwell* (1871) IV. 239 Assassinative truculent-flunky head in steeple-hat worn brown.

assassinator (ə'sæsɪneɪtə(r)). [n. of agent f. ASSASSINATE, on L. analogies; cf. 16th c. F. *assassinateur.*] One who assassinates; an assassin.

1676 BATES *Immort. Soul* xii. (R.) The assassinators of kings. **1704** *Lond. Gaz.* No. 4029/3 Looked upon..as Assassinators.

assassinatress (ə'sæsɪneɪtrɪs). [f. prec. + -ESS.] A female assassin.

1869 OUIDA *Puck* xxix. 360 She, the Faustine, the Assassinatress, the Hell-born.

†**a'ssassinay.** *Obs.* [? ad. F. **assassinée* ppl. sb., or mispr. for *assassinacy.*] Assassination.

a **1641** BP. MOUNTAGU *Acts & Mon.* v. §7. 320 This villanous assassinay by Bassus committed upon his kinsman.

†**a'ssassinist.** *Obs. rare*[−1]. [f. ASSASSIN + -IST.] An advocate of assassination.

1612 T. JAMES *Jesuits Downf.* 6 Bloudy garboyles and cruelties is threatned to all nations by these Assassinists.

†**a'ssassinment.** *Obs. rare.* [a. 16th c. F. *assassinement* (= It. *assassinamento*), f. *assassiner*; see ASSASSIN *v.*] Assassination.

1577 S. PATERICKE *Gentillet's Agst. Machiavel* (1602) 228 A palliation or coverture, for all assassi[n]ments, murders, and vengeances.

†**a'ssassinous,** *a. Obs.* [f. ASSASSIN + -OUS. (No equivalent form is recorded in F. or It.)] Of the nature of assassins; murderous.

1623 in COCKERAM. **1648** MILTON *Observ. Art. Peace* Wks. 1851, 566 To murder them in the basest and most assassinous manner.

†**'assate,** *v. Obs. rare*[−1]. [f. L. *assāt-* ppl. stem of *assāre* to roast.] To roast.

1657 TOMLINSON *Renou's Disp.* 602 Tragacanthum and Arabick should be assated before commixtion.

assation (æ'seɪʃən). ? *Obs.* [a. F. *assation* (16th c.), n. of action f. L. *assāre* to roast, f. *assus* roast.] Roasting or baking.

1605 TIMME *Quersit.* I. x. 40 Mercuriall spirites..do vanish away by their assation. **1650** SIR T. BROWNE *Pseud. Ep.* (ed. 2) 151 In the assation or roasting, it [an egg] will sometimes abate a dragme. **1727–51** CHAMBERS *Cycl.*, *Assation*, in respect of culinary matters, is more frequently called *roasting*. **1815** T. PEACOCK *Headlong Hall* 66 The malignant adhibition of fire and all its diabolical processes of elixion and assation.

†**'assature.** *Obs.*[−0] [ad. L. *assātūra* roast meat, f. *assāre*: see prec. and -URE.] 'A roast or roasted meat.' Bailey 1731.

assault (ə'sɔːlt), *sb.* Forms: 3 **asaȝt,** 3–7 **asaut, assaut,** 4 **asauȝt,** 4–6 **asaute, asawt(e, assalt,** 5 **a sawt(e, a-saute,** 5–6 **assaute, -awte,** 6 **a saute, a saulte,** 5– **assault.** [a. OF. *asaut* (later *assaut*), cf. Pr. *assalt*, It. *assalto*, Sp. *asalto*:—late pop. L. **adsaltus*, f. the simple *saltus* leap, which took the place of its L. equivalent *ad-, assultus*, deriv. of *adsilīre*, when the latter gave place to the analytical *ad-salīre*: see ASSAIL. The original *asaut* was altered (with an eye to the Latin), *c* 1530, to *assault*. Already in 13th c. aphetized to *saut*, whence in 16th c. SAULT q.v.]

1. a. *gen.* An onset or rush upon any one with hostile intent; an attack with blows or weapons.

1297 R. GLOUC. 380 Vor trauayl of þe foul asaȝt. *c* **1314** *Guy Warw.* 74 Thou schalt gif the first asaut Opon the Almaundes. **1382** WYCLIF *Acts* xix. 29 Thei maden a sawt..in to the teatre. *c* **1400** *Destr. Troy* XXVI. 10271 A folke þat was fell, fuerse of assaute. **1591** SHAKS. *1 Hen. VI*, IV. i. 24 In which assault, we lost twelue hundred men. **1611** BIBLE *1 Macc.* iv. 8 Neither be ye afraid of their assault. **1877** LYTTEIL *Landm.* III. i. 101 To guard the shores of Gaul against the assaults of these northern buccaneers.

b. *spec.* **assault (of** *or* **at arms)**: an attack made upon each other by two fencers, etc., as an exercise or trial of skill; and, in a wider sense (after F. *assaut d'armes*), a display of hand-to-hand military exercises.

1694 SIR W. HOPE *Swordman's Vade M.* 68 He should take his Lessons and Assault in his Cloaths and walking Shoes. **1771** J. OLIVIER *Fencing* 141 An assault is the resemblance of a single fight with swords, where you perform..all the thrusts and all the parades that you learned by lessons. **1851** *Handbill* 27 Jan., Assault of Arms..at the Swan Hotel, Hastings. **1884** *Daily News* 26 May 5/6 Military Assault-at-Arms in aid of Charity, Kensington Town Hall.

2. The sudden rush or charge of an attacking force against the walls of a city or fortress; a storm; *esp.* in the phrases ***to make*** or ***give assault, to win, gain, take,*** or ***carry by assault.***

1297 R. GLOUC. 409 Hii sette Roberd Courtehose..in þe Est syde, þe asaut vor to do. **1375** BARBOUR *Bruce* XVII. 474 The assalt haf thai levit all. **1480** CAXTON *Chron. Eng.* v. (1520) 45 b/2 The kynges men gave a greate assaute unto the castell. **1530** PALSGR. 619/1, I make a saulte to a towne. *c* **1532** LD. BERNERS *Huon* 519 They went to the castell of

Iaffet and toke it with assaulte. **1685** *Lond. Gaz.* 24 Aug. 1/2 The Enemy gave several Assaults to the Outworks. **1872** YEATS *Growth Comm.* 180 He took Goa by assault.

3. An unlawful attack upon the person of another. (In *Law* a menacing word or action is sufficient to constitute an *assault*, the term *battery* being techn. added when an actual blow is inflicted.)

1447-8 SHILLINGFORD *Lett.* (1871) 90 Affrayes assautes and other riotous mysgovernaunce. **1581** LAMBARDE *Eiren.* II. iii. (1588) 135 An Assault..can not be performed, without the offer of some hurtfull blow, or at the least of some fearefull speach. **1590** GREENE *Arcadia* (1616) 47 Without either assault or any such batterie. **1768** BLACKSTONE *Comm.* III. 120 If one lifts up his cane, or his fist, in a threatning manner at another; or strikes at him, but misses him; this is an assault. **1849** MACAULAY *Hist. Eng.* I. iii. 296 A soldier therefore by knocking down his colonel, incurred only the ordinary penalties of assault and battery.

4. An attack upon institutions, opinions, or customs; an endeavour to overthrow them by argument or by hostile measures.

c **1449** PECOCK *Repr.* I. xiii. 71 For that he knowith me admytte and allowe the writingis..he makith aȝens me this assaut. *a* **1674** CLARENDON (J.) After some unhappy assaults upon the prerogative by the parliament. *a* **1704** LOCKE (J.) Theories built upon narrow foundations are very hard to be supported against the assaults of opposition. **1841** MYERS *Cath. Th.* IV. §22. 291 The assaults which are made upon them by natural and scholastic scepticism.

5. *transf.* and *fig.* Hostile approach, attack, onset.

1508 FISHER *Wks.* (1876) 277 Abidynge the sharpe assautes of deth. **1814** WORDSW. *Excurs.* v. 689 Unshaken bears the assault Of their most dreaded foe, the strong south-west. **1856** KANE *Arct. Exp.* I. xx. 245 In the polar zone the assault [of the climate] is immediate and sudden.

6. *esp.* An attack by spiritual enemies; a temptation to evil. (The earliest use in Eng.)

c **1230** *Ancr. R.* 196 þer þes deofles assauz beoð ofte strengest. **1486** CAXTON *Curial* 8 Thassaultes of whyche I am enuyronned. **1671** MILTON *Samson* 845 Hear what assaults I had, what snares besides, What sieges girt me round. **1877** SPARROW *Serm.* iii. 32 The enemy makes there his subtlest and strongest assault..and thus the man falls.

†**7.** A love-proposal, a wooing. *Obs.*

1599 SHAKS. *Much Ado* II. iii. 120 Inuincible against all assaults of affection. **1611** —— *Cymb.* I. vi. 150 The King my Father shall be made acquainted Of thy Assault.

8. Applied *attrib.* to equipment or troops used in making an assault, as ***assault boat, craft, ship, troops***; **assault course**, a course of training in assault; also ***assault practice***.

1915 *Bayonet Fighting* (*H.M.S.O.*) 1 To obtain efficiency with the bayonet, the men..should frequently carry out the Final Assault Practice. **1916** *Bayonet Training* vi. 26 The 'points' will also be practised..on dummies placed, as a preparation for the Final Assault Course, in positions of increasing difficulty. **1941** *War Illustr.* 18 Apr. 398 Collapsible boats of wood and canvas, known as assault boats, much larger than the rubber boats, are used when a number of troops are to be carried across water. **1943** *Combined Operations* ii. 16 (*caption*) Assault Course. In the battle schools, British troops are trained under realistic conditions. *Ibid.* 17 Landing craft are carried by infantry landing ships, originally known as assault ships. **1943** *Hutchinson's Pict. Hist. War* July 247/2 As the assault craft headed towards the beaches, everything was very quiet. **1945** *Daily Tel.* 12 June 1/1 Assault troops of the Australian Ninth Division..quickly established beachheads against almost no resistance. **1959** *Times* 8 Sept. 4/2 Rotodyne vertical take-off and landing aircraft..will be able to carry 70 fully equipped assault troops.

assault (əˈsɔːlt), *v.* Forms: 5-6 **assawte**, 6 **a saute, assaute, assalt**, 7 **assult**, 6- **assault**. *Aphet.* 5-7 SAULT, etc. q.v. [a. OF. *asaute-r*, cogn. w. It. *assaltare*, Sp. *asaltar*, Romanic type *ad-, assaltāre*, f. L. *ad* to, at + *saltāre* to leap, spring, which took the place of the L. equivalent *ad-, assultāre*, freq. of *ad-silīre*. Cf. prec. and ASSAIL.]

1. To make a violent hostile attack by physical means upon (a person, army, etc.); to commit an unlawful or criminal assault upon the person of (see ASSAULT *sb.* 3). ***to assault a city*** or ***fortress***: (in mod. usage) to attack it by a sudden rush of armed men, to storm.

c **1450** *Merlin* iv. 69 Yef he me assawte with werre. **1513** BRADSHAW *St. Werburge* 163 As the kynges were sautynge this forsayd cite. **1604** SHAKS. *Oth.* v. ii. 258 Speake with me, Or, naked as I am I will assault thee. **1611** BIBLE *Acts* xvii. 5 And assaulted the house of Iason. **1685** R. BURTON *Eng. Emp. Amer.* i. 21 His Horsemen..assulted Atahaliba's people. **1722** DE FOE *Moll Fl.* (1840) 269 He should commit him to Newgate for assaulting the constable. **1860** FROUDE *Hist. Eng.* V. xxvi. 206 The next morning Norwich was assaulted. **1884** *Daily News* 23 June 5/3 Two lads of nine were accused of assaulting a little boy of three.

b. *fig.* or *transf.*

1622 R. HAWKINS *Voy. S. Sea* (1847) 63 The gownes being well soked, every man..tooke one, and assaulted the fire. **1709** POPE *Let. H. Cromwell* May 7 Wks. 1837 V. 66 'Tis a mercy I do not assault you with a number of original Sonnets and Epigrams.

2. To attack with hostile words; to speak or write directly against; = ASSAIL *v.* 4. *arch.* or *Obs.*

1561 T. N[ORTON] *Calvin's Inst.* I. 18 To shew yᵉ quicknesse of their witt in assalting the truthe of God. **1670** COTTON *Espernon* I. II. 83 The Leaguers..wish'd they had never assaulted the Duke by the way of writing.

3. To attack with reasoning or argument; to address with the object of persuading, convincing, or controverting; = ASSAIL *v.* 5. *arch.* or *Obs.*

1551-6 ROBINSON tr. *More's Utopia* 15 To assault me until he..persuaded me. *a* **1674** CLARENDON *Hist. Reb.* (1702) I. v. 464 Hoping..that they would not..have thought fit to assault him with a Newer Declaration.

4. Of things: To come roughly against, so as to batter, injure, or hurt; to dash against; = ASSAIL *v.* 7.

1667 MILTON *P.L.* II. 953 A universal hubbub..Assaults his eare. **1781** GIBBON *Decl. & F.* III. xlviii. 25 His vessel was assaulted by a violent tempest. **1850** LYNCH *Theo. Trin.* xii. 230 The roaring of the waves..assaults our ear.

5. Of physical or mental states, as of disease: To come upon, attack, invade. *arch.* or *Obs.*

1594 T. B. *La Primaud. Fr. Acad.* II. 365 Gowtie persons ..be not assaulted with such great and vehement floods of waters. **1774** MRS. CHAPONE *Improv. Mind.* II. 20 When we find ourselves assaulted by this infirmity.

6. To assail with temptations; to tempt, try. *arch.* or *Obs.*

1529 MORE *Comf. agst. Trib.* II. Wks. 1197/1 Nor all the deuilles in hell so strong to inuade and assawte him, as god is to defende him. **1585** ABP. SANDYS *Serm.* (1841) 263 Satan ceaseth not to assault our faith. **1714** ADDISON *Spect.* No. 598 ¶7 Levity of Temper..opens a Pass to his Soul for any Temptation that assaults it.

7. *absol.* chiefly in sense 1. (In quot. 1575 *A saute* may be the sb. used interjectionally.)

1489 CAXTON *Faytes of Armes* I. ix. 23 To teche hem bettre in all thynges to fighte and to sawte. **1575** CHURCHYARD *Chippes* (1817) 106 A saute, a saute, wee lye ore longe in trenche. **1595** SHAKS. *John* II. i. 408 Say, where will you assault? **1667** MILTON *P.L.* XI. 657 By Batterie, Scale, and Mine, Assaulting.

b. To attack in fencing: see ASSAULT *sb.* 1 b.

1694 SIR W. HOPE *Swordman's Vade M.* 69 When People assault, it is commonly with Blunts.

assault, in phr. *to be* or *go assault*: see ASSAUT.

assaultable (əˈsɔːltəb(ə)l), *a.* Also 6 **assaut-**; and see aphet. SAULTABLE. [f. prec. vb. + -ABLE. Cf. It. *assaltevole.*] Capable of being assaulted, open to assault.

1548 HALL *Chron.* (1809) 737 They bet the walles so, with great ordinaunce, that they made the town assautable. **1649** (17 Sept.) CROMWELL *Lett.* (Carl.) To make breaches assaultable, and by the help of God to storm them. **1829** S. TURNER *Hist. Eng.* III. II. xix. 589 The place was found not to be assaultable.

assaulted (əˈsɔːltɪd), *ppl. a.* [f. as prec. + -ED.] Assailed, attacked.

1601 CORNWALLYES *Ess.* II. xxix. (1631) 40 It makes the assaulters weake, the assaulted strong. *c* **1660** JER. TAYLOR *Life of Christ* xi. Wks. 1822 III. 52 So long as the assaulted person is in actual danger.

assaulter (əˈsɔːltə(r)). Also **assaultair, -tour.** [f. ASSAULT *v.* + -ER¹. Cf. OF. *assauteur*, AF. *assaultour*, also occas. followed in Eng. spelling.] One who assaults, an attacker or assailant.

1548 HALL *Chron. Hen. VIII* an. 16 (R.) The assaulters to deuise all maner of engynes for the assaulting. **1566** KNOX *Hist. Ref.* Wks. 1846 I. 212 And receaved the first assaultairis upon the poyntis of thare spearis. **1583** STANYHURST *Aeneis* II. (Arb.) 58 The Troians..the assaultours with weak force vaynely repulsed. **1796** MISS BURNEY *Camilla* VIII. ix. Admiration is a dangerous assaulter of diffidence. **1837** CAMPBELL *Song of Greeks* ii. 154 For we've sworn by our Country's assaulters, By the virgins they've dragged from our altars.

assaulting (əˈsɔːltɪŋ), *vbl. sb.* [f. ASSAULT *v.* + -ING¹.] Hostile onset, attack, assault.

1548 [see prec.] **1561** HOLLYBUSH *Hom. Apoth.* 44 b, When a man perceyueth the assaultinge of the ague. **1675** SHEPPARD *Grand Abridgm.* s.v. *Battery*, Menacing beginneth the breach of the Peace, Assaulting, which every Battery doth imply, increaseth it, and Battery accomplisheth it. **1707** SIR W. HOPE *New Meth. Fencing* (1714) 232 Laws to be observed upon the Weekly Assaulting Days.

aˈssaulting, *ppl. a.* [f. as prec. + -ING².] That assaults; attacking, assailing.

1567 DRANT *Horace Epist.* I. i. Cj, To master thyne assaltynge fyttes. **1797** HOLCROFT tr. *Stolberg's Trav.* II. ci. (ed. 2) 433 Defending himself against an assaulting lion. **1879** in *Cassell's Techn. Educ.* IV. 139 The assaulting troops.

assaultive (əˈsɔːltɪv), *a.* [f. ASSAULT *v.* + -IVE.] Liable or wishing to commit an assault.

1955 *Sci. News Let.* 2 July 4/1 She became assaultive, wanted to kill herself and had delusions of persecution. **1961** E. HUNTER *Mothers & Daughters* II. 213 The moment the jacket was removed..she became assaultive.

†**aˈssaut**, *adv.* (*adj.*), prop. *phrase*. *Obs.* Forms: 5 **a sawt**, 5-7 **assaut**, 6 **asawte, assault.** [a. F. *à saut* to leaping: see *saut* (sense 10) in Littré.] In phr. ***to go*** or ***be assau(l)t***: to seek the male, to rut.

c **1400** *Bk. Huntynge, MS. Bodl.* No. 546, viii. 38 The fyxene of þe wolf is a sawt ones yn þe ȝeer. **1552** HULOET, Go asawte..which is the desyre betwene the male kynd, and the female kynde, *Catulio*. **1580** BARET *Alv.* A 630 To go assault ..*Catulio*. **1601** HOLLAND *Pliny* XVI. xxv, When as Nature seemeth to goe proud or assaut, and is in the rut and furious rage of love.

†**aˈssavour**, *v. Obs.* [a. OF. *assavoure-r*, earlier *asavorer*, cogn. with Pr. *assaborar*, It. *assaporare*, a late L. or Romanic compound, f. *ad* to + *sapōrāre* to season, flavour, in late L. to savour, relish, f. *sapōr-em* relish, SAVOUR.] To relish, enjoy the taste of.

1483 CAXTON *Gold. Leg.* 30/4 The propre body of jhesu ..[to] receyve and assavoure devoutly. *Ibid.* 364/3 She herd the sermons ententyuely and assaueured them more swetely.

assay (əˈseɪ), *sb.* Forms: 4 **assai**, 4-5 **assay(e**, 4-7 **assaie, assaye**, 6 **a saie, assey(e**, 4- **assay**. Also aphetic SAY, and refashioned ESSAY, q.v. [a. OF. *assai, assay*, var. of *essai, essay*, cogn. with Pr. *essai, assai, assag*, Sp. *asayo*, Cat. *assatg*, It. *assaggio* (also Cat. *ensatg, ensaig*, Sp. *ensayo*, Pg. *ensaio*):—L. *exagium* 'weighing,' but used in Romanic in wider sense of 'examination, trial, testing'; f. L. *ex-agĕre, exigĕre* to weigh, try, prove, measure, adjust, ascertain, examine, inquire into. For the sense of the L. cf. *exāmen* = *exagmen*: see EXAMINE; for the form cf. *contāgium* = *contāmen* f. *con-tangĕre, naufragium* f. *frangĕre*. Fr. *essai* = It. *assaggio*:—L. *exagium* may be compared to Fr. *ai* = OIt. *aggio*:—L. *habeo*. The etymological form from L. *ex-* was in *es-*, but in Romanic this was by confusion with other prefixes made *as-* and *en-*. In Fr. the etymological *essai* has now quite ousted *assai*, and in Eng., since the end of the 16th c., ESSAY has similarly taken the place of *assay*, exc. in the 'assay of metals,' and uses founded upon it. An aphet. SAY was very common down to 17th c.]

I. The action or process of trying, trial *generally*.

1. The trying (of a person or thing); trial imposed upon or endured by any object, in order to test its virtue, fitness, etc. *Obs.* exc. as fig. use of 6.

1330 R. BRUNNE *Chron.* 341 Noblie regned he here, bi profe and gode assaies. *c* **1386** CHAUCER *Wife's Prol.* 290 But folk of wyves maken non assay, Til thay ben weddid. *c* **1450** *Merlin* xiv. 219 Now lete se youre cheualrye, for now be ye come to the assay. *c* **1500** W. DE WORDE *Communyc.* C iij, Whan thou of all thy frendes haste made assaye Thou shalte fynde none lyke to me. **1603** SHAKS. *Meas. for M.* III. i. 164 Angelo had neuer the purpose to corrupt her; onely he hath made an assay of her vertue. **1711** BUDGELL *Spect.* No. 307 ¶12 To make an Assay of his Parts in Geometry. **1868** RUSKIN *Pol. Econ. Art.* Add. 211 A great assay of the human soul.

†**2.** 'Trial,' tribulation, affliction. *Obs.*

1375 BARBOUR *Bruce* II. 412 The King..Wes set in-till full hard assay. *c* **1430** LYDG. *Bochas*, Their pacience put at fell assayes. **1596** SPENSER *F.Q.* I. vii. 27 Sorrowfull assay, Which..almost rent her tender heart in tway. **1671** MILTON *P.R.* I. 263 My way must lie Through many a hard assay even to the death.

†**3.** Experiment. ***put it in assay***: make the experiment, try it. *Obs.*

c **1374** CHAUCER *Compl. Venus* 62 Let the jelouse put hit in assay. **1525-30** MORE *De quat. Nouiss.* Wks. 77/1 Yf thou putte it in a saie and make a proofe. **1644** MILTON *Educ.* Wks. 1738 I. 140 It may prove much more easy with assay than it now seems at distance. **1768** STERNE *Sent. Journ.* (1778) I. 84 'Tis an assay upon human nature.

†**4.** Experience. *Obs.*

1387 TREVISA *Higden* (Rolls Ser.) I. 73 Schort witted men and litel of assay. *c* **1449** PECOCK *Repr.* II. xi, þe doom of experience and of assay.

†**5.** The faculty of trying or judging of things.

c **1394** *P. Pl. Crede* 537 þanne haue y tynt all my tast, touche and assaie.

II. Trial *specifically*.

6. a. The trial of metals, by 'touch,' fire, etc.; the determination of the quantity of metal in an ore or alloy; or of the fineness of coin or bullion.

c **1386** CHAUCER *Clerkes T.* 1110 If that thay were put to such assayes The gold of hem hath now so badde alayes With bras, that..It wolde rather brest in two than plye. *a* **1500** *Songs on Costume* (1849) 52 Thyng counterfeet wol faylen at assay. **1600** HAKLUYT *Voy.* (1810) III. 316 To get some of that their copper for an assay. **1724** SWIFT *Drapier's Lett.* ii. Wks. 1761 III. 31 An assay was made of the coin. **1798** *Phil. Trans.* LXXXVIII. 424 The valuable minerals are soon pointed out by assay. **1813** WELLINGTON in Gurw. *Disp.* X. 194, I haue requested Sir Charles Stuart to have an assay made of them at the Portuguese Mint. **1881** RAYMOND *Mining Gloss.* s.v., Both assays and analyses may be either qualitative or quantitative..The assay value of gold and silver ores is usually determined in Troy ounces.

b. Esp. in ***biological assay*** (= *bio-assay*), the determination of the strength of a substance by means of a test on an organism, usu. in comparison with the effect of a standard preparation.

1922 BURN & DALE *Rep. Biol. Stand.* I. 50 We do not assume that it will be necessary to make a new batch of the Standard for the assay of every batch of the commercial extract. **1927** BURN & ELLIS in *Pharmaceut. Jrnl.* 9 Apr. 384/1 (*title*) The Biological Assay of the Specific Alkaloid of Ergot. **1928** H. H. DALE in J. H. Burn *Methods Biol. Assay* p. x, The most serious difficulty in biological assay is that due to the variability of the living reagent. **1961** *Lancet* 22 July 214/1 The daily urinary loss of vitamin B_{12}..was measured in three patients by microbiological assay.

7. The metal or substance to be assayed.

1837 EDE *Pract. Chem.* 10 The assay is moistened and made to adhere to the flux and heated with it. **1879** RUTLEY *Stud. Rocks* x. 158 To get this colouration the assay should not be previously reduced.

†**8.** The trial of weights, measures, quality of bread, etc. by legal standard. *Obs.* exc. *Hist.*

1601 F. TATE *Househ. Ord. Ed. II*, §24 (1876) 17 The clarke of the market..shal take the assay of al manner of mesures, waightes and elnes within the vierge. **1631** *Chart. 6 Chas. I*, in Bingham *Rep.* V. 341 Assize and assay of bread, wine, and beer. **1751** CHAMBERS *Cycl.*, *Assay* of weights and measures signifies the trial or examination of common weights and measures.

†**9.** *Venery.* Trial of 'grease of a deer.' *Obs.*

c **1340** *Gaw. & Gr. Knt.* 1328 Serched hem at þe asay, summe þat þer were. **1612** DRAYTON *Poly-olb.* xv. 244 Nor tooke so rich assaies. (*Note.* Breaking up of Deare brought into the Quarry.)

10. The trial of anything by taste, tasting. *arch.*

1477 NORTON *Ord. Alch.* (Ashm. 1652) v. 73 Yet of some parts seperable, A Tast maie well be Convenable..to make assay Whether they be well wrought or nay. **1561** T. N[ORTON] *Calvin's Inst.* III. ii. (1634) 276 Being before.. without judgment of taste to take assay of them. **1616** SURFL. & MARKH. *Countr. Farm* 610 As concerning the tasting of wine..it is good to make the assay at such time as the North-East winde bloweth. **1667** MILTON *P.L.* IX. 747 Whose taste, too long forborn, at first assay Gave elocution to the mute. **1823** LAMB *Elia* Ser. I. xii. (1865) 98 That Guyon must take assay of the glorious bait.

†**11.** *fig.* A taste, a foretaste. *Obs.*

1594 J. KING *Jonah* (1864) 56 A taste and assay beforehand of that everlasting and utter darkness. **1605** SHAKS. *Lear* I. ii. 47 But as an essay, or taste of my vertue.

†**12. a.** The act, latterly perhaps nothing more than complimentary, of tasting the food or drink before giving it to an exalted personage. *Obs.* exc. *Hist.*

1547 in Strype *Eccl. Mem.* II. App. I. A 7 A sumptuous dinner, and the chief mourner served with assays and al other service. **1548** HALL *Chron.* (1550) 14 The esquier whiche was accustomed to sewe and take the assaye before kyng Rychard. **1602** CAREW *Cornwall* (1723) 137 b, Serued with kneeling assay, and all other rites due to the estate of a Prince. **1641** PRYNNE *Antipathie* 200 Hee made Dukes and Earles to serve him with Wine, with assay taken.

b. *cup of assay*: a small cup with which assay of wine, etc. was taken.

c **1530** in Gutch *Coll. Cur.* II. 283 Twoo litill Cuppis of asseye silvar and gilt. **1548** HALL *Chron.* (1550) 212 The Maior of London claymed to serue the quene with a cuppe of golde and a cuppe of assay of the same. **1852** THACKERAY *Esmond* II. ii. (1876) 171 In this state she had her train carried by a knight's wife, a cup and cover of assay to drink from, and fringed cloth.

III. A trying to do something, an attempt.

13. An attempt, an endeavour. *arch.*

c **1386** CHAUCER *Chan. Yem. Prol. & T.* 696 Yet wol I make assay The second tyme, that ye mow taken heede. *c* **1450** *Merlin* vi. 100 He..that was ferthest from the assaye of this swerde. **1625** BACON *Seditions, Ess.* (Arb.) 395 A kinde of shaking off the yoake and Assay of disobedience. **1684** BUNYAN *Pilgr.* II. 32 She and her companions made a fresh assay to go past them. **1725** POPE *Odyss.* IV. 535 Perilous th' assay, unheard the toil, T' elude the prescience of a God by guile. **1876** BLACKIE *Songs Relig.* 64 O! it is a hard assay For the reach of human clay.

†**14.** Putting forth of one's strength or energy, best effort. *arch. to do his assay*: to put forth all his might, do his best. *Obs.*

c **1385** CHAUCER *L.G.W.* 1590 Prayinge him that he most doon his assay To gete the flese of golde. **1393** GOWER *Conf.* I. 68 He hath put all his assay To winne thing which he ne may get. **1605** SHAKS. *Macb.* IV. iii. 143 Their malady conuinces The great assay of Art. **1634** A. HUISH, Endeavouring with our strength and whole assay, Our God to praise. **1797** COLERIDGE *Christabel* I, Deep from within she seems half-way To lift some weight with sick assay.

†**15.** An attack, an assault. *Obs.*

1375 BARBOUR *Bruce* XIV. 34 In vaveryng fyrth arivit thai Saufly, but bargane or assay. *c* **1400** *Destr. Troy.* VIII. 3903 Paris was ffull siker at asaye, and a sad knight. **1513** DOUGLAS *Æneis* VIII. i. 13 The first chiftanis for assay or defens. **1596** SPENSER *F.Q.* v. iv. 23 To have wrought unwares some villainous assay. **1599** SHAKS. *Hen. V*, I. ii. 151 Galling the gleaned Land with hot Assayes. **1602** —— *Ham.* II. ii. 71 To giue th' assay of Armes against your Maiestie. **1705** HICKERINGILL *Priest-cr.* IV. 211 The next Essay and Assay that I make against Priest-craft, shall be to Disarm it for ever.

†**16.** A first tentative effort, in learning or practice. *Obs.*

1560 *Disob. Child* in Hazl. *Dodsl.* II. 284, I went to school, And of my Latin primer I took assay. **1613** R. C. *Table Alph., Preamble*, forespeech..entrance, or assay. **1624** CAPT. SMITH *Virginia* Pref. I Our practices haue hitherto beene but assayes, and are still to be amended. **1677** GILPIN *Dæmonol. Sacra* (1867) 247 These are his first assays with young men.

†**17.** A trial specimen; a sample. *Obs.*

1581 LAMBARDE *Eiren.* IV. xvi. (1588) 580, I labour to bee short, and therfore I giue but an assaie of each thing. **1675** COLLINS in Rigaud *Corr. Sci. Men* I. 212 Be pleased to thank him for those assays of his method already sent.

IV. Quality as determined by trial.

18. †**a.** Approved quality, proof, temper of metal, etc. *Obs.* **b.** Standard of fineness in the precious metals.

c **1430** *Syr Generides* 6037 Ne had his helme be goode of assay He had died the same day. **1436** *Pol. Poems* (1859) II. 196 Instrumentis of werre of beste assay. **1596** SPENSER *F.Q.* I. ii. 13 Purfled with gold and pearle of rich assay. **1820** G. CAREY *Funds* 99 As twenty-two carats are to the gross weight so is the assay or real fineness to the quantity.

†**19.** *fig.* Character, temper. *Obs.*

1393 GOWER *Conf.* III. 356 That outward feignen youthe so And ben within of pouer assay. **1579** J. STUBBES *Gaping Gulf* A vij, To be of one assaie or touche with the Idolatrous and trayterous Israelits.

†**20.** Sounding; depth as ascertained by it. *Obs.*

1436 *Pol. Poems* (1859) II. 186 Havenesse grete and godely bayes, Sure, wyde, and depe, of gode assayes.

V. Phr. **at all assays.** (Also *at all assay*, *at every assay.*)

†**21.** At every trial, in every crisis, juncture, or time of need; passing imperceptibly into: At all events, in any case; on every occasion, always. *Obs.*

c **1360** *Yesterday* 166 in *E.E.P.* (1862) 137 Put þi trust in godus Mercie. Hit is þe best at al assay. *c* **1400** *Test. Love* I. (1560) 274/1, I have thee found at all assayes..to be readie. *c* **1485** *Digby Myst.* (1882) I. 531 Ye shal me fynde plesant at euery assaye. **1570** *Marr. Wit & Sc.* v. iv. in Hazl. *Dodsl.* II. 389 God speed us well, I will make one at all assays. **1577** tr. *Bullinger's Decades* (1592) 135 God..our present deliuerer and ayder at all assayes. **1612** WOODALL *Surg. Mate* Wks. 1653, 153 Words..which might serve at all assayes, or upon all occasions. **1658** USSHER *Ann.* VI. 164 He had at all assayes, ever upheld their State, against their enemies.

†**22.** (Armed, ready) *at all assays*: ready for every event. *Obs.*

1553 UDALL *Roister D.* (Arb.) 36 Shall we sing a fitte?.. *Dou.* I am at all assayes. **1594** *2nd Rep. Faustus* in Thoms *E.E. Rom.* (1858) III. 408 Four Janisaries horsemen armed at all assaies. **1603** FLORIO *Montaigne* I. xlviii. (1632) 155 The Roman gentlemen armed at all assayes.

VI. *Comb.* in names of things used in or connected with assaying; as ***assay-balance***, ***-beam***, ***-furnace***, ***-house***, ***office***, ***-oven***; **assay-ton** (see quot.). Also ASSAY-MASTER, q.v.,

1746 *Phil. Trans.* XLIV. 245 The flat Pieces of Glass, often placed under the Scales of an Essay-Balance. **1753** CHAMBERS *Cycl. Supp.*, *Assay-Ballance.* **1863** *Proc. Amer. Phil. Soc.* IX. 226 The recent receipt of two assay beams at the Mint. **1707** *Lond. Gaz.* No. 4313/3 Without..the accustomary Charges of making Essay Furnaces. **1773** *Act 13 Geo. III.* c. 52 §4 Such Silver Vessel, Plate, or manufactured Silver shall be marked..with the Mark of the Company within whose Assay Office such Plate shall be assayed and marked. **1851** *San Francisco Herald* 1 Feb. 2/1 Arrangements for opening the United States Assay Office in this city, are being rapidly completed. **1853** in Mrs. C. Clacy *Lady's Visit to Gold Diggings* xv. 233 The quantity of gold taken to the Assay-office, during four consecutive weeks, amounting to less than four thousand ounces. **1869** 'MARK TWAIN' *Innoc. Abr.* xviii. 179 The cargoes of 'crude bullion' of the assay offices of Nevada. **1622** MALYNES *Anc. Law-Merch.* 284 Comming to the Assay-house, there we found diuers gentlemen desirous to see the manner of making of Assayes of Gold and Siluer. **1683** PETTUS *Fleta Min.* I. (1686) 8 There are many sorts of Assay-Ovens which Assayers made use of. **1881** RAYMOND *Mining Gloss.*, *Assayton*, a weight of 29166⅔ grams. Each milligram of gold or silver obtained from one assay-ton of ore represents one ounce troy to the ton of 2000 pounds avoirdupois.

assay (əˈseɪ), *v.* Forms: 4 asaie, (asyghe), 4–5 asay(e, 4–6 assaye, 4–7 assaie, (5 asse), 5–6 assey(e, 6 assai, asey, (assy), 4– assay. Also aphetic SAY, and refashioned ESSAY, q.v. [a. OF. *a(s)saye-r*, *a(s)saie-r*, also *essayer*, cogn. with Sp. *asayar*, Pr. *essaiar*, *assaiar*, *assatjar*, It. *assaggiare* (cf. also Pr. and Pg. *ensaiar*, Sp. *ensayar*, Cat. *ensajar*):—late L. or early Romanic **exagiāre*, f. *exagium*: see ASSAY *sb.* In later Fr. the etymological form *essayer* is alone found; this was introduced into Eng. by Caxton, and, except as applied to the testing of metals, *assay* is now an archaic form of ESSAY. An aphet. SAY was formerly common.]

I. To put to the test.

1. a. *trans.* To put to the proof, try (a person or thing); to test the nature, excellence, fitness, etc. of. *Obs.* exc. as fig. use of 4.

1330 R. BRUNNE *Chron.* 219 He said he wild asay þer hors alle in a mile. **1340** HAMPOLE *Pr. Consc.* 1399 In þis world liggis twa ways, Als men may fynd þat þam assays. *a* **1450** *Knt. de la Tour* (1868) 27 After dyner y wille assaie my wiff, and bidde her lepe into the basin. **1513** MORE *Rich. III.* (1641) 395 Every man assaid his armour and proved his weapon. **1545** ASCHAM *Toxoph.* (Arb.) 20 Therfore did I take this little matter in hande to assaye myselfe. **1671** MILTON *P.R.* II. 233, I shall..his strength as oft assay. **1791** COWPER *Odyss.* VIII. 27 With which they should assay his force.

†**b.** with *object clause. Obs.*

c **1385** CHAUCER *L.G.W.* 487 That al here lyf ne don nat but asayen How many women they may done a shame. *c* **1450** LONELICH *Grail* xxvii. 300 Only to asayen what he wolde do. **1513–75** *Diurn. Occurr.* (1833) 59 To assy ȝif thair ladderis wer convenient and lang aneuch. **1611** BIBLE *Transl. Pref.* 7 To assay whether my talent..may be profitable in any measure to Gods Church.

†**2.** *intr.* To make trial (*of*). *Obs.*

c **1386** CHAUCER *Frankl. T.* 839, I wole of hym assaye At certeyn dayes yeer by yeer to paye. *c* **1394** *P. Pl. Crede* 647 A-say of her sobernesse. **1576** THYNNE in *Animadv.* App. 108, I manye tymes with deeper muse assayed.

†**3.** *trans.* To try by touch; to 'feel' by handling. *lit.* and *fig. Obs.*

1366 MAUNDEV. viii. 91 On that mount appeared Crist to Seynt Thomas..and bad him assaye his woundes. *c* **1374** CHAUCER *Boeth.* I. vi. 26 Suffre me to touche and assaie þe stat of þi þouȝt by a fewe demaundes. **1398** TREVISA *Barth. De P.R.* III. xxiii. (1495) 70 Olde men and wyse chese the veynes of the arme to assaye the puls.

4. a. *trans.* To test the composition of (an ore, alloy, or other metallic compound) by chemical means, so as to determine the amount of a particular metal contained in it; to determine the degree of purity of one of the precious metals.

c **1440** *Morte Arthure* 2347, I sende hyme the somme, assaye how hyme likes! **1697** LUTTRELL *Brief Rel.* IV. 239 The goldsmiths are to meet to assay the new money coyned at the Tower. **1754** CRAMER (*title*) Elements of the Art of Assaying Metals in Theory and Practice. **1818** ACCUM *Chem. Tests* 104 To assay it for lead. **1879** G. GLADSTONE in *Cassell's Techn. Educ.* IV. 146/1 A small piece..is cut off each ingot that has to be assayed.

b. *fig.* To test as metal.

c **1400** HYLTON *Scala Perf.* (W. de W. 1494) xxiv, Tyll thou be assaid and purifyed by the fyre of desire in devoute prayer. **1834** SOUTHEY *Doctor* clx. (1862) 404 Sterling merit ..he can now understand and value, having..the means of assaying it.

c. To show (a certain yield) by assay; to yield on assay. Also *absol.*

1882 *Rep. Prec. Metals U.S.* 305 Assay as high as $100 to the ton. **1892** *Graphic* 26 Mar. 387/1 A 'pocket'..which assays a good many ounces to the ton. **1927** *Sunday Times* 13 Feb. 2 Ore,..assaying as high as 7·3 dwts. (31s.).

d. To test the strength of a substance by means of a test on an organism (see ASSAY *sb.* 6 b); so ***assayed*** ppl. a.

1922 BURN & DALE *Rep. Biol. Stand.* I. 51 A comparison of each batch with its accurately assayed predecessor should suffice. **1928** *Lancet* 20 Oct. 820/1 Drugs..can be assayed with a sufficient degree of accuracy by biological methods. **1962** *Ibid.* 6 Jan. 24/1 Tissue-culture methods have been used for some time to assay the effect of drugs on normal and neoplastic cells.

†**5.** *trans.*, *absol.*, and *intr.* with *of.* To try by tasting. *spec.* To taste food or drink before it is offered to a prince or lord. *Obs.* exc. *Hist.*

1377 LANGL. *P. Pl.* B. XVI. 74, I prayed pieres to pulle adown an apple..and suffre me to assaye what sauoure it hadde. **1393** *Ibid.* C. VII. 357 Ich haue good Ale, godsyb gloton, wolt þow assaye? *c* **1460** *Bk. Curtasye* 751 in *Babees Bk.* (1868) 325 þo Coke assayes þe mete vngryȝt, þo sewer he takes and kouers on ryȝt. **1522** *World & Child* in Hazl. *Dodsl.* I. 266 At the Pope's-Head sweet wine assay. *a* **1529** SKELTON *El. Rummyng* 397 Of thyne ale let us assay. **1693** ROBERTSON *Phraseol. Gen.* 154 To assay or taste before or first, *Prægustare.* **1859** TURNER *Dom. Archit.* III. iii. 80 The Carver then entered the hall..and at once commenced the cautious process of assaying.

†**6.** *trans.* To try the depth of, sound. *Obs.*

1665 MANLEY *Grotius' Low-C. Wars* 337 He sent Count Solre to assay and sound the Issell.

†**7.** *trans.* To try, try on (clothes). *Obs.*

1592 LYLY *Mydas* v. iii. 64 Apollo is..assaying on some Shepherd's coate. **1631** DEKKER *Match Mee* II. Wks. 1873 IV. 156 Assay this glove, Sir.

†**8.** *trans.* To practise by way of trial. *Obs.*

1377 LANGL. *P. Pl.* B. XVI. 106 And did him assaye his surgerye On hem þat syke were. **1477** EARL RIVERS (Caxton) *Dictes* 18 Assaye the meanes to redresse him. **1596** SPENSER *F.Q.* I. viii. 2 Deare Sir your mighty powres assay. **1671** MILTON *P.R.* I. 143 Let him tempt and now assay His utmost subtlety. *a* **1725** POPE *Odyss.* xix. 675 Their strength and skill the suitors shall assay.

†**9.** *trans.* and *absol.* To try or examine, for the sake of information. *Obs.*

1393 LANGL. *P. Pl.* C. IV. 5 Ich shul asaye hure myself and sothliche apose. **1387** TREVISA *Higden* (1865) I. 229 þe emperour assaied and founde sooþ all þat þey seide. **1481** CAXTON *Myrr.* I. v. 20 The auncyent faders wold..assaye the werkis of our Lord. **1622** R. HAWKINS *Voy. S. Sea* (1847) 127 Assaying our pumpe to know if our shippe made more water then her ordinary.

†**10. a.** *trans.* To try to know or learn; to inquire.

1393 LANGL. *P. Pl.* C. XVII. 164 He suffrede me and seide 'assay hus oþer name.' **1401** *Pol. Poems* (1859) II. 41 This he doth in dede asseye of hem that knowith. **1664** BUTLER *Hud.* II. iii. 314 He knew..Which Socrates and Chærephon In vain assaid so long agone.

†**b.** To try to attain to, endeavour after. *Obs. rare.*

1597 DANIEL *Civ. Wares* I. xlix, For every prince seeing his danger neere, By any meanes his quiet peace assaies.

†**11.** *trans.* and *absol.* To have proof of; to learn or know by experience. *Obs.*

1340 *Ayenb.* 142 Herte þet þis heþ a-sayd naȝt ne willieþ more. *c* **1374** CHAUCER *Troylus* IV. 1076 Thow hast nat yit assayed al hire wit. **1413** LYDG. *Pylgr. Sowle* III. x. 56 No man knoweth the peyne but he that hath assayed. **1483** CAXTON *Gold. Leg.* 93/4 Yf thou hast preued and assayed that I am the temple of god byleue it. **1597** SHAKS. *Lover's Compl.* 155 Who ever shunn'd by precedent The destined ill she must herself assay?

II. To try with afflictions, temptations, force, etc. In some senses apparently influenced by *assail.*

†**12.** *trans.* To try with afflictions, to subject to 'trials.' *Obs.*

c **1400** *Rom. Rose* 2688 Thou shalt wel by thy silf see That thou must nedis assaid be. **1480** CAXTON *Chron. Eng.* I. (1520) 6/2 After that God had assayed hym [i.e. Job] in his patience he lyved an .C. and 40 yere. **1596** SPENSER *F.Q.* I. ii. 24 O, how great sorrow my sad soule assaid!

†**13.** To try with temptations or things that influence; to tempt; to try to gain over. *Obs.*

1532 MORE *Confut. Tindale* Wks. 563/2 The diuel..letted not to assai Job againe and againe for al the pacience that he founde in him. **1589** GREENE *Menaph.* (Arb.) 57 To assay him by curtesie before hee assayled him with rigour. **1611** SPEED *Hist. Gt. Brit.* IX. xviii. (1632) 913 Catesby whether hee assayed him, or assayed him not, reported vnto them. **1614** RALEIGH *Hist. World* II. 547 Then did he assay them with goodly words, accompanied with gifts.

†**14. a.** To try the mettle of (any one) in fight, to try to conquer; *hence* to attack, assault, assail.

1375 BARBOUR *Bruce* III. 376 Sa hard anoy thaim then assayit, Off hungir, cauld, with schowris snell. *c* **1400** *Rowland & Ot.* 797 Be Mahoun.. I scholde assaye his Body. *c* **1440** *Generydes* 6074 He thought not hym for to Asse. *a* **1470** TIPTOFT *Caesar's Comm.* xiii. (1530) 17 Theyr enemies lept sodenly out.. in so much as they assayd them that bare the banners. *c* **1500** *Lancelot* 569 His purpos Is.. planly to assay Your lond, with mony manly man of were. **1582–8** *Hist. James VI* (1804) 176 These of Edinburgh.. went to assaye the castell of Merchestoun, with some peeces of ordinance. **1676** HOBBES *Iliad* XII. 51 Exhorting them the Trenches to assay.

†**b.** To challenge to a trial of strength, skill, etc.

1602 SHAKS. *Ham.* III. i. 14 Did you assay him to any pastime?

†**c.** *fig.* To attack anything difficult: cf. ASSAIL.

1605 DRAYTON *Man in Moone* 435 She the high Mountaynes actively assayes. **1643** DENHAM *Coopers Hill* 303 Thinks not their rage so desperate t' assay An Element more merciless than they.

†**15.** To assail: **a.** with words, or arguments; to accost, address. *Obs.*

1513 DOUGLAS *Æneis* IV. x. 96 Eneas.. Gan stert on fut, and fast his feris assayit. Awalk anon, get vp my men in hy. **1603** SHAKS. *Meas. for M.* I. ii. 186 Bid her selfe assay him.

†**b.** with love-proposals. *Obs.*

c **1550** *Dane Hew* 17 in Hazl. *E.P.P.* III. 135 And thought alway in his minde.. how he might her assay, And if she would not to say him nay. **1591** SPENSER *Virgils Gnat* 491 Th' other was with Thetis love assaid. **1598** SHAKS. *Merry W.* II. i. 26 What an unwaied Behauiour hath this Flemish drunkard pickt.. that he dares In this manner assay me?

III. To try to do, attempt, venture.

16. *trans.* To attempt, try to do (anything difficult).

c **1300** *K. Alis.* 3879 Now let seo gef ony is so hardy That durste hit him asyghe. **1382** WYCLIF *Heb.* xi. 29 The which thing Egipciens asayinge weren deuourid. **1513** DOUGLAS *Æneis* II. xii. (xi) 117 Wilfull all aventuris newlingis to assay. **1593** SPENSER *Sonn.* li, Never ought was excellent assayde Which was not hard t' atchive and bring to end. **1647** SPRIGG *Ang. Rediv.* I. vi. (1854) 54 It was resolved first to assay that. **1826** SCOTT *Woodst.* ii, The stranger paused, as if uncertain whether he should demand or assay entrance.

†**17.** *intr.* or with *inf.* **a.** To set oneself (*to do* something), to address or apply oneself. *Obs.*

1330 R. BRUNNE *Chron.* 47 For to com tille Inglond sone suld he assay. *c* **1400** *Destr. Troy* II. 382 Þat he go shuld, Soiorne þere a season, assay when hym lyke. **1541** ELYOT *Image Govt.* 13 All noble men assaied to folowe hym. **1611** BIBLE *Deut.* iv. 34 Hath God assayed to goe and take him a nation from the midst of another nation? **1665–9** BOYLE *Occas. Refl.* v. ix. (1675) 330 He fits them to the various tempers of the Persons he assays to work upon.

b. To make the attempt, to endeavour (the issue being conceived as uncertain); to do one's best. Generally with *inf.*

1370 *Lay-Folks Mass-Bk.* App. iv. 626 Noþeles · I wol assay. **1382** WYCLIF *2 Macc.* ii. 24 So we temptiden, or assayeden, for to abregge in to oo boke, thingus comprehendid.. in fyue bookis. **1535** COVERDALE *Jonah* i. 13 Neuerthelesse, the men assayed with rowinge, to brynge the shippe to londe. **1620** *Jrnls. Pilgrims* (1848) 30 For Cod we assayed, but found none. **1791** COWPER *Iliad* IX. 727 Him Œneus also.. with earnest prayers Assay'd to soften. **1868** FREEMAN *Norm. Conq.* (1876) II. x. 521 The King's strength was failing, but he assayed to show himself in the usual kingly state.

†**c.** To venture, make bold. With *inf. Obs.*

a **1400** *Cov. Myst.* 26 This frute to ete I xal asayn. **1579** FENTON *Guicciard.* (1618) 282 It is very manifest, that he neuer durst assay to oppresse vs without that vnion. **1605** *Play of Stucley* (1878) 191 So both our spies and friends dare not assay To hang out signal, nor come near the Port. **1678** BUNYAN *Pilgr.* I. (1862) 136 Then they assayed to look.

assayable (ə'seɪəb(ə)l), *a.* [f. ASSAY *v.* + -ABLE.] That may be assayed or tested.

1859 LEWES *Phys. Com. Life* II. ix. 236 Sensation is not tangible, assayable, like gold. **1883** *Act 46 & 47 Vict.* lv. §10 British plate by law assayable in such office.

assayed (ə'seɪd), *ppl. a.* [f. ASSAY *v.* + -ED.] Tried, tested.

1440 *Promp. Parv.* 15 A-sayyd, *Temptatus, probatus.* **1611** COTGR., *Esprouvé*, Proved, tried,.. assayed. **1863** J. MURPHY *Comm. Gen.* xxii. 1 Such assaying of the will and conscience is worthy both of God the assayer, and of man the assayed.

assayer (ə'seɪə(r)). Also 5 **assayar**, 5–7 **assaier**, **-or**, **-our**. [a. AF. *assaior*, *-our*, f. *assayer* to ASSAY. See -ER[1].]

1. One who tries, finds out by trial, or attempts.

1398 TREVISA *Barth. De P.R.* v. xlii. (1495) 158 Wyse men and assayers telle that.. that gutte.. is alwaye founde voyde and empti. *c* **1449** PECOCK *Repr.* I. xi. 58 As experience wole nedis proue to eche asaier. **1828** CARLYLE *Misc.* (1857) I. 173 The Assayers have Christian dispositions.

2. One who assays metals.

[**1423** *Act 2 Hen. VI*, xii, Et que ceux assaiour, controllour soient vaillantes, credible et expertz persones eiantes notorie science en la mestiere d'orfeour et de mynt.] **1618** PULTON transl., And that the Assaier and Comptroller be expert men. **1641** *Termes de la Ley* 27 Assayer is an officer of the Mint appointed by the Statute of 2. H. 6. cap. 12. **1796** PEARSON in *Phil. Trans.* LXXXVI. 410 The Assayers observe it from charges of lead with silver. **1852** MCCULLOCH *Taxation* II. vi. §2. 275 The offence of counterfeiting.. the marks, stamps, &c., impressed on plate by the assayers, was formerly felony. **1860** W. WHITE *Wrekin* xxvi. 272 Borax is the flux of assayers.

3. An officer who tastes food before it is served to a prince or lord, a fore-taster (L. *prægustātor*). (This sense of the word seems to have originated in a corruption of, or confusion with, ASSEOUR, 'he who sets the table,' f. F. *asseoir* 'to seat, set,' apparently the original name of this officer, referring to another duty: see also ASSEWER.)

[*c* **1315** *Househ. Ord. Ed. II*, transl. 1601 (1876) §26 The kinge shal have a squier surveiour and warden of the viandes for his mouth, and to take the assay at his table [Fr. *asseour de sa table*]. *ibid.* §37 Three esquiers assaiors of the messe [Fr. *asseours de la messe*] in the hal, ought to sett the messes in the halles, and that with as good advisement as thei can, so as men of state and others be servid according to their estate. *ibid.* §§48, 49, 50 The asseour of the kinges table.] ? *c* **1400** *K. Robt. Cysille* in Hazl. *E.P.P.* I. 276 Thou schalt ete on the grownde, Thyn assayar schalle be an hownde. **1693** W. ROBERTSON *Phraseol. Gen.* 154 An Assayer or tryer, He that assayeth or tasteth first, *Prægustator.* **1861** *Our Eng. Homes* 60 The assayer and his office.

assaying (ə'seɪɪŋ), *vbl. sb.* [f. ASSAY *v.* + -ING[1]]

1. The action of trying or proving; trial.

c **1375** WYCLIF *Serm.* xvi. Sel. Wks. 1871 II. 271 Assaiyng of a þing shulde teche for to know þat þing. **1398** TREVISA *Barth. De P.R.* XVII. liii. (1495) 634 Knowlege and assayeng of wyne. **1580** BARET *Alv.* A 618 A proofe: a trying: an assaying, *Tentamen.*

2. *spec.* The trial of metals.

1727–51 CHAMBERS *Cycl.*, *Assaying* is more particularly used by moneyers and goldsmiths. **1740** MRS. DELANY *Autobiog.* (1861) II. 82 Then to the Tower and Mint—the assaying of the gold and silver is very curious. **1838** HALLAM *Hist. Lit.* I. I. ix. §23 The chemical part of metallurgy, and especially what relates to assaying, is treated with great care.

b. *attrib.*

1800 HENRY *Epit. Chem.* (1808) 374 An assaying furnace. **1828** CARLYLE *Misc.* (1857) I. 173 It passed smoothly through the critical Assaying-house.

†**3.** *Mus.* A preliminary flourish; 'tuning up.' *Obs.*

1693 W. ROBERTSON *Phraseol. Gen.* 154 An Assaying or flourishing with a weapon before one begin to play. **1706** PHILLIPS, *Assaying*, a Term us'd by Musicians for a Flourish before they begin to Play.

assayle, var. ASSALE, *Obs.*, sale; obs. f. ASSAIL.

a'ssay-,master. [see ASSAY *sb.*] The master of an assay-house; an officer appointed to assay coin, gold and silver plate, etc.

1647 HAWARD *Crown Rev.* 22 Assay Master: Fee, 100*m.* **1662** PETTY *Taxes & Contr.* 26 Reports of the ablest Saymasters. **1692** LUTTRELL *Brief Rel.* II. 623 Sir John Brattle, essay master of the mint, is dead. **1701** *Lond. Gaz.* No. 3714/1 An Act for appointing Wardens and Assay-Masters, for Assaying Wrought Plate. **1784** C. BURNEY in *Parr's Wks.* (1828) VII. 394 You, who are my Assay Master, and separate my dross from the sterling ore.

asscaunce, obs. form of ASKANCE *adv.*

assch-, obs. spelling of ASH- and ASCH-.

asscomfite, var. ASCOMFIT *v. Obs.* to discomfit.

asse, obs. f. ASH (tree), and ASH *sb.*[2] (cinder).

asse, obs. dial. f. ASK *v.*

†**a'sseal**, *v. Obs.* Forms: 3–5 **asele**, 3–4 **acele**, 4–5 **aseel**, 5 **assele**, **-ale**. [Later form of *as-seele*, *a-sele*, for earlier **ansele* (see A- *pref.* 10), *ensele*, a OF. *enseele-r*, *-sele-r*, *anseele-r*:—late L. *insigillāre*, f. *in* in upon + *sigillum* seal (see ENSEAL).]

1. To set one's seal to (a document).

1297 R. GLOUC. 510 He made of the olde lawes is Chartre.. and aselede it [*printed* is] vaste inou. **1388** WYCLIF *Esther* iii. 12 Lettris aseelid with the ring of the kyng. **1492** *Bury Wills* (1850) 80 Myn testament.. with my sealle asselid.

2. To seal up.

1297 R. GLOUC. 496 Hor bernes dores acelede, and al clene out hom caste. *c* **1305** *Pains of Hell* in *O.E. Misc.* 228 Þe angel him schewed.. A put aseled wiþ seuen seles. **1388** WYCLIF *Dan.* xii. 9 The wordis ben closed and aseelid.

3. *fig.*

1388 WYCLIF *Wisd.* ii. 5 No turnyng aȝen of oure ende is; for it is aseelid, [*marg.*] by a stoon put on the bodi of the deed man biried. **1430** LYDG. *Chron. Troy* III. xxiv, With his worde the sentence was assealed.

†**'ass-ear.** *Herb. Obs.* [f. ASS *sb.*] Obsolete name of the Comfrey (*Symphytum officinale*), in Fr., *oreille d'âne.*

1585 in *Nomenclator* 137. **1611** COTGR., *Consire*, the hearbe Comfrey, Consound, Asse eare, Knitbacke, Backwort.

†**'assecle.** *Obs. rare.* [ad. L. *assecla*, f. *ass-*, *adsequi* to follow after.] Attendant, follower.

1616 SHELDON *Mirac. Antichr.* 325 (L.) It mattereth not with the pope and his assecles.

†**'asseclist.** *Obs.* [f. L. *assecla* + -IST.] = prec.

? **1607** in Nichols *Prog. Q. Eliz.* III. 632, I was the Aseclist that did attend her Weft to her vitall web, her breathing scope.

†**assec'tation.** *Obs.*[–0] [ad. L. *assectātiōn-em*, n. of action f. *assectāri*, freq. of *assequi*: see ASSECLE.] The action of following after or attending upon.

1656 in BLOUNT *Glossogr.*

†**assector.** *Obs.*[–0] [? for L. *assecūtor* or *assectātor*, nn. of agent f. *assequi*, *assectāri*.] 'A companion, a follower.' Cockeram 1623.

†**asse'curance.** *Obs. rare*[–1]. [ad. med.L. *assecūrāntia*, f. *assecūrāre*: see ASSECURE and -ANCE. Cf. It. *assicuranza*.] Assurance.

1616 SHELDON *Mirac. Antichr.* 320 (R.) What may be thought of those assecurances which they give?

†**assecu'ration.** *Obs. rare*[–1]. [ad. med.L. *assecūrātiōn-em*, n. of action f. *assecūrāre*: see next and -ATION.] The action of making sure; assurance.

a **1656** BP. HALL *Rem. Wks.* (1660) 268 Such a fiduciall persuasion as cannot deceive us, nor be liable to falsehood. But how far reaches this assecuration?

†**asse'cure**, *v. Obs.* [ad. med.L. *assecūrā-re*, f. L. *as-* = *ad-* to, completely + *sēcūr-us* SECURE, sure. Cognate with ASSURE, through OF. *aseürer*.] To make secure, sure, or safe; to assure, secure.

1594 HOOKER *Eccl. Pol.* VI. vi. §1 III. 89 Sin is not helped but by being assecured of pardon. **1597** DANIEL *Civ. Wares* III. xxiv, Think you that any meanes under the Sunne, Can assecure so indirect a course?

†**asse'curit**, *ppl. a. Sc. Obs.* [f. prec. + *-it* = -ED.] Assured, constant.

1501 DOUGLAS *Pal. Hon.* Prol I. viii, Quhais hie curage and assucurit cure Causis the eirth his fruits till expres Diffundant grace on euerie creature.

†**asse'cution.** *Obs.* [n. of action f. L. *assecūt-* ppl. stem of *assequi* to overtake, obtain: see ASSEQUENT.] The action of obtaining, acquirement.

c **1630** JACKSON *Creed* IV. III. iii. Wks. III. 393 Desires of pleasing himself in.. the assecution of any higher prized good. **1726** AYLIFFE *Parerg.* 115 Because such Living is immediately void by his Assecution of a second Benefice.

(-)assed, var. ARSED *ppl. a.*

†**'assedate**, *v. Sc. Law. Obs.* [f. med.L. *assedāre*, f. F. *asseoir*: see ASSESS.] To let on lease.

1545 *Aberdeen Reg.* V. 19 (JAM.) He assedat his fisching.

assedation (æsɪ'deɪʃən). *Sc. Law.* ? *Obs.* [n. of action f. prec.] A letting out on lease, a lease.

1457 *Act 14 Jas. II* (1597) §72 Our Soveraine Lord sall ratifie and apprieve the said assedation. *c* **1550** SIR J. BALFOUR *Practicks* (1754) 27 Ane contract.. sic as ane assedatioun of landis. **1651** CALDERWOOD *Hist. Kirk* (1843) II. 532 An assedatioun of the fruicts of the bishoprick.

asseege, assege, var. ASSIEGE *v. Obs.* to besiege.

assegai, recent variant of ASSAGAI *sb.*

†**a'sseize**, *v. Obs. rare*[–1]. [f. *as-* = A- *pref.* 11 + SEIZE *v.*] To seize upon, seize.

1590 MARLOWE *Edw. II*, I. ii. 238 Then laid they violent hands upon him.. and his goods asseized.

†**'assel(e.** *Obs. rare*[–1]. [a. OF. *essele* (mod. *aisselle*):—L. *axilla* armpit; or, for earlier Eng. *axle*, *eaxle*, *exle*, shoulder, between which and the OF. there was an early confusion.]

c **1450** *Merlin* vii. 116 The speres on their asseles, theire sheldes be-fore her bristes. [Cf. JOINV. in Littré 'le glaive dessous s'essele et l'escu devant li.]

assele, var. ASSEAL *v. Obs.* to seal.

asself (ə'sɛlf), *v.* [f. AS- *pref.* + SELF.] To take to oneself, appropriate, adopt.

1632 G. FLETCHER *Christ's Tri.* 9 Yet this is better, to asself the blame. **1659** FULLER *App. Inj. Innoc.* (1840) 631 If he cite the words, with commendation.. he as-selfeth them. **1884** *Secular Rev.* 237 Just as the stomach and other chylopoietic viscera build up our bodies by asselfing aliment.

asseller, obs. form of AXILLAR.

†**a'ssemblable**, *a. Obs. rare*[–1]. [a. OF. *assemblable*; cf. late L. *assimilābilis*, f. *assimilāre*: see ASSEMBLE *v.*[2] and -ABLE.] Like; *subst.* fellow.

c **1520** *Dial. Creat. Moral.* 96 (Halliw.) Every thinge that berithe life, desyreth to be conjoynyd to his assembleable.

assemblage (ə'sɛmblɪdʒ). [a. F. *assemblage* (Cotgr.), f. *assembler*: see ASSEMBLE *v.*[1] and -AGE.]

1. A bringing or coming together; a meeting or gathering; the state of being gathered or collected.

a **1730** E. FENTON *Ep. Lambard* (R.) In sweet assemblage every blooming grace Fix love's bright throne in Teraminta's face. **1768** BLACKSTONE *Comm.* I. I. i. 13 In consequence of this lucky assemblage. **1868** FREEMAN *Norm. Conq.* (1876) II. x. 507 From the first assemblage of the thegns at York.

2. The joining or union of two things; conjunction. *Obs.* exc. as techn. term in various *techn.* uses: the joining, putting together of parts (in *Carpentry* or of a machine); a collection (e.g. of artefacts); a work of art consisting of miscellaneous objects fastened together.

1727–51 CHAMBERS *Cycl.* s.v., The assemblage of two bones for motion, is called articulation. *Ibid.*, The carpentry of some Indians..where the assemblage is made without either nails or pins. **1728** THOMSON *Spring* 8 With innocence and meditation join'd In soft assemblage. **1849** WEALE *Dict. Terms, Assemblage*, in carpentry and joinery, framing, dovetailing, etc. *a* **1875** KNIGHT *Dict. Mech.* I. 171/1 This system of interchangeability and assemblage..is one of the most beautiful triumphs of modern mechanism. **1958** *Listener* 6 Nov. 752/2 The success of the total effect was due to the cutting and assemblage of the recordings under the composer's care. **1959** J. D. CLARK *Prehist. S. Afr.* ii. 55 The preservation of more complete faunal assemblages. **1961** *N.Y. Times* 4 Oct. 42/2 An 'assemblage' is a work of art made by fastening together cut or torn pieces of paper, clippings from newspapers, photographs, bits of cloth, fragments of wood, metal,..shells or stones, or even objects such as knives and forks,..automobile fenders, steel boilers, and stuffed birds and animals. **1963** *Listener* 7 Feb. 254/2 His [*sc.* John Latham's] assemblages do not strike me as random, when considered as arrangements of forms and planes.

3. A number of persons gathered together; a gathering, concourse. (Less formal than *assembly*.)

1741–2 H. WALPOLE *Lett. H. Mann* 22 (1834) I. 93 It was an assemblage of all ages and nations. **1809** PINKNEY *Trav. France* 48 The assemblage of ladies being very numerous. **1877** LYTTEIL *Landm.* IV. ii. 193 An assemblage of mighty heroes.

4. A number of things gathered together; a collection, group, cluster.

a **1704** LOCKE (T.) All that we amass together in our thoughts is..the assemblage of a great number of positive ideas. **1748** ANSON *Voy.* II. xii. 260 Opposite..is an assemblage of rocks. **1833** HT. MARTINEAU *Fr. Wines & Pol.* i. 13 Of the chesnut woods nothing remained but an assemblage of bare poles.

†**a'ssemblance**[1]. *Obs.* Also 5 **a-semlaunvs**. [a. F. *assemblance*, cogn. with It. *assembranza*:—late L. *assimulāntia*, f. *assimulāre*: see ASSEMBLE *v.*[1] and -ANCE.] Assemblage, assembling, assembly.

c **1485** *Digby Myst.* (1882) III. 387 Were þe kyng of flesch her with his a-semlaunvs! **1547** HOOPER *Answ. Bp. Winchester* Wks. 175 Paul..would in this assemblance the gospel to be preached. **1596** SPENSER *F.Q.* v. iv. 21 To weete the cause of their assemblaunce.

†**a'ssemblance**[2]. *Obs.* [a. Fr. *assemblance*, taken in sense of ASSEMBLE *v.*[2] In OF. *l'assemblance* occurs for *la semblance*. Cf. It. *assimiglianza* resemblance.] Semblance, appearance, show.

1485 CAXTON *Chas. Gt.* 207 Whyche was of fyn yuorye after thassemblaunce of a man. **1597** SHAKS. *2 Hen. IV*, III. ii. 276 Care I for..the stature, bulke, and bigge assemblance of a man? giue mee the spirit.

†**a'ssemblant**. *Obs. rare*[−1]. [cf. prec. with *semblance, -ant*, and It. *assimigliante* like.] = prec.

1523 LD. BERNERS *Froiss.* I. ccciv. 452 They came before the towne..and made great assemblant to assaut it.

†**assem'blation**. *Obs. rare*[−1]. [irreg. f. ASSEMBLE *v.*[1] + -ATION.] Assembling, meeting.

a **1733** NORTH *Examen* I. iii. ¶126 The Time and Place of the Assemblation was generally notified.

assemble (ə'sɛmb(ə)l), *v.*[1] Forms: 3–4 **asemle**, 4 **asemble**, 5 **assemle, -ele, -bill, -myll**, 6 **-bul**, 4– **assemble**. See also aphet. SEMBLE *v.*[1] [a. OF. *a(s)semble-r*, cogn. with Pr. *assemblar*, Sp. *asemblar*, It. *assemblare, -brare*:—L. *ad-, assimulā-re*, in its late sense of *simul cogĕre*, f. *ad* to + *simul* together.] Occas. strengthened by *together*.

1. *trans.* To bring together (persons) into one place or company; to gather, collect, convene.

c **1250** *Gen. & Ex.* 3865 God [bad] semelen folc and gon, And foren hem smiten on ðe ston. **1297** R. GLOUC. 360 And amorwe hem lete asemly [*printed* asely] wyþ mylde herte ynou. *a* **1330** *Otuel* 72 Tho lette Garsie asemlen anon, Alle hise sarazins echon. *c* **1400** *Destr. Troy* XI. 4577 To assemble on yche side soudiours ynogh. **1529** RASTELL *Pastyme* Brit. (1811) 127 And semblyd an other hoste. **1699** DRYDEN *Knts. T.* I. 456 Thou mayst..Assemble ours and all the Theban race. **1812** J. & H. SMITH *Rej. Addr.* xiii. (1873) 119 This tenth day of October Again assembles us in Drury Lane.

2. a. To bring together (things) into one place or mass, to collect; †*formerly*, to heap up, amass.

c **1374** CHAUCER *Boeth.* III. vii. 80 Yif þou enforcest þe to assemble moneye. **1483** CAXTON *Gold. Leg.* 249/3 Whan thou assemblest peyne thou encreacest his glorye. **1534** LD. BERNERS *Gold. Bk. M. Aurel.* (1546) N vij, They assemble by litel and littell diuers thynges. **1659** LEAK *Water-wks.* 24 That the Sun shining upon the said Burning Glasses may assemble the raies of the Sun within the said Vessels. *a* **1790** FRANKLIN *Autobiog.*, These proverbs..I assembled and formed into a connected discourse. **1855** BAIN *Senses & Int.* III. ii. §23 We also assemble, into one recollection, many widely scattered periods of our past history.

b. To put together (the separately manufactured parts of a composite machine or mechanical appliance); also with the machine as obj. Also in extended use.

1852 *Harper's Mag.* V. 158/1 When the several parts are all finished, the operation of putting them together so as to make up the musket from them complete, is called 'assembling the musket'. **1865** *Mech. Mag.* 31 Mar. 200/2 When all these parts are assembled together. **1888** *Sun* 21 Mar. (Farmer), The steel forgings have been made and turned over to our ordnance officers to assemble into guns. **1909** *Westm. Gaz.* 28 Apr. 2/2 Structural steel is imported punched, riveted, and assembled to be set up. **1909** *Ibid.* 16 Sept. 5/1 If all the parts are not there when the time comes to assemble the chassis. **1923** *Ibid.* 15 Sept., Assembling and packing cycle bells. **1961** K. REISZ *Technique Film Editing* (ed. 9) 278 *Assemble*, to carry out the first process in film editing, namely, to collect together the required shots and join them in provisional order, thus producing a rough cut.

†**3. a.** To join together, unite (two things or persons, one thing *to* or *with* another). *Obs.*

1393 GOWER *Conf.* II. 186 By that cause the godhede Assembled was to the manhede In the virgine. *Ibid.* III. 107 Assembled with astronomy Is eke that ilke astrology. **1483** CAXTON *G. de la Tour* L viij b, Syth that god hath assembled them no man mortal ouȝt to separe them.

†**b.** To couple (sexually). *Obs.*

c **1386** CHAUCER *Pars. T.* ¶831 That thay be assemblid bycause that they ben maried. **1393** GOWER *Conf.* I. 291 Two serpentes in his waie..Assembled were.

4. *refl.* in sense of next.

1302 *Pol. Songs* 188 The webbes and the fullaris assembleden hem alle. *c* **1425** WYNTOUN *Cron.*, þe barnage off Scotland, at þe last, Assemlyd þame. **1611** BIBLE *1 Kings* viii. 2 All the men of Israel assembled themselves unto king Solomon. **1801** STRUTT *Sports & Past.* II. ii. 82 Crowds of people assemble themselves upon the banks.

5. *intr.* To come together into one place or company; to gather together, congregate, meet.

a **1300** *Cursor M.* 7410 His shepe to-gedir walde assemble samme. *c* **1325** *E.E. Allit. P.* B. 1364 þat alle þe grete vpon grounde schulde..assemble at a set day. *c* **1450** *Merlin* i. 1 Thei assembleden to-gedir. **1538** STARKEY *England* 52 Cytes and townys, wherto they myght assembul. **1606** G. W[OODCOCKE] *Hist. Justine* 79 b, All the women assembled into the Temple of Venus. **1667** MILTON *P.L.* XI. 663 Grey-headed men and grave, with Warriours mixt Assemble. **1791** MRS. INCHBALD *Simp. Story* IV. x. 132 A confusion of persons a[s]sembling towards the apartment. **1849** MACAULAY *Hist. Eng.* I. 186 Driven from the towns, they assembled on heaths and mountains. **1860** MASSEY *Hist. Eng.* III. xxv. 33 The Parliament assembled in November.

†**6.** *esp.* To meet in fight; to join battle, make an attack or charge. (So in OFr.) *Obs.*

c **1350** *Will. Palerne* 3425 To hem of þe cite a sembled he þanne & fauȝt þan so ferscheli. **1375** BARBOUR *Bruce* XV. 421, I sall assembill on hym..All thouch ȝhe hald him neuir sa stout. *c* **1500** *Lancelot* 1083 To-giddir thar assemblit al the ost: At whois meting many o knycht was lost. **1513** DOUGLAS *Æneis* X. xii. 112 Athir man assemblit face for face [L. *seque viro vir contulit*].

†**7.** *trans.* To encounter, attack, assail. *Obs. rare.*

c **1532** LD. BERNERS *Huon* 613 Then they assembeled Brohart on all sydes.

†**a'ssemble**, *v.*[2] *Obs.* Also 5 **assamble**. [a. OF. *a(s)semble-r*, either referred in meaning to L. *assimulāre, adsimilāre* to liken (see ASSIMILATE); or confused by Englishmen with *ressembler*: see RESEMBLE. Cf. It. *assimigliare* to resemble, compare.] To liken, compare; to be like to, resemble.

1483 CAXTON *Gold. Leg.* 114/3 For the world assambleth the see. **1549** LATIMER *7 Serm. bef. Edw. VI* (Arb.) 151 Bribes may be assembled to pitch. **1550** BALE *Image Both Ch.* Sel. Wks. 1849. 379 The other be assembled unto most filthy locusts.

a'ssemble, *sb. Mil.* [ASSEMBLE *v.*[1] (sense 5) in the imperative mood, used as the name of a command or signal.] The second beat of the drum, or other signal, ordering soldiers to strike their tents and stand to their arms. Cf. ASSEMBLY 9.

1883 *Army Corps Orders* in *Standard* 22 Mar. 3/3 No bugle sounds are to be used..except the 'cease fire' and the 'assemble.'

assemble, obs. form of ASSEMBLY.

assembled (ə'sɛmb(ə)ld), *ppl. a.* [f. ASSEMBLE *v.*[1] + -ED.] Gathered into one place or company; put together.

1591 SHAKS. *1 Hen. VI*, I. i. 139 Whom all France, with their chiefe assembled strength, Durst not presume to looke once in the face. **1718** POPE *Iliad* II. 968 Assembled armies oft have I beheld. **1833** I. TAYLOR *Fanat.* ix. 398 The worship of an assembled nation. **1894** *Harper's Mag.* July 256/2 The partly assembled gun. **1907** *Westm. Gaz.* 9 Nov. 14/2 The vertically assembled differential case is being gradually superseded by the horizontally assembled case.

‖**assemblée** (asɑ̃ble). [Fr.; see ASSEMBLY.] Var. ASSEMBLY (esp. sense 7).

1712 SWIFT *Jrnl. to Stella* Let. xxxviii (1948) II. 460 Was last night at Lady Betty Germain's assemblée. **1787** MATY tr. *Riesbeck's Trav. Germ.* II. xxxi. 47 [In Hungary] every town with four or five houses in it, has its *assemblées*, and *redoutes*. **1938** *Times Lit. Suppl.* 5 Mar. 153/1 Mr. Tourtellot is prepared to join the ranks of the admiring *assemblée* and to gaze at her with uncritical eyes.

†**a'ssemblement**. *Obs.* [a. OF. *a(s)semblement*, f. *assembler*: see ASSEMBLE *v.*[1] and -MENT.] An assembly, assemblage, gathering.

1470 HARDING *Chron.* xciv, Whome Oswald mette with greate assemblement. *a* **1564** BECON *Demands Holy Script.* Wks. (1844) 613 What is the day of the Lord? The great assemblement, court, and parliament of all men. **1645** DIGBY *Nat. Bodies* xxv. (1658) 289 The complex assemblement..of all the causes, that concur to produce this effect.

assembler (ə'sɛmblə(r)). [f. ASSEMBLE *v.*[1] + -ER[1]; cf. OF. *assembleor, -eur*, n. of agent f. *assembler*: see ASSEMBLE *v.*[1]] One who assembles.

1. One who brings together, collects, or convenes.

1635 PERSON *Varieties* I. Introd. 2 The builder of cities, assembler of men. **1780** BURKE *Refl. Exec.* Wks. IX. 273 None of..the assemblers of the mob..have been convicted.

2. One who takes part in an assembly; *e.g.* a member of the Westminster Assembly of Divines.

1647 *Assembly-man* in *Harl. Misc.* (1745) V. 94/4 Yet it is some Relief to a sequestered Person to see two Assemblers snarl for his Tithes. *a* **1660** HAMMOND *To Cheynel* Wks. I. 193 (R.) Your confession of faith which you say shall be published by your assemblers. **1710** SHAFTESB. *Charac.* IV. §3 (1737) I. 148 If they can produce..Visionary Assemblers to attest a story of a Witch upon a Broomstick.

3. One who assembles a machine or its parts.

1898 *Cricket & Football Field* 1 Oct. 3 'Assemblers'—men who buy [cycle] frames..then put in whatever fittings they or their customers may be inclined to use. **1908** *Daily Chron.* 21 Feb. 10/6 Arc lamp assemblers. **1909** *Ibid.* 21 Aug. 6/6 One cannot get such a cycle ready made, but a good assembler can build it up.

4. The mechanism of a linotype machine which assembles the matrices and space bands to form a line of type. Also *attrib.*

1902 *Encycl. Brit.* XXXIII. 523/2 They are set up in proper order in the assembler block. **1905** C. T. JACOBI *Printers' Handbk.* (ed. 3) 93 When the line is accidentally overset..it is necessary to remove some of the matrices from the assembler. **1908** J. S. THOMPSON *Mechanism of Linotype* (ed. 3) ii. 15 The assembler shute spring..should be curved so as to tend to throw the bottom of the matrix towards the assembler wheel. **1925** J. R. ROGERS *Linotype Instruct. Book* 1 Beginning with the touch of a finger upon a Keybutton.. a matrix is released and falls by gravity upon a constantly running belt which delivers the matrix into the 'assembler'.

5. *Computing.* **a.** A program for converting instructions written in low-level symbolic code or assembly language into machine code. Cf. COMPILER 1 b.

1959 *Jrnl. Assoc. Computing Machinery* II. 139 Instead of absolute binary output, this assembler produces a SQUOZE deck. **1967** *Computer Group News* Jan. 4/2 An assembler operates almost on a symbol-by-symbol basis. **1970** O. DOPPING *Computers & Data Processing* xix. 305 The difference between a compiler and an assembler is explained. **1975** *Sci. Amer.* May 38/3 An assembly-language program must be translated into machine language before it is committed to a memory; this conversion is accomplished by an assembler, which checks the assembly-language program for certain types of errors and, if none are found, produces the desired machine-language code. **1979** D. R. HOFSTADTER *Gödel, Escher, Bach* (1980) x. 291 This program, called an assembler, accepts mnemonic instruction names, decimal numbers, and other convenient abbreviations which a programmer can remember easily, and carries out the conversion into the monotonous but critical bit-sequences. **1984** J. HILTON *Choosing & using your Home Computer* 165/2 Assembler packages will usually only work with a disk drive.

b. = *assembler language* in sense 6.

1979 *Sci. Amer.* Apr. 75/2 Simple languages called assemblers replace the binary notation with symbols that are more concise and more easily remembered. **1985** *Personal Computer World* Feb. 238/3 People who are not familiar with assembler should consult a book before they start.

6. Special Combs.: **assembler code, language** *Computing* = *assembly language* s.v. ASSEMBLY IV; **assembler program** *Computing* = sense 5 above.

1975 *Austral. Computing Jrnl.* July 78/1 Another potential hazard occurs when the programmer writes structured source code and the compiler generates unstructured *assembler code. **1985** *Personal Computer World* Feb. 230/3 The first listing is the assembler code. **1968** *New Scientist* 11 Jan. 79 The makers offer a library of programs to go with it [*sc.* a desk computer], including..an *assembler language, and a general mathematics library. **1979** W. S. CAELLI *Microcomputer Revolution* p. xii, Till recently most microcomputer programs had to be written in assembler language. **1977** *Sci. Amer.* Sept. 152/3 The translation is done by the computer itself with an '*assembler' program. **1985** *Personal Computer World* Feb. 39/1 (Advt.), Integral linker allows assembler programs to be linked together. **1980** C. S. FRENCH *Computer Sci.* xxv. 189 The manufacturer provides a program called an assembler or assembler program which translates the assembly language into machine code.

a'ssembling, *vbl. sb.* [f. as prec. + -ING[1].] Gathering together, meeting. Also in obs. senses: **a.** Attack, onslaught. **b.** Union of two, coupling.

1375 BARBOUR *Bruce* XII. 515 The remanant..That mycht cum to the assembling. *c* **1386** CHAUCER *Pars. T.* ¶830 Whan thay take noon reward in her assembling but only to the fleischly delit. *c* **1450** LONELICH *Grail* xiii. 539 He sawgh twey batailles..That weren redy to the assemblyng. **1611** BIBLE *Heb.* x. 25 Not forsaking the assembling of our selues together. **1855** MACAULAY *Hist. Eng.* III. 205 The Parliaments of Ireland had then no fixed place of assembling. **1894** *Harper's Mag.* July 252/1 The assembling, as the process of shrinking on the various parts which go to make up the modern cannon is called. **1926** *Time* 14 June 34/2 In 1924 he profited $25,000,000 by shipping parts to district assembling plants.

assembling (əˈsɛmblɪŋ), *ppl. a.* [f. as prec. + -ING².] That assemble, gathering.

1619 FINETT *Let.* in *Eng. & Germ.* (1865) 63 The now assembling powres of the Archdukes. **1697** DRYDEN *Georg.* IV. 802 Straight issue thro' the Sides assembling Swarms.

assembly (əˈsɛmblɪ). Forms: 4–5 **assemblee,** 4–6 **assemblé,** 5 **assemblié, -blay,** 6 **-blie,** 5– **assembly.** See also aphet SEMBLY. [a. OF. *a(s)semblee,* sb., f. fem. pa. pple. of *assembler*: see ASSEMBLE *v.*¹ and -Y². Cf. *army*.]

I. The action or fact of assembling, the state of being assembled.

1. a. Gathering together, meeting; the state of being collected or gathered; = ASSEMBLAGE 1.

1413 LYDG. *Pylgr. Sowle* v. v. 76 The byrdes..syttynge in assemble vpon an hye tre. **1436** *Pol. Poems* (1859) II. 152 The duk of Burgayn..Mad greet assembillé in landes wyd. *c* **1500** *Lancelot* 267 Mony assemblay that gawane gart be maid To wit his name. **1641** *Termes de la Ley* 187 Unlawfull assembly is where people assemble themselves together to doe some unlawfull thing against the peace. **1876** GREEN *Short Hist.* viii. §6. 521 A Triennial Bill enforced the assembly of the Houses every three years.

b. The assembling of troops; freq. *attrib.* Cf. sense III.

1917 H. W. YOXALL *Jrnl.* 18 Sept. in *Fashion of Life* (1966) iv. 37 Went with..two runners to peg out our assembly area. .. The marking-out of the assembly position was not difficult. **1918** E. S. FARROW *Dict. Mil. Terms* 42 The assembly position must be far enough to the rear to enable [etc.]. **1919** *King's Royal Rifle Corps Chron. 1916* 62 The Battalion..proceeded to the assembly trenches. **1923** KIPLING *Irish Guards* I. 324 The Battalion moved nearer their assembly-areas.

c. The action or method of assembling a machine or composite article; the parts so assembled.

1914 *Engineering Mag.* XLVII. 6 The boards travel.. down the line, growing in completeness as they move, each 'team' working simultaneously on opposite sides of the board, adding some step to the assembly. *Ibid.* 882/2 Axles to be placed in chassis assembly at the Highland Park shops are lifted up off the chain-line. **1922** *Autocar* 10 Nov. 983 Arrol-Johnston gear assembly, showing how the whole can be removed without disturbing the box itself...Rear axle assembly. **1935** *Discovery* June 183/2 The assembly of an ordinary electric-lampholder consisting of eighteen parts. **1937** *Ibid.* June 187/1 The glass envelope housing the electrode assembly. **1948** 'N. SHUTE' *No Highway* ii. 43 The port tailplane and elevator, the port landing wheel assembly. **1962** A. NISBETT *Technique Sound Studio* 247 The whole assembly can be very light in weight and may be cheap to produce.

Also *attrib.*, as ***assembly-belt*** (also *fig.*), ***-plant, -room, -shop***; **assembly-line** (orig *U.S.*), a group of machines and workers concerned with the progressive assembly of some product; also *attrib.* and *fig.*

1938 AUDEN & ISHERWOOD *On Frontier* 17 The assembly-belt is like an army on the move. **1945** SINCLAIR LEWIS *C. Timberlane* (1946) i. 13 He had a wife unremittingly productive of babies, for whose assembly-belt production he felt only accidentally responsible. **1914** *Engineering Mag.* XLVII. 858/2 The study of the finishing and assembling of front-axle components shows how labor-costs may be.. reduced..by the use of sliding assembly lines, chain-driven for the final assembling, but having the partial assemblies moved by hand. **1926** *Sci. Amer.* July 41/1 The illustration shows the chassis on the assembly line. **1943** S. C. MENEFEE *Assignment* (1944) I. v. 103 The assembly-line method of putting bombers together has great possibilities. **1945** *Reader's Digest* Oct. 82/2 The syndicate developed an assembly-line method of producing beef. **1955** *20th Cent.* June 548 From the top of a school assembly line they are carried by their parents or the State to a conveyor belt that runs through the spiry city [*sc.* Oxford] for three years or so. **1931** *Economist* 28 Feb. 432/1 The project to build an assembly plant at the new port of Gdynia has not been carried any further. **1897** *Outing* (U.S.) XXX. 279/2 They are then polished, nickelplated,..and sent to the assembly-room to take their places in the wheel. **1914** *Auto-motor Jrnl.* 21 Mar. 362/1 It is only because every part is dead true before it reaches the assembly shop.

d. The assembling of parts of a film or sound recording. Also *attrib.*

1949 W. H. OFFENHAUSER *16-Mm. Sound Motion Pict.* x. 328 Editing and assembly are loose and broad terms customarily used to describe the processes that occur between the original records and the release prints. **1960** O. SKILBECK *Film & T.V. Terms* 12 *Assembly*, rushes of a film joined together in script scene order, with spare takes and number boards eliminated; but not, as yet, edited. **1962** A. NISBETT *Technique Sound Studio* 246 *Copy editing*, the copying of selected extracts from recorded material into sequence on a main programme assembly tape.

†**2.** The coming together of two persons or things; meeting, conjuction, union. Cf. ASSEMBLAGE 2.

c **1325** *E.E. Allit. P.* A. 759 My makelez lambe..Me ches to hys make, al-þaȝ vnmete Sum tyme semed þat assemblé. **1330** R. BRUNNE *Chron.* 51 Vnder Southamptone was þer assemble, Of Harald & Hardknoute. **1483** CAXTON *Gold. Leg.* 255/4 The unyte and assemble of the flesshe of oure lord and of oure lady.

†**3.** Hostile meeting, onslaught, attack. *Obs.*

1375 BARBOUR *Bruce* XII. 491 He gert trwmp vp to the assemble. *c* **1400** *Destr. Troy* xv. 6299 He was..sonest in assembly in þe sad fyght. *a* **1500** *Lancelot* 3336 The Knycht ..Wich at the first assemble in this sted Wencussith all. **1535** STEWART *Cron. Scot.* II. 454 Ane scharpar sembla ȝit wes thair neuer sene.

II. The company assembled.

4. A gathering of persons; a number of people met together; a concourse, throng.

1330 R. BRUNNE *Chron.* 73 Þe bisshop corouned hir þore, bifor þat faire semble. **1377** LANGL. *P. Pl.* B. Prol. 216 Barones an burgeis..I seiȝ in þis assemble. **1486** CAXTON *Curial* 10 Kepe you ferre fro suche an assemblee. **1543** *Necess. Doctr.* F j b, Ecclesia, that is to saye, an assemble of people called out from other. **1601** SHAKS. *Jul. C.* III. ii. 19 If there bee any in this Assembly, any deere Friend of Cæsars. **1711** ADDISON *Spect.* No. 1 ¶5, I sometimes pass for a Jew in the Assembly of Stock Jobbers. **1825** *Bro. Jonathan* I. 286 The assembly broke up.

5. a. *esp.* A gathering of persons for the purpose of deliberation and decision; a deliberative body, a legislative council.

1366 MAUNDEV. iii. 16 Thei holden here Grete Conseilles and here Assembleez. *c* **1440** *Morte Arth.* 1578 Salle he never..sitt in þe assemblé, in syghte wyth his feris. **1534** MORE *On the Passion* Wks. 1302/1 Therefore agreed thys greate assemble that they would not take hym on the holye daye. **1681** NEVILE *Plato Rediv.* 72 A Government consisting of a Prince and a Popular Assembly. **1718** POPE *Iliad* I. 77 The assembly seated, rising o'er the rest, Achilles thus the king of men address'd. **1878** GLADSTONE *Prim. Homer* 125 The Achaian assemblies were in general regularly summoned by the heralds.

b. Hence in various specific or historical uses: ***Assembly*** or ***General Assembly***: the name given to the legislature in some of the United States of America. ***General Assembly*** of the Church of Scotland: the representative body which meets annually to direct its affairs; other Presbyterian bodies elect similar councils. ***National Assembly*** of France: the popularly-elected branch of the legislature. ***Primary Assembly***: (see quot.). ***Westminster Assembly*** of Divines, appointed by the Long Parliament in 1643, to aid in settling the government and liturgy of the Church of England (whence *The Assembly's Catechism*).

a **1572** KNOX *Hist. Ref.* IV. 344 The General Assembly of the Church..holden in December [1561] after the Queen's Arrival. **1643** MILTON *Divorce* Introd., To the Parliament of England, with the Assembly. **1688** *Col. Rec. Pennsylv.* I. 223 The Comittee presented to this board three bills which was brought to them from yᵉ Assembly. **1759** ROBERTSON *Hist. Scotl.* I. III. an. 1560 The first general assembly of the church..was held this year. **1794** J. GIFFORD *Louis XVI* 212 The inhabitants of every district in France, preparatory to the election of delegates, hold what is called a primary assembly, where they choose a prescribed number of electors, who are to act for the whole in the choice of a representative to the states. **1839** *Penny Cycl.* XV. 255/2 Mirabeau was now acknowledged as the chief leader in the National Assembly.

6. a. A gathering of persons for religious worship; a congregation.

1600 SHAKS. *A.Y.L.* III. iii. 50 We haue no Temple but the wood, no assembly but horne-beasts. **1641** HINDE *J. Bruen* xxvii. 83 To bring in such able and godly Ministers..into the publike Assembly. *a* **1748** WATTS *Hymn*, Lord, how delightful 'tis to see A whole assembly worship thee.

b. *spec.* In schools, a general gathering of staff and pupils (usu. before lessons begin) for worship or other purposes.

1932 [see *school assembly* s.v. SCHOOL VI 16 a]. **1943** *Times Educ. Suppl.* 25 Dec. 622/1 The day begins quietly with assembly. **1955** E. BLISHEN *Roaring Boys* III. 114 At assembly the head announced that it was going to be a fine year. **1968** 'P. HOBSON' *Titty's Dead* i. 14 The bell for Assembly clanged through the school. **1984** S. TOWNSEND *Growing Pains A. Mole* 141 Lousy stinking school started today... Pandora and I held hands in assembly.

7. A gathering of persons for purposes of social entertainment. (The public assembly, which formed a regular feature of fashionable life in the 18th century, is described by Chambers (*Cycl.* 1751) as 'a stated and general meeting of the polite persons of both sexes, for the sake of conversation, gallantry, news, and play.' Private assemblies corresponded in some respects to the modern 'reception' or 'at-home.')

1590 SHAKS. *Com. Err.* v. i. 60 Haply in priuate. *Adr.* And in assemblies too. **1603** —— *Meas. for M* I. iii. 9, I haue euer lou'd the life remoued, And held in idle price to haunt assemblies. **1718** *Free-thinker* No. 2. 10 He will find admittance into all the crowded Balls and Assemblies. **1764** FOOTE *Patron* I. (1774) 9 You know this is his day of assembly, I suppose you will be there. **1865** H. PHILLIPS *Amer. Paper Curr.* II. 167 Gaiety pervaded the American camp..and an assembly was organized. **1883** *Scotsman* 15 Jan. 1/1 (*Advt.*) Citizen Assemblies. Fancy Dress Ball in aid of the Royal Infirmary.

†**8.** A collection of things; = ASSEMBLAGE 4.

1642 HOWELL *For. Trav.* (Arb.) 51 An assembly of huge crags and hils. **1699** EVELYN *Acetaria* (1729) 149 A very plentiful assembly of Sallet-Herbs.

III. A military call by drum or bugle. Cf. ASSEMBLE *sb.*

1727–51 CHAMBERS *Cycl.*, *Assembly* is also used..for the second beat of the drum. On hearing this, the soldiers strike their tents, roll them up, and then stand to their arms. The third beating is called the *march*, as the first is called the *general*. **1803** SIR J. NICHOLLS in Gurw. *Wellington Disp.* II. 394 The generale was beat at half-past four, the assembly at half-past five.

IV. *Comb.*, **assembly-ground,** a place where birds assemble esp. for mating; **assembly house** (*a*) = *sembly-house* (SEMBLY 4); (*b*) a house in which assemblies (see sense 7) were held; **assembly language** *Computing*, a low-level programming language that corresponds closely to the machine language of a computer but employs mnemonics and labels in place of numerical codes and operands; **assembly-man,** a member of an Assembly (see sense 5); **assembly-place,** a place in which an assembly is held; *spec.* = *assembly-ground*; **assembly program** *Computing* = ASSEMBLER 5 a; **assembly routine** *Computing*, (*a*) a routine which assembles other routines; (*b*) a routine for converting symbolic code into machine code, usu. as a task within a larger program; cf. ASSEMBLER 5 a; **assembly-room,** a room in which assemblies (see sense 7) were formerly held, and in which balls, concerts, and similar entertainments are now given.

1906 E. SELOUS in *Zoologist* X. 419 There were, too, some good examples of the deportment of Ruffs on the assembly-ground. **1920** H. ELIOT HOWARD *Territory in Bird Life* v. 173 In the first place, there are the assembly grounds to which the birds repair season after season; and then, on the assembly grounds, there are the territories. **1502** in *Oxf. Univ. Statutes* (1888) 217 In Domo vocata *le Assemblie-House* in Universitate prædicta. **1749** B. M. CAREW *Apol. for Life* 28 He saw a fine House, and demanding whose it was, they told him it was the Assembly-House [in Maryland]. **1762** O. GOLDSMITH *Life R. Nash* 46 People of fashion [at Bath] make public breakfasts at the assembly-houses. **1964** *Honeywell Gloss. Data Processing* 3/2 *Assembly language*, the machine-oriented programming language (e.g. EASY, ARGUS) belonging to an assembly system. **1965** *Times* 7 Jan. 14 Manufacturers today are expected to supply..a fairly simple assembly language which makes it possible to instruct the machine without recourse to its own confusing language of zeros and ones. **1979** J. E. ROWLEY *Mechanised In-House Information Syst.* I. 52 Assembly languages are powerful, and make for easier program construction than machine codes. **1983** *Listener* 12 May 38/1 Assembly-language programming is still an exceedingly cryptic business. **1647** in *Harl. Misc.* (1745) V. 93/1 (*title*) The Assembly-man. **1837** HALIBURTON *Clockm.* Ser. I. xxxii. 347 He sot up for an Assembly-man. **1875** WINGATE in *N. Amer. Rev.* CXX. 161 An assembly-man came to his room..to receive the price of his vote. **1684** BAXTER *12 Argts.* §16 28 Separatists, such as the Assembly-men had been. **1936** *Discovery* Sept. 263/1 The last occasion in which a new assembly-place in this country was chosen was in 1919. **1941** J. S. HUXLEY *Uniqueness of Man* ix. 198 Assembly-places [of birds] for mating. **1955** R. K. RICHARDS *Arithmetic Operations in Digital Computers* xii. 379 An 'assembly program' is..used to assemble the sections and compute the actual storage locations and addresses from the symbolic notation. **1961** LEEDS & WEINBERG *Computer Programming Fund.* ii. 50 We define the assembly program as a program capable of translating some other program from the coder-acceptable programming language to the computer-acceptable machine language. **1984** *Byte* Nov. 524/2 The instruction set considered legal by the assembler is that specified by Motorola for the MC68000. The editor lets you create 68000 assembly programs and regular text files. **1744** JOHNSON *L.P.*, *Savage* Wks. III. 298 Nor could she enter the assembly-rooms..without being saluted with some lines from The Bastard. **1862** THACKERAY *Four Georges* ii. 99 Every country town had its assembly-room. **1951** *Proc. R. Soc.* A. CCVI. 541 An assembly routine is one which may be used to organize the input of a whole programme, marshalling the various sub-routines in suitable places in the store, and making the necessary adjustments in the orders. The method of inserting extra print orders was originated by M. V. Wilkes, who also constructed the first assembly routine. **1984** *Byte* May 371/3 The program must check for the occurrence of an overrun. Upon finding one, the assembly routine sets a flag that can be read by the BASIC program once the data collection is finished.

assence, -cial, obs. ff. ESSENCE, -TIAL.

assend, pa. pple. of ASHEND *v. Obs.* to disgrace.

assend, assent, obs. forms of ASCEND, ASCENT.

†**assenel, -yke.** *Obs.* Glossed in *Promp. Parv.* (1440) by L. *squilla* 'sea-leek, sea-onion.'

assent (əˈsɛnt), *v.* Forms: 3–5 **asent(e, acent(e,** 4–6 **assente,** 4– **assent.** *Aphet.* 4–5 **sent.** (*Pa. t.* and *pple.* 4–5 **assent, assent.**) [a. OF. *a(s)sente-r*:—L. *assentāre* (*-āri*), irreg. freq. of L. *assentīre* (*-īri*), f. *as-* = *ad-* to + *sentīre* to feel, perceive, think, whence also F. *assentir*, used in OF. beside *assenter*, and now the only form.]

1. a. *intr.* To give the concurrence of one's will, to agree *to* (a proposal), to comply with (a desire). *Arch.* in general sense, and commonly replaced by *consent*, exc. as said of the sovereign *assenting* to a measure, or as in 4. (Rare obs. const. *for*.)

1297 R. GLOUC. 96 Þe maydenes wolde raþer dye, þan acente þer to. *c* **1385** CHAUCER *L.G.W.* 1596 The kyng assentede to his bone. **1450** MYRC 1644 Ȝef þow ley on hym more Thenne he wole asente fore. **1576** LAMBARDE *Peramb. Kent* (1826) 329 The Maister assented easily to their desire. **1670** LD. NORTH in Somers *Tracts* (1748) I. 2 Having assented to a Publication. **1771** *Junius Lett.* xliv. 237 The constitutional duties of a house of Commons are..to propose or assent to wholesome laws. **1864** TENNYSON *En. Ard.* 126 Would Enoch have the place? And Enoch all at once assented to it. **1863** COX *Inst. Eng. Govt.* II. iii. 341 The Lords passed a resolution, to which the King assented.

b. without prepositional const. *arch.*; see prec.

c **1350** *Will. Palerne* 2692 He swor his oþ · þat he a-sent nold. **1393** LANGL. *P. Pl.* C. v. 98 So alle myne claymes ben quyt · by so þe kynge asente. **1611** BIBLE *Luke* xxiii. 24 Pilate gaue sentence [*marg.* assented] that it should be as they required. **1878** B. TAYLOR *Pr. Deukalion* II. ii. 65 Assent, and the future is sure.

†**c.** with *inf. Obs.*

1382 WYCLIF *Judith* xii. 10 Go, and sweteli moue this Ebru, that..she sente to dwelle with me. **1393** LANGL. *P. Pl.* C. III. 170 To be maried for monye · mede hath a-sented. *c* **1485** *Digby Myst.* (1882) IV. 297 And thou wert well assent To let it ren owt most plenteosly. **1611** SPEED *Hist. Gt. Brit.* IX. xx. (1632) 979 The summe assented to be gathered was sixescore thousand pounds.

†**d.** *trans.* (elliptically) To agree to, sanction. *Obs.*

a **1641** STRAFFORD *Lett.* II. 120 If it shall be thought fit.. I assent it with all my heart. **1675** TRAHERNE *Chr. Ethics* xx. 329 Godliness, and honesty, need nothing but to be maintained and assented by the prince.

†**2. a.** *intr.* To come to an agreement as to a proposal; to agree together, determine, decide. Const. *to, into. Obs.*

c **1300** *Beket* 1107 To this consail everechone assentede. *c* **1386** CHAUCER *Man of L.T.* 246 They sworen and assenten every man To lyf with hir and dye. *c* **1440** *Bk. Curtasye* in *Babees Bk.* 316 Þo clerke of kechyn, countrollour, Stuarde, coke, and surueyour, Assenten in counselle.. How þo lorde schalle fare at mete. **1470–85** (ed. 1634) MALORY *Arthur* (1816) I. 107 Into this counsel the five kings assented.

†**b.** *esp.* in *pa. pple.* Come to agreement, come to a conclusion or resolution, agreed. *Obs.*

c **1350** *Will. Palerne* 538 Whan sche so was a-sented · sche seide sone after. *c* **1400** *Destr. Troy* XXXIII. 13008 The Rebellis..þat were assent to the slaght of his sure fader. *c* **1430** *Syr Generides* 2025 Thoo baronnes were assented sone Al hir will forto doone. **1528** MORE *Heresyes* IV. Wks. 276/1 Yf the worlde were assented therunto.

†**c.** *trans.* To agree, determine, decide upon (a thing proposed). *Obs.*

c **1300** *K. Alis.* 1480 They assentyn, by on assent, A riche croune of red gold. *c* **1386** CHAUCER *Doctor's T.* 146 Whan that assented was this cursed reed. **1591** LAMBARDE *Arch.* (1635) 143 No matter shall be assented, but at the least there assent thereunto foure Councellors.

†**3. a.** *intr.* To conform in practice, submit, yield (*to*). *Obs.*

1340 HAMPOLE *Pr. Consc.* 4386 He sal þam turment þat wille noght til his law assent. **1375** BARBOUR *Bruce* I. 169 Schir Ihon the balleol..Assentyt till him, in all his will. *c* **1400** *Apol. Loll.* 84 To assent is better þan for to offer þe fatnes of schep. *a* **1520** *Myrr. Our Ladye* 7, I laboure to kepe the wordes..as farre as oure language wyll well assente. **1636** HEALEY *Epictetus' Man.* xxvii. 33 To curbe thy minde from too quicke assenting to thine eye.

†**b.** *trans.* with cognate object. *Obs.*

1615 T. ADAMS *Leaven* 105 They..that..subscribe and assent obedience to his hests.

4. a. To give or express one's agreement with a statement or matter of opinion; to agree to an abstract proposition, or a proposal that does not concern oneself, or involve one's own action. Const. *to* (*with, unto*, obs.). The ordinary modern use as distinguished from CONSENT.

c **1380** WYCLIF *Three Treat.* 24 Crist wole not assent with thes, for thei may not be sothe. **1393** LANGL. *P. Pl.* C. I. 190 Al þe route of ratons · to þys reison a-sentede. *c* **1450** LONELICH *Grail* xlviii. 49 To this word assentyd ful foure and twenty. **1612** WOODALL *Surg. Mate* Wks. 1655 Pref. 2 This opinion is also assented unto by holy Scriptures. **1712** ADDISON *Spect.* No. 411 ¶4 We see, and immediately assent to the Beauty of an Object. **1718** *Free-thinker* No. 90. 243 My readers will readily assent to the Truth of what I have observed. **1874** F. HALL *N. Amer. Rev.* CXIX. 329 Assenting to the premises, we reject the conclusion.

b. without prepositional const.

1528 MORE *Heresyes* I. Wks. 126/1 Which thinge bicause I daily se, I assented. **1611** BIBLE *Acts* xxiv. 9 The Iewes also assented, saying that these things were so. **1735** POPE *Prol. Sat.* 201 Damn with faint praise, assent with civil leer. **1873** BLACK *Pr. Thule* iii. 40 She assented with a gracious smile.

†**c.** *with* or *to* a person, i.e. to his opinion. *Obs.*

1632 HEYWOOD *Iron Age* I. I. i, Æneas, your aduise assents with vs. **1695** WOODWARD *Nat. Hist. Earth* (1723) 25 Some ..fully assent to me herein. **1783** WATSON *Philip III* (1793) II. VI. 255 They undoubtedly assented to the king in the opinion he entertained.

†**5.** *refl.* in prec. senses. *Obs.*

c **1374** CHAUCER *Boeth.* III. xi. 95, I assent[e] me quod I. *c* **1400** *Destr. Troy* x. 4241 All assentid hom sone, þat his saw herd. **1447–8** SHILLINGFORD *Lett.* (1871) 51 To which bothe parties..aggreed and assented ham. **1470–85** MALORY *Arthur* (1816) II. 98 'I assent me thereto,' said sir Palomides.

assent (əˈsɛnt), *sb.* Forms: 4–5 **asent(e, acent(e,** 5 **assente,** 4– **assent.** *Aphet.* 4–5 **sent(e.** [a. OF. *a(s)sent, a(s)sente*, f. *assenter*: see prec.]

1. The concurrence of the will, compliance with a desire. *arch.* and repl. by *consent*, exc. as in next.

a **1300** *Cursor M.* 4955 Ye solde him out of myn assent. *a* **1330** *Otuel* 47 And Ich wele ben at acent, That thou sschalt wedde Belecent. **1418** ABP. CHICHELE in Ellis *Orig. Lett.* I. 2. I. 5 He hath ȝiven his assent therto. **1739** T. SHERIDAN *Persius* II. 31 By what do you propose to purchase the Assent of the Gods? **1814** SCOTT *Ld. Isles* VI. iii, There Bruce's slow assent allows Fair Isabel the veil and vows.

2. Official, judicial, or formal concurrence of will; sanction; the action or instrument that signifies such concurrence.

c **1386** CHAUCER *Doctor's T.* 204 Thurgh thassent of this juge Apius. **1461** J. PASTON in *Lett.* 408 II. 35, I wyll nothyng graunt withowt the under shreves assent. *a* **1672** WREN in Gutch *Coll. Cur.* I. 247 All those, whose votes were known to depend upon his will, gave their assents. **1737** POPE *Horace Epist.* II. ii. 30 Laws, to which you gave your own assent. **1863** COX *Inst. Eng. Govt.* I. vi. 48 A bill does not become an Act of Parliament until it has received the Royal assent. **1877** BURROUGHS *Taxation* 407 Those who sign such written assents may withdraw.

†**3.** The concurrence of a number of persons in sentiment or purpose; accord. *Obs.*

c **1325** *E.E. Allit. P.* A. 94 Thay songen wyth a swete asent. *c* **1440** *Morte Arth.* (Roxb.) 72 Through the sente of all..Ganne the kynge a lettre make. **1480** CAXTON *Chron. Eng.* liv. 38 Crouned and made kyng by assent of the britons. *c* **1500** *Lancelot* 421 And one of them, with al ther holl assent. Saith, etc. **1718** POPE *Iliad* I. 31 The Greeks in shouts their joint assent declare.

b. *esp.* in phrases ***by*** or ***with one assent, common assent.*** *arch.* exc. as influenced by senses 2 and 5.

c **1300** *K. Alis.* 1480 They assentyn, by on assent. *c* **1320** *Sir Beues* 1713 Be comin acent, Ther was comin parlement. *c* **1485** *Digby Myst.* II. 477 Let vs both by on assent go to the busshopys. **1538** STARKEY *England* 11 Thys cyvyle lyfe was a polytyke ordur..stablyschyd by commyn assent. **1611** BIBLE *2 Chron.* xviii. 12 The prophets declare good to the king with one assent. **1843** CARLYLE *Past & Pr.* (1858) 182 Travelling with one assent on the broad way.

†**4.** Opinion. *Obs.*

1377 LANGL. *P. Pl.* B. IV. 187 Ȝif ȝe bidden buxomnes, be of myne assente. *c* **1386** CHAUCER *Merch. T.* 288 Men most enquere (this is myn assent) Wher sche be wys, or sobre, or dronkelewe. *c* **1435** *Torr. Portugal* 1359, I cord with that assent. **1559** *Myrr. Mag., Dk. Suffolk* xviii. 1 The Lords and Commons both of like assent.

5. Agreement with a statement, an abstract proposition, or a proposal that does not concern oneself; mental acceptance or approval. (The ordinary modern use, as distinguished from CONSENT.)

c **1534** tr. *Polyd. Verg. Eng. Hist.* (1846) I. 169 Which thinge [he]..sayde not withoute the aspiration and assent of the Hollie Spirit. **1659** PEARSON *Creed* (1839) 2 This assent, or judgment of any thing to be true. **1794** SULLIVAN *View Nat.* I. 15, I must honestly confess my full assent to the doctrine. **1843** MILL *Logic* Introd. (1868) 5 Our assent to the conclusion being grounded on the truth of the premises.

b. in the formal phrase ***assent and consent.***

1574 tr. *Littleton's Tenures* 9 a, Provinge his assent and consente of such endowemente. **1875** STUBBS *Const. Hist.* I. xiv. 143 The deliberate assent and consent of a parliament.

†**aˈssent,** *pa. pple. Obs.* [App. f. SEND; but spelt like prec. word: cf. ASEND *v.*] Used frequently by Gower, app. in the two senses: Sent forth; sent for.

1393 GOWER *Conf.* I. 343 This Climestre him had assent. *Ibid.* II. 54 Therupon of one assent The maidens weren anone assent. *Ibid.* III. 327 He let sommone a parlement, To which the lordes were assent.

assentaneous (æsənˈteɪnɪəs), *a. rare*⁻¹. [f. late L. *assentāne-us* (f. *assentīri*) + -OUS: cf. *consentaneous.*] Inclined to assent, deferential.

1834 LANDOR *Exam. Shaks.* Wks. 1846 II. 276 Finding thee docile and assentaneous.

†**aˈssentant,** *ppl. a.* and *sb. Obs.* [a. OF. *a(s)sentant*, pr. pple. of *a(s)senter*: see ASSENT *v.* and -ANT. Now replaced by ASSENTIENT.]

A. *adj.* Assenting, consenting; agreeing.

[*a* **1400** *Relig. Pieces fr. Thornt. MS.* 89 Noghte assent-and to syne.] *c* **1400** *Test. Love* I. (1560) 277/1, I was drawe to bee assentaunt. **1480** CAXTON *Chron. Eng.* cxcv. 171 All tho that were assentant to the same quarel.

B. *sb.* [the adj. used *absol.*] One who assents or consents to; an abettor, partisan.

1562 LEIGH *Armorie* (1597) 113 b, When God the father had expulsed the prince of pride, with his assentantes, from heauen. **1622** MABBE tr. *Aleman's Guzman D' Alf.* II. 333 The Accessary was to have as much as the Principall; the Assentant as the Assaylant.

assentation (æsənˈteɪʃən). [a. F. *assentation* (Cotgr.), ad. L. *assentātiōn-em*, n. of action f. *assentāri*: see ASSENT *v.* and -ATION.] The action of assenting to the opinions of another; *esp.* obsequious or servile expression or act of assent.

1481 EARL WORC. *Tulle on Friendsh.* Cj/2 To gete the same benyvolence by meane of flaterye and assentacyon is right..shamefull. **1542** UDALL *Erasm. Apophth.* (1877) 203 Which assentation is the southing of eche bodies tale and saiynges, and holding vp their yea and nay. **1603–5** SIR J. MELVIL *Mem.* (1735) 24 A certain Discretion..free both from Sawciness and Assentation. **1749** CHESTERF. *Lett.* 190 II. 205 Abject flattery and indiscriminate assentation degrade. **1829** SOUTHEY in *Q. Rev.* XXXIX. 381 More noted for courtly assentation to King James than for anything else. **1859** I. TAYLOR *Logic in Theol.* 265 A safer anchorage may be found than..the shoal of mindless assentation.

assentatious (æsənˈteɪʃəs), *a. rare.* [f. prec.: see -TIOUS.] Ready to assent, given to assentation.

1860 J. KENNEDY *Swallow Barn* ii. 34 A respectable, assentatious stranger, one who listens well.

assentator (æsənˈteɪtə(r)). [a. L. *assentātor*, n. of agent f. *assentāri*: see ASSENT *v.* and -ATOR.] One who assents to or connives at; one who expresses obsequious or flattering assent.

1531 ELYOT *Gov.* II. xiv. (1557) 139 Other there be which, in a more honest term, may be called assentatours or folowers. **1871** SWEET tr. *Gregory's Past.* 149 The assentator, who is ready to pass over what he ought to punish.

assentatorily (əˈsɛntətərɪlɪ), *adv. rare*⁻¹. [f. next + -LY²: cf. L. *assentātōriē.*] Flatteringly, obsequiously.

a **1626** BACON *Wks.* II. 246 (R.) I have no purpose, vainly or assentatorily, to represent this greatness [of Britain].

assentatory (əˈsɛntətərɪ), *a. rare*⁻⁰. [f. L. **assentātōrius*, in adv. *assentātōriē*: see ASSENTATOR and -ORY.] Of or befitting an assentator; flattering, obsequious.

assented (əˈsɛntɪd), *ppl. a.* [f. ASSENT *v.* + -ED¹.] Applied to bonds or stocks deposited under an agreement by which the owners assent to some proposed change affecting their amount, nature, or status. (Webster 1961.)

1907 M. ROLLINS *Money & Investments* 11 *Assented Stocks* (*or Bonds*), in the event of a corporation passing through a reorganization where the security holders are requested to give 'assent' to a certain plan..some banking house..is usually selected to receive the securities. **1957** *Economist* 7 Sept. 866/1 Operators therefore went largely for the most readily available stocks—Dawes assented and the Young assented. **1959** *Ibid.* 16 May 659/1 Most of the bonds are quoted in an 'assented' form, but those British subjects who have held on to 'non-assented' bonds for surtax purposes will have to sell to foreign residents to avoid tax on the accrued interest that becomes payable once assent to the debt settlement is given.

assenter (əˈsɛntə(r)). [f. ASSENT *v.* + -ER. Cf. ASSENTOR.] One who gives assent or acquiescence.

1634 SIR T. HERBERT *Trav.* 337 (T.) Seemingly an assenter to their meschanteries. *a* **1674** CLARENDON *Hist. Reb.* (1720) III. I. x. 108 As Witnesses only..not as Assenters. *a* **1859** DE QUINCEY *Pope* Wks. IX. 39 A careless and indolent assenter to such doctrines..as his own Church put forward.

assentient (əˈsɛnʃənt), *ppl. a.* and *sb.* [ad. L. *assentient-em*, pr. pple. of *assentīri* to ASSENT. Takes the place of the earlier ASSENTANT.]

A. *adj.* Assenting, approving, accordant.

1851 NICHOL *Archit. Heavens* 271 [They] could obtain assentient hearers for the doctrine. **1866** J. ROSE *Ovid's Met.* 49 To this the powers marine assentient are.

B. *sb.* One who assents or agrees; an assenter.

1859 SMILES *G. Stephenson* 241 Lords Derby and Sefton ..were found among the assentients to the London and Birmingham line. **1860** *Lit. Ch.-man* VI. 45 We find..fifty assentients in the Lower House.

assenting (əˈsɛntɪŋ), *vbl. sb.* [f. ASSENT *v.* + -ING¹.] The action of giving assent, acquiescence.

1651 HOBBES *Leviath.* II. xxvi. 149 Faith of Supernaturall Law, is..only an assenting to the same. **1670** VAUGHAN in *Phœnix* 1721 I. 422 A Juror kept his Fellows a Day and a Night without any reason or assenting.

aˈssenting, *ppl. a.* [f. as prec. + -ING².] Giving assent. Also in arch. or obs. use: Giving consent; agreeing; deferential.

1483 CAXTON *Cato* G v b, That thou were partyner and assentyng to the fayte. **1752** CHESTERF. *Lett.* 284 III. 300 You must be respectful and assenting, but without being servile. **1878** E. WHITE *Life in Christ* Pref. 5 The assenting voice of a great multitude.

aˈssentingly, *adv.* [f. prec. + -LY².] In an assenting manner; so as to express assent.

1552 HULOET, Assentinglye, accordyngly, or by agreamente, *Concorditer.* **1561** T. N[ORTON] *Calvin's Inst.* I. 6 Wil assentingly and willingly yeld himself to serue God. **1753** RICHARDSON *Grandison* (1781) III. xii. 90 He assentingly bowed. **1872** GEO. ELIOT *Middlem.* IV. 226 'Truly, my dear,' said Mr. Bulstrode assentingly.

†**aˈssention.** *Obs. rare*⁻¹. [ad. L. *assensiōn-em*, n. of action f. *assens-* ppl. stem of *assentīri* to ASSENT: cf. OF. *assension.* See -TION, -SION, freq. interchanged in 17th c.; cf. next.] Assent.

1660 STANLEY *Hist. Philos.* (1701) 476/2 As to Assention grounded on a firm belief of any Physical dogm.

assentist, obsolete variant of ASSIENTIST.

assentive (əˈsɛntɪv), *a. rare*⁻¹. [f. ASSENT + -IVE, by form-assoc. with *invent-ive*, etc. The etymological forms would be *assensive* and *assentative.*] Inclined to assent, assenting, assentaneous.

a **1743** SAVAGE *Wks.* II. 196 (JOD.) May that lip assentive warmth express!

aˈssentiveness. [f. prec. + -NESS.] Inclination to assent, or defer to the opinions of others.

1876 FARRAR *Marlb. Serm.* iv. 35 We may..become false ..by timidity, even by a mere social assentiveness.

assentment (əˈsɛntmənt). *arch. rare.* [a. OF. *as(s)entement*, f. *assenter*: see ASSENT *v.* and -MENT.] An act of assenting; agreement, consent (*obs.*); assent.

1490 CAXTON *Eneydos* xi. 41 By one comyn assentmente the goddis haue assembled theym selfe. **1646** SIR T. BROWNE *Pseud. Ep.* I. vii. 26 Whose argument is but precarious and subsists upon the charity of our assentments. **1818** COLEBROOKE *Obligat.* I. 45 A true assent implies.. perfectly free use of power..to give assentment.

assentor (ə'sɛntɔ:(r)). [Specific legal form of ASSENTER: see -OR.] An assenter; *spec.* applied to those who, in addition to the proposer and seconder, subscribe the nomination-paper of a candidate in a parliamentary or other election.
1880 McCARTHY *Own Times* lix. 307 A proposer and seconder and eight assentors. **1883** *Pall Mall G.* 27 June 3/1 One of his proposers..was an episcopalian Protestant, while several of his assentors are Presbyterian farmers.

assenycke, -yke, obs. forms of ARSENIC: see also ASSENEL.

assenyhe, obs. var. ENSIGN *sb.*: see A- *pref.* 10.

†**asseour.** *Obs.* [OF. '*Asseour*, en parlant du service de la table, *qui fait asseoir*,' Godefroy; f. *asseoir* to seat, set.] An officer who superintended the laying of the king's table for dinner. Cf. ASSAYER 3 and ASSEWER.
[*c* **1315** *Househ. Ord. Ed. II*, transl. 1601 (1876) §§49–51 The asseour of the kinges table.] **1448** in Hearne *R. Glouc.* 462 Sir William Martelle, the kynge's asseore, take eke was ther.

†'**assequent,** *ppl. a. Obs. rare*[−1]. [ad. L. *assequent-em*, pr. pple. of *assequi*, f. *as-* = *ad-* to + *sequi* to follow.] Following, subsequent.
1657 MACALLO *99 Canons* (1659) 35 The assequent or following marks of Phlegm are, etc.

assert (ə'sɜ:t), *v.* [f. L. *assert-* ppl. stem of *asserĕre* (f. *ad* to + *serĕre* to join, put) to put one's hand on the head of a slave, either to set him free or claim him for servitude, *hence*, to set free, protect, defend; to appropriate, claim; to affirm, declare, state. Cf. also med.L. *assertāre* (freq. of *asserĕre*) to affirm.]
I. To grant or ensure liberty, to protect.
†**1.** *trans.* To bring into freedom, set free. (Cf. L. *asserere in libertatem.*) *Obs. rare.*
1638 CHILLINGW. *Relig. Prot.* I. iv. §13. 196 He that could assert Christians to that liberty which Christ and his Apostles left them. **1699** BP. PATRICK *Comm. Numb.* xxiii. 22 (T.) The people of Israel..were asserted by God into a state of liberty.
†**2.** To maintain the cause of, take the part of; to champion, protect, defend. *Obs.* exc. with *cause* as object (where it passes into 5).
1652 W. CARTWRIGHT *Offspr. Mercy* 19 His [Christ's] father's foreknowledge..asserted his death from casualty. **1655** FULLER *Ch. Hist.* VI. §32 III. 283 Engaged to assert their good Patron..in his just vindication from this unjust aspersion. **1667** MILTON *P.L.* I. 25 That..I may assert th' eternal Providence, And justifie the wayes of God to men. **1705** STANHOPE *Paraphr.* III. 53 God..could not so receive and assert an Impostor. **1718** POPE *Iliad* II. 339 Sedition silence, and assert the throne. **1814** SCOTT *Wav.* iv, The cause that I shall assert I shall dare support in every danger.
II. To lay claim to.
3. *trans.* To claim (something) as belonging *to* (oneself or another); to declare one's right to, or possession of. *arch.*
1652 NEEDHAM tr. *Selden's Mare Cl.* 210 Julius Cæsar did assert to himself a Dominion over British Isle and Sea. **1836–7** SIR W. HAMILTON *Metaph.* xxxviii. (1870) II. 374 The few who assert to man a knowledge of the infinite.
†**4.** To lay claim to, claim. *Obs.*
1649 MILTON *Eikon.* Wks. 1738 I. 393 Their Principles too much asserted Liberty. **1656** BRAMHALL *Replic.* vii. 292 Here is no power asserted, no punishment to be inflicted.. but only politicall. **1714** GAY *Trivia* I. 4 When to assert the Wall, and when resign. **1791** COWPER *Iliad* XXIII. 764 The fourth awarded lot..Meriones asserted next, The golden talents.
5. To maintain practically, insist upon, or vindicate, a (disputed) claim to (anything).
1649 HOWELL *Pre-em. Parl.* 11 How infinitely necessary the Parlement is, to assert, to prop up, and preserve the Public Liberty. **1667** MILTON *P.L.* VI. 157 A third part of the Gods, in Synod met Thir Deities to assert. **1769** *Junius Lett.* xxxv. 164 A generous people..dare openly assert their rights. **1835** MARRYAT *Jac. Faithf.* xlvi, He who would assert his independence.
6. *to assert oneself*: to insist upon the recognition of one's rights or claims, and take means to secure them.
1879 MRS. OLIPHANT *Within Precincts* xxxviii, He was all the more anxious not to lose her..that she had thus asserted herself. **1883** WACE *Gosp. & Witn.* iv. 80 That agnostic philosophy which now asserts itself so loudly.
III. To declare, state.
7. *trans.* To declare formally and distinctly, to state positively, aver, affirm: **a.** a thing *to be*, or *that* it is.
a **1604** HANMER *Chron. Irel.* (1633) 21 Polycronicon assirteth..that they came to the North of Ireland in Vespasian's time. **1691** RAY *Creation* (R.) Nothing is more ..unworthy a natural philosopher than to assert any thing to be done without a cause. **1750** HARRIS *Hermes* I. ii. (1786) 16 To assert [is]..to publish some Perception either of the Senses or the Intellect. **1857** RUSKIN *Pol. Econ. Art* 15 Would you not at once assert of that mistress, that she knew nothing of her duties?
b. with pronominal obj. standing for a clause.
1661 BRAMHALL *Just Vind.* iii. 46 Which is all that we assert. **1795** SEWEL *Hist. Quakers* I. Pref. 9, I have endeavoured to assert nothing but what I had good authority for. **1867** FREEMAN *Norm. Conq.* (1876) I. App. 650 It is not directly asserted, but it seems to be implied.
c. with sb. as object.
1667 MILTON *P.L.* v. 798 Those Imperial Titles which assert Our being ordain'd to govern. **1839** KEIGHTLEY *Hist. Eng.* II. 37 She asserted her innocence in the strongest terms. **1862** H. SPENCER *First Princ.* I. v. §27 (1875) 99 Common Sense asserts the existence of a reality.
†**8.** To declare or affirm the existence of.
1660 STANLEY *Hist. Philos.* (1701) 184/1 He likewise asserteth Faith and Imagination. **1724** A. COLLINS *Gr. Chr. Relig.* 264 Justin Martyr asserts a double sense of some prophesies.
†**b.** To bear evidence of, bespeak. *Obs. rare.*
1823 LAMB *Elia* I. xviii. (1865) 138 Their air and dress asserted the parade.
†**9.** To declare the extent of, to state. *Obs.*
1675 OGILBY *Brit.* Pref. 4 Some have deviated..in Asserting the Distance. **1677** MOXON *Mech. Exerc.* (1703) 170 No size for..the Puppets can be well asserted.

†**a'ssert.** *Obs. rare.* [f. prec. vb.] Assertion, declaration.
1649 G. DANIEL *Trinarch. Hen. V.* lii, Treason strongly back't In the Assert of Language. **1655** LESTRANGE *K. Chas. I*, 79 His assert being entred upon record.

assert, obsolete form of ASSART.

assertable (ə'sɜ:təb(ə)l), *a.* Also -ible. [f. ASSERT *v.* or L. *assertā-re* + -A)BLE.] Capable or worthy of being asserted or maintained.
1837 CARLYLE *Fr. Rev.* I. I. VII. xi. 222 The king either has a right, assertible as such to the death..or he has no right.

†**asser'tation.** *Obs. rare*[−1]. [ad. med.L. *assertātiōn-em*, n. of action f. *assertā-re*: see ASSERT. Cf. *dissertation.*] Affirmation, assertion.
a **1535** MORE *Wks.* 141 (R.) Bothe y[e] confuting of theirs, and..the assertacion of our owne.

assertative (ə'sɜ:tətɪv), *a. rare.* [f. med.L. *assertāt-* (see prec) + -IVE] = ASSERTIVE.
1846 MORELL *Philos. 19th C.* I. 218 As assertative of the great fundamentals of morality. **1883** *Chicago Advance* 18 Oct., Their treatment is necessarily assertative or dogmatic.

asserted (ə'sɜ:tɪd), *ppl. a.* [f. ASSERT *v.* + -ED.] Claimed, maintained; positively stated.
1685 DRYDEN *Thren. August.* xviii, Th' asserted Ocean rears his reverend Head. **1805** SOUTHEY *Madoc in Azt.* i. Wks. V. 206 Every beast of rapine had retired From man's asserted empire. **1875** WHITNEY *Life Lang.* ix. 170 To see.. how close the asserted correspondences are.

asserter (ə'sɜ:tə(r)). [f. as prec. + -ER[1]: cf. also ASSERTOR.] One who asserts.
1. One who maintains or defends; a champion.
1643 MILTON *Divorce* Introd. (1851) 12 Our wonted prerogative of being the first asserters in every great vindication. **1728** YOUNG *Love Fame* IV. (1757) 110 The Crown's asserter, and the People's friend. **1833** I. TAYLOR *Fanat.* x. 458 A strenuous asserter of apostolic authority.
2. One who makes positive declarations.
c **1449** PECOCK *Repr.* III. xix. 411 As oonli therof teller, asser[t]er, or witnesser. **1818** COBBETT *Resid. U.S.* 84 He is a bold asserter; and very few of his statements proceed upon actual experiments. **1865** MOZLEY *Mirac.* i. 211 *note*, According to which the Church was an infallible asserter.

assertible: see ASSERTABLE.

asserting (ə'sɜ:tɪŋ), *vbl. sb.* [f. as prec. + -ING[1].] The action of laying claim to, maintaining, or declaring; assertion. (Now mostly gerundial.)
1644 MILTON *Judgm. Bucer* (1851) 302 The asserting of our just Liberties. **1673** *True Worship of God* 52 Our standing up..when the Creed is read, is an asserting of it.

a'sserting, *ppl. a.* [f. as prec. + -ING[2].]
1. That asserts; affirming, declaring, maintaining.
1848 R. HAMILTON *Sabbath* iii. 68 The Lord Jesus was himself the asserting Lawgiver. **1878** T. SINCLAIR *Mount* 93 New protestant, and more than protestant, asserting thinkers.
2. *self-asserting*: insisting on one's own rights or claims; egoistic; assuming.
1865 DICKENS *Mut. Fr.* xvi. 263 With a self-asserting air. **1879** GEO. ELIOT *Theo. S.* xviii. 317 These..self-asserting men.

assertion (ə'sɜ:ʃən). Also 6 ads-, assercion. [(? a. F. *assertion*, 14th c. in Littré), ad. L. *assertiōn-em*, n. of action f. *asser-ĕre* to ASSERT; see -ION[1].]
†**1.** The action of setting free, liberation. *Obs.*
1552 HULOET, Assertion, or libertie, or fredome, *Vindiciæ*. *a* **1707** BEVERIDGE *Priv. Th.* I. (1730) 67 Redemption from the Slavery of Sin, and Assertion into Christian Liberty.
2. The action of maintaining a cause or defending it from hostile attack; vindication. *arch.*
1532 MORE *Confut. Tindale* Wks. 661/2 Hys moste famous booke of the assercion of the sacramentes. **1604** W. STOUGHTON (*title*) An Assertion for true and Christian Church Policie. **1644** MILTON *Educ.* Wks. 1738, 135 Having my mind..half diverted in the pursuance of some other assertions. **1828** SCOTT *F.M. Perth* I. 59 Flinching from the assertion of his daughter's reputation.
3. a. Insistance upon a right or claim.
1660 R. COKE *Power & Subj.* 6 The Kings of England had exercised their jurisdiction in the assertion of their regal power. **1792** *Anecd. W. Pitt* III. xliii. 134 The present bill might be looked upon as a bill of concession..At the same time it was a bill of assertion. **1876** GREEN *Short Hist.* vii. §5 (1882) 394 The duties..on cloth and sweet wines were an assertion of her right of arbitrary taxation.
b. *self-assertion*: insistence on a recognition of one's own rights or claims.
1847 LD. LINDSAY *Chr. Art.* I. Introd. 209 The self-assertion of the Teutonic over the classic element of modern Europe. **1870** LOWELL *Among my Bks.* II. (1873) 299 The haughty and defiant self-assertion of Dante.
4. The action of declaring or positively stating; declaration, affirmation, averment.
c **1449** PECOCK *Repr.* 411 Ech conclusioun, in to whos fynding..mannys resoun..withoute assercioun of eny other creature may come to. **1582** R. ROBINSON (*title*) Leland's Learned and true Assertion of the Original Life, Actes and Death of..Prince Arthure. *a* **1784** *Johnsoniana* (1836) 399 Assertion is like an arrow shot from a long bow; the force with which it strikes depends on the strength of the arm that draws it. **1884** CHURCH *Bacon* i. 26 To show gross credulity and looseness of assertion on the part of the Roman Catholic advocate.
5. A positive statement; a declaration, averment. †*head assertion* (obs.): a fundamental principle, an axiom.
1531 ELYOT *Gov.* (1875) 8 Nowe to conclude my fyrste assercion or argument. **1535** JOYE *Apol. Tindale* 31 Adding this adsercion of his owne brayne. **1599** SANDYS *Europæ Spec.* (1632) 24 So in their Art also they have certain Head Assertions, which as indemonstrable principles they urge all men to receive and hold. **1798** FERRIAR *Var. Man.* in *Illustr. Sterne* 196 Authors have believed assertions without enquiry. **1822** HAZLITT *Table-t.* II. vi. 120 A sweeping, unqualified assertion ends all controversy.
6. *Comb.* **assertion-sign** *Logic*, the sign introduced by G. Frege in 1879 to indicate that the signs following it express a proposition which is asserted to be a true judgement; the same sign used in related senses; also in extended use of other signs considered equivalent in function.
[**1903** B. RUSSELL *Princ. Math.* §477 The sign of judgment (*Urtheilstrich*) does not combine with other signs to denote an object.] **1906** —— in *Amer. Jrnl. Math.* XXVIII. 160, I have adopted from him [*sc.* Frege] the assertion-sign. *Ibid.* 161 The sign '⊢' is called the assertion-sign; it may be read 'it is true that' (although philosophically this is not what it means). **1910** WHITEHEAD & RUSSELL *Principia Math.* i. 8 The sign '⊢', called the 'assertion-sign', means that what follows is asserted. It is required for distinguishing a complete proposition, which we assert, from any subordinate propositions contained in it but not asserted. **1922** tr. *Wittgenstein's Tractatus* 4. 442 Frege's assertion sign '⊢' is logically altogether meaningless. **1947** H. REICHENBACH *Elem. Symbolic Logic* vii. 336 In written language the assertion sign is supplied by the period at the end of a sentence, meaning: the writer asserts the sentence. **1953** G. E. M. ANSCOMBE tr. *Wittgenstein's Philos. Investig.* I. §22 Frege's assertion sign marks the *beginning of the sentence.* Thus its function is like that of the full-stop.

a'ssertional, *a. rare.* [f. prec. + -AL[1].] Of, pertaining to, or of the nature of, assertion.
a **1864** WEBSTER cites LATHAM.

†**a'ssertionate,** *v. Obs. rare*[−1]. [f. as prec. + -ATE[3].] To make assertion, to ASSERT. (The latter was apparently not yet in use.)
1593 NASHE *Christ's T.* (1613) 31 Once more I will assertionate, vertue hath no enimy but pryde. **1623** in COCKERAM.

†**a,ssertio'nation.** *Obs.*[−0] [n. of action f. prec.]
1623 COCKERAM *Dict.* II, An Auouching, *Assertionation*.

assertive (ə'sɜ:tɪv), *a.* [f. as if ad. L. **assertīvus*; cf. Fr. *assertive-ment* Cotgr., It. *assertivo* Florio: see ASSERT *v.* and -IVE.]
1. Of the nature of, or characterized by, assertion; declaratory, affirmative; positive, dogmatic.
1562 [see ASSERTIVELY]. *a* **1619** FOTHERBY *Atheom.* II. xii. §2. 336 By the assertiue testimonie..of the Corinthians. **1661** GLANVILL *Sceps. Sci.* 15 As assertive and dogmatical as if they were omniscient. **1711** GREENWOOD *Eng. Gram.* 225 Not to make this Mark (?)..at the Ending or Conclusion of an Assertive Sentence. **1856** MAURICE *Serm. John* i. 8 The broad, simple assertive tone, 'In the beginning was the Word.'
2. Characterized by mere assertion; (see quot.)
1849 ABP. THOMSON *Laws of Th.* (ed. 2) 305 The assertive judgment is one of which we are fully persuaded ourselves, but cannot give grounds for our belief, that shall compel men in general to coincide with us.
3. *self-assertive* = self-ASSERTING *ppl. a.*
1865 DICKENS *Mut. Fr.* 24 Reginald..being too aspiring and self-assertive a name.

a'ssertively, *adv.* [f. prec. + -LY[2].] In an assertive manner, by way of assertion, positively, dogmatically.
1562 BP. EXETER in Strype *Ann. Ref.* I. xxxi. 348 Which they all with one universal consent have assertively written. **1653** MANTON *Exp. James* iii. 2 Wks. IV. 277 Or you may take it positively and assertively..'If you offend not in word you are perfect.' **1860** GOODWIN *Ess. & Rev.* (ed. 2) 250 If he speaks of the same phenomena assertively, we are bound to suppose that things are as he represents them.

a'ssertiveness. [f. as prec. + -NESS.]
1. Tendency towards assertion or self-assertion.
1881 PERKIS *Wanted an Heir* 79 In gait there was a crispness and assertiveness. **1883** MISS BRADDON *Gold. Calf* xxvii. 317 Brian..talked with loud assertiveness of the right of genius to do what it likes.

2. Special Comb. **assertiveness training** orig. *U.S.*, a technique by which diffident persons are trained to behave (more) assuredly.

1975 *Ms.* Mar. 109/2 Jean Withers..organized an Assertive Rap Group and edited a brochure on *assertiveness training. **1977** J. F. FIXX *Compl. Bk. Running* ii. 14 Zen, transcendental meditation, assertiveness training, est and similar movements are all directed at making us fulfilled human beings. **1977** C. MCFADDEN *Serial* (1978) iii. 13/1 She'd like to take assertiveness training but was afraid Harvey wouldn't let her. **1982** S. TOWNSEND *Secret Diary A. Mole* (1983) 43 My mother has gone to a woman's workshop on assertiveness training.

assertor (əˈsɜːtɔː(r), -ə(r)). [a. L. *assertor*, n. of agent f. *asserĕre*: see ASSERT *v.* and -OR. Cf. also ASSERTER.]

†**1.** (In L. senses) **a.** One who liberates a slave. **b.** One who lays claim to a slave. *Obs.*

1566 PAINTER *Pal. Pleas.* I. 22 That Claudius the assertor ..shoulde haue the keping and placing the mayde. **1678** CUDWORTH *Intell. Syst.* I. ii. §32. 482 Called Σωτὴρ and Ἐλευθέριος, Saviour and Assertour.

2. One who maintains or defends; a champion, vindicator, advocate.

1647 J. HARE *St. Edw. Ghost* in *Harl. Misc.* (1746) VIII, The Greeks and Gauls were..famous Assertors of their Liberties. **1872** FREEMAN *Norm. Conq.* (1876) IV. xvii. 96 Archbishop John was a rigid Assertor of ecclesiastical discipline.

3. One who makes a positive statement.

1646 SIR T. BROWNE *Pseud. Ep.* 206 Wherein indeed Aristotle playes the Aristotle, that is, the wary and evading assertor. **1797** *Encycl. Brit.* (*Astronomy*) II. 493/1 The imputation must return upon the assertor. **1853** DE MORGAN in Bowen *Logic* ix. (1870) 286 Which the assertor is afterwards at liberty to deny.

assertorial (æsəˈtɔərɪəl), *a. Logic.* [f. L. *assertōri-us* (f. *assertor*; see prec.) + -AL¹.] Of the nature of assertion, affirming that a thing *is*; as distinguished from *problematical* (that it *may* be) and *necessary* or *apodictical* (that it *must* be). Hence **asserˈtorially** *adv.*, in assertorial manner, in affirmation.

1863 tr. *Saisset's Ess. Relig. Philos.* I. 281 Judgments.. problematical, assertorial, and apodeictic. **1877** CAIRD *Philos. Kant* II. xviii. 637 The practical reason will thus give assertorial value to the problematical results of theory. *Ibid.* II. xiii. 499 No perception..of objects beyond the sphere of sense, on which the understanding might be used assertorially.

asserˈtoric, *a. Logic.* [f. as ASSERTORIAL *a.* + -IC.] = ASSERTORIAL *a.* Also as *sb.*, a proposition of this type.

1889 in *Cent. Dict.* **1905** *Athenæum* 8 Apr. 439/2 One kind of propositions, viz. assertorics. **1929** N. K. SMITH tr. *Kant's Crit. Pure Reason* 110 The assertoric proposition deals with logical reality or truth.

assertorical (æsəˈtɒrɪkəl), *a.* [f. as ASSERTORIAL *a.* + -ICAL; cf. F. *assertorique.*] = ASSERTORIAL *a.* Hence **asserˈtorically** *adv.* = ASSERTORIALLY.

1838 F. HAYWOOD tr. *Kant's Crit. Pure Reason* 233 A possible intuition, whereby objects can be given to us out of the field of sensibility, and the understanding used assertorically beyond the same. **1869** J. MARTINEAU *Ess.* II. 190 The next sentence is..rendered assertorically. **1870** BOWEN *Logic* v. 121 Judgments are..pure. A is B. Assertorical.

aˈssertorily, *adv.* ? *Obs.* [f. next + -LY².] By way of assertion, assertively, assertorially.

a **1679** T. GOODWIN *Wks.* (1864) IX. 246 An ocular demonstration of what hath been but assertorily delivered.

assertory (əˈsɜːtərɪ), *a.* [ad. L. *assertōrius*, f. *assertor* ASSERTOR: see -ORY.]

1. Of the nature of, or characterized by, assertion; assertive, affirmative.

1639 ROUSE *Heav. Univ.* v. (1702) 69 Having a commission that is Promulgatory and Assertory of what is past. *a* **1733** NORTH *Exam.* I. iii. ¶93. 188 The greatest Part of these assertory Transactions. **1810** COLERIDGE *Friend* VI. viii. (1867) 319 The mode..in Lord Bacon is dogmatic, i.e. assertory.

b. *esp.* in ***assertory oath***: one taken in support of a present statement, as distinguished from a *promissory oath*, which guarantees a future action.

1617 COLLINS *Def. Bp. Ely* II. x. 502 How many oaths are taken in Courts daily, both assertory and promissory. **1652** MARBURY *Comm. Habak.* (1868) 202 An oath..is assertory when we do call God to witness against our souls, if we affirm not the truth. **1823** BENTHAM *Not Paul* 258 By an oath every one understands at first mention an assertory, not a promissory declaration; by a vow, a promissory, not an assertory one.

2. in *Logic.* = ASSERTORIAL.

1837 SIR W. HAMILTON *Metaph.* xxiii. (1859) II. 70 The cognition, therefore, is assertory, inasmuch as the reality of that, its object, is given unconditionally as a fact. **1838** —— *Logic* xiv. (1866) I. 260 A proposition is called Assertory, when it enounces what is known as actual.

assertress (əˈsɜːtrɪs). [f. ASSERTOR + -ESS; cf. *actress.*] She who asserts, a female assertor.

1656 J. HARRINGTON *Oceana* Introd. 35 The most obstinate Assertress of her Liberty.

†**aˈsservant,** *v. Obs.*⁻⁰ [a. OF. *aservantir*, f. *à* to + *servant* SERVANT.] To reduce to the position of a servant.

1611 COTGR., *Asservissement*, An asservanting, inthralling.

†**asserˈvation.** *Obs. rare.* [n. of action f. L. *asservāt-* ppl. stem of *asservā-re*, f. *ad* to + *servāre* to keep.] The action of keeping, preservation.

1621 H. AINSWORTH *Annot. Pentat.* Num. xix. 9 For an asservation, a keeping, that is. **1657** TOMLINSON *Renou's Disp.* 491 A heap of green simples by long asservation, putrefie.

†**aˈsserve,** *v. Obs.* [a. OF. *a(s)servir* to serve, deserve:—L. *asservīre*, f. *ad* to + *servīre* to serve.]

1. a. To serve, attend to (a person). **b.** (?) To serve up (a dish).

c **1330** *MS. Laud.* No. 108, 104 b, þare he miȝte beo al one To aservi Godes wille. *c* **1470** *Househ. Ord.* (1790) 66 Nor to suffer theyre owne servauntes muche conversaunt ∴ whyles the Kinge specially shal be asservinge. *a* **1500** *To serve a Lord* in *Babees Bk.* 369 The kerver..most asserve [? assewe] every disshe in his degre. **1731** BAILEY, *Asserve*, to serve to.

2. To deserve, merit.

c **1325** *MS. Coll. Trin. Oxon.* 57 (Halliw.) Ich thonky the ..That ich it have aserved In atte the ȝatis to wende. *a* **1400** *Leg. Rood* (1871) 147 Vche mon schal haue as þei a serue.

†**aˈsservile,** *v. Obs.* [f. AS- *pref.*¹ + SERVILE *a.*] To make servile or subservient.

1619 *Sacrilege Sacr. Handled* 88 To asseruile the Gospell to his vile appetites. **1686** W. DE BRITAINE *Hum. Prud.* §17. 80, I cannot asservile my self to the Humour of other Men.

asservilize (əˈsɜːvɪlaɪz), *v. rare.* [f. as prec. + -IZE. Cf. *servilize.*] To make servile, reduce to serfdom.

1877 OWEN *Wellesley Disp.* Introd. 29 Which, by excluding the citizen of a whilom native State from office, tended to debase and asservilize him.

assess (əˈsɛs), *v.* Also 5 accesse, 5–6 assesse, 6–7 assease, 7 ascease. *Aphet.* CESS, SESS, q.v. [a. OF. *assesse-r*:—late L. *assessā-re*, frequentative of *assidēre* to sit by (*e.g.* as an assessor or assistant-judge), in late L. to fix or apportion a tax, to assess, f. *ad-* to + *sedēre* to sit. In mod.Fr. *asseoir* (:—L. *assidēre*) is used in this sense: cf. ASSIZE *v.*]

1. *trans.* To settle, determine, or fix the amount of (taxation, fine, etc.) to be paid by a person or community, or by each member of a community.

1447–8 SHILLINGFORD *Lett.* (1871) 81 Half a dym which was assessed and payd. **1581** LAMBARDE *Eiren.* IV. xvi. (1588) 580 The same Justices..shall assesse the Fine at their wils and pleasures. **1628** COKE *On Litt.* 33 a, Found the value of the land..and assessed damages for the deteyning of the Dower. **1852** MᶜCULLOCH *Taxation* Introd. 12 Taxes..that admit of being fairly assessed and collected.

2. To determine the amount of and impose (taxation, fine, etc) *upon* (a person or community).

1495 *Act 11 Hen. VII*, iv, Suche fynes and amerciamentis as upon them shalbe cessid. **1531** *Dial. Laws of Eng.* II. ix. (1638) 75 The neighbours by assent assesse a certaine summe upon every inhabitant. **1876** GREEN *Short Hist.* vi. 319 A forced loan was assessed upon the whole kingdom.

3. a. To impose a fine or tax upon (a person, community, or property); to lay under contribution; to tax, fine. Const. *in*, *at* the amount.

1494 FABYAN VII. 344 And after sessyd theym at greuouse fynys. **1564** HAWARD *Eutrop.* VI. (1584) 52 He..assessed hym to pay a great summe of mony. **1660** R. COKE *Power & Subj.* 180 An Englishman shall be assessed in a deeper mulct. **1711** STEELE *Spect.* No. 53 ¶10 Where each Person shall be assessed but at two Shillings and six Pence. **1839** KEIGHTLEY *Hist. Eng.* I. 298 Each county was assessed in a certain number of carpenters, masons and tylers. **1863** COX *Inst. Eng. Govt.* III. ii. 602 John Hampden was assessed twenty shillings.

b. *fig.*

1804 W. TAYLOR in *Ann. Rev.* II. 220 Several of our country historians..might be assessed for tributary materials.

4. To estimate officially the value of (property or income) for the purpose of apportioning its share of taxation.

1809 BAWDWEN tr. *Domesday Bk.* 245 Each one..was assessed at as much as a house in the city. **1842** *Penny Cycl.* XXIV. 112/1 After assessing the annual income of each person. **1870** *Daily News* 18 Apr., Woodlands may be assessed..upon the amount for which they might reasonably be expected to let. Tithes should be assessed on the commuted value.

5. *transf.* To evaluate (a person or thing); to estimate (the quality, value, or extent of), to gauge or judge.

1934 in WEBSTER. **1948** *Assessment of Men* (U.S. Office of Strategic Services) 3 A number of psychologists and psychiatrists attempted to assess the merits of men and women recruited for the Office of Strategic Services. **1955** *Bull. Atomic Sci.* Apr. 108/2 It is impossible even for a scientist of genius to assess a lost opportunity of which he was unaware. **1958** I. MURDOCH *Bell* iii. 41 How could he assess her like this because of something which had happened in the past? **1963** *B.S.I. News* May 14/2 Both specifications..include the Bacharach or Shell smoke scale for use in assessing smoke density. **1968** S. HILL *Gentleman & Ladies* vi. 81, I doubt if she could assess a human situation very accurately, I doubt if she would know where the truth of a matter lay. **1976** *Daily Mirror* 16 July 2/3 The 300 British citizens left in Uganda 'know the risks they are running, and have assessed them,' he said. **1979** J. HELLER *Good as Gold* (1980) v. 197 Dressing at his locker, he assessed the damage to his flesh, bones, and systems from the track.

†**aˈsess(e,** *sb. Obs.*; but see the aphet. CESS, SESS. [f. prec.] = ASSESSMENT.

1576 LAMBARDE *Peramb. Kent* (1826) 183 Conteining the assesse of such particular watch and warde. **1586** J. HOOKER *Girald. Irel.* in *Holinsh.* II. 78/2 Vpholders of all Irish enormities, wringing from the poore tenants euerlasting sesse. **1649** *Princely Pelican* ix. (1702) 294 Taking off Assesses, Levies, and Free-quarterings.

assessable (əˈsɛsəb(ə)l), *a.*; also 9 -ible. [f. ASSESS *v.* + -ABLE.] Capable of being assessed, liable to assessment.

1777 BURROW *Rep.* II. 991 (Jod.) Whether the lord of a manor is assessable to the poor rates. **1818** COLEBROOKE *Obligat.* I. 37 If no assessible damages can arise from the non-execution of it. **1882** *Daily News* 29 Aug. 6/5 A rate.. at 1*s.* in the pound on all property assessable.

assessably (əˈsɛsəblɪ), *adv.* [f. prec. + -LY².] In a way liable to assessment; ratably.

1864 in WEBSTER.

assessed (əˈsɛst), *ppl. a.* [f. ASSESS *v.* + -ED.]

1. Fixed or apportioned by assessment. ***assessed taxes***: those on inhabited houses, male servants, carriages, horses, mules, dogs, horse-dealers, hair-powder, armorial bearings, and game.

1796 PITT in *Ld. Auckland's Corr.* (1862) III. 364 Additional payment on the assessed taxes. **1842** *Penny Cycl.* XXIV. 111/2 The assessed annual value. **1852** MᶜCULLOCH *Taxation* II. vi. 272 The duties on armorial bearings, carriages, horses, and horse-dealers, dogs, game certificates, servants, and windows, are called, for what reason it is not easy to imagine, the 'assessed taxes.'

2. Subject to taxation, taxed, fined.

1552 HULOET, Assessed person, or he that is assessed or taxed, *Census*.

assessee (əsɛˈsiː). [f. ASSESS *v.* + -EE¹.] One whose property or income is assessed.

1726 *Laws of Sewers* 194 The Assessees of the Lands held by the Adventurers under the Trustees. **1959** *Economist* 7 Mar. 883/2 The expenditure of wives and minor children will be aggregated with that of the assessee even where their incomes are separate.

assessing (əˈsɛsɪŋ), *vbl. sb.* [f. as ASSESSED *ppl. a.* + -ING¹.] The action of fixing the amount of or apportioning taxation, etc.; assessment.

1447–8 SHILLINGFORD *Lett.* (1871) 80 Accessyng and levy was mad amonge the sayde Bysschoppis tenantes. **1622** LEY in *Fortesc. Papers* 175 About the assessing of the prices of wynes. **1635** *Act 10 Chas. I* (Irish) 9 At the time of the said assessings.

aˈssessing, *ppl. a.* [f. as prec. + -ING².] That assesses or fixes assessments.

1865 *Pall Mall G.* 21 Nov. 9 The assessing jury.

assession (əˈsɛʃən). [ad. L. *assessiōn-em*, n. of action f. *assess-* ppl. stem of *assidēre*: see ASSESS. Cf. (in sense 2) AF. *assesseaunce.*]

1. A sitting beside or together; a session.

1560 J. DAUS tr. *Sleidane's Comm.* 374 b, Whome he commaunded that..in the assession..they shoulde exhibite the confession of the doctrine wrytten. **1731** in BAILEY. **1852** BP. FORBES *Nicene Creed* 11 Of His Assession, that He 'sitteth at the right hand of the Father.'

†**2.** = ASSESSMENT. *Spec.* In the Duchy of Cornwall, the action of assessing and letting to rent the lord's demesnes, which was done at a court held for the purpose; also attrib. in ***assession-court***, ***-roll***. Also **aˈssessioning** *vbl. sb.* and *ppl. a.*; **assessionable** (əˈsɛʃənəb(ə)l) *a.*, occas. **aˈssessional** *a.*, applied to seventeen manors of the Duchy in which the lands were let by courts of assession. *Obs.*

1447–8 SHILLINGFORD *Lett.* (1871) 98 The tenants of his saide fee were not warned to come..to the assession therof. **1820** J. SCARLETT in G. Concanen *Rep. Rowe* v. *Brenton* (1830) App. 77 There is no custom stated for the free tenants to attend the assession-court, only the conventionaries. **1820** BROUGHAM *Ibid.*, They have done enough to differ the present case, of tendering the assession-roll, from the circumstances under which it was tendered before. **1828** BARNEWALL & CRESSWELL *Rep. King's Bench* VIII. 740 The seventeen manors hereafter mentioned as assessionable manors. *Ibid.* 750 A roll called an Assession Roll, which purported to be an account of the acts done by certain assessors in the 7 Edw. 3., under a commission to them by John Earl of Cornwall. **1830** G. CONCANEN *Rep. Rowe* v. *Brenton* (*title*), The right to minerals in the assessional lands of the duchy of Cornwall. *Ibid.* Introd. 23 The mode of letting the lands of the assessional manors by the assessioning commissioners. *Ibid.*, The assessioning of the same manors occurred at intervals of less than seven years. *Ibid.* 36 The conventionary tenants of the seventeen assessionable manors of the Duchy. **1839** *Penny Cycl.* XIV. 390/1 The courts..were called assessions, or courts of assession. The course usually was to let the land until the next assession. **1848** *Act 11 & 12 Vict.* c. 83 (*title*) An Act to confirm the Awards of Assessionable Manors Commissioners.

a'ssessionary, *a.* ? *Obs.* [f. prec. + -ARY.] Of or pertaining to assession or assessors.
1602 CAREW *Cornwall* (R.) One of the answers of the jury upon their oaths at the assessionary court.

assessment (əˈsɛsmənt). Also 6–7 **assessement**. See aphet. SESSMENT. [f. ASSESS *v.* + -MENT, prob. in AF. *assessement.*] The action of assessing; the amount assessed.

1. The determination or adjustment of the amount of taxation, charge, fine, etc., to be paid by a person or community.
1548 HALL *Chron. Hen. VIII*, an. 24 (R.) The assessement of whiche fines were appoynted to Thomas Cromwell. **1591** in Heath *Grocers' Comp.* (1869) 85 That 8000*l.* should be levied out of the Halls of the Cittie, by an equal and indifferent assessmente. **1764** BURN *Hist. Poor Laws* 196 Charges..to be raised by an assessment on the several parishes, in proportion to the number of poor they send to the said house. **1861** PEARSON *E. & Mid. Ages Eng.* 181 Even adultry is still matter of assessment.

2. The scheme of charge or taxation so adjusted.
a **1700** in Somers *Tracts* I. 509 Such of the said Corporation as usually join in making By-laws, Assessments or Rates. **1865** H. PHILLIPS *Amer. Paper Curr.* II. 26 An assessment was prepared, based upon the supposed population of the Colonies.

3. The amount of charge so determined upon.
1611 COTGR., *Quottité*, an even assessement, a rate or to-quot imposed. **1662** PEPYS *Diary* 15 Dec., To speak about my assessment of 42*l.* to the Loyal Sufferers. **1867** PEARSON *Hist. Eng.* I. 48 To see that these assessments were not excessive.

4. Official valuation of property or income for the purposes of taxation; the value assigned to it.
c **1540** *Plumpton Corr.* 239, I marvill greatly that your said manor shold be so highley charged..I could never se no writing of the sesment therof. **1600** HOLLAND *Livy* 31 (R.) The manner of equall contribution..proportionably to the assessment and rate of men's goods. **1842** *Penny Cycl.* XXIV. 112/1 Income arising from some sources, being capable of direct assessment, cannot be concealed.

5. a. *fig.* in gen. sense: Estimation, evaluation.
a **1626** BP. ANDREWES *Serm.* (1856) I. 458 It hath been held no way safe for us to make our own assessment. **1853** GROTE *Greece* II. lxxxvii. XI. 367 In the comparative assessment of Hellenic forces.

b. *Educ.* The process or means of evaluating academic work; an examination or test. Cf. *continuous assessment* s.v. CONTINUOUS *a.* 3.
1956 H. LOUKES *Secondary Modern* iv. 112 What is needed is..to find new means of assessment. **1965** *Nursing Times* 5 Feb. 205/1 Agreement was reported upon the payment of £5 to nurses in non-psychiatric hospitals upon passing the preliminary or hospital examination or assessment. **1972** *N.Z. News* 26 Jan. 3/5 The Post Primary Teachers' Association is pressing for internal assessment in place of the examination at fifth form level. **1985** *Washington Post* 18 June B4/5 Test scores and core curriculum are not the answers... That is why individual assessments are necessary.

6. *attrib.* and *Comb.*, as ***assessment board, centre; assessment-work***: (see quot.).
1870 *Daily News* 18 Apr., Establishing County Assessment Boards, with power to hear..appeals from the Union Assessment Committees. **1881** RAYMOND *Mining Gloss.*, *Assessment-work*, the work done annually on a mining claim to maintain possessory title. **1948** *Assessment of Men* (U.S. Office of Strategic Services) x. 473 As a means of training graduate students as well as physicians..we cannot conceive of a better system than that provided by an *Assessment center. **1976** *West Lancs. Even. Gaz.* 8 Dec. 3/4 Members of the county committee accepted a report which included a £403,000 new assessment centre for the school. **1983** *Listener* 4 Aug. 24/3 Debbie had been sent to the assessment centre to escape her father's incestuous attentions.

assessor (əˈsɛsə(r)). Also 4–7 **-sour**, 5 **accessour**. [a. OF. *assessour* (mod. *assesseur*), cogn. with Pr. *assessor*, Sp. *asesor*, It. *assessore*:—L. *assessōr-em* (in cl. L.) an assistant-judge, (in late L.) one who assesses taxes, n. of agent f. *assidēre*: see ASSESS *v.* and -OR.]

1. One who sits beside; *hence*, one who shares another's position, rank, or dignity.
1667 MILTON *P.L.* VI. 670 Whence to his Son, Th' Assessor of his Throne, he thus began. **1701** W. WOTTON *Hist. Rome* (Commod.) i. 186 Gone up to Heaven, to be a Companion and an Assessor with the Gods. **1842** DE QUINCEY *Philos. Herodot.* Wks. IX. 211 He justifies his majestic station as a brotherly assessor on the same throne with Homer.

2. One who sits as assistant or adviser to a judge or magistrate; *esp.* a skilled assistant competent to advise on technical points of law, commercial usage, navigation, etc. (The earliest sense in Eng.)
c **1380** WYCLIF *Wks.* (1880) 33 Newe religious assessours of þes vnkunnynge worldely prelatis. **1413** LYDGATE *Pylgr. Sowle* I. xi. 8 Come to oure jugementes, to here and to see as assessours, that ryght be performed. **1496** *Dives & Paup.* (W. de W.) v. xviii. 220/2 The Juge, the aduocate, the accessour. **1636** FEATLY *Clavis Myst.* ix. 113 How religious then ought Judges to be, who are Almighty God's assessours. **1756** NUGENT *Gr. Tour* I. 102 He has his assessors who sit with him, when there are any complaints to be heard. **1810** BENTHAM *Packing* (1821) 6 The body of unlearned assessors, termed Jurors or Jurymen. **1883** *Law Times* 20 Oct. 409/1 The court on the trial of a patent case may call in the aid of a specially qualified assessor.

3. a. One who assesses taxes. **b.** One who officially estimates the value of property or income for purposes of taxation.
1611 COTGR., *Tauxeur*, a rater, taxer, assessor. *a* **1618** RALEIGH *Arts of Empire* 63 (T.) The assessors of taxes may be elected of the meaner sort of the people. **1835** REEVE *De Tocqueville's Democr. Amer.* I. v. 119 In New England the assessor fixes the rate of taxes. **1852** MCCULLOCH *Taxation* i. iv. 37 The assessors having no means of learning whether individuals have 130*l.*, 140*l.*, or 150*l.* a year.

4. *transf.* or *fig.* in prec. senses.
1625 HART *Anat. Ur.* I. ii. 21 Other accidents..are called ..assessors or assistants to the disease. **1722** WOLLASTON *Relig. Nat.* ix. 173 Bodily inclinations and passions [where reason] allows them to be as it were assessors to it upon the throne, are of admirable use in life. **1841** DE QUINCEY *Homer* Wks. VI. 350 Pisistratus summoned seventy men of letters..as critical assessors upon these poems.

assessorial (æsɛˈsɔərɪəl), *a.*; also 8 **assyss-**. [f. L. *assessōri-us*, f. *assessor*: see prec. and -AL¹.] Of or pertaining to an assessor or assessors.
1726 DE FOE *Hist. Devil* (1822) 17 The assyssorial tribunal of Poland. **1849** LEWES *Robespierre* 116 Begging your assessorial and provostal majesty's pardon.

a'ssessorship. [f. ASSESSOR + -SHIP.] The office, position, or function of an assessor.
1831 CARLYLE *Sart. Res.* II. iv, His progress..towards any active Assessorship is evidently of the slowest. **1883** A. B. HOPE *Worship & Ord.* 127 Guided by the assessorship of Archbishops Sumner and Tait.

†**a'ssessory**, *a. Obs.* [ad. L. *assessōri-us*: see prec.] = ASSESSORIAL.
1609 BIBLE (Douay) *Ps.* lxxiv. *comm.*, Christ with his Apostles, and other *assessorie* judges wil praise and thanke God.

‖**a'ssestrix.** *Obs.*⁻⁰ [L., fem. of *assessor*: see -TRIX.] A woman who sits by, a female assistant.
1623 in COCKERAM.

†**a'sseth(e**, *sb. Obs.* Forms: 4 **aseeth, a seeth**, 4–5 **aseth, a-seth, assethe**, 5 **a seth, a-sethe, asethe, aseyth, asseth, (assete, assetz)**. *Aphet.* **seth(e**. See also ASSYTH for the northern forms. [a. OF. *a(s)set* (pronounced aˈseθ), also *ases*, *asez*, sb., orig. the same word as *asez*, *assez* adv. 'enough':—late L. *ad satis*, for cl. L. *sat*, *satis*, 'enough' (see ASSETS). In the phrase *satis facĕre*, OF. *aset fere*, *fere aset*, 'to make amends,' the adv. was treated as a sb. 'amends,' nom. *ases* (*asez*), objective *aset*, which was the form adopted in Eng. As final *-t* in OF. was = (θ) (cf. *faith*, *poortith*), *aseth* was the reg. ME. spelling. The word had no connexion in Eng. with *assets*, and was obsolete before the latter came into English use.]

Satisfaction; compensation, amends, reparation, expiation. ***to make*** or ***do asseth*** (= OF. *fere aset*, L. *satis facĕre*): to satisfy (desires), expiate (sin), make atonement (*to* a person *for* a wrong).
1340 HAMPOLE *Pr. Consc.* 3610 Thurgh assethe makyng, Als thurgh penance of fre[n]des and fastyng. *c* **1375** WYCLIF *Serm.* v. Sel. Wks. 1869 II. 237 To make aseþ for mannis synne. **1377** LANGL. *P. Pl.* B. XVII. 237 If it suffice nouȝte for assetz [*other MSS.* asseth]..Mercy..wil make good the remenaunte. **1382** WYCLIF *1 Sam.* iii. 14 The wickidnes of hys hows shal not be doon a seeth. **1388** —— *Mark* xv. 15 Pilat, willynge to make aseeth [**1382** to do ynow] to the puple. **1430** LYDG. *Chron. Troy* IV. xxxviii, To make assete by oblacyon For the thefte. **1436** *Test. Ebor.* (1855) II. 217 They sall have amendis and asseth for thare losse. **1461** *Paston Lett.* 408 II. 36 Compelle hem to make amendes and sethe to the pore peple. **1494** FABYAN VI. cxciv. 199 He made a seth and amendes to Goddes pleasure.

†**a'ssethe**, *v.* [f. prec. sb. Cf. also ASSYTHE.] To satisfy.
1481 EARL WORC. *Tulle on Friendsh.* B iv, To assethe the same desire. ? **1481** CAXTON *Orat. G. Flamineus* F iv, I have be redy in every place to assethe your lyefful desires.

assets (ˈæsɪts). [a. late Anglo-Fr. *assets* (Littleton §714), early AF. *asetz* (Britton I. xvi. §5), OF. *asez* enough, cogn. w. Pr. *assatz*, OSp. *asaz*, Pg. *assaz*, *assas*, It. *assai*:—late pop. L. *ad satis* 'to sufficiency,' substituted for simple *satis* 'enough.' The origin of the English use is to be found in the Anglo-French law phrase *aver assetz* 'to have sufficient,' viz. to meet certain claims; whence *assets* passed as a technical term into the vernacular. It was originally singular but was soon (from its final *-s*, and collective sense) treated as plural, and in modern use has a singular *asset*.]

1. *Law.* Originally: Sufficient estate or effects; *esp.* 'Goods enough to discharge that burthen, which is cast upon the executor or heir, in satisfying the testator's or ancestor's debts and legacies' Cowell. Chiefly in phrase ***to have assets.***
1531 *Dial. Laws of Eng.* II. xlix. (1638) 154 If this man have assets by discent from the ancestor. **1574** tr. *Littleton's Tenures* §714 Vnlesse that he hath Assets by discent in Fee simple. **1671** F. PHILIPPS *Reg. Necess.* 413. **1691** SOUTHERNE *Sir A. Love* III. i. (1721) 212, I shall fall like an Executor without assets. **1768** BLACKSTONE *Comm.* II. 244 This deed, obligation, or covenant, shall be binding upon the heir, so far forth only as he had any estate of inheritance vested in him by descent from that ancestor, sufficient to answer the charge..which sufficient estate is in law called assets. **1876** DIGBY *Real Prop.* v. §2. 216 The heir of the tenant in tail was not bound by his ancestor's alienation..unless he had assets (lands in fee simple equivalent to those which had been granted away) by descent from his ancestor.

2. By extension applied to: Any property or effects liable to be applied as in sense 1, without regard to its being *sufficient*. (Still *sing.* in 17th c., but now a *collective plural*.)
assets in hand: effects in the hands of executors which are applicable to discharge the testator's debts.
1583 BABINGTON *Commandm. To Gentl. Glamorg.*, An advouson in respect of the patron, is accounted no assets.. because it is not valuable. **1601** *Act 43 Eliz.* iv. §7 Any of them, havynge Assettes in Law or Equitie, see the same assettes will extende. **1705** COLLIER *Ess.* III. 104 He left not assids enough to bury him. **1870** PINKERTON *Guide Administr.* 39 If there are not sufficient assets in hand to pay all the debts of the Estate.

3. *Law* and *Comm.* Effects of an insolvent debtor or bankrupt, applicable to the payment of his debts; and by extension: All the property of a person or company which may be made liable for his or their debts. The Dr. and Cr. sides of a Balance Account contain 'Assets' and 'Liabilities' respectively. (In this sense always used as *plural*, with singular *asset* applied to a single item appearing on the debit side.)
1817 JAS. MILL *Brit. India* I. I. v. 89 The assets or effects of the London Company in India fell short of the debts of that concern. **1855** H. SPENCER *Psychol.* (1872) II. VII. viii. 382 Cheques and bills are accepted and passed on without enquiring whether there are assets to meet them. **1868** *Pall Mall G.* 23 July 4 The chances of a dividend depend upon the realization of two assets, one a large debt due by a trustee of the bank, and the other, etc. *Mod.* The former of these is a very doubtful asset.

4. *fig.*
1675 WYCHERLEY *Pl. Dealer* II. (1735) 55, I, that am a relict of known plentiful assets and parts, who understand myself and the law. **1690** DRYDEN *Amphitr.*, No more may be expected from him to Night, when he has no Assets. **1884** *Daily News* 9 June 3/2 The high character which the corps has won for..trustworthiness is in itself a valuable asset.

5. Special Comb. **asset card** *U.S.* = *debit card* s.v. DEBIT *sb.* 3; **asset stripping**, the practice of selling off the assets of a company (esp. one recently taken over) in order to make a profit, without regard for the company's future; hence **asset-stripper**.
1975 *Asset card [see *debit card* s.v. DEBIT *sb.* 3]. **1986** *U.S. Banker* Mar. 42/3 The solution..—moving the $2 billion asset card business to..South Dakota—ushered in a new era in interstate banking. **1972** *Observer* 8 Oct. 15/2 The *asset stripper's aim is to find a company rich in assets but down on its luck. **1984** *Financial Times* 21 Jan. 24 'We were asset-strippers,' Mr. Rowland recalls proudly. According to one former plantations stockbroking analyst, 'Some of his bidding tactics were controversial.' **1972** *Observer* 8 Oct. 15/1 *Asset stripping has become the short cut to great wealth for young men with a burning ambition to make as much money as possible, with as little effort as possible. **1977** *Guardian Weekly* 23 Oct. 21/3 Inquires in detail into Slater Walker's forays into industry but finds little evidence of industrial efficiency but plenty of asset stripping. **1983** *Listener* 18 Aug. 28/2 The financiers Humpage hoodwinks are either patricianly incompetent or else sharkishly bent and intent on making a quick asset-stripping killing.

assett, obsolete form of ASHET.

asseure, obsolete form of ASSURE.

assever (əˈsɛvə(r)), *v. arch.* [ad. L. *assevērāre* to assert seriously, f. *as-* = *ad-* to + *sevērus* serious, severe. Cf. It. *asseuerare* (Florio 1598).] To asseverate: **a.** a thing *to be*, or *that* it is.
1581 CAMPION in *Confer.* IV. (1584) D d iij, The Jewes asseuering the obseruation of the lawe..to be necessarie. **1603** HARSNET *Pop. Impost.* xxiii. 166 We do not Asserver that the Devil cannot say a Troth. **1637** BASTWICK *Litany* II. 8 King James absolutely assevers..that the Pope is Antichrist.

b. with *simple obj.*
a **1618** SYLVESTER *Job Tri.* III. 268 O! that my words (the words I now assever) Were writ. **1690** LOCKE *Hum. Und.* II. xxvii. §8 Wks. 1727 I. 145, I had heard many Particulars.. assever'd by People hard to be discredited. **1826** E. IRVING *Babylon* II. VII. 222 The question being..assevered of the vision generally.

†**a'sseverance.** *Obs. rare*⁻¹. [f. as next; see -ANCE.] An asseveration.
1574 WHITGIFT *Def. Answ.* iii. Wks. 1851 I. 345 These bold asseverances in matters most untrue are so common.

†**a'sseverant**, *a. Obs.*⁻⁰ [ad. L. *assevērānt-em*, pr. pple. of *assevērāre*: see ASSEVER and -ANT.] Asseverating, solemnly asserting.

†**a'sseverantly**, *adv. Obs.* [f. prec. + -LY². Cf. L. *assevērānter*.] By way of asseveration.
c **1555** HARPSFIELD *Divorce Hen. VIII* (1878) 122 Not spoken asseverantly but opinionatively, and by the way of allegation. **1600** ABP. ABBOT *Exp. Jonah* 562 To speak an untruth voluntarily and asseverantly, had been a shameful thing.

asseverate (əˈsɛvəreɪt), *v.* [f. L. *assevērāt-* ppl. stem of *assevērāre*: see ASSEVER and -ATE³.] To affirm solemnly, assert emphatically, declare positively, avouch, aver: **a.** with *subord. cl.*

1791 D'ISRAELI *Cur. Lit.* 36 They asseverated they saw no child. **1860** B. POWELL *Ess. & Rev.* (ed. 2) 141 If the most numerous ship's company were all to asseverate that they had seen a mermaid.

b. with *simple obj.*

a **1847** R. HAMILTON *Rew. & Punishm.* viii. (1853) 406 If the doctrine of the preceding argument be true, let it be asseverated. **1876** E. MELLOR *Priesth.* iv. 179 To asseverate his previous statement with increased emphasis.

a'sseverating, *ppl. a.* [f. prec. + -ING².] That asseverates; solemnly declaring or confirming.

1838–9 HOOD *Popping Quest.* 19 With an asseverating thump on the table.

a'sseve,ratingly, *adv.* [f. prec. + -LY².] By way of asseveration or solemn affirmation.

1880 HARDY *Trumpet-Maj.* III. xxxviii. 187 He laid his hand asseveratingly upon his breast.

asseveration (ə,sɛvə'reɪʃən). [ad. L. *assevērātiōn-em*, n. of action f. *assevērāre*: see ASSEVER and -ATION. Cf. It. *asseueratione* (Florio 1611).]

1. The action of asseverating; solemn affirmation, emphatic assertion, positive declaration, avouchment.

1564 *Brief Exam.* ****** ij b, You so confidently bare the matter downe with your vndoubted asseueration. **1605** BACON *Adv. Learn.* I. 26 Men ought.. to propound things sincerely, with more or lesse asseueration, as they stand in a man's own iudgement, prooued more or lesse. **1781** COWPER *Convers.* 59 Asseveration blustering in your face, Makes contradiction such a hopeless case.

2. That which is asseverated; a solemn or emphatic declaration or assertion.

a **1556** CRANMER *Wks.* I. 67 Such abominable and beastly asseverations as you never heard. **1658** T. WALL *God's Revenge* 25 The wise man's constant asseveration, by pride only cometh contention. **1753** SMOLLETT *Ct. Fathom* (1784) 152/2 Incensed at this asseveration, which he was not prepared to refute. **1855** MACAULAY *Hist. Eng.* IV. 520 In spite of the solemn asseverations of his wife and his servants.

3. Emphatic confirmation of a statement; a word or phrase used to express confirmation; an oath.

1602 T. FITZHERB. *Apol.* 11 a, I do first make the same asseueration as before vpon my Saluation. **1644** BULWER *Chiron.* 57 Both Hands smitten together.. doth affirme with Rhetoricall asseveration. *a* **1675** STERRY *Freed. Will* 167 It is brought.. with a twofold Asseveration; 'Yea, even.' **1841** DICKENS *Barn. Rudge* (C.D. ed.) 146 The sergeant rejoined with many choice asseverations that he didn't.

asseverative (ə'sɛvərətɪv), *a.* [f. L. *assevērāt-* (see ASSEVERATE) + -IVE, as if ad. L. **assevērātīvus.*] Of, pertaining to, or characterized by asseveration.

1837 *Chamb. Jrnl.* 6 May 117 We here omit a couple of words of an asseverative character.

a'sseveratory, *a.* ? *Obs. rare*⁻¹. [f. as prec. + -ORY.] = prec.

a **1733** NORTH *Exam.* (1740) 247 (D.) Diverse warm and asseveratory answers.

†**a'ssevering,** *ppl. a. Obs.* [f. ASSEVER *v.* + -ING².] Asseverating, solemnly affirmative.

a **1733** NORTH *Exam.* I. iii. ¶23. 137 He affirmed.. in the most assevering Manner he could.

†**a'ssewer.** *Obs.* [A difficult word: used on the one hand as identical with ASSEOUR, he who sets the table; on the other identified with SEWER, as if it were a compound of the latter, or the latter an aphetic form of *assewer*. (*Sewer* occurs earlier.) Cf. also ASSAYER 2.] An officer who superintended the placing of a banquet on the table, or who himself carried in and arranged the dishes; a sewer. (In the *Househ. Ord.* of Edw. IV it interchanges with *Sewer*, and represents the *Asseour* of the *Househ. Ord.* of Edw. II, transl. in 1601 *Assayer*.)

1478 *Liber Niger Edw. IV* in *Househ. Ord.* (1790) 45 Twentie Squires attendantes on the Kinges person.. to helpe serue his table.. as the Assewer will assigne. *a* **1483** *Ibid.* 36 *A sewar for the Kynge.* He receveth the metes by sayes and saufly so conveyeth it to the King's bourde.. he seweth at one mele, and dyneth and soupeth at another mele. .. Item, if the King's surveyour lacke, then this assewer, with the clerke of countrolment and the clerk of Kychyn, and the master cooke for the mouthe, shall go see the King's servyse.

assh-: for words so spelt in 14–15th c., see under ME. form in ASCH-, or modern in ASH-.

assh(e, obsolete form of ASH *sb.*¹, ASK *v.*

'ass-head. [See ASS *sb.*¹ 2 and HEAD.] A stupid fellow, a blockhead.

1550 BALE *Apol.* 61 O absolute ass-heade.. and wytlesse ydyote. **1589** *Hay any Work* 36 As verye an Asshead as John Catercap. **1601** SHAKS. *Twel. N.* v. i. 212 An Asse-head, and a coxcombe.

'ass-,headed, *a.* [f. prec. + -ED.] Stupid.

1532 MORE *Confut. Barnes* VIII. Wks. 736/1 Thys felowes folishe apishenesse, and al hys asseheded exclamacions. **1609** DOULAND *Ornithop. Microl.* 65 Asse-headed ignorance.

Hence also **'asseheaddinesse,** or blockishnesse.' Minsheu 1617.

assibilate (ə'sɪbɪleɪt). *v.* [f. L. *assībilāt-* ppl. stem of *ads-*, *assībilāre*, f. *ad* to + *sībilāre* to hiss. Cf. F. *assibiler*.] To give a sibilant or hissing sound to.

1844 DONALDSON *Varron.* 218 Two different values of the Greek ζ, which was a dental, either assibilated (as σδ) or softened (as δς). **1861** *Proc. Amer. Phil. Soc.* VIII. 361 The second step consists in *y* being assibilated in *sh*.

assibilation (ə,sɪbɪ'leɪʃən). [n. of action f. prec.: see -ATION.] Pronunciation with a sibilant or hissing sound.

1850 *Proc. Amer. Philol. Soc.* IV. 262 The assibilation of the final guttural is a matter far too important to be discussed incidentally. **1861** *Proc. Amer. Phil. Soc.* VIII. 361 The first step in the modern English assibilation of *t* and *d*. **1933** JESPERSEN *Essentials Eng. Gram.* v. 57 Assibilation.. is the name of the development of new [ʃ, ʒ, tʃ, dʒ] from combinations with [j].

Assidæan, -ean, -ian (æsɪ'diːən). [f. Gr. Ἀσιδαῖ-οι (ad. Heb. *ḥăsīdīm*, holy ones, saints) + -AN.] **a.** *orig.* One of those Jews who, under the leadership of Mattathias, defended the purity of their worship against the attempts of Antiochus Epiphanes to introduce idolatry. **b.** in later usage: A member of a Jewish sect professing peculiarly intimate communion with God; more commonly *Chasidim*.

1382 WYCLIF *2 Macc.* xiv. 6 Thei that ben said Assideys [COVERDALE, Assidei; **1611** Asideans] of Jewis, to whom Judas Machabeus is souereyn. **1611** BIBLE *1 Macc.* ii. 42 A company of Assideans. **1834** *Penny Cycl.* II. 502/1 The Assidians, or Chasidim.

†**'assidence.** *Obs. rare*⁻¹. [f. L. *assidēnt-em*: see next and -ENCE.] Constant attendance.

a **1656** BP. HALL *Rem. Wks.* (1660) 248 None of God's children upon earth want the assidence and ministration of those blessed Spirits.

†**'assident,** *a.* and *sb. Obs.* [ad. L. *assidēnt-em*, pr. pple. of *assidē-re* to sit by: see ASSESS *v.* and -ENT.] **A.** *adj.* Constantly attendant; usually accompanying though not inseparable from (a disease). **B.** *sb.* [sc. symptom.]

1753 CHAMBERS *Cycl. Supp.* s.v., A dry rough tongue, thirst, and watching, are Assident signs in an ardent fever. *Ibid.*, Assidents differ from Pathognomonics, which are inseparable from the disease. [So in REES *Cycl.* 1819.]

†**a'ssidual,** *a. Obs.* Also 5 **assedual, assyduel.** [a. OF. *assiduel*, f. L. *assiduus* ASSIDUOUS: see -AL¹.]

1. Of persons or agents: = ASSIDUOUS 1.

a **1400** [see ASSIDUALLY]. **1599** SANDYS *Europæ Spec.* (1632) 142 Assiduall horse-leeches which neuer lin sucking it. **1651** *Father Sarpi* (1676) 96 More devout and attentive .. and particularly in meditation more assidual.

2. Of actions: = ASSIDUOUS 3.

1622 MALYNES *Anc. Law-Merch.* 255 Sulphur and Mercury.. doe ingender.. by an assiduall concoction. **1678** JORDAN *Tri. Lond.* in Heath *Grocers' Comp.* (1869) 519 The assidual wishes of.. Your heartily humble Servant.

†**a'ssidually,** *adv. Obs.* [f. prec. + -LY².] Constantly, continually, assiduously.

a **1400** *Cov. Myst.* 388 And assedually wachith me be dayes and nythis. **1483** CAXTON *Gold. Leg.* 430/2 To kepe & absteyne them assyduelly from alle synne. *c* **1485** *Digby Myst.* (1882) v. 256 Ffor in hym thei Ioye assiduly.

†**a'ssiduate,** *a. Obs.* [f. *assiduāt-* ppl. stem of *assiduāre* to apply constantly, f. *assiduus*: see ASSIDUOUS and -ATE³.] Continually exercised, constant, assiduous.

1494 FABYAN VI. cxli. 129 By the assyduat laboure of his holy wyfe. **1658** SLINGSBY *Diary* (1836) 207 It was my assiduate care therefore to remove all such subtile witnesses.

†**a'ssiduately,** *adv. Obs.* [f. prec. + -LY².] Constantly, continually, assiduously.

1490 CAXTON *Eneydos* vi. 26 Oute of her fayr swete eyen .. flowed teeris assyduatly. **1635** HEYWOOD *Hierarch.* VI. 351 But run into contempt assiduately.

assidue: see ARSEDINE.

assiduity (æsɪ'djuːɪtɪ). [(? a. F. *assiduité*), ad. L. *assiduitātem*, n. of quality f. *assiduus*: see -ITY.]

1. Constant or close attention to the business in hand, unremitting application, persistent endeavour, perseverance, diligence.

1605 BACON *Adv. Learn.* II. xxiii. §37 Some measure things according to the labour and difficulty or assiduity which are spent about them. **1712** HUGHES *Spect.* No. 316 ¶6 The labour and assiduity with which Tully acquired his eloquence. **1866** GEO. ELIOT *F. Holt* III. xl. 105 Not one to fail in a purpose for want of assiduity.

2. Persistent endeavour to please, obsequious attention. *arch* exc. as in b.

1630 NAUNTON *Fragm. Reg.* (Arb.) 38 And could not brook the obsequiousnesse and assiduity of the Court. **1720** SWIFT *Fates Clergym.* Wks. 1755 II. II. 27 His lord was.. attended by him with the most abject assiduity. **1825** *Bro. Jonathan* II. 287 Full of serene, delicate, reverential assiduity.

b. *esp.* in *pl.* Constant attentions.

1683 D. A. *Art Converse* 98 To be rid of our troublesome assiduities. **1748** SMOLLETT *Rod. Rand.* lv. (1804) 389 To vanquish her coldness and suspicion by my assiduities. **1847** H. ROGERS *Ess.* I. v. 242 And even declined, with cold and averted eye, the assiduities of their zealous love.

†**3.** Continual recurrence or repetition, frequency.

1611 COTGR., *Assiduité*, assiduity, frequencie, oftennesse. **1626** DONNE *Serm.* iv. 36 To dishonour miracles by the assiduity and frequency and multiplicity of them. **1668** CULPEPPER & COLE *Barthol. Anat.* III. i. 323 The Magnitude is various, according to the condition of the Organs and dignity of the Actions, their Assiduity and Magnitude.

assiduous (ə'sɪdjuːəs), *a.* [f. L. *assidu-us* (f. *assidē-re* to sit by: see ASSESS *v.*; lit. 'sitting down to,' hence 'closely applying to') + -OUS.]

1. Of persons or agents: Constant in application to the business in hand, persevering, sedulous, unwearyingly diligent.

1660 JER. TAYLOR *Duct. Dubit.* II. ii. vii. §3 Christ.. commands us to be perfect, that is.. to be assiduous in our prayers. **1711** ADDISON *Spect.* No. 311 ¶5 Those assiduous Gentlemen who employ their whole Lives in the Chace. **1876** GREEN *Short Hist.* iii. §7 (1882) 148 He was assiduous in his attendance on religious services.

2. Constantly endeavouring to please, obsequiously attentive. *arch.*

a **1725** POPE *Odyss.* VI. 89 The queen, assiduous, to her train assigns The sumptuous viands. **1750** JOHNSON *Rambl.* No. 104 ¶13 Few can be assiduous without servility.

3. Of actions: Unremitting, persistent, constant.

1538 LELAND *Itin.* I. Introd. 20 By infinite Variete of Bookes and assiduus reading of them. **1667** MILTON *P.L.* XI. 310 To wearie him with my assiduous cries. **1711** ADDISON *Spect.* No. 10 ¶1 Follies that are only to be killed by a constant and assiduous Culture. **1849** MACAULAY *Hist. Eng.* I. 491 Baxter's life was chiefly passed.. in the assiduous discharge of parochial duties.

†**4.** Of things: Constant, regular. *Obs.*

1661 EVELYN *Fumifug.* Misc. Writ. (1805) I 217 The Election of this constant and assiduous food, should something concerne us.

a'ssiduously, *adv.* [f. prec. + -LY².] With close or constant application, sedulously.

1627 J. FORBES in *Quiver* (1880) 301, I prayed also assiduously that it would please Him to root out of my heart .. every root of bitterness. **1753** SMOLLETT *Ct. Fathom* (1784) 183/1 His sister assiduously attended him in his recovery. **1855** MACAULAY *Hist. Eng.* III. 425 He set himself assiduously to drill those new levies.

a'ssiduousness. [f. as prec. + -NESS.] Close or constant application, assiduity.

1637 *Sidney State Papers* II. 509 (L.) Persons that will have the patience to understand and press with art and assiduousness.

†**a'ssiege,** *v. Obs.* Forms: 3–4 **asege,** 4 **aseege,** 4–6 **assege,** 5–6 **-yege,** 6 **-aige, -eige,** 5–7 **assiege.** [a. OF. *asegier* (mod. *assiéger*), cogn. with Pr. *assetiar*, *assetjar*, Sp. *asediar*, It. *assediare*:—late L. *assediāre* f. *as-* = *ad-* to, at + *sedium* (cf. *obsidium*) sitting, SIEGE.] To besiege, lay siege to, beleaguer, beset.

1297 R. GLOUC. 184 Kyng Arture and ys poer aseged hym wyþoute. *c* **1386** CHAUCER *Knts. T.* 23 And how asegid was Ypolita The faire hardy quyen of Cithea. **1483** CAXTON *Gold. Leg.* 158/3 They had assyeged Jherusalem. **1522–4** *Diurn. Occurr.* (1833) 8 And assaigit the castell of Wark. **1632** J. HAYWARD *Eromena* 160 She was assieged, and in danger to bee lost.

†**a'ssiege,** *sb. Obs.* Also 4 **asseege,** 4–5 **assege,** 6 **assige.** [f. prec. Not in Fr.] A siege.

1375 BARBOUR *Bruce* XVII. 270 He.. To the toune ane assege set. **1469** SIR J. PASTON in *Lett.* 621 II. 375, I have herde.. werse tydynges syn the assege by gan. **1589** IVE *Fortif.* 5 The Winde and Seas alteration is such, that an Assige at Sea cannot be continued. **1598** FLORIO, *Oppugnatione*.. an assiege [not in ed. 1611].

†**a'ssieged,** *ppl. a. Obs.* [f. as prec. + -ED.] Besieged, beleaguered, beset.

1383 WYCLIF *Sel. Wks.* (1871) III. 274 To vitele þes men asegid. **1535** STEWART *Cron. Scot.* I. 102 In flesche assegit with foul faminitie. **1596** SPENSER *F.Q.* II. xi. 15 Th' assieged castles. **1614** RALEIGH *Hist. World* II. v. i. §2. 268 And left the Mutineers to be cut in pieces by the assieged.

assiegement (ə'siːdʒmənt). *arch.* [f. as prec. + -MENT.] A besieging or beleaguering, a siege.

1587 FLEMING *Contn. Holinshed* III. 965/2 The assiegement of those two townes, Bullongne and Muttrell. **1839** BAILEY *Festus* (1848) 64/2 They vanish from the assiegement of the saints.

†**a'ssieger.** *Obs. rare*⁻¹. [f. as prec. + -ER¹.] A besieger.

1584 T. HUDSON tr. *Du Bartas' Judith* III. (1613) 254 (D.) No lesse to keep, then coole th' assiegers pride.

†**a'ssieging,** *vbl. sb.* [f. as prec. + -ING¹.] A besieging, siege.

c **1450** LONELICH *Grail* xiii. 140 Tholomes.. hath there leid asegeng. **1582–8** *Hist. James VI* (1804) 229 All their prouisioun for asseging of the castell. **1606** B. BARNES *Bks. Offices* 202 Towards the assieging of any cities or forts.

assientist (æsɪ'ɛntɪst). In 8 assentist. [f. next + -IST; cf. F. *assientiste*, and Sp. *a(s)sentista*, after which the earlier form was *assentist*.] One of the parties to an Assiento contract; a shareholder in an Assiento company.

1713 *Lond. Gaz.* No. 5132 1 With Priviledges beyond what any former Assentists ever enjoy'd. **1719** W. WOOD *Surv. Trade* 280 The supplying the Spaniards with Negroes, has proved a Loss to other Assientists. **1876** BANCROFT *Hist. U.S.* II. xxxv. 390 The assientists might introduce as many more[slaves] as they pleased.

‖**assiento, asiento** (əˈsjɛntəʊ, æsɪˈɛntəʊ). [Sp. *asiento* (Minsheu), mod. *asiento*, settlement, contract.] 'A contract, or conuention between the king of Spain and other powers, for furnishing the Spanish dominions in America with negro slaves' (J.). *spec.* That made between Great Britain and Spain at the peace of Utrecht in 1713.

1714 *Lond. Gaz.* No. 5213/3 The Assiento, or Contract for allowing the Subjects of Great Britain the Liberty of Importing Negroes into the Spanish America. **1876** BANCROFT *Hist. U.S.* II. xlii. 555 The English slave-trade began to attain its great activity after the assiento treaty.

‖**assiette** (aˈsjɛt). [Fr. = seat, site.] In *Bookbinding*, A composition laid on the cut edges of books previous to gilding them.

1869 *Eng. Mech.* 1 Oct. 37/2 Assiette..is composed of Armenian bole, 1 lb.; bloodstone, 2 oz.; and galena, 2 oz.

assification (ˌæsɪfɪˈkeɪʃən). [n. of action, f. as ASSIFY: see -FICATION.] The action of making an ass of (a person); asinine act.

1823 *Blackw. Mag.* XIV. 576/2 The last assification I shall notice..would settle the business in the most scrupulous court *de Lunatico inquirendo*. **1879** C. M. YONGE *Magnum Bonum* III. xxxii. 682, I ruined you all..with that assification.

assify (ˈæsɪfaɪ), *v.* [f. ASS *sb.*[1] + -(I)FY.] To make an ass of, turn into an ass. (*Jocular.*)

1804 SOUTHEY in Robberds *Mem. W. Taylor* I. 515 Instead of oxifying or assifying myself. *c* **1800** 'P. PINDAR JUN.' (*title*) An Assified Mare: the London Mare turned Ass.

assige, variant of ASSIEGE *sb. Obs.* a siege.

assign (əˈsaɪn), *v.* Forms: 3-6 **assygn(e**, 3-7 **assigne**, 4 **a sign, asegne, asingne**, 4-6 **assine**, 5 **asyne, a-cyne, asigne, assygne**, 5-6 **assyg(e**, 6 **assyne, asein**, 7 **essign**, 5- **assign.** *Aphet.* 5 **syne.** [a. OF. *a(s)signe-r, a(s)siner, a(s)sene-r*:—L. *ad-, assignāre*, f. *ad* to + *signāre* to make a sign, f. *signum* sign.] *Prim. sign.* To mark out to.

I. To allot, appoint, authoritatively determine.

1. *trans.* To allot as a share, portion, or allowance (*to*); to appoint, apportion, make over.

1340 *Alex. & Dind.* 321 We han a sertaine somme asingned of ȝerus. **1393** GOWER *Conf.* III. 117 To every monthe..of signes twelve He hath..Assigned one in speciall. **1513** DOUGLAS *Æneis* III. ii. 140 Assynging ilk ane propir houss and aucht. **1570** J. PHILLIP in Farr *S.P.* (1845) II. 529 And vnto his elected churche A pleadge of loue assinde. **1599** GREENE *Poems* (1861) 317 By 'signing want and poverty thy share. **1667** MILTON *P.L.* IX. 231 The work which here God hath assign'd us. **1794** S. WILLIAMS *Hist. Vermont* 152 The most laborious services were assigned to the female. **1807** CRABBE *Par. Reg.* I. 130 Has a small space for garden-ground assign'd.

2. To transfer or formally make over to another. In modern *Eng. Law* the appropriate word to express the transference of *personal* property (including chattels real), *e.g.* leaseholds, railway shares, furniture, as distinguished from *real* property.

1297 R. GLOUC. 314 Wat thyng he adde assygned ys tueye bretheren al so. *c* **1400** *Apol. Loll.* 82 þei..þat occupien men toward her end a bout..assining of þer goodis. **1522** *Bury Wills* (1850) 117 The residue of all my goodes..I assign to myn executors to pay dettes. **1660** STANLEY *Hist. Philos.* (1701) 369/1 He essigned the School to Aristaeus. **1748** JOHNSON in *Boswell* (1831) I. 167, I assign to him the right of copy of an Imitation of the Tenth Satire of Juvenal. **1862** HOOK *Lives Abps.* II. ii. 88 Some land which had been newly assigned to the monastery.

3. To allot (a place) *to* a person; to appoint or set it apart for a purpose.

1393 GOWER *Conf.* II. 10 But me was never assigned place. *c* **1400** *Destr. Troy* II. 508 And he assignet hir a seite. **1439** *E. E. Wills* (1882) 116 My body to be beryed..yn suche place as I haue assyngned. **1622** in *Fortesc. Papers* 189 To have places assigned where your marchants might erect forts. **1762** GOLDSM. *Cit. World* xxxiii. (1837) 131, I was assigned my place on a cushion on the floor. **1855** PRESCOTT *Philip II*, I. vii. (1857) 116 He assigned to his men their several posts.

4. a. To allot or appoint *to* a person (those that shall perform certain functions in relation to him).

1340 HAMPOLE *Pr. Consc.* 4189 Til hym sal assygned be A gude angelle. **1350** *Will. Palerne* 580 þenne had þis menskful Melior maydenes fele asegned hire to serue. *c* **1400** *Destr. Troy* IV. 1136 With a soume of soudiours assignet vs. **1506** *Ord. Crysten Men* (W. de W.) IV. v. 177 Unto them assygne not an other confessour. *a* **1656** BP. HALL *Rem. Wks.* (1660) 52 The Lords Assigned us five very worthy Lawyers. **1826** SCOTT *Woodst.* (1832) 180 England will not long endure the rulers which these bad times have assigned her.

b. To make over a convict as an unpaid servant.

1827 P. CUNNINGHAM *Two Years in N.S. Wales* II. xxviii. 188 Convict servants are now assigned on application being made for them in a printed form to the land board. **1837** [see ASSIGNED]. **1843** *Penny Cycl.* XXV. 138/2 Female convicts were assigned..in the capacity of domestic servants.

†**5.** To appoint authoritatively, prescribe (a course of action). *Obs.*

c **1485** *Digby Myst.* II. 214 Make thi curse As I shall assyng the by myn aduysse. **1533** MORE *Answ. Poysoned Bk.* Wks. 1048/2 They assygned him..what maner a miracle thei wold haue him do. *c* **1550** *Lusty Juv.* in Hazl. *Dodsl.* II. 59 Thou must love..thy neighbour as thyself, because he hath so assigned. **1607** TOPSELL *Four-f. Beasts* 103 Simeon Sethi ..assigneth them rather to be eaten in Winter time.

6. To appoint, designate, ordain, depute (a person) for an office, duty, or fate. *Obs.* exc. in *Law.*

1297 R. GLOUC. 502 He assigneth the bissop of Winchestre ther to. *c* **1470** *Three 15th C. Chron.* (1880) 72 The Duke of Exceter was syned for kepe the see ayenes the Erle of Warwike. **1489** *Plumpton Corr.* 81, I have assigneed my servant..to levy and receive such rents. *a* **1547** EARL SURREY *Æneis* II. (R.) Assigning me To the altar. **1712** BUDGELL *Spect.* No. 404 ¶7 They assign themselves to what they are not fit for. **1768** BLACKSTONE *Comm.* I. 482 If the founder has appointed and assigned any other person to be visitor.

†**7.** To appoint, direct, send (a person) *to* a place; to consign. *Obs.*

1413 LYDG. *Pylgr. Sowle* V. xiv. 80 Assignyng his company, euerych in to his place. **1567** DRANT *Horace Epist.* I. vii. D v, At length to bed to take a nap he, fraighted, was assynde. **1611** BIBLE *2 Sam.* xi. 16 He assigned Vriah vnto a place where hee knewe that valiant men were.

8. a. To fix, settle, determine, or authoritatively appoint (a time or temporal limit).

c **1305** *St. Swithin* in *E.E.P.* (1862) 46 Hi assignede a dai þerto. **1485** CAXTON *Chas. Gt.* 220 The day of bataylle..was assygned on bothe partyes. **1553** T. WILSON *Rhet.* 42 We would assigne God his tyme. **1708** SWIFT *Predict.* 1708 Wks. 1755 II. I. 153 In this month likewise an ambassador will die in London; but I cannot assign the day. **1883** J. GILMOUR *Mongols* xvii. 202 A hell to the duration of which no period is assigned.

†**b.** To fix the time and place of (a meeting).

1558 FORREST *Grysilde Sec.* 89 A Cowrte he assigned at Dunstaple, To which was summoned goode Grysildis.

†**9.** To make an assignation or appointment with (a person) *to do* a thing. *Obs.*

1470-85 MALORY *Arthur* (1817) X. ii, I assigne you to mete me in the medowe. *Ibid.* (1816) I. 187 And there this night I had assigned my love and lady to have slept with me.

10. To determine, lay down as a thing ascertained.

1664 POWER *Exp. Philos.* II. 93 Who all assign its Altitude to be but about 27 inches. **1772-84** COOK *Voy.* (1790) IV. 92 Who sailed round it, and assigned its true position. **1817** CHALMERS *Astron. Disc.* i. (1852) 24 Who shall assign a limit to the discoveries of future ages?

II. To point out, show.

11. a. To point out exactly, designate, specify.

1377 LANGL. *P. Pl.* B. IV. 126 And til seynt Iames be souȝte þere I shal assigne. **1533** MORE *Debell. Salem* Wks. 952/1 Folk whom I neither assigne bi name, nor as yet know not who they be. **1660** BARROW *Euclid* I. xxxiv. *Schol.*, To draw a parallel to a right line given, thro' the point assigned. **1714** GROVE *Spect.* No. 601 ¶2, I shall therefore endeavour to assign some of the principal Checks upon this generous Propension. *c* **1854** STANLEY *Sinai & Pal.* v. 251 The special locality which Jewish tradition has assigned for the place.

b. *spec.* in *Law.*

1672 MANLEY *Cowell's Interpr.* s.v., To assigne false Judgment..is to declare how and where the Judgment is unjust. To assigne Waste is to show wherein especially the Waste is committed.

†**12.** To exhibit, display, present. *Obs.*

1398 TREVISA *Barth. De P.R.* VI. xv, The faderis herte is sore greuyd, yf eny rebelnesse is assignid [*presentatur*] in his children.

III. To ascribe, attribute.

13. To ascribe, attribute, or refer, as belonging *to* or originating in.

1541 R. COPLAND *Guydon's Quest. Cyrurg.*, The memory of the herte..is assygned in the partye that is vnder the ioynt that is vnder the arme pytte. **1835** MACREADY *Remin.* I. 461 The various spots assigned to the words and actions of our Saviour. *a* **1849** HOR. SMITH *Addr. Mummy* iii, Tell us..To whom should we assign the Sphinx's fame. **1875** SCRIVENER *Lect. Grk. Test.* 9 Whose date may be assigned with certainty to the fourth and fifth centuries.

14. To ascribe (a reason) *to* or as accounting *for* anything.

1489 CAXTON *Faytes of Armes* IV. vii. 246 Many good raisons that dyuine right assigneth thereto. **1655** FULLER *Ch. Hist.* IX. IV. 383 Sundry reasons are assigned of Mr. Cartwright's silence. **1769** *Junius Lett.* xxiv. 132 To justify my assigning that motive to his behaviour. **1792** *Anecd. W. Pitt* I. v. 122 No reason can be assigned for the Queen of Hungary's refusing the terms.

15. To bring forward, allege, offer, suggest (something as a reason, etc.).

a **1665** J. GOODWIN *Filled w. the Spirit* (1867) 380 This is that which we now assign for a reason. **1780** COXE *Russ. Disc.* 42 They assigned the insecurity of the roads as their reason for coming..by sea. **1790** PALEY *Hor. Paul.* i. §3, I cannot assign a supposition of forgery.

†**IV.** [f. *as-* = A- *pref.* 11 + SIGN *v.*] To sign. *Obs.*

1563 ABP. SANDYS in Strype *Ann. Ref.* I. xxxv. 389 The bill..was..sent up in the docket to be assigned by the Queen. **1633** H. COGAN *Pinto's Voy.* vi. 15 A safe conduct, written and assigned with thine own hand.

†**assign**, *sb.*[1] *Obs.* [see different senses.]

1. Appointment, command. [f. ASSIGN *v.*]

1633 P. FLETCHER *Purple Isl.* II. xliii, Soon as the gate opes by the Kings assigne.

2. A sign, portent. [f. SIGN *sb.*; cf. ASSIGN *v.* IV.]

1601 WEEVER *Mirr. Mart.* C viij b, To the Frenchmen, this assigne was sent, Disaster, fatall, inauspicious.

¶ for DESIGN.

a **1641** FINETT *Philoxenis* (1656) 50 His so gracious notice and furtherance of their assignes.

assign (əˈsaɪn), *sb.*[2] Also 5-7 **assigne.** [ME. *assigne* (three syllables), a. F. *assigné*, pa. pple. of *assigner* to ASSIGN, has split into two forms in mod.E. *assign* and *assignee*. In the former, ME. *-e* (like final *-e* from other sources) became mute in 15th c., and disappeared in mod.E. (Cf. *avow(e*, F. *avoué*:—L. *advocātus*; *costive*, F. *costivé*:—L. *constipātus*, etc.) In the latter, final *-e* was preserved through the influence of law French, and was at length analogically written *-ee*. (Cf. *avowee, advowee*, beside *avow(e)*.) The 15th c. *assigne* might represent either pronunciation, and belongs equally to *assign* and *assignee*. Cf. ASSIGNEE.]

†**1.** One who is appointed to act for another, a deputy, agent, or representative; = ASSIGNEE 1. *Obs.*

1526 *Ord. R. Househ.* 224 Their servants, factors, or assignes. **1594** HOOKER *Eccl. Pol.* v. (1863) 413 [We] are but delegates or assignes to giue men possession of his graces. **1714** *Fr. Bk. of Rates* 31 As the Owner, or his Deputy, or Assign shall desire.

2. One to whom a property or right is legally transferred; = ASSIGNEE 2. Esp. in the phrase *heirs and assigns*: see quot. 1865.

c **1450** *Pol. Rel. & L. Poems* (1866) 24 To thyne heyres & assygnes alle-so. **1590** SWINBURN *Testaments* 74 To him and his assignes for terme of life. **1710** STEELE *Tatler* No. 200 ¶ 11 Made payable to..her Assigns. **1844** WILLIAMS *Real Prop. Law* (1877) 64 Thus, a purchaser from him in his lifetime, and a devisee under his will, are alike assigns. **1865** NICHOLLS *Britton* II. xvi. I. 312 It was in favour of bastards that the word assigns [F. *assignez*] was first devised.

†**3.** An appurtenance, a belonging. *Obs. rare.*

1602 SHAKS. *Ham.* v. ii. 157 Six French Rapiers and Poniards, with their assignes as Girdle, Hangers, or so.

assignability (əˌsaɪnəˈbɪlɪtɪ). [f. next: see -BILITY.] Capability of being assigned.

1884 *Law Times* 23 Feb. 301/1 The effect of the Judicature Act on the assignability of *choses in action.*

assignable (əˈsaɪnəb(ə)l), *a.* [f. ASSIGN *v.* + -ABLE.]

1. That may be assigned or allotted; legally transferable.

1809 TOMLINS *Law Dict.* s.v. *Assignment*, A bond is assignable for a valuable consideration paid. **1868** M. PATTISON *Academ. Org.* §4. 66 A fixed number of scholarships..assignable among the colleges.

2. That may be designated or specified.

1659 PEARSON *Creed* (1839) 178 Being thus the Alpha..he was before any time assignable. **1793** SMEATON *Edystone L.* §239 No assignable power..could lift one of these stones. **1848** MILL *Pol. Econ.* I. 82 Without assignable limit.

3. That may be referred as belonging *to* or originating in; attributable.

1673 *Lady's Call.* I. ii. §15 The correcting of som particular passions are more immediately assignable to other virtues. **1869** PHILLIPS *Vesuv.* viii. 235 Thus three relations of volcanic energy are assignable to geographical conditions.

4. That may be alleged as accounting for.

1659 PEARSON *Creed* (1839) 36 There is no other cause assignable of the rain but God. **1817** COLERIDGE *Biog. Lit.* I. i. 8 In the truly great poets..there is a reason assignable.. for every word.

assignably (əˈsaɪnəblɪ), *adv.* [f. prec. + -LY[2].] In a manner capable of being assigned.

1674 N. FAIRFAX *Bulk & Selv.* 45 If so be, that which is neither to be shown here nor there, nor to be understood every where, be assignably no where.

‖**assignat** (ˈæsɪgnæt, asiˈɲa). [Fr., ad. L. *assignātum*, pa. pple. of *assignāre* to ASSIGN.] Paper money issued by the revolutionary government of France, on security of the state lands. Cf. ASSIGNATION 4.

1790 BURKE *Fr. Rev.* Wks. V. 415 Is there a debt which presses them? Issue assignats. Are compensations to be made?..assignats. Is a fleet to be fitted out? Assignats. **1876** FAWCETT *Pol. Econ.* III. ii. 449 Issuing inconvertible notes in the form of assignats.

†ˈ**assignate**, *ppl. a. Obs. rare*⁻¹. [ad. L. *assignātus*: see prec.] Assigned, specified.

1471 RIPLEY *Comp. Alch.* (Ashm. 1652) v. 150 Blacknes.. ys Of kyndly Commyxyon to the tokyn assygnate.

assignation (æsɪgˈneɪʃən). [a. OF. *assignacion* (14th c. in Littré), ad. L. *assignātiōnem*, n. of action f. *assignāre*: see ASSIGN *v.* and -ATION.]

1. The action of allotting; apportionment.

1600 HOLLAND *Livy* 919 (R.) As touching the appointment and assignation of those provinces. **1673** *Lady's Call.* I. ii. §13 Since Gods assignation has thus determined subjection to be the womens lot. *a* **1716**

BLACKALL *Wks.* 1723 I. 132 Not a Matter of Choice, but of divine Assignation. **1878** BOSW. SMITH *Carthage* 73 To hold out visions of assignations of public land..to the multitudes.

2. The action of legally transferring a right or property (see ASSIGN *v.* 2); formal transference. Also **a.** formal declaration of transference; **b.** the transferred interest. (Now usually ASSIGNMENT.)

1579 FENTON *Guicciard.* IV. (1599) 176 And sent them foorthwith the assignation of the Castle. **1605** BACON *Adv. Learn.* II. §10 Alexander made..a liberal assignation to Aristotle of treasure. **1621** R. JOHNSON *Way to Glory* 29 Hee had but the assignation and lease of tythes. **1754** ERSKINE *Princ. Sc. Law* (1809) 342 All moveable rights are transmissible by simple assignation. **1809** TOMLINS *Law Dict.*, *Assignation* is when simply any thing is ceded, yielded and assigned to another.

†3. The setting apart of certain revenue to meet a claim. Also **a.** the mandate granting the money; **b.** the amount thus set apart, a pension, allowance.

1489 *Acts Jas. IV*, xxiv, Quhatsumeuer assignatioun or gift be made thairupon under the preiue seill. *a* **1626** BACON *Lopez' Treason* (T.) He had obtained an assignation of 50,000 crowns to be levied in Portugal. *a* **1674** CLARENDON *Hist. Reb.* III. XIII. 343 They settled an Assignation of six thousand Livers by the Month upon the King, payable out of such a Gabel. **1747** *Gentl. Mag.* 13 Jan., The payment of the assignations of the purveyors..of the army.

4. Paper currency; a negotiable document representing and secured by revenue or property; a bill, an *assignat.*

a **1674** CLARENDON *Hist. Reb.* III. XVI. 601 The custom of that Country, [Holland]..being to make their payments in Paper by Assignations. **1747** *Gentl. Mag.* 13 Jan., It is not possible it should be satisified by paper or any assignation.

†5. Appointment or designation to office. *Obs.*

1432 *Paston Lett.* 18. I. 32 The namyng, ordeignance and assignacion beforesaid. **1593** BILSON *Govt. Christ's Ch.* 111 If they be called by Christ, read their assignation from Christ. **1656** BRAMHALL *Replic.* v. 202 Their successors have assignation to particular charges.

†6. Authoritative appointment, prescription, order. *Obs.*

a **1400** *Cov. Myst.* 93 Be [= by] prayour grett knowleche men recure And to this I counselle ȝou to ȝeve assygnacion. **1480** CAXTON *Chron. Eng.* IV. (1520) 37 b/1 Seynt Laurence at the assygnacion of his mayster the pope departed this tresour about Rome. **1544** BALE *Sir J. Oldcastell* in *Harl. Misc.* (Malh.) I. 276 Temporall payne, which I am worthy to suffer as an heretike, at the assignacion of my most excellent chrysten Prince. **1605** BACON *Adv. Learn.* I. vii. §6 Making assignation..for re-edifying of cities.

7. **a.** The appointment of a particular time or place; *esp.* the arrangement of the time and place for an interview; an appointment, tryst.

1660 JER. TAYLOR *Duct. Dubit.* II. ii. vi. §51 This assignation of a definite time. **1680** CROWNE *Mis. Civ. War* II. 16 'Twou'd have spoil'd An assignation that I have to-night. **1854** J. ABBOTT *Napoleon* (1855) II. xii. 197 Compelled to make assignations with as much secrecy as two young lovers.

‖**b.** A summons to appear in court. (Fr.)

1884 *Pall Mall G.* 31 Mar. 3/1 And have served assignations upon..the Comtes de Paris and de Bardi.

8. The action of attributing as belonging to or originating in; attribution of origin.

1603 SIR C. HEYDON *Jud. Astrol.* xxi. 477 He concludeth against the assignation of phlegme to the Moone. **1782** T. WARTON *Rowley Enq.* 68 (T.) Happy to find this assignation of Stonehenge..ascertained by so authentick an historian. **1865** T. WRIGHT in *Athenæum* No. 1979. 441/3 The true assignation of the bronze weapons.

†9. A pointing out, indication, assignment (of a cause, etc.). *Obs.*

1615 CROOKE *Body of Man* 178 His Assignation of the vse of the Bladder of Gall. **1667** *Phil. Trans.* II. 511 A very ingenious assignation of the cause of that variety.

10. *attrib.* (sense 7), ***assignation house*** (U.S.), a brothel.

1870 OLIVE LOGAN *Bef. Footlights* 538 Denounced the National theatre as the vilest of 'assignation houses'. **1943** R. OTTLEY '*New World A-Coming*' 28 Don't come..bothering me with any more protests about assignation houses until you can bring concrete evidence of such houses.

assigned (əˈsaɪnd), *ppl. a.* [f. ASSIGN *v.* + -ED.] Allotted, appointed, prescribed, specified, etc.: see the vb.

c **1374** CHAUCER *Boeth.* I. iv. 16 By certeyne day assigned. **1758** *Month. Rev.* 35 Certain assigned quantities. **1837** J. LANG *New S. Wales* II. 31 The assigned servant of a respectable Scotch family residing near Sydney. **1862** H. SPENCER *First Princ.* I. iii. §17. (1875) 56 Its motion as measured from an assigned position.

assignee (æsɪˈniː), *ppl. a.* and *sb.* Also 5 asigne, assygne, 5–6 assigne. [a. OF. *a(s)signé*, pa. pple. of *assigner* to ASSIGN. *Assign* sb.² and *assignee* both represent the ME. *assigne*; in the former the final *-e* has become mute in popular use, in the latter it has been retained in legal use through the influence of law French, and at length refashioned as *-ee*. (The 15th c. instances of *assigne* belong equally to ASSIGN *sb.*²)]

A. *ppl. a.* Assigned, appointed.

1494 FABYAN VII. 488 Chargynge his lordes with theyr assygnes sowdyours, to mete with hym..at the cytie of Arras.

B. *sb.*

1. One who is appointed to act for another; a deputy, agent, or representative. = ASSIGN *sb.*² 1.

1419 H. STAFFORD in Ellis *Orig. Lett.* III. 28. I. 65 Swych as ȝe left assigne of ȝoures. **1494** FABYAN VII. 316 If the cytie were not by kynge John, or his assygneys, rescowyd. *c* **1600** NORDEN *Spec. Brit., Cornw.* (1728) 65 A howse..occupied by the assignees of the Bishop of Exon. **1713** STEELE *Englishm.* No. 15. 99 To Nestor Ironside, Esq.; or in his absence to the Englishman, his Assignee. **1809** WELLINGTON in Gurw. *Disp.* V. 229 That the assignee is the real agent of the party claiming the debt.

2. One to whom a right or property is legally transferred or made over; = ASSIGN *sb.*² 2.

1467 *Bury Wills* (1850) 47 To his heyrys and assigneis for euermoore. **1613** *E. Kirke's Will* in *Spenser's Wks.* (1882) III. Introd. 113 The saide Richard his heires and Assignees. *Ibid.*, To haue and to houlde to her and to her Assignes. **1768** BLACKSTONE *Comm.* II. 327 In assignments he parts with the whole property, and the assignee stands to all intents and purposes in the place of the assignor. **1876** DIGBY *Real Prop.* x. § 1. 380 The assignee of the lease has the same interest as the lessee (his assignor).

3. ***assignees in bankruptcy***: those to whom the management, realization, and distribution of a bankrupt's estate is committed, on behalf of the creditors.

1687 *Lond. Gaz.* No. 2294/4 Several of the Creditors.. nominated Assignees. **1768** BLACKSTONE *Comm.* II. 480 Assignees, or persons to whom the bankrupt's estate shall be assigned, and in whom it shall be vested for the benefit of the creditors. **1843** MILL *Logic* VI. ix. §5 The official assignees in bankruptcy.

4. A convict assigned as unpaid servant to a colonial settler.

1843 *Penny Cycl.* XXV. 139/2 It is comparatively difficult to obtain another assignee,—easy to obtain a hired servant.

assigneeism (æsɪˈniːɪz(ə)m). [f. prec. + -ISM.] The practice of appointing assignees.

1883 CHALMERS & HOUGH *Bankr. Act* Introd. 8 The extension of official assigneeism to the country generally.

assiˈgneeship. [f. as prec. + -SHIP.] The position or office of assignee.

1829 LAMB in *Life & Lett.* Wks. 1865 xvii. 161 Advancement to an assigneeship. **1884** *Sat. Rev.* 5 July 2/1 This burdensome and impossible assigneeship.

assigner (əˈsaɪnə(r)). [f. ASSIGN *v.* + -ER¹. Cf. OF. *assigneur*, and see ASSIGNOR.] One who assigns, allots, apportions, etc.: see the vb.

1667 *Decay Chr. Piety* (J.) The Gospel is..the assigner of our tasks. **1682** SCARLETT *Exchanges* 227 He may chuse which of the Assigners he pleases, to demand Satisfaction of. **1859** MERIVALE *Rom. Emp.* IV. xxxv. 186 The assigner of the military colonies.

assigning (əˈsaɪnɪŋ), *vbl. sb.* [f. as prec. + -ING¹.] The action of the vb. ASSIGN; assignation, allotment, appointment.

1580 HOLLYBAND *Treas. Fr. Tong.*, *Assignation d'argent*, an assigning of money. *a* **1709** ATKINS *Parl. & Pol. Tracts* (1734) 256 These great Officers, who had the assigning of Sheriffs. **1751** JOHNSON *Rambl.* No. 160 ¶2 The power of assigning to others the task of life.

assignment (əˈsaɪnmənt). Also 4–7 -ement, 5 -ament, assygnement. [a. OF. *assignement*, ad. late or med.L. *assignāmentum* (whence *assignament*), f. *assignāre*: see ASSIGN *v.* and -MENT.]

1. The action of appointing as a share, allotment.

1460 CAPGRAVE *Chron.* 198 Was assigned to the qween his modir a dowary, that men had no mende of swech assignament. **1628** COKE *On Litt.* 36 a, An assignement of Dower..may be made of more then a third part. **1850** MERIVALE *Rom. Emp.* II. xx. 394 Assignment of lands to the veterans.

2. Legal transference of a right or property (cf. ASSIGN *v.* 2); the document that effects or authorizes the transference.

1592 WEST *Symbol.* A iiij. §104 To avoid or frustrate the foresaid grants and assignements. **1668** CHILD *Disc. Trade* (1698) 137 No Debts, after Assignment, to be liable to any Attachments. **1768** [see ASSIGNEE 2]. **1861** GOSCHEN *For. Exch.* 35 *A* will not be able to pay *B* by giving him an assignment on *C*.

†3. **a.** = ASSIGNATION 3. *Obs.*

c **1460** FORTESCUE *Abs. & Lim. Mon.* (1714) 34 The poor Man had rather have a 100 Marks in hand, than a 100 Pound by any Assignement. *a* **1674** CLARENDON *Hist. Reb.* I. II. 15[He] had drawn assignments and anticipations upon the Revenue. **1678** *Trans. Crt. Spain* 121 To accept the pensions and assignments which he injoys.

†**b.** = ASSIGNATION 4. *Obs.*

1622 MALYNES *Anc. Law-Merch.* 335 Paiments by assignement in Banke without handling of moneys. **1708** *Lond. Gaz.* No. 4496/4 Lost.., one Order of the Bankers Assignments, No. 1783, for 4*l.* 7*s.* 8*d.* per Ann.

4. The allotting of convicts as unpaid servants to colonists; the condition of such service.

1843 *Penny Cycl.* XXV. 139/2 The operation of assignment in respect to female convicts is even worse. **1845** DARWIN *Voy. Nat.* xix. (1879) 445 The years of assignment are passed away with discontent and unhappiness.

†5. Appointment to office, nomination, designation; setting apart for a purpose. *Obs.*

1447 BOKENHAM *Lyvys of Seyntys* 56, I am the aungel the which at assignement Of God am comaundyde thy kepre to be. **1532** MORE *Confut. Tindale* Wks. 632/2 By gouernours of hys assignement. *a* **1600** HOOKER (J.) The only thing which maketh any place publick, is the publick assignment.

†6. Appointment, command, bidding. *Obs.*

1393 GOWER *Conf.* III. 15 Went..By his faders assignement To make a wer. **1494** FABYAN VII. 346 By his assygnement, the erle of Glowcetyr was than lodgyd within the cytie. **1611** SPEED *Hist. Gt. Brit.* Concl., Nations fulfilling their times by Heauens asignement. **1744** *Life Boyle* in *Penny Cycl.* V. 297/2 Had he been permitted an election, his choice would scarce have altered God's assignment.

†7. Appointment or arrangement of day and place for a meeting; an assignation. *Obs.*

1670 COTTON *Espernon* II. v. 213 In expectation..of an assignment from you, of a day, and place.

8. Attribution as belonging or due *to.*

a **1704** LOCKE (J.) This institution, which assigns it to a person, whom we have no rule to know, is just as good as an assignment to no body at all. **1847** LEWES *Hist. Philos.* (1867) II. 398 By his assignment of definite functions to definite organs.

9. Allegement, statement (of a reason).

1651 JER. TAYLOR *Clerus Dom.* 5 An assignment..must be made of certain reasons. **1817** JAS. MILL *Brit. India* II. v. iv. 426 The assignment of these reasons.

10. A pointing out, specification.

1646 SIR T. BROWNE *Pseud. Ep.* 44 The Philosophical assignment of the cause. **1868** SKEAT *Mœso-Goth. Gloss.* Pref. 4 The assignment of the passage in which they occur.

†11. An assigned measure, a definite amount. *Obs.*

1519 HORMAN *Vulg.* 29 All bestz be withyn a certaine assignement of theyr quantite. **1533** ELYOT *Cast. Helth* (1541) 8 Increase..in quantitie or qualitie over..their natural assignement.

12. [Cf. ASSIGN *v.* 16.] The act of signing, signature.

1598 *Wills & Inv. N.C.* II. (1860) 332 Upon the assignment of a generall acquittance.

13. A task assigned to one; a commission or appointment. orig. *U.S.*

c **1848** GARLAND in W. C. Church *Ulysses Grant* (1897) iii. 45 Lt. Grant can best serve his country..under this assignment. **1897** *Scribner's Mag.* Aug. 232/2 The reporters ..were waiting to be sent off on their first assignments before getting breakfast. **1898** *Daily News* 4 Jan. 3/1 Here a man goes out on an assignment and if the person sought does not wish to express his views, he comes back empty-handed. **1910** C. E. MULFORD *Hopalong Cassidy* xvii. 99 At first his assignment had pleased, but as hour after hour passed with growing weariness, he chafed more and more. **1949** F. MACLEAN *Eastern Approaches* III. vi. 373 His next assignment [as an officer helping partisans] was in enemy-occupied Albania. **1964** G. L. COHEN *What's Wrong with Hospitals?* i. 17 The nursing profession has therefore perfected its own technique of fragmentation: 'task assignment'. This enables one patient's needs to be split up among many nurses. **1967** *Oxford Mag.* 10 Feb. 205/2, I set them [*sc.* Canadian students] an exercise and they bring me an assignment.

assignor (æsɪˈnɔː(r)). *Law.* [f. ASSIGN + -OR, refashioned form of AF. *-our*; = F. *assigneur.*] One who assigns or makes over a right or property. (Correlative with *assignee.*)

1668 CHILD *Disc. Trade* (1698) 137 After such Assignment it shall not be in the power of any Assignor to.. discharge the Debt. **1875** POSTE *Gaius* III. 431 Any creditor intermediate between the original assignor and the final assignee.

ˈassilag. Dial. name of the Stormy Petrel.

1698 M. MARTIN *Voy. St. Kilda* 63 (JAM.) The assilag is as large as a linnet. **1768** PENNANT *Zool.* II. 518 The Assilag ..breeds on the coast of Kerry, and in St. Kilda.

assimilability (əˌsɪmɪləˈbɪlɪtɪ). [f. next: see -BILITY.] Capability of being assimilated.

c **1819** COLERIDGE in *Rem.* (1836) II. 274 Whether a word was invented under the conditions of assimilability to our language or not. **1881** *Nature* XXIV. 283 To determine their relative assimilability.

assimilable (əˈsɪmɪləb(ə)l), *a.* and *sb.* [ad. late L. *assimilābilis*, f. *assimilāre*: see ASSIMILATE.]

A. *adj.* 1. That may be appropriated as nourishment.

1667 BOYLE *Orig. Formes & Qual.*, Such assimilable juices. **1859** LEWES *Sea-side Stud.* 208 Very simple organisms find assimilable food in the element they live in.

2. That may be likened or compared *to.*

1847 TODD *Cycl. Anat. & Phys.* IV. 107/2 This intrinsic change seems assimilable to that effecting softening of fibrinous clots in the veins. **1862** H. SPENCER *First Princ.* I. v. §30 (1875) 106 Agencies less assimilable to the familiar agencies of men and animals.

B. as *sb.* That which is assimilable.

1646 SIR T. BROWNE *Pseud. Ep.* 386 Meeting no assimilables wherein to react their natures.

‖**assimilado** (əsɪmɪˈlɑːdəʊ). [Pg., pa. pple. of *assimilar* to assimilate.] Used as *sb.* to designate an African in Portuguese East and West Africa who has been admitted to Portuguese citizenship. Also *attrib.*

1953 *N.Y. Times* 15 Jan. 3/1 In Portuguese East Africa, he said, a native wishing to become a member of the European group had to be officially recognized as an 'assimilado'. **1953** *Wall St. Jrnl.* 24 July 4/5 It's even possible for a Mozambique native to become a full Portuguese citizen. About 4,000 Africans have reached this 'assimilado' status. **1958** *Spectator* 30 May 679/3 The Portuguese *assimilado* system. **1961** *Economist* 6 May 550/1 Out of a black population of 4½ million, Angola has 30,000 *assimilados* who enjoy the basic rights denied to their fellows.

†**a'ssimilant**, *ppl. a.* and *sb. Obs.* [ad. L. *assimilānt-em*, pr. pple. of *assimilāre*: see ASSIMILATE and -ANT.] **A.** *adj.* Assimilating. *rare* —0.

B. *sb.* An assimilating agent.
1684 tr. *Bonet's Merc. Compit.* VI. 195 The more these Humours are heated..the more willingly they turn to the Assimilants side.

a'ssimilate, *pple.* and *sb.* Also 7 -ulat. [ad. L. *assimilātus*: see next.] †**A.** *pple.* Likened, compared. *Obs.* **B.** *sb.* †**1.** That which is like. *Obs.* **2.** Something which has been assimilated (see ASSIMILATE *v.* 7).
1671 *True Non-Conf.* 463 How then can our necessary undertaking..be assimulat to that precedent. **1691** E. TAYLOR *Behmen's Theosoph. Philos.* ii. 357 When the will findeth its assimilate.
1935 *Ann. Reg. 1934* 56 Work on the transport of assimilates and other dissolved substances. **1936** *Nature* 14 Nov. 851/2 The movement of assimilate in seedling tomato plants.

assimilate (əˈsɪmɪleɪt), *v.*; also 7-8 -ulate. [f. L. *assimilāt-* ppl. stem of *assimilā-re* to liken, f. *ad-* to + *simil-is* like: cf. F. *assimiler*, 16th c.]
I. To make or be like.
1. a. *trans.* To make like *to*, cause to resemble.
1628 BP. HALL *Old Relig.* 195 Religion..doth more assimilate and vnite vs to that vnchangeable Deity. **1721** R. KEITH *T. à Kempis' Vall. Lillies* i. 5 Thou art assimilated to the holy Angels. **1865** DICKENS *Mut. Fr.* x. 346 Observe the dyer's hand, assimilating itself to what it works in. **1866** (13 Mar.) BRIGHT *Reform, Sp.* (1876) 344 To assimilate our law in this respect to the law of Scotland.
b. with *with.* (In this const. some influence of II is apparent; as not only *resemblance*, but also *alliance* or *incorporation* is implied.)
1849 RUSKIN *Sev. Lamps* vi.§16. 178 Stains, or vegetation, which assimilate the architecture with the work of Nature. **1865** MILL *Repr. Gov.* 52 Whose education and way of life assimilate them with the rich.
c. without prepositional const.: To make alike.
1785 COWPER *Task* IV. 328 The downy flakes..Softly alighting upon all below, Assimilate all objects.
d. *Philol.* To render (a sound) accordant, or less discordant (*to* another sound in the same or a contiguous word). Also *intr.*
1854 *Proc. Philol. Soc.* V. 200 In our own language..it is to be expected that some traces of the law of assimilated vowels should appear. **1871** H. J. ROBY *Gram. Latin Lang.* I. I. viii. 48 Before *s*, *d* is assimilated or falls away. **1946** E. A. NIDA *Morphology* ii. 43 Nasal consonants assimilate regressively according to the point of articulation of the following consonant.
2. a. *intr.* To be or become like *to*, resemble.
1837 LYTTON *Athens* II. 189 Whose courage assimilated to their own. **1849** MISS MULOCH *Ogilvies* xxxii. (1875) 244 That outward empressement which sometimes assimilates to affectation.
b. with *with.* (See note to 1 b.)
1768 BLACKSTONE *Comm.* V. 408 Which revenues..do always assimilate, or take the same nature, with the antient revenues. **1851** D. MITCHELL *Fresh Glean.* 245 It yet more assimilates with the character of New England scenery.
3. *trans.* To bring into conformity *to*, adapt. *arch.*
1664 H. MORE *Apol.* 501 That the Body of Christ assimilated itself to the Regions it passed in his Ascension. **1748** RICHARDSON *Clarissa* (1811) IV. 245 This lady..half-assimilates me to her own virtue. **1791** MACKINTOSH *Vind. Gall.* Wks. 1846 III. 35 Absolute monarchies..assimilate every thing with which they are connected to their own genius.
4. *intr.* (for *refl.*) To conform *to*, act in accordance *with. arch.*
1792 *Anecd. Pitt* III. xliv. 177 The honest American, that will not assimilate to the futility and levity of Frenchmen. **1795** COLERIDGE *Friend* III. xvi. (1867) 214 With whose prejudices and ferocity their unbending virtue forbade them to assimilate.
5. *trans.* To liken, compare, put into the same class. Const. *to*, *with.*
1616 R. C. *Times' Whis., etc.* (1871) 118 To these 4 brutes ..Foure kindes of men we may assimilate. **1774** GOLDSM. *Nat. Hist.* (1862) I. v. 22 Which we can assimilate with no shells that are known. **1794** J. HUTTON *Philos. Light, etc.* 114 To assimilate things upon fallacious grounds. **1855** H. SPENCER *Psychol.* (1872) I. II. vii. 255 A mouse's squeak assimilates itself in thought with sounds of high pitch. **1869** LECKY *Europ. Morals* II. iv. 273 Marcus Aurelius mournfully assimilated the career of a conqueror to that of a simple robber.
†**6.** *trans.* To resemble, be like, take after. *Obs.*
1578 BANISTER *Hist. Man* I. 17 The Image of it [the Larynx] assimulateth a Shield. **1652** GAULE *Magastrom.* 139 The reason that children..assimulate their nurses more than their mothers. **1661** K. W. *Conf. Charac.* (1860) 30 He much assimulates the Saracen's head without Newgate.
II. To absorb and incorporate.
7. a. To convert into a substance of its own nature, as the bodily organs convert food into blood, and thence into animal tissue; to take in and appropriate as nourishment; to absorb into the system, incorporate. Cf. ASSIMILATION 4.
1578 BANISTER *Hist. Man* v. 64 Those thynges were.. assimulated, and made like to nourish, and restore the body. **1677** HALE *Prim. Orig. Man.* I. iii. 85 The Fire assimulates the Stubble, and converts it into Fire. **1732** ARBUTHNOT *Rules Diet* 309 Aliment that is easily assimilated or turned into Blood. **1869** MRS. SOMERVILLE *Molec. Sc.* I. i. 14 Vegetables decompose it [carbonic acid], assimilate the carbon and set the oxygen free.
b. *fig.*
a **1631** DONNE *Select.* (1840) 28 The understanding believer, he [the adversary] must chaw, and pick bones, before he come to assimilate him, and make him like himself. **1751** JOHNSON *Rambl.* No. 95 ⁋20 Falsehood by long use is assimilated to the mind, as poison to the body. **1850** MERIVALE *Rom. Emp.* (1865) I. II. 73 His mind had no power to assimilate the lessons of history.
8. a. *intr.* To become of the same substance; to become absorbed or incorporated into the system.
1626 BACON *Sylva* §680 Birds be commonly better meat than beasts, because their flesh doth assimilate more finely. **1658** A. FOX tr. *Wurtz' Surg.* I. iii. 12 Stitch none of the loose pieces of flesh, they will assimilate no more. **1866** DICKENS *Uncomm. Trav.* xvi. 115/1 The nightly pint of beer, instead of assimilating naturally.
b. *fig.*
1761 CHURCHILL *Rosciad* Wks. 1763 I. 23 He stands aloof from all..And scorns, like Scotsmen, to assimilate. **1864** J. H. NEWMAN *Apol.* 350, I am a foreign material, and cannot assimilate with the Church of England.
¶ Occas. for ASSIMULATE, q.v.

a'ssimilated, *ppl. a.* [f. prec. + -ED.] Rendered similar, made like *to*; taken in and appropriated as nourishment.
1797 BEWICK *Birds* (1847) I. Introd. 20 Screened..by an arrangement of colours happily assimilated to the places which they most frequent. **1848** CARPENTER *Anim. Phys.* 24 This assimilated fluid has to be conveyed into every part of the body.

a'ssimilateness. ? *Obs.* [f. ASSIMILATE *ppl. a.* + -NESS.] 'Likeness.' Bailey 1731.

assimilating (əˈsɪmɪleɪtɪŋ), *vbl. sb.* [f. ASSIMILATE *v.* + -ING[1].] The action of the vb. ASSIMILATE; assimilation.
1779 SHERIDAN *Critic* I. i. (1883) 152 The poverty of your own language prevents their assimilating. **1881** *Daily News* 18 Aug. 6/5 Assimilating of the Law of Exchange.

a'ssimilating, *ppl. a.* [f. as prec. + -ING[2].] That assimilates.
1651 *Rawleigh's Apparition* 84 There is *vis assimulatrix*, an assimulating power. **1829** S. TURNER *Hist. Eng.* IV. II. xxxvii. 563 The Spanish writers and their assimilating partisans.

assimilation (əˌsɪmɪˈleɪʃən). Also 7-8 -ulation. [prob. a. F. *assimilation*, ad. L. *assimilātiōn-em*, n. of action f. *assimilāre* to ASSIMILATE; but it may have been taken directly from the L.]
1. a. The action of making or becoming like; the state of being like; similarity, resemblance, likeness.
1605 TIMME *Quersit.* I. xv. 74 The elimentary or nourishing humour of life..is called the assimilation or resemblance of the nourishment and nourished. **1660** STANLEY *Hist. Philos.* (1701) 180/1 Wisdom..is nothing else but an Assimulation to the Deity. **1830** SIR J. HERSCHEL *Stud. Nat. Phil.* 302 The assimilation of gases and vapours. **1869** LUBBOCK *Preh. Times* viii. 277 Ten times fifty years must elapse before their complete assimilation can be effected.
b. *Philol.* The action of assimilating or fact of being assimilated: see ASSIMILATE *v.*
1850 *Proc. Philol. Soc.* IV. 89 The law for the assimilation of vowels..will account for the introduction of an *o* in *biodhmur*,..before the *u* of the final syllable. **1871** B. H. KENNEDY *Public Sch. Lat. Gram.* 18 Complete Assimilation occurs, when, of two meeting Consonants, the former becomes the same as the latter. **1885** COOK tr. *Siever's O.E. Gram.* §86. 38 A partial assimilation of the basic vowel to the following sound. **1936** *Language* XII. 246 An assimilation is produced by the replacement of some phoneme or phonemes by other phoneme or phonemes shortly to be uttered.
2. The becoming conformed *to*; conformity *with. arch.*
1677 HALE *Prim. Orig. Man.* II. vii. 197 If they escape a total Assimulation to the Country where they thus are mingled. **1794** SULLIVAN *View Nat.* II. 75 In assimilation with all, M. Macquer thinks that, etc.
3. The action of likening, comparison.
4. a. Conversion into a similar substance; *esp.* the process whereby an animal or plant converts extraneous material into fluids and tissues identical with its own; absorption of nutriment into the system. (By some physiologists restricted to the final stage of this conversion, which takes place after the absorption of digested fluids by the lymphatics and blood-vessels.)
1626 BACON *Sylva* §877 Frictions..make better Passages for the Spirits, Bloud, and Aliments..All which help Assimulation. **1727-51** CHAMBERS *Cycl.* s.v., Assimilation we see in flame, which converts..fuel into its own firy and luminous nature. **1836** TODD *Cycl. Anat. & Phys.* 144/1 Assimilation..is the ultimate term of nutrition. **1880** GRAY *Bot. Text Bk.* iii. §4. 85 Vegetable assimilation..being the conversion of inorganic into organic matter, takes place in all ordinary vegetation only in green parts.
b. *fig.*
1790 BURKE *Fr. Rev.* 114 Which, by a bland assimilation, incorporated into politics the sentiments which beautify and soften private society. **1871** FREEMAN *Hist. Ess.* Ser. I. i. 36 The first Teutonic settlement involved, whether by extirpation or assimilation, the..driving out of the earlier British.
†**5.** *Path.* The supposed conversion of the fluids of the body to the nature of any morbific matter. *Obs.*
1864 WEBSTER cites PARR. **1881** *Syd. Soc. Lex.*, *Assimilation destructive*, a term formerly used to express what is known now as *Metabolism*.
6. *Psychol.* The process whereby the individual acquires new ideas, by interpreting presented ideas and experiences in relation to the existing contents of his mind. Used with some manner of qualification or specification by various writers.
1855 H. SPENCER *Psychol.* I. II. viii. 267 Knowing a feeling is the assimilation of it to past kindred exactly like it. **1873** G. H. LEWES *Problems of Life & Mind* 190 Since interpretation means mental assimilation, the significance of the phenomena must depend upon the pre-perceptions and pre-conceptions which they arouse. **1896** G. F. STOUT *Analyt. Psychol.* II. 118 Assimilation there must always be, inasmuch as the existence of a given experience coincides with the re-excitement of some preformed disposition. **1897** C. H. JUDD tr. *Wundt's Outlines Psychol.* 227 Assimilations, or associations between the elements of like compounds. *Ibid.* 228 Assimilations are a form of association that is continually met with, especially in the case of intensive and spacial ideas. **1923** W. MCDOUGALL *Outl. Psychol.* 397 By some psychologists who followed Locke's way of 'ideas', yet saw that 'ideas' cannot be generated by association alone.. assimilation was made the fundamental mode of growth.
7. *Geol.* The absorption of extraneous matter by an igneous magma.
1903 R. A. DALY in *Amer. Jrnl. Sci.* XV. 270 The 'marginal assimilation' theory of plutonic intrusion..a hypothesis of slow caustic action by magmas that have advanced into the overlying earth-crust by their own energetic solvent action. **1909** A. HARKER *Nat. Hist. Igneous Rocks* iii. 83 On the *assimilation hypothesis*, still supported by some French geologists, an igneous rock-magma is supposed to be capable of melting and incorporating freely the solid rocks which it encounters.

assimilationist (əˌsɪmɪˈleɪʃənɪst). [f. ASSIMILATION + -IST.] One who advocates the integration of different races, cultural groups, etc.
1928 L. WIRTH *Ghetto* p. ix, The ghetto becomes the physical symbol for that sort of moral isolation which the 'assimilationists'..are seeking to break down. **1930** *Times Lit. Suppl.* 23 Jan. 51/3 General Smuts is not an assimilationist. The whites must not impose their civilization on the natives. **1942** L. B. NAMIER *Conflicts* 132 The 'emancipation' movement of the 'assimilationists' arose in the individualist era; it knew only Jews, but no Jewish nation.
b. *attrib.* or *quasi-adj.*
1934 W. STEED *Hitler* iv. 126 The younger Jews..revolted inwardly against assimilation, and denounced assimilationist doctrine.

assimilative (əˈsɪmɪleɪtɪv), *a.*; also 6-7 -ulative. [a. F. *assimilatif, -ive*, ad. late L. *assimilātīv-us*: see ASSIMILATE *v.* and -IVE.]
1. a. Of, characterized by, or tending to assimilation.
1528 PAYNELL *Salerne Regim.* 2 C j b, Ruddy fleshe wytnesseth fortitude of vertue assimilative. **1669** W. SIMPSON *Hydrol. Chem.* 66 The fifth or last digestion, viz. the assimilative ferment of the solid parts of the body. **1846** H. ROGERS *Ess.* (1860) I. 170 He made the contents of books his own by..the powerful assimilative processes of his own intellect.
b. *spec.* in *Philol.* (cf. ASSIMILATION 1 b).
1936 *Language* XII. 246 In consonantal clusters it is common to find that the posterior consonant exerts an assimilative influence upon the preceding. **1946** E. A. NIDA *Morphology* ii. 29 If assimilative changes are quite extensive in some pattern of the language, the related sets are frequently described as 'vocalic harmony'.
2. That may be or has been assimilated.
1837 SOUTHW. SMITH *Philos. Health* II. x. 160 To this crude sap..sugar and mucus, assimilative substances, are super-added. **1847** in CRAIG.

a'ssimilator. [n. of agent, on L. analogies, f. ASSIMILATE. Cf. F. *assimilateur.*] He who or that which assimilates.
1734 SALE tr. *Koran* Prel. Disc. §8. 169 The Moshabbehites, or Assimilators; who allowed a resemblance between God and his creatures. **1880** C. CLOUGH in *Geol. Mag.* 433 (*title*) The Whin Sill of Teesdale as an Assimilator of the Surrounding Beds.

assimilatory (əˈsɪmɪlətərɪ), *a.* [f. L. *assimilāt-* (see ASSIMILATE *v.*) + -ORY, as if ad. L. **assimilā-tōri-us*.] = ASSIMILATIVE 1.
1856 in WEBSTER. **1881** VINES in *Nature* XXIII. 562 The ..products of its assimilatory activity. **1921** E. SAPIR *Language* viii. 186 This assimilatory change was regular, i.e., every accented long *o* followed by an *i* in the following syllable automatically developed to long *ö*.

†**a'ssimile**, *v. Obs.* Also 6 -ule. [a. F. *assimiler* (16th c. in Littré), ad. L. *assimilāre* to liken, f. *ad-* to + *similis* like.] To make like, to liken; to resemble. Earlier by-form of ASSIMILATE.
1547 BOORDE *Brev. Health* 32 By it he is assimiled to the immortall God. **1548** RECORDE *Urin. Physick* xi. (1651) 100 Horn white..hath his name of the thing that it assimuleth most. **1583** STUBBES *Anat. Abus.* II. 49 To be compared and assimiled to the husbandman.

†**a'ssimilize**, *v. Obs. rare*⁻¹. [f. F. *assimiler*, or L. *assimilāre* (see prec) + -IZE.] = ASSIMILATE.
1654 GAYTON *Fest. Notes* III. iii. 79 Assimilize..to the Flanders breed.

†**a'ssimulate**, *v. Obs.* [f. *assimulāt-* ppl. stem of *assimulāre*, according to Lewis and Short only a copyists' variant of *assimilāre* in sense of *simulāre* 'to feign, counterfeit': see ASSIMILATE *v.*] To simulate, feign, or counterfeit.
1630 J. TAYLOR (Water P.) *Wks.* III. 120/1 Which Rackets did assimulate the shapes..of Men, women, fowles, beasts. **1652** GAULE *Magastrom.* 321 All noted for assimulating of religion.

†**assimu'lation.** *Obs. rare*⁻¹. [ad. L. *assimulātiōn-em*, n. of action f. *assimulāre*: see prec. and -ATION.] Simulation, counterfeiting, pretence.
c **1450** LONELICH *Grail* xlvii. 66 Cristened to ben be fals assumylaciown. **1721** in BAILEY.

†**'assinat.** *Obs. rare*⁻¹. [? a. F. *assignat.*] ? Security, guarantee.
1652 C. STAPYLTON *Herodian* VIII. 63 Th' Assinats (he knew) they sought to have.

assine, obsolete form of ASSIGN.

assinego: see ASINEGO.

†**assinuate**, *v. Obs.* Corrupt form of INSINUATE.
1742 FIELDING *J. Andrews* I. vi. (1815) 17 Do you intend to assinuate that I might be as old as your mother?

‖**assise** (a'siːz). *Geol.* [mod.Fr. = layer (of rock); the same word as ASSIZE *sb.*, q.v.] A geological formation consisting of parallel beds of rock agreeing in their organic remains.
1882 GEIKIE *Text-bk. Geol.* VI. 635 Two or more such zones, united by the occurrence in them of the same characteristic species or genera, may be called beds or an assise.

assish ('æsɪʃ), *a. rare.* [f. ASS *sb.*¹ + -ISH.] Asinine, stupid.
1587 GOLDING *De Mornay* xxi. (1617) 371 The said Assish report of the Asses head is scarce worth the disproofe.

'assishly, *adv. rare.* [f. prec. + -LY².] In asinine manner; on an ass.
1612 SHELTON *Quix.* I. vii. I. 47 That ever any Knight Errant carried his Squire assishly mounted.

'assishness. [f. as prec. + -NESS.] Asinine quality, stupidity.
1611 FLORIO, *Asinita*, Assishnesse, blockishnesse. **1623** MABBE *Aleman's Guzman D'Alf.* 113 See in what ample manner their Assishnesse extendeth itselfe.

Assisian (ə'siːsɪən, -'zɪən), *a.* and *sb.* Also **Assisan.** [See -AN.] **A.** *adj.* Of or pertaining to the town of Assisi in central Italy; *spec.* of St. Francis of Assisi. **B.** *sb.* An inhabitant of Assisi. ***The Assisian***, St. Francis.
1870 MRS. OLIPHANT *Francis of Assisi* i. 18 This absolute penury must have struck the sick fancy of the young Assisan [*sc.* St. Francis]. *Ibid.* iv. 66 The Assisan bishop, who knew something of the temper of the lords of Umbria. *Ibid.* xvii. 281 As anxious as the Assisans that the head-quarters of the Order at the Portiuncula should be the future shrine of the saint. **1893** F. THOMPSON *Poems* 72 The Assisian, who kept plighted faith to three, to Song, to Sanctitude, and Poverty. **1905** *Athenæum* 30 Sept. 431/1 She—like the Assisian.. exhibited on her own body the Stigmata. *a* **1907** F. THOMPSON *St. Ignatius Loyola* (1909) iii. 76 Another story recalls the Assisian Saint. **1923** G. K. CHESTERTON *St. Francis* iii. 52 The Papal cause..aroused enthusiasm among a number of young Assisians. *Ibid.* 53 The legal authority of the Assisian magistrates.

assist (ə'sɪst), *v.* Also 6 **assyst.** [a. F. *assiste-r* (15th c. in Littré), ad. L. *assist-ĕre*, f. *ad-*, *as-* to + *sistĕre* to take one's stand.]
I. To stand to or by; to be present.
†**1.** *intr.* To take one's stand *to* or towards a place; *fig.* to stand *to*, abide by (an opinion). *Obs.*
c **1565** R. LINDSAY *Chron. Scot.* (1728) 2 A great Part of the Nobility assisted to his Opinion. **1646** J. G[REGORY] *Notes & Obs.* (1650) 74 Assisting especially..to the East.
†**2.** *trans.* To stand or remain near, to stand by; to attend, escort. *Obs.*
1525 LD. BERNERS *Froiss.* II. clvii. [cliii.] 429 The quenes lytter..was assysted with the duke of Thourayne, and the duke of Burbone. *a* **1650** CRASHAW *Sospetto d'Her.* ix, Three vigorous virgins, waiting still behind, Assist the throne of th' iron-sceptred king.
†**3. a.** *trans.* To take one's place with (a person), join, accompany, attend. Also *absol. Obs.*
1553 T. WILSON *Rhet.* 11 b, It was no mastery for David, beyng assisted with God..to overthrowe this one man. **1607** SHAKS. *Cor.* V. vi. 156 Yet he shall haue a noble Memory. Assist. **1610** —— *Temp.* I. i. 57 The King, and Prince, at prayers, let's assist them.
†**b.** To attend upon (a sick person or the period of his illness) with religious ministrations. (Cf. F. *assister un malade*: lui donner des soins; l'exhorter à bien mourir. Littré.) *Obs. rare.*
1664 EVELYN *Freart's Archit.* Ep. Ded. 18 His Sickness.. was assisted by his Director the R. P. de Sainct Jure.
4. a. *intr.* To be present (*at* a ceremony, entertainment, etc.), whether simply as a spectator, or taking part in the proceedings. (In the former case, 'to be present *at* without taking part in,' now treated as a French idiom.)
1626 C. POTTER *Father Paul's Hist.* I. 32 The Counsellors assembled to assist at a solemn Masse. **1705** ADDISON *Italy* (1767) 29 The Duke of Lorrain used often to assist at their midnight devotions. **1765** WILKES *Corr.* (1805) II. 163 Last Saturday I assisted at the great festival. **1837** J. H. NEWMAN *Proph. Office Ch.* 96, I quote the words of Cornelius Mussus ..who assisted at the Council of Trent. **1849** MACAULAY *Hist. Eng.* I. 53 The congregation may be said to assist as spectators rather than as auditors. **1854** THACKERAY *Newcomes* II. 103 The dinner at which we have just assisted. **18..** DICKENS *Seven Poor Trav.* 12 And assisted—in the French sense—at the performance of two waltzes. **1873** *Q. Rev.* CXXXV. 183 The sane and sober must simply 'assist,' in the French sense, i.e. stand by and say nothing.
†**b.** Const. *to* (after Fr. *assister à*). *Obs.*
1603 FLORIO *Montaigne* (1634) 392 Having all day long assisted to the ceremonies, and publike banket. **1677** *Govt. Venice* 229 Three Senators always assisting in the Prince's name to all Transactions and Decrees of that Court.
†**5.** *trans.* To be present at, take part in. *Obs.*
1603 FLORIO *Montaigne* II. xii. (1632) 292 Wont to sacrifice their owne children..and with cheerefull and pleasant countenance to assist that office.
II. To aid, help.
6. *trans.* To help, aid: **a.** a person in doing something; frequently with adv. or advb. phr. denoting that in which the assistance is given. **b.** a person in necessity; **c.** an action, process, or result. To second, support; to succour, relieve; to further, promote.
1547 J. HEYWOOD *Wit. & Folly* (1846) 25 To assyst man gods comandments to fulfyll. **1683** *Brit. Spec.* 77 Displeased with them for having assisted the rebellious Gauls. **1711** STEELE *Spect.* No. 27 ¶6 When I assist a friendless Person. **1711** POPE *Rape Lock* V. 56 The sprites survey The growing combat, or assist the fray. **1777** SIR W. JONES *Seven Fount.* 52 He read, assisted by a taper's ray. **1837** E. HOWARD *Old Commodore* I. v. 186 Assist the chaplain down the poop-ladder. **1843** LEVER *Jack Hinton* xxv, He assisted me on with my great-coat. *Ibid.* xxvii, As I assisted her from the carriage, I could not but mark the flashing brilliancy of her eye. **1855** —— *Sir Jasper Carew* xxix, He assisted me off with my coat. **1860** TYNDALL *Glac.* I. §24. 170 A desire to..assist me in my observations. **1864** MRS. GASKELL *Wives & Dau.* (1866) I. v. 47 'May I help you to potatoes?' or, as Mr. Wynne would persevere in saying, 'May I assist you to potatoes?' **1881** MRS. J. H. RIDDELL *Senior Partner* II. xi. 228 'It's no use my trying to put in a friendly oar', said Mr. McCullagh, assisted perhaps to this last figure of speech by the sight of an outrigger spinning down the stream. **1885** *Mod.* Rest assists digestion. The rumours will not assist his election. 'Could you assist a poor man with a copper, Sir?' **1924** ROSE MACAULAY *Orphan Island* xi, Miss Smith..was assisted from her hammock.
7. a. *absol.* and *intr.*
1514 BARCLAY *Cyt. & Uplondyshm.* 10 Whan God assysteth, man worketh not for nought! **1606** SHAKS. *Ant. & Cl.* IV. xv. 31 Helpe me, my women..Assist. good Friends. **1697** DRYDEN *Virg. Georg.* IV. 9 If Heav'n assist, and Phœbus hear my call.
b. with (*to* obs.) *in* or *inf.*
1649 J. KENT in Ellis *Orig. Lett.* II. 295 III. 340 The ordinary hangman..was commanded to assist to the King's death. **1704** NELSON *Fest. & Fast., St. James* Collect ii. (T.) That they might mutually assist to the support of each other. *a* **1745** BROOME *Notes to Odyss.* (J.) She agreed to assist in the murder of her husband. **1860** FROUDE *Hist. Eng.* V. xxiv. 33 Barlow..whose indiscretion had already assisted to ruin Cromwell.
c. Of the dealer's partner in the game of euchre: to order the adoption of the suit of the card turned up as trump.
1878 *Encycl. Brit.* VIII. 654/2 If the first hand passes, the second may say 'I assist', which means that the dealer (his partner) is to take up the trump. *Ibid.* 655/1 A player can declare to play alone when he or his partner orders up, or when his partner assists.

a'ssist, *sb.* Now chiefly *N.Amer.* [f. prec.]
1. a. An act of assistance; aid, help.
1597 G. MARKHAM *Devoreux* f. 15ʳ, st. 84, I hop'd, by her assist, this fourth Henrie. **1607** DAY *Trav.* 3 *Eng. Brothers* (1881) 6 Now your assists To helpe the entrance of our history.
1923 *Daily Mail* 5 May 8 The supporting bid, the assist, ..and 'the switch' assume a new value. **1957** W. H. WHYTE *Organ. Man* viii. 107 An assist from others can help a lot. **1958** B. ULANOV *Hist. Jazz* vii. 73 He usually played second cornet back of Oliver's lead, an alternately delicate assist and blasting support. **1966** *New Yorker* 4 June 18 (Advt.), Credit Hart Schaffner & Marx tailors with a skilful assist.
b. With qualifying word: a device, power, or force that provides assistance (to a system or an operation), esp. as ***power assist***. orig. *U.S.*
1967 *Automotive World* Apr. 22/2 The conventional hydraulic brakes are still effective, even when the power assist from the vacuum system fails. **1969** *New Yorker* 1 Nov. 10/2 (Advt.), Grand luxury car... Pampers you with a full range of power assists. **1972** *Sci. Amer.* Jan. 46/1 A favorable planetary alignment enabling a spacecraft to receive a gravity assist from Jupiter. **1979** *Ibid.* Feb. 26/3 The good landlord..serves mild and bitter at the needed rate with a beer engine or with a power assist. **1985** *Which Computer?* Apr. 46 The system offers a wide range of standard reporting functions and operator assists.
2. a. *Baseball.* 'The act of a player who handles the ball in assisting to put an opposing player out; also the credit given by the scorer to a player so assisting' (*Dict. Americanisms*).
1877 *Constit. Nat. League Baseball* 40 An assist should be given to each player who handles the ball in a run-out or other play of this kind. **1896** KNOWLES & MORTON *Baseball* 101 The fielder who handles the ball in sufficient time to aid in retiring a base-runner is credited with an assist. **1917** C. MATHEWSON *Sec. Base Sloan* xiv. 187 Five strike-outs, three assists and no errors was considered a fine record.
b. Also in *Ice Hockey*, the act of taking a direct part in the action (esp. by making the scoring pass) which results in a team-mate scoring a goal; the credit awarded for this. Similarly in other sports. *N. Amer.*
1925 *Mail & Empire* 9 Feb. 8/1 He attacked continuously and was rewarded by two goals and an assist. **1934** F. W. HEWITT *Down Ice* xi. 124 When a player scores a goal an 'assist' shall be credited to any player taking part in the play leading up to the scoring of the goal... An assist cannot be credited to any player when a goal is scored from a rebound off a goal-keeper. **1955** *Spectator* (Hamilton, Ont.) 25 Jan. 15/4 Montreal Canadiens..collect more assists per goal than any other club. **1967** *Boston Herald* 1 Mar. 16/1 K. C. Jones was the top play-maker with 12 assists. **1977** *Time* 12 Sept. 45/1 It was an unheralded Briton..who led the Cosmos to victory in Soccer Bowl-77 with a goal and an assist. **1984** *Toronto Star* 28 Mar. B4/1 Barry Pederson scored four goals..and added an assist.

assistance (ə'sɪstəns). Forms: 4–6 **assystence**, 6 **assistence**, 6–7 **-aunce**, 6– **-ance**. [a. F. *assistance*, f. *assister*: see ASSIST *v.* and -ANCE.]
†**1.** The being or remaining near; presence, attendance. *Obs.* except as assumedly French.
a **1520** *Myrr. Our Ladye* 78 Ryghtful men are strengthed ..by more nere assystence of aungels to them. **1528** MORE *Heresyes* I. Wks. 145/2 The perpetual..assistence of Christ with his church. **1644** MILTON *Judgm. Bucer* Wks. 1738 I. 272 His sumptuous burial..solemnized with so great an assistance of all the University. **1883** *Pall Mall G.* 5 Nov. 3 The 'assistance' of the Government at the ceremony.
2. *collect.* (rarely *pl.*) Persons present, bystanders, audience. *Obs.* exc. as recently re-adopted from Fr.
1491 CAXTON *Vitas Patr.* (W. de W.) I. xvi. 21 a/1 Whyche the holy angelles bare in to heuen in the presence of the assystences. **1596** LODGE *Marg. Amer.* 136 Weeping [so] piteously..that the whole assistance became compassionate. **1651** *Father Sarpi* (1676) 8 Difficult propositions..by him maintained before that venerable assistance. **1881** G. SCOTT junr. *Eng. Ch. Archit.* i. 8 The altar, in full view of all the assistance.
3. a. The action of helping or aiding in an undertaking or necessity; furtherance, succour; *also*, the help afforded, aid, support, relief. Formerly often in *pl.*
1398 TREVISA *Barth. De P.R.* I. (1495) 3 By the goode grace, helpe and assystence of almyghty god. **1494** FABYAN an. 1267 (R.) Roger, with the assystence of the mayre..toke the sayd rasccall. **1594** SHAKS. *Rich. III.* IV. ii. 4 Thus high, by thy aduice, and thy assistance, is King Richard seated. **1659** HAMMOND *On Ps.* cviii. 12 All other assistances, beside that of heaven, being utterly unsufficient. **1740** CIBBER *Apol.* (1756) II. 79 Notwithstanding these assistances the expence of every play amounted to fifty pounds. **1858** O. W. HOLMES *Aut. Breakf. T.* viii. 70 Many people can ride on horseback who find it hard to get on and to get off without assistance.
b. *ellipt.* for *National Assistance* (see NATIONAL *a.*).
1956 A. WILSON *Anglo-Saxon Att.* II. i. 244 Ten quid's not going to put us on Assistance. **1959** *New Statesman* 1 Aug. 125/2 The forthcoming increases will be a temptation to the 'casual' labourer who has a large family to shift from earnings to assistance.
†**4.** *collect.* (rarely *pl.*) A body of helpers: see ASSISTANT *sb.* 3. (Cf. *accountance, acquaintance.*)
1564 in Strype *Ann. Ref.* I. II. xli. 463 To every parish belongeth..an assistance, being thirteen persons, to consist of such only as had before been church-wardens and constables. **1611** in Gutch *Coll. Cur.* I. 106 The chief magistrate..was a Portgrave or Reve..and his assistances Burgesses. **1679** T. OATES *Myst. Iniq. Jesuits* 17 Give notice ..to the Assistance at Rome, or to the Father-General. **1692** E. SETTLE *Tri. Lond.* in Heath *Grocers' Comp.* (1869) 555 Then twelve Gentlemen Ushers, and after them the Court of Assistance.

assistancy (ə'sɪstənsɪ). Also 7–8 **assistency.** [f. ASSISTANT *sb.*: see -ANCY.] The position of an assistant.
1608 T. FITZHERBERT *Let.* 23 Aug. (1948) 29 You have confirmed Mʳ Singleton in his Assistency. **1757** A. BUTLER *Lives Saints* III. I. 328/1 The general..has five assistants nominated by the general congregation, who prepare all matters to his hands, each for the province of his Assistency. **1790** W. MACLAY *Jrnl.* 3 May (1890) vii. 255 There is a prospect of Tench Coxe succeeding Duer in the assistancy of the Treasury. **1884** *Lancet* 27 Dec. (Advt.), Wanted an Assistancy, or to manage a Branch. **1909** *Practitioner* Nov. 723 Thirty years ago the average medical man took an assistancy directly he was qualified. *Ibid.*, Qualified men.. are..not available for assistancy work.

assistant (ə'sɪstənt), *a.* and *sb.* Forms: 5–6 **assystent**, 5–7 **assistent**, 6– **-ant.** [a. F. *assistant*, pr. pple. of *assister* (formerly also, as sb., *assistent*), ad. L. *assistent-em*, pr. pple. of *assistĕre* to ASSIST. See -ANT, -ENT. The current spelling follows the Fr. and not L. analogy.]
A. *adj.*
†**1.** Standing or remaining by, present, accompanying. *Obs.*

1485 CAXTON *St. Wenefr.* 12 She rested not..to preche and enfourme them that were assistent with holy and blessid exhortacions. **1550** CRANMER *Sacrament* I. 45 Christ hath promised in both sacraments to be assistent with us. **1625** HART *Anat. Ur.* I ii. 21 These accidents are called assistant or accompanying. **1677** *Govt. Venice* 42 They see the Senat assistant at the killing of a Bull on Holy-Thursday.

2. Present to help; aiding, helpful, auxiliary (*to*).

a **1400** *Cov. Myst.* 240 But angelys were to hym assystent. *c* **1465** *Eng. Chron.* (1856) 31 Stirid the peple to be assistent ..to the..amendement of the myschiefs. **1570** HOLINSHED *Scot. Chron.* (1806) II. 316 Which by turns should be assistant to the queen. **1720** GIBSON *Farrier's Guide* I. v. (1738) 56 The third pair are..very assistant in the Office of Chewing. **1858** GEN. P. THOMPSON *Audi Alt.* I. xvii. 56 Animals assistant to man.

3. In *comb.* (either as adj., or as sb. in apposition.) ***assistant curate***, see CURATE 2; ***assistant master, mistress*** (in a school); ***assistant professor*** (chiefly U.S.); ***assistant stage-manager***.

1710 *Lond. Gaz.* No. 4735/3 The Office of Assistant-Master of the Ceremonies. **1844** *Reg. & Ord. Army* 289 The Assistant-Surgeon's Tent is to be pitched in its vicinity. **1851** C. CIST *Cincinnati* 304 In September..he received the appointment of assistant professor of mathematics. **1872** *Schoolmaster* 6 Jan. 4/1 Wanted..an Assistant Master, Ex P.T., for Canal-street Wesleyan Schools, Derby. *Ibid.*, Wanted, in a Mixed School, an ex P.T., as Assistant Mistress. **1898** L. MERRICK *Actor-Manager* iii. 38 He was to be described on the playbills as 'Assistant Stage-manager'. **1902** A. C. BENSON *Schoolmaster* 29 As to corporal punishment, the doubtful privilege of dispensing it is, at my own School, not conceded to the assistant-masters. **1905** [see ASSOCIATE *ppl. a.* 1]. **1952** M. MCCARTHY *Groves of Academe* (1953) iv. 74 All these, on the instructorial or assistant-professor level, constituted the bulk of Jocelyn's faculty.

B. *sb.*

†**1.** One who is present, a bystander; one who takes part in an assembly. Usually in *pl. Obs.*

1483 CAXTON *Cato* A iv b, Thus shalt thou be honoured of thassistentis in thy companye. **1590** GREENE *Arcadia* (1616) 70 The assistants greeued to see [it]. **1638** CHILLINGW. *Relig. Prot.* I. vi. §41. 363 Having your Service in such a language as the Assistants generally understand not. **1768** STERNE *Sent. Journ.* (1775) IV. 219 It is not at all astonishing that every convivial assistant should go home cherry-merry. **1781** GIBBON *Decl. & F.* II. 11 The growing circumference was observed with astonishment by the assistants.

2. One who gives help to a person, or aids in the execution of a purpose; a helper, an auxiliary; a promoter; *also*, a means of help, an aid.

1541 R. COPLAND *Guydon's Quest. Cyrurg.*, What condycions ought the assystentes..of the pacyent haue? *a* **1631** DONNE *Six Serm.* i. (1634) 11 Those great assistants of the Reformation, Luther and Calvin. **1774** MRS. CHAPONE *Improv. Mind* II. 167 Make use of numbers and rhymes merely as assistants to memory. **1851** H. SPENCER *Soc. Statics* v. §5 Unpractised assistants at surgical operations often faint.

3. *spec.* **a.** A deputy-judge. **b.** An official auxiliary to the Father-General of the Jesuits. †**c.** Obsolete name of the 'superintendent' among Wesleyan Methodists. **d.** ***Court of Assistants***: certain senior members who manage the affairs of the City of London Companies. **e.** A shop assistant (see SHOP *sb.*).

1611 COTGR., *Assessoriat*, th' office..of a Judge Laterall, Assistant, or Assesseur. **1622** FLETCHER *Sp. Curate* III. i, The Assistant sits to-morrow. **1679** T. OATES *Myst. Iniq. Jesuits* 7 And there is Choice made of some other Fathers, who..are called his Assistants..One is stiled the Assistant of France, a second of Spain. **1685** in *Antiquary* Oct. (1881) 149/2 Mr. Maior and 4 or 5 of ye Aldermen, with as many of ye assistants as please. *a* **1791** WESLEY *Wks.* (1872) VIII. 319 The Assistant [is] that Preacher in each Circuit who is appointed..to take charge of the societies and the other Preachers therein. **1829** HEATH *Grocer's Comp.* 27 The Courts of Assistants..were compelled to hold their meetings..at various places. **1853** MRS. GASKELL *Ruth* I. iv. 110 Her eldest son..was an assistant in a draper's shop. **1908** *Rep. Truck Committee* (Cmd. 4442-4) 132/2 The smartest assistant is the one who can sell to customers worthless goods.

†**a'ssistantly**, *adv. Obs. rare*[−1]. [f. ASSISTANT *a.* and *sb.* + -LY[2].] In manner of an assistant.

a **1641** BP. MOUNTAGU *Acts & Mon.* 44 He hath assistantly been present with the work of his hands.

a'ssistantship. Also 7 -nceship. [f. as prec. + -SHIP.] The office or position of assistant.

1696 in *Col. Rec. Penn.* I. 498 Desired of the Governor to be acquitted of his Assistanceshipp. **1879** *Schoolmaster* 2 Aug. (*Advt.*) Wanted Assistantship, by non-Certificated Teacher.

assisted (əˈsɪstɪd), *ppl. a.* [f. ASSIST *v.* + -ED.] Aided, helped. *spec.* Applied to subsidized passages for emigrants.

1853 *14th Gen. Rep. Colonial Land & Emigration Commissioners* (1854) 139 Remittances may be made for either of the following objects:—*Assisted passages.*—To assist the nominees in paying the expense of their passage and out-fit. *Free passages.* **1856** *16th Gen. Rep. Emigration Commissioners* 9 Emigration from the United Kingdom, which we shall divide into 'unassisted', or that of which the expense is defrayed out of private or local funds, and 'assisted', or that which is carried on by this Board with funds derived from the Colonies (at present the Australian only) to which the emigrants are sent. **1888** C. M. YONGE *Our New Mistress* xvi. 148 A number of papers about Australia, assuring me of all the advantages of emigration, promising me..an assisted passage. **1937** *Jrnl. R. Aeronaut. Soc.* XLI. 275 An aircraft with the assisted take-off, and therefore not requiring the maximum power output of the engine. **1945** *Guide Educ. System* (Min. Educ. Pamph. No. 2) 57 *Assisted School*, school not maintained by, but receiving some financial assistance from, an L.E.A. **1954** P. K. KEMP *Fleet Air Arm* xx. 216 Brown..successfully took off in about half the length of the flight deck. For this he had an assisted take-off with rockets. **1946** *Encycl. Brit.* XV. 470/1 Assisted passage schemes have been arranged which considerably reduce the cost of travel to the settler.

†**a'ssistency.** *Obs.* Also 7 ads-. [f. L. *assistent-em*, pr. pple. of *assistĕre* to ASSIST, as if ad. L. **assistentia.*] Helpfulness; assistance.

1642 SIR E. DERING *Sp. on Relig.* xvi. 83 Let him ordaine and censure, but with due assistency. **1676** PERRINCHIEF *Chas. I.* (1693) 230 And as in an Ecstasie to have left His senses without its Adsistency.

assister (əˈsɪstə(r)). Also 6 **assistar**; and see ASSISTOR. [f. ASSIST *v.* + -ER[1].]

1. He who is present at or takes part in an assembly, ceremony, etc. *arch.* (Cf. ASSIST *v.* 4, 4 b.)

1705 STANHOPE *Paraphr.* I. 34 The Assisters at this Ceremony. **1728** MORGAN *Algiers* I. iii. 68 The numerous assembly of Bishops who are upon record, as assisters at the African Councils. **1853** DE QUINCEY *Wks.* XIV. vii. 206 The lay spectator or assister.

2. He who or that which gives help, or assists in doing something; = ASSISTANT *sb.* 2.

1535 STEWART *Cron. Scot.* II. 248 That he sould be assistar to that cryme. **1634** MASSINGER *Very Wom.* II. iii, You may be a great assister in my ends. **1681** *Phil. Collect.* XII. 23 The natural heat that is..the constant assister of this motion. **1721** SWIFT *S. Sea Proj.* xxix, We gentlemen are your assisters. **1841** LANE *Arab. Nts.* III. 239 A lover unto whom there is no assister or helper save the morning.

a'ssistful, *a.* ? *Obs.* [f. ASSIST *v.* + -FUL, prob. after *helpful* (which is f. *help* sb. + -FUL).] Helpful.

1600 CHAPMAN *Iliad* v. 120 If ever in the cruel field thou hast assistful stood. **1720** GIBSON *Dispens.* I. §2 (1734) 34 [Milk] sometimes proves very assistful in ripening Tumors.

assisting (əˈsɪstɪŋ), *ppl. a.* [f. as prec. + -ING[2].]

†**1.** Situated near, bordering. *Obs. rare.*

1579 FENTON *Guicciard.* VI. (1599) 230 Fontarabia with the other places assisting vpon the Occean sea.

†**2.** Present, attendant. *Obs.*

1670 COTTON *Espernon* III. XII. 647 After midnight, the Duchess..got up to be assisting at this Holy Ceremony.

3. Giving aid, helpful, auxiliary (*to*). *arch.*

1653 MILTON *Hirelings* Wks. (1851) 366 God's assisting Spirit. **1702** *Lond. Gaz.* No. 3815/2 The Assisting Ships shall have no greater Shares..than has been accustomed. **1794** GODWIN *Cal. Williams* 210 These men might be in some way assisting to me. **1804** MITFORD *Harmon. Lang.*, Through means of an assisting power.

assistive (əˈsɪstɪv), *a. rare*[−0]. [ad. med.L. *assistīvus*, in *assistīva mulier* a kind of nun.] Assistant.

a'ssistless, *a. poet.* [f. as ASSISTFUL: see -LESS; cf. *resistless.*] Without assistance, helpless.

1720 POPE *Iliad* XVI. 970 Stupid he stares, and all assistless stands.

assistor (əˈsɪstɔː(r)). Variant of ASSISTER, used in legal phraseology: see -OR.

1602 FULBECKE *1st Pt. Parall.* 93 The counsellor, commandor, or assistor are..guilty of homicide. **1768** BLACKSTONE *Comm.* IV. 38 Any assistance whatever given to a felon, to hinder his being apprehended..makes the assistor an accessory.

assite, variant of ACCITE *v. Obs.* to cite.

assith-, -ment, obs. forms of ASSYTH, -MENT.

assize (əˈsaɪz), *sb.* Forms: 3-5 **asise**, 3-6 **assyse**, 4 **assys**, 4-6 **asyse**, **assiss(e**, 5 **assis**, **assyze**, **acyse**, **asyce**, 6 **assyce**, **-ies**, 3-9 **assise**, 5- **assize**. *Aphet.* 4-6 **syse**, 6 **sise**: see also SIZE. [a. OF. *asise*, *assise*, 'act of sitting down, sitting, seat, siege; act of setting, settlement, fixation of imposts, assessment; appointment, regulation; regular mode, manner;' substantive use of fem. sing. of *a(s)sis*, pa. pple. of *asseoir*, OF. *aseeir* 'to sit at, set down, settle, assess':—L. *assidēre* to sit at, sit down to: cf. ASSESS. Analogous to sbs. in *-ata*, *-ada*, Fr. *-ée*, from pa. pples. It is not clear whether the intrans. idea of 'a sitting,' or the trans. one of 'a thing settled,' was the original sense; perhaps both were equally early: see Stubbs *Const. Hist.* §160, where the suggestion is also made that in the latter sense *assize* was used to translate OE. *ȝesetniss*, ME. *isetnesse*, statute. In the sense of 'assessment,' *assise* was early corrupted to *acise*, *accise*, now corruptly EXCISE. In that of 'measurement' aphetized as SIZE.]

I. Legislative sitting, statute, statutory measure or manner.

†**1.** A sitting or session of a consultative or legislative body. *Obs.*

Applied in OF. to the sitting of the King's Council, but perhaps not in Eng. See next sense.

[*Jus Municipale Normann.* I. v. vi. (in Du Cange) Assise est une assemblée de plusieurs sages hommes en la Cour del Prince, en laquelle cen qui y sera jugié, doit avoir perdurable fermeté.]

†**2. a.** The decree or edict made at such a sitting. *Obs.* exc. *Hist.*

Applied specifically in Eng. Hist to various formal edicts, named sometimes from the place where they were made, sometimes from the subject with which they were concerned; e.g. *Assize of Clarendon, Assize of Arms, Assize of the Forest, Assize of Measures, Assize of Bread and Ale*, etc. ***Assizes of Jerusalem***, the code of jurisprudence for the new kingdom of Jerusalem, established by the Crusaders in 1099.

[**1164** HOVEDEN, Assisæ Henrici Regis factæ apud Clarendonum.] **1330** R. BRUNNE *Chron.* 301 þe chartre of franchise conferm it ȝow he salle, & of þe first assise as his fader gaf it alle. **1590** RECORDE, etc. *Gr. Arts* (1646) 316 The reason of the Statute of Assise of Bread and Ale. **1642** CHAS. I. *Answ. Decl. Both Houses* 1 July 41 Assises (or Assesements) of Arms. **1768** BLACKSTONE *Comm.* II. 66 By an ordinance in 27 Hen. II. called the assise of arms, it was provided that every man's armour should descend to his heir. **1855** MILMAN *Lat. Chr.* (1864) V. IX. vii. 349 Their code of law was the Assises of Jerusalem. **1875** STUBBS *Const. Hist.* I. xiii. 573 The formal edicts known under the name of Assizes, the Assizes of Clarendon and Northampton, the Assize of Arms, the Assize of the Forests, and the Assizes of Measures, are the only relics of the legislative work of the period [of Henry II.]

†**b.** Hence *gen.* Ordinance, appointment, regulation, established order. ***rent of assize*** (in the Assizes of Clarendon 1164, *Assisus reditus*): a fixed rent. *Obs.*

1303 R. BRUNNE *Handl. Synne* 804 Come blelyche to þe seruyse Whan holy chyrche settyþ asyse. *c* **1320** *Seuyn Sages* 2490 Thine seuen wise, That han i-wrowt ayen the assise. **1523** FITZHERB. *Surv.* 11 b, Also it is to be enquered, who be fre tenauntes..and what they yelde by the yere of rent of Assise.

†**3.** *esp.* Ordinances regulating weights and measures, and the weight and price of articles of general consumption (*assisæ venalium*); e.g. the *Assize of Measures* in reign of Henry II, *Assize of Bread and Ale* 51 Henry III, etc. Also *gen.* Rule of trade. *Obs.* exc. *Hist.*

a **1330** *Poem temp. Edw. II.* (1849) lxxiii, Somtyme wer marchants That trewly bout and sold, Now is thilk assise i-broke. **1473-4** *Act 12 & 13 Edw. IV.* in *Oxf. & Camb. Enactmts.* 9 The kepyng of assise of brede, wyne, and ale. **1601** TATE *Househ. Ord. Edw. II.* §15 He shal cause offendors which have broken thassise to be punished. **1609** SKENE *Reg. Maj.* 149 They keip not..the assise (lawes) anent the bread, wyne, aill and fleshe. **1768** BLACKSTONE *Comm.* IV. 157 The assize of bread, or the rules laid down by law, and particularly by statute 31 Geo. II. c. 29. and 3 Geo. III. c. 11. for ascertaining it's price in every given quantity. **1821** J. Q. ADAMS in C. Davies *Metr. Syst.* III. (1871) 89 The act of 51 Henry III. (1266), is called the assize of bread and of ale.

4. The statutory regulation or settling of the price of bread and of ale, with reference to that of grain, in accordance with the aforesaid ordinances.

1447-8 SHILLINGFORD *Lett.* (1871) 91 Thine predecessours have had assize of bred and of ale. **1577** HARRISON *England* I. II. xviii. 294 In these markets..assises of bread..are not anie whit looked unto. **1638** PENKETHMAN (*title*) Artachthos; or Assis of Bread. **1876** ROGERS *Pol. Econ.* xx. 12 The assize of bread, that is the regulation of its price by the price of wheat.

5. The standard of quantity, measure, or price ordained by such ordinances; *hence*, customary, required, or prescriptive standard.

a **1400** *Leg. Rood* (1871) 80 þan was it schorter þan þe assise. **1466** *Paston Lett.* 549 II. 268 For vii. barels bere, xviis. vid. For a barel of the grettest assyse iiis. iiii*d*. **1556** *Chron. Grey Friars* (1852) 2, Xxxv. men..sworne to mayntayne the assies in London. **1622** CALLIS *Stat. Sewers* (1647) 25 They presented the said Were to be over high and ..inhaunced above the ancient assize. **1710** LUTTRELL *Brief. Rel.* VI. 586 Last week a baker was convicted for selling bread under the assize. **1768** BLACKSTONE *Comm.* I. 275 It was ordained that..the custody of the assise or standard of weights and measures shall be committed to certain persons. **1813** *Examiner* 15 Mar. 160/1 The Lord Mayor..has ordered the price of Bread to rise half an assize. **1821** J. Q. ADAMS in C. Davies *Metr. Syst.* III. (1871) 229 Laws regulating the assize of casks.

†**6.** *Hence*: Measurement, dimensions. *Obs.* (Now SIZE.)

c **1430** *Syr Tryam.* 1557 'A lytulle lower, syr,' seyde hee.. Now are we bothe at oon assyse. **1481-90** HOWARD *Househ. Bks.* 293 Iiij. peces of redde wusted of the grettest asyse. **1567** DRANT *Horace Epist.* A iij, Put out no puffes, nor thwackyng words, words of to large assyce. **1624** BP. MOUNTAGU *Gagg* To Reader 6 A pretty little Whip-Jacke of less than ordinary assise, in a blew Jacket.

†**7.** Measure, extent (of things immaterial). *Obs.*

1625 BP. MOUNTAGU *App. Cæsar.* 316 The power of the keyes are to both alike in equall assise. *a* **1641** —— *Acts & Mon.* 83 A false surmise, that Prophecies and Promises be of like assise. **1655** LESTRANGE *Chas. I.* 166 Every event, of any considerable assise.

†**8.** Mode, manner, fashion; quality. *Obs.*

c **1325** *E.E. Allit. P.* B. 844 As in þe asyse of Sodomas to seggez þat passen. *c* **1350** *Will. Palerne* 4451 It is geinli greiþed in a god asise. **1393** GOWER *Conf.* III. 144 First they ..ben hard, and thilke assise Betokeneth in a king constaunce. *c* **1460** *Emare* 830 Shypmen..Dyght her takull on ryche acyse.

†**9.** Site, situation, position. *Obs.*

c **1400** *Rom. Rose* 900 Floures..of many gise Sett by compas in assise. *Ibid.* 1237 Ther nas a poynt, trewely, That it nas in his right assise. **1491** CAXTON *Vitas Patr.* II. 194 b/2 In all other thynges he kepte the myddell assyse.

†**10.** ? Commodity; article; manner of thing. *Obs.*

c **1300** *K. Alis.* 7074 Whan ther comes marchaundise, With corn, wyn, and steil, othir other assise.

II. A trial in which sworn assessors or jurymen decide questions of fact; a judicial inquest.

11. a. Orig. applied to: All legal proceedings of the nature of inquests or recognitions, fiscal, civil, or criminal.

Esp. the *Grand* or *Great Assize*, recognition as to the right of the claimant in a writ of right, substituted in the reign of Henry II for trial by battle, the assizes of *Mort d'ancestre*, *Novel disseisin*, and *Darreine presentment*, named in Magna Carta.

[*c* **1290** BRITTON III. iv. §28 Qe le tenaunt se puse mettre en juree a la semblaunce de graunt assise, *i.e.* that the tenant may put himself on a jury after the manner of a great assize.] **1297** R. GLOUC. 429 False sueryars of assyses. **1330** R. BRUNNE *Chron.* 64 He was chefe justise, Agayn þe erle Godwyn he gert sette assise. **1876** DIGBY *Real Prop.* ii. §2. 73 The cause..was decided either by the duel, or, under the great improvement of the law effected by an ordinance of Henry II..by the grand assize; that is, by the verdict of twelve milites of the neighbourhood, chosen by four other milites summoned by the sheriff for the purpose.

b. Hence, an action to be decided by such a trial; also applied to the writ by which it is instituted.

[*c* **1481** LITTLETON *Tenures* §233 Il poit aver Assise de Novel disseisin envers le tenant.] *c* **1574** *Transl.* He may have an Assise of novel disseisin against the tenant. *a* **1626** BACON *Maxims Com. Law* ii. (1630) 6 And the disseisee bring his assize in the Court of the Lord. **1641** *Termes de la Ley* 28 b, Assise is a writ, and it lyeth where any man is put out of his lands, tenements..and so disseised of his freehold. **1649** SELDEN *Laws of Eng.* I. lxvii. (1739) 158 In case the Lord would hold the Wardship longer than the full age of the Heir, an Assize did lie against the Lord. **1768** BLACKSTONE *Comm.* III. 221 An assise of nusance is a writ, wherein it is stated that the party injured complains of some fact done. **1876** DIGBY *Real Prop.* ii. §9. 97 The writ of assize of Mort d'Ancestor was perhaps instituted by the ordinance called the Assize of Northampton, A.D. 1176.

12. a. Hence (usually in *pl.*): The sessions held periodically in each county of England, for the purpose of administering civil and criminal justice, by judges acting under certain special commissions (chiefly and usually, but not exclusively, being ordinary judges of the superior courts, or, since 1875, of the Supreme Court).

It was provided by Magna Carta that the judges should visit each county once every year to take assizes (*i.e.* try writs of assize) of novel disseisin, mort d'ancestre, and darreine presentment (so that the jury who constituted the Grand Assize (see 11) might not be obliged to travel from remote corners of England to appear in court at Westminster). Thence the names *assizes*, and *justices* or *judges of assize*, still retained by these circuit courts and itinerant judges, after their judicial functions have been greatly extended in various directions, especially in that of the trial of felonies and offences.

[**1215** *Magna Carta*, Duos Justiciarios..qui..capiant in comitatu et in die et loco comitatus assisas predictas.] *c* **1386** CHAUCER *Prol.* 314 Justice he was ful often in assise, By patent, and by pleyn commissioun. *c* **1538** STARKEY *England* 190 Thos wych haue authoryte in the sessyons and Sysys. **1577** tr *Bullinger's Decades* (1592) 191 At Sessions or Assises, parties appeare and sue one an other. *a* **1626** BACON *Use Com. Law* (1635) 18 The third commission that the judges of circuits have is, a commission directed to themselves onely and the Clerk of Assize to take assizes, by which they are called Justices of Assize, and the office of those justices is to doe right upon writs called assizes, brought before them by such as are wrongfully thrust out of their lands. *a* **1674** CLARENDON *Hist. Reb.* II. VI. 150 Some few Counties, whither the King sent some Judges of Assize. **1758** JOHNSON *Idler* No. 46 ⁋4 Finery for the assizes and horse-races. **1827** HALLAM *Const. Hist.* (1876) II. viii. 16 The judges of assize were directed to inculcate on their circuits the necessary obligation of forwarding the King's service by complying with his writ. *Mod.* Tried for murder at the Maidstone assizes.

b. *attrib.* *assize-ball*, *-week*; **assize sermon**, a sermon preached at the holding of assizes.

1624 SANDERSON *Serm.* (1681) I. 103, I..desired for this assise-assembly to choose a text as near as I could of equal latitude with the assise-business. **1832** F. TROLLOPE *Dom. Manners* xiv. 215 The dancing was not quite like..what we see at an assize or race-ball in a country town. **1853** MRS. GASKELL *Ruth* I. i. 13 The assize-balls had been discontinued. **1857** THACKERAY *Fitz-boodle's Prof.* Misc. Wks. IV. 29 Confounded new policemen and the assize-courts prevent that. **1699** SEWALL *Letter-book* (1886) I. 216 Mr. Noyes..preached an excellent Assize Sermon. **1859** READE *Love me Little* iii, Shall you go to the assize sermon? **1812** SIR S. ROMILY in *Examiner* 7 Sept. 573/2 The duty of a Sheriff was..to ride..before the Judges, into an Assize town. **1628** EARLE *Microcosm.* xxviii. 61 He is fearful of being Sheriff of the Shire..and dreads the Assize-week as much as the prisoner. **1845** *Ainsworth's Mag.* VII. 503 Some years ago..I acted in Lancaster during the assize week.

13. In Scotland: **a.** A trial by jury.

1375 BARBOUR *Bruce* XIX. 55 [Thai] war with ane assiss thar ourtane. *a* **1605** SIR J. MELVIL *Mem.* (1683) 128 He went through the street to the Tolbooth to undergo his assize. **1609** SKENE *Reg. Mag.* Table 61 Ane Assise may proceid agains ane man absent being lawfullie summoned. **1651** CALDERWOOD *Hist. Kirk* (1843) II. 67 If the offender abide an assise, and by the same be absolved.

b. The jury or panel.

1513–75 *Diurn. Occurr.* (1833) 108 The names of the assyiss are thir; the erle of Cassillis, etc. **1574** tr. *Littleton's Ten.* 48 b, This name assise, sometime is put for the Jury. **1609** SKENE *Reg. Maj.* 157 Of them quha spares the ritch men, and summons the pure men to passe vpon the assise. *Ibid.* Table 61 The Assise in the breive of richt, is of twelue sworne men. **1715** BURNET *Own Time* (1766) I. 31 The fact being only referred to the jury or assize as they call it.

†**14.** Judgement, sentence; deliverance of opinion. *Obs.*

a **1300** *Cursor M.* 19344 Vr eldrin god did Iesu rise..þe quilk ȝe hang wiþ fals assise. *c* **1314** *Guy Warw.* 13 Herkeneth now, hou seith the wise? Y schal you schewe bi this asise. **1426** AUDELAY *Poems* 49 Thus sayd David forsoth in the Sautere, And verefyus in asise the love of our Lord. *c* **1570** THYNNE *Pride & Lowl.* (1841) 18 Perchaunce an issue hereon may be ioynt, Whereon thassise foorthwith we may award. **1643** SIR T. BROWNE *Relig. Med.* II. §14 Let us call to assize the loves of our parents.

15. With *great*, *last*, etc.: The Last Judgement.

a **1300** *Cursor M.* 22780 For to deme baþe ded and quik.. Al þat sal be at þat asise. **1340** HAMPOLE *Pr. Consc.* 5514 Þe haythen men at þat grete assys Sal þan be halden als men rightwys. *a* **1400** *Cov. Myst.* 60 Ȝoure soulys may thei save at the last asyse. **1413** LYDG. *Pylgr. Sowle* I. v. 5 The grete assises, at which oure noble gloryous kyng wyl descende presentely in his owne persone. **1598** SYLVESTER *Du Bartas* I. ii. (1641) 18/1 Where life still lives, where God his Sises holds. **1620** DEKKER *Christ's Coming* in Farr *S.P.* (1848) 172 That Lord by his own subiects crucified, So at his grand assize comes glorified. **1730** BEVERIDGE *Priv. Th.* I. 77 At the great Assizes of the World. **1812** COMBE (Dr. Syntax) *Pictur.* VIII. 29 Till summon'd to the last assize.

†**16.** *transf.* The office of judge, the action of judging, censorship. *Obs.*

1641 MILTON *Ch. Govt.* II. iii. (1851) 158 The Roman censor, a civil function, to that severe assise of surveying and controuling the privatest and sliest manners of all men and all degrees had no jurisdiction..no punitive force annexed. **1675** HOBBES *Odyss.* 90 The judges..who had elected been By publick vote, of games to hold assize.

III. Isolated senses from French.

†**17.** Siege, besieging. (So in OF.) *Obs. rare.*

c **1430** *Syr Generides* 8889 Generides by manly asise Hath beseged the tone of Vise..That noon may passe out I-wis.

†**18. a.** Fixation of imposts, imposition, tax. *Obs.* (See EXCISE, a corrupt form of this word.)

1642 HOWELL *For. Trav.* (Arb.) 74 When one hath seene the *Tally* and *taillage* of France, the *Milstone* of Spaine, the *Assise* of Holland..hee will blesse God, and love England better ever after.

†**b. assize-herring**, a royalty of one thousand herrings due three times a year during the season to the kings of Scotland from each boat engaged in the herring fishery. *Obs.*

1597 *Act 15 James VI.* §237 The..assise herring perteinis to our Soveraine Lorde, as ane part of his customes, and annexed propertie. **1673** H. STUBBE *Further Vind. Dutch War* App. 128 The King could not alienate the Royalty of the Assize-herring, by the Laws of Scotland.

†**a'ssize**, *v.* *Obs.* [a. AF. *assiser*, f. *assise* ASSIZE *sb.*]

†**1.** *trans.* To set, place.

1393 GOWER *Conf.* III. 122 The which [stars] upon his heved assised He bereth. *Ibid.* 126 Right so ben devised The signes twelve, and stonde assised. *a* **1420** *Pallad. on Husb.* I. 430 Assise And yote on it tilpavyng playne and strong.

2. To fix, ordain, appoint.

1393 GOWER *Conf.* III. 228 The king..hath therof a time assised. *Ibid.* I. 181 Two cardinales he hath assised..That with his doughter shulden go.

3. To determine, decide, judge.

c **1399** *Pol. Poems* (1859) II. 11 Ȝit natheles the lawe stant assised Of mannys wit to be so resonable.

4. To assess, value, rate.

1393 GOWER *Conf.* Prol. I. 5 That this prologue is so assised. **1624** BP. MOUNTAGU *Gagg* 2 It is a Prophecy; and Prophecies are assised at obscurity.

5. To assess. **a.** To fix the amount of (a tax). **b.** To value for the purposes of taxation.

1523 LD. BERNERS *Froiss.* I. ccccix. 712 In tyme past, whan Gaunt was assyned, Andwarpe was of lyhte valur. *Ibid.* II. xlix. (R.) Taxes and tallages [were] assysed in cytees and good townes.

6. To regulate or fix (weights, measures, prices, etc.) according to an ordinance or standard.

1566 PAINTER *Pal. Pleas.* I. 15 If the people will haue victuals and corne at that price, whereat it was assised and rated in time past. *c* **1638** *Ord. Priv. Counc.* in Penkethman *Artachthos* H ij b, When the second Wheat is at 3*l.* the Quarter, he may make and assize his Bread, as if the same Wheat were at 3*l.* 6*s.* the Quarter. **1638** *Chart. Goldsm. Co.* in A. Ryland *Gold & Silver Wares* (1852) 191 Persons, who shall bring..any weight called troy weight to be assized, according to his Majesty's standard.

assizement (ə'saɪzmənt). [f. ASSIZE *v.* + -MENT.] The action of assizing; the statutory inspection of weights and measures, or fixing of the price of articles of consumption.

1864 WEBSTER cites SIMMONDS.

assizer, -or (ə'saɪzə(r)). Also 4–6 **assisour**, 7 **assyser**, 8 **asyser**. *Aphet.* 4 **sysour**: see SIZAR. [a. AF. *assisour*, n. of agent f. *assiser* to ASSIZE.]

1. *Eng. Hist.* One of those who constituted the assize or inquest, whence the modern jury originated; a sworn recognitor.

a **1330** *Pol. Songs* (1839) 344 Assisours that comen to shire and to hundred, Damneth men for silver. **1393** LANGL. *P. Pl.* C. III. 59 Sysours and somners · shereuyes and here clerkes. *c* **1400** *Gamclyn* 864 The twelve sisours that weren of the queste, They schul ben hanged this day, so have I reste. **1617** DANIEL *Hist. Eng.* 169 Murtherers, fighters, false assisors, and other such malefactors.

2. *Scotch Law.* A juryman. *Obs.* exc. *Hist.*

1436 *Act 13 James I.* i. §2 Al Jugis sal ger þe assisoures swere..þat þai nothir haf tane na sal tak mede. **1609** SKENE *Reg. Maj.* 13 All the assisours sall sweare, that..they sall nocht laine nor conceale the trueth. **1709** *Royal Procl.* (Scotl.) in *Lond. Gaz.* No. 4522/2 We require..our Sheriffs, that they cause sufficient..Men to Compear before our.. Judges..for being Asysers and Witnesses. **1873** BURTON *Hist. Scot.* V. liv. 45 John Kirkcaldy, a cousin of Grange, had gone to Dunfermline..to act as an assizer or juryman.

3. An officer who had charge of the Assize of Weights and Measures, or who fixed the Assize of Bread and Ale, or of other articles of consumption.

1751 CHAMBERS *Cycl.*, *Assiser*..of weights and measures, is an officer who has the care and oversight of those matters.

assizing (ə'saɪzɪŋ), *vbl. sb.* [f. ASSIZE *v.* + -ING[1].] The action of regulating (weights and measures, prices, etc.) by a standard.

c **1638** *Ord. Priv. Counc.* in Penkethman *Artachthos* H ij b, That they observe and keep the good and antient custome, in making, assizing, and selling of all sorts of their Bread. **1860** in *Morn. Star* 20 May, There has been no assizing of weights in this town for four years.

asskrie, variant of ASCRY *v.* *Obs.*

assmay, -ayhe, var. of ASMAY *v.* *Obs.*

†**a'ssobre**, *v.* *Obs.* [? f. A- *pref.* 11 + SOBER.] *trans.* To make sober; *intr.* To become sober.

1393 GOWER *Conf.* III. 11 But if I mighte netheles Of suche a drinke..have o receite, I shulde assobre. *Ibid.* 16 Thus I rede thou assobre Thine herte.

associability (ə,səʊʃə'bɪlɪtɪ). [f. next: see -BILITY.] The quality of being associable.

1855 H. SPENCER *Psychol.* I. II. viii. (1872) 260 There is considerable associability of co-existences with sequences. **1865** MASSON *Rec. Brit. Philos.* 252 The associability of nerve-currents.

associable (ə'səʊʃ(ɪ)əb(ə)l), *a.* [a. F. *associable*, f. *associer* to ASSOCIATE: see -ABLE.]

†**1.** That may be associated with, companionable.

1611 COTGR., *Associable*, Companable, sociable, associable, fit to hold fellowship with.

2. That may be associated or connected in thought (*with*).

1855 H. SPENCER *Psychol.* I. II. viii. (1872) 259 The relations which enter into relation with one another are.. most easily associable. **1870** PROCTOR *Other Worlds* iii. 57 Effects which seem associable with their comparative proximity to the sun's orb.

3. *Phys.* Of nerves, muscles, etc.: Liable to be affected by sympathy with other parts.

a'ssociableness. [f. prec. + -NESS.] = ASSOCIABILITY.

1847 in CRAIG

associate (ə'səʊʃɪət), *ppl. a.* and *sb.* Also 4 **-cyat**, 6–8 **-ciat**, 7 **associat**. [ad. L. *associātus*, pa. pple. of *as-*, *ad-sociāre* to join together with, f. *ad* to + *socius* sharing, united, allied. Used at first as pa. pple. of the vb. ASSOCIATE; see next.]

A. *ppl. a.* = ASSOCIATED.

1. Joined in companionship, function, or dignity.

1398 TREVISA *Barth. De P.R.* II. v. (1495) 32 Angels ben ..assocyat and couplyd togyders in the joyefull companye of god. **1590** MARLOWE *Edw. II.* IV. iii, With him is Edmund gone associate? **1603** KNOLLES *Hist. Turkes* (1638) 33 Christ our Sauiour, equall and associate to his Father. **1822** *N. Amer. Rev.* XIV. 51 M. Stuart, Associate Professor of Sacred Literature in the Theological Seminary at Andover. **1844** BROUGHAM *Brit. Const.* xix. §6 (1862) 377 The Supreme Court..is composed of a president and six associate judges. **1896** J. L. FORD *Lit. Shop* (ed. 3) vi. 62 Mr. Johnson..in his capacity of associate editor of the *Century Magazine*. **1900** *Daily News* 14 Nov. 6/3 Associate-editor of the 'Engineer'. **1905** *N.Y. Even. Post* 25 Dec., The additional class is that of associate professors. All assistant professors under the old order were made 'associate'. **1931** H. F. PRINGLE *T. Roosevelt* II. xii. 432 The *Outlook* office where the ex-President was an associate editor.

2. Joined in league, allied, confederate.

1600 HOLLAND *Livy* xxv. xiii. 556 All the associate and confederate [*sociis*] cities thereabout. **1667** MILTON *P.L.* x. 395 While I..Descend through Darkness..To my associate Powers. **1725** POPE *Odyss.* XVI. 367 Amphinomus survey'd th' associate band. **1795** SOUTHEY *Joan of Arc* IX, If ought of patriot enterprise required Associate firmness.

3. United in the same group or category, allied; concomitant.

1750 JOHNSON *Rambl.* No. 90 ⁋9 They want some associate sounds to make them harmonious. **1765** TUCKER *Lt. Nat.* II. 407 Faith, understood in the most comprehensive sense, as including the two associate virtues. **1880** GARRETSON (*title*) A System of Oral Surgery..Surgery of the Mouth, Jaws, and Associate Parts.

B. *sb.* [the adj. used absolutely.]

1. One who is united to another by community of interest, and shares with him in enterprise, business, or action; a partner, comrade, companion.

1533 MORE *Apol.* xliv. Wks. 914/2, I woulde not greatly wish to be..their associate in anye suche confederacies. **1663** GERBIER *Counsel* B v b, Collonel Rushner and his assotiates in Holland, their proposalls concerning waterworks. **1725** POPE *Odyss.* IX. 200 My dear associates, here indulge your rest. **1849** MACAULAY *Hist. Eng.* I. 651 These men, more wretched than their associates who suffered death.

2. A companion in arms, ally, confederate.
1548 GRAFTON *Chron. Edw. III.* an. 12 (R.) For the receyuing of him, his associates and armie. **1601** HOLLAND *Pliny* I. 39 This hapned the yeare before the war of our Associates. **1849** W. IRVING *Mahomed's Succ.* vii. (1853) 26 His associates soon turned the tide of the battle.

3. One who shares an office or position of authority with another; a colleague, coadjutor. *spec.* An officer of the Superior Courts of Common Law in England, 'whose duties are to superintend the entering of causes, to attend sittings at nisi prius, and there receive and enter verdicts,' etc. (Warton.)
(In accordance with the statutes of Edward I and Edward II, the commissions of the judges on circuit were accompanied by *writs of association*, directing certain persons (usually the clerk of assize and his subordinate officers) to *associate* themselves with the justices and serjeants in order to take the assizes. (Stephens.) Up to 1879 there were 3 Associates in London, and 8 in the provinces, one for each Circuit. By the Supreme Court of Judicature Act of that year, the Associates in London were abolished, and made Masters of the Supreme Court.)
1552 HULOET, Associat in auctoritie, or put in ioynt commissioun, *Assessor.* *a* **1586** SIDNEY (J.) They persuade the king..to make Plangus his associate in government. **1685** *Lond. Gaz.* No. 2014/6 The Mayor, Associate, Justices of the Peace, Aldermen. **1862** ARCHBOLD *Practice* (Prentice) I. 15 (ed. 13) There is an Associate in each Division appointed by the Chief Justice and Chief Baron respectively.

4. One who is frequently in company with another, on terms of social equality and intimacy; an intimate acquaintance, companion, mate.
1601 WEEVER *Mirr. Mart.* A vj, No meane Cumrades, no base associates. **1678** BUNYAN *Pilgr.* I. 41 One of my Lords most intimate associates. **1851** HELPS *Friends in C.* I. 111 We become familiar with the upper views, tastes, and tempers of our associates.

5. One who belongs to an association or institution in a subordinate degree of membership, without the honours and privileges of a full member or 'Fellow.'
Commonly expressed by A.: as A.R.A., Associate of the Royal Academy, A.L.S. Associate of the Linnæan Society.
1812 *Examiner* 9 Nov. 714/2 [They] have..been elected Associates of the Royal Academy. **1831** BREWSTER *Newton* (1855) II. xix. 207 The eight foreign associates of the Academy of Sciences.

6. A thing placed or found in conjunction with another.
1658 SIR T. BROWNE *Hydriot.* 24 A way to make wood perpetual, and a fit associat for metal. **1879** G. GLADSTONE in *Cassell's Techn. Educ.* IV. 111/1 It is an almost constant associate of lead that we look for our supply of British silver.

7. *Psychol.* An idea, or other mental content, connected with another by any of the forms of association.
1700 LOCKE *Hum. Und.* II. xxxiii. §5 (R.) The one [idea] no sooner at any time comes into the understanding but its associate appears with it. **1880** W. JAMES *Coll. Ess. & Rev.* (1920) 207 In the trance-subject's mind any simple suggestion will be both believed and acted on, because none of its usual associates are awakened. **1931** *Brit. Jrnl. Psychol.* XXI. 279 The effect of partial elimination of associates on order of precedence in respect of memory.

associate (ə'səʊʃɪeɪt), *v.* Also 5 -siat. [f. prec.: the pa. pple. and pa. t. *associat(e* were in use before the present tense, or the pa. t. and pple. *associated.* Cf. the earlier ASSOCIE from Fr.]

1. *trans.* To join (persons, or one person *with* (*to* arch.) another), *in* (*to* obs.) common purpose, action, or condition; to link together, unite, combine, ally, confederate.
1398 [see ASSOCIATE *ppl. a.* 1.] **1494** FABYAN v. cxxvii. 107 He..associate vnto hym certeyn wanton persones. **1548** UDALL, etc. *Erasm. Par. Mark* viii. 34 (R.) Yf he intende to be associate wyth me in blisse. **1561** T. N[ORTON] *Calvin's Inst.* Table Quot., She was associated unto him in marriage. **1642** ROGERS *Naaman* 436 To associate him to the worke which himselfe and Paul went about. **1724** SWIFT *Drapier's Lett.* Wks. 1755 V. II. 72 None but papists are associated against him. **1761** HUME *Hist. Eng.* I. xvi. 394 The troops.. associating to them all the disorderly people. **1867** FREEMAN *Norm. Conq.* (1876) iv. 232 Arnulf associated his son with him in his government.

b. To elect as associate: see ASSOCIATE *sb.* 5.
1806 SOUTHEY in *Ann. Rev.* IV. 582 He..was associated to the royal Academy there. **1859** ALLIBONE *Biogr. Dict.* I. 43/1 The Royal College of Physicians associated him [Akenside] as a licentiate.

2. *trans.* To join, combine in action, unite (things together, or one thing *with* another). (Mostly *refl.* or *pass.*)
1578 BANISTER *Hist. Man* v. 70 The thyrd veyne of the ventricle is very small, not associated with any Arterie. **1660** BOYLE *New Exp. Phys.-Mech.* Digress. 352 The inspired Air ..does there associate it self with the Exhalations of the circulating Blood. **1751** JOHNSON *Rambl.* No. 158 ¶7 Faults are endured without disgust when they are associated with transcendent merit. **1855** BAIN *Senses & Int.* II. i. §7 The muscles..act in groups, being associated together by the organization of the nervous centres. **1878** HUXLEY *Physiogr.* 72 This vapour is intimately associated with the other constituents of the atmosphere.

b. To connect in idea.
1760 H. BROOKE *Fool of Qual.* (1859) I. 110 They associate the ideas of pain to those lessons. **1850** MCCOSH *Div. Govt.* I. iii. (1874) 64 The very name of God is associated in the human mind with fear. **1870** M. CONWAY *Earthw. Pilgr.* xvii. 213 Who could associate rose-leaves with hell-fires?

3. *refl.* in sense of 4. Const. as in 1, 2.
1494 FABYAN VI. ccxii. 228 Algarus..the whiche assosiat hym with Gryffyne, kynge or duke of Walys. **1611** BIBLE *Isa.* viii. 9 Associate your selues, O ye people, and yee shalbe broken in pieces. **1769** ROBERTSON *Chas. V.* III. XI. 340 He associated himself as a member of their fraternity. **1788–94** GIBBON *Misc. Wks.* (1814) I. 2 By associating ourselves to the authors of our existence.

b. To make oneself a partner in (a matter).
1881 GLADSTONE in *Times* 17 May 7/3 It is for me..to associate myself with the answer previously given by the Under-Secretary.

4. *intr.* **a.** To combine for a common purpose, to join or form an association.
1653 BAXTER *Chr. Concord.* 107 Those Congregations whose Ministers refuse to Associate. **1770** BURKE *Pres. Discont.*, When bad men combine, good men must associate. **1832** HT. MARTINEAU *Ireland* i. 8 As many as..sixteen tenants associated in one lease.

b. To keep company or have intercourse (*with*).
1644 MILTON *Judgm. Bucer* (1851) 313 Any dishonest associating they permit. **1728** THOMSON *Winter* 205 Let me associate with the serious night. **1754** CHATHAM *Lett. Nephew* iv. 20 Be sure to associate with men much older than yourself. **1868** GEO. ELIOT *F. Holt* 40 The Rector.. associated only with county people.

†**5.** *trans.* To join oneself to (a person): **a.** To accompany, escort, attend. *Obs.*
1548 HALL *Chron. Hen. VII.* an. 34 (R.) He shoulde have associated him in hys iourney. **1592** SHAKS. *Rom. & Jul.* v. ii. 5 A bare-foote Brother..to associate me, Here in this Citie visiting the sick. **1609** *Man in Moone* (1857) 108 The Parasite, associating the Glutton to the gate, entereth. **1657** BROME *Queene's Exch.* III. 499 And who associates him?

†**b.** To keep company or consort with. *Obs.*
1581 MARBECK *Bk. of Notes* 1108 Therfore shal man leaue father and mother and associate his wife. **1590** J. GREENWOOD in *Confer.* III. 63 If I associat a theife & Communicate in his euill.

†**c.** To act as associate or assistant to. *Obs.*
1627 SMITH *Seaman's Gram.* viii. 36 The Lieutenant is to associate the Captaine.

†**d.** of things: (cf. 2.) To accompany, join.
1578 BANISTER *Hist. Man* v. 70 The Arterie associatyng this veyne. **1613** HEYWOOD *Braz. Age* I. Wks. 1874 III. 181 Those torturing pangues That should associate death. **1691** RAY *Creation* (1714) 277 It is necessary that the large trunks of the Veins and Arteries should not associate each other.

a'ssociated, *ppl. a.* [f. prec. + -ED.]

1. Joined in companionship; united in action or purpose, sharing in dignity or office, allied. ***Associated Press*** (abbrev. *A.P.*), an association of American newspapers.
1611 COTGR., *Associé*, Associated, accompanied, consorted. **1656** (*title*) Agreement of the Associated Ministers and Churches of the Counties of Cumberland and Westmoreland. **1835** SIR J. ROSS *N.-W. Pass.* vi. 89 My associated though junior officer. **1849** *New Orleans Picayune* 9 May 2/2 The Associated press..occupy the telegraph many hours. **1879** [see A III]. **1881** *Echo* 31 Jan. 3/6 The New York Associated Banks. **1948** *Daily Ardmoreite* (Okla.) 25 Apr. 11/1 A poll conducted by the Associated Press. **1955** *Times* 29 June 7/5 Details of the programmes which will be transmitted by the Associated Broadcasting Company when commercial television begins in September were announced. **1958** *Daily Tel.* 30 June 13/4 Associated-Rediffusion, the main ITV company for London.

2. Connected in thought, mentally related.
1748 HARTLEY *Observ. Man* I. iv. §1 ¶94 The factitious, associated nature of these Pleasures. **1877** LYTTEIL *Landm.* III. iv. 119 Nothing but the name and the associated monuments to help us.

3. Combined locally, circumstantially, or in classification (*with*); occurring in combination. ***associated movements***: those 'having no connexion with the essential act calling them forth, but coincident or consensual with it' (*Syd. Soc. Lex.* 1881).
1830 LYELL *Princ. Geol.* I. 250 With associated beds of finer ingredients. **1839** MURCHISON *Silur. Syst.* I. xxii. 275 The combustion of lignite and coal producing a long continued heat, which has acted upon the associated shale. **1845** DARWIN *Voy. Nat.* xviii. (1852) 424 The almost entire absence of associated grasses [in New Zealand] may perhaps be accounted for by the land having been aboriginally covered with forest trees.

a'ssociatedness. [f. prec. + -NESS.] The quality of being associated.
1862 F. HALL *Hind. Philos. Syst.* 226 Giving to the subject of right notion the characteristic of associatedness with the affection that has taken the form of it, i.e. of its object.

associateship (ə'səʊʃɪət-ʃɪp). [f. ASSOCIATE *sb.* + -SHIP.] The position or status of an associate.
1846 *Calendar of King's Coll. Lond.* Index, Rules for the Associateship. **1862** THORNBURY *Turner* I. 257 Up to 1799 (his Associateship year) Turner had exhibited sixty-two pictures.

associating (ə'səʊʃɪeɪtɪŋ), *vbl. sb.* [f. ASSOCIATE *v.* + -ING[1].] The action of the vb. ASSOCIATE; association, union for a common purpose. (Now mostly gerundial.)
1644 [see ASSOCIATE *v.* 4 b.]. **1653** GAUDEN *Hierasp.* Pref. 11 They deny any Nationall Church in any larger associatings of Christians. **1863** MILL *Utilit.* 59 By associating the doing right with pleasure.

a'ssociating, *ppl. a.* [f. as prec. + -ING[2].] That associates; uniting; connecting in thought. ***associating fibres*** = ***association fibres*** (see next, sense 9).
1646 GAULE *Cases Consc.* 27 It is the assembling or associating Witch. **1683** *Lond. Gaz.* No. 1859/5 The Plots and Machinations of..Associating Men. **1823** LAMB *Elia* (1860) 360 Or what associating league to the imagination can there be between the seers and the seers not, of a presential miracle? **1885** *Harper's Mag.* Mar. 640/1 One set serves to connect the cells of different areas of the cortex (the 'associating fibres').

association (əˈsəʊʃɪ-, əˌsəʊsɪˈeɪ ʃən). Also 7 -tiation. [ad. L. *associātiōn-em*, n. of action f. *associāre*: see ASSOCIATE and -ATION. Cf. mod.F. *association*, perhaps the immediate source.]

1. a. The action of combining together for a common purpose; the condition of such combination; confederation, league.
1535 BP. WINCHESTER in Strype *Eccl. Mem.* I. App. lxv. 160 Me seemeth the word *association* soundeth not well. **1584** in Heath *Grocers' Comp.* (1869) 84 To the better corroboration of this our loyall bond and association. **1660** R. COKE *Power & Subj.* 48 A solemn oath of association for the restoring of it. **1746** SMOLLETT *Reproof* 53 Engag'd in firm association, stood, Their lives devoted to the public good. **1856** KINGSLEY *Lett.* (1878) I. 474 Association will be the next form of industrial development.

b. ***deed of association***: the specific document setting forth the particulars of a proposed 'limited liability company.' ***articles of association***: see ARTICLE *sb.* 9.
1866 CRUMP *Banking* ii. 43 On its being proposed to start a banking company on the 'limited liability' principle..at least seven persons must sign a deed of association.

2. A body of persons who have combined to execute a common purpose or advance a common cause; the whole organization which they form to effect their purpose; a society; *e.g.* the British Association for the Advancement of Science, the National Football Association, the Church Association, the Civil Service Supply Association.
a **1659** CLEVELAND *Poems* (1677) 117 Many Sects twisted into an Association. **1863** FAWCETT *Pol. Econ.* II. vi. 220 If land was owned and cultivated by associations of labourers. **1879** (*title*) Report of the Somersetshire Association of Congregational Churches.

†**3.** A document setting forth the common purpose of a number of persons, and signed by them as a pledge that they will carry it into execution. *Obs.*
1586 *Lett. to E. Leycester* 18 Your oth made in the association. **1682** *Lond. Gaz.* No. 1714/6 That Seditious Paper, the *Association*, lately found in the Earl of Shaftsbury's Closet. **1772** *Hist. Rochester* 185 Three men who had forged an association. **1855** MACAULAY *Hist. Eng.* IV. 251 Dropping the Association into a flowerpot.

4. Union in companionship on terms of social equality; fellowship, intimacy.
1660 BOYLE *Seraph. Love* iii. (1700) 33 Thus Self-denial is a kind of Holy Association with God. **1761** SMOLLETT *Gil Blas* XII. vi. (1802) III. 382 The nobility would be profaned by my association. **1872** SANFORD *Eng. Kings* 330 He had become habituated to..grossness and immorality in his daily associations.

5. a. The action of conjoining or uniting one person or thing with another.
1774 SIR J. REYNOLDS *Disc.* vi. (1876) 390 The spark that without the association of more fuel would have died.

b. *Chem.* The aggregation of molecules to form a loosely-bound complex.
1895 *Bull. Philos. Soc. Washington* XII. 158 They behave as simple oxide molecules, capable of arranging themselves in different associations according to physical circumstances. **1904** *Amer. Jrnl. Sci.* XVII. 427 Molecular weights of liquids, with a few words about association. **1940** *Chambers's Techn. Dict.* 553/1 *Molecular association*, the relatively loose binding together of the molecules of a liquid or vapour in groups of two or more.

6. *Law.* The appointment of additional legal officials to act as colleagues on any occasion; the writ appointing them. (Cf. ASSOCIATE, *sb.* 3.)
1613 SIR H. FINCH *Law* (1636) 319 Association is a writ for other to be associate into their company, as fellow Iustices together with them. **1809** TOMLINS *Law Dict.* s.v., The King may make an association unto the sheriff upon a writ of *re disseisin*.

7. a. The mental connexion between an object and ideas that have some relation to it (*e.g.* of similarity, contrariety, contiguity, causation). ***phr. association of ideas.***
1690 LOCKE *Hum. Und.* II. xxxiii. §7 That there are such associations of them [ideas] made by custom in the minds of most men, I think no body will question. **1700** *Ibid.* (ed. 4) II. xxxiii. 221 Of the Association of Ideas. **1759** J. ADAMS in *Wks.* (1850) II. 68 The principle in nature is imitation, association of ideas, and contracting habits. **1779** JOHNSON *L.P., Cowley* (1816) 56 Words being arbitrary must owe their powers to association, and have the influence, and that only, which custom has given them. **1855** BAIN *Senses & Int.* I. ii. §20 The simple act of seizing food implies..the mental association of the appearance of the food with the

satisfying of the feeling [of hunger]. **1890** W. JAMES *Princ. Psychol.* I. xiv. 555 Association occurs as amply between impressions of different senses as between homogeneous sensations. **1894** G. T. LADD *Psychol.* xiii. 264 The very limited nature of the application of the so-called laws of the association of ideas to the entire mental life. **1905** E. B. TITCHENER *Exper. Psychol.* II. i. 192 We show him a word; he is to react when the word has suggested something, no matter what. The word *sea* may arouse the idea of land or water or ships or some particular sea or some particular incident at sea,—anything it likes. Associations of this sort are termed, technically, *free* associations. **1938** R. S. WOODWORTH *Exper. Psychol.* xv. 340 In free association the laws of association are supposed to have full sway. **1958** HAYWARD & HARARI tr. *Pasternak's Dr. Zhivago* II. ix. 262 Through an unaccountable association of ideas started by the sight of the real town outside the window..Yury remembered the distant panorama of the town.

b. Psychol. ***laws of association***, see quot. 1897²; ***mediate association***, association by unconscious or unnoticed intermediaries; ***simultaneous, successive association***, forms of association of ideas in which the process of connexion is simultaneous or falls into two stages. Also *attrib.*, as ***association philosophy, psychology, test, theory, time***.

1820 T. BROWN *Lect. Phil. Human Mind* II. xl. 346 The other supposition..ascribes our trains of ideas to associations previous to the suggestion itself,—to laws of association in short, in the sense in which that phrase is distinguishable from laws of suggestion. **1833** J. S. MILL in *Monthly Repos.* VII. 663 The association-philosophy as taught by Hartley. *a* **1856** W. HAMILTON *Lect. Metaph. & Logic* (1860) IV. xxx. 122 Our Cognitions, Feelings, and Desires are connected together by what are called the *Laws of Association*. **1864** J. S. MILL *Let.* 3 Apr. in D. Duncan *Life & Lett. H. Spencer* (1908) 115 You and Bain..have succeeded in affiliating the conscious operations of mind to the primary unconscious organic actions of the nerves, thus filling up the most serious lacuna..in the association psychology. **1890** W. JAMES *Princ. Psychol.* I. xiv. 558 The difference [between the apperception-time and the reaction-time], called by Wundt the *association-time*, amounted, in the same four persons, to 706, 723, 752, and 874 thousandths of a second respectively. **1897** C. H. JUDD tr. *Wundt's Outlines Psychol.* 13 Intellectualistic psychology has in the course of its development separated into two trends... The logical theory... The association-theory. *Ibid.* 225 The following forms were discriminated: association by similarity and contrast, and association by simultaneity and succession. These class-concepts gained by a logical dichotomic process were dignified with the name 'laws of associations'. **1924** J. RIVIERE et al. tr. *Freud's Coll. Papers* II. 13 Association test. **1938** [see sense 7a]. **1959** *Listener* 29 Oct. 722/2 He [*sc.* Jung] used what were called association tests... The subject of the experiment was given a number of stimulus words and asked to react with another word or phrase to each.

8. An idea or recollection linked in the mind or memory with some object of contemplation, and recalled to the mind in connexion with it.

1810 COLERIDGE *Friend* (1865) 27 Why should..the holiest words with all their venerable associations be profaned. **1862** TROLLOPE *Orley F.* xlii. 306 A man could have no pleasant associations with a place unless he had made money there. **1879** MCCARTHY *Own Times* II. 62 One association of profound melancholy clings to that great debate.

9. *Physiol.* Used *attrib.*, as ***association area, centre, field, link, path, sphere***, of those portions of the cortex of the brain which connect the sensory and motor areas, and are supposed to be concerned with ideation, etc.; ***association fibres*** (in *Funk's Stand. Dict.* 1900), nerve fibres connecting different areas of the brain cortex, as distinguished from the commissural fibres; so ***association organ, system***.

1880 H. C. BASTIAN *Brain as Organ of Mind* xxiii. 452 The connecting, or, as Meynert terms them, the 'association system' of fibres of the Brain. **1890** W. JAMES *Princ. Psychol.* II. xviii. 75 During waking hours every centre communicates with others by association-paths. **1901** ALLCHIN *Man. Med.* III. Physiol., Introd. 31 A portion of the 'association' field of the cortex. **1902** *Encycl. Brit.* XXXI. 742/1 The areas of intervening cortex, arriving at structural completion later than the..sense-spheres, are called by some association-spheres. **1902** W. JAMES *Var. Relig. Exper.* xvi. 427 Other alienists..have explained 'paranoiac' conditions by a laming of the association-organ. **1904** J. MCCABE tr. *Haeckel's Wonders of Life* i. 13 In 1894 Flechsig showed that there are four central sense-regions.. in the gray cortex of the brain, and four thought-centres ('association-centres', or phroneta). **1909** *Cent. Dict.* Suppl., Association area. **1932** *Brit. Jrnl. Psychol.* XXIII. 22 These lesions [of brain tissue] represented interference with association links. **1952** *Sci. News* XXIII. 63 Histologically, we recognize in the so-called association areas [of the brain] the structures responsible for linking sensory stimuli with motor response.

10. A personal connection or link; esp. *attrib.* in ***association book, copy***, a volume showing some mark of personal connection with the author or a former owner (of note).

1882 *Gentl. Mag.* CCLII. 92 Speaking of books with an association reminds us of that most destructive craze of the present day, the collection of book-plates. **1901** *Munsey's Mag.* Oct. 80/1 His remarkable collection of 'Association Books'. **1912** *Times* (weekly ed.) 7 June 444 The collection is chiefly remarkable for what are termed in America 'association books'. **1914** *W. M. Murphy's Catal. Bks.* 19 Jan. 5 Association Copy. **1918** *Times* 21 Feb. 3/3 It is very rich..in what Americans call 'association books', such as the copy of 'Vanity Fair' which Thackeray sent to Charlotte Brontë. **1928** *N. & Q.* 12 May 341/2 Presented by Sir Walter Scott to Lydia White in 1808—double association of good interest.

11. Applied to the game of football played according to the rules of the Football Association formed in 1863, as distinguished from the Rugby game. (Cf. *soccer*, SOCKER.)

1867 *Routledge's Handbk. Football* 53 Football Association Rules. **1873** *Football Annual* 16 To play *with the feet* is the main object of Association Football. Hands should not, and must not be used. **1880** *Times* 12 Nov. 4/4 The Association game [of football] is, perhaps..more scientific. **1885** SHEARMAN & VINCENT *Football* 30 In the Association game no collaring, and therefore no running with the ball, is allowed. *Ibid.* 45 Before the days of the Rugby Union and Association rules. *Ibid.* 53 The ball..is several ounces heavier than an Association ball. **1920** K. R. G. HUNT (*title*) Association football.

12. *Ecol.* A group of associated plants within a formation (see FORMATION 5 b).

[**1807** HUMBOLDT & BONPLAND *Essai sur la Géographie des Plantes* 13 La Géographie des plantes..c'est cette science qui considère les végétaux sous les rapports de leur association locale dans les différens climats.] **1900** B. D. JACKSON *Gloss. Bot. Terms* 25/2 Plant Associations. **1909** GROOM & BALFOUR tr. *Warming's Œcology of Plants* xxxv. 145 An association is a community of *definite floristic composition* within a formation. **1911** A. G. TANSLEY *Types Brit. Veg.* 10 Thus each of the types of vegetation, woodland, scrub and grassland, within a given formation, is a plant-association. **1916** F. E. CLEMENTS *Plant Succession* vi. 128 The association as usually understood becomes what is here termed the consociation, in so far as it is a climax community. This is the association with a single dominant. **1918** G. E. NICHOLS in *Trans. Connecticut Acad.* XXII. 275 In any unit area where more than one association is represented, the associations, taken collectively, constitute an association complex.

a,ssoci'ational, *a.* [f. prec. + -AL¹.] Of or pertaining to (an) association. ***Associational School***: those philosophers who hold the doctrine of associationism.

1815 *Boston Q. Rev.* 56 in Pickering *Dict. Amer.*, [Students in divinity] must..pass through the associational or presbyterial examination. **1847** BUSHNELL *Chr. Nurture* vi. (1861) 148 A kind of associational instinct. **1899** W. JAMES *Talks* xii. 119 The laws of memory..are incidents of our associational constitution. **1951** R. FIRTH *Elem. Social Organization* ii. 43 The associational standard is applied to the way in which it affects social relations.

a,ssoci'ationalism = ASSOCIATIONISM.

a,ssoci'ationalist = ASSOCIATIONIST.

associationism (ə,səʊʃɪ'eɪʃənɪz(ə)m). [f. ASSOCIATION + -ISM.] The doctrine that mental and moral phenomena may be accounted for by association of ideas.

1875 *Encycl. Brit.* II. 732/2 To account for the fact of synthesis in cognition, in express opposition to associationism. **1882** *Athenæum* 28 Jan. 118/1 Points where Mill's mind emancipated itself from the narrow range of associationism in psychology. **1890** W. JAMES *Princ. Psychol.* I. x. 338 All the individual thoughts and feelings which have succeeded each other 'up to date' are represented by ordinary Associationism as in some inscrutable way 'integrating' or gumming themselves together.

a,ssoci'ationist. [f. as prec. + -IST.]

1. One who belongs to an association. Also *attrib.* or as *adj.* = next.

1851 S. JUDD *Margaret* II. i. (1871) 160 Groups of.. industrious associationists. **1881** E. PURCELL in *Academy* 22 Jan. 56 The wretched Church Associationist is reduced to auricular confession.

2. One who holds the doctrine of associationism.

1862 R. PATTERSON *Ess. Hist. & Art* 55 The beautiful.. instead of being, as the Associationists affirm, merely a chameleon-like phantasm. **1876** *Mind* I. 322 It is only with a very small part..of what is distinctive in the teaching of the associationist philosophers that we are at present concerned. **1880** W. JAMES *Coll. Ess. & Rev.* (1920) 209 The English associationist school..had also represented choice and decision as nothing but the resultant of different ideas failing to neutralize each other exactly. **1881** —— *Will to Believe* (1897) 128 The strict associationist school..under the domination of Mill, Bain, and Spencer dominated us but yesterday. **1882** *Athenæum* 28 Jan. 119/1 Prof. Bain..the last of the Associationists. **1886** A. WEIR *Hist. Basis Mod. Europe* xii. 500 The associationist psychology. **1890** W. JAMES *Princ. Psychol.* I. x. 353 The chain of distinct existences into which Hume thus chopped up our 'stream' was adopted by all of his successors as a complete inventory of the facts. The associationist Philosophy was founded. **1951** E. E. EVANS-PRITCHARD *Social Anthropology* iii. 44 When anthropologists even as recent as Tylor and Frazer looked to psychology for aid it was to associationist psychology that they looked.

associationistic (ə,səʊʃɪeɪʃə'nɪstɪk), *a.* [f. ASSOCIATIONIST + -IC.] Of or relating to associationism or associationists.

1901 W. JAMES *Mem. & Stud.* (1911) vii. 148 All psychology, whether animistic or associationistic, was written on classic-academic lines. **1935** *Brit. Jrnl. Psychol.* XXV. 277 We are here making use of the associationistic 'meaning theory'.

associative (ə'səʊʃɪətɪv), *a.* [f. L. *associāt-* (see ASSOCIATE) + -IVE, as if ad. L. **associātīvus*.] **1.** Of, pertaining to, or characterized by association.

1881 RAE in *Contemp. Rev.* Feb. 233 The associative principle in the arrangements of economical life.

2. *Psychol.* Of, pertaining to, characterized by, or subserving, the association of ideas. (Cf. ASSOCIATION 7.)

1812 COLERIDGE in *Omniana* II. 13 The fancy, or the aggregative and associative power. **1864** J. S. MILL *Lett.* (1910) II. 7 He [*sc.* Spencer] has a great mastery over the obscurer applications of the associative principle. *a* **1873** —— *Three Ess. Relig.* (1874) 199 When analysed to the bottom on the principles of the Associative Psychology, the brain..is, like matter itself, merely a set of human sensations either actual or inferred as possible. **1923** J. S. HUXLEY *Ess. of Biologist* i. 24 Through associative memory, present behaviour is modified by past experience. **1957** *New Biol.* XXIV. 123 Associative learning—a term which covers both classical conditioned reflexes and learning by trial and error.

3. *Math.* Governed by or stating the condition that where three or more quantities are connected together by operators, the result is independent of the grouping of the quantities as long as their order is unchanged, e.g. that $(a \times b) \times c = a \times (b \times c)$.

1844 W. R. HAMILTON in *Proc. R. Irish Acad.* II. 430 It will be found that another important property of the old multiplication is preserved, or extended to the new, namely, that which may be called the *associative* character of the operation, and which may have for its type the formula $Q. Q^{I}\ Q^{II}.\ Q^{III},\ Q^{IV} = QQ^{I}.\ Q^{II}\ Q^{III}\ Q^{IV}$. **1870** B. PIERCE *Linear Associative Algebra* 21 The associative principle of multiplication may be adopted, namely that the product of successive multiplications is not affected by the order in which the multiplications are performed, provided that there is no change in the relative position of the factors... This is quite an important limitation, and the algebras which are subject to it will be called associative. **1924** [see BOOLEAN *a.*]. **1964** N. N. HANCOCK *Matrix Analysis Electr. Machinery* ii. 7 There may be more than two matrices in a product and in such cases matrix multiplication is associative. **1975** I. STEWART *Concepts Mod. Math.* v. 73 We say that our method of combining functions satisfies the associative law.

Hence **a'ssociatively** *adv.*; **associa'tivity**, †**associativeness** *Math.* the property of being associative.

1878 *Amer. Jrnl. Math.* I. 50 The associativeness of such symbols arises from the circumstance that the definitions of α, β, γ,.. determine the meanings of $\alpha\beta$, $\alpha\gamma$, &c. **1880** CYPLES *Hum. Exp.* v. 110 So as to represent associatively. **1926** *Trans. Amer. Math. Soc.* XXVIII. 222 The present direct method of finding the conditions for associativity is far more complicated than our earlier direct method. **1965** J. J. ROTMAN *Theory of Groups* i. 4 Must we postulate more intricate associativity axioms in order to do without parentheses? **1979** D. R. HOFSTADTER *Gödel, Escher, Bach* (1980) ii. 56 The commutativity and associativity of multiplication.

associator (ə'səʊʃɪeɪtə(r)). Also 7 -er. [n. of action on Latin type f. ASSOCIATE or L. *associāre*.] He who or that which joins in association; a confederate, companion; a member of an association.

1616 PURCHAS *Pilgr.* (1864) 126 Another Nayro, who with his Associaters kill him. **1683** *Lond. Gaz.* No. 1857/5 All Conventiclers, Covenanters, Associators, and all other Traytors. **1750** HARRIS *Hermes* II. i. (1786) 229 The natural Associators with Articles are..common Appellatives. **1876** BANCROFT *Hist. U.S.* V. xii. 456 Congress..called on the associators in Philadelphia..to join the army.

associatory (ə'səʊʃɪə,tərɪ), *a.* [f. prec.: see -ORY.] Having the quality of associating.

1880 CYPLES *Hum. Exp.* ii. 39 The associatory activity of the senses.

†**a'ssocie**, *v. Obs.* Also 4 **assossie**, 5 **-cye**. [a. OF. *associe-r* (13th c. in Littré):—L. *associā-re*: see ASSOCIATE.] Early equivalent of ASSOCIATE *v.*

1. *trans.* To unite, place, or bring (a person or oneself) into companionship or alliance with another; = ASSOCIATE *v.* 1, 3.

c **1380** WYCLIF *Sel. Wks.* (1871) III. 329 He is irreguler þat sittiþ in place as associed wiþ þe domesman. **1388** —— *1 Kings* xxii. 50 *marg.*, Josephat nolde be assossied with him.. in nauey. **1447** BOKENHAM *Seyntys* 97 He..assocyied hym on to ther cumpanye. **1480** CAXTON *Chron. Eng.* ccxxi. 212 Robert..assocyed vnto hym Syr Rogger the Mortimer.

2. *intr.* To enter into confederacy; = ASSOCIATE 3.

1441 *Plumpton Corr.* Introd. 57 They had assocyed to the number of DCC persons or thereabouts.

associes (ə'səʊs(ɪ)iːz). *Ecol.* [mod.L., irreg. f. L. *associāre*: see ASSOCIATE *ppl. a.* (cf. quot. 1926).] (See quot. 1916.)

1916 F. E. CLEMENTS *Plant Succession* vi. 136 The associes is the developmental equivalent of the association... It is composed of two or more consocies, *i.e.*, developmental consociations, just as the association consists of two or more consociations. Like the association, it is based upon life-form, floristic composition, and habitat, but differs from it in as much as all of these are undergoing constant or recurrent developmental changes. **1926** TANSLEY & CHIPP *Stud. Vegetation* ii. 19 The three higher ranks..we distinguish from the corresponding climax communities by using the suffix *-es*, thus *associes, consocies, socies*. **1964** V. J. CHAPMAN *Coastal Vegetation* i. 11 The *associes, consocies* and *socies* are their equivalents in a sere (succession).

†**a'ssogue.** *Obs.* [a. F. *assogue* (in same sense), a. Sp. *azogue*, Pg. *azougue*, quicksilver, ad. Sp. Arab. *az-zaouga* (P. de Alcala) = Arab. *az-zāūq*, i.e. *az* = *al* the, *zāūq*, ad. Pers. *zhīwah* quicksilver.] A Spanish vessel carrying

quicksilver to America for use in the silver-mines.
1692 *Lond. Gaz.* No. 2760/2 The two Assogues Ships designed to have sailed..for New Spain. **1762** *Gentl. Mag.* 118 Outward bound flotas, assogues, or register ships.

assoil (ə'sɔɪl), *v.* Forms: 3–4 asoyl-en, -y, asoil-en, -y, 3–6 asoyle, -oile, 4 asoyli, -lye, asoilie, assoill-en, -i, assoil-en, 4–6 assoyle, assoille, 4–7 assoile, 5 assole, 5–7 assoyl, 6 asoylle, 5– assoil. *Scotch* 5 assolyhe (= assolȝe), 6 assolye, assoilȝe, -ye, -ze, 7 assolzie, -oylle, 7– assoilzie. *Aphet.* 5–6 soile, soyle. [f. OF. *a(s)soille* pres. subj., *a(s)soil* pres. indic. of *a(s)soldre, a(s)soudre*:—L. *absolŭĕre* = *absolvĕre* to absolve, f. *ab* from + *solvĕre* to loose. Other forms of the infinitive in OF. (the first two also in AF.) were *a(s)soilier, a(s)soiler, a(s)soillir, a(s)solir*, as if:—L. **absoluēre*. L. '*solŭĕre* gave OF. '*solre*, '*soldre*, as '*batŭĕre*, '*quatŭŏr* gave *batre, quatre*, and *voluĕrunt*, *'*volŭĕrunt* gave *volrent, voldrent*; with the variants *a(s)soilier, a(s)oillir*, compare other OF. double forms, as *tesir, taire*:—L. *tacēre*, **tacĕre*, and *plesir, plaire*:—L. *placēre*, **placĕre*. Subsequently refashioned in Fr. as *absoudre*, and in Eng. as ASSOIL, which paved the way for the modern ABSOLVE, formed directly from the L after 1500. The Fr. *l mouillé*, lost in Eng., was as usual retained in Scotch, and symbolized by *lȝ, lyh, ly*, now corrupt'y written *lz*, whence the current *assoilzie* (əs'ɔɪljɪ, ə'sɔɪlɪ).]

I. To assoil a person.

1. To absolve from sin, grant absolution to, pardon, forgive; = ABSOLVE 2. '*Whom God assoil!*' (OF. *que Dieu assoille!* L. *quem Deus absolvat!*): an ejaculatory prayer for the departed. *arch.*
1297 R. GLOUC. 464 No man, bote þe pope one, hem asoyly ne myȝte. **1340** *Ayenb.* 172 Þet he habbe power him to asoyli and him penonce to anioyni. *c* **1340** *Gaw. & Gr. Knt.* 1882 Of absolucioun he on þe segge calles, & he asoyled hym. **1426** *Pol. Poems* II. 131 As wele on his ffader side, Henry the fifth, whom God assoille, as by Kateryne quene of Englond, his modir, whom God assoile. **1610** HOLLAND *Camden's Brit.* I. 564 Pray devoutly for the soule whom God assoile. **1638** *Penit. Conf.* vii. (1657) 132 God remitting whomsoever the Priest assoileth. **1816** SCOTT *Antiq.* xxvi, 'God assoilzie her!' ejaculated old Elspeth..'His mercy is infinite.' *c* **1840** DE QUINCEY *Autobiog. Sk.* Wks. II. 102 Oxford might avail to assoil me.

b. *of, from* the sin. *arch.*
1297 R. GLOUC. 501 The pope of alle hor sunnes asoileth alle the Barons & kniȝtes. **1393** LANGL. *P. Pl.* C. XXII. 185 To asoylye men of alle manere synnes. **1508** FISHER *Wks.* I. 44 Be assoyled clene from synne of theyr ghostly fader. **1551** ABP. HAMILTON *Catech.* 151 b (JAM.) The wordis of absolutioun..I assoilye the fra thi synnis. **1596** DRAYTON *Legends* iv. 857 Secretly assoyling of his sin. **1664** H. MORE *Myst. Iniq.* 112 Acquitted and assoiled from the guilt of all our sins.

c. from purgatory. (Cf. senses 2 and 5.) *arch.*
1483 CAXTON *Gold. Leg.* 21/1 And assoylle the synnars whan thou descendest into helle. **1828** SCOTT *F.M. Perth* II. 299 He will be freed from purgatory the sooner that good people pray to assoilzie him.

†2. To absolve or set free from excommunication or other ecclesiastical sentence. *Obs.*
1362 LANGL. *P. Pl.* A. III. 139 Heo þat ben Curset in Constorie counteþ hit not at a Russche..Heo is asoyled as sone as hire-self lykeþ. *c* **1450** *Merlin* xxvii. 560 The londe was assoiled by the legat. **1611** SPEED *Hist. Gt. Brit.* IX. viii. (1632) 578 Vntil he were assoyled of his excommunication. **1660** R. COKE *Power & Subj.* 206 If any Bishop do excommunicate any person..the King may write to the Bishop, and command him to assoyl, and absolve the party. **1691** BLOUNT *Law Dict.*, *Assoile* (*absolvere*) Signifies to deliver, pardon, or set free from an Excommunication.

†3. To set free, discharge, or release (*of, from* obligations, liabilities); = ABSOLVE 5. *Obs.*
1366 MAUNDEV. iii. 18 To whom God ȝaf his pleyn Power, for to bynde and to assoille. **1382** WYCLIF *1 Macc.* x. 29 Now y assoile you, and alle Jewis, of tributis. **1460** CAPGRAVE *Chron.* 143 The same Pope..cursed him, and asoiled al his barones fro that feith whech they had mad to him. **1483** CAXTON *Gold. Leg.* 266/2 She..was assoilled of her vowe. **1650** S. CLARKE *Eccl. Hist.* (1654) I. 507 A lawful oath, from which no man can assoile you.

4. To acquit (a person) of a criminal charge, to pronounce not guilty, to clear; = ABSOLVE 4. Const. *of, from. arch.* (see b.)
1528 MORE *Heresyes* III. Wks. 211/2 Than may the iudges acquite and assoyle the defendaunt. **1548** UDALL, etc. *Erasm. Par. Matt.* xviii. 92 Whom Cesar doth condemne, God sumtime doth assoyle. **1647** (11 Mar.) CROMWELL *Let.* xxv. (Carl.) The houses did assoil the army from all suspicion. *a* **1667** JER. TAYLOR *Serm.* (1678) 88 Many persons think themselves fairly assoiled, because they are..not of scandalous Lives. **1832** LAMB *Lett.* II. (1841) 82 If the candlestick be not removed, I assoil myself.

b. *esp.* in *Sc. Law*, where *assoilzie* (i.e. *assoilȝie, assoilyie*) is still the proper term for: To acquit by sentence of court.
1603–5 SIR J. MELVIL *Mem.* (1735) 155 Being assoilzied he continued the greatest Favourite at Court. **1609** SKENE *Reg. Maj.* IV. xxviii. (JAM.) The malefactour assoilyied at the instance of the partie. *a* **1691** SIR G. MACKENZIE in *Stewart's Trial* (1753) 143 The chief actor must be first discussed, and either found guilty or assoilzied. **1800** A. CARLYLE *Autobiog.* 235 Clear in their judgement that the panel should be assoilzied and the Presbytery taken to task. **1865** *Morn. Star* 5 Dec., The action could not be maintained, and the defendants were entitled to be assoillzied.

5. To release, deliver, set free; to discharge. Const. *of, from. arch.*
1401 *Pol. Poems* (1859) II. 38 When ye han assoiled me.. In truth I shall soile thee of thine orders. **1502** ARNOLD *Chron.* 280 The sayd bysshop now beyng cardynal, was assoiled of his bisshoprich of Wynchester. **1596** SPENSER *F.Q.* I. x. 52 Till from her bands the spright assoiled is. **1658** USSHER *Ann.* VI. 400 To assoile all the sea craft of Thracia from the power and jurisdiction of Philippus. *a* **1845** HOOD *Open Quest.* xv, What harm if men who burn the midnight-oil..Seek once a week their spirits to assoil? **1850** MRS. BROWNING *Wks.* I. 330 Death's mild curfew shall from work assoil.

II. To assoil a thing.

†6. To unloose the knot of (difficulty or doubt); to clear up, solve, or resolve; = ABSOLVE 6. *Obs.* (In this sense freq. *soyle, soil* in 16th c. Cf. SOIL *v.*)
c **1374** CHAUCER *Boeth.* V. iii. 154 Þat þei mowen assoilen and vnknytten þe knot of þ is questioun. **1377** LANGL. *P. Pl.* B. III. 236 Þis asketh dauid; And dauyd assoileth it hymself. **1485** CAXTON *Trevisa's Higden* (1527) 1 This questyon and doubte is easy to assoyle. **1513** DOUGLAS *Æneis* VII. ii. 138 The pepill..thar petitiouns gettis assolȝeit heir. **1548** UDALL, etc. *Erasm. Par. Mark* xi. 28 Soyle me this question. *a* **1593** H. SMITH *Serm.* 259 Nebuchadnezzar cannot assoile his owne dreame. **1602** WARNER *Alb. Eng.* XIII. lxxvii. 318 Sybil assoiling Oracles in Caue. **1696** WHISTON *Th. Earth* (1722) 65 Fewer difficulties in the..Books themselves, than in the..very Comments which ought to assoil 'em.

†7. To refute (an objection or argument). *Obs.*
c **1370** WYCLIF *Wks.* (1880) 388 Argumentisþat may not be asoylid. *c* **1449** PECOCK *Repr.* I. xix. 78 A good clerk couthe not assoile the firste obieccioun. **1655** GURNAL *Chr. in Arm.* II. 587 For the fuller assoyling this objection. **1721** STRYPE *Eccl. Mem.* I. xxxviii. 300 To confute the pope's primacy..and to assoyl Pole's arguments.

8. To purge oneself from, purge, expiate, atone for. (From 1, 2.) *arch.*
1596 SPENSER *F.Q.* IV. vi. 25 Well weeting how their errour to assoyle. **1601** HOLLAND *Pliny* I. 453 To expiate and assoile the carnage and execution don vpon the enemies. **1693** W. ROBERTSON *Phraseol. Gen.* 162 To assoil crimes or accusations—i.e. to free himself from them. **1879** E. ARNOLD *Lt. Asia* VIII. (1881) 228 Let each act Assoil a fault or help a merit grow.

†9. To acquit oneself of, or discharge (an obligation). (From 3.) *Obs. rare.*
1596 SPENSER *Daphn.* lxxvii, Till that you come where ye your vowes assoyle.

†10. To discharge, get rid of, dispel (a thing). (From 5.) *Obs. rare.*
1596 SPENSER *F.Q.* IV. v. 30 In seeking him that should her payn assoyle. *Ibid.* III. i. 58 She soundly slept, and carefull thoughts did quite assoile.

¶ *Catachr.* for SOIL, *sully.*
1845 DISRAELI *Sybil* 290 Is it that the world has assoiled my soul? Yet I have not tasted of worldly joys.

†**a'ssoil**, *sb. Obs. rare.* [f. prec. vb.] Solution, explanation.
1589 PUTTENHAM *Eng. Poesie* (Arb.) 198 By way of riddle (Enigma) of which the sence can hardly be picked out, but by the parties owne assoile.

a'ssoiler (ə'sɔɪlə(r)). [subst. use of AF. *assoiler* to ASSOIL.] Absolving (from excommunication).
1813 *Ann. Reg.* 279/2 Sir Samuel Romilly..stated that he had applied for a writ of assoiler on account of the plaintiff. [Cf. **1553** FITZHERB. *Nat. Brev.* 63 b, Leuesque ad maunde ses lettres de assoiler le partie.]

†**assoiling** (ə'sɔɪlɪŋ), *vbl. sb. Obs.* [f. ASSOIL *v.* + -ING[1].]

1. The action of absolving, absolution.
c **1380** WYCLIF *De Eccl.* iii. Sel. Wks. 1871 III. 345 Many heresies, as of assoilingis and indulgencis, and cursingis, wiþ feyned pardons. **1387** TREVISA *Higden* Rolls Ser. V. 415 Monkes myȝte use þe offys of assoillynge [L. *absolvendi*]. **1642** JER. TAYLOR *Episc.* (1647) 317 The publike assoyling of penitents.

2. The resolving of a difficulty, solution.
1619 FAVOUR *Antiquitie* 72 For the triall of all controversies, and assoyling all doubts. **1678** CUDWORTH *Intell. Syst.* 209 For the assoilling of which Difficulty (seeming so formidable at first sight).

3. The refutation or answering of an objection.
1382 WYCLIF *Wisd.* viii. 8 The soilingis [*v.r.* asoilyngis] of argumentis. *c* **1449** PECOCK *Repr.* II. xi. 208 For answere and assoiling to the firste argument. *a* **1679** T. GOODWIN *Wks.* (1863) VII. 406 Assoiling or answer to one of the greatest difficulties or objections.

assoilment (ə'sɔɪlmənt). [f. ASSOIL *v.* + -MENT; perh. a. AF. **assoillement*.]

1. The action or condition of absolution from sin, guilt, censure, or accusation.
1611 SPEED *Hist. Gt. Brit.* IX. viii. 51 They did absolue him; but..this assoilement was not so much the Epilogue of his olde, as the Prologue of his new Tragicall vexations. **1664** H. MORE *Myst. Iniq.* 12 Assoilment from guilt. *c* **1840** DE QUINCEY *Autobiog. Sk.* Wks. II. 102 To win for me..a station of purification and assoilment.

†2. Discharge, acquittal (of a duty). *Obs.*
1649 JER. TAYLOR *Gt. Exemp.* III. xvii. 73 It is a sufficient assoilment of this part of his duty.

†3. Solution of a difficulty; reconciliation of conflicting statements. *Obs.*
a **1679** T. GOODWIN *Wks.* 1863 V. 460 The second part of this assoilment or reconciliation of Haggai and Paul.

¶ *Catachr.* for: Soil, defilement.
1876 FARRAR *Marlb. Serm.* xxv. 249 He will cleanse from your repentant souls this daily assoilment of unwilling sin.

assoilzie, Scotch form of ASSOIL *v.*

†**a'ssoin(e**, *sb. Obs.* Also 3 **asoyne, assoyne**, 4 *Sc.* **assonȝe**. [Variant of ESSOIN, a. OF. *essoigne, essoine*: see A- *pref.* 10, AS- *pref.*[2]] An excuse; a legal excuse put in for non-appearance.
1297 R. GLOUC. 539 Giffardes asoyne. *a* **1300** *Cursor M.* 2266 Þat schending is wit-outen soyne [*v.r.* soygne, *Trin. MS.* assoyne]. *c* **1300** *K. Alis.* 6051 Thider com withowten assoyne, Two quenes of Amazoyne. *c* **1375** ? BARBOUR *St. Thomas* 52 Þat al..Suld but assonȝe cume to þat feste.

†**a'ssoin(e**, *v. Obs.* Forms: 3 **asunien, asonien**, 3–5 **asoyne**, 4 **assoyne, assoine**, 4–6 *Sc.* **assonȝe, -zie, yie**, 7 **assoygne**. [variant of ESSOIN *v.*, a. OF. *essoigner*: see prec.]

1. *trans.* To excuse; to offer or put in an excuse for non-appearance of.
c **1230** *Ancr. R.* 64 Uor swuch hit mei beon þat ȝe schulen asunien [*v.r.* aseinen, asonien] ou. *c* **1330** *Florice & Bl.* 67 Ne scholde no weder me assoine. *c* **1380** WYCLIF *Sel. Wks.* (1871) 440 Worldliche excusasioun shal not þenne assoyne. **1513** DOUGLAS *Æneis* XIII. Prol. 133 How think we he assonzeis [*v.r.* essonȝies] him to astart. **1646** GAULE *Cases Consc.* 65 Such as are absent, and have no care to be assoygned.

2. *intr.* To excuse oneself, decline, refuse.
c **1440** *Promp. Parv.* 15 Assoynynge or refusynge. *c* **1470** HENRY *Wallace* x. 365 With gret inwy to Wallace fast he raid; And he till him assonyeit nocht for thi.

assommon: see ASSUMMON *v. Obs.* to summon.

assonance ('æsənəns). [a. F. *assonance* (cf. Sp. *asonancia*), as if ad. L. **assonāntia*, f. *assonāre* to sound to, respond to, f. *as-* = *ad-* to + *sonāre* to sound.]

1. Resemblance or correspondence of sound between two words or syllables.
1727 CHAMBERS *Cycl.* s.v., Assonance..where the words of a phrase, or a verse, have the same sound or termination, and yet make no proper rhyme. **1855** MILMAN *Lat. Chr.* (1864) IX. XIV. vii. 222 The numerals are so nearly akin that there would be a close assonance if not identity in the words. **1870** LOWELL *Study Wind.* 327 Homer..seems fond of playing with assonances. **1879** FARRAR *St. Paul* I. 623 Incessant assonances and balances of clauses and expressions.

2. a. *Pros.* The correspondence or riming of one word with another in the accented vowel and those which follow, but not in the consonants, as used in the versification of Old French, Spanish, Celtic, and other languages.
1823 T. ROSCOE *Sismondi's Lit. Eur.* (1846) I. iii. 85 Assonance or the rhyming of the terminating vowels. **1837** HALLAM *Hist. Lit.* I. ii. 165 In their lighter poetry the Spaniards frequently contented themselves with assonances ..as *duro* and *humo, boca* and *cosa*. **1861** MARCH *Eng. Lang.* (1862) 403 The rule of assonance..requires the repetition of the same vowels in the assonant words, from the last accented vowel inclusive. Thus *man* and *hat, nation* and *traitor, penitent* and *reticence*, are assonant couples of words. **1879** H. NICOL in *Encycl. Brit.* IX. 633 In the Roland such assonances occur.

b. In extended use: = *half-rhyme*; the correspondence or rhyming of one word with another in the final (sometimes also the initial) consonant, but not in the vowel. Also applied by philologists, in studying rhyming pairs of words (i.e. with identical vowel), to final consonants of such similarity of articulation as to be acceptable, with poetic licence, in a rhyming position.
1917 R. GRAVES *Let. c.* 22 Dec. in W. Owen *Lett.* (1967) 595 You [*sc.* Wilfred Owen] have found a new method and must work it yourself—those assonances instead of rhymes are fine. **1920** E. BLUNDEN in *Athenæum* 10 Dec. 807/1 The discovery of final assonances in place of rhyme may mark a new age in poetry. **1934** C. DAY LEWIS *Hope for Poetry* iii. 17 His [*sc.* Wilfred Owen's] one innovation is the constant use of the alliterative assonance as an end rhyme—(mystery, mastery; killed, cold). *Ibid.* x. 72 Owen's alliterative assonance. **1948** G. L. BROOK *Harley Lyrics* 20 Assonance sometimes takes the place of rhyme; the most frequent examples are of *m* : *n* and *ng* : *nd* (e.g. *tyme* : *pyne*). **1960** E. G. STANLEY *Owl & Nightingale* 112 An example..of assonance on dentals. **1960** D. S. R. WELLAND *Wilfred Owen* vi. 116 Not only in its use of the 'mean/moan/men' assonance does this passage anticipate 'Insensibility'.

3. A word or syllable answering to another in sound.
1882 FARRAR *Early Chr.* I. 491 Clopas or Chalpai is a Hebrew name, of which Alphæus is the current assonance.

4. *transf.* Correspondence more or less incomplete.
1868 J. STIRLING in *N. Brit. Rev.* XLIX. 387 With an assonance to reality everywhere. **1876** LOWELL *Among my Bks.* Ser. II. 41 Assonance between facts seemingly remote.

'**assonancy.** ? *Obs.* [ad. Sp. *asonancia*: see prec.] = ASSONANCE 1.
1770 BARRETTI *Lond. to Genoa* III. 272 Their poets search studiously after such assonancies and scatter them often in the scenes of their dramas.

assonant ('æsənənt), *a.* and *sb.* [a. F. *assonant*, or Sp. *asonante*, ad. L. *assonānt-em*, pr. pple. of *assonāre*: see prec.]

A. *adj.* Corresponding in vowel-sound; characterized by assonance.

1727–51 CHAMBERS *Cycl.*, *Assonant Rhymes*..a kind of verses common among the Spaniards. **1845** R. FORD *Handbk. Trav. Spain* i. 191 *Amor* and *razon* are assonants. **1861** [see ASSONANCE 2]. **1864** SKEAT *Uhland's Poems* Pref., Such words as *famous*, *sailor*, *neighbour*, etc., may be used as assonant.

B. *sb.* [sc. word.]

1834 *Penny Cycl.* II. 510/1 In English, *hardy*, *manly*, and *carry*, would be assonants. **1862** *Guardian* 5 Feb. 136/2 *Enchantments*, *morasses*, *vastness*, and *unstable* are English assonants, as all containing an accented *a*, followed by an unaccented *e*. **1904** BRANDIN & HARTOG *Bk. Fr. Pros.* I. iv. 47 *Bergère* and *pimprenelle* are assonants..the 'Symbolistes' have reintroduced assonance into poetry.

assonantal (æsə'næntəl), *a.* [f. ASSONANT *a.* and *sb.* + -AL[1].] Of or pertaining to assonance.

1852 *Fraser's Mag.* XLV. 651 Assonantal rhymes..are of not unfrequent occurrence. **1881** *Blackw. Mag.* Apr. 482 *note*, The assonantal rhythm which satisfies Spanish ears. **1925** D. CORKERY *Hidden Ireland* vii. 179 They had, perforce, to use the simpler assonantal metres. **1938** R. GRAVES *Coll. Poems* p. xv, Internal assonantal rhyme (*heather*, *wither*).

asso'nantic, *a.* [irreg. f. as prec. + -IC.] = prec.

1881 LD. LYTTON in *19th Cent.* Nov. 782 An assonantic theory which commends itself to the ear of the poet.

assonate ('æsəneɪt), *v.* [f. L. *assonāt-* ppl. stem of *assonāre*: see ASSONANCE and -ATE.] To correspond in sound, *esp.* in vowel-sound; to rime in assonance.

[**1623** COCKERAM, *Assonate*, to sound or ring like a bell.] **1656** BLOUNT *Glossogr.*, *Assonate*, to sound together, to answer by sound. **1879** H. NICOL in *Encycl. Brit.* IX. 633 The accented vowels being those which rhyme or assonate. **1880** —— in *Academy* 24 July 57/3 Such a metre..is assonating heroic verse. **1952** R. CAMPBELL *Lorca* 40 We could assonate the word 'filbert' with it [*sc.* 'winter']. **1966** BENNETT & SMITHERS *Early ME. Verse & Prose* 291, [rð] and [rd] do not commonly assonate in ME texts.

assonȝe, var. ASSOIN(E *sb.* and *v. Obs.*

as 'soon, a'ssoon, *advb. phr.* Forms: 3–4 als son(e, 4–5 also sone, alsone, 5 asoune, 5–7 assoone. The two words *as soon* were commonly written as one from 15th to 18th c., both with, and without, following *as*; cf. Fr. *aussitôt(que*. See other instances under ALSOON.

?**1475** *Plumpton Corr.* 30 Asoune as they may be gotten. **1485** CAXTON *Paris & V.* 13 Assone as they myght. **1581** SIDNEY *Def. Poesie* (1622) 510 Assoone as he might see those beasts well painted. **1760** T. HUTCHINSON *Hist. Col. Mass. Bay* i. (1765) 58 Assoon as they knew the terms.

Beside the obvious sense (see AS A 3–5, and SOON), *assoon* had also the meaning: As soon as might be, immediately, forthwith. (Fr. *aussitôt*.)

a **1300** *Cursor M.* 339 He..said wit[h] word, and als son [*later* als sone, also soone] All his comament was don. **1340** HAMPOLE *Pr. Consc.* 4102 þus sal ende þe dignité of Rome; And als sone aftir sal anticrist come. *c* **1420** *Sir Amadace* lvii. (1842) 50 Alsone his lord he metes. **1585** JAMES I *Ess. Poesie* (Arb.) 23 He stays assone, and in his mynde doeth cast, What way to take.

†**a'ssopiate**, *v. Obs. rare.* [irreg. f. F. *assopir* (Cotgr.), mod. *assoupir*, or It. *assopire*, f. L. *as-* = *ad-* to + *sopīre* to lull asleep: see -ATE[3].] To lull, calm, assuage, lay at rest, put an end to.

a **1649** *Scotch Acts Chas. I* (1814) V. 667 (JAM.) Not intended as ane justificatione of the band, for..all of that kynd wes already assop[i]at. **1684** J. MORISON *Struys' Voy.* 66 The Captain gave me fair words, and assopiated the Quarrel between Me and Myself.

assort (ə'sɔːt), *v.* [a. OF. *assorter* (mod. *assortir*), f. *à* to + *sorte* SORT, kind; cf. It. *assortare* (Florio), *-ire*.]

1. *trans.* To distribute (things, *rarely* persons) into groups, as being of like nature or intended for the same purpose; to arrange in sorts, classify.

1490 CAXTON *Eneydos* xv. 54 And chose theym one from the other for to assorte theym. **1611** COTGR., *Assortir*, To sort, assort..order severall things handsomely; also, to furnish, or store with all sorts of. **1774** BURKE *Sp. Amer. Taxation* Wks. II. 420 The colleagues whom he had assorted at the same boards. **1803** MISS PORTER *Thaddeus* xiv. (1831) 128 Assorting some parcels on the counter.

2. *trans.* To class, place (a thing or person) in the same group *with* others.

1833 I. TAYLOR *Fanat.* v. 89 The companions with whom we found ourselves assorted. **1861** DICKENS *Gt. Expect.* I. 259 He would..assort it with the fabulous dogs and veal-cutlets as a monstrous invention.

3. *intr.* To fall into a class, take one's place fitly; to be of a sort, match, suit *well* or *ill with*.

1800 W. TAYLOR in *Month. Mag.* X. 424 His *Muse* assorts ill with the personages of Christian mythology. **1837** SIR W. HAMILTON *Metaph.* xxxvii. (1870) II. 335 Finding that it is harmonious,—that it dovetails and naturally assorts with other parts.

4. *intr.* To consort, keep company, associate *with*.

1823 LAMB *Elia* Ser. II. vii. (1865) 284, I could abide to assort with fisher-swains. **1861** PYCROFT *Agony Point* vii. (1862) 81 She assorted with those of an age at which, etc.

5. *trans.* To furnish with an assortment.

[Cf. **1611** in 1.] *a* **1797** BURKE (T.) The well-assorted warehouses of dissenting congregations. *Mod.* We have sent orders for some white goods to assort our store.

assortative (ə'sɔːtətɪv), *a.* [f. ASSORT *v.* + -ATIVE.] That assorts; ***assortative mating***, non-random mating, mating on the basis of the possession by the partners of similar characteristics, circumstances, etc.

1897 K. PEARSON in *Phil. Trans. R. Soc.* 1896 A. CLXXXVII. 258 Preference of individuals with an organ or characteristic of given size for mates with the same or another organ or characteristic of a size, the average of which differs from the..population average. This type of sexual selection which may be spoken of as assortative mating is measured mathematically by the coefficient of correlation between the two organs or characteristics in mated pairs. **1902** *Encycl. Brit.* XXXIII. 637/1 Assortative mating exists when individuals which mate are not paired at random, but a definite correlation is established between the characters of one mate and those of the other. **1955** *New Biol.* XVIII. 37 In a few animal species negative assortative mating, that is to say a tendency of like to mate with unlike, has been observed. Positive assortative mating occurs in flowering plants which are fertilized by insects.

†**a'ssorte**, *sb. Obs. rare*[−1]. [f. ASSORT *v.* or its F. original.] A company, group.

c **1400** *Sowdone Bab.* 1997 Sitte down here by one assorte.

assorted (ə'sɔːtɪd), *ppl. a.* [f. prec. + -ED.] Arranged in sorts, classified; matched, suited, fitted; furnished with all sorts. Also, comprising various sorts.

a **1797** BURKE (T.) No way assorted to those with whom they must associate. [See ASSORT 4.] **1814** SOUTHEY *Roderick* II. Wks. IX. 14 In wedlock to an ill-assorted mate. **1844** MACREADY *Remin.* II. 240 Put by my assorted papers. **1897** G. B. SHAW *Theatres in Nineties* (1932) III. 246 Dickens..made desperate efforts to take his assorted heroines quite seriously by resolutely turning off the fun. **1937** D. L. SAYERS *Busman's Honeymoon* xv. 302 'Will you have some of these little biscuits? Dear me, what a remarkable variety!'.. 'They come assorted in boxes.'

a'ssortedness. [f. prec. + -NESS.] The condition of being (well or ill) assorted or matched.

1859 G. MEREDITH *R. Feverel* I. iv. 55 An outraged future bearing with it a life-long ill-assortedness.

a'ssorter. *U.S.* [f. ASSORT *v.* + -ER[1].] One who assorts.

1897 *Scribner's Mag.* Jan 17/2 The assorter, who distributes the bundles [of goods] into lots to go to the different parts of the city. **1915** W. HOLT *Beacon for Blind* vii. 70 He was anxious to bring deaf and dumb assorters into the Post Office.

assorting (ə'sɔːtɪŋ), *vbl. sb.* [f. ASSORT *v.* + -ING[1].] Assortment; the supplying of the sorts of which there is a deficiency.

1883 *Daily News* 22 Oct. 7/1 The new orders are only small, and for assorting-up purposes.

assortment (ə'sɔːtmənt). [f. ASSORT *v.* + -MENT; cf. F. *assortiment*, It. *assortimento*.]

1. The action of assorting; assorted condition; arrangement or classification into classes or kinds.

1611 COTGR., *Proprieté*..a handsome or comelie assortment. **1714** R. JOHNSON *Noctes Nottingh.* 8 (T.) Of better direction for the assortment and certainty of structure. **1765** TUCKER *Lt. Nat.* II. 652 If a certain lucky assortment of corpuscles could produce me into being. **1866** HOWELLS *Venet. Life* (1883) I. iv. 72 The absence of quantity and assortment in his wares. *Mod.* She was engaged in the assortment of her crewels.

2. A group of things of the same sort; a class formed by assorting. *spec.* in *Forestry* (see quots.). Also *attrib.*

1759 ADAM SMITH *Format. Lang.* in *Mor. Sent.* (1797) II. 407 Those classes and assortments, which, in the schools, are called genera and species. **1774** BURKE *Sp. Amer. Taxation* Wks. II. 431 In such heterogeneous assortments, the most innocent person will lose the effect of his innocency. **1896** W. R. FISHER *Schlich's Man. Forestry* V. I. v. 248 The various pieces into which a tree may be converted by the woodcutter are termed rough assortments of timber. **1953** *Brit. Commonw. Forest Terminol.* I. 13 *Assortment table*, a volume table in which the volumes are differentiated according to size classes or other criteria affecting utilization.

3. An assorted set, whether of different varieties of the same thing (as 'an assortment of silks') or of various things (as 'an assortment of goods'); a variety of sorts adapted to various requirements.

1791 HAMILTON *Berthollet's Dyeing* II. II. 357 To produce an assortment of shades. **1823** LAMB *Elia* (1860) 416 Having by us a tolerable assortment of these gift-horses. **1823** F. COOPER *Pioneer* viii. (1869) 36/2 Enough to furnish, in the language of the country, as assortment for a store. **1869** J. MARTINEAU *Ess.* II. 60 Such as the sample is, will the entire assortment be.

†**a'ssot**, *v. Obs.* Forms: 2 asottie, 4 asote, 4–5 assote, 6–8 assot. [a. OF. *a(s)soter*, f. *à* to + *sot* fool, SOT.]

1. *intr.* To become or act like a fool; to become infatuated, foolishly fond, madly in love.

c **1175** *Lamb. Hom.* 17 Gif þu hine iseȝe þet he wulle asottie to þes deofles hond. **1393** GOWER *Conf.* III. 235 That he ne assote To chaunge for the womanhed The worthinesse of his manhed. *Ibid.* 281 Eke I not for what emprise I shulde assote upon a nonne.

2. *trans.* To make a fool of, infatuate, befool.

1393 GOWER *Conf.* III. 237 Thilke firy rage Of love, which the men assoteth. **1583** STUBBES *Anat. Abus.* 110 See how drunkenesse assotteth a man. *a* **1626** BP. ANDREWES *Serm.* (1856) I. 348 They assot themselves, they will not conceive aright of their estates. ?**1741** *Squire of Dames* xxvii. in Dodsl. *Poems* (1770) IV. 130 As couthful fishers at the benty brook, By various arts assot the seely fry.

3. in *pa. pple.* **assotted.** Infatuated.

c **1380** *Sir Ferumb.* 2007 þow ert a-sotid. **1393** GOWER *Conf.* III. 270 The riche..Assoted were upon her love. **1474** CAXTON *Chesse* 114 Loth..was assoted by moche drynkynge of wyn. **1525** LD. BERNERS *Froiss.* II. ccxxxvii. (ccxxxiii) 736 The kynge was so asotted on this syr Hugh Spenser. **1610** GWILLIM *Heraldry* III. xvii. (1660) 209 So much were the Israëlites assotted in Idolatry.

†**a'ssote**, *a. Obs.* Also 6 assott. [(3 syllables in Gower) ? a. OF. *a(s)soté*, pa. pple. of *assoter* (see prec.); or short for *assotted*.]

1393 GOWER *Conf.* I. 235 She made Hercules so nice Upon her love, and so assote. **1579** SPENSER *Sheph. Cal.* Mar. 25 Willye, I wene thou bee assott.

assouerit, obs. Sc. form of ASSURED *ppl. a.*

assowe, var. ASWOUGH *adv. Obs.* a-swoon.

assuade (ə'sweɪd), *v.* ? *Obs. rare.* [f. AS- *pref.*[1] + L. *suadēre* to advise.] *trans.* To present as advice, to urge persuasively.

1806 W. TAYLOR in *Ann. Rev.* IV. 240 A chance of assuading his own better judgment on the multitude.

assuage (ə'sweɪdʒ), *v.* Forms: 3–7 **aswage**, 4–5 **asuage**, 5–8 **asswage**, 4– **assuage**. *Aphet.* 5–7 **swage**: see SUAGE. [a. OF. *a(s)souage-r*, *-agier*, Pr. *a(s)suaviar*, f. L. type **assuāviāre*, f. *ad* to + *suāvis* sweet, agreeable. Cf. *abridge*, *aggrege*, *allege* (L. *abbreviāre*, *aggraviāre*, *alleviāre*).]

I. *trans.*

1. To soften, mitigate, calm, appease, allay (angry or excited feelings).

1330 R. BRUNNE *Chron.* 300 His wrath forto asuage. *c* **1420** *Pallad. on Husb.* IV. 883 But yf he bite hir in his rage, Let labouryng him his melancoly swage. **1513** MORE *Rich. III*, Wks. 35/2 The displeasure of those that bare him grudge..was well asswaged. **1642** ROGERS *Naaman* 32 God hath asswaged his pride, and tamed him. **1777** WATSON *Philip II* (1793) II. XIV. 229 They omitted nothing in their power to assuage his resentment. **1857** BUCKLE *Civiliz.* viii. 500 That secular spirit which, in every country, has assuaged religious animosities.

2. To pacify, appease, calm (the excited person).

c **1325** *E.E. Allit. P.* C. 3 When heuy herttes ben hurt wyth heþyng..Suffraunce may aswagen hem. **1596** SPENSER *F.Q.* v. ii. 47 But Artegall him fairely gan asswage. **1598** FLORIO, *Propitiare*..to asswage God with sacrifice. **1706** ADDISON *Rosamond* II. vi, Kindling pity, kindling rage At once provoke me, and asswage. **1763** SIR W. JONES *Caissa* Poems (1777) 33 So may thy prayers assuage the scornful dame. **1858** HAWTHORNE *Fr. & It. Jrnls.* I. 295, I shall..assuage and mollify myself a little after that uncongenial life of the consulate.

†3. To relax, modify, moderate (a harsh law, etc.).

c **1300** *Beket* 1454 That the King wolde..aswagi the lithere lawes. **1483** CAXTON *Gold. Leg.* 287/1, I pray the..that thou asuage uppon hym the sentence of dampnacion.

4. To mitigate, alleviate, soothe, relieve (physical or mental pain); to lessen the violence of (disease).

1393 GOWER *Conf.* I. 267 That shulde assuage The leper. *c* **1400** *Rom. Rose* 2815 Thus Swete-Thenkyng shalle aswage The peyne of lovers. **1561** T. N[ORTON] *Calvin's Inst.* III. 206 Then were there ministred other plaisters to asswage such peines. **1605** BACON *Adv. Learn* II. xxii. §1 They need medicine..to assuage the disease. **1725** POPE *Odyss.* II. 29 The rest with duteous love his griefs asswage. **1868** MILMAN *St. Paul's* xix. 481 Perhaps no man has assuaged so much human misery as John Howard.

5. To appease, satisfy (appetites, desires).

c **1430** LYDG. *Venus-Mass* in *Lay Folk's Mass-Bk.* 394 Water or wyne..asswage the grete dryhnesse of ther gredy thruste. **1697** DRYDEN *Virg. Georg.* II. 791 The good old God his Hunger did asswage With Roots and Herbs. **1812** COMBE (Dr. Syntax) *Picturesque* x. 57 His thirst assuage With tea that's made of balm or sage. **1856** MRS. STOWE *Dred* II. xxvii. 278 So the fearful craving of his soul for justice was assuaged.

6. *gen.* To abate, lessen, diminish (*esp.* anything swollen). *arch.* or *Obs.*

c **1430** LYDG. *Min. Poems* 64 His olde gyltis bothe to asoft and swage. **1494** FABYAN VII. ccxxxvi. 273 Short of body, and therwith fatte; the whiche to aswage he toke ye lesse of metis. *c* **1525** SKELTON *El. Rummyng* 10 For her visage It would aswage A mannes courage. **1667** PEPYS *Diary* 20, 21 Dec., My poor wife is in mighty pain, and her face miserably swelled..My wife is a little better, and her cheek asswaged. **1774** J. BRYANT *Mythol.* II. 284 The Dove..brought the first tidings that the waters of the deep were aswaged.

II. *intr.*

†7. Of passion, pain, appetite, etc. (from senses 1, 2, 4, 5): To become less violent, to abate. *Obs.*
1330 R. BRUNNE *Chron.* 78 Of his crueltes he gynnes forto assuage. *c* **1386** CHAUCER *Merch. T.* 838 His sorwe gan aswage. **1509** HAWES *Past. Pleas.* XVIII. xvi, The great payne of love May not aswage tyl death it remove. **1607** TOPSELL *Four-f. Beasts* 57 Their lust asswageth till another time. **1722** DE FOE *Plague* 191 The plague being come to a crisis, its fury began to assuage.

8. *gen.* To grow less, diminish, decrease, fall off, die away; to abate, subside. *arch.* or *Obs.*
c **1430** *Hymns to Virg.* (1867) 79 Take hede..How fast ȝoure ȝouþe dooþ asswage. **1523** LD. BERNERS *Froiss.* I. xxviii. 42 Kyng Phylippes enterprise of yᵉ sayd Croysey beganne to asswage and waxe cold. **1611** BIBLE *Gen.* viii. 1 And the waters asswaged. **1677** MOXON *Mech. Exerc.* 242 The Fire in Lime burnt, Asswages not, but lies hid. **1858** MOTLEY *Dutch Rep.* Introd. v. 17 As the deluge assuaged.

†**aˈssuage**, *sb. Obs. rare*⁻¹. [f. prec.] = next.
1596 FITZ-GEFFREY *Sir F. Drake* (1881) 15 His griefe, impatient of asswage.

assuagement (əˈsweɪdʒmənt). Also 6 aswage-, 6–7 asswage-. [a. OF. *a(s)souagement*: see ASSUAGE *v.* and -MENT.]
1. The action of assuaging; the condition of being assuaged; mitigation, alleviation, relief, abatement.
1561 T. N[ORTON] *Calvin's Inst.* III. 213 Yᵉ faithfull haue aswagement of their sorrowe, in considering the purpose of god. **1638** BAKER *Lett. Balzac* (1654) IV. 52 To read there the continuation of your sickness, could not..be any asswagement of mine. **1871** BROWNING *Balaust.* 555 And for assuagement of these evils—nought!
2. An assuaging medicine or application, a lenitive, sedative, alleviative.
1599 A. M. *Gabelhouer's Bk. Physic* 255/1 [Recipe for] An assuagement for the Face. **1833** I. TAYLOR *Fanat.* v. 116 Assuagements of the dread which the belief in purgatory inspired. **1858** CARLYLE *Fredk. Gt.* I. II. vi. 78 Medicinal assuagements, from the Lübeck ship-stores.

assuager (əˈsweɪdʒə(r)). In 6–7 assw-. [f. ASSUAGE *v.* + -ER¹.] He who, or that which, assuages.
1564 BAULDWIN *Mor. Philos.* (Palfr.) iii. (1595) 4 An asswager of wrong ought greatly to be honoured. **1605** TIMME *Quersit.* I. xiii. 53 Red ocre..is an asswager of things ..and a great mittigator of all griefes and paines.

assuaging (əˈsweɪdʒɪŋ), *vbl. sb.* [f. as prec. + -ING¹.] Assuagement.
1580 HOLLYBAND *Treas. Fr. Tong.*, *Addoulcissement*, an assuaging, an appeasing. **1824** SCOTT *St. Ronan's* iii, Many other acts of moderating authority they performed, much to the assuaging of faction.

aˈssuaging, *ppl. a.* [f. as prec. + -ING².] **a.** Giving relief or mitigation. **b.** Abating, subsiding.
1651 E. PRESTWICH *Hippol.* 89 Th' asswaging waters left behind The Earth with slime and rubbish clad. **1801** SOUTHEY *Thalaba* I. vii, She had not wept till that assuaging prayer. **1879** GEO. ELIOT *Theo. Such* ii. 36 To raise the assuaging reflection.

assuasive (əˈsweɪsɪv), *a.* and *sb.* ? *Obs.* [f. AS- *pref.*¹ + *-suasive*, as in *persuasive* (cf. ASSUADE); but confused in sense with ASSUAGE.]
A. *adj.* Soothingly persuasive; soothing.
1708 POPE *St. Cecilia* 25 Music her soft assuasive voice applies. *a* **1762** LADY MONTAGUE *Poems* (1785) 63 There blend your cares with soft assuasive arts There sooth the passions, there unfold your hearts. **1791** COWPER *Iliad* XV. 485 Sprinkling with drugs assuasive of his pains. **1854** DICKENS *Hard Times* III. iii. 282 His so quiet and assuasive father-in-law.
B. *sb.* A soothing medicine or application.
1829 *Jrnl. Naturalist* 77 The lenient assuasives of our forefathers seeming unequal to contention with the constitutions of these days.

†**assubˈject**, *v. Obs.* [a. F. *assubjectir* (16th c.), mod. *assujétir*, *-jettir*, f. *as-* = *à* to + *subject* (mod. *sujet*) SUBJECT.] To subdue, reduce to subjection.
1579 FENTON *Guicciard.* (1618) 142 An earnest desire to assubiect it to himselfe. **1656** EARL MONM. *Advt. fr. Parnass.* 125 People newly assubjected, easily rebel, if they be forced to change their religion.

assubjugate (əˈsʌbdʒ(j)ʊgeɪt), *v.* [f. *as-* = A- *pref.* 11 + SUBJUGATE.] To reduce to subjugation.
1606 SHAKS. *Tr. & Cr.* II. iii. 202 No, this thrice worthy and right valiant Lord Must not..assubiugate his merit.. By going to Achilles. **1883** F. M. CRAWFORD *Dr. Claudius* 239 Which not only disarmed resistance, but assubjugated the consent of the advised.

†**aˈssubtile**, *v. Obs. rare*⁻¹. [a. OF. *assubtiller*, *-ier*, refash. form of *assoutiller*, *-ier*, cogn. with It. *assottigliare*, f. Latin type **adsubtīliāre*, f. *ad-* to + *subtīlis* SUBTLE.] To subtilize.
1589 PUTTENHAM *Eng. Poesie* I. iii. (Arb.) 23 Much abstinence..assubtiling and refining their spirits.

†**assubˈtiliate**, *v. Obs.* [f. OF. *assubtilli-er* (see prec.) + -ATE³.] To subtilize, refine, rarify.
1548 VICARY *Prof. Treat.* or *Englishm. Treas.* (1641) 72 Our Quintessence doth assubtiliate the Blood. **1582** HESTER *Phiorav. Secr.* I. xxxviii. 45 The second operation..[in gout] is to assubtiliate the grosse and rotten humors.

as-ˈsuchness. [f. *as such* (SUCH 38 c) + -NESS.] Absolute existence or possession of qualities, independently of all other things whatever; the character of a thing when viewed as it is in itself, regardless of anything else.
1909 W. JAMES *Pluralistic Universe* ii. 47 It [*sc.* Bradley's Absolute] is us, and all other appearances, but none of us *as such*, for in it we are all 'transmuted', and its own as-suchness is of another denomination altogether. **1962** *Times Lit. Suppl.* 4 May 311/3 Mr. Middleton..has a beautiful love and respect also just for the as-suchness of things: the sniffing man in the restaurant.

†**assueˈfaction.** [(? a. F. *assuefaction* in Cotgr.), ad. L. **assuēfactiōnem*, n. of action f. *assuēfacĕre* to make accustomed, f. *assuētus* (see next) + *facĕre* to make.] The action or process of accustoming; the fact of becoming, or state of being, accustomed or used to a thing; use, habituation.
1644 DIGBY *Nat. Bodies* xxxviii. §6 The Antipathy of Beasts towards one another may be taken away by assuefaction. **1661** EVELYN *Fumifug.* Misc. Writ. (1805) I. 223 Such as by assuefaction have made the rankest poysons their most familiar diet. **1682** SIR T. BROWNE *Chr. Morals* (1756) 99 Forget not how assuefaction unto anything minorates the passion from it.

†**aˈssuete**, *a. Obs.*⁻⁰ [ad. L. *assuētus*, pa. pple. of *assuēscĕre*, f. *as-* = *ad-* to + *suēscĕre* to accustom.] 'Accustomed, practised, enured, exercised by long continuance.' Blount *Glossogr.* 1656.

ˈassuetude. [ad. L. *assuētūdo*: see prec. and -TUDE.] Accustomedness.
1626 BACON *Sylva* §67 Assuetude of things hurtful, doth make them lose their force to hurt. **1830** MARRYAT *King's Own*, xxxvi, To whose..beauty, from assuetude, he had.. been blind. **1873** *Contemp. Rev.* XXII. 699 The petrified assuetudes and porcelain effeminacies of the Chinese. **1890** *Daily News* 15 Nov. 5/6 At the same time..the effect of assuetude may become apparent.

†**aˈssuffer**, *v. Obs. rare*⁻¹. [? f. A- *pref.* 11 + SUFFER *v.*] To suffer, allow.
c **1425** WYNTOUN *Cron.* VII. ix. 589 And fourty dayis assuffryd ware þai þame for þat passage to purway.

assumable (əˈsjuːməb(ə)l), *a.* [f. ASSUME *v* + -ABLE.] That may be assumed.
1784 FRANKLIN in *Ann. Reg.* (1817) 383/2 Others object to the title as not properly assumable by any but General Washington. **1854** HOOKER *Himal. Jrnls.* I. xiii. 309 It is further assumable.

aˈssumably, *adv.* [f. prec. + -LY².] As may be assumed or taken for granted, presumably.
1883 *Athenæum* 12 May 613/2 It is also, assumably, indebted to the rendering of Madame Sarah Bernhardt. *Ibid.* 20 Oct. 505/3 Sufferings which will assumably unfit him for future happiness.

assume (əˈsjuːm), *v.* [ad. L. *as-*, *ad-sūmĕre* to take to oneself, adopt, usurp, f. *ad* to + *sūmĕre* to take. In 15–16th c. the pa. pple. was ASSUMPT.]
I. To take unto (oneself), receive, accept, adopt.
1. *trans.* To take to be with one, to receive into association, to adopt into partnership, employment, service, use; to adopt, take.
1581 SAVILE *Tacitus' Agric.* (1622) 186 Into whose train being assumed hee was..well liked. **1607** *Schol. Disc. agst. Antichr.* I. i. 44 Paule forbiddeth to assume the weake to the controuersies of disputation. **1641** THORNDIKE *Prim. Govt. Ch.* 113 [He] assumed S. Augustine to assist him. **1674** PLAYFORD *Skill of Mus.* III. 29 The lowest note of that fifth assume for your Key. **1861** TRENCH *Sev. Ch. Asia* 94 Revealed religion assumes them into her service. **1868** *Perthsh. Jrnl.* 18 June, Mr. Mark..has been assumed as a Partner in the Edinburgh Branch of the Business.
b. *esp.* To receive up into heaven. (The earliest use in Eng.; cf. ASSUMPTION 1, 1 b). *arch.* or *Obs.*
1436 *Pol. Poems* (1859) II. 204 He us assume, and brynge us to the blisse. *a* **1520** *Myrr. Our Ladye* 309 Thow arte assumpte aboue all thynges, wyth Iesu thy sonne, Maria. **1600** ABP. ABBOT *Exp. Jonah* 189 As when Enoch and Elias were assumed up into heaven. **1751** CHAMBERS *Cycl.* s.v. *Assumption*, The Holy Virgin was assumed or taken into heaven.
†**c.** Of things. *rare.*
1508 FISHER *Wks.* I. 134 Whan stones be assumpte for the reedyfyenge of cytees or toures. **1695** WOODWARD *Nat. Hist. Earth* II. (1723) 85 All these [bodies] were assumed up..into the Water, and sustained in it.
†**2.** To adopt, choose, elect, to some position. (So in L.) Often with the idea of elevation; cf. ASSUMPTION 2. *Obs.*
1502 ARNOLD *Chron.* 280 He was assumpte to the state of cardynal. **1621** QUARLES *Esther* (1717) 96 Her Unkles love assum'd her for his own. **1670** G. H. tr. *Hist. Cardinals* II. III. 177 He was assum'd to the Papacy.
†**3.** To take into the body (food, nourishment, etc.). So in L.; cf. ASSUMPTION 4. *Obs.*
1620 VENNER *Via Recta* viii. 184 Afterwards vpon meats taken againe, let there be assumed a draught of..Beere. **1657** *Phys. Dict.*, *Assumed*, taken inwardly.

II. To take upon oneself, put on, undertake.
4. *trans.* To take upon oneself, put on (a garb, aspect, form, or character).
1447 BOKENHAM *Lyvys of Seyntys* 46 That be hem oure nature assumpt shul be To ye secunde persone of ye trinite. **1599** SHAKS. *Hen. V*, Prol. 6 Then should the Warlike Harry ..Assume the Port of Mars. **1659** PEARSON *Creed* (1839) 229 Thus the whole perfect and complete nature of man was assumed by the word. **1697** DRYDEN *Virg. Georg.* IV. 587 The slipp'ry God will..various Forms assume. **1780** COWPER *Progr. Err.* 582 Habits are soon assumed. **1791** HAMILTON *Berthollet's Dyeing* I. I. I. i. 4 Mercury with a larger quantity of oxygen assumes a red colour. **1860** MOTLEY *Netherl.* (1868) I. i. 5 The Netherland revolt had therefore assumed world-wide proportions.
b. To invest oneself with (an attribute).
1667 MILTON *P.L.* III. 318 Reign for ever, and assume Thy merits. **1797** GODWIN *Enquirer* I. vi. 38 Intellect assumed new courage. **1841** MYERS *Cath. Th.* IV. §11. 245 These Doctrines assume at once a reasonableness and an importance.
5. To take to oneself formally (the insignia of office or symbol of a vocation); to undertake (an office or duty).
1581 SAVILE *Tacitus* (1596) 214 Assuming the markes and ornamentes of the Roman gouernors. **1628** COKE *On Litt.* 7 b, Which title of Dominus Hiberniæ, he assumed. **1640** in Rushw. *Hist. Coll.* III. (1692) I. 44 Mr. Speaker assumed the Chair. **1786** BURKE *Art. W. Hastings* Wks. 1842 II. 156 Justified in immediately assuming the government. **1863** MRS. OLIPHANT *Sal. Ch.* i. 6 The community which he had assumed the spiritual charge of. **1869** FREEMAN *Norm. Conq.* (1876) III. xii. 180 He assumed the monastic habit.
†**b.** with *upon* and refl. pron. (Cf. 'To take upon oneself'). *Obs.*
1530 PALSGR. 439/1 To assume upon the this great charge. **1578** THYNNE *Perf. Ambass.* in *Animadv.* Introd. 60, I could not..assume such enterprize upon me. **1675** BROOKS *Gold. Key* Wks. 1867 V. 224 The curse..he assumed upon himself of his own accord.
6. (with *inf.*) in *Law.* To undertake, give an undertaking.
1602 FULBECKE *2nd Pt. Parall.* 21 That A...did assume to carrie his horse..ouer the water of Humber sound and safe. **1641** [see ASSUMPSIT]. **1795** Wyllie *Amer. Law Rep.* 74 The appellee pleaded that he did not assume.
III. To take as being one's own, to arrogate, pretend to, claim, take for granted.
7. *trans.* To take to oneself as a right or possession; to lay claim to, appropriate, arrogate, usurp.
1548 HALL *Chron. Hen. VII*, an. 1 (R.) This Lambert might assume..the person and name of one of kyng Edward the fourthes chyldren. **1627** FELTHAM *Resolves* I. vi. Wks. 1677, 7 Such..think there is no way to get Honour, but by a bold assuming it. **1715** BURNET *Own Time* (1766) I. 345 Murray assumed to himself the praise of all that was done. **1833** I. TAYLOR *Fanat.* x. 461 That disposition..to assume ..intolerant jurisdiction over other men's conduct. **1849** MACAULAY *Hist. Eng.* II. 126 The king assumed to himself the right of filling up the chief municipal offices.
8. To take to oneself in appearance only, to pretend to possess; to pretend, simulate, feign.
1602 SHAKS. *Haml.* III. iv. 160 Assume a Vertue, if you haue it not. **1790** BURKE *Fr. Rev.* 14 Ignorant both of the character they leave, and of the character they assume. **1853** LYTTON *My Novel* VI. xxiv, The scepticism, assumed or real, of the ill-fated aspirer.
9. (with *inf.*) To put forth claims or pretensions; to claim, pretend.
1714 *Spect.* No. 630 ¶16 As Gentlemen (for we Citizens assume to be such one day in a Week). **1781** GIBBON *Decl. & F.* lviii, Witnesses who had or assumed to have knowledge of the fact. **1823** LAMB *Elia* Ser. II. xxiv. (1865) 406 Sage saws assuming to inculcate content.
10. *trans.* To take for granted as the basis of argument or action; to suppose: **a.** *that* a thing is, a thing *to be*.
1598 BARCKLEY *Felic. Man* (1631) 680 Plotinus alwaies assumeth that beatitude and eternity goeth ever together. **1660** BARROW *Euclid* I. xlviii. *Schol.*, We assumed in the demonstration of the last Proposition *CD* = *BC*. **1841** MYERS *Cath. Th.* III. §25. 91 To assume that we have the most accurate possible translation. **1868** PEARD *Water-farm.* x. 103 The entire length of our farm is assumed to be about thirty-two miles.
b. a thing.
1646 SIR T. BROWNE *Pseud. Ep.* 273 His labours are rationall, and uncontroulable upon the grounds assumed. **1790** PALEY *Hor. Paul.* i. 1 Assuming the truth of the history. **1869** FREEMAN *Norm. Conq.* (1876) III. xiii. 294 William assumes the willingness of the Assembly.
11. *Logic.* To add the minor premiss to a syllogism. Cf. ASSUMPTION 12.
1628 T. SPENCER *Logic* 294 The antecedent is assumed, when the words of it are barely repeated in the second proposition, or assumption. **1655** FULLER *Ch. Hist.* IX. vi. §25 V. 86 Thus the Major may propound what it pleaseth, and the Minor assume what it listeth. **1837** SIR W. HAMILTON *Logic* xv. (1866) I. 285 The distinctive peculiarity of the minor premise,—that of being a subordinate proposition,—a proposition taken or assumed under another.

assumed (əˈsjuːmd), *ppl. a.* [f. prec. vb. + -ED.]
1. Taken to or upon oneself; appropriated; usurped.
1624 GATAKER *Transubst.* 189 Angels in assumed bodies can [not] be wounded. **1794** PALEY *Evid.* II. vi. §22 He was sitting in judgement in that assumed capacity.
2. Pretended, 'put on.'
1813 SCOTT *Rokeby* I. xiv, Assumed despondence bent his head. **1849** P. CUNNINGHAM *Handbk. Lond.* (1850) 547 Mendicants who live on assumed sores.

3. Taken for granted, adopted as a basis of reasoning.

1810 BENTHAM *Packing* (1821) 132 The assumed root ascribed to the corruption was nothing worse than casual irregularity. **1852** MCCULLOCH *Taxation* I. iv. 124 The answer to the question.. depends materially on the assumed rate of interest.

assumedly (ə'sjuːmɪdlɪ), *adv.* [f. prec. + -LY².] As is assumed or taken for granted, presumably.

1881 *Daily News* 10 Mar. 2/1 The point of order.. was assumedly designed to ascertain whether the Chairman was justified. **1882** H. NORMAN in *Fortn. Rev.*, The smaller acts of his life, assumedly the best indexes of a man's character.

† **'assument,** *sb.*¹ *Obs. rare.* [ad. L. *assūmentum*, f. *assuĕre* to sew on: see -MENT.] Something tacked on, an addition.

[**1642** JER. TAYLOR *Episc.* (1647) 177 [It].. is not found in the Greek, but is an *assumentum* for exposition of the Greek.] **1731** LEWIS *Hist. Eng. Bible* 9 (T.) This assument or addition.. he never could find anywhere but in this Anglo-Saxonick translation.

† **a'ssument,** *ppl. a.* and *sb.*² *Obs.* [ad. L. *assūment-em*, pr. pple. of *assūmĕre* to ASSUME; see -ENT.] **A.** *adj.* Assuming. *rare*⁻⁰. **B.** *sb.* One who assumes or takes.

1657 TOMLINSON *Renou's Disp.* 735 Two spoonfuls or thereabouts according to the age of the assument.

assumer (ə'sjuːmə(r)). [f. ASSUME *v.* + -ER¹.] One who assumes or takes to himself; who makes claims, pretensions, or suppositions.

1600 CHAPMAN *Iliad* XIII. 350 A lance that singled out this great assumer. **1657** TOMLINSON *Renou's Disp.* 170 They doe not commaculate the fingers of the assumer. **1875** WHITNEY *Life Lang.* x. 196 Enough to exclude the assumer from the ranks of scientific linguists.

a'ssuming, *vbl. sb.* [f. as prec. + -ING¹.]

1. The action of the vb. ASSUME; assumption.

1641 SMECTYMNUUS *Vind. Answ.* §9. 104 If this.. be onely an assuming them into the fellowship of consulting. **1857** KEBLE *Euchar. Ador.* 32 His first assuming of the title.

2. Arrogation, pretension, presumption. *arch.*

1602 B. JONSON *Poetaster* (T.) The vain assumings Of some, quite worthless of her sovereign wreaths. **1742** RICHARDSON *Pamela* IV. 132 All Assumings and Pride.. would have been grievous to me.

assuming (ə'sjuːmɪŋ), *ppl. a.* [f. as prec. + -ING².] Taking much upon oneself; taking for granted that one has a right to do so and so.

1695 *Remarks Late Serm.* (ed. 2) 25 With such assuming and reiterated Boldness. **1790** BURKE *Fr. Rev.* 40, I have seen very assuming letters, signed, Your most obedient, humble servant. **1863** LADY D. GORDON *Lett. Egypt* (1875) 284 Bill.. was thought rather assuming, because he was asked in church and lawfully married.

assumingly (ə'sjuːmɪŋlɪ), *adv.* [f. ASSUMING *ppl. a.* + -LY².] In an assuming manner, presumptuously.

1839 J. P. SMITH *Scripture & Geol.* 215 What I may, not assumingly, call the whole body of geologists. **1927** *Scots Observer* 12 Mar. 3/5, I ken him fine commented the other assumingly.

a'ssumingness. [f. ASSUMING *ppl. a.* + -NESS.] The quality of being assuming.

a **1832** BENTHAM in *L. Hunt's Lond. Jrnl.* No. 4. 29 A form of imperiousness somewhat less annoying.. which may be called assumingness.

† **a'ssummon,** *v. Obs.* Also 5-6 assom(m)on. [? f. A- *pref.* 11 + SUMMON *v.*] To summon.

c **1450** *Crt. of Love* xxv, But were ye not assomoned to appere. *c* **1594** DANIEL *Sonn.* xl. in Arb. *Garner* III. 611 That grace.. Doth her, unto eternity assommon. **1607** *Barley-Breake* (1877) 7 And to locke hands one doth them all assummon.

assumpsit (ə'sʌmsɪt). [L. = 'he has taken upon himself,' perf. ind. of *assūmĕre* to ASSUME.]

1. A taking upon oneself, an undertaking; *spec.* in *Law.* **a.** A promise or contract, oral or in writing not sealed, founded upon a consideration. **b.** An action to recover damages for breach or non-performance of such contract.

1612 WARNER *Alb. Eng.* I. iv. 14 Hercules.. accepts the assumpsit, and prepares the feend-like fish to tame. **1641** *Termes de la Ley* 30b, Assumpsit is a voluntary promise made by word by which a man assumeth and taketh upon him to performe or pay any thing to another. **1768** BLACKSTONE *Comm.* III. 157 The assumpsit or undertaking of the defendant. **1853** WHARTON *Pa. Digest* 150 Assumpsit lies against a corporation on an implied contract.

† 2. An assumption, a taking for granted. *Obs.*

a **1628** F. GREVILLE *Sidney* (1653) 95 He saw the vast body of the Empire.. under this false assumpsit, to have laid the bridle on the neck of the Emperor. *Ibid.* 105 Upon these and the like assumpsits he resolved.

† **a'ssumpt,** *pa. pple.* and *sb. Obs.* [ad. L. *assūmptus*, pa. pple. of *assūmĕre* to ASSUME.]

A. *pa. pple.* Assumed, taken up, raised, elevated, elected. (Used as pa. pple. of the vb. *assume.*)

1447 [see ASSUME *v.* 4.] **1483** CAXTON *Gold. Leg.* 255/1 Therby he understode that she was assumpt in to heuen. **1502** ARNOLD *Chron.* (1811) 280 He was assumpte to the state of cardynal. **1553-87** FOXE *A. & M.* (1596) 1027/2 Jesus is asaumpt, or taken awaie into heauen.

B. *sb.* A thing assumed, an assumption.

1553-87 FOXE *A. & M.* II. 357 He.. first of all denied the Bishop's assumpt. **1570** BILLINGSLEY *Euclid* I. xix. 28 An Assumpt is a Proposition taken of necessitie to the helpe of a demonstration, the certainty whereof is not so plaine, and therefore nedeth it selfe first to be demonstrated. **1638** CHILLINGW. *Relig. Prot.* I. i. §12. 39 The summe of all your Assumpts.. is this.

† **a'ssumpt,** *v. Obs.* [f. prec. Cf F. *assumpter.*]

1. To receive into association; = ASSUME *v.* 1.

1595 HUBBOCKE *Apol. Infants Unbapt.* 25 The child is assumpted into the association and fellowship of the blessed Trinitie. **1627** H. BURTON *Bait. Pope's Bull* 93 As being assumpted into the individuall vnity with Christ.

b. *esp.* To receive up into heaven; = ASSUME *v.* 1 b.

1530 PALSGR. 751/2 Our Ladye was assumpted. **1582** N.T. (Rhem.) *Acts* i. 11 This Iesus which is assumpted from you into heaven. **1607** J. DAVIES *Summa Tot.* (1876) 19 But how remou'd, God knowes; I cannot proue, Assumpted, some suppose.

2. To elect or elevate to office; = ASSUME *v.* 2.

a **1581** CAMPION *Hist. Irel.* xiv. 47 From thence assumpted Bishop of Lismore. **1629** L. OWEN *Spec. Jesuit.* 33 Pope Gregory.. being assumpted to S. Peters chaire.

3. To take to oneself, put on, assume.

1572 BOSSEWELL *Armorie* II. 22 And assumpted, or tooke to his Armes.. a Crosse Siluer, in a field vert. **1579** FULKE *Heskins's Parl.* 143 His humaine nature.. is assumpted of the worde of God. **1611** CHESTER *K. Arthur* (1878) 61 Vnto himselfe he hath assumpted.. A Crosse of Siluer.

† **a'ssumpted,** *ppl. a. Obs.* = ASSUMED.

1565 JEWEL *Repl. Harding* (1611) 273 Christ after condition of nature assumpted, suffered death in Body. **1624** GATAKER *Transubst.* 107 As angels in assumpted bodies are said to bee seene.

† **a'ssumpting,** *vbl. sb. Obs.* Assumption.

1565 CALFHILL *Answ. Treat. Crosse* (1846) 153 The same divine nature, after the assumpting of flesh, to remain notwithstanding incircumscriptible.

assumption (ə'sʌmʃən). Also 4-6 -cyon, -tyowne, etc. [ad. L. *assūmptiōn-em*, n. of action f. *assūmĕre*: see ASSUME *v.* and -TION. Cf. also OF. *asompsion* 13th c., *assomption* 16th c. As with other such words (cf. *advent*, *annunciation*), the specific ecclesiastical use was the earliest in Eng.]

I. The action of taking to oneself; reception, adoption.

1. The action of receiving up into heaven; ascent to or reception into heaven.

1577 HANMER *Anc. Eccl. Hist.* (1619) 21 The wonderfull resurrection of our Saviour, and his assumption into the heavens. **1627** tr. *Bacon's Life & Death* (1651) 15 He.. lived after the Assumption of Elias, sixty yeares. **1850** TENNYSON *In Mem.* lxxxiii, Can hang no weight upon my heart In its assumptions up to heaven.

b. *esp.* The reception of the Virgin Mary into heaven, with body preserved from corruption, which is a generally accepted doctrine in the Roman Catholic Church. Also the feast held annually on the 15th of August in honour of this event.

1297 R. GLOUC. 570 After þe Assumption þe vifte day iwis, He dude him in þe se at Douere. *c* **1430** *Hymns to Virg.* (1871) 474 þat holi assumpcioun Of his blessid modir. *a* **1520** *Myrr. Oure Ladye* 5 From tyme of her sonnes passyon vnto her assumpcyon. **1674** BREVINT *Saul at Endor* 143 Her other Solemn and great Feast, which they call the Assumtion. **1884** ADDIS & ARNOLD *Cath. Dict.* s.v., The denial of the Blessed Virgin's corporal assumption into heaven, though by no means contrary to the faith, is still so much opposed to the common agreement of the Church, that it would be a mark of insolent temerity.

† 2. Elevation to office or dignity. *Obs.*

1642 JER. TAYLOR *Episc.* (1647) 160 A distinction of orders.. and assumptions to them respectively. **1687** N. JOHNSTON *Assur. Abb. Lands* 94 The news of.. the Assumption of Queen Mary to the Crown.

3. Reception into union or association; incorporation, inclusion; adoption. *arch.* or *Obs.*

1617 COLLINS *Def. Bp. Ely* II. x. 425 How the flesh and humane nature of Christ may be worshipped, by the priuiledge of their assumption into his Godhead. **1661** *Origen's Opin.* in *Phœnix* (1721) I, Those Parts of Matter.. in their innumerable Assumptions and Adoptions into other Bodies. **1774** WARTON *Eng. Poetry* xlv. (1840) III. 151 It is evident that the prose psalms of our liturgy were chiefly consulted.. by the perpetual assumptions of their words. **1811** L. HAWKINS *C'tess & Gertrude* 244 The assumption into Lady Luxmore's confined house.. of Mr. Sterling.

† 4. The taking of food, etc. into the body. *Obs.*

1599 B. JONSON *Ev. Man out of Hum.* III. iii. 43 The most gentlemanlike use of tabacco.. the delicate sweete formes for the assumption of it. *c* **1645** HOWELL *Lett.* I. v. 9 (T.) To the nutrition of the body there are two essential conditions required, assumption and retention.

II. The action of taking for or upon oneself.

5. The taking upon oneself of a form or character; formal taking of office or position.

1646 SIR T. BROWNE *Pseud. Ep.* 238 The assumption of humane shape, had proved a disadvantage unto Sathan. **1768** H. WALPOLE *Hist Doubts* 108 Before Richard's assumption of the crown. **1866** ROGERS *Agric. & Prices* I. v. 121 The festival following the assumption of the Bachelor's degree.

b. The form or character assumed.

1871 *Athenæum* 15 Apr. 471 Madame Pauline Lucca.. has appeared in two of her best assumptions.

6. *Law.* A promise or undertaking, either oral or in writing not sealed.

1590 SWINBURN *Testaments* 229 The promise or assumption made by the testator. **1853** WHARTON *Pa. Digest* 75 A principal is not liable for the assumptions of an agent who exceeds his authority.

7. The action of taking possession of, appropriation. ***arms of assumption*** = ASSUMPTIVE arms.

1754 ERSKINE *Princ. Sc. Law* (1809) 53 Particular localities were assigned in every benefice, to the extent of a third, called the assumption of thirds. *a* **1832** MACKINTOSH *Revol. of* 1688 Wks. 1846 II. 313 The assumption of the whole legislative authority. **1870** R. FERGUSON *Electr.* 7 Steel therefore has a force which.. resists the assumption of magnetism.

8. The action of laying claim to as a possession, unwarrantable claim, usurpation.

1647 CRASHAW *Steps to Temple* (1858) 79 We to the last Will hold it fast, And no assumption shall deny us. **1796** BURKE *Regic. Peace* Wks. 1842 II. 287 This astonishing assumption of the publick voice of England. **1872** BLACK *Adv. Phaeton* xvi. 216 That calm assumption of the virtues of meekness and patience was a little too much.

9. A taking too much upon oneself, a laying claim to undue importance; arrogance.

1606 SHAKS. *Tr. & Cr.* II. iii. 133 In self-assumption greater Then in the note of judgement. **1814** SCOTT *Wav.* xlix, His usual air of haughty assumption. **1856** R. VAUGHAN *Mystics* (1860) I. 97 On consideration of his services to priestly assumption.

10. The taking of anything for granted as the basis of argument or action.

1660 STANLEY *Hist. Philos.* (1701) 145/2 He used Arguments not by Assumption, but by Inference. **1794** SULLIVAN *View Nat.* II. 74 It steers clear of the fatal assumption of physical elements, merely upon the grounds of mathematical conclusions. **1874** SAYCE *Compar. Philol.* vi. 254 The assumption of pronominal roots.. might mean anything or nothing.

11. That which is assumed or taken for granted; a supposition, postulate.

a **1628** F. GREVILLE *Sidney* (1652) 58 He had no hope of bringing these curious assumptions to pass. **1693** DRYDEN *Juvenal* x. (J.) Hold! says the Stoick, your assumption's wrong. **1798** WELLINGTON in Gurw. *Disp.* I. 4 This assumption is directly at variance with the general tenor of the public records. **1856** FROUDE *Hist. Eng.* II. viii. 201 Language which was only pardonable on the assumption that it was inspired.

12. *Logic.* The minor premiss of a syllogism.

1588 FRAUNCE *Lawiers Log.* I. iii. 19 The assumption was this, 'But Paris is idle.' **1628** T. SPENCER *Logic* 276 Here we haue the.. assumption vniversally affirmatiue. **1837-8** SIR W. HAMILTON *Logic* xv. (1866) I. 281 The other premise, which enounces the application of the general rule.. is called the Minor Premise, the Minor Proposition, the Assumption, or the Subsumption.

assumptionist (ə'sʌm(p)ʃənɪst). [f. ASSUMPTION + -IST.]

1. One who bases his arguments on assumption.

1891 G. A. DENISON *Let.* 9 Mar. in *Fifty Years at East Brent* (1902) 344 He is a remarkable assumptionist—he is no logician.

2. *R.C. Ch.* A member of the congregation entitled Augustinians of the Assumption, 'which had its origin in the College of the Assumption, established at Nîmes, in France, in 1843' (*Cath. Encycl.*).

1898 *Westm. Gaz.* 30 Sept. 6/2 An article in the *Croix* by its editor, the Assumptionist Father Bailly. **1901** *Daily News* 7 Jan. 4/7 The Assumptionists, who have played such an infamous part in French politics the last three years.

assumptious (ə'sʌmʃəs), *a. rare.* [f. ASSUMPTION: see -TIOUS.] Given to assumption, assuming. Hence **a'ssumptiousness**, tendency to take too much upon oneself.

1878 MRS. H. WOOD *Pomeroy Abb.* I. viii, 'When she has shaken down into her place, and'—'Become less assumptious you would say.' **1870** *Pall Mall G.* 3 June, The 'assumptiousness' which Mr. Beresford Hope attributed to the First Commissioner of Works.

assumptive (ə'sʌmtɪv), *a.* [ad. L. *assūmptīvus*: see ASSUMPT *a.* and -IVE.] Characterized by assumption.

1. Characterized by being assumed or taken to oneself. ***assumptive arms*** in *Her.* (see quot.)

1611 GUILLIM *Heraldrie* iii. 261 Armes Assumptiue.. are such as a man of his proper right may assume as the guerdon of his valorous seruice, with the approbation of his Soueraigne and of the Herauld. **1787** PORNY *Heraldry* 11 Assumptive Arms.. are taken up by the caprice or fancy of Upstarts. **1831** LANDOR *Ct. Julian* (1846) II. 509 The gaudy trappings of assumptive state.

2. Of the nature of an assumption; taken for granted.

c **1650** NEEDHAM *Case Commonw.* 23 As to the Assumptive part of this Objection, which insinuates, etc. **1837** SIR W. HAMILTON *Metaph.* v. (1877) I. 82 A purification of the intellect from all assumptive beliefs.

3. Apt to take to oneself, appropriative.

1829 *Westm. Rev.* Oct. 490 That plastic species of intellect, which may be termed the assumptive or.. assimilative.

4. Apt to take things for granted.

1856 *Q. Rev.* Sept. 399 The negligent and assumptive habits of the literary biographers. **1882** HARDY *Two on Tower* II. v. 72 A woman's forethought is so assumptive.

5. Making undue claims, assumptious, arrogant.
1879 Miss Bird *Rocky Mount.* 206 An American is nationally assumptive, an Englishman personally so. 1881 *Echo* 13 Jan. 2/5 The assumptive tone of the speech.

a'ssumptively, *adv.* [f. prec. + -LY[2].] In assumptive manner, by way of assumption.
1859 in Worcester.

assurance (əˈʃʊərəns). Also 4 **asseurance, -ouerans,** 4–6 **assuraunce,** 5–6 **-ans.** *Aphet.* SURANCE, q.v. [a. OF. *asseürance* (mod. *assurance*), f. *asseürer* to ASSURE. Cf. It. *assicuranza*, Sp. *aseguranza*, Eng. ASSECURANCE: see -ANCE.]

I. The action of assuring.
* *Of making certain.*

1. A promise or engagement making a thing certain; a formal engagement, pledge, or guarantee.
c1386 Chaucer *Man of Lawes T.* 243 Wol ye maken assuraunce, As I schal say, assentyng to my lore? 1490 Caxton *Eneydos* xxvii. 99 He is departed wyth thyne assuraunce. 1601 Shaks. *Twel. N.* I. v. 192 Plight me the full assurance of your faith. 1623 Bingham *Xenophon* 78 The Macrons asked..whether they would giue assurance of that they said; Who answered, they were readie to giue, & take assurance. 1853 Robertson *Serm.* Ser. III. viii. 110 A symbol and assurance of the Divine pardon.

b. *esp.* An engagement guaranteeing peace and safety; terms of peace. *Obs.* exc. *Hist.*
1513–75 *Diurn. Occurr.* (1833) 277 Thair was assurance and trewis tane betuix the Inglis and Scottismen. 1577 Holinshed *Chron.* III. 1214/1 [They] came in to the lord lieutenant, submitting themselues to him, and were receiued into assurance. 1653 Holcroft *Procopius* III. 110 The rest of the Army..took assurances and yeilded to Totilas. 1873 Burton *Hist. Scot.* VI. lxx. 191 Hamilton was angry that assurances should have been given to the Covenanters.

†2. A marriage engagement, betrothal. *Obs.*
1494 Fabyan vii. 496 The Flemynges..had constrayned theyr erle to be assured, by bonde of assurance, unto yᵉ doughter of Kyng Edward. 1579 Gosson *Sch. Abuse* (Arb.) 31 Wooing allowed by assurance of wedding. 1601 Holland *Pliny* I. 550 In knitting vp of marriages, and assurance making. 1641 *Life Wolsey* in *Harl. Misc.* (1793) 105 The Lord Piercys assurance to Mrs. Anne Bullen.

3. A positive declaration intended to give confidence.
1609 Rowlands *Knaue of Clubs* 36 This assurance take, Some satisfaction I in part will make. 1719 De Foe *Crusoe* I. 303 He gave me all the Assurances that the Invention and Faith of Man could devise. 1880 McCarthy *Own Times* III. xl. 202 He was probably quite sincere in the assurances he repeatedly gave.

** *Of making secure.*

4. *Law.* The securing of a title to property; the conveyance of lands or tenements by deed; a legal evidence of the conveyance of property.
1583 Stubbes *Anat. Abus.* II. 33 In times past when men dealt vprightly..sixe or seuen lines was sufficient for the assurance of any peece of land whatsoeuer. 1648 Sheppard (*title*) The Touchstone of Common Assurances and Conveyances. 1768 Blackstone *Comm.* II. xix. II. 294 The legal evidences of this translation of property are called the common assurances of the Kingdom; whereby every man's estate is assured to him. *Ibid.* II. 367 Copyhold estate..cannot possibly be transferred by any other assurance.

5. The action of insuring or securing the value of property in the event of its being lost, or of securing the payment of a specified sum in the event of a person's death; insurance.
Technically, the present usage is to differentiate life-*assurance*, and fire- and marine-*insurance*; though, as will be seen from the quotations, *assurance* was the original term in reference to marine risks.
1622 Malynes *Anc. Law-Merch.* 159 To haue a regard what winde must serue, and the true season of the yeare, which maketh a difference in the price of assurance. 1642 Fuller *Holy & Prof. St.* II. i. 51 Some keep an Assurance-office in their chamber. 1692 *Lond. Gaz.* No. 2747/4 Lost..a Police of Assurance made upon the Ship Olive-Branch. 1755 Magens *Insurances* II. 254 Assurance or Insurance is a just and faithful Compact, by which one, or more, in Consideration of the Payment of a Sum of Money agreed on, called the Insurance Premium, takes upon himself all the Dangers which may or shall happen to the Ship, Vessel, Effects, and Property of another. 1883 *Daily News* 18 Sept. 1/4 (*Advt.*) The Employers' Liability Assurance Corporation. 1883 *Sc. Prov. Inst. Prospect.*, Yearly payments for Assurance of £100 at death.

II. The state of being sure or assured.

†6. Objective certainty; = ASSUREDNESS 1. *Obs.*
c1485 *Digby Myst.* (1882) II. 387, I can not beleve that thys ys of assurans. 1509 Hawes *Past. Pleas.* xxxi. xvii, Wo worth the trust without assuraunce. 1603 Knolles *Hist. Turks* (1621) 538 New friends of more assurance.

7. Security.
1559 *Myrr. Mag., Dk. York* vii. 4 Liung hopeles of his liues assuraunce. 1570 T. Wilson *Demosth.* 13 *marg.*, Things wrongfully gotten haue none assurance. 1576 Lambarde *Peramb. Kent* (1826) 141 To sende..unto a place of most assuraunce all such as hee had taken prisoners. 1622 Heylin *Cosmogr.* i. (1682) 158 The Fortifications being weak, and of ill assurance. 1839 Keightley *Hist. Eng.* I. 427 The King's ascent to the crown and assurance therein.

8. Subjective certainty; a being certain as to a fact, certitude; confidence, trust.
1375 Barbour *Bruce* xi. 309 In hys hye cheuelry Thai had assouerans, trast trewly. c1374 Chaucer *Troylus* v. 1259 O trust, O feith, O depe asseuraunce! 1601 Cornwallyes *Ess.* II. xxix, It is as naturall in men to purchase hope as assurance. 1605 Shaks. *Macb.* IV. i. 83 But yet Ile make assurance double sure, And take a Bond of Fate. 1843 Mill *Logic* II. vi. §3 We can have full assurance of particular results. a1842 Tennyson *Two Voices* 315 The doubt would rest, I dare not solve..Assurance only breeds resolve.

b. in *Theol.* (See quot.)
1651 C. Cartwright *Cert. Relig.* I. 251 The Doctrine of Protestants concerning assurance of salvation..viz. that a man may have this assurance. 1852 Sir W. Hamilton *Disc.* (1853) 508 Assurance, Personal Assurance, Special Faith, (the feeling of certainty that God is propitious to me,—that my sins are forgiven).

9. Self-confidence, self-reliance; confidence of manner, steadiness, intrepidity.
1594 T. B. *La Primaud. Fr. Acad.* II. 263 Assurance is a certaine perswasion..whereby wee are confirmed in danger against euilles that threaten vs. 1603 Knolles *Hist. Turks* (1621) 72 Jaques..with his Flemings, received the charge with great assurance. 1734 tr. *Rollin's Rom. Hist.* (1827) II. 352 To inspire him with a noble assurance so necessary for those that are born to command. 1751 Johnson *Rambl.* No. 147 ¶8 The benefits of publick education, and the happiness of an assurance early acquired.

10. In a bad sense: Hardihood, audacity, presumption, impudence.
1699 Bentley *Phal.* 281 Quote Authors they had never read, with an Air of Assurance. 1709 Swift *Vind. Bickerstaff* Wks. 1755 II. I. 174 Several of my friends had the assurance to ask me, whether I was in jest? 1771 *Junius Lett.* lxiii. 323 The barrister has not the assurance to deny it flatly. 1832 Ht. Martineau *Hill & Vall.* ii. 23, I should like to know where you picked up so much assurance.

†**a'ssurancer.** *Obs.* [f. prec. + -ER[1].] One who gives assurances; one who makes great professions.
1592 Chettle *Kind-Harts Dr.* (1841) 28 Such a rare obscure assurancer, to worke what not wonders in phisicke.

assurant (əˈʃʊərənt). [f. ASSURANCE: see -ANT.] One who insures his life, or takes out a policy of insurance.
1863 *Circ. Comm. Union Assur.* Dec., The importance of this to intending Assurants will be readily perceived.

†**a'ssurantly,** *adv. Obs.* In 7 **asseur-.** [f. ASSURANCE, as if on an adj. *assurant*; cf. *confidence, confidently.*] With assurance, confidently.
1619 Sir I. Wake *Let.* in *N. & Q.* Ser. II. VII. 285 The astrologer doth asseurantly affirme that, etc.

†**a'ssurd,** *v. Obs. rare.* [a. OF. *assourd-re*, earlier *assord-re* 'jaillir,' app.:—L. *ads-, assurgĕre*, to rise to, rise up, arise (cf. ASSURGE); but in OF. mixed up (cf. the form *axordre*) with *essordre, exurdre*:—L. *exsurgĕre* to rise up, spring up: see A- *pref.* 9, AS- *pref.*[2]] To burst forth, break out.
c1525 Skelton *Garl. Laurell* 302 Then he assurded into this exclamacyon.

assure (əˈʃʊə(r)), *v.* Also 4 **aseure, asseure,** (*Sc.* **assower**), 5 **asure,** 6 **assurre.** [a. OF. *aseürer* (mod. *assurer*), cogn. with Pr. *assegurar*, It. *assecurare*:—late L. *adsēcūrāre*, f. *ad* to + *sēcūrus* safe: see ASSECURE, SECURE, and SURE.]

†1. *trans.* To render safe or secure (from attack or danger); to secure. *Obs.*
1413 Lydg. *Pylgr. Sowle* iv. xxx. (1483) 80 He hath no more to care fore..but his propre persone. whiche he wil assuren as ferforth as he may. c1500 *Lancelot* 1573 Yhour cuntre and yhour lond he wil assure. 1595 Bedingfield *Hist. Florence* 2 Neither was..Bretagne..assured from suche invasion. 1614 Raleigh *Hist. World* v. i. §6. 564 The Romans, the better to assure themselves, cut a deep trench.

†b. To secure to oneself, make sure of. *Obs.*
1581 Savile *Tacitus' Agric.* (1622) 191 Being of opinion rather to keep and assure the places suspected. a1674 Clarendon *Hist. Reb.* II. vi. 26 To assure that City to his Service.

c. To make safe *from* or *against* (*of* obs.) risks; to insure. *esp.* in mod. usage *to assure life*: to secure the payment of a specified sum in the event of death. Also *absol.* (Cf. ASSURANCE 5.)
c1385 Chaucer *L.G.W.* 1629 Of whiche no creature Save only she ne myghte hys lyf assure. 1481 Caxton *Myrr.* III. viii. 147 The fruytes..ben..more assured of tempestes and other greuaunces. 1852 McCulloch *Comm. Dict.* 755 Persons assuring their own lives. —— 756 Those who assure with this Company will participate in the profits. 1884 *Manch. Exam.* 26 June 5/1 If they could be assured against any unpleasant consequences.

2. To make secure against change or overthrow; to make stable, establish securely.
1494 Fabyan II. xxx. 22 The whiche condicions well and suerly vpon the Dukes partie..assured. 1586 T. B. *La Primaud Fr. Acad.* 621 Force, feare, and the multitude of his gard, assure not the estate of a prince so well, as the good-will..of his subjects. 1678 Dryden *Œdipus* Epil. 29 As weak States each other's Pow'r assure, Weak Poets by Conjunction are secure. 1848 Lytton *Harold* (1862) 102 The two chiefs who most assured his throne.

†3. To secure or make sure the possession or reversion of; to convey property by deed. *Obs.*
1572 *Act 14 Eliz.* xi. §5 in *Oxf. & Camb. Enactments* 33 All such Houses and Groundes may be granted dimised and assured. c1590 Marlowe *Faustus* v. 54 And with my proper blood Assure my soul to be great Lucifers. 1611 Bible *Lev.* xxvii. 19 He shal adde the fift part of the money of thy estimation vnto it, and it shall be assured to him. 1670 Cotton *Espernon* I. I. 41 He assur'd to himself the whole Countrey of Champagne.

†4. To make sure for marriage, affiance, betroth, or engage. *Obs.*
1393 Gower *Conf.* I. 190 He wol her wedde, and upon this Assured eche til othir is. 1494 [see ASSURANCE 2.] 1581 Savile *Tacitus' Agric.* 242 He assured to me his daughter.

5. To make certain the occurrence or arrival of (an event); to ensure.
1622 T. Scott *Belg. Pismire* 4 To assure a better life hereafter. 1697 Dryden *Virg. Georg.* I. 284 Yet is not the Success for Years assur'd. 1863 Mrs. C. Clarke *Shaks. Char.* i. 10 Nothing which shall assure the accomplishment of her purpose. 1878 B. Taylor *Deukalion* I. ii. 27 Forever shall betray it and assure My coming triumph.

6. To make certain (a thing doubtful). *arch.*
1682 Dryden *Relig. Laici* 6 Not to assure our doubtful way. 1832 Lewis *Use & Ab. Pol. Terms* Introd. 2 Assuring the results or detecting the fallacies.

†7. *trans.* To guarantee: a. (a thing *to* a person); to promise as a thing that may be depended on. *Obs.*
c1400 *Destr. Troy* xix. 8001 All þo couenandes to kepe..This he sadly assurit at the same tyme. 1447 Bokenham *Seyntys* 31 They hym assuryd with scryptyre and seel Evere cloos to kepyn al hys counseel. c1450 *Merlin* xxvi. 482 Assureth me youre feith to holde me companye. 1624 Capt. Smith *Virginia* (1629) 74 The President assuring the King perpetual love. 1680 *Life Edw. II* in *Harl. Misc.* (1793) 36 He assures a reformation.

b. a person *from* a thing. *rare.*
1820 Scott *Ivanhoe* iv, I will assure you from all deaths but a violent one.

†c. *absol.* or with *subord. cl.* To give a guarantee, promise, pledge oneself. *Obs.*
c1386 Chaucer *Doctor's T.* 143 This juge..made him to assure He schulde telle it to no creature. c1400 *Destr. Troy* xxvi. 10475 He assentid full sone, asurit with hond. c1450 *Merlin* x. 145 Than thei swore and assured to-geder that neuer shulde thei be gladde till thei were avenged.

8. *trans.* To give confidence to, confirm, encourage.
1375 Barbour *Bruce* vi. 225 His gentill hert and vorthy Assurit him intill that neide. c1386 Chaucer *Clerkes T.* 37 Youre humanité Assureth us and giveth us hardynesse. 1477 Earl Rivers *Dictes* 83 His corage, by the whiche he shalbe the more assured in all his nedis. 1591 Spenser *Bellay's Vis.* vii, By more and more she gan her wings t' assure. 1611 Bible *1 John* iii. 19 And hereby we..shall assure our hearts before him. 1853 Robertson *Serm.* Ser. III. v. 76 A pure man forgives, or pleads for mercy, or assures the penitent.

†b. *refl.* (in sense of c.) *Obs.*
1370 *Lay-Folks Mass-Bk.* App. iv. 223 In Marie · I me a-seure. 1625 Bacon *Ess., Atheism* (Arb.) 339 Man, when he resteth and assureth himselfe, vpon diuine Protection. 1641 Warmstry *Blind Guide* 18 To assure our selves upon that promise of our Lord Jesus.

†c. *intr.* To have confidence, trust, rely. *Obs.*
1375 Barbour *Bruce* xi. 309 In hys hey cheualry Thai assoweryt rycht soueranly. c1374 Chaucer *Troylus* I. 681 As frend fullich yn me assure, And tel me plat what is thencheson. c1420 *Pallad. on Husb.* v. 185 Towarde nyght in restyng thai assure.

†d. *refl. & intr.* To be so bold as, dare, venture.
c1385 Chaucer *L.G.W.* 908 Late no gentyl woman hyre assure To pottyn hire in swich an aventure. 1513 Douglas *Æneis* xi. xv. 95 He na langar durst..Assure for to debait hym with his speir.

9. *trans.* To make (a person) sure or certain (*of* a fact, or *that* it is).
1393 Gower *Conf.* III. 186 That ye me wolde assure and say With such an othe, as ye woll take. a1555 Latimer *Wks.* (1845) II. 491 By him I could assure you, if I had time. c1590 Marlowe *1st Pt. Tamburl.* II. iii; Thy words assure me of kind success. 1611 Bible *2 Tim.* iii. 14 Continue thou in the things which thou hast learned, and hast been assured of. 1658 *Whole Duty Man* iv. §2 (1684) 38 The use of oaths being to assure the persons to whom they are made. 1843 Mill *Logic* III. xvii. §1 To consider how we are to assure ourselves of its truth. 1879 Miss Braddon *Vixen* III. 287 What can I do to assure you of my love?

b. *refl.* and *pass.* To feel certain or satisfied.
1484 Skelton *Death Edw. IV.* 17 Who to lyue euer may himselfe assure? 1538 Starkey *England* 154 Of thys we may be assuryd. 1596 Spenser *F.Q.* I. vii. 52 Assure your selfe, I will not you forsake. 1767 Fordyce *Serm. Yng. Wom.* I. i. 9 Be assured it proceeds from real regard. 1826 Scott *Woodst.* iv, Assure yourself, sir..that his sagacity saw in this man a stranger. 1870 Bryant *Homer* iv. I. 105 Be at least assured That all the other gods approve it not.

10. To tell (a person) confidently as a thing that he may trust (*that* it is, or *of* its being).
1513 More *Rich. III.* Wks. 43/1, I assure him quod the Archebishoppe..it will neuer bee soo well as wee haue seene it. 1598 Shaks. *Merry W.* II. ii. 109 *Quick.* I think you have charms..*Fal.* Not I, I assure thee. 1704 Hearne *Duct. Hist.* (1714) I. 439 Thucydides assures us 't was built 5 years after Syracuse. 1712 Steele *Spect.* No. 508 ¶5, I assure you these are things worthy your consideration. 1876 Green *Short Hist.* viii. §2 (1882) 477 The Spanish ambassador..was assured that no effectual aid should be sent to the Palatinate. *Mod.* He assured us of his own willingness to go.

†b. with second object. *Obs.*
1644 Slingsby *Diary* (1836) 127 The man..that assured me the truth of it. a1718 Penn *Life* Wks. 1726 I. 22 Their Age no Antiquary living can assure us.

†11. *trans.* To state positively, to affirm. *Obs.*
1535 Coverdale *Jer.* xxix. 23 This I testifie and assure. 1587 Fenner *Def. Ministers* B ij b, When the people is..secure, to bee more diligent in assuring threatninges. 1598 Greenwey *Tacitus' Ann.* III. ii, I will not assure either of those things. a1677 Barrow *Serm. Virt. Faith*, About which neither Socrates nor Seneca could assure anything.

†b. with *subord. cl.* or *inf. phr. Obs.*

1509 FISHER *Wks.* (1876) 293 Whether slepynge or wakyng she could not assure. **1638** HEYWOOD *Wise Wom.* IV. i. Wks. 1874 V. 329 If hee assure to know mee, I'le out face him. **1708** SWIFT *Predict. for 1708* Wks. 1755 II. I. 150, I cannot..so confidently assure the events will follow exactly as I predict them.

† **a'ssure**, *sb. Obs.* [f. prec. vb.] Assurance.
c **1374** CHAUCER *Anel. & Arc.* 331 To profre a newe assure. **1658** USSHER *Ann.* VI. (1683) 745 Not taking any meat without assure.

assured (əˈʃʊəd), *ppl. a.* and *sb.* Also 5 **assewred, -rid, asseured,** 6 **adsured**; *Sc.* 4–6 **assouerit,** 6 **assurit.** [f. ASSURE *v.* + -ED.]

A. *ppl. a.*

†**1.** Made safe, secured; safe, secure. *Obs.*
1375 BARBOUR *Bruce* x. 187 Quhen feldis..Chargit with corne assouerit var. **1475** CAXTON *Jason* 78 He helde him wel assured in his palais. **1525** LD. BERNERS *Froiss.* II. clxiii. [clx.] 453 Whanne he thought to haue been moste assuredest on the heyght of fortunes whele. **1614** RALEIGH *Hist. World* II. v. iii. §6. 375 In some plentifull and assured place.

2. Made sure or certain.
1430 LYDG. *Chron. Troy* I. vi, Your owne assured man. **1559** *Myrr. Mag., Dk. York* x. 5 For ayde wherin I knit assured bandes. **1614** RALEIGH *Hist. World* v. ii. §2 Being thought so much the more assured to their master. **1882** *Pall Mall G.* 13 July 2/1 Many of the charters to carry coal.. being made upon an assured return cargo.

†**3.** Engaged, covenanted, pledged. *arch.* or *Obs.*
1426 *Pol. Poems* (1859) II. 136 Phelip..Duc of Burgoyne, assured eke and sworne. **1570** HOLINSHED *Scot. Chron.* (1806) II. 244, 700 English horsemen, besides the assured Scots horsemen. **1600** in *Shaks. C. Praise* 38 Your assured friend Charles Percy. *a* **1672** in Wood *Life* (1848) 86 *note*, Your honor's most asurid to do you servis, Thos. Baskeruile.

†**4.** Engaged for marriage, betrothed. *Obs.*
1474 CAXTON *Chesse* 14 A right fayr mayde which was assured and handfast vnto a noble yonge gentilman. **1580** LYLY *Euphues* (Arb.) 466 You muse Philautus to see Camilla and me to bee assured. **1590** SHAKS. *Com. Err.* III. ii. 145 This drudge..call'd me Dromio, swore, I was assur'd to her.

5. Certified, verified, certain, sure.
1574 tr. *Marlorats Apocalips* 50 An assured testimonie of Christes Godhead. *c* **1712** *Advt.* in *Spect.* (ed. Morley) 905 An Assured Cure for Leanness. **1853** RUSKIN *Stones Ven.* II. v. §29. 142 The assured facts are, that both the shafts of the pillars..were, etc.

6. Satisfied as to the truth or certainty of a matter, confident.
1523 LD. BERNERS *Froiss.* I. ix. 7 Whan she knewe she was in the Empyre, she was better assured than she was before. **1596** SHAKS. *Merch. V.* I. iii. 30, I will be assured I may: and that I may be assured, I will bethinke mee. **1703** MAUNDRELL *Journ. Jerus.* (1732) 137 A Man had need be well assur'd of his Credit. **1851** HELPS *Friends in C.* I. 108 The great thing to be assured of in social knowledge.

7. Full of self-assurance, self-possessed, confident, bold; in a bad sense: Self-satisfied, presumptuous.
1475 CAXTON *Jason* 30 b, The moste asseured of them began to tremble. **1685** EVELYN *Mem.* (1857) II. 253 Of an assured and undaunted spirit. **1714** *Spect.* No. 573 ⁋2 He.. began to proceed with such an assured easy air. **1734** WATTS *Reliq. Juv.* (1789) 48 With an air of assured ignorance. **1839** CARLYLE *Chartism* iv. (1852) 18 Leave with assured heart the issue to a higher Power!

B. *sb.* (sometimes with pl. in *-s*). A person whose life or goods are insured by the payment of a premium.
1755 MAGENS *Insurances* I. 138 The Assureds on their part represented: That all the Effects shipped for this Account ought to be included in this Risk. **1861** *Times* 26 Dec., The assured or their agents, though concerned in the shipment. **1884** *Law Times Rep.* 16 Feb. 764/1 Liabilities of T., as an insurer, to the other members of the association as assureds.

assuredly (əˈʃʊərɪdlɪ), *adv.* [f. prec. + -LY².]

1. Certainly, surely, undoubtedly; in very truth.
a **1400** *Chester Pl.* II. 50 One of them thou arte assuredlye. **1578** in Campbell *Chancellors* (1857) II. xlv. 268 Yours assuredly, W. Burleigh. **1758** PULTNEY in *Phil. Trans.* L. 517 It will almost assuredly rain. **1849** MACAULAY *Hist. Eng.* II. 230 Assuredly James did not mean to say anything cruel or insolent.

2. With assurance or confidence, confidently.
1508 FISHER *Wks.* (1876) 309 [She] confessed assuredly, that in the sacrament was conteyned Cryst Ihesu. **1557** RECORDE *Whetst.* B iij b, Trust thereto adsuredly. **1640–1** *Kirkcudbr. War-Comm. Min. Bk.* (1855) 15 We expect, assuredlie, that ye will use all possible diligence. **1853** ROBERTSON *Serm.* Ser. III. xvi. 205 If a man sincerely and assuredly thinks.

assuredness (əˈʃʊərɪdnɪs). [f. as prec. + -NESS.]

1. Objective certainty; = ASSURANCE 6.
1570 T. NORTON *Nowel's Catech.* (1853) 151 He continued and maintained the assuredness of his promises. **1680** H. MORE *Apocal.* Pref. 14 That there may be no distrust of the assuredness of our Interpretation. **1851** RUSKIN *Mod. Paint.* II. III. II. iii. §25 That which is doubtful ..has strength, sinew, and assuredness, built up in it by fact.

2. Subjective certainty, certitude, confidence, trust; = ASSURANCE 7.
1561 T. N[ORTON] *Calvin's Inst.* I. 14 To fasten in their harts that assurednesse that godlinesse requireth. *a* **1679** T. GOODWIN *Wks.* 1864 VIII. 266 In all faith there is..an assuredness of the things that I do believe.

3. Self-confidence, firmness of mind, intrepidity; hardihood, audacity. Cf. ASSURANCE 8, 9.
1581 SAVILE *Tacitus' Agric.* (1622) 202 With an assurednesse and great grace in his countenance. **1613** SIR E. SACKVILLE in *Guardian* No. 133 (1756) II. 199 Being verily mad with anger, the lord Bruce should thirst after my life with a kind of assuredness. **1647** COTTRELL *Davila's Hist. Fr.* (1678) 16 To encounter with..assuredness any opposition. **1748** RICHARDSON *Clarissa* (1811) II. i. 3 To give us women a little air of vanity and assuredness at public places.

† **a'ssurely**, *adv. Obs.* [prob. a confusion of *assuredly* and *surely*: *assure* adj. has not been found in Eng., though *asseur* is common in OF.] Assuredly, surely.
1589 HORSEY *Trav.* (1857) App. 339 [He would] contynew his lov and favour towards me assewrely.

† **a'ssurement.** *Obs.* [a. F. *assurement*, f. *assurer*: see ASSURE *v.* and -MENT.] Assurance.
c **1532** LD. BERNERS *Huon* 412 He made promyse and assurement that he wolde neuer come here more.

assurer (əˈʃʊərə(r)). [f. ASSURE *v.* + -ER¹.]

1. He who, or that which, gives assurance.
1607 HIERON *Wks.* I. 221 The conscience of my former course is the assurer..of my happinesse. **1650** ELDERFIELD *Tythes* 43 Preserver, defender, assurer, protector of a man.

2. One who gives security or indemnifies in case of loss; an insurer or underwriter; = ASSUROR.
1827 *Edin. Rev.* XLV. 499 The real assurer..engages..he will..give him a certain sum for the policy. **1841** *Mar. Insur. Policy* in *Penny Cycl.* XXI. 407/1 The adventures and perils which we the assurers are contented to bear. **1874** *Policy of Neptune Mar. Insur. Co.*, By Agreement between the Assured and Assurer in this policy.

3. One who takes out a policy of assurance; one who insures his life. (A more recent use.)
1865 *Spectator* 30 Sept. 1097 At age thirty-five, one out of one hundred..accepted assurers died. **1869** *Daily News* 20 Aug., Such old offices..unfairly overcharge the prudent young assurer.

† **a'ssurge**, *v. Obs.* [ad. L. *assurgĕre* to rise up, f. *as-* = *ad-* to + *surgĕre* to rise.] To rise up, arise.
1556 ABP. PARKER *Psalter* xciii, The stremes assurge with griesly waues. **1657** TOMLINSON *Renou's Disp.* 305 Its caule assurges to the height of a Cubit. **1670** MAYNWARINGE *Vita Sana* x. 102 Some..will have the difference of bodies to assurge out of these Principles.

assurgency (əˈsɜːdʒənsɪ). [f. ASSURGENT: see -ENCY.] The quality of being assurgent; the disposition to rise or raise oneself.
1664 BAXTER *Life & Times* I. 126 My nature..may find itself insufficient for..assurgency to the attempting of difficult things. *a* **1834** COLERIDGE *Lit. Rem.* (1839) IV. 167 The continual assurgency of the spirit through the body.

assurgent (əˈsɜːdʒənt), *a.* and *sb.* [ad. L. *assurgent-em*, pr. pple. of *assurgĕre*: see above.]

A. *adj.*

1. Rising, ascending; in *Bot.* rising obliquely.
1578 BANISTER *Hist. Man* I. 12 By..which assurgent line, this present bone is..deuided. **1757** PULTNEY in *Phil. Trans.* L. 66 The antheræ are thick and assurgent. **1848** DANA *Zooph.* 195 Animals..with the sides expanded, explanate, and assurgent.

2. Seeking ascendancy, aggressive.
1881 *Times* 29 Apr., A rich..and assurgent priesthood.

B. *sb.* He who or that which rises up.
1791 E. DARWIN *Bot. Gard.* I. 109 Emerging from infernal night, The bright Assurgent rises into light.

assuring (əˈʃʊərɪŋ), *vbl. sb.* [f. ASSURE *v.* + -ING¹.] The action of the vb. ASSURE; making sure, assurance. In obs. sense: Betrothal.
1530 PALSGR. 195/2 Assuryng, *assurement.* **1579** LYLY *Euphues* (Arb.) 84 That a maryage should be solemnised, where never was any mention of assuring. **1655** GURNALL *Chr. in Arm.* III. (1669) 341/1 The promise is an Assuring-office to secure him his adventure. *a* **1866** J. GROTE *Exam. Util. Philos.* iii. 51 Such assurings do not produce..as much effect as we should expect.

a'ssuring, *ppl. a.* [f. as prec. + -ING².] **1.** That assures or gives confidence.
1866 *Build. News* No. 583. 147/1 The experiment [was] far from assuring.

2. That takes out a policy of assurance.
1891 *Charity Organis. Rev.* VII. 262 Each assuring member secured a small payment at death.

a'ssuringly, *adv.* [f. prec. + -LY².] In an assuring manner; so as to give confidence.
1877 F. ROBINSON *Tito's Troubl.* in *Casquet of Lit.* V. 197/1 'Oh, not this week,' said the master assuringly.

assuror (əˈʃʊərɔː(r)). [f. ASSURE *v.*, repr. an AF. *assurour, OF. *asseureor: see -OR.] A legal form of the word ASSURER, used in the specific sense of: One who assures or insures any one's life or property; an underwriter.
1622 MALYNES *Anc. Law-Merch.* 166 The Assurors are to aunswere the damage of the goods laden therein. **1819** REES *Encycl.*, *Assurors* are not answerable for what damages arise through the negligence..of the master or seamen.

asswage, common f. ASSUAGE in 16–18th c.

assweeten, variant of ASWEETEN *v. Obs.*

asswithe, asswythe, variants of ASWITHE.

† **'assy**, *a. Obs.* [f. ASS¹ + -Y.] Asinine.
1583 STUBBES *Anat. Abus.* 51 How unseemelie (I will not say, how assy) a fashion that is.

assyde, obs. form of ASIDE.

assyege, variant of ASSIEGE *v. Obs.* to besiege.

assygn(e, assyne, assyng(e, obs. ff. ASSIGN.

assyl, obs. form of AXLE.

† **A'ssyriac**, *a. Obs.* [Cf. SYRIAC.] = next.
1801 HAGE *Babylon. Inscr.* 17 Both show their Assyriac origin. *Ibid.* 19 A dialect of the more antient Assyriac.

A'ssyrian (əˈsɪrɪən), *a.* and *sb.* [See -AN.] **A.** *adj.* Of the country Assyria; *absol.* its language. **B.** *sb.* A native of Assyria.
1591 SPENSER *Virg. Gnat* 98 Steeped in Assyrian dye. **1815** BYRON *Heb. Mel.* XXII. i, The Assyrian came down like the wolf on the fold.

Assyriology (əˌsɪrɪˈɒlədʒɪ). [See -(O)LOGY.] The study of the language, history, and antiquities of Assyria. **Assyriological** (-əʊˈlɒdʒɪkəl), *a.*, pertaining to Assyriology. **Assyriologist** (-ˈɒlədʒɪst), **A'ssyriologue**, a student of Assyriology.
1865 *Reader* 4 Mar. 250/3 The Institute bestowed its last biennial prize upon an Assyriologist. **1828** *N. Amer. Rev.* CXXVII. 157 The cognate grounds of Egyptology and Assyriology. **1881** *N. Y. Nation* XXXII. 405 In an article.. upon English Assyriological studies. **1884** PLUMPTRE in *O.T. Comm.* IV. 415 Mr. Sayce, M. Oppert, and the other Assyriologists. **1880** CHEYNE *Isaiah* II. 161 Mr. George Smith, the Assyriologue.

Assyro- (əˈsɪrəʊ), comb. form of ASSYRIAN *a.*, as **Assyro-Babylonian** *a.*, of or pertaining to both Assyria and Babylonia; *spec.* designating an ancient Semitic language of Mesopotamia; hence as *sb.*, = AKKADIAN *sb.* 1.
1835 [see MEDO-]. **1888** A. H. SAYCE *Hittites* ii. 22 A large collection of clay tablets..in the Assyro-Babylonian language. **1932** W. L. GRAFF *Lang.* xi. 400 The only East Semitic language known is Akkadian, which was spoken in Ancient Babylonia and Assyria and is therefore sometimes called Assyro-Babylonian. **1952** O. R. GURNEY *Hittites* iii. 82 The Hittite and Assyro-Cappadocian texts.

assys(e, assyst, obs. forms of ASSIZE *sb.*, ASSIST.

assyte, variant of ACCITE *v. Obs.* to cite.

† **a'ssyth**, *sb. Sc. Obs.* Also 4 **asyth,** 5 **assithe, asith,** 6 *aphet.* **sith.** [northern and esp. Sc. form of ASSETH(E *sb.*] **a.** Satisfaction. **b.** Satisfaction for wrong done, reparation, compensation. *to make assyth*: to satisfy; to make reparation.
c **1375** ? BARBOUR *St. Johannes* 601 He had nocht quhare-of to tak To mak asyth to þat beggar. *c* **1425** WYNTOUN *Cron.* VIII. xviii. 105 And thowcht full Assyth to ta' And Vengeance of þe Brwis. **1439** *E.E. Wills* (1883) 119 Make dew assithe for allmaner land that is holden by me or in my name wrongfully. *a* **1450** *York Myst.*, *Skinners* P v b, To hym will I make asith agayne. *a* **1600** *Ps.* lxxxiii. in *Poems 16th C.* (JAM.) Your bludie boist na syth can satisfie.

† **a'ssyth(e**, *v. Sc. Obs.* Also 4 **assith,** 5 **asythe,** 6 **assyith,** *aphet.* **sith.** [north. form of ASSETHE *v.*]

1. To satisfy.
c **1375** ? BARBOUR *St. Georgis* 118 Gold and siluir..At mycht assith fullely þare wil. *c* **1465** in *Eng. Gilds* 381 Foundyn defectyf, and after that asythed and contented. **1535** BELLENDENE *Cron. Scot.* IX. xxviii. (JAM.) The Kyng was nocht full sithit with his justice.

2. To compensate, make compensation to; *esp.* for an offence or injury done.
c **1375** ? BARBOUR *St. Justina* 489 Assith me Of þe lange seruice I haf mad þe. **1424** *Act 2 Jas. I.* (1597) §46 Assyth the partie skaithed and compleinand. **1609** SKENE *Reg. Majest.* 111 He sall not onely assyth the partie, bot also tynes his office for zeare and day.

† **a'ssything**, *vbl. sb. Sc. Obs.* [f. prec. + -ING¹.] The giving of satisfaction for an offence.
1708 J. CHAMBERLAYNE *St. Gt. Brit.* II. III. v. (1743) 408 Nor does the King's Remission in Scotland free from assything, any more than his pardon in England forecloses an appeal.

assythment (əˈsaɪðmənt). *Sc.* Forms: 6 **assyithment,** *aphet.* **sithement,** 7 **asyth-,** 8 **assith-,** 7– **assyth-, assythement.** [f. ASSYTH(E *v.* + -MENT.] Satisfaction for an injury done; compensation, reparation, indemnification.
1535 BELLENDENE *Cron. Scot.* XIV. xi. (JAM.) In sithement of his ransoun. **1597** *Acts Sc. Parl.* (Jas. I) §46 (*title*) Anent remissions to be giuen, and assyithment of partie. **1753** CHAMBERS *Cycl. Supp.*, *Assithment* is the same with what, in the English Law, is called *Man-Bote.* **1828** SCOTT *F.M. Perth* xxi, The amount of an assythment may be recovered out of Ramorny's estate. **1832** AUSTIN *Jurispr.* xv. (1879) I. 397 By the law of Scotland the wife and family of the slain have still the right to bring a civil action for assythement.

ast, obs. or dial. pa. t. of ASK *v.*

astaat(e, obs. form of ESTATE.

astable, -lish, obs. forms of ESTABLE, -LISH.

astable (ə-, eɪˈsteɪb(ə)l), *a.* [f. A- 14 + STABLE *a.*] Not stable. In *Electr.* (see quot. 1960).
1951 *Electronic Engin.* XXIII. 481/2 An astable multivibrator is synchronized by line frequency pulses at a multiple of line frequency. **1952** *Proc. Inst. Radio Engin.* XL. 1531/2 The operation of this circuit may be monostable, bistable, or astable (oscillatory), depending on the nature of the emitter load. **1953** *Electronic Engin.* XXV. 239 A form of astable pulse generator..has been used by several workers. **1960** COOKE & MARKUS *Electronics & Nucl. Dict.* 26/2 *Astable circuit*, a circuit that alternates automatically and continuously between two unstable states. *Ibid.*, *Astable multivibrator*, a multivibrator in which each tube alternately conducts and is cut off.

astacian (əˈsteɪʃ(ɪ)ən). *Zool.* [f. L. *astac-us*, Gr. ἀστακός lobster, crayfish + -IAN.] A crustacean of the lobster kind. **astacite** (ˈæstəsaɪt), **astacolite** (əˈstækəlaɪt), a fossil crustacean resembling a lobster or crayfish (*Penny Cycl.* 1834).

astalde, pa. t. and pple. of ASTELL *v. Obs.*

astale, var. ESTALE *v. Obs.* = mod.F. *étaler*.

†**aˈstand**, *v. Obs.* For forms see STAND *v.* [OE. *astandan*, f. A- *pref.* 1 + *standan* to STAND; cf. OHG. *arstantan*, MHG. *erstân*, mod.G. *erstehen*. But in some of the senses *a-* appears to represent *on-* (incl. *ond-*), *at-*. Cf. AN-, AT-, ONSTAND.]

1. To stand up.
a **1000** *Beowulf* 3117 Syþðan he eft astód. **1250** LAY. 6495 þat deor up astod.

2. To come to a stand, stop, arrive.
c **1314** *Guy Warw.* 47 At the girdel the swerd astode. *c* **1400** *St. Alexius* 288 þo it was liȝt At Rome hy gonne astonde.

3. To remain standing; to continue, abide, persist. Cf. ONSTAND.
c **1000** *Ags. Gosp.* Luke xxiii. 23 And hiȝ astodon [*Lindisf.* on-stodon]. *c* **1300** *Beket* 2015 The Clerkes..if hi wolleth her astonde, Swerie the king true to be. *c* **1400** *St. Alexius* (Laud) 234 þat sholde hem lere..where he were a-stonde.

4. *trans.* and *absol.* To withstand. Cf. ATSTAND.
1250 LAY. 4240 Alle þaie þat astode: hii fulde to grunde. *c* **1330** *Pol. Songs* 338 Theih bien londes and ledes, ne may hem non astonde. *c* **1400** *Chron. Eng.* in Ritson II. 61 The kyng was ateoned stronge, That Corineus astod so longe.

a-starboard (əˈstɑːbɔəd), *adv. phr. Naut.* [A *prep.*[1] + STARBOARD.] On or toward the starboard or right side of the ship when looking forward. ***to put the helm a-starboard***: to bring the rudder to the port side, making the vessel turn to the left.
1627–30 [see A-PORT]. **1762** FALCONER *Shipwr.* II. 49 The helm a-starboard flies. **1878** *Daily News* 18 Sept. 2/3 The helm was put hard astarboard to counteract the effects of the tide on the port bow.

a-stare (əˈstɛə(r)), *adv. phr.* [A *prep.*[1] + STARE.] Staring; prominent.
1855 BROWNING *Men & Wom.* I. 140 One stiff blind horse, his every bone a-stare, Stood stupified. **1873** MISS BROUGHTON *Nancy* vi. 47 The tulips are all a-blaze and a-stare.

†**aˈstart**, *v. Obs.* Forms: 3 asteorte, 5 asstart, 4–6 astert(e, astart(e. *Pa. t.* 3 astirte, -orte, -urte, 4–5 astert(e, asterted. [f. A- *pref.* 1 up + START *v.* In sense 3 prob. for ATSTART.]

1. *intr.* To start up.
1205 LAY. 26045 þe eotend up a-sturte [**1250** vp a-storte]. *c* **1380** *Sir Ferumb.* 3399 Op a-sterte þe route anon. **1423** JAMES I *King's Q.* II. xxi, Anon astert The blude of all my body to my hert. **1596** SPENSER *F.Q.* III. ii. 29 Out of her bed she did astart.

2. *intr.* To start into existence, happen, fall out; with *dative* of the person, afterwards taken as *object*, and hence *trans.* To happen to, befall.
1393 GOWER *Conf.* II. 151 Though such an happe of love asterte. *Ibid.* I. 66 That thing shall never me asterte..To make her any feigned chere. **1579** SPENSER *Sheph. Cal.* Nov. 187 No daunger there the shepheard can astert.

3. *intr.* To start off, get away, escape.
1250 LAY. 4262 Ech man þat mihte a-steorte in to one borewe [**1205** And he æt-sturte]. *c* **1386** CHAUCER *Frankl. T.* 294 He seeth he may nat fro his deeth asterte. *c* **1430** LYDG. *Bochas* VII. v. 169b, He might not asterte, He was so pursued. **1509** HAWES *Past. Pleas.* (1845) 65 You have me fettered; I may not asterte. *a* **1541** WYATT *Poet. Wks.* (1861) 31 Let not this song from thee astart.

b. To remove, withdraw, desist.
c **1400** *Song of Roland* 68 Wyn went be-twen them, non did astert. *c* **1450** LONELICH *Grail* xxxviii. 230 But to God ȝoven preysenges, and not a-sterte. **1572** FORREST *Theoph.* 334 Ye shall fynde me fyrme..not onse to astarte.

4. *trans.* (*orig.* with *dat.*) To escape, avoid, shun.
c **1374** CHAUCER *Troylus* v. 1343 If ought amys mastart, [*v.r.* me start] Foryeve it me. *c* **1386** —— *Freres T.* 14 Ther might astert [*v.r.* astirte] him no pecunial peyne. *c* **1450** LONELICH *Grail* xxxi. 404 Thanne schal thyn enemy neuere the asterte. **1575** TURBERV. *Venerie* 138 [I] must needes please him by my death, I may it not astarte.

a-start (əˈstɑːt), *advb. phr.* [A *prep.*[1] + START.] With a start, suddenly.
1721 WODROW *Corr.* (1843) II. 582 The Commissioner came out a start to the Assembly. **1880** SWINBURNE *Thalassius* 372 His heart, As out of sleep suddenly struck astart, Danced.

†**aˈstartle**, *v. Obs. rare.* [f. A- *pref.* 11 + STARTLE *v.*] To startle.
1681 GLANVILL *Sadducismus* 138 They are presently a-startled and amazed at the saying. **1682** H. MORE *Annot. Glanvill's Lux O.* 104 That astartling name of Sandolphon.

astasia (əˈsteɪsɪə). *Med.* [mod.L., a. Gr. ἀστασία unsteadiness, f. ἄστατος unstable, never standing still (ἀ- priv. + στατός standing): see -IA[1].] †**a.** Dysphoria. (Dunglison 1842.) *Obs.* **b.** [ad. Fr. *astasie.*] Inability to stand, as a hysterical disorder. So ***astasia-abasia***, inability to stand or walk. Cf. ABASIA.
[**1888** P. BLOCQ in *Archives de Neurologie* XV. 24 Sur une Affection caractérisée par de l'Astasie et de l'Abasie.] **1890** *N.Y. Med. Jrnl.* LII. 612/2 Those symptoms, then, of difficulty in standing..and ataxia of movement for the act of walking, but not for other muscular acts, corresponded..to the condition described by Blocq under the title *astasia* and *abasia*. **1891** [see ABASIA]. **1960** HINSIE & CAMPBELL *Psychiatric Dict.* (ed. 3) 74/1 Although astasia-abasia is not confined to any single psychiatric group, it is probably most common in conversion hysteria.

†**aˈstate.** *Obs.* [early variant of ESTATE (OF. *estat*:—L. *status*), with atonic *ă* for atonic *ĕ*.]
[*c* **1225** *Hali Meid.* 13 Scheaweð in hire estat of þe blisse undeadlich.] *c* **1230** *Ancr. R.* 178 Sik mon haueð two swuðe dredfule aestaz. *Ibid.* 160 þeos þreo astaz. [*Ibid.* 204 Euerich efter his stat.] **1482** CAXTON *Chron. Eng.* ccli. 321 The kyng in his astate clad in blewe. *a* **1520** *Myrr. Our Ladye* 85 They that ar in dygnite and astate of power are called goddes.

astatic (əˈstætɪk), *a. Electro-Magn.* [f. Gr. ἄστατ-ος unstable (f. ἀ priv. + στα- to stand) + -IC.] Having no tendency to remain in a fixed position. ***astatic needle***: one so situated or arranged as to be unaffected by the earth's magnetism.
1827 J. CUMMING *Man. Electro Dynamics* i. 13 The moveable conductors..are astatic; that is, they are so constructed as not to be affected by the magnetic influence of the earth. **1832** U. K. S. *Nat. Phil.* II, *Electro-Magnet.* xi. §193 The moveable conductor..may be rendered astatic or independent of terrestrial influence. **1870** R. FERGUSON *Electr.* 252 An upright galvanometer with the astatic needles loaded. **1940** *Chambers's Techn. Dict.* 56/1 *Astatic galvanometer*, a moving-magnet galvanometer in which the magnets form an astatic system. **1962** T. AXSON in G. A. T. Burdett *Automatic Control Handbk.* VI. §10 This fundamental characteristic of not tending to any one position has given rise to the name 'Astatic' voltage relay.

aˈstatically, *adv.* [f. prec. + -AL[1] + -LY[2].] In an astatic manner.
1864 in WEBSTER.

astatine (ˈæstətɪn, -iːn). *Chem.* [f. Gr. ἄστατ-ος unstable (see ASTASIA) + -INE[5].] A radioactive element of short half-life, which is rare in nature but can be made artificially; the heaviest element of the halogen group. (Formerly called ALABAMINE and ANGLO-HELVETIUM.) Symbol At, atomic number 85, principal isotope 211.
1947 D. R. CARSON et al. in *Nature* 4 Jan. 24/1 We propose to call element 85 'astatine' from the Greek ἄστατος, unstable. Astatine is in fact the only halogen without stable isotopes. The corresponding chemical symbol proposed is 'At'. **1950** F. GAYNOR *Conc. Encycl. Atomic Physics* 21 *Astatine*, a very rare radioactive element..first announced by Allison and Murphy under the name *alabamine* in 1929; also referred to formerly as eka iodine. *Ibid.*, The name astatine was officially adopted by International Union of Chemistry and announced by the American Chemical Society on September 23, 1949. **1950** N. V. SIDGWICK *Chem. Elements* II. 1260 *Element No. 85* (*Astatine*). There seems to be no doubt now that this element has been obtained as artificial product of nuclear bombardment.

astatki (æˈstætkɪ). [ad. Russ. *ostátki* (pronounced aˈstatkiː), pl. of *ostátok* remainder.] The waste product of the distillation of Russian petroleum atomized with steam and made combustible for use as fuel. Also *attrib.*
1885 *Jrnl. Soc. Chem. Ind.* IV. 78/1 Petroleum residuum or astatki is the only fuel employed in distilling petroleum at Baku. **1902** *Encycl. Brit.* XXXI. 646/1 Large quantities of refuse were produced—known by the Russian name of *astatki*. *Ibid.* 646/2 Practically all the steam power in South Russia..is now raised from *astatki* fuel.

†**aˈstaunch**, *v. Obs. rare*[−1]. [a. OF. *estanchier*, cogn. with Sp. *estancar*:—late L. *stancāre* to STAUNCH.] To staunch, satisfy.
c **1430** LYDG. *Min. Poems* 30 (Halliw.) One to chese to hir delite, That may better astaunche hir appetite.

aˈstay, *v. Obs. rare.* [a. OF. *estaye-r* (mod.F. *étayer*) to support; see STAY *v.*] To stay, stop.
1513–75 *Diurn. Occurr.* (1833) 70 To astay the said tumult.

a-stay (əˈsteɪ), *advb. phr. Naut.* [A *prep.*[1] + STAY *sb.*] A phrase used of the anchor when, in heaving in, the cable is at an acute angle, so as to have a position similar to that of one of the ship's stays. Cf. A-PEAK.
1867 in SMYTH *Sailor's Word-bk.*

†**aˈstays**, *advb. phr. Naut. Obs.* [A *prep.*[1] + STAYS.] = ABACKSTAYS, ABACK *sb.*; also called *by the backstays, by the stays, by the lee.*
1622 R. HAWKINS *Voy. S. Sea* (1847) 123 Another more forcible tooke us astayes; which put us in danger. **1671** *Lond. Gaz.* No. 544/3 Discovering the length of his ship, which the little wind had brought a stayes.

Astbury (ˈæstbərɪ). The surname of John *Astbury* (1688–1743), used (esp. *attrib.*) to designate a type of Staffordshire pottery; also in ***Astbury-Whieldon*** (see quot. 1929).
[**1874** W. CHAFFERS *Collect. Hand Bk. Marks Pottery* 141 Pottery. Staffordshire..Astbury.] **1904** A. H. CHURCH *Eng. Earthenware* (ed. 2) 55 A two-handled loving cup with design in white relief on a red body the whole glazed with a yellow lead glaze was sold..under the designation of Astbury ware. **1929** H. READ *Staffs. Pottery Figures* (Plate 17, *caption*), The term 'Astbury type' is used for those figures in which the decoration depends mostly on a use of coloured clays; the term 'Astbury-Whieldon type' when this technique is combined with decoration in coloured glazes. **1962** *V. & A. Mus. Internat. Art Treasures Exhib.* 62/2 Two Astbury figures in creamware splashed with manganese.

†**aˈsteal**, *v. Obs. rare.* [for ATSTEAL, f. AT *pref.*[2] + STEAL, OE. *stelan.*] *intr.* To steal or slip away (with *dative* = from).
c **1325** *E.E. Allit. P.* B. 1524 Neuer steuen hem a-stel, so stoken is hor tonge.

a-steep (əˈstiːp), *advb. phr.* [A *prep.*[1] + STEEP.] To steep, steeping or soaking. Also *fig.*
1589 *Pappe w. Hatchet* (1844) 14 Elderton swore he had rimes lying a steepe in ale. **1672** RANEW in Spurgeon *Treas. Dav.* xxxix. 3 Laying it asteep in..quickening meditation.

asteer (əˈstɪə(r)), *adv.*, prop. *phr.*, *Sc.* [A *prep.*[1] + *stere* early form of STIR.] Stirring, up and moving about, out of bed; in commotion.
1535 STEWART *Cron. Scot.* (1858) I. 121 Within schort quhile he maid it all on steir. **1785** BURNS *Halloween* xx, Wha was it but Grumphie Asteer that night! **1818** SCOTT *Leg. Montrose* vi, The haill Hielands are asteer.

asteism (ˈæstiːɪz(ə)m). *Rhet.* [ad. L. *asteïsmus*, a. Gr ἀστεϊσμός refined witty talk, f. ἀστεῖος of the city, polite, f. ἄστυ city.] Genteel irony, polite and ingenious mockery.
1589 PUTTENHAM *Eng. Poesie* (Arb.) 200 Asteismus or the Merry scoffe, otherwise the ciuill iest. **1675** TULLY *Let. Baxter* 35 Yet one Asteisme in it must not be omitted. **1753** CHAMBERS *Cycl. Supp.*, Asteism, a genteel irony, or handsome way of deriding another. **1815** [So *Encycl. Brit.* III. 5.]

ˈ**astel.** Also 4–5 astell(e, -yl. [a. OF. *astelle*, *astele*, splinter, split, shingle, thin board:—late L. *hastella* a thin stick, dim. of *hasta* spear, shaft.]

†**1.** A slip of wood; a splinter, a chip; split wood.
a **1330** *Sir Otuel* 1547 With a nastell schide he slewe þam doun. **1440** *Promp. Parv.* 16 Astelle, a schyyd (*v.r.* astyl schyde) *Teda, astula.* **1472** *Paston Lett.* 710 III. 71 Make fagottes and astell and lete alle your grete..trees stande.

2. *Mining.* 'A board or plank, an arch or ceiling of boards over the men's head in a mine, to protect them.' Weale, *Dict. Terms.*

†**aˈstell**, *v. Obs.* Pa. t. and pple. 1–3 asteald(e, astald(e. [OE. *astęllan*, f. A- *pref.* 1 + *stęllan* to place.] To set up, set on foot, establish.
c **885** K. ÆLFRED *Oros.* II. iv. §6 Héo wære tó bisene a-steald. *c* **1175** *Lamb. Hom.* 19 Hu he erest astalde þeos woreld. **1205** LAY. 8950 Grið þer heo astalleden [**1250** makede]. *Ibid.* 27060 þæ astalden þer flem.

astellabre, obs. form of ASTROLABE.

†**aˈstench**, *v. Obs. rare*[−1]. [OE. *astęncan, f. A- *pref.* 1 + *stęncan* to STENCH. Cf. G. *erstänken.*] To assail with stench.
c **1225** *St. Marhar.* 12 Stute nu..to astenchen me wið þe stench þat of þi muð stiheð.

astent, obs. Sc. f. EXTENT: see AS- *pref.*[3].

astent(e, pa. t. of ASTINT *v. Obs.* to stop.

asteorve, var. ASTERVE *v. Obs.* to STARVE.

aster (ˈɑːstə(r), æ-). [a. L. *aster*, a. Gr. ἀστήρ star.]

†**1.** A star. *Obs.* as Eng.
1603 FLORIO *Montaigne* I. xxi. (1632) 47 The revolutions ..and carrols of the asters and planets. **1706** [see 2].

2. *Bot.* A large genus of the N.O. *Compositæ*, with showy radiated flowers, of which the N. American species are especially numerous. The only indigenous British species is the Sea Starwort or Michaelmas Daisy (*A. Tripolium*).
1706 PHILLIPS, Aster, a Star; also the Herb Star-wort, Spare-wort, or Cod-wort. *a* **1761** MRS. DELANY *Autobiog.* (1861) III. 507 A little pale purple Aster with a yellow thrum. **1864** BRYANT *Autumn Walk* iii, And the purple aster waves In a breeze from the land of battles.

3. China aster: a flower (*Callistephus chinensis*) allied to and resembling the asters proper.

1794 MARTYN *Rousseau's Bot.* xxvi. 392 Chinese Aster is an annual plant, with ovate angular leaves. **1859** JEPHSON *Brittany* xvi. 268 A fine show of China asters in full bloom.

4. *Cytology.* **a.** A star-shaped achromatinic structure surrounding the centrosome of a cell during mitosis. **b.** The star-shaped grouping of the chromosomes during mitosis.

1879 E. KLEIN in *Q. Jrnl. Microscop. Soc.* XIX. 414 We pass..to large nuclei..in which the deeply-stained fibrils are arranged like a single aster ('Monaster'), apparently terminating freely at the periphery, but connected into a central network... Next, we trace these [fibrils] into a nuclei without a membrane in which the fibrils are similar in appearance to the preceding ones, but arranged as a double aster ('Dyaster'). **1888** ROLLESTON & JACKSON *Anim. Life* p. xxv, A star or aster with a pronucleus as a centre. **1909** J. W. JENKINSON *Exper. Embryol.* 107 Each sperm forms its own aster, and these combine with one another to form various irregular mitotic figures (triasters, tetrasters, and so on). **1920** L. DONCASTER *Introd. Study Cytology* iii. 31 The centrosome with its system of rays is called an *aster*, and the two asters with the sheaf of fibres connecting them are the achromatic or mitotic spindle. **1963** *New Scientist* 7 Feb. 305 When an egg is fertilised, two structures called asters appear in the cell and a spindle forms between them.

-aster (-'æstə(r)), a. L. *-aster*, suffix of sbs. and adjs., expressing incomplete resemblance, hence generally pejorative (Diez); e.g. L. *philosophaster* a petty philosopher, *oleaster* a wild or bastard olive, *surdaster* a little deaf. Extensively used in Rom. langs. (It. *-astro*, Sp. *-astro*, *-astre*, Pr. *-astre*, OF. *-astre*, mod.F. *-âtre*), esp. in F. as adj. suffix, e.g. *bleuâtre* bluish, *blanchâtre* whitish, etc. In Eng. only in words from L. or Romance, e.g. *astrologaster*, *grammaticaster*, *oleaster*, *poetaster*, *politicaster*.

asteraceous (æstə'reɪʃəs), *a. Bot.* [f. mod.L. *Asterăceæ*, f. *aster* star: see -ACEOUS.] Belonging to the *Asteraceæ* or *Compositæ*; composite.

1876 HARLEY *Mat. Med.* 378 The florets of an asteraceous flower.

astereognosis (əˌstɛriːɒg'nəʊsɪs, -ˌstɪəriːəʊ-). *Med.* [mod.L., f. A- 14 + STEREOGNOSIS.] Inability to recognize the shapes and special relationships of objects, *esp.* as a symptom of disorder of the central nervous system. Also **astereog'nosia**.

1900 in DORLAND *Med. Dict.* 82/2. **1912** *Proc. R. Soc. Med.* V. (Neurol.) 150 *(title)* Case of Asteriognosis, probably due to a Lesion of the Posterior Columns in the Cervical Region. **1941** *Brit. Jrnl. Psychol.* XXXI. 334 This case of astereognosia,..offers no support whatever to the assumption of a psycho-physical process conveying more than mere sensory qualities.

‖**a'steria.** [L.] A precious stone mentioned by Pliny; either the *Asteriated sapphire* (see below) or Cymophane. Cf. ASTROITE, ASTERITE.

1646 SIR T. BROWNE *Pseud. Ep.* 137 Asteria, or some kinde of *Lapis stellaris.* **1874** WESTROPP *Prec. Stones* 66 Asteria..is undoubtedly the cymophane, or chrysoberyl cat's-eye.

†**a'sterial**, *a. Obs.* [f. Gr. ἀστέρι-ος starry (f. ἀστήρ star) + -AL¹.] **a.** Of or connected with the stars. **b.** Star-like; asteriated.

a **1708** T. WARD *Eng. Ref.* (1716) 298 (D.) If the deep learn'd asterial quacks Paint Time to life in almanacks. **1686** PLOT *Staffordsh.* 191 Perforated..with foliated or asterial inlets.

‖**Asterias** (ə'stɪərɪæs). *Zool.* Pl. -æ. [mod.L., a. Gr. ἀστερίας starry, f. ἀστήρ star. A sing. *asteria* has been sometimes used.] A genus of Echinoderms, containing the common Five-rayed Star-fish, with allied species. **asterialite** (ə'stɪərɪəlaɪt) [see -LITE], a fossil star-fish. **asterid** ('æstərɪd), **asteridian** (æstə'rɪdɪən), an animal belonging to the *Asteridæ* or star-fish family.

1794 SULLIVAN *View Nat.* II. 175 Asteriæ and entrochi.. have a starry appearance. **1847** CARPENTER *Zool.* §1012 The common Asterias, or Star-fish. **1876** BENEDEN *Anim. Parasites* 43 Delle Chiaie has lately observed on an asteria a *Nereis squamosa.* **1883** tr. *Nordenskiöld's Voy. Vega* 74 Asterids of many kinds.

asteriated (ə'stɪərɪeɪtɪd), *ppl. a.* [f. Gr. ἀστέρι-ος starry + -ATE + -ED.] Radiated; with rays diverging from the centre, as in a star.

1816 CLEAVELAND *Min.* 194 Asteriated sapphire.. presents a very peculiar reflection of light in the form of a star, with six radii. **1868** DANA *Min.* 138 A variety having a stellate opalescence, when viewed in the direction of the vertical axis of the crystal, is the Asteriated Sapphire (*Asteria* of Pliny).

‖**asterion** (ə'stɪərɪən). [mod.L., a. Gr. ἀστέριον starry, f. ἀστήρ star.] †**a.** *Herb.* Name of a plant of doubtful identity. **b.** in *Phys.* (See quot.)

c **1000** *Sax. Leechd.* I. 164 Genim þysse wyrte bergean þe we asterion nemdon. **1614** MARKHAM *Cheap Husb.* Table, Asterion, is an Herb growing..on walls..It hath yellow flowers like Foxgloves, and the leaves are round and blewish. **1878** BARTLEY *Topinard's Anthrop.* II. ii. 224 Asterion, point behind the mastoid process, where the parietal, occipital and temporal bones meet.

asterisk ('æstərɪsk). Also (4 **asterichos, -icus**), 7 **asterisque, -iske,** (**-ick**), 7–9 **-isc.** [ad. L. *asteriscus*, a. Gr. ἀστερίσκος, dim. of ἀστήρ star: see -ISK.]

1. A little star.

1682 SIR T. BROWNE *Chr. Mor.* 38 Add one ray unto the common lustre..and prove not a cloud but an asterisk.

2. *transf.* Anything shaped or radiating like a star; *spec.* in *Eastern Ch.* a star-shaped instrument of gold or silver placed above the chalice and paten to prevent the veil from touching the elements.

1708 *Phil. Trans.* XXVI. 77 An Irregular Coralline-stone, naturally Engrav'n with Asterisks. *a* **1733** NORTH *Lives* I. 274 The lanthorn is in the centre of an asterisk of glades. **1872** O. SHIPLEY *Gloss. Eccl. Terms*, The veil [*aer*]..is placed over the asterisk, and covers both chalice and paten.

3. *esp.* The figure of a star (*) used in writing and printing. **a.** as a reference to a note at the foot or margin of the page, **b.** to indicate the omission of words or letters, **c.** to distinguish words and phrases as conjectural, obscure, or bearing some other specified character, **d.** as a dividing mark, or for similar typographical purposes.

[**1382** WYCLIF *2 Chron.* Prol., Wher euer ȝe seen asterichos ..there wijte ȝe of Ebrue added, that in Latyne bokis is not had. **1387** TREVISA *Higden* V. 55 A signe þat hatte asteriscus and is i-shape liche a sterre.] **1612** BRINSLEY *Pos. Parts* Pref. (1669) 4 For the necessary questions..I have set an Asterisk upon them. **1645** M. CASAUBON *Temp. Evils* 47 Set out as imperfect with three asteriscs. **1656** BLOUNT *Glossogr.*, *Asterisque.* **1796** PEGGE *Anonym.* (1809) 289 The asterisks in Drake's Eboracum are intended for Archbishop Lancelot Blackburne. **1824** J. JOHNSON *Typogr.* II. iii. 51 The Asterisk divides each verse of a Psalm into two parts.

'**asterisk,** *v.* [f. prec.] To mark with an asterisk, to star.

a **1733** NORTH *Exam.* (1740) 279 (D.), I need not asterisk the quaint words and expressions. **1864** *Glasgow Daily Her.* 24 Sept., Additions written on the blank pages..and often asterisked where they are intended to be taken in.

asterisked ('æstərɪskt), *ppl. a.* [f. ASTERISK *v.* + -ED.] Marked with an asterisk; printed with asterisks replacing omitted letters or words.

1897 *Westm. Gaz.* 20 July 2/2 An asterisked speech [in 'Hansard']. **1911** C. MACKENZIE *Passionate Elopement* xx. 183 All the world was deeply engrossed in reading about his asterisked self and his asterisked neighbour.

asterism ('æstərɪz(ə)m). [ad. Gr. ἀστερισμός a marking with stars, a constellation, f. ἀστήρ star: see -ISM.]

1. A group or cluster of stars; a constellation.

1598 CHAPMAN *Bl. Beggar* Plays 1874, 12 All set in number and in perfect form, Even like the Asterisms fix'd in heaven. **1774** J. BRYANT *Mythol.* I. 341 The zodiac, and its asterisms. **1869** DUNKIN *Midn. Sky* 151 Cepheus was one of the old forty-eight asterisms.

†**2.** *loosely*, A star, or anything shaped like one.

1657 REEVE *God's Plea* 55 Oh that Mercy is such a bright Star, and yet that we have neither observed the Asterism, nor, etc. **1743** tr. *Heister's Surg.* 19 There are other [Compresses] again in the form of an Asterism.

3. A group of three asterisks placed thus (⁂) to direct attention to a particular passage. *Rarely*, a single asterisk (*) so used.

1649 G. DANIEL *Trinarch.* xvi, This full Quotation, by an Asterisme Set in the margent of a middle Page. **1796** MORSE *Amer. Geog.* I. 193 To which an asterism (*) is prefixed. **1871** RINGWALT *Encycl. Print.* 48 *Asterism*, three asterisks placed in this manner [⁂].

4. *Min.* (Also in mod.L. form *asterismus.*) An appearance of light in the shape of a six-rayed star seen in some crystals, as in star sapphire.

1879 RUTLEY *Stud. Rocks* x. 135 This asterismus is due to the presence of included microliths or small crystals.

aste'rismal, *a.* [f. prec. + -AL¹.] Of or pertaining to asterisms or constellations.

1840 H. H. WILSON *Vishnu Pur.* 224 The cycle comprehends..sixty-seven lunar-asterismal months.

†**aste'ristic**, *a. Obs. rare.* [f. as prec.: see -ISTIC.] Of or pertaining to constellations; starry.

1652 URQUHART *Jewel* Wks. 1834, 241 An asteristick ouch, wherein were inchased fifteen several diamonds. *Ibid.* 259 Asteristick and planetary influences.

†'**asterite.** *Obs.* [ad. L. *asterītes*, a. Gr. ἀστερίτης. The L. form is more usual.] A gem known to the ancients; cf. ASTRION, ASTERIA.

1398 TREVISA *Barth. De P.R.* XVI. xvii. (1495) 559. Asterites is a precyous stone..Therin is closyd as it were a sterre. **1635** SWAN *Spec. Mund.* (1670) 258 The Astarite is a clear shining chrystalline stone, having in the midst the image of a full moon. **1677** HALE *Prim. Orig. Man.* 328 The Configurations of Asterites, of Crystals, of Salts.

astern (ə'stɜːn), *adv.* (*prep.*), orig. *phr.*, *Naut.* [f. A *prep.*¹ + STERN, the hinder part of a ship.]

A. *adv.* **1.** Of position: In or at the stern.

1675 HOBBES *Odyss.* 61 Then he astern sate down and governed. *a* **1826** HOOD *Wee Man* x, Good sir, you must not sit a-stern, The wave will else come in.

2. Hence, in the rear, behind (at any distance).

1627 SMITH *Seaman's Gram.* ix. 45 To lay an anchor.. ahead, and another asterne. **1692** *Lond. Gaz.* No. 2811/3 The Rupert being about a mile a-stern. **1725** DE FOE *Voy. round World* (1840) 350 A gale of wind right astern. **1845** DARWIN *Voy. Nat.* iii. (1879) 43 They made all sail..and soon left the horse astern.

b. *astern of*: in the rear of (a ship).

1634 SIR T. HERBERT *Trav.* 3 A Barbarian man of warre ..came asterne of us. **1707** LUTTRELL *Brief Rel.* VI. 168 One of the biggest..men of war..sunk down a stern of him. **1865** DICKENS *Mut. Fr.* i. 3 Keeping halt his boat's length astern of the other boat.

3. Of motion: To the rear, backward; stern foremost. Said of a ship or boat.

1681 *Lond. Gaz.* 1628/1 Soon after the Algerine fell a stern. **1857** EMERSON *Poems* 29, I, Alphonso, live and learn, Seeing Nature go astern. **1858** J. MANSFIELD in *Merc. Mar. Mag.* V. 19 She came round with head to wind, when she backed astern.

B. *prep.* At the stern or rear of (a ship).

1675 HOBBES *Odyss.* 150 Dolon's spoils astern his ship he plac'd.

astern, var. *austerne*, obs. f. AUSTERE.

asternal (ə'stɜːnəl), *a. Phys.* [f. A- *pref.* 14 + mod.L. *stern-um* breast-bone, ad. Gr. στέρνον chest + -AL¹.] Not joined to the breast-bone.

1847 TODD *Cycl. Anat. & Ph.* IV. 652/1 The asternal ribs.

asteroid ('æstərɔɪd), *a.* and *sb.* [ad. Gr. ἀστεροειδής star-like, f. ἀστήρ star: see -OID.]

A. *adj.* **1.** Star-shaped, star-like.

1854 DALLAS *Anim. Kingd.* (1856) 52 The asteroid polypes are all compound animals. **1880** WALLACE *Isl. Life* xiv. 296 The woody Asteroid forms.

2. *Zool.* Of, belonging to, or characteristic of the Asteroidea.

1888 ROLLESTON & JACKSON *Anim. Life* 5 The Asteroid larva closely resembles the Holothurioid. **1900** F. A. BATHER et al. *Echinoderma* 3 No sharp line can be drawn between Asteroid and Ophiuroid structure.

B. *sb.*

1. Name given to the numerous minute planetary bodies revolving round the sun between the orbits of Mars and Jupiter; called also *planetoids* and *minor planets*.

1802 HERSCHEL in *Phil. Trans.* XCII. 228 From this, their asteroidical appearance, if I may use that expression..I shall take my name, and call them Asteroids. **1875** PROCTOR *Exp. Heaven* 114 Not a year passes without the recognition of two or three and sometimes ten or twelve..asteroids.

†**2.** A meteor. *Obs.*

1830 GOODRICH (P. Parley) *Sun Moon and Stars* lvii. (1837) 296 By the term 'November Asteroïds' it is the shooting or falling stars that are spoken of. **1849** MRS. SOMERVILLE *Connex. Phys. Sc.* xxxvii. 447 They [the meteorites] are asteroids revolving about the sun.

3. Hence applied to a kind of fire-work.

1875 *Times* 4 Nov. 1/6 (*Advt.*) Rockets with pearl stars.. Asteroids changing colours while sailing through the air.

4. *Zool.* A star-fish of the class Asteroidea.

1841 E. FORBES *Brit. Starfishes* 1. 3 The Crinoids as analogues of the Polypes are lower than the Asteroids. **1888** ROLLESTON & JACKSON *Anim. Life* 563 The apical system of plates is well defined in the young Asteroid. **1900** F. A. BATHER et al. *Echinoderma* 14 The Asteroids were probably the last group to branch off from the fixed Echinoderms. **1921** *Chamber's Jrnl.* XI. 502/1 The mauve of these beautiful asteroids blends perfectly with the soft gray sands of the North Pacific.

asteroidal (æstə'rɔɪdəl), *a.* [f. prec. + -AL¹.] Of or pertaining to asteroids.

1868 LOCKYER *Heavens* 238 Meteoric and asteroidal rings. **1881** PROCTOR *Poetry Astron.* x. 355 The asteroidal family.

†**aste'roidical**, *a. Obs.* [f. as prec. + -ICAL.] = prec.

1802 [see ASTEROID *sb.* 1.]

asterophyllite (ˌæstərəʊ'fɪlaɪt). *Palæont.* [f. Gr. ἀστήρ, ἀστερο-, star + φύλλον leaf + λίθος stone.] A fossil plant, with leaves arranged in whorls, found in the coal formations of Europe and America.

1847 in CRAIG (as Latin). **1851** RICHARDSON *Geol.* 192.

astert, var. ASTART *v. Obs.* to escape.

†**a'sterve**, *v.*¹ *str. Obs.* Forms: 1 ***asteorfan**, 2–3 **asteorven**, 3–4 **asterve**. *Pa. pple.* 1 **astorfen**, 3 **astorve(n.** [OE. *asteorfan*, f. A- *pref.* 1 + *steorfan* (str. intr.): see STARVE. Cf. OHG. *arstërpan*, *istërban*, MHG. *ersterben.* Before 1400 the strong and weak forms were levelled in *asterve*, which did not survive long enough to become *astarve*; cf. STARVE, and mod.G. *ersterben.*] *intr.* To die, *esp.* of hunger; to starve.

c **1000** ÆLFRIC in Wright *Voc.* 61/1 *Sideratus* vel *ictuatus*, færunge astorfen. *c* **1230** *Ancr. R.* 326 He not hweðer he schulle þet ilke daie uerliche asteoruen. *a* **1250** *Owl & Night.* 1200 3if deor schule ligge astorve. *c* **1380** *Sir Ferumb.* 3058 Schamly for to asterue þer for hungre.

†**a'sterve**, *v.*² *wk. Obs.* Forms: 1 **asterfan, astyrfan, astærfan**, 4 **asterve**. [OE. *astęrfen*, f. A- *pref.* 1 + *stęrfen* (weak trans.): see STARVE. Cf.

OHG. *arsterpan*, MHG. *ersterben*, and see prec.] *trans.* To kill, destroy; to starve out.
c975 *Rushw. Gosp.* Matt. xv. 13 Wæstmaseten þa þe ne sette fæder min.. astærfed bið. a1000 *Crist* (Grein) 192 Stánum astyrfed. 1340 *Ayenb.* 240 He ssel.. wyþdraȝe þe metes and þet weter uor to asterue.. þe castel. þe castel of þe wombe.. is asterued be uestinges.

†**a'steynte**, *v.* (only in pa. t.) *Obs.* [f. OF. *esteindre* (mod. *éteindre*), pa. pple. *esteint*:—L. *extinguĕre, extinct-um*, to EXTINGUISH.] To put out, extinguish.
c1450 LONELICH *Grail* l. 442 A gret rein.. halfendel the flawme fully asteynte.

†**a'steynte**, *ppl. a. Obs.* [Perhaps for *atteynte*: see ATTAINT *a.*; or ? pa. pple. of ASTENCH, = 'caused to stink, stinking'; cf. *aseint, asench, adreint, adrench.*]
c1300 *K. Alis.* 880 He! fyle asteynte horesone! To misdo was ay thy wone.

‖**asthenia** (æsθɪ'naɪə). Rarely '**astheny**. *Path.* [mod.L., a. Gr. ἀσθένεια, f. ἀσθενέ-ς weak, f. ἀ priv. + σθένος strength.] Lack of strength, diminution of vital power, weakness, debility. **asthe'nology**, scientific consideration of diseases arising from debility (Mayne *Exp. Lex.* 1853). **asthe'nopia** [Gr. ὤψ, ὦπα eye], weakness of sight.
1802 *Med. & Physical Jrnl.* VII. 246 Nervous diseases from direct asthenia. 1830 *Edin. Encycl.* XIV. 10 Asthenia including those diseases which consist in a diminution of the nervous energy. 1859 WORCESTER, *Astheny.* 1862 BELLEW *Afghan.* 390 The typhus character was proved by the extreme asthenia. 1875 WALTON *Dis. Eye* 345 Asthenopia quickly occurs. 1933 *Brit. Jrnl. Psychol.* July 22 Perseveration due simply to mental asthenia and lack of spontaneity. 1938 S. BECKETT *Murphy* iv. 49 That long hank of Apollonian asthenia.

asthenic (æs'θɛnɪk), *a.* and *sb. Path.* [ad. Gr. ἀσθενικός: see prec.] **A.** *adj.* **a.** Of, pertaining to, or characterized by asthenia; weak, debilitated; weakening.
1789 NATH. FOSTER *Parr's Wks.* (1828) VII. 466 Are you sure that your diathesis is purely asthenic. 1852 T. ROSS tr. *Humboldt's Trav.* I. iii. 136 Bleeding, evacuating, and all the asthenic remedies.
b. Applied to a type of physique (see quot. 1937).
1925 W. J. H. SPROTT tr. *Kretschmer's Physique & Character* I. ii. 19 Three ever-recurring principal types of physique have emerged.. which we will call 'asthenic', 'athletic', and 'pyknic'. 1927 HENDERSON & GILLESPIE *Text-bk. Psychiatry* VII. 118 The thin, visceroptotic 'asthenic' type. 1937 [see ATHLETIC *a.* 3].
B. *sb.* One who is asthenic.
1893 in *Funk's Stand. Dict.* 1925 E. & C. PAUL tr. *Janet's Psychol. Healing* I. III. 389 Deschamps finds it necessary to admit that, under the influence of strong emotion, an asthenic can perform actions which are beyond his powers at ordinary times. 1925 W. J. H. SPROTT tr. *Kretschmer's Physique & Character* I. ii. 21 The essential characteristic of the type of the male asthenic is.. a deficiency in thickness combined with an average unlessened length.

as'thenical, *a.* [f. prec. + -AL[1].] = prec.
1819 LAWRENCE *Lect. Man* (1844) 369 No symptom of the asthenical malady which characterizes Albinos.

asthenolith (æs'θɛnəʊlɪθ). *Geol.* [f. as next + -LITH.] The material in the asthenosphere.
1929 B. WILLIS in *Bull. Geol. Soc. Amer.* XL. 311 An asthenolith may be defined as a body of magma formed in consequence of a rise of temperature in the asthenosphere because of concentration of heat energy.

asthenosphere (æs'θɛnəʊsfɪə(r)). *Geol.* [f. Gr. ἀσθεν-ής weak (f. Gr. ἀ- priv. + σθένος strength) + -O + SPHERE *sb.*] (See quot. 1914.)
1914 J. BARRELL in *Jrnl. Geol.* XXII. 659 The theory of isostasy shows that below the lithosphere there exists in contradistinction a thick earth-shell marked by a capacity to yield readily to long-enduring strains of limited magnitude... Its comparative weakness.. is its distinctive feature. It may then be called the sphere of weakness—the *asthenosphere.* 1915 *Ibid.* XXIII. 43 The weakest part of the asthenosphere is of the order of one-hundredth of the maximum strength of the lithosphere. 1922 *Encycl. Brit.* XXXI. 214/1 A yielding but not necessarily molten layer, Barrell's asthenosphere.. which lies some 80 to 100 m... below the general surface of the geoid. 1966 *New Scientist* 10 Mar. 635/1 The seat of crustal upheavals may be the so-called 'asthenosphere' or low-velocity layer in the Earth's upper mantle.

asthma ('æsθmə, 'æsmə). Forms: 4–7 **asma**, (4 **asmy**), 7 **astma**, 6– **asthma**. [a. Gr. ἆσθμα, -ματ-, f. ἄζ-ειν to breathe hard, ἄ-ειν to blow. Smart and Walker give the pronunciation ('æstmə).]
1. Difficulty of breathing; *spec.* a disease of respiration, characterized by intermittent paroxysms of difficult breathing, with a wheezing sound, a sense of constriction in the chest, cough, and expectoration.
1398 TREVISA *Barth. De P.R.* VII. xxix. (1495) 243 Dyffy-culte and hardnes of brethynge hight Asma. *Ibid.* 244 Thre manere of Asmyes. 1578 LYTE *Dodoens* 776 The shortnesse of breath called asthma. 1634 R. H. *Salerne Regim.* 205 The matter that causeth Asma. 1741–3 WESLEY *Extr. Jrnl.* (1749) 20 He seemed to be dying of an asthma. 1861 E. MAYHEW *Dogs* 101 Asthma is spasm of the bronchial tubes.

2. *attrib.* **asthma herb** *Austral.* (see quot. 1887).
1887 MOLONEY *Forestry W. Afr.* 411 Australian Asthma-Herb (*Euphorbia pilulifera*, L.). 1889 J. H. MAIDEN *Useful Native Plants Australia* 183 Queensland Asthma Herb.

†'**asthmasy**. *Obs. rare*[−1]. [cf. Gr. ἀσθμάζ-ειν and ἀσθμαίν-ειν, to breathe hard.] = ASTHMA.
1599 A. M. *Gabelhouer's Bk. Physic* 102/2 Asthmasye, or shortnes of breath.

asthmatic (æsθ'mætɪk), *a.* and *sb.* Also 6 **asmatycke**, **-icke**, **asthmatyke**, **-ique**, **-icke**, 7–8 **-ick**. [ad. L. *asthmaticus*, a. Gr. ἀσθματικός: see ASTHMA and -IC.] **A.** *adj.*
1. Affected with or suffering from asthma.
1542 BOORDE *Dyetary* xxxv. (1870) 296 A dyete for.. asthmatyke men. 1582 HESTER *Phiorav. Secr.* III. cxi. 135 Giuen in the broth of a Chickin vnto those that are Asmaticke. 1775 H. WALPOLE *Last Jrnls.* 14 Mar., Asthmatic and unhealthy like her father. 1861 WYNTER *Soc. Bees* 459 An asthmatic patient.
2. a. Of or pertaining to asthma.
1620 VENNER *Via Recta* iii. 61 The Asthmatick passion.. is a short and painfull fetching of breath. 1872 BLACK *Adv. Phaeton* xxiv. 328 Interrupted by a fit of asthmatic coughing.
b. Good against asthma.
1880 M. COLLINS *Th. in Gard.* I. 53 An asthmatic balsam that is 'truly efficacious and pleasant.'
3. *fig.* Puffing, wheezy.
1806 J. BERESFORD *Miseries* I. x. 242 An asthmatic pair of bellows. 1853 KANE *Grinnell Exp.* cxi, The asthmatic old steam-tug.
B. *sb.* A person suffering from asthma.
1610 BARROUGH *Physick* II. vii. (1639) 82 You must give unto the Asthmatickes.. Antidotes. 1871 NAPHEYS *Prev. & Cur. Dis.* III. vii. 891 Why should the close air of a crowded room be balmiest of airs to some asthmatics?

asth'matical, *a.* [f. prec. + -AL[1].] = prec.
a1639 WOTTON *Let.* in *Reliq.* (1685) 467 Asthmatical straitness of respiration. 1862 *Athenæum* 30 Aug. 264 Almost all the men were asthmatical.

asth'matically, *adv.* [f. prec. + -LY[2].] After the manner of one suffering from asthma.
1812 L. HUNT in *Examiner* 21 Dec. 815/1 The waves heave rather asthmatically. 1859 GEO. ELIOT *A. Bede* II. xviii. 168 Old Burge.. leaned forward coughing asthmatically.

‖**asthore** (æs'θɔː(r)). *Anglo-Ir.* [Irish, f. *a* O + *stór* treasure.] My treasure; (my) darling.
1894 SOMERVILLE & ROSS *Real Charlotte* III. xli. 132 Come in out o' the rain, asthore. a1896 J. TODHUNTER in E. A. Sharp *Lyra Celtica* (1896) 170 Sure it's our complaint that's on us, asthore, this day. 1897 ROSS & SOMERVILLE *Silver Fox* v. 64 'Oh, asthoreen,' wailed his mother... 'Take the cup o' tay, asthore, don't be talkin' that way.' 1906 A. P. GRAVES in C. V. Stanford *Nat. Song Bk.* 156 I've found my bonny babe a nest On Slumber Tree: I'll rock you there to rosy rest, Astore Machree!

astiȝ, astigh, variants of ASTYE *v. Obs.*

astigmatic (æstɪg'mætɪk), *a. Phys.* [f. Gr. ἀ priv. + στίγμα, -ματ- point + -IC.] **1.** Pertaining to or characterized by astigmatism.
1849 TODD *Cycl. Anat. & Phys.* IV. 1468/2 An astigmatic lens. 1879 HARLAN *Eyesight* vi. 82 The astigmatic cornea.. has different curvatures in directions at right angles to each other.
2. Of an artificial lens: correcting astigmatism.
1881 *Ophthalmic Rev.* Nov. (Advt.), Every description of Astigmatic, Cylindrical and Sphero-Cylindrical Spectacle Lenses. 1958 *Listener* 6 Nov. 728/2 This distortion is immediately removed if his pictures are photographed through a one-degree astigmatic lens at an axis of fifteen degrees off the vertical.

astigmatism (ə'stɪgmətɪz(ə)m). [f. as prec. + -ISM.] **1. a.** A structural defect in the eye (see quot.), which prevents the rays of light from being brought to a common focus on the retina.
1849 G. B. AIRY in *Trans. Camb. Philos. Soc.* VIII. 361 Twenty years ago, I had the honour of submitting to this Society a statement of the effects of a mal-formation in my own left eye. The nature of the effect was this: that the rays of light coming from a luminous point and falling upon the whole surface of the pupil do not converge to a point at any position within the eye, but converge in such a manner as to pass through two lines at right angles to each other, (a geometrical phenomenon, to which the term *astigmatism* was very happily affixed by the present Master of Trinity College [Whewell]). 1862 J. LAURENCE in *Med. Times* 1 Nov. 474/1 Correction both of the astigmatism and the ametropia. 1878 FOSTER *Phys.* III. ii. 411 The cause of astigmatism is.. unequal curvature of the cornea.
b. *Optics.* A similar defect in a lens.
1859 PARKINSON *Optics* iv. 48 When a pencil of rays is reflected or refracted at the surface of a medium, the reflected or refracted rays will not, in general, pass accurately through one point. This peculiarity is sometimes called astigmatism. 1892 J. T. TAYLOR *Optics Photogr.* xxiii, Astigmatism is a serious fault for a lens to possess in any marked degree.
2. *fig.*
1934 G. BOTTOMLEY in *Ess. & Stud.* XIX. 142 This mental astigmatism.. was not noticed while the fires of great genius flamed high.

astilbe (ə'stɪlbiː). *Bot.* [mod.L. (F. Hamilton (*olim* Buchanan), 1825), f. Gr. ἀ- priv. (A- 14) + στίλβη, fem. of στίλβος glittering (στίλβειν to glitter).] A plant of a genus of perennials of the family Saxifragaceæ with terminal clusters of small white or red flowers.
1843 A. GRAY in *London Jrnl. Bot.* II. 123 Three species belong to a single and highly natural genus, for which the name of *Astilbe* must be retained. *Ibid.* 124 The stamens of the original *Astilbe* are probably sometimes double the number of the sepals. 1863 —— *Man. Bot. N. United States* 142 *Astilbe*, false goatsbeard. 1956 *Dict. Gardening* (*R. Hort. Soc.*) (ed. 2) I. 215/1 The Astilbes grow well in rich garden soil if it is moist in summer. 1959 *Listener* 14 May 866/3 Aruncus and astilbe.. and many primulas are suitable.

astiler, obs. form of ASHLAR *sb.*

†**a'stint**, *v. Obs.* Forms: 1 **astynt-an**, 2–4 **astynt-en**, 3 **astunt-en** (**y**), 4 **astent**. For inflexions, see STINT. [OE. *astyntan*, f. A- *pref.* 1 + *styntan* to STINT.]
1. *trans.* To bring to a standstill, to cause to cease or stop.
c700 *Epinal Gl.* (Sweet) 488 *Hebetatus* astyntid. c1230 *Ancr. R.* 72 þeone kuðen heo neuere astunten hore cleppe. c1330 *Arth. & Merl.* 835 So noble swerdes dent, That hem astint. 1480 CAXTON *Chron. Eng.* ccxii. 198 Tho were al maner plees of the kynges benche astent.
2. *intr.* To stop, stay.
c1230 *Ancr. R.* 80 Heo schal tunen hire muð þ te swote breð.. astunte wiðinnen. c1380 *Sir Ferumb.* 1109 Er þay come to Mantrible neuere þay ne astente.
3. *intr.* To cease, desist, leave off.
1250 LAY. 31891 þo astunte þe cwaolm. c1380 *Sir Ferumb.* 1842 He nel neuere a-stynte.

†**a'stipulate**, *v. Obs.* [f. L. *astipulāt-* ppl. stem of *a(d)stipulā-ri*, f. *ad* to + *stipulāri* to bargain, covenant. Cf. ADSTIPULATE, -ATION, in mod. treatises on Rom. Law.]
1. *intr.* To make an agreement or stipulation; to assent or agree (*to*).
1548 HALL *Chron. Hen. VII* an. 10 (R.) He nothynge denyed, but.. did astipulate and agree to all thinges layed to hys charge. 1634 JACKSON *Creed* VII. xx. Wks. VII. 176 So the prophet astipulateth in the name of his God. 1652 BP. HALL *Invis. World* II. §1 All.. have astipulated to this truth.
2. *trans.* To agree or assent to.
1658 J. ROBINSON *Eudoxa* ix. 50 Several of Hippocrates Aphorisms.. do astipulate the same.

†**a,stipu'lation**. *Obs.* [ad. L. *astipulātiōn-em*, n. of action f. *astipulāt-*: see prec. and -ATION.]
1. The action of agreeing to a proposal; agreement, bargain.
1594 R. PARSONS *Conf. Next Success.* I. v. 84 The astipulation and promises made on both sides. 1628 BP. HALL *Hon. Maried Clergie* III. §10. 802, I.. by the consent and astipulation of my princes.. consigne to them, that monasterie.
2. The action of assenting to what has been alleged; a confirming statement.
1618 *Hist. P. Warbeck* in *Harl. Misc.* (1793) 96 The council.. found.. his reasons of defence manifest astipulations of the matter. 1708 MOTTEUX *Rabelais* IV. xxxii, By the Testimony, and Astipulation of the brute Beasts.

†**a'stir**, *v. Obs.* Forms: 1 **astyri-**, **astiri-an**, 2 **astiri-**, **asteri-**, 3 **asturi-en**, 5 **astere**, 6 **asteir**. [OE. *astyri-an*, f. A- *pref.* 1 up, out + *styrian* to STIR; cogn. w. OHG. *irsturen*, MHG. *erstürn* to stir up.] To stir up, move, disturb, excite, physically or emotionally.
c1000 *Ags. Gosp.* John v. 4 þæt water wæs astyred. —— Mark xv. 11 þa astyredon þa bisceopas þa meneȝu. c1175 *Lamb. Hom.* 95 He sake ne asterde. 1205 LAY. 28786 Astured wes al þas þeode strongliche swiðe. 1567 *Test. K. Hen. Stewart* in *Sc. Poems 16th C.* II. 262 My solace, sorow, sobbery to asteir.

astir (ə'stɜː(r)), *adv.*, orig. *phr.* [A *prep.*[1] + STIR *sb.* Not in any Dict. of 18th c.: not in Todd 1818, Craig 1847, Webster 1864. First in northern writers; perh. anglicized from Sc. ASTEER, q.v.] Stirring. **a.** *esp.* Out of bed, up and moving about.
[1805 WORDSW. *Waggoner* I. 23 Hush, there is some one on the stir!] 1823 LOCKHART *Reg. Dalton* I. vii. (1842) 34 Astir by eight o'clock. 1831 SCOTT *Cast. Dang.* ii, It is lucky.. we have found our friends astir. 1833 HT. MARTINEAU *Briery Crk.* iii. 46 The whole village was early astir. 1850 MRS. STOWE *Uncle Tom's C.* xxx. 281 Now it is morning, and everybody is astir. 1871 M. COLLINS *Mrq. & Merch.* II. vi. 163 Early as it is, the world is astir.
b. *gen.* In motion. **c.** *fig.* In excitement.
1837 CARLYLE *Fr. Rev.* v. v. II. 314 All kings and kinglets.. are astir; their brows clouded with menace. 1856 KANE *Arct. Exp.* II. i. 17 All hands are astir with their [the winds'] novel influences. 1870 F. WILSON *Ch. Lindisf.* 34 The village is astir with sea-faring men. 1878 HUXLEY *Physiogr.* 62 When there is much wind astir.

†**a'stirbroad**, *adv. Obs.* [? f. A *prep.*[1], STIR *v.*, and ABROAD.] Stirring abroad, moving from place to place.
1643 HORN & ROBOTHAM *Gate Lang. Unl.* xix. §224 The grasshopper.. singeth astirbroad: the cricket at home.

†**astite, as tite**, *advb. phr. Obs.* Chiefly *north.* Forms: 4 **als tit(e**, **als tyte**, **als tyd**, 4–5 **alstite**; 4 **as tit**, 4–5 **as tyt**, **as tyte**, **as tyd**, 5 **astyht**, 5–7 **astite**. The two words *as tite* were commonly written as one from 15th to 17th c. (cf. ASFAST, ASSOON.)

Beside the obvious import (see AS, A 3, 5, and TITE), it had the sense: As quick as might be, immediately (Fr. *aussitôt*).

[**1325–1420** See other instances under ALSTITE.] *c* **1320** R. BRUNNE *Medit.* 436 þow shalt haue of vs þe deþ astyte. *c* **1330** *Amis & Amil.* 1046 And lepe astite opon a stede. *c* **1435** *Torr. Portugal* 641 A! theff! yeld the astyt. *c* **1450** LONELICH *Grail* xxii. 12 Al this schal I the tellen astyht. **1674** RAY *N. Countr. Wds.* 2 *Astite*, Anon, shortly, or as soon.

astiune: see ASTRION.

astod(e, pa. t. of ASTAND *v. Obs.*

as-told-to, *adj.* (and *sb.*) *phr.* Chiefly *U.S.* [f. phr. *as told to*, qualifying a book-title.] *attrib.* Of a biographical account, etc.: written by a professional author using material gathered from personal conversation with the subject. Also *absol.* as *sb.*, a book or article of this nature.

[**1928** (*title*) My life is in your hands by Eddie Cantor as told to David Freedman.] **1966** *Listener* 22 Sept. 428/2 His 'autobiography', so-called, put together by Alex Haley, a journalist, was intended to be an 'as told to' book, with every word.. sanctioned by Malcom [X]. **1975** *New Yorker* 1 Dec. 52/2 Butchers are ready for the big time, the talk shows, the as-told-tos, throwing out the first ball—the whole side of beef. **1977** *Rolling Stone* 5 May 47/2 He sat down with poet Tom Clark.. to tape an 'as-told-to' biography.

astomatous (əˈstɒmətəs), *a.* [see next.] Having no mouth; applied in *Zool.* to the *Astomata* or 'mouthless' animals, a division of the Protozoa, comprising the *Gregarinidæ* and *Rhizopoda*.

1855 OWEN *Inv. Anim.* 669 Astomatous Infusoria.. have no true or determinate mouth.

astomous (ˈæstəməs), *a.* [f. Gr. ἄστομ-ος mouthless (f. ἀ priv. + στόμα, -ματ-, mouth) + -OUS.] Having no mouth, astomatous; applied chiefly in *Bot.* to those Mosses in which the urn does not open by the detachment of the operculum.

1857 HENFREY *Bot.* §319 In what are called Astomous Mosses there is no deciduous operculum. **1880** GRAY *Bot. Text-bk.* 398 Astomous, without a stoma or mouth.

†**aˈstonate**, *ppl. a. Obs.* [north. f. ASTONÈD, with *-ate* written for *-et*, *-it*: see -ATE.] Astounded.

1513 DOUGLAS *Æneis* XII. xi. 113 (*ed.* 1710) Turnus astonate stude doun in studying [*ed.* 1874, astonyst stude dum.]

†**astone, astun** (əˈstʌn), *v. Obs.* Forms: 3–6 **aston-e(n, 4 astune, astoune, 5 astoon, astown, 5–6 astoyne, astoun, 6 astonne, 6–7 aston, 7–8 astun** (some of these only in pa. pple.). [The etymology and form-history present points of difficulty. To all appearance, *astone, astune, astoune*, was a. OF. *estone-r, estuner, estouner* (now *étonner*) to stun, strike senseless, stupefy, shock, astonish:— L. **extonāre*, f. *ex* out + *tonāre* to thunder: cf. cl. L. *attonāre* to strike with a thunderbolt, stun, stupefy. See A- *pref.* 9. The nature of its relation to STUN is as yet doubtful; connexion with mod.G. *staunen, erstaunen*, uncertain.

The form-history is rendered more difficult by the ME. habit of spelling *on* for *un* (cf. *son, sun; ton, tun; done, dun; some, sum; won, wont, etc.*), which probably obtained here, since Gower rhymed *astone, sone* (= OE. *sunu*, son), Chaucer *astoned, woned* (= OE. *wunod*, wont), and 18th c. writers had still *astun*. OF. *o, u*, sometimes gives Eng. *u* as in *tun, gum, sum*; sometimes *ou, ow* (through *ū*) as in *crown, sound, round, confound*; hence the forms *astun, astoun*; the late *aston* seems, like *astony, astonish*, to have been influenced by later F. *estonner*; *astoon* may have been a phonetic spelling of *astūn*; *astoyne* is unexplained. STUN (q.v.) is of later appearance, and so far as evidence goes, seems to be an aphetic form of *astun*. These words do not appear to have any connexion with OE. *stunian* to resound (the sense 'impingere' was only a bad guess of Junius, repeated by Lye, etc.); but, both in meaning and form, it is difficult to consider them not related to G. *staunen, erstaunen*, a modern word adopted in 18th century from Swiss *stūne*, for which German scholars would seek a Teutonic etymology: see Grimm, Kluge. From *astone* and its pa. pples. *astoned, astun'd, astound*, have arisen the variants *astony, astonied*, whence again *astonish, astonished*, with their derivatives; also a new vb. *astound*, and pple. *astounded*, with their derivatives. To *astun, astony, astonish, astound*, are thus all of common origin.]

1. *trans.* To stun; to strike senseless with a blow, or partially senseless with a loud noise; to paralyse a limb with anæsthetics; to paralyse action, strike powerless, stupefy.

1340 *Ayenb.* 130 þise byeþ uour strokes of þondre þet astoneþ þane zeneȝere and makeþ ssake. *c* **1450** LONELICH *Grail* xiv. 314 Of that strok astoned he was. *c* **1532** LD. BERNERS *Huon* 493 With this mall I shall astone them all. **1543** TRAHERON *Vigo's Chirurg.* IV. 160 Some commaund to astoyne the member before incisyon. **1547** BOORDE *Brev. Health* cclxxi. 90 b, The one legge and the one arme is benomed or astonned. **1576** T. N[EWTON] *Lemnie's Touchst. Complex.* (1633) 99 Some do so astone the limmes of them that touch them, that they have no feeling.. a good while after. **1612** DRAYTON *Poly-olb.* xviii. 291 Who with the thundring noyse.. Astund the earth.

2. To daze (the eyes). *rare.*

c **1385** CHAUCER *L.G.W.* (MS. G g. Camb.) 164 His face schon so bryhte That with the glem a-stonede was the syhte.

3. To smash or shiver with a blow.

1440 *Promp. Parv.*, Astoynyn, or brese werkys (*v.r.* astoyn or brosyn), *Quatio, quasso.*

4. To strike mute with amazement, overwhelm one's presence of mind; to confound, astound; to astonish.

c **1374** CHAUCER *Boeth.* IV. v. 133 The moeueable poeple is a-stoned of alle þinges þat comen selde. *c* **1400** *Destr. Troy* IV. 1203 þe grekes on þe ground were greatly astoynet. **1440** *Promp. Parv.*, Astonyd, as mannys wytte, *Attono.* **1565** JEWEL *Repl. Harding* (1611) 276 Only to astonne and amaze the simple. *a* **1677** BARROW *Serm.* Wks. 1716 I. 342 Would it not astone a mind so pure?

5. *intr.* To be amazed, to be full of astonishment. (Cf. G. *erstaunen.*)

1393 GOWER *Conf.* III. 54 He drad him of his owne sone, That makith him wel the more astone.

†**astoned, astunned** (əˈstʌnd), *ppl. a. Obs.* Forms: 3–7 **astoned, 4 astuned, astouned, 5 astonyd, astownyd, 5–6 astooned, astoyned, 4–6 astonned, 6–7 astond, 7 astund, 7–8 astunned.** [Pa. pple. of prec. vb., pronounced in ME. (aˈstunəd, aˈstund); but sometimes, like other ME. words in *-und*, lengthened to (aˈstuːnd), and spelt *astound, astownd*; see ASTOUND *ppl. a. Astoyned* in 15–16th c. is an unexplained variant, perhaps mixing *astoned* and *astonyed.*]

1. Stunned, benumbed, stupefied, insensible.

c **1300** *St. Margar.* 290 þe folc.. ful adoun for drede & leye þer as hi were astoned & as hi were dede. *c* **1330** *Arth. & Merl.* 6297 Hors and man astuned lay. **1485** CAXTON *Chas. Gt.* 76 So astoned that the eyen in hys heed were al troubled of the payne. **1578** LYTE *Dodoens* 383 The same.. dissolueth the blood that is astonde or fixed. **1624** QUARLES *Job Mil.* (1717) 187 Astun'd with sorrows. **1735** SOMERVILLE *Chase* III. 253 Prostrate he lies Astunn'd and impotent.

2. Stupid.

c **1374** CHAUCER *Boeth.* IV. iii. 122 Yif he be slowe and astoned.. he lyueth as an asse.

3. Stricken with consternation or amazement, so as to lose presence of mind; amazed, overwhelmed, confounded; astonished.

1297 R. GLOUC. 396 Her hors were al astoned, & nolde after wylle Sywe noþer spore ne brydel. *c* **1386** CHAUCER *Clerks T.* 281 No wonder is thogh that she were astoned [astoned–⁵ *v.r.* astonyd, -yed].. Sche neuere was to swiche gestis woned. *c* **1400** *Destr. Troy* XXIII. 9488 All astonyt þai stode starond aboute. *c* **1500** *Virgilius* in Thoms *E.E. Rom.* (1858) II. 26 Virgilius was a stoned and merueyled greatly thereof. **1543** GRAFTON *Cont. Harding* 494 At whiche questyon all the lordes sat sore astonned, musynge muche. *c* **1550** CHEKE *Matt.* xiii. 54 In so much yᵗ yᵉⁱ weer astooned. **1576** GASCOIGNE *Compl. Philom.* (Arb.) 89, I stood astoynde. *a* **1677** BARROW *Serm.* (1686) III. xxxii. 352 He will be astond, and will say, In truth great is the God of Christians.

astonied (əˈstɒnɪd), *ppl. a.* Forms: 4–5 **astoneyd, 4–6 -yed, 5 -eyed, 5–6 astoyned, astonnyed, -ied, 6– astonied.** *Aphet.* **4 stoneyd, stoneȝid.** [A variant of prec.; pa. pple. of ASTONY *v.* (Various writers have apparently fancied this word to be a derivative of *stony*, and used it as = *petrified*, in the transferred senses 2, 3, 4.)]

†**1.** Stunned, stupefied, deprived of sensation; primarily by a blow, but subseq. also by anæsthetics, cold, etc.; insensible, benumbed, paralysed.

c **1386** [see ASTONED 3]. *c* **1450** *Merlin* x. 164 He fill to the grounde astonyed. **1523** LD. BERNERS *Froiss.* I. clxiii. 201 Sir Edwarde.. strake hym suche a stroke on the helme with his swerde, that he was astonyed. **1578** LYTE *Dodoens* 451 The body and greeved place is only astonied, or made asleepe for a season. **1580** BARET *Alv.* B 544 Benummed or astonied, a sleepe, without sence or feeling, *Torpidus.* **1601** HOLLAND *Pliny* II. 323 Their feet will be immediatly benummed and astonied. **1603** KNOLLES *Hist. Turks* (1621) 87 The Sultan .. gave him such a blow upon the head, as might have killed a bull, so that the Emperour.. astonied, fell down from his horse. **1611** COTGR., *Gourdi*, Benummed, astonied, stonnied.

†**b.** Of parts of the body: Rendered powerless, or functionless. Of the teeth: 'set on edge.' *Obs.*

c **1350** *Med. MS.* in *Archæol.* XXX. 373 To veynes astonyid.. ful of myth. **1388** WYCLIF *Ecclus.* xxx. 10 Thi teeth schulen be astonyed. **1398** TREVISA *Barth. De P.R.* XIX. lxxiii. (1495) 903 Synewes that ben astonyed other shronken.

2. Deprived for the moment of the power of action, dazed, paralysed. *arch.*

c **1350** *Will. Palerne* 880 Stifly astoneyd for ioye. **1388** WYCLIF *Prov.* xvi. 30 With iȝen astonyed. **1494** FABYAN V. cxxvii. 108 They were so astonyed, that they myght not goo one foote forwarde. **1535** COVERDALE *Job* xxxvii. 1 My hert is astonnied, and moued out of his place. **1596** R. LINCHE *Poems* (1877) 60 Stone-astonied, like a Deare at gaze. **1667** MILTON *P.L.* IX. 890 Adam.. Astonied stood and Blank, while horror chill Ran through his veins. **1850** MRS. BROWNING *Poems* I. 319 And I astonied fell and could not pray.

3. Bewildered, filled with consternation, dismayed. *arch.*

c **1386** CHAUCER *Knts. T.* 1503 This Emelye astoneyd was, And seide, 'What amounteth this, allas!' **1440** *Promp. Parv.*, Astonyed or a-stoyned yn mannys wytte, *Attonitus, consternatus, stupefactus, perculsus.* **1594** *Mirr. Policie* (1599) D, The part of a stout man is not to be astonied and cast downe in aduersity. **1611** BIBLE *Ezra* ix. 3, I rent my garment and my mantle.. and sate downe astonied. **1674** GOULDMAN *Lat. Dict.*, *Stupefio*, to be abashed or astonied.

1873 MISS BROUGHTON *Nancy* i. 2 Might well hold up his hands in astonied horror.

4. Greatly surprised, amazed, astonished. *arch.*

c **1400** *Test. Love* III. (1560) 296 b/2 Hugelye tho was I astonied of this suddain adventure. **1535** COVERDALE *2 Chron.* vii. 21 Euery one that goeth by, shall be astonnyed at this hye house. **1611** CHESTER *Dialogue* (1878) 127 Within the night they shine so gloriously, That mans astonied senses they do feed. **1790** WOLCOTT (P. Pindar) *Ep. J. Bruce* Wks. 1812 II. 353 The public eye astonied stare. **1857** MISS WINKWORTH *Tauler's Life* 70 Your brethern in the convent were much astonied at you.

†**aˈstoniedness.** *Obs.* [f. prec. + -NESS.] Insensibility or benumbedness of body; stupor or torpor of mind.

1580 BARET *Alv.* B 541 Astoniednesse or dulnesse of the minde.. *Stupor*.. Benummednesse or astoniednesse, *Torpor.* **1611** COTGR., *Stupeur*, Stupor, numnesse.. astoniednesse.

†**aˈstoning**, *vbl. sb. Obs.* [f. ASTONE *v.* + -ING¹.] = ASTONISHING. Cf. ASTONYING.

c **1374** CHAUCER *Boeth.* I. ii. 9 Why art þou stille. Is it for schame or for astonynge? **1440** *Promp. Parv.*, Astonynge or a-stoynynge yn wytte.

astonish (əˈstɒnɪʃ), *v.* Also 6 **astonysshe.** Aphetized in 7 to STONISH. [An alteration (not found before 1500) of earlier *astony*, as if this represented a F. **estonnir, estonissant*. Perhaps such a form had arisen in Anglo-Fr.: Palsgrave has 'astonysshyng, *estonissement*,' Godefroy a ppl. adj. *estoni.*]

1. †**a.** To deprive of sensation, as by a blow; to stun, paralyse, deaden, stupefy. *Obs.*

1530 PALSGR. 439/1, I astonysshe with a stroke upon the heed, *Jestourdis.* **1550** DK. SOMERSET in Coverdale *Spir. Perle* (1588) Pref. A. iv b, Medicines that doth but astonishe the sore place. **1600** HOLLAND *Livy* XLII. XV. 1124 The one smote the king upon the head, the other astonished his shoulder. **1616** *Withals' Dict.* 597 A kind of fish that hath power to astonish the hands of them that take it, *Torpedo.* **1635** PEMBLE *Wks.* 52 The Stoikes.. did rather astonish than conquer them [*i.e.* desires and passions].

†**b.** To set the teeth on edge. *Obs.*

1656 RIDGLEY *Pract. Physic* 321 Teeth astonished. The cause is a sowre tast. *The cure*: Purslane chewed.

†**2.** To stun mentally; to shock one out of his wits; to drive stupid, bewilder. *Obs.*

1530 PALSGR. 438/2, I astonysshe, I dull one, I take from him the quicknesse of his wytte. **1600** HOLLAND *Livy* II. xii. 40 The king.. as if he had been distracted, was almost astonished at the sight.

†**3.** To shock one out of his self-possession, or confidence; to dismay, terrify. *Obs.*

1535 COVERDALE *Jer.* ii. 12 Be astonished (o ye heauens), be afrayde, and abashed at soch a thinge. **1601** SHAKS. *Jul. C.* I. iii. 56 When the most mightie Gods, by tokens, send Such dreadfull Heraulds to astonish vs.

4. To give a shock of wonder by the presentation of something unlooked for or unaccountable; to amaze, surprise greatly. Also *absol.*

1611 BIBLE *Matt.* vii. 28 The people were astonished at his doctrine. **1653** HOLCROFT *Procopius* I. 7 Cabades.. seeing it, was astonisht, and all the Persians with him. **1776–88** GIBBON *Decl. & F.* xliv. (1813) VIII. 83 The Romans.. astonished the Greeks by their sincere and simple performance of the most burthensome engagements. **1844** MACAULAY *Chatham, Ess.* (1852) 729 Weymouth had a natural eloquence, which sometimes astonished those who knew how little he owed to study. **1904** L. T. MEADE *Love Triumphant* III. i, There might come to you a knowledge which would astonish and terrify.

†**aˈstonishable**, *a. Obs.* [f. prec. + -ABLE.] Calculated to astonish, surprising, wonderful.

1603 HARSNET *Pop. Impost.* xix. (*title*) 110 The Astonishable power of Nick-names. **1657** REEVE *God's Plea* 276 Men have rare endowments, and astonishable demeanour.

astonished (əˈstɒnɪʃt), *ppl. a.* Also 6 **-ist**, 7 **-isht.** [f. ASTONISH + -ED.]

†**1.** Bereft of sensation; stunned, benumbed. *Obs.*

1576 BAKER *Gesner's Jewell Health* 50 a, The water doth lyke recover astonished or benummed partes of the body. **1615** CROOKE *Body of Man* 460 Who lay.. apoplecticall or astonished. **1658** ROWLAND *Mouffet's Theat. Ins.* 1106 This cures the nerves relaxed, contracted, astonished.

†**2.** Stunned or paralysed mentally, bereft of one's wits; stupefied, bewildered. *Obs.*

1513 DOUGLAS *Æneis* VIII. iii. 59 Pallas, astonyst of sa hie a name. **1580** SIDNEY *Arcadia* (1622) 5 Musidorus.. had his wits astonished with sorrow. **1670** MILTON *Hist. Brit.* II. 502 Blind, astonished, and struck with superstition as with a planet; in one word, Monks.

3. Filled with consternation; dismayed. *arch.*

1653 CRASHAW *Sacr. Poems* 147 Th' astonish'd nymphs their flood's strange fate deplore. **1697** DRYDEN *Virg. Georg.* iv. (R.) With rage inflam'd astonish'd with surprize. **1790** BURNS *Tam O'Shanter*, But Maggie stood right sair astonish'd.

4. Amazed, full of surprised wonder.

1718 POPE *Iliad* VII. 105 This fierce defiance Greece astonish'd heard. **1781** GIBBON *Decl. & F.* III. 228 Beaten to death with sticks, before the eyes of the astonished emperor. **1810** SOUTHEY *Kehama* XXIII. ix, The towers of Yamenpur Rise on the astonish'd sight.

astonishedly (əˈstɒnɪʃtlɪ), *adv.* [f. prec. + -LY².] In an astonished manner; with astonishment.

1612–15 BP. HALL *Contempl.* (R.) Was it, that thy amazedness..astonishedly waited for the success? **1628** EARLE *Microcosm.* xiii. (Arb.) 35 Hee neuer heares any thing more astonishtly than what hee knowes before. **1882** *Daily Tel.* 11 Apr., Delightedly and, I may add, astonishedly young.

aˈstonishedness. ? *Obs.*⁻⁰ [f. prec. + -NESS.] Astonishment, amazement.

1530 PALSGR. 195/2 Astonysshednesse, *frayevr.*

astonisher (əˈstɒnɪʃə(r)). [f. ASTONISH *v.* + -ER¹.] He who or that which astonishes: see quot.

1871 RINGWALT *Encycl. Print.* 20 Better known as the Exclamation Point. Printers term it the Astonisher, and.. the Scarer. **1881** *Times* 27 Oct., A true Hibernian astonisher.

astonishing (əˈstɒnɪʃɪŋ), *vbl. sb.* [f. as prec. + -ING¹.] †**a.** Deprivation of sensation; paralysis, benumbment. *Obs.* **b.** Dismaying. *arch.* **c.** Surprised wonder.

1530 PALSGR. 195/2 Astonysshing, *estonnissement.* **1563** HYLL *Arte Garden.* (1593) 95 The cramp, the Apoplexie, the astonishing and the trembling of the members. **1597** DANIEL *Civ. Wares* II. lviii, He kneeles him downe with some astonishing. **1608** HIERON *Wks.* I. 712/1 To the astonishing and amazement of the mightie. **1820** MAIR *Tyro's Dict.* (ed. 10) 6 *Exanimatio*, an astonishing, a disheartening.

aˈstonishing, *ppl. a.* [f. as prec. + -ING².]
†**a.** Stunning, benumbing, paralysing. *Obs.* †**b.** Stupefying, confounding, bewildering. *Obs.* **c.** Filling with wonder, surprising, wonderful.

1612 WOODALL *Surg. Mate* Wks. 1653, 52 Them that have convulsions, or any astonishing disease. **1628** EARLE *Microcosm.* vi. 15 Some astonishing bombast, which men only till they understand are scared with. **1690** LOCKE *Hum. Und.* §4 What incredible and astonishing actions do we find ..tumblers bring their bodies to. **1712** ADDISON *Spect.* No. 315 ¶9 Circumstances that are both credible and astonishing. **1795** BURKE *Corr.* (1844) IV. 296 It is an age of astonishing events. Nothing happens in the ordinary course. **1879** B. TAYLOR *Germ. Lit.* 64 The marvelous legendary growths which collect around certain names, have an astonishing vitality.

aˈstonishingly, *adv.* [f. prec. + -LY².] In an astonishing manner; to an astonishing degree; amazingly, surprisingly.

1668 HOWE *Bless. Righteous* Wks. 1834, 227/2 Considerations that would render this astonishingly strange. **1803** W. TAYLOR in *Ann. Rev.* I. 744 Wherever bills of exchange originated, they are become astonishingly numerous.

aˈstonishingness. [f. as prec. + -NESS.] The quality of being astonishing.

1731 in BAILEY.

aˈstonishment. [f. as prec. + -MENT.]
†**1.** Loss of physical sensation, insensibility; paralysis, numbness, deadness. *Obs.*

1576 BAKER *Gesner's Jewel Health* 153 b, It avayleth also in the hote joynt aches..in causing an astonishment to those places. **1607** TOPSELL *Four-f. Beasts* 431 Those which are troubled with any deafness or astonishment in any part of their bodies. **1656** RIDGLEY *Pract. Physic* 234 There is astonishment of the Leg by compression of the Nerves.

†**b.** 'Setting on edge' of the teeth. *Obs.*

1616 SURFL. & MARKH. *Countr. Farm* 176 Purcelane eaten doth cure the roughnesse and astonishment of the teeth.

†**2.** Loss of sense or 'wits'; being out of one's wits or at one's wits' end; mental prostration, stupor. ***wine of astonishment***: stupefying wine. *Obs.*

1611 BIBLE *Ps.* lx. 3 To drinke the wine of astonishment [*Genev.* giddines]. **1667** MILTON *P.L.* I. 316 If such astonishment as this can seize Eternal spirits. **1725** DE FOE *Voy. round World* (1840) 271, I had a kind of astonishment upon me for a great while.

3. Loss of presence of mind, coolness, or courage; dismay, consternation, dread. *arch.*

a **1586** SIDNEY (J.) With no less wonder to us than astonishment to themselves. **1596** SPENSER *F.Q.* V. iii. 26 They stricken were with great astonishment, And their faint hearts with senseless horror queld. **1733** BAILEY *Erasm. Colloq.* (1877) 381 A man under an astonishment betwixt the hope of life and the fear of death. **1861** ALFORD in *Life* (1873) 339 Let not the astonishment of your present grief supersede your zeal for God's work.

4. Mental disturbance or excitement due to the sudden presentation of anything unlooked for or unaccountable; wonder temporarily overpowering the mind; amazement.

1594 T. B. *La Primaud. Fr. Acad.* II. 401 Epicures & Atheists, must needs be driuen into an astonishment at this. **1630** MILTON *On Shaks.*, Thou in our wonder and astonishment Hast built thy selfe a livelong monument. **1712** ADDISON *Spect.* No. 412 ¶2 We are flung into pleasing astonishment at such unbounded views. **1798** FERRIAR *Illustr. Sterne* i. 6 The splendid scenes beheld with astonishment by Europe. **1874** BLACK *Pr. Thule* 47 He looked at her for a moment in astonishment.

5. An object of astonishment; a cause of sudden consternation or wonder.

1611 BIBLE *Deut.* xxviii. 37 Thou shalt become an astonishment, a prouerbe, and a by-worde. **1666** PERRINCHIEF *Serm. Westm.* 7 Nov. 32 [It] makes his Memory an execration, and his Name an astonishment. **1792** T. JEFFERSON *Writ.* (1859) III. 459 Mr. Carmicheal's silence has been long my astonishment.

astony (əˈstɒnɪ), *v. arch.* Forms: 3 **astoney,** 3–5 **astonie, -ye,** 6 **astunnye,** 6– **astony.** [A variant of ASTONE, of difficult explanation; perh. the ending is due to OF. pa. pple. *estoné, estonné.* The instance in the *Ayenbite* may be only the inf. in *-ie* of *astone*: it has pr. tense *aston-eth.*]

1. *trans.* = ASTONE; to stun, paralyse, astound, amaze.

1340 *Ayenb.* 126 Hou it ssolde ous ssende and astonie. *Ibid.* 257. *c* **1375** WYCLIF *Serm.* Sel. Wks. 1871 II. 113 þes wordis astonyeden hem. **1386** CHAUCER *Clerk's T.* 260 This soden cas this man astonyed so [So 2 MSS.; astoneyd⁻¹, astoned⁻³]. **1388** WYCLIF *Isa.* xxi. 4 Myn herte fadide, derknessis astonieden me [**1382** dercnesses stoneid maden me]. **1401** *Pol. Poems* (1859) II. 51 With her sterne stounes [they will] astonye al the erthe. **1526** TINDALE *Matt.* xxviii. 4 The kepers were astunnyed. **1557** *K. Arthur* (Copland) I. xvi, A myghty stroke upon the helme whyche astonyed hym sore. **1593** NASHE *Christes Teares* (1613) 10 O Ierusalem.. that stonest, and astoniest thy Prophets with thy peruersnesse. **1646** H. LAWRENCE *Comm. & Warre w. Angels*, His word was with power, which astonied the auditours. [Later instances, see ASTONIED.]

2. *intr.* (? or *absol.*) (Cf. ASTONE 5.) *rare.*

1850 MRS. BROWNING *Poems* I. 195 She stares at the wound where it gapes and astonies. [A rhyme to *Adonis.*]

†**aˈstonying,** *vbl. sb. Obs.* [f. prec. + -ING¹.] = ASTONISHING, ASTONISHMENT; see their senses.

1388 WYCLIF *Amos* iv. 6 Y gaf to ȝou astonying [**1382** eggyng] of teeth in all ȝoure cities. **1576** BAKER *Gesner's Jewel Health* 131 a, The person troubled with ..the astonying of partes. **1580** HOLLYBAND *Treas. Fr. Tong.*, *Effray*..feare, astonying, abashing, amasing. **1607** HIERON *Wks.* I. 457 With blindnesse and with astonying of heart. **1666** WALLIS in I. Mather *Rem. Provid.* 84 Besides a present astonying or numness, had no other hurt.

astoop (əˈstuːp), *advb. phr.* [A *prep.*¹ + STOOP *sb.*] In an inclined or leaning position.

1644 NYE *Gunnery* (1670) 13 Taking the Cauldron from off the fire, and setting it astoop, so that the lees and dregs ..may not with any water run over the brims of the vessel. **1720** GAY *Poems* (1745) II. 51 Heigh day! my darling wine astoop!

†**aˈstore,** *v. Obs.* [a. OF. *estore-r, estaure-r* to construct, repair, restore, furnish:—late pop. L. ˈ*staurāre*, for L *instaurāre* to erect, repair, renew, refresh. Hence the aphetic STORE *v.* now in use.]

1. To repair, restore, mend.

c **1300** *Alexander* in *Rouland & Vern.* (1836) Introd. 24 And [I yeld] Ich a thousand pounde and more, Your harmes for to astore.

2. To furnish, fit out, provide, store.

1297 R. GLOUC. 375 þe nywe forest..he louede ynou, And astored yt wel myd bestys. **1340** *Ayenb.* 112 þet bread tuies ybake huermide he astoreþ his ssip. **1440** *Promp. Parv.*, Astoryn, or instoryn wyth nedefulle thyngys, *Instauro.* **1530** PALSGR. 439/1 This house is astored of all things.

†**aˈstore,** *sb. Obs.* [a. OF. *estor* (med.L. *instaurum*) provision, f. *estorer*: see prec. Cf. the aphetic STORE.] Provision, stock of provisions.

c **1330** *Arth. & Merl.* 8068 To kepe wele her charrois, Her astore and her harnois.

†**a-ˈstore,** *advb. phr. Obs.* [App. A *prep.*¹ in + STORE.] In great number; in a heap; together.

c **1300** *K. Alis.* 2110 He ladde to-fore Gode knyghtis and doughty astore. *Ibid.* 5002 Every wilde dere astore, Hy mowen by cours ernen tofore. *c* **1320** *Seuyn Sages* (W.) 926 Men unkek gate and halle-dore, Barons entrede in astore.

†**ˈastorgy.** *Obs. rare*⁻¹. [ad. Gr. ἀστοργία, f. ἄστοργος, f. ἀ priv. + στοργή natural affection, love.] Want of natural affection.

1648 JOS. BEAUMONT *Psyche* xxii. 107 (D.) Upon an Ostrich, more unnatural Than barbarous She, rode meagre Astorgy.

astound (əˈstaʊnd), *ppl. a. arch.* Forms: 4 **astuned,** 4–6 **astouned,** 5 **astownyd,** 6 **astownd,** 6 **astound.** [A phonetic development of ASTONED, *astun'd*, ME. (aˈstunəd, aˈstund), by lengthening and subsequent diphthongizing of the *u*, as happened in *bound, found, ground, round*, OE. *bunden, funden, grund*, OF. *rond.* The result was to dissociate *astūnd, astound* from *astone, astun*, and to make it appear as an independent adjective.]

†**1.** Stunned, stupefied. *Obs.*

c **1315** SHOREHAM 88 Ase a mesel ther he lay Astouned in spote and blode. *c* **1330** *Arth. & Merl.* 6297 Hors and man astuned lay. **1596** SPENSER *F.Q.* I. ix. 35 His hollow eyne Lookt deadly dull, and stared as astound.

2. Confounded, distracted; amazed; astounded. *arch.*

c **1440** *Generydes* 4013 Where with the Sowdon was astownyd sore. **1596** SPENSER *F.Q.* I. viii. 5 With staring countenance..as one astownd. **1600** FAIRFAX *Tasso* XIX. lxv, Vafrine..with griefe and care Remain'd astound. **1633** P. FLETCHER *Purple Isl.* XII. xl, Earth astound, Bids dogs with houls give warning. **1810** SCOTT *Lady of L.* II. xxxi, Ellen, dizzy and astound As sudden ruin yawned around. **1881** ROSSETTI *Bal. & Sonn.* 126 Astound of the fearful sight.

astound (əˈstaʊnd), *v.* [f. *c* 1600 from the prec., either by treating it as a simple adj., and forming a factitive vb. on it, as in *round*, to *round*, or by taking it as the contracted form of a pa. pple. *astounded*, which implied a vb. *to astound.* (Cf. ME. *send* = *sended*, pa. pple. of SEND *v.*) The latter view is supported by the facts that the pple. *astounded* (see next) appears much earlier than the other parts of the verb, and that our earliest instance of the latter shows *astound* as (contracted) pa. tense. Analogous changes appear in the vb. *sound, sounded*, for OF. *soner, suner, souner*, ME. *soun*, pa. t. *souned, soun'd*, and in several other words. (Cf. esp. the vulgar *drownd, drownded*, for *drown, drown'd.*)]

†**1.** To deprive of consciousness, stupefy. *Obs.*

1600 FAIRFAX *Tasso* IX. xxiii, No weapon on his hard'ned helmet bit, No puissant stroke his senses once astound. **1727** THOMSON *Summer* 1138 The lightnings flash a larger curve, and more The noise astounds.

2. To shock with alarm, surprise, or wonder; to strike with amazement.

1634 MILTON *Comus* 210 These thoughts may startle well, but not astound The virtuous mind. **1642** —— *Apol. Smectymn.* (1851) 306 It was intended to astound and to astonish the guilty Prelats. **1837** J. HARRIS *Gt. Teacher* 367 Who could..have dazzled and astounded the world with celestial visions. **1851** H. SPENCER *Soc. Statics* xxxii. §6 Very intimate friends occasionally astound him by quite unexpected behaviour.

astounded (əˈstaʊndɪd), *ppl. a.* [f. ASTOUND *ppl. a.*, the *-ed* marking more distinctly its participial character; cf. *content, contented*, etc., and see prec., of which this is now the pa. pple.]

†**1.** Stunned, stupefied. *Obs.* **2.** Shocked mentally, amazed; confounded with surprise and wonder.

c **1440** *Destr. Troy* XXII. 9171 With langur of lust, and of loue hote, He was stithly astondid, stird into þoght. **1596** DRAYTON *Legends* iii. 199 Astounded with a mightie blow, I stood awhile insensible of payne. **1810** SOUTHEY *Kehama* XIX. xi, Abashed, confounded..yea all astounded In over-powering fear and deep dismay. **1824** DIBDIN *Libr. Comp.* 688 We are..astounded at the enormous prices which the greater part of them produce.

aˈstounding, *ppl. a.* [f. as prec. + -ING².] Shocking with surprise or wonder, amazing.

1586 MARLOWE *1st Pt. Tamburl.* Prol., Threatening the world with high astounding terms. **1599** B. JONSON *Cynthia's Rev.* (T.) The third is your soldier's face, a menacing and astounding face. **1642** MILTON *Apol. Smectymn.* (1851) 306 It was an astounding prayer. **1855** DK. BUCKHM. *Crt. Geo. III*, III. 450 The astounding climax came in the shape of the surrender of the Austrian army at Ulm.

aˈstoundingly, *adv.* [f. prec. + -LY².] In an astounding manner; amazingly.

1826 MISS MITFORD *Village* Ser. II. (1863) 273 Affrontingly gracious or astoundingly impertinent by fits and starts. **1865** DICKENS *Lett.* II. 228 His memory is astoundingly good.

astoundment (əˈstaʊndmənt). [f. ASTOUND *v.* + -MENT.] The condition of being stricken with amazement; profound astonishment.

1810 COLERIDGE *Friend* (1818) III. 260 In wonder, says Aristotle, does philosophy begin: and in astoundment, says Plato, does all true philosophy finish. **1823** LAMB *Elia* xviii. 93/1 The fountains..which I have made..to the astoundment of the young urchins my contemporaries.

†**aˈstounedness.** *Obs.* [f. *astouned* (early form of ASTOUND *ppl. a.*) + -NESS.] The quality of being 'astound,' or astounded; mental stupefaction from terror, surprise, or alarm.

1549 CHALONER tr. *Erasm. Moriæ Enc.* N iv a, Little lacked that they were not chaunged throughe astounednesse into stones.

astown(e, astoyne, -d: see ASTONE, -ED, ASTOUND.

†**ˈastracism.** *Obs. rare.* [? from some confusion of ASTERISK, ASTERISM.] An asterism or constellation; an asterisk.

1590 MARLOWE *2nd Pt. Tamburl.* IV. iii. Above the three-fold astracism of heaven. **1695** W. LOWNDES *Silver Coin* 6 Some have derived it [*sterling*] from a Star or Astracism.

a-straddle (əˈstræd(ə)l), *advb. phr.* [A *prep.*¹ + STRADDLE *v.*] In a straddling position, with the legs stretched out widely across something. ***a-straddle of***: bestriding.

1703 CIBBER *She wou'd, etc.* I. i. (1736) 4 A-straddle we got and so rode after him. **1823** GALT *Entail* I. xxvi. 224 The tongs..were placed upright astraddle in front of the grate. **1873** W. MAYO *Never Again* xxiv. 314 Strong-minded philanthropists..astraddle of the biggest and most rampant hobbies.

astragal (ˈæstrəgəl). Also 7 **astrigal.** [(? a. F. *astragale*), ad. L. *astragalus*, a. Gr. ἀστράγαλος a huckle-bone (in *pl.* dice), a moulding in the capital of a column, a leguminous plant. See also ASTRAGALUS.]

1. *Phys.* The ball of the ankle-joint; the huckle-bone; = ASTRAGALUS 1. Hence in *pl.* (as in Gr.): Dice, which were orig. huckle-bones.

1727–51 CHAMBERS *Cycl., Astragal*..a bone of the heel. **1850** LEITCH *Müller's Anc. Art* §391 Eros as Ganymedes' conqueror at the game of astragals.

2. a. *Arch.* A small moulding, of semicircular section, sometimes plain, sometimes carved with leaves or cut into beads, placed round the top or bottom of columns, and used to separate the different parts of the architrave in ornamental entablatures. Also *attrib.*

1563 SHUTE *Archit.* C j a, Nowe at the toppe of Scapus, you shall make Astragalus. **1651** DAVENANT *Gondibert* II. vi. xlvi, From the astrigal To the flat frieze. **1789** SMYTH tr. *Aldrich's Archit.* (1818) 89 An astragal..has berries often cut on it. **1862** RICKMAN *Goth. Archit.* 14 The torus when very small becomes an astragal. **1872** SHIPLEY *Gloss. Eccl. Terms* 402 *Roundel*, a bead or astragal moulding.

b. (See quot. 1940.)

1858 *Skyring's Builders' Prices* 33 Astragal sashes. **1940** *Chambers's Techn. Dict.* 56/2 *Astragal*, a specially shaped bar used for connecting together glazing bars or sheets of glass in a window. *Ibid., Astragal tool*, a special tool..used in wood-turning for turning beads and astragals.

3. *Gunnery.* A ring or moulding encircling a cannon about six inches from the mouth.

1656 BLOUNT *Glossogr., Astragal*..is therefore transferred to the canon. **1692** in Smith's *Seaman's Gram.* II. vi. 94 The Astragal, or Cornice Ring. **1862** GRIFFITHS *Artill. Man.*, Muzzle Astragal and Fillets.

4. (See quot.) ? *Obs.*

1725 BRADLEY *Fam. Dict.* s.v. *Tyles*, Scallop or Astragal are used in some places for weather Tyling. **1751** CHAMBERS *Cycl.* s.v. *Tyle*, Scallop or astragal Tyles are..like plain tiles, only their lower ends are in form of an astragal.

astragalar (ə'strægələ(r)), *a.* *Phys.* [f. ASTRAGAL-US + -AR.] Of or pertaining to an astragalus.

1854 OWEN in *Circ. Sc.* Org. Nat. I. 218 The astragalar part..would seem to include the scaphoid. **1866** HUXLEY *Preh. Rem. Caithn.* 146 The astragalar articular surfaces.

†**a'stragalize.** *v. Obs.*–⁰ [ad. Gr. ἀστραγαλίζειν, f. ἀστράγαλος: see ASTRAGAL and -IZE.] 'To play at dice.' Cockeram 1623. 'To play at Dice, Huckle-bones, or Tables.' Blount *Gl.* 1656.

a'stragaloid, *a. rare.* [f. Gr. ἀστράγαλ-ος (see prec.) + -OID.] Shaped like an astragalus.

astragalomancy (ə'strægələʊ,mænsɪ). [f. as prec. + -MANCY; cf. Gr. ἀστραγαλόμαντις.] Divination by means of dice or huckle-bones.

1640 E. CHILMEAD tr. *Ferrand's Ερωτομανια* xxiii. 178, I shall omit to speak here of Astragalomancy, that was done with Huckle bones. **1652** in GAULE *Magastrom.* 166. **1693** URQUHART *Rabelais* III. xxv, Amply disclosed unto you..by astragalomancy. **1853** *Encycl. Brit.* III. 780/2 Astragalomancy..was practised in a temple of Hercules in Achaia. **1962** C. L. WRENN in Davis & Wrenn *Eng. & Med. Studies* 312 Pauly-Wissowa..also treats of astragalomancy.

‖**astragalus** (ə'strægələs). [L., a. Gr. ἀστράγαλος: see ASTRAGAL.]

1. *Phys.* The ball of the ankle-joint, the upper bone of the foot, on which the tibia rests.

1541 R. COPLAND *Guydon's Quest. Cyrurg.*, Astragallus..is in maner as yᵉ nut of a crosbow rounde on eche syde. **1696** PHILLIPS *Astragal*; *Ibid.* ed. 1706 *Astragalus.* **1855** HOLDEN *Hum. Osteol.* 210 The astragalus is the keystone of the arch of the foot, and supports the whole weight of the body.

2. *Bot.* An extensive genus of leguminous plants, of which *A. verus* produces gum tragacanth, and three British species are known as Milk-vetch.

1548 TURNER *Names of Herbs* 17 Astragalus..may be called in english peaserthnut. **1862** BELLEW *Afghan.* 199 Several varieties of astragalus and other leguminous plants.

†**a'strain,** *v. Obs.* Also 4–5 **astreyn,** 5 **estrayne.** [a. OF. *astreign-* stem of *astreindre, astraindre*:—L. *astringĕre* to ASTRINGE.] To bind; to put under obligation; to restrain.

c **1400** *Apol. Loll.* 52 He may astreyn himsilf a ȝer to dwel wiþ a man to serue him. **1483** CAXTON *Gold. Leg.* 363/4 Jhesus..was taken, estrayned, haled forth, and mocked. **1594** CAREW *Tasso* (1881) 108 And free in place Will die, ere base cord hand and foot astraine.

a-strain (ə'streɪn), *advb. phr.* [A *prep.*¹ + STRAIN.] On the strain, straining.

1856 MRS. BROWNING *Aur. Leigh* VI. 328 Eyes..with conscious lids astrain In recognition. **1870** MORRIS *Earthly Par.* II. III. 164 A-strain, All gifts of that sweet time to gain.

astrakhan (æstrə'kæn). **a.** The skin of still-born or very young lambs from Astrakhan in Russia, the wool of which resembles fur. **b.** A kind of cloth used chiefly as an edging or trimming for garments.

1766 EARL MARCH in *Selwyn & Contemps.* II. 116 My black silk coat lined with an Astrakan. **1859** W. BOYD *Swartzen*, With a muff..Of chinchilla, fitch, opossum, Astrakhan. **1887** *Cassell's Fam. Mag.* Oct. 698/1 The curled cloths or woollen Astrachans used for trimmings and for entire jackets. **1898** *Daily News* 23 Mar. 5/6 Mr. Gladstone..closely muffled up in a brown astrachan-lined overcoat. **1904** *Tailor & Cutter* 4 Aug. 479 Astrachan: A cloth made of worsted material, with a long and closely-curled pile, in imitation of the fur of that name. **1958** HAYWARD & HARARI tr. *Pasternak's Dr. Zhivago* I. vi. 183 Her astrakhan cape hung open over the..quaking layers of her double chin. **1965** *Which?* Mar. 96/2 Most astrakhan cloth is imitation fur, usually made from wool and mohair. For coats, hats, trimmings.

astral ('æstrəl), *a.* (and *sb.*) [ad. L. *astrālis*, f. *astr-um* star: see -AL¹.]

A. *adj.* 1. a. Of, connected with, or proceeding from the stars; consisting of stars, starry.

1605 TIMME *Quersit.* I. iv. 14 Those things which are simply formall are astrall and spirituall. *a* **1652** J. SMITH *Sel. Disc.* x. 501 There needs no fatal necessity or astral impulses. **1862** RAWLINSON *Anc. Mon.* I. vii. 139 The religion was to a certain extent astral. **1861** SIR F. PALGRAVE *Norm. & Eng.* III. 331 Astral showers covered the heavens.

b. ***astral spirits***: those formerly supposed to live in the heavenly bodies, variously represented as fallen angels, souls of dead men, and spirits originating in fire.

1647 H. MORE *Song of Soul* Notes 143/2 Neither Astrall spirit nor Angel can prevail against one ray of the Deity. **1769** WESLEY *Wks.* (1872) III. 358 All his [Glanvill's] talk of 'aërial and astral spirits' I take to be stark nonsense. **1851** CARLYLE *Sterling* I. viii, Who could..as the Alchymists professed to do..distil you an 'Astral spirit' from the ashes.

2. Star-shaped, star-like. ***astral lamp***: one resembling an Argand lamp, with the oil contained in a flattened ring, and so contrived that uninterrupted light is thrown upon the table below it.

1671 GREW *Anat. Plants* I. iv. §5 Sometimes they [the Hairs] are Astral as upon Lavender. **1831** *Encycl. Amer.* VII. 398/1 In the astral and sinumbral lamps..the oil is contained in a large horizontal ring. **1834** I. TAYLOR *Sat. Even.* iv. 47 Shines only with an astral lustre. **1852** HAWTHORNE *Blithed. Rom.* II. vi. 100 The glow of an astral-lamp was penetrating mistily through the white curtain.

3. *Theosophy.* Pertaining to or consisting of a supersensible substance considered to be next above the sensible world in refinement and held to pervade all space. So ***astral body***, the ethereal counterpart or shadow of a human or animal body.

[**1691** R. KIRK *Secret Commonw.* (1815) i. 9 That what the Low-countrey Scotts calls a Wreath..is only exuvious Fumes of the Man approaching Death, exhal'd and congeal'd..and called astral Bodies, agitated as Wild-fire with Wind.] **1877** HELENA P. BLAVATSKY *Isis Unveiled* in *Secr. Doctrine* (1888) II. 74 When those circulations—which Eliphas Levi calls 'currents of the astral light'—in the universal ether..take place in harmony with the divine spirit, our earth..enjoys a fertile period. **1880** ANNA KINGSFORD in Maitland *A. Kingsford* (1913) I. 401 In man the astral fluid becomes transformed into human life at the moment of conception. *Ibid.*, All they whose bodies have decomposed leave, or have left, their shadow in the astral space. **1881** SINNETT *Occult World* 162 Even our astral bodies, pure ether, are but illusions of matter so long as they retain their terrestrial outline.

4. *Cytology.* Of or pertaining to an aster.

1896 E. B. WILSON *Cell* ii. 74 The contractile elements are formed by certain of the astral rays which grow into the nucleus. **1901** CALKINS *Protozoa* iii. 82 In others they [*sc.* the rays] are focussed in a central or 'astral' granule (*Gymnosphæra, Actinophrys, Sphærastrum*, etc.), which in some cases has been seen to divide like a centrosome and to form an amphiaster. *Ibid.* viii. 278 In some cases this structure resembles the astral system of Metazoa. **1910** *Encycl. Brit.* VII. 714/2 The remaining radiations at the two poles of the spindle are the 'astral rays'.

B. *sb.* 1. An astral lamp. Also *attrib.*

1838 *Knickerbocker* XII. 57 As she drew the flowers on the centre-table more under the light of the astral. *c* **1860** WHITTIER *Maud Müller* xlvii, The weary wheel to a spinnet turned, The tallow candle an astral burned. **1883** *N.Y. World* in *Glasg. Week. Her.* 9 June 8/3 An ordinary tin can..in which astral oil is sold.

2. An astral body.

1880 ANNA KINGSFORD in Maitland *A. Kingsford* (1913) I. 400 The Astral is not an entity, for it cannot reproduce itself. It is an imprint only, a shadow, a reflect, an echo. **1888** HELENA P. BLAVATSKY *Secr. Doctrine* (ed. 2) I. 639 Our more intimate astral, or inner man.

'astrally, *adv.* [f. prec. + -LY².] **a.** In an astral manner; according to the stars. **b.** In, or through the powers of, the astral body.

1671 SALMON *Syn. Med.* I. i. 1 Astrological Medicine is that which teacheth Astrally..how to..Cure all..Diseases. **1886** *Sat. Rev.* 4 Dec. 751 Whether the Thibetan Adepts go spooking astrally through the world. *c* **1900** W. B. YEATS *Lett.* (1954) 344 Our thaumaturgists..called her up astrally, and told her to leave him.

a-strand (ə'strænd), *advb. phr.* [A *prep.*¹ + STRAND.] On the strand, stranded.

1810 SCOTT *Lady of L.* VI. xiii, The tall ship..Amid the breakers lies astrand. **1878** J. MILLER *Songs of Italy* 24 You lie like a seaweed well astrand.

astrange, obsolete form of ESTRANGE.

†**a'strangle,** *v. Obs.* [a. OF. *estrangle-r* (mod. *étrangler*), cogn. with Pg. *estrangular*, It. *strangolare*:—L. *strangulā-re*, ad. Gr. στραγγαλά-ειν, στραγγαλίζειν to STRANGLE, f. στραγγάλη halter. Cf. ESTRANGLE, in Caxton from continental French, and the aphetic STRANGLE.] To strangle, suffocate.

1297 R. GLOUC. 342 Mossel he dude in to hys mouþ..Hyt byleuede amydde hys þrote, astrangled he was ryȝt þere. **1340** *Ayenb.* 50 He ȝernþ to þe þrote..him uor to astrangli. *c* **1400** *Test. Love* III. (1560) 296 b/1 It hath nigh mee astrangled.

†**a'straught,** *ppl. a. Obs.* [f. after *distraught*, as if from a vb. **astract*; cf. *asposit.*] Distraught, distracted.

1564 GOLDING *Justine* 179 (R.) At her syght he was so astraught, that..he made peace with the Massiliens. **1583** —— *Calvin on Deut.* cxvii. 721 Needes must wee bee astraught or rather utterly blockish.

†**a'straughted,** *pa. pple. rare*⁻¹. = prec.

1565 GOLDING *Ovid's Met.* III. 504 (1567) 37 Astraughted like an image made of marble stone he lyes. [Ovid, *Met.* III. 418 *Adstupet*..]

†**a'stray,** *v. Obs.* [var. ESTRAY (see A- *pref.* 9), a. OF. *estraier*, according to P. Meyer, cogn. w. Pr. *estraguar*:—L. **extrāvagāre*, f. *extra* out of bounds + *vagāre* to wander. Chiefly found in pa. pple. *astraied* = OF. *estraié*: cf. ASTRAY *adv.*, ESTRAY *v.*, and the aphetic STRAY.]

1393 GOWER *Conf.* II. 132 This prest was drunke and goth astraied. **1556** ABP. PARKER *Psalter* cxix. 110 Offend thy law yet will I not: to renne from it astraid. **1584** T. HUDSON *Judith* ii. 352 (D.) They astraid From God their guide,

†**a'stray,** *sb. Obs.* [variant of ESTRAY, a. AF. *estray*, q.v.] A stray beast; an estray.

1440 *Promp. Parv.* 16 Astray, or a best that goythe astray.

astray (ə'streɪ), *adv.* or *a.* Forms: 3 **o strai,** 3–4 **on stray,** 5 **on the straye, of stray;** 4 **astreyey, a-strayey;** 4–5 **a-stray,** 6 **astraie, -aye, -aigh,** 5– **astray.** [Already in 14th c. often written *o stray, on stray, of stray*, as if f. A *prep.*¹ + STRAY; but of *stray* as a separate sb. no early instances have been found; so that *astray* was perhaps orig. the OF. pa. pple. *estraié, estrayé*, 'strayed' (see ASTRAY *v.*, and cf. the southern form *astrayey*, 1380) with *-e* lost (first in the north), used as a predicative adjective, and thence as an adv., and confused with forms like *a-float, a-sleep, a-loft.* As adj. the simple STRAY is now used: cf. *alive, live* (fish), *asquint, squint* (eyes).]

1. Out of the right way, away from the proper path, wandering.

a **1300** *Cursor M.* 6827 þi faas beist þou findes o strai [*v.r.* on stray]. *c* **1325** *E.E. Allit. P.* A 1161 When I schulde start in þe strem astraye. **1375** BARBOUR *Bruce* XIII. 195 Mony a steid Fleand on stray. *c* **1380** *Sir Ferumb.* 3730 Rennyngge a-streyey þar on þe waye. *Ibid.* 5532 Ynowe [stedes] þay founde withoute gon, A-strayey on þe grene. *a* **1400** *Chester Pl.* 63 Loke and tell, and yf thou maye, Starres standinge one the straye. *c* **1420** *Anturs of Arth.* xl, Opon a startand stede he strikes oute of stray. *c* **1450** *Merlin* x. 158 And saugh an horse go a-stray. **1590** SHAKS. *Mids. N.* III. ii. 358 And lead these testie Riuals so astray. **1810** SCOTT *Lady of L.* II. xxvi, Why urge thy chase so far astray?

2. Away from the right; in or into error or evil.

1535 COVERDALE *Ps.* lxii. 3 They go astraie & speake lyes. **1548** UDALL *Erasm. Par.* Pref. 4 So ferre gone astraigh from Christe. **1591** SHAKS. *Two Gent.* I. i. 109 Nay, in that you are astray. **1767** FORDYCE *Serm. Yng. Wom.* I. i. 17 One young lady going astray shall subject her relations to..discredit and distress. **1867** FREEMAN *Norm. Conq.* I. vi. 478 Evil counsellors had led him astray.

†**a'strayly,** *adv. Obs.* [f. ASTRAY + -LY.] Astray.

1440 *Promp. Parv.* 16 Astrayly, *Palabunde.*

‖**astre.** [a. OF. *astre, aistre* (mod.F. *âtre*) 'hearth,' of unknown origin.

(See Brachet *âtre*, Littré *âtre, êtres*, Diez *piastra.* The med.L. *astrum*, in the same sense, is quoted by Du Cange only from English authors, as if formed on AF. *astre.*)]

A hearth, a home. Hence **astrer** (see quot.)

[**1292** BRITTON II. xxxviii. §6 Chescun communer qi ad astre en mesme la vile.] ? *a* **1500** in Utterson *Pop. Poetry* II. 78 (Halliw.) Bad her take the pot..And set it aboove upon the astire. **1576** W. LAMBARDE *Peramb. Kent* (1826) 507 Astre, that is to say, the stocke, harth, or chimney, for fire. **1686** PLOT *Staffordsh.* 278 They have the privilege of the Astre, or herth for fire, in the Mansion house. **1865** NICHOLS *Britton* II. 155 *note*, An astrer..was a peasant householder, residing at the hearth or home where he was bred. **1882** ELTON *Orig. Eng. Hist.* 191 [In] Montgomeryshire..Auster-land is that which had a house upon it in ancient times.

astream (ə'striːm), *adv.* and *pred. a.* [f. A *prep.*¹ + STREAM.] In a stream; that streams, streaming, flowing.

1763 C. SMART *Song to David* st. 85, Glorious the northern lights astream. **1925** G. MURRAY tr. *Eumenides* 51 Joy be a-stream in your ways, as the fire that bloweth A-stream from beacon and brand. **1928** BLUNDEN *Undertones of War* 299 Their rosy scarves are spied astream. **1929** C. K. SCOTT-MONCRIEFF tr. *J.-R. Bloch's —— & Co.* (1930) I. iv. 43 Two or three marauding brigs..arrived one after another, their backs astream with water. **1930** R. CAMPBELL *Adamastor* 79 Round which, astream through flowering vales.. The great Zambezis wreathe their coils.

†**a'strean**, *a. Obs. rare*⁻¹. [f. Gr. ἀστραῖ-ος starry (cf. L. *Astræus, Astræa*) + -AN.] Of or belonging to the stars.
1647 HOWELL *Lett.* III. ix. (1726) 425 Every Star in Heaven..is coloniz'd and replenish'd with Astrean Inhabitants.

astrelabre, obs. form of ASTROLABE.

†**a'strength**, *v. Obs.* [f. A- *pref.* 1 + STRENGTH *v.*] To strengthen, establish, confirm.
c **1250** *Kent. Serm.* in *O.E. Misc.* (1872) 32 þerefore sal hure beliaue bie þe betere astrengþed. **1297** R. GLOUC. 180 He..bygan to astrengþy ys court.

†**a'stretch**, *v. Obs.* For forms see STRETCH *v.* [OE. *astręccan*, f. A- *pref.* 1 + *stręccan* to STRETCH; cogn. w. OHG. *arstrecchan*, mod.G. *erstrecken.*] To stretch forth, reach out, extend.
c **1000** ÆLFRIC *Hom.* II. 194 Astrece ðine hand ofer ða sæ. Moyses ða astrehte his hand. *a* **1420** OCCLEVE *MS. Soc. Antiq.* No. 134. 262 (Halliw.) His hyȝe vertu astreccheth With bokis of his ornat endityng e. **1440** *Promp. Parv.*, Astretchyn or arechyn, *Attingo.*

astrict (ə'strɪkt), *v.* Also 7–9 **adstrict.** [f. L. *astrict-* ppl. stem of *astringĕre* to ASTRINGE.]
1. *trans.* To bind up, confine within narrow limits, compress; *hence*, to render costive.
1548 HALL *Chron.* 239 The Course of water astricted.. will flow and burst out in continuance of tyme. **1650** tr. *Bacon's Life & Death* 42 The Stomach..to be..Astricted or bound, not Loose. **1863** C. WALTON in *N. & Q.* Ser. III. IV. 406 A little globe, so contracted, astricted, and narrowed, that, etc.
2. To bind by moral or legal obligation.
1513–75 *Diurn. Occurr.* (1833) 108 His fader was astrictit be souerties in parliament. **1688** *Ess. Magistr.* in *Harl. Misc.* I. 7 Tied to the same rules they were adstricted to. **1880** MUIRHEAD *Gaius* III. §87 Whether a man..be astricted to the inheritance by necessity of law.
3. To restrict, tie down, limit *to.*
1588 A. KING *Canisius' Catech.* H v. b, Yᵉ monethes..war æqualI to yᵉ cowrse of yᵉ moon: ȝeit war thay nocht astricted yairto. **1619** *Sacrilege Sacr. Handled* 6 Holy meates were astricted to only holy persons. **1836–7** SIR W. HAMILTON *Metaph.* xl. (1870) II. 403 The mind is thus astricted to certain necessary modes or forms of thought.
4. *Sc. Law.* To restrict in tenure. See ASTRICTED.

†**a'strict**, *a. Obs. rare*⁻¹. [ad. L. *astrictus*; see prec.] Compressed, concise.
1631 WEEVER *Anc. Fun. Mon.* 8 An Epitaph is..an astrict pithie Diagram.

a'stricted, *ppl. a.* [f. ASTRICT *v.* + -ED.] Confined, restricted; *spec.* in *Sc. Law* applied to lands held on such terms that the tenant must take grain grown upon them to be ground at a particular mill, paying a toll called *multure* or *thirlage.*
1656 FERGUSSON *On Coloss.* 130 That astricted dispensation under the Old Testament. **1754** ERSKINE *Princ. Sc. Law* (1809) 229 Thirlage may be extinguished by a charter of the astricted lands. **1819** J. GREIG *Rep. Affairs Edinb.* 37 Astricted multures payable by the brewers.

a'stricting, *ppl. a.* [f. as prec. + -ING².] That astricts; binding, restricting.
1837 C. LOFFT *Self-form.* I. 284 An adstricting business or profession.

astriction (ə'strɪkʃən). Also 6–7 **adstriction.** [ad. L. *a(d)strictiōn-em*, n. of action f. *astringĕre* to ASTRINGE. Cf. F. *astriction*, 16th c. in Littré.]
1. The action of binding or drawing close together, esp. the soft organic tissues; the state of being thus bound; constriction; constipation.
1568 TURNER *Herbal* II. 110 a, Seth the gall if the disease requyre great adstriction or bindyng..in wyne. **1655** CULPEPPER *Riverius* II. i. 63 This Disease is also begot by adstriction..of the Optick Nerves. **1732** ARBUTHNOT *Rules Diet* 268 Subject to Astriction of the Belly. **1853** MAYNE *Exp. Lex.*, *Astriction*, term for the act of using, or the state produced by the use of, astringent medicines; also for constipation.
†**2.** Astringent quality, astringency. *Obs.*
1551 TURNER *Herbal* (1568) 94 The roote is full of iuice, bytyng wyth a certayne astriction. **1662** CHANDLER *Van Helmont's Oriatr.* 251 The tast of astriction, or an earthly sharpness or harshness. **1750** PRINGLE in *Phil. Trans.* XLVI. 552 Endued with Qualities of..Astriction, and the like.
†**3.** Moral or legal binding; obligation, bond. ? *Obs.*
1536 BELLENDENE *Cron. Scot.* (1821) I. 56 He wald bind him..under quhat astrictionis thay plesit. *a* **1631** DONNE *Aristeas* (1633) 141 Linked together by astriction of firme amity. **1643** MILTON *Divorce* xiii. (1851) 53 Hence will not follow any divine astriction more then what is subordinate to the glory of God.
4. Restriction; *spec.* obligation to have grain ground at a particular mill: see ASTRICTED.
1619 *Sacrilege Sacr. Handled* 6 If astriction to holy and Ceremoniall persons..maketh a thing truely Legall and Ceremoniall. **1836** S. LAING *Resid. Norway* i. 48 In Norway there is no astriction to mills.

astrictive (ə'strɪktɪv), *a.* (*sb.*) Also 6–7 **adst-.** [f. L. *astrict-* (see ASTRICT *v.*) + -IVE, as if ad. L. **astrictīvus.* Cf. F. *astrictif*, 16th c. in Littré.]
A. *adj.* †**1.** Binding, obligatory. *lit.* and *fig.*
c **1555** HARPSFIELD *Divorce Hen. VIII.* (1878) 155 Being a law astrictive and preceptive. *a* **1659** OSBORN *Machiavel* (1673) 358 Becoming, like Juglers Knots, no ways astrictive to the more Potent.
2. Having a tendency to draw together or contract organic tissue; astringent, styptic.
1562 BULLEYN *Bk. Simples* 67 b, This tree..is adstrictive of nature. **1601** HOLLAND *Pliny* II. 48 It is astrictiue and will strengthen a weak stomack. **1669** W. SIMPSON *Hydrol. Chym.* 20 Vitriol..is also stiptick and astrictive.
B. as *sb.* An astringent.
1657 TOMLINSON *Renou's Disp.* 607 So many astrictives.

a'strictively, *adv.* [f. prec. + -LY².] Astringently.
1634 T. JOHNSON tr. *Parey's Chirurg.* XXVI. xlii. (1678) 657 Aluminous waters taste very astrictively.

†**a'strictly**, *adv. Obs. rare*⁻¹. [f. ASTRICT *a.* + -LY².] Closely, strictly.
1585 JAMES I. *Ess. Poesie* (Arb.) 21 Noght..that eyther I, or any others behoued astricktly to follow it.

†**a'strictory**, *a. Obs. rare*⁻¹. [ad. L. *astrictōrius*, f. *astrict-*: see ASTRICT *v.* and -ORY.] Astrictive, astringent.
1620 VENNER *Via Recta* vii. 109 They..corroborate..the stomacke, by their light astrictory faculty. **1731** in BAILEY.

astride (ə'straɪd), *adv.*, *prep.*, and *adj.*, orig. *phr.* [f. A *prep.*¹ + STRIDE.]
A. *adv.* **a.** In a striding position; with the legs stretched wide apart, or so that one leg is on each side of some object between, as when a person is on horseback. ***astride of***: bestriding.
1664 BUTLER *Hud.* II. ii. 764 Does not the Whore of Bab'lon ride Upon her horned Beast astride? **1785** COWPER *Tirocin.* 366 The playful jockey scow'rs the room..astride upon the parlour broom. **1854** THACKERAY *Newcomes* xxx. I. 297 The way in which the impudent little beggar stands astride, and sticks his little feet out. **1860** SMILES *Self-Help* viii. 209 Sitting astride of a house-roof.
b. *transf.* and *fig.*
1709 SWIFT *T. Tub* ix. 110 When a man's fancy gets astride on his reason. **1839–42** ALISON *Hist. Europe* (1850) XII. lxxix. §57. 48 Napoleon's central position astride on the Elbe.
B. *prep.* With one leg on each side of, bestriding.
1713 *Guardian* No. 112 (1756) II. 118 It is my intention to sit astride the dragon upon Bow steeple. **1883** ROE in *Harper's Mag.* Dec. 49/1 Astride his grandpa's cane.
C. *adj.* Of a seat on horseback: belonging or proper to one riding astride.
1889 in *Cent. Dict.* **1907** *Daily Chron.* 25 Oct. 3/5 Makers of riding habits are going to make a special effort to show that the 'astride' seat can be made elegant. **1930** S. G. GOLDSCHMIDT *Fellowship of Horse* ix. 132 Some say that astride riding is safer. **1931** *Times Lit. Suppl.* 26 Nov. 944/4 The Dianas of our modern horse-shows will be mildly surprised to learn..that the astride seat is impossible for women.

astridge, obs. form of OSTRICH.

a'striferous, *a.* ? *Obs.* [f. L. *astrifer* (f. *astri-* comb. form of *astrum* star + *-fer* bearing) + -OUS.] Bearing or containing stars, starry.
1656 in BLOUNT *Gloss.* **1677** GALE *Crt. Gentiles* II. IV. 508 That vast space between Earth and the astriferous Heaven.

a'strigerous, *a.* ? *Obs.*⁻⁰ [f. L. *astriger* (f. *astri-* star + *-ger* bearing) + -OUS.] = prec.
1731 in BAILEY.

astringe (ə'strɪndʒ), *v.* Also 6–7 **adstringe**, 7 **astring.** [ad. L. *a-*, *ad-stringĕre*, f. *ad* to + *stringĕre* to tie, bind.]
1. *trans.* To bind together, draw close (the organic tissues); to constrict, compress; *hence*, to render costive, constipate.
1562 BULLEYN *Bk. Simples* 41 b, Ivy is of a contrary.. facultie, adstringyng, binding. **1607** TOPSELL *Serpents* 789 Cobweb adstringeth..and closeth up wounds. **1620** VENNER *Via Recta* vi. 95 They coarctate the breast, and astringe the belly. **1725** BRADLEY *Fam. Dict.*, *Vinegar*..will so much astringe the Fibres of the whole Body. **1875** H. WOOD *Therap.* (1879) 25 Every living soft tissue..may.. have its tonicity increased, or be astringed.
†**2.** *intr.* To become constricted or compressed.
1603 HOLLAND *Plutarch's Mor.* 819 (R.) The moister anything is..given it is to cold, to astringe and congeal.
†**3.** *trans.* To bind morally or legally; to put under obligation or necessity; to oblige. *Obs.*
1523 *State Papers Hen. VIII*, I. 119 Your Grace is not astringed or bounden to any charge. **1635** [GLAPTHORNE] *Lady Mother* v. ii, Natures does astring a dewteous child To obey his parent. **1752** LAW *Spir. Love* I. 32 The desire, as astringing, always begets a resistance equal to itself.

astringency (ə'strɪndʒənsɪ). Also 7 **adstr-.** [f. ASTRINGENT: see -ENCY.]
1. Astringent quality.
1601 HOLLAND *Pliny* II. 510 Astringencie of Vitrioll. **1743** tr. *Heister's Surg.* 46 Caustic Medicines, which act by their great astringency. **1881** A. GRIFFITH in *Sci. Gossip* No. 203. 249 The astringency of tea is due to the tannin present.
†**2.** Astriction, astricted state. *Obs.*
1669 W. SIMPSON *Hydrol. Chym.* 344 [It] gives a gentle astringency to the Membranous Parts.
3. *fig.* Harshness, sternness, austerity.
1823 GALT *Entail* II. xix. 179 The doubtful credit of any wiser person might produce the same astringency. **1865** DRAPER *Int. Devel. Europe* xxi. 504 The lank-haired Puritan ..his face corrugated with religious astringency.

astringent (ə'strɪndʒənt), *a.* and *sb.* [a. F. *astringent*, ad. L. *astringentem*, pr. pple. of *astringĕre*: see ASTRINGE and -ENT.]
A. *adj.*
1. Having power to draw together or contract the soft organic tissues; binding, constrictive, styptic.
1541 R. COPLAND *Galyen's Terap.* 2 Hj b, I cal austere.. a lytell adstryngent. **1620** VENNER *Via Recta* vii. 146 It is astringent, and therefore effectual to stop the laske. **1855** BAIN *Senses & Int.* II. ii. §14 Astringent substances act on the skin and on the mucous membranes generally.
2. *fig.* Severe, austere, stern.
1820 BYRON *Juan* V. clvii, Their chastity..Is not a thing of that astringent quality, Which in the North prevents precocious crimes.
†**3.** Constipated, costive. *Obs.* Cf. ASTRINGENCY 2.
1662 R. MATHEW *Unl. Alch.* §76. 98 There are some such whom it hath purged most of all, which otherwise have been most astringent.
B. *sb.* An astringent medicine or substance.
1626 BACON *Sylva* §66 Blood is stanched..by astringents. **1830** LINDLEY *Nat. Syst. Bot.* 195 The root of Statice caroliniana is one of the most powerful astringents.

a'stringently, *adv.* [f. prec. + -LY².] In an astringent manner.
1865 BUSHNELL *Vicar. Sacr.* Introd. (1868) 24 The definitions operate astringently.

astringer (ə'strɪndʒə(r)). [f. ASTRINGE *v.* + -ER¹.] That which astringes, an astringent.
1662 R. MATHEW *Unl. Alch.* §75. 97 When through impatience he had got some violent astringer..he was all torn in his Limbs.

astringer, var. AUSTRINGER, keeper of goshawks.

astringing (ə'strɪndʒɪŋ), *ppl. a.* [f. ASTRINGE *v.* + -ING².] Binding together, astringent.
1752 LAW *Spir. Love* I. (1816) 25 The first property of nature..is an attracting, astringing, and compressing desire.

a'stringingness. *rare*⁻⁰. [f. prec. + -NESS.] Astringent quality, astringency.
1731 in BAILEY.

‖'**astrion.** *Obs.* [L., dim. of Gr. ἀστήρ star.] A kind of precious stone; 'no description can better suit the asteriated crystals of sapphire, which exhibit a brilliant six-sided star in its centre' (Westropp). Cf. ASTERIA, ASTROITE.
[*c* **1300** *Land Cokaygne* in *E.E.P.* (1862) 158 Carbuncle and astiune.] **1398** TREVISA *Barth. De P.R.* XVI. xv. 558 Astrion is a precyous stone of Ynde nyghe lyke to crystall. **1567** MAPLET *Gr. Forest* 3 Astrion is a gem..in whose centre ..a certaine light is seene shining. **1601** CHESTER *Love's Mar.* lxxxviii. (1878) 101 Euidos, Iris, Dracontites, and Astrion. **1874** WESTROPP *Precious Stones* 65 Astrion—star sapphire.

†**a'stripotent**, *a. Obs. rare*⁻¹. [f. L. *astri-* comb. form of *astrum* star + *potent-em* powerful.] Having power over or ruling the stars.
?*a* **1500** *MS. Harl.* 2251. 80 b (Halliw.) The high astripotent auctor of alle.

astro- ('æstrəʊ), repr. Gr. ἀστρο- stem and comb. form of ἄστρον 'star.' In compounds formed in Greek itself, as *astronomy*, ἀστρονομία; in others formed in L.; and in many of mod. formation: as **astro-'alchemist**, one who mingled astrology and alchemy; **astrobi'ology**, a branch of biology concerned with the discovery or study of life on the celestial bodies; (*astrobiology* (ad. F. *astrobiologie* (R. Bertholet)) and *astrobiological* also occur in *Mind* (1934) XLIII. 269 and *Mind* (1937) XLVI. 116 applied to a pseudo-metaphysical interpretation of certain ancient beliefs of the Chaldeans); **astro'botany** [ad. Russ. *astrobotanika* (Tikhov 1945)], the study of plant organisms on the celestial bodies; hence **astro'botanist**; **,astro-chrono'logical** *a.*, pertaining to the chronology and periods of the heavenly bodies; **astro'compass**, a form of compass for determining the direction of true north relative to the stars; used for correcting the errors of magnetic or gyroscopic compasses; **,astro-dy'namics** (see quot. 1955); **astro-fix**, the process or an act of determining the position of an aircraft by observation of the stars; **astro-hatch** = ASTRODOME; **,astroli'thology**, the scientific study of meteoric stones (1850 Sowerby *Pop. Min.* 218); **astro'magical** *a.*, pertaining to star-divination, astromantic; **,astropha'nometer** [Gr. φανός bright, τὸ φανόν brightness: see -METER], obs. equivalent of ASTROMETER (1830 *Edin. Encycl.* III. 1); '**astrophile**, a lover of the stars (also *fig.*);

astro'phobia, fear of the influence of the stars; ˌastro-pho'tometer, an apparatus for measuring the intensity of a star's light; hence ˌastrophoto'metrical *a.*; astro'phyllite [Gr. φύλλον leaf + -ITE], an orthorhombic mineral of yellow colour and micaceous composition, occurring sometimes in stellate groups (Dana); **astro'physical** *a.*, relating to stellar physics, or the study of the physical structure of the stars; **astro'plankton**, living material, postulated by Liebig, Kelvin and others but not yet observed, drifting in space; **astro-shot** (*colloq.*), **astro-sight**, an observation of the stars for the purpose of determining the position of an aircraft in flight; ˌastro-the'ology, that part of theology which may be deduced from the study of the stars; a religious system founded upon the observation of the heavens.

1876 M. COLLINS *Midn. to Midn.* III. iv. 29 The *astroälchymist regarded him with contemplative compassionate eyes. **1955** *Sci. News Let.* 13 Aug. 107/2 Among operational sciences and skills..would be..*astro-biology. **1958** C. C. ADAMS et al. *Space Flight* x. 240 The International Mars Committee..surveyed astrobiology, spectroscopic evidence of vegetation on Mars [etc.] **1952** *Sci. News Let.* 5 Jan. 2 There is much attention [in the Soviet Union] to what is called *astrobotany. **1956** *Newsweek* 22 Oct. 26/2 Gabriel Tikhov, Soviet '*astrobotanist', reports confirmation of his theory that higher forms of vegetation, similar to trees, exist on Mars. **1851** *Househ. Wds.* Mar. 545 Who is to check his *astro-chronological computation? **1951** *Gloss. Aeronaut. Terms* (*B.S.I.*) III. 10 *Astro-compass, a non-magnetic instrument which gives the direction of true north relative to a celestial body. **1955** *Sci. News Let. 13 Aug.* 107/1 *Astrodynamics, dealing with 'the dynamic flight behavior of space vehicles'. It would include the performance kinetics and dynamics, stability and control of spacecraft, similar to aerodynamics in aeronautics. **1941** J. A. HAMMERTON *ABC of RAF* 111 If the aircraft is over cloud and with clear sky above, the navigator may use the stars and get an '*astro' fix. **1944** 'N. SHUTE' *Pastoral* iv. 97 He said 'Navigator to captain. Can you get her up above this for an astro fix?' **1941** A. O. POLLARD *Bombers over Reich* x. 140 White frost..on the *astrohatch. **1944** *Times* 18 Jan. 6/3 Over the target area one engine was put out of action and the astro-hatch shattered. **1652** GAULE *Magastrom.* 73 In *astromagicall diviners.. when astrologicall magick had its first possession among men. **1708** MOTTEUX *Rabelais* Prol., I have..look'd out whatever all the *Astrophyles..have thought. **1903** *Daily Chron.* 6 June 5/2 Dr. Anderson..refuses..the name of astronomer... As he makes his observations with the naked eye from his own study window, with merely a pocket telescope..he prefers the name astrophil. **1936** L. PEARSALL SMITH in *S.P.E. Tract* XLVI. 204 The fever of perfection is not catching; and if it be foolish for these astrophils to hitch their wagons (in Emerson's phrase) to this remotely glittering star, surely they cannot reasonably be supposed to inflict any serious damage on the solar system. **1871** ALGER *Future Life* 604 Bitten by some theological fear which has given him the *astrophobia. **1876** CHAMBERS *Astron.* 481 An elaborate catalogue of 206 conspicuous stars arranged progressively in the order of brightness as determined by an *astro-photometer. **1878** *Astron. Soc. Notices* XXXVIII. 65 On a new *astrophotometrical method. **1881** C. YOUNG *Sun* 166 The new *astrophysical observatories at Potsdam and Meudon. **1954** J. B. S. HALDANE in *New Biol.* XVI. 25 One of the earliest parties to land on the moon should be able to look for *astroplankton, that is to say spores and the like, in dust from an area of the moon which is never exposed to sunlight. **1946** V. TEMPEST *Near Sun* i. 15 An *Astro-shot is a check on navigation that is made by the use of a sextant and the stars. **1943** G. L. CHESHIRE *Bomber Pilot* i. 10 To check ..by visual pin-point if possible: if not, by taking drifts or *Astro sights. **1714** DERHAM (*title*) *Astro-Theology, or a Demonstration of the Being and attributes of God, from a survey of the heavens. **1882** *Q. Rev.* July 131 The astro-theology of Chaldæa.

astroblast ('æstrəʊblɑːst, -æ-). *Anat.* [f. ASTRO- + -BLAST.] A primitive cell that develops into an astrocyte.

1901 in DORLAND *Med. Dict.* (ed. 2). **1940** GLADSTONE & WAKELEY *Pineal Organ* xxv. 382 Section through the spinal cord of a..chick embryo..*b.* supportive spongioblast, *c.* astroblast, or displaced epithelial cells.

†**a'strobolism.** *Med. Obs.* [ad. L. *astrobolismus*, a. Gr. ἀστροβολισμός, f. ἀστροβολίζεσθαι to be sun-stricken, f. ἄστρο-ν star + βολίζ-ειν to smite. Cf. F. *astrobolisme.*] Sudden paralysis attributed to the malign influence of a planet or star; sunstroke; blasting of plants in the dog-days.

1721 BAILEY, *Astrobolism*, a Blasting or Planet Striking. **1853** in MAYNE *Exp. Lex.*

astrocyte ('æstrəʊsaɪt). *Anat.* [f. ASTRO- + -CYTE.] **a.** A star-shaped cell of the neuroglia tissue in the central nervous system. **b.** A star-shaped bone corpuscle (1893 in *Funk's Stand. Dict.*).

1898 E. L. BILLSTEIN tr. *P. Stöhr's Text-Bk. Histology* (ed. 2) v. 170 The neuroglia principally consists of nucleated elements, the glia-cells... There are two kinds of glia-cells, ependymal cells and astrocytes. **1934** E. A. SHARPEY-SCHAFER *Histology* (ed. 13) xviii. 191 Protoplasmic cells.. radiating processes spring from the cytoplasm; hence the names astrocyte and spider-cell, by which these neuroglia-cells are also known. **1945** W. E. LE GROS CLARK *Tissues of Body* (ed. 2) xiii. 367 Scattered throughout the grey and white matter of the central nervous system are stellate cells. .. They are divided into two categories, protoplasmic astrocytes..and fibrous astrocytes.

astrocytoma (ˌæstrəʊsaɪ'təʊmə). *Path.* Pl. -mata, -mas. [mod.L., f. prec. + -OMA.] A tumour consisting wholly or largely of astrocytes.

1930 D. S. RUSSELL & H. CAIRNS in *Jrnl. Path. & Bacteriol.* XXXIII. 389 The tumour described is evidently a fibrillary astrocytoma. **1961** *Lancet* 16 Sept. 657/1 Well-differentiated astrocytomas. **1962** *Ibid.* 6 Jan. 25/2 Several astrocytomata have also been treated with derivatives of melphalan and with chlorambucil.

astrodome ('æstrəʊdəʊm). *Aeronaut.* [f. ASTRO- + DOME *sb.*] A transparent dome on the top of the fuselage of an aircraft from within which astronomical observations can be made.

1941 *Aeropl. Spotter* 16 Jan. 23 (*caption*) Astro Dome. **1942** *We speak from the Air* xi. 34 As second pilot I was in the astro-dome keeping a look-out all round. **1943** *Times* 11 Mar. 2/5 The astrodome was shot away; and the bomb doors would not close.

astrogeny (ə'strɒdʒɪnɪ). [f. ASTRO- + Gr. -γένεια birth, origin.] The doctrine of the origin or evolution of the stars; astrogony.

1880 WEBSTER cites H. SPENCER.

astrognosy (ə'strɒgnəsɪ). [ad. mod.L. *astrognōsia*, f. Gr. ἀστρο- star + -γνωσία = γνῶσις knowledge.] Knowledge of the stars; *spec.* that part of astronomy which treats of the fixed stars.

[**1753** CHAMBERS *Cycl. Supp.*, *Astrognosia.*] **1871** OTTÉ tr. *Humboldt's Cosm.* 30 (*Heading*) Astrognosy (The Domain of the Fixed Stars).

astrogony (ə'strɒgənɪ). [f. ASTRO- + Gr. -γονία production.] The doctrine of the generation or formation of the stars; stellar cosmogony. Hence **astro'gonic** *a.*

1869 *Eng. Mech.* 17 Dec. 329/1 Saturn is the only exception to physical astrogonic law. *Ibid.*, I spoke of cosmogony and astrogony. **1881** *Dublin Rev.* Ser. III. V. 236 Pesch's dissertation on astrogony.

astrographic (æstrəʊ'græfɪk), *a.* [f. ASTROGRAPHY + -IC, after *photographic.*] Of, pertaining to, used in, or produced by astrography.

1893 *Westm. Gaz.* 5 June 6/3 With the astrographic equatorial 722 photographic plates..were taken. **1895** *Athenæum* 8 June 743/1 The shutter of the astrographic dome was torn off and blown into the courtyard. **1895** H. H. TURNER in *Oxf. Univ. Gaz.* 11 June 588/1 The De la Rue Astrographic Telescope is in good order and has been in.. use throughout the year. **1903** —— *Astrographic Chart* 13 The real work of the Astrographic Chart consists in measuring the positions of the stars, which will tell us ultimately their motions. **1946** *Nature* 17 Aug. 221/2 A better system for astrographic work is the Schmidt camera, in which the aberrations of a spherical mirror are removed by a figured plate at its centre of curvature.

astrography (ə'strɒgrəfɪ). [f. ASTRO- + Gr. -γραφία writing, description.] 'The science of describing the stars' J.; the mapping of the heavens.

1740 B. MARTIN *Bibl. Techn.* xvii. 325 *Uranology*..may be considered under the following branches: *Heliography*.. *Astrography.* **1810** J. GREIG (*title*) Astrography; or the Heavens displayed.

astroid ('æstrɔɪd), *a.* and *sb.* [f. Gr. ἀστροειδής star-like, f. ἀστήρ star: see -OID.] **A.** *adj.* Star-shaped, star-like (cf. ASTEROID *a.*).

1909 in WEBSTER.

B. *sb. Geom.* A hypocycloid with four cusps.

1897 H. LAMB *Infinit. Calculus* ix. §138 The 'four-cusped hypocycloid'..is sometimes called the 'astroid'.

astroite ('æstrəʊaɪt). [ad. L. *astroītes* (Pliny), f. Gr. ἀστρο- star: see -ITE.] *lit.* A 'star-stone.'

1. A gem known to the ancients, apparently the same as the ASTRION.

1601 HOLLAND *Pliny* xxxvii. ix. (R.) As touching astroites, manie make great account of it. **1617** MINSHEU, *Astroite*, a precious stone. **1675** OGILBY *Brit.* 12 Star-like Stones called Astroyts, formerly of great esteem. **1750** *Leonardus' Mirr. Stones* 68 Astroites, Astrion, Asterias, or Asterites, is a white Stone approaching to Christal.

†**2.** Any star-shaped mineral or fossil, *e.g.* the joints of pentacrinites. *Obs.*

1610 HOLLAND *Camden's Brit.* I. 536 Stones called Astroites, which resemble little starres joyned with one another. **1724** DE FOE, etc. *Tour Gt. Brit.* (ed. 4) II. 326 (D.) Certain stones about the breadth of a silver peny and thickness of an half-crown, called astroites or star-stones, being fine pointed like a star and flat. **1728** LEWIS in *Phil. Trans.* XXXV. 491 Stones resembling Shells of the Escallop and Cockle kind..with some Astroites.

3. *Zool.* A species of madrepore.

1708 in *Phil. Trans.* XXVI. 77 The Astroite, an Irregular Coralline-stone, naturally Engrav'n with Asterisks. **1794** SULLIVAN *View Nat.* II. 175 Those of the coral class as madrepores, millepores, astroites. **1848** DANA *Zooph.* vii. §112. 110 The Porites..graduate into the Astræoporæ, and thence to the Astroites.

astrolabe ('æstrəleɪb). Forms: 4– **astrolabe**; 4–5 **astre-, astrylabe, astre-, astra-, astro-, astrilabie, -labye; astre-, astro-, astel-labre, astro-laboure,** 5 **astyllabyre, astyrlaby,** 6 **astroloby, -ie,** 7 **astralobe (astrolable).** [a. OF. *astrelabe*, and ad. med.L *astrolabium*, f. Gr. ἀστρολάβον (in same sense), orig. adj. 'star-taking' (sc. instrument), f. ἄστρον star + λαβ- take. The forms in *astre-*, etc. were of OF. origin, as also the ending *-labe*; *-labie, -laby*, was prob. adaptation of med.L. *-labium*, and *-labre* of a med.L. corruption **-labrum*, after *candelabrum*, etc.]

An instrument formerly used to take altitudes, and to solve other problems of practical astronomy.

The actual form and structure of the astrolabe of course varied greatly with the progress of astronomy, and the purposes for which the instrument was intended; its most complex form, as described by Tycho Brahe, passed into the modern EQUATORIAL. The chief types were:

a. A portable ARMILLA, or arrangement of armillary circles.

b. A planisphere, representing the circles of the heavens in the plane of the equinoctial, with movable sights.

c. A graduated brass ring with movable label or index turning upon the centre, used simply to take altitudes (the *Sea Astrolabe*).

1366 MAUNDEV. xvii. 180, I my self have mesured it by the Astrolabre. *c* **1386** CHAUCER *Miller's T.* 23 (Harl. MS. *c* 1415) His almagest..his astrylabe [*other 15th c. MSS.* astrelabie, -labre, astellabre, astro-laboure]. *c* **1391** —— *Astrol.* Prol. 1 To lerne the tretis of the astrelabie..A suffisaunt astralabie as for owre orizonte [*also, passim*, astrolabie, astrilabie]. **1393** GOWER *Conf.* III. 64 With him his astrolabe he name, Which was of fine gold precious With points and cercles merveilous. **1440** *Promp. Parv.*, Astyllabyre, instrument (**1499** Astyrlaby), *Astrolabium.* *c* **1525** SKELTON *Speke Parrot* 137 In the astroloby To pronostycate. **1594** BLUNDEVIL *Exerc.* (7th ed.) III. II. viii. 387 Having taken the Meridian altitude..with your Astrolabe or Quadrant. **1594** J. DAVIS *Seaman's Secr.* (1607) 2 The Astrolabie and Quadrant being instruments very vncertaine for Sea observations. *a* **1626** BP. ANDREWES *Serm.* (1856) I. 255 Never a Chaldean of them all could take it with his astrolabe. **1834** *Penny Cycl.* II. 525 Hipparchus is the first who can be supposed to have made use of an astrolabe. **1837** WHEWELL *Hist. Induct. Sc.* III. iv. §3 (1857) I. 156 To ascertain the position of the sun with regard to the ecliptic..an instrument called astrolabe, was invented, of which we have a description in Ptolemy.

astrolabical (æstrəʊ'læbɪkəl), *a.* [f. prec. + -ICAL.] Of, or pertaining to, an astrolabe.

1613 PURCHAS *Pilgr.* IV. x. I. 344 By his own Astrolabicall observation.

astrolatry (ə'strɒlətrɪ). [f. ASTRO- + Gr. λατρεία worship: see -LATRY. Cf. mod.F. *astrolâtrie.*] The worship of the heavenly bodies.

1678 CUDWORTH *Intell. Syst.* 593 Creature-worship, now vulgarly called idolatry..astro-latry, and demono-latry. **1877** SHIELDS *Final Philos.* 483 Astronomy..having groped through the two preceding stages of astrolatry and astrology.

†**'astrolog, -logue.** *Obs.* [a. F. *astrologue*, ad. L. *astrolog-us*, a. Gr. ἀστρολόγ-ος astronomer; prop. adj. 'telling the stars.'] = ASTROLOGER.

1375 BARBOUR *Bruce* IV. 707 It war gret mastry Till ony astrolog to say, This sall fall heir, and on this day. *c* **1508** DUNBAR *Lament* x, Art magicianis and astrologis, Rethoris, logitianis, theologis. *a* **1723** D'URFEY *Plague Impert.* (D.) I am a physician too..an astrologue infallible.

a'stroloˌgaster. ? *Obs.* [ad. It. *astrologastro* 'a foolish lying astrologer,' f. *astrologo* ASTROLOGER: see -ASTER.]

1622 HEYLIN *Cosmogr.* III. (1673) 113/1 At last every Astrologaster or Figure flinger was called a Chaldæan. **1686** GOAD *Celest. Bod.* III. iii. 456 Therefore we give the Poet leave..to call us Astrologasters.

†**'astrologe.** *Obs.* Also 4 **a'strology**, and in L. form **astro'logia.** [a. OF. *astrologe*, corruption of *aristoloche* (*aristoloche, astroloche*), by confusion with the more familiar word.] The herb ARISTOLOCHIA.

1393 GOWER *Conf.* III. 132 His herbe is astrology, Which folweth his astronomy. **1548** TURNER *Names of Herbes* 83 *Bistorta*..is called in the south countrey Astrologia. **1608** TOPSELL *Serpents* 622 The root of aram, and astrologe..is most effectual against the bitings of serpents. **1706** PHILLIPS, *Astrologe*, otherwise call'd Birthwort, and Hart-wort.

astrologer (ə'strɒlədʒə(r)). [f. ASTROLOGY, or perhaps from *astrolog-ien, -an* (*a'strologen* in Chaucer), by substitution of -ER, the native ending of the agent, for the F. *-ien.* Cf. ASTRONOMER.]

†**1.** An observer of the stars, a practical astronomer. *Obs.* (When *astrologer* and *astronomer* began to be differentiated, the relation between them was, at first, the converse of the present usage.)

1382 WYCLIF *Bible* Pref. Ep. (1850) 66/1 Astronomers, astrologerys, fisissians. **1440** *Promp. Parv.* 16 Astrologere, *Astrologus.* **1581** MARBECK *Bk. of Notes* 77 The Astrologer is he that knoweth the course and motions of the heavens, and teacheth the same, which is a virtue, if it passe not his bondes, and he become of an Astrologer an Astronomer. *a* **1625** BOYS *Wks.* (1630) 645 An Astrologer expert in his art, fortelleth an eclipse of the Sunne. **1676** EVELYN *Mem.* (1857) II. 115 Dined with me Mr. Flamsted, the learned astrologer and mathematician, whom his Majesty had established in the new Observatory in Greenwich Park.

†**2.** Applied to the cock, as watchman of the night and announcer of the sunrise. *Obs.*

c **1374** CHAUCER *Troylus* III. 1366 Whan that the cok, commune astrologer, Gan to his brest to bete, and afftyr, crowe. **1430** Lydg. *Chron. Troy* I. vi. **1444** *Pol. Poems* (1859) II. 216 Comoun astrologeer, as folk expert weel knowe.. Sumtyme hih and sumtyme he syngith lowe.

3. One who professes astrology in the modern sense; who pretends to judge of the influence of the stars upon human affairs.

1601 Holland *Pliny* VII. lvi. (R.) The above-named astrologers affirmed, that a man could not possibly passe the space of 90 degrees from the ascendent or erection of his nativities. **1611** Bible *Dan.* i. 20 Ten times better then all the Magicians and Astrologers that were in all his Realme [Wyclif, witches; Purvey, astronomyens; Coverdale, charmers; *Genev.* astrologians]. **1722** De Foe *Mem. Caval.* 1 Under the government of what star [I was born] I was never astrologer enough to examine. **1875** B. Taylor *Faust* I. 232 The astrologer Nostradamus was born at St. Remy.

†**astro'logian**, *sb.* and *a.* *Obs.* Also 4 astrologen, 4–6 -ien. [a. OF. *astrologien*, f. *astrologie*, or L. *astrologia*, as if ad. L. **astrologiānus*; cf. *chrestien*, *italien*, etc. Subseq. assimilated to L. spelling: cf. *theologian.* (Accented *a'strologen*, *-ian*, from 14th to 17th c.)]

A. *sb.* A professor of astrology, an ASTROLOGER.

c **1386** Chaucer *Wife's Prol.* 324 The wise Astrologen [*so 3 MS.*; -ien 2; -es 1] daun Ptholomé. *c* **1391** —— *Astrol.* Prol. 2, I nam but a lewd compilatour of the labour of olde Astrolog[i]ens. **1483** Caxton *Cato* Dij, He made all hys astrologiens to be gadred.. to gyder. **1570** Dee *Math. Pref.* 25 The common and vulgare Astrologien, or Practiser. **1583** Bible *Dan.* ii. 2 The inchanters, and the astrologians, and the sorcerers. **1630** J. Taylor *Wks.* I. 68/1 The Jewes, th' Egyptians, Caldies, Persians, Devised Arts and were Astrologians. **1693** *Phil. Trans.* XVII. 799 These excluded the Astrologians and Diviners from their Habitations.

B. *adj.* Dealing with astrology, astrological.

1621 Burton *Anat. Mel.* I. ii. I. iv, Amongst those astrologian treatises. **1646** Gaule *Cases Consc.* 26 The Astrologian, Starre-gazing, Planetary, Prognosticating Witch.

astrologic (æstrəʊ'lɒdʒɪk), *a.* and *sb.* [Ultimately ad. Gr. ἀστρολογικ-ός of an astrologer, f. ἀστρολόγ-ος (see ASTROLOGY and -IC); probably immediately after F. *astrologique* or med.L. *astrologic-us*.]

A. *adj.* Of or belonging to astrology or astrologers.

1648 Jos. Beaumont *Pysche* XIX. cix, Persians Astrologick Skill. **1686** Goad *Celest. Bod.* II. xiii. 333 Making iii Aspects in Astrologic account. **1762** Churchill *Ghost* I. Poems 1769 I. 162 That ancient people.. Gaz'd on the Stars, observ'd their motions, And suck'd in Astrologic notions.

†**B.** *sb. pl.* (after med.L. *astrologica*, Gr. τὰ ἀστρολογικά; in quot. title of a treatise) Matters or facts of astrology.

1569 J. Sanford *Agrippa's Van. Artes* 72 Julius Firmicus in his Astrologikes. **1671** Salmon *Syn. Med.* I. i. 5 The three aforesaid Books, immediately following the Astrologicks.

astro'logical, *a.* [f. prec. + -AL[1].]

1. Of the nature of, or dealing with, astrology.

a. In the earlier sense: Astronomical.

1591 Percivall *Sp. Dict.*, *Astrologal*, Astronomical, Astrological. **1646** Sir T. Browne *Pseud. Ep.* 34 Many excellent discourses, Medicall, Naturall, and Astrologicall. **1704** Hearne *Duct. Hist.* (1714) I. 13 Whoever looks for the New Moon in the Astrological Calendar, will often find Easter observ'd a week too late.

b. Pertaining to astrology, as now applied.

1591 Nashe (*title*) Wonderfull, strange and miraculous, Astrological Prognostication for this yeer of our Lord God. **1834** *Penny Cycl.* II. 528 In the second century, the whole world was astrological; and even Ptolemy was infected.

astro'logically, *adv.* [f. prec. + -LY[2].] In an astrological manner; by or according to astrology.

1603 Sir C. Heydon *Jud. Astrol.* xi. 252 [He] seeketh Astrologically to be satisfied vnto his questions. **1659** Gadbury (*title*) Nativity of the late King Charles, astrologically and faithfully performed. **1869** Dircks in *Eng. Mech.* 2 Apr. 25/2 Mankind rank astrologically as being of four temperaments.

astrologize (ə'strɒlədʒaɪz), *v.* [f. Gr. ἀστρολόγ-ος (see ASTROLOG) + -IZE. Gr. had ἀστρολογέειν and ἀστρονομίζειν.]

1. To examine or work out by astrology.

a **1733** North *Exam.* II. iv. ¶ 136. 301, I have elsewhere astrologised this Case of the Faction prevailing at Oxford.

2. *intr.* To practise or study astrology. *rare*—⁰.

1755 in Johnson.

†**astro'logo'mage.** *Obs.* *rare*—¹. [f. Gr. ἀστρολόγο-ς (see ASTROLOG) + μάγος Magian, MAGE.] An astrological diviner or wizard.

1635 Heywood *Hierarch.* VII. 445 And as in these, so likewise in past ages, He wanted not his Astrologomages.

a'strologous, *a.* [Cf. *homologous*, etc.] = ASTROLOGICAL.

1817 Byron in *Lett.* cclviii. (1866) 335 The month of my birth—and various other astrologous matters.

astrologue: see ASTROLOG.

astrology (ə'strɒlədʒɪ). Forms: 4–7 astrologie, 4– astrology. [a. F. *astrologie* (14th c. in Littré), ad. L. *astrologia*, a. Gr. ἀστρολογία 'account of the stars,' f. ἀστρολόγ-ος 'telling of the stars,' subst. 'one who tells of the stars, an astronomer,' f. ἄστρον star + -λογος speaking, telling, f. λέγ-ειν to tell, speak. Ἀστρολόγος and ἀστρολογία were the earlier terms in Gr.; subsequently ἀστρονόμος and ἀστρονομία were introduced: see ASTRONOMY. *Astrologia* was likewise the earlier and pop. word in L., where also *astronomia* took its place as the scientific term, while *astrologia* passed into the sense of 'star-divination.' In OF. and ME. *astronomie* seems to be the earlier and general word, *astrologie* having been subseq. introduced for the 'art' or practical application of astronomy to mundane affairs, and thus gradually limited by 17th c. to the reputed influences of the stars, unknown to science. Not in Shakspere.]

1. *gen.* Practical astronomy; the practical application of astronomy as an art to human uses; *esp.* (in later usage) to the prediction of events natural or moral.

The original distinction between Astronomy the *science*, and Astrology the *art*, is clearly expressed by Gower *Conf.* III. 105–135. Chaucer's *Treatise on the Astrolabe* was a work of 'astrology,' *i.e.* practical astronomy.

'Astrology' was of two kinds:

†**a.** ***Natural Astrology***: the calculation and foretelling of natural phenomena, as the measurement of time, fixing of Easter, prediction of tides and eclipses; also of meteorological phenomena. *Obs.*

1375 Barbour *Bruce* IV. 693 Astrology, Quhar-throu clerkis.. May knaw coniunctione of planettis. *c* **1391** Chaucer *Astrol.* Prol. 3 A gret part of the general rewles of theorik in astrologie. **1570** Dee *Math. Pref.* 23 Astrologie, is an Arte Mathematicall. **1649** Bp. Hall *Cases Consc.* III. ii. (1654) 178 Naturall Astrology, when it keepes it selfe within its due bounds is lawfull. **1669** Worlidge *Syst. Agric.* (1681) 264 The use of this part of Astrology.. by the Farmer as by the Sayler.

This sense (exc. in *Hist.*) became obs. in 17th c., all the regular physical phenomena passing into the domain of ASTRONOMY, and those that concerned the presumed influence of the moon and planets on the weather, etc., being called ASTRO-METEOROLOGY.

b. ***Judicial Astrology***: the art of judging of the reputed occult and non-physical influences of the stars and planets upon human affairs; star-divination, astromancy. (The only meaning of 'Astrology' since end of 17th c.)

'*Judiciary* or *Judicial* Astrology, which we commonly call simply *Astrology*, is that which pretends to foretell moral events, *i.e.* such as have a dependence on the free will and agency of man; as if that were directed by the stars.' Chambers *Cycl.* 1727.

[**1393** Gower III. 107 Assembled with astronomy Is eke that ilke astrology, The which in jugements accompteth Theffect, what every sterre amounteth.] *c* **1560** G. Gylby (*title*) An Admonition against Astrology Judiciall, and other curiosities that reygne now in the World[transl. Calvin]. **1597** Bp. Hall *Sat.* II. vii, Thou damned mock art, and thou brain-sick tale Of old astrology. **1649** —— *Cases Consc.* III. ii. (1654) 179 That other Calculatory, or figure-casting Astrology is presumptuous and unwarrantable. **1652** W. Rowland (*title*) Judicial Astrology judicially condemned. **1765** Tucker *Lt. Nat.* II. 466 Astrology is the pretended knack of telling fortunes by the stars. **1845** J. Saunders *Pict. Eng. Life* 175 In astrology.. the heavens were divided into twelve parts or houses. **1869** *Daily News* 9 Dec., Yesterday .. a curious action for trespass was brought by a herbalist and astrologer.. illustrating the manner in which astrology flourishes in London at the present time.

†**2.** = ASTRONOMY 1. Cf. ASTROLOGER 1. *Obs.*

1660 Stanley *Hist. Philos.* (1701) 246/2 A Boy or ignorant fellow knows not that the Sun is greater than the Earth, because he is ignorant of Astrology. **1807** Robinson *Archæol. Gr.* III. xxv. 330 The writers of fables say that Οὐρανὸς.. was the Father of all the Gods, and.. the inventor of Astrology.

astrology. *Herb.*: see ASTROLOGE.

astromancer ('æstrəʊ,mænsə(r)). *rare.* [f. next + -ER; cf. *necromancer*.] A diviner by the stars.

1652 Gaule *Magastrom.* 335 Of astromancers turning pantomancers, etc.

astromancy ('æstrəʊ,mænsɪ). *rare.* [ad. med.L. *astromantia*, a. Gr. ἀστρομαντεία, f. ἀστρο- star + μαντεία divination: see -MANCY.] Divination by the stars; 'astrology' in the modern sense.

1652 Gaule *Magastrom.* 165 What difference betwixt astromancy, magomancy, or magastromancy.. and all these?

astromantic (æstrəʊ'mæntɪk), *a.* and *sb.* [ad. (ultimately) Gr. ἀστρομαντικ-ός pertaining to an ἀστρόμαντις, f. ἄστρο- star + μάντις diviner.]

A. *adj.* Of or pertaining to astromancy.

1660 H. More *Myst. Godl.* VII. xvii. 360 Three fine Fools so goodly gay in their Astromantick Disguises.

B. *sb.* A professor of astromancy; an astromancer.

1652 Gaule *Magastrom.* 63 Whether the skilfullest astromantick.. be not convinced.

astro-meteorology (,æstrəʊ,miːtɪə'rɒlədʒɪ). [f. ASTRO- + METEOROLOGY.] The investigation of the (alleged) influence upon the weather, climate, etc. of planetary and stellar phenomena, such as sun-spots, phases of the moon, comets, meteors, planetary conjunctions. This was a branch of the older *natural astrology*; and the term is often applied to a pretended prognostication of the weather, which is no better than modern 'astrology.'

[**1753** Chambers *Cycl. Supp.*, *Astrometeorologia*, the art of foretelling the weather, and its changes, from the aspects and configurations of the moon and planets.] **1862** *Scot. Rev.* 402 Men had transformed Astro-meteorology into meteorology, or weather-lore into the science of the Atmosphere.

Hence **astrometeorological** (,æstrəʊ ,miːtɪərəʊ'lɒdʒɪkəl), *a.*, and **astrometeorologist** (,æstrəʊ,miːtɪə'rɒlədʒɪst).

1693 *Phil. Trans.* XVII. 893 Earthquakes he shews.. to be caused by the Stars, according to the Principles of the Astro-meteorological Art. **1864** *Intell. Observ.* No. 32. 104 The Astro-meteorologists, as they call themselves. **1866** *Lond. Rev.* 1 Dec. 596/2 Lunarists, cyclists, and astro-meteorologists.. have been utterly baffled in their vaticinations. **1869** F. Pratt in *Eng. Mech.* 19 Mar. 587/3 My only connection with Zadkiel was one of opposition to him in the Astro-Meteorological Society.

astrometer (ə'strɒmɪtə(r)). [f. ASTRO- + Gr. μέτρον measure.] An instrument for measuring the apparent relative magnitude of the stars.

1830 in *Edin. Encycl.* II. 582. **1867–77** Chambers *Astron.* 748 A useful astrometer for determining star-magnitudes.

astrometry (ə'strɒmɪtrɪ). [f. ASTRO- + Gr. -μετρία measurement.] The measurement of the apparent relative magnitude of the stars.

1867–77 Chambers *Astron.* 913.

astromyen, var. form of ASTRONOMIEN.

astronaut ('æstrəʊnɔːt). [f. ASTRO- + Gr. ναύτ-ης sailor, after AERONAUT.]

1. Name given to a space ship. *rare*—¹.

1880 P. Greg *Across the Zodiac* I. 27 In shape my Astronaut somewhat resembled the form of an antique Dutch East-Indiaman.

2. One who travels in space, i.e. beyond the earth's atmosphere; a student or devotee of astronautics. Cf. COSMONAUT.

1929 *Jrnl. Brit. Astr. Assoc.* June 331 That first obstacle encountered by the would-be 'Astronaut', viz., terrestrial gravitation. **1954** *N.Y. Times* 4 Apr. E9/7 The escape velocity from the earth is 25,000 miles an hour, yet astronauts talk glibly of achieving it, though they are fully aware of the heat that will be generated. **1957** P. Moore *Sci. & Fiction* xvii. 171 The astronauts taking off for the planet Hesikos remain standing upright. **1961** *Times* 6 May 8/3 President Kennedy spoke to Commander Alan Shepard by radiotelephone a few minutes after the astronaut was delivered by helicopter to the deck of the aircraft carrier Lake Champlain. **1962** J. Glenn in *Into Orbit* 4 We Astronauts have a mission... We are helping to break the bonds that have kept the human race pinned to the earth. **1966** *Electronics* 31 Oct. 39 Should a single goal—such as a manned landing on Mars in the 1980's—be chosen for the nation's space program once the Apollo astronauts have landed on the moon? **1971** *International Herald Tribune* 3 June 1 American astronauts and Soviet cosmonauts today swapped anecdotes about their experience in space exploration.

astronautics (æstrəʊ'nɔːtɪks). [ad. F. *astronautique* (coined by J. H. Rosny aîné (pseud. for J. H. H. Boëx-Borel) (1856–1940) in 1927; see *N. & Q.* (1960) CCV. 312 ff. and *Amer. Speech* (1961) XXXVI. 169 ff.): see -IC 2; cf. AERONAUTICS.] The art or science of locomotion outside the earth's atmosphere. Hence **astro'nautical** *a.*, pertaining to or concerned with astronautics or astronauts.

1929 *Jrnl. Brit. Astr. Assoc.* June 332 Prof. Oberth.. has just been awarded the £80 prize offered for the most successful solution of the 'astronautical' question. **1929** *Mech. Engin.* (*A.S.M.E.*) Nov. 864/2 (*title*) Astronautics. **1931** *Internat. Cycl. Aviation Biogr.* s.v. Robert Esnault-Pelterie: This volume [*sc.* R. Esnault-Pelterie's *L'Astronautique* (Paris, 1930)] affords a most thorough groundwork upon which the future development of the science of 'Astronautics' will doubtless depend. **1932** *Times Lit. Suppl.* 16 June 439/3 France has a Committee of Astronautics. **1952** *Jrnl. Brit. Interplanetary Soc.* May 126 The term 'astronautical engineer' cannot yet have the same significance as 'aeronautical engineer'.. although one day we feel sure it will have. **1960** *Times* 21 Mar. 13/6 There is need for an international law of astronautics.

astronavigation (,æstrəʊnævɪ'geɪʃən). [f. ASTRO- + NAVIGATION.] Determination of the position and course of aircraft by means of observation of the stars; applied also to the possible or actual use of this means in vehicles travelling in space. Also ,**astro'navigator**, an air pilot, or automatic air-piloting machine, using astronavigation.

1942 W. Simpson *One of our Pilots is Safe* ii. 46 We had neither the sextant nor the detailed knowledge necessary for astro-navigation. **1949** *Aeronautics* Jan. 52/1 When the weapon enters the area of enemy held territory.. an automatic astro-navigator will take over. **1958** *Daily Mail* 10 Nov. 4/3 The huge 'astro-navigation trainer', a planetarium sort of thing which taught the space navigator to determine his position by measuring the position of the earth and the moon with respect to the immovable background of the fixed stars.

astronomer (əˈstrɒnəmə(r)). Forms: 4–6 **astronomyer**, 5–6 **astronomier**, 5– **astronomer**. [Formed on ASTRONOMY, or rather on the earlier *astronomy-en* by substituting the native agent-ending -ER for F. *-en, -an*. Afterwards contracted so as to seem formed directly on Gr. ἀστρονόμ-ος, or F. *astronome* + -ER. Cf. *astrolog-er, philosoph-er*.]

One who studies astronomy; one skilled in the knowledge of the heavenly bodies. ***Astronomer Royal***: the official title of the astronomer who has charge of one of the royal, or national, observatories of Great Britain.

1366 MAUNDEV. v. 45 In that Contree ben the gode Astronomyeres. **1480** CAXTON *Chron. Eng.* I. (1520) 6/1 Athlas ye great astronomyer. **1523** LD. BERNERS *Froiss.* I. xlii. 57 Kyng Robert of Cicyle..was a great astronomyer. **1530** PALSGR. 644/2, I nombre, as an astronomer doth his thing by augorisme. **1580** LUPTON *Too Good to be True* (Wright) Chesse, the astronomer's game, and the philosopher's game. *a* **1704** LOCKE (J.) Astronomers no longer doubt of the motion of the planets about the sun. **1742** YOUNG *Nt. Th.* IX. 771 An undevout Astronomer is mad. **1838** *Penny Cycl.* X. 297 Flamsteed was appointed [1674] astronomer royal, or, as the warrant ran 'astronomical observator,' and carried on his observations at the queen's house in Greenwich Park. **1874** MOTLEY *Barneveld* I. i. 28 Protecting the astrologer, when enlightened theologians might have hanged the astronomer.

b. In early use it included the 'astrologer'; and, when the two terms began to be differentiated, was sometimes distinctively so used: see ASTROLOGER.

1388 WYCLIF *2 Chron.* xxxiii. 6 He hadde with hym astronomyers and enchaunteris..that disseyven mennus wittis. *a* **1577** GASCOIGNE *Fruites of Warre* (R.) These astronomers thinke, where Mars doth raigne, That all debate and discorde must be rife. **1606** SHAKS. *Tr. & Cr.* v. i. 100 When he performes, astronomers foretell it. **1611** TOURNEUR *Ath. Trag.* v. i, Thou ignorant Astronomer Whose wand'ring speculation seekes among The planets for men's fortunes.

c. astronomer's ring: a modification of the *Sea Astrolabe*. **astronomer's staff**: the ALMUCANTAR-STAFF.

1551 RECORDE *Pathw. Knowl.* II. Pref., The arte of measuryng by the astronomers staffe, and by the astronomers ryng. [**1570** DEE *Math. Pref.* 19 The helpe of his..Staffe Astronomicall. **1594** BLUNDEVIL *Exerc.* VII. xxxvi. 712 Seeke by your Astronomicall Ring..to know what houre it is.]

astronomic (æstrəʊˈnɒmɪk), *a.* [a. F. *astronomique*, ad. L. *astronomic-us*, a. Gr. ἀστρονομικ-ός, f. ἀστρονομία: see ASTRONOMY and -IC.] **a.** Of or belonging to astronomy.

1712 BLACKMORE *Creation* II. (J.) Can he not pass an astronomick line? **1789** COWPER *Queen's Visit* xix, More than astronomic eyes. **1857** H. MILLER *Test. Rocks* iv. 159 All theologians have now received the astronomic doctrines.

b. = ASTRONOMICAL *a.* 1 b. *colloq.*

1949 E. BOWEN *Heat of Day* xvii. 297 North African spring teemed with pursuits and astronomic surrenders, with a victoriousness hard, still, not to associate with the enemy. **1969** *Daily Tel.* 23 Apr. 18 What astronomic sum would be necessary for that today—£50,000 a year? **1973** *Times Lit. Suppl.* 7 Dec. 1492/2 The need for astronomic speeds is rare. *Ibid.* 1492/3 Astronomic data compiled on a computer can be extracted. **1986** *Washington Post* 23 Jan. A23/5 Today nearly 60 percent of all black children are born out of wedlock. Imagine the astronomic percentages in many inner cities.

astroˈnomical, *a.* [f. prec. + -AL¹.]

1. a. Connected with, bearing upon, dealing with astronomy. (Cf. an *Astronomical* Society with an *astronomic* fact.) ***astronomical year***: one of which the length is determined by astronomical observations, apart from conventional reckoning. ***astronomical ring, staff***: see ASTRONOMER c.

1556 RECORDE *Cast. Knowl.* Pref. 11 If Astronomicall accompt were not. **1588** A. KING *Canisius' Catech.* I. iij, According to ye astronomicall calculation. **1692** BENTLEY *Boyle Lect.* ii. 47 Aratus the Cilician, in whose Astronomical Poem this passage is now extant. **1818** HAZLITT *Eng. Poets* i. (1870) 12 There can never be another Jacob's Dream. Since that time the heavens have gone further off, and grown astronomical. **1855** LEWIS *Early Rom. Hist.* v. §11 A solar eclipse..on the 21st of June in the astronomical year 399 B.C.

b. Of figures, distances, etc.: immense, similar in magnitude to those used in astronomy.

1899 *Daily News* 7 Oct. 8/2 He..excused his delay on the ground that in stock-taking..they discovered that they omitted one credit line of thirty thousand pounds. Such familiarity with astronomical finance made Mr. Rylands somewhat irritable. **1934** G. B. SHAW *Too True to be Good* Pref. p. 7 The odds against a poor person becoming a millionaire are of astronomical magnitude. **1947** *Evening News* 23 Apr. 2/1 Britain 'owes' astronomical sums in war-debts to India and Egypt. **1953** E. HYAMS *Gentian Violet* i. 9 The value of stage, film, broadcasting and other rights was astronomical.

2. *ellipt.* as *sb. pl.*

[**1594** BLUNDEVIL *Exerc.* I. xxvii. 73 Multiplication of Astronomical Fractions.] **1706** PHILLIPS, Astronomical Numbers or Astronomicals. See Sexagesimal Fractions. **1751** CHAMBERS *Cycl.*, *Astronomicals*, a name used by some writers for sexagesimal fractions, on account of their use in astronomical calculations.

3. *Comb.*, as ***astronomical clock***: a clock which keeps sidereal time; ***astronomical telescope***: a telescope designed for astronomical use, commonly one not giving an upright image (opp. *terrestrial telescope*); ***astronomical triangle***: 'a triangle on the celestial sphere whose vertices are the pole, the zenith, and the observed body' (Webster 1961); = *celestial triangle*; ***astronomical unit***: the mean distance between the earth and the sun (approx. 93 million miles), used as a unit for measuring distances within the solar system.

1856 D. LARDNER *Handbk. Astr.* I. vi. 136 The rate of the astronomical clock is so regulated that [etc.]. **1904** GOODCHILD & TWENEY *Technol. & Sci. Dict.* 31/1 *Astronomical clock*, a clock keeping sidereal time. It indicates 0 h. 0 m. 0 s. when the first point of Aries crosses the meridian. **1882** *Encycl. Brit.* XIV. 594/2 We can now understand the working of the ordinary *astronomical telescope*... The object glass furnishes an inverted but real image of a distant body, *within our reach*. **1917** A. H. HOLT *Man. Field Astr.* ii. 10 This spherical triangle..is so much used in field astronomy that it is called the astronomical triangle. *Ibid.* 11 Each part of the astronomical triangle, with the exception of the angle of the star, may be expressed in terms of the observer's position on the earth's surface (latitude) or the co-ordinates of the star. **1909** *Cent. Dict.* Suppl. s.v. *Unit*, Astronomical unit. **1963** JERRARD & MCNEILL *Dict. Sci. Units* 20 *Astronomical unit*.. approximately equal to the mean distance between the sun and the earth ($1{\cdot}496 \times 10^{11}$m)... Radar determinations carried out since 1960 indicate the astronomical unit will soon be known to an accuracy better than 1 in 10^6.

astroˈnomically, *adv.* [f. prec. + -LY².] In an astronomic or astronomical manner; according to astronomy or astronomic principles.

1649 BP. HALL *Cases Consc.* III. i. (T.) Images astronomically framed. **1794** SULLIVAN *View Nat.* I. 219 Astronomically speaking, the greatest cold should be felt at the latter end of December. **1856** KANE *Arct. Exp.* II. 404 The headlands..were generally determined astronomically.

†**astronomien, -an.** *Obs.* Also **-yen, astromyen.** [a. OF. *astronomien*, f. *astronomie* or L. *astronomia*, like *chrestien, italien*, as if repr. a. L. **astronomiānus*. *Astromyen* was a phonetic reduction. Cf. *astrologien, -an*.] The earlier word for ASTRONOMER (including *astrologer*).

c **1300** *K. Alis.* 136 He is an astromyen. *c* **1340** HAMPOLE *Prose Tr.* 9 Astronomyenes byhaldes þe daye, and þe houre, and þe poynte þat man es borne in. **1388** WYCLIF *Matt.* ii. 1 Lo! astromyenes camen fro the eest to Jerusalem. **1393** GOWER *Conf.* II. 230 Which was an astronomien, And eke a great magicien. **1483** CAXTON *Gold. Leg.* 403/2 The kyng.. assemblid lx astronomyens. *c* **1500** *Partenay* 12 Neuer better astronomian might be.

astronomize (əˈstrɒnəmaɪz), *v.* [f. ASTRONOMY: see -IZE.] *intr.* To pursue astronomy; to act or speak astronomically.

1682 SIR T. BROWNE *Chr. Morals* (1756) 97 Thus they astronomiz'd in caves. **1684** T. BURNET *Th. Earth* III. 44 It is a great question..whether Moses did either philosophize or astronomize in that description. **1848** H. ROGERS *Ess.* I. vi. 311 Thales..astronomising as he walked.

astronomy (əˈstrɒnəmɪ). Forms: 3–7 **astronomie**, 3 **astronomiȝe**, 4 **astronemy**, 4–6 **astronomye**, (5 **astrony**,) 6 **astronamye**, 4– **astronomy**. [a. OF. *astronomie* (11th c. in Littré), ad. L. *astronomia*, a. Gr. ἀστρονομία, n. of quality f. ἀστρονόμ-ος 'star-arranging,' 'one who arranges or classes the stars'; f. ἀστρο-ν star + -νομος 'distributing, arranging, ' f. νέμ-ειν to distribute, arrange, order. Ἀστρονόμος was a later word than ἀστρολόγος, and probably at first applied to those who mapped out the constellations; hence, both in Gr. and L., *astronomia* was a later and more scientific term than *astrologia*, which at length acquired the modern sense of *astrology* or star-prognostication. But in OF. and early Eng., *astronomie* seems to have been the term first used, and to have embraced the whole field of the ancient *astrologia*. Subseq. *astrologie* was adopted for the *art* or *practice* of astronomy, and gradually, though not completely before the 17th c., *astronomy* and *astrology* took their current senses.]

The science which treats of the constitution, relative positions, and motions of the heavenly bodies; that is, of all the bodies in the material universe outside of the earth, as well as of the earth itself in its relations to them.

1205 LAY. 24298 Þe craft is ihate Astronomie [**1250** *adds* in oþer kunnes speche]. *c* **1250** *Gen. & Ex.* 792 And hem lerede, witterlike, Astronomiȝe and arsmetike. **1340** HAMPOLE *Pr. Consc.* 7606 Gret clerkes of clergy, Þat has bene lered in astronemy And knawes þe constellacyouns. **1432–50** tr. *Higden* VII. ii. (1879) VII. 271 A man instructe gretely in astrony and in geometry. **1481** CAXTON *Myrr.* I. xiii. 39 Astronomye, whiche is of all clergye the ende. **1570** BILLINGSLEY *Euclid* v, Introd. 126 The whole arte of Astronomy teacheth to measure proportions of tymes and mouinges. **1605** TIMME *Quersit.* I. i. 1 The Ægyptians had a most singular knowledge of Astronomy. **1869** DUNKIN *Midn. Sky* 1 Astronomy has for ages been one of the most popular of the sciences.

†**b.** In earlier usage it included also the alleged relations of the heavenly bodies to human action, subseq. distinguished as ASTROLOGY. *Obs.*

c **1300** *K. Alis.* 137 Astronomye and nygremauncye. **1393** LANGL. *P. Pl.* C. XXII. 244 To seo and to seye · what sholde by-falle..As astronomyens þorw astronomye. **1494** FABYAN VII. 490 So lernyd in astronomy yᵗ she toke vpon her to shewe thynges to come. **1540** BOORDE *(title)* The pryncyples of Astronamye the whiche diligently perscrutyd is in maner a pronosticacyon to the worldes end. *c* **1600** SHAKS. *Sonn.* xiv, Not from the stars do I my judgment pluck, And yet methinks I have astronomy. **1728** DE FOE *Syst. Magick* I. i. 21 In Astronomy the first soothsayers found the secret influences of the stars upon the surface of the earth.

For the distinction between *astronomy* and *astrology* in early use, see ASTROLOGY.

astrophanometer, -phile, etc.: see ASTRO-.

†ˈ**astrophel.** *Obs.* [perh. corruption of *astrophyllum* = star-leaf; Nares suggests of *Aster Tripolium*.] Name of a plant mentioned by Spenser, which has not been identified.

1591 SPENSER *Daphn.* 346 Feede ye hencefoorth on bitter astrofell. —— *Astrophel* 186 That hearbe of some, Starlight is cald by name..From this day forth do call it Astrophel.

ˌ**astrophoˈtography.** [f. ASTRO- + PHOTOGRAPHY.] The photography of celestial bodies. So ˌ**astrophotoˈgraphic, -ˈgraphical** *adjs.*, of, pertaining to, used in, or produced by astrophotography. Also ˌ**astroˈphotograph** *sb.*

1858 SUTTON & WORDEN *Dict. Photogr.* 28 *Astrophotography*, a convenient name for the application of Photography to the delineation of the planets and constellations. **1889** WINTERHALTER *(title)* The International Astrophotographic Congress. **1892** *Pall Mall Gaz.* 9 Aug. 2/1 The astrophotographic telescope. *Ibid.*, The new astrophotographical telescope is..controlled by an electric current. **1903** A. M. CLERKE *Problems in Astrophysics* 5 Astrophotography is an art, and has a technique of its own. **1938** *Times Lit. Suppl.* 3 Dec. vi/2 A vision of the exposed night sky—shown in over 30 astrophotographs.

astrophysical, *a.* (Later examples: see ASTRO- and next.)

1956 *Nature* 18 Feb. 299/2 The explanation lies in the advance of radio technology as well as in astrophysical phenomena at radio wave-lengths. **1958** *New Scientist* 20 Nov. 1299/2 The Soviet Union's most powerful telescope, the 48-inch reflector at the Crimean Astrophysical Observatory.

astrophysics (æstrəʊˈfɪzɪks). [f. ASTRO- + PHYSICS.] That branch of astronomy which treats of the physical or chemical properties of the celestial bodies. Hence **astroˈphysicist**, a student of astronomical physics.

1869 E. DUNKIN *Midnight Sky* 201 As a subject for the investigations of the astro-physicist, the examination of the luminous spectras of the heavenly bodies has proved a remarkably fruitful one. **1890** *Sat. Rev.* 9 Aug. 176/1 The new science of 'astrophysics'. **1901** NEWCOMB *Stars* i. 10 The astronomer, or astrophysicist as he now calls himself. **1933** *Discovery* May 165/1 Some time ago it seemed to be the belief of the astrophysicists that the age of the stars and of the galactic system must be much greater than that of the earth. **1938** R. W. LAWSON tr. *Hevesy & Paneth's Man. Radioactivity* (ed. 2) xxvi. 289 The results of their observations [of cosmic radiation] are no less important in astrophysics than in atomic research. **1946** *Nature* 23 Nov. 764/2 A modern laboratory for spectroscopic research—a most important branch in connection with future developments in astrophysics. **1962** *Sci. Survey* V. 70 Astrophysicists—those who apply physics to astronomical problems—have provided a coherent account of the life history of the stars.

astropyle (ˈæstrəʊpaɪl). *Zool.* [f. Gr. ἄστρον star + πύλη gate.] A tubular aperture or funnel-like membranous projection found in some radiolarians.

1887 E. HAECKEL *Radiolaria* in *Rep. Challenger* XVIII. I. p. iv, This osculum is closed by a radiate cover (astropyle or operculum radiatum). **1888** ROLLESTON & JACKSON *Anim. Life* 876 Or again there is a main oral aperture or astropyle. .. The astropyle consists of a tubular proboscis, rising from the centre of a radially striated disc or operculum. **1901** CALKINS *Protozoa* iii. 70 The Cannopylea, in which the membrane around the pores is drawn out into funnel-like projections termed astropyles.

astroscope (ˈæstrəskəʊp). [f. ASTRO- + Gr. -σκοπος observer.] An astronomical instrument formerly in use, 'composed of two cones, on whose surface the constellations with their stars were delineated.' Chambers *Cycl. Supp.*

1675 SHERBURNE *Sph. Manilius* C ij b, These Instruments are not true Astroscopes. **1753** CHAMBERS *Cycl. Supp.* s.v., The astroscope is the invention of Wil. Schukhard, formerly professor of mathematics at Tubingen..in 1698. **1867–77** CHAMBERS *Astron.* 913.

†**aˈstroscopy.** *Obs.* [f. ASTRO- + Gr. -σκοπία observation.] Observation of the stars. (J.)

†**aˈstrose**, *a. Obs.* [ad. L. *astrōsus* (Isidore), f. *astrum* star.] Ill-starred.

1731 in BAILEY.

astrosphere (ˈæstrəʊsfɪə(r)). *Biol.* [ad. G. *astrosphäre* (H. Fol 1891, in *Anatomischer Anz.*

VI. 273), f. ASTRO- + SPHERE.] **a.** The central portion of the aster exclusive of the astral rays; the centrosphere. **b.** The whole aster exclusive of the centrosome.

1896 E. B. WILSON *Cell in Development & Inheritance* Gloss. 333 Astrosphere..1. The central mass of the aster, exclusive of the rays, in which the centrosome lies..(Fol, 1891, Strasburger, 1892). 2. The entire aster exclusive of the centrosome..(Boveri, 1895). **1901** CALKINS *Protozoa* 278 This structure resembles the astral system of Metazoa, in consisting of an outer spherical mass with radiating processes (astrosphere).

astrote, a-strout, obs. forms of ASTRUT.

Astroturf (ˈæstrəʊtɜːf). Also **astroturf, astro-turf.** [f. *Astro*dome (see def.) + TURF *sb.*[1]] A proprietary name for a kind of artificial grass surface (first used in the Astrodome indoor sports stadium at Houston, Texas).

1966 *Daily Tel.* 21 Apr. 16/6 Houston had spent £11 million building its mammoth, air-conditioned Astrodome... Now..[they are] spending £180,000 on a carpet of synthetic turf, called..Astroturf. **1968** *Official Gaz.* (U.S. Patent Office) 3 Dec. TM6/2 Astroturf. For plastic materials in the form of fibers, filaments, ribbon-like extrusions. **1968** *Trade Marks Jrnl.* 11 Dec. 2164/2 Astroturf... Ropes, string, nets and sacks..tents, awnings (textile), tarpaulins, sails, padding and stuffing materials..and raw fibrous textile materials. Monsanto Company. **1975** FELTON & FOWLER *Best, Worst, & Most Unusual* 280 Campsites.. carpeted with astroturf. **1975** *Telegraph* (Brisbane) 2 Oct. 22/5 Near the pool is a putting green of astro-turf. **1977** *New Yorker* 12 Sept. 59/1 He and Henny..sat down in a couple of lawn chairs on a green Astroturf lawn. **1986** *Washington Post* 25 Jan. C5/3 He couldn't wait to test the Bourbon Street Theory on the Superdrome astroturf.

Hence **ˈastroturfed** *a.*, carpeted with Astroturf.

1984 *Times* 9 Oct. 13/1 They were speaking on the astro-turfed roof terrace of Lloyd Webber's Soho offices.

†**aˈstroy,** *v. Obs.* Forms: 2-3 **astruȝe,** 2-4 **astrue,** 4 **astroie.** Also aphetic STROY. [a. OF. *estrui-re*, cogn. w. It. *struggere*:—late pop. L. ˈ*strŭere* for *distrŭere* to DESTROY.] To destroy.

c **1200** *Trin. Coll. Hom.* 211 Swo heneð and astruȝeð þe riche men þe wrecches. *c* **1330** *Arth. & Merl.* 6756 That eueriche baroun loke his pas, And aspie hem bi tropie, And so fond hem to astroie. **1340** *Ayenb.* 17 Prede astruþ..alle þe graces..þet byeþ ine manne.

†**aˈstructive,** *a. Obs. rare*$^{-1}$. [f. L. *astruct-* (ppl. stem of *a(d)strŭere*, f. *ad* to + *strŭere* to build) + -IVE.] Building up, erecting, constructive.

a **1656** BP. HALL (O.) The true method of Christian practice is first destructive, then astructive.

a-strut (əˈstrʌt), *advb. phr.* Forms: 4 **a-strout,** o strut, one strowte, 5 **on strut,** 5-6 **a strote,** 6 **a strute, a strutte,** 6-8 **astrut,** 5- **a-strut.** [A *prep.*[1] + STRUT *sb.*]

1. Sticking out, projecting stiffly; protruding, swollen, puffed up. *arch.*

c **1330** *Pol. Songs* 336 The knif stant a-strout. *c* **1400** *Sir Isumbras* 620 His eghne stode one strowte. **1532** MORE *Confut. Tindale* Wks. 589/1 Theyre belyes standinge a strutte with stuffing. **1606** *Choice, Chance, etc.* 28 With his armes astrut, like a Scarcrow in a peas-garden. **1785** COWPER *Task* v. 268 Inflated and astrut with self-conceit.

†**2.** Stubbornly. *Obs.*

1330 R. BRUNNE *Chron.* Pref. 194 þei schoued, þei þrist, þei stode o strut. *c* **1460** *Towneley Myst.* 49, I rede no man from him dray, In way, ne stand on strut.

3. On the strut, strutting, walking grandiosely.

†**aˈstuce,** *sb. Obs. rare*$^{-1}$. In 6 **austuce.** [a. OF. *astuce*, ad. L. *astūtia*, n. of quality f. *astūtus* ASTUTE.] Astuteness.

1548 *Compl. Scot.* 87 Be there austuce..thai furnest vitht money baitht the parteis aduersaris.

†**aˈstuce,** *a. Obs. rare*$^{-1}$. [a. OF. *astus, -uz, -uce, -ut*, ad. L. *astūtus* ASTUTE.] Astute.

1549 *Compl. Scot.* xi. 97 Sedusit be ther astuce and subtil persuasions.

astucious (əˈstjuːʃəs), *a.* Also **-tious.** [ad. F. *astucieux*, f. *astuce, astucie*: see prec.] Astute.

1823 SCOTT *Quentin D.* ix, Like all astucious persons, as desirous of looking into the hearts of others as of concealing his own. **1846** MRS. JAMESON *Char. Wom.* I. 72 The astutious lady of Belmont with her magic potions.

aˈstuciously, *adv.* [f. prec. + -LY[2].] Astutely.

18.. SCOTT, Marked you how astuciously the good father eluded the questions?

astucity (əˈstjuːsɪtɪ). [f. ASTUCIOUS; cf. *ferocious, ferocity*.] Astuteness.

1837 CARLYLE *Fr. Rev.* I. iii. (1872) III. 19 With astucity, with swiftness, with audacity! **1851** —— *Sterling* III. v. (1872) 211 He was a man..great only in..speciosities, astucities.

astun(e, see ASTONE.

astunde, for *a stunde*: see STOUND.

astunt, variant of ASTINT *v. Obs.* to stop.

Asturian (əˈstjʊərɪən), *a.* and *sb.* [ad. Sp. *asturiano*; cf. L. *Astur, -uris* Asturian.] **A.** *adj.* Of or pertaining to Asturias, an ancient province of northern Spain (now Oviedo), or its inhabitants; *spec.* designating a culture, remains of which have been found in Asturias (see quots.). **B.** *sb.* **1.** A native or inhabitant of Asturias. **2.** The Castilian dialect spoken by natives of Asturias.

1612 T. SHELTON tr. *Cervantes' Don Quixote* (1896) I. III. ii. 132 There likewise served in the Inne an Asturian Wench. *Ibid.* 136 He stretched forth his armes to receive his beautifull Damzell the Asturian. **1834** *Penny Cycl.* II. 539/1 The Asturian farmers also plant..scarlet-runners together with the Indian corn. *Ibid.* 540/1 The Asturians speak the Castilian language. **1875** *Encycl. Brit.* II. 824/2 There is a special clan among the Asturians called the Baqueros. **1887** *Ibid.* XXII. 350/2 *Castilian Dialects..Asturian*—The Asturian idiom, called by the natives *bable*, is differentiated from the Castilian by the following characters [etc.]. **1924** C. D. MATTHEW tr. *H. Obermaier's Fossil Man in Spain* x. 349 Protoneolithic phases in Europe... The only such phase known in Spain is the Asturian, which..is post-Azilian and pre-Neolithic in age. *Ibid.*, The cultural phase which the present writer has styled the 'Asturian'. **1959** *Chambers's Encycl.* V. 452/2 On the north coast of Spain are found the middens of the Asturians who hunted land game and collected shell-fish on the shore during late mesolithic times.

asturt, variant of ASTART *v. Obs.* to escape.

astute (əˈstjuːt), *a.* [(? a. F. *astut*) ad. L. *astūtus*, lengthened form of *astus* crafty, cunning.] Of keen penetration or discernment, esp. in regard to one's own interests; shrewd, subtle, sagacious; wily, cunning, crafty.

1611 COTGR., *Astut*, astute, crafty, subtill, wyly, guilefull. **1634** SIR M. SANDYS *Prudence* 168 Wee terme those most Astute, which are most Versute. [Not in JOHNSON 1755.] **1829** I. TAYLOR *Enthus.* x. 258 The astute atheism of Greece and Rome. **1878** BOSW. SMITH *Carthage* 331 He had, with the astute fickleness of a barbarian, come to a secret understanding with Scipio.

aˈstutely, *adv.* [f. prec. + -LY[2].] In an astute manner; with keen penetration, shrewdly.

1826 SYD. SMITH *Wks.* (1867) II. 112 He sets himself to comment astutely upon the circumstances. **1851** SIR F. PALGRAVE *Norm. & Eng.* I. 296 Louis astutely evaded the contest.

aˈstuteness. [f. as prec. + -NESS. Before this was in use, the L. *astūtia* was occas. employed.] The quality of being astute; keenness of penetration or discernment; mental subtlety, shrewdness.

[**1802** BENTHAM *Wks.* X. 396 Could this mass of law by any *astutia* be construed to come under title Poor.] **1843** VAUGHAN *Age Gt. Cities* 152 The astuteness acquired in the exercise of this greatest of free schools. **1865** MAFFEI *Brig. Life in It.* II. 89 The astuteness of the Pontifical police.

†**aˈsty(e,** *v. Obs.* Forms: 1-2 **astīȝan,** 3 **astyen, astye.** *Pa. t.* 1 **astaȝ,** 2 **astah, asteh.** [OE. *astīȝan*, f. A- *pref.* 1 up, away + *stīȝan* to go, proceed, ascend; cogn. with Goth. *ussteigan*, OHG. *arstîgan*, mod.G. *ersteigen*.]

1. To go up, ascend.

c **950** *Lindisf. Gosp.* John vii. 8 Ic ne astiȝo [Vulg. *ascendo*] to doeȝe symbel ðissum. *c* **1175** *Lamb. Hom.* 91 Crist aras of deaðe and..astah to heofene. *c* **1275** *Passion Our Lord* 624 in *O.E. Misc.* 55 Er he wolde astyen to heuene. *c* **1380** *Sir Ferumb.* 2971 By þat was Gyoun vp a-stoȝe: oppoun þe laddre an heȝ.

b. To rise with its summit.

c **1175** *Cott. Hom.* 227 Enne stepel..swa háhcne þat his rof astiȝe up to hefenne.

c. To rise in arms.

1297 R. GLOUC. 317 He was in fere Of Edmondes tueye breþeren..laste hii gonne astye.

2. To go or come down, descend.

c **975** *Rushw. Gosp.* John ii. 12 Ðona astaȝ [*Ags. & Hatton*, fóron; Vulg. *descendit*]..he & moder his. *c* **1175** *Cott. Hom.* 241 Ic am cwuce bread þe astah fram hefene. *c* **1200** *Trin. Coll. Hom.* 111 Ðe heuene abeh and dun asteh.

†**aˈstying,** *vbl. sb. Obs.* In 2 **astiunge.** [f. prec. + -ING[1].] Ascension.

c **1220** *Lofsong Ure Louerd* in *Cott. Hom.* 209 þine wurðful astiunge into heouene.

astyl, var. ASTEL, *Obs.*, a splinter.

astylar (əˈstaɪlə(r)), *a.* [f. Gr. ἀ priv. + στῦλ-ος pillar + -AR.] Without columns or pilasters.

1842 in GWILT. **1845** *Penny Cycl.* 1st Supp. I. 148/1 We had no examples of such astylar class of design, until it was introduced by Mr. Barry, in the Travellers' Clubhouse.

astyllabyre, astyrlaby, obs. ff. ASTROLABE.

aˈstyllen. *Mining.* A small dam in an adit or level to prevent the full passage of the water.

1849 in WEALE *Dict. Terms.*

astyte, variant of ASTITE *adv. Obs.*

a-sudden (əˈsʌd(ə)n), *advb. phr.* [A *prep.*[1] + SUDDEN.] Of a sudden, suddenly.

1875 B. TAYLOR *Faust* I. iv, A-sudden stood I in a glowing sphere. **1880** *Contemp. Rev.* Apr. 642 And, asudden, witching Spring Into her bosom sucks the snow.

†**aˈsue,** *v. Obs. rare*$^{-1}$. In 4 **asiwe.** [a. OF. *a(s)suivre*:—late L. *assequĕre*, for cl. L. *assequi* (see ASSEQUENT); cf. *pursue*.] To follow after.

c **1300** *K. Alis.* 2494 Quyk asiweth him al his men.

†**aˈsum,** *v. Obs. rare*$^{-1}$. [a. OF. *a(s)somme-r, -umer*:—late L. *assummā-re* to sum up, f. *as-* = *ad-* to + *summa* total.] To consummate, complete.

1340 *Ayenb.* 168 Huanne hi habbeþ al asummed, þanne verst ham þingþ þet hit is al to aginne.

asunder (əˈsʌndə(r)), *adv.*, orig. *phr.* Forms: 1 **on sundran,** 1-4 **o sunder(e,** 5 **on sondre, one sondyre, on sundre;** 4 **asondri, asyndre,** 4-5 **asondry,** 4-6 **asondur, -dre,** 5 **a-sundyr, -dir, asondyr, -dir,** 5-6 **asonder,** 6 **a sundre, asundur,** 6- 8 **a sunder, assunder,** 4- **asunder.** See also *in* SUNDER (*ensunder*) in same sense. [OE. phr. *on sundran* 'in or into a separate position or condition': see A *prep.*[1] and SUNDER.]

†**1.** In or into a position apart or separate; apart.

a **1000** *Cædmon's Gen.* (Gr.) 842 Sæton on sundran. *c* **1000** *Ags. Gosp.* Mark vii. 33 Ða nam he hine onsundran [*Lindisf.* sundurlice] of þære meniȝu. *c* **1160** *Hatton G.* ibid., Asundre. **1548** COVERDALE *Erasm. Par. Gal.* i. 15 But me called he a sonder to be his preacher.

2. Of two or more things: Apart or separate from each other: **a.** in position.

1330 R. BRUNNE *Chron.* 282 þei er o sundere. *c* **1386** CHAUCER *Prol.* 493 Wyd was his parisch, and houses fer asondur. *c* **1420** *Pallad. on Husb.* IV. 133 Sowe hem..half a foote asonder. **1563** SHUTE *Archit.* E iiij b, How far and how nere the pillers shalbe set a sunder. **1611** HEYWOOD *Gold. Age* IV. i. Wks. 1874 III. 57 Heer's a coyle to keep fire and tow a sunder. **1777** JOHNSON *Lett.* 183 II. 2 We are now near half the length of England asunder. **1867** FROUDE *Short Stud.* (1872) I. 23 Wide asunder as pole and pole.

b. in direction or motion.

c **1250** *Gen. & Ex.* 116 Ðe ðridde dai..was water and erðe o sunder sad. *c* **1330** *Amis & Amil.* 309 Now we asondri schal wende. *c* **1450** *Merlin* ix. 140 They wolde not departe on sondre. **1613** SHAKS. *Hen. VIII*, v. i. 112 My Chaffe And Corne shall flye asunder. **1719** YOUNG *Revenge* IV. i, Unhand her—Murder! Tear them asunder. **1855** MACAULAY *Hist. Eng.* III. 685 Lochiel..while forcing them asunder, received a wound.

3. Apart from each other in character, or in one's judgement or consideration; separately as objects of thought. ***to know asunder***: to distinguish. *arch.*

c **1386** CHAUCER *Somp. Prol.* 8 Freres and feendes been but litel asunder. *c* **1525** SKELTON *Agst. Scottes* 96 Know ye not suger and salt asondyr. **1592** SHAKS. *Rom. & Jul.* III. v. 82 Villaine and he be many Miles assunder. **1699** BENTLEY *Phal.* 217 The several words taken asunder have nothing Poetical in them. **1722** DE FOE *Plague* (1756) 264 It was impossible to know them assunder.

4. Of one thing: Into separate parts; in two, in pieces; *esp.* with *break, burst, cut, rend, tear*, etc.

[**1340** HAMPOLE *Pr. Consc.* 888 Wormes sal ryve hym in sondre.] *c* **1450** LONELICH *Grail* xiv. 199 Bothe palettes and scheldes he to-craked asondir. *c* **1440** *Gesta Rom.* 253 He kutte ensundre alle his clothis. **1526** TINDALE *Acts* i. 19 Brast a sondre in the myddes. **1586** T. B. *La Primaud. Fr. Acad.* 136 To rent and break a sunder our good and sure friendship. **1641** J. JACKSON *True Evang. Temper* i. 85 If she will saw me asunder, let her. **1862** STANLEY *Jew. Ch.* (1877) I. v. 95 The rending asunder of the veil which overhung the temple.

†**aˈsunder,** *v. Obs.* Forms: 1 **asundri-an,** 4 **assunder,** 4- **asunder.** [OE. *asundrian*, f. A- *pref.* 1 + *sundrian* to SUNDER.] To put asunder, separate, divide.

a **1000** *Cod. Exon.* 98 a (Bosw.) Se déaþ asundraþ líc and sáwle. *c* **1440** *Gesta Rom.* 206 He was asunderid fro alle his men. **1580** TUSSER *Husb.* (1878) 37 A plough beetle..Great clod to asunder. **1593** R. BARNES *Parthen.* ii. in Arb. *Garner* V. 409 Thou could not be persuaded that my wits Could once retire so far from Sense asundered.

aˈsundering, *vbl. sb. rare.* [f. prec. + -ING[1].] The action of putting asunder; separation.

1881 BUCHANAN *God & Man* III. 244 After death's asundering.

asunderness (əˈsʌndənɪs). [f. ASUNDER *adv.* + -NESS.] The state of being asunder; separateness.

1843 *Blackw. Mag.* LIII. 765 What the Germans would call the *Auseinanderseyn*..the asunderness, of things.

asuni-en, var. ASSOIN *v. Obs.* to excuse.

asur(e, obs. form of ASSURE and AZURE.

a-sware, obs. form of A-SQUARE.

a-swarm (əˈswɔːm), *advb. phr.* [A *prep.*[1] + SWARM.] Swarming.

1830 *Blackw. Mag.* XXVII. 947 A shower of natural leaf-born flies a-swarm in the air. **1840** BROWNING *Sordello* I. 147 Tutti Santi, think, a-swarm With Ghibellins, and yet he took no harm! **1882** SWINBURNE *Tristr. Lyonesse* 281 Shines yet with fire..From tossing torches round the dance aswarm. **1890** J. A. SYMONDS *Essays* i. 166 The atmosphere ..was aswarm with them.

†**a-'swash**, *advb. phr. Obs.* Also 6 **a sosshe, a shosshe.** [Derivation of *swash, sosh*, unknown; A- is evidently the prep., as in *aslant, across*, etc.]

1. Slantingly, obliquely, crosswise, aslant.

1530 PALSGR. 831 A sosshe as one weareth his bonnet, *a gyngoys.* **1575** TURBERV. *Falconrie* 277 You must cut it off.. a slope, and (as they say) aswashe. **1611** COTGR. s.v. *Chamarre*.. Worne aswash, or skarfewise.

2. With scorn, contemptuously. Cf. ASKANCE *adv.* 2.

1530 PALSGR. 614 Se how she loketh ashosshe, or aswasshe, is she nat a prowde dame. **1611** COTGR., *De guingois*.. huffingly, swaggeringly, aswash.

a-sway (ə'sweɪ), *advb. phr.* [A *prep.*[1] + SWAY.] Swaying, bending from side to side.

1858 MORRIS *Harpdon's End* 99 On some broad stream, with long green weeds a-sway. **1880** SWINBURNE *Stud. Song* 113 A ship on the waters.. poised softly for ever asway.

a-sweat (ə'swɛt), *advb. phr.* [A *prep.*[1] + SWEAT.] Sweating, moist.

1879 J. LONG *Æneid* II. 730 The Dardan shore So oft asweat with blood.

†**a'sweeten**, *v. Obs. rare.* In 7 assw-. [f. A- *pref.* 11 (improperly written *as-*, after *as-sure*, etc.) + SWEETEN.] To sweeten, make less bitter.

1599 SANDYS *Europ. Spec.* (1632) 232 That rigour of Iustice, which the bountifulnesse of this Mercy did mitigate and assweeten.

aswell, obs. way of writing *as well*: see AS C 2.

†**a'swelt**, *v. Obs.* 3-4. *Pa. t.* aswalt. [OE. *asweltan*, f. A- *pref.* 1 + *sweltan* to die: see SWELT *v.*] *intr.* To perish, die, become extinct.

c **1230** *Ancr. R.* 216 Gif þe gulchecuppe weallinde bres to drincken.. þet he aswelte wiðinnen. **1250** LAY. 27474 Cnihtes þar aswalten. *c* **1300** *K. Alis.* 6638 That theo snow for the fuyr no malt, No the fuyr for theo snow aswelt.

†**a'sweve**, *v. Obs.* [OE. *aswębban* (= *aswefian*), f. A- *pref.* 1 + *swębban* to put to sleep: see SWEVE *v.*] *trans.* To put to sleep; to stun; in OE. to put to death.

a **1000** *Judith* 322 (Sweet *Reader*) Ealdhettende sweordum aswefede. *c* **1384** CHAUCER *H. Fame* 549 So astonyed and a-sweued Was euery vertu in my heued.

†**a'swike**, *v. Obs.* 1-3. *Pa. t.* aswác. [OE. *aswícan*, to betray, desert, abandon, f. A- *pref.* 1 + *swícan* to fail, fall short, deceive: see SWIKE *v.* But ME. *aswike* corresponds in sense to the OE. intrans. verb *ȝeswícan* to leave off, cease, desist.] To cease, desist.

c **975** *Rushw. Gosp.* Matt. v. 29, 30 Gif þanne þin eȝe.. aswicað þe [*Ags.* æswicie, aswice, *Hatton* aswikie, aswike]. **1205** LAY. 16112 þa aswac worden Merlin þe wise. *c* **1220** *Leg. St. Kath.* 2186 þis swifte pine þat aswikeð se sone.

a-swim (ə'swɪm), *advb. phr.* [A *prep.*[1] + SWIM.] Swimming, afloat.

1663 in Spalding *Troub. Chas. I* (1829) 44 The soldiers.. were all a-swim through the water that came in at the holes and leaks of the ship. **1870** MORRIS *Earth. Par.* I. I. 125 The shallow flowing sea.. set the wrack a-swim.

†**a'swind**, *v. Obs.* 1-4. *Pa. t.* aswond. *Pa. pple.* **aswunde(n, aswounde.** [OE. *aswindan*, f. A- *pref.* 1 away + *swindan* to languish.]

1. *intr.* To languish away, vanish, perish.

c **885** K. ÆLFRED *Boeth.* xxxiii. §4 þýlæs.. ealle oþre ȝesceafta aswindað. *c* **1175** *Lamb. Hom.* 133 Sum [of þe sede feol] among þeornen and þer aswond. **1250** LAY. 17940 Sealde he aswint þat to him seolue trestep. *a* **1250** *Owl & Night.* 1572 Al thi sputing schal aswinde.

2. in *pa. pple.* Languishing, worn out; enervated.

c **885** K. ÆLFRED *Boeth.* xl. §4 Hwý ȝe swá unnytte sión & swá aswundene? **1205** LAY. 22254 þat his folc gode aswunden [**1250** aswonde] ne laie þere. *a* **1250** *Owl & Night.* 534 Vor ich nam non aswunde wrecche. *c* **1350** *Leg. Rood* (1871) 52 ȝe beþ neih aswounde.

a-swing (ə'swɪŋ), *advb. phr.* [A *prep.*[1] + SWING.] Swinging, swaying to and fro.

1876 DOWDEN *Poems* 35 Airy bells, a-swing Through half a summer day. **1880** L. WALLACE *Ben-Hur* 232 Ships a-swing at their moorings.

†**a'swink**, *v. Obs. rare*[−1]. [f. A- *pref.* 1 + SWINK *v.*, OE. *swincan.*] To labour for, toil for.

c **1300** *Beket* 1665 ȝoure mete ȝe mowe aswynke.

a-swirl (ə'swɜːl), *adv.* or *pred. a.* [f. A- *pref.* 2 + SWIRL.] In a swirl, swirling.

1909 H. G. WELLS *Tono-Bungay* IV. iii. 490 The water all a-swirl with the wash of shipping. **1915** C. C. MARTINDALE *In God's Army* 125 Despite the.. mists that set the imagination a-swirl. **1924** R. CAMPBELL *Flaming Terrapin* vi. 34 The breeze.. passed by with golden locks aswirl.

†**a'swithe, as swithe**, *advb. phr. Obs.* Also 4-5 **alswithe, asswyþe, aswythe.** This, besides its literal meaning 'as quickly,' had the sense: As quickly as possible, immediately. (See AS A III, and cf. ASFAST, ASSOON, ASTITE.)

[**1375-1521**; see quotations under ALSWITHE.] *c* **1320** R. BRUNNE *Medit.* 1016 Ryȝt wyth þat wurde aswyþe she ryst. *c* **1340** *Gaw. & Gr. Knt.* 1400 To soper þay ȝede as-swyþe. *c* **1386** CHAUCER *Man of L.T.* 539 Thou schalt be slayn as swithe. *c* **1420** *Pallad. on Husb.* IV. 623 A sithe Made for lupyne is upp to honge aswithe.

†**a'swolkeness.** *Obs.* [OE. *asolcennesse*, f. *asolcen* idle, pa. pple. of *aseolcan*, 'torpescere' + -NESS.] Sloth, laziness.

c **1000** WULFSTAN *Addr. Eng.* (Sweet *Reader* 111) þurh bisceopa asolcennesse. *c* **1175** *Lamb. Hom.* 83 Forwunded, mid spere of prude.. mid onde, mid aswolknesse.

a-swoon (ə'swuːn), *advb. phr.* Forms: 4-5 **aswoune, aswounne, aswowne, a swowen, a swoun(e, a swown(e,** 5 **a-swoone,** 7- **aswoon, a-swoon.** [Also written *a swoune*, expanded *on swoune*, and most commonly from 1325 to 1500 *in swoune, in swowne*, after 1500 *in a swown(e, sown(e, swoon*; as if f. A *prep.*[1] + SWOON *sb.* But as this sb. does not otherwise appear in early use, *aswowne* was perhaps by mistaken analogy for *aswown* (cf. *adowne, adown*), *aswowen* = *iswowen*, OE. *ȝeswóȝen*; in which case *aswoon* and ASWOUGH are of identical origin: see the latter, and SWOON *sb.*]

In a swoon or faint. *to fall aswoon*: to faint away.

c **1386** CHAUCER *Sqrs. T.* 466 And fil to grounde anon And lith aswowne [*v.r.* a swounne, a swowne, on swoune], deed and lyk a stoon. *c* **1400** *Rom. Rose* 1804 A-swoone I felle, bothe deed & pale. **1483** CAXTON *Gold. Leg.* 217/3 Yf the moder be a swowne of the payne. **1535** STEWART *Cron. Scot.* I. 408 Mony fell in swoun. **1637** RUTHERFORD *Lett.* 110 (1862) I. 276 My faith was fallen aswoon and Christ but held up a swooning man's head. **1860** S. DOBELL in *Macm. Mag.* Aug. 326 A-swoon With fear. **1865** CARLYLE *Fredk. Gt.* III. VIII. iii. 15 Wilhelmina, faint, fasting, sleepless all night, fairly falls aswoon.

aswooned (ə'swuːnd), *ppl. a.* [Due to mixture of *aswoon* (which, in the Chaucer instance, the other MSS. read) and *swooned*, in ME. *iswouned.*] A-swoon, swooned.

[Cf. *c* **1385** CHAUCER *L.G.W.* 1342 Twenti tyme Iswounyd hath sche thanne (*v.r.* y-swowned, i-swowned, i-swonyd, swouned, swowned, -yd, yswounded).] *c* **1386** —— *Clerkes T.* 1023 (Harl. MS.) Whan sche this herd, aswoned doun sche fallith [*Six-text*, aswowne, aswounne, a swowne, in swowe]. **1878** B. TAYLOR *Deukalion* II. v. 85 The Past, that 'mid her ruins lay a-swooned.

†**a'swough, aswow(e**, *adv.* (or *ppl. a.*) Also 4-5 **asuowe, aswo, aswou, aswowe, aswogh, assowe.** [Interchanging in 14th c. with *on swowe, in swowe*, as if f. A- *prep.*[1] + SWOUGH *sb.*; but perhaps originally = *iswowe*:—*iswowen*:—OE. *ȝeswóȝen* senseless, fainted, pa. pple. of *swóȝan* to overgrow, choke, in the phrase 'to fall *iswowen, iswowe*, or *aswowe*' to fall in a faint; cf. *aslope, awake, athirst.*] In a swoon; = A-SWOON.

[Cf. *c* **1000** ÆLFRIC *Hom.* II. 336 Se læȝ.. ȝeswóȝen betwux þam ofsleȝenum. **1205** LAY. 3074 He feol iswowen (**1250** hi-swoȝe); *c* **1300** *St. Brandan* 10 And ful adoun i-suoȝe; *c* **1380** *Sir Ferumb.* 2497 For hungre þai fulle y-sowe. *c* **1350** *Will. Palerne* 87 And fel doun on swowe.] *c* **1320** R. BRUNNE *Medit.* 490 Aswo she fyl doun yn þe felde. *c* **1330** *Arth. & Merl.* 3304 Sir Arthour was aswowe. *c* **1420** *Chron. Vilod.* 496 Hurre moder adoune assowe dudde falle. **1460** *Lybeaus Disc.* 1171 Aswogh he fell adoun.

a-'swound, *advb. phr. arch.* Also 6-7 **asound.** [Corruption of *a-swown*, the earlier form of A-SWOON: see SWOON and SWOUND. Apparently not connected with the earlier *aswounde* from ASWIND.] In a swoon.

1634 ROW *Hist. Kirk* (1842) 466 He was in hazard of falling a-sound.

a-swowing: see SWOWING.

†**a'sye**, *v. Obs.* Forms: 1 **asíȝan**, 3 **asye-n.** *Pa. t.* 1 **asáh**, 2-3 **aseh.** [OE. *asíȝan*, f. A- *pref.* 1 + *síȝan*: see SYE *v.*] To sink down; to 'set.'

1024 *O.E. Chron.* (Laud. MS.) He mid þam dynte niðer asáh. *c* **1200** *Trin. Coll. Hom.* 109 þe sunne of rightwisnesse.. eft aseh alse sunne to-glade. *c* **1275** in *O.E. Misc.* 90 Al we schullen a-syen, and seo to þe nede.

asyghe, obs. form of ASSAY.

a'syle. *Obs.* exc. *poet.* Also 4-6, 20 **asile.** [a. F. *asile, asyle*, ad. L. *asȳlum*: see below.] The earlier form of ASYLUM *sb.* (in senses 1, 2, 3).

1382 WYCLIF *2 Macc.* iv. 34 Counseilide hym for to go forth of asile. **1542** BECON *Pathw. Prayer* Wks. 1843, 128 Fly unto prayer as unto an holy anchor, or sure asile. **1594** *Zepheria* xxxix. in Arb. *Garner* V. 85 A harbour where they looked for asile. **1725** tr. *Dupin's Eccl. Hist. 17th C.* I. II. iii. 40 The Asyles having occasion'd great Abuses in Greece. **1925** HARDY *Human Shows* 45 When an inner court outspreads As 'twere History's own asile.

asyllabic (æ-, eɪsɪ'læbɪk), *a.* [f. A- *pref.* 14 + SYLLABIC *a.*] Not syllabic; not constituting a syllable; = ASYLLABICAL *a.*

1827 S. LEE *Hebr. Gram.* ix. 169 This letter, when Paragogic, is.. asyllabic, and is mostly found between two nouns in the state of construction. **1953** C. E. BAZELL *Ling. Form* v. 50 A single phoneme (e.g. Latin *i*) may occur in syllabic or in asyllabic function.

asyllabical (æsɪ'læbɪkəl), *a.* [f. A- *pref.* 14 + SYLLABICAL.] Not constituting a syllable.

1751 WESLEY *Wks.* (1872) XIV. 153 The formatives הֿ, ֿי, ו, are termed Asyllabical.

asylum (ə'saɪləm), *sb.* Pl. **asylums** (also in senses 1, 2, **asyla**). Forms: 5-7 **asilum,** 7 **assylum,** 8 **azylum,** 7- **asylum.** [a. L. *asȳlum*, a. Gr. ἄσυλον refuge, sanctuary, neut. of adj. ἄσυλος inviolable, f. ἀ priv. + σύλη, σῦλον right of seizure. Cf. ASYLE.]

1. A sanctuary or inviolable place of refuge and protection for criminals and debtors, from which they cannot be forcibly removed without sacrilege.

c **1430** LYDG. *Bochas* II. xxviii. 65 a, A territory that called was Asile. This Asilum.. Was a place of refuge and succours.. For to receyue all foreyn trespassours. **1600** HOLLAND *Livy* I. viii. 7 Romulus.. set up a sanctuarie or lawlesse church, called Asylum. **1673** CAVE *Prim. Chr.* I. vi. 145 How far those Asyla's and Sanctuaries were good and useful. **1727-41** CHAMBERS *Cycl.* s.v., We read of asylums at Lyons and Vienne among the ancient Gauls. **1807** ROBINSON *Archæol. Gr.* III. ii. 197 Some were asyla for all men, and others were appropriated to particular persons and crimes.

2. *gen.* A secure place of refuge, shelter, or retreat.

1642 SIR E. DERING *Sp. on Relig.* xvi. 87 They have bin the *Asylum* for superstition. **1691** WOOD *Ath. Oxon.* II. 729 He fled to Oxon, the common Asylum of afflicted royalists. **1728** MORGAN *Algiers* II. v. 318 A Port, where his Ships might find an Azylum. **1855** MILMAN *Lat. Chr.* II. III. vi. 76 The monasteries were not as yet the asyla of letters.

3. *abstr.* Inviolable shelter; refuge, protection.

1725 tr. *Dupin's Eccl. Hist. 17th C.* I. II. iii. 40 The Senate was oblig'd to confine the Right of Asylum to Nine Temples. **1814** BYRON *Lara* II. viii, Beneath his roof They found asylum oft but ne'er reproof.

4. A benevolent institution affording shelter and support to some class of the afflicted, the unfortunate, or destitute; *e.g.* a 'lunatic asylum,' to which the term is sometimes popularly restricted.

1776 PENNANT *Tour Scot.* II. 307 When the grievous distemper of the leprosy raged.. our ancestors erected asyla for those poor wretches. **1866** G. MACDONALD *Ann. Q. Neighb.* vii. (1878) 115 Miss Oldcastle thought she was out of her mind, and spoke of an asylum. **1879** HARLAN *Eyesight* v. 56 Three hundred of these persons [victims of Egyptian Ophthalmia] were cared for in an asylum.. in Paris.

asylum (ə'saɪləm), *v. rare.* [f. the sb.] *trans.* To give protection to; to place in an asylum. Also *refl.*

1794 J. COURTENAY *Pres. State Manners, Arts, & Politics of France & Italy* 43 Th' assassin *asylums* himself in the Church, And we see him in every fine portico lurch. **1843** *Times* 8 Mar. 5/3 Do they wish to spill blood—they have only to play a few pranks—get asylum'd a month and a day. **1866** J. B. ROSE tr. *Ovid's Fasti* II. 139 Crime thou asylum'd, crime ejecteth he.

asymbolia (æsɪm'bəʊlɪə). *Path.* [ad. G. *asymbolie* (C. Finkelnburg 1870, in *Berl. klin. Wochenschrift* 19 Sept. 461), f. A- *pref.* 14 + SYMBOL *sb.*[1]: see -IA[1].] Inability to understand or use words or signs: a form of aphasia.

1876 in DUNGLISON *Dict. Med. Sci.* **1912** *Jrnl. Abnormal Psychol.* VI. 218 When the nature of those objects (*symbolia*) was tested, grave errors were committed by the patient and she was absolutely unable to name any of them... Asymbolia was therefore complete.

asymbolic (æsɪm'bɒlɪk), *a.* [see the senses.]

1. 'One escaping scot-free.' Cockeram 1623. [f. L. *asymbol-us*, a. Gr. ἀσύμβολ-ος not contributing (f. ἀ priv. + συμβολαί contribution, share) + -IC, after *symbolic.*]

1678 in PHILLIPS. **1742** in BAILEY.

2. Not symbolic. [f. A- *pref.* 14 + SYMBOLIC.]

1685 MACKENZIE *Relig. Stoic* vii. 60 Asymbolic qualities.

asym'bolical, *a.* [f. as prec.: see -ICAL.] Not symbolical.

1660 STANLEY *Hist. Philos.* 253/1 The Symbolical.. are more easily transmutated into one another than the assymbolical. **1678** J. J[ONES] *Brit. Ch.* 188 Wholly asymbolical and contrary to the nature of such a Church.

†**a'symmetral**, *a. Obs.* [f. Gr. ἀσύμμετρ-ος incommensurable, disproportionate (see SYMMETRY) + -AL[1].] **a.** Incommensurable. **b.** ASYMMETRICAL.

c **1630** JACKSON *Creed* IV. viii. Wks. IV. 125 Their degrees are of another size and ofttimes asymmetral with the former. **1680** H. MORE *Apocal. Apoc.* 350 The Word of God.. with which these times not squaring, they are called Incommensurable or Asymmetral. **1706** in PHILLIPS.

a,symme'tranthous, *a. Bot.* [f. Gr. ἀσύμμετρ-ος (see prec.) + ἄνθος flower + -OUS.] Having asymmetric flowers. (Allman.)

asymmetric (æsɪ'mɛtrɪk), *a.* [f. Gr. ἀ priv. + SYMMETRIC: see prec.] **a.** = next.

1878 GURNEY *Crystallog.* 56 Forms with asymmetric faces occur in crystals of Topaz. **1881** *Syd. Soc. Lex.* s.v., In Botany an organ is said to be asymmetric, when it cannot be divided into two similar halves by a vertical plane.

b. *Chem.* Exhibiting, pertaining to, or affected by asymmetry (sense 2 b below); = *stereo-*

isomeric. Spec., ***asymmetric synthesis*** (see quots.). Cf. *optical isomerism*.

1875 *Jrnl. Chem. Soc.* XXVIII. 862 The author [*sc.* J. H. van't Hoff] proceeds to show that combinations which possess an atom of carbon combined with four different univalent groups, and which he terms an asymmetric atom, present anomalies with respect to isomerism. **1881** *Nature* XXIV. 41 One asymmetric carbon atom, *i.e.* an atom directly united with four different radicles. **1885** *Encycl. Brit.* XIX. 314/2 A carbon atom combined with four different atoms or compound radicals may therefore be called an asymmetric carbon atom. **1902** *Ibid.* XXVI. 722/1 The number of modifications of an asymmetric compound—which is not itself symmetric—is 2^n, where *n* is the number of such carbon atoms. **1904** *Jrnl. Physical Chem.* VIII. 528 By asymmetric synthesis is meant the synthesis of a substance containing an asymmetric carbon under such conditions that there shall be formed an excess either of the dextrorotatory or of the lævorotatory compound. **1949** *Thorpe's Dict. Appl. Chem.* IX. 117/2 A molecule containing one asymmetric carbon atom possesses two isomeric structures, which are mirror images of each other. *Ibid.* 118/1 Asymmetric syntheses involving photochemical reactions under the influence of circularly polarised light have been successfully attempted. **1962** P. J. & B. DURRANT *Adv. Inorg. Chem.* viii. 237 A rotating molecule may..be regarded as a spinning top, and on this analogy a polyatomic molecule may be placed in one of the four following classes: a. Symmetric tops. b. Spherical tops. c. Linear molecules. d. Asymmetric tops.

asy'mmetrical, *a.* [Gr. ἀ priv. + SYMMETRICAL: cf. prec.] Not symmetrical, out of proportion, with the parts not arranged correspondingly.

1690 BOYLE *Chr. Virtuoso* II. 8 Truths..asymmetrical, or unsociable, that is, such as we see not how to reconcile with other things evidently and confessedly true. **1880** GUNTHER *Fishes* 23 Flat-fishes are in fact nothing but asymmetrical Cod-fishes.

asy'mmetrically, *adv.* [f. prec. + -LY².] Not symmetrically, without symmetry.

1877 HUXLEY *Anat. Inv. An.* Introd. 14 [They] give rise to symmetrically or asymmetrically disposed processes.

asymmetro'carpous, *a. Bot.* [f. Gr. ἀσύμμετρ-ος (see above) + καρπός fruit + -OUS.] Having asymmetric fruit. (Allman.)

†**a'symmetrous**, *a. Obs. rare.* [f. as ASYMMETRAL + -OUS.] = ASYMMETRICAL.

1661 LOVELL *Hist. Anim. & Min.* 102 [Panthers have] various colour, and an asymmetrous body.

asymmetry (ə'sɪmɛtrɪ). [ad. Gr. ἀσυμμετρία, n. of quality f. ἀσύμμετρος: see SYMMETRY.]

1. *Math.* The relation of two quantities which have no common measure, as 1 and $\sqrt{2}$; incommensurability. ? *Obs.*

a **1652** J. SMITH *Sel. Disc.* 4. 100 Equality, proportion, symmetry and asymmetry of magnitudes. **1675** COLLINS in Rigaud *Corr. Sci. Men* II. 264 The method of shunning asymmetries mentioned in Des Cartes. **1796** in HUTTON *Math. Dict.* I. 162.

2. a. Want of symmetry, defective correspondence between things or their parts, disproportion.

1664 EVELYN *Freart's Archit.* Ep. Ded. 8 The assymmetrie of our Buildings. **1672** J. WORTHINGTON in *Mede's Wks.* Introd. 32 There was an asymmetry and disproportion in the subservient Faculties. **1877** HUXLEY *Anat. Inv. An.* viii. 530 Male Cephalopods are distinguished..by the asymmetry of their arms. **1948** GLASSTONE *Physical Chem.* xii. 904 The influence on the velocity of the ion is known as the relaxation effect, or sometimes as the asymmetry effect, because it arises from the lack of symmetry in the electrical atmosphere of a moving ion.

b. *Chem.* Lack of symmetry in the spatial arrangement of atoms or groups in a molecule; = *stereo-isomerism*.

1875 *Jrnl. Chem. Soc.* XXVIII. 862 He [*sc.* J. H. van't Hoff] has deduced the following rules... Derivatives of optically active combinations lose their rotatory power when the asymmetry of their carbon-atoms disappears. **1885** *Encycl. Brit.* XIX. 314/1 What peculiarity of constitution can give a molecule this helicoidal asymmetry? **1902** *Ibid.* XXVI. 721/1 The doctrine of asymmetry may be extended to elements other than carbon. **1959** *Chambers's Encycl.* III. 357/2 When two of the four attached groups are similar, as in propionic acid,..the asymmetry vanishes together with the possibility of optical isomerism.

a'symphony. ? *Obs.* [ad. Gr. ἀσυμφωνία, f. ἀσύμφωνος inharmonious: see SYMPHONY.] Want of harmony, discord.

1656 in BLOUNT *Glossogr.*

asymptomatic (əsɪmptəʊ'mætɪk), *a. Path.* [f. A- *pref.* 14 + SYMPTOMATIC *a.*] Without symptoms; producing or exhibiting no symptoms.

1932 in DORLAND *Med. Dict.* (ed. 16). **1962** *Lancet* 13 Jan. 67/1 Splenectomy has not been indicated to control these asymptomatic blood changes.

asymptosy (ə'sɪmtəsɪ). *Math.* [f. Gr. ἀ priv. + συμπτωσία coincidence: see next.] The quality of being asymptotic.

1656 tr. *Hobbes' Elem. Philos.* (1839) 199 Asymptosy depends upon this, that quantity is infinitely divisible.

asymptote ('æsɪmtəʊt). *Math.* [ad. (ultimately) Gr. ἀσύμπτωτος not falling together, f. ἀ priv. + σύν together + πτωτ-ός apt to fall. Cf. F. *asymptote.*]

A line which approaches nearer and nearer to a given curve, but does not meet it within a finite distance. A rectilinear asymptote may be considered as a tangent to the curve when produced to an infinite distance. Also *fig.*

1656 tr. *Hobbes' Elem. Philos.* (1839) 200 Asymptotes.. come still nearer and nearer, but never touch. **1796** HUTTON *Math. Dict.* I. 162 Two parabolas, placed with their axes in the same right line, are asymptotes to one another. **1860** FARRAR *Orig. Lang.* 117 Language, in relation to thought, must ever be regarded as an asymptote. **1867** DENISON *Astron. without Math.* 238 [A hyperbola's] legs continually approach two straight lines called asymptotes which are in fact the outline of the cone itself, but never reach them.

b. *attrib.* quasi-*adj.*

a **1714** GREW (J.) Asymptote lines..produced infinitely will never meet.

asymptotic (æsɪm'tɒtɪk), *a.* [f. prec. + -IC, after Gr. πτωτικός.] **1.** *Math.* = next.

1671 *Phil. Trans.* VI. 3065 Asymptotick spaces.. comprised between two lines, which being infinitely prolonged do never meet. **1881** MAXWELL *Electr. & Magn.* I. 167 The equi-potential surfaces have each of them an asymptotic plane.

2. ***asymptotic freedom*** (Particle Physics): an absence of coupling between quarks and gluons which is approached as their energy increases but is never attained.

[**1973** GROSS & WILCZEK in *Physical Rev. Lett.* 25 June XXX. 1343 We have found that they [*sc.* non-Abelian gauge theories] possess the remarkable feature..of asymptotically approaching free-field theory. Such asymptotically free theories will exhibit, for matrix elements of currents between on-mass-shell states, Bjorken scaling.] **1973** *Physical Rev.* D 15 Nov. VIII. 3646/1 In the case of pure gauge theories asymptotic freedom provides no constraint. **1974** *Physics Rep.* XLV. 133 The discovery of asymptotic freedom has opened new avenues in strong interaction theory. **1976** *Sci. Amer.* Nov. 56/3 Ultraviolet freedom is also known as asymptotic freedom, because the state of completely independent movement is approached asymptotically and never actually achieved. **1979** *Nature* 29 Mar. 408/2 QCD loses its property of asymptotic freedom if there are more than 16 quark flavours. **1981** M. GELL-MANN in J. H. Mulvey *Nature of Matter* viii. 172 This notion of 'asymptotic freedom' suggested by the theory has been amply confirmed by experiment.

asymp'totical, *a. Math.* [f. as prec. + -ICAL.] Of, pertaining to, or of the nature of an asymptote.

1704 *Phil. Trans.* XXV. 1700 Assymptotical Curves. **1854** H. MILLER *Sch. & Schm.* xvii. (1857) 383 Not an asymptotical progress, but destined from the beginning to furnish a point of union.

asymp'totically, *adv.* [f. prec. + -LY².] In the manner of an asymptote.

1675 GREGORY in Rigaud *Corr. Sci. Men* II. 277 Whether asymptotically approached..may be worth consideration. **1879** J. TYNDALL *Frag. Sci.* (ed. 6) II. xv. 418 The theory is not a thing complete from the first, but a thing which grows, as it were asymptotically, towards certainty. **1886** A. B. BRUCE *Mirac. Element in Gospels* i. 42 A moral ideal which in the natural order of things can never be more than asymptotically approximated. **1959** E. PULGRAM *Introd. Spectrogr. Speech* viii. 63 The resonance curve of a damped sonator..approaches asymptotically, but never reaches, a zero level of power.

asynapsis (æ-, eɪsɪ'næpsɪs). *Biol.* [f. A- *pref.* 14 + SYNAPSIS.] Absence of synapsis; failure of chromosomes to pair in meiosis. Hence **asy'naptic** *a.*

1930 G. W. BEADLE in *Cornell Univ. Agr. Exp. Sta. Mem.* CXXIX. (*title*) Genetical and Cytological Studies of Mendelian Asynapsis in *Zea mays.* **1937** C. D. DARLINGTON *Rec. Adv. Cytol.* (ed. 2) vii. 291 In 'asynaptic' maize which has as a rule no pairing of chromosomes at meiosis, the progeny nevertheless show the results of normal crossing-over. **1949** DARLINGTON & MATHER *Elem. Genetics* v. 110 A so-called asynaptic gene often..produces a general reduction in the crossing-over of all the chromosome pairs when homozygous.

asynartete (ə'sɪnɑːtiːt), *a.* and *sb. Pros.* [ad. Gr. ἀσυνάρτητος not connected (also used *subst.* of verses), f. ἀ priv. + συν-αρτά-ειν to knit together.] **A.** *adj.* Not connected; consisting of two members having different rhythms. **B.** *sb.* A verse of this nature. Hence **asynartetic** (əˌsɪnɑː'tɛtɪk), *a.*

[? **1792** BURNEY *Parr's Wks.* (1828) VII. 412 Which follows another asynartetum, which also ends with ithyphallic.] **1830** tr. *Aristoph. Wasps* 122 *note*, The metre.. is an asynartete of Iamb. and Troch. **1847** GROTE *Greece* II. xxix. (1862) III. 77 Combinations of the dactyl, trochee and iambus, analogous to the asynartetic verses of Archilochus.

asynchronism (ə'sɪŋkrənɪz(ə)m). [f. A- *pref.* 14 + SYNCHRONISM.] Want of synchronism; non-correspondence in time. **a'synchronous** *a.*, not coinciding in time.

1875 HAYDEN *Dis. Heart* 7 Asynchronism between its movements and those of the lungs. **1748** HARTLEY *Observ. Man* I. ii. §7 ¶74 When the Contractions of the Ventricles are once become asynchronous and inharmonious to those of the Auricle. **1912** G. KAPP *Electricity* viii. 219 To the late Professor Ferraris of Turin belongs the merit of having discovered a principle of alternating current working by which the motor may be started by the alternating current itself without bringing it first up to the speed of synchronism. Motors of this kind are called 'asynchronous' or 'non-synchronous' motors. **1940** *Chambers's Techn. Dict.* 582/2 *Non-synchronous motor*..an a.c. motor which does not run at synchronous speed... Also called *asynchronous motor.* **1962** *Gloss. Terms Autom. Data Processing* (*B.S.I.*) 9 *Asynchronous working*, the performance of a sequence of operations, such that each operation starts as a result of a signal that the previous operation has been completed or that the equipment required for the next operation is now available.

‖**asyndeton** (ə'sɪndɪtən). [L., a Gr. τὸ ἀσύνδετον, subst. use of ἀσύνδετος unconnected, f. ἀ priv. + σύνδετος, vbl. adj. f. συν-δέ-ειν to bind together.] A rhetorical figure which omits the conjunction. **asyndetic** (æsɪn'dɛtɪk), *a.*, characterized by asyndeton, not connected by conjunctions; Hence **asyn'detically** *adv.*

1589 PUTTENHAM *Eng. Poesie* (1869) 185 Asyndeton, or the Loose language..as thus: I savv it, I said it, I vvill svveare it. **1740** B. MARTIN *Bibl. Techn.* 145 Asyndeton the Cop'latives denies. Faith, Justice, Truth, Religion, Mercy dies. **1879** tr. *Meyer on 1 Cor.* xiv. 1 Διώκετε τὴν ἀγάπην.. asyndetic, but following with all the greater emphasis upon the praise of love. **1928** in *Funk's Standard Dict.* **1959** M. SCHLAUCH *Eng. Lang. in Mod. Times* ii. 57 The possibility.. of attaching adjectival relative clauses asyndetically to the main one.

asyne, obs. form of ASSIGN.

asynergy (ə'sɪnədʒɪ). *Path.* Also **asy'nergia**. [f. A- *pref.* 14 + SYNERGY.] Lack of co-ordination of parts or organs normally acting in harmony.

1860 MAYNE *Expos. Lex.* 1406/2 Asynergia. **1900** DORLAND *Med. Dict.* **1907** *Practitioner* Dec. 851 The laryngitis of singers..is made evident..by muscular troubles (vocal asynergy). **1934** H. C. WARREN *Dict. Psychol.* 22/2 *Asynergia*, a term introduced in 1899 by J. Babinski to describe the underlying symptom of cerebellar deficit, i.e. an inability to carry out complex motor acts involving harmonious cooperation of separate muscle groups.

asyntactic (æsɪn'tæktɪk), *a.* [f. Gr. ἀσύντακτ-ος (f. ἀ priv. + σύντακτος, vbl. adj. f. συν-τάσσειν to range together) + -IC (after *syntactic*).] Loosely put together, irregular, ungrammatical.

1880 M. PATTISON *Milton* vi. 70 The same asyntactic disorder is equally found in History of Britain.

asyse, obs. form of ASSIZE *sb.*

‖**asystole** (ə'sɪstəliː). *Path.* [mod.L., f. Gr. ἀ priv. + συστολή contraction: see SYSTOLE.] Cessation of the functional contraction of the heart. **a'systolism** [= F. *asystolie* (Beau)], see quot.

1870 GEE *Auscult.* xxi. 237 Asystolism..that remarkable group of symptoms which is characteristic of an enduring inability in the right ventricle to empty itself. **1876** BALFOUR *Dis. Heart* iii. 87 Asystole, in which the aortic blood-pressure suddenly falls below that necessary for the maintenance of life, because the left ventricle ceases to act.

asyth, -ment, obs. form of ASSYTHE, -MENT.

at (æt, ət), *prep.* Forms: 1–2 æt, 2–3 et (ed), 3–6 att, 5 ate, atte, 2– at. [Common Teut.; OE. *æt* is cogn. with OS. *at*, OFris. (*at*) *et*, ON. *at*, OHG. *az*, Goth. *at*; also with L. *ad* to, at, Skr. *adhi* near. Lost in mod.G. and Du., where its place is largely taken by *to* (G. *zu*, Du. *toe*), as is also the case in s.w. Eng. dialects; in Scandinavian, on the other hand, *to* is lost, and its place largely taken by *at*, e.g. as sign of the infinitive mood, which is also the case in north. Eng. dialect. In OE. (as in the other Teut. langs.) *æt* governed the dative, only exceptionally the accusative. It was also compounded with many verbs: see AT- *pref.*¹, all of which are now obs. In ME. it coalesced with various cases of the 'definite article' in *atte, atten, attere*, 'at the'; so also *attam* 'at them.'

c **1175** *Lamb. Hom.* 167 Deð is attere dure. *c* **1175** *Cott. Hom.* 231 Me sceold ánon eter gat ȝemete. *c* **1225** *Hali Meid.* 7 Heuene atten ende. *c* **1250** *Moral Ode* in *E.E.P.* (1862) 26 Ded is ate dure. *a* **1300** *Cursor M.* 5694 And attam con þair fader frain. *c* **1386** CHAUCER *Prol.* 125 After the scole of Stratford atte bowe. [See others below.]]

At is used to denote relations of so many kinds, and some of these so remote from its primary local sense, that a classification of its uses is very difficult. Only a general outline can be here given; its idiomatic constructions with individual words must be looked for under the words themselves, e.g. AIM, ANGRY, APT. It will be observed that when a verb is construed with *at*, the same construction usually obtains with the cognate sb. and adj., and when *at* is used with an adjective, it is generally used also with a derived sb.; thus *to envy, envy, envious* at, *apt, aptness* at, etc. The arrangement of the senses here adopted is:—I. Local position. II. Practical contact, engagement, occupation, condition, etc. III. Position in a series or graduated scale, rate, price, etc. IV. Time, order, consequence, cause, object. V. In other adverbial phrases. VI. With the infinitive mood. VII. Followed by other prepositions.

I. Local position; answering the question *Where?* (passing into *Whereby? Whence? Whither?*)

At expresses the position reached by completed motion *to*, or that which is left by motion *from*: lines drawn *to* a point, *from* a point, or *through* a point, meet or intersect *at* the point. Hence, with certain verbs, *at* comes into contact with *through, from,* or *of, to,* and *toward.* See 10–15 infra.

* *Simple place or position.*

1. a. The most general determination of simple localization in space, expressing, strictly, the simple relation of a thing to a point of space which it touches; hence, usually determining a point or object with which a thing or attribute is practically in contact, and thus the *place* where it is, when this is either so small as to be treated as a mere point, or when the exact relation between the thing and the place is not more particularly expressed by the prepositions *close to, near, by, about, on, in, over, under,* etc., all of which may at times be covered by *at*.

a **1000** *Cædmon's Gen.* (Gr.) 2426 Æt burhȝeate sittan. **1175** *Lamb. Hom.* 35 On snawe up et minne chinne. *Ibid.* 73 Et þe chirche dure, and..et þe fonstan. *c* **1200** Ormin 781 He stod..att Godess allterr. *c* **1250** *Gen. & Ex.* 1366 At a welle wiðuten ðe tun. *c* **1300** *K. Alis.* 4175 He set at his owne table. *c* **1325** *E.E. Allit. P.* B. 1187 At vch brugge a ber-fray. *c* **1386** Chaucer *Wyf's Prol.* 6 Housbondes atte chirch dore I have had fyve. *a* **1400** *Sir Perc.* 489 Made he no lett at ȝate, dore ne wykett. **1571** Digges *Pantom.* I. xix, At C and D the situation is all one, but at E it somewhat differeth, as you may behold in this figure. **1660** Barrow *Euclid* I. ii, At a point given A, to make a right line AG equal to a right line given BC. **1787** G. White *Selborne* vii. (1789) 21 To cut and deliver the materials at the spot. **1883** *Sc. Monthly* Dec. 34/2 These streamers seem to converge at a point beyond the zenith.

b. Used with the cardinal points of the compass, as *at the East(ward)*, to indicate parts of the country. *U.S.*

1636 John Winthrop jr. *Let.* 7 Apr. in *Mass. Hist. Soc. Coll.* (1863) 4th Ser. VI. 515 If Mr. Mayhew hath bought the provisions at the east. **1646** John Winthrop snr. *Let.* 19 Sept. in R. C. Winthrop *Life & Lett. J. Winthrop* (1867) II. xxiii. 357 Some hurt was done here..much fish and salt lost at eastward. **1692** in *Essex Inst. Hist. Coll.* XLII. 142 Marke How that is now dead, who dyed at the Eastward. **1782** S. A. *Let.* 12 Feb. *Ibid.* I. 13/2 My company being at the Sotherd, the money was drawn for them for 3 months. **1851** Hawthorne *Ho. Sev. Gables* xiii. 210 A still unsettled claim to a very large extent of territory at the eastward. **1883** J. Quincy *Figures of Past* (1884) 343 Characteristic of slave-holders when upon their good behavior at the North.

c. *Naut.* Indicating the quarter of the wind. *U.S.*

1635 R. Mather *Jrnl.* (1850) 18 Afore noone the wind waxed strong at north. **1732** Franklin *Poor Rich. Alm.* *1733* 10 Clouds and winds at southwest. **1780** Wm. Heath *Let.* 30 July in *Mass. Hist. Soc. Coll.* (1905) 7th Ser. V. 93 The wind which now blows at east. **1848** J. F. Cooper *Bee-hunter* II. xiv. 203 The wind stood at the westward.

d. Used superfluously after *where. U.S.* and *Brit. dial.* (see *E.D.D.*).

1859 Bartlett *Dict. Amer.* (ed. 2), *At* is often used superfluously in the South and West, as in the question 'Where is he at?' **1899** A. Nicholas *Idyl of Wabash* 34 Where does he live at? **1903** *N.Y. Sun* 8 Nov. 6 The business world wants rest. It wants to know where it is at. **1911** E. Ferber *Dawn O'Hara* xx. 294 This is where I get off at. **1914** G. Atherton *Perch of Devil* i. 8 She..disliked..not knowing where she was at.

2. With proper names of places: Particularly used of all towns, except the capital of our own country, and that in which the speaker dwells (if of any size), also of small and distant islands or parts of the world.

Cf. *in* the Isle of Wight, *on* Inchkeith, *at* St. Helena, *at* Malta, *at* the English Lakes, *at* the Cape, *in* Cape Colony. Formerly used more widely: *at* Ireland, *at* London.

755 *O.E. Chron.*, His lic liþ æt Wintanceastre. **1205** Lay. 5 He wonede at Ernleȝe. **1258** *Eng. Procl. Hen. III*, §7 Witnesse vs seluen æt Lundene, þane Eȝtetenþe day on þe Monþe of Octobre. *c* **1300** *K. Alis.* 4423 The tole that was at Greece y-sought! *c* **1386** Chaucer *Prol.* 62 And foughten [hadde he] for oure faith at Tramassene. **1387** Trevisa *Higden* Rolls Ser. VII. 183 In þese dayes a famous clerk..was at Ireland. **1641** *Vind. Smectymn.* §13. 128 James at Hierusalem. **1675** Brooks *Gold. Key* Wks. 1867 V. 589 He is in a far country, he is at the Indies. **1742** Richardson *Pamela* III. 151 Be not overthoughtful about what may happen at London. **1849** Macaulay *Hist. Eng.* II. 120 The Parliament met at Edinburgh. *Mod.* Did he graduate at Oxford or Cambridge?

3. *At* a person (L. *apud*): †**a.** In personal contact with; in the immediate presence or company of. *Obs.* (repl. by *with, by, beside, in presence of, before*).

(*At* is still used with a person in other senses, as 12–14, 17, 25, 35, 36.

1205 Lay. 25290 We weoren..at Ardure þan kinge. **1366** Maundev. v. 38 The soudan may lede..mo than 20000 men of armes..and thei ben alle weys at him. **1382** Wyclif *John* i. 1 The word was at God..This was in the bigynnynge at God. *c* **1430** *Syr Tryam.* 613 And at sir Roger ȝende we wylle dwelle. *c* **1500** *Merch. & Son* in Halliw. *Nug. P.* 28 Y schall be hastely at yow ageyn with the myght of Mary mylde!

†**b.** *fig.* In sensory or perceptional contact with; before, in the sight of, in the eyes of, in the estimation of. *Obs.*

a **1300** *E.E. Psalter* xxxviii. 13 Cumelinge I am at þe..als al mi fadres be. **1388** Wyclif *ibid.*, Y am a comelyng at thee..as all my fadris. *c* **1400** *Apol. Loll.* 105 Religioun clene at God, & at þe Fader, is þis, to visite þe fadirles & modirles. *c* **1449** Pecock *Repr.* 296 At God it is possible a riche man to entre into the kingdom of heven. **1493** *Festyvall* (W. de W. 1515) 93 b, Forsothe thou hast founde grace at our lorde. **1580** Tusser *His Beleefe* xx, At God of Heaven there is forgivenesse of our sins.

c. *ellipt.* In active or aggressive contact; applying to, soliciting, pestering, assailing. Cf. 17. Cf. also *Sc. Nat. Dict.*, *at* (sense 1).

1612 Brinsly *Lud. Lit.* iii. (1627) 21 Some of their parents..will bee at me..to helpe their reading of English. **1741** Richardson *Pamela* I. 198 Mrs. Jewkes is mightily at me, to go with her. **1842** FitzGerald *Let.* 31 Mar. (1889) I. 94 Alfred [Tennyson] is busy preparing a new volume for the press: full of doubts, troubles &c. The reviewers will doubtless be at him. **1899** E. Wharton *Greater Inclin.* iv. §3. 111 All his people are at him, you see—oh, I know *their* little game! Trying to get him away from me.

4. The preceding sense (3 a) is now partly represented by the elliptical construction with possessive case: At (a person's) house. Fr. *chez*, Ger. *bei*.

1562 J. Heywood *Prov. & Epigr.* (1867) 110 Whan I at the shoemakers shall shoes assay. **1591** Shaks. *1 Hen. VI*, I. iv. 20 Thou shalt finde me at the Gouernors. **1711** Steele *Spect.* No. 114 ¶1 We had Yesterday at Sir Roger's a Set of Country Gentlemen who dined with him. *Mod.* We met at her father's.

5. *At*, as distinguished from *in* or *on*, is sometimes used to express some practical connexion with a place, as distinguished from mere local position: cf. *in* school, *at* school; *in* or *on* the sea, *at* sea; *in* prison, *at* the hotel.

In such phrases the article is often omitted, e.g. *at home, at church, at college, at court, at town, at market.*

a **1000** *Beowulf* 3851 Hiȝelác Hreþling þǽr æt hám wunode. **1340** *Ayenb.* 56 At cherche kan God his uirtues sseawy. *c* **1460** *Towneley Myst.* 310 Som at yllehowse I fande. **1556** *Chron. Grey Friars* (1852) 65 Raynyd atte the yelde halle, &..condemnyd. **1606** Shaks. *Ant. & Cl.* II. vi. 25 Weele speake with thee at Sea. At land, thou know'st How much we do o're-count thee. **1694** Echard *Plautus* 50 My master Amphitryon's now at bed with Alcmena. **1754** C'tess Shaftesb. in *Priv. Lett. Ld. Malmesbury* I. 81, I was twice at Court before, the same week. **1758** *Dodsley's Coll. Poems* (1766) V. 210 At market oft for game I search, Oft at assemblies, oft at church. **1793** Smeaton *Edystone L.* §316 The light may be seen at sea much stronger..than it can from a great elevation at land. **1835** Crabbe *Par. Reg.* II. 456 No Sunday-shower, Kept him at home. **1840** Dickens *Old C. Shop* x, What the parson at chapel says. **1884** *Times* 7/1 He was sent to be a boarder at the school for six months.

6. *At* an occurrence or event: *i.e.* at the place of its occurrence and taking some part in it; assisting or present at.

a **1000** *Beowulf* 1239 Æt þǽre béor-þeȝe. *c* **1175** *Lamb. Hom.* 27 Hwet wule mon et scrifte? **1205** Lay. 1871 Þer wes muchel folc at þere wrastlinge. *c* **1300** *K. Alis.* 1096 Thou schalt at her bridale beon. **1432–50** tr. *Higden* (1865) I. 193 The consuetude was in that tyme women to be at cownselles amonge the men. **1610** Shaks. *Temp.* II. i. 97 When we were at Tunis at the marriage of your daughter. **1711** Steele *Spect.* No. 2 ¶1 He fills the Chair at a Quarter Session with great abilities. *Ibid.* ¶2 He is at a Play. **1848** Thackeray *Van. Fair* (1880) 255 He asked..whether he had been at the battle.

7. Defining the point or part of a body where any thing is applied; hence, sometimes, hanging or attached by; sometimes defining more generally the side or direction on which the thing is, as 'a dog *at* his heels,' 'the friend *at* your left hand.'

a **1000** *Cædmon's Gen.* (Gr.) 636 Hire æt heortan læȝ æppel unsælȝa. *c* **1230** *Ancr. R.* 414 Sitte ȝe..ston-stille ed Godes fet. *c* **1300** *K. Alis.* 2142 Siweth me at my taile. *c* **1325** *E.E. Allit. P.* B. 155 Byndez byhynde at his bak boþe two his handez. *c* **1450** *Merlin* xxii. 380 At the foote of the castell. **1613** Purchas *Pilgr.* II. xii. 177 At the Temple doore were two Lions tied at two chaines. **1631** Weever *Anc. Fun. Mon.* 815 The Seale..hanging at the parchment by a silke string. **1711** Addison *Spect.* No. 3 ¶9 Liberty with Monarchy at her right hand. **1712** Budgell *Spect.* No. 365 ¶14, I have nothing more at heart than the honour of my dear countrywomen. **1766** Goldsm. *Vic. W.* xii. (1857) 72 Yonder comes Moses, with..the box at his back. **1870** Trollope *Ph. Finn* 401 You have the ball at your feet. *Mod.* He wears it at his watch chain. Too old to be at his mother's apron string. An infant at the breast.

8. Of distance: e.g. *at* hand, *at* a distance, *at* arm's length, *at* a hundred yards.

1526 Tindale *Matt.* iii. 1 Repent: the kyngdome of heuen is at honde [Wyclif, neiȝe]. **1594** Greene *Fr. Bacon* Wks. 1831 I. 161 We are all ready at an inch. **1658** Ussher *Ann.* 749 They fought with them at hand, and afar off. **1671** Milton *Samson* 348 To save himself against a coward arm'd At one spear's length. **1796** Nelson in Nicolas *Disp.* II. 215 The Corsican privateers keep at such a distance..I wish two could be directed to be always at my elbow. *c* **1817** Hogg *Tales & Sk.* V. 49 They held Dame Reason at the staff's end. **1884** A. Forbes in *Eng. Illust. Mag.* Jan. 239/2 The long resistance..had held his soldiers at arm's length.

9. Expressing the relation of an attribute to a particular place or part: e.g. 'sick *at* heart,' 'out *at* elbows.'

c **1000** *Crist* (Gr.) 539 Hát æt heortan. **1605** Shaks. *Lear* II. iv. 10 A man ouerlustie at legs. **1735** Thomson *Liberty* II. 121 Withered at the root. **1742** Richardson *Pamela* III. 172, I wish at my Heart, the Gentlemen..would pursue such measures. **1825** Waterton *Wanderings* III. iii. 255 The sight of the snake had..turned him sick at stomach. **1849** Macaulay *Hist. Eng.* II. 43 The late king had been at heart a Roman Catholic.

** *Passing into* through, by.

10. Defining the point *at* which anything enters, or issues, and hence the channel *through* or *by* which entrance or exit is effected.

a **1000** *Batt. Fin.* 16 (Gr.) Eodon æt óðrum durum. *c* **1175** *Lamb. Hom.* 5 He rad in et þan est ȝete. *c* **1220** *Sawles Warde* in *Cott. Hom.* 251 Snikeð in ant ut neddren..et muð ant et earen, ed ehnen ant ed neauele. *c* **1320** *Seuyn Sag.* (W.) 1449 And spak out ate windowe. **1483** Caxton *G. de la Tour* D vj b, The theef that cometh in atte back dore. **1595** Shaks. *John* v. vii. 29 Now my soule hath elbow roome; It would not out at windowes, nor at doores. **1711** Steele *Spect.* No. 32 ¶2 Find an Hole for him to creep in at. **1848** Thackeray *Van. Fair* (1880) 118 He looked in at the dining-room window. *Mod.* Smoke issued forth at several orifices. He entered at the front door.

*** *Passing into* from, of.

†**11.** Determining the source *from* which anything comes, and *at* which we seek it: e.g. *To ask, inquire, seek, learn, take, get, obtain, find, have, receive, buy, earn, win, suffer,* at. *Obs.* or *dial.* (repl. by *of, from*) exc. in (b.) the expanded phrases *at the mouth* or *hands of*.

c **1000** *Ags. Gosp.* Matt. xi. 29 Leorniað æt me. —— xxv. 28 Anymað ðæt pund æt hym. *c* **1175** *Lamb. Hom.* 33 þu most biȝeten milce et þine drihtene. *c* **1250** *Gen. & Ex.* 2697 Mai he no leue at hire taken. *c* **1320** *Seuyn Sag.* (W.) 3103 At the lady the ryng he hase. **1375** Barbour *Bruce* XII. 484 Thai ask mercy, bot nocht at ȝou. *a* **1400** *Chester Pl.* 194 Receive my sonne nowe at me. **1513** Douglas *Æneis* III. ii. Argt., How that Eneas socht ansueir at Apollyne. **1535** Coverdale *Judith* x. 7 They axed no question at her, but let her go. **1618** M. Baret *Horsemanship* I. Pref. 4 Nature [hath] given to the Ant, such prouidence, that Man is wished to learne at her. **1794** J. Hutton *Philos. Light, etc.* 38 For that purpose, we must inquire at nature. **1883** J. Sime *Hist. All-Israel* vii. 170 He was making a similar inquiry..at other maidens.

b. 1768 Sterne *Sent. Journ.* (1778) I. 132, I took it kindly at her hands. **1855** Macaulay *Hist. Eng.* III. 397 All that they had..suffered at the hands of the Tories. **1884** *Eng. Illust. Mag.* Feb. 303/1 He took at their hands the most outrageous treatment.

**** *Passing into* to.

12. With certain verbs of motion: Indicating attainment of a position at, e.g. *to end, stop, arrive, land* at a point; hence, determining the point *to* which the motion extends.

†**a.** *simply* = 'to.' *Obs.*

c **1000** *Ags. Gosp.* Matt. xxv. 43 Ge ne comon æt me. *c* **1400** *Destr. Troy* VI. 2674 Hit plesit wele þe pepull at Parys to wende. *c* **1400** *Sege off Melayne* 505 Thay wolde noghte come att Parische To thay had offerde to Seyne Denys. **1528** More *Heresyes* III. Wks. 203/1 The vniuersitie, where he was..ere he came at you. **1537** ? Tindale *Exp. John* 13 We wyl neuer come more at scoole. *c* **1601** W. Watson *Decacord.* 180 To come at the holy altar.

†**b.** *esp.* Into the presence of, into personal contact with, near to; in *to come* at (L. *accēdere*): to approach, come near, have to do with. *Obs.*

c **1532** Ld. Berners *Huon* 630, 'I charge the..that thou come no more at her, beware that thou fallest not in amours with her.' **1535** Coverdale *Ex.* xix. 15 No man come at his wife [Wyclif, Neiȝe ye not to ȝoure wyues]. **1611** Shaks. *Wint. T.* II. iii. 32 He hath not slept to night; commanded None should come at him. **1678** R. L'Estrange *Seneca's Life*, He would not let Piso come at him.

c. With idea of intervening space traversed: Even to, as far as; in *to come* (arch.), *arrive, land* at.

c **1300** *K. Alis.* 1428 The thridde day..He aryved at Cysile. **1340** Hampole *Pr. Consc.* 7732 In fallyng, A thowsand yhere..Ar it come at the erth. *c* **1400** *Sir Perc.* 1819 Tille he come at a way By a wode ende. **1552** *Bk. Com. Prayer, Burial Off.*, When they come at [1559 to] the graue, the Priest shall say. **1611** Bible *Luke* viii. 26 They arriued at the countrey of the Gadarenes. **1612** Brinsly *Lud. Lit.* 61 When they come at the Passiue, let them doe the like. **1684** Bunyan *Pilgr.* II. 183 Then they came at an Arbor, warme and promising much Refreshing. **1712** F. T. *Meth. Shorthand* 6 Without taking off the Pen 'till you come at a Vowel. **1870** Jevons *Elem. Logic* xxiii. 191 To arrive at exactly the same results.

d. With idea of obstacles or difficulties intervening: esp. in *to come, get* at = to reach.

1530 Tindale *An Answer, etc.* (1850) 120 Worldly tyrants, at whom no man may come, save a few flatterers, etc. **1711** Steele *Spect.* No. 2 ¶4 That great man has as many to break through to come at me, as I have to come at him. *Ibid.* No. 115 ¶5 Food and Raiment are not to be come at, without the Toil of the Hands. **1711** Addison *Ibid.* No. 131 ¶1 The Sport is the more agreeable where the Game is the harder to come at. **1742** Richardson *Pamela* III. 199 There was no coming at her here, under my Mother's Wing. *c* **1815** Miss Austen *Northang. Abb.* (1848) 40 'My dear Isabella, how was it possible for me to get at you?' **1840** Dickens *Old C. Shop* ii, Stooping down to get at his ear.

***** *Passing into* towards.

13. Of motion directed *towards*: In the direction of, towards, so as to get *at*; often with hostile intent, 'against'; in *to run, rush, go, have, throw, shoot, let drive, aim, etc.* at.

a **1400** *Octouian* 976 Swych twenty n'ere worth a slo At me to fyght. *a* **1400** *Sir Perc.* 1701 His swerde drawes he, Strykes at Percevelle. *c* **1485** *Digby Myst.* (1882) v. 629 Be-gynne ye, and haue at yowe. **1590** Shaks. *Com. Err.* II. ii. 136 Wouldst thou not spit at me. **1596** —— *1 Hen. IV*, II. iv. 217 Foure Rogues in Buckrom let driue at me. **1613** —— *Hen. VIII*, I. i. 142 We may out-runne..that which we run at. **1663** Butler *Hud.* I. i. 356 To shoot at foes, and sometimes pullets. **1714** Addison *Spect.* No. 579 ¶7 The Dogs flew at him with so much fury. **1849** MACAULAY *Hist. Eng.* I. 231 A great blow was about to be aimed at the Protestant religion. *Ibid.* 617 Once they were seen and fired at.

b. Of bodily action and gesture; in *to point, look, stare, swear, shout, grumble, mock, laugh, etc.* at.

c **1400** *Sir Isumb.* 625 The qwene..at hym faste loghe. **1596** SPENSER *F.Q.* I. v. 30 Hungry Wolues continually did howle, At her abhorred face. **1711** STEELE *Spect.* No. 144 ¶2 That Patience of being stared at. **1840** DICKENS *Old C. Shop* ix, Ugly faces that were frowning over at her. **1854** THACKERAY *Newcomes* xvii. I. 163 Look at the horseman in Cuyp's famous picture. [Cf. also 36.]

c. Of mental aim, allusion, hint, conjecture, etc. *esp.* with verbs of speaking, with implication of indirect attack. See also TALK *v.* 3 d.

1656 *Artif. Beauty* (1662) 4 Eyes over-curious to find fault at Art. **1682** in *Harl. Misc.* (1793) 439 Secrets..which now we can only conjecture at. **1711** ADDISON *Spect.* No. 112 ¶6 The Parson is always preaching at the 'Squire. **1711** BUDGELL *Spect.* No. 116 ¶2, I have before hinted at some of my Friend's Exploits. **1749** CHESTERF. *Lett.* 194 II. 230 He ..thinks every thing that is said meant at him. **1818** MOORE *Fudge Fam. in Paris* vi. 61 This touch at our old friends, the Whigs. **1863** COWDEN CLARKE *Shakes.-Char.* v. 133 The latter..always make her speak *at* her husband. **1863** TROLLOPE *Rachel R.* II. iv. 78 Had he been then present, she would have risen up and spoken at him, as she had never spoken before.

14. Of motion or action directed towards the attainment or acquisition of: **a.** *lit.* in *to snatch, clutch, catch, reach, make, etc.* at.

1590 SHAKS. *Mids. N.* III. ii. 29 Briars and thornes at their apparell snatch. **1593** —— *2 Hen. VI*, I. ii. 11 Put forth thy hand, reach at the glorious Gold. **1711** ADDISON *Spect.* No. 159 ¶6 Catching at every thing that stood by them. **1711** STEELE *Spect.* No. 450 ¶1 All Men..make at the same common thing, Money. *Prov.* Drowning men catch at straws.

b. *fig. To aim, aspire, endeavour, etc.* at.

1591 SHAKS. *Two Gent.* II. vi. 30 Ayming at Siluia as a sweeter friend. **1711** STEELE *Spect.* No. 2 ¶4 Crowds who endeavour at the same end with himself. **1709** —— *Tatler* No. 22 A thousand that can dress genteelly at a mistress. **1777** WATSON *Philip II* (1793) I. I. 19 That power at which he had aspired. **1811** MISS AUSTEN *Sense & Sens.* (1846) 38 You will be setting your cap at him now. **1840** DICKENS *Old C. Shop* xi, 'Strangers are nothing to me,' said the young fellow, catching at the words.

II. Of action, position, state, condition, manner.

15. With things which are the objects or centres of special activities, and are more or less put for the activities themselves: *at meat* = eating; *at the bar* = acting as a barrister, or as one on trial; *at grass* = grazing; *at the stake, wheel, plough,* etc.; *at bat*: see BAT *sb.*[2] 3 d.

a **1000** *Beowulf* 2224 Æt þæm áde wæs eþ-ȝesýne swát-fáh syrce. *c* **1220** *Hali Meid.* 37 Seoð þe cat at the fliche and te hund at te huide. **1297** R. GLOUC. 285 To be of bold word atte mete. **1377** LANGL. *P. Pl.* B. VI. 104 And ben his pilgryme atte plow for pore mennes sake. *c* **1449** PECOCK *Repr.* III. ii. 283 To spend it at the wijn. **1611** BIBLE *Jer.* l. 11 As fat as the heifer at grass. **1773** JOHNSON in *Boswell* (1831) III. 91 He must be a great English lawyer, from having been so long at the bar. **1811** MISS AUSTEN *Sense & Sens.* (1846) 263 And idled away the mornings at billiards. **1880** FROUDE *Bunyan* 4 His father brought him up at his own trade.

b. Sometimes with the idea of instrumentality.

c **1375** WYCLIF *Serm.* xxxvi. Sel. Wks. 1869 I. 97 We may see þis at eye. *c* **1440** *Morte Arth.* 449 Thowe moste spede at the spurs. **1483** CAXTON *Gold. Leg.* 24/1 No man demanded of that they sawe atte eye. **1641** CAVENDISH *Wolsey* (1825) I. 66 Thou shalt espy at thine eye the wonderful work of God. **1763** C. JOHNSTON *Reverie* I. 212 He foils the Devil at his own weapons. *Mod.* To contest it at sword's point.

c. Hence in designations, as *barrister-at-law, serjeant-at-arms, assault-at-arms*, etc.

1711 ADDISON *Spect.* No. 89 ¶1 He is a serjeant at law. **1761** HUME *Hist. Eng.* (1826) II. xv. 377 Four thousand men at arms. **1884** *Daily News* 6 Feb. 2/2 The Speaker, attended by the Serjeant-at-Arms and the Chaplain.

d. By (auction or sale; retail or wholesale). orig. *U.S.* Cf. AUCTION *sb.* 2.

1726 *Boston News-Let.* 3 Mar., Valuable books, many more than a thousand, to be sold at auction. **1825** NEAL *Bro. Jonathan* I. 12 The education, which they had been laying in, at wholesale, during the summer season. **1860** [see AUCTION *sb.* 2]. **1900** DRANNAN *On Plains & Mts.* 476 As soon as we arrived at San Francisco we commenced selling our horses at private sale. **1932** GRAYSON *Leaders* 135 They got the land at $2 an acre and immediately offered it at auction. **1967** PHILIP WILSON (*title*) Art at Auction. The Year at Sotheby's and Parke-Bernet, 1966–67.

16. With actions in or with which one is engaged: as *at dinner, at work, at play*.

1440 *Sir Eglamour* 230 At my jurney wolle Y bee. **1591** SHAKS. *Two Gent.* II. i. 46 As she sits at supper. **1610** —— *Temp.* v. i. 185 This Maid, with whom thou was't at play. **1712** ADDISON *Spect.* No. 415 ¶6 This..has set men at work on Temples. **1821** BYRON *Sardan.* III. i. 424 Myrrha! what, at whispers With my stern brother? **1835** CRABBE *Par. Reg.* I. 575, I trace the matron at her loved employ. **1872** *Daily News* 1 Aug., The case..is still at hearing.

b. *at it*: hard at work, fighting, etc.; busy.

1606 SHAKS. *Tr. & Cr.* v. iii. 95 They are at it [*i.e.* fighting], harke. **1666** PEPYS *Diary* 5 Mar., I was at it till past two o'clock on Monday morning. **1884** *Times* 3 Mar. 5/2 After having the wound dressed he was at it again.

17. After many verbs expressing action: *to work, toil, labour, play* at (a thing or action); *to pull, nibble, kick, tear, knock, drum* at (a thing). (Cf. 3 c.)

a **1300** *E.E. Psalter* cxxxix. 6, I might noght at it. *c* **1300** *K. Alis.* 660 To play at bal. *c* **1510** *Cocke Lorelles Bote* 14 Than every man pulled at his ore. **1588** SHAKS. *L.L.L.* v. ii. 326 When he plaies at Tables. **1594** T. B. *La Primaud. Fr. Acad.* II. 575 An Apparitour rapping at their doore. **1884** *Times* 30 Jan. 9/5 She saw him working at the Memoirs. **1884** *Longm. Mag.* Feb. 445 The secret anxiety that was gnawing at her heart. *Mod.* To play at fighting; to work hard at clearing a path.

18. Connecting adjectives of occupation and proficiency, or their substantives, with a thing or action.

a **1000** *Beowulf* 1910 Hord-weorþunge hnáhran rince sæm-ran æt sæcce. **1610** SHAKS. *Temp.* III. i. 20 My Father Is hard at study. **1663** BUTLER *Hud.* I. i. 25 Mighty he was at both of these. **1711** STEELE *Spect.* No. 2 ¶4 Very aukward at putting their Talents within Observation. **1855** MACAULAY *Hist. Eng.* III. 320 In agility and skill at his weapons he had few equals. *Mod.* Diligent at his lessons; readiness at replying.

19. Of posture, position: e.g. *at gaze, at bay, at right angles*.

1535 STEWART *Cron. Scot.* II. 608 Thair tha stude rycht lang at thair defence. **1593** SHAKS. *Lucr.* 1149 The poor frighted deer, that stands at gaze. *c* **1680** STERRY *2nd Posth. Vol.* 319 He lieth at wait to catch your Hearts. *a* **1843** SOUTHEY *Wks.* (1858) 174/1 Here, ere they reach'd their ships, they turn'd at bay. **1840** DICKENS *Old C. Shop* v, In some of the vessels at anchor. **1869** PHILLIPS *Vesuv.* vii. 191 Section at right angles to the axis.

20. Of state, or condition of existence: e.g. *at rest, peace, ease, liberty, a loss*, etc.

c **1300** *K. Alis.* 3108 Than mowe ye beon at ese. **1375** BARBOUR *Bruce* XIX. 77 To se at myscheiff sic a knycht. **1470–85** (1634) MALORY *Arthur* (1816) II. 398 Sir Launcelot..found them all at a great array. **1594** SHAKS. *Rich. III.* I. i. 133 Whiles Kites and Buzards play at liberty. **1649** BLITHE *Eng. Improv. Impr.* (1653) 115 No man.. would be either at want of Firing, or Timber. **1671** MILTON *Samson* 598, I shall shortly be with them at rest. **1707** *Lond. Gaz.* No. 4343/4 You have not..left them at Uncertainty. **1709** POPE *Let. H. Cromwell* 17 July, I..was utterly at a loss how to address myself. **1710** STEELE *Tatler* No. 264 ¶8 At liberty to talk. **1711** ADDISON *Spect.* No. 122 ¶2 One..who is..at Peace within himself. **1882** *Athenæum* 1 July 24 [They] were sometimes at fault.

21. Of mutual relations: e.g. *at war, at variance, at strife, at accord, at one, at daggers drawn*.

c **1305** *St. Dunstan* 143 in *E.E.P.* (1862) 39 Þis tuei bischopes and seint Dunstan were al at one rede. *c* **1325** *Cœur de L.* 1369 We ben at on acord. **1493** *Festyvall* (W. de W. 1515) 35 b, An other Knyght and this man fell at debate. **1539** TONSTALL *Serm. Palme Sond.* (1823) 36 Howe the apostels fell at contention amonge them selfes. **1559** *Homilies* II. xviii. 504 When they be at hate betwixt themselves? *c* **1600** SHAKS. *Sonn.* xlvi, Mine eye and heart are at a mortal war. **1671** MILTON *Samson* 1585 What cause Brought him so soon at variance with himself. **1853** THACKERAY *Eng. Hum.* 65 Truth and lies always at battle. **1868** ROGERS *Pol. Econ.* vi. 58 They have been at cross purposes when they should have been at one.

22. Of mode, manner, measure, extent, etc.

c **1280** *Fall & Passion* 85 in *E.E.P.* (1862) 15 Hi [the Jews] seid at one mouþe · þat he wolde destru temple. *c* **1325** *Cœur de L.* 571, I spak to hym at wurdes fewe. *c* **1380** *Sir Ferumb.* 1894 Terry him ansuerede þan ! at schorte wordes & rounde. *c* **1449** PECOCK *Repr.* I. viii. 40 Alle tho gouernauncis..ben groundid at fulle..in the inward book. **1548** UDALL, etc. *Erasm. Par. Mark* i. (1552) 119 Leused and sette at large. **1601** SHAKS. *Twel. N.* I. i. 27 Shall not behold her face at ample view. **1646** SIR T. BROWNE *Pseud. Ep.* I. viii. 29 Their accounts are not to be swallowed at large. **1682** DRYDEN *Medal* Ep. Whigs, The Picture drawn at length. **1795** COLERIDGE *Conc. ad Pop.* Ess. 1850 I. 87 The people at large exercise no sovereignty. **1857** BUCKLE *Civiliz.* vi. 298 The preceding specimens have not been taken at random.

23. Of conditioning circumstance: e.g. *at peril, risk, hazard, expense, charge*; *at an advantage, disadvantage*, etc.

c **1380** *Sir Ferumb.* 3485 At al perils wil y go. **1712** ADDISON *Spect.* No. 553 ¶1 To be at the charge of it himself. **1749** FIELDING *Tom Jones* v. vi. (1840) 57 Pursue her at the hazard of his life. **1866** CRUMP *Banking* xi. 250 To supply its place at a loss. **1869** FREEMAN *Norm. Conq.* III. xii. 114 At all risks, at all sacrifices, to keep Normandy in full possession.

24. Of relation to some one's will or disposition: e.g. *at his will, pleasure, mercy, desire, discretion, disposal, command, orders, call, nod, beck*, etc. (Allied to 7, 8; cf. *at his elbow, at his call, at his beck, at his will.*)

1250 LAY. 9411 Weder him stod at wille [**1205** an wille]. *a* **1300** *Cursor M.* 3546 Broþer, atty will all sal be. *c* **1450** *Merlin* xxii. 401 'Sir'..'I will it be at youre volunte.' *c* **1532** LD. BERNERS *Huon* 457 To make your marchaundise at your pleasure. **1652** NEEDHAM tr. *Selden's Mare Cl.* 425 To remain at his judgement and award. **1825** T. JEFFERSON *Autobiog.* Wks. 1859 I. 3 The King's Council..held their places at will. **1849** MACAULAY *Hist. Eng.* I. 252 Their votes were at his disposal.

III. Of relative position in a series or scale, degree, rate, value.

25. Defining special point in a series at which one begins, stops, ends, etc.

c **1300** *E.E. Poems* (1862) 18 First at prude I wol be-gin. *Ibid.* 20 Be-ginne at his heued. *c* **1386** CHAUCER *Prol.* 42 At a knight than wol I first begynne. **1535** COVERDALE *Ezek.* ix. 6 Then they begane at the elders, which were in the Temple. **1536** R. BEERLEY in *Four C. Eng. Lett.* 35 Sume..begenynge at the mydes, and sume when yt ys allmost done. **1873** WILLIAMSON *Chem.* xvi. §107 At about 250°C. it [sulphur] is an opaque mass..At still higher temperatures it again becomes perfectly liquid..It boils at 490°C. *Mod.* With the thermometer standing at ninety in the shade.

b. *esp.* with superlatives.

c **1325** *Cœur de L.* 132 The wynd..servede hem atte the beste. *c* **1449** PECOCK *Repr.* I. xvii. 99 To be at uttrist examyned. *c* **1460** *Three 15th C. Chron.* (1880) 59 She..put him dyverse tymes at the worste. **1596** SHAKS. *Tam. Shr.* IV. ii. 73 Trauaile you farre on, or are you at the farthest? **1876** TREVELYAN *Macaulay* i. 7 He was rewarded by seeing Johnson at his very best.

c. *ellipt.* (*advb. phr.*) = taken *at best, most, least*, etc.

a **1661** FULLER *Life H. Smith* in *Smith's Wks.* 1866 I. 7 Wholly concealed or at the best uncertain. **1775** SHERIDAN *Rivals* Pref. (1883) 78 At least double the length of any acting comedy. **1818** BYRON *Juan* I. cxvi, You..have been, At best, no better than a go-between. **1882** PROCTOR in *Knowledge* No. 41. 178 Two, or at the outside, three miles.

26. Of rate or degree, *at* which a thing is done.

c **1200** ORMIN 4730 Þatt þu beo swinncfull att tin mahht. **1330** R. BRUNNE *Chron.* 43 He halp our Kyng..at his myght. *c* **1380** WYCLIF *Sel. Wks.* (1871) III. 289 Seynt Gregory and Seynt Austin fledden at al here power to be bischopis. *c* **1450** HENRYSON *Moral Fab.* 19 Hee would doe vs pleasing, At his power. **1710** POPE *Let. Wycherley* 15 Apr., If I am to go on at this rate. **1758** JOHNSON *Idler* No. 19 Jack Whirler always dines at full speed. **1840** DICKENS *Old C. Shop* i, Carrying me along with it at a great pace. **1882** *Athenæum* 24 June 793 She lived and worked at high pressure.

27. Of price or value.

c **1325** *Cœur de L.* 362 He set his stroke at nought. **1330** R. BRUNNE *Chron.* 174 A quarter whete was at twenty mark. *c* **1375** WYCLIF *Antecrist* 132 Wiþ knyȝtes at robes and fees ..to leden her bridelis. *c* **1460** *Towneley Myst.* 29 Thi felowship set I not at a pyn. **1602** SHAKS. *Ham.* IV. iii. 60 If my loue thou holdst at ought. **1615** E. S. *Britain's Buss* in Arb. *Garner* III. 631 Addesses, for Cooper's work, 6 at two shillings. **1663** GERBIER *Counsel* 68 Twelve inches at six pence an inch. **1791** BOSWELL *Johnson* (1826) I. 67 A man might live in a garret at eighteen-pence a week. **1849** MACAULAY *Hist. Eng.* I. 417 Wheat was at seventy shillings the quarter. **1868** FREEMAN *Norm. Conq.* (1876) II. x. 484 Stories like these must be taken at what they are worth. *Mod.* To set at nought their counsel.

28. Of reference to a standard generally = *according to*.

c **1430** *Syr Generides* 1409 At my witting..I trespassed neuer. **1483** CAXTON *G. de la Tour* K j b, Euery good woman ought to be meke and humble at the exemplary of the blessyd Vyrgyne Mary. **1855** MACAULAY *Hist. Eng.* III. 232 By land or by water at their choice.

IV. Of time, order, occasion, cause, object.

29. Introducing the time *at* which an event happens: **a.** with the time named.

c **1230** *Ancr. R.* 46 At al þe oþre tiden. *c* **1250** *Gen. & Ex.* 1641 At set time he sulden samen. **1477** EARL RIVERS (Caxton) *Dictes* 20 Atte grete day of Jugement. **1586** BRIGHT *Melanch.* xviii. 111 From three at after noone till nine at night. **1611** SHAKS. *Cymb.* I. iii. 31 At the sixt houre of Morne, at Noone, at Midnight. **1697** DRYDEN *Virg. Georg.* III. 248 Late at Night, when Stars adorn the Skies. **1712** STEELE *Spect.* No. 450 ¶7 All I have to say at present. **1758** JOHNSON *Idler* No. 19 Mr. Whirler..will be at home exactly at two. **1853** THACKERAY *Eng. Hum.* 91 Addison left off at a good moment.

b. with the time indicated by an event: At the time of, on the occasion of.

c **1200** ORMIN 707 Att te come off Sannt Johan. *c* **1230** *Ancr. R.* 20 Et te one psalme ȝe schulen stonden..& et te oðer sitten. *c* **1400** *Sir Perc.* 1531 Thay mone At thaire metyng. **1663** GERBIER *Counsel* C viij b, At the return of the Army. **1673** RAY *Journ. L. Countr.* 2 A town..at our being there, but thinly inhabited. *c* **1720** DE FOE *Mem. Cavalier* (1840) 209 Our men..gave them a shout at parting. **1849** MACAULAY *Hist. Eng.* I. 172 At the Restoration Hyde became chief minister.

30. Introducing the age *at* which one is.

a **1400** *Cov. Myst.* 383 At fourten yer sche conseyved Criste. *c* **1590** MARLOWE *Faustus* (2nd vers.) 13 At riper years, to Wittenberg he went. *a* **1626** BACON *Max. & Uses Com. Law* 31 If he were at full age. **1711** ADDISON *Spect.* No. 93 ¶2 The minor longs to be at age. **1844** DISRAELI *Coningsby* III. i. 89 He was Pope as Leo X. at thirty-seven.

31. Of nearness or distance in time, interval.

c **1200** ORMIN 1893 Att twenntiȝ daȝhess ende. *c* **1300** *K. Alis.* 1184 Theo knyghtis armed heom at ones. **1551** ROBINSON tr. *More's Utopia* 98 Vpon truste to be payed at a daye. **1673** RAY *Journ. L. Countr.* 39 We arrived at four hours end. **1716** *Lond. Gaz.* No. 5472/4 A Note..at three Months after Date. **1840** DICKENS *Old C. Shop* viii, I must begin at once, I see that.

32. Of the number of times, turns, or occasions.

c **1300** *K. Alis.* 6608 He beoreth at ones..Ten men over theo flod. *c* **1532** LD. BERNERS *Huon* 409 And deliuerid them to one man by .ii. louys atones. **1666** J. SMITH *Old Age* (ed. 2) 83 To do that at twice, and to be three or four times as long about it. **1668** HALE *Pref. Rolle's Abridgm.* 3 May go far at one Essay to provide a fit law. **1711** STEELE *Spect.* No. 155 ¶3 Being seen toying by two's and three's at a time. **1758** J. S. *Le Dran's Observ. Surg.* (1771) 124 Two Ounces of Manna..to be taken at three Doses. *Mod.* To complete the business at two sittings.

33. Of order: e.g. *at first, at last, at length, at the conclusion*, etc.

a **1000** *Beowulf* 89 Þe hine æt frumsceafte forð onsendon. **1297** R. GLOUC. 155 Atte laste þis Saxones by gonne forto fle. *c* **1300** *K. Alis.* 1668 Now at the erst, the messangers Buth y-come. *c* **1384** CHAUCER *H. Fame* 2155 Atte last y saugh a man. **1591** SHAKS. *1 Hen. VI.* I. ii. 71 She takes vpon her brauely at first dash. **1611** BIBLE *Matt.* xxvi. 60 At the last came two false witnesses. **1788** T. JEFFERSON *Writ.* (1859) II. 493 It is at length signed this day. *Mod.* At first, I thought otherwise. Home at last!

34. Introducing the occasion on which a fact or action ensues, and *hence* the occasioning circumstance, or cause.

c **1300** *K. Alis.* 4637 He starf at the furste tidyng. **1303** R. BRUNNE *Handl. Synne* 901 At hys cunsel.. Halewede þey al þat yche ȝere. *c* **1430** *Freemasonry* 23 At these lordys prayers they cownterfetyd gemetry. *c* **1532** LD. BERNERS *Huon* 455 He was ioyfull, and blyssyd hym at the vertue of that stone. **1574** tr. *Marlorats Apocalips* 33 They bee caryed aboute like babes at euery blast of doctrine. **1600** FAIRFAX *Tasso* I. xxix. 3 At my request this war was undertake. **1711** ADDISON *Spect.* No. 124 ¶4 It is at his Instance that I shall continue my rural speculations. **1795** SOUTHEY *Joan of Arc* VI. 50 At their voice He drew the strong bolts back. **1812** KEATS *Lamia* 627 Do not all charms fly at the mere touch of cold philosophy?

35. Introducing the occasion or cause of an emotion: e.g. ***astonished, dismayed, delighted, grieved at***; to ***rejoice, mourn at; joy, surprise at***, etc.

1366 MAUNDEV. xxviii. 287 Thei maken ioye and gladnesse at hire dyenge. **1596** SPENSER *F.Q.* I. vi. 9 All stand amazed at so uncouth sight. **1611** SHAKS. *Cymb.* I. i. 15 Not a Courtier.. hath a heart that is not Glad at the thing. **1655** FULLER *Ch. Hist.* IX. §5 IV. 264 Aggrieved at this Ecclesiasticall Power. **1671** MILTON *Samson* 1603, I sorrow'd at his captive state. **1727** POPE *Dunc.* I. 26 Mourn not, my Swift! at ought our Realm acquires. **1849** MACAULAY *Hist. Eng.* I. 175 Terrified at the completeness of their own success. **1853** KANE *Grinnell Exp.* xlviii. 445 Impatient at the delays.

36. Introducing what is at once the exciting cause and the object of active emotions: e.g. *envy, hate, wrath*. Uniting the senses of 13 b and 35.

c **1325** *Metr. Hom.* 78 The fende at him had grete enuye. *c* **1430** *Syr Tryam.* 885 At Tryamoure had he tene. **1535** COVERDALE *Zach.* vii. 12 Wherfore the Lorde of hoostes was very wroth at them. **1607** SHAKS. *Timon* III. iii. 13 I'me angry at him. **1704** POPE *Let. Wycherley* 26 Dec., Continued by envy at his success and fame. **1737** WHISTON *Josephus' Wars* IV. v. §4 They all had indignation at the judges. **1742** RICHARDSON *Pamela* IV. 47 He brought it to me himself, and was angry at me.

†**37.** Introducing the reason or consideration: in ***at reverence of*** = out of respect to. *Obs.*

1425 *Paston Lett.* 5 I. 21 John, atte reverence of your right worthy persone, hathe cesed. *c* **1465** *Eng. Chron.* (1856) 60 Othir thyngis.. the whiche atte reverence of nature and of wommanhood shul not be reherced. *a* **1575** ABP. PARKER *Corr.* 51 At the reverence of God, I pray you.. help that I be not forgotten.

V. 38. In many idiomatic phrases arising out of the preceding senses, which see separately treated, or under the word governed by *at*: e.g. ***at any*** RATE, ***at*** STAKE, AT HOME, AT ONE, AT ONCE. ***at all***: see ALL *a.* 9 b; ***at that***: see THAT *dem. pron.* 5 c.

1557 *Ord. Hospitalls* F vj b, Children abrode at Nurse. **1589** PUTTENHAM *Eng. Poesie* (Arb.) 287 To set vpon Darius at the sodaine. *a* **1622** WITHER *Brit. Remembr.* 146 The World.. Hath so intangled us at unaware. **1674** MARVELL *Reh. Transp.* II. 234 Fain to sell them all at second-hand. **1681** in Arb. *Garner* I. 440 The King at unawares falls upon them. *a* **1718** PENN *Tracts* Wks. 1726 I. 869 They[the Quakers] were at a word in Dealing. **1742** RICHARDSON *Pamela* IV. 312, I shall be glad to take you at your word. *a* **1782** BP. NEWTON *Wks.* II. iii. 78 Cain taking him at an advantage.. slew him. **1817** MAR. EDGEWORTH *Love & Law* I. iv, Scotch!—not Irish native, at-all-at-all. **1859** MASSON *Milton* I. 703 At all events, Milton had seen.. the greatest of living Dutchmen. **1877** GOLDW. SMITH in *Contemp. Rev.* Dec. 122 The aristocratic conspiracy, for such at bottom it was. **1883** *Manch. Guard.* 22 Oct. 5/2 The questions at issue between the Hovas and the French.

VI. With the infinitive mood.

†**39.** Introducing the infinitive of purpose (the original function also of *to*; cf. Fr. *rien à faire*, nothing *to* do, nothing *at* do, nothing ADO). *Obs.* exc. *dial.*

Corresponding to ON. *at* (Da. *at*, Sw. *att*) in *gefa at eta* to give one *at* eat, i.e. *to* eat; but not, like it, used with the simple infinitive; the nearest approach to which was in the phrase 'That is *at* say' = Fr. *c'est à dire*.

? **1280** Kemble's *Cod. Dipl.* II. 186 Na man sal have at do. *c* **1314** *Guy Warw.* 88 That he cum with the at ete. *c* **1325** *Metr. Hom.* 46 Þat es at say, to mak the sin for sin. **1330** R. BRUNNE *Chron.* 34 Was he not so hardy at stand to bataile. **1340** HAMPOLE *Pr. Consc.* 5234 Þus sal he com doun at sitte þare. **1440** *Lay-Folks Mass-Bk.* C 278 Be redy at answere hym. *c* **1460** *Towneley Myst.* 181 We have othere thynges at do. **1470** HARDING *Chron.* Pref. I Lordes sonnes bene sette .. To scole at lerne. [*Modern Westmorl. dial.* A bit o' summat at eat.]

VII. Before other prepositions or adverbs.

40. With prepositions. Cf. AFTER D I. *Obs.* exc. in ***at about***, at approximately.

c **1386** CHAUCER *Frankl. T.* 492 At after soper fille they in tretee. ? *c* **1400** *MS. Rawlinson* C 258 (Halliw.), I trust to see you att-after Estur. **1594** SHAKS. *Rich. III.* IV. iii. 31 Come to me Tirrel soone, at [*Ff.* and] after Supper. **1843** G. BORROW *Bible in Sp.* I. ii. 26 At about seven o'clock in the evening we reached Aldea Gallega. *a* **1882** TROLLOPE *Autobiogr.* (1883) I. ix. 214, I have been paid at about that rate. **1915** V. WOOLF *Voyage Out* iii. 37 At about that hour he reappeared. **1929** D. H. LAWRENCE *Paintings* sig. B1r, At about the time of our Elizabethans. **1945** E. WAUGH *Bridesh. Rev.* II. v. 272 My divorce case.. was due to be heard at about the same time.

†**41.** With adverbs. *Obs.* or *dial.*

c **1440** *Morte Arth.* 3181 To hafe pete of þe Pope, þat put was at-undere. **1513** DOUGLAS *Æneis* VIII. viii. 35 Nor ȝit the Troiane power put at under. *a* **1641** STRAFFORD in Southey's *Common-pl. Bk.* II. (1849) 183 Casting them aside at after. **1675** BROOKS *Gold. Key* Wks. 1867 V. 33 It will keep grace at an under. **1863** ATKINSON *Whitby Gloss.* s.v., Ploughing first, sowing at after.

† **at, 'at** (ət), *rel.pron., adv., conj. Obs.* exc. *dial.* [A worn-down form of *that*, perhaps from ON. *at* (used in precisely the same senses), perh. independently developed in the northern dialect, in which it was very common in 14–15th c.; rare, even in Scottish writers, after 1500; but still in regular use in northern dialect speech.]

A. *adv.* or *conj.* = 'that.'

c **1325** *Metr. Hom.* 73 Sainte Makary hard say, At thai wald come. *c* **1425** *Seven Sag.* (P.) 1909, I graunt wel at hit so be. *a* **1440** *Sir Degrev.* 1210 Loke at thou come at that tyme. *c* **1480** *Plumpton Corr.* Introd. 65 For so much as I, Thomas Lord Clifford and of Westmerland am enformed at a nisi prius is like to pas. **1513** DOUGLAS *Æneis* (1710) IV. Prol. 139 Willing at thou and thay may haue the sicht Of heuynnys blys. **1657** BROME *Queene's Exch.* II. i. 477 And at we find you we'l our selves bestir. [*a* **1885** *North dial.* I sed 'at I wad, and I did.]

b. Formerly blended with *ne* into *atten, attyn*, 'that not, but that.' (= L. *quin.*)

c **1340** *Cursor M.* 1440 (Fairf.), Ne muȝt ham help no halihede, attyn to hel þai most nede. *Ibid.* 6130 Was na hous .. attyn þer was dede mon in liggande.

B. *rel. pron.* That; who, which; what.

a **1300** *E.E. Psalter* xxx. 16 Outtake me.. at ere filyhand me fra þa. *c* **1340** *Cursor M.* 3248 (Fairf.), Al atte [*other MSS.* þat] camels ten muȝt bere. *c* **1380** WYCLIF *Sel. Wks.* III. 417 Þo freris were served of þat at þei craven. **1429** EARL SALISB. in *Wills & Inv. N.C.* 69 *note*, Grete costages and expences at I haue hadd now of late. *c* **1480** LD. CLIFFORD in *Plumpton Corr.* Introd. 65 All other Christen men att this writing sall here or see. *c* **1500** *Carpenter's Tools* in Halliw. *Nug. P.* 15 That at I sey it shall be sure. **1879** G. MACDONALD *Sir Gibbie* II. xvii. 290 'To onything 'at's richt, Gibbie wants nae perswaudin'.'

[**at,** freq. misread or misprinted for AC *conj.* but.

1297 R. GLOUC. 256 At vpe Gode's wylle yt ys. *c* **1400** *Ywaine & Gaw.* 132 At tel to me and thi felawes, Al thi tale.]

at, obsolete form of ATE, pa. t. of EAT.

At, AT, A.T.: see A.T.S. (as separate entry).

at-, *pref.*[1] [:—OE. *æt-*.] The preposition AT in composition, with force of 'at, close to, to'; frequent in OE., and retained in some words in ME., as *at-stand(en* to stand close to, 'adstare,' *at-rech(en* to reach to, get at, *at-fore(n* before, *at-hind(en* behind. In the oldest Eng. the prefix was *æt-* only when it bore the stress accent (i.e. in sbs. and adjs.); *ot-*, (*oþ-*, *oð-*,) when unaccented (in vbs. and prepositions): thus, *'ætgræpe* grasping at, apprehensive, *ot'grípan*, *oþ'grípan*, to grip at, *oð'beran* to bear to, bring, *oð'íewan* (Goth. *a'taugjan* to show). Northumbrian had sometimes *æd-*, *od-*: cf. ATEW. The forms *oþ*, *oð*, seem to have arisen in an early assimilation of *ot-* to *óþ-*, *óð-*, from *anð-*, the old accented form of AND-, *ond-*, occurring in the prep. *óð*, the meaning of which was not far removed from that of *æt-*, *ot-*. But in later OE. the strong form *æt-* (ME. *at-*, in south. dial. *et-*) was extended to all compounds, without regard to the position of the stress. Mod.Eng. has lost all these compounds, exc. that *a'twíte* survives in *twit*. *Atone* is a modern formation of a different kind.

at-, *pref.*[2] [:—OE. *æt-*.] Representing earlier OE. *oþ-*, *oð-*, unaccented form of *úð-* 'away, from' = Gothic *unþa-* in *unþa-þliuhan* to flee away, G. *ent-* (in part), OHG. *int-*, in *entfliehen*, OHG. *intfliohan*, Du. *ont-* in *ontvlieden* to flee away. This *oð-*, *oþ-*, from *úð-*, being phonetically levelled with *óð-* from *anð-*, and *ot-* the unaccented form of *æt-* being assimilated to the latter (see prec.), these three prefixes ran together in form, and when at a later time the accented form *æt-* took the place of its own weak form *ot-*, *oþ-*, *oð-*, it also usurped the place of *oð-* from *anð-*, and *oð-* from *úð-*, *unþ-*. The last of these was by far the most frequent in use: hence the most common sense of *at-* prefix in ME. is 'from, away' = Gothic *unþa-*, Ger. *ent-*, as in *at-bear* to bear away, *at-flee* to flee away, *at-go* to go away. As *úð-*, *oþ-*, had nearly the same sense as *æf-*, *of-*, these verbs in *at-* often take the place of corresponding vbs. in *of-*, as OE. *oð-beran*, *æt-beran*, = *of-beran* to bear away, ME. *at-come* = OE. *of-cyman* to come off, escape, etc. Several new compounds of this type arose in ME., and it was even irregularly extended to Fr. words, as in ATSCAPE, refashioned from *ascape*, OF. *escaper*. All these are now obsolete.

at-, *pref.*[3] Assimilated form of L. *ad-* to, before *t*, used in all modern words from Latin. In OF. *ad-*, *at-*, was reduced to *a-*, and so introduced into ME., but afterwards refashioned as *at-*, after L. spelling, both in Fr. and English, e.g. L. *attingĕre*, OF. *ateindre*, later *atteindre*, ME. *ataindre*, mod. *attainder*. The Eng. has also taken *at-* where Fr. retains the simple *a-*, as in OF. *atorné*, mod. *atourné*, ME. *atorney*, mod. *attorney*. The *t* was also erroneously doubled in various words in *at-* with prefix *a-* from other sources, as *a(t)tame*, *a(t)tray*, *a(t)troke*. See AD- *pref.*[2]

-at, *suffix.* **1.** The original form of -ATE[1], surviving in a number of words, as *commissariat* (1), *concordat*, *diplomat*, *format*, *quadrat*, *secretariat* (also *-ate*). Most of these are loan-words from French.

2. Representing the 3rd pers. sing. pres. tense ending of Latin verbs of the first conjugation, as *ægrotat*, *habitat*.

‖**atabal** (atə'bal). Also 7 **ataballe**, 8 **attaball**. [a. Sp. *atabal*, a. Arab. *aṭ-ṭabl*, i.e. *al* the, *ṭabl* a drum. (Also in F. *attabale*)] A kind of kettle-drum or tabour used by the Moors.

1672 DRYDEN *Conq. Granada* I. i. (1725) 32 From the Streets sound Drums and Ataballes. **1781** GIBBON *Decl. & F.* III. lxviii. 723 The martial music of drums, trumpets, and attaballs. **1811** SCOTT *Roderick* I. xix, Then answered kettle-drum and atabal.

atabrine, var. ATEBRIN.

atacamite (ə'tækəmaɪt). *Min.* [f. *Atacama*, a province of Chili, where found + -ITE, min. form.] A bright green ore, an oxychloride of copper, found in Chili, Australia, and at St. Just in Cornwall.

1837–68 DANA *Min.* 121. **1869** PHILLIPS *Vesuv.* x. 280 Atacamite has been found incrusting lavas.

atactic (ə'tæktɪk), *a.* [f. Gr. ἄτακτος not arranged (f. ἀ priv. + τακτός, vbl. adj. f. τάσσ-ειν to arrange) + -IC.] **1.** Of language: Not syntactic.

1842 *Chamb. Jrnl.* 30 July 218 In this manner syntactic and atactic forms have been respectively formed.

2. *Path.* Of or pertaining to or afflicted with ataxia.

1880 W. JAMES *Feeling of Effort* 20 in *Anniv. Mem. Boston Soc. Nat. Hist.*, The special case of the limb being completely anæsthetic, as well as atactic. **1956** JAKOBSON & HALLE *Fundamentals of Lang.* II. iv. 74 In one variety of aphasia.. sometimes.. labeled 'atactic', the word is the sole linguistic unity preserved... All other sound-sequences are either alien and inscrutable to him or he merges them into familiar words by disregarding their phonetic aberrations.

3. Characterized by or exhibiting irregularity in the spatial arrangement of parts in a molecule. Cf. ISOTACTIC *a.*, SYNDYOTACTIC *a.*

1957 *Chem. Abstr.* 15993 [Abstract of art. by G. Natta et al. in 1957 *Gazz. Chim. Ital.* LXXXVII]. Stereospecific polymerization... First syntheses of isotactic and atactic polypropene. **1957** *Technology* July 176/2 The side groups are situated quite at random along the chain; this type of combination is termed 'atactic'.. atactic polypropylene is a rubbery material freezing below −30 deg. C.

ataghan ('ætəgæn). [variant of YATAGHAN, q.v.] A long dagger worn by Turks and Moors in their belt in a scabbard of silver or gold.

1813 BYRON *Giaour* 355 Each turban I can scan, And silver-sheathed ataghan. **1851** HAWTHORNE *Twice-told T.* II. xx. 278 He still wore beneath his vest the ataghan.

† **a'take,** *v. Obs.* 3–5. *Pa. t.* **atok**. *Pa. pple.* **atake(n.** [f. A- *pref.* 1 + TAKE.] To overtake; get at, catch.

c **1300** *Beket* 1963 This messager ne miȝte noȝt atake hem mid no ginne. *c* **1330** *Arth. & Merl.* 468 Al that Fortiger atok He let to-drawe. **1382** WYCLIF *Lev.* xxvi. 5 The thresshynge of repyn tilthes shal atake the vyndage. *c* **1386** CHAUCER *Freres T.* 84 Sire, quod this Sompnour, haile, and wel atake! *c* **1440** *Partonope* 6390 And then he sayd, Syr, wele atake!

† **ata'lantis**. *Obs.* Brief title of a romance [prob. after Bacon's *New Atlantis*] satirizing those who had effected the Revolution of 1688 (see first quot.); hence *gen.* a secret or scandalous history.

1709 MRS. MANLEY (*title*) Secret Memoirs and Manners of several Persons of Quality of both Sexes from the New Atalantis, an Island in the Mediterranean. **1785** R. CUMBERLAND in *Observer* No. 109 ¶3 He has a court-atalantis of his own, from which he can favour you with some hints of sly doings amongst the maids of honour. **1789** (*title*) The Naval Atalantis; or a Display of the Characters of such Flag Officers, etc.

ataman, var. HETMAN.

1835 *Court Mag.* VI. 82/1 'We may not do this,' replied one of the Cossacks, 'without the consent of our Ataman.' **1920** *Glasgow Herald* 18 Aug. 7 The Ataman of the Don Cossacks. **1924** *Blackw. Mag.* Feb. 171/2 The Ataman had been waiting a mile away.. for the last of the attacking party to come in. **1950** E. H. CARR *Bolshevik Revol.* I. 294 At the head of each community was an elected ataman.

atamasco lily (ætə'mæskəʊ). Also † **attamusco**. [N. Amer. Ind.] A plant, *Zephyranthes atamasco*, of the south-eastern U.S., bearing a single lily-like flower.

[**1629** PARKINSON *Parad.* 87 *Narcissus Virgineus*. The Virginia Daffodil... The Indians in Virginia do call it

Attamusco.] **1743** CATESBY *Carolina* I. App. 112 The Attamusco Lilly is a native of Virginia and Carolina. **1760** J. LEE *Introd. Bot.* App. 305 Atamasco Lily, *Amaryllis.* **1813** MUHLENBERG *Catal. Plants* 34 Atamasco lily; Car. Georg. Pen.; fl. Jun. **1956** *Dict. Gardening* (*R. Hort. Soc.*) (ed. 2) IV. 2307 Atamasco Lily..perianth 2¾ to 4½ in. long, white or white flushed pink..United States, from Missouri and Virginia to Florida.

† **a'tame**, *v. Obs.* Also in 6 **att-**. [f. A- *pref.* 1 + TAME *v.*; substituted for OE. *atęmian*, when *tęmien* was assimilated in form to TAME *a.*] To tame, subdue.

[*c* **885** K. ÆLFRED *Gregory's Past.* xlvi. 345 And atemiað hira lichoman.] **1340** *Ayenb.* 153 Huanne þise uour deles byeþ atamed. *c* **1400** *Sowdone Bab.* 935 These hethen houndes we shal a-tame. *c* **1525** SKELTON *Agst. Venom. Tongues* 2 Men said they [Women] could not their tunges atame. **1530** PALSGR. 439/2 He was as wylde as a bucke, but I have made hym as attamed as a lambe.

atame, atar: see ATTAME, ATTAR.

atane, *obs.* northern form of ATONE *v.*

atap, var. ATTAP.

ataractic, -axic (ætə'ræktɪk, -'æksɪk), *a.* [f. Gr. ἀτάρακτος not disturbed, calm + -IC; cf. ATARAXY.] **a.** Calm, serene.

1941 H. MILLER *Colossus of Maroussi* i. 90 Mycenae.. reared in anthropophagous luxury, reptilian, ataraxic, stunning and stunned.

b. *Med.* Of drugs: inducing calmness, tranquillizing. Hence as *sb.*, a drug of this kind.

1955 H. D. FABING in *Neurology* V. 327/1 The Epicureans were especially fond of the term 'ataraxia' which meant *freedom from confusion, peace of mind*... It is proposed, therefore, that drugs of this type be designated *ataraxics*, and that the adjectival form, *ataractic*, be used to describe this therapeutic property in drugs. *Ibid.* 328/2 Proposal is made to adopt the generic term, *ataraxics*, for pharmacological agents such as chlorpromazine, rauwolfia compounds, Frenquel, and others, which bring about *ataraxy*, or freedom from confusion. *Ibid.* 609/2 Why can't some new tools be devised to screen potential new ataractic drugs? **1956** *Newsweek* 21 May 68/1 The other tranquilizers ..are all known as ataractics. **1957** *Times* 12 Mar. 6/6 The rapidly increasing use of drugs described as 'tranquillizers' and 'ataraxics'..has become a cause of concern in many countries. **1957** *New Scientist* 12 Dec. 26/1 So-called ataractic drugs—that can cure the 'incurable' mental case.

ataraxy ('ætəræksɪ). Also 7 **ataraxie**, and in L. form **ataraxia** (ætə'ræksɪə). [ad. Gr. ἀταραξία impassiveness, f. ἀ priv. + ταράσσ-ειν to disturb, stir up. Cf. F. *ataraxie* (Cotgr.).] Freedom from disturbance of mind or passion; stoical indifference.

1603 FLORIO *Montaigne* (1634) 281 Ataraxie..is the condition of a quiet and setled life. **1864** R. BURTON *Dahome* II. 98 The ataraxy and the *comme il faut* calm that characterises the more refined Anglo-Tropical mind. **1882** *Sat. Rev.* 20 May 624 They go their way unmolested and have attained to literary *ataraxia*.

atarned, pa. t. and pple. of ATREN *v. Obs.*

ataunt (ə'tɔːnt), *adv.* [a. F. *autant* as much.]

†**1.** As much as possible, to the full, thoroughly. (Cf. Palsgrave 'I quaught, I drinke all out, *Je boys dautant*.') *Obs.*

c **1325** *E.E. Allit. P.* A. 179 Þat stonge myn hert ful stray atount. *c* **1430** LYDG. *Min. Poems* 167 A dronken foole that sparithe for no dispence To drynk ataunt til he slepe at table. *c* **1520** W. DE WORDE *Treat. Galaunt* (1860) 17 Talewes and talkynge, and drynkynge ataunte.

2. *Naut.* With every mast standing and fully rigged; with all sails set. (Also *ataunto*, *all-ataunto*.)

1622 R. HAWKINS *Voy. S. Sea* (1847) 52 A fayre gale of wind..so that wee might beare all a taunt. **1836** MARRYAT *Midsh. Easy* (1863) 193 Not one soul of you puts his foot on shore until we are again all ataunto. **1867** J. MACGREGOR *Voy. Alone* 58 All was ataunt again, and then the two yachts started.

atavic (ə'tævɪk), *a.* [ad. F. *atavique*, f. L. *atavus*; see next and -IC.] Of or pertaining to a remote ancestor.

1866 HUXLEY *Preh. Rem. Caithn.* 159 The brachycephaly of the Norman-French colonists of Quebec, can only come from their atavic ancestors, the Belgæ.

atavism ('ætəvɪz(ə)m). [a. F. *atavisme*, f. L. *atav-us* a great-grandfather's grandfather, an ancestor; cf. *av-us* grandfather.] Resemblance to grand-parents or more remote ancestors rather than to parents; tendency to reproduce the ancestral type in animals or plants.

1833 J. RENNIE *Sci. Gardening* 113 Children often resemble their grandfathers or grandmothers more than their immediate parents..This propensity is termed Atavism by Duchesne. **1872** BAGEHOT *Physics & Pol.* 218 Some mysterious atavism—some strange recurrence to a primitive past.

b. *Path.* Recurrence of the disease or constitutional symptoms of an ancestor after the intermission of one or more generations.

atavistic (ætə'vɪstɪk), *a.* [f. prec.: see -ISTIC.] Of or pertaining to atavism; atavic.

1875 *N. Amer. Rev.* CXX. 275 The social and the atavistic influence. **1915** W. S. MAUGHAM *Of Human Bondage* xxvi. 108 Some atavistic inheritance of the cave-dweller. **1922** JOYCE *Ulysses* 676 The sporadic reappearance of atavistic delinquency. **1932** E. WAUGH *Black Mischief* v. 168 Was it some atavistic sense of a caste, an instinct of superiority, that held him aloof?

Hence **ata'vistically** *adv.*

1884 *N. Amer. Rev.* Sept. 253 The ancient types crop out atavistically. **1897** E. P. EVANS *Evol. Ethics* i. 33 The lower classes..reflect atavistically the ideas and passions of primitive man. **1926** *Blackw. Mag.* Apr. 446/2 Some of them bolted atavistically up the nearest tree.

ataxic (ə'tæksɪk), *a.* [mod. f. next; cf. F. *ataxique*, and see -IC. Not on Gr. analogies.] Characterized by ataxy, *esp.* in *Path.* by disturbance of the natural animal functions; irregular. *ataxic fever*: malignant typhus fever.

1853 in MAYNE *Exp. Lex.* **1877** ERICHSEN *Surg.* (ed. 7) 295 An ataxic state of the muscles. **1880** M. DRYSDALE in *Med. Temp. Jrnl.* Oct. 7 Ataxic or adynamic symptoms are frequently seen.

ataxy (ə'tæksɪ, 'ætæksɪ). Also 7 **ataxie**; in sense 2 often as L. **ataxia**. [ad. Gr. ἀταξία, f. ἀ priv. + τάξις arrangement, order, f. τάσσ-ειν to arrange.]

†**1.** Want of order or discipline; irregularity, confusion, disorderliness. *Obs.* in gen. sense.

1615 BYFIELD *On Coloss.* ii. 10 (1869) 205/2 There is [no] ataxy among those glorious creatures [*i.e.* angels]. **1634** CANNE *Necess. Separ.* (1849) 207 A mere ataxy, or confused chaos. *a* **1733** NORTH *Exam.* III. viii. ¶70 If it had been slipt over, he must have blamed his own Ataxy in the Disposition.

2. *Path.* Irregularity of the animal functions, or of the symptoms of disease. *locomotor ataxy*: inability to co-ordinate the voluntary movements, constitutional unsteadiness in the use of legs, arms, etc.

1670 MAYNWARINGE *Vita Sana* i. 13 There ariseth Distempers, Ataxies and discord. **1684** tr. *Bonet's Merc. Compit.* VIII. 305 A Woman very subject to vapours and ataxies of the animal spirits. **1855** H. SPENCER *Psychol.* (1872) I. I. ii. 5 An early stage of ataxy. **1878** A. HAMILTON *Nerv. Dis.* 208 Locomotor ataxia..often occurs among seafaring men who have fallen overboard.

atayn, ataynt, obs. f. ATTAIN, -T.

at-bat (æt'bæt). *N. Amer. Baseball.* [f. the phr. *at bat* s.v. BAT *sb.*[2] 3 d.] A player's turn at the bat; also, the official time at bat, used in calculating a batter's average.

1941 J. KIERAN *Amer. Sporting Scene* 86 From 'One Old Cat' to the last 'At Bat', was there ever a guy like Ruth? **1961** COBB & STUMP *My Life in Baseball* vii. 96 Over the course of that 4-game New York series, I had a double, two triples, a homer, and three singles in 13 at-bats for a ·534 figure. **1968** *Globe & Mail* (Toronto) 10 July 26/5 In that one inning alone, Mays tied one All-Star record for most official at-bats. **1978** *Detroit Free Press* 14 Apr. D3/2 Jackson hit a three-run homer in his first at-bat. **1984** *Gainesville* (Florida) *Sun* 26 Mar. 23/1 In his first at-bat..Wilson doubled home the tie-breaking run.

†**at'bear**, *v. Obs.* [OE. *ætberan* (*oðberan*), f. AT- *pref.*[1], [2] + *beran* to BEAR.]

1. [f. AT-[1].] *trans.* To bear to, to bring. (In OE.)

a **1000** *Daniel* (Gr.) 538 He wundor maniȝ for men ætbær.

2. [f. AT-[2].] *trans.* To bear away, carry off.

a **1000** *Beowulf* 4261 Hió þæt lic ætbær. ? *c* **1350** *MS. Digby* No. 86. 123 (Halliw.) A wonder thing he sey him thar, A wolf his other child atbar.

†**at'blench**, *v. Obs.* [f. AT- *pref.*[2] + BLENCH *v.*, OE. *blencan* to deceive, escape.] *intr.* To escape.

c **1275** *Sinners Beware* in *O.E. Misc.* 79 And cunnen atblenche From sathanases wrenche. *c* **1275** *Death* 8 *ibid.* 168 From þe dreorie deað ne mai nomon at-blenche.

†**at'blow**, *v. Obs. rare.* [f. AT- *pref.*[1] + BLOW, OE. *bláwan*: cf. ABLOW.] *intr.* To blow (at).

? *a* **1400** *MS. Linc.* A. i. 17. 128 (Halliw.) The tourmentours atblewe at hyme.

†**at'braid**, *v. Obs.* [OE. *ætbreȝdan*, (*oðbreȝdan*) f. AT- *pref.*[2] + *breȝdan* to wrench: see ABRAID *v.*] *trans.* To draw or snatch away.

a **1000** *Guthlac* (Gr.) 826 Se éðel uðgenge wearð Adame and Evan..oðbroden. *c* **1000** *Ags. Gosp.* Matt. xiii. 12 þæt þe he hæfð him bið ætbroden. *a* **1250** *Owl & Night.* 1380 Ah ȝef heo is atbroide thenne, He is unfele and forbrode.

†**at'break**, *v. Obs.* Also 3 **et-**; for inflexions see BREAK *v.* [f. AT- *pref.*[2] + BREAK *v.*, OE. *brecan*. Cf. G. *entbrechen*, Du. *ontbreken*.] *intr.* (with *dat.*) To break away, escape (from).

1205 LAY. 1346 Neðelas Brutus at-bræc [**1250** at-brac]. *c* **1230** *Ancr. R.* 172 His þrelles etfluwen him & etbreken him ut. *a* **1250** *Passion Our Lord* in *O.E. Misc.* 44 Er he were him at-broke him þuhte ful long.

†**at'burst**, *v. Obs.* [OE. *ætberstan*, (*oðberstan*) f. AT- *pref.*[2] + *berstan* to BURST.] *intr.* (with *dat.*) To burst away, escape (from).

c **1000** ÆLFRIC *Gen.* xiv. 13 Ða ætbærst him sum man. *c* **1200** ORMIN 14734 All swa summ Ysaac attbrasst Unnwundedd & unnwemmedd. *c* **1250** *Bestiary* 672 in *O.E. Misc.* 21 Ðis elp..tus atbresteð ðis huntes breid.

atch, obsolete form of ADZE.

atcha, atchoo, var. ATISHOO.

atchaar, variant of ACHAR.

atchcan, atchkan, var. ACHKAN.

atchea-, atche-, atch'ment, intermed. forms between ACHIEVEMENT and HATCHMENT.

atcherne, obsolete form of ACORN.

atchieve, -ment, obs. ff. ACHIEVE, -MENT.

†**atchison** ('ætʃɪsən, 'eɪtʃɪ-). *Obs.* exc. *Hist.* Also 7 **acheson, -ison**. [Sc. pronunciation of *Atkinson*, name of the assay-master of the Edinburgh Mint in the beginning of James VI's reign. (Jamieson.)] A copper coin, coated with silver, coined in the reign of James VI, equal in value to eight pennies Scots or two-thirds of an English penny.

1605 ARMIN *Foole upon F.* (1880) 14 A sallet of an atchison price, which in our money was three farthings. **1657** COLVIL *Whigs Supplic.* (1751) 68 Achisons, Babees and Placks. **1773** RUDDIMAN *Introd. Anderson's Diplom.* 137 (JAM.) The first whitish colour, which discovers itself in these atchisons, seems to indicate that they are mixed with a little silver, or laid over with that metal.

†**at'come**, *v. Obs. rare*[−1]. [f. AT- *pref.*[2] + COME, OE. *cuman*. Cf. Ger. *entkommen*, Du. *ontkomen*.] *intr.* To come away, escape.

c **1220** *Rel. Ant.* I. 234 Dun til helle licten ne gan, ðe ðridde dai off deadd atkam.

†**at'creep**, *v. Obs. rare*[−1]. [f. AT- *pref.*[2] + CREEP, OE. *creópan*. Cf. Ger. *entkriechen*, Du. *ontkruipen*.] *intr.* To creep away.

1205 LAY. 5671 And qualden alle þa ilke þe aniht weoren atcropene [**1250** awei crope].

†**at'dare**, *v. Obs. rare*[−1]. [f. AT- *pref.*[2] + *darien*, *dearien*: see DARE *v.*[2]] *intr.* (with *dat.*) To escape by hiding (from).

c **1275** *Pains of Hell* 224 in *O.E. Misc.* 153 Nis þer non þat heom atdareþ.

‖**Ate** ('eɪtiː). [L., a. Gr. ἄτη.] Infatuation, mad impulse; personified by the Greeks as goddess of mischief and authoress of rash destructive deeds.

1587 GOLDING *De Mornay* xvii. 271 Homer speaketh of a Goddesse whom he calleth *Até*, that is Waste, Losse, or Destruction. **1617** COLLINS *Def. Bp. Ely* II. ix. 405 Ill newes flyes apace, the Ate still out-running the Litae. **1725** POPE *Iliad* XIX. 92 Not by myself but vengeful Ate driven. **1819** BYRON *Proph. Dante* I. 117 Death and Até range O'er humbled heads.

ate, obs. f. OAT, HATE; var. ETE, *Obs.*, food.

ate (ɛt, *occas.* eɪt), pa. t. of EAT *v.*

-ate, *suffix*[1], formerly *-at*, forming sbs. derived from L. sbs. in *-ātus* (*-ato-* and *-atu-*), *-ātum*, *-āta*, and their modern Romanic representatives.

1. In popular words which lived on into OFr., L. *-ātus*, *-ātum*, became (through *-ato*, *-ado*, *-ad*, *-ed*, *-et*) *-é*, as *cūrātus*, *senātus*, *avocātus*, *stātus*, *peccātum*, OF. *curé*, *sené*, *avoué*, *esté*, *péché*; learned words, adapted from Latin, took *-at*, as in *estat*, *prelat*, *primat*, *magistrat*. After 13th c. many of the popular words were refashioned with *-at*, as *sené*, *senat*, *avoué*, *avocat*; and all new words have been thus formed, e.g. *assassinat*, *attentat*, *épiscopat*, *palatinat*, *professorat*, *syndicat*. In Eng. these were originally adopted in their Fr. form, *estat*, *prelat*, etc.; after 1400, *-e* was added to mark the long vowel, *estate*, *prelate*, etc., and all later words from Fr. took *-ate* at once. After these, Eng. words are formed directly on L., as *curātus* 'curate,' or on L. analogies, as *alderman-ate*, cf. *triumvir-ate*. In meaning, words in *-ate* are chiefly: **a.** Substantives denoting office or function, or the persons performing it, as *marquisate*, *professorate*, *episcopate*, *syndicate*, *aldermanate*. **b.** Participial nouns, as *legate* 'one deputed,' *prelate* 'one preferred,' *mandate* 'a thing commanded,' *precipitate* 'what is thrown down.' **c.** Chemical terms, denoting salts formed by the action of an acid on a base, as *nitrate*, *acetate*, *sulphate*, *carbonate*, *alcoholate*, *ethylate*. In the 18th c. chemists said *plumbum acetatum* 'acetated lead,' lead acted on by vinegar, whence substantively *acetatum* the acetated (product), the 'acetate'; cf. *precipitate*, *sublimate*, *distillate*. (In the dog-latin of pharmacy, *acetas*, *-ātis*, is ignorantly put for *acetātum*.)

2. In some words, *-ate* = F. *-ate*, ad. L. or It. *-āta*, as in *pirate*, *frigate*.

-ate, *suffix*[2], formerly *-at*, forming participial adjectives from L. pa. pples. in *-ātus*, *-āta*, *-ātum*, being only a special instance of the adoption of L. pa. pples. by dropping the inflexional endings, e.g. *content-us*, *convict-us*, *direct-us*, *remiss-us*, or with phonetic final *-e*, e.g.

complēt-us, *finīt-us*, *revolūt-us*, *spars-us*. The analogy for this was set by the survival of some L. pa. pples. in OF., as *confus*:—*confūsus*, *content*:—*contentus*, *divers*:—*diversus*. This analogy was widely followed in later Fr., in introducing new words from Latin; and both classes of Fr. words, i.e. the popular survivals and the later accessions, being adopted in Eng., provided Eng. in its turn with analogies for adapting similar words directly from L., by dropping the termination. This began about 1400, and as in -ATE[1] (with which this suffix is phonetically identical), L. *-ātus* gave *-at*, subsequently *-ate*, e.g. *desolātus*, *desolat*, *desolate*, *separātus*, *separat*, *separate*. Many of these participial adjectives soon gave rise to causative verbs, identical with them in form (see next), to which, for some time, they did duty as pa. pples., as 'the land was *desolat(e* by war;' but, at length, regular pa. pples. were formed with the native suffix *-ed*, upon the general use of which these earlier participial adjs. generally lost their participial force, and either became obs. or remained as simple adjectives, as in 'the *desolate* land,' 'a *compact* mass.' (But cf. *situate* = *situated*.) So *aspirate*, *moderate*, *prostrate*, *separate*; and (where a vb. has not been formed), *innate*, *oblate*, *ornate*, *sedate*, *temperate*, etc. As the Fr. repr. of L. *-atus* is *-é*, English words in *-ate* have also been formed directly after Fr. words in *-é*, e.g. *affectionné*, *affectionate*.

2. As with Eng. *-ed*, L. ppl. adjs. in *-ātus* were also formed on nouns, etc., when no other part of the vb. was required, as *cauda* tail, *caudātus* tailed, and often with negatives, as *sensus* sense, *insensātus* unprovided with sense. In modern times these have been liberally adopted in Eng., and on their analogy, or that of corresponding Fr. words in *-é*, new words are constantly formed where L. actually had not the formation, as *apiculate*, f. *apiculus* a little point; *lunulate*, f. *lunula* little moon; *roseate*, f. *roseus* rosy; *angustifoliate*, f. *angustum* narrow + *folium* leaf.

3. Many words, originally adj., are also used substantively, e.g. *delegate*, *reprobate*, *precipitate*, *carbonate*, *alcoholate*, and have gone to reinforce the number of the earlier sbs. in -ATE[1], q.v.

-ate, *suffix*[3], a verbal formative, used to english L. verbs of the first conjugation, and to form Eng. verbs on other L. words or elements. This use originated in the formation of verbs from the participial adjs. in *-ate* mentioned under -ATE[2].

1. In OE., verbs had been regularly formed on adjectives, as *hwít hwítian*, *wearm wearmian*, *bysiȝ bysȝian*, *drýȝe drýȝan*, etc. With the loss of the inflexions, these verbs became, by the 15th c., identical in form with the adjs., e.g. to *white*, *warm*, *busy*, *dry*, *empty*, *dirty*, etc.

2. In Latin, vbs. were also freely formed on adjectives, as *siccus siccāre*, *clārus clārāre*, *līber līberāre*, *sacer sacrāre*. This prevailed still more extensively in Fr., e.g. *sec sècher*, *clair clairer*, *content contenter*, *confus confuser*, etc. Thence also Eng. received many verbs, which by the 15th c. were identical in form with their adjectives, e.g. to *clear*, *humble*, *manifest*, *confuse*, etc.

3. On these analogies Eng. adjectives formed from L. pa. pples. began generally, in the 16th c., to yield verbs of identical form, e.g. adj. *direct*, vb. *to direct*; adj. *separate*, vb. *to separate*; adj. *aggravate*, vb. *to aggravate*: precisely analogous to adj. *busy*, vb. *to busy*; adj. *content*, vb. *to content*.

4. These verbs, though formed immediately from participial adjectives already in English, answered in form to the pa. pples. of L. verbs of the same meaning. It was thus natural to associate them directly with these L. verbs, and to view them as their regular Eng. representatives.

5. This once done, it became the recognized method of englishing a Latin verb, to take the ppl. stem of the L. as the present stem of the Eng.; so that Eng. verbs were now formed on L. pa. pples. by mere analogy, and without the intervention of a participial adjective. In accordance with this, *fascinate*, *concatenate*, *asseverate*, *venerate*, and hundreds of others, have been formed directly on the participial stems of L. *fascināre*, *concatēnāre*, *assevērāre*, *venerāri*, etc., without having been preceded by a cognate adjective. In the case of many words introduced in the 16th c., evidence is wanting to show whether the vb. was preceded by, or contemporaneous with, the ppl. adj. in *-ate*.

6. These Eng. vbs. in *-ate* correspond generally to Fr. vbs. in *-er* (:—L. *-āre*), as Eng. *separate*, *create*, F. *séparer*, *créer*: this in its turn gave an analogy for the formation of Eng. verbs from French; as F. *isoler* (ad. It. *isolare*:—L. *insulāre*), Eng. *isolate*; F. *féliciter*, Eng. *felicitate*.

7. Latin vbs. in *-āre* might, analogically, have been formed on many words, on which they were not actually formed; wherever such a vb. might have existed, a F. vb. in *-er*, and an Eng. vb. in *-ate*, are liable to be formed. Thus *nōbilitas* gave in L. *nōbilitāre*, the Eng. representative of which is *nobilitate*; *fēlīcitas*, which might have given *fēlīcitāre*, has given F. *féliciter* and Eng. *felicitate*; and *capācitas*, which might have given L. *capācitāre* and F. *capaciter*, has actually given Eng. *capacitate*. Hence numerous modern verbs, as *differentiate*, *substantiate*, *vaccinate*; including many formed on modern or foreign words, as *adipocerate*, *assassinate*, *camphorate*, *methylate*.

(It is possible that the analogy of native verbs in *-t*, with the pa. pple. identical in form with the infinitive, as *set*, *hit*, *put*, *cut*, contributed also to the establishment of verbs like *direct*, *separat(e*, identical with their pa. pples.)

-ate, *suffix*[4], in *Chem.*: see -ATE[1] 1 c.

atebrin ('ætɪbrɪn). Also (chiefly U.S.) **atabrine**. (Both are proprietary terms.) [ad. -ATE[1] 1 c + BRIN(E.] A synthetic antimalarial drug, quinacrine dihydrochloride; also called MEPACRINE.

The word is recorded from 1913 but was not applied to the anti-malarial drug discovered by the German chemists H. Mauss and F. Mietzsch in 1930 (when it was known by the laboratory name of 'Erion') until 1932. See 1933 *Klinische Wochenschrift* 19 Aug., 1276–8.

[**1913** *Trade Marks Jrnl.* 12 Mar. 390 *Atebrin.* Chemical Substances Prepared for Use in Medicine and Pharmacy.. The Bayer Comp., Limited, Manchester.] **1932** *Lancet* 16 Apr. 826/1 Atebrin, originally called erion, has been produced recently by the makers of plasmoquine. **1933** *Discovery* Apr. 118/1 Atebrin, made by the chemists Mietzsch and Mauss..in some experiments..has been more successful than quinine in curing and preventing relapses [of malaria]. **1935** F. STARK *Let.* 17 Mar. in *Coast of Incense* (1953) i. 91 Decided it must be malaria—took masses of atebrin. **1945** *Times* 1 Sept. 4/3 The sick had few medical supplies and no quinine or atebrin. **1948** *Chem. Abstr.* *1937–46* Index 4073/1 Atabrine. **1957** *New Yorker* 29 June 75/1 The only malaria suppressive available for the Buna campaign was quinine; even atabrine, itself now an outmoded weapon against the disease, was not on hand. **1961** J. HELLER *Catch-22* (1962) xxxviii. 391 I'm sorry about making such a fuss about those Atabrine tablets on the way over. If you want to catch malaria, I guess it's your business, isn't it?

atechnic (ə'tɛknɪk), *a.* and *sb. rare.* [f. A- *pref.* 14 + TECHNIC; cf. Gr. ἄτεχνος, f. ἀ priv. + τέχνη skill, art.] **A.** *adj.* Not having technical knowledge. **B.** *sb.* (*sc.* person.)

1869 HAMERTON in *Fortn. Rev.* 1 May 579 An atechnic, a man not technically instructed. **1876** —— *Etching & E.* 399 Difficult to convey to the atechnic reader.

a'techny. ? *Obs.* [ad. Gr. ἀτεχνία; see prec. Cf. mod.F. *atechnie.*] Ignorance of art, unskilfulness.

1731 in BAILEY.

†**a'tee,** *v. Obs.* For forms see TEE *v.* [OE. *ateón*, f. A- *pref.* 1 + *teón* to draw = OS. *atiohan*, OHG. *arziohan*, Ger. *erziehen*, Goth. *ustiuhan*.]

1. *trans.* and *intr.* To drag or draw away, to withdraw.

Beowulf 1537 Siðþæt se hearm-scaða tó Heorute atéah. *c***885** K. ÆLFRED *Bæda* (Sweet *Reader* 49) Ðæt hé menn atuȝe from sinna lufan. *c***1200** *Trin. Coll. Hom.* 199 Þanne we ateð, þat þe iuele fondeð us.

2. *trans.* To handle, treat; to maltreat.

*c***1000** *Ags. Gosp.* Matt. xxvii. 7 Hu hiȝ sceoldon þæs Hælendes wurð ateon. *c***1200** *Trin. Coll. Hom.* 205 His holi lichame was..for ure gulten reuliche atoȝen. **1205** LAY. 12096 Þat weoren æi wimman Swa wræcchelichen atoȝene [**1250** a-towen].

ateign, atein, obsolete forms of ATTAIN.

ateil, variant of ATTEAL, *Obs.*

‖**ateknia** (ə'tɛknɪə). *Med.* [mod.L., a Gr. ἀτεκνία, f. ἀ priv. + τέκνον child.] Childlessness, barrenness.

1874 [see AGALACTIA].

†**'atel,** *a. Obs.* [OE. *atol*, *atul*, *atel*, cogn. w. ON. *atall* fierce, dire.] Terrible, hideous, foul.

a **1000** *Beowulf* 1700 Atol yða ȝeswing. *c***1200** ORMIN 13678 He..warrþ till atell defell þær. *c***1230** *Wohunge* in *Cott. Hom.* 275 Þa harde atele hurtes.

atelectasis (ætɪ'lɛktəsɪs). *Path.* [mod.L., f. Gr. ἀτελής imperfect (f. ἀ priv. + τέλος completion) + ἔκτασις extension.] Imperfect dilatation, *esp.* of the lungs of newly-born children.

1859 TODD *Cycl. Anat. & Phys.* V. 263/1 Atelectasis of that portion of the lung. **1877** ROBERTS *Handbk. Med.* I. 406 Atelectasis strictly refers only to lungs which are more or less in their fœtal condition.

atelectatic (ˌætɪlɛk'tætɪk), *a. Path.* [f. ATELECTASIS.] Characterized by atelectasis. Also **ate'lectic** *a.*

1875 GAMGEE tr. *Hermann's Human Physiol.* 159 The lungs left to themselves contain no air: they are *atalectic* [sic], like the lungs of the fœtus before it has 'breathed'. **1880** FLINT *Princ. Med.* (ed. 5) 187 Occlusion of the bronchi immediately connected with the atelectatic spots can be demonstrated.

ateleiosis, ateliosis (ətɛlɪ'əʊsɪs, ətɛlaɪ-, ətiːl-). [f. A- 14 + TELEIOSIS.] Dwarfism; defective or arrested development. Hence **atelei'otic, -li'otic** *a.* Also as *sb.*, a person suffering from ateleiosis.

1902 HASTINGS GILFORD in *Medico-Chirurg. Trans.* LXXXV. 306 This delay of growth and development is so evidently the main feature, that I have suggested that the disease should receive a name which emphasizes this fact. I have proposed that it should receive the name of Ateleiosis. *Ibid.* 345 It is probable that ateleiotic dwarfs of the second class may be distinguished from all other dwarfs by their physiognomy alone. **1910** *Clinical Jrnl.* 7 Dec. 140/1 A sexual ateleiotic who begat a family of children who, except one who was an asexual ateleiotic, were normal. **1913** *Proc. R. Soc. Med.* VI. I. Clin. 197 (*title*) Ateleiosis in a Man, aged 45. **1932** J. S. HUXLEY *Probl. Rel. Growth* iv. 131 In ateliotic dwarfs, the proportions of the limbs to the trunk and of the limb-segments to each other are not affected.

atelene ('ætɪliːn), *a. Crystallog.* [f. Gr. ἀτελ-ής (see ATELECTASIS).] Imperfect; wanting regular forms in the genus.

1859 in WORCESTER.

†**'atelich,** *a. Obs.* Forms: 1 atolíc, atelíc, 2–3 (e)atelich, 3 etilich, attelich. Compared **-luker, -lukest**. [OE. *atol-*, *atelíc*, f. *atol*, ATEL + *-líc*: see -LY[1].] = ATEL.

*c***1175** *Lamb. Hom.* 41 Eateliche to bihaldene. *c***1220** *Hali Meid.* 41 Makede of heh engel eatelukest deouel. *c***1275** MAPES *Body & Soul* 343 The bodi ther hit lay on bere, An atelich thing.

†**'ateliche,** *adv. Obs.* [f. as prec.: see -LY[2].] Frightfully, horribly.

*c***1275** *Death* in *O.E. Misc.* 180 So me wule sathanas ful ateliche brede.

‖**atelier** ('atəˌlje). [F. *atelier*, cogn. with Pr. *astelier*, f. *astelle* small plank: see ASTEL. Cf. Sp. *astillero* 'a docke to build ships on' (Minsheu 1623), f. *astilla* 'rafter, lath, chip.'] A workshop; an artist's or sculptor's studio.

1840 THACKERAY *Paris Sk. Bk.* (1872) 33 He [the artist] arrives at his 'atelier.' **1882** *Chamb. Jrnl.* 82 The great atelier where wheel and lathe were humming.

†**a'tell,** *v. Obs.* [OE. *atęllan*, f. A- *pref.* 1 + *tęllan* to TELL; cogn. w. OHG. *arzellan*, Ger. *erzählen*.] *trans.* To reckon up, count up.

*c***885** K. ÆLFRED *Boeth.* viii, Gif ðú nú atellan wilt ealle ðá blíþnessa. *c***1200** *Trin. Coll. Hom.* 113 And ne mai þeroffe be stille, ne mid worde hem atellen. **1297** R. GLOUC. 171 And atel al her god.

Atellan (ə'tɛlən), *a.* and *sb.* Also **Att-**. [ad. L. *Atellānus*, f. *Atella*, a town in Campania.] **A.** *adj.* Of or pertaining to Atella, which was famous for its popular satirical and, in later times, licentious farces; *hence*, farcical, ribald.

1600 P. HOLLAND tr. *Livy* VII. 251 The Actours in the Atellane interludes. **1647** R. STAPYLTON *Juvenal* 106 Of whom some Attelan or ridiculous jeering rimes were made. *c***1710** SHAFTESB. *Charac.* (1749) II. 170 Their Fescennin and Atellan way of Wit was in early days prohibited. **1938** R. GRAVES *Coll. Poems* 166 And what Atellan orgies of the soul Were celebrated then among the rocks They testify themselves in books That rouse Atellan laughter.

B. *sb.* A dramatic composition of this kind.

1621 BURTON *Anat. Mel.* III. i. I. i. 257 Many old poets.. did write Fescennines, Attellanes, and lascivious songs. **1875** A. W. WARD *Hist. Dram. Lit.* I. i. 10 The ribald jests of Atellanes and mimes.

Also †**Ate'llanican** *a.* [L. *Atellānicus*], = ATELLAN.

1607 TOPSELL *Four-f. Beasts* 183 Tiberius Cæsar..was called 'Hircus vetulus,' in the Atellanican comœdie.

atelo- ('ætɪləʊ), comb. form of Gr. ἀτελής imperfect, f. ἀ priv. + τέλος end, completion; used in many mod.L. terms of physiology, indicating some structural imperfection, as **atelo'glossia**, imperfect development or malformation of the tongue; **-'gnathia**, of the jaws; **-my'elia**, of the spinal marrow; **-'stomia**, of the mouth.

‖**a tempo** (a 'tɛmpəʊ). *Mus.* [It., lit. 'in time'.] A direction to perform a passage, etc., in the tempo indicated, as ***a tempo rubato***, ***giusto***, etc. Also, a direction to return to the previous tempo.

1740 GRASSINEAU *Mus. Dict.* 6 *Atempo giusto*, signifies to sing or play in an equal, true and just time. **1834** *Penny Cycl.* II. 549/2 *A tempo*, in music..signifies, that after any change in motion, by retardation or acceleration, the original movement is to be restored. **1886** R. DUNSTAN *Man. Mus.* III. 70 Terms of Pace, or Speed..*A tempo*, in strict time (used after *Accel.*, *Rall.*, or *Rit.*).

a-temporal (ə'tɛmpərəl), *a.* [f. A- *pref.* 14 + TEMPORAL.] Free from limits of time, timeless.
1870 D. SIMON *Dorner's Pers. Christ* II. II. 273 Humanity is taken up into this..a-temporal sphere.

atempre, atemper, etc., obs. ff. ATTEMPER, etc.

Aten ('ɑːtən). Also **Aton.** [ad. Egyptian *ìtn.*] One of the names of the sun in ancient Egypt; the name by which the sun or solar disc was worshipped particularly during the reign of Amenophis IV (Akhnaten) in the 14th century B.C. Hence **'Atenism, 'Atonism**, worship of the Aten.
[**1841** G. WILKINSON *Manners & Customs Anc. Egyptians* ser. II. I. xiii. 297 The name Atin-re cannot fail to call to mind Attin, or Atys, the Phrygian Sun.] **1877** *Encycl. Brit.* VII. 738/1 Amenophis IV..introduced a new religion, the worship of Aten, the solar disk. **1906** J. H. BREASTED *Hist. Egypt* xviii. 360 Already under Amen-hotep III an old name for the material sun, 'Aton', had come into..use, where the name of the sun-god might have been expected... Under the name of Aton, then, Amen-hotep IV introduced the worship of the supreme god. **1925** J. W. JACK *Date of Exodus* i. 20 There is..no connection between the Atenism of that king [*sc.* Akhnaten] and the religion of Israel. **1933** *Times Lit. Suppl.* 22 June 419/2 The period of the Aten heresy.. which may be said to cover a little more than half-a-century down to 1346 B.C. **1935** W. EMPSON *Poems* 12 Stand, wolf-chased Phoebus..Aton of maggots of reflected girder. **1939** A. TOYNBEE *Study Hist.* VI. 328 (*heading*) Atonism. **1961** A. GARDINER *Egypt of Pharaohs* ix. 222 A curious addition states that the Mnevis-bull of Hēliopolis should likewise be buried in the Aten's city, another sign how dependent the new Atenism was upon one of the oldest of Egypt's religious cults.

†**a'tend**, *v. Obs.* Also 3-4 **attend**, 4 **atent.** [late OE. *atęndan*, f. A- *pref.* 1 or 4 + *tęndan* to TIND; cf. earlier OE. *ontęndan.*]
1. *trans.* To set on fire, kindle.
[**994** *O.E. Chron.* (Laud), Hi mid fyre ontendan woldon.] **1006** *Ibid.* Hi..atendon heora beacna. *c* **1200** *Trin. Coll. Hom.* 107 Leomene fader..for þan þe he sunne atend. *c* **1380** *Sir Ferumb.* 2413 A candlee he attendeþ. *c* **1400** *Beryn* 2727 A stoon, that is so hote of kynde That what thing com forby, anoon it woll a tend.
b. *fig.*
c **1175** *Lamb. Hom.* 95 Heortan þet calde weren..beon atende to þan heofenliche biboden. *a* **1250** *Passion Our Lord* 661 *O.E. Misc.* 56 Hi weren of þe holy goste attende.
2. *intr.* To take fire.
1398 TREVISA *Barth. De P.R.* XVII. iv, Þis tre 'Abies' atenteþ ful sone, and brenneþ with lyȝte leye.

†**a'tene**, *v. Obs.* [f. A- *pref.* 1 + TEEN, OE. *tíenan, týnan*, to vex.] To irritate, vex, annoy.
c **1320** *Sir Beves* 2601 The dragoun was atened stronge That o man him scholde stonde so longe. *c* **1380** *Sir Ferumb.* 114 He was atened of his envy. *a* **1400** *Chron. Eng.* 61 in Ritson *M.R.* II. 272 The kyng wes ateoned stronge That Corineus astod so long.

atenkt, obs. form of ATTAINT *ppl. a.*

atent, variant of ATEND and ATTENT, *Obs.*

A tent. *U.S.* [f. the letter A, from its shape.] A tent with sides sloping downwards from a ridge pole.
1863 GRAY & ROPES *War Lett.* (1927) 187 Beside them was a lot of negro laborers (not even soldiers) in brand new A tents. **1888** *Century Mag.* Jan. 447/2 Three wall tents.. and twice as many 'A' or 'wedge' or common tents. **1904** ELIZ. ROBINS *Magnetic North* xvi. 284 Down in the desolate hollow a ragged A tent sagged away from the prevailing wind. **1933** CHELEY *Camping Out* 432 An 'A' tent is almost as easy to pitch, especially if it is hung on a ridge rope tied between two trees.

ater-: see ATTER-.

Aterian (ə'tɪərɪən), *a.* [ad. F. *atérien* (M. Reygasse 1922, in *Rec. de Notices & Mém. Soc. Arch. Constantine* LIII. 171), f. Bir el *Ater* in Algeria + -IAN.] Of or pertaining to a form of Mousterian culture found in northern Africa. Also *ellipt.* as *sb.*
1928 V. G. CHILDE *Most Ancient East* ii. 28 This specialized Mousterian found from Morocco to Egypt is designated Atérian. **1931** *Man* XXXI. 83 (*caption*) A specialized Mousterian industry with 'Aterian' affinities. **1941** F. R. WULSIN *Prehist. Archæol. N.W. Afr.* iv. 58 This site shows that the Aterian not only grew out of the archaic Mousterian, but that it followed the archaic Mousterian very closely, with no appreciable time interval between. **1946** G. CATON-THOMPSON in *Jrnl. R. Anthrop. Inst.* LXXVI. 88/2 The Aterian industry, which appears to be centred in North-West Africa, has been described as a Mousterian with the addition of the tanged point. This is an understatement. It habitually includes other artifacts equally unfamiliar or rare in the Mousterian.

‖**à terre** (a tɛr), *adv.* and *adj. phr.* [Fr.] On the ground; *spec.* in *Ballet.* Also *fig.* (cf. TERRE-À-TERRE).
1922 BEAUMONT & IDZIKOWSKI *Man. Class. Theatr. Dancing* 19 When the entire base of the foot touches the ground, the foot is said to be *à terre.* If we speak of..the *third* position, etc. it is understood that the position is *à terre*, that is, with both feet *flat on the ground.* **1926** D. H. LAWRENCE *Plumed Serp.* ix. 149 Without aim or purpose, they lived absolutely *à terre*, down on the dark, volcanic earth. **1951** *Ballet Ann.* V. 138/2 One dancer indeed is so indifferent that while the position demands that the *corps de ballet* should be on *pointe*, she is firmly *à terre.* **1961** *Times* 13 Apr. 16/7 She has a lightness and effortless purity, à terre and in elevation.

Atestine (ə'tɛstɪn, -aɪn), *a.* and *sb.* [ad. L. *Atestīnus* of Ateste + -INE[1].] **A.** *adj.* Of or pertaining to the ancient city of Ateste in north-eastern Italy (now Este); *spec.* designating the pre-Roman culture of Ateste. **B.** *sb.* An inhabitant of Ateste.
1924 D. RANDALL-MACIVER *Villanovans & Early Etruscans* ii. 4 Immediately north of the Po were the *Atestines*... To avoid race-names we have chosen this word in preference to 'Euganean'. **1931** *Antiquity* V. 386 In the later tombs we have figured bronzes of Atestine style admittedly of early 5th century age. **1957** *Encycl. Brit.* VIII. 733/2 The close cousinship of the Bolognese Villanovans and the Atestines is proved by the complete identity not only of the burial rite, cremation, but of the forms and details of their graves. *Ibid.* 734/1 The third period, especially the first half of the 5th century B.C., marks the zenith of Atestine art.

†**a'tew**, *v. Obs.* Forms: 1 **ætéawan, ætéowan, ætíewan, ætýwan,** (**ædeawan, odeawan, oðíewan,**) 2 **atywen, -ewen, -eawen, -awen.** [f. AT- *pref.*[1] + *éawan* (*íewan*, etc.) to show; cogn. w. Goth. *ataugjan*, f. *at* at, to + *augjan* f. *augo* in OE. *éage* eye; *ætíewan*, with umlaut, was the regular form phonetically.]
1. *trans.* (and with obj. clause) To show.
a **1000** *Cædmon's Gen.* (Gr.) 540 Þu oðíewest. *c* **1000** *Ags. Gosp.* Matt. xvi. 1 Þæt he him sum tacen of heofone ætywde [*Lindisf.* ædeawde, *Hatton* æteawde]. **1154** *O.E. Chron.* an. 1137 §7 Ure Dryhten atywede ðæt he was hali martir. *c* **1175** *Cott. Hom.* 225 Þanne bið atáwed min rén boȝe.
2. *intr.* (for *refl.*) To show oneself, appear.
a **1000** *Elene* (Gr.) 163 His béacen..þe me swá léoht oðýwde. *c* **1000** *Ags. Gosp.* Matt. ii. 13 Þá ætýwde Drihtnes engel Iosepe [*Lindisf.* ætdeaude, *Rushw.* æteawde]. *c* **1160** *Hatton G.* ibid., Þa atewede Drihtnes engel Iosepe.

a'teynt, *a. Obs.* [See ATTAINT. Perhaps in this sense to be referred to OF. *éteint*, earlier *esteint* 'stifled' (by heat, etc.):—L. *extinctus*: see EXTINCT.] Exhausted, overpowered.
c **1325** *Cœur de L.* 6131 In the hete they wer almost ateynt. *c* **1380** *Sir Ferumb.* 3612 Ys sted wax al ateynte.

†**at'fall**, *v. Obs.* Also 3 **etf-**. [OE. *ætfeallan*, f. AT- *pref.*[2] + *feallan* to FALL; cogn. w. OS. *antfallan*, OHG. *intfallan*, G. *entfallen*, Du. *ontvallen.* Cf. OE. *oðfeallan.*] *intr.* To fall away; to fall down, drop (with *dat.* = from).
a **1000** *Ord. Dunsetas* §5 (Bosw.) Healf wér ðǽr ætfealþ. **1205** LAY. 4237 Here tir wes at-fallen. *c* **1230** *Ancr. R.* 342 Auh me is..moni crume etfallen. *c* **1250** *Serm.* in *O.E. Misc.* 187 To deþe he ȝef him for us alle, þo we weren so stronge at-falle.

†**at'fare**, *v. Obs.* [f. AT- *pref.*[2] + FARE, OE. *faran*; cf. AFARE, and OE. *oðfaran*; cogn. w. G. *entfahren*, OHG. *infaran*, Du. *ontvaren.*] To go away, escape (with *dat.* = from).
a **1000** *Cædmon's Exod.* (Gr.) 64 Siððan hi féondum oðfaren hæfdon. **1205** LAY. 27072 Þa Romanisce men þe þer at-faren mihten.

†**at'flee**, *v. Obs.* Also 3 **etf-**; for inflexions see FLEE. [OE. *ætfléon*, f. AT- *pref.*[2] + *fléon* (= *fléohan*) to FLEE; cogn. w. G. *entfliehen*, OHG. *intfliohan*, Goth. *unpaþliuhan.*] *intr.* To flee away (with *dat.* = from).
c **1000** ÆLFRIC *Job* (Bosw.) Ic ána ætfléah. *c* **1200** ORMIN 19639 Ec þe Laferrd Crist attflæh Forr þe to gifenn bisne Þatt tu mihht flen. *c* **1230** *Ancr. R.* 172 His þrelles etfluwen him. *a* **1250** *Owl & Night.* 37 Min heorte atflith. **1250** LAY. 27072 Þe Romanisse me[n] þat at-flowen were.

†**at'fong**, *v. Obs.* For forms see AFONG *v.* [OE. *ætfón*, f. AT- *pref.*[2] + *fón* (pa. t. *feng*) to seize: see FONG, FANG. Cf. G. *entfangen*, MHG. *entpfahen.*] To seize upon.
a **1000** *Laws of Hlothere & Eadric* §7 (Bosw.) Gif se ágend hit eft ætfó. **1205** LAY. 15359 Þa cnihtes hit atfengen and ane while heo heolden.

†**at'fore**, *prep. Obs.* Forms: 1 **ætforan,** 1-3 **-en,** 2-3 **etforan, -en,** 3 **atforen, etfor, at vore,** 3-4 **atfore.** [OE. *ætforan*, f. *æt*, AT *prep.* + *foran* in front, properly dative of *for*: see AFORE.]
1. In front of, before.
c **1000** *Ags. Gosp.* John xix. 13 And sæt æt-foran ðam dómsetle. *c* **1175** *Lamb. Hom.* 41 Heȝe treon eisliche beor-ninde etforen helle ȝete. **1297** R. GLOUC. 358 Hys baner, Þat men at vore hym bere.
2. In the presence of, in the sight of, before.
c **1175** *Cott. Hom.* 225 Rich[t] wis et-foran gode. *Ibid.* 229 Et-for har alra ȝesychðe. **1258** *Eng. Procl. Hen. III.* §8 Ætforen ure isworene redesmen. *c* **1305** *St. Lucy* 79 in *E.E.P.* (1862) 103 Sire Iustise atfore þe.
3. Before in time or order. *rare.*
c **1230** *Ancr. R.* 226 Þeo þet beoð her etforen iseid.

†**at'go**, *v. Obs.* [OE. *ætgán, -gangan, -gǫngan*, f. AT- *pref.*[1], [2] + *gán*, *gangan* to GO.]
1. [f. AT- *pref.*[1]] *intr.* To go to, approach, L. *accēdere.* Only in OE.
a **1000** *Azarius* (Gr.) 183 Hét hie..néar ætgongan.
2. [f. AT- *pref.*[2] Cf. G. *entgehen*, OHG. *intkân*, Du. *ontgaan.*] *intr.* (with *dat.* = from) To go away, pass away, depart.
c **1175** *Lamb. Hom.* 35 Mon aldeð and his daȝes him at-gað. *c* **1300** in Wright *Lyric P.* xxxv. 74 Whet may I sugge, bote wolawo! When mi lif is me at-go?

ath, athe, obsolete forms of OATH.

a þa = 'until': see ATHAT and A *prep.*[3]

Athabascan, var. ATHAPASCAN.

athalamous (ə'θæləməs), *a. Bot.* [f. Gr. ἀ priv. + θάλαμ-ος bed + -OUS.] Of lichens: Having no conceptacles or spore-shields on the thallus.
1847 in CRAIG.

athamantin (æθə'mæntɪn). *Chem.* [see -IN.] A crystalline substance, $C_{24}H_{30}O_7$, with a rancid soapy odour and bitter taste, procured from the roots and seeds of *Athamanta oreoselinum.*
1863 in WATTS *Dict. Chem.* I. 430.

athamaunte, obsolete form of ADAMANT.

athambia (ə'θæmbɪə). *rare*[−1]. [a. Gr. ἀθαμβία imperturbability.] Imperturbability.
1956 S. BECKETT *Godot* I. 42 From the heights of divine apathia divine athambia divine aphasia loves us.

Athanasian (æθə'neɪʃ(ɪ)ən), *a.* and *sb.* [f. *Athanasius*, name of the famous archbishop of Alexandria in the reign of the emperor Constantine: see -AN.] **A.** *adj.* Of or pertaining to Athanasius, *esp.* in ***Athanasian Creed***, that beginning with the words '*Quicunque vult*,' which has been attributed to his authorship.
1781 GIBBON. *Decl. & F.* III. xxxvii. 537 He [*sc.* Gundamund] recalled the bishops, and restored the freedom of Athanasian worship. **1823** C. LAMB (Let. of Elia to R. Southey) in *London Mag.* VIII. 402/1 T.N.T., a little tainted with Socinianism..and ——, a sturdy old Athanasian. **1850** NEWMAN *Difficulties Anglicans* i. 23 The same popular voice..may..dispense with the Athanasian Creed altogether. *Ibid.* i. 24 It will be obvious to allege that, ..provided we hold fast this 'scriptural fact', it matters not whether we be Athanasians, Sabellians, Tritheists, or Socinians.
B. *sb.* An adherent of the doctrines of Athanasius. **Atha'nasianism**, the principles or doctrines of the Athanasian Creed. **Atha'nasianist**, an adherent of this creed.
1586 T. ROGERS 39 *Art.* (1854) 92 The Nicene, Athanasian, and Apostolical Creeds. **1724** WATERLAND *Athan. Creed* (T.) To call one side Athanasians, and the other side Arians. **1777** PRIESTLEY *Matt. & Spir.* I. Pref. 21 Athanasianism..will..appear to have been merely Oriental philosophy in its origin. **1873** *Spectator* 8 Feb. 171/2 What Athanasianists regard as the Gospel of Christ.

athanasy (ə'θænəsɪ). [ad. L. *athanasia*, a. Gr. ἀθανασία; f. ἀ priv. + θάνατος death.] Deathlessness, immortality.
[**1829** SOUTHEY *Sir T. More* II. 395 My verses..had none of the *athanasia* in their composition.] **1870** LOWELL *Study Wind.* 346 Is not a scholiastic athanasy better than none?

athanor ('æθənɔː(r)). *Alch.* Also **acanor**; and in 5 **athenor**, 7 **athanar.** [ad. Arab. *attannūr*, i.e. *at* = *al* the, *tannūr* furnace, according to Dozy, a. Heb. or Aramaic *tannūr*, f. root *nūr* fire. Also in Fr. *athanor*, Sp. *atanor*, pipe of a fountain.] A digesting furnace used by the alchemists, in which a constant heat was maintained by means of a tower which provided a self-feeding supply of charcoal. Also *fig.*
1471 RIPLEY *Comp. Alch.* (Ashm. 1652) v. 149 Thy Fornace..Whych wyse men do call Athenor. **1610** B. JONSON *Alch.* II. iii, In the lent heat of Athanor. **1651** BIGGS *New Disp.* §141 They are not therefore digested in the Athanor of our Œconomy. **1752** JOHNSON *Rambl.* No. 199 ¶3, I have sat whole weeks without sleep by the side of an athanor, to watch the moment of projection. **1863** in WATTS *Dict. Chem.* I. 430.

Athapascan, -paskan (æθə'pæskən), *a.* and *sb.* Also **-bascan, -baskan,** †**-pasca.** [f. Cree *Athapaskaw*, lit. 'grass or reeds here and there' (Webster) + -AN.] **A.** *adj.* Of or pertaining to a widely spread people of North American Indians or their language.
[**1776** *Cumberland House Jrnl.* 27 June (Hudson Bay Rec. Soc., 1951) I. 60 He says that he supposed there were an hundred Canoes of them, the chiefest part A 'Thopuskow Indians.] **1846** J. SCOULER in *Edin. New Philos. Jrnl.* XLI. 171 An inspection of the vocabularies of the languages spoken on the north-west coast, will aid us in defining the limits of the Athabascan family. **1877** L. H. MORGAN *Ancient Soc.* I. i. 10 It leaves in the Upper Status of Savagery the Athapascan tribes of the Hudson's Bay Territory. **1915** R. H. LOWIE in *Amer. Anthrop.* XVII. 239 All the Siouan, or all the Athabaskan, or all the Southwestern systems. **1933** BLOOMFIELD *Language* iv. 72 The Athabascan family covers all but the coastal fringe of northwestern Canada [etc.].
B. *sb.* **1.** A member of this people.
1846 J. SCOULER in *Edin. New Philos. Jrnl.* XLI. 170 To the west of the Rocky Mountains, the Athabascans, under the names of Tacullies or Carriers, occupy the country called New Caledonia. **1851** R. G. LATHAM *Ethnol. Brit. Colonies* vi. 257 To separate, not only Caribs from

Algonkins, or Peruvians from Athabascans, but Peruvians from Caribs [etc.]. **1871** L. H. MORGAN *Syst. of Consanguinity* v. 231 The Athapascans depend for subsistence upon fish and game. **1877** *Encycl. Brit.* VI. 448/1 The still more important myth of the north-west Athapascas. **1910** *Ibid.* I. 814/2 The Athapascan covered all north-western Canada with his open and portable birch-bark canoe. **1938** R. H. LOWIE *Hist. Ethnol. Theory* viii. 121 The Canadian Athabaskans are introduced as 'vigorous, but poorly endowed'.

2. The language of this people.

1889 in *Cent. Dict.* (s.v. *Athabaskan*). **1932** A. HUXLEY *Brave New World* vi. 120 Extinct languages, such as Zuñi and Spanish and Athapascan. **1933** *Publ. Mod. Lang. Assoc.* XLVIII. 620 In Athabascan..the idea 'to carry' is expressed by different verbs according to whether the load is light or heavy. **1965** *Canad. Jrnl. Linguistics* Spring 78 Languages of sure affiliation, e.g. Sarcee (Athapaskan).

† **a that**, *adv.* and *prep. Obs.* Also **aþet**. [Worn-down f. OE. *óþ-þæt* = till that. Cf. A *prep.*[3]]

A. *conj. adv.* Until, till.

c **1175** *Lamb. Hom.* 23 Ic wille liggen a þet ic beo ealdre. *c* **1230** *Ancr. R.* 152 Heo hit healden euer ihud, vort tet heo [*v.r.* aðat ha] comen biuoren him.

B. *prep.* Until, till.

c **1175** *Lamb. Hom.* 119 Alle daȝen aþet endunge þissere weorlde. *c* **1230** *Ancr. R.* 134 And wunien uort heo deie [*v.r.* aðet dead] þerinne.

† **'atheal**, *a. Obs.* [f. Gr. ἄθε-ος without God, denying God (f. ἀ priv. + θεός God) + -AL[1]. Cf. F. *athée*] Atheistic.

1612 T. JAMES *Jesuits Downf.* 33 This most vile, Atheall, and heathenish assertion.

† **'athean**, *a. Obs.* [f. as prec. + -AN.] = prec.

1611 BROUGHTON *Require Agr.* 37 Yee teach your children athean traditiones. **1625** GIL *Sacred Philos.* (title-p.) Iewish, Athean, and hereticall Infidelity.

atheism ('eɪθiːɪz(ə)m). Also 6 **athisme**. [a. F. *athéisme* (16th c. in Littré), f. Gr. ἄθεος: see ATHEAL and -ISM. Cf. It. *atheismo* and the earlier ATHEONISM.] Disbelief in, or denial of, the existence of a God. *Also*, Disregard of duty to God, godlessness (*practical* atheism).

1587 GOLDING *De Mornay* xx. 310 Athisme, that is to say, vtter godlesnes. **1605** BACON *Adv. Learn.* I. i. §3 A little or superficial knowledge of philosophy may incline the mind of man to atheism. **1711** ADDISON *Spect.* No. 119 ¶5 Hypocrisy in one Age is generally succeeded by Atheism in another. **1859** KINGSLEY *Lett.* (1878) II. 75 Whatever doubt or doctrinal Atheism you and your friends may have, don't fall into moral Atheism.

atheist ('eɪθiːɪst), *sb.* (and *a.*) Also 6 **atheyst**, 6–7 **athist(e**. [a. F. *athéiste* (16th c. in Littré), or It. *atheista*: see prec. and -IST.]

A. *sb.* **1.** One who denies or disbelieves the existence of a God.

[*a* **1568** COVERDALE *Hope of Faithf.* Pref. Wks. II. 139 Eat we and drink we lustily; to-morrow we shall die: which all the epicures protest openly, and the Italian *atheoi*.] **1571** GOLDING *Calvin on Ps.* Ep. Ded. 3 The Atheistes which say ..there is no God. **1604** ROWLANDS *Looke to it* 23 Thou damned Athist..That doest deny his power which did create thee. **1709** SHAFTESB. *Charac.* I. I. §2 (1737) II. 11 To believe nothing of a designing Principle or Mind, nor any Cause, Measure, or Rule of Things, but Chance..is to be a perfect Atheist. **1876** GLADSTONE in *Contemp. Rev.* June 22 By the Atheist I understand the man who not only holds off, like the sceptic, from the affirmative, but who drives himself, or is driven, to the negative assertion in regard to the whole Unseen, or to the existence of God.

2. One who practically denies the existence of a God by disregard of moral obligation to Him; a godless man.

1577 HANMER *Anc. Eccl. Hist.* 63 The opinion which they conceaue of you, to be Atheists, or godlesse men. **1660** STANLEY *Hist. Philos.* 323/2 An Atheist is taken two ways, for him who is an enemy to the Gods, and for him who believeth there are no Gods. **1667** MILTON *P.L.* I. 495 When the Priest Turns Atheist, as did Ely's Sons. **1827** HARE *Guesses* Ser. I. (1873) 27 Practically every man is an atheist, who lives without God in the world.

B. *attrib.* as *adj.* Atheistic, impious.

1667 MILTON *P.L.* VI. 370 The Atheist crew. **1821** LOCKHART *Valerino* II. xi. 316 Borne from its wounded breast an atheist cry Hath pierced the upper and the nether sky.

atheistic (eɪθiː'ɪstɪk), *a.* [f. prec. + -IC.]

1. Of or befitting an atheist; pertaining to or involving atheism.

1634 HABINGTON *Castara* (1870) 78 Who will with silent piety confute Atheisticke Sophistry. **1871** R. H. HUTTON *Ess.* I. 45 A vague, general dread that Science..is atheistic in its tendency.

2. Of the nature of an atheist; denying the existence of a God; godless, impious.

1677 GALE *Crt. Gentiles* III. 179 A wide gate for atheistic blasphemous wits to impute to him the greatest sins. *a* **1711** KEN *Poet. Wks.* (1721) II. 136 The Atheistick Fools who God deny. **1871** TYNDALL *Fragm. Sc.* II. xiv. 368 The moral doctrine taught by this 'atheistic' leader.

athe'istical, *a.* [f. as prec. + -ICAL.]

1. Of or belonging to atheists.

1603 HOLLAND *Plutarch's Mor.* 1315 Beastly cogitations and Athisticall discourses. **1666** EVELYN *Mem.* (1857) II. 19 The public theatres..were abused to an atheistical liberty. **1718** J. CHAMBERLAYNE *Relig. Philos.* (1730) Pref. Let., A great many Atheistical Books. **1830** MACKINTOSH *Eth. Philos.* Wks. 1846 I. 75 The atheistical opinions of Hobbes.

2. = ATHEISTIC 2.

1588 *Marprel. Epist.* (1843) 42 Ignorant and atheistical dolts. **1692** BENTLEY *Boyle Lect.* 6 In the mouths of atheistical men.

athe'istically, *adv.* [f. prec. + -LY[2].] In an atheistical manner; as befits an atheist, impiously; with a leaning towards atheism.

1655 GURNALL *Chr. in Arm.* II. 251 Being by a neighbour excited to thank God for a rich crop of corn..atheistically replied, 'Thank God? nay rather, thank my dung-cart.' **1785** REID *Intell. Powers* VI. vi. 460 No man however atheistically disposed. **1878** E. WHITE *Life in Christ* 296 To conclude..atheistically, that there is no mind in nature.

athe'isticalness. ? *Obs.* [f. as prec. + -NESS.] The quality of being atheistic; godlessness.

1654 HAMMOND *Fundam.* Wks. I. 500 (R.) Lord, purge.. out of all hearts that profaneness and atheisticalness. **1667** H. MORE *Div. Dial.* IV. xv. (1713) 319 By reason of their Ignorance, Atheisticalness and Idolatry.

† **athe'isticness.** *Obs. rare*[−1]. = prec.

1691 BEVERLEY *Mem. Kingd. Christ* 12 The Spirit of Debauchery, Prophaness, and Atheisticness, that is.. abroad.

atheize ('eɪθiːaɪz), *v.* [f. Gr. ἄθε-ος (see ATHEAL) + -IZE.]

1. *intr.* To speak, write, or act as an atheist.

1678 CUDWORTH *Intell. Syst.* 23 Empedocles Atheized in the same manner that Democritus did.

2. *trans.* To render atheistic or godless; to make an atheist of. Hence: **atheized** *ppl. a.*

1678 CUDWORTH *Intell. Syst.* 59 The Atheized and Adulterated Atomology. *a* **1711** KEN *Hymnotheo* Wks. 1721 III. 63 Lewd Company..By impious Talk his Spirit atheize. **1865** GROSART *Palmer's Mem.* Introd. 2 Who..have sought to atheize England's Second Thinker [Bacon].

'atheizer. [f. prec. + -ER[1].] One who atheizes, or renders atheistic.

1678 CUDWORTH *Intell. Syst.* Pref., The First Atheizers of this Ancient Atomick Physiology.

† **'athel**, *sb.*[1] *Obs.* Forms: 1 **æðel-u** *pl.*, 3 **æðele, aðele** *pl.*, ? **athel** *sing.* [OE. *æðel-u, -o*, neuter pl. of **æðel* = OS. *aðali* n., OHG. *adal* n., MHG., mod.G., Du. *adel* 'good family, noble descent, nobility,' ON. *aðal* 'family, race, kind,' f. root **aþ* Aryan *ăt*, not in Gothic. The orig. signification seems to have been 'race, ancestry' as in ON. (cf. the cognate ETHEL, OE. *éðel*, 'ancestral land, patrimony, *patria*'), which was specialized in W.Ger. as 'distinguished race, good family, nobility': cf. specific use of G. *geschlecht*, and of *family* in 'county families.']

Ancestry, origin; *spec.* noble ancestry, nobility; *hence*, honour, dignity, might, power.

Beowulf 790 He eower æðelu can. *c* **885** K. ÆLFRED *Boeth.* XXX. ii, His æðelo bioþ má on þam mode, ðonne on þam flæsce. **1205** LAY. 2938 þa ældede þe king & wakede an aðelan [**1250** failede his mihte]. —— 10629 He leoseden heore aðele. —— 9263 þe eorl Aruiragus mid æðele help his broðer. —— 12915 His aðelen weore store. *c* **1300** in Wright *Lyric P.* viii. 33 In uch an hyrd thyn athel ys hyht.

athel, var. ETHEL, *Obs.*, patrimony.

† **'athel**, *a.* and *sb.*[2] *Obs.* Forms: 1–2 **æðele**, 1–3 **eðele**, 3 **æðel**, 3–4 **aþel(l**, 3–5 **aðel(e**, 5 **athil**, 4–5 **haþel(le**, 5 **hathill**, 6 **hatell**. [Common Teut.: OE. *æðele*, *ęðele*, = OS. *eðili*, OFris. *ethel*, *edel*, OHG. *edili*, MHG. *edele*, mod.G., Du. *edel*, OTeut. **aþali-s*, of good family, f. **aþal* race, family: see prec. Cf. L. *generōsus* f. *genus*.]

A. *adj.*

1. Of persons: Noble by birth or character, eminent, illustrious, renowned.

a **1000** *Cædmon's Gen.* (Gr.) 1182 Se eorl wæs æðele. *c* **1200** ORMIN 612 Nemmnedd..Affterr summ aþell mann. *c* **1250** *Owl & Night.* 632 Lutle children..Bothe chorles an ek athele. *c* **1325** *E.E. Allit. P.* B. 761 'Now aþel lorde,' quoth Abraham. *c* **1440** *Morte Arth.* 988 One of þe hathelest of Arthur knyghtez. *c* **1450** *Holland's Houlate* III. 4 (JAM.) The athil Emprour annon nycht him neir.

2. Of things, actions, etc.: Noble, excellent, splendid, fine, pleasant, 'grand.'

a **1000** *Cædmon's Gen.* (Gr.) 1533 Æðelum stencum. —— *Exod.* 227 Æðelan cynnes. **1205** LAY. 10031 þat lond wes swiðe æðele. *c* **1325** *E.E. Allit. P.* B. 1276 þat condelestik.. of aþel golde. *c* **1340** *Gaw. & Gr. Knt.* 1654 Aþel songez.

3. *Comb.*, as **athelmod**, noble-minded.

1205 LAY. 23255 Walwæin wes ful aðelmod.

B. *sb.*[2] One who is noble; a lord, chief.

1205 LAY. 10092 Coil þe king, þe wes Bruttene aðel. *c* **1340** *Gaw. & Gr. Knt.* 2056 þe haþel..þat haldez þe heuen vpon hyȝe. *c* **1450** *Gaw. & Gologras* III. 20 (JAM.) Thair wes na hathill sa heich, be half ane fute hicht. **1515** *Scot. Field* 330 in *Chetham Misc.*, That every hatell should him hie, in hast ..To Bolton.

† **'athel(e**, *v. Obs.* [In 13th c. *aðelien*, f. ATHEL *a.*; cf. OE. *ȝe-aðelian*, OHG. *ant adaljan*, MHG. *edelen*.] To honour, dignify.

1205 LAY. 2815 Alcne godne mon he æðelede. *Ibid.* 6651 Elidur..Mid muchelen ædmeden æðelede his broðer.

† **at-'hele**, *v. Obs. rare*[−1]. In 2–3 **et-hele**. [f. AT- *pref.*[2] + HELE *v.*, OE. *helan*, to conceal.] *trans.* To hide away.

c **1200** *Trin. Coll. Hom.* 63 þe man..þe sume of his sinnes forleteð, and sume et-heleð.

atheling ('æθəlɪŋ). *Obs.* exc. *Hist.* Also 1–3 **æðeling**, 4–8 **adelyng, -ing**, 9 **etheling, ætheling.** [OE. *æðeling*, f. *æðel* noble family + *-ing* belonging to; = OS. *eðiling*, OFris. *etheling*, *edling*, OHG. *adaling*. (In med.L. *adal-*, *adelingus*.)]

A member of a noble family, a prince, lord, baron; in OE. poetry often used in pl. for 'men' (*viri*); in later writers often restricted as a historical term to a prince of the blood royal, or even to the heir apparent to the throne.

a **1000** *Crist* (Gr.) 158 Crist nerȝende! wuldres æðeling! —— *Gen.* (Gr.) 1161 Héht him céosan æðelingas. **1057** *O.E. Chron.* (Laud), On þisum ȝeare com Ædward æðeling Eadmundes sunu cynges hider to lande. **1205** LAY. 5375 Heo axeden aðelinges war leye þa kinges. **1297** R. GLOUC. 354 þe kunde eir, þe ȝonge chyld, Edgar Aþelyng. Wo so were next kyng bykunde, me clupeþ hym Aþelyng. **1387** TREVISA *Higden* Rolls Ser. I. 277 Comounliche he þat comeþ of kynges blood is i-cleped Adelyngus. **1756** NUGENT *Montesquieu's Spir. Laws* XXX. xix. (1758) II. 384 Six hundred sous for the murder of an adeling. **1844** LINGARD *Anglo-S. Ch.* (1858) I. ii. 91 Ethelings, or princes of the blood. **1861** HOOK *Lives Abps.* I. iii. 142 In the Atheling Alchfrid, Wilfrid had a friend. **1867** FREEMAN *Norm. Conq.* (1877) I. 493 The Ætheling was taken to Ely.

athematic (æ-, eɪθɪ'mætɪk), *a.* [f. A- 14 + THEMATIC *a.*] **1.** *Gram.* Of verb-forms: having suffixes attached immediately to the verb-stem without a connecting (thematic) vowel; also used of nouns (see quot. 1959). Hence used of languages which have such verb-forms.

1894 W. M. LINDSAY *Lat. Lang.* viii. 454 In Latin almost every athematic verb becomes thematic in 1 Sg. Pres. Ind. **1959** A. CAMPBELL *O.E. Gram.* xi. 255 Place-names of Celtic origin seem frequently to adopt the forms of the athematic nouns in OE, having gen. sg. in *-e*, otherwise no endings, e.g. a. and d.s. *Cent* Kent.

2. *Mus.* Lacking, or not composed of, deliberate themes.

1935 *Musical Times* Oct. 942/1 The three main forces of the universe..are each symbolised, not by themes—because the music [of Hábas] is athematic—but by the character of the thematic material and the orchestration. **1959** *Listener* 22 Oct. 704/2 The symphony is described by the composer [*sc.* Gerhard] as 'athematic' (the literal antonym of 'thematic'), from which it is obvious that each part, while indispensable to the whole, is meaningless when divorced from its context. **1960** *20th Cent.* Nov. 460 Webern.. adopted Schönberg's serial technique to organize this athematic music.

‖ **Athenæum** (æθɪ'niːəm). Also **-eum**. Mod. pl. **-æums**. [a. L. *Athenæum*, a. Gr. Ἀθήναιον, (the temple) of Ἀθήνη, goddess of wisdom, Minerva.]

1. *Gr. Antiq.* The temple of Athene in ancient Athens, in which professors taught their students, and orators and poets rehearsed their compositions. (Similar institutions, with the same name, were afterwards established at Rome and Lyons.)

1727–51 CHAMBERS *Cycl.* s.v., The Athenæa were built in the form of amphitheatres.

2. In modern times often used as a title for:

a. An association of persons interested in scientific and literary pursuits, meeting for the purpose of mutual improvement; a literary or scientific club.

1807 *Monthly Anthol.* May 226 The Trustees with their associates are made a body corporate by the title of the Proprietors of the Boston Athenæum. **1847** HOWE *Ohio* 390 The atheneum was commenced as a library company. **1864** in WEBSTER. **1882** E. K. GODFREY *Nantucket* 13 The Athenaeum and other literary societies.

b. A building or institution in which books, periodicals, and newspapers are provided for use; a literary club-room, reading-room, library. Esp. the Athenæum Club in London.

1799 (*title*) Laws and Regulations of the Athenæum in Liverpool. **1807** SOUTHEY *Lett. from England* II. xl. 224 The history of their [*sc.* Liverpool's] Athenæum is a striking instance of their spirit:—by this name they call a public library, with a reading-room for the newspapers and other journals. **1822** J. FLINT *Lett. Amer.* 112 The Atheneum, or reading-room, is much frequented. *Mod.* The Manchester Athenæum. **1834** H. C. ROBINSON *Diary* 14 Mar. (1967) 132 When the alarm of the cholera took place two years ago he gravely proposed turning the Athenaeum into a cholera hospital. **1845** *Ainsworth's Mag.* VII. 424 It would almost seem that the Athenæum had a personal quarrel with Mr. Pettigrew. **1887** W. S. GILBERT *Ruddigore* (1899) III. p. 38 Who found Athenæums and local museums. **1936** *N. & Q.* CLXX. 386/1 Thackeray..was more of the Athenaeum type.

c. A periodical devoted to the interests of literature, science, and art, e.g. *The Athenæum*, published in London.

1835 DICKENS *Let.* 11 Jan. (1965) I. 54, I can't get an Athenæum, a Literary Gazette—no not even a penny Magazine. **1848** H. C. ROBINSON *Diary* 5 Aug. (1967) 248 There is in the *Athenaeum* a severe article as respects Talfourd's style.

Athenian (əˈθiːnɪən), *a.* and *sb.* Also 6 **Attenian**. [ad. L. *Athēn-iensis* a. and sb. (whence OE. *Athēniense* sb. pl., the Athenians), f. L. *Athēnæ*, Gr. Ἀθῆναι Athens + -IAN; cf. Gr. Ἀθηναῖος Athenian.] **A.** *adj.* Of or pertaining to Athens, the leading city of ancient Greece, now the capital of Greece. Cf. ATTIC *a.* and *sb.*[1] Also *transf.* and *fig.*

1590 SHAKES. *Mids. N.* I. i. 12 Stirre vp the Athenian youth to merriments. **1673** MILTON *Death of Fair Infant* st. 2, l. 9 in *Poems* 17 Aquilo his charioter By boistrous rape th' Athenian damsel got. **1791** BOSWELL *Johnson* I. 32 For an Athenian blockhead is the worst of all blockheads. *a* **1822** SHELLEY *Homer's Hymn to Minerva* 2 in *Poet. Wks.* (1907) 694 Athenian Pallas! tameless, chaste, and wise. **1840** E. BULWER *Let.* in C. H. Shattuck *Bulwer & Macready* (1958) 157 The Scotch of Macfinch &c had better be looked over by one more learned than I am in that Athenian tongue. **1851** R. W. BROWNE *Hist. Class. Lit.* II. xiv. 121 The Greek orator, or rather..the Athenian orator, for oratory flourished only in Athens, composed..his speech in private, before he delivered it. **1953** D. F. POCOCK tr. *Durkheim's Sociol. & Philos.* ii. 57 The Roman or the Athenian ideals were closely related to the particular organizations of these two cities.

B. *sb.* A native or inhabitant of Athens; also (see quot. 1638) the speech of this people.

[*c* **893** ÆLFRED tr. *Orosius* 78/22 Sona swa Atheniense wiston. *a* **1490** SKELTON tr. *Diod. Siculus* I. 40 The Athenyensis conferme this oppynyon.] **1526** TINDALE *Acts* xvii. 21 All the Attenians an straungers whych were there gave them selves to nothynge els but other to tell or to heare newe tydynges. **1539** *Cranmer's Bible* Acts xvii. 21 All the Athenians & straungers which were there. **1550** T. NICOLLS (*title*) The hystory writtone by Thucidides the Athenyan. **1590** SHAKES. *Mids. N.* IV. ii. 31 If I tell you, I am no true Athenian. **1638** R. BRATHWAIT *Barnabees Jrnl.* sig. B5 To Oxford came I... Each thing ther's the Muses Minion, Queenes College-Horn speakes pure Athenian. **1643** JOHN TAYLOR *Let. sent to London* 13, I would have gone to a fellow that conjures with a paire of sheares and a Sieve, sure that grave Athenian would have told me all. **1788** GIBBON *Decl. & F.* VI. lxii. 255 The Athenians are still distinguished by the subtlety and acuteness of their understandings. **1877** L. H. MORGAN *Ancient Soc.* II. xiv. 349 Bachoven has collected and discussed the evidence of female authority..among the ..Athenians.

athenk-, -yng: see ATHINK, -ING.

atheoˈlogian. ? *Obs.* [f. A- *pref.* 14 + THEOLOGIAN.] One who is no theologian; one destitute of theological knowledge.

1603 HAYWARD *Answ. Doleman* ix. (T.) They of your society [Jesuits]..are the only atheologians, whose heads entertain no other object but the tumult of realms.

atheological (ˌeɪθiːəʊˈlɒdʒɪkəl), *a.* [f. A- *pref.* 14 + THEOLOGICAL.] Opposed to theology. **aˌtheoˈlogically** *adv.*, in opposition to theology.

a **1641** BP. MOUNTAGU *Acts & Mon.* 46 Zwinglius, the father, forger, and fosterer of many atheologicall fancies. **1880** SWINBURNE *Stud. Shaks.* App. (ed. 2) 234 The curt atheological phrase of the Persian Lucretius, 'one thing is certain, and the rest is lies.' *a* **1641** BP. MOUNTAGU *Acts & Mon.* 94 As some atheologically conceive.

atheology (eɪθiːˈɒlədʒɪ). [f. Gr. ἄθεο-ς without God + -λογία discourse.] Opposition to theology.

1678 CUDWORTH *Intell. Syst.* 61 Nothing else but a Philosophical Form of Atheology, a Gigantical and Titanical Attempt to dethrone the Deity. **1878** E. WHITE *Life in Christ* 524 The atheology of the scientific luminaries.

†**ˈatheonism.** *Obs. rare*$^{-1}$. [Formation irregular; perh. after It. *atheo* (cf. *Draco, Draconism*); see quot. 1568 in ATHEIST 1.] = ATHEISM.

c **1534** *Pol. Verg. Eng. Hist.* (1846) I. 165 Godd would not longe suffer this impietie, or rather atheonisme.

atheous (ˈeɪθiːəs), *a.* [f. Gr. ἄθε-ος godless (see ATHEAL) + -OUS.]

†**1.** Atheistic, impious. *Obs.*

1612 BP. HALL *Contempl.* I. 12 It is an ignorant conceit, that enquiry into nature should make men atheous. **1671** MILTON *P.R.* I. 487 Suffers the Hypocrite or atheous Priest To tread his Sacred Courts. **1792** D. LLOYD *Voy. Life* III. 46 In atheous men conscience becomes a scourge.

2. Not dealing with the existence of a God. (Intended to convey a purely privative sense, as distinguished from the negative *atheistic*.)

1880 *19th Cent.* Mar. 503 If I might coin a word, I should say that science was atheous, and therefore could not be atheistic..conversant simply with observed facts and conclusions drawn from them, and in this sense..atheous, or without recognition of God.

ather, obs. form of EITHER and OTHER.

atherine (ˈæθəraɪn). Also 8 **athorine**. [ad. mod.L. *atherīna*, a. Gr. ἀθερίνη a kind of smelt.] Name given to various species of smelt.

[**1753** CHAMBERS *Cycl. Supp.*, *Atherina*..is a small fish of the length and thickness of a finger.] **1770** *Phil. Trans.* LX. Introd. 14 The Gwiniad and Athorine. **1854** BADHAM *Halieut.* 285 The argentina, or Tiber pearl-fish, is strikingly like the atherine or sea smelt.

athermancy (əˈθɜːmənsɪ). *Physics.* [f. Gr. ἀθέρμαντος not heated: see next.] Athermanous quality; the power of stopping radiant heat.

1863 ATKINSON *Ganot's Physics* (1877) §422 Athermancy ..corresponds to opacity for light. **1870** M. WILLIAMS *Fuel of Sun* §111 The quantitative athermancy of flame.

athermanous (əˈθɜːmənəs), *a. Physics.* [f. Gr. ἀ priv. + θερμαν- stem of θερμαίν-ειν to heat (f. θέρμη heat) + -OUS.] Not permeable by radiant heat.

1863 TYNDALL *Heat* iii. 79 An athermanous body which stops the radiation. **1871** B. STEWART *Heat* §206 This substance is..athermanous, that is to say opaque for heat.

athermic (əˈθɜːmɪk), *a.* [ad. F. *athermique*, f. A- 14 + Gr. θέρμη heat + -IC.] **a.** That is not pervious to heat or heat-rays. Cf. ADIATHERMIC *a.* **b.** Without fever or rise of temperature (Dorland 1900). **c.** (See quot. 1909.)

1862 *Catal. Internat. Exhib.* II. XIII. 16 Melloni's apparatus for illustrating the athermic and diathermic character of minerals. **1909** WEBSTER, *Athermic*, heatless; as, an athermic motor.

‖**atheroma** (æθəˈrəʊmə). *Path.* [L., a. Gr. ἀθήρωμα, -ματ-, f. ἀθήρη = ἀθάρη groats, porridge.] **a.** An encysted tumour containing matter resembling oatmeal-gruel or curds. **b.** Fatty degeneration of the arterial coats.

1706 PHILLIPS, *Atheroma*..does not cause Pain, nor change the Colour of the Skin. **1875** WALTON *Dis. Eye* 94 The ophthalmic artery was found to have undergone atheroma.

atheromatous (æθəˈrɒmətəs), *a. Path.* [f. Gr. ἀθηρωματ- (see prec.) + -OUS.] Of, pertaining to, or of the nature of, atheroma.

1676 WISEMAN *Surgery* (J.) Feeling the matter fluctuating, I thought it atheromatous. **1724** HOUSTOUN in *Phil. Trans.* XXXIII. 10. **1877** ROBERTS *Handbk. Med.* I. 37 Atheromatous or calcareous degeneration of the arteries.

atherosclerosis (ˌæθərəʊsklɪəˈrəʊsɪs). *Path.* [ad. G. *atherosklerose* (F. Marchand 1904, in *Verh. d. Kongr. f. Innere Med.* XXI. 58), f. Gr. ἀθήρη = ἀθάρη (see ATHEROMA) + -O + SCLEROSIS.] A form of arteriosclerosis with atheromatous degeneration of blood-vessel walls; = ATHEROMA b. Hence **ˌatheroscleˈrotic** *a.* and *sb.*

1910 *Jrnl. Amer. Med. Assoc.* LV. 546/1 (*title*) Atherosclerosis in Youth of 17 with Pulmonary Tuberculosis and Chronic Nephritis. [By] M. Simon. **1914** *Trans. Assoc. Amer. Physicians* XXIX. 513 Our knowledge of atherosclerotic processes in dogs is scant. **1958** *New Scientist* 25 Dec. 1582/3 Among the atherosclerotics, only three did not benefit. **1962** *Lancet* 28 Apr. 889/2 Most aneurysms of the abdominal aorta are probably a result of the atherosclerotic and degenerative changes in the media of the vessel wall. **1964** *Listener* 20 Feb. 311/2 Atherosclerosis ..is known to be associated with certain biochemical abnormalities in the blood—raised levels of serum cholesterol and other components.

†**a-ˈthester**, *v. Obs.* [OE. *aþeóstrian*, f. A- *pref.* 1 + *þeóstrian*: see THESTER *v.*] To grow dim, darken, become obscure.

c **885** K. ÆLFRED *Boeth.* ix, þonne aðeóstriaþ ealle steorran. *c* **1175** *Cott. Hom.* 239 Si sunne and se mone aþestreð for godes brictnesse. **1205** LAY. 2860 Enne blase of fure, þe neuer ne aþeostrede.

athet, a þet, variant of ATHAT *adv. Obs.* till.

athetesis (æθɪˈtiːsɪs). [a. Gr. ἀθέτησις, f. ἀθετεῖν (see ATHETIZE *v.*).] In textual criticism: the rejection (of a passage) as spurious.

1887 J. S. REID in *Classical Rev.* June 135/2 He is judiciously conservative and takes no notice of such extravagant *atheteses* as those put forward by Lütjohann in a paper on the *Cato Maior*. **1888** LEAF *Iliad* II. 435 Aristarchos' athetesis of 614–7 has been generally accepted, but..on inadequate grounds. **1962** WACE & STUBBINGS *Compan. to Homer* 222 There are two grades of rejection: complete omission, and athetesis which denotes the sort of suspicion which would lead a modern editor to consider the use of square brackets.

†**aˈtheticize**, *v. Obs. rare*$^{-1}$. [irreg. f. Gr. ἀ priv. + θετικός positive + -IZE: cf. ἄθετος set aside, invalid.] To set aside, invalidate.

1701 BEVERLEY *Glory of Grace* 51 Might he not even Atheticize, and Disannul Sin, and bring it even to nothing?

athetize (ˈæθɪtaɪz), *v.* [f. Gr. ἄθετος set aside + -IZE: formed to render Gr. ἀθετεῖν to set aside, reject as spurious.] *trans.* To set aside (a passage) as spurious. Hence **ˈathetizer**.

1886 JEVONS in *Jrnl. Hellenic Stud.* VII. 306 The solution is to athetize B 35–41 [of the *Iliad*]. **1888** LEAF *Iliad* II. 435 The opening passage (1–30) contains an unusual number of lines which have been suspected on undeniably valid grounds since the time of Aristarchos, who athetized no less than fourteen. **1889** *Athenæum* 26 Oct. 553/1 Dr. Leaf.. controverts with success the athetizers and abjudicators of Homeric verses. **1962** WACE & STUBBINGS *Compan. to Homer* 223 He used the *obelus* as Zenodotus had done, and he added other signs, especially the κεραύνιον..to mark groups of athetized lines.

athetosis (æθɪˈtəʊsɪs). *Path.* [f. Gr. ἄθετος without position or place + -OSIS.] A form of cerebral palsy, chiefly affecting children, characterized by continuous slow involuntary movements of the extremities. Hence **athetoid** (ˈæθɪtɔɪd), **athetotic** (æθɪˈtɒtɪk) *adjs.*, pertaining to or characteristic of athetosis.

1871 W. A. HAMMOND *Treat. Dis. Nervous Syst.* 654 Under the name of athetosis..I propose to describe an affection which..is mainly characterized by an inability to retain the fingers and toes in any position. **1875** *Proc. Amer. Neurol. Assoc.* I. 193 (*title*) A case of athetoid affection. **1882** *Edin. Med. Jrnl.* XXVII. 971 (*title*) Athetosis and athetoid movements in the insane. **1897** *Trans. Amer. Pediatric Soc.* IX. 158 In the analysis of 151 cases of cerebral paralysis in children..he found..athetosis six times. **1898** DAWSON WILLIAMS *Med. Dis. Inf.* 562 The general character of athetotic movements. **1910** *Practitioner* July 64 The right side of the face was then noticed to be paretic in its lower half, and there were athetoid movements of the right arm and leg. *Ibid.* 99 In some cases of hemiplegia due to encephalitis, choreiform or athetotic movements have been observed in the affected limbs. **1962** *Lancet* 26 May 1131/2 Although the athetosis ceased within fifteen minutes, respiration did not drop to 16 for ninety minutes.

†**at-ˈhind(en**, *adv.* and *prep. Obs.* [OE. *æthindan*; cf. *ætforan* and *bihindan*.] Behind.

1016 *O.E. Chron.* (Bosw.) Se cyning férde him æthindan. *a* **1275** *Prov. Alfred* 349 in *O.E. Misc.* 123 Seiet him faire biforen, fokel at-henden.

†**aˈthink**, *v. Obs.* 3–4. Also 3 **aþinche**, 4 **athynke**, **othenke**. *Pa. t.* 3 **aþohte**. [Worn-down f. OFTHINK, f. OF- + *þyncan* to seem: see A- *pref.* 3.] impers. ***it athinks me***: it repents me.

1250 LAY. 3364 Hofte hit bi-falleþ, þat eft him aþincheþ [**1205** of-þincheþ]. *Ibid.* 13221 Constantines deaþe, þat him sore a-þohte. **1377** LANGL. *P. Pl.* B. XVIII. 89 Sore it me athynketh For þe dede þat I haue done. **1382** WYCLIF *Gen.* vi. 7 It othenkith [5 *MSS.* athinkith; **1388** repentith] me to haue maad hem.

†**aˈthinking**, *vbl. sb.* [f. prec.] Repentance.

1382 WYCLIF *1 Sam.* xv. 29 Thur3 athenkynge [**1388** bi repentaunce] he shal not be bowid.

athirst (əˈθɜːst), *ppl. a.* Forms: 1 **of-þyrst(ed**, 3–4 **of-þurst**; 4 **afurst**, 5 **afforst**; 4 **athrist, -yst**, 4–6 **athurst(e, athrust**, 5–6 **athyrst(e**, 6– **athirst**. [Worn-down form of OE. *ofþyrst*, for *ofþyrsted*, pa. pple. of *ofþyrstan* to suffer thirst, be very thirsty. Cf. A- HUNGERED, and A- *pref.* 3.]

1. Suffering from, or oppressed by, thirst; thirsty.

a **1000** *Soul* (Gr.) 40 Ic ofþyrsted wæs..gástes drynces. *c* **1200** *Trin. Coll. Hom.* 199 þe neddre beð of-þurst..and drinkeð. *c* **1300** *Vox & Wolf* 273 He wes hofthurst swithe stronge. *c* **1305** *St. Kenelm* in *E.E. Poems* (1862) 56 Aþurst hi were for werinisse. *c* **1320** *Cast. Love* (Halliw.) 1654 When I was afurst 3e 3eve me dryng. **1398** TREVISA *Barth. De P.R.* v. xxxviii. (1495) 153 A drye stomake is sone athryst. *c* **1480** *Robt. Devyll* 20 If ye be a thrust ye shall drynke nowe. *a* **1500** *Frere & Boy* 21 in Hazl. *E.P.P.* III. 61 Nor halffe ynowh therof he had, Oft he was afforst. **1535** COVERDALE *Judges* iv. 19 Geue me a litle water to drynke, for I am a thyrst. **1697** DRYDEN *Virg. Georg.* III 213 And, when athirst, restrain 'em from the Flood. **1805** SOUTHEY *Madoc in W.* v. Wks. V. 43 Fatigued and hungry and athirst.

2. *fig.* Eager, earnestly desirous, longing (*for*).

1480 CAXTON *Chron. Eng.* lxxv. 59 To hem that ben a thyrste hys worde shal be Gospell. **1535** COVERDALE *Ps.* xlii. 1 My soule is a thurste for God. **1642** FULLER *Holy & Prof. St.* I. ix. 23 He is athirst to know the issue of the matter. **1877** L. MORRIS *Epic Hades* II. 132 Bold young hearts, Athirst for fame of war.

athirt, obs. or dial. form of ATHWART.

†**a-this-half, a-this-side**, *advb. phr.* (also prepositional). [see A *prep.*[1] 3.] On this side (of).

1297 R. GLOUC. 217 The companye a thes half much anethered was. *c* **1380** *Sir Ferumb.* 4315 A þys syde þ^e^ toun. **1482** *Monk of Evesham* (Arb.) 61 Athishalfe domys daye.

†**athletary**, *a. Obs. rare*$^{-1}$. [f. next + -ARY.] Of or pertaining to athletes.

1660 WATERHOUSE *Arms & Arm.* 103 The Greeks in their ..athletary agonies.

athlete (ˈæθliːt). [ad. L. *āthlēta*, ad. Gr. ἀθλητής, n. of agent f. ἀθλέ-ειν to contend for a prize, f. ἆθλος contest, ἆθλον prize. Before *c* 1750 always in L. form, which is still occas. used in sense 1.]

1. A competitor in the physical exercises—such as running, leaping, boxing, wrestling—that formed part of the public games in ancient Greece and Rome.

1528 PAYNELL *Salerne Regim.* E iij b, Porke..nourisheth mooste: wherof those that be called athlete [= -æ] haue beste experience. **1683** CAVE *Ecclesiastici* 235 A Bishop, not an Athleta or Champion. **1741** DELANY *David* (T.) Dioxippus, the Athenian athlete. **1756** MISS TALBOT in *Mrs. Carter's Lett.* (1808) I. 390 We have looked in Johnson for *Athlete*, no such word there. **1868** M. PATTISON *Academ. Org.* §5. 241 The barbarised athlete of the arena. **1877** BRYANT *Ruins Italica* ii, But where the combatant With his bare arms, the strong athleta where?

2. One who by special training and exercise has acquired great physical strength; one whose profession it is to exhibit feats of strength and activity; a physically powerful, robust, vigorous man.

1827 SCOTT in *Lockhart* lxxiii. (1842) 654 He was a little man, dumpled up together..Though so little of an athlete, he nevertheless beat off Dr. Wolcott. **1881** PHILLIPPS-

WOLLEY *Sport in Crimea* 280 The jump.. was easily within the powers of the most third-rate athlete.

3. *fig.*

1759 ADAM SMITH *Mor. Sent.* VII. §2 (R.) Having opposed to him a vigorous athlete, over whom.. the victory was more glorious and equally certain. **1876** LOWELL *Poet. Wks.* (1879) 470 The long-proved athletes of debate.

4. ***athlete's foot***, a popular name for tinea or ringworm of the foot.

1928 *Lit. Digest* 22 Dec. 16/1 Athlete's foot.. from which more than ten million persons in the United States are now suffering. **1942** *Lancet* 18 July 75/2 After what we have been told about the shortage of phenol and its derivatives no-one over here is likely to begin trials of a remedy for 'athlete's foot' (tinea interdigitalis), advocated in America, which consists of equal parts of phenol and camphor.

athletic (æθ'lɛtɪk), *a.* and *sb.* Also 7 **-ique**. [ad. L. *āthlētic-us*, Gr. ἀθλητικός, f. ἀθλητής: see prec. and -IC.] **A.** *adj.*

1. Pertaining to an athlete, or to contests in which physical strength is vigorously exercised. Also *fig.*

1636 SANDERSON *Serm.* Ad Aul. (1681) II. 58 Ὑπωπιάζω.. is an Athletique Pugilar word. **1691** RAY *Creation* (1704) Ded. 3 Your Athletic Conflicts with the greatest of Temporal Evils. **1748** *Phil. Trans.* XLV. 607 For the baiting of wild beasts, or other athletic diversions. **1875** HELPS *Anim. & Masters* v. 131 He was never much given to athletic pursuits.

2. Of the nature of, or befitting, an athlete; physically powerful, muscular, robust.

1659 HAMMOND *On Ps.* lxxiii. 4 An athletick health and habit of body. **1751** CHESTERF. *Lett.* 268 III. 231 He is an athletic Hibernian, handsome in his person. **1877** FIELD *Killarney to Gold. Horn* 121 That little brook.. an athletic leaper would almost clear at a single bound.

3. In Kretschmer's system, designating a type of physique characterized by well-developed muscles (see quots.); mesomorphic.

1925 W. J. H. SPROTT tr. *Kretschmer's Physique & Character* I. ii. 24 The male athletic type is recognised by the strong development of the skeleton, the musculature and also the skin. **1937** R. H. THOULESS *Gen. & Social Psychol.* (ed. 2) vi. 109 [Kretschmer] divides men into three physical types: the *athletic* (large muscle and bones), the *asthenic* or *leptosomatic* (lean, flat-chested, and narrow-shouldered), and the *pyknic* (with tendency to rounded contours of face and body).

†**B.** *sb.* **a.** = ATHLETICS. **b.** An athlete. *Obs.*

1605 BACON *Adv. Learn.* II. x. §1 Art of activity, which is called athletic. **1696** J. EDWARDS *Exist. & Prov. God* I. 25 Some celebrated athletick that is famous for his nimbleness of feet. **1817** JAS. MILL *India* I. II. vii. 315 The magistrate.. shall retain in his service.. jesters, and dancers, and athletics.

¶ See also ATHLETICS.

ath'letical, *a.* ? *Obs.* [f. as prec. + -AL[1].] Of or pertaining to an athlete; vigorous, athletic.

1593 G. HARVEY *Pierces Super.* Wks. (Gros.) II. 264 Vnto whom.. I can wish.. no lesse then athleticall health. **1615** W. HULL *Mirr. Maj.* 118 Neither Lillies nor Roses are wanting to her Athleticall crowne. **1656** TRAPP *Comm. 2 Tim.* ii. 5 Not he that had an athletical ability, but he that wrestled best.

ath'letically, *adv.* [f. prec. + -LY[2].] In athletic manner; in the direction of athletics.

1750 CHATHAM in Lady Chatterton *Mem. Gambier* (1861) I. iii. 40 Don't.. fancy you can do all the Admirabilis and I do so athletically. **1883** *Times* 23 Jan. 6/2 Upper Boys [of Eton].. athletically inclined.

athleticism (æθ'lɛtɪsɪz(ə)m). [f. ATHLETIC + -ISM.] The practice of, or devotion to, athletic exercises; training as an athlete.

1870 *Daily News* 24 Nov., The controversy about athleticism at the Universities and the Public Schools. **1881** *Macm. Mag.* XLIII. 290 Athleticism.. ought to be a valuable ally in promoting habits of temperance and sobriety.

athleticize (æθ'lɛtɪsaɪz), *v.* [f. ATHLETIC *a.* + -IZE.] *trans.* To make athletic.

1896 *Godey's Mag.* Apr. 447/1 Are we to be so athleticized that we will disdain all fripperies? **1897** *Eclectic Mag.* Oct. 523 France, superficially, has become Anglicized, athleticised.

ath'letics. [ATHLETIC *a.* used in pl. on the analogy of *mathematics*, etc. Cf. L. *āthlētica*.] The practice of physical exercises by which muscular strength is called into play and increased.

1727-51 CHAMBERS *Cycl.* s.v. *Gymnastics*, Dancing, Spheristics, Athletics, Wrestling. **1868** M. PATTISON *Academ. Org.* 316 Pretending to think that cricket, boating, and athletics, as now conducted, are only recreations.

athletism ('æθliːtɪz(ə)m). [f. ATHLETE + -ISM.] The characteristic qualities of an athlete.

1866 *Reader* 3 Nov. 904 Recipes for attaining athletism.

athlothete ('æθləʊθiːt). [ad. Gr. ἀθλοθέτης, f. ἆθλο-ς contest, ἆθλο-ν prize + θέτης one who places. Cf. mod.F. *athlothète*] The awarder of prizes, judge, or steward in the public games.

1850 LEITCH *Müller's Anc. Art* §425 A female flute-player.. before an athlothete.

Athoan (æ'θəʊən), *a.* [f. Gr. Ἀθῶος of Athos + -AN.] Of or pertaining to Athos, the most easterly of the three peninsulas of Chalcidice in Macedonia, or to the 'Holy Mountain' at the eastern end of this peninsula, or to the monasteries of Athos (cf. ATHONITE).

1869 H. F. TOZER *Highl. Turkey* I. v. 119 The new iconostase.. is composed partly of Tenian and partly of Athoan marble. **1939** A. TOYNBEE *Study Hist.* IV. 361 An artist whose art would appear to be the antithesis of the rigid canon of the Athoan iconists.

athodyd ('æθəʊdɪd). *Aeronaut.* [f. *A*ero- + *th*ermo*dy*namic *d*uct.] A jet engine deriving its propulsive power from the combustion of fuel in a duct or tube into which air is admitted and compressed as a result of forward speed. Now usu. called *ram-jet*.

1945 *Westinghouse Engineer* Mar. 51/1 The continuous-firing duct engine is relatively little known but is credited to Lorin of France in 1913. It has been under development principally in England under the.. name of 'athodyd'. **1946** *Air Reserve Gaz.* July 7/1 The athodyd engines at the tailplane tips are highly efficient at speed. **1950** *Jrnl. R. Aeronaut. Soc.* Apr. 217/1 The principle of the ram-jet or athodyd has been understood for a number of years.

†**at-'hold**, *v.* *Obs.* Also 2-3 **et-hold**; for inflexions, see HOLD *v.* [f. AT- *pref.*[2] + HOLD *v.*; in OE. *oðhealdan*. Cf. G. *enthalten*, Du. *onthouden*.]

1. *trans.* To withhold, keep back (something).

c **885** K. ÆLFRED *Gregory's Past.* xlix. 377 Oððe ʒif hwelc folc bið mid hungre ʒeswenced, & hwá his hwæte ʒehyt & oðhielt. *c* **1175** *Lamb. Hom.* 91 Heo walden sum of heore ehte etholdan þam apostlan. **1205** LAY. 12483 Ofte ʒe us habbeð at-halden þat gauel. *c* **1300** *Beket* 1749 Seint Thomas athuld the lettre.

2. To detain, restrain (a person).

c **1230** *Ancr. R.* 374 Bitternesse of þisse liue.. ethalt ham urom blisse. *c* **1314** *Guy Warw.* 60 He gan to.. wepe with his eyghen therfore. He him might no lenge at held.

3. To keep (a thing) in one's possession, to retain.

c **1200** *Trin. Coll. Hom.* 63 þat we ne athelde none [synne] on ure heorte. *c* **1230** *Ancr. R.* 286 God haueð etholden to him sulf.. wurðschipe & wreche. *c* **1330** *Florice & Bl.* 367 Thou shalt.. Thi golde cop with þe at holde.

4. To keep, retain (a person) in attendance.

c **1200** *Trin. Coll. Hom.* 123 Gode menisshe.. he [God] understant and mid him athalt. **1297** R. GLOUC. 124 þo kyng of hys men at huld wuche he wolde. *c* **1330** *Arth. & Merl.* 618 This clerkes.. With the king weren at held.

5. To keep in existence, maintain, preserve.

c **1220** *Hali Meid.* 13 And iþis world.. athalt hire burðe ilicnesse of heuenliche cunde. **1250** LAY. 769 Somme he sloh, somme he bond, þe beste he cwic at-heold.

6. To keep in consideration, observe, give heed to.

c **1175** *Lamb. Hom.* 47 þeo þe ihereð godes weordes and heom athaldeð. *c* **1250** *Owl & Night.* 392 The niʒtingale in hire thoʒte At-hold al this. *c* **1275** *Passion Our Lord* 364 in *O.E. Misc.* 47 I-hereþ myne word, And heo wel atholdeþ.

7. To lay fast hold of, put under arrest.

a **1230** *St. Juliana* 41 Ich hit am þat sum chearre wes þurh þe wise Salomon ethalden [*v.r.* feste bitunet]. *c* **1275** *Passion Our Lord* 535 in *O.E. Misc.* 52 Nu wolden heo [þe gywes] hyne at-holden þat scop alle þing.

Athole brose. [*Athole, Atholl*, a district in Perthshire.] See BROSE b and *Sc. Nat. Dict.*

at home, at-home (æt'həʊm), *advb. phr.* and *sb.* Also 1 **æt hám**, 3 **atom**. [See AT *prep.* and HOME.]

A. *advb. phr.*

1. At one's home, in one's own house.

a **1000** *Beowulf* 2500 Ge æt hám ʒe on herʒe. *c* **1225** *St. Margarete* 180 þe were betere habbe bileued atom. **1483** CAXTON *G. de la Tour* E j b, Ryote and noyse shalle all day be at home. **1711** STEELE *Spect.* No. 24 ¶6 The Misfortune of never finding one another at home. **1840** DICKENS *Old C. Shop* vi, There was only Mrs. Quilp at home.

b. Prepared to receive visitors accessible to callers.

1829 WARREN *Diary Physic.* xix, The servant brought up the cards of several of his late colleagues. 'Not at home, sirrah! Harkee— ill—ill,' thundered his master. **1880** *Etiq. of Good Soc.* 103 In the country a bride's first appearance in church is taken as a sign that she is 'At home.' **1883** J. HATTON in *Harper's Mag.* Nov. 830/2 The President makes it a point to be 'at home' on Sunday afternoons.

2. (As opposed to ABROAD): **a.** In one's immediate neighbourhood, near at hand. **b.** In one's own country.

c **885** K. ÆLFRED *Oros.* I. x. §3 Oþer æt ham beon heora lond to healdanne. **1594** SHAKS. *Rich. III*, I. i. 134 No newes so bad abroad as this at home. **1884** *Daily News* 5 Feb. 4/8 Everything.. done by the Government at home and abroad.

3. At ease, as if in one's own home. Hence *fig.* Thoroughly familiar or conversant *with*, well-practised *in*. Hence also **at-homeish, -ly, -ness, at-home-ness**, etc.

1840 DICKENS *Old C. Shop* vi, That kind of acting had been rendered familiar to him by long practice, and he was quite at home in it. **1849** MACAULAY *Hist. Eng.* I. 365 They never felt themselves at home in our island. *Mod.* His genial manner made me feel quite at home with him. **1843** LEVER *J. Hinton* I. 135 Whose.. indescribable air of at-homeishness bespoke them as the friends of the family. **1880** *Dimplethorpe* II. 66 What an air of at-home-ness there was about her.

4. *Cribbage.* See HOME *sb.*[1]

B. *sb.* A reception of visitors, for whose entertainment the host or hostess, or both, have announced that they will be 'At home' during certain hours, in the course of which the visitors may call and leave as they please.

1745 H. WALPOLE *Lett. G. Montagu* 12 Lady Granville, and the dowager Strafford have their At-home's, and amass company. **1883** J. HATTON in *Harper's Mag.* Nov. 844/2 Among the notable 'at homes' of London.. are the Tuesdays at Mr. Alma-Tadema's.

-athon: a combining form, barbarously extracted f. MAR)ATHON, used occas. in the U.S. (*talkathon, walkathon*), rarely in Britain, to form words denoting something carried on for an abnormal length of time. (*Amer. Speech* (1934) IX. 76, 317/2.)

Athonite ('æθənaɪt), *a.* [f. L. **Athōnis* of Athos, f. *Athōs*, f. Gr. Ἄθως + -ITE[1].] = ATHOAN *a.*; esp. of or pertaining to the monasteries of Athos. Also as *sb.*

1887 J. A. RILEY *Athos* xi. 163 St. Athanasius the Athonite was a Georgian by nation, who came from Trebizonde to Mount Athos about the year 950, and founded the Lavra in 963 or 964. **1935** *Times Lit. Suppl.* 10 Oct. 621/3 Frescoes so characteristic of Athonite Churches. **1957** *Oxf. Dict. Chr. Ch.* 101/2 A curious rule of the Athonite monks forbids women, or even female animals, to set foot on the peninsula. **1963** *Sunday Times* (Colour Mag.) 5 May 5/2 A.. representative of the Athonite police force.. scrutinized my letter of ecclesiastical recommendation.

athort, Sc. form of ATHWART.

a-three: in three: see A *prep.*[1] 6.

1297 R. GLOUC. 437 Henry hys ost aþre delde.

athrepsia (ə'θrɛpsɪə). *Path.* [ad. Fr. *athrepsie* (Parrot 1874, in *Progrès Méd.* 24 Oct. 637/1), f. A- 14 + Gr. θρέψ-ις nourishing + -IA[1].] Malnutrition, esp. in infants; marasmus.

1885 R. & F. BARNES *Syst. Obstetric Med.* II. iii. 122 *Athrepsia* is a frequent morbid state in the new-born. **1905** *Med. Ann.* 407 There would appear to be such a condition as 'athrepsia', or marasmus which is not dependent upon any discoverable source.

a-thrill (ə'θrɪl), *advb. phr.* [A *prep.*[1] + THRILL.] In a thrill, thrilling.

1879 *Cornh. Mag.* May, *Susanna* i, Hedges seem trembling with life.. the whole place is athrill. **1881** E. ARNOLD *Ind. Poetry* 101 Then Jymul's supple fingers.. Set athrill the saddest wire of all the six.

athrist, -ust, athurst, obs. forms of ATHIRST.

†**a'throat**, *v.* *Obs. rare*$^{-1}$. [f. A- *pref.* 1 (or 6) + THROAT *v.*] To throttle, strangle.

c **1400** *Test. Love* II. (1560) 284 b/2 If thou wolt algates wyth superfluitie of riches be athroted.

a-throb (ə'θrɒb), *advb. phr.* [A *prep.*[1] + THROB.] Throbbing.

1857 MRS. BROWNING *Aur. Leigh* v. 175 That blue vein athrob on Mahomet's brow. **1882** SWINBURNE *Tristr. Lyon.* 70 One heart on flame, Athrob with love and wonder.

athrocyte ('æθrəʊsaɪt). *Cytology.* [f. Gr. ἀθρόος crowded, collected + -CYTE.] A cell having the property of absorbing and retaining solid particles. Hence **athro'cytic** *a.*; **ˌathrocy'tosis**, the capacity for such absorption.

1938 *Chem. Abstr.* 2631 The athrocytic function among the Hirudinea... Athrocytic cells (athrocytes) are found in renal or celomic organs, and serve to maintain the constancy of compn. of the interior fluids of the animal... Athrocytosis is the absorption by living cells of submicroscopic electroneg. particles. **1948** *Lancet* 24 July 150/2 In blackwater fever.. some emphasise the pigment and athrocytic aspect. **1951** G. BOURNE *Cytol. & Cell Physiol.* (ed. 2) xi. 481 The proximal convoluted tubules have the capacity for storing vital dyes and other particulate matter (athrocytosis).

a-throng (ə'θrɒŋ), *advb. phr.* [A *prep.*[1] + THRONG.] In a throng; thronged, crowded.

c **1300** *K. Alis.* 3409 Alle weore dryven athrang. **1881** PALGRAVE *Vis. Eng.* 83 A mazy forest.. a-throng with ruddy limbs.

†**a'thrysm, a'thrusem**, *v.* *Obs.* [OE. *aþrys(e)mian*, f. A- *pref.* 1 + *þrysmian* to suffocate. (*Athrusm* had Fr. *u* (y): the mod. form would be *athrism*.)] To suffocate, stifle, choke, kill.

c **885** K. ÆLFRED *Oros.* v. iv. §3 Hi hine on his bedde asmoredan and aþrysemodon. *c* **1220** *Sawles Warde* in *Cott. Hom.* 251 Euch aþrusmeð oðer. *c* **1230** *Ancr. R.* 40 þine brihte blissful sune þet te Gyus wenden vorto aþrusemen.

athum, earlier f. OTHEM, *Obs.*, son-in-law.

†**a-thus-gate**, *phr. Obs.* [See A *prep.*[1]] In this way, thus.

c **1460** *Towneley Myst.* 233 Stemmate regali, kyng athusgate me of Pila.. I am ordand to reyn upon Juda.

athwart (ə'θwɔːt), *adv.* and *prep.* Also 6 **athirt**, 7 **athawart, atwart**. *Sc.* 6 **athourt, -rcht**, 6-9 **athort**. [f. A *prep.*[1] + THWART; the latter was in earlier use as an adv.; *a-thwart* was formed like *about*, *across*, and other adverbs in *a-*; there was also an early OVERTHWART.]

A. *adv.*

1. Across from side to side, transversely; usually, but not necessarily, in an oblique direction.

1611 CORYAT *Crudities* 294 Yron beames that come athwart or acrosse from one side to the other. **1646** SIR T. BROWNE *Pseud. Ep.* 333 The Asse having .. a crosse made by a black list down his back, and another athwart, or at right angles down his shoulders. **1702** W. J. *Bruyn's Voy. Levant* xxxvi. 140 All these stones are laid a-thwart over the breadth of the chamber. **1879** TENNYSON *Lover's T.* 10 The cloud .. sweeps athwart in storms.

b. *Naut.* From side to side of a ship.

1762-9 FALCONER *Shipwr.* II. 174 The fore-sail right athwart they brace. **1858** in *Merc. Mar. Mag.* V. 317 A .. framework, extending fore and aft and athwart.

†**2.** Across in various directions, about. (*Northern*: still in Scotch.)

c **1500** *Partenay* 169 Thorught the wodes went, athirt trauersing. *a* **1662** BAILLIE *Lett.* (1775) I. 83 (JAM.) There goes a speech athort .. dissuading the king from war with us.

3. Across the course (of anything), so as to thwart or oppose progress.

1594 CAREW *Huarte's Exam. Wits* x. (1596) 145 If nature .. haue no impediment cast athwart to stop her. **1790** COWPER *Iliad* III. 91 And with his spear Advanced athwart push'd back the Trojan van.

4. *fig.* In opposition to the proper or expected course; crosswise, perversely, awry.

1596 SHAKS. *1 Hen. IV*, I. i. 36 All athwart there came A Post from Wales, loaden with heauy Newes. **1603** —— *Meas. for M.* I. iii. 30 And quite athwart Goes all decorum. **1876** MORRIS *Sigurd* III. 213 Turned the steadfast athwart.

5. In the form of a cross, crosswise. ? *Obs. rare.*

1607 *Schol. Disc. agst. Antichr.* I. iii. 154 They clappe their armes athwarte, to expresse a crosse.

B. *prep.* [the adv. with object expressed.]

1. From side to side of, transversely over, across: **a.** of motion.

c **1470** HENRY *Wallace* in Masson *3 Cent. Eng. Poet.* 114 A locklat bar was drawn athwart the door. **1513-75** *Diurn. Occurr.* (1833) 323 The fisches wes blawin athort the gait. **1623** LISLE *Ælfric on O. & N.T.* 10 Moses then led them .. athwart the red sea. **1712** POPE *Rape Lock* II. 82 The stars that shoot athwart the night. **1846** KEBLE *Lyra Innoc.* (1873) 124 A-thwart the field, the rooks fly home.

b. of position or direction.

1588 SHAKS. *L.L.L.* IV. iii. 135 Nor neuer lay his wreathed arms athwart His louing bosome. **1615** HEYWOOD *Four Prent.* I. Wks. 1874 II. 240 Skarfe-like these athwart my breasts I'le weare. **1830** TENNYSON *Mariana* ii, She .. glanced athwart the glooming flats.

†**2.** Across in various directions, to and fro over, all over. (Only in north. dial.; still in every day use in Scotland as *athort*.)

1548 *Compl. Scot.* vi. 38 The borial blastis .. hed chaissit the fragrant flureise .. far athourt the feildis. *a* **1662** BAILLIE *Lett.* (1775) I. 32 (JAM.) Posts went forth athort the whole country. [*Mod.Sc.* Lazy loons stravaguing athort the kintrae.]

3. *Naut.* Across or transversely to the course or direction of. †*athwart the fore foot*: (a cannon-ball fired) across in front of a ship's bows, as a signal for her to bring to. *to run athwart*: to run into sidewise; cf. A 1 b.

1693 LUTTRELL *Brief Rel.* III. 70 A French privateer .. whom he run athawart and sunk him. **1693** *Lond. Gaz.* No. 2926/3 The Wind being Northerly .. with a great Swell and strong Tide; The Frigats were obliged to Moor athwart it. **1793** SMEATON *Edystone L.* §167 *note*, A vessel .. being laid athwart the Jetty Head. **1865** DICKENS *Mut. Fr.* iii. 284 Athwart the steamer's bows.

4. Across the direction of, so as to meet or fall in with; hence *fig.* into the notice or observation of.

1622 R. HAWKINS *Voy. S. Sea* 232 If this Spanish shippe should fall athwart his King's armado. **1642** FULLER *Holy & Prof. St.* II. vi. 71 Be not proud if that chance to come athwart thy seeing side, which meets with the blind side of another. **1817** COLERIDGE *Poems* 70 Ye sweep athwart my gaze. **1849** ROBERTSON *Serm.* I. ii. (1866) 34 The image .. comes athwart his every thought.

5. Across the course of, so as to oppose.

1667 MILTON *P.L.* II. 683 That dar'st .. advance Thy miscreated Front athwart my way. **1748** SMOLLETT *Rod. Rand.* iii. (1804) 10 If you come a-thwart me, 'ware. **1860** MAURY *Phys. Geog. Sea* v. §298 Mountains which lie athwart the course of the winds.

6. *fig.* **a.** In opposition to.

1644 MILTON *Areop.* (Arb.) 39, I have seen this present work, and finde nothing athwart the Catholick faith. **1865** CARLYLE *Fredk. Gt.* V. XIV. iii. 182 Honest to the bone, athwart all her prejudices.

b. *catachr.* Through, across.

a **1719** ADDISON (J.) Athwart the terrors that thy vow Has planted round thee, thou appear'st more fair.

C. *Comb.* **athwart-hawse**, phrase used of a ship's position across the stem of another ship at anchor; hence prep. phr. **athwart-hawse of**; **athwart-ship** *a.*, **athwart-ships** *adv.*, from side to side of the ship; **athwart-wise**, athwart.

1709 *Lond. Gaz.* No. 4543/2 He .. laid her on Board under her Boltsprit, directly athwart her Hawse. **1813** SOUTHEY *Nelson* v. 150 Anchoring athwart-hawse of the Orient. **1718** STEELE *Fish Pool* 177 Two bulk-heads .. running athwart-ships. **1879** W. WHITE in *Cassell's Techn. Educ.* IV. 363/1 An athwartship section of the lower part of a ship. **1868** HAWTHORNE *Amer. Note-Bk.* (1879) II. 223 And now lies athwartwise.

athymy ('æθɪmɪ). *Path.* [ad. Gr. ἀθυμία, f. ἀ priv. + θυμός spirit.] Despondency, dejection.

1853 in MAYNE *Exp. Lex.*

athyr, obs. form of EITHER and OTHER.

athyrst(e, obs. form of ATHIRST.

-atic, *suffix*, forming adjs., (= Fr. *-atique*) ad. L. *-āticus*, a particular case of the suffix *-ic-us*, 'of, of the kind of' (see -IC), appended to pa. ppl. stems of verbs; as in *errā-re* to wander, *errāt-um*, *errātic-us* of wandering nature, *volātic-us* of flying kind, *vēnātic-us* of hunting kind; also used with sbs., e.g. *aqua* water, *aquāt-us* watered, watery, *aquātic-us* of watery kind, *Asiātic-us*, *fānātic-us* (*fānum* temple), *silvātic-us* (*silva* wood), *umbrātic-us* (*umbra* shade). Thence also neuter sbs. as *viāticum* 'what belongs to the way (*via*).' In late L. and Romanic, the subst. use received great extension: it survives phonetically in the Fr. and Eng. -AGE, in *umbrage, vantage, breakage*. The adjectives in *-atic*, as *aquatic, Asiatic, fanatic, lunatic, lymphatic*, are all of modern introduction; they are to be distinguished from words in which the suffix is *-ic* only, as *dramat-ic, hepat-ic, muriat-ic, pirat-ic, pneumat-ic, prelat-ic*.

†**a'tiffe**, *v. Obs. rare.* [? a. OF. *atife-r* (15th c. *attiffer*) f. *à* to + OF. *tifer* to adorn, deck out, trick out, perh. f. L.Ger. (Du.) *tippen* to cut the ends of the hair, to trim, f. *tip*, TIP. (Burguy, Diez.) In mod.F., *attifer* is familiar, often rather ironical, and said chiefly of dressing the head; cf. Eng. *titivate*.] To adorn, deck (the person).

c **1230** *Ancr. R.* 420 þauh heo atiffe hire nis nout muchel wunder. *Ibid.* 360 Let oðre atiffen hore bodi.

†**a'tiffement.** *Obs. rare*$^{-1}$. [f. prec. vb., or a. OF. *atifement* (*attiffement* in Cotgr. 1611): see -MENT.] Adornment, decoration.

1330 R. BRUNNE *Chron.* 152 A pauillon of honour, with riche atiffement.

†**a'til, a'tyl**, *v. Obs.* [a. OF. *atillier*, cogn. with Pr. *atilhar*, It. *attillare*, Sp. *atildar, atilar*, according to Diez:—L. **adtitulāre*, f. *ad* to + *titulus* (a title, sign), in late L. and It. *titolo* a prick, a point, the dot of an *i*, Sp. *tilde* a little prick, the mark over *ñ*, a jot, a TITTLE. Hence, the primary idea was 'to finish to a *t*, to the last tittle.' In 17th c. Fr. *attiler* and *attifer* were synonymous: 'to deck, prank, trick, trim, adorn,' Cotgr.]

To deck out, dress, equip, arm completely.

1297 R. GLOUC. 184 To þys batayle hii come .. atyled wel ynou. *Ibid.* 525 Richard the marschal Vpe is stede iarmed is & atiled thoru out al.

2. *refl.* To address or apply oneself. (So OF. *s'atillier à*.)

1297 R. GLOUC. 191 þe knyȝtes atyled hem aboute in eche syde In feldes and in medys to preue her bachelerye.

†**'atil, 'atyl**, *sb. Obs.* [a. OF. *atil, atyl*, f. *atillier*: see prec.] Equipment, gear.

1297 R. GLOUC. 102 Schippes and here atyl. *Ibid.* 349 He ber þe croune, & huld þe deys, myd oþer atyl also.

-atile, *suffix* forming adjs. (= mod.F. *-atile*), ad. L. *-ātilis*, consisting of the suffix *-ilis* (see -ILE) 'denoting possibility and quality,' appended to ppl. stems in *-āt-* of verbs in *-āre*, as in *volātus* flying, *volātilis* used to fly, Eng. *volatile*: also with sbs. as *aquātilis*, Eng. *aquatile, fluviatile, umbratile*, all of modern introduction, and nearly synonymous with those in -ATIC.

a-tilt (ə'tɪlt), *advb. phr.* [A *prep.*¹ (in sense 2, perh. AT *prep.*) + TILT.]

1. Tilted up, set on tilt, in such a position that it is just ready to fall over. Also *fig.*

1562 J. HEYWOOD *Prov. & Epigr.* (1867) 194 We apply the spigot, till tubbe stande a tilte. **1735** POPE *Donne Sat.* iv. 176 In that nice moment, as another lye Stood just a-tilt. **1881** PAYN *Grape fr. Thorn* xiv, Sitting with his chair atilt.

2. In phr. *to run* (or *ride*) *a-tilt*: i.e. in an encounter on horseback with the thrust of a lance. Now usually *fig.* of controversial encounters. Const. *at, with, against*. [The origin of *a-* is here uncertain.]

1591 SHAKS. *1 Hen. VI*, III. ii. 51 Breake a Launce, and runne a-Tilt at Death. **1608** *2nd Pt. Def. Reas. Refus. Subscript.* 52 [He] taketh heart to run at Tilt a fresh. **1702** S. PARKER *Tully's De Fin.* 31 Impetuously as they run atilt against other people. **1862** SIR H. TAYLOR *St. Clem. Eve* III. iii. Wks. 1864 III. 149 He rode a-tilt and smote the scaly Dragon. **1873** BURTON *Hist. Scot.* V. lv. 94 A paper in defense of queen Mary's honour, in which he ran atilt with Buchanan.

atimy ('ætɪmɪ). [ad. Gr. ἀτιμία, f. ἄτῑμος dishonoured, f. ἀ priv. + τῑμή honour.] Public disgrace; *spec.* deprivation of civil rights. (A transference of the Greek word, in its technical sense.)

1847 GROTE *Greece* II. xi. III. 134 Those who had been condemned by the archons to atimy (civil disfranchisement).

a-tingle (ə'tɪŋg(ə)l), *advb. phr.* [A *prep.*¹ + TINGLE.] Tingling.

1855 BROWNING *Men & Wom.* I. 27 Till the stalks of it seem a-tingle.

-ation (-'eɪʃən), the particular form of the compound suffix -T-ION (*-s-ion, -x-ion*), which forms nouns of action from L. pples. in *-āt-us* of vbs. in *-āre*, Fr. vbs. in *-er*, and their English representatives. As mentioned under -TION (q.v.), the living form of L. *-ātiōn-em* in OF. was *-aisun, -eisun*, whence ME. *-aisun, -eisun, -esun*, mod. *-eason, -ison*; cf. *ratiōn-em, reisun*, REASON; *ōrātiōn-em, ureisun*, ORISON. All F. words in *-ation* (OF. *-aciun*, ME. *-aciun, -acioun, -acyon*) were of later and literary introduction from Latin, though many of them already existed before the earliest introduction of F. words into English, where, in theological writings, *passiun* occurs *c* 1175, and *sauvaciun c* 1225. In French, vbs. in *-er*:—L. *-āre*, far outnumber all others; they also constitute the type on which all recent verbs are formed; hence, nouns in *-ation* exceed in number not only the early words in *-sun, -çun, -ssun*, but all the other forms of *-tion*. In English, they number more than 1500 in modern use; the obsolete examples amount to several hundred more: see, within a few pages, *apostrophation, apparation, appendication, apprecation, appunctuation, aquation, argutation, ariolation, artation, asperation, aspernation, assectation, assecuration, assedation, assemblation*. A few have no accompanying verb in English use, e.g. *constellation, duration, lunation, negation, oration, ovation*; the great majority have a verb in *-ate*, e.g. *cre-ate, -ation, moder-ate, -ation, satur-ate, -ation*; some are formed on Gr. vbs. in -IZE (of which the L. was, or would be, *-izāre*, Fr. *-iser*), or their imitations, e.g. *organize, -ation, civilize, -ation*: the remainder have a vb. without suffix, derived through Fr., either with or without modification; e.g. *modi-fy, -fication, appl-y, -ication, publ-ish, -ication, prove, probation; alter-ation, caus-ation, cit-ation, commend-ation, consult-ation, embark-ation, fix-ation, form-ation, not-ation, plant-ation, quot-ation, tax-ation, tempt-ation, vex-ation, visit-ation*. To the mere English speaker the latter have the effect of being formed immediately on the Eng. verbs *alter, cause, embark, fix, plant, tax, vex, visit*, etc.; and *-ation* thus assumes the character of a living Eng. suffix. Hence, it comes to be applied to verbs not of Fr. origin, as in *starv-ation, flirt-ation, bother-ation, backward-ation*. For the meaning, see -TION; words in which *-ation* is, or seems to be, merely added to the verb, are synonymous with the verbal substantive in *-ing*; already in 17th c. the use of *vexation, visitation*, etc. instead of *vexing, visiting*, etc. (*flirtation, starvation* had not yet been heard of) was ridiculed thus:

1638 RANDOLPH *Amyntas* I. iii. 32 *Thestylis.* But what languages doe they speake, servant? *Mopsus.* Several languages, as Cawation, Chirpation, Hootation, Whistleation, Crowation, Cackleation, Shriekation, Hissation. *The.* And Fooleation!

a-tiptoe (ə'tɪptəʊ), *advb. phr.* [see A *prep.*¹] On tiptoe, on the tips of one's toes (either to raise oneself higher, or to move about noiselessly).

1576 R. SCOT *Hop Gard.* 45 They must stand longwyse, as it were a tiptoe. **1647** R. STAPYLTON *Juvenal* 98 She sure must stand a-tipto for a kisse. **1751** SMOLLETT *Per. Pic.* lxxxi, 133 He stood a tiptoe to view himself in the glass. **1868** GEO. ELIOT *Sp. Gipsy* 224 Moving a-tiptoe, silent as the Elves.

†**a'tire**, *v. Obs.* [OE. *ateorian*, f. A- *pref.* 1 + *teorian* to TIRE.] To become weary, cease, fail.

c **1000** *Ps.* (Spl.) xi. 1 (Bosw.) Ateorode háliȝ. *c* **1200** *Trin. Coll. Hom.* 29 Vnwreste þu best ȝef þu wreche ne secst .. ȝief mihte þe ne atiereð.

atishoo, atichoo (a'tɪʃ(j)uː), *int.* and *sb.* A representation of the characteristic noises accompanying a sneeze.

[**1873** R. BROUGHTON *Nancy* iii. 41, I sneeze loudly and irrepressibly. Atcha! Atcha!] **1878** *Punch* 26 Jan. 36 A cough tears your ludgs, but a sneeze tears you through—A'd—goodness!—it's cubbi'g—a-tschoo—A-tischoo! [**1878** *Hood's Comic Ann.* 54 I've got such a cold. Er-tchiou—ertchiou!] **1892** ZANGWILL *Childr. Ghetto* I. 112 Ezekiel sneezed. It was a convulsive 'atichoo'. **1910** *Punch* 30 Nov. 383 There, that's all right. A-a-a-tishoo! **1960** *Times* 8 Jan. 11/4 A sneeze may still mean the onset of a pestilential cold in the head and the thought prevents our taking a proper pleasure in our involuntary atishoos.

-ative, ad. F. *-atif, -ative*, L. *-ātīvus*, consisting of adj. suffix *-īvus* (see -IVE) appended to ppl. stems in *-āt-* of vbs. in *-āre*, e.g. *dēmonstrāre* to point out, *dēmonstrāt-īvus* 'having the attribute or habit of pointing out, tending to point out.' Only a few were used in Latin, but the analogy is extensively followed in the modern languages. In the majority of instances, as in *demonstrate*, *demonstrative*, adjs. in *-ative* belong to vbs. in *-ate*; cases like *represent*, *-ative*, *affirm*, *-ative*, *figure*, *figurative*, in which the Eng. vb. represents (through Fr.) the present stem of the Latin, have afforded a formal analogy for *talk*, *talk-ative*.

A few adjs. of this class are moreover formed directly from sbs. in -TY, as if from an intervening verb in *-tate*, which does not exist; e.g. AUTHORITY, (**authoritate*), *authoritative*; so *qualitative*, *quantitative*.

Atkins ('ætkɪnz). Also **Mister Atkins.** [See THOMAS 3.] = *Tommy Atkins* (*s.v.* TOMMY 7).

1892 KIPLING *Barrack-r. Ballads* 6 Oh it's Tommy this, an' Tommy that, an' 'Tommy, go away'; But it's 'Thank you, Mister Atkins', when the band begins to play. **1898** *Westm. Gaz.* 1 Nov. 4/3 Our citizen soldiers have been unduly agitated... Pathetic pictures have been drawn in the imagination of our sturdy civilian 'Atkinses' of wives left weeping. **1901** 'LINESMAN' *Words by Eyewitness* i. 3 Private Atkins.. is from the masses himself. **1928** E. WEEKLEY *Eng. Lang.* vii. 47 *Padre*, father, adopted in the sense of priest by the natives of India and then acquired from the natives by Mr. Atkins.

atlantad (æt'læntəd), *adv. Phys.* [f. as next + *-ad*, taken as advb. termination (? after Gr. -δε towards).] Towards the atlas (vertebra); towards the upper part of the body.

1825 J. LIZARS *Extr. Dis. Ovaria* 15 The intestines.. were pushed atlantad and dorsad, or upwards and backwards.

atlantal (æt'læntəl), *a. Phys.* [f. Gr. ἀτλαντ-, stem of ἄτλας (see ATLAS *sb.*[1]) + -AL[1].] Of or belonging to the atlas; also used by some for: Of or belonging to the upper part of the body.

1803 *Edin. Rev.* III. 105 Dr. Barclay therefore proposes the words *atlantal* and *sacral* instead of *superior* and *inferior*. **1839** TODD *Cycl. Anat. & Phys.* III. 245/1 The atlantal portion of the body. **1854** OWEN in *Orr's Circ. Sc.* Org. Nat. I. 197 The atlantal neurapophyses.

Atlantean (ætlæn'tiːən), *a.* [f. L. *Atlantē-us*, f. *Atlant-*: see prec. and -EAN.] Pertaining to, or having the supporting strength of, Atlas.

1667 MILTON *P.L.* II. 306 With Atlantean shoulders fit to bear The weight of mightiest Monarchies. **1863** MRS. C. CLARKE *Shaks. Char.* iv. 100 The mainspring and Atlantean support of the entire structure.

‖**atlantes** (æt'læntiːz), *sb. pl. Arch.* [L., a. Gr. Ἄτλαντες, pl. of Ἄτλας: see ATLAS *sb.*[1]] Figures or half-figures of men used instead of columns to support an entablature.

1706 in PHILLIPS. **1835** *Penny Cycl.* III. 25/1 The Atlantes of this temple [of Jupiter Olympius, at Agrigentum] were twenty-five feet high.

Atlantic (æt'læntɪk), *a.* and *sb.* Also (4 **athlant**), 7 **athlanticke, atlanticke**, 7–8 **-ick.** [ad. L. *Atlanticus*, a. Gr. Ἀτλαντικός, f. Ἄτλαντ-: see ATLAS *sb.*[1] and -IC.] **A.** *adj.*

1. a. Of or pertaining to Mount Atlas in Libya, on which the heavens were fabled to rest. Hence applied to the sea near the western shore of Africa, and afterwards extended to the whole ocean lying between Europe and Africa on the east and America on the west.

1601 HOLLAND *Pliny* I. 51 This river [Guadiana].. falleth into the Spanish Atlantick Ocean. **1626** COCKERAM, *Athlanticke Sea*, is the Mediterranean, or a part thereof. **1732** LEDIARD *Sethos* II. 4 The Phœnicians.. pass'd.. into the Hesperian or Atlantick ocean. **1878** HUXLEY *Physiogr.* 178 The southern part of the Atlantic basin.

b. *fig.* Far-reaching, distant; *transf.* in U.S.: Eastern.

1650 H. MORE *Enthus. Tri., etc.* (1656) 112 Which no man were able to smell out, unlesse his nose were as Atlantick as your rauming and reaching fancy. **1790** BURKE *Fr. Rev.* Wks. V. 430 Mr. Bailly will sooner thaw the eternal ice of his atlantick regions, than restore the central heat to Paris. **1800** WEEMS *Washington* (1877) 163 Northern and southern—atlantic and western.

c. Of or pertaining to countries bordering on the Atlantic Ocean, in recent times esp. with reference to the political alliances of these countries.

1776 H. WALPOLE *Let.* 17 Apr. (1904) IX. 349, I now submit to recall my thoughts to America... The army that was to overrun the Atlantic continent, is not half set out yet. **1931** H. G. WELLS *Work, Wealth & Happiness* (1932) viii. 305 We of the Atlantic world are too disposed to be ungrateful to the vast experiments Communism has made. **1944** W. LIPPMANN *U.S. War Aims* 80 In addition to the United States, the United Kingdom, and France.. the Atlantic Community includes.. [the South American countries],.. Australia, Belgium,.. Canada, [etc.]. **1960** R. L. C. FITZGIBBON *Kissing had to Stop* xii. 220 She [*sc.* Britain] could become.. the junior partner of an omnipotent Atlantic bloc. **1961** *Listener* 5 Oct. 493/1 Granted that Americans are not interested in Atlantic union, the emotional value to them of European union is enormous.

d. Crossing the Atlantic Ocean.

1839 *S. Lit. Messenger* V. 5/2 The packet owners have carried the Atlantic mail.. for twenty years. **1858** *Harper's Mag.* Oct. 700/2 We had learned articles proving that the Atlantic cable could never succeed under the existing conditions. **1895** KIPLING *Devil & Deep Sea* in *Day's Work* (1898) 141 Her crew signed and signed again with the regularity of Atlantic liner boatswains.

†**2.** = ATLANTEAN. *Obs.*

1631 BRATHWAIT *Whimzies* 139 His Atlanticke shoulders are his supporters. **1652** L. S. *People's Liberty* vi. 11 Neither can one man.. be so Atlantick, as to bear upon his shoulders the government of the Universe.

†**3.** Of the nature or size of an atlas; atlas-like.

1768 JOHNSON in *Boswell* (1831) II. 539 The maps.. fill two Atlantic folios.

4. Applied by Blytt to one of the successive periods of vegetation in Scandinavia after the glacial period, and later by others to the climate of other areas.

1876 [see ARCTIC *a.* 3]. **1935** *Discovery* July 198/1 The following climatic phase of the Postglacial period, the 'Atlantic Period', was considerably damper than the Boreal. **1959** J. D. CLARK *Prehist. S. Afr.* vii. 169 The Makalian Wet Phase probably equates in time with the warm Atlantic stage in Northern Europe, between *c.* 5,500 B.C. and *c.* 2,500 B.C. **1960** B. W. SPARKS *Geomorphology* ix. 216 Godwin has distinguished the following phases in the development of the Fens... *The pre-Boreal period*.. approximately 8300 to 7600 B.C... *The Boreal period.* From about 7600 to 5500 B.C. .. *The Atlantic period.* The period 5500 to 3000 B.C. was one of increasing dampness and of extensive peat formation. **1964** G. MANLEY in Watson & Sissons *Brit. Isles: Syst. Geogr.* 162 This event [*sc.* the breaking of the last land bridge between Britain and the continent] is commonly associated with the onset of 'Full-Atlantic' conditions, notably the mild winters that resulted from the broadening of the North and Irish Seas.

5. Phrases: ***Atlantic Alliance*** = *Atlantic Pact*; also the countries concerned in the Atlantic Pact; ***Atlantic Charter***, a declaration of eight common principles in international relations, drawn up by the British Prime Minister, Winston Churchill, and President Franklin D. Roosevelt, on behalf of the British Empire and the U.S.A., at their meeting in the Western Atlantic in August 1941; ***Atlantic Pact***, an agreement made in 1949 to ensure the defence of countries with seaboards on the North Atlantic (cf. N.A.T.O.); ***Atlantic States***, those of the United States situated on the Atlantic coast; ***Atlantic Wall***, the line of fortifications constructed by the Germans to defend the Atlantic coast of Europe in the war of 1939–45.

1958 *New Statesman* 15 Feb. 185/3 Does the Atlantic alliance come first—or the principles it is pledged to uphold? **1941** *Hutchinson's Pict. Hist. War* 9 July–30 Sept. 150/1 The President of the United States and the British representative in what is aptly called the Atlantic Charter, have jointly pledged their countries to the final destruction of the Nazi tyranny. **1958** *New Statesman* 1 Feb. 130/3 The verbal flaying of the clumsy, the ruthless persecution of the unfortunate—these have more in common with Buchenwald than with the Atlantic Charter. **1949** *Times* 19 Mar. 5/2 The Atlantic Pact is much more than an American guarantee of Europe.. it is a cooperative venture which will call for equal efforts. **1789** *Deb. Congress U.S.* (1834) I. 153 The policy of taxing the navigation of the Atlantic States for the purpose of encouraging their agriculture. **1832** J. P. KENNEDY *Swallow Barn* II. xiv. 233 Old Nick.. is falling into the sere and yellow leaf, especially in the Atlantic states. **1961** KURATH & MCDAVID (*title*) The Pronunciation of English in the Atlantic States. **1944** *Hutchinson's Pict. Hist. War* 12 Apr.–26 Sept. 189/1 The first ramparts of Hitler's so-called Atlantic Wall were breached.

B. *sb.* The Atlantic ocean; also *fig.* [For the 14th c. *athlante*, cf. F. *atlante*, Atlas, also inhabitant of the mythic Atlantis (an island placed by the Greeks in the far West).]

1387 TREVISA *Higden* Rolls Ser. I. 53 Þe see of occean of athlant [*oceanus Atlanticus*]. *a* **1711** KEN *Hymnotheo* Wks. 1721 III. 331 Down on the Earth it in Atlanticks rain'd. **1865** MASSON *Rec. Brit. Philos.* iv. 388 'Feelings' or 'phænomena of feeling' is an indiscriminate Atlantic of a phrase.

atlanto- (æt'læntəʊ), comb. form of ATLAS *sb.*[1] (in the physiological sense), as in *atlanto-axial*, etc.

1839 TODD *Cycl. Anat. & Phys.* III. 457/1 The atlanto-occipital articulation. **1881** MIVART *Cat* 55 The ventral atlanto-axial ligament connects the ventral arch of the atlas with the centrum of the axis.

Atlantosaurus (æt,læntə'sɔːrəs). *Palæont.* [mod.L., f. Gr. Ἄτλας, -αντος (see ATLAS *sb.*[1]) + -O- + σαῦρος lizard.] An extinct genus of huge dinosaurian reptiles of the sub-order Sauropoda; also, a reptile of this genus.

1877 O. C. MARSH in *Amer. Jrnl. Sci.* XIV. 514 The gigantic Dinosaur, *Atlantosaurus montanus*.. is.. from the upper Jurassic... It is the representative of a distinct family, which may be called *Atlantosauridæ*. In the type genus, *Atlantosaurus*, one of the most important characters is the pneumaticity of the vertebræ. **1882** *Cliftonian* Nov. 289 We have seen what gigantic representatives of the race this *Atlantosaurus*, and even our Iguanodon were. **1884** J. FISKE *Excurs. Evolut.* i. 12 Professor Marsh has lately discovered the atlantosaurus of Colorado, nearly one hundred feet in length and thirty feet in height,—the largest land animal as yet known. **1893** *Graphic* 11 Feb. 134/1 A view of the thigh-bone of the atlantosaurus.

Atlas ('ætləs), *sb.*[1] Pl. **atlases.** [a. L. *Atlās*, *-antem*, a. Gr. Ἄτλας, -αντα; name of one of the older family of gods, who was supposed to hold up the pillars of the universe, and also of the mountain in Libya that was regarded as supporting the heavens. Hence the various fig. uses.]

1. One who supports or sustains a great burden; a chief supporter, a mainstay.

1589 NASHE in *Greene's Menaph.* Ded. (Arb.) 17, I dare commend him to all that know him, as.. the Atlas of Poetrie. **1618** *Barneveld's Apol.* C iv b, You.. make your selfe the Atlas, and sustainer of the whole state of Holland. **1883** M. HOWLAND in *Harper's Mag.* Mar. 598/1 We brokers are the Atlases that bear the world upon our shoulders.

b. *Arch.* (See ATLANTES.)

2. *Phys.* The first or uppermost cervical vertebra, which supports the skull, being articulated above with the occipital bone. (So in Gr.)

1699 *Phil. Trans.* XXI. 180 The Union by the Atlas, is not so firm and compact as in the other Vertebræ. **1842** E. WILSON *Anat. Vade M.* 9 The Atlas is a simple ring of bone, without body, and composed of arches and processes.

3. A collection of maps in a volume. [This use of the word is said to be derived from a representation of Atlas supporting the heavens placed as a frontispiece to early works of this kind, and to have been first used by Mercator in the 16th c.]

1636 (*title*) Atlas; or a Geographic Description of the World, by Gerard Mercator and John Hondt. **1641** EVELYN *Mem.* (1857) I. 28 Visited the famous Hondius and Bleaw's shop, to buy some maps, atlasses, etc. **1729** FLAMSTEED (*title*) Atlas Cœlestis. **1812** WOODHOUSE *Astron.* ix. 63 Celestial Atlases also, or maps of the Heavens.

4. A similar volume containing illustrative plates, large engravings, etc., or the conspectus of any subject arranged in tabular form; *e.g.* 'an atlas of anatomical plates,' 'an ethnographical atlas.'

1875 FORTNUM *Maiolica* vi. 53 The details of all these methods are illustrated on the 3rd table of his atlas of plates.

5. A large square folio resembling a volume of maps; also called *atlas-folio*.

6. A large size of drawing-paper.

1712 *Act 10 Anne* in *Lond. Gaz.* No. 5018/3 For all Paper called Atlas fine 16*s.* per Ream, Atlas ordinary 8*s.* **1879** SPON *Workshop Rec.* 1, Atlas, 33 × 26 inches.

7. *Comb.* or *Attrib.*, as **atlas beetle**, a gigantic olive-green lamellicorn beetle (*Chalcosoma Atlas*), found in the East; **Atlas-like** *a.* (or *adv.*), like, or after the manner of, Atlas; **atlas moth** (*Saturnia Atlas*), a very large foreign moth.

a **1649** DRUMM. OF HAWTH. *Wks.* (1711) 3/2 That Atlas-like it seem'd the heaven they beared. **1868** WOOD *Homes without H.* xiv. 280 That magnificent insect the Atlas Moth.

atlas ('ætləs), *sb.*[2] *arch.* or *Obs.* [a. (ultimately) Arab. *aṭlas* 'smooth, bare,' thence 'smooth silk cloth,' f. *ṭalasa* to rub smooth, delete. Cf. in same sense It. *raso* shaved, satin. Also in G. *atlas* satin.] A silk-satin manufactured in the East.

1687 *Lond. Gaz.* No. 2273/7 Atlasses 549 pieces. **1706** T. BAKER *Tunbr. Walks* I. i, Fat city-ladies with tawdry atlasses. *c* **1710** in J. Ashton *Soc. Life Reign Q. Anne* (1882) I. 167 One Purple and Gold Atlas Gown. **1766** J. H. GROSE *Voy. E. Indies* (1772) I. 117 Their Atlasses or satin flowered with gold and silver.

atlas ('ætləs), *v.* [f. ATLAS *sb.*[1]] *trans.* To support after the manner of Atlas: **a.** to prop up; **b.** to carry on one's shoulder or head.

1593 NASHE *Christes T.* (1613) 121 To ouerthrow both thy cause and my credite at once, by ouer-Atlassing mine inuention. **1859** *All Y. Round* No. 35. 203 An Armenian, atlasing a square coop of some forty barn-door fowls.

atlasite ('ætləsaɪt). *Min.* [f. ATLAS *sb.*[2]; given in Ger. in 1865.] An ore of vitreous or silky lustre, consisting of carbonate, with a little chloride, of copper, which is perhaps a mixture of AZURITE and ATACAMITE. (Dana.)

atlatl ('æt(ə)læt(ə)l). [Amer. Indian (Nahuatl) *atlatl* spear-thrower.] A throwing-stick used by American Indians and Eskimos.

1871 E. B. TYLOR *Prim. Cult.* I. ii. 60 The highest people known to have used the spear-thrower proper are the Aztecs. Its existence among them is vouched for.. by its name 'atlatl'. **1910** F. W. HODGE *Handbk. Amer. Indians* II. 746/1 *Throwing stick.* This implement, called also throwing board, dart sling, and atlatl, is an apparatus for hurling a lance, spear, or harpoon at birds and aquatic animals. **1933** A. A. MORRIS *Digging in Southwest* iv. 45 The bow and arrow had not yet come into use, but instead game and enemies were reduced by long darts hurled with an *atlatl*.

atle, var. ETTLE *v. Obs.* to intend, purpose.

†**at'lead**, *v. Obs.* [OE. *ætlǽdan* (cf. earlier *oplǽdan*), f. AT- *pref.*[2] + *lǽdan* to LEAD.] *trans.* To lead or take away (with *dat.* = from).

a **1000** *Ags. Ps.* cxxxv. 11 He Israhelas ealle oðlædde of Ægyptum. *c* **1000** ÆLFRIC *Gen.* xxxi. 26 Ðæt ðu ætlæddest me mine dóhtra. **1205** LAY. 3200 Þat Leir kinge hire fæder heo him wold atleden. **1250** *Ibid.* 4654 Þat Brenne wolde.. mi leofman me at-leade.

†**at'let**, *v. Obs.* Also 2–3 **etlet.** [f. AT- *pref.*[2] + LET, OE. *lǽtan*; cogn. with G. *entlassen*, OHG.

intlagan, Du. *ontlaten*.] *trans.* To let away, let go from consideration: *hence*, **a.** to neglect, disregard; **b.** to remit, pardon.

c **1200** *Moral Ode* 257 in *Lamb. Hom.* 175 þet oðer monnes wif lof · his aȝen et-lete. *c* **1200** *Trin. Coll. Hom.* 69 Edie ben alle þo : þe here giltes ben atleten.

† **at'lie**, *v. Obs.* For forms, see LIE *v.*[1] [OE. *ætlicgan*, f. AT- *pref.*[2] + *licgan* to LIE.] *intr.* To lie idle or fallow (with *dat.* = from).

c **1000** ÆLFRIC *Gram.* Pref., þæt godes feoh ne ætlicge. *c* **1200** *Trin. Coll. Hom.* 161 Atlai þat lond unwend, and bicam waste. *Ibid.*, þat londe, þat is longe tilðe atleien.

'atlo-, at'loido, comb. forms of ATLAS, formed on imperfect analogy: see ATLANTO-. **atloi'dean** *a.* (similarly formed) = ATLANTAL.

1840 G. ELLIS *Anat.* 275 A posterior atlo-axoid ligament ..The ligaments, which connect the arch of the atlas to the occipital bone, are named occipito-atloidean. **1857** BULLOCK *Cazeaux's Midwif.* 223 The atloido-axoid articulation.

† **at-low**, *advb. phr. Obs. rare*[−1]. [app. f. on analogy of *atfore*, before.] Below.

c **1460** *Towneley Myst.* 133 Othere lord is none atlowe, Bothe man and beest to hym shalle bowe.

† **at'lutien**, *v. Obs.* Also 3 etl-. [OE. *ætlútian*, f. AT- *pref.*[2] + *lútian*: see LOUT *v.*] *intr.* To hide away, lurk, escape notice.

c **1000** ÆLFRIC *Judges* iv. 18. *c* **1230** *Ancr. R.* 316 ȝif þer out etluteð. *Ibid.* 400 'Non est qui se abschondat a calore ejus:' nis non þet muwe etlutien þet heo ne mot him luuien.

‖ **atman** ('ɑːtmæn). *Hindu Philos.* [Skr. *ātmán* essence, the highest personal principle of life; cf. OE. *ǽðm, éðm* breath, ETHEM.] The self or soul; the supreme principle of life in the universe.

1785 C. WILKINS tr. *Bhagvat* xiii. 105 He who beholdeth all his actions performed by *Prăkrĕĕtĕĕ*, nature, at the same time perceiveth that the *Ātmă* or soul is inactive in them. **1859** J. R. BALLANTYNE *Christianity contr. w. Hindu Philos.* p. xxiii, The soul (*ātman*) is spoken of as an entirely different entity from the mind (*manas*). **1867** F. M. MÜLLER *Chips* I. iii. 70 For *âtman*, originally breath or spirit, comes to mean Self and Self alone. **1933** J. BAILLIE *Life Everl.* v. 139 The soul of man is *atman*, and *atman* is Brahma, the one supreme reality. **1945** A. HUXLEY *Time must have Stop* xxx. 275 'Devotion can be defined as the search for the reality of one's own Atman.' And the Atman, of course, is the spiritual principle in us, which is identical with the Absolute.

atmidometer (ætmɪ'dɒmɪtə(r)). [f. Gr. ἀτμίς, -ίδ- vapour + μέτρον measure: see -(O)METER.] = ATMOMETER.

1830 in *Edin. Encycl.*

atmology (æt'mɒlədʒɪ). *Physics.* [f. Gr. ἀτμό-ς vapour: see -(O)LOGY.] That branch of science which treats of the laws and phenomena of aqueous vapour. **at'mologist**, one skilled in, or a professed student of, atmology (in Webster 1864). **atmological** (ætməʊ'lɒdʒɪkəl), *a.*, of or pertaining to atmology.

1837 WHEWELL *Hist. Induct. Sc.* (1857) I. 255 An atmological doctrine by Watt. *Ibid.* II. 378 These we may include under the term Atmology.

atmolysis (æt'mɒlɪsɪs). *Physics.* [f. Gr. ἀτμό-ς vapour + λύσις setting free, release; cf. *analysis*.] The (partial) separation of gases or vapours of unequal diffusibility. **atmolyse, -ze** ('ætməʊlaɪz) [cf. *analyse*], to perform atmolysis. **'atmolyser, -zer**, an instrument for effecting it.

1866 T. GRAHAM *Absorpt. Gases* 1 The agency of atmolysis is therefore very limited in parting the oxygen and nitrogen of atmospheric air. **1876** *Catal. Sci. App. S. Kens.* 344 Atmolyser, an instrument for the separation of gases by diffusion..through a porous septum.

atmometer (æt'mɒmɪtə(r)). *Physics.* [f. Gr. ἀτμό-ς vapour + μέτρον measure: see -METER.] An instrument for determining the amount of evaporation from a moist surface in a given time.

1815 *Edin. Rev.* XXIV. 348 Mr. Leslie has invented another instrument which..he has named the Atmometer. **1878** HUXLEY *Physiogr.* 69 Meteorologists occasionally measure the rapidity of evaporation by means of.. atmometers.

atmosphere ('ætməsfɪə(r)), *sb.* Also 7 **-sphære, -sphear.** [ad. mod.L. *atmosphæra*, f. Gr. ἀτμό-ς vapour + σφαῖρα ball, sphere.]

1. a. The spheroidal gaseous envelope surrounding any of the heavenly bodies. **b.** *esp.* The mass of aeriform fluid surrounding the earth; the whole body of terrestrial air.

The name was invented for the ring or orb of vapour or 'vaporous air' supposed to be exhaled from the body of a planet, and so to be part of it, which the *air* itself was not considered to be; it was extended to the portion of surrounding air occupied by this, or supposed to be in any way 'within the sphere of the activity' of the planet (Phillips 1696); and finally, with the progress of science, to the supposed limited aeriform environment of the earth or other planetary or stellar body. (It is curious that the first mention of an *atmosphere* is in connexion with the Moon, now believed to have none.)

1638 WILKINS *New World* I. x. (1707) 76 There is an Atmosphæra, or an Orb of Gross, Vaporous Air immediately encompassing the Body of the Moon. **1677** PLOT *Oxfordsh.* 4 That subtile Body that immediately incompasses the Earth, and is filled with all manner of exhalations, and from thence commonly known by the name of the Atmosphere. **1692** BENTLEY *Boyle Lect.* 208 The sun and planets and their atmospheres. **1751** CHAMBERS *Cycl.* s.v., Among some of the more accurate writers, the *atmosphere* is restrained to that part of the air next the earth, which receives vapours and exhalations; and is terminated by the refraction of the sun's light. **1867** E. DENISON *Astron. without Math.* 56 The earth's atmosphere decreases so rapidly in density, that half its mass is within $3\frac{1}{2}$ miles above the sea; and at 80 miles high there can be practically no atmosphere. **1881** STOKES in *Nature* No. 625. 597 In the solar atmosphere there is a cooling from above.

2. *transf.* A gaseous envelope surrounding any substance.

1863 WATTS *Dict. Chem.* I. 431 Thus we speak of the atmosphere of oxygen which spongy platinum attracts to its surface, or of the reduction of a metal in an atmosphere of hydrogen. **1876** TAIT *Rec. Adv. Phys. Sc.* xiii. 321, I shall simply put this atmosphere of coal gas..outside the bulb.

3. † **a.** A supposed outer envelope of effective influence surrounding various bodies; esp. ***electrical atmosphere***, that surrounding electrified bodies (*obs.*). **b.** ***magnetic atmosphere***, the sphere within which the attractive force of the magnet acts.

1668 *Phil. Trans.* III. 851 Notes and Trials about the Atmospheres of Consistent Bodies. **1727-51** CHAMBERS *Cycl.*, *Atmosphere* of Solid or Consistent Bodies, is a kind of sphere formed by the effluvia, or minute corpuscles, emitted from them. **1750** FRANKLIN *Lett.* Wks. 1840 V. 228 The additional quantity [of electrical fluid] does not enter, but forms an electrical atmosphere.

4. a. *fig.* Surrounding mental or moral element, environment. Also, prevailing psychological climate; pervading tone or mood; characteristic mental or moral environment; fascinating or beguiling associations or effects.

1797-1803 FOSTER in *Life & Corr.* (1846) I. 163 An extensive atmosphere of Consciousness. **1817** COLERIDGE *Biog. Lit.* I. iv. 84 The original gift of spreading the tone, the *atmosphere*, and with it the depth and height of the ideal world around forms, incidents. **1828** SCOTT *F.M. Perth* ii. (1878) 36 He lives in a perfect atmosphere of strife, blood, and quarrels. **1854** W. C. ROSCOE in *Prospective Rev.* X. 398 [Shakespeare] leaves his meaning to rest in great measure on the atmosphere that hangs about his language, rather than on its dictionary meaning and grammatical construction. **1859** MILL *Liberty* 116 Genius can only breathe freely in an atmosphere of freedom. **1869** M. ARNOLD in *Cornhill Mag.* Nov. 600 Being in love changes for the time a man's spiritual atmosphere. **1884** [see EFFECT *sb.* 3 b]. **1884** 'VERNON LEE' *Euphorion* I. 27 Their intellectual atmosphere was as clear as our own. *a* **1902** S. BUTLER *Way of all Flesh* (1903) vi. 27 Genial mental atmosphere. **1922** G. SANTAYANA *Solil. in England* ix. 30 What governs the Englishman is his inner atmosphere, the weather in his soul. **1923** H. G. BAYNES tr. *Jung's Psychol. Types* v. 230 The religion of the last two thousand years..has, thereby, created an atmosphere which remains wholly uninfluenced by any intellectual disavowal. **1923** WODEHOUSE *Inimit. Jeeves* xii. 130, I never know, when I'm telling a story, whether to cut the thing down to plain facts or whether to..shove in a lot of atmosphere. **1934** L. SIEVEKING *Stuff of Radio* I. ix. 90 *Together* the music of the orchestra, the aeroplane and sea sounds, and the dialogue of the three men, created genuine 'atmosphere', evoked emotion. **1948** J. R. SUTHERLAND *Pref. 18th c. Poetry* i. 1 Hobbes and Locke..were subjecting the intellectual atmosphere to a sort of air-conditioning process.

b. *spec.* Applied to the background sounds that evoke a particular mood, impression, setting, etc., in a broadcast programme, etc. Also *attrib.*

1941 *B.B.C. Gloss. Broadc. Terms* 4 *Atmosphere*, sounds forming the acoustic background incidental to an event such as a race meeting, procession, etc. Hence *atmosphere microphone*, microphone specially placed to pick up such sounds. **1961** K. REISZ *Technique Film Editing* (ed. 9) ii. 186 The sound editor can do little more than choose a piece of accompanying atmosphere music from his library. **1962** A. NISBETT *Technique Sound Studio* ii. 42 A record of courtroom 'atmosphere' completed the picture by providing an occasional cough or shuffling noise. *Ibid.* viii. 141 At this point, in order to maintain the fullest continuity, we can do a crossfade which keeps the atmosphere running throughout the pause.

5. The air in any particular place, *esp.* as affected in its condition by heat, cold, purifying or contaminating influences, etc.; = AIR *sb.* 4.

1767 FORDYCE *Serm. Yng. Wom.* I. vi. 239 The suffocating atmosphere of..a small apartment. **1858** HAWTHORNE *Fr. & It. Jrnls.* I. 126 No amount of blaze would raise the atmosphere of the room ten degrees.

6. A pressure of 15 lbs. on the square inch, which is that exerted by the atmosphere on the earth's surface.

1830 LYELL *Princ. Geol.* I. 396 Congealed under the pressure of many hundred, or many thousand atmospheres. **1881** LUBBOCK in *Nature* No. 618. 411 Hydrogen was liquefied by Pictet under a pressure of 650 atmospheres.

7. *Comb.* **atmosphereful** *sb.* (cf. *bucketful*); **atmosphereless** *a.*, without an atmosphere.

1879 BLACK *Macleod of D.* xxiii, A whole atmosphereful of pheasants. **1858** J. BENNET *Nutrition* iii. 75 Our cold satellite, the atmosphereless moon.

'atmosphere, *v.* [f. prec. sb.] To surround like, or as with, an atmosphere.

1881 PALGRAVE *Vis. Eng.* 197 The deep uneasy lurid gloom That atmosphered usurping sway. **1882** W. C. SMITH in *Gd. Words* 103 Hunter's religious convictions.. were atmosphered in a fine spirit of reverence.

'atmosphered, *ppl. a.* [f. ATMOSPHERE *v.*] Having or provided with atmosphere (sense 4).

1920 *Times Lit. Suppl.* 12 Feb. 103/2 The scenes..are no less sharp and clear and 'atmosphered'. **1962** *Listener* 1 Feb. 224/3 The amorphous and exquisitely atmosphered landscapes.

† **atmos'pherial**, *a. Obs.* [cf. *aerial*.] = next.

1709 T. ROBINSON *Nat. Hist. Westmorld.* 9 Until the atmospherial heat rarifies the nitrous part of the fog. **1728** EARBERY tr. *Burnet's State of Dead* II. 77 The.. Atmospherial Air around us.

atmospheric (ætməs'fɛrɪk), *a.* [f. ATMOSPHERE *sb.* + -IC; cf. Gr. σφαιρικός.]

1. Of the nature of, or forming, the atmosphere.

1783 T. HENRY (*title*) Effects produced by various Processes on Atmospheric Air. **1860** MAURY *Phys. Geog. Sea* vi.§346 The earth itself, or the atmospheric envelope by which it is surrounded.

2. Existing, taking place, or acting in the air.

1789 A. BENNET *New Exper. Electr.* 103 It may be proper to mention such theory of atmospheric electricity as appears to me consonant to the general operations of nature. **1835** *Penny Cycl.* III. 36/2 The action of the sun and moon must produce certain small atmospheric tides. **1872** BLACK *Adv. Phaeton* xxi. 301 The wildest atmospheric effects became visible. **1876** PAGE *Advd. Text-bk. Geol.* ii. 43 There would have been..greater atmospheric moisture. **1934** *Discovery* Mar. 68/2 A report..on fog and atmospheric pollution. **1947** *Archit. Rev.* CI. 139/1 Heavy atmospheric pollution occurs in most of the larger towns in this country, with consequent detriment to health and environment.

3. Caused, produced, or worked by the action of the atmosphere.

atmospheric engine, a steam-engine in which the piston was forced down by the pressure of the atmosphere, after the condensation of the steam that caused it to rise. ***atmospheric line***, the equilibrium line on the indicator-card of a steam-engine. ***atmospheric pressure***, that exerted by the atmosphere on the earth's surface, 14·7 (roughly 15) lbs. to the square inch. ***atmospheric railway***, one worked by the propulsive force of compressed air or by the formation of a vacuum; a pneumatic railway.

1822 BURROWES *Cycl.* X. 229/2 The atmospheric engine of Newcomen. **1853** KANE *Grinnell Exp.* viii. (1856) 61 The Polar glacier must be regarded as strictly atmospheric in its increments.

4. Evoking or designed to evoke an atmosphere (sense 4).

1908 [see AVIATE *v.*] **1927** *Melody Maker* Sept. 942 (Advt.), Modern atmospheric music by the World's most eminent writers. **1946** *Ann. Reg. 1945* 343 An atmospheric story, 'The Seventh Veil', broke all box-office records. **1963** *Punch* 20 Feb. p. vii/1 Visually beautiful, atmospheric little tragedy about the love of a guilt-ridden childlike man.

atmos'pherical, *a.* [f. as prec. + -ICAL.]

1. = ATMOSPHERIC 1. *arch.* (*Atmospherical air* was so called at first to distinguish it from other gases also called *air*: see AIR *sb.* 2.)

1664 POWER *Exp. Philos.* II. 99 By Atmosphærical Air, I understand such as we constantly breathe and live in. **1816** FARADAY *Exp. Res.* i. 2 The atmospherical air being perfectly excluded.

2. = ATMOSPHERIC 2.

1666 BOYLE in *Phil. Trans.* I. 182 The Extent of the Atmospherical Changes. **1824** DICK *Chr. Philos.* 317 Hail, rain, snow, dew, and other atmospherical phenomena.

3. = ATMOSPHERIC 3.

1661 BOYLE *Spring of Air* I. iv. (1682) 11 There is much of the Atmospherical pressure—if I may so speak, taken off. **1829** T. FORSTER (*title*) Illustrations of the Atmospherical Origin of Epidemic Diseases.

4. Subject to atmospheric influences. *rare.*

1728 POPE *Let. Swift* in *Swift's Wks.* (1761) VIII. 85 If I lived in Ireland, I fear the wet climate would endanger..my humour, and health; I am so atmospherical a creature.

atmos'pherically, *adv.* [f. prec. + -LY[2].] As regards atmosphere or (*fig.*) surrounding influence.

1871 *Daily News* 23 Jan., To-day, atmospherically, has been..dull. **1874** EMERSON *Ess.* xvi. 210 A man should not go where he cannot carry his whole sphere or circle with him —not bodily..but atmospherically.

atmospherics (ætməs'fɛrɪks). [pl. of ATMOSPHERIC *a.* used as *sb.*] Atmospheric disturbances of electrical origin causing interference with communication in wireless telegraphy, television, etc. Also occas. without final *-s*.

1905 A. Y. FORREST in J. Erskine-Murray *Handbk. Wireless Telegr.* (1907) x. 181 Upon changing over to the Fessenden interference preventer, the terrific atmospheric was cut down to such an extent that I was enabled to receive the report. **1913** *Year-bk. Wireless Telegr.* 334 No signal nor atmospheric can put it out of action. **1915** *Wireless World* Apr. 55/1 To protect the condenser from strong 'atmospherics', a spark gap should be connected to the two plates of the condenser. **1919** R. STANLEY *Text-bk. Wireless Telegr.* I. 173 Irregular noises are produced in the receiver telephones which seriously interfere with the reception of the regular signals; they are due to 'Atmospherics', or 'strays', or Xs. **1934** *Discovery* Mar. 73/2 The Air Ministry chose this wavelength because it is only in this region that uninterrupted communication, free from all possibility of interference and atmospherics can be depended upon at all times. **1947** CROWTHER & WHIDDINGTON *Sci. at War* i. 15 The atmospherics are a very brief phenomenon. **1947** *Sci. News* IV. 58 It is an accepted fact that 'atmospherics' are produced also by a radiation which comes to us direct from the centre of the Galaxy.

atmospherology (,ætməsfɪə'rɒlədʒɪ). [f. ATMOSPHERE *sb.*: see -(O)LOGY.] Scientific investigation of the atmosphere, or a treatise upon it.

1859 WORCESTER cites BESWICK.

ato, obsolete form of A-TWO.

atocha (ə'təʊtʃə). *U.S.* [Sp.] Esparto. Also *attrib.*, as ***atocha grass, plant.***

1869 *Rep. U.S. Commissioner Agric. 1868* 262 There are two classes of this plant, the 'atocha', properly so called, and the coarse or 'bastard' atocha... The atocha grass, which is called esparto, is not cut like ordinary grass, but is pulled up from its socket. *Ibid.* 264 It is at about this elevation [*sc.* 3,500 feet] where the snow usually commences, that the atocha plant ceases to grow.

atoȝen, pa. pple. of ATEE *v. Obs.*

atoke ('ætəʊk). [G. (E. Ehlers *Die Borstenwürmer* (1868) II. 453), ad. Gr. *ἄτοκος*, f. *ἀ-* priv. (A- 14) + *τόκος* birth.] The sexless part of certain polychætous worms. Hence **atokal** ('ætəkəl), **atokous** ('ætəkəs) *adjs.*, non-sexual; producing only asexual progeny.

1896 *Cambr. Nat. Hist.* II. 277 Ehlers employed the term 'epitokous', whilst he called the 'Nereid' phase 'atokous', under the impression that the worm did not become mature in this condition. **1903** J. S. KINGSLEY tr. *Hertwig's Zool.* 311 The atoke..forms chains of dimorphic individuals which later separate. **1904** *Jrnl. R. Microsc. Soc.* Apr. 183 The total length [of the marine worm palolo] averages 400 mm., about one-fourth of which is in the anterior atokal part. **1916** [see EPITOKOUS *a.*].

†**at-old**, *adj. phr. Obs.* Also **at-eald.** [f. AT- *pref.*[2] + OLD; a unique combination, of which the prefix may be compared to OE. *úð-* in *úðwita* an extra-wise man, a sage.] Too old.

c **1200** *Trin. Coll. Hom.* 125 His [Zacharie's] woreldes make was teames atold, and unberinde. *Ibid.* 133 Two lif holi men..þe weren boðe teames ateald.

atole (ə'təʊliː). *U.S.* [Amer.-Sp., f. Nahuatl *atolli.*] A kind of corn or other meal; gruel or porridge made of this.

1716 in *S.W. Hist. Q.* XXXI. 56 They make large pots in which to keep water, make *atole*, and to preserve other things. **1798** tr. *Peyrouse's Voyage* 86 A breakfast of barley meal..It is boiled in water; the Indians give this food the name of *atole.* **1844** J. GREGG *Commerce of Prairies* I. 153 A sort of thin mush, called *atole*, made of Indian meal, is another article of diet. **1946** R. PEATTIE *Pacific Coast Ranges* 41 All partook of a morning meal of atole.

‖**atoll** (ə'tɒl, 'ætɒl). In 7 **atollon.** [adoption of the native name *atollon, atoll*, applied to the Maldive Islands, which are typical examples of this structure; prob. = Malayalam *aḍal* 'closing, uniting' (Col. Yule).]

A coral island consisting of a ring-shaped reef enclosing a lagoon. Darwin's theory, now generally accepted, is that the lagoon occupies the place of a submerged island.

1625 PURCHAS *Pilgrims* II. 1648 Every Atollon is separated from others, and contaynes in itselfe a great multitude of small Isles..Each of these Atollons are inuironed round with a huge ledge of rocks. **1832** LYELL *Princ. Geol.* II. 285 In the centre of each atoll there is a lagoon from fifteen to twenty fathoms deep. **1859** DARWIN *Orig. Spec.* xii. (1873) 324 Such sunken islands are now marked by rings of coral or atolls standing over them.

b. *Comb.* and *Attrib.*

1842 DARWIN *Coral Reefs* 107 An atoll-shaped bank of dead rock. *Ibid.* 169 True atoll-structure. **1845** —— *Voy. Nat.* xx. 468 The foundations, whence the atoll-building corals sprang.

atom ('ætəm), *sb.* Forms: (4 **attomus, athomus,** 6-7 **atomus,**) 5-7 **attome,** 6-7 **attom,** 6-8 **atome,** 7- **atom.** [a. F. *atome*, ad. L. *atom-us* 'an atom'; also 'the twinkling of an eye,' a. Gr. *ἄτομ-ος*, subst. use of *ἄτομ-ος*, adj. 'indivisible,' f. *ἀ* priv. + *-τομ-ος* 'cut,' from strong stem of *τέμ-ν-ειν* to cut. In 16th c. chiefly used in the L. and Gr. forms *atom-us, atom-os*, with pl. *atomi.* About 1600 the F. form *atome* came into general use, and was at length anglicized to *atom.*]

I. In philosophical and scientific use.

In senses 2 and 3 now generally held to consist of a positively charged nucleus, in which is concentrated most of the mass of the atom, and round which orbit negatively charged electrons.

1. A hypothetical body, so infinitely small as to be incapable of further division; and thus held to be one of the ultimate particles of matter, by the concourse of which, according to Leucippus and Democritus, the universe was formed.

1477 NORTON *Ord. Alch.* (in Ashm. 1652) v. 79 Resolving in Attomes [the 15th c. form is uncertain: the MSS. (16th and 17th cc.) have *attomis, atomes, attoms, anotamies.*] **1546** LANGLEY *Pol. Verg. De Invent.* I. ii. 4 b, Epicurus one of Democritus dysciples putteth two Causes Atomos or motes and Vacuitie or Emptinesse; of these he saith the foure Elementes come. **1603** HOLLAND *Plutarch's Mor.* 807 Epicurus saith: That the principles of all things be certeine Atomes. **1606** BRYSKETT *Civ. Life* 170 Epicures opinion.. that the falling of his motes or *Atomi* should breed necessitie in our actions. **1709** SWIFT *Trit. Ess.* Wks. 1755 II. I. 139 That the universe was formed by a fortuitous concourse of atoms. **1837** WHEWELL *Hist. Induct. Sc.* (1857) I. 48 The technical term, Atom, marks sufficiently the nature of the opinion. According to this theory, the world consists of a collection of simple particles, of one kind of matter, and of indivisible smallness..and by the various configurations and motions of these particles, all kinds of matter and all material phenomena are produced.

2. In Nat. Phil. ***physical atoms***: the supposed ultimate particles in which matter actually exists (without reference to their divisibility or the contrary), aggregates of which held in their places by molecular forces, constitute all material bodies.

1650 CHARLETON *Paradoxes* Prol. 14 The imperceptible Emissions, streaming in a semi-immaterial thread of Atomes from sublunary bodies. **1777** PRIESTLEY *Matt. & Spir.* i. (1782) I. 11 By an atom..I mean an ultimate component part of any gross body. **1871** TYNDALL *Fragm. Sc.* I. ii. 35 Atoms are endowed with powers of mutual attraction.

3. ***chemical atoms***: **a.** The smallest particles in which the elements combine either with themselves, or with each other, and thus the smallest quantity of matter known to possess the properties of a particular element.

1819 CHILDREN *Chem. Anal.* 437 The composition of hypo-sulphuric acid must be, 2 atoms of sulphur, 5 of oxygen. **1868** CHAMBERS *Encycl.* I. 527 What the chemist regards as an atom in his science, may not be an ultimate and indivisible atom in a physical point of view; the chemical atom, though incapable of division as a chemical atom, may still be composed or built up of many physical atoms. **1873** WILLIAMSON *Chem.* §85 Each atom of oxygen in water is combined with two atoms of hydrogen.

b. The smallest quantity in which a group of elements, called a radical, forms a compound corresponding to one formed by a simple element, or behaves like an element; thus the smallest known quantity of a chemical compound.

1847 *Nat. Encycl.* III. 395 The Benzoyle atom is formed of twenty-one elementary atoms—C_{14} H_5 O_2. **1873** WILLIAMSON *Chem.* §8, N H_4 is a radical, analogous to potassium, and N H_4 is capable in many compounds of taking the place of K: N H_4 is called an atom of Ammonium.

II. In popular use.

4. From sense 1, as the nearest popular conception to the atoms of the philosophers: One of the particles of dust which are rendered visible by light; a mote in the sunbeam. *arch.* or *Obs.*

1605 Z. JONES *De Loyer's Specters* 27 Atomes signifie motes in the Sunne. **1627** DRAYTON *Aginc.* (1631) 61 Bils and Axes play As doe the Attoms in the Sunny ray. **1784** COWPER *Task* I. 361 The rustling straw sends up a frequent mist Of atoms. **1821** BYRON *Two Fosc.* III. i, Moted rays of light Peopled with dusty atoms.

5. The smallest conceivable portion or fragment of anything; a very minute portion or quantity, a particle, a jot: **a.** of matter.

c **1630** DRUMM. OF HAWTH. *Poems* (1633) 166 Like tinder when flints atoms on it fall. **1644** DIGBY *Nat. Bodies* vi. (1658) 54 Little attomes of oyl..ascend apace up the week of a burning candle. **1835** SIR J. ROSS *N.-W. Pass.* xxxiv. 477 There was not an atom of water.

b. of things immaterial. ***logical atom***: one of the essential and indivisible elements into which some philosophers hold that statements can be analysed.

c **1630** DRUMM. OF HAWTH. *Poems* (1656) 136 We as but in a Mirrour see, Shadows of shadows, Atomes of thy Might. **1651** HOBBES *Leviath.* III. xliii. 331 Casting atomes of Scripture, as dust before mens eyes. **1866** G. MACDONALD *Ann. Q. Neighb.* i. 2, I do not feel one atom older than I did at three and twenty. **1873** C. S. PEIRCE in *Mem. Amer. Acad. Arts & Sci.* IX. II. 343 The logical atom, or term not capable of logical division, must be one of which every predicate may be universally affirmed or denied... A logical atom, then, like a point in space, would involve for its precise determination an endless process. **1918** [see ATOMISM 1 b]. **1958** G. J. WARNOCK *Eng. Philos. since 1900* v. 54 Russell's world of indefinitely numerous, independent logical atoms is the metaphysical opposite of Bradley's Absolute.

c. *esp.* in ***to smash, shiver,*** etc., ***to*** or ***into atoms.*** Cf. also BLOW *v.*[1] 24 a.

1664 H. MORE *Myst. Iniq.* 495 They would nimbly take a-pieces and consume to Atomes any such Terrestrial consistency of flesh and bloud. **1705** OTWAY *Orphan* v. vii. 2114 If but your word can shake This World to Atomes. **1851** [see SMASH *v.*[1] 2]. **1874** HELPS *Soc. Press.* iii. 51 Which should shiver into atoms some of our present most potent ideas. **1905** A. CONAN DOYLE *Return of Sherlock H.* 226 His second bust..had been smashed to atoms where it stood.

6. a. A very minute or microscopic object (without implying that it is a particle of anything else); anything relatively very small; an atomy.

1633 HERBERT *Ch. Milit.* in *Temple* 184 The smallest ant or atome knows thy power. **1664** POWER *Exp. Philos.* I. 26 Her eyes are two such very little black Atoms. **1884** ROE in *Harper's Mag.* Mar. 616/1 A saucy little atom of a bird.

b. *attrib.*

1742 YOUNG *Nt. Th.* IV. 421 And shall an atom of this atom-world Mutter, in dust and sin, the theme of heaven? **1813** L. HUNT in *Examiner* 15 Feb. 104/1 The swarm Of atom bees.

III. Of time. (Already in Gr. *ἄτομος* (1 Cor. xv. 22), L. *atomus* = 'twinkling of an eye,' and regularly fixed in value in med.L.; see Du Cange.)

†**7.** The smallest mediæval measure of time; = $\frac{15}{94}$ of a second. *Obs.*

According to the table of Papias in Du Cange—

47 atoms of time	= 1 ounce	= 7½ seconds (modern)
8 ounces	= 1 ostent	= 1 minute ,,
1½ ostents	= 1 moment	= 1½ minutes ,,
2⅔ moments	= 1 part	= 4 minutes ,,
1½ parts (or 4 moments)	= 1 minute	= 6 minutes ,,
2 minutes	= 1 point	= 12 minutes ,,
5 points	= 1 hour	= 1 hour ,,

Thus an hour was equal to either 5 points, 10 minutes, 15 parts, 40 moments, 60 ostents, 480 ounces, or 22560 atoms.

1398 TREVISA *Barth. De P.R.* IX. ix. (1495) 354 An vnce of tyme conteynyth seuen and forty attomos. *Ibid.* xxi. 359 Dyuydynge..of tyme passyth no ferder than Athomus.

IV. attrib. and *Comb.* **a.** attrib., as ***atom-dance***; also loosely used *attrib.* for *atomic*, as ***atom age, bomb*** (so ***atom-bomb*** v., ***-bombing*** vbl. sb.), ***scientist, spy.*** **b.** instrumental, as ***atom-born***; also, used with the sense of *atomic energy*, as ***atom-driven, -powered,*** and of ***atomic weapons,*** as ***atom-free.*** **c.** Objective, as ***atom-splitting.*** **d.** Similative, as ***atom-like.*** Also **atom-smasher** *colloq.*, an apparatus for accelerating charged particles; so ***atom-smashing*** vbl. sb.; **atom-theory**: the theory that accounts for the properties of bodies by the shape, position, etc. of their atoms.

1946 *Daily Tel.* 24 Sept. 3/7 A pre-vision of interplanetary travel in the *atom age. **1945** *Times* 7 Aug. 4/1 An impenetrable cloud of dust and smoke had covered the target area after the *atom bomb had been dropped at Hiroshima. **1945** *Evening News* 13 Aug. 1 (*headline*) Ultimatum to Japs: Accept by 6 p.m.—or be atom-bombed. **1946** *Britannica Bk. of Year* 832/1 Atom bombing. **1948** *John o' London's Weekly* 15 Oct. 491/2 The story concerns a group of survivors in the ruins of atom-bombed Los Angeles. **1953** C. DAY LEWIS *Ital. Visit* ii. 30 Gleefully brush past atom-bomb cauliflowers [*sc.* cloud-shapes]. **1819** SHELLEY *Ode to Heaven* 485 The abyss is wreathed with scorn At your presumption, *atom-born. **1878** GEO. ELIOT *Coll. Breakf. Party* 191 You saw the facial *atom-dance. **1950** *Jane's Fighting Ships 1950–51* Add. 5/2 Plans for an *atom-driven submarine..are reported. **1958** *Listener* 18 Dec. 1026/2 The creation of an atom-free zone in central Europe. **1890** W. JAMES *Princ. Psychol.* I. x. 348 The enjoyment of the *atom-like simplicity of their substance *in sæcula sæculorum* would not to most people seem a consummation devoutly to be wished. **1953** *Encounter* Oct. 59/2 An American *atom physicist. **1949** *Air Trails* 21 May 21 *Atom-powered bombers! How soon? How big? What shape? **1953** *Ann. Reg. 1952* 403 On 14 January the first official announcement was made in the United States about the production of an atom-powered aircraft carrier. **1945** *Sci. News Let.* 17 Nov. 312/3 *Atom scientists federate to help Congress. **1937** *Lit. Dig.* 12 June 17/3 The Westinghouse *atom-smasher will look like a gigantic aluminum pear. **1932** *Ibid.* 28 May 26/1 *Atom-smashing has been accomplished before, and it seems to be still only a laboratory wonder. **1942** *Electronic Engin.* Sept. 166/1 Several types of accelerator have been developed for providing high velocity particles with which to bombard the nuclei of atoms—a practice popularly known as 'atom smashing'. **1960** *New Statesman* 2 Jan. 8/1 With the aid of their big atom-smashing machines, other Americans manufactured fragments of anti-matter. **1939** *Discovery* Apr. 181 (*caption*) A New Type of *Atom-Splitting. **1946** *War Illustr.* 4 Jan. 572 (*caption*) Japanese Atom-Splitting Device. **1959** *Listener* 19 Mar. 514/2 The ideological *atom spies. **1871** R. H. HUTTON *Ess.* I. 40 Why do scientific men attach..less and less [credit] to the *atom-theory of matter?

†**atom** ('ætəm), *v. Obs.* [f. prec. sb.] To reduce to atoms, to atomize.

a **1678** FELTHAM *On Luke* xiv. 20 (R.) When he is atom'd into flying dust, he has prepared his substitute. **1648** EARL WESTMRLD. *Otia Sacra* (1879) 78 Attom'd into dust.

atom, obsolete form of AT HOME.

atomare (ætə'mɛə(r)). [f. ATOM *sb.*; cf. F. *hectare*, and see ARE *sb.*[3]] An area, or geometrical figure, supposed to be formed by a combination of ultimate atoms: see ATOMECHANICS.

1867 *Mining Jrnl.* Dec., According as the figures thus formed, or atomares, are composed of equilateral triangles, or squares, the elements are divided into two orders, trigonoids (or metalloids) and tetragonoids (or metals).

atomatic (ætə'mætɪk), *a. rare.* [irreg. formed as if on a Gr. *ἀτοματ-*, which does not exist; cf. *schism, -atic, prism, -atic.*] = ATOMIC.

1862 R. PATTERSON *Ess. Hist. & Art* 10 Those substances which are the most ethereal in their atomatic structure.. vibrate most readily. **1881** WILLIAMSON in *Nature* No. 618. 414 An atomatic formula of its composition.

atomechanics (,ætəmɪ'kænɪks). [f. ATO(M + MECHANICS.] The mechanics of atoms; chemistry considered as the mechanical interaction of ultimate atoms.

1867 *Mining Jrnl.* Dec., The science of atomechanics, or chemistry considered as the mechanics of the panatoms..In 1856 and 1857 Hinrichs communicated a memoir upon atomechanics to various *savants* and academies in Europe.

atomed ('ætəmd), *ppl. a.* ? *Obs.* [f. ATOM *v.* + -ED.] Reduced to or consisting of very fine particles.

1627 DRAYTON *Aginc., etc.* 185 In those bleake mountaines can you liue, where..attom'd mists turne instantly to hayle?

atomic (əˈtɒmɪk), *a.* and *sb.* [f. ATOM *sb.* + -IC. (Mod.L. *atomicus*, F. *atomique*.)]

A. *adj.*

1. Of or pertaining to atoms. ***atomic heat***: see HEAT *sb.* 2 e; ***atomic mass*** (= *atomic weight*): the mass of an atom, usually expressed in ***atomic mass units*** (in one scale, a unit equal to $\frac{1}{16}$ of the mass of an oxygen atom, or *spec.* of the oxygen isotope ^{16}O; since 1960, when it was formally adopted by the International Union of Pure and Applied Physics, equal to $\frac{1}{12}$ of the mass of the principal isotope of carbon, ^{12}C), abbrev. *a.m.u.*, *amu*; ***atomic number***: (of a chemical element) the number of unit positive charges present in the nucleus of its atom, being the physical property which determines the position of the element in the periodic table; symbol Z; ***atomic structure*** (see quots.); ***atomic weight*** in *Chem.*: the weight of an atom of an element (or radical), as compared with that of an atom of hydrogen, which is taken as unity; also the sum of the weights of the atom of a compound; combining equivalent; (after the adoption of oxygen as a standard) the ratio between the weight of one atom of the element and $\frac{1}{16}$ of the weight of an atom of oxygen (see WEIGHT *sb.*[1] 10 d, and *atomic mass*, above); ***atomic volume*** of a body: the space occupied by a quantity of it proportional to its atomic or molecular weight.

1692 J. EDWARDS *Remark. Texts* 229 According to their hypothesis..this *atomick bustle was from eternity. **1819** CHILDREN *Chem. Anal.* 285 The *atomic composition of pyromucic acid. **1898** S. W. HOLMAN *Matter, Energy, Force & Work* 153 The terms **atomic masses, combining masses*, etc., are likewise used instead of 'atomic weights', [etc.]. **1946** *Electronic Engin.* May 153/1 This discovery accounted for the large discrepancy between the actual atomic mass of neon (20.2) and the..view that such masses should be whole numbers. **1955** *Gloss. Terms Radiology* (*B.S.I.*) 18 Atomic mass unit..Abbreviation: amu. **1958** MANSFIELD *Elem. Nucl. Physics* i. 10 The *atomic mass M*, not to be confused with the molecular weight, is the mass of an isotope in atomic mass units. Numerically the atomic mass and mass number differ by less than 1 part in 100. In fact, the mass number is obviously the atomic mass rounded off to an integer. **1962** *Nature* 19 May 621/1 Some confusion of meaning..could be avoided if 'atomic mass' were reserved for the species of matter now known as nuclides and 'atomic weight' were used only in its traditional connotation, that is, for elements. **1963** JERRARD & MCNEILL *Dict. Sci. Units* 20 The masses of atoms and molecules are generally given in atomic mass units. These units are based on a scale in which the mass of the carbon isotope C_6^{12} is taken to be 12. **1821** T. THOMSON in *Ann. Phil.* N.S. I. 5 The following table exhibits the numbers assigned to the atom of these bodies... They approach very nearly to the other *atomic numbers contained in the table. **1913** H. G. J. MOSELEY in *Phil. Mag.* 6th Ser. XXVI. 1028 Table I. N atomic number. *Ibid.* 1031 We are therefore led by experiment to the view that N is the same as the number of the place occupied by the element in the periodic system. This atomic number is then for H 1. **1958** MANSFIELD *Elem. Nucl. Physics* i. 4 The *atomic number Z*, is the number of protons in the nucleus and, since the atom as a whole is electrically neutral, this also equals the number of the electrons. **1897** W. F. MAGIE tr. *C. Christiansen's Elem. Theor. Physics* i. 48 (*heading*) On the Molecular and *Atomic Structure of Bodies. **1938** R. W. LAWSON tr. *Hevesy & Paneth's Man. Radioactivity* (ed. 2) viii. 79 The theory of atomic structure has cleared up many points on the origin and nature of the individual types of rays. **1850** DAUBENY *Atom. The.* ix. 279 Supposing that all bodies were of the same specific gravity, the atomic weight of each would represent the relative size of its atoms, or in other words, its *atomic volume. **1820** T. THOMSON in *Ann. Phil.* XVI. 329 The greater number of chemical writers in this country have adopted the *atomic weights assigned by Wollaston. **1821** *Ibid.* N.S. I. 3 We found reason to conclude that the atomic weight of every body is a multiple of the weight of an atom of hydrogen. **1827** A. FYFE *Elem. Chem.* II. 493 The atomic weights are given both according to the oxigen and hydrogen scale. **1942** J. D. STRANATHAN *Particles* v. 169 Results obtained with the new mass spectrograph..made it certain that atomic weights are in general not quite whole numbers; but they are very close to whole numbers. *Ibid.* 182 It is rather fortunate that 99·76% of all O is of atomic weight 16. **1962** *Nature* 19 May 621/2 The chemist..needs to know the average mass of the mixture of nuclidic species which constitute the element. This is the quantity that has been called the atomic weight of the element.

2. About or concerned with atoms. In Physics and extended uses (senses 2 c, d, e) the early quots. refer to the *theory* of atomic structure and to various theoretical applications. Cf. ATOM IV.

a. *Philos.* Formerly, pertaining to or designating the doctrine taught by Leucippus, Democritus, and Epicurus: see ATOM *sb.* 1 and ATOMISM. In modern philosophy: unanalysable, irreducible, ultimate, essential; also, of a sentence: without conjunctions or other connective words.

1678 CUDWORTH *Intell. Syst.* Pref. 6 The Atomick Physiology..the foundation of the Democritick Fate. **1809** W. IRVING *Knickerb.* (1861) 7 The great atomic system taught by old Moschus..revived by Democritus of laughing memory; improved by Epicurus..and modernized by the fanciful Descartes. **1912** L. WITTGENSTEIN *Let.* (to Russell) in *Notebks. 1914–16* (1961) 120, I believe that our problems can be traced down to the *atomic* propositions. **1918** B. RUSSELL in *Monist* 523 An atomic proposition is one which does mention actual particulars, not merely describe them but actually name them. **1922** tr. *Wittgenstein's Tract. Log.-Phil.* 31 An atomic fact is a combination of objects (entities, things). **1929** WITTGENSTEIN in *Knowledge, Exper. & Realism* (Aristotelian Soc. Suppl., Vol. IX) 163 The propositions which represent this ultimate connexion of terms I call, after B. Russell, atomic propositions. **1933** *Mind* XLII. 38 Similar to the species of geometry, we might have in logic 'a logic of atomic propositions' and 'a logic of molecular propositions'. **1948** B. RUSSELL *Human Knowl.* II. ix. 145 We give the name ' atomic sentence' to one not containing logical words. **1956** G. RYLE in Ayer et al. *Revol. Philos.* 10 The analysis of compound propositions into their simple elements, the conjunctionless or 'atomic' propositions.

b. *Chem.*, esp. as ***atomic theory***, the doctrine that elemental bodies consist of aggregations of indivisible atoms of definite relative weight; that the atoms of different elements unite with each other in fixed proportions; and that the latter determine the fixed proportions in which elements and compounds enter into chemical combination with each other.

1811 J. DALTON (*title*) Observations on Dr. Bostock's Review of the Atomic principles of Chemistry. **1880** CLEMENSHAW tr. *Wurtz' Atom. The.* 26 From the year 1804 the atomic theory inspired all Dalton's labours.

c. Applied to research and researchers in atomic energy, structure, etc. (e.g. ***atomic physics***, ***physicist***, ***scientist***); to apparatus (e.g. ***atomic furnace***, ***pile*** (see PILE *sb.*[3]), ***reactor***) used to disintegrate atomic nuclei; and to ships, industrial plant, etc., deriving power or driving-force from the harnessing of atomic energy (***atomic-powered*** ppl. a.).

1882 J. TYNDALL in *Knowledge* II. 371/1 (*title*) A problem in atomic physics. **1914** H. G. WELLS in *Century Mag.* LXXXVII. 343/2 The new atomic aëroplane became indeed a mania. *Ibid.* 571/1 The swift aëroplane, with its atomic engine as noiseless as a dancing sunbeam. **1925** F. J. REYNOLDS *Marvels of 1924* 24 The specialty of Dr. Robert A. Millikan..is atomic physics and he has done as much as any other American in this branch. **1933** *Discovery* May 154/2 The quantum of action..taken together with the existence of the elementary particles, forms the foundation of atomic physics. **1945** W. DAVIS (*title*) Atomic Power Plants of the Future. **1945** *War Illustr.* 9 Nov. 439/1 (*caption*) An atomic-powered locomotive;..an atomic power-house;..a streamlined atomic-powered liner. **1946** *Sci. News Let.* 23 Mar. 187 Atomic scientist warns against misinterpretation. **1949** *Jrnl. R. Aeronaut. Soc.* Oct. 1013 A British atomic physicist. **1949** *Atomics* Aug. 3 This work is particularly aimed at building an atomic power plant that will..provide steam. **1950** *Amer. Speech* XXV. 24 The surprising thing about *pile* and *reactor* is that only a few alternatives have ever been used for them: *nuclear furnace*, *atomic furnace*, *atomic-energy machine*. **1950** *Sat. Even. Post* 22 July 26 (*headline*) We're betting our shirts on the atomic submarine. **1952** *Jane's Fighting Ships 1952–53* p. vii/1 The second atomic submarine will be of the same general design as the nuclear-powered *Nautilus*. *Ibid.*, Her [*sc.* the submarine's] power plant will use a different kind of atomic reactor. **1953** *Ann. Reg. 1952* 403 In June President Truman was present at the laying of the keel of the first atomic-powered submarine *Nautilus*. **1955** *Times* 4 July 5/1 The heat from the Atomic Energy Authority's six new reactors (atomic furnaces). **1958** *Listener* 11 Dec. 992/1 Fourth atomic reactor at Calder Hall comes into operation. **1959** *Times* 16 Sept. 10/2 The Soviet atomic icebreaker Lenin left Leningrad to-day on her maiden voyage into the Baltic. **1962** *Ibid.* 4 Apr. 15/1 There is every promise that the Sizewell nuclear power station..will be the first atomic installation to produce electricity as cheaply as the most modern conventional power station.

d. ***atomic energy***: the energy released by the fission of the atomic nuclei of certain heavy elements such as uranium 235 or plutonium or by the fusion of light nuclei; also *attrib.*

1906 *Nature* 9 Aug. 357/2 Nevertheless, there is a sense in which it may be said that we are profiting by atomic energy. **1914** H. G. WELLS *World set Free* i. 40 Holsten..was destined to see atomic energy dominating every other source of power. **1921** *Flight* XIII. 299/2 This is indeed the beginning of the liberation of atomic energy. **1924** *Sci. Amer.* Aug. 120/1 Atomic energy is the phrase of the hour. **1946** A. BOYD *U.N. Handbk.* v. 72 The member states had all nominated their representatives to the Atomic Energy Commission by May 1946. **1953** *Economist* 14 Nov. 505/1 The White Paper sets out to describe the kind of organisation to which the Government has decided to entrust the development of atomic energy.

e. Of weapons: deriving their destructive power from the partial conversion of such energy, as ***atomic bomb*** (hence as vb., to attack with this type of bomb, ***-bombing*** vbl. sb.; ***atomic bomber***, an aircraft designed to carry atomic bombs), ***device***, ***shell***, etc. Cf. HYDROGEN *bomb*. Also, of, pertaining to, possessing, or employing atomic weapons, as ***atomic club***, ***control***, ***warfare***.

1914 H. G. WELLS *World set Free* ii. 96 The three atomic bombs, the new bombs that would continue to explode indefinitely. **1917** S. STRUNSKY in *Yale Rev.* Jan. 295 When you can drop just one atomic bomb and wipe out Paris or Berlin, war will have become monstrous and impossible. **1925** *Punch* 11 Feb. 152/2 When, like the bursting of atomic bombs, Cats call to cats and Toms miaul to Toms. **1932** H. NICOLSON *Public Faces* xii. 325 We must now assume that a single atomic bomb is capable of destroying all matter within a circumference of seventy to eighty miles from the point of explosion. **1944** G. B. SHAW *Everyb. Polit. What's What* xxxii. 286 Neither Vril nor Prospero's magic nor flying islands have ever existed, nor has the atomic bomb yet been invented. **1945** *Times* 7 Aug. 4/1 President Truman announced..yesterday that the first atomic bomb had been dropped 16 hours before by an American aircraft on Hiroshima. **1945** *Reader's Dig.* Dec. 2/2 The atomic-bombers of nation A may be on their way to bomb nation B while their own homeland is being turned into a crematorium. **1945** *War Illustr.* 28 Sept. 345 (*title*) I Visited the First City to be Atomic Bombed. *Ibid.* 9 Nov. 438/1 The results of the atomic bombing of Hiroshima and Nagasaki. **1946** *Ibid.* 4 Jan. 572/1 The manufacture and storage of atomic weapons. *Ibid.* 18 Jan. 604/3 Our Royal Navy is rushing plans to revolutionize the fleet to resist atomic warfare. **1946** *Jane's Fighting Ships 1944–45* p. iv/2 The possibility of ships mounting guns that fire atomic shells, to say nothing of the potentialities of the atomic torpedo. **1948** *Ann. Reg. 1947* 250 No progress was made in the discussions on the problem of atomic control. **1954** *Ann. Reg. 1953* 376 The main spring test was made on 17 March with an 'atomic device' having about three-quarters of the power of the bombs dropped on Hiroshima and Nagasaki, but containing less fissionable material. **1955** *Bull. Atomic Sci.* Mar. 79/2 Atomic weapons do not belong to a dream world. **1955** KOESTLER *Trail of Dinosaur* 238 The only deterrent against atomic aggression is an atomic stockpile. **1957** *Times Lit. Suppl.* 1 Nov. 654/4 Can atomic attack be circumscribed? **1958** *Times* 1 July 10/4 The French Ministers, as had been expected, last night emphasized their wish to see France become a member of the 'atomic club'. **1958** *Economist* 25 Oct. 297/2 If the Chinese had missiles with atomic warheads opposite Formosa now.

f. In journalistic and colloquial use: of the age, era, etc., marked by the various applications of atomic energy.

1945 *War Illustr.* 9 Nov. 439 Wonders of the Atomic Age in the not-too-distant future. **1946** A. BOYD *U.N. Handbk.* i. 25 It is already clear that the arrival of the 'atomic age' has brought in its train the possibility of outbursts of destruction on an incomparably greater scale [than in the war of 1939–45]. **1950** *Amer. Speech* XXV. 27 The 'Atomic Era' will depend, both as a new term and a new thought, upon the use the generality of us give it. **1959** *New Statesman* 19 Dec. 874/2 What are you to do about all the new long atomic-age words?

3. Of persons: Adhering to the atomic philosophy.

1691 RAY *Creation* (1714) 41 These mechanick theists have quite outstripped..the atomick atheists. **1850** DAUBENY *Atom. The.* i. 46 That vantage ground which the atomic philosopher possesses over the rival theorist.

4. Atom-like in size; minute, tiny.

1809 PEARSON in *Phil. Trans.* XCIX. 319 These atomic globules are quite different. **1866** ROGERS *Agric. & Prices* I. ii. 28 The means of measuring changes almost atomic.

5. Of the nature of atoms; simple, elemental.

1881 LOCKYER in *Nature* No. 617. 391 Whether the temperature produces a simpler form, a more atomic condition of the same thing.

6. Forming phraseological *combs.* with *sbs.*, as (senses 1, 2) **atomic beam** (see quot. 1962); **atomic clock**, an instrument which attains extreme accuracy by measuring time in terms of the vibration-rate of molecules of ammonia or cæsium atoms; **atomic hydrogen**, hydrogen dissociated into atoms; so **atomic-hydrogen (arc) welding**, a form of arc-welding in which hydrogen is dissociated into atoms by passing through an electric arc and then recombines, thus supplying intense heat; hence ***atomic-hydrogen torch***, etc.; (senses 2 c, d, e) **atomic power**.

1928 *Physical Rev.* XXXI. 646 The increase of the divergence of the atomic beam upon reflection at the crystal surface may obviously be due to any of several causes. **1962** *Gloss. Terms Nucl. Sci.* (*B.S.I.*) 10 *Atomic beam*, gas atoms emerging from a small aperture into a high vacuum and collimated by one or more additional apertures so as to form a narrow beam. **1938** *Jrnl. Optical Soc. Amer.* July 215 (*title*) Experimental Study of the Rate of a Moving Atomic Clock. **1958** *Times* 14 Oct. 5/3 The caesium atomic clock, which is on exhibition at the British clock and watch industry's display in the Goldsmiths' Hall, London. **1962** E. BRUTON *Dict. Clocks & Watches* 15 The most accurate atomic clock or frequency standard ever made employs as its 'pendulum' the vibration of the caesium atom, which is at 9,192,631,770 cycles a second. **1915** I. LANGMUIR in *Jrnl. Amer. Chem. Soc.* XXXVII. 428 (*heading*) Diffusion of Atomic Hydrogen away from the Wire. **1930** H. CHATLEY *Princ. Rocket Propulsion* 5 Esnault-Pelterie..discusses the possibility of using atomic hydrogen as the propellant but little is known of this highly active material. **1933** *Welding Industry* June 141 Atomic-Hydrogen arc welding, which originated in America..is rapidly finding favour. **1914** H. G. WELLS in *Century Mag.* LXXXVII. 704/2 The year of crisis that followed the release of atomic power. **1945** *Daily Tel.* 7 Aug. 1/1 Congress would be asked to investigate how atomic power might be used to maintain the future peace. **1953** *Economist* 14 Nov. 507/2 The argument is also gaining ground that a shortage of coal will compel Britain to turn to atomic power for marginal supplies of electricity, regardless of cost.

†**B.** *sb.* An adherent of the atomic philosophy.

1678 CUDWORTH *Intell. Syst.* Pref., Other Philosophick Atheists..before those Atomicks, Epicurus and Democritus.

atomical (əˈtɒmɪkəl), *a.* [f. as prec. + -ICAL.]

1. Concerned with atoms; = ATOMIC *a.* 2, 3.

1664 POWER *Exp. Philos.* I. 57 The Controversie twixt the Peripatetick and Atomical Philosophers. **1866** FERRIER *Lect. Grk. Philos.* I. viii. 170 Doctrines of the Atomical philosophers.

2. Of or pertaining to atoms; = ATOMIC *a.* 1.

1660 INGELO *Bentiv. & Ur.* (1682) II. 206 The parts of this Atomical Composition still marching away, and other succeeding in their rooms. **1836** TODD *Cycl. Anat. & Phys.* I. 58/2 The microscopical and atomical structure of fat.

3. Tiny, very minute.

1646 SIR T. BROWNE *Pseud. Ep.* 53 Their powders and Atomicall divisions. **1752** LISLE *Observ. Husb.* 11 Minute, atomical, imperceptible bodies.

a'tomically, *adv.* [f. prec. + -LY².] In accordance with the principles of atomic philosophy; also in other senses of the adj.

1678 CUDWORTH *Intell. Syst.* Pref. 7 Divers of the Italicks, and particularly Empedocles, physiologized atomically. **1888** *Athenæum* 18 Aug. 214/2 Ourselves atomically constituted in body, soul..and spirit..we are in constant rapport with external influences of similar kinds. **1955** *Bull. Atomic Sci.* May 191/3 The example..cited, amphibious landings in the face of an atomically armed foe, presents no greater difficulties than defense of a shore line against an atomically armed invader.

atomician (ætə'mɪʃən). *rare.* [f. ATOMIC: see -ICIAN.] = ATOMIST 1.

1859 in WORCESTER.

†**a'tomicism.** *Obs. rare*⁻¹. [f. ATOMIC + -ISM.] The atomic philosophy: see ATOMIC *a.* 2.

1678 CUDWORTH *Intell. Syst.* 59 That Philosophy..made up of..Atomicism and Corporealism complicated together, is essentially Atheistical.

atomicity (ætə'mɪsɪtɪ). *Chem.* [f. ATOMIC + -ITY.] **1. a.** The combining capacity of an element (or radical), *i.e.* the number of atoms of hydrogen, or other monovalent element, with which one of its atoms normally combines.

Thus the atomicity of chlorine is 1 (or chlorine is a monad) because it forms with hydrogen H Cl; and that of carbon is 4 (or carbon is a tetrad) because it forms with hydrogen C H_4. Atomicity has also been called *equivalence, quantivalence, adicity*, and (now usually) *valency*.

1865 *Reader* 1 Apr. 372 The word atomicity has been invented for the purpose of describing those properties of atoms which were described by the word 'equivalence.' **1873** COOKE *Chem.* 284 The number of these replaceable atoms measures what is called the atomicity of the compound.

b. The number of atoms in the molecule of an element (Webster 1900).

2. In modern philosophy: capacity for being reduced to or analysed into atomic propositions or other elements; cf. ATOMIC A. 2 a, ATOMISM 1 b.

1929 A. N. WHITEHEAD *Process & Reality* III. i. 333 A prehension, considered genetically, can never free itself from the incurable atomicity of the actual entity to which it belongs. **1940** B. RUSSELL *Inq. Meaning & Truth* xii. 169 Can we construct an adequate language in which the principle of atomicity holds? **1959** —— *My Philos. Devel.* x. 118 The principle of atomicity is stated by Wittgenstein in the following terms: 'Every statement about complexes can be analysed into a statement about their constituent parts, and into those propositions which completely describe the complexes' (*Tractatus*, 2.0201).

atomism ('ætəmɪz(ə)m). [f. ATOM *sb.* + -ISM.]

1. a. Atomic philosophy; the doctrine of the formation of all things from indivisible particles endued with gravity and motion.

1678 CUDWORTH *Intell. Syst.* 16 This spurious and counterfeit atomism of his [Anaxagoras']. **1865** *Q. Rev.* Jan. 29 The Atomism of the philosopher of Abdera.

b. In modern philosophy: the theory that all statements, propositions, situations, etc., are composed of mutually independent, simple, primary, and irreducible elements; the elucidation and study of these elements; spec. *logical atomism*.

1914 B. RUSSELL *Sci. Method in Philos.* 16 The philosophy which I wish to advocate may be called logical atomism or absolute pluralism, because while maintaining that there are many things, it denies that there is a whole composed of those things. **1918** —— in *Monist* 497 The reason that I call my doctrine *logical* atomism is because the atoms that I wish to arrive at as the..last residue in analysis are logical atoms and not physical atoms. **1956** D. F. PEARS in Ayer et al. *Revol. Philos.* 49 You see how the theory of logical atomism develops. You begin with statements, subject them to analysis and find that they are built up out of parts.

2. The doctrine of the action of individual atoms.

1836 *Athenæum* No. 434. 142 Unstable atomism is to give to the Church and the State new solidity and unity. **1879** BARING-GOULD *Germany* II. 260 He repudiated altogether Liberal atomism, the doctrine that all social and political economy must start from the individual.

3. *Psychol.* (See quot. 1934.)

1883 F. H. BRADLEY *Logic* II. II. i. 276 The philosophy of Experience is psychological Atomism. **1934** H. C. WARREN *Dict. Psychol.* 23/1 *Psychological atomism*, the theory of mind which assumes that experiences are composed of elementary psychic units or atoms.

atomist ('ætəmɪst). [f. ATOM *sb.* + -IST.]

1. a. One who holds the principles of atomism.

1610 HEALEY *St. Aug. City of God* 438 Of the Atomists, some confound all, making bodies of coherent remaynders. **1678** CUDWORTH *Intell. Syst.* 846 The old Religious Atomists. **1880** CLEMENSHAW tr. *Wurtz' Atom. The.* 27 The atomists of the seventeenth century..had revived..the ancient conception of the Greek philosophers.

b. An adherent or student of logical atomism Cf. ATOMISM 1 b.

1941 *Mind* L. 166 They may themselves choose to be called Logical Atomists or Logical Positivists, or may repudiate all such titles. **1956** P. F. STRAWSON in Ayer et al. *Revol. Philos.* 97 Atomists and Positivists alike accepted the skeleton language of the new mathematical logic.

2. A student or exponent of the atomic theory. See ATOMIC *a.* 2.

1869 PHILLIPS *Vesuv.* x. 270 Symbols of chemical constitution, on which there is still some want of agreement among atomists.

atomistic (ætə'mɪstɪk), *a.* [f. prec. + -IC.]

1. a. Of or pertaining to atomists or atomism.

1809 COLERIDGE *Friend* I. 121 It is the object of the mechanical atomistic philosophy to confound synthesis with synartesis. **1877** E. CAIRD *Philos. Kant* II. xi. 443 The atomistic doctrine of the existence of a vacuum.

b. Of or pertaining to logical atomism. See ATOMISM 1 b.

1918 B. RUSSELL in *Monist* 496 The logic which I shall advocate is atomistic, as opposed to the monistic logic of the people who..follow Hegel. When I say that my logic is atomistic, I mean that I share the common-sense belief that there are many separate things.

2. Consisting of separate atoms.

1874 SAYCE *Comp. Philol.* vi. 214 Instead of starting with atomistic individuals, we must start with..the community. **1875** D. SIMON *Dorner's Pers. Christ* I. II. 123 To conceive the world..as an atomistic multiplicity without unity.

3. Of or pertaining to psychological atomism. See ATOMISM 3.

1883 *Encycl. Brit.* XX. 60/2 Such a statement is liable to all the objections already urged against what we may call atomistic psychology. *a* **1910** W. JAMES *Some Probl. Philos.* (1911) iv. 87 To such an atomistic plurality the associationists reduce our mental life. **1940** R. S. WOODWORTH *Psychol.* (ed. 12) ii. 38 An atomistic psychology attempts to explain any total activity by analysing it into its elements.

ato'mistical, *a.* ? *Obs.* [f. as prec. + -ICAL.] = ATOMISTIC 1.

c **1700** *Gentl. Instruc.* 427 (D.) The atomistical hypothesis does not weaken the force of my reason. **1716** M. DAVIES *Crit. Hist.* 104 The Atomistical Poet Lucretius.

ato'mistically, *adv.* [f. prec. + -LY².] In atomistic manner; as composed of distinct atoms. (*spec.* in *Psychol.*)

1874 tr. *Van Oosterzee's Chr. Dogm.* lxxiv. 400 So little can it [mankind] be atomistically individualised in its sins. **1881** E. THOMAS tr. *Lange's Materialism* III. 215 Matter.. whether we conceive it atomistically or as a continuum. **1924** A. S. PRINGLE-PATTISON *Locke's Human Und.* p. xx, This start with sensations, atomistically conceived as simple or particular ideas..is a presupposition of the older psychology, common to Locke, Berkeley, and Hume. **1935** K. KOFFKA *Princ. Gestalt Psychol.* vii. 271 Atomistically considered, there is no disparate point on the right side.

atomization (ˌætəmaɪ'zeɪʃən). [n. of action f. ATOMIZE: see -ATION.] **1.** The process of reducing to very minute particles, *spec.* in *Med.* of reducing liquids to a fine spray.

1866 H. BEIGEL *On Inhalation* v. 49 The minuteness of atomization. **1871** NAPHEYS *Prev. & Cure Dis.* III. iv. 688 This method is called the atomization of fluids. **1875** H. WOOD *Therap.* (1879) 522 The use of drugs by atomization ..A solution of the medicine is broken up by a mechanical contrivance into a fine spray and projected into the back of the mouth.

2. *transf.* The process of reducing or dividing into small units; fragmentation.

1935 *Archit. Rev.* LXXVIII. 86/2 The characteristically capitalist atomization of society into isolated economic units. **1953** A. K. C. OTTAWAY *Educ. & Soc.* v. 98 The break-down or 'atomization' of the process into one operation per worker leads to a lack of interest. **1954** KOESTLER *Invis. Writing* xxii. 244 There are various answers to this—atomisation, dispersion, the sorry end of all independent Communist splinter-groups.

atomize ('ætəmaɪz). *v.* [f. ATOM*sb.* + -IZE.]

†**1.** *intr.* To hold the doctrines of the atomic philosophy. *Obs.*

1678 CUDWORTH *Intell. Syst.* I. i. §26 Other ancient Atomists did Atomize as well as he but they did not atheize.

2. a. *trans.* To reduce to atoms, or to an atom; to belittle.

1845 MOZLEY *Blanco White* Ess. 1878 II. 130 Strange and melancholy is the idea that atomises truth.

b. To reduce (a liquid) to very small particles or to the condition of spray.

1865 *Lancet* 25 Feb. 203/2 He believed that atomising the fluids was unnecessary, on the ground that they could be introduced in the simplest manner by ordinary inhalation. **1902** *Encycl. Brit.* XXXI. 646/2 Utilizing the waste product [of petroleum] as fuel by spraying or atomizing it with steam.

3. To damage or destroy with an atomic weapon. *colloq.*

1945 *Daily Mirror* 11 Aug. 1/3 Nagasaki, the second.. Japanese city to be 'atomised'. **1961** A. WILSON *Old Men at Zoo* ii. 90 Poor old Rackham's looking quite down in the mouth now that we aren't all going to be atomized into eternity.

'atomized, *ppl. a.* [for ANATOMIZED; cf. ATOMY¹.] †**1.** Existing as a skeleton. *Obs. rare*⁻¹.

1633 LD. BROOKE *Hum. Learn.* cxx, Whereby their abstract formes yet atomis'd May be embodied.

2. Reduced to a fine spray; also, (of a solid) reduced to minute particles.

1865 MORELL MACKENZIE in *Lancet* 25 Feb. 202/2 (*heading*) On the treatment of chronic disease of the lungs by the inhalation of atomised liquids. **1870** T. HOLMES *Syst. Surg.* (ed. 2) IV. 530 The inhalation of 'atomised fluids', or spray. **1926** *Punch* 26 May p. ix (Advt.), An electro-vaporiser secures a perfectly atomised gas for starting. **1958** *Gloss. Terms Powders (B.S.I.)* 5 *Atomized powder*, (a) powder produced by the dispersion of molten metal or other material by spraying under conditions such that the material breaks down to powder, (b) powder produced by disintegration of a material through internal rupture caused by rapid change of external pressure.

3. Damaged or destroyed by an atomic weapon. *colloq.*

1950 G. GREENE *Third Man* x. 95 Tainted, like the soil of an atomised town.

4. *transf.* Disunited, dissociated; having lost social unity.

1942 J. S. HUXLEY in *Polit. Q.* XIII. 387 A dingy, discontented, and atomized black proletariat. **1945** KOESTLER *Yogi & Commissar* III. iii. 215 Europe east of the Alps is atomized and in a state of political, economical, ideological chaos. **1949** I. DEUTSCHER *Stalin* iv. 98 But the atomized mass of Moslem labourers did not lend itself easily to propaganda or organization.

atomizer ('ætəˌmaɪzə(r)). [f. ATOMIZE + -ER¹.] He who or that which atomizes; *spec.* an instrument for reducing medicinal liquids to a fine spray.

1865 MORELL MACKENZIE in *Lancet* 25 Feb. 203/1 The author observed that his own atomiser is very simple and can be used very easily. The liquid is driven from a fine glass pipe on to a projection in a bell-shaped tube, by the descent of a piston. **1875** H. WOOD *Therap.* 95 Applied by means of the atomizer. **1904** [see next, sense 2]. **1930** *Engineering* 3 Jan. 3/1 The quantity of fuel supplied to each atomiser is regulated on the by-pass principle.

'atomizing, *ppl. a.* [f. as prec. + -ING².] **1.** Reducing to atoms; individualizing.

1847 BUSHNELL *Chr. Nurt.* viii. (1861) 219 This atomizing scheme of piety.

2. Reducing to a fine spray.

1867 B. DURHAM in *Chicago Med. Jrnl.* XXIV. 245 (*title*) Atomizing instruments. **1894** *Jrnl. Amer. Med. Assoc.* XXIII. 973 Topical treatment of the air passages, with exhibition of a new atomizing vaporizer. **1904** GOODCHILD & TWENEY *Technol. & Sci. Dict.* I. 33/1 Atomiser or atomising carburetter. **1951** *Good Housek. Home Encycl.* 204/1 An atomising jet is needed, and the paraffin oil is burnt as a vapour.

atomless ('ætəmlɪs), *a. poet.* [see -LESS.] Without atoms, without leaving an atom, entire.

1839 BAILEY *Festus* xxxii. (1848) 351 Hath perished atomless.

atomology (ætə'mɒlədʒɪ). [f. Gr. ἄτομο-ς ATOM *sb.* + -λογία discourse: see -LOGY.] The science or philosophy which treats of the nature of atoms.

1678 CUDWORTH *Intell. Syst.* Pref. 7 Anaxagoras his Homœomery or Similar Atomology, was but a Degeneration from the..Genuine Atomology of the Ancient Italicks.

atomy¹ ('ætəmɪ). [f. ANATOMY by aphæresis of *an-*, due to its being taken for the indef. article, as, by similar treatment of *a-*, the forms *natomy, nathomy*, were also in early use. In the concrete and popular senses of the word this contracted form was formerly quite established; but is now only illiterate or jocular.]

1. An anatomical preparation, an anatomized body; *esp.* a skeleton.

1728 GAY *Beggar's Op.* II. i, He is among the Otamys at Surgeon's Hall. **1755** SMOLLETT *Quix.* (1803) IV. 148 My bones..will be taken up smooth, and white, and bare as an atomy. **1823** F. COOPER *Pioneer* xiii. 146 His sides..looked just like an atomy, ribs and all.

2. An emaciated or withered living body, a walking skeleton.

1597 SHAKS. *2 Hen. IV.* v. iv. 33 [Quarto; folio 1623 has 'anatomy'] You starved blood-hound!.. Thou atomy, thou! **1681** R. KNOX *Hist. Ceylon* 124 Consumed to an Atomy, having nothing left but skin to cover his Bones. **1864** MRS. LLOYD *Ladies Polcarrow* 149 'We should have wasted to atomies if we had a-stayed in that terrible bad place any longer,' said Ursula.

b. *fig.* or *transf.* of things.

1848 DICKENS *Dombey* 86 Withered atomies of teaspoons.

atomy² ('ætəmɪ). Also 7 **attomé, -mye.** [f. *atomi*, pl. of *atomus* (formerly in learned use; see ATOM *sb.*), by treating it as an English singular. Perhaps influenced also by ATOMY¹ 2. Cf.

1596 FITZ-GEFFREY *Sir F. Drake* (1881) 99 Anatomize me into atomies. **1611** BARKSTED *Hiren* (1876) 86 The kingly Eagle strikes through Atomie, Those little moates that barre him from the Sun.]

1. An atom, a mote.

1595 MARKHAM *Sir R. Grinuile*, Thicker then in sunne are Atomies, Flew bullets. **1600** SHAKS. *A.Y.L.* III. ii. 245 It is as easie to count Atomies as to resolue the propositions of a Louer. **1620** *Swetnam Arraigned* (1880) 37, I would hew thy flesh Smaller then Attomés. **1879** TENNYSON *Lover's T.* 65 A broad And solid beam of isolated light, Crowded with driving atomies.

b. *fig.*

1614 OVERBURY *A Wife, &c.* (1638) 266 Circumstances are the Atomies of Policie.

2. A diminutive or tiny being, a mite, a pigmy.

1591 SHAKS. *Rom. & Jul.* I. iv. 57 Drawne with a teeme of little Atomies Ouer mens noses. **1605** P. WOODHOUSE *Flea* (1877) 19 If with this atomye I should contend. **1863** KINGSLEY *Water Bab.* (1878) viii. 369, I suppose you have come here to laugh at me, you spiteful little atomy.

Aton, var. ATEN.

atonable, atoneable (ə'təʊnəb(ə)l), *a.* [f. ATONE *v.* + -ABLE.] That may be atoned for.
a **1679** T. GOODWIN *Wks.* (1863) V. 424 The expiation of such sins.. made atoneable by such occasional sacrifices. **1870** SMITH *Syn. & Antonyms, Inexpiable.. Ant.* Expiable, Pardonable, Atoneable.

atonal (ə'təʊnəl, æ-, eɪ-), *a. Mus.* [f. A- 14 + TONAL *a.*] Applied to a style of composition in which there is no conscious reference to any scale or tonic. So **a'tonalism** *sb.*, **a'tonalist** *sb.* and *a.*, **ato'nality** *sb.*, **a'tonally** *adv.*
1922 A. E. HULL in *Musical Opinion* Oct. 48/1, I have been working for two years at a system of non-tonal harmony, which I had long been unable to christen. Now, after visiting no less than seven foreign countries I not only find that the thing is widely known as Atonality, but [etc.]. *Ibid.* 48/3 Keyboard chord-writing as well as linear, tonal as well as Atonal. **1923** *Mus. Assoc. Proc. 1922–3* 67 We find the principle of polytonality or atonality superseding the old key system. **1928** *Daily Express* 25 June 10/6 Eugene Goossens himself said recently that 'modern music composition has come to an impasse in its trend towards laboratory atonalism'. **1929** P. C. BUCK *Hist. Mus.* iii. 34 Nor as a means of destroying the key-scale as the atonalists of today are using it. **1930** *Mus. Assoc. Proc.* 97 To write atonally in a harmonic form at present is to produce a thought 'heterodyne'. **1936** *Scrutiny* V. 153 Atonalism would seem to be an adequate medium for the expression of certain precious, morbid, esoteric sensibilities. *Ibid.* The fact that the works of the most relentless of the atonalists, Webern, rarely last more than a minute or so.. is surely significant. **1952** B. ULANOV *Hist. Jazz Amer.* (1958) xxiii. 330 He can teach almost anything.. from counterpoint to atonalist formations. **1958** *Times Lit. Suppl.* 4 July 372/3 What began as atonality is now called dodecaphony.. or.. serialism. **1958** *Listener* 18 Dec. 1051/1 Schönberg who was also writing atonally in such a work as the *Five Pieces* for orchestra. **1963** *Ibid.* 14 Feb. 313/3 Luigi Dallapiccola, an atonalist who has remained faithful to his country's abiding concern for melody.

at once (æt'wʌns), *advb. phr.* Also 3 **at enes**, 3–6 **at ones**, 4 **at oones, at onis, atonys**, 4–6 **atones, -is, attones, -is**, 5 **at oonys, atte ones, attonys**, 6 **atons, att onis, attonce**, 6– **at once**. *North.* 4–6 **atanes, -is, atans**, 6 **atanse**. [AT *prep.* and ONCE, ME. *anes, ones*, gen. of ONE, used in sense of OE. *áne* adv., 'one time, once,' instrumental case of *án*.]
†**1.** At one stroke, heat, etc.; with one sweep; once for all. *Obs.*
a **1300** *E.E. Psalter* xxi. 15 Als watre outyet I am at anes. *c* **1374** CHAUCER *Troylus* v. 41 Were it not bet at oones for to dye, Than, etc. **1579** SPENSER *Sheph. Cal.* Feb. 38 You deemen the Spring is come attonce.
†**2.** In (or into) one heap, company, or body; together. *Obs.*
a **1300** *Havelok* 1294 That I fadmede al at ones Denemark. *c* **1350** *Will. Palerne* 5178 Alphouns & his broþer, & here worþi wiues þat were alle at onis. **1387** TREVISA *Higden* (1865) I. 227 ȝif þe stone is oon, telle what craft brouȝt hym vppon; ȝif meny st[on]es, telle where þey ioyne attones. *c* **1430** *Hymns Virg.* (1867) 123 The folke schall com alle attonys. **1508–13** W. DE WORDE *Bk. Keruynge* in *Babees Bk.* 269 Holde these thre endes atones, & folde them atones. **1579** SPENSER *Sheph. Cal.* Mar., Mought her neck bene ioynted attones, She shoulde haue neede no more spell.
3. At one and the same time; simultaneously. (At first scarcely distinguishable from the prec.)
c **1230** *Ancr. R.* 420 Ne ne nime, at enes, to ueole disceplines. *c* **1385** CHAUCER *L.G.W.* 294 Full sodeynly they stynten al atones [*v.r.* attones, at ones]. **1483** CAXTON *Gold. Leg.* 410/1 Eche man myght haue foure wyues wedded att-ones. **1552** LYNDESAY *Monarche* 5027 Sic treasour.. In erth had neuir no kyng att onis. **1576** GASCOIGNE *Steele Glass* (Arb.) 70 More clothes attones than might become a king. **1677** MOXON *Mech. Exerc.* (1703) 31 At once, you will have two Sides of your Shank forged. **1714** *Spect.* No. 599 ⁋1 As I had had many Coquettes recommended to me.. I let them in all at once. **1870** BRYANT *Homer* IV. I. 121 The gods Bestow not all their gifts on man at once.
4. With the temporal sense weakened: In one and the same act, position, condition, circumstances, manner, degree; equally, both.
1588 A. KING *Canisius' Catech.* 6 b, Mother of god, and ane virgine baithe atanse. **1692** E. WALKER *Epictetus' Mor.* iv, Be rich, and yet true Happiness attain; That is, at once, be very wise and vain. **1709** SWIFT *Trit. Ess.* Wks. 1755 II. I. 140 He was at once the judge and the criminal. **1862** STANLEY *Jew. Ch.* (1877) I. xiii. 259 The background at once of the history and of the geography of Palestine.
†**5.** At one time or turn, at each time, every time, at a time. *Obs.*
1563 SHUTE *Archit.* F ij a, The encreasing from . 15 . to . 60 . foote increased by . 5 at ones. **1585** LLOYD *Treas. Health* D viij, Put into the eye a lytle atons.
6. Immediately, straightway.
1531 TINDALE *Exp. & Notes* (1849) 179 The apostles were clear-eyed, and espied antichrist at once. *a* **1774** GOLDSM. *Surv. Exp. Philos.* (1776) I. 311 This effectually destroys the steam at once. **1812** T. JEFFERSON *Writ.* (1830) IV. 176 If this be their purpose.. it ought to be met at once.

at one (ætwʌn), *advb. phr.*; formerly often written in comb. **aton, atoon, atone, attone** (ə'toːn), as a simple *adv.* [found in 13th c. along with the fuller phrases *at one assent, at one accord*, and soon treated as repr. a simple idea, and written *aton, a ton, at-on*; in northern writers *at ane, a tane, atane*. For the sense cf. AT *prep.* 20. With vbs. of rest, as *to be at one*, and vbs. of motion, as *to bring, make, set at one*; whence the vb. ATONE.]
1. In a position of unity of feeling; in harmony, concord, or friendship; opposed to *at variance, at odds*. Sometimes implying a previous state of dissension, and thus = Agreed, reconciled. *arch.*
a **1300** *K. Horn* 925 At on he was wiþ þe king. *c* **1400** *Gamelyn* 166 And went and kist his brother, and than they were at oon. *a* **1440** *Sir Degrev.* 435 Y rede ye be at ane Or there dey any moo. **1535** COVERDALE *2 Sam.* xxi. 14 After this was God at one with the londe. **1557** N. T. (Genev.) *2 Cor.* v. 20 We praye you in Christes stede, that ye be atone with God. **1596** SPENSER *F.Q.* II. i. 29 So beene they both atone. **1830** COLERIDGE *Ch. & St.* 257 Am I at one with God, and is my will concentric with that holy power? **1881** BUCHANAN *God & Man* I. 171 The maiden, in her sweet.. content, was at one with Nature.
2. Into a state of harmony or unity of feeling. **to bring, make, set at one**: to harmonize, reconcile. *arch.* (having been mostly replaced by ATONE *v.*)
c **1300** *Beket* 1707 That hi were At one ibrouȝt. *c* **1386** CHAUCER *Clerkes T.* 381 If gentilmen.. Were wroth, sche wolde brynge hem at oon. *c* **1475** *Stans Puer* in *Babees Bk.* 28 Wrathe of children is sone ouergone, Withe an apple the parties be made atone. *c* **1540** BECON *Christm. Banq.* Wks. 1843. 75 God the Father is.. set at one with us for his sake. **1643** HORN & ROBOTHAM *Gate Lang. Unl.* xciii. §911 They that are fallen out (at ods) must be reconciled (atoned, set at one). **1611–1881** BIBLE *Acts* vii. 26 And would haue set them at one again [so TINDALE, COVERDALE, CRANMER, *Geneva*; WYCLIF, acordid hem in pees; *Rhem.* reconciled them vnto peace].
3. Of the same opinion (as to a matter), of one mind, unanimous, agreed.
c **1320** *Cast. Loue* 492 Þer ne ouȝte no dom forþ gon, Er þen þe foure ben a-ton. At-on heo moten at-stonden alle. **1677** HALE *Contempl.* (1688) 62 Is it possible that we should be at one in these points, in which yourselves do disagree? **1877** PAGE *De Quincey* II. xviii. 43 On one or two points the writer was not wholly at one with him.
†**4.** Of the same effect, amounting to the same.
1697 DAMPIER *Voy.* (1729) I. 14 Whether it rained or shined it was much at one with us.
†**5.** In one company, together. (? Only in Spenser.)
1591 SPENSER *Teares Muses* 418 And all her Sisters.. With lowd laments her answered all at one. **1596** —— *F.Q.* IV. ix. 30 The warlike dame was on her part assaid Of Claribell and Blandamour attone. *Ibid.* IV. iv. 14 The knights in couples marcht with ladies linckt attone.
6. *Comb.* †**atonemaker**, one who sets at one persons at variance, a reconciler; †**atonemaking**, reconciliation; **at-oneness**, the state of being at one (*with*), harmonious relationship.
1533 TINDALE *Wks.* (1850) III. 275 There is but one media-tour.. And by that word vnderstand an attonemaker, peace maker, and brynger into grace and favour. **1548** COVERDALE *Erasm. Par. Heb.* vii. 27 For what manour of atonemakers were they, which themselfes had nede to be made at one with god. **1611** COTGR., *Conciliation*, a reconcilement .. an attone-making. **1877** FURNIVALL *Leopold Shaks.* Introd. 121, I see him at last passing into at-oneness with God and man. **1960** C. DAY LEWIS *Buried Day* iv. 81 The strange at-one-ness between myself and the boat. **1962** *Listener* 25 Oct. 659/1 A sense of at-oneness with the universe.

atone (ə'təʊn), *v.* Also 6–8 **attone**. [f. the prec. advb. phr. in its combined form as repr. a simple idea, and 16th c. pronunciation. Short for the phrase 'set or make at one'; cf. *to back, to forward, to right*, etc., and the compounds *at-one-maker, at-one making*, under prec. Assisted by the prior existence of the vb. to ONE = make one, put at one, unite, L. *unīre*, F. *unir*; whence *onement* was used already by Wyclif. From the frequent phrases 'set at one' or 'at onement,' the combined *atonement* began to take the place of *onement* early in 16th c., and *atone* to supplant *one* vb. about 1550. *Atone* was not admitted into the Bible in 1611, though *atonement* had been in since Tindale.]
I. Of unity of disposition.
1. *trans.* To set at one, bring into concord, reconcile, unite in harmony: **a.** contending persons. (*Obs.* exc. as revived by etymological writers.)
1593 SHAKS. *Rich. II*, I. i. 202 Since we cannot attone you, you shall see Iustice designe the Victors Chiualrie. **1611** SPEED *Hist. Gt. Brit.* IX. vii. 65 The new Pope.. sends a Cardinall Deacon to attone the two mightie Kings of France and England. **1643** MILTON *Sov. Salve* 9 The king and parliament will soon be attoned. **1675** DRYDEN *Aureng-zebe* III. 1136 The King and haughty Empress.. If not atton'd, yet seemingly at Peace. **1845–6** TRENCH *Huls. Lect.* Ser. I. ii. 30 Him in whom God and man were perfectly atoned.
†**b.** differences, quarrels. To compose, appease.
1555 *Fardle Facions* I. vi. 92 Those battayles are attoned by the women.. For when they be ones comen into the middle.. the battaile sodenly ceaseth. **1565** J. HEYWOOD in *Casquet Lit.* IV. 232/2 The constable is called to atone the broil. **1624** HEYWOOD *Gunaik.* IV. 167 She presently.. attonde the discord. **1702** ROWE *Tamerlane* III. i. 1096 Could I attone The fatal Breach 'twixt thee and Tamerlane.
†**2.** *intr.* To unite, come into unity or concord.
1600 SHAKS. *A.Y.L.* V. iv. 116 Then is there mirth in heauen When earthly things made eauen Attone together. **1607** —— *Cor.* IV. vi. 72 He and Auffidius can no more attone Then violent'st Contrariety.
3. *trans.* To reconcile or restore to friendly relations: **a.** one who is alienated by a sense of wrong or offence received: To conciliate, propitiate, appease. *arch.*
a **1617** BAYNE *On Eph.* (1658) 11 Now he [God] is atoned and reconciled by Christ. **1698** DRYDEN *Æneid* III. 45 With pray'rs and vows the Driads I attone. **1718** POPE *Iliad* I. 89 So heaven, atoned, shall dying Greece restore. **1809** *Let.* in Dk. Buckhm. *Crt. Geo. III* (1855) IV. 391/3 To atone Lord Wellesley for the mortification he must have experienced.
†**b.** the offender: To restore by forgiveness to favour or friendly relations, to make at peace with.
1642 J. JACKSON *Bk. Consc.* 54 There can be no sound peace of Conscience, till we be atoned and reconciled to God.
4. Whence, *absol.* To make reconcilement or propitiation: **a.** *for* the offender.
1682 DRYDEN *Relig. Laici* 89 If sheep and oxen could atone for men. *a* **1700** —— *Dram. Wks.* (1761) III. 18 The Oracle of Appius, and the Witchcraft of Erictho will somewhat attone for him [Lucan].
b. *for* the offence. (Here the idea of reconciliation or reunion is practically lost sight of, under that of legal satisfaction or amends.)
1665 GLANVILL *Sceps. Sci.* Addr. 28 Need to plead it to attone for the imperfection of this Address. **1710** PALMER *Proverbs* xi, Fine language will never atone for want of manners. **1711** STEELE *Spect.* No. 20 ⁋7 Nothing can atone for the Want of Modesty. **1771** *Junius Lett.* liv. 288 He.. has a multitude of political offences to atone for. **1873** BLACK *Pr. Thule* xix. 315 She would.. give him a chance of atoning for the past.
5. *trans.* (by omission of *for*) To expiate, make amends for (a fault or loss).
1665 GLANVILL *Sceps. Sci.* 76 [This] I hope will attone the Digression. *a* **1677** BARROW *Serm.* (1687) I. xxxi. 430 Other sacrifices.. did in their way propitiate God and atone sin. **1799** SHERIDAN *Pizarro* V. iv, I will endeavour to atone the .. errors. **1837** LYTTON *Athens* II. 223 They endeavoured to atone the loss by the pursuit of Artabazus.
†**b.** To make expiation for (the offender). *Obs.*
1650 W. BROUGH *Sacr. Princ.* (1659) 29 For thy dear Sons sake.. By whom the world is attoned, O let me be reconciled to Thee. **1717** L. WELSTED *Wks.* (1787) 105 No victim can atone the impious age.
II. Of physical, expressional, or artistic unity.
†**6.** *trans.* To join in one, unite together. *Obs.*
1609 HEYWOOD *Bryt. Troy* IV. xx, Their long diuided bodies they attone, And enter amorous parley. **1615** CHAPMAN *Odyss.* IX. 266 High built with pines, that heaven and earth attone. **1672** DAVENANT *Mistress* (1673) 322 Your Eies and Hair atone the day and Night.
b. *fig.* To bring into artistic or logical harmony; to harmonize.
1691 E. TAYLOR tr. *Behmen's Theos. Phil.* 203 The contrary properties in him are.. so attoned and in harmony. **1827** HARE *Guesses* I. 233 To atone our ideas with our perceptions.
c. *absol.* To produce a harmony of significance.
1862 TRENCH *Mirac.* Introd. 76 That attempt to reconcile and atone between revelation and science, which, etc.
7. *intr.* †**a.** To come together, unite. *Obs.*
1611 HEYWOOD *Gold. Age* II. i, You neuer shall with hated men attone.
b. To harmonize in character or appearance.
1649 G. DANIEL *Trinarch., Rich. II.* 122 The Glorious flowers wch best attone Within a Chaplett. **1844** LD. HOUGHTON *Mem. Many Sc.* 106 Welcome such thoughts! They well atone With this more serious mood.

atone (ə'təʊn), *sb.* [f. prec. vb.]
†**1.** Agreement, reconciliation. *Obs.*
1595 SPENSER *Col. Clout* 843 For how should else things so far from attone.. Be ever drawne together into one. **1638** HEYWOOD *Rape Lucr.* (1874) 185 Tullia.. hath not yet by reconcilement made Attone with Phœbus.
2. Reparation, expiation. (Archaism with mod. sense.)
1868 BUCHANAN *Wallace* I. iii, Oh injured Wallace! Would Heaven but lend me one day's life to do Atone to thee.

atoned (ə'təʊnd), *ppl. a.* [f. ATONE *v.* + -ED.] Made one, united; reconciled; propitiated, expiated.
1611 COTGR., *Concilié*.. attoned, vnited, accorded. **1634** HEYWOOD *Maidenh. Lost* I. Wks. 1874 IV. 113 Conditions of attoned peace 'Twixt vs and Naples. **1697** DRYDEN *Æneid* (1806) II. 223 Ev'n haughty Juno.. At length aton'd, her friendly pow'r shall join.

atonement (ə'təʊnmənt). Also 6 **attonment**, 6–7 **attonement**. [In use a verbal sb. from ATONE, but apparently of prior formation, due to the earlier sb. *onement* and the phrase 'to be atone' or 'at onement.' Cf. the following:
1533 Q. CATH. PARR *Erasm. Comm. Crede* 162 To reconcile hymselfe and make an onement with god. **1599** BP. HALL *Sat.* III. vii. 69 Which never can be set at onement more. **1555** *Fardle Facions* II. xii. 298 The redempcion, reconciliacion, and at onement of mankinde with God the father.]
†**1.** The condition of being *at one* with others; unity of feeling, harmony, concord, agreement.
1513 MORE *Rich. III* Wks. 41 Having more regarde to their olde variaunce then their newe attonement. **1554**

PHILPOT *Exam. & Writ.* (1842) 330 What atonement.. is there betwixt light and darkness. **1610** HEALEY *St. Aug. City of God* 763 Beasts should live at more attonement and peace betweene them-selves. **1611** SPEED *Hist. Gt. Brit.* VI. xxv. (1632) 129 After three great and dangerous Battles came to an attonement. **1623** COCKERAM, *Atonement*, quietnesse.

†**2.** The action of setting at one, or condition of being set at one, after discord or strife: **a.** Restoration of friendly relations between persons who have been at variance; reconciliation. *Obs.*

1513 MORE *Edw. V* Wks. 40 Of which.. none of vs hath any thing the lesse nede, for the late made attonemente. **1577** HOLINSHED *Chron.* II. 98 At length an attonment was concluded betwixt him and the king. **1594** SHAKS. *Rich. III*, I. iii. 36, I Madam, he desires to make atonement Betweene the Duke of Glouster, and your Brothers. **1632** MASSINGER *Maid of Hon.* V. ii, As a perfect sign of your atonement with me, You wish me joy. **1685** MORDEN *Geog. Rect.* 201 The atonement made by Hannibal.. between Bruneus and his Brother.

†**b.** The settling *of differences*, staunching *of strife*; appeasement. *Obs.*

1605 *Play of Stucley* (1878) 227 There shall be now atonement of this strife. **1622** HEYLIN *Cosmogr.* I. (1682) 215 Made Umpire for the atonement of some differences betwixt Henry.. and John.

†**c.** The means or agent of appeasement. *Obs.*

1752 LAW *Spir. Love* (1816) II. 69 Water is the proper atonement of the rage of fire; and that which changes a tempest into a calm, is its true atonement.

3. *spec.* in *Theol.* Reconciliation or restoration of friendly relations between God and sinners.

1526 TINDALE *2 Cor.* v. 18 God.. hath geven unto us the office to preache the atonement. *a* **1569** KYNGESMILL *Man's Est.* vi. (1580) 28 If God did.. vouchsafe to make atonement with us. **1611** BIBLE *Rom.* v. 11 Our Lorde Iesus Christ, by whom we haue now receiued the atonement [WYCLIF, reconcilyng, *or accordyng*; TINDALE, CRANMER, attonment; COVERDALE, attonement; *Genev.* atonement; *Rhem. & Revised*, reconciliation]. **1650** S. CLARKE *Eccl. Hist.* (1654) I. 29 We must not come to make an attonement with God.. before we have made attonement with our Brother. **1852** [See in 4 ¶].

4. Propitiation of an offended or injured person, by reparation of wrong or injury; amends, satisfaction, expiation.

1611 BIBLE *Job.* xxxiii. 24 Deliuer him from going downe to the pit; I haue found a ransome [*marg.* atonement]. **1711** ADDISON *Spect.* No. 8 ¶7 The best Atonement he can make for it, is to warn others. **1768** BLACKSTONE *Comm.* I. 131 No suitable atonement can be made for the loss of life, or limb. **1875** STUBBS *Const. Hist.* III. xx. 494 No atonement is offered to their injured dignity.

b. *Theol.* Propitiation of God by expiation of sin.

1611 BIBLE *Lev.* i. 4 It shall be accepted for him to make atonement for him. **1714** ADDISON *Spect.* No. 580 ¶3 The High-Priest.. having made an Atonement for the Sins of the People. **1876** NORRIS *Rudim. Theol.* I. iii. 61 The old word atonement.. has by a true instinct been deepened into the idea on which it rests, and has come to carry with it the idea of propitiation or expiation.

¶ As applied to the redemptive work of Christ, *atonement* is variously used by theologians in the senses of *reconciliation*, *propitiation*, *expiation*, according to the view taken of its nature. (Not so applied in any version of the N.T.)

1630 PRYNNE *Anti-Armin.* 158 Saued onely by meanes of his aduocation and attonement. **1836** J. GILBERT *Chr. Atonem.* (1852) VII. 199 The efficacy of the Christian atonement is deduced solely from the appointment of it by God. **1847** H. MILLER *First Impr.* i. 5 A Scottish religious controversy of the present time regards the nature and extent of the atonement. **1852** ROBERTSON *Serm.* Ser. IV. xlvi. 345 The atonement between God and man consisted of two parts: God atoned to man by the work of Christ; man atoned to God by the work of the Christian ministry. **1860** E. D. GRIFFIN in *Disc. & Treat. Atonem.* 149 Atonement is that which was adapted to prevent punishment, or that which came in the room of punishment, and laid a foundation for our discharge from every part of the curse. **1860** C. BURGE *ibid.* 437 The necessity of some atonement in order that sinners may be consistently pardoned.

5. *Comb.* †**atonement-maker**, one who makes atonement, a reconciler or mediator; †**atonement-making**, reconciliation, propitiation; **atonement-money**, money paid in expiation of offences.

c **1540** BECON *New-Y. Gift* Wks. 1843, 314 There is one Atonementmaker between God and men. **1587** GOLDING *De Mornay* vi. 70 Men were forbidden to vtter the vncommunicable name of God.. saue onely in the daies of attonementmaking. **1611** BIBLE *Ex.* xxx. 16 And thou shalt take the atonement money of the children of Israel.

a'tonementist. [f. prec. + -IST.] One who holds the Calvinistic doctrine of the Atonement.

1836 J. GILBERT *Chr. Atonem.* (1852) vii. 208 Urged as inconsistent with the views of atonementists.

atoner (əˈtəʊnə(r)). [f. ATONE *v.* + -ER¹.] One who atones; a reconciler; an expiator.

1719 D'URFEY *Pills* (1872) I. 108 Oh Joy too fierce to be exprest, Thou sweet atoner of Life's greatest Pain. **1860** MAURICE *Lect. Apoc.* v. 95 The Lamb that was slain.. the perfect Atoner of man with the Father of Light. **1881** W. NICOLL *The Saviour* xxiii. 378 The atoner for souls must be sinless.

†**a'toneside, a'toside,** *advb. phr. Obs.* [*a t'one side* = on the one side: see A *prep.*¹ and ONE.] On one side, on the one side.

1600 HOLLAND *Livy* XXX. xxxiv. 764 They cast them atoside [*ejecerunt*]. *Ibid.* XXXVII. xi. 950 Those vessels which lay atone side upon the land. **1621** MOLLE *Camerar. Liv. Lib.* III. xx. 217 The third made that which remained to hang a tone-side.

atonic (əˈtɒnɪk), *a.* and *sb.* [ad. med.L. *atonic-us*, f. Gr. ἄτον-ος without tone (f. ἀ priv. + τόνος stretch, strain, stress, tone, f. τείν-ειν to stretch); see -IC.] **A.** *adj.*

1. *Pros.* Not having an accent, unaccented; *usually*, not bearing the stress or syllabic accent, as 'the atonic syllables of a word,' 'an atonic vowel.'

1878 KITCHIN tr. *Brachet's Etym. Fr. Dict.* §50 Every atonic Latin vowel, in the last syllable of a word disappears in French.

2. *Path.* Wanting tone; characterized by want of tone or nervous elasticity in the system.

1792 *Gentl. Mag.* May 448 Recommended in the atonic gout. **1843** C. WILLIAMS *Princ. Med.* iii. §494 Atonic enlargement of the capillaries. **1861** *Sat. Rev.* 7 Sept. 240 We live in what is delicately called an atonic age. Medical science is devoted constantly to the task of fanning into a sickly flame the sparks of life.

B. *sb.*

1. *Pros.* A word or element of speech not having an accent. (Used *spec.* in Greek Grammar of the words ὁ, ἡ, οἱ, αἱ, ἐν, ἐς, εἰς, ἐκ, ἐξ, εἰ, οὐ, ὡς.)

1727–51 CHAMBERS *Cycl.* s.v. *Accent*, Words which have no accent are called Atonics. **1874** PARRY *Grk. Gram.* 172 Ten monosyllables (called Atonics or Proclitics) have no accents.

2. *Med.* 'A remedy having power to allay excitement.' *Syd. Soc. Lex.* 1881.

1864 in WEBSTER.

atonicity (ætəˈnɪsɪtɪ). [f. ATONIC *a.* + -ITY.] The fact or quality of being atonic (in various senses).

1900 DORLAND *Med. Dict.* 85/2 *Atonicity*, atonic quality. **1930** L. BLOOMFIELD in *Curme Vol. Ling. Stud.* 54 This usage does not reflect old atonicity.

atoning (əˈtəʊnɪŋ), *ppl. a.* [f. ATONE *v.* + -ING².] Reconciling; making reparation for offences; expiating.

1609 ARMIN *Maids More-cl.* (1880) 107 Two hearts relenting, Thine penetrable, through attoning pittie. **1814** SOUTHEY *Roderick* XV. Wks. IX. 137 Who on the Cross Gave his atoning blood for lost mankind. **1879** GEO. ELIOT *Theo. Such* 122 Dion's atoning friendliness has a ring of artificiality.

a'toningly, *adv.* [f. prec. + -LY².] In an atoning manner; by way of expiation of an offence.

1864 SWINBURNE *Atalanta* 1647 Being just, I had slain their slayer atoningly.

atony (ˈætənɪ). *Path.* [a. F. *atonie* (14th c.), ad. med.L. *atonia*, a. Gr. ἀτονία, n. of state f. ἄτονος: see ATONIC.] Want of tone, relaxed condition: enervation, languor. Also *fig.*

1693 *Phil. Trans.* XVII. 659 This Atony of the Glandules of the Brain. **1751** CHAMBERS *Cycl.*, *Atony*, in medicine, a want of tone or tension; or a relaxation of the solids of a human body; occasioning a loss of strength, faintings, &c. **1847** tr. *Geo. Sand's Wks.* VI. 141 Ennui is the languor of the soul, an intellectual atony.

atonys, obsolete form of AT ONCE.

atop (əˈtɒp), *adv.* and *prep.* [A *prep.*¹ + TOP; formerly written *divisim*.]

A. *adv.* On or at the top, above.

1658 ROWLAND *Mouffet's Theat. of Ins.* 912 Boil them.. in an earthen vessel, take off the skim a top. **1779** in *Phil. Trans.* LXIX. 534 A black mass a-top, and a metallic mass at bottom. **1877** M. ARNOLD *Sohrab & R.* Sel. Poems (1882) 37 From the fluted spine atop, a plume Of horsehair waved.

b. followed by *of*.

1672 PENN *Spir. Truth* 120 Set atop of Christ, that is, over His Head. **1708** MRS. CENTLIVRE *Busie Body* IV. ii, You are a-top of the House, and you are down in the Cellar. **1883** W. SIKES in *Harper's Mag.* Feb. 349/1 A round hole in the greensward atop of the cliff.

B. *prep.* [by omission of *of*.] On the top of.

1655 GURNALL *Chr. in Arm.* 14. xviii. (1669) 67/1 Float a-top the waves. **1713** DERHAM *Phys.-Theol.* Addr. 6 Sideways, not under or a-top the Spear. **1868** HAWTHORNE *Amer. Note-Bks.* (1879) I. 179 Rushing atop the waves.

atopy (ˈætəpɪ). *Med.* [ad. Gr. ἀτοπία unusualness, f. ἄτοπος unusual (ἀ- priv. + τόπος place).] A form of hypersensitivity in which acute reactions occur, on exposure to the antigen, in some special organ or tissue. So **'atopic, a'topic,** *a.*, (*a*) out of place (Webster 1909); (*b*) *Med.* pertaining, relating to, or characterized by atopy.

1923 A. F. COCA in *Jrnl. Immunol.* VIII. 166 The group of abnormal hypersensitiveness includes.. those idiosyncrasies that are controlled by the dominant gene... This latter sub-group evidently needs a special term by which it may be conveniently designated, and this need is satisfactorily met with the word atopy, which was.. suggested by Professor Edward D. Perry. *Ibid.* 167 (*heading*) Atopic hyper-sensitiveness. **1925** COCA & GROVE *Ibid.* X. 448 It will be convenient to introduce here a term with which to designate the specifically reacting substances in the serum of atopic individuals... We would like to suggest the noncommittal term 'atopic reagin'. **1948** J. H. BLACK *Vaughan's Practice of Allergy* vi. 37 *Atopy* will be used in this volume.. to indicate that group of allergic phenomena in which a reagin mechanism can be demonstrated... Atopic eczema can thus be differentiated from contact eczema. **1964** S. DUKE-ELDER *Parsons' Dis. Eye* (ed. 14) xix. 275 An Atopic Cataract which tends to develop rapidly, appears frequently in sufferers from severe and widespread skin diseases—atopic eczema, [etc.].

-ator (eɪtə(r)), *suffix.* See -OR 2 b, c.

atornde, pa. t. of ATREN *v. Obs.*

‖**à tort et à travers** (a tɔr e a travɛr), *advb. phr.* [Fr., lit. 'wrongly and across'.] At random, haphazardly; without fixed principle.

1749 LD. CHESTERFIELD *Let.* 24 Oct. (1774) I. 479 Pray speak it [*sc.* Italian] in company, right or wrong, *à tort ou à travers.* **1778** F. BURNEY *Diary* 25 July (1842) 21 They were .. afraid of praising *à tort et à travers*, as their opinions are liable to be quoted. **1834** J. S. MILL in *Monthly Repos.* VIII. 391 That kind of philosophic pedantry, which, when it has got hold of a few truths which it conceives to be a test of superiority over the vulgar, applies them *à tort et à travers.* **1856** C. M. YONGE *Daisy Chain* I. i. 47 She found herself going *à tort et à travers* all the morning. **1921** G. B. SHAW in *Times Lit. Suppl.* 17 Mar. 178/2 It bristles with mad hyphens *à tort et à travers.*

atoside, variant of ATONESIDE.

†**a'touch,** *v. Obs. rare*⁻¹. [a. OF. *atouche-r*, earlier *-ier*, f. *à* to + *touchier* to TOUCH.] To touch, come in contact with.

1483 CAXTON *Gold. Leg.* 248/3 Sore vexed with tooth ache, and he atouched this wode and anone the ache was gone.

†**a'touchment.** *Obs rare*⁻¹. [a. OF. *atouchement*, f. *atoucher*: see prec. and -MENT.] Touch.

1483 CAXTON *Gold. Leg.* 430/2 That euer he felte ony atouchemente, tatche, or spotte, of mortal crysme.

†**a'tour,** *sb. Obs.* Forms: 3 aturn, 4–5 atour(e, -owr(e, attour. [a. OF. *aturn*, *-ourn*, *-ur*, *-our* (mod. *atour*), vbl. sb. f. *atourner*: see ATURN.]

1. Attire, array, dress.

c **1220** *Hali Meid.* 23 For þi is hare aturn se briht. *c* **1300** *K. Alis.* 6834 Ne saughe he never so faire atoure. *c* **1400** *Rom. Rose* 3717 Nor of robe, nor of tresour.. neithir of hir riche attour. **1475** CAXTON *Jason* 115 b, That poure creature habylled with ryall atours.

2. Military equipment or preparation.

1375 BARBOUR *Bruce* XVII. 717 The schipmen.. pressit with that gret atour Toward the wall. **1480** CAXTON *Ovid's Met.* XII. v, For t' avenge it, he made redy alle his atowr.

atour (əˈtaʊr), *prep.* and *adv.* *Sc.* Forms: 4 a-toure, at-oure, 4–5 **atoure**, 6 **attoure**, **attouir**, 9 **atower**, 4– **attour**, **atour.** [Only Scotch, exc. in the quotations from *Alisaunder* and *Sir Beves.* App. f. AT *prep.* + *our*, *ower*, Sc. form of OVER. In Barbour's *Bruce* OUTOUR is used in the same sense, as if *at-* were corrupted from *out.* In his *Saints' Lives* it rimes many times with *fower*, 'four,' never with Fr. *ou* in *hour*, *honour*; nor does the sense suit Fr. *autour*, or OF. *entour*, around, about.]

A. *prep.*

1. Of position: Over.

1375 BARBOUR *Bruce* XIII. 353 Bannokburne, that sa cummyrsum was.. mycht nane atour it ryde. **1423** JAMES I *King's Q.* III. viii, Thaire hudis all.. atoure thair eyen hang. *c* **1425** WYNTOUN *Cron.* IV. xix. 64 Atoure the Peychtys kyng regnand. **1535** STEWART *Cron. Scot.* I. 9 To fair attour the flude. **1826** J. WILSON *Noct. Ambr.* Wks. 1855 I. 149 Loupin atower the sopha. **1837** R. NICOLL *Poems* (1842) 85 The sunshine creeps atour the crags.

2. Of degree, quantity, or number: Over, more than, beyond.

1375 BARBOUR *Bruce* II. 368 And he hym-selff, atour the lave, Sa hard and hewy dyntis gave. *Ibid.* XX. 434 Nocht.. atour ten. *c* **1475** *R. Coilyear*, Ane man he traistit in, maist atour all vther thing. **1609** SKENE *Reg. Maj.* 139 Attour the space of ane zeare, and ane day.

b. *by and atour*: over and above, in addition to.

c **1600** in *Orig. Paroch. Scot.* (1851) I. 517 Three chalders of victual.. by and attour the ministeris stipend. **1824** SCOTT *Redgaunt.* xii, By and attour her gentle havings.

3. Over an obstacle, restriction, prohibition: In defiance of, in spite of.

1535 STEWART *Cron. Scot.* II. 12 How the Pechtis crownit ane King attouir forbidding. *Mod. Sc.* (Jamieson) I'll do this attour ye.

†**4.** ? Over against.

c **1375** ? BARBOUR *St. Adrian* 380 Furth come campyonis foure, & al stud Adryane atoure.

B. *adv.*

1. Over and above, moreover, in addition, besides.

c **1320** *Sir Beves* 2137 Atour, a seide, in is contre Icham a erl and also is he. *c* **1375** ? BARBOUR *St. Marcus* Prol. 1 ȝete suld I here a-toure Spek of þe ewangelistis foure. **1558** KENNEDY *Compend. Tract.* in *Misc. Wodr. Soc.* (1844) 108 Attouir, it is to be notit. **1663** in Spalding *Troub. Chas. I* (1829) 42 Attour, they are of intolerable greediness.

b. In same sense, the phrases *by atour, by and atour, more atour (mairatour)*.

c **1300** *K. Alis.* 4511 Ded buth my prynces be atour. *a* **1500** *Lancelot* 1775 And mor atour he shall Have O thing. **1725** A. RAMSAY *Gent. Sheph.* (1844) 31 By an attour..twa quey cawfs, I'll yearly to them give. **1794** BURNS *Wks.* 137 Bye attour, my gutcher has A hich house and a laigh ane.

2. ? All over, everywhere.

a **1475** *R. Coilyear* 469 His plaitis properlie picht attour with precious stanis. **1513** DOUGLAS *Æneis* VII. vi. 68 Quhy suld I dred or spayr To purches help..attour allquhair?

† **a'tourement.** *Obs. rare*⁻¹. [a. OF. *atornement, -ournement*, f. *atourner*; assimilated in form to ATOUR *sb.*] Attire, clothing, vesture.

1481 CAXTON *Myrr.* I. xvi. 50 This clerenesse..callyd ayer spyrituel..where the angels take their araye and atourement.

atowen, pa. pple. of ATEE *v. Obs.* to maltreat.

atoxyl (əˈtɒksɪl). *Chem.* [G. (1902), as trade name regd. by Ver. Chem. Werke, Charlottenburg, f. A- 14 + TOX(IC *a.* + -YL.] An organic arsenical compound (esp. as formerly used hypodermically in skin diseases).

Equivalent names include arsamin and soamin.

1906 *Daily Chron.* 18 Sept. 3/4 The treatment of the patients was based on the simultaneous use of atoxyl and strychnine. *Ibid.* 21 Dec. 5/3 Professor Koch decided to employ atoxyl injections of half a gramme. **1911** *Allbutt's Syst. Med.* IX. 104 Optic atrophy caused by arsenical injections, in the form of atoxyl. **1920** J. M. H. MACLEOD *Diseases of Skin* 111 Arsacetin and orsudan have the advantage over atoxyl of being more stable and capable of being boiled without decomposition. **1943** *Endeavour* Apr. 41/1 The organic arsenicals, atoxyl, salvarsan, neo-salvarsan. **1957** A. H. DOUTHWAITE *Hale-White's Materia Medica* (ed. 30) 383 Pentavalent Arsenicals. *Sodii Aminoarsonas* (B.P.C.). Synonym, Atoxyl. **1964** S. DUKE-ELDER *Parsons' Dis. Eye* (ed. 14) xxiii. 352 *Arsenic* is specially liable to cause optic atrophy, usually total, when administered in the form of pentavalent compounds such as atoxyl or soamin.

ATP (eɪtiːˈpiː). *Biochem.* Also **A.T.P.** [Abbrev. of *a*denosine *t*ri*p*hosphate.] = *adenosine triphosphate* s.v. ADENOSINE b.

1939 [see ADENOSINE b]. **1953** *Sci. Amer.* Sept. 102/2 ATP delivers a phosphate to an amino acid, thereby creating an amino acid acylphosphate. **1956** [see *phosphoenolpyruvate* s.v. PHOSPHO-]. **1964** W. G. SMITH *Allergy & Tissue Metabolism* viii. 86 The energy can be released from ATP by its reconversion to ADP and inorganic phosphate. **1976** *Ann. Rev. Microbiol.* XXX. 6 We were able to isolate from the frog eggs several milligrams of ATP. **1983** *Oxf. Textbk. Med.* II. xiii. 7/1 Energy in the form of ATP is used to maintain the integrity of cell structures, to fuel the pumps for maintenance of ionic gradients, and to bring about muscle shortening.

Hence **ATPase** (eɪtiːˈpiːeɪz), an enzyme that hydrolyses ATP to adenosine diphosphate and inorganic phosphate.

1946 *Jrnl. Biol. Chem.* CLXIII. 340 We conclude that the ATPase is contained only in a fraction of the myosin. **1975** *Sci. Amer.* Dec. 35/1 We had been working with normal *E. coli* bacteria, and we decided..to try certain mutant strains that lack the enzyme ATPase. **1982** J. F. VAN PILSUM in T. M. Devlin *Textbk. Biochem.* xxi. 1007 The sliding filament model of muscle contraction involves the ATPase activity of the globular portion of the myosin molecule. **1984** J. F. LAMB et al. *Essent. Physiol.* (ed. 2) i. 23 The current view of this pump is that it is a large phospholipid molecule in the surface membrane of the cell, which has ATPase (ability to split ATP) properties.

† **atrabilar, -'laire**, *a. Obs.* [a. F. *atrabilaire*, ad. med.L. *ātrabīlārius*, f. L. *ātrabīlis*: see ATRABILE, ATRABILIAR.] = ATRABILARIOUS.

1597 LOWE *Art Chyrurg.* (1634) 147 Ulcers Cankerous are ingendred of a humor atrabilar. **1738** WARBURTON *Div. Legat.* I. 360 More subject to atrabilaire Disorders.

atrabilarian (ætrəbɪˈlɛərɪən), *a.* and *sb.* [f. med.L. *ātrabīlāri-us* (see prec.) + -AN.]

A. *adj.* = ATRABILARIOUS; 'replete with black choler.' J.

1678 CUDWORTH *Intell. Syst.* 792 An Hypochondriacal or Atrabilarian Distemper. **1732** ARBUTHNOT *Rules Diet* 298 Melancholy or atrabilarian Constitutions. **1831** HEIDIGER *Didoniad* v. 130 His pristine prompt atrabilarian Commands.

B. *sb.* An atrabilious man, a hypochondriac.

† **atrabi'laric**, *a. Obs.* [irreg. f. med.L. *ātrabīlārius* or F. *atrabilaire* (see above) + -IC; prob. after *melancholic*, etc.] = ATRABILIOUS.

1620 VENNER *Via Recta* (1650) 97 Sausages..are most hurtfull to the cholerick and atrabilarick.

atrabilarious (ætrəbɪˈlɛərɪəs), *a.* [f. med.L. *ātrabīlāri-us* (see ATRABILE) + -OUS.] **a.** Of or pertaining to black bile. **b.** Atrabilious, melancholy, hypochondriacal; splenetic, acrimonious.

1684 tr. *Bonet's Merc. Compit.* III. 49 An Atrabilarious humour is but enraged and irritated by using hot things. **1732** ARBUTHNOT *Rules Diet* 367 Atrabilarious dry Constitutions. **1882** J. HAWTHORNE *Fort. Fool* I. xx, Kate Roland was defending Mr. Sinclair against a rather atrabilarious onslaught from Miss Vivian.

† **atrabi'lariousness.** *Obs.*⁻⁰ [f. prec. + -NESS.] = ATRABILIOUSNESS.

1731 in BAILEY.

† **atra'bilary**, *a. Obs.* [ad. med.L. *ātrabīlāri-us*, or F. *atrabilaire.*] = ATRABILARIOUS.

1672 COLES, *Atrabilary*, troubled with Melancholly. **1684** tr. *Bonet's Merc. Compit.* XI. 377 Let Atrabilary Melancholists use it. **1751** [see ATRABILE].

† **'atrabile.** *Obs.* [a. F. *atrabile*, in 16th c. *atrebile* (= It. *atra'bile*), ad. L. *ātra bīlis*, used to transl. Gr. μελαγχολία black bile, melancholy, and treated in later times as a single word, as in the mod. langs.; hence the late adjs. *ātrabiliārius, ātrabīlārius*. (Of these the former is on the whole the more regular, though both are supported by L. analogies: cf. *viridārium* and *viridiārium*.]

lit. Black bile, 'a term anciently used for an imaginary fluid, thick, black, and acrid,' supposed to be secreted by the renal or atrabiliary glands, or by the spleen, and to be the cause of melancholy (*Syd. Soc. Lex.*); *hence*: Melancholy, spleen. (Also used in L. form *ātra bīlis*.)

1594 CAREW *Huarte's Exam. Wits* (1616) 85 *Choler adust*, or *atrabile*, of which Aristotle said, That it made men exceeding wise. **1639** G. DANIEL *Vervic.* 638 To see my Phlegme, or Atra bilis rise. **1727-51** CHAMBERS *Cycl.*, *Atrabilis* was one of the great humours of the ancient physicians; whence arose the *atrabilary*, one of their temperaments; answering to what we call *melancholy*.

atrabiliar (ætrəˈbɪlɪə(r)), *a.* [f. after earlier F. *atrabiliaire*, or mod.L. *ātrabiliārius*: see prec.] = ATRABILIOUS.

1831 CARLYLE *Sart. Res.* I. ix, In my atrabiliar moods. **1877** MORLEY *Crit. Misc.* Ser. II. 102 Of nervous atrabiliar constitution.

atrabili'arious, variant of preceding.

1761 *Brit. Mag.* II. 359 Active and alert, with an atrabiliarious aspect.

atrabiliary (ætrəˈbɪlɪərɪ), *a.* [ad. mod.L. *ātrabiliāri-us* (in It. *atrabiliario*), f. *ātra bīlis*: see ATRABILE and -ARY.] **a.** Of or pertaining to black bile; 'applied to the renal or supra-renal glands or capsules, and to the arteries and veins by which they are supplied.' *Syd. Soc. Lex.* **b.** = ATRABILIOUS.

1725 BRADLEY *Fam. Dict.* s.v. *Lentils*, Subject to atrabiliary Distempers. **1830** *Edin. Encycl.* I. 839 Called renal, or suprarenal glands, and from the blackish fluid they contain atrabiliary capsules. **1839** HOOPER *Med. Dict.* 1179 An atrabiliary young man.

atrabilious (ætrəˈbɪlɪəs), *a.* [f. L. *ātra bīlis* (see ATRABILE) + -OUS, after L. *bīliōsus* BILIOUS.] Affected by black bile or 'choler adust'; melancholy, hypochondriac; splenetic, acrimonious.

1651 BIGGS *New Disp.* ¶220 Some æruginous or atrabilious. **1816** SOUTHEY *Ess. Mor. & Pol.* (1832) I. 270 It would make the English..fonder of life, less atrabilious. **1849** LOWELL *Biglow P.* Wks. 1879. 179/1 A hard-faced, atrabilious, earnest-eyed race. **1866** CARLYLE *Remin.* (1881) II. 206 My atrabilious censures.

atra'biliousness. [f. prec. + -NESS.] The quality of being atrabilious.

1882 *Spectator* 8 Apr. 462 The atrabiliousness of Carlyle's attitude towards human life.

† **atra'bilous**, obs. variant of ATRABILIOUS.

1681 tr. *Willis' Rem. Med. Wks.*, *Atrabilous*, belonging to the black bile or melancholy, or to the melancholic humour.

atrament (ˈætrəmənt). [ad. L. *ātrāmentum* blacking, ink, f. **ātrā-re* to blacken, f. *āter* black.] Blacking, ink; any similar black substance, as the 'ink' of the cuttle-fish.

1398 TREVISA *Barth. De P.R.* XIX. xxxiii. (1495) 879 Attrament is made of sote. **1661** LOVELL *Hist. Anim. & Min.* 195 Being in dainger, they [cuttle-fish] cast forth their atrament. **1678** R. RUSSELL *Geber* I. iii. 8 There are divers Atraments and they are found of divers Colour. **1834** ALLAN *Min.* 15 Atrament Stone..is a mixture of the sulphate and peroxide of iron..of a dark brick-red colour.

† **atramen'taceous**, *a. Obs. rare*⁻¹. [f. L. *ātrāmentum* (see prec.) + -ACEOUS.] Of the nature of ink, inky.

1713 DERHAM *Phys.-Theol.* IV. ii. 94 The Vitreous, and Crystalline Humours—and Atramentaceous Mucus.

atramental (ætrəˈmɛntəl), *a.* [f. as. prec. + -AL¹.] Of or pertaining to ink; ink-.

1646 SIR T. BROWNE *Pseud. Ep.* VI. xii. 336 If we inquire in what part of vitriol this Atramentall and denigrating condition lodgeth. **1662** EVELYN *Sylva* (1679) 29 That the sap should be..so flat and pallid in the Atramental Galls.

† **,atramen'tarious**, *a. Obs. rare*⁻¹. [f. L. *ātrāmentāri-us* pertaining to ink (*ātrāmentārium* an ink-stand) + -OUS.] Inky.

1717 SLARE in *Phil. Trans.* XXX. 566 They degenerate into a deep Purple, or even to an Atramentarious Colour.

atra'mentary, *a. rare.* [ad. L. *ātrāmentāri-us*: see prec.] Belonging to ink; written, printed.

1613 JACKSON *Creed* II. xxxi. Wks. II. 145 To communicate..by these dumb characters or atramentary instructors.

† **atramen'titious**, *a. Obs. rare*⁻¹. In 7 atrim-. [f. L. *ātrāment-um* (see above) + -ITIOUS.] Of the nature of blacking or ink.

1650 BULWER *Anthropomet.* xxii. 255 The Moores might possibly become Negroes; receiving atrimentitious impression by the power and efficacy of imagination.

atramentous (ætrəˈmɛntəs), *a.* Also 7 **attrim-.** [repr. L. **ātrāmentōs-us*, f. *ātrāment-um*: see above, and -OUS.] Inky, ink-like, black as ink.

1646 SIR T. BROWNE *Pseud. Ep.* 336 The second way whereby bodies become black, is an Atramentous condition. **1669** W. SIMPSON *Hydrol. Chym.* 38 Not that the solution of Nitre or Salt, contributed anything to this attrimentous curdling. **1683** *Phil. Trans.* XIV. 489 [Brine] becomes Atramentous with galls. **1713** DERHAM *Phys.-Theol.* IV. ii. 92 Snails send out their Eyes..like atramentous spots, fixed at the end of their Horns.

atran, pa. t. of ATRIN *v.*, ATRINE *v. Obs.*

atrap, var. of ATTRAP *v. Obs.*, to entrap, catch.

† **'atrate.** *Obs.*⁻⁰ [ad. L. *ātrātus*, ppl. adj. f. *āter* black.] 'One cladde in blacke, a mourner.' Cockeram 1623.

atraumatic (æ-, eɪtrɔːˈmætɪk), *a.* [f. A- 14 + TRAUMATIC *a.*] Not causing trauma or injury; applied *spec.* to surgical instruments or techniques that minimize injurious effects.

1934 in WEBSTER. **1950** K. W. STARR in *Brit. Surg. Practice* VIII. 140 *Atraumatic sutures.* In plastic procedures on nerves, blood-vessels, tendons, [etc.]..the finest atraumatic needle (8–20 millimetres) is required. **1957** A. V. PARTIPILO *Surg. Technique* (ed. 6) i. 33 An atraumatic technique avoids pinching, pulling, crushing, twisting, and tearing of the tissues.

† **a-'travers**, *adv.* and *prep. Obs.* Also 5 **attrauerse.** [a. F. *à travers.*] **A.** *adv.* Crosswise, sidewise. **B.** *prep.* Across.

1430 LYDG. *Chron. Troy* III. xxiii, And goth to him attrauerse. **1483** CAXTON *Gold. Leg.* 34/4 A crosse..of sonde a travers the Angle. **1659** LEAK *Water-wks.* 14 They must be soldered a travers above the great Pipes.

† **a'tray**, *v. Obs.* Also 4–5 **atrey.** [f. A- *pref.* 1 + TRAY *v.*, OE. *treȝian.*] To vex, trouble.

c **1320** *Seuyn Sages* (W.) 1867 Swithe sore sche him atraid. *c* **1330** *Kyng of Tars* 605 He sturte him up..In his herte sore atrayyed. *a* **1400** *Cov. Myst.* 350 We were of hym so sore atreyd.

† **a'treach**, *v. Obs. rare.* [f. AT- *pref.*¹, ² + REACH; cf. AREACH.]

1. To reach or get at with a weapon; to strike.

c **1330** *Arth. & Merl.* 4827 Who so evir he at raught Tombel of hors he him taught.

2. To seize or snatch away.

c **1300** in Wright *Lyric P.* x. 37 Al my ro were me at-raht.

† **'atred**, *ppl. a. Obs. rare*⁻¹. [f. L. *ātr-um* (*āter*) black + -ED. Cf. ATRATE.] Coloured black.

1638 T. WHITAKER *Blood of Grape* 76 (T.) Yellow choler or atred, or a mixture of both.

† **a'trede**, *v. Obs. rare.* [f. AT- *pref.*² + *rede*, READ; lit. 'to give advice away from.' Possibly for *out-read* (as edited by Tyrwhitt, though all MSS. have *at-*); cf. ATOUR *prep.*] To outdo in counsel.

c **1374** CHAUCER *Troylus* IV. 1456 Men may the wise atrenne, and nought atrede. *c* **1386** —— *Knts. T.* 1591 Men may the eelde at-renne, but nat at-rede.

† **a'treet, a'trete**, *adv. Obs.* Also 4 **atrayt.** [a. F. *à trait* at a draught. The spelling after 1500 would have been *atreat.*] At one draught, continuously; straight off, distinctly.

1340 *Ayenb.* 50 Þe wombe zayþ, þou sselt et longe and atrayt. **1388** WYCLIF *Nehem.* viii. 8 Thei redden..distinctli, *ether atreet*, and opynli to vndurstonde. **1440** *Promp. Parv.* 17 Atreet (**1499** atrete), *Tractatim, tractim, distincte.*

a-tremble (əˈtrɛmb(ə)l), *advb. phr.* [A *prep.*¹ + TREMBLE.] In a trembling state.

1856 MRS. BROWNING *Aur. Leigh* VI, My hands a-tremble, as I had just caught up My heart to write with. **1876** DOWDEN *Poems* 151 A whisper fine In the leaves a-tremble.

† **a'tren**, *v. Obs.* Forms: 3 *Pa. t.* **atarnde, -ærnde, -ornde**, 4–5 *Inf.* **atrenne.** [f. AT- *pref.*² + OE. *rennan* (weak): see RUN. Cf. G. *entrennen.* Properly causal, but confused with the intr. ATRIN, q.v.] *intr.* To run away, escape (with *dat.* = from).

1205 LAY. 26638 Þa eorles biuoren heom aneuste atarnden. **1297** R. GLOUC. 539 The Constable vnnethe Atarnde aliue. *Ibid.* 419 He atornde as vaste as he myȝte. **1374-86** CHAUCER [see under ATREDE].

‖ **atresia** (əˈtriːʃ(ɪ)ə). *Path.* [mod.L., f. Gr. ἄτρητος not perforated, τρῆσις perforation.]

1. Occlusion or closure of a natural channel of the body.

1807 in MORRIS & KENDRICK *Edin. Med. Dict.* **1866** T. PEACOCK *Malform. Heart* 60 Atresia of the orifice..of the pulmonary artery.

2. Disappearance by degeneration, as of the follicles in the mammalian ovary.

1903 *Jrnl. R. Microsc. Soc.* Aug. 485 In the ferret, ovulation does not occur in the absence of coition, without which the follicles undergo atresia. **1962** *New Scientist* 7 June 506/3 The others [*sc.* egg cells] are eliminated from the ovary at different stages of development by a process of spontaneous degeneration known as atresia.

Hence **a'tresic, a'tretic** *adjs.*, pertaining to or resulting from atresia; imperforate.

1897 *Lippincott's Med. Dict.* 101/1 *Atresic*, characterised by atresia. **1903** *Nature* 20 Aug. 384/2 Other atresic follicles are reduced to fibrous tissue or remain cystic. **1903** *Jrnl. R. Microsc. Soc.* Aug. 485 The atretic follicle differs from the developing corpus luteum in the absence of any discharge to the exterior. **1962** *New Scientist* 7 June 506/3 No distinction was made between normal and atretic egg cells.

atrey, variant of ATRAY *v.*, ATRY *v. Obs.*

atrial ('eɪtrɪəl), *a. Phys.* [f. L. *ātri-um* (see ATRIUM) + -AL[1].] Of or belonging to the *atrium*.

1869 HUXLEY *Classif. Anim.* 31 In these animals [*Ascidioida*] there is an atrial system.

† **a'tride**, *v. Obs. rare*[−1]. [f. AT- *pref.*[2] + OE. *rídan* to RIDE. Cf. MHG. *entrîten*, Du. *ontrijden*.] *intr.* To ride away, escape.

1205 LAY. 31439 He at-ræd, þe seint Oswald biswac.

† **a'trin**, *v. Obs.* Forms (only in pa. t.): 1–3 ætarn, 3 attrann, 3–4 atarn. [OE. *ætrinnan*, *ætirnan*, f. AT- *pref.*[2] + OE. *rinnan* or *irnan*; cf. OE. *oðrinnan*; cogn. with G. *entrinnen*: see RUN.] *intr.* To run away, escape (with *dat.* = from). Also causal, for ATREN.

a **1000** *Boeth. Metr.* xx. 138 [He] þære eorþan æfre ne oðrinneð. *c* **1000** ÆLFRIC *Gen.* xxxix. 13 þa ætarn he ut. *c* **1200** ORMIN 1424 þatt bucc attrann Ut inntill wilde wesste. *c* **1315** SHOREH. 149 Thes ilke screawe into helle God at arn.

† **a'trine**, *v. Obs.* Forms: 1 æthrín-an, 3 atrin-en, etrin-en, attryne. 1 *Pa. t.* æthrán, 2–3 atran. [OE. *æthrinan*, f. AT- *pref.*[1] + *hrínan* to touch: see RINE and ARINE.]

1. To touch.

c **1000** *Ags. Gosp.* Matt. xxiii. 3 Nellaþ hig þá mid heora fingre æthrinan. **1205** LAY. 1554 ʒif he hine mid sweorde atran. *c* **1275** *Passion Our Lord* 582 in *O.E. Misc.* 53 Jhesus ..forbed þat heo attryne ne scolde his honde.

2. *fig.* **a.** To touch, concern; **b.** to befall.

c **1230** *Ancr. R.* 50 Ich write muchel uor oðre, þat noðing ne etrineð ou. *c* **1275** *Sinners Beware* 258 in *O.E. Misc.* 80 Bute he do bi preostes lore..Ne schal him no god attryne.

atriopore ('eɪtrɪəʊpɔə(r)). *Zool.* [f. ATRIUM + Gr. πόρος passage, PORE *sb.*[1]] The posterior opening of the atrium or cavity in the body of the lancelet.

1892 *Athenæum* 13 Aug. 227/2 There are no buccal cirri, and, so far as can be made out, no atriopore [in a certain specimen of Amphioxus]. **1896** KIRKALDY & POLLARD *Boas's Text Bk. Zool.* 355.

atrioventricular (ˌeɪtrɪəʊvɛn'trɪkjʊlə(r)), *a. Anat.* [f. *atrio-*, comb. f. ATRIUM + VENTRICULAR *a.*] Of or belonging to the atrial and ventricular cavities of the heart.

1879 *St. George's Hosp. Rep.* IX. 93 The heart showed.. very slight thickening of the atrio-ventricular valves. **1962** *Lancet* 12 May 990/2 In a few experiments a sling of rubber tubing was placed in the atrioventricular groove.

a-trip (ə'trɪp), *advb. phr. Naut.* [f. A *prep.*[1] + TRIP: as if 'on the trip, starting, ready.']

1. Of yards: Swayed up, ready to have the stops cut for crossing. Of sails: Hoisted from the cap, sheeted home, and ready for trimming. Smyth *Sailor's Word-bk.* 1867.

1626 G. SANDYS *Ovid's Met.* XI. 228 Then hoise their Yards a trip, and all their sailes. **1726** PENHALLOW *Ind. Wars* (1859) 53 They got their mainsail atrip.

2. Of an anchor: Just raised perpendicularly from the ground in weighing.

1796 DIBDIN *Poor Jack*, From the moment the anchor's atrip. **1849** W. IRVING *Columbus* III. 68 One ship, with anchor atrip and sails unfurled, waited to receive Nicuesa.

† **a'trist**, *v. Obs. rare*[−1]. [f. A- *pref.* 1 + *trist* = TRUST *v.*] To trust.

c **1400** *Apol. Loll.* 96 Veyn supersticoun..þat men atristun in.

atrium ('eɪtrɪəm). [L.] *Pl.* atria, atriums.

1. A court. **a.** The central hall or court of a Roman house. **b.** A covered court or portico in front of the principal doors of churches, etc.

1577 tr. *Bullinger's Decades* (1592) 340 The third parte was called Atrium, the court. **1791** ADAM *Rom. Antiq.* (1807) 522 In the atrium the nuptial couch was erected. **1853** RUSKIN *Stones Ven.* II. iv. §65 A large atrium or portico is attached to two sides of the church.

c. In a modern house, a central hall or glassed-in court that may be used as a sitting-room, having rooms opening off it, sometimes at more than one level. Chiefly *N. Amer.*

The 1864 example forms a bridge between the ancient and modern senses.

1864 G. O. TREVELYAN *Competition Wallah* xii. 446, I was present lately at an entertainment given by the Maharaja of Nilpore. The dancing went on in a sort of atrium in the centre of the palace, while the host..inspected the scene.. from the gallery. **1900** in WEBSTER. **1962** *Archit. Rec.* Oct. 140/2 You enter a nice atrium with the living room on one side. **1970** *Globe & Mail* (Toronto) 25 Sept. 35/4 (Advt.), Large bungalow... Atrium in garden setting with hanging flower baskets, for either basking in the sun or dining under the stars. **1977** *N.Z. Herald* 5 Jan. 2-17/4 (Advt.), The ultimate in executive family living, 4 brms, 2 baths, office, central atrium, private swimming pool. **1986** *Southern Living* Feb. 135 The Simon house is entered through the atrium, where a skylight and glass doors provide natural lighting.

d. In a public building, a usu. skylit central court rising through several storeys and surrounded by galleries at each level with rooms (shops, offices, etc.) opening off them. orig. *U.S.*

1967 *Interiors* July 69/1 The unsuspecting visitor enters the..hotel..through a dark-brown tunnel-like entrance. He then walks smack into..a 24-story atrium full of breathtaking fantasy. *Ibid.* 69/2 The five elevators.., elongated bubbles of glass..glide soundlessly up and down powerful concrete columns shooting through the atrium. **1976** J. C. STARBUCK (*title*) Atriums: a bibliography on an architectural vogue. **1976** J. ARCHER *Not Penny More* xii. 126 The gambling rooms, which were added in 1910, are linked by an atrium to the Salle Garnier in which operas and ballets are performed. **1979** *Daily Tel.* 20 Apr. 18 The owner of the block..plans to have five floors as a 'retail atrium'. **1982** *Times* 8 May 4/5 The Waverley market will have..two atria.

2. *Phys.* **a.** Either of the two upper cavities (*left* and *right* atrium) of the heart into which the veins pour the blood. **b.** In the Tunicata: A large cavity into which the intestine opens.

1870 NICHOLSON *Zool.* (1880) 382 From the stomach an intestine is continued, which..opens into the bottom of a second chamber called the 'cloaca' or 'atrium.' **1880** GUNTHER *Fishes* 119 Each atrium is supported externally by a small bone.

atro- ('ætrəʊ), comb. form of L. *āter* black, as in *atrorubent* reddish-black, *atrosanguineous* of a dark blood-red colour.

1697 LHWYD in *Phil. Trans.* XXVII. 467 All black, or atrorubent. **1881** *Syd. Soc. Lex.*, *Atrosanguineous.*

† **a'troce**, *a. Obs.* [a. F. *atroce*, ad. L. *atrōcem*: see ATROCIOUS *a.*] Atrocious.

a **1733** NORTH *Exam.* II. iv. ¶54 The..atroce Wickedness of these Doings. *Ibid.* v. ¶124 This most atroce Machine.

atrochal ('ætrəʊkəl), *a. Zool.* [f. A- 14 + TROCHAL *a.*] Having no definite rings of cilia.

1880 F. M. BALFOUR *Comp. Embryol.* I. 274 The atrochal forms are to be regarded as larvæ which never pass beyond the primitive stage of uniform ciliation. *Ibid.*, The atrochal larvæ are not common.

atrocious (ə'trəʊʃəs), *a.* [f. L. *atrōci-* (nom. *atrox*) fierce, cruel, f. *āter* black + -OUS.]

1. Characterized by savage enormity; excessively and wantonly cruel; heinously wicked: **a.** of actions. **b.** of persons or agents.

1669 HONYMAN *Surv. Naphtali* II. 203 If it [a fault] be atrocious and landdefiling. **1772** PENNANT *Tours Scot.* (1774) 252 Here all atrocious criminals were excluded. **1833** I. TAYLOR *Fanat.* vi. 21 Human nature..may become atrocious in a degree that confounds every distinction between human and diabolical wickedness. **1845** DARWIN *Voy. Nat.* ii. (1879) 24 Atrocious acts which can only take place in a slave country.

†2. Stern, terrible, fierce; extremely violent. *Obs.*

1735 THOMSON *Liberty* II. 305 The fierce, atrocious frown of sinewed Mars. **1733** CHEYNE *Eng. Malady* I. vi. §10 Nervous Diseases..with higher, and more numerous and atrocious Symptoms.

3. *colloq.* Very bad, shocking, execrable.

Mod. What an atrocious pun!

a'trociously, *adv.* [f. prec. + -LY[2].] In an atrocious manner; with heinous wickedness or cruelty; shockingly.

1765 BP. LOWTH *Lett. Warburton* ii, Abusing me infamously and atrociously. **1831** ALFORD in *Life* (1873) 67 The letter had an atrociously long sentence in it.. **1859** T. TROLLOPE *Tuscany* ix. 137 The populace..were atrociously incited to crimes of the deepest dye.

a'trociousness. [f. as prec. + -NESS.] The quality of being atrocious; heinousness.

1731 in BAILEY. **1750** JOHNSON *Rambler* No. 8 ¶8 Withdraws his attention from the atrociousness of the guilt. **1793** tr. *Beccaria's Ess. Crimes* xiii. 49 The credibility of a witness is less as the atrociousness of the crime is greater.

atrocity (ə'trɒsɪtɪ). [(? a. F. *atrocité*,) ad. L. *atrōcitātem*, n. of quality f. *atrox* fierce, cruel.]

1. Savage enormity, horrible or heinous wickedness.

1534 MORE *On the Passion* Wks. 1294/2 For the atrocyte of the story..almost euerye childe hathe heard. *a* **1674** CLARENDON (J.) They desired justice might be done upon offenders, as the atrocity of their crimes deserved. **1863** GARDINER *Hist. Eng.* I. 253 If the atrocity of their design was hidden from their eyes.

2. Fierceness, sternness, implacability. *arch.*

1635 NAUNTON *Fragm. Reg.* 183 The atrocity of her father's nature. **1865** BARING-GOULD *Werewolves* v. 54 They besiege it with atrocity, striving to break in the doors.

3. An atrocious deed; an act of extreme cruelty and heinousness.

1793 T. JEFFERSON *Writ.* (1859) IV. 14 To defend themselves from the atrocities of a vastly more numerous and powerful people. **1880** MCCARTHY *Own Times*, The deeds which have ever since been known as 'the Bulgarian atrocities.' **1915** *Sphere* 22 May 197 The British report on German atrocities in Belgium. **1918** W. OWEN *Let.* 25 Oct. (1967) 589, I have found in all these villages *no evidence of German atrocities*. The girls here were treated with perfect respect.

4. *colloq.* with no moral reference: A very bad blunder, violation of taste or good manners, etc.

1878 *Hatton Corr.* Pref. 4 Their diction and their spelling, and the fearful atrocities committed in the latter.

5. *attrib.* and *Comb.*, as ***atrocity-monger*** (so ***-mongering*** vbl. sb. and ppl. a.), ***atrocity propaganda, story***.

1896 *Westm. Gaz.* 18 Feb. 1/2 The massacres were a tale, either grossly exaggerated or altogether invented by atrocity-mongering journals. **1897** *Ibid.* 28 Aug. 2/3 We should be very cautious about accepting these atrocity stories. **1899** *Ibid.* 18 Oct. 3/3 In the words of General Colley, is not all this atrocity-mongering calculated to 'make our soldiers either cowards or butchers'? **1905** A. BENNETT *Tales of Five Towns* I. 94 You see roundabouts, swings,.. atrocity booths, quack dentists. **1914** E. A. POWELL *Fighting in Flanders* v. 129 Let them hear our side of this atrocity business. **1930** G. B. SHAW *What I really wrote about War* p. ix, The atrocity mongers who are using Belgium as a stick to beat Germany. **1937** KOESTLER *Spanish Testament* iv. 84 We know how much harm the preposterous atrocity propaganda engaged in by both sides caused during the Great War.

‖ **à trois** (a trwa), *phr.* [Fr.] Arranged for or shared by three persons; in a group of three. Cf. MÉNAGE À TROIS.

1881 L. TROUBRIDGE *Jrnl.* 31 Dec. in J. Hope-Nicholson *Life amongst Troubridges* (1966) xii. 158 A cheery dinner *à trois* and a quietly nice evening. **1897** G. B. SHAW *Let.* in J. Dunbar *Mrs. G. B. S.* (1963) x. 153, I bar the seaside *à trois*. **1962** *Observer* 18 Feb. 27/2 He lives *à trois* with a worried, irritating wife and a niece whom he loves like an incestuous father. **1966** L. DAVIDSON *Long Way to Shiloh* v. 72 We were sitting taking lemon tea *à trois*.

† **a'troke**, *v. Obs.* Also att-. [f. A- *pref.* 1 + OE. *trucan*: see TROKE *v.*] To fail, become faint.

c **1315** *Bodl. MS., Laud Misc.* No. 108 lf. 1 (Halliw.), I nelle nouʒt fastinde late him go That heo beon overcome And attrokien bi the weie. **1460** in *Pol. R. & Love Poems* (1866) 221 Him atroketh his breth And þe soule a-wey geth.

atropal ('ætrəpəl), *a. Bot.* = ATROPOUS.

1871 GRAY *Bot. Text-bk.* 524.

atrophiated (ə'trəʊfɪeɪtɪd), *ppl. a.* [f. ATROPHY + -ATE + -ED.] = ATROPHIED.

1634 T. JOHNSON tr. *Parey's Chirurg.* XXIX. (1678) 711 Every part which hath not his motion remaineth languid and atrophiated. **1836** TODD *Cycl. Anat. & Phys.* I. 117/1 The right [ovary]..atrophiated and useless.

atrophic (ə'trɒfɪk), *a.* [f. Gr. ἄτροφ-ος (see ATROPHY *sb.*) + -IC.] = ATROPHOUS.

1865 C. JONES *Year-bk. Med.* 86 Atrophic degeneration of the Spinal Cord. **1876** tr. *Wagner's Gen. Pathol.* 252 Tissues ..atrophic or flaccid.

atrophied ('ætrəfɪd), *ppl. a.* Also 6 **atrofied**. [f. ATROPHY + -ED.] Affected with atrophy; starved, wasted, emaciated. Also *fig.*

1597 LOWE *Art Chyrurg.* (1634) 59 The bodie.. becommeth atrofied and leane. **1836** TODD *Cycl. Anat. & Phys.* II. 79/2 The muscles..for want of use are more or less wasted and atrophied. **1876** BANCROFT *Hist. U. S.* VI. 533 The people, weary of atrophied institutions, yearn for fuller knowledge of the rules of right.

atrophous ('ætrəfəs), *a.* [f. Gr. ἄτροφ-ος (see next) + -OUS.] Characterized by atrophy.

1877 ROBERTS *Handbk. Med.* (ed. 3) I. 397 Atrophous emphysema is merely due to wasting of the septa.

atrophy ('ætrəfɪ), *sb.* [a. F. *atrophie*, ad. L. *atrophia*, Gr. ἀτροφία, n. of state f. ἄτροφος ill-fed, not nourished, f. ἀ priv. + τροφή nourishment.]

1. A wasting away of the body, or any part of it, through imperfect nourishment: emaciation.

1620 VENNER *Via Recta* viii. 189 Which..bringeth the body into a deformed Atrophie or consumption. **1667** MILTON *P.L.* XI. 486 Moon-struck madness, pining atrophy. **1862** TRENCH *Mirac.* xix. 323 A partial atrophy, showing itself in a gradual wasting of the size of the limb.

2. *fig.*

1653 JER. TAYLOR *Serm. Year* Ded., We..fear the people will fall to an Atrophy, then to a loathing of holy food. **1782** J. TRUMBULL *M'Fingal* IV. (1795) 102 By fatal atrophy of purse. **1840** CARLYLE *Heroes* (1858) 315 For the Scepticism ..is..a chronic atrophy and disease of the whole soul.

atrophy ('ætrəfɪ), *v.* [f. prec. sb.] *lit.* and *fig.*

1. *trans.* To affect with atrophy, to starve.

1865 MILL in *Westm. Rev.* XXVIII. 9 Organs are strengthened by exercise and atrophied by disuse. **1876** HAMERTON *Intell. Life* II. v. 428 A constant and close pressure atrophies the higher mind.

2. *intr.* To become atrophied or abortive.

1865 LIVINGSTONE *Zambesi* xi. 222 The horns, mere stumps not a foot long, must have atrophied. **1883** G. ALLEN *Col. Clout's Gard.* xxi. 121 As the fruit ripens, one of them [the seeds] almost always atrophies.

atrophying ('ætrəfɪɪŋ), *ppl. a.* [f. ATROPHY *v.* + -ING[2].] That atrophies; spec. ***atrophying cirrhosis***, cirrhosis characterized by shrinkage and shrivelling of the organ.

1886 *Brit. Med. Jrnl.* 2 Oct. 650/2 Atrophying cirrhosis was diagnosed.

atropine ('ætrəʊpaɪn). *Chem.* and *Med.* Also atropin. [f. *atropa* deadly nightshade, f. Gr. Ἄτροπος 'inflexible,' name of one of the Fates.] **a.** A poisonous alkaloid found in the Deadly Nightshade and the seeds of the Thorn-apple. **atropia** (ə'trəʊpɪə), synonym of prec. **atropic** (ə'trɒpɪk), *a.*, of or pertaining to atropine, as in *Atropic acid.* **atropinism** ('ætrəʊpɪˌnɪz(ə)m) = ATROPISM. **'atropiˌnized**, *ppl. a.*, poisoned by atropine. **atropism** ('ætrəʊpɪz(ə)m), poisoning by atropine.

1836 R. D. & T. THOMSON *Records of General Sci.* IV. 149 *Atropin may be obtained in a crystalline state by dissolving it in the smallest possible quantity of boiling water. **1842** T. GRAHAM *Elem. Chem.* III. ix. §4. 982 Atropine, in all parts of Atropa Belladonna.. possesses the power to dilate the pupil of the eye. **1877** MRS. H. KING *Discip., Ruffini* (ed. 3) 19 The deadly drops of atropine Are mixed into the water and the wine. **1908** *Practitioner* Mar. 364 Atropin should be instilled into the eye to dilate the pupil. **1927** HALDANE & HUXLEY *Animal Biol.* ix. 198 Stimulating substances, such as atropin, caffein, etc. **1835** *Penny Cycl.* III. 50/1 *Atropia is insoluble in cold water. **1863** WATTS. *Dict. Chem.* I. 474 *Atropic acid.. is said to resemble benzoic acid in form and volatility. **1876** BARTHOLOW *Mat. Med.* (1879) 311 The remarkable similarity in the symptoms of *atropinism and of scarlatina. **1875** H. WOOD *Therap.* 243 *Atropinized animals.

b. *attrib.* and *Comb.*

1879 *St. George's Hosp. Rep.* IX. 477, I prescribed atropine drops. **1920** *Chambers's Jrnl.* 11 Sept. 654/1 In England atropine-poisoning is mostly accidental.

atropinization (əˌtrɒpɪnaɪ'zeɪʃən). [f. ATROPIN(E + -IZATION.] The condition of being affected by atropine; the process of atropism.

1880 W. JAMES in *Annivers. Mem. of Boston Soc. Nat. Hist.* 14 Slight atropinization of one eye might cause such strong accommodative innervation. **1949** H. W. FLOREY et al. *Antibiotics* I. vii. 303 After atropinization the blood pressure was raised by from 20 to 30 mm. Hg. **1964** S. DUKE-ELDER *Parsons' Dis. Eye* (ed. 14) xviii. 244 The most effective treatment is to intensify atropinization in order to allay the inflammatory congestion.

atropous ('ætrəpəs), *a. Bot.* [f. Gr. ἄτροπ-ος not turned (f. ἀ priv. + τρόπος turn) + -OUS.] Of ovules: Not inverted, erect (see quot.).

1839 LINDLEY *Introd. Bot.* 219. **1857** HENFREY *Elem. Bot.* §237 Where the nucleus is straight and the micropyle is at the end opposite the attachment of the funiculus, and the chalaza next the placenta, such an ovule is called atropous.

atrous ('eɪtrəs), *a. rare. Nat. Hist.* [f. L. *āter*, *ātro-* black + -OUS.] Of a jet black colour.

†**a'trout**, *v. Obs.* [f. AT- *pref.*[2] + ROUT *v.*, OE. *hrútan.*] *intr.* To rush away, escape (with *dat.* = from).

a **1250** *Owl & Night.* 1166 Þu ne miht nohwar atrute. **1297** R. GLOUC. 78 Þer nas prince vnneþe þat hym myȝte atroute. *c* **1305** *Pilate* 242 in *E.E.P.* (1862) 117 Hi neþerste no whar at-route.

†**a'try**, *v. Obs.* Also 4 attrie, 5 ? atrey. [f. TRY *v.*, a. OF. *trier*; the origin of the prefix is doubtful: perh. intensive after native vbs.]

1. *trans.* To try, as a judge.

1330 R. BRUNNE *Chron.* 80 Chefe justise he satte, þe sothe to atrie. *Ibid.* 245 Þe rightes he did attrie of þo þat wrong had nomen.

2. *intr.* To try, test, as with a touch-stone.

c **1485** *Digby Myst.* (1882) III. 983 With many a temtacyon we tochyd hym to atrey to know whether he was god or non.

a-try (ə'traɪ), *advb. phr. Naut.* [? A *prep.*[1] + TRY.] Of a ship in a gale: Kept by a judicious balance of canvas with her bows to the sea.

1611 COTGR., *Cappéer*, A ship to lye a-try. **1628** DIGBY *Voy. Medit.* (1868) 86 We tooke in our fore course and lay a trie with our maine course. *a* **1733** NORTH *Lives* (1826) II. 316 Sometimes a-try and sometimes a-hull we busked it out. **1867** in SMYTH *Sailor's Word-bk.*

A.T.S., abbrev. of *Auxiliary Territorial Service* for women (1938–48). Often with pronunc. (æts), whence the *colloq.* sing. form **At**, **AT**, **A.T.**, a member of the A.T.S. Cf. AUXILIARY *a.* 1 b.

1939 *War Illustr.* 18 Nov. p. iii/1 Wartime Abbreviations .. A.T.S.—Auxiliary Territorial Service. **1940** *New Statesman* 13 Apr. 486 It looks as though, while democratising the army, we are aristocratising the A.T.S. **1941** *Ibid.* 6 Dec. 469 You would not become an adventuress In the ranks of adventurous A.T.S., Where brave girls cook for the Sergeants' Mess And the batwoman busily bats. **1942** *Ann. Reg. 1941* 90 The Wrens, the Waafs, and the Ats. .. The two former had no difficulty in filling their ranks from volunteers. The Ats, however, .. were not so popular. **1944** *Lancet* 15 Apr. 516/1 The ATS with one accord Say 'Ma'am' when they address her, And though this is an ugly sound It does not much distress her. *Ibid.* 517/1 (*heading*) Rehabilitation for ATS. **1958** J. BETJEMAN *Coll. Poems* 94 As beefy ATS Without their hats Come shooting through the bridge.

†**at'sake**, *v. Obs. Pa. t.* 1 ætsóc, 2–3 atsoke. [OE. *ætsacan*, f. AT- *pref.*[2] + *sacan*: see ASAKE.]

1. *intr.* To deny.

c **1000** *Ags. Gosp.* Luke viii. 45 Ða hiȝ ealle æt-socon. **1205** LAY. 6101 Þa Densce men dunriht atsoken þat heo to Brutlonde nolden mare Senden gold. *c* **1275** *Passion* 293 in *O.E. Misc.* 45 Peter at-sok and seyde, awaryed mote heo beo.

2. *trans.* To deny, abjure, renounce.

c **1000** *Ags. Gosp.* Mark xiv. 72 Þriwa ðu me æt-sæcst. **1205** LAY. 28210 To ðæi ich atsake hine here.

†**at'scape**, *v. Obs. rare*[−1]. [f. AT- *pref.*[2] + *scape*, aphetized form of ASCAPE, ESCAPE; after *atflee*, *atrin*, *atslip*, etc.] To escape.

c **1300** in Wright *Lyric P.* xxxv. 75 Iesu .. do thou me, Atscapen peyne ant come to the.

†**at'seek**, *v. Obs. rare*[−1]. In 3 atsechen. [f. AT- *pref.*[1] + OE. *sécan* to SEEK; or for earlier ASEEK.] To seek for.

1205 LAY. 13322 And þere Densemonne king þas Denen wulle atsechen [**1250** seek].

atseet, pa. t. of ATSIT *v. Obs.*

†**at'shake**, *v. Obs. rare*[−1]. In 3 atscec-en. [f. AT- *pref.*[2] + OE. *sceacan* to SHAKE, to flee; cf. also ASHAKE.] *intr.* To flee away.

1205 LAY. 26516 Hit is eo[w] muchel scorne þat ȝe wulleð atscecen [**1250** fleon].

†**at'shoot**, *v. Obs.* [f. AT- *pref.*[2] + OE. *sceótan* to SHOOT. Cf. G. *entschieszen*, Du. *ontschieten.*] *intr.* To shoot away (with *dat.* = from).

a **1250** *Owl & Night.* 44 Hire horte was so gret, þat wel neȝ hire fnast at-schet. *Ibid.* 1621 Þah mi lif me beo at-schote.

†**at'sit**, *v. Obs.* Inflexions, see SIT. [OE. *ætsittan*, f. AT- *pref.*[1] + *sittan* to SIT; cf. also ASIT.]

1. *intr.* To remain sitting, stay, abide.

905 *O.E. Chron.*, þa ætsæton ða Centiscan þær be æftan.

2. To sit against, withstand, disobey. (with *dat.*)

1297 R. GLOUC. 174 In ys ryȝt hond ys lance he nom .. Hym ne myȝte atsytte non. *a* **1300** *Havelok* 2200 Hise bode ne durste non atsitte. *c* **1320** *Cast. Loue* 235 Þo he Godes heste at-seet, And eke þo he þe appel eet.

†**at'slike**, *v. Obs. rare*[−1]. [f. AT- *pref.*[2] + OE. **slícan*, cogn. w. MLG. *slîken*, OHG. *slîchan*: see SLIKE *v.* Cf. G. *entschleichen.*] To slip away.

c **1325** *E.E. Allit. P.* A. 574 Her sweng wyth lyttel atslykez.

†**at'slip**, *v. Obs. rare*[−1]. *Pa. pple.* 3 etslopen. [f. AT- *pref.*[2] + OE. *slúpan* to SLIP; see ASLIP.] *intr.* To slip away; cf. ASLOPE.

c **1230** *Ancr. R.* 148 Al min hope were etslopen.

†**at'spring**, *v. Obs.* [OE. *ætspringan*, f. AT- *pref.*[2] + *springan* to SPRING; cogn. w. OHG. *intspringan*, Du. *ontspringen*: cf. ASPRING.] To spring forth; to spring into existence, originate.

a **1000** *Beowulf* 2247 Ðonne blod æt-sprang. *c* **1320** *Cast. Loue* 152 O þat of hem to weren at-sprong þe noumbre of þe soulen þat from heuene felle.

†**at'stand**, *v. Obs.* Also 2–3 ets-, 3 eds-: for inflexions see STAND *v.* [OE. *ætstandan*, f. AT- *pref.*[1] + *standan* to STAND; cf. ASTAND. With senses 3, 4, cf. G. *entstehen*, Goth. *andstandan*, Du. *ontstaan.*]

1. *intr.* To stand still, remain, stay.

c **1000** ÆLFRIC *Oswald* (Sweet *Reader* 101) Se post ána ætstód ansund. *c* **1175** *Lamb. Hom.* 129 Heo .. ne mehten þer naleng etstonden. **1297** R. GLOUC. 367 After betere wind hii moste þere atstonde.

2. To come to a stand; to stop.

c **1000** *Ags. Gosp.* Luke viii. 44 Ða æt-stod sona þæs blodes ryne. **1205** LAY. 23982 Hit [the sword] at his breoste atstod. *c* **1300** *Beket* 2375 Er he com to Canterbure: he nolde no whar atstonde.

3. To make a hostile stand, to resist, withstand.

c **1230** *Ancr. R.* 248 Edstond: þuruh hwat strencðe? **1297** R. GLOUC. 355 Vor he at stode .. And drof the Englysse men aȝen.

4. with *dat.* becoming at length *trans.* To stand to: **a.** To withstand, resist. **b.** To stand close to; to press. (L. *instare.*)

c **1220** *Sawles Warde* in *Lamb. Hom.* 255 Etstont þen feont and he flið anan riht. **1297** R. GLOUC. 44 Hym ne myȝte non at stonde. *c* **1330** *Amis & Amil.* 1728 Begged hem mete and drink also, When hem most ned atstod.

†**at'stert**, *v. Obs.* Forms: 3 atstirt-en, atstert-en, etstert-en. *Pa. t.* æt-, atsturt(e, atsterte. [f. AT- *pref.*[2] + *stert-en*: see START *v.* and ASTART *v.* Cf. G. *entstürzen.*]

1. *intr.* To start away, escape.

1205 LAY. 4264 He æt-sturte in to are burje. *c* **1230** *Ancr. R.* 332 Þet wrecche best selden etstertеð.

2. *trans.* (i.e. with dative obj.) To escape from.

c **1220** *Leg. St. Kath.* 699 Tu schalt sone atstirten [*v.r.* etsterten] al þe strengðe of þis strif. *c* **1230** *Ancr. R.* 370 We þolien þe soule vuel uorte etsterten vlesches vuel.

†**at'stunt**, *v. Obs.* Also 3 etst-. [f. AT- *pref.*[1] + *stunten*: see STINT *v.* and ASTINT *v.*]

1. *trans.* To bring to an end, to put a stop to.

1205 LAY. 31903 Hu þat ufel wes atstunt. *c* **1220** *St. Marherete* 15 Ha nanes weis ne schulen .. etstunten ne etstonden þe strencðe of mine swenges.

2. *intr.* To stop, stay, remain.

c **1230** *Juliana* 50 Þah an etsterte us; tene schulen etstunten. **1297** R. GLOUC. 168 So he was fram Euerwyk aboute an ten myle, He at stunte.

†**at'stutte-n**, *v. Obs.* [f. AT- *pref.*[1] + *stutten*: see STIT.] *intr.* To remain, stay.

c **1220** *Leg. St. Kath.* 23 Se wide him wex weorre .. in a londe, Ylirie het, þ tear he atstutte.

atsuki, obs. var. ADZUKI.

atta ('ætə). *Anglo-Indian.* [Punjabi *aṭṭa.*] Wheaten flour or meal.

1860 W. H. RUSSELL *Diary India* II. 206 Each man with his *viaticum* of atta in skin-bags tied over his hips. **1920** *Blackw. Mag.* Oct. 445/2 Sacks of atta for the troops. **1937** H. W. TILMAN *Ascent of Nanda Devi* iv. 31 Coolie food .. could be bought locally; that is rice, atta (wheat flour) and satu.

attaboy ('ætəbɔɪ), *int. slang* (chiefly *U.S.*). Also **at-a-boy**, **ata boy**. [Said to represent careless pronunc. of *that's the boy!* (BOY *sb.*[1] 2 c).] An exclamation expressive of encouragement or admiration. Hence **attagirl**, etc., as *nonce-wds.*

1909 *Amer. Mag.* May 40/2 Back of Chance's war cries, 'At-a-boy', or 'Now ye're pitching', may be hidden a whole command to his team. **1917** C. MATHEWSON *Sec. Base Sloan* xxii. 298 'Ata boy!' called the Damascus catcher. **1924** P. MARKS *Plastic Age* iv. 26 Suddenly one of the girls .. caught the bag deftly... 'Ray! Ray! Atta girl! Hot dog! Ray, ray!' **1925** H. L. FOSTER *Trop. Tramp Tourists* 101 The marines rose from their chairs to encourage the new performer: 'Attaboy, soldier! Attaboy! Shake 'em doggies!' **1927** *Blackw. Mag.* July 4/2 Cries, also, of 'Attaboy!' leave no doubt that the greeting is not entirely British. **1929** WODEHOUSE *Summer Lightning* xv. 286 'Give me two minutes to get the car out and five to make the trip and I'll be with you.' ''At-a-boy!' said Millicent. ''At-a-baby!' said Hugo. **1932** JAMES JOYCE in *New Statesman* 27 Feb. 261/1 Attagirl! **1936** AUDEN & ISHERWOOD *Ascent of F6* II. iii. 101 Chin up! Kiss me! Atta Boy! Dance till dawn among the ruins of a burning Troy! **1946** H. CROOME *Faithless Mirror* x. 102 I'm celebrating. Atta girl! **1958** J. BETJEMAN *Coll. Poems* 153 Look at that little mite with *Attaboy* Printed across her paper sailor hat.

attach (ə'tætʃ), *v.* Also 4 **atache**, 4–7 **attache**. *Sc.* 6 **atteche**, **atteiche**. [a. OF. *atachie-r* (mod. *attacher*), cogn. with It. *attaccare*, Sp. *atacar*; f. *à* to, at + a radical which is found also in *détacher* DETACH, and is connected by Diez and Littré with the Genevese *tache*, Sp., Pg. *tacha*, a round-headed nail, a TACK, q.v. Thus *lit.* 'to tack to.' See Diez, Littré, Skeat.

The development of signification seems to have been thus: 1. The regular OF. sense was 'to fasten,' as in mod.Eng., where however this sense is of quite recent adoption from mod.F. 2. The earlier Eng. sense of 'arrest, seize,' arose in AF. and Eng., as an elliptical expression for '*attach* by some tie to the control or jurisdiction of a court,' i.e. so that it shall have a *hold* on the party. A man might thus be *attaché* or 'nailed,' *par le cors* by his body, *par ses avers et par ses chateus* by his goods and chattels, *par pleges* by sureties for his appearance (Britton). In the first two cases the *attachment* consisted in *arrest* and *detention.* 3. The It. equivalent is *attaccare*: in the 16th c. the It. *attaccare battaglia* to *join* battle, *attaccarsi a* to fasten (oneself) upon, 'attack,' was first imitated with F. *attacher*, and then adapted in Fr. as *attaquer*; whence Eng. ATTACK, and occasional 17th c. use of *attach* (see 4 *infra*).]

I. To arrest, lay hold of, seize, 'nail'; indict.

1. *Law.* To secure for legal jurisdiction and disposal, to place or take under the control of a court; to arrest or seize by authority of a writ of attachment: **a.** a person. (See quot. 1691.)

1362 LANGL. *P. Pl.* A. II. 212 Eke wepte and wrong hire hondes whon heo was a-tachet. *c* **1380** *Sir Ferumbr.* 4517 'Ribaux,' saide he, 'ich ȝow attache, Aȝeld ȝow anon to me.' **1531–2** *Act 23 Hen. VIII*, ii, Euery shiriffe .. shall attache the saide offenders. **1581** *Acts Jas. VI* (1814) 226 (JAM.) Power to atteiche and arreist the personis transgressouris. **1590** SHAKS. *Com. Err.* IV. i. 6 Therefore make present satisfaction, Or Ile attach you by this Officer. **1615** G. SANDYS *Trav.* 108 Often they attach poore innocents, when they cannot apprehend the guiltie. **1691** BLOUNT *Law Dict.* s.v. *Attach*, He, who Arrests, carries the party Arrested to another higher person to be disposed of forthwith; he that attacheth, keeps the party attached, and presents him in Court at the day assigned in the Attachment. **1814** SCOTT *Wav.* xxxi, The means .. of attaching this suspicious and formidable delinquent.

Const. *for*, *of*.

1494 FABYAN VII. 415 Guy, his sone, was attachyd for the same and sent to pryson. **1649** MILTON *Eikon.* 83 The Peers gave .. thir consent .. to attaching the Bishops of High Treason. **1715** BURNET *Hist. Ref.*, He was attached of heresy. **1823** SCOTT *Peveril* v, I attach thee of the crime of which thou hast but now made thy boast. **1852** MISS YONGE *Cameos* II. xvii. 183 The Earl Marshal attached Gloucester for high treason.

b. property, goods.

1330 R. BRUNNE *Chron.* 158 Þe godes attached waren to þe kyng of Cipres Isaac. **1523** FITZHERB. *Surv.* 28 If any of these sayde officers fynde any maner of catell .. they maye attache theym and cease theym as streyes. **1613** SHAKS. *Hen. VIII*, I. i. 95 France .. hath attach'd Our Merchants goods at Burdeux. **1853** WHARTON *Pa. Digest* 168. §66 Choses in action of the wife cannot be attached for the husband's debt. **1882** C. SWEET *Dict. Law Terms* s.v. *Attachment*, To attach property is to seize it, or place it under the control of a Court.

†**2.** To indict before a tribunal, accuse, charge.

c **1450** HENRYSON *Mor. Fab.* 34 Be thou attached with thift or with treason .. Thy cheer changes. **1513** DOUGLAS *Æneis* XII. Prol. 266 Welcum celestiall myrrour and aspy, Attechyng all that hantis sluggardy! **1534** LD. BERNERS *Gold. Bk. M. Aurel.* (1546) K k viij, They wolde .. elles attache vs for fooles. **1589** NASHE *Anat. Absurd.* 36 They shall not easily be attached of any notable absurditie. **1653**

M. CARTER *Hon. Rediv.* (1660) 81 In which Parliament, the King attaches Earl Godwin, for that he had kil'd his Brother.

†3. *transf.* To seize, lay hold of. **a.** Said *fig.* of death, sickness, love, passion, misfortune. *Obs.*

1533 ELYOT *Cast. Helth* (1541) A iv, If they had bene.. attached with envy and covaytise. **1550** BALE *Image Both Ch.* III. xix. §13 Hastely shall death attache them. **1610** SHAKS. *Temp.* III. iii. 5, I..am my selfe attach'd with wearinesse. **1681** W. ROBERTSON *Phraseol. Gen.* 173 A sore sickness attached or attacked him.

†**b.** *lit.* To seize with hands, claws, or talons. *Obs.*

1588 SHAKS. *L.L.L.* IV. iii. 375 Euery man attach the hand Of his faire Mistresse. **1611** GUILLIM *Heraldrie* III. xv. 137 The Lion..lesse able to attach and rend his Prey. **1649** SELDEN *Laws of Eng.* I. lxvi. (1739) 144 The strength of the Canon-Law growing to its full pitch, after a long chase attached the prey.

II. †4. To attack. *Obs.* (So in 16th c. F. from It.)

1627 *Lisander & Cal.* III. 41 The Archduke threatned to attach Reyne Berk with a siege. **1666** KILLIGREW *Urbin* v, The walls are every where attach'd.

III. *trans.* To tack on, fasten, affix, connect.

5. a. To tack on; to fasten or join (a thing *to* another, or *to* a spot), by tacking, hooking on, tying, stitching, sticking, etc.

1802 PALEY *Nat. Theol.* viii. (1827) 458/2 The shoulder-blade..is bedded in the flesh; attached only to the muscles. **1828** SCOTT *F.M. Perth* xix, The hundred points or latchets which were the means of attaching the doublet to the hose. **1855** MACAULAY *Hist. Eng.* xii. III. 201 A huge stone, to which the cable..was attached. **1878** HUXLEY *Physiogr.* 77 By attaching to the apparatus a tube which dips beneath water. **1879** G. FENNELL in *Cassell's Techn. Educ.* IV. 76/2 The young of the oyster..attach themselves immediately to the first clean, hard substance they meet with.

†**b.** To fasten (the eyes), keep fixed *on* an object.

1663 GERBIER *Counsel* C v a, I did not attach my Eyes onely on the generallity of Objects, but did exactly consider some particulars worthy of note.

6. a. To connect or join on functionally (e.g. a person *to* a company, expedition, etc.) Often *refl.*

?*a* **1700** ROGERS (J.) The great and rich depend on those whom their power or their wealth attaches to them. **1781** COWPER *Charity* 16 God..By various ties attaches man to man. **1808** SCOTT *Mem.* in *Lockhart* i. (1842) 16/2 That I should seriously consider to which department of the law I was to attach myself. **1873** TRISTRAM *Moab* i. 8 A Bedouin who had attached himself to us. **1876** GREEN *Short Hist.* ii. §7 (1882) 95 The second attached himself to the Dukes of France.

b. *Mil.* and *Naval.* To allocate for service *to* a particular unit: chiefly *pass.*

1802 C. JAMES *Mil. Dict.* s.v., Officers and non-commissioned officers are said to be attached to the..army, regiment, [etc.]..with which they are appointed to act. **1909** *Regs. for Mobilization* 8 The equipment..which he would take with him when transferred or attached to another unit.

7. a. To join in sympathy or affection *to* a person, place, etc. Often in pass. *to be attached to.*

1765 GOLDSM. *Ess.* 14 (L.) To form the manners and attach the mind to virtue. **1816** MISS AUSTEN *Emma* III. x. 341 When I was very much disposed to be attached to him. **1833** HT. MARTINEAU *Brooke F.* ix. 109 How she kept her father's house in order..how she attached her little brothers to her. **1853** LYTTON *My Novel* IX. viii, I resolved again to attach myself to some living heart.

b. *esp.* To cause to adhere to oneself in sympathy or affection; to win or attract the attachment of.

1811 MISS AUSTEN *Sense & Sens.* III. i. 224 So totally unamiable, so absolutely incapable of attaching a sensible man. **1814** —— *Lady Susan* xiv. (1879) 230 His account of her attaching Miss Mainwaring's lover. **1861** PEARSON *E. & Mid. Ages of Eng.* xxvi. (L.) Enemies whom no defeat could intimidate, and no peace attach. **1865** CARLYLE *Fredk. Gt.* III. IX. iv. 102, I return you all..except Charles Douze, which attaches me infinitely.

8. a. To fix (anything immaterial) *to*; to affix a name, description, property, or adjunct of any kind.

1812 *Examiner* 30 Nov. 768/1 A most diabolical attempt to attach the guilt of murder to two men innocent of the crime. **1843** MILL *Logic* I. vi. §2 Certain properties to which mankind have chosen to attach that name. **1879** B. TAYLOR *Germ. Lit.* 111 To this treasure a curse is attached. **1883** E. PAYNE in *Law Times* 27 Oct. 432/2 The magistrates' licence ..is attached to a particular house. **1884** SIR C. BOWEN in *Law Times Rep.* 12 Apr. 197/1 The liability which English law attaches to contracts.

b. *refl.* To fasten itself on; to adhere, cleave, stick *to*.

1861 MILL *Utilit.* 41 No reason why all these motives.. should not attach themselves to the utilitarian morality, as completely..as to any other. **1875** BRYCE *Holy Rom. Emp.* v. 51 Legends which attached themselves to the name of Charles the Emperor.

9. To add or bestow as an attribute, to attribute; to view as pertaining or appropriate *to*.

1837 DISRAELI *Venetia* I. x. (1871) 50 Little credibility.. should be attached to such legends. **1855** PRESCOTT *Philip II*, I. viii. 134 The importance they attached to their own services. **1870** JEVONS *Elem. Logic* xxxiii. 292 Different people attach different meanings to the words. **1879** LUBBOCK *Addr. Pol. & Educ.* iii. 49 Only thirteen attach any weight at all to scientific subjects in the examinations.

IV. *intr.* (for *refl.*) To adhere, stick, cling, remain adherent.

10. To fix or fasten itself upon as an obligation or liability; to fall, or come *upon*, and adhere to.

1780 BURKE *Econ. Ref.* Wks. III. 338 It is..just..that the loss should attach upon the delinquency. **1852** MCCULLOCH *Taxation* II. vi. 284 The stamp duties have a tendency to facilitate the transactions on which they attach. **1863** KINGLAKE *Crimea* I. 491 Blame attaches upon Lord Aberdeen's Cabinet for yielding.

11. To adhere *to*, as an appertaining quality or circumstance; to be incident *to* (formerly *on*).

1791 BOSWELL *Johnson* (1816) I. 233 For that the right of Chieftainship attached to the blood of primogeniture, and, therefore, was incapable of being transferred. **1812** SOUTHEY *Lett.* (1856) II. 312 Without any farther suspicion ..than attaches to all works written in an age of physical credulity. **1818** SIR G. DALLAS in *Parr's Wks.* (1828) VII. 191 The just veneration that attaches on your opinions. **1859** *Ecce Homo* iii. 22 All the advantages which attach to hereditary monarchy.

12. To take legal effect, come into legal operation in connexion with anything.

1818 COLEBROOKE *Obligations* I. 93 If the whole obligation do not attach, the whole of it fails. **1829** SOUTHEY in *Q. Rev.* XLI. 385 Wherever they should make their settlement, there the laws of England attached. **1844** WILLIAMS *Real Prop. Law* (1877) 235 The wife's right to dower accordingly attached. **1848** ARNOULD *Mar. Insur.* (1866) I. I. i. 16 When the liability of the Underwriter commences, the technical mode of expressing this is by saying that 'the policy attaches.' **1876** DIGBY *Real Prop.* iii. §II. 123 To give the tenure the character of tenure by knight-service, and consequently to cause the incidents of wardship and marriage to attach.

†**a'ttach**, *sb. Obs.* [f. prec. vb.]

1. The act of laying hold of, apprehension by writ, arrest.

1601 WEEVER *Mirr. Mart.* E vij b, The meanes for my attach. **1607** HEYWOOD *Wom. Kilde* Wks. 1874 II. 102, I am made the vnwilling instrument of your attach and apprehension. **1641** *Termes de la Ley*, *Attach* is a taking or apprehending by command or writ.

2. *fig.* A seizure or attack of disease, etc.

1674 J. B[RIAN] *Harv.-Home* §4. 23 Free from attaches Of sickness, weakness, in no part feel aches.

3. A tie, attachment; a thing attached.

1663 SIR G. MACKENZIE *Relig. Stoic* xiii. (1685) 117 Have the weakest attachs to this life. **1694** *Ladies' Dict.*, An attache is, as much as to say..one thing fasten'd to another. **1742** in BAILEY.

attachable (ə'tætʃəb(ə)l), *a.* [f. ATTACH *v.* + -ABLE.]

1. Liable to arrest or legal seizure: see ATTACH *v.* 2.

a **1579** SIR N. BACON (*title*) An Argument to show that the persons of noblemen are attachable by law for contempts in the High Court of Chancery. **1755** MAGENS *Insurances* II. 102 The Goods on board..shall be more particularly bound and attachable for the same. **1884** *Law Rep.*, *Q. Bench* XII. 525 No attachable debt was in existence at the date.

2. Capable of being tacked on, annexed, added, attributed as an adjunct *to* anything.

1856 RUSKIN *Mod. Paint.* III. IV. viii. §21 The terms 'true' and 'false' are..attachable to the opposite branches. **1876** J. H. NEWMAN *Hist. Sk.* I. I. ii. 50 A throne, to which wheels were attached, and horses attachable. **1879** T. MARKS *Gt. Pyr.* 26 Any theoretical importance, attachable to them.

3. Capable of personal attachment (to others).

1865 CARLYLE *Fredk. Gt.* VI. XVI. vi. 196 Voltaire is, by nature, an attached or attachable creature.

a'ttachableness. [f. prec. + -NESS.] Capability of attachment.

1876 MISS SEDGWICK *Live & let Live* 199 She had sterling qualities of truth, honesty, and attachableness.

attaché (ə'tæʃeɪ). [Fr., pa. pple. of *attacher* to ATTACH.] One attached to, connected with, on the staff of, another person or thing; *spec.* one attached to the suite of an ambassador.

1835 H. GREVILLE *Leaves fr. Diary* 55 To offer this post to Fraser, now paid attaché at Vienna. **1859** MASSON *Milton* I. 404 [He] had come up to London and become an attaché of the court. **1876** A. ARNOLD in *Contemp. Rev.* June 42 One is surprised to see English attachés skating in Tehran. **1883** *Scot. Rev.* Sept. 282 The attachés of a leading daily paper in New York.

Hence, **attachéship** [see -SHIP].

1834 *Tait's Mag.* I. 440/1 *Attachéship* is, in fact, too onerous a calling for any man to adopt. *Ibid.* 440/2 The Honourable Arthur is promoted to *paid* attachéship. **1857** THACKERAY *Fitzbood. Prof.* Wks. IV. 26. **1882** *Standard* 25 Oct. 5/4 Colonel T. Gonne..has accepted the Military Attachéship at Constantinople.

attaché case (ə'tæʃeɪkeɪs, ə'tæʃiːkeɪs). A small rectangular case (orig. such as those used by attachés) for carrying papers, documents, and the like.

1904 *Army & Navy Co-op. Soc. Price List*, 'Attaché' cases. Green and brown leather, double-action lock. **1918** H. WALPOLE *Green Mirror* II. i. 146 The two young men in perfect attire and attaché cases. **1946** M. DICKENS *Happy Prisoner* vi. 106 Mary Brewer burst in at the door, carrying her little fibre attaché case.

attached (ə'tætʃt), *ppl. a.* [f. ATTACH *v.* + -ED.]

1. Arrested, seized under warrant of attachment.

1611 COTGR., *Saisi*, seised, laied hold on..attached, arrested. **1751** CHAMBERS *Cycl.* s.v. *Attaching*, He that attaches keeps the party attached.

†2. Seized, attacked (with sickness, passion, etc.).

1552 HULOET, Attached wyth syckenes. **1579** LYLY *Euphues* (Arb.) 66 Attached of loue. *a* **1619** FOTHERBY *Atheom.* II. vi. §3 (1622) 253 Attatched with a dangerous sicknesse.

3. Tacked on, fastened by a material union *to*.

1841 DE QUINCEY *Homer & Hom.* Wks. VI. 387 Homer introduces horses only as attached to the chariots. **1860** TYNDALL *Glac.* I. §3. 30 Moving the staff with such fragments attached to it.

b. *Zool.* Fixed to a spot during life, stationary, as opposed to 'free'; **c.** *Arch.* Joined to a wall, etc., instead of standing clear, or 'detached.'

1854 WOODWARD *Man. Mollusca* (1856) 7 Most of them [Mollusca] are attached, or have no means of moving from place to place. **1879** G. SCOTT *Lect. Archit.* I. 149 The attached and detached shafts may be used alternately.

4. Joined functionally.

1859 TENNENT *Ceylon* I. IV. viii. 493 A cemetery.. attached to the city. **1879** RUSKIN *Lett. Clergy* 4 Are the clergymen..simply the attached and salaried guides of England?

5. Joined by taste, predilection, affection, or sympathy *to*; partial, fond, affectionate, devoted.

1793 T. BEDDOES *Math. Evid.* 9 Readers, attached to these speculations, will find abundant entertainment. **1823** BYRON *Juan* XII. xxxv, Fred really was attach'd. **1849** MACAULAY *Hist. Eng.* II. 165 The theological system to which his family was attached. **1853** LYTTON *My Novel* X. ii, Paulina became excessively attached to her. **1857** LIVINGSTONE *Trav.* xii. 215 The Barotse are strongly attached to this fertile valley. **1860** FROUDE *Hist. Eng.* V. xxix. 508 Ardent Protestants side by side with the attached friends of Mary.

6. Incident *to*.

1852 MCCULLOCH *Taxation* I. iv. 129 The inconveniences attached to duties on expenditure.

attachedly (ə'tætʃɪdlɪ), *adv.* [f. prec. + -LY².] With attachment; affectionately, devotedly.

1801 W. TAYLOR in Robberds *Mem.* I. 369 Yours attachedly, William Taylor, Jun.

attacher (ə'tætʃə(r)). [f. ATTACH *v.* + -ER¹.] One who attaches; one who arrests under a writ of attachment.

c **1440** *Promp. Parv.* 14 A-rester, or a-tacher, or a catcherel. **1609** SKENE *Reg. Maj.* 76 Sic sould be attachers, at command of the Judge, quhen it is necessare to attach sic men. **1641** PRYNNE *Antipathie* 45 If such Attachers be Clerkes Beneficed, they shall be suspended from their Office.

attaching (ə'tætʃɪŋ), *vbl. sb.* [f. ATTACH *v.*]

1. The action of arresting; arrest, seizure.

1543 GRAFTON *Contn. Harding* 437 After whose attachynge and imprysonmente, the realme was set in more quyetnes. **1576** A. HALL *Acc. Quarrel* (1815) 21 A warrant ..for the attaching of Smalley. **1863** COX *Inst. Eng. Govt.* III. ii. 593 *note*, 3 Edw. I. c. 35 prohibits bailiffs of liberties from attaching persons not subject to their jurisdictions.

2. The action of joining to. (Mostly gerundial).

1747 in *Col. Rec. Penn.* V. 149 The attaching these Indians and their Friends to the English Cause.

a'ttaching, *ppl. a.* [f. as prec. + -ING².]

1. That attaches persons to oneself; engaging.

1813 MISS BURNEY *Diary* VII. 10 Mdme. de Staël's Mémoires..are so attaching, so evidently original and natural. **1867** BP. SALISBURY *Charge* 11 That most attaching of friends, Dr. Arnold.

2. That adheres or pertains *to*; incident.

a **1858** DE QUINCEY *Autobiog. Sk.* Wks. I. vii. 205 The peculiar circumstances attaching to a royal ball. **1879** R. DOUGLAS *Confucian.* iii. 78 The..ceremonies attaching to the social distinctions.

a'ttachingness. [f. prec. + -NESS.] The quality of being attaching: engagingness.

1808 W. TAYLOR in Robberds *Mem.* II. 219 It..has all the attachingness of romance.

attachment (ə'tætʃmənt). Also 5 *aphet.* **tachement.** [a. F. *attachement*: see ATTACH *v.* and -MENT.] The action of attaching, the condition of being attached.

I. Apprehension, seizure.

1. a. The action of apprehending (a person) and placing him under the control of a court of law; now, especially used of arrest for contempt of court. (With subjective or objective genitive: cf. APPREHENSION 2.)

1447-8 SHILLINGFORD *Lett.* (1871) 77 Have had, used, and enjoyed..attacheaments, arestes. **1521** WOLSEY in Ellis *Orig. Lett.* I. 64 I. 178 The attachement of the late Duke of Bukingham. **1720** SHADWELL *Humourist* IV, I'll follow and apprehend him, and his attachment will secure me **1827** HALLAM *Const. Hist.* (1876) I. v. 269 The house had the same power of attachment for contempt. **1876** DIGBY *Real Prop.* vi. 286 To enforce the decrees of the Chancellor by attachment, that is, by arrest and imprisonment for contempt of court.

b. The writ or precept commanding such apprehension.

1468 *Paston Lett.* 567 II. 296, I am sore troblyd with Bedston..be the wey of tachements owte of the Chauncer. **1586** J. HOOKER *Girald. Irel.* in *Holinsh.* II. 128/2 If anie one of the parlement house be serued, sued, arrested, or attached by anie writ, attachment, or minister of the Kings bench. **1691** BLOUNT *Law Dict.* s.v., An Attachment sometimes issues out of a Court Baron. **1784** DE LOLME *Const. Eng.* I. xi. 109 If he does not appear, an attachment is issued against him. **1883** MRQ. SALISBURY *Sp. in Parl.* 17 July, The captain was brought up under an attachment, and, refusing to relieve the men, was committed.

2. The taking of property into the actual or constructive possession of the judicial power. ***foreign attachment***: 'legal seizure of the goods of foreigners, found in some liberty (*e.g.* the City of London) to satisfy their creditors within such liberty.'

1592 MANWOOD *Coll. Lawes Forest* 99 The first maner of Attachement is, to Attache a man by his goodes and Cattels. **1622** MALYNES *Anc. Law-Merch.* 424 The Common Law of England doth not vse the course of Attachments, as is vsed by the Custome of the Citie of London. **1809** TOMLINSON *Law Dict.* s.v., A foreign attachment cannot be had when a suit is depending in any of the courts at Westminster. **1842** WHITTOCK *Compl. Bk. Trades* 220 In cases of insolvency, the Factor ought immediately to lay 'attachments' and advise his employers of it. **1875** MAINE *Hist. Inst.* ix. 276 It seems probable that Distress was gradually lost in and absorbed by Attachment and Distringas.

3. In *Forest Laws* (see quot.).

1592 MANWOOD *Coll. Lawes Forest* 90 In the said court of Attachments the officers there do nothing but receiue the Attachments of the Foresters. **1768** BLACKSTONE *Comm.* III. 71 The court of attachments, or wood-mote..is to be held before the verderors of the forest..and is instituted to enquire into all offenders against vert and venison. **1809** TOMLINS *Law Dict.* s.v., The lower court is called the *attachment*, the middle one the *swainmote*; the highest, *the justice in Eyre's seat.*

†**4.** *fig.* Arrest, confinement. *Obs.*

1606 SHAKS. *Tr. & Cr.* IV. ii. 5 To bed, to bed: sleepe kill those pritty eyes, And giue as soft attachment to thy sences, As Infants empty of all thought.

II. Fastening, connexion, tie.

5. The action of fastening or tacking on.

1859 OWEN *Classif. Mamm.* 65 The rest of the cranium is modified..for the attachment of muscles to work the jaw. **1860** TYNDALL *Glac.* I. §18. 131 His mode of attachment was new to me. **1867** A. BARRY *Sir C. Barry* ix. 315 Ingenious provisions for attachment of girders.

6. The fact or condition of being fastened on or to; connexion.

1817 R. JAMESON *Min.* 130 Werner understands by attachment, the connection of single crystals with massive minerals, and the aggregation of crystals together.

7. The fact or condition of being attached by sympathy; affection, devotion, fidelity.

a **1704** T. BROWN *Sat. Antients* Wks. 1730 I. 21 We discover nothing of him..that deserves our attachment. **1791** BURKE *App. Whigs* Wks. 1842 I. 511 He governed by party attachments. **1814** SCOTT *Wav.* (1817) II. xx. 302 The lover's eye discovered the object of his attachment. **1855** PRESCOTT *Philip II*, I. i. 2 His early attachments..were with the people of the Netherlands.

8. That whereby a thing is attached; a fastening, tie, or bond.

1801 *Phil. Trans.* XCI. 15 The attachments between the nerve and pericardium were completely divided. **1859** TENNENT *Ceylon* I. I. iii. 105 The falling timber..dragging those behind to which it is harnessed by its living attachments. **1874** LYELL *Elem. Geol.* xix. 330 A continuous pavement formed by the stony roots or 'attachments' of the Cruroidea.

9. Something attached to any object, an adjunct.

a **1797** H. WALPOLE *Geo. II* (1847) III. vi. 157 The whole body of Whigs were cantoned out in attachments to the Dukes of Newcastle and Bedford. **1876** *Catal. Sci. App. S. Kens.* §3405 Compass attachment to the Theodolite. *Mod.* The Eolian attachment to the pianoforte.

10. *Mil.* and *Naval.* The fact or condition of being attached to a particular unit.

1904 *Regs. for Mobilization* (Provisional) I. 12 Units which do not exist as such in peace are completed in officers by special appointments, and as regards other ranks by reservists, attachments from other corps, and transfers from existing units. **1914** *Daily Express* 5 Oct. 5/1 Each man wearing an armlet indicating his attachment to these special siege batteries. **1955** *Times* 5 Aug. 7/1 Numbers of Egyptian officers and men have recently been serving on attachment with the British forces in the Zone.

attack (ə'tæk), *v.* Also 7 **attaque, attacque.** [a. F. *attaque-r*, 16th c. ad. It. *attaccare*: see ATTACH. Not in Shaks., nor in Cotgr. under F. *attaquer.*] *trans.* in all senses.

1. a. To fasten or fall upon with force or arms; to join battle with, assail, assault. (The ordinary word to describe offensive military operations.)

1600 HOLLAND *Livy* I. 3 Being attackt with war from the Sabines. **1660** BLOUNT *Boscobel* I. (1680) 15 Lambert with a far greater number of Rebels attaqu'd him. **1684** *Scanderbeg Rediv.* v. 117, 2000 Janisaries..were sent out to Attacque a small Castle. **1776–88** GIBBON *Decl. & F.* xliii. (1813) VII. 359 The strong towns he successively attacked. **1876** GREEN *Short Hist.* i. §5 (1882) 43 The Danes were the same people in blood and speech with the people they attacked.

b. *absol.*

a **1755** CANE *Campaigns* (J.) Those that attack generally get the victory, though with disadvantage of ground.

2. To set upon with hostile action or words, so as to overthrow, injure, or bring into disrepute.

1643 MILTON *Sov. Salve* 32 Under colour of a pretended partie..the Parliament is attaqued. **1656** COWLEY *Misc.* (1669) 30 Some care bestow On us..Attacqu'ed by Envy, and by Ignorance. **1678** OWEN *Mind of God* I. 10 Religion was attacqued or disturbed withal. **1771** *Junius Lett.* lix. 309 Who attacks the liberty of the press? **1798** FERRIAR *Illustr. Sterne* ii. 25 Rabelais attacked boldly the scholastic mode of education. **1858** DE QUINCEY *Whiggism* Wks. VI. 173 He attacked the Archbishop of Dublin..in a rancorous tone.

3. To assail with temptations.

1673 *Lady's Call.* I. i. §20 Finding it their interest to corrupt him with money, they were yet so possest with the reverence of his vertues, that none durst undertake to attaque him. *Ibid.* I. v. §23 There are few more frequently attaqued then women of quality.

4. To enter upon a work of difficulty, with the intention of conquering or completing it.

1812 SHELLEY *Let.* 17 Dec. (1964) I. 216 Mrs. Shelley is attacking *Latin* with considerable resolution. **1871** *Trans. Amer. Inst. Min. Engin.* I. 201 Finding the ore, making all roads, shafts, drifts, etc., which will enable the miner to attack it. **1872** BLACK *Adv. Phaeton* xxi. 296 They will have to attack some hard work. **1875** *Times* 20 Apr. 5/6 We have never been able to attack those parts of the sun's surroundings.

5. Of disease: To seize upon, begin to affect.

1677 HALE *Prim. Orig. Man.* 318 Diseases, Disorders, Weaknesses, Sicknesses, Harbingers and Forerunners of Death attaquing his Bodily Constitution. **1863** KEMBLE *Resid. Georgia* 40 Rheumatism..attacks indiscriminately the young and old.

6. Of physical agents: To begin to act upon destructively, to begin to destroy, devour, waste, decompose, or dissolve.

1842 *Penny Cycl.* XXIV. 232/2 White ants..often attacking the wood-work of houses. **1871** B. STEWART *Heat* I. i. §20 Hydrofluoric acid..attacks the glass where the wax has been scratched off. **1878** HUXLEY *Physiogr.* 208 The columns, when attacked [by boring molluscs], must have been washed by the sea. **1879** P. DELAMOTTE in *Cassell's Techn. Educ.* IV. 89/1 The mordants used in the dyeing are apt to attack the leather.

7. *Mus. intr.* and *trans.* (See quot. and cf. ATTACK *sb.* 7.)

1835 *Court Mag.* VI. 264/1 The instruments do not *attack* properly—that is to say, they do not come in simultaneously with sufficient precision to form a sharp, crisp chord, as if proceeding from a single instrument. **1967** *Oxford Mail* 27 Nov. 6/1 Those boys from the Chapel Royal and St. Paul's ..attack their leads with the confidence of professionals.

attack (ə'tæk), *sb.* Also 7 **attaque, attacque.** [f. the vb., or a. F. *attaque*: cf. It. *attacco.* (Not in Shaks., Cotgrave, Cockeram: once in Milton.)]

1. a. The act of falling upon with force or arms, of commencing battle; an offensive operation; an onset, an assault. The common military term; opposed to *defence.*

1667 MILTON *P.L.* VI. 248 The dire attack Of fighting Seraphim. **1678** BUTLER *Hud.* III. i. 1084 And bravely scorn to turn their backs Upon the desperatest attacks. **1693** *Mem. Count Teckely* I. 41 The Grand Vizier endeavoured to maintain the Attacques. **1703** *Lond. Gaz.* No. 3913/2 The Enemy..made a Salley out of the Town against Major General Dedem's Attack. **1789** BENTHAM *Princ. Legisl.* xiii. §2 To compare the means of attack and defence. **1849** MACAULAY *Hist. Eng.* v. I. 601 Monmouth..conceived that a night attack might be attended with success.

b. *ellipt.* for: Point of attack, attacking force.

1709 LUTTRELL *Brief Rel.* VI. 460 All the cannon..will begin to play as to morrow from the 3 several attacks.

2. a. *fig.* The offensive part in any contest or match; *e.g.* the bowling in *Cricket*, a move directed to gain a point in *Chess*, etc.

1822 BURROWES *Cycl.* III. 345/2 It is not always necessary in the attack to have them [queen and rook] near the adversary's king. **1871** M. COLLINS *Mrq. & Merch.* II. x. 294 [He] taught her the Mortimer attack in the Evans gambit. **1882** *Daily Tel.* 19 May (*Cricket*), Spofforth and Palmer being entrusted with the attack.

b. Lacrosse. ***the attack***: the 'attack fields' collectively; ***attack field***: see quot. 1892.

1885 E. T. SACHS *Lacrosse for Beginners* 43 As matches are played, the ball falls more often to the defence than to the attack. *Ibid.* 52 The Attack Fields. These two players play rather forward of centre. **1892** G. A. HUTCHISON *Outdoor Games* 507 The players stand all down the field, from goal-keeper to goal-keeper, a defence man watching one of the opposite attack. *Ibid.* 508 The three men nearest the opponents' goal (they are called the 'home' first, second, and third, first being nearest the goal) should practice throwing at goal... The two players next nearest are called the 'attack fields'. **1902** *Westm. Gaz.* 28 Apr. 7/3 His place in the attack field.

3. An assault with hostile or bitter words, or action intended to overthrow, injure, or defame.

1751 JOHNSON *Rambl.* No. 144 ¶2 The attack upon a rising character. **1804** MAR. EDGEWORTH *Mod. Griselda* x. Wks. 1832 XI. 320 Griselda..established herself upon a couch, and began an attack upon Emma. **1850** LYNCH *Theo. Trin.* ix. 169 Some who have braved with forehead of flint public attack. **1876** GREEN *Short Hist.* v. §2 (1882) 227 The knights of the shire united with the burgesses in a joint attack on the royal council.

4. *fig.* The commencing of operations in order to perform any difficult work. So, *jocularly*, upon dinner, viands, etc.; cf. 6.

1812 COMBE (Dr. Syntax) *Pictur.* XVII. 62 The Doctor then..pronounced the grace..The fierce attack was soon begun. **1874** FURNIVALL *Rep. E. Eng. Text Soc.* 26 The attack [of the Society] is weakest at the farthest point, Anglo-Saxon. **1875** *Times* 20 Apr. 5/5 The Committee of the Royal Society laid so much stress upon this part of the attack that no less than three instruments were devoted to it.

5. An invasion or access of disease; a fit or bout of illness.

1811 HOOPER *Med. Dict.* s.v. *Asthma*, Its attacks are most frequent during the heats of summer. **1878** SEELEY *Stein* III. 543 He suffered from attacks of overpowering giddiness.

6. The commencement of destructive or dissolving action by any physical agent.

1842 *Penny Cycl.* XXIV. 224/1 The attacks of this animal [Teredo] upon piles. **1871** TYNDALL *Fragm. Sc.* viii. §7. 187 To..initiate the attack of the oxygen.

7. *Mus.* [after It. *attacca.*] The action or manner of beginning a piece, passage, or phrase, in respect of precision and clarity. Also, more generally in the arts, brilliance of style, decisive rendering. Cf. sense 4.

1871 *Monthly Pkt.* Oct. 401 Their splendid 'attack', no dropping in one after another... They knew how to look at their music and the conductor both at once. **1879** GROVE *Dict. Mus.* I. 100 *Attack*, a technical expression for decision and spirit in beginning a phrase or passage. **1891** *Durham Univ. Jrnl.* 11 Nov. 216 There was a certain want of precision in the attack. **1905** *Westm. Gaz.* 12 Dec. 3/2 Mr. Runcie has fancy, verve, and what artists call 'attack'. **1906** B. STOKER *Personal Rem. H. Irving* II. li. 84 In this play Irving was very decided as to the 'attack'. He had often talked with me about the proper note to strike at the beginning of the play. **1938** A. L. HASKELL *Ballet* vii. 198 Riabouchinska is not a purely classical dancer, lacking the necessary hardness and attack. **1956** I. DEAKIN *At Ballet* 206 *Attack*: In ballet it has the meaning of the deliberation behind the performance of the various steps. **1961** G. MILLERSON *Technique Telev. Production* iii. 45 The face would merge into the background—the picture would lack 'attack'—appear flat. **1962** *Listener* 13 Sept. 409/2 One cannot imagine a performance more remarkable for attack, verve, clarity of articulation, and gradations of tone colour.

8. *attrib.* and *Comb.*, as (sense 1) ***attack-aircraft-carrier***, ***attack-bomber***, ***-division***, ***-formation***, ***-order***, ***-practice***; (sense 5) ***attack-rate***.

1899 *Daily News* 6 Mar. 8/5 Small-pox breaks out, and.. the attack rate is..limited to exactly 10 per cent. in each class. *Ibid.* 27 Dec. 8/4 We..marched four or five miles in regular attack formation. **1901** *Westm. Gaz.* 8 July 7/3 One officer, two non-coms., and twenty men, who march eleven miles and finish at Stickledown Ranges with the attack practice. **1923** KIPLING *Irish Guards* II. 179 The Companies dressed in attack-order. **1932** AUDEN *Orators* II. p. 76 1st Army: 15 attack divisions, 2 ordinary divisions. **1952** *Amer. Speech* XXVII. 4 Search planes, dive bomber, attack bomber. **1957** *Jane's Fighting Ships 1957–58* 407/3 It is the intention to build six nuclear powered, attack aircraft carriers. **1961** *Lancet* 26 Aug. 473/2 Another outbreak of respiratory-syncytial-virus infection, again with a peak attack-rate in infants under 7 months.

attackable (ə'tækəb(ə)l), *a.* [f. ATTACK *v.* + -ABLE; but Fr. has had *attaquable* since 16th c.] Capable of being attacked, assailable.

1813 *Examiner* 15 Mar. 170/2 His conceit..is his most attackable point. **1860** *Cornh. Mag.* II. 713 A substance not attackable by common acids. **1868** HELPS *Realmah* xvii, Every compromise is easily attackable.

attacked (ə'tækt), *ppl. a.* Also 7– **attackt.** [f. ATTACK *v.* + -ED.] Assaulted.

1685 *Lond. Gaz.* 17 Aug. 1 We almost ruined the Flanks of the attackt Bastions.

attacker (ə'tækə(r)). Also 7 **attaquer.** [f. ATTACK *v.* + -ER[1]: cf. F. *attaqueur*, 16th c.] One who attacks, an assailant.

1664 PEPYS *Diary* 4 June, Prince Rupert, the boldest attaquer in the world. **1779** FORREST *Voy. N. Guinea* 228 The attackers boarded her. **1882** M. ARNOLD in *19th Cent.* Aug. 229 The attackers of the established course of study.

attacking (ə'tækɪŋ), *vbl. sb.* [f. ATTACK *v.*] The action of falling upon with hostile intent.

1696 LUTTRELL *Brief Rel.* II. 48 To assist at the attacking of the prince of Orange. **1876** GREEN *Short Hist.* v. §3 (1882) 229 Ockham had not shrunk..from attacking the foundations of the Papal supremacy.

a'ttacking, *ppl. a.* [f. as prec. + -ING[2].] That attacks; assailing, acting on the offensive.

1833 *Reg. Instr. Cavalry* I. 144 The Attacking File. **1856** FROUDE *Hist. Eng.* III. 144 Easy for an attacking army to force a passage.

†**a'ttacted,** *a. Obs.* [f. L. *attact-us* touched + -ED.] Touched upon, briefly handled.

1656–81 in BLOUNT *Glossogr.*

attain (ə'teɪn), *v.* Forms: 4 **ateyn(e, ateine, ateign,** 4–5 **atteygne, atteigne,** 4–6 **atteyne,** 5–6 **attayne,** (5 **ataine**), 5–7 **atteine, -aine,** 6– **attain.** *Pa. pple.* **attained;** also 4–6 **ateynt,** etc.: see ATTAINT. [a. OF. *ataign-, ateign-*, stem of *ataindre, -eindre*:—L. *attingĕre* to touch on, get at, reach, f. *ad-, at-*, to + *tangĕre* to touch.]

I. *trans.* To touch, strike, attaint. (All *Obs.*)

†**1.** To get at with a blow, strike, hit; = ATTAINT I. *Obs.*

1475 CAXTON *Jason* 16 And with his spere was atteyned of the king..by suche a might that he percid the shelde.

†**2.** To touch upon (a matter), mention, treat of, deal with. *Obs.* (So L. *attingere* and OF. *ateindre.*)

1447–8 SHILLINGFORD *Lett.* (1871) 42 The mater is attainyd at large in the comyn lawe.

†**3.** To catch or detect in an offence, convict, condemn, ATTAINT. *Obs.* [Common sense of OF. *ateindre*: cf. Britton I. xxvii. §1 La forme de *atteyndre* nostre pes enfreynte. 'The manner of

convicting offenders for breach of our peace'; see also s.v. ATTAINOR.]

1330 R. BRUNNE *Chron.* 49 Knoute . . siþen ateyned Edrik þorgh treson of old . . Edrik was hanged on þe toure, for his trispas. 1340 HAMPOLE *Pr. Consc.* 5332 To reprove þam [his enmys] at þe last day, And to atteyn þam. *c* 1350 *Harl. MS.* No. 4196. 164 *St. James* 39 Pharisenes . . went for to wit of his [Christ's] thewes, For to atteyn him in sum thing þat þai might wrye him to the king. *c* 1400 *Ywaine & Gaw.* 1601 He es ateyned for traytur, And fals and lither losenjoure.

II. *trans.* To come so near as to touch, to overtake, reach, catch.

†4. To approach so as to touch, encroach on. *Obs.*

1382 WYCLIF *Prov.* xxiii. 10 Ne ateyne thou [1388 Touche thou not] the termes of litle childer.

†5. To overtake, come up with, catch up, get at or within reach of, catch. *Obs.*

1393 GOWER *Conf.* III. 128 The fire is hote . . And brenneth what he may atteigne. *c* 1450 *Merlin* xviii. 278 Thei . . began to pursue the hoste so that thei ateyned hem at a passage. *Ibid.* xvii. 272 The saisnes . . slowgh alle that thei myght atteyne. 1485 CAXTON *Chas. Gt.* 182 Them that they attayned dyd them neuer hurte after. 1622 BACON *Hen. VII*, 174 The Earle . . pursued with all celeritie . . hoping to have ouer-taken the Scottish King . . but not attaining him.

6. To reach by motion, to arrive at, 'gain' (a point aimed at).

c 1585 *Faire Em.* III. 811 We quickly shall attain the English shore. 1616 R. C. *Times' Whis.* VI. 2667 By this time we th'appointed place attainde. 1805 SOUTHEY *Madoc in W.* I. Wks. V. 7 Now had they almost attain'd The palace portal. 1854 J. ABBOTT *Napoleon* (1855) II. xviii. 336 The heroic marshal, however, attained the opposite shore.

b. To reach (an age or time).

1826 PRAED *Poems* (1865) I. 255 Sir Lidian had attained his sixteenth year.

7. To reach, arrive at, gain, accomplish, by continued effort (an end or purpose, a position, state, or personal quality).

a 1300 *Cursor M.* 1114 Þat he ne sal caim dede [= Cain's death] a-teign. 1393 GOWER *Conf.* III. 184 That he his purpose might atteigne. *c* 1400 *Pol. Poems* (1859) II. 8 If thou myghtest parfit pes atteigne. 1574 tr. *Marlorat's Apocalips* 3 Of whiche thyng we may now atteyne manifest knowledge. 1651 HOBBES *Leviath.* I. v. 21 Reason is not . . borne with us . . but attayned by Industry. 1660 R. COKE *Power & Subj.* 262 Yet were they so far from attaining their ends. 1738 WESLEY *Psalms* li. xi, Let me the Life Divine attain. 1839 KEIGHTLEY *Hist. Eng.* II. 32 His fame would never probably have attained its present eminence.

8. To come into the possession of, to gain by effort, acquire, obtain (a possession; not now used of a material thing). *arch.*

c 1386 CHAUCER *Frankl. T.* 47 Pacience . . venquysseth . . Thynges þat rigour sholde neuere atteyne [*v.r.* atteigne, ateyne]. 1477 EARL RIVERS (Caxton) *Dictes* 13 By whiche ye atteyne helpe of the holy gost. 1513 MORE *Edw. V*, 4 He attained the Crowne and Scepter of the Realme. 1523 LD. BERNERS *Froiss.* I. xxvi. 38 To atteyne therby the towne of Berwike. 1532 MORE *Confut. Tindale* Wks. 825/1 Manasses . . dyd penaunce and attained mercy. 1639 ROUSE *Heav. Univ.* x. (1702) 138 He teacheth them to attain a kingdom. 1653 HOLCROFT *Procopius* II. 48 Her Husband, who at first attained her Bed by violence. 1863 COX *Inst. Eng. Govt.* I. vii. 80 To concur with the Prince of Orange in attaining a free Parliament.

†9. To get to know, 'get at,' find out. *Obs.*

c 1374 CHAUCER *Boeth.* II. i. 31 Þou hast now knowen and ataynt þe doutous or double visage of . . fortune. *Ibid.* III. iii. 69 Þat fals beaute . . is knowe and a-teint in þilke þinges. 1483 CAXTON *Cato* E iiij, Secretes that humayne nature may not attayne, knowe, ne understonde. 1571 DIGGES *Pantom.* II. xxiv. P ij, To attayne the quantitie of this longer portion, ye shall thus worke. 1655 FULLER *Ch. Hist.* III. v. §26 II. 180 Not well attaining his meaning. 1666 —— *Hist. Camb.* (1840) 105 About this time, for I cannot attain the certain year.

III. *intr.* (The distance of the point reached, or the effort made, is more distinctly expressed by the *intr.* const. with *to, unto.*)

10. To come so far as, succeed in coming to, get (*to*). ***to attain to*** = reach, arrive at. *arch.*

c 1325 *E.E. Allit. P.* A. 547 Bygyn at þe laste . . Tyl to þe fyrste þat þou at-teny. *c* 1430 LYDG. *Min. Poems* 4 To the Blakhethe whan the did atteyne. 1535 COVERDALE *Joshua* xvii. 16 We shal not be able to atteyne vnto the mountaynes. 1608 ARMIN *Nest Ninn.* (1842) 18 With much adoe they attained thether againe. 1611 BIBLE *Acts* xxvii. 12 If by any meanes they might attaine to Phenice. 1810 SCOTT *Lady of L.* I. vii, Nor nearer might the dogs attain.

†b. Without locomotion: To reach. *Obs.*

1587 GOLDING *De Mornay* xi. 161 God . . atteineth to them without putting himself foorth. 1646 SIR T. BROWNE *Pseud. Ep.* v. vi. 241 The second lay so with his backe towards the first, that his head attained about his bosome.

†c. To come by succession, descend (*to*). *Obs.*

1413 LYDG. *Pylgr. Sowle* IV. vii. 61 To whome the synne of Adam hath atteyned by very succession and descent.

†d. To happen (*to*). ***to attain to*** = overtake, befall. *Obs.*

1529 MORE *Comf. agst. Trib.* III. Wks. 1217/2 We shall nede no rehersal of any harme that . . maye attaine thereto.

11. To live on (*to* a time or age).

1535 COVERDALE *2 Esdras* xi. 17 There shal none after y[e] atteyne vnto thy tyme. 1611 BIBLE *Gen.* xlvii. 9 And haue not attained vnto the dayes of the yeeres of the life of my fathers. *Mod.* He has attained to years of discretion.

12. To reach, or arrive at, a state, condition, purpose, possession; to succeed in reaching. Cf. 7, 8.

c 1375 WYCLIF *Serm.* ix. Sel. Wks. 1869 I. 23 No conquerrour myȝte atteyne to Lordship of al þis erþe. *c* 1386 CHAUCER *Clerkes T.* 391 Sche may unto a knave childe atteigne By liklihed, sith sche nys not bareigne. 1490 CAXTON *Eneydos* vi. 26 He sholde attayne to thende of his desire. 1535 COVERDALE *Ps.* cxxxviii. 5 Soch knowlege is to wonderfull . . for me, I can not atteyne vnto it. 1609 D. ROGERS in *Digby Myst.* (1882) Introd. 24 It cannot be attaynd vnto in this liffe. 1710 PRIDEAUX *Tithes* ii. 47 Infallibility . . being what no Man can attain unto. 1782 COWPER *Lett.* 11 Nov., To see your trees attain to the dignity of timber. 1876 GREEN *Short Hist.* ii. §6 (1882) 90 Few boroughs had as yet attained to power such as this.

†b. with *inf.* of purpose. *Obs.*

1523 LD. BERNERS *Froiss.* I. xv. 15 Where as he thought to . . attaigne to haue any company of men of warre. 1662 FULLER *Worthies* (1840) III. 372 He . . attained to be a most accomplished person.

†13. = 9, but with *to, unto. Obs.*

1530 PALSGR. 439/2, I study tyll my braynes ake to perceyve this mater, but I can nat attayne to it. 1577 HOLINSHED *Chron.* III. 1168/1 Neither they nor I haue yet atteined to their names. 1628 COKE *On Litt.* Pref., The certain time wee cannot yet attain unto.

†IV. Senses influenced by, or derived from, L. *attinēre. Obs.*

†14. *intr.* To extend as far as, stretch, reach (*to*).

c 1350 *Will. Palerne* 5497 Here riȝt arm redeli ouer Rome ateyned. 1432–50 tr. *Higden* (1865) I, The see Tyren atteynethe to Ytaly [L. *attinet ad Italiam*]. *c* 1530 LD. BERNERS *Arth. Lyt. Bryt.* (1814) 252 Wyth great chaines of yren attaining fro one house to an other.

†15. *intr.* To matter, concern, pertain *to*. *Obs.*

c 1374 CHAUCER *Boeth.* II. vii. 59 What atteiniþ fame to swiche folk.

a'ttain, *sb.* [f. prec. vb.] = ATTAINMENT: a. The action of attaining; b. The thing attained.

1559 *Myrr. for Mag., Dk. Suffolk* viii. 4 There is more glory in The keping thinges than is in their attayne. 1665 GLANVILL *Sceps. Sci.* xxiv. (J.) Crowns and diadems, the most splendid terrene attains. 1925 HARDY *Human Shows* 141 A painter of high attain.

attain, obsolete northern form of ATONE *v.*

1630 NAUNTON *Fragm. Reg.* (Arb.) 30 To appease and attain them.

attainability (əˌteɪnəˈbɪlɪtɪ). [f. next: see -BILITY.] The quality of being attainable; an attainable circumstance or condition of things.

1810 COLERIDGE *Friend* (ed. 3) III. 97 Faith in its attainability and hopes of its attainment. 1845 KINGSLEY *Lett. & Mem.* I. 137 Hovering between nine shillings a week and the workhouse, the sum of all attainabilities this side of heaven. 1847 GROTE *Greece* II. xxxvii. IV. 524 Despair as to the attainability of certain knowledge.

attainable (əˈteɪnəb(ə)l), *a.* [f. ATTAIN *v.* + -ABLE. Cf. OF. *ataignable.*] Capable of being attained (in various senses of the verb).

1647 PETTY *Adv. Learn.* in *Harl. Misc.* (1810) VI. 4 Things . . attainable by the help of memory. 1712 ADDISON *Spect.* No. 513 ⁋5 The highest pitch of perfection attainable in this life. 1776 ADAM SMITH *W.N.* I. I. vi. 51 *note*, The rate of profit attainable. 1856 KANE *Arct. Exp.* I. i. 18 To its most northern attainable point. 1881 RUSKIN *Morn. in Florence* 47 The shop-window with its unattainable splendours, or too easily attainable trifles.

a'ttainableness. [f. prec. + -NESS.] The quality of being attainable.

1656 JEANES *Fuln. Christ* 279 The attainablenesse of this progressive fulnesse. 1707–8 BERKELEY in Fraser *Life* (1871) 600 Rational desires are vigorous in proportion to the . . attainableness of their object. 1871 ALGER *Future Life* 469 A similar conception of the attainableness of heaven.

†**attainant**, *a. Obs.* [a. OF. *a(t)taignant* proper to attain an end.] Suitable, appropriate.

1494 FABYAN 2 To my dull wytte it is nat atteynaunt.

attainder (əˈteɪndə(r)). Forms: 5 **attaynder**, 6 **atteindor**, **attendre**, **attaindour**, 6–7 **-or**, 7 **attender**, 6– **attainder**. [Subst. use of OF. *ataindre, ateindre*, inf., to ATTAIN, also to strike, touch, affect, accuse, convict, condemn:—L. *attingĕre* to touch upon, strike, attack, etc.; subsequently warped in meaning by erroneous association with F. *taindre, teindre*, to dye, stain:—L. *tingĕre, tinguĕre* to imbue, dye, TINGE, TAINT.]

1. The action or process of attainting: *orig.* as in ATTAIN *v.* 3; in later usage, the legal consequences of judgement of death or outlawry, in respect of treason or felony, viz. forfeiture of estate real and personal, corruption of blood, so that the condemned could neither inherit nor transmit by descent, and generally, extinction of all civil rights and capacities. From the false derivation referred to above, the second of these was looked upon as the essence of Attainder, which is defined by the lawyers as 'The stain or corruption of blood of a criminal capitally condemned, the immediate inseparable consequence by the Common Law, on the pronouncing of the sentence of death' (Tomlins, etc.). See also ATTAINT *v.* 6.

Bill or *Act of Attainder*: one introduced or passed in the English Parliament (first in 1459) for attainting any one without a judicial trial.

1473 WARKW. *Chron.* 12 At the parleament aboue seide . . alle other attayndresses that were made in Kynge Edwardes tyme were anulled. 1584 POWEL *Lloyd's Cambria* 150 The Attaindour of Edward the last Duke of Buckingham. *a* 1626 BACON *Max. & Use Com. Law* 29 Upon attainder of treason the King is to have the land, although he be not the Lord of whom it is held. *a* 1649 DRUMM. OF HAWTH. *James III*, Wks. (1711) 44 The king might . . by their attenders reward the services of many of his necessitous friends. 1768 BLACKSTONE *Comm.* II. 251 By attainder for treason or other felony, the blood of the person attainted is so corrupted, as to be rendered no longer inheritable. 1844 WILLIAMS *Real Prop. Law* (1877) 23 All attainders are now abolished. 1864 WEBSTER *Dict.* s.v., By the constitution of the United States, no bill of attainder shall be passed; and no attainder of treason (in consequence of a judicial sentence) shall work corruption of blood or forfeiture, except during the life of the person attainted.

b. The instrument of attainting; Act of Attainder.

1587 FLEMING *Contn. Holinshed* III. 952/2 As in their atteindor was speciall mention made.

†2. *fig.* a. Condemnation, sentence; foul or dishonouring accusation or allegation. *Obs.*

1588 SHAKS. *L.L.L.* I. i. 158 He that breakes them . . Stands in attainder of eternall shame. 1593 —— *Rich. II*, IV. i. 24 Either I must, or haue mine honor soyl'd With th'Attaindor of his sland'rous Lippes.

†b. Stain of dishonour. *Obs.*

1594 SHAKS. *Rich. III*, III. v. 32 He liu'd from all attainder of suspects. 1752 JOHNSON *Rambl.* No. 192 ⁋7 A resumption of ancestral claims, and a kind of restoration to blood after the attainder of a trade.

†**a'ttaindrie.** *Obs. rare*[−1]. [f. prec., assimilated to sbs. in -RY.] Attainder, attainting.

1628 COKE *On Litt.* 37 a, So long as that attaindrie standeth in force.

†**a'ttaindure.** *Obs.* Also **attendure**. Confusion of ATTAINDER and ATTAINTURE.

1577 HOLINSHED *Chron.* III. 928/1 The king hauing purchased of the cardinall after his attendure . . his house at Westminster. 1677 PLOT *Oxfordsh.* 353 Upon the attaindure of John Earl of Lincoln, and Edmund his brother.

attained (əˈteɪnd), *ppl. a.* [f. ATTAIN *v.* + -ED.] Reached, got at; †touched, hit, struck (*obs.*).

1596 CHAPMAN *Iliad* XI. 175 He wounded takes his horse, attain'd with shaft or lance. 1861 MILL *Utilit.* 57 The degree of virtue attained.

attainer (əˈteɪnə(r)). [f. ATTAIN *v.* + -ER[1].] One who attains or reaches any object of effort.

1610 HEALEY *St. Aug. City of God* 754 The finall good doth immediately make the attainer blessed.

a'ttaining, *vbl. sb.* [f. as prec. + -ING[1].]

1. The action of getting at by continued effort; reaching, acquiring.

1570 ASCHAM *Scholem.* (Arb.) 95 For the . . perfit atteyning of any tong. 1638 SANDERSON *Serm.* II. 121 To the more ready attaining to this Christian unanimity. 1875 B. TAYLOR *Faust* I. iii. 52 Lo! it waits for thy attaining!

2. That which is attained; an attainment.

1615 DANIEL *Queens Arcad.* (1717) 161 Our Longings never stay With our Attainings, but they go beyond.

attainment (əˈteɪnmənt). [f. ATTAIN *v.* + -MENT; cf. OF. *ataignement*, mod. *atteignement.*]

†1. Encroachment. (Cf. ATTAIN *v.* 4.) *Obs.*

1384 in Arnold *Chron.* (1811) 19 Landis and tenementis . . free and quyt of alle maner axions, axing, and attenement.

2. The action or process of attaining, reaching, or acquiring by effort. (No *pl.*)

1549 *Bk. Com. Prayer Edw. VI*, Holy Com. (1852) 311 Towards the attainment of everlasting salvation. 1636 HEALEY *Epictetus' Man.* xxix. 34 Dost thou ayme at the attainment of wisedome? 1872 YEATS *Growth Comm.* 294 The primary object of their voyages was often impossible of attainment.

3. That which is attained or acquired by continued effort; *esp.* a personal acquirement or accomplishment.

a 1680 GLANVILL (J.) Men that count it a great attainment to be able to talk much. 1736 AINSWORTH *Lat. Dict.* (1751) Pref. 12 A man of good attainments. 1824 DIBDIN *Libr. Comp.* 55 A prelate and poet of very distinguished attainments.

b. more *abstractly*. (No *pl.*)

1831 CARLYLE *Sart. Res.* II. iv, No mortal's endeavour or attainment will . . content [him]. 1868 M. PATTISON *Academ. Org.* §3. 47 The cause of the inefficiency of the teaching in Oxford in the old days was . . the low standard of attainment in the place.

attainor (əˈteɪnə(r), -ɔː(r)). *Law.* [a. AF. *atteignour* = OF. *atteigneur*, f. *atteign-ant*, pr. pple. of *atteindre*: see ATTAIN.] One of the twenty-four jurors in the ancient process of ATTAINT.

[1292 BRITTON IV. ix. §4 Si acun bie a fere atteyndre acuns jurours, si fet a prendre garde quant des jurours et queus furent en l'assise, issi qe chescun jurour eit deus atteignours al meyns.] 1865 NICHOLS transl., When any one desires to attaint any jurors, it must be seen how many and what jurors were upon the assise, so that each juror may have two attainors at least.

†**a'ttaint**, *ppl. a. Obs.* Forms: 4–5 **ateynt**, **ataynt**, **atteynt**, **-aynt**, (4 **atenkt**) 5 **atteint**, 6–8 **attaint**. [a. OF. *ateint, ataint*, mod. *atteint*, pa. pple. of *a(t)teindre* to ATTAIN, formed like *teindre, teint, joindre, joint*, etc., and not from L.

attactus. (Cf. *peindre*, *peint*, for L. *pictus*.) Hence, erroneously latinized in med.L. as *attinctus*, and referred, in England at least, to L. *tinctus* 'dyed, stained,' an etymological fancy which warped the meaning of the word and its derivatives.]

1. Convicted, attainted. Used *orig.* as pa. pple. of ATTAIN, subseq. of ATTAINT *v.*; also as adj.

1303 R. BRUNNE *Handl. Synne* 12628 Þat we be neuer more ateynt For fals shryvyng. **1393** GOWER *Conf.* III. 340 Atteint they were by the lawe And demed for to honge and drawe. *c* **1460** *Launfal* 761 Fyle atayte traytour! **1642** *Declar., Votes, etc. conc. Magaz. at Hull* 14 That..he, or they, be in no wise convict or attaint of high Treason. **1768** BLACKSTONE *Comm.* IV. 373 He is then called attaint, *attinctus*, stained, or blackened. He is no longer of any credit or reputation.

2. Affected with sickness, passion, etc.; infected.

1303 R. BRUNNE *Handl. Synne* 3065 Wyþ pryde are swyche men ateynte. *c* **1315** SHOREHAM 103 That he ne schel soffry ther hys [wo], As he [is] here atenkt. *c* **1500** *Blowbol's Test.* in Halliw. *Nug. P.* 1, I trow he was infecte certeyn With the faitour..Or with a sekenesse called a knave ateynt.

3. Overcome with heat, weariness, or fatigue; overpowered, exhausted. [In this sense perhaps partly due to F. *éteint*.]

c **1325** *Cœur de L.* 6131 In the hete they wer almost ateynt. *c* **1380** *Sir Ferumb.* 333 If he beo þer in batail atteynt : þou lest þy los þerfore. *Ibid.* 3612 Ys sted wax al ateynte. **1430** LYDG. *Chron. Troy* I. ix, With weriness atteynt. **1470–85** (1634) MALORY *Arthur* (1816) II. 276 And suffered him till he was nigh attaint, and then he ran upon him.

attaint (əˈteɪnt), *v.* Forms: 4–6 ataynt(e, 5–6 ateynt(e, atteynt, (attend), 5–7 attaynt, atteint, (6 attent) 6– attaint. *Aphetic* TAINT. [f. ATTAINT *ppl. a.* (cf. to *convict*), which was also used as pa. pple. of this, for a considerable time, till *attainted* took its place. *Attaint* had thus originally some of the early senses of *attain*; but its subseq. development was affected by its being associated in fancy with TAINT *v.*[1] (F. *taindre*, *teindre*, pa. pple. *taint*, *teint*:—L. *tingĕre*, *tinctus*, to steep, dye, stain), with which its aphetic form coincided; so that in some senses, it passed into the latter vb.]

I. To touch, get at; = ATTAIN.

†**1.** To touch, get at with a blow, to hit in tilting; = ATTAIN *v.* 1. *Obs.*

1523 LD. BERNERS *Froiss.* I. ccclxv. 597 The seconde course they met and attaynted. *Ibid.* II. clxviii. [clxiv.] 470 They ran togider, and tainted eche other on yͤ helmes. **1530** PALSGR. 439/2, I atteynt, I hyt or touche a thyng, *Jattayngs*. He attaynted hym upon the myddes of the helmet.

†**2.** To get at the facts, find out, ascertain; = ATTAIN *v.* 9. *Obs.*

1489 CAXTON *Faytes of A.* IV. xiii. 266 The causes that ben obscure and hidd may be therby attainted and knowen.

II. To convict, prove, accuse, condemn.

†**3.** To convict, prove guilty. *Obs.*

c **1340** *Cursor M.* (Fairf.) 5512 Ȝou be-houys to wirke ful quaynte and in þaire dedis ham attaynt. **1440** *Promp. Parv.* 16 Atteyntyn, *Convinco*. **1499** *Plumpton Corr.* 141 Parkin Warbek and other iij were arreyned..They all were attended, and judgment given. **1768** BLACKSTONE *Comm.* IV. 79 That the accused be..upon sufficient proof attainted of some open act by men of his own condition.

†**4.** To prove (a charge). *Obs.*

1609 SKENE *Reg. Maj.* 21 Gif it be otherwaies attainted (or proven).

†**5.** *Old Law.* To convict a jury of having given a false verdict; to bring an action to reverse the verdict of a jury as false. *Obs.*

[**1292** BRITTON IV. ix. §4 Se il avent qe les jurours de acune petite assise eynt fet..faus serment..purrount il estre atteintz en plusours maneres. **1865** NICHOLS transl., If it happens that the jurors in any petty assise have taken a false oath, they may..be attainted in several ways.] **1528** PERKINS *Prof. Bk.* v. §383 (1642) 166 Before that this verdict be attainted by the heire in a writ of attaint. **1667** E. CHAMBERLAYNE *St. Gt. Brit.* I. III. viii. (1743) 194 The Punishment of Petty-Jurors attainted of giving a verdict contrary to evidence, wittingly, is severe.

6. To condemn (one convicted of treason or felony) to death, corruption of blood, and extinction of all civil rights and capacities; to subject to ATTAINDER, whether by judicial sentence, or by Act of Parliament without a judicial trial. (Influenced by its erroneously assumed relation to TAINT, whence the idea of 'corruption of blood.')

c **1340** *Cursor M.* (Fairf.) 1114 He þat flemed first adam..he..sal caym sone a-taynt. **1473** WARKW. *Chron.* 1 A parleament, at whiche were atteynted Kynge Herry and all othere that fledde with hym. **1551** T. WILSON *Logike* 16 All such as use deceipt in bargayning..and shalbe atteinted there-upon as fellones. **1679** HOBBES *Dial. Com. Laws*, To be attainted is, that his Blood be held in Law as stained and corrupted. **1704** *Lond. Gaz.* No. 4013/4 Edward Patchell..attainted of Murther in the City of Chester. **1790** BURKE *Fr. Rev.* 31 Do they mean to attaint and disable backwards all the kings that have reigned before the Revolution, and consequently to stain the throne of England with the blot of a continued usurpation? **1844** BROUGHAM *Brit. Const.* xiii. (1862) 195 On Edward IV's victory, they [Parliament] unanimously attainted Henry IV.

7. To accuse *of* crime or dishonour. *arch.* (Also in OF.)

1586 T. B. *La Primaud. Fr. Acad.* 227 How processe ought to proceede against those that are attainted of it [*i.e.* adultery], and how such as are convicted thereof are to be punished. **1609** SKENE *Reg. Maj.* 24 Gif any man..salbe attaynted and convict of such alienation. **1819** SCOTT *Ivanhoe* II. xv. 265 Rebecca..being attainted of sorcery..doth deny the same. **1883** HOWELL *Undisc. Country* I. 71 Who are you to attaint me of unworthy motives?

III. To lay hold of (as sickness), affect, infect.

8. To touch, strike, or seize upon, as a disease or other bodily or mental affection; to affect.

[*a* **1400** *Cov. Myst.* (1841) 223 If dedly syknes have you ateynt.] *c* **1534** tr. *Pol. Verg. Eng. Hist.* (1846) I. 199 Ethelwolphus..was attainted with an easie sicknes. **1591** GREENE *Maiden's Dr.* (1861) 277 And like to one whom sorrow deep attaints. **1598** *Hist. Parismus* I. (1661) 267 Which sight attainted her heart with such grief. **1603** KNOLLES *Hist. Turks* (1621) 561 His foule disease, continually attainting him with intolerable paines. **1688** DRYDEN *Brit. Rediv.* 175 The same shivering sweat his lord attaints.

†**9.** (Influenced by TAINT): To affect with any contagion; to infect. *Obs.*

c **1525** SKELTON *Col. Clout* 902 They be so attaynted With coveytous and ambycyon. **1536** BELLENDENE *Cron. Scot.* (1821) II. 102 That he suld fall in Pelagius heresyis; howbeit all othir Scottis kingis afore him war nevir attentit with sic thingis. **1591** SHAKS. *1 Hen. VI*, v. v. 81 My tender youth was neuer yet attaint With any passion of inflaming loue. **1631** BP. WEBBE *Pract. Quietnesse* (1657) 84 If thou be attainted with any of these evil properties.

10. (In full sense of TAINT): To touch or impregnate with something corrupting; to infect with corruption, poison, etc.

1580 [see ATTAINTED 4]. **1608** J. KING *Serm. 1 Chron.* xxix. 26–8, 23 Dead flies wil atteint the sweetest ointments of Apothecaries. **1645** QUARLES *Sol. Recant.* xii. 77 When secret Vlcers shall attaint thy breath. **1849** DE QUINCEY *Mail Coach* Wks. IV. 290 Even to have kicked an outsider might have been held to attaint the foot.

b. *fig.* To sully (lustre, purity, etc.).

1596 SPENSER *F.Q.* I. vii. 35 Phoebus golden face it did attaint, As when a cloud his beames doth over-lay. *Ibid.* IV. i. 5 Lest she with blame her honour should attaint. **1718** POPE *Iliad* VI. 564 How would the sons of Troy..Attaint the lustre of my former name? **1856** MILMAN in *Q. Rev.* XCIX. 6 No breath of calumny ever attainted the personal purity of Savonarola.

11. (Blending the preceding with fig. use of 7.)

1642 MILTON *Apol. Smect.* (1851) 288 Wherein a good name hath bin wrongfully attainted. **1815** SOUTHEY *Roderick* VIII. 15 His mother's after-guilt attainting not the claim legitimate he derived from her.

attaint (əˈteɪnt), *sb.* Forms as in vb.; also 6 atteinct. [a. OF. *ateinte*, *atainte*, sb. from fem. of *ateint*, pa. pple. of *ateindre*; see ATTAINT *ppl. a.*]

1. The act of touching or hitting; *spec.* a 'hit' in tilting. *arch.*

1525 LD. BERNERS *Froiss.* II. clxviii. (clxiv.) 473 The first course, they strake eche other on their helmes a great attaynt. **1600** CHAPMAN *Iliad* XVII. 6 Nor to pursue his first attaint Euphorbus' spirit forbore. **1819** SCOTT *Ivanhoe* ix, Both the others failed in the attaint. **1820** —— *Monast.* (1867) 458/1 *note*, Attaint was a term of tilting used to express the champion's having attained his mark; or in other words, struck his lance straight and fair against the helmet or breast of his adversary.

†**2.** *fig.* A dint, a blow (of misfortune, etc.). *Obs.* [Cf. Fr. les atteintes de la mauvaise fortune, etc.]

1655 JENNINGS *Elise* Epist. Ded., Generous hearts laugh at the attaints of fortune.

3. *Vet. Surgery.* A blow or wound on the leg of a horse caused by over-reaching, or by a blow from another horse's foot.

1523 FITZHERB. *Husb.* §113 Atteynt is a sorance, that commeth of an ouer-rechynge, yf it be before; and if it be behynde, it is of the tredynge of an other horse. **1607** TOPSELL *Four-f. Beasts* 313 Of an upper Attaint or over-reach upon the back sinew of the shanke. **1751** CHAMBERS *Cycl.* s.v., The farriers distinguish *upper attaints* given by the toe of the hindfoot upon the sinew of the fore-leg, and *nether attaints*, or over-reachers, on the pastern-joint.

4. *Old Law.* The conviction of a jury for giving a false verdict; a legal process instituted for reversing a false verdict and convicting the jurors.

This was done by a grand jury of twenty-four; 'for the law wills not that the oath of one jury of twelve men should be attainted or set aside by an equal number, or by less indeed than double the number.' (BRACTON, in TOMLINS.)

[**1292** BRITTON IV. xi. §1 (*title*) Ou gist Atteynte. **1865** NICHOLS transl., In what cases an attaint lies.] **1528** PERKINS *Prof. Bk.* v. §383 (1642) 166 The heire hath defeated the verdict by attaint. **1577** HARRISON *England* I. II. iv. (1877) 101 Now and then the honest yeomen..shall be sued of an atteinct and bound to appeare at the Starre chamber. **1768** BLACKSTONE *Comm.* III. 351 Another species of extraordinary juries, is the jury to try an attaint; which is a process commenced against a former jury, for bringing in a false verdict. **1827** HALLAM *Const. Hist.* (1876) II. viii. 31 The ancient remedy, by means of attaint, which renders a jury responsible for an unjust verdict, was almost gone into disuse.

5. = ATTAINDER.

1603 DRAYTON *Heroic. Ep.* vi. 140 Those great Lords, now after their Attaints, Canonized amongst the English Saints. **1692** BEVERLEY *Concil. Disc.* 7 The Court of Honour, where Attaints are purg'd off, and Blood, as they speak, restor'd.

6. *fig.* Imputation or touch of dishonour, stain upon honour, lustre, purity, or freshness.

1592 DANIEL *Compl. Rosamond* (1717) 38 Her Legend justifies her foul Attaint. *c* **1600** SHAKS. *Sonn.* lxxxii, Thou ..maiest without attaint o're-looke The dedicated words. *a* **1850** ROSSETTI *Dante & Circ.* I. (1874) 197 Among the faults..Are two so grave that some attaint is brought Unto the greatness of his soul thereby. *a* **1850** JEFFREY in Ld. Cockburn *Lett.* II. ccx, I have faith in races, and feel that your blood will resist such attaints.

†**7.** ? Exhaustion, weariness, fatigue. Cf. ATTAINT *a.* 3. *Obs.*

1599 SHAKS. *Hen. V*, IV. Cho. 39 Nor doth he dedicate one iot of Colour Vnto the wearie and all-watched Night; But freshly lookes, and ouerbeares Attaint, With cheareful semblance. [*Perh. here* = stain upon freshness.]

attainted (əˈteɪntɪd), *ppl. a.* [f. ATTAINT *v.* + -ED; taking place of the earlier ATTAINT.]

†**1.** Hit, struck. *Obs.*

1558 WARDE *Alexis' Secr.* (1568) 18 a, One of the Mariners so attainted with the stroke of a gone that he had his arme brused and broken.

2. Subjected to ATTAINDER.

1596 SPENSER *State Irel.*, There are more attaynted landes, concealed from her Majestie. **1618** BOLTON *Florus* III. xxiii. 254 The goods of attainted Citizens. *a* **1797** H. WALPOLE *Mem. Geo. III* (1845) I. iv. 53 Clemency..to some attainted Jacobite families. **1868** MILMAN *St. Paul's* ii. 33 To abstain from all communion with the attainted prelate.

†**3.** Touched or affected with sickness, passion, etc.

1509 HAWES *Past. Pleas.* XIX. xiii, How your hert is faynted, Wyth fervent love so surely attaynted. **1593** G. HARVEY *New Let.* in *Archaica* (1813) II. 12 So attainted with the French pox.

†**4.** Tainted, corrupted. *Obs.*

1580 TUSSER *Husb.* lxxv. viii, Where meate is attainted, there cookrie is naught. **1580** BARET *Alv.* A 694 Attaynted and stinkyng fleshe.

aˈttainting, *vbl. sb.* [f. as prec. + -ING[1].] Conviction.

1395 PURVEY *Remonstr.* (1851) 54 For shame of opin leesyng and ateyntynge of falsnesse by Jesu Crist.

attaintment (əˈteɪntmənt). [f. as prec. + -MENT.] Conviction; attainder.

1549 LATIMER *Serm. bef. Edw. VI* (Arb.) 144 And [= if] arrainement maye be tourned in to attayntement. **1715** ASHMOLE *Antiq. Berks* (1723) I. 45 Upon whose Attaintment that sacrilegious Prince re-annexed it to the Crown.

attainture (əˈteɪntjʊə(r)). [f. ATTAINT *v.*, after (Eng.) med.L. *attinctūra*, f. *attinctus*, when this was used to translate OF. *atteint*.]

1. = ATTAINTMENT, ATTAINDER.

1538 LELAND *Itin.* VII. 71 It was the Lord Lovel's Pocession. Sens by Attainture it cam by gift to Knolls. **1580** BARET *Alv.* A 694 Attaynture, or bloud stained and corrupted, *Sanies*, *Tinctura*, *Attinctura*. **1593** SHAKS. *2 Hen. VI*, I. ii. 105 Her Attainture will be Humphreyes fall. *a* **1655** R. HALL in Fuller *Ch. Hist.* v. III. 110 At his attainture the King's Officers seised on all he had.

2. *fig.* Imputation of dishonour; stain.

1608 CHAPMAN *Byron's Trag.* Plays 1873 II. 268 Without the least attainture of your valour. **1644** MILTON *Judgm. Bucer* (1851) 304 Their pure unblamable Spirits..they must attaint with new Attaintures.

attal, var. ETTLE *v. Obs.* to intend, purpose.

attam, ME. coalesced form = *atþam* at them.

†**aˈttame**, *v. Obs.* Also 4–5 **atame**. [a. OF. *atame-r*:—L. *attāminā-re* to lay hands on, attack, violate, f. *at-* = *ad-* to, at + *tāmināre*, f. *-tāmen* = **tagmen* touch, from *tangĕre*, *tag-*, to touch. Cf. mod.F. *entamer*. For *att-* see AT- *pref.*[3]]

1. *trans.* To cut into; to penetrate, pierce.

c **1314** *Guy Warw.* 261 The smallest scale that on him is, No wepen no may atame. *c* **1440** *Morte Arth.* 2175 The boustous launce þe bewelles attamede. **1494** FABYAN VI. clxi. 154 At the hede of the fysshe shall be fyrste attamyd [L. *a capite aggrediendus est*].

2. To pierce (a cask, etc.) so as to let the liquor run out; to broach. Hence **attamed** *ppl. a.*, **attaming** *vbl. sb.*

1393 LANGL. *P. Pl.* C. xx. 68 He vnbokelede hus boteles, and boþe he a-tamede. *c* **1425** *Leg. Rood* (1871) 210 He let atame hys pyement tunne. **1440** *Promp. Parv.* 16 Attamyn a wesselle wyth drynke, or abbrochyn, *Attamino*, *depleo*. *Ibid.* Atthamynge of a wesselle wyth drynke, *Attaminacio*. Athamyd, *attaminatus*.

3. To attack, lay hands on, meddle with.

c **1430** LYDG. *Bochas* IV. xxiii. 121 a, It is not holsome with goddes to playe, Nor their puissaunce presumteously to attame. *c* **1450** *'Chaucer's' Dreme* 1128 That a queene Of your estate..In any wise shoulde be attamed.

4. To enter or venture upon, begin, undertake. (Cf. *fig.* uses of *attack*, *broach*.)

c **1386** CHAUCER *Nonnes Preestes Prol.* 52 Right anon his tale he hath attamed. *a* **1420** OCCLEVE *De Reg. Princ.* 2795 Hem deynethe not an accioun atame At comon lawe. *c* **1430** LYDG. *MS. Soc. Antiq.* No. 134. 8 (Halliw.) He schulde anone atame Another of newe.

b. with *inf.*

1430 LYDG. *Chron. Troy* I. ii, And gan also attempten and attame..A new towre to edify agayne. *c* **1430** —— *MS. Soc. Antiq.* No. 134. 1 Sithen Adam dide atame The frute to ete.

†**aˈttaminate**, *v. Obs.*[—0] [f. L. *attāmināt-* ppl. stem of *attāmināre*: see prec.] 'To defile, also to meddle with.' Blount *Glossogr.* 1681.

attap ('ætəp). Also **adap, atap.** [Native word.] The name used in Malayo-Javanese regions for any palm-fronds used in thatching, *esp.* those of the palm *Nipa fruticans*; hence, a thatch made of these. Also *attrib.*

[**1672** BALDÆUS *Ceylon* 164 Het Huys is van Leem gemaakt, ende gedekt met *Atap*, ofte bladeren von Palmeer-boomen.] **1817** RAFFLES *Java* I. iv. 166 In the maritime districts *átap*, or thatch, is made almost exclusively from the leaves of the *nipa* or *búyu*. *Ibid.*, The leaves of the *gêbang*.. are too large and brittle to form durable *átap*. **1886** *Jrnl. Anthrop. Inst.* XV. 293 The roof is thatched with the common Brettam attaps in the same way as Malay houses. **1897** *Blackw. Mag.* Nov. 637/2 Overhead lizards ran in the attap thatch. **1924** *Chambers's Jrnl.* 72/1 The atap-thatched, pile-perched native hutches. **1928** *Daily Express* 13 Mar. 12/2 The coolie women of Bangkok, who cook their food.. over an open fire in front of their 'atap' houses. **1951** 'N. SHUTE' *Round Bend* iii. 89 The little atap village was just by the strip.

attaque, obs. form of ATTACK.

attar ('ætə(r)). Also 9 **atar**, and OTTO, q.v. [a. Pers. *ʿaṭar* perfume essence, *ʿaṭar-gul* essence of roses, ad. Arab. , *ʿiṭr*, pl. , *ʿuṭūr*, *ʿoṭōr*, aroma, f. *ʿaṭara* to breathe perfume.] A very fragrant, volatile, essential oil obtained from the petals of the rose; fragrant essence (of roses).

1798 PENNANT *Hindostan* II. 238 That luxury of India, the Attar of Roses. **1825** MACAULAY *Milton, Ess.* I. 6 These poems differ from each other, as atar of roses differs from ordinary rose water. **1873** T. HARDY *Madding Crowd* xxiii. (1882) 175 That buzz of pleasure which is the attar of applause.

b. The full Persian *Attar-gul* is sometimes used.

1813 BYRON *Br. Abydos* I. x, The Persian Atar-gul's perfume. **1876** BROWNING *Pacchiarotto* 228 The true half-brandy, half-attar-gul.

† **a'ttask**, *v. Obs. rare*⁻¹. [f. TASK, with A- *pref.* 11 written *at-*.] To take to task, to blame.

1605 SHAKS. *Lear* I. iv. 366 (Qo. 2) Attaskt for want of wisedome. [*Folio* 1623, at task.]

† **a'ttaste**, *v. Obs.* Forms: 4–5 **atast(e**, 5–6 **attast(e.** [a. OF. *ataste-r*, cogn. w. It. *attastare*:—Romanic **attaxitā-re*, f. *at-* = *ad-* to + **taxitāre*: see TASTE.] To taste, experience: **a.** *trans.*

c **1374** CHAUCER *Boeth.* II. i. 30 þat þou drynke and atast[e] some softe and delitable þinges. *a* **1400** *Cov. Myst.* 31 Out of this blysse sone xal ȝe go.. And sorwe ȝe xal atast. **1559** *Myrr. for Mag.* (James I.) xviii, Attaste no poyson.

b. *absol.* or *intr.*

c **1400** *Beryn* 458 This is his owne staff, þou seyist; þerof he shal a-tast. *c* **1460** J. RUSSELL *Bk. Nurture* 648 in *Babees Bk.* 161 Shrympes well pyked.. þat youre lord may attast.

atte, obs. f. AT *prep.*; also ME. comb. for *at þe*, at the.

atteal ('æti:l). *Ornith.* Also 7 **atteille, ateil, awteal(e**, 9 **a-teal.** A species of duck of the Orkney and Shetland Isles, identified by some with the Widgeon.

1600 *Act 16 Jas. VI*, xxiii, Termigants, wyld-Dukes, Teilles, Atteilles, Goldings.. or any sic kynde of fowlles. **1653** URQUHART *Rabelais* I. xxxvii, River-fowle, teales and awteales. **1809** EDMONSTON *Zetland Isl.* II. 255 (JAM.) *Anas Ferina*, A-teal, Pochard, Great-headed Wigeon. **1813** LOW *Fauna Orcad.* 145 (JAM.) Another bird of the teal-kind here called Atteal.. is very small, brown or dusky above, and a yellowish belly.

atteche, -eiche, obs. Sc. forms of ATTACH.

† **a'ttediate**, *v. Obs. rare*⁻¹. [f. late L. *attædiāt-* ppl. stem of *attædiāre*, f. *at-* = *ad-* to + *tædium* weariness; cf. obs. F. *attédier* (Cotgr. 1611).] To be tedious to; to tire, weary.

1603 FLORIO *Montaigne* III. viii. (1632) 529 As if he feared to attediate and molest us with their multitude.

† **attedi'ation.** *Obs. rare*⁻¹. [? a. obs. F. *attédiation* (Cotg. 1611), f. *attædiāt-*: see prec.] The action of wearying or fact of being wearied.

1485 CAXTON *Chas. Gt.* 2 There shalle be founden.. the mater of whyche the persone shall haue desyre to here or rede without grete atedacyon.

atteigne, atteine, obs. forms of ATTAIN.

attemper (ə'tɛmpə(r)), *v.* Also 4–6 **attempre**, (4 **entempre**). [a. OF. *atempre-r*, *atremper* (mod. *attremper*):—L. *attemperāre*, f. *at-* = *ad-* to + *temperāre* to temper, qualify, arrange, regulate.]

1. To qualify by admixture; to modify or moderate by blending with something of different or opposite quality; to temper.

1393 GOWER *Conf.* III. 201 Which [justice], for to escheue cruelte, He mote attempre with pite. **1483** CAXTON *Gold. Leg.* 44/2 The love attempered the sorow. **1528** PAYNELL *Salerne Regim.* L iiij b, A lyttell pellitorie and persly, to attempre the coldenes of the forsayde thynges. **1666** J. SMITH *Old Age* (ed. 2) 20 There is scarce any condition so evil, that is not attempered with some good. **1762** H. WALPOLE *Vertue's Anecd. Paint.* (1786) IV. 315 The most perfect taste in architecture, where grace softens dignity, and lightness attempers magnificence. **1851** TRENCH *Poems* 27 If sweet with bitter, pleasure with annoy, Were not attempered still.

2. To modify the temperature of; to make (air, etc.) warmer or colder.

c **1374** CHAUCER *Boeth.* I. i. 8 What attempriþ þe lusty houres of þe fyrste somer sesoun. **1658** EVELYN *Fr. Gard.* (1675) 87 You may give them a gentle stove, and attemper the air with a fire of charcoal. **1717** POPE *Eloisa to Abel.* 63 Those smiling eyes attempering every ray. **1846** HAWTHORNE *Mosses* I. i. 3 The shadow of the willow tree.. attempered the cheery western sunshine.

3. To moderate, mitigate, assuage (passion or harshness); to soothe, mollify, appease (the excited person).

c **1386** CHAUCER *Melibeus* ¶548 The angry man maketh noyses, and the pacient man attempereth and stilleth him. **1483** CAXTON *Gold. Leg.* 206/4 Cezar, amende thy maners and attempre thy commaundementis. **1494** FABYAN VI. clxxxii. 180 He somwhat attempred his fury and crueltie. **1625** BACON *Anger, Ess.* (Arb.) 565 How the.. Habit, To be Angry, may be attempred, and calmed. **1770** LANGHORNE *Plutarch* (1879) I. 87/1 The genius of Numa.. softening and attempering the fiery dispositions of his people. **1882** SHORTHOUSE *J. Inglesant* lxxvi. II. 3 The wild passions and deeds of men are so attempered and adjusted.

4. To restrain, control, govern. Also *refl.* ? *Obs.*

c **1380** *Sir Ferumb.* 164 Entempre þou beter þy tonge. **1393** GOWER *Conf.* I. 333 Attempre thy corage Fro wrath. **1477** EARL RIVERS (Caxton) *Dictes* 40 Attemper you from covetise. **1548** UDALL, etc. *Erasm. Par. Mark* iv. 24 Always attempering thy self as much as thou canst.

5. To regulate, control, order, arrange. *arch.*

c **1374** CHAUCER *Boeth.* IV. i. 111 þere haldeþ þe lorde of kynges þe ceptre of his myȝt and attempereþ þe gouernementes of þis worlde. **1539** CRANMER in Strype *Cranmer* (1694) App. 244 The Holy Ghost hath so ordered and attempered the Scriptures. **1662** MORE *Antid. Ath.* II. ii. (1712) 43 Its Motion and Posture would be so directed and attemper'd, as we.. would have it to be. **1792** *Childr. Thespis* 115 She moves and attempers the springs of the Mind.

6. To make fit or suitable *to*; to accommodate or adapt in quality *to*. Also *refl.*

1393 GOWER *Conf.* I. 87 There may no welth ne pouerte Attempren hem to the deserte Of buxomnesse. **1545** JOYE *On Daniel* v. H viij b, They wolde attemper and drawe Gods worship and religyon unto their own profites. **1656** TRAPP *Comm. Matt.* xi. 17 Attempering their discourses to the hearers' capacities. **1860** PUSEY *Min. Proph.* 128 God often attempers Himself and His oracles to the conditon of men.

b. *intr.* (for *refl.*) To adapt oneself *to*. *rare.*

1809 J. BARLOW *Columb.* II. 85 The tribes.. attempering to the clime, Still vary downward with the years of time.

7. To attune, bring into harmony. Const. *to.*

1579 SPENSER *Sheph. Cal.* June 8 Byrds of euery kynde To the waters fall their tunes attemper right. **1633** P. FLETCHER *Poet. Misc.* 55 All in course their voice attempering. **1725** POPE *Odyss.* IV. 24 High airs, attemper'd to the vocal strings. **1879** H. N. HUDSON *Shaks.* 36 Horatio hits the key-note of the part, and attempers us to its influences.

8. To temper (metal).

1869 *Eng. Mech.* 20 Aug. 488/3 The process of hardening steel is called tempering or attempering.

attemperally, -aly, var. of ATTEMPRELY *adv.*

a'ttemperament, -perment. [f. prec. after Lat., or Eng. and Fr. analogies: see -MENT. Cf. OF. *atemprement.*] The bringing to a proper temper; mixture in due proportions.

1630 BRATHWAIT *Eng. Gentl.* (1641) 355 An attemperament of both those indisposed fancies.. by seasoning them both with an indifferent temper. **1836** *Tracts for Times* lxvii. 5 The efficacy of the whole depends upon the attemperament of the several portions. **1864** WEBSTER, *Attemperment.*

† **a'ttemperance.** *Obs.* Also 4–6 **-peraunce**, 6 **-praunce, atemperance.** [a. OF. *atemprance*, f. *atemprer*: see ATTEMPER and -ANCE.]

1. Temperance, moderation.

c **1386** CHAUCER *Pers. T.* ¶759 Attemperaunce, that holdith the mene in alle thinges. *a* **1450** *Knt. de la Tour* (1868) 131 Of so noble attemperaunce, that she kepte her husbonde.. oute of wrathe. **1560** DAUS tr. *Sleidane's Comm.* 60 a, These people handled the matter with more attemprance.

2. = ATTEMPERAMENT.

c **1374** CHAUCER *Boeth.* IV. vi. 144 þis attemperaunce noryssiþ and brynggeþ furþe al þinge þat brediþ lyfe in þis worlde. **1555** *Fardle Facions* I. ii. 33 Through the attemperaunce of that moysture and heate.

3. The blending or attuning of sounds, harmony.

1481 CAXTON *Myrr.* I. xii. 37 Of this science of musyque cometh alle attemperaunce.

4. Temperament, natural constitution.

c **1374** CHAUCER *Boeth.* IV. vi. 138 As men were wont to demen or speken of complexiouns and attemperaunces of bodies. *Ibid.* þe leche þat knoweþ þe manere and þe attemperaunce of heele and of maladie.

† **a'ttemperate**, *ppl. a. Obs.* [ad. L. *attemperātus*, pa. pple. of *attemperāre*: see above, and cf. the earlier ATTEMPRE.]

1. Temperate, moderate, well-regulated.

c **1386** CHAUCER *Pers. T.* ¶407 (Tyrwhitt), Attemperat [*v.r.* attempree] speche. **1477** EARL RIVERS (Caxton) *Dictes* 36 Be attemperate at thy mete. **1534** LD. BERNERS *Gold. Bk. M. Aurel.* (1546) Hij, This good emperoure was.. attemperate in his exercyses.

2. Of climate, etc.: Temperate, equable, mild.

c **1300** *St. Brandan* 55 The londe Attemperate ne to hote ne to colde. **1480** CAXTON *Descr. Brit.* 47 The attemperate hete and colde that is therein. **1523** LD. BERNERS *Froiss.* II. ccxxiv. (R.) The ayre was more attemparate there.

3. Well-proportioned.

1485 CAXTON *Chas. Gt.* 198 Hyr mouth was wel composed with an attemperat roundenes.

attemperate (ə'tɛmpəreɪt), *v.* [f. prec. ppl. adj.]

† **1.** To moderate or regulate; to accommodate or adapt (*to*); = ATTEMPER 5, 6. *Obs.*

c **1561** VERON *Free Will* 62 a, Christ did attemperat and order his answers according to the persons that he did talke withal. **1644** HAMMOND *Pract. Catech.* (J.) Hope must be proportioned and attemperate to the promise. *a* **1711** KEN *Psyche* Poet. Wks. 1721 IV. 303 Love best attemperates both Food and Sleep.

2. To modify in temperature; to make warmer or colder as may be required; = ATTEMPER 2.

1605 TIMME *Quersit.* II. vii. 134 It will attemperate and dissolve the most hard ise. **1756** C. LUCAS *Ess. Waters* III. 347 We may use our warm baths, properly attemperated.. in all weather. **1875** [see ATTEMPERATING *ppl. a.*]

† **a'ttemperately**, *adv. Obs.* Also 5 **-oraunt-**, 5–6 **-atly.** [f. ATTEMPERATE *a.* + -LY².] Temperately, with moderation; suitably, properly.

c **1420** *Pallad. on Husb.* II. 159 Now spek of goode lande.. As welny rare attemporauntly mete. **1525** LD. BERNERS *Froiss.* II. xliv. 143 He spake so attemperatly, and so good Frensshe. *a* **1551** DK. SOMERSET in Foxe *A. & M.* 736/1 We do study to do al things attemperatly.

a'ttemperating, *vbl. sb.* [f. ATTEMPERATE *v.* + -ING¹.] Suitable modification or regulation.

1684 tr. *Bonet's Merc. Compit.* XIV. 514 A convenient Diet.. for attemperating of the offending Matter.

a'ttemperating, *ppl. a.* [f. as prec. + -ING².] That attempers, modifies, or regulates.

1684 tr. *Bonet's Merc. Compit.* IV. 120 It is better then to use attemperating and moderately moist things. **1875** URE *Dict. Arts* I. 273 Air or water is the attemperating agent.

attemperation (ə,tɛmpəreɪʃən). [f. L. *attemperāt-* (see above) and -ATION.] The action of attempering or regulating; suitable modification; *spec.* in *Rhet.* (see quot.)

1620 VENNER *Via Recta* 7 The better sustentation, and attemperation of our spirits. **1723** SHAW *Bacon's Wisd. Ancients* (1860) 223 Effected.. by proper and exquisite attemperations of nature. **1753** CHAMBERS *Cycl. Supp.*, *Attemperation*.. the casting a restriction, or softening, on something said, by the formulas, *Fama es, ut perhibent.*

attemperator (ə'tɛmpəreɪtə(r)). [n. of agent (after L. analogies) f. L. *attemperāre*: see above and -OR.] That which attempers; *spec.* in *Brewing*, an arrangement for regulating the temperature of the fermenting wort, and of the malting-rooms.

1854–7 MUSPRATT *Chem.* I. 253/2 The mashing attemperator.. can be so managed to preserve the heat at any temperature. **1876** *Encycl. Brit.* (ed. 9) IV. 275 The attemperator consists of a series of pipes fixed within the tun.. It should be possible to run hot or cold water through these pipes.

† **a'ttemperature.** *Obs.* [f. L. *attemperāt-* after *temperature*: see ATTEMPER and -URE.] Due regulation of temper; attempered condition.

1635 BRATHWAIT *Arcad. Pr.* II. 136 The happy disposure and attemperature of his distempered humour. **1658** SLINGSBY *Diary* 198 This Christian attemperature and composure.

attempered (ə'tɛmpəd), *ppl. a.* Also 5 **-prid**, 6 **-pred.** [f. ATTEMPER + -ED.]

1. Qualified by due admixture; fitly blended.

1481 CAXTON *Myrr.* II. iv. 68 Two somers and two wynters.. so attemprid that there is alway verdure. **1555** *Fardle Facions* Pref. 13 Obscure and doubtfully attempred Responcions. **1866** PUSEY *Mirac. Prayer* 15 His own all-wise laws of attempered justice and mercy.

2. Modified in temperature, equable, mild.

c **1430** LYDG. *Min. Poems* 3 The ayre attempered, the wyndes smowth and playne. **1730** THOMSON *Autumn* 28 Attemper'd suns arise.

3. Of persons: Tempered in character, well-balanced, subdued, sober.

1474 CAXTON *Chesse* 53 He was noble and wyse and more attempered than other. **1815** SOUTHEY *Roderick* xv. 23 Draw on with elevating influence.. the attempered mind.

4. Suitably modified, harmonized, attuned.

1796 COLERIDGE *Poet. Wks.* I. 157 Harmonize The attemper'd organ.

5. Of metals: Tempered. Also *fig.*

1852 TENNYSON *Wellington* v, A man of well-attemper'd frame. **1864** NEALE *Seaton. Poems* 9 Well-attemper'd sword.

† **6.** Having temper or disposition; constituted.

1627 FELTHAM *Resolves* II. lxxii. (1677) 313 Nor can men so attempered, injoy themselves in all the smiles of Fortune.

† **a'ttemperel**, *a. Obs. rare.* [Only in Harl. MS. of Chaucer; ? error.] = next.

c **1386** CHAUCER *Melib.* ¶22 Attemperel [*six-texts:* attempre(e, -pere, atempre, a-tempre] wepyng is no thing defended.. But though attemperel wepyng be graunted, outrageous wepynge certes is defended.

† **a'ttempre**, *a. Obs.* Also 4–5 **atempre(e.** [a. OF. *atempré* pa. pple. of *atemprer* to attemper.]

1. Temperate, moderate, well-regulated.

1340 *Ayenb.* 254 Yef þou louest to bi sobre and atempre.. zete ane brydel to þine couaytises. *c* **1374** CHAUCER *Boeth.* II. iv. 40 þi wif þat is attempre of witte. *c* **1386** —— *Nonne Pr.*

T. 18 Attempree [*v.r.* attemper, -pre(e] diete was al hir phisik.

2. Of climate, etc.: Temperate, equable, mild. *c* **1400** MAUNDEV. xiv. 157 Ynde the more..is a fulle hoot Contree; and Ynde the lesse, is a fulle atempree contrey. **1426** *Pol. Poems* (1859) II. 139 Thatempre wedir lusty and benigne. **1555** *Fardle Facions* II. xi. 260 Ayre..so attempre and pure.

†**a'ttemprely,** *adv. Obs. rare.* Also **-perely, -elly, -ally, -aly.** [f. prec. + -LY².] Temperately. *c* **1386** CHAUCER *Sompn. T.* 345 (Ellesm.) Ffor goddes loue drynk moore attemprely [*v.r.* a-temperelly, attemperelly, -aly]. ? *a* **1450** *MS. Linc.* A i. 17. 35 (Halliw.), He es gretly to commend that in reches lyffez attemperally.

attempt (əˈtɛmt), *v.* Also 7 **attemp, attemt.** [a. OF. (14th c.) *attempte-r*, Latinized spelling of *attenter* = Pr. *attentar*, It. *attentare*:—L. *attemptāre*, *attentāre*, to strive after, try, attack, f. *at-* = *ad-* to, at + *tempt-*, *tentāre*, to try, test, freq. of *tendĕre* to stretch. See also the rarer ATTENT.]

I. To try, endeavour, essay.

1. *trans.* To make an effort, to use one's endeavour to do or accomplish some action: **a.** with *inf.* To endeavour, try, essay. **1513** BRADSHAW *St. Werburge* 100 The foresayd wylde gees attempten by no way To hurte theyr fruytes. **1596** SHAKS. *Merch. V.* II. i. 39 You must..either not attempt to choose at all, Or sweare, etc. **1681** DRYDEN *Abs. & Achit.* I. 228 Him he attempts with studied arts to please. **1810** COLERIDGE *Friend* (1865) 82 The truths we may attempt to communicate. **1850** MᶜCOSH *Div. Govt.* II. ii. (1874) 168 Phenomena in which science never attempts to discover law.

b. with *vbl. sb.*, *noun of action*, or *pronoun* representing them: To try, essay. **1538** STARKEY *England* 22 Many..wych wythout profyt had attemptyd the same. **1558** Q. ELIZ. in Strype *Ann. Ref.* I. App. i. 2 Not to attempt..chaunge of any ordre or usage presently establyshed. **1604** SHAKS. *Oth.* v. ii. 255 Vnkle, I must come forth. *Gra.* If thou attempt it, it will cost thee deere. **1611** BIBLE *Pref.* 2 Whosoeuer attempteth anything for the publike. **1754** HUME *Hist. Eng.* iv, To embolden her to attempt extorting the right of investitures. **1802** MAR. EDGEWORTH *Moral T.* (1816) I. 216 Without attempting any reply. **1876** GREEN *Short Hist.* i. §3 (1882) 22 To attempt the conversion of the English.

c. *absolutely.* **1603** SHAKS. *Meas. for M.* I. iv. 79 Our doubts..make vs loose the good we oft might win, By fearing to attempt.

2. *ellipt.* To essay to engage with or have to do with, to try to accomplish or attain (any action or object of activity, *esp.* one attended with risk or danger); to venture upon, try one's fortune with. *c* **1534** tr. *Polyd. Verg. Eng. Hist.* (1846) I. 81 The battayle was soe fearselie attempted as whoe shulde say eche mann thrested other's life. **1691** RAY *Creation* (1704) 192 Courage and Hardiness to attempt the Seas. **1701** *Stanley's Hist. Philos.* Biogr. 2 Stanley was not the first who had attempted this Province. **1858** in *Merc. Mar. Mag.* V. 189 The vessel must not attempt the port, but continue at sea.

†**3.** To try to use or in use; to try the effect or operation of, make trial of. *Obs.* **1563** FOXE in *Latimer's Serm. & Rem.* (1845) Introd. 15 Some also there were which attempted the pen against him. **1692** WASHINGTON tr. *Milton's Def. Pop.* Wks. 1738 I. 539 After they..had attempted all other ways and means. **1770** *Junius Lett.* xxxix. 195 Everyone of these remedies has been ..attempted.

II. To try to influence or move.

†**4.** To try with afflictions. *Obs.* **1525** LD. BERNERS *Froiss.* II. cxxx. [cxxvi.] 369 Sir Olyuer of Clyssone, whom I can nat loue nor neuer dyde, nor he me (who shall attempte me with rygorous wordes). **1550** DK. SOMERSET *Pref. Coverdale's Spir. Perle* (1588) A v, It pleased God for a time to attempt vs with his scourge, and to proue if we loued him. **1650** JER. TAYLOR *Holy Dying* iii. §4 (1727) 72 O Pain, in vain do'st thou attempt me.

5. To try with temptations, try to win over, seduce, or entice; to tempt. *arch.* **1513** BRADSHAW *St. Werburge* 191 Sore attempted by his gostly enemy. **1667** MILTON *P.L.* x. 8 God..Hinder'd not Satan to attempt the minde of Man. **1691** NORRIS *Pract. Disc.* 26 They attempt us, as the Devil did Adam. **1859** TENNYSON *Vivien* 20 It made the laughter of an afternoon That Vivien should attempt the blameless King.

b. Const. *to do* something, *to* an action, course, etc. **1513** BRADSHAW *St. Werburge* 191 The bedyls of Belial attempted full fast The erle and his countesse to kepe theyr opinion. **1596** SPENSER *F.Q.* v. xi. 63 Why then will ye, fond dame, attempted bee Unto a stranger's love? *a* **1670** HACKET *Abp. Williams* I. (1693) 119 His Highness should not be attempted to recede from the Religion. **1773** BERRIDGE *Chr. World Unm.* (1815) 22 Nothing will be found, I fear, to attempt a man to be a thief.

†**6.** To endeavour to obtain or attract. *Obs.* **1607** SHAKS. *Timon* I. i. 126 This man of thine attempts her loue. **1749** JOHNSON *Van. Hum. Wishes* in *Boswell* (1816) 172 Shall..No cries attempt the mercy of the skies?

†**7.** To try to move, to seek to influence (by reasoning, entreaty); to address with urgency. *Obs.* *a* **1547** EARL SURREY *Æneid* IV. (R.) Lefull it is for the For to attempt his fansie by request. **1596** SHAKS. *Merch. V.* IV. i. 421 Deare sir, of force I must attempt you further, Take some remembrance of vs as a tribute. **1671** MILTON *Samson* 1457, I have attempted, one by one, the lords..With supplication prone and father's tears, To accept of ransom for my son. **1673** CAVE *Prim. Chr.* III. ii. 261 She had been oft attempted..by the perswasions of good men.

III. To try with violence or force, make an attack upon.

8. *intr.* (with *indirect passive*) To make an attempt of hostile nature, an attack, or assault *upon* (an enemy, a fortress, life, property, an institution, etc.). Fr. *attenter sur. Obs.* (now 'to make an attempt upon,' or as 9.) **1636** *Ariana* 90 That wicked desire in you to attempt upon her honour. **1645** CROMWELL *Lett. & Sp.* (1871) I. 179 We look to be attempted upon euery day. **1658–9** in Burton *Diary* (1828) III. 482 If..your interest be attempted upon. **1697** CONGREVE *Mourn. Bride* IV. vii, Look that she attempt not on her life.

†**b.** To attempt *nothing*, *the like*, upon = to make *no*, *the like*, attempt upon. Fr. *rien attenter sur. Obs.* **1613** SHAKS. *Hen. VIII*, III. ii. 17 If you cannot Barre his accesse to' th' King, neuer attempt Anything on him. *c* **1613** W. BROWNE *Elegy* in *Overbury's Wks.* (1856) 12 Attempt the like on his unspotted fame. **1745** in *Col. Rec. Penn.* V. 5 Something will be attempted upon Us this Winter by the Enemy.

9. *trans.* To try to master, take by force, or overthrow; to attack, assail, assault: **a.** an enemy, fortress, etc. *arch.* **1605** ROWLANDS *Hell's Br. Loose* 32 With courage now let vs our selues addresse, Attempting on the sodaine Munster Towne. **1719** DE FOE *Crusoe* (1858) 207 How I should escape from them, if they attempted me. **1770** LANGHORNE *Plutarch* (1879) I. 169/2 They attempted the Capitol by night. **1813** *Examiner* 22 Feb. 120/2 The Bank was attempted, but it was saved by the soldiery.

b. in various fig. and transf. senses. *arch.* **1562** J. HEYWOOD *Prov. & Epigr.* (1867) 26 What attempth you, to attempt vs, To come on vs before the messenger thus? **1612** DRAYTON *Poly-olb.* xv. 239 That no disordered blast attempt her braided haire. **1749** CHESTERF. *Lett.* 210 II. 303 The former would not have attempted..the liberties of Rome. **1796** MORSE *Amer. Geog.* II. 67 Those rash hands which attempted his father's crown.

†**c.** To make an attack upon the chastity of, to try to ravish or seduce. *Obs.* **1607** TOPSELL *Four-f. Beasts* 3 Apes that attempt women. **1610** GUILLIM *Heraldry* III. vii. (1660) 136 The Judges.. who attempted Susanna. **1741** RICHARDSON *Pamela* (1824) I. xviii. 29 When one of our sex finds she is attempted.

d. *to attempt the life of*: to try to take the life of, try to kill. **1743** J. MORRIS *Serm.* iii. 73 The unbelieving Jews frequently attempted the life of Jesus. **1883** *L'pool Daily Post* 31 Dec., The life of Mr. Forster was repeatedly attempted.

attempt (əˈtɛmt), *sb.* [f. prec. vb.]

1. a. A putting forth of effort to accomplish what is uncertain or difficult; a trial, essay, endeavour; effort, enterprise, undertaking. **1548** UDALL, etc. *Erasm. Par. Heb.* vi. 3 (R.) If God be favourable vnto our attemptes. **1660** STANLEY *Hist. Philos.* (1701) 80/1 Tolerance raiseth us to high Attempts. *c* **1680** SIR T. BROWNE *Tracts* 155 For such an attempt there wanteth not encouragement. **1711** STEELE *Spect.* No. 168 ¶5 It is a worthy Attempt to undertake the cause of distrest Youth. **1751** JOHNSON *Rambl.* 165 ¶7 The first attempts of a new claimant. **1860** TYNDALL *Glac.* I. §18. 122 The weather was sufficiently good to justify an attempt.

b. *esp.* The effort in contrast with the attainment of its object; effort merely, futile endeavour. **1605** SHAKS. *Macb.* II. ii. 11 They haue awak'd, And 'tis not done: th' attempt, and not the deed, Confounds vs. **1784** COWPER *Task* v. 369 The State that strives for Liberty, though foiled..Deserves at least applause for her attempt. **1877** LYTTEIL *Landm.* IV. x. 257 These conflicting notions are only the result of attempts at interpretation.

c. Const. *to do*, *at* (*of* obs.) *doing*. **1711** ADDISON *Spect.* No. 18 ¶2 Some attempts of forming Pieces upon Italian Plans. **1754** SHERLOCK *Disc.* (1759) I. iii. 136 The vain Attempts of Men to dive into the Mysteries of God. **1876** GREEN *Short Hist.* viii. §5 (1882) 509 An attempt to vest the government of the Church in the King.

d. phr. *to make an attempt* (*to give attempt*, obs.): to make an effort, to try (*to do* a thing). *c* **1534** tr. *Pol. Verg. Eng. Hist.* II. (1846) 27 When as they might with better lucke geve newe attempt. **1580** NORTH *Plutarch* (1595) 236 After many attemptes made. **1632** LE GRYS *Velleius* 133 Cinna..dared give attempt upon those things which no honest man ever durst thinke. **1703** MAUNDRELL *Journ. Jerus.* (1732) 142 Made another attempt this day to see the Cedars. **1849** MACAULAY *Hist. Eng.* I. 177 He made a feeble attempt to restrain the intolerant zeal of the House of Commons.

†**2. a.** The thing attempted, object aimed at, aim. **1610** GUILLIM *Heraldry* III. ii. (1660) 107 His noble courage and high attempts atchieved. **1790** PALEY *Hor. Paul.* Rom. ii. 17 His design and attempt was to sail.. immediately from Greece.

b. A concrete result of an attempt. **1871** L. W. M. LOCKHART *Fair to See* xxiii, His first attempt [*sc.* a letter] ran thus.

3. An effort to accomplish an object by force or violence: †**a.** A warlike enterprise; an attack, assault, onset. *Obs.* or *arch.* **1584** ALLEN in *Edin. Rev.* (1883) 378 No man can charge us of any attempt against the realm. **1603** KNOLLES *Hist. Turks* (1621) 56 The King following, gave no attempt unto the citie, for that he knew to be but vaine. **1605** SHAKS. *Macb.* III. vi. 39 Hee Prepares for some attempt of Warre. **1665** MANLEY *Grotius' Low-C. Wars* 629 These strong attempts of the Enemy did not terrify the Hollanders.

b. A personal assault made upon a person's life, a woman's honour, etc. Now usually requiring specification: 'an attempt upon the life of,' etc. **1593** SHAKS. *Lucr.* 491, I see what crosses my attempt will bring. **1603** —— *Meas. for M.* III. i. 267 The Maid will I frame, and make fit for his attempt. **1611** —— *Cymb.* I. iv. 128 A Repulse, though your attempt (as you call it) deserue more. *Mod.* Another attempt upon the life of the Czar.

†**c.** *fig. Obs.* **1662** MORE *Antid. Ath.* III. xv. (1712) 135 That all the Species of things..came first out of the Earth, by the omnifarious attempt of the particles of the matter upon one another. **1673** CAVE *Prim. Chr.* I. iii. 51 Coming off from all the attempts of adversity with victory and triumph.

†**4.** Temptation, seduction. *Obs.* **1611** BIBLE *Ecclus.* ix. 4 Vse not much the companie of a woman that is a singer, least thou be taken with her attempts. **1667** MILTON *P.L.* IX. 295 To avoid Th' attempt it self, intended by our Foe. For hee who tempts..at least asperses The tempted with dishonour foul.

attemptability (əˈtɛmtəˈbɪlɪtɪ). [f. next: see -BILITY.] The quality of being attemptable, capability of being attempted. **1840** CARLYLE *Heroes* (1858) 351 Short way ahead of us it is all dim; an unwound skein of possibilities.. attemptabilities, vague-looming hopes.

attemptable (əˈtɛmtəb(ə)l), *a.* In 7 **-ible.** [f. ATTEMPT *v.* + -ABLE.] That may be attempted; liable or open to attempts. **1611** SHAKS. *Cymb.* I. iv. 65 Vouching..his [Mistress] to be more Faire, Vertuous, Wise, Chaste..and lesse attemptible, than any the rarest of our Ladies.

†**a'ttemptate.** *Obs.* Also **attemptat.** [a. OF. (14th c.) *attemptat* (mod. *attentat*), as if ad. L. **attempt-*, *attentātus*, sb., f. *attempt-*, *attentāre*, to ATTEMPT. See also ATTENTATE.]

1. An attempt, endeavour. **1531** ELYOT *Gov.* Proem (1544) A ijb, I have nowe enterprised to describe in our vulgar tunge the forme of a juste publike weale..which attemptate is not of presumption. **1589** PUTTENHAM *Eng. Poesie* (Arb.) 160 Many other like words borrowed out of the Latin and French..as..*attemptat* for *attempt*.

2. *esp.* A violent or criminal attempt; an attack, assault, outrage, raid, incursion. (So F. *attentat.*) **1524** *State Papers Hen. VIII*, IV. 122 To represse any attemptate that might be made against the said King. *c* **1570** MARY Q. SCOTS in H. Campbell *Love-lett.* (1824) 269 To repair the wrangis and attemptatis committit aganis me their soverane. **1721** STRYPE *Eccl. Mem.* IV. 364 He called..for redress of the attemptates committed by the Greams.

†**attemp'tation.** *Obs. rare*⁻¹. [ad. L. *attemptātiōn-em*, n. of action f. *attemptāre* to ATTEMPT. See also ATTENTATION.] An attempting. **1425** *Paston Lett.* 5 I. 21 The attemptacion of diverses matieres a geyn summe frendes of the seyd John.

attempted (əˈtɛmtɪd), *ppl. a.* [f. ATTEMPT *v.* + -ED.] Tried, essayed, endeavoured; assailed, attacked; *also*, tempted, tested, put to trial (*obs.*). **1513** BRADSHAW *St. Werburge* (1848) 197 The erle sore attempted by his gostly ennemy. **1535** HEN. VIII in Strype *Eccl. Mem.* I. App. lxiii. 155 By long attempted experience in searching the truth. **1596** SPENSER *F.Q.* I. vi. 46 Lewd lusts, and late attempted sin. **1642** MILTON *Apol. Smect.* Wks. (1851) 271 To secure and protect the weaknesse of any attempted chastity. **1838** ARNOLD *Hist. Rome* (1848) I. 151 The charge of treason and attempted tyranny.

attempter (əˈtɛmtə(r)). Also 6–7 **-or, -our.** [f. as prec. + -ER¹; or a. OF. (14th c.) *attempteur*.]

1. One who attempts or essays anything. **1598** FLORIO, *Saggiatore*..an attempter, a tryer. **1646** SIR T. BROWNE *Pseud. Ep.* Pref., The exceeding difficulty, which..the obscurity of the subject..must often put upon the attemptor. **1798** W. TAYLOR in *Month. Rev.* XXVI. 247 An attempter of Italian comedy. **1837** DICKENS *Pickw.* (1842) II. 73 Any attempt..will recoil on the head of the attempter.

†**2.** One who makes a violent or criminal attempt (against a person, institution, etc.), an assailant; one who attempts the virtue of a woman. *Obs.* **1580** SIDNEY *Arcad.* (1622) 184 They resisted, and by our helpe draue away, or slue those murdering attempters. **1581** LAMBARD *Eiren.* II. vii. (1588) 265 If upon an attempt of Burghlarie..the attemptors take it [the money] away..it is a full and complete Burghlarie. **1609** tr. *Sir T. Smith's Commw. Eng.* 133 Such an attemptour hath had warning.. of the danger, into which hee falleth by such attempt. **1671** MILTON *P.R.* IV. 602 The attempter of thy Father's throne, And thief of Paradise. **1741** RICHARDSON *Pamela* (1824) I. xviii. 29. **1748** —— *Clarissa* (1811) III. 273 It would be a miracle if she stood such an attempter.

†**3.** A tempter. *Obs.* **1645** MILTON *Tetrach.* Wks. (1851) 207 Which his conscious attempters doubtlesse apprehended sooner then his other auditors. **1665–9** BOYLE *Occas. Refl.* IV. i. (1675) 170 Instead of looking upon the attempter as his Friend.

attempting (əˈtɛmtɪŋ), *vbl. sb.* [f. as prec. + -ING¹.] The action of making an effort, trying; attempt, endeavour. **1556** PHAËR *Æneid* IV. Liij, Quaking..her huge attemptings to pursue. **1641** MILTON *Ch. Govt.* II. Wks. (1851) 145 Though of highest hope, and hardest attempting.

1784 ANDERSON in *Phil. Trans.* LXXV. 21 The attempting to climb it was at the risk of my life.

a'ttempting, *ppl. a.* [f. as prec. + -ING[2].] Endeavouring, enterprising, venturous.
c1630 RISDON *Surv. Devon* §144 (1810) 158 Sir Humphry Gilbert..was of an high attempting spirit.

†**a'ttemptingly**, *adv. Obs.* [f. prec. + -LY[2].] By way of attempt or essay, tentatively.
1598 FLORIO, *Tentatamente*, feelingly, by tryall, attemptingly, by assay.

†**a'ttemption.** *Obs. rare*$^{-1}$. [irreg. for *attemptation*.] An attempt.
1565 R. LINDSAY *Hist. Scot.* (1728) 33 The English Attemptions were punished in the last Battle.

†**a'ttemptive**, *a. Obs. rare.* [irreg. f. ATTEMPT + -IVE.] Given to bold attempts; venturous.
1603 DANIEL *Panegyr. King* vi, This great nation.. Attemptive, able, worthy, generous. 1603 —— *Def. Rhyme* (1717) 7 The gallant Proffers of attemptive Spirits.

attemptless (ə'tɛmtlɪs), *a. rare.* [f. ATTEMPT *sb.* + -LESS.] Without attempting; inert.
1586 MARLOWE *1st Pt. Tamburl.* II. v, And rest attemptless, faint, and destitute?

attemptor, -tour, obs. var. ATTEMPTER.

atten, ME. for *at-þen* 'at the': see AT *prep.*

attend (ə'tɛnd), *v.* Forms: 4-6 **atende**, 5-6 **attende**, 6- **attend**. Aphetic 4- TEND. [a. OF. *atendre* (mod. *att-*):—L. *at-*, *adtendĕre*, f. *ad* to + *tendĕre* to stretch: see AT- *pref.*[3]]

Prim. sign. To stretch to (still in OFr.); *hence*, to direct the mind or observant faculties, to listen, apply oneself; to watch over, minister to, wait upon, follow, frequent; to wait for, await, expect. In almost every variety of meaning it is, or has been, both *trans.* and *intr.*, the latter construed with *to, unto, on, upon*, and having *indirect passive*, as: we must *attend to* this, this must be *attended to*.

I. To direct the ears, mind, energies to anything.

1. To turn one's ear to, listen to. **a.** *trans. arch.*
a1300 *Cursor M.* 21803 Qua-sum þe tale can better a-tend. 1513 DOUGLAS *Æneis* II. x. Argt., Into this nixt cheptur ȝe may attend Off Priame King of Troy the fatale end. 1611 SHAKS. *Cymb.* I. vi. 142, I do condemne mine eares that haue So long attended thee. 1715 POPE *Iliad* I. 510 But, goddess! thou thy suppliant son attend. 1808 SCOTT *Marmion* v. xxi, My tale Attend.

b. *intr.* (Const. *to, unto.*)
1447 BOKENHAM *Seyntys* Introd. 3 As they shul heryn wych lyst attende. 1594 SHAKS. *Rich. III*, III. i. 13 Your Grace attended to their Sugred words. 1611 BIBLE *Ps.* xvii. 1 O Lord, attend vnto my crie. 1715 POPE *Iliad* I. 61 Thus Chryses pray'd: the favouring power attends. 1842 J. H. NEWMAN *Par. Serm.* VI. xx. 318 Every one must..attend his best.

2. To turn the mind to, give consideration or pay heed to, regard, consider. †**a.** *trans. Obs.*
1432-50 tr. *Higden* (1865) I. 47 Hit is to be attendede that alle the worlde..is diuided in to iij. partes. 1514 BARCLAY *Cyt. & Uplondyshm.* 45 If they see a fault, they will it not attende. a1644 QUARLES *Sol. Recant.* v. i. 22 Attend thy footsteps when thou drawest near The house of God. 1775 TRUMBULL in Sparks *Corr. Amer. Rev.* (1853) I. 5, I shall.. attend your request.

b. *intr.* with *to.*
1678 GALE *Crt. Gentiles* III. 121 Some said..that the action of sin was not from God; attending to the very deformity of sin, which is not from God. 1711 STEELE *Spect.* No. 262 ¶9 Beauties or Imperfections which others have not attended to. 1852 MCCULLOCH *Taxation* I. iv. 135 Were the justice of the case only attended to.

†**3.** *to attend from*: to turn the mind from, beware of. (L. *attendere ab.*) *Obs. rare.*
c1375 WYCLIF *Serm.* Sel. Wks. 1869 I. 223 [Crist] biddiþ attende from false prophetes [Vulg. *Matt.* vii. 15 *Attendite a falsis prophetis*].

4. To turn the energies to, give practical heed to, apply oneself to, look after. †**a.** *trans. Obs.*
a1400 *Cov. Myst.* 259 To provyde, Lord, for thi comyng, With alle the obedeyns we kan atende. 1523 FITZHERB. *Husb.* §7 If a man attende not his husbandrye, but goo to sporte or playe. 1649 SELDEN *Laws of Eng.* II. xiii. (1739) 69 That himself might attend his own security. 1715 POPE *Iliad* III. 527 The maids..dispersing, various tasks attend. 1798 W. TAYLOR in *Month. Rev.* XXV. 578 The agriculture is every where sedulously attended.

b. *intr.* with *to.*
c1315 SHOREHAM 82 Gode atende to my socour. c1450 LONELICH *Grail* xxii. 207 ȝif thow attenden wilt to his servise. 1502 *Ord. Crysten Men* (W. de W.) I. iv. (1506) 46 Unto that attendeth well the deuyll. 1833 HT. MARTINEAU *Manch. Strike* vi. 65 She was attending very diligently to her work. 1853 A. MORRIS *Business* vi. 127 Worldly affairs are attended to at the cost of men's salvation.

†**c.** with *upon. Obs.*
1611 BIBLE *Rom.* xiii. 6 They are Gods ministers, attending continually vpon this very thing. 1689 BURNET *Tracts* I. 79 Captains..are not obliged to attend upon the Service.

†**d.** with *inf.* To apply oneself, endeavour. *Obs.*
1523 WHITTINTON *Vulg.* 1 Yf a carpenter without compasse, rule, lyne, and plummet sholde attende to square tymbre. 1597 DANIEL *Civ. Wares* III. ii, First, he attends to build a strong conceipt Of his usurped powre.

†**e.** with *subord. cl.* To give heed, take care, look.
1612 MONIPENNIE *Chron.* in *Misc. Scot.* I. 38 The Scots were very..vigilant all night, and attended that their enemies should not escape.

II. To watch over, wait upon, with service, accompany as servant, go with, be present at.

5. To direct one's care to; to take care or charge of, look after, TEND, guard. †**a.** *trans. arch.* or *Obs.*
c1420 *Pallad. on Husb.* I. 511 It wol thyne oxen mende.. yf thai the fyre attende. 1611 SHAKS. *Cymb.* I. vi. 197 They are in a Trunke Attended by my men. 1641 R. B. K. *Liturgy & Mass-Bk.* Pref. 1 Another quarter of our walls, which to him appeared more weake and lesse attended. 1725 POPE *Odyss.* III. 538 Leave only two the gally to attend. 1856 KANE *Arct. Exp.* II. i. 10 They attend their lamps with assiduous care.

b. *intr.* with *to.*
1796 NELSON in Nicolas *Disp.* (1845) II. 199 This will enable me better to attend to all the services. 1850 LYTTON *My Novel* III. xvi, The clergyman had his own flock to attend to.

6. *trans.* To apply oneself to the care or service of (a person); *esp.* to watch over and wait upon, to minister to (the sick). Of a medical man: To pay professional visits to (a patient).
1572 FORREST *Theoph.* 244 A bushoppe..havinge great numbers to pasture..which to his powre he attended. 1596 SPENSER *F.Q.* I. x. 41 The fift had charge sick persons to attend. 1722 DE FOE *Plague* 82 Hired nurses who attended infected people. 1732 POPE *Mor. Ess.* III. 270 Prescribes, attends, the med'cine makes, and gives. 1832 BABBAGE *Econ. Manuf.* xv. 141 The chemist..never attends his customers.

7. To wait upon, as servant or attendant; *also*, to wait upon (a personage) in obedience to an authoritative summons.
1469 *Paston Lett.* 614 II. 360 Attendid as wurshepfully as evir was Quene a forn hir. 1591 SHAKS. *Two Gent.* I. iii. 27 His companion..Attends the Emperour in his royall Court. 1849 MACAULAY *Hist. Eng.* ix. II. 546 The Lord Mayor and the Sheriffs of London were also summoned to attend the King.

b. *intr.* To be present in readiness for service, or in answer to an authoritative summons.
1514 BARCLAY *Cyt. & Uplondyshm.* 47 Rebukes..For not attending and fayling of thy tide. 1697 DRYDEN *Virg. Georg.* IV. 539 Officious Nymphs, attending in a Ring.

c. with *on, upon* (formerly *of*).
?1499 *Plumpton Corr.* 135 If it please you..to appoynt fryday or satterday..I shall then attend of you. a1547 EARL SURREY *Æneid* IV. (R.) And at the threshold of her chamber dore, The Carthage lords did on the quene attend. a1674 CLARENDON (J.) He was required to attend upon the committee. 1808 SCOTT *Marmion* I. viii, Twenty yeomen.. Attended on their lord's behest.

8. To follow, escort, or accompany, for the purpose of rendering services. (Used specifically of those who act as ladies or gentlemen in waiting to royal personages.) **a.** *trans.*
1653 WALTON *Angler* Ep. Ded. 3 If common Anglers should attend you, and be eye-witnesses of the success. 1750 JOHNSON *Rambl.* No. 115 ¶10 Permission to attend her to publick places. 1855 PRESCOTT *Philip II*, I. ii. 21 The Portuguese infanta..was attended by a numerous train of nobles. 1883 *Times* 13 Feb., Their Royal Highnesses..left for London this morning, attended by Mdlle. Heim.

b. *intr.* with *on, upon*; and *absol.*
1591 SHAKS. *Two Gent.* II. iv. 121 Wee'll both attend vpon your Ladiship. 1600 SHAKS. *A.Y.L.* v. i. 66 Trip Audry, trip Audry, I attend, I attend. 1619 *Treas. Anc. & Mod. Times* II. 516/2 So [the Queene] attended upon with the Nobilitie, came downe. 1801 SOUTHEY *Thalaba* VII. xxx, Following the deep-veil'd Bride Fifty female slaves attend. 1883 G. MACDONALD *Sir Gibbie* II. v. 84 Attending on drunk people and helping them home.

9. *Mil.* and *Naut.* To accompany or wait upon for hostile purposes, so as to defeat an enemy's plans. (*trans.*, and *intr.* with *to.*)
a1674 CLARENDON (J.) He was..strong enough to have stopped or attended Waller in his western expedition. 1804 NELSON in Nicolas *Disp.* (1845) V. 484 Cruizing off Cadiz for the purpose of attending to L'Aigle, and securing the approach of our Convoy. 1805 —— *ibid.* VII. 59 The Enemy [has three vessels of war]..If this is so, a Force is necessary of Line-of-Battle Ships and Frigates to attend them.

10. Of things: To follow closely upon, to accompany. (Now only of things immaterial.) **a.** *trans.*
1615 MARKHAM *Eng. Housew.* Pref., My poor prayers shall to my last gasp labour to attend you. 1697 DRYDEN *Virg. Georg.* I. 422 What Cares must then attend the toiling Swain. 1712 STEELE *Spect.* No. 449 ¶3 With a Frankness that always attends unfeigned Virtue. 1751 FIELDING *Amelia* II. vi. Wks. 1784 VIII. 239 Our food was attended with some ale. 1860 TYNDALL *Glac.* I. §18. 130 The loss of our track would be attended with imminent peril.

b. *intr.* with *on, upon.*
1606 SHAKS. *Tr. & Cr.* II. ii. 134 All feares attending on so dire a project. a1847 R. HAMILTON *Rew. & Punishm.* iv. (1853) 149 Destruction and misery attend on wicked doings.

†**11.** *causal.* To follow up, accompany, conjoin, associate (one thing *with* another). *Obs.*
1605 BACON *Adv. Learn.* II. xxiii. §7 [I] have also attended them with brief observations. 1748 ANSON *Voy.* II. xiii. 278 The Governor..had returned a very obliging answer..and had attended it with a present of two boats. 1775 BURKE *Sp. Conc. Amer.* Wks. III. 64 We have carefully attended every settlement with government.

12. To present oneself, for the purpose of taking some part in the proceedings, at a meeting for business, worship, instruction, entertainment. **a.** *trans.* e.g. *to attend* church, school, a lecture, a meeting, a funeral, the sittings of a court, also a *place* of worship.
1646 ROW *Hist. Kirk* Introd. (1842) 17, I had bein in Edinburgh..attending his Majestie's Counsell. 1770 LANGHORNE *Plutarch* (1879) I. 177/1 Pericles also attended the lectures of Zeno. 1831 CARLYLE *Sart. Res.* II. iii, Andreas too attended Church. 1849 MACAULAY *Hist. Eng.* I. 177 It was made a crime to attend a dissenting place of worship. 1884 *Edin. Daily Rev.* 18 Oct. 2/9 The meeting was attended by some of the leading agriculturists. *Mod.* Did you attend the funeral? To attend school regularly.

b. *intr.* Const., *on* the proceedings (*obs.*), *at* the place.
1660 STANLEY *Hist. Philos.* (1701) 35/2 [They] attended on his Funerals. 1764 REID *Wks.* I. 40/1 They pay fees for the first two years, and then they..may attend gratis. *Mod.* He attends regularly at the City Temple.

III. To wait for, await, expect.

13. *trans.* To look out for, wait for, await: †**a.** a person or agent, or his coming. *Obs.*
1475 CAXTON *Jason* 30 b, They sette hem in araye..and attended frely and fast a fote the preu Jason. 1586 T. B. *La Primaud. Fr. Acad.* 104 To stand still in their places, and so to attend their enimies. 1658 SIR T. BROWNE *Hydriot.* iv. (1736) 45 Contriving their Bodies..to attend the Return of their Souls. 1749 SMOLLETT *Regic.* II. i. (1777) 26 Here I attend The king—and lo! he comes.

b. a future time, event, result, decision, etc. *arch.*
1513 BRADSHAW *St. Werburge* (1848) 39 Attendynge oportunyte to take them in a trayne. 1642 ROGERS *Naaman* 358 They must attend the moving of the waters. 1713 ADDISON *Cato* II. i. 9 And Rome attends her fate from our resolves. 1866 HOWELLS *Venet. Life* 128 The countryman, taking shelter at the stern of his boat, attended the shot.

†**c.** *ellipt.* with *clause*: To wait to see or learn, to await the issue. *Obs.*
1589 *Late Voy. Sp. & Port.* (1881) 82 Attending if any strangers would unburthen them. 1699 TEMPLE *Hist. Eng.*, And attended what would be the Issue of this..Convulsion of the State.

†**14.** *fig.* (Of things.) To remain for, be reserved for, be in store for, 'await.' **a.** *trans. Obs.*
1612 WOODALL *Surg. Mate* Wks. 1653, 3 The Trapan.. onely attendeth the Fractures of the Cranium. a1704 LOCKE (J.) The state that attends all men after this. 1734 tr. *Rollin's Anc. Hist.* (1827) I. 72 The prize attended the victor.

†**b.** *intr.* with *for. Obs.*
1578 T. N. tr. *Conq. W. India* Pref. 4 Would you now in your old daies be an Emperor, considering that your Sepulchre attendeth for you?

†**15.** To look forward to, expect. **a.** *trans. Obs.*
1483 CAXTON *Gold. Leg.* 162/2 The grete prouffite that he attended of hym. 1581 SAVILE *Tacitus' Agric.* (1622) 191 The souldier..attended an end for that yeere of his trauell. 1614 RALEIGH *Hist. World* II. v. iii. §14. 430 The Capuans relying on..the succours attended from Hannibal. 1692 RAY *Disc.* II. v. (1732) 285 So dreadful a Tempest that all the People attended therein the very End of the World.

†**b.** *intr.* with *for. Obs. rare.*
1581 SAVILE *Tacitus' Agric.* (1622) 195 The Britans.. attending for nothing els but reuenge or seruitude.

†**16.** *intr.* To wait, tarry, stay. *Obs.*
1560 DAUS tr. *Sleidane's Comm.* 260 a, They would.. attende, vntyl suche tyme as the Emperour had aduertised them. 1605 VERSTEGAN *Dec. Intell.* ii. (1628) 36 Attending at the sea ports..for conuenient winds. 1736 *Col. Rec. Penn.* IV. 98 The two Members..now attending for an Answer. 1768 STERNE *Sent. Journ.* (1775) I. 30 The lady attended as if she expected I should go on.

†**b.** *fig.* Of things. *Obs.*
1596 *Edw. III*, I. ii, Albeit my business urgeth me, It shall attend while I attend on thee.

†**IV.** *trans.* To intend. *Obs.* [So OF. *atendre*, occas. for *entendre*. Cf. ATTENT.]
1455 *Paston Lett.* 239 I. 331 They never attendyde hurt to his owne persone. 1655 GURNALL *Chr. in Arm.* IX. §1 (1669) 184/2 Very unlikely to do real good to the souls: alas, it is not that he attends.

†**a'ttend**, *sb. Obs. rare*$^{-1}$. [f. prec.; cf. OF. *atende.*] Attendance.
1594 GREENE *Look. Glasse* (1861) 117 To give attend on Rasnis excellence.

attend, var. ATEND *v. Obs.*, to kindle.

attend, obs. corrupt f. ATTAINT *v.*

†**a'ttendable**, *a. Obs. rare*$^{-1}$. [f. ATTEND *v.* + -ABLE; or a. OF. *attendable*, glossed 'abydyng' in Du Guez.] Giving attention, attentive.
1547 BOORDE *Brev. Health* Pref. 3 b, Maysters of Chierurgy ought to be..dylygent and attendable about theyr cures.

attendance (ə'tɛndəns). Also 4-6 **attendaunce**, 5 **atendans, -ance**, 6 **attendans.** [a. OF. *atendance*, f. *atendre*: see ATTEND *v.* and -ANCE.]

†**1.** The action or condition of applying one's mind or observant faculties to something; = ATTENTION 1. *Obs.*
c1374 CHAUCER *Troylus* I. 339 No thing askith so grete attendaunces, As doth your lay. c1485 *Digby Myst.* (1882) III. 1306 My lugges anon gyffe a-tendans. 1533 BELLENDENE *Livy* v. (1822) 453 The Gaulis gaif sic attendance to him, that he wes notit and knawin to all thare armye. 1612 T. TAYLOR *Comm. Titus* ii. 6 Men generally think that..

attendance vnto the word, is for old age. **1790** CATH. GRAHAM *Lett. Educ.* 56, I would advise the tutor..not to press his young pupil to give attendance, when he is eagerly engaged with some other favourite pursuit.

†**2.** The action or condition of turning one's energies to; assiduous effort; = ATTENTION 2. *Obs.*

c **1400** MAUNDEV. xxii. 232 Every man ȝeveth..so gode attendance to his servyse. **1533** BELLENDENE *Livy* IV. (1822) 447 And tuke mare attendance and care to ordoure thame. **1674** OWEN *Holy Spirit* (1693) 103 Commands for our Attendance unto such Duties.

3. The action or condition of waiting upon, accompanying, or escorting a person, to do him service; ministration, assiduous service. ***in attendance***: waiting upon, attending.

c **1386** CHAUCER *Wife's T.* 77 A man shall winne us best with flaterie; And with attendance..Ben we ylimed. *c* **1400** *Epiph.* (Turnb. 1843) 114 Or wer ther any ladees hur abowte..Or maydons doyng any attendaunce. **1598** R. T[OFTE] in *Shaks. C. Praise* 25 Giving attendance on my froward Dame. **1605** SHAKS. *Lear* II. iv. 246 Why might not you, my lord, receiue attendance From those that she cals Seruants. **1745** DE FOE *Eng. Tradesm.* I. xxii. 208 Reputation for..good attendance on his customers. **1855** PRESCOTT *Philip II*, I. iii. (1857) 54 The lords and ladies in attendance gathered round the queen. **1860** DICKENS *Uncomm. Trav.* vi, Your waiter reproachfully reminds you that 'attendance is not charged for a single meal.'

fig. **1833** I. TAYLOR *Fanat.* iv. 75 The malign emotions are found in close attendance.

4. The action or condition of an inferior in waiting the leisure, convenience, or decision of a superior.

c **1461** *Paston Lett.* 423 II. 67 He wole gef a tendance unto you for to have summe letter from you. **1542** BRINKLOW *Complaynt* xviii. (1874) 42 How long shal men wayte and geue attendance vpon rulers, before thei can come to the spech of them! **1750** JOHNSON *Rambl.* No. 108 ¶10 Compelled by want to attendance and solicitation. **1821** COMBE (Dr. Syntax) *Wife* I. 264 The poor are never seen to wait In vain attendance at their gate.

5. In senses 3, 4 the phrases ***to wait attendance*** (obs.), ***to dance attendance***, occur = 'to attend'; the latter usually with some shade of sarcasm or contempt.

1562 J. HEYWOOD *Prov. & Epigr.* (1867) 166 He daunceth attendance. **1590** MARLOWE *Edw. II*, I. iv, Nobles..That wait attendance for a gracious look. **1621** BURTON *Anat. Mel.* III. ii. II. iv, Shut him out of doors once or twice, let him dance attendance. *a* **1704** T. BROWN *Com. View* Wks. 1730 I. 164 Why should the loadstone complain of the iron for not dancing attendance after it. **1850** THACKERAY *Pendennis* lvi. 477 What was he about dancing attendance here?

6. The action of coming or fact of being present, in answer to a summons, or to take part in public business, entertainment, instruction, worship, etc.

c **1460** FORTESCUE *Abs. & Lim. Mon.* (1714) 112 Nedyn not to have grete Wag[e]s for their Attendaunce to this Conceile. **1658** *Whole Duty Man* xi. §12 (1683) 90 The many attendances the creditor is put to in pursuit of it. **1725** POPE *Odyss.* VIII. 12 The King in council your attendance waits. **1855** PRESCOTT *Philip II*, I. i. 5 Charles..sent to require his son's attendance at Brussels. **1876** GREEN *Short Hist.* vii. §6 (1882) 401 The Catholics withdrew from attendance at the national worship. *Mod.* The number of attendances recorded in the School Register.

†**7.** Waiting, delay. *Obs.*

1614 RALEIGH *Hist. World* IV. iii. §v. 492 Compelled..to put the matter in hazard without further attendance. **1664** EVELYN *Sylva* 71 Spring-woods..have been let rest till..thirty years, and have prov'd highly worth the attendance.

†**8.** Waiting for, expectation. *Obs.*

a **1600** HOOKER (J.) That which causeth bitterness in death, is the languishing attendance and expectation thereof. *a* **1641** FINETT *Philoxenis* (1656) 164 Resting..in attendance of their Lords Plate, not yet come.

†**9.** A body of attendants, train of servants, retinue. *Obs.*

1607 HIERON *Wks.* I. 228 Two or three of her attendance looked out. **1696** LUTTRELL *Brief Rel.* IV. 44 The Venetian ambassadors, with an attendance of about 40 noblemen. **1779** JOHNSON *L.P.*, *Pope* (1787) IV. 91 So many wants, that a numerous attendance was scarcely able to supply them.

10. The body or number of persons present to take part in any proceedings.

1835 J. WILSON in *Life* (1878) iii. 89 The attendance at the stated services of the mission is greater than..ever. **1882** *Daily Tel.* 17 May, Greatly increased interest in the match should be represented..by a greatly increased attendance.

11. *Comb.*, as **attendance allowance**, a social security benefit (superseding the *constant attendance allowance* s.v. CONSTANT *a.* 6d) payable to (those who care for) any severely disabled person who needs constant attendance at home; **attendance centre**, a non-residential institution run by a local authority which a young offender may be required by a court to attend for a prescribed number of hours (see quot. 1982); **attendance-officer**, one whose duty it is to see that children attend school.

1969 *Hansard Commons* (Written Answers) 7 July 165 The Government's proposals to introduce a new *attendance allowance for the very severely disabled, including housewives. **1972** *Whitaker's Almanack 1973* 498/2 The Act of 1970..provides for the payment of a tax-free attendance allowance to the severely disabled... The full rate..is paid to those in need of a great deal of attention or supervision both by day and by night. **1986** *Times* 2 Apr. 11/3 I'm a carer. I get a £20-a-week attendance allowance. **1948** *Act* 11 & 12 *Geo. VI* c. 58 §19(1) Where a court..has power..to impose imprisonment on a person who is not less than twelve but under twenty-one..the court may, if it has been notified..that an *attendance centre is available..order him to attend at such a centre..for such number of hours..as may be..specified. **1965** *Listener* 27 May 793/2 The suggestion is that 'treatment' may be carried out..by an improved Probation Service, attendance centres, or out-patients departments of mental hospitals. **1979** *Daily Tel.* 2 Nov. 10 Experiments with mixed attendance centres for offenders aged 14 to 16, are planned by the Government. **1982** *Criminal Justice Act* c. 48 §16(2) In this Act 'attendance centre' means a place at which offenders under 21 years of age may be required to attend and be given under supervision appropriate occupation or instruction. **1884** *Pall Mall G.* 17 June 1/1 A blind eye..should be an indispensable qualification in an *attendance officer.

†**a'ttendancy.** *Obs.* Also 7 **-ency.** [f. prec.: see -NCY.]

1. The condition of giving heed; attention.

a **1679** T. GOODWIN *Wks.* 1863 VII. 396 Our attendancy to this very discrimination..may have a great influence.

2. The giving of attendance.

1594 HOOKER *Eccl. Pol.* VII. 442 Of honour, another part is attendancy; and therefore..angels are spoken of as his attendants.

3. = ATTENDANCE 9.

1586 FERNE *Blaz. Gentrie* 322 With as great an attendancy of friendes and seruants as..shalbe fit.

4. The quality of accompanying, adjoining, or following on; attendant relation.

a **1626** BACON *Max. & Use* xxv. (1630) 89 To name land by the attendancy they have to other lands more notorious.

5. An accompaniment, an attendant thing.

1654 WARREN *Unbelievers* 47 There was..equivalency in respect of the adjuncts or attendencies.

6. Waiting for, expectation.

1646 H. LAWRENCE *Comm. & W. Angels* 154 A certaine..attendancy, or looking after some good thing desired.

attendant (əˈtɛndənt), *a.* and *sb.* Also 4–6 **-aunt.** [a. OF. *attendant*, pr. pple. of *attendre*, earlier *atendre*, to ATTEND.]

A. *adj.*

†**1.** Turning the attention, giving earnest heed; watchful, observant, attentive. *Obs.*

1432 *Paston Lett.* 18. I. 34 Attendant and obeissant in accomplishing therof. **1509** HAWES *Past. Pleas.* XVI. lxxi, Her servaunt To obtayne her love is so attendaunt. **1649** SELDEN *Laws Eng.* II. xiii. (1739) 73 To have the King..attendant upon his Advice.

2. Waiting upon, accompanying, or following, in order to do service; ministrant.

c **1485** *Digby Myst.* (1882) III. 1872 In good soth we byn a-tenddawntt. **1575** (*title*) Robert Laneham's Letter..from a freend officer attendant in the Court. **1667** MILTON *P.L.* VIII. 149 Other Suns..With thir attendant Moons thou wilt descrie. **1828** SCOTT *F.M. Perth* xxviii, From the attendant flotilla rang notes of triumph.

b. Const. *to* (obs.), *on, upon.*

1393 GOWER *Conf.* II. 172 As damiselles attendaunt To the goddesses. **1531–2** *Act 23 Hen. VIII*, v. §4 Officers..attendant to you in and aboute the due execucion of this our commission. **1675** TRAHERNE *Chr. Ethics* xxx. 473 His guardian angels alwaies attendant on him. **1849** MACAULAY *Hist. Eng.* iii. I. 314 Fresh meat was never eaten even by the gentlemen attendant on a great Earl.

†**3.** *Law.* Dependent on; owing duty or service to.

1393 GOWER *Conf.* I. 214 To whom the lond was attendant As he, whiche heir was apparant. *c* **1400** *Destr. Troy* VII. 3369 Yles ynow are attendant to Troy. **1528** PERKINS *Prof. Bk.* v. §424 The tenant in dower..shall be attendant unto them by the rate and portion of the rent. **1641** *Termes de la Ley* 31 His wife shal be endowed of the land, and shee shall be attendant to the heire of the third part of 1. d.

4. Accompanying, in a dependent position; closely consequent or resulting. Const. *on, upon.*

Attendant Keys in *Mus.*: the keys or scales on the fifth above, and fifth below (or fourth above), any key-note or tonic, considered in relation to the key or scale on that tonic.

1617 COLLINS *Def. Bp. Ely* I. v. 220 Miracles come from no inhaerent power..from a circumstant rather, or an attendant. **1750** JOHNSON *Rambl.* No. 77 ¶11 To show innocence and goodness with such attendant weaknesses. **1833** HT. MARTINEAU *Brooke F.* vi. 72 The suffering and death attendant upon war. *Mod.* The attendant circumstances.

5. Present at any public proceeding or at the place in which it is held.

1588 LAMBARDE *Eiren.* II. ii. 101 Ecclesiasticall persons (if they be not attendant upon diuine seruice) may be arrested for the Peace. **1880** tr. *Daudet's Fromont & Risler* I. ii. 12 The round of fêtes with their attendant crowds.

B. *sb.*

1. One who waits upon, accompanies, or follows another in order to render service; one of a retinue or train; a servant, satellite, subordinate companion.

1555 *Fardle Facions* I. v. 57 He laied all the faulte vpon the ministres and attendauntes. **1604** SHAKS. *Oth.* IV. iii. 8 Dismisse your Attendant there. **1780** HARRIS *Philol. Enq.* (1841) 480 This author was a constant attendant upon the person of this great prince. **1822** BYRON *Juan* VII. lxxii, Two..ladies, who With their attendant aided our escape.

b. *transf.* or *fig.*

1667 MILTON *P.L.* VII. 547 Least sin Surprise thee, and her black attendant, Death. **1793** SMEATON *Edystone L.* §129 Hancock's Sloop, which I had before made use of as an attendant. **1837** WHEWELL *Hist. Induct. Sc.* (1857) I. 301 Jupiter also has attendants.

2. 'One that waits the pleasure of another.' J.

1684 T. BURNET *Th. Earth* (J.) To give an attendant quick despatch is a civility.

3. Something that accompanies in a circumstantial relation; an accompaniment, close consequent.

1607 *Schol. Disc. agst. Antichr.* I. i. 56 [The Crosse] is vsed by vs, as an attendant vpon the Sacrament. **1660** WATERHOUSE *Arms & Arm.* 36 They had their Crowns, Chayns, Rings, like our attendants of Knighthood. **1737** POPE *Hor. Epist.* II. i. 247 The laugh, the jest, attendants on the bowl. **1869** J. COLERIDGE *Keble* iv. 65 Melancholy is a common attendant on poetic genius.

4. One who is present at any public proceeding or at the place in which it is held.

1641 HINDE *J. Bruen* xxx. 95 The attendants..of such Wakes. *a* **1745** SWIFT (J.) A constant attendant at all meetings relating to charity. **1882** PICTON *Cromwell* ii. 26 His parents were certainly diligent attendants at church.

5. *Law.* (See A 3.)

a'ttendantly, *adv. rare.* [f. prec. adj. + -LY[2].] After the manner of an attendant.

1578 BANISTER *Hist. Man* I. 6 Reason..whereon..the senses continually as ministers attendantly should wayte.

attended (əˈtɛndɪd), *pa. pple.* [f. ATTEND *v.* + -ED.] Waited upon, accompanied, frequented.

1603 KNOLLES *Hist. Turkes* (1638) 53 Andronicus..secretly fled..attended vpon only with a few of his trusty seruants. **1846** DE QUINCEY *Shelley* Wks. VI. 24 A dreadful storm, attended by thunder and columns of lightning. *Mod.* A well-attended church.

a'ttendedness. *rare.* [f. prec. + -NESS.] The condition of being attended or accompanied.

1862 F. HALL *Hindu Philos. Syst.* 215 There is need..of perception of invariable attendedness.

attendee (ætɛnˈdiː). orig. and chiefly *U.S.* [f. ATTEND *v.* + -EE[1].] One who (merely) attends a meeting, conference, etc.; = ATTENDANT *sb.* 4.

1961 in WEBSTER. **1967** W. E. J. BREEDLOVE *Swinging Set* vi. 79 The only attendees who bother with clothes. **1972** *Phys. Bull.* Oct. 577/1 Such a gathering can be satisfactory to both organizers and attendees only if it is run efficiently. **1974** *Summerville* (S. Carolina) *Jrnl.* 24 Apr. 1/5 Concert attendees are requested to be in their seats by 8:15 p.m. **1980** *Financial Times* 3 Apr. 4/7 Some attendees view this flexibility as an opportunity to negotiate favourable terms. **1983** *ICL News* Jan. 11/3 Diana is still a regular attendee at Shareholders' meetings.

attender (əˈtɛndə(r)). [f. as ATTEND *v.* + -ER[1].]

1. One who gives heed or attention; an observer.

1660–3 J. SPENCER *Prodigies* (1665) 287 Crazy brains..are not seldom the most curious attenders of such things as these. **1876** M. ARNOLD *Lit. & Dogma* 49 Attending to conduct..makes the attender feel that it is joy to do it.

2. He who (or that which) attends or waits upon, *esp.* to render service; a ministrant, attendant.

1461–83 *Ord. R. Househ.* 83 One page..to be labourer and attender. **1594** DANIEL *Cleop.* (1717) 290 Go my Maids, my Fortune's sole Attenders. **1612** WOODALL *Surg. Mate* Wks. 1653, 342 The attenders of the sick. **1635** STAFFORD *Fem. Glory* (1869) 117 On whose lookes, words, and actions, Modesty is a diligent attender. **1681** GLANVILL *Sadducismus* I. (1726) 40 These mischievous spirits..are more constant Attenders..upon the Actions and Inclinations of such, whose Genius and Designs prepare them for their Temptations.

3. = ATTENDANT *sb.* 4.

1704 J. BLAIR in Perry *Hist. Coll. Amer. Col. Ch.* I. 96, I was a constant attender at Councils. **1882** MCQUEEN in *Macm. Mag.* XLVI. 164 Tobacco and pipes are not provided..each attender bringing his own supply.

†**a'ttender,** *v. Obs. rare*[−1]. [prob. a. F. *attendre* in the sense of 'tend, attend to,' confused with the idea of *tender*: see TENDER *v.*[2]] To treat with kindly attention or regard.

1550–3 *Decaye Eng.* in *Supplic.* 96 We desyre you sumwhat to attender the premisses.

attending (əˈtɛndɪŋ), *vbl. sb.* [f. ATTEND *v.* + -ING[1].] The action of the vb. ATTEND; attendance, attention.

1611 COTGR., *Attendue*, An attendance, or attending. **1880** CYPLES *Hum. Exp.* vi. 153 Cases..where the attending wholly ceases.

a'ttending, *ppl. a.* [f. as prec. + -ING[2].]

1. Listening, attentive.

1592 SHAKS. *Rom. & Jul.* II. ii. 167 Like softest Musicke to attending eares. **1793** SOUTHEY *Tri. Woman* 119 Hush'd are all sounds, the attending crowd are mute. **1884** *Athenæum* 27 Sept. 395/2 Defining a mind as an attending subject.

2. Waiting to do service, ministrant, attendant.

1588 SHAKS. *L.L.L.* IV. iii. 231 My Loue, (her Mistres) is a gracious Moone; Shee (an attending Starre). **1720** POPE *Iliad* XXIII. 49 Th' attending heralds..With kindled flames the tripod-vase surround.

3. Accompanying in a circumstantial relation; closely consequent.

1683 CREECH *Lucretius* I. 13 *note*, Cartes proposes his Ambient attending Circle..to solve the Phenomenon of Motion. **1812** L. HUNT in *Examiner* 12 Oct. 641/1 To lose sight of all attending circumstances.

†**a'ttendment.** *Obs. rare.* [a. OF. *atendement* waiting, expectation, f. *atendre* to ATTEND: see -MENT. But in sense 1 prob. for *entendement*,

which in early use embraced the sense of *attendement* also: cf. ATTEND *v.* IV, and ATTENT.]

1. Sense, meaning. (Cf. *double entendre.*)

1430 LYDG. *Chron. Troy* IV. xxxiv, Therein was double attendement, He spake but one and yet he mente twayne.

2. A thing that attends, *pl.* surroundings.

1646 SIR T. BROWNE *Pseud. Ep.* 372 He passed his daies in tears, and the uncomfortable attendments of hell.

attendress (ə'tɛndrɪs). ? *Obs. rare.* [f. ATTENDER + -ESS.] A female attendant, a waitress.

1662 FULLER *Worthies* (1840) III. 103 A female attendress at the table .. applied herself wholly to him.

attendure, var. ATTAINDURE, *Obs.*, attainder.

attent (ə'tɛnt), *ppl. a.* [ad. L. *attentus*, pa. pple. of *attendĕre* to ATTEND; cf. It. *attento*, and OF. *attentement.*] Earnestly or eagerly directed towards the perception of anything: said of the eyes, ears, mind, or whole man; intent, attentive, full of attention (*to*, *upon*).

1482 *Monk of Evesham* (Arb.) 25 For al degreys and condycyons of alle crystyn pepulle, and more attente for hys enmyes .. he made meruailous prayers. **1534** MORE *On the Passion* Wks. 1346/1 Thoughte vppon with a myndefull and attent mynde. **1535** COVERDALE *2 Chron.* vii. 15 Myne eares shal be attente vnto prayer in this place. **1651** HOBBES *Leviath.* I. ii. 6 Long and vehemently attent upon Geometricall Figures. **1699** DRYDEN *Wife's T.* 310 As judges on the bench more gracious are, And more attent to brothers of the bar. **1867** BUSHNELL *Mor. Uses Dark Th.* 132 To be alive and thoroughly attent to evils about our path.

† **a'ttent**, *sb. Obs.* Also 3–5 **atent(e**, **attente**. [a. OF. *atente*, now *attente*, act of attending, in various senses = Pr. *atenta*:—L. **attenta* sb., f. fem. of pa. pple. *attentus* (analogous to nouns in -*āta*): see ATTENT *a.* Already in OF. confused with *entente*, *antente*, and used in senses proper to the latter, whence sense 3, the earliest and most frequent in Eng.]

1. Attention; care, heed.

c **1450** HENRYSON *Mor. Fab.* 29 But to the end attent hee tooke no more. **1596** SPENSER *F.Q.* VI. ix. 37 And kept her sheepe with diligent attent. **1652** NEEDHAM tr. *Selden's Mare Cl.* 469 After all this attent on his Majestie's part, and so long deliberation on their's.

2. ? Expectation.

c **1430** *Seven Sages* (P.) 87 And that wole do so by myn attente, That ȝe no schal nouȝt repente.

3. Intention, aim, purpose.

c **1230** *Ancr. R.* 252 Al his attente is uorte unuestnen heorten. **1376** *E.E. Gilds* 74 þis ffraternite is be-gonnen in þis atent. *a* **1400** *Cov. Myst.* 4 Abraham toke with good atent His sone Ysaac. **1450** MYRC 953 þou .. Leuest also in fulle a tent How þat holy sacrament, Is I-ȝeue to mon kynne.

† **a'ttent**, *v. Obs. rare*⁻¹. [ad. L. *attent-āre* less correctly *attemptāre*: see ATTEMPT *v.*] Variant of ATTEMPT. (Cf. *account*, *accompt.*)

1620 QUARLES *Feast Wormes* 648 With oft-repeated labours, oft attented, They .. deepely delu'd the furrow'd seas.

a'ttentat(e. ? *Obs.* [Variant of ATTEMPTATE, assimilated to L. *attentatus*, and mod.F. *attentat.*]

† **1.** A criminal attempt or assault of any kind. *Obs.*

1622 BACON *Hen. VII*, 92 Their detestation of Popular Attentates, upon the Person or Authoritie of Princes. **1691** WOOD *Ath. Oxon.* II/316 This most execrable Attentate. **1721** STRYPE *Eccl. Mem.* III. xliii. 354 Commissioners for redress of attentates on both sides.

2. An attempt to gain an unauthorized advantage in law: see quot.

1701 ATTERBURY *Add. 1st Ed. Rights Convoc.* 35 An Attentat, i.e. a Criminal Endeavour of exerting a Power, which was superseded and laid asleep. **1726** AYLIFFE *Parerg.* 100 Attentates .. such Proceedings as are made in a Court of Judicature, (pending Suit) and after an Inhibition is decreed .. Those Things which are done after an Extra-judicial Appeal, may likewise be stiled Attentates.

† **a'ttentate**, *v. Obs.*⁻⁰ [f. L. *attentāt-*: see ATTENT *v.* and -ATE³.] = ATTEMPT; 'to attempt, assay, or prove.' Blount *Glossogr.* 1656.

† **atten'tation**. *Obs.* [ad. L. *attentātiōn-em*, n. of action f. *attentāre*: see ATTENT *v.*] = ATTEMPTATION; 'a trying or essaying.' Bullokar 1676.

a **1670** HACKET *Abp. Williams* i. 99 (D.) The Devil that spies the first spark of attentation, and blows it into a flame.

† **a'ttentful**, *a. Obs. rare.* [f. ATTENT *sb.* + -FUL.] Full of attention, attentive. **a'ttentfully** *adv.*, attentively.

1513 DOUGLAS *Æneis* XIII. viii. 13 The gret capitane Enee .. Attentfully behaldand euery wycht.

attentik, obs. form of AUTHENTIC.

attention (ə'tɛnʃən). [ad. L. *attentiōn-em*, n. of action f. *attendĕre* to ATTEND. Used by Chaucer in transl. from Latin, then not found till *c* 1600; not in Fr. till 16th c.]

1. a. The action, fact, or state of attending or giving heed; earnest direction of the mind, consideration, or regard; *esp.* in phr. ***to pay*** or ***give attention***. The mental power or faculty of attending; *esp.* with *attract*, *call*, *draw*, *arrest*, *fix*, etc.

c **1374** CHAUCER *Boeth.* II. i. 29 After þat she hadde gadred .. myn attencioun she seide þus. **1593** SHAKS. *Rich. II*, II. i. 6 The tongues of dying men Inforce attention. **1667** MILTON *P.L.* I. 618 Attention held them mute. **1771** *Junius Lett.* xlix. 253 The attention I should have paid to your failings. **1871** SMILES *Charac.* i. (1876) 21 They still arrest the attention. **1878** SEELEY *Stein* III. 478 He marked with attention all that appeared from other pens.

b. *Metaph.* (See quot.)

1690 LOCKE *Hum. Und.* II. xix. (1695) 119 When the Ideas that offer themselves are taken notice of, and, as it were, registred in the Memory, it is Attention. **1762** KAMES *Elem. Crit.* (1833) 483 Attention is that state of mind which prepares one to receive impression. **1838** SIR W. HAMILTON *Logic* xxx. II. 136 Attention is the voluntary direction of the mind upon an object, with the intention of fully apprehending it.

2. Practical consideration, observant care, notice.

1741 CHESTERF. *Lett.* 77 I. 213 They have attention to every thing, and always mind what they are about. **1816** F. NAYLOR *Hist. Germ.* I. II. xv. 775 *note*, To soften the rude manners of an uncultivated people by a benignant attention to their morals. **1882** *Daily Tel.* 4 May (*Markets*), Oats met with a moderate amount of attention at Monday's prices.

3. The action of attending to the comfort and pleasure of others; ceremonious politeness, courtesy. Often in *pl.* spec. ***to pay attention*** or ***one's attention to***: to court.

1752 CHESTERF. *Lett.* 285 III. 305 Nice and scrupulous, in points of ceremony, respect, and attention. **1774** *Ibid.* 26. I. 96 A well-bred man .. takes care that his attentions for you be not troublesome. **1849** C. BRONTË *Shirley* ii. 18 To 'pay attention,' as they say, to some young lady. **1855** PRESCOTT *Philip II*, I. ii. 25 Philip received all the attentions which an elegant hospitality could devise.

† **4.** A matter of attention, a consideration. *rare.*

1784 J. BARRY *Lect. Art* iv. (1848) 156 Distances, lines, angles, and other mechanical subordinate attentions. *Ibid.* v. 185 The chiaroscuro and the other attentions of the composition should be calculated.

5. a. 'A cautionary word used as a preparative to any particular exercise or manœuvre.' C. James *Mil. Dict.* ***to come to attention***: to assume a prepared military attitude; so ***to stand at attention***.

1792 *Rules & Regs. for Formations of H.M.'s Forces* 6 Upon the word *Attention*, no one shall have materially lost his dressing in the line. **1820** COMBE (Dr. Syntax) *Consol.* I. 145 He attention's look display'd As he was wont on war's parade. **1833** *Reg. Instr. Cavalry* I. 10 On the word *Attention*, the hands are to fall smartly upon the outside of the thighs; the right heel to be brought up in a line with the left; and the proper unconstrained position of a soldier .. resumed. **1870** *Daily News* 1 Oct., Yonder sergeant of Zouaves .. comes promptly to attention when an officer addresses him.

b. ***to stand (at, to) attention***: to stand in the military attitude assumed at the word of command 'Attention!' Also ***to draw oneself up, spring***, etc., ***to attention***.

1859 WHYTE MELVILLE *Holmby House* (1860) xviii. 276 He .. stood gaunt and dripping at 'attention'. **1866** —— *Cerise* (ed. 3) I. i. 11 Like a soldier who springs to 'attention'. **1879** H. HARTIGAN *Stray Leaves* ser. II. 146 He drew himself up to attention, and performed the lance exercise. *Ibid.* 181 The old man was standing at attention. **1892** KIPLING & BALESTIER *Naulahka* 259 A trooper .. stood to attention at the horse's head. **1895** *Cornhill Mag.* Dec. 633 He .. saluted, and stood at attention. **1899** *Allbutt's Syst. Med.* VIII. 8 Make the patient 'stand attention'.

6. *attrib.* and *Comb.*

1898 TITCHENER *Primer Psychol.* v. 88 The attention-wave rises and falls at short intervals: attention fluctuates. **1901** —— *Exper. Psychol.* I. II. viii. 197 The attention period (the time-interval from maximum to maximum of sensation). *Ibid.* 198 A continuous attention-strain. **1902** W. JAMES *Let.* 20 Apr. (1920) II. 164 It is an uplifting thought that truth is to be told at last in a radical and attention-compelling manner. **1934** *Jrnl. Social Psychol.* V. 313 Results which present conflicting records of the attention-spans of the subjects observed. **1949** *Mind* LVIII. 125 The book is written with grace and humour, and in an attention-holding way. **1964** L. S. HULTZÉN in D. Abercrombie et al. *Daniel Jones* 90 Attention-calling modifications tend to occur.

attentional (ə'tɛnʃənəl), *a.* [f. ATTENTION + -AL.] Of or pertaining to attention as a psychological concept.

1896 TITCHENER *Outl. Psychol.* vi. 132 The passive attention of the animal or the child is the first stage of attentional development. **1901** —— *Exper. Psychol.* I. II. 206 The experiments on attentional time-displacement form one of the most interesting .. chapters of experimental psychology.

attentive (ə'tɛntɪv), *a.* (Also 7 **attemptive.**) [a. F. *attentif*, *-ive* (16th c. in Littré), perhaps altered from the earlier *ententif*, *-ive*, after L. *attentus*, *attentio*; cf. the next word, in which the *at*-form appears earlier, and see ENTENTIVE, INTENTIVE, TENTIVE.]

1. a. Steadily applying one's mind, observant faculties, or energies; giving or evincing careful consideration; intent, heedful, observant.

[*c* **1374** CHAUCER *Boeth.* II. i. 29, I was ententif to herkene hire.] **1577** HELLOWES *Gueuara's Chron.* 10, I admonishe .. great lordes, to be magnificent in their giftes, and verie attemptiue in their commaundements. **1596** SHAKS. *Merch. V.* v. i. 70 Your spirits are attentiue. **1622** T. SCOTT *Belg. Pismire* 41 Diligent and attentiue at their workes. **1711** ADDISON *Spect.* No. 3 ¶ 4 The news .. to which she was exceedingly attentive. **1866** G. MACDONALD *Ann. Q. Neighb.* viii. (1878) 134 A more attentive and devout worshipper was not in the congregation.

b. Of or pertaining to attention as a psychological concept.

1890 BALDWIN *Handbk. Psychol.* v. 69 A strong effort of attentive thought. **1890** W. JAMES *Princ. Psychol.* I. xi. 420 All forms of attentive effort would be exercised at once. **1892** J. SULLY *Human Mind* I. iv. 75 The region of clear consciousness or of attentive consciousness. *Ibid.* ix. 301 The process of attentive integration is really more complex than is here supposed. **1898** TITCHENER *Primer Psychol.* v. 84 The attentive state. **1901** —— *Exper. Psychol.* I. II. viii. 186 There are serious differences of opinion concerning the nature of the attentive consciousness. **1934** *Jrnl. Social Psychol.* V. 314 An investigation of the attentive activity of preschool children.

2. Assiduous in ministering to the comfort or pleasure of others, giving watchful heed to their wishes; polite, courteous.

c **1570** TURBERV. *To late friend* (R.) Beware That you attentiue be on hir. **1709** ADD. & STEELE *Tatler* No. 81 ¶ 3, I saw most of them attentive to three Sirens. *Mod.* Very attentive to the ladies.

a'ttentively, *adv.* Also 4–6 **-ifly**, **-ifely**. [orig. a variant of the earlier ENTENTIVELY, assimilated to L. *attentè*; in later usage f. ATTENTIVE + -LY². Cf. aphet. TENTIVELY.] With attention; with steady application of mind, energies, or senses; with careful consideration; observantly, heedfully.

1382 WYCLIF *Joshua* xxii. 5 That ȝe kepen attentifly [Vulg. *attente*] .. the maundement. **1477** EARL RIVERS (Caxton) *Dictes* 39 The wyseman thenketh on the wele of his saule .. attentyuely. **1659** *Gentl. Call.* (1696) 2 A Manual .. frequently and attentively perused.

1790 BOSWELL *Johnson* (1848) 228/2 He listened to it very attentively. **1876** GREEN *Short Hist.* vi. §4 (1882) 312 The physical aspects of society were cared for as attentively as its moral.

a'ttentiveness. [f. as prec. + -NESS. Cf. the earlier ENTENTIVENESS, TENTIVENESS.] The quality of being attentive; heed, attention.

1549 CHALONER tr. *Erasm. Moriæ Enc.* E ij b, Vouchsafe me your eares and attentivenesse. *a* **1656** HALES *Gold. Rem.* (1688) 31 To have held your attentiveness with new and quaint conceits. **1742** RICHARDSON *Pamela* III. 404 Polly heard me with more attentiveness than I expected. **1820** *Indicator* 11 Oct. (1822) 6 Their .. spirits carry them away from a proper attentiveness to others. **1921** *Contemp. Rev.* Sept. 366 A wider degree of attentiveness involving eye, ear, and the gregarious instinct.

attently (ə'tɛntlɪ), *adv. arch.* [f. ATTENT *a.* + -LY².] Attentively, with heed or attention.

1562 N. WINGATE *Tractate* (1835) 6 To watch attently and continually upon your flock. **1647** JER. TAYLOR *Dissuas. Popery* ii. (1686) 158 Say your prayers or offices attently, reverently and devoutly. **1866** NEALE *Seq. & Hymns* 137 Listen attentlier yet.

attenuable (ə'tɛnjuːəb(ə)l), *a.* ? *Obs.* [f. L. *attenuā-re* to ATTENUATE: see -BLE.] That may be attenuated or made thinner.

1658 SIR T. BROWNE *Hydriot.* iii. 29 The attenuable parts ascend.

attenuant (ə'tɛnjuːənt), *a.* and *sb.* Also 8 **-ent**. [a. F. *atténuant*, ad. L. *attenuāntem*, pr. pple. of *attenuāre to* ATTENUATE: see -ANT.]

A. *adj.* Having the property of attenuating; *spec.* in *Med.* of thinning the humours or secretions.

1603 HOLLAND *Plutarch's Mor.* 642 (R.) They put into the stomach those things that be attenuant. **1756** C. LUCAS *Ess. Waters* III. 151 The attenuent diluting .. qualities of the water. **1855** DORAN *Hanover Q.* II. i. 11 [Eringo] root was attenuant and deobstruent.

B. *sb.* A drug or agent having this property.

1725 HUXHAM in *Phil. Trans.* XXXIII. 392 One seasonable vomit .. acting as an Attenuant. **1830** LINDLEY *Nat. Syst. Bot.* 67 The fruit of .. Belleric Myrobalan is an astringent, tonic, and attenuant.

attenuate (ə'tɛnjuːeɪt), *v.* [f. L. *attenuāt-* ppl. stem of *attenuāre*, f. *at-* = *ad-* to + *tenuāre* to make thin, f. *tenuis* thin. Cf. F. *atténuer*, 12th c.]

1. To make thin or slender in girth or diameter (*e.g.* by natural or artificial shaping, drawing out, wearing down, starving, physical decay).

1530 PALSGR. 440/1, I attenuate, I make thynne, *Jattenue.* **1621** BURTON *Anat. Mel.* I. ii. III. x. (1651) 111 They crucifie the soul of man, attenuate our bodies. **1668** CULPEPPER & COLE tr. *Barthol. Anat.* I. xvii. 47 The Ureters in their progress are not attenuated within, as other Vessels are. **1794** SULLIVAN *View Nat.* I. 47 This shell also being attenuated .. the surface of the earth will tumble in. **1848** MRS. JAMESON *Sacr. & Leg. Art* (1850) 203 The wasted unclad form is seen attenuated by vigils. **1876** BANCROFT *Hist. U.S.* III. iii. 344 To attenuate them by gently drawing them out.

2. a. To make thin in consistency, to separate the particles of a substance, to diminish density, rarefy.

1594 PLAT *Jewell-ho.* I. 40 Earth beeing attenuated becommeth water. **1691** E. TAYLOR *Behmen's Theos. Phil.* 187 The Suns lustre attenuateth the gross air. **1756** C. LUCAS *Ess. Waters* I. 48 Burning spirits .. are oils attenuated and subtilised by the action of fermentation. **1762** tr. *Duhamel's Husb.* I. iii. 5 Salt, for example, may attenuate earth. **1874** [see ATTENUATED 2.]

b. *spec.* in *Med.* To render thinner (the humours or concretions of the body).

1533 ELYOT *Cast. Helth* II. xiv. (R.) Dry figges..havinge power to attenuate or make humours currant. **1605** TIMME *Quersit.* I. xiii. 64 O[y]le of pepper doth attenuat..tartarus matters in the body. **1797** DOWNING *Disord. Horn. Cattle* 13 These medicines..powerfully attenuate the cloggy disposition of the blood.

3. *fig.* To weaken or reduce in force, effect, amount; in value, estimation; (*obs.*) to extenuate.

1530 PALSGR. 440/1 He hath attenuat my power. **1579** LYLY *Euphues* (Arb.) 49 The delightfulnesse of the one will attenuate the tediousnesse of the other. *c* **1645** HOWELL *Lett.* (1650) I. 335 The Mahometans..attenuated their numbers in Asia. **1660** A. SIDNEY in *Four C. Eng. Lett.* 119 To aggravate that, which he doth intend to attenuate. **1850** *Q. Rev.* June 15 Some Notes..intended to attenuate the authority of the Christian philosopher. **1869** LECKY *Europ. Mor.* I. i. 117 To attenuate..his own appetites and emotions.

4. *intr.* To become slender, thinner, or weaker.

a **1834** COLERIDGE (in Webster), The attention attenuates as its sphere contracts.

5. *Electr.* To introduce attenuation; in *pass.*, to be subjected to attenuation. Cf. ATTENUATION 4.

1886 LORD RAYLEIGH in *Phil. Mag.* 5th Ser. XXII. 490 If we had the means of observing the passage of signals at various points of a long cable, we should find them not merely retarded..as we recede from the sending end, but also attenuated. **1892** HEAVISIDE *Electr. Papers* II. 133 The act of reflection attenuates. *Ibid.* 346 During transmission along the circuit, the vibrations are attenuated. **1959** *Chambers's Encycl.* VII. 696/2 The lower part of the Heaviside layer is of particular importance..because it is in this region that radio waves used for long-distance communication are attenuated.

attenuate (əˈtɛnjuːət), *ppl. a.* [ad. L. *attenuātus*, pa. pple. of *attenuāre*: see prec.] Made thin.

1. Slender, thin; tapered, reduced to thinness.

1848 DANA *Zooph.* 161 Tentacles numerous, attenuate, diaphanous. **1864** MRS. H. WOOD *Shad. Ashlydyat* (1878) 433 She saw the white and wan face, the attenuate hands. **1880** GRAY *Bot. Text-bk.* 398 *Attenuate*, slenderly tapering or narrow.

2. Thin in consistency, rarefied; refined.

1626 BACON *Sylva* §938 Such a rare and attenuate substance, as is the spirit of living creatures. **1647** H. MORE *Song of Soul* III. Pref./1 The life of the body..hinders us of the sight of more attenuate phantasmes. **1879** G. MEREDITH *Egoist* I. xiv. 255 The idea is too exquisitely attenuate.

a'ttenuated, *ppl. a.* [f. ATTENUATE *v.* + -ED.]

1. Made thin or slender in girth or transverse thickness (by natural shaping, mechanical reduction, starving, or wasting); tapered off; fine-drawn.

1677 PLOT *Oxfordsh.* 107 From the basis there issue..five tails of serpents, waved and attenuated. **1742** YOUNG *Nt. Th.* I. 179 The spider's most attenuated thread. **1840** HOOD *Up Rhine* (1869) 250 The venerable pastor thrust his attenuated fingers into the flame. **1853** KANE *Grinnell Exp.* I. (1856) 484 As attenuated as parchment.

2. Made thin in consistency; rarefied, diluted.

c **1610** CHAPMAN *Hymne to Hermes* 58 Steele..did raise..the attenuated baies To that hot vapor. **1635** N. CARPENTER *Geog. Del.* II. ix. 148 The vapours are too much attenuated and rarified. **1823** LAMB *Elia* I. iii, Attenuated small beer. **1874** MOSELEY *Astron.* lxix. 202 A huge ring of attenuated matter..girds the planet. **1876** M. DAVIES *Unorth. Lond.* 74 That most attenuated of all things, the shadow of a shade. *fig.* **1827** *Gent. Mag.* XCVII. II. 494 A more attenuated and enlarged standard of thought.

3. Weakened in intensity, force, effect, value.

1828 CARLYLE *Misc.* (1857) I. 217 A certain attenuated cosmopolitanism had taken place of the old insular home feeling. **1882** *Manch. Guard.* 22 Sept. 5 An 'attenuated' or modified bacteria.

† **a'ttenuater, -or.** *Med. Obs.* [f. as prec. + -ER[1].] = ATTENUANT *sb.*

1684 tr. *Bonet's Merc. Compit.* III. 89 Decoctions of Guaiacum and other attenuaters. **1783** C. BRYANT *Flora Diæt.* 99 The plant was in high esteem formerly as an attenuater.

a'ttenuating, *ppl. a.* [f. as prec. + -ING[2].] Making thinner; in *Med.* = ATTENUANT *a.*

1616 SURFL. & MARKH. *Countr. Farm* 552 Such as haue need of a fine and attenuating nourishment. **1822** BURROWES *Cycl.* II. 550/1 Caryophyllaceæ..are reckoned astringent, attenuating and detersive.

attenuation (əˌtɛnjuːˈeɪʃən). [ad. L. *attenuātiōn-em*, n. of action f. *attenuāre* to ATTENUATE: see -ATION. Cf. F. *atténuation*.] The action of attenuating; attenuated condition.

1. The making thin or slender in transverse measure; diminution of thickness; emaciation.

a **1631** DONNE *Select.* (1840) 265 Neither in a superfluous and cumbersome fatness, nor in an uncomely..attenuation. **1849** MURCHISON *Siluria* iii. 60 The omissions of certain deposits in some parts, and their attenuation in others. **1870** DISRAELI *Lothair* vi. 20 His stature seemed magnified by the attenuation of his form.

2. The making less dense; diminution of density. *spec.* in brewing and distilling.

1594 PLAT *Jewell-ho.* I. 40 All those elements doo onely differ in attenuation and condensation. **1646** SIR T. BROWNE *Pseud. Ep.* 159 Heat doth..rarifie that body [*i.e.* air], and by attenuation..disposeth it for expulsion. **1732** ARBUTHNOT *Rules of Diet* 273 The Attenuation of the Aliment makes it perspirable. **1873** WATTS *Fownes' Chem.* 576 The diminished density, or attenuation of the wort. **1882** W. T. BRANNT tr. *Thausing's Beer* 707 The decrease in density [of the beer-worts] is called attenuation. **1956** *New Biol.* XXI. 17 Beers..which are satisfactory in respect of attenuation.

3. The process of weakening, as if by dilution; diminution of characteristic force. *spec.* of a disease, or of the pathogenicity of a micro-organism. Also *attrib.*

1868 M. PATTISON *Academ. Org.* §5. 149 The process by which the results of philosophy are rendered popular is not one of attenuation but of translation. **1882** *Manch. Guard.* 22 Sept. 5 The gradual 'attenuation' of disease germs. **1944** C. D. DARLINGTON in *Nature* 5 Aug. 167/1 In the attenuation process, the nucleus is mutafacient with respect to the virus. **1964** M. HYNES *Med. Bacteriol.* (ed. 8) vi. 62 The virulence of a given organism can often be reduced by physical means such as drying or heat. The reduction of virulence is known as attenuation.

4. *Electr.* The decrease in amplitude of an electrical signal or current. Also *attrib.*

1887 HEAVISIDE in *Electrician* 24 June 143/2 The idea of attenuation, expressed in a more roundabout manner in terms such as diminution of amplitude, and so forth, is nothing new; the *word* 'attenuation' I found Lord Rayleigh use, and at once adopted it myself. **1931** *B.B.C. Year-Bk.* 436/2 *Attenuation Factor*, a factor indicating the rate of reduction in amplitude of an ether wave as the distance from the point of origin increases. **1931** *Wireless World* 2 Sept. 228/1 The attenuation of the higher modulation frequencies. **1935** *Discovery* Sept. 278/2 The cut-off or attenuation of television signals, due to intervening obstructions.

† **attenuative**, *a.* and *sb. Med. Obs.* [f. L. *attenuāt-* (see ATTENUATE *v.*) + -IVE.] **A.** *adj.* Attenuating, attenuant. **B.** *sb.* An attenuating agent, an attenuant.

1656 RIDGLEY *Pract. Physick* 105 The spleen cannot endure Attenuatives. **1684** tr. *Bonet's Merc. Compit.* VI. 211 Its heat and attenuative virtue.

attenuator (əˈtɛnjuːeɪtə(r)). *Electr.* [f. ATTENUATE *v.* + -OR.] A device which introduces attenuation.

1924 *Wireless World* 3 Sept. 643 The mechanical filter, or as it has sometimes been termed..the mechanical attenuator. **1931** *B.B.C. Year-Bk.* 436/2 *Attenuator*, an arrangement of calibrated resistances to introduce loss into a circuit. **1963** B. FOZARD *Instrumentation Nucl. Reactors* x. 122 Variation of the over-all gain is effected by the use of switched resistance attenuator networks.

attenuity (ætəˈnjuːɪtɪ). [f. ATTENUATE after *tenuity*.] = TENUITY I.

1830 *Blackw. Mag.* XXVIII. 387 Not so much as the taperest wine-glass wire-woven into almost invisible attenuity. **1861** *Temple Bar* III. 437 No cotton-yarn of such attenuity as this can be..woven. **1898** *Echo* 22 June 1/4 Drawing his thin willowy form..to its full attenuity.

† **'atter**, *sb. Obs.* or *dial.* Forms: 1 **átr, átor, attor, ættor,** 1–6 **ater,** 1–9 **atter;** also 3 **aterr,** 4 **attere,** 4–5 **attur, hoter,** 5 **hatter,** 5–6 **attir,** 5–7 **attyr,** 6 **atir, etter.** [Common Teut.: with OE. *átr, átor, attor*, cf. OHG. *eitar, eittar*, mod.G. *eiter*, OS. *êtar*, ON. *eitr*, (Sw. *etter*, Da. *edder*,) Du. *eyter, etter*. The original long vowel (giving ME. *ōter*) has been irregularly shortened in Eng., as also in other of the modern languages.]

† **1.** Poison, venom, *esp.* that of reptiles. *Obs.*

c **1000** *Sax. Leechd.* II. 112 Wiþ fleoȝendum atre & ælcum æternum swile. *c* **1175** *Lamb. Hom.* 169 Atter meind mid wine. **1377** LANGL. *P. Pl.* B. XII. 256 And alle þe oþer..enuenymeþ þorgh his attere. *c* **1400** *Destr. Troy* III. 920 And withdroghe the deire of his dere attur. *fig. c* **1175** *Lamb. Hom.* 75 Þan depliche atter þet þe alde deouel blou on Adam. *c* **1230** *Ancr. R.* 80 Habbeð wlatunge of þe muðe þet speoweð ut atter.

† **2.** Gall; *fig.* bitterness. *Obs.*

a **700** *Epinal Gloss.* 141, *Corpus* 297, *Bile*, átr. *c* **1175** *Lamb. Hom.* 23 A lutel ater bitteret muchele swete. *c* **1320** *Cast. Loue* 1150 Atter heo him dude to drinke i-meynt wᵗ eisil. *c* **1430** *Hymns to Virg.* (1867) 24, I may drede at my departynge þat it wole be attir & ille.

3. Corrupt matter, pus, from a sore, ulcer, abscess, etc. Still in *Sc.* and *north. dial.*

1398 TREVISA *Barth. De P.R.* IV. vii. (1495) 90 Vnkynde blood and hoter. **1483** CAXTON *Gold. Leg.* 326/1 Of kyrnellys and botches of his face..ranne grete plente of blood and atter. **1535** COVERDALE *Job* ii. 7 And scraped of the etter off his sores with a potsherde. **1601** HOLLAND *Pliny* II. 422 Ears that run attyr. **1643** HORN & ROBOTHAM *Gate Lang. Unl.* xxv. §318 A green wound..rotted into a gory venemous atter. **1864** ATKINSON *Whitby Gloss.*, *Atter* or *Atteril*, the matter of a sore..The tongue is said to be covered with 'a dry white atter,' when furred with fever.

† **'atter**, *v. Obs.* [OE. *ǽtrian, ættrian*, f. prec.]

1. To poison, envenom. Also *fig.*

c **885** K. ÆLFRED *Oros.* III. ix. §18 For ȝeǽtredum ȝescótum. *c* **1175** *Lamb. Hom.* 75 Hore loking..hore smelling, heore feling was al iattret. *c* **1230** *Ancr. R.* 84 Oðer speche soileð..ac þeos attreð þe heorte & te earen boðe.

2. To mix with gall, embitter.

c **1400** *Destr. Troy* VI. 2286 Or all so myght aunter to atter for euer.

atter, obsolete form of OTTER.

† **'attercop.** *Obs.* or *dial.* Forms: 1 **attorcoppa,** 1–5 **attercoppe,** 4 **atturcoppe, addurcop,** 5 **attyrcope, -coppe,** 6 **att-, addircop,** 7 **attercob,** 9 **attercap,** 4–9 **attercop.** [OE. *attorcoppa*, f. *átor*, *attor*, poison + *coppa*, deriv. of *cop* top, summit, round head, or *copp* cup, vessel; in reference to the supposed venomous properties of spiders. Cf. also Du. *spinne-cop* 'spider,' and COB-WEB, formerly *cop-webbe*; whence it appears probable that the simple *coppa* was itself = 'spider.']

1. A spider.

c **1000** *Sax. Leechd.* I. 92 Wiþ attorcoppan bite. *a* **1250** *Owl & Night.* 600 Wat etestu..Bute attercoppe and fule vliȝe? ? *c* **1350** *MS.* in *R. Brunne's Chron.* (Hearne) Pref. 200 An atturcoppe cum owte..and bote hem by the nekkus ..þat II. of hem weron deed. **1382** WYCLIF *Isa.* lix. 5 The webbis of an attercop [**1388** an yreyn]. *a* **1400** *Metr. Gloss.* in Wright's *Voc.* 177 *Aranea*, addurcop. *c* **1425** WYNTOUN *Cron.* VIII. xi. 46 Alsa kobbyd in his crope As he had ettyn ane attyrcope. *a* **1450** *Knt. de la Tour* (1868) 63 The attercoppe..makithe his nettes to take the flyes. **1658** ROWLAND *Mouffet's Theat. Ins.* 1058 The English[call it] Attercop, Spider, Spinner. **1691** RAY *N. Countr. Wds.* 139 Attercop.

2. *fig.* Applied to a venomous malignant person.

c **1505** KENNEDIE *Flyting* 523 Thow irefull attircop, Pilate, apostata. **1881** W. PATTERSON *Antrim Gloss.* (E.D.S.) *Attercap*, cross-grained, ill-natured person, 'Ya cross attercap, ya.'

3. Misapplied to: A spider's web.

1530 PALSGR. 193/1 Addircop, or a spinner's web, *araignee*. **1674** RAY *N. Countr. Wds.* 3 An Attercob, A Spiders Web. *Cumberland*. **1873** R. FERGUSON *Cumberld. Dial.* (E.D.S.).

attere, ME. coalesced f. *at the*: see AT *prep.*

atteril, dial. variant of ATTER *sb.*

† **'attering**, *ppl. a. Obs.* [f. ATTER *v.* + -ING[2].] Poisoning, venomous.

c **1440** *Epiph.* (Turnb. 1843) 154 On face and hondis thei had gret nayles And grette hornes and atteryng taylys.

† **'atterlich**, *a. Obs. rare*[−1]. [OE. *áterlíc*: see ATTER *sb.* and -LY[1].] Venomous; bitter.

c **1050** in Wright *Voc.* (W.) /414 *Gorgoneo*, Aterlicum oððe biter. *c* **1230** *Ancr. R.* 212 þe atterluche deouel.

† **'atterliche**, *adv. Obs. rare*[−1]. [f. prec.: see -LY[2].] Bitterly.

c **1400** *St. Alexius* (Laud 463) 143 Þo she of swounyng ros, Atterliche hir agros.

† **'atterling.** *Obs. rare*[−1]. [f. ATTER *sb.* + -LING.] A venomous malignant person, a shrew.

c **1430** in *Babees Bk.* (1868) 38 Meekely þou him answere, And not as an attirling.

† **'atterlothe.** *Herb. Obs.* [OE. *átor-, attorláðe*, f. ATTER *sb.* + *láð* hostile.] An antidote to poison, an alexipharmic. Applied *spec.* to several different plants: see quot.

c **1000** *Sax. Leechd.* I. 148 Ðeos wyrt þe man *galli crus*, & oðrum naman attorlaðe nemneð. *c* **1000** ÆLFRIC *Gloss.* in Wright *Voc.* (W.) /133 *Venenifuga*, atterlaðe. *c* **1050** *Gloss.* ibid. /358 *Bettonica*, aterlaðe. *c* **1230** *Ancr. R.* 274 Gif hit to swuð swelle..drinc þeonne atterloðe. *c* **1250** *Voc. Plants* in Wright *Voc.* /558 *Morella*, atterloþe.

† **a'tterminate**, *v. Obs. rare*[−1]. [f. L. *attermināre*: see ATTERMINE *v.* and -ATE[3].] To attermine. Hence **a'tterminated** *ppl. a.*

1738 *Hist. Crt. Excheq.* vi. 99 Payments of atterminated Debts.

† **a,ttermi'nation.** *Obs. rare*[−1]. [n. of action f. prec.: see -ATION.] Appointment of a term for the payment of a debt; = ATTERMINEMENT.

1738 *Hist. Crt. Excheq.* v. 100 If he did not pay according to the Attermination.

a'ttermine, *v.* ? *Obs.* Also 5 **aterm-.** [a. OF. *atermine-r*, ad. L. *atterminā-re*, f. *at-* = *ad-* to + *termināre* to set bounds to, f. *terminus* bound, limit. See AT- *pref.*[3]] To settle the limit or term of, fix a future date for; *esp.* to adjourn payment of (a debt) till a day fixed. Hence **a'ttermining** *vbl. sb.* = next word.

1413 LYDG. *Pylgr. Sowle* v. i. 74 Many honderd yeres.. whiche though the nombre be vnknowen to man, yet it is atermyned at a certeyne ende in the siȝt of god. **1618** PULTON *Coll. Stat.* 27 Edw. I, Such as will purchase Attermining of their Debts. **1809** TOMLINS *Law Dict.*, *Attermining* the granting a time or term for payment of a debt.

† **a'tterminement.** *Obs. rare*[−1]. [a. AF. *atterminement*, OF. *aterm-*, f. *aterminer*: see prec. and -MENT.] Adjournment of the payment of a debt to a fixed future date.

[**1299** *Act 27 Edw. I, De Lib. perqu.*, Ceux qux voudrount purchaser attermynement de lour dettez soyent envoyez al escheqer.] **1543** BERTHELET transl., Suche as wyl purchase attermynemente of theyr dettes.

† **'attern**, *a. Obs.* or *dial.* Also 3 **hatterne.** [OE. *ǽtren, ættren, ættern*, f. *átor*: see ATTER *sb.* and -EN[1].] Venomous, poisonous; malignant.

c **950** *Lindisf. Gosp.* Matt. xii. 34 Cynn æterna, hu maga ȝe godo spreca? **1205** LAY. 16084 He þurh atterne [**1250** hatterne] drench dæð scal iþolien. **1868** HALLIWELL *Dict.*, *Attern*, fierce, cruel, snarling. *Gloucester*.

† **'atterness.** *Obs. rare*⁻¹. [f. prec. + -NESS.] Malignity, bitterness.
c **1230** *Ancr. R.* 196 þe ueond kundeliche eggeð us to atternesse, as to prude, to ouerhowe, to onde, & to wreððe.

† **a'tterr,** *v. Obs.* [a. F. *atterre-r*, or It. *atterrare*, f. *à* to + F. *terre*, It. *terra*, L. *terra* earth.] To bring to the ground, humble.
1598 SYLVESTER *Du Bartas* II. Ded. (1641) 74 Your renown alone Atterrs the stubborn and attracts the prone. **1614** —— *Bethulian* IV. 2 Judith the while, trils Rivers from her eyes, Atterrs her knees.

† **'atterrate,** *v. Obs.* [f. It. *atterrare* 'to fill or dam vp with earth' (Florio 1598), f. *a.* to + *terra* earth. Cf. OF. *aterrer, aterrir* in same sense.] To fill up with earth, *esp.* with alluvial earth.
1673 RAY *Journ. Low Countr.* 7 Filling up and atterrating (to borrow that word of the Italians) the skirts and borders of the Sea. **1757** DA COSTA in *Phil. Trans.* L. 234 If these effects proceed from local deluges, recedings of the sea, gulphs atterrated, etc.

† **atte'rration.** *Obs.* [n. of action f. prec.: see -ATION.] The action of filling up with earth; the washing up of alluvial soil.
1686 PLOT *Staffordsh.* 113 All valleys rise by atterration, i.e. by Earth continually brought down from the tops of Mountains by Rains and Snows. **1713** DERHAM *Phys-Theol.* 53 No accidental Currents and Atterrations of the Waters themselves..could ever have made or found so long and commodious Declivities and Channels. **1757** DA COSTA in *Phil. Trans.* L. 235 Producible by local deluges, atterrations.

† **'attery, 'attry,** *a. Obs.* or *dial.* Forms: 2–3 attri, 3 attriȝ, 3–6 attrie, 4 attre, 4–5 attry(e, 5–9 attery. [f. ATTER *sb.* + -Y¹.]
1. Venomous, poisonous.
c **1000** *Sax. Leechd.* I. 152 Gif hwa mid his fet of stepð ættriȝ bansnacan. *c* **1220** *Hali Meid.* 15 Earewen idrencte of an attri haliwei. *c* **1230** *Ancr. R.* 288 His teð beoð attrie, ase of ane wode dogge.
2. Mixed with gall, bitter. *lit.* and *fig.*
c **1230** *Ancr. R.* 188 þet attri drunc þet me ȝef him, þeo him þurste o rode. *Ibid.* 190 þauh hit þunche attri, hit is þauh healuwinde.
3. Malignant, malicious, spiteful.
c **1200** ORMIN 9785 All fulle off attriȝ lund And fulle of bitterr spæche. *c* **1386** CHAUCER *Pers. T.* ¶ 509 Thanne cometh of ire attry anger. **1535** STEWART *Cron. Scot.* II. 493 With atrie visage and with glowrand ene. **1868** HALLIWELL *Dict., Attery*, irascible, choleric. *West.*
4. Full of morbid or bloody matter.
1535 STEWART *Cron. Scot.* III. 431 With bludie woundis so attrie and reid. **1868** HALLIWELL *Dict., Attery*, purulent. *East.*

attest (ə'tɛst), *v.* [a. F. *atteste-r*, OF. *atester*, ad. L. *attestā-ri*, f. *at-* = *ad-* to + *testā-ri* to bear witness, f. *testis* witness.]
1. a. *trans.* To bear witness to, affirm the truth or genuineness of; to testify, certify. Const. *simple obj., subord. cl., inf. phr.*, or *absol.*
1596 SPENSER *F.Q.* II. i. 37 Live thou! and to thy mother dead attest That cleare she dide from blemish criminall. **1667** MILTON *P.L.* IX. 367 Thy constancie..who can know, Not seeing thee attempted, who attest? **1718** POPE *Iliad* III. 569 Ye Trojans..Hear and attest! **1725** —— *Odyss.* XIX. 211 Idomeneus, whom Ilian fields attest Of matchless deed. **1875** J. CURTIS *Hist. Eng.* 154 The merit of the English bowmen..is strongly attested by Froissart.
b. formally (*a*) by signature, (*b*) by oath.
1665 MANLEY *Grotius' Low-C. Wars* 463 The publick Instruments of this League..were solemnly attested with publick Joy. **1670** MILTON *Hist. Eng.* VI. (1851) 262 For fear or hope of reward they attested what was not true. **1708** SWIFT *Bickerstaff Det.* Wks. 1755 II. I. 163, I will assert nothing here, but what I dare attest. **1836** [see ATTESTER].
2. *transf.* of things: To be evidence or proof of, testify to, vouch for.
1599 SHAKS. *Hen. V.* I. Cho. 16 Since a crooked Figure may Attest in little place, a Million. **1794** SULLIVAN *View Nat.* II, Physical appearances attest the high antiquity of the globe. **1876** GREEN *Short Hist.* i. §4 (1882) 37 Forty-five works remained after his death to attest his prodigious industry.
3. *intr.* To bear witness, testify *to*.
1672 WILKINS *Nat. Relig.* 302 To the reasonableness of this, several of the wisest heathens have attested. **1875** SCRIVENER *Lect. Grk. Test.* 15 The principal witnesses which attest to it.
4. *trans.* To call to witness. *arch.* or *Obs.* (So in Fr.)
1606 SHAKS. *Tr.& Cr.* II. ii. 132 But I attest the gods, your full consent Gaue wings to my propension. **1796** T. JEFFERSON in Sparks *Corr. Amer. Rev.* (1853) IV. 483, I attest everything sacred and honorable to the declaration. **1880** BLACKMORE *M. Anerley* III. i. 8 Flamborough had called to witness Filey, and Filey had attested Bridlington.
5. To put (a man) on his oath; *techn.* among 'Friends,' to put him on his solemn declaration. Also, to administer the oath of allegiance to a military recruit (see quot. 1812); used esp. in connection with the 'Derby Scheme' of 1915. Also *intr.*, to enrol oneself as ready for military service when called up.
1685 *Col. Records Penn.* I. 148 It was against their methods to take an Oath, but if he pleased to be attested, according to yᵉ Laws of the Province, they would attest him. *Ibid.* Then he was attested thus: Thou dost Solemnly declare in yᵉ Presents of God, and before this board, that thou will truly and Justly performe yᵉ office of yᵉ King's Collector. **1812** WELLINGTON in Gurw. *Disp.* IX. 153 They are to be attested according to the following form..I, A.B. do make oath, etc. **1915** LD. DERBY in *Times* 20 Oct. 10/1 They would be medically examined, and, if found fit, attested there and then. **1917** J. H. WORRALL *Tribunal Hand-bk.* 128 Police magistrates who..will not..see that the attested man before them is shorn of justice, because, unfortunately for him, he attested. **1922** *Encycl. Brit.* XXX. 212/2 In Oct. 1915, the 'Derby Scheme' or 'Group System' was initiated by Lord Derby... Between Oct. 25 and the middle of Dec. 2,000,000 men were attested under this system.

attest (ə'tɛst), *sb.* [f. prec. vb.]
1. Evidence, testimony, witness.
1606 SHAKS. *Tr. & Cr.* v. ii. 122 (*Qo.*) A credence in my heart..That doth inuert th' attest [*Folio* that test] of eyes and eares. **1646** SIR T. BROWNE *Pseud. Ep.* (1650) 143 Nor will the attest or prescript of Philosophers..be a sufficient ground. **1830** WORDSW. *Egypt. Maid*, Here must a high attest be given, What Bridegroom was for her ordained by Heaven.
2. Attesting signature, attestation.
1649 SELDEN *Laws Eng.* II. Pref. (1739) 6 The attests of the King's Chaplain and his Scribe, do shew also that they were not all Members of the House of Lords.

attestable (ə'tɛstəb(ə)l), *a.* [f. as prec. + -ABLE.] That may be attested or borne witness to.
1768 WALES in *Phil. Trans.* LX. 108 Circumstances.. attestable by too great a cloud of witnesses to be disputed.

attestant (ə'tɛstənt), *ppl. a.* and *sb.* [ad. L. *attestānt-em*, pr. pple. of *attestāri* to ATTEST: see -ANT.] **A.** *ppl. adj.* Attesting, bearing witness. **B.** *sb.* One who attests (by signature), an attester.
1880 H. COOTE *Gild of Knts.* 8, A MS. deed to which these knights are attestants.

† **a'ttestate,** *sb. Obs. rare.* Also 7 **-at.** [f. L. *attestāt-* ppl. stem of *attestāri* to ATTEST: see -ATE¹.] An attestation, testimony, proof.
1630 LORD *Banians* Ep. Ded., Let it be an attestate of my acknowledgments to you. **1656** EARL MONM. *Advt. fr. Parnass.* 134 The true attestat of Guicchardin..that it is more usual for an officer to run hazard, then for a merchant to break.

† **a'ttestate,** *v. Obs. rare*⁻¹. [f. as prec.: see -ATE³.] To attest.
1652 SPARKE *Prim. Devot.* (1663) 523 Which the sacred Scripture most contracts, and best attestates.

attestation (ætɪ'steɪʃən). [a. F. *attestation*, ad. L. *attestātiōn-em*, n. of action f. *attestāri* to ATTEST: see -ATION.]
1. The action of bearing witness; the testimony borne; evidence, proof.
1598 FLORIO *Testatione*, an attestation or bearing witnes. **1631** MASSINGER *Beleeve as you list* II. ii, The reasons this man urges To prove hymselfe Antiochus..And the attestation of his cuntriemen. **1788** REID *Act. Powers* I. v. 524 No necessary truth can have its attestation from experience. **1869** GOULBURN *Purs. Holiness* iv. 31 He wrought every sort of cure in attestation of his claims.
b. Formal testimony or confirmation by signature, oath, etc.; *esp.* the verification of the execution of a deed or will by the signature of the testator in the presence of witnesses.
1674 *Ch. & Crt. of Rome* 13 That strange Solemnity of Attestation, the apprecating Destruction to those of his Family. **1768** BLACKSTONE *Comm.* II. 307 The last requisite to the validity of a deed is the attestation, or execution of it in the presence of witnesses. **1824** W. IRVING *T. Trav.* II. 13, I bowed down, and kissed the turf, in solemn attestation of my vow. **1858** LD. ST. LEONARDS *Handy Bk. Prop. Law* XVIII. 136 The attestation should be..in this form:—Signed by the above-named testator, in the presence of us present at the same time, who have hereunto signed our names.
†**2.** The action of calling to witness. *Obs.*
1547 *Homilies* I. *Of Swearing* G j b, When men make faithful promises with attestacion of the name of God. **1741** BETTERTON in Oldys *Eng. Stage* vi. 91 In Swearing or.. Attestation of any Thing to the Verity of what you say.
3. The administration of an oath, *e.g.* of the oath of allegiance to a military recruit.
1812 WELLINGTON in Gurw. *Disp.* IX. 153 They are to receive pay from the date of their attestation. **1844** *Regul. & Ord. Army* 307 Showing the date and term of his enlistment, and of his attestation.

attestative (ə'tɛstətɪv), *a.* [f. L. *attestāt-* ppl. stem of *attestāri* to ATTEST: see -ATIVE.] Of the nature of, or pertaining to, attestation.
a **1832** BENTHAM *Wks.* (1838) I. 374 Attestative satisfaction: arising from establishing truth by evidence against a false statement prejudicial to one. **1827** I. TAYLOR *Transm. Anc. Bks.* (1859) 207 Mutually attestative evidence of thousands of witnesses.

attestator (ætɪ'steɪtə(r)). ? *Obs.* [n. of agent after L. analogies (cf. It. *attestatore*, Florio) f. L. *attestāri*: see ATTEST *v.* and -OR.] = ATTESTER.
1598 FLORIO, *Testatore*, a witnes, an attestator, a testifier. **1789** in J. Downes *Rosc. Angl.* 16 The persons whom the clergyman mentioned as attestators to his character.

attested (ə'tɛstɪd), *ppl. a.* [f. ATTEST *v.* + -ED.] **a.** Sworn, vouched for, certified, proved.
1611 COTGR., *Attesté*, attested, protested, avouched, affirmed. **1711** F. FULLER *Med. Gymn.* 86 Its effects..are numerous, and some of 'em very well attested. **1873** TRISTRAM *Moab* vii. 116 An attested friend of these gentlemen.
b. Of cattle or milk: approved by authority as free from disease.
1934 *Hansard Commons* CCXC. 1131 Our programme providing..for the payment of premiums to attested herds should..bring us perhaps 1,000 herds in the first year.

attester, -or (ə'tɛstə(r), -ɔː(r)). [f. as prec. + -ER¹, -OR.] One who attests, bears witness, or vouches for.
1598 FLORIO, *Testatrice*, a woman witnes, or attester. **1663** J. SPENCER *Prodigies* (1665) 226 Suspicion of deceit of sight or imagination in the Attestors. **1705** STANHOPE *Paraphr.* II. 607 Credible Attesters of it to Others. **1836** T. DAVIES in *Brit. Annual* 322 The mode of attesting an agreement, where the attestor could not write his name.

attesting (ə'tɛstɪŋ), *vbl. sb.* [f. as prec. + -ING¹.] Attestation.
1661 SANDERSON *Episc.* 19 For the attesting of any other part of Ecclesiastical Story. **1663** GERBIER *Counsel* (1664) 47 In the attesting of Bills..not to pass his eyes slightly over them.

a'ttesting, *ppl. a.* [f. as prec. + -ING².] That bears witness to; that calls to witness (*obs.*).
1720 POPE *Iliad* XVIII. 587 Alternate each th' attesting sceptre took. **1725** —— *Odyss.* XIV. 176 What I speak attesting Heaven has heard. *a* **1859** DE QUINCEY *Wks.* XIII. 310 Under the attesting record of Pope's own sign and seal.

attestive (ə'tɛstɪv), *a. rare.* [f. as prec. + -IVE.] Attesting, furnishing evidence.
1859 in WORCESTER.

attestment (ə'tɛstmənt). *rare.* [f. as prec. + -MENT.] Attestation, testimony, proof.
1850 NEALE *Mediæv. Hymns* 155 Thus they gain their true attestment As the people's chiefs in fight.

† **a'ttex,** *v. Obs. rare*⁻¹. [ad. L. *attexĕre*, f. *at-* = *ad-* to + *texĕre* to weave.] To weave on, add.
1654 KEEK in *Sir T. Browne's Relig. Med.* To Rdr. (1672) 71 The bookseller would not be denied these notes to attex to it.

atteyn, -ant, -ment, obs. ff. ATTAIN, etc.

Attic ('ætɪk), *a.* and *sb.*¹ [ad. L. *Atticus*, Gr. Ἀττικός of Attica.]
A. *adj.* **1.** Of or pertaining to Attica, or to its capital Athens; Athenian. *Formerly* = Greek.
1599 *Broughton's Lett.* 46 You..that arrogate to your selfe the Atticke Science [*i.e.* knowledge of Greek.] **1607** DEKKER *Knts. Conjur.* (1842) 75 No Atticke eloquence is so sweete. **1835** THIRLWALL *Greece* III. xviii, A wooden theatre still sufficed for the Attic drama.
2. Having characteristics peculiarly Athenian; *hence*, of literary style, etc.: Marked by simple and refined elegance, pure, classical. ***Attic salt*** or ***wit*** (L. *sal Atticum*): refined, delicate, poignant wit. ***Attic faith***: inviolable faith.
1633 *Batt. Lutzen* in *Harl. Misc.* (Malh.) IV. 185 Written in a stile so attick..that it may well be called the French Tacitus. **1738** POPE *Epil. Sat.* II. 85 While Roman Spirit charms, and Attic Wit. **1760** STERNE *Tr. Shandy* V. iii, Triumph swam in my father's eyes, at the repartee: the Attic salt brought water into them. **1830** T. HAMILTON *Cyr. Thornton* (1845) 49 The true attic pronunciation inculcated in Mrs. Blenkinsop's academy. **1864** M. ARNOLD in *Cornh. Mag.* Aug. 164 Well, but Addison's prose is Attic prose.
3. ***Attic base*** in *Arch.*: a base used for Ionic, Corinthian, and occasionally for Doric columns, consisting of an upper and lower torus divided by a scotia and two fillets. ***Attic order***: a square column of any of the five orders.
[**1563** SHUTE *Archit.* E iiij a, That piller which Vitruuius nameth Atticurga or Attica.] **1601** HOLLAND *Pliny* XXXVI. xxiii, Pillars..of the Atticke fashion..be made with foure corners, and the sides are equall. **1727–51** CHAMBERS *Cycl.* s.v., The Attic is the most beautiful of all the bases. **1823** P. NICHOLSON *Pract. Build.* 493 The base is attic, as it is in most of the Roman antiques.
B. *sb.*¹ A native of Attica, an Athenian (author).
1699 BENTLEY *Phal.* 390 A time when the Atticks were as unlearned as their neighbours.

attic ('ætɪk), *sb.*² (orig. *adj.*). [a. F. *Attique*, ad. L. *Atticus*: see prec.]
1. A decorative structure, consisting of a small order (column and entablature) placed above another order of much greater height constituting the main façade. This was usually an Attic order, with pilasters instead of pillars; whence the name.
[**1676** FÉLIBIEN *Princ. Archit.* 481 Nous appellons aussi *Attique* dans nos bastimens un ordre que l'on met sur un autre beaucoup plus grand..Ce petit ordre n'a ordinairement que des Pilastres d'une façon particuliere, qui est à la maniere Attique dont le nom luy a esté donné.] **1696** [not in ed. 1678] PHILLIPS, *Attick*, we call Attick in our Buildings a little Order plac'd upon another much greater: for that, instead of Pillars, this Order has nothing but Pilasters of a particular Fashion and Order which is call'd Attick. **1760** RAPER in *Phil. Trans.* LI. 804 The height of the attic [in the Pantheon] above the cornice it stands upon, is 27 feet 2¾ inches. **1874** J. FERGUSSON *St. Paul's* in *Contemp. Rev.* Oct. 750 The introduction of an Attic over the main Order.
2. *attrib.* quasi-*adj.* in ***Attic storey***: originally the space enclosed by the structure described in prec. sense; *hence*, the top storey of a building,

under the beams of the roof, when there are more than two storeys above ground. So *attic-floor*, *-room*, etc.

1724 De Foe, etc. *Tour Gt. Brit.* (1769) I. 74 The Rustic and Attic Stories are 12 Feet high each. **1769** *Phil. Trans.* LIX. 72 They have no Attic story, only ware-houses, and one floor over them. **1831** Carlyle *Sart. Res.* I. iii, The attic floor of the highest house.

3. The highest storey of a house, or a room in it; a garret. *Humorously*, the 'upper storey,' the brain.

1817 Byron *Beppo* xxv, His wife would mount, at times, her highest attic. **1855** Macaulay *Hist. Eng.* III. 464 Betaking himself with his books to a small lodging in an attic. **1870** Alford in *Life* (1873) 467 Tolerably well all day, but the noise in the attic unremoved.

4. *Anat.* The upper part of the tympanum of the ear.

1889 J. Leidy *Elem. Treat. Human Anat.* (ed. 2) xvi. 893 The attic of the tympanum is a pyramidal cavity above the atrium with which it communicates by a horizontal, fore and aft oval aperture. **1891** *Med. Ann.* 159 Pathological Changes in the External 'Attic' of the Tympanic Cavity. **1900** Dorland *Med. Dict.* 87/1 *Attic*, the part of the tympanum that is situated above the atrium.

† **'Attical, 'Attican**, *a. Obs. rare*; = Attic *a.*

a **1660** Hammond *Serm.* 12 (T.) The common Attical acception of it. **1610** Healey tr. *Vives' Comm. St. Aug. City of God* (1620) 75 Gellius (not Aulus with the Attican nights).

† **a'ttice**, *v. Obs.* Forms: 5 **atyse, -ise,** 6 **attise, -yse, -ice.** [a. OF. *atisier*, *-icier*, *-icher* (mod. *attiser*), cogn. with Pr. *atizar*, Sp. *atizar*, Pg. *atiçar*, It. *attizare*:—late L. or Romanic **attitiāre*, lit. 'to put the brands of a fire closer together,' f. *at-* = *ad-* to + *titio* brand. See at- *pref.*[3] Cf. entice.] To stir up, instigate, urge to a course of action; to gain over, allure, entice.

c **1450** *Merlin* xxi. 366 He hath me atised to bataile. **1490** Caxton *Eneydos* xii. 46 Crye mercy vnto the goddis .. atyse and drawe theym by sacrifyces. **1509** Barclay *Ship of Fooles* (1570) 245 Thou makest youth such as thou doest attice To lese the vertue of manhood. **1557** Paynell *Barclay's Jugurth* 50 Attysed to the prodycion of their master.

† **a'tticement.** *Obs. rare*$^{-1}$. In 5 **atyse-.** [a. OF. *atisement* (13th c. in Littré), f. *atisier*: see prec. and -ment.] Instigation, enticement.

1483 Caxton *Gold. Leg.* 248/4 By thatysement of the deuyll he had his wyf suspecte of a knyghte.

Atticism ('ætɪsɪz(ə)m). [ad. Gr. Ἀττικισμός.]

1. Siding with, or attachment to, Athens.

1628 Hobbes *Thucyd.* viii. xxxviii, Tydeus and his accomplices were put to death for atticism. **1837** Thirlwall *Greece* IV. xxxi. 188 The charge of Atticism.

2. The peculiar style and idiom of the Greek language as used by the Athenians; *hence*, refined, elegant Greek, and *gen.* a refined amenity of speech, a well-turned phrase.

1612 T. James *Corrupt. Script.* ii. 68 Which yet for the stile and Atticismes comes a great deale short of Baronius commendation. **1642** Milton *Apol Smect.* Wks. 1851, 268 They made sport, and I laught, they mispronounc't and I mislik't, and to make up the atticisme, they were out, and I hist. **1792** Newcome *Eng. Bible Trans.* 279 (T.) An elegant atticism which occurs[in] *Luke* xiii. 9. **1813** *Examiner* 10 May 298/1 Such a man would accuse Thucydides of false grammar on account of his atticisms.

Atticist ('ætɪsɪst). [ad. Gr. Ἀττικιστ-ής: see -ist.] One who affected Attic style. Hence **Atti'cistic** *a.*

1835 *Penny Cycl.* III. 63/1 The name of Atticists was given to this artificial class of writers. **1881** *Athenæum* 2 Apr. 461/3 Phrynichus, the second century Atticist. **1919** H. J. Cadbury *Style of Luke* i. ii. 38 The gulf between New Testament Greek in general and Attic or Atticistic Greek is .. being exaggerated. **1934** A. Toynbee *Study Hist.* I. i. B. ii. 25 This phase of Hellenic history is commonly called 'the Hellenistic Age', but 'the Atticistic Age' is the proper name for it.

Atticize ('ætɪsaɪz), *v.* [ad. Gr. Ἀττικίζειν: see -ize.] Hence **Atticizing** *vbl. sb.* and *ppl. a.*

1. *intr.* To side with or favour Athens.

1753 W. Smith *Thucyd.* viii. (R.) Put to death .. for atticizing. **1849** Grote *Greece* ii. liv. VI. 618 The Thebans destroyed the walls of Thespiæ .. on the charge of atticizing tendencies.

2. To affect Attic style; to conform to Athenian or (in wider sense) Greek habits, modes of thought, etc. **a.** *intr.* **b.** *trans.*; whence **Atticized** *ppl. a.*

1610 Healey tr. *Vives' Comm. St. Aug. City of God* (1620) 631 Pherecrates, a man wholly atticizing. **1669** Gale *Crt. Gentiles* i. i. ii. 9 What is Plato but Moses Atticizing? **1846** Grote *Greece* i. xi. I. 227 The Atticised worship of the Eleusinian Dêmêter.

† **a'ttiguous,** *a. Obs.* [f. L. *attigu-us* (f. *attingĕre*: see attinge) + -ous.] Touching, contiguous.

1672 in Coles. **1721** in Bailey. (Not in J.)

Hence **a'ttiguousness,** in Bailey 1731.

† **a'ttincture.** *Obs. rare*$^{-1}$. [ad. med.L. *attinctūra*, f. *attinctus*, erroneous latinization of OF. *atteint*.] = attainture.

c **1580** J. Hooker *Sir P. Carew* in *Archæol.* XXVIII. 128 Whether anye attincture, statute, or alyenacion were made by anye of the auncesters of this gentleman.

† **'attinency.** *Obs.* [f. L. *attinēnt-em* belonging to, pr. pple. of *attinēre* to hold on to, belong to, relate to: see -ency.] The quality of belonging to; relationship.

1610 Guillim *Heraldry* ii. v. (1660) 64 In Attinency we be distinguished in Consanguinity and Affinity.

† **a'ttinge,** *v. Obs.* [ad. L. *attingĕre* to touch on, f. *at-* = *ad-* to + *tangĕre* to touch. Cf. attain, in origin the same word.]

1. To touch upon, come in contact with.

1656 Blount *Glossogr.*, *Attinge*, to touch lightly or softly; to mention or handle briefly, to reach to, to arrive or come to. **1657** Tomlinson *Renou's Disp.* 534 It helps and delights all parts it attinges. **1666** J. Smith *Old Age* (ed. 2) 78 Because they [the teeth] might the better attinge one anothers bodies. **1742** in Bailey [from Blount].

2. To touch in relationship.

a **1639** Spottiswood *Hist. Ch. Scot.* iv. (1677) 202 The Con-sanguinity standing betwixt Bothwell and his wife .. they mutually attinging others in the fourth degree.

3. To affect, influence.

1640 Bp. Reynolds *Of Passions* xxxii. (1826) VI. 247 The pollution of the soul .. attinging the ultimate disposition of the Body.

† **a'ttingence.** *Obs.* [f. L. *attingent-em*: see attingent and -ence.] Effect, influence, incidence of one thing upon another.

1678 Gale *Crt. Gentiles* III. 47 There is no executive power in God distinct from his Wil: his concurse in regard to its active attingence is no more than his simple volition.

† **a'ttingency.** *Obs.* [f. as prec.: see -ency.] Attingent quality; effective contact, operation.

1642 tr. *Ames' Marrow Div.* 32 A passive attingency of the Divine will. **1675** Baxter *Cath. Theol.* i. iii. viii. 28 We must call our selves Patients, and think of the Attingency of his Active essence with its effects, by some Analogie of Corporeal Attingency, contact, and impressed moving force.

a'ttingent, *a.* and *sb.* [f. L. *attingentem*, pr. pple. of *attingĕre*: see attinge.] **A.** *adj.* Touching, in contact. † **B.** *sb. Obs.* That which comes in contact.

1578 Banister *Hist. Man.* i. 37 The sides are attingent to the sides of ye vj and iiij bones [of the foot]. **1657** Tomlinson *Renou's Disp.* 302 With hard pricks it punges its attingents. **1895** M. H. N. Story-Maskelyne *Crystallogr.* ii. §15. 16 To each octant there will correspond three adjacent octants, which have each one axial plane in common with the original octant; three attingent octants, in contact with it only along an axis.

attir, -ling, variants of atter, -ling.

‖**attirail, attiral.** *Obs.* [F. *attirail*, f. *attirier* attire *v.*[1] + *-ail*, repr. L. *-āculum*, as in *gubernāculum*, *gouvernail*.] Apparatus, gear.

1611 Cotgr., *Attelements*, th' attirals, harnesses, geeres or furniture, belonging to draught horses, or oxen. **1790** Roy in *Phil. Trans.* LXXX. 160 The whole attirail was transported from place to place, in a four-wheeled spring carriage.

attire (ə'taɪə(r)), *v.*[1] Forms: 3–5 **atire,** 4–6 **atyre,** 6–7 **attyre,** 4– **attire.** See also aphet. tire *v.*[2] [a. OF. *atire-r*, earlier *atirier* to arrange, put into order, array, equip, dress, deck, cogn. w. Pr. *atieirar*, formed on the phrase *a tieira*, OF. *à tire* 'into row or order,' f. Pr. *tieira* (*teira*, *tiera*), It. *tiera*, OF. *tire* (*tiere*), row, rank, order, series, suite, train; of uncertain origin: see tier.

(See article by H. Nicol in *Trans. Philol. Soc.* (*Proc.* 19 Dec. 1879). Connexion with OHG. *ziari* 'beauty, adornment,' is still doubtful.)]

† **1.** To put in order, put to rights. *Obs.*

1330 R. Brunne *Chron.* 10 Into þe waise þam fro he tombled top ouer taile. His knyghtis vp him lyft, and did him eft atire. *c* **1400** *Destr. Troy* v. 2013 Þai .. knitten vp þe saile, Atyrit þe tacle.

† **2.** To prepare, equip, fit out. *Obs.*

1330 R. Brunne *Chron.* 207 What dos þe Kyng of France? atires him gode nauie [Langtoft, *attyre sa navye*]. *a* **1440** *Ipomydon* 535 Turnementis atyred in the felde, a M. armed with spere and shelde.

† **3.** To equip (the person, a horse): **a.** for war: To arm. *Obs.*

1297 R. Glouc. 547 & newe kniȝtes made, & armede & attired hom, & hor bedes ȝerne bade. *c* **1400** *Destr. Troy* vii. 2995 A palfray of prise, prudly atyrit. **1593** Drayton *Ecl.* iv. 99 That did streight Limbs in stubborn Steele attire.

b. with dress or clothing: To dress, adorn, array. (Now only literary, and chiefly *refl.* and *pass.*)

c **1350** *Will. Palerne* 1705 Sche .. borwed boiȝes cloþes & talliche hire a-tyred tiȝtli þerinne. *a* **1450** *Knt. de la Tour* cviii. 145 And atyred hem selff with thaire riche and fresshe atyre. **1526** Tindale *1 Pet.* iii. 5 After this manner in the olde tyme did the wholy women .. tyre them selves. **1593** Shaks. *2 Hen. VI.* ii. iv. 109 It will hang vpon my richest Robes, And shew it selfe, attyre me how I can. **1699** Dryden *Pal. & Arc.* iii. 69 His shoulders large a mantle did attire. **1859** Tennyson *Enid* 770 To greet her thus attired.

c. To dress (the head, *mostly* of women). *arch.*

c **1400** *Destr. Troy* vii. 3026 The here atiret in tressis trusset full faire. **1595** Spenser *Amoretti* xxxvii, Her golden tresses, She doth attyre vnder a net of gold. **1611** Bible *2 Kings* ix. 30 Shee painted her face, and tyred her head, and looked out at a window. **1859** Tennyson *Enid* 62 This too the women who attired her head .. Told Enid.

† **4.** To 'dress' venison for food. *Obs.*

c **1320** *Sir Tristr.* i. xliii, Yond lith a best unflain, Atire it as thou wold.

† **a'ttire,** *v.*[2] *Obs.* [a. F. *attire-r*, f. *à* to + *tirer* to draw.] To draw to itself, attract.

1549 Chaloner *Erasm. Moriæ Enc.* T ij b, The myght of God .. ravisheth and attyreth all thyngs to itself.

attire (ə'taɪə(r)), *sb.* Forms: 3–4 **atyr,** 4–7 **atir(e, atier,** 5–6 **atyre,** 6–7 **attyre,** 4– **attire.** [f. attire *v.*[1]] (With the senses cf. apparel, array.)

† **1.** Equipment of man or horse, outfit for war.

1250 Lay. 3275 Mid his fourti cniȝtes, and hire hors and hire atyr. *c* **1350** *Will. Palerne* 1147 Alle tristy atir þat to batayle longed. *c* **1440** *Sir Isumb.* 413 Alle the atyre that felle to a knyghte.

† **2.** Personal adornment, or decoration; 'get up.' Also (with *pl.*) an ornament. *Obs.*

1382 Wyclif *Ezek.* xxiii. 40 Ourned with wommans atyre [Vulg. *mundo muliebri*]. **1568** Bible (Bishops') *Isa.* iii. 18 The gorgiousnesse of ye attyre about their feete. **1621** Molle *Camerar. Liv. Lib.* iv. vi. 240 Dressings, bracelets, and attires. **1642** Fuller *Holy & Prof. St.* v. i. 358 Commonly known by her whorish attire: As crisping and curling.

3. Dress, apparel.

c **1300** *K. Alis.* 173 Ladies and damoselis .. In faire atire. **1393** Langl. *P. Pl.* C. iii. 15 To telle of hure atyre · no tyme haue ich nouth. **1553** T. Wilson *Rhet.* Pref. A iij b, Having neither house to shroude them in, nor attyre to clothe their backes. **1601** Shaks. *Jul. C.* i. i. 53 And do you now put on your best attyre? And do you now cull out a Holyday? **1767** Fordyce *Serm. Yng. Wom.* I. ii. 73 They plead religious principles for the form of their attire. **1859** Geo. Eliot *A. Bede* 62 The most conspicuous article in her attire was an ample checkered linen apron.

† **b.** (with *pl.*) A dress. *Obs.*

1586 J. Hooker *Girald. Irel.* in *Holinsh.* II. 130/1 Awaie with his English attires, and on with his brogs, his shirt and other Irish rags. **1597** Hooker *Eccl. Pol.* v. lxxix. §5 Threescore and seuen Attires of Priests. **1787** Miss Burney in *Diary & Lett.* III. 367 Two new attires, one half, the other full dressed.

† **4.** Head-dress, head-gear; *spec.* (in 16–17th c.) a head-dress of women. Also aphet. tire. *Obs.* (In this sense fancifully connected with *tiara.*)

c **1380** *Sir Ferumb.* 3704 Helm & heued wyþ al þe atyre In-to þe feld it fleȝ. **1483** *Cath. Angl.*, Atyre of þ^e hede, *tiara.* **1530** Palsgr. 195/2 Atyre for a gentilwomans heed, *atour.* **1583** Babington *Commandm.* (1590) 275 The bracelets and the bonets, the attires of the head and the slops, the headbands, etc. **1611** Rich *Honest. Age* (1844) 37 These Attyre-makers that within these forty yeares were not knowne by that name, and but nowe very lately they kept their lowzie commoditie of periwygs, and their other monstrous attyres, closed in boxes, they might not be seene in open show.

5. *Venery* and *Her.* The 'head-gear' of a deer.

1562 Leigh *Armorie* (1597) 52 He renueth his attire euerie year. **1610** Guillim *Heraldry* iii. xiv. **1727** Bradley *Fam. Dict.* s.v., The Heralds call the Horns of a Stag or Buck his Attire. **1736** Dale in *Phil. Trans.* XXXIX. 384 The Present which I herewith make you, is the Head, or rather the Attire (as it is called in Heraldry) of the Moose-Deer. **1857** *Fraser's Mag.* LVI. 211 The terms for the attire of a Buck, according to the old woodmen, are the bur, the beam, the brow-antlier, the back-antlier, the advancer, palm, and spellers or spillers.

† **6.** The furniture (of a house). *Obs.*

c **1325** *Metr. Hom.* 86 A pouer hous was son purvaide, And pouer atir tharin was layde.

7. *fig.* The plants which clothe and deck the earth; the covering of animals, *esp.* when beautiful; the external surroundings, 'apparel' or 'garb' of anything immaterial.

1610 Guillim *Heraldry* iii. x. 148 Choisest attires of the Garden. **1647** Cowley *Mistr. Weeping* i, Let not ill Fortune see Th' attire thy sorrow wears. **1667** Milton *P.L.* vii. 501 Earth in her rich attire Consummate lovly smil'd. **1798** Coleridge *Anc. Mar.* iv. iii, Within the shadow of the ship I watched their rich attire .. They coiled and swam, and every track Was a flash of golden fire.

† **8.** In plants: The name given by Grew to the parts within the floral leaves or corolla, especially the stamens (*seminiform attire*), and the florets of the disk in Composite flowers (*florid attire*). *Obs.*

1671 Grew *Anat. Plants* i. v. (1682) 35 The Flower. The general parts whereof are most commonly three; *sc.* the *Empalement*, the *Foliation*, and the *Attire*. *Ibid.* 37 The *Attire*, I find to be of two kinds, *Seminiforme* and *Florid*. **1676** *Ibid.* iv. ii. i. §3 In all Flowers with the Florid Attire, as of Marigold, Daisy and the like. **1725** in Bradley *Fam. Dict.* s.v. **1751** in Chambers *Cycl.* s.v. [from Grew].

attired (ə'taɪəd), *ppl. a.* [f. attire *v.* + -ed.]

† **1.** Equipped, furnished, fitted out, prepared. *Obs.*

1330 R. Brunne *Chron.* 148 A schip þer was of London, richely atired [Langtoft, *de riche atiffement*]. *c* **1485** *Digby Myst.* (1882) iii. 360, I am a-tyred in my tower to tempt you þis tyde.

2. Dressed, clad.

c **1350** *Will. Palerne* 5043 Þe clergie .. riȝt gailiche atyred. **1588** Shaks. *Tit. A.* v. iii. 30 Why art thou thus attir'd? **1791** Cowper *Iliad* xviii. 473 Charis, Vulcan's well-attired spouse. *Mod.* A woman plainly but decently attired.

† **3.** Adorned, decked. *Obs.*

c **1325** *E.E. Allit. P.* B. 114 Ay þe best byfore & bryȝtest atyred. *a* **1450** *Knt. de la Tour* 39 Riche atyred of perles and presious stones.

4. *Venery* and *Her.* Furnished with horns.

1572 Bossewell *Armorie* ii. 59 An hartes heade cabazed d'Or, attyred verte. **1661** Morgan *Sph. Gentry* i. vi. 94

When the horns of a deer are of another colour from the head, it is called Attired. **1864** BOUTELL *Heraldry Hist. & Pop.* x. 62 A stag is attired of his antlers.

5. *fig.* Wrapped, clothed; adorned, arrayed.

1599 SHAKS. *Much Ado* IV. i. 146 For my part, I am so attired in wonder, I know not what to say. **1756** BURKE *Subl. & B.* Wks. 1842 I. 49 The rose and the apple blossom are both beautiful, and the plants that bear them are most engagingly attired.

attirement (əˈtaɪəmənt). [a. OF. *atirement*, f. *atirier* to ATTIRE + -MENT.] Outfit, dress, apparel; †furniture, decoration, adornment (*obs.*).

1566 PAINTER *Pal. Pleas.* I. 45 So she tare the attirement from her head and body. **1583** GOLDING *Calvin on Deut.* 628 They tooke vp their lampes, their perfumes, their attyrementes. **1596** *Edward III*, III. iii. 44 Bring forth A strong attirement for the prince my son. **1867** HOWELLS *Ital. Journ.* 58 It is the kindest and charitablest of attirements, this white veil.

attiring (əˈtaɪərɪŋ), *vbl. sb.* [f. ATTIRE *v.*]

1. The action of fitting out, accoutring, dressing, apparelling.

c **1350** *Will. Palerne* 1941 For [to] telle þe a-tiryng of þat child þat time. **1611** RICH *Honest. Age* (1844) 26 This strange atiring of themselues. **1678** PHILLIPS, *Attiring*, a dressing, or apparrelling, from *Tiara*, a Persian ornament for the Head. **1836** *Chamb. Jrnl.* 6 Aug. 217 A certain smartness in the attiring of the neck.

2. a. Dress, apparel, trappings of a horse. **b.** Head-dress. **c.** Personal ornament. **d.** *fig.*

1552 HULOET, Attirings yt gentilwomen weare on their heades, *Ridemicula*. **1583** STANYHURST *Æneid* III. (Arb.) 89 Thee Troian atyring And Troian weapons. **1596** DRAYTON *Legends* i. 123 Putting her rich Gems and attyrings on. **1631** WEEVER *Anc. Fun. Mon.* 697 The exoticke forme of their attiring. **1859** W. GREGORY *Egypt in* 1855–6 I. 33 Dromedaries, with their leopard-skin attirings.

3. The 'attire' of a stag or deer.

1678 PHILLIPS, *Attiring*, a term of Heraldry. Also among Hunters the Branching Horns. **1742** BAILEY, *Attiring*, the branching Horns of a Buck.

4. *Comb.* †**attiring-house, -room** (*obs.*) = TIRING-HOUSE, -ROOM, the room or place where players attire or dress themselves for the stage; **attiring-room**, also a dressing-room, generally.

1647 *Assembly-man* in *Harl. Misc.* (1745) V. 94/1 This Assembly is the two Houses Attiring-room, where the Lords and Commons put on their Vizards and Masks of Religion. **1656** TRAPP *Comm. 1 Tim.* v. 645/1 Follow stage-players into their attiring-house. *a* **1661** FULLER *Life H. Smith* in *Smith's Wks.* (1866) I. 7 As few did take notice of their coming out of their attiring-house, so their well acting on the stage commanded all eyes to observe their returning thereunto. **1756** C. LUCAS *Ess. Waters* III. 346 Fit houses.. furnished with warm stoves, and attiring rooms.

†**a'ttitle**, *v. Obs. rare.* [a. OF. *atitele-r* 12th c., later *atitrer* (mod. *att-*):—L. *at-*, *adtitulāre* to name, entitle, in med.L. to dedicate, f. *ad.* to + *titulāre* to entitle, f. *titulus* title.] To name, name after; to dedicate.

1393 GOWER *Conf.* II. 157 But yet her sterres bothe two Saturne and Jupiter also They have.. Attitled to her owne name. *Ibid.* III. 118 This Aries out of the twelve Hath Marche attitled for him selve.

attitude (ˈætɪtjuːd). [a. F. *attitude*, ad. It. *attitudine* (1) fitness, adaptation, (2) disposedness, disposition, posture:—med.L. *aptitūdin-em* fittedness, fitness, n. of quality f. *aptus* fitted, fit: see APTITUDE. Originally a technical term of the Arts of Design, substituted for the earlier *aptitude c* 1710; thence extended into general use.]

1. In *Fine Arts*: The 'disposition' of a figure in statuary or painting; *hence*, the posture given to it. (Now merged in 2.)

1668 J. E[VELYN] tr. *Freart's Perf. Peinture* Advt., Though we retain the words, *Action* and *Posture*..the tearm *Aptitude* [F. *attitude*] is more expressive. And it were better to say the *Disposition* of a Dead Corps than the *Posture* of it, which seems a Tearm too gross; nor were it to speak like a Painter, to say, this Figure is in an handsome *Posture*, but in a graceful *Disposition* and *Aptitude* [F. *attitude*]. The Italians say *Attitudine*. **1686** AGLIONBY *Paint. Illustr.* iii. 107 The Painter must also vary his Heads, his Bodies, his Aptitudes. **1695** DRYDEN *Dufresnoy's Art of Painting* §4 The business of a painter in his choice of attitudes [DUFRESN. *positurae*]. **1705** ADDISON *Italy* 340 The several Statues that we see with the same Air, Posture, and Aptitudes. **1718** PRIOR *Ded. Ld. Dorset*, Bernini would have taken His Opinion upon the Beauty and Attitude of a Figure. **1721** in BAILEY. **1755** in JOHNSON: the only sense.

2. a. A posture of the body proper to, or implying, some action or mental state assumed by human beings or animals. ***to strike an attitude***: to assume it theatrically, and not as the unstudied expression of action or passion.

1725 DE FOE *Voy. round World* (1840) 153 He took the two men and put them in the same attitude. **1775** HARRIS *Philos. Arrangem.* (1841) 346 These various positions peculiar to animal bodies, and to the human above the rest, (commonly known by the name of attitudes). **1832** HT. MARTINEAU *Each & All* i. 4 She stood with her arms by her side in the attitude of waiting. **1862** STANLEY *Jew. Ch.* (1877) I. vi. 121 He stands in the Oriental attitude of prayer. **1883** J. GILMOUR *Mongols* xviii. 211 You will find him..striking pious attitudes at every new object of reverence.

b. *fig.* Of inanimate things, conceptions, etc.

1744 AKENSIDE *Pleas. Imag.* I. 30 The gayest, happiest attitude of things. **1750** JOHNSON *Rambl.* No. 96 ¶10 To copy the mien and attitudes of Truth. **1831** CARLYLE *Sart. Res.* I. iv, The remainder [of his sentences] are in quite angular attitudes, buttressed-up by props (of parentheses and dashes).

c. *Aeronaut.* (See quots.) Also *attrib.*

1910 R. FERRIS *How it Flies* 455 *Attitude*, the position of a plane as related to the line of its travel. **1914** *R. Engineers' Jrnl.* Nov. 311 *Attitude*, an aeroplane's or wing's position relative to the direction of motion through the air. **1953** *Flight* 17 July 78/2 The automatic pilot..applies control movements proportional to the attitude changes. **1962** J. GLENN in *Into Orbit* 209 The capsule's attitude would have to be near-perfect when the rockets fired, or the angle of re-entry would be affected.

d. *Dancing.* A posture or disposition of the body; spec. a form of arabesque (see quot. 1957).

1721 J. WEAVER *Lectures upon Dancing* 137 Dancing is an elegant, and regular Movement, harmonically composed of beautiful Attitudes, and contrasted graceful Postures of the Body. *Ibid.* 145 *Attitude* is a Posture, or graceful Disposition of the Body, in Standing; Sitting; or Lying. **1830** R. BARTON tr. *Blasis' Code of Terpsichore* II. v. 74 That particular position technically termed attitude is the most elegant, but at the same time the most difficult which dancing comprises. **1911** [see ARABESQUE *sb.* 4]. **1922** BEAUMONT & IDZIKOWSKI *Man. Class. Theatr. Dancing* 27 There are an infinite number of *attitudes*, so that they depend on the taste of the professor or *chorégraphe*. **1957** G. B. L. WILSON *Dict. Ballet* 32 *Attitude*, position derived from the statue of Mercury by Giovanni da Bologna.

3. Settled behaviour or manner of acting, as representative of feeling or opinion.

1837 CARLYLE *Fr. Rev.* I. ii. II. 20 In the Senate house again, the attitude of the Right Side is that of calm unbelief. **1876** GREEN *Short Hist.* vi. §2 (1882) 278 That the misrule had been serious was shown by the attitude of the commercial class.

4. a. ***attitude of mind***: deliberately adopted, or habitual, mode of regarding the object of thought.

1862 H. SPENCER *First Princ.* I. i. §1. 4 Much depends on the attitude of mind we preserve while listening to, or taking part in, the controversy. **1832** TREVELYAN in *Life Macaulay* (1876) I. v. 254 With regard to our Eastern question the attitude of his own mind is depicted in the passage on Burke. **1881** *Athenæum* No. 2811. 328/1 A necessary accompaniment of the allegorical attitude of the mind.

b. = ***attitude of mind*** above. Cf. senses 2 b, 3.

a **1873** MILL *Three Ess. Relig.* (1874) 126 Along with this change in the moral attitude of thoughtful unbelievers towards the religious ideas of mankind, a corresponding difference has manifested itself in their intellectual attitude. **1909** TITCHENER *Lectures Exper. Psychol. Thought-Processes* iii. 112 Attitude, the background of meaning or reference against which a mental process is seen, may [etc.]. **1922** H. E. PALMER *Eng. Intonation* p. viii, We all recognize immediately..each of the attitudes associated with the tones. **1937** G. W. ALLPORT *Personality* (1938) xi. 294 Both *attitude* and *trait* are indispensable concepts... Ordinarily *attitude* should be employed when the disposition is bound to an object or value, that is.., when it is aroused by a well-defined class of stimuli, and when the individual feels toward these stimuli a definite attraction or repulsion. **1941** *Punch* 3 Sept. 203/1 The attitude of ordinary people.. towards mathematics..may be summed up as the same as their attitude to the police force. **1948** KRECH & CRUTCHFIELD *Theory & Probl. Social Psychol.* v. 151 Many psychologists regard the study of attitudes as the central problem of social psychology. **1958** G. J. WARNOCK *Eng. Philos. since 1900* 169 A marked capacity for abstract thought is compatible with an 'attitude to life' entirely ordinary, or even dull.

5. *Lit. Criticism. spec.* in the use of I. A. Richards, 'the non-overt impulse to action involved in the poetic experience of the reader'.

1925 I. A. RICHARDS *Princ. Lit. Crit.* xv. 112 These imaginal and incipient activities or tendencies to action, I shall call attitudes. *Ibid.* xvi. 132 For it is the attitudes evoked which are the all-important part of any experience.

6. *attrib.* and *Comb.*, as ***attitude measurement, research, scale, study, test, theory; attitude-taking*** vbl. sb.

1904 W. JAMES *Mem. & Stud.* (1911) vi. 140 Spencer's 'Ethics' is a most vital and original piece of attitude-taking in the world of ideals. **1929** THURSTONE & CHAVE *Measurement of Attitude* p. xii, The true allocation of an individual to a position on an attitude scale is an abstraction. *Ibid.* i. 1 (*heading*) Theory of attitude measurement. **1934** *Jrnl. Social Psychol.* V. 387 The attitude test was administered again. **1935** H. C. WARREN *Dict. Psychol.* 24/1 *Attitude scale*, a scale for measuring degrees of attitude upon a particular question. **1940** *Mind* XLIX. 228 In the Introduction Ross divides attempted definitions of ethical terms into 'attitude-theories' and 'consequence-theories'. **1941** *Jrnl. Social Psychol.* XIII. 429 (*heading*) On the use of certain qualitative methods of attitude research. **1958** *Listener* 28 Aug. 308/3 All types of attitude-studies could contribute something. **1960** *Language & Speech* III. 223 Attitude measurement..seemed a promising technique. *Ibid.*, Osgood's semantic differential..was the attitude-measuring technique used in the experiment. **1960** *Times Rev. Industry* Jan. 54/1 Attitude and motivation research assesses what qualities of the product give it its appeal to some consumers and not to others.

attitudinal (ætɪˈtjuːdɪnəl), *a.* [f. It. *attitudine* + -AL[1].] Pertaining or relating to attitudes. *spec.* in *Psychol.*

1831 HEIDIGER *Didon.* I. 30 Which argued attitudinal instruction Beyond belief, in nauticals ashore. **1909** TITCHENER *Lectures Exper. Psychol. Thought-Processes* v. 181 The different *Aufgaben* come to consciousness, in part, as different feels of the whole body... I find..that these attitudinal feels are touched off in all sorts of ways. *Ibid.* 248 We may not..infer that the attitudes and the attitudinal constituents of the thoughts..are vestigial derivatives of visual imagery. **1935** H. C. WARREN *Dict. Psychol.* 24/1 *Attitudinal* (or *attitude*) *test*, a phrase applied somewhat broadly to numerous tests of non-intellectual mental traits. **1941** *Jrnl. Social Psychol.* XIII. 455 Inconsistency, both of the attitudinal and merely verbal sort, appeared often enough to demand some explanation. **1960** *Language & Speech* III. 223 (*heading*) Attitudinal meanings conveyed by intonation contours. **1962** A. C. GIMSON *Introd. Pronunc. Eng.* x. 253 (*heading*) The Attitudinal Function of Intonation.

ˌattitudiˈnarianism. [f. prec. + -ISM.] The study and excessive use of attitudes.

1803 W. TAYLOR in *Month Mag.* XV. 324 It displays all the attitudinarianism of sophistry. **1853** RUSKIN *Stones Ven.* III. ii. §78 The absence of posture-making in the works of the Pre-Raphaelites, as opposed to the Attitudinarianism of the modern school.

attitudinarian (ˌætɪtjuːdɪˈnɛərɪən). [f. as prec. + -ARIAN; cf. *valetudinarian.*] **1.** One who studies and practises attitudes.

1754–6 COWPER in *Connoisseur* No. 138 Those buffoons in society, the Attitudinarians and Face-makers. These accompany every word with a peculiar grimace or gesture. **1831** J. BOADEN *Life Mrs. Jordan* I. xiii. 310 Dancing was certainly more strictly a science, and either the *jumper* or the *attitudinarian* undervalued by the masters of the art. **1870** *Contemp. Rev.* XV. 281 The attitudinarians of the Ritualistic Churches.

2. *attrib.* or quasi-*adj.*

1823 *Examiner* 9 June 379/2 When an artist intends only to give some dashes of luxuriant colour and hints of attitudinarian character,..we will not think of wishing for the presence of higher qualities.

attitudinization (ætɪˌtjuːdɪnaɪˈzeɪʃən). [f. next: see -ATION.] = ATTITUDINIZING *vbl. sb.*

1871 ALGER *Future Life* 523 What is right..will be done in spite of all..spiritual attitudinizations.

attitudinize (ætɪˈtjuːdɪnaɪz), *v.* [f. It. *attitudine* (see above) + -IZE.]

1. *intr.* To practise attitudes studiously or excessively; to strike an attitude; to pose, posture.

1784 JOHNSON in *Boswell* (1831) V. 220 He had a great aversion to gesticulating in company. He called once to a gentleman who offended him in that point, 'Don't attitudinise.' **1833** HT. MARTINEAU *Loom & Lug.* II. iv. 74 Sobbing and attitudinizing and looking dolorously. **1837** DICKENS *Sk. Boz.* (1837) II. 103 The elegant Sparkins attitudinized with admirable effect.

2. *fig.* To practise affected and self-conscious deportment, or to speak or write in a corresponding manner, in order to produce an effect upon spectators.

1864 *Fraser's Mag* Apr. 404 When Audley Egerton attitudinizes and works out the regulation of an iron exterior and an iron heart. **1879** FROUDE *Cæsar* xiv. 194 In every line that he wrote Cicero was attitudinising for posterity. **1882** *Atl. Monthly* July 105 Even the leaders of the Southern Confederacy sometimes attitudinized for an awe-stricken world to see.

3. To go to excess in representing attitudes in painting or sculpture.

attiˈtudinizer. [f. prec. + -ER[1].] One who practises or depicts attitudes. (*Contemptuous.*)

1824 *Blackw. Mag.* XV. 635 My first flame was a flaunting, airy, artificial attitudinizer. **1833** J. S. MILL in *Monthly Repos.* VII. 68 The French painters..must all be historical; and they are, almost to a man, attitudinizers. **1881** L. STEPHEN in *Cornh. Mag.* Apr. 411 He is no attitudinizer.. He is as simple, honest, and soundhearted, as he is tender and impassioned.

attiˈtudinizing, *vbl. sb.* [f. as prec. + -ING[1].] The practice or assumption of attitudes; posturing; mode of action purposely assumed.

1813 H. & J. SMITH *Rej. Addr.* 59 The brisk locomotion of Columbine or the tortuous attitudinizing of Punch. **1869** BLACK *In Silk Attire* I. xiii, To throw off the cold attitudinizing of life.

attiˈtudinizing, *ppl. a.* [f. as prec. + -ING[2].] That practises or assumes attitudes of body, conduct, or mind; posturing.

1853 MACREADY in *Four C. Eng. Lett.* 511 The morbidly acute sensibility..of Hamlet to be frozen up..in a declaiming and attitudinising statue or automaton. **1879** GEO. ELIOT *Theo. Such* v. 113 An attitudinizing deference.

attjar, variant of ACHAR.

1798 WILCOCKE *Voy. E. Indies* I. 237 When green it [the Mango] is made into Attjar.

attle (æt(ə)l). *Mining.* Also **attal, adall, addle.** [Etymology uncertain: cf. ADDLE.] 'Rubbish, deads, refuse, or stony matter; impure off-casts in the working of mines.' Weale *Dict. Terms* 1849.

attle, var. ETTLE *v. Obs.* to purpose, intend.

†**a'ttol**, *v. Obs. rare*[−1]. [ad. L. *attollĕre*, f. *at-* = *ad-* to, completely + *tollĕre* to raise.] To raise or lift up. Hence **a'ttolled** *ppl. a.*

1578 BANISTER *Hist. Man* I. 28 These Processes are so attolled, and prominent.

†**a'ttolerance.** *Obs. rare*[−1]. [f. A- *pref.* 11 + TOLERANCE *sb.*] Permission, allowance.

1676 *Elgin Law-paper* in E. Dunbar *Soc. Life* (1865) 177 The attolerance granted..to the said crafts.

attollent (ə'tɒlənt), *a.* and *sb.* [ad. L. *attollentem*, pr. pple. of *attollĕre*: see ATTOL *v.*] **A.** *adj.* Raising, lifting up; *spec.* applied to muscles whose function is to raise various parts of the body. (The L. *attollens* is chiefly used.) **B.** *sb.* A muscle of this kind.

1713 DERHAM *Phys.-Theol.* IV. ii. 98 The Magnitude and Strength of the Attollent Muscle. **1751** CHAMBERS *Cycl.*, *Attollents*, or attollent muscles, are otherwise called *levators*.

attomy, attonce, attone, obs.: see ATO-.

attorn (ə'tɜːn), *v. Law.* Forms: 5–7 **attourne**, 6–7 **-urne, -orne,** 7 **-urn,** 6– **attorn.** [a. OF. *atorne-r, aturne-r, atourne-r* (whence law Latin *attornāre*) to turn, turn to, assign, attribute, dispose, arrange, order, appoint, constitute, ordain, decree, f. *à* to + *tourner* to TURN. The analogical spelling is *a(t)turn*; but under the influence of med.L. *attornāre*, the late AF. became *attorner*, whence *attorn* passed into the Eng. law-books.]

1. *trans.* To turn over to another; to assign, transfer (goods, tenants' service, allegiance, etc.).

[**1292** BRITTON II. 46 Ne voloms nous mie qe seignur puse attourner le homage et le service de soen tenaunt a qi qe ly plera.] **1649** SADLER *Rights Kingd.* 16 (T.) In some case a lord might atturn and assign his vassal's service to some other. **1676** MARVELL *Wks.* III. 147 A good Christian.. cannot attorn and indenture his conscience over, to be represented by others. **1691** BP. ST. ASAPH *God's Transf. Power* I. i. §44 This being follow'd by the People's attorning their Allegiance. **1727** *Cowell's Interpr.* s.v., To *Attorn* or turn over Money and Goods: i.e. to assign or appropriate them. **1865** NICHOLS *Britton* II. 46.

2. *intr.* (for *refl.*) In *Feudal Law*: To transfer oneself (*i.e.* one's homage and allegiance) from one lord to another; to yield allegiance, or do homage to, as lord. Also *fig.*

1611 SPEED *Hist. Gt. Brit.* IX. xiii. 94 The Gascoignes.. had sent into England to shew causes why they should not atturne to the Duke. **1650** B. *Discollim.* 13 Shall they do honestly to atturn, and do homage and fealty without a legall *Salvo*? **1863** *Possibilities of Creat.* 370 How sottish the soul would become were it required to attorn to the Devil. **1883** HEALY in *Pall Mall G.* 28 Dec. 1/2 Mr. Parnell.. has shown an undisguised contempt for every effort to compel him to attorn to British opinion.

3. *Mod. Law.* To agree formally to be the tenant of one into whose possession the estate has passed; to do some act which constitutes a legal acknowledgement of the new landlord.

1458 *Lease* in Ld. Campbell *Chancellors* (1857) I. xxii. 322 The said Joyes hath attourned to the said Sir John. **1574** tr. *Littleton's Tenures* 110 a, The more common attournement is to saye, sir I attorne to you by force of the same graunt, or I become your tenant, etc. **1628** COKE *On Litt.* 27 b, Hee shall not be compelled to atturne. **1853** WHARTON *Pa. Digest* II. 161 Tenant who attorns under mistake may defend against lessor. **1879** *Echo* 12 Apr. 3/3 The defendant.. had never recognised the plaintiff as his landlord, and never 'attorned' to the tenancy.

b. So *to attorn tenant.*

1844 WILLIAMS *Real Prop. Law* (1877) 247 He could refuse to attorn tenant to the purchaser. **1871** *Daily News* 23 May, Notice is given to the tenantry not to attorn tenant or pay rent to any person except Mr. Richard Wallace.

attorney (ə'tɜːnɪ), *sb.*[1] Forms: 4 **aturne, -orne, attourne,** 4–8 **att(o)urney,** 5–8 **attorny,** 6 **aturney, atturnie, -eye, -eie, attornay,** 6–7 **atturny,** 5– **attorney.** [a. OF. *atorné, aturné, atourné*, pa. pple. masc. of *atourner* to ATTORN, in sense of 'one appointed or constituted,' whence all the specific uses. (The statement found in the law dictionaries for the last 200 years, that the word means one 'who acts *in the turn* of another,' is a bad guess.) For spelling cf. ATTORN.]

†**1.** One appointed or ordained to act for another; an agent, deputy, commissioner. In later times only *fig.* and perhaps with conscious reference to sense 2. *Obs.*

[**1303** R. BRUNNE *Handl. Synne* 5503 So shulde eche aturne seriaunt, But many one holde no cunnaunt.] **1347** *Ord. R. Househ.* 9 Clerkes, attorneys of the Victualles in sondry shiers. *c* **1430** LYDG. *Bochas* VIII. vi. (1554) 181 a, From occupacion hys rest for to take Hys atturney Maximian he doth make. *c* **1440** *Promp. Parv.*, Atturneye, *suffectus, attornatus.* **1590** SHAKS. *Com. Err.* v. i. 100, I will attend my husband.. for it is my Office, And will haue no atturney but my selfe. **1642** ROGERS *Naaman* 382 His Minister, whom he hath made.. his Attorney to receiue our acknowledgement.

2. (*attorney in fact, private attorney.*) One duly appointed or constituted (by *letter* or *power of attorney*) to act for another in business and legal matters, either *generally*, as in payment, receipt, and investment of money, in suing and being sued, etc., or in some *specific* act, which the principal, by reason of absence, is unable to perform in person. Hence the contrast between 'in person' and 'by attorney,' frequent also in fig. senses.

[**1292** BRITTON VI. x. §1 Des attournez sount acuns generals, acuns especials. (NICHOLS transl., Of attorneys, some are general and some special.)] **1466** *Mann. & Househ. Exp.* 344 Paid to John Smythe of Yipswych, his attorney in the kervelle of the marchaundyse, viijs. iiijd. **1600** SHAKS. *A.Y.L.* IV. i. 94 Then in mine owne person, I die. *Ros.* No faith, die by Attorney. **1628** COKE *On Litt.* 52 a, A fem may be an Attorney to deliuer seisin to her husband. **1642** FULLER *Holy & Prof. St.* II. xix. 124 None may appear in Gods service by an Atturney. **1839** *Penny Cycl.* XIII. 449/1 An attorney, unless power be specially given him for that purpose, cannot delegate his authority or appoint a substitute. *Mod.* 'Received payment. (Signed) *John Smith*, by his Attorney *William Taylor*.'

3. (*attorney-at-law, public attorney.*) A professional and properly-qualified legal agent practising in the courts of Common Law (as a *solicitor* practised in the courts of Equity); one who conducted litigation in these courts, preparing the case for the barristers, or counsel, whose duty and privilege it is to plead and argue in open court.

(This sense slowly disengaged itself from the preceding, as a body of professional legal agents was recognized and incorporated. The actual duties and privileges of the *Attorney-at-Law* also varied with time and place; in earlier times, as still in some of the United States of America, the distinction between *attorney* and *counsel* did not exist. (Cf. next sense.) From an early period the name was often used reproachfully as almost = 'knave or swindler': see quotations under **b**. By the Judicature Act of 1873, the title, never used in Scotland, was abolished in England, 'attorneys' being merged in the 'Solicitors of the Supreme Court.')

c **1330** *Pol. Songs* 339 Attourneis in cuntré theih geten silver for noht. [**1402** *Act* 4 *Hen. IV*, xviii, Ordeignez est et establiz qe toutes ces attournees soient examinez par les Justices & par leur discretion leur nouns mys en rolle. (*transl.* It is ordained that all attorneys be examined by the Justices, and that at the discretion of these their names be entered on the roll.)] **1467** J. PASTON in *Lett.* 569 II. 299 He is an attorny.. in the Baylys Coort of Yermouthe. **1536** WRIOTHESLEY *Chron.* (1875) I. 57 An atturney of the lawe and felowe of Graies Inne. *a* **1617** HIERON *Wks.* II. 177 There needs no professed atturney to open his inditement. **1712** STEELE *Spect.* No. 456 ¶4 The Law of the Land is his Gospel, and all his Cases of Conscience are determined by his Attorney. **1768** BLACKSTONE *Comm.* III. iii. III. 25 An attorney at law answers to the procurator, or proctor, of the civilians and canonists. **1836** DICKENS *Pickw.* xx, Messrs. Dodson and Fogg, two of his Majesty's Attorneys of the Courts of King's Bench and Common Pleas at Westminster, and Solicitors of the High Court of Chancery. **1873** *Act 36 & 37 Vict.* lxvi. §87 From and after the commencement of this Act all persons admitted as solicitors, attorneys, or proctors of or by law empowered to practise in any Court, the jurisdiction of which is hereby transferred to the High Court of Justice or the Court of Appeal, shall be called Solicitors of the Supreme Court.

b. *a* **1400** WM. OF NASSINGTON *Spec. Vite*, MS. Bodl. 48. lf. 166 A fals atorne Ffor he foloweþ wᵗ al his myȝt As wel a wrong ple as a riȝt. *c* **1538** STARKEY *England* iv. 119 Justyce schold not be so defettyd.. by euery lyght and couetouse Sergeant, Proktor or Attornay. **1732** POPE *Mor. Ess.* III. 274 Vile attorneys, now an useless race. *a* **1784** JOHNSON in *Boswell* (1831) I. 385 Johnson observed, that 'he did not care to speak ill of any man behind his back, but he believed the gentleman was an attorney.' **1837** CARLYLE *Fr. Rev.* III. VII. v, Attorneys and Law-Beagles, which hunt ravenous on this Earth.

4. *transf.* An advocate, pleader, mediator. ? *Obs.*

1537 ? TINDALE *Exp. St. John* 21 We haue an aduocate and intercessour, a true attourney with the father. **1563** *Homilies Gd. Friday* I, He sytteth on the right hande of his father, as our proctoure and atturneye, pleading and suyng for vs. **1594** SHAKS. *Rich. III*, IV. iv. 413 Therefore, deare Mother, Be the Atturney of my loue to her; Pleade what I will be, not what I haue beene.

5. Specific title of the law officer of various councils, etc. and the clerk of various courts: see also ATTORNEY-GENERAL.

1494 FABYAN VII. 633 In which fray a gentylman, beynge the quenys attourney, was slayen. **1587** FLEMING *Contn. Holinshed* III. 1286/2 Nicholas Bacon esquier, attourneie of the court of wards. **1633** T. STAFFORD *Pac. Hib.* i. 27 Appointing two sufficient men to bee Clearkes or Attornies to that Councell. **1786** BEATSON *Ann. Reg.* III. 84 King's Remembrancer.. has under him eight attornies or sworn clerks. **1868** CHAMBERS *Encycl.* I. 540/1 The master of the crown office.. is called the 'Coroner and Attorney for the Queen.'

6. *the King's Attorney*: earlier (descriptive) designation of the legal officer now called ATTORNEY-GENERAL. ***Mr. Attorney***, the 'style' used in addressing (formerly also in speaking *of*) him.

1414 *Act* 2 *Hen. V*, iv, Attournes du Roy. **1546** BERTHELET transl., The kynges Atturney, on the contrary, Vrg'd on the Examinations. **1613** SHAKS. *Hen. VIII*, II. i. 15 The kings Atturney, on the contrary, Vrg'd on the Examinations. **1660–1** MARVELL *Corr.* 16 Wks. 1872–5 II. 47 Yesterday I carryed it [the warrant] to Mr. Atturny's. *a* **1674** CLARENDON *Hist. Reb.* I. IV. 280 The King's Atturney. **1689** SIR R. SAWYER in *Tryal Bps.* 91 You have heard this charge which Mr. Attorney has been pleased to make against the Bishops. **1856** *Times* 26 May, *Witness.* I'll tell you, Mr. Attorney. *Sir A. Cockburn, Att. Gen.*, Don't 'Mr. Attorney' me, Sir! answer my question.

7. *attrib.*, as in ***attorney-cunning***, etc.: see 3 b.

1839 CARLYLE *Chartism* v. 138 Shiftiness.. attorney-cunning is a kind of thing that fancies itself.. to be talent. **1865** —— *Fredk. Gt.* III. x. vi. 269 Kingship was not a thing of attorney mendacity.

a'ttorney, *sb.*[2] Also 5 **atorne,** 6 **atturneie, -ourney,** 7 **-urney.** (In 7 *Sc.* **actorney, -ay.**) [a. OF. *atournée, attornée, actournée*, 'action of attorning, function of the attorney,' sb. fem. from pa. pple. = L. **attornāta* (but actually latinized in med.L. as *attornātio, attornātus* 4th decl., whence OF. *atorné* in same sense.]

†**1.** The action of appointing a legal representative, legal commission, procuration. (The phrase 'by attorney' perh. orig. belonged to this.)

1594 SHAKS. *Rich. III*, v. iii. 83, I, by Attourney, blesse thee from thy Mother. **1609** SKENE *Reg. Maj.* 168 For ilk actorney, and commission twa shillings. **1635** QUARLES *Emblems* v. vi. (1718) 270 Mine eye, by Contemplations great attorney, Transcends the crystal pavement of the skie.

Now used only in,

2. ***letter*** or ***warrant of attorney***: a legal document by which a person appoints one or more persons to act for him as his attorney or attorneys, either ***generally*** or in a ***specific*** transaction. ***power of a.***: the authority conferred by such a document, now used also for the document itself.

[*a* **1432** in Rymer *Fœdera* X. 500 Habet Literas Regis de Generali Attornatu.] **1461** *Paston Lett.* 408 II. 37, I wold a new dede and letter of atorne were mad. **1586** J. HOOKER *Girald. Irel.* in *Holinsh.* II. 145/2 They deliuered.. their letters of atturneie vnto their said agents. **1611** COTGR., *Attournée*, a letter of Atturney. **1750** CARTE *Hist. Eng.* II. 369 Letters of protection and attorney being still granted. **1753** HANWAY *Trav.* (1762) II. I. vii. 35 By his order.. or by virtue of his power of attorney. **1858** LD. ST. LEONARDS *Handy-bk. Prop. Law* XXII. 175 Payments and acts by any trustee.. under a power of attorney.

a'ttorney, *v.* [f. the sb.] To perform by attorney or proxy.

1611 SHAKS. *Wint. T.* I. i. 30 Their Encounters (though not Personall) hath been Royally attornyed with enter-change of Gifts.

a'ttorneydom. [See -DOM.] The body of attorneys collectively or abstractly. (*Contemptuous.*)

1881 *Standard* 22 Aug. 5/2 The narrow and captious argument of 'attorneydom.' **1882** *Society* 7 Oct. 16/2 A strong element of what Mr. John Bright has been pleased to call attorneydom.

attorney-general.

†**1.** *gen.* A legal representative or deputy acting under a general commission or 'power' of attorney, and representing his principal in all legal matters: opposed to ***attorney special*** or ***particular***. Plural: ***attorneys general***. *Obs.*

[**1292** BRITTON VI. x. §2 Touz attournez generals purrount lever fins et cirographer. (NICHOLS transl., All general attorneys may levy fines and make chirographs.)] **1593** SHAKS. *Rich. II*, II. i. 203 Call in his Letters Patents that he hath By his Atturneyes generall to sue His Liuerie. **1717** BLOUNT *Law Dict.* s.v., Atturney General is he, who by general authority is appointed to manage all our affairs or Suits.. Attorney Special or Particular is he that is imployed in one or more Causes particularly specified.

2. spec. ***Attorney-General, Attorney General***: a legal officer of the state empowered to act in all cases in which the state is a party. In England, Ireland, Isle of Man, most of the British Colonies and settlements, and in the United States, the title of the first ministerial law-officer of the government, also of his or her Majesty's attorney in the duchies of Lancaster and Cornwall, and county palatine of Durham. Plural (better): ***Attorney-Generals***.

The designation began in England, where this officer was at first merely the king's attorney (see above 6), called from the reign of Edward IV, 'the king's general attorney,' to distinguish him from those appointed to act on special occasions, or in particular courts. The descriptive designation seems to have grown into a title during the 16th c. The A.G. is now a member of the Ministry (but not of the Cabinet), and usually has a seat in the House of Commons.

1533–4 *Act 25 Hen. VIII*, xvi. §2 The kinges generall attorney, and general Solicitour, which for the time is. **1585** in Somers *Tracts* (1809) I. 214 Then began John Popham Esq. her Majestys Attorney-general, as followeth. **1614** SELDEN *Titles Hon.* 31 Sʳ John Dauis Knight, his Maiesties Attorny Generall for Ireland. **1708** *Lond. Gaz.* No. 4482/3. *a* **1733** NORTH *Life Bar. Guildf.* (1742) 18 His admission into the Conversation of Mr. Attorney-General Palmer.. proved of great use to him.. For Mr. Attorney.. was a very great Book Lawyer. **1812** *Examiner* 25 May 334/1 Attorneys-General, Judges, and Hangmen. **1812** L. HUNT *ibid.* 24 Aug. 529/1 Attorney-Generals should be restricted.

Hence, **attorney-generalship.**

1871 *Daily Tel.* 6 Nov., Might have seen the Attorney-Generalship filled once more by the Member for Richmond. **1876** in *N. Amer. Rev.* CXXIII. 384 The nomination of Mr. O'Conor as a candidate for the attorney-generalship.

a'ttorneyism. [See -ISM.] The practice of attorneys, or that attributed to the 'rascally attorney'; unscrupulous cleverness. (*Vituperative.*)

1837 CARLYLE *Fr. Rev.* (1871) III. VII. v. 258 Vanish, then, thou rat-eyed Incarnation of Attorneyism. **1864** —— *Fredk. Gt.* IV. II, Instinctively abhorrent of attorneyism and the swindler element. **1884** *Sat. Rev.* 28 June 835/2 The peculiarity, however, of that kind of cleverness which.. is called attorneyism, is that it frequently overreaches itself.

a'ttorneyship. [See -SHIP.]

1. The acting as an attorney for another; proxy.

1591 SHAKS. *1 Hen. VI*, v. v. 56 Marriage is a matter of more worth, Then to be dealt in by Atturney-ship. **1598** FLORIO, *Procuraria*..the doing or managing of another mans busines by atturneyship. **1763** CHURCHILL *Poems* Ded., But you my Lord renounced Attorneyship.

2. The profession and practice of an attorney; also = ATTORNEY-GENERALSHIP.

1611 COTGR., *Attournance*, an atturneyship, or, the following of a cause by an Atturney. **1634** in *3rd Rep. R. Com. Hist. MSS.* 283/1 Succeeding in the atturneyship your countriman Noy. **1861** SPEDDING *Bacon* I. 266 Christmas passed away without any resolution concerning the Attorneyship.

attornment (əˈtɜːnmənt). *Law.* Forms: see ATTORN *v.* [a. OF. *atournement*, f. *atourner*: see ATTORN and -MENT.]

1. A turning over; transference, assignment.

1650 ELDERFIELD *Tythes* 251 The attournment or making them over to man to be received by him.

2. *spec.* The transference of his homage and service by a tenant to a new feudal lord; *hence*, legal acknowledgement of the new landlord.

1531 *Dial. Laws of Eng.* I. xx. (1638) 35 The feoffee hath right..to the rents, if there be atturnements. **1602** FULBECKE *1st Pt. Parall.* 10 No attournement can make an euill graunt to bee good. **1768** BLACKSTONE *Comm.* II. v. II. 72 The lord also could not alienate his seignory without the consent of his tenant, which consent of his was called an attornment. **1876** DIGBY *Real Prop.* v. §3. 227 The necessity for attornment was done away with by 4 Anne, c. 16.

†**aˈttouch**, *v. Obs.* [a. F. *attouche-r* to touch on, f. *à* to + *toucher*, OF. *tochier* to touch.] To touch (lightly). Hence **attouching** *vbl. sb.*, **attouchment**, the action of touching lightly, contact. (All in Caxton only.)

c **1480** CAXTON *Ovid's Met.* XIV. i, And [Circe] attouchyd the water in fanstosme & syth departed. **1483** —— *G. de la Tour* D vj, So many euylle dedes bicomen by foolisshe attouchementis. **1491** —— *Vitas Patr.* (W. de W.) I. i. 6/2 He embracyd and kyssyd her, In makynge fowle attowchynges.

attouir, attour, var. ATOUR *adv.* and *prep.*

†**aˈttourne**, *v. Obs.* [? phonetic var. of *retourne*, *return*.] = RETURN.

c **1386** CHAUCER *Knts. T.* 1237 (Wright) The day approcheth of her attournyng [*Six-text*, retournynge]. **1470** HARDING *Chr.* x, He woulde..with Troyans to their lande attourne.

†**aˈttoxicated**, *ppl. a. Obs. rare*⁻¹. [f. L. *at-*, *ad-* to + *toxicāre* to poison.] = Intoxicated.

1604 T. WRIGHT *Passions Mind* II. iii. §1. 70 A villanous Passion of Love..with an attoxicated delight imprisoneth the affection.

attract (əˈtrækt), *v.* [f. L. *attract-* ppl. stem of *attrah-ĕre* to draw to, f. *at-*, *ad-* to + *trahĕre* to drag, draw. Formed on analogy of the verbs *abstract*, *contract*, which preceded it in use, and had been formed on the ppl. adjs. *c* 1400.]

To draw to or towards oneself. Only *trans.*

†**1.** To draw in, take in by drawing or suction: **a.** fluids, nourishment, as the vessels of the body do; To absorb.

1540 RAYNALD *Birth Man.* 7 b, An attractife power..geuen to the wombe, to attracte and drawe towards itselfe the seede. **1652** FRENCH *Yorksh. Spa* xi. 96 The internal vessels being heated will more strongly attract, and expell.

b. the breath; To inhale. (cf. L. *pulmo attrahens ac reddens animam.*)

1610 GUILLIM *Heraldry* III. xvii. (1660) 209 Animals that do attract and deliver their breath more strongly. **1667** *Phil. Trans.* II. 603 To speak inwardly, as do the *Ventriloqui*, by attracting the Breath.

†**c.** ideas; To take in. (Cf. 'swallow.') *Obs.*

1593 NASHE *Christ's T.* 181 A hundred thousand times more then thought can attract, or supposition apprehend.

†**2.** To draw to or toward oneself by taking hold of; to pull, drag in. *Obs.*

1669 BOYLE *Cont. New Exper.* II. (1682) 16 That the Thumb sticking in the angle *P*, the rest of the fingers may attract the Lever *L*, and so force, etc. **1677** HALE *Prim. Orig. Man.* 222 Out of the History of Moses touching the Universal Flood, and the History of Deucalion, Ovid made up his first Book, attracting in a great measure to the latter what was written of the former by Moses.

3. To draw to itself by invisible influence: †**a.** Said of medical applications, as a poultice. *Obs.*

1563 T. GALE *Antidot.* I. 2 Medicines which do drawe and attracte be of whote temperature and subtyle partes.

b. Said of physical forces: the word appropriated to the action of all bodies upon each other under the influence of gravitation, of electrical and magnetic bodies upon certain substances, and the like.

1627 SMITH *Seaman's Gram.* ii. 11 Iron nailes would attract the Compasse. **1646** SIR T. BROWNE *Pseud. Ep.* II. iv, Jet and amber attracteth straws and light bodies. **1670** *Phil. Trans.* V. 2041 This Substance is Electrical, attracting (to speak with the Vulgar,) when heated, straw, Feathers, etc. **1727–51** CHAMBERS *Cycl.* s.v., Every particle in nature is proved to attract every other particle. **1834** MRS. SOMERVILLE *Connex. Phys. Sc.*, The sun attracts all the planets..inversely as the square of their distances from its centre.

c. Said of influencing the will and action of men or animals, so as to cause them to come near; *e.g.* to draw them by expected advantages, curiosity, admiration, sympathy.

1568 GRAFTON *Chron.* (1809) II. 131 Secretly to enuegle and attract such persons of yᵉ nobility to ioyne with and take her part. **1703** MAUNDRELL *Journ. Jerus.* (1732) 69 It has attracted the City round about it. *a* **1744** POPE (J.) What nymph could e'er attract such crowds as you! **1874** HELPS *Soc. Press.* ii. 15 A great capital attracts great talent. **1879** LUBBOCK *Sci. Lect.* i. 9 Color, scent, and honey are the three characteristics by which insects are attracted to flowers. **1884** *Manch. Exam.* 9 June 5/1 The cricket ground..had never previously attracted such large gatherings.

d. Said of drawing to oneself parasites, disease, damp, dust, the shafts of wit, criticism, etc., by exposing a surface which intercepts them, or by presenting conditions favourable to their settlement.

1771 *Junius Lett.* liv. 281 Private vices have not dignity sufficient to attract the censure of the press. *Mod.* Conditions which attract fever; likely to attract the cholera.

4. Hence (from 3 c, d), without any material movement: **a.** To draw forth or excite towards oneself the pleasurable emotions of a person, so that he 'feels drawn' to the source of attraction, and takes pleasure in dwelling upon it in contemplation or thought. (Either the person or emotion may be the object.)

1601 SHAKS. *Twel. N.* II. iv. 89 'Tis that miracle, and Queene of Iems That nature prankes her in, attracts my soule. **1667** MILTON *P.L.* x. 152 Adornd She was indeed, and lovely to attract Thy Love. **1836** KINGSLEY *Lett.* (1878) I. 36 The beauty of the animate and the human began to attract me. **1876** GREEN *Short Hist.* iii. §2 (1882) 118 John ..had a strange gift of attracting friends and of winning the love of women.

b. To draw forth, and fix upon oneself the attention (of eyes, ears, mind), or notice, of others.

1692 DRYDEN *Eleonora* 169 A wife..Made to attract his eyes, and keep his heart. *a* **1808** PORTEUS *Lect.* I. ii. (R.) A new star..attracted the notice of those illustrious strangers. **1860** TYNDALL *Glac.* I. §2. 20 Our attention was attracted by a singular noise.

5. To pilfer or steal. *slang.*

1891 KIPLING *Light that Failed* vii. 135 'Do they [*sc.* the students] still steal colours at lunch-time?' 'Not steal Attract is the word... I'm good—I only attract ultramarine; but there are students who'd attract flake-white.' **1933** 'E. CAMBRIDGE' *Hostages to Fortune* 24 He 'attracted' some timber and built a boat house.

†**aˈttract**, *sb. Obs.* Also 7 attraict. [Formed after F. *attrait*, in 17th c. *attraict*, but going back in spelling to L. *attractus* (4th decl.), the original of the Fr.] Attraction; chiefly in *pl.* attractive qualities, charms.

1633 EARL MANCH. *Al Mondo* (1636) 198 Shee on her part corresponds, and with a willing assent glides after these attracts. **1671** MRS. BEHN *Amorous Pr.* III. i. 364 Oh Madam ask your eyes, Those powerful attracts. **1673** H. STUBBE *Furth. Vind. Dutch War* 27 The Image of some Hero, which is all life, charm, and attract.

aˌttractaˈbility. *rare.* [f. next: see -BILITY.] The quality or fact of being attractable.

1794 SIR W. JONES *Asiat. Philos.* in *Asiat. Res.* IV. 177 A corpuscle destitute of that natural attractibility [*sic*].

attractable (əˈtræktəb(ə)l), *a.* [f. ATTRACT *v.* + -ABLE.] Capable of being attracted. Hence **attractableness**.

1799 KIRWAN *Geol. Ess.* 492 Contains no part attractable by the magnet. **1879** RUTLEY *Stud. Rocks* x. 157 A metallic globule..attractable by the magnet.

attractant (əˈtræktənt). [f. ATTRACT *v.* + -ANT¹.] That which attracts; a substance used to attract.

1926 *Jrnl. Econ. Entomology* XIX. 546 It soon became evident that if the fundamentals of 'attractants' and repellents were to be studied, special apparatus for measuring or recording the responses of insects of these substances must be developed. **1953** *Brit. Commonw. Forest Terminol.* I. 14 *Attractant*, a substance attractive to insects, rodents, etc., used in population surveys or in control traps or baits. **1955** *Sci. Amer.* Aug. 76/3 It is neither an attractant nor a repellent to unconditioned salmon. **1959** *Times* 9 Jan. 13/2 The attractive scents of female butterflies are produced by scattered gland cells... Other examples are the sexual attractants of cockroaches.

attracˈtation. *Obs.* Bad form of ATTRACTION.

1634 T. JOHNSON tr. *Parey's Chirurg.* XIV. vi, A dolorifick ligation causes a greater attractation of blood and spirits.

attracted (əˈtræktɪd), *ppl. a.* [f. ATTRACT *v.* + -ED.] Drawn to or towards (the agent), drawn in or up. (In various senses of the vb.)

1610 GWILLIM *Heraldry* III. v. (1660) 119 A certain attracted fume drawne up on high by the operation of the Sunne. **1656** tr. *Hobbes' Elem. Philos.* 1839 Breath, that is to say attracted air. **1809** CRABBE *Tales* 37 Like all attracted things, he quicker flies, The place approaching where the attraction lies. **1856** TYNDALL *Fragm. Sc.* (1871) I. xiii. 374 The attracted end of the needle.

†**aˈttractical**, *a. Obs. rare*⁻¹. [f. ATTRACT, on incorrect analogies: cf. *tactical*.] Of the nature of attraction; 'attractional.'

1691 RAY *Creation* (1714) 93 Some stones are endued with an electrical or attractical vertue.

attracting (əˈtræktɪŋ), *vbl. sb.* [f. as prec. + -ING¹.] The action of drawing; attraction.

1563 T. GALE *Antidot.* II. 13 A power and vertue of healing and attracting. **1611** COTGR., *Attraiement*, an attracting, or drawing unto. [Now chiefly gerundial.]

aˈttracting, *ppl. a.* [f. as prec. + -ING².] That attracts: **a.** physically; **b.** emotionally, attractive (? *obs.*). Hence **aˈttractingly** *adv.*

1661 MORGAN *Sph. of Gentry* III. v. 53 The..attracting songs of the Syrens. **1753** RICHARDSON *Grandison* I. iv. 16 The most attracting ornament in it. *c* **1790** IMISON *Sch. Art* II. 163 Place the two attracting poles..on the middle of one of the bars. **1850** DAUBENY *Atom. The.* iv. 117 The attracting force of the atom of a given body. **1876** GEO. ELIOT *Dan. Der.* VII. lv. IV. 103 She had been attractingly wrought upon by the refined negations he presented to her.

attraction (əˈtrækʃən). [a. F. *attraction*, 16th c. (in 13th c. *attration*), or ad. L. *attractiōn-em*, n. of action f. *attrahĕre*: see ATTRACT *v.* and -TION.]

I. The action of drawing or sucking in.

†**1.** The drawing in or absorption of matter by any vessel of the body; the taking in of food. *Obs.*

1533 ELYOT *Cast. Helth* (1541) 46 Augmentation of heat, wherby hapneth the more attraction of thynges to be digested. **1585** LLOYD *Treas. Health* N ij, Debylitie of attraction in ye milte. **1621** BURTON *Anat. Mel.* I. i. II. v, Attraction is a ministering faculty, which as a loadstone doth iron, draws meat into the stomach, or as a lamp does oil.

†**2.** The drawing in of the breath, inspiration, inhalation. *Obs.*

1610 GWILLIM *Heraldry* III. xxii. (1660) 232 It behoveth they should have both Attraction and Respiration. **1638** VENNER *Tobacco* 411 Not sucking it into your windepipe and throat, with a sudden, or strong attraction.

II. The action or faculty of drawing to or towards the subject; the force that so draws; the fact of being so drawn.

†**3.** *Med.* The action of drawing humours, etc.; *concr.* an application that so draws, a poultice, etc.

1541 R. COPLAND *Galyen's Terap.* 2 H iv, The vsage of the herbe..for to make vyolent attraction. **1656** RIDGLEY *Pract. Physic* 14 Attractions must be applyed, as Pigeon's dung, Sope.

†**4.** Pulling, dragging, traction. *Obs.*

1578 BANISTER *Hist. Man* II. 39 Neither do they [Cartilages]..be extended by Attraction, as doe the Ligamentes.

5. a. The action of a body or substance in drawing to itself, by some physical force, another to which it is not materially attached; the force thus exercised.

1607 SHAKS. *Timon* IV. iii. 439 The Sunnes a Theefe, and with his great attraction Robbes the vaste Sea. **1626** BACON *Sylva* §704 Similitude of Substance will cause Attraction, where the Body is wholy freed from the Motion of Gravity. **1692** BENTLEY *Boyle Lect.* vii. 243 Attraction is an Operation, or Virtue, or Influence of distant Bodies upon each other through an empty Interval, without any Effluvia or Exhalations or other corporeal medium to convey and transmit it. **1722** WOLLASTON *Relig. Nat.* v. 79 Attraction, according to the true sense of the word, supposes one body to act upon another at a distance, or where it is not. **1837** BREWSTER *Magnet.* 265 A reciprocal tendency to unite, which is designated, and sometimes thought to be explained, by the merely descriptive word *attraction*.

Hence: The appropriate term for all the physical actions of this nature; (in every case *attraction* is used to name the *power* or *force* inferred, as well as the simple action of which we are cognizant).

b. ***magnetic attraction***: the action of a magnet or loadstone in drawing and attaching iron to itself. ***electric attraction***: the similar action of electrified substances upon certain other bodies.

1626 BACON *Sylva* §906 The Drawing of Amber and Iet, and other Electrick Bodies, and the Attraction in Gold of the Spirit of Quick-silver. **1665** GLANVILL *Sceps. Sci.* 14 To solve the motion of the Sea, and Magnetick Attractions. **1686** DRYDEN *Hind & P.* 370 Two magnets, heaven and earth, allude to bliss; The larger loadstone that, the nearer this; The weak attraction of the greater fails. **1849** MRS. SOMERVILLE *Connex. Phys. Sc.* xxviii, The attraction between electrified and unelectrified substances is merely a consequence of their altered state.

c. ***attraction*** of ***gravity*** or ***gravitation***: that which exists between all bodies, and acts at all distances, with a force proportional to their masses, and inversely proportional to the square of their distance apart.

1727 CHAMBERS *Cycl.* s.v., The attraction of gravity is one of the greatest and most universal principles in all nature. **1843** MILL *Logic* III. xiv. §2 Brought under the one law of the mutual attraction of all particles of matter. **1858** SIR J. HERSCHEL *Astron.* §564 In so far as their orbits can remain unaltered by the attractions of the planets. **1865** TYNDALL *Fragm. Sc.* II. i, With gravity there is no selection: no particular atoms choose, by preference, other particular atoms as objects of attraction.

d. ***molecular attraction***: that which takes place between the molecules of bodies, and acts only at infinitely small distances. ***attraction of cohesion***: that by which the particles composing a body are kept together. ***attraction of adhesion***: that by which certain substances, when brought into contact, stick together. ***capillary***

attraction: that whereby a liquid is drawn up or ascends through a hair-like tube.

1727 CHAMBERS *Cyclopædia* s.v., That which does not extend to sensible distances .. a late ingenious author chuses to call the *attraction of cohesion*. **1788** REID *Act. Powers* I. vi, The powers of corpuscular attraction, magnetism, electricity, gravitation. **1813** DAVY *Agric. Chem.* ii. (1814) 35 Attraction of cohesion .. enables fluids to rise in capillary tubes .. hence it is sometimes called capillary attraction. **1837** WHEWELL *Hist. Induct. Sc.* (1857) II. 50 Usually called capillary or molecular attraction. **1854** SCOFFERN in *Orr's Circ. Sc.* Chem. 2 Attraction which is effective only at insensible distances .. has been called *contiguous attraction*.

e. ***chemical attraction*** = AFFINITY 9.

1790 NICHOLSON *Chem.* vii. (*title*) On the Attractions exerted between Bodies, particularly those which the Chemists call Elective Attractions. **1813** DAVY *Agric. Chem.* 35 Chemical attraction, the power by which different species of matter tend to unite into one compound. **1831** T. P. JONES *Convers. Chem.* xx. 208 Both the compounds will be decomposed by the mutual interchange of their constituents, and two new compounds will be formed. All instances of this kind are said to result from *double elective attraction*, or *complex affinity*. **1865** TYNDALL *Fragm. Sc.* II. i, That molecular attraction which we call chemical affinity.

f. *fig.* Personal influence, figured as magnetic.

1750 JOHNSON *Rambl.* No. 160 ⁋5 Many natures .. seem to start back from each other by some invincible repulsion. There are others which immediately cohere whenever they come into the reach of mutual attraction. **1876** HAMERTON *Intell. Life* IX. v. 323 The subtle, but powerful attraction of the greater mind over the less.

6. The action of causing men or animals to come to one by influencing their appetites or desires; or of encouraging the visits of things by providing fit conditions for their settlement.

1742 POPE *Dunc.* IV. 75 And all the nations summoned to the throne .. None need a guide, by sure attraction led. *Mod.* The attraction of the disaffected to his standard.

7. The action of drawing forth interest, affection, or sympathy; the power of so doing; attractive influence.

1767 FORDYCE *Serm. Yng. Wom.* II. xiii. 256 Place your glory in .. kind attraction. **1848** CLOUGH *Armours de Voy.* II, There are two different kinds .. of human attraction: One which simply disturbs, unsettles, and makes you uneasy. **1884** V. LEE in *Contemp. Rev.* XLV. 33 Boars and stag hunts had no attraction for quiet men of business.

8. A quality which draws forth the interest or admiration; an attracting quality. (Chiefly in *pl.*)

1608 SHAKS. *Per.* v. i. 46 She, questionless, with her sweet harmony And other choice attractions, would allure. **1711** STEELE *Spect.* No. 41 ⁋5 She had new Attractions every time he saw her. **1750** JOHNSON *Rambl.* No. 72 ⁋11 The ornament of superficial attractions. **1824** DIBDIN *Libr. Comp.* 158 By no means destitute of typographical attractions.

9. A thing or feature which draws people by appealing to their desires, tastes, etc.; *esp.* any interesting or amusing exhibition which 'draws' crowds. (Littré, in his Supplement, says that this 'English sense' of attraction began to be borrowed in French about the era of the Great Exhibitions, and had then, in 1869, become quite current.)

1829 *Harlequin* 20 June 43 These performances, though possessing much novelty, did not prove sterling attractions. **1832** *Rep. Sel. Committee Dram. Lit.* 45 You may draw as beautiful a picture, but not so as to produce that sort of scenic effect which is the great attraction. **1862** W. ADAMS *Guide I. Wight* (1873) 108 The Pier is of course the great 'lion' and main attraction of the place. *a* **1885** *Mod.* The Health Exhibition has been the great attraction of the season (1884).

10. attraction sphere = CENTROSPHERE (*a*).

1896 E. B. WILSON *Cell in Developm. & Inher.* 36 The centrosome .. lies outside, though near, the nucleus, in the cyto-reticulum, surrounded by a granular, reticular, or radiating area of the latter known as the *attraction-sphere* or *centrosphere*. *Ibid.* 334 *Attraction-sphere*, the central mass of the aster from which the rays proceed.

Hence **a'ttractionless**, *a.* void of attractions, unattractive.

1882 *Glasg. Her.* 24 Nov. 4/1 The bare, attractionless area.

a'ttractionally, *adv.* [Implies an adj. *attractional*.] In manner of, or by way of, attraction.

1883 *American* VI. 172 The advance and retreat of the water react attractionally upon the plummet.

†**a'ttractionist.** *Obs.* [f. prec. + -IST.] One who accounted for phenomena by a theory of attraction.

1748 *Lond. Mag.* 583 The attractionists were in raptures with that which they perceived .. in electrical bodies.

attractive (əˈtræktɪv), *a.* and *sb.* Also 7 **attrective.** [a. F. *attractif, -ive* (14th c.), cogn. with Pr. *atractiu*, It. *attrattivo*, f. as if repr. L. **attractīvus*, f. *attract-*: see ATTRACT *v.* and -IVE.]

A. *adj.* Having the attribute of attracting; apt or tending to attract.

†**1.** Having the attribute of drawing or sucking in; absorptive. *Obs.*

1540 [see ATTRACT *v.* 1]. **1620** VENNER *Via Recta* viii. 192 By debilitie of the digestiue facultie, or of the Attractiue. **1621** BURTON *Anat. Mel.* I. i. II. v, This attractive power is very necessary in plants, which suck up moisture by the root. **1713** C'TESS. WINCHELSEA *Misc. Poems* 91 Vapours Which .. rise In Clouds to the attractive Brain.

†**2.** *Med.* Having the property of 'drawing' matter or humours. *Obs.*

1547 BOORDE *Brev. Health* xlvii. 22 b, For aches and peyne in the armes use seare clothes that be attractyve. **1597** J. T. *Serm. Paules Crosse* 46 A sore bitten with a venemous beast, can not be healed, except by an attractiue medicine. **1608** TOPSELL *Serpents* 630 Drawing or attractive plaisters. **1786** CHAMBERS *Cycl.* (Rees), *Attractives*, or *attractive remedies* .. which are to be externally applied.

†**3.** Having the property of drawing to itself by contact. *Obs.*

1607 TOPSELL *Four-f. Beasts* 81 The tongue of a Cat is very attractive and forcible like a file, attenuating by licking the flesh of a man.

4. Having the property of drawing to itself by some physical force bodies not materially attached to it; of the nature of attraction.

1603 HOLLAND *Plutarch's Mor.* 1337 There is not in that voidnesse any puissance attractive of bodies. **1656** tr. *Hobbes' Elem. Philos.* (1839) 527 The attractive power of the loadstone. **1695** BLACKMORE *Pr. Arth.* II. 466 It feels th' attractive Earth's Magnetick Force. **1794** HERSCHEL in *Phil. Trans.* LXXXV. 46 Sir Isaac Newton has shewn that the sun, by its attractive power, retains the planets of our system in their orbits. **1879** PRESCOTT *Sp. Telephone* 67 The intensity of the attractive impulses.

b. *fig.* Drawing as by magnetic influence.

1602 SHAKS. *Ham.* III. ii. 117 Here's Mettle more attractiue. **1642** BP. ANDREWES *Pattern Cath. Doctr.* 109 Love is the lode-stone attractive of love.

5. Having the quality of drawing (living beings) by influencing their will and action.

1590 SHAKS. *Mids. N.* II. ii. 91 She hath blessed and attractiue eyes. **1601** HOLLAND *Pliny* Ep. Vespas., Although your gentlenesse and humanitie be one way attrective, and induceth me to draw neare unto your presence. **1730** SOUTHALL *Buggs* 32 My Liquor has an attractive as well as the destructive Quality, and thereby does bring out and destroy every live Bugg. **1862** MILL *Utilit.* 60 The repelling influence of pain as well as the attractive one of pleasure.

6. Having the quality of attracting attention, interest, affection, or other pleasurable emotion; interesting, engaging, pleasing, winning, alluring. (Now the most frequent use.)

1602 WARNER *Alb. Eng.* Epit. (1612) 389 By his attractiue vertues .. confirmed to him the hearts of all his Subiects. **1630** BRATHWAIT *Eng. Gentl.* (1641) 410/2 Decency, the attractivest motive of affection. **1817** SCOTT *Rob Roy* i, Interesting and attractive for those who love to hear an old man's stories of a past age. **1859** *Sat. Rev.* 23 July 103 It tells it in a style almost as attractive as a novel. **1878** OUIDA *Friendship* I. 85 'Do you think her attractive?' 'No, not at all.'

B. *sb.*

†**1.** *Med.* A 'drawing' medicament. *Obs.*

1607 TOPSELL *Serpents* 619 The safest way .. to cure the poyson, is by attractives. **1656** RIDGLEY *Pract. Physic* 288 Set Cupping glasses to it; also other Attractives. **1786** [see A 2].

†**2.** That which draws like a magnet. Also *fig.*

1581 R. NORMAN (*title*) The new Attractive, containing a short Discourse of the Magnet or Loadstone, now first found out. **1614** RALEIGH *Hist. World* II. (1736) 267 The impiety of men is the forcible attractive of God's vengeance. *a* **1652** J. SMITH *Sel. Disc.* vii. 359 That powerful attractive which by a strong and divine sympathy draws down the virtue of heaven into the souls of men.

†**3.** A thing or circumstance which attracts attention, or interest, or draws people to see it; an 'attraction.' *Obs.*

1598 B. JONSON *Ev. Man in Hum.* III. iii. 34 And, then, the dressing Is a most maine attractive! **1765** DODDRIDGE in *Mem.* viii. §4. (1823) 221 God has removed so powerful an attractive from earth.

†**4.** A quality that attracts morally or through pleasurable emotions; *esp.* an attractive personal quality. *Obs.* (A very favourite word in the 17th and 18th centuries; now replaced by ATTRACTION.)

1635 NAUNTON *Fragm. Reg.* in *Harl. Misc.* (1793) 187 He had very fine attractives, as being a good piece of a scholar. **1706** COLLIER *Refl. Ridic.* 194 The Women that are caught by these Attractives, must be very silly. **1712** STEELE *Spect.* No. 302 ⁋4 The attractives of her Beauty. *a* **1805** BEDDOME *Disc.* in Spurgeon *Treas. Dav.* Ps. lxiii. 8 The powerful attractives of divine grace.

a'ttractively, *adv.* [f. prec. + -LY[2].] In an attractive manner, in a manner that attracts, or draws; by way of or with attraction.

1604 DRAYTON *Moyses* 1578 ('Ord. MS.' L.) And their glad ears attractively retain With what at Sinai Abraham's God had told. **1648** ROUS *Balm of Love* 3 Attractively amiable. **1871** SIR J. HERSCHEL *Fam. Lect. Sc.* 286 A medium attractively, and not repulsively elastic. **1878** ROFFE *Handbk. Shaks. Mus.* 18 The song was most attractively given.

a'ttractiveness. [f. as prec. + -NESS.] Attractive quality; aptness to draw to itself.

1673 *Phil. Trans.* VIII. 6136 The .. body will emulate Amber in brightness and the attractiveness of straw. **1684** in Birch *Hist. Royal Soc.* IV. 268 Observing the attractiveness of hot iron. *a* **1716** SOUTH *Serm.* VII. xiv. 293 (T.) The same attractiveness in riches, the same relish in sovereignty. **1869** SEELEY *Lect. & Ess.* vii. 190 The liveliness and attractiveness which interest boys.

attractor (əˈtræktə(r)). Also 7–8 **-er.** [Noun of agent (on Latin analogies), f. ATTRACT.]

1. That which attracts or draws to itself.

1646 SIR T. BROWNE *Pseud. Ep.* 81 Amber draweth them not .. they cannot rise unto the Attractor. **1713** DERHAM *Phys.-Theol.* 32 *note*, Which attraction .. of the lesser Bodies to that greater and most prevalent Attracter the Earth, is called their Gravity. **1859** MERIVALE *Rom. Emp.* V. xli. 65 The seven hills were themselves great attractors of rain.

2. One who draws by sympathy or moral force.

1641 SMECTYMNUUS *Answ. Humb. Rem.* (1653) 90 The chiefe attractor of the rebellious party. **1654** WHITLOCK *Mann. Eng.* 343 (T.) True attracters of love.

†**a'ttractory**, *a. Med. Obs. rare*$^{-1}$. [ad. L. *attractōrius*, f. *attract-*: see ATTRACT *v.* and -ORY.] Acting as an attractor (of humours, etc.).

1684 tr. *Bonet's Merc. Compit.* VI. 159 In this [fever] especially Hippocrates propounded his attractory Broths.

attrahent (ˈætrəhənt), *a.* and *sb.* [ad. L. *attrahent-em*, pr. pple. of *attrahĕre* to draw to: see ATTRACT *v.*] **A.** *adj.* That attracts, drawing, attracting. **B.** *sb.* (sc. agent.)

1661 LOVELL *Hist. Anim. & Min.* 518 The humours, which easily follow the attrahent medicament. **1665** GLANVILL *Sceps. Sci.* xv. 127 The motion of steel to its attrahent. **1786** CHAMBERS *Cycl.* (Rees) s.v., Attrahents are the same with what we otherwise call drawers, ripeners, maturantia, etc.

‖**attrait** (atrɛ). *Theol.* [Fr., f. *attraire* to attract.] The means by which God draws souls to Himself, vocation; inclination, attraction.

1908 F. VON HÜGEL *Mystical Element of Religion* I. iv. 131 (*heading*) Catherine and Tommasa Fiesca: their difference of character and *attrait*. **1911** —— *Let.* 11 Jan. in M. de la Bedoyere *Life* (1951) II. xi. 254 Souls of a mystical *attrait* .. will also tend to find, in so far as they are dominated by their specific religious *attrait*, all the *other non-religious contingencies and activities of* man's life, a weariness and an irritation. **1936** E. UNDERHILL *Worship* xiv. 309 A Quaker Meeting does not merely provide a suitable environment, within which individuals can follow in the silence their own devotional *attrait*. **1970** O. CHADWICK *Victorian Church* II. iv. 182 He was not in such plentiful supply as to warrant stationing him in the country unless he had a special attrait in that direction. **1978** *Church Times* 8 Dec. 13/1 Other Western countries .. have lost or ignored the deep *attrait* to simplicity which showed itself in such things as Georgian houses [etc.]. **1984** *Kairos* No. 10. 8 To help others, they must be conversant with a diversity of methods [of prayer] and sensitive to diversity of attrait.

†**a'ttrap**, *v.*[1] *Obs.* [a. F. *attrape-r*, OF. *atraper*, f. *à* to, at + *trappe* TRAP.] To catch in, or as in, a trap; to entrap.

1524 *State Pa. Hen. 8*, VI. 258 To practise and attrapp Mons. de Bourbon. **1588** A. KING *Canisius' Catech.* 36 He .. hes strowed all our wayes with girnes, to attrape our saules. **1681** DINELEY *Tour in Irel.* in *Trans. Kilkenny Archæol. Soc* Ser. II. II. 24, I have seen his hunts men halter, at-trap, and put ropes upon ye heads of good bucks.

†**a'ttrap**, *v.*[2] *Obs.* Chiefly in pa. pple. **attrapped, attrapt.** [f. A- *pref.* 11 + TRAP *v.*] Furnished with trappings. (Said of a horse.)

1580 BARET *Alv.* A 704 Attrapped royally, *Instratus ornatu regio.* **1596** SPENSER *F.Q.* IV. iv. 39 And all his steed With oaken leaves attrapt. **1600** HOLLAND *Livy* 858 (R.) Shall your horse bee attrapped and barbed more richly? **1693** ROBERTSON *Phraseol. Gen.* 178 Attrap, *Phaleris ornare.*

†**a'ttray**, *v. Obs. rare*$^{-1}$. [a. F. *attrai-re, attrayant*:—L. *attrahĕre* to ATTRACT. Cf. *betray*.] To attract, draw away.

1579 BAKER *Guydon's Quest. Cyrurg.* 40 The third intention wherefore bleeding is made, is for to attray.

†**a'ttrayant**, *a. Obs. rare*$^{-1}$. In 5 **atr-**. [a. F. *attrayant*, OF. *atrayant*, pr. pple. of *a(t)traire* to attract.] Attracting.

1475 CAXTON *Jason* 61 The gracioуse atrayans regardes that she gaf afte times unto the preu Jason.

†**attrec'tation.** *Obs.* Also 7 **attract-.** (attrection in Cockeram.) [ad. L. *attrectātiōn-em*, n. of action f. *attrectā-re* to touch, handle, f. *at-* = *ad-* to + *tractāre* to handle.] Touching, handling, feeling with the hands.

1615 CROOKE *Body of Man* 237 What through the affluence of humours, what through attrectation. **1623** COCKERAM, *Attrection*, a handling, or feeling. **1663** *Flagellum* or *O. Cromwell* (1672) 176 Which like .. the apples of Sodom, vanished and perished in the Attrectation.

a'ttribuate, *pa. pple. Obs.* [f. F. *attribué*: see -ATE[2].] By-form of ATTRIBUTE *ppl. a.*

1541 R. COPLAND *Guydon's Quest. Cyrurg.*, Their mater is attribuate to them at the very begynnynge of theyr creacyon.

†**a'ttribue**, *v. Obs.* [a. F. *attribue-r* (14th c. in Littré), ad. L. *attribuĕre*.] To ATTRIBUTE.

1481 CAXTON *Tulle of Old Age*, Hit must be attribued and remitted unto the Greekyssh bokes and langage. **1483** —— *Gold. Leg.* 87/4 To attrybue it to the mercy of God. **1489** —— *Faytes of A.* I. vi. 14 To the seygnourye of a [= one] Cyte he attrybued and gate so many other.

attributable (əˈtrɪbjʊtəb(ə)l), *a.* [f. ATTRIBUTE *v.* + -ABLE.] Capable of being attributed or ascribed, *esp.* as owing to, produced by.

1665 GLANVILL *Sceps. Sci.* xii. 65 Not strictly attributable to any thing without us. **1678** EVELYN *Silva* (ed. 3) Pref., Experiments justly Attributable to several Members of the Royal Society. **1843** MILL *Logic* III. xvii. §4 How much is attributable to that cause.

attributal ('ætrɪbjuːtəl, ə'trɪb-), *a.* [f. ATTRIBUTE *sb.* + -AL.] Of the nature of an attribute.

1894 *Standard* 30 July 6/6 Why do not Welshmen take as surnames..the attributal adjectives by which they are known? William Thomas, distinguished by Tynawern (the house in the wood) would always be identified as William Tynawern. **1902** *Jrnl. Amer. Folk-lore* Jan.-Mar. 14 It is oftentimes difficult to discover their identities, since they bear many attributal or descriptive names.

†**a'ttributary**, *a.* *Obs. rare*⁻¹. [On form-analogy of *tributary*.] To be attributed.

1650 CHARLETON *Paradoxes* 58 As if the whole energy of the act were soly attributary to himself.

†'**attribute**, *ppl. a. Obs.* [ad. L. *attribūt-us*, pa. pple. of *attribuĕre*, f. *at-*, *ad-* to + *tribuĕre* to assign, bestow, grant, yield, deliver. After the formation of the verb *to attribute*, the regular *attributed* gradually took its place as pa. pple., and *attribute* not being needed as an adj. became obs. Cf. -ATE².] Attributed; assigned, given.

1398 TREVISA *Barth. De P.R.* I. (1495) 5 Power is approprid to the fader . to the sone wysdome is attrybute: and to the holy ghost is attrybute grace. **1539** TONSTALL *Serm. Palme Sund.* (1823) 51 All these honorable names be attribute by theym vnto hym. **1599** THYNNE *Animadv.* 48 Heccate, which name is attribute to Diana.

attribute ('ætrɪbjuːt), *sb.* [prob., in the main, a subst. use of ATTRIBUTE *ppl. a.*, though the L. *attribūtum* (neuter sb. from the pa. pple. *attribūtus*), common in theological language, or its F. adaptation *attribut* (14th c. in Littré), may well have been the prototype.]

1. A quality or character ascribed to any person or thing, one which is in common estimation or usage assigned to him; hence, *sometimes*, an epithet or appellation in which the quality is ascribed.

a **1400** *Cov. Myst.* 193 To the Sone connynge doth longe expres, Therwith the Serpent dyd Adam asay..Thus the secunde person attrybute Was only towchyd by temptacion. **1589** PUTTENHAM *Eng. Poesie* (Arb.) 44 The verie *Etimologie* of the name [God]..declaring plainely the nature of the attribute, which is all one as if we sayd *good*. **1596** SHAKS. *Merch. V.* IV. i. 195 Mercy is aboue this sceptred sway..It is an attribute to God himselfe. **1660** STANLEY *Hist. Philos.* 3/2 The attribute of Wise..was conferr'd upon the rest in respect of their moral Rules and Practice. **1846** WRIGHT *Ess. Mid. Ages* II. xiii. 88 It is surprising how soon historical personages become invested with romantic attributes.

†**2.** Distinguished quality or character; honour, credit, reputation ascribed. (Cf. the parallel use of *quality*, *rank*, *position*, etc. in 'a person of *quality*,' i.e. '*quality* worth naming.') *Obs.*

1602 SHAKS. *Ham.* I. iv. 22 It takes From our achievements..The pith and marrow of our attribute. **1606** —— *Tr. & Cr.* II. iii. 125 Much attribute he hath, and much the reason, Why we ascribe it to him. *c* **1690** TEMPLE *Heroic Virt.* Wks. 1731 I. 194 Cæsar..possessed very eminently all the Qualities..that enter into the composition of an Heroe, but failed of the Attribute or Honour.

3. A material object recognized as appropriate to, and thus symbolic of, any office or actor; *spec.* in *Painting*, *Sculpture*: A conventional symbol added, as an accessory, to denote the character or show the identity of the personage represented.

1596 SHAKS. *Merch. V.* IV. i. 191 His Scepter shewes the force of temporall power, The attribute to awe and Maiestie. **1705** ADDISON *Italy* Rome, The sculptor, to distinguish him, gave him what the medallists call his proper attributes, a spear and a shield. **1727-41** CHAMBERS *Cycl.* s.v. *Attributes*, The Club is an attribute of Hercules. **1814** WORDSW. *Excurs.* v. 492 A crown, an attribute of sovereign power. **1880** WALDSTEIN *Pythag. Rhegion* 19 A..remnant of marble, which shows that he also held a long attribute in his left hand. **1883** Q. VICTORIA *More Leaves* 6 A small room full of his rifles and other implements and attributes of sport.

4. A quality or character considered to belong to or be inherent in a person or thing; a characteristic quality.

1836-7 SIR W. HAMILTON *Metaph.* viii. (1870) I. 151 *Attribute* is a word properly convertible with *quality*, for every quality is an attribute and every attribute is a quality; but in our language, custom has introduced a certain distinction in their application. Attribute is considered as a word of loftier signification, and is, therefore, conventionally limited to qualities of a higher application. Thus, for example, it would be felt as indecorous to speak of the qualities of God, and as ridiculous to talk of the attributes of matter.

(This distinction is hardly borne out by historical usage. Originally, 'the attributes of God' was preferred probably because men assumed no knowledge of the actual *qualities* of the Deity, but only of those more or less fitly 'attributed' him; i.e. 'attributes' in sense 1. But the exalted sense 2 may have associated itself with the expression in the minds of many who used it. J. A. H. M.)

[Cf. 1400 and 1596 in sense 1.] **1603** HOLLAND *Plutarch's Mor.* 26 All other fabulous fictions and attributes given unto them [the Gods]..have been devised only to give contentment to the readers. **1605** BACON *Adv. Learn.* I. vi. §1 The attributes and acts of God, as far as they are revealed to man. **1692** BENTLEY *Boyle Lect.* vi. 208 Neither Matter, nor Motion as its Attribute and Property, can have existed from all Eternity. **1713** DERHAM *Phys.-Theol.* 72 Demonstrations of the Being and Attributes of God. **1825** MᶜCULLOCH *Pol. Econ.* I. 2 An attribute or quality of those articles only which it requires some portion of voluntary human labour to produce. **1860** PUSEY *Min. Proph.* 208 Truth, wisdom, power, justice, holiness and other attributes ..have in God their real being; in creatures a shadow of being only. **1868** FREEMAN *Norm. Conq.* (1876) II. ix. 359 Endowed with all the highest attributes of the statesman.

b. *rarely applied to*: A bodily quality.

1820 SCOTT *Monast.* xxiv, Beauty was an attribute of the family. **1862** TROLLOPE *Orley F.* xix. 130, I will begin with her exterior attributes.

c. in *Logic*, That which may be predicated of any thing; a quality, mode of existence, affection; *strictly* an essential and permanent quality.

1785 REID *Int. Powers* 440 Every attribute is what the ancients called an universal. **1843** MILL *Logic* I. ii. §4 Whiteness, again, is the name of a quality or attribute of those things. **1870** BOWEN *Logic* i. 8 The Concept is the Intuition stripped of its contingent or unessential attributes or marks.

5. *Gram.* Sometimes used for: A word denoting an attribute; an attributive word; a predicable. *esp.* in *Sentence Analysis*: = Attributive adjunct, *i.e.* an adjective, or a word, phrase, or clause, performing the function of an adjective.

1808 MIDDLETON *Grk. Article* (1855) 56 By Attributes Mr. Harris means Adjectives, Verbs, and Participles. **1867** MORELL *Eng. Gram.* (ed. 3) 53 The attribute to the noun, *i.e.* the adjective or whatever takes the place of the adjective. **1873** J. CURTIS *Analysis* 5 The subject may be enlarged by an attribute.

attribute (ə'trɪbjuːt), *v.* [f. the prec. ppl. adj., which continued for some time to act as the pa. pple. of this, alongside of *attributed*. The poets down to Dryden and Scott show the pronunciation *attri'bute* or '*attribute*, as in the ppl. adj. and sb.]

I. As an external act.

1. To assign, bestow, give, concede, yield *to* any one, as his right (property, title, authority, worship, honour). *arch.* or *Obs.*

1523 LD. BERNERS *Froiss.* I. 375 These two townes were attributed to Flaunders by reason of gage. **1537** HEN. VIII in Strype *Cranmer* (1694) App. 49 Whether this word Sacrament be, and ought to be, attribute to the Seven only? **1565** T. RANDOLPH in Ellis *Orig. Lett.* I. 184 II. 201 All honor that maye be attributed unto anye man by a wyf. **1620** MELTON *Astrolog.* 62 Idolatry is a Diuine Worship, attributted to Idols. **1771** *Junius Lett.* xlix. 255 The power of depriving the subject of his birthright [was] attributed to ..the legislature.

b. To give or ascribe in assertion (praise or honour).

1563 SHUTE *Archit.* F ij b, To whom vndoubtedly, the praise and commendation is chiefly to be attrybuted. **1605** BACON *Adv. Learn.* II. xxii. §15 What celsitude of honour Plinius Secundus attributeth to Trajan in his funeral oration.

2. To add to the representation of a personage, the conventional symbolic 'attribute.' *rare.*

1756 J. WARTON *Ess. Pope* (1782) I. ii. 25 The trite and obvious insignia of a river God are attributed.

II. As a mental act.

3. To ascribe *to* as belonging or proper; to consider or view as belonging or appropriate *to*.

1538 STARKEY *England* 45 In the felycyte of man you put dyverse degres, to some attrybutyng more, and to some les. **1667** MILTON *P.L.* XI. 836 God attributes to place No sanctity, if none be thither brought By men. **1678** CUDWORTH *Intell. Syst.* I. iv. xxiv. 409 They..attribute the Highest place to that which is divine. **1832** LEWIS *Use & Ab. Pol. Terms* Introd. 6 A sense is attributed to them which was never intended.

†**4.** *to attribute* (*much*), etc.: to ascribe great importance *to*, to hold in high estimation. *Obs.*

1586 *Let. to Earle Leycester* 32, I attribute not so much to mine owne iudgement. **1611** BIBLE *Pref.* 4 Epiphanius.. doeth attribute so much vnto it [the LXX], that he holdeth the Authours thereof..for Prophets. **1667** MILTON *P.L.* VIII. 565 Attributing overmuch to things Less excellent. *Ibid.* IX. 320 Eve, who thought Less attributed to her Faith sincere.

5. To ascribe as a quality or 'attribute' belonging, proper, or inherent. (To attribute wisdom to one = to hold that he is wise.)

1534 MORE *Answ. Pois. Bk.* Wks. 1121/1 To attribute to hys manhed yᵗ property which onely is appropried to his godhed, is to confounde bothe yᵉ natures in Christ. **1611** BIBLE *Job* i. 22 In all this Iob sinned not, nor charged God foolishly [*marg.* attributed folly to God]. **1638** WILKINS *New World* I. (1684) 172 Such a strange Efficacy in the Bread of the Eucharist, as their Miraculous Relations do Attribute to it. **1862** MILL *Utilit.* 42 The sort of mystical character which ..is apt to be attributed to the idea of moral obligation.

6. To ascribe, impute, or refer, as an effect *to* the cause; to reckon as a consequence of.

1530 PALSGR. 440/1, I attrybute, I ascrybe the cause of a mater to one cause or other, *J'attribue*. **1626** DK. BUCKHM. in Ellis *Orig. Lett.* I. 329 III. 234, I cannot attribute this honour to any desert in me. **1794** SULLIVAN *View Nat.* I. 39 To the deluge he attributed the changes of the earth. **1876** GREEN *Short Hist.* vi. §1 (1882) 268 The shrivelled arm of Richard the Third was attributed to witchcraft.

7. To ascribe *to* an author as his work.

1599 THYNNE *Animadv.* 15 [They] whiche attribute that choyse of armes to Chaucer. **1628** PRYNNE *Cens. Cozens* 29 Others attribute the inuention of them to St. Hierome. **1728** NEWTON *Chronol. Amended* i. 86 The people of the Island Corcyra attributed the invention of the Sphere to Nausicaa. **1816** SINGER *Hist. Cards* 157 To Gutenberg..we are inclined to attribute that which is said to be in the characters afterwards used by Albert Pfister at Bamberg. **1854** (*title*) Edward III: a Play attributed to Shakespeare.

8. To assign in one's opinion *to* its proper time or place.

1567 *Triall Treas.* (1850) 27 To the ende he semeth to attribute that thing When men be asociate with treasures celestiall. **1601** HOLLAND *Pliny* I. 75 They attribute the birth of the Muses in the wood Helicon. **1875** SCRIVENER *Lect. Grk. Test.* 12 Several copies which may fairly be attributed to the fourth century.

†**9.** With *complement*: To allow any one the 'attribute' of; to hold him to be.

1649 G. DANIEL *Trinarch. Hen. IV*, 192 When a Naturall Motley makes a Hood Vnto a Man, wee attribute him wise.

a'ttributed, *ppl. a.* [f. prec. + -ED. (Scott accented '*attributed*.)] Given as an attribute or appropriate possession; ascribed as proper to.

1808 SCOTT *Marm.* IV. Introd., If mortal charity dare claim The Almighty's attributed name. **1854** [see ATTRIBUTE *v.* 7].

attributeless ('ætrɪbjuːtlɪs), *a.* [f. ATTRIBUTE *sb.* + -LESS.] Without attributes.

1894 *Thinker* VI. 448 The Vedântin is more drawn by the fascination of that attributeless immensity. **1924** *Expositor* Feb. 107 Esoterically he holds that nothing is real but the attributeless Brahman.

a'ttributer. *rare.* [f. ATTRIBUTE *v.* + -ER¹.] One who attributes; an imputer.

1611 COTGR., *Imputeur*..a putter of things vpon, an attributer of things vnto others.

a'ttributing, *vbl. sb.* [f. as prec. + -ING¹.] The action of ascribing as an attribute; attribution.

a **1631** DONNE *Select.* (1840) 36 We banish..all attributing of any power, to any faculty of our own.

attribution (ætrɪ'bjuːʃən). [a. F. *attribution*, 14th c. ad. L. *attribūtiōn-em*, n. of action f. *attribuĕre* to ATTRIBUTE.] The action of attributing; the result in which this action is embodied.

I. The (external) action of bestowing.

1. The action of bestowing or assigning (in fact); bestowal. *arch.* or *Obs.*

1467 J. TIPTOFT, EARL. WORC. in *MS. Harl.* 69 No. 17 Reserving always to the Queenes Highnes and the Ladyes there present, the Attribution and Gifte of the Prize. **1650** T. GOODWIN *Wks.* (1862) IV. 446 The communication and attribution of the same rights, privileges, attributes. **1829** LANDOR *Imag. Conv.* (1846) I. 249 Although the Graces in none of their attributions are benignant to him.

2. Ascription in word or statement.

1649 ROBERTS *Clavis Bibl.* 39 By a gratefull Attribution, or Ascribing such names and titles unto God. **1667** *Decay Chr. Piety* v. §18. 233 We..never suspect these glorious attributions may be no more than complement or flattery. **1876** BANCROFT *Hist. U.S.* V. v. 389 The biographer's attribution of special merit to Colonel Reed.

II. The (internal) action of ascribing or imputing.

3. The assigning or ascribing of a character or quality as belonging or proper to any thing.

1651 WITTIE tr. *Primrose's Pop. Err.* IV. 246 Attribution of this power and dominion to them. **1774** T. WARTON *Eng. Poetry* (1840) I. Diss. i. 14 The attribution of prophetical language to birds. **1837** WHEWELL *Hist. Induct. Sc.* XVII. iv. §2 The attribution of sexes to plants. **1838** SIR W. HAMILTON *Logic* v. (1866) I. 77 As these qualities or modes are only identified with the thing by a mental attribution, they are called attributes.

b. *self-attribution*: ascription of honour or credit to oneself.

1649 ROBERTS *Clavis Bibl.* 184 Not to give themselves to sensual pleasures, Luxury, Vain-glory, Self-attributions.

4. The ascribing of an effect to a cause, of a work to its author, date, place, or of date and place to a work. *esp.* in *Art-criticism*: The ascription of a work of art to its supposed author.

a **1665** J. GOODWIN *Filled w. the Spirit* (1867) 335 Though the same attribution..be made unto God..wherein the action is ascribed unto God. **1805** ELLIS *E.E. Metr. Rom.* (ed. Bohn) 75 *note*, Few mistakes are more usual than the attribution of early pieces to the copyists. **1864** *Reader* 27 Feb. 261/2 That any one has been yet tempted to follow his attributions. **1881** SAINTSBURY *Dryden* i. 19 The blundering attribution of Dryden and his rivals to Corneille and Racine. **1882** J. EVANS in *Nature* XXV. 549 Of John Hyrcanus.. there are numerous copper coins of undoubted attribution.

†**5.** *Rhet.* The qualifying of words by attributive adjuncts; giving of epithets. *Obs.*

1589 PUTTENHAM *Eng. Poesie* III. xvii. (Arb.) 193 *Epitheton* or the Quallifier, otherwise the figure of Attribution.

6. *Logic.* Predication of an attribute.

1860 ABP. THOMSON *Laws of Th.* §60 To say that man is mortal is an act of Attribution. **1870** BOWEN *Logic* v. 128 In each of the other forms the attribution is conditional.

III. A thing attributed.

7. Anything ascribed in one's opinion or estimation, *e.g.* ascribed name, appellation, credit, character, property, quality, meaning, or sense of a word. Also in early use = ATTRIBUTE 2. ? *Obs.*

1596 SHAKS. *1 Hen. IV*, IV. i. 3 Such attribution should the Douglas haue, As not a Souldiour of this seasons stampe, Should go so generall currant through the world. **1615** T. ADAMS *Two Sonnes* 68 Many and excellent are the attributions wᶜʰ the Scripture giveth us—as Friends,

Children, Heirs, &c. **1738** Warburton *Div. Legat.* II. 237 To which Species of Gods it was an honorary Attribution.

†8. An attributive word or adjunct, an 'attribute.' (So in L.) *Obs.*

1589 Puttenham *Eng. Poesie* III. xvii. (Arb.) 193 Sometimes wordes suffered to go single, do giue greater sence and grace than words quallified by attributions do.

9. Authority or function granted (to a ruler, minister, delegate, court). (From mod. French.)

1796 Morse *Amer. Geog.* II. 376 The legislative body shall determine the number and attributions (or functions) of the ministers. **1849** Grote *Greece* II. xlvi. V. 482 Trials for homicide were only a small part of its attributions. **1865** Mill *Repr. Govt.* 125/2 Within the limits of its attributions, it makes laws which are obeyed by every citizen.

attributive (æˈtrɪbjuːtɪv), *a.* and *sb.* [a. F. *attributif, -ive* (Cotgr.), f. L. *attribūt-* (see attribute *a.*) + -ive, as if ad. L. **attribūtīvus*.]

A. *adj.*

†1. Characterized by attributing. *Obs.*

1606 Shaks. *Tr. & Cr.* II. ii. 58 (*Qo.*) The will dotes that is attributive [*Folio*, inclineable] To what infectiously it selfe affects, Without some image of th' affected merit.

2. *Logic.* That assigns an attribute to a subject.

1849 Abp. Thomson *Laws of Th.* (1860) §77. 134 Attributive [judgment] where an indefinite (i.e. undistributed) predicate is assigned to the subject. **1870** Bowen *Logic* v. 110 In Attributive Judgments the Predicate is actually thought only connotatively, as a Mark or attribute of the Subject, and not denotatively, as the name of a class of things.

3. *Gram.* That expresses an attribute.

c **1840** Douglas *Eng. Gram.* (1876) 16 Attributive adjectives are those which express the quality of an object, as, a kind friend. **1875** Whitney *Life Lang.* x. 207 Nearly all attributive words were inflected. **1881** Mason *Eng. Gram.* 145 When to a noun or pronoun we attach an adjective, or what is equivalent to an adjective..this adjective or its equivalent stands in the *Attributive Relation* to the noun or pronoun, and is said to be an *Attributive Adjunct* to it.

4. So-assigned, so-ascribed (by those who essay to assign the authorship of a painting or work of art). Cf. *ascriptive, putative,* and attribution 4.

1866 Howells *Venet. Life* xiv. 206 An attributive Veronese.

B. *sb.* An attributive word, one that denotes an attribute. Applied by Harris and others to adjectives, verbs, and adverbs; by most modern grammarians only to adjectives and their equivalents.

1750 Harris *Hermes* I. vi. (1786) 87 Attributives are all those principal Words, that denote Attributes, considered as Attributes. *Ibid.* 94 All Attributives are either Verbs, Participles, or Adjectives. **1858** Marsh *Eng. Lang.* ix. 193 A radical, which in its simplest form and use, serves only as an attributive, in other words as an adjective, may be made to denote the quality which it ascribes, or an act by which that quality is manifested or imparted, and thus become a noun or a verb. **1881** Mason *Eng. Gram.* 18 Both Verbs and Adjectives express notions of the actions and attributes of things. Verbs *assert* the connection of the thing and its action or attribute; Adjectives *assume* this connection. To borrow a word from Mechanics, the Verb is a *Dynamic Attributive*, the Adjective is a *Static Attributive*.

a'ttributively, *adv.* [f. prec. + -ly[2].] In an attributive way; as an attribute.

1853 J. W. Gibbs *Philol. Stud.* xi, Any substantive may have a word or phrase joined to it attributively. *Mod.* In *house dog*, and OE. *hús-carl*, the simple substantive 'house' is used *attributively*, instead of an adjective or genitive case.

a'ttributiveness. *rare.* [f. as prec. + -ness.] The quality of being attributive.

1861 L. Alexander tr. *Dorner's Pers. Christ* I. I. 24 A position fluctuating between self-sustenance and attributiveness [Ger. *Selbstständigkeit und Eigenschaftlichkeit*].

attrimentous, obs. form of atramentous.

attrist (əˈtrɪst), *v.* ? *Obs.* [a. F. *attriste-r*, f. *à* to + *triste*:—L. *tristis* sad.] To make sad, sadden.

1680 Sir W. Waller *Div. Medit.* (1839) 103 Some aires and tunes..sensibly attrist, others comfort. **1791** H. Walpole in *Miss Berry's Jrnl. & Corr.* I. 307 Your tender nature is not made for such spectacles; and why attrist it without doing any service.

attrite (əˈtraɪt), *ppl. a.* [ad. L. *attrītus*, pa. pple. of *atterĕre*, f. *at-* = *ad-* to, at + *terĕre* to rub.]

1. Worn or ground down by friction. ? *Obs.*

1654 Jer. Taylor *Real Pres.* 40 A thing may be..chewed though it be not attrite or broken. **1667** Milton *P.L.* x 1073 Or by collision of two bodies, grinde The Air attrite to Fire.

2. *Theol.* Having attrition: see attrition 4.

1625 Ussher *Answ. Jesuit* 91 A man in confession, of attrite is made contrite by vertue of the keyes. **1817** *Tracts for Day* i. 10 The Ephesian converts again, moved by fear and therefore attrite, came and confessed.

attrited (əˈtraɪtɪd), *ppl. a.* [f. prec. + -ed.] Worn down by continued friction. Also *fig.*

1760 Sterne *Tr. Shandy* (1770) III. 50 So glazed, so contrited and attrited was it with fingers and with thumbs in all its parts. **1866** J. Rose *Ovid's Met.* 47 The stream..Rolling and bubbling through attrited sand. **1872** M. Collins *Pr. Clarice* I. xiv. 206 The traveller..gets his individuality toned down, gets a softened and attrited character.

a'ttriteness. ? *Obs.* [f. attrite *a.* + -ness.] 'The being much worn.' Bailey 1731.

attrition (əˈtrɪʃən). Also 4–6 -icioun, -ycyon, etc. [ad. L. *attrītiōn-em*, n. of action f. *attrīt-*: see attrite and -ion[1]. The theological sense 4 was earliest in Eng.]

1. The action or process of rubbing one thing against another; mutual friction.

1601 Holland *Pliny* I. 490 They make shift for to rub and grate one wood against another, and by this attrition there fly out sparkes. **1776** Priestley in *Phil. Trans.* LXVI. 230 Some..think that heat is produced in the lungs by the attrition of the blood in passing through them. **1822** Imison *Sc. & Art.* I. 70 When the mill is too slowly fed..the stones, by their attrition, are apt to strike fire.

fig. **1656** Bp. Hall *Occas. Medit.* (1851) 34 The dangerous attritions of stubborn and wrangling spirits. **1782** V. Knox *Ess.* (1819) II. lxviii. 55 Nor have yet become callous by attrition with the world.

2. a. The action or process of rubbing away, wearing or grinding down, by friction.

1601 Holland *Pliny* II. 466 Polished by that rubbing and attrition which it meets withall, in the course and stream of the water. **1718** J. Chamberlayne *Relig. Philos.* I. iv. §6 The Attrition or Breaking of the Food. **1830** Lyell *Princ. Geol.* I. 250 Pebbles and sand..decrease in size by attrition.

fig. **1682** Sir T. Browne *Chr. Morals* (1756) 58 The compage of all physical truths is not..always so closely maintained, as not to suffer attrition. **1858** Max Müller *Chips* (1880) II. xxvii. 354 Contact with English society exercises a constant attrition on the system of castes.

b. *Mil.* The wearing down of the enemy's strength and morale by unremitting harassment, esp. in phr. ***war of attrition.***

1914 *Sphere* 21 Nov. 181/1 This is a war of attrition, in which each side tries to wear down the other. **1915** Kitchener *Memorandum* in Lloyd George *War Mem. D. Lloyd George* (1933) I. xii. 435 The end of the War must come through one of the two following causes: (1) by a decisive victory..or (2) by attrition. **1918** E. S. Farrow *Dict. Mil. Terms* 45 *Attrition*, in a military sense, the act of wearing away the enemy's strength, increasing his mortality list, and lowering his morale. **1919** Haig *Desp.* 21 Mar. (1919) 326 The rapid collapse of Germany's military powers ..would not have taken place but for that period of ceaseless attrition. **1927** W. S. Churchill *World Crisis 1916–18* I. ii. 45 The only method of waging war on the Western Front was by wearing down the enemy by 'killing Germans in a war of attrition'. **1958** *Listener* 13 Nov. 791/3 Nor did Montgomery, unfairly scornful though he is of generalship in the first world war, disdain tactics of attrition at times.

fig.

1930 *Daily Express* 30 July 3/7 Fine weather at the Oval may mean an endurance test—perhaps a full week of slow batting and attack by process of attrition.

3. *Surg.* a. Rubbing away of the skin or tissue; excoriation, abrasion. b. Comminuted fracture. (With quot. 1585 cf. OF. *attrice* hæmorrhoid.)

1543 Traheron *Vigo's Chirurg.* vi. 184 A greate medicine in all wrestyngs and attritions of lacertes. **1585** Lloyd *Treas. Health* M ij, Hemorroydes and attrycions in the fundament. **1634** T. Johnson tr. *Parey's Chirurg.* xv. i. (1678) 327 They call it Attrition, when the bone is broken into many small fragments. **1853** Mayne *Exp. Lex.*, *Attrition*..(*Surg.*) violent crushing of a part. **1875** H. Wood *Therap.* (1879) 582 Whenever surfaces become sore by attrition, or chafe.

4. *Theol.* An imperfect sorrow for sin, as if a bruising which does not amount to utter crushing (*contrition*); 'horror of sin through fear of punishment, without any loving sense, or taste of God's mercy' (Hooker), while *contrition* has its motive in the love of God. (A sense invented by scholastic theologians in 12th c.; the earliest in Eng.)

c **1374** Chaucer *Troylus* I. 557 Thou..wailist for thi synne and thyn offence, And hast for ferde caught attrition. **1506** *Ord. Crysten Men* IV. iii. 171 Attrycyon..is a maner of contrycyon unparfyte. **1765** Tucker *Lt. Nat.* II. 65 Three stages in the passage from vice to virtue: attrition, contrition, and repentance. The first is a sorrow for the mischiefs men have brought upon their own heads by their ill doings. **1875** H. E. Manning *Mission H. Ghost* i. 16 Sacramental grace to raise our sorrow from attrition to contrition.

attritional (əˈtrɪʃənəl), *a.* [f. attrition + -al.] Characterized by attrition.

1847–9 *Todd's Cycl. Anat.* IV. 530/1 The preliminary breaking up of structure which appears to be chiefly physical or attritional in the normal cartilage. **1960** *Times* 20 Feb. 10/2 McMorris..delved into the archives of slow-scoring. .. Attritional cricket is his speciality.

attritive (əˈtraɪtɪv), *a.* *rare.* [f. L. *attrīt-* see attrite), as if ad. L. **attrītīvus*.] Characterized by attrition, wearing away.

c **1850** H. Miller *Rambles Geol.* ii. (1858) 246 Subjected to some further attritive process.

attritor (əˈtraɪtə(r)). *rare.* [f. as prec. + -or.] He who or that which rubs away or wears down.

1818 *Art Preserv. Feet* 49 Another with his eradicator, a third with his attritor, all radical cures for corns.

attritus (əˈtraɪtəs). *rare.* [f. as prec. after *detritus*.] Matter produced by rubbing away or wearing down.

1837 Carlyle *Fr. Rev.* III. iv. (1871) I. 71 When..the World is all decayed down into due attritus of this sort.

attrokien: see atroke *v.*

attroopment (əˈtruːpmənt). *rare.* [a. F. *attroupement*, f. *attrouper* to assemble tumultuously, f. *à* to + *troupe* troop, crowd.] A disorderly or tumultuous troop or crowd.

1795 W. Taylor in *Month. Rev.* XVIII. 540 In a nation truly free there are not attroopments of houseless Lazaroni, as at Naples. **1822** —— in *Month. Mag.* LIII. 103 Nominated by attroopments of people.

attry, variant of artry and of attery *a.* *Obs.*

attuition (ætjuːˈɪʃən). *Psychol.* [f. L. *ad* (see ad-) + tuition after *intuition*.] A hypothetical apprehension higher in order than mere animal sensation and lower than human perception. Hence **attu'itional, a'ttuitive** adjs. So **attuent** (æˈtjuːənt), *a.* [L. *tuent-*, pres. pple. of *tuēri* to look at], that has the function of, or is characterized by, attuition; **a'ttuit**, something of which one becomes conscious by attuition; **attuite** (æˈtjuːɪt) *v. trans.*, to become conscious of (an object) by attuition; **a'ttuitively** *adv.*, by attuition.

1884 'Scotus Novanticus' *Metaph. Nova et Vetusta* 6 This word (Attuition) is here coined, in order to indicate that state of Consciousness which lies between Sensation-proper and Perception-proper. *Ibid.* 11, I may now define *Attuition* to be the reflex co-ordination of the elements or units of Sensation into an image or synopsis: it is a synthesis *in* and *for* the Conscious Subject. *Ibid.*, The range and character of attuitional intelligence. *Ibid.* 29 The Will then has now affirmed the attuited totality in perception as a one totality. *Ibid.* 49 The Attuent consciousness at the moment of receiving the 'impression' of Extension, locates it as outside itself. *Ibid.* 143 An animal is attuitively conscious of the *à posteriori* categories, but it cannot categorize, because it cannot affirm. They are present to it as sense-attuits. **1888** J. Martineau *Study Relig.* I. II. i. 180 In the higher quadrupeds..a state is reached which may be called Attuition, marked by discrimination of particular objects from each other in space..but without corresponding discrimination of them from the attuent subject. *Ibid.* 184 How I should feel if I were..reduced to the 'attuent' condition, I find it impossible to judge. **1896** W. Caldwell *Schopenhauer's System* iii. 157 Our consciousness of other things—*i.e.*, our *attuitive* knowledge. **1902** *Encycl. Brit.* XXX. 677/2 Supposing..that a man, or a dog, through association 'attuites' sequence and invariableness of succession.

attune (əˈtjuːn), *v.* [f. at- *pref.*[3] + tune *v.*; probably suggested by atone.]

1. a. To bring into musical accord. Const. *to.*

1596 Spenser *F.Q.* II. xii. 76 Gan all the quire of birdes Their diverse notes t'attune unto his lay. **1725** Pope *Odyss.* xvii. 312 For Phemius to lyre attuned the strain. **1814** Wordsw. *Wh. Doe* I. 327 Fancies wild: To which with no reluctant strings Thou hast attuned thy murmurings. **1867** Macfarren *Harmony* iv. (1876) 144 Were all the notes perfectly attuned to the true natural scale.

b. *fig.* To bring into harmony or accord.

1727 Thomson *Summer* 1365 Social friends Attun'd to happy union of soul. **1849** Freeman *Archit.* 90 The mind attuned to grace and harmony.

2. To bring (a musical instrument) to the right pitch; to tune. Also *fig.*

1728 Thomson *Spring* 1116 Harmony itself Attuning all their passions into love. **1866** Argyll *Reign Law* v. 276 The physical causes which have 'attuned' a material organ so as to catch certain ethereal pulsations in the external world. **1875** B. Taylor *Faust* I. xxi. 186, I hear the noise of instruments attuning.

3. To make tuneful or melodious.

1667 Milton *P.L.* IV. 265 Aires, vernal aires..attune The trembling leaves. *c* **1750** Shenstone *Ruin'd Abbey* 14 Birds ..Attune from native boughs their various lay. **1796** Coleridge *Dejection*, Joy lift her spirit, joy attune her voice.

†4. *Wireless Telegr.* To tune in. *Obs.*

1899 R. Routledge *Discov. 19th C.* (ed. 13) 546 A Geissler tube, when its circuit is properly attuned, can be lighted up by the magneto-electric disturbances propagated without material contacts, and this itself would constitute a method of signalling to a distance. **1901** *Westm. Gaz.* 23 Dec. 5/1 The message..would reach every attuned recorder within that distance. **1902** *Ibid.* 30 Apr. 12/2 Inventions covering the attuning of transmitters and receivers.

attune (əˈtjuːn), *sb.* *rare.* [f. prec. vb.; cf. *accord*, to *accord*.] Tuneful accord, harmony.

1850 Mrs. Browning *Poems* II. 290 The new generations that cry In attune to our voice..'God,' 'Liberty,' 'Truth.'

a'ttuned, *ppl. a.* [f. attune *v.* + -ed.] Brought into harmony, or to right musical pitch, harmonious, accordant.

1596 Spenser *F.Q.* I. xii. v, [They sung] In well attuned notes a joyous lay. **1796–7** Coleridge *Autumn. Even.*, No more your sky-larks melting from the sight Shall thrill the attuned heart-string with delight. **1833** I. Taylor *Fanat.* x. 501 The chords of a nicely attuned heart.

attunement (əˈtjuːnmənt). [f. as prec. + -ment.] An attuning or bringing into harmony.

1866 Alger *Solit. Nat. & Man* IV. 348 The healthy attunement of the discordant faculties and forces of the soul.

atturn, atturney, obs. ff. attorn, -ey.

attyn, *Obs.* 'that not,' L. *quin*: see at *conj.*

‖**atua** (ˈatua, əˈtuːə). Also **akua**. Earlier forms: 8 **eatua** (erron.), 9 **hotooa**. [Maori, Raratongan, Tahitian, Samoan *atua*, Tongan *'otua*,

Hawaiian *akua*.] A Polynesian name for a supernatural being, god, or demon.

1769 Cook *Jrnl.* 28 June (1955) I. 113 Near the great Morie were many large Altars..on [which] were exposed meat for Eatua or God. **1773** *Ibid.* 17 Sept. (1961) II. 234, I then asked if they sacrificed men to the Eatua. **1773** J. Hawkesworth *Acct. Voy. Disc. S. Hemisphere* II. I. xv. 165 It was a representation of Mauwe, one of their Eatuas, or gods of the second class. **1817** J. Martin *Account of Natives of Tonga Islands* II. xviii. 103 Hotooas, gods, or superior beings, who have the power of dispensing good and evil to mankind. **1832** A. Earle *Narr. Resid. N.Z.* (1966) 178 The natives say, 'It is Atua, the Great Spirit, coming into them, and eating up their inside.' **1851** J. C. Richmond in Scholefield *Richmond-Atkinson Papers* I. 103 Though he may have some faith in the atonement as a charm to exorcise 'atuas'..his Xtianity does not go a great deal further. **1884** Lady Martin *Our Maoris* ii. 35 He..told us that an Atua Maori,—that is to say, a man who professes to be possessed by a spirit,—had been disturbing the neighbourhood. **1902** E. Clodd *T. H. Huxley* iv. 160 The 'atuas' include gods good and evil, home and foreign, as well as the souls of men. **1928** W. Baucke *Where White Man Treads* (ed. 2) 211 Each tohunga diagnoses after his own skill, and in the ripeness of his wisdom applies what his atua has revealed to him.

a-tumble (əˈtʌmb(ə)l), *advb. phr.* [A *prep.*[1] + TUMBLE *v.*] In tumbling condition, tossing.

1881 W. C. Russell *Sailor's Sweeth.* II. i. 75 The sea was all a-tumble with the breeze.

†**aˈturn**, *v. Obs.* [In sense 1, a. OF. *aturne-r*, *-orner*, *-ourner*, f. *à* to + *turner*:—L. *tornāre* to round off, f. *tornus*, Gr. τόρνος lathe; cf. ATOUR *sb.* and ATTORN.]

1. *trans.* To attire, array, dress, prepare fitly.

c **1220** *Sawles Warde* in *Cott. Hom.* 257 Ich iseo a sonde cumen..leofliche aturnet.

2. To turn. (*a-* is perh. for *y-* = *ȝe*: see A *particle*.)

c **1230** *Ancr. R.* 284 [Er] ure Louerd..þuruh his grace, habbe hire swuch aturned and imaked. *c* **1330** *Poem temp. Edw. II*, li, Thus is the ordre of knight Aturned up & down.

aturn, early f. ATOUR *sb. Obs.* dress, attire.

a-twain (əˈtweɪn), *advb. phr. arch.* Forms: 4 **a-twayn**, 4–5 **a-twene**, **atweyn(e**, 7 **atwaine**, 6– **atwain**. [f. A *prep.*[1] + TWAIN. Cf. A-TWO.]

1. In or into two parts; in two.

1377 Langl. *P. Pl.* B. vii. 116 And pieres for pure tene pulled it atweyne. *c* **1485** Digby Myst. (1882) I. 540 A sharpe Sward of Sorowe shall cleve hir hert atweyn. **1634** A. Huish, Now earth's black mantle's cut atwaine. **1870** Morris *Earthly Par.* II. III. 344 Upon a stone the ring smote, and atwain It broke.

2. Away from each other, asunder. Cf. ATWIN.

1870 Morris *Earthly Par.* II. III. 74 This bitter morn That joy and me atwain hath torn.

†**aˈtwape, atwappe**, *v. Obs. rare.* [f. AT- *pref.*[2] + **wapp-en*, of unknown meaning.] *intr.* To escape (with *dative* = from).

c **1325** *E.E. Allit. P.* B. 1205 Er þay at-wappene moȝt þe wach. *c* **1340** *Gaw. & Gr. Knt.* 1167 What wylde so atwaped wyȝes þat schotten, Watz al to-raced & rent.

aˈtweel, *phr. Sc.* ? Contracted from *wat weel* = 'wot well'; sometimes aphetized to *'tweel*.

1768 Ross *Helenore* 21 (Jam.) Atweel I danc'd wi' you on your birth day. **1794** Burns *Wks.* IV, 'Tweel thou know'st na' every pang Wad wring my bosom. **1816** Scott *Antiq.* xxxix, Atweel I wad fain tell him.

atween (əˈtwiːn), *prep.* and *adv. arch.* and *dial.* Forms: 5 **atwen(e**, **a-twene**, 5–6 **attwen(e**, 7– **atween**; aphetic 'TWEEN. [f. A *prep.*[1] + *-twene*, *-tween*, stem of BE-TWEEN, on analogy of *afore before*, *among bimong*, and other twin forms already in OE. *Atween* is the usual form in north. dial., but only a poetic archaism in the literary language.]

A. *prep.* Between.

c **1400** *Pol. Rel. & L. Poems* (1866) 27 A-twene theis tweyn a gret comparison. *c* **1485** *Digby Myst.* (1882) I. 442 Atwen myn armys now shall I the embrace. **1579** J. Stubbes *Gaping Gulf* C v, Assured peace attwene them. **1748** Thomson *Cast. Indol.* I. ii, A season atween June and May. **1842** Tennyson *Oriana*, Thou comest atween me and the skies.

†**B.** *adv.* In between, between whiles. *Obs.*

1595 Spenser *Col. Clout* 83 A bonie swaine, That Cuddy hight, him thus atweene bespake. **1596** —— *F.Q.* IV. vii. 35 From her faire eyes wiping the deawy wet..and kissing them atweene.

†**aˈtwend**, *v. Obs.* [f. AT- *pref.*[2] + OE. *wendan* to go; cf. OE. *oðwendan*.] *intr.* To go away, escape (with *dative* = from).

a **1000** *Cædmon's Gen.* 403 (Gr.) Uton oþwendan hit nu monna bearnum! **1205** Lay. 19564 Feole þer atwenden touward þan norðenden. *a* **1250** *Owl & Night.* 1425 Heo mai hire guld atwende.

†**aˈtwin**, *v. Obs. rare*[−1]. [f. A *pref.* 1 + ME. *twinnen* to divide, separate.] To separate, part.

? *a* **1400** *MS. Laud* No. 486 (Halliw.) The grete drede that the saule ys inne, Whan the bodye and yt schal atwynne.

†**a-ˈtwin**, *advb. phr.*[1] *Obs.* Forms: 4 **o twynne**, **o tuyn**, **o twyne**, **a twyne**, **a twyny**, **atwinn(e**, 4–5 **atwynne**, **atwin**, 4–6 **atwyn**. [f. A *prep.*[1] + TWIN, a. ON. *tvinn* 'two and two, in pairs, two different things'; also *tvinni* (indecl.) two. ? Or from TWIN *v.* to separate: cf. ATWIN *v.*]

1. Away from each other, asunder, apart.

1303 R. Brunne *Handl. Synne* 9177 Þe same oure atwynne þe wonede. **1330** —— *Chron.* 101 Neuer þei were o twynne, vntille ded þam slouh. **1382** Wyclif *Acts* xv. 39 Forsoth dissencioun is maad, so that thei departiden a twyny [*v.r.* a twynne. **1388** a twynny. *c* **1449** Pecock *Repr.* I. vii. 32 Grammer and dyuynyte ben ij. facultees atwin and asundir departid. *c* **1500** *King & Barker* 127 in Hazl. *E.P.P.* (1864) 10 Owr kyng and the barker partyd feyr a twyn.

2. In two, in twain.

c **1460** *Lybeaus Disc.* 1962 And karf..hys hedde atwynne.

a-twin (əˈtwɪn), *advb. phr.*[2] *rare*[−1]. [f. TWIN after AKIN.] In the relation of twin *with*.

1879 M. Conway *Demonol.* I. III. xi. 418 The monster sent by one..is ethically atwin with the snake created by the other.

†**aˈtwind**, *v. Obs.* 1–3. *Pa. t.* **atwand**, **atwond**. *Pa. pple.* **atwunden**, **atwonde**. [OE. *ætwindan*, f. AT- *pref.*[2] + *windan* to WIND.] *intr.* To escape (with *dative* = from); to depart, cease.

c **1000** Ælfric *Job* i. 16 (Bosw.) Ic ána ætwánd. *c* **1200** Ormin 8003 Þatt Crist ne shollde muȝhenn himm [Herod] Onn ane wise attwindenn. *c* **1250** *Gen. & Ex.* 3058 Moyses ..helde up is hond, And al ðis vnweder ðor atwond.

a-twist (əˈtwɪst), *advb. phr.* [A *prep.*[1] + TWIST.] On the twist, twisted, askew.

1754 Smeaton in *Phil. Trans.* XLVIII. 534 This plate being set a little atwist. **1835** Beckford *Recoll.* 171 His limbs all atwist, and his mouth all awry.

atwitch (əˈtwɪtʃ). *adv.* or *pred. a.* [f. A *prep.*[1] + TWITCH *v.*[1]] Twitching; jerking.

1910 J. Farnol *Broad Highway* II. v. 219 That hoary head all a-twitch with eagerness. **1957** J. Frame *Owls do Cry* xi. 46 The four poplars..atwitch with trickle of air.

†**aˈtwite**, *v.*[1] *Obs.* Forms: *Inf.* 1 **ætwítan**, 3 **etwite**, 3–6 **atwite**, 4 **atwyȝte**, 4–6 **attwyte**. *Pa. t.* 1–3 **ætwát**, **-witen**, 3 **etwat**, 4 **atwot**. [f. AT- *pref.*[1] + OE. *wítan* to blame, reproach; cf. OE. *oðwítan*. The modern TWIT, formerly *twite*, is an aphetized form of this word.]

1. To cast an imputation upon, reproach, upbraid, blame, taunt, twit; **a.** with double object (acc. and dative): To reproach a thing *to* a person.

a **1000** *Beowulf* 2304 Siþðan [him]..Gúðláf and Osláf ..ætwiton weána dǽl. **1205** Lay. 19594 Sexisce men..mine unhæle me atwiten. *c* **1320** *Seuyn Sages* (W.) 1876 And hire misdedes hire atwot. *c* **1430** Lydg. *Bochas* IV. xiv. (1554) 113 a, Thyng most slaundrous theyr nobles tatwite.

b. a person *of* a thing, or *that*, etc.

c **885** K. Ælfred *Boeth. Metr.* xxvii. 5 Hwý oðwíte ȝe wyrde eowre, þæt hío ȝeweald nafað? *c* **1230** *Ancr. R.* 70 Ne ne etwiteð him of his unðeau. *c* **1330** *Florice & Bl.* 485 Thilke dai schal neuer be That men schal at wite me That I schal ben of loue untrewe. *c* **1524** in Hazl. *E.P.P.* III. 25 Of gredynes lest men the wolde attwite. **1530** *Calisto & Melib.* in Hazl. *Dodsl.* I. 85, I marvel greatly thou dost me so atwite Of the doubt, that thou hast of my secretness.

c. with simple personal obj.

c **1000** *Ags. Ps.* lxxiii. 17 Fynd ætwítað fæcne Drihtne. **1205** Lay. 26584 Ofte heo heom atwiten. *c* **1315** Shoreham 106 So may God answerye the Wanne thou hym atwyst. *c* **1430** Lydg. *Bochas* VII. iv. (1554) 167 b, Who is defouled, none other should atwite.

¶ A weak pa. t. *atwytede* occurs, and an anomalous pa. t. and pple. *atwist* after *wit* to know.

1297 R. Glouc. 33 Þis word..atwytede hym & ys stat.. He yt vnderstod, þat ys child at wiste ys pouerte. *c* **1314** *Guy Warw.* 251 And thou in thine halle me sle, For traisoun it worth atwist the.

†**aˈtwite**, *v.*[2] *Obs. rare*[−1]. [f. AT- *pref.*[2] + OE. *wítan* to go, proceed.] To depart, go away.

c **1250** *Gen. & Ex.* 1649 And god at-wot in-to hise liȝt.

†**aˈtwiting**, *vbl. sb. Obs.* [f. ATWITE *v.*[1] + -ING[1].] Reproaching; reproach, taunt.

1340 *Ayenb.* 194 Hi ham..ziggeþ zuo vele atuytinges. *c* **1460** Russell *Bk. Nurture* 273 in *Babees Bk.* 139 To alle þe lordes haue ye a sight for groggynge & atwytynge.

a-twitter (əˈtwɪtə(r)), *advb. phr.* [A *prep.*[1] + TWITTER.] In a twitter, twittering.

1833 *Blackw. Mag.* 848 Eaves all a-twitter with swallows.

atwixt (əˈtwɪkst), *prep. arch* or *dial.* Forms: 4–5 **atwyxen**, **-ixen**, **-ix(e**, 5 **-yxyn**, **-exyn**, **athwyx**, 4– **atwixt**; aphetic 'TWIXT. [f. A- *pref.* 2 + *-twix(t*, stem of *betwixt*; cf. *atween*. For the variations, see BETWIXT.] Between.

c **1374** Chaucer *Troylus* v. 472 Atwixt noone and prime. *c* **1440** *Promp. Parv.* 17 A-twyxyn, atwexyn, atwyxt, *Inter.* **1464** Edw. IV in *Paston Lett.* 493 II. 166 Maters..in debate athwyx the seid John Paston and William Yelverton. **1475** *Bk. Noblesse* 25 Trewes..atwixen Charles the vij[th]..and your predecessour Harry the sext. **1566** Gascoigne *Jocasta* (1587) 104 Then I atwixt them both wil throw my selfe. **1870** Morris *Earthly Par.* III. IV. 383 The yellow sand They kissed atwixt the sea and land.

a-two (əˈtuː), *advb. phr. arch* and *dial.* Forms: 1 **on tú**, **on twá**, 3–4 **atuo**, 4–5 **atwoo**, 4–6 **a to**, **ato**, 5 **o-two**, 6 **atoo**, 3– **atwo**, **a-two**. [OE. *on tú*, *on twá*, in two: see A *prep.*[1] and TWO *numeral a.* While *a-twain* is only a literary archaism, *a-two* is also in modern dialects; the regular prose form is *in two*.]

1. In or into two parts; a-twain. *arch.*

c **885** K. Ælfred *Oros.* I. x. §3 Híe heora here on tú [*v.r.* on twá] todǽldon. **1297** R. Glouc. 375 Rychard..brec þer hys necke atuo. *c* **1420** *Chron. Vilod.* 862 Alle þe gables of the shippe þey broston a to. **1605** Camden *Rem.* (1637) 291 A mouse in time may bite atwo a cable. **1876** Morris *Sigurd* I. 49 Sawed Sigmund..till the stone was cleft atwo.

†**2.** Away from each other, apart, asunder. *Obs.*

c **1270** *Assumpcion* 263 Sithen we ben parted atwo. *c* **1425** *Seven Sages* (P.) 3053 Thay token leve and wente o-two. *c* **1450** Lonelich *Grail* xv. 604 Kysseth me er that we now departen atwo.

atwond, atwot, pa. t. of ATWIND, ATWITE *v.*

†**atˈwrench**, *v. Obs.* Also 3 **et-**. [f. AT- *pref.*[2] + *wręncan* to deceive by artifice, f. *wręnc* trick.] *intr.* To escape by wile (with *dative* = from).

c **1200** *St. Marhar.* 15 Ȝef ha þus..þauieð ant þolieð ant weneð þah to etwrenchen. *c* **1250** *Owl & Night.* 812 The fox ..wenth eche hunde at-wrenche.

atypic (əˈtɪpɪk), *a.* [f. A- *pref.* 14 + TYPIC.] Not typical, not conformable to the ordinary type.

atypical (æ-, eɪˈtɪpɪkəl), *a.* [f. A- 14 + TYPICAL *a.*] Not typical; not conformable to the ordinary type. Hence **atypiˈcality**, the quality of not being typical; **aˈtypically** *adv.*, in an atypical manner.

1885 C. H. Fagge *Princ. Med.* I. 100 Carcinomata can be ..distinguished from other epithelial growths by their being 'atypical'. **1916** *Times* 25 Oct. 7/3 The cases up to this time were mostly mild and atypical. **1917** C. R. Payne tr. *Pfister's Psychoanalytic Method* I. xi. 292, I have also found the serpent atypically as allusion to the pretendedly poisonous tongue of the wife. **1918** *Sat. Westm. Gaz.* 13 Apr. 11/1 She, ..something atypically for a woman, appears to be more interested in places than people. **1935** *Proc. Prehistoric Soc.* I. 152 The stations in Crimea and Transcaucasia..have yielded exclusively rather atypical flake implements. **1957** *Archivum Linguisticum* IX. 83 The atypicality of *-o* in feminines. **1959** B. Wootton *Soc. Sci. & Soc. Path.* v. 161 Criminologists have interested themselves more in the heavy incidence of crime upon the young than in the relatively atypical late entrants. **1964** S. Duke-Elder *Parsons' Dis. Eye* (ed. 14) xiv. 143 Three atypically large viruses of ophthalmic interest.

atyse, var. ATTICE *v. Obs.* to instigate, entice.

au-, in ME. was commonly written for AV-, and sometimes for AW-, which see for words and forms not entered under AU-.

au, obs. form of OWE *v.*

aualk, aualle: see AWAKE, AFALLE.

‖**aubade** (oˈbad). [Fr., ad. Sp. *albada*, f. *alba* dawn: see -ADE.] A musical announcement of dawn, a sunrise song or open-air concert.

1678 Phillips, *Aubades* (French), Songs, or Instrumentall music, sung, or playd under any ones Chamber window in the morning. **1867** *Standard* 3 Jan. 5/7 The annual aubade, or salute of drums, took place on Monday afternoon. **1873** Longf. *Emma & Eginh.* 111 Till the crowing cock..Sang his aubade with lusty voice and clear.

‖**aubain** (obɛ̃). [Fr.; med.L. *Albānus*; etymol. unknown: see Littré.] A non-naturalized foreigner subject to the right of *aubaine*.

1882 Brace *Gesta Christi* 194 The aubains..of the Middle Ages seem to have been in almost the same position with serfs.

‖**aubaine** (oˈbɛn). [Fr.: see prec.] (See quots.)

1727–51 Chambers *Cycl.* s.v., An embassador..is not subject to the right of *aubaine*. **1866** Haydn *Dict. Dates*, *Aubaine*, a right of French Kings, which existed from the beginning of the monarchy, whereby they claimed the property of every stranger who died in their country, without having been naturalised, was abolished by the national assembly in 1790; re-established by Napoleon; and finally annulled July 14, 1819.

aube, obs. form of ALB.

‖**auberge** (oˈbɛrʒ). Also 7 **alberge**. [Fr.:—*alberge*, earlier *helberge*, 11th c. *herberge*, a. MHG. *herberge*, OHG. *heri-berga*, lit. 'army-shelter,' camp, tent, inn: cf. G. *herberge*, and HARBOUR.] An inn, a place of accommodation for travellers.

1615 G. Sandys *Trav.* 195 The alberges of the Knight Hospitallers of St. Johns. **1777** Shuckburgh in *Phil. Trans.* LXVII. 533 We had dined in a most miserable auberge. **1871** Tyndall *Fragm. Sc.* II. i. 2 At an auberge near the foot of the Rhone glacier.

Hence ‖**auberˈgiste**, keeper of an auberge. †**auˈbergical** *a.* (nonce-wd.).

1775 H. Walpole *Lett. C'tess Ossory* I. 178 Some tender swain had written..his fair one's name in this usual aubergical exclamation. **1766** Smollett *Trav.* 25 The aubergistes impose upon us shamefully.

aubergine (ˈəʊbə(d)ʒiːn). [Fr., dim. of *auberge*, variant of *alberge* 'a kind of peach' (Littré), ad. Sp. *alberchigo*, *alverchiga*, 'an apricocke'

(Minsheu 1623).] **a.** The fruit of the Egg-plant, *Solanum esculentum*, resembling a goose's egg in size and shape, and usually of purple colour; also called *brinjal*.

1794 STEDMAN *Surinam* (1813) I. xii. 320 The aubergines are a species of fruit which grows in the shape of a cucumber. **1811** *Monthly Mag.* XXXII. 258 The tomato, the aubergine, and several other culinary plants. **1883** *St. James's Gaz.* 20 Dec. 5/2, I wonder also that the aubergine did not remind him of another kitchen fruit.

b. A purple colour resembling that of the fruit. Also *attrib.* and as *adj.*

aubergine purple, a shade of purple found in Oriental porcelain.

1895 *Windsor Mag.* I. 109/1 An aubergine silk lining. **1898** *Daily News* 29 Sept. 3/4 Cashmere in a tone of Burgundy that is sometimes called aubergine, from the deep reddish mauve of the vegetable. **1903** *Daily Chron.* 31 Oct. 8/4 Aubergine..is a tint with some claret and a touch of violet in it. **1906** S. W. BUSHELL *Chinese Art* II. 23 The deep purple, or *aubergine* (*ch'ieh tzŭ*), of the Chun-chou wares. **1909** *Daily Chron.* 29 Jan. 4/5 Aubergine coloured cloth. **1927** *Daily Tel.* 5 Apr. 13/3 Examples of the Ming dynasty ..vases, jardinières, bowls,..an aubergine fish-bowl.

† **aubifane.** *Obs. rare*⁻¹. [a. F. *aubifoin* 'the weed Blew-bottle, Blew-blaw, Corne-flower, Hurt-sickle' (Cotgr. 1611), of unkn. origin.] The Corn Blue-bottle (*Centaurea Cyanus*).

1622 PEACHAM *Compl. Gent.* (1634) X v, The 5th colour is Sable, or Black, and signifieth, in Flowers, the Aubifane.

‖ **aubin** (obẽ). [Fr., = OF. *hobin* (applied also to the horse itself), according to Diez f. Eng. HOBBY.] 'A kind of broken gait, or pace, between an amble and a gallop; reputed a defect in a horse.' Chambers *Cycl. Supp.* 1753.

aubrietia (ɔːˈbriːʃ(ɪ)ə). Also very freq. in erron. form **aubretia**. [mod.L., f. the name of Claude *Aubriet* (1668–1743), after whom it was named by Adanson in 1763: see -IA[1].] The common name of a member of the genus *Aubrieta* of spring-flowering dwarf perennial plants belonging to the family Cruciferæ, of trailing habit, bearing flowers of various shades of purple, grown as a rock plant or garden edging.

'Aubrieta is the original spelling of the generic name but the form Aubrietia has been so generally used that it has come into common speech and we retain that form as the common name' (R. Hort. Soc. *Dict. Gardening*, 1956, I. 222/1).

1829 in LOUDON *Encycl. Plants* (1836) 544. **1870** W. ROBINSON *Alpine Flowers* I. 48 Look at what we could do with the dwarf green Iberises, Helianthemums, Aubrietias, Arabises, [etc.]. **1883** F. M. PEARD *Contrad.* I. 227 Lilac aubretias clamber up the meadows behind Titian's house. **1911** 'A. MARSHALL' *Eldest Son* xxx, The station-master's arabis and aubrietia were making a fine show.

auburn (ˈɔːbɜːn), *a.* Forms: 5–7 **aborne, -ourne,** 6 **alborne, auberne, aberne,** 6–7 **auborn(e, abourn, aburn(e,** 9 **auburne,** 8– **auburn;** also 6 **abron, abrun(e,** 7 **abroun, abrown.** [a. OF. *alborne, auborne*:—L. *alburnus* (= *subalbus*, Du Cange) nearly white, whitish. In 16–17th c. written *abron, abrune, abroun* (cf. APRON, *aperne*), which prob. originated, or at least encouraged, the idea that *auburn* was a kind of *brown* (an etymology actually adopted by Richardson), and so helped to modify the signification of the word.]

orig. Of a yellowish- or brownish-white colour; *now*, of a golden-brown or ruddy-brown colour.

1430 LYDG. *Chron. Troy* II. xv, Aborne heyr crispyng for thicknesse. **1481** CAXTON *Myrr.* II. xvii. 103 The rayes of the sonne make the heer of a man abourne or blounde. **1533** ELYOT *Cast. Helth* (1541) 2 Heare blacke or darke aburne. **1547** BOORDE *Brev. Health* lvi. 25 Alborne heare and yelowe heare commethe of a gentyl nature. **1576** T. N[EWTON] *Lemnie's Touchst. Complex.* (1633) 58 Faire aburne or chesten colour. **1580** BARET *Alv.* A 715 Light auborne, *subflauus, subrutilus*. **1591** PERCIVALL *Sp. Dict.*, *Rojo*, abrun headed, *Subrufus*. **1599** HALL *Sat.* III. v. 8 Whose curled head With abron locks was fairely furnished. *a* **1649** DRUMM. OF HAWTH. *Jas. I* Wks. 1711, 16 His hair was abourn, a colour between white and red. *a* **1697** in Masson *Milton* (1859) I. 275 'He had light brown hair,' continues Aubrey,—putting the word 'abrown' ('auburn') in the margin by way of synonym for 'light brown.' **1808** SCOTT *Marm.* v. ix, And auburn of the darkest dye, His short curled beard and hair. **1859** GEO. ELIOT *A. Bede* 61 The rays..lit up her pale red hair to auburn.

b. *absol.* quasi-*sb.*

1852 D. MOIR *Christm. Musings* v. Wks. II. 254 Thy tresses in the breeze Floating their auburn.

Aubusson (obysõ). [Name of a manufacturing town, dept. Creuse, France.] Tapestry made at Aubusson, *esp.* a carpet made of this, more explicitly ***Aubusson carpet***.

[**1774** H. WALPOLE *Descr. Strawberry-Hill* 102 The bed is of tapestry of Aubusson, festoons of flowers on a white ground, lined with crimson silk.] **1851** *Illustr. Exhibitor* p. xxx, Tapestry, carpets, [etc.]... Castel, E., France, Aubusson carpet. **1866** *Argosy* Jan. 142 The elegant Aubusson carpet. **1900** E. GLYN *Visits Eliz.* (1906) 110 The room..is hung with aubusson. **1927** J. B. PRIESTLEY *Adam in Moonshine* vi. 101 Wasn't that the dreadful hairy, smelly one [*sc.* a Russian conspirator] who spoilt your Aubusson? **1961** *Connoisseur* Dec. p. lii, Fine Aubusson Carpets and Rugs.

auch, variant of AC *conj. Obs.* but.

'auchlet. *Sc.* ? *Obs.* [f. *aucht*, EIGHT + -LET *dim.*, or LOT, a part (Jamieson).] A measure, the eighth part of a boll: cf. *firlot*, the fourth part.

1796 *Acc.* in Scott *Old Mort.* Introd. (1862) 8 To Four Auchlet of Ait meal 3*s.* 4*d.* **1819** *Caled. Mercury* 1 Nov. (JAM.) The auchlet..usually contained two pounds more than the present stone does.

aucht, Sc. form of AUGHT and EIGHT.

‖ **au courant** (o kurɑ̃). [Fr.] Acquainted with what is going on; aware of current developments: usu. const. *with* or *of*.

1762 GIBBON *Jrnl.* 13 Oct. (1929) 162 Having neglected my Journal from the 14th of September, I was forced to bestow some days to put myself *au courant*. **1830** J. S. MILL *Let.* 20 Aug. in *Wks.* (1963) XII. 59 They are quite eager to place me *au courant* of all their proceedings. **1885** *Law Q. Rev.* Apr. 138 To keep themselves fairly *au courant* with what was being decided in the various Courts. **1928** *Daily Tel.* 23 Oct. 11/3 It would have been wiser if the United States had been kept au courant of the negotiations from the very outset. **1962** *Listener* 8 Mar. 427/2 He also believed that Chambers 'has a set of spies here in Rome'—to be *au courant* what Robert is doing.

† **auct,** *ppl. a. Obs. rare.* [ad. L. *auctus*, pa. pple. of *augēre* to increase.] Increased, enlarged.

1652 GAULE *Magastrom.* 86 Of stars auc't and diminute.

† **'auctary.** *Obs.* Also 7 **auctuarie.** [ad. L. *auctārium*, f. *auct-*: see prec. and -ARIUM.] An addition or augmentation; something superadded.

1580–1646 in T. Craufurd *Univ. Edin.* 137 (JAM.) An large auctary to the library. **1621** MOLLE *Camerar. Liv. Lib.* Pref., In this Volume comprehended, with a large Auctuarie. **1653** BAXTER *Saint's R.* I. vi. (1662) 63 God gives us outward things, as auctaries, as overplus, or above measure.

auctentyke, obs. form of AUTHENTIC.

aucthor, -itie, -ize, obs. f. AUTHOR *sb.*, -ITY, etc.

† **auc'tifical,** *a. Obs.*⁻⁰ [f. L. *auctific-us* (f. *auct-us* increase + *-ficus* making) + -AL[1].] 'That makes an increase or augmentation.' Blount 1656.

auction (ˈɔːkʃən), *sb.* [ad. L. *auctiōn-em* 'increase,' n. of action f. *augēre* to increase, already in L. use for 'a sale by increase of bids.' (Not in Fr.)]

† **1.** The action of increasing; increase, growth.

1692 RAY *Disc.* II. iv. (1732) 124 The Actions of Nutrition, Auction and Generation. **1696** PHILLIPS, *Auction*, in Physic, Nourishment whereby more is restor'd than was lost.

2. a. A public sale in which each bidder offers an increase upon the price offered by the preceding, the article put up being sold to the highest bidder. Called in Scotl. and north of Engl. a *roup*.

('To sell or put up *at* auction' is a common const. in U.S.; in England goods are 'sold *by* auction,' 'put up *to* auction.')

1595 WARNER *Plautus' Menæch.* v. vii. (R.) The auction of Menæchmus..when will be sold Slaves, household goods, etc. **1678** PHILLIPS (App.), *Auction*, a making a publick Sale, and selling of Goods by an Outcry. **1692** SIR C. LYTTELTON in *Hatton Corr.* (1878) II. 169 Many auctions..of yᵉ best collections [of pictures]. **1758** JOHNSON *Idler* No. 5 ¶6 Ladies, who must run to sales and auctions without an attendant. **1860** MOTLEY *Netherl.* I. i. 14 His carpets..were disposed of at auction. **1876** ROGERS *Pol. Econ.* xiii. 21 These ..were put up from time to time to auction.

fig. **1849** MACAULAY *Hist. Eng.* II. 216 Then followed an auction..On one side the king, on the other the Church, began to bid eagerly against each other.

b. = *auction bridge* (BRIDGE *sb.*[2] b). Also *attrib.*

1908 W. DALTON *Auction Bridge* p. iv, If you are accustomed to play Bridge for 6*d.* points, or £2 10*s.* per 100, play Auction for £1 per 100. **1918** A. BENNETT *Pretty Lady* xxviii. 196 Auction afterwards? **1929** M. C. WORK *Complete Contract Bridge* p. xi, Slowly but surely auction players began to realize that the new game had attractions. **1930** J. B. PRIESTLEY *Angel Pavement* xi. 580 They were now playing their third rubber of auction.

c. *Auction Bridge.* The act or process of bidding; a bid made in this way.

1908 'AUCTIONEER' *Auction Bridge for Three or Four Players* 31 The player who wins the auction takes the dummy as his partner. **1927** L. HATTERSLEY *Contract & Auction Bridge Clarified* (ed. 2) i. 20 The Auction begins with the first declaration after each deal and continues until the final pass. **1958** *Listener* 2 Oct. 541/2 North bid Three Clubs and East became the declarer in Six Diamonds after this auction: *South* No bid [etc.].

d. Phr. ***all over the auction***, everywhere. *Austral. slang.*

1930 K. S. PRICHARD *Haxby's Circus* v. 63 'Did I step on it, Doc?' Will asked. 'Step on it? You waltzed all over the bloomin' auction.' **1960** 'N. SHUTE' *Trustee from Toolroom* i. 11 You'd be surprised at the number of letters that there are —all over the auction.

3. A public sale of somewhat similar character.

(It has been the custom in some places to set up an inch of lighted candle, the last bidder before the wick falls becoming purchaser of the property. In a *Dutch auction*, property is offered at a price beyond its value, the price being gradually lowered till some one accepts it as purchaser.)

1673 MARVELL *Reh. Transp.* II. 234 As in an Auction, to be sold by Inch of Candle. **1728** YOUNG *Love of Fame* iv. (1757) 115 The writing tribe, who shameless auctions hold Of praise, by inch of candle to be sold. **1881** *Daily News* 29 Dec. 6/4 The captain sells the fish by auction, putting the highest price on the basketful to be sold, and gradually lowering it till some one closes with his offer.

† **4.** The property put up to auction. *Obs.*

1732 POPE *Mor. Ess.* iii. 119 Ask you why Phryne the whole auction buys? Phryne foresees a general excise.

5. *attrib.*, as in ***auction-house, -mart, -pulpit, -room, -sale***; **auction bridge, pool**: see BRIDGE *sb.*[2] b, POOL *sb.*[3]

1682 *Lond. Gaz.* No. 1716/4 There is daily attendance given at the *Auction-house. **1810** BENTHAM *Packing* (1821) 121 The magnificent edifice, now erecting..under the name of the *Auction Mart. **1767** J. WEDGWOOD *Let.* 31 May (1965) 55 Everybody would be apt to stroll into an *Auction room. **1775** JOHN ANDREWS *Lett.* (1866) 81 The soldiers.. took quarters..in Gould's auction room or store. **1791** BOSWELL *Johnson* 8 Apr. 1775 A certain celebrated actor was just fit to stand at the door of an auction-room with a long pole, and cry 'Pray gentlemen, walk in'. **1936** V. A. DEMANT *Christian Polity* ii. 36 The auction-room flavour of our secular moralities. **1820** *Deb. Congress U.S.* I. 367 The evils arising from *auction sales. **1888** [see SALE *sb.*[2] 1 b]. **1898** *Daily News* 3 Mar. 3/3 Auction sale of rights of patronage was absolutely prohibited.

auction (ˈɔːkʃən), *v.* [f. prec. sb. Cf. L. *auctiōn-āri* in same sense.] To sell by auction. Hence **auctioned** *ppl. a.*

1807 CRABBE *Par. Reg.* II. 349 An auctioned bed, with curtains neat and new. **1884** J. STEPHENS in *Contemp. Rev.* May 689 And auctioned off their consciences to the Ministerial bidder.

auctionary (ˈɔːkʃənərɪ), *a.* ? *Obs.* [ad. L. *auctiōnārius*: see AUCTION and -ARY.] Of or pertaining to an auction.

1693 DRYDEN *Juvenal's Sat.* vii. (R.) With auctionary hammer in thy hand..and knocking thrice.

auctioneer (ɔːkʃəˈnɪə(r)), *sb.* [f. AUCTION + -EER[1]. (Cf. med.L. *auctiōnārius, auctiōnātor*, one who increases the price, a regrater.)] One who conducts sales by auction.

1708 in KERSEY. **1762** *Lond. Mag.* XXXI. 296 An Auctioneer and a Fishmonger. **1841** BORROW *Zincali* I. iv. II. 289 He had perhaps talked more than an auctioneer during a three days' sale.

attrib. **1865** CARLYLE *Fredk. Gt.* III. x. i. 200 To describe this Crown-Prince Mansion..with auctioneer minuteness.

auctio'neer, *v.* [f. prec. sb.] To sell by auction. Hence **auctioneering** *vbl. sb.*

a **1733** NORTH *Lives* (1826) III. 290 Mills, with his auctioneering, atlasses and projects, failed. **1785** COWPER *Task* III. 756 Estates are landscapes, gazed upon awhile, Then advertised, and auctioneer'd away. **1880** MUIRHEAD *Gaius* 456 *Argentarius*..combined auctioneering with banking.

† **'auctive,** *a. Obs. rare*⁻¹. [f. L. *auct-* (see AUCT) + -IVE, as if ad. L. **auctīvus*.] Characterized by increase or growth.

1634 T. JOHNSON *Parey's Chirurg.* I. i. (1678) 52 The Natural [faculty] is parted into the nutritive, auctive, and generative. **1678** PHILLIPS (App.) *Auctive*, apt to grow or increase.

‖ **auctor** (ˈɔːktɔː(r)). *Rom. Law.* [a. L. *auctor*: see AUTHOR *sb.*] The person who warrants the right of possession; *hence*, a seller, vendor.

1875 POSTE *Gaius* III. 401 His auctor, or the person from whom he deduced his title.

auctor, -ice, -yte, obs. ff. AUTHOR, -ESS, -ITY.

† **aucto'ration.** *Obs.*⁻⁰ [ad. late L. *auctōrātiōn-em*, n. of action f. *auctōrāre, -āri*, to hire oneself out.] 'A binding one's self an apprentice or servant.' Bailey 1731.

auctorial (ɔːkˈtɔərɪəl), *a.* [f. L. *auctor* AUTHOR *sb.*: see -ORIAL.] Of or pertaining to an author. (Cf. AUTHORIAL *a.*)

1821 *Examiner* 300/1 Pricked to it..by auctorial jealousy. **1900** M. H. SPIELMANN *Ruskin* 65 What is his reflection on his own auctorial life? **1926** A. BRENT SMITH *Studies & Caprices* 153 Auctorial bias. **1949** WELLEK & WARREN *Theory of Lit.* iii. 27 Eliot makes the judgment of responsibility depend on both auctorial intention and historic effect.

† **auc'torizate, autor-,** *ppl. a.* [ad. med.L. *auctōrīzāt-us* authorized; cf. F. *autorisé*, in 16th c. *auctorisé*. See -ATE[1].] **1.** *pa. ppl.* Authorized. **2.** *adj.* Of established authority, accredited.

1548 UDALL, etc. *Erasm. Par. John* xix. 10 To punishe transgressours of the lawe am I auctorisate. **1558** KENNEDY *Compend. Tract.* in *Misc. Wodr. Soc.* (1844) 109 The maist ancient and autorizate authoris.

aucuba (ˈɔːkjʊbə). *Bot.* [Japanese name.] **1.** A well-known hardy evergreen diœcious shrub (*Aucuba Japonica*, N.O. *Cornaceæ*), with laurel-like leaves usually blotched with pale yellow, grown for ornamental purposes.

1819 REES *Cycl.* III, *Aucuba*, a large Japanese tree.. introduced by Mr. John Grœfer in 1783. **1862** S. PARTRIDGE *Eng. Months* 10 The aucuba shows in the shrubbery his broadening leaf Spotted with gold.

2. ***aucuba mosaic*** [MOSAIC *a.*[1]], a mosaic disease which attacks the leaves of solanaceous plants.

1922 H. M. QUANJER in *Rep. Internat. Potato Conf.* 136 On account of its resemblance to the variegation of Aucuba japonica, I call it Aucuba-mosaic [of potato]. **1936** *Nature* 21 Mar. 500/2 It was not..possible to distinguish serologically the viruses of tobacco mosaic, aucuba mosaic and tomato streak.

†**'aucupable,** *a. Obs.*—⁰ [ad. late L. *aucupābilis*, f. *aucupāri*: see next and -BLE.] 'Fit for birding and fowling.' Bailey 1731.

aucupate ('ɔːkjʊpeɪt), *v.* ? *Obs.* [f. L. *aucupāt*-ppl. stem of *aucupāri*, *-āre*, f. *aucup-em* (nom. *auceps* = *aviceps*) bird-catcher, f. *avi-s* bird + *capěre* to take.] *lit.* To go a bird-catching; *fig.* (as in L.) to lie in wait for, hunt after, gain by craft.

1630 R. H. in *J. Taylor's* (Water P.) *Wks.* A v b/1 To aucupate great fauours from Apollo. **1834** *Gentl. Mag.* CIV. I. 66 To aucupate benefices, by cajoling the Patrons.

aucu'pation. ? *Obs.*—⁰ [ad. L. *aucupātiōn-em*, n. of action f. *aucupā-ri*: see prec.] 'Hunting after a thing.' BULLOKAR 1616. 'Birding or fowling; also gain, advantage.' Blount *Gl.* 1656.

audacious (ɔːˈdeɪʃəs), *a.* [f. L. *audāc(i-*, nom. *audax*, bold, daring, f. *audēre* to dare: see -ACIOUS. Cf. F. *audacieux*, Cotgr. 1611.]

1. Daring, bold, confident, intrepid.

1550 NICOLLS *Thucydides* II. cvi. 67 More bolde and audacious in this thing, wherein we have much experyence. **1698** DRYDEN *Ovid's Iphis* (T.) Big was her voice, audacious was her tone:—The maid becomes a youth. **1712** STEELE *Spect.* No. 436 ¶9 Miller had an audacious Look, that took the Eye. **1826** SCOTT *Woodst.* (1832) 178 All eyes turned to the audacious speaker.

b. *transferred* to things.

1609 B. JONSON *Sil. Wom.* II. v, My Wife must be accomplished with courtly and audacious Ornaments. **1855** MOTLEY *Dutch Rep.* I. i. (1866) 51 The audacious and exquisitely embroidered tower of the townhouse.

2. Unrestrained by, or setting at defiance, the principles of decorum and morality; presumptuously wicked, impudent, shameless.

1591 SHAKS. *1 Hen. VI*, III. i. 14 Such is thy audacious wickednesse. **1612** WARNER *Alb. Eng.* I. i. 2 As he and his audacious crew, the Tower of Babel reare. **1649** MILTON *Observ. Art. Peace* Wks. 1738 I. 357 But we are told, We embrace Paganism and Judaism in the arms of Toleration. A most audacious calumny! **1722** DE FOE *Moll Fl.* (1840) 286, I grew more hardened and audacious than ever. **1825** *Bro. Jonathan* II. 259 Like an audacious profligate, as he was.

†**3.** Inspiring boldness. *Obs. rare.*

a **1625** FLETCHER *Wom. Prize* II. v. (T.) They have got metheglin, and audacious ale, And talk like tyrants!

au'daciously, *adv.* [f. prec. + -LY².]

1. Fearlessly, boldly; with confidence and courage.

1588 SHAKS. *L.L.L.* v. ii. 104 Yet feare not thou, but speake audaciously. **1855** MOTLEY *Dutch Rep.* VIII. (1858) 47 The honor of having battled audaciously..in behalf of human rights.

2. Presumptuously, impudently, shamelessly.

1611 SPEED *Hist. Gt. Brit.* VII. iv. (1632) 205 [He] committed more audaciously those vices. **1850** MERIVALE *Rom. Emp.* xxviii. III. 287 He audaciously transmitted a mandate to Rome, requiring that these titles should be acknowledged.

au'daciousness. [f. as prec. + -NESS.]

1. Boldness, confidence, daring.

1601 HOLLAND *Pliny* II. 494 The audaciousnesse of the artificer, who ventured to make so huge and monstrous works. **1825** T. JEFFERSON *Autobiog.* Wks. 1859 I. 75 As much a man as either of her colleagues, in audaciousness, in enterprise, and in the thirst of domination.

2. Reckless daring; = AUDACITY 2.

1599 *Mirr. Policie* 25 Fortitude..reduceth feare and audaciousnesse to mediocritie. **1742** MIDDLETON *Cicero* (ed. 3) II. vi. 17 In an act so mad..his audaciousness could not get the better of his fears.

3. Presumptuousness, effrontery, impudence, shamelessness; = AUDACITY 3.

1599 *Warn. Faire Wom.* II. 1493 He should with such audaciousness presume To baffle Justice. *a* **1639** WHATELEY *Prototypes* I. iv. (1640) 42 A grievous audaciousnesse..that hee would leape over the poles as it were which God had fixed. **1838–9** *Hood's Own, Jubb Lett.* 53 As Mr. Davis had the audaciousness to own to.

audacity (ɔːˈdæsɪtɪ). Forms: 5 audacite, 5–6 -yte, 6–7 -itie, 7 -itye, 6– audacity. [f. L. *audāc-em* AUDACIOUS + -ITY; see -ACITY: cf. It. *audacita* (Florio 1611).]

1. Boldness, daring, intrepidity; confidence.

1432–50 tr. *Higden* (1865) I. 61 Euery thynge is of more animosite and audacite in his universalle then in his parte parcialle. **1538** COVERDALE *N.T.* Ded., It doth..encourage me now likewyse to use the same audacity toward your grace. **1601** HOLLAND *Pliny* II. 454 Such is the audacitie of man, that hee hath learned to counterfeit Nature. **1714** STEELE *Lover* (1723) 30 Some..have relapsed from the Audacity they had arrived at, into their first Bashfulness. **1839–42** ALISON *Hist. Europe* lvii. §9 Under the eye of the Emperor..nothing was impracticable to their audacity.

b. Bold departure from the conventional form; daring originality.

1859 JEPHSON *Brittany* viii. 104 The beauty of its [a tower's] details and the audacity of its construction. **1878** TAIT & STEWART *Unseen Univ.* Introd. 21 In strength and happy audacity of language.

2. Boldness combined with disregard of consequences; venturesomeness, rashness, recklessness.

1531 ELYOT *Gov.* (1580) 163 Audacitie..is an excessiue and inordinate trust, to escape all daungers. **1660** STANLEY *Hist. Philos.* (1701) 622/1 Fortitude is different from Audacity, Ferocity, inconderate Temerity. **1840** MACAULAY *Clive* 9 Neither climate nor poverty..could tame the desperate audacity of his spirit.

3. Open disregard of the restraints of decorum or morality; effrontery, impudence, shamelessness.

1545 JOYE *Exp. Daniel* vii. (R.) With the most arrogant audacite thei dare alter..and expowne Gods lawes and gospell at their plesures. **1865** LIVINGSTONE *Zambesi* vi. 140 His Excellency was shocked at her audacity, and reprimanded her.

4. Boldness in the concrete, a bold creature.

1658 SIR T. BROWNE *Hydriot.* 39 Those audacities, that durst be nothing, and return into their Chaos again.

†**au'daculous,** *a. Obs.* [f. L. *audāculus*, dim. of *audax* bold + -OUS.] A little bold or daring.

1603 SIR C. HEYDON *Jud. Astrol.* xxi. 429 The ignorance hereof hath caried him too farre in this audaculous dispute.

audad, var. AOUDAD.

Audenesque (ˌɔːdəˈnɛsk), *a.* [f. the name of W. H. *Auden* (b. 1907), + -ESQUE.] Resembling in matter, style, or quality the works of Wystan Hugh Auden, poet and critic.

1940 *Scrutiny* IX. 291 Facetious quasi-ballads in the Audenesque mode. **1944** *Horizon* IX. 209 The point of this little Audenesque folly is that history has revealed to us the volcano under the Victorian world.

‖**au désespoir** (o dezɛspwar). [Fr.] In despair.

1766 C. ANSTEY *New Bath Guide* i. 9 My Spirits flag, my Life and Fire Is mortify'd *au Desespoir*. **1768** STERNE *Sent. Journ.* I. 142 Monsieur his master was *au desespoire* for her re-establishment from the fatigues of her journey. **1801** *Wynne Diaries* 6 Sept. (1940) III. iii. 62 Mrs. Otway has been a widow ten days... She does not seem au desespoir. **1859** TROLLOPE *Bertrams* II. v. 109 Some time since she was giving advice that it should be broken off, and now she was *au désespoir* because that result had been reached.

Audi (əʊdɪ). *Archæol.* Applied *attrib.* to remains of the lower Aurignacian period resembling those found at l'Abri *Audi*, a rock-shelter near Les Eyzies, Dordogne, France, and to the culture they represent. Also *absol.*

1921 M. C. BURKITT *Prehist.* iv. 72 In the Audi tool, the pointed knife edge is produced by a flake struck off the flint, this edge being sometimes trimmed. **1927** PEAKE & FLEURE *Hunters & Artists* iv. 42 The characteristic Audi tool is found with considerable frequency throughout most Lower Aurignacian deposits. **1932** *Antiquity* VI. 192 In France the Aurignacian culture is divisible into five stages: the Audi, the Châtelperron, [etc.].

audibility (ɔːdɪˈbɪlɪtɪ). [f. next: see -BILITY.] The quality of being audible, capability of being heard, distinctness to the ear; audible capacity.

1669 WORLIDGE *Syst. Agric.* (1681) 300 The Audibility of Sounds are certain Prognosticks of the temper of the Air. **1709** in *Phil. Trans.* XXVI. 372 The Sound..very little less in respect to its Audibility; but much more mellow. **1856** EMERSON *Eng. Traits* 75 No man can claim to usurp more than a few cubic feet of the audibilities of a public room.

audible (ˈɔːdɪb(ə)l), *a.* and *sb.* [ad. med.L. *audībilis*, f. *audīre* to hear: see -BLE.]

A. *adj.*

1. Able to be heard, perceptible to the ear.

1529 MORE *Comf. agst. Trib.* III. Wks. 1259/1 The ioyes of heauen are..to mans eares not audible. **1667** MILTON *P.L.* XI. 266 Eve..with audible lament Discover'd soon the place of her retire. **1742** RICHARDSON *Pamela* III. 229, I had rather have their silent Prayers, than their audible ones. **1858** O. W. HOLMES *Aut. Breakf. T.* xi. 110, I tried to speak twice without making myself distinctly audible.

†**2.** Able to hear. *Obs. rare.*

1603 H. CROSSE *Vertues Commw.* (1878) 120 The minde is nothing so tentible at a good instruction, nor the eare so audible, as at a vaine and sportiue foolerie.

B. *sb.* [the adj. used *absol.*] A thing capable of being heard.

1626 BACON *Sylva* §269 The species of audibles seem to be carried more manifestly through the air than the species of visibles. **1794** TAYLOR *Plotinus* xxix, The auditory sense knows audibles.

'audibleness. [f. prec. + -NESS.] The quality of being audible; audibility.

1612–15 BP. HALL *Contempl. N.T.* IV. iii. (1833) 188 Zaccheus stood: and what if the desire of more audibleness raised him to his feet? **1881** *Ch. Bells* 29 Jan. 143/2 [In reading there should be] 1. Correctness. 2. Audibleness.

audibly (ˈɔːdɪblɪ), *adv.* [f. as prec. + -LY².] In audible manner, so as to be heard, aloud.

1635 JACKSON *Creed* VIII. xxix. 338 All the rest..had been visibly and audibly fulfilled. **1805** SOUTHEY *Madoc in Azt.* XIII. Wks. V. 287 Which made her heart with terror and delight Throb audibly. **1860** TYNDALL *Glac.* I. §11. 80 Audibly muttering his doubts as to our ability to reach the top.

audience (ˈɔːdɪəns). Forms: 4–6 **audiens,** 5 **audenes, -yence, awdiens, -yens, -yence,** 5–6 **audyens,** 4– **audience.** [a. F. *audience* (13th c.), refash. form after L. of OF. *oiance*:—L. *audientia*, n. of quality f. *audient-em*, pr. pple. of *audīre* to hear: see -ENCE.]

I. Audience (*abstractly*). *No plural.*

1. The action of hearing; attention to what is spoken. ***to give audience***: to give ear, listen.

c **1374** CHAUCER *Troylus* v. 235 Now I am gon, whom yeve ye audiens? *c* **1485** *Digby Myst.* (1882) II. 156 We beseche yow of audyens. **1549** *Compl. Scot.* xvi. 138, I refuse to gyf eyris or audiens to thy accusations. **1607** SHAKS. *Cor.* III. iii. 40 List to your Tribunes. Audience: Peace I say. **1657** REEVE *God's Plea* Ep. Ded. 14 To put audience into his ears, compassion into his eyes. **1849** MACAULAY *Hist. Eng.* I. 406 These teachers easily found attentive audience.

2. a. The state or condition of hearing, or of being able to hear; hearing. ***in*** (***open, general***) ***audience*** (obs.): so that all may hear, publicly.

c **1386** CHAUCER *Melib.* ¶83 Many folk..conseilled him the contrary in general audience. **1470–85** MALORY *Arthur* (1816) I. 86 He said, in open audience: 'This is your place.' **1640** *Abel Rediv., Musculus* (1867) I. 300 And uttereth these words in the audience of the congregation. **1814** CARY *Dante* 290 Thou in his audience shouldst thereof discourse.

†**b.** with objective genitive. *Obs. rare.*

1626 AILESBURY *Passion-Serm.* 1 Saint Paul..gained the audience of unspeakable mysteries.

3. Judicial hearing. ***Court of Audience*** or ***Audience Court***: an ecclesiastical court, at first held by the archbishop, afterwards by learned men, called Auditors, on his behalf. The Audience Court of Canterbury is now merged in the Court of Arches. *arch.* or *Obs.*

c **1425** WYNTOUN *Cron.* VIII. x. 28 He cald til þe audiens Of Edward. *c* **1500** *Lancelot* 1649 That thi pupIe have awdiens With thar complantis. **1541** *Act 33 Hen. VIII*, xxxi, Constrained for appeles to resort to the audience of Canturbury. **1726** AYLIFFE *Parerg.* 192 The Court of Audience held in Pauls Church in London. **1809** TOMLINS *Law Dict.* s.v., The archbishop of York hath, in like manner, his court of audience.

4. Formal hearing, reception at a formal interview: see 6.

1377 LANGL. *P. Pl.* B. XIII. 434 Shulde none harlote haue audience · in halle ne in chambres. **1599** SHAKS. *Hen. V*, I. i. 91 The French Embassador vpon that instant Crau'd audience. **1743** TINDAL *Rapin's Hist.* xvii. II. 140 Being admitted to audience. *Mod.* The ambassador had audience of her majesty.

attributively.

1753 HANWAY *Trav.* (1762) I. VII. xc. 412 The throne in the audience-chamber is of velvet. **1878** H. STANLEY *Dark Cont.* I. xv. 398 The court before the audience-hall.

II. An audience. *With plural.*

†**5.** *gen.* An occasion of hearing. *Obs.*

1426 *Paston Lett.* 7 I. 26 In any sermon or other audience, in your cherche or elles where.

6. A formal interview granted by a superior to an inferior (especially by a sovereign or chief governor) for conference or the transaction of business. Const. *of, with.*

audience of leave: interview for the purpose of taking leave, farewell interview.

1514 EARL WORC. in Ellis *Orig. Lett.* II. 69 I. 233 The king ..gave me a good and longe audiens. *a* **1674** CLARENDON *Hist. Reb.* III. XII. 253 The embassadours declined any formal audiences. **1711** STEELE *Spect.* No. 298 ¶5, I dropped him a Curtsy, and gave him to understand that this was his Audience of Leave. **1770** *Junius Lett.* xli. 216 He had a right to demand an audience of his sovereign. **1844** DISRAELI *Coningsby* IV. xv. 184, I had an audience..with the Spanish Minister.

7. a. The persons within hearing; an assembly of listeners, an auditory.

1407 W. THORPE *Examin.* (R.T.S.) 51 There was no audience of secular men by. **1519** *Four Elem.* in Hazl. *Dodsl.* I. 46 Such company..Will please well this audience. **1667** MILTON *P.L.* VII. 31 Fit audience find, though few. **1714** BYROM *Spect.* No. 597 ¶9 The rest of the Audience were enjoying..an excellent Discourse. **1817** MOORE *Lalla R.* (1824) 128 He here looked round, and discovered that most of his audience were asleep. *Mod.* He lectured to large audiences in New York.

b. *transf.* The readers of a book.

1855 H. REED *Lect. Eng. Lit.* vii. (1878) 225 'Pilgrim's Progress'..has gained an audience as large as Christendom. **1883** G. HAMILTON in Mrs. Rollins *New Eng. Bygones* Pref. 1 This book is published with no thought of an audience.

c. *transf.* Listeners to radio programmes or viewers of television.

1928 *B.B.C. Handbk. 1929* 259 The audience for broadcast entertainment has already far outstripped in size any other audience in the world. **1936** *B.B.C. Ann.* 85/2 The audience for the daily broadcasts to schools constitutes another special section of the public. **1952** *Ann. Reg. 1951* 400 Television's *For the Children*..won an avid audience.

d. *attrib.* and *Comb.*, as ***audience participation***, sharing by an audience in a broadcast programme, etc.; ***audience-rating***, assessment of the audience of a radio or television programme; ***audience research*** (cf. *listener research*), see quot. 1951; hence ***audience-researcher***.

1812 *Dramatic Censor for 1811* 99 The hall, or audience part of the House, to comprise the segment of a circle. **1940** E. MCGILL *Radio Directing* x. 201 On audience-participation broadcasts the script is no more than a guide-post. *Ibid.* 203 An audience-participation program should never be built around a person who is not a ready improviser. **1940** *Q. Jrnl. Speech* Feb. 134 Experimental productions may teach the playwright..the importance of audience-reactions in the revision of a script. **1948** *Penguin Music Mag.* Feb. 52 Intelligent audience-participation is more and more possible. **1950** L. A. G. Strong *Which I Never* ii. 48, I was thinking less of intrinsic quality, of skill, than of what I believe is termed audience appeal. Box-office. **1950** *Times* 6 Sept. 2/5 An analysis by the B.B.C. Audience Research Department of the social grades of listeners. **1951** *B.B.C. Year Book* 144 The BBC maintains an Audience Research Department to advise it on the habits, tastes, and opinions both of listeners and of viewers. **1955** Koestler *Trail of Dinosaur* 91 The radio performances of a Bach cantata and of a sobbing crooner are compared on the same scale of audience-rating. **1959** *Observer* 8 Feb. 18/3 I.T.V. ..is now estimated by the audience-researchers to have an average daily audience or viewing public of 5,250,000.

† **8.** A place of hearing, an audience-chamber. *Obs.*

1596 Danett *Commines' Hist. Fr.* (1614) 344 He had built a publike audience, where himselfe heard the sutes of all men.

9. A court, either of government or justice, in Spanish America; *also*, the territory administered by it. (Sp. *audiencia*.)

[**1622** R. Hawkins *Voy. S. Sea* (1847) 158 It hath his governour, and *audiencia*, with two bishoppes.] **1727–51** Chambers *Cycl.* s.v., New Spain comprehends three audiences, those of Gaudalajara, Mexico, and Guatimala. **1777** Robertson *Amer.* II. 393 Supreme direction of civil affairs was placed in a board, called The Audience of New Spain.

† **'audiencer, -'cier.** *Obs.* [a. F. *audiencier*, ad. med.L. *audientiārius*, f. *audientia*: see prec.] 'An Officer in the Chancerie, that examines, or heares read, all letters patents, etc., before they passe the seale..receives the fees of the seale,' etc. (Cotgr. 1611.)

1611 Cotgr. s.v. *Droict*, Due vnto th' audienciers of Chanceries. **1752** Carte *Hist. Eng.* III. 681 The president Richardot, and the audiencer Verreicken [were commissioners] for the archduke Albert.

† **'audiency.** *Obs. rare*⁻¹. [ad. L. *audientia*: see prec.] Right to be heard.

1626 Bp. Andrewes *Serm.* (1856) I. 106 Moses and Elias were there in the mount, and resigned up both their several audiencies. [Cf. 'This is my beloved Son; hear him.']

audient ('ɔːdɪənt), *a.* and *sb.* [ad. L. *audientem*: see audience.]

A. *adj.* Listening, giving heed to sounds.

1839 *Blackw. Mag.* XLV. 111, I trembled..At critic grinders, and the audient yawn. **1856** Mrs. Browning *Aur. Leigh* vii. 849 Music, verse, For thrilling audient souls.

B. *sb.* A hearer or listener; *spec.* a hearer of the gospel, not yet a member of the church.

1612 Heywood *Apol. Actors* i. 22 Nor did the audients hold themselves disgraced Of turfe and heathy sods to make their seates. **1647** *Power of Keys* v. 126 Three yeares shal they continue among the Audients. **1819** Rees *Encycl.* III, *Audients*, or *Auditors*, in Ecclesiastical History, an order of cataechumens..not yet admitted to baptism.

† **audi'entiary.** *Obs. rare*⁻¹. [ad. med.L. *audientiārius*: see audiencer.] = audiencer.

1628 tr. *Camden's Hist. Eliz.* iv. (1688) 586 Lodowick Verrekeim, Audientiary and principal Secretary.

† **'audiently,** *adv. Obs. rare*⁻¹. [f. audient + -ly².] So as to be heard, audibly, aloud.

1575 *MS. Eccl. Proc. Durh.*, [He] did hear the said Jenet say audiently.

audile ('ɔːdaɪl), *a.* and *sb.* [Irreg. f. L. *audīre* to hear + -ile.] **A.** *adj.* Pertaining to or received through the auditory nerves. Of a person: of or pertaining to an audile.

1897 *19th Cent.* Aug. 229 The phenomena..may be dichotomised as (1) audile, (2) visual. The audile subdivide into (1) Footsteps. (2) Voices..(3) Raps..(4) and (5) Noises ..(6) A detonating noise. **1909** *Daily Chron.* 22 Feb. 4/7 Unless you are a microcephalous idiot, you are either Audile, Motile, or Visile. **1919** E. Barker in H. G. Wells *Outl. Hist.* xv. 86/2 Homer..is audile, not visual. **1956** H. Read *Art of Sculpture* iv. 71 Thus there are visual types, tactile types, and audile types.

B. *sb.* A person in whom auditory images are predominant over motile and visual presentations.

1886 *Mind* July 415 M. Paulhan, an audile, declares..he can represent the auditory images of *i* and *u* while the motor presentation of *a* is being presented. **1917** J. Adams *Student's Guide* 23 Some prefer to learn through the eye, others like to learn through the ear, still others through the sense of touch. The first kind are called *visuals*, the second *audiles*, the third *tactiles*.

audio ('ɔːdɪəʊ). [Absol. use of audio-.] Sound, esp. recorded or transmitted sound; a signal or signals representing this; sound recording and reproduction.

1934 *Wireless World* 22 June 426/2 The division between radio and audio at 10 kilocycles is quite arbitrary. **1937**, etc. [see video *sb.* 3]. **1940** *Broadcasting* 1 June 32 In addition to *video*, television employs *audio* (= sound signals). **1962** *Radio-Electronics* Dec. 64/3 Audio is recorded on the top edge of the tape. **1967** *National Observer* (U.S.) 3 July 13 The audio—the spoken message—was put, by tape, on the special 'beeper' system that is available to all commercial radio stations. **1979** *Daily Tel.* 28 Aug. 11/4 As soon as the abuse begins, blow..with the whistle about an inch from the mouthpiece. This means..that its originator gets a very painful blast of audio. **1982** *Giant Bk. Electronics Projects* i. 6 The audio was 80% hum, 20% ham. **1984** *Mail on Sunday* (Colour Suppl.) 2 Dec. 6/2 (Advt.), It's the first stacking system to fully integrate the latest developments in hi-fi audio and video.

audio- ('ɔːdɪəʊ). [Combining form, f. L. *audī-re* to hear + -o; cf. audiometer.] **I. audio-active** *a.*, of or pertaining to interactive language learning, esp. in a language laboratory, in which the student is able to listen and respond to course material through a headset linked to a tape recorder or teacher's console; **audio-ca'ssette**, a cassette of audiotape; **audio disc**, a record or disc, esp. a compact disc, on which a sound recording has been made; **audio-frequency**, a frequency capable of being perceived aurally; abbrev. A.F., a.f.; **audio'genic** *a.*, caused by sounds of high frequency, *spec.* of a seizure so induced; **'audiogram** [see -gram], the diagram traced by an audiometer; **audio-lingual** *a.*, pertaining to both listening and speaking (as opp. reading and writing), esp. with reference to the teaching and learning of language; hence **audio-'lingualism, audio-'lingualist**; also **audio-'lingually** *adv.*; **audi'ology**, the science or study of hearing; hence **audi'ologist**, one who specializes in audiology; **'audiophile** [see -phil], a devotee of high-fidelity reproduction of sound (chiefly *U.S.*); **,audio'spectrogram**, a tracing or the like produced by an audiospectrograph; a diagram showing how the frequency components of a sound change with time; **,audio'spectrograph**, an instrument for analysing sound; a diagram traced by this instrument; **,audio-spec'trometer** (see quot. 1957); **audio-visual** *a.*, pertaining to both hearing and vision, esp. of mechanical aids to teaching (see quot. 1959).

1963 *AV Communication Rev.* XI. 36/1 **Audioactive* (*adj.*), listening-speaking practice; also facilities in which students are equipped with headphones, preamplifier, and microphone by means of which the student's voice is amplified and carried simultaneously to his own headphones as he speaks. **1964** J. B. Hilton *Lang. Laboratory in School* vi. 80 The headsets can be audio-active or not at the wish of the pupil. **1968** *Jrnl. Assoc. Teachers of Russian* XVII. 4 In an incredibly short period we have shifted the emphasis of our teaching from 'traditional' attitudes to an audio-active approach. **1975** D. L. Forrester in P. S. Green *Language Laboratory in School* 6 The student's situation is essentially the same as in the simplest audio-active lab. **1971** *Author* LXXXII. 114 Instead of increasing investment in new books, or diversifying into *audio-cassettes,..they [*sc.* the publishers] should put their money into the places where the public goes for their wares. **1983** *Listener* 18 Aug. 34/3 Now you can get a music centre with two audio-cassette heads to facilitate the copying of cassettes as well as discs. **1970** *Audio* Sept. 96/1 Some experts will..take the view that *audio disks made with the new techniques will exchange one set of problems for others. **1983** *Fortune* 21 Mar. 8/1 The digital audio disc player and its companion, the audio Compact Disc, are arriving in the U.S. **1913** *Proc. Inst. Radio Engin.* I. 102 The *audio-frequency produced is equal to the difference in the fundamental oscillation frequencies. **1916** *Wireless World* Aug. 344 (*title*) The Design of the Audio Frequency Circuit of Quenched Spark Transmitters. **1918** W. H. Eccles *Wireless Telegr.* (ed. 2) 487 A.F. Abbreviation for 'Audio Frequency'. **1919** E. W. Stone *Elements of Radiotelegr.* 17 Frequencies from 25 to 10,000 cycles per second are termed audio frequencies. **1936** *Electronics* Jan. 44/2 Resistance coupled a-f amplifiers. **1941** *B.B.C. Gloss. Broadc. Terms* 4 Audio-Frequency: Rate of oscillation corresponding to that of sound audible to the normal human ear (i.e. within the range of about sixteen cycles per second to about fifteen thousand cycles per second). **1943** *Electronic Engin.* XVI. 69 No single curve can be taken as universally representative of the distribution of speech energy throughout the audio frequency band. **1941** C. T. Morgan & H. Waldman in *Jrnl. Compar. Psychol.* XXXI. 1 (*title*) 'Conflict' and *Audiogenic Seizures. **1959** *Chambers's Encycl.* XI. 334/1 These so-called audiogenic seizures..perhaps have more in common with epileptic convulsions than with neurotic manifestations as ordinarily understood. **1930** *Archives of Otolaryngology* XII. 760 An *audiogram is a graphic representation of hearing capacity. **1945** *Electronic Engin.* XVII. 451 Audiograms, i.e. plots of hearing acuity against frequency, taken from a large number of deaf people. **1960** N. Brooks *Language & Lang. Learning* 201 Audio-lingual. Since the words aural and *oral* cannot be dependably distinguished in spoken English, the term **audio*-lingual is proposed instead. **1962** *Mod. Lang. Jrnl.* Nov. 307/2 If language teachers do not reincorporate an unobtrusive grammatical content into the audio-lingual method, they may..come to merit the appellation..'little men with tape recorders'. **1977** D. M. Taylor et al. in H. Glass *Lang., Ethnicity & Intergroup Relations* iv. 100 The traditional grammar-translation methods and even the newer audio-lingual approaches..have generally proved less than satisfactory. **1984** *Jrnl. Res. in Reading* VII. 3 The role and influence of the audiolingual component on the learning process. **1961** *Hispania* Mar. 148/2 Let us urge greater moderation in the assumptions and claims of *audio-lingualism. **1976** E. W. Stevick *Memory, Meaning & Method* x. 155 Audiolingualism sets the learner to work on prefabricated and neatly packaged meanings presented primarily as words of the native and target languages. **1979** *Mod. Lang. Jrnl.* Dec. 423/2 These trends—the post-World War II audiolingualism, the mentalistically oriented cognitivism, and..eclecticism—have been reflected in the way Hebrew has been taught in North American Hebrew schools. **1961** *Hispania* Mar. 148/2 The oft-repeated claim of the *audio-lingualists that 'language is speech; language is not writing.' **1977** *Language* LIII. 503/2 S argues that neither the audio-lingualists nor the cognitivists are on the right track. **1974** *French Rev.* XLVIII. 20 The George Sherer experiment..was to compare proficiency results between *audio-lingually and traditionally taught students. **1947** Hallowell Davis *Hearing & Deafness* i. 4 '*Audiology', meaning the science of hearing seems to be a useful name for this field. *Ibid.* [S. R. Silverman] xiv. 363 In consultation with the clinical audiologist (a person trained in meeting problems of deafness) he [*sc.* the otologist] is prepared to suggest whatever measures are indicated. **1952** *Lancet* 15 Nov. 967/1 In clinical audiology the normal unit of intensity is the decibel. **1951** *High-Fidelity* I. 4 (*title*) *Audio-Phile's Bookshelf. **1953** *Electronic Engin.* XXV. 306 An 'audiophile' whose desire is to achieve high quality reproduction. **1968** *McGraw-Hill Yearbk. Sci. & Technol.* 56/2 (*caption*) *Audiospectrograms of three white-crowned sparrows, from a wild-caught bird [etc.]. **1978** *Nature* 31 Aug. 888/1 Rates for complete cycles of wing movement, consisting of two openings and two closings, were calculated from audiospectrograms. **1954** *Ohio Jrnl. Sci.* LIV. 298 *Audio-spectrographs of the song of *N. ensiger*. *Ibid.* 303 A tape recording of the song of *Neoconocephalus ensiger* (Harris) was analyzed by means of an audio-spectrograph. **1962** *Science Survey* XVII. 278 The sounds must be recorded because only then can they be examined by the oscillogram and audio-spectrograph. **1952** Benson & Hirsh in *Jrnl. Acoust. Soc. Amer.* XXIV. 453 (*title*) A simplified *audiospectrometer. **1957** *New Scientist* 9 May 26/2 The panoramic audiospectrometer shows the frequencies present in a sound at any given instant... A second type of audiospectrometer called the 'Sonagraph' graphs the variation in frequency with time for a part of the sound. **1937** Townsend & Stewart (*title*) *Audio-visual aids for teachers. **1959** L. M. Harrod *Libr. Gloss.* (ed. 2) 26 *Audio-visual aids*, material such as gramophone records, tape recordings and various visual aids used as an adjunct to teaching.

II. Independent use of prec. as a quasi-sb. used *attrib.*: of or pertaining to frequencies within the range of audibility; relating to the reproduction, transmission, or reception of sound. Also **audio secretary**, a secretary who does audio typing; **audio typist**, one who types directly from material previously recorded (as on magnetic tape); hence **audio typing** *vbl. sb.* and *ppl. a.*

[**1924** Gibson & Cole *Wireless of To-day* 11 *Audio*, within the limits of audition.] **1930** *Proc. Inst. Radio Engin.* XVIII. 159 If..the radio tubes obtain their grid and plate voltage from the same points supplying the first audio tube [etc.]. **1935** *Discovery* Sept. 277/2 They are providing ever better products and service to enable the listening public to get more enjoyment from the 'audio' programmes..and will be ready to cater for those who wish..to see such 'video' items as may become available. **1937** *Ibid.* Nov. 331 (*caption*) Audio Transmitter. **1943** *Gloss. Terms Telecommunic.* (*B.S.I.*) 3 *Audio range*, the range of frequencies audible to the normal human ear. **1948** *Audio Visual Guide* XIV. 7 (*title*) A brief survey of currently available audio equipment. **1958** *Observer* 20 Apr. 10/5 A closer understanding between audio engineers and musicians. **1959** *Times* 3 Sept. 14/1 The audio-typing pool. *Ibid.*, Most kinds [of tape-recording machines] enable the employer to dictate letters into a hand microphone... With the help of another machine..an 'audio-typist' completes the process. **1960** *Times* 14 Jan. 19/4 Two audio channels—each with a bass 'woofer' and treble 'tweeter' to cover the extremely wide compass of stereo sound. **1962** H. E. Beecheno *Introd. Bus. Stud.* viii. 75 By audio-typing methods he can dictate material when he is free. **1966** *Daily Tel.* 19 Aug. 20/2 Nearly all studiously avoid the term 'typing pool'. Instead, 'audio room' or 'the typing service unit' is preferred. **1968** *Evening Standard* 2 Dec. 12/6 (Advt.), Audio sec[retary] reqd. for super job with international manager. **1969** *Times* 5 Dec. 18/6 (Advt.), Audio secretary required by Executive of rapidly expanding Company of Consultants in Belgravia. **1977** *Wandsworth Boro' News* 7 Oct. 21/3 (Advt.), Solicitors require Audio Secretary for Partner. **1982** *Financial Times* 25 June 23/3 Legal-audio-secretaries can name their own price at the moment.

audiometer (ɔːdɪ'ɒmɪtə(r)). [f. L. *audī-re* to hear + Gr. μέτρον measure: see -(o)meter.] An instrument for measuring the sensitivity of the ear to sounds of different frequencies.

1879 *Daily News* 31 Dec. 5/4 This sonometer has been used by Dr. Richardson to measure minute differences in hearing under the name of the Audiometer. **1879** B. W. Richardson in *Proc. R. Soc.* XXIX. 65 Professor Hughes' new Instrument for the Measurement of Hearing; the Audiometer. *Ibid.* 70 The world of medicine..is under a deep debt of gratitude to Professor Hughes for his simple and beautiful instrument, which I have christened the audimeter, or less correctly but more euphoniously, the audiometer. **1884** *Health Exhib. Catal.* 145/2 Audiometer for testing the amount of hearing possessed by the deaf. **1919** *Trans. Amer. Otol. Soc.* XV. 24 The pitch range audiometer as we have it today, measures the tonal range from 30 double vibrations to 10,000 double vibrations; that is, the practical range of hearing. **1959** *Chambers's Encycl.* VI. 721/1 Audiometers are of two types: one tests hearing for speech and the other acuity for pure-tones of the kind produced by tuning-forks.

Hence **audi'ometry**, the testing and measurement of the sense of hearing; **,audio'metric** *a.*, of or pertaining to audiometry; **,audiome'trician, audi'ometrist**, one who specializes in audiometry.

1889 *Cent. Dict.*, Audiometry, audiometric. **1924** *Volta Rev.* Jan. 10 (*title*) Audiometric Measurements and Their Uses. **1931** *Lancet* 4 July 20/2 A method of audiometry by tuning-forks. **1948** *Hansard Commons* CCCCXLV. W.A. 221 To recruit trained audiometrists to ensure the suitable allocation of the aural aids. **1952** *Lancet* 15 Nov. 967/2 Any worker who was to be exposed continuously to a noise of more than 90 decibels' intensity should have his hearing tested by modern audiometric methods before starting work and at intervals afterwards. **1963** *Hark!* IV. 70 They were helped by the loan of equipment for free hearing tests, with two audiometricians in attendance throughout the displays.

audion (ˈɔːdɪɒn). *Radio.* [Coined in 1906 by C. D. Babcock, assistant to the inventor, Lee de Forest; f. L. *audīre* to hear + *-on*.] A former trade name for a three-electrode thermionic valve, used as a detector and an amplifier. (*Disused.*)

1911 LEE DE FOREST *U.S. Pat.* 995,126 1/2, O represents an oscillation detector.. herein shown as an audion. **1914** E. H. ARMSTRONG in *Electrical World* 12 Dec. 1149 (*title*) Operating Features of the Audion. **1916** *Chambers's Jrnl.* 63/1 The audion, or wireless lamp, which plays such a part in wireless telephony between Arlington, Hawaii, California, Paris and other distant parts.

audiotape (ˈɔːdɪəʊteɪp). Also as two words and with hyphen. [f. AUDIO- + TAPE *sb.*[1]] **a.** Magnetic tape on which sound can be recorded. **b.** A length of audiotape; a sound recording on tape.

1958 *Jrnl. Soc. Motion Picture & Television Engineers* LXVII. 738/3 Video tape is different from the introduction of audio tape in radio. **1961** *Ibid.* LXX. 419/2 A ¼-in. audio-tape composite track is finally transferred to the original soundtrack of the edited video-tape master. **1964** M. MCLUHAN *Understanding Media* II. xxix. 291 Audio tape and video tape were to excel film eventually. **1977** *Lancet* 21 May 1116/2 The service has operated its own production centre for audiotapes and slides. **1982** T. BARR *Acting for Camera* IV. xxvi. 190 He sits at the tape recorder, starting and stopping the audio tape as needed. **1983** *Brit. Med. Jrnl.* 16 July 201 Input methods—that is keying in via typewriter keyboard, audiotape recording, and two types of written.. forms. **1984** *Listener* 13 Dec. 38/3 Why not try the 30-minute audio-tape?

Hence as *v. trans.*, to record (sound, speech, etc.) on tape; ˈ**audiotaped** *ppl. a.*

1974 *Florida FL Reporter* XIII 53/3 A brief audiotaped speech sample. **1981** FERGUSON & HEATH *Lang. in U.S.A.* IV. 408 Each interview was audio-taped. **1984** *Lang. & Communication* IV. 289 All responses were audiotaped.

audiphone (ˈɔːdɪfəʊn). [f. L. *audī-re* to hear + Gr. φωνή sound. (Improperly formed after *telephone*, 'that which sounds afar,' from Gr. -φωνος sounding, that sounds; whereas *audiphone* seems intended to mean 'that which hears sound.')] An instrument which, pressed against the upper teeth, enables the deaf to hear more distinctly.

1880 *Scribner's Mag.* Feb. 637 The audiphone will prove to be of great value to deaf mutes, as it enables them to hear their own voices. **1882** AGNES CRANE in *Leisure H.* July 412 The audiphone, a fan-like instrument which materially alleviates certain phases of deafness.

audit (ˈɔːdɪt), *sb.* Forms: 5–6 **awdite**, 5–7 **audite**, 6 **-yte**, 7 **-itt**, 6– **audit**. [ad. L. *audītus* a hearing, n. of action f. *audīre* to hear.]

1. *gen.* A hearing, an audience; *esp.* a judicial hearing of complaints, a judicial examination. *arch.*

1598 FLORIO, *Vdita*, the sence of hearing. Also an audite. **1649** MILTON *Eikon.* v. 49 With his orisons I meddle not, for hee appeals to a high audit. **1683** CAVE *Ecclesiastici* 90 The death of Arsenius.. was not defendable at a fair Audit. **1784** COWPER *Task* IV. 610 Whoso seeks an audit here Propitious, pays his tribute.. and his errand speeds. **1880** RUSKIN in *19th Cent.* Nov. 758 Whose last words.. gave to Scott's heart the vision and the audit of the death of Elspeth of the Craigburn-foot.

2. Official examination of accounts with verification by reference to witnesses and vouchers. (Accounts were originally *oral*: cf. Matt. xxv. 19–30; Luke xvi. 2–7.)

1435 in Heath *Grocers' Comp.* (1869) 417 A dyner maad to the newe maistres and the Companye atte audite. **1589** *Pasquil's Ret.* D iij, I meane to be Clarke of their Audit. **1622** MARKHAM *Decades War* v. vi. 2 Many Subtreasurers.. skilfull in Audit and matter of account. **1704** J. BLAIR in Perry *Hist. Coll. Amer. Col. Ch.* I. 98 The Gov[r]. & Council in a solemn audit examined & past the accounts of the revenue. **1860** FROUDE *Hist. Eng.* xxix. V. 474 An annual audit of the books of all collectors.

3. *fig.* A searching examination or solemn rendering of accounts; *esp.* the Day of Judgement.

1548 UDALL, etc. *Erasm. Par.* Pref. 14 The generall daie of accumpte and audite to bee made at the throne of God. **1606** DEKKER *Sev. Sins* I. (Arb.) 15 Those heapes of Siluer .. will be a passing bell.. calling thee to a fearefull Audit. **1747** HERVEY *Medit.* II. 9 One who walks on the Borders of Eternity, and is hasting continually to his final Audit. **1839** DE QUINCEY *Recoll. Lakes* Wks. 1862 II. 179 The awful temper of the times.. had summoned to an audit, even the gay.

4. A periodical settlement of accounts between landlord and tenants; a yearly, half-yearly, or quarterly rent-paying; *hence*, receipts, revenue (*obs.*).

1489 *Plumpton Corr.* 87 He will have a generall awdite, where ye, & all other, shall have your lesses out. **1523** FITZHERB. *Surv.* 8 To make a true accompt therof at the lordes audyte. **1616** *Pasquil & Kath.* I. 62 When the Lord my Fathers Audit comes, wee'l repay you againe. **1625** BACON *Riches, Ess.* (Arb.) 235 A Nobleman.. that had the greatest Audits, of any Man in my Time. **1880** *Daily News* 13 Dec. 6/5 The audits on his Irish estates had just been held.

5. A statement of account; a balance-sheet as prepared for the auditor; *lit.* and *fig. arch.* or *Obs.*

c **1550** *Lusty Juv.* in Hazl. *Dodsl.* II. 100 Your owne secret conscience shall then give an audit. **1613** SHAKS. *Hen. VIII*, III. ii. 141 You haue scarse time To steale from Spirituall leysure a briefe span To keepe your earthly Audit. **1619** LD. DONCASTER *Let.* in *Eng. & Germ.* (1865) 174 You may give his Majesty an auditt of the time I have spent. **1654** FULLER *Two Serm.* 6 When he casteth up his Audit, he shall finde himselfe a great loser.

6. *attrib.*, as in ***audit-book***, ***-day***, ***-office***; **audit ale**, ellipt. *audit*, ale of special quality brewed (at certain Colleges in the English Universities), originally for use on the day of audit; **audit-house**, **-room**, a building or room appendant to a cathedral, used for the transaction of business; **audit trail**, (*a*) *Accounting*, a means of verifying the detailed transactions underlying any item in an accounting record; (*b*) *Computing*, a record of the computing processes which have been applied to a particular set of source data, showing each stage of processing and allowing the original data to be reconstituted; a record of the transactions to which a database or a file has been subjected; cf. TRACE *sb.*[1] 12 a.

1823 BYRON *Age of Bronze* xiv, But where is now the goodly audit ale? **1872** OUIDA *Gen. Matchmaking* 34 Are you going to smoke and drink audit on that sofa all day? *a* **1679** T. GOODWIN *Wks.* (1863) VI. 487 Their own audit-book, in which losses and gains are written. **1553** T. WILSON *Rhet.* 15 b, Behynde hand with their reckenynges at the audite day. **1689** WHELER *Ch. Prim. Chr.* x. 115 Sermon at Ten in the Audit-house. **1884** *Govt. Offices*, Exchequer and Audit Department, Somerset House. **1726** FIDDES *Wolsey* 94 The Chapter-house.. is commonly used as the Audit Room of the Canons. **1954** *Jrnl. Accounting* July 41/2 It is significant that the actual and projected uses of electronic equipment today do provide an adequate '*audit trail'. **1962** *Data Processing Yearbk. 1962–63* 156/2 The auditor.. can ascertain whether the system contains adequate audit trails. **1964** T. W. MCRAE *Impact of Computers on Accounting* vi. 173 It is up to the firm being audited to provide an adequate audit trail so that both they and their external auditor can satisfy themselves as to the make-up of any balance. **1985** *Personal Computer World* Feb. 124/2 Popovich expects the drive will satisfy 'a real need for archival and audit trail data'.

audit (ˈɔːdɪt), *v.* [f. prec. sb.]

1. *trans.* To make an official systematic examination of (accounts), so as to ascertain their accuracy.

1557 *Ord. Hospitalls* B iv b, Auditors generall.. to Audite .. thaccompts of all other officers. **1726** AYLIFFE *Parerg.* 283 Bishops Ordinaries.. auditing all Accounts.. take twelve Pence and no more. **1856** FROUDE *Hist. Eng.* I. 153 With subscribed funds, regularly audited.

2. To examine, 'hear' (a pupil). *rare.*

1805 W. TAYLOR in *Ann. Rev.* III. 511 He audited catechumens.

†**3.** *gen.* To calculate, reckon. *Obs.*

1655 FULLER *Ch. Hist.* II. x. §40 I. 353 All things being audited proportionably. **1667** *Decay Chr. Piety* ix. §19. 306 And audit what real profit accrues to them from the expence of so many precious hours.

†**4.** *intr.* To draw up or render an account. *Obs.*

1640 BP. HALL *Chr. Moder.* 20/2 It will be wofully audited for. **1712** ARBUTHNOT *John Bull* (1727) 89 Let Hocus audit; he knows how the money was disbursed.

5. *trans.* and *intr.* To attend (a course or other form of instruction) in order to participate without the need to earn credits by writing papers, etc. *U.S.*

1933 *Bull. Ohio State Univ. Coll. Arts & Sci.* 14 Mar. 16 A student in the University may audit a course without additional fee... One not a student in the University may be admitted as an auditor.. subsequently paying the fees required in the College in which he desires mainly to audit. **1948** *Bull. Ohio State Univ. Catal. 1948–49* 325 No credit will be recorded for courses audited. **1969** *Computers & Humanities* IV. 74 As an introduction to software design, I audited a class in compiler-writing and implemented a portion of the class projects. **1974** A. LURIE *War between Tates* ii. 28 She audited his undergraduate lectures; she waylaid him in the department office. **1980** *Early Music Gaz.* Apr. 15/1 The brochure states that 'participants can either be active or audit'. **1985** *New Yorker* 4 Nov. 63/1 He .. studied with Millard Meiss.., and he audited lectures or seminars given by.. other notable art historians.

audit, obsolete form of ADIT.

audited (ˈɔːdɪtɪd), *ppl. a.* [f. prec. + -ED.] Of accounts: Submitted to official examination.

1819 J. GREIG *Rep. Affairs Edin.* 30 The Audited Accounts of the City's Revenue.

auditing (ˈɔːdɪtɪŋ), *vbl. sb.* [f. as prec. + -ING[1].] Official examination of accounts; reckoning up.

1659 *Gentl. Call.* (1696) 2 To his own account and joy in the auditing of the harvest, as also to the glory of God.

audition (ɔːˈdɪʃən), *sb.* [? a. F. *audition*, 14th c. *audicion*, ad. L. *audītiōn-em*, f. *audīre* to hear.]

1. a. The action of hearing or listening.

1660 STANLEY *Hist. Philos.* (1701) 257/1 The act of the Object, and the act of Sense itself, as Sonation and Audition .. differ only intentionally. **1881** FITCH *Lect. Teaching* viii. 252 What may be called audition—the listening to French sentences and rapidly interpreting them.

b. A trial hearing or performance of an actor, singer, etc., seeking employment.

1881 *Scribner's Monthly* May 122/1 The director of the Académie de Musique.. fixed a day for her *audition* at the theatre. **1908** *Evening News* 18 June 3/3 When she was nineteen she was given an 'audition' at the Santa Cecilia Conservatoire. **1926** *Westm. Gaz.* 30 Jan., The plaintiff gave auditions to several girl saxophonists to fill the vacancy. **1933** P. GODFREY *Back-Stage* xv. 190 The chorus-girl gets her jobs by attending auditions.

2. The power or faculty of hearing.

1599 A. M. *Gabelhouer's Bk. Physic* 63/1 It draweth all out which is in the Eares, and administreth good auditione. **1867** TYNDALL *Sound* ii. 74 The insect-music lying quite beyond his limit of audition.

3. An object of hearing, something heard; cf *vision.*

1762 H. WALPOLE *Corr.* (1837) II. 133, I went to hear it for it is not an *apparition* but an *audition*.

audition (ɔːˈdɪʃən), *v.* [f. the sb.] **1.** *trans.* To give an audition to (an applicant); to test by means of an audition.

1935 *Punch* 18 Sept. 325/3 'Players who wish to be auditioned..' *B.B.C. Advertisement.* **1958** *Sunday Times* 26 Jan. 20/4 Here the sixty-eight-year-old playwright auditions Jacqueline Foster for a part. **1959** *Times* 14 Sept. 5/1 When I auditioned English dancers for the London production.

2. *intr.* To undergo an audition; to be tested by means of an audition. orig. *U.S.*

1937 *Variety* 17 Mar. (*heading*) Ice-Skater auditions in Rockefeller Plaza to ag[en]cy 14 floors up. **1938** *Amer. Speech* XIII. 194 Candidates for radio work at first are given an audition; later they simply *audition*. **1955** BEGLEY & MACCRAE (*title*) Auditioning for TV: How to prepare for success as a television actor.

auditive (ˈɔːdɪtɪv), *a.* [a. F. *auditif*, *-ive*, f. L. *audīt-* ppl. stem of *audīre* to hear: see -IVE.] Of or pertaining to the sense of hearing; auditory.

1611 COTGR., *Auditif*, auditiue, of a hearing propertie or facultie. **1634** T. JOHNSON tr. *Parey's Chirurg.* I. x. (1678) 15 That [spirit] which is conveyed to the Auditory passage, is called the Auditive or Hearing. **1880** LE CONTE *Monoc. Vision* 10 The 8th pair—auditive nerve—is specially organized to respond to sound-vibrations.

auditor (ˈɔːdɪtə(r)). Forms: 4–6 **audytour(e**, 4–7 **-itour**, 5 **-ytor**, **awdyter**, 5– **auditor**. [a. AF. *auditour* = F. *auditeur* (substituted for OF. *oeor*), ad. L. *audītor*, f. *audīre* to hear: see -OR.]

1. A hearer, listener; one of an audience.

c **1386** CHAUCER *Sompn. T.* 229 Workers of Goddes word, not auditours. **1590** SHAKS. *Mids. N.* III. i. 81 What, a Play toward? Ile be an auditor. **1621** BURTON *Anat. Mel.* Democr. 58 No parish to contain above a thousand auditors. **1752** JOHNSON *Rambl.* 195 ⁋1 He that long delays a story, and suffers his auditor to torment himself with expectation. **1863** MARY HOWITT tr. *F. Bremer's Greece* I. viii. 264 The galleries were.. filled with auditors.

2. a. One who learns by oral instruction; an attendant on lectures, a disciple; in *Eccl. Hist.* a catechumen; cf. AUDIENT *sb.*

1483 CAXTON *Gold. Leg.* 425/1 He made al the audytours of the cristen feyth to be put to deth. **1589** *Pasquil's Ret.* B iiij, As the Auditors of the Philosophers did in times past. **1691** WOOD *Ath. Oxon.* I/326 Bodley.. was an auditor of Chevalerius in Hebrew. **1851** TORREY *Neander's Ch. Hist.* I. 502 The great mass, consisting of the exoterics, were to constitute the Auditors.

b. One who audits a course, etc.: see AUDIT *v.* 5. *N. Amer.*

1933 [see AUDIT *v.* 5]. **1937** *Bull. Univ. Kentucky* June 14 Auditors. In lecture and recitation courses.. $1.00 per credit hr. **1964** *Bull. Univ. Kentucky Gen. Catal. 1964/5* 28/2 All auditors are charged the same fee that they would pay for credit. **1987** *Washington Post* 8 Feb. E3/6 Several of the older passengers earned credits for their efforts, although most had attended as auditors.

3. (From the fact that accounts were formerly vouched for orally) An official whose duty it is to receive and examine accounts of money in the hands of others, who verifies them by reference to vouchers, and has power to disallow improper charges.

1377 LANGL. *P. Pl.* B. xix. 458 Of my reue to take Al þat myne auditour, or elles my stuwarde Conseilleth me by her acounte. **1469** J. PASTON in *Lett.* 631 II. 388 Send downe.. to some awdyter, to take acomptys of Dawbneys byllys. **1557** *Ord. Hospitalls* B iv b, There shall also be chosen Auditors generall of the Accompts. **1607** SHAKS. *Timon* II. ii. 165 Call me before th' exactest Auditors, And set me on the proofe. **1832** BABBAGE *Econ. Manuf.* xxxi. 313 The public ought to have auditors on their part, and the accounts should be annually published.

fig. **1393** GOWER *Conf.* II. 191 Upon thilke ende of our accompte, Which Crist him self is auditour. **1533** MORE *Apol.* i. Wks. 845/2 No such man wil ouer me be so sore an auditour.. as to charge me with any great losse.

4. a. One who listens in a judicial capacity and tries cases brought before him for hearing; *spec.* the official presiding in the archbishop's Audience Court (see AUDIENCE 3).

1640 BP. REYNOLDS *Passions* vi. 42 In matter of Action, and of Iudicature, Affection in some sort is an Auditor or Iudge. **1706** *Lond. Gaz.* No. 4230/1 Signior Caprara, one of the Auditors de Rota. **1726** AYLIFFE *Parerg.* 192 The Auditor, or Official of Causes and Matters in the Court of Audience of Canterbury.

b. (See quot.)

1919 MOORE-ANDERSON *Sir Robert Anderson* i. 4 Of his University life [at Trinity Coll., Dublin] he.. cherished pleasant memories.. associated with the College Historical

Society, of which he became Auditor, a position corresponding to that of President of the Union at Oxford or Cambridge.

auditorial (ɔːdɪˈtɔərɪəl), *a.* [f. L. *audītōri-us* AUDITORY + -AL[1].]

1. = AUDITORY *a.*

1859 in WORCESTER. [Cf. next word.]

2. Of or pertaining to auditors of accounts; connected with an audit.

1883 *Manch. Guard.* 12 Oct. 4/6 The auditorial investigation at the River Plate Bank.

audiˈtorially, *adv.* [f. prec. + -LY[2].] In auditorial manner, by means of hearing or listening.

a **1881** ROLLESTON *Mem.* (1884) 910 Obtaining orally, or rather auditorially, what it would have cost him more time to obtain..by reading.

auditorium (ɔːdɪˈtɔərɪəm). [a. L. *audītōrium* lecture-room, audience, neut. of adj. *audītōrius* used subst.: see AUDITORY and -ORIUM.]

1. a. The part of a public building occupied by the audience; in ancient churches, the 'nave.' Also (*U.S.*) applied to the entire building.

1727–51 CHAMBERS *Cycl., Auditory, Auditorium*..was that part of the church where the *audientes* stood to hear, and be instructed. **1854** W. IRVING *Let.* 22 Nov. in P. M. Irving *Life & Lett.* (1864) IV. 158, I mingled in the crowd, and heard Bancroft's erudite address from the 'auditorium'. **1881** *Daily News* 12 Sept. 2/3 Every part of the auditorium, the boxes, upper circle, and gallery. **1928** F. HURST *President is Born* iv. 35 Bek..arranged his one-man [water-colour] show in the Auditorium of the Tallahassee High School. **1929** H. G. WELLS *King who was King* viii. 248 The lights in the auditorium [of the cinema] go up. **1954** *Manch. Guardian Weekly* 18 Feb. 8/4 Joe's first stop was Charleston, West Virginia, where..he drew a good crowd of 2,800 to an auditorium that had seats for 3,517.

b. *attrib.*

1898 J. HOLLINGSHEAD *Gaiety Chron.* ii. 50 The room belonged to the *auditorium* side of the curtain. **1908** *Westm. Gaz.* 7 July 10/1 The design of the Auditorium building is in the Renaissance style of architecture.

‖**2.** The reception-room of a monastery. (Med.L.)

1863 J. MORISON *St. Bernard* II. ii. 196 In the 'auditorium,' or talking-room of the monastery.

auditorship (ˈɔːdɪtəʃɪp). [see -SHIP.] The office or position of auditor.

1779 JOHNSON *L.P., Halifax* ¶10 With a grant to his nephew of the reversion of the auditorship of the Exchequer. **1875** WINGATE in *N. Amer. Rev.* CXX. 145 The duties of the auditorship are comparatively unimportant.

auditory (ˈɔːdɪtərɪ), *a.* [ad. L. *audītōrius* pertaining to hearing or hearers, f. *audītor*: see AUDITOR and -ORY.]

1. a. Pertaining to the sense or organs of hearing; received by the ear.

1578 BANISTER *Hist. Man* I. 10 That part of the temple bones, where the auditorie hole is sited. **1646** SIR T. BROWNE *Pseud. Ep.* 253 Three small bones in the Auditory Organ..Incus, Malleus, and Stapes. **1724** SWIFT *To Delany* Wks. 1755 IV. I. 46 From each ear, as he observes, There creep two auditory nerves. **1813** W. TAYLOR in *Month. Mag.* XXXV. 139 A habit of attending to auditory ideas.

b. in *Comb.*

1936 J. KANTOR *Objective Psychol. Gram.* iii. 32 Comparative grammar deals with auditory-vocal mass phenomena abstracted from the linguistic adjustments of the persons *using* such languages. **1964** M. A. K. HALLIDAY et al. *Linguistic Sciences* iii. 59 The term 'consonant'..is..an auditory-articulatory label.

2. Belonging to the auditorium of a theatre, etc.

1740 CIBBER *Apol.* (1756) I. 231 If the auditory part were a little more reduced to the model of that in Drury Lane.

ˈauditory, *sb.* [ad. L. *audītōrium* (see above). Sense 1, the earliest in Eng., was the latest in L.]

1. An assembly of hearers, an audience.

c **1380** WYCLIF *Sel. Wks.* (1871) III. 426 Nouþer wolde I graunte hit..byfore auditorie þat I trowed schulde be harmed þerby. **1548** LATIMER *Serm. Plough* I. 68 Here is a learned auditory: yet for them that be unlearned I will expound it. **1715** BURNET *Own Time* (1766) I. 188 He chose to preach to small auditories. **1855** MACAULAY *Hist. Eng.* IV. 525 A loud moan of sorrow rose from the whole auditory.

2. A place for hearing; the part of a building occupied by the audience; an auditorium.

1548 UDALL, etc. *Erasm. Par. Matt.* xiii. 2 (R.) The sande of the bancke and the bryncke of the bancke, made as though it were a rounde auditory. **1730** A. GORDON *Maffei's Amphit.* 22 That Place we call *Auditory*, from our hearing therein. **1884** *Pall Mall G.* 19 Jan. 4/2 The stage is divided from the auditory by a solid brick wall.

†**3.** A lecture-room; a philosophical school. *Obs.*

1606 G. W[OODCOCKE] *Hist. Justine* G g v b, His felow-scholers..taxed him, in the auditory, for not observing his word. **1643** SIR T. BROWNE *Relig. Med.* I. §36 Another scruple..much disputed in the Germane auditories. **1774** T. WARTON *Eng. Poetry* II. 130 (T.) A provision, that he should..not suffer Ovid's Art of Love..to be studied in his auditory.

†**4.** The office of an auditor of accounts. *Obs.*

1611 SPEED *Hist. Gt. Brit.* VI. xlvi. 160 The Count also of priuate reuenewes had his Rationall or Auditory of priuate State in Britain: to say nothing..of other officers of inferiour degrees.

auditress (ˈɔːdɪtrɪs). [f. AUDITOR: see -ESS.] A female hearer or auditor.

1667 MILTON *P.L.* VIII. 51 Adam relating, she sole auditress. **1767** FORDYCE *Serm. Yng. Wom.* I. i. 34 You, my honoured auditress. **1874** PAYN *Best Husb.* I. viii. 144 Skill in getting his somewhat cooked accounts passed by an auditress in the High Court of Love.

auˈditual, *a.* [f. L. *audītu-s* sense of hearing + -AL[1]; cf. L. *vīsuālis* VISUAL, f. *vīsus*.] Of or belonging to the sense of hearing; auditory.

1653 BROME *City Wit* I. i, I disclaime my hearing. I defie my audituall part. **1666** G. ALSOP *Maryland* (1869) 37 Must now..whisper softly in the auditual parts of Mary-Land.

†**ˈauditur(e.** *Obs.* [a. F. *auditoire*, ad. L. *audītōrium*.] Scotch form of AUDITORY.

1549 *Compl. Scot.* iv. 29 The vniuersal auditur of oure realme. **1566** KNOX *Hist. Ref.* Wks. 1846 I. 137 He passyd to the pulpett, but the auditure was small.

Audubon (ˈɔːdəbən). The name of J. J. *Audubon* (1785–1851), American ornithologist, used *attrib.* or in the possessive case of certain birds.

1837 TOWNSEND in *Jrnl. Acad. Nat. Sci. Phila.* VII. 191 Audubon's Warbler..inhabits the forests of the Columbia river. **1909** WEBSTER s.v. *shearwater*, The Manx shearwater ..and the Audubon's shearwater..common about the West Indies, Florida coasts, etc., are small species. **1933** *Discovery* Feb. 62/2 The petrel known as Aud[u]bon's shearwater is sometimes confused with the capped petrel, 'Le Diablotin', owing to the fact that both birds have the same colloquial name in the different islands [*sc.* Dominica and Grenada].

aue-board: see AWE *sb.*[2]

auen, obs. form of OWN, EVEN.

auer, auete, obs. ff. OVER, EFT.

†**auf(e.** *Obs.* Also 7 **aulfe, auph,** 8 *dial.* **awf.** [a. ON. *álfr* (cogn. w. OE. *ælf*) elf, fairy; but apparently not applied in Eng. to the *elves* themselves.] An elf's child, a goblin child, a changeling left by the fairies; *hence,* a misbegotten, deformed, or idiot child, a half-wit, simpleton. The earlier and more etymological form of OAF[1].

1621 BURTON *Anat. Mel.* III. ii. IV. i. (1651) 519 A very monster, an aufe imperfect. **1627** DRAYTON *Agincourt, etc.* 119 Say that the Fayrie left this Aulfe, And tooke away the other. **1659** BROME *Eng. Moor* III. ii. 43 The Arsivarsiest Aufe that ever crept into the world. **1678** DRYDEN *Kind Kpr.* I. i. 11 You Auph you, do you not perceive? *c* **1750** TIM BOBBIN *Eawther & Buk*, What an awf wur I t' pretend rime weh yo!

‖**au fait** (o ˈfɛ), *advb. phr.* [Fr.; *au* at the, to the, *fait* fact, point, question, under discussion.] In phr. ***to be au fait in*** or ***at***: to be well instructed or 'up to the mark' in, thoroughly conversant with, expert or skilful in. ***to put a person au fait of*** (= F. *mettre au fait de*): to instruct thoroughly in. Also const. *to*, or (most freq. in recent use) *with*.

a **1743** LD. HERVEY *Mem.* (1952) v. 221 Your Majesty being *au fait* of all transactions..for these last ten years. **1748** H. WALPOLE *Lett. H. Mann* II. 255 Being *au fait* he went up to him at Ranelagh and apostrophized him. **1821** *New Monthly Mag.* II. 220 Yet, to be *au fait* at nonsense, is no easy matter. **1828** A. GRANVILLE *Autobiog.* II. 286, I..will put you *au fait* of all the circumstances of the case. **1849** C. BRONTË *Shirley* I. vi. 157 For the benefit of those who are not 'au fait' to the mysteries of the 'Jew-basket' and 'Missionary-basket',..these 'meubles' are willow-repositories. **1859** DE QUINCEY *Incognito* Wks. XI. 11 The gallant troops were not quite *au fait* in the art of loading. **1881** *Daily News* 7 Mar. 2/3 (*Boat-race*), Not quite so *au fait* at the work as Mr. West. **1906** *Nature* 13 Sept. 485/1 The author is..not *au fait* with any up-to-date work. **1916** T. E. LAWRENCE *Let.* 22 Dec. (1938) 213, I hope..to run up first to Feisal and so put you au fait with his intentions. **1936** *Punch* 3 June 624/2 Now Daniel would have been perfectly *au fait* with such a situation.

†**auˈfer,** *v. Obs.* [ad. L. *aufer-re*, f. *au-* = *ab-* from + *ferre* to bear.] To take away, withdraw, remove.

1587 M. GROVE *Pelops & Hipp.* (1878) 16 We thee auferre such blisse. **1631** *Celestina* vi. 74 That is not auferred which is but deferred.

‖**aufgabe** (ˈaʊfgabə). [G.] A task, an assignment; used esp. in *Psychol.* Cf. TASK *sb.*

1902 W. JAMES *Var. Relig. Exper.* xvi. 389 The notion is thoroughly characteristic of the mystical level, and the *Aufgabe* of making it articulate was surely set to Hegel's intellect by mystical feeling. **1909** —— *Pluralistic Universe* vi. 238 This amount is the datum or *gabe* which reality feeds out to our intellectual faculty; but our intellect makes of it a task or *aufgabe*. **1917** M. A. MAY in *Arch. Psychol.* XXXIX. 2 *Aufgabe*..There are two gross meanings: (1) The problem set by the experimenter, the instructions given, and (2) the problem understood and actualized by the observer or subject.

‖**Aufklärung** (ˈaʊfklɛːrʊŋ). [G., 'enlightenment'.] Enlightenment (sense 2), illuminism; the name given to a European intellectual movement in the 18th c. laying claim to extraordinary intellectual illumination and enlightenment. So **ˈAufklärer** *pl.*, the members of this movement.

1801 H. CRABB ROBINSON in E. J. Morley *Crabb Robinson in Germany 1800–1805* (1929) 49 Till the *Aufklärer* or Enlighteners—contrived to draw to themselves the larger body. **1842** J. S. MILL *Let.* 22 Aug. in *Wks.* (1963) XIII. 543, I hope to hear from yourself somewhat more about the Berlinische Aufklärung from personal knowledge. **1856** [see ILLUMINISM]. **1865** J. H. STIRLING *Secret of Hegel* I. p. xix, Those remnants of the *Aufklärung*, of Eighteenth Century Illumination, which still exist among us. *Ibid.* p. xxii, The one principle of the Aufklärung, its single outcome—the Right of Private Judgment. **1933** J. BAILLIE *Life Everlasting* (1934) viii. 259 Humanism had its real fruitage in the *Aufklärung*.

‖**au fond** (o fɔ̃), *advb. phr.* [F.] At bottom, basically, essentially.

1782 LADY DERBY *Let.* 1 Jan. in Duke of Argyll *Intimate Society Lett. of 18th C.* (1910) I. 280 Prince Hen: says he [*sc.* Prince Ernest of Prussia] is charming, but *au fond* he is french. **1847** GEO. ELIOT *Let.* 10 May (1954) I. 235 But *au fond*, dear Mary, I have no impiety in my mind at this moment. **1890** G. B. SHAW in *World* 19 Nov. 23/2 If you know your Don Giovanni *au fond.* **1933** M. LUTYENS *Forthcoming Marriages* 182 *Au fond* every man is a hunter, a cave-man.

aufyn, var. ALFIN, *Obs.*, bishop in chess.

†**auge,** *v. Obs. rare*[−1]. [ad. L. *augē-re* to increase.] *trans.* To increase.

1542 BOORDE *Dyetary* xii. 266 It doth auge and augment the heate of the lyuer.

†**auge,** *sb. Astr. Obs.* [a. OF. *auge* (also in It. and Sp.), a. Arab. *awj*, 'height, top, summit, higher apsis of sun or planet.']

1. The highest point of the apparent course of the sun, moon, or a planet; *fig.* culmination, climax; = APOGEE 2, 3.

1617 COLLINS *Def. Bp. Ely* II. ix. 405 They were in the Auge, or in the Zenith, in their first loue. *a* **1679** T. GOODWIN *Wks.* (1864) VIII. 445 The promises..in the Old Testament..were in their prime, in their auge.

2. The 'high apsis' in the orbit of the moon or any planet; i.e. the point at which it is at its greatest distance from the earth; = APOGEE 1.

1594 BLUNDEVIL *Exerc.* III. I. viii. 287 Auges..be certaine imagined points in the heaven, notifying the furthest distance of any Orbe or Spheare from the Center of the world. *Ibid.* VII. xliv. 730 His [the moon's] slow motion is when he is in the point called Auge or Apogeon.

3. Extended to both apsides.

1681 WHARTON *Mut. Empires* Wks. (1683) 131 When the Auges, (or Absides) of the Planets are changed from one Sign to another. **1751** CHAMBERS *Cycl., Auges*, two points in a planet's orbit, otherwise called *apsides*. One of the auges is particularly denominated the *apogee*, the other *perigee*.

4. The orbit of a planet; = APSIS 1.

1601 HOLLAND *Pliny* I. 10 Those eccentrique circles or Epicycles in the stars, which the Greeks call Absides..Now euery one of the planets haue particular Auges or circles aforesaid by themselues.

Augean (ɔːˈdʒiːən), *a.* [f. L. *Augēas*, Gr. Αὐγείας: see -AN.] Abominably filthy; *i.e.* resembling the stable of Augeas, a fabulous king of Elis, which contained 3,000 oxen, and had been uncleansed for 30 years, when Hercules, by turning the river Alpheus through it, purified it in a single day.

1599 MARSTON *Sco. Villanie* III. Proem 210 To purge this Augean oxstall from foule sinne. **1775** P. SCHUYLER in Sparks *Corr. Amer. Rev.* (1853) I. 4, I shall have an Augean stable to clean there. **1866** ALGER *Solit. Nat. & Man* IV. 389 To cleanse the augean bosom of the world by turning through it a river of pure enthusiasm.

augelite (ˈɔːdʒɪlaɪt). *Min.* [f. Gr. αὐγή lustre + λίθος stone: see -LITE.] A hydrous phosphate of alumina of pale red colour and pearly lustre.

1868 DANA *Min.* 580.

‖**augen** (ˈaʊgən). [pl. of G. *auge* EYE *sb.*[1]] Applied to a variety of gneissic rock containing eye-shaped masses of feldspar or quartz; porphyritic gneiss; esp. ***augen-gneiss.***

1885 A. GEIKIE *Text-bk. Geol.* (ed. 2) vii. 132 Porphyritic gneiss or Augengneiss, in which large eye-like kernels of orthoclase are dispersed. **1910** *Encycl. Brit.* XII. 149/2 When large felspars, of rounded or elliptical form, are visible in the gneiss, it is said to have augen structure. *Ibid.* 352/2 The larger crystals are converted into lenticular or elliptical 'augen'. **1925** N. E. ODELL in E. F. Norton *Fight for Everest 1924* III. iii. 297 It would certainly appear that the augen variety [of gneisses] were the younger and intrusive facies. **1940** C. M. RICE *Dict. Geol. Terms* 27/2 *Augengneiss*, a general term for gneissose rocks,..containing 'eyes', i.e., phacoidal or lenticular crystals, or aggregates, which simulate the porphyritic crystals of igneous rocks.

augend (ˈɔːdʒɛnd). [a. G. *augend* (H. Schubert *Arithmetik und Algebra* (*a* 1898)), ad. L. *augendus* (sc. *numerus*), gerundive of *augēre* to increase: see -END.] The quantity to which an addend is added.

1898 T. J. MCCORMACK tr. *Schubert's Math. Ess. & Recreations* 10 It has been proposed to call the number which is regarded in addition as the passive number or the one to be changed, the augend, and the other which plays the active part..the increment. **1946** A. W. BURKS in *Theory & Techniques Design Electronic Digital Computers* (Univ. Penn.) (1947) I. VIII. 2 If the right hand digits of the addend and augend are *either* both 1's *or* both 0's, make the right-hand digit of the sum 0. **1953** *Proc. IRE* XLI. 1245/2 The arithmetic element of our computer is simply an accumulator... Addition of numbers is performed by first entering one of the numbers (the augend) in the accumulator and then giving the command to add, at the same time entering the other number (the addend). **1977** [see ADDEND].

auger (ˈɔːgə(r)), *sb.*[1] Forms: α. 1 **nabfogár, nabogár, -gaar, -gér, nafogár, nafegár,** 2-3 **nauegar, navegar, -gor,** 3-6 **nauger,** 4-5 **nagere,** 6 **nagare, nauguayre.** β. 5-8 **augur,** 6 **awgure, -ar,** 7 **augar, -oer, -ure, -or, awgor, oagar, -er,** 7-9 **augre,** 6- **auger.** [OE. *nafu-gár*, f. *nafu* 'nave' (of a wheel) + *gár* piercer, borer, spear; lit. 'nave-borer,' a compound found also in other Teutonic idioms; cf. OHG. *nabugêr, nabigêr, nagibêr,* MHG. *nabeger, neg(e)ber,* mod.G. *näber, neber,* LG. *naviger, näviger,* Du. *avegaar (eveger, egger),* ON. *nafarr.* The original *-af-* passed through *-av-* to *-aw-, -au-,* as in OE. *hafoc,* now *hawk,* and the initial *n-* has been lost, as in *adder,* through confusion of *an nauger, a nauger, an auger.* The latter change has taken place also in Dutch, and one analogous to the former in German.]

1. A carpenter's tool for boring holes in wood, etc., having a long pointed shank with a cutting edge and a screw point, and a handle fixed at right angles to the top of the shank, by means of which the tool is worked round with both hands.

c **700** *Epinal Gloss.* 1010 *Terebellus,* nabfogar. *c* **875** *Erfurt Gl.* naboger. *c* **725** *Corpus Gl.* 2002 nabogaar. *a* **1000** in Wright *Voc.* (W.) /44 *Rotrum,* nabogar. *Ibid.* /106 *Terebrum,* nafegar. *Ibid.* /241 *Foratorium,* nafogar. *a* **1100** *Ibid.* /333 Nauegar. *a* **1200** *Ibid.* /550 Navegar. *a* **1300** W. DE BIBLESW. in Wright *Voc.* 170 *Par terere* [glossed] wymble (nauger). *a* **1400** *Chester Pl.* I. 107 With this axe that I beare This perscer and this nagere. *a* **1500** in Wright *Voc.* (W.) /616 *Terebrum,* an augur or a persour. **1523** FITZHERB. *Husb.* §3. 12 An augurs bore. **1523** —— *Surv.* xxv. (1539) 48 To boore an hole with an nauger. **1556** *Inv.* in French *Shaks. Geneal.* (1869) 472 One axe, a bill, iiij nagares. **1572** *Inv.* in *Midl. C. Hist. Coll.* II. 363 Item three naugers. **1601** HOLLAND *Pliny* I. 490 To bore a hole into them with an augoer. **1607** SHAKS. *Cor.* IV. vi. 87 Your Franchises..confin'd Into an Augors boare. **1611** COTGR., *Villette,* a little Turrell, or Coopers oagar. **1677** MOXON *Mech. Exerc.* (1703) 94 The Augre hath a handle and bit. Its office is to make great round holes. **1746** *Brit. Mag.* 12 Something like an Augur or Cheese-borer. **1823** P. NICHOLSON *Pract. Build.* 235 The Auger is the largest of all tools which are used for boring wood. **1848** DE QUINCEY *Wks.* IX. 282 To bore with an augre in a ship's bottom. **1881** *Mechanic* §265 The auger..is a gimlet on a large scale.

2. An instrument for boring in the soil or strata of the earth, having a stem which may be lengthened as the perforation extends.

1594 PLAT *Div. Sorts Soyle* 29 A piercing Augur to search into the bowels of the earth. **1643** WOOD in Prynne & Walk. *Fiennes's Tr.* (1644) App. 11 Below that a firme strong Rocke, and that he had searched purposely with an Awgor. **1784** E. DARWIN in *Phil. Trans.* LXXV. 2 Till some sand was brought by the auger. **1879** WRIGHTSON in *Cassell's Techn. Educ.* I. 175 The auger or boring apparatus..looked upon..as saving excavation.

3. 'A large spiral bit used to mix a material and force it through a die (as in a brickmaking machine or a meat grinder); the rotating helical member of a screw conveyor' (Webster 1961). Hence as *v. trans.*, to convey by an auger.

1934 WEBSTER, *Auger,* a rotating screwlike device for advancing chaff in some forms of spiral conveyors; a large spiral bit used to mix a material and force it through a die, as in a brick or a sausage machine. **1960** *Farmer & Stockbreeder* 5 Jan. 74/3 Oats are shovelled or augered into the feed mixer until a flashing light indicates the feed mixing drum is full. *Ibid.* 8 Mar. 42/2 Regulated auger feed from food hoppers to mangers. **1963** *Gloss. Terms Agric. Machinery* (*B.S.I.*) 82 *Auger conveyor,* a grain conveyor in which material is moved by the screwing action of a helix inside a tube or trough.

4. *Comb.* **auger-hole,** the hole drilled by an auger; **auger-shell,** the shell of the molluscous genus *Terebra.* Also *auger-bit, -stem,* etc.

1601 DENT *Pathw. Heaven* (1831) 305 To creep into an auger-hole to hide their heads. **1677** MOXON *Mech. Exerc.* (1703) 154 Should the augure-hole be too wide, the Shank would be loose in it. **1813** MAR. EDGEWORTH *Patronage* (1833) I. ii. 37, I could have squeezed myself into an Auger-hole once, when you blundered. **1881** RAYMOND *Mining Gloss., Auger-stem,* the bar to which a drilling-bit is attached. **1883** *Century Mag.* July 329/2 The 'augur stem,' an iron bar perhaps eight feet long screwed into the bit. **1615** CROOKE *Body of Man* 762 The first paire are called Styloglossi or the Auger-tongue Muscles. **1757** BORLASE in *Phil. Trans.* L. 52 Pierced with the teredo, or augur-worm.

Auger (ˈoʒe), *sb.*[2] [Name of P. V. *Auger,* French physicist (b. 1899).] Used *attrib.* in ***Auger effect, electron*** (see quot. 1962).

[**1930** G. WENTZEL in *Physik. Zeitschr.* XXXI. 1007/2 Den wir erläutern wollen..am Auger-Effekt.] **1931** *Chem. Abstr.* XXV. 3911 This reviews quantum processes such as.. the Auger effect. **1949** M. G. E. COSYNS et al. in *Proc. Physical Soc.* LXII. 803 The criterion..is that slow electrons should be admitted as Auger electrons only if the beginning of the track can be certainly identified within 1 micron of the end of the meson. **1962** *Newnes Concise Encycl. Nuclear Energy* 53/1 *Auger effect,* the non-radiative transition of an atom from an excited electronic energy state to a lower state with the emission of an electron... The electron ejected in the Auger effect is known as an Auger electron.

‖**auget, -ette** (oʒe, ɔːˈdʒɛt). [Fr., dim. of *auge* trough:—L. *alveus* basin.] **a.** A wooden pipe containing the powder used in exploding a mine. James *Mil. Dict.* 1816. **b.** 'The priming tube used in blasting.' Raymond *Mining Gl.* 1881.

augh! (ɔːx), *int. Sc.* An exclamation of disgust; = faugh!

1853 READE *Chr. Johnstone* 31 'Augh!' cried she, 'just a' sugar an saut butter thegither.'

†**aught,** *sb.*[1] *Obs.* exc. *dial.* Forms: 1 **æht,** *pl.* **æhta,** 2-3 *prop. pl.* **æhte, ehte, eahte, echte,** 3 **eiȝte, aihte, ahte, aȝte,** 4 **eyghte, eighte, ehte, aghte, aȝt, auht(e, auchte, auȝt(e, aughte, haut, ahut,** 5 **aght, aught,** 6- (*Sc.*) **aucht.** [Common Teutonic: OE. *æht* is cogn. with OHG. *éht,* Goth. *aiht-s*; f. *ágan* to own, possess, pa. t. *áhte.* The ME. form with final *-e* is perhaps the OE. plural *ǽhta* 'possessions, property,' used collectively, and at length as a sing. In Scotch *aucht* (ɑxt) is still a living word.]

1. Possession; that which one possesses as his own; property.

c **1000** *Ags. Gosp.* Mark x. 22 He hæfde mycele æhta. *c* **1160** *Hatton G.* ibid., He hæfde mycele ehte. *c* **1175** *Cott. Hom.* 233 Hit is muche sunne if mon echte luuieð. **1205** LAY. 1311 Muchel ahte heo hæfden biwunnen. *c* **1230** *Ancr. R.* 214 Eorðlich eihte, nis buten eorðe & asken. *c* **1300** *Cursor M.* 3395 Bitwene his childre he delt his auȝt. *c* **1300** *K. Alis.* 6884 He highth hem aughtte and gret nobleys. *c* **1320** *Seuyn Sag.* (W.) 1101 He went hom with that eighte. *c* **1460** *Towneley Myst.* 11 To gif away my warldes aght. **1513** DOUGLAS *Æneis* III. ii. 140 Assynging ilk ane propir houss and aucht. **1609** SKENE *Reg. Maj.* Table 81 The best aucht, sould be given to the maister. **1823** SCOTT *Quentin D.* I. vii. 126 The surest gear in their aught. **1862** in Hislop *Prov. Scot.* 36 Better saucht wi' little aucht than care wi' mony cows.

†**2.** *esp.* Live stock, cattle. *Obs.*

c **1200** *St. Marharete* 2 Ant wiste..othe felt hire foster motheres ahte. **1297** R. GLOUC. 537 Sir Jon Giffard nom to him is quic eiȝte ech on. *a* **1300** *Cursor M.* 6765 Ox or ass, or cou or scepe, Hors or ani oþer aght [*v.r.* aȝt, auht, auȝt].

†**3.** *Comb.*, as ***aught-greedy*** (in 2 *eiht-gradi*), ***aughtless*** (in 2 *aihteles*). *Obs.*

c **1200** *Trin. Coll. Hom.* 29 To þe eiht-gradi men þe deuel runeð on his herte and þus queð. Ȝef þu best aihteles þu best unwurð and loð.

aught (ɔːt), *sb.*[2] (*pron.*), *adv.*, *adj.* Forms: α. 1 **áwiht, áwuht, áwyht, áwht, áuht, áht,** 1-3 **awiht, awht, aht,** 3 **æht,** 3-5 **auht,** 4 **aȝt, aght, auȝht, aut, (ahut),** 4- **aught.** β. 1 **ówiht, ówuht,** 3 **oht,** 3-5 **oȝt, ocht, ouht, out,** 3-6 **oght,** 4 **ouȝt, (ohut, hout),** 4-5 **oucht, owcht,** (9 *dial.* **owt**), 4- **ought.** γ. 2-3 **eawiht,** 3 **eawicht, eawet, eawt, ewt.** [f. OE. *á, ó,* ever + *wiht* creature, being, wight, whit, thing; *lit.* 'e'er a whit,' 'anything whatever'; cogn. with OFris. *âwet, âet,* OS. *êowiht,* OHG. *eowiht, iowiht, iawiht, iewiht,* MHG. *ieht, iht, iewet, iwet, iet, iut,* Du. *iet* in *iets.* Already in OE. the full *á-wiht* was phonetically contracted through several stages to *áht,* whence regularly Me. *ōht, ōght,* mod. *ought,* the usual form in Eng. writers from 1300 to 1550. But there must also have been a form *awht, aht,* with the orig. long *á* shortened before the two consonants, whence regularly (as in *caught, taught,* etc.) ME. *aht, aght,* mod. *aught,* the spelling now preferred as distinguishing this word from *ought* vb. In Shaks., Milton, Pope, *ought* and *aught* occur indiscriminately. The EE. *eawiht, ewt* seem to point to an OE. *ǽwiht* with umlaut.]

A. *sb.* (*pron.*) Anything whatever; anything. In interrogative, negative, and conditional sentences.

α. Forms *áwiht, aught.*

a **1000** *Ags. Ps.* lviii. 8 Nafast þú for áwiht ealle þéoda. —— cxiii. 14 Ne mágon hí áwyht ȝehýran. —— cxliii. 4 Þæt þú him áht wið æfre hæfdest. *c* **1175** *Lamb. Hom.* 103 Ȝif he awiht delan wule. *c* **1230** *Ancr. R.* 194 Er þan hi ham aȝt yeue. *a* **1300** *Cursor M.* 4836 If we might find here aught to sell. **1388** WYCLIF *Prov.* x. 4 To gete auȝt [*v.r.* ony thing] bi leesyngis. **1574** tr. *Marlorats Apocalips* 114 Those..can-not bereeue them of aught that is theirs. **1593** SHAKS. *Rich. II,* II. iii. 73 Before I make reply to aught you say. **1702** POPE *Jan. & May* 790 Excuse me, dear, if aught amiss was said. **1773** GOLDSM. *Stoops to Conq.* III. i. (1854) 60 For aught I know to the contrary. **1859** TENNYSON *Vivien* 239 Unfaith in aught is want of faith in all.

β. Form *ought. arch.*

c **1175** *Lamb. Hom.* 65 Ȝif eni mon mis-deð us oht. *c* **1300** *Cursor M.* 4144 Quar-for suld we of oght be ferd? **1375** BARBOUR *Bruce* I. 251 Gyff man bad his thryll owcht do. **1382** WYCLIF *Gal.* vi. 3 If ony man gessith him silf for to be ouȝt. **1387** TREVISA *Higden* (Rolls) III. 39 Ȝif out schulde be wiþdrawe of þis law or put out more þerto. **1413** LYDG. *Pylgr.* I. ii. 3 Yf thou canst ought alledgen. **1583** STUBBES *Anat. Abus.* II. 83 Whether he be ought or naught. **1601** SHAKS. *All's Well* v. iii. 281 It might be yours or hers for ought I know. **1728** POPE *Dunc.* I. 24 Grieve not, my Swift, at ought our realm acquires. **1845-6** TRENCH *Huls. Lect.* I. i. 9 Who that knows ought of what is going forward.

†γ. Forms *eawiht, eawet, eawt, ewt. Obs.*

c **1175** *Lamb. Hom.* 3 Ȝif eni man seid eawiht to eou. *c* **1220** *Leg. St. Kath.* 1193 For to drehen eawt. *Ibid.* 997 Butin ewt to leosen.

†**B.** *adj.* (Attributive use of prec. Cf. *naught* = worthless, found much earlier.) Anything worth, something worth; worthy, estimable, valiant, doughty. *Obs.*

[**1086** *O.E. Chron.* 222 An man þe hym sylf aht wære.] **1205** LAY. 8141 Ahte cniht wes Auelin. *Ibid.* 4348 Þu eær muchele ahtere. *Ibid.* 18426 And æuerælc ocht [**1250** oht] mon: sterkliche heom legge on. *a* **1250** *Owl & Night.* 1477 Ȝef he is wurthful and aht man. **1297** R. GLOUC. 183 Al þe bachelerye, þat aȝt was in þe lond. *Ibid.* 459 As godemen & aȝte. *Ibid.* 569 Auȝte men inowe. **1340** *Alex. & Dind.* 936 Whan he is eldure of age · þat auht is his strenke. *c* **1340** *Gaw. & Gr. Knt.* 2215 If any wyȝe oȝt wyl wynne hider fast.

C. *adv.* [The accusative of the sb. used adverbially, as in '*somewhat* fresh,' etc.] To any extent, in any degree, in any respect, 'anything,' at all.

c **1205** LAY. 7027 Ȝif heo wes awiht hende. *c* **1300** *Beket* 109 'If he me wolde spousi oȝt.' *c* **1340** *Cursor M.* (Gött.) 3828 'Knau ȝe aut,' he said, 'laban?' *c* **1386** CHAUCER *Can. Yem. Prol.* 44 Can he ought telle a mery tale or tweye. *a* **1460** *Towneley Myst.* 62 Or thay flytt oght far us fro. **1577** HARRISON *England* I. II. xxiii. 353 When rain doth ought annoie them. **1659** FIELDER in Burton *Diary* (1828) IV. 129 It is against the order of your house to interpose aught. **1790** COWPER *Odyss.* II. 373 Neither wise Are they, nor just, nor aught suspect the doom. **1870** MORRIS *Earthly Par.* I. I. 47 But none the glittering evil valued aught.

D. *Comb.* **aughtways** *adv.*, any way, in any wise.

1878 J. THOMSON *Plenip. Key* 26 Let none be aughtways backward..To echo fervently this hymn of mine.

aught, pa. t. of *agan*: see OWE, OUGHT.

aught(e, obs. and dial. form of EIGHT.

†**ˈaughtly,** *adv.* and *a. Obs.* Forms: **2 ahtlice,** 3 **aht-, ohtliche,** 4 **autly.** [f. AUGHT *a.* + -LY.]

A. *adv.* Estimably, worthily, nobly.

a **1121** *O.E. Chron.* (Laud MS.) an. 1071 And he hi ahtlice út lædde. **1205** LAY. 1591 He wende onȝean sone & he ohtliche feaht. *Ibid.* 31142 He wes ahtliche under-uon.

B. *adj.* Worthy, estimable.

c **1325** *E.E. Allit. Poems* B. 795 Watz non autly in ouþer, for aungels hit wern.

†**ˈaughtship.** *Obs. rare*[−1]. In 3 **ohtscipe.** [f. AUGHT *a.* + -SHIP.] Valour, worth.

1205 LAY. 24671 Bute he icostned weoren: þrie inne compe · & his oht-scipen [**1250** manede] icudde.

augite (ˈɔːdʒaɪt). *Min.* [ad. L. *augītes* (Pliny), a. Gr. αὐγίτης, prob. an inferior variety of turquoise, f. αὐγή lustre: see -ITE.] One of the aluminous varieties of the mineral PYROXENE, consisting chiefly of silica, magnesia, iron, and lime; it has a greenish, brownish, or pure black colour, and occurs mostly in volcanic rocks.

(Formerly taken in a wider sense as synonymous with *pyroxene*; while 'the *Augite* of Werner included only the black mineral of igneous rocks—the *volcanic schorl* of earlier authors.' Dana.)

[**1786** CHAMBERS *Cycl.* (Rees), *Augites*..a kind of gem, of a pale green colour.] **1804** *Phil. Trans.* XCIV. 302 In many of the ancient lavas of Somma, large augites are imbedded. **1807** J. MURRAY *Chem.* III. 574 Augite has also considerable resemblance to the olivin. **1854** F. BAKEWELL *Geol.* 86 The solid volcanic rock lava, if it contain a large proportion of augite, becomes dark-coloured.

augitic (ɔːˈdʒɪtɪk), *a. Min.* [f. prec. + -IC.] Of, pertaining to, or characterized by, augite.

1843 HUMBLE *Dict. Geol.*, Augitic Porphyry..containing crystals of augite and Labrador felspar. **1862** DANA *Man. Geol.* 86 Igneous rocks—the feldspathic..and the augitic.

auglet, ? obsolete variant of AGLET.

1594 NASHE *Unfort. Trav.* 16 A blacke budge edging of a beard on the vpper lip, and the like sable auglet of excrements in the rising of the ancle of my chinne.

augment (ˈɔːgmənt), *sb.* Also 6 **agment.** [a. F. *augment* (14th c.), ad. L. *augmentum* increase, f. *augēre* to increase: see -MENT.]

†**1.** Increase, extension, augmentation. *Obs.*

1430 LYDG. *Chron. Troy* I. v, In augment of thy wo. **1501** DOUGLAS *Pal. Hon.* Prol. I. x, In the is rute and agment of curage. **1599** THYNNE *Animadv.* 71 To seeke the augmente and correctione of Chawcers Woorkes. **1677** PLOT *Oxfordsh.* 132 That though indeed there be an augment in some petrifications, yet that it is not so in all. **1696** PHILLIPS, *Augment*..an encreasing.

2. *Gram.* The prefixed vowel (in Sanskrit *ă*, in Greek ε) which characterizes the past tenses of the verb in the older Aryan languages. (Sometimes applied to any prefix supposed to be of analogous use, *e.g.* the *ge-* of past participles in German.)

(In Greek, when the ε remains separate, it is called the *syllabic augment*; when it forms, with a following vowel, a long vowel or diphthong, the *temporal augment.*) Hence **augmentless** *a.*, wanting the verbal augment.

a **1771** GRAY in *Corr.* (1843) 226 The *y* which we often see prefixed to participles passive, ycleped, yhewe, etc...is the old Anglo-Saxon augment. **1861** JELF *Grk. Gram.* I. §171 The augment is employed in the indicative mood only of all the *historic* tenses. **1879** Whitney *Skr. Gram.* §585 The augment is a short *a*, prefixed to a tense stem.. The augment is a sign of past time. *Ibid.* §587 The accentuation of the augmentless forms.

augment (ɔːgˈmɛnt), *v.* Forms: 4 **aument**, 6 **agg-, auge-**, 5– **augment**. [a. F. *augmente-r* (14th c.), earlier *aumenter*, cogn. with It. *aumentare*, Sp. *aumentar*:—L. *augmentā-re* to increase, f. *augment-um*: see prec.]

1. *trans.* To make greater in size, number, amount, degree, etc.; to increase, enlarge, extend.

c **1460** Fortescue *Abs. & Lim. Mon.* (1714) 116 Hou our Navye may be mayntenyd, and augmentyd. **1561** T. N[orton] *Calvin's Inst.* iv. xiv. (1634) 634 *marg.*, The power which Sacraments have in augmenting Faith. **1601** Holland *Pliny* I. 58 [The Tiber] is augmented with two and forty riuers. **1763** J. Brown *Poetry & Mus.* §5. 66 The Chords of the Lyre were augmented gradually from four to forty. **1816** Scott *Old. Mort.* 217 The insurgents were intent upon augmenting and strengthening their forces.

2. *intr.* To become greater in size, amount, degree, intensity, etc.; to increase, grow, swell.

c **1400** *Rom. Rose* 5600 For to encrese, and not to lesse, For to aument and multiplie. **1475** Caxton *Jason* 51 The bruit of preu Jason augmentid and encresid from day to day. **1589** Greene *Menaph.* (Arb.) 39 The grasse hath his increase, yet never anie sees it augment. **1697** Dryden *Virg. Georg.* i. 466 The Winds redouble, and the Rains augment. **1869** Tyndall *Light* §436 The polarizing angle augments with the refractive index of the medium.

†**3.** *trans.* To increase or add to the resources of; to enhance in circumstances. *Obs.*

c **1460** Fortescue *Abs. & Lim. Mon.* (1714) 93 To augment his Realme in Rycesse, Welth, and Prosperyte. **1529** Wolsey in *Four C. Eng. Lett.* 11 Aggmentyng my lyvyng, and appoyntyng such thyngs as shuld be convenient for my furniture. **1601** Cornwallyes *Essayes* ii. xxxvi. (1631) 117 Thou augmentest their state purchasing a blessing upon their house and life.

†**4.** *trans.* and *refl.* To raise (a person) in estimation or dignity; to exalt. *Obs.*

1567 *Trial Treas.* in Hazl. *Dodsl.* III. 273 Labour yourself to advance and augment. **1655** Fuller *Ch. Hist.* iii. ii. §43 II. 84 Theobald.. was augmented with the title of *Legatus natus.*

†**b.** *intr.* To rise in estimation or dignity. *Obs.*

1534 Ld. Berners *Gold. Bk. M. Aurel.* I v b, With a littell fauour ye wyll exalt, augement, and grow into gret prid.

5. *Her.* (*trans.*) To make an honourable addition to (a coat of arms).

1655 Fuller *Ch. Hist.* iv. II. 357 The Armes of London were augmented with the addition of a Dagger. **1864** Boutell *Heraldry Hist. & Pop.* xiii. 95 The Scottish Baronets.. were authorized to augment their own arms.

†**6.** To multiply (mathematically). *Obs.*

1571 Digges *Pantom.* iii. iii. Q ij, The Solide content of a Cylinder is gotten by augmenting the base in his altitude. **1593** Fale *Dialling* 31 Augment the Sine of the Complement repeated, by the Sine of the doubtfull Arke: an the product arising thereof.. shall be the distance, etc.

augmentable (ɔːgˈmɛntəb(ə)l), *a.* [f. prec. + -able.] †**a.** Capable of increasing. *Obs.* **b.** Capable of being increased.

1471 Ripley *Comp. Alch.* xi. iii. (Ashm. 1652) 182 Ryche ys he whych any parte hath in store Of our Elixers whych be augmentable infynytly. **1775** Harris *Philos. Arrangem.* Wks. 1841. 306 Every multitude is infinitely augmentable.

augmentation (ɔːgmənˈteɪʃən). Also 5 **avmentacion**, 5–6 **augmentacyon, -cion**, etc. [a. OF. *aument-*, *augmentacion* (mod. *-tion*), ad. late L. *augmentātiōn-em*, n. of action f. *augmentāre*: see augment *v.* and -ation.]

1. The action or process of augmenting, making greater, or adding to; extension, enlargement.

1463 *Bury Wills* (1850) 29 To haue the seyd iii *s.* iiij *d.* to the avmentacion of his lif loode. **1586** Thynne in *Animadv.* Introd. 73 Both the historie of England & Scotland were half printed before I set pen to paper to enter into the augmentation.. of them. **1656** tr. *Hobbes' Elem. Philos.* (1839) 165 The composition therefore of proportions is not in this case the augmentation of them. **1853** Kane *Grinnell Exp.* xxxv. (1856) 313 Refraction, with its preternatural augmentation of the visual hemisphere, revisited us.

†**2.** The action or process of raising in estimation or dignity; exaltation, honouring. *Obs.*

1494 Fabyan v. cxxiii. 100 And to the augmentacion of theyse wordis [he] shortly after restored to hym all such cyties. **1558** in Strype *Ann. Ref.* I. App. iv. 5 Every augmentation.. of such men in authority.. is an encouragement of those of their sect. **1611** Bible *2 Macc.* v. 16 Dedicated by other kings, to the augmentation and glory and honour of the place.

3. The process of becoming greater; growth, increase.

?*c* **1486** *Bk. St. Albans, Her.* in Dallaway *Sc. Her.* App. 110 The first son.. is in hoope of augmentacion and encressyng of his patrimony. **1656** Ridgley *Pract. Physic* 10 Old men are lesse nourished; also generation and augmentation ceaseth. **1825** McCulloch *Pol. Econ.* iii. §7. 334 The.. excessive augmentation of their numbers.

4. Augmented state or condition; increased size, amount, degree, etc.; increase.

1533 Elyot *Cast. Helth* (1541) 46 Therof commeth augmentation of heat. **1630** Naunton *Fragm. Reg.* (Arb.) 49 Some generall Learning, which by diligence he enforced to a great augmentation. **1794** Godwin *Cal. Williams* 50 The vices of Mr. Tyrrel in their present state of augmentation. **1825** T. Jefferson *Autobiog.* Wks. 1859 I. 71 The result was an augmentation of the revenue.

5. That by which anything is augmented; an addition, increase.

1576 (*title*) Ane Compendious Buik of godlie Psalmes and spirituall Sangis.. with augmentation of sindrie gude and godlie Ballatis, not contenit in the first editioun. **1601** Shaks. *Twel. N.* iii. ii. 85 More lynes then is in the new Mappe, with the augmentation of the Indies. **1872** F. Duncan *Roy. Regt. Artill.* xxix. 381 Augmentations to the Regiment in the form of other battalions.

6. *Her.* An honourable addition to a coat of arms, either quartered with the family arms, or borne upon an escutcheon or canton.

1662 Fuller *Worthies* (1840) I. 275 Authorized.. to bear three Turks' heads, as an augmentation to his arms. **1864** Boutell *Heraldry Hist. & Pop.* xiii. 93 Complicated Augmentations.. were granted by Henry VIII to his successive Consorts.

7. *Med.* 'The period between the commencement and height of a fever.' Mayne *Exp. Lex.* 1853.

8. *Mus.* The repetition of a subject (*esp.* in fugues) in notes double or quadruple those of the original.

1597 Morley *Introd. Mus.* 24 Augmentation proceedeth of setting the signe of the more prolation in one part of the songe onely, and not in others. **1674** Playford *Skill Mus.* i. vii. 24 A Large, Long, Breve, Semibreve.. are Notes of Augmentation. **1869** Ouseley *Counterp.* xv. 104 Imitation by augmentation is often introduced into fugues.

9. *Sc. Law.* Increase of stipend obtained by a Scottish parish minister by an action (*Process of A.*) in the Court of Teinds, against the titular or beneficiary, and heritors.

1653 Milton *Hirelings* Wks. (1851) 370 As Glebes and Augmentations are now bestow'd. **1816** Scott *Antiq.* (1879) II. xxxi. 139 A dreadful proser, particularly on the subject of augmentations, localities, tiends. **1868** Chambers *Encycl.* I. 548 By 48 Geo. III. c. 138, it is enacted that no Augmentation shall be granted.. till the expiration of 20 years from any Augmentation subsequent to the act.

10. Augmentation Court, ***Court · of Augmentation*(*s*, or ellipt. *The Augmentation***: a court established by 27 Hen. VIII, for determining suits and controversies in respect of monasteries and abbey-lands; so called because, by the suppression of monasteries, it largely augmented the revenues of the Crown. Dissolved by 1 Mary, sess. 2, cap. 10, and its records kept in the ***Augmentation Office***. **augmentationer**, an officer of this court.

1542 Brinklow *Complaynt* x. (1874) 24 Saue me from the court of the Augmentacyon! **1550** Latimer *Serm. bef. Edw. VI*, I. 244, I speak to you, my masters, minters, augmentationers. **1587** Fleming *Contn. Holinshed* III. 977/1 Edward North knight, chancellor of the augmentation. **1884** *Athenæum* 4 Oct. 423 The zeal that he showed in saving the records of the Augmentation Office [in 1834].

11. (*Army*). Promotion ***by augmentation*** (*sc.* of the number of officers): promotion by the issue of an additional commission, instead of by purchase of one previously existing. (Obsolete in use since the abolition of purchase.)

augmentative (ɔːgˈmɛntətɪv), *a.* and *sb.* [a. F. *augmentatif*, *-ive* (14th c.), f. L. *augmentāt-* ppl. stem of *augmentāre* to augment: see -ive.]

A. *adj.*

1. Having the property of augmenting, increasing, or adding to; in *Metaph.* = ampliative.

1502 *Ord. Crysten Men* (W. de W. 1506) i. vii. 78 Augmentatyf of grace and of benedyccyon. **1677** Gale *Crt. Gentiles* II. iv. 266 God.. cannot fal under any mutation.. augmentative or diminutive. **1857** T. Webb *Intell. Locke* vi. 113 Augmentative Judgments.. add to our conception of the subject a predicate which is not contained in it. **1858** Marsh *Eng. Lang.* v. 106 Words inflected in the weak or augmentative manner.

2. *Gram.* **a.** Of a formative suffix or prefix: Augmenting or increasing in force the idea conveyed by a word. **b.** Of a word: Augmenting the properties of the term whence it is derived, or generally expressing augmentation of an idea. (Augmentative *words* are generally formed by the addition of augmentative *affixes*.)

1641 R. Brooke *Eng. Episc.* i. v. 19 The preposition *In*.. in other compounds (as *incipere, inflammare*).. they call *augmentative.* **1711** J. Greenwood *Eng. Gram.* 173 Augmentative Words, or such as encrease the Signification. **1848** Latham *Eng. Lang.* iv. ii. 211 For the word *wizard*, from *witch*, see the Section on Augmentative forms.

B. *sb.* An augmentative formative or word.

1804 W. Taylor in *Ann. Rev.* II. 632 Some nations have used the word *bull* as an augmentative. **1848** Latham *Eng. Lang.* iv. xv. 287 Compared with *capello* = 'a hat,' the Italian word *capellone* = 'a great hat' is an Augmentative.

augˈmentatively, *adv.* [f. prec. + -ly².] By way of augmentation or addition.

1726 Ayliffe *Parerg.* 339 Not.. by way of Limitation, but Augmentatively and by way of Accessory.

augˈmented, *ppl. a.* [f. augment *v.* + -ed.]

1. Made greater, increased, intensified.

1605 Thynne in *Animadv.* Introd. 112 Your augmented Kingdomes. **1667** Milton *P.L.* vi. 280 Or some more sudden vengeance.. Precipitate thee with augmented paine. **1859** Mill *Liberty* 180 The augmented price.

2. *spec.* **a.** *Her.* Of coats of arms: Having an additional charge granted as an honourable distinction. **b.** *Mus.* Of an interval: greater by a chromatic semitone than a perfect, or than a major, interval of the same name: opp. to *diminished.* **c.** *Bot.* Increased by the addition of other parts.

1776 J. Lee *Introd. Bot.* (ed. 3) 404 Auctus calyx, augmented, having a Series of distinct Leaves, shorter than its own, that surround its Base. **1825** [see fifth *sb.* 2 a]. **1864** Boutell *Heraldry Hist. & Pop.* xxviii. 434 Examples of augmented shields. **1869** Ouseley *Counterpoint* 9 The augmented fourth or tritone is an interval peculiarly abhorrent to strict Counterpoint. **1947** A. Einstein *Mus. in Rom. Era* ix. 100 The Sanctus, which leaves the major key of F by way of an augmented fifth chord. **1954** *Grove's Dict. Mus.* (ed. 5) IV. 522/1 An augmented interval, so limited, is a chromatic interval regarded as a perfect or a major diatonic interval extended by adding to it a chromatic semitone.

augˈmentedly, *adv.* [f. prec. + -ly².] In increased measure, in a greater degree.

1805 E. H. Seymour in Halliw. *Shaks.* V. 440 *Twice-blessed*.. [means] blessed augmentedly, blessed supremely, or in a great degree.

augmenter (ɔːgˈmɛntə(r)). Also 6 **-tour**, 6–7 **-tor.** [orig. a. F. *augmenteur*, f. *augmenter* vb.; in later use f. augment *v.* + -er¹.] He who or that which augments, makes greater, or adds to; *spec.* a magnifying glass.

1534 Ld. Berners *Gold. Bk. M. Aurel.* (1546) G g viij b, Augmentours of the common welth. **1603** Knolles *Hist. Turks* (1638) 189 Amurath.. the great avgmentor of their kingdome. **1702** *Phil. Trans.* XXIII. 1359 The bristles.. were when viewed with a large Augmenter all spicated. **1839** J. Rogers *Antipopopr.* Introd. ¶ 16 His wife is.. the lessener of his pain, and the augmenter of his pleasure.

augˈmenting, *vbl. sb.* [f. augment *v.* + -ing¹.] Augmentation, increase. (Now gerundial.)

1537 ? Tindale *Exp. St. John* 78 They beleue it an augmentynge of synne. **1702** *Lond. Gaz.* No. 3812/3 As to the augmenting of the Army. **1830** Lyell *Princ. Geol.* (1875) I. i. xii. 245 Its effect in somewhat augmenting the quantity of antarctic ice.

augˈmenting, *ppl. a.* [f. as prec. + -ing².] Making greater, magnifying; increasing.

1658 Sir T. Browne *Gard. Cyrus* iii. 144 He that would exactly discern the shop [= shape] of a Bees mouth, need observing eyes, and good augmenting glasses. **1812** Crabbe *Tales* xvi. Wks. 1834 V. 156 Then came augmenting woes.

†**augˈmention.** *Obs.* [f. augment on mistaken analogy; cf. *invent-ion*.] = augmentation 2.

1634 Sir T. Herbert *Trav.* 187 In augmention of fashion they very orderly cut and pinke their skin.

augmentive (ɔːgˈmɛntɪv), *a.* and *sb. rare.* [f. augment *v.* + -ive: cf. *arrestive*, etc.] = augmentative (which shows the more usual type).

1413 Lydg. *Pylgr. Sowle* iv. xxvii. 72 The sowle hath also power nutritif and augmentif. **1602** W. Watson *Decacord.* 305 For the most advancement of our nobles, and augmentive florish of the whole common wealth. **1816** J. Gilchrist *Philos. Etym.* 115 The augmentives are *ard, est, er, some, ous*, etc.

augmentor (ɔːgˈmɛntɔː(r)). [f. augment *v.* + -or.]

1. var. augmenter.

2. *Physiol.* Applied to a nerve or nerve cell by the stimulation of which the cardiac contractions are increased. Also *attrib.*

1902 *Nature* 6 Nov. 3 The anabolic inhibitory and the katabolic augmentor parts. **1907** *Practitioner* Nov. 692 The imperfectly oxygenated blood has to be sent through the heart and other muscles oftener per minute than healthy blood; the augmentor nerve is, therefore, called into action.

3. A substance which increases the action of an auxetic substance although unable itself to initiate cell-division.

1915 Stedman *Med. Dict.* (ed. 3) 90/2 *Augmentor*, a hypothetical substance supposed to increase the action of an auxetic or a kinetic. **1918** J. A. Thomson in *New Statesman* 26 Jan. 400/1 The dying away in autumn and winter produces substances ('auxetics') which later on promote.. an increasing quantity of certain other substances ('augmentors') which give more power to the elbow of the first.

augoer, augre, augur(e, obs. ff. auger.

‖**au grand sérieux** (o grɑ̃ serjø), *advb. phr.* [F.] In all seriousness: const. to treat, take a matter, a person, etc., *au grand sérieux.* Cf. au sérieux.

1849 Thackeray *Pendennis* I. xvi. 139 Pen.. took the matter *au grand serieux*, with the happy conceit and gravity of youth. **1865** Mrs. Gaskell *Wives & Daughters* (1866) II. v. 48 You mustn't go and take me *au grand sérieux.* **1930** *Times Lit. Suppl.* 9 Oct. 800/2 The author.. is being treated *au grand sérieux*.. to an extent which he does not quite merit. **1936** C. S. Lewis *Alleg. Love* iv. 163 They all took Chaucer's love poetry *au grand sérieux.*

au gratin: see gratin.

augrim(e, -isme, -ym(e, obs. ff. algorism.

augur ('ɔːgə(r)), *sb.* Also 6–7 **augure.** [a. L. *augur*, earlier *auger*; perh. f. *av-is* bird + *-gar*, connected with *garrire* to talk, *garrulus* talkative, and Skr. *gar* to shout, call, show, make known; but Fick would derive it from *augēre* to increase, promote, etc.; cf. *auctor* AUTHOR *sb.*]

1. A religious official among the Romans, whose duty it was to predict future events and advise upon the course of public business, in accordance with omens derived from the flight, singing, and feeding of birds, the appearance of the entrails of sacrificial victims, celestial phenomena, and other portents.

1549 HOOPER *Commandm.* vi. Wks. (1852) 327 There were some called augures, that by observation of the birds of the air..made men believe they knew things to come. **1719** D'URFEY *Pills* (1872) III. 78 Having like an Augur watched, Which way he took his flight. **1879** FROUDE *Cæsar* iii. 21 The College of Augurs could declare the auspices unfavourable, and so close all public business.

2. Hence extended to: A soothsayer, diviner, or prophet, generally; one that foretells the future.

1593 DRAYTON *Eclogues* i. 7 Philomel, the augure of the Spring. **1647** R. STAPYLTON *Juvenal* 115 The Phrygians, Cilicians, and Arabians were very skilfull augurs, or diviners by the flight of birds. **1718** POPE *Iliad* I. 131 Augur accursed! denouncing mischief still, Prophet of plagues, for ever boding ill!

augur ('ɔːgə(r)), *v.* [f. prec. sb.; or a. F. *augure-r* (14th c.), ad. L. *augurāri*, f. *augur*; see prec.]

1. *trans.* To prognosticate from signs or omens; to divine, forbode, anticipate.

1601 B. JONSON *Poetaster* I. i, I did augur all this to him beforehand. **1775** BURKE *Sp. Conc. Amer.* Wks. III. 56 They augur misgovernment at a distance and snuff the approach of tyranny. **1827** SCOTT *Surg. D.* i. 25 The Docter..hastened down stairs, auguring some new occasion for his services. **1852** D. MITCHELL *Bat. Summer* 70 Who augured from the very fact, a state of quietude.

b. Of things: To betoken, portend, give promise of.

1826 SCOTT *Mal. Malagr.* i. 54 It seems to augur genius. **1843** LYTTON *Last Bar.* I. i. 32 Whose open, handsome, hardy face augured a frank and fearless nature.

2. *intr.* (or with *subord. cl.*) To take auguries; to conjecture from signs or omens; to have foreknowledge or foreboding.

1808 SCOTT *Marm.* III. xv, Not that he augur'd of the doom, Which on the living closed the tomb. **1840** GEN. P. THOMPSON *Exerc.* (1842) V. 119 What have the cock-sparrows to do with it; do we augur from them, as the Romans did from chickens? **1877** SPARROW *Serm.* xxiii. 308 He may augur the gust is coming, but cannot prevent it.

3. *esp.* (with *well* or *ill*) **a.** Of persons: To have *good* or *bad* anticipations or expectations *of*, *for*.

1803 WELLINGTON in Gurw. *Disp.* II. 275, I augur well from this circumstance. **1849** MACAULAY *Hist. Eng.* I. 544 Fletcher, from the beginning, had augured ill of the enterprise. **1859** JEPHSON *Brittany* vi. 69 As I looked at his good-natured face I augured well for my reception.

b. Of things: To give *good* or *bad* promise. [Perh. *ill* was orig. a sb. = evil.]

1788 T. JEFFERSON *Writ.* (1859) II. 506 One vote, which augurs ill to the rights of the people. **1810** SCOTT *Lady of L.* III. vii, All augured ill for Alpine's line. **1855** PRESCOTT *Philip II* (1857) 68 A reverential deference, which augured well for the success of his mission.

4. *trans.* (also with *in*) To induct into office or usher in with auguries; to inaugurate.

1549 LATIMER *Serm. bef. Edw. VI* (Arb.) 46 Numa Pompilus, who was augured and created king [of] the Romaynes next after Romulus. **1865** *Reader* 11 Feb. 157 Profuse promises have augured in its birth.

augur, variant of AUGURE, *Obs.*, augury.

augural ('ɔːgjʊərəl), *a.* [ad. L. *augurālis*, f. *augur*: see AUGUR *sb.* and -AL[1].]

1. Of or pertaining to augurs or augury.

1513 DOUGLAS *Æneis* IX. i. 51 Wyth wordis augurall.. Onto the flude anone furth steppis he. **1598** GREENWEY *Tacitus' Ann.* II. iii, Going out the Augurall gate. **1683** CAVE *Ecclesiastici* 193 The augural Portent of the flight of Birds. **1770** LANGHORNE *Plutarch* (1879) I. 167/2 They discovered ..the augural staff of Romulus. **1850** LEITCH *Müller's Anc. Art* §169 The consecrated enclosure for the observation of auspices,—the augural templum.

2. Significant of the future; betokening either good or ill; lucky or ominous.

1600 HOLLAND *Livy* VII. xxvi. 266 The God..that sent unto him from above that augurall foule [*præpetem*]. **1677** GALE *Crt. Gentiles* II. III. 65 Aristotle saith that sternutation was an augural signe. **1863** BROWNING *Sordello* v. Wks. III. 408 Moody music augural of woe.

augurate ('ɔːgjʊəreɪt), *sb.* [ad. L. *augurātus*, f. *augurāt-* ppl. stem of *augurāri* to predict from omens, f. *augur*: see prec. and -ATE[1].] The office of augur; the augurship.

1741 MIDDLETON *Cicero* I. v. (1742) 331 Tell me..since Nepos is leaving Rome, who is to haue his brother's Augurate. **1859** MERIVALE *Rom. Emp.* (1865) VI. xlix. 108 The formal dignity of the Augurate.

†**'augurate,** *v. Obs.* [f. L. *augurāt-*: see prec. and -ATE[3].] Hence **augurating,** *vbl. sb.*

1. *intr.* To perform the duties of augur; to take the auguries, observe and predict from omens.

1678 CUDWORTH *Intell. Syst.* 713 Navius having performed his Augurating Ceremonies, replied, that the thing might be done.

2. *trans.* (and with *subord. cl.*) To infer or conjecture from omens, to divine.

[**1623** COCKERAM *Eng. Dict.* II, *Bewitch*..Augurate.] **1652** EARL MONM. *Warrs Fland.* (1654) 167 Should not we, then .. augurate good success to our undertakings? **1759** FRANKLIN *Ess.* Wks. 1840 III. 507 They should augurate, from the excellence of his character, that his administration would be excellent. **1765** TUCKER *Lt. Nat.* I. 10 Whence he may augurate that I have a larger scheme in reserve.

3. *trans.* To inaugurate; cf. AUGUR *v.* 4.

1623 (Feb.) BARGRAVE *Serm.* (1624) 3 That Memorable Redemption of mankind..he himselfe augurated by the solemne Sacrament of his last Supper.

†**augu'ration.** *Obs.* [ad. L. *augurātiōn-em*, n. of action f. *augurāt-*: see prec. and -ATION.] The practice of prognosticating the future by observing the flight of birds and other phenomena; augury; *gen.* omen, prognostic, token.

1569 J. SANFORD *Agrippa's Van. Artes* 50 Emonge those gaineful Artes of Diuination, be reckened..Augurations. **1614** RALEIGH *Hist. World* I. (1736) 93 Parnassus, the Inventor of Auguration. *a* **1674** CLARENDON *Hist. Reb.* III. x. 9 Transported with this happy auguration, he left Jersy.

†**'augure**[1]. *Obs.* Also 7 **augur.** [a. F. *augure* (12th c.), ad. L. *augurium* (substituted for the popular OF. *aür*, *eür* = mod. *heur* in *bonheur*, *malheur*).] By-form of AUGURY.

1475 *Bk. Noblesse* 59 To lerne and know by augures, and divinacions of briddis. **1603** FLORIO *Montaigne* I. xxi. (1632) 47 As a good Augur or foreboding of a martiall minde. **1666** EVELYN *Mem.* (1857) III. 178 With which happy augure permit me..to subscribe myself, etc.

†**'augure**[2]. *Obs.* [for *auger* phonetic var. ALGERE; cf. Du. *aalgeer*, *elger*.] Eel-spear.

1616 SURFL. & MARKH. *Countr. Farm* 508 The augure.. a sharpe instrument of yron made thinne with many sharpe teeth, and so striken into holes or muddie banks, vvhere they vvill many times catch a great aboundance of Eeles.

augured ('ɔːgəd), *ppl. a.* [f. AUGUR *v.* + -ED.] Predicted, foretold, anticipated, foreseen.

1823 BYRON *Island* I. vii, Others scoff'd his augur'd miseries.

†**'augurer.** *Obs.* Also 7 **agurer.** [a. OF. *augurere*, *-eour*:—L. *augurātor*, *-ātōrem*, n. of agent f. *augurāt-*: see AUGURATE and -OR.] = AUGUR *sb.* 1.

c **1400** *Apol. Loll.* 95 Augureris we calle þoo þat tentun to þe garring & fliyng of briddus. **1601** SHAKS. *Jul. C.* II. ii. 37 What say the Augurers? **1607** —— *Cor.* II. i. 1 The Agurer tels me, wee shall haue Newes to night. **1624** GEE in Somers' *Tracts* (1810) III. 78 The ceremonies of augurers.

augurial (ɔː'gjʊərɪəl), *a.* [ad. L. *auguriālis* (synonym of *augurālis*) f. *augurium* AUGURY.] Pertaining to augury, augural.

1513 DOUGLAS *Æneis* VII. iv. 85 Cled in rial rob auguriall. **1646** SIR T. BROWNE *Pseud. Ep.* I. iv. 16 Auguriall and Tripudiary divinations. **1855** BAILEY *Mystic* 119 Augurial rites Of volant fowl.

†**au'gurian,** *a. Obs. rare*[−1]. [f. L. *auguri-us* (see prec.) + -AN.] = prec.

1513 DOUGLAS *Æneis* XII. v. 59 From the hevin..Ane takyn hes scho schawin auguriane.

auguring ('ɔːgərɪŋ), *ppl. a.* [f. AUGUR *v.* + -ING[2].] Divining, presaging, prophetic.

1606 SHAKS. *Ant. & Cl.* II. i. 10 My powers a Cressent, and my Auguring hope Sayes, it will come to' th' full.

†**'augurism.** *Obs.* [f. AUGUR + -ISM.] Augury.

1590 LODGE *Euphues Gold. Leg.* in Halliw. *Shaks.* VI. 41 If augurisme be authenticall..it cannot bee but such a shadow portends the issue of a substance. **1607** TOPSELL *Four-f. Beasts* (1658) 68 Then did the Priest divide the intrails, that so he might make his augurism. **1658** *Wom. Never Vexed* III. i. in Hazl. *Dodsl.* XII. 143 There shall no augurism fright my plain dealing.

†**'augurist.** *Obs.* [f. as prec. + -IST.] An augur.

1623 in COCKERAM *Dict.* II. **1630** J. TAYLOR (Water P.) *Fearf. Summer* Wks. I. 60/2 Propheticke Augurists.

†**'augurize,** *v. Obs.* [f. as prec. + -IZE.] To augur, predict from omens. Hence: **'augurizer,** an augur. **'augurizing,** *vbl. sb.* and *ppl. a.*

1596 FITZ-GEFFREY *Sir F. Drake* (1881) 106, I augurize this shall be done ere long. **1603** J. SAVILE *Salut. K. James* in Arb. *Garner* V. 635 When one..Could augurise aright, foresee, foresay. **1652** GAULE *Magastrom.* 178 The Roman augurizers, the French druids. *Ibid.* 305 Tush! quoth Hercules: the best augurizing is to fight valiantly for our countrey. *Ibid.* 319 Augurizing and aruspicall diviners.

augurous ('ɔːgjʊərəs), *a. rare.* [f. AUGUR + -OUS.] Presaging, foreboding, full of forebodings.

1600 CHAPMAN *Iliads* XVIII. 191 Presaging in their augurous hearts the labours that they mourn'd A little after. **1848** CONINGTON *Æschylus' Agamem.* 109 Wherefore is this constant fear..Still before my augurous bosom flitting?

augurship ('ɔːgəʃɪp). [f. AUGUR *sb.* + -SHIP.] The office, or term of office, of an augur.

1618 BOLTON *Florus* I. v. 14 Hence the Augurship became sacred among the Romans. **1862** MERIVALE *Rom. Emp.* (1865) VII. lvi. 89 Priesthoods and augurships were bestowed on veteran dignitaries.

augury ('ɔːgjʊərɪ). [a. OF. *augurie*, ad. L. *augurium*: cf. AUGURE.]

1. The art of the AUGUR: the practice of divining from the flight of birds, etc.; divination.

c **1374** CHAUCER *Troylus* IV. 88, I have eke foundyn by astronomye, By sort, and by augury eke truly..That fere and flaum on al the toun shal sprede. **1602** SHAKS. *Ham.* V. ii. 230 Not a whit, we defie Augury..If it be now, 'tis not to come: if it bee not to come, it will bee now. **1718** POPE *Iliad* XVII. 259 Ennomus, in augury renown'd. **1846** ARNOLD *Hist. Rome* I. i. 6 Enquired of the gods by augury.

b. Skill in divining from omens; prophetic skill.

1591 SHAKS. *Two Gent.* IV. iv. 73 Thy face, and thy behauiour, Which (if my Augury deceiue me not) Witnesse good bringing vp. **1611** BEAUM. & FL. *Philaster* I. i, If he give not back his crown again, upon the report of an elder-gun, I have no augury.

2. An augural observation, ceremony, or rite.

1742 MIDDLETON *Cicero* II. vi. 85 The onely one of the College, who maintained the truth of their auguries, and the reality of divination. **1861** HOOK *Lives Abps.* I. v. 223 To put down pagan observances, auguries, phylacteries, and incantations. **1875** STUBBS *Const. Hist.* I. ii. 30 The priests ..took the auguries and gave the signal for onset.

3. An omen drawn by augury; a prognostic, portent, significant token of any kind.

1612 DRAYTON *Polyolb.* xii. 206 From their flight strange auguries shee drew. **1656** COWLEY *Acme & Sept.* iii, The God of Love..Sneez'd aloud, and all around The little Loves..Bow'd, and bless'd the Augury. **1718** POPE *Iliad* XXIV. 388 Jove..from the throne on high Dispatch'd his bird, celestial augury! **1876** GEO. ELIOT *Dan. Der.* II. xi. 87 The appropriateness of the event seemed an augury.

4. *fig.* Foreboding from tokens, presentiment, anticipation.

1783 T. BLAND in Sparks *Corr. Amer. Rev.* (1853) IV. 25, I am led to form the most pleasing augury of our future greatness. **1871** BROWNING *Balaust.* 2300 Be not extravagant in grief, no less! Bear it, by augury of better things!

5. *fig.* Indication or signification of the future afforded by any thing; presage, promise.

1797 GODWIN *Enquirer* I. xvi. 156 Tameness is the characteristic of most fatal augury. **1843** PRESCOTT *Mexico* II. i. (1864) 68 He resigned himself..with a docility that gave little augury of his future greatness.

†**'auguryne.** *Obs. rare*[−1]. [formed on L. or OF. *augur* by mistaken analogy.] An augur.

c **1400** MAUNDEV. xv. 167, I have seen of Paynemes and Sarazines, that men clepen Augurynes, that..wolde telle us the prenosticaciouns of thinges that felle aftre.

august (ɔː'gʌst), *a.* [ad. L. *augustus* consecrated, venerable, prob. f. *augur*, as if 'consecrated by augury, auspicious'; perh. influenced in use by association with *augē-re* to increase, magnify. Cf. mod.F. *auguste* (not in Cotgrave).]

1. Inspiring mingled reverence and admiration; impressing the emotions or imagination as magnificent; majestic, stately, sublime, solemnly grand; venerable, revered.

1664 H. MORE *Apol.* 486 The ancient Philosophers look'd upon this Universe as one August Temple of God. **1712** ADDISON *Spect.* No. 414 ¶4 There is generally in Nature something more Grand and August, than what we meet with in the Curiosities of Art. **1795** BURKE *Let.* Wks. 1842 II. 244 Never was so beautiful and so august a spectacle presented to the moral eye. **1855** MACAULAY *Hist. Eng.* IV. 534 The funeral was long remembered as the saddest and most august that Westminster had ever seen. **1869** J. MARTINEAU *Ess.* II. 149 [It] renews its ancient glance with an auguster beauty.

2. Venerable from birth or position; of stately dignity; dignified, worshipful, eminent, majestic. (Sometimes complimentary or perfunctory.)

1673 DRYDEN *Marr. à la Mode* v. i, Since he is King..He looks so grand and so august. *a* **1720** J. SHEFFIELD (Dk. Buckhm.) *Wks.* (1753) II. 141 And made obeisance to that august Assembly. **1821** BYRON *Two Fosc.* IV. i, To mingle with a body so august. **1860** TRENCH *Serm. Westm.* xiv. 152 We have a human sufferer in Him—the augustest indeed that ever shared our flesh and blood. **1864** H. AINSWORTH *Tower* 231 Your august father was a prince of high and noble qualities.

August ('ɔːgəst), *sb.* Forms: 4 **auguste, augst,** 5 **aust,** 4– **august.** [In form *aust* a. OF. *aoust* (mod. *août*):—L. *augustus* (see prec.); in current form, from the L.; in form *augst* partially latinized.] The eighth month of the year, so named after Augustus Cæsar, the first Roman emperor.

1097 *O.E. Chron.* (Laud MS.) Fram midde sumeran for neah oð August. *c* **1325** *E.E. Allit. P.* A. 39 In auguste in a hyȝ seysoun. **1393** GOWER *Conf.* III. 370 Till augst be passed and septembre. *c* **1450** *Merlin* ix. 132 It was feire wedir..as stille as aboute aust. **1591** SHAKS. *1 Hen. VI*, I. i. 110 The tenth of August last. **1870** MORRIS *Earthly Par.* I. II. 551 And August came the fainting year to mend With fruit and grain.

august ('ɔːgəst), *v.* [f. prec. sb. after F. *aoûter.*] To ripen, bring to fruition.

1693 [see AUGUSTED]. **1855** BAILEY *Mystic* 55 He for..dear nations toiled, And augusted man's heavenly hopes.

Au'gustal, *a. Hist.* [ad. L. *Augustālis*, f. *Augustus*: see -AL[1].] Of or pertaining to the emperor Augustus, or to his worship; imperial. ***Augustal Prefect*** (L. *præfectus Augustalis*), the title of the prefect of Egypt.

1658 USSHER *Ann.* 809 The Augustal Principality, that is of governing after his own will..he [Tiberius] obtained afterwards. **1730** A. GORDON *Maffei's Amphith.* 346 The Augustal Priests. **1731** *Hist. Litteraria* II. 57 The great power that was lodged in the Augustal Praefect of Egypt. **1907** W. G. HOLMES *Age of Justinian & Theodora* II. vii. 475 The Augustal Praefect resigned the control of all Egypt for that of Alexandria and the adjacent country.

Augustan (ɒ'gʌstən, ɔː-, ə-), *a.* (and *sb.*) [ad. L. *Augustānus*, f. *Augustus*: see -AN.]

A. *adj.*

1. Connected with the reign of Augustus Cæsar, the palmy period of Latin literature.

1704 ROWE *Ulysses* Ded., Favour and Protection which it [Poetry] found in the famous Augustan Age. **1859** MERIVALE *Rom. Emp.* (1871) V. xl. 52 In the Augustan period this outer area was only partially occupied.

2. Hence applied to the period of highest purity and refinement of any national literature; and *gen.* Of the correct standard in taste, classical. Also, applied *spec.* to 17th and 18th cent. English literature; and *absol.*

1712 J. OLDMIXON *Refl. on Dr. Swift's Let.* 19 King Charles the Second's Reign, which probably may be the Augustan Age of English Poetry. *a* **1745** SWIFT *Thoughts on Var. Subjects* in *Wks.* (1897) I. 284 Charles the Second's reign..is reckoned, though very absurdly, our Augustan age. **1759** GOLDSMITH *Bee* 24 Nov. No. 8. p. 235 (*title*) An Account of the Augustan Age of England. **1772** H. WALPOLE *Let.* 21 July (1904) VIII. 184 What a figure will this our Augustan age make; Garrick's prologues, epilogues, and verses, Sir W[illiam] Chambers's *Gardening*, Dr. Nowel's sermon. **1819** *Pantolog.* s.v., The reign of queen Anne is often called the Augustan age of England. **1849** RUSKIN *Sev. Lamps* vii. §7. 190 We must first determine what buildings are to be considered Augustan in their authority. **1861** M. ARNOLD *On Transl. Homer* i. 29 Chapman translates his object into Elizabethan, as Pope translates it into the Augustan of Queen Anne. **1916** G. SAINTSBURY (*title*) The Peace of the Augustans. *Ibid.* 389 To see the beauties, to hear the music, and to taste the sweetness or the tartness, the bitter and the salt, of Augustan poetry. **1952** I. JACK (*title*) Augustan satire. Intention and idiom in English poetry 1660–1750.

3. Of the town of Augusta Vindelicorum or Augsburg, where in 1530 Luther and Melanchthon drew up their confession of Protestant principles.

1565 SHACKLOCK tr. *S. Hosius's Hatchet of Heresies* 71 *margin*, In his Apologie of the Augustane confession. *c* **1645** HOWELL *Lett.* (1650) 23 Som embracing..the Augustane, and som the Helvetian confession. **1796** MORSE *Amer. Geog.* I. 281 They adhere to the Augustan Confession.

B. *sb.* A writer of the Augustan age (of any literature).

1882 *Athenæum* 25 Nov. 692/3 A picture of the later Augustans [*i.e.* writers of the reign of Queen Anne].

Augustanism (ɔː'gʌstənɪz(ə)m). [f. AUGUSTAN *a.* + -ISM.] The condition of being Augustan.

1903 T. WATTS-DUNTON in *Chambers's Cycl. Eng. Lit.* III. 5/1 [Gray's] chief poem, the famous elegy, furnishes a striking proof of the poet's slavery to Augustanism. **1904** *Athenæum* 16 Jan. 73/1 The period of Augustanism in English literature—that age of acceptance which began after Milton and ended with Gray and Collins. **1955** J. LAWLOR in *Ess. & Stud.* VIII. 61 This is the real achievement of Augustanism..the imposition of order, the self-possession of the artist.

Auguste ('aʊgʊst). [Adopted in Fr. spelling *auguste*, f. G. *August* (*der dumme August* circus clown).] A type of circus clown (see quots.).

The 'explanation' of the origin of the word in quot. 1935 is one of several unsubstantiated stories. Robert, *Dict. de la Langue Franç.*, regards Fr. *auguste* as a noun that has arisen by antonymy from the adj. *auguste* 'august, majestic', but evidence is lacking.

1910 W. J. LOCKE *Simon the Jester* iv. 42 Auguste..is the generic name of the clown in the French Hippodrome. **1935** *Observer* 15 Dec. 13/3 The Auguste is the man with the battered bowler hat, his jacket on back to front..who always gets the worst of it... The name is supposed to have come about this way: A century ago an English clown, playing in Germany, had the novel idea..of going into the circus with a battered hat and his clothes all wrong. The audience began shouting out, 'August! August!' (The German phrase, 'dumme August' is equivalent to our word 'zaney' or 'addle-pate'.) And the name has stuck to this day. **1950** *Oxf. Jun. Encycl.* IX. 139/1 In the late 19th century a new type of clown appeared in the circus. He was called an 'auguste', and wore ill-fitting ordinary clothes..and a large bulbous red nose.

† **Augu'stean**, *a. Obs. rare.* [f. L. *Augustē-us* of Augustus + -AN.] = AUGUSTAN.

1678 CUDWORTH *Intell. Syst.* 368 Manilius, who lived in the same Augustean age. **1690** [ATTERBURY] *Pref. to Second Part of Mr. Waller's Poems* sig. A4, I question whether in Charles the Second's Reign, English did not come to its full perfection; and whether it has not had its Augustean Age, as well as the Latin.

'augusted, *ppl. a.* [f. AUGUST *v.*; cf. F. *aoûté*.]

1693 EVELYN *De la Quint. Compl. Gard.*, *Augusted*, is a Term used to signifie any thing that is Sun burnt..and is turned ripe and yellow like Corn in August..An Augusted branch is a Branch of a Summers Growth, that is just hard'ned, and has done growing.

† **augu'steity**. *Obs. rare.* [f. L. *augustē-us* (taken as = *augustus*) + -ITY.] Augustness.

1633 T. ADAMS *Comm. 2 Pet.* i. 11 He exalteth himself above all that is called God..above all augusteity. *a* **1639** S. WARD *Serm.* (1862) 5 (D.) Advanced above all Augusteity.

Augustin(e (ɔː'gʌstɪn, 'ɔːgəstɪn), *sb.* (and *a.*) [a. F. *Augustin*, or ad. L. *Augustinus*, name of the great Latin father. See also AUSTIN.] A member of the monastic order named after St. Augustine.

c **1400** *Rom. Rose* 7463 Frere prechours ben good men alle ..So been Augustins. **1631** WEEVER *Anc. Fun. Mon.* 314 The Abbey of the Friers Augustines. **1708** *Lond. Gaz.* No. 4427/13 The Church of the barefooted Augustins.

Augustinian (ɔːgʌ'stɪnɪən), *a.* (and *sb.*) [f. L. *Augustīn-us* (see prec.) + -IAN.]

1. Of or pertaining to St. Augustine or his doctrines, the prominent tenets of which were immediate efficacy of grace and absolute predestination. *sb.* An adherent of these doctrines.

1674 HICKMAN *Hist. Quinquart.* 36 But what was.. become of the Augustinian spirit? **1851** J. TORREY *Neander's Ch. Hist.* (Bohn) IV. 379 The Augustinian doctrine of election. **1860** J. GARDNER *Faiths of World* 263 This notion of human freedom was denied by the Augustinians.

2. Belonging to (*sb.* one of) the order of Augustines.

1602 W. WATSON *Decacord.* 75 Dominicans, Augustinians, and other poore religious Friers. **1875** T. LINDSAY in *Sund. Mag.* June 589 The Augustinian monks in Brussels. **1882** *Athenæum* 3 June 692/3 A house of Augustinian canons.

3. Adhering to (*sb.* an adherent of) Augustine the Bohemian.

1645 PAGITT *Heresiogr.* (1647) 30 Augustinians..affirme the entrance into Paradice to have been shut up untill Augustine the Bohemian opened it for..those that were of his sect.

Augu'stinianess, a female disciple of St. Augustine. **Augu'stinianism**, **Au'gustinism**, the doctrines held by him and his followers.

1853 FABER *All for Jesus* 140 Veronica the Augustinianess. **1830** MACKINTOSH *Eth. Philos.* (1867) 356 The Calvinism, or rather Augustinianism, of Aquinas. **1883** *Athenæum* 3 Feb. 148/3 [In] the eighteenth epistle..Augustinism is directly opposed.

† **au'gustious**, *a. Obs. rare.* [f. L. *august-us* AUGUST, on mistaken analogy: cf. *illustrious*.] Grand, magnificent, AUGUST.

a **1670** HACKET *1st Serm. Incarn.*, The most Augustious Temple in the world. —— *Abp. Williams* 169 These augustious preparations would be ridiculously disappointed.

augustly (ɔː'gʌstlɪ), *adv.* [f. AUGUST *a.* + -LY[2].] In a manner calculated to inspire reverential awe or wonder; grandly, majestically.

1667 G. C. in *H. More's Div. Dial.* Pref. (1713) 9 That which makes Des Cartes his Philosophy look so augustly on't. **1742** YOUNG *Nt. Th.* II. 688 Undarken'd by despair, Philander, thus, augustly rears his head. **1861** *Sat. Rev.* 6 Apr. 340/1 What are the pediments of the Parthenon.. beside this augustly simple image?

au'gustness. [f. as prec. + -NESS.] August quality; supreme majesty, grandeur, or stateliness.

1758 H. WALPOLE *R. & Noble Authors* (1806) IV. 52 Daunted at the augustness of such an assembly. **1871** BROWNING *Pr. Hohenstiel* 1903 Truth, Right, And other such augustnesses.

auh (ɒh), *int.* expressing disgust.

1732 FIELDING *Miser* III. v, Auh! what an animal!

auh, variant of AC *conj. Obs.* but.

auht(e, obs. form of AUGHT, EIGHT; pa. t. of *agan*: see OUGHT.

auhtend, obs. form of EIGHTH.

auk (ɔːk). Also 8 **alk**, 8–9 **awk**. [cogn. with Sw. *alka*, Da. *alke*:—ON. *álka*.] Any bird of the family *Alcidæ* of diving birds, predominantly black, white, or grey in colour, inhabiting mainly the colder parts of the northern oceans and characterized by short wings, tail, and legs, and webbed feet. The auks include the guillemot, puffin, razor-bill, little auk, and the extinct and flightless great auk.

[**1580** TUSSER *Husb.* (1878) 140 Ill husbandry drowseth At fortune so auke: Good husbandry rowseth himselfe as a hauke.] **1674** [see RAZOR-BILL 1 a]. **1678** RAY *Willughby's Ornith.* 323 The Bird called the Razor-bill in the West of England, the Auk in the North, the Murre in Cornwal. **1796** MORSE *Amer. Geog.* II. 17 The alks build upon rocks. **1856** KANE *Arctic Exp.* I. xxiv. 320 Wounded awks. **1865** GOSSE *Land & Sea* (1874) 44 That rarest of British birds, the great auk. **1866** EDMONDSTON *Orkney Gloss.* 4 *Auk*, the common guillemot. **1802**, **1894** [see GARE-FOWL].

auk(e, -ly, -ness, -ward, obs. ff. AWK, etc.

auklet ('ɔːklɪt). [f. AUK + -LET.] Applied to any of various species of small auk.

1886 R. RIDGWAY *Man. N. Amer. Birds* 13 Simorhynchus pusillus (Pall.) Least Auklet. **1901** R. C. LEHMANN *Anni Fugaces* 135 The last Great Auk..left..Two orphaned Auklets in their shell. **1956** R. PETERSON et al. *Field Guide Birds Brit. & Europe* (ed. 2) 297 Paroquet auklet..Crested auklet.

aul, var. AOUL.

Aularian (ɔː'lɛərɪən), *a.* and *sb.* [f. late L. *aulāri-us* belonging to the *aula*, Gr. αὐλή, hall + -AN.] **A.** *adj.* Of or belonging to a hall. *spec.* Pertaining to or characteristic of a hall in a collegiate university, esp. in respect of its power of self-administration. **B.** *sb.* At English universities: The member of a hall (as distinguished from the member of a college).

a **1695** WOOD *Life* (1848) 302 Afterwards Dr. Adams [Principal of Magdalen Hall] entertained the vice-chancellor and Aularians with a glass of wine. *c* **1849** *Stranger's Guide Oxford* (ed. 6) 92 As the foundation of this establishment marks a new era in the academical annals of this University, it is not without reason..that..the name of *New College* should still attach to this erection. Before this period, however, the Aularian system was generally prevalent. **1871** *Daily News* 13 Jan., The 'inmates,' or 'aularians,' had prevailed at the University. **1895** RASHDALL *Universities Europe Mid. Ages* II. 624 Aularian Statutes at Oxford. *Ibid.* 626 Even these Oxford Statutes which had for their very object to assert the authority of the University and of the Principals contain traces of the old Aularian self-government.

'aulary ('ɔːlərɪ), *a. rare.* [ad. late L. *aulārius*: see AULARIAN *a.* and *sb.* and -ARY[1].] Of or relating to the halls in a university.

1845 LD. CAMPBELL *Chancellors* (1857) I. xxiv. 351 Aulary Statutes for the government of the University.

aulbe, obs. form of ALB.

auld (ɔːld, *Sc.* ɑːld), *a. dial.* Also **aud.** [mod.Sc. and north Eng. descendant of OE. *ald*, which became in midl. dial. in 13th c. OLD.] = OLD; as in ***auld lang-syne***, 'old long-since,' old long-ago (used subst.); ***Auld Reekie***, 'Old Smoky,' a sobriquet of Edinburgh; ***auldfarrand***, 'favouring,' *i.e.* resembling the old or adult, having the manners or sagacity of age; ***auld-warld***, old-world.

[**950–** see ALD.] **1375** BARBOUR *Bruce* I. 17 Aulde storys that men redys. **1692** 'JACOB CURATE' *Scotch Presb. Eloq.* iii. 101 Now billy Jonah, wilt thou go to Nineveh for ald lang syne [*marginal note*, old kindness]. **1702** THORESBY *Diary* I. 352 Saw..a child of three years old fill its pipe of tobacco, and smoke it as audfarandly as a man of three score! **1721** RAMSAY *Poems* 72 [*title*] The Kind Reception. *To the Tune of* Auld lang syne. **1788** [see LANGSYNE]. **1818** SCOTT *Hrt. Midl.* xl, My best service to all my friends at and about Auld Reekie! **1827** SCOTT *Two Drovers* i. in *Chron. of Canongate* I. xiii. 303, I am Hugh Morrison from Glenae, come of the Manly Morrisons of auld langsyne. **1848** KINGSLEY *Alt. Locke* (1881) I. 91 Foolish auld-warld notions about keeping days holy. **1896** G. B. SHAW in *Our Theatres in Nineties* (1931) II. 140 That smile may have meant sentimental memories of auld lang syne. **1901** W. LAIDLAW *Poetry & P.* 58 On auld lang syne I'll stand and ponder.

aule, obs. form of AWL.

aulete ('ɔːliːt). [ad. Gr. αὐλητής, f. αὐλέ-ειν to play the flute, f. αὐλός flute.] A flute-player.

1850 LEITCH *Müller's Anc. Art* § 131 Ismenias the aulete.

auletic (ɔː'lɛtɪk), *a. rare.* [ad. Gr. αὐλητικός, f. αὐλητής: see prec. and -IC.] Of or pertaining to a flute-player or flute.

1731 in BAILEY.

aulf(e, variant of AUFE, obs. form of OAF[1].

aulgorism(e, obs. form of ALGORISM.

aulic ('ɔːlɪk), *a.* and *sb.* [ad. F. *aulique*, or L. *aulicus*, a. Gr. αὐλικός, f. αὐλή court: see -IC.]

A. *adj.* Of or pertaining to a court; courtly.

The *Aulic Council*, in the old German Empire, was the personal council of the Emperor, forming one of the two supreme courts of the Empire; it heard appeals from the courts of Germanic states, and was dissolved, with the Empire, in 1806. The name is now given to a council at Vienna, managing the war-department of the Austrian Empire.

1701 *Lond. Gaz.* No. 3719/3 Baron Seylern..has notified to the Imperial Diet the Decrees of the Aulick Council. **1853** DE QUINCEY *Wks.* XIV. ii. 17 Investing the.. homeliness of Æsop with aulic graces and satiric brilliancy.

B. *sb.* The ceremony observed in the Sorbonne in granting the degree of doctor of divinity, when, after a harangue from the chancellor, the new doctor received his cap and presided at a disputation.

† **'aulical**, *a. Obs.* [f. as prec.: see -ICAL.] = prec.

1602 W. WATSON *Decacord.* 233 Some to be aulicall, others martiall, others rurall. **1651** *Reliq. Wotton.* 41 Maners ..without which no man shall be eminent in the aulicall function.

† **'aulicism**. *Obs. rare*[−1]. [f. AULIC *a.* + -ISM.] A courtly phrase or turn of expression.

1633 T. ADAMS *Comm. 2 Peter* i. 15 God affects not aulicisms and courtly terms.

aulmoniere: see AUMONIERE.

auln-, ault- (in various words): see AL-.

† **'aultel, 'aultelle.** *Obs.* Also 6 altel. [either a. OF. *altel* (now *autel*), or a diminutive form after L. sbs. in *-ellum.*] An altar; a small or inferior altar.

1555 [see ALTEL]. **1556** *Chron. Grey Friars* (1852) 59 They shulde have..no communyone at no aultelle in the church but at the hye awlter.

aum (ɔːm). A modern English variant form of *aam*: see AAM for etymology and earlier quots.

1502 ARNOLD *Chron.* [see quot. 1717 under AAM.] **1852** MCCULLOCH *Dict. Comm.* 35 [In Amsterdam] the *aam* liquid measure = 4 ankers = 41 English wine gallons. *Ibid.* 649 [In Hamburg] 1 aum = 4 ankers = 32 English imperial gallons. **1863** W. BALDWIN *Afr. Hunting* 369 He helped considerably to lighten our half-aum of Pontac.

aumail (ɔː'meɪl). *rare.* [Archaistic refashioning of AMEL *sb.*, after Spenser's pa. pple. *aumayld*: see AMELED.] Enamel.

[**1596** SPENSER *F.Q.* II. iii. 27 In gilden buskins..entayld With curious antickes, and full fayre aumayld.] **1824** WIFFEN *Tasso* XX. xlii, Smote him where with gold and rich aumaile [It. *smalto*] Gay on the helm flamed his barbaric crown.

aumble, -ynge, etc., obs. forms of AMBLE, etc.

aumbry(e, -bery, -bray, -brey, -brie, archaic spellings of AMBRY.

aumener(e, -monere, aumner, obs. forms of ALMONER.

aument, -acion, obs. ff. AUGMENT, -ATION.

† **'aumere.** *Obs. rare*⁻¹. [Cf. the forms *almar, -er, -owr,* under ALMONER[1] 1.] = ALMONER.

?*c* **1400** in *Dom. Arch.* III. 133 The aumere a rod schall haue in honde, As offyce of almes y understonde.

aumery, -rie, -ry, obs. or dial. ff. AMBRY.

aumes-, aums-ace, obs. forms of AMBS-ACE.

‖ **au mieux** (o mjø), *advb. phr.* [Fr., lit. 'at the best'.] On the best of terms *with* (someone); on very intimate terms.

1848 THACKERAY *Van. Fair* li. 450 Both attachés of the embassy..declared that they were *au mieux* with the charming Madame Ravdonn. **1849** — *Pendennis* I. xxxviii. 374, I thought you used to be *au mieux* in that quarter. **1953** E. M. FORSTER *Hill of Devi* 145 The Maharajah, out of sheer mischievousness, accused him of being *au mieux* with a lady.

‖ **aumil** ('ɔːmɪl, 'ɑːmɪl). [Urdū (prop. Arab.) *ʻāmil*, operator, agent, *spec.* 'revenue-collector,' agent-noun f. Arab. *ʻamala* to act, perform an office.] A native collector of revenue in India; also called *amaldar*, AMILDAR.

1800 WELLINGTON in *Wellesley Disp.* 200 He had repeatedly applied..for the necessary purwannahs to your several aumils. **1808** *Cobbett's Weekly Pol. Reg.* XIII. 1006 They soon find themselves beset with new aumils and peculators.

Hence (by confusion of *aumil* and *amaldār*): **aumildar** (with same sense).

1778 ORME *Brit. Mil. Trans.* (1803) III. 496 Frauds in the management of the aumildar or renter. **1799** WELLINGTON in *Wellesley Disp.* 772 To sell the office of aumildar.

‖ **aumônière.** Also aulm-. [Fr.; = ALMONER[2], q.v.] A purse formerly carried at the girdle.

1834 PLANCHÉ *Brit. Costume* 89 Berengaria..is represented with a small pouch called an *aulmonière.* **1874** AINSWORTH *Merry Eng.* I. I. ii. 22 She was likewise provided with an aulmoniere, or silken purse. **1883** D. GOODALE in *Harper's Mag.* July 241/1 The little plush aumônière.

aumulet, obs. f. OMELET *sb.*; cf. F. *aumelete*, 16th c.

‖ **aumusse.** *Obs. rare*⁻¹. [Fr. *aumusse, aumuce*: see AMICE[2].] The grey fur amice.

1708 MOTTEUX *Rabelais* IV. l, It is the Likeness of a Pope ..I know it by the Triple-Crown, his Furr'd Aumusse, etc.

‖ **au naturel** (o natyrel), *advb. phr.* [F.] In the natural state; cooked plainly; uncooked; undressed.

1817 *Blackw. Mag.* Nov. 192/2 They in general speak with great contempt of our national partiality for roast beef and potatoes 'au naturel'. **1827** DISRAELI *Vivian Grey* v. xv. 303 To say the truth, I think it [*sc.* the make-up] is *au naturel.* **1860** *Leisure Hour* 22 Nov. 186/2 With good round paunch *au naturel.* **1862** THACKERAY *Philip* I. xvi. 300, I..forget whether it was a cold dagger *au naturel*, or a dish of hot coals *à la Romaine*, of which they partook. **1905** MRS. H. WARD *Marriage W. Ashe* x. 181 You would have preferred ankles *au naturel!*

aunc-, aund- (in various words): see AN-.

† **'auncel.** *Obs.* Forms: 4-5 **aunser(e, auncere, aunselle,** 5-7 **auncel(le,** 6-7 **ancel,** 7 **awnsel.** [a. AF. *aunselle, auncelle*, apparently for *launcelle* (*l-* having been mistaken for the article), ad. It. *lancella* a little balance, dim. of *lance* balance:—L. *lanx, lancem*, a plate, a scale of a balance. So called probably in contrast to the 'Balancia domini regis,' or *Great Beam* of the king.

This important suggestion is due to Mr. J. A. Kingdon, late Master of the Grocers' Company, which company, originally called *Pepperers*, were charged with the custody of the King's Beam. In their records *Balauncer* and *Aunsell* appear as surnames in 13-14th c.; *Ballance* is also a surname.]

A kind of balance and weight formerly used in England.

(See the accounts of 17th c. writers below: that of Cowell, being given as hearsay, and connected with an absurd derivation from *hand-sale*, must be accepted with caution. Later explanations simply follow Cowell.)

1314 *MS. Letter-bk.* in Riley *Mem. Lond.* Introd. 22 Thomas the aunseremaker. **1351-2** *Act 25 Edw. III*, v. §9 Une pois qest appelle Aunselle. [*transl.* 1618 Pulton *Statutes* 155 Whereas great damage and deceit is done to the people ..by a weight which is called Auncel: it is accorded and established that this weight called auncell..shalbe wholly put out.] **1356** in Riley *Mem. Lond.* 283 One balance called an *auncere*..2 balances called *aunceres.* **1362** LANGL. *P. Pl.* A. v. 132 Þe pound þat heo peysede [by] · peisede a quartrun more þen myn Auncel dude · whon I weyede treuþe [*v.r.* Aunsel, B. auncere, aunser, C. auncel]. **1429** ABP. CHICHELEY in Wilkins' *Concilia* III. 516 Constitutio..pro abolitione ponderis vocati *le Auncell Weight*..Præcipue dicto pondere *le Auncell scheft* seu *pounder*..doloso quodam stateræ genere. **1429** *Act 8 Hen. VI*, v.§1 Le pois appelez Auncell. **1502** ARNOLD *Chron.* (1811) 191 Ther beth iij. maner weyghtis, that is to wete, troy weyght, auncell weyghtis, and lyggynge weyght..Another Weyght Ys called auncels shafte, and this weyght is forboden by statute of parlement, and also hooly chirche hath cursed alle thoo that beyen or sellen by that auncel weyght. **1607** COWELL *Interpr., Awncell* weight, as I have been informed, is a kinde of weight with scoles hanging or hooks fastened at each end of a staffe, which a man lifteth up upon his forefinger or hand and so discerneth the equalitie or difference betweene the weight and the thing weied..It may probably be thought to be called *awnsell* weight (quasi *hand sale* weight) because it was and is performed by the hand, as the other is by the beame. And if I should draw it from the Greeke, ἀγκών i. *cubitus*, the part of the arme from the elbowe to the fingers ends, I might chalenge a good warrand. *a* **1640** JACKSON *Creed* XI. xxvi. Wks. 1844 X. 502 The ancel weight or balance (which most of you have seen) wherein one pound weight put upon the one end of the balance will counterpoise a stone weight put upon the other end. **1641** *Termes de la Ley* 34 Auncell weight. **1656** DU GARD *Gate Lat. Unl.* §534. **1678** PHILLIPS, *Awnsel* weight. **1691** BLOUNT *Law Dict.*, *Auncel* Weight (*quasi* Hand sale weight, or from Ansa, *i.* The handle of the Ballance).

‖ **aune** (oːn). [Fr.; for etymol. see ALNAGE.] An ell; an obsolete French cloth measure, which varied in length in different localities.

1706 *Lond. Gaz.* No. 4218/3 Five Auns of Shalloon. **1812** J. SMYTH *Pract. Customs* 111 To measure..Linen, in order to check the quantity of Aunes or Ells marked thereon.

aune, -ing, obs. forms of AWN, -ING.

aungel(e, -yke, obs. forms of ANGEL *sb.*, etc.

Aunjetitz ('aʊnjətɪts). The German form of the name of a village near Prague, Czechoslovakia, applied attrib. to the remains found there of an important Early Bronze Age culture and to the culture itself.

1925 V. G. CHILDE *Dawn Europ. Civilization* xii. 191 The first original bronze age civilization of Central Europe is called, after the great cemetery south of Prague, the Aunjetitz culture. *Ibid.* 191 Typical Aunjetitz mug. **1949** *Proc. Prehist. Soc.* XV. 99 The first effective European adoption of distinctive bronze-pin types..took place in the Early Bronze Age of Central Europe, primarily in the Aunjetitz culture with its centre in Bohemia.

aunsetter, -estre, obs. forms of ANCESTOR *sb.*

aunsion, obs. form of ANCIENT.

1447-8 SHILLINGFORD *Lett.* 101 Hit was aunsion demene.

aunt (ɑːnt). Forms: 3-6 **aunte,** 5 **awnt,** 5- **aunt;** 3-7 **(mi, thi) naunt(e,** 9 *dial.* **noant.** [a. OF. *aunte, ante*, cogn. with Pr. *amda*, Lombard. *amida*:—L. *amita*. In Eng. a mistaken division of *mine aunt*, as *my naunt*, occurs in literature from 13th to 17th c., and still dialectally; cf. *nuncle* for *uncle*, and *auger, apron*, etc. (Some mod.F. dialects have also *nante* (*ma nante* = *mon ante*); the modern F. *tante*, found already in 13th c., perhaps originated, in the language of the nursery, from OF. *t'ante* 'thy aunt.')]

1. a. The sister of one's father or mother. Also, an uncle's wife, more strictly called an *aunt-in-law.*

1297 R. GLOUC. 571 Sir Gui de Mountfort, that was..is aunte sone. *a* **1300** *Cursor M.* 24675 His moder was þi naunt. *c* **1460** *Towneley Myst.* 82 Elezabethe, myn awnt dere. **1473** MARG. PASTON in *Lett.* 716 III. 78 Recomaunde me to..my naunte. *a* **1556** CRANMER *Wks.* II. 329 Aunt and aunt-in-law, niece and niece-in-law. **1598** SHAKS. *Merry W.* IV. ii. 76 My Maids Aunt the fat woman of Brainford. **1711** ADDISON *Spect.* No. 7 ¶4 A Maiden Aunt..who is one of these antiquated Sybils. **1834** GEN. P. THOMPSON *Exerc.* (1842) III. 45 *note*, What might have happened afterwards, is only known to those who can tell what would have come to pass if your aunt had been your uncle.

b. (in U.S.) Used endearingly of: Any benevolent practical woman who exercises these qualities to the benefit of her circle of acquaintance; cf. Sp. *tia*, and see AUNTHOOD. Also used *dial.* (see E.D.D.) as 'a term of familiarity or respect applied to elderly women, not necessarily implying relationship'. Also *transf.* Cf. AUNTIE b.

Universal aunt is taken from the name of a bureau in London undertaking such services, e.g. conducted tours, errands, as might be rendered by a maiden aunt. Cf. AUNTHOOD.

1793 [see UNCLE *sb.* 2 b]. **1861** MRS. STOWE *Pearl of Orr's Isl.* 21 These universally useful persons receive among us the title of 'aunt' by a sort of general consent..They are nobody's aunts in particular, but aunts to human nature generally. **1921** *Star* 28 Feb. 4/5 (headline) Professional Aunts on Hire. **1921** *Times* 15 Oct. 13/5 This sort of universal aunthood to the whole neighbourhood... It has been left to our own day to adopt her [*sc.* Miss Mulock's] idea in the more direct and concrete form of 'Universal Aunt'. **1928** H. WILLIAMSON *Pathway* xvii. 376 'I..thought I would look in, Aunt Connie.' 'Please don't call me Aunt Connie. I'm sorry to be so explicit.' **1944** H. G. WELLS *'42 to '44* 144 Jane Austen is one of my dearest aunts. **1959** *Observer* 11 Jan. 15/1 There is an element of knight-errantry in the investigations with which *Shopper's Guide* and *Which?* continue to plough their way through the labyrinth of consumers' goods... We, the public, are at last being championed by a battalion of scientific aunts. **1962** 'J. LE CARRÉ' *Murder of Quality* ii. 21 She..became..their guide, friend and universal aunt.

† **c.** Formerly used by alumni of Oxford and Cambridge as a title for the 'sister university.'

1655 FULLER *Ch. Hist.* II. I. 308 The Sons of our Aunt are loth to consent, that one who was taught in Cambridge, should teach in Oxford. **1701** PEPYS *Corr.* 403 An humble present of mine, though a Cambridge man, to my dear Aunt, the University of Oxford.

d. *U.S.* (See quots.)

1835 LONGSTREET *Georgia Scenes* 110 'There they are, Aunt Glory.' *Footnote*: 'Aunt' and 'Mauma'..are terms of respect commonly used by children to aged negroes. **1869** *Atlantic Monthly* Oct. 479/2 A pleasant, industrious 'Aunt Sally', a mulatto. **1904** HARBEN *Georgians* 106 A negro woman, Aunt Amanda,..passed in and out.

† **2.** An old woman; a gossip. *Obs.*

1590 SHAKS. *Mids. N.* II. i. 51 The wisest Aunt telling the saddest tale.

† **3.** A bawd or procuress; a prostitute. *Obs.*

1607 MIDDLETON *Michaelm. Term.* III. i, Wks. X. 470 She demanded of me whether I was your worships aunt or no. Out, out, out! **1663** *Parson's Wedd.* III. i, in Hazl. *Dodsl.* XIV. 448 Yes, and follow her, like one of my aunts of the suburbs. **1678** DRYDEN *Kind Kpr.* I. i, The easiest Fool I ever knew, next my Naunt of Fairies in the *Alchymist.*

4. Aunt Sally. a. A game much in vogue at fairs and races, in which the figure of a woman's head with a pipe in its mouth is set up, and the player, throwing sticks from a certain distance, aims at breaking the pipe.

1861 *Times* (*Derby Day*), Aunt Sally..this fashionable and athletic sport..is rather overdone than otherwise. **1884** *Pall Mall G.* 15 Aug. 4/1 Aunt Sallies and skittles for those who prefer such attractions.

b. A nickname for a wicket-keeper in cricket. *colloq.*

1898 G. GIFFEN *With Bat & Ball* 239 Practice may improve an 'Aunt Sally'..but unless he has natural genius ..a lad is not likely to become a star wicket-keeper. **1927** *Observer* 29 May 28/1 A 'keeper'..who combines batsmanship with all the 'Aunt Sally's' excellencies.

c. *fig.* An object of unreasonable or prejudiced attack.

1898 G. B. SHAW in *Sat. Rev.* 30 Apr. 592/2 This comes of an author making no serious attempt to get to the point of view of the character he professes to have dramatised—of simply conspiring with the stupid section of the pit to make an Aunt Sally of it. **1958** *Oxf. Mag.* 1 May 398/2 Palpable gross hits at a favourite Aunt Sally, modern psychology.

5. *my* (*sainted*) *aunt!* and similar phrases, as trivial exclamations.

1888 *Boy's Own Paper* Summer No. 35/2 'My aunt!' exclaimed Guy, with a start. **1888** KIPLING *Story of Gadsbys* (1889) 66 Prince Kraft a stable-boy—Oh, my Aunt! **1919** J. BUCHAN *Mr. Standfast* viii. 168 My holy aunt! The General disguised as Charlie Chaplin! **1921** WODEHOUSE *Jill Reckless* 301 'My sainted aunt!' he said slowly. **1928** A. HUXLEY *Point Counter Point* x. 163 Rampion..turned up his eyes. 'Oh, my sacred aunt!' he said.

6. Special collocations: ***Aunt Edna***, used of a typical theatre-goer of conservative taste; ***Aunt Emma***, used in croquet of a typically unenterprising player (or play); ***Aunt Fanny***, in various slang phrases expressing negation or disbelief.

1953 T. RATTIGAN *Coll. Plays* II. p. xii, Let us invent a character, a nice, respectable, middle-class, middle-aged, maiden lady, with time on her hands and the money to help her pass it... Let us call her Aunt Edna... Now Aunt Edna does not appreciate Kafka... She is, in short, a hopeless lowbrow. **1958** N. F. SIMPSON *Resounding Tinkle* in *Observer Plays* 241 The author..leans forward..to make simultaneous overtures of sumptuous impropriety to every Aunt Edna in the house. **1960** E. P. C. COTTER *Tackle Croquet this Way* 66 Whatever happens don't become an Aunt Emma player. **1963** *Croquet* Aug. 3/1 Aunt Emma is banished for ever. **1967** *Ibid.* Aug./Sept. 13/2 He played too much 'Aunt Emma'. **1945** M. DICKENS *Thurs. Afternoons* i. 69 She's got no more idea how to run this house than my Aunt Fanny. **1946** J. IRVING *Royal Navalese* 24 Tell that to my old Aunt Fanny. **1954** 'G. CARR' *Death under Snowdon* v. 54 'Agree my Aunt Fanny,' retorted the other loudly.

aunter, -tre, -trous, etc., obs. ff. *aventure*, ADVENTURE *sb.*, etc.

†**'aunters**, *adv. Obs.* or *dial.* Also 4 **auntre**, 5 **aventurs, awnturs**, 9 **anters**. [f. *aunter, aventure*, ADVENTURE *sb.*: the *-s* (orig. wanting) seems to be genitival, and the word parallel to the contemporary *of aventure*; cf. also *per adventure* (in ME. *paraunter*) and the later *per-hap-s*.]

†**a.** At a venture, at all risks, in any case, at all events. *Obs.* **b.** Peradventure, perhaps.

c **1325** *Cœur de L.* 3878 Auntre, they swore hym hool oth To be hys men. *a* **1450** *Syr Eglamore* 1211 The chylde.. Was aventurs in the felde. *Ibid.* 213 For oon the beste knyghtes art thou, That in thys londe ys levyd now, Awnturs [*Other MSS.* owther] ferre or nere. **1691** RAY *N. Countr. Wds.* 4 *Aunters*, Peradventure, or, in case, if it chance. **1807** J. STAGG *Poems* 54 Or anters in yon mouldering heap, Some luivelier female form I weep.

aunthood ('ɑːnthʊd). [f. AUNT + -HOOD.] The relationship of aunt.

1862 MISS MULOCH *Dom. Stories* 373 This sort of universal aunthood to the whole neighbourhood was by no means disagreeable to Miss Milly.

auntie, aunty ('ɑːntɪ). [see -IE, -Y⁴.] **a.** A familiar, endearing form of *aunt*.

1792 BURNS *Young Lassie*, My auld Auntie Katie upon me taks pity. **1850** MRS. STOWE *Uncle Tom's C.* xxvi, Ask Aunty to come and cut it for me. **1863** *Little People* (Mozley) iv. 37 A little voice called after her, 'Auntie! you've not given me a real good kiss!'

b. In U.S.: 'A familiar term, often used in accosting an elderly woman.' Bartlett *Dict. Amer.* 1860. Applied esp. to a Negress. Also used in Britain, formerly only *dial.* (see E.D.D.), as a term of familiarity or respect applied to an elderly woman. Now increasingly used (*a*) in some social classes by a younger person of an unrelated older family friend, (*b*) *transf.* of an institution, etc., considered to be of conservative style or approach; *spec.* the B.B.C. Cf. AUNT 1 b.

1835 J. H. INGRAHAM *South-West* II. 241 Nor are planters indifferent to the comfort of their gray-headed slaves... They always address them in a mild and pleasant manner as 'Uncle' or 'Aunty'. **1852** *Knickerbocker* Oct. 326 So long as the race of good old colored 'aunties' do the cooking. **1865** G. W. NICHOLS *Story Gt. March* 132 [To Negro woman] 'What was it that struck you, aunty?' **1883** *Harper's Mag.* Oct. 728/2 The negro no longer submits with grace to be called 'uncle' and 'auntie' as of yore. **1931** A. HUXLEY *Music at Night* 134 The *Times* finds it profitable to employ someone..to talk to us every morning about our dear old Culture-Aunties and Uncles. **1937** PARTRIDGE *Dict. Slang* 20/2 *Auntie*..like *uncle*, used by children for a friend of the house. **1938** E. BOWEN *Death of Heart* III. vi. 439 'Rightie-o, auntie,' said the driver. **1958** J. CANNAN *And be a Villain* i. 31, I saw about Uncle Edmund in auntie *Times*. **1959** *Guardian* 14 Oct. 6/2 A part-time teacher..paid her children's 'auntie' £2 a week to take them for afternoon walks. **1959** J. BRAINE *Vodi* xxi. 231 Honestly, that woman's magazine stuff, just the sort of advice these damned aunties give. **1960** WILLMOTT & YOUNG *Family & Class in Lond. Suburb.* i. 4 The East End is a different class altogether—people there call you Dad or Uncle or Auntie. **1962** *Listener* 22 Mar. 529/1 The BBC needs to be braver and sometimes is. So let there be a faint hurrah as Auntie goes over the top. **1968** *Woman* 27 Jan. 18/3, I had read..about Mollie Dundas's unit for autistics at this hospital. Mollie was in urgent need of voluntary 'aunties', substitute mother figures, to work with her in treating them. *Ibid.* 3 Feb. 15/2 At this clinic I had been an 'auntie'..for some months.

auntly ('ɑːntlɪ), *a.* [cf. *motherly*: see -LY¹.]

1844 LADY S. LYTTELTON *Lett.* (1873) 337 My best regards and Auntly blessing to my nephew. **1846** SARA COLERIDGE *Mem. & Lett.* II. 68 This is a very motherly and auntly tale.

auntship ('ɑːnt-ʃɪp). [see -SHIP.] = AUNTHOOD.

1870 LUBBOCK in *Illustr. Lond. News* 1 Oct., On the Sandwich Islands uncleship, auntship, cousinship were ignored.

‖**au pair** (o pɛr, əʊ pɛə(r)). [F., on equality.] Applied to an arrangement between two parties by which mutual domestic services are rendered formerly without consideration of money payment; *esp.* of a young girl learning the language of a foreign country while rendering certain services in return for hospitality. Also *attrib.* Hence as *sb.*, a person who is 'au pair'.

1897 *Girl's Own Paper* 16 Oct. 63/1 An arrangement.. frequently made is for an English girl to enter a French, German or Swiss school and teach her own language in return for joining the usual classes. This is called being *au pair*. **1928** *Sunday Express* 22 July 15 To have a German lady on 'au pair' terms in my house to teach German to my children in return for education in English. **1960** *Oxford Times* 1 Jan. 2/2 *Au pair* to help with young children. **1962** *Times* 22 May 13 An agency for placing *au pair* girls. **1967** *Guardian* 3 July 5/5 The au pair's Italian boy friend.

‖**au pied de la lettre** (o pje də la lɛtr), *phr.* [Fr., lit. 'to the foot of the letter'.] Exactly, down to the last detail; literally.

1782 H. WALPOLE *Let.* 10 Nov. (1904) XII. 368 The Romans..loved to be obeyed *au pied de la lettre*. **1854** MRS. GASKELL *North & South* (1855) II. vi. 78 Some one had told you that stolen fruit tasted sweetest, which you took au pied de la lettre, and off you went a-robbing. **1863** *Blackw. Mag.* Feb. 192/1 She does not always intend that we should believe her *au pied de la lettre*. **1936** A. HUXLEY *Eyeless in Gaza* xiii. 173 A purely figurative and metaphorical sanctity taken *au pied de la lettre*.

‖**aura** ('ɔːrə). [L., a. Gr. αὔρα breath, breeze.]

1. A gentle breeze, a zephyr.

1398 TREVISA *Barth. De P.R.* XI. xv. (1495) 400 Aura is lyghte wynde meuyd. **1635** SWAN *Spec. M.* v. §2 (1643) 88 Such a gale as is commonly called Aura. **1731** in BAILEY.

2. a. A subtle emanation or exhalation from any substance, *e.g.* the aroma of blood, the odour of flowers, etc.

1732 BERKELEY *Alciphr.* II. 35 After which [*i.e.* the flying off of the volatile salt or spirit] the Oil remains dry and insipid, but without any sensible diminution of its weight, by the loss of that volatile essence of the soul, that æthereal aura. **1836** TODD *Cycl. Anat.* II. 466/2 Fecundation is attributable to the agency of an aura from..the seminal fluid.

b. *fig.* Also, a distinctive impression of character or aspect.

1859 J. HOLLAND *Gold Foil* 110 Wrapped in the aura of his ineffable love. **1876** EMERSON *Ess.* Ser. II. i. 28 The condition of true naming, on the poet's part, is his resigning himself to the divine aura which breathes through forms. **1901** *Harper's Mag.* XLI. 808/2 Tragedy is as old as story-writing itself—the *aura* thereof being the very breath of every great drama since Eden. **1921** *Glasgow Herald* 25 Aug. 5 The genteel aura of the upper circle. **1959** *Economist* 27 June 1164/2 No such charges were brought against Mr Strauss, though his Wall Street aura rankles with progressive Democrats.

c. A supposed subtle emanation from and enveloping living persons and things, viewed by mystics as consisting of the essence of the individual, serving as the medium for the operation of mesmeric and similar influences. So **'aural** *a.*³

1870 P. B. RANDOLPH *Seership!* (1884) 77 Peculiar substances can be charged with the efflux or aura of the human being. **1918** VIOLET TWEEDALE *Veiled Woman* vii. 83 [His] personality happens to be very distasteful to me. Our auras don't blend. **1920** ROSE MACAULAY *Potterism* III. i, Unless..the immortal soul wraps itself about in some aural vapour that takes the form it wore on earth.

3. *Electr.* †**a.** = Electrical atmosphere: see ATMOSPHERE *sb.* 3 (*obs.*). **b.** The current of air caused by the discharge of electricity from a sharp point, *e.g.* from those of the electrical whirl.

1737 FRANKLIN *Lett.* Wks. 1840 VI. 2 Divers species of earthquakes, according to the different position, quantity, etc., of this imprisoned aura. **1810** COLERIDGE *Friend* VI. vii. (1867) 317 A fourth composes the electrical aura of oxygen, hydrogen, and caloric. **1863** ATKINSON *Ganot's Physics* §742 On approaching the hand to the whirl while in motion, a slight draught is felt, due to the movement of the electrified air..This draught or wind is known as the electrical aura.

4. *Path.* A sensation, as of a current of cold air rising from some part of the body to the head, which occurs as a premonitory symptom in epilepsy and hysterics.

1776–83 CULLEN *First Lines* (1827) II. 424 Aura Epileptica. **1875** H. WOOD *Therap.* (1879) 353 The patient should..inhale it at once whenever the aura is felt.

aural ('ɔːrəl), *a.*¹ [f. prec. + -AL².] Of or pertaining to the aura.

1869 *Eng. Mech.* 5 Nov. 191/2 Magnetic power depends.. upon the aural condition of the atmosphere.

aural ('ɔːrəl), *a.*² [f. L. *aur-is* ear + -AL¹. (L. would prob. have been *aurīlis*.)] = AURICULAR.

1. Of or pertaining to the organ of hearing.

1847 LEWES *Hist. Philos.* (1853) 251 Acting on the aural nerve. **1878** A. HAMILTON *Nerv. Dis.* 124 Deafness is..the result of the destructive aural disease.

2. Received or perceived by the ear.

1860 *Sat. Rev.* No. 252. 247/2 Continental cities, where he had seen and suffered from ocular, aural, or nasal nuisances. **1863** GEO. ELIOT *Romola* III. xvii. 175 Aural acquaintance with Latin phrases.

aurally ('ɔːrəlɪ), *adv.* [f. AURAL *a.*² + -LY².] Auricularly, by the ear.

1883 R. STORRS *Amer. Ann. Deaf & D.* July 145 To confer speech upon those who have never in any measure caught its clue aurally.

auramine ('ɔːrəmɪn, -iːn). *Chem.* [G. (proprietary, 1884), f. L. *aur-um* gold + AMINE.] A synthetic yellow dyestuff of the diphenylmethane series.

1884 *Jrnl. Chem. Soc.* XLVI. 1450 Auramine..is the first artificial yellow dye which can be fixed on the vegetable fibre with tannic acid like aniline dyes... Auramine also becomes fixed on wool, giving colours of great purity. **1888** *Jrnl. Chem. Soc.* LIV. 156 Commercial auramine is the hydrochloride of a base obtained by the action of ammonium chloride on tetramethyldiamidobenzophenone. **1920** CROSS & BEVAN *Textbk. Paper-Making* (ed. 5) ix. 269 Auramine Yellow, very largely employed in paper dyeing, stands near but not in this group, being a derivative of diphenylmethane. **1963** *Lancet* 5 Jan. 24/2 It is analogous to the detection of isolated tubercle bacilli in sputum after their staining with an auramine-rhodamine dye combination.

aurantia (ɒ'rænʃɪə). [L. *aurantia*: see ORANGE *sb.*¹] An orange-yellow dye colour; see also quot. 1940.

1877 *Jrnl. Chem. Soc.* XXI. 310 Aurantia... This dyestuff ..produces splendid orange tints on wool and silk. **1892** WOODBURY *Encycl. Photogr.* 62 *Aurantia*, a beautiful orange dye, the ammonia salt of an acid. It is used as a sensitiser in orthochromatic photography. *Ibid.*, To make an aurantia screen for orthochromatic photographic purposes. **1940** *Thorpe's Dict. Appl. Chem.* (ed. 4) IV. 14/2 *Aurantia*..is a dyestuff, but is of more importance as an explosive.

aurantiaceous (ɔːˌræntɪ'eɪʃəs), *a. Bot.* [f. mod.L. *aurantiāceæ*, f. *aurantium*, latinized adaptation of ORANGE: see -ACEOUS.] Of or belonging to the N.O. *Aurantiaceæ*, which includes the trees that bear oranges, lemons, and similar fruits.

1837 *Penny Cycl.* VII. 214/1 Citrus, a genus of aurantiaceous plants. **1873** WATTS *Fownes' Chem.* 778 The coniferous and aurantiaceous orders.

‖**aurata** (ɔː'reɪtə). [a. L. *aurāta*, pa. pple. fem. (used subst.) of *aurāre* to gild, f. *aurum* gold.] A gold-coloured fish; prob. the Gilthead or Golden Maid (*Crenilabrus tinca*), a variety of Wrasse.

c **1520** ANDREWE *Noble Lyfe* in *Babees Bk.* 230 A Aurata is a fysshe in the see that hathe a hede shinynge lyke golde. **1854** BADHAM *Halieut.* 42 Open sea fish..such as *e.g.* auratas.

aurate ('ɔːreɪt). *Chem.* [f. L. *aur-um* + -ATE⁴.] A compound of auric oxide with a base.

1838 *Penny Cycl.* XI. 292/1 Auric acid..combines with potash, soda, and barytes, to form..aurates. **1862** PEPPER *Play-bk. Metals* 207 Aurate of ammonia, or fulminating gold.

aurated ('ɔːreɪtɪd), *ppl. a.*¹ [f. L. *aurāt-us* gilded (see AURATA) + -ED.] Resembling or containing gold; gold-coloured, gilded. In *Chem.* Combined with auric acid (*obs.*).

1864 in WEBSTER.

'aurated, *ppl. a.*² [A bad form of AURITED.] 'In Conchology, having ears as in the pecten or scallop shell.' Craig 1847.

1843 in HUMBLE *Dict. Geol.*

†**'aureal,** *a. Obs.* [a. OF. *aureal*, f. L. *aureus* golden, gilded: see -AL¹.] Golden, gilded; yielding gold, auriferous.

1587 M. GROVE *Poems* (1878) 86 The tree with aureal fruit. *c* **1600** NORDEN *Spec. Brit., Cornw.* (1728) 18 The aureall brookes of Scotlande.

aureate ('ɔːriːət), *a.* Also 4–7 **aureat**, 6 **aureait**. [ad. L. *aureātus* decorated with gold, f. *aureus*: see prec. and -ATE².]

1. Golden, gold-coloured.

c **1450** *Crt. Love* 817 With aureat seint about her sides clene. **1599** A. M. *Gabelhouer's Bk. Physic* 378/2 This præcious aureate or goulden water. **1845** D. MOIR in *Blackw. Mag.* LVIII. 410 The aureate furze..lent its peculiar perfume.

2. *fig.* Brilliant or splendid as gold, *esp.* in literary or rhetorical skill; *spec.* designating or characteristic of a highly ornamental literary style or diction (see quots.).

1430 LYDG. *Chron. Troy* Prol., And of my penne the traces to correcte Whiche barrayne is of aureat lycoure. *c* **1505** DUNBAR *Gold. Terge* viii, Zour [Homer and Cicero's] aureat tungs had baith bene all to lyte, For to compyle that paradyce compleit. **1625** PURCHAS *Pilgrims* II. 1847 If I erre, I will beg indulgence of the Pope's aureat magnificence. **1819** T. CAMPBELL *Spec. Brit. Poets* I. II. 93 The prevailing fault of English diction, in the fifteenth century, is redundant ornament, and an affectation of anglicising Latin words. In this pedantry and use of '*aureate terms*', the Scottish versifiers went even beyond their brethren of the south. **1908** G. G. SMITH in *Camb. Hist. Eng. Lit.* II. iv. 93 The chief effort was to transform the simpler word and phrase into 'aureate' mannerism, to 'illumine' the vernacular. **1919** J. C. MENDENHALL *Aureate Terms* i. 7 Such long and supposedly elegant words have been dubbed 'aureate terms', because..they represent a kind of verbal gilding of literary style. The phrase may be traced back..in the sense of long Latinical words of learned aspect, used to express a comparatively simple idea. **1936** C. S. LEWIS *Allegory of Love* vi. 252 This peculiar brightness..is the final cause of the whole aureate style.

aureation (ˌɔːriː'eɪʃən). [f. AUREATE *a.* + -TION.] The condition of being aureate in literary style.

1908 G. SAINTSBURY in *Camb. Hist. Eng. Lit.* II. viii. 219 Undue aureation and undue beggarliness being equally avoided. **1936** C. S. LEWIS *Allegory of Love* vi. 251 The aureation of his allegories.

aureity (ɔː'riːɪtɪ). [f. L. *aure-us* golden + -ITY.] The peculiar properties of gold; goldenness.

1824 COLERIDGE *Aids Refl.* App. C. (1858) I. 379 The properties peculiar to gold were..generalized in the term Aureity. **1847** LEWES *Hist. Philos.* (1867) II. 219 Having no more objective existence than the lapidity of stone, the aureity of gold.

aurelia (ɒ'riːlɪə, ɔː-, ə-). [a. It. *aurelia* 'the [silk] worm when shut up in his pod' (Baretti); from fem. of *aurelio* 'shining like gold, yellow, golden; also the little wings of butterflies' (Florio 1598); f. L *aurum* gold; thus synonymous with *chrysalis*, Gr. χρυσαλλίς, f. χρυσός gold.]

1. *Ent.* The chrysalis or pupa of an insect, *esp.* of a butterfly. (Now scarcely in use, chrysalis being the ordinary term.)

1607 TOPSELL *Serpents* 669 All Caterpillers are not converted into Aureliaes. **1667** BOYLE *Orig. Formes & Qual.*, Then Aurelia's (or husked Maggots), and then Butterflies. **1713** DERHAM *Phys. Theol.* VIII. v. 409 They retire to Places of Safety..and put on their Aurelia or

Chrysalis State. **1854** H. MILLER *Footpr. Creat.* viii. (1874) 152 An intermediate period of apparent death as an inert aurelia.

†**2.** The Gold-flower (*Heliochrysum Stœchas*). *Obs.*

1598 FLORIO [*Aurelia*, the herb called Mothweede, or golden Floweramour, or golden Stœchados or Cudweede], *Eliocriss*, the gold flower or herbe Aurelia.

3. *Zool.* A genus of phosphorescent marine animals of the class *Acalephæ*.

1876 BENEDEN *Anim. Parasites* 33 Alex. Agassiz once found a Hyperina on the disc of an Aurelia.

au'relian, *a.* and *sb.* [f. prec. + -AN.]

A. *adj.* Of or pertaining to an aurelia; *gen.* gold-coloured, golden.

1791 E. DARWIN *Bot. Gard.* I. 134 Glad Zephyr..pausing flings Soft showers of roses from Aurelian [? butterfly] wings. **1883** C. HOLDER in *Harper's Mag.* Jan. 181/2 The..dysmorphosa..illumines it with a light of deep aurelian hue.

B. *sb.* A collector and breeder of insects, especially of butterflies and moths; a lepidopterist.

1778 M. HARRIS (*title*), Aurelian; or, Natural History of English Insects, namely, Moths and Butterflies..and their standard names, as given and established by the Society of Aurelians. **1816** KIRBY & SP. *Entomol.* (1843) II. 244 A butterfly called by Aurelians the large Skipper.

‖**aureola** (ɔːˈriːələ). [L., fem. (sc. *corona*) of adj. *aureolus* golden, prop. 'somewhat golden,' dim. of *aureus*, f. *aurum* gold. In sense 1 taken as equivalent to *coronula* 'little crown,' as to which see quot. 1626.]

1. *Mediæval* and *R.C. Ch.* The celestial crown won by a martyr, virgin, or doctor, as victor over the world, the flesh, or the devil; the special degree of glory which distinguishes these.

(According to Josephus Angles in Du Cange, the *aureola* or *coronula* of virgins is white, that of martyrs red, that of doctors green.)

1483 CAXTON *Gold. Leg.* 348/1 The vyrgyns shall haue the crowne that is callyd Aureola. **1626** DONNE *Serm.* (1640) 743 Because in their Translation, in the Vulgat Edition of the Roman Church, they find in Exodus xxv. 25 that word *Aureolam.* Facies Coronam *aureolam*, Thou shalt make a lesser Crowne of gold; out of this diminutive, and mistaken word, they have established a Doctrine, that besides those *Coronæ aureæ*, Those Crowns of gold, which are communicated to all the Saints from the Crown of Christ, some Saints have made to themselves, and produced out of their owne extraordinary merits, certaine *Aureolas*, certaine lesser Crownes of their own..And these *Aureolaes* they ascribe onely to three sorts of persons, to Virgins, to Martyrs, to Doctors. **1640** *Canterbur. Self-Convict.* Postcr. 21 That..the keeping of the three Monastick vowes doth deserve an augmentation, as ye call it, an Aureola above common happinesse. **1702** DODWELL in *S. Parker's Tully de Fin.* B ij b, The Schoolmen themselves allow such publick Endeavours a Title to an Aureola of a Doctor.

2. = AUREOLE *sb.* 2, 3.

1727–51 CHAMBERS *Cycl.*, *Aureola*, the crown of glory, given by painters and statuaries, to saints, martyrs, and confessors. **1877** FARRAR *Thy Youth* iv. 40 Though no visible aureola gleam as yet around their brows.

3. = AUREOLE *sb.* 4, 5.

1871 tr. *Schellen's Spectr. Anal.* §51. 227 The magnificent corona or aureola burst into view..round the black edge of the moon. **1884** WOOLSON in *Harper's Mag.* Jan. 190/2 She floated into the..breakfast-room in an aureola of white lace.

aureole (ˈɔːriːəʊl), *sb.* [ad. L. *aureola*; see prec. Cf. OF. *aureole* adj. 'golden,' mod.F. *auréole* sb.]

1. = AUREOLA 1.

c **1220** *Hali Meid.* 23 Þe meidenes habben upo þat [*i.e.* the champion's crown] a gerlaunde(sche) schinende schenre þen þe sunne, Auriole ihaten o latines ledene. **1413** LYDG. *Pylgr. Sowle* v. iii. (1483) 93 Seynt Powle claymed by the deth that he suffred the Aureole of martirs; by gods word that he preched and taught besily he must..were also the aureole of prechours. *c* **1440** HYLTON *Scala Perf.* (W. de W. 1494) lxi, Thyse thre werkes..shull haue specyall mede whyche they callen aureole. **1502** *Ord. Crysten Men* (W. de W. 1506) v. vii. 422 Glorye accedentall excellent and synguler, the whiche glorye is named and called aureole, the whiche is as moche to say as a lytell crowne. **1884** ADDIS & ARNOLD *Cath. Dict.*, *Aureole*..is defined as a certain accidental reward added to the essential bliss of heaven, because of the excellent victory which the person who receives it has attained during his warfare upon earth.

2. *Art.* Properly: The gold disc surrounding the head (or ? the whole figure) in early pictures, and denoting the glory of the personage represented; *hence*, applied by some to **a.** The radiant circle of light depicted around the head; by others to **b.** The oblong glory, or *vesica*, with which divine figures are surrounded.

Didron (*Iconographie Chrétienne* p. 109) by a strange blunder takes *aureola* for a diminutive of *aura* 'emanation, exhalation,' and defines it as a mantle of light emanating from and enveloping the body, as distinct from the *nimbus*, which he confines to the head. This definition, which reverses the historical use both of *aureola* and *nimbus*, is not accepted in France (see Littré), but has been copied by Fairholt, and various English Dictionaries.

a. **1848** MRS. JAMESON *Sacr. & Leg. Art* (1850) 12 The glory round the head is properly the nimbus or aureole. **1860** O. MEREDITH *Lucile* II. VI. §2 In the light of the aureole over her head. **1871** ROSSETTI *Jenny* 230 The gilded aureole In which our highest painters place Some living woman's simple face.

b. **1851** *Didron's Chr. Iconog.* (transl. by E. J. Millington) I. 107 The aureole surrounds the entire body. **1880** E. VENABLES in Smith's *Dict. Chr. Antiq.* s.v. *Nimbus*, The aureole (*aureola*, the golden reward of special holiness) may be defined as the nimb of the body, as the ordinary nimbus is that of the head.

3. *fig.* A glorifying halo.

1852 J. H. NEWMAN *Univ. Educ.* 363 In his beaming countenance Philip had recognized the aureol of a saint. **1861** O. W. HOLMES *Elsie V.* 344 The aureole of young womanhood had not yet begun to fade from around her. **1869** LECKY *Europ. Mor.* II. iv. 281 The aureole which the genius of Theodoric cast around his throne. **1871** R. H. HUTTON *Ess.* I. 326 Shrinking infirmity and self-contempt, hidden in a sort of aureole of revelations abundant beyond measure—that was St. Paul.

4. *transf.* An actual halo of radiating light; *esp.* in *Astr.* that seen in eclipses.

1857 B. TAYLOR *N. Trav.* xxv. 256 All faces..tinged by the same wonderful aureole, shone as if transfigured. **1861** LYTTON *Str. Story* II. 383 There, on the threshold, gathering round her bright locks the aureole of the glorious sun, stood Amy. **1871** PROCTOR *Light Sc.* 105 The glorious aureole of light seen around the sun during total eclipses.

5. *transf.* or *fig.* in wider sense.

1842 MRS. BROWNING *Grk. Chr. Poets* (1863) 89 An inseparable aureole of sweet sound. **1867** MISS BRADDON *Aur. Floyd* iv. 34 Bulstrode's ideal woman..crowned with an aureole of pale auburn hair.

6. *Geol.* The belt of metamorphosed rocks surrounding an igneous intrusion.

[**1884** A. J. JUKES-BROWNE *Student's Handbk. Physical Geol.* II. xii. 442 By French writers the term *aureole* has been introduced to designate the concentric zone of metamorphosed rock which surrounds an intrusive mass of igneous rock.] **1896** J. F. KEMP *Handbk. Rocks* 126 *Aureole*, the area surrounding an igneous intrusion that is affected by contact metamorphism. **1905** J. GEIKIE *Structural & Field Geol.* xv. 214 The zone or aureole of altered rocks surrounding a large batholith of granite may be a mile or more in width.

aureole (ˈɔːriːəʊl), *v.* [f. AUREOLE *sb.*] *trans.* To encircle with or as with an aureole or halo. Chiefly in *pa. pple.*

1888 *Macm. Mag.* July 188 Their forms are intertwined with rainbows and aureoled with light. **1896** MARY COWDEN-CLARKE *My Long Life* 13 His seraph-like face,..aureoled by its golden hair. **1905** C. KERNAHAN *Visions* 240 The cloud-rack which aureoled the moon. **1933** L. A. G. STRONG *Sea Wall* 258 The slanting rays of the sun aureoled it with mellow gold.

aureoled (ˈɔːriːəʊld), *ppl. a.* [f. AUREOLE *sb.* + -ED[2]: cf. F. *auréolé.*] Encircled with an aureole.

1860 MISS MULOCH in *Macm. Mag.* II. 40 This, this is *Thou*. No idle painter's dream Of aureoled, imaginary, Christ. **1878** B. TAYLOR *Deukalion* II. iv. 76 Aureoled faces.

aureolin (ˈɔːrɪəlɪn, ɔːˈriːəlɪn). [f. L. *aureol-us* (see above) + -IN.] A transparent yellow pigment.

1879 ROOD *Chromatics* 57 Pigments which approximate to pure yellow in hue, such as gamboge and aureolin. **1882** *Sci. Gossip* 1 Mar. 49.

aureoline (ˈɔːrɪəlaɪn), *a. rare.* [f. as prec. + -INE.] Gold-coloured, golden-hued.

1881 *Daily News* 14 Apr. 5/2 More or less aureoline preparations filled the windows of the barbers' shops.

aureomycin (ˌɔːriːəˈmaɪsɪn). [f. L. *aure-us* golden + Gr. μύκ-ης fungus + -IN[1].] Name of an antibiotic substance, chlortetracycline, derived from the mould *Streptomyces aureofaciens*, or produced artificially, and used in medical treatment esp. of lung and rickettsial diseases.

1948 B. M. DUGGAR in *Ann. N.Y. Acad. Sci.* LI. 177 We are concerned with a species of the established *Streptomyces*, for which the name *Streptomyces aureofaciens* is being proposed... The antibiotic (aureomycin) from this species of mold will be evaluated. **1948** *Lancet* 16 Oct. 618/1 Aureomycin, derived from a strain of *Streptomyces aureofaciens* and effective against numerous gram-positive and gram-negative organisms..has been obtained as a yellow crystalline hydrochloride. **1949** H. W. FLOREY et al. *Antibiotics* II. 1533 The action of aureomycin was thought to be bacteriostatic rather than bactericidal. **1949** *Britannica Bk. of Yr.* 687/1 *Aureomycin*,..a golden-coloured antibiotic related to streptomycin, and effective in some diseases where streptomycin and penicillin fail.

aurequere, var. of OURWHERE *adv.* anywhere.

‖**au reste** (o rɛst), *phr.* [F.] As for the rest.

1619 J. CHAMBERLAIN *Let.* 26 June in T. Birch *Court & Times Jas. I* (1848) II. 176 *Au reste*, he is fallen to his old diet. **1752** H. WALPOLE *Let.* 6 June (1903) III. 97 *Au reste*, he is just where he was. **1825** H. WILSON *Memoirs* I. i. 22 'Au reste,' continued Julia, 'some day, perhaps soon, you shall know all about me.' **1853** C. BRONTË *Villette* I. xi. 193 Au reste it was only the most temporary expedient in the world.

ˈaureus. (ˈɔːrɪəs). Pl. aurei (-aɪ). [L., substantival use (sc. *nummus*) of *aureus* golden, f. *aurum* gold.] **1.** A Roman gold coin of the late republic and empire, of the value of 25 silver denarii.

1609 HOLLAND *Amm. Marcell.* xx. iv. 149 He..promised unto them all throughout five *aurei* apeece. *a* **1666** EVELYN *Diary* c 7 May an. 1645 (1955) II. 398 As to Coynes & Medails..10 Asses make the Roman Denarius,..10 Denarius's an Aureus. **1895** G. ALLEN *The Woman who Did* xv. 162 His profile was clear-cut, like Trajan's on an aureus. **1940** *Oxoniensia* V. 142 The donation of..an *aureus* of Hadrian, and a *siliqua* of Gratian. **1959** *Chambers's Encycl.* X. 127/2 Constantine gave it a last reform, introducing an aureus of gold of 72 to the pound which lasted to the end of the empire.

†**2.** (See quot.) *Obs.*

1658 ROWLAND *Mouffet's Theat. Ins.* 1055 Take Birthwort round and long, each one aureus. **1881** *Syd. Soc. Lex.*, *Aureus*, a weight of a drachm and a half.

‖**au revoir** (‖o rəvwar, əʊrəvˈwɑː(r)). [F., = lit. 'to the seeing again', i.e. in anticipation of seeing (meeting) you again.] An expression implying farewell for the present; hence as *sb.*, a farewell of this kind. Also occurs in slang abbrevs. ***aurev.***, ***au 'voir***, and as a malapropism in the form ***au reservoir***.

1694 N. H. *Ladies Dict.* 15/1 He must kiss his Landlady.., and so parting, says *a Revoir*, Madam, till I see you again. **1761** CHESTERF. *Let. to his Son* 6 Dec. (1774) 455 *Au revoir*, as Sir Fopling says, and God bless you. **1801** MARIA EDGEWORTH *Belinda* II. xv. 117 Instead of adieu, I shall only say—*Au revoir!* **1853** 'C. BEDE' *Adv. Verdant Green* x. 93 I'm going now in search of an appetite, and I should advise you to take a turn round the Parks and do the same. *Au reservoir!* **1905** *Daily Mail* 5 Aug. 6/1 The King and Queen, after an au revoir of ceremonious courtesy, left for their own yacht. **1921** T. E. LAWRENCE *Let.* 1 Oct. (1938) 334 This life goes on till February 28 next year. Au 'voir. **1922** JOYCE *Ulysses* 418 Au reservoir, Mossoo. Tanks you. **1924** GALSWORTHY *White Monkey* I. viii. 59 Oh! Well! You'll bob in anyway. Aurev! **1948** S. G. SPAETH *Hist. Pop. Mus. in Amer.* (1960) vi. 221 That lilting waltz..appeared in 1892, and in the following year Harry Kennedy made his lasting gift to barber-shop quartets with *Say Au Revoir but Not Goodbye.*

auric (ˈɔːrɪk), *a.*[1] [f. L. *aur-um* gold + -IC.] Of or pertaining to gold. Applied in *Chem.* to compounds in which gold combines as a triad, e.g. *Auric Iodide* Au I_3, *Auric oxide* (or *acid*), Au_2O_3.

1838 *Penny Cycl.* XI. 292/1 Teroxide of Gold..has been called *auric acid.* **1876** BARTHOLOW *Mat. Med.* (1879) 209 These auric preparations promote the appetite.

auric (ˈɔːrɪk), *a.*[2] [f. AURA + -IC.] Of or pertaining to an aura.

1889 in *Cent. Dict.* **1910** *Westm. Gaz.* 13 Apr. 5/2 An auric veil. **1921** GALSWORTHY *To Let* I. vi. 62 Why! Look at their photographs of auric presences. **1956** R. M. LESTER *Towards Hereafter* iii. 39 Every one of us has auric radiations.

aurichalcite (ɔːrɪˈkælsaɪt). *Min.* [f. (by Böttger 1839) *aurichalcum*, erroneous spelling (after *aurum* gold) of L. *orichalcum* 'yellow copper ore, or the brass made of it,' a. Gr. ὀρείχαλκον 'mountain-copper.' So called, because, when reduced, it yields brass, 'a gold-coloured alloy of copper and zinc,' whence Sage in 1791 had suggested its possible identity with the '*aurichalcum* of the ancients' (Dana.) Some authors write *orichalcite*, but as the false etymology influenced the choice of the name, Dana retains *auri-*.]

A cuprous hydrozincite, of pale green, verdigris, or sky-blue colour.

1844–68 DANA *Min.* 712.

auricle (ˈɔːrɪk(ə)l). [ad. L. *auricula* external ear, ear-lap, dim. of *auris* ear: cf. F. *auricule.*]

1. The external ear of animals. Formerly sometimes restricted to the lower lobe or 'lap' of the human ear.

1653 BULWER *Anthropomet.* viii. 144 A certaine Nation, whose Auricles are so great, that they hang down to their shoulders..Where men had not onely hanging Eares, but broad and large Auricles. **1748** HARTLEY *Observ. Man* I. ii. §5 ¶64 The Auricle and *Meatus Auditorius* are cartilaginous. **1874** ROOSA *Dis. Ear* 53 The auricle..has as its functions the reception, reflection, and condensation of the waves of sound.

b. *trans.* An 'ear' or ear-hole.

1859 HAWTHORNE *Fr. & It. Jrnls.* II. 300 The penitent..poured his sins through a perforated auricle into this unseen receptacle.

2. A process shaped liked the lower lobe or 'lap' of the human ear; a lobe; *esp.* in *Bot.* and *Conch.* (Cf. AURICULATE.)

1665 *Phil. Trans.* I. 87 A stone..having three Auricles or crisped Angles. **1851** RICHARDSON *Geol.* viii. 242 The auricles are the processes on each side of the umbones. **1861** MRS. LANKESTER *Wild Fl.* 74 The upper leaves..embracing the stem by pointed auricles.

3. Name of the two upper cavities of the heart, which, in mammals, birds, and reptiles, receive blood from the veins and lungs respectively. (Fishes have only one auricle.)

1664 POWER *Exp. Philos.* I. 40 In this Cartilaginous Pericardium [of the Lamprey]..is likewise the Auricle co-included. **1748** HARTLEY *Observ. Man* I. ii. §7 ¶74 The contraction of the Auricle of the Heart. **1847** YOUATT *Horse* xi. 239 Called auricles, from their supposed resemblance to the ear of a dog.

4. A kind of ear-trumpet for the deaf.

1864 WEBSTER cites MANSFIELD.

ˈauricled, *ppl. a.* [f. prec. + -ED[2].] Furnished with an auricle or auricles, auriculate.

1821 S. GRAY *Brit. Plants* II. 3 Leaflets sub-auricled at the base. **1872** OLIVER *Elem. Bot.* II. 212 A straggling deciduous shrub, with..auricled leaves.

auricomous (ɔːˈrɪkəməs), *a.* [f. L. *auricom-us* (f. *auri-*, comb. form of *aurum* gold + *coma* hair) + -OUS.] Of or pertaining to golden hair.
1864 in *N. & Q.* Ser. III. VI. 282 The Auricomous Fluid of another professor. **1882** MISS BRADDON *Mt. Royal* II. ix. 182 The auricomous tangles..or the flaxen fringe.

‖**auricula** (ɔːˈrɪkjʊlə). [L.: see AURICLE.]
1. = AURICLE 1.
1691 RAY *Creation* II. (1701) 271 The outward ear or Auricula.
2. (See quot.)
1877 HUXLEY *Anat. Inv. An.* ix. 574 In the Echinoida, ambulacral plates of the oral margin of the corona are produced into five perpendicular perforated processes, which arch over the ambulacra and are called the auriculæ.
3. *Bot.* (Formerly also *auriculus.*) A species of Primula, also called Bear's-ear, named from the shape of its leaves; formerly a great favourite with flower-fanciers, producing under cultivation trusses of many blooms, the corollas often powdered with white or grey.
1655 *Antheologia* 4 Marigolds, Wall-flowers, Auriculusses. **1713** *Flying-Post* 20 Oct., The finest Collection of Aurickelouses that are in England. **1728** THOMSON *Spring* 533 Auriculas, enrich'd With shining meal o'er all their velvet leaves. **1807** CRABBE *Par. Reg.* I. 151 Tulips tall-stemmed and pounced auriculas rise.
4. A genus of pulmoniferous molluscs, found chiefly in brackish swamps in the tropics.
1843 in HUMBLE *Dict. Geol.* **1856** WOODWARD *Fossil Shells* 11 The auriculas live on the sea-shore, or in salt marshes.

auricular (ɔːˈrɪkjʊlə(r)), *a.* and *sb.* Also 6 aurycular(e. [ad. med.L. *auriculāris*, f. *auricula*: see prec. and -AR¹. Cf. F. *auriculaire*, 16th c.]
A. *adj.* **1.** Of or pertaining to the ear.
1649 BULWER *Pathomyot.* II. ii. 108 Having the auricular muscles bigger than ordinary. **1850** SIR W. JARDINE *Humming Birds* I. 48 Forming auricular tufts of the same colour.
2. Perceived by the ear; audible.
1579 G. HARVEY *Letter-Bk.* (1884) 61 Quippinge notorious or auricular iybinge on every hande. **1605** SHAKS. *Lear* I. ii. 99 You shall..by an Auricular assurance haue your satisfaction. **1654** LESTRANGE *Chas. I* (1655) 92 So suddain a death afforded him not the respiration of auricular contrition.
†**b.** Hearsay, oral, traditional. *Obs.*
1605 BACON *Adv. Learn.* I. iv. §11. **1626** —— *Sylva* §326 The Alchemists call in..auricular traditions, feigned testimonies of ancient authors and the like.
c. *esp.* (in ***auricular confession***): Addressed to the ear; told privately in the ear.
1542 BRINKLOW *Complaynt* xix. (1874) 46 That auryculare confessyon, which is the preuy chamber of treason. **1651** C. CARTWRIGHT *Cert. Relig.* I. 164 The Popish confession is auricular (as it is called), secret, in the eare of a Priest. **1839** HALLAM *Hist. Lit.* (1847) II. 22 The practice of auricular confession brought with it an entire science of casuistry.
†**3.** Addressing, affecting, or employing the ear only (to the exclusion of mental apprehension).
1589 PUTTENHAM *Eng. Poesie* (Arb.) 172 Reaching no higher then th'eare and forcing the mynde little or nothing ..is the office of the auricular figures. **1638** MEDE *Rev. God's House* 54 (T.) By hearing is meant in this place not auricular hearing but practical. **1740** CIBBER *Apol.* (1756) I. 74 Not mere auricular imitators of one another.
4. ***auricular witness***: one who relates what he has heard. (Cf. *ocular*, and F. *témoin auriculaire.*)
1642 HOWELL *For. Trav.* (Arb.) 13 One eye-witness is of more validity than ten auricular. **1878** *Daily News* 9 Jan. 6/1 Alluded to as an auricular witness by the *Estafette*.
5. Pertaining to the auricle of the heart.
1870 ROLLESTON *Anim. Life* 101 This 'pericardial' or 'auricular' membrane. **1872** HUXLEY *Phys.* ii. 42 The moment the auricular systole is over.
6. Shaped like an auricle.
1857 BULLOCK *Cazeaux's Midwif.* 21 A semilunar articular surface..called the auricular facet. **1872** NICHOLSON *Palæont.* 211 Tubular spines..abundant upon the auricular expansion.
B. *sb.* An auricular organ or part. *spec.* **a.** A tuft of feathers covering the orifice of a bird's ear. **b.** The little finger, as the one most easily inserted in the ear: cf. Fr. *doigt auriculaire*.
1797 BEWICK *Brit. Birds* (1847) I. 12 The plumage..plain on the auriculars. *a* **1845** HOOD *Tale Trumpet* iii, For each auricular Was deaf as a post. **1874** COUES *Birds N.-W.* 126 A post-ocular stripe just over the auriculars.

au'ricularly, *adv.* [f. prec. + -LY².] In auricular manner: **a.** In one's ear, in a whisper (see AURICULAR *a.* 2); †**b.** So as to affect the ear only (see AURICULAR *a.* 3); **c.** By means of auricles.
1589 PUTTENHAM *Eng. Poesie* (Arb.) 182 Your figures that worke auricularly by exchange. **1667** *Decay Chr. Piety* vii. §4. 260 These will soon confess, and that not auricularly, but in a loud and audible voice. **1847** CRAIG, *Auricularly stem-clasping*, having auricles at the base clasping the stem; applied to leaves.

auriculate (ɔːˈrɪkjʊlət), *ppl. a.* [f. L. *auricula* AURICLE + -ATE².] Furnished with auricles or ear-like appendages.
1. *Bot.* Of leaves: Having at the base a pair of small, blunt projections, shaped like the lower lobe of the human ear.
1713 PETIVER in *Phil. Trans.* XXVIII. 54 With auriculate Leaves. **1857** HENFREY *Elem. Bot.* §88 If a sessile leaf has a cordate base, it becomes auriculate or eared.
2. *Conch.* Having an ear-shaped projection or process on one or both sides of the *umbones* or bosses, as in certain bivalves.
1854 WOODWARD *Man. Mollusca* II. 233 *Producta*..shell free, auriculate. **1872** NICHOLSON *Palæont.* 211 The shell is auriculate, or furnished with ear-like expansions.

auriculated (-eɪtɪd), *ppl. a.* [f. prec. + -ED.] = prec. ***auriculated*** (or ***sociable***) ***vulture***: a species of vulture which has a fleshy crest extending from each ear along the side of the neck.
1711 PETIVER in *Phil. Trans.* XXVII. 385 Having auriculated..Radish-like Leaves. **1809** G. SHAW *Zool.* VII. 24 The auriculated Vulture or Oricou.

auriculately, *adv.* [f. as prec. + -LY².] In auriculate manner.
1858 DRURY *Useful Pl. India* 470 Auriculately sagittate, eared at the base, so as to give the leaf the appearance of the head of an arrow.

auriculo- (ɔːˈrɪkjʊləʊ), comb. f. of AURICLE [f. L. *auricula*], as in ***auriculo-temporal***, ***-ventricular***, etc.
1836 TODD *Cycl. Anat. & Phys.* I. 330/2 The auriculo-ventricular orifice is an oblique slit. **1881** MIVART *Cat* 273 The auriculo-temporal nerve.

au'riculoid, *a.* [f. L. *auricul-a* + -OID.] Shaped like an auricula or auricle: cf. AURICULA 4.
1856 WOODWARD *Man. Mollusca* III. 397 The most remarkable land-shells..are the great auriculoid Bulimi.

aurielet, obs. form of OREILLET.

aurient, obs. form of ORIENT.

auriferous (ɔːˈrɪfərəs), *a.* [f. L. *aurifer* (f. *auri-* comb. f. *aurum* gold + *-fer* producing) + -OUS.] Containing or yielding gold; *lit.* and *fig.* Hence **auriferously** *adv.*
1727 THOMSON *Summer* 648 Whence many a bursting stream auriferous plays. **1849** MURCHISON *Siluria* i. (1867) 18 Those slaty rocks which bear the chief auriferous quartz-veins. **1855** DICKENS *Dorrit* II. xvi. 390 Only one thing sat otherwise than auriferously..on Mr. Dorrit's mind.

‖**aurifex** (ˈɔːrɪfɛks). [L., f. *auri-* gold + *-fex* maker, worker.] A worker in gold; a goldsmith.
1862 *Athenæum* 30 Aug. 276 The tutelary aurifex to whom has been attributed the chair of King Dagobert himself.

aurific (ɔːˈrɪfɪk), *a.* [f. L. *auri-* gold + *-fic-us* making: cf. mod.F. *aurifique.*] Producing gold.
1667 BOYLE *Orig. Formes & Qual.*, An Aurifick Powder. **1671** J. WEBSTER *Metallogr.* xxix. 365 Seed of an aurifick or argentifick nature. **1881** in *Syd. Soc. Lex.*

aurification (ˌɔːrɪfɪˈkeɪʃən). [n. of action f. AURIFY: see -ATION. Also in mod.F.] Working in gold; *spec.* the stopping of a tooth with gold.
1881 *Times* 2 Feb. 12/1 Technically described as dental autoprothesis with aurification.

auriflamb(e, obs. form of ORIFLAMME.

auriform (ˈɔːrɪfɔːm), *a.* [f. L. *auri-s* ear + -FORM.] Shaped like an (usually the human) ear.
1816 KIRBY & SP. *Entomol.* (1843) II. 239 Two auriform respiratory organs. **1836** TODD *Cycl. Anat. & Phys.* I. 691/2 Two auriform appendages.

aurify (ˈɔːrɪfaɪ), *v.* [f. L. *auri-* comb. f. *aurum* gold + -FY, L. *-ficāre* to make. Cf. F. *aurifier.*] *trans.* and *intr.* To turn into gold.
1652 Ashmole's *Theat. Chem.* 369 Made full pure And aurified. **1687** *Turkish Spy* IV. xx. 354 Mercury..aurifies the very seed of Gold. **1800** LAMB in *Lett.* (1837) vi. 54 Guineas that now lie ripening and aurifying in..some undiscovered Potosi.

‖**auriga** (ɔːˈraɪgə). [L.] A charioteer. †**a.** *fig.* Leader (*obs.*). **b.** *Astr.* One of the northern constellations, the Waggoner. †**c.** *Phys.* The fourth lobe of the liver (*obs.*). †**d.** *Med.* A bandage for the sides (*obs.*).
c **1430** LYDG. *Min. Poems* (1844) 139 Tyl blissed Austyn, by goostly elloquence Was trewe Auriga of foure gospelleeris. **1868** AIRY *Pop. Astron.* i. 7 The bright star Capella..in the constellation Auriga.

au'rigal, *a.* *rare*⁻⁰. [ad. L. *aurīgālis*: see prec. and -AL¹.] Of or pertaining to a charioteer.
1864 in WEBSTER.

aurigation (ɔːrɪˈgeɪʃən). [ad. L. *aurīgātiōn-em*, n. of action f. *aurīgāre* to drive a chariot.] The action or art of driving a chariot or coach.
1623 in COCKERAM. **1849** DE QUINCEY *Mail Coach* Wks. IV. 332 All the skill in aurigation of Apollo himself.

Aurignac, name used *attrib.* (See next.)
1863 C. LYELL *Geol. Evidences Antiquity of Man* x. 192 The Aurignac cave adds no new species to the list of extinct quadrupeds. **1875** *Encycl. Brit.* II. 336 [The bones of] other extinct mammals, alongside of human remains and works of art, in the famous Aurignac caves of the Pyrenees. **1939** R. CAMPBELL *Flowering Rifle* II. 61 The Aurignac man could spare us better bones. **1946** F. E. ZEUNER *Dating Past* ix. 299 The foyer..contains Aurignac bone points.

Aurignacian (ɔːrɪˈnjeɪʃ(ɪ)ən), *a.* and *sb.* [ad. F. *Aurignacien* (H. Breuil 1906, in *Comptes Rendus Congr. Int. d'Anthrop.* 329), f. the place-name *Aurignac* (France) + -IAN.] **A.** *adj.* Of or pertaining to the Aurignac cave of the Pyrenees; belonging to the *Aurignac era* or *period*, that indicated by the remains and works of art found in the cave. Also *absol.*
1914 *Q. Jrnl. Geol. Soc.* LXX. p. xcviii, A bed was found, which yielded the incised drawings..as well as numerous mammalian remains and flint-implements; and this is regarded as of Aurignacian age. Immediately below the last-mentioned bed a deposit of sand..was penetrated..and this deposit, also referred to the Aurignacian, was found to contain an enormous number of bones. **1920** J. RITCHIE *Influence Man Anim. Life Scot.* VI. iii. 344 The Aurignacian painting of two Reindeer fronting each other. **1920** *Q. Rev.* Oct. 377 The course of Art, from the Aurignacian era (circa 35,000 B.C.) till to-day. **1926** *Times Lit. Suppl.* 2 Sept. 574/3 During the greater part of the upper palæolithic age the culture of Europe was what is termed Aurignacian.
B. *sb.* A man or woman of this period.
1915 R. LANKESTER *Diversions of Naturalist* xxx. 280 Bushman-like Aurignacians. **1963** E. S. WOOD *Field Guide Archæol.* II. ii. 102 Aurignacians lived in Paviland Cave, Gower (Glamorgan).

‖**au'rigo.** *Obs.* [L., var. of *aurūgo.*] Jaundice.
1398 TREVISA *Barth. De P.R.* VIII. liii. (1495) 266 The yelowe jawndes is callyd Aurigo. **1731** in BAILEY. **1795** TATE tr. *Cowley's Plants* 36 For if with gold alone the soul's inflam'd, It has th' aurigo from the metal nam'd.

aurigraphy (ɔːˈrɪgrəfɪ). [ad. med.L. *aurigraphia*, f. L. *auri-* gold + Gr. *-γραφία* writing.] 'A writing or graving in gold.' Blount *Gl.* 1656.

aurilave (ˈɔːrɪleɪv). [f. L. *auri-s* ear + *lav-* stem of *lavāre* to wash.] An instrument for cleansing the external ear and auditory meatus.
1874 ROOSA *Dis. Ear* 122 A very small sponge attached to an appropriate handle, called an aurilave.

aurin (ˈɔːrɪn). *Chem.* [f. L. *aur-um* gold + -IN.] A red colouring matter produced (by Kolbe and Schmidt in 1861) by heating phenol with oxalic acid and strong sulphuric acid.
1869 *Eng. Mech.* 19 Mar. 586/3 Rosolic acid, or aurine.. from coaltar. **1883** *Athenæum* 10 Mar. 316/2 Aurin.

auriphrygiate (ɔːrɪˈfrɪdʒɪət), *ppl. a.* [ad. med.L. *auriphrygiātus*, f. *auriphrygium* gold fringe or embroidery: cf. cl. L. *phrygio* an embroiderer in gold.] Embroidered or fringed with gold.
1814 SOUTHEY *Roderick* XVIII. Wks. IX. 164 Nor wore he mitre here, Precious or auriphrygiate. **1815** —— *Life & Corr.* (1850) IV. 107 The *auriphrygiate* is the only piece of pedantry that I acknowledge..and I was tempted to it by the grandiloquence of the word.

†**auri'pigment.** *Obs.* [ad. L. *auripigmentum* (also in Eng. use), = *auri* of gold + *pigmentum* colouring matter. Now replaced by the form ORPIMENT through Fr.] A bright yellow mineral, the trisulphide of arsenic (As_2S_3), used by painters under the name of King's Yellow. Cf. ARSENIC 1 a.
1398 TREVISA *Barth. De P.R.* XVI. vi. (1495) 555 Yf auripigment be layed to brasse it maketh the brasse whyte. **1596** W. P. *Bk. of Secrets* 9 Take Auripigmentum and red lead. **1607** TOPSELL *Four-f. Beasts* 399 Mug-wort..with auripigment, killeth wolfs and mice. **1741** *Compl. Fam.-Piece* II. i. 321 Strew upon it..Powder of Auripigmentum.

†**au'ripotent**, *a.* *Obs. rare.* [f. L. *auri-* gold + *potent-em* powerful; cf. *armipotent.*] Having gold at command; rich in gold.
a **1560** J. ROLLAND *Crt. Venus* II. 130 Thair riche array, and thair habillement..So bene, so big, and so Auripotent ..it was.

†**'auriscalp.** *Obs.* [ad. L. *auriscalpium*, f. *auri-s* ear + *scalpĕre* to scratch.] An ear-pick; a surgical probe for the ear.
[**1742** BAILEY, *Auriscalpium.*] **1819** in *Pantologia.*

auriscope (ˈɔːrɪskəʊp). *Med.* [f. L. *auri-s* ear + Gr. *-σκοπος* observing, observer.] An instrument for examining the condition of the Eustachian passage of the ear. (In Mayne *Exp. Lex.* 1853.) **auriscopy** (ɔːˈrɪskəpɪ), the use of the auriscope.

aurist (ˈɔːrɪst). [f. L. *aur-is* ear + -IST.] A specialist in regard to diseases of the ear.
1678 in PHILLIPS (App.) **1787** FORDYCE in *Phil. Trans.* LXXVIII. 32 The Egyptians..had..oculists, aurists, etc. long before the Trojan war. *a* **1845** HOOD *Tale Trumpet* xxv, The Aurist only took a mug, And pour'd in his ear some acoustical drug.

aurite ('ɔːraɪt), *ppl. a.* ? *Obs. rare*⁻¹. [ad. L. *aurītus* eared, f. *auris* ear.] Long-eared.
1654 GAYTON *Fest. Notes* I. v. 17 This beast (though by nature Aurite) was never so prick-ear'd as now.

aurited (ɔː'raɪtɪd, 'ɔːrɪtɪd), *ppl. a.* [f. prec. + -ED.] Furnished with ears or auricles; auriculate.
1748 SIR J. HILL *Hist. Anim.* 122 (JOD.) The thin aurited nautilus.

aurivorous (ɔː'rɪvərəs), *a.* [f. L. *auri-*, comb. form of *aurum* gold + *-vorus* devouring.] Gold-devouring, feeding on gold.
1783 H. WALPOLE *Lett. C'tess Ossory* I. 151 Man is an aurivorous animal. **1845** FORD *Handbk. Spain* vi. 465 The most aurivorous.. population of the peninsula.

auro- ('ɔːrəʊ), comb. form of L. *aurum* gold, used chiefly in *Chem.* and *Min.*, as in **auro-'cephalous** *a.*, having a gold-coloured head; **auro-'chloride**, a compound of auric chloride with a base, a chloro-aurate; **auro-plum'biferous** *a.*, containing lead mixed with gold; **auro-te'llurite**, an ore of tellurium containing gold and silver, SYLVANITE.
1816 CLEAVELAND *Min.* 566 Auro-plumbiferous native tellurium. **1875** BLOXAM *Chem.* 403 Aurochloride of sodium forms reddish yellow prismatic crystals.

‖**aurochs** ('aʊrɒks, 'ɔːrɒks). [a. Ger. *aurochs*, obs. form of *auerochse*:—MHG. *ûr-ochse*, OHG. *ûr-ohso*, f. *ûr* = OE. *úr*, ON. *úrr*, OTeut. **ûrus*, the *Urus*, + G. *ochs*, MHG. *ochse*, OHG. *ohso*, ox. The L. *ūrus* and Gr. *οὖρος* were adopted from the OTeut. word, of which the derivation is uncertain.]
Historically and properly, the name of an extinct species of Wild Ox (*Bos Urus* Owen, *B. primigenius* Boj.), described by Cæsar as *Urus*, which formerly inhabited Europe, including the British Isles, and survived until comparatively recent times in Prussia, Poland, and Lithuania. Since this became extinct, the name has often been erroneously applied to another species, the European Bison (*Bos Bison* Gesn., *B. bonasus* Linn.), still extant in the forests of Lithuania, in which sense it is used by some English naturalists.
In early mod.G. *aurox, aurochs*, was still applied to the *Urus*, and only since its disappearance (in 17th c.) has been popularly misapplied to the Bison, in which sense it was unfortunately adopted by some naturalists, before the facts were known. More recent authors have sought to remedy the mistake by introducing the form *Urox* (MHG. *ûr-ochse*) for the Urus, while retaining *Aurochs* for the Bison; but as *Urox* and *Aurochs* are only the earlier and later form of the same name, this is historically indefensible, and the only accurate nomenclature is to distinguish the two animals as *Urus* (or *Urox*), and *Bison* (improperly called *Aurochs*). See SCHADE *Altdeutsch. Wb.* s.v. *Wisunt*; BOYD DAWKINS, *Fossil Brit. Oxen*, in *Q. Jrnl. Geol.Soc.* XXII. I. 393.
1766 PENNANT *Brit. Zool.* (1776) I. I. ii. II. ii. 19 The *Urus* of the Hercynian forest described by Cæsar.. called by the modern Germans, *Aurochs*, i.e. *Bos sylvestris*. **1797** BARR *Buffon's Nat. Hist.* VIII. 23 The urus, or aurochs. **1835** *Penny Cycl.* IV. 463/2 The aurochs of the present day is nothing more than the Bison or Bonasus of the antients. **1869** J. GRAY *Guide Brit. Mus.* 3 The Lithuanian Bison or Aurochs.. is now nearly extinct. **1882** C. ELTON *Orig. Eng. Hist.* 59 A confused account of two distinct animals, the Aurochs or Zubr of Lithuania, and the extinct Urus which Charlemagne is said to have hunted. [Pol. *zubr* = bison.]

aurora (ɒ'rɔərə, ɔː-, ə-). [L.; = dawn, goddess of the dawn, orient. Rarely in Fr. form *aurore*.]
1. The rising light of the morning; the dawn.
1483 CAXTON *Gold. Leg.* 430/4 On the thyrd nyght after, nygh the rysyng of aurora. **1638** WILKINS *New World* I. (1684) 57, I may call it *Lumen crepusculinum*, the Aurora of the moon. **1652** URQUHART *Jewel* Wks. (1834) 235 The antarctick oriency of a western aurore.
2. *personified*, The (Roman) goddess of the dawn, represented as rising with rosy fingers from the saffron-coloured bed of Tithonus.
1587 *Myrr. for Mag., Induct.* i. 6 Sweete Aurora. **1645** MILTON *L'Allegro* 19 Zephyr with Aurora playing, As he met her once a-maying. **1718** POPE *Iliad* VIII. I Aurora now, fair daughter of the dawn.
3. *fig.* The beginning, the early period; *poet.* for 'rise,' 'dawn,' 'morn,' in same fig. sense.
1844 LINGARD *Anglo-Sax. Ch.* (1858) II. xii. 197 The virtues which had so brilliantly illuminated the aurora of their church. **1858** HAWTHORNE *Fr. & It. Jrnls.* II. 222 An aurora of mirth, which probably will not be very exuberant in its noon-tide.
4. *poet.* The East, the Orient. *rare.*
a **1649** DRUMM. OF HAWTH. *Wks.* 37/1 They make the Scythian them adore, The Gaditan, and souldier of Aurore.
5. a. A luminous atmospheric phenomenon, now considered to be of electrical character, occurring in the vicinity of, or radiating from, the earth's northern or southern magnetic pole, and visible from time to time by night over more or less of the adjoining hemisphere, or even of the earth's surface generally; popularly called the Northern (or Southern) Lights, merry-dancers, streamers, etc.
The *northern* lights, being alone conspicuous in Europe, had from the earliest periods various popular names in the northern languages; they began to attract scientific attention early in the 17th c., and were described by Gassendi in 1621 under the descriptive appellation of *aurora borealis* or 'northern dawn,' their simplest form suggesting the appearance of dawn or approaching sunrise on the northern horizon; this appellation (occasionally varied as *aurora septentrionalis*) passed into general scientific use. On the recognition of similar phenomena in the antarctic regions, these were called *aurora australis* or 'southern lights'; whence *aurora* is now used generically as the proper term for the phenomenon, without any thought of 'dawn,' and with English plural *auroras*; and this has become the ordinary prose meaning of *aurora*, the preceding senses being only poetical.
1621 [1822 BURROWES *Cycl.* s.v., On Sept. 2nd, 1621, the same phenomenon was seen all over France; and it was particularly described by Gassendus in his *Physics*, who gave it the name of *aurora borealis*.] **1717** *Phil. Trans.* XXX. 584 On February the 5th, 1716–7, at Eight at Night, an *Aurora Borealis* appeared. **1727–51** CHAMBERS *Cycl.*, *Aurora Borealis* or *Aurora Septentrionalis*, the northern dawn, or light; is an extraordinary meteor, or luminous appearence, shewing it self in the night-time, in the northern part of the heavens. **1741** *Phil. Trans.* XLI. 744 (*title*), An account of the *Aurora Australis* observed at Rome, January 27, 1740. **1788** BURNS *Wks.* II. 183 Last, she sublimes th' Aurora of the poles, The flashing elements of female souls. **1823** MOORE *Fables, Holy Alliance* i. 12, A dome of frost-work.. Which shone by moonlight—as the tale is—Like an aurora borealis. **1835** SIR J. ROSS *N.-W. Pass.* xiv. 216 There was an aurora at night. **1852** W. GROVE *Contrib. Sc.* 359 In air rarefied by the air-pump an aurora or discharge of five or six inches long could be obtained. **1855** SCOFFERN *Pract. Meteorol.* 98 After 1790 auroras became unfrequent, but since 1825 they have been on the increase. **1868** LOCKYER *Heavens* 211 Lit up by auroræ and long lingering twilights. **1870** R. FERGUSON *Electr.* 37 The appearance of auroras is invariably accompanied by magnetic irregularities.
b. ***aurora borealis***: transf.
1818 'THOS. BROWN, THE ELDER' *Brighton* I. 131 She was eclipsed by an *Aurora Borealis* in the matrimonial sphere. **1922** JOYCE *Ulysses* 469 The aurora borealis of the torch-light procession leaps.
6. The colour of the sky at the point of sunrise; a rich orange hue.
1791 HAMILTON *Berthollet's Dyeing* II. II. §4. iv. 273 For silks to be dyed of an aurora or orange colour. **1822** IMISON *Sc. & Art* II. 189 If an orange, or an aurora be required. **1862** R. PATTERSON *Ess. Hist. & Art* 33 Orange-reds, such as scarlet, nacarat, and aurora.
7. Used as the popular or trivial name of various species of animals, as of a monkey (*Chrysothrix sciurea*), a sea-anemone, and as the fancy name of varieties of various flowers, *e.g.* of a ranunculus.
1774 GOLDSM. *Nat. Hist.* (1862) I. VII. i. 508 The Samari, or Aurora; which is the smallest, and most beautiful of all monkeys that hold by the tail. **1858** G. H. LEWES *Sea Side Stud.* Index.
8. *Comb.* **aurora australis, borealis, septentrionalis**: see sense 5. **aurora-like** *a.*, like the dawn, like the aurora borealis; **aurora-parrot**, the species *Psittacus Aurora*; **aurora-pole**, one of the two points on the surface of the earth which form the centres of the luminous circles of the aurora borealis and australis; **aurora-snake**.
1877 MRS. H. KING *Discip., Ugo Bassi* II. 65 Filmy aurora-flowers Opened and died in the hour. **1580** SIDNEY *Arcad.* (1622) 139 Aurora-like new out of bed. **1879** KINGSTON *Austral. Abr.* iii. 24 Rays of light seemed, aurora-like, to shoot out from its crown. **1881** tr. *Nordenskiöld's Voy. Vega* II. xi. 40 A luminous crown.. whose centre, 'the aurora-pole,' lies somewhat under the earth's surface, a little north of the magnetic-pole.

auroral (ɔː'rɔərəl), *a.* [f. prec. + -AL¹.]
1. Of or pertaining to the dawn, eastern; *fig.* of or pertaining to the rise or first period of anything.
1552 LYNDESAY *Monarche* Prol. 148 Quhose donke impurpurit vestiment nocturnall.. He [Phebus] lefte in tyll his regioun aurorall. **1854** BADHAM *Halieut.* 529 To have begun the day with a.. crust.. like the French auroral 'biscuit de Rheims.' **1878** P. BAYNE *Purit. Rev.* ix. 361 Auroral splendours of promise.. which accompany all revolutions in their earlier stages. **1879** J. TODHUNTER *Alcestis* 61 To paint the auroral mysteries of the dawn.
2. Like the dawn in colour, brightness, freshness, soft beauty, etc.; dawning, roseate, rosy.
1827 CARLYLE *Misc.* I. 41 The auroral light of Tasso. **1863** LONGF. *Falc. Federigo* 151 Her cheeks suffused with an auroral blush. **1883** R. NOEL in *Academy* No. 577. 365/3 A radiance in auroral spirits now.
3. Of or pertaining to the aurora (borealis).
1828 in WEBSTER. **1851–9** SIR J. HERSCHEL in *Adm. Man. Sc. Enq.* 161 Note also the meteors.. within the auroral region. **1856** KANE *Arct. Exp.* I. xxxi. 421 A true and unbroken auroral arch. **1872** PROCTOR *Ess. Astron.* xiii. 179 The extreme height of the auroral light.
4. Resembling the aurora in its coruscations.
1871 PALGRAVE *Lyr. Poems* 136 Auroral flashings of wit. **1882** MYERS *Renew. Youth* 222 Hast thou.. Marked in her eyes those gleams auroral play?

au'rorally, *adv.* [f. prec. + -LY².]
1. After the manner of the dawn; roseately.
1873 BROWNING *Red. Cott. Night-C.* 117 How heaven's own pure may seem To blush aurorally.
2. After the manner of an aurora (borealis).
1882 PIAZZI SMYTH in *Nature* No. 682. 83 A space, eminently and distinctly aurorally dark, was formed near the middle of the north-east arc itself.

aurorean (ɔː'rɔəriən), *a.* [f. AURORA + -EAN. Latin might have had *aurōre-us* (*roseus*).] Belonging to dawn, or resembling it in brilliant hue.
1819 KEATS *Ode to Psyche*, At tender eyedawn of aurorean love. **1860** O. MEREDITH *Lucile* II. v. §16. 11 Aurorean clouds. **1880** SWINBURNE *Birthday Ode* 340 Ringed with aurorean aureole of the sun.

au'roric, *a.* [f. AUROR-A + -IC: not well formed.] = AURORAL 3.
1881 KINAHAN in *Nature* XXIII. 350 Auroric lights have been faint and scarce of late.

†**au'rose**, *a. Obs.*⁻⁰ [ad. L. *aurōsus*, f. *aurum*; see -OSE.] Full of gold, golden.
1731 in BAILEY.

aurous ('ɔːrəs), *a.* [f. L. *aur-um* gold + -OUS.] Of or containing gold. Applied in *Chem.* to compounds in which gold combines as a monad, e.g. *Aurous iodide* AuI. *Aurous oxide*, Au_2O.
1862 PEPPER *Play-bk. Metals* 201 Purple of Cassius, termed by Gmelin stannate of aurous oxide. **1876** HARLEY *Mat. Med.* 307 Aurous iodide is a greenish-yellow powder.

aurthwart, -wert, obs. forms of OVERTHWART.

aurulent ('ɔːrjʊlənt), *a.* [ad. L. *aurulentus*, f. *aur-um* gold: see -ULENT.] Gold-coloured.
1731 in BAILEY. **1811** G. SHAW *Zool.* VIII. 306 Aurulent humming-bird.

‖**aurum** ('ɔːrəm). [L.] Gold. Used in the names of several preparations containing or resembling gold, as **aurum fulminans** (= FULMINATE of gold), an explosive precipitate obtained by adding ammonia to a solution of auric chloride; **aurum mosaicum** or **musivum**, bisulphide of tin, known also as *bronze powder*, used by statuaries, house-painters, and paper-stainers; †**aurum potabile**, 'drinkable gold,' gold held in a state of minute subdivision in some volatile oil, formerly in repute as a cordial.
a **1500** *E.E. Misc.* (1855) 4 Pynaculs alle of aurum, Clene gold alle and summe. **1681** tr. *Willis' Rem. Med. Wks.*, *Aurum fulminans*, or thundering gold. **1794** J. HUTTON *Philos. Light, etc.* 213 Aurum fulminans may be heated to a certain degree without exploding. **1652** ASHMOLE *Theat. Chem.* 208 Bice, Vermillion, Aurum Musicum. **1822** IMISON *Sc. & Art* II. 325 Aurum Musivum is used by Japanners. **1644** QUARLES *Judgm. & Mercy* 86 Poverty.. is a sickness very catching.. The best cordial is aurum potabile. **1678** PHILLIPS, *Aurum potabile*, a Medicine made of the body of Gold it self, totally reduced, without Corrosive, into a blood-red, gummie or Hony-like substance.

auscult (ɔː'skʌlt), *v.* [ad. L. *auscultāre* to hear with attention, listen to. (*Aus-* = *aur-* in *auris* ear; the rest is doubtful.) Cf. F. *ausculter*.] = next.
c **1840** E. RIGBY in *Tweedie's Libr. Med.* VI. 55 The sound of each heart should be ausculted at the same moment. **1881** MISS BRADDON *Asph.* xxiii. 254 He ausculted me carefully, found me sound in wind and limb.

auscultate ('ɔːskʌlteɪt), *v.* [f. *auscultāt-* ppl. stem of *auscultāre*: see prec. and -ATE³.] *trans.* To listen to; *spec.* in *Med.* to examine by auscultation.
1862 THACKERAY *Philip* III. vi. 122 This practitioner studied, shampooed, auscultated Tregarvan. **1881** in *Syd. Soc. Lex.* [The only form.] **1892** STEVENSON & OSBOURNE *Wrecker* xv. 233 It was therefore necessary.. to auscultate what remained [of the ship], like a doctor sounding for a lung disease. **1908** *Practitioner* Feb. 272 The child is first auscultated in the upright position.

auscultation (ɔːskʌl'teɪʃən). [ad. L. *auscultātiōn-em*, f. *auscultāt-*: see prec. and -ATION.]
1. The action of listening or hearkening.
1634 HICKES *Lucian* (T.) You shall hear what deserves attentive auscultation. **1836** H. TAYLOR *Statesman* xxxi. 239 He who can listen with real attention to every thing that is said to him, has a great gift of auscultation. **1842** MRS. BROWNING *Grk. Chr. Poets* (1863) 64 The suggestive name of *acroases*—auscultations, things intended to be heard.
2. *Med.* The action of listening, with ear or stethoscope, to the sound of the movement of heart, lungs, or other organs, in order to judge their condition of health or disease.
1833 J. FORBES *Cycl. Pract. Med.* I. 234 The whole doctrine of auscultation as a means of diagnosis. **1872** THOMAS *Dis. Wom.* 767 Auscultation reveals a loud basic systolic cardiac murmur.

auscultative (ɔː'skʌltətɪv), *a. Med.* [f. L. *auscultāt-* (see AUSCULT) + -IVE.] Of the nature of, or pertaining to, auscultation.
1834 RAMADGE *Consump. Curable* 95 By auscultative examination. *Ibid.* (1861) 47 He displayed, unequivocally, all its auscultative signs.

auscultator ('ɔːskʌlteɪtə(r)). [a. L. *auscultātor*, n. of agent f. *auscultāre*: see prec. and -OR.]
1. *Med.* One who practises auscultation.

1833 J. FORBES *Cycl. Pract. Med.* I. 225 In the hands of an expert auscultator. **1872** THOMAS *Dis. Wom.* 77 The auscultator..bringing to his aid the double stethoscope.

‖2. Title formerly given in Germany to a young lawyer who has passed his first public examination, and is thereupon employed by Government, but without salary and with no fixed appointment. (Now called *referendar.*) Hence **auscultatorship**.

1831 CARLYLE *Sart. Res.* (1858) iv. 75 His first Law-Examination he has come-through triumphantly..he is hereby 'an Auscultator of respectability.' *Ibid.* 76 His progress from the passive Auscultatorship, towards any active Assessorship. **1884** *Sat. Rev.* 2 Feb. 146.

auscultatory (ɔːˈskʌltətərɪ), *a.* [f. L. *auscultāt-* (see AUSCULT) + -ORY.] Of or pertaining to listening, or to the medical practice of auscultation.

1651 BIGGS *New Disp.* ¶ 240 Engage nature in her passive auscultatory faculties. **1833** J. FORBES *Cycl. Pract. Med.* I. 235 The auscultatory diagnostics of cardiac diseases.

‖**au sérieux** (o serjø). *advb. phr.* [F.] Seriously (cf. SERIOUSLY *adv.*[2] 1 b). Cf. AU GRAND SÉRIEUX.

1836 J. S. MILL *Lett.* (1910) I. 104 What you write would be taken *au sérieux* and not as a mere play of intellect and fancy. **1888** W. JAMES *Let.* 29 Mar. in R. B. Perry *Tht. & Char. W.J.* (1935) I. 705 To me the argument seems irresistible, so long as we take the relation of really *intending* an object, *au sérieux*. **1962** *Times* 16 Feb. 15/1 D'Oyly Carte fanatics who are believed to take all Savoyardery *au sérieux*.

auslaut (ˈaʊslaʊt). *Philol.* [G., f. *aus-* denoting termination + *laut* sound.] The final sound of a syllable or word. Cf. ANLAUT, INLAUT.

1881 in *Imp. Dict.* **1892** *Classical Rev.* Feb. 3/2 It is further probable that the form *-endus* for *-vendus* arose primarily in verbal roots with vocalic auslaut. **1936** M. SCHLAUCH in *Science & Society* I. 34 Purely vocalic *Auslaut* is to be associated with a developed patriarchal-totemistic culture of hunting.

‖**auslese** (ˈaʊsleːzə). Also with capital initial. Pl. **-lesen**, (Anglicized) **-leses**. [Ger., lit. 'choice, selection', f. *aus* out + *lese* picking, vintage.] (Medium-)sweet wine, usu. white, made (esp. in Germany) from selected late-picked bunches of grapes (an official category of German wine); a wine of this category. Cf. BEERENAUSLESE, SPÄTLESE, TROCKENBEERENAUSLESE.

1851 C. REDDING *Hist. Mod. Wines* (ed. 3) viii. 233 Marcobrunn extends over an elevated plain between Hattenheim and Erbach, and produces also very fine wines, especially the Auslaas, which is made only in good vintages, the ripest grapes being gathered and vintaged separately. **1920** G. SAINTSBURY *Notes on Cellar-Bk.* vi. 83 Despite the wonderful first taste of the great 'Auslese' wines, I think both Hock and Moselle best as beverage drinks. **1951**, etc. [see SPÄTLESE]. **1962** *House & Garden* Jan. 55/2 Vintage port, *ausleses*, and rare domaine-bottlings are bound to be things for special occasions. **1980** P. V. PRICE *Dict. Wines & Spirits* 149 Then there are the *spätlese* or late harvested wines; then the *auslese* wines, made from bunches of grapes specially selected for ripeness among those that are late picked.

ausmoner, transp. of *aumosner*, obs. f. ALMONER.

Ausonian (ɔːˈsəʊnɪən), *a.* [f. L. *Ausonia* Lower Italy, poet. Italy, Gr. Αὐσονία poet. Italy, f. Αὔσων, son of Ulysses, who was fabled to have settled there.] Of or pertaining to Ausonia or to the Ausonians, the primitive inhabitants of middle and lower Italy; hence, Italian. Also *sb.*, a native of Ausonia, an Italian.

1607 TOPSELL *Foure-footed Beasts* 481 The Masilian and Ausonian shepherds were..afraid of this lion. **1667** MILTON *P.L.* I. 739 And in Ausonian land Men call'd him Mulciber. **1775** ASH *Dict.* Suppl., Ausonian, sb. **1821** BYRON *Proph. Dante* II. 131 p. 233 The Ausonian soil. **1826** K. H. DIGBY *Morus* 307 All that in this beautiful world is fair and lovely, mountains, woods, rivers, and Ausonian skys [*sic*]. **1850** TENNYSON *Pal. Art* in *Poems* (ed. 6) 115 Or..stay'd the Ausonian king to hear Of wisdom and of law. **1876** DISRAELI *Let. to Lady Chesterfield* 31 Mar. in Buckle *Life* (1920) V. xii. 472 The spring of Ausonian lands. **1882** *Encycl. Brit.* XIV. 344/2 The Auruncans, or Ausonians as they were termed by Greek writers.

‖**auspex** (ˈɔːspɛks). *Rom. Antiq.* Pl. **auspices**. [L., contr. for *avispex*, f. *avi-s* bird + *-spex* an observer, f. *specĕre* to behold, observe.] One who observed the flight of birds, to take omens thence for the guidance of affairs; *hence*, a director, protector; and *esp.* the person who superintended marriage ceremonies.

1598 GREENWEY *Tacitus' Ann.* (1604) 151 Shee should heare the words of the Auspices or hand-fasters. **1647** R. STAPYLTON *Juvenal* 206 An auspex to divine by the flying of the birds the future felicity of her marriage.

†**ˈauspical**, *a.* *Obs.*[−0] [ad. L. *auspicālis*, f. *auspic-em*, AUSPEX: see -AL[1].] = AUSPICIAL.

1656 in BLOUNT *Glossogr.*

†**ˈauspicate**, *a.* *Obs.* [ad. L. *auspicātus*, pa. pple. of *auspicāre*, *-āri* to take omens at the beginning of any business, to start prosperously, to begin, enter upon, f. *auspic-em*, AUSPEX.] Started with good auspices; well-omened; fortunate.

1603 HOLLAND *Plutarch's Mor.* 679 It is not an auspicate beginning of a feast..to snatch or lurch from one another. **1657** HOWELL *Londinop.* 6 Among the most auspicious names..[is] none more auspicate or glorious than Augusta.

auspicate (ˈɔːspɪkeɪt), *v.* [f. prec., or on analogy of vbs. so formed.]

†**1.** *trans.* To give omen of, betoken, prognosticate. *Obs.*

1603 B. JONSON *King's Entert.* Wks. (1838) 535/1 As ominous a comet..as that did auspicate So lasting glory to Augustus' state.

2. *intr.* To augur, prognosticate, predict.

1848 H. ROGERS *Ess.* (1860) III. 357 It were mockery to auspicate favorably so long as they continue.

3. *trans.* To initiate (a business, undertaking, etc.) with a ceremony calculated to ensure prosperity or good luck to it; to give a fortunate start to.

1611 SPEED *Hist. Gt. Brit.* IX. viii. (1632) 553 To auspicate his Temporall affaires with Spirituall deuotions. **1640** BROME *Antipodes* I. vi. 255 First, Sir, a health to auspicate our travailes, And wee'll away. **1823** LAMB *Elia* Ser. II. vi. (1865) 269 To auspicate..the filial concern, and set it agoing with a lustre. **1865** D. NASH in *Merlin* (E.E.T.S.) Pref. 6 Auspicating the foundations of cities..by human sacrifice.

4. To enter upon in a way which may be attended with good or bad consequences; to handsel, signalize (one's entrance upon).

1611 SPEED *Hist. Gt. Brit.* IX. vii. 6 Which Act was accidently hanseld, and auspicated with the bloud of many Jewes. **1796** BURKE *Regic. Peace* Wks. IX. 81 The very first acts, by which [this new Government] auspicated its entrance into function. **1834** SIR H. TAYLOR *Artevelde* I. II. v, Can the son better auspicate his arms Than by the slaying of who slew the father?

5. To begin, commence, start; to inaugurate.

1652 SPARKE *Prim. Devot.* (1663) 97 Whence all the rest auspicate their Gospel. **1831** *Crayons fr. Commons* 41 Long ere the purse and mace Were auspicated to proclaim the state Which fortune will'd on Henry Brougham should wait. **1876** BANCROFT *Hist. U.S.* I. iv. 125 The London company merits the praise of having auspicated liberty in America.

†**6.** *intr.* To make a start or commencement. *Obs.*

a **1670** HACKET *Cent. Serm.* (1675) 582 Let me auspicate from the Text and Authority of Holy Scripture.

†**ˈauspicately**, *adv.* *Obs. rare*[−1]. [f. AUSPICATE *a.* + -LY[2].] In accordance with omens.

1609 HOLLAND *Amm. Marcell.* XXII. viii. 197 Great cities ..founded auspicately by the direction of bird flight.

ˈauspicating, *vbl. sb.* [f. prec. + -ING[1].] = next.

1652 GAULE *Magastrom.* 189 Whether augurizing, auspicating, and aruspicinating..were not founded upon magick.

†**auspiˈcation**. *Obs. rare.* [n. of action f. L. *auspicāt-*: see AUSPICATE *a.* and -ATION.] The taking of auspices, getting of favourable omens.

1652 GAULE *Magastrom.* 4 Their sacrificing to the starres, in an auspication of the years fertility. *Ibid.* 296 He took auspication from a bird that sate before them.

†**ˈauspicator**. *Obs. rare*[−1]. [n. of agent (on L. analogies) f. L. *auspicāt-*: see prec. and -OR.] One who takes auspices, an augur.

1652 GAULE *Magastrom.* 330 The pullarian auspicator, would needs be presaging clean contrary to his tokens.

†**ˈauspiˌcatory**, *a.* *Obs. rare*[−1]. [f. prec.: see -ORY.] Of or pertaining to auspication.

1734 SALE *Koran* Prel. Disc. §iv. (1850) 42 This auspicatory form..[is] believed to be of divine original.

auspice (ˈɔːspɪs). Now usually in pl. **auspices** (ˈɔːspɪsɪz). [a. F. *auspice* (14th c.), ad. L. *auspicium* the action or function of the AUSPEX.]

1. An observation of birds for the purpose of obtaining omens; a sign or token given by birds.

1533 BELLENDENE *Livy* IV. (1822) 319 Na plebeane micht have auspicis, that is to say, thay micht nocht divine. **1652** GAULE *Magastrom.* 307 Taking an auspice..it was told him, &c. **1770** LANGHORNE *Plutarch* (1879) I. 172/2 The auspices which were taken when he was appointed. **1868** MILMAN *St. Paul's* ii. 20 All sortileges, auspices, divinations, and other works of the devil were forbidden.

2. *gen.* Any divine or prophetic token; prognostic, premonition; *esp.* indication of a happy future.

1660 R. COKE *Power & Subj.* 186 The glorious Cesar Henry..whom God may make to command with happy auspices. **1796** BURKE *Regic. Peace* iii. Wks. VIII. 327 This auspice [the publication of a pamphlet] was instantly followed by a speech from the throne, in the very spirit..of that pamphlet. **1848** R. HAMILTON *Sabbath* ii. 50 What was the auspice and relief which words like these brought to his soul! **1855** MACAULAY *Hist. Eng.* III. 20 A life which had opened under the fairest auspices.

3. Prosperous lead; propitious influence exerted on behalf of any undertaking; patronage, favouring direction; *esp.* in phr. ***under the auspices of.***

a **1637** B. JONSON (J.) Great father Mars..By whose high auspice Rome hath stood So long. **1667** DRYDEN *Ann. Mirab.* 1150 That Town..Which by his Auspice they will nobler make. **1790** BURKE *Fr. Rev.* 135 The whole has been done under the auspices..of religion and piety. **1844** LINGARD *Anglo-Sax. Ch.* (1858) II. xi. 168 Published under the auspices of the Royal Society of Literature. **1865** LIVINGSTONE *Zambesi* xvi. 337 An experiment begun under his enlightened auspices.

†**4.** A lucky or well-omened introduction. *Obs.*

1688 DRYDEN *Brit. Rediv.* 50 That James this running century may view, And give his son an auspice to the new.

auspicial (ɔːˈspɪʃəl), *a.* [f. L. *auspici-um* AUSPICE + -AL[1].]

1. Of or pertaining to auspices or augury.

1646 SIR T. BROWNE *Pseud. Ep.* IV. v. 193 That Auspiciall principle..that the left hand is ominous. **1828** CHATFIELD *Teut. Antiq.* Pref. 10 A fondness for auspicial rites.

2. Well-omened, fortunate, auspicious.

1614 (22 Dec.) *Stationers' Reg.* (Arb.) III. 559 The auspiciall government of Frederick the Prince Palatine. **1853** *Scot. Rev.* I. 84 Attaching undue importance to the auspicial favour of aristocratic names.

†**auˈspiciate**, *v.* *Obs. rare*[−1]. [f. as prec. + -ATE[3].] Variant of AUSPICATE *v.* (sense 4).

1640 YORKE *Union Hon.* 15 an. 1296 There to auspiciate his entrance to a conquest of Scotland.

†**auˈspicinator**. *Obs. rare*[−1]. [f. L. *auspicium*; cf. L. *haruspicium*, *haruspicina*, and Eng. *vaticinator*.] = AUSPICATOR, AUSPEX.

1652 GAULE *Magastrom.* 190 Augurs and auspicinators.

auspicious (ɔːˈspɪʃəs), *a.* [f. as prec. + -OUS.]

1. Ominous, *esp.* of good omen, betokening success, giving promise of a favourable issue.

1614 SELDEN *Titles Hon.* 155 An auspicious flight of an Eagle towards him. **1742** YOUNG *Nt. Th.* VIII. 202 Beneath auspicious planets born. **1823** J. THACHER *Mil. Jrnl. Amer. Rev.* 155 The splendid achievement of General Gates is auspicious to his preferment.

b. Of persons: Predicting or prognosticating good.

1702 ROWE *Ambit. Step-Moth.* II. ii. 662 Auspicious Sage, I trust thee with my Fortune. **1879** CHR. ROSSETTI *Seek & Find* 239 The aspect of jubilant auspicious angels.

2. Favourable, favouring, conducive to success.

1610 SHAKS. *Temp.* V. i. 314 I'le..promise you calme Seas, auspicious gales. **1858** SEARS *Athan.* II. xii. 248 The results ..have a direct and auspicious bearing on the great subject.

b. Of persons: Showing favour, propitious, kind.

1601 SHAKS. *All's Well* III. iii. 8 And fortune play vpon thy prosperous helme As thy auspicious mistris. **1756** C. LUCAS *Ess. Waters* I. Ded., Auspicious Heaven saw our distresses and dangers. **1871** ROSSETTI *Poems* 10 Fair with honorable eyes, Lamps of an auspicious soul.

3. Favoured by fortune, prosperous, fortunate.

1616 BULLOKAR, *Auspicious*, lucky, fortunate. **1664** H. MORE *Myst. Iniq.* 241 But *Harvest* sometimes has a more auspicious sense. **1804** in Gurwood *Disp.* III. 419 We.. have reposed for five auspicious years under the shadow of your protection.

auˈspiciously, *adv.* [f. prec. + -LY[2].] In an auspicious manner; with favourable omen, prospect, or result; fortunately, happily.

1596 DRAYTON *Legends* i. 421 Whom then I did auspiciously perswade, Once more with Warre to fright the English Fields. **1719** YOUNG *Revenge* II. i, Thus far it works auspiciously. **1855** MACAULAY *Hist. Eng.* III. 586 Schomberg had opened the campaign auspiciously.

auˈspiciousness. [f. as prec. + -NESS.] The quality of being auspicious; favourable prospect for the future, promise of success.

1649 JER. TAYLOR *Gt. Exemp.* II. Add. xi. 24 Having thus commenced with the auspiciousnesse of religion, they had better hopes their just affaires would succeed. **1884** *Manch. Exam.* 8 Nov. 5/1 The auspiciousness of this beginning was more than confirmed.

†**ˈauspicy**. *Obs.* [ad. L. *auspicium* AUSPICE.] The drawing of omens from birds.

1603 SIR C. HEYDON *Jud. Astrol.* xvii. 356 Auspicie was rather an inuention of pollicie. **1628** *Powerf. Favorite* 120 He consulted with his Auspicy to know what it presaged. **1687** SHADWELL *Juvenal's Sat.* x. *note*, Who interpret *dextro pede* 'with most prosperous Auspicies.'

Aussie (ˈɒsɪ, in Australia ˈɒzɪ), *sb.* and *a.* *colloq.* [Hypocoristic, f. AUSTRALIAN *sb.* and *a.*: see -IE.]

1. (An) Australian.

1917 *Harefield Park Boomerang* 16 Mar. 3 Send us a barrel of Aussy's shypoo. **1918** (*title*) Aussie. The Australian Soldiers' Magazine. *Ibid.* 2/1 A certain Aussie Unit. **1919** *Athenæum* 8 Aug. 727/2 [The soldier]..gave nicknames to the Overseas troops, as 'Aussies', 'Diggers', or 'Dincums' for Australians. **1931** I. L. IDRIESS *Lasseter's Last Ride* i. 7 Fred Colson, a cheerful Aussie bushman. **1957** S. HOPE *Diggers' Paradise* 78 Most Aussies, contrary to popular belief, are town-dwellers.

2. Australia.

1917 *Harefield Park Boomerang* 18 Apr. 9/2 That a passage to 'Aussie' [*sic*] they'll get, Is considered an 'odds-on' bet. **1918** *Australian at Weymouth* 2 July 8/2 He soon returns to Aussie with his 'better half'. **1928** W. SMYTH *Jean of Tussock Country* xxiii. 215 You meet a few bums from Aussie. **1956** F. B. VICKERS in *Coast to Coast* 72 You're in Aussie now. Not your country.

Aust, obs. form of AUGUST.

austempering (ɔːˈstɛmpərɪŋ), *vbl. sb.* *Metallurgy.* [f. AUS(TENITE[2] + TEMPERING *vbl.*

sb.] A quenching process used in the manufacture of steel or cast iron (see quot. 1949).

1937 E. S. Davenport in *Steel* 29 Mar. 42/1 The heat treating process known as 'austempering' consists essentially of heating steel to an appropriate temperature above the critical range to render it austenitic. **1949** R. T. Rolfe *Dict. Metallogr.* 17 *Austempering*, a patented heat treatment involving the controlled hot-quenching of steel (or cast iron), which has previously been heated above the transformation range, so as to give rise to austenite.

Austen, variant of Austin, Augustinian.

Austenian (ɔː'stiːnɪən), *a.* and *sb.* **A.** *adj.* Of or pertaining to Jane Austen, novelist, 1775–1817, or her writings. **B.** *sb.* = Austenite[1]. So **Austenish** ('ɔːstɪnɪʃ) *a.*, characteristic of Jane Austen's work; **Austenite**[1] ('ɔːstɪnaɪt), an admirer of Jane Austen's writings.

1898 J. Jacobs *Jane Austen's Emma* Introd. p. vii, If 'Emma' is not the most striking of Jane Austen's works, it is the most Austenish. **1901** *Westm. Gaz.* 11 Dec. 3/1 The Austenian topography seems to me tolerably complete. **1903** *Daily Chron.* 16 May 3/7 With Mr. Perugini Austenites will have a quarrel. **1928** *Observer* 22 Jan. 6 The claim that this unknown book is at least better than 'Sense and Sensibility' is calculated to prejudice Austenians against it from the outset. **1963** *Times* 7 Mar. 15/5 To the perfect Austenite Mr. Liddell's method of approach will be a delight and a provocation.

austenite[2] ('ɔːstɪnaɪt). *Metallurgy.* [a. F. *austenite* (Osmond 1896, in *Bull. Soc. d'Encourag. de l'Industrie* 738), f. the name of Sir William C. Roberts-*Austen* (1843–1902): see -ite[1].] (See quot. 1910[1].) Hence **auste'nitic** *a.*, containing austenite.

1902 [see troostite 2]. **1905** *Nature* 18 May 69/1 The polyhedral or 'austenitic' type of structure has never been obtained alone in a pure carbon steel... The austenitic structure appears to be that of the nose of the tool in actual use. **1910** *Encycl. Brit.* XIV. 804/2 Austenite is the name of the solid solution of an iron carbide in allotropic γ-iron. *Ibid.*, On cooling into region 6 or 8 austenite should normally split up into ferrite and cementite, after passing through the successive stages of martensite, troostite and sorbite. **1922** *Nature* 24 June 818/1 The gamma-iron lattice of austenitic steels is enlarged by dissolved carbon. **1937** [see austempering *vbl. sb.*]. **1947** *Nature* 11 Jan. 50/1 Austenitic irons have found a number of industrial uses. **1966** *Economist* 1 Oct. 80/1 Austenitic steel S-bends.

‖**auster** (ɔːstə(r)). Also 6 **austure**. [L.; cf. L. *urĕre*, *ustum*, to burn, Gr. αὔειν to dry, kindle.] The south wind; *hence*, the south.

c **1374** Chaucer *Boeth.* ii. iii. 39 Yif þe cloudy wynde auster blowe felliche. **1535** Stewart *Cron. Scot.* I. 354 Throw couetyce culd neuir ȝit be content Of all the Austure and the Orient. *c* **1630** Drumm. of Hawth. *Poems* Wks. (1711) 38/1 To dry the weeping Auster's tears. **1762–9** Falconer *Shipwr.* ii. 243 Auster's resistless force all air invades.

auster, variant of astre, hearth, home.

austere (ɔː'stɪə(r)), *a.* (*sb.*) Forms: 4 **auster**, 7 **-eer**, 4– **austere**; also 4 **austerene**, **awsterne** (**hausterne**), 4–6 **austerne**, 6 **austrun**, **astern**. [a. OF. *austere* (14th c. in Littré), ad. L. *austērus*, a. Gr. αὐστηρός making the tongue dry and rough, *hence*, harsh, severe, f. αὔειν to dry. The adscititious *-n*, common in 14–16th c., is perhaps due to contact of form and sense with *stern* adj.; cf. quot. 1388 in sense 3. The appearance of the senses in Eng. does not correspond to the logical development in Gr.]

A. *adj.* **1.** Uniting astringency with sourness or bitterness; harsh in flavour, rough to the taste.

1541 R. Copland *Galyen's Terap.* 2 H j b, I cal austere.. a lytell adstryngent. **1601** Holland *Pliny* Gloss., *Austere*, harsh or hard, as in fruits vnripe, and hard wines of hedge grapes. **1664** Evelyn *Pomona* Advt. (1729) 78 Austere Fruit ..no better than a sort of full succulent Crabs. **1784** Cowper *Task* i. 122 The bramble, black as jet, or sloes austere. **1854** Hooker *Himal. Jrnls.* I. vi. 143 Both ripen austere and small fruits.

†**2.** Of colour: Dingy, sombre. (So in L.) *Obs.*

1680 H. More *Apocal. Apoc.* 227 A Chrysoprasus: a Gemm of an austere colour.

3. Harsh to the feelings generally; stern in manner or appearance; rigorous, judicially severe.

1330 R. Brunne *Chron.* 54 Þei dred þe kyng folle sore, for he was fulle austere. **1382** Wyclif *Luke* xix. 21, I dredde thee, for thou art an austerne [**1388** a stern] man.. I am an hausterne [**1388** a stern] man. *c* **1425** Wyntoun *Cron.* v. ix. 664 Persecutiowne, Ðat wes austere and fellowne. **1513** Douglas *Æneis* x. xii. 59 Wyth astern fyry ene. **1535** Stewart *Cron. Scot.* II. 371 With drawin swordis and with austrun face. **1656** Bp. Hall *Breath. Devout Soul* (1851) 192 O thou, who justly holdest thyself wronged with the style of *an austere Master*. **1873** Browning *Red Cott. Night-C.* 248 They would be gentle, not austere.

b. Stern in warfare, grim.

1330 R. Brunne *Chron.* 28 Werred on Athelstan with oste fulle austere. *Ibid.* 263 Þe folk.. wer first auster and smerte. **1852** Miss Yonge *Cameos* (1877) I. xxx. 250 Simon, Count de Montfort, an austere warrior.

†**c.** *transf.* Rugged, forbidding. *Obs.*

1686 Cotton *Montaigne* (1877) I. 75 Difficulties.. render it austere and inaccessible.

4. Severe in self-discipline or self-restraint, stringently moral, strict, abstinent.

c **1375** Wyclif *Serm.* i. Sel. Wks. 1869 I. 1 An ypocrite þat shewide him to the world boþe austerne and clene. **1601** Shaks. *Alls Well* iv. iii. 59 Which holy vndertaking with most austere sanctimonie, she accomplisht. **1772** Priestley *Nat. & Rev. Relig.* (1782) I. 319 John.. led a remarkably austere life. **1855** Macaulay *Hist. Eng.* xiii. III. 249 To these austere fanatics a holiday was an object of positive disgust.

5. Grave, sober, serious.

1667 Milton *P.L.* ix. 272 Eve.. With sweet austeer composure thus reply'd. **1858** Longf. *M. Standish* 31 Men in the middle of life, austere and grave in deportment.

6. Severely simple in style, unadorned; without any luxury.

1597 Hooker *Eccl. Pol.* v. (1632) 390 This austere repast they took in the Euening. **1795** Mason *Ch. Mus.* i. 47, I demand no austere solemnity of strain; but I would reject all levity of air. **1852** Conybeare & H. *St. Paul* (1862) I. ix. 280 The austere comfort of an English jail.

B. as *sb.* An austere substance.

1760 Rutty *Phil. Trans.* LI. 471 Galls and other austeres.

au'sterely, *adv.* [f. prec. + -ly[2].] In an austere manner; with harshness; sternly, strictly, severely; grimly; rigorously, abstinently.

c **1375** Wyclif *Serm.* Sel. Wks. 1869 I. 256 God shal seie, austernli; Of þi mouþ Y juge þee. **1513** Douglas *Æneis* xii. vi. 121 Rycht austernly has he thrawin the brand. **1610** Shaks. *Temp.* iv. i. 1 If I haue too austerely punish'd you. **1799** S. Turner *Anglo-Sax.* (1828) I. 391 Alfred at first received them austerely. His manner was afterwards softened. **1858** De Quincey *Autobiog. Sk.* Wks. I. 134 My mother.. recoiled austerely from all direct communication with her servants. **1865** *Daily Tel.* 28 Dec. 5/4 The back lanes of Genoa are full of austerely-gorgeous palaces.

au'stereness. [f. as prec. + -ness.] Austerity.

1. Harshness or astringent sourness to the taste.

1676 Beal in *Phil. Trans.* XI. 585 An austerenes that must be allay'd.. with a little Sugar. **1751** Chambers *Cycl.* s.v. *Austerity*, Austereness of taste.

2. Harshness, sternness, severity; severe self-discipline, moral strictness.

1579 Tomson *Calvin's Serm. Tim.* 392/2 S. Paul condemned them that through austernesse of life.. serued God. **1646** Sir T. Browne *Pseud. Ep.* 372 If an indifferent and unridiculous object could draw his habituall austerenesse unto a smile. **1829** J. H. Newman in Spurgeon *Treas. Dav.* Ps. cxix. 75, I saw thy face In kind austereness clad.

austerity (ɔː'sterɪtɪ). Forms: 4 **austerité**, **austernete**, 7 **austeritie**, 7– **austerity**. [a. OF. *austerité* (14th c. in Littré), ad. late L. *austēritātem* (cf. Gr. αὐστηρότης), f. *austērus* austere: see -ity.]

1. Harshness to the taste, astringent sourness.

1634 T. Johnson tr. *Parey's Chirurg.* xxvi. vii. (1678) 632 Acerbity and austerity. **1676** Beal in *Phil. Trans.* XI. 585 A wild black Plum.. of no harsh or unpleasant austerity. **1718** Quincy *Compl. Disp.* 80 Sage.. has an Austerity upon the Palate.

2. a. Harshness to the feelings; stern, rigorous, or severe treatment or demeanour; judicial severity.

1340 Hampole *Pr. Consc.* 5376 Þe gret austerité, þat Crist sal shew þan day. *c* **1380** Wyclif *De Papa* Wks. (1880) 471 Seculer prinsis shulden teche to drede god by austernete and worldly drede. **1579** E. K. in *Spenser's Sheph. Cal.* Feb. *Gloss.*, Dismayed at the grimnes and austeritie of his countenaunce. **1614** Raleigh *Hist. World* ii. (1736) 532 He gave presence.. with such austeritie, that no man durst presume to spit or cough in his sight. **1775** Burke *Sp. Conc. Amer.* Wks. 1842 I. 181 Notwithstanding the austerity of the Chair.

b. *transf.* Rigour; rugged sternness. *arch.*

1713 *Lond. & Count. Brewer* ii. (1743) 149 Before the Austerity of the Winter renders such a damp watery Place too chilly. **1817** Byron *Manfred* iii. iv. 33 Which soften'd down the hoar austerity Of rugged desolation.

3. a. Severe self-discipline or self-restraint; moral strictness, rigorous abstinence, asceticism.

1590 Shaks. *Mids. N.* i. i. 90 Or on Dianaes Altar to protest For aie, austerity, and single life. **1655** Fuller *Ch. Hist.* ii. iii. I. 271 The Monks.. whose primitive over-Austerity in Abstinence was turned now into Self-sufficiency. **1750** Johnson *Rambl.* No. 141 ¶6 To dissipate the gloom of collegiate austerity. **1856** Mrs. Stowe *Dred.* xxvii. II. 274 The rigid austerity of his life.

b. *esp.* in *pl.* Severely abstinent or ascetic practices.

1664 H. More *Myst. Iniq.* xviii. 69 Several other Anti-christian Austerities. **1739** Wesley *Wks.* (1872) I. 178 By holiness meaning, not fasting or bodily austerities. **1851** Sir J. Stephen *Hist. France* xvii. II. 174 The cell and the austerities of an anchorite.

4. a. Severe simplicity; lack of luxury or adornment.

1875 Mrs. Charles in *Sund. Mag.* June 586 The very bareness and austerity.. was to the Gothic soldiers a proof of hidden treasure. **1883** Coan in *Harper's Mag.* June 125/2, I should restrict this austerity to the dyspeptics.

b. Applied *attrib.*, esp. during the war of 1939–45, to clothes, food, etc., in which non-essentials were reduced to a minimum as a war-time measure of economy. Also *absol.*

1942 *Times Weekly* 2 Dec. 14/2 A General Limitation Order—.. which suggests that the United States have got quite a way on the road to austerity. **1942** *Times of India* 31 Dec. 8/4 The first of a fleet of 'austerity' buses has just been completed in Britain... Fittings are kept to essentials and anything approaching luxury has been.. cut out. **1944** *Times* 16 Feb. 8/3 Mr. Dalton.. said that austerity clothing was not unsaleable. On the contrary, many men evidently thought that at 20 coupons austerity suits were a good bargain. **1951** R. Knox *Stimuli* iv. 9 There is a real humility in imitating a God who was born in a utility nursery, and laid in an austerity cradle to match it.

†**au'sterulous**, *a.* *Obs.*$^{-0}$ [f. L. *austērul-us*: see -ulous.] 'Somewhat harsh.' Bailey 1731.

Austin ('ɔːstɪn), *a.* and *sb.* Also 4–6 **Austyn(e**, 6–7 **-en**, 7 **-ine**. [Syncopated f. *'Augustin*, *'Augstin*. (No *Aoustin* cited in OF.)]

1. = Augustinian.

c **1384** Wyclif *De Eccl.* Sel. Wks. 1871 III. 353 Austyns seien þat þei weren many hundrid wynter bifore oþere freris. **1861** A. B. Hope *Eng. Cathedr. 19th. C.* 232 The church of the Austin Friars.

†**2.** 'Doing Austins': see quot. *Obs.*

c **1812** *Oxoniana* I. 5 Some traces of this practice [*disputationes in Augustinensibus*] still remain in the University exercises, and the common phrase of scholars 'doing Austins' has a direct allusion to it.

†**'Austiner.** *Obs.* Variant of prec.

1466 *Paston Lett.* 549 II. 270 Given to the Austeners at the chapter at Yarmouth.

Austinian (ɔː'stɪnɪən), *a.* Of or pertaining to John Austin (1790–1859) and his theory of government. Hence **Au'stinianism.**

1875 H. J. S. Maine *Lect. Early Hist. Institutions* xii. 362 The Austinian conception of Sovereignty has been reached through mentally uniting all forms of government in a group by conceiving them as stripped of every attribute except coercive force. **1882** *Encycl. Brit.* XIV. 357/2 The Austinian definition of law as a command creating rights and duties. **1917** H. J. Laski *Stud. Probl. Sovereignty* ii. 66 It goes back to that passionate Erastianism of Luther which was the only answer he could make to the Austinianism of Rome. **1921** *Contemp. Rev.* Dec. 858 The unified, mechanical, Austinian State.

austral ('ɔːstrəl), *a.* Also 6 **aws-**, **australl**. [ad. L. *austrālis*, f. *Auster* south wind: see -al[1].]

1. Belonging to the south, southern; *also*, influenced by the south wind, warm and moist. ***austral signs***: the six signs of the zodiac from *Libra* to *Pisces*.

1398 Trevisa *Barth. De P.R.* xiii. xxvi. (1495) 459 Fysshe of that kynde that hyghte Austral aryse whan the sterres that hyght Pliades begynne to go doune. **1541** R. Copland *Guydon's Quest. Cyrurg.*, An australl day, that is to say hote and moyste. **1635** Heywood *Hierarch.* iii. 185 If the Australl horne be any thing erected, it signifieth a South winde. **1881** Maxwell *Electr. & Magn.* II. 19 Austral magnetism is the imaginary magnetic matter which prevails in the southern regions of the earth.

2. Of or pertaining to Australia or Australasia.

1823 W. C. Wentworth *Australasia* 21 Grant that yet an Austral Milton's song.. flow deep and rich along;—An Austral Shakspeare rise. **1835** *Penny Cycl.* III. 122/2 The Austral negroes may be considered as still living in the lowest state of civilization. **1855** W. Howitt *Land, Labour, & Gold* I. 43 Every servant in this Austral Utopia thinks himself a gentleman. **1898** E. E. Morris (*title*) Austral English. A Dictionary of Australasian Words, Phrases, and Usages. **1904** *Westm. Gaz.* 30 Mar. 7/2 The Austral Club at 44, Queen's House, St. James' Court, Buckingham Gate. **1912** (*title*) The Austral Avian Record. A scientific journal devoted primarily to the study of the Australian avifauna. **1967** S. I. Tucker *Protean Shape* 279 [In 1793] Austral English was barely born.

Australasian (ɔːstrə'leɪʃ(ɪ)ən), *a.* and *sb.* [f. *Australasia*, ad. F. *Australasie* (f. L. *austrālis* southern + *Asia*) + -an; given originally, by De Brosses, to one of his 3 divisions of the alleged *Terra Australis*: now used to include Australia and its adjoining islands.] **A.** *adj.* Of or belonging to Australasia. **B.** *sb.* A native or colonist of Australasia.

[**1756** De Brosses *Hist. Navig. aux Terres Australes* Pref. 2 La division de la terre australe y étoit faite, relativement à ces trois mers, en Magellanique, Polynésie, et Australasie. **1766** Callander *Terra Australis* I. 49 (transl. De Brosses) The first[division] in the Indian Ocean south of *Asia*, which for this reason we shall call *Australasia*.] **1802** G. Shaw *Zool.* III. 506 Other Australasian Snakes. **1819** Syd. Smith *Wks.* (1867) I. 268 The Australasians grow corn. **1838** *Dublin Rev.* July 276 New Zealand is included in the vast diocese of our Australasian Bishop. **1937** D. Cowie *N.Z. from Within* 253 [New Zealand] refuses to allow the term 'Australasian' to be used in her hearing. **1940** *Chambers's Techn. Dict.* 60/2 *Australasian region*, one of the primary faunal regions into which the land surface of the globe is divided; includes Australia, New Guinea, Tasmania, New Zealand, and the islands south and east of Wallace's line.

Australasiatic (ˌɔːstrəleɪʃɪ'ætɪk), *a.* [f. *Australasia* (see Australasian) + Asiatic *a.*] Consisting of or characterized by a mixture of Australian and Asiatic elements. Also *absol.* (? *Obs.*)

1819 *New Whig Guide* in *Blackw. Mag.* V. 96 Craf-callee, which is a kind of Australasiatic Delos. **1890** *Cornhill Mag.* July 98 It was neither Cockney nor Yankee, but a nasal blend of both..: in a word, it was Australasiatic of the worst description.

australene ('ɔːstrəliːn). *Chem.* [f. L. *austrāl-is* austral + -ene.] The chief constituent of

English turpentine-oils, prepared from the turpentine of *Pinus australis*, which turns the plane of polarization to the right; also called *austraterebenthene*.

1863 in WATTS *Dict. Chem.* V. 921.

Australia Day. The anniversary of the day, 26 January 1788, on which Governor Phillip founded the settlement at Sydney Cove; an annual public holiday in Australia celebrating this.

1911 *Sydney Morning Herald* 23 May 6/3 In arrogantly setting up an Australia Day of its own, with no historical or other reference to our universal Australia Day, January 26, that Church assumes a prerogative it has no right..to exercise. **1921** *Argus* (Melbourne) 28 Jan. 7/7 Among the Australia Day celebrations in London today was a service organised by the Rev. Arthur West..at Saint Dunstan's-in-the-East. **1932** *Sydney Morning Herald* 27 Jan. 10/6 For more than 100 years the day has been commemorated as Anniversary Day, but the State Cabinet decided that it should be observed in future as Australia Day. **1977** *Weekly Times* (Melbourne) 19 Jan. 70/3 Major league championships will be played..during the Australia Day holiday weekend—January 29, 30 and 31. **1981** A. J. BURKE *Pommies & Patriots* 38 Joe Lyons..sponsored the change of name from Foundation Day to Australia Day in 1932.

Australian (ɔːˈstreɪlɪən, ɒ-), *sb.* and *a.* [ad. F. *australien*, f. L. *austrālis*, in *Terra Australis* 'southern land,' the title given, from 16th c., to the supposed continent and islands lying in the Great Southern Ocean, for which *Australia* was at length substituted (see Flinders, 1814, *Voyage to Terra Australis*, I. Introd. p. iii, *footnote*.) With the gradual restriction of *Terra Australis* and 'Australia' to New Holland (see *Penny Cycl.* 1835 s.v.), *Australian* has been similarly restricted.]

A. *sb.* †**1.** A native of the *Terra Australis*, including Australasia, Polynesia, and 'Magellanica'. *Obs.* **2. a.** An aboriginal native of, *later*, also, a colonist or resident in, the island-continent of Australia.

1693 *New Discov. Terra Incogn. Austral.* 163 It is easie to judge of the incomparability of the Australians with the people of Europe. **1766** CALLANDER *Terra Australis* (De Brosses) II. 280 One of the Australians, or natives of the Southern World, whom Gonneville had brought into France. **1815** *Ann. Reg.* 546 Like most Australians their legs did not bear the European proportion to the size of their heads and bodies. **1880** *Daily News* 25 Nov. 5/2 Herbert it seems is an Australian, or at least has been living in Australia.

b. ***New Australian***, a recent immigrant resident in Australia, esp. one from Europe.

1926 J. DOONE (*title*) Timely Tips for New Australians. **1952** MITCHELL in *Chambers's Shorter Eng. Dict.* Suppl., *New Australian*, an immigrant, usually a European; first applied to displaced persons from the Baltic countries. **1959** *N.Z. Listener* 9 Jan. 3/2 The hero of the story, Nino Culotta, is a New Australian—or what is now known as a Naussie.

3. *absol.* uses of the adj. (contextual sense editorially inserted in square brackets).

1850 E. WARD *Jrnl.* 3 Oct. (1951) 40 Australians [ships]..are not common enough to meet on the high seas. **1896** N. NEWNHAM-DAVIS *Three Men & God* 123 The additional felicity of exercising an old bucking Australian [horse] belonging to the Master. **1901** *Westm. Gaz.* 4 June 12/1 That well-known collector..had a collection of Australians [stamps] alone worth £10,000. **1930** *Economist* 8 Nov. 866/2 The improving tendency of Australians [shares]. **1945** C. L. B. HUBBARD *Observer's Bk. Dogs* 21 Sydney Silky dogs are frequently crossed with Australians [Australian terriers].

B. *adj.* **a.** Of or belonging to Australia.

1814 R. BROWN in Flinders *Voy. Terr. Austr.* II. 535 The collection of Australian plants. **1839** *Penny Cycl.* XIV. 363 The Alfourou and Australian races. *a* **1885** *Mod.* Proposed confederation of the Australian colonies.

b. In specific combinations with sbs., as **A. ballot** (see quot. 1903); **A. bluebell creeper**, an evergreen vine of the genus *Sollya* with blue flowers; **A. cattle-dog** (see quots.); **A. cranberry**: see CRANBERRY 2; **A. crawl**: see CRAWL *sb.*[1] c; **A. currant**: see CURRANT 3; **A. English**, the form of English used by the inhabitants of Australia; the characteristic features which distinguish this form; **A. honeysuckle**, any of several plants of the genus *Banksia* (see HONEYSUCKLE 3 a); **A. kelpie**: see KELPIE[2]; **A. lady-bird** (see quots.); **A. mahogany**, any of several eucalypts having hard red timber (Webster, 1909); **A. National Football**, the official name for Australian Rules football (see *A. rules* below); **A. rules**, regulations governing a football game having certain characteristics of both association and rugby football, with eighteen players on each side; also, the game itself; **A. terrier**, a type of terrier bred in Australia, resembling the English wire-haired breeds.

1888 *Nation* (N.Y.) 2 Aug. 91/2 By introducing the secret '*Australian ballot' in Congressional elections..the use of bribery in the choice of Congressmen might be discouraged to some extent. **1903** A. B. HART *Actual Government* 74 The so-called Australian ballot system, under which all the candidates appear upon one ballot, prepared and distributed by the state, and the voter indicates on the ballot his choice of candidates. **1896** T. W. SANDERS *Encycl. Gardening* (ed. 2) 368 *Sollya* (*Australian Bluebell Creeper). **1916** H. L. G. VAN WIJK *Dict. Plantnames* II. 81/2 Australian blue bell creeper. **1926** *Australian Encycl.* II. 453/1 A blending of the native bred dog..and the smooth-haired Scotch sheep-dog. ..Such is the *Australian cattle-dog. **1945** C. L. B. HUBBARD *Observer's Bk. Dogs* 20 Australian Cattle Dog. Australian Heeler. This is an Australian manufactured breed much resembling a miniature Alsatian. **1940** A. G. MITCHELL in *Southerly* July 11 (*heading*) *Australian English. **1953** BAKER *Australia Speaks* 7 Scores of people have rallied to the cause of sorting out the intricacies of Australian English. **1967** *Guardian* 11 Jan. 18/8 There is Australian English, and American English, and Indian English, and West African English, and West Indian English—recognisable..as a matter of idiom and accent. **1985** *English World-Wide* VI. I. 36 (*heading*) Australian (and NZ) English. **1881** *Encycl. Brit.* XII. 140/2 *Australian or heath honeysuckle is the Australian *Banksia serrata*. **1898** MORRIS *Austral Eng.* 18/2 *Banksia*,..the so-called *Australian Honeysuckle*. **1902** *Encycl. Brit.* XXVII. 636/2 One of the most notable examples of the use of insect allies is the case of the *Australian Lady Bird, *Adalia cardinalis*. **1952** MITCHELL in *Chambers's Shorter Eng. Dict.* Suppl., *Australian ladybird*, a small blue and orange beetle introduced into California in 1888 to combat the cottony-cushion scale. **1948** T. CORKHILL *Gloss. Wood* 19 *Australian Mahogany. *Dysoxylon fraseranum*. Also called Australian Rosewood. Reddish colour and fragrant. Characteristics of red cedar. Very durable and stable. Used for general purposes, furniture, aircraft. **1927** *Argus* (Melbourne) 9 Aug 10/6 The name of the council..was altered to that of the *Australian National Football Council, and all of the States will place before the word 'football' in the title of their organisations the words 'Australian National'. **1968** EAGLESON & MCKIE *Terminol. Austral. Nat. Football* I. 12 This does not mean..that Australian National Football is the most frequently used term... In the community at large, Australian Rules would undoubtedly be the most common term. **1925** *Australian Encycl.* I. 479/1 Of matches under *Australian (then known as Victorian) rules seven were won and 12 were lost. **1933** *Bulletin* (Sydney) 22 Mar. 30 The Australian rules football carnival in Sydney next August. **1958** *Australian Encycl.* IV. 134/2 Generally, it [*sc.* Australian football] is known as the Australian Game, National Football, or Australian Rules. **1909** WEBSTER, *Australian terrier. **1910** *Encycl. Brit.* VIII. 378 (*caption*) Australian Terrier. **1928** F. T. BARTON *Kennel Encycl.* 26 The so-called Australian terriers are nothing more or less than inferior specimens of the Yorkshire terriers. **1966** *Weekly News* (N.Z.) 1 June 40 Australian terrier..a low-set, compact, active little dog which may be silver-grey with tan markings, or sandy.

Hence, **Australioid** (ɔːˈstreɪlɪɔɪd), *a.*, also **Australoid** (ˈɔːstrəlɔɪd), of the ethnological type of the aborigines of Australia. Also as *sb.*

1864 *Reader* No. 103. 771/1 Australioid rather than Australian. **1869** LUBBOCK *Preh. Times* xii. 378 The Australoid type contains all the inhabitants of Australia, and the native races of the Deccan. **1884** *Sat. Rev.* 26 July 118 Proving the existence of Australioid blood in our veins. **1910** *Encycl. Brit.* II. 748/2 It is also probable that the Australoid family extends into south Arabia and Egypt. **1913** H. JOHNSTON *Pioneers in Australasia* ii. 49 The ancestors of the Tasmanians and Australoids were driven forth into the forests of Africa and southern Asia... The Australoids..became the native race of the Australian continent.

Australiana (ɔːˌstreɪlɪˈɑːnə). [f. *Australia* + ANA *suff.*] Things relating to or characteristic of Australia.

1855 *Putnam's Monthly Mag.* V. 598 Australiana. The Campbell Town Election. **1886** R. HENTY (*title*) Australiana or my early life. By..first white native of the first settlement of Victoria, Australia. **1941** BAKER *Dict. Austral. Slang* 6 *Australiana*, Australian cultural or artistic life; the record of the country's culture and history. **1958** *Times* 7 Aug. 9/7 There is a growing interest in Australiana. **1962** *Listener* 4 Oct. 510/2 The September number of *The London Magazine*..consists of Australiana. **1967** S. H. COURTIER *See who's Dying* iii. 36 He collects books, original editions, early Australiana and that sort of thing.

Australianism (ɔːˈstreɪlɪənɪz(ə)m). [f. AUSTRALIAN + -ISM.] An idiom or mode of expression peculiar to Australian English; an attitude of mind characteristic of Australia or an Australian. So **Austraˈlasianism**.

1891 *Daily News* 26 June 5/2 He appears to think that our speech is in danger of being invaded by Australianisms. **1891** *Harper's Mag.* July 215/1 The coming degradation of the English language by the invasion of Australasianisms. **1905** *Daily Chron.* 22 Nov. 6/7 There are 'Australianisms' enough to make a dictionary an essential for the proper understanding of an Antipodean journal. **1911** E. M. CLOWES *On Wallaby* vii. 179 One place in Melbourne..where the Frenchman, the German,..and Russian throw off the garment of Australianism, and eat, look, and speak like men of their own country. **1965** G. MCINNES *Road to Gundagai* xvi. 281 They would prove their Australianism by rallying to England's defence.

Australianize (ɔːˈstreɪlɪənaɪz), *v.* [f. AUSTRALIAN + -IZE.] *trans.* To naturalize as an Australian; to make Australian in habits, customs, etc. So **Auˈstralianized** *ppl. a.*

1883 *St. James's Gaz.* 10 May, Are the latter wronged..in having to become for instance, 'Australianized'? **1888** D. B. W. SLADEN *Australian Ballads* 280 Even in his own particular line of 'Australianised Calverley'. **1908** H. JONES in Hetherington *Life & Lett.* (1924) 213 She is, I think, the wife of an old Scot who has been Australianized.

Australianness (ɔːˈstreɪlɪənnɪs). [f. as prec. + -NESS.] The condition of being Australian or having qualities peculiar to Australia or its inhabitants.

1954 *Landfall* VIII. 27 An essential Australianness which is apt to recede when too deliberately pursued. **1960** *Encounter* May 28 The British migrant..must not..attack the country itself or its Australianness.

australite (ˈɔːstrəlaɪt). *Min.* [ad. G. *australit* (F. E. Suess 1901, in *Jahrb. d. K.K. Geol. Reichsanstalt 1900* L. 194), f. AUSTRAL *a.* + -ITE[1].] A form of tektite found in Australia and neighbouring countries. Cf. BILLITONITE, TEKTITE.

1909 *Geol. Mag.* VI. 411 Occurrences of the related 'obsidianites' (referred to by Professor Weinschenk as Billitonite and Australite) in the Malay Peninsula. **1916** *Bull. U.S. Nat. Mus.* XCIV. p. x (*caption*) Australites and an obsidian button from Australia. **1936** *Geogr. Jrnl.* LXXXVIII. 287 Tektites under various names are found in many parts of the world, but those which are peculiar to Australia, designated australites, appear to be more numerous as well as much more distinctive than any other class.

†**ˈaustralize,** *v.* ? *Obs. rare*⁻¹. [f. AUSTRAL *a.* + -IZE.] To point southward.

1646 SIR T. BROWNE *Pseud. Ep.* II. ii. (1686) 44 Steel and Iron conveniently placed do Septentrionate at one extream and Australize at another. **1656** in BLOUNT *Glossogr.*

Australopithecus (ɔːˌstreɪləʊˈpɪθɪkəs). [mod.L., f. L. *austrālis* southern + Gr. πίθηκος ape.] In full *Australopithecus africanus*, a form of anthropoid ape known from fossil remains discovered at Taung in Bechuanaland in 1924 (cf. TAUNG). Hence **Auˌstraloˈpithecine** *a.* and *sb.*, pl. -s; also in mod.L. form *Australopithecinæ*.

1925 R. A. DART in *Nature* 7 Feb. 195, I propose that the first known species of the group be designated *Australopithecus africanus*. **1937** *Ann. Reg. 1936* 52 A Pleistocene skull of Australopithecus type..was found near Johannesburg. **1940** *Jrnl. R. Anthrop. Inst.* LXX. 23 The diminutive gap which separates the Australopithecine group proper from human status. **1947** *Lancet* 14 June 837/1 Later, more remains of the same type of creature were discovered..and these are now all regarded as representatives of a common sub-family, the Australopithecinae. **1953** *N.Y. Times* 3 Jan. 16/7 A small and aberrant..specimen of Paranthropus, one of the South African apemen or Australopithecines.

Australorp (ˈɔːstrəlɔːp). [f. AUSTRAL(IAN + ORP(INGTON.] (See quot. 1929.)

1922 *Daily Mail* 9 Dec. 14 (Advt.), Australorps imported. Australian Black Orpingtons. World's Record Layers—1,750 eggs 6 birds, 12 months. **1929** E. BROWN *Poultry Breeding* I. x. 259 *Australorps.* The fowls to which this name is given in Britain are very nearly the type of the original Black Orpington... When brought over to Europe a few years ago the name here employed was applied to..distinguish them from those which had been so markedly changed. **1965** *Sunday Mail Mag.* (Brisbane) 3 Oct. 14/1 Australorp..This bird is of medium size, has a white skin, a single comb, and beautiful black plumage.

Austrasian (ɔːˈstreɪʃ(ɪ)ən), *a.* and *sb.* [f. med.L. *Austrasia, Ostrasia* + -AN.] **A.** *adj.* Of or pertaining to the Germanic part of the Frankish empire east of the Rhine. **B.** *sb.* A native or inhabitant of Austrasia.

1781 GIBBON *Decl. & F.* III. xxxviii. 598 The remote province was separated from his Austrasian dominions, by the intermediate kingdoms of Soissons, Paris, and Orleans. **1833** S. A. DUNHAM *Hist. Eur. Middle Ages* II. i. 13 He restored Brunehild to the Austrasians. **1874** STUBBS *Constit. Hist.* I. i. 9 The Austrasian domination was more purely Germanic than the Neustrian which it superseded. **1924** *Public Opinion* 27 June 618/3 The Moroccan divisions of her army stood as unshakable as Austrasian Franks.

Austrian (ˈɔːstrɪən, ɒ-), *a.*[1] and *sb.* [f. *Austria* (= G. *Oesterreich* Eastern Kingdom) + -AN.] **A.** *adj.* Of or pertaining to Austria, a country in central Europe. **B.** *sb.* A native or inhabitant of Austria.

1620 *Two very lamentable Relations* [ad fin.], The true neather Austrian Euangelicall Committees and Ambassadours. **1660** A. MOORE *Compend. Hist. Turks* 566 Turacous led Ferdinands main Battel, strengthened on one side with the Stirian, on tother with the Austrian Horse. *Ibid.*, The Stirians were worsted by the Transilvanians, and Bodoes left wing being mostly unexpert Souldiers, were likewise overthrown by the Austrians. **1701** JOHN SAVAGE *Knolles's Turkish Hist.* II. 224 In the year 1670, the Austrian Troops entred Hungary. **1741** *Defence of Rights of House of Austria* 27 To this Purpose the Austrians had..offered large Sums of Money. **1807** W. COXE *Hist. House of Austria* I. I. ix. 145 The Imperial investiture established the indivisibility of the Austrian territories. *Ibid.* II. 980 The elector, at the head of..10,000 Austrians, and 6,000 Polish cavalry, marched towards Holstein. **1876** [see SLAVONIAN *sb.* 2]. **1935** CICELY HAMILTON *Mod. Austria* i. 2 More than one frontier of the Austrian state is a barrier between those who may one day be enemies. *Ibid.* ix. 126 The Italian march halted, arrested by no more than 30,000 Austrians.

†**ˈaustrian,** *a.*[2] *Obs. rare*⁻¹. [f. L. *Austr-* (*Auster*) south + -IAN.] Southern, austral.

1638 QUARLES *Eleg. Lady Luckyn* xiv, The Queen of light, Rob'd with full Glorie in her Austrian skies.

Austric (ˈɔːstrɪk), *a.* [ad. G. *austrisch* (W. Schmidt *Die Mon-Khmer-Völker* (1906) 70), f. L. *Austr-* (see AUSTRIAN *a.*[2]) + -IC.] Designating or pertaining to a family of languages comprising the Austro-Asiatic and Austronesian families.

1927 [see AUSTRO-²]. **1933** BLOOMFIELD *Language* iv. 71 Some scholars believe both the Munda and the Mon-Khmer families to be related to the Malayo-Polynesian family (forming the so-called Austric family of languages).

austrich, -idge, obs. forms of OSTRICH.

†**'austrine**, *a. Obs.* [a. F. *austrin* (Cotgr.), ad. L. *austrīnus*, f. AUSTER.] Southern, austral.

1635 HEYWOOD *Hierarch.* iii. 169 Under the feet of Aquarius, lieth the Great Austrine [*printed* Austriue] Fish.

austringer ('ɒstrɪndʒə(r)). *Falconry*. Also **astr-**, **ostr-**. [Also spelt *ostringer*, a corruption of earlier *ostregier*, *ostreger*, a. OF. *ostruchier*, *austruchier* (*autrucier*, *autoursier*):—late L. **austurcārius*, f. *austurcus*, also *austorius*, *ostorius*, in OF. *hostur*, *ostour*, now *autour*, the goshawk. For corruption of *ostreger* to *ostringer*, *austringer*, cf. *messenger*, *passenger*, *porringer*, etc.] A keeper of goshawks. See also OSTRINGER.

1486 *Bk. St. Albans* b v b, They be calde Ostregeris that kepe Goshawkys, or Tercellis. **1575** G. TURBERVILLE *Falconrie* 63 Falconers and Ostregers. **1601** SHAKS. *All's Well* v. i. (*Stage direction*) Enter a gentle astringer. **1670–1717** BLOUNT *Law Dict.* s.v. *Austurcus*, We usually call a *Faulkoner* who keeps that kind of Hawks, an *Ostringer*. **1695** KENNETT *Par. Antiq.* ix. 117 Sent beyond sea with the Kings Austringers and Falconers.

Austro-¹ ('ɔːstrəʊ), combining form of AUSTRIAN *a.*¹ and *sb.*.

1832 J. H. STOCQUELER *Fifteen Months' Pilgrimage* II. iv. 98 It marks to the traveller proceeding northward the boundary of Austro-Papal influence. **1851** *Fraser's Mag.* Feb. 141/2 The Austro-Russian ascendancy over Germany. **1866** *Macm. Mag.* XIV. 387 The state of public opinion which preceded the Austro-Prussian war. **1868** *Amer. Ann. Cycl.* 57/2 The whole Austrian monarchy is now officially called the Austro-Hungarian empire. **1910** *Westm. Gaz.* 9 Apr. 2/1 The links between Italy and her ally can hardly be strengthened without provoking a fresh outburst of Austrophobia in Italy, or weakened without making the Austrophobes rather more dangerous. **1920** *Q. Rev.* July 204 The endeavours of far-seeing Austro-German patriots. **1954** KOESTLER *Invisible Writing* xxiii. 254 The so-called teachings of the so-called Austro-Marxist school.

Austro-² ('ɔːstrəʊ), combining form of AUSTRAL *a.* and of AUSTRALIAN.

1869 A. R. WALLACE *Malay Archipelago* i. 14 We can draw a line among the islands, which shall so divide them that one half shall truly belong to Asia, while the other shall no less certainly be allied to Australia. I term these respectively the Indo-Malayan, and the Austro-Malayan divisions of the Archipelago. **1899** A. H. KEANE *Man Past & Present* v. 145 Sumbawa and Celebes..are..included in the Austro-Malayan zoological and botanical regions. **1927** G. A. GRIERSON *Ling. Survey India* I. I. ii. 32 This 'Austric Family'..he [*sc.* W. Schmidt] divided into two subfamilies, the 'Austro-Nesian' and the 'Austro-Asiatic'. **1936** *Discovery* Jan. 20/1 The Austro-Malayan sub-region. *Ibid.* July 205/2 The Mon-Khmer branch of the great linguistic family known as Austroasiatic.

austromancy ('ɔːstrəʊmænsɪ). [f. L. *Auster* south wind + Gr. μαντεία divination: see -MANCY.] Divination from observation of the winds.

1656 in BLOUNT *Glossogr.*

Austronesian (ɔːstrəʊ'niːʃ(ɪ)ən), *a.* [f. G. *austronesisch* (W. Schmidt 1899, in *Mitteil. Anthrop. Ges. Wien* XXIX. 248/1). f. L. *austr(ālis* southern + -O + Gr. νῆσ-ος island: see -IAN.] = MALAYO-POLYNESIAN *a.*

1903 *Amer. Anthropol.* V. 164/1 Father Schmidt..accepts that part of his [*sc.* Müller's] theory which sees in the Melanesians a mixed race sprung from the Papuan aborigines and Austronesian (Malayo-Polynesian) immigrants. **1927** [see prec.]. **1958** *Times* 6 Nov. 7/2 Bennett ..considers that beyond doubt the cradle of Maori origins lies 'somewhere in south-east Asia' while Malaya itself is the homeland of the Austronesian family of languages.

austrun, obs. form of AUSTERE.

austuce, variant of ASTUCE, *Obs.*, astuteness.

austure, obs. form of AUSTER.

Austyn, aut, obs. ff. AUSTIN, AUGHT.

autacoid ('ɔːtəkɔɪd), *a.* and *sb.* [f. Gr. αὐτ-ός self + ἄκ-ος remedy + -OID.] (Of, pertaining to, or designating) a drug-like substance produced by the organs of internal secretion.

1914 E. A. S. SCHÄFER in *Internat. Congr. Med. 1913* II. ii. 21 A convenient Greek derivative to denote this quality is 'acoid'..and to further denote that these principles are formed within and by the body, i.e. are natural, we may employ the prefix 'aut-'. We thus get the complete expression *autacoid substance* to denote any druglike principle which is produced in or can be extracted from the internally secreting organs. **1928** *Daily Express* 6 July 6 These are chemical substances of a drug-like character distributed by the circulation of the blood, to act where they are needed upon various organs and tissues. They are best referred to as 'autacoids'... Among the best known of the autacoid substances are adrenaline..thyroxine..insulin.

†**au'tæsthesy**. *Obs.* [f. Gr. αὐτ(ο- self + αἴσθησις perception, sensation.] Self-consciousness.

1642 H. MORE *Song of Soul* I. II. xxv, Autæsthesy's divided into tway. *a* **1652** J. SMITH *Sel. Disc.* viii. 387 To preserve an unhallowed autæsthesy and feeling sense of themselves.

†**au'tangelist**. *Obs.*⁻⁰ [f. Gr. αὐτάγγελ-ος, f. αὐτ(ο- self + ἄγγελος messenger.] 'One who is his own Messenger.' Bailey 1742.

autantitypy (ɔːtæn'tɪtɪpɪ). [f. Gr. αὐτ(ο- self + ANTITYPY.] 'The positive notion of an insuperable power in body of resisting compression; ultimate or absolute incompressibility.' Sir W. Hamilton *Dissert.* in *Reid's Wks.* 847.

autarch ('ɔːtɑːk). [ad. Gr. αὔταρχος, f. αὐτ(ο-self, by oneself, independently + ἀρχός ruler.] An absolute ruler; = AUTOCRAT.

1865 *Daily Tel.* 28 Feb. 4/4 The great autarchs of history.

autarchic (ɔː'tɑːkɪk), *a.*¹ [f. AUTARCHY¹ + -IC.] Absolute, despotic.

1893 in *Funk's Standard Dict.* **1936** [see AUTARKIC *a.*].

autarchic, *a.*², var. AUTARKIC *a.*

autarchy ('ɔːtɑkɪ). [ad. Gr. αὐταρχία, f. αὔταρχος: see AUTARCH and -Y.]

1. Absolute sovereignty, despotism.

1665 M. N. *Medela Medicinæ* sig. A5 Epist. ded., Who.. are so confident, as to attempt an Autarchie in Physick, and long for an opportunity to oppress and trample upon the nobler sort of Philosophers and Physicians. **1692** WASHINGTON tr. *Milton's Def. Pop.* Wks. 1738 I. 467 A certain Government, which he calls an Autarchy, of which he makes God the only Judg. *Ibid.* 468 That absolute and imaginary Right of Sovereignty, that Autarchy. **1838** F. LIEBER *Man. Pol. Ethics* I. II. xii. 411, I call autarchy that state in which public power, whole and entire, unmitigated and unmodified, rests..in the hands of a monarch, or the people, or in aristocracy.

2. Self-government.

1691 G. B. (*title*) Autarchy or the Art of Self-Government.

autarchy, var. AUTARKY.

autarkic (ɔː'tɑːkɪk), *a.* Also (irreg.) **autarchic**. [f. next (cf. AUTARKY) + -IC.] Of, pertaining to, or characterized by autarky; (economically) self-sufficient.

1883 L. F. WARD *Dynamic Sociology* I. vii. 466 Stages in the inception, development, and progress of social aggregation..1, the solitary, or autarchic, stage. **1936** *Economist* 11 Jan. 74/1 The world must retrace its..steps towards arbitrary autarkic divisions. **1936** R. F. HARROD in *Times* 1 Dec. 12/3 Since the autarchic States tend generally to be autarkic also, genuine confusion may be caused.. unless the spellings are kept distinct. **1939** A. G. B. FISHER *Econ. Self-Suff.* 22 Any attempt to carve the earth's surface into suitable large-scale autarkic blocs must..mean serious conflict. **1958** *Economist* 26 July 269 The itch..to make the sterling area into more of an autarkic block.

autarky ('ɔːtɑkɪ). In 7 **-archie**; 9– **-archy**.[ad. Gr. αὐτάρκεια, f. αὐτάρκης self-sufficient, f. αὐτ(ο- self + ἀρκέ-ειν to suffice.]

a. Self-sufficiency.

1617 SAMUEL WARD *Balme from Gilead* 18 The Autarchie and selfe-sufficiencie of God. **1635** H. VALENTINE *Foure Sea-Sermons* 10 It may as well stand upon its bottome, and boast an Autarchie, and selfe sufficiencie. *c* **1643** *Maximes Unfolded* 4 Autarchie or selfe sufficiency. **1657** J. TRAPP *Commentary Ezra, Neh., Psalms* 669 [Ps. xxxiv. 10] These have an autarkie, a self-sufficiency, such as godliness is never without. **1863** D. SIMON *Dorner's Pers. Christ* II. III. 66 To the Kantian *practical* autarchy, the dogma of the Godman is unnecessary. **1951** HOGGART *Auden* v. 150 He may deny the necessity for any metaphysic, and retreat into a cold intellectual autarchy. **1957** T. S. ELIOT *On Poetry* i. 23 A general *autarky* in culture simply will not work: the hope of perpetuating the culture of any country lies in communication with others.

b. *spec.* (A policy of) economic self-sufficiency in a political unit.

1934 *Sun* (Baltimore) 11 Apr. 10/3 Internationalism.. would at least check the present steady drive toward.. autarchy, political isolationism and Fascism. **1939** J. HOPE SIMPSON *Refugee Question* 5 The doctrine of 'autarky'..has materially affected normal international trade.

Hence **'autarkist** *sb.*, one who advocates or practises autarky. Also *attrib.*

1938 *New Statesman* 15 Jan. 75/1 The only chance of inducing the autarkist countries to open their frontiers to the free flow of goods and money. **1939** A. G. B. FISHER *Econ. Self-Suff.* 14 The autarkist is not greatly interested in higher standards of living.

autecology (ɔːtiː'kɒlədʒɪ) [ad. G. *autökologie* (Schröter, 1898), f. AUT(O-¹ + ECOLOGY.] The study of the ecology of an individual plant or species, opp. SYNECOLOGY. Hence ˌ**auteco'logical** *a.*

1910 FLAHAULT & SCHRÖTER *Phytogeogr. Nomencl.* (IIIrd Internat. Bot. Congr.) 24 Oecology thus includes the study of the habitat conditions and the adaptation-phenomena of the single species (Autecology). **1926** H. H. ALLEN in Tansley & Chipp *Aims & Methods Stud. Veg.* xxii. 370 The high-mountain vegetation provides, further, much valuable material for autecological work. **1932** FULLER & CONARD tr. *Braun-Blanquet's Plant Sociol.* v. 81 The chief interests of most ecologists have centred in autecology, the life relations of the individual plant.

autem. *Old. Cant.* A church. Hence **autem mort**, a married woman, **autem cackler**, a Dissenting preacher. See Harman's *Caveat*, B.E. *Dict. Cant. Crew*, Grose, Farmer & Henley *Slang*.

autenkid, *ppl. a. Obs.* [Corrupt f. *autentik*, or *autenticat*.] Authenticated.

c **1400** *Apol. Loll.* 15 Materis to be..confermid, canonizid, autenkid.

autentik, -ycal, etc., obs. ff. AUTHENTIC, etc.

auter(e, -ir, -re, obs. forms of ALTAR.

autergy, variant of AUTURGY.

†**aute'xousious**, *a. Obs. rare*⁻¹. [f. Gr. αὐτεξούσι-ος (see next) + -OUS.] Exercising free-will.

1678 CUDWORTH *Intell. Syst.* 220 As autexousious or freewilled, they should have a power of determining themselves.

†**autexousy**. *Obs. rare*⁻¹. [ad. Gr. αὐτεξουσία independent power, f. αὐτ(ο- (see AUTO-¹) + ἐξουσία power, authority.] Free will.

1678 CUDWORTH *Intell. Syst.* 55 Asserting the τὸ ἐφ' ἡμῖν, Autexousie, or Liberty from Necessity.

†**au'thent**. *Mus. Obs.* In 6 **autenta**. [ad. med.L. *aut(h)ent-a*, ad. Gr. αὐθέντ-ης: see AUTHENTIC.] = AUTHENTIC B 5.

1597 MORLEY *Introd. Mus.* Annot., To the autentas they give more liberty of ascending then to the Plagæ..euery autenta may go a whole eight aboue the finall key. **1609** DOULAND *Ornithop. Microl.* 13 An Antiphone is newly found, which..hath not the rising of an Authent in the middle.

authentic (ɔː'θɛntɪk), *a.* (and *sb.*). Forms: 4–5 **auctentyke**, 4–7 **autentik(e**, 5 **-yk**, 5–6 **-icke**, **-yke**, 6 **attentik**, **awtentyke**, 6–7 **aut-**, **authentique**, **-ike**, **-icke**, 6–8 **-ick**, 6– **authentic**. [a. OF. *autentique* (13th c.), ad. L. *authentic-us*, a. Gr. αὐθεντικός 'of first-hand authority, original,' f. αὐθεντία 'original authority,' and αὐθέντης 'one who does a thing himself, a principal, a master, an autocrat,' f. αὐτ(ο- self + -ἕντης (cf. συνέντης = συνεργός fellow-worker). In 15th c. mis-spelt after L. *auctor*; in 16th assimilated to the orig. Greek. The development of meaning is involved, and influenced by med.L. and Fr.; senses 3 and 4 seem to combine the ideas of 'authoritative' and 'original.']

A. *adj.*

†**1. a.** Of authority, authoritative (*properly* as possessing original or inherent authority, but also as duly authorized); entitled to obedience or respect. *Obs.*

1340 HAMPOLE *Pr. Consc.* 7116 Saint Austyn..Whase wordes er auctentyke. **1382** WYCLIF *Isa.* Prol., No goostli vndurstondyng is autentik, no but it be groundid in the text opynli. *a* **1420** OCCLEVE *De Reg. Princ.* 125 The bible, Whiche is a booke autentyke and credible. **1595** CHAPMAN *Banq. Sence* (1639) 31 Let autentique Reason be our guide. **1630** NAUNTON *Fragm. Reg.* (Arb.) 62 We have an authentique Rule to decide the doubt. **1682** NORRIS *Hierocles* 20 To esteem their Sentences as authentick as Laws. **1724** SWIFT *Drapier's Lett.* Wks. 1755 V. II. 105 Some short plain authentick tract might be published for the information both of petty and grand-juries. **1849** FITZGERALD tr. *Whitaker's Disput.* 332 That is called authentic, which is sufficient to itself, which commends, sustains, proves itself, and hath credit and authority from itself.

†**b.** of persons. *Obs.*

1523 LD. BERNERS *Froiss.* I. ccccxxvii. 749 One of the moost autentyke men of the court of parlyment. **1710** PRIDEAUX *Orig. Tithes* iii. 160 Doth not appear in any Authentic writer.

†**2. a.** Legally valid, having legal force. *Obs.*

1401 *Pol. Poems* (1859) II. 80 Of her lettris and of her sele, if autentike thei weren. **1466** *Paston Lett.* 554 II. 284 Divers old deeds, some without date, insealed under autenticke seales. **1671** FLAVEL *Fount. Life* vi. 15 What is done by Commission is Authentick. **1723** SHEFFIELD (Dk. Buckhm.) *Wks.* (1753) I. 130 Under the broad authentic seal of heav'n.

†**b.** Of persons: Legally or duly qualified, authorized, licensed. *Obs.*

c **1450** HENRYSON *Mor. Fab.* 35 Hee is Autentike and a man of age, And hes great practicke of the Chancellarie. **1540** *Act 32 Hen. VIII*, xxv, With the approbacions and testimonies of fowre sundrie notaries autentique thervnto subscribed. **1601** SHAKS. *All's Well* II. iii. 14 Of all the learned and authenticke fellowes. **1610** B. JONSON *Alch.* II. iii, Why, h'is the most autentique dealer I'these commodities!

3. a. Entitled to acceptance or belief, as being in accordance with fact, or as stating fact; reliable, trustworthy, of established credit. (The prevailing sense; often used in contradistinction to *genuine*, esp. by writers on Christian Evidences, while others identify 'authentic' and 'genuine.' See sense 6.)

1369 CHAUCER *Bk. Duchesse* 1086 Though her stories be autentike. **1485** CAXTON *Trevisa's Higden* IV. xxvii. (1527) 174 This is founden in no cronycle that is auctentyke.

1532-3 *Act 24 Hen. VIII*, xii, By diuers sondrie olde autentike histories, and cronicles it is manifestlie declared and expressed. **1735** SOMERVILLE *Chase* II. 125 If some stanch Hound, with his authentick Voice Avow the recent Trail. **1739** CHESTERF. *Lett.* 35 I. 117 *Authentic* means *true*; something that may be depended upon, as coming from good authority. **1796** BP. WATSON *Apol. Bible* ii. 183 A *genuine* book is that which was written by the person whose name it bears as the author of it. An *authentic* book is that which relates matters of fact as they really happened. **1858** HAWTHORNE *Fr. & It. Jrnls.* II. 178 Some portrait.. reckoned authentic, which the early painters followed.

b. of persons (or agents).

1561 T. NORTON tr. *Calvin's Inst.* III. 327 To discredit so many authentike witnesses. **1638** SUCKLING *Aglaura* Epil. (1646) 59 When an authentique watch is shewn, Each man windes up and rectifies his own. *c* **1645** HOWELL *Lett.* (1650) I. 375 Some of the authentickest annalists. **1797** HOLCROFT tr. *Stolberg's Trav.* IV. xci. (ed. 2) 5 He is an authentic writer.

†**4.** Original, first-hand, prototypical; as opposed to *copied*. *Obs.*

1581 LAMBARDE *Eiren.* III. iv. (1588) 370 According to the Originall and Autentique Records. **1610** BP. CARLETON *Jurisd.* 72 They would send for the autentike copies of the Nicen Councell. **1667** MILTON *P.L.* IV. 719 On him who had stole Joves authentic fire. **1728** NEWTON *Chronol. Amended* vi. 369 The book..was originally copied from Authentic writings. **1822** S. ROGERS *Italy, Florence* 16 To steal a spark from their authentic fire.

5. Real, actual, 'genuine.' (Opposed to *imaginary*, *pretended*.) *arch.*

1490 CAXTON *Eneydos* vii. 32 To be closed and enuyronned wyth wallis autentyke. **1664** POWER *Exp. Philos.* III. 188 An Authentick discouragement to the promotion of the Arts and Sciences. *a* **1704** T. BROWN *Epigr.* Wks. 1730 I. 128 Well might the sage philosophers of old Their justling atoms for authentic hold. **1845** CARLYLE *Cromwell* (1871) I. 66 A faint, authentic twilight.

6. Really proceeding from its reputed source or author; of undisputed origin, genuine. (Opposed to *counterfeit*, *forged*, *apocryphal*. Cf. note, sense 3.)

1790 PALEY *Hor. Paul.* I. 1, I believe the letters authentic, and the narration in the main to be true. **1824** DIBDIN *Libr. Comp.* 27 Every authentic piece from the pens of Tyndal and Coverdale. **1880** *Daily News* 16 Dec. 5/3 Authentic documents artfully falsified.

†**7.** Belonging to himself, own, proper. *Obs.*

1596 CHAPMAN *Iliad* VIII. 74 Then Nestor cut the gears With his new-drawn authentic sword. **1649** MILTON *Eikon.* xxviii. [For justice] to put her own authentic sword into the hands of an unjust and wicked man.

†**8.** Acting of itself, self-originated, automatic.

1765 TUCKER *Lt. Nat.* I. 545 The spontaneous or authentic motions of clock-work.

9. *Mus.* Of ecclesiastical modes: Having their sounds comprised within an octave from the final. (For this application, see Grove *Dict. Mus.* I. 105.) Also, composed in an authentic mode. ***authentic cadence***: that form of perfect cadence in which the (major) chord of the dominant immediately precedes that of the tonic. Opp. to PLAGAL *a.*

1730 PEPUSCH *Harmony* x. 80 One of the Parts is in the Authentick, and the Other in the Plagal Mode of the Key we compose in. *a* **1789** BURNEY *Hist. Mus.* II. ii. 81 Guido uses the terms authentic and plagal for the modes. **1806** CALLCOTT *Mus. Gram.* 160 The Dominant..derives its name from the ancient Church Tones, in which it was the Fifth in the Authentic, and the Octave in the Plagal Scales, but always a Fifth above the final or modern Tonic. **1873** BANISTER *Music* §128 The perfect (formerly termed Authentic) Cadence, or Full Close, consists of the Major Triad on the Dominant, followed by the Triad on the Tonic. **1879** GROVE *Dict. Mus.* I. 105/2 'Ein feste Burg' and 'Eisenach' are examples of 'authentic' melodies, and the Old 100th and Hanover of 'plagal' ones. **1880** *Ibid.* II. 18/1 When first employed in polyphonic music, the Authentic scale was usually transposed.

B. *sb.*

†**1.** An authoritative book or document. *Obs.*

1599 THYNNE *Animadv.* 42 The proper signyficatione of 'autenticke' is, 'a thinge of auctorytye or credit allowed by menne of auctorytye, or the originall or fyrste archetypum of any thinge.' **1602** FULBECKE *Pandects* 25 Scripture, the authentike of Religion.

†**2.** An original (document). *Obs.*

1599 [See in sense 1]. **1608** *2nd Pt. Def. Reas. Refus. Subscr.* 86 Which is to confounde the measure and the mesured..the authentick, and some copie or notes taken out of it. **1655** FULLER *Ch. Hist.* I. 42 Principall and Interest, Authenticks and Transcripts, are all imbezzelled.

3. The ***Authentics***: title given to a collection of the New Constitutions of Justinian.

1614 SELDEN *Titles Hon.* 21 Iustinians Nouells (which they call authentiques). **1725** tr. *Dupin's Eccl. Hist. 17th c.* I. II. ii. 25 Frederick II. in the year 1220, made an Authentick which is inserted in the Justinian Code. **1744** *Notes to Peere Williams' Rep.* (1826) 52 They are called Novels, because they are new laws; and Authenticks, because they are translated authentically from the Greek tongue.

†**4.** One whose opinion is entitled to acceptance; an authority. *Obs. rare.*

1713 ADDISON *Guardian* No. 115 No critick has ever.. been looked upon as an authentick, who did not shew by his practice that he was a master of the theory.

†**5.** *Mus.* = Authentic mode; see A 9. *Obs.*

1609 DOULAND *Ornithop. Microl.* 13 Whilest they discend from a Fift to the finall Note, they are Authentickes.

†**au'thentic**, *v.* *Obs.* *rare*$^{-1}$. [ad. F. *authentique-r*: see AUTHENTICATE.] By-form of AUTHENTICATE (in passage cited, in sense 3 b).

c **1595** DANIEL *Sonnets* 52 But I must sing of thee, and those fair eyes Authentic shall my verse in time to come.

au'thentical, *a.* *arch.* Forms: 6 **autentycal**, 6–7 **-ical**, **-icall**, **authenticall**, 6– **authentical**. [f. AUTHENTIC *a.* + -AL[1].]

1. = AUTHENTIC *a.* 1.

1562 BULLEYN *Sorenes* 31 a, By the rules, and autenticall counsaill, of learned Phisicions. **1608** *2nd Pt. Def. Reas. Refus. Subscr.* 83 No scripture is Canonical but that which is Authentical, and carrieth credit in it self and of it self, without dependance of any other writinge. **1651** HOBBES *Leviath.* II. xxvi. 143 The Authenticall Interpretation of Law is not that of writers. **1710** PRIDEAUX *Orig. Tithes* v. 258 Published, and commanded to be observed as Authentical.

b. **1537** *Inst. Chr. Man* H iij b, In the writinges of any autenticall doctour or auctour of the church. **1599** B. JONSON *Ev. Man out of Hum.* IV. iii, By the Judgment of the most authentical Physicians.

2. = AUTHENTIC *a.* 2.

c **1531** *Pol. Rel. & L. Poems* (1866) 34 By the autorite of my lorde of london vnder his Autentycal seale. **1615** T. ADAMS *Lycanthr.* 29 Having first martyr'd them, then held disputation whether the act was authenticall. *a* **1679** T. GOODWIN *Wks.* (1861) I. 315 A formal, sure, legal, authentical interest.

3. = AUTHENTIC *a.* 3.

1541 BARNES *Wks.* (1573) 328/1 Authenticall hystories doth make mention, that, etc. **1677** HALE *Prim. Orig. Man.* II. vii. 181 A vigorous and authentical Tradition. **1716** T. WARD *Eng. Ref.* 247 Rome this Version does allow For most Authentical and True. **1861** W. MILL *Applic. Panth. Princ.* (ed. 2) 175 In the most authentical copies now extant.

b. **1553-87** FOXE *A. & M.* III. 381 The testimony of any authentical Writer. *a* **1619** FOTHERBY *Atheom.* I. iv. §1, More authenticall witnesses. **1666** FULLER *Hist. Camb.* (1840) 117 What authentical authors had attested the king's words.

4. = AUTHENTIC *a.* 4.

1586 FERNE *Blaz. Gentrie* 136 The worde Marque, in that autenticall tongue signified the Vttermost partes. **1594** HOOKER *Eccl. Pol.* I. (1617) 9 That Law..is as it were an authenticall, or an originall draught. **1638** SANDERSON *21 Serm.* Ad. Aul. viii. (1674) 121 The original record only is authentical and not the transcript. **1814** CARY *Dante's Parad.* xxxiii. 51 Into the ray authentical Of sovran light.

5. = AUTHENTIC *a.* 5.

1609 B. JONSON *Sil. Wom.* III. ii, Shee is the onely authenticall courtier, that is not naturally bred one, in the citie.

6. = AUTHENTIC *a.* 6.

1624 GATAKER *Transubst.* 43 He citeth these confessed counterfeits as authenticall Authors. **1845** SHAW *On Conf. Faith* i. (1848) 20 The Scriptures..have come down to us uncorrupted, and are, therefore, authentical.

7. *Mus.* = AUTHENTIC *a.* 9.

1597 MORLEY *Introd. Mus.* Annot., Euery song which about the beginning riseth a fift aboue the finall key, is of an autenticall tune. **1609** DOULAND *Ornithop. Microl.* 13 All the odde tones are *Authenticall*, all the euen *Plagall*.

au'thentically, *adv.* [f. prec. + -LY[2].]

†**1.** With authority, authoritatively; with legal validity, in proper legal form. *Obs.*

1577 G. HARVEY *Letter-bk.* (1884) 56 A former Composition solemely and autentically agreid uppon. *a* **1652** J. SMITH *Sel. Disc.* vi. viii. (1821) 262 To declare his mind authentically to them, and dictate what his truth was. **1757** BURKE *Abridgm. Eng. Hist.* Wks. X. 286 Now for the first time authentically known by the name of England. **1798** W. TAYLOR in *Month. Rev.* XXVII. 501 Its promises are more authentically proclaimed.

2. With evidence of truth or certainty, so as to be accepted or relied upon; credibly.

1590 C. S. *Right Relig.* 26 How can they proue those counsels to be autentically true? **1681** in Somers' *Tracts* II. 125 When our Grievances shall be authentically proved. **1767** BARRINGTON in *Phil. Trans.* LVII. 212, I was most authentically informed..that several of them were caught. **1883** FROUDE in *Contemp. Rev.* XLIV. 1 A few pages will contain all that can be authentically learnt of..Shakspeare.

3. Actually, genuinely, really.

1658 SIR T. BROWNE *Gard. Cyrus* Wks. II. 524 Authentically differenced. **1840** CARLYLE *Heroes* (1858) 252 All old Poems, Homer's and the rest, are authentically Songs. **1858** —— *Fredk. Gt.* I. II. i. 49 An authentically noble human figure. *a* **1850** ROSSETTI *Dante & Circ.* I. 247 The possibility..of these sonnets being authentically by Dante and Forese.

†**au'thenticalness.** *Obs.* [f. as prec. + -NESS.] Authentical quality; authenticity.

1. Authoritativeness, original authority.

a **1652** J. SMITH *Sel. Disc.* VI. xiii. (1821) 295 They might seem to weaken the authenticalness of the divine oracles. **1655** FULLER *Hist. Camb.* 25 Although some copies and transcripts of them were reserved; yet..such carried not authenticalness with them.

2. = AUTHENTICITY 2.

1637 WINSTANLEY *Eng. Poets* 147 These additions.. obtain not equal authenticalness with what was set forth by Mr. Cambden himself. **1725** *Brice's Week. Jrnl.* 6 Aug. 4 The Two following Stories..For the Authenticalness of either I cannot answer.

3. = AUTHENTICITY 3.

1667 *Treaty* in Magens *Insurances* (1755) II. 523 Countersigns..whereby their Authenticalness may the better appear, and that they may not in any wise be falsified. **1702** ADDISON *Dial. Medals* (1751) 8 Descanting upon the rarity and authenticalness of the several pieces that lie before them. *a* **1859** L. HUNT in *Athenæum* 7 July (1883) 18 Mrs. Iago asked me the other day about its authenticalness.

authenticate (ɔːˈθɛntɪkeɪt), *v.* [f. med.L. *authenticā-re*, *authenticāt-*, to make authentic, f. *authentic-us*; also in It. *autenticare*, Sp. *autenticar*, Fr. *authentiquer*.] To make or prove authentic.

1. *trans.* and *refl.* To invest (a thing) with authority; to render authoritative.

a **1733** NORTH *Lives* II. 339 They want antiquity to authenticate their ceremonies. **1768** BLACKSTONE *Comm.* I. 32 The Clementine constitutions..were..authenticated in 1317 by..John XXII. **1829** I. TAYLOR *Enthus.* iv. (1867) 80 Christianity authenticates the voice of conscience.

2. To give legal validity to; to render valid, establish the validity of.

1653 *Nissena* 64 An Order from his Majesty, authenticated and sealed by his Kingly Seal. **1768** BLACKSTONE *Comm.* I. 323 A tax..of service to the public in general, by authenticating instruments. **1817** JAS. MILL *Brit. India* I. ii. (1840) I. 63 They recommended, as the best mode of authenticating the privilege, that it should be incorporated in a fresh renewal of their charter.

3. To establish the title to credibility and acceptance: **a.** of a statement, or **b.** of a reputed fact.

a. **1654** COKAYNE *Dianea* I. 15 Oleandro replied, he.. could authenticate his Maximes by examples. **1664** POWER *Exp. Philos.* II. 135 To authenticate and make good his Hypothesis. **1856** DOVE *Logic Chr. Faith* I. i. §2. 63 If the conclusion..is not authenticated by the real occurrence.

b. **1662** H. STUBBE *Ind. Nectar* ii. 13 Those ways, which are authenticated by Physicians. **1778** ROBERTSON *Hist. Amer.* II. v. 60 Were not all the circumstances of this extraordinary transaction authenticated by the most unquestionable evidence. **1823** LAMB *Elia* (1860) 298 A room, which tradition authenticated to have been the same.

4. To establish the claims of (anything) to a particular character or authorship; to establish the genuineness of; to certify the authorship of.

1852 LD. COCKBURN *Jeffrey* I. 285 We went through the whole work, authenticating all his papers. **1865** GROTE *Plato* I. iv. 155 Aristophanes authenticates..not merely the Leges, but also the Epinomis, and the Epistolæ.

b. with *subord. cl.*

1860 PUSEY *Min. Proph.* 535 The usual formula..with which the prophets authenticated, that they spake not of themselves, but by the Spirit of God.

†**au'thenticate**, *ppl. a.* *Obs.* *rare*$^{-1}$. [ad. L. *authenticāt-us*: see prec.] = AUTHENTICATED.

1572 *Schole House Wom.* 862 in Hazl. *E.P.P.* IV. 138 The trueth is knowen, as in this case, By holy writ autenticate.

au'thenticated, *ppl. a.* [f. AUTHENTICATE *v.* + -ED.] Invested with authority, validity, correctness, truth, genuineness; certified.

1846 GEO. ELIOT tr. *Strauss's Life of Jesus* I. I. iv. §32. 203 It is an authenticated point that the assessment..did not take place..under Herod. **1862** DANA *Man. Geol.* 605 Authenticated instances of this are wanting. **1874** BOUTELL *Arms & Arm.* ii. 10 Unfounded conjectures in place of authenticated facts.

au'thenticating, *ppl. a.* [f. as prec. + -ING[2].] That authenticates.

1787 ELPHINSTON *Propriety*, The alluring and authenticating picture drawn by the hand ov Truith. **1817** BENTHAM *Ch. Eng.* (1818) Introd. 218 Without any authenticating date.

authentication (ɔːˌθɛntɪˈkeɪʃən). [n. of action f. AUTHENTICATE: see -ATION.]

1. The action or process of authenticating.

1788 T. JEFFERSON *Writ.* (1859) II. 543 So numerous are the writings..that their authentication..would occupy the greater part of his time. **1847** C. ADDISON *Contracts* I. i. §1 (1883) 19 The use of seals for the authentication of contracts and writings. **1868** M. PATTISON *Academ. Org.* §5. 308 The interpretation and authentication of ancient documents.

2. The condition of being authenticated.

1860 DICKENS *Uncomm. Trav.* xv, Politeness..forbade my doubting them [ghost stories], and they acquired an air of authentication.

authenticator (ɔːˈθɛntɪkeɪtər). [n. of agent f. AUTHENTICATE, on L. analogy.] He who authenticates, who guarantees a thing as valid, true, or reliable.

1863 J. MURPHY *Comm. Gen.* ii. 8–14 That Moses was not merely the authenticator, but the composer of this.. document of Genesis.

authenticity (ɔːθənˈtɪsɪtɪ). Also 7 **authentity**. [f. AUTHENTIC *a.* + -ITY. Cf. mod.F. *authenticité*.] The quality of being authentic, or entitled to acceptance,

1. as being authoritative or duly authorized.

1657 TRAPP *Comm. Job* i. 1 Sufficiently asserting the authentity and authority of this Book. **1858** HAWTHORNE *Fr. & It. Jrnls.* II. 254 He proved the authenticity of his mission.

2. as being in accordance with fact, as being true in substance.

1762 H. WALPOLE *Vertue's Anecd. Paint.* (1786) I. 53 The portrait..was rather a work of command and imagination than of authenticity. **1790** BOSWELL *Johnson* V. ix. 295 What I have preserved..has the value of the most perfect authenticity. **1830** J. POYNDER in *Academy* 21 Oct. (1876) 410/1 The value of the evidence must, of course, depend entirely on its authenticity. **1868** FREEMAN *Norm. Conq.* (1876) II. App. 663 The fact at once stamps its authenticity.

3. as being what it professes in origin or authorship, as being genuine; genuineness.

1760 HUME in *Four C. Eng. Lett.* 243 With regard to the authenticity of these fragments of our Highland poetry. **1790** PALEY *Hor. Paul.* I. 3 As to the authenticity of the epistles, this argument .. is nearly conclusive. **1855** MILMAN *Lat. Chr.* (1864) II. IV. i. 175 *note*, Though not free from interpolation yet there seems no reason to doubt its authenticity.

4. as being real, actual; reality.

1851 MARIOTTI *Italy in 1848*, 116 A voucher for the authenticity of deeds of wanton cruelty.

¶ By some writers, especially on the Christian evidences, *authenticity* has been confined to sense 2, and *genuineness* used in sense 3.

†**au'thenticly**, *adv. Obs.* For forms see AUTHENTIC *a.* [f. AUTHENTIC *a.* + -LY[2].] = AUTHENTICALLY.

1483 CAXTON *Gold. Leg.* 261/1 Saynt Austyn sheweth autentyckly in a Sermon. **1542** HEN. VIII *Declar. Scots* 198 Regesters and recordes iudicially and autentiquely made. **1583** GOLDING *Calvin on Deut.* Pref. Ep. 1 As their writings do autentikely, fully, and sufficiently, witnesse. **1648** FAIRFAX, etc. *Remonstr.* 32 Publikely and authentickly avowed. **1737** WHISTON *Josephus' Antiq.* Dissert. i, He could learn no way so authenticly as from this testimony.

†**au'thenticness.** *Obs.* [f. AUTHENTIC *a.* + -NESS.] Authentic quality; authenticity.

1. Authoritativeness, authority: = AUTHENTICITY 1.

1629 DONNE *Serm.* xxiv. 238 Another manner of credit and authentiquenesse then that which the Canonists speak of. **1655** GURNALL *Chr. in Arm.* iii. (1669) 286/2 Who will say that the Proclamation of a Prince hath its authentickness from the Piller it hangs on in the Market Cross?

2. = AUTHENTICITY 2, 3.

1634–46 ROW *Hist. Kirk* (1842) 479 Sundrie old papers .. that did verie much prove to the authenticknes of the old registers of the Kirk. **1695** WOODWARD *Nat. Hist. Earth* III. ii. (1723) 180 The Authentickness of the Mosaick Writings. **1709** W. SMITH in *Thoresby's Corr.* II. 171 Who vouch for the credit and authenticness of that which is usually called Chapernay's Charter. **1743** M. TOMLINSON *Protest. Birthr.* 18 A diligent Search into the Authentickness, Veracity, and Sense of the sacred Writings.

auther, -ir, obs. forms of EITHER.

authigenic (ɔːθɪ'dʒɛnɪk), *a. Geol.* [ad. G. *authigene* (E. Kalkowsky 1880, in *Neues Jahrb. f. Mineralogie* 4), f. Gr. αὐθιγενής born on the spot, native + -IC.] Originating where found (see quots.). Cf. ALLOTHIGENIC *a.*

1888 F. H. HATCH in J. J. H. Teall *Brit. Petrogr.* (Gloss.), *Authigenic*, a term applied by Kalkowsky to a mineral constituent, to denote that it came into existence with, or after, the rock containing it. **1890** C. R. VAN HISE in *Bull. Geol. Soc. Amer.* I. 231 It has been seen that much if not all of the mica is authigenic. **1893** A. GEIKIE *Text-bk. Geol.* (ed. 3) 65 Such crystals, which are obviously more ancient than those forming the general mass of the rock, have been called *allogenic*, while those which belong to the time of formation of the rock, or to some subsequent change within the rock, are known as *authigenic*.

authology, obs. form of AUTOLOGY.

author ('ɔːθə(r)), *sb.* Forms: 4–6 **autour**, 4–7 **autor**, 5 **awtor**, **autere**, 5–6 **auctoure**, **-tore**, **actour**, **-tor**, 5–7 **auctour**, **-tor**, 6 **aucthour**, 6–7 **aucthor**, 6–8 **authour**, 6– **author**. [a. AF. *autour* = OF. *autor*, later *auteur*, ad. L. *auctor*, agent-noun f. *augēre* to make to grow, originate, promote, increase. Already in 14th c. F., occasionally written *auct-* after L., which became the ordinary spelling in Eng. in 15–16th c., and was further corrupted to *act-*, from med.L. confusion of *auctor* and *actor*. The spelling *auth-* seems to have been at first a scribal variant of *aut-* (cf. *rhetor*, *rethour*) in 15–16th c. F., and appeared in Eng. *c* 1550, being at first applied to the form *auctour* so as to make *aucthour*. It is impossible to say to what extent these factitious spellings affected the spoken word, or when the modern pronunciation was established.]

1. *gen.* The person who originates or gives existence to anything: **a.** An inventor, constructor, or founder. Now *obs.* of things material; exc. as in b.

c **1384** WYCLIF *De Eccl.* ix, *Sel. Wks.* 1871 III. 359 Þis [lawe] mut passe alle oþir siþ þe auctor is þe beste. *c* **1386** CHAUCER *Parson's Tale* 808 The auctour [*v.r.* auctor, actour, autere] of matrimonye, that is Crist. **1447** BOKENHAM *Seyntys* Introd. 1 The efficyent cause is the auctour Wych .. doth hys labour To acomplyse the begunne matere. **1576** LAMBARDE *Peramb. Kent* (1826) 297 One Robert Creuequer, the authour of the Castle. **1663** GERBIER *Counsel* C iij a, The Author of the Piazza. **1699** *Lond. Gaz.* No. 3532/4 (*Advt.*) The Author of the Rich Cordial called Nectar and Ambrosia, is Removed to Mr. Hugh Newmans. **1766** GOLDSM. *Vic. W.* xxix. (1857) 211 The Authour of our religion. **1865** MILL *Liberty* ii. 18/1 The authors and abettors of the rule.

b. (*of all*, *of nature*, *of the universe*, etc.) The Creator.

c **1374** CHAUCER *Troylus* III. 1016 But o þou Ioue, o autour of nature! *c* **1400** *Apol. Loll.* 44 Crist, autor of al þing. **1508** FISHER *Wks.* I. 198 Auctour and maker of all thynges. **1714** ADDISON *Spect.* No. 571 ⁋7 The great Author of Nature. **1853** ROBERTSON *Serm.* Ser. III. iv. (1872) 55 The Father the Author of our being .. He is the Author of all life.

c. He who gives rise to or causes an action, event, circumstance, state, or condition of things.

1413 LYDG. *Pylgr. Sowle* I. xvii. 14 An open lyer and autour of al falshede. *c* **1440** *Gesta Rom.* II. v. (1838) 287 Auctore of pride is the fende; auctor of concupiscence of eyene is the worlde. **1606** SHAKS. *Ant. & Cl.* II. vi. 138 The immediate Author of their variance. **1609** SKENE *Reg. Maj.* 6 Ane lover, and ane auctor of peace. **1653** HOLCROFT *Procopius* I. 15 Authour of the mischiefs. **1865** MILL *Liberty* ii. 16/1 The authors of such splendid benefits. **1884** *Chr. World* 5 June 417/1 The author of the Zulu war.

†**d.** He who authorizes or instigates; the prompter or mover. *Obs.*

1570 ASCHAM *Scholem.* (Arb.) 69 Som .. in Courte were authors that honest Citizens .. shoulde watche at euerie gate. **1578** TIMME *Calvin on Gen.* 159 Neither will I be the author to give liberty. **1588** SHAKS. *Tit. A.* I. i. 435 The Gods .. forfend, I should be Authour to dishonour you! **1656** HOBBES *Liberty, etc.* (1841) 214 Author, is he which owneth an action, or giveth a warrant to do it.

2. *spec.* †**a.** One who begets; a father, an ancestor. *Obs.* (exc. in *author of his being*: cf. 1 c.)

c **1300** *K. Alis.* 4519 My riches, and my tressours, And alle hath do myn autors. **1660** BLOOME *Archit.* A b, Tuscanus, who is reported to be the generall Author of the Germans. **1718** POPE *Iliad* VI. 254 The honour'd author of my birth and name. **1823** LAMB *Elia* Ser. I. i. (1865) 9 Old Walter Plumer (his reputed author). **1850** THACKERAY *Pendennis* xxvii. (1863) 227 The author of her being, her persecuted .. murdered father.

3. a. *esp.* and *absol.* One who sets forth written statements; the composer or writer of a treatise or book. (Now often used to include *authoress*.)

c **1380** WYCLIF *Wks.* (1880) 267 ȝif holy writt be fals, certis god autor þer-of is fals. *c* **1385** CHAUCER *L.G.W.* 88 Of manye a geste As autours seyn. **1432–50** tr. *Higden* (1865) I. 7 A tretys, excerpte of diverse labores of auctores. **1509** BARCLAY *Shyp of Folys* (1874) II. 26 The noble actor plinius. **1578** LYTE *Dodoens* 499 Wherof both Turner and this Aucthor do write. **1678** R. LESTRANGE *Seneca's Mor.* To Reader, My Choice of the Authour, and of the Subject. **1726** GAY *Fables* I. x, No author ever spar'd a brother; Wits are game-cocks to one another. **1771** BURKE *Corr.* (1844) I. 275, I am not the author of Junius, and .. I know not the author of that paper. **1818** BYRON *Beppo* lxxii, One hates an author that is all author, fellows In foolscap uniforms turned up with ink, So very anxious, clever, fine, and jealous. **1880** *Sat. Rev.* 20 Nov. 653 What size will the author's writings attain when she gets beyond her studies?

b. *elliptically* put for: An author's writings.

1601 SHAKS. *Twel. N.* II. v. 175, I will reade politicke Authours. **1727** SWIFT *To Earl Oxf.* Wks. 1755 III. II. 42 Cheap'ning old authors on a stall. **1759** ROBERTSON *Hist. Scotl.* I. II. 141 Acquainted with the Greek and Roman authors. **1865** *Sat. Rev.* 5 Aug. 168/1 The names of authors whom they never read.

4. The person on whose authority a statement is made; an authority, an informant. (Usually with *poss. pron.* 'my, his author.') *arch.* or *Obs.*

c. **1384** CHAUCER *H. Fame* 314 Non other auttour [*v.r.* auctour, authour] a-legge I. *c* **1440** *Partonope* 392 That ys french which ys myn auctoure. **1529** MORE *Dyaloge* 88 b, I wold se a better author therof than such an heretyque as Luther. **1697** DAMPIER *Voy.* (1729) I. 350 Islands that abound with Gold and Cloves, If I may credit my Author Prince Jeoly, who was born on one of them. **1784** REID *Let.* in *Wks.* I. 63/2, I suspected that the gentleman who was my author had given some colouring to this story.

†**5.** One who has authority over others; a director, ruler, commander. *Obs.*

1382 WYCLIF *Gal.* iv. 2 He is under tutours and actouris [*v.r.* autours; **1388** tutoris; Vulg. *auctoribus*.]

6. *attrib.* and in *Comb.* See also AUTHOR-CRAFT. Frequent in appos. use.

1711 SHAFTESB. *Charac.* (1737) I. 214 To recommend this author-charactor to our future princes. *Ibid.* 226 Wherever the author-practice and liberty of the pen has .. prevail'd. *a* **1806** D. WORDSWORTH *Tour Scotland* in *Jrnls.* (1941) I. 297 The author-tourists have quarrelled with the architecture of it. **1830** LAMB *Corr.* cxiii. 317 How comfortable to author-rid folks. **1835** *Court Mag.* VI. 51/1 His peculiarity as an author-actor. **1860** DICKENS *Lett.* (1881) III. 195 All through my author life. **1865** *Macm. Mag.* Dec. 156 Author-created visitants. **1898** *Daily News* 21 May 2/2 My friend the author-statesman. **1903** *Book Lover* Sept. 4/1 The author-artist has been as successful with his pen as with his brush. **1905** *Daily Chron.* 16 Dec. 8/5 The brilliant young author-manager. **1909** *Westm. Gaz.* 15 Dec. 1/2 There was only one author-producer in his experience in whose judgment the actor could always trust implicitly. **1922** JOYCE *Ulysses* 449 *Bloom.* Well, I follow a literary occupation. Author-journalist.

†**7.** The editor of a journal. *Obs.*

1697 *Flying Post* May 18–20 Printed by T. Snowden .. for the Author. **1724** *Brit. Jrnl.* (*imprint*) London: Printed for T. Warner, at the Black Boy in Pater-Noster-Row, where Advertisements and Letters to the Author are taken in. **1753** *Jackson's Oxf. Jrnl.* I. 5 May *ad fin.* Printed by W. Jackson in the High-Street, Oxford: By whom Letters to the Author, Articles of News, and Advertisements are taken.

author, *v.* [f. prec. sb.]

1. To be the author of an action; to originate, cause, occasion. *Obs.* exc. in U.S. use: to be the author or originator of (a book, play, remark, etc.).

1596 CHAPMAN *Iliad* I. 231 The last foul thing Thou ever author'dst. **1602** WARNER *Alb. Eng.* XIII. lxxviii. (1612) 322 A good God may not aucthor noysome things. **1632** SIR J. ELIOT in *Four C. Eng. Lett.* 65 The divine blessing .. which authors all the happiness we receive. **1940** *Time* 15 Apr. 55/2 Her father .. authored several successful plays and movies. **1957** W. C. HANDY *Father of Blues* xxi. 288 He once authored the famous Ziegfeld Midnight Roof productions. **1959** M. CHAMBERLIN *Dear Friends & Darling Romans* (1960) viii. 182 The saying was authored by some husband. **1967** *Boston Sunday Herald* 30 Apr. VI. 2/6 She has authored a reference book on the Genus Ilex in China.

†**2.** To be the author of a statement; to state, declare, say. *Obs.*

1602 WARNER *Alb. Eng.* Epit. (1612) 352 Brute is authored to haue arriued in this Iland .. in the year of the worlds age 2855. **1632** MASS. & FIELD *Fatal Dowry* IV. ii, More of him I dare not author.

†**'authorage.** *Obs. rare.* [f. AUTHOR *sb.*; cf. *brokerage*, etc.] = AUTHORSHIP.

1652 *F. Greville's Life of Sidney* Ded., Not pretending to the Authorage.

†**au'thorament.** *Obs. rare*[−1]. [ad. L. *auctōrāment-um*, in med.L. *autōrāmentum*, f. *auctōrāre* to bind, oblige, f. *auctor* in sense of 'vendor.'] An obligation, binding provision, stipulation.

1607 *Schol. Disc. agst. Antichr.* I. Contents 2, It sinneth against a maine authorament of the 2. command.

†**'authorative**, *a. Obs. rare*[−1]. [f. med.L. *autōrāre*, *auctōrāre*, to be author, authorize: see -ATIVE.] Of the nature of authority, authoritative.

1645 *Mod. Answ. Prynne's Reply* 46 For any authorative power of jurisdiction that Synods .. have.

author-craft ('ɔːθəkrɑːft, -æ-). Skill as an author, or its exercise.

1816 SCOTT *Antiq.* xiv, The mysteries of author-craft. **1824** *Westm. Rev.* Jan. 223 High examples .. of this species of authorcraft. **1840** CARLYLE *Heroes* ii. (1858) 234 All art and authorcraft are of small amount to that. **1851** DIXON *W. Penn* vii. (1872) 60 An attempt in author-craft which brought him into conflict with men.

†**'authorer.** *Obs. rare*[−1]. [f. AUTHOR *v.* + -ER[1].] Originator, instigator.

a **1556** CRANMER *Wks.* II. 190 The authorers and procurers of these seditions.

authoress ('ɔːθərɪs). Forms: 5 **aucteuresse**, 6–7 **auctr-**, **authresse**, 8 **authouress**, 7– **authoress**. Also 5 **auctorice**, 6 **auctrice**. [f. AUTHOR *sb.* (in its successive forms) + -ESS. Not in Fr. The 15–16th c. *auctorice*, *auctrice*, ad. L. *auctrix*, *-tricem*, is strictly a distinct formation: see -TRICE.] A female author: **a.** an originator, causer; **b.** a leader; **c.** a mother, creatress; **d.** *esp.* a female literary composer. (Now used only when sex is purposely emphasized; otherwise, in all the senses, and especially the last, *author* is now used of both sexes.)

a. 1494 FABYAN V. cxxvi. 107 Brunechield, that had been auctorice of so manyfold mischefes. **1523** *State Papers Hen. VIII*, IV. 87 The oonly auctrice of ferme peax bitwene bothe realmes. **1612** WARNER *Alb. Eng.* VII. xxxvi. 176 Only thou art Auctresse of such ill. **1632** J. HAYWARD *Eromena* 32 She was the authresse of all the mischiefe. **1645** J. G[OODWIN] *Innoc. & Truth Tri.* 63 If all the errors .. should be charged upon the way of Presbyterie, as the Authoresse and Foundresse of them. **1718** POPE *Iliad* XXIV. 970 Others cursed the authoress of their woe.

b. 1583 STANYHURST *Aeneis* I. (Arb.) 29 Of this valiant attempt a woomman is authresse. **1654** EARL ORRERY *Parthen.* (1676) 532 The Authoress of shedding so much Blood.

c. *c* **1603** CHAPMAN *Iliad* VI. 277 The great helm-mover thus received the auth'ress of his kind: 'My royal mother.' *a* **1779** COOK *Voy.* (1790) IV. 1491 Who, they say, is a female, and the supreme authoress of nature.

d. 1478 CAXTON *Prou. Crist. de Pisan* Coloph., Of these sayynges Cristyne was aucteuresse. **1724** SWIFT *Corinna* Wks. 1755 III. II. 154 At twelve a wit and a coquette .. Turns auth'ress, and is Curll's for life. **1825** SOUTHEY in *Q. Rev.* XXXI. 384 Upon this, the authoress has been misinformed. **1865** *Reader* 4 Mar. 254 The authoress has read a deal and travelled a deal.

authorial (ɔː'θɔərɪəl), *a.* Also **autorial**. [f. AUTHOR *sb.*; after words from L. *-ōrius*: see -ORIAL. *Autorial* is a futile variation; L. analogies would give *auctorial*.] Pertaining to an author (of books).

1796 RITSON in *Four C. Eng. Lett.* 346 A mass of error both typographical and authorial. **1816** SCOTT *Antiq.* xiv, I am a total stranger to authorial vanity. *a* **1847** POE *E. A. Lewis* Wks. 1864 III. 248 The autorial merits of Mrs. Lewis. **1882** *Athenæum* 1 Apr. 405/2 There is a good deal to be said, after all, for the authorial 'we.'

au'thorially, *adv.* [f. prec. + -LY[2].] After the manner of an author (of books).

1844 TUPPER *Twins* xxiii. 170, I was, authorially speaking, behind the door.

†**au'thorical**, *a. Obs.* [f. AUTHOR *sb.*, after *oratorical*, etc.; not on L. analogies.] Of or pertaining to an author, or to one who is an authority.

1564 BAULDWIN *Mor. Philos.* (Palfr.) v. 4 Which they understand not, without some authoricall direction. **1837** *Athenæum* No. 503. 437 Mere authorical backslidings.

†**au'thoridate**, *v. Obs. rare*[−1]. [? for *authoritate* (cf. med.L. *auctōritāre*); or f. L. *dare*,

datum, to give.] To attribute to an author, to father *on*.

1652 URQUHART *Jewel* Wks. 1834. 198 Authoridating this [proverb] on Paul, the first on Solomon, etc.

'authoring, *vbl. sb.* [f. AUTHOR *v.* + -ING[1].] Book-writing.

1742 FIELDING *J. Andrews* II. i. Wks. 1784 V. 105 Initiated into the science of authoring.

'authorish, *a. rare*$^{-1}$. [f. AUTHOR *sb.* + -ISH; cf. *amateurish*.] Somewhat author-like.

1825 LAMB in *Final Mem.* viii. 257 Yet hath it an authorish twang about it.

authorism ('ɔːθərɪz(ə)m). [f. as prec. + -ISM.] The position or character of a writer of books.

1761 H. WALPOLE *Corr.* (1837) II. 90 He [Burke] is a sensible man, but has not worn off his authorism yet. **1805** MISS SEWARD in Polwhele *Trad. & Recoll.* (1826) II. 569 His restless spirit and thirst of authorism. *c* **1824** MISS FERRIER *Let.* in *Daily News* 29 Dec. (1881) 2/2, I could not bear the fuss of authorism!

authoritarian (ɔːˌθɒrɪˈtɛərɪən), *a.* and *sb.* [f. AUTHORITY + -ARIAN; cf. *trinitarian*.]

A. *adj.* Favourable to the principle of authority as opposed to that of individual freedom.

1879 *Daily News* 28 June 2/6 Men who are authoritarian by nature, and cannot imagine that a country should be orderly save under a military despotism. **1882** *Contemp. Rev.* Sept. 459 Communists of the 'Authoritarian' type.

B. *sb.* One who supports the principle of authority.

1883 *Times* 2 Jan. 3/1 [Gambetta] was accused of being an authoritarian. **1884** SEELEY in *Encycl. Brit.* XVII. 226/1 A lover of liberty, not an authoritarian.

authoritarianism (ɔːˌθɒrɪˈtɛərɪənɪz(ə)m). [f. AUTHORITARIAN + -ISM.] Authoritarian principles.

1909 in WEBSTER. **1914** STREETER *Restatement & Reunion* ii. 47 Logical arguments in defence of authoritarianism. **1927** *British Weekly* 30 June 285/3 A decided drift towards authoritarianism, whether Catholic or fundamentalist. **1940** *Mind* XLIX. 100 The camouflage of spirituality in which the champions of authoritarianism disguise the essential materialism of their doctrines.

authoritative (ɔːˈθɒrɪˌteɪtɪv), *a.* Also 7 autor- [f. AUTHORITY: see -ATIVE.]

1. Of authority, of the nature of authority, exercising or assuming power; imperative, dictatorial, commanding.

1605 *Answ. Supp. Disc. Rom. Doc.* 38 What authoritative Sermons to the Religious..they vsed. **1659** PEARSON *Creed* (1741) 44 God's authoritative or potestative power. *a* **1733** NORTH *Lives* III. 132 He was diligent and in acting authoritative. **1749** FIELDING *Tom Jones* (1775) III. 160 The first time Thwackum ever wrote in this authoritative stile. *a* **1850** ROSSETTI *Dante & Circ.* II. (1874) 264 Its authoritative minuteness in matters which ladies now-a-days would probably consider their own undisputed region.

2. Possessing due or acknowledged authority; entitled to obedience or acceptance.

1653 GAUDEN *Hierasp.* To Reader 40 An authoritative ministry. **1664** H. MORE *Myst. Iniq.* 449 A number sufficient to constitute an Authoritative Church. **1833** I. TAYLOR *Fanat.* viii. 301 A written and authoritative canon of faith. **1871** MARKBY *Elem. Law* §42 *note*, Opinions which are not in a forensic sense authoritative. **1880** MUIRHEAD *Gaius* Introd. 22 The authoritative edition is that of Mommsen.

3. Proceeding from a competent authority.

1809 COBBETT *State Trials* I. 323 To all which both of us do give our authoritative decree and sanction. **1812** J. HENRY *Camp. agst. Quebec* 54 No firing without authoritative permission. **1853** MARSDEN *Early Purit.* 265 An authoritative declaration of pardon.

au'thoriˌtatively, *adv.* [f. prec. + -LY[2]] In an authoritative way or manner, with authority exercised or possessed; on due or good authority.

1621 BP. MOUNTAGU *Diatribæ* 119 They have had [to do with tithes]..but not either primarily or authoritatively. **1647** *Power of Keys* ii. 6 Authoritatively he gave him the keyes. **1808** BENTHAM *Sc. Ref.* 7 An authoritatively reported example. **1855** MILMAN *Lat. Chr.* (1864) V. IX. viii. 452 *note*, The Council of Lateran..first authoritatively proclaimed transubstantiation. **1860** FROUDE *Hist. Eng.* V. xxiv. 36 Entitled to speak authoritatively.

authoritativeness (ɔːˈθɒrɪˌteɪtɪvnɪs). [f. as prec. + -NESS.] The quality of being authoritative.

1659 CRADOCK *Knowl. & Pract.* II. v. (1673) 39 The Majesty of the Style, the Authoritativeness, and Godlike manner of speaking. **1861** GEO. ELIOT *Silas M.* 58 That self-possession and authoritativeness of voice and carriage which belonged to a man who thought of superiors as remote existences.

authority (ɔːˈθɒrɪtɪ, ɒ-, ə-). Forms: 3–5 autorite, 4–6 autoryte, 5–6 auctorite, -itee, 5 awtoryte, 5–6 auctoryte, 5–7 autoritie, auctoritie, -ity, 6 auctorytye, -ety, awtoritee, aucthoritie, -ytye, -ity, authorite, 6–7 authoritie, 6–8 autority, 7 aucthorytie, 5– authority. [a. F. *autorité*, early ad. L. *auctōritas, -tātem*, f. *auctor*: see AUTHOR *sb.* and -ITY. The Fr. was also spelt *auctorité* from 12th to 16th c., and *authorité* in 16th, whence the successive Eng. forms.]

I. Power to enforce obedience.

1. a. Power or right to enforce obedience; moral or legal supremacy; the right to command, or give an ultimate decision.

1393 GOWER *Conf.* I. 257 The pope..Of his papall auctorite Hath made and yove the decre. **1480** CAXTON *Chron. Eng.* III. (1520) 20/1 They chose another man the whiche sholde have more auctoryte..and they called hym dictator. **1590** *Harl. Misc.* (Malh.) II. 176 He hath aucthoritie over all kinges and princes. **1598** BARRET *Theor. Warres* IV. iv. 113 Their Colours..represent the authoritie Royall. **1603** SHAKS. *Meas. for M.* II. ii. 118 Proud man, Drest in a little briefe authoritie,..Plaies such phantastique tricks before high heauen, As makes the Angels weepe. **1665** BOYLE *Occas. Refl.* IV. xi. (1675) 233, I allow lawful Authority a Jurisdiction over my Actions, that I deny it over my Opinions. *a* **1680** BUTLER *Rem.* (1759) I. 251 Authority is a Disease and Cure, Which Men can neither want, nor well endure. **1872** RUSKIN *Eagle's Nest* §94 If ever you find yourselves set in positions of authority.

b. *in authority*: in a position of power; in possession of power over others.

c **1460** FORTESCUE *Abs. & Lim. Mon.* (1714) 108 Men that were in grete Auctorite. **1551–6** ROBINSON tr. *More's Utop.* 15 Nowe placed in aucthorytye and called to honoure. **1611** BIBLE *Prov.* xxix. 2 When the righteous are in authoritie, the people rejoyce. **1722** SEWEL tr. *Hist. Quakers* (1795) I. Pref. 12 Speaking to persons in authority. **1878** HOPPS *Jesus* x. 36 The people in authority..would try to stop him.

2. a. Derived or delegated power; conferred right or title; authorization.

(The relation to sense 1 is seen in 'by the (king's) authority, by authority of the King.')

c **1375** WYCLIF *Serm.* Sel. Wks. 1869 I. 56 Reprovede him sharpli bi autorite of God. *c* **1400** *Apol. Loll.* 8 If he pronounce wiþout autorite..aȝennis þe lordis wille. **1483** RICH. III in Ellis *Orig. Lett.* II. 49 I. 153 Upon auctorite or commission yeven unto him. **1535** COVERDALE *Mark* xi. 28 By what auctorite dost thou these things, and who gaue the this auctorite. **1790** BURKE *Fr. Rev.* 6 To open a formal public correspondence..without the express authority of the government under which I live. **1831** CARLYLE *Sart. Res.* III. vii, He carries in him an authority from God.

b. with *inf.* Conferred right *to do* something.

1535 COVERDALE *Ezra* vii. 24 Ye shall haue no auctorite to requyre taxinge & custome. **1559** BP. SCOT in Strype *Ann. Ref.* I. App. vii. 13 By commission from him, prestes hathe aucthorytie to forgyve sin. **1719** YOUNG *Revenge* IV. i, Am I not your wife? Have I not just authority to know That heart? **1855** PRESCOTT *Philip II* Pref. 8, I also obtained the authority of Prince Metternich to inspect the Archives of the Empire. **1858** LD. ST. LEONARDS *Handy-bk. Prop. Law* IV. 20 The authority to sell does not include a power to receive the purchase-money.

3. Those in authority; the body or persons exercising power or command. (Formerly in *sing.* = Government; a Local Sanitary Authority or similar body is also spoken of as 'the authority.')

1611 BIBLE *1 Pet.* iii. 22 Angels, and authorities, and powers being made subject vnto him. **1652** NEEDHAM tr. *Selden's Mare Cl.* Ep. Ded. 1 The Supreme Autoritie of the Nation, the Parlament of the Common-wealth of England. **1682** LUTTRELL *Brief Rel.* I. 233 Authority has thought fitt ..to prosecute the offenders for the same. **1760** T. HUTCHINSON *Hist. Coll. Mass. Bay* iii. (1765) 395 The authority treated him kindly, and sent him home. **1833** I. TAYLOR *Fanat.* x. 456 The conduct of the authorities. **1859** MILL *Liberty* 172 It is a proper office of public authority to guard against accidents. **1865** LIVINGSTONE *Zambesi* xx. 403 The Mozambique authorities. **1870** *Statutes* V (Tramways Act) 491 Orders authorising the construction of tramways.. may be obtained by (1) The local authority of such district. **1880** *Sat. Rev.* 25 Dec. 809 The actual authorities of the Post Office. **1909** *Westm. Gaz.* 8 Sept. 2/3 The Port of London Authority is a thoroughly practical body of men. **1951** *Good Housek. Home Encycl.* 189/2 It is usually possible to obtain the free services of one through the local Health Authority.

II. Power to influence action, opinion, belief.

4. Power to influence the conduct and actions of others; personal or practical influence.

c **1410** HOCCLEVE *Mother of God* 92 Syn thou art of swich auctoritee Lady pitious. *c* **1449** PECOCK *Repr.* V. ix. 531 Hiȝe in wisdom and in auctorite and in fame. **1542** BRINKLOW *Complaynt* i. (1874) 7 Them which beare any auctoryte..in the cowncel or Parlament. **1673** *Lady's Call.* I. i §20 Such an autority there is in vertue, that where 'tis eminent, 'tis apt to controle all loose desires. **1705** ADDISON *Italy* Ded., With your Lordship's Interest and Authority in England. **1792** *Anecd. W. Pitt* III. xliv. 202 It is your duty, my Lords, as the grand hereditary council of the nation..to feel your own weight and authority. **1818–60** WHATELY *Commonpl. Bk.* (1864) 125 The person, body, or book, in favour of whose decisions there is a certain presumption, is said to have, so far, authority.

5. Power over, or title to influence, the opinions of others; authoritative opinion; weight of judgement or opinion, intellectual influence.

c **1386** CHAUCER *Sqrs. T.* 474 Preued..As wel by werk as by Auctoritee. **1481** CAXTON *Myrr.* III. xii. 160 Good clerkes ..of grete auctoryte. *a* **1677** BARROW *Serm.* (1683) II. viii. 119 The auctority of the ancients doth more prevail with me. **1724** A. COLLINS *Gr. Chr. Relig.* Pref. 18 Is there anything that..stifles the light of truth, but autority? **1794** SULLIVAN *View Nat.* II. 231 The proper way of reasoning from authority, that what seems true to some wise men, may upon that account be esteemed somewhat probable. **1865** MILL *Liberty* ii. 21/2 He is either led by authority, or adopts..the side to which he feels most inclination.

6. Power to inspire belief, title to be believed; authoritative statement; weight of testimony. Sometimes weakened to: Authorship, testimony.

1303 R. BRUNNE *Handl. Synne* 1239 Seynt Poule þat sagh Goddys pryvyte, He seyþ yn hys autoryte A feyre wurd vs for to save. **1494** FABYAN I. i. 8 Therof is founde lytell auctoryte. **1586** THYNNE in *Animadv.* Introd. 73 Untill I may see good authoritie to disproove it. **1710** PRIDEAUX *Orig. Tithes* v. 253, I deny not Ingulph's autority to be good, but for his Copy there is his autority only. **1875** SCRIVENER *Lect. Grk. Test.* 12, I have been recently informed on excellent authority. *a* **1885** *Mod.* Do not accept news on the authority of the evening papers.

7. The quotation or book acknowledged, or alleged, to settle a question of opinion or give conclusive testimony.

c **1230** *Ancr. R.* 78 Þen ilke autorite, þet..schal beon vre strencðe..aȝein þes deofles turnes. *c* **1386** CHAUCER *Freres Prol.* 12 Lete auctoritès, in Goddes name, To preching and to scoles of clergie. *a* **1535** MORE *Confut. Barnes* VIII. Wks. 770/2 Hys fyrst authorite be these words of saynte Austyne in hys fyftieth sermon. **1608** SHAKS. *Per.* III. ii. 33 By turning o'er authorities. **1706** POPE *Lett.* Wks. 1736 V. 55 To corroborate these observations by some great authorities ..in Tully and Quintilian. **1876** GREEN *Short Hist.* Pref. 6 Giving in detail the authorities for every statement.

8. a. The person whose opinion or testimony is accepted; the author of an accepted statement. **b.** One whose opinion *on* or *upon* a subject is entitled to be accepted; an expert in any question.

1665 GLANVILL *Sceps. Sci.* 77 To confront such celebrated Authorities. **1855** PRESCOTT *Philip II.* I. II. vi. 210 Historians in a season of faction are not the best authorities. **1860** R. WILLIAMS *Ess. & Rev.* 59 Egyptian authorities continue the reign of Menephthah later. **1867** A. J. ELLIS *E.E. Pronunc.* I. iii. 65 Wallis is the great authority for the fully developed pronunciation of the XVIIth century. **1871** BLACKIE *Four Phases* i. 1 A great utilitarian authority. *a* **1885** *Mod.* Who, may I ask, is your authority for the statement? A. B. He is no authority!

9. *Comb.*, as ***authority-maker***.

1678 CUDWORTH *Intell. Syst.* I. v. 893 These justice-makers and authority-makers pretend to derive their factitious justice from Pacts and Covenants.

authorizable ('ɔːθəˌraɪzəb(ə)l), *a.* Forms: 6 autorysabyl, auctorizable. [In sense 1, a. OF. *au(c)torisable*, or med.L. *auctōrīzābilis*, f. *auctōrīzāre*; in sense 2, f. AUTHORIZE + -ABLE.]

†**1.** *actively.* Having the faculty of authorizing.

1530 *Declar.* in Strype *Eccl. Mem.* I. xvii. 131 From no power or consent autorysabyl of any secular prince. **1590** SWINBURN *Testaments* 48 The propertie of auctoritie, or auctorizable consent, is to concurre with the acte.

2. *passively.* Capable of being authorized.

1877 M. ARNOLD *Last Ess. Ch.* 207 Authorisable forms of burial service.

authorization (ˌɔːθəraɪˈzeɪʃən). [f. AUTHORIZE: see -ATION. (Also in mod.F.)] The conferment of legality; formal warrant, or sanction.

1610 HEALEY *St. Aug. City of God* 63 Ordained by..the authorization of the Chiefe Priest. **1827** BENTHAM *Ration. Evid.* Wks. 1843 VII. 484 Authorization does away the fraud: what is authorized is legalized. **1835** J. HARRIS *Gt. Teacher* (1837) 133 A mere adoption and authorization of pre-existing opinions. **1859** MERIVALE *Rom. Emp.* xlviii. V. 435 Without a special authorization from the chief.

authorize ('ɔːθəraɪz), *v.* Forms: 4 autorize, -yse, 4–5 -ise, 4–6 auctorize, -yse, -ise, 6 auctorish(e, -eise, authoriss, -ish, aucthorishe, 7 -ize, -ise, 6– authorise, -ize. [a. F. *autorise-r*, in 14–16th c. commonly *auctoriser*, also in 15–16th c. *authoriser*, ad. med.L. *auctōrīzāre*, f. *auctor* author: see -IZE. The phonetic history follows that of AUTHOR *sb.*, *auctorize* being the usual form down to *c* 1575. In 16th c. accented *auc'torise*, which led to the form *auc'torish* after *nourish, perish*: see -ISH[2].]

I. To authorize a thing.

†**1.** To set up as authoritative; to acknowledge as possessing final decisiveness. *Obs.*

1401 *Pol. Poems* (1859) II. 80 Thou autorisest ȝour pride aȝenes his holi werkes. **1579** TOMSON *Calvin's Serm. Tim.* 509/2 To the end the word of God may be authorized, and men know that we must be heard. **1620** SHELTON *Quix.* III. xvii. 116 Let the Courtier..authorize his Prince's Court with Liveries.

†**2.** To give legal force to; to make legally valid.

1464 EDW. IV in *Paston Lett.* 493 II. 165 Inacted and auctorised in the parlement next holden. **1567** DRANT *Horace Epist.* II. i. Gj, Tables..Deuysed and auctorished by well knowne Romanes ten. **1644** *Vind. Treat. Monarchy* iv. 27 Being authoritative, they authorize the Instrument, and give him an unresistance. **1692** DRYDEN *St. Euremont's Ess.* 87 New Titles to Authorize a new Power.

3. To give formal approval to; to sanction, approve, countenance.

c **1383** WYCLIF *Sel. Wks.* (1871) III. 326 Crist and alle his seyntis..autoriseden it. —— *De Eccl.* viii. *ibid.* 357 Whanne þe pope auansiþ a shrewe, he autorisiþ his shrewidnesse. **1567** DRANT *Horace's Arte Poet.* A iij, Who hath to iudge, autorish, reule, All maner speache at will. *c* **1600** SHAKS. *Sonn.* xxxv, Authorizing thy trespas with compare. **1749** CHESTERF. *Lett.* 211 II. 305 The Season in which Custom seems..to authorise civil and harmless Lies under the name of compliments. **1865** MILL *Liberty* 15 The gentlest and most amiable of philosophers..authorised the persecution of Christianity.

b. Of things: To afford just ground for, justify.
1603 FLORIO *Montaigne* (1634) 525 The issue doth often aucthorize a simple conduct. **1656** COWLEY *Davideis* IV. Wks. 1710 II. 460 If Human Strength might authorize a Boast. **1660** DRYDEN *Astræa Red.* 178 Till some safe crisis authorise their skill. **1748** ANSON *Voy.* Introd., These reasons alone would authorize the insertion of those papers. **1831** SCOTT *Cast. Dang.* i, More..than the coldness of the weather seemed to authorise.

†**4.** To vouch for the truth or reality of; to confirm by one's authority. *Obs.*
1393 GOWER *Conf.* III. 167 This I finde eke of recorde, Which the cronique hath auctorized. **1489** CAXTON *Faytes of A.* III. i. 169 The more that a werke is wytnessed..the more it is auctorysed and more auctentyke. **1605** SHAKS. *Macb.* III. iv. 66 A womans story, at a Winters fire, Authoriz'd by her Grandam. **1646** SIR T. BROWNE *Pseud. Ep.* 75 Multiplying obscurities in nature, and authorising hidden qualities that are false.

II. To authorize a person.

5. To endow with authority, place in authority; to commission.
1494 FABYAN V. xcvii. 71 After that he of this Realme was auctorysyd for kynge. **1548** UDALL, etc. *Erasm. Par. Matt.* iii. 17 Did manyfestly auctoryse his sonne. **1676** BULLOKAR, *Authorize*, to put in authority, or give power unto. **1770** *Junius Lett.* xli. 216 Will you..tell the world by what law..you were authorized? [See AUTHORIZED.]

†**b.** To hold as an authority. *Obs. rare.*
1535 STEWART *Cron. Scot.* II. 141 He had sic credens of the king, And wes with him auctoreist than so hie.

†**c.** To accredit. *Obs. rare.*
1579 FULKE *Confut. Sanders* 536 Neither is the credite of such late writers—sufficient to authorise them for such.

†**d.** To patronize, countenance. *Obs. rare.*
1713 *Guardian* No. 10 ¶3 For this reason I shall authorise and support the gentleman.

†**6.** *refl.* **a.** To claim authority for oneself; to plume oneself. **b.** To found one's authority *upon*.
1581 SIDNEY *Def. Poesie* (Arb.) 31 The Historian..loden with olde Mouse-eaten Records, authorising himselfe (for the most part) vpon other histories. *a* **1586** —— (J.) Making herself an impudent suitor, authorizing herself very much, with making us see, that all favour and power depended upon her.

7. To give legal or formal warrant to (a person) *to do* something; to empower, permit authoritatively.
1571 *Wills & Invent. N.C.* (1835) 353, I appoint and aucthorishe hym to call for and receyue..all suche debts. **1571** LD. BURLEIGH in Ellis *Orig. Lett.* I. 200 II. 261 We will, & by warrant herof authoriss you to procede. **1660** R. COKE *Power & Subj.* 249 To authorize any forreigne Prince to invade or annoy him or his Countries. **1796** MORSE *Amer. Geog.* I. 148 His Majesty may authorize the governor to fix the time and place. **1855** MACAULAY *Hist. Eng.* IV. 551 A royal message authorising the Commons to elect another Speaker.

b. Of things: To give satisfactory ground to.
1794 SULLIVAN *View Nat.* I, Nothing which can authorise us to suppose it formed in the sea. **1843** MILL *Logic* III. xxi. §3 Past experience of mortality authorizes us to infer both.

authorized (ˈɔːθəraɪzd), *ppl. a.* [f. prec. + -ED.]
1. Possessed of authority, acknowledged as authoritative; thoroughly established; highly esteemed.
c **1399** *Pol. Poems* (1859) II. 13 Cassodre, whos writinge is auctorized, Seith. *c* **1534** *Pol. Verg. Eng. Hist.* (1846) 27 Pomponius Lætus..the moste authorised of late writers. **1784** J. BARRY *Lect. Art* vi. (1848) 209 The most authorised and surest observations which have fallen in my way. **1810** COLERIDGE *Friend* (1865) 30 Received and authorized opinions.

2. Placed in (*obs.*) or endowed with authority.
1483 CAXTON *G. de la Tour* K vj, Knyghtes auctorysed and renommed. **1613** WITHERS *Abus. Stript* I. vi, More vile In men authoriz'd, than in those that be Borne to a lower fortune or degree. **1648** MILTON *Tenure Kings* 235 The dragon gave to the beast his..authority; which beast so authorized most expound to be the tyrannical powers and kingdoms of the earth. *Mod.* The arrangement was made by your own authorized agent.

3. Legally or duly sanctioned or appointed. ***Authorized Version*** of the Bible: a popular appellation of the version of 1611. (The *Great Bible* 1540, and *Bishops' Bible* (after 1572), actually bore on their titles 'authorized and appointed,' but that of 1611 has never claimed to be 'authorized.') ***authorized capital*** (see quots.).
1480 CAXTON *Ovid's Met.* XV. iv, A cyte rych and auctorysed in thy lynage. **1538** STARKEY *Eng.* 181 That by no prerogatyfe he usurpe upon the pepul any authorysyd tyranny. **1794** PALEY *Evid.* II. ii. (1817) 24 Authorized assurances of the reality of a future existence. **1824** DIBDIN *Libr. Comp.* 32 What is called our authorized version. **1879** RUSKIN *Lett. Clergy* 39 This piece of authorized mockery. **1911** W. THOMSON *Dict. of Banking* 39/2 *Authorised capital*, the capital of a company as authorised by its memorandum of association. **1917** W. H. WALKER *Corporation Finance* ii. 25 The state..limits the number of shares or the par value of the shares which the company may issue, and this limit is known as 'authorized capital'. **1930** *Economist* 5 Apr. 784/1 Resolutions are to be considered to increase the authorised share capital to £8,000,000.

†**'authorizement.** *Obs.* [f. AUTHORIZE; cf. med.L. *auctōrizāmentum*.] Authorization.
1594 J. KING *On Jonah* (1864) 45 Without authorisement and confirmation from them.

authorizer (ˈɔːθəraɪzə(r)). [f. as prec. + -ER¹.] One who authorizes (in various senses).
1607 T. SPARKE *Persuas. Unity* 63 The meaning either of the book or of the authorisers therof. *a* **1619** DONNE *Biathan.* (1644) 29 A strong Authorizer, if not an Authour. **1681** H. MORE *Exp. Daniel* ii. 51 The Instigator or Authorizer of the War. **1861** *Athenæum* 29 June 861 They seem to have acted as agents..and reported back to their authorizers.

'authorizing, *vbl. sb.* [f. as prec. + -ING¹.] The giving of authority; sanctioning.
1523-4 *Act 14-15 Hen. VIII.* v, For the further authorising of the same Letters Patents. **1697** *Let. Memb. Parl. conc. Convoc.* 41 The authorizing of the Books of Common Prayer.

'authorizing, *ppl. a.* [f. as prec. + -ING².] That authorizes.
1881 *Echo* 28 June 1/3 A copy of the authorising Acts may be inspected at the office.

authorless (ˈɔːθəlɪs), *a.* [f. AUTHOR *sb.* + -LESS.]
1. Without admitted author; anonymous.
1713 *Guardian* No. 133 The false aspersions some authorless tongues have laid upon me. **1869** *Spectator* 3 July 797 After 1715 his works were apparently authorless, or issued under fictitious and assumed names.

2. Without originator; uncreated.
1862 F. HALL *Hindu Philos. Syst.* 64 The Sánkhyas..would have it [the Veda] to be authorless.

3. Void of authors or writers.
1879 B. WHEATLEY *Catal. Med. Chirurg. Soc. Libr.* Pref. 13 A long interval of authorless years.

authorling (ˈɔːθəlɪŋ). [f. AUTHOR *sb.* + -LING.] A petty author; an insignificant writer.
1771 SMOLLETT *Humph. Cl.* 836 A parcel of authorlings. **1828** *Q. Rev.* XXXVII. 418 The surviving Grub-street authorling. **1850** WHIPPLE *Ess. & Rev.* (ed. 3) II. 89 Weak manikins and dapper authorlings who mistake indigestion for inspiration.

authorly (ˈɔːθəlɪ), *a.* [f. AUTHOR *sb.* + -LY¹; cf. *fatherly*.] Proper to authors, authorial.
1784 COWPER *Let. Unwin* 1 Nov. (R.) He keeps his own authorly secrets. **1834** GEN. P. THOMPSON *Exerc.* (1842) III. 90 The authorly rule..appears to be to insert the possible maximum of stops.

authorship (ˈɔːθəʃɪp). [f. AUTHOR *sb.* + -SHIP.]
1. Occupation or career as a writer of books.
1710 SHAFTESB. *Charac.* (1870) I. 347 Patentees, with a sole commission of Authorship. **1771** SMOLLETT *Humph. Cl.* (1815) 148, I saw none of the outward signs of authorship. **1817** COLERIDGE *Biog. Lit.* 113 The profession of literature, or, to speak more plainly, the trade of authorship. **1857** H. REED *Lect. Brit. Poets* v. 160 The term of his authorship belongs..to the time of Queen Elizabeth.

2. The dignity or personality of an author; cf. *lordship*.
1782 COWPER *Lett.* 23 Nov., My authorship is undoubtedly pleased when I hear that they are approved. **1853** TUPPER *Heart* xvi. 155 Such..was not my authorship's intention.

3. Literary origin or origination (of a writing).
1825 LD. COCKBURN *Mem.* 318 To deny his authorship of them. **1831** BREWSTER *Newton* (1855) II. xv. 75 A question ..respecting the authorship of the review. **1834** H. N. COLERIDGE *Grk. Poets* 284 To doubt the individual authorship of the Iliad. **1870** *Echo* 11 Nov., To hunt for a correct solution of the authorship of Junius.

4. *gen.* Origination or instigation of an action, state of affairs, etc. Cf. AUTHOR *sb.* 1.
1884 *Leeds Merc.* 24 Oct. 4/4 He did not..expressly charge [him]..with the authorship of the riots at Aston Park.

†**'authrix.** [Cf. L. *auctrix*.] = AUTHORESS.
1650 CHARLETON *Paradoxes* 74 A certaine Naturall sensation, the immediate Authrix of all sympathy.

autism (ˈɔːtɪz(ə)m). *Psychiatry.* [ad. mod.L. *autismus* (also used), f. Gr. αὐτός self + -ISM.] A condition in which a person is morbidly self-absorbed and out of contact with reality. So **au'tistic** *a.*, of, pertaining to, or characterized by this; *sb.*, a person thus affected; also **au'tistically** *adv.*
1912 BLEULER in *Amer. Jrnl. Insanity* LXIX. 874 When we look more closely we find amongst all normal people many and important instances where thought is divorced both from logic and from reality. I have called these forms of thinking *autistic*, corresponding to the idea of schizophrenic autismus. *Ibid.* 884 The unconscious can think logically or autistically. **1912** A. HOCH *Ibid.* 888 The chief traits which had existed before the mental breakdown were those which I at that time called the shut-in tendencies —tendencies to which Professor Bleuler has recently applied the term autism. **1916** C. E. LONG tr. *Jung's Coll. Papers Analyt. Psychol.* vi. 203 Autism (Bleuler) = Auto-eroticism (Freud). For some time I have employed the concept of *introversion* for this condition. **1922** WOODWORTH *Psychol.* xix. 508 Daydreaming..is an example of what is called 'autistic thinking', which means thinking that is sufficient unto itself, and not subjected to any criticism. Autistic thinking gratifies some desire and that is enough for it. **1962** *Guardian* 15 Nov. 6/6 London County Council has opened an experimental unit at the health centre in Guildford Street for the treatment and diagnosis of autistic children. **1963** *New Scientist* 25 Apr. 184/1 Childhood autism—sometimes inaccurately called childhood schizophrenia. **1968** *Woman* 27 Jan. 24/2 There are over 4,000 diagnosed autistics in this country. *Ibid.* 56/4 Our hospital..is by no means the only one with an autistic unit.

autly, variant of AUGHTLY *a. Obs.* worthy.

‖**auto** (ˈaʊtəʊ), *sb.*¹ [Sp. and Pg.:—L. *actu-s* act.]
1. A play. Cf. ACT *sb.* 7.
1779 H. SWINBURNE *Trav. Spain* iii. 9 Autos and mysterios are prohibited on the theatres of Madrid. **1848** MRS. JAMESON *Sacr. & Leg. Art* (1850) 339 Calderon founded on it one of his finest autos, the 'Magico Prodigioso.'

2. for AUTO-DA-FÉ. Cf. ACT *sb.* 9.
1727-41 CHAMBERS *Cycl.* s.v. *Act*, They usually contrive the Auto to fall on some great festival. **1823** BYRON *Age Bronze* vii, The faith's red 'auto,' fed with human fuel.

auto (ˈɔːtəʊ), *sb.*² **1.** Colloq. abbrev. of AUTOMOBILE *sb.* after F. *auto*; also *attrib.* and *Comb.*; **auto court** *U.S.*, a MOTEL. See also AUTO-².
1899 *Boston Herald* 9 July 6/3 The accident to Mr. W. K. Vanderbilt's 'auto'. **1901** *Daily Colonist* (Victoria, B.C.) 30 Oct. 6/1 These auto enthusiasts are trying hard. **1902** *Aeronautical World* (U.S.) 1 Oct. 60/1 Cycles, autos and all other contrivances for rapid transit. **1910** *Daily Chron.* 12 Mar. 6/4 The auto-manufacturing business. **1922** *Hotel World* 11 Mar. 6/2 The chamber of commerce of Santa Barbara, Cal., fathers an 'auto camp'. **1925** *Beaver* Sept. 201/2 All our 'tourists' report..the auto camps doing a roaring business. **1927** *Blackw. Mag.* Nov. 646/2 The auto-trip to Ixtlan del Rio. **1928** *Sunday Express* 24 June 8/2, I was raised in Canada sixty odd years ago, when..the country was not safe for slick auto-tourists. **1930** R. MACAULAY *Staying with Relations* xix. 274 Sign-boards.. telling travellers about hotels and auto-camps. **1934** J. M. CAIN *Postman always rings Twice* i. 9 A half-dozen shacks that they called an auto court. **1962** *Economist* 20 Oct. 277/2 This demand..has surprised many automen.

2. Abbrev. of AUTOTYPE 2. *rare.*
1882 SWINBURNE *Lett.* (1960) IV. 309 The autos gave great satisfaction.

3. Abbrev. of AUTOBIOGRAPHY. *rare.*
1940 V. WOOLF *Writer's Diary* 6 Jan. (1953) 323, I suppose the origin of many of the new middle aged autos.

auto (ˈɔːtəʊ), *v. U.S.* Shortened form of AUTOMOBILE *v.* So **autoing** (ˈɔːtəʊɪŋ), *vbl. sb.*
1909 *Cent. Dict.* Suppl., *Autoing*, the use of automobiles for business or pleasure traveling. **1916** *Sphere* 12 Feb. 180/3, I find the following commentary on new verbs in the New York *Outlook*: '..''Thursday we autoed to the country club.'' ' **1919** MENCKEN *Amer. Lang.* 110 *Auto* is almost unknown [in England], and with it the verb *to auto*. **1940** BRYANT & AIKEN *Psychol. of English* 84 We plan to *auto* through the mountains.

auto-¹ (ˈɔːtəʊ), repr. Gr. αὐτο- 'self, one's own, by oneself, independent-ly,' combining form of αὐτός self. Exceedingly common in Gr.; in L. only in a few words adopted from Gr. without analysis, as *autochthones*, *autographus*, *automatus*; more common in med.L.; and largely used in the mod. langs. In Eng., to a certain extent, a living element, prefixable to scientific terms denoting action or operation, whence occasionally to others, in combinations that are more or less nonce-words. In free composition as a prefix element, its chief meanings are: (*a*) of oneself, one's own; self-; (*b*) self-produced or -induced (pathologically) within the body or organism; (*c*) spontaneous, self-acting, automatic (cf. esp. b below).

Such are: **auto-'abstract**, a speaker's own abstract of an address or speech prepared for publication; **ˌauto-aggluti'nation** [G. (A. Klein 1902, in *Wiener Klinische Wochenschrift* XV. 415/1)], spontaneous agglutination, esp. produced by auto-antibodies; **auto-'antibody**, an antibody which is produced by an organism and which reacts against some constituent of that organism; **auto-catalepsy**, catalepsy self-produced; **autoca'talysis** *Chem.*, catalysis of a reaction by one of its own products; hence **auto'catalyst**, a substance or organism capable of autocatalysis; **autocata'lytic** *a.*, **-ally** *adv.*; **autoclastic** (-ˈklæstɪk), *a. Geol.* [CLASTIC *a.*], of a rock, composed of its own fragments produced by crushing or granulation; **ˌauto-colli'mation**, collimation of an instrument by means of its own parts; so **auto'collimating** *ppl. a.*, that collimates by means of its own parts; **auto'collimator**, an instrument with an autocollimating eyepiece (Webster, 1934); **auto-coprophagous** *a.*, eating its own dung; **auto-criticism**, criticism of oneself or one's own works; **autocytotoxin** (-saɪtəʊˈtɒksɪn) [CYTOTOXIN], a cytotoxin formed in the body; **ˌautodiag'nosis**, diagnosis of one's own disease; hence **ˌauto-diag'nostic** *a.*, of or pertaining to autodiagnosis; **auto-di'gestion** = AUTOLYSIS; also, self-destruction of plant tissue; **ˌauto-'follow, -'following** *Radar*, automatic following; a system in which a radar beam automatically follows the object from which echoes are received; also *attrib.*; cf. *automatic following* (AUTOMATIC *a.* 2); **'autofrettage** [a. F.

autofrettage, self-hooping; cf. FRETTAGE], the process of strengthening a tube, esp. the barrel of a gun, by applying internal pressure in order to raise the limit of strain; hence **'autofrettaged** *a.*; **'autograft** *Surg.*, a graft of skin or other tissue taken from a person's own body (Dorland, 1913); **ˌautohyp'nosis** [HYPNOSIS 2], **auto'hypnotism**, a self-induced hypnotic condition; so **ˌautohyp'notic** *a.* and *sb.*; **ˌauto-hypnoti'zation**, the inducing of hypnosis by auto-suggestion; **ˌauto-i'mmunity**, the state produced by the presence either of auto-antibodies or of lymphoid cells sensitized against some constituent of the subject's own tissues; so **auto-immune** *a.*, characterized by auto-immunity; **ˌauto-immuni'zation**, (*a*) immunization from within the body; self-immunization (Dorland, 1900); (*b*) the production of auto-immunity; **auto-in'fectant** *sb.*, an agent of auto-infection; **auto-infection**, self-infection; **auto-in'fective** *a.*, or of pertaining to auto-infection; **auto-infra-glottic** *a.*, of what is below one's own glottis; **auto-inoculation**, self-inoculation, whence **auto-inoculable** *a.*; **auto-in'toxicant**, a toxic substance generated in the system; also *fig.*; **auto-intoxi'cation**, poisoning by or resulting from toxin produced within the body; also *fig.*; hence **auto-in'toxicate** *v. trans.*; **autokinesis** (ˌɔːtəʊkaɪˈniːsɪs), (*a*) = AUTOKINESY (Mayne, Suppl. (1860) *autocinesis*); (*b*) the apparent movement of a stationary object; hence **autokinetic** (-kaɪˈnɛtɪk) *a.*; **auto-laryn'goscopy**, examination of one's own larynx, whence **auto-laryngo'scopic** *a.*, **auto-laryn'goscopist**; **au'tologous** *a.*, derived from the same organism; **ˌautolumi'nescence**, the spontaneous emission of light from certain radioactive substances; **auto'photograph** = AUTORADIOGRAPH; **auto'poisoning**, poisoning caused by a virus formed within the body; **auto'poisonous** *a.*, that is poisonous to the organism within which it is formed; **auto-portrait**, a portrait drawn by any one of himself; **auto-portraiture**, portraiture of oneself; **auto-prothesis**, self-produced or spontaneous prothesis; **auto'psychic** *a. Psychol.* [ad. G. *autopsychisch* (C. Wernicke 1892, in *Pathologie des Nervensystems* (1893) 166)], of or pertaining to self-consciousness or awareness of oneself; **auto-psychology**, psychological study of oneself; **ˌautopsy'chography**, psychography of oneself; so **ˌautopsy'chographize** *v. intr.*, to give the psychography of oneself; **autoro'tation** *Aeronaut.*, unpowered rotation, esp. that of the rotor of a rotorcraft; so **autoro'tate** *v. intr.*; **'autoscript**, a communication received by a medium in the form of automatic writing; **'auto-sex** *a.*, **'autosexed** *a.*, **ˌauto'sexing** *ppl. a.*, applied to any breed of poultry in which the sexes are distinguishable at hatching; so *autosex-linkage*, etc.; **autosoteric** (-səʊˈtɛrɪk), *a.*[Gr. σωτηρία salvation], relating to salvation by oneself; so **auto'soterism**; **autotelic** (-ˈtɛlɪk) *a.*, having or being an end or purpose in itself (see quot. 1901); **ˌauto'therapy**, treatment of one's own infirmity; hence **auto'therapist** *sb.*; **ˌautoto'xæmia, -toxemia**, the presence of autotoxin in the blood; **ˌautotransplan'tation**, transplantation of tissue from one site to another in the same individual; **autotrophic** (-ˈtrɒfɪk), *a.* [Gr. τροφός + -IC. Cf. Gr. τροφικός nursing, tending], self-nourishing; of a plant, as distinguished from parasitic and saprophytic; of a lake (see quot. 1927); hence **'autotroph(e**, an autotrophic organism; **autotropism** (ɔːˈtɒtrəpɪz(ə)m), *Bot.* [TROPISM], (see quots.). So *auto-burglar*, etc.

1903 *Nature* 15 Jan. 253/2 It is pleasing to note that a considerable number of these are auto-abstracts, for this method of summarising is the only one which ensures that the really essential points in the various investigations are brought forward. **1910** *Practitioner* Feb. 234 The older the infection the more noticeable is the tendency to clump (auto-agglutination). **1960** L. PICKEN *Organiz. Cells* iii. 66 In another phase it may aggregate spontaneously, undergoing auto-agglutination. **1910** *Lippincott's Med. Dict.* 101/1 *Auto-antibody*, an antibody against products of the individual in which it is formed. **1943** *Brit. Jrnl. Exper. Pathol.* XXIV. 122 It seems appropriate to look upon the cold agglutinin in atypical pneumonia as an auto-antibody. **1964** HUMPHREY & WHITE *Immunology* (ed. 2) 448 *Auto-antibody*, antibody reacting with constituents of the subject's own tissues. **1965** *New Scientist* 11 Mar. 628/3 Since rheumatoid factor activity is directed against the individual's own IgG, it too may be regarded as 'auto-antibody'. **1884** READE *Singleheart* v. 105 No drunkard and auto-burglar to drain the wife's purse. **1851** KINGSLEY *Yeast* Epil., Unattributable even to auto-catalepsy. **1891** *Jrnl. Chem. Soc.* LX. 1151 Autocatalysis... The presence of a salt of the acid, for instance the sodium salt, in the solution, retards the formation of the lactone very considerably, and the amount of free acid in the solution, as determined alkalimetrically, remains constant for days together. **1913** DORLAND *Med. Dict.* (ed. 7), *Autocatalysis*.., catalysis, or alteration of the velocity of a reaction, produced by products formed during the course of the reaction. **1940** *Chambers's Techn. Dict.* 61/1 *Autocatalysis*, reaction or disintegration of a cell or tissue, due to the influence of one of its own products. **1940** C. S. SHERRINGTON *Man on his Nature* v. 163 And the gene? A protein system containing auto-catalysts? **1952** G. H. BOURNE *Cytol. & Cell Physiol.* (ed. 2) ix. 392 The suggestion has been advanced that viruses are complex auto-catalysts. **1913** DORLAND *Med. Dict.* (ed. 7) Autocatalytic. **1939** *Ann. Reg. 1938* 376 Certain plant viruses.. may be a new type of autocatalytic protein. **1965** PHILLIPS & WILLIAMS *Inorg. Chem.* I. x. 370 A typical autocatalytic curve for the decomposition of a solid. **1949** *New Biol.* VII. 60 The actual flower-promoting hormone.. accumulates autocatalytically at the growing points once it has been formed. **1891** H. L. SMYTH in *Amer. Jrnl. Sci.* 3rd Ser. XLII. 331 The two orotechnic actions have produced great developments of autoclastic schists. That is, schists formed in place from massive rocks by crushing and squeezing, without intervening processes of disintegration or erosion, removal and deposition. **1903** LAMPLUGH *Geol. Isle of Man* 70 The autoclastic structure occurs where strata of different characters are in juxtaposition. **1961** J. CHALLINOR *Dict. Geol.* 15/2 *Autoclastic rock*, a rock formed by the breaking up of a part of a rock-mass within itself. **1915** R. A. HOUSTOUN *Treatise on Light* vii. 106 The Abbe or Auto-collimating Spectrometer.. performs the functions of both telescope and collimator. **1946** *Nature* 24 Aug. 275/1 The auto-collimating spectrograph consists of solid glass prisms of 6-in. aperture. **1932** MCCAW & CAZALET tr. *O. von Gruber's Photogrammetry* vii. 139 By autocollimation on one of the surfaces of the first pair the line of collimation is brought into parallelism with the picture axis. **1938** *Geogr. Jrnl.* XCI. 388 To effect auto-collimation with a scale in the focus of the telescope. **1951** *Engineering* 6 July 9/3 The probe arm.. is observed by sighting an autocollimator on to a mirror fixed to [it]. **1880** SWINBURNE in *Fortn. Rev.* 719 Obscurity.. proper to such autocoprophagous animals. **1884** *Pall Mall G.* 20 June 11/1 Another literary curiosity is an auto-criticism of 'Christie Johnstone' [by Chas. Reade]. **1902** *Science* 2 May 697 In a few instances autocytotoxins for blood-cells have been produced. **1894** GOULD *Dict. Med.*, *Autodiagnosis*.., self-diagnosis; the morbid impression sometimes possessed by a patient that he is affected with some particular disease. **1903** *Med. Record* LXIII. 169/1 The same hand must not be used for autodiagnostic purposes all the time. **1890** BILLINGS *Med. Dict.*, *Autodigestion*, self-digestion of stomach by gastric juice. **1896** *Jrnl. Chem. Soc.* LXX. 616 In autodigestion, xanthine-like substances are formed. **1913** S. M. BAKER in *Ann. Bot.* XXVII. 172 The well-known phenomenon of 'auto-digestion' shown by the fruit bodies of most species of *Coprinus*. **1962** *Lancet* 22 Dec. 1313/1 It allows for the progress of autodigestion over a wide range of pH. **1948** TAYLOR & WESTCOTT *Princ. Radar* iv. 62 Auto-follow systems.. have found many applications... Any equipment which needs to track one selected target only usually benefits considerably by being fitted with auto-following. **1961** *Aeroplane* CI. 75/1 Auto-follow is manually initiated by means of 'rolling-ball' type controls, which are used to set the initial position of the auto-follow track symbols on the airways displays. **1946** *Jrnl. Inst. Electr. Engin.* XCIII. III. 17/1 (*heading*) Auto-following Radar Sets. **1920** *Proc. U.S. Naval Inst.* Dec. 1969 Investigation.. has been made at the Central Laboratory of the French Navy, under the name of 'Autofrettage', literally self-hooping or auto-hooping... The pressure of autofrettage is limited to such a pressure that.. there shall not be developed any new permanent deformations in the interior layer. **1950** *Engineering* 28 Apr. 479/3 Autofrettage is the art of inducing elasticity in a tube at pressures which otherwise cause overstrain. **1933** *Jrnl. Iron & Steel Inst.* CXXVIII. 620 Some details are given of the tests applied to the autofrettaged tubes used in the construction of the pressure pipes. **1919** J. S. DAVIS *Plastic Surgery* ii. 16 An autograft is a graft obtained from the same individual. **1955** *Sci. News* XXXV. 104 Skin grafts are only permanently successful when the skin is taken from another area of the patient's own body—an autograft. **1903** S. S. COHEN *Syst. Physiol. Therap.* VIII. 275 Auto-hypnosis.. relieves the cortex of the corrective restraint imposed in the waking condition by the contact of the senses with the outer world. **1941** 'REBECCA WEST' *Black Lamb & Grey Falcon* I. 209 'I will sit here and look at the maps,' said my husband, who is much given to that masculine form of auto-hypnosis. **1913** DORLAND *Med. Dict.* (ed. 7), *Autohypnotic*.. 1. Pertaining to self-induced hypnotism. 2. One who can put himself into a hypnotic state. **1955** R. BLESH *Shining Trumpets* (ed. 3) v. 101 It is a possessive spell, seemingly auto-hypnotic upon the singer, which is projected. **1894** GOULD *Dict. Med.*, *Auto-hypnotism*.., mental stupor induced by dwelling intensely upon some all-absorbing delusion. **1924** W. B. SELBIE *Psychol. Relig.* ii. 49 He [*sc.* the Shaman] is regularly consecrated to the office through initiation and other methods, which produce a kind of auto-hypnotism, trance, or alternate personality. **1902** *Encycl. Brit.* XXXII. 53/2 They [*sc.* our witch-burning ancestors] could scarcely have reasoned otherwise.. in certain cases of hysteria and autohypnotization. **1952** *Proc. Third Congr. Internat. Soc. Hematology* 120 The development of an autoimmune, anti-red cell mechanism. **1962** *New Scientist* 27 Sept. 668/1 A typical case.. of severe autoimmune disease, systemic lupus erythematosus. **1904** *Dunglison's Dict. Med. Sci.* (ed. 23) 114/2 *Autoimmunity*, immunity.. effected by the unaided powers of the organism. **1961** *New Scientist* 17 Aug. 383/2 This concept of immunization against the body's own constituents has been termed auto-immunity. **1967** J. R. ANDERSON et al. *Autoimmunity* ii. 33 The term autoimmunity is used.. to indicate the occurrence of an immune response resulting in the production of antibody and/or sensitized lymphoid cells capable of reacting with normal endogenous antigenic body constituents. **1907** *Practitioner* Nov. 653 These cases [of pulmonary tuberculosis].. will be found.. to show 'high phases' and 'low phases', corresponding with waves of auto-immunisation. **1952** *Proc. Third Congr. Internat. Soc. Hematology* 132 By some obscure mechanism the phenomenon of autoimmunization develops and becomes injurious to the person's own red cells. **1887** A. M. BROWN *Anim. Alkaloids* p. iii, Their action as auto-infectants. **1878** T. BRYANT *Pract. Surg.* I. 135 Auto-infection.. is not seen equally in all the sorts of infectious tumours. **1887** A. M. BROWN *Anim. Alkaloids* 136 The body escapes disturbance and disintegration by processes purely auto-infective. **1872** COHEN *Dis. Throat* 45 A series of auto-infra-glottic examinations. **1874** VAN BUREN *Dis. Urin. Org.* 19 Auto-inoculation is the proper test. *Ibid.* Auto-inoculable. **1900** DORLAND *Med. Dict.*, *Auto-intoxicant*, a poison generated within the system. **1909** *Nation* 29 Apr. 427/2 They have ceased to get very much excited since they have learned that selfishness and greed are auto-intoxicants. **1902** W. JAMES *Var. Relig. Exper.* i. 13 If we adopt the assumption,.. Carlyle was undoubtedly auto-intoxicated by some organ or other, no matter which. **1887** A. M. BROWN *Anim. Alkaloids* p. v, Lessons on Auto-intoxication in Disease. **1893** *Times* 3 Oct. 9 The practice of introspection not rarely results in autointoxication or the generation of doubts and perplexities that work like poison in the blood. **1901** H. H. FOSTER in *Amer. Jrnl. Psychol.* Jan. 160 The common starting point of auto-intoxication theories is the influence of certain products of decomposition of living substance upon the continuance of cell activity. **1928** GALSWORTHY *Swan Song* I. vii. 55 You suffer from auto-intoxication in that House [i.e. Parliament]. **1900** DORLAND *Med. Dict.*, *Autokinesis*, voluntary motion. **1949** *Jrnl. R. Aeronaut. Soc.* LIII. 943/2 When only the tail light of an aircraft is visible auto-kinesis may occur. **1959** *New Scientist* 19 Feb. 389/2 An optical illusion known as autokinesis may confuse the pilots... If you stare at a stationary object for a few seconds it appears to move. *a* **1884** KNIGHT *Dict. Mech.* Suppl. 56/2 *Autokinetic telegraph*, an English name for a form of municipal telegraph for fire-alarms, police, etc. **1934** H. C. WARREN *Dict. Psychol.* 26/2 Autokinetic illusion. **1966** *Daily Tel.* 16 Aug. 18/4 Autokinetic reactions.. occur when a person fixes his eye on an illuminated object in an otherwise empty field of vision. **1870** A. DURHAM in *Syst. Surg.* IV. 527 By Auto-laryngoscopy, or by the examination of the Larynx of some living subject. **1872** COHEN *Dis. Throat* 35 The practice of the auto-laryngoscopist. **1921** STEDMAN *Med. Dict.* (ed. 6) 99/2 Autologous. **1958** *Immunology* I. 206 Incubated.. in heparinized autologous plasma. **1962** *Lancet* 27 Jan. 194/1 The dose of autologous marrow had been so very small. **1904** *Sci. Amer.* 7 May 366/1 Prof. Barker showed a number of photographs which had been developed by the autoluminescence of the minerals which he exhibited. **1938** R. W. LAWSON tr. *Hevesy & Paneth's Man. Radioactivity* (ed. 2) xxiv. 242 The rays from radium, themselves invisible, are able to excite substances to emit visible light... This is most strikingly manifested in the phenomenon of autoluminescence. **1904** *Nature* 25 Feb. 403 Thorium with less than a trace of actinium produces an auto-photograph. **1924** *Chambers's Jrnl.* 773/2 Constipation is.. responsible for more ultimate disease or auto-poisoning than anything else. *a* **1909** *Buck's Handbk. Med. Sci.* IV. 184 (Cent. D. Suppl.), Autopoisonous. **1828** *Edin. Rev.* XLVIII. 468 The auto-portrait they present. **1881** *Times* 2 Feb. 12/1 Dental autoprothesis with aurification. *a* **1909** *Buck's Handbk. Med. Sci.* V. 27 (Cent. D. Suppl.), Consciousness is a function of the associative mechanism and may be considered in its threefold relationship to the outer world, the body and self—allopsychic, somatopsychic, and autopsychic. **1941** *Brit. Jrnl. Psychol.* Jan. 232 The amnesia was already less marked, and autopsychic orientation largely restored. *c* **1833** W. H. BROOKFIELD *Let.* in H. Tennyson *Memoir* (1897) I. v. 126 At autopsychography I am not good, if I had any idiopsychology to autopsychographize. **1940** E. GILL *Autobiogr.* 7 The only kind of autobiography I can possibly write must be an autopsychography, a record of mental experience. *a* **1850** ROSSETTI *Dante & Circ.* I. (1874) 1 The *Vita Nuova* (the Autobiography or Autopsychology of Dante's youth). **1920** *Flight* XII. 1194/2 Below 15° the aerofoil remains at rest, but at high angles it auto-rotates, slowly at first, and then more quickly. **1938** *Jrnl. R. Aeronaut. Soc.* XLII. 578 The lifting screw in this case autorotates and is not engine driven. **1918** *Rep. & Mem. Advis. Committee for Aeronaut.* No. 549 p. 4 The speed of auto-rotation is very nearly proportional to the wind speed. **1935** *Times* 4 Mar. 11/3 Speed lift is obtained by autorotation and the whole of the engine power is available for speed. **1909** *Review of Reviews* Feb. 121/1 Autoscript from 'F. W. H. Myers'. **1909** *Daily Chron.* 19 Feb. 6/5 A friend of mine who has a remarkable faculty of automatic writing sends me the following autoscript which she received this morning. **1936** tr. A. L. HAGEDOORN in *Scient. Rep. VIth World's Poultry Congress* III. 54 (*title*) The autosexing Barnevelder, and the autosexing Leghorn, two new breeds. *Ibid.*, The author started.. to produce an autosexing Barnevelder by adding the barring factor to the ordinary laced brown Barnevelder. **1936** M. PEASE *Ibid.* 59 On Brown stripe downs the barred factor in the homozygous state (male) produces a far greater effect than it does in the heterozygous state (female)... This is the principle underlying auto-sexlinkage. *Ibid.*, Directions are given for the making of new auto-sexlinking breeds. **1941** *Poultry Sci.* XX. 317/1 Auto-sex linkage is a name given to the phenomenon of simple and positive sex differences apparent among baby chicks of a fixed breed, not crossbreds. *Ibid.* 317/2 The third.. method for distinguishing sex at hatching is the production of auto-sexing (self-sexing) varieties. **1951** *Catal. of Exhibits, South Bank Exhib., Festival of Britain* 112/1 Live autosexed chicks. **1894** Autosoteric [see *heterosoteric* s.v. HETERO-]. **1909** B. B. WARFIELD *Calvin as Theologian* iii. 31 The logic of Socinianism gave us.. an auto-soteric religion. *Ibid.* ii. 18 There is nothing against which Calvinism set its face with more firmness than.. auto-soterism. **1901** BALDWIN *Dict. Philos. & Psychol.* I. 96/1 Autotelic is suggested as serving, in the phrases autotelic function, process, &c., the meaning indicated by the German Selbstzweck. **1932** T. S. ELIOT *Sel. Essays* I. ii. 24 No exponent of criticism.. has.. ever made the preposterous assumption that criticism is an autotelic activity. **1958** *Times Lit. Suppl.* 12 Sept. 507/1 The autotherapists, conscious or unconscious, who compulsively at the end of each day make their confessions to their journal. **1933** H. G. WELLS *Shape of Things to Come* II. §8. 197 This great German mind.. was incapable of autotherapy, and let its sickness have its way with it. **1890** BILLINGS *Med. Dict.* Autotoxæmia. **1924** *Psyche* July 67 A form of blood poisoning due to the development of autotoxaemia from over indulgence in flesh foods. **1909** *Jrnl. Exper. Med.* XI. 177 Besides my own the only successful autotransplantations of these glandules in dogs are, perhaps, the two in puppies reported by Pfeiffer, Hermann, and Mayer. **1920** *Ibid.* XXXII. 113 (*title*) Homeotransplantation and autotransplantation of the spleen in rabbits. **1938** S. MORGULIS tr. *A.I. Oparin's Origin of Life* viii. 206 These autotrophic organisms can be compared..to the green autotrophes, even to the simplest algae. *Ibid.* 207 This fairly isolated group of living things must have arisen..at the same time when the first autotrophes capable of photosynthesis appeared. **1954** *New Biol.* XVII. 61 Organisms able to subsist entirely on inorganic nutrients are known as autotrophs ('self-feeders'); they are relatively common among the sulphur bacteria. **1959** *Chambers's Encycl.* II. 317/2 The autotrophes, which include the green plants, possess the ability to trap and harness for their own purposes energy from the inorganic world outside. **1901** I. B. BALFOUR in *Rep. Brit. Assoc. Advancem. Sci.* 820 The root-difference between plants and animals is one of nutrition. Plants are autotrophic, animals heterotrophic. **1927** BIRGE & JUDAY in *Amer. Philos. Soc. Proc.* LXVI. 371 Many lakes..are dependent wholly on internal sources and may be called *autotrophic*—they receive water directly from rain and from a very limited drainage which has passed through a sand filter. **1947** *Endeavour* VI. 173 Nitrogen-fixing blue-green algae are the most completely autotrophic organisms known. **1898** *Nat. Science* June 387 By autotropism is implied the inherent tendency of vegetable organs to grow in a straight line. **1908** H. DRIESCH *Sci. & Philos. of Organism* I. I. 158 'Autotropism', that is, the fact that branches of plants always try to reassume their proper angle with regard to their orientation on the main axis, if this orientation has been disturbed.

b. Used frequently in the names of self-acting mechanisms, machines, instruments, etc.; **auto-a'larm**, a radio receiving device which in time of distress gives audible automatic warning of the need for help; **auto-'analyser**, an automatic apparatus for performing (chemical) analyses; **auto-change, -changer**, a device which automatically places a record on the turntable of a record-player when the previous record has finished playing; **'autocode** *Computers* (see quots.); **auto-con'verter** *Electr.* = *auto-transformer*; **'autoflare** *Aeronaut.*, a mechanism for automatically preparing an aircraft to land (see quots.); **auto-focus**, a device by means of which an enlarger, camera, or the like is automatically focused; also *attrib.* or quasi-*adj.*; hence ***auto-focusing***; **auto-trans'former**, a transformer or compensator in which a part of the primary coil is used as a secondary, or a part of the secondary as a primary coil.

1885 *Jrnl. Chem. Soc.* XLVIII. 854 New Pile, or Auto-accumulator. **1895** S. P. THOMPSON *Polyphase Electric Currents* x. 186 The auto-transformer (or 'one-coil' transformer) merely consists of a coil of wire wound on an iron core, and connected across the mains. **1902** W. J. DIBDIN *Public Lighting* 176 The auto-valve, which is not affected by condensation or grit. **1904** *Electr. Rev.* 17 Sept. 459 (Cent. D. Suppl.), An 'oil-break auto-starter' switch. **1927** *Glasgow Herald* 18 July 10 The object of the auto-alarm is to ensure that the call shall be received by the smaller ships and that no wireless distress calls shall be missed by any ship owing to the operator being off duty. **1928** *B.B.C. Handbk. 1929* 427/2 *Auto-transformer*, a transformer either in radio or audio frequency in which the primary and secondary windings are formed by one and the same coil having three connections to it. **1943** *Gloss. Terms Electr. Engin. (B.S.I.)* 38 *Auto-transformer*, a transformer in which the primary and secondary windings have a common part or parts. **1944** *Gramophone* Apr. 174/3 (Advt.), H.M.V. Autochange Radiogram. *Ibid.*, Specially constructed Connoisseur Radiogram with twin auto changers. **1949** *Q. Jrnl. Forestry* XLIII. 26 A new model..auto-scythe, with independent wheel drive was demonstrated cutting bracken. **1957** *Times Survey Brit. Aviation* Sept. 2/5 Auto-stabilization is fitted to simplify the pilot's tasks. **1958** V. DRUMM in M. L. Hall *Newnes Compl. Amat. Photogr.* 312 When the two systems are coupled together, auto-focus to get the approximate position, and manual focusing for the final fine touch, it is very satisfactory. *Ibid.*, A test for auto-focus enlargers. *Ibid.* 313 If the enlarger is auto-focus, try altering the focus slightly, and see if the image can be improved. **1959** *New Scientist* 25 June 1375/2 Some of the [computer] machine-makers have gone as far as building into their later machines an 'autocode' by which the advanced types can automatically adapt the programme codes of previous models. **1959** *Listener* 29 Oct. 731/1 (Advt.), *Four* speed autochanger. **1959** 'ELLIS PETERS' *Death Mask* i. 17 We hadn't got an auto-change on the old radiogram. **1960** *Ann. N.Y. Acad. Sci.* LXXXVII. 6/6 The development of the Auto-Analyzer has made available an instrument for rapid, precise colorimetric analysis of various biochemical components. **1960** *Times Rev. Industry* Aug. 53/2 Emission of air from the nozzles is controlled by the aircraft's electro hydraulic autostabilizer. **1962** *Engineering* 26 Jan. 137 Auto-ignition is now virtually standard on gas cookers. **1962** *Lancet* 2 June 1162/1 Urea was measured by autoanalyser ('Technicon'). **1962** *Listener* 7 June 986/2 We can just say let the letter 'A' stand for the set of instructions, and then we can, in our programme, simply write 'repeat "A" fifty times'. This instruction is what is called an auto-code, which the computer will itself translate into the fully detailed instructions. **1962** *New Scientist* 12 July 84/3 The autoflare system (the system which puts the aeroplane into the landing attitude at the right moment). **1963** *Times* 19 Apr. 11/6 On the Trident and VC 10 it is proposed to use the equipment in stages, the first being autoflare, in which the aircraft is brought down to the height at which it levels off for landing, leaving the pilot to put the aircraft down. **1967** KARCH & BUBER *Offset Processes* iv. 123 It is linked with an 'autofocussing' system.

c. *Biol.* In comp. with *-ploid*, as AUTOPOLYPLOID, AUTOTETRAPLOID: having sets of chromosomes derived from a single species (opp. *allo-*).

auto-² ('ɔːtəʊ). abbreviation of AUTOMOBILE used as comb. form, chiefly in the names of vehicles, as ***autobus***, ***autocar***, ***automotor***, etc. See also AUTO *sb.*², AUTOCYCLE.

1895 *Daily News* 30 Nov. 5/1 To apply the new principle of the 'auto-motor' to road-waggons, heavy drags, hunting-traps, and stage-coaches. **1895** *Westm. Gaz.* 17 Dec. 3/1 We congratulate the police authorities..on having convicted the owner of an autocar for proceeding along a road at a pace exceeding three miles an hour. **1896** (*title*) The Automotor Journal. **1897** *N.Y. Herald* 19 Sept. 2/1 The introduction of an efficient autocab service in the streets of Paris. **1899** *N.Y. Jrnl.* 17 June 5/2 The New York Auto-Truck Company. **1899** *Westm. Gaz.* 4 July 6/3 The auto-conveyances of members of Parliament. **1899** *Boston Herald* 12 July 6/5 We should have the new words..auto-bus, [etc.]. **1900** *Engineering Mag.* Aug. 733 The auto-waggon, which provides just that rapid and cheap form of independent direct transport [etc.]. **1904** *Westm. Gaz.* 23 Sept. 7/3 Mr. W. K. Vanderbilt, junior's auto-boat 'Mercédès the Sixth'. **1908** A. BENNETT *Buried Alive* iv. 88 Two commissionaires were helping him into an auto-cab. **1918** W. STEVENS *Let.* 30 Apr. (1967) 208, I must wait..for an auto-bus back to Johnson City. **1927** *Chambers's Jrnl.* 375/2 You can..explore the French side..from end to end by safe, strong, comfortable autocar. **1927** *South America* May 137/2 The auto-coach is much needed to replace the horse-coach. **1941** KOESTLER *Scum of Earth* 206 The regular autobus line Bergerac-Bordeaux still functioned.

auto-analysis (ˌɔːtəʊə'nælɪsɪs). [f. AUTO-¹ + ANALYSIS.] Self-analysis; *esp.* exploration by a person of his own conscious or unconscious mind. Hence **auto-'analyst**, one who engages in auto-analysis.

1894 W. WALLACE *Proleg. to Hegel's Philos.* (ed. 2) xvii. 209 The method of mathematics or mechanics..is analytic or synthetic—but not auto-analysis or auto-synthesis. **1917** C. R. PAYNE tr. *Pfister's Psychoanalytic Method* xii. 346 Finally he submitted to autoanalysis and found it was the melody of Beethoven to Goethe's verse: 'Mit Männern sich geschlagen'. *Ibid.*, This also occurred to the autoanalyst in a moment. **1928** *Daily Tel.* 3 Jan. 8/5 The tradition..that the keepers of journals are more..intent on auto-analysis.

autobahn ('ɔːtəʊbɑːn). Pl. **autobahnen, autobahns.** [G., f. *auto* (AUTO-²) + *bahn* path, road, f. MHG. *ban(e)*, MLG., MDu. *bāne*, usually related to OHG. *bano*, MHG. *ban(e)* death, OE. *bana* BANE *sb.*¹] In Germany, a fast motor road; = MOTORWAY.

1937 *Sunday Times* 18 Apr. 33/2 In the last six months or so there has sprung up from several quarters a demand for motorways, or autobahnen or autostrade—meaning..new roads for the exclusive use of motor traffic. **1940** D. E. STEVENSON *English Air* I. iv. 35 The Continental roads were the ones for speed—the long straight roads of France, and those new German *Autobahn.* **1941** *Hutchinson's Pict. Hist. War* 14 May–8 July 156 (*caption*) Autobahn bridge near Mannheim extensively damaged after a raid by the R.A.F. **1955** *Times* 14 June 7/5 It was easy for a Hitler or a Mussolini to drive great autobahns or autostradas through their respective countries.

autobasidiomycete (ˌɔːtəʊbə'sɪdɪəʊmaɪ'siːt). *Biol.* [G. (O. Brefeld *Untersuchungen aus d. Gesammtgeb. d. Mykologie* (1889) VIII. 185), f. AUTO-¹: see below.] A fungus belonging to the Autobasidiomycetes, a division of the Basidiomycetes, including mushrooms, toadstools, and related fungi having an autobasidium.

1895 M. C. COOKE *Introd. Study of Fungi* II. x. 115 The Basidiomycetes are arranged in two groups: (1) The Protobasidiomycetes..(2) the Autobasidiomycetes, in which the basidia are not septate, and bear a definite number of basidiospores. **1933** *Ann. Reg. 1932* 57 Wakayama's demonstration that the chromosome numbers in thirty-four Autobasidiomycetes are either two, four, or six. **1937** GWYNNE-VAUGHAN & BARNES *Struct. & Dev. Fungi* (ed. 2) 326 The Autobasidiomycetes include between 12,000 and 13,000 species; they are cosmopolitan in distribution.

autobasidium (ɔːtəʊbə'sɪdɪəm). *Biol.* [f. AUTO-¹ + BASIDIUM.] A basidium that has no septum.

1902 WEBSTER Suppl., *Autobasidium*, an undivided basidium, characteristic of the *Autobasidiomycetes*, one of the two groups into which the Basidiomycetes are sometimes divided. **1928** C. W. DODGE tr. *Gäumann's Compar. Morphol. Fungi* xxv. 412 The basidia in which nuclear division is not followed by formation of septa are called auto- or holobasidia. **1940** *Chambers's Techn. Dict.* 602 *Autobasidium*, a basidium which does not become septate.

autobi'ographal, *a. rare.* [See AUTO-¹.] = AUTOBIOGRAPHICAL.

1845 LD. CAMPBELL *Chancellors* (1857) IV. xci. 246 The following autobiographal account of these occurrences.

autobi'ographer. [See AUTO-¹.] One who writes the story of his own life.

1821 *Q. Rev.* XXIV. 361 He merely describes his own [thoughts]..just as a real autobiographer might do. **1829** C. MATHEWS *Mem.* IV. ii. 23 Mr. Rattle, Autobiographer in Embryo. **1878** SEELEY *Stein* III. 476 The praise of an autobiographer is to reveal what it is the virtue of a man to keep secret.

autobiographic (ˌɔːtəʊbaɪəʊ'græfɪk), *a.* [see AUTO-¹.]

1. Of the nature of autobiography.

1827 T. J. DIBDIN *Reminisc.* II. viii. 326 My life, ladies and gentlemen! (that is, my autobiographic life) is now drawing towards its close. **1850** CARLYLE in *Athenæum* 18 June (1881) 815/3 An excellent good book, by far the best of the autobiographic kind I remember. **1870** LOWELL *Among my Bks.* Ser. II. (1873) 26 The writings of Dante..are all..autobiographic.

2. Of the character of an autobiographer.

1864 *Reader* 28 Apr. 512/1 Was he never..autobiographic? Did he never make entries in..a sort of diary?

ˌautobio'graphical, *a.* [See AUTO-¹.]

1. Belonging to, connected with, autobiography.

1831 CARLYLE *Sart. Res.* II. ii, These Autobiographical times of ours. **1878** SEELEY *Stein* III. 499 For its autobiographical value, I translate the substance of this Memoir.

2. = AUTOBIOGRAPHIC 1, 2.

1829 *Gentl. Mag.* XCVII. II. 526 An auto-biographical sketch of the life of a poet. **1880** L. STEPHEN *Pope* viii. 186 Pope takes advantage of the suggestions in Horace to be thoroughly autobiographical.

ˌautobio'graphically, *adv.* [f. prec. + -LY².] In the way or manner of autobiography.

1864 in WEBSTER. **1883** *Sat. Rev.* 29 Dec. 839 Writing in the present tense and autobiographically.

autobiographist (ˌɔːtəʊbaɪ'ɒgrəfɪst). [f. AUTO-¹ + BIOGRAPHIST.] = AUTOBIOGRAPHER.

1840 *Fraser's Mag.* XXII. 579 We must first describe this volunteer autobiographist. **1850** *Tait's Mag.* XVII. 525/2 Our autobiographist betakes himself to London. **1920** *Westm. Gaz.* 26 Nov. 8/2 Too indiscreet a candour in autobiography..may..involve unfortunate consequences upon the autobiographist.

autobiography (ˌɔːtəʊbaɪ'ɒgrəfɪ, -bɪ'ɒg-). [f. AUTO-¹ + BIOGRAPHY *sb.* Neither this nor any of its derivatives are in Todd 1818; only *Autobiography* in Craig 1847.] The writing of one's own history; the story of one's life written by himself.

1797 *Monthly Review* 2nd Ser. XXIV. 375 It is not very usual in English to employ hybrid words partly Saxon and partly Greek: yet *autobiography* would have seemed pedantic. **1809** SOUTHEY in *Q. Rev.* I. 283 This very amusing and unique specimen of autobiography. **1828** CARLYLE *Misc.* (1857) I. 154 What would we give for such an Autobiography of Shakspeare. **1859** B. POWELL *Ord. Nat.* 252 Geology (as Sir C. Lyell has so happily expressed it) is 'the autobiography of the earth.'

autobus, autocar: see AUTO-².

autocarpous (ɔːtəʊ'kɑːpəs), *a. Bot.* [f. Gr. αὐτο- self + καρπός fruit + -OUS.] '(A fruit) Consisting of pericarp alone having no adnate parts.' Gray. Also **auto'carpian** *a.*

1847 in CRAIG.

autocentric (ɔːtəʊ'sɛntrɪk), *a.* [f. AUTO-¹, after EGOCENTRIC *a.*] Centred in the self; making oneself the centre (see quot. 1889). Hence **auto'centrism**, the possession of an autocentric attitude or outlook.

a **1866** J. GROTE *Moral Ideals* (1876) 189 Becoming cosmocentric instead of autocentric in our knowledge. **1889** J. VENN *Empirical Logic* xxv. 572, I should be inclined to mark the above distinction by the words *autocentric* and *coinocentric*..the distinction between two attitudes which we may adopt in our practice. In the one case the agent is supposed to make himself the centre of his own speculation and consequent action. **1927** T. BURROW *Social Basis of Consciousness* II. vii. 188 The type of individual who upon the initial stimulus to defence has recourse to a tactic of unconditional retreat..is the autocentric individual. **1931** K. E. KIRK *Vision of God* 489 As long ago as 1906, he had fixed upon 'autocentrism' as the clue to the complexities of Newman's character.

autocephalous (ɔːtəʊ'sɛfələs), *a.* [f. Gr. αὐτοκέφαλ-ος (f. αὐτο- independent + κεφαλή head) + -OUS.] *lit.* Having a head or chief of its own. Of bishops and churches: Independent of archiepiscopal or patriarchal jurisdiction.

1863 NEALE *Liturgiol.* 289 Georgia had its own autocephalous metropolitan. **1881** G. SIMCOX in *Academy* 2 Apr. 237 Autocephalous churches like that of Cyprus.

autochrome ('ɔːtəʊkrəʊm), *a.* and *sb. Photogr.* (Disused.) [f. Gr. αὐτο- (see AUTO-¹) + χρῶμα colour.]

A. *adj.* Defining a process and a plate used in colour-photography, invented by Messrs. Lumière of Lyons; also, a slide produced by this process.

1907 *Daily Chron.* 12 July 6/4 The new plates are called 'The Autochrome Plates'. **1907** *Brit. Jrnl. Photogr.* 2 Aug. 573/1 The Lumière 'Autochrome' Plates. **1920** *Glasgow Herald* 1 Mar. 13 A series of autochrome slides.

B. *sb.* A photograph produced by this process.

1907 *Brit. Jrnl. Photogr.* 2 Aug. 573/1 The reproduction of Lumière 'Autochromes' on 'Uto' paper. **1910** *Westm. Gaz.* 16 Apr. 14/2 An excellent collection of autochromes.

autochthon (ɔː'tɒkθən, -əʊn). Pl. **autochthons**, or in L. form **autochthones** (ɔː'tɒkθəniːz). [a. Gr. αὐτόχθων sprung from that land itself, f. αὐτο (see AUTO-¹) + χθών, χθονός, earth, soil.]

1. *lit.* A human being sprung from the soil he inhabits; a 'son of the soil.'

1646 SIR T. BROWNE *Pseud. Ep.* 274 There was therefore never any Autochthon, or man arising from the earth but

Adam. **1660** INGELO *Bentiv. and Ur.* II. (1682) 83 [They] suppose men to be Autochthones, Intelligent Mushromes. **1879** JEFFERIES *Wild Life in S.C.* 147 He loves the earth on which he walks like a true autochthon.

2. *Hence* in *pl.* The earliest known dwellers in any country; original inhabitants, aborigines.

1741 WARBURTON *Div. Legat.* II. 28 They thought themselves Autochthones. **1851** D. WILSON *Preh. Ann.* (1863) I. ix. 279 But for the evidence of history, the Norse population of the Orkneys would appear to be autochthones. **1858** GLADSTONE *Homer* I. 205 Greek tradition..placed the Pelasgians first in the Peloponnesus as autochthons.

3. *transf.* and *fig.* Original inhabitants or products.

1837 CAMPBELL *To Sp. Patriots* ii, Ye Are worse than common fiends from Heaven that fell, The baser, ranker sprung, Autochthones of Hell! **1879** LE CONTE *Elem. Geol.* 553 The Pliocene Autochthones were destroyed.

4. *Geol.* An autochthonous rock formation; opp. ALLOCHTHON.

1942 M. P. BILLINGS *Struct. Geol.* x. 181 Rocks of the foreland..are said to be *autochthonous*—that is developed where found; these rocks are sometimes called the autochthon. **1957** [see ALLOCHTHON]. **1961** J. CHALLINOR *Dict. Geol.* 15/1 The 'autochthon' is essentially a rock-succession that, as a whole, has not been translated by tectonic movement (it forms part of the foreland); but it may show..autochthonous folding, within itself.

5. An indigenous plant.

1893 in *Funk's Stand. Dict.* **1916** B. D. JACKSON *Gloss. Bot. Terms* (ed. 3) 40/2 *Autochthon*,..a native plant, not an introduction.

autochthonal (ɔːˈtɒkθənəl), *a.* [f. prec. + -AL[1].] Autochthonic, autochthonous.

1829 T. PEACOCK *Misfort. Elphin* 93 The autochthonal justice of our agrestic kakistocracy. **1869** FARRAR *Fam. Speech* iv. (1873) 117 These autochthonal peoples.

autochthonic (ɔːtɒkˈθɒnɪk), *a.* [f. as prec. + -IC.] Native to the soil, aboriginal, indigenous.

1845 FORD *Handbk. Spain* i. 52 The old autochthonic Iberians. **1860** ABP. THOMSON *Outl. Laws Th.* 285 To consider both Greek and Indian philosophy as autochthonic.

autochthonism (ɔːˈtɒkθənɪz(ə)m). [f. as prec. + -ISM.] Birth from the soil of a country, or aboriginal occupation of it.

1857 GLADSTONE *Oxf. Ess.* 43 Argolis and Arcadia.. disputing with Athens the palm of autochthonism.

auˈtochthonist. *rare.* [f. as prec. + -IST.] One who believes in the existence of autochthons.

1879 *De Quatrefages' Hum. Spec.* 185 No other part of the globe seems to justify, to such an extent, the opinions of autochthonists.

autochthonous (ɔːˈtɒkθənəs), *a.* [f. as prec. + -OUS.] **a.** = AUTOCHTHONIC.

1805 W. TAYLOR in *Ann. Rev.* III. 309 If the English have this great predilection for autochthonous bread and butter. **1860** *Sat. Rev.* X. 149/1 Most of them [the Red Indians] believe themselves to be autochthonous. **1879** B. TAYLOR *Germ. Lit.* 13 A native autochthonous German literature.

b. *transf.* in *Path.*; (see quot.)

1876 tr. *Wagner's Gen. Pathol.* 189 An autochthonous or primitive thrombus is one which remains confined in the part in which it first arose, especially in the heart.

c. *Geol.* [f. G. *autochthon* (K. W. von Gümbel 1888), see ALLOCHTHONOUS *a.*] Consisting of or formed from indigenous material (opp. ALLOCHTHONOUS); applied to organic deposits and rock formations originating *in situ*.

1900 in J. F. KEMP *Handbk. Rocks* (ed. 2) 126. **1916** C. C. FORSAITH in *Bot. Gaz.* LXII. 33 Autochthonous peat (that type of peat which represents the amassing of successive generations of plants in..constant, but stagnant..water). **1928** K. E. CARPENTER *Life in Inland Waters* viii. 207 In place of the 'autochthonous' (home-produced) sediments.. we have 'allochthonous' material of drifted fragments from shore-living plants. **1935** E. B. BAILEY *Tectonic Essays* iii. 34 In tectonics, an autochthonous fold is one that is made of untravelled indigenous rocks. **1946** *Q. Jrnl. Geol. Soc.* CI. 207 It is considered that for the most part the Downtonian and Dittonian vertebrate faunas were not autochthonous, but were of freshwater origin.

autochthonously (ɔːˈtɒkθənəslɪ), *adv.* [-LY[2].] In an autochthonous manner.

1885 *Encycl. Brit.* XVIII. 361/2 The larger number of maladies do not arise autochthonously or 'under a whole skin', they are generated by certain morbific causes. **1953** HINSIE & SHATZKY *Psychiatric Dict.* (ed. 2) 60/2 The heart ..continues to beat for a time after it has been removed from the body. It is then said to function autochthonously.

autochthony (ɔːˈtɒkθənɪ). [f. AUTOCHTHON + -Y.] Autochthonous condition; aboriginal occupation.

1846 GROTE *Greece* I. vi. I. 146 The fancy of one or a few great families branching out widely..was more popular.. than that of a distinct autochthony in each of the separate districts. **1879** *De Quatrefages' Hum. Spec.* 179 The partisans of the autochthony of nations.

¶ *erron.* for *autoctony* 'suicide.'

1652 URQUHART *Jewel* Wks. (1834) 243 By taking away the sword, hindred the desperate project of that autochthony.

†**ˈautocide.** *Obs. rare*[−1]. [irreg. f. AUTO-[1] + L. *-cīda* slayer.] A self-destroyer, a suicide.

1635 PERSON *Varieties* III. 155 Such autocides and selfe murtherers.

autoclave (ˈɔːtəkleɪv). [a. F. *autoclave*, f. Gr. αὐτο- (see AUTO-[1]) self + L. *clāvus* nail (or) *clāvis* key; hence = 'a self-fastening apparatus.'] **1.** A kind of French stew-pan with a steam-tight lid.

1880 FRISNELL in *Soc. Arts Jrnl.* 444 Strong cast-iron vessels, enamelled inside, and known as 'autoclaves.'

2. A vessel for carrying out chemical reactions at high temperatures under pressure; an apparatus for sterilizing by steam at high pressure.

1876 *Jrnl. Chem. Soc.* XXX. 451 Saponification of Neutral Fats in Autoclaves. **1886** *Ibid.* L. 112 High Pressure Digesters (Autoclaves) for Chemical Laboratories... The apparatus consists of a cylindrical copper vessel, provided with a cover, which is firmly fastened down by a screw. **1919** *Modern Hospital* XII. 281 (*title*) High-pressure dressing sterilizers or autoclaves. **1931** *Forestry* V. 141 The nutrient medium..is made up and sterilized in an autoclave. **1946** *Electronic Engin.* XVIII. 317 The phosphors..are prepared in autoclaves at high temperature and under pressure of some thousand atmospheres.

Hence **ˈautoclave** *v. trans.* and *intr.* (Webster, 1934); so **ˈautoclaving** *vbl. sb.* and *ppl. a.*, **ˈautoclaved** *ppl. a.*

1929 *Biochem. Jrnl.* XXIII. 1052 The preparation of 'bios' used was an autoclaved solution of marmite. **1943** *Electronic Engin.* XV. 394 A number of steatite bodies.. were investigated by autoclaving. **1955** J. G. DAVIS *Dict. Dairying* (ed. 2) 844 Autoclave at a pressure of 15 lb. per sq. in. for 20 min[utes]. **1960** *Times* 19 Aug. 2/5 Spray drying and autoclaving techniques. **1965** *Economist* 5 June 1176/2 Siporex is an autoclaved light weight aerated concrete product.

autocopyist (ɔːtəʊˈkɒpiːɪst). [f. AUTO-[1] + COPYIST.] An apparatus for producing facsimile copies of written matter. (Disused.)

1888 *Encycl. Brit.* XXIV. 697/2 In principle the autocopyist is like the hektograph. **1907** *Daily Chron.* 21 Jan. 3/5 Sketch maps..have been reproduced by means of an autocopyist.

autocorrelation (ˌɔːtəʊkɒrɪˈleɪʃən). [f. AUTO-[1] + CORRELATION.] A correlation between all the elements of a series and those separated from them by a given interval (see quot. 1951). Also *attrib.* Hence **ˌautoˈcorrelator**, an apparatus for computing autocorrelations.

1950 *Jrnl. Acoust. Soc.* XXII. 677 (*title*) Autocorrelation analysis of speech sounds. **1951** *Amer. Jrnl. Psychol.* LXIV. 258 An autocorrelation is simply a correlation computed between all items of a series, and the items that follow any given item by one, two, three, or more steps, or by corresponding time-intervals. *Ibid.* 262 The autocorrelator is directly connected to the output. **1956** J. WHATMOUGH *Lang.* v. 76 The quantitative criterion..might be established by some electrical apparatus, such as an autocorrelator. **1965** *Math. in Biol. & Med.* (*Med. Res. Council*) I. 37 The computer is being used to apply the mathematical techniques of autocorrelation and cross-correlation to the interpretation of the EEG in the treatment of temporal lobe epilepsy.

autocracy (ɔːˈtɒkrəsɪ). [ad. Gr. αὐτοκράτεια, n. of state f. αὐτοκρατής: see AUTOCRAT. Cf. mod. F. *autocratie*.]

†**1. a.** Self-sustained or independent power. *Obs.*

1655 LESTRANGE *Chas. I* 121 The king of Sweden..had prospered to an autocracy, a self-subsistence, and so needed no participants..in the hazard. *a* **1716** SOUTH *Serm.* VIII. 285 (T.) [The Divine Will] moves not by the external impulse..of objects, but determines itself by an absolute autocracy. **1755** JOHNSON, *Autocrasy*, independent power.

†**b.** Of states: Possession of the right of self-government, political independence; = AUTONOMY.

1864 WEBSTER cites BARLOW.

2. a. Absolute government.

1855 MERIVALE *Rom. Emp.* xlviii. V. 418 Caius..had inherited his autocracy. **1855** MILMAN *Lat. Chr.* (1864) V. IX. viii. 376 Unrepining subjection under the religious autocracy of the Pope.

b. *transf.* Controlling authority or influence.

1855 H. SPENCER *Psychol.* (1872) II. VII. ii. 314 The establishment of this autocracy among the faculties. **1860** FARRAR *Orig. Lang.* ii. 36 The autocracy of philosophic bodies.

c. Autocrats collectively; the realm of autocrats.

1905 *Smart Set* Sept. 125 Of all the fish that swim or swish In ocean's deep autocracy There's none possess such haughtiness As the codfish aristocracy. **1928** *Manch. Guardian Weekly* 19 Oct. 301/2 She is credited with wiser views of Russian policy than were commonly found in the heads of that fated autocracy.

3. *Med.* The controlling influence exerted by nature or the vital principle on disease.

1864 WEBSTER cites DUNGLISON.

autocrat (ˈɔːtəkræt). [a. F. *autocrate*, ad. Gr. αὐτοκρατής ruling by oneself, absolute, f. αὐτο- (see AUTO-[1]) + κράτος, κρατε- might, power, authority; cf. κρατύς strong, cogn. w. Goth. *hardus*, Eng. *hard.*] A monarch of uncontrolled authority; an absolute, irresponsible governor; one who rules with undisputed sway. (***Autocrat of all the Russias***, a title of the Czar.)

1803 SOUTHEY in *Ann. Rev.* I. 89 An embassy sent by the Directory, or the Corsican autocrat. **1851** H. SPENCER *Soc. Stat.* v. §6 The Russian noble is alike a serf to his autocrat, and an autocrat to his serf. **1853** LYNCH *Self-Improv.* vi. 149 The will is no autocrat to have his bidding done at once. **1858** O. W. HOLMES (*title*) The Autocrat of the Breakfast Table.

autocratic (ɔːtəʊˈkrætɪk), *a.* [ad. F. *autocratique*, f. *autocrate*: see prec. and -IC.] Of the nature of, or pertaining to, an autocrat; absolute in authority, despotic.

1823 BYRON *Juan* x. xlix, The fair Czarina's autocratic crest. **1867** PEARSON *Hist. Eng.* I. 49 The tax on salt..was farmed out to almost autocratic contractors. **1878** BOSW. SMITH *Carthage* 177 Hamilcar received the command with autocratic powers.

autoˈcratical, *a.* [f. as prec. + -AL[1].] = prec.

1801 LD. COLCHESTER *Diary & Corr.* I. 290 The haughtiness of the Autocratical Empire. **1828** LANDOR *Imag. Conv.* (1846) I. 185 A sage, too autocratical to be taught anything by sages of another class.

autoˈcratically, *adv.* [f. prec. + -LY[2].] In autocratic manner, absolutely, despotically.

1860 GOSSE *Rom. Nat. Hist.* 2 Regions where he reigns autocratically. **1875** MAINE *Hist. Inst.* iii. 86 Whether popularly or autocratically governed.

autocratism (ɔːˈtɒkrətɪz(ə)m). [f. AUTOCRAT + -ISM.] The principles or practices of autocrats.

1848 *Fraser's Mag.* XXXVII. 96 To liberal sentiments he united the instincts of autocratism. **1916** V. HORSLEY in S. Paget *Life* (1919) III. iii. 315 It is interesting to appreciate the sensation of an autocratism. **1952** V. GOLLANCZ *My Dear Timothy* 316 How difficult it is to overcome an autocratism native to one's temperament.

autocrator (ɔːˈtɒkrətɔː(r)). ? *Obs.* [a. Gr. αὐτοκράτωρ one's own master, an absolute ruler.] = AUTOCRAT (and in earlier use).

1789–96 MORSE *Amer. Geog.* II. 88 The emperor, or autocrator of Russia. **1832** AUSTIN *Jurispr.* (1879) I. vi. 213 That our own king was monarch and autocrator in Hanover.

†**autocraˈtoric,** *a. Obs.* [ad. Gr. αὐτοκρατορικός: see prec. and -IC.] = AUTOCRATIC. †**autocraˈtorical** *a.* = prec.

1678 *Hist. Indulg.* in G. Hickes *Spir. Popery* (1680) 74 The Autocratorick..Power of making Laws. **1659** PEARSON *Creed* (1741) 297 The Father, Son, and Holy Ghost..have the same autocratorical power. **1769** W. JACKSON in *Month. Rev.* XLII. 171 Their..autocratorical automatous author.

†**auˈtocratress.** *Obs. rare*[−1]. [fem. of AUTOCRATOR: see -ESS.] A female autocrat.

1762 *Ann. Reg.* 227/2 We Catharine II..autocratress of all the Russias.

†**auˈtocratrice.** *Obs. rare.* [a. F. *autocratrice*, ad. *autocratrix*: see next.] = prec.

1767 CHESTERF. *Lett.* 410 IV. 251, I do not think that the Autocratrice of all the Russias will be trifled with.

autocratrix (ɔːˈtɒkrətrɪks). [Latinized feminine of AUTOCRATOR, assumed as a title by Catharine II of Russia.] A female autocrat; the title of the empresses of Russia ruling in their own right.

1762 *Gentl. Mag.* 382 Autocratrix of all the Russias. **1844** JEFFREY *Contrib. Edin. Rev.* I. 375 The celebrated Autocratrix, Catherine II.

ˈautocratˌship. [See -SHIP.] Position as an autocrat; autocracy.

1864 in WEBSTER.

autocritical (ɔːtəʊˈkrɪtɪkəl), *a.* [f. AUTO-[1] + CRITICAL *a.* Cf. *auto-criticism* s.v. AUTO-.] Critical of oneself or one's own work.

1642 C. HERLE *Fuller Answ. to Ferne* 14 Thats the peculiar Priviledge of Gods word to be autocritical, its own last judge. **1821** *Blackw. Mag.* X. 116 We differ..from the autocritical junto who are willing to dictate to *us*. **1850** L. HUNT *Autobiogr.* I. p. vi, Coleridge's *Literary Life* is professedly autocritical. **1957** R. CAMPBELL *Coll. Poems* II. 132 No autocritical confession Could be extracted.

autocross (ˈɔːtəʊkrɒs). [f. AUTO-[2] + CROSS(-COUNTRY.] A form of cross-country racing for motor vehicles.

1965 *Observer* 5 Sept. 13/4 Rallies are a doomed sport... The future lies with autocross, a form of cross-country motor racing with private cars on private estates. **1966** *Pubn. Amer. Dial. Soc.* 1964 XLII. 2 *Autocross*, an automotive competition like a gymkhana, except that there are fewer obstacles and greater speeds involved.

autocue (ˈɔːtəʊkjuː). [f. AUTO-[1] + CUE *sb.*[2]] The name of a script device, placed out of range of the camera, which prints the words to be spoken by a speaker on television as an aid to his memory.

1958 I. BROWN *Words in our Time* 22 The autocue is..one of the gadgets introduced by television. The speaker or recorder of news has in front of him a screen over which his text passes. Thus he can read without looking down or fidgeting with papers. **1967** P. PURSER *Twentymen* xi. 70 The revised pieces were then typed up for the Autocue prompting machine.

autocycle (ˈɔːtəʊsaɪk(ə)l). [f. AUTO-[2] + CYCLE *sb.*] A cycle propelled by a motor; a motor-cycle. So **ˈautocyclist**, one who rides an autocycle.

1905 *Daily Chron.* 21 July 5/5, 86 miles an hour. Wonderful Performance on an Autocycle. **1920** *Daily Mail* 29 Nov. 8 The Autocraft Board, which has an Auto-cycle section. **1958** *Oxford Mail* 7 Feb. 7/5 Auto-cyclist..killed yesterday when the auto-cycle he was riding was involved in a collision with a Land Rover.

‖**auto-da-fé, -de-fé** (ˌautoda'fe). Plural **autos-da-fé**; improperly **auto-da-fés**. [The former, Pg. (also used in Fr.); the latter, Sp. (Pg. *da* of the, Sp. *de* of) = judicial sentence or act of (the) faith. Cf. ACT *sb.* 9. (The Portuguese form was first known in England.)]

1. A judicial 'act' or sentence of the Inquisition.

1723 *Lond. Gaz.* No. 6207/1 There will be an Auto da Fé in the Church of the Monastery of St. Dominick [in Lisbon]. **1817** BYRON *Juan* I. xxxii. *note* Wks. (1846) 594/2 Little less than an auto-da-fé was anticipated.

2. The execution of a sentence of the Inquisition; *esp.* the public burning of a heretic. Also *transf.*

1727–41 CHAMBERS *Cycl.*, *Act of Faith*, *Auto da fe*..a solemn day held by the inquisition, for the punishment of heretics, and the absolution of the innocent accused. **1771** FLETCHER *Checks* Wks. 1795 II. 278 Papists call their burning of those whom they call heretics an *auto de fe*. **1839** KEIGHTLEY *Hist. Eng.* I. 333 The Inquisition, with its horrible autos-da-fé. **1876** BANCROFT *Hist. U.S.* II. xliii. 575 Busy in celebrating auto-da-fés and burning heretics. **1917** KIPLING *Diversity of Creatures* 148 Evidently this was their established *auto-da-fé*. *a* **1930** D. H. LAWRENCE *Last Poems* (1932) 175 Help! Help! they want to burn my pictures, They want to make an *auto da fe*!

autodidact ('ɔːtəʊdɪˌdækt) [ad. Gr. αὐτοδίδακτος self-taught.] One who is self-taught.

[**1534** MORE *On Passion* Wks. 1388/1 Saynte Hierome tearmeth theym Autodidactons..of themselues learned.] **1748** *Europ. Mag.* V. 270 This gentleman..is supposed to be an autodidact. **1883** *Blackw. Mag.* Mar. 393 As a painter, Rossetti was essentially an autodidact.

autodidactic (ˌɔːtəʊdɪ'dæktɪk), *a.* [f. AUTODIDACT + -IC.] Self-taught; acquired by teaching oneself; pertaining to self-teaching.

1847 S. AUSTIN tr. *Ranke's Hist. Ref.* III. 586 Autodidactic artisans. **1878** *Tinsley's Mag.* XXIII. 293 Autodidactic studies. **1886** *Contemp. Rev.* Feb. 293 He [*sc.* Menzel] was from the beginning an auto-didactic realist; he drew and painted as he saw. **1966** *English Studies* XLVII. 201 Whitman was largely a self-educated journalist whose Self, at the top of its autodidactic voice, brought into poetry many of the ideas of the time.

autodrome ('ɔːtəʊdrəʊm). [f. AUTO-² + Gr. δρόμος race-course.] A motor-racing track or circuit.

1935 EYSTON & LYNDON *Motor Racing* i. 7 An autodrome was opened at Linas-Montlhèry, near Paris. **1957** S. MOSS *In Track of Speed* xi. 139 The Argentine autodrome was a short twisty one of just under 2¼ miles. **1963** *Times* 25 Apr. 3/7 The new Ferrari formula one car amazed experts by its speed at the Monza autodrome today.

autodynamic (ˌɔːtəʊdɪ'næmɪk), *a. Physics.* [mod. f. Gr. αὐτο-δύναμ-ος powerful in itself + -IC; cf. F. *autodynamique.*] Operating by its own power; *esp.* in ***autodynamic elevator***: a machine for raising weights, worked by a falling column of water.

autodyne ('ɔːtəʊdaɪn). *Radio.* [f. AUTO-¹ + -DYNE.] An electric oscillating circuit in which the same valve is used for rectification and generation of oscillations. Also *attrib.*

1918 W. H. ECCLES *Wireless Telegr.* (ed. 2) 497 Autodyne Reception, Self-Heterodyne Reception, are names given to those modes of beat reception in which the auxiliary oscillations are generated within windings and condensers that are essential parts of ordinary receiving circuits. **1943** *Gloss. Terms Telecommunic.* (*B.S.I.*) 72 *Autodyne oscillator*, a receiving device which generates the local oscillations required for beat reception in addition to performing its other functions, such as amplification or detection. **1961** *Times Rev. Industry* Apr. 18/2 The autodyne is a kind of rotary converter where 'feed back' is used to control the operation of the device.

autœcious (ɔː'tiːʃ(ɪ)əs), *a. Bot.* Also **autecious**, **autoicous**. [f. Gr. αὐτός same + οἰκία house: see -IOUS.] **a.** Of parasitic fungi: inhabiting the same host throughout their life. **b.** Having both sexual organs on the same plant; monœcious.

1882 VINES *Sachs's Bot.* 332 Such forms [of parasitic fungi] as these are said to be heterœcious (metœcious), to distinguish them from those..which inhabit the same host throughout their whole life (autœcious). **1900** B. D. JACKSON *Gloss. Bot. Terms*, *Autoicous*, in Bryophytes, the male and female inflorescences on the same plant.

auto-erotic (ˌɔːtəʊɛ'rɒtɪk), *a.* [f. AUTO-¹ + EROTIC *a.*] Pertaining to auto-erotism. Hence **auto-e'rotically** *adv.*

1898 HAVELOCK ELLIS in *Alienist & Neurol.* Apr. 260 Among auto-erotic phenomena..we must further include those religious sexual manifestations for an ideal object, of which we may find evidence in the lives of saints. **1914** *Lancet* 9 May 1303/2 When the auto-erotic impulse of the child first turns to an external object that impulse is bisexual. **1927** HENDERSON & GILLESPIE *Text-bk. Psychiatry* VI. 115 But in some individuals the development of the libido's object-direction may be arrested at an intermediate stage (the autoerotic or the homosexual). **1933** J. C. FLUGEL *Hundred Yrs. Psychol.* IV. viii. 284 A certain amount of libido always finds its satisfaction auto-erotically. **1954** KOESTLER *Invisible Writing* 362 Auto-erotic indulgences may quickly become an addiction.

auto-erotism (ˌɔːtəʊ'ɛrətɪz(ə)m). *Psychol.* Also **-e'roticism.** [f. AUTO-¹ + EROTISM, EROTICISM; cf. G. *autoerotismus* (Freud 1899, *Let.* to W. Fliess 9 Dec. in *Aus d. Anfängen d. Psychoanalyse* (1950) 324).] Spontaneous erotism, self-erotism; sexual gratification aroused or obtained by oneself, i.e. not with another person; masturbation. (Cf. ALLO-EROTISM.)

1898 HAVELOCK ELLIS in *Alienist & Neurol.* Apr. 260 (title of paper), Auto-Erotism, a Psychological Study. *Ibid.*, By 'auto-erotism' I mean the phenomena of spontaneous sexual emotion generated in the absence of an external stimulus proceeding, directly or indirectly, from another person. **1900** —— *Studies Psychol. Sex* II. 125 In a wide sense.. auto-erotism may be said to include those transformations of repressed sexual activity which are a factor of some morbid conditions as well as of the normal manifestations of art and poetry. **1916** Auto-eroticism [see AUTISM]. **1952** V. GOLLANCZ *My Dear Timothy* 198 A common or garden tendency to masochistic autoerotism. **1954** [see ALLO-EROTISM]. **1955** C. S. LEWIS *Surprised by Joy* xi. 160 The first and deadly error..turning religion into a self-caressing luxury and love into auto-eroticism. **1963** in A. Heron *Towards Quaker View of Sex* ii. 16 It can firmly be said that autoeroticism (the name given by psychologists to masturbation) is a normal phase of human development.

autofacture. [See AUTO-¹.] Self-making.

1868 *Daily Tel.* 29 May, A self-made man—so far as humanity is capable of autofacture.

autogamous (ɔː'tɒgəməs), *a. Bot.* [f. Gr. αὐτο- (see AUTO-¹) + γάμος marriage: see -OUS.] Characterized by self-fertilization.

1889 in *Cent. Dict.* **1925** *Glasgow Herald* 20 June 4 Distomum hepaticum is an autogamous hermaphrodite.

autogamy (ɔː'tɒgəmɪ). *Bot.* [f. Gr. αὐτο- self + -γαμία marriage; cf. Gr. αὐτόγαμος willingly married. First formed in G. (A. Kerner 1876, *Die Schutzmittel der Blüthen*).] **1.** Self-fertilization. **autogamic** (ɔːtəʊ'gæmɪk) *a.*, characterized by, or fit for, autogamy.

1877 DARWIN *More Letters* (1903) II. 413, I wish that I had used some such terms as autogamy, xenogamy, etc. **1878** OGLE tr. *Kerner's Flowers* 9, I understand by autogamy the fecundation of a flower by the pollen from the andrœcium of the same flower. **1880** GRAY *Bot. Text-bk.* vi. §4. 216 Autogamy, the application and action of a flower's pollen upon its own pistil. **1881** MOORE in *Jrnl. Bot.* X. 85 Small open [flowers] with a modification of the stigmas rendering them autogamic.

2. *Biol.* Fusion of sister-cells or of pairs of nuclei within a cell. Hence **auto'gamic** *a.*

1900 K. PEARSON *Gram. Sci.* (ed. 2) 437 Is there any form of sexual selection such as autogamy, endogamy, apolegamy, or homogamy, using these terms in their broadest senses? *Ibid.* 501 Variations do not occur accidentally or in isolated instances; autogamic and assortative mating are realities. **1940** *Chambers's Techn. Dict.* 61/1 *Autogamy*, the fusion of sister-cells, or of two sister-nuclei.

autogeneal (ɔːtəʊ'dʒiːnɪəl), *a.* Erron. **-ial.** [f. Gr. αὐτο-γενής, -ές self-produced (see -GEN¹) + -AL¹.] **a.** Self-begotten, self-produced. **b.** Produced by oneself.

1656 BLOUNT *Glossogr.*, *Autogeneal*, self-begotten. **1864** W. HARDY *Waurin's Chron.* I. 63 Our author has not here constructed..an autogenial version of the Brut d'Engleterre.

autogenesis (ɔːtəʊ'dʒɛnɪsɪs). [f. AUTO-¹ + -GENESIS.] Origination within the organism.

1890 BILLINGS *Med. Dict.*, *Autogenesis*.., spontaneous generation.

ˌautoge'netic, *a.* [f. prec.; see -GENETIC.]

1. *Med.* Developed by or due to autogenesis; produced within the organism. Hence **ˌautoge'netically** *adv.*

1886 *Brit. Med. Jrnl.* 10 Apr. 694/1 Autogenetic puerperal fevers. Mental worry from illicit pregnancies and clandestine marriages was a common source of autogenetic empoisonment. *Ibid.*, Some septic poison, either from without or autogenetically, might cause the same series of symptoms.

2. *Physical Geogr.* (See quot.)

1902 WEBSTER Suppl., *Autogenetic* (*Phys. Geol.*), pertaining to, controlled by, or designating, a system of self-determined drainage. *Autogenetic drainage*, a system of natural drainage developed by the constituent streams through headwater erosion. *Autogenetic topography*, a system of land forms produced by the free action of rain and streams on rocks of uniform texture.

autogenic (ɔːtəʊ'dʒɛnɪk), *a.* [f. as AUTOGENEAL *a.* + -IC.] = AUTOGENOUS *a.* in various senses (in quot. 1890 = self-induced). Also *spec.* in *Ecology* (see quot. 1931).

1875 URE *Dict. Arts* I. 274 In Devonport dockyard, the autogenic process has been largely used. **1890** MERCIER *Sanity & Insanity* xiii. 343 The melancholy..is a spontaneous and autogenic melancholy. **1931** [see ALLOGENIC *a.* 2]. **1946** A. G. TANSLEY *Introd. Plant Ecology* iv. 46 The first species to occupy the area will..in most cases give way to others..until a relatively stable equilibrium is reached between the vegetation and its habitat. This kind of succession is called the development of vegetation (autogenic succession). *Ibid.* xiii. 157 The accumulation of humus..is a direct reaction of the plant community itself upon its habitat (autogenic factor).

autogenous (ɔː'tɒdʒɪnəs), *a.* [f. Gr. αὐτογενής (see prec.) + -OUS.] Self-produced, independent. Applied *spec.* **a.** in *Phys.* to parts of the skeleton developed from independent centres of ossification; **b.** in *Path.* to the essential elements of morbid tissues; **c.** to a process of soldering in which the ends of metal are themselves melted, and so joined. Also applied to a process of welding in which metals are united by melting their edges together, any added welding-metal being of the same composition. Hence **autogenously** *adv.*

1846 OWEN in *Brit. Assoc. Rep.*, Those parts..usually developed from distinct and independent centres, I have termed 'autogenous.' **1860** F. GALTON *Vac. Tour* 426 Let us hope that a united Italy may develop..an autogenous form of social life. **1878** T. BRYANT *Pract. Surg.* I. 102 Capable of secreting their own contents..autogenous cysts, as Sir J. Paget calls them. **1879** SPON *Workshop Rec.*, Autogenous Soldering, or burning together. **1883** *J. W. Queen's Electr. Catal.* 16 A case of insulite, having a lid of the same material autogenously soldered in. **1930** *Engineering* 7 Feb. 163/2 The oxygen is chiefly required..for autogenous welding. **1961** J. N. ANDERSON *Appl. Dental Mat.* (ed. 2) xiii. 116 Sweating..is sometimes referred to as autogenous welding.

autogeny, autogony (ɔː'tɒdʒɪnɪ, -'ɒgənɪ). [f. Gr. αὐτογενής, -γόνος, self-produced: see prec.] A mode of spontaneous generation; (see quot.).

1875 SCHMIDT *Desc. & Darw.* 320 Haeckel's hypothesis of Autogony. **1876** tr. *Haeckel's Hist. Creat.* I. 339 In spontaneous generation..we must first distinguish two essentially different kinds, viz. *autogeny* and *plasmogeny*. By autogeny we understand the origin of a most simple organic individual in an inorganic formative fluid.

autogiro (ˌɔːtəʊ'dʒaɪərəʊ). Also **autogyro.** [f. AUTO-¹ + It., Sp. *giro* GYRE *sb.*] The proprietary name (in spelling *-giro*) of a type of aircraft, deriving its lift mainly from a system of freely rotating horizontal vanes, and capable of landing in a very small space.

1923 *Flight* 24 May 275 Some tests have recently been carried out at Getafe, near Madrid, with an extremely interesting and original type of machine, the invention of a young Spanish engineer, Don Juan de la Cierva. This machine is known as the 'Autogiro', and is what might be described as being midway between the aeroplane and the helicopter. **1927** *Observer* 17 Apr. 10/2 The wider range of control promised by such types as the 'autogyro'. **1930** *Flight* 4 Apr. 391/1 The Autogiro stands quite alone in the aircraft market, as it is the most unorthodox. **1960** STUBELIUS *Balloon* 277 Autogiros were in use up to about 1943. Today, when the design is obsolete, the word *autogiro* occurs only in historical contexts. **1962** *Listener* 21 June 1075/2 A single-seater autogyro.

'autogram. [Cf. *telegram*: after the introduction of this there was a rage for saying *autogram, paragram*, etc.] = AUTOGRAPH.

1881 C. LOWE *Bookseller's Catal.* No. 60. 3 An Autogram of the Ayrshire Poet.

autograph ('ɔːtəgrɑːf), *sb.* (and *a.*). [ad. L. *autographum*, Gr. αὐτόγραφον, neut. (used subst.) of adj. αὐτόγραφος written with one's own hand, f. αὐτο- by oneself + -γραφος writing, written. In 17–18th c. often in L. or Gr. form. Cf. F. *autographe* adj. in Cotgr.]

A. *sb.* **1. a.** That which is written in a person's own handwriting; the author's own manuscript.

1640–4 SIR S. D'EWES in Rushw. *Hist. Coll.* III. (1692) I. 311 Particulars..drawn out of the Autographs themselves. **1659** BP. WALTON *Consid. Considered* 61 The autographa of the sacred Penmen. *a* **1733** NORTH *Exam.* Pref. 14 Memoirs ..of which he hath the Autographon. **1794** SULLIVAN *View Nat.* II. 238 The Autograph, or original manuscript of the law. **1839** HALLAM *Hist. Lit.* III. iii. §27 The letter is imperfect, some sheets of the autograph having been lost. **1892** W. W. SKEAT *12 Facs. O.E. MSS.* 10 The MS. of Piers Plowman is corrected with minute care, and seems to be an autograph of the author.

b. *abstr.* A person's own handwriting.

1858 HAWTHORNE *Fr. & It. Jrnls.* I. 139 Poems of Tasso in his own autograph. **1868** *Digby's Voy. Medit.* Pref. 37 Entirely in the autograph of Sir Kenelm.

2. A person's own signature. Hence *attrib.* An ***autograph-book*** (or ***-album***) freq. contains occasional verses, etc., as well as a person's signature.

1791–1817 D'ISRAELI *Cur. Lit.* (Rtlg.) 439 The French editor..has given the autograph of her name. **1808** *Monthly Pantheon* I. 665/1 Another learned collector purchases a work..because some learned man's name or *autograph*, according to the modern fashionable literary nomenclature, is written on the title page. **1838** DICKENS *Lett.* (1880) I. 13 Left our autographs and read those of other people. **1841** F. A. KEMBLE *Let.* 26 Dec. in *Records of Later Life* (1882) II. 148, I am not an autograph collector. **1858** O. W. HOLMES *Autocrat* i. 6 One of the lady-boarders..sent me her autograph-book. **1858** QUEEN VICTORIA *Let.* 15 Feb. in *Dearest Child* (1964) 45 Never mind about my sheet of the autograph album. **1861** SALA *Tw. round Clock* 117 The register becomes an autograph-book of..illustrious signatures. **1870** 'F. FERN' *Ginger-Snaps* 203 If there is an intolerable nuisance, it is your persistent autograph-hunter. **1879** B. F. TAYLOR *Summer-Savory* xxvi. 209 The writer hopes the reader's name is not found in many autograph albums. **1959** I. & P. OPIE *Lore & Lang. of Schoolchildren* vii. 117 American children's film-star rhymes..seem to be slicker, more of the autograph-album variety. **1966** *Guardian* 12 Aug. 6/6 Will it only be television that will bring the autograph-hunters to the stage door?

3. A copy produced by autography.
1868 *People's Mag.* Jan. 62 (*title*) Vegetable Autographs.

B. *adj.* Written in the author's own handwriting. Also used of a painting done by the painter himself, not by an imitator.
1832 Coleridge *Table T.* 164 Autograph copies of some of the apostles' writings. **1878** Seeley *Stein* III. 503, I must at least greet you with an autograph letter. **1958** *Times Lit. Suppl.* 5 Sept. 490/1 Some of the Madonnas..must be wholly or in large part autograph.

'autograph, *v.* [f. prec. sb.]
1. a. To write with one's own hand. **b.** To copy or reproduce by autography. Hence **'autographed** *ppl. a.*
1818 *Gentl. Mag.* LXXXVIII. I. 160/2 The sixth plate is written music, or, as the Lithographers denote it, autographed music. **1882** *Athenæum* 18 Mar. 341/2 Both [books] were autographed and intended for practical purposes only.
2. To write one's autograph on or in; to sign.
1837 *Blackw. Mag.* XLI. 281 Don Carlos might long ere now have autographed his decrees, Yo el Rey, from..the Escurial. **1883** *Graphic* 3 Nov. 452 He autographs the Admiral's book.

†**au'tographal,** *a. Obs.* [f. as prec. + -AL[1].] = AUTOGRAPH *a.* ***autographal name*** = signature.
1715 Bennet *39 Art.* 177 The autographal names of eleven bishops. **1716** M. Davies *Ath. Brit.* II. 376 Memorials Autographal..of the Stage-Poet, Christopher Marlow.

'autographed (-grɑːft, -æ-), *ppl. a.* [f. AUTOGRAPH *v.*] In senses of the verb.
1818 [see AUTOGRAPH *v.* 1]. **1901** *Daily Chron.* 10 July 3/5 Autographed photographs of celebrities. **1908** Ld. Rosebery in Begbie *Life W. Booth* (1920) II. xxviii. 398 Send me your autographed photograph.

autographic (ɔːtəʊ'græfɪk), *a.* [f. AUTOGRAPH; cf. Gr. γραφικός pertaining to writing.] **1.** Of or pertaining to autography; of the nature of an autograph: written in the author's own handwriting.
1810 *Ann. Reg. 1808* 118 The manuscript..is an autographic note, written by the late Lord Bute. **1824** *New Monthly Mag.* XI. 221 Judging from the autographic obituary before me. **1868** Sir J. Herschel in *People's Mag.* Jan. 62 Autographic representations of fungi on glass. **1875** Ure *Dict. Arts* III. 133 Autographic ink..must be fatter and softer than that applied directly to the stone. **1879** Farrar *St. Paul* II. 611 The Epistle to the Galatians [was] also autographic.
2. *Path.* (See quot.)
1894 Gould *Dict. Med., Autographic..Skin*, a condition of vaso-motor paralysis, usually in hysterical patients, in which markings made upon the skin form quite persistent and intensely red traces. *A. woman*, one with an *Autographic Skin.*

auto'graphical, *a. arch.* [f. as prec. + -ICAL.] = prec. (also used for AUTOBIOGRAPHICAL. *Obs.*).
1656 in Blount *Glossogr.* **1673** Hickeringill *Greg. Father Greyb.* 286 The autographical Copy..laid up in that famous Library. **1825** *Gentl. Mag.* XCV. I. 349 The Autographical Journal of Christopher Columbus. **1837** Whewell *Hist. Induct. Sc.* I. 370 A kind of autographical account of the way in which the author was led to his views.

auto'graphically, *adv.* [f. prec. + -LY[2].] In autograph, by means of autography.
1673 Hickeringill *Greg. Father Greyb.* 292 In what Language was the New Testament first indited? In Greek, all of them Autographically. **1841** Dickens *Lett.* (1880) I. 42, I am glad to shake you by the hand again autographically. **1880** *Times* 5 Oct. 6/6 Making the colours of nature print..autographically upon the plate.

autographism (ɔː'tɒgrəfɪz(ə)m). *Path.* [f. AUTOGRAPH *sb.* + -ISM.] A condition of the skin in which tracings leave an elevated mark. Hence **au'tographist.** Cf. AUTOGRAPHIC *a.* 2.
1890 *Globe* 13 June 6 Autographism, as this phenomenon is called, is believed to be due to a nervous susceptibility which may exist for years in a patient. **1894** Gould *Dict. Med., Autographist..*, one who has an autographic skin.

'autogra,phize, *v. colloq.* [Cf. *botanize*, etc.] To collect autographs. **'autogra,phizer**, a collector of autographs.
1824 Dibdin *Libr. Comp.* 108 More than one hungry autographiser of my acquaintance.

autography (ɔː'tɒgrəfɪ). [f. AUTOGRAPH; cf. Gr. -γραφία writing.]
1. The action of writing with one's own hand; the author's own handwriting.
1644 Bulwer *Chirol.* 82 By the old autography of the Hand. **1723** S. Mather *Vind. Bible*, The date of the autography. **1870** Spurgeon *Treas. Dav.* Ps. xlvii, Every expert would here detect the autography of the Son of Jesse.
2. Reproduction of the form or outline of anything, by an impression from the thing itself; 'nature printing'; *esp.* a process in lithography by which a writing or drawing is transferred from paper to stone.
1864 in Webster.
†**3.** = AUTOBIOGRAPHY. *Obs.*
1661 Glanvill *Van Dogm.* A viij b, Nor doth the last Scene yield us any more satisfaction in our autography, for we are as ignorant how the Soul leaves the light, as how it first came into it.
4. Autographs collectively.
1788 Thane (*title*) British Autography, a Collection of Fac-Similes of the Handwritings of..Illustrious Persons.

autogravure (,ɔːtəʊgrə'vjʊə(r)). [f. AUTO-[1] + F. *gravure*, after *photogravure*.] A photo-mechanical modification of the etching process. Used *attrib.* in ***autogravure process***. Also, a picture produced by this process.
1885 *Athenæum* 31 Jan. 156/3 Plates, produced by the autogravure process of the Autotype Company. **1888** *Chambers's Encycl.* I. 606 *Autogravure*, a peculiar process of photo-engraving patented by J. R. Sawyer, London, on November 12, 1884. **1889** *Guardian* 23 Jan. 137/1 An autogravure from Correggio.

autogyro, var. AUTOGIRO.

autoharp ('ɔːtəʊhɑːp). [f. AUTO-[1] + HARP *sb.*[1]] A musical instrument of the zither type provided with dampers to facilitate the production of arpeggio effects.
1882 C. F. Zimmermann *U.S. Pat. 257,808* 1/1 A harp so provided..I term an 'autoharp'. *Ibid.*, The autoharp..may be used for accompaniment to the voice or another musical instrument. **1893** *U.S. Pat. 490,407*, I, Christian Henry Eisenbrandt..have invented certain new and useful Improvements in Hammers for Autoharps... My invention relates to means for striking chords on such stringed instruments as the autoharp. **1894** *Work* 23 June 365/2 An autoharp can be bought from almost any dealer in musical instruments. **1897** Mary Kingsley *W. Africa* 82 Captain Heldt..produced an autoharp, an instrument upon which he was himself proficient. **1958** *Times* 13 Oct. 3/4 The autoharp, a kind of sweet-toned zither.

autoist ('ɔːtəʊɪst). *U.S.* [f. AUTO *sb.*[2] 1 + -IST.] One who uses or drives an automobile, a motorist.
1903 *Sci. Amer.* 21 Feb. 134/1 Bills giving equal rights to autoists and the drivers of horses. **1904** *N.Y. Globe* 29 Mar. 4 A protest against the young lawbreakers who stone autoists.

†**auto'kinesy.** *Obs.* Also autoch-. [ad. Gr. αὐτοκῑνησία, n. of quality f. αὐτοκίνητος: see next.] Self-movement, spontaneous motion.
1678 Cudworth *Intell. Syst.* I. iii. §33. 159 A simple internal energy or vital autokinesie, which is without.. Consense and Consciousness. *Ibid.* v. 668 Self-activity or autochinesie was in order of nature before the local motion of body which is heterochinesie.

†**,autoki'netical,** *a. Obs.* [f. Gr. αὐτο-κῑνητ-ος self-moved (f. αὐτο-κινέ-ειν to have the power of motion in oneself) + -ICAL.] Self-moving, possessed of spontaneous activity.
1642 H. More *Poems* (1647) 87 But that each soul's Autokineticall Is easily shown.

autolatry (ɔː'tɒlətrɪ). In 7 as L. **autolatria**. [f. Gr. αὐτο- self + λατρεία worship.] Self-worship.
a **1625** Boys *Wks.* (1630) 453 That insolent cariage of such spirits..is rather *autolatria*, worshipping themselves. **1866** Ld. Strangford *Select.* (1869) II. 300 His sty of epicurean autolatry. **1871** Farrar *Witn. Hist.* i. 22 *note*, The autolatry of Max Stirner, with its motto, *Quisque sibi Deus.*

autolithography (,ɔːtəʊlɪ'θɒgrəfɪ). [f. AUTO-[1] + LITHOGRAPHY.] A form of lithographic printing in which the drawing, etc., is first made on transfer paper, then put on stone for printing (see also quot. 1967). Hence **auto'lithograph** *v. trans.*, to produce or reproduce by this process; **auto'lithograph** *sb.*, a picture or print produced by autolithography; **,autolitho'graphic** *a.*, of or belonging to this process.
1874 M. A. Lenoir (*title*) The Lenoir Collection of original French portraits at Stafford House. Autolithographed by Lord Ronald Gower. *Ibid.* Pref., This collection of portraits which I have attempted to reproduce in autolithography. *Ibid.*, Autolithographic copies aiding me in the production of these Autolithographs. **1895** *Daily News* 22 Nov. 6/5 An autolithograph by Mr. Whistler. **1967** E. Chambers *Photolitho-offset* xvii. 264 Any image which is produced directly on to a stone, metal or plastic surface and uses lithographic principles to provide the printing medium, comes within the general classification of autolithography.

autological (ɔːtəʊ'lɒdʒɪkəl), *a.* [ad. G. *autologisch* (K. Grelling & L. Nelson 1907, in *Abhandl. Fries'schen* II. *Schule* 307), f. AUTO-[1] + LOGICAL *a.*] (See quots. 1926, 1947). Opp. HETEROLOGICAL *a.*
1926 F. P. Ramsey in *Proc. Lond. Math. Soc.* XXV. 358 Let us call adjectives whose meanings are predicates of them, like 'short', autological; others heterological. **1947** H. Reichenbach *Elements Symb. Logic* (1948) vi. 220 Let us comprise as autological all properties whose names have the property they denote. **1952** R. L. Wilder *Introd. Found. Math.* iii. 75 Is the adjective 'heterological' either autological or heterological?

autology (ɔː'tɒlədʒɪ). [f. AUTO-[1] + -LOGY.] Self-knowledge, scientific study of oneself.
1633 Featly in P. Fletcher *Purple Isl.* To Readers, He that would learn Theologie must first studie autologie. The way to God is by our selves. *c* **1645** Howell *Lett.* (1650) III. 16 Well vers'd in Autology, in that lesson *Nosce Teipsum*. **1873** D. Hamilton (*title*) Autology: an inductive system of mental science. *Ibid.* 3 This system..is called Autology because it is man's own knowing of himself.

autolysis (ɔː'tɒlɪsɪs). *Biol.* [ad. G. *autolyse* (M. Jacoby 1900, in *Zeitschr. physiol. Chem.* XXX. 160), f. Gr. αὐτο- (see AUTO-[1]) + λύσις a loosening.] **a.** Self-acting disintegration of tissue. **b.** The destruction of cells of the body by the action of their own enzymes. Hence **au'tolysate**, a substance produced by autolysis; **autolyse** ('ɔːtəʊlaɪz) *v. intr.* and *trans.*, to undergo or cause to undergo autolysis; **au'tolysin** [-IN[1]], a substance that produces autolysis (Webster, 1934); **autolytic** (ɔːtəʊ'lɪtɪk) *a.*, belonging to or of the nature of autolysis.
1902 *Jrnl. Chem. Soc.* LXXXII. 35 After autolysis, the same organs yield solutions which hinder blood-clotting. **1902** *Science* 28 Nov. 858 Autolytic ferments. **1903** Flexner *Ibid.* 3 July 15 An acute lobar pneumonia in which the inflammatory exudate..failing to autolyze perfectly cannot absorb, and hence undergoes organisation. **1911** *Encycl. Brit.* XX. 922/1 Autolysis is a disintegration of dead tissues brought about by the action of their own ferments, while degeneration takes place in the still living cell. The study of autolytic phenomena..has thrown much light on these degenerative processes. **1927** Zinsser & Grinnell in *Jrnl. Bacteriol.* XIV. 307 Reactions in guinea pigs to the pneumococcus autolysate are examples of true allergic sensitization. **1932** J. S. Huxley *Probl. Rel. Growth* vi. 173 The autolysing agencies which operate at metamorphosis. **1933** *Times Lit. Suppl.* 12 Oct. 695/3 Injecting into animals varying quantities of a saline extract of autolysed homologous muscle. **1949** Florey *Antibiotics* I. i. 46 Secondary lysis is very possibly associated with the release of autolytic enzymes. **1964** M. Hynes *Med. Bacteriol.* (ed. 8) xi. 166 This process destroys an autolysin which can otherwise completely lyse a saline suspension of the organisms in a few hours.

†**'automa.** *Obs.* Erroneous singular of *automata* (cf. *stoma, stomata*, etc.) for AUTOMATON; cf. AUTOMATE, AUTOME.
1625 B. Jonson *Staple of News* III. ii, It is an Automa, runnes vnder water. **1669** Flamsteed in Rigaud *Corr. Sci. Men* II. 82 That the time be measured with exact and rectified Automas.

automacy (ɔː'tɒməsɪ). [f. AUTOMATIC, prob. after mod.F. *automatie*: see -ACY. Gr. has αὐτοματία accidentality, chance.] The condition or state of being an automaton; automatic quality.
1882 Wigan in Proctor *Nat. Stud.* 131 Human minds.. performing by a sort of automacy all the ordinary functions.

automaker ('ɔːtəʊmeɪkə(r)). *N. Amer.* [f. AUTO *sb.*[2] 1 + MAKER.] A manufacturer of motor vehicles; a company that manufactures motor vehicles.
1947 *Fortune* May 204/2 It [*sc.* Ford] has found that forty-four years of faithful manufacturing has rolled up a tremendous fund of good will that few..other auto makers could match. **1959** *Time* 25 May 86/2 (*heading*) Automaker Knudsen. **1969** *Sci. Amer.* Nov. 2 We at Renault are one of the few automakers to make a car that's better than the horse. **1970** *Edmonton* (Alberta) *Jrnl.* 14 July 4/3 The automakers maintain that they have no choice but to stick with the internal combustion engine. **1976** *Washington Post* 19 Apr. A23/2 Between 1972 and 1974, the automaker British Leyland lost almost 25 per cent of its production owing to strikes. **1986** *Financial World* (U.S.) 18 Feb. 17 If you want to buy a specialty automaker with noncyclical earnings growth, you'll look at BMW or Volvo.

automat ('ɔːtəmæt). [G., f. F. *automate* AUTOMATE *sb.*] **1.** = AUTOMATON.
1671 R. Bohun *Wind* 44 Air is a body so fluid, and tractable..that if it once be set a going, it as a kind of perpetuall Automat, continues the motion. **1887** *Blackw. Mag.* Oct. 518 Such is not the action of flesh and blood..but ..of some fabulous species of automat. *a* **1930** D. H. Lawrence *Last Poems* (1932) 186 The automat has no soul to lose.
2. A cafeteria in which food is obtained from compartments by the insertion of a coin or token. *U.S.*
1903 *Sci. Amer.* 18 July 49/2 [*in photograph of restaurant*] Automat. **1909** Webster, *Automat*, a café or restaurant in which orders are automatically delivered to customers, who place coins or tokens in slots. **1919** F. Hurst *Humoresque* 48 Waldorf! You've got a fine chance. You mean the Automat, and two spoons for the ice-cream. **1921** Wodehouse *Jill the Reckless* xiv. 208 The Automat?.. The food's quite good. You go and help yourself out of slot-machines, you know. **1951** *Amer. Speech* Oct. 166 Probably the 'Automat', a self-serving institution supplying food, gave special impetus to the extension of the suffix *-mat.*
3. An automatic slot-machine.
1908 *Daily Chron.* 11 Jan. 4/6 A very commendable feature has just been introduced into several German schools. Automats were placed in the courtyards, which, for a small coin, deliver hot or cold milk. **1958** *Times* 14 July 11/5 Next month..an 'automat' at the station [*sc.* New York subway] will receive the passengers' soiled clothes and return them, spotlessly dry-cleaned, the same day.

†**au'tomatal,** *a. Obs. rare*[−1]. = AUTOMATIC.
1682 H. More *Annot. Glanvill's Lux O.* 129 The whole Universe is..the Automatal Harp of that..true Apollo.

†**au,toma'tarian,** *a. Obs.*[−0] [f. L. *automatāri-us* (f. *automat-on*: see -ARY) + -AN.] = next.
1656 Blount *Glossogr., Automatarian*, of or belonging to the art of making Clocks, or such things as seem to move of themselves.

†**au'tomatary**, *a. Obs.* [see prec.] AUTOMATIC.
1652 URQUHART *Jewel* Wks. (1834) 266, I can no better compare him then to an automatary engine. **1653** —— *Rabelais* I. xxiv, Automatarie Engines..moving of themselves.

†**'automate**, *sb.* and *a. Obs.* [a. F. *automate* (Cotgr.), ad. L. *automaton, -um.*]
A. *sb.* = AUTOMATON.
a **1649** DRUMM. OF HAWTH. *James III* Wks. 61 Taken with admiration of watches, clocks, dials, automates. *a* **1751** BOLINGBROKE *Hum. Knowl.* i. (R.) We pronounce our fellow animals to be automates, or we allow them instinct.
B. *adj.* [Cf. F. *automate*, adj.] = AUTOMATIC.
1818 SOUTHEY in *Q. Rev.* XIX. 18 His scheme of a Royal Garden comprehended..artificial echos, automate and hydraulic music.

automate ('ɔːtəmeɪt), *v.* orig. *U.S.* [Back-formation f. next or f. AUTOMATION; cf. AUTOMATE *sb.* and *a.*] **1.** *trans.* To apply automation to; to convert to largely automatic operation; to introduce automatic control to (the manufacture of a product, etc.).
1954 *N.Y. Times* 4 May (*heading*) Huge Sums to Be Spent to Automate Plants. **1959** *Listener* 5 Nov. 762/2 In theory.. management in steel has the right to automate the mills without interference. **1961** *Times* 3 Oct. (Computer Suppl.) ii/5 The first stage in 'automating' a production plant is to increase mechanization. **1962** *Listener* 17 May 855/1 It is natural that we should try to programme, or automate, part of the teacher's work [by the use of teaching machines].
2. *intr.* or *absol.*
1955 *Controller* Dec. 602/2 PanAm Automates. **1962** *Economist* 19 May 693/1 Those days saw the country 'automating' considerably faster than it is doing now. **1967** *Listener* 23 Feb. 248/1 The more we automate, the greater the resources needed.

'automated, *ppl. a.* orig. *U.S.* [Back-formation f. AUTOMATION.] **1.** In senses of the verb (see prec.).
1952 *Cleveland* (Ohio) *Plain Dealer* 13 Apr. 12 Another 'automated' line, less spectacular than the block line, machines the cylinder head. **1954** *Economist* 6 Nov. 466 (*heading*) Automated Giants. **1962** *Observer* 15 July 3/5 An automated laundry which washes, rinses and irons in a continuous process. **1962** *Cath. Gaz.* Nov. 320/1 A society is automated when its production is dominated by machines to the extent that machines are given a priority over men in the performance of human tasks. **1967** KARCH & BUBER *Offset Processes* xii. 506 A Lawson automated-spacing power paper cutter.
2. Special collocation: ***automated teller machine*** (orig. *U.S.*) = *automatic teller machine* s.v. AUTOMATIC *a.* 2; abbrev. *A.T.M.* s.v. A III. 1.
1974 *Computers & People* Aug. 35/1 Installations of cash-dispensing and *automated teller machines in proliferation by both thrifts and commercial banks. **1986** *Amer. Banker* 13 Aug. 4/2 He's been actively shopping bank certificate of deposit rates, and uses your automated teller machines often.

automath ('ɔːtəʊmæθ). *rare.* [ad. Gr. αὐτομαθής, f. αὐτο- self + -μαθής learned, f. μανθ-άν-ειν, μαθ- to learn.] A self-taught person, an autodidact.
1759 YOUNG *Conject. Orig. Comp.* 292 Those Automaths, those self taught Philosophers.

automatic (ɔːtə'mætɪk), *a.* [f. Gr. αὐτόματ-ος (see AUTOMATON) + -IC.] Of the nature of, or pertaining to, an automaton.
1. *lit.* Self-acting, having the power of motion or action within itself.
1812 SIR H. DAVY *Chem. Philos.* 180 In the universe, nothing can be said to be automatic. **1876** FOSTER *Phys.* (1879) Introd. 2 We may therefore speak of the amœba as being irritable and automatic. (*Note.* Automatic..has recently acquired a meaning almost exactly opposite to that which it originally bore, and an automatic action is now by many understood to mean nothing more than an action produced by some machinery or other. In this work I use it in the older sense, as denoting an action of a body, the causes of which appear to lie in the body itself.)
2. a. Self-acting under conditions fixed for it, going of itself. Applied *esp.* to machinery and its movements, which produce results otherwise done by hand, or which simulate human or animal action, as an 'automatic mouse.' ***automatic direction finder***, one in which the bearing is determined automatically; ***automatic following*** (see AUTO-*following*); ***automatic landing*** (*Aeronaut.*), a landing in which the pilot is guided by instruments and not by visual observation; ***automatic machine***, spec. a slot machine; ***automatic observer*** (*Aeronaut.*) (see quot. 1950); ***automatic parachute*** (see quot. 1951); ***automatic pilot***, a device in an aircraft for maintaining a set course and height (cf. AUTOPILOT); ***automatic stabilizer***, a device in an aircraft for maintaining a set attitude; cf. *auto-stabilizer* (AUTO-[1] b); ***automatic teller (machine)*** (orig. *U.S.*), a machine (usu. linked to a computer) that automatically provides cash or performs other functions of a bank cashier when a special card is inserted; cf. *A.T.M.* s.v. A III. 1; ***automatic train control***, a system which in appropriate circumstances provides an audible warning in the driver's cab of a locomotive; ***automatic transmission*** (cf. TRANSMISSION d), an automatic gear-changing system in a motor vehicle; ***automatic volume control*** (abbrev. *A.V.C.*), also ***automatic frequency control*** (abbrev. *A.F.C.*), ***gain control*** (*A.G.C.*): devices used in radio for regulating a frequency or signal; ***automatic writing*** (see 6).
1940 *Chambers's Techn. Dict.* 61/2 Automatic direction-finder. **1951** *Gloss. Aeronaut. Terms* (*B.S.I.*) III. 27 *Automatic direction finder*, an airborne equipment designed to indicate automatically the bearing of a continuous-wave ground beacon relative to the bearing of the aircraft. **1946** *Jrnl. Inst. Electr. Engin.* XCIII. III. 17/1 Automatic-following radar..was of the essence of the A.A. gunnery successes against flying bombs. **1950** *Gloss. Terms Radar* (*B.S.I.*) 7 *Automatic following*, automatic aiming with the addition of automatic range measurement. **1935** *Proc. Inst. Radio Engineers* XXIII. 1125 (*title*) Automatic Frequency Control. *Ibid.* 1133 (*diagram*) From AFC bias. **1930** *Proc. Inst. Radio Engineers* XVIII. 633 Those components.. which fade in and out..can be maintained at what approaches a constant level by means of the automatic gain control. **1942** *Electronic Engin.* XV. 216 A fault of most communications receivers is the inability to use A.G.C. when the B.F.O. is switched on. **1938** *Jrnl. R. Aeronaut. Soc.* XLII. 505 No mention had been made of the automatic landing, which seemed to represent the development of this science which was now engaging the attention of American experts. **1958** *Times* 17 Oct. 3/4 More than 2,000 completely automatic landings, some in thick fog and others in strong cross-winds, have been made. **1903** SHAW *Man & Superman* I. 14 A box of matches will come out of an automatic machine when I put a penny in the slot. **1872** YEATS *Techn. Hist. Comm.* 370 Automatic machinery [for].. the drilling and boring of metal. **1936** *Aircraft Engin.* Dec. 330/2 An 'automatic observer' was not employed from considerations of weight. **1950** *Gloss. Aeronaut. Terms* (*B.S.I.*) I. 41 *Automatic observer*, an apparatus for recording automatically the readings of a specified set of instruments in flight. [**1919** *E. R. Calthrop's Aerial Patents Book* 24 The 'Guardian Angel' Parachute, in all its different types, is instantly automatic.] **1951** *Gloss. Aeronaut. Terms* (*B.S.I.*) III. 13 *Automatic parachute*, a parachute which is withdrawn from its pack by a static line. **1916** *Aeronautics* 13 Sept. 175 The Sperry automatic pilot. **1921** *Ibid.* 3 Feb. 76/2 The automatic pilot..enables the pilot of an aeroplane to leave the machine entirely to its own devices. **1944** 'N. SHUTE' *Pastoral* iv. 91 Marshall sat motionless at the controls, flying upon the automatic pilot. **1842** W. GROVE *Corr. Phys. Forces* 57 Automatic or self-registration of periodical phenomena. **1909** *Flight* 17 July 434/2 The automatic stabiliser must.. show a strong and immediate tendency to return to its proper normal working position under all conditions. **1950** *Gloss. Aeronaut. Terms* (*B.S.I.*) I. 41 *Automatic stabilizer*, an automatic pilot adjusted to provide increased aerodynamic stability to the aircraft. **1802** PALEY *Nat. Theol.* iii, The difference between an animal and an automatic statue. **1971** *Amer. Banker* 31 Aug. 8/3 Depositors seal their deposits in envelopes which are provided and insert them in the 'automatic teller', which flashes a Thank You sign and issues a receipt. **1977** *Science* 18 Mar. 1116/1 Automatic teller machines (ATM's) for commercial banking being developed are in various stages of pilot testing. **1983** *N.Y. Times* 15 May 15 About 1,300 automatic teller machines are now in use at American supermarkets. *a* **1885** *Mod.* A Sewing Machine with automatic tension. **1912** *Railway Gaz.* 12 July 40/2 Automatic Train Control Demonstration. .. The ramps are so electrically connected that either of two signals are given on the engine—a clear signal or a danger —..as the train proceeds. **1936** *Economist* 25 Jan. 178/2 Security against collisions of this kind can only be provided by a combination of track-circuiting..and automatic train control. **1946** W. H. CROUSE *Automotive Mechanics* xvii. 403 The Hydra-Matic drive, supplied on Cadillac and Oldsmobile cars as special equipment, combines the fluid drive with an automatic transmission that has four forward and one reverse speed. **1961** *Autocar* 29 Sept. 471/1 A conventional clutch and three-speed gearbox costs..less than an automatic transmission. **1930** *Proc. Inst. Radio Engineers* XVIII. 321 The severe fluctuation of the signal.. indicates the desirability of some form of automatic volume control. **1933** *Pract. Wireless* 25 Nov. 545 The way in which A.V.C. operates does not seem to be widely understood.
b. Of a firearm: furnished with mechanism for successively and continuously loading, firing, and ejecting a cartridge as long as ammunition is supplied.
1877 *Independent* (U.S.) 5 July 20/2 Smith & Wesson's automatic revolvers. **1902** *Encycl. Brit.* XXX. 401/2 In the modern 'automatic' machine gun the loading, firing, extracting, and ejecting are all performed automatically by the gun itself. *Ibid.* XXXII. 649/2 No nation has yet armed her forces with an automatic rifle. *Ibid.* 658/2 The Colt Automatic Pistol, calibre ·38.
c. Of a telephone exchange or system: operated by automatic switches (opp. *manual*). Also, designating a telephone instrument fitted with a dial.
1879 M. D. CONNOLLY et al. *U.S. Pat. 222,458*, We.. have jointly invented a certain new and useful Automatic Telephone-Exchange..so constructed and arranged that any member of the exchange may..place himself in direct communication with any disengaged member of the exchange. **1914** W. ATKINS *Princ. Automatic Telephony* 1 In an automatic system of telephony it is required that the subscriber shall be able to obtain connection with any other subscriber without the intervention of an operator at the exchange. **1934** *Discovery* Mar. 58/2 The automatic telephone..has not been an unqualified blessing. **1955** *Oxf. Jun. Encycl.* VIII. 433/2 In an automatic exchange, the connexion to the required line is made by mechanical selectors.
3. Of animal actions: Like those of mechanical automatons; not accompanied by volition or consciousness, 'mechanical.'
1748 HARTLEY *Observ. Man* I. Introd., The Motions are called automatic from their Resemblance to the Motions of Automata, or Machines, whose Principle of Motion is within themselves. **1855** BAIN *Senses & Int.* I. ii. §18 The winking of the eyes is essentially automatic. **1871** tr. *Pouchet's Universe* 106 The automatic nature of insects has only been maintained by those who have never observed them.
4. Not characterized by active intelligence; merely mechanical.
1843 J. MARTINEAU *Chr. Life* (1876) 60 To rest in mere automatic regularities. **1855** MILMAN *Lat. Chr.* II. III. vi. 95 Mechanical and automatic acts of devotion.
5. Relating to automatons; AUTOMATICAL.
c **1860** WRAXALL tr. *R. Houdin* v. 50 He gave me the automaton I was to repair..I began my first automatic labours.
6. *Spiritualism.* Of or pertaining to automatism (sense 4); performed by unconscious, subconscious, or occult action.
1883 W. S. MOSES *Spirit-Teachings* Introd. 1 Automatic Writing is a well-known method of communication with the invisible world of what we loosely call Spirit. **1884** *Proc. Soc. Psychical Research* II. 226, I wished to know if I were myself an automatic writer, or so-called writing medium. **1889** BARKWORTH in *Proc. Soc. Psychical Research* Dec. 85 It is only the execution and not the initiation of the movements which is automatic, the suggestion for them being external to the subject's own personality. **1890** W. JAMES *Princ. Psychol.* I. viii. 209 Certain trance-subjects who were also automatic writers. **1934** *Archit. Rev.* LXXV. 215/1 Mr. Cooper's picture, on the other hand, might almost be a piece of automatic writing.
7. *Art.* Applied to a form of painting performed by the technique of 'automatism' (see AUTOMATISM 5).
1951 A. HILL *Painting out Illness* xi. 74, I deny that true automatic pictures can be produced while both the eye and hand in subconscious conjunction are said to be 'employed'. **1960** E. H. GOMBRICH *Art & Illusion* x. 358 The modern painter may use what he calls 'automatic painting', the creation of Rorschach blots, in order to stimulate the mind ..towards fresh inventions.

automatic (ɔːtə'mætɪk), *sb.* [f. prec.]
1. Abbreviation of *automatic pistol, gun*, etc.: see AUTOMATIC *a.* 2b.
1902 *Sears Catal.* (ed. 112) 305/2 Forehand Perfection Automatic, small frame, rebounding lock. **1914** G. ATHERTON *Perch of Devil* II. vii. 269 I've even bought an automatic. I suppose..I should call it a gun. **1920** *Blackw. Mag.* Aug. 154/1 A German automatic hung at his side. **1945** *Diamond Track* (*Army Board, N.Z.*) 35/1 Everything was thrown into it—grenades, automatics, bayonets, and rifle butts.
2. A machine, tool, etc., that is operated automatically.
1909 in WEBSTER. **1914** *Machinery* (Engin. Ed.) XX. 468 (*title*) Making shrapnel cases on the Cleveland automatic. **1917** *Amer. Machinist* XLVII. 17 Automatics used advantageously in the making of starter parts. **1921** *Conquest* II. 125 The full advantage of automatics will only be appreciated when a large number of automatic exchanges have been erected. **1930** *Engineering* 7 Mar. 309/2 The machine tool display..covers automatics of various types, bending machines, sheet-metal working machines, drills [etc.]. **1949** *Jrnl. R. Aeronaut. Soc.* LIII. 428/2 Failures of the automatics may be more dangerous than the human failures they are designed to prevent.
3. A motor vehicle, esp. a car, which has automatic transmission. orig. *U.S.*
1949 *Newsweek* (U.S.) 24 Oct. 65/1 (*heading*) Ford's automatic. **1966** *Motoring Which?* Oct. 124 The only automatic we have tested is the little Dutch-built Daf. **1984** *Which? Car Suppl.* Oct. 17/2 The BX range has recently been expanded with the inclusion of a diesel version, and there will be estates and automatics soon.

auto'matical, *a.* [f. as AUTOMATIC *a.* + -ICAL.]
1. *prop.* Having reference to or connected with things automatic.
1665 *Surv. Aff. Netherl.* 178 Ships that (according to the Automatical proposal) could manage themselves.
2. = AUTOMATIC.
1586 BRIGHT *Melanch.* xiii. 66 Automaticall instruments. **1788** PASQUIN *Childr. Thespis* (1792) 159 Automatical, heavy, dull, sombrous, half crazy. **1830** *Edin. Encycl.* II. 66/2 Automatical rope-dancers or tumblers.

auto'matically, *adv.* [f. prec. + -LY[2].]
1. In automatic manner; like an automaton; by spontaneous, or apparently spontaneous, action.
1858 GLADSTONE *Homer* II. 276 Which [three-legged stands] he is carefully fitting with wheels, in order that they may automatically take their places. **1874** tr. *Lommel's Light* 10 Apparatuses have been invented which automatically approximate the points..as they are burnt away.
2. Without active thought or volition; unconsciously, involuntarily, mechanically.
1853 *Scot. Rev.* I. 123 Actions..at first voluntary may come by habit to be automatically performed. **1859** GEO. ELIOT *A. Bede* 104 Lisbeth automatically obeying her old habits, began to put away the breakfast things.

automaticity (ɔːˌtɒmə'tɪsɪtɪ). [f. AUTOMATIC + -ITY.] Automatic condition or nature.
187. D. FERRIER *Funct. Brain* 213 Man..in whom volition is predominant and automaticity plays only a subordinate part in the motor activities.

automation (ɔːtə'meɪʃən). [irreg. f. AUTOMATIC *a.* + -ATION.] Automatic control of the manufacture of a product through a number of successive stages; the application of automatic control to any branch of industry or science; by extension, the use of electronic or mechanical devices to replace human labour.

The example of *automation* found in some copies of the 1669 edition of S. Patrick's *Brief Account of the New Sect of Latitude-Men* is a misprint for *automaton* (see *Amer. Speech* (1959) XXXIV. 236). The coinage of the modern word is usually attributed to Delmar S. Harder (U.S.).

1948 *Amer. Machinist* 21 Oct. in *McGraw-Hill Encycl. Sci. & Technol.* I. 676/2 *Automation*, the art of applying mechanical devices to manipulate work pieces into and out of equipment, turn parts between operations, remove scrap, and to perform these tasks in timed sequence with the production equipment so that the line can be put wholly or partially under pushbutton control at strategic stations. **1953** *Manch. Guardian Weekly* 3 Dec. 15/2 Many factories are spending large sums on 'automation', that is, the adoption of automatic machines working together with little labour. **1954** *Economist* 29 May 712 Mechanisation—promoted to the exalted station of 'automation'—now consists essentially in the use of bigger and faster machine tools. **1955** *Times* 3 Aug. 8/7 The group of resolutions on automation..says the technological advances will present the trade union movement with new opportunities, but these opportunities will be attended by new and complex human, social and economic problems. **1957** *Technology* July 182/1 Automation is now well known to be the automatic control of mechanized systems, although the term is used somewhat vaguely to cover many different aspects of control and communication, especially in the industrial situation. **1964** *Ann. Reg. 1963* 181 The demand for skilled labour and the substitution of unskilled labour by automation was increasing faster than the training and education of the Negro.

automatism (ɔː'tɒmətɪz(ə)m). [f. AUTOMAT-ON + -ISM; cf. Gr. αὐτοματισμός that which happens of itself, and F. *automatisme*.]

1. The quality of being automatic, or of acting mechanically only; involuntary action. *Hence*, the doctrine attributing this quality to animals.

1838 *Blackw. Mag.* XLIII. 605 The Cartesian doctrine of the automatism of the whole animal kingdom. **1857** T. Webb *Intell. Locke* viii. 154 Whatever is done from blind Impulse is Automatism rather than Action. **1879** Mallock *Life worth Living* 171 The unity or dualism of existence, the independence or automatism of the life and will of man.

2. Mechanical, unthinking routine.

1882 in *Med. Temp. Jrnl.* No. 52. 154 Nowhere, perhaps, is medical automatism seen..more commonly than in our Lunatic Asylums.

3. The faculty of independently originating action or motion. (From the original sense of *automaton*.)

1876 Foster *Phys.* I. iii. (1879) 111 Automatism, *i.e.* the power of initiating disturbances or vital impulses, independent of any immediate disturbing event or stimulus from without, is one of the fundamental properties of protoplasm. **1882** Romanes in *Nature* XXV. 335 The hypothesis of conscious automatism is nothing more than an emphatic restatement of the truth, that the relation between body and mind is a relation which has so far proved inconceivable.

4. Any psychic phenomenon that appears spontaneously in consciousness; any action performed subconsciously or unconsciously, undirected by the mind or will of the normal personality; also, the mental state in which these phenomena occur.

1884 Myers in *Proc. Soc. Psychical Research* II. 223 In the graphic automatism of mental abstraction and the graphic automatism of cerebral disease, the passages written are usually very *short*. **1886** E. Gurney et al. *Phantasms of Living* I. ii. 76 The planchette-writing obtained through the automatism of a young child. **1889** Barkworth in *Proc. Soc. Psychical Research* Dec. 85 We have..instances of complete automatism in the case of the sleep-walker who goes through a variety of complicated actions entirely self-suggested. *a* **1901** Myers *Human Personality* (1903) I. Gloss. s.v., Sensory automatism will thus include visual and auditory hallucinations; motor automatism will include messages written without intention.

5. *spec.* A technique in surrealist painting (see quot. 1958).

[**1935** D. Gascoyne tr. A. Breton in *Short Survey Surrealism* iv. 61 *Surrealism*, pure psychic automatism, by which it is intended to express, verbally, in writing, or by other means, the real process of thought.] **1948** H. Read in *Philos. Mod. Art* (1952) I. ii. 53 Applying Freudian methods to the problems of artistic creation, Breton evolved a theory and..practice of aesthetic automatism which is the essential feature of surréalisme. **1958** M. L. Wolf *Dict. Painting* 25 *Automatism*, in *art*, the principle of creation without the interference of thought... Practically, it is the unfettered stroke of *brush* or *pencil*, with no direction, will, or control exercised by the conscious mind.

automatist (ɔː'tɒmətɪst). [f. prec.: see -IST.]

1. One who holds the doctrine of automatism (1).

1882 Goldw. Smith in *Pop. Sci. Monthly* XX. 768 Though not a declared automatist, Mr. Spencer is a necessarian.

2. One who is subject to automatism; a medium; in *Art*, one whose technique is based upon automatism (sense 5). Also *attrib.*

1885 Myers in *Proc. Soc. Psychical Research* III. 41, I have seen an automatist writing page after page in ordinary handwriting, and then a page in mirror-writing. *a* **1901** —— *Human Personality* (1903) I. 28 The ordinary consciousness of the automatist appears to be suspended; he passes into a state of trance. **1920** W. B. Yeats in *If I were Four & Twenty* (1940) 43 He gathered the opinions, as he believed, of spirits speaking through a great number of automatist and trance speakers. **1959** *Listener* 2 July 26/2 Exhibitions by their own artists, in the international idioms of pure Abstract, Abstract-Concrete, Tâchiste, Automatist [etc.].

automatization (ɔː,tɒmətaɪ'zeɪʃən). [f. AUTOMATIZE *v.* + -ATION.] The action of making or condition of being made automatic or automatically controlled.

1924 *Psyche* July 87 The pointing method in localization ..does not tend so readily toward automatization. **1932** *Discovery* Oct. 336/2 The initial effect [of noise] tends to wear off very rapidly, mainly in consequence of automatization of the task. **1937** C. G. Philp *Conquest of Stratosphere* x. 82 The instruments were designed to work automatically as far as possible..and the degree of automatization reached a high standard. **1964** E. A. Nida *Toward Sci. Transl.* vi. 128 Languages..develop in the direction of automatization.

automatize (ɔː'tɒmətaɪz), *v.* [a. F. *automatise-r*, f. *automate* AUTOMATON: see -IZE. Cf. Gr. αὐτοματίζειν to act of itself.]

1. To reduce to an automaton. *rare.*

1837 [Implied at AUTOMATIZED *ppl. a.*]

2. To make or render automatic or automatically controlled; to introduce automation. orig. *U.S.*

1952 *Sci. Amer.* Sept. 152/3 The estimated cost of complete instrumentation of a new modern plant to automatize it as fully as possible. **1955** *Atlantic* June 14/2 Only a war, he believes, could automatize industry overnight.

So **au'tomatized** *ppl. a.*, (*a*) reduced to an automaton; (*b*) provided with or using automatic devices.

1837 Carlyle *Misc.* (1857) IV. 2 Man; forced to exist, automatised, mummy-wise. **1956** *Sci. News Let.* 7 July 9/3 Petroleum production is more highly automatized today than any other industry. **1959** *Times* 9 Oct. 20/4 It [*sc.* the plant] is so highly automatised that it employs only 350 persons. **1960** *Commentary* June 470/2 A rich, heavily automatized society.

automatograph (ɔːtəʊ'mætəgrɑːf, -æ-). [f. Gr. αὐτόματος acting of itself + -γραφος writing, writer, -GRAPH.] A scientific form of the planchette, used for recording the involuntary movements of the hand and arm. Hence **auto'matogram**.

1892 J. Jastrow in *Amer. Jrnl. Psychol.* Apr. 400 This apparatus enables us to record all movement in the horizontal plane, and, inasmuch as its chief purpose is to write slight involuntary movements, we have given it the name of the *automatograph* and may speak of such a record as an *automatogram*. **1901** Titchener *Exper. Psychol.* I. I. 95 Automatograph. This consists of a light but strong board,.. carrying at one end a small block of wood,..hollowed out to take the elbow, and pierced at the other end by a circular hole, through which the stylus passes.

automaton (ɔː'tɒmətən). Also 7–8 **automatum**. Pl. **automata, -atons**. [a. Gr. αὐτόματον, neut. of adj. αὐτόματος acting of itself, also adopted in L. as *automaton*, *-atum*. See also AUTOMA, AUTOMATE, AUTOME.]

1. *lit.* Something which has the power of spontaneous motion or self-movement.

a **1625** Beaum. & Fl. *Bloody Bro.* IV. i, [It] doth move alone, A true automaton. *a* **1797** Burke *Ess. Drama* Wks. X. 153 The perfect Drama, an automaton supported and moved without any foreign help, was formed late and gradually.

Thus applied also to:

2. A living being viewed materially.

1645 Digby *Nat. Bodies* xxiii. (1658) 259 Because these parts [the mover and the moved] are parts of one whole; we call the intire thing automatum, or se movens, or a living creature. **1686** Boyle *Notion Nat.* 305 These living Automata, Human bodies. **1713** *Guardian* (1756) II. 186 To be considered as Automata, made up of bones and muscles, nerves, arteries and animal spirits. **1880** Huxley *Cray-Fish* iii. 127 And such a self-adjusting machine, containing the immediate conditions of its actions within itself, is what is properly understood by an Automaton.

3. A piece of mechanism having its motive power so concealed that it appears to move spontaneously; 'a machine that has within itself the power of motion under conditions fixed for it, but not by it' (W. B. Carpenter). In 17–18th c. applied to clocks, watches, etc., and *transf.* to the Universe and World; now usually to figures which simulate the action of living beings, as clock-work mice, images which strike the hours on a clock, etc.

1611 Coryat *Crudities*, The picture of a Gentlewoman whose eies were contrived..that they moved up and down of themselves..done by a vice which the Grecians call αὐτόματον. **1645** Evelyn *Mem.* (1857) I. 205 Another automaton strikes the quarters. **1660** H. More *Myst. Godl.* II. iii. 37 God will not let the great Automaton of the Universe be so imperfect. *c* **1790** Imison *Sch. Art* I. 284 Those automata..do by little interstices, or strokes, measure out long portions of time. **1832** Babbage *Econ. Manuf.* v. 38 Automatons and mechanical toys moved by springs.

4. A living being whose actions are purely involuntary or mechanical.

1678 Cudworth *Intell. Syst.* I. i. §41. 50 Consequently that themselves were but machines and automata. **1691** Ray *Creation* I. (1777) 165 Nor can it well consist with his veracity to have stocked the earth with divers sets of automata. **1777** Priestley *Matt. & Spir.* (1782) I. §22. 283 Descartes..made the souls of brutes to be mere automata.

5. A human being acting mechanically or without active intelligence in a monotonous routine.

1785 Betsy Sheridan *Jrnl.* (1960) 72 Mrs. Dexter..says the Goths in her neighbourhood had the impudence to think of your playing second to that Automaton Mrs Kennan. **1796** Stedman *Surinam* I. ix. 200 The whole party [of slaves] was a set of scarcely animated automatons. **1844** Disraeli *Coningsby* IV. xi. 167 'Do you think so?' said the Princess..'Have these automata, indeed, souls?' **1873** Symonds *Grk. Poets* v. 140 How could a Spartan, that automaton of the state..excel in any fine art?

6. *Comb.* and *Attrib.*, as in ***automaton figure, lips***, etc.; **automaton-like** *a.* and *adv.* resembling or like an automaton.

1770 T. Jefferson *Corr.* Wks. 1859 I. 194 Your periagua ..will meet us, automaton-like, of its own accord. **1801** Strutt *Sports & Past.* III. ii. 149 Automaton figures made of wood. **1866** G. Macdonald *Ann. Q. Neighb.* xxvi. 451 Her lips, with automaton-like movement, uttered the words.

automatonism (ɔː'tɒmətənɪz(ə)m). [f. AUTOMATON + -ISM.] = AUTOMATISM 1.

1925 Yeats *Vision* I. iv. 78 [Shelley] was subject to an *automatonism* which he mistook for poetic invention, especially in his longer poems. **1947** *Nature* 18 Jan. 80/2 Anyone who has dealings with a tame raven will find it difficult to dispense with the word 'intelligence' in any analysis of its conduct. Is it automatonism when it tweaks the cat's tail?

automatous (ɔː'tɒmətəs), *a.* [f. Gr. αὐτόματος (see AUTOMATON) + -OUS.]

1. Acting spontaneously; having power of self-motion.

1769 W. Jackson in *Month. Rev.* XLII. 171 Their great, ineffable, autocratorical, automatous author. **1808** Knox & Jebb *Corr.* I. 427, I long to be set at work, but I am not automatous: I need to be wound up. **1871** Farrar *Witn. Hist.* i. 36 He may accept the nebular hypothesis, but..must he not admit that the fluid haze was not automatous?

2. Of the nature of an automaton: **a.** 'self-acting' mechanically; **b.** acting involuntarily without conscious determination.

1646 Sir T. Browne *Pseud. Ep.* v. xviii. (1686) 212 Clocks or Automatous organs. **1682** —— *Chr. Mor.* (1756) 34 They who are merely carried on by the wheel of such inclinations are but the automatous part of mankind. **1867** W. Smith *Lat.-Eng. Dict.*, *Automatarius*..of or pertaining to an automaton, automatous.

†**'autome.** *Obs.*—[0]. Variant, perh. Fr., of erroneous form AUTOMA = AUTOMATON.

1656–81 in Blount *Glossogr.*

autometry (ɔː'tɒmɪtrɪ). [f. AUTO-[1] + Gr. -μετρία measurement.] **a.** Self-measurement, self-estimation. **b.** Measurement of the parts of a figure in terms of its entire height. **autometric** (ɔːtəʊ'mɛtrɪk), *a.* [see -IC], of or pertaining to autometry.

1829 Southey *Sir T. More* (1831) II. 278 You judge of others by yourselves, and therefore measure them by an erroneous standard whenever your autometry is false. **1874** *Edin. Rev.* No. 285. 191 Autometric division or delineation of figures in terms of their entire height.

automnesia (ɔːtɒm'niːzɪə). *Psychol.* [f. Gr. αὐτο- (see AUTO-[1]) + μνῆσις memory: see -IA[1].] (See quots. *a* 1901.)

1897 tr. *Ribot's Psychol. Emotions* 153 By some phenomenon of affective automnesia, this same event reproduced itself. *a* **1901** Myers *Human Personality* (1903) I. Gloss., *Automnesia*, spontaneous revival of memories of an earlier condition of life. *Ibid.* II. 139 Littré..describes what he calls the 'affective automnesia'—or spontaneously arising flow of emotion.

automobile ('ɔːtəməbiːl), *a.* and *sb.* Also (formerly) **auto-mobile**. [a. F. *automobile* (1876 in Littré Suppl.), f. Gr. αὐτός self + F. *mobile*: see AUTO-[1] and MOBILE *a.*] **A.** *adj.* That moves by means of mechanism and power within itself; esp. of a vehicle, self-propelling as distinguished from horse-drawn.

1883 H. Greer *Dict. Electricity* 48 There are half a dozen systems of electric traction..in use... An auto-mobile car, with isolated rails. **1886** *Harper's Mag.* June 25/2 These vessels..besides their equipment of auto-mobile torpedoes, are provided with powerful batteries. **1895** *Daily News* 15 Oct. 5/3 Signor Cleto Brena has arrived at Naples with his automobile carriage from Milan. **1902** *Encycl. Brit.* XXXI. 12/1 France has undoubtedly led in the development of the light automobile vehicle.

B. *sb.* A self-propelled vehicle; a motor vehicle.

1895 *Pall Mall Gaz.* 15 Oct. 2/3 Three miles an hour gives the automobile little chance of displaying the powers it doubtless enjoys. **1902** *Encycl. Brit.* XXXI. 11/1 On the Continent of Europe and in the United States the usual expression for these vehicles [*sc.* motor-cars] is 'automobile'. **1934** H. G. Wells *Exper. Autobiogr.* II. viii. 543 The bicycle was the swiftest thing upon the roads in those days, there were as yet no automobiles.

attrib. **1896** *Manch. Guardian* 24 Sept. 10/1 The Automobile Club of France. **1901** *Daily News* 16 Feb. 6/1 The French have shown themselves keenly interested in the subject of auto-mobile races. **1903** [see TRIAL *sb.*[1] 2 a].

'automobile, *v.* [f. prec.] *intr.* To travel or ride in an automobile or motor car; to drive. Hence

auto'mobiling *vbl. sb.*, the action or practice of using an automobile; also *attrib.*
1898 *Cosmopolitan* Sept. 485/1 Mr. Tiffany assures the writer that he finds 'automobiling' more interesting than coaching. **1901** W. R. H. TROWBRIDGE *Lett. her Mother to Eliz.* xii. 54 Blanche spent the morning.. automobiling with the Vicomte and the Marquise. **1903** *N.Y. Times* 19 Dec. 9 Here is a hat for the skating girl and the automobiling woman. **1924** *Public Opinion* 24 Oct. 403/2, I have lately automobiled in Cornwall, Devonshire, Somerset and adjoining counties. **1932** *New Yorker* 9 Apr. 59/2 Yachting on the Trollfjord,.. automobiling in the Baltic Capitals.

automobilism (ɔːtəʊ'məʊbɪlɪz(ə)m). [f. AUTOMOBILE *sb.* + -ISM after F. *automobilisme.*] The use of automobiles or motor vehicles.
1896 *Harper's Weekly* 31 Oct. 1075 We lack France's superb roads; and American automobilism is likely to be hampered in various rural sections of the country. **1898** *Cosmopolitan* Sept. 483/2 As a sport, automobilism now occupies the foremost rank. **1899** *Motor-Car World* Oct. 8/1 Automobilism will be the method of locomotion of the future. **1953** *Archit. Rev.* CXIV. 246 The shopping pedestrian, the morning coffee-taker, the cash-and-handshake dealer, certainly need protection from automobilism.
So **automobilist** (ɔːtəʊ'məʊbɪlɪst), one who uses an automobile or motor vehicle, a motorist.
1897 *Daily News* 26 July 5/5 The hour's rest at St. Germain was improved by the automobilists to see that their machines were in order. **1902** C. N. & A. M. WILLIAMSON *Lightning Conductor* 114 The old peasant.. exclaimed that if all automobilists were like us there would never be complaints. **1907** 'F. MILTOUN' (*title*) The Automobilist Abroad.

automobility (ˌɔːtəʊməʊ'bɪlɪtɪ). [f. AUTOMOBILE *sb.* + -ITY.] **1.** The use of automobiles or motor vehicles as a mode of locomotion or travel.
1903 *Times Lit. Suppl.* 16 Oct. 295/3 To come.. upon a book.. packed with suggestions for the well-being of the walker is, in this year of grace and automobility, no small joy. **1926** *Daily News* 29 Oct. 6/7 The automobility of society.. has helped many Englishmen to discover England.
2. Mobility by means of an automobile or motor vehicle.
1909 *Westm. Gaz.* 18 Mar. 2/3 The interesting experiment of conveying troops by motor vehicles to Hastings.. proves what may be called the automobility of a defensive force. **1926** *Blackw. Mag.* Mar. 309/2 The small expedition, being totally inadequate to its purpose, achieved nothing but automobility.

automolite (ɔː'tɒməlaɪt). *Min.* [f. Gr. αὐτόμολος going by oneself, subst. 'a deserter' (f. αὐτο- by oneself + μολεῖν to come, go) + -ITE; so named by Ekeberg (1806) in allusion to the unexpected appearance of zinc in connexion with spinel.] A variety of zinc-spinel or GAHNITE.
1843 HUMBLE *Dict. Geol., Automalite.* **1868** DANA *Min.* 149 Automolite is found at Fahlun, in talcose schist.

automorphic (ɔːtəʊ'mɔːfɪk), *a.* [f. Gr. αὐτομορφ-ός self-formed, f. αὐτο- self + μορφή form. (After *anthropomorphic.*)] **1.** Characterized by automorphism (sense 1). **auto'morphically** *adv.*, in automorphic manner.
1873 H. SPENCER *Stud. Sociol.* vi. 114 The conception which anyone frames of another's mind, is inevitably more or less after the pattern of his own mind—is automorphic. *Ibid.* 115 He interpreted them automorphically.
2. Math. ***automorphic function*** [ad. G. *automorphe funktion* (F. Klein 1890, in *Nachrichten v. d. königlichen Ges. d. Wissenschaften, Göttingen 1890* Mar. 94).] (See quot. 1892.)
1892 W. BURNSIDE in *Proc. London Math. Soc. 1891–2* XXIII. 49 On a class of automorphic functions. *Ibid.* 52, I have used the phrase 'automorphic function', as introduced by Professor Klein, to denote generally any function which is unchanged by the substitutions of a discontinuous group, whatever be the nature of the group. **1898** E. T. WHITTAKER in *Phil. Trans.* (1899) CXCII. 1 The only automorphic functions known hitherto which have been applied to uniformise forms whose genus is greater than unity, are those given by certain sub-groups of the modular group. **1902** —— *Mod. Analysis* 339 Two classes of automorphic functions are known by which this uniformisation may be effected.
3. *Cryst.* [ad. G. *automorph* (C. E. M. Rohrbach 1885, in *Mineral. u. Petrograph. Mittheilungen* VII. 18).] = IDIOMORPHIC *a.*
1888 F. H. HATCH in J. J. H. Teall *Brit. Petrogr.* 435 The mineral constituents of rocks are said to be idiomorphic in so far as they are bounded by faces peculiar to the species. The word is synonymous with Rohrbach's 'automorphic'.

auto'morphism. **1.** The ascription of one's own characteristics to another.
1873 H. SPENCER *Stud. Sociol.* vi. 117 Our interpretations must be automorphic; and yet automorphism perpetually misleads us.
2. *Math.* (See quots.)
1903 *Science* 5 June 904 Class of a group and degree of transitivity, automorphism, representation, index notation. **1955** L. MIRSKY *Introd. Linear Algebra* iv. 125 An automorphism of a linear manifold $\mathfrak{M}$ is an isomorphism of $\mathfrak{M}$ with itself. *Ibid.*, A linear transformation of a finite-dimensional linear manifold onto itself is an automorphism. **1959** M. HALL *Theory of Groups* vi. 86 The automorphism group A (C) is cyclic. **1959** G. & R. C. JAMES *Math. Dict.* 221/1 An isomorphism of a set with itself is an automorphism. An automorphism of a group is an inner automorphism if there is an element t such that x corresponds to x^* if and only if $x^* = t^{-1}xt$; it is an outer automorphism if it is not an inner automorphism. **1965** J. J. ROTMAN *Theory of Groups* iv. 76 *Definition.* A homomorphism $f{:}G \to G$ is called an endomorphism of G; an isomorphism $f{:}G \to G$ is called an automorphism of G.

automotive (ɔːtəʊ'məʊtɪv), *sb.* and *a.* [f. AUTO-[1] + MOTIVE *a.*] †**A.** *sb.* [a. F. *automotive.*] A self-propelled vehicle (in quots., an early kind of helicopter).
1865 C. H. TURNOR *Astra Castra* 256 This journal—this indispensable *Moniteur* to the aerial automotive. *Ibid.* 344 MM. Ponton d' Amécourt and de la Landelle were constructing their small automotives.
B. *adj.* **a.** Of or pertaining to an automobile or automobiles. **b.** Self-propelled.
1898 tr. *L. Lockert's Petroleum Motor-cars* p. ix, His work .. is read with satisfaction by all amateurs of automotive touring. **1901** (*title*) The Automotor and Horseless Vehicle Pocket-Book of Automotive Formulæ. **1922** *Public Opinion* 7 Sept. 222/1 He chugged up the street in an automotive contraption. **1938** W. WILKINSON *Puppets through America* xiv. 156 In spite of all its cars, its crowded streets and its cheap stores for automotive workers, Detroit has a splendid oasis in the white stone Merrick Public Library. **1956** A. H. COMPTON *Atomic Quest* 355 Airplane and automotive manufacture.

automotor: see AUTO-[2].

autonoetic (ˌɔːtəʊnəʊ'ɛtɪk), *a.* [f. Gr. αὐτο- self + νοητικός perceptive; cf. Gr. αὐτονόητος self-understood.] Self-perceiving.
1883 G. WYLD (*title*) Clairvoyance; or, the Auto-noetic Action on the Mind.

auto'nomasy. Derived in mod. Dicts. from Gr. αὐτός self + ὀνομασία naming, and explained as the use of a common name in a connexion in which it acquires an accepted specific sense; *e.g.* 'town' for 'London,' 'river' for 'Thames,' in 'He is in town, and has gone across the river (to Lambeth)'; it being held that 'town,' 'river' here virtually name themselves 'London,' 'Thames.' But as this is a strained etymology, and the word exactly corresponds in meaning to ANTONOMASIA, it seems more reasonable to suppose that it is a mere mistake due to a turned *n* (= *u*) in printing.

auto'nomian, *a.* ? *Obs.*[—0] [f. AUTONOMY + -AN.] = next.
1864 in WEBSTER.

autonomic (ɔːtəʊ'nɒmɪk), *a.* and *sb.* [f. AUTONOMY: see -IC.] **A.** *adj.* **a.** Of, pertaining to, or possessing, autonomy; self-governing, independent.
1832 AUSTIN *Jurispr.* I. v. 185 Laws autonomic or autonomical are laws made by subjects as private persons in pursuance of legal rights. **1854** HICKOK *Sci. Mind* 207 Reason is thus ever autonomic; carrying its own law within itself.
b. *Physiol.* Functioning independently of the will; ***autonomic nervous system*** (see quots. 1898).
1898 J. N. LANGLEY in *Jrnl. Physiol.* XXIII. 241 The 'autonomic' nervous system means the nervous system of the glands and of the involuntary muscle. *Ibid.* 270, I propose the term'autonomic nervous sytem' for the sympathetic system and the allied nervous system of the cranial and sacral nerves, and for the local nervous system of the gut. **1940** R. S. WOODWORTH *Psychol.* (ed. 12) xii. 419 *The autonomic nerves.* These are the nerves that run to the heart, blood vessels, lungs, stomach, intestines, and other viscera... These nerves are composed of extra-slender nerve fibres, which grow out from cells in the brain stem and cord. **1966** *Lancet* 24 Dec. 1415/1 Individuals can gain cortical control over various autonomic nervous symptoms.
B. *sb. Physiol.* A part of the autonomic nervous system.
1929 F. H. GARRISON *Hist. Med.* (ed. 4) xiii. 696 Adrenalin, the hormone governing the sympathetic autonomic. *Ibid.*, The two opposing autonomics of the sympathetic system control the ductless glands and the visceral organs made up of smooth (involuntary) muscle.

auto'nomical, *a.* [f. as prec. + -ICAL.] = prec.
1659 BAXTER *Key for Cath.* II. iii. 402 Them that would.. make the Church to be autonomicall.. or chief Governour of it self. **1865** MAFFEI *Brigand Life* I. 313 Taking away from the Neapolitans their autonomical government.

auto'nomically, *adv.* [f. prec. + -LY[2].] In autonomic manner; by right of self-government.
1832 AUSTIN *Jurispr.* (1879) II. xxviii. 541 Laws made autonomically or by private authority. **1863** D. SIMON *Dorner's Pers. Christ* II. III. 314 So far as it [*i.e.* the sensuous principle] works autonomically.

autonomism (ɔː'tɒnəmɪz(ə)m). [f. AUTONOMY + -ISM.] **1.** The principle or system of autonomy or self-government.
1874 FISKE *Cosmic Philos.* II. 205 The two feelings known to the Greeks as Pan-Hellenism and Autonomism, represented respectively by Athens and by the Doric communities.
2. *Biol.* 'The theory that the forms into which animals and plants develop are determined by an inward agency' (*Cent. Dict.* Suppl., 1909).

autonomist (ɔː'tɒnəmɪst). [f. AUTONOMY: see -IST.] An advocate of autonomy. Also *attrib.*
1865 *Pall Mall G.* 25 Nov. 4 The priests and so-called autonomists and Liberal Conservatives [sat] on the right [in the Croatian Diet]. **1871** *Daily News* 5 Jan., Provincial Landtags are the centre of autonomist resistance.

autonomistic (ɔːtɒnə'mɪstɪk), *a.* [-IC.]
1. *Politics.* Of or pertaining to autonomism (sense 1).
a **1870** GEN. R. E. LEE in *Westm. Gaz.* (1898) 25 May 3/1 The Autonomistic Cabinet.
2. *Biol.* Of or pertaining to autonomism (sense 2) or the theory of self-determined development.
1904 *Biol. Bull.* (Mass.) Sept. 201 They [*sc.* changes] resemble in character certain of the phenomena which have led Driesch to assume the existence of an autonomistic principle or entelechy governing form.

autonomize (ɔː'tɒnəmaɪz), *v.* [f. as AUTONOMIST: see -IZE.] To make autonomous; to confer the right of self-government upon.
1878 *Daily News* 29 Jan. 2/4 If Bulgaria were to be autonomised.

autonomous (ɔː'tɒnəməs), *a.* [f. Gr. αὐτόνομ-ος making or having one's own laws, independent (f. αὐτο- self, own + νόμος law) + -OUS.]
1. Of or pertaining to an autonomy.
1800 W. TAYLOR in *Month. Mag.* VIII. 600 With an autocratic, not an autonomous, constitution. **1861** C. KING *Antique Gems* (1866) 237 The autonomous coins of Sybaris.
2. Possessed of autonomy, self-governing, independent. In *Metaph.*: see AUTONOMY 1 c.
1804 W. TAYLOR in *Ann. Rev.* II. 244 If the [Irish] nation was to become autonomous. **1851** D. WILSON *Preh. Ann.* (1863) I. II. i. 313 The autonomous Greek cities in Asia Minor. **1868** BAIN *Ment. & Mor. Sc.* 736 The absolutely good Will must be autonomous—*i.e.*, without any kind of motive or interest.
3. *Biol.* **a.** Conforming to its own laws only, and not subject to higher ones. **b.** Independent, *i.e.* not a mere form or state of some other organism.
1861 H. MACMILLAN *Footn. Page Nat.* 158 Some of these productions may not be autonomous, some may seem to pass into each other by intermediate forms. **1881** *Syd. Soc. Lex.* s.v. *Autonomy*, Anatomy and physiology are autonomous, since the phenomena presented by animals and plants are not at present referable to chemical, physical, or other laws. **1882** T. DYER in *Nature* 23 Feb. 391 The view that they [lichens] are autonomous organisms.

autonomously (ɔː'tɒnəməslɪ), *adv.* [-LY[2].] In an autonomous position, as an autonomous state, etc.
1881 G. S. HALL *German Culture* 183 We must know and autonomously will to follow non-egoistic absolute ends as essentially our ends. **1897** GLADSTONE *Eastern Crisis* 14 Why should not Crete be autonomously united with Greece, and yet not detached in theory from the body of the Ottoman Empire?

autonomy (ɔː'tɒnəmɪ). [ad. Gr. αὐτονομία the having or making of one's own laws, independence, noun of quality f. αὐτόνομος: see AUTONOMOUS *a.*]
1. Of a state, institution, etc.: The right of self-government, of making its own laws and administering its own affairs.
(Sometimes limited by the adjs. *local*, *administrative*, when the self-government is only partial; thus English boroughs have a local autonomy, the British colonies an administrative autonomy; 'political autonomy' is national independence.)
1623 COCKERAM, *Autonomy*, liberty to liue after ones owne law. [**1681** H. MORE *Exp. Daniel* vi. 237 His successour granted an Αὐτονομία to the Jews, viz. liberty of living according to their own laws.] **1793** W. TAYLOR in *Month. Rev.* XI. 336 A protest in behalf of the Right of Autonomy in the name of all the independent states of Europe. **1846** GROTE *Greece* I. xiv. I. 443 The inhabitants of Sigeium could not peaceably acquiesce in this loss of their autonomy. **1880** MCCARTHY *Own Times* IV. 482 It [Bulgaria] was to have, as to its interior condition, a sort of 'administrative autonomy,' as the favourite diplomatic phrase then was.
b. Liberty to follow one's will, personal freedom.
1803 W. TAYLOR in *Ann. Rev.* I. 384 The customers of a banker can desert to a rival at will, and thus retain.. an autonomy of conduct.
c. *Metaph.* Freedom (of the will); the Kantian doctrine of the Will giving itself its own law, apart from any object willed; opposed to *heteronomy*.
1817 COLERIDGE *Biog. Lit.* 70 Kant.. was permitted to assume a higher ground (the autonomy of the will) as a postulate deducible from the unconditional command.. of the conscience. *a* **1871** GROTE *Eth. Fragm.* ii. (1876) 45 Kant .. means by Autonomy, that there are in this case no considerations of pleasure or pain influencing the will.
2. *Biol.* Autonomous condition: **a.** The condition of being controlled only by its own laws, and not subject to any higher one. **b.** Organic independence.
1871 H. MACMILLAN *True Vine* 79 Each branch is a little plant in itself.. having its own autonomy, feeding, growing, and propagating as an individual. **1881** *Syd. Soc. Lex.* s.v., The several tissues of the body, as the muscles and nerves, have some properties which they possess in common with all the other tissues, and others which are peculiar to

themselves, governed by special laws, and not subject to the laws affecting the rest of the system. In this respect they have an autonomy of their own.

3. A self-governing community (cf. *a* monarchy).

1840 tr. *Ranke's Popes* (1849) I. 11 All those autonomies wherewith the world was filled..one after another, stoop and disappear.

autonym (ˈɔːtənɪm). [f. Gr. αὐτο- self + ὄνυμα = ὄνομα name.] 'A book published under the author's real name.' O. Hamst *Mart. Bibliogr.* 1867. Also, one's own name as distinguished from a pseudonym, esp. the real name of an author; also *attrib.*

1895 *Daily News* 23 Dec. 5/1 Autonym works, anonymous works, and special works.

autopathic (ɔːtəʊˈpæθɪk), *a.* [f. Gr. αὐτο- self + παθικός pertaining to suffering.] Of or pertaining to disease inherent in a living being itself.

1881 J. Simon in *Nature* No. 616. 373 Causes of death.. autopathic and exopathic. On the one hand, there is the original and inherited condition under which to every man born there is normally assigned eventual old age and death.

†**auˈtopathy.** *Obs. rare.* [ad. Gr. αὐτοπάθεια, n. of state f. αὐτοπαθής self-feeling or experiencing, f. αὐτο- self + -παθής feeling.] (See quot.)

1647 H. More *Song of Soul* I. III. lxvi, Base fear proceeds from weak Autopathy. *Ibid.* note (D.), Autopathy denotes the being self-strucken; to be sensible of what harms us, rather than what is absolutely evill.

autophagous (ɔːˈtɒfəgəs). *Med.* [f. Gr. αὐτοφάγ-ος (f. αὐτο- self + φαγ-εῖν to eat) + -ous.] Self-devouring. **autophagy** (ɔːˈtɒfədʒɪ) [cf. F. *autophagie*], the feeding upon oneself, sustenance of life during the process of starvation by absorption of the tissues of the body.

1881 in *Syd. Soc. Lex.*

autophoby (ɔːˈtɒfəbɪ). *rare.* [f. auto-[1] self + Gr. -φοβία fear.] Fear of referring to oneself.

1827 Hare *Guesses* 102 This shrinking from the use of the personal pronoun, this autophoby, as it may be called.

autophone (ˈɔːtəʊfəʊn). Also **autophon.** [f. auto-[1] + -phone.] **1.** A type of barrel-organ (see quot. *a*1875). (Disused.)

1852 *Reports Juries 1851 Exhib.* 332/2 A barrel-organ, called an Autophon. *a* **1875** Knight *Dict. Mech.* I. 192/1 *Autophon*, a barrel-organ, the tunes of which are produced by means of perforated sheets of mill-board. **1878** in *Design & Work* 2 Mar. 275/3 Autophone.

2. [ad. F. *autophone* (Mahillon, 1880).] A musical instrument that produces sound through the vibration of its constituent material (see quots.).

1937 F. W. Galpin *Textbk. Europ. Mus. Instr.* 27 The various sound-producers were classed as *Autophones* or self-vibrators. *Ibid.* 52 The representative instrument in the plucked type of *Autophones* is the *Crembalum* or Jew's-harp. **1954** *Grove's Dict. Mus.* IV. 489/2 Under Auto- or Idiophones..we find not only the xylophone..but also the marimba..and the marimba gongs.

Hence **autoˈphonic** *a.*[2]

1937 F. W. Galpin *Textbk. Europ. Mus. Instr.* 29 Autophonic Instruments or self-vibrators, i.e. instruments of solid substance which, owing to their elastic nature, have a sonority of their own, which is emitted in waves when they are struck, plucked, or stimulated by friction or air.

autophony (ɔːˈtɒfənɪ). *Med.* [ad. Gr. αὐτοφωνία, n. of quality f. αὐτόφωνος self-sounding, f. αὐτο- self, one's own + φωνή voice.] Observation by a practitioner of the peculiarities of resonance of his own voice, when he places his head close to the chest of a patient, and speaks loudly. **autophonic** (ɔːtəʊˈfɒnɪk), *a.*[1], pertaining to autophony.

1862 H. Fuller *Dis. Lungs* 124 Autophony, either directly or through the intervention of a stethoscope..in aid of the diagnosis of thoracic disease. *Ibid.*, The inference that autophonic resonance would vary with the density of the contents of the thoracic cavity.

ˌ**autophˈthalmoscope.** [f. Gr. αὐτο- self + ὀφθαλμός eye + σκοπός observer.] = autoscope 1.

1875 Walton *Dis. Eye* 281 Such is the principle of the autophthalmoscope of Coccius.

autopiano (ˌɔːtəʊpɪˈænəʊ). [f. auto-[1] + piano *sb.*[2]] A piano with a playing apparatus.

1905 *Connoisseur* XIII. 41 (Advt.), The —— 'Autopiano' is a Pianoforte of excellent tone..played with music roll. **1928** *Sunday News* 17 June 4/4 Their sale bargains including several auto-pianos.

auto-pilot, autopilot. *Aeronaut.* [f. auto-[1] + pilot *sb.*] = automatic *pilot.*

1935 *Flight* 10 Jan. 42/2 No information is available concerning the degree of accuracy which the 'Autopilot' will give in bumpy weather. **1943** *Times* 21 Sept. 4/5 Because its electronic mechanism is hyper-sensitive, the auto-pilot corrects immediately the slightest deviation in the course or balance of a bomber in the midst of cross-currents. **1956** *Spaceflight* I. 24/1 Under the control of an autopilot, the whole thrust unit can be deflected up to 5 degrees from the rocket's centre-line.

‖**autopista** (ˈɔːtəʊpiːstə). [Sp., f. *auto* (auto-[2]) + *pista* track (see piste[2]).]

In Spain and Spanish-speaking countries, a fast motor road; = motorway.

1955 'S. Marlowe' *Second Longest Night* vii. 61 A four-lane superhighway [in Venezuela]... 'Some *autopista*,' he said. **1963** *Economist* 2 Nov. 491/1, 204 kilometres of *Autopistas* [in Spain]. **1967** *Daily Tel.* 15 Mar. 14/4 After several years' delay Spain's first *autopista*, or through motorway, linking Barcelona to the French frontier is to be built.

autopisty (ˈɔːtəʊpɪstɪ). *rare*[−0]. [f. Gr. αὐτόπιστ-ος credible in itself (f. αὐτο- self + πιστός trustworthy, credible) + -y[3].] Credibility on internal evidence.

autoplast (ˈɔːtəʊplæst). [f. auto-[1] + -plast.] **a.** *Embryol.* An autogenous cell as distinguished from a cleavage cell. **b.** *Plant Physiol.* A chlorophyll granule.

1883 E. Ray Lankester in *Encycl. Brit.* XVI. 682/2 In addition to the layer of cleavage cells..additional cells are formed.., each cell having a separate origin, whence they are termed 'autoplasts'. **1885** [see *trophoplast* s.v. tropho-].

autoplasty (ˈɔːtəʊplæstɪ). *Surg.* [f. Gr. αὐτόπλαστ-ος self-formed + -y[3]. Cf. F. *autoplastie.*] Repair of wounds or diseased parts by means of tissue taken from other parts of the same body. **autoplastic** (ɔːtəʊˈplæstɪk), *a.*, of or pertaining to autoplasty.

1853 in Mayne *Exp. Lex.*

autoplate (ˈɔːtəʊpleɪt). *U.S.* [f. auto-[1] + plate *sb.*] A curved stereotype for newspaper printing, made by an autoplate machine; also, the machine itself; ***autoplate machine***, a machine for automatically casting, shaving, and bevelling stereotypes.

1901 *Sci. Amer.* Suppl. LII. 21591/1 The Autoplate—an automatic stereotyping machine. **1902** *Westm. Gaz.* 22 May 9/1 The Autoplate, a wonderful revolution in stereotyping. **1902** *Census Bulletin* 28 June 51 (Cent. D. Suppl.), A device known as the autoplate was invented in 1900 by means of which the time required for casting plates was..reduced. **1963** *Times* 17 Apr. 3/5 Junior Autoplate Casting Equipment is available.

autopolyploid (ˌɔːtəʊˈpɒlɪplɔɪd). *Biol.* [f. auto-[1] + polyploid.] A polyploid having its sets of chromosomes derived from a single parent species. Hence **autoˈpolyploidy**, the condition or occurrence of such a polyploid.

1928 [see allopolyploidy]. **1930** E. Müntzing in *Hereditas* XIII. 293 Auto-polyploids, however, are generally less stable than the diploid parents. **1930** [see allopolyploidy]. **1945** *Lancet* 14 July 47/2 Colchicine possesses the property of arresting cells in the process of mitotic division at a stage when the chromosomes have divided and the cytoplasm is undivided, so that a cell with a double complement of chromosomes results... This process of doubling is called autopolyploidy, and the products autopolyploids. **1952** *New Biol.* XIII. 31 These shoots have 48 chromosomes instead of the usual 24, four of each chromosome being present in place of the original pair. .. Polyploids of any sort which have thus originated from one parental species are called 'autopolyploids'.

autopsic (ɔːˈtɒpsɪk), *a.* [f. mod.L. *autopsia* autopsy + -ic.] Of or pertaining to autopsy; based on personal observation; *spec.* in *Med.*, obtained by means of the post-mortem examination of a body. Also **auˈtopsical** *a.*

1881 L. Putzel in *von Ziemssen's Cycl. Med.* Suppl. 561 Basing his opinion upon the autopsical examination of five patients. **1886** *Alienist & Neurol.* July 533 The autopsic and the combined ante-mortem testimony to his insanity was not more confirmatory.

autopsical, obs. variant of autoptical.

autopsorin (ɔːtɒpˈsɔːrɪn). *Med.* [f. Gr. αὐτο- self, own + ψώρα cutaneous disease + -in.] Some of a patient's own virus administered homœopathically by way of remedial treatment in cases of itch, smallpox, cancer, etc.

1853 in Mayne *Exp. Lex.*

autopsy (ˈɔːtɒpsɪ, -ˈtɒpsɪ), *sb.* [ad. mod.L. *autopsia* (also used in Eng.), a. Gr. αὐτοψία, n. of quality f. αὔτοπτ-ος seeing (or seen) for oneself (see auto-[1], optic); cf. F. *autopsie.*]

1. Seeing with one's own eyes, eye-witnessing; personal observation or inspection.

1651 Wittie tr. *Primrose's Pop. Err.* I. xiv. 53 Or by autopsie, when by our observation, wee get a certaine knowledge of things. **1858** De Quincey *Miracles* Wks. VIII. 237 The defect of autopsy may be compensated by sufficient testimony of a multitude.

2. Dissection of a dead body, so as to ascertain by actual inspection its internal structure, and *esp.* to find out the cause or seat of disease; post-mortem examination.

1678 Cudworth *Intell. Syst.* I. iii. 161 The Cartesian attempts to solve the motion of the heart mechanically seem ..confuted by autopsy and experiment. **1859** Mahony *Mod. Lat. Poets* ii. 548 Had an autopsia taken place after his death. **1881** *Times* 22 Sept. 4/1 The physicians' autopsy [of President Garfield] shows the bullet to be nowhere near where it was supposed to be.

b. *fig.* Critical dissection.

1835 *Hist. Eng.* in *Lardner's Cab. Cycl.* IV. viii. 375 He [James I.] is, moreover, one of the least inviting subjects of moral autopsia. **1879** Miss Braddon *Vixen* III. 143 This autopsy of a fine lady's poem.

autopsy (ˈɔːtɒpsɪ, ɔːˈtɒpsɪ), *v.* [f. autopsy *sb.*] *trans.* To perform an autopsy on or make a post-mortem examination of (a body).

1900 *Jrnl. Exper. Med.* V. 257 One of the pigs was killed and autopsied, with the result that its organs..were found to be entirely free of lesions. **1919** Sachs in S. Paget *Sir V. Horsley* II. iv. 190 It was the first walrus that had been autopsied in London for many years. **1969** *Nature* 19 Apr. 287/1 The rats..were autopsied on the thirteenth day of pregnancy.

autoptic (ɔːˈtɒptɪk), *a.* [ad. Gr. αὐτοπτικός, f. αὔτοπτος: see autopsy *sb.* and -ic.] Of, or of the nature of, an eye-witness; based on personal observation.

1849 Alford *Grk. Test.* I. 48 Undoubted marks of autoptic testimony. **1861** *Jrnl. Sacr. Lit.* XIV. 196 Canon Stanley, who in this case is an autoptic witness.

auˈtoptical, *a.* [f. as prec. + -al[1].] = prec.

1651 Biggs *New Disp.* ¶38 The autopticall unsuccessefulnesse of their own practice. **1675** Evelyn *Terra* (1729) 26 My autoptical observations of the several earths. **1861** *Jrnl. Sacr. Lit.* XIV. 168 The style changes from the autoptical to the purely historical.

auˈtoptically, *adv.* [f. prec. + -ly[2].] In an autoptic manner; by actual inspection.

1646 Sir T. Browne *Pseud. Ep.* 342 It would autoptically silence that dispute out of which side Eve was framed. **1661** Glanvill *Van. Dogm.* 174 That the galaxy is a meteor..the telescope hath autoptically confuted.

autopticity (ɔːtɒpˈtɪsɪtɪ). [f. autoptic + -ity; cf. *authenticity.*] Autoptic quality or nature.

1861 *Jrnl. Sacr. Lit.* XIV. 169 If we attend to his style, it will be observed that its autopticity coincides with the use of the first person plural.

autor, -ial, -ity, etc., obs. ff. author *sb.*, etc.

autoradiograph (ɔːtəʊˈreɪdɪəʊgrɑːf), *sb.* [f. auto-[1] + radiograph.] An image of an object produced on a sensitive film by the radioactivity of the object itself. Hence as *v. trans.*, to produce an autoradiograph of. Also ˌ**autoradiˈography** [F. *autoradiographie*], the production of an autoradiograph; ˌ**autoradioˈgraphic, -ical** *adjs.*, pertaining to or involving autoradiography; ˌ**autoradioˈgraphically** *adv.* Cf. *radio-autograph.*

1903 *Dublin Rev.* July 170 Auto-radiographs of thorium. **1941** *Physical Rev.* LX. 688/1 Recently autoradiography has been of value in tracer studies of biological substances. **1943** *Amer. Mineralogist* XXVIII. 459 The elements are arranged in the order of decreasing suitability for autoradiographic study. **1947** *Nature* 9 Aug. 193/2 Suppose now that a layer of tissue one cell thick is to be autoradiographed. **1955** G. A. Boyd *Autoradiogr. in Biol. & Med.* i. 7 In 1940, Hamilton [et al.]..used radioiodine to study the thyroid autoradiographically. **1956** *Nature* 25 Feb. 379/1 To prepare radioactive streptomycin for autoradiographical studies of its distribution in the body. **1958** *New Scientist* 2 Jan. 24/1 The tool material on the metal is sufficiently radioactive to darken the film in its neighbourhood and thus takes its own photograph. This is called an autoradiograph. **1965** G. J. Williams *Econ. Geol. N.Z.* xiii. 207/2 Autoradiographs show the radioactivity to be confined to the carbonaceous material which is clearly epigenetic in origin.

autorizate, variant of auctorizate.

‖**autoroute** (ˈɔːtəʊruːt). [F., f. *auto* (auto[2]) + *route* road (see route *sb.*).] In France, a fast motor road; = motorway.

1963 H. Slesar *Bridge of Lions* (1964) vii. 105 The lights of Paris were behind them. Ahead, on the six-lane *autoroute*, lay Versailles. **1966** *Guardian* 30 Dec. 7/6 Those..monster housing estates that sprout along the *autoroutes* outside Paris.

autoschediasm (ɔːtəʊˈskɛdɪæz(ə)m). [ad. Gr. αὐτοσχεδίασμα, f. αὐτοσχεδιάζειν to act, speak, etc. off-hand, f. αὐτοσχέδιος personally near, hand to hand, off-hand.] Something done off-hand, extemporized, or hastily improvised. **autoschediastic** (ˌɔːtəʊskɛdɪˈæstɪk), *a.* [Gr. αὐτοσχεδιαστικός], done on the spur of the moment, hasty, extemporary. ˌ**autoschediˈastical,** *a.* = prec. **autoschediaze** (ɔːtəʊˈskɛdɪeɪz), *v.* to extemporize, improvise.

1842 Kingsley *Lett.* (1878) I. 62 Pardon Auto-schediasms of paper and obscurity of style. **1823** Parr *Wks.* (1828) VII. 159 Remember, the verses are merely autoschediastic. **1662** E. Martin *Lett.* 21 (T.) My autoschediastical and indigested censure of St. Peter's primacy. *a* **1859** De Quincey in Page *Life* II. 174 To autoschediaze or improvise is sometimes in effect to be forced into a consciousness of creative energies.

autoscope (ˈɔːtəskəʊp). [f. Gr. αὐτο- self + σκοπός observer.] **1.** 'An instrument invented by Coccius for the self-examination of the eye.' *Syd. Soc. Lex.* 1881. **autoscopy** (ɔːˈtɒskəpɪ) [Gr. -σκοπία observation], the use of this instrument.

2. (See quot. *a*1901.)

1900 *Daily News* 10 Apr. 6/2 The so-called Divining Rod ..is only one of many 'autoscopes', which perhaps bring into observation what is passing in the mysterious entity styled 'the subconscious self'. ***a*1901** MYERS *Human Personality* (1903) I. Gloss., *Autoscope*, any instrument which reveals a subliminal motor impulse or sensory impression; *e.g.* a divining rod, a tilting table, or a planchette.

autosemantic (ˌɔːtəʊsɪˈmæntɪk), *a.* (*sb.*). *Philol.* [ad. G. *autosemantisch* (A. Marty 1908, *Untersuchungen zur Grundlegung d. allgemeinen Grammatik und Sprachphilosophie* II. i. 206), f. AUTO-[1] + SEMANTIC *a.*] Of a word or phrase: having meaning outside a context; meaningful in isolation; categorematic. Opposed to SYNSEMANTIC *a.* Also *absol.* (A distinction first proposed by the Austrian philosopher A. Marty as a correlate in linguistics of the distinction in logic between *categorematic* and *syncategorematic*.)

1929 *Year's Wk. Eng. Stud. 1927* 47 Funke..classifies the units of speech under two heads, termed Autosemantic and Synsemantic, the former constituting the semasiological units of speech, i.e. those which give complete expression of psychic phenomena which are communicable in themselves. .. Autosemantics correspond to the three basic types of sentence and are not necessarily themselves single words. **1931** G. STERN *Meaning & Change of Meaning* iv. 86 We have to distinguish not only between autosemantic and synsemantic expressions, but also between autosemantic and synsemantic meanings. **1931** W. WORSTER tr. *Jørgensen's Treat. Formal Logic* III. xiii. 239 The word 'and' is syncategorematic or synsemantic. It *may* however, also occur as categorematic or autosemantic, as..in the assertion: '"And" is a conjunction.' **1962** S. ULLMANN *Semantics* ii. 44 Full words are 'autosemantic', meaningful in themselves, whereas articles, prepositions,..and the like are 'synsemantic', meaningful only when they occur in the company of other words.

autosite (ˈɔːtəʊsaɪt). [f. Gr. αὐτόσιτος bringing one's own provisions, f. αὐτός self + σῖτος food.] The larger twin of a double fœtal monster, which supplies nourishment to the smaller (called the parasite); also, a single monster capable of independent life. Hence **auto'sitic** *a.*, that is, or is of the nature of, an autosite.

1848 DUNGLISON *Dict. Med. Sci.* (ed. 7), *Autosite*.., a single monster, capable of deriving nourishment from its own proper organs, in contradistinction to *Omphalosite*. **1894** GOULD *Dict. Med.*, Autosite. *Ibid.*, Autositic.

autosome (ˈɔːtəsəʊm). *Biol.* [f. AUTO-[1] + Gr. σῶμα body.] A chromosome other than a sex-chromosome. Hence **auto'somal** *a.*, of, belonging to, or designating an autosome.

1906 T. H. MONTGOMERY in *Trans. Amer. Philos. Soc.* XXI. 97, I here employ the following nomenclature ..*Autosome* (*autosoma*), the non-aberrant chromosomes that I have previously called *ordinary chromosomes*. **1930** R. A. FISHER *Genetical Theory Nat. Selection* iii. 51 The autosomal and the sex-linked mutations. **1950** E. B. FORD *Stud. Heredity* iii. 32 The sex chromosomes..do not differ from the autosomes except that they carry, among others, the genes which decide whether development shall proceed along male or female lines. **1967** *New Scientist* 19 Oct. 178/1 Normally, the autosomal chromosomes occur in pairs.

autostrada (ˈɔːtəʊstrɑːdə). Pl. **-strade** (-strɑːdeɪ), **-stradas**. [It., = motor road, f. *auto* (AUTO-[2]) + *strada* road, f. L. *stratum* (see STRATUM).] In Italy, a fast motor road; = MOTORWAY.

1927 *Daily Tel.* 15 Nov. 7/1 It will be a 'speedway' pure and simple, somewhat on the lines of the Italian Autostrada. **1937** *Sunday Times* 10 Jan. 27/4 Ten years ago, when the first of the Italian autostrade were built..the powers-that-be in this country might have displayed similar foresight in the planning of the new bypasses and main roads in this country. **1937** *Daily Herald* 16 Apr. 18/2 Those wonderful motor toll-roads, the autostradas, dead straight and with no cross-overs, are of non-skid concrete. **1955** [see AUTOBAHN].

autostylic (ɔːtəʊˈstɪlɪk), *a. Phys.* [f. Gr. αὐτο- one's own + στῦλ-ος pillar + -IC.] Applied to skulls in which the mandibular arch is suspended by its own proper pier, the quadrate.

1880 GUNTHER *Fishes* 71 An autostylic skull.

auto-suggest (ˌɔːtəʊsəˈdʒɛst), *v.* [Back-formation from next.] *trans.* To produce, remove, or influence, by auto-suggestion. Also *intr.*

1921 *Discovery* Nov. 296/2 We are suffering from toothache and wish to autosuggest it away. **1926** W. R. INGE *Lay Thoughts* III. viii. 230 The name Coué, which till lately would have auto-suggested a tale of adventure in the Australian bush, has now become famous in connection with the newest school of psychotherapy. **1936** *Discovery* Aug. 254/1 Intellectual preconceptions..which.. autosuggest to the subject [*sc.* a dowser or diviner] some coherent..scheme of interpretation with which his subsequent muscular reflexes..concur. **1945** *Salt* 12 Feb. 37/2, I guessed Bill was auto-suggestin' for all he was worth.

ˌauto-suˈggestion. [AUTO-[1].] Suggestion originating from oneself; *spec.* in *Psychol.*, the subconscious realization of an idea suggested to oneself for adoption. (Cf. SELF-SUGGESTION 2.)

1890 W. JAMES *Princ. Psychol.* II. xxvii. 601 When the [hypnotic] subject obeys it is by reason of the 'operator's suggestion'; when he proves refractory it is in consequence of an 'auto-suggestion' which he has made to himself. **1890** *Standard* 12 Apr. 5/5 The greatest criminals..may be the responsible victims of a 'suggestion', or even of an 'auto-suggestion'. **1894** *Trans. Obstet. Soc.* XXXV. 246 Women may come to feel cravings by a process of auto-suggestion, especially in their first pregnancy. **1907** J. COATES (*title*) Self-Reliance: Practical Studies in Personal Magnetism, Will-power and Success, through Self-help or Auto-Suggestion. **1921** *Punch* CLX. 238/2 Though we cannot all of us be born at Newmarket, we can by auto-suggestion and psycho-analysis..persuade ourselves that we have been born there.

So **ˌauto-suˈggestible** *a.*, capable of being influenced by auto-suggestion; **ˌauto-suggestiˈbility**, the capacity of being thus influenced; **auto-suˈggestionist**; **auto-suˈggestive** *a.*, arising from or due to auto-suggestion.

1900 DORLAND *Med. Dict.*, *Autosuggestibility*, a peculiar mental state with loss of will, in which suggestions become easy. **1907** *Mind* XVI. 608 Hysterical persons are abnormally auto-suggestible. *Ibid.* 609 The auto-suggestibility preponderates in the severer cases. **1908** E. WORCESTER et al. *Relig. & Med.* 102 The auto-suggestionist must have the intellectual acquisitions in connection with the idea which he seeks to realize. **1910** *Athenæum* 5 Mar. 273/2 An hysterical girl under autosuggestive influences. **1926** ROGER FRY *Transformations* 1 Honesty is..very difficult to come at, since in this matter we are all excessively auto-suggestible.

autotetraploid (ˌɔːtəʊˈtɛtrəplɔɪd). *Biol.* [f. AUTO-[1] + TETRAPLOID.] A tetraploid having four sets of chromosomes produced by doubling the chromosome number of a single diploid species. Hence **ˌautoˈtetraploidy**, the condition or occurrence of such a tetraploid.

1930 J. B. S. HALDANE in *Jrnl. Genetics* XXII. 363 The self-sterile *Dahlia variabilis* behaves in some respects at least as an autotetraploid. **1942** J. S. HUXLEY *Evolution* iii. 87 The normal diploid complement of chromosomes of a species may become doubled (autotetraploidy). **1949** DARLINGTON & MATHER *Elem. Genetics* vi. 135 The allotetraploid stands at one extreme; the *autotetraploid*, the product of doubling a homozygous diploid such as a tomato, stands at the other.

autotheism (ɔːtəʊˈθiːɪz(ə)m). [mod. f. Gr. αὐτόθεος very God (f. αὐτο- self + θεός God) + -ISM.]

1. The doctrine of God's self-subsistence. *spec.* The ascription of this attribute to the Second Person of the Trinity, as being 'God of himself,' and not merely 'God of God.'

1582 N.T. (Rhem.) *John* x. 29 *note*, Caluins Autotheisme, holding that Christ took his person of the Father, but not his substance. **1656** BLOUNT *Glossogr.*, s.v. Calvin's autotheism signifies that point of Doctrine which Calvin held, which is, That God the Son is not *Deus de Deo*, God from God. **1742** in BAILEY.

2. Self-deification.

*a*1619 FOTHERBY *Atheom.* I. viii. §3 He fell into Autotheisme: professing himselfe a God. **1874** tr. *Van Oosterzee's Chr. Dogm.* 248 Pantheism becomes autotheism, and leads to self-adoration.

autotheist (ɔːtəʊˈθiːɪst). [f. as prec.: see -IST.] **a.** 'One who believes God's self-subsistence.' Bailey 1731. **b.** One who makes himself his own god; a deifier of himself.

1855 KINGSLEY in *Alt. Locke* (1881) Pref. Mem. 62 To mistake more and more the voice of that very flesh of his.. for the Voice of God, and to become without knowing it an autotheist. **1866** LD. STRANGFORD *Select.* (1869) II. 299 The Eastern and the Western autotheist alike give full play to their fancy.

autotheistic (ɔːtəʊθiːˈɪstɪk), *a.* [f. AUTOTHEIST + -IC.] Of or pertaining to the autotheists or to autotheism.

1854 *Fraser's Mag.* XLIX. 708 There is this boundless difference between the healthy and godly 'subjective' style, and the unhealthy autotheistic subjective style. **1868** *Contemp. Rev.* IX. 75 Emerson's doctrine, too, is.. essentially autotheistic. **1872** A. M. FAIRBAIRN *Ibid.* XX. 49 In principle they [*sc.* the Hindu philosophies] might be Theistic, Auto-Theistic, Pantheistic or Atheistic.

autotomic (ɔːtəʊˈtɒmɪk), *a.* [f. Gr. αὐτο- self + -τομ-ός cutting + -IC.] Self-intersecting.

1879 THOMSON & TAIT *Nat. Phil.* I. I. §137 The trace on the tangent plane, however complicatedly autotomic it may be, is a finite closed curve or polygon.

autotomy (ɔːˈtɒtəmɪ). [f. AUTO-[1] + -TOMY.] The casting off or ejection of some part or parts of the body as a reflex action peculiar to some animals when disturbed or in order to escape. Hence **auˈtotomize** *v. intr.*, to practise autotomy; *trans.* to cast off; **auˈtotomizing** *vbl. sb.*; **auˈtotomous** *a.*, pertaining to or of the nature of autotomy.

1898 *Proc. Zool. Soc. 1897* 911 The autotomous break occurs between femur and coxa. *Ibid.*, The autotomy of the jumping-legs takes place at the femoro-trochanteric suture. **1899** *Q. Rev.* July 281 The self-mutilation (autotomy) met with in lizards. **1901** T. H. MORGAN *Regeneration* 153 In this way the arm may be autotomized, piece by piece, to its very base. **1930** *Discovery* May 166/1 An allied action is seen when the spider has cast a leg. It has lately been discovered that this familiar a[u]totomy is not, in arachnids, the reflex action it was formerly supposed to be. **1941** J. STEINBECK *Log* in *Sea of Cortez* (1958) xxviii. 267 Two large, hairy grapsoid crabs..were..difficult to catch, and when caught, battled fiercely and ended up by autotomizing.

autotoxin (ɔːtəʊˈtɒksɪn). [f. AUTO-[1] + TOXIN.] A poisonous substance formed within the body. So **autoˈtoxic** *a.*, of, pertaining to, or caused by an autotoxin.

1894 GOULD *Dict. Med.*, *Autotoxin*.., any product of tissue-metamorphosis within the organism that has a toxic effect upon that organism. **1903** *Med. Record* 30 May 857 (Cent. D. Suppl.), We believe the excitant is a toxic or autotoxic agent. **1907** *Times Lit. Suppl.* 5 Dec. 371/3 Thus regarded, senility is an autotoxic phenomenon. **1938** H. BELLOC *Great Heresies* 235 We say that an organism has become 'auto-toxic' when it is beginning to poison itself.

autotype (ˈɔːtətaɪp). [f. Gr. αὐτο- (see AUTO-[1]) self + τύπος type, impress, print, f. τυπ- to strike, after *prototype*, etc.]

1. A 'type' of the thing itself, a true impress of the original; a reproduction in facsimile.

1853 KINGSLEY *Misc.* I. 299 The utterance must be..the outward and visible autotype, of the spirit which animates it. **1880** SWINBURNE *Stud. Shaks.* iii. 202 The type of Angelo.. an autotype of the huge national vice of England.

2. A process of permanent photographic printing, which reproduces photographs or works of art in monochrome; a facsimile produced by this process. Also *attrib.* or as *adj.*

1869 *Pall Mall G.* Supp. 20 Dec. 1 It is illustrated with autotype and other photographs after engravings. **1878** *Prospectus of the 'Autotype Company,'* The public need no longer be content with fading photographs; ask for 'Autotypes' or 'Chromotypes.' **1881** *Athenæum* 16 Apr. 521/2 These days of autotype and heliogravure.

'autotype, *v.* [f. prec. sb.] To reproduce by autotype process.

1883 *Philadelphia Even. Tel.* No. 1306 To autotype certain manuscripts and documents. **1884** *Athenæum* 4 Oct. 434/1 A portrait of Jane Austen..autotyped for this work.

autotypic (ɔːtəʊˈtɪpɪk), *a.* [f. AUTOTYPE + -IC.] **1.** Of, pertaining to, or reproduced by the autotype process (see AUTOTYPE 2).

1885 *Athenæum* 14 Mar. 351/3 The 'Little Devil's Bridge' ..could hardly be surpassed in autotypic reproduction.

2. Of the nature of an autotype or reproduction of an original.

1904 G. S. HALL *Adolescence* I. 124 Man..is more autotypic than he knows, reproducing in his representation of the human form the type of his own race.

autotypography (ˌɔːtəʊtɪˈpɒgrəfɪ). [f. AUTO-[1] self + TYPOGRAPHY.] A process by which drawings made on gelatine are transferred to soft metallic plates, which can be afterwards used for printing.

autotypy (ɔːˈtɒtɪpɪ, ˈɔːtəʊtaɪpɪ). [f. AUTOTYPE + -Y.] The process of reproducing in autotype.

autoxidize (ɔːˈtɒksɪdaɪz), *v. Biochem.* [f. AUTO-[1] + OXIDIZE *v.*] *intr.* To oxidize by direct combination with oxygen at ordinary temperatures (Webster, 1909). Hence **autoxiˈdizable** *a.*, capable of oxidizing by contact with the air; **autoxiˈdation, -iˈzation**, oxidation by direct combination with oxygen; **auˈtoxidator**, a substance in an active cell, oxidizable by water.

1883 *Science* 30 Mar. 229/2 Autoxidation in living vegetable cells. *Ibid.*, Autoxidizable substances,..those bodies which, at a low temperature, and by the action of free, passive oxygen, can be oxidized. *Ibid.* 230/1 In every active cell, autoxidators are formed; that is, substances which, at a low temperature, and by the action of molecular oxygen, can be oxidized in the presence of water. **1948** *Jrnl. Brit. Interplan. Soc.* VII. 142 The so-called autoxidation process which is based on the alternate oxidation and reduction of certain organic compounds. **1956** *Nature* 21 Jan. 129/1 It is characteristic of N-dialkylhydroxylamines to autoxidize very rapidly in aqueous alkali. *Ibid.* 17 Mar. 527/2 All of these ferric chelates..are very rapidly autoxidizable.

autozooid (ɔːtəʊˈzəʊɔɪd). *Zool.* [f. AUTO-[1] + ZOOID *sb.*] The normal zooid in Alcyonarians, as distinguished from the siphonozooid.

1881 [see *siphonozooid* s.v. SIPHONO-]. **1888** *Athenæum* 3 Mar. 279/3 Dr. G. H. Fowler [read a paper] on a new Pennatula from the Bahamas, the most interesting feature of which was the presence of immature autozooids at the dorsal end of the leaves. **1940** *Chambers's Techn. Dict.* 63/2 *Autozooid*, in *Anthozoa*, an ordinary typical zooid.

autre, obs. form of ALTAR.

†**'autume,** *v. Obs. rare*[−1]. [ad. L. *autumāre* to say aye, affirm.] To affirm, assert.

1661 HICKERINGILL *Jamaica* 69 Above what the most favouring presage can expect or autume.

autumn (ˈɔːtəm). Forms: 4–6 **autumpne**, 6 **authum**, 6–7 **autumne**, 7 **autome**, 7– **autumn**. [a. OF. *autompne* (mod. *automne*), ad. L. *autumnus* (also written *auctumnus*), of doubtful etymology. See Lewis and Short.]

1. a. The third season of the year, or that between summer and winter, reckoned astronomically from the descending equinox to the winter solstice; i.e. in the northern hemisphere, from September 21 to December 21. Popularly, it comprises, in Great Britain, August, September, and October (J.); in North America, September, October, and November (Webster); in France 'from the end of August to the first fortnight of November' (Littré); in the southern hemisphere it corresponds in time to the northern spring.

The astronomic reckoning retains the Roman computation; the antiquity of the popular English usage is seen in the name *Midsummer Day*, given to the *first day* of the Astronomical Summer, and in the OE. *midsumormónað* 'June,' *midwinter* 'winter-solstice, Christmas.'

c **1374** CHAUCER *Boeth.* IV. vii. 144 Autumpne comeþ aȝeyne heuy of apples. **1526** TINDALE *Jude* 8 Trees rotten in authum. **1596** SHAKS. *Tam. Shrew* I. ii. 96 Though she chide as loud As thunder, when the clouds in Autumne cracke. **1653** WALTON *Angler* 204 In Autome, when the weeds begin to..rot. **1795** SOUTHEY *Joan of Arc* I. 292 When the leaves Fell in the autumn. **1864** TENNYSON *Aylmer's F.* 610 Autumn's mock sunshine of the faded woods.

b. *poet.* The fruits of autumn; 'harvest.'

1667 MILTON *P.L.* v. 394 Rais'd of grassie terf Thir Table was..And on her ample square, from side to side, All Autumn pil'd. *a* **1749** PHILIPS (J.) The starving brood, Void of sufficient sustenance, will yield A slender autumn.

2. *fig.* A season of maturity, or of incipient decay.

1624 DONNE *Serm.* ii. (1640) 13 In heaven it is always Autumn; his mercies are ever in their maturity. **1770** LANGHORNE *Plutarch* (1879) I. 219/2 The very autumn of a form once fine Retains its beauties.

3. *Comb.* **a.** attrib., as ***autumn fruit, leaf, tide***; **b.** instrumental, as ***autumn-brown, -tinted***; **c.** locative (of time), as ***autumn-flowering, -sown***. **autumn-bells**, English name of *Gentiana pneumonanthe*; **autumn-fly** (see quot.); **autumn-spring**, a spring in autumn.

1597 GERARD *Herball* II. ciii. 355 Calathian Violet..is called..in English *Autumne bell flowers. **1866** WHITTIER *Snow-Bound* 21 Hill-sides *autumn-brown. **1896** T. W. SANDERS *Encycl. Gardening* 86 [*Crocus*] Plant..*autumn-flowering species in Aug. & Sept. **1861** HULME *Moquin-Tandon* II. IV. i. 234 The *Autumn Fly (*Conops Calcitrans*, Linn.)..bites the legs, especially on the approach of rain. **1620** VENNER *Via Recta* vii. 116 Lesse hurtfull then other *Autumne fruites. **1713** C'TESS. WINCHELSEA *Misc. Poems* 4 *Autumn-Leaves, which every Wind can chace. **1765** *Museum Rusticum* IV. l. 227 The winter frosts will have broke down the clods on to the roots of the *autumn-sown rye. **1883** *Daily News* 25 June 5/8 The autumn-sown wheat needed rain. **1960** *Farmer & Stockbreeder* 2 Feb. 115/1 Grazing autumn-sown wheat the following spring reduces the subsequent yield of grain. **1639** FULLER *Holy War* III. xi. (1840) 133 This short prosperity, like an *autumn-spring, came too late..to bring any fruit to maturity. **1870** MORRIS *Earthly Par.* I. II. 485 The changing year came round to *autumn-tide. **1884** J. HATTON in *Harper's Mag.* Feb. 346/1 *Autumn-tinted branches. **1795** SOUTHEY *Joan of Arc* III. 380 Wither'd leaves which *autumn winds Had drifted in.

autumn (ɔːtəm), *v.* [ad. L. *autumn-āre* to bring on autumn, (in late L.) to ripen; cf. AUGUST *v.*]

a. *trans.* To bring to maturity. **b.** *intr.* To come to maturity, ripen.

1771 *Muse in Miniature* 31 That life's fair spring may autumn into age.

autumnal (ɔːˈtʌmnəl), *a.* [ad. L. *autumnālis*, f. *autumnus* AUTUMN: cf. F. *automnal*, 16th c.]

1. Of, belonging or peculiar to, autumn.

autumnal equinox: the time when the sun crosses the equator as it proceeds southward. ***autumnal point***: the point at which the celestial equator is intersected by the ecliptic as the sun proceeds southward; the first point in Libra. ***autumnal signs***: the signs Libra, Scorpio, and Sagittarius. ***autumnal star*** (Gr. ἀστὴρ ὀπωρινός): Sirius.

1636 HEALEY *Theophrast.* To Reader, Posidion was the last Autumnall Moneth in the Attick yeere. **1678** HOBBES *Nat. Phil.* Wks. 1845 VII. 101 From the autumnal equinox to the vernal, there be one hundred and seventy-eight days. **1667** MILTON *P.L.* I. 302 Thick as Autumnal Leaves that strew the Brooks In Vallombrosa. **1791** COWPER *Iliad* v. 7 Bright and steady as the star Autumnal. **1855** MACAULAY *Hist. Eng.* III. 427 The autumnal rains of Ireland are usually heavy.

2. Maturing or blooming in autumn.

1574 T. NEWTON *Health Mag.* 52 Quinces among Autumnal fruictes are reckened..bindinge. **1727** BRADLEY *Fam. Dict.* s.v. *Flower*, Let him also plant..autumnal Crocus and Colchicums. **1861** MISS PRATT *Flower. Pl.* V. 273 Autumnal Squill..is a somewhat rare plant.

3. *fig.* Past the prime (of life).

1656 *Artif. Beauty* 59 When her own [haire], now more withered and autumnall, seemed less becoming her. **1728** YOUNG *Love Fame* v. (1757) 137 Autumnal Lyce carries in her face *Memento mori*. **1838** DICKENS *Old C. Shop* 38 Miss Melissa might have seen five and thirty summers or thereabouts, and verged on the autumnal.

auˈtumnally, *adv.* [f. prec. + -LY².] In an autumnal manner, with autumnal hues.

1872 M. COLLINS *Pr. Clar.* II. 130 Trees..autumnally tinted.

†**auˈtumnian**, *a. Obs.* [f. L. *autumn-us* AUTUMN + -IAN.] = AUTUMNAL.

1606 DEKKER *Sev. Sins* I. (Arb.) 11 And like Autumnian leaues dropt to the ground. **1610** *Histriom.* I. 270 Reach me the bowle with rich Autumnian Juice.

autumnity (ɔːˈtʌmnɪtɪ). ? *Obs.* [ad. L. *autumnitātem* the season or produce of autumn: see -ITY.] Autumn quality or conditions.

1599 BP. HALL *Sat.* III. i. 60 Thy furnace reeks Hot steams of wine; and can aloof descrie The drunken draughts of sweet autumnitie.

autumnize (ˈɔːtəmnaɪz), *v. rare.* [f. AUTUMN *sb.* + -IZE.] To make autumnal (in appearance).

1829 JESSE *Jrnl. Natur.* 109 When first the maple begins to autumnize the grove.

autumny (ˈɔːtəmɪ), *a.* [f. AUTUMN *sb.* + -Y¹.] Redolent of autumn, characteristic of the autumn season.

1916 C. S. LEWIS *Let.* 27 Sept. (1966) 30 The country at home was beginning to look nice and autumn-y with dead leaves in the lanes. **1926** *Glasgow Herald* 16 July 9 The air was distinctly 'autumny'. **1928** D. H. LAWRENCE *Let.* 12 Sept. (1962) II. 1089 Mountains are beginning to be misty and a bit damp and silent and autumny. **1941** E. BOWEN *Look at all those Roses* 112 The crushed, autumny grass.

autunite (ˈɔːtʌnaɪt). *Min.* [named (in 1852) from *Autun*, in France + -ITE.] A hydrous phosphate of lime and uranium, of citron- or sulphur-yellow colour; also called *lime-uranite*.

1852 BROOKE & MILLER *Phillips' Elem. Introd. Min.* 519 *Autunite*..found in crystals, massive, and investing other minerals, in granite at St. Symphorien near Autun. **1868** DANA *Min.* 586. **1957** *Financial Times Ann. Rev. Brit. Industry* 39/3 Others [*sc.* secondary ore minerals] from which smaller amounts of uranium have been produced, are ..the phosphates autunite and torbernite.

auturgy (ˈɔːtədʒɪ). Also 7 **autergy**. [ad. Gr. αὐτουργία, n. of quality f. αὐτουργός working oneself, f. αὐτο- (see AUTO-¹) self + ἔργον work.] Self-action, independent activity.

1651 BIGGS *New Disp.* Pref. 10 Nature's Autergie, not a whit belowe her self. **1656** BLOUNT *Glossogr.*, *Auturgie*, working with his own hand.

auxanography (ˌɔːksəˈnɒgrəfɪ). *Microbiol.* [ad. F. *auxanographie* (M. W. Beijerinck 1889, in *Archives Néerl. des Sci. Exactes* XXIII. 367), f. Gr. αὐξάν-ειν to increase + -OGRAPHY.] A method of studying the effects and interactions of various substances in promoting or inhibiting the growth of micro-organisms, by inducing diffusion gradients of the substances in agar plates on which the micro-organisms are grown. Hence **auˈxanogram**, a plate culture used in auxanography; ˌ**auxanoˈgraphic** *a.*

1905 GOULD *Dict. New Med. Terms* 108/2 *Auxanogram*, a pure plate culture of microbes which has been prepared by Beyerinck's auxanographic method in which the colonies indicate which one of several nutrient media is best suited to their growth. *Ibid.* 109/1 *Auxanography*, a method devised by Beyerinck for ascertaining which nutrient media are suitable for a growing microbe. Plate cultures of bad media ..are stippled with drops of solutions, the nutrient properties of which are to be tested. The species of microbe under examination will then develop strong colonies only on those spots where the requisite pabulum is present. **1949** H. W. FLOREY *Antibiotics* I. i. 35 The auxanogram method which consists in spreading one organism evenly on the surface of a solid medium and sowing the other at points or in streaks on it. **1949** G. PONTECORVO in *Jrnl. Gen. Microbiol.* III. 122 Sixty years ago..Beyerinck (Beijerinck) described a technique..for the study of the nutritional requirements of micro-organisms. The 'auxanographic' technique, as he called it, has gone almost unnoticed. *Ibid.*, The first kind of test, based on the promotion of growth, could perhaps be termed 'positive' auxanography.

auxanometer (ˌɔːksəˈnɒmɪtə(r)). [f. Gr. αὐξάνειν to increase + -OMETER.] An instrument for measuring growth in plants.

1878 MASTERS *Henfrey's Elem. Bot.* (ed. 3) 612 Where great accuracy and the measurement of minute spaces [in growth] are demanded, recourse must be had to special instruments called Auxanometers. **1887** BATESON & DARWIN in *Jrnl. Linn. Soc., Bot.* XXIV. 2 The increase in length was measured by means of an auxanometer-lever.

‖**auxesis** (ɔːkˈsiːsɪs). *Rhet.* [L., a. Gr. αὔξησις increase, amplification, f. αὐξ-άν-ειν to increase.]

1. Amplification: †**a.** A gradual increase in intensity of meaning. *Obs.* **b.** Hyperbole.

1577 H. PEACHAM *Gard. Eloq.* N. iiij (T.) By this figure, auxesis, the orator doth make a low dwarf a tall fellow..of pebble stones, pearls; and of thistles, mighty oaks. **1589** PUTTENHAM *Eng. Poesie* (Arb.) 226 Auxesis, or the Auancer ..as..He lost besides his children and his vvife, His realme, renovvne, liege, libertie and life. **1657** J. SMITH *Myst. Rhet.* 55 Auxesis, when we increase or advance the signification of a speech. **1751** CHAMBERS *Cycl.*, *Auxesis*, a figure whereby any thing is magnified too much.

2. *Biol., Plant Physiol.* (See quots.)

1848 DUNGLISON *Dict. Med. Sci.* (ed. 7) 96/2 *Auxesis*, augmentation, increase. **1900** B. D. JACKSON *Gloss. Bot. Terms* 28/1 *Auxesis*, (1) dilatation or increase in the valves of Diatoms, etc.; (2) new formation of organs (Czapek); (3) predominance of leaves, hairs, etc., on a particular side (Pfeffer). **1903** A. J. EWART tr. *Pfeffer's Physiol. of Plants* II. 73 The term 'auxesis' (*photoauxesis*) may be used to denote the predominant formation of leaves, roots, or hairs upon a particular side. **1940** *Nature* 9 Nov. 618/1 Botanists do still distinguish between *auxesis* or growth by expansion, and *merisis* or growth by cell-multiplication. **1953** *Faber Med. Dict.* 53/1 *Auxesis*, increase in size by cell expansion without cell division.

auxetic (ɔːkˈsɛtɪk), *a. Rhet.* [ad. L. *auxēticus*, Gr. αὐξητικός, f. αὐξητός, vbl. adj. of αὐξ-άν-ειν to increase.] **1.** Of, pertaining to, or characterized by auxesis; amplifying. †**auˈxetical** *a.*, = prec. **auˈxetically** *adv.*, by auxesis or amplification.

1740 T. HUTCHINSON *Cerem. Law* 8 *note*, Superadded—προσετέθη—this auxetic power is also observable in the epistle to Philemon *v.* 19. **1723** S. MATHER *Vind. Bible* 375 Thence it appears what an auxetical hyperbole Vossius used. **1652** URQUHART *Jewel* Wks. (1834) 292 Speeches extending a matter beyond what it is, auxetically, digressively.

2. *Biol., Plant Physiol.* Of or pertaining to a substance which stimulates cell growth. Also as *sb.*, such a substance.

1913 DORLAND *Med. Dict.* (ed. 7) 123/1 *Auxetic.* 1. Stimulating cell proliferation. 2. A substance which stimulates cell proliferation. **1918** [see AUGMENTOR 3].

auxetophone (ˈɔːksətəfəʊn). [f. Gr. αὐξητός that may be increased + φωνή sound.] A pneumatic recorder for a phonograph; also, a phonograph fitted with this recorder; an amplifying instrument. (Disused.)

1904 *Daily Chron.* 9 June 4/6 The Hon. C. A. Parsons.. has recently amused himself by devising a little valve called the auxetophone which promises..to advance the phonograph. **1907** *Ibid.* 6 Aug. 4/7 An instrument..known as the Auxetophone, gives..vocal and instrumental selections. **1934** A. Q. CARNEGIE in G. L. Parsons *Scientific Papers of C. A. Parsons* III. 244 In its perfected form, the auxetophone gave results, thirty years ago, which in volume and quality..have only just been approached by the electric gramophone and wireless loud-speakers of the last few years.

†**auˈxiliant**, *a. Obs.* [ad. L. *auxiliāntem*, pr. pple. of *auxiliāri* to help, assist, f. *auxili-um* help.] Affording help or assistance, auxiliary.

a **1631** DONNE *Select.* (1840) 111 Therefore we call them auxiliant graces, helping graces. **1677** GALE *Crt. Gentiles* II. IV. 92 The auxiliant or assistant Power.

auxiliar (ɔːgˈzɪlɪə(r)), *a.* and *sb. arch.* [ad. L. *auxiliār-is*, f. *auxili-um* help: see -AR¹.]

A. *adj.* AUXILIARY, helpful, assistant (*to*).

1583 *Exec. Treason* (1675) 38 The same Forces with other auxiliar Companies..landed. **1659** *Instruct. Oratory* 30 The Auxiliar verbs. **1718** POPE *Iliad* II. 987 Th' auxiliar troops and Trojan hosts appear. **1814** WORDSW. *Excurs.* IV. 1242 Subservient still to moral purposes, Auxiliar to divine.

B. *sb.* An AUXILIARY, helper, assistant; something which helps towards a purpose.

1670 MILTON *Hist. Brit.* Wks. 1738 II. 23 Two Cohorts more of Auxiliars..they quite intercepted. **1750** HARRIS *Hermes* I. iii. (1786) 25 Auxiliars, as when for *Bruti*, or *Bruto*, we say, *of Brutus, to Brutus*. **1859** G. MEREDITH *R. Feverel* II. xiii. 274 They could not have contracted alliance with an auxiliar more invaluable.

auxiliary (ɔːgˈzɪlɪərɪ), *a.* and *sb.* [ad. L. *auxiliārius*, f. *auxili-um* help: see -ARY¹.]

A. *adj.* Const. *to*.

1. a. Helpful, assistant, affording aid, rendering assistance, giving support or succour.

1605 BACON *Adv. Learn.* II. viii. §2 Mixed [mathematics] hath for subject some..parts of natural philosophy, and considereth quantity determined, as it is auxiliary and incident unto them. **1686** PLOT *Staffordsh.* 11 Calling upon the auxiliary name of Jesus to help her well home. **1857** BUCKLE *Civilis.* ii. 108 In a well-balanced mind, the imagination and the understanding..are auxiliary to each other.

esp. **b.** in warfare. See B. 2. Also in the names of various special ancillary services as: ***Auxiliary Air Force*** (formed 1917), ***Auxiliary Fire Service*** (formed 1937, absorbed in National Fire Service 1941), ***Auxiliary Territorial Service*** (formed 1938, replaced by the Women's Royal Army Corps in 1949) (see also A.T.S., separate entry).

1603 HOLLAND *Plutarch's Mor.* 404 To send unto him auxiliarie souldiers. **1862** MERIVALE *Rom. Emp.* (1865) VII. lvi. 109 Two auxiliary cohorts were cut to pieces. **1917** *Act 7 & 8 Geo. V.* c. 51 §6 It shall be lawful for His Majesty to raise and maintain an Air Force Reserve and an Auxiliary Air Force. **1925** *Times* 19 Feb. 17/3 The City of London Auxiliary Air Force Squadron..one of the first to be formed under the scheme for home defence against air attack. **1937** *Mem. on Emerg. Fire Brigade Organ.* (*Home Office*) 11 The Auxiliary Fire Service is one which should make a considerable appeal to many men. **1938** *Army Orders* Sept. 9 Our will and pleasure is that there shall be formed an organization to be designated the Auxiliary Territorial Service; Our further will and pleasure is that women may be enrolled in this Service. **1939** *War Illustr.* 23 Sept. p. iii/1 W.A.T.S. (Women's Auxiliary Territorial Service.) *Ibid.* 14 Oct. 151 (*caption*) Dame Helen Gwynne Vaughan, Director of the Auxiliary Territorial Service. **1940** *Ann. Reg. 1939* 86 The fighter and general reconnaissance squadrons of the Auxiliary Air Force had been called up. **1940** *Hutchinson's Pict. Hist. War* 2 Oct.–26 Nov. 168 Men of the Auxiliary Fire Service have been fully tested by raid conditions.

c. in *Grammar*: see B. 3. Formerly applied to any formative or subordinate elements of language, *e.g.* prefixes, prepositions; cf. AUXILIAR *sb.*

1677 PLOT *Oxfordsh.* 282 Expressing the auxiliary Particles of the English language, by distinct points and places about the radical or integral words. **1750** HARRIS *Hermes* (1841) 178. **1762** STERNE *Tr. Shandy* V. xliii. 146 The verbs auxiliary..are, *am, was, have, had, do, did, make*, etc. **1834** SOUTHEY *Doctor* I Our auxiliary verbs give us a power which the ancients, with all their varieties of mood, and inflections of tense, never could attain.

2. a. Subsidiary to the ordinary, additional. ***auxiliary language***, a language, esp. one invented for the purpose (*e.g.* Esperanto), used as a means of communication by speakers from two different language groups; an artificial language (see ARTIFICIAL *a.* 5).

a **1687** PETTY *Pol. Arith.* ii. (1691) 49 Auxiliary Seamen, are such as have another Trade besides, wherewith to maintain themselves, when they are not employed at Sea. **1869** SIR E. REED *Ship-build.* ii. 43 To employ side-keels, which are..known as 'drift-keels,' 'auxiliary keels,' 'bilge-keels.' **1877** W. THOMSON *Voy. Challenger* II. i. 14 There is an auxiliary eye on each of the maxillæ. **1905** *Westm. Gaz.* 15 Aug., Esperanto aims at becoming a generally accepted 'auxiliary language'. **1939** *Nature* 29 Apr. 717/1 The value of an auxiliary language as an agency for world peace.

b. *Music.* (See quot.)

1864 WEBSTER, *Auxiliary scales*, the six keys or scales, consisting of any key major, with its relative minor, and the relative keys of each. **1873** BANISTER *Music* §225-6 Auxiliary notes are notes one degree above or below essential or unessential notes, preceding such notes, either with or before the accompanying harmony..The *Appoggiatura*, *Acciaccatura*, etc., are examples of such notes.

B. *sb.*

1. One who renders help or gives assistance; a helper, assistant, confederate, ally; *also*, that which gives help, a source or means of assistance.

1656 COWLEY *Davideis* IV. Wks. 1710 II. 439 He Rains and Winds for Auxiliaries brought. **1660** JER. TAYLOR *Duct. Dubit.* I. ii. Wks. IX. 79 Suspected to take in auxiliaries from the spirits of darkness. **1769** ROBERTSON *Chas. V*, V. II. 250 The appearance of such a vigorous auxiliary..was at first matter of great joy to Luther. **1862** MARSH *Eng. Lang.* iv. 67 A knowledge of certain other languages is a highly useful auxiliary in the study of our own.

2. *Mil.* (usually in *pl.*) Foreign or allied troops in the service of a nation at war.

1601 R. JOHNSON *Kingd. & Commw.* 193 They maintaine three sorts of soldiers..the third are Auxiliaries, which serue for pay. **1692** DRYDEN *St. Euremont's Ess.* 23 When Xantippus, a Lacedæmonian, arrived with a Body of Auxiliaries. **1862** MERIVALE *Hist. Rom. Emp.* (1865) VII. lvi. 109 A Gaul and a Roman happened to challenge one another to wrestle; the legionary fell, the auxiliary mocked him.

3. *Gram.* A verb used to form the tenses, moods, voices, etc. of other verbs.

They include *auxiliaries* of periphrasis, which assist in expressing the interrogative, negative, and emphatic forms of speech, viz. *do* (*did*); auxiliaries of tense, *have, be, shall, will*; of mood, *may, should, would*; of voice, *be*; of predication (i.e. vbs. of incomplete predication which require a verbal complement), *can, must, ought, need*, also *shall, will, may*, when not auxiliaries of tense or mood.

1762 STERNE *Tr. Shandy* V. xlii. 145 The use of the Auxiliaries. **1835** *Penny Cycl.* III. 160/1 After the verb *to be*, the next in importance among the auxiliaries is the verb *to have*. **1878** MORRIS & BOWEN *Eng. Gram. Exerc. Prim.* 70 In deciding whether a verb is an auxiliary or not, it is necessary to decide whether it marks the time or the manner of action of another verb, or whether it makes the subject, or thing spoken of, the doer or sufferer of the action. If it does none of these things, then it is no auxiliary.

4. *Math.* A quantity introduced for the purpose of simplifying or facilitating some operation, as in equations or trigonometrical formulæ.

† **au'xiliate**, *v. Obs.* [f. L. *auxiliāt-* ppl. stem of *auxiliāri*: see above.] To help, assist.

1656 in BLOUNT *Glossogr.* **1657** TOMLINSON *Renou's Disp.* 150 Whose tenuity that we may auxiliate. **1667** WATERHOUSE *Fire Lond.* 34 A just and severe judgement..auxiliated and perfected by concurrence of circumstances.

† **auxili'ation.** *Obs. rare*⁻¹. [ad. L. *auxiliātiōn-em*, n. of action f. *auxiliāri*: see AUXILIANT and -ATION.] Assistance, help.

1657 TOMLINSON *Renou's Disp.* 472, I have in three books, by Gods auxiliation, briefly..composed all medicinal matter.

† **au'xiliatory**, *a.* and *sb. Obs.* [f. L. *auxiliātor*, n. of agent f. *auxiliāri.*] = AUXILIARY.

1599 SANDYS *Europæ Spec.* (1632) 139 The purchasing of Masses both auxiliatorie and expiatorie. **1657** TOMLINSON *Renou's Disp.* 499 It is a special auxiliatory in..inflammations. **1678** CUDWORTH *Intell. Syst.* I. iv. §32. 501 God..hath about himself Innumerable Auxiliatory Powers.

auxin ('ɔːksɪn). *Plant Physiol.* [G. (F. Kögl & A. J. Haagen Smit 1931, in *Proc. Sect. Sci. Kon. Akad. v. Wetenschappen* XXXIV. 1416), f. Gr. αὔξ-ειν to increase + -IN¹.] An organic substance which promotes and directs the growth of plant cells; a growth hormone.

1934 *Brit. Chem. Abstr.* A. 1332/1 Plant growth substances. X. Constitution of auxin-*a* and -*b*. **1936** *Ann. Reg. 1935* 56 Auxin *a* is an organic hydroxy-acid, Auxin *β* is a keto-acid. **1937** *Discovery* June 174/1 Putting a block of auxin-charged agar on one side of a coleoptile stump. **1937** WENT & THIMANN *Phytohormones* 4 The term *auxins*..will be arbitrarily restricted to those substances which bring about the specific growth reaction which is conveniently measurable by the curvature of *Avena* coleoptiles. **1955** *Sci. News Let.* 16 July 44/1 A plant growth hormone called auxin controls the shedding of leaves in the fall and the dropping of fruit when it is ripe.

auxochrome ('ɔːksəʊkrəʊm). [G. (O. N. Witt 1888, in *Ber. d. Deut. Chem. Ges.* XXI. I. 325), f. Gr. αὔξ-ειν to increase + -O + χρῶμα colour.] Any salt-forming group that, when combined with a chromogen, produces a dyestuff. Hence **auxochromic** (-'krəʊmɪk), **auxochromous** (-'krəʊməs), *adjs.*, defining such groups.

1892 COLLIN & RICHARDSON tr. *Nietzki's Chem. Org. Dyestuffs* i. 13 The chromophoric quinone group confers strong acid properties on the auxochromic hydroxyl group. **1893** *Athenæum* 15 July 100/1 They [*sc.* chromogens] become true dyestuffs by the introduction of..what Witt terms auxochromes. **1902** *Brit. Jrnl. Photogr.* 11 Apr. 299 Auxochromic groups. **1902** *Encycl. Brit.* XXVII. 564/2 Such compounds containing chromophorous groups are termed chromogens, because, although not dyestuffs themselves, they are capable of generating such by the further introduction of salt-forming atomic groups—*e.g.*, OH, NH_2. These Witt terms auxochromous groups. **1953** J. RAMSBOTTOM *Mushrooms & Toadstools* ix. 102 Other groups (–OH, –OCH_3, –CO_2H, NH_2), known as auxochromes, modify this basal colour in various ways.

auxospore ('ɔːksəʊspɔː(r)). *Bot.* [f. Gr. αὔξ-ειν to increase + -O + σπόρος, σπορά SPORE.] A spore formed in diatoms by the union of two cells or by the excessive growth of an individual cell. Also, the resting-spore of the diatoms.

1884 MASTERS & BENNETT *Henfrey's Elem. Bot.* (ed. 4) 425 The individuals must..constantly diminish in size, until the original size is restored by the production of auxospores. **1888** *Encycl. Brit.* XXIV. 126/2 *Diatomaceæ*... Reproduction, vegetative by division or by means of asexually-produced spores (auxospores). **1904** G. S. WEST *Brit. Fresh-water Algæ* 269 A normal auxospore can be regarded as one produced by the conjugation of two cells (or gametes), those produced without conjugation being parthenogenetic.

auxotroph ('ɔːksəʊtrəʊf, -trɒf). *Genetics.* [f. L. *aux-ilium* help + -O + Gr. τροφή nourishment.] A mutant bacterium, fungus, etc., which has an additional nutritional requirement compared with the original strain; a naturally occurring bacterium with a requirement for a specific nutrient.

1950 DAVIS & MINGIOLI in *Jrnl. Bacteriol.* LX. 17 The terms 'auxotrophic'..and the corresponding noun 'auxotroph' are suggested for convenience in denoting biochemical mutants with increased nutritional requirements. **1953** *Ann. N.Y. Acad. Sci.* LVI. 844 Algae, like autotrophic bacteria, may be divided into auxotrophs and non-auxotrophs. **1971** M. ALEXANDER *Microbial Ecol.* v. 109 Auxotrophs are ubiquitous, and though their proliferation denotes that their needs are satisfied, the level of growth factors in nature and their significance..have been the subject of only modest inquiry, except in water and soil. **1976** *Ann. Rev. Microbiol.* XXX. 92 Other auxotrophs such as those requiring amino acids, purines, and pyrimidines do not assume a colonial or semicolonial growth habit if the biochemical supplement in the medium is limiting. **1980** *Nature* 3 Jan. 106/1 The fact that we were able to detect auxotrophs among the bacterial strains tested suggests that certain vitamin and amino acid requirements do not necessarily represent a selective disadvantage to the bacteria that possess them.

Also **auxo'trophic** *a.*, of, pertaining to, or being an auxotroph; **auxo'trophically** *adv.*; **au'xotrophy**, the state or condition of being auxotrophic.

1950 Auxotrophic [see above]. **1953** *Ann. N.Y. Acad. Sci.* LVI. 839 The relative incidence of auxotrophy in coastal and oceanic phytoplankton species. **1968** W. HAYES *Genetics of Bacteria & their Viruses* (ed. 2) x. 210 Auxotrophic mutants of bacteria are..widely used in biochemical as well as in genetic research. **1973** R. G. KRUEGER et al. *Introd. Microbiol.* xv. 412/2 Each of the auxotrophic strains was spread separately in large numbers..on plates of synthetic medium lacking the necessary nutritional supplements needed for the repair of defects caused by auxotrophy. **1976** *Ann. Rev. Microbiol.* XXX. 45 Since many exoproteins lack cysteine, starvation of *cys*⁻ mutants for their auxotrophic requirement appears to offer a potential method for separating exoprotein synthesis from general cellular protein synthesis. *Ibid.* 395 A problem that has long hampered *Caulobacter* workers in the efficient isolation of auxotrophically marked strains is the relative resistance to mutagenesis exhibited by several *Caulobacter* species. **1977** R. Y. STANIER et al. *Gen. Microbiol.* (ed. 4) 35 Auxotrophy, represented by an absolute requirement for one or more vitamins, is characteristic of many photoautotrophic algae and bacteria. **1982** *Jrnl. Bacteriol.* CLI. 708 Mutants of *Escherichia coli* K-12 auxotrophic for thiamine phosphates were produced in stepwise fashion.

auxunge, obs. form of AXUNGE.

av-. From the Norman Conquest (rarely before) to *c* 1625, *v* was treated merely as an initial *shape* of the letter *u*, which had the phonetic value of both *u* and *v*, e.g. *vnto* unto, *vile* vile, *ouer* over, *full* full, *loue* love. Hence, during this period, *au-* was commonly written for *av-*. All such words are here entered under AV-.

ava, ava' (ə'vɑː), *phr. Sc.* [worn-down form of *of all*: see A *adj.*³ and OF.] Of all; at all.

1768 ROSS *Helenore* 145 (JAM.) She neither kent spinning nor carding, Nor brewing nor baking ava'. *a* **1796** BURNS *Answ. Poet. Epist.* xii, This pleased them warst ava.

‖**ava** ('ɑːvə), *sb.* Native name in the Sandwich Islands of a species of Cordyline yielding an intoxicating liquor; also applied to the liquor itself, and *gen.* to any intoxicant spirit.

1831 TYERMAN & BENN. *Voy.* II. xxix. 43 Drinking ava, a rank inebriating spirit. **1845** DARWIN *Voy. Nat.* xviii. 410 The dark-green knotted stem of the Ava, so famous in former days for its powerful intoxicating effects. *Ibid.* 412 All the ava (as the natives call all ardent spirits) was poured on the ground.

avadavat. Corruption of AMADAVAT, q.v. [The latter is itself a corruption of *Ahmadābād*, name of a town in Goojerat. Col. Yule.]

[**1698** FRYER *Acc. E. India & P.* 116 In Amidavad small Birds, who..Fifty in a cage, make an admirable Chorus.] **1735** ALBIN *Nat. Hist. Birds* Supp. 72 Amaduvad. **1878** BESANT & RICE *Celia's Arb.* I. iii. 34 Avvadavats, Japanese sparrows, lovebirds.

† **'avage, 'avisage.** *Obs.* [Cf. F. *avage* 'droit que les exécuteurs de la haute justice levaient en argent ou en nature en quelques lieux, et certains jours de marché' (Littré).] A payment made by tenants of the manor of Writtel, Essex, for the privilege of feeding pigs in the manor woods.

1670 in BLOUNT *Law Dict.*

avail (ə'veɪl), *v.* Forms: 4-7 au-avail(e, au-avayle, 4-5 au-availl(e, aveile, 5-6 au-avaylle, avayl, aduayle, 4- avail. *North.* 4-5 avalȝe, awaill, awailȝe, awayle, 5-6 awale: see AV-. [Not in Fr.; apparently formed on the simple VAIL *v.* (ad. F. *vaille*, f. *valoir* to be worth:—L. *valēre*) as if this were an aphetic form; cf. *gree, agree, mount, amount*, etc. Both vb. and sb. were occas. spelt *advayle* in 15-16th c. on assumed L. analogies: see AD- *pref.* 2. In senses 1-3 chiefly in negative or interrogative sentences.]

I. Regular senses.

1. a. *intr.* To have force or efficacy for the accomplishment of a purpose; to be effectual, serviceable, or of use; to afford help.

a **1300** *Cursor M.* 90 Quat bote is to sette traueil On thyng þat may not auail. **1494** FABYAN VII. 357 But all aduayled ryght nought. **1567** MAPLET *Gr. Forest* 23 Zellicum.. availeth against venome. **1583** STANYHURST *Aeneis* II. (Arb.) 68 This labor..too no great purpose auayleth. **1667** MILTON *P.L.* XI. 312 But prayer against his absolute Decree No more availes than breath against the winde. **1718** POPE *Iliad* VII. 176 Nor aught the warrior's thundering mace avail'd. **1818** SCOTT *Rob Roy* i, 'Words avail very little with me, young man,' said my father. **1836** J. GILBERT *Chr. Atonem.* iii. 69 No ingenuity can avail to confound them.

† **b.** of persons. *Obs.*

c **1450** LONELICH *Grail* xx. 204 Thanne of his knyhtes he axede counsaille, ȝif to that roche they cowden owght availle. **1542** UDALL *Erasm. Apophth.* 4, I auaile moche more, saieth he, in that I teach all thother Phisicians.

c. † ***avalȝe que valȝe*** (mod.F. *vaille que vaille*): let it avail what it may, come what may. *Obs.*

1375 BARBOUR *Bruce* IX. 147 Thai wuld defend, avalȝe que valȝe. [**1552** LYNDESAY *Papyngo* 161, I wyll, said scho, ascend, vailȝe quod vailȝe.]

2. *intr.* To be of value, profit, or advantage.

1375 BARBOUR *Bruce* I. 336 For knawlage off mony statis May quhile awailȝe full mony gatis. **1538** STARKEY *England* 37 What avaylyth hyt to have ryches..to hym wych can not by wysdome use them. **1583** STANYHURST *Aeneis* II. (Arb.) 46 Whilst counsel auayled, Then we were of reckning. **1844** DISRAELI *Coningsby* VII. vii. 275 What avail his golden youth, his high blood..if they help not now?

3. *trans.* (the obj. was at first *dative*.) To be of use or advantage to; to benefit, profit; to help, assist: **a.** a person.

a **1300** *Cursor M.* 7992 þou folu it [consail], þe sal it a-wail. *c* **1384** CHAUCER *H. Fame* 363 Al hir compleynt..avayleth hir not a stre. **1465** *Paston Lett.* 498 II. 175 They [will] not [be] so avaylled as they weene. **1611** BIBLE *Esther* v. 13 All this auaileth me nothing, so long as I see Mordecai the Iew sitting at the kings gate. **1742** RICHARDSON *Pamela* IV. 209 What avails it me to oppose them? **1816** J. WILSON *City of Plague* II. v. 89 Right pious words! but they will not avail thee.

† **b.** a thing (*e.g.* a cause, disease). *Obs.*

c **1374** CHAUCER *Troylus* I. 20 If this may done gladnesse To any louer, and his cause aueile. **1576** BAKER *Gesner's Jewell Health* 89 b, This also much avayleth and helpeth any passion of the bodie.

† **4.** *refl.* To benefit or advantage oneself. *Obs.*

1787 G. WHITE *Selborne* v. (1789) 14 They availed themselves greatly by spinning wool.

5. esp. ***to avail oneself of*** (in Shaksp., elliptically, ***to avail of***): **a.** to benefit oneself or profit by; to take advantage of, turn to account. (With *indirect passive*, esp. in U.S.)

1603 SHAKS. *Meas. for M.* III. i. 243 But how of this can shee auaile? **1667** MILTON *P.L.* XII. 515 Then shall they seek to avail themselves of names, Places, and titles. **1860** TYNDALL *Glac.* I. §1. 1, I..availed myself of my position to make an excursion into North Wales. **1861** EMERSON *Cond. Life* 24 Power..must be availed of, and not by any means let off and wasted. **1899** *Westm. Gaz.* 25 Aug. 4/1 It is now definitely settled that the Admiralty..will avail of the opportunity..for the renewal of the subsidies. **1927** *Daily Tel.* 30 Aug. 8/6 The wonderful system of drainage is being availed of.

b. to make use of, use, employ.

1768 STERNE *Sent. Journ.* (1778) I. 119 La Fleur availed himself but of two different terms of exclamation in this encounter. **1838** Dickens *Lett.* (1880) I. 7, I have availed myself of the very first opportunity of writing.

6. *to avail upon* (a person): to take advantage of, impose upon. *rare.*

1866 Carlyle *Remin.* (1881) II. 115 Very independent where mere rank etc. attempted to avail upon him.

7. *causal.* To give (a person) the benefit or advantage of; hence *ellipt.* to give him the advantage of knowing, to inform, assure *of.* (Only in U.S.)

1785 T. Jefferson *Corr.* Wks. 1859 I. 418 It will rest, therefore, with you, to avail Mr. Barclay of that fund. **1789** —— *Writ.* (1859) III. 22, I shall avail government of the useful information I have received from you. *a* **1794** Witherspoon *Wks.* IV. 296 (Bartlett), The members of a popular government should be continually availed of the.. condition of every part. **1843** Mrs. Trollope *Barnabys in Amer.* xviii. 119 'We should have got no invites, you may be availed of that, I expect.'

II. Isolated senses after L. *valēre.*

†**8.** *intr.* To do well, prosper, profit. *Obs.*

1523 Ld. Berners *Froiss.* I. viii. 6 Your besynesse shall auayle moche the better. **1560** Whitehorne *Arte Warre* (1573) 98 b, To take the commoditie from the enemie, that he availe not by the things of thy country. **1563** Hyll *Arte Garden.* (1593) 44 Al such partes which may be holpen by cooling, may with the iuice of it.. annointed on those places, greatly auaile.

†**9.** *trans.* To be worth or equivalent to. *Obs.*

1582–8 *Hist. Jas. VI* (1804) 25 A ressonabill pecuniall sowme, availling a thowsand punds money of Scotland. **1598** Barret *Theor. Warres* III. ii. 70 One shot well bestowed, auayleth many vnaduisedly spent.

avail (ə'veɪl), *sb.* Forms: 5–8 **au-availe,** 5–7 **au-avayle,** 5 **au-availle, au-avayll(e,** 5–6 **advail(le, advayle,** 5– **avail.** *North.* 5 **awayle, awaylle, aweyle,** 6 **availl, avale.** See Av-. [f. prec. vb.; or perhaps on vail *sb.*, which seems, however, to be later, and may itself be an aphetic form of this.]

1. Beneficial effect; advantage, benefit, profit. *arch.* or *Obs.* exc. as in 4.

c **1420** *Pallad. on Husb.* I. 850 For anntes eke an oules herte availe is To putte upon her bedde. *Ibid.* III. 497 Croppe and tail To save.. is thyne advail. **1489** Caxton *Faytes of A.* I. xxiv. 76 Thus they may lette more than doo eny auayll. **1600** Tourneur *Transf. Metam.* lxiii, Both usde their blades unto so good availe. **1694** *Lond. Gaz.* 2959/3 Which Horses.. are to be rouped.. to the best avail. **1871** *Daily News* 24 July, Taking avail of the cover.

†**b.** *to have at avail*: i.e. at an advantage. *Obs.*

1470–85 Malory *Arthur* I. xxiii, Hym thought no worship to haue a knyght at suche auaille, he to be on horsbak and he on foot. *c* **1500** in Furniv. *Percy Folio* I. 107 So shalt thou nott skape.. I have thee nowe at avayle.

†**2.** Assistance, help, aid. *Obs.* exc. as in 4.

c **1450** Lonelich *Grail* xiii. 475 And ȝit kepte Tholome to his availles, In his refrescheng, twey batailles. **1556** Abp. Parker *Ps.* ix. 10 For their aduayle thou wilt not fayle, All them that thee do seeke. **1640** Sanderson *21 Serm.* Ad. Aul. xii. (1673) 169 Furtherance or avail towards the attaining of that end.

†**3.** Value, estimation. *Obs.* or *arch.*

1513 Douglas *Æneis* IX. Prol. 50 The cur, or mastis, he haldis at small availl. **1631** J. Taylor (Water P.) *Fort. Wheele* (1848) 13 They hold your blessinge in no more avayle, Then is the flapping of a fox his taile! **1846** Sir W. Hamilton *Logic* (1866) II. App. 252 It is only as indefinite that particular, it is only as definite that individual and general, quantities have any (and the same) logical avail.

4. *of avail*: of advantage or assistance in accomplishing a purpose, effective, effectual. ***of no avail, without avail***: ineffectual. ***to little avail***: with little effect, ineffectually, to little purpose.

c **1450** *Crt. of Love* 116 Cloth of gold.. And other silk of easier availe. *a* **1704** Locke (J.) Truth, light upon this way, is of no more avail to us than errour. **1810** Southey *Kehama* XI. 11 The impervious mail, The shield and helmet of avail. **1814** Chalmers *Evid. Chr. Revel.* i. 12 The highest sagacity is of no avail, when there is an insufficiency of data. **1817** Jas. Mill *Brit. India* II. IV. v. 177 He found all he could urge without avail. **1862** Grote *Greece* xl. III. 434 Bows and arrows were of little avail. **1881** Buchanan *God & Man* I. 281 This he did, but to little avail.

5. *concr.* (chiefly *pl.*) Profits or proceeds of business transactions; remuneration or perquisites of employment. Cf. vails. (*Obs.* exc. *U.S.*)

c **1449** Pecock *Repr.* 392 A riȝt forto.. haue certeyn fruytis or sum othir avail. **1483** Caxton *G. de la Tour* M. viij, [He] promysed hym.. grete auaylles and prouffytees. **1568** T. Howell *Arb. Amitie* (1879) 83 The Marchant.. Doth ioy for gaine of his auailes. **1601** Holland *Pliny* II. 476 This [Minium] setleth down to the bottom of the water.. and the painters take it for their auailes. *a* **1733** North *Exam.* II. iv. ¶59. 260 Which.. is no small Availes of a Discoverer that has the selling the Copies. **1860** Hawthorne *Marble Faun* (1879) II. xviii. 180 The avails are devoted to some beneficent.. purpose.

avail(e, avayle, var. avale *v. Obs.* to go down.

availability (əˌveɪlə'bɪlɪtɪ). [f. next: see -bility.]

1. The quality of being available; capability of being employed or made use of.

1803 W. Taylor in *Ann. Rev.* I. 439 It is not in celebrity ..but in availability that he places importance. **1862** R. Patterson *Ess. Hist. & Art* 224 The distance and difficulty of access to the minerals are formidable impediments to their availability.

b. *spec.* in U.S. 'That qualification in a candidate which implies or supposes a strong probability of his success, apart from substantial merit,—a probability resulting from mere personal or accidental popularity.' J. Inman in Bartlett *Dict. Amer.*

1848 *N.Y. Herald* May (in Bartlett *Dict. Amer.*), Availability, not merit or qualifications, is the only requisite to secure a nomination. **1870** Lowell *Study Wind.* 158 He was.. nominated for his availability,—that is, because he had no history.

2. *concr.* That which is available.

1867 O. W. Holmes *Guard. Angel* I. iv. 64 His list of possible availabilities in the matrimonial line. **1876** Blackmore *Cripps* III. x. 170 Against the gate-post she settled her most substantial availability, and exerted it.

available (ə'veɪləb(ə)l), *a.* Also 5–6 **advayl-, au-avayl-,** 6–7 **auail-, au- avayle-, au- availeable.** [f. avail *v.* + -able.]

I. That may avail. *arch.*

1. Capable of producing a desired result; of avail, effectual, efficacious. *arch.* or *Obs.* exc. as in b.

1502 *Ord. Crysten Men* (W. de W. 1506) III. iii. 162 Y^t^ wyll make his prayers avaylable. **1585** Abp. Sandys *Serm.* (1841) 67 That the mass is a sacrifice available for quick and dead. **1605** Timme *Quersit.* I. iii. 63 That oyle.. being as auailable against the falling sicknesse as vitriol. *a* **1699** Lady Halkett *Autobiog.* 32 Nothing I could do could be available.

b. in *Law.* Valid.

1451 *Scotch Hom.* in Rymer's *Foedera* (1710) XI. 291 Most advaylable in the Law. **1574** tr. *Littleton's Tenures* 106 a, A release is not avaylable to the tenant.. but where a privitye is betwene him, and him y^t^ releaseth. **1622** Malynes *Anc. Law-Merch.* 453 After which the bill is held as confessed and au[a]ileable. **1768** Blackstone *Comm.* II. 275 And all charges by him lawfully made.. shall be good and available in law. **1876** Digby *Real Prop.* v. §1. 207 Leasehold interests became rights of property (or rights available not only against the lessor, but also against all the world).

2. Of advantage; serviceable, beneficial, profitable (*to, unto*). *arch.* (The last quotation passes into 3.)

1474 Caxton *Chesse* II. v. Div, To be pietous in herte.. is avaylable to alle thyng. **1598** Barret *Theor. Warres* I. ii. 13 It shall be wonderfull auaileable for him to reade Histories. **1614** Raleigh *Hist. World* II. IV. vii. §1. 248 His Mother Veturia, and Volumnia his Wife.. were more auaileable to Rome, than was any force of Armes. **1836** *Recoll. Ho. Lords* xvi. 389 Where fair argument is available to his side of the question.. he does not have recourse to sophistry.

II. That may be 'availed of.'

3. Capable of being employed with advantage or turned to account; *hence*, capable of being made use of, at one's disposal, within one's reach.

1827 Faraday *Exp. Res.* xli. §12. 226 This quantity is.. wholly available in the liquid when used as a bleaching agent. **1833** I. Taylor *Fanat.* x. 476 The epistle to the Romans.. is available as proof. **1860** Tyndall *Glac.* I. §12. 86 We spent every available hour upon the ice. **1868** Rogers *Pol. Econ.* xv. 213 Lenders.. wish.. to have their assets as available as they can. **1868** Freeman *Norm. Conq.* II. 386 There was no available candidate of the old princely line.

a'vailableness. [f. prec. + -ness.]

†**1.** Capability of producing a desired result; efficacy. *Obs.*

1677 Hale *Prim. Orig. Man.* 225 The efficacy, or availableness, or accommodation, or suitableness of these Reductives to the end proposed.

2. = availability 1, 1 b.

1837 J. H. Newman *Proph. Off. Ch.* 41 The accuracy and availableness of their existing Tradition. **1841** Emerson *Conserv.* (1875) II. 274 It goes for availableness in its candidate and not for worth.

a'vailably, *adv.* [f. as prec. + -ly².]

†**1.** Effectively, serviceably, advantageously. *Obs.*

1530–1 *Act 22 Hen. VIII*, xv, His said free pardon.. shall be.. taken.. most beneficially and auailablye to all.. his sayed subiectes. **1655** Gouge *Comm. Heb.* xiii. 1 How to do any thing acceptably to God, or availably to his own salvation.

2. So as to be capable of being employed.

1875 Whitney *Life Lang.* x. 197 Such means as lie most availably at hand. **1879** G. Macdonald *P. Faber* II. vii. 114 The moment his property was his availably.

†**a'vailant,** *a. Obs. rare.* [f. avail *v.* + -ant after ppl. adjs. from Fr.] = availing.

c **1420** *Pallad. on Husb.* XII. 126 A serpent skynne doon on this tree men lete Avaylant be to save it in greet hete.

availer (ə'veɪlə(r)). [f. as prec. + -er¹.] One who avails, is serviceable or helpful.

1598 Florio, *Giouatore*, an auayler, a helper, a succorer.

†**a'vailful,** *a. Obs.* [f. avail *sb.* + -ful.] Of much avail, of advantage; serviceable, profitable. (A good word, taking up the earlier sense of available.)

1598 Florio, *Giouéuole*, helpefull, auailefull, profitable. **1603** —— *Montaigne* (1634) 463 Beautie is the true availefull advantage of women. **1650** H. Brooke *Conserv. Health* 169 Riding is availful for the stomach.

†**a'vailfully,** *adv. Obs.* [f. prec. + -ly².] With good effect, with advantage, profitably.

1603 Florio *Montaigne* III. vi. (1632) 505 The Hungarians did very availefully bring them [war-chariots] into fashion. *Ibid.* 524 Availefully to employ the same.

a'vailing, *vbl. sb.* [f. avail *v.* + -ing¹.] The action of the vb. avail; benefiting, profiting.

1562 J. Heywood *Prov. & Epigr.* (1867) 180 Great losse, small auaylyng.

a'vailing, *ppl. a.* [f. as prec. + -ing².] Advantageous, profitable; of beneficial efficiency.

c **1420** *Pallad. on Husb.* I. 562 To faat hem is avayling and plesaunte. **1850** Mrs. Browning *Substitution* Poems I. 327 Speak Thou, availing Christ! **1862** Ruskin *Unto this Last* 118 A truly valuable or availing thing is that which leads to life with its whole strength.

availingly (ə'veɪlɪŋlɪ), *adv.* [f. availing *ppl. a.* + -ly².] In an availing manner; so as to avail or profit.

1853 Faber *Ess. Lives of Saints* 116 Its intrinsic beauty pleads availingly with the man of letters. **1871** *Contemp. Rev.* XIX. 136 Neither the royal Placet,.. nor the right to convene synods, could be availingly employed.

availment (ə'veɪlmənt). [f. avail *v.* + -ment.] The fact of being beneficially effective.

1699 Boyer *Fr. Dict.* (1759) s.v., It is of little availment with me, *Cela ne me sert presque à rien.* **1865** Bp. Forbes *Nourishm. Soul* vii. 76 Prayer.. gives to us great availment with God.

†**a'vailsome,** *a. Obs.* [f. avail *sb.* + -some; cf. *troublesome.*] Of avail, serviceable, effectual.

1619 Sclater *Exp. Thess.* (1627) II. Ep. Ded., [If in] furtherance of Faith.. this poore paines may be auailesome.

‖**aval.** [F., f. phr. *à val* at the bottom:—L. *ad vallem*: see avale *v.*] An endorsement (*lit.* a writing 'at the bottom') on a commercial document, guaranteeing payment of it.

1880 Ld. Blackburn in *Law Rep., Appeal* V. 772 An indorsement.. by what was called an aval.. either on the bill itself or a separate paper.

avalanche ('ævəlɑːnʃ, -lænʃ, ævə'lɑːnʃ, -'lænʃ), *sb.* [a. F. *avalanche*, dial. form of *avalance* 'descent,' f. *avaler*: see avale. *L'avalanche* also appears dialectally as *la valanche*, It. *valanca, valanga*; also *lavanche, lavange*, either a purely phonetic transposition, or due to association with It. *lava* torrent, gully, f. *lavare* to wash.]

1. A large mass of snow, mixed with earth and ice, loosened from a mountain side, and descending swiftly into the valley below.

[**1765** *Nat. Hist.* in *Ann. Reg.* 86/1 The Clergyman.. percieving a noise towards the top of the mountains, looked up, and descried two valancas driving headlong towards the village. **1766** Smollett *Trav.* xxxviii. 337 Scarce a year passes in which some mules and their drivers do not perish by the valanches.] **1771** Pennant *Tour Scotland* 111, I have seen these *spates*.. lie cross the roads, as the *avelenches*, or snow-falls, do those of the *Alps.* **1787** *Monthly Rev.* LXXVII. 533 They were also apprehensive of exposing themselves to the *Avalanches*, which are frequently tumbling from the summit of the mountain. **1789** Coxe *Trav. Switz.* xxxviii. II. 3 We crossed some snow, the remains of a last winter's Avalanche. **1817** Byron *Manfr.* I. ii. 75 Ye avalanches, whom a breath draws down. **1870** H. Macmillan *Bible Teach.* ii. 31 The muffled roar of a distant avalanche.

2. *transf.* and *fig.*

1850 Mrs. Stowe *Uncle Tom's C.* xxxviii. 334 Overwhelmed by the avalanche of cruelty and wrong which had fallen upon her. **1850** Carlyle *Latter-d. Pamphl.* v. (1872) 153 Unable longer to endure such an avalanche of forgeries. *c* **1854** Stanley *Sinai & Pal.* (1858) Introd. 41 This mass of ruins.. rolled down in avalanches of stones.

3. *Comb.* and *attrib.*, as ***avalanche-like, -theory***; **avalanche lily,** any one of several large erythroniums found near the snow-line in N. America.

1877 Rosenthal *Muscles & Nerves* 122 Pflüger spoke of it as an avalanche-like increase in the excitement within the nerves. **1912** A. O. Wheeler *Selkirk Mts.* 74 The avalanche lilies.. which follow the edges of the glaciers. **1952** in *Jrnl. Canad. Ling. Assoc.* (1956) II. 28 The grass was starred with white anemones and yellow avalanche lilies. **1963** W. S. Avis et al. *Dict. Canad. Eng.* (*Intermediate*) 58/2 *Avalanche lily*, the dogwood violet of the Rockies. **1881** *Syd. Soc. Lex.*, He explains this by the avalanche theory, according to which nervous influence gathers force as it descends.

avalanche ('ævəlɑːnʃ, -lænʃ), *v.* [f. avalanche *sb.*] *intr.* To descend in or like an avalanche. Also *trans.*, to carry by or as by an avalanche.

1872 'Mark Twain' *Roughing It* iv. 16 We avalanched from one end of the stage[-coach] to the other. **1897** *Daily News* 31 Mar. 6/5 He was gently avalanched downstairs into the street. **1899** Somerville & 'Ross' *Irish R.M.* 244, I avalanched down the companion. **1923** *Daily Mail* 23 June 7 The boulders on the edge are continually avalanching down. **1957** Clark & Pyatt *Mountaineering in Britain* x. 178 They had nearly completed the ascent and reached a cornice when a snow step avalanched.

avalanchine (ævə'lɑːnʃɪn, -lænʃ-), *a. rare.* [f. AVALANCHE *sb.* + -INE.] Of the nature of, or like, an avalanche.

c **1860** W. GASPEY *Doom Creat.*, Crushed are the seats of early state 'Neath Ruin's avalanchine weight.

avalanchy ('ævəlɑːnʃɪ, -lænʃɪ), *a.* [f. AVALANCHE *sb.* + -Y[1].] Liable to descend in or be swept by an avalanche.

1893 FENN *In Alpine Valley* I. vi. 117 Rather an avalanchy place, this. **1894** *Contemp. Rev.* Aug. 218 Snow-slopes, of which one was rotten and avalanchy. **1925** T. H. SOMERVELL in E. F. Norton *Fight for Everest: 1924* III. vi. 356 The steep ice cliffs of the North Col are safer than the avalanchy slopes.

† **a'vale**, *v. Obs.* Forms: 4–8 **au- avale**, 4–6 **auaile**, 5–6 **au- avayle**, 6 **advale**, **auayl**, **aueyle**, 7 **avail**. *North.* 4–5 **awale**, 6 **awail**. See also aphet. VALE *v.* [a. OF. *avaler*, f. phr. *à val*:—L. *ad vallem* to the valley; = Pr. *avalar*, It. *avallare*; cf. AMOUNT *v.*, F. *amonter*, f. *à mont*, L. *ad montem*. For the spelling *advale*, see AD- *pref.* 2.]

1. *intr.* Of persons: To descend; to come, go, or get down; to dismount, alight. (Often with redundant *down*; cf. *ascend up*.)

c **1400** MAUNDEV. xxvi. 266 Summe of the Jewes han.. avaled down to the Valeyes. *c* **1425** WYNTOUN *Cron.* IX. viii. 140 Owre a bra down awaland. **1483** CAXTON *Gold. Leg.* 160/3 A corde by which he aualed doun and was saued. **1509** HAWES *Past. Pleas.* 6 When Phebus in the west Gan to avayle. **1596** SPENSER *F.Q.* II. ix. 10 They..from their sweaty coursers did avale. *Ibid.* IV. iii. 46 Out of her coch she gan availe.

2. *trans.* To descend, come down (a hill, etc.).

1494 FABYAN VII. 489 The sayd hoost of Flemynges aualyd yͤ mount in a secret wyse.

3. *intr.* Of things: To sink, flow, or drop down.

c **1374** CHAUCER *Boeth.* IV. vi. 143 Þe heuy erþes aualen by her weyȝtes. **1483** CAXTON *Gold. Leg.* 144/2 The precious blood aualed by the shafte of the spere upon hys hondes. **1509** HAWES *Past. Pleas.* 92 The droppes.. Whiche from her eyen began to advale. **1596** SPENSER *F.Q.* I. i. 21 But when his later spring gins to avale, Huge heapes of mudd he [Nilus] leaves.

b. To sail down stream, or away on an ebb tide.

a **1547** EARL SURREY *Æneid* IV. 387 To flight Was armde the fleet all redy to avale. **1551** BODENHAM *Voy. Scio* in Arb. *Garner* I. 33, I vailed down that night ten miles, to take the tide in the morning.

4. *transf.* and *fig.* To lower oneself, submit, yield.

1484 CAXTON *Chyualry* 78 Auaryce..maketh noble courage to descende and auale. **1525** LD. BERNERS *Froiss.* II. xxix. 84 Whiche castell after aueyled to me.

5. *trans.* To cause to descend, fall, or sink; to let down, lower; to send or direct downwards.

c **1314** *Guy Warw.* 80 His hauberk was al to tore And his nasel avaled bifore. *c* **1400** *Rom. Rose* 1803 The thridde arowe.. Into myn herte he dide avale. *a* **1450** *Knt. de la Tour* (1868) 113 [Rahab] aualed hem by a corde from.. the toune walles. **1523** LD. BERNERS *Froiss.* I. ccclxxiv. 619 Drawe vp your ankers and aueyle your sayles. **1579** SPENSER *Sheph. Cal.* Jan. 73, Phœbus gan auaile His weary waine. **1770** LANGHORNE *Plutarch* (1879) I. 118/2 He ordered that the rods should be avaled in respect to the citizens.

6. To lower (the visor of a helmet), to uncover; *hence*, to take off, doff (hat, cap, etc.).

c **1330** R. BRUNNE *Chron.* 97 Ilk auailed his helme, & to conseile drowe. *c* **1386** CHAUCER *Miller's Prol.* 14 He wold avale nowther hood ne hat. *c* **1420** *Anturs of Arth.* xxxii, He auaylet vppe his viserne. **1544** BALE *Sir J. Oldcastell* in *Harl. Misc.* (Malh.) I. 272 All the clergye..avayling their bonnettes. **1557** *K. Arthur* (Copland) v. xii, Yͤ kyng aualed his vyser with a meke and noble countenance.

7. *fig.* To degrade, abase, humble; to lower.

c **1430** LYDG. *Bochas* II. i. (1554) 41 a, Fortune..Auailed hym from his royall see. **1551–6** ROBINSON tr. *More's Utop.* 146 One that hath aualed the heighe nature of hys soule to the vielnes of brute beastes bodies. *a* **1639** WOTTON in *Reliq.* (1651) It pleased him to..avale his goodness, even to the giving of his friend secret directions.

† **a'vale**, *sb. Obs. rare.* In 6 **auail**. [f. prec.]

a. Abasement, humiliation. **b.** ? Descent, disembarkation.

c **1505** DUNBAR, The lang availl on humil wyse. *a* **1547** EARL SURREY in Tottell's *Misc.* (Arb.) 16 Furdering his hope, that is his sail Toward me, the swete port of his auail.

avale, obs. form of AVAIL.

† **a'valing**, *vbl. sb. Obs.* [f. prec. *v.* + -ING[1].] Descending, descent; declivity.

c **1380** *Sir Ferumb.* 984 At aualyng of an hulle: þe frensche han þey of-take. *c* **1430** LYDG. *Bochas* I. i. (1544) 1 b, Rivers ..In their upspringing and avayling down. **1523** LD. BERNERS *Froiss.* I. xviii. 23 They..ordeyned iii. great battelles, in the auaylynge of the hyll.

avalite ('ævəlaɪt). *Min.* [ad. G. *avalit* (1884), f. *Avala*, name of a mountain near Belgrade, its locality + -ITE[1].] A green earthy mineral containing chromium oxide.

1889 in *Cent. Dict.* **1896** CHESTER *Dict. Min.*

avalone, var. ABALONE.

avanc, var. AFANC.

avance, -se, obs. forms of ADVANCE, AVENS.

avancers: see AVANTERS.

avang(e, pa. t. of AFONG *v. Obs.* to receive.

‖ **avania** (ævə'niːə). Also 8 **avarria**, **avaria**. [In common use in the Levant, but of uncertain language and origin; in It. and Pg. *avanía*, F. *avanie*, mod.Gr. ἀβανία, Arab. and Turk. *awānī*, also found as *awārī* (Devic), and in Bocthor *ʿawān*, and *ʿawānia*. See below. Also in 17th c. anglicised as AVENY, q.v.]

An imposition by the (Turkish) government, a compulsory tax, government exaction, 'aid,' 'benevolence' (Marsh); *spec.* (as applied by Christians) an extortionate exaction or tax levied by the Turks. Hence **avanious** *a.*, extortionate.

1687 RYCAUT *Hist. Turks* II. 251 The trading Christian enjoyed the privilege of their Capitulations with..less frequent Avanias. *Ibid.* II. 62 Their extravagant Exactions, and Avanious Practices. **1703** MAUNDRELL *Journ. Jerus.* (1721) 93 Their perpetual extortion and Avarria's. *a* **1733** NORTH *Lives* II. 420 False and extortious demands which they call Avanias. *Ibid.* III. 1 *title*, The avanious demand of the Tunis Basha. **1751** CHAMBERS *Cycl.*, Avaria.

[The etymology of *avania* has been variously sought in Arabic, Persian, Turkish: see Devic, in Littré's *Suppt.*, and G. P. Marsh, *Notes and Additions* to Wedgwood. The variant Arabic form *awārī* (whence Eng. *avaria, avarria*, above) as well as original correspondence of meaning, suggests a connexion with It. *avaria*—see AVERAGE *sb.*[2]: in fact Mr. Marsh proposed the derivation of the latter from this word. But on the other hand, the various and uncertain forms of the word in Arabic may be merely adaptations of Fr. *avarie* or It. *avaría*, assimilated to native words or roots (e.g. *awār* oppression, injustice, *hawān* contempt, etc.) 'The plur. *aavaniet* is now in popular use in Syria, to express government exactions, the singular signifying *aid, help*, just as *benevolence* in Europe sometimes meant a compulsory tax' (Marsh). The word has been adopted in It. and Pg. in the transferred sense: It. *avanía* 'an undeserved wrong, a secret grudge, an insulting injury' (Florio); Pg. *avanía* 'wrong, injury' (Vieyra).]

avant, obs. form of AVAUNT.

‖ **avant-** (ə'vɑːnt, -æ-, avɑ̃). [F. *avant* before, cogn. with Pr. *avant*, It. *avanti*:—L. *abante*, f. *ab* from + *ante* before. See AVAUNT. The *t*, which was pronounced in OF., was retained much longer in English. In words in early use *ava(u)nt* was worn down to *vant-*, *van-*, and sometimes to *vaw-*, *va-*.]

In a few combinations, partly French, partly hybrid; as † **avantalour** [AFr.], one who goes before; † **avant-darter**, transl. L. *antepīlānus*; **avant-fossé** [Fr.], the ditch on the outer side of a counterscarp, dug at the foot of the glacis; **avant-peach** [F. *avant-pêche*], an early variety of peach. See also AVANT-BRACE, -COURIER, etc.

1601 TATE *Househ. Ord. Ed. II*, §90 Their shalbe a forger [F. *avantalour*] in the kinges houshold..No man shalbe avant alour who hath forjured the Court. **1600** HOLLAND *Livy* VIII. viii. 286 This battaillon..they called Antepilani (avant-darters). **1611** COTGR., *Avant-pesche*, th' Auant-peach or hastie peach. **1719** LOUDON & WISE *Compl. Gard.* 283 The Avant Peaches, or Forward Peaches.

avantage, obs. form of ADVANTAGE.

† **a'vant-brace**, **a'vawmbrace**. *Obs.* [a. OF. *avant-bras*, f. *avant* before + *bras* arm. Normally *a'vaunt*, whence *a'vaun-*, *a'vaum-*, *a'vawm-brace*, much more usual in the aphetic forms VAMBRACE, VANTBRACE.] Armour for the front of the arm.

c **1440** *Morte Arth.* 2568 Þe avawmbrace vrayllede with silver.

avant-courier (ə'vɑːnt-, -'vænt-, ə'væn-, 'ɑːvən-, -'ævən-, 'avɑ̃,kʊrɪə(r)), *sb.* Forms: 7 **avauntcourrier**, **avant-currier**, **-curror**, **-coureur**, 9 **avant courier**. [Fr. *avant-coureur*, with the latter word modified as in COURIER *sb.* Aphetized in 16th c. as *vaunt-*, *vant-currer*; from 17th c., VAN-COURIER, q.v. (The two first-given pronunciations are historical in Eng.; but many have affected to treat the word both in spelling and pronunciation as modern French, whence the *avant-coureur* of 1670, and the mongrel third pronunciation now prevalent.)]

One who runs or rides before; a herald; *esp.* (in 17th c.) in *pl.* the scouts, skirmishers, or advance-guard of an army.

1603 KNOLLES *Hist. Turks* (1621) 217 Having suffered 2000 of the enemies horse (the avaunt-courriers of the Turks armie) to passe by him. **1658** CLEVELAND *Rustic Ramp.* Wks. (1687) 494 Ten Lances of the Avant Currors rout them. **1670** COTTON *Espernon* I. III. 110 The Avant Coureurs of the Duke of Mayenne's Army. **1810** COLERIDGE *Friend* I. v. (1867) 18 The avant-courier rode at full speed into the court.

b. *transf.* or *fig.*

1611 FLORIO, *Etesij*, windes blowing very stiffly..called of mariners the Auant curriers. **1649** BRAMHALL *Fair Warning* vi. Wks. III. 262 These are prognostics of ensuing storms, the avant-couriers of seditious tumults. **1860** FROUDE *Hist. Eng.* V. xxv. 97 A set of noisy declaimers, avant couriers, as they called themselves, of the crown.

avant-'courier, *v.* [f. prec. sb.] To herald.

1870 LOWELL *Among my Bks.* Ser. I. (1873) 167 In a triumphal car, avant-couriered by a band of music.

† **a'vanters**, **avancers**, *sb. pl. Obs.* [? f. F. *avant* before.] Part of the numbles of a deer.

c **1340** *Gaw. & Gr. Knt.* 1342 Eft at þe gargulum bigynez on þenne, Ryuez hit vp radly ryȝt to þe biȝt, Voydez out þe a-vanters. **1486** *Bk. St. Albans* E vij b, Oon croke of the Nomblis lyth euermoore Under the throote bolle of the beest be foore That called is auancers.

‖ **avant-garde** (avɑ̃gard), † **a'vant-,guard**. Forms: 5 **au-**, **avaunt-**, **aduantgard(e**, **avantgaird**, 7 **au-**, **avant-**, **avaunt-**, **avan-guard**, **-gard**, 8–9 **avant-garde**. [a. F. *avant-garde*, f. *avant* before + *garde* GUARD. Formerly anglicized, *avaunt-*, and *-guard*; sense 1 is now archaic or obs., being replaced by the aphetic VANGUARD; cf. *(ar)rear-guard*.]

1. The foremost part of an army; the vanguard or van.

1470–85 MALORY *Arthur* I. xv, Lyonses and Pharyaunce had the aduant garde. **1582–8** *Hist. Jas. VI* (1804) 40 The gentillmen of the surname of Hamiltoun were on the Queenes avantgaird. **1630** HAYWARD *K. Edw. VI*, 18 Next followed the avauntguard. **1664** S. CLARKE *Tamerlane* 8 Odmar led the avanguard. **1796** *Campaigns* 1793–4 I. I. ii. 12 Gen. Stengel..commanded the avant garde of Valence's army. **1800** COLERIDGE *Wallenstein* III. vii, Mid full glasses Will we expect the Swedish Avantgarde.

2. The pioneers or innovators in any art in a particular period. Also *attrib.* or as *adj.* Hence **avant-'gardism**, the characteristic quality of such pioneering; **avant-'gardist(e)** (-ɪst), such a person; also *attrib.*

1910 *Daily Tel.* 1 July 14/6 The new men of mark in the *avant-garde*. **1925** *League of Composers' Rev.* Jan. 26 He used rather questionable methods of calling attention to himself..publishing wild manifestoes in the *avant-garde* magazines. **1940** GRAVES & HODGE *Long Week-End* xii. 197 At Paris..British and American literary *avant-gardistes* fraternized or came to blows. **1947** *University Observer* I. 1. 19 There is a terrible striving always to be *avant-garde*: to 'discover' Henry James, T. S. Eliot, Melville or the more obscure modern English poets. **1947** *Horizon* Dec. 299 A literature without an *avant-garde* soon becomes a literature without a main body. **1950** A. KOESTLER in *God that Failed* I. 31 Their policy..in cultural matters [was] progressive to the point of *avant-gardism*. **1953** *Archit. Rev.* CXIII. 149/2 For avant-gardist architecture produces..characterless buildings. **1967** *Spectator* 3 Nov. 547/3 What baffles me about our various well-meaning avant-gardes is their prodigious appetite for punishment. **1967** *Times* 23 Nov. 13/3 They resembled a group of avant-gardists who seemed not quite to know where they were going.

† **a'vant-,lay**. *Hunting. Obs.* Also 5 **avaunt-elay**, 7 **advaunt-reley**. [f. F. *avant* before, in front + OF. *alais*, *eslais*, and *relais*: see ALLAY *sb.*[2], RELAY.] The laying on of fresh hounds to intercept a deer already chased by others.

1486 *Bk. St. Albans* E viij b, Even at his comyng yf thow lett thy howndys goo While the oder that be behynde fer arn hym froo That is a vauntelay. **1606** *Ret. fr. Parnass.* II. v. in Hazl. *Dodsl.* IX. 149 There other huntsmen met him with an ad[v]auntreley. *a* **1630** J. TAYLOR (Water P.) *Wks.* I. 93/1 Auaunt-laye, Allaye, Relaye [see ABATURE].

a'vant-,mure. *Obs.* exc. *Hist.* Also 6–7 **avaunt-**. [a. F. *avant-mur* fore-wall. Commonly aphetized in 16–17th c. to *vanmure*, VAMURE, q.v.] The outer wall of a fortress, or in circumvallation. Hence **avaunt-mure** *v. Obs.*

1530 PALSGR. 440/2, I avauntmure, I make a wall by fore the walles of a towne, *Je auant mure*. This towne is strongely avauntmured. **1611** COTGR., *Avant-mur*, an auant-mure; fore-wall, out-wall, or outward-wall. **1693** W. ROBERTSON *Phraseol. Gen.* 179 An Avaunt-mure, or a Fortress before a wall, *Antemurale*.

avanturine, variant of AVENTURIN(E.

† **a'vant,ward**. *Obs.* Also **avaunt-**, **avawm-**, **awaward**. [a. ONF. *avantwarde*, = central F. *avant-guarde*, now *avant-garde*: cf. ARREARWARD. Aphetized in 13th c. as *vauntwarde* (1297), *vaumwarde* (1330), *vauwarde* (1401), VAWARD (1435–1625, common in Shaks.), VANWARD.] = AVANT-GARDE, VAN-GUARD.

1375 BARBOUR *Bruce* XIII. 169 Thar awaward ruschit was. *c* **1440** *Morte Arth.* 324, I salle have the avanttwarde wytterly my selvene. *Ibid.* 3169 The avawmwarde voydez theire horsez. **1480** CAXTON *Chron. Eng.* ccxliv. 298 That he wold graunte hym that day the auauntward in his batayle.

Avar ('ɑːvɑː(r), 'eɪvɑː(r)). **1.** A member of a Turkic people, prominent in south-eastern Europe from the 6th to the 9th c. A.D.; also, their language. Also *attrib.* **2.** ('ævɑː(r)). Also **Awar**. A member of a people of the North Caucasus; also, their language.

1788 GIBBON *Decl. & F.* IV. xlii. 229 He imparted to the senate his resolution..to purchase the friendship of the Avars. *Ibid.*, But the virtue or treachery of an Avar betrayed the secret enmity and ambitious designs of their countrymen. **1881** *Jrnl. R. Asiatic Soc.* XIII. 293 My ride took me through the Avâr-speaking country. *Ibid.*, It is written by the one in Avâr, by the other in Russian. **1882** FREEMAN *Lect. Amer. Audiences* 339 The Empire which had beaten back the Persian and the Avar lost its provinces to the Saracen and the Bulgarian. **1920** H. G. WELLS *Outline of Hist.* VI. xxxi. §1 The Avars and Slavs struck down from the Danube country towards the Adriatic. **1934** A. TOYNBEE *Study Hist.* III. 25 The transitory Avar ascendency was the making of the Slavs. **1951** W. K. MATTHEWS *Languages of*

U.S.S.R. v. 89 Awar has..fifty phonemes, only five of which are vowels.

Hence **Avarian** (əˈvɑːrɪən) *a.*, of or pertaining to the Avars (both senses); also *absol.*, the language of the Avars.

1875 C. HENEAGE tr. *M. von Thielman's Journey in Caucasus* II. 286/2 Avarian guides. **1889** *Jrnl. R. Asiatic Soc.* XXI. 729 *Til* meant 'black' in Avarian. *Ibid.* 731 The importance of the Avarian domination..has hardly been sufficiently appreciated. **1902** *Encycl. Brit.* XXVII. 341/2 The Avarian is a sort of inter-tribal tongue. **1909** WEBSTER s.v., *Avarian rings*, vestiges of Avarian fortifications formed by stakes surrounding a settlement.

avaria: see AVANIA, AVERAGE *sb.*[2]

avarice (ˈævərɪs). Forms: 3–4 **auaris, -ise,** 4–5 **averyce, -ys,** 4–6 **-ice, avaryce,** 4– **avarice.** *Sc.* 5 **awarys, awerys,** 6 **auereis.** [a. OF. *avarice*, ad. L. *avāritia*, f. *avārus* greedy: see -ICE[1].] Inordinate desire of acquiring and hoarding wealth; greediness of gain, cupidity.

a **1300** *Cursor M.* 10112 Þe world has tuynne to his ascyse, þat es auaris, and couaytise. *c* **1386** CHAUCER *Pers. T.* ¶671 Coveitise is for to coveit swiche thinges as thou hast not; and avarice is to witholde and kepe swiche thinges as thou hast, without rightful nede. *c* **1425** WYNTOUN *Cron.* VI. xx. 28 Pryd, Falshud, and Covatys He held at wndyr, and Awarys. **1549** *Compl. Scotl.* (1872) 64 Quhou kyng midas gat tua asse luggis on his hede, be cause of his auereis. **1643** SIR T. BROWNE *Relig. Med.* II. §13 To me avarice seems not so much a vice, as a deplorable piece of madnesse. **1766** GOLDSM. *Vic. W.* (1876) 159 Avarice was his prevailing passion. **1812** COMBE (Dr. Syntax) *Pictur.* x. 36 Pale av'rice may his heart possess, The bane of human happiness.

b. *fig.* Eager desire to get or keep for oneself.

c **1386** CHAUCER *Pers. T.* ¶670 Avarice ne stont not oonly in lond ne in catel, but som tyme in science and in glorie. **1709** POPE *Ess. Crit.* 579 Be niggards of advice, on no pretense; For the worst avarice is that of sense. **1764** GOLDSM. *Trav.* 264 And all are taught an avarice of praise. **1775** BURKE *Sp. Conc. Amer.* Wks. 1842 I. 189 This avarice of desolation, this hoarding of a royal wilderness.

avaricious (ævəˈrɪʃəs), *a.* Also 6 **-ycyouse,** 6–8 **-itious.** [a. F. *avaricieux, -euse*, f. *avarice*, as if ad. L. **avāritiōsus*.] Immoderately desirous of accumulating wealth; greedy of gain, grasping; *fig.* eager to possess or accumulate.

1474 CAXTON *Chesse* III. iv. G j, The auaricious wolf. **1531** ELYOT *Gov.* (1834) 210 His cruel and avaricious appetite. **1660** R. COKE *Power & Subj.* 72 Nor will avaricious rich men fail to pretend poverty. **1762** H. WALPOLE *Vertue's Anecd. Paint.* (1786) II. 71 Queen Elizabeth was avaricious with pomp; James I. lavish with meanness. **1809** W. IRVING *Knickerb.* IV. vii. (1849) 230 We are naturally..avaricious after imaginary causes of lamentation.

avaˈriciously, *adv.* [f. prec. + -LY[2].] In an avaricious manner.

1611 COTGR., *Avarement*, avariciously. **1682** NORRIS *Hierocles* Pref. 19 Neither spends his Goods prodigally.. nor yet keeps them avariciously. **1767** REID *Let.* in *Wks.* I. 49/2 Avariciously amassing knowledge. *a* **1859** DE QUINCEY *Ceylon* Wks. XII. 36 Avariciously to anchor our hopes on a pearl fishery.

avaˈriciousness. [f. as prec. + -NESS.] The quality of being avaricious; greediness of wealth.

1560 in Spottiswood *Hist. Ch. Scot.* III. (1677) 168 Avariciousness and solicitude of mony is no less to be damned.

†**avaˈrition.** *Obs. rare*$^{-1}$. [irreg. f. *avaritious* = AVARICIOUS; cf. *ambition, -ious*.] = prec.

1622 PEACHAM *Compl. Gent.* (1661) 157 Gold Colour signifieth Avarition.

†**ˈavarous,** *a. Obs.* or *dial.* Forms: 4–5 **au-averous(e,** 6 **avarus,** 4–7 **avarous.** [a. OF. *averos, -us*, f. *aveir, avoir*, possession: see AVER *sb.* Subsequently confused with F. *avare*, and so spelt.] Avaricious.

1303 R. BRUNNE *Handl. Synne* 5578 Swyþe coveytous And a nygur and auarous. *c* **1386** CHAUCER *Pers. T.* ¶673 The avarous man hath more hope in his catel than in Jhesu Crist. **1388** WYCLIF *1 Cor.* vi. 10 Nether theues, nether auerouse men. *c* **1450** *Merlin* vi. 106 He ȝaf to hem that were auerouse, golde and siluer. **1513** DOUGLAS *Æneis* III. i. 83 Flee from this auarus kingis cost. **1658** LENNARD tr. *Charron's Wisd.* I. xxxix. §6 (1670) 132 So avarous is he of misery.

†**ˈavarously,** *adv. Obs.* [f. prec. + -LY[2].] Avariciously, greedily.

1382 WYCLIF *Job* xxvii. 8 If auerously he take. **1432–50** tr. *Higden* VI. xxviii. (1879) VII. 219 Men eitynge avarousely. **1580** BARET *Alv.* A 713 Avarously or couetously, *Auarè*.

avascular (əˈvæskjʊlə(r), eɪ-), *a. Physiol.* [f. A-14 + VASCULAR *a.*] Lacking or deficient in vascularity or blood vessels.

1900 DORLAND *Med. Dict.* 89/1 *Avascular*, not vascular. **1908** *Practitioner* June 771 An avascular area on the bladder is exposed. **1963** *Lancet* 19 Jan. 133/1 The wound flaps were under some tension, and avascular necrosis of the wound margins developed.

avast (əˈvɑːst), *phr. Naut.* [prob. a worn-down form of Du. *hou'vast, houd vast*, hold fast: cf. Du. *hou* stop! stay! and *houvast* cramp-iron.] Hold! stop! stay! cease!

1681 OTWAY *Soldier's Fort.* IV. i, Hoa up, hoa up; so, avast there, Sir. **1727–51** CHAMBERS *Cycl.*, *Avast*, a term frequently used on board a ship, signifying to stop, hold, or stay. **1748** SMOLLETT *Rod. Rand.* xli, 'Avast there friend, none of your tricks upon travellers.' **1836** MARRYAT *Midsh. Easy* xix. 70 'Avast heaving,' said Gascoigne.

avatar (ɑːvəˈtɑː(r), æ-, ˈævətɑː(r)). [ad. Skr. *avatāra* descent, f. *ava* down + *t'r-, tar-*, to pass over.]

1. *Hindu Myth.* The descent of a deity to the earth in an incarnate form.

1784 SIR W. JONES in *Asiat. Res.* I. 234 The ten Avatárs or descents of the deity, in his capacity of Preserver. **1858** BEVERIDGE *Hist. India* II. IV. ii. 28 The fifth avatar, called Varuna, because in it Vishnu assumed the form of a dwarf.

2. Manifestation in human form; incarnation.

1815 SCOTT *Paul's Lett.* (1839) 325 A third avatar of this singular emanation of the Evil Principle [Bonaparte]. **1878** R. SAYLER in *N. Amer. Rev.* CXXVI. 94 McClellan was.. the very god of war, in his latest avatar.

3. Manifestation or presentation to the world as a ruling power or object of worship.

1859 MASSON *Milton* I. 226 The avatar of Mathematics had not begun. *Ibid.* 447 Glad that the avatar of Donne, as an intermediate power between Spenser and Milton, was so brief and partial. **1883** *Harper's Mag.* Mar. 541/1 The Baireuth festivals..the completest and most characteristic avatars of art our century can shew.

4. *loosely*, Manifestation; display; phase.

1850 L. HUNT *Autobiog.* ii. (1860) 36 She ended with enjoying, and even abetting, this new avatar of the Church militant. **1880** L. STEPHEN *Pope* ii. 29 Wit and sense are but different avatars of the same spirit.

avaunce, obs. form of AVENS.

avaunce, -se, etc., obs. forms of ADVANCE, etc.

†**aˈvaunt,** *sb.*[1] *Obs.* Forms: 4–6 **au- avant,** 4–7 **au- avaunt(e,** 5 **awaunte,** 6 **advaunt(e,** (*Sc.* **awant).** [f. AVAUNT *v.*[1]]

1. A boast, vaunt; boasting, vain-glory.

c **1380** *Sir Ferumb.* 355 Yf þou þyn auaunt perforny myȝt. *c* **1380** WYCLIF *Three Treat.* 35 Thei tellen to greet auaunt, that thei ben charious to the puple. *c* **1430** *Life St. Katherine* 56 Not in auant of pryde, bot in mekenesse. **1553** BRENDE *Q. Curtius* III. 25 These wordes he spake with greater avaunt then trueth.

2. *esp.* in phr. ***to make avaunt***: to boast, declare confidently or arrogantly; = AVAUNT *v.*

c **1340** *Alex. & Dind.* 570 Of more make ȝe avaunt..þan ȝe mow forþen. **1465** *Paston Lett.* 512 II. 206 They make ther awaunte were that I may be goten I schul dye. **1553–87** FOXE *A. & M.* (1596) 342/2 The saide Bishop dooth make his auaunt, that he had full power to create and depose kinges. *a* **1600** *Parl. Byrdes* 228 in Hazl. *E.P.P.* III. 179 For the Crowe spake the Cormoraunt, And of his rule made great avaunt.

3. Promise.

c **1325** *E.E. Allit. P.* B. 664, I a-vow verayly þe avaunt þat I made, I schal..sende to Sare a soun & an hayre.

†**aˈvaunt,** *sb.*[2] *Obs.* [A substantive use of AVAUNT *adv.* or *int.* taken as a name for itself; cf. *alarm, assemble* sb.] The order to be off.

1596 BP. BARLOW *Three Serm.* iii. 132 The diuell tempted him, but he gaue him the auaunt, with the sworde of the spirit. **1613** SHAKS. *Hen. VIII*, II. iii, To give her the avaunt! **1711** SHAFTESB. *Charac.* (1737) I. 232 The defiance or avant [to Satan] shou'd run much after this manner.

†**aˈvaunt,** *v.*[1] *Obs.* Forms: 4–6 **au- avaunt(e,** 4–7 **avant,** 6 **advant, -uant, -vaunte,** (*Sc.* **awant).** [a. OF. *avante-r, avaunte-r*, f. *à* to, here intensive + *vanter*:—late L. *vānitāre* to boast (Augustine), freq. of **vanāre* to lie (in Pr. and It.), f. *vānus* vain, empty. For the form *advant* see AD- *pref.* 2. In OF. as in Eng. mostly refl., *s'avanter*.]

1. *trans.* To speak boastfully or proudly of: **a.** To glory in, boast of (an action); **b.** To speak proudly of, praise, commend (a person).

1303 R. BRUNNE *Handl. Synne* 8309 And þat ys nat þe synne leste, Avaunte þy synne to hym þat þou sest. *c* **1440** *Bone Flor.* 299 Wyth mekyll worschyp they hym avaunt. *c* **1380** *Sir Ferumb.* 42 Þat nyȝt was Charl[es proude]..& auaunted his kniȝtes olde. **1556** J. HEYWOOD *Spider & Fl.* lxxvi. 10 When he at end (to them) had it a vaunted.

c. with *compl.* To boast, declare confidently (*to be*).

c **1374** CHAUCER *Boeth.* I. i. 5 Whereto auaunted(e) ȝe me to be weleful. **1513** BRADSHAW *St. Werburge* (1848) 212 That I may the auaunt A gentill Werburge.

2. *refl.* To boast, brag, glory, vaunt oneself. Const. *of, for.*

1340 HAMPOLE *Pr. Consc.* 4298 His disciples..Sal þam avant, and þam self hald Better of lif. *c* **1386** CHAUCER *Melib.* ¶585 Prudence had herd hire housbond avaunte him of his richesse. **1547** *Homilies* I. III. ii. 28 When a man avaunteth not himself for his own righteousness. **1580** BARET *Alv.* A 714 To auaunt himselfe prowdely, *Gloriari insolenter.*

b. with *subord. cl.* or *inf. phr.*

c **1315** SHOREHAM 118 To segge that ich hyt maky can.. Dar ich me nauȝt avanty. *c* **1386** CHAUCER *Wife's T.* 158, I dar me wel avaunte, Thy lif is sauf. **1483** CAXTON *Gold. Leg.* 28/2 Evyl peple auaunte them to haue don myracles. **1553–87** FOXE *A. & M.* (1684) II. 95 He so avanted himself, that he had slain a Lutheran Priest.

3. *intr.* in sense of 2.

1471 RIPLEY *Comp. Alch.* v. (Ashm. 1652) 154 As they make boste of and avaunte. **1569** J. SANFORD *Agrippa's Van. Artes* 182 b, In this serpente lette him then auaunte, that glorieth in knowledge. **1573** COOPER *Thesaur.*, *Glorior*..to auaunt or boast, to thende to haue praise.

b. with *subord. cl.* or *inf. phr.*

1473 SIR J. PASTON in *Lett.* 722 III. 85 He shall not avaunt that evyr he spake with hym. **1553** BRENDE *Q. Curtius* VIII. 5 Advauntyng the notable victorye at Cheronese to be his dede. **1576** GASCOIGNE *Philomene* (Arb.) 89, I might aduant Of al his speech to knowe the plaine entent.

†**aˈvaunt,** *v.*[2] *Obs.* Also 6 **advant.** [f. AVAUNT *adv.*, but also influenced probably by AVAUNT *v.*[1] 1 and ADVANCE *v.* In sense 3, apparently from the interjectional sense *away! be off!*]

1. *intr.* To go or come forward, advance.

c **1400** *Beryn* 1972 Somtyme thowe wolt auaunte, & som tyme wolt arere. **1596** SPENSER *F.Q.* II. iii. 6 To whom avaunting in great bravery.

2. *trans.* To raise, ADVANCE.

1393 GOWER *Conf.* I. 246 To knighthode more and more Prowesse avaunteth his corage. *c* **1400** *Melayne* 1575 The kynge callede sir lyonelle, And a-vauntede hym full heghe. **1605** [see ADVANT *v.*[2]].

3. To be off, go away, depart.

1549 COVERDALE *Erasm. Par. Jude* 21 That they should not avaunt..into the dongeon of eternal damnacion. **1601** CHESTER *Love's Mart.* xii. (1878) 83 It causeth them from thence for to auaunt.

avaunt (əˈvɔːnt, əˈvɑːnt), *adv., int.*, etc. Forms: 4–7 **auaunt,** 5–8 **au- avant,** (5 **a-want),** 4– **avaunt.** [a. F. *avant* to the front, forward, before:—L. *ab ante* 'from before,' used in late L. for the simple *ante*; cf. *arrear*.]

†**A.** *adv.* Forward, to the front. *Obs.*

c **1400** *Rom. Rose* 3958 With that word came Drede avaunt. *Ibid.* 4793 Never the more avaunt, Right nought am I thurgh youre doctrine. **1415** *Pol. Poems* (1859) II. 125 Lete every man preve hym silfe a good man this day, and avant baneres. *c* **1440** *Arthur* 444 Than seyd Arthour, 'Auaunt Baner, & be Goo.'

B. *interjectionally.* orig. and lit.: Onward! move on! go on! *Hence*, Begone! be off! away!

c **1485** *Digby Myst.* (1882) III. 925 A-wantt, a-want þe, onworthy wrecchesse! *c* **1525** SKELTON *Agst. Garnesche* 112 Avaunt, Avaunt, thou sloggysh. **1607** CHAPMAN *Bussy D'Amb.* Plays 1873 II. 55 Auant about thy charge. **1687** CONGREVE *Old Bachelor* III. vi, No! No! Avaunt! I'll not be slabbered and kissed now. *a* **1725** POPE *Odyss.* XIX. 80 Avaunt, she cried, offensive to my sight! **1849** C. BRONTË *Shirley* II. ii. 43 Accosted me as Satan, bid me avaunt.

C. *prefix.* Forward, fore-. See later spelling AVANT-, also the aphetic forms VANT-, VAN-.

avauntage, obs. form of ADVANTAGE.

†**aˈvauntance.** *Obs. rare.* [a. OF. *avantance*, n. of action f. *avanter*: see AVAUNT *v.*[1] and -ANCE.] Boasting, self-glorification.

1393 GOWER *Conf.* I. 123 The vice cleped Avauntance. *Ibid.* 131 In armes lith none avauntance.

†**aˈvaunter.** *Obs.* Forms: 5 **avauntour,** 6 **-ure, advaunter.** [a. OF. *avanteur, -our*, n. of agent f. *avanter*: see AVAUNT *v.*[1]] A boaster.

c **1374** CHAUCER *Troylus* III. 260 Avauntour and a lier, all is one. **1496** *Dives & Paup.* (W. de W.) VIII. v. 327 The auaunter of hymselfe is worse than the lacker of hymselfe. *c* **1530** LD. BERNERS *Arth. Lyt. Bryt.* (1814) 440 For I neuer saw so good a knight and so lytel auauntere. **1553** BRENDE *Q. Curtius* VIII. 5 Being over great an advaunter of hymselfe.

†**aˈvaunting,** *vbl. sb.* [f. AVAUNT *v.*[1] + -ING[1].] Boasting, self-glorification, vaunting.

c **1380** *Sir Ferumb.* 352 Þat auantyngge þat þou hast mad. **1528** MORE *Heresyes* IV. Wks. 256/1 In the vaine auaunting of hys own false boast and prayse.

†**aˈvaunting,** *ppl. a. Obs.* [f. as prec. + -ING[2].] Boastful, vain-glorious.

1494 FABYAN VII. 280 In ye moste auauntynge maner.

†**aˈvauntment.** *Obs. rare*$^{-1}$. [a. OF. **avantement*, n. of action f. *avanter*: see AVAUNT *v.*[1] and -MENT.] Boasting, self-glorification.

1303 R. BRUNNE *Handl. Synne* 4579 Fyrst ys pryde, as þou wel wost, Auauntement, bobaunce, and bost.

†**aˈvauntry.** *Obs.* Also 4 **-arie,** 5 **-erye.** [a. OF. **avanterie*, n. of quality f. *avanteur*: see AVAUNTER and -Y.] Boastfulness, boasting.

1330 R. BRUNNE *Chron.* 194 Rebuke him for þat ilk of þat auauntrie. **1393** GOWER *Conf.* I. 124 That I may never..Of love make avauntarie. **1491** CAXTON *Vitas Patr.* I. i. 4 a/2 Lete us flee vayne glory, pryde and auaunterye.

avawmbrace, avawmwarde: see AVANT-.

avawnetage, obs. form of ADVANTAGE.

†**aˈvay, aˈvey,** *v. Obs.* Also 4 (*north.*) **awaye.** [a. OF. *avie-r*, pres. sing. *aveie*, to put one on his way, start, guide, direct, instruct, cogn. with Pr. and Sp. *aviar*, It. *avviare*:—Romanic **adviāre*, f. *ad* to, *viam* way: cf. F. *envoyer*, OF. *envier, enveier*:—L. **inviāre*. Cf. AVYE.]

trans. To instruct, inform, teach. (Frequent in Shoreham; erron. printed by Wright *aneye, anaye*.)

c **1315** SHOREHAM 19 Ther he set atte soupere, And..Of sothe he ham aueyde. *Ibid.* 158 For swythe wel he [the devil] was auayd Of mannes stad. *c* **1325** *E.E. Allit. P.* A. 709 Quo con rede, He loke on bok & be awayed.

†a'vayment. *Obs.* In 3 aueyment, 4 *Sc.* **awayment.** [a. OF. *aveiement* (later Parisian *avoiement*), f. *aveier*: see AVAY and -MENT.] Instruction, information; *also* (legal) declaration.

[The later sense is common with OF. *avoie-*, *aveiement*: Godefroy suggests confusion with *avoement* AVOWMENT.]
c **1315** SHOREHAM 77 Of spou[se] hoth thys aueyment Louketh ȝou for hordome. *c* **1425** WYNTOUN *Cron.* VIII. v. 113 Ðis dwne, and þe awaymentis Consawyd full in þare intentis.

ave ('eɪviː, 'ɑːveɪ), *int.* and *sb.* Forms: 3–7 **aue,** 7 **auee,** 5– **ave.** [a. L. *avē*, 2nd sing. imp. of *avēre* to be or fare well, used as an expression of welcome or farewell. (In earliest use = *Ave Maria.*)]

A. *int.* Hail! welcome!—Farewell! adieu!

1377 LANGL. *P. Pl.* B. XVI. 151 Aue raby, quod þat ribaude .. And kiste hym. **1850** TENNYSON *In Mem.* lvii, And 'Ave, Ave, Ave,' said, 'Adieu, adieu' for evermore.

B. *sb.*

1. a. A shout of welcome. **b.** A farewell.

1603 SHAKS. *Meas. for M.* I. i. 71 Their lowd applause, and Aues vehement. **1611** HEYWOOD *Gold. Age* I. i. Wks. 1874 III. 8 The people .. Have shrild their Auees high. **1634** SIR T. HERBERT *Trav.* 191 And for her Ave her sacrifice is bettered with .. Jewels her kindred throw upon her.

2. Short for AVE MARIE, q.v.

c **1230** *Ancr. R.* 18 Wendeð ou to vre Leafdi onlicnesse, & cneoleð mid fif auez. *c* **1330** *Kyng of Tars* 1116 Ur ladi with an avè he grette. *c* **1430** *Freemasonry* 622 Say thy pater noster and thyn ave. **1596** SPENSER *F.Q.* I. iii. 13 Every day .. thrise nine hundred Aves, she was wont to say. **1808** SCOTT *Marm.* I. xxvi, He sleeps before his beads Have marked ten aves.

b. *Ave-bell*: that rung at the hours when Aves are to be said.

1635 PAGITT *Christianogr.* III. (1636) 88 Dayly after three toulings of the Ave Bell. **1849** ROCK *Ch. of Fathers* III. ix. 336 The Ave bell, morning and evening, was instituted by Constitutions of 1347.

3. a. The time of ringing the Ave-bell. **b.** The beads on a rosary corresponding to the number of Aves repeated.

1463 *Bury Wills* (1850) 29 The seid chymes to goo also at the avees. *Ibid.* 42 A peyre bedys of sylvir wᵗ x. avees and ij. patern[oste]ris of sylvir and gilt.

†'ave, *v. Obs. rare*⁻¹. [f. prec.; cf. to *salvo*.] To greet with shouts of *Ave*; to hail, acclaim.

1611 HEYWOOD *Gold. Age* III. i. Wks. 1874 III. 47 Wher's that Godhead With which the people Auee'd thee to heauen?

aveer, variant of AVER *sb. Obs.* property.

aveile, obs. form of AVAIL.

†'avelinges, *adv. Obs. rare*⁻¹. [? f. AVELONGE, with termination assimilated to advs. in -LINGS.] In an oblong or oval shape.

1577 *Durham Wills* (1860) 14 Eache to have half a yarde of lyninge clothe cut avelinges, in the stede of huddes.

†a'vell, *v. Obs.* [ad. L. *āvell-ĕre*, f. *ā-* = *ab-* away, off + *vellĕre* to pull away, tear off.] To pull or tear away, pull up.

1530 *State Papers Hen. VIII*, I. 357 [It] hath takyn suche rotys, that the same can (never) be auellyd. **1651** BIGGS *New Disp.* ⁋232 Avelling the .. membrane lining the chest.

Avellan (ə'vɛlən, 'ævələn), *a.* and *sb.* Also **avell-, avelane.** [ad. L. *Avellānus* of Avella or Abella, a town in Campania famous for its fruit-trees and nuts. Cf. Sp., It. *avellana* sb., OF. *avelin* adj., *avelaine* sb., mod.F. *aveline* sb.]

A. *adj.* Of Avella; filbert-, hazel-; cf. L. *Avellāna nux.*

1398 TREVISA *Barth. De P.R* XVI. viii, Adamas .. passeþ neuer þe quantite of a note avelane [**1535** walnut]. **1875** BLACKMORE *A. Lorraine* III. xxvii. 340 From the size of an avellan-nut to that of a small castane.

B. *sb.* A filbert- or hazel-nut. (See also quot. 1610.)

1398 TREVISA *Barth. De P.R.* VII. lxvii. (1495) 285 Grete nottes & Auellanes. **1610** MARKHAM *Masterp.* II. clxxiii. 484 Auellane, which we call the ashes of nut-shells burnt.

b. *attrib.* in *Her.*, as applied to a kind of cross.

1611 GWILLIM *Heraldrie* III. i. 190 A Crosse Auellane. **1727** BRADLEY *Fam. Dict.*, *Avelane* .. the Form of a Cross, which resembles four Filberts in their Husks or Cases, joined together at the great End.

†'avelonge, awe-, awey-, *a. Obs.* [? a. Icel. *aflangr* (cf. Da. *aflang*, Sw. *aflång*), itself a late adaptation of L. *oblongus* OBLONG.] Oblong or oval; drawn out of the square.

c **1440** *Promp. Parv.* 17 Auelonge (*v.r.* awelonge, **1499** aweylonge), *oblongus. Ibid.* 517 Warpyn, or wex wronge or avelonge, as vesselle, *oblongo.* ? *a* **1500** *Harl. MS.* No. 1002, 119 *Oblongo*, to make auelonge. **1828** CARR *Craven Dial.* I. 14 *Avelang*, elliptical, oval.

Ave Maria (see below), **Ave Mary** ('eɪviː'mɛərɪ). [L. and It. See AVE.] The *Hail Mary!* the angelic salutation to the Virgin (*Luke* i. 28), combined with that of Elizabeth (*v.* 42), used as a devotional recitation, with the addition (in more recent times) of a prayer to the Virgin, as Mother of God; so named from its first two words.

The words are: 'Ave [Maria] gratia plena, Dominus tecum; benedicta tu in mulieribus; et benedictus fructus ventris tui [Jesus; Amen]. Sancta Maria, Mater Dei, ora pro nobis peccatoribus nunc et in hora mortis nostræ.' (The words *Jesus, Amen*, were added by Pope Urban IV, 1261–66. They are now omitted, since the addition of the prayer first sanctioned by Pius V, 1568.)

(Of the Latin the usual Eng. pronunciation is ('eɪviːmə'raɪə), but ('ɑːveɪmə'riːə) after Italian, or 'restored Latin,' is common; some poets have ('mɑːrɪə) after L. precedents.)

c **1230** *Ancr. R.* 46 Þritti Pater nostres, & aue Maria efter euerich Pater noster. *c* **1365** CHAUCER *ABC* N., An Avemary or twey. **1552** ABP. HAMILTON *Catechism* (1884) 273 The Salutatioun of the Angel Gabriel, callit the *Ave Maria*: 'Hail Marie ful of grace, our lord is with the, blissit art thow amang wemen, and blissit is the fruit of thi wambe.' **1593** SHAKS. *3 Hen. VI*, II. i. 162 Numb'ring our Aue-Maries with our Beads. **1621** BURTON *Anat. Mel.* II. ii. IV. (1676) 180/1 To say so many paternosters, avemarias, creeds. **1765** TUCKER *Lt. Nat.* II. 414 Mumbling over Paternosters and Ave Mary's. **1876** S. CURTIS in *N. Amer. Rev.* CXXIII. 52 Death gives him time only to recite an Avemaria and a Paternoster.

b. = AVE *sb.* 2 a, 3 a.

1599 SANDYS *Europæ Spec.* (1632) 6 The devotion advised is the Ave Marie, and the Bell which rings to it hath also that name. **1835** *Penny Cycl.* III. 166/1 Ave Maria is in Italy .. about half an hour after sunset .. In many churches .. the bells are also rung at the first dawn of day, and this is called in Italy the morning Ave Maria.

avenaceous (ævɪ'neɪʃəs), *a.* [f. L. *avēnāce-us*, f. *avēna* oats: see -ACEOUS.] Of the nature of, or belonging to, oats; in *Bot.* belonging to the *Avenæ* or Oat-grasses, including the cultivated oats.

1775 ASH, *Avenacious.* **1847** in CRAIG.

†'avenage. *Obs.* [a. F. *avenage*, f. *aveine*, *avoine*:—L. *avēna* oats; cf. med.L. *avēnāgium.*] A payment in oats made to a landlord or feudal superior.

1594 NORDEN *Spec. Brit.* Essex (1840) 9 Barstable .. yeeldeth greate store of ottes .. whence her Maᵗⁱᵉ hath greate store of prouision of auenage. **1693** W. ROBERTSON *Phraseol. Gen.* 182 Avenage, or an homage of oats, *Avenarium tributum.* **1742** BAILEY, *Avenage*, Oats paid to a Landlord instead of other Duties.

†'avenant, *a.* and *sb. Obs.* Forms: 4–5 **au-avenant, -aunt(e,** 4 **auinant.** *North.* 4–5 **avenand, -aund, -ond(e, awenand, (auonand).** [a. OF. *avenant*, pr. pple. of *avenir* to arrive, happen, succeed, to suit, befit, become:—L. *advenīre*, f. *ad-* to + *venīre* to come.]

A. *adj.* **1.** Convenient, suitable, agreeable.

c **1300** *K. Alis.* 6333 They no haveth camayle, no olifaunt, No kow, no hors avenaunt. **1375** BARBOUR *Bruce* III. 41 Tharfor me thynk maist awenand To withdraw ws. *c* **1440** *Morte Arth.* 2627 Aketouns avenaunt for Arthur hym selfene.

b. with *inf.* Fit, able *to.* Cf. OF. *avenant à.*

c **1400** *Octouian* 923 No dosyper nas so avenaunt To stonde hys strok.

2. Handsome, comely, graceful; pleasant.

1340 HAMPOLE *Pr. Consc.* 5020 Þair bodys sal be semely .. With avenand lymes. *a* **1440** *Sir Degrev.* 1309 'Syre duke avenaunt I pray the hold couvenaunt.' **1481** CAXTON *Myrr.* I. xiv. 45 A lytil man is ofte wel made and auenaunt.

B. *sb.* That which suits one; convenience, purpose. ***at*** or ***to one's avenant***: at one's convenience or pleasure, as suits one.

c **1400** *Ywaine & Gaw.* 3174 He said, That war noght mine avenant. *a* **1440** *Sir Degrev.* 370 One the morow sire Degrevvant Dyght him at is avennaunt.

†'avenantly, *adv. Obs.* [f. prec. adj. + -LY².] Suitably, agreeably, pleasantly.

c **1350** *Will. Palerne* 3784 Armed at alle points and avenantli horsed. *Ibid.* 4884 Alphouns .. auenauntli him grette.

†a'venary, -ery. *Obs.* [a. AF. *avenerie*, = OF. *avenière*:—L. **avēnāria*, f. *avēnārius*: see next.] The office of the avener.

1601 TATE *Househ. Ord. Edw. II*, §56 And receve livery of hay, oates, and littere from the office of the avenery. **1627** R. PERROT *Jacobs Vowe* 48 Payable unto his Avenary. **1631** POWELL *Tom All Trades* 168 The Master of the Horse preferrs to the Avenanarie [*sic*] and other Clarkeships offices.

avence, obs. form of AVENS.

†a'vener. *Obs.* exc. *Hist.* Forms: 5 **aueyner,** 5–8 **avener,** 7 **avenor, -our, -ar,** (9 **aveynor**). [a. OF. *avenier*, *avener*, oat-merchant:—L. adj. *avēnārius* pertaining to oats.] A chief officer of the stable, who had charge of the provender for the horses.

[**1282** *Petit. in Tower Lond.*, Sive Accipitrariorum, sive falconariorum, sive Avenariorum.] *a* **1400** in Wright *Voc.* 176 *Abatis*, avener. *c* **1460** *Bk. Curtasye* in *Babees Bk.* (1868) 305 Þe Aueyner schalle ordeyn prouande .. For þo lordys horsis. **1576** *Exp.* in Nichols *Progr. Q. Eliz.* II. 51 The Avener, equiries and all others of the stable. **1671** F. PHILIPPS *Reg. Necess.* 223 The Equirries and Avenors. **1727** *Hist. Reg.*, *Chron. Diary* 26 Appointed Avener and Clerk Martial to the King. **1861** *Eng. Home* 80 He gave to the aveynor the coarse lentil bread baked for that purpose.

aveng, pa. t. of AFONG *v. Obs.* to take.

avenge (ə'vɛndʒ), *v.* Forms: 4–6 **auenge,** (4 **awenge**), 5 **avenie** (= *je*), 5–6 **aduenge,** 5– **avenge.** [a. OF. *avengier* (3rd s. pr. *avenge*), f. *à* to + *vengier*:—L. *vindicāre* to claim as one's own, avenge: see VINDICATE. The pref. *a-* was often in the 15–16th c. expanded to *ad-*, after assumed Latin analogies; cf. *advertise*, *advance*, *advowson.*]

1. To take vengeance, inflict retributive punishment, exact satisfaction, or retaliate, on behalf of (an injured person, violated right, etc.); to vindicate. Const. *on*, *upon*, *of* (arch.), *against* (arch. or obs.), (*over* obs.) the offender; *of*, *against* the offence (*arch.*). **a.** *trans.*

1377 LANGL. *P. Pl.* B. xx. 382 Now kynde me auenge. *c* **1450** *Merlin* x. 155 He wolde his felowe a-venge yef he in eny wyse cowde. **1526** TINDALE *Luke* xviii. 3 Avenge [WYCLIF, venge] me of myne adversary. **1591** SHAKS. *1 Hen. VI*, I. iv. 94 Remember to auenge me on the French. **1655** MILTON *Sonn.* xviii, Avenge, O Lord, thy slaughtered saints. **1799** SHERIDAN *Pizarro* II. iv, Go, and avenge your fallen brethren. **1866** NEALE *Seq. & Hymns* 74 Thou shalt avenge Thy right.

b. *refl.* (on one's own behalf.)

c **1380** *Sir Ferumb.* 1029 Auenge þe her-of eft sone. **1481** CAXTON *Myrr.* III. xiii. 162 Thus auenged he hym on her. **1587** GOLDING *De Mornay* xvi. 259 Brute Beasts .. they ad-uenge themselues. **1861** HOOK *Lives Abps.* I. vii. 377 Edwy had the power to avenge himself upon Dunstan.

fig. **1837** DISRAELI *Venetia* I. ix, He .. avenged himself at these moments for his habitual silence before third persons.

c. *passively.* (Chiefly with reflexive sense.)

c **1375** WYCLIF *Antecrist* 126 Crist was suffryng & forȝaue, & þei wolen be awengid. *c* **1440** *Syr Gowghter* 448 On the he will avenied be. **1483** CAXTON *Gold. Leg.* 418/2, I shal be aduengyd agenst the. **1535** COVERDALE *Ps.* cxix. 84 When wilt thou be auenged of my aduersaries? **1667** MILTON *P.L.* IX. 143 Hee to be aveng'd .. Determin'd to advance into our room A Creature form'd of Earth.

d. *intr.* (refl. pron. omitted) To take vengeance.

1535 COVERDALE *Isa.* i. 23, I must ease me of myne enemies, and a venge [**1611** auenge me] vpon them. **1611** BIBLE *Lev.* xix. 18 Thou shalt not auenge [COVERDALE, thyself], nor beare any grudge against the children of thy people.

2. *trans.* To take vengeance, inflict retributive punishment, or retaliate on account of, or to exact satisfaction for (a wrong or injury, or the feelings of resentment caused by it). Const. as in 1.

1377 LANGL. *P. Pl.* B. XVIII. 101 For be þis derkenesse ydo his deth worth avenged. **1483** CAXTON *G. de la Tour* H vij, For to auenge his grete yre. **1541** BARNES *Wks.* (1573) 289/1 The which God shall aduenge full straitly ouer you. **1611** BIBLE *Hosea* i. 4, I will auenge the blood of Iezreel vpon the house of Iehu. **1790** BURKE *Fr. Rev.* 112 To avenge even a look that threatened her with insult. **1860** MASSEY *Hist. Eng.* III. xxix. 267 Private grudges were avenged.

†3. To take vengeance upon. *Obs.*

1633 BP. HALL *Hard Texts* 206 Thy mercy in blessing and forgiuing thy people, and thy judgment in avenging thine enemies. **1666** [see AVENGING *vbl. sb.*]

¶ Neither in earlier, nor even in modern, usage is the restriction of *avenge* and its derivatives to the idea of just retribution, as distinguished from the malicious retaliation of *revenge*, absolutely observed, although it largely prevails.

a'venge, *sb. arch.* [f. prec. vb.] Execution of vengeance; retributive punishment, retaliation (either upon an offender, or on account of a wrong).

1568 Q. ELIZ. in H. Campbell *Love-lett. Mary Q. Scots* (1824) App. 12 Fearing his avenge when he shall come to age. *a* **1603** T. CARTWRIGHT *Confut. Rhem. N.T.* (1618) 668 That for Gods glory in the avenge of Idolatry .. there should be no rain for a time. **1880** *Lit. World* 31 Dec. 453/1 A Spanish avenge for the death of Mary Queen of Scots.

avengeance (ə'vɛndʒəns). ? *Obs.* [f. as prec. after *vengeance*.] Avenging; vengeance.

1535 COVERDALE *Isa.* lxi. 1 The daye of yᵉ avengeaunce of oure God. **1708** J. PHILIPS *Cyder* II. (1726) 49 This neglected, fear Signal Avengeance.

avenged (ə'vɛndʒd, -ʒɪd), *ppl. a.* [f. AVENGE *v.* + -ED.] (One) on whose behalf vengeance is taken.

1850 MRS. BROWNING *Poems* II. 7 Bring the avengèd's son anear.

avengeful (ə'vɛndʒfʊl), *a.* [f. AVENGE *sb.* + -FUL.] Full of vengeance, vengeance-taking.

1591 SPENSER *Tears of Muses* 8 Ioues auengefull wrath. **1649** tr. *Alcoran* 73 God will be avenged on him, he is omnipotent, and avengfull. **1763** CHURCHILL *Duellist* I. 95 Fearing his avengeful rod. **1841** D'ISRAELI *Amen. Lit.* I. 19 His avengeful queen cast the mother .. into the river.

avengement (ə'vɛndʒmənt). Also 5–7 **au-,** 6 **adv-.** [a. OF. *avengement*, f. *avengier*: see AVENGE *v.* and -MENT.] Infliction of retributive punishment, exaction of satisfaction, vengeance.

1494 FABYAN cl. (R.) In auengement of his sayd lordes deth. **1535** *Goodly Primer* (1848) 64 Drawn to .. avengement, wrath, or such other vices. **1670** MILTON *Hist. Eng.* IV. (1851) 167 Thir full avengement upon Ecfrid. **1795**

T. TAYLOR *Apuleius* (1822) 212 He..enjoyed the most grateful avengement of corrupted nuptials. **1826** E. IRVING *Babylon* II. 319 The Lord, in all his avengements, hath..an eye to..the reformation of the wicked.

avenger (əˈvɛndʒə(r)). [f. AVENGE *v.* + -ER[1].]

1. He who avenges (the injured or the injury).

1535 COVERDALE *Isa.* xli. 14 The holyone of Israel thine avenger [WYCLIF, aȝeen biere]. —— *Josh.* xx. 5 Yf the auenger of bloude [WYCLIF, blood wreker, venger] folowe vpon him. **1741** MIDDLETON *Cicero* (1742) III. XI. 265 The avenger of so many treasons. **1818** BYRON *Ch. Har.* IV. 130 Time, the avenger, unto thee I lift My hands and eyes. **1876** GREEN *Short Hist.* i. §1 (1882) 2 Every freeman was his own avenger.

†**2.** He who takes vengeance on, or punishes (the offender). Cf. AVENGE *v.* 3. *Obs.*

1388 WYCLIF *Ps.* viii. 3 That thou destrie the enemy and avengere [**1382** veniere]. *a* **1625** BOYS *Wks.* (1630) 878 And they be called Auengers in that they persecute the friends of God. **1667** MILTON *P.L.* x. 241 Ere this he had return'd, with fury driv'n By his Avenger.

avengeress (əˈvɛndʒərɪs). [f. prec. + -ESS.] A female avenger.

1596 SPENSER *F.Q.* III. viii. 20 That cruell queene avengeresse. **1855** SINGLETON *Virgil* II. 123 The guilty doth th' avengeress..Tisiphone, Torment in mockery.

avenging (əˈvɛndʒɪŋ), *vbl. sb.* [f. AVENGE *v.*] The action of the vb. AVENGE; avengement.

1541 ELYOT *Image Govt.* 166 The auengeyng of his displeasure. **1666** BP. NORWICH *Serm.* 7 Nov. 27 Even in the avenging of conquer'd Enemies Moderation is advantagious. **1883** *Athenæum* 1 Dec. 700/1 The story of a villain, of his victims, and of their avenging.

aˈvenging, *ppl. a.* [f. as prec. + -ING[2].] That avenges or has as its attribute to avenge.

1596 SPENSER *F.Q.* I. vii. 47 The bitter dint of his auenging blade. **1667** MILTON *P.L.* VII. 184 Whose just avenging ire Had driven out th' ungodly from his sight. **1781** GIBBON *Decl. & F.* II. 119 An avenging Deity. **1836** HOR. SMITH *Tin Trump.* (1876) 183 Wielding the avenging thunder.

aˈvengingly, *adv.* [f. prec. + -LY[2].] In an avenging manner, with vengeance, vengefully.

1824 GALT *Rothelan* III. VI. vii. 71 The same day that he so avengingly visited Sir Amias. **1843** *Blackw. Mag.* LIII. 305 Avengingly out from the cloud Come the levin, the bolt, and the ball!

aveniform (əˈviːnɪfɔːm), *a.* [f. L. *avēna* oats + -FORM.] Having the form or appearance of oats, oat-like.

1881 in *Syd. Soc. Lex.*

avenin (əˈviːnɪn). [f. as prec. + -IN.] The nitrogenous principle of the oat.

1863 WATTS *Dict. Chem.* I. 476 Avenin..[is] probably identical with legumin.

†**aˈvenom**, *v. Obs.* [a. OF. *avenime-r* = *envenimer*: see A- *pref.* 10, and cf. ANVENOM.] To poison.

c **1314** *Guy Warw.* 98 His armes alle a-venimed beth.

avenor, corrupt form of AVENER.

avenous (əˈviːnəs), *a.* [f. A- *pref.* 14 + L. *vēn-a* vein + -OUS. *Avenious* (Mayne *Exp. Lex.* 1853) is a bad form.] Without veins, veinless.

1881 in *Syd. Soc. Lex.*

avens (ˈævənz). *Herb.* Forms: 3–5 **avence**, 5 **avance, avans**, 6 **avaunce**, 6–7 **auens**, 6– **avens**. [a. OF. *avence*; in med.L. *avencia, -ancia, -antia*; origin unknown.] Popular name of two species of the genus *Geum* (N.O. *Rosaceæ*), the Wood Avens or Herb Bennet (*G. urbanum*), formerly used medicinally and to give a clove-like flavour to ale, and Water Avens (*G. rivale*); also applied to the subalpine Mountain Avens (*Dryas octopetala*).

c **1250** in Wright *Voc.* (W.) /555 *Avencia*, avence, harefot. *c* **1420** *Liber Cocorum* (1862) 42 Rede nettel crop and avans also. *a* **1500** *Rel. Ant.* I. 53 Tak avaunce, matfelon, yarow. **1578** LYTE *Dodoens* 133 The leaues of Sanamunda, Auens, or Herbe Bennet, are rough. **1616** SURFLET *Countr. Farm* 182 Costmarie and Auens..haue the taste of Pepper and Cloues. **1858** KINGSLEY *Misc.* I. 176 The avens—fairest and most modest of all the water-side nymphs..with a soft blush upon her tawny cheek. **1863** BARING-GOULD *Iceland* 190 The pale mountain avens with its sunny heart.

†**aˈvent**, *v. Obs.* [a. AF. *avente-r* (= OF. *esventer*, mod.F. *éventer*):—Romanic **exventare*, f. L. *ex* out + *ventus* wind.]

1. *trans.* To air, to refresh with cool air, *esp.* by opening the front of the helmet so as to admit it; *hence*, to open (the helmet) for this purpose.

1375 BARBOUR *Bruce* VI. 305 That of his basnet than had tane To awent hym [*v.r.* tak the air] for he wes hate. *c* **1400** *Destr. Troy* xv. 7090 He voidet his viser, auentid hym seluyn. *c* **1440** *Bone Flor.* 1941 As he schulde hys helme avente, A quarell smote hym. *c* **1450** *Merlin* xx. 335 Thei were well refresshed and a-vented.

2. *refl.* and *intr.* To come out or escape into the open air; *fig.* to escape from confinement. Hence **aventing** *vbl. sb.*

c **1375** WYCLIF *Serm.* (Sel. Wks. 1869) I. 219 Whanne þei ben aventid..Goddis lawe lymyteþ how þes wyndis shulen passe awei. *c* **1380** —— *De Pseudo-Freres* Wks. (1880) 319 It were good to many men þat ben closid in þise ordris þat þei disporteden hem in þe world. for siche auentyng many times fordoiþ enuye, ire & lust.

aventail, -ayle (ˈævənteɪl). Forms: 4–9 **aventail(e, -ayle**, 4–5 **aventaille, -ale, avantaille, adventayle**. [a. AF. **aventail* = OF. *esventail* air-hole, f. *esventer* (see prec.): the Lat. type is **exventaculum* (cf. *prōpugnāculum*). For the form in *adv-*, see AD- *pref.* 2.]

The movable front or mouthpiece of a helmet, which may be raised to admit fresh air.

c **1340** *Gaw. & Gr. Knt.* 608 Wyth a lyȝtli vrysoun ouer þe auentayle. *c* **1374** CHAUCER *Troylus* v. 1558 As he drough a kynge by th' avantaille. *a* **1400** *Octouian* 1153 Hys adventayle he gan unlace. **1460** *Lybeaus Disc.* 1618 Pysane, aventayle, and gorgere. **1805** SCOTT *Last Minstr.* II. iii, And lifted his barred aventayle. **1842** *Blackw. Mag.* LII. 171 With pierced aventails for the eyes and mouth.

†**aventine** (ˈævəntaɪn). [ad. L. *Aventīnus* (sc. *mons*) one of the seven hills of Rome.] *fig.* A secure position, a 'strong tower.' (*Obs.*)

a **1625** BEAUM. & FL. (in Webster) Into the castle's tower, The only Aventine that now is left him. **1626** MASSINGER *Rom. Actor* I. i, I expect No favour from him. My strong Aventine is That great Domitian.

†**aˈventre**, *v. Obs.* Probably an alteration of *afeutre*, a. OF. *afeutrer* to FEWTER = to set (a spear) in the rest.

1557 *K. Arthur* (Copland) IV. xviii, He dressed his shelde, and they auentred their speres. **1596** SPENSER *F.Q.* III. i. 28 Her mortal speare She mightily aventred towards one, And downe him smot. *Ibid.* IV. vi. 11 And eft aventring his steele-headed launce Against her rode.

†**aˈventure**. *Obs.* [a. OF. *aventure* (see ADVENTURE *sb.*), used spec. in Eng. law-books of death by accident pure and simple, as distinguished from *mesaventure*, in which some amount of negligence is implied.] (See quot.)

[**1292** BRITTON I. viii.] **1672** MANLEY *Interpr., Aventure*..is a Mischance, causing the death of a Man, without Felony; as when he is suddenly drowned or burnt, falling into the Water or Fire. **1809** [So in TOMLINS *Law Dict.*].

aventure, obs. form of ADVENTURE *sb.* and *v.*

aventurine, -in (əˈvɛntjʊərɪn). Also **avant-**. [a. F. *aventurine*, ad. It. *avventurino*, f. *avventura* chance; so called from its accidental discovery.]

1. A brownish-coloured glass interspersed with small gold-coloured spangles, manufactured first at Murano, near Venice. Also called *artificial aventurine, aventurine glass, gold flux.*

1811 PINKERTON *Petral.* II. 461 With an effect resembling aventurine. **1883** W. WILLIAMS in *Gentl. Mag.* July 94 Aventurine..is a kind of glass of a pale brownish colour, brown pink I should call it. Bedded and suspended in this are innumerable brilliant gold-like spangles.

2. *transf.* A variety of quartz, spangled with yellow scales of mica, resembling the preceding in appearance.

1858 TENNANT *Catal. Brit. Foss.* 77 Earthy Minerals—Rock Crystal, Amethyst, Cairngorm, Avanturine. **1861** C. KING *Ant. Gems* (1866) 63 The true Aventurine, or Goldie-stone..takes a high polish. **1863** WATTS *Dict. Chem.* I. 476 Aventurin or Avanturin.

3. The colour or appearance of aventurine.

1791 HAMILTON *Berthollet's Dyeing* II. II. III. vii, The wax is coloured..for aventurine or gold-colour with orpiment.

4. *attrib.* **aventurine glass** (see 1); **aventurine glaze**, a glaze for porcelain which produces a similar gold-spangled brown colour; **aventurine felspar** or **sunstone**, a mixture of oligoclase and orthoclase spangled with yellowish or reddish crystals; **aventurine quartz** (see 2).

1875 URE *Dict. Arts* I. 277 Aventurine glass owes its golden iridescence to a crystalline separation of metallic copper from the mass coloured brown by the peroxide of iron. **1816** CLEAVELAND *Min.* 269 Aventurine Feldspar..contains little spangles or points, which reflect a brilliant light.

avenue (ˈævɪnjuː), *sb.* Also 7 **advenue, avenew(e, avennue**. [a. F. *avenue* sb. from fem. pa. pple. of *avenir*:—L. *advenīre*, f. *ad* to + *venire* to come (after which spelt *advenue* by some in 16–17th c.). Occas., in 18th c., accented *aˈvenue*.]

†**1.** The action of coming to; approach. *Obs.*

1639 SALTMARSH *Pract. Policie* 23 The first heate you raise by your avenues and addresses will coole.

2. *gen.* A way of access or approach; a passage or path of entrance or exit. (Formerly a regular military term.) Now chiefly *fig.*

1600 HOLLAND *Livy* XXXV. I. 917 Hermeum, where is the advenue [*transitus*] out of Bœotia into the Iland of Eubœa. *a* **1672** WOOD *Life* (1848) 26 Col. Legge..with the reere guarded the towne and avenews. **1678** BUTLER *Hud.* III. i. 1500 With holy water, like a sluice To overflow all avenues. **1800** STUART in *Wellesley Disp.* (1877) 577 It becomes incumbent on us to watch..this avenue to India. **1921** WODEHOUSE *Indiscr. Archie* i. 12 You did not irremediably close all avenues to a peaceful settlement. **1926** *Sat. Rev.* 16 Oct. 446/2 He..explores every avenue which may lead him to a point of vantage whence to view his life in its new meaning. **1927** *Rev. Eng. Stud.* Oct. 432 Our politicians are said to deal with *dominant issues* and to *explore avenues.*

fig. **1603** HOLLAND *Plutarch* 160, I have prevented thee (ô Fortune) I have stopped up all thy avenewes. **1655** LESTRANGE *Chas. I*, 8 To whom we dare not think the advenue's of eternal blessednesse precluded. *c* **1742** C. WESLEY in Southey *Wesley* (1846) I. xiii. 370 *note*, Guard each avenue to thy flutt'ring heart, And act the sister's and the Christian's part. **1876** GREEN *Short Hist.* ix. §9. 697 To Scotland the Union opened up new avenues of wealth.

3. The chief approach to a country-house, usually bordered by trees; *hence*, any broad roadway bordered or marked by trees or other objects at regular intervals. Sometimes used of the trees alone, with tacit disregard of the road they overshadow.

(The current literal sense, app. introduced by Evelyn.)

1654 EVELYN *Diary* 25 Aug., The avenue was vngraceful. **1664** —— *Sylva* Advt., That this may yet be no prejudice to the meaner capacities let them read for *avenue*, the principal walk to the front of the house, or seat. **1669** WORLIDGE *Syst. Agric.* (1681) 321 *Avenues*, Ways or Passages, or Rows or Walks of Trees. **1707** FARQUHAR *Beaux' Strat.* IV. i, Drawn by the Appearance of your handsome House..and walking up the Avenue. **1859** GEO. ELIOT *A. Bede* 111 Arthur Donnithorne passed under an avenue of limes and beeches. **1862** STANLEY *Jew. Ch.* (1877) I. iv. 74 The avenue of sphinxes leading to the huge gateway.

4. A fine wide street. (Used *esp.* in U.S.)

1858 HAWTHORNE *Fr. & It. Jrnls.* II. 209 They hardly look like streets at all, but, nevertheless have names printed on the corners, just as if they were stately avenues. *a* **1885** *Mod.* Northumberland Avenue leading to the Thames Embankment.

5. The ambulacrum or double row of pores for the protrusion of the tube-feet in sea-urchins.

1841 E. FORBES *Brit. Starfish* 152 There are five pairs of avenues; they run from mouth to anus. **1870** ROLLESTON *Anim. Life* 141 Along the medial line of each radial avenue.

ˈavenue, *v.* [f. prec. sb.] To make into an avenue; to form avenues in; to line.

1865 *Cornh. Mag.* Aug. 224 The too-fragrant exotics which avenue its lengths.

avenued (ˈævɪnjuːd), *ppl. a.* [f. AVENUE *sb.* or *v.*] Furnished with or having an avenue or avenues.

1870 RUSKIN *Verona* §31 One paradise of lovely pasture and avenued forest of chestnut and blossomed trees. **1899** *Daily News* 7 Nov. 3/5 An open, avenued, highly-cultivated plateau.

†**ˈaveny**. *Obs.* Anglicized form of AVANIA; cf. F. *avanie.*

1676 TEONGE *Diary* (1825) 161 Afrayd least an aveny (fine) should have been layd on them. **1682** WHELER *Journ. Greece* IV. 298 One runs the risque of having the Barque burned, and an Aveny set upon you besides. **1682** LUTTRELL *Brief Rel.* (1857) I. 177 The Turks..lay greater avenies [*printed* avenue's] on that trade than ever.

aver (ˈeɪvə(r)), *sb. Obs.* exc. *dial.* Forms: *α.* 4 **aueyr, auere, haver**, 4–5 **auer**, 5 **aveer, hawere**. *Pl.* 5 **auers, averys**. *β.* 5 **auoyre, havoire, auoir, hauoyr, havyoure, havur**, 5–6 **hauour, hauoir**, 6 **hauor, avyoure**. In sense 3 in *Sc.* 6 **avir**, 6– **aver**, 8– **aiver**. [a. OF. *aveir, aver*, mod.F. *avoir*, possession, property, stuff, 'stock,' cattle, domestic animals, beasts of burden; lit. 'having,' subst. use of *aveir, avoir*:—L. *habēre* to have. So It. *avere* 'substance, goods, stocke, chattle' (Florio); Sp. *averes, haveres*, pl., 'goods, wealth, substance'; whence med.L. *aver, avere, averium, averum*, 'substance, goods,' and *avera, averia*, pl. (in Anglo-Lat.), 'beasts, cattle,' sing. *averum, -ium*, sometimes *averia*, 'beast,' *averius, affrus, affer*, 'beast of burden, draught-horse.' Eng. had only the Norman form *aveyr, aver*, bef. 1400; the 15th c. introduced *avoir* from literary French, from Caxton onward *havoir, havor*, HAVOUR (q.v.) in sense 1. The earlier *aver* was retained in north. dial. only in a special sense (3).]

1. a. *coll. sing.* Possession, property, estate, wealth; money.

α. **1330** R. BRUNNE *Chron.* 124 In suilk felonie gadred grete auere. *c* **1340** HAMPOLE *Prose Tr.* 24 Muchelle haver of worldely goodis. **1393** LANGL. *P. Pl. C.* VII. 32 þat men wende ich were, as in aueyr, riche. *c* **1450** *Merlin* xi. 167 Thei boughten londes and rentes..with the auer that was departed. **1496** *Dives & Paup.* (W. de W.) VII. iv. 279/2 Unryghtfull occupyenge of ony..auer in this worlde, is called theeft. ? **1558** *Sir Lambervell* 150 in Furniv. *Percy Folio* I. 149, I am a knight without hawere.

β. *c* **1400** *Rom. Rose* 4723 Havoire withoute possessioun. *c* **1410** LOVE *Bonavent. Mirr.* xxiv. (Gibbs MS.) 53 All worldly ryches as in Aver [**1530** *W. de Worde*, hauoyr]. *c* **1450** *Merlin* xx. 357 All the grete auoir that thei hadde conquered. **1483** *Act 1 Rich. III*, iv. §1 Persones of noo substaunce ne havur. **1529** MORE *Comf. agst. Trib.* III. Wks. 1221/1 A manne of some hauor and substaunce. **1600** HOLLAND *Livy* XXXV. xxii. 900 Of any havoir, worth and worship.

b. *plural.* Possessions, goods, riches.

c **1440** *Partonope* 775 Gold and ryche averys. *c* **1450** *Merlin* vi. 106 As sone as he hadde the grete auers.

2. *pl.* Farm-stock, cattle, domestic animals of any kind, beasts.

Common in Anglo-French and Anglo-Latin; though no vernacular instances have been found, the next sense must have arisen out of it.

[**1292** BRITTON II. xxiii. §6 Cum il deit aver pasture a totes maneres des avers, et ne ly soit mie suffert for qe a une manere de avers. (*i.e.* When he ought to have pasturage for all kinds of *avers* (beasts), and he is allowed to have it only for one manner of *avers.*) ? *a* **1300** *Reg. Majest.* IV. xxvii, Averia, id est, animalia muta (transl., *Avers*, that is, dumb-animals). *c* **1481** LITTLETON *Tenures* §71 Si come jeo bayle a vn home mes brebits a compester sa terre, ou mes bœfs a arer la terre, et il occist mes auers. (*c* **1574** transl., If I lend to one my Sheepe to tathe his Land, or my Oxen to plow the Land, and he killeth my Cattell.)]

3. *sing.* A beast of burden, a draught ox or horse; hence, *spec.* a horse used for heavy work, a cart-horse; and in later usage, in ***north. dial.***, an old or worthless horse.

[*a* **1259** M. PARIS in T. Walsingham *Gesta* (1867) I. 259 Juravit idem Abbas Willelmus, se centum equos uno anno in diversis partibus Abbathiæ [perdisse], quorum alii erant manni, alii vero runcini, alii Summarii, alii veredarii, alii vero averii. **1285** *Stat. Westm.* 2 c. 18 Vicecomes liberet ei omnia catalla debitoris, exceptis bobus et affris carucæ. (**1618** PULTON transl., All the Cattells of the debtor, sauing onely his Oxen and beasts of his Plough.)]*c* **1505** DUNBAR *Flyting* 229 And cager aviris castis bayth coillis and creilis. **1536** BELLENDENE *Cron. Scot.* (1821) II. 269, I sall gar him draw like ane avir in ane cart. **1599** JAMES I *Basil. Doron* (1603) 62 A kindely auer will never become a good horse. **1674** RAY *N. Countr. Wds., Average*.. deduced from the old word *Aver* [Averium] signifying a labouring beast. **1691** BLOUNT *Law Dict.* s.v. *Affri* (transl. Spelman), In Northumberland, to this day, they call a dull or slow Horse, a *False aver*, or *Afer.* **1820** SCOTT *Monast.* (1867) 521/1 An auld jaded aver to ride upon.

aver (ə'vɜː(r)), *v.* Pples. **averred, averring.** Forms: 4–7 **auer,** 6–7 **au- averre,** 7–8 **averr,** 6– **aver.** [a. F. *avérer*, cogn. with Pr. *averar*, It. *avverare*:—late L. **advērāre* to make true, verify, prove to be true, f. *ad* to (factitive) + *vērus* true. Sense 2 was the earlier in Fr.]

† **1.** *trans.* To declare true, assert the truth of (a statement). *Obs.*

c **1380** WYCLIF *Wks.* (1880) 306 We auer þis what iude seiþ of apostataes. **1602** WARNER *Alb. Eng.* XI. lxv. (1612) 280 Loue is a lordly Feast, he writes, and I the same auerre. **1634–46** ROW *Hist. Kirk* (1842) 106 That youths doe not maintaine fals opinions, howbeit averred by Aristotle or other profane authors.

† **2.** To prove true, confirm, verify. *Obs.*

1548 (ABP.) ABBOT in Strype *Eccl. Mem.* II. I. xv. 122 This lying Jesuit can shew no letter.. to aver this his calumniation. *a* **1593** H. SMITH *Wks.* (1867) II. 60 That answer.. seemeth to aver the truth of that which I say. **1603** KNOLLES *Hist. Turks* 132 Onely so farre as shall be.. by the authority of good Histories to be auerred. **1678** *Trans. Crt. Spain* 52 If the Crime be averred, the Criminal will be so too.

3. *Law.* To prove or justify a plea; to offer to justify an exception pleaded; to make an averment. Const. as in 4.

1490 *Act 4 Hen. VII*, xx, The pleyntif.. may averre that the said recovere.. was had by covyne. **1586** J. HOOKER *Girald. Irel.* in *Holinsh.* II. 180/2 The appellant was demanded whether he would auerre his demand or not; who when he had affirmed that he would, the partie defendant.. did answer as did the other, that he would auerre it by the swoord. **1676–7** MARVELL *Corr.* 286 Wks. 1875 II. 520 He cannot averre against the Record of his conviction. **1847** C. ADDISON *Contracts* I. i. § 1 (1883) 19 No one can be permitted .. to aver or to prove anything in contradiction to what he has solemnly and deliberately avowed by deed.

4. To assert as a fact; to state positively, affirm. **a.** *trans.* with simple obj.

1583 STANYHURST *Aeneis* III. (Arb.) 84 What sooth thee virgin auerreth, Shee frams in Poëtry. **1691** RAY *Creation* I. (1704) 159, I shall only averr what myself have sometimes observed. **1839** JAMES *Louis XIV*, IV. 46 What one author avers upon the subject, another denies.

b. with *complement* or *inf. phr.*

1509 HAWES *Past. Pleas.* v. xi, The Latyn worde whyche that is referred Unto a thynge whych is substancyall, For a nowne substantyve is wel averred. **1581** SIDNEY *Def. Poesie* (Arb.) 52 How often doe the Phisitians lye, when they auer things good for sicknesses. **1699** BENTLEY *Phal.* 384 Which being.. within the reach of my own Knowledge, I do averr to be a Calumny. **1829** I. TAYLOR *Enthus.* iv. (1867) 100 Is a mystic prediction averred to be unfulfilled?

c. with *subord. cl.* Cf. quot. 1490 in 3.

1624 GATAKER *Transubst.* 80 Both averre that the Elements in the Eucharist after consecration retaine.. the same nature and substance. **1798** COLERIDGE *Anc. Mar.* II. iv, They all averr'd I had killed the Bird That brought the fog and mist. **1838** DICKENS *Nich. Nick.* xxx, The shopman averring that it was a most uncommon fit.

d. *absol.* quasi-*intr.*

1599 GREENE *George a Gr.* (1861) 264 But, gentle King, for so you would aver, And Edwards betters, I salute you both. **1852** MISS YONGE *Cameos* II. xiii. 145 On good authority as he avers.

5. To assert the existence or occurrence of. *arch.*

1611 SHAKS. *Cymb.* v. v. 203 Auerring notes Of Chamber-hanging, Pictures. **1641** MILTON *Ch. Discip.* Wks. 1738 I. 15 Æsop's Chronicles auer many stranger Accidents. **1673** CAVE *Prim. Chr.* I. ix. 278 Augustine both avers the custom and gives the reason. **1845** R. HAMILTON *Pop. Educ.* ix. 214 Hobbes.. strongly avers this prerogative of the Ruler.

aver, obs. form of A-FIRE and EVER.

aver-, in some compound terms pertaining to feudal usage, appears to be connected with AVERAGE *sb.*[1] Of these terms, we have only the explanations (usually inferences from the assumed derivation) offered by legal editors of 16th and 17th centuries, which are of very doubtful value:—

† **1. aver-corn.** ? Corn paid as a feudal due or in lieu of service.

[**1263** *Charter* in Thorn *Chron.* 1912/2 Quoddam servitium annuum quod *avercorn* vocatur, sub mensura minus certa.] **1670** BLOUNT *Law Dict., Aver-corn*, is such Corn, as by Custom is brought by the Tenants Carts or Carriages to the Lords Granary or Barn. ? **1695** KENNETT *Gloss., Aver-corn* a reserved rent in corn paid to religious houses by their tenants or farmers.

† **2. averland.** ? Land subject to 'average.'

1670 BLOUNT *Law Dict., Averland*, Item Cellarius libere solebat capere omnia sterquilinia ad suum opus in omni vico, nisi ante ostia eorum qui habebant *Averland*. Mon. Angl. I. par. fol. 302. a. It seems to have been such Land as the Tenants did plow and manure, cum averiis suis, for the proper Use of a Monastery or Lord of the Soil: [*Chron. J. de Brakelonda* 75] Quod autem nunc vocatur *Averland*, fuit terra rusticorum, which was subject to Averages, or the Lord's Carriages.

† **3. averpenny.** ? Money paid in lieu of 'average.' (Cf. AVERAGE[1] quot. 1206.)

1253–1378 *St. M. Magd. Coll. MS.* in *4th Rep. R. Com. Hist. MSS.* (1874) 459/1 [Richard ii. 1378, 12 May. Confirmation to the Knights Hospitallers of charters granted to the Templars by Henry iii in 1224, and 1253; of which charters the latter.. exempts them from all taxes and tolls, including] wardepeny et averpeny et hundredepeny et borghelpeny et thethingepeny. **1579** RASTELL *Expos. Term.* 26 *Averpeny*, that is to bee quite of diuers summes of money for the kinges auerages. **1691** BLOUNT *Law Dict., Averpeny* (quasi average-peny) is Money contributed towards the Kings Averages, or Money given to be freed thereof.

† **4. aver-silver.** ? = averpenny. (Halliwell suggests: 'A custom or rent so called, originating from the cattle, or *avers* of the tenants of the soil.')

'**average,** *sb.*[1] *Old Law.* Forms: 5– **average;** *Sc.* 6 **avarage, arage, average, aryage,** 6–9 **arriage.** [In OF. *average* (Godef.) and med. (Anglo-) L. *averagium*, apparently the same as *avera* in Domesday Book, explained by Spelman as 'one day's work which the king's tenants gave to the sheriff.' In the vernacular form, only in Scotch, where also phonetically worn down to *arage* (cf. *laverok, lark, favorand, farrand*), and spelt *arriage* in association with *carriage*. Origin uncertain.

Early explanations evidently treated *avera* as latinized form of OF. *ovre, œvre* work. Sir J. Skene referred it to *aver* 'beast of burden,' and so explained the meaning; but his proposed explanation (since repeated in the Law Dicts.) is hardly supported by the early use of *averagium* and OF. *average*. Danish *hoveri* 'average, soccage-duty,' suggested by Wedgwood, is (with its Romance suffix) a more recent word than *averagium*, and not possibly its source. Mr. C. I. Elton, from the actual use of *avera*, is disposed to revert to the idea of referring it to OF. *ovre, œvre*, its form being perhaps affected by the use of *avere, aver*, for property and cattle. He compares *averagium* with F. *ouvrage*, and med.L. *operagium*.]

Some kind of service due by tenants to the feudal superior. Explained in the Law Dictionaries, since Sir J. Skene, as 'service done by the tenant with his beasts of burden' (see above). Known chiefly in the phrase 'arriage and carriage,' retained in Scotch leases till 20 Geo. II, but having in later times no definitely ascertained meaning.

[**1085** *Domesday Bk.* I 9 b (Kent) In Berham hundredo.. de auera, id est servitium, LX solidi. —— I 132 b (Herfordsh.) In seruitio regis inuenit unam aueram et inwardum, sed iniuste et per vim. *c* **1200** JOCELIN DE BRAKELOND *Chron.* in T. Arnold *Memorials St. Edmund's Abbey* (Rolls Ser. 1890) I. 303 Solebant autem homines villæ, jubente celerario, ire apud Laginghehe [Lakenheath] et reportare avragium de anguillis de Sutreia [Southrey], et sæpe vacui redire et ita vexari sine aliquo emolumento celerarii. **1206** *Fine Rolls of 8 John* (Elton *Tenures of Kent* 366) Ita ut xenia et aueragia et alia opera quæ fiebant de terris iisdem conuertentur in redditum denariorum ægros alentem. *c* **1300** *Custumal Manor of Wye* in S.R. Scargill-Bird *Custumals Battle Abbey* (Camden Soc. 1887) 123 Præter prædicta averagia sunt in æstate de liberis jugis xxxiij averagia, scilicet inter Hokeday et Gulam Augusti. **1371** *Indenture betw. Earl Menteith & C'tess. Fife* (JAM.) Cum auaragiis et caragiis.] **1489** *Acts Jas. IV* (3 Feb.) vii, All landes, rentes, custumez, burrow malez, fermes, martes, mutoun, poultre, average, cariage, and vtheres dewiteis. **1534** *MS.* in *Regr. Off.* (JAM.) That he should pay a rent of 20*l.* usual mony of the realm; 4 dozen poultrie, with all aryage and carriage, and do service use and wont. **1549** *Compl. Scot.* xv. 125, I am maid ane slaue of my body to ryn and rashe in arrage and carraige. **1597** SKENE *De Verb. Sign.* (JAM.), *Arage*.. vtherwaies *Average*, signifies service quhilk the tennent aucht to his master, be horse, or carriage of horse. **1641** *Termes de la Ley* 33 b. **1754** ERSKINE *Princ. Sc. Law* (1809) 191 Clauses were formerly thrown into most tacks, obliging tenants to services indefinitely, under the name of arriage and carriage, or services use and wont. **1818** SCOTT *Hrt. Midl.* viii, Regular payment of mail-duties, kain, arriage, carriage, etc. **1835** *Tomlins' Law Dict., Arriage and carriage*, indefinite services prohibited by 20 Geo. II. c. 50 §21, 22.

average ('ævərɪdʒ), *sb.*[2] Forms: (5 **auerays**) 7 **auer- avaridge,** 7 **averige,** 8 **avirage,** 5– **average.** [Appears first *c* 1500: the corresponding term in F. is *avarie*, Cotgr. 1611 *avaris* (? plural), Catalan *averia*, Sp. *averia* (also found as *haberia*), Pg. and It. *avaria*; also in Du. *avarij, haverij*, Ger. *hafarei, havarie*, Da. *havari*, all from the Romance langs. The earliest instances occur in connexion with the maritime trade of the Mediterranean; but the derivation is uncertain (see below). The Eng. *auerays* (plural) in Arnold's Chron. (if not a misprint) was probably meant for the F. word; the form *average* (also in Arnold's Chron.) is confined to English, and evidently formed on the model of *lodemanage* (pilotage), *primage*, etc.: see -AGE.]

I. Maritime use.

† **1.** *orig.* A duty, tax, or impost charged upon goods; a customs-duty, or the like. *Obs.*

(The original use of *avaria, averia, avarie* in the maritime codes, ordinances, and records of the Mediterranean.)

[*a* **1200** *Assises of Jerusalem* xlii (Pardessus I. 277), Et sachies que selui [aver] qui est gete ne doit estre conté fors tant com il cousta o toutes ses avaries (*transl.*) Know that that property which is thrown overboard shall be reckoned only at what it cost with all its charges: in Venetian version *dazii e spese*, i.e. duties and expenses). *c* **1250** *Consulado del Mar* lix. (1791) Lo nôlit è les avaries (i.e. the freight and charges). **1777** ROBERTSON *Hist. Amer.* (1783) III. 425 The Averia, or tax paid on account of convoys to guard the ships sailing to and from America.] **1502** ARNOLD *Chron.* 180 And ouer that alle maner of grauntis.. of youre custumes or subsidyes or auerage.. be voyd and in none effecte. **1667** E. CHAMBERLAYNE *St. Gt. Brit.* I. III. i. (1743) 146 The goods of Clergymen are discharged.. from Tolls and Customs of Average, Pontage, Murage, Pavage. **1760** BURN *Eccl. Law* (1797) III. 204 Ecclesiastical persons ought to be quit and discharged of tolls, customs, avirage, pontage, paviage, and the like.

2. Any charge or expense over and above the freight incurred in the shipment of goods, and payable by their owner. (In this sense it still occurs in ***petty average***, and the now inoperative phrase, ***average accustomed*** in Bills of Lading: see quotations 1540 and 1865.)

1491 in Arnold *Chron.* 112 And ouer that to pai or doo pay all maner auerays as wel for Burdeux as for Thamys. **1540** *Act 32 Hen. VIII*, xiv, Fraight in any shipp.. for euery tonne homewardes xiijs. iiij*d.*, and for primage and lode-manage of euery tonne vi*d.* stirling, with all auerages accustumed after thold use and custume of English Shippes. **1670** BLOUNT *Law Dict., Average*, is also a little Duty, which those Merchants, who send Goods in another Mans Ship, do pay to the Master of it, for his care over and above the Freight; for in Bills of Lading it is expressed—Paying so much Freight for the said Goods, with Primage and Average accustomed. **1682** SCARLETT *Exchanges* 253 Then he.. may receive the goods, paying the Shipper his Freight and Avaridge; but if there be extraordinary Avaridge, or if the goods be damaged, then the sum of the damage, and of the extraordinary Avaridge, must be deducted from the sums that D, E and G are to receive, they being as Bodomerers or Assurers. **1865** J. LEES *Laws Brit. Ship.* (ed. 9) 203 The term 'average' [in bills of lading] applies to certain small charges, called *petty* or *accustomed* averages, of which, generally, one-third falls to the ship, and two-thirds to the cargo. Both these indefinite terms.. are often adjusted at a precise sum for the voyage.

3. *spec.* The expense or loss to owners, arising from damage at sea to the ship or cargo.

[**1556–84** See *Guidon de la Mer*, Pardessus V. 387. **1611** COTGR., *Avaris*, decay of wares, or merchandise; leckage of wines; also, the charges of the cariage, or measuring thereof.] **1622** MABBE *Aleman's Guzman D' Alf.* II. 127 To defray the charges of averige; for it will not be alwaies faire weather. [**1664** SPELMAN, *Averagium*.. à Gall. *avaris*.. est detrimentum, quod vehendis mercibus accidit; ut fluxio vini, frumenti corruptio, mercium in tempestatibus ejectio. Quibus addunt vecturæ sumptus, et necessariæ aliæ impensæ.] **1755** MAGENS *Insur.* I. 347 Suppose that of this Silver, during the Voyage ¼ had been diminished.. that is an Average or Loss, whatever it is called, of 25 per Cent. *Ibid.* II. 74 An Action for the Damage or Decay of any Ships or Goods, that are insured, generally called Average, must be brought within a Year and a half at furthest, if such Average happened within the limits of Europe or Barbary. **1848** ARNOULD *Mar. Insur.* (1866) I. I. v. 234 The word 'Average,' as employed in this clause, means 'partial loss by sea damage.'

4. a. The incidence of any such charge, expense, or loss; *esp.* the equitable distribution of expense or loss, when of general incidence, among all the parties interested, in proportion to their several interests.

particular average is the incidence of the partial loss or damage of ship, cargo, or freight, through *unavoidable accident*, upon the individual owners (or insurers) of these respective interests.

general average is apportionment of loss caused by *intentional* damage to ship (*e.g.* cutting away of masts or boats), or sacrifice of cargo and consequent loss of freight, or of expense incurred by putting into a port in distress, by acceptance of towage or other services, to secure the general safety of ship and cargo; in which case contribution is made by the owners (or insurers) of ship, cargo, and freight in proportion to the value of their respective interests.

(In connexion with Maritime Law and Marine Insurance this has come to be the prevailing sense of the word. Its first known occurrence is in the 14th c. Civil Statute of Cataro (Pardessus V. 97), where it is enacted that anything given as a present or 'Christmas-box' (*pro strena*), or paid in tribute (*pedocia*), with the consent of the majority, for the good of the vessel, shall be shared by way of average (*illud dividatur per avariam*). Cf. quot. 1603, 1727.)

1598 W. PHILLIP *Linschoten's Trav.* in Arb. *Garner* III. 413 In their ships there is no Average. For when there happeneth any loss, or that any goods are thrown overboard, he standeth to the loss that oweth the goods without any more accounts, etc. **1603** *Act 1 Jas. I*, xxxii, The Master, Owner, and Shipper, payinge the same [rate for repair of Dover Harbour], shall have allowance of the Marchants, according to the rate of the Goods in the same Shippe, Vessell, or Crayer, by way of Average. **1607** COWELL *Int.*, *Average*..is also used for a certaine contribution that merchants and others doe every man proportionably make toward their losses, who have their goods cast into the sea for the safe-gard of the shippe, or of the goods and lives of them in the shippe in time of a tempest. **1622** MALYNES *Anc. Law-Merch.* 136 In such a case, when goods by stormes are cast ouer-boord, it shal not be made good by contribution or aueridge, but by the Masters owne purse: For if hee over-burthen the Ship above the true marke of lading, hee is to pay a fine. **1697** *Lond. Gaz.* No. 3339/4 All Persons the Freighters of the Ship call'd the St. Jago Briganteen..which was cast away..upon the Coast of Portugal, are desired to go to the Jamaica Coffee-House..to sign an Instrument of a general Average, in order to receive their Dividend of the Goods saved. **1715** *Ibid.* No. 4872/3 The whole must come into a general Average, that every one concerned in the Loss may receive a due Proportion of what is saved. **1727** CHAMBERS *Cycl.* s.v. *Average* or *Averidge*, Such sum shall be divided among the several claimers by way of average, in proportion to their respective interests and demands. **1881** *Shipping Gaz.* 29 Mar. 7/1 Defendants said that as by what had happened they had lost their freight, they were entitled to claim a contribution, by way of General Average, on account of the loss of freight.

b. *Attrib.* and *Comb.*, as **average-adjuster, -stater**, one whose profession it is to adjust the claims and liabilities of all parties concerned in a case of General Average, and to make up an **average-statement** showing the same; **average bond**, a guarantee given to the master of the ship by the consignees of a cargo liable to General Average, by which they undertake that if he delivers the cargo, they will pay the general average contribution as soon as its amount is authoritatively determined.

1865 J. LEES *Laws Brit. Ship.* (ed. 9) 354 Or the documents and vouchers are placed in the hands of a professional average-adjuster to prepare an average statement. *Ibid.* 347 A general average loss is that which has been sustained by some part of the ship or cargo for the safety and preservation of the whole. **1883** *Standard* 19 May 2/8 Mr. —— ..who was described as an 'average adjustor.'

II. Transferred use.

5. *transf.* The distribution of the aggregate inequalities (in quantity, quality, intensity, etc.) of a series of things among all the members of the series, so as to equalize them, and ascertain their common or mean quantity, etc., when so treated; the determination or statement of an arithmetical mean; a medial estimate. Now only in phrases ***at an average, on an average***.

1735 BERKELEY *Querist* (R.) Whether..Birmingham alone doth not upon an average circulate every week..the value of 50,000*l.* **1758** DYCHE & PARDON, *Average*, the taking of several things together, and considering the profit of the one and the loss of the other, so as to make a mean or common price. **1787** G. WHITE *Selborne* i. 3 Our wells, at an average, run to about sixty-three feet. **1843** CARLYLE *Past & Pr.* (1858) 121 Under such conditions and averages as it can. **1878** HUXLEY *Physiogr.* 188 Earthquake-shocks occur, on an average, about three times a week.

6. a. The arithmetical mean so obtained; the medium amount, the generally prevailing, or ruling, quantity, rate, or degree; the 'common run.'

[Not in CHAMBERS *Supp.* 1753. **1755** JOHNSON, *Average*, 4. A medium, a mean proportion. (No quot.)] **1802** PALEY *Nat. Theol.* xxvi. (R.) Looking to the average of sensations ..the preponderancy is in favour of happiness. **1860** MAURY *Phys. Geog. Sea* iii. § 185 The month's average of wrecks has been as high as three a day. **1860** ABP. THOMSON *Laws Th.* § 125 Where a mean is taken, without any need for arranging the several observations according to their approach to it, it has been called an average. **1867** LADY HERBERT *Cradle L.* iii. 92 The hotel itself is..very much above the average. **1874** REYNOLDS *John Bapt.* i. § 2. 15 To predict the future, not only in its averages or in the law of its evolution, but in its detail.

b. spec. in *Cricket*. The mean number of runs per innings scored by a batsman, or the mean cost in runs per wicket achieved by a bowler, during a season, tour, etc.

1845 W. DENISON *Cricketer's Companion* (ed. 2) 113 Many of our finest bats have had their average diminished. *Ibid.* (*heading*) Averages for 1844. **1854** F. LILLYWHITE *Guide to Cricketers* 74 Mr. H. Lampson..Bowling average, per innings, 2 and 13 over. **1870** *Baily's Monthly Mag.* Oct. 85 In 1868 his batting average was 52 and 5 over. **1967** *Whitaker's Almanack* 982 (*heading*) Batting and bowling averages.

Hence **avera'garian** (*nonce-wd.*).

1864 *Cornh. Mag.* Aug. 219 The averagarians usually give the statistics of murders, suicides, and marriages, as proof of the periodic uniformity of events.

[Few words have received more etymological investigation: see Diez, Dozy, Littré, Wedgwood, E. Müller, Skeat, etc., and especially the fruitful researches of the late G. P. Marsh in the American edition of Wedgwood (New York 1861). The latter has conclusively shown that, as a maritime term, *avaria, averia*, was first used in the Mediterranean, and that its original meaning was *duty* charged upon goods. In connexion with this cf. also quotations from Muratori *Chron. Parmense* (in Du Cange s.v. *Averia*), e.g. *Conscenderint lembum Averiæ ad excipiendos prædictos galeones*, 'they went on board the *revenue* cutter to intercept the aforesaid galleons.' These results quite dispose of the two derivations suggested in Diez from Ger. *hafen* haven, and Arab. *ʿawâr* loss, damage, the latter being merely a mod. Arabic translation and adaptation of the western term in its latest sense. Mr. Marsh's connexion of the word with the Arabic or Turkish *avania, avaria*, is of great weight; but as said under AVANIA, that word is more probably adopted from the Franks. May not *averia* be a derivative of It. *avere*, OF. *aveir*, property, goods (see AVER *sb.*), in sense of 'charge on property or goods'? Compare such terms as *tonnage, poundage, pollage* (charge on *polls*). The chief difficulty lies in the early It. form *avaria*, not *averia*, and F. *avarie*: the Catalan has however been *averia* since 13th c.: see Marsh on Sp. and Catalan use of the word, and *Averia, Avaria* in Du Cange. It is to be noted that OF. *avarie* was used of other than maritime dues or charges; in a document dated Nicosia, 18 March 1468, in De Mas Latrie, *Histoire de Chypre* III. 276, the owner of a mill is bound 'de paier l'ensencive (= cens) de l'abaie de Bibi, et tout autre avarie que le dit moulin paie aujourdhui.' Cf. also certain uses of *avérage* in Godefroy.]

†**average**, *sb.*³ *Obs.* or *dial.* Forms: 6 **averaige, averish**, 7–8 **average**. [Etymol. uncertain: see quot. 1674. No such sense of med.L. *averagium* or OF. *average*. Cf. ARRISH.] (See quot.)

1537 *Reg. Leases Dean & Chapt. York* I. 74 The averaige of the said cloises. *c* **1615** *MS. Crt. Bk. Riccall Yorksh.*, No goodes or cattell to depasture in the towne feildes in averish tyme. **1669** WORLIDGE *Syst. Agric.* (1681) 321 *Average*, the feeding or Pasturage for Cattle especially the Edish or Roughings. **1674** RAY *N. Countr. Wds.* 3 *Average*, the breaking of corn fields; Eddish, Roughings..It may possibly come from *Haver* signifying Oates; or from *Averia*, beasts, being as much as feeding for cattal, pasturage. **1788** W. MARSHALL *Yorkshire* (1796) II. 151 Average, a provincial term for the eatage of arable land, after harvest.

average ('ævərɪdʒ), *a.* [attrib. use of AVERAGE *sb.*², in sense 5.]

1. Estimated by average; *i.e.* by equally distributing the aggregate inequalities of a series among all the individuals of which the series is composed.

1770 *Month. Rev.* 235 The average price of corn. **1776** ADAM SMITH *W.N.* I. I. v. 37 *note*, The average rent of the best arable land. **1797** HOLCROFT tr. *Stolberg's Trav.* IV. xcv. (ed. 2) 327 The average summer heat of these countries. **1849** MACAULAY *Hist. Eng.* I. 309 The average income of a temporal peer was estimated..at about three thousand a year. **1851** *Coal-trade Terms Northmbld. & Durh.* 4 Average Weight.—The mean weight of a tub of coals at a colliery for any fortnight, upon which the hewers' and putters' wages are calculated..usually obtained by weighing two tubs in each score.

2. a. Equal to what would be the result of taking an average; medium, ordinary; of the usual or prevalent standard.

1803 W. TAYLOR in *Ann. Rev.* I. 423 The manufacturer has to deal with the average poor, with the spendthrift and the sparethrift. **1812** *Examiner* 5 Oct. 629/2 Of corn..there is not an average crop. **1858** GLADSTONE *Homer* III. 16 These districts by no means represent the average character of Greece. **1859** MILL *Liberty* 119 The honour and glory of the average man is, that he is capable of following that initiative. **1868** RUSKIN *Pol. Econ. Art* ii. 89 A modern drawing of average merit.

b. Used with *sensual* [tr. F. (*l'homme*) *sensuel moyen*.]

1882 [see SENSUAL A. 4 a]. **1894** G. B. SHAW in *Fortnightly Rev.* Feb. 263 The average sensual boy comes out the average sensual man. **1937** A. HUXLEY *Ends & Means* xiv. 297 Only the disinterested mind can transcend common sense and pass beyond the boundaries of animal or average-sensual human life. **1950** —— *Themes & Variations* 71 Samuel Pepys's day-by-day record of how the average sensual man comports himself. **1968** R. AMBERLEY *Incitement to Murder* i. 10 If an average sensual man, he was also an average kindly man.

3. *Comb.*, ***average-sized*** adj.

1851 H. MELVILLE *Moby Dick* III. ii. 340 An average-sized male. **1960** *Farmer & Stockbreeder* Suppl. 29 Mar. 9/1 They all fit an average-sized head.

average ('ævərɪdʒ), *v.* [f. AVERAGE *sb.*² in sense 5; = 'calculate or estimate by average'; cf. *to proportion, square, cube, double*, etc.]

1. *trans.* To estimate, by dividing the aggregate of a series by the number of its units, (*at* so much); to take the average of; to form an opinion as to the prevailing standard of.

1831 SOUTHEY in *Q. Rev.* XLIV. 382 His Sunday congregation was averaged at about six hundred persons. **1851** H. SPENCER *Soc. Stat.* xxxii. § 6 By averaging the characters of those whom he personally knows, he can form a tolerably correct opinion of those whom he does not know. **1852** SIR W. HAMILTON *Disc.* 444 Averaging the Battel dues paid by each at thirty shillings, there results, etc. **1881** M. TWAIN *Pr. & Paup.* xxii. 257 The blacksmith averaged the stalwart soldier with a glance, then went muttering away.

2. *ellipt.* for: To average itself at, or be averaged at; to amount to, or be, on an average.

1769 WASHINGTON *Diaries* (1925) I. 314 A fat wether—it being imagind..would average the above weight. **1806** FESSENDEN *Orig. Poems* 113 Each paper..Will average at a hundred lies. **1821** BYRON *Juan* III. xv, They all had cuffs and collars And averaged each from ten to a hundred dollars. **1822** W. SPENCE *Pol. Econ.* Pref. 33 Fixing the annual sum to be paid by each parish at what it has averaged for the past five or ten years. **1832** HT. MARTINEAU *Ella of Gar.* i. 2 These visits averaged about one in the life-time of each laird. **1856** FROUDE *Hist. Eng.* (1858) I. i. 21 Wheat..averaged in the middle of the fourteenth century tenpence the bushel. **1859** MASSON *Milton* I. 452 The sale of the book..averaged a thousand copies a year.

3. *ellipt.* for: To do, gain, take (or almost any verb of which the meaning may be inferred from the context) on an average; to accomplish (in any kind of action) an average amount of (so much).

1822 DE QUINCEY *Conf.* (1862) 200 So much this surgeon averaged upon each day for about twenty years. **1881** *Daily News* 10 Dec. 3/1 The hard-worked officers..have been averaging eighteen hours' work per diem.

4. *intr.* with *out*: To work out so as to produce an average. Also *trans.* in corresponding sense.

1914 G. B. SHAW *Misalliance* 41 Averages out the human race. Makes the nigger half an Englishman. Makes the Englishman half a nigger. **1922** *Times Lit. Suppl.* 28 Sept. 610/4 The particular obstacles will vary from time to time and from species to species, but on the whole will average out. **1928** *Britain's Industr. Future* (*Liberal Ind. Inquiry*) v. xxxi. § 5. 446 Any attempt to average out burdens. **1934** G. B. SHAW *Too True to be Good* III. p. 97 In the army these things average themselves out.

'**averagely**, *adv.* [f. AVERAGE *a.* + -LY².] According to the average; ordinarily; in accordance with the usual or prevalent standard.

1832 CHALMERS *Pol. Econ.* iv. 112 The price, averagely speaking, is in the inverse proportion to the quantity. **1844** R. CHAMBERS *Vest. Creat.* (1845) 344 No averagely constituted human being would. **1875** *Cornh. Mag.* Dec. 694 Averagely young and agreeable.

averageness ('ævərɪdʒnɪs). [f. AVERAGE *a.* + -NESS.] The fact or condition of being average; ordinariness, mediocrity.

1925 *Glasgow Herald* 18 June 9 The minister occupies a position in which the averageness of his ability is necessarily exposed to more general remark. **1961** *Encounter* Oct. 76/2 Gordon Comstock..finally sinks in a morass of wage-earning, aspidistra-garnished, lower-middle-class averageness.

averager ('ævərɪdʒə(r)). [f. AVERAGE *sb.*² + -ER¹.] An average adjuster.

1884 *Manch. Exam.* 22 Mar. 4/6 An action brought by the executors..of an averager.

avercalye, var. CAPERCALYE, Wood Grouse.

aver-corn: see AVER-.

Averel, -il, -ylle, early forms of APRIL.

†'**averene**. *Obs. Sc.* Some kind of custom. Cf. AVERAGE *sb.*²

1625–49 *Acts Chas. I* (1814) V. 627 (JAM.) With powar to —vptak the tollis, customeis, pryngilt, averene, entreissilver, gadgeing silver.

averice, -yce, obs. forms of AVARICE.

†**a'verify**, *v. Obs. rare*⁻¹. [f. A- *pref.* 11 + VERIFY.] To prove true, verify.

1502 ARNOLD *Chron.* (1811) 132 Your said suppliaunt.. wil doo it good and be then redy to auerify it.

averin ('eɪvərən). *Sc.* Also **averan, -en, aiverin, avern**. [Etymol. unknown.] The cloudberry or knoutberry (*Rubus chamæmorus*).

1768 ROSS *Helenore* 26 (JAM.) She..spies a spot of averens ere lang. *c* **1795** *Perths. Statist. Acc.* ix. 237 (JAM.) Picking up here and there a plant of the rubus chamaemorus (the averan or Highland oidh'rac). **1881** *Blackw. Mag.* July 109 Does the reader know the cranberry and the avern?

averish *sb.*: see AVERAGE *sb.*³

'**averish**, *v. Obs.* or *dial.* [f. prec.] To consume the eddish, arrish, or average.

Mod. dial. of Burford, Hull, He is going to buy some of our pigs to averish (or haverish) the corn.

averland: see AVER-.

averment (ə'vɜːmənt). Also 5–7 **averrement**. [a. F. *avere-, averrement*, f. *averer*: see AVER *v.* and -MENT.]

1. The action of proving; establishment as true or genuine, by argument or evidence.

1429 HEN. VI in Rymer *Fœdera* (1710) X. 411 Not bound to eny maneres of acconte..or to any Averrement as therefore. **1599** SANDYS *Europæ Spec.* (1632) 128 Which their adversaries producing in averment of their opinions, they were not able..to reply to. *a* **1626** BACON (J.) To avoid the oath, for averment of the continuance of some estate, which is eigne, the party will sue a pardon.

2. *Law.* Formal offer to prove or justify a plea; the proof or justification offered, verification.

1514–5 *Act 6 Hen. VIII*, iv, All outlawries had contrary to this Acte be advoyded by averrement. **1613** SIR H. FINCH *Law* (1636) 359 Entrie plea..must be offered to be proued true. By saying in the plea, *Et hoc patr' natus est verificare*, which we call an auerment. **1765** TUCKER *Lt. Nat.* II. 156 If he happens to demur by averment, when he should have concluded to the contrary, judgment shall go against him. **1809** TOMLINS *Law Dict.*, *Averment* is either general or particular; general, which concludes every plea, etc. containing matter affirmative, and ought to be with these words, *and this he is ready to verify*. Particular averment is when the life of the tenant for life, or of tenant in tail, etc. is averred.

3. The action of positively declaring as true; assertion, affirmation.

1633 PRYNNE *Histriom.* 489 (R.) Playes are the nourishers of delight: by the express averment of Mr. George Whetston. **1694** ? SHERLOCK *Provid. God* 83 The Faith of the Nation being engaged for the Truth of it, by the Envoys Averment thereof. **1817** SCOTT *Rob Roy* 28 After an effort or two to support their consequence by noise and bold averment.

4. A positive statement, assertion, or declaration.

c **1629** in Rushw. *Hist. Coll.* (1659) I. 592 Which averment of Sir John Elliots was attested by Sir Thomas Wentworth.

1794 PALEY *Evid.* I. viii. (1817) 155 Two out of the four Gospels contain averments..which..fix the time and situation of the authors. **1834** GEN. P. THOMPSON *Exerc.* III. 105 The old averments, that the landlords will be ruined.

Avern (əˈvɜːn). *poet.* [a. F. *Averne* 'the pit of hell' (Cotgr. 1611), ad. L. *Avernus* (sc. *lacus*), = Gr. ἄορνος (λίμνη) the birdless (lake), f. ἀ priv. + ὄρνις bird.] *orig.* A lake in Campania, the poisonous effluvium from which was said to kill birds flying over it. *transf.* The infernal regions.

1599 GREENE *Alphon.* (1861) 227 Pluto, king of dark Avern.

Avernal (əˈvɜːnəl), *a.* (and *sb.*) [a. F. *Avernal* 'hellish' (Cotgr.), ad. L. *Avernālis*, f. *Avernus*: see prec. and -AL[1].] **A.** *adj.* Of the nature of, or belonging to, Avernus; infernal. **B.** *sb.* An inhabitant of Avernus, a devil. **A'vernian** *a.* = prec. adj.

c **1578** GASCOIGNE *Devyll's Will*, The Courte Auernall. *Ibid.*, Pamachios..doth cause all his Auernals, forked tipes and annointed Gentlemen to come to the readynge of the Deuylls Testament and last Wyll. **1660** STANLEY *Hist. Philos.* (1701) 603/1 Avernal places, so termed, for that they are pernicious to Birds. **1853** F. NEWMAN *Odes of Horace* 57 Through all the house Avernal waters sprinkling. **1864** WEBSTER, *Avernian.*

averous, variant of AVAROUS *a. Obs.*

†**ave'royne.** *Herb. Obs. rare*$^{-1}$. [a. AF. *averoine* = OF. (13th c.) *avroigne*, Picard *avrogne*, mod.F. *aurone*:—L. *abrotonum*, a. Gr. ἀβρότονον.] Southernwood (*Artemisia abrotonum*).

c **1350** *Med. MS.* in *Archæol.* XXX. 350 Aueroyne he take wt owte lettynge, Qweche is callyd soþernwoode also.

averpenny: see AVER-.

averrable (əˈvɜːrəb(ə)l), *a.* [f. AVER *v.* + -ABLE.] **a.** Capable of being verified or proved true (*obs.*). **b.** Capable of being averred, asserted, or declared.

1562-3 *Act 5 Eliz.* vi, Fees to the clere yerely value of three thowsande powndes averrable..by Bookes of Subsidies. **1588** J. HARVEY *Probl. Proph.* 125 In case we would entertaine..the Glosse..as averrable. **1846** SPENCE *Equit. Jurisd.* I. 497 Express trusts were..capable of being declared simply by word, or in legal language were averrable.

†**a'verral.** *Obs.* [f. AVER *v.* + -AL[2].] Averment.

1611 COTGR., *Confirmation*..an auouching or auerrall of a thing for truth.

averred (əˈvɜːd), *ppl. a.* [f. AVER *v.* + -ED.] **a.** Verified (*obs.*). **b.** Asserted, maintained.

1641 *Vind. Smectymn.* §13. 161 The averred Episcopacy of Timothy and Titus. **1818** COLEBROOKE *Import Col. Corn* 93 Well averred facts.

averring (əˈvɜːrɪŋ), *vbl. sb.* Averment.

1528 PERKINS *Profit. Bk.* ii. §147 To take advantage of this deed by averring of the deliverie of the same.

Averroist (ævəˈrəʊɪst). Also 8-9 **Averrh-**. [f. *Averroes* or *Averrhoes* (see below) + -IST.] One of a sect of peripatetic philosophers who appeared in Italy some time before the restoration of learning, and adopted the leading tenets of Ibn Roshd or Averrhoes, an Arabian philosopher born at Cordova, viz. that the soul is mortal, or (as others stated it) that the only immortal soul is a universal one, from which particular souls arise, and into which they return at death. Hence **Ave'rroism, Averro'istic** *a.*

1753 CHAMBERS *Cycl. Supp.*, *Averrhoists*..yet protested to submit to the christian theology..But the corpuscular philosophy now introduced into Italy, seems almost to have extinguished Averrhoism. **1837** HALLAM *Hist. Lit.* (1847) II. 6 The Averroistic notion of an universal human intelligence. **1877** E. THOMAS *Lange's Materialism* I. 179 Averroism prepared the way for the new Materialism.

†**ave'rruncal**, *a. Obs. rare.* [f. *Averrunc-us* an averter (of evil), name of deity (cf. next) + -AL[1].] Averting evil.

1705 *Phil. Trans.* XXV. 2107 Averruncal, Prophylactic and Polycharactaristick Statues.

averruncate (ævəˈrʌŋkeɪt), *v.* ? *Obs.* [f. L. *āverruncāt-* ppl. stem of *āverruncāre* to ward off, avert, remove (evils, ill-luck, etc.), f. *ā*, *ab* off + *verruncāre* to turn. Erroneously explained in 17th c. from *ab* off + *ēruncāre* to weed out, whence sense 2.

This mistake began in mod.L. or Fr.: Cotgrave (1611) has '*averronquer*, to purge, or weed; to turne, put, or take away euill; to divert mischiefes; also to appease'; where the perverted sense is put first. Bailey (1731) essayed to accommodate the spelling to the new sense, by entering the fictitious variant *aberuncate*, adopted from him by Johnson, and later dictionaries. No such compound as *ab-ē-runcāre* is warranted by Latin analogies.]

1. *prop.* To avert, ward off.

1663 BUTLER *Hud.* I. i. 758 Sure some Mischief will come of it, Unless by Providential Wit, Or Force, we averruncate it. [*ed.* 1694 has the erroneous Annotation: '*Averruncate*..though it appear ever so Learned..means nothing else but the Weeding of Corn.' (Cf. **1693**, sense 2.)]

2. *improperly.* (See quotations.)

1623 COCKERAM, *Aueruncate*, to take away that which hurts, to weed. **1693** W. ROBERTSON *Phraseol. Gen.* 183 *Averruncate*; to weed..to cut or take away that which hurteth; to weed ground, to prune or dress vines, etc. Hence to avert or take away; to appease or attone. **1731** BAILEY, *Aberuncated*, pulled up by the roots, weeded. **1755** JOHNSON, *Averruncate*, to root up; to tear up by the roots. *Aberuncate* [*averunco* Lat.], to pull up by the roots; to extirpate utterly. [Subseq. Dicts. have *Aberuncate* (or *Aberruncate*), and *Averruncate*.]

averruncation (ævərʌŋˈkeɪʃən). [a. Fr. *averroncation* (Cotgr. 1611), f. L. *āverruncāre*: see prec.]

1. *prop.* The warding off or averting (of evils).

1660 STANLEY *Hist. Philos.* (1701) 401/2 From these are sent to men, dreams and presages of sickness, and of health..to these pertain expiations and averruncations, and all Divinations. **1658** J. ROBINSON *Eudoxa* x. 52 Averruncation of Epidemical Diseases, by Telesmes.

2. *improperly.* (See quotations.)

1656 BLOUNT *Glossogr.*, *Averruncation*, a scraping or cutting off, as men do vines. **1731** BAILEY, *Averruncation*, a scraping, cutting off, a lopping off the superfluous branches of trees. **1755** JOHNSON, *Averruncation*, the act of rooting up any thing. **1821** DE QUINCEY *Conf.* (1862) 21 His decree of utter averruncation to the simple decoration overhead.

averruncator (ævərʌŋˈkeɪtə(r)). [n. of agent f. AVERRUNCATE in the improper sense 2.] An instrument for cutting off the branches of trees at a height above the head, consisting of a pair of pruning shears, or a knife-blade working within a hook, mounted on a pole and worked by a string or wire.

1842 in BRANDE. **1864** in WEBSTER (*Averruncator*, and *Aberuncator*). **1878** R. THOMPSON *Gardener's Assist.* 71 By means of an averruncator branches more than an inch in diameter and at the height of 12 or 15 feet from the ground may be cut off without using a ladder or steps.

†**a'versable**, *a. Obs. rare*$^{-1}$. [ad. L. *āversābilis* before which one is obliged to turn away, f. *āversārī*: see AVERSATE and -BLE.] Abominable.

1663 SIR G. MACKENZIE *Relig. Stoic* xiii. (1685) 117 The most aversable ill in nature.

a'versant, *a.* [ad. L. *āversāntem*, pr. pple. of *āversārī.*] †**1.** Disinclined, averse. *Obs. rare*$^{-1}$.

1657 TOMLINSON *Renou's Disp.* 262 With such..humidity that it makes the ventricle aversant to it.

2. *Her.* Turned to show the back (said of a right hand).

1830 ROBSON *Brit. Herald* III. Gloss., *Aversant*, or *Dorsed*; as, a right hand *dorsed* or *aversant*, when turned to shew the back part. **1889** ELVIN *Dict. Her.*

†**'aversate**, *v. Obs. rare*$^{-1}$. [f. L. *āversāt-* ppl. stem of *āversārī* to turn oneself from, turn away, reject, freq. (deponent) of *āvertĕre* to AVERT.] To turn away from, regard with aversion, reject.

1725 BAILEY *Erasm. Colloq.* 371 Aversating their Meat-offerings, abhorring their Fasts.

aversation (ævəˈseɪʃən). *arch.* [ad. L. *āversātiōn-em*, n. of action f. *āversāt-*: see -ATION.]

†**1.** The action of turning away; the turning of one's back in flight. *Obs.*

1600 CHAPMAN *Iliad* XXII. 213 Thrice have I compassed This great town..with aversation That out of fate put off my steps. **1673** *Regul. Pract. Physick* 27 Allowed Fees he may freely take, and that not with aversation or blushing.

†**2.** A moral turning away, estrangement. *Obs.*

1651 JER. TAYLOR *Course Serm.* I. ii. 25 An habituall aversation from God. **1659** PEARSON *Creed* (1839) 460 Our natural corruption consisting in an aversation of our wills.

3. = AVERSION 4. (With same const.) *arch.*

1613 CHAPMAN *Bussy D' Amb.* Plays 1873 II. 142, I had an auersation to this voyage. **1625** BACON *Friendship, Essays* (Arb.) 163 Secret Hatred, and Auersation towards Society. **1630** NAUNTON *Fragm. Regalia* (Arb.) 18 Her aversation to grant Tirone the least drop of her mercy. **1648** *Eikon Bas.* (1824) 278 To entertain aversation or dislike of Parliaments. **1649** MILTON *Eikon.* ix. Wks. (1851) 402 No great aversation from shedding blood. **1672-5** COMBER *Comp. Temple* (1702) 373 An aversation for that which he saith is evil. **1737** WHISTON *Josephus' Wars* II. xix. §6 The aversation God had to the city. **1863** EMERSON in Thoreau *Excurs.* 13 His aversation from English and European manners.

4. = AVERSION 6.

1730 BEVERIDGE *Priv. Th.* I. 111 As the Promises of God are to be the Object of my Hope, so are His Threatenings to be my Fear and Aversation.

averse (əˈvɜːs), *a.* and *sb.* Also 7 **avers.** [ad. L. *āversus*, pa. pple. of *āvertĕre* to AVERT. Cf. OF. *avers*, in which L. *āversus* and *adversus* seem to have combined.]

A. *adj.* †**1.** Turned away, averted; turned in the backward or reverse direction. *Obs.*

1682 SIR T. BROWNE *Chr. Mor.* 90 Two faces averse, and conjoined Janus-like. **1697** DRYDEN *Virgil* (1806) III. 274 The tracks averse a lying notice gave. **1703** ROWE *Fair Penit.* I. i. 109 With looks averse and Eyes that froze me.

†**b.** quasi-*adv.* = AVERSELY 1. *Obs.*

1607 TOPSELL *Four-f. Beasts* 440 The hair [of the Oryx] groweth averse..forward toward his head. **1610** GWILLIM *Heraldry* III. xiii. (1660) 161 If the Horse be not mounted, he fights averse. **1814** CARY *Dante* (Chandos) 238 That star, which views Now obvious, and now averse, the sun.

†**2.** Lying on the opposite side. *Obs.*

1667 MILTON *P.L.* IX. 67 On the Coast averse From entrance or cherubic watch..Found unsuspected way.

†**3.** In the rear, behind. (So in L.) *Obs.*

1646 SIR T. BROWNE *Pseud. Ep.* III. i. 107 The situation of the genitalls is averse.

4. Turned away in mind or feeling; actuated by repugnance; habitually opposed, disinclined.

1597 DANIEL *Civ. Wares* I. xxvi, And of a spirit averse, and overthwart. **1671** MILTON *Samson* 1461 Some much averse I found and wondrous harsh. **1744** HARRIS *Three Treat.* III. II. (1765) 233 That Law..which leads the Willing, and compels the Averse.

b. Const. *from*, *to*.

The use of the prep. *to*, rather than *from*, after *averse* and its derivatives, although condemned by Johnson as etymologically improper, is justified by the consideration that these words express a mental relation analogous to that indicated by *hostile*, *contrary*, *repugnant*, *hostility*, *opposition*, *dislike*, and naturally take the same construction. *Aversion* in the sense of an action, which would properly be followed by *from*, is now obsolete. Examination of many instances shows that *from* has been used by Donne, Speed, R. Burton, Milton, Bp. Mountagu, Sir T. Browne, Evelyn, Hale, Dryden, Pope, Johnson, Southey, Motley, Lowell, and J. R. Green; *to* by Heylin, Walton, Boyle, Locke, South, Addison, Steele, De Foe, D. North, Richardson, H. Walpole, Gibbon, Burke, Buckle, Mill; whilst Sir E. Sandys, Jer. Taylor, Barrow, Clarendon, Swift, Hume, Macaulay have used both. Shakspere does not use the word.

1611 BIBLE *Micah* ii. 8 As men auerse from warre. **1639** ROUSE *Heav. Univ.* viii. (1702) 105 Make thee averse to God's teaching. **1761** HUME *Hist. Eng.* II. xxiii. 75 Licentious tyrants..equally averse from peace and from freedom. *a* **1771** GRAY *Poems* (1775) 7 What Cat's averse to fish? **1849** MACAULAY *Hist. Eng.* II. 32 He had been averse to extreme courses. **1876** GREEN *Short Hist.* iv. §3 (1882) 175 His impulses were generous, trustful, averse from cruelty.

c. with *inf.* Disinclined, unwilling, reluctant.

1646 SIR T. BROWNE *Pseud. Ep.* IV. viii. 198 We are not averse to acknowledge, that some may distill..into the winde-pipe. **1777** WATSON *Philip II* (1793) II. XII. 83 Averse at this time to declare herself openly. **1864** R. BURTON *Dahome* 8 Even the grass is, from idleness, averse to wave.

†**5.** Of things: Of opposed nature, adverse. *Obs.*

1623 MASSINGER *Dk. Milan* II. i, Tell me rather That the earth moves; the sun and stars stand still; Or anything that is averse to nature. **1651** HOBBES *Leviath.* II. xviii. 91 What Opinions and Doctrines are averse, and what conducing to Peace. **1657-83** EVELYN *Hist. Relig.* (1850) I. 217 Whatever prejudices ill education..or other averse accidents may have produced.

†**B.** *sb.* The back, the hinder part (so L. *āversum*); the reverse of a coin. *Obs.*

1654 LESTRANGE *Chas. I*, 122 Before fortune had ever forsaken him, or shewed him her averse. **1658** W. BURTON *Itin. Anton.* 58 A Coyn..in the averse of which we read, etc.

†**a'verse**, *v. Obs.* [f. prec.] To turn away.

1652 GAULE *Magastrom.* 137 Man's liberty, or freewill, either to prosecute or averse.

†**a'versed**, *ppl. a. Obs.* [f. prec. + -ED.] Turned away, averted; opposed, hostile.

1609 B. JONSON *Masques* (1692) 351 My Face avers'd. **1644** DIGBY *Nat. Bodies* XXX. (1658) 325 Shadow..must of necessity lie aversed from the illuminant. **1686** GOAD *Celest. Bod.* II. vii. 250 Obliging aversed Parties to a Truce.

aversely (əˈvɜːslɪ), *adv.* [f. AVERSE *a.* + -LY[2].]

1. In the reverse or opposite direction.

1651 DAVENANT *Gondib.* II. iv. lxii, Hubert his arm westward aversely stretched. **1823** LAMB *Elia* Ser. I. xii. (1865) 100 My face turned to the window aversely from the bed.

b. Backwardly.

1646 SIR T. BROWNE *Pseud. Ep.* 137 It is emitted aversly or backward. *Ibid.* 261 *Clunatim*, or aversly. **1658** —— *Hydriot.* 34 They kindled the pyre aversly, or turning their face from it.

2. With aversion or dislike; repugnantly.

1643 MILTON *Divorce* iii. Wks. (1851) 26 All the faculties..appeare to be so ill and so aversly met. **1691** BAXTER *Nat. Churches* x. 41 Aversly suspicious of National Churches.

a'verseness. Also 7 **aversnes(s, aversenesse.** [f. as prec. + -NESS.] The quality or state of being averse; a mental attitude of opposition, disfavour, dislike, or repugnance; = AVERSION 4.

1623 T. SCOT *Highw. God & King* 11 With most..obstinate auersenesse. **1654** COKAYNE *Dianea* IV. 316 His complaints against the aversenesses of heaven. **1689** LOCKE *Toleration* i. Wks. 1751 II. 250 Unreasonable averseness of mind.

b. Const. as in AVERSION 4 b, c.

1611 SPEED *Hist. Gt. Brit.* VI. xlii. (1632) 146 His auersnes from so dangerous an ambition. **1622** in Rushw. *Hist. Coll.* (1659) I. 71 Considering all the aversness unto it of the Infanta. **1666** PEPYS *Diary* 14 Dec., The House..showing all manner of averseness to give the king money. **1683** LORRAIN *Muret's Rites Fun.* 152 Such an horror and averseness for the corruption of the Dead. **1741** MIDDLETON *Cicero* (1742) II. VIII. 362 Caesar's averseness to restore him. **1748** RICHARDSON *Clarissa* (1811) I. xx. 145, I am sorry for your averseness to this match. **1765** TUCKER *Lt. Nat.* II. 381 An invincible averseness against all supernatural interposition. **1863** COX *Inst. Eng. Govt.* II. iii. 327 It is not from any averseness to them [special verdicts] in juries.

aversion (ə'vɜːʃən). Also 7 avertion. [(? a. F. *aversion*, 16th c. in Littré) ad. L. *āversiōn-em*, n. of action f. *āvers-*: see AVERSE and -ION[1].]

†**1.** The action of turning away oneself, one's eyes, etc.; *spec.* in *Rhet.* (as in L.) = APOSTROPHE[1] 1.

1611 SPEED *Hist. Gt. Brit.* IX. xii. (1632) 691 Which auersion or defection [of the Scots] was augmented vpon private quarrels. **1656** DU GARD *Gate Lat. Unl.* §687 An Aversion or Apostrophe, wherein the speech is turned from the hearers to somthing els. **1668** HOWE *Bless. Righteous* (1825) 167 Nor permits the aversion of the beholder's eye.

†**2.** The action of averting, warding off, or getting rid of. *Obs.*

1664 EVELYN *Silva* (1776) 417 Whatever is Exitial to Men is so to trees; for the Avertion of which they had, of old, recourse to the Robigalia. **1684** tr. *Bonet's Merc. Compit.* XIV. 504 The Humours..are to be purged in the beginning, at which time aversion is the most desired.

†**3.** A moral turning of oneself away, estrangement (*from*). *Obs.*

1596 BELL *Surv. Popery* III. v. 281 Which is an auersion from God of infinite maiestie. **1691** NORRIS *Pract. Disc.* 307 Sin..is an Aversion from God.

4. a. An averted state of mind or feelings; a mental attitude of opposition or repugnance; a fixed, habitual dislike; an antipathy.

1651 HOBBES *Gov. & Soc.* iii. §31. 55 Good and Evill are names given to things to signefie the inclination, or aversion of them by whom they were given. **1713** STEELE *Englishm.* No. 52. 332 There are among Brute Creatures many natural Aversions and Antipathies. **1855** PRESCOTT *Philip II*, I. II. vi. 204 Coldness and silence intimated too plainly the aversion of the inhabitants.

b. Const. (*towards*, *against*, obs.), *from*, *to* (*for*), *infin.* See AVERSE 3 b.

a **1626** BACON (J.) His aversion towards the house of York. **1690** LOCKE *Hum. Und.* I. iii. (1695) 16 Nature..has put into Man a desire of Happiness, and an aversion to Misery. **1712** ADDISON *Spect.* No. 538.⁋3 An unconquerable aversion which some stomachs have against a joint of meat. **1759** DILWORTH *Pope* 85 Having no aversion to go by different names, she was called Sapho. **1771** *Junius Lett.* xlii. 224 The king of France's present aversion from war. **1855** MACAULAY *Hist. Eng.* IV. 34 One for whom William felt an intense personal aversion. **1878** SIMPSON *Sch. Shaks.* I. 96 Philip's aversion to pirates.

5. *transf.* of things.

?*c* **1800** tr. *Fourcroy* (Webster) Magnesia, notwithstanding this aversion to solution, forms a kind of paste with water.

6. An object of dislike or repugnance.

1678 WYCHERLEY *Pl.-Dealer* II. i. 15 For, if anything be a Womans Aversion, 'tis Plain-dealing from another Woman. **1732** FIELDING *Miser* I. i. Wks. 1784 II. 385 Mrs. Susan Crossstitch, whom you know to be my utter aversion. **1821** BYRON *Juan* III. xciv, A drowsy frowsy poem call'd 'The Excursion,' Writ in a manner which is my aversion.

7. *attrib.*, as **aversion therapy, treatment**, therapy or treatment designed to render a particular habit repugnant to someone addicted to it.

1950 LEMERE & VOEGTLIN in *Q. Jrnl. Stud. Alcohol* XI. 199 (*title*) An evaluation of the aversion treatment of alcoholism. **1956** *Brit. Med. Jrnl.* 13 Oct. 854/2, I have been unable to find any previous record of a fetishist who responded favourably to aversion therapy. **1965** *Listener* 28 Jan. 143/1 One method of so-called aversion therapy is to associate the stimulus that one wants to get rid of with something unpleasant, such as forced vomiting or electric shocks.

aversionist (ə'vɜːʃənɪst). [f. AVERSION 4 + -IST.] One who has a strong aversion or repugnance towards something.

1938 C. MORGAN *Flashing Stream* p. xix, The experience of sex is, in her case, what Nature intended it to be and what in women not aversionists it is—a delight, and not an act of self-sacrifice. **1961** P. MASON *Common Sense about Race* IV. ii. 149 A determined aversionist..has recently argued that the dislike which he himself clearly feels must be a biological function which only emerges at puberty.

†**a'versive**, *a. Obs. rare*[−1]. [f. L. *āvers-us* AVERSE + -IVE, as if ad. L. **āversivus*.] Characterized by aversion; of opposed tendency.

1597 DANIEL *Civ. Wares* VII. lxxviii, They could not fashion otherwise Those strong-bent humors, which aversive grew.

†**a'versively**, *adv. Obs. rare*[−1]. [f. prec. + -LY[2].] With aversion; in a backward direction.

1624 CHAPMAN *Hymn to Hermes* 398 The tracks of oxen..aversively Converted towards the Pierian hills.

avert (ə'vɜːt), *v.* Also 6 advert. [a. OF. *avert-ir*:—late L. *āvertĕre*, for cl. L. *āvertĕre* to turn away or aside, f. *ā-* = *ab-* from + *vertĕre* to turn. OF. *avertir* represented both L. *āvertĕre* and *advertĕre*, whence *avert* in ME. also = ADVERT, which see for the eventual differentiation of the forms and senses.]

1. *trans.* To turn away: †**a.** a thing. *Obs.*

a **1400** *Cov. Myst.* 88 Mayde most mercyfulle..A verte of[f] the anguysche that Adam began.

b. a person *from* a place, thing, or course of action; to draw away, withdraw. *arch.*

c **1555** HARPSFIELD *Divorce Hen. VIII* (1878) 66 To averte and deflect him from this enterprise. **1674** tr. *Scheffer's Lapland* xxvi. 122 The Priests avert them from so doing. **1697** DRYDEN *Virg. Georg.* II. 239 Mighty Cæsar, whose victorious Arms..Avert unwarlike Indians from his Rome. **1862** TROLLOPE *Orley F.* xv, How fatal it might be to avert her father from the cause while the trial was still pending.

†**c.** *fig.* To turn away in mind or inclination; to alienate, estrange. *Obs.* or *arch.*

1532 MORE *Confut. Tindale* Wks. 607/2 Saynte Peter was once from God auerted, and sinnefully turned away. **1594** HOOKER *Eccl. Pol.* IV. xii. §6 For fear of averting them from the Christian faith. **1633** *Primer Virg. Mary* 258 Pilate..said to them, you haue presented vnto me this man, as auerting the people. **1877** [see AVERTED].

†**2.** *refl.* To turn oneself away. *Obs.*

1541 BARNES *Wks.* (1573) 360/1 Hee that doth beleeue, and auerte hym selfe from hys sinnes.

3. *intr.* (by omission of refl. pron.) To turn away. *arch.* or *Obs.*

1483 CAXTON *Gold. Leg.* 73/1 Yf ye auert and torne fro me. **1607** TOPSELL *Serpents* 754 To hate and avert from that which is evill. **1805** SOUTHEY *Madoc in Azt.* XII, And from that hideous man Averting, to Ocellopan he turn'd.

4. *trans.* To turn away (the face, eyes, thoughts).

1578 *Ps.* li. in *Sc. Poems 16thc.* II. 115 Fra my sinnes advert thy face. **1605** SHAKS. *Lear* I. i. 214 Therefore beseech you T' auert your liking a more worthier way. **1667** MILTON *P.L.* XII. 108 Till God at last..withdraw His presence..and avert His holy Eyes. **1837** WHEWELL *Hist. Induct. Sci.* (1857) I. 195 The thoughts were thus intentionally averted from those ideas.

5. To turn away anything about to befall, *esp.* things threatened or feared; to prevent the incidence or occurrence of; to ward off.

1612 WARNER *Alb. Eng.* I. v. 17 And so auert our ire. **1686** DRYDEN *Hind. & P.* III. 872 Avert it Heaven! nor let that plague be sent. **1791** COWPER *Iliad* VI. 20 None interposed To avert his woeful doom. **1849** MACAULAY *Hist. Eng.* I. 201 Any expedient which might avert the danger.

†**6.** To oppose; to view with aversion. *Obs.*

1635 PERSON *Varieties* II. iv. 62 Our moderne astronomers, averting this Aristotelian opinion, have found, etc. **1646** SIR T. BROWNE *Pseud. Ep.* I. iii. 8 Averting the errors of Reason. **1667** *Decay Chr. Piety* vi. §9. 251 The nature of mankind doth certainly avert both killing and being kill'd.

¶ *catachr.* for EVERT and REVERT.

1533 BELLENDENE *Livy* (1822) 334 His hous and biggingis ..suld be avertit and cassin doun to the ground. **1540** *Act 32 Hen. VIII*, xxix, Landes..shall..be descendable, remaine, auert, come, and be inheritable.

avertebrated (ə'vɜːtɪbreɪtɪd), *a. rare*[−1]. [f. A- *pref.* 14 + VERTEBRATED.] Invertebrate.

1860 *Encycl. Brit.* XXI. 974/2 Very few avertebrated animals are vermiparous.

averted (ə'vɜːtɪd), *ppl. a.* [f. AVERT *v.* + -ED.]

1. Turned away, turned aside.

1704 SWIFT *Batt. Bks.* (1711) 263 The Belt of the averted Antient. **1807** CRABBE *Village* I. 289 Impatience mark'd in his averted eyes.

2. Turned away in mind; unfavourable, unpropitious. *arch.*

1618 BOLTON *Florus* (1636) 99 The gods of Carthage now averted, carried him a diverse way. **1877** L. MORRIS *Epic Hades* I. 16 Appease Zeus and the averted Gods.

a'vertedly, *adv.* [f. prec. + -LY[2].] In an averted manner or position; unfavourably.

1867 W. SMITH *Lat. Dict.*, *Aversim*..avertedly, sideways. **1873** MRS. WHITNEY *Hitherto* xxviii. 312 Richard was silent; not avertedly; he was simply not outwardly responsive.

averter (ə'vɜːtə(r)). [f. AVERT *v.* + -ER[1].] He who or that which averts, or turns aside.

1621 BURTON *Anat. Mel.* II. v. I. iv, Averters and purgers ..to divert this rebellious humour and turn it another way. **1875** FARRAR *Seekers* II. v. 248 The averters of evil.

avertible (ə'vɜːtɪb(ə)l), *a.* Also -able. [f. as prec. + -IBLE.] That may be averted; preventable.

1658 OSBORN *Jas. I* (1673) 502 No ways avertible but by his Death. **1874** GREG *Rocks Ahead* Pref. 26 However avertable, they will not be averted. **1880** KINGLAKE *Crimea* VI. viii. 171 The evils thus superadded may in one sense be called 'avertible.'

avertiment, obs. form of ADVERTISEMENT.

‖**avertin**[1] (avɛrtɛ̃, 'ævətɪn). [Fr. (13th c. *avertin*, *auvertin*, 16th c. *advertin*), f. *avertir* to turn away, AVERT.] **a.** A vertiginous disease in sheep more usually called *tournis*. **b.** Mental disease which renders the patient obstinate and furious; crazy sullenness.

1864 in WEBSTER.

Avertin[2] (ə'vɜːtɪn). *Med.* Also avertin. [G. (trade-name, 1927), f. AVERT *v.* + -IN[1]; cf. G. *avertieren* to avert, ward off.] The trade-name of an anæsthetic drug.

1927 *Chem. Abstr.* 2154 (*title*) Clinical experiences with avertin. **1929** F. J. MORRIN in *Irish Jrnl. Med. Sci.* Apr. 183 Within the past year, I have used avertin anæsthesia in 54 cases. **1930** *Lancet* 7 June 1264/1 Avertin by itself procures in most cases the desired deep sleep.

averting (ə'vɜːtɪŋ), *vbl. sb.* [f. AVERT *v.* + -ING[1].] The action of turning away.

1628 BP. DAVENANT *Serm. Westm.* 5 *Apr.* 12 The remoouall of such heauie iudgements..and the auerting of more heauie. **1812** *Examiner* 12 Oct. 652/2 A kind of averting of the eye.

a'verting, *ppl. a.* [f. as prec. + -ING[2].] That turns away; causing aversion, repellent.

c **1811** FUSELI *Lect. Art* iv. (1848) 444 A figure as mannered in form and attitude as averting by stern severity.

avertion, obs. form of AVERSION.

avertive (ə'vɜːtɪv), *a.* [f. AVERT *v.* + -IVE.] Designed to avert or ward off.

1889 *Cornhill Mag.* May 491 A series of avertive and violent sweeps of a table-napkin. **1895** *Q. Rev.* July 211 We are not convinced that the heraldic animals were originally 'avertive' amulets.

avertress (ə'vɜːtrɪs). [f. AVERTER + -ESS.] A female who averts.

1838 *Blackw. Mag.* XLIII. 259 'Twas thine in youth to seek the tomb, Avertress of thy husband's doom!

†**averty**, *a. Obs.* [a. OF. *averti* prudent, pa. pple. of *avertir*:—L. *advertĕre* to turn attention to, ADVERT.] Well-advised, prudent, cautious.

1330 R. BRUNNE *Chron.* 260 A knyght fulle auerty gaf þam þis ansuere. **1375** BARBOUR *Bruce* VIII. 162 The kyng..That wes ay wiss and a-verty.

†'**avery, -ey.** *Obs.* A corruption of AVENERY.

c **1480** *Liber Niger Edw. IV* in *Househ. Ord.* (1790) 69 Other provender in the averey. **1667** E. CHAMBERLAYNE *St. Gt. Brit.* I. II. xii. (1743) 100 The accompts of the..avener, being chief clerk of the avery. **1783** AINSWORTH *Lat. Dict.* (Morell), The king's Avery.

Avesta (ə'vɛstə). = ZEND-AVESTA. Hence **A'vestan, A'vestic** *adjs.*, of or belonging to the Avesta; *sbs.*, the language of the Avesta.

1807 W. JONES *Sixth Discourse on Persians* in *Wks.* (1807) III. 113 A learned follower of Zeratusht..assured me, that the *letters* of his prophet's book were properly called *Zend*, and the *language*, *Avestà*. **1856** W. D. WHITNEY in *Amer. Oriental Jrnl.* V. 352 The Avesta is written in a language to which..the name of *Zend* has been given... If it should be regarded as still practicable to change the common usage, and give the language a more appropriate designation, none ..could be found so simple, and open to so few objections, as *Avestan*... The Avestan, then, is an ancient Persian language. *Ibid.*, General considerations..refer us to a time as early as the first half of the thousand years before Christ as being that of the Avestan language. **1888** *Encycl. Brit.* XXIV. 775/2 Although the Avesta is a work of but moderate compass..there..exists no single MS. which gives it in its entirety. **1888** JOSEPH WRIGHT (*title*) Elements of the comparative grammar of the Indo-Germanic languages. A concise exposition of the history of Sanskrit, Old Iranian (Avestic and Old Persian), Old Armenian,..by Karl Brugmann. **1906** L. C. CASARTELLI *Sketches in Hist.* viii. 216 Paulinus di San Bartolommeo..not only defended the genuineness of the Avestic language, but even indicated.. its affinity with the Sanskrit. **1914** E. J. RAPSON *Ancient India* ii. 31 Avestan forms are, from the etymological point of view, manifestly later than Vedic forms. **1932** W. L. GRAFF *Lang. & Languages* x. 370 Two dialects, Old Persian and Avestan or Zend.

†**ave'trol.** *Obs.* [Formation obscure: cf. OF. *awotron* 'enfant adulterin' (Godefroy), and *avoltre*:—L. *adulter-um* (see ADULTER).] A bastard.

c **1300** *K. Alis.* 2693 Whar artow, horesone! whar?.. Thou avetrol, thou foule wreche. *c* **1320** *Seuyn Sag.* (W.) 1107 What than was he [the child] an auetrol?

†**a'veugle**, *v. Obs.* [a. F. *aveugle-r*, f. *aveugle*:—pop. L. *aboculus* eyeless, blind, f. *ab* away, wanting + *oculus* eye (like *ā-mens* mindless).] To blind, hoodwink; (cf. *inveigle*).

1543 in *Calend. St. Papers* IX. 287 Whom they aveugled so with fayre words and sayings. **1547** SIR W. SHARINGTON in Froude *Hist. Eng.* V. xxv. 132 So seduced and aveugled by the lord admiral.

†**a'vex**, *v. Obs.* [f. VEX *v.* The nature of the *a-* prefix is uncertain.] To annoy, distress, VEX.

a **1400** *Cov. Myst.* 375 My dowtefull beleve ryght Sore me avexit. **1482** *Monk of Evesham* (Arb.) 95 So a vexid ther of that he was madde and owte of hys mynde.

avey, -ment (*aney* in Shoreham): see AVAY.

†**a'veyn.** *Obs.* [a. F. *aveine* (mod. *avoine*):—L. *avēna*.] Oats.

1475 *Bk. Noblesse* 69 Aveyn for hors-mete.

aveyner, -or, variants of AVENER, *Obs.*

avian ('eɪvɪən), *a.* [f. L. *avi-s* bird + -AN; cf. *apian*.] Of or pertaining to birds.

1870 ROLLESTON *Anim. Life* Introd. 49 Peculiarities which distinguish the Avian from the Reptilian organism. **1879** *Cornh. Mag.* June 722 The avian system of architecture.

aviarist ('eɪvɪərɪst). [f. next: see -IST.] The keeper of an aviary.

1883 W. GREENE *Parrots in Captiv.* Introd. 9 Where the aviarist lives in the country.

aviary ('eɪvɪərɪ). [ad. L. *aviārium*, f. *avi-s* bird: see -ARIUM.] A large cage, house, or inclosure, in which birds are kept.

1577 HARRISON *England* III. ii. 17 Our costlie and curious aviaries. **1662** FULLER *Worthies* (1840) II. 263 Lincolnshire may be termed the aviary of England, for the wild fowl therein. **1713** *Guardian* No. 49 (1756) I. 215, I look on the beaus and ladies as so many paraquets in an aviary. **1849**

MACAULAY *Hist. Eng.* I. 310 The more than Italian luxury of Ham, with its busts, fountains, and aviaries.
b. *fig.* **1647** WARD *Simp. Cobler* 9 What pity it is, that that Country.. should now become the Aviary of Errors to the whole world. **1810** COLERIDGE *Friend* (1865) 46 The statute of libel is a vast aviary, which encages the awakening cock.. no less than the babbling magpie and ominous screech-owl.

aviate (ˈeɪvɪeɪt), *v.* [Back-formation from AVIATION.] *intr.* To navigate the air in an aeroplane; to fly. Also *trans.*
1887 tr. *J. Verne's Clipper of Clouds* iv. 36 Mr. Aviator.., you who talk so much of the benefits of aviation, have you ever aviated? **1900** *Manch. Guardian* 4 Apr. 9/2 In the event of the sudden failure of the aviating mechanism. **1908** *Punch* 21 Oct. 305/2 'To aviate' is nauseous enough, and 'planing', in the atmospheric study of country-house parties, is pretty bad. **1943** C. H. WARD-JACKSON *Piece of Cake* 11 *To aviate*, to fly, to fly flashily, to show-off when flying. **1959** W. E. JOHNS *Biggles at World's End* i. 22 The obsolete crates we're expected to aviate.

aviation (eɪvɪˈeɪʃən). [ad. F. *aviation*, irreg. f. L. *avis* bird + -ATION.] Aerial navigation by means of an aeroplane; the science of powered flight. Also *attrib.*
1866 J. S. HARRY tr. *Nadar's Right to Fly* xvi. 82 The cause of Aviation. **1870** *Ann. Rep. Aeronaut. Soc* 11 Men do not consider the subject of 'aërostation' or 'aviation' to be a real science. **1891** *Daily News* 27 Aug. 5/1 The frequency of the term 'aviation' as a synonym for aerial navigation. **1908** *Daily Report* 12 Sept. 4/4 Santos-Dumont.. won the first aviation prize. **1910** R. FERRIS *How it Flies* 455 *Aviation* —Flying by means of power-propelled machines which are not buoyed up in the air, as with gas bags. **1911** *Daily Express* 13 June 1/3 The Home Secretary has issued an order prohibiting aviation in specified areas. **1916** *Sci. Amer. Suppl.* 3 June 357 (*title*) Aviation sickness; its symptoms and cure. **1920** *Flight* 26 Feb. 252/1 The Anglo-American Oil Co., Ltd., announce the present retail price of.. Pratt's aviation spirit, 4*s.* 1½*d.* per gallon. **1920** W. H. WILMER (*title*) Aviation Medicine in the A.E.F. **1928** *Lancet* 7 Apr. 714/1 Aviation or aviators' sickness.. a train of complex symptoms occurring in those who take the air. **1957** *Technology* Mar. 8/1 Some of the men from whose wisdom he will benefit have been in aviation almost from the beginning. **1960** *Times* 18 Oct. 13/7 What used to be the School of Aviation Medicine at San Antonio has been the Aerospace Medical Centre for a year now.

aviator (ˈeɪvɪeɪtə(r)). [ad. F. *aviateur*, f. L. *avis* bird + *-ateur* -ATOR.] †**1.** A heavier-than-air aircraft. Also *attrib. Obs.*
1891 *Brooklyn Morning Jrnl.* 22 July 1/6 (Funk), Mr. Maxim's invention is called an Aviator. It is in form like a huge kite of silk, to which hangs a platform carrying the engines and the screw propellers. **1895** *Knowledge* 2 Dec. 276/1 Mr. Maxim represents gunnery and the aviator flying machine. **1908** V. SILBERER in *Aeronaut. Jrnl.* July 51/1 A flying machine or aviator, however well constructed and furnished with such a motor.
2. a. The pilot of an aeroplane.
In early use, as distinguished from an aeronaut, *i.e.*, a balloonist.
1887 [see AVIATE *v.*]. **1896** *Westm. Gaz.* 15 Sept. 1/3 Intending aviators and aeronauts. **1909** *Ibid.* 26 Oct. 1/3 Other 'aviators'—the word has forced itself into the vocabulary, and it seems futile to resist it any longer—had other machines. **1911** *Yorks. Post* 3 Aug. 9/6 At height of 1,000 metres an aviator can find a submarine.
b. aviator's (or **aviators'**) **ear** = AERO-*otitis media*; **aviator's** (or **aviators'**) **sickness**, see AVIATION (quot. 1928).
1937 Aviator's ear [see AERO-*otitis media*]. **1916** *Sci. Amer. Suppl.* 3 June 357/2 What distinguishes aviators' sickness from mountain sickness is that the symptoms persist during descent and are aggravated after landing.
Hence **ˈaviatress, -trice, -trix**, a female aviator or pilot.
1910 *Daily Chron.* 5 Jan. 1/7 The aviatrice made a bad turn. **1911** *Aero* June 74/2 Various articles on the subject of 'Aviatresses' which have appeared from time to time. **1927** *Glasgow Herald* 29 Sept. 11 The English aviatrix, Miss Evelyn Spooner.

Avicennia (ævɪˈsɛnɪə). Also **avicennia.** [Named after *Avicenna*, Arabian physician (980–1037): see -IA[1].] A plant of the genus so named, esp. *A. tomentosa*, the white mangrove.
1829 LOUDON *Encycl. Plants* 522. **1871** KINGSLEY *At Last* II. xiii. 211 The statelier Avicennias, or white mangroves. **1883** *Encycl. Brit.* XV. 481/2 The 'white mangrove', *Avicennia*, a verbenaceous plant.

avicide (ˈævɪsaɪd). *nonce-wd.* [f. L. *avi-s* bird + -CIDE.] The slaughter of birds, bird-shooting.
1834 L. HUNT in *Lond. Jrnl.* No. 22 A stout fellow, in a jacket and gaiters and the rest of the costume of avicide.

avicolous (əˈvɪkələs), *a.* [f. L. *avis* bird + *-colus* inhabiting + -OUS.] Living, as parasites, on birds.
1895 D. SHARP in *Cambr. Nat. Hist.* V. xv. 349 The greater portion of the avicolous species have two claws.

avicular (əˈvɪkjʊlə(r)), *a. rare.* [f. L. *avicula*, dim. of *avis* + -AR.] Of or pertaining to small birds.
1857 *Fraser's Mag.* LVI. 631 The avicular millennium in the paradise of Walton Hill.

‖**avicularium** (əˌvɪkjuːˈlɛərɪəm). *Zool.* Pl. **-a.** [mod.L., f. *avicula*: see prec. and -ARIUM.] Name given to small prehensile processes shaped like birds' heads with a movable mandible, which snap incessantly, found on the cells of many Polyzoa. **aˌvicuˈlarian** *a.*, of or pertaining to avicularia.
1856 GOSSE *Marine Zool.* II. 4 They have been commonly called 'Bird's-head processes,' *avicularia.* **1873** DARWIN *Orig. Spec.* vii. (ed. 5) 194 The presence of the upper or fixed beak alone serves to determine its avicularian nature.

aviculture (ˈeɪvɪˌkʌltjʊə(r)). [f. L. *avi-s* bird + *cultūra* tending.] Rearing of birds; bird-fancying.
1880 *Daily Tel.* 14 Oct. 5 The object of the display [a bird-show] was to encourage aviculture. **1883** in *Lond. Soc.* July.

aviculturist (eɪvɪˈkʌltjʊərɪst). [f. AVICULTURE + -IST.] One who practises aviculture; a bird-fancier.
1904 *Nature* 31 Mar. 507/2 His work forms an excellent history of these beautiful birds, and is alike interesting to the field naturalist and the aviculturist. **1923** *Glasgow Herald* 23 Oct. 6 Probably Mr Farrar thinks that only aviculturists will concern themselves with his writing.

avid (ˈævɪd), *a.* [a. F. *avide*, ad. L. *avidus*, f. *avēre* to long for, crave.] Ardently desirous, extremely eager, greedy. Const. *of*, *for*, rarely *inf.*
1769 FR. BROOKE *Em. Montague* (1784) IV. ccvi. 118 The human heart is.. avid of pleasure and of gain. **1835** LYTTON *Rienzi* iv. iii, The most avid desire of personal power. **1866** J. ROSE *Ovid's Met.* 183 Or dragon avid for his prey.

avidin (ˈævɪdɪn). *Biochem.* [f. AVID *a.* + -IN[1], from its 'avidity' for biotin.] A protein in raw white of egg which combines with and inactivates biotin.
1941 R. E. EAKIN et al. in *Jrnl. Biol. Chem.* CXL. 536 The name 'avidin' seems appropriate for this protein; this term is suggested by its peculiar biotin-binding capacity. **1945** *Lancet* 5 May 568/1 Avidin is a protein constituent of egg-white which inactivates biotin by forming a complex with it.

avidious (əˈvɪdɪəs), *a. rare.* [f. L. *avid-us* or F. *avide.* As in some other obsolete words in *-idious* e.g. *splendidious*, the *-ious* is due to imitation of words in which it is etymological: see -IOUS.] = AVID *a.*
1534 WHITTINTON *Tullyes Offyces* I. (1540) 12 The auydious desyres of honour. **1550** BALE *Sel. Wks.* (1849) 418 With all avidious greediness. **1865** *Athenæum* No. 1959. 658/3 A sharp, avidious, cunning-looking man.

aˈvidiously, *adv.* [f. prec. + -LY[2].] = AVIDLY.
1546 LELAND *New Y. Gift* K iij b (T.) Avydyously we drynke the wynes of other landes. **1550** BALE *Image Both Ch.* G viij b, Nothing is more avydyouslye to be desyred.

avidity (əˈvɪdɪtɪ). Also 5 **avidite.** [a. F. *avidité* (16th c. in Littré), ad. L. *aviditātem*, n. of quality f. *avidus* AVID: see -ITY.]
1. Ardent desire, extreme eagerness, greediness.
c **1449** PECOCK *Repr.* II. xvii. 251 Deuocioun and avidite whiche men.. hadden into goostli techingis. **1667** *Phil. Trans.* II. 491 The dog.. fell a gnawing of them with a strange avidity. **1785** REID *Int. Powers* II. iv, Philosophers have an avidity to know how we perceive objects. **1833** I. TAYLOR *Fanat.* vi. 175 The mere avidity of gold. **1871** TYNDALL *Fragm. Sc.* II. ii. 11 Magazines, which I used to read with avidity when a boy.
b. *transf.* of things.
1646 SIR T. BROWNE *Pseud. Ep.* III. xvii. 149 The avidity of that part dilateth it selfe, and receiveth a second burden. **1854** SCOFFERN in *Orr's Circ. Sc.* Chem. 340 The avidity for oxygen manifested by sulphurous acid.
2. *ellipt.* Greediness of gain, graspingness, avarice.
1662 J. BARGRAVE *Pope Alex. VII* (1867) 44 He shewed no small rapacity or (to give it a milder term) avidity. **1796** MORSE *Amer. Geog.* I. 737 Nature never offered to the avidity of mankind.. such rich mines as those of Potosi. **1884** *United Presb. Mag.* Mar. 99 Raised at the same time the rents and the avidity of the landlords.

avidly (ˈævɪdlɪ), *adv.* [f. AVID + -LY[2].] Greedily, with intense eagerness.
1856 T. TROLLOPE *Girlh. Cath. de Medici* 71 The talk going on around her, which Catherine's sharp and active intellect was then avidly seizing. **1860** *Sat. Rev.* No. 255. 326/2 Premonitory symptoms of dissolution are avidly discounted by post-obit dealers.

†**avidous** (ˈævɪdəs), *a. Obs.* [f. L. *avid-us* + -OUS. Cf. AVIDIOUS.] = AVID.
1542 BOORDE *Dyetary* ix. 252 Mannes mynde is so auydous althoughe he haue eate ynoughe. **1607** TOPSELL *Serpents* 795 Your avidous and covetous mindes.

†**aˈvidulous**, *a. Obs.*—[0] [f. L. *avidul-us*, dim.] 'Somewhat greedy.' Bailey 1731.

†**a-ˈvie**, *advb. phr. Obs.* Forms: 6 **auy, avy,** 7 **a-vy,** 6–7 **auie, avie, a vie.** [f. A *prep.*[1] + VIE *sb.*] In rivalry or emulation.
1509 BARCLAY *Ship of Fooles* (1570) 32 There as beastes to striue and drinke auy. **1598** GREENWEY *Tacitus' Ann.* III. iii, The accusers and witnesses had spoken a vie against her. **1644** BULWER *Chiron.* 10 That most eminent Oratour would often contend and strive avie with Roscius.

aviette (eɪvɪˈɛt). [Fr., f. *avi*(*on* AVION + -ETTE.] An engineless aeroplane or glider. (Disused.)
1912 *Daily News* 1 June 1/4 It is called an aviette competition, an aviette being a flying machine propelled by muscular force alone. **1923** *Westm. Gaz.* 7 Apr., The 'Aviette', as the new glider with an auxiliary motor threatens to call itself.

†**aˈview**, *v. Obs.* Forms: 5–6 **avew(e,** 6 **aview(e, aweue,** 6 **advewe, -view.** [Cf. F. *aveuer*, *avuer*, to follow with the eye (a term of the chase), f. *à* to + *vue* view, sight, and see VIEW *sb.* and *v.* For the spelling *adv.*, see AD- *pref.* 2.] To view or inspect officially; to survey, reconnoitre; in Spenser simply = to view.
1494 FABYAN VII. 505 The sessynge whiche they had auewyd and sessed for y[e] xxx M. men. **1523** LD. BERNERS *Froiss.* I. xl. 55 They rode to aviewe y[e] englyssh hoost. **1530** PALSGR. 441/1 Who shal avewe [*Qui avisera a*] the partycion of these landes? **1596** SPENSER *F.Q.* v. iii. 20 All which when Artegall.. well advewed.. He could no longer beare.

avifauna (ˈeɪvɪˌfɔːnə), *sb.* [f. L. *avi-s* bird + FAUNA.] Collective term for the various kinds of birds found in any district or country; the 'Fauna' so far as concerns birds.
1874 COUES *Birds N.-W.* Introd. 10 The Avi-fauna proper of the region is not rich. **1883** M. WATKINS in *Academy* 8 Sept. 164/1 The claims of all pretenders to join the British Avifauna are strictly examined.

avifaunal (ˈeɪvɪˌfɔːnəl), *a.* [f. AVIFAUNA + -AL.] Of or pertaining to avifauna.
1889 in *Cent. Dict.* **1933** *Geogr. Jrnl.* LXXXI. 315 Some influence on avifaunal distribution.

avigato, variant of AVOCADO.

Avignon Berry (əˈvɪnjən). [So called from Avignon in France.] The fruit of the *Rhamnus infectorius*, and kindred species, used for dyeing yellow, and for making the pigment *sapgreen.*
1727–51 CHAMBERS *Cycl.*, *Avignon-Berry*, called also *French Berry*.. is somewhat less than a pea; its colour is green approaching towards yellow.

†**aˈvile**, *v. Obs.* Also 4 **avyle.** [a. OF. *avile-r* (= mod. *avilir*), cogn. with Pr., Sp. *avilar*, It. *avvilire*, *-are*:—Romanic **advilāre*, f. L. *ad* to + *vīlis* cheap, worthless, base.]
1. *trans.* To make vile, defile, dishonour, debase.
1297 R. GLOUC. 495 The bissopes.. amansede all the, That avilede holi chirche. *c* **1325** *E.E. Allit. P.* B. 1151 He þe vesselles avyled þat vayled in þe temple. *a* **1670** HACKET *Abp. Williams*, Pinch it into an epitome, you mangle the meaning and avile the eloquence.
2. To humble, degrade, abase.
a **1617** HIERON *Wks.* (1634) II. 65 Dauid was exceedingly auiled and cast downe in himselfe. **1632** SANDERSON *Serm.* I. 304 To exalt the papacy.. and to avile the secular powers.
3. To hold cheap or in small esteem, to depreciate.
1610 B. JONSON *Masques* (1692) 356 Want makes us know the price of what we avile. **1656** TRAPP *Comm. Acts* xxv. 19 These cocks.. know not the price of that pearl, and do therefore avile it.
4. To speak contemptuously of; to vilify.
1615 T. ADAMS *Lycanthr.* 13 So easy is it to avile and revile, so hard to convince. *a* **1617** HIERON *Wks.* 1634 II. 435 To curse him, that is, either to reuile him or to auile him.

†**aˈvilement.** *Obs. rare*—[1]. [f. prec. + -MENT; cf. OF. *avilement*, mod. *avilissement.*] A rendering, or treating as, vile.
a **1617** HIERON *Wks.* 1634 II. 390 Thoughts.. such as tend to the auilement and abasement of our selues.

avine (ˈeɪvaɪn), *a.* [f. L. *av-is* bird + -INE; cf. *ovine.*] = AVIAN.
1881 G. STABLES in *Boys' Own P.* 458 Avine architecture.

avintaine: read *a* VINTAINE, a score.

‖**avion** (avjɔ̃). [F. *avion*, f. *aviateur* AVIATOR, app. after *ballon* BALLOON *sb.*[1]] A flying-machine, esp. a French war aeroplane.
1898 *Sci. Amer.* 27 Aug. 137 The 'Avion' [*sc.* flying-machine of C. Ader (1841–1925)] in its position of flight. **1915** T. F. FARMAN in *Blackw. Mag.* Apr. 435/1 How many avions the French and British military authorities possessed when war broke out. **1927** *Chambers's Jrnl.* 258/2 Less easy prey they may be for the avions. **1935** J. JOYCE *Let.* 16 July (1966) III. 369 An avion letter from Bailly.

avionics (eɪvɪˈɒnɪks), *sb. pl.* [f. AVI(ATION + ELECTR)ONICS.] **a.** Const. as *sing.* The application of electronics in aeronautics and astronautics; electronics as developed for these areas. **b.** Const. as *pl.* Electrical and electronic equipment in an aircraft or spacecraft, or used in connection with their flight.
1949 *Aviation Week* 17 Oct. 28/2 'Avionics' is a new word, coined by *Aviation Week* as a simple and much needed term to describe generically all the applications of electricity to the field of aeronautics. **1965** *Guardian* 7 Apr. 20/3 There might be a programme to produce a more advanced avionics package (radar and electronics) which would fit into the existing air frame. **1969** *New Scientist* 10 Apr. 72/3 Let's buy American aircraft and save money by putting in our own avionics! **1971** *Times* 8 Dec. 23/6 Their employers announced plans to withdraw from the avionics market. **1976** H. WILSON *Governance of Britain* iv. 103 There was a no less strong argument for linking the production of highly sophisticated aircraft with avionics generally, the production of missiles and other associated electronic industries. **1981** *Australian* 15 Apr. 25/3 Distributors said

they frequently had to strip all avionics out of brand new Nomads and replace them.

Hence **avi'onic** *a.*

1949 *Aviation Week* 14 Nov. 29/1 Avionic devices, such as autopilots, bombsights, computers, gyros..radios, radars, etc. **1959** *Ibid.* 7 Dec. 67/1 Rapid growth by many avionic companies has brought with it related problems. **1966** *Economist* 16 Apr. 253 (Advt.), Britain's largest manufacturer and exporter of avionic equipment. **1969** *Telegraph* (Brisbane) 24 May 7/5 Australia's F111s would be equipped with the F111 Mark 1 avionic system. **1976** *Proc. R. Soc. Med.* LXIX. 251/2 Helicopters..have increasingly complex avionic fits all generating heat within the cockpit. **1984** *AGARD Conf. Proc.* No. 361. XXIX. 1 (*heading*) Automatic error detection and recovery techniques in onboard intelligent units for space and avionic application.

avirage, obs. form of AVERAGE.

†**a'vire**, *v. Obs. rare*⁻¹. [a. OF. *avire-r*, f. *à* to + *virer* to turn, to VEER.] To turn.

c **1440** *Morte Arth.* 3164 Towarde Viterbe this valyant avires the reynes.

†**avi'roun**, *adv. Obs.* [prob. a. AF. **aviroun*, variant of OF. *environ* around: see ENVIRON, and A- *pref.* 10.] Round about.

c **1300** *K. Alis.* 2672 Quykliche to Tebie toun: They wenten and segedyn aviroun. *c* **1320** *Syr Beves* 2533 In this contre aviroun A mette with a vile dragoun.

avirulent (æ'vɪrjʊlənt, eɪ-), *a.* [f. A- 14 + VIRULENT *a.*] Not virulent.

1900 in DORLAND *Med. Dict.* **1949** FLOREY et al. *Antibiotics* I. xxxiii. 1094 Iland (1946) found that an avirulent strain was more effective in this respect than the virulent strains. **1960** *New Biol.* XXXI. 72 In 1928.. Griffith..discovered that an avirulent and normally harmless strain of pneumococcus was changed into a virulent strain when injected into mice together with some virulent pneumococci that had been thoroughly killed by heating.

avis(e, etc., obs. form of ADVICE, ADVISE, etc.

avisage: see AVAGE.

†**a'vision.** *Obs.* Forms: 3-4 auisiun, **awision, a visyon**, 3-5 **aysyon, -ion**, 4-5 **avision**, 4-6 **au-avisioun**, 5 **avysioun, auicion, -yon, aduision, -uysion**, 6 **-uysyon**. [a. OF. *avision, -iun*, app. f. *à* to + *vision, -iun*, by form-association with *aviser, avisement*, etc. As in the other words of the *avise*-ADVISE group, the pref. *a-* was often written *ad-* in 15th c.]

1. A vision, dream.

a **1300** *Cursor M.* 4516 Pharaon..commanded be-for him bring Clerc and knithe, erle and baron To sceu til his a-uisiun. *c* **1386** CHAUCER *Nonne Pr. T.* 294 A litil or he was mordred..His mordre in his avysioun he say. *a* **1450** *Knt. de la Tour* 48 She awoke of her traunce and auicion. **1513** DOUGLAS *Æneis* III. i. 69 Beseiking this auisioun worth happy.

2. Warning or monition (given in a dream).

1297 R. GLOUC. 255 þe kyng þys auyson, þat þe angel hym seyde, þe oþer tolde priuelyche. **1525** LD. BERNERS *Froiss.* II. cciv. [cc.] 627 Preace thou forthe and shewe them thine aduysyon, for thou shalte be herde.

aviso (ə'vaɪzəʊ). Pl. **-os** (17th c. **-o's**). See also ADVISO. [a. Sp. *aviso* advice, intelligence, also an advice-boat:—late L. *advisum*: see ADVICE, which is the Eng. cognate. In 16th c. refashioned as ADVISO, which is now obs.]

†**1.** Intelligence, information; a notification, dispatch, or formal advice. *Obs.*; = ADVICE 8.

1634 HABINGTON *Castara* (Arb.) 102 This vault shall furnish thee With more aviso's, then thy costly spyes. **1654** LESTRANGE *Chas. I*, 6 His first act..was to dispatch Aviso's of his Father's decease to forein Princes.

2. An ADVICE-BOAT.

1714 *Let.* in C. King *Brit. Merch.* (1721) III. 225 An Aviso or Pacquet-Boat. **1870** *Daily News* 16 Sept., The light frigates and a few avisos and gunboats.

avisy, variant of ADVISY.

†**a'vitaile.** *Obs. rare*⁻¹. [f. F. *avitailler*, f. *à* to + *vitaille* VICTUAL.] Provisions, victuals.

1592 WYRLEY *Armorie* 125 No avitaile had they for to dine.

avital (ə'vaɪtəl, 'ævɪtəl), *a.* ? *Obs.* [f. L. *avīt-us* of or pertaining to the *avus*, grandfather + -AL¹. More analogically formed than the two following words; cf. *marital, fraternal.*] Ancestral, ancient, of long standing.

1611 SPEED *Hist. Gt. Brit.* IX. vi. (1632) 509 To maintaine those Auitall Customes to the vttermost. **1641** PRYNNE *Antip.* 22 The said Lawes and Avitall customes.

avitaminosis (ə,vaɪtæmɪ'nəʊsɪs, eɪ-, -,vɪt-). Pl. **-oses** (-'əʊsiːz). [mod.L., f. A- 14 + VITAMIN + -OSIS.] A condition resulting from a deficiency of one or more vitamins. Also used *spec.* (*avitaminosis A, B*, etc.): deficiency of the vitamin specified. Cf. DEFICIENCY *disease*.

1914 *Lancet* 9 May 1328/2 The author [*sc.* C. Funk] states that this publication [sc. *Die Vitamine*] is the first attempt at a representation of our knowledge about vitamines and avitaminoses... By the word avitaminoses, coined by the author, is understood what is called in English 'deficiency diseases'. **1923** *Nature* 26 May 728/1 Contribution to the study of B avitaminosis in the pigeon. **1931** *Lancet* 14 Mar. 624/1 (*title*) A Multiple Avitaminosis. A disease which is claimed to be a multiple food deficiency. *Ibid.* 624/2 Multiple partial avitaminoses..are probably all too common among native races the world over and are the abundant fruit of poverty.

avitic (ə'vɪtɪk), *a.* [f. as AVITAL *a.* + -IC.] = AVITAL *a.*

1865 *Pall Mall G.* 3 July 1/1 The old or 'avitic' Constitution.

†**a'vitous**, *a. Obs.*⁻⁰ [f. as prec. + -OUS.] = prec.

1731 in BAILEY.

avives (ə'vaɪvz), *sb. pl.* ? *Obs.* [a. F. *avives* (also *vives*), a. Sp. *avivas, adivas*, ad. Arab. *aḍ-ḍībah*, with same meaning, lit. *al-*, the, *ḍībah* she-wolf.] A swelling of the parotid glands in horses; the strangles; called also VIVES.

1616 SURFL. & MARKH. *Countr. Farm* 139 The horse hauing drunke much, or watered verie quickly after his heat ..doth beget the Auiues. **1639** T. DE GREY *Compl. Horseman* 40 Auyues [*printed* Auynes]. **1725** BRADLEY *Fam. Dict., Vives, Avives*, or *Fives*, all one Disease in a Horse, being certain flat Kernels, much like unto Bunches of Grapes growing in a Cluster..They center from the Ears and creep downwards.

‖**avizandum, avis-** (ævɪ'zændəm). *Sc. Law.* [gerund of med.L. *avizāre, avisāre*, to consider, ADVISE.] Consideration. ***to take a case into*** or ***to avizandum***, is for a judge to take it for private consideration outside the court.

1861 TRAYNER *Lat. Phr.* in *Sc. Law* 33 A process is said to be at avizandum when the Judge after debate is considering it with a view to decision. **1884** *Law Rep., Appeal* IX. 307 After argument..his Lordship made avizandum with the cause.

avize, -ful, -ment, obs. forms of ADVISE, etc.

avocado (ɑːvəʊ'kɑːdəʊ, now æv-). Also 7 **avogato**, 8 **avocato**, 9 **avigato**. [Sp. *avocado* advocate, substituted by 'popular etymology' for the Aztec *ahuacatl* (Tylor), of which a nearer form in Sp. is *aguacate*; F. *aguacat* and *avocat*, in Eng. also *avigato* and, corruptly, *alligator* (pear).] **a.** The fruit of a West Indian tree (*Persea gratissima*); a large pear-shaped fruit, called also ALLIGATOR PEAR.

1697 DAMPIER *Voy.* (1729) I. 203 The Avogato Pear-tree is as big as most Pear-trees..the Fruit as big as a large Lemon. **1763** GRAINGER *Sugar-cane* I. 422 And thou green avocato, charm of sense, Thy ripened marrow liberally bestow'st. (*Note.* The *avocato, avocado, avigato*, or as the English corruptly call it, *Alligator-pear.*) **1830** LINDLEY *Nat. Syst. Bot.* 30 Much esteemed in the West Indies under the name of the Avocado Pear. **1861** [see ALLIGATOR² 4]. **1864** WEBSTER, *Avigato.* **1829** MARRYAT *F. Mildmay* xviii. (Rtlg.) 174 Abbogada pears (better known by the name of subaltern's butter).

b. The green colour of the flesh of an avocado. In full, ***avocado green***. Also as *adj.*

1947 *House & Garden* Sept. 89/1 Brighten a dining foyer with a floor of Persimmon plastic tiles, paint its walls Avocado Green, its ceiling white. **1963** *New Yorker* 15 June 78 Made..of fine Sanforized cotton in..Avocado with Lime, or Black with White. **1974** *Anderson* (S. Carolina) *Independent* 19 Apr. 12B/1 (Advt.), 1 Hoover portable washer avocado green. **1976** *National Observer* (U.S.) 1 May 3/5 (Advt.), [Lamp-] shade & base in one color: Avocado, Bone White or Ebony. **1978** *Detroit Free Press* 5 Mar. C20/6 (Advt.), Avocado green washer.

†**a'vocament.** *Obs.* [ad. L. *āvocāment-um*, f. *āvocāre*: see AVOCATE.] A calling off, a distraction; = AVOCATION in proper sense.

1673 O. WALKER *Educ.* (1677) 216 Those states seem.. best which have the fewest avocaments from Religion.

avocat(e, obs. form of ADVOCATE.

†**'avocate**, *v. Obs.* [f. L. *āvocāt-* ppl. stem of *āvocāre* to call off or away, f. *ā, ab*, off + *vocāre* to call. In sense 2 f. F. *avoquer*, later *advoquer*, ad. L. *advocāre*: see ADVOKE, ADVOCATE *v.*¹]

1. To call away, withdraw, distract, divert (*from*).

1543 BECON *David's Harp* Wks. (1843) 266 Whereby they might be avocated and called away from sin. **1641** PRYNNE *Antip.* Ep. 14 Temporall meanes, & honour..avocate and hinder them from preaching. **1752** SHENSTONE *Wks. & Lett.* III. 192, I have avocated my thoughts, and fixed them for a while upon common amusements.

2. To call to a higher tribunal; = ADVOCATE *v.*¹ 2.

1649 LD. HERBERT *Hen. VIII*, 259 (T.) Seeing now all proceeding in England inhibited, the cause avocated to Rome, Campegius recalled. **1679** BURNET *Hist. Ref.* 120 Must avocate the business to be heard in the court of Rome.

†**'avocating,** *ppl. a.* [f. prec. + -ING².] Calling away, distracting.

1643 PRYNNE *Power Parl.* I. Pref. (ed. 2) A ij, So farre forth, as..avocating Imployments would permit. **1660** BOYLE *Seraph. Love* iv. (1700) 27 Laborious and avocating Duties.

avocation (ævəʊ'keɪʃən). [ad. L. *āvocātiōn-em*, n. of action f. *āvocāre*: see AVOCATE and -ATION. In sense 5 f. AVOCATE *v.* 2, and = OF. *avocation*, ad. L. *advocātiōn-em*: see ADVOCATION.]

I. (= L. *āvocātio.*)

1. The calling away or withdrawal (of a person) from an employment; diversion of the thoughts. *arch.* or *Obs.*

a **1617** HIERON *Wks.* 1634 II. 271 The many auocations and withdrawments from good which they are sure to meet with. **1642** JER. TAYLOR *Episc.* (1647) 363 Which could by no meanes make recompense for the least avocation of them from their Church imployment. *c* **1645** HOWELL *Lett.* VI. 11, I could be larger, but for a sudden auocation to business. **1758** GRAY in *Poems* (1775) 270 Try, by every method of avocation and amusement, whether you cannot..get the better of that dejection.

2. The condition of being called away, or having one's attention diverted; distraction.

a **1646** TWISSE in *Mede's Wks.* IV. lxx. 846 The care whereof is apt to cause avocation and disturbance in that *Unum necessarium*. **1768** BLACKSTONE *Comm.* I. 26 Too long an avocation from their private concerns and amusements. **1844** S. MAITLAND *Dark Ages* 327 He devoted himself, with less avocation, to prayer.

3. That which has the effect of calling away or withdrawing one from an occupation. *Hence*, A minor or less important occupation, a by-work (πάρεργον).

1642 FULLER *Holy & Prof. St.* IV. ix. 281 Heaven is his vocation, and therefore he counts earthly employments avocations. **1752** JOHNSON *Rambl.* No. 194 ¶11 He.. appears to hear me, but is soon rescued from the lecture by more pleasing avocations. **1794** GODWIN *Cal. Williams* 203 Upon some avocation, however, a noise I believe in the passage, the turnkey went. **1879** FURNIVALL *Rep. New Shaks. Soc.* 9 If its editor's new vocation (school-mastering) had left him time for the avocation of finishing his task for us.

4. But as, in many cases, the business which called away was one of equal or greater importance (see quot. in a., where *avocation* is rightly used), the new meaning was improperly foisted upon the word: Ordinary employment, usual occupation, vocation, calling.

a. **1660** BOYLE *New Exp. Phys.-Mech.* Proem 19 The onely [experiments] wherewith my Avocations will allow me to entertain your Lordship in this Letter. **1794** SULLIVAN *View Nat.* II, In the hurry of avocations for the necessities of life, little was the time he could apply to abstract speculations. **1804** WELLINGTON in Gurw. *Disp.* III. 557 Prevented by other avocations of extensive national importance, from a residence in Mysore. **1840** MACAULAY *Ranke, Ess.* (1854) II. 552/2 Found, even in the midst of his most pressing avocations, time for private prayer.

b. **1761** *New Comp. Fest. & Fasts* xxxvi. §2. 353 When a universal weakness and decay enfeebles us from even the common avocations of life. **1815** MOORE *Lalla R.* (1824) 337 Poetry was by no means his proper avocation. **1865** DICKENS *Mut. Fr.* ii. 280 My avocation is in London city. **1858** BUCKLE *Civiliz.* (1873) II. viii. 498 War and religion were the only two avocations worthy of being followed.

II. (= L. *advocātio.*)

5. The calling of a cause or action before itself by a superior court; = ADVOCATION 2.

1529 DR. BENNET *To Wolsey* in Burnet *Hist. Ref.* (1679) I. Rec. 80 His Holiness may..the more boldly deny Avocations to the Cæsareans. **1683** BURNET *Hist. Ref. Abr.* 49 The Queen's Agents pressed hard for an Avocation. **1856** FROUDE *Hist. Eng.* II. ix. 312 His unjust avocation of the cause to Rome.

avocational (ævə'keɪʃənəl), *a.* [f. AVOCATION + -AL.] Of or pertaining to an avocation, hobby, or leisure-time pursuit; that occupies one's leisure; existing apart from or in addition to one's regular occupation.

1940 D. E. SUPER (*title*) Avocational interest patterns. **1947** J. C. RICH *Materials & Methods Sculpture* xi. 357 Soap is an inexpensive, readily available and easily worked material that is steadily gaining in popularity as a wholesome and interesting avocational carving medium. **1949** R. K. MERTON *Social Theory* vi. 163 Their [*sc.* intellectuals'] activities may be vocational or avocational... The fact that John Stuart Mill spent many years in the India Office does not rule him out as an intellectual. **1966** L. & G. POOLE *One Passion, Two Loves* 7 The introduction..concluded many years of avocational study.., and marked the beginning of purposeful research for the writing of *One Passion, Two Loves*. **1979** *Sci. Amer.* Apr. 19/1 Physicists with an avocational interest in the martial arts.

Hence **avo'cationally** *adv.*

1952 GERTH & MARTINDALE tr. *Weber's Anc. Judaism* xv. 393 The..rabbi..exercising his function as advisor and counsel in matters of ritual avocationally, that is, alongside his secular occupation. **1986** *N.Y. Times* 16 Mar. VI. II. 69/1 We who deal avocationally with anthropophagi, such as sharks, endeavor to cut our losses by calculating our risks.

avocative (ə'vɒkətɪv), *a.* and *sb.* [f. L. *āvocāre*: see AVOCATE and -ATIVE.]

A. *adj.* Calling off or away.

1835 in KNOWLES.

B. *sb.* Anything which calls away.

a **1677** BARROW *Exp. Creed* (L.) All other incentives to virtue and avocatives from vice.

avocatory (ə'vɒkətərɪ), *a.* and *sb.* [ad. med.L. *āvocātōrius*, f. *āvocāre*: see AVOCATE and -ORY. Also in F. (lettre) *avocatoire.*]

A. *adj.* Recalling, that recalls. ***letters avocatory***: letters by which a sovereign recalls his subjects from a foreign state with which he is at war, or bids them desist from illegal proceedings.

1666 *Lond. Gaz.* No. 99/1 His Imperial Majesty hath sent out his Avocatory Mandates to the States of the Empire. **1758** *Hist. Europe* in *Ann. Reg.* 50/1 Letters avocatory were issued notifying..that if they did not..disperse their armies ..they were put under the ban of the Empire.

B. *sb.* (in L. form) Avocatory letter or mandate.

1689 LUTTRELL *Brief Rel.* I. 498 The imperial avocatoria was published..requireing all the subjects of the empire engaged in the service of France forthwith to quitt the same. **1751** CHAMBERS *Cycl.*, *Avocatoria*, a mandate of the emperor of Germany, directed to some prince or subject of the empire, to stop his unlawful proceedings in any cause brought by way of appeal before him.

avocet, -set (ˈævəʊˌsɛt). Also 7–8 **avosetta**, 9 **avocetta**. [a. F. *avocette*, ad. It. *avosetta*.] One of the Wading birds (*Grallatores*), allied to the Snipes and Stilts, specially distinguished by its flexible upturned beak.

[**1674** RAY *Water Fowl* 94 Avosetta Italorum: Recurvirostra.] **1766** PENNANT *Brit. Zool.* (1812) II. 143 An Avoset that we shot weighed thirteen ounces. **1771** —— *Tour. Scotl.* (1790) 13 Numbers of Avosettas, called there yelpers from their cry. **1863** *Sat. Rev.* 284 Drainage has banished the avoset..and the godwit from our eastern marshes. **1881** M. WATKINS in *Academy* 27 Aug. 163/2, 1840 was the last year in which the avocet is known to have bred in England.

‖**avodiré** (ævəʊˈdɪəreɪ). Also **avodire**. [Fr.] The smooth-textured hardwood of light colour from a large West African tree (*Turræanthus africanus* or *T. vignei*) of the mahogany family; also, the tree itself.

1934 A. L. HOWARD *Man. Timbers World* 44 Light-weight, white wood..offered for sale as African white mahogany... Among the best of these timbers it is now possible to name Avodire, which possesses a golden-yellow colour, with a firm, clean grain, capable of giving a very smooth surface. **1935** *Archit. Rev.* Oct. 160/3 A corner fitting, veneered with avodire, consisting of a radio-gramophone and copious record storage. **1936** *Nature* 9 May 790/1 The following woods amongst others have been used [for the liner *Queen Mary*]..Avodiré (*Turreanthus africana*).

Avogadro (ævəʊˈgɑːdrəʊ). *Chem.* The name of the Italian scientist Count Amedeo *Avogadro* (1776–1856), used esp. *attrib.* or in the possessive case of his hypothesis that equal volumes of all gases at the same temperature and pressure contain equal numbers of molecules. Also ***Avogadro('s) constant, number***: the number of molecules in a mole (MOLE *sb.*[7]) (see quot. 1958).

1871 *Jrnl. Chem. Soc.* XXIV. 1247/1 Avogadro's law. *Ibid.* 300 *On the Law of Avogadro.*—The relation of this law —viz., that 'equal volumes of different gases contain, under like conditions, equal numbers of molecules', to the mechanical theory of gases, has lately been the subject of.. discussion. **1874** J. P. COOKE *New Chem.* ii. 37 Avogadro's law declares that all gases contain, under like conditions of temperature and pressure, the same number of molecules in the same volume. **1895** C. S. PALMER tr. *Nernst's Theoret. Chem.* v. 148 We know the gas pressure of all well-defined chemical substances, which are subject to Avogadro's rule. **1902** *Encycl. Brit.* XXVI. 739/1 Avogadro's theorem is directly applicable to dilute solutions. **1927** WEBSTER Addenda, Avogadro number. **1958** BALLENTYNE & WALKER *Dict. Named Effects* 9 *Avogadro's Number*, the number of individual atoms in a gramme-atom, of ions in a gramme-ion or of molecules in a gramme-molecule... The accepted value is $6{\cdot}023 \times 10^{23}$. **1959** *Chambers's Encycl.* I. 746/1 Since molecules have now lost their hypothetical character, it seems preferable to refer to Avogadro's theorem rather than Avogadro's hypothesis or law.

avoid (əˈvɔɪd), *v.* Forms: 4–7 **au- avoide, -oyde**, 5 **awoyde**, 5–6 **aduoyde, -voyde**, 6 **advoid, awode**, 6–7 **auoyd, auoid**, 6– **avoid**. [a AF. *avoide-r* = OF. *esvuidier, évuider* (see A- *pref.* 9), to empty out, clear out, quit, get quit of, banish, f. *es* out + *vuidier*, f. *vuit, vuide*, empty: see VOID *v.* and *a.* Cf. the sense development of EVACUATE *v.* For the spelling *adv-* see AD- *pref.* 2.] In several senses formerly occasionally strengthened by *out, away*; cf. *to clear out, away*.

I. To empty a thing (of what is in it); to make, become, or be empty.

†**1.** *trans.* To make (a vessel, place, person) void or empty; to empty, clear, free, rid (*of*). *Obs.*

1382 WYCLIF *Ecclus.* xiii. 6 He shal lyue with thee, and auoide thee out [Vulg. *evacuabit te*; **1611** make thee bare]. *c* **1430** LYDG. *Min. Poems* 16 Hertis avoydyng of alle ther hevyness. *c* **1500** *Yng. Childr. Bk.* in *Babees Bk.* 23 Sone A-voyd þou thi trenchere. **1531** ELYOT *Gov.* II. vii. (1557) 105 Commanded the chambre to be avoided. **1601** TATE *Househ. Ord. Ed. II*, §94 (1876) 56 To avoid the court of al manner of such people.

2. To make void or of no effect; to refute, disprove. In *Law*, to defeat (a pleading); to invalidate, 'quash' (a sentence, agreement, document, etc.)

c **1375** WYCLIF *Serm.* Sel. Wks. 1871 II. 167 How wickide men sclaundriden [Crist] and he avoydide þer blame. **1514–5** *Act 6 Hen. VIII*, iv, All outlawries had contrary to this Acte be advoyded. **1581** FULKE in *Confer.* II. (1584) I iij b, This answere is a senseles cauil, which is easily auoyded. **1628** COKE *On Litt.* 43 a, The Statute intended not to auoid the feoffment. **1768** BLACKSTONE *Comm.* II. 308 How a deed may be avoided, or rendered of no effect. **1858** LD. ST. LEONARDS *Handy-bk. Prop. Law* VIII. 59 If the advowson is purchased with a corrupt view, that may avoid the purchase.

†**3.** *intr.* (for *refl.*) Of benefices: To become void, to fall vacant. *Obs.*, but cf. AVOIDANCE.

1521 *Mem. Ripon* (1882) I. 183 To have their turne when it fortun to advoide agayn. **1726** AYLIFFE *Parerg.* 112 If a Person takes a Bishoprick, it does not avoid by Force of that Law of Pluralities, but by the antient Common Law.

II. To empty things out of a place, etc., to remove, to quit.

†**4.** To empty out, clear out, put away, remove (the contents of anything). *Obs.*

1398 TREVISA *Barth. De P.R.* VII. xliv. (1495) 257 The matere shall be auoyded and pourgyd wyth couenable medicyne. **1563** HYLL *Arte Garden.* (1593) 136 Little furrowes..to auoyd the moisture and raine. **1641** PRYNNE *Antip.* I. i. 28 His Images and Pictures..should be pluckt down and avoided out of all Churches.

†**b.** To eject by excretion; to void. (Said loosely also of snakes sloughing their skin.) *Obs.*

1562 COOPER *Answ. Priv. Masse* (1850) 208 The sanctified bread..passeth into the belly, and is avoided out of the body. **1598** HAKLUYT *Voy.* I. 97 It causeth vrine to be avoided in great measure. **1604** JAMES I *Counterbl.* (Arb.) 104 Forced to auoyde muche winde out of your stomacke. **1691** RAY *Creation* (1714) 28 So they avoid their skins unbroken. *Ibid.* (1701) 145 They avoid them [pebbles] by siege.

†**c.** To get rid of, clear away, do away with, put an end to (things immaterial). *Obs.*

1382 WYCLIF *2 Cor.* iii. 7 The whiche glorie is auoydid [Vulg. *evacuatur*]. *c* **1485** *Digby Myst.* (1882) I. 90 Ffor to a-voide a-wey all interrupcion. **1561** HOLLYBUSH *Hom. Apoth.* 14 a, The same doth avoyde horsenesse. **1685** BAXTER *Paraphr. N.T.* Acts xv. 17 There was then no Judge of such controversies..to avoid and end them.

†**5.** To get rid of, expel, banish, dismiss, send or drive away (a person *from, out of* a place). *Obs.*

1460 CAPGRAVE *Chron.* 178 That this Petir [Gaveston] schuld be a voyded. **1494** FABYAN VII. ccxxxviii. 276 He auoyded yᵉ munkys out of the house of Aumbrisbury. **1529** RASTELL *Chron.* (1811) 106 He myght not clerely avoyed them the lande. **1540** HYRDE *Vives' Instr. Chr. Wom.* (1592) B iij a, Avoide all mankinde away from her. **1643** PRYNNE *Power Parl.* II. 19 They would avoyd all aliens and strangers out of it [the City].

b. *refl.* in sense of next. *arch.* or *Obs.*

a **1300** *Cursor M.* 3622 Avoyde scho hir, and vmbethoght. *a* **1400** *Cov. Myst.* 131 Avoyd ȝow hens out of this place. **1808** SCOTT *Marm.* VI. xxxii, Avoid thee, Fiend!

†**6.** *intr.* To move or go away, withdraw, depart, quit; to give place, retire, retreat. *Obs.*

a **1400** *Cov. Myst.* 131 Avoyd, seres, and lete my lorde the buschop come. *a* **1529** SKELTON *Vox Pop.* vii. 45 Or els, for non payeing the rent, Avoyde at our Ladye daye in Lent. **1599** HAKLUYT *Voy.* II. I. 35 Thinking to auoid by the swiftnes of his horse. **1615** G. SANDYS *Trav.* 72 The Musicians spent so much time in vnseasonable tuning, that he commanded them to auoid. **1763** PRIOR *Alma* III. 253 And both as they provisions want, Chicane, avoid, retire, and faint.

†**b.** Const. *from, out of, forth of. to avoid* (from a horse): to dismount. *Obs.*

1485 CAXTON *Paris & V.* 26 Eche body avoyded oute of the chambre. **1535** COVERDALE *Matt.* xvi. 23 Auoyde fro me, Sathan. **1570–87** HOLINSHED *Scot. Chron.* (1806) I. 351 Quicklie avoiding from his horse. **1611** BIBLE *1 Sam.* xviii. 11 Dauid auoided out of his presence.

†**c.** *transf.* of water, wind, etc. To escape, run out or away. *Obs.*

1483 CAXTON *Gold. Leg.* 305/3 The see Ocean..auoydeth twyes and gyueth way to the peple. **1523** FITZHERB. *Surv.* xxxv. (1539) 53 Make a great dyche..that the water may auoyde. **1610** MARKHAM *Masterp.* II. cxxi. 424 If you put a hollow quill therein..the winde will auoyd the better.

†**7.** *trans.* To depart from, leave, quit (a place); to dismount from (a horse). *Obs.*

1447–8 SHILLINGFORD *Lett.* (1871) 91 They wolle avoyde theire dwellyng places. **1481** CAXTON *Reynard* (1844) 105 Ye commaunded them to auoyde your Court. **1557** *K. Arthur* (Copland) VII. xxxiv, The Kynge auoyded his hors. **1660** *Trial Reg.* 160 Desired that strangers might avoid the room.

III. To keep away from, keep from, keep off.

8. (the usual current sense—a natural extension of 7): To leave alone, keep clear of or away from, shun; to have nothing to do with, refrain from: **a.** a person or place.

(The first quotation may belong to 5, hardly to 4.)

c **1384** WYCLIF *De Eccl.* Sel. Wks. 1871 III. 353 Men shulden avoide þis frere. **1530** PALSGR. 441/1 Never have to do with hym, if thou mayst avoyde hym. **1697** DRYDEN *Virg. Georg.* IV. 579 And Sheep, in Shades, avoid the parching Plain. **1722** DE FOE *Plague* 131 Avoiding the towns, they left ..Newington on the right hand. **1857** BOHN'S *Handbk. Prov.* 323 Avoid a slanderer as you would a scorpion. *Mod.* Avoiding Scylla, he fell into Charybdis.

b. a thing, course of action, etc.

c **1450** *Pol. Rel. & L. Poems* (1866) 28 Mowth and tongge avoydyng alle outrage. **1681** DRYDEN *Abs. & Achit.* II. 483 Still thou mayst live, avoiding pen and ink. **1722** DE FOE *Moll. Fl.* (1840) 148, I ventured to avoid signing a contract. **1767** FORDYCE *Serm. Yng. Wom.* I. i. 36 Take care to avoid every appearance of partiality.

9. To escape, evade (things coming towards one); to keep out of the way of.

1530 PALSGR. 441/1 That was wel avoyded, *cela estoyt bien eschappé*. **1541** BARNES *Wks.* (R.) Can you deuise for to auoyde hys vengeaunce? **1594** SHAKS. *Rich. III*, III. v. 68 T'auoid the Censures of the carping World. **1661** LOVELL *Hist. Anim. & Min.* 92 Wormes creep out of the earth to avoide them [moles]. **1714** *Spect.* No. 578 ¶11 The King had perished..had he not avoided his Pursuers. **1808** SCOTT *Marm.* V. xviii, They deemed it hopeless to avoid The convoy of their dangerous guide.

†**10.** To prevent, to obviate, to keep off. *Obs.*

1608 PLAT *Gard. Eden* (1653) 54 Northerly windes may be avoyded by some defence. **1664** POWER *Exp. Philos.* II. 129 Which will avoid..multiplicity of terms for the future. **1831** CARLYLE *Sart. Res.* III. v, That the Body..be decently interred, to avoid putrescence.

†**11.** Obs. or arch. const. of senses 8–10: with *subord. cl.* To avoid *that*; with *inf.* To avoid *to do*.

1570–87 HOLINSHED *Scot. Chron.* (1806) II. 124 To avoid that none..that had offended the laws, should be received into anie of their dominions. **1599** HAKLUYT *Voy.* II. I. 23 Because he by that meanes would auoid to marry with Alice. **1600** HOLLAND *Livy* X. xv. 361 He avoided App. Claudius to be his companion in government. **1853** F. NEWMAN *Odes of Horace* 185 Horace..in praising the emperor and congratulating Marcellus, avoids to make either seem his main subject.

†**aˈvoid**, *a.* *Obs.* [f. prec. vb.; on apparent analogy of *void* vb. and adj. or ? contr. of *avoided*; cf. *devoid*.] Empty, void; free or rid (*of*). *Obs.*

1488 *Plumpton Corr.* 66 The clarkship therof standeth avoyd. **1514** BARCLAY *Cyt. & Uplondyshm.* 3 The ploweman resteth avoyde of all busynesse.

†**aˈvoid**, *sb.* *Obs.* [f. AVOID *v.*]

1. The withdrawal of dishes (after meals).

1494 *Ord. R. Househ.* 113 All that is dispended for..the greete avoides at feestes. **1577** HARRISON *England* I. II. v. 124 They do not their mantels from them untill supper be ended, and the avoid doone.

2. Excretion, evacuation.

1502 ARNOLD *Chron.* (1811) 150 Nott to ete nor dryncke out of noo vessel but in the same that he made hys avoid in.

avoidable (əˈvɔɪdəb(ə)l), *a.* [f. AVOID *v.* + -ABLE.]

1. Liable to be made void or become invalid; voidable. ? *Obs.*

a **1677** HALE (J.) The charters were not avoidable for the king's nonage. **1818** COLEBROOKE *Obligations* I. 228 The acts of a madman, lunatic, or idiot..are void or avoidable.

†**2.** To be avoided or shunned. *Obs.*

1610 HEALEY *St. Aug. City of God* 752 If those evills make it avoydable, what is become of the blisse? **1744** HARRIS *Three Treat.* (1841) 57 Another division of things external; that is, pursuable, avoidable, and indifferent.

3. Capable of being avoided or escaped.

1638 CHILLINGW. *Relig. Prot.* I. iii. §52 If the cause of it be some voluntary and avoidable fault, the Errour is it selfe sinfull. **1859** MILL *Liberty* 176 From idleness or from any other avoidable cause.

avoidably (əˈvɔɪdəblɪ), *adv.* [f. prec. + -LY[2].] In an avoidable manner.

1833 HT. MARTINEAU *Briery Crk.* Summ. 155 An expenditure which avoidably exceeds the revenue is a social crime.

†**aˈvoidal.** *Obs. rare.* [f. AVOID *v.* + -AL[2].] An avoiding.

1695 *Def. Vind. Depr. Bps.* 28 He should have made the avoidal of the feared evils certain.

avoidance (əˈvɔɪdəns). Forms: 4–6 **au-avoydaunce**, 5 **avoydans**, 6 **advoidance**, 6–8 **au-avoydance, auoidance**, 6– **avoidance**. [f. AVOID *v.* + -ANCE; prob. (from the date) in AFr.]

†**1. a.** The action of emptying a vessel, etc., or of emptying away its contents; *hence*, a clearing away, removal; ejection, excretion. *Obs.*

1398 TREVISA *Barth. De P.R.* VII. lxix. (1495) 290 Leest there be to grete auoydaunce. *c* **1430** *Freemasonry* 712 From spyttynge and snyftynge kepe the also, By privy avoydans let hyt go. **1548** GESTE *Pr. Masse* 85 For..advoidance of ymage worshyp. **1577** *Test. 12 Patriarchs* 108 [God] hath assigned ..the belly to the avoidance of the stomach. **1627** SPEED *Eng. Abridged* x. §3 Wolues, for whose auoydance Edgar the peaceable did impose a yearely Tribute. **1661** MORGAN *Sph. Gentry* IV. iii. 36 Until..Supper and Avoydance be done and accomplished.

†**b.** A means of emptying; an outlet. *Obs.*

1602 CAREW *Cornwall* 122 a, A great standing water..fed by no perceyved spring, neither having any avoydance. **1625** BACON *Build., Ess.* (Arb.) 553 Fountaines, Running..from the Wall, with some fine Auoidances.

2. The action of making void or of no effect; voidance, invalidation, annulment. (Esp. in *Law*.)

1628 COKE *On Litt.* 261 b, If a man in auoydance of a fine ..alleage that hee was out of this Realme in Spaine, at the time of leuying of the fine. *a* **1832** MACKINTOSH *Hist. Rev.* Wks. 1846 II. 119 Some members were threatened with the avoidance of their elections. **1855** MILMAN *Lat. Chr.* (1864) V. IX. iv. 246 The obsequious clergy..pronounced at once the avoidance of the marriage.

†**3.** The action of vacating an office or benefice.

1642 SIR E. DERING *Sp. on Relig.* 90 After the death, or other avoidance of a Bishop.

4. The becoming void or vacant, vacancy (of an office or benefice); also *ellipt.* the right to fill up the vacancy.

1462 *Paston Lett.* 440 II. 90 That I may have the presentacion of the next avoydaunce for a newew of myn. **1594** PLAT *Jewell-ho.* III. 64 A learned Vintner and worthie to haue the next auoydance of Bacchus his chaire. **1660** R. Coke *Power & Subj.* 268 That Patron who should simonically promote any Clerk should not only forfeit that avoidance, but the advowson. **1858** Beveridge *Hist. India* II. v. iv. 347 The avoidance of the office of said governor-general by death. **1879** Maclear *Celts* xi. 170 On each avoidance of the abbacy, to fill up the situation from founder's kin.

†**5.** The action of dismissing a person or bidding him quit; dismissal, removal. *Obs.*

a **1631** Donne *Aristeas* (1633) 111 The King having made avoydance of those hee esteemed not necessary. **1650** Fuller *Pisgah* II. xi. 232 By the avoidance of this servant divine providence made a way for Elisha.

†**6.** The action of quitting; withdrawal, departure, exit. *Obs.*

a **1555** Latimer *Serm. & Rem.* (1845) 293 The bishop.. commanded avoidance. **1613** Hayward *Norm. Kings* 86 By voluntary avoidance out of the Realme. **1635** Swan *Spec. M.* (1670) 418 They make present avoidance from their holes.

7. a. The action of avoiding or shunning anything unwelcome, or of holding aloof from a person.

1610 Donne *Pseudo-mart.* 343 For avoydance of scandall is Divine law. **1615** Bp. Hall *Contempl.* xix. v. (1796) II. 261 Some things may be yeelded for the..avoidance of others misconstruction. **1684** Baxter *Cath. Commun.* 30 Must we let Men Excommunicate one another, and call all to mutual avoidance? **1876** Green *Short Hist.* iii. §2 (1882) 120 There was no public avoidance of the excommunicated King.

b. *Anthropology.* The custom prevalent among many primitive tribes by which one member of a family is forbidden to meet and address another member.

[**1865** Tylor *Early Hist. Man.* x. 287 Their object seems to be in general the avoidance of intercourse or connexion between parents-in-law and children-in-law... But the reasons for this avoidance are not clear.] **1889** —— in *Jrnl. Anthrop. Inst.* XVIII. 247 If the customs of residence and the customs of avoidance were independent, or nearly so, we should expect to find their coincidence following the..law of chance. *a* **1899** J. J. Atkinson *Primal Law* (1903) 269 Avoidance would arise at the same time between mother-in-law and son-in-law. **1903** *Lancet* 22 Aug. 532/2 The conditions in which he lived with the female members of his own family gave origin to the curious etiquette of 'avoidances' which is still to be found amongst some savage races. **1958** A. R. Radcliffe-Brown *Method Soc. Anthrop.* I. v. 122 In many primitive societies the relation established between two groups of kin by a marriage between a man of one group and a woman of the other is one which is expressed by customs of avoidance.

avoider (ə'vɔɪdə(r)). [f. avoid *v.* + -er[1].]

†**1.** 'The person that carries any thing away. The vessel in which things are carried away.' J. *Obs.* Cf. voider.

2. One who avoids or shuns.

1613 Fletcher *Hon. Man's Fort.* iv. i. (T.) Good sir..you were wont to be a curious avoider of woman's company.

avoiding (ə'vɔɪdɪŋ), *vbl. sb.* [f. as prec. + -ing[1].] The action of emptying or getting rid of (*obs.*), of making void or invalid, of shunning or keeping aloof from; avoidance.

1494 Fabyan v. lxxxiv. 62 In aduoydyng of gretter daunger. **1586** Bright *Melanch.* xiii. 67 For avoiding of rivers of water out of drowned fens. **1627** *Lisander & Cal.* I. 9 She prevented him..with such premeditated avoidings, that he judged she had knowledge of his designe. *a* **1716** Blackall *Wks.* (1723) I. 71 He will not rigorously insist on his Bargain but will..consent to the avoiding it.

a'voidless, *a. poet.* [f. avoid *v.* (or *sb.*) + -less.] That cannot be avoided or escaped, inevitable; that cannot be made void, indefeasible.

a **1668** Davenant *Philos. Disq.* (1673) 334 Avoidless ills we to no purpose feare. **1698** Dryden *Ovid's Met.* x. (T.) She too, when ripen'd years she shall attain, Must, of avoidless right, be yours again. **1850** Blackie *Æschylus* I. 93 Justice upon thy head the stony curse Shall bring avoidless.

avoidment (ə'vɔɪdmənt). [f. avoid *v.* + -ment.] The action of avoiding; avoidance.

1882 *St. James' Gaz.* 14 Apr. 7 In the International Handicap..the notice of avoidment has been overlooked.

avoir, obs. variant of aver *sb.*

avoirdupois (,ævədə'pɔɪz). Forms: 4 **auoirdepeise, auer de peis, 4–7 avoir de pois, 5 haberdepase, 6 auerdepaise, auer de poiz, haberdepoys, -poise, 6–7 hauer de pois, haberdepois, 7 averdepois, aver-, haberdupois(e, haverdupois(e, 8 hauer-du-pois, 7- avoirdupois.** [A recent corrupt spelling of *avoir-de-pois*, in early OF. and AF. *aveir de peis* 'goods of weight,' f. OF. *avoir, aveir*, property, goods, aver, *de* of, *pois, peis* (= Pr. *pes, pens*, It. *peso*):—L. **pēsum, pensum*, weight. The first word had the variant forms of the simple aver, and the pronunciation remains 'aver; the Norman *peis* was from 1300 varied with, and *c* 1500 superseded by, the Parisian *pois*. The best modern spelling is the 17th c. *averdepois*; in any case *de* ought to be restored for *du*, introduced by some ignorant 'improver' *c* 1640–1650.]

†**1.** Merchandise sold by weight. *Obs.* (*c* 1600.)

c **1300** *E.E. Poems* (1862) 154 ȝur gret packes of draperie, auoir-depeise, and ȝur wol sackes. **1388** Wyclif *Ezek.* xxvii. 16 Thei settiden forth in thi marcat gemme, and purpur.. and cochod, ether auer de peis [**1382** chodchod, that is, precious marchaundise]. [**1392** *Act 16 Rich. II*, i. §2 Toutz marchants..qe achater ou vendre voillont bledz, vinz, avoir de pois, char, pesson, & toutz autres vivres & vitails.] **1502** transl. in Arnold *Chron.* (1811) 34 Cornes, wynes, auerdepaise, flesh, fishe, or odur vitayles. **1598** Hakluyt *Voy.* I. 137 To exercise other marchandises, as of Hauer de pois, and other fine wares, as sarcenets, lawnes, cindalles, and silke. **1618** Pulton tr. *Act 27 Edw. III*, Staple x, That Wools, and all manner auoir de pois, be weighed by the ballance. **1691** Blount *Law Dict., Avoir du Pois*..signifies such Merchandises as are weighed by this weight, and not by Troy-weight.

2. (More fully ***avoirdupois weight***) The standard system of weights used, in Great Britain, for all goods except the precious metals, precious stones, and medicines.

The a. pound contains 7000 grains. The a. weight of the United States agrees with that of Great Britain in the pound, ounce, and dram; but the hundredweight contains in U.S. 100, in G.B. 112 lbs., and the ton of 20 cwt. differs accordingly.

1485 *Inv.* in *Ripon Ch. Acts* 367, j par balance cum ponderibus de haberdepase. **1532–3** *Act 24 Hen. VIII*, iii, Lawfull weyght, called haberdepois. **1543** Recorde *Gr. Artes* (1575) 202 An other weight called Haberdepoise, in whiche 16 ounces make a pounde. **1594** Plat *Jewell-ho.* III. 7 Vveightes that may agree vvith the auer de poiz. **1619** Dalton *Countr. Just.* lxv. (1630) 143 In this Averdepois weight..112 pounds make a hundred weight. **1631** Brathwait *Whimzies* 16 A trite discourse of weights and measures: most ponderously dividing them into troy and averdepois. **1647** Ward *Simp. Cobler* (1843) 39 Weigh Rules by Troyweight, and not by the old Haber-du-pois. **1650** B. *Discollim.* 16 Weighed..at the..publick beam..not at..every Shop-keeper's *Aver-du-pois.* **1656** Du Gard *Gate Lat. Unl.* §536 Avoir-du-pois, wherewith wares are bought and sold. **1667** E. King in *Phil. Trans.* II. 450, 49 ounces (Haver de pois weight) of blood. **1669** Boyle *Cont. New Exp.* I. xxxiii. (1682) 112 Haberdupoise weight. **1701** J. Jones in A. J. Ellis *E.E. Pron.* I. iii. 220, *h* may be sounded in halleluiah, habiliment, hauer-du-pois, etc. **1755** *Phil. Trans.* XLIX. 184 So great a weight as twenty-six pounds avoirdupoize. **1806** Vince *Hydrost.* ii. 21 A cubic foot of rain water weighs 1000 ounces avoirdupoise. **1831** Carlyle *Sart. Res.* II. viii, The weakest can stand under thirty stone avoirdupois.

3. Weight; degree of heaviness. (Common in U.S.)

1597 Shaks. *2 Hen. IV*, II. iv. 276 The weight of an hayre will turne the Scales betweene their Haber-de-pois. **1680** *Hon. Cavalier* 26 To make it more than *Aver-du-pois.* **1883** *Atl. Monthly* May (*Football*), Avoirdupois and strength are at a premium for rushing, blocking, and tackling.

avoirdupois (as prec.), *v. rare*[−1]. [f. the sb.] To have the avoirdupois weight of, to weigh.

1854 Badham *Halieut.* 231 A huge African fish..has been known to avoirdupoise one hundred and forty pounds.

†**a'voke,** *v. Obs.* [In sense 1, ad. L. *āvocāre*, after *revoke*, etc. In sense 2, a. MF. *avoquer* = *advoquer*, ad. L. *advocāre*: see advoke.]

1. To call away. *rare.*

1623 Cockeram, *Auoke*, to call [*printed* fall] from, or backe againe. **1639** R. Baillie *Lett.* (1775) I. 183 Absence.. not much remarked..if their negligence or ado's or misconduct did avoke them.

2. = advoke, advocate *v.*[1] 2.

1529 Dr. Bennet *To Wolsey* in Burnet *Hist. Ref.* (1679) I. Rec. 80 Dangers to follow, both to himself and to the See Apostolick, if his Holiness..should avoke the cause.

†**a'vokement.** *Obs. rare*[−1]. [f. avoke + -ment: cf. avocament.] A calling off or away.

1637 Bastwick *Litany* III. 19 Declining all avokements and hinderances from this holy imployment.

avoket, -ette, obs. forms of advocate *sb.*

†**'avolate,** *v. Obs.* [f. L. *āvolāt-* ppl. stem of *āvolāre* to fly off or away, f. *ā, ab* off + *volāre* to fly.] To fly off, escape, exhale, evaporate.

1673 *Phil. Trans.* VIII. 6024 Yet must not all the spirits avolate. **1709** Blair *ibid.* XXVII. 73 Wherever these Particles avolate freely.

†**avo'lation.** ? *Obs.* [n. of action f. prec.: see -ation.] The action of flying away; escape, exhalation, evaporation.

1650 Sir T. Browne *Pseud. Ep.* v. xxiii. (1686) 224 The avolation of the light and favillous particles. **1684** Boyle *Porousn. Anim. Bod.* ii. 6 There being a great waste..by the avolation of invisible steam. **1757** Walker in *Phil. Trans.* L. 129 This cremor..bearing a considerable heat without avolation. **1824** Galt *Rothelan* I. I. iv. 30 He was..but for a certain avolation of the eye, when looked steadily in the face, of a goodly aspect.

avolitional (ævəʊ'lɪʃənəl), *a.* [f. a- *pref.* 14.] Not volitional, independent of volition.

1855 J. R. Reynolds *Diagn. Dis. Brain* ix, Simply an exaggeration of avolitional motility.

avondbloem(etje): see aandblom.

avong(e, var. afong *v. Obs.* to seize, receive.

avoset, variant of avocet.

avou, obs. form of avow.

avouch (ə'vaʊtʃ), *v.* Forms: 4–6 **au- avouche, 5–7 auouch, -owch, 6–7 advouch, 7 auoch, 5- avouch.** [a. OF. *avochier*, ad. L. *advocāre*. In living use *advocāre*, by regular phonetic change, became in OF. *avoer, avouer*; but as Latin continued in legal use, and the technical terms became to some extent popularized, *advocāre*, in its technical senses of 'call upon as defender, guarantor,' etc., was subsequently made French, as *avochier, avocier, avoker*, which thus became to a certain extent a more technical synonym of *avoer*; so in Eng. with *avouch, avow*. Cf. vouch.]

I. To appeal or refer for confirmation to some warrant or authority.

†**1.** trans. ***to avouch a thing upon one***: to call or cite him as warrant or authority for it; to prove, declare, or state it on his authority. *Obs.*

1393 Gower *Conf.* I. 295 And that I durst right wel avouche Upon her selfe, as for witnesse. **1494** Fabyan v. civ. 79, I am in dought because of the sayinge of Ranulphe, Monke of Chestre, whiche auowchyth it vpon Wyllyam, wryter of Historyes of Kynges.

†**2.** To certify (an account) by reference to, and comparison with, vouchers. *Obs.*

1540 *Househ. Ord. Hen. VIII* in *Thynne's Animadv.* Introd. 35 The Clerkes-Comptrollers to goe with him to take the said Remaines to be advouched with him, what the expence shall rise to. Item..the Booke of Comptrollment.. shall be put yearly into the Exchequer, to be advoucht to the Cofferers account.

†**3.** To appeal to, cite, or allege, as warrant, authority, or testimony. *Obs.*

1573 G. Harvey *Letter-bk.* (1884) 26 Reasuns he usid none against me, but only avouchid and maintainid M. Osburns. **1579** Fulke *Heskins's Parl.* 220 In none of them can I reade that whiche he auoucheth out of him. *a* **1619** Fotherby *Atheom.* I. vi. §2 Making God himselfe a lyer: as auouching of him, as a witnesse vnto their lye. **1628** Coke *On Litt.* 216 b, For proofe of their opinion they auouch many successions of authorities. *a* **1718** Penn *Life* Wks. 1726 I. 42, I shall avouch the Authorities.

†**4.** To establish upon testimony, to prove. *Obs.*

1588 Thynne in *Animadv.* Introd. 92 Whiche I will sufficiently advouche, yf Instances be called for at my handes. **1596** Spenser *State Irel.* 490 The certainty of things in times so far from all knowledge, cannot be justly avouched. **1664** Power *Exp. Philos.* I. 56 Every hair of our head is as a little quill or horn, hollow and transparent. Which seems to be further avouched also by the burning of hair. **1678** R. Barclay *Apol. Quakers* II. §10. 43 It is by this Spirit, that they avouch themselves to have been converted to God.

II. To give one's own warrant or assurance; to guarantee, confirm.

5. *intr.* To give assurance, guarantee, vouch.

1532 Hen. VIII in Burnet *Hist. Ref.* II. 169 Subscribed with your Holiness's hand, which avouched to confirm the sentence, and not to revoke the commission. **1705** De Foe *Mrs. Veal* Wks. 1840 V. 341, I can avouch for her reputation.

6. *trans.* To vouch to the certainty of, vouch for, guarantee.

1548 Udall *Erasm. Par.* Pref. 5 Voices avouched to haue come from heauen. *a* **1626** Bacon *Max. & Uses Com. Law* (1635) 63 The seller must bring one to avouch his sale. **1649** Milton *Eikon.* xxviii. 520 Ambrose avouch'd it for the Law of God. **1754** Mackenzie in *Phil. Trans.* XLVIII. 820 There are bad accounts from Nicomedia, but none well avouched. **1868** Milman *St. Paul's* viii. 179 The authority of Erasmus avouches the accomplished scholarship of Pace. **1876** E. Mellor *Priesth.* iv. 175 A miracle avouched by the testimony of those who drank the wine.

III. To declare as a thing for which one can bring vouchers.

7. To declare as a thing one can prove, or upon which one offers his own express testimony as a personal witness; to affirm, assert. Now strictly of matters of fact upon which one can give first-hand evidence, formerly also of matters of inference or opinion, on which one might speak with 'authority.'

1494 Fabyan vii. ccxxiii. 249 More ouer he avouched, that yᵉ see of Lyncoln belonged to the see of Yorke. **1562** Grindal *Let.* Wks. 1843, 253, I pray you let me understand, whether it may be certainly avouched that the king of Navarre..is killed. **1587** Fleming *Contn. Holinshed* III. 383/1 Declared vnto him, that there was a gentleman of qualitie..that would auouch it to his face. **1604** T. Wright *Climact. Years* 16, I..haue knowne a man, almost with halfe his lungs rotten with a consumption, and yet boldelie auowch that he was strong. **1624** Bedell *Lett.* vii. 111 Loe how plainly Saint Augustine auoucheth Purgatorie. **1691** Wood *Ath. Oxon.* II/62, I constantly avouch that what I have writ is the truth. **1821** Byron *Juan* III. xxxviii, He did not know (alas! how men will lie!) That a report..Avouch'd his death. **1840** Thackeray *Paris Sk. Bk.* (1872) 96 Millions again were ready to avouch the exact contrary. **1845** R. Hamilton *Pop. Educ.* vi. 129 The true principle is avouched. **1852** Miss Yonge *Cameos* I. xl. 342 His own deposition, as three Cardinals avouched that he had made it before them.

b. *intr.* To state, declare, assert.

1577 Vautroullier *Luther's Ep. Gal.* 288 So Paule seemeth to auouch in this place. **1681** J. Collins *Glanvill's Sadducism.* Pref., As I have heard him earnestly avouch.

IV. To declare to be one's own, to acknowledge, avow.

8. *trans.* To acknowledge (or claim) solemnly as one's own: **a.** a person. *arch.*

1579 TOMSON *Calvin's Serm. Tim.* 320/2 God auoucheth vs and taketh vs for his children. **1600** HAKLUYT *Voy.* (1810) III. 300 Not being our subjects, nor by vs any way to be avouched, maintained, or defended. **1611** BIBLE *Deut.* xxvi. 17–18 Thou hast auouched the Lord this day to be thy God ..And the Lord hath auouched thee this day to be his peculiar people. **1861** TRENCH *Sev. Ch. Asia* 183 He was one of God's hidden ones, but now he is openly avouched.

†**b.** a thing. *Obs.*

1597 MORLEY *Introd. Mus.* Ded., So wil I not auouch for mine that which by your censure shal be condemned. **1606** BP. CARLETON *Tithes* v. 26 a, Tithes are euer holy to God.. both dedicated to him by man, and aduouched by himselfe.

9. To acknowledge or take the responsibility of an action: **a.** To acknowledge, sanction, confirm the act of a subordinate agent. *arch.*

a **1553** UDALL *Royster D.* III. ii, Adde what so ever thou canst..And I will avouche it what so ever it bee. **1577** HOLINSHED *Chron.* III. 905/2 He..might speake things that his maister would not auouch. **1597** DANIEL *Civ. Wares* III. lxxix, He for whom thou dost this villanie..will not avouch thy fact. **1647** SPRIGG *Ang. Rediv.* Apol. (1854) 5 That they should..own and avouch them as having been done in their name and by their authority. **1834** SIR H. TAYLOR *Artevelde* II. v. ii. (1849) 254 Dukes and regal potentates, whose power May currently avouch her doubtful deeds.

b. To acknowledge (any act) as one's own; to admit, confess, own to. *arch.*

1606 BRYSKETT *Civ. Life* 76 The offences done to men may be auouched before Princes and magistrates in iudgement, as no wrongs, but lawfull acts. **1655** FULLER *Ch. Hist.* IX. vi. V. 77 Suppose a poor Lay Catholick..to purchase one of these Rhemish Testaments, he durst not avouch the reading thereof. **1862** TRENCH *Eng. Past & Pr.* iii. (ed. 9) 119 Milton in his prose works frequently avouches the peculiar affection to the Italian literature and language which he bore.

10. To acknowledge (a charge), confess, avow.

1649 MILTON *Eikon.* Wks. 1738 I. 391 Under that excuse avouches himself openly the general Patron of most notorious Delinquents. **1825** SCOTT *Betrothed* iii, The first time that I have heard one with a beard on his lip avouch himself a coward. **1883** A. FORBES in *19th Cent.* Oct. 721 Men..who avouch that they are..plotting for the disruption of the Union.

V. Combining IV with II.

11. To acknowledge and support or justify; to make good, establish, prove (*with*).

1599 MARLOWE *Edw. II*, v. iv. 2371 And will avouch his saying with the sword. **1700** in *Coll. Rec. Penn.* I. 604 All which several charges hee is readie to avouch and prove. **1852** MISS YONGE *Cameos* II. xiii. 146 Richard..offered to avouch his innocence with his sword.

†**a'vouch**, *sb. arch.* [f. prec. vb.] Guarantee, assurance.

1602 SHAKS. *Ham.* I. i. 57, I might not this beleeue, Without the sensible and true auouch Of mine owne eyes. **1860** J. KENNEDY *Rob of Bowl* xiii. 139 What he recounts.. you have his own avouch for.

avouchable (əˈvaʊtʃəb(ə)l), *a.* [f. AVOUCH *v.* + -ABLE.] Able to be avouched.

1594 CAREW *Huarte's Exam. Wits* (1616) 96 It is a matter not auouchable. **1651** FULLER *Life H. Smith* in *Smith's Wks.* 1866 I. 9 Incapable by weakness or any avouchable impediment. **1655** —— *Ch. Hist.* I. iii. Wks. I. 67 The most avouchable Evidence of Christianity flourishing in this Island in this Age. [In mod. Dicts.]

avouched (əˈvaʊtʃt), *ppl. a.* [f. AVOUCH *v.* + -ED.] Vouched for; acknowledged, avowed.

1637 GILLESPIE *Eng.-Pop. Cerem.* Ep. A iv, Professed Papists and avouched Atheists. **1846** GROTE *Greece* I. xiii. (1862) I. 207 Matter of fact generally unquestionable, though little avouched as to details.

avoucher (əˈvaʊtʃə(r)). Also 6 **advoucher**. [f. as prec. + -ER[1].] One who avouches.

1570 DEE *Math. Pref.* 1 Plato..the constant auoucher, and pithy perswador of *Verum, Bonum*, and *Ens.* **1583** FULKE *Defence* xix. 544 The most impudent advoucher.. that ever became a writer. **1664** POWER *Exp. Philos.* II. 133 This opinion hath many eminent Advocates and Avouchers. **1678** *Trans. Crt. Spain* 98 The Secretary..may likewise be an avoucher of the truth of what I say. [In mod. Dicts.]

a'vouching, *vbl. sb.* = next.

1580 HOLLYBAND *Treas. Fr. Tong.*, *Approbation*, approuing or auouching.

avouchment (əˈvaʊtʃmənt). [f. as prec. + -MENT.] The action of avouching; assurance, guarantee; positive declaration, assertion.

1574 tr. *Marlorat's Apocalips* 16 The auouchment of the truth. **1649** MILTON *Eikon.* i. Wks. (1851) 340 The avouchment of that which is so manifestly untrue. **1677** GILPIN *Dæmonol.* (1867) 131 The positiveness of avouchments..in such cases, where we want sufficient reason to support what we affirm. **1715** M. DAVIES *Icon Libel.* I. 124 Notwithstanding his avouchments to the contrary. *a* **1884** W. WARD in *Spectator* No. 2911, 487/2 In innumerable past instances the avouchments of memory have been true.

†**a'vouchy.** *Obs. rare*[−1]. [f. AVOUCH; cf. *warranty*, etc.] Avouching, avouchment.

1631 J. BURGES *Answ. Rejoined* Ep. Ded. 3 By avouchie of this Branch of truth against the opinions of some.

‖**avoué** (avue). [F.:—L. *advocātus*; = Eng. AVOWE, ADVOWEE.] A patron.

1851 SIR F. PALGRAVE *Norm. & Eng.* I. 561 He was also Avoué of Centulla.

†**a'vour(e**, *sb.*[1] *Obs. rare.* [erroneously for *avourie*, AVOWRY; if not for OF. *avoeor, avoeur, avoueur*, of which the proper Eng. form is *avower*, while the OF. in the first quotation would be *avoeresse*.] = AVOWRY 2.

c **1400** *Sowdone Bab.* 2390 God and seynte Mary myn avoure! **1868** STANLEY *Westm. Ab.* 158 Round his [Henry VII's] tomb stand his nine accustomed *Avours* or guardian saints, to whom he calls and cries. [HENRY VII; *Instr. for Tomb* in Bell's *Handbk. Westm. Ab.* 33 The same to be filled with ymages, specially of our said avouries.]

†**a'voure**, *sb.*[2] *Obs. rare*[−1]. [for AVOWER.] (Legal) Avowal, answer for.

1596 SPENSER *F.Q.* VI. iii. 48 To make avoure Of his lewd words and deedes which he had done.

avourie, -y, obs. form of AVOWRY.

avouter(e, etc., obs. form of ADULTER, etc.

avow (aˈvaʊ), *v.*[1] Forms: 2 **auouh(en**, 3 **awou**, 3–7 **au- avowe**, 5 **awowe**, 5–7 **aduow(e**, 6– **avow**. [a. OF. *avoue-r, avoer*:—L. *advocā-re* to call to, call upon; *esp.* to call in as a defender or patron (cf. ADVOCATE): *hence*, in feudal times, to call upon or own as defender, patron, client, or person in some way related, to acknowledge as ours in some relation; afterwards extended to things. Often semi-latinized to *advow* in 15–16th c., a corruption which has become permanent in the derivative ADVOWSON. Cf. AVOUCH.]

1. *trans.* To own or acknowledge (a person) as one's own.

(In the first example it may mean literally 'call to thyself.')

c **1220** *Ureisun* in *Cott. Hom.* 197 Auouh mine soule hwon ich of þisse liue uare. **1467** *Bury Wills* (1850) 50, I will..that myn executors avowe hym in his suet. **1580** NORTH *Plutarch* (1676) 2 His Father knew him, and avowed him for his Son. **1600** HAKLUYT *Voy.* (1810) III. 176 Not our subiects, nor by vs any way to be advowed. **1619** LD. DONCASTER in *Eng. & Germ.* (Camd. 1865) 147 Giving me commission to say what I would..wherein he promised to avow me.

†**2.** refl. *to avow (oneself) on or upon*: to put oneself under the protection or patronage of, to claim the authority of, to affiliate oneself upon. *Obs.*

1577 HOLINSHED *Chron.* III. 900/2 Certeine aduowing themselues on you, haue assailed and taken by force the citie of Rome. **1602** CAREW *Cornwall* 135 b, Our Foy Gallants.. auowing themselves vpon the Earle of Warwicke.

†**3.** *trans.* To own (the deeds of an agent); to sanction, approve. *Obs.*

1530 PALSGR., 418/1, I advowe or make good, *Jaduoue*.. What so euer he promyse in my name I wyll advowe it. **1628** T. SPENCER *Logick* 3 We have the frequent vse of learned men to avow it. **1651** HOBBES *Leviath.* II. xviii. 90 Be contented to avow all the actions he shall do.

4. *trans.* To declare (as a thing one can vouch for); to affirm, maintain (a thing which others might deny). Const. *simple obj.*, *subord. cl.*, *absol. Obs.* or *arch.*, but surviving in some uses of VOW.

a **1300** *Cursor M.* 7307 For-soth i sai, and sal a-wou, Ful sare yee sal repent yow. **1393** GOWER *Conf.* III. 191 Tullius his tale avoweth And saith. **1476** SIR JOHN PASTON in *Lett.* 778 III. 164 [They] offryd to afferme and advowe my tytell for goode. **1533** MORE *Debell. Salem* Wks. 992/1 Ryghte worshipful folk, that before me aduowed it in hys face. **1596** DANETT *Commines' Hist. Fr.* (1614) 339 De Clerieux.. aduowed his report to be true for them both. **1611** BIBLE *Pref.* 8 Wee affirme and auow that the very meanest translation of the Bible in English..containeth the word of God. **1759** FRANKLIN *Ess.* Wks. 1840 III. 272 Avowing proprietary and deputy-government reasons for such his refusal. **1805** SCOTT *Last Minstr.* I. xi, As bards avow.

†**b.** To vouch for, guarantee. *Obs.*

1530 PALSGR. 441/2, I avowe, I warrant or make good, or upholde as in marchaundyse or such lyke..Take this clothe of my worde, I avowe it for good.

5. *trans.* To own, acknowledge, admit, or confess (facts, statements, or opinions, that one might himself conceal or deny). Const. as in 4.

1330 R. BRUNNE *Chron.* 320 If he wille avowe alle his wikked sawe. *c* **1386** CHAUCER *Chan. Yem. Prol. & T.* 89, I wol nought avowe what I say, And therfor kep it secré I yow pray. *c* **1440** *Promp. Parv.* 19 A-vowyn, or stonde by the forsayde worde or dede, *Advoco.* **1460** CAPGRAVE *Chron.* 182 Sche accused a certeyn knyte, whech cam to the Kyng and avowid every word. **1659** *Gentl. Call.* ix. §3 This little tract ..must avow to come upon that uncivil yet friendly errand. **1667** DRYDEN *Ann. Mirab.* 545 As when fiends did miracles avow, He stands confess'd e'en by the boastful Dutch. **1778** JOHNSON in *Boswell* (1816) III. 294 Many a man thinks, what he is ashamed to avow. **1855** PRESCOTT *Philip II*, I. II. viii. 235 The boldness with which he avowed his opinions.

6. *refl. and pass.* To confess one's identity, declare oneself.

1465 *Paston Lett.* 533 II. 249 William Nawton is here with me, but he dare not ben avowyd. **1621** MOLLE *Camerar. Liv. Libr.* I. vi. 16, I affirme and auow myselfe, that I am Liegeman..of Ferdinand. **1769** SIR W. DRAPER in *Junius Lett.* xxiv. 114 Avow yourself, and prove the charge. **1837** S. MAITLAND *12 Lett.* (1841) 81 The gentlemen who have avowed themselves as the instigators of the new edition.

7. *Law.* To justify or maintain (an act done, *spec.* a distress, for rent taken in one's own right).

1528 PERKINS *Profit. Bk.* ii. §122 If in a Replevin the defendant avow for a Rent charg in another place. **1540** *Act 32 Hen. VIII*, ii. §9 The next heire..shall haue..liberty.. to sue demaunde, aduowe, declare, or make, the sayd titles, claymes, prescriptions. **1617** MINSHEU s.v. *Avowrie*, He that took the Distresse, justifying or maintaining the act, is said to auow, and that is called his Auowrie. **1809** TOMLINS *Law Dict.* s.v. *Avowry*, Where tenant in tail aliens in fee, the donor may avow upon him.

†**avow** (əˈvaʊ), *v.*[2] *Obs.* Forms: 4–7 **avow(e**, ? also 6 **aduowe**. [a. ? OF. *avoue-r, avoer* (Palsgr. *aduouer*), f. *à* to + *vouer*:—late Lat. *vōtāre* (cf. Pr. *vodar*, and cl.L. *dē-vōt-āre*), freq. of *vovē-re*, *vōt-um*, to vow. Already in OF. the two vbs. *avouer* were confounded; Littré has only that from *advocāre*.]

1. *trans.* To put (one) to a vow or oath, to bind with a vow (*to* some act, *to do* something).

1303 R. BRUNNE *Handl. Synne* 7647 þese lordynges, þat avowe here men to do swych þynges. **1382** WYCLIF *Acts* xxiii. 14 With deuocioun we han avowid vs to no thing tastinge, til we slen Poul. [Vulg. *devotione devovimus nos nihil gustaturos.*]

2. To devote, consecrate, dedicate by a vow (a person or thing *to* God, or *to* some solemn purpose).

1382 WYCLIF *Lev.* xxvii. 16 If the feelde..he auowe [Vulg. *voverit*] & halowe to the Lord. *a* **1450** *Knt. de la Tour* (1868) 107 To avowe her children vnto God and holy chirche. **1533** BELLENDENE *Livy* I. 49 Tullus..avowit XII preistis..to be perpetualy dedicate to Mars. **1583** A. CONHAM in *Babington's Commandm.* To Reader***b, Hee.. as it were aduowed himselfe a man to the Lord, to serve in his Tabernacle.

3. *intr.* (from *refl.*) To bind oneself by a vow, to take a vow (*to* an act or *to do* something).

c **1325** *E.E. Allit. P.* C. 333, I dewoutly awowe þat veray betz halden Soberly to do þe sacrafyse. **1483** CAXTON *G. de la Tour* C. iij b, She..repentyd her and auowed to many pylgremages. **1531** *Dial. Laws Eng.* II. liv. (1638) 164 If a man avow never to eat white meat. **1603** H. CROSSE *Vertues Commw.* (1878) 13 The three Romans..who for the safeguard of their Countrey auowed to dye.

b. *absol.* or with *subord. cl.* To make a vow.

c **1400** *Melayne* 733, I a-vowe to mylde marie..I sall noghte leve the soo. *c* **1440** *Promp. Parv.* 19 Auowyn, or to make auowe, *Voveo.* **1493** *Festyvall* (W. de W. 1515) 93 He that hath avowed or ioyned in penaunce must fast the even. **1594** R. PARSONS *Confer. Success.* I. v. 109, I do promisse and auow to euery one of you..that I wil kepe, etc.

4. *trans.* **a.** with *cogn. obj.* To vow.

1393 LANGL. *P. Pl.* C. VIII. 13 Ich haue a-vowed vowes fourty · and for-ȝut hem a morwe. **1483** CAXTON *Gold. Leg.* 285/3 Auowe ye vowes and yelde them to god.

b. with *ordinary obj.*: To vow to give, keep, observe, do; to promise or undertake with a vow.

c **1374** CHAUCER *Anel. & Arc.* 355 And unto Mars avoyth sacrifice. *a* **1450** *Knt. de la Tour* (1868) 11 Than she avowed chastite. **1539** *Act 31 Hen. VIII*, vi, Suche as haue auowed religion. **1601** R. JOHNSON *Kingd. & Commw.* 218 Auowing continual war against the Abessine Christians.

avow (əˈvaʊ), *sb.*[1] *arch.* Forms: 4–5 **avou, avowe**, 5 **auough**, 6 **advow**, 7– **avow**. [f. AVOW *v.*[2], on analogy of vow *v.* and *sb.*

(In OF. the two verbs *avouer* seem to have been quite identified (cf. *alouer* ALLOW). The sb. *aveu*, whose form is best explained by comparing it with *veu, vœu*:—L. *vōtum*, seems to belong in sense to *avouer*:—*advocāre*; whereas the Eng. sb. *avow* was in early times used only in sense of AVOW *v.*[2]:—**advōtāre*. The connexion of the Eng. with the Fr. sb. is thus rendered doubtful.)]

1. A vow, a solemn promise made to a deity, etc.

a **1300** *Cursor M.* 10203 For-þi to godd a-vou þai gaf. **1330** R. BRUNNE *Chron.* 112 He brak his avowe, þat he to God had suorn. *c* **1440** *Promp. Parv.* 19 A-vowe, *votum.* *c* **1465** *Chevy Chase* I The perse owt off northombarlonde an avowe to god mayd he. **1493** *Petronylla* (Pynson) 24 In hir auough made unto chastyte. **1493** *Festyvall* (W. de W. 1515) 79 Four cursyd knyghtes..made theyr avowe togider to sle Thomas. **1531** *Dial. Laws Eng.* II. xxii. (1638) 103 There is a promise that is called an Advow. **1655** JENNINGS *Elise* 74, I could not address my avows to a more accomplished subject. **1828** SCOTT *F. M. Perth* III. 45 I make mine avow, by the Red Rover's soul! that he shall eat his writ.

†**2.** A thing vowed; a votive offering. *Obs.*

1388 WYCLIF *Acts* xxiv. 17 To do almes dedis to my folc, and offryngis, and auowis. *c* **1400** MAUNDEV. ix. 105 Ther thei ȝolden up here avowes.

†**a'vow**, *sb.*[2] *Obs. rare*[−1]. [subst. use of AVOW *v.*[1]] Avowal, sanction.

1697 DRYDEN *Virgil* (1806) IV. 234 What, without thy knowledge and avow, Nay more, thy dictate, durst Juturna do?

avowable (əˈvaʊəb(ə)l), *a.* [f. AVOW *v.*[1] + -ABLE. Cf. mod.F. *avouable.*] Capable of being avowed: †**a.** To be sanctioned, or approved of (*obs.*). **b.** To be acknowledged, confessed, or declared.

1602 SEGAR *Honor Mil. & Civ.* I. xxix. 38 No souldier departing from his Ensigne without leaue can be excused, nor his absence auowable. **1624** DONNE *Devotions* 209 (R.) The proceedings may be apert, and..avowable. **1825** BENTHAM *Ration. Rew.* 119 This is not an avowable reason.

a'vowableness. [f. prec. + -NESS.] The quality of being avowable.

a **1631** DONNE *Serm.* lv. (1640) 549 To enquire into the nature and avowablenesse and exemplarinesse of this.

avowal (ə'vaʊəl). [f. AVOW *v.*[1] + -AL[2].] An act of avowing; acknowledgement, declaration; unconstrained admission or confession.

[**1727-31** BAILEY, *Avowsal*.] **1732** BARCLAY, *Avowal*. **1741** RICHARDSON *Pamela* I. 136 O frightful!..here's an Avowal of the matter at once. **1845** R. HAMILTON *Pop. Educ.* viii. 199 The Dissenters..have fallen behind their avowals. **1855** PRESCOTT *Philip II*, I. ii. ix. 252 A plain avowal of his sentiments.

avowance (ə'vaʊəns). ? *Obs.* [a. OF. *avouance*, f. *avouer*: see AVOW *v.*[1] and -ANCE.]

1. The action of the avowant; the maintaining or making good of a claim or statement.

1642 SIR E. DERING *Sp. on Relig.* 19 If now you want any of them here, to make avowance of their Petition. **1662** FULLER *Worthies* I. 142 In avowance of the latter it sheweth more Burrow-towns then any Shire..in Mercia.

2. The action of acknowledging; public acknowledgement or confession.

a **1603** T. CARTWRIGHT *Confut. Rhem. N. T.* 134 An open avowance and profession of the doctrine of Antichrist.

avowant (ə'vaʊənt). [a. F. *avouant*, pr. pple. (used subst.) of *avouer*: see AVOW *v.*[1]] In *Law*, A challenger; a person making cognizance, or admitting that he distrained goods belonging to another, but maintaining his right to do so.

1529 *Act 21 Hen. VIII*, xix. §2 Every avowaunt and every other person..that make any such avowrie. **1598** KITCHIN *Courts Leet, etc.* (1675) 214 Then the Avowant shall recover damages. **1768** BLACKSTONE *Comm.* III. 147 Which bond shall be assigned to the avowant or person making cognizance. **1816** Taunton *Law Rep.* VI. 526 An avowant in replevin for rent was obliged to shew a title in fee.

†**avowe.** *Obs.* Also 3 avow. [a. OF. *avoué*, *avoé* (12th c.), *avoet* (11th c.):—L. *advocāt-us*: see ADVOCATE *sb.* As in *assign* and other words, the final *-e* became mute in ME., leaving *avow*. In 15th c. Fr. it was occas. spelt by the clerks *advoué*, whence the later Eng. ADVOWEE. (See AD- *pref.* 2.)] An advocate, patron, or protector; *esp.* a patron saint.

1297 R. GLOUC. 475 God and Seinte Marie, and Sein Denis al so, and alle the avowes [*printed* abowes] of this churche, in w[h]as ore ich am ido. *c* **1300** *Beket* 2129 Alle the avows of the churche. *c* **1300** *K. Alis.* 3160 Hendely they bysechith thé That thou beo heore avowé. *c* **1490** *Lyt. Geste* IV. in Ritson *Rob. Hood* I. 42 'Where is your abbay, when ye are at home, And who is your avowé?'

avowed (ə'vaʊd), *ppl. a.*[1] [f. AVOW *v.*[1] + -ED.]

1. Acknowledged, owned, plainly declared.

1340 [see AVOWRY 4]. **1556** J. HEYWOOD *Spider & F.* lii. 35 Arms..In harolds books a vowde. **1659** *Gentl. Call.* (1696) 41 A man of such an avowed brutality. **1793** T. JEFFERSON *Writ.* (1859) IV. 12 For the avowed purpose of committing hostilities on us. **1858** FROUDE *Hist. Eng.* III. xvi. 362 The avowed leaders were..the bishops.

2. Self-acknowledged, declared by himself.

1651 HOBBES *Leviath.* III. xxxvi. 231 He is a Prophet avowed. **1792** *Anecd. W. Pitt* III. xliv. 197 An avowed enemy to American independency. **1824** DIBDIN *Libr. Comp.* 224 Lord Somers was the avowed Editor.

†**a'vowed,** *ppl. a.*[2] *Obs.* [f. AVOW *v.*[2] + -ED.] Vowed.

1720 WELTON *Suff. Son of God* I. x. 279 The Avowed Poverty of St. Francis..The Spiritual Repasts of this Sacred Vow.

avowedly (ə'vaʊɪdlɪ), *adv.* [f. prec. + -LY[2].] In an avowed manner; with open declaration or acknowledgement; confessedly, openly.

1656 COWLEY *Davideis* III. (1669) 108 *note*, That he should go..avowedly to Achis Court so soon after the defeat of Goliah. **1791** MACKINTOSH *Vind. Gall.* Wks. 1846 III. 88 An avowedly hostile tribunal. **1858** GLADSTONE *Homer* III. 18 The avowedly mythical..character of the delineation.

avowedness (ə'vaʊɪdnɪs). ? *Obs.* [f. as prec. + -NESS.] The quality of being avowed, openness.

1673 *Lady's Call.* I. i. §19 The frequency and avowedness of a fashion. **1695** *Prot. Relig. Motive Rev.* 13 To assert their Religion with the more Courage and Avowedness.

avower[1] (ə'vaʊə(r)). [f. AVOW *v.*[1] + -ER[1].] One who avows.

1623 BP. HALL *Serm. Chapell Earle Exceter* (1627) 526 Set out by the stile of the Promiser and Avower. **1668** DRYDEN *Ess. Dram. Poetry* in Arb. *Garner* III. 529 A bold avower of his own virtues. **1783** AINSWORTH *Lat. Dict.* (Morell), An avower, *Qui aliquid affirmat*.

†**a'vower**[2]. *Obs.* [a. F. *avouer* (see AVOW *v.*[1]), inf. used subst.] Avowing, avowal.

[Cited as yet only in form AVOURE and ADVOWER, q.v.]

a'vowing, *vbl. sb.*[1] [f. AVOW *v.*[1] + -ING[1].] Acknowledgement, avowal.

1687 M. CLIFFORD *Notes Dryden's Poems* ii. 6, I might have spared..you your avowing. *a* **1718** PENN *Life* Wks. 1726 I. 137 An open avowing..of these Things.

†**a'vowing,** *vbl. sb.*[2] [f. AVOW *v.*[2]] Vowing.

c **1420** (*title*) The Avowynge of King Arther, etc. *Ibid.* ix, I a-vow, sayd Kaye, to ride þis forest or day. *Ibid.* lxvi. Of þi thryd a-vowyng telle me quych is hit?

†**a'vowment.** *Obs.* [a. OF. *avoe-*, *avouement*, f. *avouer*: see AVOW *v.*[1] and -MENT.] Acknowledgement, avowal. (Cf. also AVOWRY 6.)

1581 LAMBARDE *Eiren.* II. v. (1588) 183 Whether any persons doe take others to their Auowment and protection. **1685** *Lond. Gaz.* No. 2017/3 To make the Avowments of our Faith and of our Allegiance unto your most Sacred Majesty.

†**a'vowre,** *v. Obs.* [Only in loc. cit., where it seems to be a mistaken use of the Fr. infinitive *avouer*, or extension of the synonymy of *avow* and *avower* sb. to the vb.] To vow, devote.

a **1560** PHAËR *Æneid* VIII. (1573) X iv, O Juno most of powre! Euen all to thee he kild, and on thine altars did auowre.

avowry (ə'vaʊrɪ). Forms: 4 avoerie, 4-7 auowrie, avowrie, 5-6 -rye, 5-7 auowry, advowry, 6 advoury, -uowry(e, 6-7 avourie, -ry, 5- avowry. *Aphet.* 4-5 vory. [a. OF. *avoerie*, *avouerie*, *avourie*, *avorie*, AF. *avowerie*, f. *avoueur*, OF. *avoeor*, n. of agent f. *avouer* (see AVOW *v.*[1] and -RY); the office of the *avoueur*, *avoué*, or patron. In 15-16th c. F. frequently spelt by clerks *advouerie* (see Cotgrave), whence in 16th c. Eng. commonly *advowry*, esp. when = *advowson*; but in the senses retained in 18-19th c., the influence of AVOW *v.* has made *avowry* the current form.]

†**1.** The function of an *avoué*, ADVOWEE, advocate, or patron; patronage, protection. *Obs.*

1330 R. BRUNNE *Chron.* 260 Saue condite vs gyue, þorgh þi lond to go in þin auowrie.

2. Advocacy, protection or authority *personified*: a protector, a patron; *esp.* a patron saint, chosen for one's advocacy in heaven. (Rarely *attrib.*)

1387 TREVISA *Higden* Rolls Ser. IV. 219 Julius Cesar þat was his [Catiline's] patroun and his vorie, and pleded for hym. **1483** CAXTON *Gold. Leg.* 328/4 Thankynge to almyghty god and to Saynt Johan his avowry. **1528** ROY *Satire* (1845) S. Frances their advowry. **1549** LATIMER 7 *Serm. Edw. VI* (Arb.) 193 Awaye with these auowryes. Let god alone be oure auowry. **1611** SPEED *Hist. Gt. Brit.* VII. ii. (1632) 198 These Germanes that worshipped Herthum the Mother-earth for their Auowrie Goddesse. **1849** ROCK *Ch. of Fathers* II. vii. 489 Close to the corpse were carried the four banners of the dead person's 'avowries.'

†**3.** Patronage or right of presentation to a benefice; advowson. *Obs.*

1660 R. COKE *Power & Subj.* 204 Benefices..which were of the advowry of people of the holy Church. *Ibid.* 205 The Archbishopricks and other dignities elective..of his avowry.

†**4.** Avowal or acknowledgement as one's own.

1340 *Ayenb.* 101 His zone be adopcioun, þet is be avoerie, zuo þet he ssel bi yhealde vor his zone avoud.

5. (From Eng. vb. AVOW[1], in its legal sense): The answering for or avowal of an act done; *esp.* the plea whereby one who distrains for rent *avows* the act and justifies it.

1531 *Act 21 Hen. VIII*, xix, Alleaging in the said auowrie ..the same manors, lands and tenements. **1662** SIR A. MERVYN *Sp. Irish Aff.* 37 The Law will allow an Avowry without Atturnment, where he hath no means to compel the Test to atturn. **1768** BLACKSTONE *Comm.* III. 234. **1876** DIGBY *Real Prop.* vii. §1. 316 *note*, He is said to make *avowry* if he justifies in his own right..and to make *cognisance* if he justifies in the right of another.

†**6.** (Due to the confusion between the two verbs AVOW): A vowing, swearing, solemn declaration, or oath. *Obs.*

1587 FLEMING *Contn. Holinshed* III. 1020/1 All which their promises and auowries they performed. **1593** BILSON *Govt. Christ's Ch.* 204, I convent your owne consciences, which of our auowries standeth on the surest ground.

avowter(e, -trie, -tresse, etc., obs. forms of ADULTER, etc.

†**a'voy,** *int. Obs.* Also 4 **avoi, auoy.** [a. OF. *avoi*, *avoy!* of uncertain origin.] Exclamation of surprise, fear, remonstrance.

[*c* **1193** BENEDICT. PETRIB. in *Mater. Hist. Becket* Rolls Ser. II. 5 'Auoy!' inquit, 'quid est quod dicis?'] *c* **1300** *Beket* 2066 'Avoi! Sire preost!' he seide. *c* **1325** *E.E. Allit. P.* B. 863 Avoy! hit is your vylaynye. *a* **1330** *Florice & Bl.* 480 Auoy! [printed by D. Laing *anoth*] dameisele, quaþ Blaunche-flour. *c* **1386** CHAUCER *Nonne Pr. T.* 88 Avoy quod she, fy on yow hertelees. **1393** GOWER *Conf.* III. 332 Avoy my lorde, I am a maide.

avoyd(e, obs. form of AVOID.

‖**avoyer** (avwaje, ə'vɔɪə(r)). Also 6-8 advoyer. [Fr.: perh. connected with *avoué*; but the form has not been explained.] The French title of the first magistrate of some of the Swiss Cantons, dating from the time when their chief towns were free imperial cities. Used in Berne till 1794. **avoyership**, the position or office of an avoyer.

1586 T. B. *La Primaud. Fr. Acad.* (1589) 588 In some places they have Advoyers, or Bourg-maisters, as in the Cantons of Switzerlande, and in the free Townes of Germanie, which acknowledge an Emperor. **1689** BURNET *Tracts* I. 25 In a competition for the Advoyer-ship. **1704** ADDISON *Italy* (1733) 278 Avoyer, or Doge of the Commonwealth. **1707** *Lond. Gaz.* No. 4350/3 The Advoyer ..of the Town of Berne. **1835** *Penny Cycl.* IV. 304 Berne.. a schultheiss or avoyer was the chief magistrate.

avulse (ə'vʌls), *v.* [f. *āvuls-* ppl. stem of *āvellĕre*, f. *ā*, *ab* from + *vĕllere* to pull, pluck.] To pull or pluck off, tear away.

a **1765** SHENSTONE *Odes* 258 As though..ev'ry bough Like that the Trojan gather'd once, avuls'd, Were by a splendid successor supply'd.

avulsion (ə'vʌlʃən). [ad. L. *āvulsiōn-em*, n. of action f. *āvuls-*: see prec. and -ION[1].]

1. The action of pulling off, plucking out, or tearing away; forcible separation.

1622 PEACHAM *Compl. Gentl.* viii. 69 By avulsion or division of the Sea..Sicily was divided and severed from Italy, Cyprus from Syria. **1708** J. PHILIPS *Cider* I. 24 The thronging Clusters thin By kind Avulsion. **1775** T. JEFFERSON *Corr.* Wks. 1859 I. 201 On condition of everlasting avulsion from Great Britain. **1822** LAMB *Lett.* II. (1841) 22 Did the Eyes come away kindly with no Œdipean avulsion.

2. A part torn off, a detached portion.

1678 CUDWORTH *Intell. Syst.* I. iv. §25. 420 Certain parts of God, or decerptions and avulsions from Him. **1809** J. BARLOW *Columb.* VIII. 280 Crash your curst continent, and whirl on high The vast avulsion vaulting thro' the sky.

3. *Law.* The sudden removal of land, by change in a river's course or by the action of flood, to another person's estate; in which case, contrary to the rule respecting *alluvion* or gradual accretion of soil, it remains the property of the original owner.

1864 in WEBSTER. **1880** MUIRHEAD *Gaius* 456 Alluvion.. distinguished from avulsion.

avuncular (ə'vʌŋkjʊlə(r)), *a.* [f. L. *avuncul-us* maternal uncle, dim. of *avus* grandfather + -AR.] **a.** Of, belonging to, or resembling, an uncle.

1831 LANDOR *Rupert* Wks. 1846 II. 571 Love..Paternal or avuncular. **1854** THACKERAY *Newcomes* I. v. 50 Clive in the avuncular gig is driven over the downs.

b. (*humorously*) Of a pawnbroker: see UNCLE. Also *absol.*

1832 *Fraser's Mag.* V. 85 My only good suit is at present under the avuncular protection. **1859** SALA *Gaslight & D.* iii. 37 If you enter one of these pawnshops..you will observe these peculiarities in the internal economy of the avuncular life. **1922** JOYCE *Ulysses* 417 Avuncular's got my timepiece.

Hence **a'vuncularism** (*joc.*), recourse to a pawnbroker; **avuncu'larity**, the state of being an uncle; **a'vuncularly** *adv.*, in the manner of an uncle.

1859 D. G. ROSSETTI *Let.* 15 Feb. (1965) I. 348, I have only been saved from further 'avuncularism' by a visit of old Plint, who has bought two..drawings. **1937** A. L. ROWSE *R. Grenville* ii. 28 The pleasures of avuncularity. **1957** *Economist* 7 Sept. 824/1 The classical picture here is of Lord Woolton avuncularly presiding over the rapidly growing Young Conservatives.

avunculate (ə'vʌŋkjʊlət). *Anthropology* [f. L. *avuncul-us* maternal uncle + -ATE[1] 1 a.] The special relationship existing in some societies between a maternal uncle and his sister's son; maternal uncles regarded as a collective body.

1920 R. H. LOWIE *Prim. Soc.* v. 81 Ethnologists describe under the heading of *avunculate* the customs regulating in an altogether special way the relations of a nephew to his maternal uncle. *Ibid.* vii. 171 The Omaha are patrilineal now, but their having the avunculate proves that they once traced descent through the mother, for on no other hypothesis can such a usage be explained. **1927** *Observer* 17 July 6/4 This particular group of Melanesians is almost entirely lacking in the typical institutions of the region, the dual organisation, the avunculate. **1932** R. F. FORTUNE *Sorcerers of Dobu* i. 62 Dobu practices the avunculate, inheritance from mother's brother to sister's son. **1937** *Times Lit. Suppl.* 27 Feb. 145/1 It is a little surprising to find the mother's brother—in his collective capacity sometimes known as the 'avunculate'—so much under an obligation to do the honours.

avunculize (ə'vʌŋkjʊlaɪz), *v. rare.* [f. as AVUNCULAR *a.* + -IZE, cf. *patronize*.] To act like an uncle.

1662 FULLER *Worthies* II. 14 Seeing he was sisters son to blackmouth'd Sanders, it is much that he doth not more Avunculize in his bitterness against Protestants.

†**a'vye,** *v. Obs.* Also 5 **awye.** [a. OF. *avie-r*:—Rom. **adviāre*: see AVAY.] To send away, dismiss; *refl.* To take one's way.

c **1440** *Morte Arth.* 3717 Sir Arthure and Gawayne avyede theme bothene. *c* **1485** *Digby Myst.* (1882) III. 500, I wol a-wye sovereyns; and soiettes I dys-deyne.

†**avyn'sime.** *Obs.* In 5 **auyzeme, auynsime.** Error for *quynsime*, QUINZIÈME.

1480 CAXTON *Chron. Eng.* VII. (1520) 121 b/2 The auyzeme of Paske kynge Edwarde..made Edwarde his fyrst sone prynce of Wales. *c* **1500** *Partenay* 1981 Within thys Auynsime be ye retornyng.

avyowre, obs. variant of AVER *sb.*

Avyryle, early form of APRIL.

avys(e, -ness, etc., obs. ff. of ADVICE, -ISE, etc.

avysioun, variant of AVISION, *Obs.*

aw (ɔː), *int.* An exclamation usually expressing mild remonstrance, entreaty, commiseration, disgust, or disapproval.

1852 STOWE *Uncle Tom* viii. 39/2 'Ugh? aw! like enough!' grunted his complaisant acquaintance. **1902** J. J. BELL *Wee Macgreegor* viii. 76 'He sudna ha'e boastit.' 'Aw, Lizzie!' **1911** J. C. LINCOLN *Cap'n Warren's Wards* xix. 312 Aw, let me alone. **1928** W. SMYTH *Jean of Tussock Country* v. 46 'Aw—yes, you want a job!' the manager muttered. *Ibid.* v. 47 'Can you ride?'..'Aw—you can.' **1932** 'SPINDRIFT' *Yankee Slang* 9 Aw! Shucks, forget it—to tender thanks for courtesy or kindness is to provoke this phrase.

aw, obs. form of AWE, OWE, OUGHT.

aw- was frequently written in ME. for AU-, e.g. *awght, awditorie*; and in Scotch for AV-, as in *awail, awoid.* For such forms see AU-, AV-.

awa, Sc. form of AWAY.

awabi (ə'wɑːbɪ). [Jap.] The Japanese abalone or sea-ear (*Haliotis gigantea*).

1889 in *Cent. Dict.* **1924** *Glasgow Herald* 12 May 11 Soochon awaibi, and a whole gamut of marvels taking days to concoct. **1934** E. BLUNDEN *Choice or Chance* 10 And ice may marry well with beer, And—what, they serve *Awabi* here? **1962** *Times Lit. Suppl.* 15 June 440/3 Sensual figures of the almost naked awabi fishergirls in another famous triptych of Utamaro's.

AWACS ('eɪwæks). *Mil.* (orig. *U.S.*). Also Awacs. [Acronym, f. the initial letters of *A*irborne *W*arning *a*nd *C*ontrol *S*ystem.] An airborne long-range radar system for detecting other aircraft, including low-flying ones, and controlling weapons directed against them.

1966 *Electronics* 8 Aug. 47/1 Two companies received the go-ahead to proceed with the next study phase on the airborne warning and control system (Awacs). **1970** *Sci. News* 7 Feb. 149/1 Joining Safeguard on the upswing are such projects as the AWACS (Airborne Warning Alert Command System), a flying radar station to warn of a missile attack. **1977** *R.A.F. News* 30 Mar. 11/3 A British contribution to a Nato AWACS force..will be very costly. **1977** *New Yorker* 10 Oct. 167/1 One project the President was devoting his attention to was..the proposed sale of an Airborne Warning and Control System (AWACS) to Iran. **1986** *Daily Tel.* 16 Dec. 28/1 The Labour Government chose Nimrod in preference to AWACS in March 1977.

await (ə'weɪt), *v.* Forms: 3 **awaitie**, 3–6 **awate**, 3–7 **awaite**, 4 **aweyte**, 4–5 **aweite**, 3–6 **awayte**, 6 **awayt, awaight, adwate**, 6– **await**. [a. ONF. *awaitie-r* (OF. *aguaitier*) to lie in wait for, watch, observe, f. *à* to + *waitier* (OF. *guaitier*, mod. *guetter*) to watch, ad. OHG. *wahtên*, mod.G. *wachten*: see WAIT *v.* With the development of meanings, cf. ATTEND *v.*]

†**1.** To keep watch, watch for; *esp.* to watch stealthily with hostile purpose; to lie in wait for, waylay. **a.** *trans. Obs.*

c **1230** *Ancr. R.* 174 Me awaiteð ou..as me deð þeoues þet beoð ibroken to chirche. *c* **1320** *Cast. Loue* 767 Vre fo þat vs awayteþ day and niht. **1382** WYCLIF *Ex.* xxi. 13 Who forsothe is not aweytid [*insidiatus*]. **1475** CAXTON *Jason* 133 How Jason..was awayted in a wood and assaylled. **1530** PALSGR. 441/2, I awayte, I lye in wayte of a person to marke what he dothe or sayeth, *Je aguayte.* **1634** *Malory's Arthur* (1816) II. 413 Sir Agravaine..awaited queen Guenever and sir Launcelot, for to put them to a rebuke and shame. **1671** MILTON *Samson* 1197 Your ill-meaning politician lords.. Appointed to await me thirty spies.

†**b.** *refl. Obs.*

1297 R. GLOUC. 49 Þe kynges broþer and þe Erl of Kent al so..Awatede him to þilke ost, þat þe Emperour inne was.

†**c.** *intr.* usually with *inf. Obs.*

c **1230** *Ancr. R.* 174 Leste he..awaitie uorte worpen upon ou his crokes. *a* **1300** *Cursor M.* 899 Wommon to stynge awayte þou shal. *c* **1386** CHAUCER *Sompn. T.* 344 Ther is ful many an eyghe and many an eere Awaytand on a lord, and he not where. *c* **1440** *Gesta Rom.* 224 He awaytid and caste him, in alle that euere he myght, for the dethe of his fadir. **1530** PALSGR. 441/2 Let him awayte hardely, for.. he may happe to be taken sleper. **1596** DRAYTON *Legends* ii. 141 Thou seest who doth awaite, T' intrap thy Beautie.

†**2.** *trans.* To watch for a chance of doing, contrive, plan, plot (harm of some sort) *to* a person. *Obs.*

c **1400** *Rom. Rose* 7525 He awaited nothing, But to deceive Faire-Welcoming. *c* **1430** *Syr Gener.* 2560 To awaite him shame. *c* **1450** LONELICH *Grail* lvi. 330 Forto donȝow swich dishonowr, Owther ȝow velonye to awayten.

†**3.** To watch, look at, observe, notice. **a.** *trans.*

c **1350** *Will. Palerne* 1711 Sche a-wayted wel þe white bere skinnes. *c* **1400** *Apol. Loll.* 92 Ȝe schal not a wat dremis. *Ibid.* 93 A waytiþ not þeis Egipcian daies. *c* **1449** PECOCK *Repr.* II. xiii. 226 It is diligentli to be awaitid whether the feend entermetith him.

†**b.** *intr.* or with *subord. cl.* To look, take note. *Obs.*

c **1300** *Beket* 85 Out he ȝeode forte awaite what that wonder were. *c* **1350** *Will. Palerne* 2415 Eche wiȝh wol aweite after þe white beres. **1393** LANGL. *P. Pl.* C. XVIII. 62 Awaite hoo haþ moost neede.

†**4.** To watch over, look after, attend to. **a.** *trans.*

c **1340** *Cursor M.* (Trin.) 5416 Þus coude Ioseph..Awayte his lord þe kyngus prow. **1393** LANGL. *P. Pl.* C. VII. 279 Yf ich sente ouer see my seruaunt..my profit to a-waite.

†**b.** *intr.* with *on, inf. phr.*, or *subord. cl.* To keep watch, give heed, take care, endeavour. *Obs.*

? *c* **1430** ? LYDG. in *Rel. Ant* I. 158 Well a-waytyng to fulfyll anoon What thi soverain commandith the to done. **1484** CAXTON *Curial* 1 Thou awaytest frely on thyn owne pryuat thynges. **1489** CAXTON *Faytes of A.* II. xxxix. 163 Ought always to awayte of all theire powere to dryue and sette theire enemyes a grounde. **1531** ELYOT *Gov.* (1580) 180 Accompteth hym a beast..and awaighteth diligently to trust him with nothing. **1603** H. CROSSE *Vertues Commw.* (1878) 15 Awaiting that voluptuousnesse haue no preheminence in the soule.

†**5.** To wait upon, as a servant or attendant, to attend. **a.** *trans. Obs.*

1393 GOWER *Conf.* III. 22 His cokes ben for him affaited, So that his body is awaited, That him shall lacke no delite. *a* **1547** EARL SURREY *Aeneid* IV. 174 Then issued she, awayted with great train. **1641** J. JACKSON *True Evang. Temper* iii. 175 His Baptismall Laver [was] awaited by a Dove. [Cf. 1671 in 1.]

†**b.** *intr.* with *on, upon*; or *absol. Obs.*

1393 GOWER *Conf.* III. 70 Where as this guiler faste by Upon this god shall prively Awaite. *c* **1400** *Epiph.* (Turnb. 1843) 125 To se on the non other a watyng But beestes. *c* **1500** *To serve a Lord* in *Babees Bk.* (1868) 368 The servitours to be redy to awayte. **1523** LD. DACRE in *St. Papers* (1836) IV. 65 Horsemen, to adwate upon hym. **1600** TOURNEUR *Transf. Met.* lii, Awaited on by Truth, his Page, full kind. **1742** POPE *Dunc.* IV. 117 On whom three hundred gold-capt youths await.

†**6.** *intr.* To wait *upon* to transact business. *Obs.*

1448 SHILLINGFORD *Lett.* (1871) 62 Y wold awayte upon hym there as sone as he hadde dyned. **1489** *Plumpton Corr.* 83 To assigne a place, wher..I might awayte upon you.

7. To wait for (a coming event or person). **a.** *trans.* (This and 8 a are the only current senses.)

1393 GOWER *Conf.* III. 258 The tigre his time awaiteth In hope for to cacche his pray. **1542–3** *Act 34 & 35 Hen. VIII*, ix. §1 Awaiting..the comming of the said great botes. **1667** MILTON *P.L.* IV. 550 Betwixt these rockie Pillars Gabriel sat ..awaiting night. **1876** GREEN *Short Hist.* iv. §3 (1882) 179 King Bruidi awaited them at the head of the Picts. **1878** SEELEY *Stein* III. 464, I shall await your answer with the greatest eagerness.

†**b.** *intr.* with *on, for*; or *absol.*: to WAIT. *Obs.*

c **1386** CHAUCER *Frankl. T.* 571 Aurelius.. Awaiteth nyght and day on this myracle. **1393** GOWER *Conf.* III. 319 Every man with great desire Awaiteth upon his coming. **1530** PALSGR. 441/2, I have awayted here for you this houre. **1677** R. CARY *Chronol.* I. I. I. xii. 45 They awaited until 29 Days were accomplished. **1725** POPE *Odyss.* VI. 169 In dubious thought the King awaits. **1821** SCOTT *Kenilw.* vii, The acclamations..of the commons who awaited without.

†**c.** with *for* = 'look out' for, expect. *Obs.*

1591 SHAKS. *1 Hen. VI*, I. i. 48 Posteritie, await for wretched yeeres. **1608** HIERON *Wks.* (1624) I. 689 Both to trust vnto and awaite for thy saluation.

8. To be in store for, be reserved for. **a.** *trans.*

1593 SHAKS. *2 Hen. VI.* I. iv. 35 What fates await the Duke of Suffolke? **1727** DE FOE *Apparitions* iv. 34 What may await us behind the dark curtain of futurity. **1849** MACAULAY *Hist. Eng.* I. 632 Honors and rewards which he little deserved awaited him.

†**b.** *intr.* (with *for* or *inf.*) *arch.*

1633 BP. HALL *Hard Texts* 382 That glory which awaits for thee. **1861** PYCROFT *Agony Point* xxvi. (1862) 247 The duties that awaited to try his powers.

†**a'wait**, *sb. Obs.* Forms: 4–6 **awayte, aweyte**, 4–7 **awaite, awayt**, 5 **avayte**, 7 (**awate**), 4–8 **await**. [a. ONF. *await, aweit*, (OF. *aguait*, mod. *aguets*), f. *await-, aguaitier*: see prec.]

1. A lying in wait or waylaying with hostile intent; ambush, ambuscade; a snare, plot.

1387 TREVISA *Higden* Rolls Ser. IV. 165 Delyvered out of þe awaytes [*ab insidiis*] of his owne moder. **1460** CAPGRAVE *Chron.* 317 Where was leyd gret awayte on the Kyng to his destruccion. **1491** CAXTON *How to Die* 12 The temptacyons of the deuyll and his ryghte subtyl awaytes and fallaces. **1526** TINDALE *Acts.* ix. 24 There awayte [WYCLIF, the aspies of hem] wer knowen of Saul. **1611** *ibid.*, Their laying awaite [**1881** *Revised*, their plot] was known of Saul. **1677** HOBBES *Dial. Com. Laws* 184 The killing by awayt, or of malice prepensed. **1691** BLOUNT *Law Dict.*, *Await* seems to signify what we now call *waylaying*, or lying in *wait*, to execute some mischief. **1867** in SMYTH *Sailor's Word-bk.*

b. *in await*: in ambush; with *be, sit, stand, lay, lie*. So *upon await*.

c **1386** CHAUCER *Nonne Pr. T.* 405 Homicides..That in awayte lyn to morther men. **1393** GOWER *Conf.* III. 311 For hate is ever upon await. *c* **1440** *Gesta Rom.* 8 Deth..stondith euermore redy in awaite, for to shete his dart. **1580** SIDNEY *Arcadia* (1622) 185 There in await had he laid these murtherers. **1600** FAIRFAX *Tasso* v. xviii. 78 The hidden deuill, that lies in close awate To win the fort of vnbeleeuing man. **1610** HOLLAND *Camden's Brit.* I. 400 Many frames wherin shooters..and slingers were set in await.

2. Watching, watch, watchfulness; heed, caution. ***to have*** or ***take good await***: to take good heed. ***to set good await***: to watch carefully.

c **1374** CHAUCER *Troylus* III. 408 In aweyte alwey, and in fere. **1430** LYDG. *Chron. Troy* I. viii, They sette good awayte On euery syde leste there were deceyte. **1461** *Paston Lett.* 399 II. 22 Take good awayte to your person. **1523** LD. BERNERS *Froiss.* I. xliv. 60 The fronters towarde Fraunce were euer in good awayt. **1531** ELYOT *Gov.* (1580) 97 They should haue good awayt that they spake not in such familiar facion..as..before.

b. ***to have*** or ***keep*** (a person) ***in await, to make*** or ***lay await on***: to keep a look-out upon, to watch suspiciously.

c **1386** CHAUCER *Monkes T.* 735 No man trust upon hir favour longe, But have hir in awayt for evermo. —— *Mauncip. T.* 45 A good wyf..Schuld not be kept in noon awayt. **1469** *Paston Lett.* 609 II. 351 He myght not speeke with you, ther was made so gret awayte upon hym and upon you boothe. **1523** LD. BERNERS *Froiss.* I. cccvi. 459 His men hadde him in suspect, and layed great awayt on him.

3. Waiting, expectation. *rare.*

1557 *Primer, Dirige* Ps. xxix, With long awaite I loked after our Lorde: and he intended unto me.

awaited (ə'weɪtɪd), *ppl. a.* [f. AWAIT *v.* + -ED.] Waited or looked for, expected.

1670 MILTON *Hist. Eng.* I. Wks. (1851) 9 The awaited revenge of those whose friends they had slain. **1814** SOUTHEY *Roderick* XVIII. Wks. IX. 169 He gave the awaited signal.

a'waiter. ? *Obs.* Also 4 **awaitour**, 4–6 **awayter.** [a. AF. **awaitour* (= OF. *aguaiteor, aguetteur*), f. *awaitier*: see AWAIT *v.* and -ER[1].]

†**1.** One who lies in wait. *Obs.*

c **1374** CHAUCER *Boeth.* IV. iii. 121 Yif he be a preue awaitour. **1548** UDALL etc. *Erasm. Par. Luke* xx. 20 The subtile awaiters to haue taken him in a trippe.

†**2.** An attendant. *Obs.*

1398 TREVISA *Barth. De P.R.* XVII. clxxx. (1495) 721 A vynyerde is lefte in wynter wythout keper or awayter. **1543** GRAFTON *Contn. Harding* 595 The kynges awayters were in coates of whyte and grene.

3. One who awaits or waits for.

a'waiting, *vbl. sb.* [f. AWAIT *v.* + -ING[1].]

†**1.** Lying in wait; ambush, plot. *Obs.*

c **1380** *Prymer* 101 in Maskell *Mon. Rit.* II, Delyuer us Fro the aweitingis of the fend. **1552** *Godly Prayers* in *Liturg. Q. Eliz.* 249 The deceitful awaiting of the most subtle serpent.

†**2.** Attendance, attention. *Obs.*

c **1374** CHAUCER *Anel. & Arc.* 250 Youre awaytinges.. Uppon me þat ye callid your mastresse. *c* **1400** *Epiph.* (Turnb. 1843) 101 With a waytyng and wonder besy cure.

3. Waiting, expectation. *arch.*

1607 HIERON *Wks.* I. 220 An intentiue awaiting for the Consolation of Israel. **1868** LONGF. *Dante's Parad.* XXIII. 17 Brief the space..From my awaiting.

awakable (ə'weɪkəb(ə)l), *a.* [f. next + -ABLE.] Liable to be awakened or aroused.

1844 *Blackw. Mag.* LV. 631 The tiger..lies sleeping, but always awakable, in every man's heart.

awake (ə'weɪk), *pred. a.* [Short for *awaken*, original pa. pple. of AWAKE *v.*; the full form occurs sporadically in 17th c.]

1. Roused from sleep, not asleep. ***wide awake***: thoroughly roused from sleep.

a **1300** [see AWAKE *v.* 1 *a.*] **1581** MARBECK *Bk. of Notes* 770 Men scarcely know, whether they be a wake or a sleepe. **1611** BIBLE *Luke* ix. 32 When they were awake [not in earlier versions, nor elsewhere in 1611], they saw his glory. **1639** SLINGSBY *Diary* (1836) 41 As she lay awaken in the night. **1820** KEATS *St. Agnes* xxxiv, She still beheld Now wide awake, the vision of her sleep.

2. *fig.* In activity; vigilant, watchful, on the alert.

1618 BOLTON *Florus* (1636) 9 That..the flame preserved there alive, might ever keepe awake for safegard of the State. **1681** DRYDEN *Abs. & Achit.* II. 682 Grudge his own rest, and keep the world awake. **1714** ADDISON *Spect.* No. 580 ¶9 Such a Consideration should be kept awake in us at all times. **1800** *Let.* in Trevelyan *Life Macaulay* I. i. 43 We want to have all our faculties awake.

b. ***to be awake to*** (anything): to be fully conscious of it, to appreciate it fully. Cf. *alive.*

1813 MISS AUSTEN *Pride & Prej.* xi. 48 As much awake to the novelty of attention in that quarter as Elizabeth herself. **1879** FROUDE *Cæsar* x. 109 He was awake to the dangers.

awake (ə'weɪk), *v.* Pa. t. **awoke** (ə'wəʊk), formerly also **awaked**. Pa. pple. **awoke** and **awaked.** Forms: α. (1 **awæcn-an**, see below and cf. AWAKEN). *Pa. t.* 1–3 **awóc**, 3–4 **awok**, 4 **awook**, (6 *Sc.* **awoik**), 3– **awoke.** *Pa. pple.* 1 **awacen**, 3 **awake**, 7 **awaken**, (*poet.*) **awoken**, 8– **awoke.** β. 1 **awaci-an**, 3 **awaki-en, awakie**, 4 **awaki, -ye**, 4– **awake**, (5 *Sc.* **awalk**). *Pa. t.* 1 **awacode**, 3–9 **awaked.** *Pa. pple.* 1 **awacod**, 4– **awaked.** [In this, as in the simple WAKE, q.v., two early verbs are mixed up; the form-history being complicated with that of AWAKEN, as the sense-history is with that of AWECCHE. 1. For the intransitive vb., OE. has *awæcnan, awóc, awacen*, compound of *wæcnan, wóc, wacen*, the present stem having a formative *-n-, wak-n-.* (Cf. Goth. *fraihn-an, frah, fraihans.*) This present began already in OE. to be treated as a weak vb., with pa. t. *awæcnede*; whence mod.E. *awaken, awakened.* As the earliest texts have *onwæcnan*, the *a-* in later OE. was probably = *on-*, not A- *pref.* 1. 2. Late OE. had also a weak vb. *awacian, awacode*, in form a compound of *wacian, wacode*, to watch, keep awake, but in sense identical with *awæcnan*, and perhaps originating in a confusion of the two. This gave M. and mod.E. *awake, awaked.* 3. After the weak *awakened* came into common use, as pa. t. of AWAKEN, the original relation of *awoke* and its pa. pple. to that vb. became obscured; and later instinct, in accordance with the general analogies of the language, has referred them to

AWAKE, treating them as strong equivalents of *awaked*. They are so included here. 4. Of all these forms the sense was in OE. only intrans. 'to arise or come out of sleep,' the transitive (causal) sense of 'rouse from sleep' being expressed by the derivative *awęcc(e)an*, ME. AWECCHE, Goth. *uswakjan*, mod.G. *erwecken*; but soon after 1100 *awake* began to be used in this sense also, and at length superseded *awecche*, which is not found after 1300. There has been some tendency, especially in later times, to restrict the strong pa. t. and pa. pple. to the orig. intrans. sense, and the weak inflexion to the trans. sense, but this has never been fully carried out. 5. The str. pa. pple. *awaken* was already in 13th c. reduced to *awake*, and at length became merely an adjective (mostly predicative), after which a new form from the pa. tense, *awoken*, later *awoke* was substituted; but the weak *awaked* is also in common use. (Shakspere used only the weak inflexions.)]

I. *intr.*

1. To come out of the state of sleep; to cease to sleep. (With pa. pple. belonging to the active voice, cf. *come, gone, risen*.) Cf. AWAKEN 1.

a. strong (pa. t. and pa. pple.).

c **1000** ÆLFRIC *Gen.* ix. 24 He awóc of þam slæpe. **1205** LAY. 1254 þæ awoc Brutus. *a* **1300** *Judas* in *Rel. Ant.* I. 144 Sone so Judas of slepe was awake. *a* **1300** *Oxf. Student* 61 in *E.E.P.* (1862) 42 þe clerkes awoke anon. **1513** DOUGLAS *Æneis* XIII. Prol. 154 And I for feir awoik. **1611** BIBLE *Judg.* xvi. 20 Hee awoke out of his sleepe. **1639** [see AWAKE *a.* 1]. **1866** G. MACDONALD *Ann. Q. Neighb.* xxix, I awoke to less trouble than that of my dreams.

β. weak (including the now ambiguous present).

c **1000** ÆLFRIC *Gen.* xlv. 26 Of hefeȝum slæpe awacode. **1205** LAY. 17915 Late he gon awakien [**1250** gan a-wakie]. *c* **1305** *St. Kenelm* in *E.E.P.* (1862) 56 Hi of Gloucestre schire: bigonne to awaki. *c* **1385** CHAUCER *L.G.W.* 2183 Ryght in the dawynyng awakyth she. **1393** LANGL. *P. Pl.* C. XIX. 180 Ner frentik ich awakede. *c* **1450** LONELICH *Grail* xlv. 364 þe goodman ful awaked was. *c* **1500** *Lancelot* 1047 Awalk! It is no tyme to slep. **1611** BIBLE *Gen.* xxviii. 16 And Jacob awaked out of his sleepe. **1711** ADDISON *Spect* No. 3 ¶9, I was so transported with joy that I awaked. **1714** POPE *Rape Lock* I. 16 And sleepless lovers, just at twelve, awake. **1827** JEFFREY *Let.* 97 in Ld. Cockburn *Life*, I shall come back to you like one of the sleepers awaked.

2. *fig.* To rise from a state resembling sleep, such as death, indifference, inaction; to become active or vigilant; to bestir oneself. (Used also of things personified.)

c **1450** LONELICH *Grail* xxiii. 179 Anon as he owt of his thowht awook. *a* **1541** WYATT *To my Lute* 1 My Lute awake. **1591** SHAKS. *1 Hen. VI*, I. i. 78 Awake, awake, English Nobilitie! Let not slouth dimme your Honors. **1678** *Crt. Spain* 17 They who were most concerned, awaked not. **1751** JOHNSON *Rambl.* No. 185 ¶14 Whenever he awakes to seriousness and reflection. **1842** H. E. MANNING *Serm.* (1848) I. 295 We feel as if we had awoke up to know that we had learned nothing really until now. **1867** FREEMAN *Norm. Conq.* I. v. 346 The national spirit again awoke.

3. *to awake to* (something): to become fully conscious of, to become 'alive' to.

[Cf. 1751 in sense 2.] **1872** YEATS *Growth Comm.* 233 England and France at length awoke to the value of their fisheries. **1878** BOSW. SMITH *Carthage* 358 When they awoke to their danger.

4. To be or keep awake; to be vigilant, to watch. *rare.* (Cf. WAKE.)

1602 FULBECKE *2nd Pt. Parall.* 26 The Græcians did manie times sleep, when the Romanes did awake.

II. *trans.* (taking place of earlier AWECCHE.)

5. *trans.* To arouse (any one) from sleep.

a. weak (and ambiguous present).

c **1230** *Ancr. R.* 238 Ich wolde awakien þe. *c* **1250** *O. Kent. Serm.* in *O.E. Misc.* 32 Hise deciples..a-wakede hine. **1340** *Ayenb.* 128 þe angle þet awekede zaynte Petren. **1393** LANGL. *P. Pl.* C. I. 213 And ȝe, route of ratons · of rest men a-wake. **1553–87** FOXE *A. & M.* (1596) 1761/2 Shogged her dame, and with much adoe awaked her. **1697** DRYDEN *Virg. Georg.* III. 792 No dreadful Dreams awak'd him with affright. **1775** SHERIDAN *Duenna* I. i, If you awaked her. **1859** TENNYSON *Elaine* 6 Where morning's earliest ray Might strike it, and awake her with the gleam.

β. strong. rare.

1435 *Torr. Portugal* 146 Hys hornys blast awoke hyme nowght. **1526** TINDALE *Matt.* viii. 25 His disciples came vn to him, and awoke hym sayinge: master save vs. [So **1611**.] **1879** TENNYSON *Lover's T.* 62 Owl-whoop and dorhawk-whirr Awoke me not.

6. *fig.* To rouse from a state resembling sleep; to stir up, excite, make active. Cf. AWAKEN.

1340 *Ayenb.* 128 þe holy gost awakeþ þane zeneȝere. **1563** *Homilies* II. xi. *Almsdeeds* i. (1859) 382 God's people should awake their sleepy minds. **1595** SHAKS. *John* IV. i. 26 He will awake my mercie. **1766** GOLDSM. *Vic. W.* xix, I was soon awaked from this disagreeable reverie. **1793** SOUTHEY *Tri. Wom.* 380 Such strains awake the soul to loftiest thoughts. **1813** SCOTT *Rokeby* II. xvii, But morning beam, and wild bird's call, Awaked not Mortham's silent hall.

β. a **1400** *St. Alexius* (Laud 622) 57 A man of grete pouste, þat mychel mirþe a wook. **1633** P. FLETCHER *Elisa* II. xlv, Down dead she fell; and once again awoken, Fell once again. **1872** BLACK *Adv. Phaeton* xxxi, In a fashion which awoke the ire of the Lieutenant.

†7. *refl.* To rouse oneself from sleep or inaction. *Obs.*

1205 LAY. 25556 þa þe King him awoc swiðe, he wes idræcched. **1488** CAXTON *Chast. Goddes Chyld.* 33 A slowe wyll is towched wyth a stroke of our lorde to awake him.

awaked (əˈweɪkt), *ppl. a. arch.* = AWAKENED.

1617 HIERON *Wks.* (1634) 294 An awaked conscience.

awakedness (əˈweɪkɪdnɪs, əˈweɪktnɪs). [f. AWAKED *ppl. a.* + -NESS.] An awakening from sleep; the state of being awake.

1922 D. H. LAWRENCE *Aaron's Rod* xviii. 273 That click of awakedness which is the end. **1925** A. S. M. HUTCHINSON *One Incr. Purpose* III. xi. 280 Floods through the pulses surge of thoughts on which the eyes last night were closed, causing the leap to full awakedness.

awaken (əˈweɪk(ə)n), *v.* Forms: 1 awæcn-an, 2–5 awakn-en, 3–5 awaken-e(n, 4– awaken. [OE. *a-wæcn-an*, earlier *on-wæcn-an*, f. A- *pref.* 2 + *wæcnan*, to WAKEN. For the form-history, and its complication with that of AWAKE, see the latter. In OE. *awæcnan* was a str. vb. with pa. t. and pple. *awóc, awacen*. But sometimes the present stem (being irregular) was mistaken for a weak verb, whence already in 9th c. the pa. *awæcnede*, mod. *awakened*, which is now treated as the proper pa. t., while *awoke* and its accompanying pa. pple. are referred to the originally weak *awake*. Like *awake*, this was also at first strictly intrans.; the transitive use is of comparatively recent appearance, but now (in sense 5) the most frequent.]

(In early use, rarely in the literal sense of *awake*; commonly *transf.* or *fig.* See senses 2, 3, 5. We still prefer *awaken* to *awake* in sense 5. See also the derivatives below, in which the transferred sense is the usual one in modern use.)

I. *intransitive.*

1. *lit.* = AWAKE *v.* 1.

c **885** K. ÆLFRED *Past.* 459 Ðæt we onwæcnen of slæpe. **1377** LANGL. *P. Pl.* B. XIX. 478, I awakned þere-with & wrote as me mette. **1653** *Nissena* 29 He awakened, and found himselfe void of the hopes of asking. **1818** SCOTT *Hrt. Midl.* 267 When the captive awakened, the sun was high in heaven. **1819** R. CHAPMAN *Jas. V*, 129 When the king awakened he was in a great rage.

†2. *transf.* To arise or spring into existence, originate. (The usual sense in OE.) *Obs.*

c **885** K. ÆLFRED *Oros.* III. xi. §5 Eall heora ȝewinn awæcnedon ærest fram Alexandres epistole. *a* **1000** *Crist* (Grein) 67 Nú is þæt bearn cumen, awæcned. *c* **1230** *Ancr. R.* 422 Of idelnesse awakeneð muchel flesshes fondunge.

3. *transf.* and *fig.* = AWAKE *v.* 2, 3.

1768 WESLEY *Jrnl.* 23 Apr. (1827) III. 308 Just awakening, and darkly feeling after God. **1827** CARLYLE *Misc.* I. 24 The genius of the country has awakened. **1881** *Nonconf.* 15 Sept. 867/1 A mind that has once awakened to this great and most distressing fact.

II. *transitive.*

4. *lit.* To rouse from sleep.

1513 DOUGLAS *Æneis* VIII. viii. 7 The blysfull lycht..A-walkynnit king Euander. **1596** SHAKS. *Tam. Shr.* v. ii. 42 Hath that awakened you? **1667** MILTON *P.L.* v. 672 Satan..his next subordinate Awak'ning. **1840** DICKENS *Barn. Rudge* xvii, Even this failed to awaken the sleeper.

5. *transf.* and *fig.* To rouse into activity; to stir up, excite; kindle (desire, anxiety, interest, attention, etc.); in *Theol.* to arouse to a sense of sin.

1603 SHAKS. *Meas. for M.* IV. ii. 119 Lord Angelo..thinking me remisse..awakens mee. **1651** HOBBES *Leviath.* IV. xlv. 355 To awaken..their Piety and Industry. **1767** FORDYCE *Serm. Yng. Wom.* I. i. 11, I would..awaken your ambition. **1850** MᶜCOSH *Div. Govt.* IV. ii. (1874) 499 The cry of distress..awakens compassion.

aˈwakenable, *a.* [f. prec. + -ABLE.] Capable of being awakened.

1840 CARLYLE *Chartism* iv. 20 Deep-hidden, but awakenable.

awakened (əˈweɪk(ə)nd), *ppl. a.* [f. as prec. + -ED.] Aroused from sleep, sloth, or inaction.

c **1230** *Ancr. R.* 58 Vondunge..þurh þine dede..awakened. **1658** J. ROBINSON *Eudoxa* II. 121 The awakened needle..leapeth towards its allicient. **1746** HERVEY *Medit.* (1753) I. 74 Awakened, trembling Sinners. **1795** SOUTHEY *Joan of Arc* v. 222 Awaken'd memory. **1820** KEATS *Ode to Psyche* 6 Winged Psyche with awaken'd eyes.

awakenedness (əˈweɪk(ə)ndnɪs). [f. AWAKENED *ppl. a.* + -NESS.] The condition of being awakened.

1851 J. M. CAMPBELL *Christ the Bread of Life* 44 Some measure of awakenedness on the subject of religion. **1883** MEREDITH *Poems & Lyrics Joy of Earth* 126 With awakenedness of glee To feel stern joy her origin.

awakener (əˈweɪk(ə)nə(r)). [f. AWAKEN + -ER[1].] He who or that which awakens.

1598 FLORIO, *Risuegliatore*, an awakener, a larum in a clocke. **1797** GODWIN *Enquirer* I. vii. 58 Society is the true awakener of man. **1858** STANLEY *Arnold* I. vi. 246 Merely as awakeners and reminders to myself. **1860** S. WILBERFORCE *Addr. Cand. Ordin.* 112 An awakener of dull..conscience.

aˈwakening, *vbl. sb.* [f. as prec. + -ING[1].]

1. A rising from sleep, or (in modern use, more commonly) from sloth, inaction, or indifference.

1592 SHAKS. *Rom. & Jul.* (*Qo.* 2) v. iii. 258 Ere the time Of her awakening. **1646** *Bury Wills* (1850) 187 To continue vntill the generall awakeninge day. **1873** SYMONDS *Grk. Poets* vii. 186 The awakening of the whole English nation to activity. **1878** *Masque of Poets* 17 Dreams divine end in awakenings dull. *c* **1882** SARAH STOCK *Life Abund.* 8 The spring, Nature's great awakening.

2. An arousing from sleep or its semblance.

1684 R. ALLEYNE (*title*) A Rebuke to Backsliders..published for the Awakening of a Sleepy Age. **1872** M. TWAIN *Innoc. Abr.* 209 These violent awakenings must have been annoying to Oliver.

aˈwakening, *ppl. a.* [f. as prec. + -ING[2].]

1. Rising as if from sleep.

1726 THOMSON *Winter* 1043 Awakening nature hears..and starts to life. **1884** *Harper's Mag.* Sept. 626/1 Awakening buds and blossoms.

2. Fitted to arouse; rousing.

1694 KETTLEWELL *Comp. Penitent* 44 Thy awakening Providences. **1736** WESLEY *Wks.* (1872) I. 42 The most awakening writer..of all the ancients. **1810** COLERIDGE *Friend* (1865) 46 The awakening cock.

awakeningly (əˈweɪk(ə)nɪŋlɪ), *adv.* [f. AWAKENING *ppl. a.* + -LY[2].] In an awakening manner; so as to awaken.

1855 in *Imp. Dict.* Suppl. **1865** MEREDITH *R. Fleming* III. xi. 176 'Hoy, Gammon!' he sang out, awakeningly to ordinary ears. **1866** —— *Vittoria* (1867) II. xx. 20 The intentness sent that last falling..note travelling awakeningly through their minds.

awakenment (əˈweɪk(ə)nmənt). [f. AWAKEN + -MENT; the Romance suffix being here used with a Teutonic verb.] An awakening.

1842 GRESLEY *For. Arden* 9 The general awakenment of learning and civilisation. **1862** D. SIMON *Dorner's Pers. Christ* II. I. 276 The awakenment of a lively feeling of need. **1871** FARRAR *Witn. Hist.* i. 7 A happy awakenment to life and energy.

aˈwaker. [f. AWAKE *v.* + -ER.] = AWAKENER.

1611 COTGR., *Susciteur*, a raiser, awaker, stirrer vp. **1685** LADY R. RUSSELL *Lett.* 22 I. 58 Never any poor creature..has had more awakers to quicken and revive the anguish of its soul than I.

awaking (əˈweɪkɪŋ), *vbl. sb.* [f. as prec. + -ING[1].] The rising, or arousing, from sleep (or its semblance).

1297 R. GLOUC. 557 Of softe awakunge hii toke lute gome. **1611** SHAKS. *Wint. T.* II. iii. 36 The cause of his awaking. **1620** VENNER *Via Recta* (1650) 304 Untimely awakings do ensue. **1870** *Daily News* 18 Aug. 2 What an awaking!

†**aˈwald, -old, -eald,** *v. str. Obs.* [f. A- *pref.* + OE. *wealdan, waldan* (see WALD *v.*); prob. a later parallel formation to the old *anw(e)ald, onw(e)ald* sb. 'power, dominion'; or for OE. *ȝewealdan*. Cf. the weak AWELD, some of the forms of which in EE. are scarcely distinguishable from those of this verb.] To have control of; to wield. (Orig. governing genitive.)

1205 LAY. 23734 Ure drihten þe alle domes awalt [**1250** weldeþ]. *c* **1220** *Leg. St. Kath.* 652 Aweald þurh þi wisdom hare worldliche wit. *c* **1305** *St. Edm.* 335 in *E.E.P.* 80 As stif as enie bord hire honden bicome..heo ne miȝte hem awolde noȝt.

awale, obs. Sc. form of AVAIL and AVALE.

†**aˈwalk,** *v. Obs. rare*[−1]. [f. A- *pref.* 11 + WALK *v.*] To walk.

1536 BELLENDENE *Cron. Scot.* (1821) I. Proem 8 Quhilk in the floure of youth..Awalkis heir amang the flouris soft.

†**a-ˈwallop,** *advb. phr. Obs. rare*[−1]. [A *prep.*[1] + *wallop*, early form of GALLOP.] At a gallop.

c **1350** *Will. Palerne* 1770 þe white beres..went a-wai a wallop as þei wod semed.

awalt (ˈɑːwəlt), *adv. Sc.* Also **awald, awelled, awart (awkward).** [Etymol. uncertain. Cf. OE. *wæltan* to roll, pa. t. in Lindisf. Matt. xxvii. 60 *awælte*, in Rushw. *awælede*; but the place of the stress makes the relationship doubtful.] (See quots.)

1799–1863 *Trans. Highl. Soc.* III. 447 (JAM.) Sheep are most apt to die awald, when it grows warm after a shower. **1854** *N. & Q.* Ser. I. IX. 209/1 When fat sheep roll over on their backs and cannot get up of themselves they are said to be lying *awkward*, in some places *awalt*, and in others *awart*. **1863** MORTON *Cycl. Agric.* II. 720 Awelled (Dumfriessh.), a sheep..lying helplessly on its back.

awame, obs. form of AAM, AUM.

awance, -se, obs. Sc. form of ADVANCE.

a-wane (əˈweɪn), *advb. phr.* [A *prep.*[1] + WANE.]

†1. In want, wanting. *Obs.*

c **1175** *Lamb. Hom.* 21 Tomarȝan hit him is awane.

2. On the wane, waning.

1876 DOWDEN *Poems* 25 No wanderer morning-moon awane.

awant, obs. Sc. form of AVAUNT.

awanting (əˈwɒntɪŋ), *ppl. a.* [The phrase *a wanting* (see A *prep.*[1] 12, 13) erroneously taken as a single word, as if from a vb. *to awant*. Chiefly in Scotch writers; cf. *amissing*.] Wanting.

1661 Burney Κέρδ. Δῶρον 105 To acquaint me with what passes, or is awanting in the Nations. **1747** T. Story *Jrnl. Life* 78 Mutual Love and Esteem was not a-wanting. **1857** H. Miller *Test. Rocks* ii. 94 The upper side of the skull is often awanting. **1877** H. Page *De Quincey* II. xvi. 24 A Greek quotation with an accent misplaced or awanting.

awaped, var. awhaped *ppl. a. Obs.* bewildered.

award (əˈwɔːd), *v.*[1] [a. AF. *awarde-r*, ONF. *ewarder*, *eswarder*, central F. *esguarder*, to observe, look at, consider, examine, decide, ordain, fix = OSp. *esguardar*, It. *sguardare*:—Romanic **exwardāre*, *-guardāre*, f. *ex* out, thoroughly + *wardāre*, *guardāre*, ad. OLG. **ward-ên* (OS. *wardôn*, OE. *wardian*, cogn. w. OHG. *wartên*, mod.G. *warten*) to watch. Cf. ward, guard.]

I. To award a thing.

†**1.** To examine a matter and adjudicate upon its merits; to decide, determine, after consideration or deliberation. *Obs.* **a.** *trans.*

1393 Gower *Conf.* III. 354 So as my court it hath awarded, Thou shalt be duely rewarded. **1480** Caxton *Chron. Eng.* cxxvii. 106, I wylle that ye award and doo ryght. **1547** J. Heywood *Wit & Folly* Introd. (1846) 30, I judge and awarde Both these pleasures of yours as one in regarde. **1686** Dryden *Hind & P.* ii. 381 Shall then the Testament award the right? **1725** Pope *Odyss.* viii. 222 Ev'n he who sightless wants his visual ray, May by his touch alone award the day.

†**b.** with *inf. phr.* or *subord. cl.*

c **1386** Chaucer *Doctor's T.* 202 This clerk schal have his thral; thus I awarde. **1480** Caxton *Chron. Eng.* cxxvii. 106, I award..that hymself and his sone wend byfore the kyng. **1725** Pope *Odyss.* viii. 557 The unwise award to lodge it in the towers.

2. To determine upon and appoint by judicial sentence.

1533 More *Debell. Salem* Wks. 983/2 The iudges a warde write to enquire of what fame and behauiour the man is. **1704** *Lond. Gaz.* No. 4049/4 A Commission of Bankrupt being awarded against William Mackdugale. *a* **1709** Sir R. Atkyns *Parl. & Pol. Tracts* (1734) 93 An Officer.. executing Process which is erroneously awarded. **1876** Green *Short Hist.* viii. §5 (1882) 502 Fines of four and five thousand pounds were awarded for brawls. **1884** *Law Times Rep.* 12 Apr. 207/1 An umpire..awarded that the local board should pay..200*l*.

3. To grant or assign (*to* a person) by judicial or deliberate decision; to adjudge.

1523 *Act 14 & 15 Hen. VIII.* ii, To award to the party complainant such amendes. **1596** Shaks. *Merch. V.* iv. i. 300 A pound of that same marchants flesh is thine, The Court awards it, and the law doth give it. **1722** De Foe *Moll Fl.* (1840) 269 It was not in his power to award me any reparation. **1851** Hussey *Papal Power* ii. 66 He awarded to the Bishop of Vienne..four neighbouring cities. **1877** Mrs. Oliphant *Mak. Flor.* iii. 65 It was his..to award everlasting praise to his friends.

†**b.** *loosely.* To furnish, give. *Obs. rare.*

1583 Stanyhurst *Aeneis* i. (Arb.) 22 Furye weapon awardeth [*furor arma ministrat*]. *Ibid.* viii. (1836) 142 Theyre labor hot they folow; toe the flame fits gyreful awarding.

†**II.** To award a person. *Obs.*

†**4.** To sentence, appoint (*to do* something). *Obs.*

1538 Starkey *England* 190 The party condemnyd.. schold ever be awardyd to pay costys. **1650** Fuller *Pisgah* 384 A tierce of Levites were awarded to waite.

†**5.** To sentence, consign (*to* custody, etc.).

1548 Udall, etc. *Erasm. Par. Heb.* vi. 2 (R.) That last judgment, which shall awarde some to eternall felicitie, and other some to euerlastyng paynes. **1602** Fulbecke *1st Pt. Parall.* 83 Yet euerie of them shall be awarded to prison. **1648** Prynne *Plea for Lords* 56 The..Lords..awarded him to the custody of the Marshall.

†**aˈward,** *v.*[2] *Obs.* [f. a- *pref.* 11 + ward *v.*]

1. *trans.* To guard.

c **1534** *Pol. Verg. Eng. Hist.* (1846) 268 The passages weare straghtlie awarded bie there enemies.

2. To ward off (blows, etc.).

1579 *Poore Knights Palace* G iij, Then Clodius, to award this blow, and to drive back this dome, etc. **1670** Evelyn *Mem.* (1857) III. 222 Dexterously, yet candidly, to award some unlucky points that are not seldom made at us. **1744** Mitchell in *Phil. Trans.* XLIII. 108 To award off this Violence of the Sun's Beams. **1783** Ainsworth *Lat. Dict.* (ed. Morell), To award, or ward off, a blow, *Ictum avertĕre*.

award (əˈwɔːd), *sb.* Forms: 3 **ougard, awgarde,** 5–7 **awarde,** 5–6 **adward,** 4– **award.** [a. AF. *award*, *-airt*, *agard* = OF. *ewart*, *eswart*, *esguart*, 'look, aspect, attention, consideration, judicial decision, arbitrament,' n. of action f. *eswarder*, *esguarder*: see award *v.*[1] The EE. forms *ougard*, *awgarde*, confuse the two F. forms in *g* and *w*; for the spelling *adv-* see ad- *pref.* 2.]

1. A decision after examination, a judicial sentence, *esp.* that of an arbitrator or umpire; the document embodying it.

a **1300** *Cursor M.* 7318 Þai seke þam-self o a gret ougard [*Fairf.* a foule awgarde], þai ask now oþer king þan me. *c* **1386** Chaucer *Pers. T.* ¶ 409 To stonde gladly to the award of hise souereynes. *c* **1425** Wyntoun *Cron.* viii. iv. 152 To gyve A-ward For ane of þa twa þan askand Ðe successyown of Scotland. **1473** Sir J. Paston in *Lett.* 732 III. 102 Sette attone by the adward off the Kyng. **1577** Holinshed *Chron.* I. 3/1 To interdict so manie..as disobeied their award. **1665** Glanvill *Sceps. Sci.* x. 52 The condemning award of that unintelligent Tribunal. **1878** Jevons *Prim. Pol. Econ.* 78 The workmen have in several instances, refused to abide by the award of the umpire.

2. a. That which is awarded or assigned, as payment, penalty, etc., by the terms of the judge's sentence or arbitrator's decision.

1596 Spenser *F.Q.* iv. x. 17 Faint-heart-fooles, whom shew of perill hard Could terrifie from fortunes faire adward. **1697** Bp. Patrick *Comm. Ex.* xiv. 17 The Annoyances on their Bodies by Frogs, and Lice..were the just awards..of God's punitive Justice. **1863** Kemble *Resid. Georgia* 134 The fatal infliction of the usual award of stripes. **1882** *Pall Mall G.* 13 May 7/2 The balance of the Geneva Award.

b. Something conferred as a reward for merit; a prize, reward, honour.

1854 *Poultry Chron.* I. 622/2 Game (cock and two hens), £1, three entries. No award for want of merit. **1930** *Jrnl. Educ.* Sept. 720 Scholarship awards... The following awards have been made to candidates who have been approved for admission to a college. **1941** [see academy 7]. **1948** *Ann. Reg. 1947* 471 For the third time since the Nobel Prizes were instituted the awards for both Physics and Chemistry have been given to British men of science.

†**3.** Keeping, care, custody, wardship. (Cf. award *v.*[2] and ward *sb.*) *Obs.*

c **1450** Lonelich *Grail* xix. 202 Nasciens in presown kepten thei there That him and his londis bothe, they hadde In here award. *Ibid.* xxiii. 150 Loke thow..Of these ȝiftes that thou haue good award. **1570** *Marr. Wit & Sc.* i. in Hazl. *Dodsl.* II. 326 To whose award all creatures are assigned.

4. Special Comb. **award-winning** *a.*, of a film, design, etc.: that has won an award or awards.

1962 *Times* 30 May 5/2 His experience in documentary, being responsible for..the *award-winning study of life in British day-schools, *I Want to Go to School*. **1980** *Jrnl. R. Soc. Arts* Apr. 302/2 One is warmed by the excellence of the 27 award-winning..schemes recognized by the Civic Trust.

awardable (əˈwɔːdəb(ə)l), *a.* [f. award *v.*[1] + -able.] Rightly or lawfully to be awarded.

1622 Callis *Stat. Sewers* (1647) 169 No Processe is there awardable against the party.

awarder (əˈwɔːdə(r)). [f. award *v.* + -er[1]; cf. OF. *awardeur*, *eswardeur*.] One who awards.

1561 Jr. Heywood *Seneca's Herc. Fur.* (1581) 20 b, O thou awarder of mens gyltes. **1735** Thomson *Liberty* ii. 369 The high awarders of immortal fame. **1824** Landor *Imag. Conv.* I. 141 The jury in this case is never the awarder of damages.

aˈwarding, *ppl. a.* [f. award *v.*[1] + -ing[2].] Giving judicial sentence, deciding.

1620 Rowlands *Nt. Raven* 20 Each of an honest friend did make his choyse, And bound themselues to their awarding voyce.

†**aˈwardment.** [f. as prec. + -ment; cf. OF. *aguardement*.] = award *sb.*

1561 T. N[orton] *Calvin's Inst.* i. vii. (1634) 21 To hang the credit that we have to the Scriptures upon the will and awardment of the Church. **1679** W. Penn *Addr. Prot.* 153 Content with the awardment of such loss or gain as they the Arbitrators think equal. **1693** W. Robertson *Phraseol. Gen.* 1167 They both stood to his awardment.

†**aˈwardship.** *Obs.* [f. as prec. + -ship.] The action of an awarder, arbitration.

c **1547** Latimer *Serm. & Rem.* (1845) 422 Promising that ..he would stand to your awardship, and now doth deny it. **1555** —— in Strype *Eccl. Mem.* III. xxix. 227 He would not that his awardship should take place.

aware (əˈwɛə(r)), *pred. a.* Forms: 1 **ȝewær,** 3 **iwar, iware, iwarre, a ware,** 4 **y-wer, ywar,** 6 **awarre,** 5– **aware.** [OE. *ȝewær* (cogn. with OHG. *gawar*, *giwar*, MHG. *gewar*, mod.G. *gewahr*), f. *ȝe* (see a- *pref.* 6) + *wær* wary, cautious: see ware.]

†**1.** Watchful, vigilant, cautious, on one's guard. *to be aware of*: to be on one's guard against. *Obs.*

1095 *O.E. Chron.*, þa þe innan þam niwan castele wæron, his ȝewær wurdon. *c* **1200** *Moral Ode* 334 Bute we wurðen us iwar, þis wereld us wile drenchen. **1250** Lay. 5520 Beyne wer iwar [**1205** warre] of þan swikedome. **1340** *Ayenb.* 100 Þet þou by wys and y-wer. **1542** Udall *Erasm. Apophth.* 337 b, To bee well aware, lest thei should..areise battaill. **1636** E. Dacres tr. *Machiavel* II. 423 They were alwayes aware of taking of townes by long sieges. **1770** Wesley *Wks.* (1872) XIII. 19 Are you all aware of..talebearing and evil-speaking? **1835** I. Taylor *Spir. Despot.* iv. 164 We must be especially aware of those fallacies.

2. Informed, cognizant, conscious, sensible. *to be aware* (*of, that*): to have cognizance, to know.

1205 Lay. 18422 Ær heo wurðen iware, we scullen heom amarre. *c* **1230** *Ancr. R.* 104 Þer of beoð iwar..þet oðer hwile þe ueond, etc. *c* **1280** *Commandm.* in *E.E.P.* (1862) 16 Be a ware whose euer wol..þat for man-is sin it is. **1489** Caxton *Faytes of A.* ii. iii. 94 Whan the dwellers there were aware of hit. **1535** Coverdale *1 Chron.* xxii. 21 Arnan loked, and was aware of Dauid. **1667** Milton *P.L.* iv. 119 Whereof hee soon aware, Each perturbation smooth'd with outward calme. **1790** Cowper *Odyss.* xix. 117 Thou wast well aware ..that I design'd To ask. **1848** W. Bartlett *Egypt to Pal.* xv. (1879) 317 The only Europeans who had preceded us.. so far as I am aware, were Straus..and Bonar. *Mod.* Are you aware that your friends are here?

†**3.** *elliptically* with *be* omitted, and simulating a verb in the imperative. (So taken by Johnson.) (Be) on your guard, (be)ware. (Cf. *Soft! Quick!*)

c **1530** *Hickscorner* in Hazl. *Dodsl.* I. 154 Aware, fellows, and stand a-room. **1575** Laneham *Let.* (1871) 28 Aware, keep bak, make room noow. *c* **1590** Marlowe *Faust.* vii. 81 Well there's the second time. Aware the third.

awaredom (əˈwɛədəm). *rare*[−1]. [f. aware *a.* + -dom.] The state of being on one's guard.

1752 H. Walpole *Lett. H. Mann* 251 III. 60, I am glad you are aware of Miss Pitt; pray continue your awaredom.

awareness (əˈwɛənɪs). [f. as prec. + -ness.] The quality or state of being aware; consciousness.

1828 D. M. Moir *Mansie Wauch* in *Blackw. Mag.* XXIV. 909/1 My awareness of the danger of riding in such vehicles. **1880** Cyples *Hum. Exp.* ii. 24 No lapse of the egoistic awareness. **1880** Miss Bevington in *Mind* No. 17. 43 The higher the organisation the keener is the awareness. **1885** *Sat. Rev.* 31 Oct. 590 The most pig-headed Englishman and the most stolid German have..an awareness (if we may be granted the word) of the existence and manners of foreign barbarians. **1904** *Daily Chron.* 16 Sept. 3/4 He has the peculiar 'awareness' of a soundly cultured Catholic. **1915** C. C. Martindale *In God's Army* 125 An ultimate awareness that right is right. **1935** W. S. Maugham *Don Fernando* xi. 229 The mystical experience is an awareness of a greater significance in the universe.

†**aˈwarie,** *v. Obs.* Forms: 1 **awerȝi-an, awierȝi-an, awyrȝe-an,** 2 **awiriȝ-en, awerie-n,** 2–3 **awereȝ-en,** 2–4 **awarie-n,** 3 **awarye-n,** 4 **awarȝe, awyrie.** [OE. *awerȝian*, *awierȝian*, *awyrȝean*, f. a- *pref.* 1 + *werȝian*, *wierȝian*, *wyrȝian*, to curse: see warie.] To curse, damn.

c **825** *Vesp. Ps.* v. 9 Awerȝed. *c* **885** K. Ælfred *Past.* 249 Awierȝed. *c* **1000** Ælfric *Gen.* viii. 21 Nelle ic awirȝean þa eorþan heononforþ. *c* **1175** *Cott. Hom.* 223 Se eorðe his awiriȝd on þine weorcum. *c* **1250** *Meid. Maregr.* xix, Ðenne spec Olibrius—awarie him sonne ant mone! *c* **1394** *P. Pl. Crede* 662 Þei wolden awyrien þat wiȝt for his well dedes.

¶ See also aworry.

†**aˈwaried(e,** *ppl. a. Obs.* [f. prec. + -ed.] Accursed.

c **1000** *Ags. G.* Matt. xxv. 41 Gewitað awyrȝyde fram me [*Rushw.* awærȝede]. *c* **1160** *Hatton G.*, Gewiteð awereȝede. *c* **1220** *Leg. Kath.* 142 Toward te awariede maumetes temple. *c* **1314** *Guy Warw.* 166 Awarid worth ye ichon. **1340** *Ayenb.* 27 Awarȝede gladnesse.

†**aˈwaring,** *vbl. sb. Obs.* [f. aware *a.* or *v.* + -ing[1].] Perception, sensation.

1674 N. Fairfax *Bulk & Selv.* 50 The soul is too high bred to give us any rational accounts of the awarings of sense, as heat, cold, wetness.

awarke, obs. form of a-work.

†**aˈwarn,** *v. Obs. rare.* [f. a- *pref.* 11 (or 6) + warn *v.*] To warn.

1596 Spenser *F.Q.* iii. x. 46 That every bird and beast awarned made To shrowd themselves.

†**aˈwarp,** *v. Obs.* Forms: *Inf.* 1 **aweorp-, awurp-, awyrp-an,** 2 **awerp-,** 2–3 **aworp-en,** 3–4 **awarp-e(n.** *Pa. t.* 1 **awearp,** 1–2 **awarp,** 3 **aweorp.** *Pa. pple.* 1–3 **aworpen,** 3 **awarpen.** [f. a- *pref.* 1 away + *weorpan* to throw (see warp); cogn. with OS. *awerpan*, Goth. *uswairpan*.]

1. To throw or cast away; to throw or cast down.

c **1000** *Ags. G.* Matt. xxvii. 5 And he awearp þa scyllingas inon þæt tempel. *c* **1160** *Hatton G.*, Awarp. *c* **1175** *Lamb. Hom.* 25 And awerpeð hine in to helle pine. *c* **1225** *St. Marher.* 5 Ha walden..awarpen me. *c* **1230** *Ancr. R.* 122 Þet a windes puf..mei auellen & aworpen into sunne.

2. To warp or twist out of shape.

c **1300** *Old Age* in *E.E.P.* (1862) 149 Eld me awarpeþ þat mi schuldern scharpiþ.

†**aˈwarrant,** *v. Obs.* [f. a- *pref.* 11 + warrant *v.*] To vouch for, warrant, guarantee.

a **1400** *Chester Pl.* 3 Some writers awarrante your matter, theirfore be boulde. **1598** Greene *Jas. IV* (1861) 188 And awarrant his preferment to a prince's service. **1608** Armin *Nest Ninn.* (1842) 26 If life were awarranted fooles.

awarys, obs. Sc. form of avarice.

awash (əˈwɒʃ), *advb. phr.* (*pred. a.*) Also 9 **a-wash** [a *prep.*[1] + wash.]

1. On a level or flush with the surface of the water, so that it just washes over.

1833 *Penny Cycl.* I. 507/1 An anchor is..'a-wash,' when the stock is hove up to the surface of the water. **1868** W. Collins *Moonst.* i. xix. (1876) 144 The South spit was just awash with the flowing tide.

2. a. Washing about, at the mercy of the waves.

1870 Reade *Put Yourself* III. 274 The rising water set everything awash. **1876** Morris *Sigurd* iv. 351 Their unmanned oars awash In the sandy waves of the shallows.

b. *fig.* Esp. const. *with*: full of or abounding in; overflowing or rife with.

1912 J. London *Son of Sun* ii. 58 If I had the backbone to go and get it I could drink my back teeth awash until I died. **1950** W. Stevens *Auroras of Autumn* 193 You see the earth again..you hear its tragic drone Rise liquidly in liquid lingerings, Like watery words awash. **1954** A. Seton *Katherine* xxi. 356 The Abbey was awash with beauty of sound, enclosed by the beauty of stone. **1968** E. Bowen *Eva Trout* (1969) ii. iii. 237 The Outer Circle swept Eva round Regent's Park, awash in the gold of early evening, running with children. **1978** P. Roth *Professor of Desire* 78 In that strangely youthful face all there is to speak of sorrow are the eyes, soft, brown, and awash with feeling even while his crisp accent refuses to betray the faintest hint of grief. **1985** *Times* 5 June 12/6 Perhaps Britain was awash with voters who wanted Wilson on a free home trial.

a-waste (əˈweɪst), *advb. phr.* [A *prep.*[1] + WASTE.] Wasting, to waste.

1850 MRS. BROWNING *Prometh. Bnd.* Poems I. 146 Thy body appears Hung awaste on the rocks.

awatch = a watch: cf. next and AWAIT *sb.*

1519 HORMAN *Vulg.* 255 Whan sowdiers be..scatred about diuers besynessis: than lyghtly they be leyde awatche for.

a-watch (əˈwɒtʃ), *advb. phr.* [A *prep.*[1] + WATCH.] On the watch, watching.

1856 MRS. BROWNING *Aur. Leigh* VII, As a dog a-watch for his master's foot.

awate, obs. form of AWAIT.

†**awater**, in or on the water: see A *prep.*[1]

a-wave (əˈweɪv), *advb. phr.* [A *prep.*[1] + WAVE.] On the wave, moving in waves; waving.

1850 MRS. BROWNING *An Island* Poems II. 183 The place is all awave with trees. **1855** BROWNING *Saul* in *Men & Wom.* II. 131 The river's awave With smooth paper-reeds.

awaward, obs. Sc. form of AVANT-GUARD.

awawns, obs. form of ADVANCE.

away (əˈweɪ), *adv.* Forms: 1 **onweȝ**, 1–2 **aweȝ**, 2 **aweiȝ**, 2–5 **awei, awey, awai**, (3 **awæi**, *Orm.* **aweȝȝ**), 4 **owai (ewai)**, 0 **wey, on-wai, on way**, (**a-vey, avay**), **aweie, aweye**, 4–5 **oway**, 4–6 **awaye**, 6 **awaie**, 4– **away**. *Sc.* 8–9 **awa**. [In its origin a phrase, ON *prep.*, and *weȝ*, WAY, i.e. *on* (his, one's) *way*, 'on' (as in 'move on'), and thus 'from this (or that) place.' Already in OE. reduced to *a-weȝ*: cf. A *prep.*[1]: the 14th and 15th c. forms in *o-*, *on-*, were northern; in ME. and mod. dialects reduced to *'way* (York Plays, *do way* = put away, Sc. *co'way*, *c'way* = come away), also in certain combinations, as *way-going*. So MHG. *enwëc* (for *in wëc*), mod.HG. dial. *ewéck*, mod.G. *weg*. In earlier Eng. used as a separable verbal prefix, standing before the vb., esp. in subordinate sentences, and compound tenses (as in G.), e.g. *Sone se ich hit awei warp*, soon as I threw it away: *he wes awæi iflozen*, he had flown away; still placed emphatically before the subject as ' away he went,' 'away went hat and wig.']

I. Of motion in place, removal.

1. On (his or one's) way; onward, on, along. Hence used also with *come*, as still in north. Eng. and Sc., where 'Come away' = 'come along, come on,' without reference to place left.

Beowulf 534 Ær he on weȝ hwurfe. **921** *O.E. Chron.* (Earle 106) þa forleton hie þa burȝ and foron aweȝ. *c* **1250** *Gen. & Ex.* 810 Abram..ferde a-wei to mambre dale. *a* **1300** *Cursor M.* 8067 Wit þe king he ferd on-wai. *c* **1500** *Rel. Ant.* I. 45 The plowman cryed, Sirs, come awaye. **1601** SHAKS. *Twel. N.* II. iv. 55 Come away, come away death, And in sad cypresse let me be laide.

2. a. From this (or that) place, to a distance.

Beowulf 4199 He onweȝ losade. **918** *O.E. Chron.*, Hira feawa on weȝ comon. *c* **1000** *Ags. Gosp.* Matt. xix. 22 þa eode he aweȝ unrót [*Rushw.* awæȝ, *Hatton* aweiȝ]. *c* **1175** *Lamb. Hom.* 21 Bute he hine driue a-wei. *a* **1300** *Cursor M.* 11262 þir angels wited þam ewai. *c* **1384** CHAUCER *H. Fame* 169 And bare hym on his bakke a way [*v.r.* awey]. **1436** *Pol. Poems* (1859) II. 156 The duk fled oway. **1526** TINDALE *John* xvi. 7 That I goo a waye. **1590** SHAKS. *Com. Err.* I. ii. 16 Get thee away. **1699** DRYDEN *Char. Gd. Parson* 74 And hungry sent the wily fox away. **1711** STEELE *Spect.* No. 136 ⁋2 My Imagination runs away with me. **1854** THACKERAY *Newcomes* xxiv. I. 224 They sail away each on his course. **1884** *Pall Mall G.* 9 Aug. 9/1 The bride's going-away dress.

b. *emphatically*.

1583 BABINGTON *Commandm.* (1590) 177 Making them ride and run, post and away. **1782** COWPER *Gilpin* xxv, Away went Gilpin, neck or nought; Away went hat and wig. **1821** KEATS *Isabel* lx, Away they went.

3. From actual adherence, contact, or inclusion; off, aside; *fig.* as in to *fall away*, to desert.

c **1160** *Hatton Gosp.* Matt. xviii. 8 Awurp hine aweiȝ fram þe. *c* **1220** *Ureisun* in *Cott. Hom.* 189 Waschen a-wai alle folkes fulþe. *c* **1385** CHAUCER *L.G.W.* 393 He with his tayl awey the flye smyteth. **1481** CAXTON *Reynard* (Arb.) 41 Scrape and dygge a way a lytyl the mosse. **1577** *St. Aug. Manuell* 18 To lay away the burden of fleshly desires. *a* **1711** KEN *Poet. Wks.* I. 361 His mournful Tears he clear'd away. **1873** LONGF. *Eliz.* 29 in *Aftermath* 51 She folded her work, and laid it away.

4. From or out of one's personal possession, with sense of parting with, deprivation, loss; *e.g.* with *put, give, take, throw*, etc.

c **1400** *Apol. Loll.* 110 þei tak a vey all þingis fro alle men. **1611** BIBLE *Gen.* xxvii. 36 Hee tooke away my birthright. **1653** WALTON *Angler* 56 It shall be given away to some poor body. **1712** ADDISON *Spect.* No. 549 ⁋3 Life..is thrown away when it is not some way useful to others. **1833** HT. MARTINEAU *Loom & Lugg.* I. vi. 93 This is not an air to take away one's appetite. **1873** LONGF. *Emma & Eginh.* 179 This passing traveller, who hath stolen away The brightest jewel of my crown to-day. *Mod.* Who gave the bride away?

5. From the actual state or condition; from existence; into extinction or termination (in most cases gradual); to death, to an end, to nothing.

1340 HAMPOLE *Pr. Consc.* 3769 Parchaunce þai er ille within, And passes away in dedely syn. *c* **1384** CHAUCER *H. Fame* 1149 They were molte awey with hete. **1526** TINDALE *Luke* ix. 12 The daye beganne to weare awaye. **1611** BIBLE *Job* xiv. 10 Man dieth, and wasteth away. —— xxxiii. 21 His flesh is consumed away. **1641** FRENCH *Distill.* ii. (1651) 60 Let that..be vapoured away to the thicknesse of honey. **1714** ADDISON *Spect.* No. 565 ⁋1 They faded away. **1816** SCOTT *Old Mort.* xxxvii, Their zeal..died gradually away. **1864** LONGF. *Falc. Federigo* 114 The petted boy grew ill, and day by day Pined with mysterious malady away.

6. From its natural use with certain verbs in the preceding senses, *away* is extended to other transitive verbs, to express a specific application of the action to **a.** removal, parting with (cf. *blow* away, *kiss* away, *boon* away), **b.** doing away with, elimination (cf. *boil* away, *refine* away, *analyse* away, *explain* away); and finally also with similar force to **c.** intransitive verbs, which are thereby rendered transitive, as 'to *sigh* away one's life,' 'to *idle* away one's time,' 'to *sleep* the day away.' There are verbs which are scarcely or not at all used without it, as 'to *while* the time away,' 'to *fool* one's money away' (to part with it like a fool).

a. *c* **1661** *Argyle's Last Will* in *Harl. Misc.* (1746) VIII. 27/1 What was got by Oppression, will be booned away by the King's Liberality. **1711** STEELE *Spect.* No. 138 ⁋3 Which can play away its Words. **1881** BLACKMORE *Christowell* xxxviii, He..kissed away the tears.

b. **1738** JOHNSON *London* 53 Explain their country's dearbought rights away. **1742** RICHARDSON *Pamela* III. 75 To split hairs and to distinguish away the Christian Duties. **1751** JORTIN *Serm.* (1771) VI. vii. 140 To purify their religion, till they refined it away. **1812** L. HUNT in *Examiner* 14 Dec. 785/2 To explain away some of the passages. **1865** MILL *Utilit.* 46 This..might be analysed away.

c. **1689** SHERLOCK *Death* iii. §7 (1731) 210 These Men have loitered away the Day. **1712** *Spect.* No. 527 ⁋2 We had whiled away three hours after this manner. **1767** WESLEY *Jrnl.* 27 July (1827) III. 284 Having a severe cold, I was in hopes of riding it away. *Ibid.* 31 Oct. 14/3 They had falsely sworn away the lives of their fellows. **1812** BYRON *Ch. Har.* II. l. Let..the loitering pilgrim..gaze..the morn..away. **1864** LONGF. *Falc. Federigo* 90 The lovely lady whiled the hours away.

¶ Being used with verbs generally, like the L. prefix *ab-*, Gr. ἀπο -, G. *weg-*, *ab-*, *hin-*, F. *en-*, (cf. *aufugĕre* to flee away, ἀποτιθέναι to put away, *wegnehmen*, *abnehmen*, to take away, *s'en aller* to go away, *enlever* to take away), *away* enters into many idiomatic phrases, e.g. *to do away* (with), *make away*, *give away* (now *give way*), *fall away*, etc., which will be found under the verbs in question.

II. Of action. [Immediately from sense 1.]

7. Onward in time, on, continuously, constantly; with idea of continuance of action and progress; e.g. ***to work away*** = to go on working.

1562 J. HEYWOOD *Prov. & Epigr.* (1867) 90, I with ale, and ale with me wag away. **1570** ASCHAM *Scholem.* I. (Arb.) 29 As you perceiue your scholer to goe better and better on awaie. **1737** M. GREEN *Spleen*, While Pan melodious pipes away. **1804** *Naval Chron.* XII *Sailors have a knack*, 'Haul away! yo ho, boys!' **1821** SCOTT *Kenilw.* xxxiii, 'Scream away if you like it.' *c* **1826** R. MACNISH *Barber of Gött.* in *Mod. Pythag.* (1838) II. 101 'Brush away, my old boy—nothing like it.' **1833** HT. MARTINEAU *Brooke F.* ix. 112 The young folks tripped it away on the grass. **1855** THACKERAY *Rose & Ring* v. (1866) 23 She capered away on her one shoe. *Ibid.* xiv. 89 He sat down and worked away, very, very hard. **1875** HELPS *Anim. & Mast.* v. 132 And kept 'pegging away,' to use a presidential expression, with all my might.

8. Straightway, forthwith, directly, without hesitation or delay; chiefly colloquial in imperative sentences, as ***Fire away!*** = proceed at once to fire, begin immediately, ***Say away*** = say on, and U.S. and Eng. colloq. ***right away*** = straightway, directly.

1535 COVERDALE *John* xvi. 12, I haue yet moch to saye vnto you, but ye can not beare it awaye. **1676** SHADWELL *Virtuoso* II. Wks. 1720 I. 332 Come..pull away. **1842** DICKENS *Amer. Notes* ii. 14 'Dinner, if you please,' said I to the waiter..'Right away?' said the waiter..I saw now that 'Right away' and 'Directly' were one and the same thing. **1883** *Pall Mall G.* 27 Sept. 10 She told him 'to report away,' that she was not afraid.

III. Of position. [From senses 2–5.]

9. Of direction: (Turned) from this (or that) direction; in the other direction.

c **1175** *Lamb. Hom.* 53 Hi beoð iturnid away from heom. *c* **1383** WYCLIF *Wks.* (1880) 8 þat turneþ a wey his eris. *c* **1440** *Apol. Loll.* 68 Turniþ away ȝour facis fro al ȝour folthis. **1712** STEELE *Spect.* No. 514 ⁋3, I turned away from this despicable troop with disdain. **1879** LOCKYER *Elem. Astron.* iii. xii. 72 The axis of rotation is inclined away from the Sun.

10. Appended to *where, there, here*, with sense of: In the direction of, about; e.g. ***there away*** = in that quarter, there about. (Now only *dial.*)

1564 *Brief Exam.* iij b, The Gentiles there away had their..common bankettes. **1641** HINDE *J. Bruen* xlvii. 152 The Witch will not looke one in the face, but shee will looke here a way and there a way. **1755** *Guthrie's Trial* 210 (JAM.) Confirming the same by many mighty works in scripture tending there away. **1815** SCOTT *Guy M.* i, The three miles..extended themselves into 'four miles or there awa.' *Mod. Sc.* Where away did you lose it? He lives here-away.

11. a. Of the position attained by removal in place: In another place; at a distance; at (a stated) distance, off. *spec.* In reference to games or matches played away from the home ground. Hence as *adj.*; also as quasi-*sb.*, a win away from home.

1712 *Spect.* No. 502 ⁋5, I shall not be able to stay away. *c* **1835** C. H. BATEMAN *Hymn*, There is a happy land Far, far away! **1850** SEARS *Athan.* vi. 53 They can see the city away through the hot and stifling air. **1866** G. MACDONALD *Ann. Q. Neighb.* i. (1878) 14 Away in the distance..glittered a weathercock. **1881** BLACKMORE *Christowell* xxxix, His home was some miles away. **1893** *Abingdon Sch. Football Club Fixture Card*, Oct. 18. St. John's School. Away. **1907** *Daily Chron.* 14 Jan. 9/1 Thirteen drawn games and three away wins. **1923** *Daily Mail* 11 Jan. 9 West Ham have played so well in recent away games. **1939** M. DICKENS *One Pair of Hands* iii. 40. He was a pools maniac... 'When I won shixteen poundsh by a lucky shot with me four awaysh' was an anecdote I never got tired of hearing. **1962** P. VAN GREENAWAY *Crucified City* x. 107 Men dreamed opium dreams spun out of eight draws or four aways. **1968** *Sunday Express* 3 Mar. 31/4 No claims are wanted on the Eight Aways Treble Chance.

b. Used with intensive force, chiefly with advs., as ***away back, down, up***, etc., = far. orig. and chiefly *U.S.* Cf. WAY *adv.* 2 b.

1818 J. PALMER *Jrnl. Trav. U.S.* 130 Perhaps away up in Canada. **1825** NEAL *Bro. Jonathan* III. 145 A..he-yankee, from 'away down east'. *Ibid.* II. 78 The family were in a bustle, with some news about a rising 'away up, in the back settlements'. **1882** SWEET & KNOX *Texas Siftings* 45 Lawler..shot a deer, away back in 1840, on the spot where the capitol now stands. **1895** G. H. HASWELL *Maister* i. 35 The 'Kelers' of Tynemouth were a recognised class away back in the days of the early charters. **1903** *Sun* (N.Y.) 26 Nov. 5 Turkeys are away up in price. **1906** *N.Y. Even. Post* 28 Apr., Manufacturers of all good cars are away behind in their deliveries. **1910** W. M. RAINE *B. O'Connor* 217 That..pony in front belongs to sheriff Forbes, or I'm away wrong. **1935** *Punch* 25 Sept. 342/3, I can remember your father away back in eighty-five, long before you were born. **1958** *Times Rev. Industry* Aug. 85/1 Large towns like Liverpool..are away down in the list [of bankruptcies].

12. Of the state or condition resulting from removal: Gone (from a place); absent; wanting.

c **1300** *Cursor M.* 9702 What is wisdome be pees awaye? *c* **1350** *Will. Palerne* 2095 And turned agein..and told he was a-weie. *c* **1386** CHAUCER *Frankl. T.* 336 The Rokkes been aweye. **1562** J. HEYWOOD *Prov. & Epigr.* (1867) 53 Three maie kepe counsayle, if two be away. **1647** COWLEY *Mistr., Spring* ii, How could it be so fair and you away? **1816** SCOTT *Antiq.* xxvii, He was like a man awa frae himsell. *a* **1885** *Mod.* I called at his office, but found him away.

13. Of the condition resulting from deprivation, loss, or extinction: Gone (from existence); vanished, destroyed, consumed; dead; fainted. (Now chiefly *dial.*)

c **1380** *Sir Ferumb.* 2504 Our bred, our wyn ys al away. *c* **1430** LYDG. *Bochas* IV. ii. (1554) 102 A blase of fire, now bright, and now away. **1535** COVERDALE *Jer.* xxxi. 15 Rachel mournynge for hir children, and wolde not be comforted, because they were awaye. **1787** BURNS *Wks.* III. 119 Your mortal Fae is now awa',—Tam Samson's dead! **1818** *Edin. Mag.* Dec. 503 (JAM.) My dochter was lang awa [= in a swoon], but whan she cam again, she tauld us, etc. *Mod.* Here's a health to them that's awa'.

IV. Elliptical uses, with a verb suppressed: simulating an imperative or (rarely) infinitive.

14. = Go away.

c **1250** *Meid. Margr.* xxxvi, Awei ye euele consilers. **1375** BARBOUR *Bruce* XVIII. 367 Otherwayis mycht thai nocht avay. **1393** GOWER *Conf.*, Away the tyranny! **1562** HEYWOOD *Prov. & Epigr.* (1867) 91 Whither awaie with my hens, foxe? **1594** *2nd Pt. Contention* (1843) 177, I will a-waie to Barnet presently. **1611** BIBLE *Ex.* xix. 24 Away, get thee downe. **1623** BINGHAM *Xenophon* 28 We must..away euery man to his lodging. **1762–9** FALCONER *Shipwr.* II. 907 Away there! lower the mizen-yard on deck. **1872** W. BUTLER *Gt. Lone Land* iii. 25 Meantime we must away.

15. = Go or get away *with*, take away.

1526 TINDALE *Matt.* xix. 15 Awaye with him, awaye with him, crucify him. [WYCLIF, Take awey, take awey.] **1549** LATIMER *Serm. bef. Edw. VI.* vii. (Arb.) 193 Awaye with these auowryes. **1577** *Test. of XII Patr.* 122 My children, away with hatred out of your hearts. **1583** BABINGTON *Commandm.* (1590) 81 Yea, wee would..bid away with it, and not abide the sight of it. **1865** DICKENS *Mut. Fr.* 191 In his honest indignation he would reply, 'Away with it!'

16. a. = Get on or along *with*, put up with; tolerate, endure, bear.

1477 SIR J. PASTON in *Lett.* 802 II. 199 My charges be gretter than I maye a weye with. **1526** TINDALE *Matt.* xix. 11 All men can not awaye with that saynge. **1530** PALSGR. 419/1, I agre with meate or drinke. I can away with it. **1577** HOLINSHED *Chron.* II. 45 He..could well awaie with bodilie labour. **1606** G. W[OODCOCKE] *Hist. Justine* 85 b, They might enure themselues..to away with hardnesse and sparing. **1621** SANDERSON *Serm.* Ad. Cl. ii. (1674) 24 He being the Father of lyes..cannot away with the Truth. **1642** SIR T. BROWNE *Relig. Med.* 98 Some..can with greater patience away with death. **1748** RICHARDSON *Clarissa* (1811) IV. 183 That saucy fleer I cannot away with. **1840** CARLYLE *Heroes* (1858) 275 Idolatry..is a thing they cannot away-with. **1869** M. ARNOLD *Cult. & An.* (1882) 42 Jacobinism..cannot away with the inexhaustible indulgence proper to culture, the consideration of circumstances, etc.

†**b.** with *infinitive*. *Obs.*

1580 NORTH *Plutarch* (1676) 183 Notwithstanding the People..could well away to live like Subjects. **1598** R. BERNARD *Terence' Andr.* I. ii, Men that be in loue, can ill away to haue wiues appointed them by others.

17. ***and away*** (= and going away again), denoting discontinuance, in ***once and away*** (now, ***once in a way***) = once, but not continuously.

1583 GOLDING *Calvin on Deut.* i. 3 Not..for once and away, but wee haue our eares beaten with it euery day. *Ibid.* xvi. 96 It is not for a pang and away. **1655** GURNALL *Chr. in Arm.* (1669) 125/1 Short hints and away, may please a Scholar.

V. *Comb.* Formerly in many separable compound verbs, as ***away-bear, away-draw, away-go, away-put, away-take, away-warp.*** Of these the ppl. adjs. and vbl. substantives were retained longest, and some, as ***away-going,*** are still in use.

c **950** *Lindisf. Gosp.* John iv. 50 Gelefde ðe monn, & aue-ȝeade. **1297** R. GLOUC. 398 Þys Cristynmen..gred preye Awey bere. *a* **1300** *E.E. Psalter* lxxxviii. 14 Whar-to, Laverd, awai-puttes þou bede mine? **1588** A. KING *Canisius' Catech.* I j, Pairtly be ye away taking of thre dayes in 400 ȝeres. **1865** *Macm. Mag.* July 275 Away-stretching leagues of brick and mortar. *Mod.* The away-going crop.

¶ Formerly sometimes used in error for WAY.

1600 HAKLUYT *Voyages* (1810) III. 481 'We set sayle, but made but little away all the day.' **1755** SMOLLETT *Don Quixote* (1803) II. 193 On these considerations Sancho arose, and went aside a good away to another tree.

away(e, -ment, north. var. of AVAY, -MENT.

awayle, awayte, obs. forms of AVAIL, AWAIT.

†a'ways, *adv. Obs.* [f. AWAY *adv.* with adverbial genitive *-s.*] = AWAY.

1556 *Chron. Grey Friars* (1852) 33 He brake aways from them and went beyend see. **1591** SPENCER *Virg. Gnat* 430 And from her farre awayes A rulesse rout..lie Wallowed in their blood. **1652** CULPEPPER *Eng. Physic* (1809) 129 The decoction..and the herb..do take them aways. [*Hereaways, thereaways,* are common in Suffolk. F. Hall.]

†a'wayward, *adv. Obs.* For forms see AWAY. [f. AWAY + -WARD.] Cf. the aphetic WAYWARD.

1. a. Turned away, or in the other direction.

1205 LAY. 8878 A-weiward he halde [**1250** hit heued heold] & nolde hit iheren. **1375** BARBOUR *Bruce* XVI. 584 The Erll with the schirreff met he Awayward with thar gret menȝe. *c* **1386** CHAUCER *Maunc. T.* 158 This Phebus gan away-ward for to wryen. *c* **1407** *W. Thorpe's Exam.* in Arb. *Garner* VI. 109 The Archbishop..turned him away-ward, hither and thither. **1577** DEE *Relat. Spir.* I. (1659) 418 Holding his face away-ward.

b. quasi-*adj.* Turned away, averted; wayward.

c **1315** SHOREHAM 2 We beth al awey-ward, That scholde her by-leve. *c* **1350** *Will. Palerne* 3985 It is a botless bale.. to willne after a wif þat is a waywarde euere. **1387** TREVISA *Higden* II. 25 ȝif þe face is a weyward from þe water.

2. Of motion: Away.

1205 LAY. 23169 Far þe awæiward [**1250** aweiward]. *c* **1380** *Sir Ferumb.* 959 Faste a-wayward gunne þay flen. *c* **1530** MORE *De quat. Nouiss.* Wks. 78/1 Our life walketh awai ward, while our death draweth toward.

†a'waywards, *adv. Obs.* [f. prec., with adverbial genitive *-s.*] = prec.

1205 LAY. 22351 Gillomar..flah, & awæwardes teh. *c* **1350** *Will. Palerne* 2188 To winne hem alle a-weiwardes fro þe white beres.

†awbe. *Obs. rare.* Perhaps = ALP[2], bullfinch.

1576 GASCOIGNE *Philomene* (Arb.) 88 The tatling Awbe doth please some fancie wel, And some like best, the byrde as Black as cole.

†'awber. *Obs. rare*[−1]. [a. F. *aubour* laburnum.] The laburnum tree (*Cytisus Laburnum*).

1684 I. MATHER *Remark. Provid.* 232 Three tall oaks, a very tall awber, etc.

awblaster, awburne, awbyrchowne, obs. forms of ARBALESTER, AUBURN, HABERGEON.

awe (ɔː), *sb.*[1] Forms: *α.* 1–2 **eȝe, æȝe,** 2 **aȝeie, ȝeie,** (**heie**), 2–3 **æie,** 2–4 **eie,** 3 **eiȝe, eȝe, eȝȝe, æiȝe,** (**eaye, heye, heiȝe**), 3–4 **eye,** 4 **eighe, eyghe, ayghe, ay, aye.** *β.* 3 **aȝe, aȝhe,** 3–4 **au, auu,** 4 **auȝe, awȝe, agh, awee,** (**hage, owe**), 5 **aghe,** 4–8 **aw,** 4– **awe.** [The actual *awe,* in 13th c. *aȝe,* was a. ON. *agi,* acc. *aga* (Da. *ave*), representing an OTeut. **agon-* wk. masc. (of which the OE. repr. would have been *aga*); but this was preceded in EE. by native forms descending from OE. *eȝe,* str. masc.,:—OTeut. **agiz* str. neut., Goth. *agis* fear, taken as if it were a str. masc. *agi-z.* (Both f. *ag-an* to fear.) The ME. *eye,* (*aye,*) and *awe,* were thus in origin and derivation distinct though cognate words, but were practically treated as dialectal variants of the same word, of which *aye* was still used in s.w. *c* 1400, while *awe* was in the n.e. *c* 1250. The sense-development is common to both. They are therefore here taken together; the examples being separated into groups *α.* (from OE. *eȝe*) and *β.* (from ON. *agi*).]

I. As a subjective emotion.

†1. Immediate and active fear; terror, dread. *Obs.*

α. c **855** *O.E. Chron.* an. 457 Þa Brettas..mid micle eȝe fluȝon. **1006** *Ibid.* (Laud MS.) Þa wearð hit swa mycel æȝe fram þam here. **1205** LAY. 18924 Mid æie vnimete [**1250** Mid heye onimete]. **1297** R. GLOUC. 507 More uor eye than vor loue. **1330** R. BRUNNE *Chron.* 220 Of non þe had ay. *c* **1330** *Arth. & Merl.* 465 Gret ayghe and dout. *Ibid.* 6429 For sorwe and drede and eighe, Thai flowen euerich his weighe.

β. a **1300** *Cursor M.* 8793 'Durst we for auu, Vr thoght gladli we wald þe scau.' *c* **1340** HAMPOLE *Pr. Consc.* 1870 Ne for luf ne awe er nane sparde. **1375** BARBOUR *Bruce* XI. 555 Cum on, forouten dreid or aw. **1589–1657** [see 4 b]. **1784** COWPER *Task* II. 722 His voice Shook the delinquent with such fits of awe.

2. From its use in reference to the Divine Being this passes gradually into: Dread mingled with veneration, reverential or respectful fear; the attitude of a mind subdued to profound reverence in the presence of supreme authority, moral greatness or sublimity, or mysterious sacredness.

α. c **950** *Lindisf. Gosp.* Matt. xxviii. 8 Mið eȝe & mið micle glædnise. *c* **1175** *Lamb. Hom.* 75 Habben heie of him ouer alle þing. **1297** R. GLOUC. 469 The child lovede him..Ne he nadde of no man: more love ne eye.

β. a **1300** *E.E. Psalter* lxxxix. 30 If sones of him for-lete mi lagh, And in mi domes noghte haves gane with agh. **1380** WYCLIF *Deadly Sins* Sel. Wks. 1871 III. 167 Wiþ awȝe þenke, mon, hou þou hafs of God bothe powere and appetit. **1413–1535** [see 4 a]. **1671** MILTON *P.R.* I. 22 To his great Baptism flocked With aw the Regions round. **1742** COLLINS *Epist.* 7 With conscious awe she hears the critick's fame. **1827** KEBLE *Chr. Year* Matrim., There is an awe in mortals' joy, A deep mysterious fear.

3. The feeling of solemn and reverential wonder, tinged with latent fear, inspired by what is terribly sublime and majestic in nature, *e.g.* thunder, a storm at sea.

β. **1756** BURKE *Subl. & B.* IV. §7 (1808) 266 Astonishment, the subordinate degrees..are awe, reverence, and respect. **1833** HT. MARTINEAU *Cinnam. & Pearls* iii. 43 She pointed with awe to a mighty object. **1851** RUSKIN *Mod. Paint.* II. III. I. xiv. §26 It is possible to conceive of terribleness, without being in a position obnoxious to the danger of it, and so without *fear*; and the feeling arising from this contemplation of dreadfulness, ourselves being in safety, as of a stormy sea from the shore, is properly called *awe.*

4. *phr.* **a.** ***to stand in awe of***: to be greatly afraid of, to dread; *later,* to entertain a profound reverence for.

(This phrase has a remarkable grammatical development; its original type was 'Awe stood to men' (*i.e.* there was fear on men's part), or, with the object of fear expressed, 'Awe of me stood to men,' and 'Awe of (*rarely* to, with) me stood men (*dat.*)'; this, 'men' being erron. taken as a nom. case, was inverted into 'Men stood awe of me,' and finally, to restore the logical sense destroyed by this misconception, 'in' was inserted, giving 'Men stood in awe of me.')

α. c **1000** *Ags. Ps.* lxxvi. 12 Eorð-cyningcum se eȝe standeð. *c* **1175** *Lamb. Hom.* 161 Mare eie standeð men of monne þanne hom do of criste. **1205** LAY. 11694 Him ne stod æie to naþing [**1250** him ne stod eye of no þing]. **1330** R. BRUNNE *Chron.* 8 He stode of him non eye. *c* **1380** *Sir Ferumb.* 408 Of C[harlis] þat ys ȝour Emperer: of whame men stondeð aye..þe soþe þou me saye.

β. c **1250** *Gen. & Ex.* 432 Caym..wurð ut-laȝe, wið dead him stood hinke and aȝe. *a* **1300** *Cursor M.* 482 Fra ful hei he fell fullaw þat of his lauerd wald stand nan aw. *c* **1320** *Seuyn Sag.* (W.) Therof ne stod him non owe. **1413** LYDG. *Pylgr. Sowle* v. xiv. 81 Of theyre lord and god to stande in awen. *c* **1460** *Towneley Myst.* 305, I stand great aghe to loke on that Justyce. **1535** COVERDALE *Ps.* cxix. 161 My herte stondeth in awe of thy wordes. *a* **1600** *Scot. Poems 16th C.* (1801) II. 170 Wee stand aw Of Gods hie magnificence. **1653** HOLCROFT *Procopius,* The King..stands in aw of a Generall directing him. **1784** (29 Feb.) COWPER *Lett.* Wks. 1876, 161 We stand in awe of we know not what.

b. ***to hold*** or ***keep in awe*** (***of***): to restrain or control by fear (of).

α. [*c* **1000** *Ags. Ps.* xciv. 10 Se þe eȝe healdeþ eallum þeodum.]

β. a **1300** *Cursor M.* 5518 Halds þam for-þi in au [*v.r.* agh, awee, awe]. **1589** R. HARVEY *Pl. Perc.* (1860) 14 Yt were good to keepe such a Cur in awe. **1602** SHAKS. *Ham.* V. i. 238 Oh, that that earth, which kept the world in awe, Should patch a Wall. **1657** J. SMITH *Mys. Rhet.* 144 Nations kept in aw of his name.

II. As an objective fact.

5. Power to inspire fear or reverence; overawing influence. *arch.*

(Arising from the originally objective genitive, 'his awe' (= awe of him), taken as possessive.)

α. c **1000** ÆLFRIC *Gen.* ix. 2 Beo eower eȝe..ofer ealle nitenu. **1205** LAY. 17965 Þu scalt habben þis lond, & þin æie beon muchel & strong.

β. c **1400** *Ywaine & Gaw.* 2411, I sal deliver hir of his aw. **1601** SHAKS. *Jul. C.* II. i. 52 Shall Rome stand vnder one mans awe? **1679** DRYDEN *Troil. & Cr.* Ep. Ded., You see, my Lord, what an Awe you have upon me. **1815** SCOTT *Ld. of Isles* II. xxv, Yet nought relax'd his brow of awe.

†6. Behaviour that inspires fear; anger, fierceness, rage. *Obs.*

α. **1205** LAY. 1897 Al was heora gristbatinge, al swa wilde bares eȝe. *Ibid.* 9702 Hehten heom mucle eiȝe ut of his æh seone. **1330** R. BRUNNE *Chron.* 37 Wrothfulle wordes of eye.

†7. Something which inspires fear; a cause of dread; a restraint. *Obs.* [ON. *agi* has also sense of 'constraint.']

α. c **825** *Vesp. Ps.* xci. 5 Ne ondredes ðu ðe from eȝe næhtlicum. **1205** LAY. 2087 For swulchen eiȝe gode heo hefden muchele drede.

β. a **1300** *Cursor M.* 1773 Þat sorwe to se was greet awe. **1330** R. BRUNNE *Chron.* 333 Jhesu þorgh his myght, blissed mot he be, Reised him vp right, & passed þat hage. **1657** in Burton Diary (1828) II. 56 The Parliament may remove such persons. This will be an awe over them.

III. *Comb.* **a.** objective with pr. pple., as ***awe-awakening, -compelling, -inspiring.***

b. instrumental with pa. pple., as ***awe-filled,*** AWE-BOUND, -STRUCK.

1849 ROCK *Ch. of Fathers* I. ii. 90 The awe-awakening sound of some early Father's voice. **1757** GRAY *Bard* 117 Her awe-commanding face. **1880** 'MARK TWAIN' *Tramp Abroad* II. xliii. 151 This awe-compelling miracle. **1889** J. H. SKRINE *Mem. E. Thring* xi. 275 The stern 'Thou shalt'.. of the law, in those awe-compelling tones. **1923** J. W. HARVEY tr. *Otto's Idea of Holy* xi. 85 'The mysterious' itself in its dual character as awe-compelling yet all-attracting. **1860** PUSEY *Min. Proph.* 397 Reverential, awe-filled faith. **1814** WORDSWORTH *Excursion* IV. 887 The simple Shepherd's awe-inspiring God. **1819** SHELLEY *Cenci* I. ii. 84 Her awe-inspiring gaze.

awe, *sb.*[2] Forms: 6 **alve,** 7 **aue,** 9 **ave,** 6– **awe, aw.** [Etym. and original form unknown: *ave* (εɪv) and *aw, awe* (ɔː), now used in Sc., point to an earlier (ɑːv). The F. *aube* is said by Littré to mean 'white wood,' from the material of which the *aubes* are made.] One of the float-boards of an undershot water-wheel, on which the water acts.

1503 *MS. Reg. Test. Ebor.* VI. 83 Lez cogges, spyndyll, awes [of Butterwich Mill]. **1532** *MS. Reg. Leases Dean & Ch. York* I. 53 Cogges, spendeles, and alves [of Otley Mill]. **1611** COTGR., *Aubes,* the short boordes which are set into th' outside of a water-mills wheele; we call them ladles, or aue-boords. *c* **1795** *Unst* in *Shetland Statist. Acc.* V. 191 (JAM.) The water falls upon the awes, or feathers of the tirl, at an inclination of between 40 and 45 degrees. **1884** REV. W. GREGOR (in *letter*), *Start-and-ave wheel,* that is a wheel on the boards or aves of which the water struck, in opposition to 'bucket-wheel.' —— J. MELROSE (in *letter*), The start is the piece of timber morticed into the rings, to which the awe is fastened.

awe (ɔː), *v.* Also 4 **agh.** [f. prec. sb.; OE. had *éȝan* (= Goth. **ógjan*) in comp. *onéȝan*; and mod.Icel. has *aga* to 'chastise': cf. AWE *sb.*[1] 7.]

1. To inspire with dread, strike fear into, terrify, daunt; to control, constrain, or restrain, by the influence of fear. (At first *impersonal.*)

1303 BRUNNE *Handl. Synne* 10283 Lytyl of Goddes veniaunce hym aweth. *c* **1340** *Cursor M.* (Fairf.) 12096 Ȝe loue na landis lagh quen ȝe ȝour childe wille noȝt agh. **1577** tr. *Bullinger's Decades* (1592) 142 They..awe their seruants to worke. **1599** SHAKS. *Much Ado* II. iii. 250 Shall quips, and sentences..awe a man from the careere of his humour. **1707** *Lond. Gaz.* No. 4372/1 Two English Men of War..who may..awe the Privateers of Barbary. **1876** GREEN *Short Hist.* viii. §10 (1882) 586 The gloomy silence of their ranks awed even the careless King with a sense of danger.

†b. said of a strategical position (cf. *overawe*).

1670 COTTON *Espernon* I. III. 128 This Town..absolutely commands the River of Dordongne, as it also at least awes that of Garonne. **1809** J. BARLOW *Columb.* VII. 570 Two British forts the growing siege outflank, Rake its wide works and awe the tide-beat bank.

2. To influence, control, or restrain, by profound respect or reverential fear.

1611 BIBLE *Prov.* xvii. 10 *marg.,* A reproofe aweth..a wise man. **1640** BP. REYNOLDS *Passions* xxix. 302 Their presence aweth us from Liberty of Sinning. **1781** GIBBON *Decl. & F.* II. xlv. 711 He was not awed by the sanctity of the place. **1835** MACREADY *Remin.* I. 464 Milton elevates, thrills, awes, and delights me.

3. To inspire with reverential wonder combined with an element of latent fear.

1753 HOGARTH *Anal. Beauty* vi. 29 The wide ocean awes us with its vast contents. **1872** JENKINSON *Eng. Lakes* 205 The traveller is awed by the frowning mass of Great End.

†4. To reverence. *Obs. rare.*

1632 BP. M. SMYTH *Serm.* 166 So they deserue to be vsed that..will not reuerence and awe the King.

Awe, obs. adaptation of F. *août* AUGUST.

1580 TUSSER *Husb.* (1878) 124 In June and in Awe swinge brakes (for a lawe).

awe, obs. form of OWE and OUGHT.

awearied (əˈwɪərɪd), *ppl. a.* [f. A- *pref.* 11 + WEARIED; cf. next.] Wearied, weary.

1604 T. WRIGHT *Passions Mind* I. vi. 24 The woolfe.. awearied with fighting..runneth away. **1848** MILLER *First Impr.* xiii. (1857) 211 Listening, somewhat awearied, to scientific music.

aweary (əˈwɪərɪ), *pred. a.* [f. A- *pref.* 11 + WEARY; cf. *ahungry,* also such pairs as *live, alive.*] Tired, weary. Const. *of.*

1552 LATIMER *Serm. Lord's Prayer* (1844) 362 Such as be aweary of this world. **1605** SHAKS. *Macb.* V. v. 49, I ginne to be a-weary of the Sun. **1653** BAXTER *Saints' R.* II. (1662) 181 Pref., When we have disputed and contended ourselves aweary. **1830** TENNYSON *Mariana,* I am aweary, aweary, I would that I were dead.

a-weather (əˈwɛðə(r)), *adv.* and *prep. Naut.* [f. A *prep.*[1] + WEATHER.]

A. *adv.* Towards the weather or windward side, in the direction from which the wind blows; *esp.* in ***helm a-weather*** (see quot. 1867); opposed to *a lee.* **B.** *prep.,* short for *a-weather of.*

1599 HAKLUYT *Voy.* II. II. 47 And keepe a weather our places of traffique. **1630** J. TAYLOR (Water P.) *Wks.* III. 38/2 Hauing much adoe to get out aweather of him. **1666** *Lond. Gaz.* No. 31/4 The Conquerors..helmed a weather, and stood for the Southward Cape. **1762–9** FALCONER *Shipwr.* II. 171 Bear up the helm a-weather! Rodmond cries: Swift at the word the helm a-weather flies. **1867** SMYTH *Sailor's Word-bk., A-weather,* the position of the helm when its tiller is moved to the windward side of the ship.

†**awe-band.** *Obs.* Also **awband.** [f. AWE *sb.*[1] (in sense of Norse *agi* 'discipline, constraint') + BAND.] A curb, check, restraint; 'a band for tying black cattle to the stake..used to keep in order the more unruly animals' (Jamieson).
1536 BELLENDENE *Cron. Scot.* (1821) II. 293 The said castel suld be ane awband aganis thame. *c* **1565** R. LINDSAY *Chron. Scot.* (1728) 182 To keep him still as an awe-band above the Governor's head. **1653** BAXTER *Peace Consc.* 159 Fears of the wrath of God..are..the awe-band of your soul.

†**awe-bound,** *ppl. a. Obs.* or *dial.* [f. AWE *sb.*[1] + BOUND; cf. prec. sb.] Bound by awe or restraint of authority; submissive, obedient.
1631 *MS. Eccl. Proc. Durh.*, He was awebound to his wife. **1864** ATKINSON *Whitby Gloss.* s.v., They were awe-bun nowther wi' God nor man.

†**a'wecche,** *v. Obs.* Forms: 1–3 **aweccan,** 3–4 **awecche.** *Pa. t.* 1–3 **awehte, aweahte, awahte,** 3 **aweihte, aweightte.** *Pa. pple.* 1–3 **aweht.** [OE. *awęcc(e)an*, cogn. with OS. *awękkjan*, OHG. *arwechhan, -wekkan, irwecchen, -weken*, MHG. *erwecken*, Goth. *uswakjan*; f. A- *pref.* 1 up + *węcc(e)an*, Goth. *wakjan*, causal deriv. of *wakan* to wake: see WECCHE. The modern spelling would have been *awetch*.]
1. *trans.* To arouse out of sleep (or swoon).
c **1000** *Ags. Gosp.* Mark iv. 38 He wæs..slapende, & hi awehton hine. *c* **1160** *Hatton G.*, Awehten. **1205** LAY. 812 Heo heom aweihten *c* **1300** *K. Alis.* 5858 The Kyng.. hastilich hymself aweightte. *c* **1300** *Vox & Wolf* 266 in *Rel. Ant.* II. 277 O frere..of here slep hem shulde awecche.
2. *transf.* and *fig.* To awaken into life or activity.
c **1000** *Ags. Gosp.* Luke iii. 8 He mæȝ of þysum stanum abrahames bearn aweccan. [So *Hatton G.*] **1205** LAY. 29285 þe wind com..and þat fur awehte. *c* **1220** *Sawles Warde* in *Cott. Hom.* 267 þvs ah mon..wið þulliche þohtes awecchen his heorte. *c* **1220** *Leg. St. Kath.* 1042 He..wið his word awahte þe liflese liches to lif.

awed (ɔːd), *ppl. a.* [f. AWE *v.* + -ED.]
1. Influenced by dread or reverence; awe-struck.
1642 ROGERS *Naaman* 40 They feele an awed and feare-full heart. **1824** MISS MITFORD *Village* Ser. I. 80 Who, after a moment's awed pause, had resumed their gambols.
†**2.** Dreaded, reverenced; cf. AWE *v.* 4. *Obs.*
1652 BP. HALL *Invis. World* III. §3 Samson..that awed champion.

†**a'wede,** *v. Obs.* Forms: 1–4 **awede,** (5 **awyede**). *Pa. t.* 1–4 **awedde.** *Pa. pple.* 1–4 **awed,** (5 **aweyde**). [OE. *awédan*, f. A- *pref.* 1 + *wédan* (see WEDE), f. *wód* mad.] *intr.* To become mad, furious, or frantic; to lose one's senses.
c **885** K. ÆLFRED *Oros.* v. x. §2 Aweddon þa nietenu and þa hundas. **1250** LAY. 4438 Of witte hii weren awed [*v.r.* amadde]. **1297** R. GLOUC. 162 He was so sori and so wroþ, þat he ney awedde. *c* **1350** *Will. Palerne* 1750 Wept as sche wold awede. **1460** *Lybeaus Disc.* 395 As men that wold awyede They made greet deray.

awedness (ˈɔːdnɪs). ? *Obs. rare.* [f. AWED + -NESS.] The state of being awed; dread, awe.
1601 R. JOHNSON *Kingd. & Commw.* 153 To..induce submissiue awednes, they hold hard hands ouer the cominaltie.

a-week (əˈwiːk), *advb. phr.* [A *prep.*[1] 8 b + WEEK; cf. *a-day*.] In every week; weekly.
1547 BOORDE *Brev. Health* §133 Ones a weke anoynt the face. **1704** CIBBER *Careless Husb.* II. i, I us'd to dine there once a-week. **1841** GEN. P. THOMPSON *Exerc.* (1842) VI. 163 The poor, the men of nine shillings a-week or less.

aweel (əˈwiːl), *conj. adv. Sc.* [weakened f. *ah well!* cf. F. *eh bien*.] Well then; well!
c **1800** J. BROWN in Ramsay *Remin.* (ed. 18) 18 Aweel, I have fund ye a bed. **1822** SCOTT *Nigel* iii. (1878) 58 'Aweel, aweel, Laurie,' said I, 'it may be as you say.'

aweful, obs. form of AWFUL.

aweȝ, awei(e, aweiȝ, obs. forms of AWAY.

†**a'weigh,** *v. str. Obs.* For forms see WEIGH *v.* [OE. *aweȝan*, f. A- *pref.* 1 + *weȝan* to WEIGH. Cf. OHG. *arwegan*, MHG. *erwegen*.]
1. To lift up, support; to bear, bear away.
a **1000** *Cædmon's Ex.* (Grein) 21 Sibbe..ða ǽr wonsǽlȝe aweȝen habbaþ. *c* **1200** *Trin. Coll. Hom.* 181 Ðe fet up aweiȝeð [þe wombe].
2. To weigh, weigh out.
c **1000** ÆLFRIC *Gen.* xxiii. 16 Abraham þa aweah feower hund scillinga seolfres. *c* **1175** *Cott. Hom.* 233 þe dunan þu awiðhst..mid þina hand.

a-weigh (əˈweɪ), *advb. phr. Naut.* [A *prep.*[1] + WEIGH.] Of an anchor: Just raised perpendicularly from the ground; = *a-peak*, *a-trip*. (Said loosely also of the vessel or its crew.)
1627 [see AWAY 2]. **1670** DRYDEN *Tempest* I. i, *Trinc.* Is the Anchor a Peek? *Steph.* Is a weigh! is a weigh. **1751** SMOLLETT *Per. P.* (1779) II. lxvii. 230 He'll as soon heave up the peak of Teneriff, as bring his anchor aweigh. **1834** M. SCOTT *Cruise Midge* (1859) 320 'We are a-weigh,' sung out the skipper.

aweing, awely: see AWING, AWLY.

†**a'weld, awild,** *v. weak. Obs.* [f. A- *pref.* 1 + OE. *węldan*, weak deriv. of *wealdan* (see AWALD *v.*); or for OE. *ȝewęldan*, cogn. with MHG. *gewalten, gewalden*.]
1. *trans.* To rule with power, control, subdue; to wield, manage.
[*c* **885** K. ÆLFRED *Gregory's Past.* xvii. 118 He hit ðonne ne mæȝe to his willan ȝeweldan (*Hatt.* ȝewealdan). *c* **1000** ÆLFRIC *Gen.* i. 28 Gefillað þa eorðan & ȝewildað hiȝ.] *c* **1175** *Lamb. Hom.* 81 He ne mei his flesc awelden. **1205** LAY. 4083 þa he mihte beren wepnen, & his hors wel awilden [**1250** muneȝi]. *Ibid.* 12084 Al weoren þa wimmen awald [**1250** awild] to þan deðe. **1387** TREVISA *Higden* (1865) I. 253 ȝif wordes failleþ, ȝiftes schal hym awelde.
2. *intr.* with *inf.* To have power, be able.
1387 TREVISA *Higden* Rolls Ser. V. 259 þey þat were lefte on lyue myȝte unneþe awelde [*vix sufficerent*] forto burye hem þat were dede.

aweless, awless (ˈɔːlɪs), *a.* Forms: α. 1 **eȝeléas,** 3 **eȝȝelæs, æielese.** β. 4 **aȝlez,** 6 **aweles,** 6–7 **awlesse, awelesse,** 7–9 **awless, aweless.** [f. AWE *sb.*[1] + -LESS, continuing the sense of OE. *eȝeléas*: see AWE *sb.*[1]]
1. Without dread; fearless, undaunted, unappalled.
α. *c* **885** K. ÆLFRED *Gregory's Past.* xxxvi. 246 Eȝeléaslicor [*adv.*] **1205** LAY. 19410 Bruttes..weoren æielese.
β. *c* **1340** *Gaw. & Gr. Knt.* 2334 How þat doȝty dredles.. stondes Armed ful aȝlez. **1595** SHAKS. *John* I. i. 266 Against whose fury..The awlesse Lion could not wage the fight. **1852** D. MOIR *Cast. Time* v. Wks. II. 392 While the keen knife the aweless Patriarch keeps Unsheathed. **1880** SWINBURNE *Stud. Song* 38 The awless lord of kings.
2. Without awe; irreverent, presumptuous, rude.
α. *c* **1200** ORMIN 6190 ȝiff þatt ȝho iss gætelæs & eȝȝelæs.
β. **1571** NORTON & SACKV. *Gorboduc* v. i. (1847) 153 Careles of countrey, and aweles of God. **1656** TRAPP *Comm. Matt.* xi. 29 Christians must not be yokeless, aweless, masterless. *a* **1700** DRYDEN (J.) With awless insolence. *a* **1849** MANGAN *Poems* (1859) 45 Where lawless force is awless master.
†**3.** That inspires no awe. *Obs.*
1594 SHAKS. *Rich. III.* II. iv. 52 Insulting Tiranny beginnes to Iutt Vpon the innocent and awelesse Throne. **1614** T. ADAMS *Pract. Wks.* (1861) I. 231 It is a lawless school where there is an awless monitor.

awelessness (ˈɔːlɪsnɪs). [f. prec. + -NESS.] The quality of being aweless; irreverence.
1583 GOLDING *Calvin on Deut.* li, Despised his goodnesse, yea..turned it into an occasion of greater awelesnesse. **1881** SHAIRP *Aspects Poetry* viii. 234 A profane audacity, an utter awelessness.

†**a'welȝien,** *v. Obs. rare.* [f. A- *pref.* 1 + OE. *welȝian, weliȝian* to enrich, f. *weliȝ* rich; or for OE. *ȝewelȝian*.] To enrich.
[*c* **1000** ÆLFRIC *Gen.* xiv. 23 Ic ȝeweleȝode Abram.] **1205** LAY. 22718 Nan swa wræcche Brut þæt he nes awælȝed.

†**a'wem,** *v. Obs.* [f. A- *pref.* 1 + OE. *węmman* to corrupt, spoil (see WEM); or for OE. *ȝewęmman*.] To corrupt, defile; to disgrace, dishonour; to impair, injure, spoil.
[*c* **1000** *Ags. Gosp.* Luke xii. 33 Ne moððe ne ȝewemð.] *c* **1175** *Lamb. Hom.* 83 ȝef ho awemmed were of hire meidenhad. **1205** LAY. 21290 Heo þohten..weorien heom mid wepnen, & Arður awæmmen. **1250** *Ibid.* 20165 þe wilde crane..wane his fliht his a-wemmid.

awen, obs. form of OWN.

awenand, Sc. variant of AVENANT.

†**a'wend,** *v. Obs.* [OE. *awęndan* (= OHG. *irwendan*, Ger. *erwenden*, Goth. *uswandjan*), f. A- *pref.* 1 + *węndan* to turn: see WEND *v.* Also for OE. *onwęndan*: see A- *pref.* 2.]
1. *trans.* To turn, turn away.
Beowulf 384 Ne mihte snotor hæleð wean onwendan. *c* **1000** *Ags. Ps.* lxxiv. 11 For hwan awendest þu wuldres ansyne? *c* **1175** *Lamb. Hom.* 109 þe alde mon nule his mod to gode awendan.
b. *fig.* To change. Also *refl.*
c **1000** ÆLFRIC *Gen.* xix. 26 Lothes wif..wearð sona awende to anum sealtstane. *c* **1175** *Lamb. Hom.* 219 Hi alle wurðon awende of þan féȝre hiwe. *Ibid.* 229 He awende water to uine. *Ibid.* 81 þe king of heuene..auenede him in to his iscefte.
2. *intr.* To turn or go away, to depart.
c **1000** *Ags. Ps.* lxxviii. 57 Hi awendan aweȝ. *c* **1175** *Cott. Hom.* 225 Were swithe maneȝe on yfele awende. *c* **1305** *St. Kenelm* in *E.E.P.* (1862) 56 Vyf myle wei hi were awend.
b. *fig.* To turn or change *to*.
c **1175** *Cott. Hom.* 223 þu eart of eorðe ȝenume . and þu awénst to eorðe . þu æart dust and þu awénst to duste.

†**a'wene,** *v. Obs. rare*—[1]. [f. A- *pref.* 1 + OE. *wénan* to WEEN; or for OE. *ȝewénan* to think.] To think; to suppose, deem.
[*c* **1000** *Ags. Ps.* lxiii. 6 Ic..on ær-merȝen on ðe eac ȝewene.] *a* **1300** *Judas* in *Rel. Ant.* I. 144 The Jewes.. awenden he were wode.

awene: see A *prep.*[1] and WENE *sb.*

awer, variant of OWHERE *adv. Obs.* everywhere.

aweriȝe, awerie, var. AWARIE *v. Obs.* to curse.

awermod, var. OVERMOD, *Obs.*, haughtiness.

awerte, -ty, Sc. var. AVERTY *a. Obs.* prudent.

awesome (ˈɔːsəm), *a.* Also 6–9 **awsome.** [f. AWE *sb.* + -SOME.]
1. Full of awe, profoundly reverential.
1598 R. BERNARD *Terence' Adelphi* v. iii, Wise and wittie, in due place awsome, louing one the other. **1815** SCOTT *Guy M.* xi, 'He did gie an awesome glance up at the auld castle.' **1880** *Daily Tel.* 2 Dec., That 'Berserker rage'..of which the Scandinavian chroniclers tell us in terms of awesome admiration.
2. Inspiring awe; appalling, dreadful, weird.
1671 RUTHERFORD *Lett.* I. cciii. (JAM.) A sight of his cross is more awsome than the weight of it. **1816** SCOTT *Antiq.* xxvi, 'It's awsome to hear your gudemither break out in that gait.' **1870** MORRIS *Earthly Par.* I. I. 256 Together did the awesome sisters cry.
3. a. In weakened sense: overwhelming, staggering; remarkable, prodigious. *colloq.* (orig. and chiefly *U.S.*).
1961 *McCall's* Aug. 173/1 He looked up to see Mrs. Kirby, awesome in a black-and-yellow polka-dotted slicker, bearing down on him. **1973** E. F. SCHUMACHER *Small is Beautiful* III. iii. 180 None of these awesome problems figure noticeably in the cosy theories of most of our development economists. **1975** *Dun's Rev.* Jan. 27 It upped the original offer of a three-year package with a 50% hike in pay and fringes to an awesome 64%. **1975** *Business Week* 24 Feb. 58/2 It was awesome when they announced a staff for their Midwest office that was larger than the number of officers we have in our corporate banking department. **1975** *Economist* 9 Aug. 84/3 A garrulous old African with an awesome memory. **1983** *Observer* 6 Feb. 18/6 The profit record is not awesome... Profits in 1982 were struck at just £8.8 million against more than £25 million in the late Seventies. **1986** *New Yorker* 13 Oct. 117/2 To begin with, there is her awesome record... Over the last thirteen years, she has won at least one major title each year—a feat no other tennis player..has accomplished.
b. In trivial use, as an enthusiastic term of commendation: 'marvellous', 'great'; stunning, mind-boggling. *slang.*
1980 L. BIRNBACH et al. *Official Preppy Handbk.* 218/1 *Awesome*, terrific, great. **1982** *Guardian* 26 Oct. 8/4 It's so awesome, I mean, fer shurr, toadly, toe-dully! **1983** *New Yorker* 19 Dec. 55 (*caption*) Third grade? Third grade is awesome. **1986** *Making Music* Apr. 15/3, I just know it'd be an awesome band.

'awesomely, *adv.* [f. prec. + -LY[2].] In an awesome manner, with awe or profound reverence. Also in weakened sense, as an intensifier. *colloq.*
1884 BROWNING in *Shaks. Show-Bk.* 1 We voice the other name [Shakspere's] Awesomely, lovingly. **1973** *Daily Tel.* (Colour Suppl.) 15 June 7/3 Turner in a long and awesomely prolific career never ceased to observe and comment on nature. **1977** *Washington Post* 27 Nov. K1 He can be awesomely arrogant sometimes. **1979** *N. & Q.* Feb. 48/1 That awesomely large body of anonymously published tales. **1986** *Washington Post* 17 Jan. A10/1 'Laundresses Carrying Linen in Town', an awesomely successful sketch,..also by Degas.

'awesomeness. [f. as prec. + -NESS.] The quality of being awesome; weirdness.
1874 *Temple Bar* XLI. 237 The corpse with nothing of the awesomeness of death about it. **1876** MRS. WHITNEY *Sights & Ins.* II. xxxii. 609 It was so dark..We just sat there and felt each other's thoughts in the awesomeness.

†**a'west,** *v. Obs.* Pa. t. and pple. **awest(e.** [OE. *awéstan*, f. A- *pref.* 1 + *wéstan* to WASTE; cf. OS. *awôstian*, OHG. *arwuostan*, MHG. *erwüesten*.] *trans.* To lay waste, to devastate.
c **885** K. ÆLFRED *Oros.* I. x. §1 Hi..ealle Egypta aweston. *c* **1175** *Lamb. Hom.* 13 Lond heo eou awesteð. **1205** LAY. 2149 He hefde moni lond a-west.

a-west (əˈwɛst), *advb. phr.* [A *prep.*[1] + WEST; cf. *a-south*.] In the west; westward.
1809 J. BARLOW *Columb.* I. 670 The tired sun scarce finds their bounds awest. *a* **1849** MANGAN *Spectre Car.* Poems (1859) 266 The moon is waning far a-west.

awe-stricken (ˈɔːˌstrɪk(ə)n), *ppl. a.* = AWE-STRUCK. (Cf. *panic-stricken*, *terror-stricken*, etc.)
1853 GROTE *Greece* II. lxxxv. XI. 210 Approaching him with awe-stricken reverence. **1876** GEO. ELIOT *Dan. Der.* I. 363 Mab looked rather awe-stricken, as if this..were something preternatural.

awe-strike (ˈɔːˌstraɪk), *v.* [f. next by analysis.] To strike with awe. Hence **awe-striking** *ppl. a.*
1832 *Athenæum* No. 253. 568 An image such as he might well have awe-struck an idolatrous crowd. **1845** KINGLAKE *Eothen* xxix. 418 Preparations..for giving us an awe-striking reception. **1850** DE QUINCEY in Page *Life* (1877) II. xvii. 71 To shock, to startle and awe-strike. **1861** THACKERAY *Lovel* iv, With that air she had often awe-stricken good, simple Mr. Bonnington.

awe-struck (ˈɔːˌstrʌk), *ppl. a.* [f. AWE *sb.* + *struck*, pa. pple. of STRIKE *v.*] Struck with, or overwhelmed by, awe, terror, reverential fear, or profound admiration tinged with latent fear.
1634 MILTON *Comus* 301, I was awe-struck, And as I past, I worshipped. **1791** COWPER *Iliad* I. 417 In presence of the royal Chief awe-struck. **1846** TRENCH *Huls. Lect.* Ser. II. iii. 180 That exclamation of the awe-struck heathen centurion. **1870** H. MACMILLAN *Bible Teach.* ii. 28 Its majesty increasing as I gazed, until at last it..completely absorbed each awestruck sense.

aweto (ə'weɪtəʊ, ə'wiːtəʊ). [Maori.] The vegetable caterpillar of New Zealand, consisting of a fungus which fastens upon caterpillars and mummifies them; dried and burnt it produces a pigment.
1889 [see *vegetable caterpillar* s.v. VEGETABLE *a.* 7]. **1896** A. B. JONES in *Pearson's Mag.* Sept. 290 The dye..was a solution of burnt or powdered resin, or wood, or the aweto.

aweue, variant of AVIEW *v. Obs.*

awey(e, aweyte, obs. ff. AWAY, AWAIT.

awful ('ɔːfʊl), *a.* Forms: α. 1 eȝefull, 3 eiful(l, eifful. β. ahefull, 4 aghful(l, 6 aufull, 7 awefull, 7–8 awfull, 7–9 aweful, 5– awful. [f. AWE *sb.*[1] + -FUL, continuing the sense of OE. *eȝefull*: see AWE *sb.*[1] Occas. compared *awfuller, -est.* With sense 4, cf. the sense-history of Gr. δεινός awful.]
I. *objectively*: Awe-inspiring.
1. Causing dread; terrible, dreadful, appalling.
α. *c*885 K. ÆLFRED *Boeth.* xviii. §2 Romane nama..wæs ..maneȝum folce swiþe eȝefull. *c*1220 *Leg. St. Kath.* 39 þurh fearlac of eiful þreates.
β. *c*1230 *Wohunge* in *Cott. Hom.* 271 To fihte aȝaines alle þe ahefulle deuiles. *c*1425 WYNTOUN *Cron.* VIII. xxix. 90 And swore mony ane awful athe. **1602** WARNER *Alb. Eng.* Epit. (1612) 360 They reared thence vnto the Saxons such awefull armies. **1722** DE FOE *Plague* 64 The other scene was awful and full of terror. **1858** HAWTHORNE *Fr. & It. Jrnls.* I. 85 Too evidently looking his awfullest. **1876** GREEN *Short Hist.* viii.§9 A series of awful massacres.
2. Worthy of, or commanding, profound respect or reverential fear.
α. *c*1000 ÆLFRIC *Deut.* x. 17 God..mihtiȝ & eȝefull.
β. *a*1300 *Cursor M.* 7869 Dauid he was an aghful man, Ful rightwisli he regnd þan. *c*1425 WYNTOUN *Cron.* VI. xviii. 50 He wes in justice richt lauchful And til hys legis all awful. **1593** SHAKS. *2 Hen. VI*, v. i. 98 An awefull Princely Scepter. *a*1656 BP. HALL *Rem. Wks.* (1660) 11 Preaching..in the most awful Auditory of the University. **1711** ADDISON *Spect.* No. 169 ¶9 Cato's character..is rather awful than amiable. **1871** MACDUFF *Mem. Patmos* xix. 264 His truth, His awful holiness.
3. Solemnly impressive; sublimely majestic.
1660 STANLEY *Hist. Philos.* (1701) 179/1 Dwell awful Silence on the shady Hills. **1706** ADDISON *Rosamond* III. i, Domes in awful pomp arising. **1853** MAURICE *Proph. & Kings* iii. 39 How awful to feel himself there..an atom amidst the infinity of nature!
4. a. *slang.* Frightful, very ugly, monstrous; and *hence* as a mere intensive deriving its sense from the context = Exceedingly bad, great, long, etc.
1809 FESSENDEN *Pills Polit., Poet. & Philos.* 2, I fear our ..nation Is in an awful situation. **1816** PICKERING *Vocab.* 42 *Awful*, Disagreeable, ugly. *New England.* In New England many people would call a disagreeable medicine, *awful*; an ugly woman, an awful looking woman... This word, however, is never used except in conversation, and is far from being so common in the sea-ports now, as it was some years ago. **1818** KEATS *Let.* 27 Apr. (1958) I. 273 It is an awful while since you have heard from me. *a*1834 LAMB *Gent. Giantess* Misc. Wks. (1871) 363 She is indeed, as the Americans would express it, something awful. **1845** FORD *Handbk. Spain* i. 28 To what an awful extent the Spanish peasant..will consume garlic. **1870** MISS BRIDGMAN *R. Lynne* II. x. 212 He writes an awful scrawl. **1873** MISS BROUGHTON *Nancy* I. 26 What an awful duffer I am! *Mod.* What an awful time you've been!
b. As *adv.* = AWFULLY *adv.* 3.
1818 J. PALMER *Jrnl. Trav. U.S.* 131 [It is] awful hot. **1832** J. ROMILLY *Cambr. Diary* 24 June (1967) 17 An awful bad sermon from Hudleston. **1848** BARTLETT *Dict. Amer.* s.v., We not unfrequently hear such expressions as 'an awful cold day'. **1865** *Punch* 11 Mar. 103/1 We heard all about the horizon Seeing sights as was awful surprisin'. **1866** A. TROLLOPE *Belton Estate* III. x. 261 It is awful lonely here, too. **1876** 'MARK TWAIN' *Tom Sawyer* ii. 17 You see, Aunt Polly's awful particular about this fence. **1923** R. D. PAINE *Comr. Rolling Ocean* iii. 39 A prairie town called Follansbee that looks awful good to me.
II. *subjectively*: Filled with awe.
†**5.** Terror-stricken; timid, timorous, afraid. *Obs.*
*c*1590 MARLOWE *Faust.* ix. 37 Monarch of hell under whose black survey Great potentates do kneel with awful fear. **1681** MANTON *Serm. Ps.* xix. 74 Wks. 1872 VII. 280 Careful to please God, and awe-ful to offend him. *a*1748 WATTS (J.) A weak and awful reverence for antiquity.
6. Profoundly respectful or reverential.
1593 SHAKS. *Rich. II*, III. iii. 76 How dare thy ioynts forget To pay their awfull dutie to our presence? **1607** TOPSELL *Serpents* 641 The whole swarm and company is kept in awful order. **1641** STOCK *On Malachi* (1865) 56 An awful child will hardly be drawn..to do aught that his father hath.. forbidden him. **1781** GIBBON *Decl. & F.* III. l. 129 At an awful distance they cast away their garments. **1846** KEBLE *Lyra Innoc.* (1873) 2 Towards the East our awful greetings Are wafted. **1879** G. MACDONALD *Sir Gibbie* xii. 74 Gibbie sat calm, awe-ful..while the storm roared.
III. *Comb.*; adverbially, as in ***awful-gleaming, -looking***, or in parasynthetic deriv., as ***awful-eyed***.
1647 H. MORE *Song Soul* Notes 147/2 Manly, and awfull-eyed Fortitude. **1870** BRYANT *Homer* I. I. 12 The awful-gleaming eye.

awfully ('ɔːfʊlɪ), *adv.* [f. prec. + -LY[2]; cf. OE. *eȝesfullíc.*] In an awful manner.
I. *objectively*: With communication of awe.
1. So as to cause terror; terribly, dreadfully.
1375 BARBOUR *Bruce* IV. 321 Than lukit he awfully thame to. **1535** STEWART *Cron. Scot.* III. 51 Richart..aufullie syne enterit in the toun, With greit distructioun baith in fyre and blude. **1687** DRYDEN *Hind & P.* I. 304 The Lyon awfully forbids the prey. *a*1839 PRAED *Red Fisherm.*, Awfully were his features wrought By some dark dream.
2. So as to command reverence, or impress the imagination; sublimely, majestically.
*a*1300 *E.E. Psalter* cxxxix. 14 Mikled ertou aghfulli. **1727** THOMSON *Summer* 187 Who, Light himself!..dwells awfully retired From mortal eye. **1858** HAWTHORNE *Fr. & It. Jrnls.* I. 198 However awfully holy the subject.
3. *slang*, as simple intensive: Very, exceedingly, extremely. [Cf. Gr. δεινῶς awfully, exceedingly.]
[**1830** GEN. P. THOMPSON *Exerc.* (1842) I. 238 He will have made an awfully bad choice if he comes to be sentenced to be hanged.] **1859** LANG *Wand. India* 154 In the way of money-making..he is awfully clever. **1878** BLACK *Green Past.* ii. 15 You'll be awfully glad to get rid of me. *Mod.* It was awfully jolly!
II. *subjectively*: With a feeling of awe; with fear, timidly; with reverential fear, reverently. *arch.*
1583 GOLDING *Calvin on Deut.* viii. 43 To walke so much the more awefully when God hath shewed himselfe so bountiful. **1665** DRYDEN *To Duchess of York* 18 The waves in ranks were cast, As awfully as when God's people pass'd. **1725** POPE *Odyss.* xxiv. 126 And tim'rous pass'd, and awfully withdrew. **1790** BURKE *Fr. Rev.* 138 Awefully impressed with an idea that they act in trust. [**1820** KEATS *Isabel* vi, His heart beat awfully against his side.]

'**awfulness.** [f. as prec. + -NESS.]
1. The quality of inspiring with awe; terribleness, dreadfulness; impressive solemnity.
*a*1300 *E.E. Psalter* cxlv. 6 Might of þine aghfulnesses sal þai sai. **1651** BAXTER *Inf. Bapt.* 131 Where will be the solemn engagement and awfulness of Baptism? **1758** S. HAYWARD *Serm.* xvi. 479 The awfulness of falling into the hands of an angry God. **1870** HAWTHORNE *Eng. Note-Bks.* (1879) I. 104 The cold awfulness of an American judge.
2. The state of being full of awe; profound reverence, awe. *arch.* or *Obs.*
*a*1617 HIERON *Wks.* 1634 II. 436 An outward submissiuenesse without an inward awfulnesse were but hypocrisie. **1703** MAUNDRELL *Journ. Jerus.* (1721) 30 Tender'd to all the Guests..with the greatest care, and awfulness imaginable. **1712** ADDISON *Spect.* No. 415 ¶6 Every thing that is Majestick imprints an Awfulness and Reverence on the Mind.

awfyn, obs. var. ALFIN, bishop in chess.

awgor, -ure, obs. forms of AUGER.

†**a'whape**, *v. Obs.* 3–6; exc. in Spenser only in pa. pple. **awaped, awapped, awhaped.** [Etymol. uncertain; nothing similar recorded in OE.; but cf. Goth. *af-hwapjan* to choke, which would be in OE. **ofhweppan.* See WHAP.] To amaze, stupefy with fear, confound utterly.
*c*1300 *K. Alis.* 899 Alisaundre was sore awaped, That he was so ascaped. *c*1385 CHAUCER *L.G.W.* 814 Hire wympil let sche falle And tok non hed, so sore sche was a-wapid [*v.r.* a-whaped, aquaped]. **1430** LYDG. *Chron. Troy* I. i, Alone, awhaped, and a mate. **1591** SPENSER *M. Hubberd* 72 Deeply doo your sad words my wits awhape.

awheel (ə'(h)wiːl), *adv.* [f. A *prep.*[1] + WHEEL *sb.*] On wheels; on a bicycle, bicycling. Cf. A-WHEELS *advb. phr.*
1887 G. B. THAYER (*title*) Pedal and Path. Across the Continent Awheel and Afoot. **1888** *Pall Mall Gaz.* 25 Oct. 5, I have looked forward to my annual trips awheel..with .. delight. **1944** *Return to Attack* (Army Board, N.Z.) 12/2 Square mile after square mile of clanking armoured vehicles, rumbling lorries, bouncing guns and limbers, and roaring motor cycles... This huge force was completely awheel.

†**a-'wheels**, *advb. phr. Obs.* [A *prep.*[1] + WHEEL(S.] On wheels.
1617 B. JONSON *Masques, Vis. Delight* Wks. (1838) 605 And will they not cry then, the world runs awheels?

†**a'whene**, *v. Obs.* [OE. *ahwǽnan*; cf. OHG. *hwenjan, hwennen*, to shake.] To vex, trouble.
*c*1000 *Sax. Leechd.* I. 116 Gyf hwylc cyld ahwæned sy. *a*1250 *Owl & Night.* 1562 The lavedies..wel sore me ahweneth.

awher(e, north. f. OWHERE *adv. Obs.* everywhere.

†**a'wherf**, *v. Obs.* Pa. t. 1 ahwearf, *pl.* -urfon, 3 awharf. [OE. *ahweorfan*, f. A- *pref.* 1 + *hweorfan* to turn: see WHARF. In OE. also trans.] To turn away, turn round.
*a*1000 *Cædmon's Gen.* (Grein) 25 Hie of sib-lufan Godes ahwurfon. *c*1340 *Gaw. Gr. Knt.* 2220 He rusched on þat rurde rapely a þrowe, and wyth quettyng awharf er he wolde lyȝt.

a-'whet, *advb. phr.* [A *prep.*[1] + WHET. (On imperfect analogy.)] In act of whetting.
1866 CONINGTON *Æneid* VIII. 283 Snakes, with fangs a-whet.

awhether, aqueþer, weakened form of THOUGH-WHETHER, nevertheless.

awhile (ə'hwaɪl), *advb. phr.* Also 5 awhyle, 6 a-wyle. [Strictly two words, OE. *áne hwíle* (for) a while, a space of time: usually written in comb. since 13th c.] (For) a short time, (for) a little.
*a*1000 *Beowulf* 3528 Nú is þínes mæȝnes blǽd áne hwíle. *a*1250 *Owl & Night.* 199 þe ule one hwile hi biþohte. *a*1300 *Cursor M.* 10135 Leue ȝoure wantounship awhile. **1538** STARKEY *England* II. iii. 203 Aftur they haue byn brought up in lernyng A-wyle. **1725** DE FOE *Voy. round World* (1840) 104 Sailing awhile to the Southward. **1810** SCOTT *Lady of L.* I. xx, Awhile she paused, no answer came.
¶ Improperly written together, when there is no unification of sense, and *while* is purely a sb.
1489 CAXTON *Faytes of A.* I. xxiii. 72 It was doon but awhyle agoon. **1872** YEATS *Growth Comm.* 102 For awhile the facilities..enabled the Venetians, etc. **1882** OUIDA *Bimbi* 44 After awhile they seemed to pacify each other.

†**a-whiles, a wiles**, *advb. phr. Obs.* [f. A- *pref.* 11 (or A *prep.*[1]) + WHILES.] At times.
1546 *Supplic. Poor Commons* 68 A wiles; we think they haue red the story of a certen man.

a-whir (ə'hwɜː(r)), *advb. phr.* [A *prep.*[1] + WHIR.] In a whir, whirring.
1865 HOLLAND *Plain T.* v. 183 All the spindles awhirr.

a-whirl (ə'hwɜːl), *advb. phr.* [A *prep.*[1] + WHIRL.] In a whirl, whirling.
1883 *Blackw. Mag.* Aug. 233 With his wits awhirl.

awhit, written together for *a whit* in 16–17th c.
1642 ROGERS *Naaman* 871 It never troubles you awhit!

†**a'wide**, *adv. Obs.* [f. WIDE, on assumed analogy to *afar, ahigh*, etc.] Wide, widely.
1609 BIBLE (Douay) *Ps.* xxxiv. 21 They opened their mouth awide upon me. **1642** H. MORE *Song of Soul* II. ii. I. xiv, She from her own self awide is led.

awiht, OE. and EE. form of AUGHT *sb.*[2]

awild, variant of AWELD *v. Obs.* to control.

†**a'wild-en**, *v. Obs. rare.* [OE. *awildian*, f. A- *pref.* 1 + **wildian*, f. *wilde* WILD *a.*] *intr.* To become wild or unruly.
*c*1230 *Ancr. R.* 176 Heo wolde elles awilden [*v.r.* awilegen] oðer leten to wel of hire suluen.

†**a'wileg-en, -ig-en**, *v. Obs.* [Perh. for an OE. **awildcian*, through **awil(d)gian* (Sievers); cf. the ON. verbs in *-ka* (Vigf. p. xxiv. 1st conj.) Thus = prec.] **a.** *intr.* To become wild or unruly. **b.** *trans.* To make wild, dazzle (the eyes).
*c*1230 *Ancr. R.* 136 þet fleschs þet awiligeð [*v.r.* wildes] so sone hit euer uetteð. *Ibid.* 282 Hwit awilegeð þe eien.

†**a'will**, *v. Obs. rare*[−1]. [f. A- *pref.* 1 (or 6) + WILL *v.*] To will.
1399 LANGL. *Rich. Redeless* III. 210 þat had awilled his wyll as wisdom him taughte.

†**a-will**, *advb. phr. Obs.* [A *prep.*[1] + WILL *sb.*] At one's will, to one's pleasure or satisfaction.
*a*1250 *Owl & N.* 1720 þe wrenne..fale manne song awille.

†**a'win**, *v. Obs.* For forms see WIN *v.* [OE. *awinnan*, f. A- *pref.* 1 + *winnan* to WIN; cf. OHG. *irwinnan*, MHG. *erwinnen.*]
1. *intr.* To labour. (Only in OE.)
*c*950 *Lindisf. Gosp.* John iv. 38 Oðero awunnon [*Ags. G.* swuncon].
2. To overcome, conquer; to win, gain, obtain.
*c*1000 *Cædmon's Dan.* (Grein) 654 Súsl wæs awunnen. **1250** LAY. 7209 þe þridden deal he awan of þisse worl[d]e riche. *a*1300 *Floriz & Bl.* 205 þilke maide to awinne. **1340** *Ayenb.* 85 þis lhordssip he..naȝt ayen ne miȝte awynne.
b. with *subord. cl.* and *absol.*
1250 LAY. 10876 Mid fihte he hadde awonne þat he was king of londe. *a*1300 *K. Horn* 1071 Ne miȝte he awynne þat he come þerinne. *c*1320 *Sir Tristr.* II. lxxxvi, Ay when thai might awinne, Ther playd Ysoude and he.

awing, aweing ('ɔːɪŋ), *vbl. sb.* [f. AWE *v.* + -ING[1].] The action of inspiring with awe.
1656 J. CHALONER *Isle of Man* in D. King *Vale Royall* IV. 32 He might have had in his eye the awing of the Natives. **1877** MORRIS *Sigurd* II. (1880) 151 The Helm of Aweing, that the Fear of earth-folk bore.

awing, aweing, *ppl. a.* [f. as prec. + -ING[2].] Causing dread, reverential fear, or solemnity.
1632 J. HAYWARD *Eromena* 188 This queene bare in her countenance..an awing majestie. **1799** S. TURNER *Anglo-Sax.* (1828) I. i. 24 The awing head of Memnon. **1881** M. LEWIS *Two Pretty G.* I. 187 There is something awing in looking down upon the great city.

a-wing (ə'wɪŋ), *advb. phr.* [A *prep.*[1] + WING.] On the wing; fluttering.
1823 J. WILSON *Noct. Ambr.* I. 293 Swallows coming awing frae God knows where. **1850** MRS. BROWNING *Poems* II. 186 The island's edges are a-wing With trees that overbranch—The sea with song-birds.

a-wink (ə'wɪŋk), *advb. phr.* [A *prep.*[1] + WINK.] Winking.
1883 E. ARNOLD *Ind. Idylls* 59 By their side..his feet upon the earth, And eyes awink, stood Nala.

awiriȝe, var. AWARIE *v. Obs.* to curse.

awise, obs. Sc. f. ADVICE, ADVISE, ADVISY.

†a'wit, *v. Obs.* Pa. t. **awiste.** [f. A- *pref.* 1 + OE. *witan* to perceive, know, 'wit.'] *trans.* **a.** To perceive, know. **b.** To watch over, command (a troop).

c1200 *Moral Ode* 15 in *Lamb. Hom.* 288 Elde me is bistolen on ær ic hit a-wuste [*rimes with* myste; *other MSS.* wiste, iwiste]. **1250** LAY. 27264 Kai awiste one [ferde].

†awk (ɔːk), *a.* (*adv.*, *sb.*) *Obs.* Also 5-7 **awke,** 6-7 **auk(e,** 7 **awck.** [prob. a. ON. *afug, öfug, öfig* (Sw. *afvig*) turned the wrong way, back foremost, cogn. with OHG. *apuh, apah,* MHG. *ebech, ebich,* mod.G. dial. *äbich,* OS. *abich, aboh*; a deriv. of *af* away, identified by Fick with OSkr. *apák, apáñch* 'turned away.' Old Northumbrian has **afuh* in *afu(h)lic* 'perverse,' in Prol. to Lindisf. Gospels; but the later use of the word was probably from ON. The phonetic change of *afug* to *awk,* is the same as in *hafoc, hawk.*] **A.** *adj.*

1. Directed the other way or in the wrong direction, back-handed, from the left hand.

c1440 *Promp. Parv.* 18 Awke or wronge, *sinister.* **1530** PALSGR. 196 Auke stroke, *reuers.* **1557** *K. Arthur* (Copl.) v. x, With an awke stroke gaue hym a grete wounde. **1634** *Malory's Arthur* I. xcvii. 172.

2. Untoward, froward, perverse, in nature or disposition.

c1440 *Promp. Parv.* 18 Awke or angry, *contrarius, bilosus, perversus.* **1567** MAPLET *Gr. Forest* 25 A preposterous maner in judging, and an awke wit. **1587** GOLDING *De Mornay* xix. (1617) 331 The awk opinions of the Stoicks. **1642** ROGERS *Naaman* 836 Our natures more crooked, inconstant, awk, and perverse. **1655** GURNALL *Chr. in Arm.* II. 533 The soul, awke and listlesse enough to any duty.

3. Out-of-the-way, odd, strange. *rare.*

c1440 *Morte Arth.* 13 Off elders of alde tyme and of theire awke dedys.

4. Untoward to deal with, awkward to use, clumsy.

1593 G. HARVEY *New Lett.,* The roughest and awkest things are not so cumbersome. **1674** N. FAIRFAX *Bulk & Selv.* 152 Birds..build nests with such an auk tool, their beak.

B. *adv.* in phrases:

1. *to ring awk*: the wrong way, backward.

1636 S. WARD *Serm.* (1862) 91 When the bells ring awke, every man brings his bucket to the quenching of this fire. **1647** WARD *Simp. Cobler* 38 The bells in all the steeples will ring awke. **1694** R. LESTRANGE *Fables* ccci, Ringing as Awk as the Bells, to give notice of the Conflagration.

2. *to sing awk*: in sinister or ill-omened wise.

1600 HOLLAND *Livy* VI. xli. 247 What if a bird sing auke or crowe crosse and contrarie [*occinuerit*]?

C. *sb.* (So the neuter of the adj. in OHG.) Backhandedness, untowardness, awkwardness.

1644 BULWER *Chiron.* 128 To fling words at his Auditors out of the Auke of utterance. **1674** N. FAIRFAX *Bulk & Selv.* 108 What we have hitherto spoken, will seem to have less of auk in it.

†'awkly, *a. Obs.* [f. AWK *a.* + -LY[1]: identical with the OE. *avu[h]líc* (see AWK), but apparently formed afresh in 16th c.] Untoward, perverse.

[c950 *Lindisf. Gosp.* Matt. *Prol.* 2 *Perversa contentio* (glossed) wiðirword *vel* flitta *vel* afvlic ȝeflit.] **1556** ABP. PARKER *Ps.* xxxvi. 2 So wilfull he goes in hys awkly deuyse.

†'awkly, *adv. Obs.* [f. AWK *a.* + -LY[2].]

1. In the wrong direction, in backhanded or lefthanded wise; *hence,* sinisterly, unluckily.

c1440 *Promp. Parv.* 18 Awkly or wrongly, *sinistre.* **1564** GOLDING *Trogus Pomp.* 18 They [the Egyptians] write their letters awkelie [*i.e.* from right to left]. **1565** —— *Ovid's Met.* v. (1593) 109 Beguild as then by birds that aukly flew. **1603** HOLLAND *Plutarch's Mor.* 148 Ignorant and untaught persons many times when fortune presenteth herselfe unto them on the right hand, receive her awkly, turning to the left side. **1639** J. CLARKE *Parœmiol.* 7 To doe any thing unluckily, awkley.

2. Perversely, untowardly.

c1440 *Promp. Parv.* 18 Awkely, or wrawely, *perverse, contrarie.* **1612** T. TAYLOR *Comm. Titus* ii. 9 Many seruants ..cast off all care of pleasing, aukly attempt and performe their businesse as at a wrong end, or with a left hand.

3. In ungainly fashion, clumsily, awkwardly.

1603 SIR C. HEYDON *Jud. Astrol.* iii. 120 His Phrase sowndes awkly in mine eares. **1662** FULLER *Worthies* I. 150 For one that undertaketh a thing awkely or ungeenly, *Camelus saltat.*

†'awkness. *Obs.* [f. AWK *a.* + -NESS.] Wrongness, irrationality, perversity, untowardness, awkwardness, ineptitude.

1587 GOLDING *De Mornay* xxxii. (1617) 558 The skilfull [man] can..by his cunning ouercome the awknesse of his stuffe. **1615** HIERON *Wks.* I. 602 A reprobate awknes to all good. **1655** GURNALL *Chr. in Arm.* xv. §1 (1669) 164/1 So much awknesse and unwillingnesse to come to God's foot. **1668** SPURSTON *Spir. Chymist* Pref. 5 Awkness to this beneficial employment. **1674** N. FAIRFAX *Bulk & Selv.* 171 By shewing the aukness or great absurdity on the other side.

awkward ('ɔːkwəd), *adv.* and *a.* Forms: 4 **awkeward,** 4-5 **aykeward, owkeward,** 4-6 **awkwarde,** 6 **awkwar, ackward, acquart, aukerward,** 6-7 **aukeward(e,** 7 **auker'd, awkerd,** 7-8 **awkard,** 8 **aukard,** 6-9 **aukward,** 6- **awkward;** 9 *dial.* **awkwart, ackart,** etc. [f. AWK *a.* + -WARD, *i.e.* 'in an awk direction'; cf. *forward, backward.* Like other adverbs in *-ward,* at length also used adjectively, cf. *to go forward, a forward motion, a forward youth.*]

†**A.** *adv.* **1.** In the wrong direction, in the wrong way. **a.** Upside down; hindside foremost. **b.** In a backward direction, with a back stroke. **c.** Asquint. **d.** In some modern dialects = AWALT, q.v. *Obs.* or *dial.*

1340 HAMPOLE *Pr. Consc.* 1541 Þe world þai all awkeward sett. c1440 *Morte Arth.* 2247 The emperour thane egerly at Arthure he strykez, Awkwarde on þe umbrere. c1470 HENRY *Wallace* I. 407 With the swerd awkwart he him gawe Wndyr the hat. **1530** PALSGR. 691/2, I feare me some house be afyre..for they rynge aukewarde. **1589** NASHE *Almond for P.* 14a, Eternitie, that knew how aukward he shoulde looke to all honesty, consulted..to make him squint-eied.

B. *adj.*

†**1.** Turned the wrong way, averted, back-handed; not straightforward, oblique. *Obs.*

1513 DOUGLAS *Æneis* IV. vii. 2 Dido agreuit ay..With acquart luik gan towart him behald. **1532** *Dice Play* 22 Who so hath not some aukerward way to help himself, but foloweth his nose..always straight forward. **1866** *Cumbrld. Border Bal.* 468 Till Græme gae Bewick an ackward stroke.

†**2.** Froward, untoward, perverse, in conduct. (Passing into 'cross-grained, cantankerous, disagreeable in behaviour,' and so into 7 b.) *Obs.*

1530 PALSGR. 305/2 Awkwarde, frowarde, *peruers.* **1548** UDALL, etc. *Erasm. Par. Matt.* xxiii. 24 Blynde guydes..of an awkwarde religion doe streigne out a gnatte, and swalowe of a camell. **1634** PRESTON *New Covt.* 310 The heart..is awkward and froward and contentious. **1678** BUTLER *Hud.* III. iii. 619 But was implacable and auker'd To all that Interlop'd and Hawker'd. **1743** FIELDING *J. Wild* I. v. (1762) 244, I haue an aukward pride in my nature. **1755** B. MARTIN *Mag. Arts & Sc.* 61 They had such aukward Notions of Things.

†**3.** Untoward, unfavourable, adverse to one's course. *lit.* and *fig. Obs.*

1587 FLEMING *Contn. Holinshed* III. 1555/1 The ackward and frowning hap of sundrie woorthie gentlemen. **1590** MARLOWE *Edw. II,* IV. vi, With awkward winds and with sore tempests driven. **1593** SHAKS. *2 Hen. VI,* III. ii. 83 Twice by aukward winde from Englands banke Droue backe againe. **1663** *Flagellum* or *O. Cromwell* (1672) 21 Which aukward beginning..sorted with a very sorry Issue.

4. a. Of things: Untoward or unfavourable for one's purpose; ill-adapted for use; clumsy in operation.

1695 WOODWARD *Nat. Hist. Earth* I. (1723) 60 The Methods they used of Agriculture..were so aukward and tedious. **1743** tr. *Heister's Surg.* 452 Perform good Cures, though in an aukward manner. **1783** POTTS *Chirurg.* II. 7 A multitude of awkward unmanageable instruments. **1857** RUSKIN *Pol. Econ. Art* 19 Awkward and unfortunate efforts ..at the development of a social system.

b. Of persons: Lacking dexterity or skill in performing their part; clumsy in action, bungling. Phr. ***awkward squad***: see SQUAD *sb.*[1] 1 b.

1530 PALSGR. 305/2 Awkwar leftehanded, *gauche.* **1672** MARVELL *Reh. Transp.* I. 270 They were as unexpert as their Souldiers aukward. **1727** SWIFT *Gulliver* III. ii. 189, I have not seen a more clumsy, aukward, and unhandy people. **1816** J. GILCHRIST *Philos. Etym.* 204 They consider him as belonging to the awkward squad. **1866** G. MACDONALD *Ann. Q. Neighb.* xii. (1878) 241 What a blundering awkward fellow I was to startle you as I did.

5. Ungraceful, ungainly in action or form; uncouth: **a.** of things, action, speech, etc.

1606 SHAKS. *Tr. & Cr.* I. iii. 149 With ridiculous and aukward action..He Pageants vs. **1711** ADDISON *Spect.* No. 299 ¶2 That they may not learn any of my aukward Tricks. **1718** POPE *Iliad* I. 770 Vulcan with awkward grace his office plies. **1865** DICKENS *Mut. Fr.* vii. 314 A variety of awkward gambols.

b. of persons.

1665 PEPYS *Diary* 15 July, The most awkerd man I ever met with in my life. **1678** T. RYMER in *Shaks. C. Praise* 366 Awkward and unsightly, as the monster in the Tempest. **1773** GOLDSM. *Stoops to Conq.* I. i, The son an aukward booby. **1840** CARLYLE *Heroes* i. (1858) 199 Large awkward gianthood.

6. a. Of things: Embarrassing, inconvenient.

1709 SWIFT *Adv. Relig.* Wks. 1755 II. I. 108 If an awkward shame..have not a greater share in this mistaken conduct. **1779** J. MOORE *View Soc. Fr.* II. 182 Both seem rather in an awkward situation. **1876** FREEMAN *Norm. Conq.* IV. xvii. 58 The two Minsters of Winchester Old and New stood in awkward neighbourhood to each other.

b. Of persons: Not at one's ease; embarrassed.

1713 STEELE *Englishm.* No. 44. 288, I am very aukward in the Endeavour. **1834** L. HUNT *Town* iii. (1848) 146 He was ..beginning to feel awkward with his Whig friends. **1845** DISRAELI *Sybil* (1863) 138 It is civilization that makes us awkward; for it gives us an uncertain position.

7. a. Of things: Not easy to deal with; requiring cautious action; *euphemistic for* 'rather dangerous.'

1860 TYNDALL *Glac.* I. §16. 118 We let ourselves down an awkward face of rock. **1872** JENKINSON *Guide Eng. Lakes* (1879) 195 The ridge is rather awkward-looking. **1881** BLACKMORE *Christowell* xi, 'Be careful, if you please, there is an awkward step here.'

b. Of persons: Dangerous to meddle with.

1863 MRS. C. CLARKE *Shaks. Char.* vi. 144 He is an 'awkward customer' when his confidence is betrayed.

c. Phr. ***the awkward age***: the time of life when one is no longer a child and yet not properly grown up. (Cf. F. *l' âge ingrat.*)

1895 *Windsor Mag.* I. 705/1 She was..at what ladies call 'the awkward age'. **1928** *Daily Mirror* 7 Dec. 11/2 'How old are you, Bobbie?' 'I'm just at the awkward age.' 'What do you call the awkward age?' 'I'm too old to cry and too young to swear.'

'awkwardish, *a.* Also 7 **ocwardish.** [f. AWKWARD *a.* + -ISH.] Rather awkward. (*Colloquial.*)

1603 FLORIO *Montaigne* I. lvi. (1632) 185 He was so changed from himselfe, and become so ocwardish. **1860** *Punch* 14 July, We may be awkwardish at first.

'awkwardly, *adv.* [f. as prec. + -LY[2].] In an awkward manner.

†**1.** Wrongly, perversely. *Obs.*

c1400 *Destr. Troy* x. 4379 At attens all folke aykewardly worshippid Minerva, a maument. *Ibid.* XIX. 8139 Sum fend ..þat onsward the owkewardly.

2. Without dexterity in action; with ill adaptation to a purpose; in a bungling or clumsy way; without ease of manner, inelegantly, ungracefully.

1663 COWLEY *Verses & Ess.* (1669) 85 Who stands not aukwardly in his own light. **1697** DRYDEN *Virg. Past.* Pref., And handle their Sheep-Hook as awkardly, as they do their Oaten-Reed. **1704** *Lond. Gaz.* No. 4064/6 Envy and Malice ..awkerdly acknowledge what they cannot deny. **1816** in *Macready's Remin.* I. 129 The plainest and most awkwardly-made man. **1867** FREEMAN *Norm. Conq.* (1876) I. App. 780 The mention of Godwine comes in very awkwardly.

3. Embarrassingly, inconveniently; dangerously.

1674 MARVELL *Reh. Transp.* II. 359 Twould go very hard and aukwardly with you. **1812** L. HUNT in *Examiner* 28 Sept. 610/1, I am aukwardly situated.

'awkwardness. [f. as prec. + -NESS.]

†**1.** Untowardness, perversity. *Obs.*

1674 N. FAIRFAX *Bulk & Selv.* 189 And to pitch upon two or more best times, for a thing to begin in, is to pitch upon one of the worser kinds of awkwardness.

2. Lack of skill or dexterity; clumsiness.

a1770 MISS TALBOT *Lett. etc.* (1808) 21 With all my awkwardness of making speeches. **1848** LYTTON *Harold* IV. iv, Tostig laughed scornfully at Harold's awkwardness.

3. Awkward manner or appearance; lack of ease and grace; inelegance.

1704 ADDISON *Italy* (1733) 37 A kind of aukwardness in the Italians. **1767** FORDYCE *Serm. Yng. Wom.* I. iii. 89 The aukwardness that is apt to adhere to young persons who are confined at home. **1815** SCOTT *Guy M.* iii, A voice whose harshness corresponded with the awkwardness of his figure.

4. Awkward circumstance or feeling; inconvenience, embarrassment, unpleasantness.

1788 PITT in G. Rose *Diaries* (1860) I. 85 The awkwardness of having Sir Joseph Yorke the companion of his honours. **1837** J. H. NEWMAN *Par. Serm.* I. xii. 155 They feel the painfulness of rebuking another, and..the awkwardness of it. **1883** BLACK *Shandon B.* xxvii, [Her] pleasant humour..dispersed these awkwardnesses.

†'awky, *a. Obs.* [f. AWK (perh. in its subst. use) + -Y.] Untoward, difficult, awkward.

1655 GURNALL *Chr. in Arm.* v. §1 (1669) 32/1 It is so awky a business..to recover the activity of grace once lost.

awl (ɔːl). Forms: 1 **æl, eal,** 1-4 **al,** 3 **el,** 3-5 **alle,** 3-7 **aule,** 4 **ele,** 6 **awle,** 6-7 **all,** 8 **aul,** 8- **awl;** also 5 **nal,** 6 **nalle,** 6-7 **nall,** 7 **naul, nawl(e.** [OE. *æl,* cognate with OHG. *ala,* MHG. *ale,* mod.G. *ahle,* ON. *alr* (cf. Skr. *árá*). The length of the vowel in the old Germanic languages is uncertain; and there is some doubt as to its being originally a Teutonic word. In 15-17th c. a mistaken division of *an awl* as *a nawl* gave the form with initial *n.*]

1. A small tool, having a slender, cylindrical, tapering, sharp-pointed blade, with which holes may be pierced; a piercer, pricker, bodkin.

c885 *Laws of Ælfred* 11 (Bosw.) þurhþyrliȝe his eáre mid eale. c1000 ÆLFRIC *Lev.* xxv. 10 þirliȝe his eáre mid ale. **1382** WYCLIF *Ex.* xxi. 6 He shal thril his eer with an alle [**1388** a nal, an al; COVERDALE, botkin; *Genev.* awle; **1611** aule]. **1483** CAXTON *Gold. Leg.* 127/2 It is harde to the stryue ayenst the alle or prycke. **1607** TOPSELL *Four-f. Beasts* 144 The worm..must be pulled out by some naul or needle. **1727** SWIFT *Gulliver* II. vi. 145 To bore little holes with a fine awl. **1865** LUBBOCK *Preh. Times* xv. (1869) 537 Awls and sinews would in our hands be but poor substitutes for needles and thread.

2. *esp.* The tool of this description used by shoemakers for piercing holes in leather. Cf. also BRADAWL (used by carpenters).

c1000 *Colloq. Monast.* 30 (Bosw.) Hwanon sceó-wyrhtan æl? c1230 *Ancr. R.* 324 A sutare [þet haueð forloren] his el. **1340** *Ayenb.* 66 More boryinde þanne zouteres eles. **1564** BECON *Early Wks.* Gen. Pref. (1843) 5 The shoemaker [giveth over] his nalle and thread. **1601** HOLLAND *Pliny* I. 331 Their horns be like a shoomakers Nall blade. **1601** SHAKS. *Jul. C.* I. i. 25 Truly sir, all that I liue by, is with the Aule. **1853** *Arab. Nts.* (Rtldg.) 639 Seated on his stool, with his awl in his hand, ready to begin work.

b. *fig.* and *proverb.* applied to the occupation of a shoemaker. Cf. *last.*

1632 B. JONSON in *Brome's North. Lasse* Introd. 9 The Cobler kept him to his nall. **1826** SCOTT *Woodst.* viii. 205 Doubt not that thou shalt be set beyond thine awl.

c. *to pack up one's awls*: cf. ALL B 7 b. (It is possible that the phrase originated with this word, or in a pun on *all* and *awl.*)

1674 COTTON *Voy. Irel.* III. 10, I then call to pay, And packing my nawls, whipt to horse, and away.

3. *transf.* A sharp spine, or boring organ.

1340 *Ayenb.* 66 þe þornhog þet ys al ywryȝe myd prikyinde eles. **1802** PALEY *Nat. Theol.* xix. §2 The awl or borer, fixed at the tails of various species of flies.

†**4.** ? A dagger. *Obs.*

1387 TREVISA *Higden* Rolls IV. 209 I-slawe with alles [*capulis*] of comune..brawlers.

5. *Comb.* **awl-bird**, provincial name of the Green Woodpecker (*Picus viridis*); **awl-shaped** *a.*, subulate; **awl-wort**, a plant (*Subularia aquatica*) so named from its leaves.

1802 G. MONTAGU *Ornith. Dict.* (1833) 385 Awl Bird. **1762** ELLIS in *Phil. Trans.* LII. 664 The female has a remarkable..awl shaped papilla. **1880** GRAY *Bot. Text-bk.* 398 *Awl-shaped*, narrow, terete or somewhat so, and attenuate from a broader base to a slender or rigid point. **1797** MILLER *Gard. Dict.* s.v. *Subularia*, Awl-wort.

†**a'wlated**, *pa. pple. Obs. rare*$^{-1}$. [f. A- *pref.* 1 (or 6) + OE. *wlǽtian*, impers. *me wlǽtað* 'it disgusts me': see WLATE.] Disgusted.

1297 R. GLOUC. 485 The king was somdel awlated..That fram so vnclene thinges eni mete him com.

awlbe, awle, obs. forms of ALB, HALL.

†**a'wlench**, *v. Obs.* [f. A- *pref.* 1 + OE. *wlęncan* (see WLENCH); or for OE. *ȝewlęncan*, = OLG. *giwlenkian*.] To make splendid, adorn.

[*c* **1000** in Thorpe *Charters* 129 (Bosw.) Gewlenced mid sum dǽle Mercna ríces.] *c* **1200** *Trin. Coll. Hom.* 163 He awlencð his daie mid cloðes more þan him seluen.

awless, variant of AWELESS.

†**awly**, *a. Obs.* Only in the early forms: 3 eilich, 4 aghlich. [f. AWE *sb.*[1]: see -LY[1]; the earlier *eilich*:—OE. **ęgelíc*, cogn. w. OHG. *egilîh*, MHG. *egelîch*. Cf. OE. *ęgeslíc*, EE. *eislich*.] Awful, dreadful, terrible.

c **1200** *Trin. Coll. Hom.* 5 þat oðer tocume of ure louerd.. ô domes dai. is swiðe eiliche. *c* **1340** *Gaw. & Gr. Knt.* 136 An aghlich mayster.

†**awly**, *adv. Obs.* Only in the early forms: 3 aȝeliche, 4 aȝly. [f. prec.: see -LY[2].] Awfully, terribly, dreadfully.

c **1230** *Ancr. R.* 56 Nu cumeð forð a feble mon and halt him þauh heiliche [*v.r.* aȝeliche]. *c* **1325** *E.E. Allit. P.* B. 937 þe aungelez..aȝly hem þratten. *Ibid.* 874.

awm(e, obs. form of AAM, AUM, AIM.

awmblare, awmiler, obs. forms of AMBLER.

awmbrie, -y, awmery, obs. forms of AMBRY.

awmener(e, -merer, awmer, awmnere, obs. forms of ALMONER.

†'**awmere**. *Obs.* [contr. of *awmenere*: see ALMONER[2]; or f. *aumes* ALMS + -ER[1].] Alms-purse.

c **1400** *Rom. Rose* 2270 Streit gloves, with awmere Of silk.

awmous, Sc. form of ALMOUS.

awmyr (*Promp. Parv.*), var. AMBER *sb.*[2]

awn (ɔːn), *sb.* Forms: 3 agune, 4–7 awne, 5 awene, (avene, nawn), 6 aane, ane, aune, 7 hawne, 8 ang, 7– awn. [apparently a. ON. *ǫgn*, pl. *agnar* str. f. (Sw. *agn*, Da. *avn(e)*; cf. OHG. *agana*, MHG. *agene*, *agne*, *ane*, mod.G. *ahne*, Goth. *ahana*. The OE. form does not occur.] The delicate spinous process, or 'beard,' that terminates the grain-sheath of barley, oats, and other grasses; extended in *Bot.* to any similar bristly growth.

a **1300** W. DE BIBLESW. in Wright *Voc.* 155 *Des arestes*, fro agunes. *c* **1375** ? BARBOUR *St. Blasius* 345 Quha-sa-euire in þare throt Seknes has, awne ore mot Ore ony-kine perplexite. *c* **1440** *Promp. Parv.* 18 Avene of corn (*v.r.* awene, awne), *arista*. *c* **1450** in Wright *Voc.* 233/2 *Hec arista*, a nawn. **1523** FITZHERB. *Husb.*§34 Polerde wheate hath noo anis. **1562** TURNER *Herbal* II. 17 a, Yᵉ barley eare..hath longe aunes. **1662** FULLER *Worthies* II. 189 Not that the Hawnes thereof are Spears to fright the Mildew from it, but advantageous Gutters to slide it away the sooner. **1737** BRACKEN *Farriery* (1756) I. xi. 103 A Brush made of a few Rye or Barley-angs. **1805** LUCCOCK *Nat. Wool* 37 The singular hooked awn, or spinous termination of the scales of the receptacle [of the teazle]. **1870** HOOKER *Stud. Flora* 230 Anthers with dorsal awns, Whortleberry, Bilberry.

b. *Comb.* **awn-like** *a.*, resembling an awn.

1879 JEFFERIES *Wild Life in S.C.* 227 The awn-like seeds of other [grasses].

awn (ɔːn), *v.*[1] [f. prec. sb.] To get rid of the awns. Cf. *to shell* (peas). Hence **awning** *vbl. sb.*

1807 VANCOUVER *Agric. Devon* (1813) 172 The awning iron is..used, previous to the last winnowing of the barley.

†**awn(e**, *v.*[2] *Obs.* [Found in Ormin only. Of obscure formation; related to Goth. *augjan*, OHG. *augan*, *ougan*, MHG. *ougen*, OS. *ôgian*, OFris. *auwa*, OE. *éawan* (cf. ATEW). Mätzner says that MHG. had also a form *ougenen* as a variant of *ougen*.] *trans.* To put before a person's eyes; to show, manifest. *refl.* To manifest oneself, appear.

c **1200** ORMIN 7649 þurrh whamm shall maniȝ dærne þohht Beon oppnedd all & awwnedd. *Ibid.* 9607 Nu sket shall Godess Sune Crist Himm awwnenn her onn eorþe.

awn (ɔːn), *v.*[3] [Back-formation from AWNING.] **a.** *intr.* To hang as or like an awning. **b.** *trans.* To cover or shelter with an awning. Said also of the awning itself. Cf. AWNED *ppl. a.*[2] So '**awning** *ppl. a.*

a **1839** GALT *Demon Destiny* (1840) VII. 48 The awning clouds were as a cavern's ceil. **1844** THACKERAY *Wks.* (1900) XIII. 213 Trafalgar Square is to be awned in. **1890** *Longm. Mag.* Apr. 630 Trust Mrs. Robson for seeing that her guests are well awned on a night like this. **1904** *Daily Chron.* 8 July 7/3 The ball rested..on the canvas that goes to awn the first floor.

awn(e, obs. form of OWN.

awnderne, -dyryn, -dyrn, obs. ff. ANDIRON.

awned (ɔːnd), *ppl. a.*[1] [f. AWN *sb.* + -ED[2].] Furnished with an awn; bearded.

1801 WITHERING *Bot. Arrangem.* III. 595 Its..awned calyx distinguishes it. **1835** LINDLEY *Introd. Bot.* (1848) II. 356 *Awned*, terminated in a hard, straight, subulate point.

awned, *ppl. a.*[2] [badly f. AWN-ING + -ED[2].] Furnished or covered with an awning; awninged.

1881 MRS. HUNT *Childr. Jerus.* 45 The chief lady..was packed into the awned tray between the mules. **1884** J. ADY in *Knowledge* 30 May 387 The awned out-of-door spaces.

awner ('ɔːnə(r)). [f. AWN *v.*[1] + -ER[1].] One who or that which awns; *spec.* a machine for removing the awns from grain.

1881 in *Imp. Dict.* **1884** J. SCOTT *Barn Implements & Machines* x. 101 Awners or Hummelling Machines..are for the purpose of removing the awns from the barley, and are indispensable on a barley-growing farm. **1930** *Engineering* 18 July 83/1 The separated grain in the first dresser is delivered into an elevator, which feeds either into a barley awner or a distributing trough, as preferred.

awning ('ɔːnɪŋ). Also (7 yawning), 8 auning. [A word of obscure origin, apparently at first only in nautical use. Probably to be referred (as by Wedgwood) to Fr. *auvent* 'a penthouse of cloth, etc. before a shop window, etc.' Cotgr., early plurals in Littré *auvens*, *auvans*, med.L. *auvanna*, *auvannus*, whence **auvan*, **auwn*, *awn*; the termination is of course Eng. -ING. E. Müller refers it to Low German *havenung*, f. *haven* harbour, in sense of 'a shelter from wind and weather'; Skeat compares 'Pers. *áwan*, *áwang*, anything suspended, *awangān* hanging, *awnang* a clothes-line'; but neither of these is applied in its own language to an awning; in particular an oriental origin seems incompatible with the history. F. *auvent* is itself of doubtful etymol. See Diez, Littré, Du Cange.]

1. A roof-like covering of canvas or similar material, used as a shelter from sun, rain, etc.; *esp.* above the deck of a vessel.

1624 CAPT. SMITH *Virginia* in *Harper's Mag.* Apr. (1884) 712/1 Wee did hang an awning (which is an old saile) to.. trees to shadow us from the Sunne. **1626** —— *Accid. Yng. Seamen* 30 A trar-pawling or yawning. **1627** —— *Seaman's Gram.* vi. 27 An Awning..is but the bots saile..brought ouer the yard and stay, and boumed out with the boat hooke. **1725** BRADLEY *Fam. Dict.* s.v. *Orange tree*, An Awning of Bass-Mats..will..keep the Sun and Winds from the Orange-Trees. **1877** A. B. EDWARDS *Up Nile* vi. 135 Too hot on deck without the awning.

2. *transf.* **a.** *Naut.* That part of the poop-deck which is continued forward beyond the bulk-head of the cabin; hence ***awning-deck(ed***. **b.** *gen.* A shelter.

1764 VEITCH in *Phil. Trans.* LIV. 292 The auning, which is a projection of the deck of the cabin to shelter from the sun or rain. **1826** H. N. COLERIDGE *West Indies* 206 An alley of the graceful bamboo..which might serve for a temporary awning. **1869** SIR E. REED *Ship Build.* xv. 294 These ships ..have a complete spar deck..and an awning-deck above this. **1879** H. CRAGGS in *Daily News* 3/3 All ocean steamers should be..awning-decked fore and aft.

Hence **awninged** ('ɔːnɪŋd), *ppl. a.* [see -ED[2]], furnished with an awning; (with ***awninged off*** cf. *railed off*). '**awningless** *a.*, without awning.

1881 E. COXON *Basil Pl.* I. 78 Before the awninged door. **1881** NICHOLSON *Sword to Share* xxiv. 174 A small portion —over the propeller—is awninged off. **1865** MISS BRADDON *Only a Clod* xxxiii. 267 In an awningless boat under a broiling sun.

awnless ('ɔːnlɪs), *a.* Without awns.

1801 WITHERING *Bot. Arrangem.* III. 595 Its awnless calyx distinguishes it. **1854** HOOKER *Himal. Jrnls.* II. xxix. 307 Black awnless unirrigated rice.

awnter, obs. form of ADVENTURE *sb.*

awny ('ɔːnɪ), *a. rare.* [f. AWN *sb.* + -Y[1].] Bearded, bristly.

1786 BURNS *Scotch Drink* iii, Aits set up their awnie horn. **1788** PICKEN *Poems* 144 (JAM.) The awny grain.

a-wobble (ə'wɒb(ə)l), *advb. phr.* [A *prep.*[1] + WOBBLE.] Wobbling.

1881 W. RUSSELL *Ocean Free-Lance* I. iii. 44 It breezed up ..and the water was all awobble with it.

awode, obs. Sc. form of AVOID.

awold, variant of AWALD *v. Obs.* See also WOLD.

†**a'wonder**, *v. Obs.* Forms: 1–2 ofwundrian, 3 awundre, 4–6 awonder. [prob. a worn-down form of OE. *ofwundrian*, pa. pple. *ofwundrad*, f. OF- *pref.* + *wundrian* to WONDER; cf. *athirst*.]

1. *impers.* It astonishes, amazes (one).

c **1250** *O. Kent. Serm.* in *O.E. Misc.* 32 Al-seþo men þet weren in þo ssipe hedde i-seghe þo miracle so awondrede hem michel. *c* **1300** *K. Alis.* 1408 That he so trust and undurstode, More a-wondrith al my blod!

2. *intr.* To be astonished or amazed. (Often with dative refl. pron.)

c **1230** *Ancr. R.* 218 Heo awundreð hire swuðe, & is of dred. *c* **1300** *K. Alis.* 5513 Ich me awonder..Hou he dar. **1513** DOUGLAS *Æneis* I. viii. 34 He and his fallow awonderis this seand.

3. *pa. pple.* Amazed, astonished, astounded.

1154 *O.E. Chron.* (Laud MS.) an. 1135 Wurþen men suiðe of uundred. *c* **1220** *Hali Meid.* 39 Of hwas wlite beoð awundret þe sunne and te mone. *c* **1350** *Will. Palerne* 310 He was wiȝtliche a-wondered & gan to wepe sore. *c* **1430** *Syr Gener.* 4852 Therof the Soudon was al a-wondred. **1513** DOUGLAS *Æneis* III. v. 30 Heirof awondrit..on I stalk.

a-work (ə'wɜːk), *advb. phr.* Also 4–5 awerke. [A *prep.*[1] + WORK.] At work, in activity; *esp.* in phr. *to set a work*.

c **1375** WYCLIF *Serm.* Sel. Wks. 1871 II. 16 Monkis and freris assenten to werris wiþouten cause and bringen þes lordis awerke, to make hem enemyes. **1483** CAXTON *Gold. Leg.* 54/4 Provostes and maystres..to sette them awerke. **1523** LD. BERNERS *Froiss.* I. ciii. 124 They helde the Englysshe archers well aworke all the day. **1600** ROWLANDS *Let. Humours Bl.* i. 47 Setting his mynt aworke to coyne false tales. **1855** BROWNING *Saul* in *Men & Wom.* II. 121 The throe That a-work in the rock, helps its labour.

†**a'worry**, *v. Obs.* In 3 awurie, (?) awarie. [OE. *awyrȝan*, f. A- *pref.* 1 + *wyrȝan* to strangle (see WORRY *v.*); cf. OHG. *arwurgjan*, mod.G. *erwürgen*.] To strangle; to worry.

c **885** K. ÆLFRED *Oros.* VI. xxxvi. §2 He hine sylfne unwitende hæfde awirȝed. *c* **1230** *Ancr. R.* 324 þe hund þet ..awurieð eihte me beateð him anonriht. *c* **1275** *Pains of Hell* in *O.E. Misc.* 149 Heo hire awarieþ al aþrep, Al so wulues doð þe scep.

†**a'worth**, *v. Obs.* In 3 awurð. [OE. *aweorþan*, *awurþan*, f. A- *pref.* 1 away + *weorþan*, *wurþan*, to become; perh. (in sense 1) for OE. *ȝeweorþan*, *-wurþan*.]

1. *intr.* To become, turn *to*.

[*c* **1000** ÆLFRIC *Gen* xxi. 18 He ȝewyrð ȝit micelre mæȝte.] **1205** LAY. 25580 Bluðeliche quað þe king! to blisse hit awurðe.

2. *intr.* To vanish, perish; to escape notice.

c **1000** *Ags. Gosp.* Matt. v. 13 Gyf þæt sælt awyrð. *c* **1230** *Ancr. R.* 200 Uor þer ich feðri on, awurðeð tene oðer tweolue.

†**a'worth**, *adv. Obs.* [f. A *prep.*[1] + WORTH; = *in worth* (in same sense).] In phr. ***to take aworth***: to take (a thing) in esteem or honour, or at its worth; *hence* **a.** to bear patiently, **b.** to look upon with indifference, disregard.

1387 TREVISA *Higden* Rolls Ser. VI. 303 þis word was hevy to þe kyng but ȝit he took it aworþ. *c* **1449** PECOCK *Repr.* III. xvi. 382 Take he it aworth in pacience as a thing irremediable bi man. **1481** CAXTON *Myrr.* II. ix. 88 Somme saye that they [mermaydens] be ffysshis And other saye that they be fowles..But take it aworth. **1535** COVERDALE *Heb.* x. 34 Ye..toke a worth yᵉ spoylinge of youre goodes. **1537** ? TINDALE *Exp. John* 23 All our..motions unto synne are pardoned and taken aworthe.

†**a'worthy**, *v. Obs.* In 3 awurðien. [OE. *awyrþian*, *-eorþian*, f. A- *pref.* 1 + *wyrþian*, *weorþian*, to honour, glorify; or for OE. *ȝewyrþian*, *-urþian*, *-eorþian*.] *trans.* To give honour or dignity to; to dignify, adorn.

[*c* **1000** *Ags. Ps.* cv. 6 He Abrahames cynn..ȝeweorðude.] **1205** LAY. 9529 And he mid wurð-scipe þas cnihtes awurðede. —— 24432 þer weoren herberȝe hæhliche awurðe[de].

†'**awous**, *a. Obs. rare*$^{-1}$. [f. AWE *sb.* + -OUS.] Awe-inspiring.

c **1675** R. GARBUTT *Serm. Adultery* 101 A powerful and awous man.

awow(e, awoyde, obs. Sc. ff. AVOW, AVOID.

a-wrack (ə'ræk), *advb. phr.* [A *prep.*[1] + WRACK.] In a state of wreck or ruin.

1627 CAPT. SMITH *Seaman's Gram.* ix. 41 If she split or sinke, she is awracke. *a* **1845** HOOD *Irish Schm.* xx, Like tears dried up with rugged huckaback, That sets the mournful visage all awrack. [The sense here is doubtful.]

†**a'wrap**, *v. Obs. rare*$^{-1}$. [f. A- *pref.* 11 + WRAP *v.*] To wrap.

1609 HEYWOOD *Brit. Troy* v. lxxix, And her young infant that was bare and thin Awraps in his Capootch.

†**a'wrath, awroth,** *v. Obs.* [f. A- *pref.* 1 + WRATH *v.*; or for OE. *ȝewráðian.*] *trans.* (and *refl.*) To make angry, enrage.

[**1070** *O.E. Chron.*, þa ȝewraðede hine..Landfranc.] *a* **1250** *Owl & Night.* 1276 Nis..noȝt so glad that hit ne awrotheth. **1250** LAY. 24834 þer wes Ardures hird hehliche awraððed.

awre, awro (?), **awro-where,** variants of OWHERE *adv. Obs.* anywhere.

†**a'wreak,** *v. Obs.* For forms see WREAK *v.* [OE. *awrecan*, f. A- *pref.* 1 + *wrecan* to WREAK.]

1. *trans.* To punish or take vengeance upon (an offence, misdeed).

1048 *O.E. Chron.* (Laud MS.) §3 Hu hi mihton þæs cynges bismer awrecan. *c* **1230** *Ancr. R.* 334 Gif þu..holdest God to nesche uorto awreken sunne. **1340** *Ayenb.* 83 Errour in batayle..is anon awreke. **1481** CAXTON *Reynard* (1844) 75, I shal awreke..this trespace.

2. *trans.* **a.** To sentence to punishment, condemn (a person). **b.** To condemn, blame, find fault with.

1205 LAY. 25194 þat ilke þat Howel haf[eð] ispeken, ne sal hit na man awreken, ah we hit scullen ilæsten. *a* **1300** *Floriz & Bl.* 661 Are hi beo to diþe awreke.

3. To avenge or revenge: **a.** *refl.* oneself; **b.** *trans.* one's aggrieved feelings (of).

c **930** *Laws of Athelstan* I. 20 (Bosw.) Gif hine hwá awrecan wille. *c* **1230** *Ancr. R.* 334 Bihold hu he awrec him of his heih engel. **1575** *Gammer Gurton* IV. ii, And sware..he would awreake his sorrowe.

c. *trans.* To avenge another person. **d.** *pass.* To be avenged or revenged (of).

a **1300** *Floriz & Bl.* 658 A-wrekeþ me wiþ Jugement. **1377** LANGL. *P. Pl.* B. VI. 204 For I am wel awroke now of wastoures þoru þi myȝte. *c* **1386** CHAUCER *Miller's T.* 566 Me were lever than alle this toun..Of this dispit awroken for to be. *c* **1430** *Syr Gener.* 1272 Glad woman shal I neuer be Til ye graunt to a-wreke me. **1586** J. HOOKER *Girald. Irel.* in *Holinsh.* II. 31/1 And she to be awreaked, did..find the means to find out this Rosamund.

†**a'wreaking,** *vbl. sb. Obs.* Revenge.

1340 *Ayenb.* 8 Non ne ssel slaȝe oþren uor a wreking.

a-wreck (ə'rɛk), *advb. phr.* [A *prep.*[1] + WRECK.] In a wrecked condition.

1878 J. MILLER *Songs of It.* 122 An ark, Sea-blown and a-wreck.

†**a'wreight,** *pa. pple. Obs.* Forms: 3 **awræht, awreþt,** 4 **awreiȝt.** [According to form this ought to be = OE. *awręht*, pa. pple. of *awręccan* to arouse, stir up; but the sense connects it with **awrench*, of which the pa. pple. would be OE. *awrenct*, ME. *awreint.* There has been a confusion of forms.] Wrenched away.

1205 LAY. 15437 Ða habbeð al mi kine-lond awræht [**1250** a-wreþt] ut of mire hond. **1387** TREVISA *Higden* Rolls Ser. II. 181 Whan þe lymes beeþ awreiȝt out of her owne places [L. *dislocantur*].

†**a'write,** *v. Obs.* For forms see WRITE *v.* [OE. *awrítan*, f. A- *pref.* 1 + *wrítan.*] To write.

c **885** K. ÆLFRED *Gregory's Past.* Introd. 5 Forðæm ðe hie næron on hiora áȝen ȝeðiode awritene. *c* **1175** *Lamb. Hom.* 87 [Moses] awrat þa alde e bi godes wissunge.

awroke, -en, pa. pple. of AWREAK *v. Obs.*

awrong (ə'rɒŋ), *adv.* [f. A *prep.*[1] + WRONG, cf. *aright.*] Wrongly, wrong, in a wrong way.

1430 LYDG. *Chron. Troy* II. x, Me to reduce whan I went a wrong. **1862** T. TROLLOPE *Marietta* I. xvi. 295 Her prayer had been heard awrong! **1878** BARING-GOULD *Myst. Suffer.* ii. 35 If the power of choosing awrong were not his.

awrthwart, obs. form of OVERTHWART.

awry (ə'raɪ), *adv.* and *a.* Forms: 4 **on wry,** 5 **on wrye,** 5–6 **a wrye, awrye,** 5–7 **a wry,** 6 **a wrie, awri,** 6–7 **awrie,** 5– **awry.** [f. A *prep.*[1] + WRY; cf. *aright, awrong.*] **A.** *adv.*

1. Away from the straight (position or direction); to one side, obliquely; unevenly, crookedly, askew.

c **1375** BARBOUR *Bruce* IV. 705 As thair bemys strekit air Owthir all evin, or on wry. **1490** CAXTON *Eneydos* xiv. 50 The stones of the walles appyeren alle awry sette. **1590** *Pasquil's Apol.* I. D b, The case standing as it dooth I cannot but draw my mouth awrie. **1607** DEKKER *Westw. Hoe* Wks. 1873 II. 294 They say Charing-crosse is falne downe..but thats no such wonder, twas old, and stood awry. **1650** BULWER *Anthropomet.* xi. 115 Lest..some crum (as we use to say) should go awry. **1714** POPE *Rape Lock* IV. 8 Not Cynthia when her manteau's pinned awry, E'er felt such rage. **1838** MARRYAT *Jac. Faithf.* ii. 9, I held my spoon awry, and soiled my clothes.

b. *to look awry*: to look ASKANCE or ASQUINT. (Cf. the senses under these words.)

c **1400** *Rom. Rose* 291 Envy..ne looked but awrie. **1573** G. HARVEY *Letter-bk.* (1884) 5, I passing bi him..he hath lookd awri an other wai. **1609** ROWLANDS *Crew of Gossips* 6 When he speakes..I'll hold my peace, and (frowning) looke awry. **1709** CHANDLER *Effort agst. Bigotry* 28 When a Church-man therefore shall in scornful Pride look awry upon..a Dissenter. **1845** DARWIN *Voy. Nat.* x. (1852) 206 Some of our party began to squint and look awry.

2. *fig.* Out of the right course or place; in a wrong manner; improperly, erroneously, amiss.

1494 FABYAN 2 To me it semyth so ferre sette a wrye In tyme of yeres. **1671** MILTON *P.R.* IV. 313 Much of the Soul they talk, but all awrie. **1850** MRS. BROWNING *Aur. Leigh* III. 543 Those who think Awry, will scarce act straightly.

b. *esp.* in phr. ***to go, run, step, tread, walk awry***: (of persons) to fall into error, do wrong; (of things) to turn out badly or untowardly, 'go wrong.'

1524 *State Papers Hen. VIII*, I. 152 To wryng and wreste the maters in to bettre trayne, if they walke a wrye. **1570** B. GOOGE *Pop. Kingd.* IV. (1880) 56 b, The very Spouse and Church of Christ, that cannot runne awry. *a* **1625** BOYS in Spurgeon *Treas. Dav. Ps.* xv. 2 Aristides was so just..that he would not tread awry. **1745** DE FOE *Eng. Tradesm.* I. ix. 65 If a tradesman but once ventures to step awry. **1858** CARLYLE *Fredk. Gt.* (1865) I. II. xi. 116 Far worse, the marriage itself went awry.

c. ***to tread the shoe awry***: to fall from virtue, break the law of chastity. Cf. F. *faux pas.*

1520–41 WYATT *Poet. Wks.* (1861) 96 Farewell all my welfare! My shoe is trod awry. **1600** HEYWOOD *2nd Edw. IV*, Wks. 1874 I. 143 King Edward's children not legitimate.. Their mother hapt to tread the shoe awry. **1662** FULLER *Worthies* (1840) III. 130 He would not stick to tell where he trod his holy sandals awry.

B. *adj.* (usually *pred.*, rarely *attrib.* Cf. WRY.)

1. Out of the right course or position; displaced, disordered, disarranged; crooked, distorted.

1658 W. BURTON *Itin. Anton.* 178 The journey will prove enormiously awry. **1728** YOUNG *Love Fame* VI. (1757) 149 What pity 'tis her shoulder is awry! **1847** BARHAM *Ingol. Leg.* (1877) 172 His features and phiz awry Show'd so much misery. **1883** *Daily News* 9 Nov. 2/1 Blinds..very different from the awry, dingy, imitation Venetians of his neighbour.

2. *fig.* Turned from the right course, wide of the mark, perverted, wrong. ***awry from***: opposed to.

1581 SIDNEY *Astr. & Stella* xxvii, With dearth of words, or answers quite awrie. **1670** MILTON *Hist. Eng.* I. Wks. (1851) 23 Nothing more awry from the Law of God..then that a Woman should give Laws to Men. **1872** BROWNING *Fifine* I, If so succeed hand-practice on awry Preposterous art-mistake.

C. *ellipt.* quasi-*vb.* To turn awry or aside.

1613 R. C. *Table Alph.*, *Swarue*, awry, erre. **1653** BROME *Mad Couple* III. i, High heeld shooes, that will awry sometimes with any Women.

awsk, obs. form of ASK *sb.* a newt.

awsterne, obs. form of AUSTERE.

awtare, -eer, -ier(e, obs. forms of ALTAR.

awtayne, var. HAUTAIN *a. Obs.* haughty.

awteal, obs. variant of ATTEAL.

awyne, obs. form of OWN *a.*

awyriȝe, -rie, var. of AWARIE *v. Obs.* to curse.

†**ax, axe,** *sb. Obs.* or *dial.* Forms: 1–2 **eax, æx, ex;** also (under AX-TREE) 3–7 **ax,** 4 **exe,** 4–6 **ex,** 5–7 **axe.** [Common Teutonic: OE. *æx-e, eax-e*, fem., is cogn. with MDu. and MLG. *asse*, from **ahse*, Du. *as*, OHG. *ahsa*, MHG. *ahse*, mod.G. *achse*, OTeut. *ahsâ-*, fem., related to Skr. *áksha*, masc., Gr. *ἄξων*, L. *axis*, Lith. *aszis*, with same sense.]

The AXLE of a wheel; the AXIS of revolution. Not found after the OE. period exc. in compounds, as ***ax-nail***, the nail or pin by which the axle-tree is fixed to a cart, and AX-TREE, q.v.

a **700** *Epinal Gloss.* 1/D 10 *Axis*, aex. *c* **885** K. ÆLFRED *Boeth.* xxxix. §7 On wænes eaxe hwearfaþ þa hweól, and sió eax stent stille. *c* **1000** ÆLFRIC *Man. Astron.* (Wr.) 16 *Axis* þat is ex. **1585** *Wills & Inv. N.C.* (1860) 112, j long wayne without wheels, ij yron ax-nailes..and two ax-trees.

†**ax, axe,** *v. Obs.* In 5 **ex.** [f. AX *sb.*] To furnish with an axle.

1481–90 *Howard Househ. Bks.* 191 For boxyng a peyre wheles, and a fely uppon a nodyr, and for exyng of a carte.

ax, obs. or dial. form of ASK *v.*

axal ('æksəl), *a.* [f. AX-IS + -AL[1]; cf. L. *crīnālis, dōtālis.*] = AXIAL (which is the usual form).

1823 P. NICHOLSON *Pract. Build.* 130 The axal section. **1830** *Edin. Encycl.* V. 520 At right angles to an axal plane. **1872** NICHOLSON *Palæont.* 161 Axal furrows.

axan, -in obs. or dial. pl. of ASH *sb.*[2]

axces, -s, -se, obs. ff. ACCESS, fit, fever, ague.

axe, ax (æks), *sb.*[1] Forms: 1 **acas, äx, eax,** 2 **æx,** 3 **eax,** (**echze**), 5 **ex(e,** (6 *Sc.* **aix**), 2– **ax,** 5– **axe;** *Pl.* **axes.** [Common Teutonic: OE. *æx* (*acs*), str. fem. for earlier **aces*, **acus*, Northumb. *acas*, cogn. with OS. *akus* (MDu. *akes*, Du. *aaks*), OHG. *acchus* (MHG. *ackes*, mod.G. *ax, axt*), ON. *öx* (gen. *axar*), Goth. *aqizi*; akin to Gr. *ἀξίνη*, and prob. to L. *ascia.* The spelling *ax* is better on every ground, of etymology, phonology, and analogy, than *axe*, which became prevalent during the 19th century; but it is now disused in Britain.]

1. A tool or instrument for hewing, cleaving, or chopping, trees, wood, ice, etc.; consisting of a squarish head, now usually of iron with a steel edge or blade, fixed by means of a socket upon a handle or helve of wood, so as to be wielded with force in striking. Also called, especially when of smaller or lighter make, a *hatchet.*

In ancient times *axes* were also made of bronze or stone (see 4), and might have the head and handle in one piece, as *coal-axes* and other special forms still have.

c **1000** *Ags. Gosp.* Matt. iii. 10 Eallunga ys seo æx to þæra treowa wurtrumum asett. [*Lindisf.* Acas, *Rushw.* axe]. *c* **1160** *Hatton G.* ibid., Syo æx. *c* **1230** *Ancr. R.* 128 Aȝein þe cul of þer eax. *Ibid.* 98 (C.) Wudemonnes echze. *a* **1250** *Owl & Night.* 658 Hong up thin ax. **1297** R. GLOUC. 490 A kene ax him sulf he huld. **1382** WYCLIF *Isa.* x. 15 Whether shal glorien the ax aȝen hym that hewith with it. **1398** TREVISA *Barth. De P.R.* XVII. clxii. (1495) 709 Cloue with an axe other wyth a sawe. *a* **1550** *Christis Kirk Gr.* xxiii, Dik with ane aix Cam furth to fell a fuddir. **1611** BIBLE *Judg.* ix. 48 Abimelech tooke an axe..and cut downe a bough. **1799** J. ROBERTSON *Agric. Perth.* 239 The bark was never allowed to be taken off below the ax, or the place where the tree was cut. **1860** TYNDALL *Glac.* I. §11. 79 Driving the iron claws of our boots into the scars [in the ice] made by the axe. **1877** BRYANT *Song of Sower* iv, Whose sounding axes gleam Beside the lonely forest-stream. **1884** *Scotsman* 4 July 5/1 The silver axe..recently presented to Mr. Gladstone by 'a few admiring friends.'

b. BRICK-AXE, HAMMER-AXE, PICK-AXE, q.v.

c. ***the axe*** (fig.): the cutting down of expenditure in the public services. Also in other extended uses, esp. the dismissal of an employee.

1922 *Glasgow Herald* 5 Oct. 7 Another class of military officers for some of whom assistance..may be needed are those who are the unhappy victims of the Geddes economy'axe'. **1923** *Times* 16 Mar. 12/1 Army and the 'axe'. Limit of safety reached... No fewer than 1,500 officers had fallen before the Geddes axe. **1958** *Economist* 1 Nov. 390/1 Capital formation should never again become the first candidate for the axe when times for restraint recur.

2. In olden warfare: A battle-axe.

1205 LAY. 2263 He lædde on his exle ane muchele wi-eax. **1375** BARBOUR *Bruce* XII. 20 [Bruce] raid..with ane ax in hande. *a* **1400** *Cov. Myst.* (1841) 270 With exys, gleyvis, and swerdys bryth. *c* **1400** *Destr. Troy* v. 1588 Armurers and arowsmythes with axes of werre. **1725** POPE *Odyss.* III. 561 The ax was held by warlike Thrasymed. **1774** JOHNSON *West. Isl.* Wks. X. 457 The Lochaber ax is only a slight alteration of the old English bill. **1869** FREEMAN *Norm. Conq.* (1874) III. xv. 463 The iron mace of the Bastard, the one weapon fit to meet..with the two-handed axe of Harold. **1874** BOUTELL *Arms & Arm.* vi. 91.

3. The headsman's axe used to decapitate condemned traitors. Hence *fig.* execution.

1450 W. SOMNER in *Four C. Eng. Lett.* 4 Ther was an exe, and a stoke, and oon of the lewdeste of the shippe badde him ley down his hedde. **1551** EDW. VI. *Lit. Rem.* (1858) II. 374 And so departed without the ax of the Toure. **1603** SHAKS. *Meas. for M.* IV. ii. 56 You sirrah, prouide your blocke and your Axe. **1719** YOUNG *Revenge* IV. i, A third..Gave to the cruel ax a darling son. **1752** HUME *Ess. & Treat.* (1777) II. 96 From the operation of the ax or wheel.

4. In *Archæology* (see quot.).

1851 D. WILSON *Preh. Ann.* (1863) I. vi. 192 The name of axe is applied to the double-edged stone implements, and to those of a wedge shape, which have the aperture for inserting the handle near the broad end. **1877** GREENWELL *Brit. Barrows* 136 A small polished green-stone axe.

5. A musical instrument; formerly esp. a saxophone, now usu. a guitar. *slang* (chiefly *Jazz* and *Rock Music*).

1955 L. FEATHER *Encycl. Jazz* (1956) 345 *Ax, axe*, horn, instrument (usually saxophone). **1956** O. DUKE *Sideman* ii. 25 You wanta make it with me tonight? Bring your ax, man, blow some. **1962** 'E. MCBAIN' *Like Love* vii. 100 The musical jargon of Hip..'he peddled the ax to buy the junk, so now he can't blow anyway.' **1967** *Melody Maker* 23 Dec. 8/5 'For Pete's sake Ali you're on now, this minute...' 'Listen, man. Don't have my axe, man.' **1969** *Rolling Stone* 17 May 8/4 While Keith bashes madly on the drums,..Pete Townsend disposes of his axe with good natured dispatch. **1976** *New Musical Express* 12 Feb. 37/3 There's not the slightest hint of killer axe interplay or dazzling musical cut and thrust. **1982** *Sounds* 11 Dec., As a flashing axe, it takes some beating.

6. phrases. **a.** ***to put the axe in the helve***: to solve a doubt, to find out a puzzle. ***to send the axe after the helve*** (= the better *to send the helve after the hatchet*). ***to have axes to grind*** (orig. *U.S. politics*): to have private ends to serve [in reference to a story told by Franklin]; now more commonly ***to have an axe to grind.***

c **1450** LONELICH *Grail* xxviii. 410 Ȝit cowde he not putten the ex in þe helve. **1547** J. HEYWOOD *Prov. & Epigr.* (1867) 80 Here I sende thaxe after the helue awaie. **1815** C. MINER *Who'll turn Grindstones?* When I see a merchant over-polite to his customers..thinks I, that man has an axe to grind. **1865** HOLLAND *Plain T.* v. 188 Little cliques and cabals composed of men who have axes to grind. **1881** *Daily Tel.* 8 June 6/2 The hands..that 'grind the axe,' and that 'pull the strings.' **1922** JOYCE *Ulysses* 624 Skin-the-Goat..evidently with an axe to grind, was airing his grievances. **1939** G. B. SHAW *Geneva* II. p. 30 Distinguished statesmen of different nations..each with a national axe to grind.

7. *Comb.* **a.** *attrib.*, as ***axe-edge, -handle, -head, -shaft***; AXE-MAN, AX-STONE, AX-FITCH, -SEED, -WORT, q.v. **b.** Also ***axe-form, -like, -shaped***, etc.

1865 SWINBURNE *Chastelard* v. ii. 202 Suppose my mouth The axe-edge to bite so sweet a throat in twain. **1865** LUBBOCK *Preh. Times* 132 In some places these horn axe-handles are numerous. **1611** BIBLE *2 Kings* vi. 5 The axe head [COVERD. the yron] fell into the water. **1851** D. WILSON *Preh. Ann.* (1863) I. vi. 184 Stone celts—and axe heads—made of hard greenstone. **1815** SCOTT *Ld. Isles* VI. xv, The axe-shaft, with its brazen clasp. **1847** TENNYSON *Princ.* II. 186 An iron will, An axe-like edge unturnable.

c. axe-adze, a double-bladed tool, consisting of an axe and adze combined; **axe-breaker** *Austral.*, name given to a tree *Notelæa longifolia*; **axe-grinding** *vbl. sb.*, having private ends to serve (see sense 5); also ***axe-grinder***; **axe-hammer**, a tool consisting of an axe and hammer combined; cf. *hammer-axe*.

1925 V. G. CHILDE *Dawn Europ. Civilization* ii. 34 From Early Minoan II the Cretans knew a curious implement with one blade parallel and the other at right angles to the shaft, called an '*axe-adze'. **1928** C. DAWSON *Age of Gods* xii. 268 The type known as an 'axe-adze', with its blades set transversely to one another, which is probably the model of the Nordic battle-axe. **1884** A. NILSON *Timber Trees N.S.W.* 133 *Axebreaker. **1889** J. H. MAIDEN *Useful Native Plants* 579 (Morris), Axe-breaker. Wood hard, close-grained and firm. **1884** G. DOLBY *Dickens* viii. 227 Willard's Hotel..with its *clientèle* of bar-loafers, swaggerers, drunkards, and '*axe-grinders' (a class of politician peculiar to Washington hotels). **1909** WARE *Passing English* 12/2 *Axe-grinders* (American). Men who grumble, especially political. **1916** E. V. LUCAS *Vermilion Box* lii. 57, I have known many journalists, but hardly one who was not either a cynic or an axe-grinder, or both. **1865** SALA *My Diary* I. 421 '*Axe-grinding' is a term borrowed from one of the most charming stories told by the great apologist of shrewd common-sense, Benjamin Franklin. **1942** *Sphere* 27 June 409/2 Criticisms in the House of Commons and the newspapers are based largely on ignorance or axe-grinding. **1681** *New Castle Court Rec.* 476 (D.A.E.), Hee would beat him out with the *ax hammer. **1928** PEAKE & FLEURE *Steppe & Sown* ii. 20 They used as their distinctive weapon a perforated axe-hammer of stone. **1950** H. L. LORIMER *Homer & Monum.* iv. 122 The bronze axe-hammer from Delphi may also come thence.

†**axe**, *sb.*[2] *Obs.* [a. F. *axe*, ad. L. *axis*.] Byform of AXIS.

1551 [see AX-TREE 3]. **1570** BILLINGSLEY *Euclid* II. def. 15. 317 A sphere..may haue infinite diameters, but it can haue but onely one axe. **1752** BEVIS in *Phil. Trans.* XLVIII. 388 The inclination of the earth's axe. **1796** HUTTON *Math. Dict.* I. 178 The chief properties of the *Axe-in-peritrochio*.

axe, ax (æks), *v.* [f. AXE *sb.*[1]]

1. *trans.* To shape or trim with an ax.

1677 MOXON *Mech. Exerc.* (1703) 246 To Ax the Brick off, with an Ax that is exactly streight on the edge. **1823** P. NICHOLSON *Pract. Build.* 389 The..stretchers in returns, which are not axed, are dressed upon the rubbing-stone.

2. To remove (officials, etc.) to save expenditure; to cut down (expenditure, etc.) by means of 'the axe'.

1922 *Glasgow Herald* 5 Oct. 7, The 'axed' officer. **1923** *Hansard Commons* CLXI. 1832 Fifteen hundred officers have been axed under the Geddes recommendation. *Ibid.* 1852 It is partly due to axing. **1923** *Daily Mail* 28 June 10 Lord Inchcape, the chairman of the Committee which recently 'axed' the expenditure of the Services in India.

axe, obs. or dial. form of ASK. See also AX.

axed (ækst), *pple.* and *a.* [f. AXE *v.* or *sb.*[1] + -ED.]

1. *ppl. a.* Shaped or dressed with an axe.

1830 *Edin. Encycl.* VI. 627 The stones are either hammered, dressed, or axed.

2. Furnished with an axe or axes.

1879 FARRAR *St. Paul* II. 551 The axed fasces of the lictors.

axel, obs. form of AXLE.

axel ('æksəl). *Skating.* Also **Axel**, **Axel Paulsen**. [f. the name of a Norwegian skater, *Axel* Rudolf Paulsen (1855–1938).] A jumping movement in skating (see quot. 1930).

1930 T. D. RICHARDSON *Mod. Figure Skating* xv. 126 An excellent figure skater, who could do an 'Axel Paulsen' jump before he could do threes to a centre. *Ibid.* 136 The ever popular half Axel or Salchow jump. It consists of a leap from an inside back edge to an outside back, and is really a loop jump on two feet. **1959** *Times* 12 Mar. 4/4 Miss J. R. H. ..gave a brilliant display, with high axels and salchows off each foot.

axeless ('ækslɪs), *a.* [f. AXE *sb.*[1] + -LESS.] Without an axe; having no axe.

1895 *Athenæum* 19 Jan. 77/3 The rocks were 'glazed in many places with a thin coating of ice', which he had to hammer off with stones. For the man was all the time axeless. **1938** *Antiquity* XII. 382 The axeless microlithic culture.

axe-man, ax- ('æksmæn). [f. AXE *sb.*[1] + -MAN.]

1. One who uses an axe in his work; a woodman.

1671 in *Essex Inst. Hist. Coll.* (1883) XX. 145 The time of meeting for ax men is to be by the sun half an hour high. **1777** *Maryland Jrnl.* 18 Mar. (Th.), Five hundred good carpenters, with ax-men and sawyers in proportion. **1785** A. ELLICOTT in C. V. Mathews *Life & Lett.* (1908) 45 From a Hill where our Axe-men are now Encamped we have a most beautiful Prospect. **1809** J. BARLOW *Columb.* VI. 371 Scalpers, and ax-men rush from Erie's shore. **1878** J. BULLER *N. Zealand* I. ii. 28 They worked as axe-men, sawyers, etc.

2. A warrior armed with a battle-axe.

1828 TYTLER *Hist. Scot.* (1864) II. 218 Every axe-man who had neither spear nor bow.

3. A guitarist, esp. one who plays in a band or group. Cf. AXE *sb.*[1] 5. *slang* (chiefly *Jazz* and *Rock Music*).

1976 *Evening Post* (Nottingham) 15 Dec. 2/4 Guitarist Albert Lee..slotted in remarkably, swapping subtle licks and fresh ideas with Joan's regular axeman Jerry Donahue. **1977** *Rolling Stone* 24 Mar. 69/2 Though Beck himself adds some screaming guitar to one selection and Devadip Carlos Santana is effectively lyrical on another, axeman Ray Gomez powers four of the cuts. **1985** *Washington Post* 15 May B7/2 He learned guitar from Fats Domino's axeman, Walter (Papoose) Nelson.

axemanship ('æksmənʃɪp). [f. AX(E)-MAN + -SHIP 2 b.] The ability of an axeman; skill in handling an axe. Also *fig.*; cf. AXE *sb.*[1] 1 c.

1893 *Field* 28 Jan. 117/3 Axemanship is so universal in Tasmania..that it is said even the bank managers..have usually one or two toes missing. **1961** *Times* 9 Feb. 5/6 When the Minister..was appointed to a great spending department it was his axemanship that was needed.

axenic (eɪ'zɛnɪk), *a. Biol.* [f. A- 14 (Gr. α priv.) + ξενικ-ός alien, strange.] (See quot. 1942.)

1942 BAKER & FERGUSON in *Proc. Soc. Exper. Biol. & Med.* LI. 116/1 The adjective *axenic* is introduced to denote a living organism that is free from all other demonstrable organisms... An axenic organism, as here defined, is a species free from any life apart from that produced by its own protoplasm. **1955** *Proc. Helminthological Soc. Washington* XXII. 49 A number of soil-dwelling nematodes, particularly of the genus *Rhabditis*, have been cultured under axenic conditions.

†**axes, axesse, axez, axis, axys**, obs. forms of ACCESS, in special sense of 'Attack; fit; ague.' In this sense the word early acquired the Eng. accent *'access*, and, its identity with *ac'cess* being forgotten, it was long treated as distinct.

1398 [See ACCESS 10]. **1423** JAMES I *Kingis Q.* lxvii, Bot tho began myn axis and turment To sene hir part, and folowe I na myght. **1530** PALSGR. 450/1 This axes hath made hym so weake. **1700** WALLACE *Acc. Orkney* 66 (JAM.) An aguish distemper, which they call the Axes.

axetre(e, variant of AX-TREE.

†**'ax-fitch**, *Herb. Obs.* Also 7 **ax-vitch**. [f. AX(E *sb.*[1] + FITCH.] A leguminous plant (*Securigera Coronilla*), a native of Southern Europe.

1562 TURNER *Herbal* II. 132 a, I call it Axsede or Axwurt (or Axfich) because..the sede..is lyke vnto a two edged axe. **1601** HOLLAND *Pliny* II. 274 *Axvitch.* **1611** COTGR., *Securidaque*, the pulse Axseed, Axwort, Axfitch, Hatchet-fitch. **1727** BRADLEY *Fam. Dict.*, *Horse-shoe*..a rare plant which has Leaves like the small Axfitch.

axial ('æksɪəl), *a.* [f. L. *axi-s* + -AL[1].]

1. Forming an axis; of the nature of an axis.

1849 MURCHISON *Siluria* v. 100 The elevation of the axial line being less. **1857** HENFREY *Bot.* §35 A true or axial root. **1872** MIVART *Anat.* 25 The skeleton of the head and trunk, which is called the Axial skeleton. **1879** S. HIGHLEY in *Cassell's Techn. Educ.* IV. 313/1 The axial ray. **1879** CARPENTER *Ment. Phys.* I. i. §23 The Cerebrum and the Axial Cord on which it is super-imposed. **1880** DARWIN *Movem. Pl.* 223 Flower-stems..being axial in their nature.

2. Of, or belonging to, an axis.

1859 B. POWELL *Order Nat.* i. §2. 45 Imagined three distinct motions..orbital, rotatory, axial. **1868** LOCKYER *Elem. Astron.* 237 With its axial direction at right angles to the direction of the slit. **1870** PROCTOR *Other Worlds* iii. 61 Axial inclination [of the planets].

3. Round, or about, an axis.

1862 H. SPENCER *First Princ.* II. xxii. §170 The axial velocity. **1871** TYNDALL *Fragm. Sc.* II. xi. 239 The earth's axial rotation.

4. *Comb.* **axial flow**: usu. *attrib.* (with hyphen) (see quots.); **axial gradient** *Zool.*, the gradual change in the intensity of metabolism along any axis of a living organism.

1889 G. R. BODMER *Hydraulic Motors: Turbines* ii. 33 The mixed-flow has been developed out of the inward-flow turbine by continuing the vanes into that part of the wheel where the water assumes a vertical direction, so that the radial flow is changed into an axial flow. *Ibid.* 43 Axial-Flow Girard Turbine..has ventilated buckets..widened at the lower end, where the outflow takes place. **1910** *Hawkins' Elect. Dict.* 25/2 *Axial Flow*, a term applied to that class of turbine in which the fluid passes through the motor in a direction parallel to its axis... Also termed *Parallel flow.* **1941** *Flight* 9 Oct. 242/2 The combustion gases, with an excess of air, are then expanded through an axial-flow gas turbine which drives the main air compressor. **1949** *Gloss. Aeronaut. Terms (B.S.I.)* II. 14 *Axial-flow compressor*, a compressor which functions by the action of alternate rows of fixed and rotating blades, radially mounted; the direction of flow through the compressor being axial. *Ibid.* 17 *Axial-flow turbine*, a turbine through which the general direction of flow is axial. **1911** C. M. CHILD in *Jrnl. Exper. Zool.* XI. 214 These facts..show very clearly that an axial gradient exists in a large number of organisms and that in many cases at least the apical or anterior region is dominant in regulation. **1926** Axial gradient [see AXIATE *a.*].

axi'ality. [f. prec. + -ITY.] The quality of being axial; axial character or state.

1884 *Times* 20 Nov. 4/5 It [the Cupola] should.. emphasize the four axes of the cross..there was in that great cathedral [St. Peter's] nothing to mark the axiality.

axially ('æksɪəlɪ), *adv.* [f. prec. + -LY[2].] In the direction of the axis, from pole to pole.

1842 W. GROVE *Corr. Phys. Forces* (ed. 6) 129 Taking a position axially, or in the line from pole to pole of the magnet. **1859** *Edin. Rev.* CIX. 530 The screw is pierced axially. **1860** MAURY *Phys. Geog. Sea* vii. §345 If a bar of iron be suspended between the poles of a magnet, it will arrange itself axially, and point towards them.

axiate ('æksɪət), *a. Zool.* [f. L. *axi-s* AXIS[1] + -ATE[2].] = AXIAL *a.*

1926 L. T. HOGBEN *Compar. Physiol.* xii. 203 The morphological differentiation of parts (axiate pattern) with reference to a given axis is preceded by the appearance of a gradient of physiological activity (axial gradient) along this axis. **1949** KOESTLER *Insight & Outlook* xi. 162 In higher organisms we find axiate gradients with the growing tip..as the dominant integrative centre.

†**'axicle.** *Obs.*[—0] [ad. L. *axiculus*, dim. of AXIS; cf. *ashlar*.] 'A little shingle or board.' Blount *Glossogr.* 1656.

axier, ? error for AXIS, or for *ax-tre*, AXLE-TREE.

1594 GREENE *Look. Glass* (1861) 136 Thy hands the axier to maintain my world.

axiferous (æk'sɪfərəs), *a. Bot.* [f. L. *axi-s* AXIS + *-fer* bearing + -OUS; cf. F. *axifère*.] Consisting of an axis only, without leaves or other appendages.

1842 in BRANDE.

axiform ('æksɪfɔːm), *a.* [f. as prec. + -FORM.] In the shape of an axis.

1847 in CRAIG.

axifugal (æk'sɪfjʊgəl), *a.* [f. as prec. + L. *fugĕre* to fly + -AL[1].] = CENTRIFUGAL; in ***axifugal force***: tendency to fly from the axis of rotation.

1740 STACK in *Phil. Trans.* XLI. 422 Suppose that God forms a Vortex cylindrical and fluid..its Points will have but an axifugal Force. **1881** in *Syd. Soc. Lex.*

axil ('æksɪl). *Bot.* [ad. L. *axilla*: see below; cf. mod.F. *axille*.] The upper angle between a leaf or petiole and the stem from which it springs; also that between a branch and the trunk.

1794 MARTYN *Rousseau's Bot.* v. 50 Branches which grow from their alæ or axils. **1872** H. MACMILLAN *True Vine* v. 210 The buds of plants almost always grow in the axil.

axil(e, -tre, obs. forms of AXLE, -TREE.

axile ('æksaɪl), *a.* [f. as if ad. L. **axīl-is*, f. *axis*; cf. L. *civīlis*, *hostīlis*.] Belonging to the axis: **a.** *Bot.* Applied to an embryo having the same direction as the axis of the seed, or a placenta in the axis of the ovary.

1845 LINDLEY *Sch. Bot.* i. (1858) 16 If it [the placenta] grows from a centre which is connected with the sides of the ovary by dissepiments..it is *axile.* **1870** BENTLEY *Bot.* 342 The embryo is said to be axile, or axial when it has the same direction as the axis of the seed. **1870** HOOKER *Stud. Flora* 314 Oxyria..embryo axile.

b. in Phys. *axile bodies*: the touch corpuscles at the termination of the sensory nerves.

1859 TODD *Cycl. Anat. & Phys.* V. 503/2 Kolliker.. prefers to call these bodies, axile corpuscles. **1881** MIVART *Cat* 22.

‖**axilla** (æk'sɪlə). Pl. **-æ**. [L., = armpit; dim. of **axula*, whence *āla*: cf. AXLE[1]. Common in late L. in form *ascella*.]

1. An armpit.

1616 A. READ *Body of Man* 152 The backe part of the shoulder top, called axilla. **1877** ROBERTS *Handbk. Med.* I. 113 The eruption appears on the..borders of the axillæ.

2. = AXIL.

1830 LINDLEY *Syst. Bot.* 247 Leaf-buds..in every axilla.

axillant (æk'sɪlənt), *a. Bot.* [f. AXILLA + -ANT[1].] Of or growing from the axil.

1883 *Encycl. Brit.* XVI. 841/2 A bud with its axillant leaf. **1899** *Nature* 15 June 149/1 Buds are protected by means of developments of the axillant leaf.

axillar ('æksɪlə(r)), *a.* (*sb.*) Also 6 **assellere**. [a. F. *axillaire* of the axilla (see -AR), formerly *aisselliere*, *-aire* (Cotgr.), ad. L. ****axillāris***, f. *axilla*, F. *aisselle*: see AXILLA.]

A. *adj.* **1.** = AXILLARY 1.

1651 WITTIE tr. *Primrose's Pop. Err.* 295 The cephalick hath its beginning..in men alwayes from the axillar veine. **1772** FORSTER *Hudson's Bay Birds* in *Phil. Trans.* LXII. 393 Shining black axillar feathers, or shoulder-knot.

2. = AXILLARY 2.

1831 MACGILLIVRAY tr. *Richard's Bot.* 185 Flowers are.. axillar, when they spring from the axilla.

B. as *sb.* (cf. F. *aisselliere*) An axillary vein.

1541 R. COPLAND *Guydon's Quest. Cyrurg.*, Veynes..two asselleres, two cubytalles, and two seynalles. **1720** HALE in *Phil. Trans.* XXXI. 9 Which Duct is..inserted by four Branches into each Axillar.

axillary ('æksɪlərɪ), *a.* [f. as prec.; see -ARY[2].]

1. Pertaining or adjacent to the armpit or shoulder.

1615 CROOKE *Body of Man* 977 The second [tacke of the backe] is called..the Axillary spondell. **1791** W. VAUGHAN *Princ. Anat.* I. 381 The Axillary artery. **1842** E. WILSON *Anat. Vade M.* 345 The axillary vein is formed by the union of the venæ comitis of the brachial artery with the basilic vein. **1871** DARWIN *Desc. Man* II. xv. 179 The white striae and spots on the axillary feathers.

2. *Bot.* Situated in, or growing from, the axil.

1786 REES *Encycl.*, *Axillary leaves*..grow out of the angles formed by the branches of the stem. **1830** LINDLEY *Nat. Syst. Bot.* Introd. 23 All Labiatæ have axillary cymes.

axin ('æksɪn). *Chem.* An oleaginous and waxy product, yielded by the large Mexican cochineal

(*Coccus axinus*), and used as a soothing ointment. **a'xinic** *a.*, of axin, as in the fatty *axinic acid.*

1873 WATTS *Fownes' Chem.* 698.

axine ('æksaɪn), *a.* and *sb. Zool.* [f. AXI-S² + -INE.] **A.** *adj.* Of or pertaining to the group of stags of which the Spotted Axis is the type. **B.** *sb.* A member of this group.

1826 GRIFFITH *Cuvier's Anim. K.* IV. 116 The Axine Group. *Ibid.* The true Axines have horns of a similar form with the Rusas.

axiniform (æk'sɪnɪfɔːm), *a.* [f. Gr. ἀξίν-η axe + -(I)FORM.] Shaped like an axe-head.

1852 DANA *Crust.* II. 769 A broad axiniform process.

axinite ('æksɪnaɪt). *Min.* [f. Gr. ἀξίν-η axe + -ITE.] A mineral belonging to Dana's epidote group of unisilicates, consisting chiefly of silica, alumina, lime, and iron, with broad acute-edged crystals somewhat resembling an axe-head.

1802 BOURNON in *Phil. Trans.* XCII. 293 *note*, Axinite, the thumerstein of Werner. **1868** DANA *Min.* 298 Axinite admits of a high polish, but is deficient in delicacy of color.

axinomancy (æk'sɪnəʊmænsɪ). [ad. L. *axīnomantīa*, a. Gr. ἀξινομαντεία, f. ἀξίνη axe + μαντεία divination.] Divination by means of an axe-head.

1601 HOLLAND *Pliny* Gloss., *Axinomantie*, a kind of magicke diuination by an ax head red hot. **1693** URQUHART *Rabelais* III. xxv, To have the truth..disclosed..by axinomancy: we want only a hatchet and a jet-stone to be laid together upon a fire of hot embers. **1870** *Archæol.* XLIII. 517.

axiolite ('æksɪəʊlaɪt). *Min.* [f. L. *axi-s* + Gr. λίθος stone: see -LITE.] (See quot.) **axiolitic** (,æksɪəʊ'lɪtɪk), *a.*, of or pertaining to axiolites.

1879 RUTLEY *Stud. Rocks* xi. 184 Termed axiolites by Zirkel..elongated lenticular and curved zones of brownish glass forming the envelope of a smaller corresponding mass of paler vitreous matter, in which incipient crystallisation or fibrous structure trends at right angles to the inner surfaces of the envelope towards a longitudinal median line. *Ibid.* The axiolitic structure visible in a rhyolite.

axiology (æksɪ'ɒlədʒɪ). *Philos.* [ad. F. *axiologie*, f. Gr. ἀξία worth, value + -OLOGY.] The theory of value. Hence **,axio'logical** *a.*, of or pertaining to or of the nature of axiology; **,axio'logically** *adv.*, according to axiological theory; **axi'ologist**, one who considers or treats of axiology.

[**1902** P. LAPIE *Logique de la volonté* v. 385 La science de la valeur et la science du bonheur: l'Axiologie et l'Eudémonologie.] **1907** W. M. URBAN in *Psychol. Rev.* XIV. 5 The term *axiological* (constructed on the analogy of the term *epistemological*), is here used to distinguish the problem of validity or evaluation of worth predicates from the psychological problem of their description and genesis. **1908** J. M. BALDWIN *Thought & Things* II. xiv. 381 In the further reading of the context preferentially and so to speak 'axiologically'. *Ibid.*, 'Axiology' is a term suggested, I think, by Professor W. M. Urban for the science of *worth-meanings* as predicates, as contrasted with 'epistemology' which treats of predicates of fact. **1926** J. LAIRD *Study Moral Theory* 33 Pure axiology, the science of values of every species. **1931** A. WOLF in W. Rose *Outl. Mod. Knowl.* xiii. 547 The frst axiological problem is: How many and what ultimate values are there? **1935** *Mind* XLIV. 295 There are..in the writings of all Objectivist axiologists chapters ostensibly directed to 'proving' some selected list of 'intrinsic' values. **1954** *Sc. Jrnl. Theol.* VII. 168 In a Biblical theology there is bound to be an axiological element; the judgment of value cannot be excluded.

axiom ('æksɪəm). Forms: 6–7 **axioma, axiome,** 5– **axiom.** [a. F. *axiome*, ad. L. *axiōma*, a. Gr. ἀξίωμα that which is thought worthy or fit, that which commends itself as self-evident, f. ἀξιόειν to hold worthy, f. ἄξιος worthy.]

1. A proposition that commends itself to general acceptance; a well-established or universally-conceded principle; a maxim, rule, law.

1485 CAXTON *Paris & V.* Prol., An axiom which in Latin expressed, *hoc crede quod tibi verum esse videtur.* **1579** LYLY *Euphues* (Arb.) 100 The Axiomaes of Aristotle. **1604** DEKKER *Honest Wh.* Wks. 1873 II. 63 That's an Axiome, a Principle. **1651** HOBBES *Govt. & Soc.* i. §2. 3 Which Axiom, though received by most, is yet certainly false. **1757** JOHNSON *Rambl.* No. 175 ¶1 The axioms of wisdom which recommend the ancient sages to veneration. **1837** J. HARRIS *Gt. Teacher* 389 The axiom known by the name of the golden rule. **1875** H. E. MANNING *Mission H. Ghost* ii. 33 It is an axiom of the human reason that God is everywhere.

†**b.** Specially restricted by Bacon to: An empirical law, a generalization from experience. *Obs.*

1626 BACON *Sylva* §2 Led by great Judgement, and some good Light of Axioms. **1627** RAWLEY in *Bacon's Ess.* (Arb.) Introd. 26 True Axiomes must be drawne from plaine Experience, and not from doubtful. **1838** SIR W. HAMILTON *Logic* xxvi. II. 47 Empirical rules (Bacon would call them *axioms.*)

†**2.** *Logic.* A proposition (whether true or false).

1588 FRAUNCE *Lawiers Log.* II. i. 86 b, An axiom or proposition..hath two partes, the bande, and the partes bound. **1656** STANLEY *Hist. Philos.* VIII. *Zeno* xx. 43 Universally negative axioms are those, which consist of an universall negative particle, and a Categorem; as, *no man walketh.* **1664** H. MORE *Myst. Iniq.* Apol. 533 Otherwise no man might dispute or pronounce a false Axiome. **1742** in BAILEY.

3. *Logic* and *Math.* 'A self-evident proposition, requiring no formal demonstration to prove its truth, but received and assented to as soon as mentioned' (Hutton).

a **1600** HOOKER (J.) Axioms, or principles more general, are such as this, that the greater good is to be chosen before the lesser. **1660** R. COKE *Justice Vind.* 16. **1785** REID *Int. Powers* I. ii, Nor are they necessary truths, as mathematical axioms are. **1807** BYRON *Hours Idlen.*, *College Exam.*, Happy the youth in Euclid's axioms tried. **1851** H. SPENCER *Soc. Stat.* II. ix. §6 The axiom that the whole is greater than its part.

axiomata media (æksɪ'əʊmətə 'miːdɪə), *phr. Philos.* [mod.L. (Bacon *Nov. Org.* (1620) I. xix. p. 51), f. pl. of Gr. ἀξίωμα AXIOM + L. *medium* MEDIUM; cf. AXIOM 1 b.] (See quot. 1934.)

1833 J. S. MILL in *Monthly Repos.* VII. 669. **1843** —— *Syst. Logic* II. VI. v. 524 The principles of Ethology are properly the middle principles, the *axiomata media* (as Bacon would have said) of the science of mind... Bacon has judiciously observed that the *axiomata media* of every science principally constitute its value. **1934** WEBSTER, *Axiomata media*, middle principles; those general principles which are above simple empirical laws, yet inferior to the highest generalizations, or to such as are taken to be fundamental. **1937** A. H. MURRAY *Philos. J. Ward* vii. 154 Philosophy wants *axiomata media.* It is only by such middle principles or mediating principles that it can hope to arrive at a view of the world in which all the knowledges of the various sciences will form a unified whole.

axiomatic (,æksɪə'mætɪk), *a.* [ad. Gr. ἀξιωματικός, f. ἀξίωμα: see AXIOM and -ATIC.]

A. *adj.* **1.** Of the nature of an axiom or admitted first principle; self-evident; indisputably true.

1797 W. TAYLOR in *Monthly Rev.* XXII. 556 The axiomatic pillars of a new code of the law of nations. **1855** H. SPENCER *Psychol.* (1872) II. VI. viii. 95 These axiomatic truths are truths recognized by the simplest order of reasoning.

2. Characterized by axioms or admitted first principles; axiomatical.

1812 SIR H. DAVY *Chem. Philos.* 32 He gave an axiomatic form to the Science.

3. Full of maxims or pithy sentences, aphoristic.

1834 SOUTHEY *Doctor* (1862) 381 The most axiomatic of English Poets. **1835** I. TAYLOR *Spir. Despot.* iii. 96 A people ..rich in axiomatic good sense.

B. *sb. pl.* A body of axioms; the study or use of axioms.

1927 E. T. WHITTAKER in *Rep. Brit. Assoc. Advancem. Sci.* 21 What we want to do, then, is to set forth the axiomatics of general relativity in the same form as we have been accustomed to give to the axiomatics of any other kind of geometry. **1959** K. R. POPPER *Logic Sci. Disc.* 320 From the formal point of view of 'axiomatics', probability can be described as a two-termed functor.

,axio'matical, *a.* [f. as prec. + -AL¹.]

†**1.** *Logic.* Pertaining to, or of the nature of, a simple statement or proposition: cf. AXIOM 2. *Obs.*

1588 FRAUNCE *Lawiers Log.* I. ii. 7 This is the first part of judgement in axioms, called axiomaticall, determining only truth and falsenes in propositions or axioms. *a* **1679** T. GOODWIN *Wks.* (1864) VIII. 403 An application axiomatical, that he is mine.

2. Of or relating to axioms, maxims, or admitted first principles.

a **1676** WHITLOCK *Mann. Eng.* 109 (T.) To front his axiomatical experiments [the book of Aphorisms] with the grand miscarriages in the practice of most able physicians. *a* **1751** BOLINGBROKE *Hum. Knowl.* i. (R.) Materials of axiomatical, scientific, and, in a word, of absolute real knowledge.

3. = AXIOMATIC 1.

1678 CUDWORTH *Intell. Syst.* I. v. 731 Axiomatical Truths. **1765** JOHNSON *Pref. Shaks.* Wks. 1816 II. 167 In his art there is no..axiomatical truth that regulates subordinate positions. **1869** *Eng. Mech.* 9 Apr. 62/1 Proving..that 'two and two make four,' or propositions equally as axiomatical.

4. = AXIOMATIC 3.

1738 OLDYS *Raleigh* (R.) That solid axiomatical vein, which is observable in other productions of Ralegh's muse.

,axio'matically, *adv.* [f. prec. + -LY².] In axiomatic manner: †**a.** (*Logic*) in the form of a simple proposition (*obs.*); **b.** as in axiom, as an admitted principle or self-evident truth.

1588 FRAUNCE *Lawiers Log.* I. ii. 9 Placing them axiomatically, syllogistically, or methodically, we argue some other thing either by explication or confirmation. *c* **1643** *Maximes Unfold.* 46 Pronounced axiomatically for truth. **1840** THACKERAY *Paris Sk. Bk.* (1872) 99 'Society,' writes the Prince, axiomatically, 'contains in itself two principles.'

axiomatize ('æksɪəmətaɪz), *v.* [f. AXIOMAT(IC *a.* + -IZE.] **1.** *intr.* To make an axiom or axioms.

1716 M. DAVIES *Athen. Brit.* II. i. 12 Here, the same excellent Historian Axiomatize's very opportunely.

2. *trans.* To render axiomatic, to give an axiomatic form to; to reduce to a system of axioms.

1934 in WEBSTER. **1943** *Mind* LII. 221 Woodger's theory is axiomatised and therefore it presents us with the answer. **1956** *Trans. Philol. Soc.* 1955 97 The attempts that are made to axiomatize linguistics. **1959** K. R. POPPER *Logic Sci. Disc.* iii. 71 A so-called 'axiomatized system'.

Hence **,axiomati'zation.**

1931 *Jrnl. Philos.* XXVIII. 283 The Russell-Whitehead axiomatization of logic is a practical convenience. **1956** *Trans. Philol. Soc.* 1955 94 Even in mathematics the possibilities of complete axiomatization have been over-estimated.

axion ('æksɪɒn). *Particle Physics.* [f. AXI(AL *a.* + -ON¹.] A neutral pseudoscalar boson with very small mass that is the quantum of a field postulated as accounting for the fact that charge-parity symmetry is rarely broken.

1978 S. WEINBERG in *Physical Rev. Lett.* XL. 223/2 A very light pseudoscalar pseudo-Goldstone boson, the 'axion'. **1978** F. WILCZEK in *Ibid.* 280/2 A special kind of Higgs boson (which we are calling the *axion*) with zero bare mass. **1978** *Nature* 6 July 22/1 Axions, new elementary particles of mass less than or comparable to electrons, might have escaped previous detection because they would be semi-weakly interacting, neutral and pseudoscalar, and hence somewhat elusive. **1984** *Ibid.* 11 Oct. 517/2 If axions comprise the dark halo of our Galaxy, laboratory experiments have recently been proposed that could detect them. **1985** *Sci. Amer.* May 61/2 The axion would interact only rarely with ordinary matter; although light, axions would be abundant enough to account for the missing mass.

axio'pistical, *a.* ?*Obs.* [f. Gr. ἀξιόπιστ-ος trustworthy (f. ἄξιος worthy + πιστός to be trusted) + -ICAL.] Trustworthy.

1611 R. BADLEY *Panegyr. V.* in *Coryat's Crudities*, His most Axiopisticall Hodœpory.

axiopisty ('æksɪəʊ,pɪstɪ). [ad. Gr. ἀξιοπιστία, f. ἀξιόπιστος: see prec.] Trustworthiness. (In mod. Dicts.)

axis¹ ('æksɪs). Pl. **axes** ('æksiːz). [a. L. *axis* axle, axle-tree, pivot, axis of the earth, heavens, etc., cogn. with OE. *eax*: see AX *sb.* Used for various figurative and transferred senses of AXLE.]

I. Axis of rotation or revolution.

1. a. The axle of a wheel. ?*Obs.*

wheel and axis, axis in peritrochio: the Wheel-and-Axle, one of the mechanical powers.

a **1619** FOTHERBY *Atheom.* II. xi. §1 The weightines of the wheele doth settle it vpon his Axis. **1725** BRADLEY *Fam. Dict.* s.v. *Windmill*, Like unto the Axis of a Cutlers Grind-Stone. **1796** HUTTON *Math. Dict.* I. 178 To construct an axis in peritrochio. **1822** IMISON *Sc. & Art* I. 37 The wheel and axis may be considered as a kind of perpetual lever.

b. *fig.* The 'pivot' on which any matter turns.

1860 MOTLEY *Netherl.* (1868) I. v. 169 The axis of the revolt was the religious question.

2. *Phys.* **a.** A tooth or process on the second cervical vertebra, upon which the head is turned. **b.** The vertebra which has the process.

1694 SALMON tr. *Diemerbroeck's Anat.* IV. xii. (1714) 249 Axis..is a name which rather befits the former vertebra, whose tooth resembles an Axle. **1701** TAUVRY *Anat.* II. xvi. 268 This second Vertebra has an Apophysis call'd the Tooth ..The Head and the first vertebra..are qualified to turn upon that Axis. **1815** *Encycl. Brit.* III. 289 Axis..the second vertebra of the neck; it hath a tooth which goes into the first vertebra and this tooth is by some called the axis. **1836** *Athenæum* No. 450. 419 The Atlas and Axis of the Ichthyosaurus are united.

3. The imaginary straight line about which a body (*e.g.* the earth or other planet) rotates; the prolongation of that of the earth on which the heavens appear to revolve.

(The ends of the axis are *poles*; thence the use of *axis* as a line from pole to pole, or from end to end: see III.)

1549 *Compl. Scot.* vi. 48 3e sal ymagyn ane lyne that passis throucht the spere lyk til ane extree of ane cart, callit axis-spere. **1635** N. CARPENTER *Geogr. Del.* I. iii. 67 The motion of an iron-wire or needle..vpon his owne Axis. ?*c* **1660** HOBBES *Physics* IV. xxvi. §6. I. 428 The earth is so carried about the sun, as that its axis is thereby always kept parallel to itself. **1849** MRS. SOMERVILLE *Connex. Phys. Sc.*, There are at least three axes at right angles to each other round any one of which..the solid..will continue to revolve for ever.

4. a. *fig.* A central prop, which sustains any system (as Atlas was feigned to sustain the revolving heavens). *Obs.*

a **1616** BEAUM. & FL. *Valentin.* v. v, I have found out axis; You know he bears the empire. **1646** SIR T. BROWNE *Pseud. Ep.* 94 The Atlas or maine axis, which supported this opinion, was daily experience.

b. *fig.* The relation between countries regarded as a common pivot on which they revolve; esp. the political association of 1936 (becoming in 1939 a military alliance) formed between Italy and Germany; later extended to that between Germany, Italy, and Japan; still later to that between other allied countries. Often used *attrib.*, as ***Axis forces, powers***, and *ellipt.* for such phrases, with consequent pl. concord. Also *transf.*, of any comparable association, or connecting common interest.

1936 *Times* 3 Nov. 15/1 The 'Rome-Berlin axis' is a conceit which has its momentary attractions. **1938** *New Statesman* 19 Feb. 274/2 He [*sc.* King Carol of Rumania] will as before try to keep one foot in the Franco-Russian camp and the other in that of the Axis Powers. **1939** *Times* 6 Feb. 11/1 (*headline*) Attacks on the Axis. **1941** *Time* 21 Apr. 34/3 The London-Washington Axis. **1942** *Times*

Weekly 7 Jan. 5 The 26 anti-Axis nations are united..in the broad conduct of the war. **1952** *Economist* 19 July 145/1 The Moscow-Peking axis. *Ibid.* 22 Nov. 531/1 One [proposal] is for an Old Vic-Stratford axis, with an exchange of productions. **1959** *New Statesman* 7 Feb. 177/1 The term 'axis' is looked on with disfavour here [*sc.* Bonn] as a reminder of the Berlin-Rome-Tokyo axis of the Nazis.

5. The geometrical line, by the revolution of a superficies about which, solids with circular section, as a globe, cylinder, cone, etc. are conceived to be generated.

(This is the ***axis of revolution***; it coincides necessarily with the axis of symmetry; thence branch II.)

1571 DIGGES *Pantom.* III. iii. Q ij b, The Axis or Altitude of the Cone. **1796** HUTTON *Math. Dict.* I. 177 If a semi-circle be moved round its diameter at rest, it will generate a sphere, whose axis is that diameter.

II. Axis of symmetrical arrangement. (Cf. 5.)

6. The straight line about which the parts of a body or system are symmetrically arranged.

axis of a balance: the line upon which it turns. ***axis of oscillation*** (of a pendulum, etc.): a horizontal line passing through the centre of the oscillation, and perpendicular to its plane (Hutton 1796). ***axis of polarization***: the central line round which the prismatic rings or curves are arranged. ***neutral axis*** (of a girder): the line where there is neither compression nor tension (Brewster).

7. *Geom.* Any line in a regular figure which divides it into two symmetrical parts, e.g., which joins opposite angles or the centres of opposite sides; in a conic section, the line from the principal vertex or vertices, perpendicular to the tangent at that point; in a curve, a straight line which bisects a system of parallel chords (called ***principal axis*** when it cuts them at right angles).

transverse axis (in the ellipse and hyperbola): that which passes through the two foci; ***conjugate axis***, that which bisects the transverse one at right angles. The axes of an ellipse are also called *major* and *minor*.

1734 *Builder's Dict.*, *Axis* of a Conic Section, is a quiescent Right Line passing through the Middle of the Figure, and cutting all the Ordinates at Right Angles. **1796** HUTTON *Math. Dict.* I. 177 *Axis*..more generally..a right line conceived to be drawn from the vertex of a figure to the middle of the base. *Ibid.* The ellipse and hyperbola have each two axes; but the parabola has only one, and that infinite in length. *Ibid.* In curves of the second order, that diameter whose parallel ordinates are at right angles to it, when possible, is an Axis. **1849** MRS. SOMERVILLE *Connex. Phys. Sc.* xxi. 201 Cut longitudinally, that is, parallel to the axis of the prism. **1853** SIR J. HERSCHEL *Pop. Lect. Sc.* iii. §13 (1873) 106 The longer axes or longest dimensions of their orbits. **1879** THOMSON & TAIT *Nat. Phil.* I. I. §120.

8. *Crystallog.* An imaginary line drawn between the centres of opposite faces or edges, or the apices of opposite angles. (See quot.)

1817 R. JAMESON *Charac. Min.* 244 Three of the cleavages are equiangular and oblique-angular, in a common axis. **1869** ROSCOE *Elem. Chem.* 192 In order to classify..crystals, the existence of certain lines within the crystal called axes is supposed, round which the form can be symmetrically built up. **1878** GURNEY *Crystallog.* 30 The straight lines or directions in the crystal which are common to two or more symmetral planes are called axes of symmetry.

9. *Optics.* **a.** A ray passing through the centre of the eye or of a lense, or falling perpendicularly on it; the line which passes through the centres of the lenses in a telescope; the straight line from the eye to the object of sight.

1701 TAUVRY *Anat.* II. vii. 205 To direct the two Optick axis's, in looking upon the same object. *c* **1790** IMISON *Sch. Art* I. 196 If the axis of both eyes are not directed to the object, that object will appear double. **1831** BREWSTER *Optics* iv. 28 In all these lenses a line..passing through the centres of their curved surfaces, and perpendicular to their plane surfaces, is called the *axis*. **1855** H. SPENCER *Psychol.* (1872) I. III. x. 380 Due convergence of the visual axes. **1871** J. DICKSEE *Perspective* 27 The axis of vision or line of direction is an imaginary line proceeding from the spectator to the perspective centre.

b. ***axis of incidence***: the line passing through the point of incidence perpendicularly to the refracting surface. ***axis of refraction***: the continuation of the same line through the refracting medium. ***axis of double refraction***: the line or direction on both sides of which double refraction takes place, but along which it does not exist.

1734 *Builder's Dict.*, *Axis* of Incidence, Refraction. **1796** HUTTON *Math. Dict.* I. 178. **1831** BREWSTER *Optics* xvii. 147 An axis of double refraction..is not like the axis of the earth, a fixed line within the rhomb or crystal. It is only a fixed direction. **1836** *Athenæum* No. 448. 381 Like calcareous spar it has one axis of double refraction.

¶ In the three following the sense tends to pass into axis of growth or direction as in branch III.

10. *Phys.* and *Zool.* The central core of an organ or organism; the central skeleton or nervous cord; the central stem or core round which polypes grow; the central column of a whorled shell.

1741 MONRO *Anat. Bones* 54 The Powers that draw it towards the Axis of the Bone. **1830** *Edin. Encycl.* XIV. 599 In other species, the organs, which are not in pairs, are arranged round a central axis. **1866** R. TATE *Brit. Mollusks* iii. 44 The axis of the shell around which the whorls are coiled. **1873** A. FLINT *Nerv. Syst.* ix. 257 The nervous matter contained in the cavity..is known as the cerebro-spinal axis.

11. *Bot.* **a.** The central column of the inflorescence or other whorl of growth. **b.** The main stem and root.

1786 REES *Encycl.*, *Axis*..a taper column placed in the centre of some flowers, or katkins, about which the other parts are disposed. **1835** J. COMSTOCK *Yng. Botanist* 239 *Axis*, centre of vegetation, as the pith of vascular plants. **1835** *Penny Cycl.* III. 184 Each cluster of leaves is a small branch without perceptible axis. **1857** HENFREY *Bot.* §42 The stem is the ascending portion of the axis. **1870** HOOKER *Stud. Fl.* 232 Erica..Seeds attached to a central axis.

12. *Physiogr.* and *Geol.* A central ridge; the central line of a valley.

anticlinal axis: the line along which two opposite planes of stratification meet in a ridge. ***synclinal axis***: the line along which they meet in a depression.

1830 LYELL *Princ. Geol.* I. 135 A line of volcanos.. parallel to the axis of the older ridge. **1849** MURCHISON *Siluria* ii. (1867) 25 These round-backed hills..rise boldly from beneath the surrounding Silurian deposits, of which they form the axis. **1854** F. BAKEWELL *Geol.* 4 The technical name given to such a centre of elevation is the 'anticlinal axis.'

III. A straight line from pole to pole (cf. 3), or from end to end, of any body.

13. *gen.* e.g. ***axis of the equator***: the polar diameter of the earth, which is also the axis of rotation; see 3. ***axis of the ecliptic***, ***of the horizon***: a diameter of the sphere passing through these circles at right angles to their planes.

1796 HUTTON *Math. Dict.*

14. *spec.* An imaginary line uniting the two poles of a magnet.

1664 POWER *Exp. Philos.* III. 158 If you divide the Magnet through a meridian, or Saw of a Segment, parallel to the Axis. **1832** U.K.S. *Nat. Philos.* II. *Magnetism* i. §6 The straight line joining the two poles of a magnet is called its axis.

15. A main line of motion, growth, extension, direction.

1818 W. LAWRENCE *Nat. Hist. Man* I. ii. (1848) 99 Its axis [of the femur] coincides with the centre of gravity of the body. **1853** KANE *Grinnell Exp.* x. (1856) 75 The axis of Baffin's Bay..is from the north by east. *Ibid.* 76 The ice, after changing its original axis of drift. **1855** OWEN *Skel. & Teeth* 6 In the direction of the bone's axis. **1867** A. BARRY *Sir C. Barry* vii. 240 The principal axis of the building.

IV. Axis of reference.

16. *Analyt. Geom.* Each of the two intersecting straight lines, by reference to which the position of a certain point, the *locus*, is determined.

(Transf. from the geometrical treatment of conic sections.)

1855 TODHUNTER *Plane. Co-ord. Geom.*

V. *Comb.* **axis-cylinder** (or **axis-band**), see quot.; *attrib.*, as ***axis-ligament***.

1839 TODD *Cycl. Anat. & Phys.* III. 592/1 A central substance of nervous matter..the axis-cylinder of Rosenthal. **1855** H. SPENCER *Psychol.* (1872) I. I. ii. 27 The central fibre, or axis-cylinder of a nerve tube. **1877** ROSENTHAL *Muscles & N.* 104 The axis-band, or axis-cylinder. **1877** BURNETT *Ear* 72 In all its motion as a lever the hammer swings about this axis-ligament as a fixed point.

axis² ('æksɪs). *Zool.* [L., an Indian quadruped mentioned by Pliny.] Name given by Buffon to an Indian deer (*Cervus axis*) known by sportsmen as the Hog-deer.

1601 HOLLAND *Pliny* VIII. xxi. I. 206 A wild beast named Axis, with a skin like a fawn. **1774** GOLDSM. *Nat. Hist.* II. 72 The horns of the axis are round, like those of the stag. **1859** TENNENT *Ceylon* I. II. i. 157 The spotted axis troops in herds as numerous as the fallow deer in England.

axised ('æksɪst), *a.* Possessing an axis.

1865 RUSKIN in *Art-Jrnl.* No. 41. 129/2 A little spinning, askew-axised thing we call a planet.

axite ('æksaɪt). [f. *-ax* in *bonax*, *primax*, names of sporting cartridges manufactured by Messrs. Kynoch (I.C.I. Metals Ltd.) + *-ite* of CORDITE.] A smokeless powder for sporting rifles, composed of strip cordite in which a little of the gun-cotton is replaced by potassium nitrate.

1904 in *Trade Mark Jrnl.* 19 Oct. **1905** *Kynoch Jrnl.* Jan.-Mar. 86 'Axite' Service cartridge. **1919** E. DE B. BARNETT *Explosives* 78 Axite..is practically Cordite M.D. to which 2 per cent. of potassium nitrate has been added. **1921** *Blackw. Mag.* Dec. 802/2 A high-velocity axite charge.

†**axle¹**. *Obs.* Forms: 1-2 eaxl, exel, 1-3 exl, 3 æxl. [Common Teut.: OE. *eaxl*, fem., = ON. *öxl* (pl. *axlir*), OHG. *ahsala*, MHG. *ahsel*, mod.G. *achsel*, OTeut. **ahslā*, from same root as **ahsâ*: see AX *sb.* Cogn. w. L. **axula*, *āla*.] The shoulder.

c **1000** *Sax. Leechd.* II. 104 Weorp ofer eaxle, oþþe betweoh þeoh. *c* **1000** *Ags. Gosp.* Luke xv. 5 He hitt set on his exla [*Hatton* eaxle] geblissiende. *c* **1175** *Cott. Hom.* 245 He hit berð an his exlun. **1205** LAY. 18032 Hengen an heore æxle mucle wi-æxe.

axle² ('æks(ə)l). Forms: 5-6 axil, 5-8 **axel**, 6-7 axell, 7 axile, 7- **axle**. For earlier forms in comb., see AXLE-TREE. [Not in OE.; found in 13th c. in the compd. *axle-tree*, ON. *öxul-tre* (synonymous with the native AX-TREE), f. ON. *öxull* masc. = Goth. **ahsuls*, OTeut. **ahsulo-z*, deriv. of *ahs-â*; thence the simple *axle* has been since taken, and used in place of OE. *æx*, *eax*: see AX *sb.*]

1. The centre-pin or spindle upon which a wheel revolves, or which revolves along with it.

a. In carriages, properly, the rounded and more slender ends of the axle-tree, or the pegs fastened into the ends of the axle-tree, on which the wheel actually revolves; but used to include the axle-tree or axle-bar, especially when this is of one piece with the axles proper, or when it revolves with the wheels.

1634 MILTON *Comus* 96 The gilded car of day His glowing axle doth allay In the steep Atlantic stream. **1703** MAUNDRELL *Journ. Jerus.* (1721) 77 It turn'd upon two hinges in the nature of Axels. **1799** TURNER *Anglo-Sax.* (1828) I. v. 70 Chariots with scythes at the Axles. **1831** J. HOLLAND *Manuf. Metals* I. 157 Iron axles are becoming almost as common as once they were rare. **1870** BRYANT *Homer* II. XVI. 132 Full many a chief Fell under his own axle from the car. **1873** *Daily News* 12 Sept. 4/3 The axle of a truck in a coal train broke.

b. A central spindle of a wheel which revolves along with it, as in the mechanical power called *wheel-and-axle*, and its applications.

1730 DESAGULIERS *Axis in Peritrochio* in *Phil. Trans.* XXXVI. 226 When we pull the Rope PA, we make the Axel ..to wind itself up upon the Rope HD. **1829** U.K.S. *Nat. Philos.* I. *Mechanics* II. vi. §50 A modification of the lever, called the axle in the wheel.

c. *fig.* (Cf. 'pivot.')

1635 AUSTIN *Medit.* 194 Since he..makes that the Axell for all his Commendations to Moove on. **1641** MILTON *Ch. Govt.* i. Wks. 1851, 98 All the moments..of humane occasions are mov'd to and fro as upon the axle of discipline.

†**2.** The BEAM of a loom, on which the warp or woven fabric is wound. *Obs.*

1635 AUSTIN *Medit.* 281 The wrought part [of a web] is fastned to, and wrapt up about the Axell.

†**3.** The imaginary line about which a planet, or other body (or, in old cosmography, the heaven), revolves. Also, *poet.*, the pole, the sky or heaven (cf. AXLE-TREE 4 b). *Obs.* exc. *poet.* (Replaced by AXIS.)

1596 FITZ-GEFFREY *Sir F. Drake* (1881) 20 None but old Atlas..Should under-prop the Axel of the west. **1635** N. CARPENTER *Geogr. Del.* I. iii. 67 The magneticall wier..will ..make a circumuolution about his owne Axell. *a* **1649** DRUMM. OF HAWTH. *Wks.* (1711) 29/1 Heaven's axile seems to bend. **1667** MILTON *P.L.* VIII. 165 The earth..With inoffensive pace that spinning sleeps On her soft Axle. **1713** YOUNG *Last Day* I. 116 The blissful earth, who late At leisure on her axle roll'd in state. **1850** MRS. BROWNING *Poet's Vow* I. xviii, Since earth on axle ran!

4. *Comb.* and *Attrib.* **axle-bar**, an iron bar serving the purpose of an axletree; **axle-bearing** (see quot.); **axle-box**, in a locomotive engine or railway carriage, the box, usually of cast iron, within which the ends of the axles revolve; **axle-counter** (see quot.); hence ***axle-counting*** vbl. sb.; **axle-grease**, (*a*) grease suitable for lubricating axles; also *fig.*; (*b*) *slang*, butter; **axle-guards**, the part of the frame in which the axle-box slides up and down as acted on by the springs; **axle-journal**, **axle-neck**, the polished end of the axle which revolves under the bearing in the axle-box; **axle-nail**, **axle-pin**, one of the two nails or pins used to fasten a cart to the axle-tree; **axle-shaft**, a driving shaft forming an extension of the axle of a wheel; †**axle-wood**, wood for axle-trees. See also AXLE-TREE.

1850 WEALE *Dict. Terms*, *Axle bearing* in locomotive engines, the gun-metal, or other metal bearing, under which the axle journal revolves [in the axle-box]. **1828** SIR H. STEUART *Planter's Guide* 258 Three stages strongly bolted to the crossbar, or axle-bed (as our workmen term it). **1871** *Daily News* 23 Feb., The wheels..sunk up to the axle-boxes. **1876** *Proc. Inst. Civ. Eng.* XLVI. 92 Ordinary grease axle-boxes weigh less than 3 cwt. the set. **1936** *Gloss. Terms Railw. Signalling* (*B.S.I.*) 7 *Axle counter*, a device for counting the number of axles of the vehicles comprising a train passing a given point. **1936** *Economist* 25 Jan. 178/2 Security against collisions of this kind can only be provided by a combination of track-circuiting (or the newer device of axle-counting) and automatic train control. **1881** *Cassell's Techn. Educ.* No. 21. 174/1 The distance of the hind axle-flaps from collars will be regulated by the width of the body across. **1878** *Rep. Indian Affairs* 366 (D.A.), Class 10. Miscellaneous articles..Axle-grease—dozen boxes. **1900** A. DILLON *Greek Kalends* 31 Oh, Comedy! Laughter gives axle-grease to the wheel o' the sun. **1919** DOWNING *Digger Dial.* 9 *Axle-grease*, butter. **1485** *Inv.* in *Ripon Ch. Acts* (1882) 373 Axilnayles, 4*d.* **1530** PALSGR. 196/1 Axilnayle, *cheuille daixevl.* **1523** FITZHERB. *Husb.* §5 Lyn-pinnes of yren in the axiltre-endes . ii . axil-pynnes of yren, or els of tough harde wodde. **1837** *Athenæum* No. 510. 565 Enabling the upright axle-shaft to turn the millstone without additional gear. **1870** ALFORD in *Life* (1873) 443, I am again down on the axle-springs and must be braced up. **1562** *Wills & Inv. N.C.* (1860) 208 Axlewayne nales. **1405** *Fabric Rolls York* (1858) 34 MM. ascelwod empto 21*s.* 6*d.* **1562** *MS. Acc. Bk. Vicars Choral, York*, Pro ii thousandes & di. axellwodde.

axled ('æks(ə)ld), *a.* [f. AXLE *sb.²* + -ED².] Furnished with an axle. (Chiefly in *comb.*)

1657 FORD *Sun's Darling* v. i. (1811) 387 The waggoner might thaw His chariot, axled with Riphaean snow. **1791** HUDDESFORD *Salmag.* ii. 32 Her coral-axled car. **1869** *Echo* 3 Dec., The crank-axled machine.

†**'axless**, *a. Obs. rare*⁻¹. [f. AX *sb.* + -LESS.] Without an axle or axles.
1598 SYLVESTER *Du Bartas* (1608) 770 To see that mighty mound Hingeless and axless turn so swiftly round.

†**'axle-,tooth.** *Obs.* or *dial.* Forms: 5 **axyl-tothe**, 7 **axill-**, **axel-**; mod. *dial.* **asil-**, **assal-**, **assle-tooth.** [a. Da. *axel* (= ON. *jaxl*) molar tooth, grinder + TOOTH: cf. Da. *axel-tand* axle-tooth.] A molar tooth, a grinder.
1483 *Cath. Angl.* 16 Axyltothe, *molaris, maxillaris.* **1607** WALKINGTON *Opt. Glasse Humors* 76 To loose an axill tooth, or an eye. **1657** TOMLINSON *Renou's Disp.* 211 His axle teeth and also his gums fell out. **1691** RAY *N. Countr. Wds.* Pref., Axeltooth, *dens molaris.* **1808** JAMIESON *Dict.*, *Asil, Asil-tooth*, the name given to the grinders, or *dentes molares*, those at the extremity of the jaw. **1875** *Lanc. Gloss.* (E.D.S.) Some co'n em wang an others assal-teeth.

axle-tree ('æks(ə)ltriː). Forms: 3–4 **axeltre**, 4–6 **axil-**, **axyl-**, 5 **axille-**, **exil-**, **exul-**, **exyl-**, 6 **assyl-tre**, **exeltree**, 6–7 **axell-**, 7 **axol-**, **axil-**, 6–8 **axel-**, 6– **axle-tree.** [ME. *axel-tre*, a. ON. *öxul-tré*, f. *öxull* AXLE + *tré* TREE, synonymous with the native AX-TREE. See AXLE².]
(*Axle-tree*, being in earlier use than the simple *axle*, formerly included the sense of that word, and of *axis*. It is now restricted to sense 1, but *axle* is not kept quite distinct from it in use: see that word.)
1. The fixed bar or beam of wood, etc., on the rounded ends of which the opposite wheels of a carriage revolve. The original and only surviving sense. ***axle-tree arms***: the ends of the axle-tree which project beyond the wheels.
a **1300** *Cursor M.* 21268 Quat quele mai be..and quat axeltre [*v.r.* axil tre, axiltree]. **1481–90** *Howard Househ. Bks.* 211 Ij. hopis to the exiltre. **1523** FITZHERB. *Husb.*§5 Lyn pinnes of yren in the axiltre endes. **1535** COVERDALE *1 Kings* vii. 30 Foure brasen wheles with brasen axeltrees. **1649** BLITH *Eng. Improv. Impr.* (1653) 167 The Beech..is very good Timber for..the Husbandman, for Axol-trees. **1755** MRS. DELANY *Diary* III. 349 No harm but to the axle-tree of their coach, which broke. **1794** W. FELTON *Carriages* (1801) I. 84 The arms of the axletree, which are made round, but rather of a conical form. **1855** MACAULAY *Fredk. Gt.* 47 [They] drove shabby old carriages till the axle-trees gave way. **1862** GRIFFITHS *Artill. Man.* 112 Axle-tree arm.
†**2.** The spindle or AXLE of any wheel; the 'axle' in the *wheel-and-axle*. *Obs.*
c **1400** MAUNDEV. xvii. 181 A wheel, that turneth be his Axille Tree. **1530** PALSGR. 196/1 Axiltre, *aixsevl.* **1659** LEAK *Water-wks.* 19 It shall make the Wheel F to turn half a turn by the Cord which is fastned to the Axletree of the said Wheel. **1664** EVELYN *Sylva* II. vi. (1776) 379 For the cogs of mills, posts to be set in moist ground, and Ever-lasting Axle-trees.
†**b.** *fig.* (Cf. *pivot, axis.*)
c **1600** *Revel. Golias*, Their chaunginge mynde on tickell axeltree, Is rold and tost about. **1646** *Unhappy Game Scotch & Eng.* 9 You make his will the very Axeltree upon which your argument turnes. **1674** MARVELL *Reh. Transp.* II. 171 A necessity..which drove the great Iron nail thorough the Axle-tree of Nature.
†**3.** A revolving or driving shaft. *Obs.*
1659 LEAK *Water-wks.* 18 A straight Axeltree of wood, a foot square, and 60-foot high.
†**4.** = AXIS: **a.** The imaginary or geometrical line which forms the axis of revolution of any body, e.g. the earth, a planet, the heavens. *Obs.*
c **1400** *Epiph.* (Turnb. 1843) 113 The axyltre betwene the polys tweyne. **1594** BLUNDEVIL *Exerc.* III. I. ii. 280 A right imaginative line, called of the Astronomers the Axletree of the world, about the which the world continually turneth like a Cart-wheele. **1606** SHAKS. *Tr. & Cr.* I. iii. 65 Strong as the Axletree In which the Heauens ride. **1633** P. FLETCHER *Purp. Isl.* IV. viii, Most like the poles in heavens Axletrees.
†**b.** *poetically* (transl. L. *axis*): The pole of the heaven; the heaven, the sky. *Obs.*
1513 DOUGLAS *Æneis* VI. ix. 3 Hir rosy chariot the fresche Aurora Amydwart of the heuynis assiltre Begouth for till wproll. **1626** G. SANDYS *Ovid's Met.* I. 7 And burne heauens Axeltree.
†**c.** The central line, e.g. the axis of vision.
1624 WOTTON *Archit.* (1672) 52 The Parts farthest from the Axel-tree, or middle Beam of the Eye.
Hence **'axletreed** *a.*, furnished with an axle-tree.
1580 TUSSER *Husb.* (1878) 36 Strong exeltred cart.

Axminster ('æksmɪnstə(r)). [The name of a town in Devonshire.] Used attrib. in ***Axminster carpet*** or ***rug***, a seamless carpet of a type originally manufactured at Axminster, noted for its thick and soft pile resembling that of a Turkey carpet. Also used *absol.*
1818 *Public Ledger & Daily Advertiser* 1 Apr. 1/4 Capital Axminster, Turkey, Brussels, and Kidderminster carpets. **1845** DISRAELI *Sybil* I. II. i. 97 The Axminster carpets.. imparted even to this palatian chamber a lively and habitable air. **1886** J. D. CHAMPLIN *Chronicle of Coach* xii. 179 Hand-made Axminsters are still manufactured at Wilton, England, and at Tour[c]oing, France. **1963** *Which?* Mar. 69/2 Axminsters..are made on looms which also put the pile tufts into position at the same time as the backing is woven... Axminster carpets always have a cut pile. **1968** D. HALLIDAY *Dolly & Singing Bird* ix. 100 Plodding over the Axminsters to arrive at a stateroom.

axo- ('æksəʊ). Short comb. form of Gr. ἄξω-ν axis, used in words in several scientific fields, as AXONEME, AXOPHYTE, etc.

axode, early pa. t. of ASK.

axoid ('æksɔɪd). [f. AX-IS + -OID.] A curve generated by the revolution of a point round an advancing axis, e.g. the cycloid.
1876 *Catal. Sci. App. S. Kens.* No. 553 Conic axoids, with corresponding spheric roulettes and profiles.

axoi'dean, *a.* [f. AXIS, on imperfect analogy.] = AXIAL.
1840 G. ELLIS *Anat.* 276 The occipito-axoidean ligament.

axolotl ('æksəlɒt(ə)l). *Zool.* [the Aztec name.] A batrachian reptile (*Siredon pisciforme*, family *Proteidæ*) found in Mexican lakes, resembling the salamander in appearance, but, like all the Proteidæ, retaining throughout life the gills of its young state.
1786 REES *Encycl.*, *Axolotl*..a singular fish found in the lake of Mexico. **1835** *Penny Cycl.* III. 187/1 Cuvier..was disposed to consider the axolotl as the tadpole of some of the larger species of American salamanders. **1855** OWEN *Skel. & Teeth* 28 The axolotl has 4 fingers and 5 toes.

axon ('æksɒn). *Anat.* Also **axone**, pl. **axones.** [ad. Gr. ἄξων axis.] †**a.** The body axis. *Obs.* **b.** A filamentous process of a nerve cell carrying outgoing nerve impulses, usually single and often very long, in contrast to the multiple, branched, and short incoming fibres or dendrites: the essential constituent of most nerves. Hence **a'xonic** *a.*
1842 DUNGLISON *Dict. Med. Sci.* (ed. 3), *Axon*, axis. **1884** WILDER in *N.Y. Med. Jrnl.* 2 Aug. 113 *Axon*, the mesal, longitudinal skeletal axis, represented in Branchiostoma and embryos by a membrano-gelatinous notochord. **1899** L. HILL *Human Physiol.* xxix. 337 Each [nerve-]fibre consists of a soft central strand of protoplasmic substance called the axon or axis cylinder. **1902** *Encycl. Brit.* XXV. 394/1 A neurone consists of three parts..(2) A single filament or axon, starting from the perikaryon. **1939** *Nature* 23 Sept. 557/2 Such an axonic fusion is a most unusual feature in animals. **1940** R. S. WOODWORTH *Psychol.* (ed. 12) viii. 250 Most nerve cells have two kinds of branches, a single axon and many dendrites.

axoneme ('æksɒniːm). [f. AXO- + Gr. νῆμα thread.] One of the threads or strands in the central portion of the contractile stalk of Vorticellidæ.
1901 G. N. CALKINS *Protozoa* 179 The strand has three threads which Entz calls *spasmoneme, spironeme,* and *axoneme.*

axonometric (,æksənəʊ'mɛtrɪk), *a.* [f. AXONOMETRY + -IC.] Of or pertaining to axonometry (esp. sense b).
1908 *R. Soc. Catal. Scient. Papers Subj. Index* I. Pure Math. 473/2 (*title*) Orthogonal axonometric foreshortened circle. **1938** *Times* 24 Jan. 19/3 Important riverside buildings, such as the Palace of Westminster..and bridges ..shown in what architects call 'axonometric' projection. **1956** W. F. GRIMES in R. L. S. Bruce-Mitford *Recent Archaeol. Excav. in Brit.* 121 (*caption*) Axonometric reconstruction of a section at Gutter Lane, Cheapside, showing the relationship of Roman deposit to medieval pits and other later features.

axonometry (æksə'nɒmɪtrɪ). [f. Gr. ἄξον- (ἄξων) axis + μετρία measurement: see -(O)METRY.]
a. Measurement of axes.
1865 *Athenæum* No. 1960. 688/2 Fundamental proposition of axonometry.
b. *spec.* in *Geom.* 'The art of making a perspective representation of figures when the coördinates of points in them are given' (*Cent. Dict.* 1889).

axonophyte (æk'səʊnəfaɪt). *Bot.* [f. as prec. + Gr. φυτόν plant.] 'An amentaceous plant, the flowers of which surround a common axis.' *Syd. Soc. Lex.* 1881.

axonost ('æksəʊnɒst). *Ichthyol.* [f. Gr. ἄξων + ὀστ-έον bone.] In fishes, one of the interspinal bones; the basal portion of a fin-ray.
1887 E. D. COPE in *Amer. Naturalist* XXI. 1017, I first used the terms axial and basilar for these segments... Those who prefer a substantive appellation for these elements may call them *axonosts* and *baseosts*... The axonost is sometimes represented by more than one segment,—*e.g.*, Dipnoi... The pelvic element so called is the axonost of this fin. **1898** A. S. WOODWARD *Outl. Vertebrate Palæont.* 21 Median fins ..rods of cartilage, each segmented into three pieces... The outer (distal) element is termed a *baseost*, the inner (proximal) element an *axonost.*

axophyte ('æksəfaɪt). *Bot.* [f. Gr. ἄξω-ν axis + φυτόν plant.] A plant that has an axis or stem.
1857 HENFREY *Bot.* §15 Higher plants exhibiting the coexistence of stem and leaf..are called Axophyta.

axoplasm ('æksəʊplæz(ə)m). *Anat.* [f. AXO- + Gr. πλάσμα (cf. PLASM 4).] The substance that surrounds the fibrils of an axon.
1900 in DORLAND *Med. Dict.* **1937** *Nature* 13 Feb. 292/2 If a giant nerve fibre [of a cephalopod] is cut, the axoplasm flows out from the sheath, showing it to be a viscous fluid. **1963** *New Scientist* 25 Apr. 188 The deeper white matter [of the brain] consists of innumerable electrical conducting fibres—semifluid threads of 'axoplasm'.

axopodium (,æksəʊ'pəʊdɪəm). *Zool.* Pl. **-dia.** [mod.L., f. AXO- + *-podium* PODIUM.] A pseudopodium, stiffened by an axial filament, found in some Heliozoa and Radiolaria.
1893 in *Funk's Standard Dict.* **1912** E. A. MINCHIN *Introd. Study Protozoa* v. 48 Pseudopodia of the radiate type are generally supported by an axial rod, a secreted structure of firm, elastic nature, and are hence known as axopodia. **1959** *Chambers's Encycl.* XI. 285/2 It has been suggested that axopodia are in origin flagella that have lost the power of rhythmic contraction.

axostyle ('æksəʊstaɪl). *Zool.* [f. AXO- + Gr. στῦλ-ος column.] 'A slender flexible rod of organic substance forming a supporting axis for the body of many Flagellates' (I. F. & W. D. Henderson, *Dict. Sci. Terms*, 1920).
1964 M. HYNES *Med. Bacteriol.*(ed. 8) xxviii. 433 The body of the parasite [*Trichomonas viginalis*] contains an axostyle (stiffening rod) which projects like a tail spine. **1965** *New Scientist* 15 July 154/2 Some single-celled animals contain a large ribbon-shaped 'axostyle', running from one end of the cell to the other, which can bend vigorously.

axotomous (æk'sɒtəməs), *a. Min.* [f. as AXOPHYTE + Gr. τομ- cutting, stem of τέμνειν to cut + -OUS.] Having a cleavage perpendicular to the axis.
1834 ALLAN *Min.* 145 Axotomous Augite Spar. **1850** ANSTED *Elem. Geol.* 204 Arsenical Pyrites..An axotomous variety.

axse, obs. form of ASK.

†**ax-seed.** *Herb. Obs.* [f. AX(E *sb.*¹ + SEED.] = AX-FITCH.
1562 [See AX-FITCH]. **1597** GERARD *Herbal* II. (1633) 1236 a, In English Ax seed, Ax woort, Ax-fitch, and Hatchet Fitch. **1611** COTGR., *Le Fer de cheval*, a kind of Axseed, or small Pulse, called Horse-shooe.

axses, -sen, obs. pl. forms of ASH *sb.*²

'ax-stone ('æksstəʊn). [f. AX(E *sb.*¹ + STONE.] A greenish variety of jade or nephrite, used, on account of its toughness, by some of the natives of South America, Polynesia, and other parts, for making their stone hatchets.
1811 PINKERTON *Petral.* I. 348. **1816** CLEAVELAND *Min.* 273.

axt, obs. or dial. pa. t. of ASK.

†**'ax-tree.** *Obs.* exc. *dial.* Forms: 3 **axtreo**, 4 **exetree**, 4–6 **extre**, 4–7 **axtre**, 5 **axetre**, 6–7 **axtree**, **axe-tree**, 6– (*Sc.*) **extree**, **aixtree.** [f. AX *sb.* + TREE, in its sense of *beam*; repr. an OE. **eax-tréow*. Cf. AXLE-TREE from ON.]
1. The AXLE-TREE of a wheel. (Still *dial.*)
a **1230** *Juliana* 56 þat axtreo stod istraht..in te twa stanene postles. **1388** WYCLIF *Ecclus.* xxxiii. 5 An extre able to turne aboute [**1611** a rolling axeltree]. *c* **1440** *Promp. Parv.* 145 Exultre, or ex tre. **1483** CAXTON *Gold. Leg.* 399/2 The one whele..fyl of fro the axtre. **1566** in *Invent.* (1815) 166 (JAM.) Twa gross culverinis..mountit upoun their stokis, quheillis, and aixtreis. **1573** COOPER *Thesaur.*, *Axis*, an extree. **1617** *Janua Ling.* 813 The axe tree..broken in the cart rut. **1675** HOBBES *Odyss.* 80 They mount into the chariot..The axtree groaned under them. *Mod. Sc.* The wheels cam off the aixtree.
†**2.** = AXLE. *Obs.*
1659 LEAK *Water-wks.* 10 If two Wheels are equal..and there be unequal Weights fastened to their Ax-trees.
†**3.** = AXIS. *Obs.*
1430 LYDG. *Chron. Troy* I. iii, The sterres..Whiche the axtree rounde aboute gone. **1551** RECORDE *Pathw. Knowl.* I. Def., A right line drawen crosse these figures..called an axe lyne, or axtre. **1603** DRAYTON *Bar. Warres* VI. v, Two stedfast Poles, Twixt which this All doth on the Axtree move. **1657** WRIGHT in *Phil. Trans.* LIII. 76 Two equal equidistant circles that have one common axtree.

axunge ('æk,sʌndʒ). Also 6–8 **auxunge**, 7–8 (L.) **axungia.** [a. F. *axunge* (mod. *axonge*), ad. L. *axungia*, f. *axis* axle + *ung-ĕre* to grease.] The rich internal fat of the kidneys, etc., especially that of geese and pigs; goose-grease, lard; also *gen.* fat, grease. †**axun'giety** = prec. **a'xungious** *a.*, lard-like, greasy. **a'xungiousness** = AXUNGE.
1541 R. COPLAND *Guydon's Quest. Cyrurg.*, The one [maner of greas] is withoutforth nere to the skynne, and that proprely is called adeps or fatnes. And yᵉ other is inwarde and nyghe to the bely, and proprely is called auxunge or fat grease. **1611** *Panegyr. V.* in *Coryat's Crudities*, Where S. Nicolas knights [*i.e.* men who have been hanged] not long before Had dropt their fat axungia to the lee. **1661** LOVELL *Hist. Anim. & Min.* 271 The axunge of cart wheeles. **1754** SMELLIE *Midwif.* I. Introd. 36 Lubricated with oil or auxunge. **1875** URE *Dict. Arts* 278 Axunge, hog's lard. **1599** A. M. *Gabelhouer's Bk. Physic* 40/2 Take the Axungietye of a Goose. *Ibid.* 45/1 Take the axungiousnes of a little boare-pigge. **1658** SIR T. BROWNE *Pseud. Ep.* III. xxvi. (1686) 139 An axungious and thicker part subsiding.

†**'axwort.** *Herb. Obs.* = AX-SEED.
1562 TURNER [see AX-FITCH]. **1591** PERCIVALL *Sp. Dict.*, *Encorvada*, Axwurt, *Securidaca.*

axyl, -tre, obs. forms of AXLE, -TREE.

ay- was formerly used indifferently with *ai-* in many words: e.g. *ayd(e, ayel(e, ayle, ayme, ayne,* *ayr, ayre, ayte, ayther, ayver*. For such, see AI-. It also interchanged frequently with EI-, EY-; and sometimes with A-, EA-, E-.

ay, aye (eɪ), *adv.* Forms: 3 **aȝȝ**, 3–4 **ai**, 5 **ei, aey**, 6 **aie**, 4– **aye**, 3– **ay**. [Early ME. *aȝȝ, ai, ei*: a. ON. *ei, ey*, cogn. with OE. *á* (:—**áw*), ME. *o, oo*, OS. *eo*, OHG. *eo, io*, MHG. *ie*, mod.G. *je*, Goth. *aiw*, acc. of *aiws* 'age, eternity':—OTeut. **aiwo-z*, cogn. w. L. *ævu-m*. Cf. Gr. ἀεί, αἰϝεί 'ever,' and αἰϝών- 'age.' Preceded in Eng. by the native *á, ó*, which also continued for several centuries as the southern form: the two were combined in the phrase 'for ay and oo.' Except in poetry, *ay* is still northern. The spelling fluctuates between *ay* and *aye*: the former is preferable on grounds of etymology, phonology, and analogy. The word rimes, in the literary speech, and in all the dialects, with the group *bay, day, gay, hay, may, way*. On the other hand, *aye* 'yes' does not rime with these, and should not be written *ay*. See AYE.]

1. a. Ever, always, continually; **b.** at all times, on all occasions. (Now only in *Sc.* and *north. dial.*)

c **1200** ORMIN 3212 Hiss drinnch wass waterr aȝȝ occ aȝȝ. *c* **1220** *Hali Meid.* 21 Ah schulen weimeres lead ai mare in helle. *c* **1250** *Gen. & Ex.* 5 Luuen god and seruen him ay. *c* **1386** CHAUCER *Monkes T.* 197 An ydolaster was he ay. *c* **1400** *Apol. Loll.* 27 He doþ ai þo þingis þat plesun God. *a* **1440** *Sir Degrev.* 40 He bare the pryes aey. *c* **1440** *Sir Gowther* (1883) 260 Hyt hong ei be his syde. **1450** MYRC 452 The ioye þat lasteþ ay. **1509** BARCLAY *Ship of Fooles* (1570) 210 Flatterers ay speake fayrest when they lye. **1562** LEIGH *Armorie* Prel., But from the light aie shrowds her selfe aside. **1605** SHAKS. *Macb.* IV. i. 134 Let this pernitious houre Stand aye accursed in the Kalender! **1724** A. RAMSAY *Tea-T. Misc.* (1733) I. 3 Its sweets I'll ay remember. **1790** BURNS *Tam O'Shanter*, And ay the ale was growing better. **1826** J. WILSON *Noct. Ambr.* Wks. 1855 I. 252 They aye behaved generously to me.

†**2.** with *comparative degree*. (Still in *Sc.*)

a **1325** *Metr. Hom.* 73 Ay the halyar that a man es, The mar lufes he meknes. **1393** LANGL. *P. Pl.* C. IV. 136 And ay þe lenger ich lete þe go · þe lasse treuthe ys with þe. *c* **1400** *Apol. Loll.* 26 Ay þe moo lusts þat þei haue here, ay þe more schal ben þer peyn. *Mod. Sc.* Things grew ay the langer, the waur [*i.e.* ever the longer, the worse].

3. Phrases: **a.** *for ay*: for ever, to all eternity. Also amplified, ***for ever and ay***; in ME. ***for ay and o***. (Only *poet.* in Eng.; in prose use in Sc.)

a **1300** *Cursor M.* 6218 þat suld vs serue for euer and ai. *c* **1374** CHAUCER *Troylus* II. 1034 But that was infynyte for ay and oo. **1590** R. HARVEY *Pl. Perc.* 24 Where I for aie will make thy praises tarry. **1598** BARRET *Theor. Warres* Pref. 6 His trauels do deserue our prayse for ay. **1706** DE FOE *Jure Div.* Pref. 36 There let it ly for ever and for ay. **1838** MRS. BROWNING *Rom. Ganges* xvi, The love will last for aye.

†**b.** *in aye*: for ever. *Obs.*

a **1300** *E.E. Psalter* lxii. 9 God oure helper in ai es he.

4. As *adj.* Eternal. *rare*$^{-1}$.

1839 BAILEY *Festus* xxv. (1848) 313 Whose flowings forth are aye and infinite.

5. In *comb.* = Ever: **a.** with pples., as ***ay-during, -living, -remaining, -running, -varied***, AY-LASTING; **b.** with adverbs, as **ay-forth**: ever onward. Also AY-GREEN.

1580 HOLLYBAND *Treas. Fr. Tong, Eternel*, euerlasting, ayduring. **1589** *Tri. Love & Fortune* III. in Hazl. *Dodsl.* VI. 192 Ay-during still thy woe. **1610** HOLLAND *Camden's Brit.* I. 386 Ay-living herbs. **1608** SHAKS. *Per.* III. i. 63 Aye-remaining lamps. **1857** EMERSON *Poems* 10 His aye-rolling orbit. **1610** HOLLAND *Camden's Brit.* I. 327 Springs ay-running by. **1649** DRUMMOND *Wks.* (1711) 30/2 Ay-varied bliss. *a* **1375** *Joseph Arim.* 126 þat he nas god ay forþ. **1375** BARBOUR *Bruce* I. 14 That it lest ay furth in memory.

ay (eɪ), *int.* Forms: 3–5 **ey**, 5 **ei**, 7 **eigh**, 7–9 **aye**, 6– **ay**. [In the later *ay me!* adopted from, or influenced by, F. *ahi, aï*, It. *ahi*; cf. OF. *aymi!* It. *ahime!* Sp. *ay de mi!* The ME. *ey, ei* was probably a natural ejaculation; nothing similar is found in OE.: the MHG. and mod.G. *ey!* is probably of independent development; and though there is greater possibility of its being an adoption of OF. *aï*, this would almost certainly have given *ay, ai*, which are not found even as variants in ME. The modern northern dial. *ay! eh!* or *eigh!* (eː) is probably the ME. *ey!*, but may be merely the earlier *a!*, as OE. *wá* is now *wae* (= weː) in the north.]

1. = Ah! O! (Now the common northern exclamation of surprise, invocation, earnestness.)

1340 *Ayenb.* 105 Ey god, huo þet couþe wel al þane zang, hou he ssolde vinde uayre notes. *c* **1386** CHAUCER *Pard. T.* 453 Ey, Goddis precious dignite! **1693** W. ROBERTSON *Phraseol. Gen.* 890 Eigh you mock me. **1863** MRS. TOOGOOD *Yorksh. Dial.*, Ay my word! I am glad to see you.

2. *ay me!* = Alas! Ah me!—an ejaculation of regret, sorrow, pity.

1591 SPENSER *Virg. Gnat* 353 Ay me, that thankes so much should faile of meed. **1671** MILTON *Samson* 331 Ay me, another inward grief awak't. **1850** MRS. BROWNING *Poems* II. 29 Ay me! how dread can look the Dead. **1860** TENNYSON *Tithonus*, Ay me! ay me! the woods decay and fall.

b. *substantively.* The ejaculation as an expression of sorrow, etc.

1607 BEAUMONT *Wom. Hater* III. i, Draw Sonnets from the melting lovers brain; Ayme's, and Elegies. **1633** T. ADAMS *Comm. 2 Pet.* i. 6 Aches and aye-mes are incident to intemperate houses.

ay, variant of AYE, yes; obs. f. ANY.

ay(e, obs. form of EGG, and AWE.

‖**ayah** ('aɪə). Also in 8 **eyah**. [a. *āya, āyā* (in various Indian vernaculars), a. Pg. *aia* (= Sp. *aya*, It. *aja*) nurse, children's governess, fem. of *aio* (Sp. *ayo*, It. *ajo*) a tutor. Introduced by the Portuguese into India, where adopted in Anglo-Indian from the vernaculars.] A native Hindoo nurse or lady's maid.

1782 *India Gaz.* 12 Oct., Eyah . . 5 Rupees a month. **1810** T. WILLIAMSON *E. Ind. Vade M.* I. 337 The female who attends a lady while she is dressing, etc. is called an Ayah. **1813** MRS. SHERWOOD *Ayah & Lady* i. 7 This Lady paid her Ayah seven rupees per month. **1848** CHAMBERS *Alfred in Ind.* 18 Ayahs, or ladies'-maids, who take care of very young children. **1852** *Lond. Jrnl.* 9 Oct. 66 Ellen's ayah or native nurse who had accompanied her to England.

ayal, variant of AIEL, *Obs.*, grandfather.

ayatollah (ˌaɪə'tɒlə). Also **Ayatollah, Ayatulla(h)**. [a. Pers., ad. Arab. *'āyatu-llāh* miraculous sign of God.] **1.** (An honorific title for) an Iranian Shiite religious leader.

1950 D. N. WILBER *Iran Past & Present* (ed. 2) ix. 211 A very few of the most important Iranian religious leaders, resident either in Iran or at the Shi'a shrines in Iraq, bear the honorary title of Ayatollah. **1952** *Islamic Rev.* Aug. 28/2 Dr. Musaddiq . . has shown remarkable courage and consistency in his campaign . . to win over the support of the people, including Ayatullah Kashani and the Muslim religious groups. **1964** R. W. COTTAM *Nationalism in Iran* xvi. 308 Ayatollah Sayyed Kazem Shariatmadari, one of three ayatollahs arrested in connection with the rioting, had earlier issued a statement. **1978** *Economist* 26 Aug. 13/2 The ayatollahs . . have not, as yet, suggested that they would use such powers to introduce Islamic law in Iran. **1978** *Daily Tel.* 8 Dec. 4/2 The Ayatulla is considered to be the most prominent religious leader within the country. **1979** *Observer* 28 Jan. 9/1 Ayatollah (the title means Gift of God) Khomeini is 78 years old. **1986** *Time* 17 Nov. 15/2 The aged Ayatullah may be too weak to provide much direct leadership anymore, but no one dares do anything of which he disapproves.

2. *fig.* A dogmatic leader; an influential or powerful person.

1979 *Observer* 15 July 2/9 Mr Frank Chapple . . said 'self-styled ayatollahs' were leading a 'conspiracy of academics and professional people to keep ordinary people and their views out of the party'. **1980** *Times Lit. Suppl.* 25 Apr. 473/3 The ayatollahs of the campuses, young and old, no longer had the same power to rouse their contemporaries. **1984** *N.Y. Rev. Bks.* 8 Nov. 8/2 An ayatollah among the nuclear warfare mullahs, he had written extensively about nuclear policy at a high level of abstraction.

ayder, -ur, obs. forms of EITHER.

aye, ay (aɪ), *int.* (*adv.*), *sb.* Forms: 6–8 **I**, 7 **ai**, 7–9 **ey**, 7– **aye, ay**. [Appears suddenly about 1575, and is exceedingly common about 1600; origin unknown. The suggestion that it is the same as AY *adv.* 'ever, always,' seems set aside by the fact that it was at first always written *I*, a spelling never found with AY. But it may have been a dialect form of that word, from some dialect in which it had passed through the senses of *always, in all cases*, to *by all means, certainly, yes* (cf. *aye but*, in sense 2 b; and the history of ALGATE), and so have been taken in literary English for a different word. It is less easy to see in it a phonetic variant or dialect form of *ya* 'yea, yes.' Spelt both *aye* and *ay*: the former is in accordance with parliamentary usage, and better on every ground. *Aye* and *eye* (which many identify in pronunciation, and which differ at most only in the 'broader' or more back sound of *aye*, are analogous diphthongal words usefully distinguished by their final *e* from the regular pronunciation of *-ay, -ey*, in *bay, day, gay, hay*, etc., and *bey, dey, grey, they, convey*, etc.: see AY.]

A. *int.* (*adv.*?) **1.** As an affirmative response to a question: Yes; even so. Common dialectally, and in nautical language; the formal word used in voting 'yes' in the House of Commons; but not used for 'yes' in modern educated speech or writing, except as an archaism.

1576 *Tyde Taryeth no Man* in Collier's *E.E. Pop. Lit.* 12 If you say I, syr, we will not say no. **1594** DRAYTON *Idea* 57 Nothing but No and I, and I and No. **1637** HEYWOOD *Royall King* II. iv, Me my Lord? *King.* Ey you my Lord. **1684** BUNYAN *Pilgr.* II. 124 Ai, ai, so I mean. **1711** J. GREENWOOD *Eng. Gram.* 159, *I* for *Yes*, is used in a hasty or merry Way, as *I Sir, I Sir.* **1743** *Lond. & Country Brew.* IV. 284 Hye, says the Victualler, I believe I shall never stand it. **1823** BYRON *Island* II. xxi, 'Ey, ey!' quoth Ben, 'not new, but news enow.' **1858** LONGF. *M. Standish* IV. 33 The shouts of the mate, and the sailors' 'Ay, ay, Sir!' **1878** *Masque of Poets* 53 The mate sprang forward and cried 'Aye, Aye!' **1882** *Daily News* 22 Feb. 2/3 *The Speaker*—I must put the question to the House, as it stands, and the House must say 'Aye' or 'No.'

2. a. Indicating assent to a previous statement, and preliminary to a further or more forcible one.

1598 B. JONSON *Ev. Man in Hum.* I. i, I, so I do. **1670** R. COKE *Disc. Trade* 46, I, and the Law . . Bars us of any future supply. **1714** ADDISON *Spect.* No. 568 ¶1 Ay, Answer that if you can, Sir. **1821** KEATS *Isabel* xxiv, To-day we purpose, ay, this hour we mount. **1826** DISRAELI *Viv. Grey* III. iv. 104 Once, ay twice. **1865** R. W. DALE *Jew. Temp.* xxi. (1877) 237 Aye, and we take the promises in their fullest and broadest meaning.

b. ***aye, but*** . . . Indicating provisional assent to a statement for the sake of rebutting it.

1589 NASHE *Almond for Parr* 4 a, I, I, my maisters, you may mocke . . but I warrant you, etc. **1640** J. DYKE *Worthy Commun.* 122, I; but you doe us wrong. **1662** DRYDEN *Wild Gallant* Wks. 1725 I. 94 He shall set thee forth I warrant thee. *Burr.* I, but where's the Money for this? **1875** H. E. MANNING *Mission H. Ghost* x. 282 Ay, but it was not only men who have so endured. We have known young girls . . rise up with the courage of confessors.

B. as *sb.* An affirmative answer or vote; in *pl.* (elliptically) those who so vote.

1589 *Marprel. Epit.* B iij, Here then is the puritans I . . and M. doctors no. **1669** MARVELL *Corr.* 127 Wks. 1875 II. 289 The ayes proved 138 and the noes 129. **1771** *Junius Lett.* xliv. 238 A simple ay or no. **1851** HT. MARTINEAU *Hist. Peace* (1877) III. IV. x. 69 The ayes were loud and multitudinous. **1857** TOULM. SMITH *Parish* 62 The whole number present . . must range themselves, aye and no, on the two opposite sides of the room. **1882** *Daily News* 30 Mar. 4/7 If the Ayes have it, Mr. Marriott's hostile resolution will be rejected.

aye, variant spelling of AY *adv.* ever.

a-year, *phrase* = in the year, per annum: see A *prep.*[1] and YEAR[1].

aye-aye ('aɪˌaɪ). *Zool.* [a. F. *aye-aye*, a. Malagasy *aï'ay'* (also dialectally *ahay, haihay*) 'supposed to receive its name from its peculiar cry,' Richardson *Malagasy Dict.*] A quadrumanous animal (*Cheiromys Madagascariensis*), nocturnal, squirrel-like, of the size of a cat, found only in Madagascar, where it was first noticed by Sonnerat, *c* 1775; it is classed with the Lemurs, but in many points approaches the Rodentia.

1781 PENNANT *Quadrupeds* (1792) II. 138 Aye-Aye S[quirrel], with broad ears . . Inhabits Madagascar . . takes its name from its cry. **1827** GRIFFITH *Cuvier's Anim. K.* III. 86 But one species of the Aye-Aye is known. **1862** *Lond. Rev.* 30 Aug. 198 The most interesting of recent acquisitions of the Zoological Society, is the Aye-Aye of Madagascar.

a-yelp (ə'jɛlp), *advb. phr.* [A *prep.*[1] + YELP.] On the yelp, yelping.

1855 BROWNING *Men & Wom.* I. 198 The Kennel's a-yelp.

ayen(e, ayenst, etc., obs. ff. AGAIN, -ST.

†**a'yenbite.** *Obs.* [f. *ayen*, AGAIN + BITE; ME. translation of L. *remorsus*.] Remorse.

1340 *Ayenb.* 1 þis boc is dan Michelis of Northgate . . þet hatte Ayenbyte of inwyt. **1878** M. COLLINS *Village Com.* II. ii. 17 That remorse, that ayenbite (to use good English), can only be felt by the spirit which has kinship to the Divinity.

ayer(e, variant of AYRE *v Obs.* to travel, march.

ayer(e[2]**, ayerie,** obs. ff. AIR *sb.*[1], HEIR, AERIE.

ayghe, variant of *aye*, AWE *sb.*[1]

ay-green ('eɪˌgriːn). *Herb.* [= *evergreen*: see AY *adv.* 5] The house-leek.

1562 TURNER *Herbal* II. 133 *a*, In English Housleke, and of some Singren, but it ought better to be called Aygrene. **1693** W. ROBERTSON *Phraseol. Gen.* 192 An Herb always green, called Ay-green, or Sea-green, Everlasting, House-leek. **1721** BAILEY, *Aigreen.* **1863** R. PRIOR *Plant-n.*, *Aye-green* . . from its conspicuous tufts of evergreen leaves.

†**'ayguous,** *a. Obs. rare*$^{-1}$. [a. OF. *aigueux*:—L. *aquōs-um* watery, f. *aqua* water.] Watery.

1541 R. COPLAND *Guydon's Quest. Cyrurg.*, The bladder . . is a receyuer of ayguous superfluytees of the kydnees.

ayhe(n, aȝe, obs. forms of AGAIN.

†**a'yield,** *v. Obs.* Forms: 1 **aᵹieldan, aᵹyldan**, 4 **ayild, aȝeld**, 5 **ayelde**. [OE. *aᵹieldan*, f. A- *pref.* 1 up + *ᵹieldan* to YIELD, give.] To yield up.

a **1000** *Soul's Complaynt* 91 þæt þu ne scyle . . riht aᵹieldan. *c* **1325** *Rembrun* 475 (Halliw.) Ayild the to this knight. *c* **1380** *Sir Ferumb.* 2444 'þef,' saide he . . 'aȝeld þe, þov schalt dye.' *c* **1450** *Paper Roll* in *3rd Rep. R. Comm. Hist. MSS.* 280/1 To ayelde up . . the seid towne of Anyoies.

ayl(e, obs. f. AIL, AISLE.

†**ay-lasting,** *a. Obs.* Forms: 4 **ay-, ai-lastand(e, ai-, ay lasting**, 7 **aye-lasting**. [See AY *adv.* 5.] Everlasting. Hence **aylastingly** *adv.*

c **1340** HAMPOLE *Prose Tr.* (1866) 1 Ay-lastande saluacyone es hopede. *c* **1340** *Alex. & Dind.* 70 Ailastinge lif. *c* **1400** *Apol. Loll.* 55 Ay lasting deþ. **1603** FLORIO *Montaigne* III. vi. (1632) 506 Aye-lasting and commendable memory. *c* **1400** *Apol. Loll.* 7 Ordeyning aylastingly þe contrary.

Aylesbury (ˈeɪlzbərɪ), the name of a town and vale in Buckinghamshire, used *attrib.* or *absol.* to designate a breed of white domestic ducks.

1854 *Poultry Chron.* I. 553/2 The Aylesbury ducks were good. **1855** *Ibid.* III. 394/1 If Ducks are kept, the Rouen or Aylesbury will answer best. **1916** A. BENNETT *These Twain* II. xiv. 264 A few white Aylesburys with gamboge beaks that intermittently quacked. **1960** *Farmer & Stock-breeder* 15 Mar. 133/1 The Aylesbury ducklings will require brooder heat for 10–14 days at 95 deg. F.

aylyng, obs. f. AILING (here = injuring, damage).

c **1400** *Destr. Troy* v. 1577 The strete by the sydes.. Was archet full Abilly for [= against] aylyng of shoures.

Aymara (ˌaɪməˈrɑː). [Bolivian Sp.; cf. Sp. *aimará*.] (A member of) an Indian people mainly inhabiting the plateau lands of Bolivia and Peru near Lake Titicaca. Also, the language of this people. Hence ˌ**Ayma'ran** *a.*

1860 W. BOLLAERT *Antiquarian Researches* 166 The Quichua is spoken from the equator to 28° S. (interrupted at 15° S. by the Aymará people)... The Aymarás are from 15° to 20° S., round Lake Titicaca. *Ibid.* 217 Aymará, spoken in Bolivia.. and in Southern Peru bears a close resemblance to Quichua. **1902** *Encycl. Brit.* XXV. 374/1 The [linguistic] families of.. South America are here given.. Aymaran, Peru [etc.]. **1921** *Glasgow Herald* 17 May 3/8 The descendants of the original peoples of the Inca Empire—the Quechuas and the Aymaras. **1954** PEI & GAYNOR *Dict. Linguistics* 24 *Aymará*, a family of 11 South American Indian languages, spoken by about 500,000 persons in Ecuador and Bolivia.

ayme, obs. form of AIM.

ayme, obs. way of writing *ay me!* see AY *int.*

aymer, obs. form of EMBER.

†**aymont.** *Obs. rare.* [a. OF. *aïmant*, in Palsgr. *aymant*, cogn. with Pr. *ayman*, *aziman*, *adiman*:—pop. L. **adimant-em*, for L. *adamant-em*.] = ADAMANT.

1340 *Ayenb.* 187 Hy byeþ harde as an aymont.

aynd, -ing, -less, Sc. forms of ANDE, etc.

†**ayne**, *a. Obs.*; but see EIGNE. [a. OF. *ainé*, earlier *aisné*, *ainsné*, f. *ains* before + *né* born. As in some other words (e.g. *assign* sb.[2]), the final *e* became mute in Eng.] First-born, eldest, EIGNE.

1483 CAXTON *Gold. Leg.* 164/4 He that entred fyrst is called ayne and grete and he that cometh after shalbe called lasse. *c* **1500** *Partenay* 1695 Ayne and eldeste.

†**ayness.** *Obs. Metaph.* [f. AY *adv.* + -NESS.] Everlastingness; applied as a special term to the 'second degree of eternity' possessed by angels and spirits.

1587 GOLDING *De Mornay* ix. (1617) 141 The measure of such things as haue a fixed and stable being, and yet haue also a certaine succession in their operations, of which sort are the vnderstanding Spirits or Angels; and this is properly called Aynesse.

a'yond, a'yont, *prep. dial.* [f. A- *pref.* 2 + YOND; cf. *beyond*, and the double forms *afore*, *before*, etc. (*Ayont* is the mod. Scotch and north. Eng. dial. form.)] Beyond, on the other side of.

1724 A. RAMSAY *Tea-T. Misc.* (1733) I. 84 Down ayont the ingle he sat. **1803–49** MANGAN *Poems* (1859) 375 Ayond the gloom of thy sunken cell. **1826** J. WILSON *Noct. Ambr.* Wks. 1855 I. 145 The flock are ayont the knowes. **1837** MARRYAT *Dog Fiend* xix, I went out to the Nab buoy, and a mile ayond it. **1855** in *Whitby Glossary.*

ayr(e, obs. form of AIR *sb.*[1], EYRE, HEIR.

ayr(e, var. AIR *sb.*[2]

†**ayre, ayere**, *v.*[1] *Obs.* [a. OF. *erre-r*, 3 sing. pres. *eire*, earlier *edrar* (in St. Leger):—L. *iterāre* to journey, proceed, march, f. *iter* journey. Cf. EYRE, ERRANT.] To march, proceed, make one's way; to move about (*as opposed to* remain still).

c **1400** *Destr. Troy* XVII. 7502 Þen Achilles cherfull, & his choise cosyn.. Ayren vnto Ector angardly sore! *c* **1440** *Morte Arth.* 455 There awes none alyenes to ayere appone nyghttys.

†**ayre**, *v.*[2] *Obs.* [variant of EAR.] To plough.

c **1400** *Destr. Troy* 175 Ayre vp the erthe on ardagh wise.

ayre, obs. bad form of YARE *a.* ready.

? *c* **1475** *Sqr. lowe Degre* 501 Anone the squyer made him ayre, And by hym selfe forth can he fare.

ayre, -ie, -y, obs. forms of HEIR, AERIE.

ayrer, variant of EYRER.

Ayrshire (ˈɛəʃə(r)), *a.* and *sb.* A breed of horned cattle named from the shire or county of Ayr in Scotland, and esteemed for dairy farming.

1856 *Farmer's Mag.* Nov. 412 Cattle, half-bred Shorthorns and Ayrshires.

aysel, -ylle, early var. EISELL, *Obs.*, vinegar.

ayth, obs. Sc. form of OATH.

ayther, obs. form of EITHER.

Ayurvedic (ˌɑːjəˈveɪdɪk), *a.* Also **ayurvedic.** [f. Skr. *āyur-veda* the science of life or medicine (traditionally regarded as ancillary to the *Atharva-veda*: see VEDA) + -IC.] Of or pertaining to the traditional Hindu science of medicine.

1917 *Antiseptic* (Madras) XIV. 389 (*heading*) How to improve Ayurvedic medicine. **1922** *Blackw. Mag.* July 96/2 *Hakims*, who had a smattering of the Yunani or the Ayurvedic system of medicine. **1937** *Discovery* May 142/2 Coconut roots are also employed in ayurvedic medicine in Ceylon and India. **1960** KOESTLER *Lotus & Robot* I. ii. 86 Every posture and exercise has both a symbolic meaning and a physiological purpose related to the tenets of ayurvedic medicine.

†**ay-when**, *adv. Obs. rare.* [f. AY + WHEN; cf. next.] At every time, always.

c **1485** *Digby Myst.* (1882) Mor. Wisd. 345 And ther-in I tempte hym ay whan.

†**aywhere**, *adv. Obs.* Forms: 1 **ǽȝhwǽr, eȝhuær, -hwer, eghwar**, 3 **aihware, aiware, eihwer**, 4 **ayquar(e, aywhare**, 5 **aywhore**, 4–5 **aywhere.** [OE. *ǽȝhwǽr*, for *ǽȝehwǽr*, cogn. with OHG. *eogihwâr*, f. *á* ever + *ȝehwǽr* everywhere, 'ubique.' See YWHERE. Thus really the equivalent of *ever-ywhere*, but in ME. phonetically reduced so as to look like a compound of AY 'ever' and WHERE; hence *ay-when*.] Everywhere.

c **1000** *Ags. Gosp.* Mark xvi. 20 Hi ða farende æȝhwar bodedon [*Lindisf.* eȝhuær; *Rushw.* eȝhwer]. *c* **1200** *Trin. Coll. Hom.* 222 He þe godes wille doð aihware. *c* **1220** *Hali Meid.* 39 Te weane eihwer passeð þe winne. *a* **1250** *Owl & Night.* 216 Ho had i-lorned wel aiware. *c* **1300** *K. Alis.* 6754 Eghwar by my weyes. *c* **1325** *E.E. Allit. P.* B. 228 On vch syde of þe worlde aywhere ilyche. *c* **1460** *Towneley Myst.* 115 To slepe aywhore. **1470** HARDING *Chron.* xcv, As myster was ay where.

azalea (əˈzeɪlɪə). *Bot.* Pl. **-as.** [a. mod.L. *azalea* (Linn.), a. Gr. ἀζαλέα, fem. of ἀζαλέος dry; so named either from the dry soil in which it flourishes, or from its dry brittle wood.] A genus of shrubby plants (N.O. *Ericaceæ*), natives of the northern hemisphere, growing in sandy soil, and blooming profusely, with showy and mostly fragrant flowers, pure white or yellow, or streaked and stained with crimson. The one British species (*A. procumbens*), found in the Scotch Highlands, is by some made a distinct genus, *Loiseleuria*.

1753 in CHAMBERS *Cycl. Supp.* **1803** J. ABERCROMBIE *Gard. Calend.* 605 Hardy kinds of flowering shrubs and trees ..Such as roses..dog-woods, azaleas. **1881** BLACKMORE *Christowell* i, The white chalice of azalea.

azaleine (əˈzeɪlɪiːn). *Chem.* Also **-in.** [f. AZALEA + -INE[5].] = ROSANILINE.

1889 in *Cent. Dict.* **1894** GOULD *Dict. Med.*, *Azalein*.. same as *Rosanilin*. **1900** G. ILES *Flame, Electricity & Camera.* 283 The dyes at present used in the preparation of orthochromatic plates are chiefly eosin,..azaleine, and croculeine.

Azan (əˈzɑːn). [Arab. *adān* invitation.] The Moslem call to public prayers, made by the crier from the minaret of a mosque.

1855 R. F. BURTON *El-Medinah* II. xvii. 142 Here he prayed, hearkening to the Azan, or devotion-call, from the roof. **1922** *Blackw. Mag.* Dec. 821/2, I was wakened by the sound of the Azan from the village mosque close by.

Azande, pl. of ZANDE.

azarole (ˈæzərəʊl). *Bot.* Forms: 7 **azeroll**, 8 **azerole**, 7–9 **azarole.** [a. F. *azerole* (written by Tournefort *azarole*), cogn. with Sp. *acerolo*, *azarolla*, Pg. *azerola*, It. *azzeruola*, ad. Arab. *az-zuʿrūr*, applied to the same fruit.] The fruit of the Neapolitan Medlar, a species of hawthorn (*Cratægus azarolus*); also applied to the tree itself, sometimes called, after Fr., **azerolier.**

1658 EVELYN *Fr. Gard.* (1675) 268 Cormes, services, azerolls, and the like. **1693** —— *De la Quint. Compl. Gard.* 67 Quinces bear almost in the same manner with Rasberries, Azeroliers, and Pomegranates. —— *ibid.* (Dict.) Azeroll-Trees, ar Garden-Haw-Trees, which are usually planted against Walls. **1725** BRADLEY *Fam. Dict.* s.v., The Azerole is indeed a kind of Medlar. **1864** MRS. WOOD *Trev. Hold* II. i. 1 Leaping a dwarf hedge of azaroles.

azedarac (əˈzɛdəræk). *Bot.* Also 8–9 **-ach.** [a. F. *azédarac*, Sp. *acedaraque*, a. Pers. *āzād dirakht* 'free (or noble) tree.' The tree and name were probably introduced into Spain and Sicily by the Arabs.]

1. A lofty tree (*Melia Azedarach*), with bipinnate leaves and large bunches of fragrant lilac-coloured flowers, a native of the East Indies, but now common in Spain, Southern France, and South America. Also known as Bead-tree, Pride of India, False Sycamore, and Holy-tree.

1753 CHAMBERS *Cycl. Supp.*, *Azedarach*..the Bead-tree. **1852** TH. ROSS *Humboldt's Trav.* II. xvi. 3 Paths bordered with azedaracs. **1878** *Masque of Poets* 30 Where clear-green chrysoberyl glows Beside azedarac in rows.

2. *Pharm.* The bark of the root of this tree used in medicine.

1853 in MAYNE.

azelaic (æzɪˈleɪɪk), *a. Chem.* [f. AZ(O- + Gr. ἔλαιον oil + -IC.] In ***azelaic acid*** = ANCHOIC *acid.*

1838 *Brit. Annual 1839* 350 Azelaic acid. **1885** REMSEN *Org. Chem.* 142 Azelaic acid, $C_7H_{14}(CO_2H)_2$. **1929** *Jrnl. Chem. Soc.* 2709 The nine-carbon member of the series, azelaic acid, occurs in two crystalline modifications.

azeotrope (əˈziːətrəʊp). *Chem.* [f. Gr. ἀ- priv. (A- 14) + *zeo-* combining form f. Gr. ζεῖν to boil + *-trope* (cf. Gr. τρόπος turning).] A mixture of liquids the boiling-point of which does not change on distillation. So **azeo'tropic** *a.*; **aze'otropism, aze'otropy**, the stage of being an azeotrope.

1911 *Jrnl. Chem. Soc.* XCIX. 998 (*title*) Formation of azeotropic mixtures of ethyl alcohol and water. **1934** WEBSTER, Azeotropism..azeotropy. **1936** *Nature* 22 Aug. 307/2 Mixtures which are 'azeotropic', because they form mixtures of minimum (or more rarely, maximum) boiling point. **1938** S. T. BOWDEN *Phase Rule & Phase Reactions* vi. 118 Ordinary ethyl alcohol and water..give rise to an azeotrope containing 96 per cent of alcohol. **1947** *Endeavour* VI. 14/2 It was in Brussels too that Lecat started his chemical researches..in the field of azeotropism.

Azerbaijani (æzəbaɪˈdʒɑːnɪ). [f. *Azerbaijan*, name of a region falling partly in Iran and partly in the U.S.S.R.] One of a Turkic-speaking people in Azerbaijan; also, their language. Also **Azerbai'jan** *a.* and *sb.*, (of or pertaining to) a native or inhabitant of Azerbaijan.

1888 *Encycl. Brit.* XXIII. 661/2 Adarbaijāni Turkish. *Ibid.*, Turki dialects (Derbendi, Adarbaijāni, Krimmi, Anadoli, and Rumili). **1911** *Ibid.* XXVII. 470/1 The Turkish nomads scattered over Persian territory are often known by the name of *Azerbaijanis* or *Adharbaijanis*, though this name is strictly applicable only to the inhabitants of the province of Azerbaijan. **1954** PEI & GAYNOR *Dict. Linguistics* 24 *Azerbaidjani*, a dialect of the Southern Turkic group of the Altaic sub-family of the Ural-Altaic family of languages. **1959** *Chambers's Encycl.* II. 16/2 The Azerbaijans, who are of Indo-Iranian origin, speak a Turkish language and are Moslem in religion.

azide (ˈæzaɪd, eɪ-). *Chem.* [f. AZ(O- + -IDE.] A salt or ester of hydrazoic acid.

1907 *Chem. Abstr.* 431 (*heading*) Communication on syntheses by means of azides. **1910** *Encycl. Brit.* III. 83/1 It is soluble in water, and the solution dissolves many metals.. with liberation of hydrogen and formation of salts (azoimides, azides or hydrazoates). **1946** *Nature* 3 Aug. 156/2 The azide retards the rate of oxidation of divalent manganese in soil. **1949** MIALL & MIALL *Dict. Chem.* (ed. 2) 61/2 The azides of the heavy metals (e.g. lead azide) are dangerously explosive.

azidothymidine (ˌeɪzɪdəʊˈθaɪmɪdiːn). *Pharm.* [f. AZIDE + -O + THYMIDINE.] A substituted derivative of thymidine that has been used to inhibit the replication of HIV, the AIDS virus, 3′-azido-3′-deoxythymidine. Abbrev. *AZT* s.v. A III.

1974 *Proc. Nat. Acad. Sci.* LXXI. 4980/1 The role of.. another thymidine analogue, azidothymidine, in interfering with C-type virus release in virus positive cells is discussed. **1986** *FDA Consumer* Feb. 34/2 Another antiviral approved for experimental testing in this country is azidothymidine. **1986** *Daily Tel.* 10 Mar. 9/3 Researchers at Wellcome are significantly reticent about any potential their new drug—azidothymidine—may hold.

Azilian (əˈzɪlɪən), *a. Archæol.* [f. *Azil* in Mas d'Azil (dept. of Ariège, France), where discoveries were made by Ed. Piette of a primitive civilization; cf. F. *époque asylienne*, etc. (f. med.L. *Asylum*: see *L'Anthropologie* (1895) VI. 151).] Of or belonging to the transition period between the palæolithic and neolithic ages. Also *sb.*

1899 A. H. KEANE *Man: Past & Present* 30 M. Piette.. states..that '13 out of 23 Phoenician characters were equally Azilian graphic signs'. **1919** H. G. WELLS *Outl. Hist.* I. x. §4. 60/1 For a time there were in Southern Europe drifting communities of some little known people who are called the Azilians. *Ibid.*, These Azilian people have left behind them a multitude of pebbles, roughly daubed with markings. **1947** J. & C. HAWKES *Prehist. Brit.* i. 22 The Azilians, who brought from the south of France a microlithic culture of Magdalenian descent.

azime, variant of AZYME.

†'**azimene**, *a. Astrol. Obs.* (See quot.)

1647 LILLY *Chr. Astrol.* xix. 118 Degrees lame and deficient (*note*, called by some Azimene degrees). **1678** PHILLIPS, *Azemen.* **1819** J. WILSON *Dict. Astrol.*, *Azimene* or Weak and Lame Degrees..when they ascend at a birth, render the native lame, blind, etc.

azimuth (ˈæzɪməθ). Forms: 4–5 **azimut, azymut**, 4–7 **azymuth**, 6 **azumuth**, (7 **azimynth, -moth**), 6– **azimuth.** [a. F. *azimut*, cogn. with It. *azzimutto*, Pg. *azimuth*, ad. Arab. *as-sumūt*, i.e. *as* = *al* the + *sumūt*, pl of *samt* way, direction, a direction or point of the compass or horizon, and the arc extending from it to the zenith. Cf. *samt-al-rā's* the direction or point over head, whence the term ZENITH. With the form *azimynth* cf. It. *aziminthi* (Florio).]

1. An arc of the heavens extending from the zenith to the horizon which it cuts at right angles; the quadrant of a great circle of the sphere passing through the zenith and nadir, called an ***azimuth-circle***.

c **1391** CHAUCER *Astrol.* I. §19 From this senyth..ther come a maner krokede strikes like to the clawes of a coppe.. kervyng ouerthwart the almikanteras. And thise same strikes or diuisiouns ben cleped azymuthz. Thise Azimutz seruen to knowe the costes of the firmament. **1594** J. DAVIS *Seamans Secr.* II. (1607) 8 Circles of Azumuths, or verticall circles, are quarters of great circles, concurring together in the Zenith. **1598** SYLVESTER *Du Bartas* (1608) 299 The almycantharats, With th' azimynths. **1651** BIGGS *New Disp.* ¶157 Severall azimuths meeting in the Zenith. **1796** HUTTON *Math. Dict.* I. 178/2 These azimuths are represented..on the globe by the quadrant of altitude. **1874** MOSELEY *Astron.* ix. 45 If a great circle..be imagined to be drawn from the zenith..to the horizon, through any star.. it is called the azimuth circle of that star.

2. The angular distance of any such circle from a given limit, *e.g.* a meridian. Hence, the ***true azimuth*** of a heavenly body is, the arc of the horizon intercepted between the north (or, in the Southern hemisphere, *south*) point of the horizon and the point where the great circle passing through the observed heavenly body cuts the horizon. Its ***magnetic azimuth*** is the arc intercepted between the magnetic meridian and this great circle.

azimuth compass: a minutely divided mariner's compass, fitted with vertical sights, used for taking the magnetic azimuth of a heavenly body. ***azimuth dial***: one whose gnomon is perpendicular to the plane of the horizon. ***azimuth mirror***: an instrument placed on the glass cover of a mariner's compass and used for taking azimuths.

1626 CAPT. SMITH *Accid. Yng. Seamen* 36 Learne to obserue..the Sunnes Azimuth and Almicanter. **1697** DAMPIER *Voy.* (1729) I. 531 The Azimuth Compass, an Instrument more peculiar to the Seamen of our Nation. **1762–9** FALCONER *Shipwr.* I. 740 The pilots now their azimuth attend. **1834** U.K.S. *Nat. Philos.* III. *Astron.* xiii. 255/1 The true azimuth, compared with the magnetic azimuth, will give the deviation of the compass.

b. ***in azimuth***: in a horizontal circular direction.

1831 BREWSTER *Optics* xiv. 123 If we turn the steel plate round in azimuth. **1879** G. PRESCOTT *Sp. Telephone* 269 The mirror is so mounted as to swing in azimuth.

3. *transf.* and *fig.* Horizontal angle, or direction; point of the compass.

1667 SIR R. MORAY in *Phil. Trans.* II. 477 Note also, at what Azimuth the Mark stands from the Gun. **1831** BREWSTER *Optics* xix. 167 Reflected from the second plate, at the azimuths 90° and 270°. **1860** MAURY *Phys. Geog. Sea* iv. §245 Wind gauges..to show the inclination, as well as the Azimuth of the wind. **1867** CARLYLE *Remin.* II. 52 How he found his way thither I know not (perhaps in a cab, if quite lost in his azimuth).

azimuthal ('æzɪˌmjuːθəl), *a.* [f. prec. + -AL[1].]

1. Of or pertaining to the azimuth; used in taking azimuths.

1654 S. FOSTER (*title*) Elliptical, or Azimuthal Horologiography. **1667** *Phil. Trans.* II. 435 The Suns Azimuthal Distance from the Meridian. **1702** WALLIS *ibid.* XXIII. 1110 The Azimuthal Points of the Horizon. **1841** BREWSTER *Mart. Sc.* III. iv. (1856) 216 A brass azimuthal quadrant.

2. In azimuth, in a horizontal circle. ***azimuthal error*** (of a transit instrument): its deviation in azimuth from the plane of the meridian.

1863 *Cornh. Mag.* VII. 383 For azimuthal error, that is for the amount that the transit deviates from the north and south line. **1876** CHAMBERS *Astron.* 668 By means of a screw a small azimuthal motion may be imparted. **1880** *Nature* XXI. 211 The azimuthal rotation of the clouds.

azi'muthally (cf. prec.), *adv.* [f. prec. + -LY[2].] In azimuth, in a horizontal circle.

1867 DENISON *Astron. without Math.* 313 Herschel's great telescope was set in a frame which also turned azimuthally.

azine ('æzɪn, -aɪn, -iːn, eɪ-). *Chem.* Also **azin.** [f. AZ(O- + -INE[5].] **a.** An organic compound containing the group =N–N=. **b.** One of a group of heterocyclic organic compounds with two, three, four, etc., nitrogen atoms in a six-atom ring (thus ***diazine***, ***triazine***, ***tetrazine***, etc.), used esp. as dyes.

1887 *Jrnl. Chem. Soc.* LII. 383 Whilst the whole group of substances..should be termed quinoxaline bases, it will be convenient to divide them into two sub-groups. 1. The quinoxalines proper.. 2. The azines, in which the nitrogen-ring is in union with two other rings. **1893** *Ibid.* LXIV. I. 15 The synthesis of azine dyes. **1910** *Encycl. Brit.* VIII. 746/2 Basic colours derived from coal-tar:..azine green [etc.]. **1959** *Chambers's Encycl.* IV. 693/1 Azine, Oxazine, Thiazine, Acridine and Pyronine dyestuffs contain a central pyrazine or similar ring. *Ibid.* 693/2 The indulines and nigrosines are important azine type dyes.

azlactone (æz'læktəʊn). *Chem.* [f. AZ(O- + LACTONE.] A lactone of an unsaturated nitrogenous hydroxy-acid. Hence **azˌlactoni'zation**.

1917 *Chem. Abstr.* 3267 Synthesis of aryl-substituted fatty acids..α-$C_{10}H_7CHO$ is converted into the *azlactone* $C_{20}H_{13}O_2N$, yellow needles. **1940** *Ibid.* 3716 The azlactonization and racemization of benzol-*l*-*p*-methoxy-phenylalanine..were studied... NaOAc increases the rates of azlactonization and racemization in each case. **1949** FLOREY et al. *Antibiotics* I. iii. 189 Certain substances, such as ether-soluble keto acids, lactones, azlactones, and esters interfered with this method. *Ibid.* II. xxii. 863 It was ascertained that azlactonization of the..amino acid took place.

azo- ('æzəʊ-). *Chem.* Short combining form of AZOTE, nitrogen. Used to form the names of:

1. *gen.* Compounds containing nitrogen, as **azo'humic**, nitrogenized humic (acid); **azo'litmin**, the principal colouring matter of litmus; **azo'leic**, an acid formed by treating oleic with nitric acid.

2. *spec.* Substitution compounds in which nitrogen takes the place of another element, as in the **azo'paraffins**, formed from the paraffins by substitution of 1 atom of nitrogen for 3 of hydrogen: e.g. *azo-methane* = hydrogen cyanide, *azo-ethane* = methyl cyanide, *azo-propane* = ethyl cyanide, etc.

3. a. *more particularly.* Compounds derived from the aromatic hydrocarbons, which contain nitrogen combined in a peculiar way, constituting the *azo-* and *diazo-* compounds, or *azo-* derivatives, e.g. *azobenzene*, *azotoluene*; *diazo-amidobenzene*, *diazo-bromide*; whence adjectives as *azoben'zoic*, etc.

1881 DARWIN *Veg. Mould* v. 242 Some of the acids, which were called long ago azohumic, are enabled to dissolve colloid silica in proportion to the nitrogen which they contain. **1863** WATTS *Dict. Chem.* III. 731 Azolitmin is a red-brown amorphous powder. **1880** CLEMENSHAW *Wurtz' Atom. The.* 219 Those very remarkable organic combinations known as *azo-* and *diazo-compounds*. **1880** FRISWELL in *Soc. Arts Jrnl.* 445 Known as the azo-yellows, oranges, and scarlets.

b. azo-colours, -dyes, a group of coal-tar colours or dyes.

1879 WITT in *Jrnl. Chem. Soc.* XXXV. 181 The variety of azo-colours in the market, and the number of patents..are constantly increasing. **1884** *Ibid.* XLVI. 237 The preparation of azo-dyes from the trisulphonic acids of β-naphthol. **1894** GOULD *Dict. Med.*, *Azo-dyes*, a well defined group of the coal-tar colors, all containing the diatomic group –N = N–, bound on either side to a benzene radical. **1902** *Encycl. Brit.* XXVII. 559/1 Azo colours which are developed..upon the fibre itself (usually cotton) by the successive application of their constituent elements. **1963** R. R. A. HIGHAM *Handbk. Papermaking* xii. 256 Azo colour pigments. Yellow, orange and red used in high-quality writings.

azoic (ə'zəʊɪk), *a.* [f. Gr. ἄζω-ος (f. ἀ priv. + ζωή life) + -IC; cf. F. *azootique*.] Having no trace of life; in *Geol.*, Containing no organic remains.

1854 PAGE *Text-bk. Geol.* 39 Azoic Period. **1873** W. THOMSON *Depths of Sea* iv. 192 The bottom of the Mediterranean at depths beyond a few hundred fathoms is nearly azoic.

azoimide (æzəʊ'ɪmaɪd). *Chem.* [f. AZO- + IMIDE.] Hydrazoic acid.

1891 *Athenæum* 24 Jan. 126/1 Prof. Curtius..has obtained the compound N_3H, to which he has given the name azoimide or hydrogen nitride. **1894** [see HYDRAZOIC *a.*].

azolla (ə'zɒlə). [mod.L.; said to be f. Gr. ἄζειν to dry + ὀλλύναι to slay.] A plant of a genus of small floating ferns of the family Azollaceæ.

1872 DOMETT *Ranolf* xiv. 221 Minute azolla-stains of ruddiest hue.

azonal (ə'zəʊnəl, eɪ-), *a.* [f. A- 14 + ZONAL *a.*; cf. Gr. ἄζωνος zoneless.] Not confined to a zone, not arranged in zones; spec. in *Soil Sci.*, ***azonal soil*** (see quot. 1938).

1896 C. MACMILLAN in *Bull. Torrey Bot. Club* XXIII. 507 There are two principal types of plant arrangement in their habitats. These are (1) Zonal and (2) Azonal... When the topographic feature is devoid of..well-marked radial symmetry the plants dispose themselves according to the azonal type. **1938** *Soils & Men: Yearbook Agric. 1938* (U.S. Dept. Agric.) 1163 *Azonal soils*, any group of soils without well-developed profile characteristics. **1952** P. W. RICHARDS *Trop. Rain Forest* ix. 210 In these cases the influence of the material from which the soil is formed overrides that of the climate giving rise to so-called azonal soils (in contrast to the climatic or zonal types).

azonic (ə'zɒnɪk), *a.* [a. Gr. ἀζωνικός (better ἄζωνος), f. ἀ priv. + ζωνή belt, zone, region: see -IC.] Not confined to a zone or region, not local.

1795 T. TAYLOR *Apuleius* (1822) 325 This order is called, by the Chaldaean theologists, azonic. **1870** EMERSON *Soc. & Solit.* viii. 163 The 'azonic' and the 'aquatic Gods.'

azoology (ˌæzəʊ'ɒlədʒɪ). [f. Gr. ἄζωος lifeless + -λογία: see -LOGY.] The scientific study of inanimate nature.

1817 *Month. Mag.* XLIII. 10 With Perception he conjoined Zoology; with Retention, Azoology.

azoospermia (əˌzəʊəʊ'spɜːmɪə). *Path.* [mod.L., f. Gr. ἄζωος lifeless + σπέρμα seed, SPERM *sb.* + -IA[1]; cf. *zoosperm*.] Absence of spermatozoa in the semen.

1889 in *Cent. Dict.* **1962** *Lancet* 27 Jan. 218/1 In three patients with oligospermia or azoospermia, we found a larger anomaly in length of the Y chromosome than normally established in our observations.

azoprotein (æzəʊ'prəʊtiːn). [G. (K. Landsteiner 1917, in *Z. Immun. Forschung* XXVI. 122), f. AZO- + PROTEIN.] 'In immunology, a protein coupled with a diazonium compound so as to form an azo derivative' (MacNalty, *Brit. Med. Dict.*, 1961).

1918 *Chem. Abstr.* 2373 Altogether 23 kinds of immune sera were prepd. [by K. Landsteiner and H. Lampl] and their action on 33 azo-proteins was investigated. **1930** *Syst. Bacteriol.* (*Med. Res. Council*) VI. 237 Landsteiner and Lampl (1917) found..a general method for preparing a long series of 'azo-proteins' particularly suitable for the study of the relationship between chemical structure and specificity. *Ibid.* 238 Precipitating antisera were prepared by the injection of these azo-proteins into rabbits. **1934** *Biol. Abstr.* 10591 Certain diazo compounds or azoproteins greatly increase tissue permeability.

azorite ('æzɒraɪt). *Min.* [f. *Azores*, the islands where found + -ITE.] A white mineral crystallizing in minute octahedrons, occurring in albitic rock; according to Hayes, a columbate of lime.

1868 DANA *Min.* 761.

azotæmia (æzəʊ'tiːmɪə). *Path.*, *Vet.* Also **azotemia.** [mod.L., f. AZOT(O- + Gr. αἷμ-α blood + -IA[1].] The presence of excessive nitrogenous waste products in the blood; a disease of solipeds resulting from this; cf. AZOTURIA. Hence **azo'tæmic** *a.*

1900 in DORLAND *Med. Dict.*, **1933** *Chem. Abstr.* 2995 (*title*) Coefficient of Maillard and the azotemic ratio of the guinea pig during acute..phosphorus poisoning. **1940** *Chambers's Techn. Dict.* 62/2 *Azotæmic* (*azotemic*) *nephritis*, nephritis in which there is retention of nitrogenous products in the blood. **1961** *Lancet* 16 Sept. 656/1 Other tests..did not separate clearly hyperparathyroid subjects from euparathyroid patients with renal stones, especially when azotæmia was present.

azote (æ'zəʊt). *Chem.* Also 8–9 **azot.** [a. F. *azote*, f. Gr. ἀ priv. + ζώ-ειν = ζά-ειν to live, ζωή life. Littré points out that this word (like *oxygen*) is not etymologically formed, since Gr. ἄζωτος means 'ungirt.'] The name given by Lavoisier, from its inability to support life, to the gas now known as *nitrogen*.

1791 E. DARWIN *Bot. Gard.* I. 73 *note*, Azote..combined with Calorique or heat, forms azotic gas..and composes two thirds of the atmosphere. **1791** HAMILTON *Berthollet's Dyeing* I. I. II, i, Azot in its elastic form constitutes.. phlogisticated gas. **1848** CARPENTER *Anim. Phys.* 25 Most plants require the element nitrogen or azote as one of the materials of their growth.

b. *fig.*

1850 MᶜCOSH *Div. Govt.* II. ii. (1874) 209 Unlike that air, all azote, of which the Atheist breathes. **1865** W. PALGRAVE *Arabia* I. 149 The noxious Wahhabee atmosphere, the purest azote of Mahometanism.

Hence: † **'azotane** [see -ANE 2 a], Davy's name for Chloride of Nitrogen. **azotine** ('æzətaɪn), a residuum of melted wool, rich in nitrogen, resulting from the action of superheated steam on mixed cotton and woollen rags. † **'azotite**, a salt of azotous acid, a nitrite. † **azotous** (ə'zəʊtəs), *a.*, nitrous. † **azoturet** (ə'zəʊtjʊərɪt), a nitride. **azotometer** (æzəʊ'tɒmɪtə(r)), an apparatus for measuring the amount of nitrogen present.

1827 FARADAY *Chem. Manip.* xix. 501 Tube syringes..for the removal of azotane. **1884** *Manch. Exam.* 20 Oct. 7/1 The residue, which has received the name of azotine..is valuable on account of its nitrogen. **1854** SCOFFERN in *Orr's Circ. Sc.* Chem. 326 Hyponitrous acid, termed by Graham..azotous, or nitrous acid. **1819** CHILDREN *Chem. Anal.* 110 Azoturet of potassium or sodium..the compound formed by heating potassium or sodium in dry ammoniacal gas. **1876** *Catal. Sci. App. S. Kens.* No. 2564 Improved Azotometer.

‖**azotea** (aθo'tea). [Sp.] The flat roof of a house, used as a place of resort in hot climates.

1824 J. R. POINSETT *Notes on Mexico* (1825) ii. 23 We next ascended to the *azotea*, (terrace roof), from whence we had a view of the harbour. **1844** J. GREGG *Commerce on Prairies* II. 102, I perceived the *azotea* of the parochial church occupied by armed men. **1921** *Chambers's Jrnl.* 257/2 Roses and carnations..trailing from every *azotea*.

azoted ('æzəʊtɪd), *a.* ? *Obs.* [f. AZOTE + -ED[2].] Nitrogenized.

1848 DUNGLISON *Dict. Med. Sci.* (ed. 7), *Azoted*, nitrogenized. **1872** AITKEN *Sci. & Pract. Med.* (ed. 6) II. 1061 In proportion as animals are fed on animal diet or on azoted substances, their urine becomes more and more loaded with lithic acid.

'azoth. *Alch.* Forms: 5 **azot**, 7 **azoch**, 7–9 **azoth.** [Corruption (ultimately) of Arab. *az-zāūq*: see ASSOGUE. Cf. F. *azoth*, Sp. *azogue*.] **a.** The alchemists' name for mercury, as the essential first principle of all metals. **b.** The universal remedy of Paracelsus. Also *fig.*

1477 NORTON *Ord. Alch.* v. in Ashm. (1652) 77 With Water of Azot to make *lac virginis.* **1610** B. JONSON *Alch.* II. iii, Your lato, azoch, zernich. **1655** T. VAUGHAN *Euphrates* 105 That glassie Azoth of Lullie. **1751** CHAMBERS *Cycl.* s.v., Paracelsus's azoth..is pretended to have been a preparation of gold, silver, and mercury. **1835** BROWNING *Paracels.* v. Wks. 1883 I. 183 Last, my good sword; ah, trusty Azoth, leapest Beneath thy master's grasp for the last time?

azotic (əˈzɒtɪk), *a. Chem.* [f. AZOTE + -IC; cf. F. *azotique.*] Of, pertaining to, or chemically compounded with, azote. †***azotic air*** or ***gas***: nitrogen. †***azotic acid***: nitric acid. Also *fig.* deadening, dulling.

1791 HAMILTON *Berthollet's Dyeing* I. I. I. iii. 55 No change of colour takes place in azotic gas. **1806** W. TAYLOR in *Ann. Rev.* IV. 720 We steep their youth in ceaseless azotic confinement. **1830** LINDLEY *Nat. Syst. Bot.* 168 The presence of azotic products in the vegetable kingdom. **1868** DUNCAN *Insect W.* Introd. 12 A strong pungent odour analogous to that of azotic or nitric acid.

azotize (ˈæzətaɪz), *v.* [f. AZOTE + -IZE.] To nitrogenize; *hence*, to deprive of oxygen, leaving nitrogen only. **ˈazotized** *ppl. a.*, nitrogenous, containing nitrogen.

1804 *Edin. Rev.* III. 421 What was formerly called..deoxygenating the system these writers term azotising. **1819** BRANDE *Chem.*, Belonging to the class of azotized basic bodies..[are] tea and coffee. **1859** CARPENTER *Anim. Phys.* vii, The Kidneys..throw off the azotized compounds which result from the decomposition of the tissues.

azoto-. A combining form of AZOTE, nitrogen; cf. AZO-.

azoturia (æzəʊˈtjʊːrɪə). *Path., Vet.* [mod.L., f. AZOT(O- + -URIA.] A condition in which the urine contains an excess of nitrogenous matter; cf. AZOTÆMIA.

1838 R. WILLIS *Urinary Diseases* I. i. 18 Of the discharge of urine which is characterized by a superabundance of Urea,—Azoturia. **1846** G. E. DAY tr. *Simon's Animal Chem.* II. vii. 307 By the term azoturia Willis understands that form of disease which is usually known as diabetes insipidus. **1953** G. BROOKE *Introd. Riding* xii. 133 Azoturia or haemoglobinuria is a disease peculiar to the horse tribe.

azoxy (ˈæzɒksɪ), *a.* [f. AZ(OTE + OXY(GEN.] Defining a compound consisting of an azo-group into which an oxygen atom has been introduced.

1873 *Jrnl. Chem. Soc.* XXVI. 1028 Azoxybenzene is obtained when a solution of azobenzene in acetic acid is heated with chromic anhydride. **1894** *Rep. Brit. Assoc. Advancem. Sci.* 245 Very interesting in point of fastness to light are the azoxy colours. **1964** N. G. CLARK *Mod. Org. Chem.* xx. 404 In the presence of bases, nitrosobenzene reacts with N-phenylhydroxylamine to give a 'bimolecular' compound, azoxybenzene.

Aztec (ˈæztɛk), *sb.* and *a.* **1.** One of a native American people first known (*c.* A.D. 1100) as inhabitants of the valleys of Mexico. Also *attrib.* or as *adj.* = ˈAztecan *a.*

1787 CULLEN tr. *Clavigero's Hist. Mexico* I. II. 112 The Aztecas or Mexicans, who were the last people who settled in Anahuac. **1814** H. M. WILLIAMS tr. *Humboldt's Researches* I. 81 The Toltecks, the Cicimecks..and the Aztecks..notwithstanding their political divisions, spoke the same language. *Ibid.* 83 Tezcatlipoca, the first of the Azteck divinities after Teotl. **1824** W. BULLOCK *Six Months Residence in Mexico* xxvi. 375, I immediately prepared for making casts of the Aztec idols and sculptures. **1824** J. R. POINSETT *Notes on Mexico* (1825) vii. 108 They all talk the Azteck, or Ottomic, and the Spanish. **1886** *Science* 5 Nov. 403/2 Its circular ornamentation is not Aztecan. **1920** *Edin. Rev.* Oct. 350 In the Aztec mind, stone was symbolic of the atonement of sin. **1922** W. R. INGE *Outspoken Essays* Ser. II. 74 The half-civilised Aztecs practised human sacrifice and cannibalism. **1965** *Canad. Jrnl. Linguistics* Spring 78 Part of the Aztecan-Tanoan phylum. **1966** *Harper's Bazaar* Sept. 58 A stunning wool weave of Aztec checks.

2. ***Aztec hop*** (also ***revenge, two-step***) (slang) = TURISTA.

1962 [see MONTEZUMA'S REVENGE]. **1970** *New Scientist* 8 Jan. 47/1 An intestinal attack known as gyppy tummy..in the Middle East;..Montezuma's revenge, Aztec two-step, and turista in Mexico. **1976** *National Observer* (U.S.) 21 Aug. 7/3 We found no health problems in San Miguel. Montezuma's revenge, or the Aztec two-step, struck us only fleetingly. **1978** J. WAMBAUGH *Black Marble* viii. 125 So long, Puerto Vallarta! With his luck he'd die of Aztec Revenge anyway, first time he had a Bibb lettuce salad.

azuki, var. ADZUKI.

‖**azulejo** (aθuˈleho). [Sp., f. *azul* blue, AZURE.] A kind of Dutch glazed tile painted in colours.

1845 R. FORD *Handbk. Spain* I. 225/1 The window..has been bricked up; it may be known by its border of *azulejos.* **1854** SCOFFERN in *Orr's Circ. Sc.* Chem. 430 The *azulejos* or coloured tiles, found in the Alhambra. **1874** O'SHAUGHNESSY *Mus. & Moonlight* 36 The quaint rich azulejos, with their own Melodious manner of bright metaphor. **1901** *Scribner's Mag.* XXIX. 449/1 The entire wall is encrusted with a mass of still brilliant tiles or 'azulejos'.

azulene (ˈæzjʊliːn). *Chem.* [f. Sp. *azul* blue + -ENE.] A liquid hydrocarbon, blue in colour, found in some volatile oils; = CERULEIN.

The term is used to cover not only the parent hydrocarbon but the class of derivatives with the same basic structure, viz. a five-ring joined to a seven-ring, isomeric with naphthalene, which has two six-rings joined together.

1874 *Jrnl. Chem. Soc.* XXVII. 1 Pure oil of wormwood (obtained from Dr. Septimus Piesse) being submitted to distillation, the greater part passed over..close upon 200°, a portion of blue oily product being obtained at a higher temperature (the *azulene* of Piesse and cœruleïn of Gladstone). **1880** [see CERULEIN]. **1956** *Nature* 21 Jan. 145/2 In the fractionation of hydrocarbons found in Copaiba balsam, we have isolated..a compound with the typical reactions of azulenes, and which we propose to call 'cario-azulene'.

azuline (ˈæzjʊlaɪn). [? f. Sp. *azul* blue + -INE; cf. F. *azurine.*] A particular shade of blue.

1864 G. GLADSTONE in *Reader* 8 Oct. 450/3 Solutions of chromium salts..litmus, azuline. **1883** M. HAWEIS in *Contemp. Rev.* 423 Shades of colour known by such names as..Magenta, Alexandra blue, azuline.

azure (ˈæʒə(r), ˈæʒ(j)ʊə(r), ˈeɪ-), *sb.* and *a.* Forms: 4 **azer**, 4–5 **asur(e**, 5 **aser(e**, **aserre**, 6 **asour**, **aisur**, 7 **azur**, 5– **azure**. [a. OF. *azur, asur* (11th c.), cogn. with Pr., OSp. *azur*, Pg., Sp. *azul*, It. *azzurro*, *azzuolo*, med.L. *azura*, *azzurum*, *azolum*, adaptations of Arabic (*al-*)*lazward*, a. Pers. *lājward*, *lāzhward*, lapis lazuli, blue colour. The initial *l* is absent in the Romance langs., apparently having been dropped along with Arabic article *al-*, or as if it were the article *l'*. It remains in med.Gr. λαζούριον, and med.L. *lazurius*, *lazur*, *lazulus*, lapis lazuli, literary forms taken directly from oriental authors or sources.]

A. *sb.* **1.** The precious stone lapis lazuli.

c **1325** *E.E. Allit. P.* B. 1411 Al in asure & ynde enaumayld. *Ibid.* 1457 Bassynes ful bryȝt of brende golde clere, Enaumaylde with azer. *c* **1374** CHAUCER *Troylus* III. 1321 A broche of golde and asure. *c* **1435** *Torr. Portugal* 351 Ther gold and sylvyr wase spred, And asur that wase blewe. **1509** BARCLAY *Ship of Fooles* (1570) 169 This tombe was..set with precious stone, Alayde with asour. **1615** G. SANDYS *Trav.* 65 Richly gilded, and adorned with Azure, and Mosaicke workmanship. **1783** W. F. MARTYN *Geog. Mag.* I. 131 About Tauris, the mineral azure is also found.

2. A bright blue pigment or dye; *ellipt.* a fabric dyed of this colour. ***a. of Almayne***: ? Prussian blue.

(Ultramarine is made from powdered lapis lazuli.)

c **1374** CHAUCER *Anel. & Arc.* 330 Youre figure Before me stante Cloothed in Asure. **1430** LYDG. *Chron. Troy* I. ii, And gan forthwith with golde and asure paint. **1502** ARNOLD *Chron.* 169 Make an hole in a tree..doo in yᵉ hole good asure of almayne..and the frute shalbe blew colour. **1552** *Act 5–6 Edw. VI*, vi. §11 All broad Plunkets, Azures, Blewes and other coloured Cloth. **1601** HOLLAND *Pliny* II. 484 Cæruleum or Azur, is a certaine sandy grit or pouder. **1875** URE *Dict. Arts* I. 874 The darkest-coloured smalts, known as King's-blue or azure.

3. *Her.* The blue colour in coats of arms, represented in engraving by horizontal lines.

a **1330** *Sire Degarré* 995 With the scheld of asur, And thre bor heuedes ther in. **1429** *Pol. Poems* (1859) II. 142 Thre flour-de-lys of gold, The fielde of asure. **1610** GWILLIM *Heraldry* I. iii. (1660) 19 Blew..in Blazon is termed Azure. **1751** CHAMBERS *Cycl., Azure*..signifies the blue colour in the coats of arms of all persons under the degree of a baron. **1838** *Penny Cycl.* XII 143/2.

4. The clear blue colour of the unclouded sky, or of the sea reflecting it. (Originally, the deep intense blue of more southern latitudes.)

1481 CAXTON *Myrr.* II. viii. 81 The colour of Asure lyke unto the heuen whan it is pure and clere. **1656** COWLEY *Davideis* II. Wks. I. 354 He cuts out a Silk Mantle from the Skies, Where the most sprightly Azure pleas'd the Eyes. **1725** POPE *Odyss.* I. 408 Celestial azure brightning in her eyes. **1823** BYRON *Island* III. iii, The vast and sullen swell Of ocean's alpine azure.

5. a. The unclouded vault of heaven.

1667 MILTON *P.L.* I. 297 Not like those steps On Heavens Azure. **1738** GLOVER *Leonidas* III. 14 Mingling its majestic front With heav'ns bright azure. **1871** PALGRAVE *Lyr. Poems* 10 Above, the crystal azure, perfect, pale.

b. *fig.*

1831 CARLYLE *Sart. Res.* II. ix, Borne aloft into the azure of Eternity. **1873** TYNDALL *Addr. Brit. Assoc.*, When you and I, like streaks of morning cloud, shall have melted into the infinite azure of the past.

B. *adj.* **1.** *Her.* Blue.

a **1450** *Syr Eglamore* 1030 He bare, Aserre, a grype of golde. ? **1650** *Don Bellianis* 16 A Knight cloathed in an azure armour. **1859** TENNYSON *Elaine* 181 Sir Lancelot's azure lions, crowned with gold.

2. a. Coloured like the unclouded sky; *orig.* of a deep intense blue, *now* usually of a soft clear bright blue, as is the sky of our more northern latitudes; sky-coloured, cerulean.

c **1505** DUNBAR *Twa Luves* xi, The hevinly aisur skyis licht. **1593** SHAKS. *Lucr.* 419 Her azure veins, her alabaster skin. *a* **1626** BACON *Sylva* §5 No Beast hath any fine Azure, or Carnation, or Green Haire. *a* **1763** SHENSTONE *Odes* (1765) 110 The little halcyon's azure plume Was never half so blue. **1813** SCOTT *Triermain* II. xxvii, Slow the dark-fring'd eyelids fall, Curtaining the azure ball. **1819** SHELLEY *Ros. & Helen* 957 It was the azure time of June.

b. (Used, like L. *cæruleus*, as an epithet of sea- and river-deities and things belonging to them.)

1697 DRYDEN *Virg. Georg.* IV. 560 High o'er the Main in wat'ry Pomp he rides His azure Carr. **1725** POPE *Odyss.* V. 426 An azure sister of the main.

3. a. *fig.* Like the unclouded sky; clear, cloudless.

1827 CARLYLE *Misc.* I. 36 Is not Klopstock, with..his azure purity..a man of taste? **1841** BREWSTER *Mart. Sc.* II. iv. (1856) 146 Those azure moments when the clouds broke from his mind.

b. *transf.* in *Jewellery* (see quot.)

1865 H. EMMANUEL *Diam. & Prec. Stones*, Sometimes..stones which are set open, or, to use the technical term, 'azur,' have the interior of the setting enamelled or painted, to throw a tint of colour into the gem.

4. *Bookbinding.* Composed of horizontal parallel lines, as a tooled or stamped design; also applied to the tool used for making such a design (cf. sense A. 3).

1894 *Amer. Dict. Printing & Bookmaking* 31 Azure tools. **1922** E. J. KIMBLE *Vocational Vocabs.* (ed. 2) 24 *Bookbinding*..azure tools. **1953** LEMAITRE & THOMPSON *Vocab. Bibliothec.* 198 Azure tooling (decoration with close parallel lines).

C. *Comb.*, as ***azure-bice*** (= bice), ***-blue***, ***-circled***; ***azure-bright***, ***-coloured***, ***-eyed***, ***-flaming***, ***-lidded***, ***-veined***; **azure-spar**, lazulite, **azure-stone**, the lapis lazuli, or lazulite.

a **1500** *E.E. Misc.* (1855) 78 Iff thou wylt preve *asure bice, if hit be good or badde. **1859** W. COLEMAN *Woodlands* (1862) 113 The pretty *Azure-blue butterfly (*Polyommatus Argiolus*). **1930** O. GOGARTY *Wild Apples* 15 And gazed out at *azure-bright pinnacled forms. **1879** TENNYSON *Lover's T.* 29 High over all the *azure-circled earth. **1617** *Wardens' Acc.* in Heath *Grocers' Comp.* (1869) 426 *Azure couloured cloathes for the poore men's gownes. **1791** COWPER *Iliad* II. 539 Minerva *azure-eyed advanced. **1929** E. BLUNDEN *Near & Far* 19 And *azure-flaming waves around rock-caves. **1820** KEATS *Eve of St. Agnes* xxx, And still she slept an *azure-lidded sleep. **1657** TOMLINSON *Renou's Disp.* 417 The *Azure-stone is most commonly in the gold mynes.

ˈazure, *v.* [f. prec.; cf. F. *azurer* (Cotgr.).] To paint, dye, or colour azure or bright blue. Hence **azuring** *vbl. sb.*

1490–1587 [see AZURED *ppl a.* 1]. **1656** W. MONTAGUE *Accompl. Wom.* 118 We azure wainscots, paint images, guild swords. **1791** HAMILTON *Berthollet's Dyeing* I. I. II. i, The silks are..azured with river-water. **1833** *Blackw. Mag.* XXXIV. 540 She saffrons the hills, and azures the mountains. **1869** *Eng. Mech.* 2 July 340/2 Aniline colours have been employed..for the azuring of the surface of the paper.

azurean (əˈzjʊərɪən), *a. rare.* [f. AZURE *a.* + -EAN (after *cerulean*).] = AZURE, AZUREOUS.

1882 *Garden* 18 Mar. 188/3 The deep azurean blue Scilla.

ˈazured, *ppl. a.* [f. AZURE + -ED; cf. F. *azuré* (16th c.).]

1. *arch.* or *Obs.* Coloured azure; = AZURE *a.* (in various senses): **a.** *pple.*

1490 CAXTON *Eneydos* xv. 57 The blewe cote of the heuens azured. **1587** FLEMING *Contn. Holinshed* III. 1335/2 Two banners of silke azured with the armes of Aniou.

b. *adj.*

1562 LEIGH *Armorie* (1597) 128 In the shield, the azured field is resembled to the mightie Ioue. *c* **1590** MARLOWE *Faust.* xiii. 109 In wanton Arethusas azur'd arms. **1604** E. G. *D'Acosta's Hist. Indies* v. xx. 384 Vpon the middest of the beard hee had a peece..of an azured stone. **1658** LENNARD *Charron's Wisd.* I. xl. §4 (1670) 146 The azured heaven..counterpointed with stars. **1833** I. TAYLOR *Fanat.* vii. 242 The deep azured night.

2. *spec.* in *Bookbinding* = AZURE *a.* 4. Also in Fr. form *azuré.*

1879 J. W. ZAEHNSDORF *Art of Bookbinding* xxii. 102 The use of lined or azuré tools are a distinctive mark of the period. **1893** S. T. PRIDEAUX *Hist. Sketch Bookbinding* i. 32 The azured tools were first used by Grolier for the bindings done in France, between 1530 and 1540; no azured tools are found on French bindings before that date. **1895** J. W. ZAEHNSDORF *Short Hist. Bookbinding* 17 *Azured Tooling*, ornamentation outlined in gold and crossed by horizontal lines in the manner of indicating azure in heraldry. **1937** RYE & QUINN *Hist. & Armorial Bookbindings Exhib. in Univ. Libr.* 36 At the base is an azured border.

azureous (əˈzjʊərɪəs), *a. rare*, [f. AZURE + -EOUS.] Of a clear blue colour; azure.

azurine (ˈæzjʊəraɪn, -ɪn), *a.* and *sb.* [a. F. *azurin* (Cotgr.); cf. It. *azzurrino* (Florio 1598), med.L. *azurīnus*: see -INE[1].]

A. *adj.* **1.** Blue, azure; according to Littré, pale blue, inclining to grey.

1600 HAKLUYT *Voy.* III. 37 (R.) They lay a color [on their wrists] which continueth dark azurine.

B. *sb.* **1.** The Blue Roach (*Leuciscus cæruleus*), distinguished by the slate-blue colour of its back.

1832 YARRELL in *Trans. Linn. Soc.* XVII. I. 8 From the prevailing blue colour of this fish I have been induced to call it the Azurine. **1875** 'STONEHENGE' *Brit. Sports* I. v. i. 306 The Azurine is another fish only found in Lancashire.

2. *Dyeing.* A base obtained from aniline black, giving a bluish black shade in printing; also the colour itself.

1878 *Jrnl. Chem. Soc.* XXXIV. 572 Azurine is characterised by the blue fluorescence of its solutions. **1894** GOULD *Dict. Med., Azurin*..Same as *Azulin.* **1902** *Encycl. Brit.* XXVII. 563/2 There are several oxidation products of aniline. The first..is..emeraldine..which by treatment with alkali yields a dark blue base called azurine.

azurite (ˈæzjʊəraɪt). *Min.* [f. AZURE + -ITE.]

1. Blue carbonate of copper, a valuable ore, closely allied to malachite.

1868 DANA *Min.* 715. **1873** WATTS *Fownes' Chem.* 398 Azurite occurs in large transparent crystals of the most intense blue.

†**2.** Obsolete name of LAZULITE.

1816 R. JAMESON *Min.* I. 341.

†**'azurn**, *a. Obs. rare*$^{-1}$. [app. f. AZURE *sb.* + -N as in *leathern, silvern*; but cf. F. *azurin*, It. *azurrino*.] = AZURE.

1634 MILTON *Comus* 893 Thick set with agate, and the azurn sheen Of turkis blue, and emerald green.

azury ('æʒərɪ, 'eɪʒ(j)ʊərɪ), *a.* [f. AZURE + -Y¹; cf. F. *azuré*.] Blue, bluish, tinted with soft clear blue.

1600 TOURNEUR *Transf. Met.* vii, The skie, whose hue was azurie. **1611** GWILLIM *Heraldry* III. vii. 116 The columbine is pleasing to the eie .. in regard of the Azurie colour thereof. **1849** C. BRONTË *Shirley* xii. 171 Fleeces of white cloud fine as azury snow.

†**'azury**, *sb. Obs.* In 6 **asure**, 7 **asurie**. [? subst. use of prec.; perh. influenced by collectives in -RY, as *embroidery*.] Azure hue or colour.

1503 HAWES *Examp. Virtue* xiv. 286 Whan we were in the ayre of asure There dyd vs mete the noble Ierarchy. **1600** TOURNEUR *Transf. Met.* xxi, Encircled them with faire imbroderie Of sacred lights in ayre-cleare azurie.

azygos, azygous ('æzɪgəs), *a.* (and *sb.*) *Phys.* [(a. or) f. Gr. ἄζυγος unyoked, not a pair. f. ἀ priv. + ζυγόν yoke: see -OUS. Cf. mod.F. *azygos*.]

A. *adj.* Fellowless, unpaired: a technical epithet of organic parts not existing in pairs. **B.** *sb.* An organic part of this description.

1646 SIR T. BROWNE *Pseud. Ep.* 183 The Azygos, or vena sine pari. **1681** tr. *Willis' Rem. Med. Wks.*, Azygos vein, is a branch of the upper trunk of the vena cava, arising on the right side. **1859** TODD *Cycl. Anat. & Phys.* V. 81/1 The pancreas is an azygous .. organ. **1870** ROLLESTON *Anim. Life* Introd. 38 An azygos orifice in the abdominal walls.

azygospore (ə'zaɪgəʊspɔə(r), ə'zɪg-, eɪ-). *Bot.* [f. A- 14 + ZYGOSPORE.] A parthenogenetic zygospore.

1889 in *Cent. Dict.* **1898** H. C. PORTER tr. *Strasburger's Bot.* 348 Although the conjugating hyphæ meet in pairs, no fusion takes place, and their terminal cells become converted directly into spores, which are termed azygospores. **1952** *New Biol.* XIII. 106 Under certain circumstances the process of zygospore formation may be interrupted, whereupon a single gametangium may give rise to a thick-walled spore which resembles closely a typical zygospore with respect to size and appearance, and is termed an azygospore.

'azygously, *adv.* [f. AZYGOS, AZYGOUS *a.* (and *sb.*) + -LY².] In azygous manner; not in pairs, singly.

1854 *Orr's Circ. Sc.* Org. Nat. I. 73 The three .. arteries .. come off azygously—that is .. not in pairs, but singly.

azyme ('æzɪm, -aɪm). Also 7 **azime**. [ad. L. *azȳmus* adj., *azyma* sb. pl., a. Gr. ἄζυμος, -μα, f. ἀ priv. + ζύμη leaven. Cf. F. *azyme* adj., *azymes* sb.] The Jewish passover cake of unleavened bread; also in *pl.* the feast of unleavened bread. Also *fig.*

[**1398** TREVISA *Barth. de P.R.* XVII. lxviii. 644 Paast made onely of mele and of water hyghte Azima.] **1582** N. T. (Rhem.) *1 Cor.* v. 7 Purge the old leaven, that you may be a new paste, as ye are azymes [WYCLIF, therf; TINDALE, *Genev.* swete breed; **1611** unleauened]. —— *Mark* xiv. 1 The Pasche vvas and the Azymes after tvvo daies. **1651** *Rawleigh's Apparition* 206 Peculiar ceremonies, to wit .. the use of their Azimes and the obligation of their first born. *fig.* **1930** T. S. ELIOT tr. *St.-J. Perse's Anabasis* 69 Under the azyme of fine weather, .. the whole feather of harvest!

Azymite ('æzɪmaɪt). [ad. L. *azȳmita*, ad. Gr. ἀζυμίτης, f. ἄζυμος: see prec. and -ITE. In F. *azymite*.] One who administers the Eucharist with unleavened bread; a name given by the Greek Church to members of the Roman Church, and to Armenians and Maronites.

1727–51 in CHAMBERS *Cycl.* **1850** TORREY *Neander's Ch. Hist.* VI. 418 The two parties called each other by the heretical names, Azymites and Prozymites.

azymous ('æzɪməs), *a.* [f. L. *azȳm-us*, a. Gr. ἄζυμος + -OUS.] Unleavened.

1727 CHAMBERS *Cycl.*, *Azymus*. **1763** *Dict. Arts & Sc.* I. 238/2 The Latin Church .. maintain, that the bread in the mass ought to be azymous.

B

B (biː). **I. 1.** The second letter of the Roman alphabet, ancient and modern, corresponding, in position and power, to the Greek *Beta*, and Phœnician and Hebrew *Beth*, whence also its form is derived; representing the sonant labial mute, or lip-voice stop consonant. The plural has been written Bees, B's, *B*s.

c **1000** ÆLFRIC *Gram.* iii. (Zup. 6) þá óðre niȝon consonantes synd ȝecwedene MVTAE, þæt synd *dumbe.* hí ne synd ná mid ealle dumbe, ac hí habbað lytle clypunge . . þás ongynnað of him sylfum and ȝeendjað on þám clypjendlícum stafum. *b, c, d, g, p, t* ȝeendjað on *e.* *c* **1375** WYCLIF *Serm.* Sel. Wks. 1871 II. 239 þis eire lernede first his a, bi, ce. **1588** SHAKS. *L.L.L.* v. ii. 42 Beauteous as Incke . . Faire as a text B. in a Coppie booke. **1610** *Chester's Tri.* (1844) Addr. 23 The chiefest part of this people-pleasing spectacle, consisted in three Bees, viz. Boyes, Beasts, and Bels. **1682** BUNYAN *Holy War* Advt., Witness my name, if Anagram'd to thee, The letters make, Nu hony in a B. **1878** *Daily News* 8 July 5/2 He pronounces his P's like B's.

2. *Phrases* relating to the letter. ***not to know a B from a bull's foot, not to know a B from a battle-dore***: to be entirely illiterate.

1401 *Pol. Poems* II. 57, I know not an A from the wyndmylne, ne a B from a bole foot. **1609** DEKKER *Guls Horne-Bk.* 3 You shall not neede to buy bookes, no, scorne to distinguish a B from a battle dore. **1660** HOWELL *Eng. Prov.* 16 He knoweth not a B. from a battle-door. **1846** BRACKENRIDGE *Mod. Chivalry* 43 There were members who scarcely knew B from a bulls-foot.

II. Used, like the other letters of the alphabet (see A, *the letter*), to indicate serial order, with the value of *second*, as quire B, the second 'quire' or sheet of a book, 'Horse Artillery, B Brigade, B and C Batteries, Woolwich;' (b., *b.*) the left-hand page or *verso* of a leaf, the second column of a page. The following uses are more special:

1. In *Music*: In England the 7th note of the scale of C major, which is called H in Germany, where B means the English B flat. B was the first note modified by a semitone in the musical scale, whence the signs ♭, originally a *b* with round bottom (= B♭, Fr. *B rond*), and ♮, originally a 𝔟 with square bottom (= B ♮, Fr. *B carré*), which since *c* 1620 have been applied as indicating 'flat' and 'natural' to all notes of the scale. A piece of music 'in B' has as its main scale that beginning with B.

[*c* **1450** *Burlesque* in *Rel. Ant.* I. 83 Every clarke . . seythe that a-re gothe before be-my.] **1597** MORLEY *Introd. Mus.* 3 Every keye hath but one cleife except b fa, b mi. **1731** SWIFT *Apollo* Wks. 1755 IV. I. 161 For he could reach to B in alt. **1873** A. COLERIDGE *Moscheles* I. 271 Mendelssohn . . played his charming Capriccio in B minor. **1879** CURWEN *Mus. Theory* 73 The fourth [note] in the key of F is B flat.

2. a. In *abstract reasoning*, *hypothetical argumentation*, *law*, etc., B is put for a second or another person or thing. (Cf. A II. 4.) **b.** In various specific applications, as (i) a blood-group (see quots.); (ii) a second-class road; (iii) a supporting film to the main feature in a cinema programme; (iv) ***B Special***: in Northern Ireland (until 1970), a member of the Ulster Special Constabulary, retained on a part-time basis (see quot. 1985); a special constable; (v) a range of international standard paper sizes (as *B1*, *B2*, etc.): see A II. 9; (vi) (the music recorded on) the supporting or less important side of a single-playing gramophone record, as ***B-side***; cf. *flip side* s.v. FLIP *sb.*^{2} 7; contr. with *A-side* s.v. A II. 10.

1797 TOMLINS *Law Dict.* s.v. *Agreement*, If a bond or note be given by A., the more effectually to enable B. to bring about a match, etc. **1870** BOWEN *Logic* 207 The two categorical formulas *A is B*, or *A is not B*. **1879** BROWNING *Dram. Lyrics* Wks. III. 92 A.'s book shall prop you up, B.'s shall cover you.

[**1910** W. L. MOSS tr. Landsteiner in *Johns Hopkins Hosp. Bull.* XXI. 65/2 In a number of cases (Group A) the serum agglutinates the corpuscles of another Group (B), not, however, those of Group A.] **1921** *Brit. Jrnl. Exper. Path.* II. 33 The Landsteiner theory that two substances, 'A' and 'B', with their corresponding agglutinins, 'a' and 'b', are concerned in the isoagglutination of human bloods has been confirmed by absorption tests. **1927, 1928** [see A II. 7]. **1948** *New Biol.* V. 69 Human beings are classified into the four categories A, B, AB or O according as to whether certain A and B substances can be detected in their red blood cells (and incidentally in other tissues).

1921 *Autocar* 29 Oct. 829/2 It is not . . intended to deal with the numbering of the B roads until that of the A roads has been completed. **1962** *Guardian* 14 July 5/2 The B road . . climbs up the Cotswolds from Stroud to Birdlip. **1967** M. CULPAN *In Deadly Vein* iii. 41 A country lane of the twenties had now been widened into a B-road between A.5 and A.6.

1949 *Here & Now* (N.Z.) Oct. 29/2 There is a current reaction against the 'big' picture; and it is a sign of the times that the Academy, one of London's repertory cinemas, has been showing two American 'B' features. **1962** *Observer* 20 May 27/6 Just that something which distinguishes the good documentary from the drab British B picture. **1967** *Listener* 7 Sept. 316/2 Things are looking up on ITV, except on farmer-and-B-film-haunted Southern.

1922 in M. Gilbert *Winston S. Churchill* (1977) IV. Compan. III. 1948 In addition there were the 'B' Specials, numbering about 20,000. **1932** *Tablet* 15 Oct. 500/1 The 'B' Specials—a force of civilians enrolled as special constables. **1985** BIGGS-DAVISON & CHOWDHARAY-BEST *Cross of St Patrick* 443 The 'A' Specials were a full-time and paid force; the 'B' Specials an occasional force with an allowance; and the 'C' Specials were unpaid. **1986** *N.Y. Times* 22 Jan. A2/4 When the [Ulster Defence] regiment was created 16 years ago to replace the B-Specials, an auxiliary police force often accused of mistreating Catholics, some Protestants reacted with two riots.

1937 E. J. LABARRE *Dict. Paper* 276/2 The B series is the first and the C and D series the second and third geometrical intermediate forms of the A series. **1962** [see A II. 9]. **1982** *Electronics* 11 Aug. 5E/1 A 5-by-7 dot-matrix impact printer that accepts B5-sized paper. **1985** *Computerworld Focus* 20 Nov. 24/3 The printer uses . . European sizes A4 and B5.

1962 *Melody Maker* 7 July 10/1 'Miracles sometimes happen' . . now turns up as the B side for Michael London's vocal disc of Acker Bilk's ' Stranger on the Shore'. **1970** J. LENNON in J. Wenner *Lennon Remembers* (1971) 106 That was the B-side of 'Hello, Goodbye'. **1984** *Sounds* 1 Dec. 24/6, I was amazed that 'Little Tickets' was relegated to a B-side and won't even appear on the LP.

3. In *Algebra*: *b.* (see A II. 5.)

III. *Abbreviations.* **1. B.** (in *Academical degrees*), Bachelor, or its Latin equivalent *baccalaureus*, as *LL.B.* (*Legum Baccalaureus*) Bachelor of Laws; ***M.B.*** Bachelor of Medicine; **B.** (*Music*), Bass, Basso; **B, BB, BBB**, black, double-, treble-black (of pencil lead); **b.**, *b.*, born; **B.** (*Chem.*), Boron; **b** *Particle Physics*, bottom; **b.** (formerly also **B**), *Cricket*, bowled by; **B. (b.)** *Cricket*, 'Byes'; **B**, breathalyser; so ***B-test***; **b, B**, bugger (or bastard) (as a euphemism, sometimes printed b——); **B.A.** (or **A.B.**), Bachelor of Arts; **B.A.B.S.** *Aeronaut.*, beam (or blind) approach beacon system, a system for approaching a landing field by means of instruments; **B.A.L.**, British Anti-Lewisite, a drug (dimercaprol) developed as an antidote to Lewisite and used also to neutralize metallic poisons, e.g. arsenic; **B. and S.**, brandy and soda; **B.A.O.R.**, British Army of the Rhine; **B.B.C.** (see as separate entry); **B.C.**, Before Christ; **B.C.**, Bad character; a mark formerly set on a soldier on his expulsion from his regiment for gross misconduct; **B.C.E.**, Before the Common Era; **B.C.-G.**, **B.C.G.**, Bacillus Calmette-Guérin, used as an anti-tuberculosis vaccine; also *attrib.*; **B.C.L.**, Bachelor of Civil Law; **B.D.**, Bachelor of Divinity; **B.D.S.T.**, British Double Summer Time; **B.E.F.**, British Expeditionary Force; **B.E.M.**, British Empire Medal; **B.E.M.**, bug-eyed monster; **BeV.**, **B.E.V.**, **bev**, *U.S.* (*b*illion electron *v*olts): a thousand million (10^9) electron volts; **B.F.**, bloody fool; **B.H.C.**, benzene hexachloride; **b.h.p.**, brake horse power; **B.L.**, Bachelor of Law, also (Fr.) *Bachelier-ès-lettres*; **B.Lit(t).**, Bachelor of Literature, Bachelor of Letters; **B.M.**, British Museum; **B.M.A.**, British Medical Association; **BMX** (see as main entry); **B.O.**, body odour; **B.O.P.**, Boy's Own Paper; **B.P.**, (*a*) British Public, esp. in ***G.B.P.***, (*b*) British Pharmacopœia: the title of a list of medicines and other preparations published under the direction of the General Medical Council; (*c*) before present, *i.e.*, counting backwards from A.D. 1800; **B.Phil.**, (less commonly) **B.Ph.**, Bachelor of Philosophy; **B.R.**, British Rail (formerly Railways); **B.S.**, Bachelor of Surgery; **B.S.**, (*slang*, chiefly *N. Amer.*), bullshit; **B.Sc.**, Bachelor of Science; **B.S.(S.)**, British Standard (Specification); **B.S.I.**, British Standards Institution; **B.S.T.**, British Summer Time; (from 1968) British Standard Time; **B.T.M.**, **b.t.m.** *colloq.*, bottom, posterior; **B.T.U.**, Board of Trade unit; **B.T.U.**, **B.Th.U.**, British thermal unit; **B.U.**, bread unit: a ration token exchangeable for bread, cakes, etc.; **B.V.** (*Beata Virgo*), The Blessed Virgin. **B.V.D.** (see as main entry); **BYO** *U.S.* and *Austral.*, 'bring your own', designating a party, restaurant, etc. where food is provided but one takes one's own drink; also **BYOB** *U.S.*, 'bring your own beer (booze, bottle, etc.)'. See also B-GIRL.

1853 C. H. WEIGALL *Art of Drawing* Advts., p. 14 *B, Black (for Shading, or free Sketching). *BB, Softer ditto (for deep Shading). *BBB, Intensely Black (for extra deep Shading). **1886** C. M. YONGE *Chantry House* I. vii. 63 We had filled whole drawing-books with . . foliage in BBB marking pencil. **1931** *Boys' Mag.* XLV. 190/1 A 'B' pencil. **1945** *Amer. Speech* XX. 309 *BABS. Blind Approach Beacon System. System for approaching landing field by radar means. **1951** *Gloss. Aeronaut. Terms* (*B.S.I.*) III. 28 Beam-approach beacon system, *abbr.* BABS. **1978** *Nature* 2 Feb. 407/1 This new quark pair is labelled t and *b for 'top' and 'bottom'. **1983** *Sci. Amer.* July 105/3 The lifetime of the *b* is predicted to be between 10^{-13} and 10^{-14} second. **1983** *McGraw-Hill Yearbk. Sci. & Technol.* *1984* 284/2 The discovery of the first *b*-flavored particle . . proves the existence of the *b* quark. **1744** in Nyren *Young Cricketer's Tutor* (1833) 111 Harris 0, *B by Hadswell. **1822** in Pycroft *Cricket Field* (ed. 6, 1873) xiii. 292 Holloway, b. Beauclerk 0. **1968** *Times* 15 Mar. 15/1 S. Comacho c. Knott, b. Brown . . 87. **1967** *Daily Tel.* 21 Oct. 20/8 (*heading*) *B-test driver fined. **1851** MAYHEW *Lond. Lab.* I. 313/1 The poor *b— is in 'stir' (prison). **1925** D. H. LAWRENCE *Let.* 17 Nov. (1962) 865 I'd have sent those Irish b's seven times to hell, before I'd have moved a single iota at their pencil stroke. **1952** N. STREATFEILD *Aunt Clara* 14 Can't 'elp bein' sorry for the poor old B. *Ibid.* 161 'Poor little B's,' he thought. **1942** *PB 5545: Office of Sci. Res. & Devel., National Defense Res. Comm.* (E. I. Du Pont de Nemours & Co.) (*title of mimeographed report*) Report on the experimental manufacture and process study of *BAL. **1943** *Hospital Corps Q.* (Washington, D.C.) XVI. 140 Persons required to enter areas specifically known to be contaminated with lewisite should apply BAL ointment sparingly to unprotected parts of the body. **1944** *Brit. Med. Jrnl.* 22 July 111/1 Recently B.A.L. ointment, which is a specific for arsenical vesicants and of great value in the treatment of the eyes, has been developed. **1964** S. DUKE-ELDER *Parsons' Dis. Eye* (ed. 14) xxvi. 379 Arsenical vesicants are neutralized by the local application of BAL ointment. *a* **1878** WHYTE-MELVILLE *Black but Comely* (1879) II. xxvii. 112 Now for a *B-and-S, one quiet cigar, and then bed. **1882** *Punch* 11 Feb. 69/1 He'll nothing drink but 'B. & S.' and big magnums of 'the Boy'. **1945** *War Illustr.* 9 Nov. 421 (*caption*) A *B.A.O.R. major examined the papers of Wehrmacht youths about to be demobilized at Staaken, near Berlin. **1881** K. MAGNUS *About Jews* i. 1 A glance at the Babylonian captivity (587–536 *B.C.E.). **1915** M. RADIN *Jews among Greeks & Romans* 15 The period . . from the end of the Babylonian Captivity to the establishment of Christianity—roughly from about 450 B.C.E. to 350 C.E. **1926** *Lancet* 29 May 1030/1 It is this attenuated bacillus *B.C.-G., or *Bacillus Calmette-Guérin* that he uses for his vaccinations of both calves and newborn infants. **1958** *Sunday Times* 23 Feb. 19/4 B.C.G. inoculation against tuberculosis. **1943** *Daily Tel.* 24 June 1/7 At 1.20 this morning (2.20 *B.D.S.T.) the state of the parties was [etc.]. **1917** W. OWEN *Let.* 9 Jan. (1967) 425 Please send the compass: 2 Manchester Regt. *B.E.F. **1939** *War Illustr.* 7 Oct. 110/1 The men of the new B.E.F. have gone to the front with smiling faces. **1941** *Ibid.* 9 May 476/2 Mr. T. H. Newton, Home Guard, *B.E.M., for securing a mine and rendering it safe. **1948** *Electronic Engin.* XX. 149 The bevatron (from *B.E.V.—billion electron volts). **1964** *Sci. Amer.* July 44/3 The six-billion-electron-volt (6-bev) electron synchrotron in Cambridge, Mass. **1925** FRASER & GIBBONS *Soldier & Sailor Words* 12 **B.F.* . . Ordinary contemptuous slang: *e.g.*, 'He's an out and out B.F.!' **1939** C. DAY LEWIS *Child of Misfortune* II. i. 137 You really are a B.F., Arthur. **1947** *Ann. Appl. Biol.* XXXIV. 347 The material used . . was crude benzene hexachloride (*B.H.C.). **1895** *Oxf. Univ. Calendar 1896* 72 *B.Litt. or B.Sc. **1909** *Cent. Dict.* Suppl., B.Lit. **1937** *Discovery* Jan. ii/1 Geraldine Coster, B.Litt. (Oxon.). **1870** GEO. ELIOT *Let.* 14 Sept. (1956) V. 116, I dare not expect to be in time for any address but the *B[ritish] M[useum]. **1954** *Grove's Dict. Mus.* III. 168/2 An Indian bas-relief . . dominated the grand staircase at the B.M. **1886** *Dict. Abbrevs.* 14 **B.M.A.*, British Medical Association. **1955** *Times* 2 June 3/6 The annual meeting of the British Medical Association, which opened yesterday at B.M.A. House. **1933** *Sat. Even. Post* 14 Jan. 91/3 Those '*B.O.' ads. I laughed at—is the joke on *me*? **1936** AUDEN & ISHERWOOD *Ascent of F6* II. iii. 96 And some I know have got B.O.: But these are not for me. **1909** R. BROOKE *Let.* 4 Sept. (1968) 176 Reading the *B.O.P. **1932** DYLAN THOMAS *Let.* Dec. (1966) 8, I . . contribute . . funny verses to the B.O.P. **1939** 'G. ORWELL' *Coming up for Air* II. ii. 58 Myself under the table with the B.O.P., making believe that the table-cloth is a tent. **1896** ELLEN TERRY *Let.* 26 Nov. in *E. Terry & Bernard Shaw* (1931) 129, I should say it would be a tremendous go with the *B.P. **1963** 'A. GILBERT' *Ring for Noose* vi. 76 The dear B.P. doesn't worry its head much about proof. **1898** *Lancet* 6 Aug. 337/2 We hold it to be incumbent upon every medical man . . to write . . upon his recipes either the words *B.P. 1898 or B.P. 1885 after each preparation. **1966** D. FRANCIS *Flying Finish* vi. 69 A printed chemist's label on the front said 'Two hundred aspirin tablets B.P.' **1946** F. E. ZEUNER *Dating Past* v. 142 Going backwards into the past, the radiation curve for the last 600,000 years . . shows a series of three summer minima between 25,000 and 115,000 years *B.P. **1923** F. W. HAYCRAFT *Degrees & Hoods World's Universities & Colleges* 1 **B.Ph.*, Bachelor of Philosophy. **1942** PARTRIDGE *Dict. Abbrevs.* 19/2 *B.Phil.*, Bachelor of Philosophy. **1966** *Rep. Comm. Inquiry Univ. Oxf.* II. 22 The B.Phil. can be taken in a number of arts and social studies subjects. **1949** *Railway Gaz.* Jan. (Index Suppl.) p. v/1 (*heading*) *B.R. Eastern Region. **1958** *Spectator* 13 June 772/1 The stock BR argument against sleepers is that they are wasteful of accommodation. **1986** *Bookseller* 25 Jan. 428/2 An eminently practical . . book, really to help you get the most out of BR and Godfrey Davis Europcar. [**1884** S. F.

PECKHAM *Rep. on Petroleum* viii. 95 The oil is subject to depreciation in value from evaporation and by leakage through the roof of the tank, by which it is converted into an emulsion locally known as 'B.S.'] **1912** J. SANDILANDS *Western Canad. Dict. & Phrase-Bk.*, **B.S.*, the initials of a very vulgar but common ejaculation, describing a story as lies and nonsense. **1965** G. JENNINGS *Personalities of Lang.* 138 At one time, oilfield workers vulgarly referred to the sludge that befouls..oil tanks as 'bullshit'. This was gradually abbreviated to 'B.S.', which the industry's trade journals primly translated into 'basic sediment'. **1969** I. BLACK in A. Chapman *New Black Voices* (1972) 372 If we stuck by our women Cooled the b.s. in barbershops..If we kept our neighborhoods clean and peaceful..Think it would make a difference? **1975** J. GOULET *Human Ape* (1977) xx. 123 Shit,..you can't be around a project like this for two years without picking up some of that B.S. **1932** *Brit. Standards Inst. Handbk.* 45 List of *B.S. Specifications. *Ibid.* 61 Subject Index to B.S. Specifications ..B.S.S. No. *Ibid.* 1 Aims and Objects of the *B.S.I. **1930** *Meteorol. Gloss.* (ed. 2) 36 *British Summer Time* (**B.S.T.*).. 9 h. G.M.T. is the same as 10 h. B.S.T. **1960** *Farmer & Stockbreeder* 22 Mar. 72/1 (*headline*) Scots F.U. Oppose B.S.T. Change. **1968** *Guardian* 17 Feb. 16/6 Sunrise times under BST. **1919** R. FIRBANK *Valmouth* xi. 188 She made a sudden dash for my *b-t-m. **1934** S. BECKETT *More Pricks than Kicks* 52 The weary proletarians at rest on B.T.M. and elbow. **1946** *Lancet* 20 July 97/2 Each bread unit is equivalent to 7 oz. of bread, 5¼ oz. of flour, or 8 oz. of flour confectionery, so the scales of *B.U. per week can be read as scales of bread in ounces per day. **1965** R. C. THOMAS et al. *Acronyms & Initialisms Dict.* (ed. 2) 148 **BYO*, party invitation notation meaning 'Bring Your Own' (Liquor). **1968** *Catering* May 12/2 One important alteration in the new Liquor Control Bill is that B.Y.O. permits for unlicensed restaurants have been abolished. **1973** *Nation Rev.* (Melbourne) 31 Aug. II. 1460/6 Most people can only eat out on any regular basis if they dine at a BYO and avoid the licensed houses. **1986** *Daily Sun* (Brisbane) 23 May 38/3 Samford Restaurant is a quaint BYO house in a venerable old home that has been renovated. **1959** *Amer. Speech* XXXIV. 155 If they decide upon a party, they throw a ball or..in some cases, a *BYOB (bring your own bottle). **1975** *New Yorker* 26 May 32/1 Our parties are not just BYOB but also BYOW (Weed) and BYOBR (Brown Rice). **1984** M. FERMAGLISH *Mollie's Rules for Socially Inept* iii. 72 As long as the invitation doesn't say 'BYOB', they'll show up.

2. *B.* or *B. flat*, a humorous euphemism for *bug* (*Cimex lectularius*).

1853 DICKENS *Househ. Words* XX. 326 A stout negro of the flat back tribe—known among comic writers as B flats. **1867** *Cornh. Mag.* Apr. 450 That little busy B. which invariably improves the darkness at the expense of every offering traveller. **1881** T. HUGHES *Rugby Tenn.* 58 An insect suspiciously like a British B. flat.

†**ba**, *v. Obs. rare.* [Prob. a nursery or jocular word, imitating the action of the lips in an infant's kiss; but cf. OF. *bae-r*, *bee-r*, to open the mouth, gape.] To kiss, as a child. In the second quot. it seems to be used substantively for the action of kissing. (Cf. OF. *baée*, opening of the mouth.)

c **1386** CHAUCER *Wyf's Prol.* 433 How mekly lokith Wilkyn our scheep! Com ner, my spouse, let me ba thy cheke. *a* **1529** SKELTON *My darling dere* 9 With ba, ba, ba, and bas, bas, bas, She cheryshed hym both cheke and chyn.

ba, early form of BO *a. Obs.* both.

baa (bɑː), *v.* Also 7–9 ba(e. [Formed in imitation of a sheep's or lamb's bleat; cf. Norm.F. *bai*, Cat. *be*, sheep.] To bleat.

a **1586** SIDNEY (J.) Like a lamb, whose dam away is set, He treble baas for help. **1607** SHAKS. *Cor.* II. i. 12 He's a Lambe indeed, that baes like a Beare. **1765** C. SMART *Phædrus* (Bohn) III. xiv. 506 You little fool, why, how you baa! This goat is not your own mamma. **1877** A. B. EDWARDS *Up Nile* vi. 138 Our sacrificial sheep..comes baaing in the rear.

baa (bɑː), *sb.* Forms: 6–7 bea, ba, (7 *Sc.* bae), 7– baa, 9 (*reduplicated*) ba-ba. [f. prec. vb.] **a.** The cry of a sheep or lamb; a bleat.

1589 *Pappe w. Hatchet* (1844) 37 They haue no propertie of sheepe but bea. *c* **1600** *Ever-Green* (1761) II. 58 With mony a Bae and Bleit. **1870** *Daily News* 11 Oct., We civic sheep have set up so loud a ba-ba that we have terrified the wolves. **1877** BLACKIE *Wise Men* 264 The snow-white lamb ..fills the solitude with tremulous baa.

b. *Comb.*, as ***bea-waymenting***, ***-wailing***; **baa(h-ling**, a little lamb; **baa-lamb**, nursery equivalent of 'lamb'; also, a toy lamb.

1580 SIDNEY *Arcadia* (1622) lxix. 77 Still for thy Dam with bea-waymenting crie. **1599** T. M[OUFET] *Silkewormes* 3 Then hairy cloathes, and wooll from Baa-lambs tore. *a* **1649** DRUMM. OF HAWTH. *Poems* Wks. (1711) 4/2 There bea-wailing strays A harmless lamb. **1854** THACKERAY *Newcomes* 2 Silly little knock-kneed baah-ling. **1871** MRS. CRAIK *Little Sunshine's Holiday* ii. 31 Little Sunshine was greatly charmed with the 'baa-lambs'. **1888** MRS. H. WARD *R. Elsmere* III. VI. xxxix. 174 The baby..was..caressing.. a woolly baa-lamb. **1906** (*title*) The baa lamb's ABC.

baad, obs. f. *bade*, pa. t. of BID.

baaing (ˈbɑːɪŋ), *vbl. sb.* [f. BAA *v.* + -ING[1].] The crying or bleating of a sheep.

1832 MARRYAT *N. Forster* xxxi, The ba-aing and bleating. **1862** MAX MÜLLER in *Macm. Mag.* Nov. 57 Can we admit.. that those who imitate the baaing of the sheep name the animal?

ˈbaaing, *ppl. a.* [f. as prec. + -ING[2].] Crying baa like a sheep; *fig.* noisily silly.

1818 KEATS *Endym.* III. 3 There are..who unpen Their baaing vanities to browse away The comfortable green and juicy hay From human pastures.

baake, obs. form of BAKE *v.*

‖**Baal** (ˈbeɪəl). Pl. **Baalim**. [Heb. *ba'al* lord.] The chief male deity of the Phœnician and Canaanitish nations; hence, *transf.* false god.

1382 WYCLIF *Judg.* ii. 13 The sones of Yrael..serueden to Baalym and Astaroth. **1535** COVERDALE *ibid.*, Serued Baal and Astaroth. **1629** MILTON *Ode Nativ.* xxii, Peor and Bäälim Forsake their temples dim. **1835** J. ANDERSON *Disc. Elijah* App. 352 The title of Baal or Lord thus bestowed upon the objects of idolatry.

b. *attrib.* as in ***Baal-priest***, ***-worship***.

1831 CARLYLE *Sart. Res.* II. ix, There are True Priests, as well as Baal-Priests. **1863** *N. & Q.* 26 Sept. 251 Baal-worship prevailed in the pre-Christian era.

baal, obs. form of BAIL *v.*

baal-fire: see BALE-FIRE.

Baalish (ˈbeɪəlɪʃ), *a.* [f. prec. + -ISH.] Of or belonging to Baal; idolatrous. (In 17th c. applied opprobriously to the Roman Catholic worship; so with the three following.)

1690 *Uzziah & Jotham* 16 Mistaken zeal..Made unforeseeing Levites, Baalish Tools.

Baalism (ˈbeɪəlɪz(ə)m). [f. BAAL + -ISM.] The worship of Baal; idolatry.

a **1625** E. CHALONER *Six Serm.* (1629) 38 Hath not superstition and Baalisme infected..our land? **1650** FULLER *Pisgah* IV. vii. 130 In the interim betwixt the Judges, Baalisme was first brought into Israel. **1862** MASSON in *Macm. Mag.* Aug. 325 Baits to idolatry and Baalism.

Baalist (ˈbeɪəlɪst). [f. BAAL + -IST.] A worshipper of Baal; *transf.* a worshipper of false gods or idols, an idolater. (Opprobriously, = Romanist.)

a **1603** T. CARTWRIGHT *Confut. Rhem. N.T.* (1618) 134 Baalists..calling for fire to bee sent. *a* **1618** SYLVESTER *Tobacco Batt.* 190 (D.) Tobacco's smoakie-mists..from the Iberian Baalists. **1642** N. WARTON in *Archæol.* XXXV. 332 (D.) Our soildiers could not forbeare dauncing in the holie quire, whereat the Baalists were sore displeased.

Baalite (ˈbeɪəlaɪt). [f. BAAL + -ITE.] = prec. **Baalitical** (beɪəˈlɪtɪkəl) *a.*, of Baal or Baalites.

1639 SANDERSON *Serm.* II. 134 Elijah once said to the Baalites, etc. **1821** KEATS *Isabel* lvii, Those Bäälites of pelf, Her brethren. **1659** W. BROUGH *Sacr. Princ.* 558 No Argument this to fall to..Baalitical Worship.

baard, 'a sort of sea vessel or transport ship.' (*Old Records.*) Bailey 1721.

baardman (ˈbɑːdmən, ‖ˈbaːrtman). *S. Afr.* Also (occas.) **ˈbaardmannetjie** (-mænətʃɪ, ‖-manəci). [Afrikaans, f. *baard* beard + *man* man.] Name given to various fishes with barbels on the lips, and/or chin, as the sea-fish *Sciæna capensis*, related to and very like the Mediterranean umbra, or the fresh-water fish *Barbus capensis*.

1853 L. PAPPE *Edible Fishes Cape of G.H.* 16 *Umbrina capensis*..Baardmannetje. Snout obtuse.., lower jaw shortest with a barbel; dorsal fins distinct... Measures from 2 to 2½ feet, and is reputed for its delicious flesh. **1902** J. D. F. GILCHRIST in *Trans. S. Afr. Philos. Soc.* XI. 226 Baardman, Baardmannetje (Pappe), Bellman (Riversdale). *Umbrina capensis*. **1907** *East London Dispatch* 5 Dec. (Pettman), *Baartman* (white-fish, barbel, catfish), a well-known ugly species of the family *Siluridae*. **1913** W. W. THOMPSON *Sea Fisheries Cape Col.* 158 Barbus capensis.. Moggel (Gouritz and Berg Rivers); Barbeel or Barm (Van Riebeeck's *Journals*); Witte-visch or White-fish; Baardman or Bartman. **1947** K. H. BARNARD *Pict. Guide S. Afr. Fishes* 122 *Cape Baardman*..False Bay to Algoa Bay. **1955** *Cape Times* 19 Sept. 9/1 One of the..anglers..landed five kob and one baardman.

baas, baate, obs. forms of BASE, BATE.

baas (bɑːs). [Du.: see BOSS *sb.*[6]] In S. Africa: a master, employer of labour. Often as a form of address.

In quot. 1625 used for a Dutch ship's captain.

1625 PURCHAS *Pilgrimes* I. II. 117 Our Baase (for so a Dutch Captaine is called). **1785** G. FORSTER tr. *Sparrman's Voy.* I. 55 The steward (or as they call him there, the *baas*) presented me with a glass of strong-bodied wine. **1850** R. G. CUMMING *Hunter's Life S. Afr.* I. i. 5 At the door he is met by the baas, or master. *Ibid* ix. 176 The Hottentot replying, 'Like so, baas.' **1920** *Chambers's Jrnl.* 25 Dec. 59/2 Jeri stated that he believed the *baas* to be bewitched. **1953** P. LANHAM *Blanket Boy's Moon* I. iii. 27 'Gently, my baases,' he whispered through quivering lips.

baasskap (ˈbɑːskap). *S. Afr.* Also erron. baaskap. [Afrikaans, = domination, lit. mastership, f. prec.] Domination, esp. of white over non-white South Africans. Cf. BOSS-SHIP.

1935 *Cape Times* 8 Nov. 8/4 Let us focus our attention on the fact that the primary consideration is whether Afrikanerdom will reach its ultimate destiny of bossism (baasskap) in South Africa. **1949** *Cape Argus* 11 June 8/3 The aim of the Broederbond is the baasskap of Afrikanerdom. **1955** *Times* 20 May 11/3 Stellenbosch is the intellectual stronghold of republicanism and the Nationalist Party. There, if anywhere, can be found disinterested advocacy of the doctrines of *apartheid* and *baasskap*. **1959** *Cape Times* 25 Apr. 7/6 The Prime Minister, Dr. Verwoerd, had previously said that the Natives should have baasskap within their own areas just as the Whites should have baasskap in their areas.

Baath (bɑːθ). *Pol.* Also **Ba'ath, Ba'th, Ba'th.** [ad. Arab. *ba'ṯ* resurrection, renaissance.] Used *attrib.* and occas. *absol.* (with *the*) to designate a pan-Arab socialist party founded by Michel Aflaq, Salah al-Din al-Bitar, and other intellectuals in Syria in 1943.

1955 *Times* 14 May 7/3 Malki..was known to be sympathetic to the Baath, or Socialist Party, and he may have led a Baathist faction within the Army. **1962** *Listener* 5 Apr. 597/1 The Ba'ath leaders are doctrinaire pan-Arabs of the frontier-smashing variety, preaching a mystical marriage of Arab unity and socialism. **1963** *Daily Tel.* 24 July 17/3 The Baath Governments in Damascus and Baghdad began today to close their ranks to combat President Nasser's new moves for leadership over the eastern Arab world... *Al Baath*, official organ of the Syrian Baath régime, says to-day [etc.]. **1971** W. LAQUEUR *Dict. Politics* 34 The *Ba'ath* has not succeeded in clarifying political issues, nor has it (so far) brought greater stability in those countries where it has achieved power. **1972** HOWAT & TAYLOR *Dict. World Hist.* 153/1 *Ba'th Party*, Arab political party, founded (1943) by Michel Aflaq and Salah al-Din al-Bitar, centred in Syria, but with branches in other Arab countries, especially Iraq, and advocating Arab unity, socialism, and neutralism. **1974** *Encycl. Brit. Macropædia* XVII. 924/2 Most authority is wielded by the ruling Ba'th ('Renaissance') Arab Socialist Party. **1981** *Economist* 24 Jan. 42/3 This belief is stated in its most extreme form in the opening words of the constitution of the Baath party, different factions of which now rule Iraq and Syria.

Hence **ˈBaathism**, the ideology of this party; **ˈBaathist** *a.* and *sb.*

1955 [see above]. **1955** *Times* 14 May 7/3 The P.P.S. and the Baathists are..at opposite ends of the ideological scale. **1962** *Listener* 5 Apr. 597/1, I remember the Ba'ath founder, Michel Aflaq, saying to me that they thought that President Nasser had become a Ba'athist. **1963** *Time* 22 Nov. 29/3 Baathism is being extended to the Syrian and Iraqi armies. **1970** *Times* 3 Apr. (Arab League Suppl.) p. x/3 Baathism.. might win an appeal in an area which will undoubtedly suffer a series of political traumas in the coming years. **1980** *Daily Tel.* 24 Sept. 4/6 Iraq, whose Ba'athist philosophy concentrates on pan-Arabism, is out to secure leadership of the Gulf and of the Arab world. **1981** *Economist* 24 Jan. 43/1 The first 'United Arab Republic'..came about in 1958 because the unionist Syrian Baathists threw themselves into the arms of Egypt's President Nasser.

†**bab.** *Obs.* A former nursery word for *dad* or *papa*. [Cf. BABA; also It. *babbo* papa, dad.]

1598 FLORIO, *Pappa*..the first word children vse, as with vs dad or daddie or bab.

bab, earlier, and now dial. form of BABE.

bab, dial. form of BOB, a bait for eels.

baba[1] (ˈbɑːbɑː, -æ-, -æ), an infantile variant of *ˈpapa*, papa. Cf. BAB.

1863 KINGSLEY *Water-Bab.* 48 Sitting down and crying for his baba (though he never had any baba to cry for).

‖**ˈbaba**[2]. [Fr.] A kind of light plum-cake. Now esp. ***rum baba, baba au rhum***, a rich cake soaked in a rum syrup.

1827 L. E. UDE *French Cook* 461 The oven must be moderately hot, as the *babas* must remain a long time in. **1846** SOYER *Gastron. Regenerator* 566 Take off the band of paper, turn the baba over upon a hair sieve, and serve either hot or cold. *c* **1864** FRANCATELLI *Cook's Guide* 298 Particular care should be taken in baking the baba to prevent its acquiring a deep colour. **1868** GOUFFE *Cookery Bk.* (1869) 533 Butter a baba-mould, 6 inches in diameter. **1933** A. CHRISTIE *Lord Edgware Dies* xiv. 126 We had a delicious omelette, a sole, a chicken and a Baba au Rhum. **1939** M. ALLINGHAM *Mr. Campion & Others* 135 Accepting a rhum-baba. **1952** B. NILSON *Penguin Cookery Book* xxiv. 417 Rum Babas. **1958** W. BICKEL tr. *Hering's Dict. Class. & Mod. Cookery* 668 *Baba au rhum*, savarin dough mixed with raisins and currants, baked in baba mould, soaked while still hot with hot syrup flavored with rum; served with rum-flavored apricot sauce. **1958** R. GODDEN *Greengage Summer* ix. 95 He explained the different kinds of cake to us: éclairs, rum babas, meringues. **1959** R. POSTGATE *Good Food Guide 1959–60* 212 A chocolate gâteau 'consisting of a baba au rhum with a milk chocolate couverture, far too rich, but delicious'.

Baba[3] (ˈbaba), *sb.* (and *a.*) [Malay.] A term used in Malaysia for a Straits-born person of Chinese descent. Also *attrib.* or as *adj.*

1858 *Jrnl. Indian Archipelago* 137 The children of Chinese by Malays..that follow their father's [name] are termed Babas. **1898** A. B. RATHBONE *Camping & Tramping in Malaya* ii. 26 The Malacca Babas..are Malacca-born Chinamen. **1933** L. AINSWORTH *Confessions Planter in Malaya* ii. 35 The man who had addressed me was what is known as a 'Ba-ba', the name given to a Straits-born Chinaman, who is usually educated in a school in the Straits Settlements and speaks English quite fluently. **1964** *Catal. National Mus. Kuala Lumpur* 3/2 A section of the gallery is given over to the Malacca Baba House—a traditional Chinese House, complete with furnishings of the bridal chamber, which was transported from Malacca and re-erected in the museum. **1964** L. A. P. GOSLING in Bastin & Roolvink *Malayan & Indonesian Stud.* xi. 203 A limited field investigation was carried out among the surviving Baba rural communities in the Trengganu Valley. **1981** *Sunday Mail* (Brisbane) 30 Aug. 39/1 Terry, a Baba (local term for Singaporeans who can trace their origins back to the Straits Chinese settlers) has had a long association with Nonya food.

ˈbabacoote. [ad. Malagasy *ˈbabaˈkoto.*] The largest species of lemur (*Lichanotus brevicaudatus*) found in Madagascar.

1880 J. Sibree *Gt. African Isl.* xiv. 270 The..Babacoote is believed by the Betànimèna tribe to be an embodiment of the spirits of their ancestors.

†**ˈbaban, ˈbabbon.** *Obs.* [Origin uncertain: apparently from infantile utterance. (The similar Celtic words are all late; some of them prob. from English.)] = BABE, BABY, 1, 2.

c **1230** *Ancr. R.* 234 Weope efter him, ase deð þet lutel baban [*v.r.* barn] efter his moder. **1570** Levins *Manip.* /163 Babbon, *pupus.*

babassu (ˌbɑːbəˈsuː). [Pg. *babaçú.*] Either of two species of palm, *Orbignya martiana* or *O. oleifera*, found in north-eastern Brazil, producing a valuable oil. Also *attrib.*

1923 W. Howarth *Mod. Brazil* vi. 88 Recent years have..added considerably to the number of oil-producing seeds and kernels, among the latter being the babassú. **1925** H. G. James *Brazil after Cent. of Independence* x. 349 The high commercial value of the oil of the babassú palm. **1933** P. Fleming *Brazil. Adv.* III. xii. 399 Only the *babassú* palms stood up proudly. **1960** A. E. Bender *Dict. Nutrition* 13/1 *Babassu oil*, edible oil from the Brazilian palm nut; similar to coconut oil and used in food, soap and cosmetics.

†**ˈbabbart.** *Obs.* [Origin unknown: cf. BOB *v.*, dialectally *bab*; the termination is prob. -ARD.] An old appellation for the hare.

c **1300** *Names of Hare* in *Rel. Ant.* I. 133 The stele-awai, the momelart, The evele i-met, the babbart.

babbelyinge, obs. form of BABBLING.

†**ˈbabber-lipped,** *a. Obs.* Also 4 **baberlipped,** 5 **babyrlyppyd.** [Origin of *babber* unknown; cf. prec., also F. *babine* lip of a horse, bear, etc., and see *blabber-lipped* (1485), *blobber-lipped.*] Having thick projecting lips.

1377 Langl. *P. Pl.* B. v. 190 He was bitelbrowed · and baberlipped also. *c* **1440** *Promp. Parv.* 20 Babbyrlyppyd, *labrosus.* **1607** *Lingua* III. vi. in Hazl. *Dodsl.* IX. 404 An old..babber-lipped..slave that, looking himself by chance in a glass, died for pure hate.

babbie, babby, Sc. and north dial. f. BABY.

†**ˈbabbin.** *Obs.* [variant of BAVIN.] A faggot or bundle of brushwood.

1711 E. Ward *Quix.* I. 412 Sancho found another Cabbin, And for his Pillow took a Babbin. **1732** *Disc. Potatoe* 33 If broom can be had, babbins or faggots of that will do.

ˈbabbiting. [f. as next + -ING[1].] A fitting of Babbit-metal.

1880 *Libr. Univ. Knowl.* II. 79 The journals being so made that the babbitting may be readily renewed.

Babbit-metal. Also **babbitt (or Babbitt) metal, Babbit's metal.** [f. name of the inventor.] A soft alloy of tin, antimony, and copper, used in journal-bearings, etc., to diminish friction. Sometimes used *ellipt.* Hence *babbitt-lined* adj.

Named after Isaac Babbitt (1799–1862).

1875 Ure *Dict. Arts, Babbit's Metal*..composed of 25 parts of tin, 2 parts of antimony, and ½ a part of copper. **1900** *Sci. Amer.* Suppl. XLIX. 20184/1 Almost any solid metal for lining bearings is called by the name of 'babbitt metal'...Ordinary soft lining, so-called babbitt metal, frequently is made up of four parts lead and one part antimony. *Ibid.*, Genuine babbitt will probably change its form more by reheating than the alloys of antimony and lead. **1909** *Westm. Gaz.* 30 Nov. 5/2 The nuts are formed by pouring molten Babbitt metal in the hollow bosses of the shoes. **1932** E. Wilson *Devil take Hindmost* viii. 46 The bronze and babbitt metal are scraped out of the connecting rods. *Ibid.* 49 A finished connecting rod..must be..bored with holes..the holes lined with white babbitt and bronze. **1937** *Times* 16 Sept. 6/5 The big end and camshaft bearings are babbitt-lined.

Babbitt (ˈbæbɪt). Also *erron.* **Babbit.** [f. the name of the (hero of the) novel by Sinclair Lewis, 1922.] A type of materialistic, self-complacent business man conforming to the standards of his set. Also *attrib.* Hence **ˈBabbittism, ˈBabbit(t)ry,** the 'Philistine' behaviour associated with this type of person. Also **ˈBabbitty** *a.*

1923 *Nation* 18 Apr. 465/2 What is it I do find? A group of American business men!..A swarm of forward-lookers! A circle of Babbitts! **1925** *Spectator* 19 Dec. 1146/2 In his controversy with M. Paul Bourget [he] reveals his almost incredible 'Babbittism'. **1926** A. Huxley *Jesting Pilate* IV. 279 At all times the vast majority of human beings has consisted of Babbitts and peasants. **1928** *Daily Express* 27 Apr. 9/3 Vancouver has been inundated with the 'Babbitry' from the South. **1931** *Times Lit. Suppl.* 5 Mar. 179/3 Engrossed in intellectual matters and contemptuous of the Babbittry around them. **1931** H. G. Wells *Work, Wealth & Happiness of Mankind* (1932) x. 453 It was an Individualist's heaven, Babbitt land. **1932** *Scrutiny* I. 3 In America there is the *Hound and Horn, The Symposium*, and the *New Republic*, all of which remind us that America is not inhabited solely by Babbitts. **1942** O. Nash *Good Intentions* 130 Every party Whether Babbitty or arty. **1957** *Listener* 14 Nov. 771/1 We Americans were known as the Babbits of the nineteen-twenties... The Russians are now the Babbits of the mid-century. **1966** *Times* 20 Sept. 11/2 This was not just a bit of Babbitry—'the biggest little place in the state'—but official grading.

babblative (ˈbæblətɪv). [f. BABBLE *v.* + -ATIVE. Cf. *talkative.*] Given to babbling; prattling, prating, loquacious.

1583 *Philotimus* (Halliw.) He was..neither to bablative withe flattery, nor to whust with morositie. *a* **1624** Bp. M. Smyth *Serm.* (1632) 265 Sad with the graue, babblatiue with praters. **1829** Southey *Sir T. More* (1831) I. 350 Professors of the arts babblative and scribblative. **1838** Carlyle in Froude *Life in Lond.* v. I. 139 Sterling particularly argumentative, babblative, and..unpleasant.

babble (ˈbæb(ə)l), *v.* Forms: 3–4 **babel,** 4–8 **-le,** 6 **-yl, -il,** 6– **babble.** [Cf. Du. and LG. *babbelen*, Ger. *pappelen* (*bappelen*), Da. *bable*, Icel. *babbla* (not known in OE., ON., OHG); F. *babill-er*, 15th c. in Littré: cf. also It. *babbolare* to play the baby. In some of these languages probably adopted from others; in none can its history be carried far back; as yet it is known in English as early as anywhere else. Probably formed (with frequentative suffix *-le*; cf. *prattle*) on the repeated syllabic *ba, ba*, one of the earliest articulate sounds made by infants, fitly used to express childish prattle. No direct connexion with *Babel* can be traced; though association with that may have affected the senses.]

I. *intransitive.*

1. To make imperfect attempts at speech, like a child; to utter inarticulate or indistinct sounds.

1362 Langl. *P. Pl.* A. v. 8 And so I babelide [*v.r.* bablide, blaberde, blaberid] on my Beodes. **1534** More *Comf. agst. Trib.* II. Wks. 1187/2 They heard her tonge bable in her head ..after that the head was fro the bodye. **1560** *Disob. Child* in Hazl. *Dodsl.* II. 295 When the child waxeth somewhat old, For meat and drink he begins to babble. **1607** Hieron *Wks.* I. 149 Nurses doe halfe chew the meate to the little ones, and doe babble with them in their owne stammering and vnperfite language. **1842** Tennyson *Dora* 132 And babbled for the golden seal, that hung From Allan's watch.

2. To talk childishly, to prattle; to talk incoherently or foolishly; to utter meaningless words.

1230 [see BABBLING *ppl. a.* 2]. **1503** Hawes *Examp. Virt.* vii. 102 For ye without wytte sholde alway bable. **1599** Shaks. *Hen. V*, II. iii. 17 (Theobald), And 'a babled of greene fields. **1610** Bp. Carleton *Jurisd.* 248 As they bable in their decretals. **1799** Sheridan *Pizarro* I. i, They only babble who practise not reflection. **1838** Dickens *Nich. Nick.* i. 4 His reason went astray..for he babbled, for a long time, about the generosity and goodness of his brother.

3. To talk excessively or inopportunely; to chatter, prate.

c **1510** Barclay *Mirr. Good Mann.* (1570) Aj, Olde men which haue vsed in time passed to bable In barbarike language. **1526** Tindale *Matt.* vi. 7 When ye praye, bable not moche, as the gentyls do. **1599** Shaks. *Much Ado* III. iii. 36 For the Watch to babble and talke..is not to be indured. **1663** Bp. Patrick *Parab. Pilgr.* 227 Ever chattering and babling as if they had obtained a patent for prating. **1847** Tennyson *Princ.* III. 237 And let me tell you, girl, Howe'er you babble, great deeds cannot die.

4. *transf.* of streams, brooks, etc.; also of young birds, and *spec.* of hounds that give tongue too loudly or without reason.

1399 *Pol. Poems* (1859) I. 395 The nedy nestlingis.. bablid with her billis. **1611** Markham *Countr. Content.* II. iii. 22 If any young Hound will..run babling away without the scent. **1777** Sir W. Jones *Pal. Fort.* 27 Echo babling by the mountain's side. **1812** Combe (Dr. Syntax) *Pictur.* xxi. (D.) And when they babble in their din, I am a special whipper-in. **1860** Tennyson *Brook*, I bubble into eddying bays, I babble on the pebbles.

†**5.** ? To waver, oscillate, quiver. *Obs.* [Perhaps a distinct word.]

c **1440** *Promp. Parv.* 20/1 Bablyn, or waveryn, *Librillo.*

II. *transitive.*

6. To repeat or utter with meaningless iteration; to speak foolishly or incoherently; to prate.

c **1418** *Pol. Poems* (1859) II. 244 To bable the Bible day and niȝt. **1548** Coverdale *Erasm. Par. Rom.* Prol., Though he babil neuer so many thinges of fayth and good workes. **1651** Wittie tr. *Primrose's Pop. Err.* IV. xlviii. 405 That which he babbles concerning the spirit of the World. **1847** Barham *Ingol. Leg.* (1877) 232 Mere unmeaning talk her parch'd lips babbled now.

7. To reveal by talking or chattering. Cf. *blab.*

1562 J. Heywood *Prov. & Epigr.* (1867) 96 Who heareth all, And all bableth. **1791–1824** Disraeli *Cur. Lit.* (1859) II. 338 The queen..impatiently babbled the plot. **1852** D. Mitchell *Dream Life* 15 Griefs too sacred to be babbled to the world.

babble (ˈbæb(ə)l), *sb.* Forms: 5–6 **bable,** 6– **babble.** See BIBBLE-BABBLE *sb.* [f. the vb. Cf. F. *babil*, 15th c. in Littré.]

1. Inarticulate or imperfect speech, such as that of infants; prattle.

1668 R. L'Estrange *Vis. Quev.* (1708) 5 The Conjurer granted my request, and the Spirit went on with his Babble. **1864** Tennyson *En. Ard.* 607 The babes, their babble. **1871** Darwin *Desc. Man* ii. 55 Man has an instinctive tendency to speak, as we see in the babble of our young children.

2. Idle, foolish, or unseasonable talk; prating.

c **1460** *Play Sacr.* 648 Avoyde fealows, I loue not your bable. **1513** More *Rich. III* Wks. 57/1 Neither mute nor ful of bable. **1658** Bramhall *Consecr. Bps.* vi. 138 He had greater matters to trouble his head withall, then Mr. Holywoods bables. **1865** Carlyle *Fredk. Gt.* X. xxi. ix. 182 A great deal of unwise babble on this subject.

3. Confused murmur, as of a stream.

1616 Beaum. & Fl. *Wit without M.* v. 164 This Sack has fill'd my head so full of bables, I am almost mad. **1870** Morris *Earthly Par.* II. III. 13 Nought he seemed to hear Save the brook's babble.

4. *Telephony.* (See quots.)

1930 *Bell Syst. Techn. Jrnl.* IX. 489 Babble is the name given to the effect produced by a number of different [telephone] circuits crosstalking into a particular circuit at a given time and producing an unintelligible murmur. **1960** *Gloss. Terms Telecommunic.* (*B.S.I.*) 152 *Babble*, the aggregate crosstalk from a number of disturbing sources.

babblement (ˈbæb(ə)lmənt). [f. BABBLE *v.* + -MENT. Cf. mod.F. *babillement* (not in Cotgr.).]

1. Incoherent, imperfect, or idle talk; thoughtless or unseasonable chatter, babble.

1644 Milton *Educ.* Wks. 1738 I. 136 Deluded all this while with ragged Notions and Babblements. **1834** Carlyle *Fr. Rev.* II. III. vii. 174 A spoken Word meaning a Thing, and not a Babblement meaning No-thing. **1860** Tyndall *Glac.* I. §23. 167 The babblement of streams.

2. Open-mouthed communication of news, secrets, etc.

1850 Blackie *Æschylus* I. 124 Lest some one hear, and, with swift babblement, Inform their ears who rule.

babbler (ˈbæblə(r)). Also 6–8 **babler.** [f. BABBLE *v.* + -ER[1]. Cf. *babelard.*]

1. A foolish or idle talker, chatterer, prater.

1530 Palsgr. 196/1 Babler, *babillart.* **1535** Coverdale *Eccles.* x. 11 A babler of his tonge. **1693** Evelyn *De la Quint. Compl. Gard.* I. 13, I do not like a great Babler, who talks of nothing but his Skill. **1781** Cowper *Expost.* 502 Babbler of ancient fables. **1860** Kingsley *Misc.* II. 162 Englishmen are no babblers; they are a dumb, dogged people.

2. One who tells too freely what he knows; a prating gossip, a teller of secrets.

1580 Hollyband *Treas. Fr. Tong, Babillard*, a babler..a tittle tattle. **1625** Bacon *Ess.* (1874) 19 For who will open himselfe to a Blab or a Babler? **1781** Cowper *Friendship* xvii, Aspersion is the babbler's trade, To listen is to lend him aid. **1822** Byron *Werner* v. i, We must have no third babblers thrust between us.

3. A hound that gives tongue too freely.

1732 Berkeley *Alciphr.* Wks. 1732 I. 169 You shall often see among the Dogs a loud Babler, with a bad Nose, lead the unskilful. **1735** Somerville *Chase* IV. 66 The vain Babbler shun, Ever loquacious, ever in the wrong.

4. Name given, on account of their harsh chattering note, to the Long-legged Thrushes.

1839 *Penny Cycl.* s.v. *Merulidæ*, Subfamily *Crateropodinæ*, Babblers. Legs remarkably long and strong, with the claws but slightly curved. **1873** Tristram *Moab* xiii. 250 The bulbul, the bush babbler, the Moabite sparrow.

5. [Rhyming slang f. *babbling brook* (also used).] A (camp) cook; esp. one who cooks for shepherds, musterers, or shearers in isolated districts. *Austral.* and *N.Z. slang.*

Baker *Austral. Lang.* (1945) 79 says that it 'was in Australian currency in 1906'.

1919 *Bulletin* (Sydney) 24 July 20/2 Two, and sometimes three, of these dishes (depends on the babbler's liver) are served each morning. **1919** Downing *Digger Dial.* 9 *Babbling brook, babbler*, an Army cook. Also *babblins.* **1928** *Bulletin* (Sydney) 12 Jan. 24/1, I am the man they call the babbler Sometimes known as the babbling brook. **1942** in Baker *Austral. Lang.* (1945) xvi. 284 It's also a fair cow when the *babbling brook* (cook) makes a *crook* (bad) stew. **1944** A. F. St. Bruno *Desert Daze* 33 Arch, the cook—oh, how that bold 'babbler' could curse. **1949** P. Newton *High Country Days* vi. 63 The 'babbler'..was in his element. **1963** *Weekly News* (Auckland) 5 June 37/1 That got us started on the 'babbling brooks'. I've got a few memories of station cooks. *Ibid.* 37/2 We worked it out that old babbler made 112,000 rock cakes during those four months.

†**ˈbabblery.** *Obs.* In 6 **babelary, bablarie, -erie.** [f. BABBLE *v.* + -RY; cf. F. *babillerie* in Cotgr.] Idle chatter, babble, prating.

1532 More *Confut. Tindale* Wks. 494/1 A longe babelary, parte to no purpose and parte plaine heresie. **1567** Drant *Horace Epist.* II. ii. H iv, He kills me with his bablarie. **1593** Stubbes *Motive Gd. Wks.* 115 Deceyve the world no longer with your bableries for filthy lucre sake.

¶ Confused with BABERY or BAUBLERY.

1583 Stubbes *Anat. Abus.* M ij b, Wherin is painted some babblerie or other of imagery woork. *Ibid.* 222 Toyes, fantasies, and bableries.

babbling (ˈbæblɪŋ), *vbl. sb.* [f. BABBLE *v.*]

1. Incoherent talk, idle chatter, babblement.

c **1380** Wyclif *Wks.* (1880) 190 Preiere of holy lif..not of babelynge of lippis. **1535** Coverdale *Prov.* x. 19 Where moch bablinge is, there must nedes be offence. **1611** Bible *Prov.* xxiii. 29 Who hath contentions? who hath babbling? **1869** Freeman *Norm. Conq.* (1876) III. xi. 11 All this prophetic talk was but the babbling of an old man.

2. *transf.* Cf. BABBLE *v.* 4.

1686 *Gentl. Recr.* I. 15 Babbling..is when the hounds are too busy after they have found a good scent. **1736** Swift *Wks.* (1841) II. 131 The little church bells shall cease their babblings. **1837** Hawthorne *Amer. Note-Bks.* (1871) I. 59 No noise..but the babbling of the stream.

†**3.** ? Wavering, oscillation. Cf. BABBLE *v.* 5.

c **1440** *Promp. Parv.* 20/1 Babelynge or wauerynge, *Vacillacio, librillacio.*

4. *attrib.*, as in ***babbling-place, -school***, etc.

1650 Sherwood, A Babbling place (where gossips meet), *caquetoire.* **1653** Milton *Hirelings* Wks. (1851) 387 Bred up for Divines in babling Schools.

ˈbabbling, *ppl. a.* [f. as prec. + -ING[2].]

1. Making imperfect efforts at speech.

1579 TOMSON *Calvin's Serm. Tim.* 187/1 The Papists will pray in a mumbling and babling sort. **1828** SCOTT *F.M. Perth* III. 85 The babbling cry of childhood.

2. Chattering, prating, foolishly talkative.

c **1230** *Ancr. R.* 100 To babelinde, and to spekefule ancren. **1588** SHAKS. *Tit. A.* IV. ii. 150 A long tongu'd babling Gossip. **1735** POPE *Prol. Sat.* 304 Such babbling blockheads. **1855** MILMAN *Lat. Chr.* (1864) II. III. v. 71 His degradation was concealed from a babbling and censorious world.

3. *transf.* Cf. BABBLE *v.* 4.

1588 SHAKS. *Tit. A.* II. iii. 17 The babling Eccho mock's the Hounds. *a* **1610** FLETCHER *Faithf. Sheph.* III. i, Here never durst the babling Cuckow spit. **1735** SOMERVILLE *Chase* I. 281 A lagging Line Of babling Curs. **1814** WORDSW. *Wh. Doe* III. 257 The scorn Of babbling winds.

ˈbabblingly, *adv.* [f. prec. + -LY².] In a babbling manner, with babblement, chatteringly.

a **1603** T. CARTWRIGHT *Confut. Rhem. N.T.* (1618) 562 Irksomely and bablingly repeated. **1862** C. S. C[ALVERLEY] *Verses & Transl.* 157 Thou shalt be a royal fountain.. From yon cavernous mountain Thou breakest babblingly.

†**ˈbabblish**, *a. Obs.* [f. BABBLE *sb.* + -ISH¹.] Full of idle talk. **ˈbabblishly** *adv.*, babblingly.

1574 WHITGIFT *Defence* 262 (R.) Is this the reuerence due to the scriptures, thus bablishly to abuse them?

babbly (ˈbæblɪ), *a.* [f. as prec. + -Y¹.] Full of babble, chattering, prating, garrulous.

1865 CARLYLE *Fredk. Gt.* IV. XII. vii. 177 'For the times are babbly [Ger. *geschwätzig*],' says Goethe, 'And then again the times are dumb.' **1868** —— in Froude's *Life* (1882) I. 317 In his babbly way.

babbon, variant of BABAN, *Obs.*, baby.

babe (beɪb). Also 5–7 **bab.** [Prob. a contraction of BABAN; cf. *Tom, Will, Gib, Hugh*, and similar pet-names. Now superseded in ordinary use by its own diminutive BABY (cf. *Tommy, Willie*, etc.), and retained chiefly as a literary and poetic word. *Babe*, and not *baby*, is used in the Bible.]

1. An infant, a young child. Phr. ***babe in arms.***

1393 GOWER *Conf.* I. 290 How this babe all bloody cried. *c* **1460** *Townley Myst.* 149 Alas, my bab, myn innocent. **1540** HYRDE *Vives' Instr. Chr. Wom.* (1592) Y v, Blessed of God from his babes age. **1557** N. T. (Genev.) *1 John* ii. 1 My babes, these thinges write I vnto you, that ye synne not. **1605** SHAKS. *Macb.* IV. i. 30 Finger of Birth-strangled Babe [*rimes*, drab, slab]. **1770** GOLDSM. *Des. Vill.* 381 And kiss'd her thoughtless babes with many a tear. **1807** CRABBE *Par. Reg.* I. (1810) 70 Recorded next a Babe of love I trace! **1912** J. N. MCILWRAITH *Diana of Quebec* vii. 94 She had brought three little children with her, one a babe in arms. **1967** *Woman* 23 Dec. 3/1 She can recall being held up to see a sparkly tree as a babe in arms.

†**2.** A doll, puppet; = BABY *sb.* 2. *Obs.*

1530 PALSGR. 196/1 Babe that children play with, *poupee*. **1579** SPENSER *Sheph. Cal.* May 240 Bearing a truss of trifles .. As bells, and babes, and glasses in hys packe. **1595** SHAKS. *John* III. iv. 58, I should forget my sonne Or madly thinke a babe of clowts were he.

3. a. *fig.* A childish person; = BABY *sb.* 5. ***babes in Christ***: newly-made converts to Christianity. Also, an inexperienced or guileless person; so ***babes in the wood*** (with overt or implied reference to the old ballad *The Children in the Wood*).

1526 TINDALE *1 Cor.* iii. 1 As vnto carnall, even as it were vnto babes in Christ. **1588** A. KING *Canisius' Catech.* 53 Wavering babs caried about with everie wind of doctrin. **1611** BIBLE *Transl. Pref.* 1 Hee was no babe, but a great clearke. **1771** WESLEY *Wks.* (1872) VI. 6 Even babes in Christ are in such a sense perfect. **1795** W. B. STEVENS *Jrnl.* 26 Mar. (1965) 245 Wishes himself at home, restrained only by Principle and a Sense of Duty—A tale to tell the Babes in the Wood! **1841** LYTTON *Night & Morning* III. v. i. 98 The uncle of the babes in the wood could hardly have been more startled by the demand! **1866** MRS. GASKELL *Wives & Daughters* I. xi. 131 Molly and her future stepmother wandered about in the gardens.. hand in hand, like two babes in the wood. **1908** 'O. HENRY' *Man Higher Up* in *Wks.* (1928) 249 You're both babes-in-the-wood. **1926** H. W. FOWLER *Mod. Eng. Usage* 40/1 In figurative use, *babe* implies guilelessness, innocence, or ignorance. **1962** J. B. PRIESTLEY *Margin Released* III. v. 191 A big ambitious novel, in which there was to be far more social criticism than the babes-in-the-woods theme might suggest.

b. A girl or woman (often as a form of address). *slang* (chiefly *U.S.*).

1915 *Dialect Notes* IV. 231 *Babe*, a pretty girl. 'She's some babe.' **1930** C. WITTKE *Tambo & Bones* iv. 143 Kiss your minstrel boy good-bye, babe, 'bye, babe, 'bye, babe. **1932** *Amer. Speech* VII. 329 Babe, a girl (usually used in direct address). **1952** S. KAUFFMANN *Philanderer* (1953) iv. 57 This Mrs. Adair.. has such hotsy-totsy cottages... Yesterday this Adair babe has an ad in the paper.

4. *Comb.* and *Attrib.*; cf. BABY *sb.* B.

1647 H. MORE *Song of Soul* III. App. lxxxvi, A young babe-soul from thence to gain. **1826** SCOTT *Woodst.* xx, We, the babe-eaters, had too many acquaintances at Brentford. **1855** TENNYSON *Maud.* II. i. 13 He came with the babe-faced lord. **1868** *People's Mag.* 1 Apr. 213 (*title of verses*) Babe-wisdom.

babee, obs. form of BABY.

ˈbabehood. *arch.* [f. BABE + -HOOD.] Infancy.

1548 UDALL, etc. *Erasm. Par.* Pref. 2 His minoritie of tendre babehood. *Ibid.* Luke ii. (R.) The strengthlesse babehoode of the body.

Babel (ˈbeɪbəl). [a. Heb. *bābel*, Babylon; associated in Genesis with the idea of 'confusion,' but not referable to any known Semitic root; according to Prof. Sayce, for Assyrian *bāb-ilu* gate of God, or *bāb-ili* gate of the gods, the Assyrian rendering of the Accadian *Ca-dimíra* (see *Trans. Soc. Bibl. Archæology* I. 298, 309).]

1. The city and tower, of which the attempted construction is described in *Genesis* ix, where the confusion of languages is said to have taken place; *hence* **a.** a lofty structure; **b.** a visionary scheme.

1382 WYCLIF *Gen.* xi. 9 Therfor was callid the name of it Babel, for there was confoundid the lippe of all the erthe. **1667** MILTON *P.L.* III. 468 And still with vain designe New Babels, had they wherewithall, would build. **1703** MAUNDRELL *Journ. Jerus.* (1721) 16 What remains of this mighty *Babel*.. is no more than twenty Foot high. **1711** STEELE *Spect.* No. 167 ¶3 The fond Builder of Babels. **1847** TENNYSON *Princ.* IV. 59 Let be Their cancell'd Babels.

2. A scene of confusion; a confused assemblage.

1625 FLETCHER *Nt. Walker* (T.) All the chambers Are a mere babel, or another bedlam. **1703** MAUNDRELL *Journ. Jerus.* (1721) 48 A mere Babel of broken Walls. **1731** SWIFT *Repeal Test Act* (T.) The whole babel of sectaries joined against the church. **1860** G. MORRIS *Poems* 173 We are only two, dear brother, in this babel wide!

3. A confused turbulent medley of sounds.

a **1529** SKELTON *El. Rummyng* 387 A clatterynge and a babell Of folys fylly. **1863** KINGSLEY *Water Bab.* i. 32 Such a noise, row, hubbub, babel, shindy, hullabaloo. **1884** *Manch. Exam.* 16 Sept. 4/7 This confused and confusing babel of.. idle objurgations.

4. *Comb.*, mostly *attrib.*, in which *babel* approaches the character of an adj. (= 'confused, turbulent,' or 'lofty, huge'), as in ***babel-confusion, -sea, -sound, -tower***; also ***babel-builder***; **babel-scheme**, a visionary project.

c **1746** HERVEY *Medit.* (1818) 39 God from on high laughs at the *Babel-builder. **1653** BAXTER *Chr. Concord* 101 Sion is not built by the *Babel-confusions. **1729** SAVAGE *Wanderer* II. v. (D.) The traitors rear their *babel-schemes. **1853** KINGSLEY *Hypatia* v. (1879) 67 The *Babel sea which weltered up and down every street. **1816** SOUTHEY *Poet's Pilgr.* I. Wks. X. 20 All disregardant of the *Babel sound. **1848** DICKENS *Dombey* (1870) I. vi. 99 *Babel towers of chimneys.

babel, obs. form of BAUBLE and BABBLE.

†**ˈbabelard.** *Obs.* [f. BABBLE *v.* + -ARD; prob. after F. *babillard.*] A babbler, chatterer.

1678 MRS. BEHN *Sir P. Fancy* I. i. 237 They [men] are the greatest Babelards in Nature.

babelary, -ery: see BABBLERY, BAUBLERY.

†**babelavante.** *Obs.* [? connected with OF. *babeler* to make sorry jests, or with BAUBLE, q.v.]

a **1400** *Chester Plays* II. 34 Sir Cayphas, harcken nowe to me, This babelavante o[u]r Kinge woulde be.

Babeldom (ˈbeɪb(ə)ldəm). [f. prec. + -DOM.] A state of things like that at Babel; noisy confusion.

1882 *Contemp. Rev.* Nov. 681 Reverence has few dedicated Temples in the Babeldom of nineteenth century England.

babelet (ˈbeɪblɪt). A tiny babe.

1867 J. MACGREGOR *Rob Roy on Baltic* 277 One of these babes carried in her arms a still smaller babelet.

babelind, obs. form of BABBLING.

ˈbabelish, *a.* [f. BABEL + -ISH.] Of the nature of a babel, noisily confused.

1605 *Camden's Rem.* (1636) 40 Brings the same to a Babellish confusion. **1656** BLOUNT *Glossogr.* s.v. *Babel*, Hence 'tis we use *babelish* for *confused*. **1825** *New Monthly Mag.* XIII. 406 He may know a Babelish confusion of languages. **1898** *Daily News* 24 Aug. 3/2 A perfectly Babelish commingling of tongues fell upon the ear.

Babelism (ˈbeɪbəlɪz(ə)m). [f. BABEL + -ISM.] Noisy confusion of speech; strange utterance.

1834 *Notices of Louth* 269 Hungry critics.. with their usual acrimony and Babelism. **1865** *Athenæum* 15 July, They forthwith read what is presented to them, reproducing to a nicety.. all the queer Babelisms.

babelize (ˈbeɪbəlaɪz), *v.* [f. BABEL + -IZE.] To make a babel of, bring to confusion.

1600 TOURNEUR *Transf. Met.* xi, Her high esteeme is of high heav'n despis'd; O see ere long her Babel Babelliz'd. **1880** B. SOLYMOS *Exp. Soudan*, To putrefy the language into several thieves' lingoes, to babelize literally.

†**ˈbabery.** *Obs.* Also 4 babeuwry, -eurie, 6 baberie. [perhaps orig. a spoken or written corruption of *babwynrie*, BABOONERY; in later use f. BABE, BABY *sb.* 4.] Grotesque ornamentation in architecture and books; grotesque absurdity.

c **1384** CHAUCER *H. Fame* 1189 (Caxton) Many subtyl compassynges, As babeuwryes [*v.r.* babeuries, rabewyures, rabewynnes] and pynnacles, Ymageryes and tabernacles. *c* **1400** *Destr. Troy* v. 1563 Ymagry ouer all.. Of bestes and babery. **1580** SIDNEY *Arcad.* Verses x. 181 Trim bookes in velvet dight With golden leaves and painted baberie. **1613** SIR E. HOBY *Counter-snarle* 13 Thus might I stuffe much paper, with many like vnsauoury Baberies. **1678** PHILLIPS *App., Babeuries* (old word), antick shapes, ridiculous forms of things. **1775** ASH, *Babery*, the finery with which children are delighted. *Babewries*, odd kind of antic works, silly things.

†**ˈbabeship.** *Obs.* [f. BABE + -SHIP.] Infancy.

1542 UDALL *Erasm. Apoph.* 172 From his tendre babe-ship.. nousleed in the preceptes of philosophie. *a* **1679** T. GOODWIN *Wks.* (1863) VII. 477 Out of their babeship.

babesiasis (bæbɪˈzaɪəsɪs). *Vet. Sci.* and *Path.* [f. as next + -IASIS.] = next.

1916 H. B. FANTHAM et al. *Animal Parasites of Man* 178 The usual symptoms of babesiasis (piroplasmosis) are high fever, loss of appetite, hæmoglobinuria, icterus, anæmia, paralysis, and death in about a week in acute cases. **1935** *Vet. Jrnl.* XCI. 449 (*heading*) Note on the treatment of canine babesiasis. **1973** *Nature* 16 Feb. 477/1 The titres of the deer sera were similar to those found in a survey for babesiasis in cattle on the island of Arran.

babesiosis (bəbiːzɪˈəʊsɪs). *Vet. Sci.* and *Path.* [f. mod.L. *Babesia* (see below), f. the name of Victor *Babès* (1854–1926), Romanian bacteriologist + -IA¹: see -OSIS.] (A disease caused by) infestation with sporozoans of the genus *Babesia*, spread by ticks and occurring in animals and occas. man with widely varying effects. Also called PIROPLASMOSIS.

1911 DORLAND *Med. Dict.* (ed. 6) 116/1 *Babesiosis*, infection with Babesia. Same as piroplasmosis. **1956** *Ann. N.Y. Acad. Sci.* LXIV. 147 In the case of babesiosis, we know transmission is by ticks belonging to the family Ixodidal. **1976** *Nature* 1 Apr. 380/2 Vaccines have been developed for protecting cattle against three parasitic diseases (babesiosis, anaplasmosis and East Coast fever). **1983** *Oxf. Textbk. Med.* I. v. 419/1 The disease.. is known as babesiosis or piroplasmosis and ranges from asymptomatic to severe, haemolytic anaemia, jaundice, haemoglobinuria, and renal failure.

babewen, -ewyn(e, obs. forms of BABOON.

Babi (ˈbɑːbiː). Also **Babee.** [Pers., f. *Bab*-ed-Din 'gate of the faith'. The name *Bab* was assumed by Mirza Ali Mohammed ibn Radhik (d. 1850), the founder of Babi.] The name of a sect originating in Persia, whose doctrine and practice include Mohammedan, Christian, Jewish, and Zoroastrian elements; = BAHA'I. Hence **ˈBabism**, the doctrine or practice of this sect; **ˈBabist** (also *attrib.* or as *adj.*), **ˈBabite**, an adherent of Babism, a Bahai.

1850 in M. L. Sheil *Glimpses Life & Manners in Persia* (1856) xi. 178 A moolla of eminence.. had been converted to Bābeeism, but had recanted. *Ibid.* 180 This year, seven Bābees were executed at Tehran for an alleged conspiracy. .. Bābeeism had spread in Tehran. **1866** *Nation* 22 June 793/2 In Teheran in 1852.. the visible remnant of the 'Babist' sect was slaughtered. *Ibid.* 794/1 The new prophet .. adopted the name of the *Bab*; that is, the gate through which alone truth is to be reached. *Ibid.* 794/2 Ali Mohammed, the founder and spiritual head of Babism. *Ibid.*, The Babists were now forbidden from making any more attempts at insurrection until the Bab should decide that the hour had come. *Ibid.* 795/1 Babism is much more in harmony with the subtle and imaginative genius of the Persian people than the Shiite Mohammedanism. **1869** *Contemp. Rev.* XII. 245 (*heading*) The Bab and Babeeism. *Ibid.* 246 He.. learned the principles and substance of the Babee doctrines. *Ibid.* 266 Faithful Babees. **1877** M. DODS *Mohammed, Buddha, & Christ* 195 The martyrs of Babism. **1896** *Daily News* 4 May 5/2 No doubt is entertained that the assassination was due to Babist fanaticism. The discontent of the Babists is due to the fact that the Shah would not allow them to succeed in establishing their religion. **1896** *Ibid.* 30 June 6/1 The Babis of Persia. **1904** *Daily Chron.* 6 Aug. 3/6 He.. spoke with hope especially of the spread of the Babists. **1911** FRAZER *Golden Bough* (ed. 3) I. vii. 402 The head of the great Persian sect of the Babites.. is held by Frenchmen, Russians, and Americans, especially by rich American ladies, to be an incarnation of God himself.

‖**Babiana** (bæbɪˈeɪnə, -ˈɑːnə). *Bot.* [mod.L., f. Du. *Babianer*, given to the plants because their subterranean stems are eaten by baboons.] A South African genus of bulbo-tuberous *Iridaceæ*, with handsome yellow, purple, or scarlet flowers.

1835 *Penny Cycl.* III. 226/1. **1882** *Garden* 27 May 358/3 Those strange Babianas which one so seldom sees in their beauty in our English gardens.

babiche (bəˈbiːʃ). *N. Amer.* [Canadian Fr., orig. Algonquian.] Thongs or thread made of raw hide, sinew, etc.

1806 S. FRASER *Let.* 30 Sept. (1960) 243 Will you be able to send me over some green skins for windows and Babich. **1836** in A. Simpson *Life Thos. Simpson* (1845) x. 189 Babiche for snowshoe lacing. **1899** O. T. MASON in *Rep. Smithsonian Inst. 1897* 732 Fine babiche or rawhide string for the webbing of the snowshoe. **1948** *Sat. Even. Post* 21 Aug. 72/4 No screws or nails are used at the joints, but *babiche* instead—rawhide thongs.

babie, babil, obs. forms of BABY, BABBLE.

babify (ˈbeɪbɪfaɪ), *v.* [f. BABY sb. + -IFY.] *trans.* To render babylike or babyish. So **ˈbabified** *ppl. a.*, invested with the character or attributes of a baby.

1862 M. E. BRADDON *Lady Audley's Secret* xviii. 64 She looked a childish, helpless, babyfied little creature. **1891** S. J. DUNCAN *Amer. Girl in London* ii. 15 Good old-fashioned names, like Nancy and Betsy, that couldn't be babified. **1912** D. H. LAWRENCE *Let.* in F. Lawrence '*Not I, but the Wind*' (1934) 27, I think you're rather horrid to H... You make him more babified—baby-fied.

‖**babillard** (babɪ'ʎɑːr, 'bæbɪlɑːd). [F., f. *babiller* to chatter: see -ARD. Cf. BABELARD, and BABBLER 4.] The CHATTERER, a small bird.

1802 in G. MONTAGU *Ornith. Dict.* (1833) 15. **1851** *Gardeners' Chron.* 581 The Babillard, a little bird of passage.

babily ('beɪbɪlɪ), *adv.* [f. BABY *sb.* + -LY².] = BABYISHLY *adv.*

1891 MEREDITH *One of our Conquerors* I. xiv. 269 A young woman more than babily aware of the existence of one particular form of naughtiness on earth. *a* **1935** T. E. LAWRENCE *Mint* (1955) 98 Crying babily (the first time for years).

babingtonite ('bæbɪŋtənaɪt). *Min.* [named after Dr. Babington, physician and mineralogist: see -ITE.] A bisilicate of iron and lime, with manganese and magnesia, found in greenish-black crystals at Arendal in Norway, and elsewhere.

1837-68 DANA *Min.* 227.

Babinski (bə'bɪnskɪ). The surname of J. F. F. *Babinski* (1857-1932), a French neurologist, applied *attrib.* to a reflex action in which the great toe remains extended or extends itself when the sole of the foot is stimulated.

1900 WALTON & PAUL in *Jrnl. Nerv. & Ment. Dis.* XXVII. 323 The Babinski reflex—deliberate and constant extension of the great toe, with or without extension and separation of other toes—is never present in health. **1901** *Jrnl. Amer. Med. Assoc.* XXXVI. 181/1 The Babinski phenomenon..consists in rather slow and deliberate extension of the great toe with or without extension..of the other toes on stroking the plantar surface. **1905** *Clinical Studies* III. 311 The Babinski sign is of importance in diagnosis, since it is 'an indication of a structural lesion of, or involving, the upper motor neuron'. **1932** FULTON & KELLER *Sign of Babinski* v. 87 The Babinski response was associated with much more marked fanning and separation of hallux and second toe.

†'**babion.** *Obs.* Also 6-7 -oun, 7 -an. [a. F. *babion* 'a babion or baboone' in Cotgr., 'a kind of small monkey' in Littré, who takes it as distinct from *babouin* BABOON, and formed on 'a radical *bab* found in *babiole*': cf. BAUBLE. It was apparently identified in Eng. with *baboon*, and seems also to be the immediate source of LG. *bavian*, Du. *baviaan*, G. *pavian*, baboon.] A baboon; an ape; applied in contempt to persons.

1599 B. JONSON *Cynthia's Rev.* I. i, Neither your..satyr, nor your hyæna, nor your babion. **1610** —— *Alch.* v. i. 14 For Babiouns, or Puppets. **1605** DRAYTON *Man in Moone* 341 The nimble Babion. **1627** —— *Mooncalf* in *Agincourt*, etc. 173 Of all the rest that most resembled man, Was an o'r-worne ill-fauoured Babian. **1624** MASSINGER *Parl. Love* IV. v, Farewell, babions.

babiroussa, -russa (bɑːbɪ'ruːsə). *Zoology.* Forms: 7 barbirousa, 8-9 babyroussa, -rouessa, babiroussa, 9 babirusa, -russa. [f. Malay *bâbi* hog + *rûsa* deer; also in Fr. and mod.L.] A species of wild hog (*Babirussa alfurus*) found in the islands of Eastern Asia, the upper canine teeth of which, in the male, pierce the lip and grow upwards and backwards like horns; also called Hog-deer, Indian hog, Horned hog.

1696 W. MOUNTAGUE *Delights Holland* 85 Barbirousa is half Hart, half Hog. **1774** GOLDSM. *Nat. Hist.* II. 112 The babyrouessa is still more remote from the hog kind than the capibara. **1883** *Athenæum* 1 Dec. 706/3 A male and two female babirussas..from Celebes. **1883** *Illust. Lond. News* 8 Sept. 243/2 We present a few sketches of the Babiroussa.. recently presented to the Society.

†'**babish,** *v. Obs.* Also 5-6 babysh(e. [? f. OF. *baubiss-* lengthened stem of *baubir* to mock, ridicule; cf. *babuse, babuise*, mockery. Perhaps influenced in use by *babish* adj.] To scoff at, scorn; to treat with contempt as mere children.

c **1460** *Towneley Myst.* 78 *Josephe.* That excusyd hir thus sothly..And babyshed me that was old. **1548** UDALL, etc. *Erasm. Par. John* vii, The Phariseis had babished the simple people with fained and colde religion. **1549** OLDE *Erasm. Par. 1 Tim.* ii. 15 We do not thus babyshe woman-kynde, as thoughe we woulde exclude them from..saluation. [Cf. Sc. '*Babbis*, To scoff, to gibe; to browbeat.' Jam.]

babish ('beɪbɪʃ), *a. arch.* [f. BABE + -ISH.]

1. Of or befitting a babe; infantile, baby-like.

1532 MORE *Confut. Tindale* Wks. 593/2 Their deedes.. verye babishe and veniall. *c* **1670** BUNYAN *Conf. Faith* Wks. 72 The actors herein have been counted babish Christians. **1855** SINGLETON *Virgil* II. 459 Her babish darts From tender hand she flung.

2. *contemptuously*, Babyish, childish, silly.

1553-87 FOXE *A. & M.* 1173/1 You babishe infantes and noddies. **1653** S. FISHER *Baby Bapt.* To Rdr. 2 Empty Answers, absolute Absurdities, Babish Baflings. **1775** ASH, *Babish*, childish, trifling.

†'**babished,** *a. Obs. rare*⁻¹. [Cf. BABISH *v.*] Made babyish or childishly silly.

1535-75 ABP. PARKER *Corr.* 199 What with my.. overmuch shamefastness, I am so babished in myself, that I cannot raise up my heart..to utter in talk, etc.

†'**babishly,** *adv.* [f. BABISH *a.* + -LY².] In the manner of a babe or infant.

a **1603** T. CARTWRIGHT *Confut. Rhem. N.T.* (1618) 147 Childishly and babishly deluded. **1625** USSHER *Answ. Jesuit* 493 Our Challenger..will hardly find one Father..that ever spake so babishly herein.

†'**babishness.** *Obs.* Babyishness.

1557 RECORDE *Whetst.* Yiij b, So were it plaine babishenesse, to couet euery morsell. *a* **1603** T. CARTWRIGHT *Confut. Rhem. N.T.* (1618) Pref. 15 This babishnesse of translation.

†'**babism.** *Obs. rare*⁻¹. [f. BABE + -ISM.] A childish practice.

1653 S. FISHER (*title*), Baby-Baptism meer Babism.

†'**bablatrice,** *nonce-wd.* ? Female babbler.

1595 *Locrine* 26 (Halliw.) O you cockatrices and bablatrices That in the woods dwell.

bable, obs. spelling of BABBLE, found also in all its derivatives: cf. prec. and next. Also obs. form of BAUBLE.

babli'aminy. *nonce-wd.* A babbler.

1608 MIDDLETON *Trick to Catch* IV. v, Wks. II. 84 Out, you babliaminy, you unfeathered, cremitoned quean.

babool, var. BABUL.

baboon (bə'buːn). Forms: 4 baboyne, babewyne, 5 babewyn, -ewin, -ewen, -wyn, -wen, baubyn, 6 babound, baboyn, babwyne, 6-7 baboune, baboone, 6- baboon. [a. F. *babuin* (13th c.), mod. *babouin*, or ad. med.L. *babewynus* (used in England 1295, see Du Cange), found also in the forms *babouinus, baboynus, babuynus* (some, if not all, of which are merely latinized from F. or Eng.); = It. *babbuino*, Sp. *babuino*. French has also *babion*, treated by Littré as a distinct word, but in Eng. identified with *baboon*, and the source of LG. *bavian*, Du. *baviaan*, HG. *pavian*, baboon. The earlier history of the word is unknown.

Diez suggests connexion with F. *babine* the thick lip of a cow, dog, monkey, compared with dial. Ger. *bäppe* muzzle. Scheler, from its application also to children, refers it to same root as *babe* or It. *babbolo*, etc.; others compare med.L. *papio* (see PAPIOUN), a kind of wild dog mentioned by Jac. de Vitriaco, and Maundevile. Finally we may compare OF. *babau, babou, baboue, babouye, baboy*, a grimace, a 'mouth,' *faire la baboue à*, to make mouths at. According to Daunon (*Hist. Lit.* xvi. 39), in 13th c., med.L. *babuinare* meant 'to paint marginal figures in MSS.,' and F. *babouin* was equivalent to *homuncio*; in the earliest known F. quotation in *Le Dit des xxiii manières de vilains* (13th c.), *li vilains babuins* is a simpleton or ninny, who gapes at the statues in front of Notre Dame while his purse is cut from behind. The original meaning, and the order of the senses, thus remain quite uncertain.]

†**1.** A grotesque figure (perhaps of a *baboon* in sense 2) used in architecture or decorative work.

[Cf. **1405** *Test. Ebor.* I. 317 Ciphus deauratus, coopertus ..de aquilis, leonibus, coronis, et aliis babonibus.] *c* **1325** *E.E. Allit. P.* B. 1409 Lyfte logges þer-ouer & on lofte coruen, Pared out of paper & poynted of golde, Broþe baboynes abof, besttes an vnder. **1430** LYDG. *Chron. Troy* II. xi, The corue knottes by craft of masonry, The freshe enbowing wᵗ verges ryght as lynes, And the housyng ful of babewines [*printed* backewines]. *c* **1440** *Promp. Parv.* 20/1 Babewyn, or babewen (**1499** babwyn, or babwen), *detippus, ipos, figmentum, chimera.* **1592** GREENE *Upst. Courtier* (1871) 38 Like a half face baubyn in brass. **1861** *Our Eng. Home* 72 Among the jewels of Edward II was a spice-plate 'enamelled with baboons.'

2. A member of one of the great divisions of the *Simiadæ* or Monkeys, distinguished by a long dog-like snout, large canine teeth or tusks, capacious cheek-pouches, and naked callosities on the buttocks; they are inhabitants of Africa, Southern Asia, and the adjacent islands.

c **1400** MAUNDEV. xxii. 238 Babewynes, Apes, Marmesettes, and othere dyverse bestes. **1481** CAXTON *Reynard* (Arb.) 98, I wende hit had be a mermoyse, a baubyn, or a mercatte. **1530** PALSGR. 196/1 Babwyne beest, *baboyn.* **1605** SHAKS. *Macb.* IV. i. 37 Coole it with a Baboones blood. **1774** GOLDSM. *Nat. Hist.* II. 354 The baboon..is from three to four feet high. **1834** [See APE 2.] **1849** MACAULAY *Hist. Eng.* iv. I. 480 His forehead low as that of a baboon.

3. *fig.* as a term of abuse; cf. *ape.*

c **1500** *Robin Hood* (Ritson) xi. 238 He then began to storm, Cries Fool, fanatick, baboon! **1592** NASHE *P. Penilesse* E j b, Is it anie discredit for me, thou great babound ..to be censured by thee? **1628** WITHER *Brit. Rememb.* I. 977 Such Apes, and such Baboones, As Parasites, and impudent Buffoones. **1678** WYCHERLEY *Pl.-Dealer* II. i. 25 No chattering, Baboons, instantly be gone.

4. *Comb.* **baboon-bird;** (see quot.)

1883 I. THURN *Indians of Guiana* 116 The bird (*Threnœdus Militaris*) called in the colony baboon-bird from the resemblance of its deep note to the 'baboon.'

baboonery (bə'buːnərɪ). Also 4 babwynrie. [Cf. F. *babouïnnerie* 'apishnesse, fopperie, foolerie' (Cotgr.), f. *babouin*: see prec. and -ERY.]

†**1.** Grotesque ornamentation: cf. BABERY. *Obs.*

1383 WYCLIF *Wks.* i. (1880) 8 ȝif þei drawen þe peple..by coryouste of gaye wyndownes..peyntyngis and babwynrie.

2. A collection or colony of baboons; cf. *rookery.*

1613 CHAPMAN *Masque Mid. Temp.* (D.) A vast, wither'd and hollow tree, the bare receptacle of the Baboonerie.

3. Baboonish condition, conduct, or behaviour.

a **1848** MARRYAT *R. Reefer* xix, The improvement..that baboonery had made toward manhood. **1857** *Nat. Mag.* II. 168 Oranges which he demolished in a style of the most perfect baboonery.

baboonish (bə'buːnɪʃ), *a.* [f. BABOON + -ISH¹.] Resembling a baboon; baboon-like.

1824 GALT *Rothelan* III. 277 The baboonish-looking visage of the Italian. **1824** MISS FERRIER *Inheritance* I. ii. (D.) A long, wrinkled, smirking, baboonish physiognomy.

†**baboonize,** *v. Obs.*⁻⁰ [f. BABOON + -IZE.]

1611 COTGR. *Babouïner*, to baboonize it; to play the monkey; to use apish or foolish tricks, or knauish prankes.

babotie, var. BOBOTIE.

‖**babouche** (bə'buːʃ). Also 7 baboushe, 9 baboosh. [a. F. *babouche* (cf. Sp. *babucha*), a. Arab. *bābūsh*, ad. Pers. *pāpōsh* a slipper, f. *pā* foot + *pōsh* covering, *pōshī-den* to cover. The change from *p* to *b* is seen also in *pasha, bashaw.*] A Turkish or oriental slipper.

1695 MOTTEUX *St. Olon's Morocco* 90 They have Shooes, or rather Slippers, without Heel's, call'd Baboushes. **1863** (*Daily paper*), Boots of red leather..encased in babouches of black leather.

baboun(e, -ound, -oyn(e, obs. ff. BABOON.

babtym, obs. form of BAPTISM.

‖**babu** ('bɑːbuː). Also 8-9 baboo. [Hindi *bābū.*] **a.** *orig.* A Hindu title of respect, answering to our *Mr.* or *Esquire*; hence, a Hindu gentleman; also (in Anglo-Indian use), a native clerk or official who writes English; sometimes applied disparagingly to a Hindu or, more particularly, a Bengali, with a superficial English education.

1782 *India Gaz.* 12 Oct. (*Subscription-list*), Cantoo Baboo ..200 Sicca Rupees. **1823** HEBER *Indian Jrnl.* 11 Oct., Some of the more wealthy baboos (the name of the native Hindoo gentleman answering to our esquire). **1854** STOCQUELER *Brit. India* 120 The sircar, baboo, purvoe, or whatever he may be called, is the chancellor of the exchequer, and it is not unseldom..that his master is his debtor. *c* **1866** A. LYALL *Old Pindaree* I'd sooner be robbed by a tall man.. Than be fleeced by a sneaking Baboo. **1931** *Times Lit. Suppl.* 5 Mar. 174/3 Robin's babu clerk. **1934** H. G. WELLS *Experiment in Autobiog.* I. vi. 309 The prose was over-elaborate and with that same flavour of the Babu, to which I have called attention.

b. babu English, the ornate and somewhat unidiomatic English of an Indian who has learnt the language principally from books. So by extension, *babu*, attrib., excessively ornate.

1878 GEO. ELIOT *Let.* 27 June (1956) VII. 33 Something more amusing—a bit of Baboo English from an Indian journal. **1889** BARRÈRE & LELAND *Dict. Slang* I. 58/2 *Baboo-English*..applied to the peculiar English which is rather written than spoken by the natives in India. **1890** FARMER *Slang* I. 86/1 *Baboo-English*... Its main peculiarity is its grandiloquence, a feature born of an attempt to adapt Western speech to Eastern imagery and hyperbole. **1925** *Weekly Westminster* 4 July 258 They irritate by their rather Babu familiarity with West End place-names. **1926** A. MAYHEW *Education of India* xii. 153 The [Indian] matriculate's mastery of English, despite all the ridicule unjustly bestowed on Babu English, is far more complete and practical than that shown by the normally intelligent and industrious English boy at the same stage. **1934** R. C. GOFFIN *S.P.E. Tract* XLI. 23 The perpetrations universally recognized as 'babu English' with its preposterously learned pretensions. **1936** C. S. LEWIS *Allegory of Love* ii. 81 The fantastical 'babu' ornaments of the style [of the *De Nuptiis*] were admired.

Hence **babudom, -ism.**

18.. *Pall Mall Gaz.* 18 July 11 Baboodom is making ready for its great protest against education or any other cess. *c* **1879** ABERIGH-MACKAY *21 Days in India* 49 However much we may desire to diffuse Babooism over the Empire. **1907** *Westm. Gaz.* 18 Dec. 1/3 The partition of Bengal supplied the simmering discontent of Babudom with a definite grievance.

‖**babu'ina.** [fem. of mod.L. *babuinus* BABOON, = F. *babouine.*] A female baboon.

1882 *Pop. Sci. Monthly* XX. 398 An old babuina.

babul, babool (bə'buːl, 'bɑːbuːl). *Anglo-Ind.* [Hind. *babūl*, *babūr*, Pers. *babūl.*] A thorny mimosa, *Acacia arabica*, common in parts of India.

1824 HEBER *Narrative* 12 Dec. (1828) I. 529 A formidable underwood of cactus and bâbool. **1849** J. H. BALFOUR *Man. Bot.* §852 A variety of Indian gum procured from *A*[*cacia*] *arabica*, is called Babul, or Babool-Gum; Babul-wood is used for tanning in Scinde. **1861** BENTLEY *Man. Bot.* 531 The barks of *A*[*cacia*] *arabica* and *A. Catechu*..are used extensively in India under the name of Babool. **1884** KIPLING *Departm. Ditties* (ed. 2, 1886) 51 In place of Putney's golden gorse The sickly *babul* blooms. **1921** *Times Lit. Suppl.* 8 Sept. 574/3 Babul seeds.

†'**baburd.** *Obs. Sc.* Also 6 bawburd. [a. F. *bâbord*, adopted from Teutonic; cf. OE. *bæc-*

bord, Ger. *bakbord*, Du. *bakboord*.] = LARBOARD.

[*c* **885** K. ÆLFRED *Oros.* I. i. §20 Burȝenda land wæs us on bæc-bord.] **1513** DOUGLAS *Æneis* V. iv. 20 Betwixt the rolk and Gyas schip On bawburd fast the innar way he leit slip. *c* **1570** R. SEMPILL *Fleming Berge*, With steirburd, babburd, luf and lie. *a* **1605** MONTGOMERIE *Poems* (1821) 238 On baburd syde, the whirling of the sand.

babushka (bəˈbuʃkə). Chiefly *N. Amer.* [Russ., grandmother, f. *baba* (peasant) woman.] A head covering folded diagonally and tied under the chin; a head-scarf.

1938 *Chatelaine* Feb. 33/2 The babushka is a peasant-sort of hood you wear over your pretty curls. **1948** F. BROWN *Murder can be Fun* (1951) vii. 106 She wore a greenish mottled *babushka* and.. stringy hair.. pushed out in front of it. **1959** *Encounter* Oct. 32/2 A voile scarf tied babushka-style.

babwen, -yn, -ynrie, obs. ff. BABOON, etc.

baby (ˈbeɪbɪ), *sb.* Forms: 4–6 **babi**, 5 **babee**, 6 **babye**, 6–7 **babie**, 4– **baby**; 6–9 *dial.* **babby**. [A pet-form of BABE (see -Y[4]), which passed into familiar use, while *babe* remained as the dignified word (e.g. in Scripture) and is now chiefly poetic.]

A. *sb.* **1. a.** An infant, a young child of either sex. (Formerly synonymous with *child*; now usually restricted to an infant 'in arms.')

1377 LANGL. *P. Pl.* B. XVII. 94 With penaunce and passioun of þat babi. **1393** GOWER *Conf.* I. 265 The yonge babies crieden alle. *c* **1475** *Babees Book* 45 Yee Babees in housholde that done duelle. **1533** BELLENDENE *Livy* v. (1822) 438 We bere na armoure aganis babbyis. **1611** SHAKS. *Wint. T.* II. i. 6 You'le kisse me hard, and speake to me, as if I were a Baby still. **1771** FENNING *Eng. Dict.*, *Baby*, a young child, distinguished from 'babe,' because that is applied to children who can both walk and speak, but this to those who can do neither. **1864** TENNYSON *En. Ard.* 194 Lightly rocking baby's cradle. **1865** DICKENS *Mut. Fr.* 3 'The fire that warmed you when you were a babby.'

b. *fig.* Applied to a person's invention, achievement, concern or responsibility; so ***to carry*** or ***hold the baby***, to be saddled with an unwelcome responsibility.

1890 *Jrnl. Soc. Arts* XLVIII. 65/1 Count Chardonnet.. was then shewing his new-born baby, which he called *soie artificielle*. **1912** *Q. Rev.* July 103 The 'bull'.. becomes a 'stale' bull, and drifts into the position frequently described as 'holding the baby'—that is to say, nursing a stock or share, perhaps for months, in the vague hope of getting rid of it some day at a profit. **1927** A. E. W. MASON *No other Tiger* xxiii. 261 He certainly has had the baby to hold all his life. **1927** *Daily Express* 8 July 6 Disclaiming responsibility for all the financial misfortunes of the country, he found himself confronted by Mr. Jack Jones, who told him that he was 'carrying the baby' anyhow. **1928** *Ibid.* 14 Jan. 11/7 If other bidders enter into competition, they find themselves run up to a high figure, and are then left to 'hold the baby'. **1935** D. L. SAYERS *Gaudy Night* vii. 153 Poor blighter. He *always* gets left with the baby. **1948** 'N. SHUTE' *No Highway* xii. 297 The Assegai, it seemed, was going to be my baby.

c. A girl; a girl-friend; a young woman: often as a form of address. *slang* (chiefly *U.S.*).

The degree of slanginess of the nineteenth-century examples is not easily determinable.

1839 F. A. KEMBLE *Jrnl. Residence Georgian Plantation* (1863) 30 'Oh massa!.. where you get this lilly alablaster baby!'.. I looked round to see if she was speaking of my baby; but no.. this superlative apostrophe was elicited by the fairness of *my skin*. **1870** D. J. KIRWAN *Palace & Hovel* (1963) xxii. 196 'Baby Hamilton' is another celebrity of the Half-World. Many stories are told about the recklessness of this girl. *Ibid.*, The 'Baby' had to leave Paris. **1901** A. M. BINSTEAD *More Gal's Gossip* v. 74 One overhears a callow youth of twenty address a still fascinating belle of forty, to whom he is giving supper, as 'Baby'. **1911** H. S. HARRISON *Queed* xiii. 167 Bad-eyed young men who congregate.. to smirk at the working girls.. 'Where you goin', baby?' **1918** C. SANDBURG *Cornhuskers* 60 My baby's going to have a new dress. **1927** H. A. VACHELL *Dew of Sea* 269 I'm beginning to thing that baby is half vamp and half floosie. **1940** *Illustr. London News* 6 Jan. 24/1 He has a 'baby', an empty-headed little chorus-girl, whom he worships.

d. A person. *slang.*

In quots. 1919, 1953 'this baby' = the speaker himself.

1899 R. WHITEING *No. 5 John St.* xxix. 306 The bounders.. think they're such awfully warm babies. **1919** R. LARDNER *Real Dope* 83 Well old pal it looks like they [*sic*] wouldn't be no front line trenchs for this baby. **1928** *Sat. Even. Post* 7 Jan. 21/1 [*wife to her husband*] 'Sure, baby,' she replied sympathetically. **1950** A. LOMAX *Mr. Jelly Roll* (1952) 57 Some terrible environments.. inhabited by some very tough babies. **1953** 'R. GORDON' *Dr. at Sea* vi. 70 Some skippers cook the log, but not this baby. **1968** *Listener* 31 Oct. 565/3 The dialogue is over, baby.

e. ***to empty, pour,*** or ***throw the baby out*** (or ***away***) ***with the bath(-water)*** (cf. G. *das Kind mit dem Bade ausschütten*), to reject the essential with the inessential, to discard what is valuable along with what is waste or useless.

1909 G. B. SHAW *Pen Portraits & Reviews* (1932) 87 Like all reactionists, he usually empties the baby out with the bath. **1911** —— *Getting Married* Pref. 186 We shall in a very literal sense empty the baby out with the bath by abolishing an institution which needs nothing more than a little.. rationalizing to make it.. useful. **1922** MRS. PATRICK CAMPBELL *Let.* 7 Jan. in *Shaw & Mrs. Campbell* (1952) 239 As to 'Relativity', I read somewhere that it is a philosophy that 'empties the baby out with the bath water'. **1939** S. SPENDER tr. *Toller's Pastor Hall* II. 84 You pour the baby out with the bath. **1957** E. GOWERS *H. W. Fowler* 14 We can rid ourselves of those grammarians' fetishes which make it more difficult to be intelligible without throwing the baby away with the bath-water.

†**2.** A doll, puppet. *Obs.*

1552 HULOET, Baby or puppet for chyldren, *Pupa*. **1563** *Homilies, Idolatry* III. (1844) 238 Puppets and babies for old fools in dotage. **1651** LILLY *Chas. I* (1774) 219 Whose father sold babies and such pedlary ware in Cheapside. **1712** STEELE *Spect.* No. 500 ¶3 Little girls tutoring their Babies. **1721** POPE *Let. Blount* 3 Oct., Sober over her Sampler, or gay over a jointed Baby.

†**3.** A small image of oneself reflected in the pupil of another's eye; hence ***to look babies***. *Obs.*

1593 *Tell-trothe's N.Y. Gift* 39 That babie which lodges in womens eies. **1621** BURTON *Anat. Mel.* III. ii. VI. v. (1651) 576 They may kiss and coll, lye and look babies in one anothers eyes. **1672** MARVELL *Reh. Transp.* I. 66 Only to speculate his own Baby in their eyes. **1682** MRS. BEHN *City Heiress* III. i, Sigh'd, and lookt Babies in his gloating Eyes.

†**4.** *pl.* Pictures in books; perh. orig. the ornamental tail-pieces and borders with cupids and grotesque figures interworked (cf. BABERY). Still in *north dial.*

1598 SYLVESTER *Du Bartas* (1621) 5 We gaze but on the babies and the cover, The gaudy flowers and edges painted over. **1618** HALES *Gold. Rem.* (1673) II. 8 Provided that, in the Tables and Maps, there were no pictures and babies. **1655** FULLER *Hist. Camb.* (1840) 39 More pleased with babies in books than children are.

5. *fig.* (contemptuously) A foolish or childish fellow. ***to smell of the baby***: to be childish.

1603 *Patient Grissil* 17 My brisk spangled baby will come into a stationer's shop. **1618** BRETON *Court. & Countrym.* 19 (D.) So long in their horne booke that, doe what they can, they will smell of the Baby till they can not see to read. **1660** MILTON *Free Commonw.* Wks. (1851) 430 If we were aught els but Sluggards or Babies.

6. *transf.* The young of an animal; cf. B. 1 a.

1883 G. ALLEN in *Knowledge* 18 Aug. 97/2 While he [the young hare] is still a baby.

7. a. *fig.* A (comparatively) tiny thing; cf. B. 1 a.

1859 JEPHSON *Brittany* vii. 88 Turrets beside which the leaning tower of Pisa is a baby.

b. Applied to a small-sized bottle, jar, etc. *slang.*

1853 *Househ. Words* VII. 123/2 A stone bottle of ardent spirits called baby for shortness and secresy. *Ibid.* 124/2 He has nabbed a 'baby'! **1909** WARE *Passing Eng.* 13 The half-bottle (2d.), which from its small size was dubbed 'baby' by all men. **1958** *Spectator* 10 Jan. 40/3 Pubs refusing to serve standard-size bottles of mineral water because they only stock 'babies'.

c. *spec.* A small car.

1920 *Punch* 27 Oct. 329/3 Triumph 1920 4 h.p. Model H, also Baby, both brand new. **1931** *Star* 8 May 13/1 One of the 'babies' was setting up such a pace that the big cars were out of the hunt.

8. *transf.* The youngest or most junior of a family, group of persons, team, etc.

1897 'P. WARUNG' *Tales Old Régime* 243 Blake was twenty-five, Clyde was twenty-four, and Entworth forty-one.. Short was the 'baby'. **1914** *Daily Express* 19 Sept. 5/1 The 'babies' of the Southern League, Croydon Common, will face Crystal Palace. *Ibid.* 20 Nov. 5/4 [He] was only eighteen years of age, and was known as 'the baby' of his company. **1925** W. DEEPING *Sorrell & Son* xxiv. §2 There was one young Pentreath,—the baby.

B. *Comb.* (in which *baby* approaches in use to an adj.)

1. General relations: **a.** appositive (*hence* = 'little, tiny'), as ***baby-boy, -figure*** (1606), ***-germ, -girl, -stream***, (and of animals) ***baby-bird, -elephant, -snake***; **b.** objective gen. with verbal sb. or pple., as ***baby-eater, -minder, -seller*** (1634), ***-worship***; **c.** similative, as ***baby-blind*** (1627), ***-mild***; **d.** attrib. (of or befitting a baby), *hence* = 'infantine, innocent,' 'little, tiny,' 'babyish, silly,' as ***baby age, brow*** (1605), ***dance, face, hand, -language, mind, -name, -play, sole, talk***; **e.** attrib. (for a baby's use), as ***baby-basket, -class, -clothes, -clouts, -harness, -linen, -things*** (1783); **f.** parasynthetic deriv., as ***baby-faced, -featured*** (1780).

1634 BAYNE *On Coloss.* 357 The *baby age of the Church. **1884** Q. VICTORIA *More Leaves* 168 The *baby-basket sent her.. when King James I. was born. **1864** KINGSLEY *Water Bab.* 279 An old song.. learnt when she was a little *baby-bird. **1627** H. BURTON *Baiting Pope's Bull* 6 Filiall, or rather *baby-blind obedience. **1605** SHAKS. *Macb.* IV. i. 88 Weares vpon his *Baby-brow, the round And top of Soueraignty. **1850** MRS. BROWNING *Poems* II. 174 *Baby-browed And speechless Being. **1873** C. M. YONGE *Pillars of House* I. ii. 24 That she might not.. [go] down to the bottom of the *baby-class. **1934** NGAIO MARSH *Man lay Dead* xii. 212 Baby-class stuff at the Yard. **1704** N. BLUNDELL *Diary* 7 July (1952) ii. 23, I opened a box of *Babby Cloths which was sent to my Wife by my Lady Webb. **1798** JANE AUSTEN *Let.* 27 Oct. (1932) I. 25 Dame Tilbury's daughter has lain in. Shall I give her any of your baby clothes? **1866** ROSSETTI *Let.* 5 Jan. (1965) II. 586 Some women preparing the grave-clothes and baby-clothes at the same time. **1770** J. LOVE *Cricket* 7 Leave the dissolving Song, the *baby Dance. **1848** KINGSLEY *Saint's Trag.* I. i. 40 Worshippers of black cats, *baby-eaters, and such like. **1864** *Reader* 14 May 626 The mind of a *baby elephant. **1713** SWIFT *Cadenus & V.* Wks. 1755 III. II. 16 A *baby face, no life, no airs. **1839** DICKENS *Nickleby* liv. 536 A *baby-faced chit of a girl. **1883** A. DOBSON in *Eng. Illust. Mag.* Nov. 79/2 That baby-faced beauty. **1959** NGAIO MARSH *Singing in Shrouds* iv. 64 Baby-faced petulance. **1780** COWPER *Progr. Error* 201 *Baby-featured, and of infant size. **1606** SHAKS. *Tr. & Cr.* I. iii. 345 The *baby figure of the Gyant-masse Of things to come at large. **1842** TENNYSON *Talking Oak* xx, She gamboll'd on the greens, A *baby-germ. **1871** M. COLLINS *Mrq. & Merch.* I. i. 16 The Marchioness had a *baby-girl. **1791** E. DARWIN *Bot. Gard.* II. 64 Feeds from its *baby-hand.. The callow nestlings. **1930** M. MEAD *Growing Up in New Guinea* 24 The child sits quietly [in the canoe]... There are no straps, no *baby harnesses to detain him in his place. **1962** *Guardian* 5 Nov. 4/3 A lightweight baby harness.. used to hold a baby in a high-chair for feeding. **1892** C. M. YONGE *That Stick* xxvii. 181 That pretty precision of utterance that children sometimes acquire when *baby language has not been foolishly fostered. **1923** H. WALPOLE *Introd.* to H. Lofting *Dr. Dolittle* p. vii, Grown-ups imagine that they can do the trick by adopting baby language and talking down to their very critical audience. **1932** *Oxf. Compan. Eng. Lit.* 756/1 It [*sc.* Journal to Stella] is a series of intimate letters.. for the most part written in baby-language. **1814** JANE AUSTEN *Mansfield Park* I. i. 6 Lady Bertram dispatched money and *baby-linen. *a* **1845** HOOD *Lycus* Poems (1858) 307 The leopard was.. *baby-mild in its feature. **1863** F. A. KEMBLE *Jrnl. Residence Georgian Plantation* App. 401 The only supervision exercised over either babies or '*baby minders' was that of the old woman left in charge of the infirmary. **1959** *Times* 8 June 13/1 Resident nannies and baby-minders. **1784** COWPER *Task* v. 190 Infirm and *baby minds. **1856** C. M. YONGE *Daisy Chain* II. v. 382 *Baby-names never ought to go beyond home. **1896** G. B. SHAW in *Sat. Rev.* 6 June 575/2 Mrs Campbell's attempt at Magda is the merest *baby-play in comparison with that performance. **1634** J. HORNE *Janua Ling.* 123 *Baby-sellers [*nugivendi*] boast and speak proudly. **1864** TENNYSON *Aylmer's F.* 186 Tender pink five-beaded *baby-soles. **1864** *Realm* 15 June 5 Ravines from which Jumna, Indus, and Ganges, yet *baby streams, gush. **1836** F. A. KEMBLE *Let.* 1 Mar. in *Rec. of Later Life* (1882) I. 43 A baby.. [is] such an interruption.. to any conversation but *baby-talk. **1850** MARG. FULLER *Wom. in 19th C.* (1862) 311 To talk baby-talk and give shallow accounts of deep things. **1861** M. B. CHESNUT *Diary* 25 Nov. (1949) 162 To me this calm, monotonous baby talk is maddening. **1933** E. ARNOT ROBERTSON *Ordinary Families* x. 215 'Pore ole pussycat!' Dru would lapse into baby-talk. **1783** AINSWORTH *Lat. Dict.*, *Baby things, *linamenta ad infantes recèns natos involvendum*. **1894** M. DYAN *All in Man's Keeping* II. x. 183 His youngest sister.. had brought her boy with her, for 'Uncle Dick' to do a little final *baby-worship.

g. Passing into *adj.* = young; small or diminutive of its kind.

1750 H. WALPOLE *Let.* 25 Feb. (1903) II. 432 All the geniuses of the age are employed in designing new plans for desserts. The Duke of Newcastle's last was a baby Vauxhall, illuminated with a million of little lamps. **1819** KEATS *Let.* 24 Jan. (1958) II. 36 My modest feathered Pen frizzles like baby roast beef. **1877** *Design & Work* 1 Dec. 602/2 Gas bags.. floating high over their heads, by means of baby screws.. and the like. **1878** *Ibid.* 16 Feb. 199/3 He was surprised at the strength displayed by the baby iron rope. **1899** *Daily News* 17 Oct. 6/6 [He] decided that her baby-jib must be responsible for the Shamrock's poor pointing. **1908** FINDLATER *Crossriggs* iv. 28 She led him out of the nursery... 'There's a babier baby than Mike,' she said. **1909** *Daily Chron.* 12 Oct. 4/4 Baby beef, which is grown so little in this country. **1917** W. PETT RIDGE *Amazing Years* vii. 93 One attractive baby grand [piano] that Millwood picked up. **1918** F. A. FORBES *Let.* in G. L. Sheil *Mother F.A.F.* (1946) vi. 69, I have in my room a baby rhododendron in full bloom. **1926** *Daily Express* 30 July 9/5 Imported films for use in 'baby' cine-cameras. **1928** *Daily Express* 11 Oct. 1/1 Wonderful improvement in the 'baby car' of seven horse-power. **1929** *Melody Maker* Jan. 15/3 You can't get a harp into a Baby Austin, whereas you can garage an Austin inside a piano. **1961** C. MCCULLERS *Clock without Hands* xiii. 249 Pounding on middle C of the baby grand piano. **1965** *Economist* 2 Oct. 70/1 Intensive beef production in the shape of barley beef or 'baby beef' started here in 1961.

2. Special combinations: **baby act** *U.S.*, (*a*) the act of a baby; (*b*) an act or statute for the protection of minors; hence ***to plead the baby act***, to enter a plea that one is not legally responsible by reason of youth or inexperience; similarly, ***to read the baby act***; **baby-blue** (orig. *U.S.*), a light shade of blue; **baby-blue-eyes** (orig. *U.S.*), the popular name of a plant of any of several species of the *Nemophila* family; **baby bonus** *Canad. colloq.*, a family allowance; **baby boom** *colloq.*, a temporary marked increase in the birth-rate, *spec.* one that occurred in the years following the war of 1939–45; the children born at the time of such an increase (cf. BULGE *sb.* 3 f); hence **baby boomer** orig. *U.S.*, a person born during the post-war baby boom; **baby-bouncer** = *baby-jumper*; **baby buggy** (*N. Amer.*), **carriage, coach** (*U.S.*), a perambulator; **baby-doll**, (*a*) = DOLL *sb.*[1] 2; (*b*) (orig. *U.S.*) a girl or woman who has the youthful and regular good looks characteristic of a doll and an ingenuous disposition; **baby-doll pyjamas**, women's pyjamas consisting of a loose-fitting top worn over short trousers; also ***baby-doll nightdress***; **baby face**, (a person with) a babyish face; **baby food**, a milk-substitute or a light diet suitable for a baby; **baby-grow**: see BABYGRO; **baby-house**, a doll's house, *also*, a toy-house barometer or hygrometer from which little dolls issue to indicate changes of weather; **baby-jumper**, a hoop or frame suspended by an elastic attachment, so that a young child secured in it may exercise its limbs; **baby lace** (see quot.); **baby-like** *a.*, babyish, infantile, *adv.* as a baby does; **baby pig disease**, hypoglycæmia of newly-born pigs; **baby powder**, a skin powder for babies; **baby-ribbon**, narrow ribbon such as that used for babies' clothes; **baby's breath, babies' breath**, the popular name of any of several delicate or sweet-scented plants, esp. *Gypsophila paniculata*; **baby's head** *slang*, a steak (and kidney) pudding; **baby show** (orig. *U.S.*), a baby exhibition with an award for the 'best'; **baby-sitter**, a person engaged to be at hand to look after a young child or children in the absence of the parents; hence **baby-sit** *v. intr.*; also *trans.* (chiefly *N. Amer.*) with child or children as obj., and in extended sense, to look after, stay with, or tend (a thing, animal, sick person, etc.); also *fig.*; **baby-sitting** *vbl. sb.* and *ppl. a.* (orig. *U.S.*); **baby-snatcher** *joc.*, a person who enters into an amorous relationship with a much younger member of the opposite sex; hence **baby-snatch** *v. intr.*, **baby-snatching** *vbl. sb.*; **baby walker** orig. *U.S.*, a device for assisting babies to learn to walk.

1837 *New Yorker* 9 Dec. 593/2 We do not defend the conduct of any man who pleads usury in bar of an honest man, neither would we if he should plead the *baby act, or minority. **1888** *Congress. Rec.* Aug., App. 440/1 [Mr. S. S. Cox] admits the authorship..but pleads the baby act, and says he was a boy when he wrote it. **1899** 'MARK TWAIN' *Man corrupted Hadleyburg* (1900) 214 When politicians come out without a blush and read the baby act in this frank way, [etc.]. **1901** *Forum* Jan. 592 One minute reading the riot act of manly independence, and the next pleading the baby-act of thoughtless irresponsibility. **1904** W. H. SMITH *Promoters* xv. 229 That's business honor, and anything else is the baby act. **1889** *Century Mag.* Mar. 748/2 The small, square manuscript sewed at the back with worsted of the pale tint known as '*baby-blue'. **1922** S. LEWIS *Babbitt* i. 4 Faded baby-blue pyjamas. **1949** A. WILSON *Wrong Set* 29 Her corn-coloured hair and baby blue eyes. **1887** *Overland Monthly* Aug. 152/1 Then, if we could have been there, we should have seen the..'*baby blue eyes' (nemophila). **1952** A. G. L. HELLYER *Sanders' Encycl. Gardening* (ed. 22) 325 *Nemophila..Menziesii*. 'Baby Blue-Eyes', white or blue, summer, spreading, California. **1945** D. DUMBRILLE *All this Difference* xix. 191 The papers are full of the manpower situation.., conscription..[and] the *Baby Bonus. **1961** [see POGEY b]. **1976** *Globe & Mail* (Toronto) 16 Dec. 1/6 Extra tax on rich to be eliminated; baby bonus to rise. **1941** *Life* 1 Dec. 73/3 Whatever the reasons, the U.S. *baby boom is bad news for Hitler. **1967** *Economist* 18 Nov. 731/2 Equally important are the spurts which demographers often cannot foresee: the 'baby booms'. The results of one such phenomenon—the wave of marriages and births after the last war—will soon be felt in full. **1971** *Sci. Amer.* July 17/3 The postwar 'baby boom' and rapid growth of the economy in the 1950's pushed the population growth rate up to 18.5 percent. **1975** *Nature* 22 May 287/1 The postwar 'baby boom' has now passed through higher education. **1983** *Daily Tel.* 30 Dec. 12/4 The particular thirst for 'white knuckle rides' probably resulted from the baby boom of the early 1960s. **1974** *Time* 21 Jan. 57/2 'We'—the *baby boomers—had the schools, the attention of the media, [etc.]. **1986** *Observer* 5 Jan. 10/3 They are stressing the importance of the baby-boomers, roughly the generation now over 25 and under 40. **1968** *Times* 11 Mar. 11/2, I have him in the *baby bouncer while I'm practising. **1890** *Dial. Notes* I. 411 *Baby buggy. **1911** *Daily Colonist* (Victoria, B.C.) 30 Apr. 4/4 Your baby buggy..is on our fourth floor. **1934** J. T. FARRELL *Young Manhood* in *Studs Lonigan* (1936) 172 He..walked past the baby-buggy where young Horn had left his baby brother. **1866** *Leisure Hour* 2 June 348/1 The specification was not such as to prevent various modifications of three-wheeled *baby-carriages. **1870** L. M. ALCOTT *Old-Fashioned Girl* (1874) xiii. 215 A young girl pushing a baby-carriage. **1903** *Sun* (N.Y.) 3 Nov. 7 It gave a chance for a lot of jokes which were so distinctively British that a baby carriage was called a 'perambulator'. **1909** EATON & UNDERHILL *Runaway Place* 155 To their astonished eyes, he seemed to slip directly through a baby carriage. **1903** *N.Y. Times* 1 Oct. 3 English *baby coaches. .. The carriages are a distinctly English idea—they dub them 'Perambulators'. *a* **1862** MRS. NESBIT *Let.* in D. Langley Moore *E. Nesbit* (1933) ii. 26, I shall bring you a *Baby doll... It has blue Eyes and flaxen hair and is dressed like a little baby in long clothes. **1893** 'SARAH GRAND' *Heavenly Twins* II. III. x. 96 It was a huge wax baby-doll, considerably battered. **1946** TENNESSEE WILLIAMS *27 Wagons* 11, I fell in love with this baby-doll. **1962** *Guardian* 8 July 16/6 The serious baby-doll face suddenly broke into laughter. **1957** *Punch* 27 Mar. 418/3 The Keystone '*Baby Doll' nightdress..is barely knee-length, and has a scooped neckline trimmed with angel lace and baby ribbon. There are also '*Baby Doll' pyjamas: gossamer jacket just covering, but no more, the brief puff panties. **1959** *Listener* 2 July 35/1 The girl..appeared curled up in Baby Doll pyjamas. **1967** J. WAINWRIGHT *Talent for Murder* 44 She was wearing a grimy, 'Baby Doll' nightdress. *a* **1700** EVELYN *Diary* 4 Nov. an. 1670 (1955) III. 564 That famed beauty (but in my opinion of a childish simple & *baby face) Madamoiselle Quirreval. **1713** Baby face [see BABY *sb.* B. 1 d]. **1888** A. C. GUNTER *Mr. Potter of Texas* xxiii. 268 'That was before her baby face came between us!' cries her ladyship, hoarsely. **1926** D. H. LAWRENCE *Plumed Serpent* ii. 48 Mrs. Burlap had hitched herself on to Kate, and from her silly, social baby-face was emitting searching questions. *Ibid.* 50 The couple from the Middle-West, that withered baby-face and that limping Judge. **1897** *Sears, Roebuck Catal.* 28/2 *Baby Foods. **1939** *Jrnl. Amer. Med. Assoc.* 4 Mar. 843/2 Libby's Homogenized Baby Foods are..suitable for use particularly during the early months of infancy. **1946** *Nutrition & Child Welfare* Oct. 6/2 There are three types of baby food. **1726** SWIFT *Gulliver* I. II. iii. 55 The Furniture of a *Baby-house. **1750** H. WALPOLE *Lett. H. Mann* 218 II. 359 The Prince is building baby-houses at Kew. **1779** MACKENZIE in *Mirror* No. 21 ¶2 The little Dutch barometers, known by the name of Babyhouses. **1801** MAR. EDGEWORTH *Good Fr. Gov.* (1831) 107, I see neither..dressed dolls, nor baby-houses. **1861** H. B. STOWE *Pearl of Orr's Isl.* I. xii. 106 Mara and Sally..were revelling in apronsful of shells and seaweed, which they bustled into the other room to bestow in their spacious baby-house. **1848** *Ann. Rep. Comm. Patents 1847* (U.S.) 47 Exercising machines, under the appellation of swings, *baby-jumpers, &c. **1849** J. R. PLANCHÉ in *Extravaganzas* (1879) III. 290 Up and down leaping, My heart is keeping, like a baby jumper—that invention new. **1872** *N.Y. Times* 24 Apr. 8 Advt. (Hoppe), Cradle, Baby-Jumper and Nursery Chair Combined. **1882** CAULFEILD & SAWARD *Dict. Needlework*, **Baby Lace*, an English pillow lace, formerly made in Bedfordshire and Buckinghamshire, and called English Lille... The name Baby Lace was given as, on account of the narrow width of the lace, it was chiefly used for trimming babies' caps. **1803** *Edin. Rev.* II. 141 *Baby-like caprice. **1858** GEN. P. THOMPSON *Audi Alt.* I. xxx. 116 If a man sees his child gored to death..does he say baby-like, 'O naughty oxen!' **1942** L. L. MADSEN in *Yearbk. Agric.* (*U.S. Dept. Agric.*) 825 (*heading*) Acute Hypoglycemia in Newborn Pigs, or So-Called *Baby Pig Disease. **1960** *Farmer & Stockbreeder* 9 Feb. 102/1 Treatment of 'Baby Pig Disease'... All the piglings in the affected litter should without delay be given glucose by mouth. **1897** *Sears, Roebuck Catal. 6th page after* p. 32, Borated Talcum *Baby Powder. **1914** G. ATHERTON *Perch of Devil* i. 63 It was ordinary 'baby powder' for the bath. **1893** *Cassell's Fam. Mag.* Feb. 175/1 Various ways in which skilful fingers can utilise the *baby ribbons. **1906** *Westm. Gaz.* 28 Apr. 14/1 Baby-ribbon velvet. **1909** *Daily Chron.* 1 June 7/5 A sandwich which was tied up with pink baby-ribbon. **1897** MRS. C. A. CREEVEY *Flowers of Field, Hill & Swamp* viii. 272 Grape hyacinth. *Baby's breath. Muscari botryoides. **1938** *Word Study* Dec. 4 New flowers are weeds whose names the florists have changed; 'baby's breath' is the old 'flowering spurge'. **1905** *Daily Chron.* 5 Sept. 4/7 'A *baby's head and two veg.'.. The grubby waitress..brings steak pudding with potatoes and greens as trimmings. **1967** K. GILES *Death in Diamonds* v. 88 He went to the counter and ordered kidney soup and a baby's head and chips. **1854** *Chambers's Jrnl.* 30 Dec. 419/2 *Baby-shows have taken place in one or two western localities. **1855** *Family Economist* Nov. 160 The stupidest exhibitions lately heard of, are the Baby-show, now being got up in this country, in foolish imitation of the same foolish thing in America. **1930** 'R. CROMPTON' *Wm's Happy Days* viii. 166 Oughter be in a baby show. **1967** *Guardian* 5 Aug. 12/8 The judging of the Baby Show had been completed. **1947** in *Amer. Speech* (1949) XXIV. 72 Offer to '*baby sit' with her little boy. **1950** *Punch* 15 Mar. 292/2 Well, this is the last Monday I baby-sit for the McClouds. **1972** *Evening Telegram* (St. John's, Newfoundland) 23 June 20/5 (Advt.), Wanted, a young woman to baby-sit a four-year-old boy. *Ibid.* 24 June 11/6 It could become a pretty costly operation to baby sit their gear, even if it is properly marked. **1973** *Philadelphia Inquirer* (Today Suppl.) 7 Oct. 26/3 He baby-sat me through about a thirty day period, literally. I was weak as a new-born kid. **1976** *Billings* (Montana) *Gaz.* 30 June 4-D/5 The commissioner said he hopes for better results in the fall, adding: 'We're getting to the point where we feel we can only babysit them for so long.' **1986** *New Yorker* 8 Sept. 40/3 Bridie felt in her purse..and found..a toy whirligig she saved for times when she babysat the kids of some of her parents' clients. **1937** C. R. WALKER *American City* 230 There are two high-school girls in the neighborhood who hire out for twenty-five cents an evening as '*baby sitters' when the family wants to go to the movies. **1951** *Times* 18 Dec. 5/4 Everybody knows what a baby-sitter is supposed to do (though, curiously enough, hardly anybody except the baby ever sees her do it). **1947** *Richmond* (Virginia) *Times-Dispatch* 4 Mar. 4/2 The Cavalier *Baby-Sitting Association, recently organized at the University of Virginia. **1949** *New Yorker* 5 Mar. 24/3 Baby-sitting having become firmly established, it was only a question of time before somebody offered to provide a similar service for dogs. **1951** *Punch* 4 Apr. 421/3 Undoubtedly one of the worst features of the baby-sitting age is the coy handing over of the fee. **1958** *Spectator* 22 Aug. 248/3 Car-owning miners and baby-sitting scholars. **1911** 'I. HAY' *Safety Match* xiv. 225 She comes trapesin' about here with a collection of middle-aged *baby-snatchers. **1930** V. SACKVILLE-WEST *Edwardians* v. 199 You don't imagine that he really cared about that baby-snatcher? Good gracious me, he was a year old when her daughter was born. **1933** M. ALLINGHAM *Sweet Danger* vii. 85, I meant the elder sister. You aren't *baby-snatching, I hope, Wright? **1939** 'N. BLAKE' *Smiler with Knife* iv. 71, I don't approve of baby-snatching. **1856** *Michigan Agric. Soc. Trans.* VII. 81 Wm. Phelps ..[exhibited] 1 *baby walker. **1967–8** *Catal. Galt Toys* 7 Galt baby walker... Designed so as not to tip up when the baby, first learning to walk, pulls himself up on the handle.

baby ('beɪbɪ), *v.* [f. prec.] **1.** *trans.* To treat as a baby.

1742 YOUNG *Nt. Th.* VI. 521 It babies us with endless toys. **1865** MRS. WHITNEY *Gayworthys* I. 240, I should like to be made much of, and tended—yes, babied.

2. *intr.* To act as if dealing with a baby.

1913 G. S. PORTER *Laddie* xi. 340 I'll wager a strong young girl like the Princess will laugh at you for babying over her.

'**babydom.** *rare.* [See -DOM.] = BABYHOOD.

1864 *Daily Tel.* 14 Sept., The young foal or filly must be raced in its babydom.

'**baby-farm.** [FARM *sb.*[2] 7.] A derogatory term for a place where the lodging and care of babies is undertaken for profit. Hence '**baby-ˌfarming** *vbl. sb.*, the keeping of such a place; also *ppl. a.*; '**baby-farmed** *ppl. a.*; '**baby-ˌfarmer.**

1868 *Brit. Med. Jrnl.* 25 Jan. 75/2 Poor-law medical officers should have a power of entering, inspecting, and regulating baby-farms. *Ibid.* 22 Feb. 174/2 Children but a few months old were fed by the less indifferent of these baby-farmers with some of their own coarse food. *Ibid.* 21 Mar. 276/1 The inquiry has for its object the determination of the extent to which Baby-Farming (as distinguished from the practice of abortion) is carried on in London. **1870** *Times* 16 June 12/4 Two children..alleged to have been brought from a baby-farming establishment. **1878** W. S. GILBERT *H.M.S. Pinafore* II. 31, I practised baby-farming. **1880** *Encycl. Brit.* XIII. 4/2 The infamous relations between the lying-in houses and the baby-farming houses of London. **1881** OGILVIE (Annandale), *Baby-farmer*, a woman who receives infants, generally illegitimate, from their parents, on the pretext of bringing them up, the object being to have the child removed from sight; one who lives by baby-farming. **1884** *Chr. World* 10 July 513/3 Baby-farming was vigorously denounced. **1896** *Daily News* 26 Apr. 2/3 The great ledger in which are kept their patiently accumulated records of the baby farmers. **1896** *Westm. Gaz.* 30 May 3/1 The baby-farmed child. **1954** T. S. ELIOT *Confid. Clerk* III. 94 You're suggesting that she ran a baby farm.

Babygro ('beɪbɪgrəʊ). Also (non-*propr.*) **babygrow, babygrow.** [f. BABY *sb.* + GRO(W *v.*] A proprietary name for a kind of all-in-one stretch garment for babies.

1959 *Official Gaz.* (U.S. Patent Office) 13 Oct. 65/2 Lisle Mills, Inc...*Babygro*..For Infants' and Children's Outer and Under Garments—Namely, Pajamas, or Sleepers, and Overalls. First use on or about May 8, 1959, on pajamas. **1960** *Trade Marks Jrnl.* 21 Dec. 1652/2 *Babygro*... Pyjamas and overalls, all for infants and children. Lisle Mills, Inc..; New York..Manufacturers. **1973** *Guardian* 22 May 13/1 Babygros are fine for the early stages. **1977** *Belfast Tel.* 22 Feb. 8/6 It channels your thoughts into a nursery, cotton buds and Baby-Gros. **1978** *Daily Tel.* 23 Nov. 19/1 He was wearing a yellow 'baby-grow' and a vest. That is all, apart from his nappy and a pair of rubber pants. **1981** *Times* 4 Aug. 3/8 Parents seeking advice on clothing can be told that a nappy, vest, babygrow and cardigan are the most needed indoors.

babyhood ('beɪbɪhʊd). [f. BABY *sb.* + -HOOD; cf. senses of *manhood*.] **a.** The period or condition of infancy. **b.** Babies collectively. **c.** Babyishness, childish folly.

1748 RICHARDSON *Clarissa* (1811) IV. 208 Had she not been known to be a female, they would not from babyhood have dressed her as such. **1860** MISS YONGE *Stokesley Secr.* iii. (1880) 262 An affront to all babyhood. **1860** GEN. P. THOMPSON *Audi Alt.* III. cxiv. 45 All the malevolence and babyhood of the country rush to display themselves.

babyish ('beɪbɪɪʃ), *a.* [f. BABY *sb.* + -ISH.] Childish, simple, silly.

1753 RICHARDSON *Grandison* (1820) I. xv. 96 To me she has a babyish look, especially when she smiles. **1868** G. DUFF *Pol. Surv.* (1868) 159 Too babyish to deserve even the semblance of consideration.

'**babyishly,** *adv.* [f. prec. + -LY[2].] In a babyish manner; childishly.

1860 *Rutledge* 29, I felt rather babyishly about it. **1884** J. GOLDSMITH *Himself Again* iii. 29 He felt, almost babyishly, that she might take him and make him what she wished him to be.

'**babyishness.** [f. as prec. + -NESS.] The quality of being babyish; childish silliness.

babyism ('beɪbɪɪz(ə)m). [f. BABY *sb.* + -ISM.]

1. Babyish condition, babyhood.

1836 J. DOWNES *Mt. Decam.* II. 232 Alas for the babyism of man, this thing of yesterday.

2. Babyishness; babyish phrase or action.

1837 *Blackw. Mag.* XLI. 280 The solemn littlenesses of Lord John Russell and the babyisms of Lord Morpeth. **1864** TENNYSON *Aylmer's F.* 539 Babyisms and dear diminutives.

babyl, obs. form of BABBLE.

babyless ('beɪbɪlɪs), *a.* [f. BABY *sb.* + -LESS.] Having no babies, without a baby.

1871 CHRISTINA G. ROSSETTI *Sing-Song* 125 Motherless baby and babyless mother. **1958** *Times* 2 Oct. 12/7 Being awake and babyless we lose no time crossing the gangway into the ship.

Babylon ('bæbɪlən), *sb.* [a. L. *Babylōn*, Gr. Βαβυλών, Heb. *Bābel*.] A magnificent city, once the capital of the Chaldee Empire; also, the mystical Babylon of the Apocalypse; whence, in modern times, applied polemically to Rome or the papal power, and rhetorically to any great and luxurious city.

1362 LANGL. *P. Pl.* A. VI. 8 Bethleem and Babiloyne, I haue ben in boþe. **1634** RAINBOW *Labour* (1635) 41 Thy great Babilons which thou hast built. **1823** BYRON *Juan* XI. xxiii, The approach..to mighty Babylon [= London].

†'**babylon,** *v.* *Obs. rare*[−1]. [f. prec. sb.] To place or establish in a magnificent abode.

1633 F. GREVILLE *Cælica* VI. xxxviii, In mortall seat of Cælica's faire heart, To babylon my selfe there, did intend.

Babylonian (bæbɪ'ləʊnɪən), *a.* and *sb.* [f. L. *Babylōni-us*, Gr. Βαβυλώνι-ος + -AN.]

A. *adj.* Of or belonging to Babylon; hence *fig.* **a.** huge, gigantic; †**b.** popish (*obs.*); **c.** (cf. *Rev.* xvii. 4) scarlet.

1637 GILLESPIE *Eng.-Pop. Cerem.* II. vii. 28 The Babylonian baggage of Antichristian Ceremonies. **1790** BURKE *Fr. Rev.* 41 The confused jargon of their Babylonian pulpits. **1821** DE QUINCEY *Confess.* Wks. I. 131 No huge Babylonian centres of commerce towered into the clouds. **1848** DICKENS *Dombey* (1870) I. v. 89 A cocked hat and a Babylonian collar.

B. *sb.* **1.** An inhabitant of Babylon; hence *fig.* †**a.** papist (*obs.*), **b.** astrologer.

1564 *Brief Exam.* *** iij, We dwell not among the Babilonians and Chaldies. **1677** GILPIN *Dæmonol.* (1867) 192 For from good bishops..they are become incurable Babylonians. **1795** SOUTHEY *Lett. fr. Spain* (1799) 76 Here the Babylonian [= Romish Church] walks the street in full dress scarlet.

2. The language of the inhabitants of Babylon.

1870 G. C. SWAYNE *Herodotus* v. 78 It is in three languages—old Persian, Babylonian, and Scythian. **1888** A.

H. SAYCE *Hittites* ii. 23 At that time Babylonian was the international language.

Babylonic (bæbɪˈlɒnɪk), *a.* [ad. L. *Babylōnicus*.] = BABYLONIAN *a.*
1614 SELDEN *Titles Hon.* 154 After the Babylonique captiuitie. **1853** KANE *Grinnell Exp.* xlix. (1856) 467 The terraces of a Babylonic tower.

†**Babyˈlonical**, *a. Obs.* [f. as prec. + -AL¹.] Of or belonging to Babylon; hence *fig.* **a.** Romish, popish, **b.** Babel-like, disorderly, tumultuous.
1535 COVERDALE *Bible* Ded., Much bound..to your grace for delivering us out of our old Babylonical captivity. **1547** *Homilies* I. x. I. (1859) 105 There raigneth all..Babylonicall confusion. **1597** J. PAYNE *Royal Exch.* 38 The Babylonicall extermination by Cyrus.

†**Babyˈlonically**, *adv.* [f. prec. + -LY².] In a Babylonish manner; sumptuously, luxuriously.
1599 NASHE *Lent. Stuffe* in *Harl. Misc.* VI. 162 He is attended upon most Babilonically.

Babylonish (bæbɪˈləʊnɪʃ), *a.* [see -ISH¹.]
1. Of, belonging to, or made at Babylon.
1535 COVERDALE *Josh.* vii. 21 A costly Babilonish [WYCLIF, reed] garment. **1738** WESLEY *Psalms* cxxxvii, Fast by the Babylonish Tide..We dropt our weary Limbs. **1861** *Sat. Rev.* 21 Dec. 645 Babylonish bricks and Assyrian bulls.
2. *fig.* †**a.** Romish, popish (*obs.*); **b.** Babel-like, confused in language.
1590 BARROW in *Confer.* i. 10 The Antichristian yoke of theis Babilonish Bishopps. **1654** GAGE (*title*), A clear Vindication of the..Parochial Ministers of England, from the..injurious nickname of Babylonish. **1663** BUTLER *Hud.* I. i. 93 A Babylonish Dialect, Which learned Pedants much affect. **1816** GILCHRIST *Philos. Etym.* 128 This is the kind of Babylonish lexicography of Johnson's Dictionary, which gives *twenty-four meanings*, or shadows of meaning, to the word *from*.

ˈBabylonism. [f. as prec. + -ISM.]
†**1.** *fig.* Popery. *Obs.*
1610 BP. HALL *Apol. Brownists* 129 They baptize the seed of them who are no members of any visible church. Mere Babylonisme. **1645** [so in PAGITT *Heresiogr.* (1661) 73.]
2. A Babylonian word or phrase.
1883 DELITZSCH in *Athenæum* 25 Aug. 239/2 A good many such 'Babylonisms'..are now to be discovered in Aramaic.

ˈBabylonize, *v. rare.* [f. as prec. + -IZE.] To make Babylonian. Hence **Babylonized** *ppl. a.*
1607 DEKKER *Wh. Babylon* Wks. 1873 II. 229 Fugitiues Whose heartes are Babylonized. **1701** BEVERLEY *Apoc. Quest.* 24 The Babyloniz'd manners of the Jews of Old.

babyˈolatry. *nonce-wd.* [f. BABY *sb.*; cf. *mariolatry*: see -LATRY.]
1846 *Chamb. Jrnl.* Feb. 129 Child-worship, or babyolatry.

babyrouessa, -roussa, obs. ff. BABIROUSSA.

babysh(e, obs. form of BABISH.

babyship (ˈbeɪbɪʃɪp). [f. BABY *sb.* + -SHIP.] **a.** = BABYHOOD. **b.** The personality of a baby.
1617 in MINSHEU. **1648** HERRICK *Hesper.* (1844) II. 48 Is it a trespass, if we three Should wend along his babyship to see? **1693** W. ROBERTSON *Phraseol. Gen.* 193 Babyship or Infancy.

†**bac¹**. *Obs. rare*⁻¹. [App. a corrupt form. Cf. OE. *béaȝ* (ME. *béȝ*, *beigh*) and ON. *baugr*, ring, armilla, etc.] A chaplet.
c **1300** in Wright *Lyric P.* xxv. 70 That thou me havest ben so fre, Thy bac of thornes, thy nayles thre.

‖**bac²** (bæk). [Fr.; see also BACK *sb.*²]
1. A flat-bottomed French ferry-boat; a ferry.
1672 COLES, *Bac*, a ferry. **1753** CHAMBERS *Cycl. Supp.*, *Bac*, in navigation, is used for a praam, or ferry-boat. **1867** in SMYTH *Sailor's Word-bk.* [Cf. 'St. Augustine's *Back*' at Bristol.]
2. In *Brewing* and *Distilling*: see BACK *sb.*²

bac³ (bæk): abbrev. of BACCARAT.
1906 B. VON HUTTEN *What became of Pam* III. x. 293, I know nothing so engrossing..as a game of bac. **1937** KOESTLER *Span. Testament* i. 23 At the Estoril Casino we came across..some playing bac, others trente-et-quarante.

bac-, obs. form of BACK-, BAK-.

‖**bacalao** (bækəˈlɑːəʊ). Also 6–7 **bacalow**, 8 **baccalio, -alao**, 9 **bacallao**. [a. Sp. *bacallao* cod-fish, according to early navigators the native name in Newfoundland or the adjacent mainland.] **a.** Cod-fish. *spec.* dried or salted cod-fish. Also in Portuguese form *bacalhau*.
1555 R. EDEN *New Worlde* III. vi. (1885) 161 Cabot him selfe named those landes *Baccallaos*, bycause that in the seas ther about he found so great multitudes of certeyne bigge fysshes..which thinhabitantes caule Baccallaos. **1598** STOW *Surv.* (Strype 1754) II. v. xvii. 362/2 Merchants trading in Spain and Portugal [export]..Pilchards, Salmon, Poor Jack or Bacalow. **1749** JACKSON *Wealth of Gt. Britain in Ocean* 54 Cod finely wet cured, are much better eating than baccalao. **1762** *Gentl. Mag.* 121 Fishing upon the banks of Newfoundland for baccalao. **1765** *Lond. Chron.* 14 Feb. 160 Large Baccalio and fine old Ling. **1885** *Blackw. Mag.* July 104/2 Consumers of the salted cod or baccalao. **1961** M. MCCARTHY *On the Contrary* (1962) 116 A golden *bacalhau* (dried cod, done with egg yolks, black olives, sauté potatoes, and onions) Portugal. **1962** *Times* 13 Apr. 19/1 *Bacalhau* is as traditional [in Portugal] as the roast beef of England.
b. *bacalao-bird.*
1865 GOSSE *Land & Sea* 44 Guillemots' eggs, in Newfoundland well known by the name of Baccalao-birds' eggs.

Bacardi (bəˈkɑːdɪ). A proprietary name for a West Indian rum produced by the Compania Ron Bacardi, originally in Cuba.
1921 *Double-Dealer* Dec. 245/2 The family gin has given out and eke the family Bacardi. **1924** R. FIRBANK *Prancing Nigger* xi. 84 A little dazed after a Ron Bacardi, he moved away. **1928** H. CRANE *Let.* 27 Mar. (1965) 320 He had completely emptied a quart of Bacardi. **1933** *Official Gaz.* (U.S. Patent Office) 26 Dec. 892/1 Compania Ron Bacardi, S.A., Santiago de Cuba, Cuba... Bacardi. For rum. **1934** *Trade Marks Jrnl.* 5 Sept. 1165 Ron Bacardi Superior.. Rum. Compania Ron Bacardi, Sociedad Anonima (a Corporation organised under the Laws of the Republic of Cuba)..Cuba City, Republic of Cuba; Rum Merchants. **1945** J. B. PRIESTLEY *Three Men in New Suits* v. 77 Some excellent pink Bacardi cocktails. **1962** *Spectator* 16 Mar. 350 Best known of all the dry white rums is Bacardi. **1971** *Bahamas* XXIII. III. 3 4 parts Drambuie 1 part Bacardi rum. **1980** A. BROWNJOHN *Night in Gazebo* v. 36 It has taken Eleven pale ales To her four bacardis-and-coke to bring her to this point of revelation.

bacare, baccare, variants of BACKARE.

bacca (ˈbækə). Also **baccah, baccer.** Colloq. clipped forms of TOBACCO. (Cf. BACCO, BACCY, BACKER.)
1824 J. WIGHT *Mornings at Bow Street* 36 She told him her new lover 'couldn't abide the smell of *baccah*'. **1835** M. H. BARKER *Tough Yarns* 10 He whips out his old quid, flings it into the fire, and we sported a fresh bit o' bacca. **1837** DICKENS in *Bentley's Miscellany* Jan. 62 Are you going to put down pipes... Or trace the progress of crime to 'baccer? **1847** E. BRONTË *Wuthering Heights* II. vii. 128 Joseph's 'bacca pipe is poison. **1920** D. H. LAWRENCE *Touch & Go* I. i. 16 They'll give you plenty to eat..and a bit of bacca.

†**ˈbaccalaur, -or.** *Obs. rare.* [ad. med.L. *baccalaureus*, corrupt form of *baccalarius* (see BACHELOR), with some imaginary reference to *bacca lauri*, the laurel berry.] = BACHELOR (Academic).
1661 RAY *Three Itin.* II. 159 Students..of the third [year] they call baccalors [at Glasgow]. **1695** KENNETT *Par. Antiq.* ix. 619 John Barber, Baccalaur of both Laws.

baccalaurean (bækəˈlɔːrɪən), *a.* [f. med.L. *baccalaure-us* + -AN.] Of or befitting a bachelor.
1845 *Bachel. Albany* (1854) 30 Precision and taste rigidly baccalaurean. **1849** J. BROWN *Horæ Subs.* Ser. I. 18 That quiet comfortable baccalaurian habitation.

baccalaureate (bækəˈlɔːrɪət). [ad. med.L. *baccalaureātus*, f. *baccalaureus*: see prec. and -ATE.]
1. a. The University degree of bachelor.
1625–49 *Sc. Acts Chas. I* (1814) V. 73 (JAM.) Degries of baccalawreatt, licentiat, and doctorat. **1702** C. MATHER *Magn. Chr.* IV. Introd. (1852) 25 The degrees of a baccalaureate and a doctorate in divinity. **1849** *Catal. Wesleyan Univ.* 22 (B. H. Hall, *College Words*), The Seniors will be examined for the Baccalaureate, four weeks before Commencement. **1895** RASHDALL *Univ. Middle Ages* I. 210 The institution of the Baccalaureate or pupil-teachership. **1907** *Elem. Sch. Teacher* Mar. 372 All of these four baccalaureates extend practically the same privileges to those who have obtained them.
b. *international baccalaureate*, an examination offered by educational institutions in many countries, intended to qualify successful candidates for higher education in their own country or abroad; the diploma or qualification awarded for passing this.
1970 *Times Educ. Suppl.* 27 Feb. 15/4 The first international baccalaureate examination will be held this year with 100 candidates from four schools. **1978** *Times* 14 Feb. 3/1 Sixth-formers at a comprehensive school will for the first time be able to start studying next autumn for an international baccalaureate that will qualify them for entry to any university in the world. **1978** *New Society* 16 Feb. 373/1 There is already a tried and tested examination that overcomes many of the faults of A levels—the International Baccalaureate. **1984** *N.Y. Times* 1 Jan. VIII. 5/1 Francis Lewis has an international baccalaureate program in Geneva, and a math and science institute associated with IBM.
2. = BACHELOR. (By Longfellow used *metri gratiâ*, perh. with reference to *laureate*.)
1696 in PHILLIPS. **1868** LONGF. *Dante's Par.* XXIV. 46 [He] as baccalaureate arms himself.
3. *attrib.* **baccalaureate degree**; quasi-*adj.* in **baccalaureate-sermon**: a farewell discourse delivered to a graduating class in some American colleges.
1864 O. W. HOLMES *Soundings fr. Atl.* 72 A baccalaureate sermon of President Hopkins. **1884** *Nonconf.* 10 July 667/1 Baccalaureate sermons are now being preached by the most eminent clergymen. **1891** D. C. GILMAN *Johns Hopkins Univ.* 66 The manifold forms in which the baccalaurate [*sic*] degree is conferred. **1968** *Globe & Mail* (Toronto) 3 Feb. B7/1 (Advt.), Registered Nurses or Registered Psychiatric Nurses with baccalaureate degree or higher, and considerable experience in nursing education.

baccalio, obs. form of BACALAO.

‖**baccara, -at** (bakərɑː). [a. F. *baccara*.] A game at cards played for money between a banker and several punters.
1866 *Daily Tel.* 13 Jan. 5/2 Baccarat, bad luck, and bankruptcy. **1883** OUIDA *Wanda* I. 190 You must not steal: you may beggar your friend at baccara. **1884** *Law Times Rep.* 30 Aug. 808/2 Baccarat, being a game of cards other than a game of mere skill, was an 'unlawful game.'

baccate (ˈbækeɪt), *a. Bot.* [ad. L. *baccātus*.]
1. Bearing berries; bacciferous, berried.
1836 in LOUDON *Encycl. Plants* Gloss.
2. Of the nature of a berry, berry-like.
1830 LINDLEY *Nat. Syst. Bot.* Introd. 31 The fruit of all Grossulaceæ is baccate.

ˈbaccated, *ppl. a.* [f. L. *baccātus*, *bācātus*, set with pearls, f. *bacca* berry, pearl: see -ATE³.]
†**1.** Set with pearls. *Obs.*
1731 in BAILEY.
2. Berried, berry-bearing.
1731 in BAILEY.

baccato- (bæˈkeɪtəʊ), comb. form of BACCATE, as in ***baccato-tuberculous***, with berry-like tubercles.
1852 DANA *Crust.* I. 203 Carapax..baccato-tuberculous.

Bacchanal (ˈbækənəl), *a.* and *sb.* Forms: 6 **bacchinall**, 7 **bachinal, bachanal(e, -nel, backenal**, 6– **bacchanal**. [ad. L. *bacchānālis*, also *băccā-*, *bācā-*, f. *Bacchus*, Gr. Βάκχος god of wine.]
A. *adj.*
1. Of or pertaining to Bacchus or his worship.
1550 NICOLLS *Thucyd.* 50 (R.) Unto whom was yearely celebrated the feast bacchanal. *a* **1789** BURNEY *Hist. Mus.* I. 61 Styles of Melopœia; (1) the Dithyrambic or Bacchanal.
2. Indulging in drunken revelry; riotously drunken, roystering.
1711 SHAFTESB. *Charac.* (1737) III. 364 A bacchinal nymph. **1762** FALCONER *To Dk. York* 144 Exulting with bacchanal rage. **1818** BYRON *Ch. Har.* IV. Ded., The bacchanal roar of the songs of exultation.
B. *sb.*
1. A priest or priestess, votary, or devotee of Bacchus; a Bacchant or Bacchante.
1590 SHAKS. *Mids. N.* V. i. 48 The riot of the tipsie Bachanals. **1594** NASHE *Unfort. Trav.* 85 Like a franticke Bacchinall, she stampt. **1853** ROBERTSON *Serm.* Ser. III. ix. 113 To them the bacchanal appeared a being half inspired.
2. A drunken reveller.
1812 BYRON *Ch. Har.* I. vi, And now Childe Harold.. from his fellow bacchanals would flee. **1841** H. SMITH *Moneyed Man* II. ix. 311, I detest myself, degraded bacchanal as I am.
3. (Usually *pl.*) A festival in honour of Bacchus. [L. *Bacchanalia*.]
1616 in BULLOKAR. **1636** HEALEY *Theophrast.* To Rdr., These were preparatives to those more solemne Bacchanals or Corrivals [? *for* Convivals]. **1705** STANHOPE *Paraphr.* III. 544 Intemperance and Excess in the Heathen Bacchanals was esteemed an Act of religious Joy.
4. An occasion of drunken revelry; an orgy.
1536 LATIMER *2nd Serm. bef. Convoc.* I. 52 The solemn and nocturnal bacchanals. **1673** *Lady's Call.* II. i. §23 That a marriage-day is but a kind of bacchanal, a more licens'd avow'd revel. **1795** BURKE *Regic. Peace* IX. 118 At their debauches and bacchanals.
fig. **1860** SIR T. MARTIN *Horace* 110 Where mists and snows..Hold reckless bacchanal.
5. A dance or song in honour of Bacchus.
1606 SHAKS. *Ant. & Cl.* II. vii. 110 Shall we daunce now the Egyptian Backenals? **1697** DRYDEN *Virg. Georg.* II. 693 Where Bacchanals are sung by Spartan Maids. **1780** COWPER *Table T.* 602 Genius danced a bacchanal.
6. A scene of revelry painted or sculptured.
1753 CHAMBERS *Cycl. Supp.*, *Bacchanalia*, *Bacchanals*, pictures or basso relievos, whereon the feast is represented, consisting chiefly of dancings, nudities, and the like. **1762** H. WALPOLE *Vertue's Anecd. Paint.* (1786) III. 32 A Bacchanal of..naked boys, sitting on a tub, the wine running out.

‖**Bacchanalia** (bækəˈneɪlɪə), *sb. pl.* [L., neut. pl. of *bacchānālis*: see prec. Formerly occas. treated in Eng. as sing., with pl. *-as*.]
1. The festival held in honour of Bacchus.
1753 CHAMBERS *Cycl. Supp.*, Tacitus gives an elegant description of the Bacchanalia. **1863** HAYDN *Dict. Dates* s.v., In Rome the Bacchanalia were suppressed, 186 B.C.
2. Drunken revelry; a tippling bout, an orgy.
1633 MARMYON *Fine Comp.* II. iv, Drinks sack, and keeps his Bacchanalias. **1684** EVELYN *Mem.* (1857) II. 210 The squibs and bacchanalia of the Lord Mayor's Show. **1880** L. WALLACE *Ben-Hur* 283 The morning after the bacchanalia.
†**3.** A drinking-song: cf. BACCHANAL *sb.* 5. *Obs.*
1651 EVELYN *Char. Eng.* Wks. (1805) 158 In taverns, chanting their dithrambicks and bestial bacchanalias.
†**4.** = BACCHANAL 6. *Obs.*
1662 J. BARGRAVE *Pope Alex. VII* (1867) 117 A bachanalia piece, dugg out of the temple of Bacchus.

Bacchanalian (bækəˈneɪlɪən), *a.* and *sb.* Also 7 **bachan-**, 8 **bacchin-**. [f. L. *bacchānāli-s*, BACCHANAL + -AN.] **A.** *adj.*
1. Of, connected with, or relating to Bacchanals.
1622 *Paradox* in *Harl. Misc.* I. 267 Scarce sufficient to make a Bacchanalian sacrifice. **1623** COCKERAM, *Bacchanalean frowes*, Women-Bacchus-Priests. **1816** *Gentl. Mag.* LXXXVI. 4 An antique vase, with Bacchanalian masks.
2. Characterized by, connected with, or given to drunken revelry; riotously drunken, roystering.

1565 STOW *Chron.* (R.) Shamelesse drunken bacchanalian women. **1609** DEKKER *Gul's Hornebk.* (1812) 21 Or else, haunting taverns, desires to take the bacchanalian degree. **1750** JOHNSON *Rambl.* No. 71 ¶6 We are importuned by the bacchanalian writers to lay hold on the present hour. **1878** H. STANLEY *Dark Cont.* I. viii. 172 Began to chant in bacchanalian tones, a song that was tipsily discordant.

B. *sb.* A bacchanal, a drunken reveller, a tippler.

1617 ASSHETON *Jrnl.* (1848) 50 All this morning we plaid the bacchanalians. *a* **1704** T. BROWN *To Yng. Lady* Wks. 1730 I. 66 Let Bacchanalians.. Hunt out champagne. **1870** ANDERSON *Missions Amer. Bd.* II. iv. 28 In all the disorder of a troop of bacchanalians.

Bacchaˈnalianism, ˈ**Bacchanalism**, bacchanalian practices, drunken revelry. **Bacchaˈnalianly** *adv.*, with drunken revelry (in Webster 1864).

1855 *Scot. Rev.* 267 To lend the power of his genius to bacchanalianism. **1858** LADY WALLACE *Fredk. Gt.* II. 214 Four years of bacchanalism.. which the Count had passed.

Bacchanalization (ˌbækənælaɪˈzeɪʃən). [f. next: see -ATION.] A turning into drunken revel.

1798 W. TAYLOR in *Month. Rev.* XXVII. 572 A bacchanalization of the eucharist.

Bacchanalize (ˈbækənəlaɪz), *v.* [a. F. *bacchanaliser* (Cotgr.): see BACCHANAL and -IZE.]

1. *intr.* To act as a bacchanal, indulge in revelry.

1656 BLOUNT *Glossogr.*, *Bacchanalize*, to rage, play mad pranks, fare like mad men. **1851** S. JUDD *Margaret* II. ii. (1871) 196 Saints bacchanalizing.

2. *trans.* To turn into drunken revelry; cf. prec.

Bacchant (ˈbækənt), *sb.* (and *a.*) [ad. L. *Bacchānt-em*, sb. (in L. fem. only: see next) f. pr. pple. of *bacchāri*, ad. Gr. βακχά-ειν to celebrate with frenzied gestures the festival of Bacchus.]

A. *sb.* A priest, priestess, or inspired votary of Bacchus; *hence*, a drunken reveller, roysterer.

1699 BOYER *Fr. Dict.* (1759), *Bacchante*, a Bacchant, a Priestess of Bacchus. **1774** *Westm. Mag.* II. 428 Bacchants reeling to the tipsy song. **1853** TRENCH *Proverbs* 134 The thyrsus-bearers are many, but the bacchants few.

B. as *adj.* Bacchus-worshipping, wine-loving.

1800 MOORE *Anacreon* iv. 15 Many a rose-lipped bacchant maid Is culling clusters in their shade. **1821** BYRON *Juan* III. xliii, Over his shoulder, with a Bacchant air, Presented the o'erflowing cup.

Bacchante (bəˈkɑːnt, -æ-, ˈbækənt, bəˈkæntiː), *sb.* (and *a.*) [a. F. *bacchante*, ad. L. *Bacchāntem*: see prec. The first pronunciation is after the Fr.; the third after It. (etc.) *baccante*, favoured perhaps by the fact that the plural (of both genders) is often *Bacchantes* (-ˈæntiːz) after L.]

A. *sb.* A priestess or female votary of Bacchus.

1797 HOLCROFT tr. *Stolberg's Trav.* III. lxxvii. (ed. 2) 170 She capered with the intoxication of a Bacchante. **1811** L. HAWKINS *C'tess & Gertr.* I. 313 Whether male or female, a bacchante, or a Silenus. **1847** LONGF. *Ev.* II. 2 To follow or guide the revel of frenzied Bacchantes.

B. *attrib.* as *adj.*: cf. BACCHANT.

1821 BYRON *Juan* IV. xcii, A Bacchante blooming visage. **1868** H. LEE *B. Godfrey* l. 283 Emmot laughed with her bacchante air.

Bacchantic (bəˈkæntɪk), *a.* [f. BACCHANT(E + -IC.] Of or pertaining to the devotees of Bacchus.

1845 HIRST *Poems* 97 With Bacchantic figures glowing. **1878** *N. Amer. Rev.* CXXVII. 53 Bacchantic dances.

bacchar, baccar (ˈbækə(r)). *Bot.* [a. L. *bacc(h)ar*, *bacc(h)aris* (also used in Eng.), a. Gr. βάκκαρις, βάκχαρις ('a Lydian word'), a plant with an aromatic root yielding oil.] A plant variously identified by botanists. (*Baccharis* is now applied to an American genus of *Compositæ*.)

1551 TURNER *Herbal* (1568) 57 a, Baccharis.. in englishe sage of hierusalem. **1601** HOLLAND *Pliny* II. 85 Bacchar is named by some Rustick-Nard. **1616** SURFL. & MARKH. *Countr. Farm* 144 Against the colicke: take Asarum bacchar. **1753** CHAMBERS *Cycl. Supp.*, *Baccharis*, *Bacchar*.. commonly called plowman's spikenard. **1855** SINGLETON *Virgil* I. 27 Her gadding ivies everywhere with baccaris, Shall earth unbosom. *Ibid.* 47 With baccar binding brow.

† **Baˈcchation.** *Obs.*—⁰ [ad. L. *bacchātiōn-em*, n. of action f. *bacchāri*: see BACCHANT and -TION.] 'Riot, drunkenness.' Blount *Glossogr.* 1656.

† **Baˈcchean**, *a. Obs.*—⁰ [f. L. *Bacchē-us*, a. Gr. Βάκχειος + -AN.] 'Belonging to Bacchus, drunken, sottish.' Blount *Glossogr.* 1656.

bacchiac (bæˈkaɪæk), *a.* [ad. L. *bacchīacus*, Gr. βακχειακός.] Of the nature of a BACCHIUS; consisting of or characterized by bacchii.

1766 R. LOWTH *Larger Confut. Bp. Hare* 36 Bacchiac and Cretic Feet. **1855** F. A. PALEY *Æschylus* 204/2 The bacchiac metre also suggests τί ταῦτα for τί τῷδε. **1857** E. S. PARRY *Terentii Comœd.* p. lix, Cretic and bacchiac measures.

Bacchian (ˈbækɪən), *a.* [f. L. *Bacchi-us*, a. Gr. Βάκχιος + -AN.] Having the attributes of Bacchus.

1850 LEITCH *Müller's Anc. Art* §203 *note*, Antinous.. is sometimes also represented as Bacchian, sitting on a panther.

Bacchic (ˈbækɪk), *a.* (*sb.*) [ad. L. *Bacchicus*, a. Gr. Βακχικός of Bacchus. Cf. F. *Bacchique*.]

A. *adj.* **1.** Of or pertaining to Bacchus or his worship.

1669 GALE *Crt. Gentiles* I. II. iii. 30 The Bacchic Music was famous throughout Asia. **1736** STUKELEY *Palæogr. Sacra* 39 (T.) The bacchick orgia were celebrated on the tops of hills. **1843** MRS. H. GRAY *Sepul. Etruria* iv. 189 Gracefully twined with branches of bacchic ivy.

2. Inspired with the frenzy of a votary of Bacchus, frenzied; riotously drunken, roystering, jovial.

1699 BURNET 39 *Art.* xxiii. (1700) 255 Women Priests.. filled with a Bacchick Fury. **1865** MISS MULOCH *Chr. Mistake* 17 He.. then broke into a broad, genial laugh, quite Bacchic. **1874** MAHAFFY *Soc. Life Greece* xi. 330 *note*, Like Bacchic maidens who draw milk and honey from the rivers.

† **B.** (*absol.* as) *sb.* A drinking-song. *Obs.*

1676 ETHEREDGE *Man of Mode* IV. i. (1684) 57 Let us have the new Bachique. *O. Bell.* That's a hard word! What does it mean, Sir? *Med.* A Catch, or drinking Song.

† ˈ**Bacchical**, *a. Obs.* = prec.

1663 J. SPENCER *Prophecies* (1665) 78 They raised up a kind of Bacchical Enthusiasm.

‖ **bacchius** (bəˈkaɪəs). [L., a. Gr. βακχεῖος (sc. πούς).] A metrical foot of three syllables, one short and two long.

1589 PUTTENHAM *Eng. Poesie* (Arb.) 134 For your foote bacchius of a short and two long ye haue.. *rĕnoūncīng*, *rĕpēntānce*, *ĕnūrīng*. **1870** JEBB *Sophocles' Electra* (ed. 2) 49/2 A bacchius (ὃς ἀμφὰκ) replacing the molossus.

‖ **Bacchus** (ˈbækəs). [L., a. Gr. Βάκχος.] The god of wine; *hence*, wine, intoxicating liquor. ***son of Bacchus***: a tippler.

c **1496** DUNBAR *Gold. Terge* 124 Bacus, the gladder of the table. *c* **1640** WALLER *Batt. Summer Isl.* 17 The sweet palmettoes a new Bacchus yield. **1747** *Scheme Equip. Men of War* 36 The more corpulent Sons of Bacchus.. might have Easy-Chairs. **1823** BYRON *Island* II. xi, The palm.. Within whose bosom infant Bacchus broods.

b. *Comb.* **Bacchus-bole**; ***Bacchus-like***.

1725 BRADLEY *Fam. Dict.*, *Bacchus-Bole*, a Flower that is not tall, but a very full, large, broad-leav'd Flower, being of a sad light Purple. **1600** *Witt's Recr.* in *Southey's Common-pl. Bk.* Ser. II. 314 They mean, then, Bacchus-like to feed.

bacciferous (bækˈsɪfərəs), *a.* [f. L. *baccifer* (f. *bacca* berry + *-fer* bearing) + -OUS: cf. F. *baccifère*.] Berry-bearing, producing berries.

1656 in BLOUNT *Glossogr.* **1668** WILKINS *Real Char.* 96 Herbs.. Bacciferous; whose seeds are included in a juicy pulpe. **1862** J. WILSON *Farming* 48 The potato.. is a bacciferous herb.

bacciform (ˈbæksɪfɔːm), *a.* [ad. mod.L. *bacciformis*, f. *bacca* berry: see -FORM. Cf. F. *bacciforme*.] Berry-shaped.

1839 in HOOPER *Med. Dict.*

baccivorous (bækˈsɪvərəs), *a.* [f. L. *bacca* berry + *-vorus* devouring: cf. F. *baccivore*.] Berry-eating, living chiefly on berries.

1661 LOVELL *Hist. Anim. & Min.* Introd., Birds which are .. baccivorous, as the Thrush. [In BAILEY, and mod. Dicts.]

bacco, baccy, vulgar abbreviations of TOBACCO.

1792 W. B. STEVENS *Jrnl.* 9 July (1965) 36 Thou hast got a Crescent like my 'Bacco Box'. **1793** C. DIBDIN in *Britannic Mag.* I. 249/1 The tender motto written fair Upon his 'bacco-box he views. **1818** R. WILBRAHAM *Gloss. Cheshire* 9 *Bacco*, tobacco. **1833** MARRYAT *P. Simple* (1863) 9 'You must larn to chaw baccy.' **1853** MRS. GASKELL *Cranford* xiii. 249 But the 'bacco, and the other things ——. **1859** T. HUGHES *Scouring White Horse* i. 8 Your bacchy's nearly out, Dick. **1860** *All Y. Round* No. 57. 161 His wife has found his 'bacco-box. **1906** KIPLING *Puck of Pook's Hill* 251 Five and twenty ponies, Trotting through the dark—Brandy for the Parson, 'Baccy for the Clerk. **1933** 'G. ORWELL' *Down & Out* xxvi. 188 [Irish tramp speaking] Dere's sixpennorth o' good baccy here!

† **bace.** *Obs.* [Cf. Sw. *bas* beating, flogging, *basa* to beat, flog, also Da. *bask* stripe, blow, *baske* to beat, strike, and mod.Sc. *baiss* to beat, drub. (Jam.)] A blow; a drubbing.

a **1560** ROLLAND *Crt. Venus* iv. 678 Swyith pak.. or ȝour bak beir a bace.

bace, bacen, obs. forms of BASE, BAKEN.

bach (bætʃ), *sb.*¹ [Shortened f. BACHELOR 4 a.] **1.** *U.S. slang.* A bachelor; ***old bach***, a confirmed bachelor. Also phr. ***to keep bach*** for earlier ***to keep bachelor's hall*** (cf. HALL *sb.* 11) = BACH *v.*

1855 *Knickerbocker* XLV. 158 The President was an 'old bach.' of some sixty-five summers. **1857** W. CHANDLESS *Visit Salt Lake* II. vi. 236 Mormons look upon a 'bach' with great suspicion.. because they consider all men should marry. **1878** I. L. BIRD *Lady's Life Rocky Mts.* (1879) ix. 157 A cabin.. where two brothers and 'a hired man' were 'keeping bach'. **1883** E. EGGLESTON *Hoosier School-Boy* xvi. 106 Don't you know.. any place where we could keep 'bach' together? **1904** W. N. HARBEN *Georgians* 188, I.. thought now was the time fer me, old bach' that I am, to.. show them ladies I'd been about.

2. *N.Z.* Also **batch.** **a.** A makeshift hut, usu. one in which a man living alone fends for himself. **b.** Now esp. a small house at the seaside or at a holiday resort.

1927 J. DEVANNY *Old Savage* 100 Bob knocked up a bunk in Fletcher's bach. **1938** F. S. ANTHONY in D. M. Davin *N.Z. Short Stories* (1953) 218, I don't wonder he comes over to my batch so often—he does get a little decent cleanliness there. **1940** F. SARGESON *Man & Wife* (1944) 29 There were a few holiday baches but they were empty now that it was well on into the autumn. **1957** J. FRAME *Owls do Cry* vi. 26 The Withers haven't a week-end bach. **1957** I. A. GORDON in *N.Z. Listener* 22 Nov. 4/3 From being a mere shed, the bach has become a place at the seaside, and today many a bach has a refrigerator and wall-to-wall carpets.

Bach (bɑːx), *sb.*² The surname of the German composer Johann Sebastian *Bach* (1685–1750), applied *attrib.* to a type of trumpet suitable for the performance of his trumpet parts.

1898 G. B. SHAW *Our Theatres in Nineties* (1932) III. 282 A whole battery of Bach trumpets. **1938** *Oxf. Compan. Music* 960/1 The Bach trumpet in A has generally given place to a shorter instrument in D.

‖ **bach** (bax), *sb.*³ [W., lit. 'little'.] A term of endearment common in Wales and the border counties, freq. following a personal name: dear, little one, friend.

1889 A. J. ELLIS *On Early Eng. Pronunc.* V. 363 Won't the old fellow learn her not to do it again, the bach! **1916** C. EVANS *Capel Sion* iii. 40 'A wanton bitch you are.' 'Dennis bach, don't say!' **1927** R. DAVIES *Withered Root* II. v. 97 Now Philip bach, don't think and talk so much. Let Reuben read you some book or something. **1936** H. VAUGHAN *Harvest Home* I. viii. 53 'Are you hurted terrible bad, Ifor bach?' she asked, stooping over the child. **1955** J. BINGHAM *Paton Street Case* ii. 42 What is the matter, Dai, *bach*? Why do you shiver in this weather? **1961** E. WILLIAMS *George* vi. 75 Look in your book, Georgie bach. **1971** 'A. BURGESS' *MF* xiv. 160 How different your voice sounds tonight, *bach*. **1986** R. W. JONES *Saving Grace* i. 10 No shortage of cash there, bach.

bach (bætʃ), *v. N. Amer.*, *Austral.*, and *N.Z. colloq.* Also **batch.** [f. prec.] *intr.* Usu. of a man: to live as a bachelor; to live alone and do one's own cooking and housekeeping. Also with *it*.

a. *N. Amer.*

1870 *Repub. Daily Jrnl.* (Lawrence, Kans.) 29 Jan. (D.A.), They 'bach'. **1878** I. L. BIRD *Lady's Life Rocky Mts.* (1879) ix. 156 The men don't like 'baching', as it is called in the wilds—*i.e.* 'doing for themselves'. **1888** *Century Mag.* Jan. 412/2 He had always 'bached it' (lived as a bachelor). **1898** *Lett. fr. Canada* vii. in *Times* 22 Nov. 6/1 'To batch' upon the prairies represents perhaps the *minimum* of pleasure in existence. **1927** P. H. PEARSON *Prairie Vikings* 13 For two years they 'bached' as huntsmen along the creek banks.

b. *Australasian.*

1898 R. RADCLYFFE *Wealth & Wild Cats* viii. 71, I had a happy time at Yalgoo, 'batching' with the son of a well-known brewer and M.P. **1900** H. LAWSON *Over Sliprails* 45, I hurried home to the tent—I was batching with a carpenter. **1905** C. CLYDE *Pagan's Love* ii. 26 You would live in a cheap lodging-house or batch with another girl. **1930** *Bulletin* (Sydney) 19 Feb. 23/1, I allus reckoned that I'd be a batchin' all me days. **1938** F. S. ANTHONY *Me & Gus* ix. 53 He batched in a tin shanty for years. **1952** J. CLEARY *Sundowners* iv. 272 Where's the rest of the household? Are you batching? **1952** R. FINLAYSON *Schooner came to Atia* x. 56 If you're prepared to bach on your own.

bacha, earlier form of *basha*, BASHAW.

Bachanal, etc., obs. forms of BACCHANAL, etc.

Bacharach (ˈbaxərax, ˈbækəræk). Also 7 **Back-rac(k, -rag, Baccharach, Bachrag, -rach.** A town on the Rhine giving its name to a wine formerly much esteemed.

c **1620** FLETCH & MASS. *Begg. Bush* v. ii, My fire-works and flap-dragons and good back-rack. **1656** BLOUNT *Glossogr.* s.v., Wines which are made there, and therefore called Bach-rag or Bacharach; vulgarly, Rhenish wines. **1678** BUTLER *Hud.* III. iii. 300 Stoutly overcome With Bachrach. **1820** SCOTT *Abbot* xv, Bacharac, of the first vintage. **1851** LONGF. *Gold. Leg.* 171 A draught from the noble Bacharach cask.

bachare, obs. form of BAKER.

† **bache.** *Obs.* Also 3 bæch, bæcch(e, 9 -bach, -batch. [Origin doubtful. Possibly a dialect form of **becch*, *betch*, answering to an OE. **bęcc*, = ON. *bekkr*, Eng. BECK:—OTeut. **bakjo-z*, cognate with OE *bęce*:—OTeut. **baki-z*, brook, rivulet, stream. The transference of meaning from *stream* to *stream-valley* would be parallel to the north Eng. and Lowland Sc. use of *-burn*, *-water*, in proper names, for the whole river-vale or dale.] The vale of a stream or rivulet.

a **1000** in Kemble *Cod. Dipl.* III. 380 Of ðām æcere in cærsa bæc [*printed* bæt], of ðām bæce in pipan. ? *a* **1200** Notes to LAYAMON III. 447 At Clent in Cu-bache [Lat. interp. *In Clent, in Convalle Bovina*]. **1205** LAY. 757 [He] ferde æfter ane bache.. wes þe wei holh & long; [**1250**] þe cleues weren stronge. *Ibid.* 2596 He bicom in a bæch þer he bale funde. *Ibid.* 21776 Of dalen& of dunen, & of bæcchen deopen. *c* **1305** *St. Kenelm* 244 in *E.E.P.* (1862) 54 Coubache me clipede þis valeye & ȝut me doþ also: In Coubache þis holi bodi lay wel menie a ȝer. *Ibid.* 289 Vnder þe þorn of Coubage. **1393** LANGLAND *P. Pl.* C. VIII. 159 Bote blostered forth as bestes, ouer baches and hulles. **1494**

FABYAN VI. clviii. 147 At Clent in Cowbacch.. whiche is to meane in Englysshe nowe vsyd, at Clent in Cow vale. **1884** J. AMPHLETT (in *letter*) The deep vale in which St. Kenelm's chapel is situated, is now called *Clatterbach* (-batch). In two other stream-vales, east of it, are fields called *Withey Batch*, and *Mare Batch*.

bachelor (ˈbætʃələ(r)). Forms: 3-6 **bacheler**, 3-7 **-iler**, 4-5 **-ilere**, **-iller**, **-illier**, **bachler(e**, **-elere**, 5- **-ylere**, **baculere**, 5-6 **bachelar**, 6 **batchellour**, **-elar**, **baccheIaure**, 6-7 **batcheler**, **-ellor**, **-eller**, **batchler**, 7 **bachelaur**, **-elour**, 7-8 **batchelour**, 8 **bachellour**, 5- **bachelor**. [a. OF. *bacheler* = Pr. *bacalar*, It. *baccalare*:—L. type *baccalāris, of doubtful origin. The later F. *bachelier* is corrupted in the termination, as is the 16th c. Eng. *bachelour*, *bachelor*: cf. ANCESTOR *sb.*, and see -OR. The original meaning being uncertain, the sense-development is also doubtful.

Of med.L. *baccalāris* only a few late instances occur (in sense 1), which might be from the mod. langs. (see Du Cange, *Bacularis*). It was, however, prob. connected with *baccalāria*, a division of land, of which the size and nature varied at different times, and with the adjectives *baccalarius*, *-aria*, applied in 8th c. to rustics male and female who worked for the *colonus* or tenant of a *mansus*. (See Deloche, *Cartulaire de Beaulieu* Introd. éclairc. xxii.) But the precise relation of **baccalāris* to these words, and its subsequent history are still uncertain. Still more doubtful is its derivation: *baccalaria* is with some probability referred to *bacca*, late L. and Romanic for *vacca* cow, through **baccālis* (cf. *ovīlis* from *ovis* sheep), in which case it might be 'grazing farm,' and *baccalarius* one employed on it, the assistant of a *colonus* who had not a *mansus* of his own; Littré (without accounting for the sense) suggests Celtic *bachall* stick (a. L. *baculus*); the Welsh *bach* 'little' must be definitely discarded, its old Celtic form being *bicc-* or *becc-*, Irish *becc*. (Thurneysen.)]

1. a. A young knight, not old enough, or having too few vassals, to display his own banner, and who therefore followed the banner of another; a novice in arms. [On this sense was founded the conjectural etymology of *bas chevalier*.]

1297 R. GLOUC. 453 Syreȝong bacheler.. þow art strong & corageus. *a* **1300** *Cursor M.* 8541 He was a borli bachelere, In alþat werld had he na pere. *c* **1386** CHAUCER *Sqrs. T.* 16 Yong, fressh, strong, and in Armes desirous, As any Bacheler [*v.r.* bachiler(e, -elere, -illier] of al his hous. **1415** *Pol. Poems* (1859) II. 125 Passe we all now in fere, duke, erle, and bachelere. *c* **1500** *Partenay* 1925 This knight is A worthi baculere. **1523** LD. BERNERS *Froiss.* I. ccIxiv. 390 Let sir Johan Chandos do by himselfe, sythe he is but a bacheler. **1818** HALLAM *Mid. Ages* (1872) I. 195 Vavassors who obtained knighthood were commonly styled bachelors.

b. Hence, ***Knight Bachelor***, a knight of the lowest but most ancient order; the full title of a gentleman who has been knighted (without belonging to any one of the specially named 'orders').

1609 tr. *Sir T. Smith's Commw. Eng.* 25 He [a banneret] being before a batcheler knight, is now of a higher degree. **1614** SELDEN *Titles Hon.* 336 These Knights.. were anciently call'd Baccalaurei, or Bachelors. **1809** TOMLINS *Law Dict.*, *Knight-bachelor* a simple knight, and not knight-banneret, or *knight of the bath*. **1883** *Whitaker's Alm.* 108 *Knights Bachelors*: a list of those Gentlemen [in number 278] who have received the honour of knighthood.

†**2.** A junior or inferior member, or 'yeoman,' of a trade-guild, or City Company. *Obs.*

(In London, their position and functions seem to have varied at different times, and in different Companies; in later times Bachelors were appointed only for ceremonial occasions, chiefly when one of the Company was chosen Lord Mayor, their duty being 'to serve in foynes and budge' on Lord Mayor's Day. So in Bye Laws of Grocers' Company of 1711.)

[**1390** *Archives of Grocers' Comp.* 76 Eslieuxz Mesteres dez Grocers Roberd Peper et Herri Hatton Bacheleres]. **1427** in Heath *Grocers' Comp.* (1869) 5 Diuerse persones ikallyd Bacheleris. **1533** WRIOTHESLEY *Chron.* (1875) I. 18 A barge also of Batchlers of the Majors crafte. **1691** BLOUNT *Law Dict.* s.v., Every Company of the Twelve, consists of a Master, two Wardens, the Livery, (which are Assistants in Matters of Council, or at the least, such as the Assistants are chosen out of) and the Bachelors, who are yet but in expectance of Dignity among them, and have their Function only in attendance upon the Master and Wardens. **1809** TOMLINS *Law Dict.* s.v., The *bachelors*, in other companies called the *yeomanry*.

3. a. One who has taken the first or lowest degree at a university, who is not yet a *master* of the Arts. (In this use, a woman may now be Bachelor of Arts, etc.)

[In this sense, latinized as *baccalarius*, subsequently altered by a pun or word-play to *baccalaureus* as if connected with *bacca lauri* laurel berry, which has sometimes been gravely given as the 'etymology.']

1362 LANGL. *P. Pl.* A. Prol. 90, I sauh þer Bisschops Bolde and Bachilers of diuyn. *c* **1386** CHAUCER *Frankl. T.* 398 His felawe.. was that tyme a Bacheler of lawe. **1577** HARRISON *England* I. II. iii. 79 They ascend higher unto the estate of batchelers of art after foure yeares. **1614** SELDEN *Titles Hon.* 55 *Dominus* is now familiar for *Sir* to euery Batcheler of Art in the Schools. **1673** RAY *Journ. Low C.* 18 Every Batcheler is called Doctissimus. **1843** SIR J. COLERIDGE in *Arnold's Life & Corr.* I. i. 9 Of the scholars several were bachelors.

†**b.** *transf.* An inexperienced person, a novice. *Obs.*

1604 T. WRIGHT *Passions Mind* IV. i. 114 Some men will dispute.. about matters exceeding their capacitie.. I haue heard these batchellors hold talke.. wilfully and obstinatly in matters of Philosophie and Diuinitie.

4. a. An unmarried man (of marriageable age).

c **1386** CHAUCER *Merch. T.* 34 Bacheleris [*v.r.* bachilers, -elerys, -elers, -illiers] haue often peyne and wo. *c* **1450** *Songs & Carols* (1847) 35 If thou be a bachelar, And bryngest hom a wyfe. **1547** J. HARRISON *Exhort. Scottes* 223 She was to olde a mayde for so yonge a bachelar. **1553** T. WILSON *Rhet.* 24 The syngle lyfe of Bacchelaures. **1607** DEKKER *Northw. Hoe* IV. Wks. 1873 III. 53 His wife!.. I haue heard him sweare he was a bachiler. **1750** JOHNSON *Rambl.* No. 18 ¶5 The unsettled, thoughtless condition of a batchelor. **1856** F. PAGET *Owlet Owlst.* 151 A series of bachelor-incumbents. **1875** WHITNEY *Life Lang.* ix. 156 Nursery.. dialect, offensive to the ears of old bachelors.

b. ***bachelor's wife***: the ideal wife of which a bachelor theorizes or dreams.

1562 J. HEYWOOD *Prov. & Epigr.* (1867) 61 Bachelers wiues, and maides children be well tought. **1726** VANBRUGH *Prov. Husb.* I. i, Ay! ay!.. Bachelors' wives, indeed, are finely governed. **1854** H. MILLER *Sch. & Schm.* (1858) 503 The 'bachelor's wife'.. occupies a large place in our literature, as the mistress of all the poets who ever wrote on love without actually experiencing it.

c. *transf.* One of the young male fur-seals which are kept away from the breeding-grounds by the adult bulls. (These are the seals which may legally be killed for their fur.)

1874 *Harper's Monthly Mag.* May 801/2 To the right and left of the breeding grounds stretch sand-beaches.. upon which the 'hollus-chickie', or the bachelor seals, lie by tens of thousands. **1884** H. W. ELLIOTT *Seal Isl. Alaska* 43 The 'hollus-chickie' or 'bachelor' seals. *Ibid.* 44 Sports and pastimes of the young 'bachelors'. **1897** D'ARCY THOMPSON in *Parl. Papers* CII. 422 We saw a body of about 200 bachelors, mostly young or old, those of intermediate 'killable' size being very few. **1898** D. S. JORDAN et al. *Fur Seals* I. 50 The bachelor seals begin to arrive at about the same time as the bulls... The older bachelors come first.

d. A size of roofing slate (see quot. 1929).

1898 in E.D.D. **1914** M. S. GRETTON *Corner of Cotswolds* ix. 175 The tiles for our roofs are called, according to their sizes, long wivets, long bachelors, short bachelors, longbecks.. muffities, long days, and short days. **1929** N. LLOYD *Building Craftsmanship* x. 93/1 Sizes of.. slates, measuring from centre of peg hole to tail, in inches, are Long bachelors 11 Short bachelors 10½.

e. *Canad.* Ellipt. for *bachelor-apartment* or *bachelor-flat* (sense 6). (Advertisers' jargon.)

1968 *Globe & Mail* (Toronto) 13 Jan. 45/1 (Advt.), Opposite High Park, Bachelors,.. 2-bedrooms and 3-bedrooms. **1970** *Ibid.* 28 Sept. 26/5 Newly decorated large bachelors; short lease. **1973** *Toronto Star* 5 Mar. 45/2 Vaughan Rd.—St. Clair, interesting bachelor, in older bldg. **1978** *Ibid.* 12 Aug. C13/3 Bachelors, 1 bedroom & 2 bedrooms.

†**5.** A maid, a single woman. *Obs. rare.*

1632 B. JONSON *Magnet. Lady* II. i, He would keep you A batchelor still.. And keep you not alone without a husband, But in a sickness.

6. *Comb.* **bachelor girl, woman**, an unmarried woman who has her own income and lives independently; also (*rare*) ***bachelor-lady***, ***-maid***; **bachelor('s)** (or **bachelors') hall**: see HALL *sb.* 11; **bachelor-like** *a.*, like, or of the nature of, a bachelor; **bachelor party**, one for men only, esp. one marking the end of a bridegroom-to-be's bachelorhood; also ***bachelor-dinner***; **bachelor-room**, a room occupied by a single man; also ***bachelor-apartment***, ***-cottage***, ***-flat***, ***-quarters***: occupied by a bachelor. (Also *attrib.* in 1 a and 4 above.)

1611 COTGR., *Bachelier*, Bachelerly, bacheler-like. **1824** W. IRVING *Braceb. Hall* II. 80 To talk in a very bachelor-like strain about the sex. **1857** DICKENS *Dorrit* II. xxx. 591 Ah, but he lived in a sweet bachelor-apartment. **1862** W. STEWART *Footsteps Beh. Him* II. 46 Never had his bachelor-room looked so bare and cheerless. **1864** DICKENS *Mut. Fr.* (1865) I. xii. 109 Mr. Mortimer Lightwood and Mr. Eugene Wrayburn.. had taken a bachelor cottage near Hampton. **1894** C. C. HARRISON (*title*) A Bachelor Maid. **1895** *Dialect Notes* I. 396 *Bachelor-girl*, a maiden lady. **1898** G. E. MITTON (*title*) A Bachelor Girl in London. **1898** WRIGHT *Eng. Dial. Dict.* I. 108/2 Bachelor woman is common, spinster being unknown. **1902** *Daily Chron.* 15 Sept. 3/6 The bachelor woman who earns from two guineas a week. **1902** *Town & Country* 4 Oct. 21/2 In Baltimore, among the first events of the autumn season was the bachelor dinner given at the Baltimore Club last Saturday in honor of Mr. John T. Love, whose marriage to Miss Ellen Jenkins George will shortly take place. **1906** *Queen* 10 Nov. 808/2 The term 'old maid' is now seldom or never heard; the expression 'bachelor girl' has taken its place. **1912** DREISER *Financier* lxxiii. 762 He occupied a bachelor apartment in North Fifteenth Street. **1921** S. MCKENNA *Educ. E. Lane* i. 42 If one of your brothers saw fit to invite *my* sister to a bachelor flat. **1922** Bachelor-party [see BINGE *sb.*]. **1924** J. M. MURRY *Voyage* xii. 229 I've been in here as a bachelor lady. **1934** H. BRIGHOUSE *Exhibit C* in *Best One-Act Plays of 1933* 35 (*stage direction*) A minimum of furnishing indicates.. that this is a bachelor flat. **1954** T. S. ELIOT *Confid. Clerk* II. 62 I've come to inspect the new bachelor quarters. **1955** *Amer. Speech* XXX 298. A way of living no doubt explains *bachelor girl* and not any consideration of gender. **1968** *Globe & Mail* (Toronto) 17 Feb. B3/1 (Advt.), Accommodation.. from bachelor apartment to 6-bedroom home.. in some of Ottawa's finest locations.

bachelor's or **bachelors' buttons** (*Herb.*): a name given to various flowers of round or button-like form; chiefly to certain cultivated double varieties of wild flowers; orig. and commonly, the double variety of a common yellow buttercup, *Ranunculus acris*; also the Tansy. ***white bachelor's buttons***: orig. a double-flowered white Ranunculus (*R. aconitifolius*); also Double White Campion (*Lychnis vespertina*), Double Sneezewort (*Achillæa Ptarmica*), Double Feverfew (*Pyrethrum Parthenium*). ***red bachelor's buttons***: Double Red Campion (*Lychnis diurna*), some species of Scabious and of *Centaurea*, the Ragged Robin (*Lychnis Flos-cuculi*), etc. See Britten and Holland *Plant Names* (1878).

1578 LYTE *Dodoens* 422 The double Goldcuppes are.. called.. Bachelers Buttons. **1592** GREENE *Upst. Courtier* (1871) 7 The bachelors buttons whose virtue is to make wanton maids weep. **1597** GERARD *Herbal* (1633) 472 The similitude these flowres have to the jagged cloath buttons anciently worne.. gave occasion.. to call them Bachelours Buttons. **1629** PARKINSON *Paradisi* v. 11 Batchelours' buttons, both white and red, are kindes of wilde Campions of a very double forme. **1872** OLIVER *Elem. Bot.* I. vii. 86 If you compare a Bachelor's Button with a wild Buttercup.

ˈbachelordom. [f. prec. + -DOM.] The estate or body of bachelors collectively.

1881 *Echo* 3 Dec. 2/4 This stronghold of bachelordom.

bachelorette (bætʃələˈrɛt). [f. BACHELOR + -ETTE.] **a.** = *bachelor girl* s.v. BACHELOR 6. orig. and chiefly *Canad.*

[**1935** *Amer. Speech* X. 315 The *Bachelorettes* is the self-explanatory name of a feminine social club in a western city.] **1965** *Saturday Night* (Toronto) Nov. 35 Articles now.. describe the delights open to the 'bachelorette' who has left her family and is in no hurry to get married. **1972** *Daily Colonist* (Victoria, B.C.) 12 Feb. 24/6 Why wasn't he dancing? 'We ran out of eligible young bachelorettes.' **1975** *Globe & Mail* (Toronto) 19 Aug. 10/5 Most of those I've done have been bachelorette parties. **1982** *Sunday Sun-Times* (Chicago) 8 Aug. Living 3 A feature story on the bachelorette's party that ran in the Sun-Times Living pages.

b. A flat or apartment for a bachelor girl. *Canad.*

1973 *Globe & Mail* (Toronto) 3 Mar. 51 Rooms to Let... A beautiful bachelorette & rooms, Bloor-Spadina area. **1978** *Ibid.* 10 Oct. 8/1 Builders of illegal bachelorettes.

ˈbachelorhood. [f. BACHELOR + -HOOD.] The state or quality of a bachelor; unmarried state.

1833 LAMB *Elia* (1860) 425 The disengaged state of bachelorhood. **1855** THACKERAY *Newcomes* xl. (D.) A long easy life of bachelorhood.

bachelorism (ˈbætʃɪləˌrɪz(ə)m). [f. BACHELOR + -ISM.] **1.** A habit or peculiarity of a bachelor.

1808 W. IRVING *Salmag.* viii. (1860) 166 His character —fertile in.. bachelorisms. **1860** J. KENNEDY *Swallow B.* 14 Chiding me roundly for certain waxing bachelorisms.

2. The condition of being a bachelor; the behaviour, conduct, or nature characteristic of this. Also ***old bachelorism***.

1834 *Blackw. Mag.* XXXV. 769 Bound in the triple steel of resolute bachelorism. **1838** *New Monthly Mag.* LIV. 442 This omission may be looked upon as by no means characteristic of old bachelorism. **1857** J. AITON *Domestic Econ.* 83 A prim correct sort of bachelorism. **1884** *American* VIII. 236 The oddest theory of voluntary old bachelorism.

ˈbachelorize, *v. rare.* [f. BACHELOR + -IZE.]

1. To take the degree of bachelor (of Arts, etc.). Hence **ˈbachelorizing** *vbl. sb.*

1742 JARVIS *Quix.* II. I. vii. (D.), I am a Salamanca bachelor of arts, and there is no bachelorizing beyond that.

2. = BACH *v.* *N.Z.*

The 1854 example is a nonce U.K. use.

1854 MRS. GASKELL *Let.* ? 8–14 May (1966) 282 Mr. Gaskell.. will form no plans, but bachelorize off comfortably guided by the wind of his own daily will. **1883** 'A LADY' *Facts: Experiences in N.Z.* ii. 8 Bachelorising, to use a Colonial term, is not a disagreeable life. **1905** P. OLIPHANT *Bill the Namer* i. 6 We had then been bachelorising, and it was decided to break up the establishment. **1906** *N.Z. Truth* 10 Mar. 5/2 Single men had either to bachelorise in their whares or board with one or another of the married men. **1924** H. T. GIBSON *That Gibbie Galoot* v. 16 He promised.. to show me a few more points in bachelorising.

bachelorly (ˈbætʃɪləlɪ), *a.* [f. as prec. + -LY.[1]] Of, or of the nature of, a bachelor, bachelor-like.

1580 SIDNEY *Arcad.* III. 237 His brother.. protesting his bachelry [1598 bachelerly] intention. **1611** COTGR., *Bachelier*, bachelerly. **1823** C. WESTMACOTT *Points of Misery* 71 A set of stout bachelorly personages.

ˈbachelorˌship. [See -SHIP.]

1. The state of being a bachelor, *i.e.* unmarried.

1591 SHAKS. *1 Hen. VI.* v. iv. 13 She was the first fruite of my Bach'ler-ship. **1833** LAMB *Elia* (1860) 365, I lay down for a brief while my solitary bachelorship.

†**2.** The state or position of a knight bachelor.

1611 COTGR., *Bachelerie*, a Bachelership: the degree, estate, condition of an Esquire or Bacheler.

3. The standing of a Bachelor of Arts, etc.

a **1656** BP. HALL *Rem. Wks.* (1660) 8 The third year of my Bachelarship. **1859** MASSON *Milton* I. 116 Bachelorship terminating with the attainment of the M.A. degree.

†**4.** Apprenticeship (see BACHELOR 3 b). *Obs.*

1611 COTGR., *Bachelarie*, bachelership, prentishood.

†**ˈbachelry**, *sb. Obs.* Forms: 3 **bachelrye**, 3-4 **bachelerie**, 4- **-ilerie**, 4-5 **-elrie**, 5 **bachelary**, **-ellerye**, **-yllerie**, **-ye**, 5-7 **-elery**, 7 **batchelary**,

-ellrie. [a. OF. *bachelerie* (still in Cotgr.), f. *bacheler* BACHELOR: see -RY.]

1. The quality of a young knight; prowess.

1297 R. GLOUC. 192 þe knyȝtes atyled hem aboute in eche syde, In feldes and in medys to preue her bachelerye. *c* **1386** CHAUCER *Maunc. T.* 21 This Phebus, that was flour of bachilerie.

2. Bachelors collectively: **a.** Young knights as a class or body. (Cf. *chivalry*.)

1297 R. GLOUC. 76 A fayr ost of þys bachelerie. *c* **1330** *Arth. & Merl.* 4099 Her schal com a bachelrie Of the to haue cheualrie. **1480** CAXTON *Chron. Eng.* clxxx. 160 Kyng edward sent after al the bachyllerye of englond [ed. 1520 (f. 121 b) bachelarie]. **1656** FINETT *For. Ambass.* 10 The Prince Palatine, attended by the Batchellrie of the Nobilitie.

b. A body of unmarried men.

? *a* **1500** *Turnam. Tottenh.* xxv. in Percy's *Reliq.*, Whych of all thys bachelery Were best worthye To wed hur. **1615** A. NICCHOLES *Marriage* (1620) B, To the Youth and Batchelary of England, hote bloods at high Reuels.

bachelry *a.*: see BACHELORLY.

Bachian ('bɑːxɪən), *sb.* and *a.* [f. BACH *sb.*[1] + -IAN.]

A. *sb.* One who admires or plays the music of Bach.

1920 E. NEWMAN in *Bach Festival Programme* 16 Apr. 5 It appears to be rooted in the nature of things that the true Bachian shall be a little condescending towards Handel. **1963** *Times* 1 Apr. 14/1 Dr.. Lofthouse is.. one of our senior Bachians. He has taken part in performances of the *Passions* and the B minor Mass. **1975** *New Yorker* 12 May 130/3 Wise Bachians, knowing that the matter of each cantata arises from the Gospel of the day for which it was written, and that words and music must be followed together, would have come armed with texts.

B. *adj.* Of, pertaining to, or characteristic of J. S. Bach or his music.

1945 MENDEL & BRODER tr. *Einstein's Mozart* (1946) xii. 206 The lessons in Bachian polyphony have borne fruit. **1960** *News Chron.* 6 June 3/1 Polyphonic meshes that are.. supremely Bachian. **1971** *Daily Tel.* 16 Aug. 6/3 The music is neither pre-Beethoven nor particularly Bachian. **1980** *Early Music* Jan. 53/1 Of course, Weiss' counterpoint cannot approach Bach's, and Weiss wrote *only* for lute, but the 'Bachian gravity' in his works is a very salient characteristic.

Bachinal, obs. form of BACCHANAL.

bachle, earlier variant of Sc. BAUCHLE *v.*

bachshish, variant of BAKSHEESH *sb.*

† **'bacil.** *Obs. rare*[−1]. [ad. L. *bacillum* or *bacillus* a small stick; see below.] A little stick.

1657 TOMLINSON *Renou's Disp.* 714 Made into Rolls and Bacils of a fingers length.

bacillar (bəˈsɪlə(r)), *a.* [ad. mod.L. *bacillāris*, f. L. *bacillus*: see -AR[1].] Of, pertaining to, or of the nature of bacilli.

1883 *Lancet* 25 Aug. 317/2 The air of these regions is not absolutely fatal to bacillar life. **1884** E. KLEIN *Micro-organisms* 72 The bacillar growth.. is thus removed from the surface. **1884** BLACKMORE *Sir Thos. Upmore* (ed. 2) II. xiv. 214 The great bacillar experiment. **1887** A. M. BROWN *Anim. Alkaloids* 122 Bacterial and bacillar biologies.

bacillary ('bæsɪlərɪ), *a.* [ad. mod.L. *bacillārius*, f. L. *bacillus* little rod. Cf. F. *bacillaire*.] Of, pertaining to, or consisting of little rods. Also, of, pertaining to, or caused by bacilli; spec. ***bacillary white diarrhœa***, a disease attacking domestic fowl.

1865 *Reader* No. 139. 242/3 The bacillary layer. **1874** M. COOKE *Fungi* 170 Numerous bacillary spermatozoids. **1875** H. WALTON *Dis. Eye* Introd. 27 External layer. Rods and cones. This is termed bacillary layer, or membrane Jacobi. **1884** *Weekly Med. Rev.* (Chicago) IX. 247 (*title*) On the bacillary doctrine of phthisis. **1894** *Lancet* 3 Nov. 1022/1 A further attempt on the part of the organism to protect itself against bacillary attack. *Ibid.* 1022/2 A drying process incompatible with bacillary life. **1908** R. T. HEWLETT *Bacteriology* (ed. 3) 351 In one type of dysentery, the so-called epidemic or bacillary form. **1909** L. F. RETTGER in *Jrnl. Med. Research* XXI. 117 The malady which for a long time I have termed fatal septicemia, and for which I would suggest the name simple or uncomplicated white diarrhea, or better still, bacillary white diarrhea, has a definite etiology. **1928** *Jrnl. Ministry Agric.* Feb. 1062 The Ministry has made arrangements for.. agglutination tests for Bacillary White Diarrhœa.. to be carried out at its Veterinary Laboratory. **1930** *Times* 17 Mar. 18/3 Coccidiosis, bacillary white diarrhœa, and other chicken diseases.

bacillicide (bəˈsɪlɪsaɪd). ? *Obs.* [f. BACILLUS + -CIDE 1.] An agent or substance that destroys bacilli. Also *attrib.* or *adj.* = **bacilli'cidal** *a.*

The usual word now is BACTERICIDE.

1885 *Disenfectants & their Use* 19 A combination of lime with chlorine, perhaps the best of all the bacillicides. **1894** *Lancet* 3 Nov. 1021/1 Antiseptic or bacillicide measures. *Ibid.* 1021/2 Bacillicide treatment. *Ibid.* 1022/2 Sunshine and pure air are the best bacillicides. **1894** GOULD *Dict. Med.*, Bacillicidal.., destructive to bacilli.

bacilliform (bəˈsɪlɪfɔːm), *a.* [ad. mod.L. *bacilliformis*, f. *bacillus*: see -FORM.] Rod-shaped.

1847-9 TODD *Cycl. Anat. & Phys.* IV. 4/1 Dividing.. into a bacilliform or fusiform polypary.

bacilluria (bæsɪˈl(j)ʊərɪə). *Path.* [f. BACILL(US + -URIA.] The presence of bacilli in the urine.

1881 *Trans. Internat. Med. Congr.* II. 157 (*title*) On Bacilluria: a Form of Urinary Disorder associated with the Discharge of Rod-shaped Bacteria with the Urine. **1906** *Practitioner* Dec. 798 A factor of extreme importance in the seasonal incidence of typhoid fever.. is the large proportion.. of convalescents from typhoid fever, who suffer from typhoidal bacilluria. **1962** *Lancet* 6 Jan. 46/1 (*title*) Bacilluria in pregnancy.

‖ **bacillus** (bəˈsɪləs). *Nat. Hist.* Pl. **bacilli.** [late L. (in Isidore), 'little rod,' dim. of *baculus*, variant of *baculum* rod, stick.] A genus of *Schizomycetæ*, microscopic vegetable organisms of the lowest grade among what were once called *Infusoria*. Separated from *Bacterium*, with which it agrees in its rod-like form, and characterized by its larger size and mode of reproduction. First described by Müller *ante* 1850; recently brought into note by the discovery of some of the species in the diseased tissues in Anthrax, and in Phthisis and other tubercular diseases. Freq. in *fig.* use.

1883 H. J. SLACK in *Knowledge* 1 June 322/1 Dr. B. Yeo estimates these bacilli as from a quarter to half a blood corpuscle in length. **1884** LANKESTER in *Pall Mall G.* 6 Oct. 2/2 The bacillus found in the lungs and expectorations of phthisical patients. **1897** 'MARK TWAIN' *Foll. Equat.* li. 494 Twenty million priests, fakeers, holy mendicants, and other sacred bacilli. **1905** W. LEE-WARNER in *Anti-Slavery Reporter* June-July 63 We must not allow this bacillus of slavery to take a more virulent form. **1907** *Jewish Chron.* 15 Mar. 19/1, I refer to the existence of anti-Semitic bacilli which poison the whole air of Russia. **1918** A. GRAY tr. *Grelling's The Crime* II. ii. 145 They found a fostering soil.. on which the bacillus of war could develop unhindered.

bacin, bacinet, obs. ff. BASIN, BASINET.

bacitracin (bæsɪˈtreɪsɪn). *Biochem.* [f. BACI(LLUS + *Trac(y*, the surname of Margaret Tracy, an American child in whom the substance was found in a wound: see -IN[1].] An antibiotic obtained from organisms of the group *Bacillus subtilis*.

1945 B. A. JOHNSON et al. in *Science* 12 Oct. 376/1 We named this growth-antagonistic strain for the patient, 'Tracy I'. When cell-free filtrates of broth cultures of this bacillus proved to possess strong antibiotic activity and to be non-toxic, further study seemed warranted. We have called this active principle 'Bacitracin'. **1949** H. W. FLOREY et al. *Antibiotics* I. x. 465 There seems to be little doubt that bacitracin is a valuable agent.. especially as it is active against some pencillin-resistant organisms. **1960** A. E. BENDER *Dict. Nutrition* 13/2 *Bacitracin*,.. of use in brewing to control infection. **1961** *Brit. Med. Dict.* 168/1 Bacitracin.. is employed in ointment form for superficial skin diseases, and in lozenges for septic throat infections.

back (bæk), *sb.*[1] Forms: 1-3 **bæc**, 3-5 **bac**, 4-6 **bak, bakke**, (4-5 **bake**, 6 **balke**), 5-7 **backe**, 4- **back**. [Common Teut.: OE. *bæc* (neuter) is cogn. with OS. *bak*, OFris *bek*, MDu. *bak*, LG. *bak*, ON. *bak*.—OTeut. **bako-(m)*; not found in Gothic or OHG., and now lost in Du. exc. in derivatives, as *achterbaks*, *bakboord*. Cf. RIDGE.]

I. Original sense.

1. *properly.* The convex surface of the body of man and vertebrated animals which is adjacent to the spinal axis, and opposite to the belly and most of the special organs. It extends from the neck and shoulders to the extremity of the backbone. † ***back and side***: all over, completely (*obs.*).

c **1000** *Ags. Ps.* cxxix. 3 Ofer minum bæce bitere ongunnon þa firenfullan facen timbrian. *c* **1200** ORMIN 4776 Lende & lesske & shulldre & bac. *c* **1340** *Gaw. & Gr. Knt.* 143 Of bak & of brest al were his bodi sturne. *c* **1400** *Rom. Rose* 7318 Til he be slayne, back & side. *c* **1440** *Promp. Parv.* 21/1 Bakke, *Dorsum*. *c* **1440** *Generydes* 2155 Ther bakkes and ther belly were soo large. *c* **1485** *Digby Myst.* (1882) I. 340, I shuld bete you bak and side. **1697** DRYDEN *Virg. Georg.* III. 650 A Snake.. His Belly spotted, burnisht is his Back. **1711** BUDGELL *Spect.* No. 161 ¶7 A Country Fellow that throws his Rival upon his Back. **1741** MONRO *Anat. Bones* 187 The.. Vertebræ of the Back. **1783-94** BLAKE *Song Innoc., Chimney-Sw.* 6 Curled like a lamb's back. **1860** DICKENS *Uncomm. Trav.* xi. (1866) 72/1 He lies on the broad of his back, with his face turned up to the sky.

2. Viewed in reference to its position or functions, as: **a.** in man, the hinder surface of the body, that which is opposite to the front or face, and which is turned upon those who are left behind. (Hence many phrases: see VI.)

c **885** K. ÆLFRED *Boeth.* ii, Ða wendon hí me heora bæc. **1382** WYCLIF *Jer.* xviii. 17 Bac and not face Y shal shewe to them. *c* **1500** *Robin Hood* (Ritson) xv. 121 And there they turnd them back to back. *a* **1552** LELAND in Keightley *Hist. Eng.* I. 429 Her faire yelow haire hung down pleyne byhynd her bak. **1597** DANIEL *Civ. Wares* II. x, Richard who lookt Fortune in the backe. **1607** SHAKS. *Timon* IV. iii. 397 Thy backe I prythee. **1611** —— *Cymb.* V. iii. 6 The Army broken, And but the backes of Britaines seen. **1873** TRISTRAM *Moab* ii. 19 At length we.. turn our backs on the outskirts of civilization.

b. that part of the body which is the special recipient of clothing (as the belly is of food); often put for the whole body in this capacity.

Orig. because simple articles of clothing cover the back completely, but are either open, or merely fastened in front.

a **1300** *Cursor M.* 5130 Clathing bath for bac and bedd. *c* **1375** WYCLIF *Serm.* Sel. Wks. 1869 I. 298 Cloþing boþ for her bedde and bak. **1549** LATIMER *Serm. bef. Edw. VI* (Arb.) 51 Borrow of thy two next neighbours, that is to say, of thy backe and thi belly. **1597** J. PAYNE *Royal Exch.* 14 Suche.. as come to decaye.. by the pryde of there backs. **1603** SHAKS. *Meas. for M.* III. ii. 23 What 'tis to cram a maw, or cloath a backe. **1840** R. DANA *Bef. the Mast* xix. 53 Without clothing to his back or shoes to his feet. **1862** TROLLOPE *Orley F.* I. 83 (Hoppe) It is from the backs and bellies of other people that savings are made with the greatest constancy.

c. the part of the body which bears burdens.

c **950** *Lindisf. G.* Matt. xxiii. 4 Hia ȝebindas.. byrðenna hefiȝa.. in scyldrum *vel* bæccum monna. *a* **1300** *Cursor M.* 3048 Hir sun a-pon hir bak sco bar. *c* **1384** CHAUCER *H. Fame* 169 And tooke his fader Anchises And bare hym on hys bakke avay. **1588** SHAKS. *Tit. A.* IV. iii. 48 Wrung with wrongs more then our backe can beare. **1613** —— *Hen. VIII*, I. ii. 50 The Backe is Sacrifice to th' load. *Mod.* The back is fitted for the burden.

d. in animals, the upper surface opposite to that on which they walk, crawl, or rest: extended from vertebrates to other walking or creeping animals.

1383 *Sir Ferumb.* 794 Tak my gode stede.. Set me be-for þe on is bak. *c* **1500** *Sir Lancelott* 39 in Furniv. *Percy Folio* I. 86 They horsses bakes brake vnder them. **1647** WARD *Simp. Cobler* 36 They might have kept his back.. had they not put him beyond his pace. **1735** SOMERVILLE *Chase* I. 376 High on their bent Backs erect Their pointed Bristles stare. **1847** CARPENTER *Zool.* §574 The lower side (of Flat-fish) is generally white, whilst the upper is brown; and the former is commonly (but erroneously) regarded as the belly of the fish, and the latter as its back. *Ibid.* §723 The insects of this family swim on their backs.

II. *transf.* The surface of things analogous in position to the (human) back; the hinder side.

3. a. *gen.* That side or surface of any part of the body or of any object, which answers in position to the back; that opposite to the face or front, or side approached, contemplated, or exposed to view; *e.g.* the back of the head, of the leg; the back of a house, door, picture, bill, tablet, etc. ***back-to-back***: advb. phr. used *attrib.*, spec. (i) of houses; also *ellipt.* as *sb.*; (ii) of an aerial system or display used in radar (see quot. 1948); (iii) of a type of combination fireplace (see quots.); (iv) chiefly *U.S.*, of events: following one upon another without a break, consecutive; also *transf.*, full, crowded.

1626 BACON *Sylva* (J.) Trees set upon the backs of chimnies do ripen fruit sooner. **1777** SHERIDAN *Sch. Scandal* II. ii, He put his name at the back of a bill. **1850** LYTTON *My Novel* III. xiii. 138 At the back of the cottage.. there are some fields. *c* **1850** *Rudim. Nav.* (Weale) 94 Back of the post, the after-face of the stern-post. **1880** L. STEPHEN *Pope* IV. 92 A great part of the Iliad [Pope's] is written upon the backs of letters. *a* **1885** *Mod.* Severely hurt about the back of the head.

1845 L. PLAYFAIR *Rep. on State of Large Towns in Lancs.* 35 Back-to-back houses cannot be considered dwellings of proper construction. **1883** *Pall Mall G.* 12 Dec. 2, 11,000'back-to-back' houses in the older parts. **1901** B. SEEBOHM ROWNTREE *Poverty* vi. 153 Back-to-back houses in which through ventilation is impossible. **1940** 'M. INNES' *There came both Mist & Snow* xix. 202 Back-to-backs are monotonous.

1948 TAYLOR & WESTCOTT *Princ. Radar* v. 79 In.. air-borne radars operating on the metre wave-lengths, the back-to-back display.. is used. The 'split' signals are then displayed on either side of the trace and equality results in the trace bisecting the signal line. *Ibid.* 80 (*caption*) Back-to-back display.. used with metric radars. **1961** *Flight* LXXX. 926/1 One of the latest Marconi long-range surveillance radars is the Type S.247, comprising two high-power ($2\frac{1}{2}$-3 MW) transmitters.. feeding a combined back-to-back aerial system.

1951 *Good Housek. Home Encycl.* 263/2 *Back-to-back Grates*, in this variant of the combination range.. the open fire is placed in the sitting-room and the cooking range at the back, in the kitchen. **1955** D. CHAPMAN *Home & Social Status* 54 The other living-room usually has a 'back-to-back' combination fireplace 'shared' with the kitchen.

1952 *N.Y. Times* 24 Aug. S1/8 Back to back doubles by Gene Woodling and Joe Collins off Early Wynn in the fourth inning produced the only tally of the day. **1968** MRS. L. B. JOHNSON *White House Diary* 24 Sept. (1970) 709 Today was one of those full, back-to-back Washington days. **1974** *Plain Dealer* (Cleveland, Ohio) 27 Oct. 1-C/4 Because he is an aggressive skater, his effectiveness would be limited in back-to-back games. **1978** *Sunday Times* 5 Mar. 18/4 Not that British workers like the night shift... They explain their acceptance of it by pointing out the social barriers to back-to-back shift working. **1984** *Tampa* (Florida) *Tribune* 5 Apr. 10C/2 The same teams and players met on back-to-back weeks.

b. Used *ellipt.*, e.g. in ***one-***, ***two-***, ***three-pair back***, a room at the back of a house on the first, second, third floor. (Cf. FRONT *sb.* 11.)

1836 [see *two-pair* s.v. TWO IV. 2]. **1838**, **1883** [see THREE-PAIR *a.*]. **1873** J. H. BEADLE *Undevel. West* xiii. 233 City pastorals, written in a third story back, by men reared in the city. **1902** HENRY JAMES *Wings of Dove* v. xii. 196 The commodious, 'handsome' room, far back in the fine old house.. the rich dusk of a London 'back'.

c. ***to talk out of*** or ***through the back of one's neck***: see NECK *sb.*[1]

4. *spec.* **a.** The convex or outer side of the hand, opposite to the palm. *Colloq.* phrases: ***the back of my hand to*** (something or somebody), a phrase implying contempt and rejection (*Sc.* and *Irish dial.*); ***to know*** (something) ***like the***

back of one's hand: to be thoroughly familiar or conversant with. **b.** The under side of a leaf, which forms the outside before it unfolds. **c.** The convex part of a book, opposite to the opening of the leaves. **d.** The thick edge of a knife or other cutting instrument, opposite to the face, or cutting edge. Hence ***back and edge***: everything, through everything, through thick and thin.

a **1300** W. DE BIBLESW. in Wright *Voc.* 147 The bac of the hand, *la claye dehoris.* *c* **1440** *Promp. Parv.* 21/2 Bakke of egge toole, *Ebiculum.* **1523** FITZHERB. *Husb.* §136 A graffynge knyfe an inche brode with a thycke backe. **1601** SHAKS. *Jul. C.* I. ii. 221 Being offer'd him, he put it by with the backe of his hand, thus. **1641** J. HOTHAM (in Long Parlt.) in Southey *Commonpl. Bk.* Ser. II. (1849) 147 'Mr. Speaker; fall back, fall edge, I will go down and perform your commands.' **1716** MRS. BEHN *Dutch Lover* II. iii, I'll have no more to do with you back nor edge. **1768** A. ROSS *Fort. Shepherdesses* 131 The back o' my hand to the spinning o 't. **1789** LIGHTFOOT *Fl. Scot.* II. 671 Fructifications in two rows upon the back of the pinnules. **1831** S. LOVER *Leg. & Stories of Ireland* 147 The back o' my hand and the sowl o' my fut to you. **1844** DICKENS *Mar. Chuz.* xii. (C.D.) 137 As he drew the back of his hand across his lips. **1863** *Bookseller's Catal.*, Fine copy, calf extra, full gilt backs, marbled edges. *a* **1885** *Mod.* The back of the leaf is lighter in colour. **1914** JOYCE *Dubliners* xiv. 199 'And have you nothing for me, duckie?' 'O, you! The back of my hand to you!' said Mrs Kernan tartly. **1943** M. MILLAR *Wall of Eyes* 154, I know him as well as I know the back of my hand. **1944** 'M. INNES' *Weight of Evidence* x. 107, I know that book like the back of my hand. **1956** M. STEWART *Wildfire at Midnight* i. 17, I know the district like the back of my hand. **1968** 'C. AIRD' *Henrietta Who?* x. 97, I know that photograph like the back of my hand.

5. a. The side of any object away from the spectator, or spectators generally, the other or farther side. ***at the back of***: behind, on the farther side of; cf. 23.

c **1645** HOWELL *Lett.* (1650) II. 19 Turning by the back of Afric to the Cape of Mozambric. **1696** *Lond. Gaz.* No. 3242/3 Yesterday appeared on the back of these Sands a Fleet. **1704** *Ibid.* No. 4060/5 Passing by the back of the Goodwin Sand. **1865** TYNDALL *Fragm. Sc.* viii. §4. 181 A plate of copper against the back of which a steady sheet of flame is permitted to play.

b. Short for BACK BLOCKS, BACK COUNTRY.

1897 D. McK. WRIGHT *Station Ballads* 57, I went poisoning out at the back. *a* **1922** C. G. TURNER *Happy Wanderer* 146 These trips from 'the Back' to the town in August are stern affairs. **1932** R. A. K. MASON in *Phoenix* (N.Z.) I. II. 9 [He] came out on the 'back', as they called the main body of the sheep-run. **1949** P. NEWTON *High Country Days* v. 48 An occasional trip out to the 'back' to pack firewood to those of the camp sites which had no bush within easy reach.

c. *pl.* (Also with capital initial.) The gardens behind colleges bordering on the river Cam at Cambridge.

1871 *London Society* XIX. 40/2 Cambridge University Life... You wander through those lovely 'backs' of colleges, which might almost be carpeted with poetry. **1882** A. G. HILL *Tourist's Guide Cambr.* 31 Some of the most charming 'bits' in England are to be seen in spring-time at the 'backs' of the colleges, where the narrow part of the Cam winds behind S. John's, Trinity, King's, Catherine's, and Queen's colleges. **1925** W. DEEPING *Sorrell & Son* xviii. 170 Sorrell and Kit made their way through Nevil's Court and across the river to the 'backs'.

†**6.** Of time: The other side of, the time after. *Obs.* or *dial.*

1673 FLAMSTEED in Rigaud *Corr. Sci. Men* II. 162, I must be.. your debtor till the back of Whitsuntide.

III. Parts of things having relation, or analogous in position, to the human back; the hinder part, rear, following.

†**7.** *pl.* Clothes. *Obs.*

1341 *Mem. Ripon* (1882) I. 224 Unum indumentum quod dicitur Bak. *c* **1350** *Will. Palerne* 2096 Alle his bakkes rente. **1377** LANGL. *P. Pl.* B. x. 362 Owre bakkes [*gloss* panni] þat moth-eten be. *c* **1386** CHAUCER *Chan. Yem. Prol. & T.* 328 A bak to walken in by day light. **1393** LANGL. *P. Pl.* C. xiv. 72 Fynde beggars bred, backes for þe colde.

†**8. a.** Armour protecting the back; a back-plate.

1648 in Rushw. *Hist. Coll.* IV. II. 1411 He saw the King.. in Naseby field having Back and Breast on. **1651** CROMWELL *Lett.* (Carl.) 26 July, It is desired we may have a thousand backs-and-breasts, and fifteen-hundred pots. **1695** BLACKMORE *Pr. Arth.* VII. 137 Some o'er brazen Backs, and Breastplates sweat.

b. *fig.* A defence, protection.

1686 W. DE BRITAINE *Hum. Prud.* vi. 29 Your own Innocency will be a Back of Steel unto you.

9. The hind part of a coat or other garment.

Mod. What is the material of the back of the vest?

10. The upright hind part of a chair, that supports the back of the sitter; and *gen.* the hinder portion of any structure.

1530 PALSGR. 196/1 Backe of a chymney, *contre cuevr de la chyminee.* **1670** G. H. *Hist. Cardinals* I. III. 78 To sit down ..upon a chair without a back. **1716–8** LADY MONTAGUE *Lett.* I. x. 34 The archduchesses sat on chairs with backs without arms. **1855** MACAULAY *Hist. Eng.* IV. 520 The back of the chimney did not seem to be firmly fixed.

11. The rear of an armed force. *arch.*

1597 SHAKS. *2 Hen. IV*, I. iii. 79 He leaues his backe vnarm'd. **1737** WHISTON *Josephus' Antiq.* XII. viii. §3 And fell upon the backs of their enemies.

†**12.** A following; a body of followers or supporters; support, backing. *Obs.*

1566 KNOX *Hist. Ref.* Wks. 1846 I. 89 Without knowledge of any back or battell to follow. **1611** SPEED *Hist. Gt. Brit.* IX. xvi. (1632) 861 Scotland.. was a special backe and second to King Henry. **1649** BP. GUTHRY *Mem.* (1702) 24 Those that were otherwise minded, would have stay'd with a thin Back. *a* **1662** BAILLIE *Lett.* (1775) I. 217 (JAM.) So Mr. Pym and his back were removed.

IV. Surfaces or parts of things analogous to the back of animals.

13. *fig.* The surface of a river, the waves, etc., which bears floating burdens. (Cf. *bosom.*)

1610 SHAKS. *Temp.* II. i. 115, I saw him beate the surges vnder him, And ride vpon their backes. **1697** DRYDEN *Virg. Georg.* III. 555 Swift Rivers are with sudden Ice constrain'd; And studded Wheels are on its Back sustain'd. **1850** CLOUGH *Dipsychus* I. v. 107 We'll take the crested billows by their backs And shake them.

14. The ridge of a hill, of the nose (*obs.*).

1615 CROOKE *Body of Man* 613 The vpper part of the Nose called *Dorsum* or the backe.. the spine or ridge of the Nose. **1863** HAWTHORNE *Old Home* (1879) 169 We now rambled about on the broad back of the hill.

15. The convex surface of any thing bent.

c **1850** *Rudim. Nav.* (Weale) 96 Compass or curved timber, the outside of which is called the *Back.*

16. *Arch.* The upper surface or edge of any horizontal or oblique beam.

1677 MOXON *Mech. Exerc.* (1703) 156 Back or Hip-molding. The backward Hips or Valley-Rafters in the way of an Angle. **1753** CHAMBERS *Cycl. Supp.* s.v., Back of a hip, among builders, denotes the two planes on the outside of the hip, lying parallel with the adjoining side and end of the roof.

17. The keel and kelson of a ship.

[**1541** R. COPLAND *Guydon's Quest. Cyrurg.*, The backe is lyke yᵉ kele of a shyp.] **1692** *Lond. Gaz.* No. 2779/3 A French Ship of 70 Guns.. has broke her back. **1883** *Contemp. Rev.* Aug. 229 A stranded ship with her back broken.

V. Technical uses. (*transf.*, *fig.*, and *elliptical.*)

18. *Leather-trade.* The thickest and best-tanned hides.

1535 *Act 27 Hen. VIII*, xiv. §5 Any lether called backes or sole lether. **1776** *Excise-bk.* in *Dorset County Chron.* 2 June (1881) Kinds of hides:—Sheep and lamb, butts and backs, calves and kipps. **1859** WORCESTER cites CRABB.

19. *Mining.* (See quots.)

1807 HEADRICK *Arran* 45 Similar cracks are formed in stratified sandstone, called by the workmen, slips, cutters or backs. **1851** *Coal-trade Terms* Northumb. & Durham 4 *Back.*—A diagonal parting in coal; a description of hitch, where the strata are not dislocated. **1875** URE *Dict. Arts* I. 280 Back in mining, that side of an inclined mineral lode which is nearest the surface of the ground. The back of a level is the ground between it and the level above.

20. *Jewellery.* (See quot.)

1879 C. HIBBS in *Cassell's Techn. Educ.* IV. 349/2 'Back' which in Jewellers' parlance means either the top or bottom side of the locket.

21. *Football.* One of the players stationed behind the 'forwards,' *e.g.* 'half-back,' 'three-quarter back'; the duty of the simple '*back*' is to defend the goal. Also in other games.

1880 *Daily Tel.* 20 Dec., One of the Northern three-quarter backs sustained an injury to his leg. **1884** *Punch* 8 March 113/1 To go into this fine manly game [of football] padded.. is enough to rouse the ire of any old 'back' alive. **1910** *Encycl. Brit.* XIII. 555/1 (*Hockey*) RB, Right Back. LB, Left Back. **1920** E. H. GREEN *Hockey* i. 1 The goal-keeper and backs require a heavier stick usually than a half back or a forward. **1968** *Sunday Times* 17 Mar. 24/6 Their backs hit a succession of long passes for Hennessey and his wings to chase.

22. *Sporting.* The action of 'backing': see BACK *v.* 9.

1859 'STONEHENGE' *Brit. Sports* 35 While his [the dog's] 'point' was perfection in beauty and rigidity, the 'back' was totally the reverse.

VI. Phrases. (Chiefly from 2 a, also 2 c.)

23. With *prepositions* :

a. ***at the back of***: behind, close behind; with the pregnant senses of supporting, following, pursuing, chasing; cf. 5. ***at the back of one's mind*** (rarely ***head***): in the underlying or remote part of one's mind. **b.** ***behind the back of***: (*emphatic for*) behind; in the absence of, out of the sight, hearing, or knowledge of; ***behind backs***, clandestinely. (See also BEHIND *prep.* 9.) **c.** † ***on*** (rarely ***of***), ***upon back*** (obs.): aback, back, backward. **d.** ***on, upon the back of***: weighing upon as a burden or incubus; falling upon as an assailant. Also *colloq.*, harassing, annoying. So ***get off my back***: stop harassing or annoying me. **e.** ***on, upon the back*** (***of***): (position) behind, in the rear (*obs.*): (motion) close behind. **f.** ***to the back***: to the back-bone, all through. **g.** ***in back of*** = ***back of*** (see BACK *adv.* 15). *U.S.*

a. *c* **1400** *Destr. Troy* v. 1902 Hade bir at his bake, and þe bankes leuyt. *c* **1430** LYDG. *Bochas* I. i. (1544) 2 b, At their backe, folowed indigence. **1523** LD. BERNERS *Froiss.* I. ccxxxiii. 324 To thentent that they might haue wynter at their backes. **1593** SHAKS. *3 Hen. VI*, II. v. 133 Edward and Richard, like a brace of Grey-hounds.. Are at our backes. **1597** —— *2 Hen. IV*, II. iv. 334 You knew I was at your back, and spoke it on purpose. **1818** BYRON *Juan* I. cxxxvii, Here's my master With more than half the city at his back. **1879** FROUDE *Cæsar* xii. 166 Cæsar had the people at his back. **1895** G. DU MAURIER in *Idler* Dec. 420/2 *Trilby*, as a name, must have been lying *perdu* somewhere, as they say, 'at the back of my head', as important things so often do. **1903** E. CHILDERS *Riddle of Sands* xxi. 226 At the back of such mind as was left me lodged the insistent thought: 'we must hurry on'. **1910** S. REYNOLDS *Alongshore* i. 5 The deep ground-rumble of London.. makes one feel continually, at the back of one's mind, the presence of the great city all around. **1930** 'J. J. CONNINGTON' *2 Tickets Puzzle* v. 61 With this at the back of his mind.. he had volunteered to carry the news.

b. *c* **1380** WYCLIF *Wks.* (1880) 281 þou puttest þi self bi-hinde þi bake. **1592** SHAKS. *Rom. & Jul.* IV. i. 28 It will be of more price, Being spoke behind your backe, then to your face. **1711** ADDISON *Spect.* No. 12 ¶2 The Mistress.. scolds at the Servants as heartily before my Face as behind my Back. **1874** MAHAFFY *Soc. Life Greece* iii. 50 They will censure her behind backs. **1883** *Statist* 21 July, While they were maturing their scheme, the Government went behind their backs and concluded an agreement.

c. *c* **1000** *Ags. Gosp.* Matt. iv. 10 Gang þu on bæc! *c* **1400** *Destr. Troy* XIV. 5957 The batell on backe was borne to þe se. *Ibid.* xv. 6520 And frusshet þere fos fer vppo backe. **1447** BOKENHAM *Seyntys* 59 She nevr of bak turnyde hyr vysayge.

d. **1605** SHAKS. *Lear* I. iv. 42, I haue yeares on my backe forty eight. **1677** GILPIN *Dæmonol.* (1867) 45 No sooner obtains he a commission against a child of God, but presently he is upon his back. **1776** GOUV. MORRIS in Sparks *Life & Writ.* (1832) I. 100 We shall have all the powers of Europe on our backs. **1832** HT. MARTINEAU *Ireland* vii. 118 Rather too much to have another [priest].. on their backs. **1880** W. H. PATTERSON *Gloss. Antrim. & Down* 4 'I'm never off his back,' *i.e.* I'm always watching and correcting him. **1889** 'MARK TWAIN' *Yankee at Court of Arthur* x. 100, I should have had the Established Roman Catholic Church on my back in a minute. **1945** BAKER *Austral. Lang.* viii. 157 *They're on your back*, they (usually officers) are overworking you, demanding too much. **1956** A. MILLER *Memory of 2 Mondays* in *Coll. Plays* (1958) 349 So I buy a car, and they're all on my back—how'd I dare buy a car! **1959** J. CARY *Captive & Free* xxxiv. 146 Well, I didn't want to get into trouble and I didn't want to have him on my back either. **1961** J. HELLER *Catch-22* (1962) xl. 414 Then stop picking on me, will you? Get off my back, will you? **1968** P. MARLOWE *Hire me a Hearse* ix. 120 If you had tried, Wilma would have phoned Peregrine Porter and told him to get you off her back.

e. **1605** in *Camden's Rem.* (1637) 195 On the backe, they make men seeme women. **1658** USSHER *Ann.* vi. 437 Upon the back of these came a thousand. **1663** BP. PATRICK *Parab. Pilgr.*, As soon as they had the house on their backs and were come into the open air. **1734** *Col. Records Penn.* III. 564 Several of the Inhabitants on the back of our Mountains. **1783** BURKE *Sp. E. India Bill* Wks. 1842 I. 293 Another reform has since come upon the back of the first. *Mod.* The child took the measles, and then on the back of that came scarlatina.

f. **1588** SHAKS. *Tit. A.* IV. iii. 47 Mettall Marcus, steele to the very backe. **1705** HICKERINGILL *Priest-Cr.* II. vi. 57 Like little Laud, Mettle to the Back.

g. **1914** 'MARK TWAIN' *What is Man?* (1917) 165 The picture represents a burning martyr.. in back of the smoke. **1925** G. P. KRAPP *Eng. Lang. in Amer.* I. 77 *Back of*.. has a variant form *in back of*, which completes the analogy to *in front of.* **1952** F. BOWERS in *Papers Bibliogr. Soc. Amer.* XLVI. 194 This pure form of analytical bibliography lies in back of and leads directly into two other divisions. **1958** J. KEROUAC *On Road* I. xiii. 102, I was spreading mustard on my lap in back of a parking-lot john.

24. With *verbs*:

a. ***to break the back of***: (*fig.*) to overburden, crush; to finish the hardest part of (a task). **b.** ***to get the back of***: to get behind, take in the rear. †**c.** ***to give back*** (obs.): to retreat, turn tail, run away. **d.** ***to give one the back***: to turn away from, disregard him. **e.** ***to give*** or ***make a back*** (at leap-frog, etc.): to bend the body so as to present a surface which may be jumped over. **f.** ***to put*** or ***set up the back***: to arch it as angry cats do; to put oneself or another into anger; to arouse. **g.** ***to turn the back***: to turn away from facing, go away, flee; ***to turn the back upon***: to turn definitely from, abandon, forsake. **h.** ***to put one's back into***, to employ the whole strength of one's back in (rowing, lifting, hauling, etc.). Also *fig.*

a. *a* **1613** SHAKS. *Hen. VIII*, I. i. 84 Many Haue broke their backes with laying Mannors on 'em For this great Iourney. **1873** *Baily's Mag.* XXIV. 45 Between them they broke the back of the Eton bowling. **1883** E. G. HOLTHAM *Eight Years in Japan* vii. 151 That I had better stick to my onward route, at any rate till I had 'broken the back' of the journey overland to Kiyōto. **1890** KIPLING *Life's Handicap* (1891) I. 48 Your flanks are unprotected for two miles. I think we've broken the back of this division. **1901** *Westm. Gaz.* 9 Mar. 4/1 The back of the fire was broken at noon. **1911** H. S. HARRISON *Queed* iv. 40 The very next day, the back of the morning's mail being broken, [etc.]. **1965** R. M. ERSKINE *Passion Flowers in Business* viii. 97 'Your labours.. must be nearing completion.' 'I've broken the back of it, oh yes!'

b. **1653** HOLCROFT *Procopius*, John.. compassed the Trachea, so that he got the Backes of the Enemy.

c. *a* **1300** *Cursor M.* 2499 þe fiue gaue bak to wine a-way. *Ibid.* 4390 He drou, sco held, þe tassel brak, þe mantel left, he gafe þe bak. *c* **1400** *Destr. Troy* XXIII. 9474 þai were boun to gyffe bake, & the bent leue. **1533** BELLENDENE *Livy* I. (1822) 50 Dredand.. to be inclusit on every side.. thay gaif bakkis. **1591** SHAKS. *Two Gent.* V. iv. 126 Thurio giue backe, or else embrace thy death. **1661** R. DAVENPORT *City Nt.-Cap* V. in Dodsl. (1780) XI. 358 Catch'd at thy word, thou giv'st back. **1783** AINSWORTH *Lat. Dict.* (Morell) s.v. *Back*, To give back, *Pedem referre.*

d. *a* **1624** BP. M. SMYTH *Serm.* (1632) 24 They gaue him the back, and became apostates. **1682** BUNYAN *Holy War* 236 Emmanuel, their Prince, has given them the back.

e. **1836** DICKENS *Pickw.* vii. 57 Stooping.. as if he were 'making a back' for some beginner at leap-frog. **1848** THACKERAY *Van. Fair* III. 13 (Hoppe) The Major was giving a back to Georgy.

f. **1728** VANBR. & CIBBER *Prov. Husb.* V. iii. 112 O Lud! how her back will be up then, when she meets me. **1845** DISRAELI *Sybil* (1863) 14 But the other great whig families.. set up their backs against this claim of the Egremonts. **1864**

Sunday Mag. I. 79 He goes his own way..if you put his back up. c **1870** H. Spofford *Pilot's W.* in *Casquet Lit.* (1877) IV. 9/1 The..cat used to put up her back at the three.

g. c **1400** *Destr. Troy* iv. 1348 The Troiens..turnyt þe bake, ffleddon in fere. **1597** Shaks. *2 Hen. IV*, i. i. 130 The shame Of those that turn'd their backes. **1605** —— *Lear* i. i. 178 To turne thy hated backe Vpon our kingdome. **1611** Bible *1 Sam.* x. 9 When he had turned his backe to go from Samuel. c **1680** Beveridge *Serm.* (1729) I. 99 If you turn your backs and refuse to..hearken. **1711** Addison *Spect.* No. 108 ¶4 Sir Roger's Back was no sooner turned but honest Will began. **1866** G. Macdonald *Ann. Q. Neighb.* xxx. (1878) 522, I never turned my back on my leader yet.

h. **1882** Stevenson *New Arab. Nts.* (1884) 301 They put their back into their work, they sang loud and louder. **1885** Rider Haggard *K. Solomon's Mines* xviii. 291 Tackle on, and put your back into it; you are as strong as two. **1889** A. Conan Doyle *Micah Clarke* iv. 28 Pull, Micah! Put your back into it! **1952** M. Laski *Village* i. 21 You can get it done in half the time if you only put your back into it.

25. *complex.* **a.** *to be* or *lie on one's back*: to be laid up, to be afflicted; also, *fig.* to be prostrate, helpless; *to lay any one on his back*, to prostrate, floor, lay low. †**b.** *to have by the back*: to lay hold of, seize. †**c.** *to take the back upon oneself*: to flee. **d.** *with* or *having one's back at* or *to the wall*: hard-pressed, struggling against odds.

a. **1655** Gurnall *Chr. in Arm.* v. (1669) 343/1 They never look up to Heaven, till God lays them on their back. **1840** Dana *Bef. Mast* (1854) xxviii. 177 He confessed the whole matter; acknowledged that he was on his back. **1841** Catlin *N. Amer. Ind.* (1844) II. xlv. 80 Sick and very feeble, having been for several weeks upon my back. **1904** *McClure's Mag.* Feb. 366/1 The employers of San Francisco are flat on their backs..; when a labor leader makes a demand we give in without a word. **1938** *New Statesman* 21 May 863/2 'Speciality selling'..is the last refuge of the man who is 'on his back'.

b. a **1555** Ridley *Wks.* 67 Else thou must be had by the back. **1597** Morley *Introd. Mus.* 146 Then brother I haue you by the backe.

c. c **1500** *Lancelot* 1488 It haith gart o thousand tak At onys apone them-self the bak.

d. **1535** Stewart *Cron. Scot.* II. 73 That we may haif thair bakis at the wall, Without defend that ar oure commoun fa. **1854** H. Miller *Sch. & Schm.* 536, I ill liked to see him with his back to the wall.

back (bæk), *sb.*² [prob. immediately a. Du. *bak* trough, tub, a. F. *bac* 'ferry boat, punt' (see BAC), also 'trough, basin, mash-tub,' in med.L. *bacus*, *baccus*, ferry boat (11th c. in Du Cange); cf. also late L. *bacca* 'vas aquarium,' Isidore; remoter origin uncertain.] A large shallow vessel (chiefly for liquids); a tub, trough, vat, cistern; *esp.* applied to those used by brewers, dyers, and picklers.

1682 *Lond. Gaz.* No. 1684/4 To be Sold, six Backs, several Stills and Worms. **1737** Miller *Gard. Dict.* s.v. *Anil*, Backs or Vats of Stone-work, well cemented. **1791** Hamilton *Berthollet's Dyeing* I. i. ii. ii. 159 Long copper or wooden vessels, called troughs or backs. **1794** G. Adams *Nat. & Exp. Phil.* I. xi. 483 The gaseous atmosphere of a back of beer in fermentation. **1811** *Mem. R. Cecil* Introd. 8 His father had in this ground several large backs of water. **1818** Scott *Rob Roy* (1818) III. 13 (Jam.) Narrowly escaping breaking my shins over a turf back and a salting tub.

back (bæk), *a.* [partly attributive use of BACK *sb.*¹ as in *back wall* = wall at the back; partly elliptical use of BACK *adv.*, as in *back rent* (cf. 'to be back with his rent'), *back years* (cf. 'for years back'); by no means distinctly separated from BACK- in *comb.*; cf. senses 1 and 2, with BACK-, 4, 5.]

I. From the sb.

1. Situated behind or in the rear, or away from the front. *back row*: of a chorus, line of dancers, etc.; in *Rugby Football*, the last line of forwards in a scrummage. Hence, **a.** sometimes with the inferred sense of ' distant, outlying, remote,' as in BACK COUNTRY, *back settlement*. Also *back area*: a region behind a field of operations (esp. *Mil.*). **b.** often with that of 'inferior, mean, obscure,' as in *back alley*, *lane*, *road*, *slum*, *street*.

c **1490** *Adam Bel* 121 in Ritson's *Anc. P.P.* 10 William opened hys backe wyndow That was in hys chambre on hye. **1535** Coverdale *Ex.* xxxiii. 23 Thou shalt se my back partes, but my face shal not be sene. **1583** Golding *Calvin on Deut.* 58 When there is still some backe nooke behinde. **1683** Ray *Corr.* (1848) 134 A small flat back claw, or toe. **1703** *Lond. Gaz.* No. 3885/4 Lost..out of a back Shead, 4 peices of Crape. **1806** W. Taylor *Ann. Rev.* IV. 886 The Ohio should..have been made the back line of boundary. **1850** Thackeray *Pendennis* vii. (1884) 65 A little morocco box, which..contained the Major's back teeth. **1870** Lowell *Study Wind.* 3 A stilted plover with no back toe. a **1885** *Mod.* The occupants of the back seats. **1887** *Lippincott's Mag.* Sept. 421 We..sot an' spit at each other, like two tom-cats on a back fence. **1894** W. S. Gilbert *Foggerty's Fairy* iii. p. 71, I should be at once relegated to the back rows[in a ballet], among the stout ones. **1897** *Encycl. Sport* I. 408/1 The wheel is made on the most favourable side by the back row bringing the ball round to the front. **1906** Gallaher & Stead *Complete Rugby Footballer* vii. 100 Advantages of the New Zealand system... Two fast men in the back row [of the scrum]. *Ibid.* 105 In the back row of the scrum we [*sc.* New Zealanders] put two of the fastest forwards and two of the best collarers that we can find. *Ibid.* 106 The side-row men press on the hookers, and the back-row men push against the lock. **1912** Mrs. Woodrow *Sally Salt* 24 She could really have believed that she could transform me from an eager back-fence prowler. **1949** R. K. Merton in Lazarsfeld & Stanton *Communications Research, 1948–9* ii. 206 Walter Winchell, who reports the Broadway version of intimate gossip across the backfence. **1952** Granville *Dict. Theatr. Terms* 21 *She came from the back row of the chorus*, said of an actress who has risen the hard way, from the smallest beginnings. **1959** *Times* 30 Nov. 3/7 The Swansea back-row gave Croker and Fitch room to move.

a. **1681**, **1783** [see BACK-LAND 2]. **1759** Franklin *Ess.* Wks. 1840 III. 420 To fall on the back settlements of Pennsylvania. **1798** Malthus *Popul.* (1817) I. 7 In the back settlements, where the sole employment is agriculture. **1923** Kipling *Irish Guards* I. p. vii, The farthest back-areas where the enemy aeroplanes harried their camps. **1937** *Times* 25 Oct. 13/4 It [*sc.* a speech] called shame on the back-area workers who shirked extra hours and thereby helped the enemy. **1940** E. C. Shepherd *Britain's Air Power* 6 The bomber..might have to travel only 50 miles from our own lines in France to the back areas of the German Army to bomb dumps. **1956** *Planning* XXII. 59 Land that has been left derelict for many years with top soil destroyed exists as a consolidated mass of weed-covered uneven land... Such areas, often referred to as 'back-areas', have to be bulldozed and scraped level.

b. c **1450** in M.E.D., Backe strete. **1542** Backe lane [see MEET *v.* 11 b]. **1613** L. Bayly *Pract. Piety* (ed. 3) 652 Seeke out these in the backe Lanes, and relieve them. **1638** in *Records Early Hist. Boston* (1878) III. 6 One acre and haulfe ..butting south west upon the back streete. **1708** *Boston News-Let.* 22–29 Mar. 2/2 There is a..dwelling house to be lett in the back-street. **1764** J. Kirby *Suffolk Traveller* (ed. 2) 280 The Back-Road from Woodbridge to Blithborough by Snape Bridge. **1842** *Times* 12 Sept. 6/2 The city police.. desert the back lanes. **1847** F. A. Kemble *Let.* 16 Dec. in *Records Later Life* (1882) III. 317 Walking up a small back street..I saw a little child..standing at a poor mean kind of pastry-cook's window. **1860** Dickens *Uncomm. Trav.* x. (1866) 67/2 A back street in the neighbourhood of Walworth. **1865** *Athenæum* 28 Jan. 124/1 Imprisoned in the back slums of Westminster. **1865** H. B. Stowe *House & Home Papers* ii. 22 A little dingy den, with a window looking out on a back-alley. **1887** *Century Mag.* July 331 The road is what is called a 'back road', and leads through woods most of the way. **1894** 'Mark Twain' *P. Wilson* xvii. 177 He said they were back-alley barbers disguised as nobilities. **1898** *Westm. Gaz.* 6 Apr. 9/3 It was indeed remarkable what a knowledge these back-street children had of flowers. **1920** W. Stevens *Let.* 2 Dec. (1967) 220 The bouquet in this month's Poetry will drive me to back alleys. **1934** E. Blunden *Mind's Eye* iii. 167 A back-alley cinema. **1957** J. L. Hodson in 'C. H. Rolph' *Human Sum* x. 192 The woman ..who goes to the back-street abortionist.

¶ In this sense formerly compared BACKER, BACKERMOST, BACKMOST. Only the last is now in ordinary use.

c. *Phonetics.* Of a sound: formed by restriction of the oral passage at the back of the mouth; formed by the back or root of the tongue. Also *Comb.*, as *back-lateral* adj.

1867 A. M. Bell *Visible Sp.* 61 The 'shut' consonants are sufficiently distinguished..by the four radical varieties 'Back', 'Front', 'Point', 'Lip'. *Ibid.* 72 The vowels..are divided into three classes of palato-lingual formations, according as the oral cavity is moulded mainly by the 'Back', the 'Front', or the 'Mixed' (Back and Front) attitudes of the tongue. The 'Back' vowels have the largest oral cavities. **1877** Sweet *Handbk. Phonetics* 11 'Back' (guttural) vowels, in which the tongue is retracted as much as possible. *Ibid.* 31 By place there are five main classes [of consonants]. (1) Back (guttural) formed by the root of the tongue and the soft palate..(2) Front (palatal)..(3) Point..(4) Teeth..(5) Lip. **1910** *Mod. Lang. Rev.* V. 91 A back-modified glide or murmur vowel develops between a long vowel and a back-lateral. **1962** A. C. Gimson *Introd. Pronunc. Eng.* iv. 41 Naming those vowels..in which the back of the tongue is raised towards the soft palate *back* vowels.

d. Phonology. *back mutation* [MUTATION 4 b], in Old English, a change in the sound of the vowels *æ*, *e*, *i*, which were diphthongized to *ea* (= *æa*), *eo*, *io*, when a back vowel stood in the following syllable.

1914 H. C. Wyld *Short Hist. Eng.* v. 74 *Back-, or u-Mutation.* All the O.E. dialects are to some extent subject to this change, which consists in diphthonging *i*, *e*, and in Mercian *æ*, when *u*, or *o* (from earlier *-an*) followed in the next syllable, e.g. *hebun becomes *heofon*. **1927** E. V. Gordon *Introd. O. Norse* 254 The OE. equivalent of ON. fracture is the so-called back mutation. **1953** L. F. Brosnahan *Some O.E. Sound Changes* 89 The phenomenon of back-mutation is based on the same process of regressive influence of one vowel on another, but the nature and effect of the influence in this case is different from that in *i*-mutation.

2. Used to distinguish that one of two things (or sets of things) which lies behind the main or front one, and is more or less subsidiary to it. In this case it is more usual to use the hyphen: see BACK- 5.

1535 Coverdale *1 Kings* vii. 8 Yᵉ back courte made betwene yᵉ house and the porche. **1592**, **1713** [see BACK ROOM *a.* a]. **1768** Sterne *Sent. Journ.* (Rtldg.) 319 Coming unexpectedly from a back parlour into the shop. **1812** T. Hall in *Examiner* 31 Aug. 551/2 Which he traced to the back kitchen. **1863** Kingsley *Water Bab.* i. 21 The back staircase from the Taj-mahal at Agra.

II. From the adv.

3. a. In arrear, overdue; behindhand. Of rent, taxes, etc. *back pay*, *payment*, payment to cover a past period of time; also *back salary*, *wages*, etc.

1525 Ld. Berners *Froiss.* II. ccvii. [cciii.] 639 To fynde syluer to mayntayne it withall, he founde out subtelly a backe tayle. **1779** W. McKendry *Jrnl.* 21 July in *Proc. Mass. Hist. Soc.* ser. ii. II. 460 [He] received 500 lashes, it being back allowance due to him. **1804** in G. L. Wardle *Rep. Charges agst. Dk. York* (1809) 542 In which case, if approved, Mr Dundas would not object to allow them back-pay. **1810** G. R. Minot *Insurrections in Mass.* (ed. 2) 59 They completed an act providing for the payment of the back taxes in specifick articles. **1811** *Records Early Hist. Boston* (1908) XXXVIII. 25 Messrs. Crane & Sohier having given up their office in the Town house.—to be notified to settle their back rent with the Treasurer. **1814** J. Mayne *Jrnl.* (1909) 128 And [the postilion] when we refused told us we had passed a bridge for which he was to take back payment, one franc. **1841** S. Warren *Ten Thous. a Year* II. v. (Hoppe) Whether you have come to any arrangement with your late opponent concerning the back-rents. **1843** Dickens *Chr. Carol* v. 159 Not a farthing less. A great many back-payments are included in it. **1888** A. C. Gunter *Mr. Potter of Texas* xviii. 225 He was paying him back wages. **1905** *N.Y. Even. Post* 29 Nov. 10 Nearly two hundred claims for back pay.

b. Belonging to past time; see also BACK NUMBER.

1808 *Sporting Mag.* XXXIII. 99/2 Your neat, elegant, and conveniently sized back volumes. **1869** *Contemp. Rev.* XI. 342 It is the duty of the resident governess..to see that the knowledge of back work is carefully kept up. **1910** 'Dehan' *Dop Doctor* (1911) xxxix. 363 To its back-files I must refer those who seek a fuller account.

†**4.** That holds one back. *Obs. rare.*

1627 Feltham *Resolves* (1647) 66 Take away from him those back feares, that would speak him still to be fragile man.

†**5.** Turning or looking backward. *Obs. rare.*

1633 P. Fletcher *Purple Isl.* in Farr's *S.P.* 197 The false back Tartars..in flying ranks, Oft backward turn.

6. Coming back, returning.

1868 B. Lossing *The Hudson* 145 They generally descend the river at the close of May, when they are called Back Shad.

7. Turned back, reversed, as in *back current*, *back smoke*; spelt backward, as in *back slang*.

1857 J. Wilson *Chr. North* I. 137 That mysterious and infernal sort, called back-smoke.

back (bæk), *v.* [f. BACK *sb.*¹]

I. To line the back of, make a back to.

†**1.** To cover the back, clothe. *Obs.*

1362 Langl. *P. Pl.* A. xi. 185 To breke beggeris bred & bakken hem [*v.r.* bak hym, bachem] with cloþis.

2. a. To put a back to, to line the back, or form the back part of.

1728 Chambers *Cycl.* I. 116/2 The French Binders..are enjoin'd by Ordonnance to back their Books with Parchment. **1793** Smeaton *Edystone L.* §220 The ashler walls were backed..with rubble stone, or with bricks. **1880** L. Higgin *Handbk. Embroidery* iv. 35 Silk, satin, or velvet.. must be backed with a fine cotton or linen lining. **1884** *Law Times Rep.* LI. 230/2 That A.B. do back and cope a hundred rods of their wall. *Mod.* This book requires to be backed.

b. *Photography.* To coat the back of (a plate) with some substance which will absorb light and so prevent halation. Hence **backed** *ppl. a.*; **backing** *vbl. sb.*, often *concr.* = the coating applied to the plate.

1878 W. de W. Abney *Emulsion Proc. in Photogr.* iv. 49 This defect is..cured by applying some non-actinic varnish to the back of the plate. This backing may be made as follows: [etc.]. **1882** W. K. Burton *A.B.C. Mod. Photogr.* 59 It is well to 'back' the plate; that is, to paint or otherwise cover it at the back with some substance which will absorb light. **1906** R. C. Bayley *Compl. Photogr.* 95 A thick coat of backing is quite unnecessary. *Ibid.* 320 If there be one purpose for which backed plates are more than ever necessary, it is in interiors.

c. *Bookbinding.* To force the backs of the sections of (an unbound book) outwards on each side so as to form grooves or ledges into which the edges of the binding boards will fit. The sheets are clamped in a press, after rounding, between two bevelled boards, and the backs struck with a hammer. Hence **backing** *vbl. sb.*; also *attrib.* in *backing-board*, *-hammer*, *-machine*.

1741 Chambers *Cycl.* s.v. *Book-binding*, Then the back is turned with a hammer, the book being fixed in a press between boards, called backing-boards; in order to make a groove for fixing the paste-boards. **1818** H. Parry *Art Bookbinding* 12 Place the backing-boards a little below the back on each side. *Ibid.* 13 The centre must only be well rubbed over with the face of the backing-hammer to make it smooth. **1846** Dodd *Brit. Manuf.* ser. vi. iv. 89 In the process of 'backing',..the book is laid on a bench,..and hammered near the back edge, with such a peculiar movement of the left hand as causes the back to become rounded while the hammering proceeds. *Ibid.*, When the book is 'backed'. It is placed between two pieces of plank called 'backing-boards' . **1879** Zaehnsdorf *Bookbinding* 44 The boards required for backing, called backing boards, should always be the same length as the book. *Ibid.* 167 *Backing Machine.*—A small machine introduced for backing cheap work. **1901** D. Cockerell *Bookbinding* 118 Rounding and backing are best done after the glue has ceased to be tacky.

3. To form the rear of, lie at the back of.

1826 Disraeli *Viv. Grey* iv. vi. 162 Its ruined castle backing the city. **1853** Kane *Grinnell Exp.* xxxi. (1856) 270 This beach is backed by rolling dunelike hills. **1878** Huxley *Physiogr.* 167 The chalk cliffs which back the beach.

II. To support at the back. (Cf. BACK *sb.* 12.)

4. To support or help mechanically, materially,

a. of persons: *orig.* with physical force, *hence* with authority, money; to uphold, aid, second.

1548 W. Patten *Exp. Scotl.* Arb. *Garner* III. 98 A troup of Demi-lances to back them. **1594** Greene *Orl. Fur.* (1599) 30 He backt the Prince of Cuba for my foe. c **1605** ? Rowley

Birth. Merl. IV. ii. 340 The Saxons which thou brought'st To back thy usurpations. **1684** BUNYAN *Pilgr.* II. 70 One, that..had taken upon him to back the Lions. **1868** FREEMAN *Norm. Conq.* (1876) II. x. 503 Demands which had been backed by an armed force. **1880** JEFFERIES *Hodge & M.* I. 79 The old uncle who had 'backed' him at the bank.

b. of things. Also *fig.*

1598 BARRET *Theor. Warres* v. i. 122 They [kingdoms] are strong by nature, when..backed with lakes, mountaines, etc. **1769** FALCONER *Dict. Marine* (1789) s.v., *To Back an anchor*, to carry out a small anchor..ahead of the large one ..in order to support it, and prevent it from loosening. **1867** SMYTH *Sailor's Word-bk.* 65 *To back a rope or chain*; to put on a preventer, when it is thought likely to break from age or extra strain. **1876** GREEN *Short Hist.* ii. §6 (1882) 91 The moral revolution..was backed by a religious revival.

c. *Mus.* To accompany (a singer). Cf. BACKING *vbl. sb.* 7 b.

1961 *Jazz Jrnl.* July 4 I've heard a record or two of Lang backing a singer.

5. To support morally (by arguments, etc.).

1612 T. TAYLOR *Comm. Titus* i. 9 (1619) 205 Which Godly course Augustine backeth. **1722** DE FOE *Moll. Fl.* (1840) 313 He backed his discourses with proper quotations of scripture. **1853** H. ROGERS *Ecl. Faith* 76 Authoritative teaching..backed by the performance of miracles?

†**6.** *refl.* To support or stay oneself. *Obs.*

1642 ROGERS *Naaman* 189 Others..backe themselves with this, That your best Preachers are no better then they should be.

7. To support one's opinions, judgements, etc., as to an undecided issue, by a wager or bet. ***to back a horse***: to bet or stake money upon his winning a race; ***to back the field***: to bet upon the aggregate of the horses in a race, against one in particular. Also *transf.* and *fig.*

1697 DRYDEN *Virg. Ecl.* iii. 44 Now back your Singing with an equal Stake. **1699** LUTTRELL *Brief Rel.* IV. 505 The lord Wharton's horse Carelesse has beaten another backt by the duke of Devon, etc. for £1900. **1817** BYRON *Beppo* xxvii, Most men (till by losing render'd sager) Will back their own opinions with a wager. **1835** MARRYAT *Jac. Faithf.* xxiii. 80 Some one backed me against another man in the ring for fifty pound a side. **1872, 1888** [see FIELD *sb.* 10 a]. **1878** *Chambers's Encycl.* V. 428 There are men..ready to lay against any horse and 'back' the 'field'. **1913** *Punch* 26 Mar. 250/2 The sanguine mood induced by backing two winners. **1922** C. L. GRAVES *Mr. Punch's Hist.* III. 15 Lord Salisbury made his remarkable speech about our having 'backed the wrong horse, i.e. Turkey, in the Crimean War'. **1940** D. WHEATLEY *Scarlet Imp.* ii. 20 They [*sc.* German industrialists] backed the wrong horse, for Hitler has been their taskmaster ever since. **1955** *Times* 9 June 6/3 Dr. Clark said he never backed greyhounds but confined his modest betting to horses.

8. ***to back up***: to stand behind with intent to support or second, to uphold or support materially or morally; esp. in *Cricket* (of a fielder): To run behind another fielder in readiness to stop the ball if he should fail to do it; (of the batsman at the bowler's end): To start in readiness for a run; and similarly in other games. Cf. BACKING *vbl. sb.* 6 c. Also without *up* (*Obs.*).

1767 R. COTTON in F. S. Ashley-Cooper *Hambledon Cricket Chron.* (1923) 184 Ye Fieldsmen look sharp... When the ball is return'd back it sure. **1840** A. BUNN *Stage* II. 239 Taglioni was engaged on unheard-of terms to 'back up' Malibran's '*off-nights*'. **1854** J. PYCROFT in F. Lillywhite *Guide to Cricketers* 14 Point should back behind short slip. **1865** M. ARNOLD *Ess. Crit.* i. (1875) 32 Let us all stick to each other and back each other up. **1879** FROUDE *Cæsar* xxi. 359 He prolonged Cæsar's command, and backed him up in everything. **1883** ABP. BENSON in *Standard* 28 June 2/3 Varied appeals to strengthen and 'back up' their own long-continued efforts. **1898** G. GIFFEN *With Bat & Ball* 238 Always back up another fieldsman if you possibly can.

9. *Sporting.* Of dogs: To follow the lead of a dog that 'points,' by falling into the same perfectly stiff or semi-cataleptic state.

1860 *Encycl. Brit.* XX. 220/1 A dog which backs another is not aware of the proximity of game at the time otherwise than by inference. **1875** 'STONEHENGE' *Brit. Sports* I. I. iii. §6. 69 Some very high-couraged dogs are very difficult to make 'back'; I have known many highly-bred ones in which the cataleptic condition was never fully developed.

III. To mount on the back of.

10. a. To mount, ride on (a horse); also, to break him in to the saddle. Also, *fig.* of the billows, etc. (Cf. To *breast* the waves.) Now *rare.*

1592 SHAKS. *Ven. & Ad.* lxx, The colt that's backed and burthened being young. **1596** —— *1 Hen. IV*, II. iii. 74 That Roane shall be my Throne. Well, I will backe him straight. *c* **1620** FLETCHER & MASS. *Trag. Barnavelt* v. iii, Back the raging waves to bring you proffit. **1623** COCKERAM *Dict.* III. s.v. *Bucephalus*, He would suffer none to backe him, but his Master. **1774** GOLDSM. *Nat. Hist.* I. i. i. (1862) 250 The French horses..must not be backed till they are eight years old. **1783** AINSWORTH *Lat. Dict.* (Morell), To back, or break a horse, *Equum domare.* **1801** SOUTHEY *Thalaba* IV. xxx, Could they have back'd the Dromedary then. **1881** SWINBURNE *Mary Stuart* I. iii. 54 If I should never more back steed alive. **1925** E. SELOUS in C. Waterton *Wanderings* p. ix, The future cavamenstrian..backed and was shortly unbacked by a cow.

b. *intr.* (See quot. 1942.)

1934 J. LILICO *Sheep-Dog Memoirs* 26 Any keen dog..can be trained to back when there are other dogs doing so. **1942** R. B. KELLEY *Animal Breeding* xv. 142 In sheep yards the dog that will 'back' probably is the most specialized... Their function is to go forward..over the tightly packed sheep's backs and, by barking vigorously, cause the leading sheep to keep moving.

†**11.** To cover (used of animals in copulation).

1658 ROWLAND *Mouffet's Theat. Ins.* 927 When as the female or she Asse would be backt.

IV. To write or print at the back of.

12. a. To countersign a warrant. **b.** To endorse a bill, or cheque. Also *U.S.* and *Sc.*, to address (a letter). **c.** To print on the back (as well as the front).

1768 BLACKSTONE *Comm.* IV. 238 The warrant of a justice of the peace in one county..must be backed, that is, signed by a justice of the peace in another..before it can be executed there. **1825** JAMIESON Suppl., *To back* (a letter), to write the direction; more generally applied merely to the manual performance. An '*ill-backit* letter'; one with the direction ill written. **1829** R. C. SANDS in *Writings* (1834) II. 136 You may as well back the paper and send what loose cash you have, besides. **1859** BARTLETT *Dict. Amer.* (ed. 2) s.v., To *back* a letter, is Western for to 'direct' it. **1888** FARMER *Americanisms* s.v., The frequently-heard commercial phrase of *to back*, in the sense of 'to endorse', literally, to write on the back of a letter, bill, or cheque. **1889** J. M. BARRIE *Window in Thrums* ix. 87 He had written a letter to David Alexander, and wanted me to 'back' it. **1903** CLAPIN *Dict. Amer.* 30 *To back*, often heard, in parts of the West and the South, in sense of to address a letter.

V. *trans.* To cause to move back, put back.

†**13.** To draw back, withdraw. *Obs.*

1578 TIMME *Calvin on Gen.* 52 If he do but a little backe his hande, all things shall by and by perish, etc.

14. a. To set, lay, or incline back.

1846 ELLIS *Elgin Marb.* I. 27 Was scooped in, and backed against the rock.

b. ***to back a sail, a yard***: to lay it aback; 'to brace the yard so that the wind may blow directly on the front of the sail, and thus retard the ship's course.' Also *absolutely.*

1707 *London Gaz.* No. 4380/3 The Firebrand.. immediately backing her Foresail, drove off. **1812** CAPT. CARDEN in *Examiner* 4 Jan. (1813) 6/1 The enemy backed and came to the wind. **1828** MOORE *Meet. of Ships* iii, Then sails are backed, we nearer come. **1847** SIR J. ROSS *Voy. S. Pole* II. 168 By backing and filling the sails we endeavoured to avoid collision with the larger masses [of ice].

15. a. To push back, cause to move back or in the opposite direction.

1781 H. HAMILTON in *Hist. MSS. Comm.* 9th Rep. App. 111 (1910) II. 227 The shallowness of the water obliged us to make a dam across both rivers to back the water into the swamp. **1812** *Examiner* 24 Aug. 533/1 One..seized the horse by the nose, backed him. **1814** SOUTHEY *Roderick* xxv, And with sidelong step Backing Orelio, drew him to the ground. **1848** DICKENS *Dombey* viii, Backing his chair a little.

b. *esp.* To propel in the opposite direction, by reversing the action; as, to back a locomotive engine, a boat; also, to ***back*** the ***oars***, and, in same sense, to ***back water.***

1769 FALCONER *Dict. Marine* (1789) s.v., *To back astern*.. is to manage the oars in a direction contrary to the usual method, so as that the boat..shall retreat. **1808** ASHE *Trav. Amer.* xxxvii. 303, I again took the helm, and ordered the men to back water with all their might. **1823** F. COOPER *Pioneer* xxvii, 'Back water,' cried Natty, as the canoe glided over the place. **1830** MARRYAT *King's Own* xlvi, Before the boats could be backed astern. **1837** —— *Dog-Fiend* xv, The smugglers backed water to stop their way. **1867** SMYTH *Sailor's Wd.-bk.* 65 A sailing vessel is backed by means of the sails, a steamer by reversing the paddles or screw-propeller. *Back her!* The order directing the engineer to reverse the movement of the cranks, and urge the vessel astern. **1884** *Manch. Exam.* 18 Sept. 5/2 Then the train was backed.

VI. *intr.* (for *refl.*) To move, go, come back.

16. a. To move back, recede, retreat backward.

1486 *Bk. St. Albans, Hawking* B vj, The terettys serue to kepe hir from wyndyng whan she backes. **1853** KANE *Grinnell Exp.* xvi. (1856) 123 Backing into wider quarters. **1860** DICKENS *Uncomm. Trav.* v. (1866) 33/2 Backing into the fireplace. **1873** G. DAVIES *Mount. and Mere* xiv. 109 The big fish slowly backed out of sight.

b. ***to back and fill*** (see FILL *v.* 4 c, d), to go backward and forward. Also *transf.* and *fig. U.S.*

1777 [see BACKING *vbl. sb.* 4]. **1848** DURIVAGE & BURNHAM *Stray Subj.* 174 The steam was well up on both boats, which lay rolling, and backing and filling, from the action of the paddles, at the dock. **1854** *Congress. Globe* 11 Dec. 57 Men will be sent to Congress who will not 'back and fill', and be on one principle for one week..and upon another principle another week. **1869** 'MARK TWAIN' *Innoc. Abr.* xxiii. 229 How in the world he [*sc.* the gondolier] can back and fill, shoot straight ahead,..is a problem to me. **1890** *Harper's Mag.* Sept. 598/2 Nimble stewards back and fill from galley to pantry. **1903** *N.Y. Even. Post* 24 Oct., The engine was backing and filling on a sidetrack.

17. To move in the reverse direction. Said of the wind when it changes in a direction opposite to the course of the sun. Opposed to *veer.* Also said of a railway train, etc.

1860 ADM. FITZ-ROY in *Merc. Mar. Mag.* VII. 40 The wind appeared to 'back,' or 'retrograde.' **1870** LOWELL *Study Wind.* 5 Did the wind back round or go about with the sun? **1894** *Idler* July 609 Sometimes he would pull out when he could hear the express coming, and make her back down to the next station. **1901** GUY BOOTHBY *Myst. Clasped Hands* iv. 75 At last the train backed into the station.

18. ***to back out***: to move backward out of a place without turning; *fig.* to draw back cautiously or tacitly from an arrangement or situation, to retreat out of a difficulty.

1807 *Deb. & Proc. U.S. Congress* 651 Our committee recommended us to recede—to back out. **1818** SCOTT *Rob Roy* viii, Determined that Morris should not back out of the scrape so easily. **1830** MARRYAT *King's Own* xxi, 'Sure your honour's in luck'..replied Barney, grinning, and backing out of the room. **1863** MRS. C. CLARKE *Shaks. Char.* ix. 226 Octavius backs out; his caution and reserve come to his rescue.

19. ***to back down***: to descend as one does a ladder; to recede downward from a position taken up. Also *fig.* Orig. *U.S.*

1849 C. LANMAN *Lett. Alleghany Mts.* xi. 90 When we got up about half way..they all three of 'em backed down and said I must not keep on. **1859** BARTLETT *Dict. Amer.* (ed. 2) 17 *To back down*, to withdraw a charge, eat one's own words; as 'I asked Jenkins, before witnesses, if he had called me a cheat; and he backed right down.' **1879** F. R. STOCKTON *Rudder Grange* x. 113 We're not going to back down. **1880** *St. James's Gaz.* 11 Oct., Unless the Government back down from their preparations at this point. **1884** *Harper's Mag.* June 66/2 Be firm, don't back down. **1934** WODEHOUSE *Right Ho, Jeeves* vii. 73 But don't tell me that when he saw how shirty she was about it, the chump didn't back down?

20. ***to back off*** (orig. U.S.). **a.** To draw back, retreat, let up. **b.** *fig.* To abandon one's intention, stand, etc.; to relent or back down. *colloq.*

1938 M. K. RAWLINGS *Yearling* iv. 37 He [*sc.* the bear] seemed to stand baffled... The dogs backed off an instant. **1954** *Amer. Speech* XXIX. 93 After you get through the traps you back off, so as to slow down. **1961** in WEBSTER (*fig.*). **1963** K. NEVILLE in D. Knight *One Hundred Yrs. Sci. Fiction* (1969) 73 'It's going to cost me near a hundred a month—that's a steep bite.' 'I still think they'll back off.' **1979** *Arizona Daily Star* 22 July A10/4 A man who took authorities to the shallow graves of two women he admitted killing backed off..from an earlier story that there were six more victims.

21. Of a building, etc.: to be so situated that the back abuts *on* a particular piece of land or property.

1891 G. M. FENN *Mahme Nousie* II. xv. 257 This opening backed on to the forest, and the escaping party passed in at once among the trees. **1921** *Edin. Rev.* Jan. 190 In St. James' Square, on which the club backs, the attack was more serious.

22. ***to back up.*** **a.** Of running water: to meet a barrier and become deeper. Of a barrier, etc.: to cause running water to accumulate and become deeper. Chiefly *U.S.* Hence **back-up** *sb.*, an accumulation of such water (Webster, 1934).

1837 *Knickerbocker* X. 409 They..descended this river to the mouth of White river; and as this was backed up by the spring freshets, the voyagers turned their course up the stream. **1842** P. PUSEY in *Jrnl. R. Agric. Soc.* III. xiii. 176 The field is subject to floods, which had backed up in the drains. **1844** W. PALIN *Ibid.* V. v. 78 An obstruction to their drainage occasioned by corn mills backing up the water to a considerable extent. **1884** [see BACKING *vbl. sb.* 4]. **1960** *Times* 7 Mar. 8/3 The enormous artificial lake..will reach 300 miles southwards, 75 miles farther than the back-up behind the present dam. **1963** R. L. CARSON *Silent Spring* vi. 55 Through the labour of the beavers, a lake backed up.

b. To move backwards; also *trans.*, to drive (a vehicle) backwards. orig. *U.S.*

1834 *Visit to Texas* viii. 116 A small log building..in the rear of which a cart was backed up on the Prairie. **1872** 'MARK TWAIN' *Sketches* 269 He then backed up against Pompey's statue, and squared himself to receive his assailants. **1883** *Harper's Mag.* Aug. 400 The wagons were backed up against the walls. **1948** A. COOKE in *Manch. Guardian Weekly* 21 Oct. 14/2 He gave the proper signals and slowly backed up.

c. *Climbing.* (See quot. 1923.)

1909 C. E. BENSON *Brit. Mountaineering* v. 139 Backing up on smooth walls is extremely tiring. **1923** G. D. ABRAHAM *First Steps to Climbing* v. 58 It may be easy to 'back up', with feet and knees on one side and back on the other.

d. *trans. Computing.* To provide back-up for; to make a duplicate copy of (a file, program, etc.), esp. to safeguard against loss or corruption of the original.

1967 *AFIPS Conf. Proc.* XXX. 776/1 A parallel DDC computer system..not only provides computer backup but 'backs up' the time-shared analog and digital input/output equipment. **1974** *Computing Rev.* June 204/2 The objective of this paper is to determine the optimum frequency for backing up a data base. **1983** *Austral. Microcomputer Mag.* Sept. 70/3 The tape drive can also be used to backup the IBM XT's hard disk.

23. *trans.* To carry on the back. *U.S.*

1840 DANA *Bef. Mast* xx, We started off every morning.. and cut wood..and after dinner..carted and 'backed' it down until sunset. **1895** *Outing* (U.S.) XXVII. 47/2 These hardy woodsmen backing packs of from eighty to one hundred pounds each.

back (bæk), *adv.* [Aphetic for ABACK *adv.*, OE. *on bæc* = into or in the rear. Not found bef. 14th c.; formerly with comparative *backer*, occas. *backermore.*]

I. In a direction to the rear.

1. *lit.* In the direction of one's back, or the back of any object in question; toward the rear; away from a forward position. Often with the vb. (*go, come,* etc.) omitted, esp. in the imperative. ***back with***: move back with, take or draw back.

a **1300** *Cursor M.* 7525 Ga, Neyder forth ne ȝeit on back. **1460** *Pol. Rel. & L. Poems* (1866) 55 With that a-noon I went me bakkermore. **1549** LATIMER *Ploughers* 17 No man yͤ loketh bakke. **1562** J. HEYWOOD *Prov. & Epigr.* (1867) 158 The bore shall backe first. **1590** R. HARVEY *Pl. Perc.* 9 Backe with that leg, Perceuall. **1810** SCOTT *Lady of L.* II. xxxiv, Back, beardless boy! Back, minion! **1851** H. STEPHENS *Bk. of Farm* 691 Language to horses..*To step backward—Back* is the only word I can remember to have heard for this motion. **1860** MAURY *Phys. Geog. Sea* viii. §378 This current which baffled and beat back this fleet.

2. Away from what is treated as the front; from the actual or ordinary position.

c **1500** *Blowbol's Test.* in Halliw. *Nug. P.* 12 To draw the bake fer out of their sight. **1611** BIBLE *Matt.* xxviii. 2 The angel of the Lord rolled back the stone. **1792** *Munchausen's Trav.* xiv. 4 The crowds who were about me retreated back. **1816** J. WILSON *City of Plague* I. ii. 132 A blast..Drives me back from the grave. *Mod.* Try to force this bolt back.

3. Away from an engagement, promise, or undertaking.

1783 AINSWORTH *Lat. Dict.* (Morell) s.v. *Back*, To go back from his word, *Fidem violare.* **1855** MACAULAY *Hist. Eng.* IV. 701 Harley and Foley..promised, with an air of confidence..but soon went back from their word. *Mod.* I accepted his offer at once, lest he should draw back.

4. Into time past, backward in time.

1711 STEELE *Spect.* No. 153 ¶2 Able to look back on Youth with Satisfaction. **1712** —— *ibid.* No. 484 ¶2 If we go back to the days of Solomon. **1748** RICHARDSON *Clarissa* (1811) VI. 95, I might have gone further back than that fatal seventh. **1854** MRS. JAMESON *Bk. of Th.* (1877) 123 In memory I can go back to a very early age.

II. In the reverse direction.

5. *lit.* In the opposite direction in space, so as to return to the place originally left. Often with vb. (*go*, etc.) omitted: cf. 1.

a **1535** MORE *Wks.* 6 (R.) To pull him back into the voluptuous brode way. **1559** *Myrr. Mag., Jack Cade* x. 6 Remoued our campe, and backe to Senocke went. *c* **1590** MARLOWE *Faust.* v. 37 If thou deny it I will back to hell. **1596** SHAKS. *Merch. V.* II. vii. 14, I will suruay the inscriptions backe againe. **1624** T. TAYLOR *Two Serm.* i. 21 Backe they will to Egypt in all haste. **1783** BURKE *Affairs Ind.* Wks. XI. 54 Send it back to Bengal for the purchase of Indian merchandise. **1852** MISS YONGE *Cameos* I. 216 Back came John in rage and fury.

6. In reversal of progress, so as to return to a former condition.

1535 COVERDALE *Jer.* xliv. 2 They wente backe to do sacrifice and worshipe vnto straunge goddes. **1752** JOHNSON *Rambl.* No. 204 ¶6 And then fall back to the common state of man. **1817** BYRON *Manfred* II. ii. 78, I felt myself degraded back to them, And was all clay again. **1867** FREEMAN *Norm. Conq.* (1876) I. App. 749 The whole country fell back into heathenism.

7. a. In reversal of action or change of any kind, so as to restore former circumstances or relations; formerly expressed by AGAIN, which is still sometimes used, and often added.

1607 SHAKS. *Cor.* I. i. 149 All From me do backe receiue the Flowre of all. **1692** E. WALKER *Epictetus' Mor.* (1737) xv, How is that lost that is but given back? **1752** JOHNSON *Rambl.* No. 193 ¶11 Three times I sent it to the printer, and three times I fetched it back. **1865** BARING-GOULD *Werewolves* v. 55 And transformed himself back again into his human shape. **1883** GILMOUR *Mongols* xvii. 203 Has any one among us died..and come back to life?

b. *ellipt.* (= come, received, put, etc. back.) To be back = F. *être de retour*.

1879 W. WARD *Philos. Theism* (1884) I. 386 My desire to be back comfortably in the warm house. *Mod.* How long have you been back? I must have them back some day.

8. In return, requital, repayment, retaliation.

1599 SHAKS. *Much Ado* IV. i. 29 What haue I to giue you back? **1601** —— *Twelfth N.* IV. iii. 18 Take, and giue backe affayres, and their dispatch. **1831** CARLYLE *Sart. Res.* II. i, With heavy penalty will it one day be required back. **1863** KINGSLEY *Water Bab.* viii. 326 She knew they would pay her back. *Mod.* Strongly tempted to answer back.

III. Of position.

9. In a position to the rear, or away from the front; at a point or distance behind.

c **1300** in *O.E. Misc.* 228 He bad him stonde bac. **1473** WARKW. *Chron.* 22 And aftyre..it aroose north-est, and so bakkere and bakkere. **1594** SHAKS. *Rich. III*, I. ii. 38 My Lord, stand backe, and let the Coffin passe. **1850** THACKERAY *Pendennis* xvi. (1884) 143 Mrs. Pendennis's visit ..which we have recorded many pages back. *Mod.* The field lies back from the road. I left him back at the second milestone.

10. In a state of check to forward motion in space, to progress in condition, to production, exhibition, or declaration.

1535 COVERDALE *2 Kings* iv. 24 Dryue forth, and keep me not bak. **1575–6** THYNNE in *Animadv.* Introd. 56 There is a huge stoone tyed at my foote, whiche keepeth me backe. **1611** BIBLE *Num.* xxiv. 11 The Lord hath kept thee back from honour. **1855** MACAULAY *Hist. Eng.* III. 255 A nation ..long kept back by a sterile soil and a severe climate. *Mod.* To keep back dispatches, main facts, essential particulars. To shade fruit trees, so as to keep the fruit back.

11. In time past; ago. Usually following a measure of time.

1796 SOUTHEY *Lett. Spain* (1799) 139 Dug up, a few years back, at Buenos Ayres. **1860** HAWTHORNE *Marble Faun* (1879) I. viii. 86 For months back. **1869** FREEMAN *Norm. Conq.* (1876) III. xi. 58 A house which, two generations back, had been ignoble. *Mod.* Far back in the Middle Ages.

12. Behind in condition, behind-hand, in arrear.

1875 *Chamb. Jrnl.* No. 133. 66 A dinnerless Sunday and a week back in their rent.

13. *U.S. slang.* Served (and drunk) alongside or together with an alcoholic drink.

1976 M. MACHLIN *Pipeline* xxxiv. 382 Doheny drank Crown Royal straight with water back. **1978** *N.Y. Times Mag.* 23 July 23/4 Somebody has to figure out why drinkers who used to order 'soda on the side' now say soda back, and why whiskey 'straight' has to be ordered straight up rather than neat.

IV. *Phrases.*

14. †***back and fore*** (arch. or dial.), ***back and forth***, ***back and forward***: backwards and forwards, to and fro. Also as *attrib. phr.*

1613 [see FORTH *adv.* 1 a]. **1653** URQUHART *Rabelais* I. xxiii, He would go back and fore along the foresaid rope. **1678** R. LESTRANGE *Seneca's Mor.* (1685) 4 All Material Benefits are tossed back and forward, and change their Master. **1816** PICKERING *Vocab.* s.v., *Back and Forth*, backwards and forwards. Ex. He was walking back and forth. This is a very common expression in New England; but it is used only in conversation. **1837** DUNLAP *Mem. Water Drinker* (ed. 2) I. 57, I am not one of your brook trout to be played back and forth with a hair line as her husband catches um. **1839** *Anecd. & Trad.* (Camd.) Young girls.. dance over the candle back and forth. **1847** LE FANU *T. O'Brien* 199 Barristers..flitted back and forward through the passages. **1857** S. H. HAMMOND *Wild Northern Scenes* 138 They would run here and there, back and forth, at full speed along the sands. **1884** ROE in *Harper's Mag.* Sept. 540/2, I will go back and forth every day. **1899** *Congress. Rec.* Feb. 1743/1 Some of you..remember when at Vicksburg our boys got so close to the Confederates that they talked back and forth. **1907** U. SINCLAIR *Industrial Republic* p. xii, I would find myself comparing..the two eras, and transposing its leading figures back and forth. **1909** E. B. TITCHENER *Text-Bk. Psychol.* I. x. 47 This back-and-forth movement will continue. **1962** *Listener* 1 Mar. 377/1 Both dangers can be avoided if there is enough back-and-forth traffic of ideas, information, and influence.

15. ***back of***: back from, behind. (Esp. in U.S.). Cf. *in back of* (BACK *sb.*[1] 23 g).

1694 in *Cal. Virginia St. Papers* (1875) I. 44 We Ranged on Ackoquane and so back of the Inhabitants and ye So[u]th. **1755** L. EVANS *Geogr. Ess.* 15 If the French settle back of us, the English must either submit to them, or have their throats cut. *Ibid.* 16 If we secure the Country back of Carolina in time. **1823** G. W. OGDEN *Lett. fr. West* 76 The uplands back of the Oak Hills of the Ohio river. **1840** DANA *Bef. Mast* ix, The mission stands a little back of the town. **1857** TOMES *Amer. in Japan* iii. 83 The country which stretches back of Shanghai. **1875** WHITNEY *Life Lang.* viii. 143 Another earlier designation of a more or less kindred conception lay back of it. **1875** SEARS *Serm. & Songs* 287 The home lies back of the Sunday School. **1899** *Westm. Gaz.* 3 May 3/2 He has ideas back of his words. **1949** E. POUND *Pisan Cantos* lxxx. 96 In the shade back of the jo-house. **1953** M. LASKI *Vict. Chaise-Longue* 21 No one could live there, back of the railways, down by the canal.

back- *in comb.* is used in many relations, substantive, adjective, and adverbial (rarely verbal), often difficult to separate, and in various senses. In some of these the combination is very loose, the use of the hyphen being almost optional.

This is especially the case, when *back* is capable of being viewed as an adj., in which aspect the hyphen would not be used, e.g. *back-yard* or *back yard*, *back-stroke* or *back stroke*. As a rule, the use of the hyphen implies that the combination (in the case in point) has not the general and purely descriptive value of the two words, but is in some respect specialized or appropriated as a specific name.

A. General senses in combination.

I. from BACK *sb.*

1. *objective.* **a.** with pr. pple., forming adjectives, as ***back-wounding***, BACK-SLAPPING. **b.** with vbl. sb., forming substantives, as ***back-breaking***, ***-scratching***. **c.** with agent-noun, as ***back-scraper***, ***-scratcher***.

1603 SHAKS. *Meas. for M.* III. ii. 197 Back-wounding calumnie. **1787** BENTHAM *Wks.* X. 168 Back-breaking which is the death of so many vessels. **1794** J. WOLCOTT (P. Pindar) *Rowl. for Oliver* Wks. II. 135 Chopsticks and backscrapers. **1834** SOUTHEY *Doctor* iv. (D.) A back-scratcher, of which the hand was ivory. **1884** *Good Wds.* June 400/2 Having borne himself so lubberly over his 'back-scratching.'

2. *instrumental* and *locative*, with pples. and adjs., forming adjs., as ***back-broken***, ***back-aching***, ***-breaking***.

1603 J. DAVIES *Microcosm.* (1876) 16 (D.) An empires lode (Which weaknesse oft back-broken vndergoes). **1837** *Athenæum* No. 827. 874 The back-broken traveller.. stretches from his camel. **1870** 'MARK TWAIN' *£30,000 Bequest* (1906) 214 Did you ever notice..how back-breaking and tiresome it was? **1883** SWINBURNE *Casquettes* xvi, The strengths reluctant of waves back-bowed. **1913** *Maclean's Mag.* May 93/2 Every Monday I have a back-breaking session with that washing machine. **1916** 'TAFFRAIL' *Pincher Martin* iii. 34 The work of shovelling the coal into bags was back-breaking. **1940** F. KITCHEN *Brother to Ox* ii. 25 What a back-aching job it was! **1958** *Times* 27 Oct. 11/3 [Potato-picking] looks so easy, and to the novice pressed into service as I am it is a back-breaking penance.

3. *attrib.* Of or pertaining to the back, used for or carried on the back, e.g. ***back-ache***, ***-cloth***, ***-clout***, ***-fin***; ***back-basket***, ***-burden***, ***-dunt***.

c **1230** *Ancr. R.* 290 Gif him stronge bac duntes. **1377** LANGL. *P. Pl.* B. x. 362 Oure bakclo̥pis [*v.r.* bakkes] þat moth-eten be. **1530** PALSGR. 196/1 Backeburden, *portee, charge.* **1601** DENT *Pathw. Heauen* 79 Tooth-ache, head-ache, backe-ache, bone-ache. **1706** PHILLIPS, *Bray*, Back-clouts for young children. **1725** DE FOE *Voy. round World* (1840) 158 She came..with a great back-burden of roots. **1775** ADAIR *Amer. Ind.* 90 Large portable back-baskets. **1863** KINGSLEY *Water-Bab.* iv. 144 With their back-fins out of the water. **1907** MASEFIELD *Tarp. Muster* xii. 132 It was 'Shift topmasts', or 'Down top-gallant yards', or some gummy backache or another all the whole day long. **1922** JOYCE *Ulysses* 40 We have nothing in the house but backache pills.

II. from BACK *a.*

4. *gen.* Lying at the back, in the rear, or behind; hinder; = BACK *a.* 1, and more commonly written as two words.

1581 MARBECK *Bk. of Notes* 86 Thou shalt see my Backe-partes, but my face shal not be seene. **1650** T. GOODWIN *Wks.* (1862) IV. 267 The back-parts of God, which we call his attributes. **1752** tr. *Gersaint's Rembrandt's Etch.* 29 The Back-view is the inner part of the Temple. **1753** HANWAY *Trav.* (1762) I. III. xxxvii. 167 The back-part of this tent. **1772** MASKELYNE in *Phil. Trans.* LXII. 106 In the back-observation..the real upper-limb will appear the lowest. **1774** WHITE *ibid.* LXV. 273 The back-wall of William of Wickham's stables.

5. *esp.* Applied to a part of a house or building which lies behind, and is usually subsidiary to the front or main part bearing the name, as ***back-building***, a building behind forming an appendage to a main building, ***back-chamber***, ***-court***, ***-drawing-room***, ***-garden*** (also *transf.* and *fig.*), ***-kitchen***, ***-parlour***, ***porch***, ***shed***, etc. See also BACK-HOUSE 1, BACK YARD.

1535 COVERDALE *Ezek.* xlii. 1 The chambre that stode ouer agaynst the backbuyldinge. **1633** FORD *Love's Sacr.* I. ii. (1839) 77 I'll meet thee..in thy lady's back-lobby. **1653** URQUHART *Rabelais* I. lv, In every back-chamber or with-drawing room. **1738** *Purefoy Lett.* 8 Oct. (1931) I. viii. 191 To mend two Pannells in the back Parlour 0–03–06. **1759** STERNE *Tr. Shandy* (1802) I. 78 To drink a bottle of wine with my father..in the back-parlour. **1784** WESLEY *Wks.* (1872) XIII. 503 She heard a knocking at the back-kitchen door. **1789** WASHINGTON *Diaries* (1925) IV. 30 A back shed, which seems to be added as the family encreases. **1811** JANE AUSTEN *Let.* 25 Apr. (1932) II. 274 We were 66..quite enough to fill the Back Draw[s] room. **1818** KEATS *Let.* 24 Mar. (1958) I. 254 To have a sort of Philosophical Back Garden. **1832** *Chambers's Edin. Jrnl.* I. 50/1 It is true..that nothing can match your back kitchen as a convenience to the servants. **1840** *Southern Lit. Messenger* VI. 734/1 He was led by the hand into the back porch. **1854** MRS. GASKELL *North & S.* i, Curled up on the sofa in the back-drawing-room. **1866** R. BALLANTYNE *Lifeboat* 5 Mr. Crumps sat in a small back-office. **1875** H. B. STOWE *We & Neighbors* liv. 480 He had leaped out of a window upon a back shed. **1878** BLACK *Green Past.* iii. 20 The back-parlour of a Ballinascroon public-house. **1889** G. B. SHAW in *Hawk* 13 Aug. 172/2 Wagner..is 'buried in the back garden, sir, like a Newfoundland dog'. **1960** R. WILLIAMS *Border Country* I. ii. §6.51 It had a built-on back-kitchen. **1963** *Times* 16 Jan. 13/1 After cultivating their own back gardens contentedly.. for 15 post-war years up to the beginning of 1961, steel-makers the world over are now preoccupied with export problems.

III. from BACK *adv.*

6. With *vbs.*, forming compound verbs, as ***back-try***, to try back or over again. *rare.*

1640–1 *Kirkcudbr. War-Comm. Min. Bk.* (1855) 83 The way..shall be tryed and baktryed.

7. With *pres. pple.*, forming adjs., as ***back-acting*** (cf. *back-acter* in B below), ***-blowing***, ***-coming***, ***-driving***, ***-glancing***, ***-going***, ***-looking***, ***-lying***.

1562 TURNER *Herbal* II. 97b, A repercussiue or back-dryuyng medicine. **1615** W. HULL *Mirr. Maj.* 48 The soule is encombred with foure back-pulling retentives. **1817** MAR. EDGEWORTH *Harrington* vi. Wks. IX. 45 With back-stepping curtsy. **1850** MRS. BROWNING *Poems* II. 347 Back-looking Memory. **1863** H. KINGSLEY *A. Elliot* I. x. 110 A long, low, back-lying house. **1924** BUCHAN *Three Hostages* xxi. 299 The body was heavy, and he was clearly a back-going beast. **1928** W. BARNES *Excavating Machinery* ii. 50 The action of a back-acting shovel is..the reverse of a standard shovel, as it digs towards the machine like a drag line.

8. With *pa. pples.*, forming adjs. (chiefly poetic), as ***back-drawn***, ***-flung***, ***-thrown***, ***-turned***, etc.

1580 SIDNEY *Arcadia* (1622) 92 With shafts shot out from their back-turned bow. **1652** URQUHART *Jewel* Wks. (1834) 226 Tossed to and again, retorted, backreverted. **1850** MRS. BROWNING *Poems* II. 74 Back-thrown on the slippery coping-stone. **1863** BARNES *Rhymes Dorset Dial.* II. 28 A-lookin up with back-flung head.

9. With *agent-nouns*, forming sbs., as BACKSLIDER; ***back-sitter***, one who sits back.

1883 in PAXTON HOOD *Scot. Char.* ii. 33 But a bauchle.. in this world, and a backsitter in the neist.

10. With *vbl. sbs.* forming sbs., as BACKSLIDING, ***back-coming***, ***-drawing***, ***-going***, ***-looking***, ***-slipping***, ***-starting***, ***-surging***, ***-turning***, etc.

1535 COVERDALE *Jer.* iii. 22 So shal I heale youre bacturnynges. **1540** —— *Fruitf. Less.* iii. Wks. 1844 I. 366 Such curious backlooking doth the Lord rebuke. **1590** SWINBURN *Testaments* 197 Of apostasie..that is to say, of back-starting from the Christian faith. **1600** ABP. ABBOT *Exp. Jonah* 523 That sigh which breatheth out sorrow, by a backe-breathing bringeth in joy. *a* **1605** SIR J. MELVIL *Mem.* (1683) 79 In her back-coming..the Earl of Bothwell rancountered her. **1663** BLAIR *Autobiog.* vi. (1848) 86 Approving my jealousy, but reproving my backdrawing. **1818** SCOTT *Rob Roy* xxxiv, A..hostage for my safe backcoming. **1858** R. CHAMBERS *Dom. Ann. Scotl.* I. 4 In all her back-surgings upon the ground she lost.

11. With *nouns of action*, forming sbs., as ***back-caper***, ***-blast***, ***-come***, ***-eddy*** (usu. *fig.*), ***-flip***, ***-flow*** also (*fig.*), ***-kick*** (also *fig.*), ***-look***, ***-march***, ***-return***, ***-somersault***, ***-step***, ***-stretch***, ***-sweep***, ***-swing*** (also *fig.*), ***-swirl***, ***-throw***.

1577 tr. *Bullinger's Decades* (1592) 314 At his back-returne into his country. **1591** Backe somersaut [see SOMERSAULT *sb.* a]. **1599** SHAKS. *Hen. V*, v. Cho. 41 Till Harryes backe returne againe to France. **1606** *Ret. fr. Parnass.* II. vi, The dog, seeing him practise his..back-caper. **1645** RUTHERFORD *Tryal & Tri. Faith* (1845) 122 When the conscience hath gotten a back-throw with the hand of the Almighty. *a*1718 PENN *Wks.* (1726) I. 454 We wish it be not the Beginning of a Back-march. 1852 GROTE *Greece* II. lxxv. IX. 479 The back-march of Agesilaus. 1865 'LEWIS CARROLL' *Alice in Wonderland* v. 64 You turned a back-somersault in at the door. 1869 *Eng. Mech.* 31 Dec. 382/2 The weight is by the back-throw from C to A restrained from lowering itself. 1884 *Health Exhib. Catal.* 72/2 For the prevention of any back-flow of water or sewage. 1899 H. G. HUTCHINSON et al. *Book of Golf & Golfers* v. 125 If the back swing is a little tied up .. the down swing and its finish are as free as we could have them. 1913 D. H. LAWRENCE *Sons & Lovers* xiii. 365 The Trent carries bodily its back-swirls and intertwinings. 1923 KIPLING *Irish Guards in Great War* I. 88 Our shrapnel, which had no back-blast. 1924 A. J. SMALL *Frozen Gold* xiii. 272 Their back-kicks went out as far as their bushy tails. 1928 T. S. ELIOT *Dial. Poetic Drama* p. xxii, The age of Shakespeare moved in a steady current, with back-eddies certainly, towards anarchy and chaos. 1934 WEBSTER, *Backswing*, the movement of the [golf] club backward to the position from which it is brought down to strike the ball. 1935 W. G. HARDY *Father Abraham* I. ii. 29 His cane cut Simil-i-una .. across the calves. Its back-flip caught Abraham just as expertly across the belly. 1936 J. C. POWYS *Maiden Castle* (1937) i. 40 The least back-eddy of remorse or shame. 1939 G. GREENE *Lawless Roads* x. 261 Mexico gave me a back kick. 1940 E. WILSON *To Finland Station* I. iii. 16 The back-flow of old instincts and interests among the purposes and hopes of the new. 1940 *Chambers's Techn. Dict.* 68/1 *Back-kick*, term applied to the violent reversal of an internal-combustion engine during starting, due to a back-fire. 1948 J. HARVEY *Plantagenets* vii. 87 The break of dynasty and the back-swing of the pendulum. 1954 J. H. FINGLETON *Ashes crown Year* iv. 45 Hole's big back-swing .. leaves him vulnerable to an in-swinger. 1966 MILLS & BUTLER *Mod. Badminton* iv. 34 For the high singles serve .. your back-swing should go back further. 1967 *Boston Sunday Herald* 30 Apr. I. 25/1 The Yanks would do back-flips to get Yaz, Tony C., or Petrocelli.

12. With other *sbs.* **a.** expressing backward direction, as ***back-bias***, **back-draught** (see B).

*a*1617 BAYNE *On Eph.* (1658) 130 Youthful lusts .. like a back-bias, did draw after themselves the understanding. 1642 ROGERS *Naaman* 550 He doth but put a back-bias upon thee; that he might weigh thy motion to himselfe.

b. expressing 'in the contrary direction,' return-, as ***back-cargo***, cargo brought on the return voyage, ***back-carriage***, ***-current***, ***-fare***, ***-freight***, ***-tonnage***.

1657 COLVIL *Whigs Supplic.* (1751) 30 He treads the back-scent, brings a glove. 1721 C. KING *Brit. Merch.* I. 361 Sending any empty Ships .. for the sake of Back-carriage. Corn has been often carry'd .. for nothing, in consideration of Back-Tunnage. 1805 W. TAYLOR in *Ann. Rev.* III. 320 Our ships incur a loss of back-freight. 1832 in Mrs. A. Mathews *Mem. C. Mathews* (1839) IV. 106 No, your honour, not unless you promise me the back-fare. 1833 TENNYSON *Poems* 36 The fish that everywhere In the backcurrent glanced and played. 1860 in *Merc. Mar. Mag.* VII. 57 It is not difficult to procure back cargo.

c. expressing reciprocation or reply, as ***back-answer*** (also as *v. trans.*), ***-echo***, **back-word** (see B).

1626 BACON *Sylva* §247 You have many Back-Eccho's to the Place where you stand. 1884 *Hull & E.C. Herald* 28 Feb. 6/6 The boy was a civil boy, and never gave a back answer. 1915 A. CONAN DOYLE *Valley of Fear* II. ii. 187 'You have your back answer quick enough.' 'Yes, I was always quick of speech.' 1921 H. WILLIAMSON *Beautiful Years* 221 No one has ever back-answered Sol Isaacs and not paid for it. 1939 G. GREENE *Confid. Agent* II. i. 184 'No more back answers,' the policeman said. 1959 P. MCCUTCHAN *Storm South* iv. 57, I didn't want to be hauled over the coals for back-answering a passenger.

d. expressing 'turned or performed backwards,' as **back-pater-noster**, BACK-SLANG.

IV. Parasynthetic derivatives, as ***back-geared***, having back gear; BACK-HANDED.

1881 *Mechanic* §596 Lathe with back-geared head.

B. Special combinations (with quotations in alphabetical order):

back-acter = *backhoe* below; cf. BACK-ACTION; **back-bar**, a bar in the chimney to hang a vessel on (Ash); **back beat** *Jazz*, a secondary beat; **back-boiler**, a boiler behind a domestic fire or cooking range; **back-box**, in *Printing*, a box on top of the upper case, usually appropriated to small capitals (Craig); **back-brand** *dial.* = BACK-LOG; **back-breaker**, (*a*) the leader of a gang of farm-labourers; (*b*) a back-breaking task, etc. (cf. BACK *sb.*[1] 24 a and BACK-A. 2); also in extended use; **back-burn** [BURN *sb.*[3] I c]: see quot. 1944; also ***back-burning***; **back burner**: on a cooking stove, a simmering-burner (BURNER 4 c), freq. set behind the front burners or boiling-rings; used *fig.*, esp. in phr. ***on the back burner*** (colloq., orig. *U.S.*), (of an issue, etc.) in the state of being (temporarily) relegated or postponed; out of the forefront of attention; deferred, pending; †**back-carry** *sb.* = BACK-BEAR; **back-casing**, in *Mining*, a temporary shaft-lining of bricks, in front of which the permanent lining is built; **back-cauter** (see quot.); **back-chain**, a chain that passes over a cart-saddle to support the shafts of a cart; †**back-chair**, a chair with a back; **back-clamp** *v.* in *Wrestling* (see quot.); **back-click**, a trick in wrestling; **back-comb** *sb.*, an ornamental comb worn at the back of the head; also *v. trans.* and *intr.*, to comb the underlying hairs of a strand towards the scalp; **back-court**, (*a*) (see BACK- 5); (*b*) in *Lawn Tennis* (see quot. 1961); also *attrib.*; **back-crawl**, in *Swimming*, a form of the crawl in which the swimmer lies on his back; **back-cross** *v. trans.* (*Biol.*), to cross (a hybrid) with one of its parents; ***back-crossing*** vbl. sb.; hence **back-cross** *sb.*, an instance or product of back-crossing; **back-cut**, in *Cricket*, a late cut; hence ***back-cut*** v. trans.; **back-cutting**, in *Civil Engin.* (see quots.); **back-double** *dial.*, a back street, a side road; **back-draught**, (*a*) a draught of air backward, a hood for producing this in a fire; (*b*) a drawing in of the breath; an act of drinking or gulping down *Sc.*; (*c*) a reverse current of water, under-tow; **back-drop** *Theatr.* (orig. *U.S.*), = BACKCLOTH 2; also *transf.* and *fig.*; **back-electro-motive force, back e.m.f.**, in *Electr. Engin.*, an electro-motive force which opposes that producing the current; **backfield**: in Baseball, the outfield (*rare* or *nonce-use*); in American football, the (positions occupied by) players behind the line of scrimmage; **backfill** *sb.*, excavated earth, etc., used in backfilling; **back-filling**, the filling in again of earth which has been removed, the earth so filled in; ; so ***back-fill*** v. (1651 in D.O.S.T.); ***back-filled*** ppl. a.; **back-flap, -fold** (= *back-shutter*); **back-flash**, the act or process of flashing back (Webster, 1934); spec. (*a*) *Forestry* (see quot. 1957); (*b*) = FLASHBACK *sb.* 2; **back focus**, in *Photogr.* (see quots.); **back-front**, the ground in an etching or engraving; **back-harrow** (see HARROW); **back-heart**, the dorsal heart or large blood-vessel of insects and other arthropoda; **back-heel** *sb.*, a trick in wrestling; **back-heel** *v.*, to throw by a back-heel; (*b*) to kick (a football) backwards with the heel; **backhoe** *U.S.*, an excavating vehicle in which the scoop is rigidly attached to the lower end of a short hinged arm at the end of a boom and is pulled towards the vehicle in operation; = *back-acter* above; †**back-hood**, hiding behind cover; **back-jamb**, a wing of a house projecting behind; **back-lift**, in *Cricket* , a backward lift given to the bat immediately before a stroke is played; in *Rugby* and *Assoc. Football*, a backward lift given to the leg when kicking a ball; **back-light**, a light coming from behind or falling upon the hinder part (Worcester 1859); **back-lighting**, in *Photogr.*, lighting coming from behind the subject; **back-lining**, in *Arch.*, the piece of a sash-frame parallel to the pulley piece and next to the jamb on either side (Gwilt 1842); **back-links**, the links in a parallel motion which connect the air-pump rod to the beam (Weale *Dict. Terms* 1849); **back-lock**, a trick in wrestling; **back-nails**, 'nails made with flat shanks, so as to hold fast, and not to open the grain of the wood' (James *Mil. Dict.* 1816); **back-overman**, in *Coal Mining*, an overman who has the immediate inspection of the workings and workmen during the *back-shift*; **back-painting** (see quot.); **back-pater-noster**, the Lord's prayer repeated backward as a charm, *fig.* a muttered curse or imprecation; **back play**, in *Cricket*, a method of play in which the batsman steps back towards the wicket and plays the ball from behind the popping crease; hence ***back-player***; **back-pressure**, in the steam-engine, the resistance of the atmosphere or waste steam to the piston; also, any resistance to the flow of a liquid or gas; also *attrib.*; **back projection** *Cinematogr.* (see quot. 1933); so ***back-projected*** ppl. adj.; †**back-reckoning**, a reckoning for past transactions or misdeeds; **back-rest**, a guide attached to the slide-rest of a turning-lathe, and placed in contact with the work to steady it; **back-rope** (of a horse) = BACK-BAND; *Naut.*, a rope leading inboard from the martingale; see also quot. 1860; **back saw** (see quot.); **back-scene**, the background of a stage scene; **back-shaft**, part of a cotton-spinning machine; **back-shift**, in *Coal Mining*, the second shift or set of hewers for the day; **backshore** (see quot. 1919); **back-shutter**, the part of a shutter which folds up behind; **back-skin**, in *Mining*, a leather covering worn by miners in wet workings; **back spacer**, a typewriter key that moves the carriage one space backward; also ***back-space key*** and *transf.*; so **back-space** *v. intr.*, to use such a key; ***back-spacing*** vbl. sb.; **back-spang** (*Sc.*), a trick or legal quirk, by which one takes advantage of another, after a bargain has been adjusted (Jam.); **back-speed**, in *Mech.*, the second speed-gear of a lathe; **back-spin** = UNDERSPIN; †**back-stand**, backing, support; **back-step**, a step back; the retrograde movement without changing front (James *Mil. Dict.* 1816); **back-stool**, a stool with a back; **back-stop**, in *Cricket* = LONG-STOP; **back-straight** (see STRAIGHT B. 3), the stretch along the side of a racecourse or stadium opposite to that in which the races end; **back-striking**, in *Agriculture*, a mode of ploughing in which the earth once turned is simply thrown back again; **back-string**, a string at the back, *e.g.* at the back of a child's pinafore; **back-sweep** (see quot.); **back-swimmer**, one that swims on his back; the hemipterous insect *Notonecta* which swims on the surface of pools; **back-tack** (*Sc. Law*), a kind of deed by which the mortgagee of land gives a lease of it to the mortgagor on condition of payment of rent till redeemed (Buchanan); †**back-timber** (*humorously* for) clothing; †**back-trade**, backward course; †**back-trick**, ? a caper backwards in dancing; **back-winter**, a return of winter after its regular time; **back-word** (in *Lanc.*), withdrawal from a promise or from an accepted invitation, also *dial.* a contradiction, rude answer; **back-worm**, a disease incident to hawks; **back-wort** (*Herb.*), old name for the Comfrey (*Symphytum officinale*).

1957 J. H. ARNISON *Pract. Road Constr.* iii. 52 The shafts for the manholes may be cut out by manual labour, and the main trench by mechanical plant such as a *back-acter [*printed* -acker] or trencher. 1963 M. J. TOMLINSON *Foundation Design & Construction* ix. 537 Small hydraulically operated tractor-mounted backacters are being used to an increasing extent for narrow and shallow trench excavation. 1976 *Jrnl.* (Newcastle) 26 Nov. (Advt.), Hymac 370 wheeled digger with back acter. 1928 *Melody Maker* Dec. 1295 (*heading*) *Back beats! 1948 *Metronome* Nov. 28 I'd rather use the high-hat as a back beat and break up the bass drum rhythms. 1977 *New Musical Express* 12 Feb. 17/1 The pedal steel, sawed-off fiddle and hammering back-beat are a joy, and the dynamics are keen. 1985 *Internat. Musician* June 53/2, I put down a backbeat and a bass line—a heavy sort of Rock'n'Roll track under what they do which is sing with drums. 1939 L. J. OVERTON *Dom. Hot Water Suppl.* iii. 12 The **Back-Boiler*, for setting in brickwork behind a kitchen range or at the back of an ordinary fireplace. 1844 W. BARNES *Poems Rural Life in Dorset Dial.* 201 We got a *back bran', dree girt logs. 1874 HARDY *Far from Madding Crowd* I. xxii. 267 The log which was to form the back-brand of the evening fire was the uncleft trunk of a tree. 1867 *People's Mag.* May 314/2 He selects one of his gang as *back-breaker. 1909 WEBSTER, *Back breaker*, a task requiring excessive exertion. 1929 F. BOWEN *Sea Slang* 5 *Backbreakers*, old-fashioned ship's pumps. 1962 *Spectator* 13 Apr. 480, I don't fancy the back-breaker or the pile-driver [in wrestling]. 1944 *Soc. Amer. Foresters: Forestry Terminol.* 10/1 **Back-burn*, denotes a controlled fire burning against the wind. 1963 *Times* 26 Apr. 14/1 With Mr. Khrushchev showing no interest in the Anglo-American proposals, the test ban, with Berlin and the Soviet evacuation of Cuba, will have to be put on the *back burner, as the Americans have it. 1966 *Time* 4 Feb. 59 That uniform gives prestige and status to a guy who's been 100 years on the back burner. 1973 *Newsweek* 19 Feb. 33 Integration has become a back-burner issue... The up-front concern now is to improve economic and social conditions for blacks. 1976 *Globe & Mail* (Toronto) 23 Nov. 11/1 The new Parti Quebecois Government will either have to raise taxes.., or put most of Rene Levesque's election promises on a back burner for the time being. 1986 *Times* 10 Mar. 2/8 He had misgivings about the GM bid for BL because under its global strategy Britain had been put on the 'backburner' for the last decade. 1878 E. S. ELWELL *Boy Colonists* 90 The '*back-burning' of the fire, which though very slow, is always the most steady and most effective. 1611 COTGR., *Cautere dorsal*, the *back cauter: or, that kinde of knife-like cauter, which cuts but on th' one side. 1649 *Bury Wills* (1850) 221 Vnto my daughter Martha two wrought *backchaires. 1713 PARKYNS *Inn-Play* (1727) 43 When your Adversary *Back-clamps you, which is when he claps his Heel in your Ham. 1867 *Standard* Apr., Graham threw his antagonist first by a '*back click.' 1865 DICKENS *Mut. Fr.* I. II. xii. 268 Ladies .. twisting their back-hair .. and many of them .. carrying their *back-combs in their mouths. 1955 'C. BROWN' *Lost Girls* xii. 130 She had back-combed her hair so that it stood out. 1960 *Sunday Express* 14 Aug. 12/2 Backcombing madly .. my favourite hairdresser .. built up some splendid, puffed out effects. 1960 *News Chron.* 13 Sept. 6/2 The trend in hair styles has been, basically, inflated .. set and back-combed into .. magnificent proportions. 1774 T. PENNANT *Tour Scotl.* I. 1 The *back courts of all these houses are level with the ground. 1784 LD. FIFE *Let.* 29 Apr. in *Ld. Fife & Factor* (1925) vii. 165, I found the Duchess of Devonshire in the Back Court, solliciting my Taylor Cook to vote for Mr. Fox. 1890 L. DOD in C. G. Heathcote *Lawn Tennis* xvi. 312 For volleying, more especially than for back-court play, it is essential that the dress should be loose. 1908 *Westm. Gaz.* 11 May 8/3 Blended judiciously with her back-court game was volleying of a vigorous order. 1961 F. C. AVIS *Sportsman's Gloss.* 253/2 *Backcourt*, that portion of the court extending from the service line in a direction away from the net. 1929 HANDLEY & HOWCROFT *Crawl-Stroke Swimming* 77 Cinema camera pictures of a number of *back-crawl exponents have shown that the majority make an eight beat kick. 1951 *Swimming* (E.S.S.A.) iii. 43 The back-crawl is the fastest of the back strokes and is the second fastest swimming stroke known. 1904 *Jrnl. R. Microsc. Soc.* Feb. 52 The correctness of Mendel's hypothesis of the purity of the germ-cells and of their production in equal numbers, is shown by *back-crossing of a hybrid with one of the parental forms... Any one of them back-crossed with the recessive parent will produce 50 p.c. pure recessives and 50 p.c. hybrids. **1915** T. H. MORGAN et al. *Mechanism Mendelian Heredity* iii. 52 If the F_1 males are backcrossed to black vestigial females only two classes result. **1919** BRIDGES & MORGAN *Contr. Genetics of Drosophila Melanogaster* 171 Two autosomal back-crosses had been completed. *Ibid.* 172 No back-cross which involved autosomal linkage had been possible. *Ibid.* 173 (*heading*) Back-Cross Test of Females, Purple Vestigial 'Coupling'. **1929** *Genetica* XI. 227 Back-crossing in peas is rather troublesome. **1931** E. B. FORD *Mendelism & Evolution* I. i. 6 Segregation will also occur if heterozygotes are mated with either of the homozygous types. Such a mating is known as a 'back cross', for it is produced when the F1 (heterozygous) generation is crossed back to one of the parents. **1845** 'N. FELIX' *Felix on the Bat* I. ii. 12 He could not make the *back cut equal to the other parts of his batting. **1898** G. GIFFEN *With Bat & Ball* 221 The back cut, the sweetest of strokes. **1954** J. H. FINGLETON *Ashes crown Year* xi. 112 Back-cutting a no-ball from Lindwall most beautifully for 4. **1842** *Back-cutting [see *side-cutting* s.v. SIDE *sb.*[1] 27]. **1940** *Chambers's Techn. Dict.* 68/1 *Back cutting*, earth obtained for a railway or canal bank, when the excavated earth does not suffice for a regular cut and fill. **1932** A. R. L. GARDNER *Tinker's Kitchen* 281 *Back-doubles = back streets. **1938** 'J. CURTIS' *They drive by Night* viii. 98 Tied up in these back doubles. **1957** L. P. HARTLEY *Hireling* 43 Leadbitter avoided the thronged main roads, steering his way through the 'back-doubles', to save time and petrol. **1976** A. HILL *Summer's End* i. 8, I left the fields behind and crossed the high street, then round the back-doubles to school. **1825** JAMIESON, We was whaslin like a blastit stirk i' the *back-draucht. **1869** *Eng. Mech.* 24 Dec. 344/1 A hood or 'back draught' is applied over the fire. **1874** G. M. HOPKINS *Notebks.* 13 Aug. (1937) 202 It [*sc.* the wave] commonly has a pitch or lurch to one side besides its backdraught. **1887** MORRIS tr. *Homer's Odyssey* v. 97 The back-draft mightily Fell on him, and..drave him out to sea. *Ibid.* XII. 218 Nor happen thou upon her [*sc.* Charybdis] when the back-draught she doth win. **1922** J. B. SALMOND *Bawbee Bowden* xii. 104 Wi' the backdraucht [he] sent a moofu' o' tea up throo his nose. **1913** *Amer. Mag.* July 103/1 When the film is run off you see the *back-drop right through him [*sc.* the Ghost] while he approaches Hamlet. **1947** D. M. DAVIN *For Rest of Lives* xliii. 215 'Antimacassars, potstands complete with ferns, occasional tables, bric-a-brac.' 'Sounds like the backdrop of a Victorian wedding photo.' **1962** *Listener* 13 Sept. 390/1 A particular contribution to any science can only be assessed against the backdrop of history. **1895** RUTHERFORD in *Trans. N.Z. Inst.* XXVIII. 190 Since dN/dt may be called the *back E.M.F. in the circuit at any instant. **1898** T. O'C. SLOANE *Stand. Electr. Dict.* 156 Counter-electro-motive Force ..*Synonym*—Back Electro-motive Force. *Ibid.*, Back Electro-motive Force of Polarization. **1901** GEIPEL & KILGOUR *Electr. Engin. Formulæ* (ed. 2) 668 When the anode and cathode are of the same metal..there is no back E.M.F., for the back E.M.F. at the one electrode is of opposite sign to that at the other, and they cancel one another. **1936** *Discovery* July 202/2 In the very small fraction of a second that the current is flowing in one direction, the back electro-motive force which opposes it has not time to form. **1911** *Collier's* 12 Aug. 21/2 From the home plate to the *back field was a marked physical retrogression, ending in three strident but barely perceptible fielders. **1923** *Outing* Mar. 287/1 Now look at the backfield, the terror of all elevens. **1944** N. MAILER in *Cross-Section* 346 They had this play built around me, where I shift into the backfield..making me eligible to hold the ball. **1970** *Globe & Mail* (Toronto) 28 Sept. 23/6 Halfback Bill Simpson, playing his first game in London's offensive backfield after being shifted from defense. **1983** *Washington Post* 10 Nov. E8 Maryland's football team practiced for the third straight day yesterday without its starting backfield. **1934** WEBSTER, *Backfill. **1975** *Daily Tel.* 16 Dec. 2/4 Excavated Materials:..used as backfill to foundations and bases in lieu of hardcore. **1901** R. STURGIS *Dict. Archit. & Building* I. 181/1 **Back-filling*,.. masonry or earth, and the like, used as a filling over the back (or extrados) of arched constructions, as tunnels and sewers. **1930** *Engineering* 29 Aug. 259/2 The trenches have to be backfilled with sand, gravel or other good clean earth. **1955** *Archit. Rev.* CXVIII. 393/3 Mineral operators, when they have finished extraction, are generally free to backfill without planning consent. **1960** *Farmer & Stockbreeder* 12 Jan. 63/2 Levelling off back-filled tile drain trenches. **1957** COOK & WELCH in *Jrnl. Forestry* LV. 265/1 '*Backflash'—the sickening or sudden death, for no apparent reason, of untreated trees in a stand where chemi-peeling has been done. **1958** *New Statesman* 1 Feb. 144/3 Spiro's ruinous past is displayed in a series of back-flashes. **1960** *Ecology* XLI. 56/2 Backflash is the movement of poison, through root grafts, from poisoned trees to unpoisoned trees. **1963** in Brown & Foote *Early English & Norse Studies* 133 These disorderly and almost randomly presented backflashes [in *Beowulf*] fed to the audience are..truly confusing to a person not saturated with the material. **1897** E. J. WALL *Dict. Photogr.* (ed. 7) 295 '*Back focus'..is the distance between the posterior lens and ground-lens. **1953** AMOS & BIRKINSHAW *Telev. Engin.* I. ix. 202 The distance between the lens and the image, known as the *back focus*. **1851** *Jrnl. R. Agric. Soc.* XII. I. 158 The windows..finished with bound shutters and *back-folds. **1752** tr. *Gersaint's Rembrandt's Etch.* 59 The *Back-front or Ground is generally foul. **1883** *Longm. Mag.* May 49 A jointed animal ..with a *back-heart, a nervous system below, and a digestive tube. **1881** *Sportsman's Year Bk.* 314 Cowan scored with a very neat *back heel. **1883** *Standard* 24 Mar. 3/7 J. Hodgson *back-heeled J. Wilson. **1922** *Weekly Dispatch* 12 Nov. 10 Roberts..back-heeled cleverly to Quinn while going at top-speed. **1928** *Engin. & Contracting* LXVII. 193/3 A new gasoline powered shovel... In changing from shovel to clamshell, *back hoe or dragline service, no additions or changes are necessary in the operating machinery. **1950** *Engin. News-Rec.* 23 Nov. 32 (*heading*) Something new in big-sewer excavation is started in Chicago... Long-boomed backhoe digs deep trench. **1984** J. UPDIKE *Witches of Eastwick* i. 52 There's this constant rumbling from the backhoes moving boulders. *c* **1450** HENRYSON *Mor. Fab.* 34 Hee played *back-hood behind from beast to beast. **1852** M. SCOTT *Tom Cringle* xviii. (1859) 506 A very handsome dining room situated in what I believe is called a *back-jamb, a sort of outrigger to the house. **1912** C. B. FRY *Cricket* (*Batsmanship*) 8 Top of the *back-lift for the cut. **1955** A. ROSS *Australia* 55 135 He is not happy against real pace. His back lift, circular rather than straight, is high. **1960** E. S. & W. J. HIGHAM *High Speed Rugby* ii. 28 Often enough during a game, you..must kick immediately. Once more, be content, at first, with a short back-lift and a short follow through. **1961** *Times* 19 Jan. 3/7 This highly mobile dangerous centre forward who was prepared to shoot on sight with scarcely any backlift. **1950** R. H. BOMBACK *Cine Data Book* 78 'Baby' Solarspot.. small size unit for modelling, *back-lighting, front and cross-lighting. *Ibid.*, General-purpose lamp, particularly suited for back-lighting. **1959** HALAS & MANVELL *Technique Film Anim.* 336 Back lighting is used on the rostrum camera beneath either a drawing or a celluloid to give a silhouette or a transparent effect. **1713** PARKYNS *Inn-Play* (1727) 53 Stand with that Toe out and Leg bent, over which he intends to take the Buttock, or *Back-lock. **1876** *Daily News* 28 Sept. 4/4 The death of a *back overman, two miners, and a driver. **1753** CHAMBERS *Cycl. Supp.*, **Back-painting*, the art of pasting of prints and other designs on glass. **1815** *Encycl. Brit.* III. 309 Back-painting, the method of painting mezzotinto prints, pasted on glass, with oil colours. *a* **1575** ABP. PARKER *Corr.* 158 Prayers, for the Queen's Majesty's prosperity and continuance; where others say their *back pater-nosters for her in corners. **1844** *Lillywhite's Illustr. Hand-Bk. Cricket* 19 Forward play..is more pleasing and graceful..than *back play. **1897** K. S. RANJITSINHJI *Jubilee Bk. Cricket* iv. 158 All the really strong back-players draw back in making back-strokes. **1860** *Encycl. Brit.* XX. 600/2 The mean *back-pressure..exceeds the pressure of condensation. *a* **1877** KNIGHT *Dict. Mech.* I. 206/2 *Back-pressure valve*, a ball or clack-valve in a pipe. **1930** *Engineering* 5 Dec. 699/2 To this station will be supplied all the surplus power generated by the back-pressure turbine. **1940** *Chambers's Techn. Dict.* 69/1 *Back-pressure*, air pressure in pipes when it exceeds atmospheric pressure. **1962** *Times* 28 Sept. 17/3 The backgrounds, whether painted or back-projected, are handsome and spare. **1933** A. BRUNEL *Filmcraft* 153 **Back projection*, projection on to a transparent surface, with the projector *behind* the screen, hidden from the view of the audience in a cinema and from the view of the camera in a studio. **1939** J. DELL *Nobody Ordered Wolves* vii. 90 Back-projection..is a process by means of which an actor in Hertfordshire can be shown in Hyde Park, or the Bois, or the plains of Tibet. By the simple expedient of placing the actor in front of a screen on which is projected a film of the required setting, and by synchronising the two cameras. **1465** *Paston Lett.* 522 II. 224 Thou comyst in with many *bak rekenyngges. **1633** BP. HALL *Hard Texts* 142 Thou callest me to a backe-reckoning for the very sins of my youth. **1711** in *Lond. Gaz.* No. 4868/4 A white Spot on the middle of his Back made by the chafing of a *back Rope. **1840** R. DANA *Bef. Mast.* xxxv. 132 Tackle [was] got upon the martingale backrope. *c* **1860** H. STUART *Seaman's Catech.* 57 The cat is hooked, by means of the back-rope, to the ring of the anchor. *a* **1877** KNIGHT *Dict. Mech.* I. 206/2 **Back-saw*, a saw whose web is stiffened by a metallic back of greater substance; as, a tenon saw. **1817** BYRON *Beppo* xli, Much like the *back scene of a play. **1879** J. ROBERTSON in *Cassell's Techn. Educ.* IV. 396/1 Between the roller-beam and the creels the *back-shaft extends to each end of the mule. **1860** *Eng.& Foreign Mining Gloss.* (ed. 2) 48 *Newcastle Mining Terms*..**Back-shift*, the second set of hewers in each day. **1919** D. W. JOHNSON *Shore Processes & Devel.* iv. 161 This zone is already well known as the foreshore. Back of it is the portion of the shore covered by water during exceptional storms only, which I propose to call the *backshore. **1937** WOOLDRIDGE & MORGAN *Physical Basis Geogr.* xxi. 322 We may thus distinguish the 'foreshore'..from the 'backshore' lying immediately at the cliff-foot. **1823** P. NICHOLSON *Pract. Build.* 218 *Back-shutters or *Back-flaps, Additional breadths hinged to the front shutters. **1915** A. J. SYLVESTER *Underwood Typewriter Manual* I. 13 The *back space key is at the upper left-hand side of the keyboard. **1919** B. DE BEAR *Typewriting from A to Z* xix. 39 Back-space once for every character and space in the title to be centred. **1907** *Jrnl. Soc. Arts* 1 Mar. 432/1 The *back-spacer key..causes the carriage to move backward one space. **1962** *Which?* Dec. 355/1 The action of the back spacer..was a little doubtful, sometimes jumping two spaces. **1919** B. DE BEAR *Typewriting from A to Z* xxii. 46 It is a question of *back-spacing after the first character has been written, so as to type the second on the same point. **1957** *Economist* 19 Oct. 205/1 A Stenorette [dictating machine]..has..automatic back-spacing and erase facilities. **1916** E. F. BENSON *David Blaize* x. 200 He chipped at it [*sc.* the ball] with a lot of *back-spin. **1920** E. R. WILSON in P. F. Warner *Cricket* ii. 84 Back spin is undercut applied to the back half of the ball, and is more easily put on with a low action. **1926** *Amer. Speech* I. 632/1 *Backspin*, when put on the ball [in golf] brings a special kind of stop shot. **1548** HALL *Chron.* (1809) 425 Lytle avayleth outward Warre, except there be a stedfast *Back-stande at home. **1562** J. HEYWOOD *Prov. & Epigr.* (1867) 203 If one *backstep be as much as foresteps three. **1762** INCE & MAYHEW *Univ. Syst. Houshold Furniture* 8/1 Four Designs of *Back Stool Chairs... Four more Designs of Back Stools. **1945** *Burlington Mag.* July 164/2 The single chair was called at first a 'back-stool'; for it was not a variation of the armchair by the removal of the arms, but a development of the stool, to which, in order to make it more comfortable, a back was added—hence the name back-stool. **1952** J. GLOAG *Dict. Furn.* 121 Although referred to in Elizabethan inventories, back stools were not in common use until the middle years of the 17th century, and the name survived during the 18th century. **1905** *Cycling* 24 May 441/3 The teeming thousands on the terraces above the *back-straight. **1952** M. DUGGAN in D. M. Davin *N.Z. Short Stories* (1953) 246 She saw them go into the bend and show again..across the back-straight. **1844** BAKER in *Jrnl. R. Agric. Soc.* V. I. 32 The land..is ploughed as the work proceeds by what is termed *back-striking. **1785** COWPER *Task* IV. 227 Misses, at whose age their mothers wore The *backstring, and the bib. *c* **1850** *Rudim. Nav.* (Weale) 120 The *top-timber sweep*, or **back sweep*, is that which forms the hollow of the top-timber. **1862** *Athenæum* No. 1830. 660 The *backswimmer ..has..the faculty of entangling air in the hairs of its body. *a* **1656** BP. HALL *Rem. Wks.* (1660) 159 Excesse in diet and clothes, in belly-cheer, and *back-timber. **1640** *Lawefulnesse Exp. into Eng.* 4 He hath followed the *back trade of our defection..The Lord therefore is still on the *back trade. **1601** SHAKS. *Twel. N.* I. iii. 131, I haue the *backe-tricke, simply as strong as any man in Illyria. **1599** NASHE *Lent. Stuffe* 13 This and euery towne hath his *backewinters or frostes that nippe it in the blade. **1649** SELDEN *Laws of Eng.* II. xl. (1739) 174 Yet like a dead Calm in a hot Spring, treasured up in store sad distempers against a back-Winter. **1881** W. D. HOWELLS *Let.* 27 Feb. in *Amer. N. & Q.* (1963) 133/1 What the Canadians call the back-winter: the two months of mud and snow that precede the spring. **1841** R. W. HAMILTON *Nugæ Literariæ* 357 'In consequence of her death, I was obliged to give a party who were to have dined with me *backword;' that is, put them off. **1937** J. B. PRIESTLEY *I have been here Before* I. 6 We ought to..charge 'em a deposit when they book rooms in advance, and then if they do give backword we're not clean out o' pocket. *a* **1682** SIR T. BROWNE *Tracts* 115 That obstinate disease of the Filander or *Back-worm. **1598** FLORIO, *Consolida maggiore*, the herbe Comfrie, Knit-backe or *backwoort.

back-action. orig. *U.S.* [BACK- A. II.] Backward or reverse action, as in a machine. Also *attrib.* and *fig.*

1845 *Knickerbocker* XXV. 406 There lurks beneath it [*sc.* the Yankee countenance] the knowledge of..some 'self-acting back-action sausage-stuffer'. **1862** LOWELL *Biglow P.* II. III. i. 99 The self-cockin', back-action style o' J. D. **1873** J. H. BEADLE *Undevel. West* 800 That sort of detraction has an awkward back-action about it. *a* **1877** KNIGHT *Dict. Mech.* 205/2 Back-action Steam-engine. **1934** *Brit. Jrnl. Psychol.* Jan. 267 By 'back action' is meant the alleged fact that the conditions which follow an act affect the bond or connection responsible for the act. **1963** J. OSBORNE *Dental Mechanics* (ed. 5) x. 204 Back action clasps will be used on premolars.

So **back-actioned** *a.*

1875 [see BAR *sb.*[1] 29 a].

backage ('bækɪdʒ). [f. BACK *sb.*[1], after FRONTAGE.] The back part of a building or row of buildings; the line or outlook of buildings or plots of land on the rear side.

1887 FENN *This Man's Wife* II. II. xviii. 92 A high wall right and left to complete the blankness of the frontage. It ought to have been called the backage; for Sir Gordon Bourne's house was very pleasant on the other side. **1892** *Pall Mall Gaz.* 22 Mar. 2/3 Converting slummy 'backages' into handsome frontages. **1894** G. DU MAURIER *Trilby* II. VI. 191 Tall trees, whose lightly-falling leaves yellowed the pavement for at least a hundred yards of frontage—or backage, rather; for this was but the rear of that stately palace.

back-along ('bækə'lɒŋ), *adv. phr. dial.* [f. BACK *adv.*] Back, in direction or time. Cf. ALONG *adv.* I c.

[**1877** *Rep. & Trans. Devonshire Assoc. Adv. Sci.* IX. 127 *Backlong* (= Backwards. Formerly). This expression is of common occurrence about Teignmouth.] **1897** T. HARDY *Well-Beloved* II. viii. 162 And when, on my way backalong, I saw you waiting hereabout again, I slipped over the wall. **1905** E. PHILLPOTTS *Secret Woman* I. ix. 83 Then I mind the time when Barbara Westaway wouldn't have him—back-along ten year or so. **1923** R. FROST *Let.* 12 Feb. (1964) 160 A good old-timer dating back along.

back-and-forth, *sb.* [see BACK *adv.* 14.] An exchange (of words, views, etc.); reciprocity, give-and-take.

1941 W. A. PERCY *Lanterns on Levee* xxii. 293 Then the man asked if he couldn't 'range fur a conference en they had a lot of back-and-forth. **1969** D. ACHESON *Present at Creation* (1970) xxi. 192 He was not good in the fast back-and-forth of a press conference. **1979** *Dædalus* Summer 14 In the back-and-forth of competing charges and counter-charges..there certainly is a fund of hypocrisy. **1980** *Guardian Weekly* 13 Jan. 16/1 We have resisted using trade, agricultural sales,..sports and cultural back-and-forth.

†**backare, baccare**, *int. phr. Obs.* [Origin doubtful; perhaps for *back there!* or *back-er* (= farther back); Nares says the allusion is to an ignorant man who affected to speak Latin, in accordance with which Webster makes the word trisyllabic.] Back! stand back! give place!

a **1553** UDALL *Roister D.* (Arb.) 16 Ah sir, Backare quod Mortimer to his sowe. **1592** LYLY *Mydas* I. ii. 10 The masculine gender is more worthy than the feminine, therefore Licio—backare. **1596** SHAKS. *Tam. Shr.* II. i. 72 Let vs that are poore petitioners speake too. Bacare, you are meruaylous forward. **1660** in HOWELL *Eng. Prov.* (as in 1553).

backband ('bækbænd). [f. BACK *sb.* I + BAND.]

1. A broad leather strap, or iron chain, passing over the cart-saddle or pad on the back of a horse, and serving to keep up the shafts of a vehicle.

1523 FITZHERB. *Husb.* §5 A cart sadel, bakbandes, and belybandes. **1727** BRADLEY *Fam. Dict.* s.v. *Cart*, The Thill hooks and back-band which hold the sides of the Cart up to the horse. **1848** THOMPSON in *Jrnl. R. Agric. Soc.* IX. II. 403 The shafts should be fixed at such a height by means of the back-band, that, etc.

2. The outside moulding on a door or window casing.

1940 in *Chambers's Techn. Dict.* **1944** C. F. DINGMAN *Estimating Building Costs* (ed. 3) ix. 202 Window trim should have dimensions and descriptions of inside casings.. backbands, scotia, etc.

†'**backbear**, *sb. Obs.* [f. BACK *sb.* 2 c + BEAR *v.*] In *Forest Laws*: The act of carrying on the back venison killed illegally. (Cf. BACK-BEREND *adj.* (*pr. pple.*))

1598 MANWOOD *Lawes Forest* xviii. §9 (1615) 134/1 Backe beare is, where any man hath slaine a wild beast..and is found carrying away of the same. **1667** E. CHAMBERLAYNE

St. Gt. Brit. I. III. vi. (1743) 186 Taken either at dog-draw . . back-bear, or bloodyhand. **1866** *Chamb. Jrnl.* 261.

back bench. [BACK- A. 4.] Any one of the benches in the House of Commons or similar assembly occupied by members who are not entitled to a seat on the front benches on either side. Usu. *attrib.* (with hyphen). Hence **ˌback-ˈbencher**, a member who occupies a seat on the back benches on either side of the house.

1874 *Gentl. Mag.* XII. 334 During the debate on the Education Act Amendment Bill Mr. Osborne found himself sitting on a back bench below the gangway, and rose thence to address the House. **1885** *Eng. Illustr. Mag.* Dec. 195/1 He affects the Liberal side, sometimes presenting himself from a back bench in the rear of the bishops. **1905** *Daily Chron.* 13 July 6/1 Back-bench Members on the Ministerial side of the House. **1910** *Busy Man's Mag.* Dec. 60 Some of the best men in Parliament are back-benchers. **1923** *Daily Mail* 23 May 6 Mr. Baldwin filled the modest rôle of a back-bencher in the House for many years. **1928** *Daily Tel.* 13 Mar. 9/3 The situation was obviously developing into general back-bench communal bickering. **1940** *Ann. Reg. 1939* 9 A man comparatively unknown to Parliament— . . a 'back-bencher'. **1959** *Economist* 3 July 19/2 The foolish notion that a back-bencher's life need be a useless one.

† **ˈback-berend,** *adj.* (*pr. pple.*) *Obs.* In 3 -inde, 6–9 -and, 7 -end, 8 -ind. [OE. *bæc-berende*, f. *bæc* back + *berende*, pr. pple. of *beran* to BEAR: see BACKBEAR *sb.*] Bearing on the back: an OE. combination, long retained as a law-term to describe a thief caught in the act of thus carrying off stolen property. Sometimes modernized as ***back-bearing***.

1292 BRITTON I. xxx. §6 Acun laroun ou robbeour seisi de soen larcyn handhabbynde et bacberinde. *c* **1550** SIR J. BALFOUR *Practicks* (1754) 37 Theives tane and apprehendit in manifest thift, sic as hand-havand and back-beirand. **1641** *Termes de la Ley* 36 b, Backberind theefe. **1822** *Edin. Rev.* XXXVI. 295 If the offender could be taken back-bearing. **1828** SCOTT *F.M. Perth* iv, Our hand-habend, our back-berand, and our blood-suits.

backbite (ˈbækbaɪt), *v.* Forms: 2–5 bac-, bakbite, 4–6 bakbyte, 5–6 bag-, bakke-, bacbyte, backbyte, 6–7 backebite, 4– backbite. *Pa. t.* 4 bac-, bakbate; 4 bacbitide, bakbited, 5 bacbyted. *Pa. pple.* 5–6 bakbyttyn, -byten, 7– backbitten; 4–6 bacbyted, 6 bak-, backe-, 6–7 backbited. [f. BACK *adv.* + BITE *v.*, i.e. to bite one on, or behind, his back.]

To detract from the character of, to slander, traduce, speak ill of: **a.** a person absent.

c **1175** [see BACKBITING *vbl. sb.*] *a* **1300** *E.E. Psalter* xxxviii. 20 þat yheldes ivels for godes bac-bate [Vulg. *detrahebant*]me. **1393** GOWER *Conf.* I. 411 Is none so good, that he ne passeth Betwene his teeth and is backbited. **1496** *Dives & Paup.* (W. de W.) VII. ii. 278/2 Mary the syster of Moses backbyted her brother. *a* **1520** *Myrr. Our Ladye* Introd. 47 Why hast thou bakbyten my handemayde adjugynge hir to be prowde? **1609** HOLLAND *Amm. Marcell.* XVII. ix. 91 With contumelious tearmes traduced and back-bitten. *a* **1791** WESLEY *Husb. & Wives* iii. 7 Wks. 1811 IX. 67 To backbite an enemy is sin; how much more to back-bite one's own yoke-fellow. **1851** HELPS *Comp. Solit.* iii. (1874) 31 People will backbite one another to any extent rather than not be amused.

† **b.** an institution, action, character, etc. *Obs.*

1382 WYCLIF *James* iv. 11 He that bakbitith his brother bakbitith the lawe. **1596** SPENSER *F.Q.* I. iv. 32 The verse of famous poets witt He does backebite. **1602** DEKKER *Satirom.* Wks. 1873 I. 209 Doe not back-bite her beauties.

c. *absolutely* or *intr.*

1377 LANGL. *P. Pl.* B. II. 80 To bakbite and to bosten and bere fals witnesse. **1597** SHAKS. *2 Hen. IV*, v. i. 36 Vse his men well Dauy, for they are arrant knaues, and will backe-bite. **1841** LANE *Arab. Nts.* III. 613 Backbite not, lest thou be backbitten.

† **backbite,** *sb. Obs.* [f. prec.] Backbiting.

1598 STOW *Survey* (Strype 1754) I. III. vi. 593/2 A stay to weake, a staff to poor, Without Backbite or pride.

backbiter (ˈbækˌbaɪtə(r)). Forms: see the vb. [f. BACKBITE *v.* + -ER[1].] One who backbites; a slanderer or secret calumniator.

c **1230** *Ancr. R.* 86 Bacbitares þe biteð oðre men bihinden. *c* **1386** CHAUCER *Pers. T.* ¶422 The bacbiter wol torne al thilke goodnes up-so-doun. **1440** *Promp. Parv.* 21/2 Bakke-bytere, *Detractor.* **1509** BARCLAY *Ship of Fooles* (1570) ¶¶iv, Backbiters which good liuers diffame. **1627** *Sp. without Doors* in Rushw. *Hist. Coll.* (1659) I. 492 Diogenes being asked what beast bit sorest, answered, Of wilde beasts, the Back-biter; of tame, the Flatterer. **1859** TENNYSON *Vivien* 673 Face-flatterers and backbiters are the same.

b. (*word-play*): A biter, or striker, on the back.

1608 TOURNEUR *Rev. Trag.* II. ii. 58 Sword thou wast neuer a back-biter yet.

backbiting (ˈbækˌbaɪtɪŋ), *vbl. sb.* Forms: 2–3 -bitunge, 4 -bytyng, -bityng, -byting, 5 -bytynge, -bitynge, -bitinge, -byting, 5– -biting. [f. as prec. + -ING[1].] The action of detracting, slandering, or speaking ill of one behind his back.

c **1175** *Cott. Hom.* 205 Cursunge, bacbitunge and fikelunge. **1303** R. BRUNNE *Handl. Synne* 3544 No custummable bakbytyng God forȝeueþ. *c* **1550** *Avyse thee Welle* in *Babees Bk.* (1868) 357 Be ware of bagbytynge, y the rede. **1685** *Gracian's Courtier's Oracle* 45 There is great difference betwixt censure and backbiting. For the one is grounded upon indifference, and the other upon malice. **1862** TROLLOPE *Orley F.* lviii. 420 Not given to backbiting.

ˈbackˌbiting, *ppl. a.* [f. as prec. + -ING[2].] That slanders or speaks ill of the absent.

1382 WYCLIF *Ps.* c. 5 The bacbitende prieueli to his neȝhebore. **1580** TUSSER *Husb.* (1878) 190 Backbiting talk that flattering blabs know wily how to blenge. **1873** MISS BROUGHTON *Nancy* II. 280 Am I to have a backbiting wife?

† **ˈbackˌbitingly,** *adv. Obs.* [f. prec. + -LY[2].] In a backbiting manner; slanderously.

1580 BARET *Alv.* B 22 Backbitingly, or slaunderously.

back blocks, backblocks, *sb. pl. Austral.* and *N.Z.* [f. BACK *a.* 1 + BLOCK *sb.* 14 d.] Land in the remote and sparsely inhabited interior. Also, land distant or cut off from a river-front. Also (esp. in sing.) *attrib.* or *adj.*; **back-blocker**, a resident in the back blocks.

Also used in Canada: there are 1910–1956 examples in the *Dict. Canadianisms.*

1872 *Glimpses Life in Victoria* iii. 31 We were doomed to see the whole of our river-frontage selected and purchased by two gentlemen newly arrived in the colony. The back blocks which were left to us were insufficient for the support of our flocks, and deficient in permanent water-supply. **1890** E. W. HORNUNG *Bride fr. Bush* xix. 298 'Down in Vic' you can carry as many sheep to the acre as acres to the sheep up here in the 'back-blocks'. **1891** 'R. BOLDREWOOD' *Sydneyside Saxon* xii. 215 One of the back-block youngsters. **1892** E. W. HORNUNG *Under Two Skies* 21 Sitting on his heels over the fire in an attitude peculiar to back-blockers. **1901** *N.Z. Illustr. Mag.* III. 254 The clean-limbed hardy backblocks-men mustering in the river arm. **1911** H. FOSTON *In Bell Bird's Lair* xi. 52 The men of the city, who had not the faintest idea of what a 'Backblock' bush road was like in the winter. **1913** B. E. BAUGHAN *Brown Bread from Colonial Oven* vii. 140 Art comes at all times scantly to the back-blocks. **1926** A. F. WEBB *Miss Peters' Special* xi. 94, I think on most back-block holdings mail day is kept as a kind of Sunday or holiday. **1930** J. DEVANNY *Bushman Burke* I. vii. 32 It is one of the back-blocker's pleasures, taking tea in the restaurants in town.

† **backblow** (ˈbækbləʊ). *Obs.* [f. BACK *sb.* and *adv.* + BLOW *sb.*]

1. A blow struck at the back or from behind.

1642 FULLER *Holy & Prof. St.* II. xix. (b) 127 A premeditated back-blow in cold bloud is base. **1857** *Househ. Words* 12 Sept. 245 Outwitted him at his own game of backblows.

2. *fig.* (Cf. AFTER-CLAP.)

1649 DRUMM. OF HAWTH. *Jas. III.* Wks. 55 So many back-blows of fortune. **1705** STANHOPE *Paraphr.* II. 456 That Reflexion fell upon his Mind with this terrible back-blow.

back-board (ˈbækbɔəd), *sb.* [f. BACK *sb.*]

† **1.** = LARBOARD. Only in OE.: see BABORD.

2. A board placed at, or forming, the back of anything, *e.g.* of a picture, a cart, a boat.

1761 *Brit. Mag.* II. 613 Artfully concealed behind the back-board of Perrott's picture. **1769** FALCONER *Mar. Dict.*, *Back-Board*, a piece of board of a semicircular figure, placed transversly in the after-part of a boat, and serving the passengers to recline against. **1877** *Tinsley's Mag.* Aug. 220 Wife and family in the ramshackle tax-cart, the little ones 'creening' over the back-board.

3. A board attached to the rim of a water-wheel to prevent the water from running off the floats into the interior of the wheel.

1864 WEBSTER cites NICHOLSON.

4. A board held or strapped across the back to straighten the figure.

1794–1801 E. DARWIN *Zoon.* III. 143 Methods of confining or directing the growth of young people . . such as back-boards. **1801** MAR. EDGEWORTH *Fr. Governess* (1831) 176 Her person had undergone all the tortures of back-boards, collars, stocks, dumb-bells. **1880** J. SOUTH *Househ. Surg.* (ed. 4) 332 Another abominable contrivance called a back-board . . by which the girl's arms were trussed behind her, in much the same way as the wings of a roast fowl.

5. 'That part of the lathe which is sustained by the four legs, and which sustains the pillars that support the puppet-bar.' Weale *Dict. Terms* 1849.

ˈbackˌboard, *v.* [f. prec.] To subject to the use of a backboard.

1855 THACKERAY *Newcomes* II. 146 If they have been lectured, and learning, and back-boarded, and practising. **1881** MISS BRADDON *Asph.* I. 144 Governessed, and preached-at, and back-boarded.

back-bond (ˈbækˈbɒnd). *Sc. Law.* [f. BACK *adv.* + BOND.] A document by which a party receiving or holding a title, *ex facie* absolute, acknowledges that he really holds in trust for a specified purpose, and binds himself to convey or account to the true owner after that purpose is served. The true owner is usually the granter of the absolute deed, hence the term *back*-bond is applied to the explanatory document executed by the grantee.

a **1645** *Acts Chas. I* (1814) V. 283 (JAM.) The dispositioune . . was cancellate:—and the provest producit the bakband, q[lk] was also cancelled. **1645** RUTHERFORD *Tryal & Tri. Faith* (1845) 246 He who is ransomed by Christ . . is under a back-bond, or a re-obligation of love, service, and obedience. **1867** A. M. BELL *Conveyanc.* 1079 A heritable security . . may also be constituted in the form of an absolute disposition qualified by a backbond.

backbone (ˈbækˈbəʊn). Forms: 3 bacbon, 4 bakbon, bakebon, 5 bakbone, 4–7 backebone, 6– backbone. (In 5–7 often two words; still sometimes hyphened.) [f. BACK *sb.* 1 + BONE.]

1. The vertebral column, the spine. *to the **backbone***: thoroughly, completely.

a **1300** W. DE BIBLESW. in Wright *Voc.* 146 Bacbon, *l'etchine.* *a* **1400** *Leg. Rood* 190 þe cros behind his bakbon þat he þolud deth uppon. **1523** FITZHERB. *Husb.* (1534) F iv b, He wyll eate soo moche, that his sydes wyll stande as hygh as his backe bone. **1647** J. HALL *Poems* 89 How many back-bones nourisht have Crawling Serpents in the grave? **1849** W. IRVING *Crayon Misc.* 165 It struck a buffalo . . broke its back-bone. **1864** DK. MANCH. *Crt. Soc. Eliz. to Anne* II. 107 Harry was English to the backbone.

2. *transf.* A main support or axis, or chief substantial part; *e.g.* the backbone of a bicycle; the chief mountain-range or water-shed of a country.

1684 T. BURNET *The. Earth* I. 142 The Appennines strike through Italy . . the back-bone of that country. **1865** TYLOR *Early Hist. Man.* vii. 162 The Cordilleras, or backbone of America. **1879** A. GALLETLY in *Cassell's Techn. Educ.* IV. 390/2 The 'back-bone' of the chenille . . is composed of several strong cotton threads.

3. *fig.* The main or important element; mainstay.

1849 COBDEN *Speeches* 64, I speak to the clothiers . . the backbone and muscle of the clothing district of England. **1871** EARLE *Philol. Eng. Tong.* §313 We are now come to the backbone of our subject. **1884** J. BENT in *Macm. Mag.* Oct. 429/2 A secret society which was the backbone of Panhellenism.

4. Strength of character, stability of purpose, resoluteness, sturdiness, firmness.

1843 C. BRONTË *Let.* 13 Oct. in Mrs. Gaskell *Life* I. 299 A pretty-looking . . young man, apparently constructed without a backbone. . . I don't allude to his corporal spine . . but to his character. **1865** *Sat. Rev.* 18 Feb. 195 A great man he . . could never have been . . for his character was destitute of backbone. **1884** *Pall Mall G.* 23 Feb. 5 [This] has completely taken the backbone out of the discount market.

ˈbackˈboned, *ppl. a.* [f. prec. + -ED: cf. L. *vertebrā-tus.*] Having a backbone; vertebrate. Also *fig.*

1860 LEWES in *Cornh. Mag.* I. 291 They are all backboned; they have all an internal skeleton. **1881** MIVART *Cat* 451 The Cat then is one of the group of backboned animals. **1940** H. G. WELLS *All Aboard* i. 27 We'll have clear-headed, back-boned, clean-minded people.

backˈboneless. *a.* [f. as prec. + -LESS.] Destitute of backbone or strength of character. Hence **backˈbonelessness.**

1882 *Standard* 3 Mar. 3/6 Backbonelessness and apathy. **1882** J. PAYN *For Cash Only* III. xlviii. 260 Mildred's pride was of the most backboneless description, a mere social conceit. **1886** *Punch* 17 July 28/2 Think of a backboneless man, unable 'to swim against the stream'. **1903** W. T. ARNOLD *German Ambitions* 89 Backboneless submissiveness to Britain. **1925** *Glasgow Herald* 1 Aug. 4/2 It [*sc.* hæmoglobin] has analogues like hæmocyanin (in many backboneless animals).

back-cap, *sb. U.S. slang. **to give one a back-cap***, to disclose or state something to one's detriment; to run down. Also as *v. trans.* (*Cent. Dict.*, 1889).

1883 'MARK TWAIN' *Life on Miss.* lii. 462 Now I didn't fear no one giving me a back-cap (exposing his past life) and running me off the job. **1903** CLAPIN *Dict. Amer.* 31 *To back cap*, to speak evil of some one, so as to spoil his game.

backcast (ˈbækɑːst, -æ-), *sb. north dial.* [f. BACK *adv.* + CAST *sb.*] A throw back; a reverse.

1818 SCOTT *Hrt. Midl.* li, She got a sair back-cast wi' the slaughter o' her husband. **1864** ATKINSON *Whitby Gloss.* s.v., A 'backkest' in an illness; a relapse.

ˈback-cast (ˈbækɑːst, -æ-), *ppl. a.* [f. BACK *adv.* + CAST *pple.*] Cast or thrown backwards.

1580 SIDNEY *Arcadia* (1622) 272 With many a backe-cast looke. **1647** H. MORE *Song of Soul* II. App. lxxxviii, Back-cast tayls [of comets] turn'd to our Evening-eye. **1821** JOANNA BAILLIE *Met. Leg., Lady G.B.* li. 3 Which to her back-cast thoughts could bring The scenes of other days.

back-chat, *sb. colloq.* [? orig. soldiers' slang; f. BACK- A. 12 c + CHAT *sb.*[1]] Impertinent or impudent replies, esp. to a superior; abuse, insulting speech; altercation, heated talk; repartee. Cf. *back-answer* (BACK- 12 c) and BACK-TALK.

1901 *Subaltern's Lett. Wife* 108 'That'll do, Sergeant Jones', I heard one of our colonial officers remark; 'I don't want any more of your back-chat.' **1922** *Daily Mail* 31 Oct. 9 It was very amusing to hear public men described as 'cabin boys' and 'kitchen staff'; it was what children described as 'calling names' and soldiers 'back-chat'. **1922** W. J. LOCKE *Tale of Triona* viii. 82 'Here you are, you blackmailing thief.' 'None of your back-chat . .' said the taximan. **1939** T. S. ELIOT *Old Possum* 36 I'd extemporize back-chat, I knew how to gag.

Hence as *v. intr.*, to use back-chat (to).

1927 H. V. MORTON in *Daily Express* 27 Apr. 11 No one back-chats to a Pacific [*sc.* railway engine] except a very shabby tank. **1930** A. BENNETT *Imperial Palace* vi. 27 The bright, jostling back-chatting world of men.

back-cloth, backcloth [BACK- A. 4.]

1. *Calico-printing.* A cloth placed between the fabric that is being printed and the 'blanket', in order to keep the latter clean. Also called BACK-GREY.

1874 W. CROOKES *Pract. Handbk. Dyeing& Calico-Printing* viii. 552 The revolution of the blanket, back-cloth, and pieces is regulated by the following contrivance. **1897** C. F. S. ROTHWELL *Print. Textile Fabrics* 34 The back tenter's work is to guide the piece and back cloth into the machine. **1901** A. SANSONE *Print. Cott. Fabrics* (ed. 2) 420 For keeping the blanket clean, the back cloth is allowed to go between the blanket and the printing cloth.

2. *Theatr.* The painted cloth hung across the back of the stage as the principal part of the scenery. Also *transf.* and *fig.*

1886 *Cornh. Mag.* Oct. 435 They gazed awestruck at the backcloth and the flies. **1926** *Spectator* 10 July 44/2 Thirty acres or so for a stage and the whole firmament of heaven for a back-cloth. **1927** *Observer* 6 Nov. 9 The background.. is not a carefully constructed scene, but only a flimsy and dim back-cloth. **1955** *Times* 31 Aug. 9/2 Hanging indeed like a backcloth to Mr. Lennox-Boyd's tour, is the policy and power of China. **1955** G. S. FRASER in J. Wain *Interpretations* 214 A river, for a Restoration poet, would be primarily.. a backcloth for pastoral.

3. *Naut.* 'A triangular piece of canvas fastened in the middle of a topsail-yard to facilitate the stowing of the bunt of the topsail' (*Cent. Dict.* 1889).

back country. Chiefly *N. Amer.*, *Austral.*, and *N.Z.* [BACK *a.* 1.] The country lying towards or in the rear of a settled district.

1746 in C. R. Woodward *Ploughs* (1941) 332 In the back Country abt Paoqualin The Cattle feed is near over. **1789** MORSE *Amer. Geogr.* 415 The mistletoe is common in the back country. **1831** J. M. PECK *Guide for Emigrants* III. 292 It.. has an abundance of excellent water, and a back country as range for stock. **1840** *N.Z. Jrnl.* 29 Aug. 209/2 Hobson is founding a town at the Bay of Islands, but we have an assurance that there is no back country there. **1844** *Bytown Gaz.* (Ottawa) 8 Aug. 2/6 A road into the interior.. would not only benefit Kingston, (so much in want of a productive back country) but would open new tracts for settlement. **1860** S. BUTLER *First Year in Canterbury Settlement* 24 Mar. (1863) iv. 47 At last I have been really in the extreme back country. **1868** *Putnam's Mag.* Nov. 562 The hotel was a roomy log-house,.. and commanded a view of the back country—a prairie stretching off into the western horizon. **1882** *Macm. Mag.* XLVI. 70/2 Driven.. into the backest of the back country. **1902** *Westm. Gaz.* 6 Aug. 2/1 The unappropriated back-country of Tunis and Tripoli. **1936** F. GERALD *Millionaire in Memories* iii. 71 Travelling through the back country with Bill Langford was an education, a 'bushman's' education. **1964** *Weekend Mag.* (Montreal) 11 July 20/2 Devil's club [is] the thorned scourge of hikers in much of British Columbia's back country.

b. *attrib.*

1775 C. DRAYTON *Let.* in *South Carolina Hist. & Geneal. Mag.* (1926) XXVII. 137 His trepanned Lordship advises the back Country people not to take up arms. **1867** LADY BARKER *Station Life* Aug. (1870) xx. 173 The distant 'back-country' ranges. **1871** E. EGGLESTON *Hoosier Schoolm.* (1872) Pref. 5 Describing life in the back-country districts. **1887** *Harper's Mag.* Jan. 328/1 In a back-country town.. there chanced to die one of the members of the community. **1901** 'LINESMAN' *Words by Eyewitness* (1902) 161 Imaginations so crude as those of the back-country Boers. **1948** *Coast to Coast 1947* 296, I was in a back-country farm in Central Otago. **1965** *Star Weekly* (Toronto) 2 Jan. 37/2 The nearest doctor was 70 miles away over a poor back-country road.

Hence **back-countryman.**

1796 *Gaz. U.S.* 19 Nov., Advt. (Th.), A new Ballet Dance, called the Back Countryman, or the New Settlers. **1845** W. G. SIMMS *Wigwam & Cabin* ser. I. iv. 22 The boatman, who.. knew by his dialect and dress that he was a back-countryman, came to his relief. **1942** MARSH & BURDON *New Zealand* 9 The shepherds, musterers, shearers and drovers, the back-countrymen of New Zealand.

back county. *U.S.* [BACK *a.* 1.] A county lying in the inland part of a state. Also *attrib.*

1775 in *Maryland Hist. Mag.* X. 317 Finding it difficult to go thro' the back County..he agreed to accept a Commission. **1788** *Massachusetts Spy* 11 Nov. (Th.), A back-county correspondent informs us that [etc.]. **1803** T. M. HARRIS *Jrnl. Tour* 6 June (1805) 59 In the back counties of Virginia. **1904** W. H. SMITH *Promoters* xx. 290 The little book agent.. was working one of the brethren from some back county in great style.

'back-date, backdate, *v.* [BACK *adv.* 4.] *trans.* To affix or assign a date earlier than the actual one to (a document, book, event, etc.); to render an enactment, agreement, etc., valid retroactively from a given date.

1946 *Sun* (Baltimore) 26 Sept. 2/2 A stenographer.. testified that.. a War Assets official dictated the memorandum last April and ordered her to back-date it to December 18, 1945. **1952** *Daily Progress* (Charlottesville, Va.) 6 Feb. 1/5 Backdating of tax returns is the major irregularity.. found in the San Francisco internal revenue office. **1957** *Ann. Reg. 1956* 4 A deadlock ensued on whether the award, if accepted, should be back-dated to the beginning of the lock-out. **1958** *Listener* 19 June 1028/1 The poems cover the years 1918–58. One might back-date them in style perhaps by ten years.

backdoor ('bæk'dɔə(r)). Also **back-door.** [f. BACK *a.* + DOOR.]

1. a. A door at the back of a building or enclosure, as opposed to the *front-door*; a secondary or private entrance.

1530 PALSGR. 196/1 Backe dore, *huys de derriere.* **1535** COVERDALE *Judg.* iii. 23 Ehud gat him out at the backe dore. **1712** ARBUTHNOT *John Bull* (1727) 58 He would stand at the door.. to keep off the duns, till John got out at the back-door. **1857** HEAVYSEGE *Saul* (1869) 106 They shall sneak in at Gibeah's back-door.

b. ***back-door trot*** (fig.); also *spec.*, diarrhœa, *dial.*

1789 D. SILLAR *Poems* 57, I fear they've [*sc.* letters have] tane the back-door trott, An' miss'd the road. **1801** *Marvellous Pleasant Love-Story* I. xiii. 176 Cooky had for certain put some jalup i' the pudding, for Master George had gotten the back-door-trot with a witness! **1886** F. T. ELWORTHY *West Somerset Word-Bk.* 37, I be saafe, nif I was vor ate very many o' they there, twid zoon gie me the back-door trot.

2. *fig.*; also *attrib.* = Unworthily secret, clandestine.

1581 G. PETTIE tr. *Guazzo's Civ. Conv.* III. 32 b The children of the right side.. proue doltes.. contrariwise, those which come in at the backe doore.. auaunce themselves. **1611** SHAKS. *Cymb.* v. iii. 45 Hauing found the backe doore open Of the vnguarded hearts. **1700** J. LAW *Counc. Trade* (1751) 276 Their back-door to let in mischief. **1805** T. JEFFERSON *Writ.* (1830) IV. 46 Our back-door counsellors. **1907** *Daily Chron.* 12 Sept. 5/3 Several makers began to do a back-door sort of business. **1957** *Economist* 28 Sept. 1012/2 France did a backdoor deal for Egyptian cotton. **1965** *New Statesman* 30 Apr. 671/3 Having safeguarded their back door with China.. the Pakistanis may be tougher about their frontiers with India.

'back-down. *colloq.* Chiefly *U.S.* [BACK *v.* 20.] A complete surrender of claims; a retreat from a position taken up or from a stand made.

1862 GRAY & ROPES *War Lett.* (1927) 35 The President's message.. seems to me clearly a case of back down. **1886** *Sat. Rev.* 25 Dec. 853 The present crisis, end as it may—in a general 'backdown' or a general war—is essentially a small business as compared with much that Europe has seen in its day. **1894** 'MARK TWAIN' *Pudd'nhead Wilson* xxi. 280 It's a clean back-down! he gives up without hitting a lick! **1961** *Guardian* 20 Sept. 16/6 Krushchev's primary aim.. was to force.. [an] American back-down at Berlin.

'back-draw. *U.S.* = DRAWBACK *sb.* 4.

1883 *Century Mag.* Oct. 815/2 There are great back-draws to the bee business, the irregularities of the flowers being chief.

backe, earlier f. BAT (the winged mammal).

backed (bækt). Forms: 5 **backyd,** 6 **backt** (*Sc.* **bakkit**), 6– **backed.** [f. BACK *sb.* and *v.* + -ED.]

1. *adj.* Provided with a back, having a back, background, or backing; used particularly in composition, e.g. ***broad-backed, pig-backed, hog-backed.***

1398 TREVISA *Barth. De P.R.* XII. xiii. (1495) 422 Scabbyd horses and sore backyd. **1530** PALSGR. 442/2 This sworde is well backed. **1602** SHAKS. *Ham.* III. ii. 397 It is back'd like a Weazell. **1670** G. H. *Hist. Cardinals* I. iii. 78 Upon a back'd chair. **1716** *Lond. Gaz.* No. 5395/4 One gray Nagg.. somewhat Pigg-backed. **1863** KINGSLEY *Water Bab.* ii. 48 Whitebeam with its great silver-backed leaves.

2. *pple.* and *a.* Supported at the back, seconded, abetted; betted on; mounted, broken in to the saddle; endorsed, printed on the back; moved or laid back. (See the verb.)

1589 *Pappe w. Hatchet* (1844) 15 Art thou so backt that none dare blade it with thee? *c* **1590** BURELL *Queen's Entry*, Far better bakkit nor ane laird. **1611** SHAKS *Cymb.* v. i. 427 Great Iupiter, upon his Eagle back'd. **1692** RAY *Dissol. World* Pref. (1732) 12 Well back'd by Divine Authority. **1725** BRADLEY *Fam. Dict.* s.v. *Rot*, Take the Horse, if he be about four Years old and back'd. **1846** *Print. Appar. for Amateurs* 42 When the paper is *backed* or has two impressions.

backen ('bæk(ə)n), *v.* [f. BACK + -EN[2]; cf. *lessen.*]

1. *trans.* To put, keep, or throw back; to throw behind, retard (in progress). *Rare* in *mod. lit.*

1649 BLITH *Eng. Improv. Impr.* (1653) 160 Yet will it so backen them that thou mayst lose a full half years growth in them. **1750** A. HILL *Wks.* (1753) IV. 361 His breast will be inflated, and majestically backen'd. **1853** FABER *All for Jesus* 55 A false doctrine.. backens devotion. **1871** NAPHEYS *Prev. & Cure Dis.* III. iv. 720 Very hot vinegar applied.. to a boil.. will sometimes 'backen' it.

2. *intr.* To move or draw back. *spec.* = BACK *v.* 17.

1748 [See BACKENING *vbl. sb.*] **1800** *Ann. Reg. 1798* Chron. 88/2 The wind, nearly south,.. backened towards the eastern board to about south-east. **1805** H. F. CARY tr. *Dante's Inferno* XVII. 283 As a small vessel, back'ning out from land, Her station quits. **1909** *Westm. Gaz.* 21 Aug. 2/2 It [*sc.* a squall] blew for a few minutes violently; then backened back to the south-east.

back-end ('bæk'ɛnd). [f. BACK *a.* + END, in the sense of either extremity. Cf. FORE-END.]

1. Of things with two ends: The hinder or rear end.

a **1617** HIERON *Wks.* II. 114 To put their sinnes into the backe end of the Wallet. **1675** WYCHERLEY *Pl. Dealer* II. i. (1735) 37 At the Back-end of a Lord's coach.

2. The later part or 'latter end' of a season; (absolutely) of the year: The late autumn, the 'fall.'

1820 *Blackw. Mag.* Oct. 3 (JAM.) When you did us the honour to stop a day or two last back-end. **1860** W. WHITE *Wrekin* 43 In his opinion the 'backend' was the best fishing season.

backening ('bæk(ə)nɪŋ), *vbl. sb.* [f. BACKEN + -ING[1].] The action of moving or drawing back.

1748 THOMPSON *Cast. Indol.* II. xlii, With back'ning shunn'd his touch, for well he knew its power.

'backening, *ppl. a.* [f. as prec. + -ING[2].] Keeping back, retarding (vegetables, crops, etc.).

1781 BARKER in *Phil. Trans.* LXXI. 353 The first three weeks of April were cold, backening, and often frosty. **1794** —— LXXXIV. 175 A very backening season.

back entry. [BACK *a.* 1, BACK- A. 5, ENTRY 7.] An entry at the back of a house or houses. Also *fig.*

1677 in *Trans. Shropshire Archæol. Soc.* (1905) V. 216 For yᵉ back entry door 24 foot. **1694** W. BURNABY tr. *Petronius's Satyricon* II. 22 We made off thro' a dirty Back-Entry. **1854** O. S. FOWLER *Home for All* 127 From the center of the room toward the back-entry door to a door into the entry. **1855** [see ENTRY 7 *fig.*]. **1912** A. BENNETT *Matador of 5 Towns* 105 He emerged at the back of the chapel and got by 'back-entries' into Aboukir Street. **1958** *Observer* 10 Aug. 2/7 Our recreation was spent in back entries.

backer ('bækə(r)), *sb.*[1] [f. BACK *v.* + -ER[1].] He who or that which backs.

1. a. A supporter; *esp.* one who bets on a horse or event; one who supports by money or credit. *spec.* One who finances the production of a play, film, etc.

1583 BABINGTON *Commandm.* 380 A backer to beare out my foule oppressions. **1838** DICKENS *Nich. Nick.* i. 1 When fortune is low and backers scarce. **1850** LYTTON *My Novel* IX. ix. 86 'Take any odds against him that his backers may give,' said L'Estrange. **1888** G. O. SEILHAMER *Hist. Amer. Theatre* I. 19 The first 'backer' of an American theatrical enterprise, to use a modern phrase, was William Hallam. **1898** J. HOLLINGSHEAD *Gaiety Chron.* 363 The risk rested entirely on my individual shoulders. I.. never had a 'backer'. **1930** *Economist* 16 Aug. 312/1 In the United States .. well-known finance houses.. have become the backers of the big American film corporations.

b. ***backer-up***: a person who backs or backs up (something or somebody) (see BACK *v.*, esp. sense 8).

1921 *Dict. Occup. Terms* (1927) §499 *Backer-up*.. assists sawyer to push wood up to power-driven circular saw. *Ibid.* §524 *Backer-up*, prepares back of copper shell received from electrotyper.. by brushing it with acid. **1922** JOYCE *Ulysses* 648 Given a backerup, if one were forthcoming. **1952** SHERBROOKE-WALKER *Khaki & Blue* vi. 56 In referring to the part-time Air Force defenders, the expressive, if homely, title of 'Backers-up' was to yield place to 'Station Personnel'. **1953** S. J. BAKER *Australia Speaks* v. 124 The accomplice of a woman who *works a ginger* on a client—i.e. robs him—is a *backer-up*, and the practice is called *backing up.*

2. *Arch.* 'A narrow slate put on the back of a broad square-headed slate when the slates begin to get narrow.' P. Nicholson *Pract. Builder* 1823.

†**3.** *Arith.* The rule of three reversed. Cf. ADVANCER 3. *Obs.* But perhaps *backer* is here the adj., q.v.

1543 RECORDE, etc. *Gr. Arts* (1640) 180 That the greater the third summe is above the first, the lesser the fourth summe is beneath the second: and this rule therefore you may call the Backer or Reverse Rule.

'backer, *sb.*[2] [f. BACK *sb.* + -ER[1].] A porter, carrier, or unloader.

'In common use in the docks.' J. M. Cowper.

backer, obs. form of BAKER.

backer, backey, vulgar contr. of TOBACCO. Also **backa, backy, bakky.** Cf. BACCA, BACCO, BACCY.

1823 E. MOOR *Suffolk Words* 13 *Backa*, tobacco. **1824** W. OLIVER *Coll. of Local Songs* 9 If he's drinking gills o' yell, or axing pennies ti buy bakky. **1825** J. T. BROCKETT *Gloss. N. Country Words* 10 Leet thee pipe, And tyek a blast o' backy! **1828** *Night Watch* II. 159, I got this letter, which I have in my backey fob, from her. **1848** DICKENS *Dombey* xxxviii. 383 'You'll smoke your pipe.. won't you?'.. 'Yes; I'll take my bit of backer.' **1863** H. KINGSLEY *A. Elliot* xxi, Bits of backer pipe. **1885** C. M. YONGE *Nuttie's Father* I. vi. 61 'It is a smoking carriage,' said Miss Nugent... 'Beautiful backy —a perfect nosegay,' said Gerard.

†**'backer,** *a. compar. Obs.* [f. BACK *a.*] Farther back, hinder, posterior.

1564 *Three 15th C. Chron.* (1880) 130 Backer parts. **1575** TURBERVILE *Falconrie* 310 Deplume hir head behinde in the backer part. **1607** TOPSELL *Four-f. Beasts* 492 A hole bored in the backer part of his crooked horn. **1621** QUARLES *Argalus & P.* (1678) 87 Her dishevell'd hair.. Hung loosly down, and vail'd the backer part.

†**'backermore,** *adv. Obs.* In 5 **bakkermore.** [See BACK *adv.* 1.] Farther back; more to the rear.

†**'backermost,** *a. superl. Obs.* or *dial.* [f. BACK *a.*; late formation on type of *hindermost, innermost*: see -MOST.] By-form of BACKMOST.

1669 *Churchw. Acc.* in *Archæol.* XXXV. 449 (D.) In the gallery at Hampton in the backermost seat. **1699** in *Phil. Trans.* XXI. 287 Some of the backermost part of which [house] is an ancient Roman building.

backet ('bækɪt). *Sc.* [a. F. *baquet*, dim. of *bac*, BACK *sb.*[2]] A shallow wooden trough used for carrying ashes, coals, mortar, salt, etc.

1789 BURNS *Capt. Grose* vi, Parritch-pats, and auld saut-backets. **1823** TENNANT *Cdl. Beaton* 154 Seeking backets and mason's auld duds.

backfall ('bækˌfɔːl). [f. BACK *adv.* and *sb.*] Hence **'backfalled** *ppl. a.*

†**1.** A 'grace' in old English music; see quot.

1676 MACE *Musicks Mon.* I. xiv. 90 To make a Back-fall Right, you are always to strike the Precedent Letter.. instead of that Letter, which is to be Back-fall'd with your Right Hand. **1878** GROVE *Dict. Mus.* I. 43 The smooth graces..include the Plain-beat or Rise, the Backfall, the Double Backfall.

2. A fall or throw on the back in wrestling. Often *fig.*

1838–9 *Hood's Own* 3 No wrestler..ever received half so many back-falls as I. **1852** DICKENS *Bleak Ho.* xxv, He will throw him an argumentative back-fall presently.

3. A lever in the coupler of an organ.

1880 E. HOPKINS in Grove *Dict. Mus.* II. 606/2 This coupler is always worked by a pedal, on pressing which the backfalls descend into position. **1881** C. EDWARDS *Organs* 71 Backfalls are usually made of mahogany.

†**'backfaller.** *Obs.* [f. BACK *adv.* + FALL *v.* + -ER[1].] One who falls back (*fig.*), a renegade.

1545 JOYE *Exp. Dan.* xi. (R.) Onias with many lyke back-fallers from God fled into Egypte.

back-fire, *sb.* [Cf. BACK-FIRING *vbl. sb.*] **1.** A fire purposely lighted ahead of an advancing prairie-fire or bushfire in order to deprive it of fuel and so extinguish it. *N. Amer.* and *Austral.*

1839 'MRS. MARY CLAVERS' *New Home* xxix. 191 There was nothing now but to make a 'back-fire'! **1905** *Terms Forestry & Logging* s.v., The back fire is intended to burn only against the wind. **1944** *Living off Land* vii. 154 To start a backfire rapidly..flame-throwers are used. **1959** *Globe & Mail* (Toronto) 23 July 2/1 Setting a backfire against a prairie fire.

2. A premature ignition or explosion in an internal-combustion engine, causing the piston to be driven in the opposite direction to that in which it should travel; also, an explosion in the exhaust-pipe of such an engine.

1897 G. D. HISCOX *Gas Engines* 86 Misfire or back-fire explosives. **1902** A. C. HARMSWORTH et al. *Motors* 169 These 'back fires' are the result of what is called 'premature ignition'. **1903** MECREDY *Dict. Motoring* s.v., An explosion in the silencer is also called, but incorrectly, a back fire. **1904** FILSON YOUNG *Compl. Motorist* ix. 215 This is necessary in order to prevent a back-fire of the engine in starting it. **1968** *Globe & Mail* (Toronto) 3 Feb. 11/2 She heard a small explosion 'like the backfire of a car'.

b. *fig.* (Also *attrib.*)

1925 A. S. M. HUTCHINSON *One Incr. Purpose* I. xx. 126 The outrageous sale of this upstart work..justified it in being the subject of back-fire notices in the critical journals. **1927** *Daily Express* 22 Sept. 2/5 If Tunney, smarting under the Billingsgate backfire,..tries to go in and knock Dempsey out.

back-fire, *v.* [f. prec. or back-formation from BACK-FIRING *vbl. sb.*] **1.** *intr.* To light a fire ahead of an advancing prairie-fire in order to deprive it of fuel. *N. Amer.*

1886 P. G. EBBUTT *Emigrant Life in Kansas* 54 We all..set to work to 'back fire' from the stables, and were only just in time to save the whole place from destruction, by burning a sufficiently wide piece of grass off, and thus stopping the rush of fire. **1912** C. DAWSON *Pioneer Tales* 291 Man learned to back-fire, and plow fire-guards, so but very few settlers lost their lives from prairie-fires. **1929** C. R. COOPER *Challenge of Bush* 237 At other points they back-fired, taking advantage of every change of wind.

2. Of an internal-combustion engine or its fuel: to ignite or explode prematurely. Also *transf.*, e.g. of a firearm.

1902 KIPLING *Traffics & Discoveries* (1904) 184 That car ..back-fired superbly. **1906** *Westm. Gaz.* 23 Oct. 4/2 Some engines are obstinate starters. Others have a nasty tendency to back-fire. **1909** *Ibid.* 13 Oct. 7/4, I think the gas had backfired. **1938** M. K. RAWLINGS *Yearling* iv. 34 Penny pulled the trigger. The explosion that followed had a sizzling sound, and Penny fell backward. The gun had back-fired. **1961** *Listener* 9 Nov. 773/3 A seventh valve, called the by-pass, that takes over momentarily if any of the other valves should back-fire.

fig. **1912** C. MATHEWSON *Pitching* xiii. 300 One of McGraw's schemes back-fired on him. **1953** *Encounter* Nov. 70/1 But the reign of terror backfired.

3. *trans.* use of prec.

1924 *Glasgow Herald* 24 June 8 The great gun backfired its charge of 1800 lb. of powder. **1929** H. V. MORTON *In Search of Scotl.* iii. 76 The horrid gelatinous mass..back-fired a dark inky fluid into the water. **1962** *Which?* Mar. 87/2 The Wastemaster [*sc.* waste-disposer], without a splashguard, tended to backfire scraps.

back-firing, *vbl. sb.* [BACK *adv.*, BACK- A. 10.]

1. The action of BACK-FIRE *v.* 1. *N. Amer.*

1889 *Bellevue* (Ida.) *Press* 14 Sept. 3/2 The process known as 'back-firing' was resorted to, which resulted in saving the threatened buildings. **1946** *Los Angeles Times* 9 Sept. I. 2/4 The blaze was stopped short of the Ridge Route by backfiring.

2. Premature ignition or explosion in an internal-combustion engine.

1897 G. D. HISCOX *Gas Engines* 86 Back-firings in the muffler and exhaust pipe. **1907** *Daily Chron.* 11 Nov. 7/4 The air enters the working cylinder in advance of the combustible mixture, thus preventing backfiring. **1929** *Daily Express* 12 Jan. 2 The sound of the report would.. have been mistaken for the backfiring of a motor-car.

‖**backfisch** ('bækfɪʃ). Also (erron.) bachfisch. [G., lit. 'fish for baking'.] A girl in late adolescence, a teenager.

1888 C. M. YONGE *Beechcroft at Rockstone* vii. 136 The reckless folly of the 'Bachfisch' about health. **1891** *Pall Mall Gaz.* 29 Aug. 3/2 Let us introduce the word 'Backfisch', for we have the Backfisch always with us. She ranges from fifteen to eighteen years of age, keeps a diary, climbs trees secretly, blushes on the smallest provocation, and has no conversation. **1920** SINCLAIR LEWIS *Main Street* xiv. 161 A Gopher Prairie housewife, married a year, and yearning for a 'Prince Charming' like a bachfisch of sixteen! **1921** R. MACAULAY *Dangerous Ages* xiii. 239 These were a mother and a *backfisch*, and they..certainly did not look so prosperous and buxom as a pre-war German mother and *backfisch* would have looked. **1966** *Observer* 6 Nov. 24/4 Marlene Dietrich..conjures up the little Berlin *backfisch*.. who auditioned for 'The Blue Angel'.

back-formation. *Philol.* [BACK- A. III. (Hence G. *rückbildung*.)] The formation of what looks like a root-word from an already existing word which might be (but is not) a derivative of the former.

1889 *N.E.D.*, *Burgle*..A back-formation from *Burglar.* **1907** *Athenæum* 5 Jan. 7/3 'Narration' is fifteenth century, 'narrative'..and 'narrator' as early as Bacon, so that, like many verbs of the same termination, it [*sc.* 'narrate'] may have been a back-formation. **1926** FOWLER *Mod. Eng. Usage* 516/1 *Scavenger*, n., is the origin, in English, from which *to scavenge* is a back-formation, the normal verb being *to scavenger.*

backfriend ('bækˌfrɛnd). [f. BACK *sb.* or *adv.* Perh. orig. a friend who 'kept back,' and did not come forward to assist, and so was no real friend.]

†**1.** A pretended or false friend; an enemy who pretends friendship; a secret or unavowed enemy. *Obs.*

1472 SIR J. PASTON in *Lett.* 692 III. 40, I harde somwhat by hym off a bakke ffrende off yowr. **1574** T. NEWTON *Health Mag.* 75 Corrupte and unpure Ayre is unto all age a greate backefriende and enemie. **1611** SPEED *Hist. Gt. Brit.* IX. xv. 772 Westmorland thought it safest to checke the Scots as the neerer and continuall backefriends. **1684** T. BURNET *Th. Earth* II. 180 As S. Jerome was an open enemy to this doctrine, so Eusebius was a back friend to it. **1725** WODROW *Corr.* (1843) III. 108 My back friend, Mr. Bruce, has now another and heavier author to deal with than I, Bishop Burnet. **1827** SOUTHEY *Life & Corr.* (1850) V. 321 But I have had backfriends..as well as enemies.

2. A friend who stands at one's back, a backer.

1599 NASHE *Lent Stuffe* (1871) 77 Faithful confederates and back-friends. **1823** SCOTT *Quentin D.* vi, I had in case of the worst a stout back-friend in this uncle of mine.

3. (*dial.*) A hangnail.

1864 *N. & Q.* Ser. III. V. 25/1 The troublesome splinters of skin which are often formed near the roots of the nails are called stepmother's blessings..back-friends.

back-front. [BACK *a.* 1, BACK- A. 5.] The rear boundary line or elevation of a building.

c **1702** CELIA FIENNES *Diary* (1888) 293 The back Front goes out into a garden or Court. **1726** LEONI *Alberti's Archit.* I. 39/2 From the middle of the Fore-front of the Work I draw a Line quite thro' to the Back-front. **1738** DEFOE & RICHARDSON *Tour thro' Gt. Brit.* (ed. 2) I. 124 On the Back-front of the House was to be a noble Range of Stoves for tender Exotic Plants. **1800** *Hull Advertiser* 28 June 3/4 The workmen employed in modernising the backfront of the house. **1805** T. THORNTON *Sporting Tour through France* (1806) II. 104 A Sporting palace... The back-front is decorated with a profusion of horns of stags, deer. **1907** *Westm. Gaz.* 29 Nov. 12/1 Downing built 'four plain square brick mansions' on it with 'back-fronts' to St. James's Park.

transf. **1790** *Loiterer* 16 Jan. No. 51, p. 8 The Lady seemed, when I saw only the back-front, a fine young woman. **1900** KIPLING in *Times* 15 Mar. 8/1 The home Government..maintain intimate relations with all sides, with the front, and the far more important 'back-front' which begins at Pretoria.

'back-furrow, *v. U.S.* [BACK *adv.*] *trans.* and *intr.* To plough (land) so that a second furrow-slice is laid against the face of the first by ploughing in the reverse direction. Also ***back-furrow*** sb., ***back-furrowing*** vbl. sb.

1855 *Trans. Ill. State Agric. Soc. 1853–4* I. 425 Plow first out from the row on both sides, then finish by *back-furrowing*, so as to leave the row a trifle higher than the surrounding surface. **1858** C. L. FLINT *Milch Cows* 191 When arrived at the end of the piece, a back furrow is turned up to the potatoes. **1861** *Trans. Ill. State Agric. Soc. 1859–60* IV. 113 Mr. K. K. Jones..had his land plowed deep, [and] back furrowed it in beds twenty-four feet wide. *Ibid.* 392 This mode of plowing (called 'back-furrowing') is always to be observed when the track of the road is plowed. **1873–4** *Rep. Vermont Board Agric.* II. 239, I plow and harrow again, and then in a few days back-furrow in ridges with a side hill plow.

backgame ('bækˌgeɪm). [f. BACK *adv.*]

1. BACKGAMMON; a 'game' at backgammon.

1718 CIBBER *Non-juror* I, A Coquett's Play with a serious Lover, is like a Back-game at Tables, all open at first. **1753** in Mrs. Barbauld *Richardson* (1804) III. 68, I must now as they say at Tables, endeavour to play a good back game.

2. *Chess.*

1750 'A. D. PHILIDOR' *Chess Analysed* 8 As his King may retire at his Bishop's Square, it is necessary to send you to a second Back-game, which will shew you how to proceed in this Case. **1800** *Hoyle's Games* 132 As his king may retire to his bishop's square, the second Back-game will show how to proceed in this case.

3. A return-game.

backgammon (bæk'gæmən). Also in 7 baggammon. [Apparently = *back-game*, *back-play* (ME. *gamen* game, play, still in 15th c.), 'because the pieces are (in certain circumstances) taken up and obliged to go *back*, that is re-enter at the table.' Always called TABLES till the 17th c. Compare the prec. word; also the following early mention of *tables* along with dice, as a *kueade gemen* (Kentish for *gamen*), a wicked gamen or game:

1340 *Ayenb.* 45 Kueade gemenes, ase byeþ þe gemenes of des, and of tables.

(The unsatisfactory point is the want of 16th c. quotations for *gamen*, which may however have survived dialectally. Cf. also the analogous *after-game* in 'after-game at Irish,' a game of similar nature. For other suggestions as to derivation, see Wedgwood, and Skeat.)]

1. A game played on a board consisting of two tables (usually united by a hinge), with draughtmen whose moves are determined by throws of the dice.

c **1645** HOWELL *Lett.* (1650) II. 105 Though you have learnt to play at Baggammon, you must not forget Irish, which is a more serious and solid game. **1676** D'URFEY *Mad. Fickle* I. i, I won 300 guineys of him t'other night at Back-gammon. **1678** BUTLER *Hud.* III. II. 1062 The Hang-man, Was like to lurch you at Back-Gammon. **1771** SMOLLETT *Humph. Cl.* (1815) 142 And play at billiards, cards, or back-gammon. **1814** SCOTT in Lockhart *Life* (1839) IV. 355 In the evening Backgammon and cards are in great request.

2. *spec.* (See quot.)

1883 *Boys' Own Bk.* 620 There are three kinds of victory —one the winning the *hit*, the second the winning the *gammon*, and the third winning a *backgammon*..If the winner has borne all his men off before the loser has carried all his men to his own table, it is a *backgammon*, and held equal to three hits or games.

3. *attrib.*, as in ***backgammon board***, ***table***.

1789 MRS. PIOZZI *Journ. France* II. 371 A backgammon table preserved behind the high altar. **1820** BYRON *Juan* V. x, Like a backgammon board the place was dotted With whites and blacks.

back'gammon, *v.* [f. the sb.; cf. quot. 1678 in 1.] To defeat at backgammon, or by winning a backgammon.

1793 *Ann. Reg.* 246 At length he by death is back gammoned.

back-gate. [BACK *a.* 1, BACK- A. 5.] A gate at the back of, or leading to the rear part of, a house or other premises.

1442 *Extr. Aberd. Reg.* (1844) I. 9 Al man that has back yettes close thaim. **1632** MASSINGER & FIELD *Fatal Dowry* IV. ii. sig. H4ᵛ Let the Coach be brought To the backe gate. **1709** STEELE *Tatler* No. 45 ⁋1, I was let in at the Back-gate of a lovely House. **1818** [see LITTLE *a.* 1 a]. **1873** E. EGGLESTON *Myst. Metrop.* xxxvi. 307 When Mrs. Ferret came home from prayer-meeting she entered by the back gate. **1905** JACK LONDON *War of the Classes* 274, I battered on the drag and slammed back gates with them, or shivered with them in box cars and city parks.

back-grey. *Calico-printing.* [BACK- A. 4, GREY *sb.* 1 b.] = BACK-CLOTH 1, GREY-BACK 6.

1896 G. DUERR *Bleaching & Calico-print.* 22 Very often unbleached pieces of cloth (called back greys) are used for the purpose of keeping the blanket from getting dirty too soon;..the 'back greys' are run between the blanket and the pieces which are being printed. **1897** C. F. S. ROTHWELL *Print. Textile Fabrics* 34 These pieces, or *back-greys* as they are called, are afterwards bleached and printed with their own patterns. **1963** A. J. HALL *Textile Sci.* iv. 204 Passing around this pressure cylinder..is a thick blanket..which is endless, a so-called 'back-grey' (unbleached calico).

background ('bækgraʊnd), *sb.* [f. BACK *a.*]

1. a. The ground or surface lying at the back of or behind the chief objects of contemplation, which occupy the *foreground.* (Formerly, the part of the stage in a theatre remote from the audience.)

1672 WYCHERLEY *Love in Wood* III. ii, Ranger retires to the background. **1799** SHERIDAN *Pizarro* I. i. (1883) 182 Elvira walks about pensively in the background. **1824** MISS MITFORD *Village* Ser. I. (1863) 109 The low cottage in the back-ground.

b. *esp.* as represented in any of the Arts of Design. *spec.* in *Photogr.* Also *attrib.*

1752 tr. *Gersaint's Etch. Rembrandt* 94 The Back-ground is always faint, the Aqua-fortis having failed. **1847** LD. LINDSAY *Chr. Art.* I. 114 The backgrounds are either architectural in the Byzantine style, or mountainous. **1858** T. SUTTON *Dict. Photogr.* 29 In taking portraits, it is generally necessary to place a background behind the sitter. This is made by stretching a sheet of canvas..and painting it of an appropriate colour in distemper. **1892** *Photogr. Ann.* II. 756 Makers of exposure meters..Background manufacturers. **1961** A. L. M. SOWERBY *Dict. Photogr.* (ed. 19) 47 The following method of preparing a background and painting it will be found reliable.

c. *fig.* Also *attrib.*

1854 STANLEY *Sinai & Pal.* Introd. 28 Egypt..is the background of the whole history of the Israelites. **1858** HAWTHORNE *Fr. & It. Jrnls.* I. 160 A statelier dome.. shining on the background of the night of Time. **1868** ROSSETTI *Let.* 7 Oct. (1965) II. 668 Immense variety of background-material for any conceivable outdoor subject. **1928** *Pref. to Coll. Papers H. Bradley* p. vii, These papers.. form a background without which his labours on the Dictionary cannot be truly judged. **1930** J. B. PRIESTLEY *Angel Pav.* iii. 138 That international English,..a language without roots and background. **1940** *Camb. Bibliogr. Eng. Lit.* I. p. xv, The Middle English Period..(ii) The Political

Background..(iii) The Social Background. **1951** G. GREENE *Lost Childhood* III. 121 A young historian..gathering..background material. **1956** 'M. INNES' *Old Hall, New Hall* I. v. 52 Do some background reading in published sources. **1961** B. R. WILSON *Sects & Soc.* p. ix, Some of the background literature of my subject.

d. A person's cultural knowledge, education, experience, environment, etc.; social surroundings.

1913 J. WEBSTER *Daddy-Long-Legs* 209, I'm glad I don't belong to such a family! I should truly rather have the John Grier Home for a background. **1923** *Ladies' Home Jrnl.* Oct. 236/3 A charming girl lacking only the 'background' that wealth makes possible. **1934** A. HASKELL *Balletomania* xi. 219 Had she possessed a background of orthodox technical training [etc.]. **1954** *Manch. Guardian Weekly* 9 Dec. 2/2 A military background is not a full and complete preparation for a Chief Executive. **1959** *Manchester Guardian* 1 Aug. 8/3 Pupils are selected by interview... Family background is a major consideration.

e. Music, sound-effects, etc., subordinated to or accompanying some other activity, esp. music used as an accompaniment to a film or broadcast programme. Chiefly *attrib.* orig. *U.S.*

1928 *B.B.C. Hand Bk. 1929* 68 A..new design of control room has been decided upon, wherein effects, echoes, background music, etc. can be mixed together. **1934** E. B. MARKS *They all Sang* xvii. 215 As the hero was wheeled to the operating room, the strains of 'You're the Cheese in My Mousetrap' would trickle into the auditorium as background music. **1937** *Printers' Ink Monthly* Apr. 49/1 *Background*, any musical or sound effect used in backing up dialog or sound. **1937** *Times* 25 Sept. 8/2 *Le Coq d'Or* was no longer a musical work 'before all else', but only a musical work heard while something else very attractive to the eye was going on. It was in fact the beginning of that process now known to the B.B.C. as 'background listening'. **1946** SCOTT GODDARD in A. L. Bacharach *Brit. Mus.* i. 28 A rachitic progeny of background music to documentary films. **1949** L. FEATHER *Inside Be-Bop* ii. 17 Vocals..with fine backgrounds and solos by Bird. **1958** *Listener* 21 Aug. 260/1 As with our own Light Programme the 'background' music or entertainment is a comfort and solace to many.

f. ***background heater*** (see quot. 1961), ***heating***.

1939 MARTIN & SPEIGHT *Flat Book* ii. 25 There are excellent gas convector or background heaters. **1951** *Good Housek. Home Encycl.* 76/1 A ½ watt per cubic foot for background heating. **1961** *Gloss. Terms Gas Industry (B.S.I.)* 62 *Background heater*, a heater normally in continuous use which supplies heat to a room at such a rate as will provide a general temperature slightly below comfort temperature.

2. a. A less prominent position, where an object is not readily noticed; retirement, obscurity.

1779 SHERIDAN *Critic* III. i. (1883) 177 Keep your madness in the background. **1849** MACAULAY *Hist. Eng.* II. 253 Political friends thought it best..that he should remain in the background. **1876** GREEN *Short Hist.* iv. §2 (1882) 174 This..may have helped to throw into the background its [Parliament's] character as a supreme Court of appeal.

b. *attrib.* or as *adj.* Keeping in the background; retiring. *colloq.*

1896 *Westm. Gaz.* 9 Dec. 2/1 A reticent, background kind of lover. **1904** *Daily Chron.* 11 Feb. 8/6 'Cultivate a background manner,' is the advice of a lady..to governesses seeking situations.

3. *Electr.* Adventitious signals or effects in the reception or recording of sound. Also *attrib.*

1927 *Radio Assoc. Official Handbk.* 70 The purity of amplification..and the silence of the 'background', owing to successful elimination of atmospherics and 'mush', is remarkable. **1942** R. C. NORRIS *Radio Engin.* ii. 35/1 This tends to introduce background noise, which would be entirely avoided if a really good aerial were in use. **1962** A. NISBETT *Technique Sound Studio* vii. 132 One of the problems which may arise when tape is re-used is a background 'chatter' from the previous recording.

4. *Physics.* The level of radiation arising from cosmic rays and other natural sources. Also *attrib.*, as **background count**, the result (in counts or pulses per unit time) of measuring such radiation.

1930 *Phil. Mag.* IX. 642 The aim..was..to deduce the relative number of electrons falling in the central spot, in one of the rings or in the continuous background. **1933** RUTHERFORD *Coll. Papers* (1965) III. 343 This radiation gives rise to an inconvenient background 'wobble' in the output from the counting chamber. **1947** *Sci. News* II. 140 If a G-M (Geiger-Müller) counter has a background of 30 pulses per minute. **1950** F. GAYNOR *Encycl. Atomic Energy* 26 Background count. **1959** C. HODDER-WILLIAMS *Chain Reaction* viii. 98 No trace of radioactivity was detected over and above the normal background count.

'background, *v.* **1.** To form a background to.

1768 S. BENTLEY *River Dove* 8 Far distant as Vision can go, High Weever back-grounds the gay scene. **1843** MRS. BROWNING *Lett. R. Horne* I. 70 Where there is no reserve of character to background it [shyness]. **1891** C. JAMES *Rom. Rigmarole* 75 The 'antique spires' of the College Chapel, backgrounded with crimson sunset. **1904** *Westm. Gaz.* 17 Nov. 4/2 Planted on to the material like a raised embroidery, and backgrounded with manipulations of tulle or chiffon. **1905** *Ibid.* 4 May 4/2 Hair..well dressed can background these [features] with such effect that the face..may become almost beauty.

2. To place in the background, to make inconspicuous. Chiefly *fig.* Opp. FOREGROUND *v.*

1891 'S. MOSTYN' *Curatica* xii. 164, I am not sure if there was *any* bread and butter; if there was, it was..ignominiously back-grounded, so that I did not see it. **1976** *Word 1971* XXVII. 125 The thesis of this article is that the perceptual salience of certain aspects of events naturally foregrounds certain actions and entities and backgrounds others in a semantically predictable manner, dictating the structure of early sentences. **1980** *Times Lit. Suppl.* 19 Sept. 1045/4 Another tradition of anthropology follows Durkheim in backgrounding the intellectual propositions and foregrounding the moral persuasions of religion.

3. To inform (someone) of the circumstances pertaining to an event, situation, or the like, esp. its causes, history, etc; to 'fill in' (FILL *v.* 15 e).

1961 *Time* 10 Feb. 13/3 Salinger 'backgrounded' reporters on the news. **1971** *Rhodesia Herald* 23 June, He has served at The Hague and is completely backgrounded on the territory and the World Court battle. **1977** *Washington Post* 13 Mar. A1 A high-ranking State Department official well backgrounded in African affairs. **1985** *New Yorker* 11 Mar. 121/2 Israel's Embassy in Washington 'backgrounded' American reporters.

backgrounder. *U.S.* [f. BACKGROUND *sb.* + -ER[1].] A handout of background publicity material. Also a press conference or interview at which a government official explains the background of an action or policy.

1957 J. BLISH *Fallen Star* ii. 32 Stuffing into my jacket the release and the 'backgrounder'. **1959** *Manch. Guardian* 11 Aug. 6/2 The information office of the United States Embassy in London has sent to newspapers what it calls a 'backgrounder' on the events in Laos. **1965** T. C. SORENSEN *Kennedy* xiii. 328 During his Christmas holiday in Palm Beach both in 1961 and 1962, he [*sc.* President Kennedy] invited the two dozen or so regular White House correspondents..to a free-wheeling three-to-four hour 'backgrounder'..dividing each session into domestic and foreign affairs discussions. **1967** *Observer* 30 Apr. 11/6 In a Saigon 'backgrounder', you are told about public health measures. **1977** *Washington Post* 17 Nov. A4/3 A high administration official held a so-called 'backgrounder' to respond to Nitze. Under the rules of the backgrounder, the high official could not be named by reporters. **1982** *N.Y. Times* 16 Mar. A6/5 Larry Speakes, the deputy press secretary, was asked if Mr. Reagan was actually unaware of Mr. Haig's 'backgrounder' on Saturday.

†**'back-guard.** *Obs.* [Cf. BACK-WARD.] Rear-guard.

c **1470** HENRY *Wallace* IX. 745 To follow thaim a bakgard for to be.

back-hair ('bæk'hɛə(r)). [f. BACK *a.*] The long hair at the back of a woman's head.

1836 *Athenæum* No. 447. 358 Their back hair underneath combed upwards. **1837** DICKENS *Pickw.* xxii, Busily engaged in brushing what ladies call their 'back-hair.'

†**'back-half.** *Obs.* Forms: 5 bac-, bak-, 5–6 backe-, 6 backhalf(e. [f. BACK *a.* + HALF.] Back side, back part, rear.

1408 WYCLIF *Gen.* xix. 6 (MS. Fairfax 2) Loth ȝede out to hem on the bachalf. *a* **1450** *Knt. de la Tour* (1868) 59 The theef that comithe in atte the dore on the backe half. **1575** LANEHAM *Lett.* 52 Too Athlants ioined togeather a backhalf.

b. *adverbially*: Backward.

1470 HARDING *Chron.* Pref. 6 Thus sette he me all bakhalfe on the tayle.

back-hand ('bæk,hænd), *sb.* (and *a.*) [f. BACK *adv.*]

A. *sb.* **1.** The hand turned backwards in making a stroke, as (at *Tennis*) in taking balls at the left hand, by stretching the right across the body, *hence* the left-hand 'play' or 'court' in the game. Hence *fig.* Phr. ***on the backhand***: backhanded.

1657 DISBROWE in Burton *Diary* (1828) II. 48 It reflects upon the Long Parliament by the back-hand..So I desire the preamble may be laid aside. *c* **1706** VANBRUGH *Mistake* v. 1, I desire the honour to keep your back hand myself. *Lopez* (*servant to Don L.*) 'Tis very kind indeed. Pray, sir, have you ne'er a servant with you could hold a racket for me too? *a* **1757** CIBBER *Careless Husb.* IV. (D.) That's odds at tennis, my lord..I'll endeavour to keep your back-hand a little. **1824** SCOTT *St. Ronan's* xix, As if I had picked you out of the whole of St. James's coffee-house to hold my back-hand. **1890** H. W. W. WILBERFORCE in C. G. Heathcote *Tennis* 261 A low ball on the back-hand is very difficult to deal with. **1948** N. H. PATTERSON *Compl. Lawn-Tennis Player* iv. 12 This wide service..catches your adversary on the backhand. *Ibid.* 14 If he has a weak backhand then try to 'paste' his forehand corner until [etc.]. *Ibid.* xiv. 117 We have all seen girls trying to use both hands when attempting to take a backhand. **1966** MILLS & BUTLER *Mod. Badminton* v. 43 Reaching to take it [*sc.* the shuttle] early on the backhand will not only save time but [etc.].

2. Handwriting with the letters sloped backwards.

Mod. newspaper, Other letters produced were written by Street in his back-hand.

B. *attrib.* as *adj.* = BACK-HANDED. Also applied to the court, etc.

1695 BLACKMORE *Pr. Arth.* x. 781 With a back hand Blow. **1886** J. DWIGHT *Lawn Tennis* v. 24 The backhand volley is made in much the same way. **1889** H. W. W. WILBERFORCE *Lawn Tennis* vi. 21 For the backhand stroke the right foot is in front. **1890** —— in C. G. Heathcote *Tennis* 268 The better volleyer of a pair should play in the back-hand court. **1908** *Westm. Gaz.* 1 May 8/3 Mr. McGregor employed his backhand volley effectively. **1921** A. W. MYERS *Twenty Years Lawn Tennis* 9 He attacked the Australian's back-hand corner. **1929** *Morn. Post* 13 July 16/3 (*heading*) The Backhand Grip. **1966** MILLS & BUTLER *Mod. Badminton* v. 43 The backhand smash can be used to put away loose returns.

'back-,hand, *v.* **1.** To take a BACKHANDER 2.

1857 G. LAWRENCE *Guy Livingstone* viii. 72 Livingstone, if you begin back-handing already, you will never be able to hold that great raking chestnut.

2. *trans.* To hit or stroke with the back of one's hand.

a **1935** T. E. LAWRENCE *Mint* (1955) II. xviii. 147 Stiffy appeared, back-handing his moustache. **1962** K. ORVIS *Damned & Destroyed* ix. 62 I'm lucky the goon-squad haven't back-handed me into a lane.

back-handed ('bæk,hændɪd), *a.* [f. prec. sb.]

1. With the back of the hand.

1813 L. HUNT in *Examiner* 15 Mar. 162/1 A back-handed pat on the cheek. **1836** MACREADY *Remin.* II. 23 A back-handed slap across the face.

2. Directed backwards, or with the hand or arm crossing the body (*i.e.* for a right-handed man from left to right), as a sword-cut; sloping backwards, as handwriting. Also as *adv.*

1889 H. W. W. WILBERFORCE *Lawn Tennis* 29 It is much more difficult to volley a high lob backhanded than forehanded. **1890** L. DOD in C. G. Heathcote *Tennis* 310, I believe myself in changing the grip of one's racket, both for fore- and back-handed strokes. **1898** *The 'House' on Sport* I. 222 The first great step in this direction [of improving polo] was the introduction of the back-handed stroke. **1922** A. E. CRAWLEY *Lawn Tennis Do's & Don'ts* 27 The receiver is in doubt whether to play it forehanded or back-handed. **1934** A. CHRISTIE *Murder on Orient Express* I. vii. 63 One would have to strike backhanded.

3. *fig.* †**a.** Keeping back one's hand, backward, remiss; **b.** Indirect, like a back-handed sword-cut.

1800 *Deb. Congress* (1851) 832/2 In a back-handed way and not in the fair regular manner. **1817** GODWIN *Mandeville* II. 180 (D.) Modesty..is often the most beggarly and back-handed friend that merit can have. **1818** SCOTT *Rob Roy* xxvi, Rob might get a back-handed lick at him. **1865** DICKENS *Mut. Fr.* xii, Having given her this back-handed reminder.

Hence **back-'handedly** *adv.*, in an indirect or back-handed manner; **back'handedness**.

1859 in WORCESTER. **1889** *Cent. Dict.*, *Backhandedly*, with the hand directed backward: as, to strike back-handedly. **1957** K. A. WITTFOGEL *Oriental Despotism* ix. 386 He backhandedly admitted that his statement did not include the 'barbarian' world of Oriental despotism.

back-hander. [f. as prec. + -ER[1].]

1. a. A blow with the back of the hand.

1803 *Censor* 1 Apr. 44 He will..'give me such a back hander, as will send me reeling a dozen yards.' **1836** MARRYAT *Midsh. Easy* (1864) 11 'Go away Sarah,' said Johnny with a backhander. **1881** E. J. WORBOISE *Sissie* xxii, A heavy backhander by way of punishment.

b. *fig.*

1862 WHYTE-MELVILLE *Inside Bar* x. (ed. 12) 363 This was obviously a back-hander at James. **1880** *World* 21 Aug. 7 The Lieutenant-General got a prompt backhander when he asked for a return of the contributions.

2. An extra glass of wine out of turn, the bottle being passed back.

1854 THACKERAY *Newcomes* II. 48, I will take a back-hander, as Clive don't seem to drink.

3. A back-handed stroke or blow. Cf. BACK-HANDED *a.* 2

1890 H. W. W. WILBERFORCE in C. G. Heathcote *Tennis* 266 Few, if any, ladies can volley with effect, and the efforts of most to take a back-hander result in nothing better than a graceful scoop. **1958** J. HISLOP *From Start to Finish* 166 *Backhander*, hitting a horse with a whip in the carrying position. **1959** *Times* 19 May 4/5 [Polo] A partial clearing gave Gracida the chance to whack in a stinging backhander.

4. A tip or bribe made surreptitiously, a secret payment. *slang.*

1960 D. STOREY *Sporting Life* II. iii. 207 That's how he hopes to get the car—from the backhander he'll get. **1962** J. TUNSTALL *Fishermen* iv. 109 A boy who helps with a few odd jobs..can collect £5 or more in backhanders. *Ibid.* v. 125 Since the man's ability does not seem to qualify him, he is..suspected of having won the job by giving a backhander. **1968** *Listener* 7 Mar. 295/1 A bit of a backhander and, boy, you're in.

back-head ('bæk'hɛd). [f. BACK *a.* + HEAD.]

a. False hair worn at the back of the head; chignon. **b.** Back part of the head.

1731 *Gentl. Mag.* I. 531 Dresses youthfully, wears back-heads. **1754** RICHARDSON *Grandison* vii. 223 (D.) Her pale pink lustring and back-head. **1836** A. WALKER *Beauty Wom.* 381 If the forehead be not large in proportion to the backhead.

back-house. [BACK *a.* 1, BACK- 5.] †**1.** A subsidiary house or building which lies behind the main house. *Obs.* exc. *dial.*

1557 *Edin. B. Rec.* III. 17 To abstene..fra all melting..of talloun within thair bak hous. *a* **1603** T. CARTWRIGHT *Confut. Rhem. N.T.* (1618) 724 The intercession by Angels lyeth (as they say) in the backhouse ditch. **1710** *Lond. Gaz.* No. 4637/4 A well built Brick House, with a Back-house and other Buildings behind. **1888** B. L. BURNETT *From Stable Boy* xxvii. 148, I was layving..without going to the zider cask in the back-houze.

2. *U.S.* A privy. Also *attrib.*

1847 in WEBSTER. **1939** C. MORLEY *Kitty Foyle* ii. 23 The chlorides Mother was always throwing into the little outdoor backhouse. *Ibid.* xvii. 161 None of that backhouse talk when Molly Scarf gets here.

backhouse, obs. f. BAKEHOUSE.

backing ('bækɪŋ), *vbl. sb.* [f. BACK *v.* + -ING[1].]

I. The action of the vb. BACK in various senses.

1. The action of supporting at the back.

1596 SHAKS. *1 Hen. IV*, II. iv. 165 Call you that backing of your friends? a plague vpon such backing! **1633** AMES *Agst. Cerem.* II. 281 For the backings of the former consequence, this reason was added. **1875** Helps *Anim. & Mast.* v. 133 My ready backing of my friend.

2. The mounting of a horse; the breaking in of a colt to the saddle.

1607 Topsell *Four-f. Beasts* 240 It is good to use your horse to backing both sadled and bare. **1783** Ainsworth *Lat. Dict.* (Morell), The backing of a horse, *equi domitura.*

3. The action of putting or moving back; a throwing back in progress; retardation.

1649 Blith *Eng. Improv. Impr.* ii. (1653) 10 A great part of that land lyeth as it were drowned..it overcomes not that backing many times till near Midsummer.

4. Motion in a backward direction, *esp.* of the wind in a direction opposed to the sun's. ***backing and filling*** (see back *v.* 16 b). *U.S.*

1686 Plot *Staffordsh.* 25 Who foretold them by the Winds backing to the Sun, i.e. opposing its course. **1777** in *Essex* (Salem, Mass.) *Inst. Hist. Coll.* (1906) XLII. 315 He was then order'd..to Stillwarter, then ordered from Stillwarter to Benington... This in the Salers Frase is Backing & filling, makes but poor way a head. **1854** *N.Y. Herald* 15 June (Bartlett), There has been so much backing and filling, not only upon the Cuban question, but upon every other. **1869** Semmes *Mem. Service Afloat* 255 The reader need no longer wonder at the backing and filling of the Iroquois around the little Sumter. **1875** Bedford *Sailor's Pocket Bk.* iv. 91 From West to South-West, South, and South-East, the change is called backing. **1884** Ingersoll in *Harper's Mag.* 876/2 Rivers would be able to dispose of their water in the full season without its backing up.

attrib. **1903** Clapin *Dict. Amer.* 31 A backing and filling policy is one which is shilly-shally, trifling, irresolute. **1949** *Amer. speech* XXIV. 172 Tickers slowed down and a series of backing and filling movements made the pattern for the day.

5. *techn.* **a.** *Printing*, 'Perfecting' a sheet already printed on one side, by printing it on the other. **b.** *Bookbinding*, Preparing the back of a book with glue, etc. before putting on the cover.

1846 *Printing Appar. Amateurs* 42 When a second impression was added at the back, which is called backing, or working the reiteration.

6. a. ***backing-down***: withdrawal, shirking. **b.** ***backing-off***: unwinding silk or cotton. **c.** ***backing-up*** in *Cricket*, etc.: see back *v.* 8. Also in other games.

1816 W. Lambert *Cricketer's Guide* (ed. 6) iii. 40 Getting behind the Wicket-keeper when the Ball is thrown in, which is called *backing up.* **1836** *New Sporting Mag.* Oct. 360 By backing up too far, he ran himself out. **1839** Ure *Dict. Arts* 369 It is necessary to turn the rim beforehand a little in the opposite direction..an operation called in technical language, the *backing off.* **1851** L. Gordon *Art Jrnl. Illust. Catal.* vi. **/2 This operation of undoing the coil is called the backing-off. **1883** *Harper's Mag.* Aug. 465/1 There's to be no backing down. **1960** *Times* 14 Nov. 4/1 The age-old principle of backing-up..was once more the basic strength of the whole [Rugby football] team.

d. ***backing-out*** (see back *v.* 18). Also *attrib.*

1819 Cartwright in *Cobbett's Wkly. Pol. Reg.* 22 May col. 1112 The Duke saw his reasons for what Mr. Cobbett calls 'backing out'. **1841** *Knickerbocker* XVII. 374 Nor would her offended dignity be appeased by the self-imposed immolations of *backing-out.* **1846** S. Smith *Theatr. Apprent.* 149, I don't come from a backing out country—I must have a showing for the money that's down. **1880** Tourgée *Invis. Empire* v. 413 In explanation of the backing-out process, he says it consisted simply in not going to any more meetings.

II. Collective appellation of that which backs, or forms a back, rear, or hinder part.

7. a. Support, succour; a body of supporters.

1818 Scott *Rob Roy* viii, A quarter whence assuredly he expected no backing. **1880** *Times* 11 Dec. 9 It is promoted by what appears to be a solid backing of landowners.

b. Musical or vocal accompaniment to a singer, esp. on a recording.

1940 *Swing* Jan. 24/3 Everyone..seems happy in the rowdy backing, which gives plenty of punch to a good old barroom song. *Ibid.* June 17 The backing is based on a riff that's been used for several other numbers lately. **1959** *Punch* 19 Aug. 60/2 Mr. B. finds the backing tedious and professes indifference to the singer's charms.

8. a. Anything used to form a back, or line the back.

1793 Smeaton *Edystone L.* §221 Not only flat backing, but Purbeck ashler in rough courses, from those quarries. **1867** Smyth *Sailor's Word-Bk.*, *Backing*, the timber behind the armour-plates of a ship. **1880** L. Higgin *Handbk. Embroidery* iv. 35 Silk, satin, or velvet..must be backed with a fine cotton or linen lining. The 'backing'..is first framed. **1884** F. Crawford *Rom. Singer* I. 219 A great pier-glass was cracked..and the metallic backing seemed to be scaling off. **1962** A. Nisbett *Technique Sound Studio* 241 *Backing*, the base on which the magnetic oxide coating of tape is carried. **1963** *Which?* Mar. 691 Carpets usually have a backing and a pile. The backing is woven, and consists of a set of warp threads (usually cotton) and a set of weft threads (usually jute). **1967** E. Short *Embroidery & Fabric Collage* i. 20 (*caption*) Padded by slitting the backing and inserting cotton wool.

b. *Photogr.* (i) (See back *v.* 2 b); (ii) ***backing paper***, a strip of opaque paper on which the celluloid film in a roll-film is mounted.

1937 S. G. B. Stubbs *Mod. Encycl. Photogr.* I. 26/1 The beginning of the film, and the gummed paper holding it to the black side of the 'backing-paper' is clearly seen in the illustration. **1958** M. L. Hall *Newnes Complete Amat. Photogr.* iv. 55, 35 mm. film is without a backing paper with numbers on it which can be viewed through a red window.

c. Scenery placed behind a door, window or other opening in a stage or film set.

1889 in *Cent. Dict.* **1937** N. Coward *Pres. Indic.* ii. 102 Backings and flats..waiting about untidily to be set in Act One. **1952** W. Granville *Dict. Theatr. Terms* 20 Window backings are often part of the general back-cloth picture of the landscape.

9. = back *sb.* 16.

1823 P. Nicholson *Pract. Build.* 225 The Backing of a Hip is the angle made on its upper edge to range with the two sides or planes of the roof between which it is placed.

10. (*dial.*) Bank, embankment.

1863 *Lancashire Fents* 3 A pretty weaver lass..seated herself on the 'backing.' **1865** B. Brierley *Irkdale* I. 136 A younger person stands upon the garden 'backing.'

11. ***backings***: refuse of wool or flax, or what is left after dressing it; in the manufacture of flax, properly, the tow that is thrown off by the second hackling. (Jamieson.) Also in form **backens** *Sc.*

1780 A. Young *Tour in Ireland* 101, 8 lb. flax for coarse linen; and 4 lb. of dressed tow, and some for *backens. Ibid.* 195 The remainder is called *backings*, and is spun into the coarsest stuff. **1783** in *Ann. Reg. 1783* (1785) 84/1 Cloth made from the refuse of Flax, and Backings of Tow. *c* **1795** *Aberd. Statist. Acc.* XIX. 207 (Jam.) The waft was spun by old women, and that only from backings or nails.

12. *Sc.* and *U.S.* (The act of writing) the address of a letter. Cf. back *v.* 12 b.

1833 *Chambers's Edin. Jrnl.* II. 112/1 The same rule applies to the backing of the letter. **1871** W. Alexander *J. Gibb* xiv. 104 It was not the mere writing that dismayed him, it was the composition..and the 'backin'.

backing ('bækɪŋ), *ppl. a.* [f. back *v.* + -ing².] That backs, or moves backward.

1862 Thornbury *Turner* I. 268 In the foreground Turner has put a backing waggon with kicking horses. **1907** *Macmillan's Mag.* July 671 A small sandy bay on the left bank, where a backing eddy ran. **1934** J. E. Lilico *Sheep Dog Memoirs* 26 The finest backing dogs I have ever seen are in the saleyards at Addington. **1945** Baker *Austral. Lang.* iii. 73 A dog trained to run across the backs of sheep when they are yarded is called a *backing dog.* **1966** *Melody Maker* 23 July 10/4 The backing group on Nina Simone's recording of 'Pastel Blues'.

back-land, backland. [back *a.* 1.] **1.** *Sc.* The back portion of a piece of ground; a building on this; *spec.* a house or tenement built behind others. (Cf. land *sb.* 8.)

1488–1927 [see D.O.S.T. and Sc. Nat. Dict.].

2. = back country.

1681 Penn *Acc. Pennsylv.* Wks. 1782 IV. 301 The back-lands being..richer, than those that lie by navigable rivers. **1783** Gouv. Morris in Sparks *Life & Writ.* (1832) I. 248 The back lands are as important in the eyes of some, as the fisheries. **1830** W. S. Moorsom *Lett. fr. Nova Scotia* 130 A few families who occupy the back-lands of Great Tracadie. **1853** in *Fourteenth General Rep. Colonial Land & Emigration Commissioners* (1854) 206 Roads leading to and from the river will be reserved for public use, and as a means of access to the back lands. **1901** A. W. Jose *Australasia* vii. 110 The West Australians..began to explore more systematically their huge backlands. **1934** S. Beckett *More Pricks* 26 Each time I see it [*sc.* Fingal] more as a back-land, a land of sanctuary.

3. *Geogr.* (See quot. 1956.)

1909 H. B. C. Sollas tr. *Suess's Face of Earth* IV. xiv. 513 The backland is not the starting-point of an active fold-forming force. The Cambrian beds lie just as undisturbed in the backland of Angara as in the foreland of Laurentia. **1956** Swayne *Concise Gloss. Geogr. Terms* 18 *Backland*, (*a*) the area between a natural levée and the base of a valley slope. (*b*) A region behind mountain ranges whether occupied by sea or land, e.g. the Pacific Ocean is described as a backland of the great fold mountains.

back-lash ('bæklæʃ). *Mech.* Also **backlash.**

a. The jarring reaction or striking back of a wheel or set of connected wheels in a piece of mechanism, when the motion is not uniform or when sudden pressure is applied. **'back-lashing** (in same sense).

1815 *Brit. Pat. 3887*, There is a great risk of breaking these wheels from the backlash or returning stroke of the engine. **1825** J. Nicholson *Oper. Mech.* 44 If a wheel is not true..it will shake, or have, what is called, back-lash. **1863** *N. Brit. Rev.* May 257 Throughout the machine, in such a case, there is too much back-lash. **1883** *Fisheries Exhib. Catal.* 33 Steering Gear..whereby the steersman is relieved from the danger of back-lash on the wheel. **1883** *Century Mag.* 381 To prevent the reel from back-lashing. *a* **1935** T. E. Lawrence *Mint* (1955) iii. xiii. 194 Two extra thou of backlash in the planet pinions of an epi-gear.

b. *transf.* and *fig.*

1921 *What Business Man should know about Printing* (W. B. Conkey Co.) 23 The entire operation of the manufacture of a book..is in one continuous line without a back-lash. **1929** *Jrnl. Commerce* (N.Y.) 6 Apr. 18/8 The backlash from the diversion of finances to speculative purposes showed its first definitely injurious effects. **1939** N. Monsarrat *This is Schoolroom* vii. 166 Another world where her hair had lustre ..and meat-pies no back-lash. **1957** *Sat. Even. Post* 29 June 58 You're going to get a backlash—segregation's going to spread. **1958** *Spectator* 1 Aug. 156/1 Why should we feel the backlash of the recession at this date? **1962** P. Brickhill *Deadline* x. 126 She learned the police had searched her room. *I* caught the backlash. **1964** *Listener* 30 July 149/2 [*Addressed to a Negro*] Could you provoke a kind of white backlash if you move in, getting your full demands laid before the public? *Ibid.* 10 Sept. 372/2 The notorious white backlash (the voters, especially of immigrant origins, who fear the Negroes will move into their jobs and depress the value of their little houses). **1964** *Publishers' Weekly* 21 Sept. 28 In the backlash of the Encyclopaedia Britannica-G. & C. Merriam merger, a secret meeting was held at the Williams Club in New York.

backless ('bæklɪs), *a.* [f. back *sb.* + -less.]

a. Without a back, having no back.

1823 *Blackw. Mag.* Oct. 470/2 Bare benches, and backless seats. **1827** Southey *Lett.* (1856) IV. 79 A car (which must not have been backless). **1882** *Harper's Mag.* LXIV. 786 Narrow backless benches.

b. Applied to a woman's garment cut low at the back.

1926 C. Beaton *Diary* 18 Oct. in *Wandering Years* (1961) 142 She [*sc.* Teddie Gerrard] innovated backless dresses and huskily croaked, 'We're so glad to see you're back, dear lady!' **1960** *Harper's Bazaar* Oct. 52 A backless, strapless foundation with a contour bust.

'backlet. *dial.* [f. back *sb.* + -let, dim. suffix.] A back yard. (Chiefly in s.w.)

1724 *Lond. Gaz.* 6253/3 A Dwelling-House, with a Backlet and Garden thereto belonging. **1884** *West. Morn. News* 28 June 4/7 The backlet..was..under the power of the flames.

'back-line, backline. [f. back *a.* + line *sb.*²] A line situated behind another or others; esp. in various games, a line marking the limit of play at the end of a court, field, etc.; also [back *sb.*¹ 21], a line of backs in football, etc.

Cf. quot. 1806 s.v. back *a.* 1.

1890 H. W. W. Wilberforce in C. G. Heathcote *Tennis* 260 He must be content to play a defensive game, and retire about a yard behind the back-line. **1960** T. McLean *Kings of Rugby* 122 Tries which set the whole of the Lions' backline clicking on all cylinders. **1963** *Times* 27 May 5/3 Ramsden, from his own backline, galloped the length of the [Polo] ground and scored a lovely goal in four confident hits. **1966** Mills & Butler *Mod. Badminton* v. 45 You must turn your right shoulder towards the backline.

'backlings, -ins, *adv. north. dial.* [f. OE. *bæcling* (f. *bæc*, back + -ling) with adverbial genitive -*s*.] Back, backwards.

[*c* **975** *Rushw. Gosp.* John vi. 66 Moniȝe ðeȝnas his from foerdun on bæcling.] **1785** Burns *Wks.* III. 254 Backlins comin..She grew mair bright.

'backlist, back list. [back *a.* 3 b.] (A catalogue of) books still available for sale by a publisher or bookseller, but no longer classified by him as 'current' or 'new'. Cf. back number.

1946 S. Unwin *Truth about Publishing* (ed. 4) 14 The most stable firms are usually those which have a strong back list of publications with a continuous and profitable sale. **1947** *Sat. Rev. Lit.* 22 Feb. 5/1 'Ferdinand the Bull'..now in its twentieth edition, is still very much on the active backlists. **1957** *Economist* 21 Sept. 939/1 Its sales usually consist of filling small orders for a large number of individual titles, many of them from the backlist. **1959** *Manchester Guardian* 5 Aug. 10/2 Those [publishers]..with well-stocked back lists have been able to go on selling..Bibles, dictionaries, classics.

back-load, back load. [back- A. 3.] An amount that can be carried on the back.

1725 Bailey *Erasm. Colloq.* (1877) 182 (D.) Return home with a backload of sanctimony. **1823** *Massachusetts Spy* 3 Dec. (Th.), A black fellow was taken up on suspicion, with a back load of live turkeys. **1854** B. Young et al. *Jrnl. Discourses* I. 255/1 You might go round exhibiting a back load of gold. **1894** *Outing* (U.S.) XXIV. 88/1 She had brought us a large back-load of wood.

back-log ('bæk'lɒg). [f. back *a.*] **a.** A large log placed at the back of the fire.

1684 I. Mather *Illustr. Provid.* v. 115 The spit..came down with the point foremost, and stuck in the back-log. **1829** J. MacTaggart *Three Years in Canada* I. 52 A..blazing fire with a maple back log. **1882** Howells in *Longm. Mag.* I. 49 A back-log big enough to smoulder..for days. **1883** Mrs. Rollins *New Eng. Bygones* 63 Brightened by a roaring backlog. **1895** H. L. Twisleton *Poems* 28 The back-log's yellow light. **1900** H. Lawson *On Track* 7 A fresh back-log thrown behind the fire. **1901** *N.Z. Illustr. Mag.* IV. 596 He cut up a lot of maire backlogs.

b. *fig.* Something in reserve, reserves, an accumulation.

1883 *Wheelman* I. 294 The back-log of raw eggs and milk beginning to take effect, the pace was improved. **1952** J. Steinbeck *East of Eden* 63 If one is accused of a lie and it turns out to be the truth, there is a backlog that will last a long time and protect a number of untruths. **1953** *Encounter* Oct. 55/2 This backlog of goodwill produced by a century of free immigration.

c. Arrears of unfulfilled orders, etc.

1932 *Sun* (Baltimore) 9 Feb. 16/5 From April through December..there was a steady decrease [in the number of unfulfilled orders] and the backlog at the year-end was the smallest in 21 years. **1947** *Times* 30 Apr. 2/1 It is argued that the prospects of making up this back-log of 500,000 cars cannot be considered good. **1954** *Economist* 25 Dec. 1079/1 The backlog of unfilled orders on manufacturers' books is growing at last. **1958** *Listener* 2 Jan. 19/2 Court cases of which there was a considerable back-log.

†'backman. *Obs. rare.* [f. back *sb.* 12.] A follower, retainer, attendant.

c **1560** *Sang agane Ladyes* in *Maitland Poems*, The lairds and ladyes ryde of the toun For feir of hungerie bakmen.

back-mark, *v. Sporting slang.* [Cf. next.] *trans.* To put (a competitor) back at the start of a race. Hence, to leave far behind in a contest.

1890 Farmer *Slang* s.v., *To be backmarked*..(pedestrian), in handicapping to receive less start from 'scratch' than previously given—even to being put back to 'scratch'. **1895** *Field* 24 Aug. 315/3 Jersey men eagerly awaited the issue of the race between the amateur champion of the world and their own island champions, not that they ever expected them to back mark Tyers. **1928** *Sunday Express* 17 June 20/3, I venture the opinion that he would readily back-mark any man in Scotland over a mile course.

back-marker. [f. *back mark* (BACK *a.* 1, MARK *sb.*[1]) + -ER[1].] One who starts from 'scratch' or has the least favourable handicap in a game, match, or race.

1895 *Daily News* 5 Sept. 7/3 The back-markers were well up in the last lap. **1899** *Westm. Gaz.* 14 Mar. 10/1 One day there was an exhibition game of billiards... Captain Johnson took 150 in 300 from Cook, and had been passed by the 'back-marker'. **1957** S. Moss *In Track of Speed* i. 13, I felt it quite an honour to be the backmarker, running into third place after a lap.

backmost ('bækməst), *a.*, *superl.* [f. BACK *a.*; a late formation after the type of *foremost*, *hindmost*: see -MOST. Cf. BACKERMOST.] Most to the back, hindmost; the opposite of *foremost*.

1782 A. MONRO *Compar. Anat.* 98 The four backmost teeth. **1874** FARRAR *Christ* II. xlii. 95 Though now the axe was uplifted, nay, though it was at its backmost poise.

back number. [BACK *a.* 3 b, NUMBER *sb.* 6.] A number of a magazine, periodical, etc., earlier than the current one; hence *colloq.* (orig. *U.S.*), one who or a thing which is behind the times, out of date, or useless.

1812 *Niles' Reg.* I. 392/2 To reprint certain back numbers of the register. **1851** MAYHEW *London Lab.* I. 308/2 The sum expended annually in the streets for back numbers of periodicals amounts to upwards of £700. **1882** G. W. PECK *Peck's Sunshine* 153 Some old back number of a girl who has no fellow who wants to go. **1890** *Harper's Mag.* Feb. 439/2 Whereas if Galen should appear among us to-day,..he would be told he was a back number. **1907** *Westm. Gaz.* 4 Dec. 2/3 There are now so many competing forms of transport..that the steamboat seems to be doomed to be what is in current terminology called a 'back number'. **1924** GALSWORTHY *White Monkey* I. iv. 27 Lady Alison..finding a certain poignancy in contact with the New Age, on Fleur's copper floor. On that floor she almost felt a back number. **1945** 'G. ORWELL' *Animal Farm* 36 Snowball had made a close study of some back numbers of the *Farmer and Stockbreeder*. **1961** *Times* 18 May 5/3 A veteran who..has already proved that he is no back-number.

attrib. **1902** KIPLING *Traffics & Discoveries* (1904) 12 These old hand-power, back-number, flint-and-steel reaping machines.

back of (or **o'**) **beyond**: see BEYOND C. b.

back of (or **o'**) **Bourke,** *phr. Austral. slang.* [f. *Bourke*, a town in the extreme west of New South Wales.] Remote inland country; the 'back of beyond'.

1918 CAMPBELL & NELSON *Dinky-Di Soldier* 26 They smile to see me ploddin' on along the Bathurst road, The long, long road that runs to back o' Bourke. **1930** *Bulletin* (Sydney) 3 Dec. 12/2 He [*sc.* the cadger] had come to town from Back o' Bourke to see the Minister about a wheat scheme. **1933** *Ibid.* 20 Dec. 20/1 Choom had come straight from the ship to the back o' Bourke on book-keeping duty.

'back-out. *U.S.* [BACK *v.* 18.] An act of backing out or withdrawing from a position; inclination to back out.

1829 *Western Souvenir 1830* 314 (D.A.), There's no back out in none of my breed. **1836** CROCKETT *Exploits & Adv. Texas* (1837) 4 Now that idea..was a sort of cornering in which there was no back out. **1888** *Boston Weekly Globe* 28 Mar. (Farmer), Mr. Barker's back-out has not much surprised me.

back-pack, *sb.* Chiefly *U.S.* [BACK- A. 3, PACK *sb.*[1] 1.] A pack carried on the back; *spec.* one consisting of a folded parachute. Also *attrib.*

1914 *Outing* (U.S.) June 312/1 By folding a blanket..it is convenient as a back-pack. **1921** *Ibid.* Mar. 254/1 How about that little back-pack tent you are going to have for your trip? **1930** C. DIXON *Parachuting* 160 (*caption*) The Back Pack is usually used. **1946** W. F. BURBIDGE *From Balloon to Bomber* iii. 45 One type [of parachute] is carried on the airman's lap..a 'back pack' fastens below the shoulders. **1966** *Economist* 23 July 353/1 The back-pack manoeuvering unit that was to have been tried out by Gemini 9. **1969** *Times* 22 July (Moon Rep.) p. i/3 The mass of the back-pack does have some effect on inertia.

Hence as *v. intr.*, to carry a pack on the back: used esp. of hiking, camping, etc. Also *trans.* So **back-packer, -packing.**

1916 H. C. KEPHART *Camping & Woodcraft* I. 143 Back-packing is the cheapest possible way to spend one's vacation in the wilderness. **1940** W. S. GILKISON *Peaks, Packs* xiii. 102 Swagging—or, if you prefer it, back-packing—is more or less an essential part of every climbing trip. **1946** *Trail & Timberline* June 88/1 (D.A.), The deplorable housing situation could never really affect a certain group of enthusiasts known as back-packers. **1956** J. D. LEECHMAN *Native Tribes Canada* 37 Whatever was not carried on the toboggans had to be backpacked. **1961** *Times* 18 July 11/6 Back-packing is the only means of transport.

back-pedalling, *vbl. sb.* [BACK *adv.* 5.]

1. *Bicycling.* The action of pressing down upon the pedal as it rises, in order to check the movement of the wheel. Also *attrib.* Hence (as a back-formation) **back-pedal** *v. intr.* and *trans.*; also as *sb. attrib.*

1887 ALBERMARLE & HILLIER *Cycling* 377 This form of clutch..does not admit of back-pedalling. **1890** *Ibid.* (ed. 3) 373 A break should always be used—it is absurd to do hard work back pedalling down-hill. **1897** *Encycl. Sport* I. 268/1 Do not back-pedal too suddenly, or you may break your chain. **1898** J. PENNELL in *Fortn. Rev.* Jan. 60 The machine can be back-pedalled. *Ibid.* 63 An endless number of back-pedalling brakes have been brought out during the last year. **1940** AUDEN *Another Time* 73 She'd a bicycle with..a harsh back-pedal brake.

2. *fig.* The checking of a forward movement, the reversing of an action.

1901 'H. MCHUGH' *John Henry* 11 You back-pedal so hard that you grab for your hat. **1927** W. E. COLLINSON *Contemp. Eng.* 32 Note here the slang use of back pedal!, vulgò also come off it, hold hard. **1950** J. DEMPSEY *Champ. Fighting* xviii. 116 They sprout bad punching habits while concentrating on blocking, parrying, back-pedalling and the like. **1955** M. GILBERT *Sky High* viii. 109 It's not quite fair to ask me if I'm happy about his handling of the case... I've got a feeling..that he's going to back-pedal on it. **1958** *Oxf. Mag.* 29 May 466/1 Is there not a trace of cold feet in this bit of back-pedalling about Keble?

back-piece ('bækpi:s). [f. BACK *sb.* or *a.*]

1. A piece of armour protecting the back. Also *fig.*

1586 LUPTON *Thous. Notable Th.* (1675) 289 If you match the lady to Scotland, you are sure to have a stout Back-piece. **1607** DEKKER *Wh. Babylon* Wks. 1873 II. 274 The hollow backe-peece of a rustie Armour. **1865** PARKMAN *Huguenots* ix. (1875) 150 Gourgues took the lead, in breast-plate and back-piece.

2. The piece which forms the back of anything.

1838 *Workwoman's Guide* vi. 173 Making a slipper by merely sewing on a front to a sole, and leaving it without any back-piece. **1851** *Art Jrnl. Catal. Gt. Exhib.* 16/3 In the centre of the back-piece [of a side-board] is a medallion.

back-plate ('bækpleɪt). [f. BACK *sb.* or *a.*]

1. A plate of armour for the back.

1656 TRAPP *Exp. Eph.* vi. 14 No mention of a back-plate because the Christian soldier should never fly. **1820** SCOTT *Monast.* xxxv, Armed with cuirass and back-plate. **1859** TODD *Cycl. Anat. & Phys.* V. 170/1 The Mud Tortoise.. has a sacrum..soldered..to the back-plate.

2. A plate placed at or forming the back.

1772 WOLLASTON in *Phil. Trans.* LXIII. 78 The cock is fastened to the back-plate of the clock itself.

Backrac(k, -rag, obs. forms of BACHARACH.

†**'back-,racket.** *Obs.* [f. BACK *adv.*] The return of a ball in tennis; *fig.* a counter-charge, 'tu quoque.'

1608 MIDDLETON *Trick to Catch* IV. i, He plays at back-racket with me. **1638** FEATLY *Transubst.* 3 Bandie the tearmes of Schismatike and Heritike..the Sorbonists to the Jesuites, and the Jesuites by back-racket to the Sorbonists.

'back-rest. [BACK- A. 3, 4.] **1.** A contrivance to support or ease the back of a person when seated or engaged in manual work (e.g. at a lathe). Also, provision for such support.

1859 HOLTZAPFFEL *Turning* IV. 20 The turner using the pole lathe..requires the back rest to steady and support his body. **1909** *Daily Chron.* 13 Nov. 9/6 Neither does it mean that the passengers have their comfort curtailed in respect of insufficient back-rest.

2. A guide attached to the slide-rest of a turning-lathe and placed in contact with the work to steady it.

1881 in *Imp. Dict.* **1907** PERRIGO *Mod. Amer. Lathe Practice* 164 There are two classes of these rests which may in a general way be called 'center rests' and 'back rests'. The center rests usually have jaws bearing upon the work at three points spaced equally around the circle, while a back rest bears upon the work generally at the back and on top only.

3. *Weaving.* A bar over which the warp passes from the warp-beam.

1894 T. W. FOX *Mech. Weaving* 369 Each warp beam.. must be parallel with back rest, breast beam, and taking-up roller.

back room. Also back-room, backroom. [BACK *a.* 2.] A room at the back of a house or other building. Also *attrib.*

1592 GREENE *Conny-catch.* (1881) 59 The gentlewoman.. brought him into a backe roome. **1713** *Guardian* No. 85 The young poets are in the back room. **1679** [see FRONT *sb.* 13]. *a* **1777** FOOTE *Cozeners* (1778) III. i. 66 And, as you see he is violent, let him have the back room, with the barr'd windows, up two pair of stairs. **1841** *Punch* July 13/2 Paddy Green intends shortly to remove to a three-pair back-room in Little Wild-street. **1904** *Daily Chron.* 17 Dec. 6/4 Little Miss Lazarus or Solomon can generally be relied upon to look after..the little back-room home.

b. *spec.* A room where (esp. secret) research is carried out. Also in extended uses. Applied *attrib.* to one who works or wields influence 'behind the scenes'. So ***backroom boy*** (colloq.), a person engaged in (secret) research.

1941 LD. BEAVERBROOK in *Listener* 27 Mar. 443/1 Now who is responsible for this work of development on which so much depends? To whom must the praise be given? To the boys in the back rooms. They do not sit in the limelight. But they are the men who do the work. Many of them are Civil Servants. **1943** N. BALCHIN (*title*) The Small Back Room. **1943** *Punch* 11 Nov. 422 (*caption*) He's one of those obscure back-room boys who have lately been so much in the limelight. **1944** *Times* 9 Aug. 2/3 The man most responsible for the development of the rocket projectile..is Group Captain John D'Arcy Bakercarr,..whose 'backroom boys' at the Ministry of Aircraft Production have worked unremittingly with him. **1945** *News Chron.* 17 May 1/1 Considerable numbers of backroom Nazis, such as bankers and industrialists, have been arrested. **1951** D. N. CHESTER *Lessons Brit. War Econ.* ii. 15 No group of back-room boys writing memoranda embodying ideal policies is likely to have much influence. **1958** *Times Lit. Suppl.* 20 June 337/3 It occurred to boys working in back rooms that if only neutrons could be released in the process a chain-reaction might be set up. **1959** *Oxf. Univ. Gaz.* 1 May 995/1 The staff..could not take on additional services to readers without increasing the arrears of essential cataloguing and other back-room work.

backs (of leather): see BACK *sb.* 18.

back scattering. *Physics.* [BACK *adv.*] The scattering of radiation in a reverse direction from an irradiated substance.

1940 *Physical Rev.* LVII. 29/2 (*heading*) Disregard of back scattering. It is frequently assumed that all electrons are scattered only in the forward direction. **1946** *Ibid.* LXX. 602 The backscattering of d-d neutrons was investigated for several materials. **1958** *New Scientist* 2 Jan. 23/1 Heavyweight atoms like those of lead give a bigger 'backscattering' than lightweight atoms such as those of aluminium. **1960** *Gloss. Atomic Terms* (*A.E.A.*) 5 *Back scattering*, the emergence of radiation from that surface of a material through which it entered, due to its collision with and reflection from atoms in the material.

Hence (as a back-formation) **back-scatter** *v. trans.*; **back scatter,** *sb.* (*a*) back scattering; (*b*) the radiation scattered in this way; hence in *Telecommunications* (see quot. 1960); also *attrib.*

1957 *Gloss. Terms Nucl. Sci.* (Nat. Res. Council, U.S.) 16/1 Back scatter. **1958** *New Scientist* 2 Jan. 23/1 The beta ray source is shielded so that only radiation backscattered by the sample can enter the counter. **1959** *Manchester Guardian* 11 Aug. 7/4 The United States Navy's successful experiments with ionospheric 'back-scatter radar', capable of detecting a nuclear explosion from thousands of miles away. **1960** *Gloss. Terms Telecomm.* (*B.S.I.*) 168 A signal received by back scattering is often referred to as back scatter. **1962** *Gloss. Terms Nuclear Sci.* (*B.S.I.*) 12 *Back scatter*, the emergence of radiation from that surface of a material through which it entered... The term is also used for the actual back-scattered radiation.

'back-,scratching, *vbl. sb. colloq.* [f. BACK- A. 1 + SCRATCHING *vbl. sb.*, in allusion to the saying, 'You scratch my back, and I'll scratch yours'.] The performance of mutual services; always with the suggestion of doubt as to the legitimacy of the transactions. So **'back-,scratcher.**

(See also *back-scratcher*, *scratching* , s.v. BACK- A. 1.)

1897 *Daily News* 9 Jan. 4/7 Does it not rather partake of the ethics of the back-scratcher and the log-roller? **1924** P. C. MACFARLANE *Tongues of Flame* xxv. 223 'That is the modern method of bribery, you know—back-scratching,' she frowned savagely. '"We've scratched your back; now you scratch ours." That's the system.' **1933** *Punch* 24 May 567/1 Mr. Hugh Walpole made the startling suggestion that contemporary criticism occasionally showed symptoms of degenerating into mutual back-scratching.

back seat. [BACK- A. 4.] A seat at the back of a vehicle. Also, esp. a seat at the back of a hall, etc., an inferior seat; hence *colloq.*, a position of inferiority or comparative obscurity (orig. *U.S.* in phr. ***to take a back seat*** (*fig.*), to occupy a subordinate place; see SEAT *sb.* 27 c).

a **1832** R. C. SANDS *Writings* (1834) II. 148 He had.. ample room wherein to adjust himself and his properties, on the back-seat[of the coach]. **1858** THACKERAY *Virginians* xx. 157 The Lady Maria had the back seat to herself. **1883** LD. RONALD GOWER *My Reminiscences* II. 234 *Le gros papa* took up all the front seat of the carriage... In the middle seats were the young Germans..and in the back seat..on which two people could have been uncomfortably seated, sat the middle-aged Englishman, Walter, and I. **1928** 'IAN HAY' *Poor Gentleman* iv. 71 I'll put you in the back seat together going home.

1859 *Harper's Mag.* June 54/2 This menagerie of..red skins, whom a score of indefatigable Coopers and Longfellows could never raise to merit a back seat in the heaven of romance. **1881** J. W. JONES in *Southern Hist. Soc. Papers* IX. 133, I tell you, those able-bodied men who are sleeping in feather beds tonight,..must be content to take back seats when we get home. **1899** H. JAMES *Awkward Age* 180 'Don't you think that's rather a back seat, as they say, for one's best?' 'A back seat?'—she wondered with a purity! 'If you don't understand,' said her companion, 'it serves me right, as your aunt didn't leave me with you to teach you the slang of the day.' **1902** M. BEERBOHM in *Around Theatres* (1924) I. 395 To enliven the milieu, on he brought a circus procession... And Oxford had to take a back seat. **1959** *Times* 22 Nov. 5/6 Those who think that the trade union movement should take a back seat in the Labour movement should think again.

b. back-seat driver, a passenger in the rear seat of a car who gives unsolicited directions to the driver. Hence, *fig.*, one who criticizes or attempts to direct without responsibility (cf. *armchair critic*); one who controls affairs from a subordinate position. Also **back-seat driving** *vbl. sb.*

1926 *Nation* (U.S.) 8 Dec. 587/1 What? No taxis..back-seat driving, back-seat kisses? **1927** *Collier's* 3 Dec. 10/1 You're just another one of them back-seat drivers. **1930** WODEHOUSE *Very Good, Jeeves!* ix. 245 Quite suddenly..the car..stopped in its tracks... The back-seat drivers gave tongue. 'What's the matter? What has happened?' **1948** *Economist* 8 May 748 What was often no more than vociferous, if irritating, back-seat driving has been.. interpreted as attempts..to seize control of the wheel. **1955** *Times* 19 Aug. 6/4 [He] replied that it was contrary to democracy for elected members to consult 'pressure groups' and 'back-seat drivers'.

back-set ('bæksɛt), *sb.* [f. BACK *adv.*]

1. A setting back; a reverse, check, relapse. (Of Sc. origin.)

1721 WODROW *Hist.* II. 555 (JAM.) The people of God have got many backsets one after another. **1816** CALHOUN *Wks.* II. 170 It would give a back set, and might..endanger their ultimate success. **1883** *American* V. 373 A backset which some good judges pronounced fatal.

2. An eddy or counter-current.

1882 *Harper's Mag.* LXV. 612 The backset caused by the overflow. **1883** *Fortn. Rev.* July 119 The back-set of some deeper-flowing stream.

ˌback'set, *v.* [f. as prec. + SET *v.*[1]]

†**1.** To set upon in the rear. *Obs.*

1573 ANDERSON *Exp. Benedictus* 71 b (T.) The Israelites ..[were] backset with Pharaoh's whole power.

2. (in U.S.) To re-plough in the autumn prairie-land ploughed for the first time in the spring.

1883 *Lisbon (Dakota) Star* Sept., Contracts for large or small areas of backsetting or stubble plowing. **1884** *Ibid.* 10 Oct., Farmers were engaged in plowing and backsetting.

'back-'settler. [f. *back settle-ment*: see BACK *a.* 1 b.] One who lives in the back settlements of a colony or new country; a settler in the back-woods.

1809 SOUTHEY in *Q. Rev.* II. 322 Individual wickedness on the part of the traders and back-settlers. **1829** —— *Sir T. More* (1831) II. 190 What to the American back-settler seems the perfection of wild independence.

backsheesh, variant of BAKSHEESH *sb.*

back-shop ('bækʃɒp). [f. BACK *a.* and *sb.*] A small and usually private shop behind the main one; a secret place of business.

1549 in *Abstracts of Protocols of Town Clerks of Glasgow* 14 Oct. (1894) I. 4 A fore booth, with booth adjoining, cellars, and a small chamber, commonly called 'ane bak chop'. **1583** GOLDING *Calvin on Deut.* cxxii. 751 When we keepe such Backeshops, it is a token that our heart is not rid quite and cleane. **1682** N. O. *Boileau's Lutrin* III. 47 Here a Bookseller in his back-shop slept. **1852** *Blackw. Mag.* XXXII. 458 Like a show table in Rundle and Bridge's back-shop.

backside. Forms: 5-6 bak-, backesyde, 6 bak-, 7 backeside, 6- backside. [f. BACK. *a.* Now pronounced as two words, exc. in sense 3 (and 2 dialectally).]

1. The hinder or back part; the back, the rear.

1489 CAXTON *Faytes of A.* I. xxiii. 72 That on the baksyde of the bataylle they be not enuahysshed. **1571** DIGGES *Pantom.* I. xxviii, The backeside of your instrument. **1641** HINDE *J. Bruen* xlvi. 147 Came out at the backside of his leg. **1728** NEWTON *Chronol. Amended* 10 Scythians from the backside of the Euxine Sea. **1858** HAWTHORNE *Fr. & It. Jrnls.* (1872) I. 36 The worst back-side lanes.

†**2.** The back premises, back yard, out-buildings, attached to a dwelling; also, the privy. Now *dial.*

1541 *Act 33 Hen. VIII*, xxxvi, Houses, with the curtilage backeside and gardeine adjoining. **1630** LORD *Banians & Persees* 79 Administring food to a young Kid in his Fathers backeside. **1704** SWIFT *T. Tub* Wks. 1768 I. 150 An authentic phrase for demanding the way to the back-side. **1804** R. ANDERSON *Cumberld. Ball.* 79 The witch weyfe begg'd in our backseyde.

3. ('bæksaɪd) The posteriors or rump.

c **1500** *Robin Hood* (Ritson) II. iv. 236 With an arrowe so broad, He shott him into the backe-syde. **1651** H. MORE *Sec. Lash Alaz.* To Rdr., As if his senses lay all in his backside, and had left his brains destitute. **1713** ADDISON *Guardian* No. 156 (1756) II. 288 A poor ant..with her head downwards, and her backside upwards. **1827** *Gentl. Mag.* XCVII. II. 522 He shall fall on his back-side.

†**4.** The under surface of a leaf; the reverse side or 'back' of a document, page, book, etc.; cf. BACK *sb.* 3, 4. *Obs.*

1547 *Act 1 Edw. VI*, v. §5 Indorsed and written on the Back-side of the said Licence. **1562** TURNER *Herbal* II. 86 b, Upon the bak syde they [Hartstongue leaves] haue as it wer smal wormes hangyng on. **1709** STRYPE *Ann. Ref.* I. viii. 116 On the backside of this paper are writ these words. **1720** *Lond. Gaz.* No. 5910/5 Lost..a Pocket-Book..writ on the backside John Bennett.

†**5.** *fig.* The reverse or wrong side; the opposite.

1645 MILTON *Colast.* Wks. (1851) 377 To endorse him on the back-side of posterity, not a golden, but a brazen Asse. **1695** CONGREVE *Love for L.* IV. xix, Just the very backside of Truth.

backsight ('bæk'saɪt). [f. BACK *adv.*]

a. In *Surveying*, a 'sight' or reading taken backwards, or towards the point of starting. **b.** The sight of a rifle nearer the stock.

1847 E. CRESY *Encycl. Civil Engineering* I. 802 Compound Levelling is..performed by taking back and forward sights. **1847** [see SIGHT *sb.*[1] 14 b]. **1851** R. GLISAN in *Jrnl. Army Life* (1874) 59 A..very heavy and costly gun, with an elevating back sight for shooting at great distances. **1859** *Musketry Instruct.* 10 Firing without using the back-sight. **1860** *All Y. Round* No. 71. 501 The back or elevating sight. **1867** MARSH in *N.Y. Nation* 9 May 373 A backsight is a sight or reading taken backwards; that is, in a direction opposite to that in which the levelling party is proceeding. **1880** *Times* 18 Oct. 4/3 In using the rifle a native rarely avails himself..of the backsight. **1953** R. J. C. ATKINSON *Field Archaeol.* (ed. 2) iii. 114 The reading to a turning-point from the *previous* level station is known as a *foresight*, and that from the *next* level station as a *backsight*.

back-slang ('bæk'slæŋ). [f. BACK *adv.*] A kind of slang in which every word is pronounced backwards; as *ynnep* for *penny*.

1860 in *Modern Slang* 256. **1862** WHEATLEY *Anagrams* 141 Back Slang..is formed by the costermongers upon anagrammatical principles; thus *look* is *cool*.

'back-ˌslapping, *ppl. a.* and *vbl. sb.* [BACK- A. 1.] Slapping the back. So **back-slapper,** a vigorously hearty person. Hence (as a back-formation) **back-slap** *v.*

1777 TWINING in *Country Clergym. 18th C.* (1882) 50 A brisk, noisy, back-slapping new man. **1884** E. H. YATES *Recollections* I. v. 186 A..good-natured vulgarian, of a dreadful back-slapping, Christian-name calling familiarity. **1920** SINCLAIR LEWIS *Main Street* xxviii. §6, Isn't the thing he lacks the back-slapping jocosity that passes for humor here? **1924** *Chicago Tribune* 1 Oct. 23/1 (*heading*) Here's a Comic Piece About a Back-Slapper. **1929** *Evening News* 4 Jan. 9/4 The back-slappers, the rib-diggers, the over hearty and the dwellers-in-the-limelight are to be avoided. **1935** SINCLAIR LEWIS *It can't happen Here* ix. 88 He grinned and knee-patted and back-slapped. **1946** *Scrutiny* XIV. 155 The blustering, hearty, back-slapping manner..is the reverse of the discreet, self-effacing and seemly behaviour which one has a right to expect of a good undertaker. **1960** J. FINGLETON *Four Chukkas to Australia* vii. 77 There were, to be true, wild jumps of elation and much back-slapping.

backslash ('bækslæʃ). *Computing.* Also **back slash.** [f. BACK- 12 + SLASH *sb.*[1]] A symbol in the form of a backward-sloping diagonal line (\) used in programming notation; a reverse solidus.

1982 *Byte* Jan. 413/1 (*caption*) Arguments enclosed in backslashes refer to disk-file operations. **1982** *Ibid.* July 146/2 In some cases, they [*sc.* commands] are bordered by special characters, such as back slashes. **1983** *Austral. Microcomputer Mag.* Aug. 19/2 A path specification must be no longer than 63 characters, including the backslash characters used to separate the directory names. **1985** *Personal Computer World* Feb. 191/1 All Knowledge Man commands proper are accessible within K-Text by prefacing them with a backslash. **1986** *Which Computer?* Oct. 59/1 The single line of topics evoked by pressing Lotus's backslash key.

backslidden (bækslɪd(ə)n), *ppl. a.* [f. pa. pple. of next.] That has relapsed (into sin).

1871 TYERMAN *Wesley* III. 410 Three weeks after he [Wesley] was at backslidden Stroud.

backslide (bækslaɪd), *v.* [f. BACK *adv.* + SLIDE *v.* (In this and its derivatives, the stress varies between ' ,and , ')] To *slide back*, in a figurative sense; to fall away from attained excellence, *esp.* of religious faith and practice; to relapse.

1581 J. BELL *Haddon's Answ. Osorius* 503 The onely righteousnesse of Fayth, from whence they were back-slyden. **1641** MILTON *Ch. Discip.* I. Wks. (1851) 2 To back-slide..into the Jewish beggery of old cast rudiments. **1835** MARRYAT *Jac. Faithf.* xxi, Did not I..backslide into intemperance and folly?

†**'backˌslide,** *sb.* [f. prec. vb.] Backsliding, apostatizing, falling away.

1586 WARNER *Alb. Eng.* III. xix. (1597) 88 The back-slide of our helplesse friends, the down-fall of our state.

backslider. [f. as prec. + -ER[1].] One who backslides or falls away from an adopted course, *esp.* of religious faith or practice; an apostate, renegade.

1581 SAVILE *Tacitus' Hist.* I. (R.) A traitor and backslider to him. **1772** PRIESTLEY *Inst. Relig.* (1782) II. 306 A backslider..is worse than one who had never known the right way. **1873** HOLLAND *A. Bonnic.* viii. 141 The backsliders are returning to their first love.

backsliding, *vbl. sb.* [f. as prec. + -ING[1].] The action of a backslider, falling away, apostasy.

1552 KNOX *Faithf. Admon.* 76 (R.) Neither yet doubting, nor backsliding, can utterly destroy and quench the faith of God's elect. **1659** MILTON *Rupt. Commw.* Wks. (1851) 401 To confess in public their backsliding from the good Old Cause. **1865** TROLLOPE *Belton Est.* ii. 22 Clerical admonitions for Sunday backslidings.

backsliding, *ppl. a.* [f. as prec. + -ING[2].] Falling away from the faith, relapsing into sin, apostate; also *lit.* sliding or slipping back.

1611 BIBLE *Hosea* iv. 16 Israel slideth backe, as a back-sliding heifer. **1816** SCOTT *Old Mort.* viii, A backsliding pastor, that has..forsaken the strict path. **1869** PHILLIPS *Vesuv.* iv. 131 Wading up the loose and backsliding slope.

Hence **backslidingness.**

1864 in WEBSTER.

'back-'speir, -spear, *v. Sc.* [f. BACK *adv.* + SPEIR, to question.] To re-examine, cross-examine. **back-speirer,** cross-examiner.

a **1689** CLELAND *Poems* (1697) 101 (JAM.) Several times affronted By slie back-spearers, and accounted An empty rogue. **1796** J. RAMSEY in Lockhart *Scott* (1839) I. 348 It is however easier to backspeir you. **1860** RAMSAY *Remin.* I. 111 'I winna be back-spiered noo, Polly Fullarton.'

'back-stabber. [BACK *sb.*[1]] One who attacks unfairly, one who attacks (a person) behind his back. Hence (as a back-formation) **back-stab** *v.*

1906 *Westm. Gaz.* 6 Jan. 15/3, I will tell you my idea of a false friend and back-stabber—to sweat the workman for personal profit and fawn on him for political profit; to promise old-age pensions for votes and, having got the votes, to refuse them. **1925** *Chambers's Jrnl.* Dec. 863/2, I, after befriending her brother..had seemed to back-stab. **1960** *Spectator* 30 Sept. 470 That party of back-stabbers and double-crossers.

†**'back-ˌstaff.** *Obs.* [f. BACK *sb.*] A peculiar kind of quadrant formerly used in taking altitudes at sea, so called because the observer turned his back to the sun.

1627 CAPT. SMITH *Seaman's Gram.* xv. 73 A Crosse staffe, a Backestaffe, an Astrolobe. **1696** in PHILLIPS; in mod. Dicts.

back stage, backstage, *sb.* and *adv.* [f. BACK *a.* 1 + STAGE *sb.* 5.] The hinder or 'upper' part of a stage; the part of a theatre behind the stage containing dressing-rooms, etc.; *fig.* 'behind the scenes' (see SCENE 7). Also *attrib.*

1898 SACHS & WOODROW *Mod. Opera Houses & Theatres* III. Suppl. 14 In order to obtain as much room as possible, and to increase the depth of space of the stage floor available for setting scenery, many theatres now have what is termed a 'back stage'... This floor space is most useful for distant 'scenes'. **1902** *Encycl. Brit.* XXXII. 823/1 The back stage has no openings or mechanism beyond certain trap-doors.. and the necessary mechanism for raising and lowering scenery. **1916** *Stage Year Book* 37 A scene dock is provided back stage prompt. *Ibid.* 38 The speed of the back stage motor varies according to the position of the controller. **1923** A. STEVENS in G. Oppenheimer *Passionate Playgoer* (1958) 154, I went backstage at the Studebaker to see Bert Williams. **1929** W. FAULKNER *Sartoris* III. 177 While the ladies are backstage washing the dinner dishes. **1950** N. CARDUS *Second Innings* 184 There are all sorts of..'back-stage' activities at Lord's. **1950** T. S. ELIOT *Cocktail Party* III. 140 Alex is seen to enter with her and pass back-stage towards the kitchen. **1958** *Times Lit. Suppl.* 31 Jan. 67/2 Mr. Barker has done justice not only to the entertainments offered by the Coliseum but also to the troubles backstage and in the board room.

backstairs ('bæk'stɛəs). [f. BACK *a.*]

1. Stairs at the back of a house; a secondary staircase.

1654 EARL ORRERY *Parthen.* (1676) 547 To lead him down a back-stairs. **1655** MRQ. WORC. *Cent. Inv.* xlviii, With Back-stairs..convenient to Servants to pass up and down. **1863** H. KINGSLEY *A. Elliot* I. x. 114 'So I hits myself down the back-stairs with a tray-full of glasses.'

2. a. *esp.* The private stairs in a palace, used for other than state visitors.

1627 *Ord. R. Househ.* (1790) 343 All access must bee.. neither by back stayres or private doores. **1682** *Lond. Gaz.* No. 1764/4 Whoever brings him to her Royal Highnesses Back-stairs, shall have a Guinea Reward. **1884** *19th Cent.* Jan. 29 A page of the back stairs of the royal palace.

b. *fig.* A secret disingenuous method of approach.

1641 SIR E. DERING *Sp. on Relig.* xi. 40, I hope we are not going up the back-stairs to *Socinianisme*. **1855** C. KINGSLEY *Westward Ho!* (ed. 2) II. x. 269 A priest of the Church of England, (whose business is not merely to smuggle sinful souls up the backstairs into heaven).

c. esp. *attrib.* Of, pertaining to, or employing underhand intrigue at court. (Occas. ***backstair.***) Also (in *attrib.* use) clandestine, underhand.

1663 E. COOKE in *11th Rep. Hist. MSS. Comm.* App. v. Dartmouth MSS. (1887) 11 Sends humble service to Legge's lady..Dick Lane, and all bedchamber backstair friends. **1697** VANBRUGH *Relapse* II, A backstair minister. **1768** GOLDSMITH *Good-Nat. Man* II. 21 Is not he a backstairs favourite, one that can do what he pleases with those that do what they please? **1770** BURKE *Pres. Discont.* Wks. 1842 I. 131 A backstairs influence and clandestine government. **1882** L. STEPHEN *Swift* 110 The back-stairs plots by which the administration of his friends was hampered. **1930** G. B. SHAW *Apple Cart* I. 31 They get amusing articles, spiced with exclusive backstairs information. **1933** N. COWARD *Design for Living* I. 19 We could carry on a backstairs affair for weeks without saying a word about it. **1935** T. S. ELIOT *Murder Cathed.* ii. 58 This is the man who was the tradesman's son: the backstairs brat who was born in Cheapside.

ba(c)kstale (*Promp. Parv.* 21/2) = BACKWARD.

backstay ('bæksteɪ). [f. BACK *a.* or *sb.*]

1. *Naut.* (often *pl.*) Long ropes, slanting a little abaft, extending from the upper mast-heads to both sides or to the 'channels' of the ship, where they are fastened to ***backstay-plates***; they serve to second the shrouds in supporting the masts under a press of sail. ***backstay-stools***: small 'channels' fixed abaft the principal ones for receiving the backstays. Cf. ABACKSTAYS, ASTAYS.

1626 CAPT. SMITH *Accid. Yng. Seamen* 29 The ships at stayes, at backe-stayes. **1627** —— *Seaman's Gram.* ix. 42 He will lay her by the lee, the staies, or backestaies, that is, when all the sailes..are not kept full..they fall upon the masts and shrowds, so that the ship goes a drift upon her broad side. **1709** *Lond. Gaz.* No. 4521/2 Our Shrouds and Back-stays cut to pieces. **1833** MARRYAT *P. Simple* (1863) 115 The captain of the maintop reports the breast backstay much chafed.

2. *gen.* A stay or support at the back; *e.g.* in *Printing*, a leather strap used to check the carriage of a printing-press.

1846 HOLTZAPFFEL *Turning* II. 634 In cutting very long screws..the object becomes so slender, that the contrivance called a backstay, is always required for supporting the work. **1864** STEPHENS in *N. & Q.* V. 313 England's shield, ally, and backstay Is the Scandia whence she issued. **1879** *Carriage Build.* in *Cassell's Techn. Educ.* IV. 175/2 The wheel-iron, bed-clip, and back-stay being in one. **1911** *Act*

1 & 2 Geo. V c. 50 §46 A back-stay or other suitable contrivance for preventing the tub running back.

3. *local.* = BACKSTER.

1830 *United Service Jrnl.* Mar. 359 How would he like walking over three miles of heavy shingle [at Dungeness] in ..a pair of back stays..? **1889** H. W. LUCY in *Time* Mar. 257 What the 'backstay' is to the inhabitant of the district around Lydd, the stilts are to the lonely dwellers in the Landes. **1901** *Pall Mall Gaz.* 27 May 6/1 The bird lovers.. follow the local fishermen's example, and wear 'back-stays' —boards, about eight inches long and five inches wide, fastened on to the boots.

backster ('bækstə(r)). A flat piece of wood or cork, strapped on the feet for walking over loose beach.

1867 in SMYTH *Sailor's Word-bk.* **1884** H. HEWLETT in *19th Century* Aug. 329 Along the coast of Pevensey Bay one may meet peasants with flat pieces of wood called 'backsters,' fastened to the soles of their boots.

backster, obs. form of BAXTER, baker.

back-stitch ('bæk,stɪtʃ). [f. BACK *adv.*] A method of sewing in which, for every new stitch, the needle enters behind, and comes out in front of, the end of the previous one. Hence **backstitch** *v.*, to sew in this way.

1611 COTGR., *Arriere-poinct*, a backe-stitch. *Arriere-poincté*, backe-stitched. **1640** J. TAYLOR (Water P.) *Praise Needle*, Whip-stitch, Back-stitch, and the Cross-stitch. **1720** *Lond. Gaz.* No. 5868/9 A piece of Holland Back-stitched with a Heart. **1841** THACKERAY *Comic Tales* II. 152 The younger ones learned the principles of back-stitch, cross-stitch, bob-stitch.

back-stone. *Lead Manuf.* [BACK- A. 4.] The piece of cast iron at the back of an ore-hearth. (Cf. PIPE-STONE 2, WORK-*stone*, and FORE-*stone*.)

1839 URE *Dict. Arts* 756.

backstone: see BAKESTONE.

'back-stop. Also backstop. [BACK *a.*, BACK- A. 4.] **a.** Something placed at the back to serve as a barrier; *spec.* a mound of earth or embankment set up behind a target on a rifle range. Also *fig.*

1851 F. STARR *20 Yrs. of Trav.'s Life* xiii. 143 The remaining shaft..broke off short, and that which when we started was a gig, was now a back stop for horses' heels. **1904** GOODCHILD & TWENEY *Technol. & Sci. Dict.* 37/1 *Back stops* (Cotton Spinning), buffers, used to prevent the mule carriage from going beyond a certain point during its inward run. **1946** *Sports Afield* Jan. 55/1 (D.A.), Put up two targets on the backstop for the second barrel practice. **1947** *Landfall* I. 43 This being the first issue of *Landfall*, there is no previous survey to provide a convenient back-stop to discussion. **1954** W. FAULKNER *Fable* (1955) 343 The railroad embankment..would serve as a backstop for what bullets neither flesh nor wood absorbed.

b. *spec.* in *Cricket.* (See BACK- B.)

1819 *Suffolk Chron.* 31 July 3/2 They were deprived of two of their best bowlers, and a back-stop. **1867** *Lillywhite's Cricketer's Companion* 120 [He is] an admirable back-stop. *Ibid.* 127 T. Moore, back-stop of the eleven.

c. *Baseball.* A fence behind the catcher to stop the ball; also, the catcher himself or his position. *U.S.*

1889 *Reach's Official Base Ball Guide* 142 Backstop must be ninety feet from home base. **1890** H. C. PALMER *Stories of Base Ball Field* 46 Tom Daly was the greatest catcher.. and a careful study of that back-stop's methods behind the bat to-day will help any young catcher.

Hence as *v. trans.*, to support, back up; to supply with necessary additional resources. *colloq.* (orig. and chiefly *U.S.*).

1956 B. HOLIDAY *Lady sings Blues* (1973) xiv. 121 Tony kept my job open. He offered to backstop me with the money I needed. **1967** *Electronics* 6 Mar. 29 (Advt.), We'll backstop your control procedures in our analytical labs. **1968** P. TAMONY *Americanisms* (typescript) No. 21. 2 An invasion of unsavory schmucks..was thrown back and frustrated by Mayor Daley's phalanx of police and National Guardsmen, backstopped by the United States Army. **1977** *N.Y. Times* 17 June A26/2 The International Monetary Fund can backstop the private system.

†**'backstress.** *Obs.* [A double feminine form; f. *backster* (= BAXTER) + -ESS: cf. *sempstress*, *songstress*.] A female baker, a woman who bakes bread.

1519 HORMAN *Vulg.* 153 A baker or backstres muste be well ware: that a..pyle of wodde be nat nere the fyre.

backstroke ('bæk,strəʊk). Also **back-stroke.** [f. BACK *adv.*] **a.** A blow or stroke in return, a recoil; **b.** a back-handed stroke.

1674 FAIRFAX *Bulk & Selv.* 96 The backstroke will be sure to give him a knocker. **1753** MISS COLLIER *Art Torment.* 167 Then may you lie snug, and..play her a most noble backstroke. **1876** EMERSON *Ess.* Ser. I. iii. 90 This back-stroke, this kick of the gun.

c. *Swimming.* A stroke in which the swimmer lies upon his back in the water. Also *attrib.*, and *ellipt.* for ***backstroke event, race***, etc.

1876 W. WILSON *Swimming* xii. 49 The slightest motion of the legs..will sustain and at the same time propel the body. This is known as the plain back stroke. **1887** *Encycl. Brit.* XXII. 769/1 Another racing back stroke is performed by lifting hands and arms out of the water at the finish of the pull downward. **1908** *Manual of Seamanship* (*H.M.S.O.*) I. 319 Then lie on your back, hold him in front of you, and swim with the back stroke, taking care to keep his face above the water. *Ibid.* 320 This method will be useful to over-arm swimmers as well as to back-stroke swimmers. **1933** *Boys' Mag.* XLII. 83/1 The order in which you learn the strokes should be—crawl, breast-stroke, life-saving back-stroke, side, overarm. **1958** *Times* 3 Nov. 2/7 Miss C. Hussey.. broke the championship record for the 100 yards junior girls' backstroke.

d. *Cricket.* A stroke made from behind the popping crease when playing back. (Usu. written as two words.) Cf. *back play* (BACK- B).

1897 K. S. RANJITSINHJI *Jubilee Bk. Cricket* iv. 168 Mere defensive back-play is easy enough. The veriest novice can make some kind of back-stroke. **1898** —— *With Stoddart's Team* (ed. 4) ix. 175 Hill's play..was remarkable for..his powerful 'back' strokes.

back-sword ('bæk'sɔəd). *arch.* [f. BACK *sb.*]

1. A sword with only one cutting edge.

1611 COTGR., *Badelaire*, a short and broad back sword. **1645** *Sacr. Decretal* 24 St. Paul's Back-sword at his side. *c* **1750** BOLINGBROKE *Pol. Tracts* 214 The backsword of Justice which cuts only on one side.

2. A stick with a basket-hilt used instead of a sword in fencing, a single-stick; *hence* **b.** fencing exercise with it.

1699 FARQUHAR *Love& Bottle* II. (1728) 30 I'm much in love with fencing, but, I think, backsword is the best play. **1747** J. GODFREY *Sc. Defence* Pref., I have purchased my knowledge in the Back-Sword with many a broken head.

3. A fencer with back-sword or single-stick.

1672 DAVENANT *Siege Rhodes* (1673) 5 To the Back-swords of London. **1779** SHERIDAN *St. Patrick's Day* I. ii. 295 A sturdy fellow..and the best back-sword in the country.

back-'swording = BACK-SWORD 2 b. **back-'swordman** = BACK-SWORD 3.

1597 SHAKS. *2 Hen. IV*, III. ii. 70, I knew him a good Back-Sword-man. **1857** HUGHES *Tom Brown* ii, The great times for back-swording came round once a-year. *Ibid.* A famous back-sword man.

back-talk. *colloq.*, orig. *dial.* = BACK-CHAT *sb.*; a retort or reply which is regarded as superfluous or impertinent.

1858 *Dialogue* in *Ulster Jrnl. Archæol.* VI. 41 Oh, indeed 'twas yerself 'at begun it, So A'll give ye back-talk till ye're tired. **1880** W. H. PATTERSON *Gloss. Antrim & Down*, *Back talk*, saucy replies from a child or an inferior. **1887** J. D. BILLINGS *Hardtack & Coffee* (1888) 150 Back talk,..which ..means answering a superior officer insolently, was a prolific cause for punishments. **1888** *Harper's Mag.* Nov. 972/1 That'll do, my friend, I don't want no back talk. **1899** KIPLING *Stalky* 204 I've heard more back-talk since this volunteerin' nonsense began than I've heard in a year in the service. **1902** G. H. LORIMER *Lett. Self-made Merchant* (1903) xiii. 177 That order for a car-load of Spotless Snow Leaf from old Shorter is the kind of back talk I like. **1921** G. O'DONOVAN *Vocations* viii, ''Twas enough to disturb any girl,' her mother said... 'I'm off communion myself this morning, with all the back talk I had with your father over it last night.'

back-to-nature. [BACK *adv.* 6.] A catch-phrase applied, chiefly *attrib.*, to a movement or enthusiast for reversion to a simpler way of life. Cf. *return to nature* s.v. RETURN *sb.* 1 h.

1915 *Univ. Oklahoman* 29 Oct. 1/5 Some of the more advanced among the Frosch are holding out for 'Back to Nature' garb. **1931** W. HOLTBY *Poor Caroline* vi. 204 He was floundering..in..a Back to Nature Phase. **1945** H. CLOSS *High are Mountains* 177 All this reforming business..if they succeeded it would be so dull. Chivalry for the..'back to nature' enthusiasts. **1967** E. S. TURNER *Taking Cure* xix. 264 Of all barefoot back-to-Nature cults, the most renowned was the one initiated by the Bavarian pastor, Father Sebastian Kneipp. **1978** *Jrnl. R. Soc. Arts* CXXVI. 201/1 Nor am I a doom-dodger or a back-to-nature boy.

back to the land. [BACK *adv.* 5.] A catch-phrase applied to schemes for turning some of the dwellers in crowded cities into rural settlers. Hence **back-to-the-lander**, a townsman thus converted into a rural worker.

[**1894** *Times* 25 Oct. 12/2 All present were interested in the common principle that it was desirable, if possible, to bring the people back to the land.] **1899** *Leisure Hour* 136/2 The cry 'back to the land' has come to sound..unreal. **1903** *Times Lit. Suppl.* 16 Oct. 296/2 The common instincts that our 'back-to-the-landers' strive to relearn with arduous art. **1904** *Daily Chron.* 16 July 4/7 This is the way the successful small holder sets about the business. But it is not the fumbling, ineffective way of the townsman Back-to-the-Lander. **1905** *Spectator* 23 Dec. 1076/1 'Back-to-the-land!' is a cry full not only of pathos, but of cogency. **1906** *Times* 15 Feb. 15/6 By doing so you may make the catchwords 'Back to the Land' a reality.

back track, *sb.* Chiefly *U.S.* [BACK *a.*] A track lying or leading towards the rear; esp. in phr. ***to take the back track***, to return or retreat; also *fig.*

1724 in *Lancaster Rec.* (1884) 230 We..kept scouts upon our back tracks to see if there would any pursue. **1802** *Balance* (Hudson, N.Y.) 6 Apr. 106 (Th.), I must have been taking the course which hunters would call the Back Track. **1837** R. M. BIRD *Nick of Woods* II. 105 I'll take the back-track, and foller after madam. **1869** *Congress. Globe* Feb. 1606/1 We all have occasionally to take the back track. None of us are so proud as never to confess that we are wrong. **1892** *Ibid.* June, App. 444/2 You are arresting progress and taking the back track on civilization. **1928** 'BRENT OF BIN BIN' *Up the Country* (1966) v. 52 There was a mountainous back track by which horsemen could avoid the big stream.

back-track, *v.* orig. and chiefly *U.S.* [f. prec.] **1.** *intr.* To return; to retrace one's steps. Also *fig.*, to go back *on*, withdraw. Hence **back-tracker**, one who returns.

1904 E. ROBINS *Magnetic North* II. 164 Now I'd advise you..to back-track home. **1946** *Nat. Geogr. Mag.* Jan. 1/2 A small group of placer miners, many of them backtrackers from the California boom, had been gathering slender winnings in the gravel beds. **1947** *Time* 6 Oct. 25/2 During the week he had to back-track on three statements. **1953** *Here & Now* (N.Z.) III. x. 28/2 A Western marshal who has to stand alone..after the townspeople he has served back-track out of their responsibilities. **1955** 'J. WYNDHAM' *Chrysalids* viii. 92 Uncle Axel backtracked a bit. 'There's no reason at all why anyone should find out.' **1959** *Listener* 12 Feb. 292/3 They had to compromise, back-track, evade, as well as leap forward. **1966** *Amer. Speech* XLI. 167 Before taking up this matter, let us back-track to the state of the knowledge of German in New England. **1967** *Spectator* 29 Dec. 804/1, I hope..that President Johnson heeds the voice of the turtle in the land and begins backtracking in Vietnam.

2. *trans.* To pursue or trace; to investigate.

1925 E. E. T. SETON *Lives of Game Animals* I. 521, I started out across the fields and 'backtracked' the man. **1928** *Nat. Geogr. Mag.* July 104 Lewis back-tracked the original route up the Missouri. **1942** W. FAULKNER *Go Down, Moses* v. 151 Too dark by that time to back-track her. **1954** M. F. RODELL *Mystery Fiction* xv. 108 Backtracking the dress, he discovered that it had been bought before and returned.

back trail. Chiefly *U.S.* [BACK *a.*] = BACK TRACK.

1832 *Polit. Examiner* (Shelbyville, Ky.) 14 July 1/4 The whites..discovered that they had taken the back trail. **1869** C. L. BRACE *New West* viii. 99 There's that darn'd mule on the back trail agin! **1908** MULFORD *Orphan* xi. 132 One of his men..knelt behind a rock, his rifle covering the back trail. **1916** 'ANZAC' *On Anzac Trail* 105 Our little party now came to the conclusion that it was time to take the back trail.

Hence **'back-trail** *v. trans.* and *intr.*

1907 R. DUNN *Shameless Diary of Explorer* xix. 260 It was swim or back trail, if we didn't like it. **1924** A. J. SMALL *Frozen Gold* i. 33 They back trailed him as far as Five Fingers and there the trail ended. **1926** R. A. BENNET *Boss of the Diamond A* 163 He circled his hat in a full-armed overhead sweep, as a signal for them to back-trail.

back-turn. *Mus.* [BACK- A. 11.] = *inverted turn*: see TURN *sb.* 5.

1801 in T. BUSBY *Dict. Mus.* s.v. *turn.* **1876** STAINER & BARRETT *Dict. Mus. Terms* s.v. *Turn*, The common turn.. takes a higher note first in the change... The back-turn taking a lower note first in the change.

back-up, backup, *sb.* [BACK *v.* 8.] **1.** A backward movement of a vehicle. Cf. BACK *v.* 22 b.

1900 G. D. HISCOX *Horseless Vehicles* xii. 262 The single lever..controls the forward speeds and the backup, doing away with the confusion arising from a multiplication of levers.

2. [BACK *sb.*[1]] *attrib.* With the back facing upwards.

1906 *Westm. Gaz.* 3 Nov. 14/1 Back-up cards imprison those beneath them.

3. See BACK *v.* 22 a.

4. = BACKING *vbl. sb.* 8.

1949 *Times Rev. Industry* Aug. 28 Welding of steel reinforcement in direct contact with the concrete..has.. been successfully used as a backup for boiler and fire box installations. **1957** *Archit. Rev.* May 320 The metal sheath walls with solid back-up.

5. Orig. *U.S.* A stand-by, reserve. Also *attrib.* *spec.* in *Computing*, (the making of) a duplicate copy of a disc, file, etc., for use in case of loss or corruption of the original.

1952 *Wall St. Jrnl.* 5 June 18 Value of the stocks, including 'back-up' supplies being held in warehouses for order filling, will total about £1 million. **1953** *N.Y. Times* 21 June 4 E Behind these advanced bases, and providing the necessary supply facilities, command posts and 'back-up' are the Marianas. **1956** W. A. HEFLIN *U.S.A.F. Dict.* 67/2 *Backup communications equipment*, alternate communications equipment. **1958** *Space Talk* (U.S.) 5 *Backup*, a substitute rocket or missile, or alternate procedure, to save time in the event of a delay or failure in launching. **1962** J. DILL in *Into Orbit* p. xviii, Nearby was Glenn's backup pilot. **1964** *CIS Gloss. Automated Typesetting* 3 A back-up computer may be located in the same plant or hundreds of miles away. **1965** *AFIPS Conf. Proc.* XXVII. 193/1 The backup procedures must be prepared for contingencies ranging from a dropped bit on a magnetic tape to a fire. **1965** *ISA Jrnl.* Dec. 44/2 The analog control panel was retained and modified slightly to serve the dual purpose of a computer backup and an analog reference for digital-analog comparisons. **1967** *Lebende Sprachen* XII. 73/2 *Backup* involves having one computer on-line and the other standing by. **1967** *Times* 28 Feb. (Canada Suppl.) 27 The infantry brigade group stationed in West Germany and its back-up brigade in New Brunswick. **1973** *BIT* XIII. 233 (*heading*) Optimal backup of data bases. **1983** *80 Microcomputing* Jan. 122/1 Make backup copies of your disks. **1983** *Austral. Microcomputer Mag.* Sept. 70/3 The backup process is supported across cartridges should a cartridge run out of space during backup. **1984** S. CURRAN *Word Processing for Beginners* viii. 84 Many systems.. automatically save the previous version of an edited file, if any, as a back-up file. **1985** *Times* 9 Apr. 19/1 The most basic of data security precautions for any individual or company employing microcomputers is the making of back-ups, duplicate copies of the diskettes that hold valuable programs and data.

'backveld. Also backveldt. [BACK- A. 4, VELDT, VELD.] In S. Africa, the primitive or unprogressive rural districts lying away from the towns. Also *attrib.* Hence **'backvelder**, a dweller in the backveld.

1905 *Spectator* 7 Jan. 5/1 We do not see why the low European or the back-veld Dutchman should be given a right to a decision on matters which they do not profess to understand. **1908** *Westm. Gaz.* 4 Mar. 2/3 The back-veldt members of Het Volk. **1911** *E. London Disp.* 28 Oct. 3 (Pettman), To present the rugged backvelder in his true colours. **1920** *Contemp. Rev.* Feb. 197 In the *dorps* and the *backveld*, society, business, religion, and politics are closely interwoven. **1926** *Glasgow Herald* 15 Dec. 12 One cannot.. expect that some of the old suspicions will not from time to time be revived by the backvelders. **1960** *Times* 8 Oct. 7/2 The ox-wagon has creaked a little farther away into the blue of the backveld.

† **'back-'ward**, *sb. Obs.* Rear-guard, rear-ward.
1205 LAY. 23814 þat wes þa bac-warde [**1250** bac-ward] **1580** HOLLYBAND *Treas. Fr. Tong., Donner sur la queuë d'vne armée*, to fall vpon the backe ward of an armie.

backward ('bækwəd), *adv.*, *a.*, *sb.* Forms: 4-6 bak-, bac-, backward(e, 5 bakeword, 6 bacewarde, (*Sc.* bakwart), 6-7 backeward, 6- backward. [orig. aphetic form of ABACK-WARD; but subseq. referred directly to BACK: see -WARD. Primarily *abackward* differed from *aback*, in expressing direction rather than completed motion; and this still to some extent distinguishes *backward* from *back*.] **A.** *adv.*

I. Towards one's back, or the back of anything.

1. a. Of motion: In the direction of one's back or of that to which one's back is turned, as *to lean, bend, fall, push, be pushed* backward.
1330 R. BRUNNE *Chron.* 190 He smote him in the helm, bakwarde he bare his stroupe. **1398** TREVISA *Barth. De P.R.* XIII. xxvi. (1495) 456 By vyolente puttynge of ayre bakward the body of the byrde meuyth forwarde. *c* **1400** *Destr. Troy* XV. 6636 Bold men bakward borne of hor horses. **1535** COVERDALE *1 Sam.* iv. 18 He fell downe bacwarde from the seate..and brake his neck. **1697** DRYDEN *Virg., Georg.* III. 174 Clouds of Sand arise, Spurn'd, and cast backward on the Follower's Eyes. **1797** HOLCROFT *Stolberg's Trav.* II. lx. 362 Short horns bent backward. **1813** *Examiner* 29 Mar. 207/1 The bending of the back bone, backward and forward. **1833** *Regul. Instr. Cavalry* I. 22 Bending backward or forward is not to be permitted.

b. With verbs of continuous motion, as *go, walk, ride*, this passes from simple direction, into a description of the constant position of the body in relation to the varying direction of motion; = With the back foremost, with the face to the rear.
a **1300** *Cursor M.* 2042 A mantil on his nec he tok & bakward ȝod, als sais þe bok. **1388** WYCLIF *Gen.* ix. 23 Sem and Jafeth..ȝeden bacward. **1561** *Calvin's 4 Godlye Serm.* iv, Like kicking and resty horses, more ready to go backwarde than forward. **1602** SHAKS. *Ham.* II. ii. 206 If like a Crab you could go backward. **1726** VANBRUGH & CIBBER *Prov. Husb.* I. i. (1735) 30 Doll puked a little with riding backward. **1842** J. H. NEWMAN *Par. Serm.* V. viii. 124 We walk to heaven backward. **1850** LYTTON *My Novel* II. xii, He turned sharply round..and, with his arm still folded on his breast, he walked backward, as if not to lose the view.

c. *to go backward*: to retire for a necessary purpose (*hence* said of the action). *Obs.*
1748 SMOLLETT *Rod. Rand.* (1804) I. xi. 59 My companion's bowels being disordered he got up in order to go backward. **1771** J. S. *Le Dran's Obs. Surg.* 185 The Patient..went backward immediately. *Ibid.* 210 No Discharge backward.

†**2.** Of position: With the back towards the front, the company, centre of attention, etc. *Obs.*
c **1460** *Bk. Curtasye* in *Babees Bk.* (1868) 302 Ne bacwarde sittande gyf noȝt þy cupe.

†**3.** Of position: Toward the back or rear of a place; away from the front. *arch.* or *Obs.*; commonly *back, to the back, at the back.*
c **1460** *Towneley Myst.* 204 Whi stand ye so bakward? **1673** WYCHERLEY *Gentl. Danc. M.* I. i. (1735) 12 You know my Chamber is backward, and has a door into the Gallery. **1715** *Lond. Gaz.* No. 5328/4 A small Scar lying backward under one of his Jaws. **1716-8** LADY MONTAGUE *Lett.* 36 I. 137 The women's apartments are always built backward, removed from sight. **1729** DESAGULIERS in *Phil. Trans.* XXXVI. 202 If the Pulley be set backwarder still. **1812** *Examiner* 19 Oct. 672/2 Some injury is also done backward.

II. Towards what is behind in position or course.

4. In the direction which, so far as concerns one's general or ordinary position, is behind one, or from which one is moving, e.g. *to look, turn the head* backward. *arch.*; commonly *back, behind.*
(*This connects the present section with* I.)
c **1386** CHAUCER *Man of L.T.* 764 Sche loketh bakward to the lond. **1388** WYCLIF *John* xx. 14 Sche turnede bacward, and sai Jhesu stondinge. *a* **1575** PILKINGTON *Exp. Nehemiah* iv. Wks. (1842) 406 Let us..not look backward but go on forth. **1611** BIBLE *Gen.* ix. 23 Shem and Iaphet..went backward [= 1 b]..and their faces were backward. **1695** LD. PRESTON *Boeth.* III. 157 That he his Eyes shan't backward cast. **1728** YOUNG *Love Fame* i. (1757) 84 Men should press forward in fame's glorious chace; Nobles look backward, and so lose the race. **1855** BROWNING in *Sat. Rev.* No. 4. 69 Whom else could I dare look backward for?

5. a. In the direction from which one has come, towards the place of starting, in the opposite direction from that in which one has advanced.
Not properly used of persons, animals, etc., where it would be ambiguous; e.g. a *ball* may roll backward, a *stream* flow backward, but a man after proceeding so far will begin to walk *back* or *in the opposite direction*, not *backward*, unless in sense 1 b. But see b.
c **1374** CHAUCER *Troylus* IV. 1525 And thou Simois.. Returne backwarde to thy well. **1517** TORKINGTON *Pilgr.* (1884) 57 We..sumtyme sealyd bakward, sumtyme forward. *Ibid.* 63 We made Sayle bakward j C myle. **1535** COVERDALE *2 Esdras* xvi. 16 Like as an arowe..returneth not bacwarde. **1589** A. MUNDAY in Arb. *Eng. Garner* (1877) I. 206 Straightway suspected the matter: and returned backward. **1673** DRYDEN *Assignat.* v. iv. Wks. 1883 IV. 464 Like some impetuous flood, which mastered once, With double force bends backward. **1802** *Chron. Scot. Poetry* IV. Introd. 37 The hope..of the Angli began to melt and flow backward. **1827** KEBLE *Chr. Year, 1st Sund. Christmas* iii, Backward force the waves of Time.

b. *backward and forward*: to and fro; also *fig.* of vacillation, uncertain speech, etc.
1581 FULKE in *Confer.* III. (1584) Y iij b, Euen nowe, you denied..and now you graunt it: you go backward and foreward. **1680** LUTTRELL *Brief Rel.* (1857) I. 57 Goeing backward and forward in his accusation. *a* **1711** KEN *Hymnotheo* Poet. Wks. 1721 III. 274 The Serpent wav'd his Carcase..Backward and forward. **1715** BURNET *Own Time* (1766) II. 234 The boy went backward and forward in his story. **1793** SMEATON *Edystone L.* §237 Carried backward and forward in the yawls every tide. **1833** MACAULAY *Mahon's War Success., Ess.* (1848) II. 93 Imputations.. utterly unfounded..were hurled backward and forward by the political disputants. **1878** HUXLEY *Physiogr.* 2 This regular backward-and-forward movement of the great mass of water.

6. In the direction of retreat. (Commonly *back.*) † *to go backward*: to recede, retreat; to relapse, backslide (obs.).
1382 WYCLIF *Psa.* xl. 14 Be thei turned al bacward. *c* **1400** *Rom. Rose* 5024 The joy that is eterne, Fro which go bakward Youthe her made. **1535** COVERDALE *Isa.* i. 4 They haue prouoked the holy one of Israel vnto anger, and are gone bacward. **1611** *ibid.* Let them be driuen backward, and put to shame. **1667** MILTON *P.L.* I. 223 The flames Drivn backward slope their pointing spires. **1821** BYRON *Sardan.* III. i. 324 They are beaten backward from the palace.

7. *fig.* Towards a worse state, implying retrogression, check, etc. (More commonly *back.*)
1583 STANYHURST *Aeneis* II. (Arb.) 55 Al things goa backward. **1601** SHAKS. *All's Well* I. i. 233 The fated skye.. doth backward pull Our slow designes. *a* **1700** DRYDEN (J.) The work went backward, and the more he strove T'advance the suit, the further from her love. **1776** ADAM SMITH *Wealth Nat.* I. I. ix. 95 It is a common..opinion that France is going backward.

8. Of time: **a.** Towards the past; **b.** In the past. (*arch.*; commonly *back.*)
1562 PILKINGTON *Haggeus* ii. Wks. (1842) 176 He bids them look backward..whole forty years. **1605** BACON *Adv. Learn.* I. v. §1 By a computation backward from ourselves. **1625** BURGES *Pers. Tithes* 55 This Statute extendeth to 40 yeares backe-ward. **1691** T. H[ALE] *Acc. New Invent.* 31 For any number of years backward. **1871** SMILES *Character* xi. (1876) 305 It glorifies the present by the light it casts backward.

III. In the reverse direction or order. [Arising out of 5.]

9. a. In a direction opposite to the normal one, the reverse way; from end to beginning.
a **1520** *Myrr. Our Ladye* 295 *Eua* turned bacwarde spellyth *aue.* **1588** SHAKS. *L.L.L.* v. i. 50 What is Ab speld backward with the horn on his head? **1674** PLAYFORD *Skill Mus.* II. 104 The first Note must be plaid with the bow drawn backward. **1839** BAILEY *Festus* (1848) 195 Rites forbid and backward-jabbered prayers. **1851** MAYHEW *Lond. Labour* I. 23 The root of the costermonger tongue.. is to give the words spelt backward.

b. *fig.* The wrong way, perversely.
1552 LYNDESAY *Papyngo* 706 Deuotely saye..The auld Placebo bakwart. **1599** SHAKS. *Much Ado* III. i. 61, I neuer yet saw man..how rarely featur'd, But she would spell him backward.

10. Phrase: *to ring bells backward*: to ring them beginning with the bass bell, in order to give alarm of fire or invasion, or express dismay.
c **1500** *Adam Bel* 346 in Hazl. *E.P.P.* II. 153 There was many an oute horne in Carlyll blowen, And the belles bacewarde did they rynge. **1590** R. HARVEY *Plain Perc.* 2, I heare the bels ring backward, and the fire runne forward. **1651** CLEVELAND *Rebel Scot* 5 Ring the Bells backward; I am all on fire. **1672** WILD *Letter* 11 [They] talk'd of Bells and Bonfires; but none..durst begin, for fear they should.. when the Parliament meet, be forced to ring the Bells backward. *a* **1832** SCOTT *Bonnie Dundee*, The bells are rung backward, the drums they are beat.

†**11.** Contrariwise, *e converso, vice versa. Obs.*
1607 BP. ANDREWES *Serm.* IV. 10 All that 'rise against,' are 'enemies,' but not backward. For enemies may be such as stand on even ground.

12. With pr. pple. forming adjectives, as *backward-bending, -curving, -facing, -gazing, -looking, -sloping.*
1932 AUDEN *Orators* II. 51 He has the same backward-bending thumb that I have. **1923** D. H. LAWRENCE *Birds, Beasts & Flowers* 142 And one intense and backward-curving frisson Seizes you. **1951** *Sci. News Let.* 18 Aug. 102/1 Backward-facing seats for passengers in airplanes are again recommended by the U.S. Air Force as a forward step in lessening injuries in case of a crash. **1952** *Jrnl. R. Aeronaut. Soc.* Feb. 91/1 There is no doubt that the backward-facing seat..offers ideal protection. **1896** KIPLING *Seven Seas* 57 Hedged in a backward-gazing world. **1846** WHITTIER *Reformer* in *Poet. Wks.* (1898) 399/1 Backward-looking son of time. **1950** H. J. MASSINGHAM *Curious Traveller* iii. 55 A few lights of experience more memorable to my backward-looking glance than others. **1962** *Listener* 5 July 28/2 Is this nostalgic, rurally romantic, backward looking art a true reflection of Australia? **1944** A. L. ROWSE *Eng. Spirit* 245 That familiar backward-sloping hand.

B. *adj.* [attrib. (often elliptical) use of the *adv.*; but analogous to adjs. in -WARD of OE. origin.]

1. In *Cricket*, directed to the back or rear. (*a*) of play or a player = *back play* (see BACK- B); (*b*) of a fieldsman or his position: farther from the line of the wicket than is standard practice, as *backward point*, the position of point when standing a little behind the line of the wicket for certain kinds of bowling.
1552 HULOET, Backwarde, *recuruus..retrorsus.* **1697** DRYDEN *Virg. Georg.* III. 48 With backward Bows the Parthians shall be there. **1844** *Lillywhite's Hand-Bk. Cricket* 18 The length to pitch your ball depends very much upon your *pace*, as well as the batsman's *style* of forward, or backward play. **1870** *New Sporting Mag.* Aug. 112 It was a great treat to see a forward player and a backward player in together. **1882** *Proper Pride* ii. 145 Many regretful backward glances. **1883** LOOMIS *Treat. Astron.* 18 The forward motion of a boat..gives to the banks an appearance of backward motion. **1904** P. F. WARNER *How we recovered the Ashes* ix. 189 Rhodes caught him easily at backward point. **1926** *Times* 19 Aug. 5/2 He had Mr. Ponsford caught at backward point. **1955** *Times* 9 May 15/1 He would certainly have benefited from a backward short leg. **1959** *Daily Mail* 20 Feb. 10/4 The ball was turned by Cowdrey sharply to backward square leg.
fig. **1860** J. YOUNG *Prov. Reason* 45 The last, dim..point in the backward stretch of the reason.

2. Directed in the opposite way; of or pertaining to return.
1604 SHAKS. *Oth.* I. iii. 38 Their backward course. **1820** KEATS *Hyperion* I. 154 With backward footing through the shade. **1870** BRYANT *Homer* I. III. 81 And takes the backward way with trembling limbs. **1884** *Gt. W. Ry. Time Tables* July 87 Available for Two Calendar Months for completion of the forward and backward journeys.

3. Done in the reverse way or order; reversed.
1725 POPE *Odyss.* II. 124 The backward labours of her faithless hand. **1726** GAY *Fables* I. xxiii. 17 She mumbles forth her backward prayers. **1878** TAIT & STEWART *Unseen Univ.* vii. §230 When the backward process has reached this germ.

†**4.** Perverse, unfavourable. *Obs.*
1583 STANYHURST *Aeneis* I. (Arb.) 18 Stil crost with destenye backward. *a* **1605** SIR J. MELVIL *Mem.* (1683) 5 Who was so glad as he, to return with this backward answer?

†**5.** Placed towards or at the back or rear. *Obs.*
1610 SHAKS. *Temp.* II. ii. 95 His forward voyce now is to speake well of his friend; his backward voice, is to vtter foule speeches. **1677** MOXON *Mech. Exerc.* (1703) 156 The backward Hips..in the way of an Angle for the back part of a Building. **1751** JOHNSON *Rambl.* No. 171 ¶9 A lodging in the backward garret of a mean house. **1819** CRABBE *T. of Hall* VII. 572 'He..lodges here—he has the backward rooms.'

6. a. Turning or hanging back from action; disinclined to advance or make advances; reluctant, averse, unwilling, loath, chary; shy, bashful.
1599 SHAKS. *Hen. V*, IV. iii. 72 Perish the man, whose mind is backward now. **1673** CRADOCK *Knowl. & Pract.* I. ii. §2 Prone to evil, and backward to good. *c* **1680** BEVERIDGE *Serm.* (1729) II. 510 Take pains with your backward hearts to bring them to it. **1704** SWIFT *T. Tub* xi. Wks. 1760 I. 123 The females were nothing backwarder in beholding. **1762** H. WALPOLE *Vertue's Anecd. Paint.* (1786) II. 77 The.. nobility were not backward with presents of the same nature. **1782** PRIESTLEY *Corrupt. Chr.* I. I. 13 The apostles were never backward to combat other Jewish prejudices. **1826** DISRAELI *Viv. Grey* I. i. 2 Percy Metcalfe..was quite as backward as Vivian; indeed, backwarder.

b. *backward in coming forward*, reluctant, shy (to do something). Cf. COME *v.* 58.
1830 *Fraser's Mag.* I. 295 Mr. Hogg..never has been.. very backward in coming forward. **1833** DICKENS *Let.* ? 10 Dec. (1965) 33 They are 'rather backward in coming forward' with the needful. **1862** TROLLOPE *Orley Farm* II. xxxvii. 291, I must say you're rather backward in coming forward. **1955** L. P. HARTLEY *Perfect Woman* xxxii. 293 He's not usually backward in coming forward, is he?

7. a. Behindhand in respect of time or progress, late.
1693 LUTTRELL *Brief Rel.* (1857) III. 15 Which will occasion the French to be 6 weeks backwarder in their preparations. **1777** HUME *Ess. & Treat.* II. 43 A very backward scholar. **1845** FORD *Handbk. Spain* §1. 21 The inns of Spain are in that backward state in which those of Sicily are. **1871** MARKBY *Elem. Law* §530 The law is here certainly in a backward condition. **1883** tr. *Renan's Recoll. Youth* 24 If a child was backward in learning to walk.

b. *esp.* of the season or crops.
1616 SURFL. & MARKH. *Countr. Farm* 28 The yeare will proue backward. **1789** MRS. PIOZZI *Journ. France* I. 8 Harvest..is extremely backward this year. **1812** *Examiner* 5 Oct. 629/2 Turnips, a fair crop, although backward. **1836** *Athenæum* No. 440. 241 The season though somewhat backward promises an abundant harvest.

8. Reaching into the past.
c **1650** *Select. Harl. Misc.* (1793) 401 A tax backward, to be paid over again. **1725** POPE *Odyss.* III. 122 Far as thy mind thro' backward time can see. **1812** BYRON *Ch. Har.* II. xxiv. Each backward year.

9. *backward scattering* = BACK SCATTERING.
1938 R. W. LAWSON tr. *Hevesy & Paneth's Man. Radio-activity* (ed. 2) iii. 47 With β-rays..an appreciable fraction of the β-particles is scattered in the backward direction; in fact..the number of electrons emitted..falls off because of this process of backward scattering. **1962** *Gloss. Terms Nuclear Sci.* (*B.S.I.*) 12 *Backward scattering*, the deflexion of particles or of radiation by scattering processes through angles greater than 90° to the original direction of motion.

C. *sb.* [The *adj.* or *adv.* used absolutely.]

†**1.** *lit.* The hinder part of the body. *Obs.*
1627 MASSINGER *Gt. Dk. Flor.* II. i, I should Have kissed her backward.

2. *poet.* The past portion (of time).
1610 SHAKS. *Temp.* I. ii. 50 What see'st thou else In the dark backward and abisme of Time? **1870** LOWELL *Study Wind.* 91 One volume of contemporary memoirs.. will throw more light into the dark backward of time than, etc.

'backward, *v.* *Obs.* exc. *dial.* Also *dial.* backard. [f. BACKWARD *a.* Cf. to *forward*.] **1.** To put or keep back, delay, retard. Hence **backwarding** *vbl. sb.*, the action of going backward; phr. ***backwarding and forwarding***, 'to-ing and fro-ing'.
1594 PLAT *Jewell-ho.* III. 3 Whereby he did greatly backward the tree in his bearing. **1642** *Declar. Lords & Comm.* 16 Nov. 4 To hinder or backward the said former undertakings. *a* **1660** HAMMOND *Serm.* xv. (R.) One that doth so clog and trash, so disadvantage and backward us. **1765** *Museum Rusticum* III. xlix. 208 It [the cutting-down of the first growth] seems therefore a backwarding of the growth of the hedge several years for no advantage. **1873** M. E. BRADDON *Lucius Davoren* III. xiv. 39 As long as she do fret and werrit herself so, she'll keep backarding of her recovery. **1892** STEVENSON & OSBOURNE *Wrecker* x. 167 And now, after all this backwarding and forwarding, and that hotel clerk, and that bug Bellairs, it'll be a change.. to see the schooner.
†**2.** To send back, return. *Obs.*
1789 B. SHERIDAN *Jrnl.* 28 Feb. (1960) 151 The enclosures which to use your own phrase I *backward* to you.

backwardation (bækwə'deɪʃən). [f. prec. vb. + -ATION (after sbs. from vbs. of Latin origin as *retard-ation*).] *Stock Exchange* term for a percentage paid by a seller of stock for the privilege of keeping back or delaying its delivery till the following account or to any other future day agreed upon.
1850 KEYSER *Law Stock Exch.*, The term Backwardation is employed when stock is more in demand than money, and a premium is given to obtain the loan of stock against its value in money. *a* **1860** C. FENN *Eng. & For. Funds* (1883) 127 Backwardation is paid by the speculator for the fall, or the Bear, in order to postpone delivery until the following account. **1880** *Society* 3 Sept. 16 The Bear a good contango loves, The Bull a backwardation. **1883** *Pall Mall G.* 11 Sept. 9/2 At the opening ⅛ backwardation to ¼ contango was charged.

†**backwardi'zation.** *Obs.* = prec.
1865 in *Public Opin.* 18 Nov. 541/2 'Backwardization' expresses.. the sum which a seller pays for not being obliged to deliver the shares at the time before agreed upon, but carry them over to the following account.

'backwardly, *adv.* [f. BACKWARD *a.* + -LY².]
1. In a backward direction.
1552 HULOET, Bowed backwardlye, *recuruue.*
†**2.** Again, over again. *Obs.*
1552 HULOET, Backwardlye.. *rursum.* **1557** N. T. (Genev.) *Gal.* iv. 9 Whervnto.. ye wil be in bondage backwardly.
†**3.** Perversely. *Obs.*
a **1586** *Answ. Cartwright* 35 How backewardely doeth he deale in this matter? **1607** SHAKS. *Timon* III. iii. 18 Does he thinke so backwardly of me now.
4. Reluctantly, unwillingly, sluggishly.
1580 SIDNEY *Arcadia* I. (J.) Though they do fly, yet backwardly do go with proud aspect. **1783** AINSWORTH *Lat. Dict.* (Morell), Backwardly, *Otiose, negligenter, remisse.* **1860** RAWLINSON tr. *Herodotus* VIII. lxxxv. IV. 330 A few only followed the advice of Themistocles, to fight backwardly.

'backwardness. [f. as prec. + -NESS.]
1. The state of being behindhand in progress or preparation.
a **1588** ABP. SANDYS *Serm.* (1841) 424 Where there is backwardness in knowledge. **1628** EARLE *Microcosm.*, *Raw Preacher* 3 His backwardness in the University. **1683** SIR W. TEMPLE *Mem.* 1672–9 Wks. 1731 I. 417 By their Forwardness, and the great Backwardness of some of the Allies. **1858** FROUDE *Hist. Eng.* III. xiv. 254 The backwardness of the English in engineering skill. **1876** FAWCETT *Pol. Econ.* I. v. 63 The poverty and backwardness of India.
b. The backward state of the season, or crops.
1684 *Lond. Gaz.* No. 1928/1 Put off, by reason of the backwardness of the season. **1719** LOUDON & WISE *Compl. Gard.* 164 Causes of the Forwardness or Backwardness of Maturity in all manner of Fruits. **1828** STEUART *Planter's Guide* 323 In regard to Backwardness in Trees.
2. Reluctance, disinclination; slowness of conception or action, sluggishness; bashfulness.
1597 T. PAYNE *Royal Exch.* 14 Cowldnes and backwardnes in religion. **1624** A. WOTTON *Runne fr. Rome* 5 To beare with my slownes and backwardnes. *a* **1665** J. GOODWIN *Filled w. the Spirit* (1867) 62 Backwardness or indisposition unto the things exhorted. **1669** PEPYS *Diary* 3 Jan., I, out of my natural backwardness, did hang off, which vexed her. **1748** SMOLLETT *Rod. Rand.* xxxix. (1804) 254 Which operation I having performed with some backwardness, she put it on. **1787** T. JEFFERSON *Writ.* (1859) II. 149 The backwardness of the States to bring money into the public treasury. **1872** FREEMAN *Norm. Conq.* IV. xviii. 141 Without any suspicion of backwardness or disloyalty.

backwards ('bækwədz), *adv.* (and *a.*) Also 6 bacwardes, *Sc.* bacwartis. [f. BACKWARD with advb. genitive *-s*; cf. OE. *hámweardes*: see -WARDS.]
A. *adv.* = BACKWARD *adv.* in its various senses. ***to bend*** or ***lean over backwards(s)*** (fig.), to go to the opposite extreme (in order to avoid a possible bias, etc.); to go almost too far in the effort to overcome one's 'inclination'. *colloq.* (orig. *U.S.*). Also in colloq. phr. ***to know*** (something) ***backwards***, to know (it) extremely well or 'inside out' (INSIDE *sb.* 4); to be very familiar with (it).
1513 DOUGLAS *Æneis* VIII. ii. 46 The streme bacwartis vp, flawis soft and styll. **1535** COVERDALE *John* xviii. 6 They wente bacwardes and fell to the grounde. **1606** *Sir G. Goosecappe* I. iv. in *Old Pl.* (1884) III. 25, I will preferre thee backwards (as many friends do) and leave their friends woorse then they found them. **1664** POWER *Exp. Philos.* I. 2 The joynts of his hinder legs.. bend backwards. **1704** STEELE *Lying Lover* IV. (1747) 60 She lies backwards, and you can't so much as see her Chamber Window. **1708** *Lond. Gaz.* No. 4432/6 [They] went into the same Coach, the Bride sitting backwards. **1715** *Ibid.* No. 5323/1 To ply forwards and backwards.. on the Coasts of Calabria. **1716** *Ibid.* No. 5446/9 A house.. with the Gardens.. and four small Tenements backwards. **1771** J. S. *Le Dran's Obs. Surg.* (ed. 4) 164 The Patient being pressed to go backwards, went behind his Tent. **1833** *Regul. Instr. Cavalry* I. 24 At the words *On the Right, backwards Wheel*, the man on the right of the rank faces to his left. **1858** W. IRVING *Washington* V. 68 He walked me backwards and forwards.. for half an hour. **1872** FREEMAN *Norm. Conq.* IV. xx. 456 Brihtric having been translated backwards to the less important Abbey of Burton. **1904** G. V. HOBART *Jim Hickey* ii. 32 The chief clerk.. knew the hotel business backwards. **1925** *Nation* (N.Y.) 13 May 537 Stambuliski leaned over backwards in his desire to satisfy Serbian demands. **1933** E. O'NEILL *Ah, Wilderness!* III. ii. 112, I know this game backwards. **1936** A. THIRKELL *August Folly* viii. 255 If you did get ill.. I know the part backwards, and I've been to all the rehearsals. **1937** *Amer. Speech* XII. 167 He is being hypercorrect, leaning over backward to be correct. **1949** L. M. EDWARDS *Sauce for Geese: Story of Nebraska Farm* 12 We all but bent over backward trying to impress everyone with the fact that tempus was fugiting. **1952** *Economist* 29 Nov. 612/1 [Broadmindedness] may.. be carried beyond the optimum of impartiality to that point of unfairness to one's own case which Americans call 'leaning over backward'. **1952** M. MCCARTHY *Groves of Academe* (1953) vi. 119 A liberal college ought to lean over backward not to fire anybody who is suspected of Communism. **1953** J. CARY *Except the Lord* xliii. 195, I had provoked in him that conscience, those scruples of justice and right, which might cause him actually to favour my enemy—to, as our transatlantic friends say, lean over backwards in obliging him. **1954** J. GRENFELL in *Turn back Clock* (1983) 102 You know it absolutely backwards, so be quiet. **1974** *Economist* 16 Feb. 35 He knows the constituency backwards. **1983** *Financial Times* 17 Sept. 16/5 An eclectic collector.., he knows the showrooms backwards.
†**B.** *adj.* = BACKWARD *a.* *Obs. rare.*
1627 BP. COSIN *Corr.* (1869) I. 119 Slack or backwards in doing his.. dutie. **1683** CAVE *Ecclesiastici* 481 Nor were.. his Party backwards to blow up the Coals.

backwash ('bækwɒʃ), *sb.* [f. BACK *adv.*] The motion of a receding wave; a backward current. Also *transf.* and *fig.*
1876 MISS BRADDON *J. Haggard's D.* I. 23 Or else the backwash would draw him into its vortex. **1884** *Chr. World* 9 Oct. 757/1 The tremendous backwash of popular enthusiasm. **1927** R. H. WILENSKI *Mod. Movement in Art* 116 The backwash of the French Impressionist technique of the 'seventies. **1955** *Sci. News Let.* 26 Mar. 200/1 These air whirlpools are not caused by either the propeller backwash or jet stream.

'backwash, *v.* [cf. prec. sb.]
1. To affect with backwash (a boat *e.g.*, with that from the oars of a boat in front).
1882 *Standard* 16 Sept. 3/6 Backwashing both bow and stroke side of the Thames boat.
2. To clean the oil from wool after combing. Hence **backwasher, backwashing** *vbl. sb.*
1775 ASH, *Backwashed*, Cleaned from the oil after combing. **1882** *Standard* 29 Dec. 2/2 A backwasher of Van mohair.. The back-washing machine at which the back-washer mentioned above had worked.

backwater ('bæ,kwɔːtə(r)), *sb.* [f. BACK *a.* or *adv.*]
†**1.** Water flowing in from behind. *Obs.*
1387 TREVISA *Higden* (Rolls Ser.) I. 57 Strengþe of ryueres and bakwateres [*impetus fluminum a tergo labentium*] dryueþ forþ þe see Euxinum alway in oon cours. **1577** HARRISON *Descr. Brit.* xii, Sundrie small creekes void of backwater.
2. Water dammed back in the channel of a swollen or obstructed river (or mill-race), or that has overflowed into shallow lagoons near it.
1629 H. BURTON *Babel no Bethel* Ep. Ded., A continuall current, that so merrily driues the Popish mills about, and sets ours in a back water or float. **1799** J. ROBERTSON *Agric. Perth* 366 To free their land from the back-water, when Loch-Lubnaig is overcharged in the rainy season. **1816** U. BROWN *Jrnl.* in *Maryland Hist. Mag.* (1916) XI. 49 [I] was obliged to pay.. for ferry over on the back water forced into said gully by the River. **1857** F. L. OLMSTED *Journey through Texas* 213 At the last freshet, the whole roof of the mill.. was covered by the back water of the river. **1878** J. H. BEADLE *Western Wilds* xxv. 399 But the Columbia often rises so as to cause back-water, giving the Willamette a variation of thirty-two feet.
3. An artificial accumulation of water dammed back for any purpose.
1792 A. YOUNG *Trav. France* 77 An artificial back-water, capable.. of sweeping out the harbour's mouth clean from all obstructions. **1861** SMILES *Engineers* II. 68 By means of sluices, supplied by an artificial backwater.
4. A piece of water without current, lying more or less parallel to a river, and fed from it at the lower end by a back-flow.
1820 *Ann. Reg. 1819* 517 The flux and reflux of Teutonic invasion.. deposited this back-water of barbarism. **1863** KINGSLEY *Water Bab.* iii. 107 The great withy pollard which hangs over the backwater. **1872** TAUNT *Map Thames* 21/2 In some of the backwaters are fine Pike. *Mod.* The back-waters of the Amazon are of enormous extent.
fig. **1879** FARRAR *St. Paul* II. 20 Paul found there on his arrival a strange backwater of religious opinion. **1907** *Westm. Gaz.* 11 Dec. 2/2 Eastern Bengal has always been somewhat of a backwater—remote, neglected, and in danger of stagnation. **1911** F. SWINNERTON *Casement* v. 171 He had lived in a backwater all his life, and his ideas.. were often out of touch with reality.
5. A creek or arm of the sea, parallel to the coast, separated by a narrow strip of land from the open sea, with which it communicates by barred outlets.
1867 in SMYTH *Sailor's Word-bk.*
6. A backward current of water.
1830 LYELL *Princ. Geol.* I. 271 The current.. is a back-water, wherein the tide.. runs nine hours towards the north, and only three towards the south. **1840** CARLYLE *Heroes* i. (1858) 198 A kind of backwater, or eddying swirl.
7. The swell of the sea thrown back from contact with a solid body, *esp.* from the paddles of steamboats; *hence*, the loss of power occasioned by it in steamboats. Also *attrib.*
1838 POE *A. G. Pym* Wks. 1864 IV. 83 Those which came from the larboard, being what are called back-water seas. *c* **1865** J. WYLDE in *Circ. Sc.* I. 370/2 The back-water cast from the paddles or screw.

'backwater, back-water, *v.* **1.** *intr.* = the phr. *to back water*: see BACK *v.* 15 b.
1828 *Examiner* 56/1 They won't backwater when he endeavours to give way. **1959** P. CAPON *Amongst those Missing* 149 The boat swung right round.. and then Harry had to back-water frantically to keep her bow-on.
2. *trans.* (See quot.)
1924 *Glasgow Herald* 30 Dec. 7/7 The Tay at Meikleour was within a few feet of the top of the banks, and huge stretches of land were submerged in consequence of the ditches being backwatered.
3. *fig.* To bring into a backwater.
1885 E. F. BYRRNE *Entangled* I. I. viii. 139 He had the keenest sense, even when carried forward by the tide of a glorified passion, that Nature may treacherously and improvidently back-water. **1920** GALSWORTHY *In Chancery* I. viii. 73 What on earth did such a woman do with her life, backwatered like this?

back-way ('bæk'weɪ). [f. BACK *a.*] A way at the back, or leading to the back, of any place; *hence*, an indirect, roundabout way, a by-path.
1577 HOLINSHED *Chron.* I. 38/2 The entries, the backwaies, and the whole situation thereof. **1660** BOND *Scut. Reg.* 10 Death.. still will have, A thousand backwayes to the grave. **1709** J. STEVENS *Quevedo's Com. Wks.* 74 He should come in the back-way.. and open the Garden Door. **1866** G. MACDONALD *Ann. Q. Neighb.* ii. (1878) 21, I would not creep out the back way.

back-wind, *v.* *Naut.* [WIND *sb.*¹] To be taken, or cause to be taken, aback. Hence **back-wind** *sb.*, a gust that lays a sail aback.
1899 *Daily News* 6 Oct. 7/3 At this stage both yachts were compelled to close haul to avoid back-winding. *Ibid.* 21 Oct. 3/4 The Columbia's [spinnaker].. behaved badly, back-winding the defender constantly. **1909** *Westm. Gaz.* 30 Jan. 9/1 A whaleboat.. capsized,.. the sail being caught by a back-wind, as the course was being changed.

back'woodish, *a.* [f. BACKWOOD(S¹ + -ISH 2.] = BACKWOODSY *a.* So **back'woodishness.**
1836 *Tait's Mag.* III. 496/1 The inn here is genuine Highland: low-built,.. backwoodish. **1855** L. OLIPHANT *Minnesota* 93 There was not a particle of backwoodishness about them. **1946** KOESTLER *Thieves in Night* 147 Our own crowd of.. men and women, mute, wary and back-woodish as we had become during this first long hard year.

backwoods ('bæk'wʊdz). [f. BACK *a.*] **a.** Wild, uncleared forest-land; e.g. that of North America. Also a remote and sparsely inhabited region.
1709 J. LAWSON *Voyage to Carolina* 139 He [*sc.* the pheasant] haunts the back Woods, and is seldom found near the Inhabitants. **1807** *Repertory* (Boston) 15 Dec. (Th.), The members from the back woods seem to be the deepest skilled and most active men in Congress. **1832** F. TROLLOPE *Dom. Manners* xv. 233 The prospect of passing a night in the back woods of Indiana was by no means agreeable. **1834** *Chambers' Jrnl.* III. 40 Your widely-circulated Journal having even reached these backwoods. **1859** MERIVALE *Rom. Emp.* (1865) IV. xxxix. 389 The latest conquests of Rome annexed the backwoods of Gaul.
b. *attrib.* Also *backwood.* Also *Comb.*, as ***backwoods-trained*** adj.; ***backwoods peer*** = next, b.
1784 J. F. D. SMYTH *Tour U.S.* I. i. 12 The American soldiery, chiefly then back-woods riflemen. **1822** J. FLINT *Lett. Amer.* 207 His live-stock soon becomes much more numerous than that of his back-wood predecessor. **1863** *Pilgr. over Prairies* II. 107 Enjoying ourselves in the approved backwoods fashion. **1905** E. W. HORNUNG *Thief in Night* 110 Parrington, the backwoods novelist.. one of the shaggiest dogs I have ever seen in evening dress. **1921** GILL & VALENTINE *Govt. & People* x. 105 'Backwoods' Peers, who take little interest in politics. **1942** W. FAULKNER *Go down, Moses* 204 Ashby.. leads a handful of troops he never saw before against an entrenched position of backwoods-trained riflemen. **1956** A. L. ROWSE *Early Churchills* 109 Lord Belasyse, who—though a backwoods Catholic peer—was not without *nous.*

back'woodsman. [f. prec. + -MAN.] **a.** A settler in the backwoods; so ***backwoodswoman***. Also *fig.*

1774 DUNMORE *Corresp.* 24 Dec. (MS.) (D.A.), The back-woods-men, who are Hunters like the Indians and equally ungovernable. **1798** *Monthly Mag.* Mar. 185/1 The Back Woodsmen, as the whites all along the interior line of the states are termed, are almost gigantic. **1803** T. M. HARRIS *Jrnl. Tour* 6 June (1805) (Th.), Most of the 'Back-wood's men', as they are called, are emigrants. **1816** in PICKERING *Vocab. U.S.* **1818** COBBETT *Resid. U.S.* (1822) 305 The habitual disregard of comfort of an American back-woodsman. **1831** CARLYLE *Sart. Res.* II. viii. 208 An American Backwoodsman, who had to fell unpenetrated forests. **1884** HIGGINSON in *Harper's Mag.* July 281/1 A plain backwoodswoman.. smoking her corn-cob pipe. **1884** W. JAMES *Let.* 30 Sept. in R. B. Perry *Thought & Char. W. J.* (1935) I. 697 My yoking of Renan with Zola may sound lacking in delicacy to French ears, but as a Yankee backwoodsman it gave me a malicious pleasure. **1905** E. W. HORNUNG *Thief in Night* 111 Raffles on his right hand, and the backwoodsman of letters on his left. **1958** *Listener* 20 Nov. 839/1 The struggles of men like Kepler and Galileo against the academic backwoodsmen in the university chairs.

b. In modern politics applied to a member of the House of Lords who rarely, if ever, attends meetings of that body, but is prepared on occasion to assert his political rights.

1909 *Daily Chron.* 11 Sept. 1/5 This speech will undoubtedly encourage the backwoodsmen in the House of Lords to take strong action. **1928** *Observer* 15 July 10/4 It has been saved by 'backwoodsmen' in the Lords from undergoing the indignity of being inspected.. by county councillors.

backwoodsy, *a.* [f. as prec. + -Y[1].] Of the nature of the backwoods.

1862 B. TAYLOR *Home & Abr.* II. 72 Wild and backwoodsy as the place appeared. *a* **1910** 'O. HENRY' *Rolling Stones* (1916) xvi. 205, I want a scrubby, ornery,.. back-woodsy, piebald gang, who never heard of finger bowls. **1951** D. RIESMAN in *American Scholar* X. 271 Such people did not want to appear backwoodsy and bigoted.

backy, var. BACKER, BACKEY.

back yard, back-yard. [BACK- A. 5.] A yard or enclosure at the back of a house. Also *fig.*

1659 in *Suffolk* (Mass., U.S.A.) *Deeds* (1885) III. §246 A back yard lying on the north side of the sajd dwelling house. **1679** BEDLOE *Popish Plot* Ep. a, Creeping into back-yards, and firing stacks of Bavins. **1771** PENNANT *Tour in Scotland 1769* 125 Land sufficient to build a house on, with gardens and back-yard. **1860** O. W. HOLMES *Prof. Breakf.-t.* x. 311 A stone with a whitish band crossing it, belonging to the pavement of the back-yard. **1882** PEBODY *Eng. Journalism* xxiii. 186 The crowing of a cock in the back-yard of a suburban villa. **1920** J. MANDER *Story of N.Z. River* I. iv. 64 When you.. have seen the backyard side of people.. you don't get upset by trifles. **1933** *Bulletin* (Sydney) 1 Feb. 11 Nine Sydney he-men out of ten get sun-tanned by lying in the back yard. *Ibid.* 13 Sept. 10/2 She worked a backyard farmlet in one of the outer suburbs. **1950** *N.Z. Jrnl. Agric.* Aug. 143/1 Few backyard henhouses appear to be planned for the number of birds they ultimately hold. **1962** *Listener* 11 Jan. 51/2 Inside the area which a substantial power regards as its own backyard, the writ of the United Nations does not run.

Hence **back'yarder** *colloq.*, (*a*) a person who keeps fowls in his backyard; a small poultry-keeper; (*b*) a fowl kept in the backyard of a house.

1922 *Daily Mail* 18 Nov. 11 Backyarders can make money out of fowls if they will feed them on the simple Karswood system. *Ibid.* 9 Dec. 14 The average total of eggs per day is seven, which.. is very good, especially as they are backyarders. **1942** *Gen.* 1 Oct. 21/1 Backyarders keep fifteen million hens according to Agriculture Ministry census.

bacon ('beɪkən), *sb.* Forms: 4 **bacoun**, 4-5 **bakoun**, 5 **bacun**, 5-6 **bakon**, 6 **baken**, 5- **bacon**. [a. OF. *bacon*, *-un* (= Pr. *bacon*, med.L. *bacōn-em*), a. OHG, *bahho*, *bacho*, MHG. *bache*, *backe*, buttock, ham, side of bacon:—OTeut. **bakon-*, cogn. w. **bako-z*, BACK *sb.*[1]; cf. ODu. *baken* bacon.]

1. The back and sides of the pig, 'cured' by salting, drying, etc. Formerly also the fresh flesh now called *pork*.

c **1330** *Poem temp. Edw. II*, 388 in *Pol. Songs* 341 For beof ne for bakoun.. Unnethe wolde eny do a char. **1377** LANGL. *P. Pl.* B. v. 194 As a bondman of his bacoun his berde was bidraueled. *c* **1386** CHAUCER *Wyf's Prol.* 217 The bacoun was nought fet for hem.. That som men fecche in Essex at Donmowe. *c* **1460** FORTESCUE *Abs. & Lim. Mon.* (1714) 73 In Fraunce, the People salten but litill meate, except their Bacon. **1523** FITZHERB. *Husb.* §121 Her [a sow's] body.. wyll be as good baken as a hogge. **1620** VENNER *Via Recta* iii. 53 Bacon is not good for them that haue weake stomacks. **1781** GIBBON *Decl. & F.* II. xxxi. 181 A regular allowance of bacon was distributed to the poorer citizens.

†**2.** The carcase of a pig; *rarely* a live pig. *Obs.*

c **1380** *Sir Ferumb.* 2696 Wyþ grys, & gees, & capouns.. Wiþ motoun, & bef & bakouns. **1549-52** in Strype *Cranmer* App. xlix. 137 Ye are like for to be taken, And quartered like a baken. **1603** KYD *Span. Trag.* (T.) A young bacon, Or a fine little smooth horse-colt. **1768** PENNANT *Zool.* I. 17 The carcases of.. 80 beeves, 600 bacons, and 600 muttons.

3. *transf.* The blubber of a whale. ? *Obs.*

1712 *Phil. Trans.* XXVII. 446 The Fat of a Whale, which we call Bacon, and out of which we boil the Train-Oyl.

†**4.** A rustic, a clown, a 'chaw-bacon.' *Obs.* (Referring, like many of the compounds, to the fact of swine's flesh being the meat chiefly consumed by the rural population of England.)

1596 SHAKS. *1 Hen. IV*, II. ii. 93 On Bacons, on, what ye knaues? Yong men must liue.

5. Phrases: **a.** ***to save one's bacon***: to escape injury to one's body, to keep oneself from harm. ***to bring home the bacon***: see BRING *v.* 1 d; .

1654 T. IRELAND *Momus Elenticus* 5 Some fellowes there were.. To save their bacon penn'd many a smooth song. **1677** W. HUGHES *Man of Sin* II. iv. 75 Farewel Transubstantiation else! but 'tis a silly shift to save their Bacon. **1691** *Weesils* i. 5 No, they'l conclude I do't to save my Bacon. **1693** in *Catal.* (fictitious) *Bks.* in *Harl. Misc.* (1745) V. 269/2 In dubiis tutior pars: Or, the broad Way to save a Man's Bacon, and damn his Soul. **1812** COMBE (Dr. Syntax) *Pictur.* VI. 22 But as he ran to save his bacon, By hat and wig he was forsaken. **1931** BELLOC *Cranmer* viii. 149 Cranmer had just saved his bacon. It had been a very close thing.

b. ***to sell one's bacon***, i.e. one's flesh or body.

1825 CARLYLE *Schiller* III. (1845) 163 To the Kaiser, therefore, I sold my bacon, And by him good charge of the whole is taken.

6. *Comb.* and *Attrib.*, as ***bacon-curer***, ***-factor***, ***-merchant***; ***bacon-flitch***, ***-ham***, ***-pot***, ***-rack***, ***-rind***; **bacon beetle**, the larder-beetle (see LARDER 3); **bacon-brains**, a clownish blockhead; **bacon-face(d**, having a fat sleek face; **bacon-farced** *a.*, stuffed with bacon; **bacon-fed** *a.*, fed on bacon, rustic, clownish; **bacon-hog, -pig**, one specially fattened for making bacon; †**bacon-man**, a curer of, or dealer in, bacon; †**bacon-picker**, opprobrious name for a glutton; †**bacon-slicer**, a rustic.

1832 W. D. WILLIAMSON *Hist. Maine* I. 171 *Dermestes Lardarius*, *Bacon Beetle. **1855** *Poultry Chron.* III. 404/2 The bacon beetle.. is a common insect in houses in April, May, and June. **1959** E. F. LINSSEN *Beetles Brit. Isles* I. 267 The infamous Bacon Beetle.. occurring in England and Ireland. Besides its association with bacon, it also occurs in hides and dead animal matter. *a* **1634** RANDOLPH *Answ. B. Jonson* Poems (1668) 56 Their *bacon-brains have such a tast, As more delights in mast. **1869** *Trans. Ill. State Agric. Soc. 1867-9* VII. 432 Hogs for *bacon-curers and city consumption. **1684** OTWAY *Atheist* I A broad shining, puff t, *Bacon-face, like a Cherubim. **1731** *Pol. Ballads* (1860) II. 223 He opulent grew, As *bacon-face Jew. *c* **1600** DAY *Begg. Bednell Gr.* (1881) 37 I'de hang this *Bacon-fac'd slave ore-thwart his shanks. **1646** G. DANIEL *Poems* Wks. 1878 I. 45 A Pheasant, *bacon-farc'd. **1596** SHAKS. *1 Hen. IV*, II. ii. 89 *Bacon-fed Knaues.. downe with them. **1462** *Test. Ebor.* (1855) II. 261 *Bakon-fliks, beffe-flicks. **1796** STEDMAN *Surinam* II. xviii. 57 Provided with a *bacon ham, hung-beef, fowls, etc. **1709** KENNETT *Erasm. Moriæ Enc.* 17 (D.) As lusty as so many *bacon-hogs or sucking calves. **1869** *Trans. Ill. State Agric. Soc. 1867-9* VII. 432 The weather became much warmer, thus lessening the demand for bacon hogs. **1884** Bacon hog [see PORKER 1]. **1707** *Lond. Gaz.* No. 4349/4 Whitfeild Miller, late of Oxford, *Bacon-man. **1653** URQUHART *Rabelais* I. Prol., A certaine gulligut Fryer and true *bacon-picker. **1833** MARRYAT *P. Simple* (1863) 195 His *bacon pigs, his porkers, his breeding sows. **1789** G. WHITE *Selborne* (1851) 209 She saves the scummings of her *bacon-pot [to make rush-lights]. **1826** MISS MITFORD *Village* II. (1863) 446 The fully stored *bacon-rack. **1606** *Wily Beguiled* in Hazl. *Dodsl.* IX. 244 Whose eyes do shine, Like *bacon-rine. **1867** FRANCIS *Bk. Angling* 28 The use of the gentle or bacon rind. **1949** E. POUND *Pisan Cantos* lxxix. 74 The bacond-rind banner alias the Washington arms floats over against Ugolino. **1580** HOLLYBAND *Treas. Fr. Tong.*, *Coënne de lard*, a *Bacon skin. **1653** URQUHART *Rabelais* I. xv, Account me a very clounch, and *bacon-slicer of Brene.

bacon *v.* (*Cath. Angl.*), ? for *baton*, BATTEN.

'bacon, *v.* Chiefly *U.S.* [f. BACON *sb.*] *trans.* To convert into bacon.

1821 I. THOMAS *Diary* (1909) II. 76 Sent Legs of Pork to be baconed. **1890** *Congress. Rec.* Aug. 8887/1 We consumed or sold our own pork, and we baconed it ourselves. **1960** *Farmer & Stockbreeder* 23 Feb. 101/1 Baconing the progeny of 40-50 Large White sows.

baconer ('beɪkənə(r)). [f. BACON *v.* + -ER.] A pig fit for being made into bacon.

1743 ELLIS *Mod. Husb.* May ix. 109 Which.. will half fat them for Porkers; or prepare them for Baconers. **1805** R. W. DICKSON *Pract. Agric.* II. 1198 The litters of.. August [being] kept till the same period in the following year, in order to be sold as baconers. **1884** *Australasian* 8 Nov. 880/2 Baconers and porkers.

Baconian (beɪ'kəʊnɪən), *a.* and *sb.* [f. Lord *Bacon*, philosopher of the 17th c. + -IAN.]

A. *adj.* **1.** Of or pertaining to Lord Bacon, or to the experimental and inductive system of natural philosophy taught by him.

1812 SIR H. DAVY *Chem. Philos.* 32 In the spirit of the Baconian School, multiplying instances and cautiously making inductions.

2. In modern times used with reference to the theory that Francis Bacon wrote the plays attributed to Shakespeare.

1874 *N.Y. Herald* 19 Sept. 11/2 This Baconian theory necessitates a compact and agreement between William Shakespeare and Lord Bacon. **1904** *Daily Chron.* 14 Jan. 3/2 If Baconianism had no more cogent evidence to encounter, the game would be in its hands. Since Bacon, on the Baconian hypothesis, certainly broke all other records, why not this one as well?

B. *sb.* **1.** An adherent of Bacon's philosophical system.

1869 *Daily News* 26 Jan., The scholastics and not the Baconians of their science.

2. One who holds that Bacon wrote the plays attributed to Shakespeare.

1874 *N.Y. Herald* 19 Sept. 11/3 It appears to me that considerable blank ammunition has been wasted in this ridiculous war between the Baconians and the Shakespearians. **1904** GARNETT *Eng. Lit.* II. 201 Baconians talk as if Bacon had nothing to do but to write his play at his chambers and send it to his factotum, Shakespeare, at the other end of the town. **1952** AUDEN *Nones* 47 Lovers of small numbers go benignly potty,.. are Millerites, Baconians, Flat-Earth-Men.

Hence **Ba'conianism**, the Baconian philosophy; the theory that Bacon wrote the plays attributed to Shakespeare. **Ba'conic** *a.*, **'Baconist** = BACONIAN *a.* and *sb.*

1834 *Edin. Rev.* LIX. 32 A sort of Baconic nomenclature. *a* **1866** J. GROTE *Exam. Util. Philos.* xvii. (1870) 264 The distinction between intuitiveness and inductiveness, pre-Baconianism, and Baconianism. **1876** BANCROFT *Hist. U.S.* II. xxi. 7 The party of Baconists had obtained great influence. **1884** W. H. WYMAN *Bibliogr. Bacon-Shakes. Controversy* 27 Judge Holmes is the apostle of Baconianism. **1904** [see sense A. 2 above].

baconize ('beɪkənaɪz), *v.* [f. BACON *sb.* + -IZE.] To make into bacon; to smoke. *lit.* and *fig.*

a **1843** SOUTHEY *Nondescripts* iv. Wks. III. 65 Pigs were made for man.. born to be brawn'd And baconized. **1864** BURRITT *Walk* 309 Magnipotent chimneys.. puff their black breathings into the.. sky above, baconising its countenance.

bacony ('beɪkənɪ), *a.* [f. BACON *sb.* + -Y[1].] Bacon-like, fatty; *spec.* in a state of fatty degeneration.

1878 KINGZETT *Anim. Chem.* 107 Diseases of the liver, the best known being so called degeneration, or bacony liver.

bacstare, obs. form of BAXTER, female baker.

bacteræmia (bæktə'riːmɪə). *Path.* Also **bacteremia**, **bacteri'æmia**. [mod.L., ad. F. *bactériémie* (Vulpian 1874, in *Compt. Rend. Soc. de Biol. 1872* IV. II. 52), f. BACTERIUM + Gr. αἷμα blood: see -IA[1].] The presence of bacteria in the blood.

1890 BILLINGS *Med. Dict.* I. 141/1 Bacteriaemia. **1910** *Lancet* 30 Apr. 1212/1 In the case of septicæmia, the somewhat ungainly terms 'bacillæmia' or 'bacteriæmia' have been proposed, or sometimes the name of the organism is appended, so that we may speak of.. a gonococcal bacteriæmia. **1933** *Ibid.* 7 Oct. 805/1 In those cases in which both bacteræmia and leucocytosis were studied, the onset of complications was preceded not only by a positive blood culture but also by a high leucocytosis. **1961** *Ibid.* 5 Aug. 296/2 This seemed particularly useful.. to allow thrombosis or bacteriæmia to subside. *Ibid.* 30 Sept. 735/2 Inflammatory renal disease.. was a possible source of the proteus bacteræmia. **1961** *Brit. Med. Dict.* 1292/1 Septicaemia.. should be distinguished from bacteraemia in which organisms appear in the blood without the severe rapid generalization of infection characteristic of septicaemia.

bacteria, *pl.* of BACTERIUM.

bacterial (bæk'tɪərɪəl), *a. Biol.* [f. BACTERIUM + -AL[1].] Of or pertaining to bacteria. Also, caused by bacteria.

1871 TYNDALL *Fragm. Sc.* II. xiii. 327 Innocent of bacterial life. **1879** M. CONWAY *Demonol.* II. IV. xix. 211 The bacterial demon of modern science. **1883** D. MACALISTER tr. *Ziegler's Text-Bk. Path. Anat.* I. xxx. 290 There are.. some bacterial diseases in which one attack protects against a subsequent one, as in the case of small-pox. **1903** *Science* XVIII. 537/2 Bacterial spot, a new disease of carnations. **1946** *Nature* 6 July 32/2 Plant disease investigations by the Plant Diseases Division [in N.Z.] covered the bacterial wilt of beans, [etc.]. **1955** *Sci. Amer.* June 85/1 Bacterial wilt, a new menace to chrysanthemums, has become serious in commercial nurseries... The infecting bacterium invades the plant's sap vessels, causes them to turn a reddish color and eventually may produce a black, soft rot of the stem and leaves.

bac'terially, *adv.* [f. BACTERIAL *a.* + -LY[2].] By, with, or in regard to bacteria.

1892 *Daily News* 16 Nov. 5/4 The Thames at Hampton was, both chemically and bacterially, in rather a bad condition, owing to the autumn decay of vegetation. **1908** *Daily Chron.* 24 July 5/5 Bacterially-infected food.

bac'terian, *a. Biol.* [f. as BACTERIAL *a.* + -AN.] = BACTERIAL *a.*

1876 tr. *Wagner's Gen. Pathol.* 342 Bacterian formation.

bacteric (bæk'tɛrɪk), *a. Biol.* [f. as prec. + -IC.] = prec.

1873 LISTER in *Nature* 10 July 212/1 Contact of a moist surface is sure to lead to Bacteric development.

bactericidal (bæk'tɪərɪˌsaɪdəl), *a. Biol.* [f. BACTERI-UM + L. *-cīda* slayer + -AL[1].] Destructive to bacteria.

1878 TYNDALL in *19th Cent.* Mar. 506 The bactericidal effects which his theory ascribes to pressure. **1881** —— *Float, M. Air* 48 All bactericidal media are therefore anti-septic.

bactericidally (bæktərɪ'saɪdəlɪ), *adv.* [f. BACTERICIDAL *a.* + -LY[2].] So as to destroy bacteria.

1899 G. NEWMAN *Bacteria* i. 24 The blue and violet rays acted most bactericidally.

bactericide (bæk'tɪərɪsaɪd). [f. BACTERIUM + -CIDE 1.] A substance that destroys bacteria.

1884 *Therapeutic Gaz.* 15 Dec. 561 [Permanganate of potash] is not a bactericide of great activity. **1894** *Athenæum* 11 Aug. 199/1 A solution of formaldehyde.. appears to be a very powerful bactericide. **1956** *Sci. News* XL. 46 These [polyphenol] substances are effective bactericides, and this accounts for the marked fall in the number of bacteria.

‖**Bacteridium** (bæktə'rɪdɪəm). [mod.L., f. BACTERIUM + Gr. -ιδιον dim. ending; cf. *antheridium*.] Davaine's name for a genus of minute organisms allied to the bacilli and bacteria.

1876 tr. *Wagner's Gen. Pathol.* 104 Davaine found bacteridia also in two examples of malignant pustule in men.

bac,terio'cidal, *a.* = BACTERICIDAL *a.*

1943 *Ann. Reg. 1942* 359 Work on bacteriocidal and bacteriostatic substances from micro-fungi.. was actively developed. **1946** *Nature* 31 Aug. 304/2 The 0·2 per cent phenol exerted marked bacteriocidal activity in 48 hours.

bacteriocin (bæk'tɪərɪəʊsɪn). *Bacteriol.* Formerly also **-ine**. [ad. F. *bactériocine* (F. Jacob et al. 1953, in *Ann. de l'Inst. Pasteur* LXXXIV. 223), f. *bactérie* BACTERIUM + *colicine* COLICIN: see -O.] Any usu. proteinaceous antibiotic produced by bacteria of one strain and active against those of another strain.

1954 *Nature* 4 Sept. 465/1 Its characteristics are more closely related to the bacteriocines. **1959** JACOB & WOLLMAN in M. H. Adams *Bacteriophages* xx. 382 The general term of *bacteriocins* has been proposed to include such antibiotics of protein nature whose production is lethal and whose action, restricted to a narrow range of related species, is conditioned by the presence of specific receptors. **1972** *Nature* 24 Mar. 144/1 The colicins, bacteriocins of strains of *Escherichia coli*, needless to say, have been more extensively studied than their counterparts in the more arcane bacterial genera. **1985** *McGraw-Hill Yearbk. Sci. & Technol. 1986* 280/1 It is.. likely that bacteriocin production is the principal means by which indigenous bacteria of the bowel and lower genitourinary tract suppress potential pathogens that attempt to colonize these two sites.

bacterioid (bæk'tɪərɪɔɪd), *a.* and *sb.* [f. BACTERIUM + -OID.] **A.** *adj.* = BACTEROID *a.*

1889 in *Cent. Dict.* **1896** HENSLOW *How to study wild Flowers* 91 The nodules found on the roots of leguminous plants contain bacterioid fungi.

B. *sb.* An organism shaped like a bacterium; *spec.* the branched form of bacteria found in the root-nodules of leguminous plants.

1898 H. C. PORTER tr. *Strasburger's Text-Bk. Bot.* I. ii. 210 These tubercles become filled with a bacterial mass, consisting principally of swollen and abnormally developed (hypertrophied) Bacterioids.

bacterio'logic, *a.* = next.

1896 *Amer. Monthly Microsc. Jrnl.* XVII. 89 (*title*) Bacteriologic results from mechanical filtration. **1898** J. MᶜFARLAND *Pathogenic Bacteria* (ed. 2) 164 The bacteriologic examination of the air. *Ibid.*, In our bacteriologic researches.

bacteriological (bæktɪərɪə'lɒdʒɪkəl), *a.* [f. BACTERIOLOGY: see -ICAL.] Pertaining to bacteriology.

1886 *Brit. Med. Jrnl.* 21 Aug. 383/1 A number of little bacteriological accessories. **1886** E. M. CROOKSHANK *Bacteriology* 3 The apparatus commonly employed in a bacteriological laboratory. **1898** R. T. HEWLETT *Bacteriology* 165 The bacteriological study of diphtheria. **1939** F. A. KNOTT *Clinical Bacteriology* i. 1 These bacteriological and serological tests are.. numerous.

b. ***bacteriological warfare***, the use, as a means of war, of bacteria to spread disease in the enemy. Cf. BIOLOGICAL *warfare*.

1924 *League of Nations Official Jrnl.* Oct. 1628 The present report deals successively with the *known* effects of chemical warfare and the *possible* effects of bacteriological warfare. **1933** *Jrnl. R. Aeronaut. Soc.* XXXVII. 827 The Geneva Gas Protocol of 1925.. prohibits bacteriological methods of warfare. **1938** *Times* 23 May 8/3 Bacteriological warfare—the scattering from the sky of germs to spread disease among the people—was out of the question. **1959** *Observer* 25 Jan. 1/1 There is a legalistic difference between bacteriological and biological warfare. The first involves the use of live germs and is forbidden by the Geneva Convention. The second involves the use of toxins derived from the germs and is permissible.

Hence **bacterio'logically** *adv.*

1892 A. C. ABBOTT *Bacteriology* 229 Typhoid fever is bacteriologically one of the most unsatisfactory of the infectious diseases. **1964** M. HYNES *Med. Bacteriol.* (ed. 8) iii. 26 A coating of hot oil is bacteriologically equivalent to dry heat.

bacteriology (bæk,tɪərɪ'ɒlədʒɪ). [f. as BACTERIDIUM: see -LOGY.] The scientific study of bacteria. **bac,teri'ologist**, a student of bacteriology. **bac,teri'oscopy**, microscopic investigation of bacteria.

1884 *Athenæum* 30 Aug. 281/2 In Germany it has become a separate study under the name of bacteriology. **1891** G. S. WOODHEAD *Bacteria* 412 Another great stand-by of bacteriologists is fuchsin. **1898** J. MᶜFARLAND *Pathogenic Bacteria* (ed. 2) 127 A very convenient simple apparatus used by bacteriologists.

bacteriolysin (bæktɪərɪ'ɒlɪsɪn, bæk,tɪərɪəʊ'laɪsɪn). Also *erron.* **-ine**. [Formed as next + -IN¹.] A substance formed in the body during an infectious disease which has the property of destroying the specific bacterium of the disease.

1900 tr. P. Ehrlich *Immunity* in *Proc. R. Soc.* LXVI. 441 The specific bacteriolysines, which dissolve the bacteria. **1908** R. T. HEWLETT *Bacteriology* (ed. 3) 157 The protection afforded by the anti-serum is therefore due to the destruction of the microbes by solution, the process being known as bacteriolysis, and the bodies which bring it about being termed bacteriolysins. **1949** H. W. FLOREY *Antibiotics* I. i. 48 He[*sc.* I. Schiller] suggested that the bacteriolysins against tubercle bacilli.. might be used therapeutically.

bacteriolysis (bæktɪərɪ'ɒlɪsɪs). [f. *bacterio-*, combining form of BACTERIUM + Gr. λύσις dissolution.] **1.** A name proposed for the artificial liquefaction of solid organic matter in sewage by means of certain bacteria.

1895 W. E. ADENEY in *Sci. Trans. R. Dublin Soc.* Sept. 544 Fermentation of gelatin, or other nitrogenous substance.. by the mixed organisms of soils and waters takes place in two perfectly distinct stages... In the first stage the organic substance is simply broken down... I shall call these two 'first' and 'second' stages of fermentation for want of better terms; new terms are, in fact, wanted to describe them properly. My friend Dr. E. A. Letts has suggested to me a term which seems to be very suitable for the first, viz. bacteriolysis. **1898** in E. C. S. MOORE *Sanitary Engineering* 474.

2. The destruction of bacteria by an antibacterial serum ('lysin' or 'antiserum').

1900 tr. P. Ehrlich *Immunity* in *Proc. R. Soc.* LXVI. 443 The Pfeiffer phenomenon of bacteriolysis. **1902** R. T. HEWLETT *Bacteriology* (ed. 2) 138 The protection afforded by the anti-serum is therefore due to the destruction of the microbes by solution, the process being known as bacteriolysis. **1906** A. C. ABBOTT *Bacteriology* (ed. 7) 568 The endotoxins.. are associated with the bacterial cells, and are only liberated through the solution of the bacteria—that is, through bacteriolysis.

bacteriolytic (bæk,tɪərɪəʊ'lɪtɪk), *a.* [Formed as prec. + Gr. λυτικός able to dissolve.] Capable of causing the destruction of bacteria; pertaining to or of the nature of bacteriolysis.

1900 in DORLAND *Med. Dict.* **1901** DUNGLISON *Med. Dict.* Suppl., *Bacteriolytic*, producing decomposition of bacteria. **1903** *Therapeutic Gaz.* 15 May 292 It was found that in nearly every case the bacteriolytic power of the blood was sufficient to destroy the typhoid bacillus. **1911** R. T. HEWLETT *Bacteriology* (ed. 4) 207 Some anti-microbic sera, *e.g.* anthrax serum, are not bacteriolytic. **1946** *Nature* 23 Nov. 745/1 (*heading*) Factors contributing to the bacteriolytic effect of species of Myxococci upon viable Eubacteria.

bacteriophage (bæk'tɪərɪəʊfeɪdʒ, -fɑːʒ). *Biol.* [ad. F. *bactériophage* (F. d'Herelle 1917, in *Comptes Rendus* CLXV. 375), f. as BACTERIOLYSIS + -PHAGE.] A minute organism or agent which destroys bacteria. Hence **,bacteri'ophagy**, the action of a bacteriophage; **bac,terio'phagal, -'phagic** *adjs.*, of, pertaining to, or having the action of a bacteriophage. Cf. PHAGE.

1921 *Chem. Abstr.* 3319 The bacteriophage of Herelle. **1922** *Lancet* 2 Sept. 515/1 Acting in an attenuated state in young, actively growing, surface cultures, the bacteriophagic principle produces bare areas amidst the growth, which are analogous to colonies and are to be looked upon as colonies of the bacteriophage. **1924** *Chem. Abstr.* 4173 Bacteriophagy. **1926** G. H. SMITH tr. *d'Herelle's Bacteriophage* 5 This.. gave a new proof that the dissolving principle actually regenerated in the course of the action. Further, it demonstrated that the principle was condensed in the form of active particles. It is to this principle that I have given the name Bacteriophage; the phenomenon of bacterial solution caused by it being termed Bacteriophagy. *Ibid.* 6 To attempt to reconcile 'bacteriolysis' and 'bacteriophagy', making them identical and co-extensive is a scientific absurdity. **1927** *Lancet* 10 Sept. 536/1 According to Bail, bacteriophagal action is due to the formation of minute (filter-passing) fragments from the bacterial cells. **1943** *Times* 29 Apr. 2/2 Minute organisms called bacteriophages, which destroy bacteria, have been rendered visible for the first time. **1944** *Electronic Engin.* XVI. 420 Another intestinal bacillus.. is seen being attacked by a crowd of small bacteriophages, the anti-bodies present in the human system that are able to defeat infection. **1957** *New Scientist* 9 May 12/1 Once inside the bacterium the nucleic acid of the bacteriophage initiates a process which culminates in the production of 100–200 new bacteriophage particles.

bacterioscopic (bæk,tɪərɪəʊ'skɒpɪk), *a.* [f. BACTERIOSCOPY + -IC.] Pertaining to bacterioscopy. Hence **,bacterio'scopically** *adv.*

1886 P. F. FRANKLAND in *Phil. Trans.* CLXXVIII. B. 119 The bacterioscopic examination of air. **1896** E. KLEIN *Micro-organisms* v. 67 (*heading*) Bacterioscopic Examination of Water. **1903** *Nature* 19 Feb. 370/2 The City Corporation has therefore caused a number of samples [of shell-fish] to be bacterioscopically examined by Dr. Klein.

bacteriosis (bæktɪərɪ'əʊsɪs). [mod.L.: see -OSIS.] Any disease of plants ascribed to the action of bacteria.

1899 G. MASSEE *Plant Diseases* 338 Bacteriosis of tomatoes. *Ibid.* 339 Pink bacteriosis of wheat. **1901** *Proc. R. Soc.* LXVII. 456 Arthur ascribes the action of bacteria in the bacteriosis of carnations to an enzyme.

bacteriostasis (bæk,tɪərɪəʊ'steɪsɪs). [f. *bacterio-*, combining form of BACTERIUM + Gr. στάσις stopping.] Inhibition of the growth of bacteria without destroying them. So **bacteriostatic** (-'stætɪk) *a.*, also as *sb.*; **bac'teriostat**, an agent that causes bacteriostasis.

1912 *Jrnl. Exper. Med.* XVI. 229 Its bacteriostatic action on the violet positive organisms is evident enough. **1918** C. H. BROWNING *Appl. Bacteriol.* v. 83 This property of inhibiting proliferation, or 'bacteriostatic action' as it has been termed by Gildersleeve.. is a remarkable phenomenon. **1920** *Jrnl. Amer. Med. Assoc.* 17 Jan. 145/1 The results of attempts to apply the selective bacteriostatic power of gentian violet to the treatment of infected wounds. The activity of the dye is described as bacteriostasis, the dye is called a bacteriostat, and its property is referred to as bacteriostatic. **1936** *Nature* 15 Aug. 295/1 Selective bacteriostasis (the inhibitory action of such substances as dyestuffs and the products of their own metabolism on the growth of bacteria and fungi). **1942** *Brit. Jrnl. Exper. Path.* XXIII. 123 (*title*) Proactinomycin: A 'Bacteriostatic' Produced by a Species of Proactinomyces. **1944** *Lancet* 17 June 792/2 Cultures whose growth is delayed or prevented by.. one of the substances called bacteriostats.

bacteriotherapeutic (bæk,tɪərɪəʊθɛrə'pjuːtɪk), *a.* [See next and THERAPEUTIC *a.*] Of or pertaining to bacteriotherapy.

1886 *Medical News* 10 July 41 Dr. Ballagi has carefully followed the bacteriotherapeutic details advised by Cantani.

bacteriotherapy (bæk,tɪərɪəʊ'θɛrəpɪ). [Gr. θεραπεία medical treatment.] Treatment of disease by introducing bacteria into the system.

1886 *Medical News* 10 July (*heading*) Bacteriotherapy of Phthisis Pulmonalis. **1949** H. W. FLOREY *Antibiotics* I. i. 5 Cantani [1885] believed that this method of bacterio-therapy might be applied to accessible infected surfaces.

bacteriotropin (bæk,tɪərɪəʊ'trɒpɪn). [f. *bacterio-*, combining form of BACTERIUM + Gr. -τροπος turning + -IN¹.] (See quot. 1910.)

1909 *Chem. Abstr.* 2180 (*title*) Tubercular immuno-opsonins (bacteriotropins). **1910** *Lancet* 25 June 1738/2 Neufeld and Rimpau drew attention to the presence in immune sera of a similar humoral substance, conditioning phagocytosis, but differing from Wright's opsonin in that it was thermostable. This they termed '*bacteriotropin*'. [In *Deut. Med. Wochenschr.* (1905) XXXI. 1610 they used the expression 'Bakteriotrope Substanzen'.—Ed.] **1961** *Brit. Med. Dict.* 169/2 *Bacteriotropin*, a heat-resisting opsonin which acts on bacteria, and which assists the phagocytes in their work. Also known as immune opsonin.

bacteritic (bæktə'rɪtɪk), *a. Med.* [f. next; see -ITIS, -ITIC.] Characterized by the (morbid) presence of bacteria.

1866 A. FLINT *Princ. Med.* 86 Bacteritic endocarditis.

bacterium (bæk'tɪərɪəm). Pl. **-a**; rarely anglicized as **bactery**. [mod.L., ad. Gr. βακτήριον, dim. of βάκτρον stick, staff.] **1.** Any of several types of microscopic or ultramicroscopic single-celled organisms very widely distributed in nature, not only in soil, water, and air, but also on or in many parts of the tissues of plants and animals, and forming one of the main biologically interdependent groups of organisms in virtue of the chemical changes which many of them bring about, e.g. all forms of decay and the building up of nitrogen compounds in the soil.

1847–9 TODD *Cycl. Anat. & Phys.* IV. 6/1 In Bacterium, the contraction is weaker. **1854** J. HOGG *Microsc.* II. i. (1867) 295 What part do the fungi, or bacteria, play in the production of.. cancer? **1884** *Health Exhib. Catal.* 155/1 Imperishable Yeast.. and Models of Yeast and Bacteries. **1908** *Daily Chron.* 6 Aug. 6/5 Dr. Stonehouse said it was a bacteria infection. **1911** J. A. THOMSON *Biology of Seasons* II. 161 Analogous, though not 'inter-regnal', is the intimate and most profitable partnership between Bacteria-like microbes and Leguminous plants, like Clover. **1956** *Nature* 11 Feb. 279/2 This trypanosomid, first isolated in bacteria-free culture by Noguchi and Tilden. **1964** M. HYNES *Med. Bacteriol.* (ed. 8) iii. 26 The foundation of modern surgery is asepsis—the creation and preservation of a bacterium-free environment.

2. bacteria bed, a contact bed (see CONTACT *sb.* 6).

1913 E. H. BLAKE *Drainage & Sanitation* xi. 369 This was the origin of the contact method of working bacteria beds—a method adopted with the septic tank. **1936** *Ibid.* (ed. 5) xi. 428 Such treatment is carried out in what are often called Bacteria Beds. These may be on the intermittent principle, in which case they are called Contact Beds, or on the continuous flow principle, in which case they are called Percolating Filters or Trickling Filters; in either case the cause of purification is aerobic bacteria.

bacteriuria (bæk,tɪərɪ'jʊərɪə). *Path.* Also **bacteruria**. [f. BACTERIUM + -URIA.] The presence of bacteria in the urine.

1889–90 H. E. KENDALL in *Maritime Med. News* (Halifax) II. 37 (*title*) Notes on two cases of bacteruria. **1900** DORLAND *Med. Dict.*, Bacteriuria. **1907** *Practitioner* Aug. 328 Septic bacteriuria.

bacterization (bæktəraɪ'zeɪʃən). [f. BACTER(IUM + -IZATION.] The process or method of treating with bacteria. So **'bacterize** *v. trans.*, **'bacterized** *ppl. a.*

1902 R. L. DEVONSHIRE tr. *Vallery-Radot's Life of Pasteur* II. i. 8 Typhoid fever, bacterization! Hospital miasma, bacterization! **1915** *Chambers's Jrnl.* Dec. 830/2 He has dealt more particularly with his latest invention—bacterised peat. **1949** FLOREY *Antibiotics* I. i. 44 In the next year Novogrudsky and his collaborators (1937).. proposed to 'bacterize' flax seeds in an endeavour to reduce fungus infection. *Ibid.*, The greatest changes could be brought about in wheat seeds by the joint bacterization with this special strain and *Azotobacter*.

bacteroid ('bæktərɔɪd), *a.* and *sb.* [f. BACTERIUM: see -OID; *bacterioid* would be a better form.] **A.** *adj.* Of the nature of, or allied to, the bacteria.

1855 GARROD *Mat. Med.* 143 A decided antiseptic, arresting the development of bacteroid organisms.

B. *sb.* A micro-organism of bacterial character; *spec.* one found (*a*) in the root-nodules of leguminous plants, (*b*) in the body of certain insects.

1878 *Parkes' Pract. Hygiene* (ed. 5) 63 Bacteria, vibriones, or microzymes... Frequently spoken of as Bacteroids. **1887** *Phil. Trans.* CLXXVIII. B. 552 The gemmules or 'bacteroids' [in the Leguminosæ]. **1898** R. T. HEWLETT *Bacteriology* 26 If the roots of a pea, bean, or vetch be examined, numerous little nodules will be found upon them; on examining these microscopically small irregular bodies are found to be present, which have been termed bacteroids. **1940** *Chambers's Techn. Dict.* 70/1 *Bacteroids*, in *Oligochaeta*, rod-like bodies of unknown function occurring in the connective tissue. **1949** in H. W. Florey et al. *Antibiotics* II. VIII. xxxi. 1024 Certain body cells of cockroaches contain gram positive micro-organisms known as bacteroids.

Bactrian ('bæktrɪən), *a.* (*sb.*) [ad. Gr. Βακτριανός, L. *Bactriānus*.] Of or belonging to Bactria, an ancient country of central Asia, lying between the Hindu-Kush and the Oxus. Also *sb.*, a native of this country.

Bactrian camel, the two-humped camel of central Asia; also *Bactrian*, ellipt.

1601 HOLLAND tr. *Pliny's Hist. World* VI. xxiii. 131 This country lieth overagainst the Bactrians. **1607** TOPSELL *Foure-Footed Beastes* 92 All those [camels] which are in India, are saide by Didimus to be bred in the Mountaines of the Bactrians,..and these are worthily called Bactrians, because they were first of all conceiued among them. *Ibid.* 94 They want hornes (I meane both the Arabian and Bactrian Camell). **1757** J. DYER *Fleece* IV. 345 O'er Bukor, Cabul, and the Bactrian vales. **1797** *Encycl. Brit.* II. 728/1 The Bactrians differed little in their manners from the Nomades. **1832** *Blackw. Mag.* XXXII. 207/2 The priests of Mithras..offered him..their Bactrian dromedaries, if he chose to depart. **1877** [see IRANIC *a.*]. **1908** *Animal Management* 276 The double humped camel, also called the 'Bactrian', is found in Turkestan, and throughout central Asia. **1912** H. G. RAWLINSON *Bactria* i. 15 The Bactrians were famous for their pithy proverbial sayings. **1927** W. J. TURNER *Aesthetes* 14 On a Bactrian Horse, T'ang period.

† '**bacul.** *Obs.* [ad. L. *baculum*.] Staff, crosier.

c **1449** PECOCK *Repr.* III. xvi. 386 Chalice, mytir, bacul.

bacule, variant of BASCULE.

baculere, obs. form of BACHELOR.

baculine ('bækjʊlaɪn), *a.* [f. L. *baculum*, *-us* rod, stick + -INE.] Of or pertaining to the rod, or to punishment by caning or flogging.

1710 HUME *Sacr. Success.* (1716) 227 This baculine objection being fairly encounter'd. **1858** THACKERAY *Virginians* I. v. 38 The baculine method was a common mode of argument.

baculite ('bækjʊlaɪt). *Palæont.* [f. as prec. + -ITE.] A genus of fossil cephalopods, with chambered cylindrical shells.

1822 PARKINSON *Fossil Org. Rem.* 166 Baculites, A multi-locular straight, or slightly bent, cylindrical, or slightly conical shell. **1841** H. MILLER *O.R. Sandst.* viii. 171 The belemnites, baculites, turrilites, of the Cretaceous group.

baculometry (bækjuː'lɒmɪtrɪ). [f. as prec. + Gr. -μετρία: see -METRY.] 'The Art of measuring accessible or inaccessible Distances, or Lines, by the help of one or more Staves.' Phillips 1706.

baculum ('bækjʊləm). *Zool.* [mod.L., f. L., stick, staff.] The penis-bone (see PENIS b).

1939 I. F. & W. D. HENDERSON *Dict. Sci. Terms* (ed. 3) 32/1 *Baculum*, the penis bone; os priapi. **1949** A. S. ROMER *Vertebrate Body* vii. 175 A *baculum*..is a heterotopic bone, which is the skeleton of the penis, found in all insectivores, bats, rodents, and carnivores, and in all primates except man.

bacun, bacynet, obs. ff. BACON, -KEN, BASINET.

bad (bæd), *a.* (and *sb.*) Also 4–6 badd(e. [ME. *badde* appears in end of 13th c., rare till end of 14th: see below. Regularly compared *badder*, *baddest*, from 14th to 18th c. (in De Foe 1721), though Shakspere has only the modern substitutes *worse*, *worst*, taken over from *evil*, *ill*, after *bad* came to be = *evil*.

Prof. Zupitza, with great probability, sees in *bad-de* (2 syll.) the ME. repr. of OE. *bæddel* 'homo utriusque generis, hermaphrodita,' doubtless like Gr. ἀνδρόγυνος, and the derivative *bædling* 'effeminate fellow, womanish man, μαλακός,' applied contemptuously; assuming a later adjectival use, as in *yrming*, *wrecca*, and loss of final *l* as in *mycel*, *muche*, *lytel*, *lyte*, *wencel*, *wench(e*. This perfectly suits the ME. form and sense, and accounts satisfactorily for the want of early written examples. And it is free from the many historical and phonetic difficulties of the derivation proposed by Sarrazin (*Engl. Studien* VI. 91, VIII. 66), who, comparing the etymology of *madde*, *mad*, earlier *amad(de*:—OE. *ȝemǣded* (see AMAD), would refer *badde* to OE. *ȝebǣded*, *ȝebǣdd*, 'forced, oppressed,' with a sense-development parallel to that of L. *captīvus*, 'taken by force, enslaved, captive,' It. *cattivo*, F. *chetif*, 'miserable, wretched, despicable, worthless.' No other suggestion yet offered is of any importance; the Celtic words sometimes compared are out of the question.]

A. *adj.* **I.** In a privative sense: Not good.

1. a. Of defective quality or worth, 'of no good'; below par, poor, worthless, 'wretched,' 'miserable'; that one does not *think much* (or anything) of.

1297 R. GLOUC. 108 Wat is vs to lete þis badde kyng Go þus o liue as a schade, þat nys worþ noþing? *c* **1350** *Will. Palerne* 5024 Of here atir for to telle to badde is my witte. *c* **1386** CHAUCER *Monk's T.* 430 [In prison] Mete and drynke he hadde..it was ful poure and badde. **1393** GOWER *Conf.* II. 47 Her sadel eke was wonder badde. *c* **1440** *Promp. Parv.* 20/2 Badde, or nowght worthe, *invalidus*. *a* **1553** UDALL *Roister D.* v. ii, Better a bad scuse then none. **1732** POPE *Horace Sat.* II. ii. 63 Nor stops, for one bad cork, his butler's pay. **1873** BLACK *Pr. Thule* xxiv. 413 Sometimes they sent him a letter; but he was a bad correspondent.

b. *bad air*: corrupt, vitiated air, which cannot sustain healthy respiration; ***bad coin, penny***: debased, false coin; also *fig*; ***bad debts***: debts that cannot be realized; ***bad food***: food deficient in nourishment. ***to go bad***: to decay. ***with bad grace***: unwillingly. Also (chiefly *dial.*), in arrears (cf. BAD *sb.* 1 b. *b*). Also ***bad egg, bad form, bad hat, bad lot***, etc.: see the sbs.

1393 LANGL. *P. Pl.* C. XVIII. 73 Men may lykne letterid men..to a badde peny. **1601** SHAKS. *Jul. C.* I. ii. 252, I durst not laugh, for feare of opening my Lippes, and receyuing the bad Ayre. **1622** MALYNES *Anc. Law Merch.* 124 If any bad debts should be made thereby. **1773** JOHN WESLEY *Jrnl.* 21 Aug. (1916) V. 522 Our income does not yet answer our expense. We were again near two hundred pounds bad. **1779** in *Proc. Wesley Hist. Soc.* (1930) XVII. 158 Destroyed a bad shilling. **1782** COWPER *Expostulation* in *Poet. Wks.* (1905) 52 Perjuries are common as bad pence. **1798** MALTHUS *Popul.* (1878) 68 Children perished..from bad nourishment. **1832** LANDER *Exp. Niger* III. xvii. 44 Our people set about loading the canoe..but with bad grace. **1855** MACAULAY *Hist. Eng.* IV. xxi, The misery caused in a single year by bad crowns and bad shillings. **1858** [see LAW *sb.*[1] 17 c (*d*)]. **1866** CRUMP *Banking* xi. 244 As the price of the article increases, so do the bad debts increase. **1881** A. B. EVANS *Leicestershire Words* 96 'I'n got a quarter *bad* in my rent.' 'His illness threw us *bad* with the clothing-club.' **1884** *St. James's Gaz.* 17 Oct. 3/2 The suffering that comes from bad food, bad air, bad clothing. **1884** *Daily News* 25 Dec. 3/4 It 'goes bad' more readily than..cooked butcher's meat. **1937** A. CHRISTIE *Dumb Witness* x. 111 Always hard up—always in debt—always returning like a bad penny from all over the world. **1962** S. E. MARTIN in Householder & Saporta *Problems in Lexicography* 155 Some bad pennies of everyday conversation are shunned by dictionaries.

c. Colloq. phrases ***not bad, not so bad, not half bad***: used (usu. pred.) of a state of things, the result of an effort, etc.: less bad than it might be (or have been); hence, by meiosis, fairly good, deserving some praise or congratulation.

1771 C. BURNEY *Pres. State Mus.* 65 The *intermezzo* was not bad; the music pretty, but old. **1810** C. STEWART tr. *Mirza Abu Taleb Khan's Travels* II. xxiv. 133 The gentlemen put up with bad food, and worse wine; and whenever I complained, they took great pains to persuade me the things were not so bad, or that the master of the house was not in fault. **1835** *Naut. Mag.* IV. 689 The idea of a sailor's *chemise* is not bad. **1838** in E. Eden '*Up the Country*' (1866) I. 129 These [letters] are five months old, but that is not so bad. **1839** *Mag. Dom. Econ.* May 332 Leaving out the cheese, the thing itself is not so very bad. **1860** *Englishwoman's Dom. Mag.* Oct. 26 'Not bad!' Bloomfield replied with a loud laugh. **1867** *Field* 6 Apr. 246/3 This is not half bad,..a fish a-piece, although we were clean till four o'clock. **1871, 1886** [see HALF *adv.* 3]. **1899** KIPLING *Stalky* 220 'Not half bad years, either,' said M'Turk. **1900** W. R. KENNEDY *Hurrah Life Sailor* xii. 180 We had bagged three bulls before breakfast, which was not so bad. **1925** W. DEEPING *Sorrell & Son* xvii. 163 'Did they make it rather beastly—for you?' 'O, not so bad, pater.' **1954** WODEHOUSE & BOLTON *Bring on Girls* i. 19 'What did you think of our little entertainment?'..'Not bad,' said Plum.

d. *colloq.* (orig. *U.S.*). Discomfited, sad, or contrite; in low spirits. Esp. in phr. *to feel bad* (*about*): to be embarrassed or unhappy about (a situation, etc.). Cf. *to feel good* s.v. GOOD *a.* 3 c.

1839 MARRYAT *Diary Amer.* 1st Ser. II. 33 *Bad* is used in an odd sense: it is employed for awkward, uncomfortable, sorry. **1871** E. EGGLESTON *Hoosier Schoolmaster* ix. 83 'Why, how do you feel?' 'Kind o' bad and lonesome, and like as if I wanted to die.' **1876** J. SMITH *Archie & Bess* 46 Mind he's aye yer faither; an' he's unco bad aboot ye. **1887** W. H. HERNDON *Let.* Jan. in E. Hertz *Hidden Lincoln* (1940) 161 Tiger felt bad about the matter. **1911** G. B. SHAW *Blanco Posnet* 405 We can do it yet if you feel really bad about it. **1942** L. HUGHES *Shakespeare in Harlem* 6, I wonder if white folks ever feel bad, Getting up in the morning lonesome and sad? **1960** E. STOPP tr. *St. Francis de Sales' Sel. Lett.* 93 Naturally, when you get news of some scandal you feel very bad about it. **1986** *Los Angeles Times* 12 Sept. v. 9/1 He had spanked his daughter... It didn't work, he said. 'She just cried more and I felt bad.'

2. Incorrect, faulty. ***bad shot***: a wrong guess.

1688 *Lond. Gaz.* No. 2309/4 He speaks but bad English. **1767** FORDYCE *Serm. Yng. Wom.* I. i. 25 They learn..to speak bad French. **1845** KINGLAKE *Eothen* viii. 137, I secretly smiled at this last prophecy as a 'bad shot.' **1849** MACAULAY *Hist. Eng.* II. 110 Some bad translations of Bossuet's works. *Mod. slang*, Oh! that's very bad form!

3. *Law.* Not valid.

1883 SIR W. BRETT *Law Rep.* XI. *Queen's B.* 561 The claim is bad. **1884** *Law Times Rep.* 12 Apr. 194/1 Such a defence was bad..and could not be sustained.

4. a. Lacking good or favourable qualities; unfortunate, unfavourable; that one does not *like*.

1393 GOWER *Conf.* I. 88 They despise The good fortune as the badde. *c* **1425** in *E.E.P.* (1862) 139 My chawnce ys bad, I trow that fortune be my fo. **1602** WARNER *Alb. Eng.* XII. lxxii. 298 He shall participate my best, that must my badder plight. **1664** H. MORE *Myst. Iniq.* 540 It will bring in a *Principle* of badder consequence. **1671** MILTON *P.R.* IV. 1 Perplexed and troubled at his bad success. **1751** JORTIN *Serm.* (1771) IV. i. 23 This is humility, but it is so only in a bad sense. **1883** *Manch. Exam.* 20 Nov. 5/5 A bad pre-eminence as the hotbeds of pulmonary diseases.

b. Possessing an abundance of favourable qualities; of a musical performance or player: going to the limits of free improvisation; of a lover: extravagantly loving. *slang.* (orig. and chiefly *U.S.*, esp. ***Jazz*** and ***Black English***).

1928 R. FISHER *Walls of Jericho* xvi. 182 This crack army o' Joshua's..walk around, blowin' horns... The way they blow on them is too bad. **1955** L. FEATHER *Encycl. Jazz* x. 345 *Bad*, adj. Good. (This reverse adjectival procedure is commonly used to describe a performance.) **1959** *N.Y. Times* 15 Nov. II. 2 Jazzmen often call a thing 'terrible' or 'bad' when they like it very much. **1971** *Black World* Apr. 87, I say *read* these poets of the Seventies. They got something bad to say. **1977** B. GARFIELD *Recoil* ii. 30 'We had all kinds of activities..that's a *bad* place.' 'When "bad" comes to mean the spectacularly good, I wonder what that tells us about ourselves?' **1980** *Time* 16 June 49 Adds longtime Fan Carolyn Collins: 'Oh man, I don't think he's changed. He got quiet for a while but he's still cool-blooded. He's still bad.' Bad as the best and as cool as they come, Smokey is remarkably low key for a soul master.

II. In a positive sense: Evil, ill, noxious.

5. Morally depraved; immoral, wicked, vicious.

(The first quot. may have sense 1: 'wretched caitiffs.')

a **1300** *Cursor M.* 1801 Þai greued þan þaa caitiues badd. **1393** GOWER *Conf.* I. 196 One Thelous..whiche al was bad; A fals knight. *c* **1440** *Promp. Parv.* 20/2 Bad, or wykyde, *Malus*. **1599** SANDYS *Europæ Spec.* (1632) 125 The baddest man among the Cardinalls is chosen to be Pope. **1609** BELL *Theoph. & Remig.* 2 Badder life and wickeder dealing was neuer more frequent. **1767** FORDYCE *Serm. Yng. Wom.* II. viii. 13 Young people..are often corrupted by bad books. **1849** MACAULAY *Hist. Eng.* II. 50 Discreet counsellors implored the royal brothers not to countenance this bad man.

6. Causing inconvenience, displeasure, or pain; unpleasant, offensive, disagreeable; troublesome, painful. ***bad blood***: harsh, angry feeling.

1515 BARCLAY *Eclogues*, Bad is the colour, the savor badder is. **1622** R. HAWKINS *Voy. S. Sea* 54 The..bad entreatie which the negros gave them. **1794** NELSON in Nicolas *Disp.* I. 412 Had not the weather been so bad. **1825** *Bro. Jonathan* I. 74 If there be any bad blood in a fellow, he will show it. **1855** MACAULAY *Hist. Eng.* III. 38 The old soldiers of James were generally in a very bad temper. **1869** Hazlitt's *Eng. Prov.*, Bad words make a woman worse. **1873** SKEAT in *Piers Pl.* (C.) Pref. 32, It is too bad to suppose that, etc.

7. Causing injury to health; injurious, hurtful, noxious, dangerous, pernicious. Const. *for*.

1653 A. WILSON *Jas. I.* Pref. 4 To remove the accrescion of bad Humours. *a* **1719** ADDISON (J.) Reading was bad for his eyes. **1855** MACAULAY *Hist. Eng.* IV. 723 He had just had a bad fall in hunting. **1861** FLOR. NIGHTINGALE *Nursing* 56 The old four-post bed with curtains is bad, whether for sick or well.

8. In ill health, suffering from disease or injury, in pain.

1748 RICHARDSON *Clarissa* (1811) IV. 259 Still very bad with my Gout. **1763** MRS. HARRIS in *Priv. Lett. 1st Ld. Malmesbury* I. 90 She was so bad yesterday that she could not open her mouth. **1840** R. DANA *Bef. the Mast* xxxii. 122 One of our watch was laid up..by a bad hand.

B. quasi-*sb.*

1. a. *absol.* That which is bad; bad condition, quality, etc.

1591 SHAKS. *Two Gent.* II. vi. 13 T'exchange the bad for better. **1670** G. H. *Hist. Cardinals* II. III. 182 A capacity of penetrating into the good and bad of an affair. **1816** WORDSW. *Sonn. Liberty* II. xlvi, So bad proceeded propagating worse.

b. ***to the bad***: (*a*) to a bad condition, to ruin; (*b*) to the wrong side of the account, in deficit.

1816 'QUIZ' *Grand Master* VIII. 25 I've really to the bad Some thousand of rupees to add. **1864** T. TROLLOPE *Lindisf. Chase* I. 46 [He] went, as the common saying expressively phrases it—to the bad. **1884** *Pall Mall G.* 6 Feb. 4 He was between £70 and £80 to the bad.

c. ***in bad***: out of favour (*with*, etc.), in bad odour. *colloq.* (orig. *U.S.*).

1911 *San Francisco Examiner* 12 June 10 You'll be on the stand today—now we're in bad if you let out anything. **1915** WODEHOUSE *Psmith, Journalist* iv. 26 Any time you're in bad. Glad to be of service. **1920** —— *Coming of Bill* II. xiv. 236, I guess this has put me in pretty bad with Mamie. **1923** E. WALLACE *Missing Million* xiii. 109 You're never satisfied till you get a man in bad. **1944** L. A. G. STRONG *Director* 63 I'm in bad with your father for the minute. **1953** K. AMIS *Lucky Jim* v. 57 This ought to put me nicely in bad with the Neddies.

2. *sb.* (with *pl.*) A bad thing, quality, etc; *rarely*, a bad person. (Not in ordinary speech.)

1592 LYLY *Mydas* v. ii. 57 An inventorie of all Motto's moveable baddes and goods. **1586** WARNER *Alb. Eng.* III. xiv. 65 That of two bads, for betters choyse he backe againe did goe. **1602** *Ibid.* x. lvii. (1612) 252 For Popes be impudent, and bads their blessings neuer mis. **1869** RUSKIN *Q. of Air* §125 But, as there is this true relation between money and 'goods,' or good things, so there is a false relation between money and 'bads,' or bad things.

C. quasi-*adv.* **a.** = BADLY. Now chiefly *U.S.*

1611 BROUGHTON *Require Agreem.* 78 Our minde holdeth all badder then we can speake. **1681** GLANVILL *Sadducismus* II. Pref., Haunted almost as bad as Mr. Mompesson's house. **1806** in *Charges agst. the Duke of York* (1809) 413 The Regt he is in did their exercise so bad that the Duke swore at them. **1816** U. BROWN *Jrnl.* in *Maryland Hist. Mag.* (1915) X. 273 Land of not much account, farm'd bad. **1846** J. J. HOOPER *Adv. Simon Suggs* vii. 94 'Pshaw!' said Suggs, 'you aint bad hurt.' **1848** THACKERAY *Van. Fair* liv. 483 I didn't do my duty with the regiment so bad. **1854** S. HALE *Lett.* (1919) 7 The children..during that time act as bad as they can! **1870** *Trans. Ill. State Agric. Soc.* VIII. 238 This speaks bad for our application of the art. **1888** *Daily Inter-Ocean* 9 Mar. (Farmer), As the case now stands, the defense want Myers, and want him bad. **1895** 'ROSEMARY' *Under Chilterns* iii. 92 Las' week there was a job doin' up at the squire's, an' I wanted to go bad. **1901** M. E. RYAN *That Girl Montana* 3 There is one thing I want in this world, and want bad. **1938** M. K. RAWLINGS *Yearling* iii. 26 The meat's bad tore up. *Ibid.* iv. 39 She's bad hurt.

b. ***bad off***: badly off; in a bad or poor condition or circumstances; esp. = POOR *a.* 1 a. *U.S. dial.*

1815 HUMPHREYS *Yankee in Eng.* 77 Bad as I am off, I wouldn't swop conditions. **1817** U. BROWN *Jrnl.* in *Maryland Hist. Mag.* (1916) XI. 371 Land full of Lime Stone..bad off for Timber and Water. **1879** TOURGÉE *Fool's Err.* xxix. 179, I told him how bad off I was. **1934** L. HELLMAN *Children's Hour* (1937) III. 121, I only came cause she's so bad off.

D. *Comb.*, as ***bad-blooded, -boding, -hearted, -looker, -looking, -tempered, -weather.***

1928 A. HUXLEY *Point Counter Point* vii. 115 Insolent, *bad-blooded young cub! **1594** GREENE *Fr. Bacon* (1861) 171 Fond Ate, doomer of *bad-boding fates. **1594** SHAKS. *Rich. III*, IV. iv. 122 Bett'ring thy losse, makes the *bad causer worse. **1827** SCOTT in Lockhart *Life* (1839) IX. 128 He was generous and far from *bad-hearted. **1930** E. WAUGH *Vile Bodies* ii. 21 Not a *bad-looker herself, if it comes to that. **1863** MISS WHATELY *Ragged Life* vii. 55 They were not a *bad-looking circle. **1914** G. B. SHAW *Pygmalion* (1916) IV, Youre not bad-looking: it's quite a pleasure to look at you sometimes. **1879** ROGET *Thesaurus* (new ed.) §901 Irascible; *bad-, ill-tempered. **1922** JOYCE *Ulysses* 218 Virtuous: but occasionally they were also bad-tempered. **1883** *Man. Seamanship for Boys' Training Ships* 48 Q. What are storm trysails? A. *Bad weather sails, fitted similar to other gaff sails. **1897** *Daily News* 15 Oct. 5/1 There are.. some redeeming features even in cyclonic or bad weather systems. **1936** J. DESCHIN *New Ways in Photogr.* ii. 29 Bad-weather photography requires more zeal on the part of the hobbyist.

†**bad, badde,** *sb. Obs. rare.* ? A cat.

c **1350** *Alexander* (ed. Stevenson) 1763 As ratons or ruȝe myse in a rowme chambre, About in beddis or in bernys, þare baddis [*v.r.* baddez] are nane. [Cf. Halliwell, '*Bad*, A rural game played with a bad-stick... It probably resembled the game of cat.' Cf. also Sc. *badrans*, BAUDRONS.]

bad, badd, obs. forms of BADE, BODE.

Badarian (bəˈdɛərɪən, -ˈɑːrɪən), *a. Archæol.* [f. *Badari*, name of district in Egypt + -AN.]

Of or designating the ancient pre-Dynastic culture, evidence of which was first discovered in the Badari region of Egypt in 1924.

1924 *Brit. Sch. Archæol. in Egypt, Catal. Antiq. at Qua* 3 Beyond are some of the bowls of this oldest culture known, which we may call Badarian. **1925** *Glasgow Herald* 29 Aug. 10/1 The Badarian civilisation was widespread and covered a long period. **1931** *Discovery* Sept. 293/2 Objects from the earlier Badarian and Tasian cultures included well-preserved examples of the delicate black 'ripple' ware.

baddeleyite (ˈbædəlɪaɪt). *Min.* [f. the name *Baddeley* (see quot. 1894) + -ITE^1.] A mineral, consisting chiefly of zirconia, found in Ceylon and Brazil, and used as a refractory material.

1894 L. FLETCHER in *Mineral. Mag.* X. 158 For this new mineral I beg to propose the name *Baddeleyite*, in honour of Mr. Joseph Baddeley, by whom the interesting dense minerals of Rakwana have been brought to the notice of the mineralogical world. **1896** A. H. CHESTER *Dict. Min.* 24 *Baddeleyite*..Zirconia, in black crystals, resembling columbite. **1955** BROWN & DEY *India's Min. Wealth* (ed. 3) v. 253 Baddeleyite (or brazilite) the natural oxide of zirconium (ZrO_2).

badder, obs. comparative of BAD.

badderlocks. *Sc.* [perh. for *Balderlocks*, f. BALDER (M. J. Berkeley in *Treas. Bot.*)]. A seaweed (*Alaria esculenta*), 'the best of all the esculent Algæ when eaten raw.'

1789 LIGHTFOOT *Fl. Scot.* 938 Eatable Fucus: Badderlocks. **1830** *Edin. Encycl.* III. 442 The great tangle.. and the badderlocks, or hen ware.

baddish (ˈbædɪʃ), *a.* [f. BAD *a.* + -ISH.] Rather bad, indifferent, inferior, poor.

1755 E. MOORE *World* No. 154 To see the Country-wife, a baddish sort of a play. **1767** Fox in *Mem. & Corr.* I. 44, I can get two actors for him, one goodish and one baddish. **1865** CARLYLE *Fredk. Gt.* VI. XVI. vi. 190 A gadding.. female, with whom poor Uncle had a baddish life.

ˈbaddishness. [f. prec. + -NESS.] Baddish quality or condition; indifference, inferiority.

1824 W. IRVING *T. Trav.* II. 144 The baddishness of the crops.

baddy (ˈbædɪ). *colloq.* (orig. *U.S.*). [f. BAD *a.* + -Y^6. Prob. shortened from BAD MAN.] A criminal or desperado (cf. BAD MAN), *esp.* a villain in a play or film, esp. a western; hence *gen.* (as a jocular designation), a person of bad character.

1937 in *Amer. Speech* (1938) Apr. 107/1 One of the screen's consistent baddies, Bruce Cabot, feels the effect of the regime of vigorous villains. **1951** J. FRAME *Lagoon* 79 We got shouted to the pictures..where we cheered the goodies and booed the baddies. **1958** *Times Lit. Suppl.* 25 Apr. 226/1 The Communists are goodies and John L. Lewis is a baddy.

bade, pa. t. of BID *v.*; obs. f. BODE *sb.* and *v.*

†**baˈdeen,** *a. Obs. rare*$^{-1}$. [a. F. *badin, -ine*, derivative of Pr. *bad-ar*:—late L. *badāre* to gape. *Badin* was in earlier usage 'silly,' as if 'gaping.' Cf. BADINAGE *sb.*] Frivolous, jesting.

1685 F. SPENCE *Medici* 453 A dialogue compleatly boufon, waggish, and badeen, between the head and the cap.

†**badelar.** *Obs. rare*$^{-1}$. [a. F. *badelaire.*] A short broad sword curved like a scimitar.

1693 URQUHART *Rabelais* III. Prol., Cutlasses, Badelars.

†**ˈbadelyng.** *Obs.* [? for *paddling*: see quot. 1603.] An early term for 'a brood' of ducks.

1486 *Bk. St. Albans* F vj a, A badelyng of Dokis. [**1603** HOLLAND *Plutarch's Mor.* 344 Dolphins..strive to be doussing, badling, and diving together with them.]

badge (ˈbædʒ), *sb.* Forms: 4–7 **bage**, 5–7 **bagge**, 7 **badg**, 5– **badge**. [First in ME.: also in 15th c. Anglo-Lat. *bagia, bagea*, from the vernacular word. Also OF. *bage*: a single instance in Godefroy, of date 1465. Of unknown origin. See conjectures in Mätzner, Wedgwood, Müller, Skeat.]

1. A distinctive device, emblem, or mark, used originally to identify a knight or distinguish his followers (= *cognizance* in *Her.*), and now worn as a sign of office or licensed employment, as a token of membership in some society, etc., etc.

c **1350** *Alexander* (St.) 4180 [The fire] tinds on tend lowe trappour of stede..Bages and baners it blemyschid. *c* **1440** *Promp. Parv.* 20/2 Bage, or bagge of armys, *Banidium.* ?*c* **1450** *MS. Lincoln* A i. 17 lf. 141 (Halliw.) He beris of golde a semely sighte, His bagges are sabylle ylkane. **1485** CAXTON *Paris & V.* (1868) 8 Came to the lystes with their badges and tokens. **1530** PALSGR., Badge of a gentylman—*la deuise dung seignevr.* **1513–75** *Diurn. Occurr.* (1833) 158 My lord regentis armes and bage. **1618** ROWLANDS *Sacr. Mem.* 50 The Crosse, which Christians for their badge do weare. **1678** *Trans. Crt. Spain* 131 To wear a badg that they may beg alms. **1800** COLQUHOUN *Comm. Thames* xi. 328 They have their names and numbers on a metal Badge. **1879** DIXON *Windsor* II. xv. 161 She tore the Lancastrian badges from her clothes.

2. *gen.* A distinguishing 'sign,' emblem, token, or symbol of any kind: **a.** *transf.* of things material.

1526 TINDALE *Acts* xxviii. 11 Whose badge was Castor and Pollux. **1597** SHAKS. *2 Hen. IV*, IV. iii. 113 The Liuer white, and pale; which is the Badge of Pusillanimitie, and Cowardize. **1705** *Lond. Gaz.* No. 4140/4 The Badges or Marks put on Houses Insured by the Friendly Society. **1774** J. BRYANT *Mythol.* I. 62 A brazier of live coals carried before him as a badge of his office. **1872** FREEMAN *Norm. Conq.* IV. xviii. 104 The fortresses, the special badges of foreign rule.

b. *fig.* of things immaterial.

1529 MORE *Supplic. Soules* Wks. 314/1 The deuils badge ..yᵉ badge we meane of malice & of a very deadli deuilish hate. **1596** SHAKS. *Merch. V.* I. i. 111 For suffrance is the badge of all our Tribe. **1719** W. WOOD *Surv. Trade* 295 Monopolies, the Badges of a slavish People. **1868** M. PATTISON *Academ. Org.* §6. 237 The degrees have become social badges. **1875** STUBBS *Const. Hist.* I. vii. 167 The possession of land has become the badge of freedom.

3. *Naval Arch.* (See quot.)

1769 in FALCONER *Dict. Marine.* *c* **1850** *Rudim. Nav.* (Weale) 94 *Badge*, a sort of ornament fixed on the quarters of small vessels near the stern, containing either a sash for the convenience of the cabin, or the representation of it. **1867** SMYTH *Sailor's Word-bk.* s.v., Quarter badges, false quarter-galleries in imitation of frigate-built ships.

4. *Comb.*, as ***badge-ticket***; **badge-man**, one who wears a badge, a licensed beggar or almsman; also, *spec.* an official porter.

1790 BURKE *Fr. Rev.* Wks. V. 352 No man ever..will glory in belonging to the Chequer No. 71, or to any other badge-ticket. **1804** W. COOKE *Mem. Charles Macklin* 11 After being some time in Dublin, he got settled as a badge-man in Trinity College. **1809** CRABBE *Tales* 16 With thickset coat of Badge-man's blue. **1904** *Daily Chron.* 30 July 7/7 They deprive the licensed porters, or 'badge' men..of work.

badge (bædʒ), *v.*^{1} [f. prec. sb.] *trans.* To mark with, or distinguish by, a badge.

1380 WYCLIF *Sel. Wks.* (1871) III. 60 þus þei ben baggid wiþ signes of ipocrysie. **1599** [see BADGED]. **1737** SWIFT *Wks.* (1761) III. 336 Badging the original poor of every parish, who begged in the streets. **1880** *Daily Tel.* 28 Oct., A hyæna ..numbered and badged by the Local Board of Works.

†**badge,** *v.*^{2} *Obs.* Also in 6 bagge. [Origin unknown; app. the source of *badger* sb.^{1} (though it may have been a back-formation from that word taken as an agent-noun). Fuller derived it from L. *bājulāre* to carry (as if a cant contraction *baj.*, cf. the modern *zoo., cab.*, etc.), but evidence is required before this can be admitted for the 15th c.] To deal as a badger; to hawk for sale; to buy up (provisions) for the purpose of selling again elsewhere; *hence*, to regrate.

1552 BP. HOOPER in Strype's *Cranmer* App. 135 The Statute of Regrators is so usid, that in many quarters of these partes it wil do little good: and in some parts, where as licence by the Justices wil not be grauntyd, the people are mouche offendid, that they shuld not, as wel as other, bagge as they were wount to do. [Cf. BADGER 1, quot. 1552.] **1605** J. DAVIES *Humour's Heav. on E.* (1876) 37 Some others followed her [*i.e.* Fortune] by badging land. **1611** in *North Riding Rec.* (1884) I. 240 Marm. Foxton of Brompton [presented] for badging of butter. **1700** R. GOUGH *Hist. Myddle* 115 His imployment was buying corne in one markett towne and selling it in another, which is called badgeing. **1729–72** JACOB *Law Dict.*, *Kidder*..one that badges, or carries corn, dead victual, or other merchandize up and down to sell.

badge *v.*^{3}, variant of BAG *v.*^{2}

badged (bædʒd), *ppl. a.* [f. BADGE *v.*^{1} + -ED.] Distinguished or marked by a badge.

1599 MARSTON *Sco. Villanie* II. vii. 207 A cart? a tumbrell? no a badged coach. **1605** SHAKS. *Macb.* II. iii. 107 Their Hands and Faces were all badg'd with blood. **1861** SALA *Tw. round Clock* 95 Maledicted by the badged Jehus.

badgeless (ˈbædʒlɪs), *a.* [f. BADGE *sb.* + -LESS.] Without badge or cognizance.

1599 BP. HALL *Sat.* IV. v. 38 To get some badge-less blew upon his backe. **1855** SINGLETON *Virgil* II. 466 Afoot with naked falchion, and unawed With badgeless buckler.

badger (ˈbædʒə(r)), *sb.*^{1} Forms: 5 **bager**, 7 (?) **bodger**, **budger**, 5– **badger**. [See BADGE *v.*^{2}, and note below.]

One who buys corn and other commodities and carries them elsewhere to sell; an itinerant dealer who acts as a middleman between producer (farmer, fisherman, etc.) and consumer; a cadger, hawker, or huckster. Still common in the dialects.

By Act 5 and 6 Edw. VI. c. 14 §7 Badgers were required to be licensed by the Justices (the origin of the hawker's license). Among the commodities in which they are said to have dealt are named corn (especially), fish, butter, and cheese. They were obnoxious to the charge of *regrating*, and hence the word is in some 17th c. vocabularies, e.g. Robertson's *Phraseol. Gen.* (196), explained as 'an ingrosser, a forebuyer, or forestaller of the market, one that buyeth corn and other provisions beforehand.'

a **1500** *Office of Mayor of Bristol* in *E.E. Gilds* 424 The bagers, such as bryngeth whete to towne, as wele in trowys, as otherwyse, by lande and by watir. **1552** *Act 5–6 Edw. VI*, xiv. §7 The Buying of any Corn, Fish, Butter, or Cheese, by any such Badger, Lader, Kidder or Carrier, as shall bee assigned and allowed to that office or doing by three Justices of peace. **1562** *Act 5 Eliz.* xii, Badgers of Corn, and Drovers of Cattle, to be licensed. **1587** FLEMING *Contn. Holinshed* III. 588/2 No badger, baker, brewer, or purueior, to buie graine, vntill an houre after the full market begin. **1610** HOLLAND *Camden's Brit.* I. 555 All the inhabitants be as it were a kind of hucksters, or badgers. **1641** BEST *Farm. Bks.* (1856) 101 The badgers come farre, many of them; wheare fore theire desire is to buy soone, that they may be goinge betimes, for feare of beinge nighted. **1674** RAY *N. Countr. Wds.*, *Badger*, such as buy Corn, or other Commodities in one place, and carry them to another. **1695** KENNETT *Par. Antiq.* Gloss. s.v. *Cart-body, Badger, Budger*, or *Bodger*, i.e. a carrier or retailer of Bodges or bags of corn. **1788** W. MARSHALL *E. Yorkshire*, *Badger*, a huckster. **1825** BRITTON *Beauties of Wiltsh.*, *Badger*, a corn-dealer. **1858** *Ladies Bever Hollow* II. iv. 68 'Our Butter fetches a penny a pound more than other people's from the badger.' **1863** ATKINSON *Whitby Gloss.*, *Badger*, a huckster; a man who goes about the country with ass and panniers, to buy up butter, eggs, and fruit, which he will sell at a near market-town; and before shops were common in every village, he dealt in needles, thread, trimmings, and the like, for which he was open to exchange. [Also in the following Glossaries of E.D.S.: *Swaledale* (Meal-seller), *Huddersf.*, *Mid Yorksh.*, *Cumbrld.* (Flour or corn-dealer; also pedlar, huckster), *Worcester*, *N. Lancash.* (Travelling huckster or dealer, cadger), *Lancash.* (Keeper of small provision shop).]

[*Note.* Conjectures as to the derivation, and possible connexion with next word, depend greatly upon the original meaning. On the assumption that this was 'corn-merchant,' *bager, badger*, has been identified with obs. F. *bladier*, 'a Marchant or Ingrosser of corne,' Cotgr. (properly Provençal = OF. *blaier, blayer*); but this is phonetically inadmissible. If, however, we assume *bager* to represent a ME. **blager*, with *l* unaccountably lost, this might represent an OF. **blaagier*, f. *blaage* (*bleage, bladage*) harvest, corn-supply, feudal due paid in corn, f. *ble, bled* in med.L. *bladum* corn, wheat. (See H. Nicol *Proc. Philol. Soc.* 19 Dec. 1879.) But no such links between F. *blaage* and Eng. *bager* are found either in F. or Eng.; so that there is positively no evidence connecting *badger* with any deriv. of F. *blé*. And indeed a consideration of the whole (46) quotations which we have for the word leads to the conviction that the *bager, badger*, had no essential connexion with corn, any more than the *lader, kidder*, or *carrier*, named along with him in the statutes, proclamations and law-books. At present it is most in accordance with the facts to take *badger* as the agent-noun from BADGE *v.*]

badger (ˈbædʒə(r)), *sb.*^{2} Also 6 **bageard**, 6–7 **badgerd**. [Only mod.Eng.: of doubtful origin. Prob. (as E. Müller suggests) from BADGE *sb.* + -ARD, in reference to the white mark borne like a badge on its forehead: cf. for the sense BAUSON and BALL *sb.*^{3}, for the formation BALLARD.

Most etymologists have assumed the identity of this with the prec. word, citing the presumed analogy of the mod.F. name of the quadruped, *blaireau*, in 15th c. *blereau*, taken as a dim. of *blaier*, meaning 'little corn-merchant *or* corn-hoarder,' an appellation arising out of popular notions of the habits of the animal, 'which, it is said, makes away with much buck-wheat' (Littré). But this derivation seems to be erroneous. No OF. *blaërel, representing a L. *blādārellus, from blādārius, is found. And it seems certain that OF. *blariau* (12-13th c.), later *bléreau*, *blaireau*, in Flanders *blairiau*, *blariau*, in Normandy *blierel*, *blérel*, compared with OF. *blarie*, *blaire* 'the bald-coot,' mod.F. dial. (Flanders, Picardy) *blarie*, *blairie*, (Normandy) *blérie*, must be referred to MDu. and Flem. *blaer* 'bald,' MDu. *blare*, Flem. *blaere*, Du. *blaar* 'a white spot on the forehead of an animal.' *Blaireau* thus corresponds exactly to *bauson*, and its analogy strongly favours the derivation of *badge-ard* from *badge*.]

1. a. A plantigrade quadruped (*Meles vulgaris*), intermediate between the weasels and the bears, found in Europe and Middle Asia; it is a nocturnal, hybernating animal, feeding on small mammals, game, eggs, fruit, and roots, and digging for itself a burrow, which it defends fiercely against attack, biting and maiming dogs with its powerful jaws. Earlier names were *brock*, and *bauson*; also *grey*. The Indian and North American species differ but slightly from the European.

1523 FITZHERB. *Husb.* §71 A bauson or a badger. **1534** MORE *Comf. agst. Trib.* II. Wks. 1183/2 Bageard. **1598** SYLVESTER *Du Bartas* (1608) 514 As the selfe-swelling Badgerd..First at the entry of his barrow fights. **1720** SWIFT *Apollo to Dean* Wks. 1755 IV. I. 20 Grey as a badger. **1741** *Compl. Fam.-Piece* II. i. 298 A Badger is known by several Names, as a Gray, a Brock, a Boreson or Bauson; the young ones are called Pigs; the Male is called the Boar, and the Female the Sow. **1877** COUES *Fur Anim.* i. 2 The cruel sport which Badgers have afforded from time immemorial. [See also 5.]

fig. **1642** FULLER *Holy & Prof. St.* II. viii. 80 Erasmus was a badger in his jeeres, where he did bite he would make his teeth meet.

b. *erron.* applied to the beaver and otter.

1591 PERCIVALL *Sp. Dict.*, *Bivaro*, a badger or brocke, *Fiber*, *castor*. **1601** CHESTER *Love's Mart.* cxvii, The watrie Badger.

c. ***Cape-*** or ***Rock-badger***: the daman (*Hyrax Capensis*). ***honey-badger***: the ratel (*Ratellus mellivorus*). *Badger* (in Australia): the wombat.

1824 GRIFFITH *Cuvier* III. 429 Dutch Colonists..call the Cape Hyrax, Klip daasie, or the Rock Badger. **1861** HULME *Moquin-Tandon* II. III. ii. 122 The Daman of the Cape.. commonly called Badger of the Rocks. **1870** NICHOLSON *Zool.* (1880) 661 The Wombat, often called by the colonists the 'badger.'

2. (in *U.S.*) Nickname of natives or inhabitants of Wisconsin.

1833 C. F. HOFFMAN *Winter in West* (1835) I. 207 A keen eyed, leather-belted 'badger' from the mines of Ouisconsin. **1856** EMERSON *Eng. Traits* iv. 54 Our 'Hoosiers,' 'Suckers,' and 'Badgers,' of the American woods.

3. a. An artificial fly (for angling); **b.** a brush (for painting or shaving) made of badgers' hair.

1787 BEST *Angling* 107 The late Badger..Dubbed with the fur off a black badger's skin.

4. a. Slang phr. ***to overdraw one's badger*** (in humorous reference to *badger-drawing*; see 5): to overdraw one's banking account.

a **1845** HOOD *Kilmansegg* (D.) His checks no longer drew the cash, Because..He had overdrawn his badger.

b. ***to draw the badger***: to entice (a badger, an opponent) to come into the open. Cf. DRAW *v.* 36, *badger-drawing* (BADGER *sb.*[2] 5).

1844 [see DRAW *v.* 36]. **1857** TROLLOPE *Three Clerks* III. iii. 50 There is a sport prevalent among the downs in Hampshire... Men and boys..congregate together on a hill side, at the mouth of a narrow hole, and proceed, with the aid of a well-trained bull-dog, to draw a badger. *Ibid.* 51 So also at Westminster—with a difference... The badger when drawn has to take his place outside the hole and fight again ..while the victorious bull-dog assumes a state of badgerdom..and in his turn submits to be baited. **1870** *Chambers's Jrnl.* 2 July 420/1 Proceed to the sick man's room, with the avowed intention of 'drawing the badger'. **1890** *Daily Chron.* 19 Sept., The Parnellite taunts regarding Balfour's indifference have at last drawn the badger.

5. *Comb.* **badger-baiting, -drawing,** the cruel sport of setting dogs to draw out a badger from its (artificial) hole, *e.g.* a barrel; hence ***badger-baiter***; **badger-dog** (= Ger. *dachshund*), a long-bodied short-legged dog used in drawing a badger from its earth; **badger-fly** (= BADGER 3 a); **badger game**, an extortion scheme in which a man is lured usu. by a woman (the *badger* or *badger-worker*) into a compromising situation and is then surprised and blackmailed by her accomplice; **badger-legged** *a.*, having legs of unequal length, as the badger was vulgarly supposed to have; **badger-like** *a.* and *adv.*, like or in the manner of a badger; **'badger-pied** *a.*, (of a foxhound) parti-coloured like a badger; hence **badger-pie**, such a hound; **badger plane** (see quot.); **badger softener** [SOFTENER 2], a badger-hair brush used in wood-graining and decorating; **Badger State** *U.S.*, the State of Wisconsin; **badger tongs**, tongs used to grasp the badger as it emerges from its hole, or to pull it out.

1818 SCOTT *Rob Roy* xiii, Go and see what is become of the *badger-baiters. **1790** *Loiterer* 6 Mar. 6 The object of this grand cavalcade had been a **Badger-baiting* on *Bullingdon-Green*. **1801** STRUTT *Sports & Past.* III. vii. §19 Badger-baiting. In order to give the better effect to this diversion, a hole is dug in the ground for the retreat of the animal; and the dogs run at him singly in succession. **1864** *Reader* No. 85. 200/1 The pug, the bulldog, and the *badger-dog. **1838** DICKENS *O. Twist* (1850) 155/2 Young lords went to see cockfighting and *badger-drawing. **1787** BEST *Angling* 105 The *Badger Fly..is an excellent killer. [**1858** *Spirit of Times* 27 Feb. 412/2 He was the 'badger' at Moll Hodge's famous 'panel' establishment, in West Broadway and was sent up for 4 years and 8 months.] **1909** in *Cent. Dict.* Suppl., *Badger game [*defined*]. **1924** G. C. HENDERSON *Keys to Crookdom* 228, I know of one case where a man alone worked a variation of the badger game on women. **1936** E. S. GARDNER *Case of Stuttering Bishop* (1937) xiv. 217 It looks too damned much like a badger game. **1962** H. KANE *Killer's Kiss* xx. 156 She stood naked... 'You're in one hell of a lot of trouble,' he said. The old badger game. *a* **1704** R. LESTRANGE (J.) His body crooked all over, big-bellied, *badger-legged. **1656** *Artif. Handsom.* 60 Poor Vulcanists, who ballance the inequality of their heels, or *badger leggs, by the..help of the shoemaker. **1651** CLEVELAND *Poems* 34 Come keen Iambicks, with your Badgers feet, And *Badger-like, bite till your teeth do meet. **1867** 'STONEHENGE' *Dogs of Brit. Islands* 101 When the colours blend or amalgamate, the hounds are said to be 'pied'. Hare, *badger, red, tan, and yellow pies are the best. **1890** *Daily News* 31 Mar. 3/2 The Wiltshire squire, whose spurs were earned with the Badminton 'badger-pies'. **1845** J. MAYER *Sportsman's Directory* (ed. 7) ix. 147 Hounds are grizzled, brindled, *badger-pied, &c., which colours are indicative of strength. **1922** R. LEIGHTON *Compl. Bk. Dog* IV. xvi. 245 The Sealyham..is..frequently whole white, but also white with brown, lemon, or badger-pied markings. *a* **1877** KNIGHT *Dict. Mech.* I. 207/2 **Badger Plane*, a panel plane whose mouth is cut on the skew, and from side to side, so as to work up close to a corner in making a rabbet or sinking. **1878** A. R. & P. VAN DER BURG *Imitation of Woods & Marbles* 4 The speckles must be immediately touched up by the *badger softener in the form of the grain by which the pores desired are obtained. **1949** *Archit. Rev.* CVI. 244 The traditional tools of the grainer and marbler are numerous... Sash tool, jamb duster, flogger, badger softener,..all have their place in the craftsman's bag. **1850** E. S. SEYMOUR *Sk. Minnesota* 86 We have abundant reason to anticipate that Minnesota.. will not lag far behind the *Badger State. **1872** SCHELE DE VERE *Americanisms* 662 Wisconsin, abounding during early days in badgers, has ever since retained the name of Badger State. **1904** *N.Y. Times* 26 July 3 The Speaker will make several speeches in the Badger State. **1859** F. FRANCIS *Newton Dogvane* I. i. 11 Dog-chains, *badger-tongs, rabbit-hutches. **1928** *Sunday Dispatch* 15 July 2 Mr. Tinker..got his badger-tongs... 'Get the tongs round his neck—quick!' said the Master..as he pushed forward the long iron instrument. **1910** *New England Mag.* July 587/2 A woman who decoys men and then her accomplice (alleged husband) blackmails them is called a '*badger-worker'

badger, *sb.*[3] [f. BADGE *sb.* + -ER[1].] One who wears a badge (of a special kind).

1890 FARMER *Slang* I. 95/1 *Badger*..6. (Wellington School). A fellow who has got his 'badge' for play in the 2nd xv. at football. **1920** *John Bull* 28 Aug. 16/1 There are idle Badgers at Elmswell, where the job of Rate Collector was going the other day. **1925** *Glasgow Herald* 23 July 7 A Doggett badger is a man to be reckoned with in the rowing world.

badger ('bædʒə(r)), *v.* [f. BADGER *sb.*[2]]

1. To make a badger of, bait like a badger; *hence*, to subject (one who cannot escape from it) to persistent worry or persecution; to pester, tease.

1794 O'KEEFE *Wild Oats* I. i, At home, abroad..you will still badger me! **1855** WOOD *Anecd. Anim. Life* 238, A 'brock'..led such a persecuted life, that to 'badger' a man came to be the strongest possible term for irritating, persecuting, and injuring him in every way. **1862** *Sat. Rev.* 8 Feb. 154 The coarse expedients by which the Old Bailey advocate badgers and confuses a nervous witness.

2. *dial.* [f. BADGER *sb.*[1]] 'To barter; to banter over a bargain; to beat down in price.'

1875 in *Whitby Gloss.*; also in *Gloss. of Manley & Corringham* (Lincolnsh.)

badgered ('bædʒəd), *ppl. a.* [f. prec. + -ED.] Persistently worried, persecuted, or pestered.

1794 J. WOLCOTT (P. Pindar) *Rowl. for Oliver* Wks. II. 163 Therefore I tremble for his badger'd bacon. **1850** THACKERAY *Pendennis* Wks. 1869 IV. 59 I'm so pressed and badgered, I don't know where to turn.

badgerer ('bædʒərə(r)). [f. as prec. + -ER[1].]

1. A dog used for badger-baiting; a badger-dog.

1876 BLACKMORE *Cripps* III. xvii. 288 The loss of her finest badgerer.

2. *dial.* 'A cheapener.' [See BADGER *v.* 2.]

1875 in *Whitby Gloss.*

'badgering, *vbl. sb.* [f. as prec. + -ING[1].]

1. Persistent worrying, persecution.

1796 BURKE *Let. to Lawrence* 16 Dec., He would rather be defeated on the Rhine or Po than suffer a badgering every day in the House of Commons. **1840** DICKENS *Barn. Rudge* (1866) I. xiii. 59 The constant badgering and worrying of his venerable parent.

2. Acting as 'badger'; still *dial.* beating down the cost.

1844 *Act 7 & 8 Vic.* xxiv. Preamb., Statutes..prohibiting ..badgering, forestalling, etc. **1875** in *Whitby Gloss.*

badgerly ('bædʒəlɪ), *a.* [f. BADGER *sb.* + -LY[1].] Badger-like; *hence*, greyish-haired, elderly.

1753 RICHARDSON *Grandison* (1781) V. xliii. 273 When I see those badgerly virgins fond of a parrot, a squirrel, a monkey.

†**'badgie, bagy, bawgy.** *Obs.* [See BADGE *sb.*, and cf. Anglo-Lat. *bagia*.] = BADGE. (Chiefly Scotch.)

1486 *Bk. St. Albans* Heraldry B ij a, Theys bastardis shall adde more bagy to his armys or take a way a bagy of armys. **1513** DOUGLAS *Æneis* II. viii. (vii.) 55 His schynyng scheild, with his bawgy tuik he. **1566** in *Q. Mary's Bedroom, Edinb. Castle, under Arms of Jas. VI*, Lord Jesu Chryst..Preserve the Birth quhais Badgie heir is borne. **1586** FERNE *Blaz. Gentrie* 205 Of fesse Bagie, fesse Target and fesse Sentally.

badging ('bædʒɪŋ), *vbl. sb.* [f. BADGE *v.*[1] + -ING[1].] The action of marking with a badge.

1764 BURN *Poor Laws* 119 Badging of the poor, we see, is much more ancient.

'badging, *ppl. a.* That gives a badge or token.

c **1600** *Timon* I. iv, I come to thee a badging messenger: Our Lord Gelasimus from the Goulden Hill Sends thee a cloake, a signe of his good will.

‖**badiaga** (bəˈdjɑːgə, bædɪˈɑːgə). [Russ. *ba'dyaga* 'river-sponge.'] A species of alga, the powder of which is used to take away the livid marks of bruises.

1753 in CHAMBERS *Cycl. Supp.* **1853** in MAYNE *Exp. Lex.*

‖**badian** ('bɑːdɪən), *sb.*[1] [a. F. *badiane*, a. Pers. and Urdū *bādyān* fennel, anise.] The Chinese or Star Anise: see ANISE 3.

1847 CRAIG *Badiane*. **1864** WEBSTER, *Badian*.

Badian ('beɪdɪən), *sb.*[2] and *a.* Also *colloq.* **Bajan, Bajun.** [shortened from BARBADIAN.] = BARBADIAN *a.* and *sb.*

1910 in W. B. Whall *Ships, Sea Songs & Shanties* 83 Sally she a 'Badian bright mulatto; Seven long year I courted Sally. **1921** *Public Opinion* 30 Sept. 325/2 On the day of Gen. Baden-Powell's arrival all the Badian boatmen struck work. *Ibid.*, The Badians have an inordinate opinion of themselves and of their island. **1958** B. HAMILTON *Too much of Water* ii. 37 'I'm going to show you what a real good Bajan rum cocktail is like.' 'What's Bajan?'..'B'badian.' *Ibid.* 38 Did you ever hear of the Bajan who told an Englishman Bados was famous for three things?

badigeon (bəˈdɪdʒən). [a. F. *badigeon*, of unknown etymol.] **a.** A mixture of plaster and freestone ground together, used by sculptors for repairing defects in their stone, and by builders for giving common plaster the appearance of stone. **b.** A mixture of sawdust and glue used by joiners for filling up holes in woodwork.

1753 in CHAMBERS *Cycl. Supp.*

‖**badinage** (badɪˈnaʒ, ˈbædɪnɪdʒ), *sb.* [a. F. *badinage*, f. *badiner* (see below) and -AGE.] Light trifling raillery or humorous banter.

1658 in PHILLIPS. **1740** CIBBER *Apol.* (1756) II. 74 The frivolous charms or playful badinage of a king's mistress. **1880** DISRAELI *Endym.* xxxvii, Men destined to the highest places should beware of badinage.

badinage, *v.* [f. prec. sb.] To banter playfully. ***to badinage away***: to get rid of by badinage.

1804 W. COOKE *Mem. Charles Macklin* 74 And the men who chose to go and *badinage* with them, did it at the peril of their character. **1861** *All Y. Round* 13 July 383 To scoff away attacks, to badinage away reforms. **1878** BLACK *Green Past.* iv. 34 She has badinaged him into the peerage.

†**badiner,** *v.* *Obs.* [a. F. *badiner*, f. *badin* silly, frivolous, jesting: see BADEEN. Irreg. adopted in inf. form.] To talk jestingly and frivolously, to banter.

1697 VANBRUGH *Relapse* IV. ii, I don't know how..to pass my time; would Loveless were here to badiner a little.

‖**badinerie** (baˈdinəˌri). [Fr., f. *badiner*; see prec.] Badinage, raillery, banter.

1712 SHENSTONE *Wks. & Lett.* II. 240 The fund of sensible discourse is limited; that of jest and badinerie is infinite.

†**badineur** (badiˈnœːr). *Obs.* [Fr. (not in Littré) n. of agent f. *badiner*; see above.] One who indulges in badinage or raillery.

1734 POPE *Let. Swift* 19 Dec., Rebuke him for it..as a badineur, if you think that more effectual.

bad lands. orig. and chiefly *U.S.* [tr. F. *mauvaises terres*: BAD *a.* 4.] Arid barren lands, esp. in certain parts of western U.S.A., characterized by erosion of the soft surface strata in varied and fantastic forms. Also *bad land*, *badland*, esp. attrib.

1852 D. D. OWEN *Geol. Surv. Wisconsin* 195 The country of the 'Bad Lands'..lying high up on White River. **1872** SCHELE DE VERE *Americanisms* 180 It is different with the *Bad Lands*, which border the Missouri for about twenty miles, and were called by the first French settlers, *Mauvaises Terres*. **1876** R. I. DODGE *Black Hills* 17 All the country south is 'bad land' or tertiary formation, much cut by deep and abrupt ravines. **1931** H. F. PRINGLE *T. Roosevelt* I. viii. 94 Until recently, buffalo had roamed the Bad Lands. **1942** C. A. COTTON *Geomorphol.* (ed. 3) 31 Bare ground is carved by rain-wash into innumerable closely-spaced, steep-sided ridges and valleys..producing an almost impassable land surface generally referred to as 'badlands' or *badland erosion*.

transf. and *fig.*

1892 *Scribner's Mag.* July 8/1 'The Bad Lands' [in Chicago] is a quarter more repellent because more pretentious than 'The Dive',..being the abode of vice and crime rather than of poverty. **1952** *Manchester Guardian Weekly* 18 Dec. 3/1 Nothing in the White House career of Harry S. Truman, pride of Boss Pendergast's political badlands of Kansas City, so well became it as his behaviour [etc.].

† **'badling.** *Obs.* [OE. *bædling*, f. *bæddel* a womanish fellow (see BAD) + -ING³.] An effeminate or womanish man.

a **1000** in Wülcker *Vocab.* 391 *Effeminati, molles,* bædlingas. *a* **1600** Pinkerton *S.P.* (1792) III. 125 (JAM.) A wregh to were a nobill scarlet goune, A badlyng, furrying parfillit wele with sable.

'badling², var. BADELYNG.

1924 *Chambers's Jrnl.* Nov. 714/1 A badling of duck flighting in from the sea, whirred down and settled in a reed-bound pool. **1926** *Daily Express* 4 Aug. 6/6 A badling of duck—there are seven of them..—come skimming over me.

badly ('bædlı), *adv.* In 3-4 **baddeliche.** [f. BAD *a.* + -LY².]

1. In a manner below the proper standard; poorly, insufficiently, defectively.

1377 LANGL. *P. Pl.* B. xv. 498 Yuel y-clothed..Badly y-bedded. **1393** *Ibid.* C. v. 55 He is bold to borwe · and baddelich he payeþ. **1838** DICKENS *O. Twist* (1850) 199/1 A mean and badly-furnished apartment. **1856** KANE *Arct. Exp.* II. iv. 50 We are so badly off for strong arms.

2. Unfortunately, unluckily, unsuccessfully.

1297 R. GLOUC. 566 So longe hom spedde baddeliche. **1595** SHAKS. *John* v. iii. 2 How goes the day with vs? *Hub.* Badly, I feare. **1883** *Law Times* 20 Oct. 407/2 A great improvement upon the former rules..which worked badly.

3. Incorrectly, faultily.

1836-9 TODD *Cycl. Anat.* II. 783/2 Badly-formed bones. **1849** RUSKIN *Sev. Lamps* ii. §14 So great a painter..would never paint badly enough to deceive. *Mod.* He speaks English very badly.

4. Immorally, wickedly, viciously, improperly.

c **1440** *Promp. Parv.* 20/2 Badly or wykkydly, *Male, inique.* **1580** SIDNEY *Arcadia* (1622) 176 Badly-diligent ministers, who often cloyed our eares with her prayses. **1602** WARNER *Alb. Eng.* IX, xlvi. 218 Labouring their Mischiefes farre and neere, Whilst Eccho and Narcissus are more badly busie heere. **1879** E. DAVIDSON in *Cassell's Techn. Educ.* I. 202/2 Indolent, irregular, and badly-conducted pupils.

5. So as to cause pain, danger, disgrace or harm of any kind; cruelly, unkindly, dangerously, noxiously, disagreeably, etc.

1799 E. STANLEY in Duncan *Nelson* (1806) 112 The French behaved very badly to them. **1828** SOUTHEY in *Q. Rev.* XXXVIII. 207 One of the Indian chiefs was badly wounded. **1884** *Manch. Exam.* 21 May 4/7 The Lancashire County Eleven were badly beaten.

6. *colloq.* with 'need, want' = Much, greatly. *Mod.* I wanted to see you very badly.

7. *dial.* quasi-*adj.* Unwell, indisposed, in ill health.

1783 AINSWORTH *Lat. Dict.* (Morell), Badly, *Malè se habens.* **1821** MRS. WHEELER *Westmrld. Dial.* 45, I wur terrable feard a meaakin mesel badly agayn. **1915** D. H. LAWRENCE *Rainbow* ii. 65 'I want my mother.'..'Ay, but she's badly.' **1966** A. E. LINDOP *I start Counting* i. 18 Your Aunt Rene Tindall says she's been badly again.

bad man. Chiefly *U.S.* [BAD *a.* 5, after Sp. *malo hombre.*] A desperado, robber, gunman; a villain (see quots.). Cf. BADDY and quots. 1599 and 1849 *s.v.* BAD *a.* 5.

1855 *Santa Barbara* (Calif.) *Gaz.* 28 June 1/4 The 'bad man' was floored by the weight of a walking stick that the quaker had been known to carry. **1859** *Brit. Colonist* (Victoria, Brit. Columbia) 22 Jan. 1/3 It was they who tacitly aided the bad men to rescue the prisoner. **1888** ROOSEVELT *Ranch Life Far West* in *Century Mag.* Feb. 504/1 The 'bad men', or professional fighters, and man-killers, are of a different stamp, quite a number of them being, according to their light, perfectly honest. **1891** E. S. ELLIS *Check 2134* ix. 59 It is much more pleasant to relate how such a young gentleman outwitted a 'bad man'. **1906** *N.Y. Even. Post* 9 Nov. 6 He even appointed a typical 'bad man'—that is, manslayer—to office as a proof of his fondness for Arizona. **1910** MULFORD *Hopalong Cassidy* i. 9 They were good bad-men and bad bad-men the killer by necessity and the wanton murderer. **1922** P. A. ROLLINS *Cowboy* iii. 54 The actual 'bad man' was 'short on conversation'... All actual bad men were wholly untrustworthy, were natural killers, moral and mental degenerates, inhuman brutes who would slay for personal gain or merely to gratify a whim. **1958** V. KELSEY *Brit. Columbia rides Star* 173 Graves of badmen who met justice-in-the-rough.

‖**badmash, budmash** (bʌd'mɑːʃ). [Pers. and Urdū, f. Pers. *bad* evil + Arab. *ma'āsh* means of livelihood.] One following evil courses; a 'bad character,' rascal.

1843 in SKIPWITH *Magistr. Guide* (Calcutta) 17. **1866** SIR T. SEATON *Cadet to Col.* II. 66 Only the 'Badmashes' are flogged. **1870** KAYE *Hist. Sepoy War* II. v. 294 A rising of the 'Budmashes' of the city.

Badminton ('bædmıntən). [Named from the Duke of Beaufort's country seat.]

1. A cooling summer drink; see quot.

1845 DISRAELI *Sybil* I. i, Waiter, bring me a tumbler of Badminton. **1853** WHYTE-MELVILLE *Digby Gr.* ix, 'Badminton,' that grateful compound of mingled claret, sugar, and soda-water. **1870** DISRAELI *Lothair* xxx. (D.) Soothed or stimulated by fragrant cheroots or beakers of Badminton.

2. A game resembling lawn-tennis, played with shuttle-cocks instead of balls. Also *attrib.*

1874 *Daily News* 25 Mar. 5 Played a game at Badminton with two ladies. **1910** *Encycl. Brit.* III. 189/2 The Badminton hall should be not less than 18 ft. high. **1966** MILLS & BUTLER *Mod. Badminton* i. 20 All badminton players are strictly amateur. *Ibid.* 22 Unfortunately, except in certain countries, badminton cannot be played outdoors because of the extreme lightness of the shuttle. *Ibid.* ii. 25 The ideal hall for a badminton court.

bad mouth, *sb. slang* (orig. *U.S.*). Also **bad-mouth.** [BAD *a.*, tr. Vai *da na ma* or similar expressions in various Afr. and W. Indian languages.] **a.** Esp. among Black speakers: a curse or spell.

1835 W. G. SIMMS *Partisan* I. xv. 190 Maybe..he has an enemy, and would have a bad mouth put upon him. **1927** R. E. KENNEDY *Gritny People* 112 She..assured him that she would be the 'las' person in dis worl' to put bad mouth on him an' roll any stone in his way.' **1948** L. D. TURNER in *Publ. Amer. Dial. Soc.* IX. 81 Employment [by the Gullahs] of groups of words for nouns..or other parts of speech (such as..*a bad mouth* 'a curse'). **1970** H. M. HYATT *Hoodoo* I. 255, I have known of people that have had the record of saying that they could put a bad mouth on you.

b. Evil or slanderous talk; malicious gossip; severe criticism.

1970 H. E. ROBERTS *Third Ear* 4/1 *Bad mouth*, the telling of stories that may be true, but which reflect adversely on a person's character or reputation. **1979** *Fortune* 12 Mar. 149/2 The bad-mouth went out over the CB network. Every accident was blamed on the anti-skid brake. **1981** *Courier-Mail* (Brisbane) 19 Mar. 5/7 Companies don't mind legitimate complaints. They don't want unhappy people telling their friends about shoddy products. Word of bad-mouth can kill them.

bad-mouth ('bædmaʊθ), *v. slang* (orig. *U.S.*). Also **badmouth.** [f. the sb.] *trans.* To abuse (someone) verbally; to criticize, slander, or gossip maliciously about (a person or thing); to disparage or 'run down'.

1941 J. THURBER in *Sat. Even. Post* 5 Apr. 9/2 He bad-mouthed everybody. **1960** D. MACDONALD *Slam Big Door* (1961) vi. 96 What..reason would he have to bad-mouth Jamison? **1968** *N.Y. Times* 2 June IV. 10/6 The Poor People's Campaign should stop bad-mouthing poverty. **1969** *Listener* 31 July 159/1 Edgar tried to think of a way to badmouth this immense son. **1975** *High Times* Dec. 9/1 When the question of legalization of pot comes up, the cop always bad-mouths the legislature for even thinking of it. **1977** *Times Lit. Suppl.* 1 July 792/1 They threw matches, they badmouthed linesmen, they hit balls into the stands. **1986** P. BOOTH *Palm Beach* xi. 180 But now Jo-Anne was a bitter enemy who could be relied on to bad-mouth her at every opportunity.

Hence **bad-mouthing** *vbl. sb.*

1972 *Daily Colonist* (Victoria, B.C.) 7 Jan. 2/2 But milk has been drunk so universally for such a long time that very few people pay any attention to this bad-mouthing. **1977** *Time* 19 Dec. 20/3 Whitlam engaged in his own share of needless bad-mouthing. **1984** *Business Rev. Weekly* 4 Feb. 45/3 We've had enough bad-mouthing in the motor industry.

badness ('bædnıs). [f. BAD *a.* + -NESS.]

1. Inferior or deficient quality; poor condition; incorrectness, faultiness; invalidity.

1539 *Househ. Ord.* in Thynne *Animadv.* Introd. 34 To make relation thereof at the Greencloth of the badnesse of the stuff. **1611** BIBLE *Gen.* xli. 19 Kine..leane fleshed, such as I neuer saw in all the land of Egypt for badnesse. **1757** BURKE *Abridgm. Eng. Hist.* Wks. X. 506 The clergy also took advantage of the badness of his title. **1825** COBBETT *Rur. Rides* 8 Nothing can more strongly prove the badness of the times. **1884** LD. BLACKBURN in *Law Rep.* IX. Appeal 620 The supposed badness of the plea.

2. Evil quality or condition; wickedness, depravity; dangerousness, noxiousness, adverseness.

1377 LANGL. *P. Pl.* B. xii. 49 Þe bewte of hir body in badnesse [*v.r.* baddenesse] she dispended. **1605** SHAKS. *Lear* III. v. 9 A reproauble badnesse in himselfe. **1748** RICHARDSON *Clarissa* (1811) I. xxvii. 189 Vilely suspicious ..from the badness of his own heart. *Mod.* Forced to retreat by the badness of the weather.

† **ba'dot,** *a. Obs. rare*⁻¹. [ad. F. *badaud* gaping fool, idler, f. Pr. *badar* to gape.] Silly.

1653 URQUHART *Rabelais* I. xvii, So sottish, so badot.

badrans, var. BAUDRONS, Sc. name for *cat.*

bae, Sc. form of BAA.

bæ- in OE. and EE. words; see BA-.

Baedeker ('beıdıkə(r)). Any of the series of guide-books issued by Karl *Baedeker* (1801-59) at Coblenz, or by his successors; also applied loosely to any guide-book. Also *fig.*

1863 *Miss Jemima's Swiss Jrnl.* 29 June (1963) ii. 23 We followed the advice of our faithful Baedeker. **1889** G. B. SHAW *London Music 1888-89* (1937) 180 Glancing through Baedeker as I bowl along Bayreuthwards I perceive [etc.]. **1920** T. S. ELIOT *Ara Vos Prec.* 14 Burbank with a Baedeker. **1935** *Chambers's Encycl.* I. 659/2 In the 20th century 'Baedeker' had become a synonym for guidebook, and there are Baedekers not merely for the principal European countries, but for Palestine and Syria [etc.]. **1948** *Landfall* II. 58 There was no place in their ample kits for a Baedeker or a book of poetry. **1959** *Listener* 30 Apr. 767/1 *Balzac et son Monde* is an indispensable Baedeker to the *Comédie Humaine.*

b. Hence ***Baedeker raid***, one of a series of raids by the German Air Force in April and May of 1942 upon places of cultural and historical importance in Britain.

1942 *Daily Mail* 1 May 4/7 The 'Baedeker' raids have put the Luftwaffe in a grave dilemma. **1942** *War Illustr.* 29 May 705 York's Guildhall as it appeared on the night of April 28 after it had been struck by incendiaries in one of Hitler's 'Baedeker raids' on Britain's cultural heritage. After the legitimate R.A.F. raids on Rostock, where the Heinkel factory and other munition works were destroyed, German officials frankly stated that the Luftwaffe would go out for every building in Britain which is marked with three stars in Baedeker's guide-books.

bael, bel (bɛl). Also 7 **beele, bille,** 9 **bhel, bēl, bél.** [Hindi *bel*, Marathi *bail*:- Skr. *bilva, vilva.*] An Indian tree, *Ægle marmelos*, or its aromatic fruit; the Bengal quince. Also, the medicinal extract of the fruit.

1618 in Foster *Eng. Factories India* (1906) 10 Greene ginger, mirabilons, and beeles. **1619** *Ibid.* 76 Mirabilons and billes in conserves. **1854** HOOKER *Himal. Jrnl.* I. 50 The Bhel fruit, lately introduced into English medical practice, as an astringent of great effect, in cases of diarrhœa and dysentery. **1874** GARROD & BAXTER *Mat. Med.* (ed. 4) 219 Indian bael has obtained much reputation in India in the treatment of diarrhœa and dysentery. **1877** SHUNKAR SINGH & GUNANAND tr. *Hist. Nepāl* 33 Every Newār girl, while a child, is married to a bēl-fruit, which after the ceremony is thrown into some sacred river. **1910** *Encycl. Brit.* III. 191/1 Bael fruit (*Aegle marmelos*). **1924** R. E. ENTHOVEN *Folklore of Bombay* III. 124 The *Palas* (*Butea frondosa*) and the *Bel* (*Aegle Marmelos*), a tree sacred to the god Shiva, are considered to be holy by the Hindus.

bætyl ('biːtıl). [ad. L. *bætulus*, a. Gr. βαίτυλος.] A sacred meteoric stone. Also in Gr.-L. form **baitylos, bætylos, -us**; also **bæ'tylion** (pl. **-ia**) (Gr. βαιτύλιον). Hence **bæ'tylic** *a.*, of the nature of a bætyl.

1854 *Encycl. Brit.* IV. 361/2 These *bætylia* were the objects of much veneration among the ancient heathens. **1884** *Proc. Soc. Psychical Research* II. 117 Aerolites were scouted as a kind of fetish *in excelsis*—a transcendental bætyl—'the image which fell down from Jupiter'. **1889** W. R. SMITH *Relig. Semites* 193 The use of baetylia, or small portable stones to which magical life was ascribed. **1901** A. J. EVANS in *Jrnl. Hellen. Stud.* XXI. 106 The rough pyramidal pillars of the Bhuta Spirit,..and many other rude 'baetyls' of the same kind..are commonly set up beneath holy trees. *Ibid.* 113 An artificial pillar image of the divinity, it may be even the actual 'baetylos' of remote tradition. *Ibid.* 118 The sanctity of baetylic stones and pillars is due to a variety of causes. **1903** *Amer. Jrnl. Archæol.* VII. 200 He found the stone cooled off, and recognizing that it was a baetyl, took it home with him. **1923** *Trans. Sc. Ecclesiol. Soc.* 97 The Clack or stone [at Clackmannan]..is a true Fetich or Baitylos. **1941** *Jrnl. Theol. Stud.* XLII. 60 Most of the few fragments [of coral] discovered at Gezer seem to have been unworked pieces, probably therefore prophylactic in purpose, and not *objets de luxe.* One white piece is of baetylic form.

baff, *sb. Sc.* [Possibly a. OF. *baffe* a blow with the back of the hand; but perh. simply imitative of the sound.] A blow with anything flat or soft, *e.g.* the palm of the hand, a soft ball, etc.

a **1800** in R. Jamieson's *Pop. Ballads* II. 382 (JAM.) His back they loundert..baff for baff. **1814** SCOTT *Wav.* lxxi, For fear some dare-the-de'il should tak a baff at them. **1854** H. MILLER *Sch. & Schm.* (1858) 11 A cannon-ball would but play baff on you.

† **baff,** *v.*¹ *Obs.* [Possibly from LG. and Du. *baffen* with same meaning; but probably directly imitative: cf. *yaff*, and dialectal *bough, buff.*]

To bark or yelp as a dog; also *transf.* of persons.

c **1440** *Promp. Parv.* 20 Baffyn as howndys *Baulo, baffo, latro.* **1570** LEVINS *Manip.* /9 To baffe, as a dog, *latrare.* **1599** NASHE *Lent. Stuffe* 37 Therewith outstept the stallfed foreman..and baft in his face. Biefe, Biefe, Biefe.

to say neither buff nor baff: see BUFF.

1542 UDAL *Erasm Apoph.* 11 [Who] beeyng of him bidden good spede, saied to hym again neither buff ne baff. **1549** LATIMER *Serm. bef. Edw. VI.* 196 When he should have comforted Christ he was aslepe, not once buffe nor baffe to him.

baff (bæf), *v.*² *Sc.* [Cf. BAFF *sb.*] To beat, strike; *spec.* in Golf, to strike the ground with the sole of the club-head in making a stroke. So **'baffing-spoon** = BAFFY.

1858 *Chambers's Jrnl.* X. 157/1 The names of the wooden-headed clubs principally used at St. Andrews..are as follows: the play-club, long-spoon, mid-spoon,..putter, and baffing-spoon. **1881** R. FORGAN *Golfer's Handbk.* 10 The 'Baffing Spoon' is so called from the sound produced by it as it smites the ground in making the stroke. *Ibid.* 33 Baff. **1890** H. G. HUTCHINSON et al. *Golf* 445 Baff.

baff-end. (See quot.)

1851 *Coal-tr. Terms* Northumbld. & Durh., *Baff-end.*—A piece of wood, 15 or 18 inches long, 5 or 6 inches broad, and from 1 to 2 inches thick, used for driving behind cribs or tubbing, to bring them to their proper position in a pit.

† **'baffing,** *vbl. sb. Obs.* [f. BAFF *v.*¹ + -ING¹.] Barking; also *fig.*

1401 *Pol. Poems* (1859) II. 53 Bot wel I wot thi baffyng.. may not menuse this seint. *c* **1440** *Promp. Parv.* 20 Baffynge or bawlynge of howndys, *Baulatus, baffatus.*

baffle ('bæf(ə)l), *v.* Forms: 6 **baffull,** 7 **baffol, -oul, -ul, -il(l, -el,** 6-9 **baffle.** [Etymology, and even immediate source, uncertain. Quoted in

1548 as Scotch, and in 1570 used by a Scotchman. Hence, naturally to be compared with Sc. *bauchle*, found in senses 1–3, from a century earlier, but itself of uncertain derivation. On the other hand we have F. *beffler* (Cotgr.) 'to deceive, mocke, or gull with faire words,' etc. (cf. sense 4), and *bafouer*, in Cotgr. *baffoüer*, 'to hoodwinke; to deceive; to besmeare; *also* to baffle, abuse, reuile, disgrace, handle basely in tearmes, give reproachfull words of or vnto.' Of these, *beffler* (in Rabelais 1533–53) is easily referred to OF. *befe, beffe* mockery, *beffer* to mock, *beferie* quibbling, deceit, = It. *beffa*, Sp. *befa*, OSp. and Pr. *bafa*, mockery, banter, It. *beffare*, Sp. *befar*, Pr. *bafar*, to mock, deride (which M. Paul Meyer would derive from Pr. *baf!* interjection expressing disdain), with which words also (though less securely) Diez and others connect *bafouer*, cited first from Montaigne, 1588–92. It is possible that two or even three distinct words are confused under *baffle*.]

I. To disgrace. [Cf. Sc. BAUCHLE, F. *bafouer*.]

†**1.** To subject to public disgrace or infamy; *spec.* to disgrace a perjured knight with infamy. *Obs.*

1548 HALL *Chron.* (1809) 559 He was content that the Scottes shoulde Baffull hym, which is a great reproache among the Scottes, and is used when a man is openly perjured, and then they make of him an Image paynted reverted with hys heles upwarde, with hys name wonderynge cryenge and blowing out of hym with hornes. **1570** in Churchyard *Chippes* (1817) 127, I will baffull your good name, sounde with the trumpet your dishonour, and paint your pictor with the heeles vpward, and beate it in despight of yourselfe. **1596** SPENSER *F.Q.* VI. vii. 27 He by the heels him hung upon a tree And bafful'd so, that all which passed by The picture of his punishment might see. [See also V. iii. 37.] **1613** BEAUM. & FL. *Hon. Man's Fort.* III. i, Have his disgrace talk for Tobacco shops, His picture bafful'd. **1660** *Gentl. Call.* v. 71 A Maxime among the Swordmen, That he that has once been baffled, is ever after an incompetent Challenger.

†**2.** *gen.* To disgrace, treat with contumely. *Obs.*

1592 NASHE *P. Penilesse* 17 b, Should we..borrow all out of others..our names should be baffuld on euerie Booke-sellers stall. **1609** BP. HALL *Dissuas. Popery* (1627) 642 A religion that baffoules all temporall princes, making them stand bare-foot at their great bishops gate. **1693** SHADWELL *Volunteers* IV. i, This confounded beau..will tell all the town what men he bafles.

†**3.** To speak to or of in terms of contempt; to vilify, 'run down.' *Obs.*

1674 MARVELL *Reh. Transp.* II. 291 You run down and Baffle that serious business of Regeneration.

II. To cheat, juggle, bewilder, confound, foil. [Cf. F. *beffler* and *bafouer*.]

†**4.** To hoodwink, gull, cheat. *Obs.*

c **1590** GREENE *Fr. Bacon* v. 83 But friends are men, and love can baffle lords. **1609** ARMIN *Ital. Taylor* (1880) 178 Such deedes must haue a reach of wit To baffill such as he. **1649** MILTON *Eikon.* 163 The Scots would not be baffl'd with the pretence of a Coronation Oath. **1653** —— *Hirelings* Wks. (1851) 360 They cry out Sacrilege, that Men will not be gull'd and baffl'd..by giving credit to frivolous Pretences of divine Right. **1726** DE FOE *Hist. Devil* II. viii. (1840) 292 He had not a mind to cheat or baffle the poor man.

†**5. a.** *intr.* To juggle, shuffle, quibble. *Obs.*

1656 *Trapp Exp. Matt.* xxv. 11 Trifling and baffling with Christ. *a* **1677** BARROW *Wks.* III. 180 (T.) To what purpose can it be to juggle and baffle for a time? *a* **1733** NORTH *Life Guilford* (1808) II. 78 (D.) The vexatious side baffled before the master, as long as he could, upon trifles.

†**b.** *to baffle out* or *away* (trans.). *Obs.*

1643 MILTON *Divorce* Introd. Wks. (1851) 12 To have eluded and baffl'd out all Faith and chastity from the marriagebed. **1653** W. MEWE in Hartlib *Ref. Commw. Bees* 47 Relicks of his goodness, whereof we have baffled away the better part.

†**6.** *trans.* To bewilder, confuse, confound. *Obs.*

1649 G. DANIEL *Trinarch., Hen. V.* 364 Let the rude Noyse of Bells enchant Dull Ears, And Bon-fires baffle Eyes. **1692** R. LESTRANGE *Josephus' Wars* I. xx. (1733) 605 And does not despair of baffling the Truth with a Trick. *a* **1704** T. BROWN *Oxf. Scholars* Wks. 1730 I. 12 Their understandings have been so baffled with phrases and distinctions.

†**7.** To confound, bring to confusion, bring to nought. *Obs.*

1649 MILTON *Eikon.* xxvii. 511 Whose sole word and will shall baffle..what all the wisdom of a Parlament hath bin deliberately framing. **1709** STEELE & ADD. *Tatler* No. 160 ¶15 To baffle Reproach with Silence. **1812** CRABBE *Parting Hour* 224 A wish so strong, it baffled his repose.

8. To defeat anyone in his efforts; to frustrate or confound his plans, to foil: **a.** a person.

1675 TRAHERNE *Chr. Ethics* xxi. 338 He is baffled from the acquisition of the most great and beautiful things. **1722** WOLLASTON *Relig. Nat.* v. 81 Both the beginnings and the ends of things..all conspire to baffle us. **1753** HOGARTH *Anal. Beauty* v. 24 An old cunning one has baffled, and outrun the dogs. **1883** FROUDE *Short Stud.* IV. I. x. 111 Baffled by a problem which he has done his best to solve.

b. actions, faculties, efforts, plans.

1692 BENTLEY *Boyle Lect.* 15 Whose Stolidity can baffle all Arguments. **1751** JOHNSON *Rambl.* No. 177 ¶8 How fatally human sagacity was sometimes baffled. **1781** J. MOORE *View Soc. It.* I. i. 4 A rapidity which baffles all description. **1849** MACAULAY *Hist. Eng.* II. 164 To baffle curiosity by dry and guarded answers. **1868** FREEMAN *Norm. Conq.* (1876) II. vii. 107 The murderer baffled pursuit.

c. Often said of the wind and weather defeating the efforts of a ship to advance.

1748 ANSON *Voy.* II. ix. 224 We were baffled for near a month..with tempestuous weather. **1833** MARRYAT *P. Simple* (1863) 102 If the wind does not baffle us, we shall weather. **1860** MAURY *Phys. Geog. Sea* viii. §378 This current which baffled and beat back this fleet.

d. In technical uses.

1883 GRESLEY *Gloss. Coal Mining, Baffle*, to brush out or mix fire-damp with air in order to render it non-explosive; a dangerous practice, and not now allowed. **1885** *Marine Engineer* 1 Apr. 3/2 The corrugations serve to break up the volume of steam, and also baffle the water passing through the condenser. **1909** WEBSTER s.v., Plates are used for baffling the steam.

†**9.** *to baffle out of*: to do out of by baffling (in various senses); to cheat, juggle, shuffle, confuse, cajole, manœuvre (one) out of anything. *Obs.*

1652 NEEDHAM tr. *Selden's Mare Cl.* 467 So bold as to..endeavour to baffle him out of his Rights. **1673** *Lady's Call.* I. v. §20. 38 He..whom the fear of suffering can baffle out of anything he thinks just and honest. **1695** *Parl. dissolved by Death P'cess Orange*? 54 They were baffled and bantered out of their Design. **1748** RICHARDSON *Clarissa* (1811) II. xxxv. 258 Parents will not be baffled out of their children by impudent gentlemen.

III. 10. *intr.* To struggle ineffectually; to move, act, or exert oneself in a futile manner. (In north. dial. MAFFLE.)

1860 *Times* 27 Feb., The ill-fated ship was seen baffling with a gale from the N.W. **1865** CARLYLE *Fredk. Gt.* IV. 103 Let the Pandours baffle about.

baffle ('bæf(ə)l), *sb.*[1] [f. prec. vb.]

†**1.** Disgrace, affront. *Obs.*

c **1645** HOWELL *Lett.* (1726) II. xiv, You will be free from all baffles and affronts. **1692** BP. ELY *Answ. Touchstone* A iij, It sculkt and durst not show its head, till they imagined that Baffle was forgot.

†**2.** A shuffle; quibbling, trifling. *Obs.*

1783 AINSWORTH *Lat. Dict.* (Morell), A baffle, *Nugæ*. It is all a baffle, *Meræ nugæ sunt*.

†**3.** Confusion, discomfiture, check. *Obs.*

1628 EARLE *Microcosm.* lxiv. 138 Other men's modesty..rescues him many times from a baffle. **1670** COTTON *Espernon* II. VIII. 373 After this baffle her Army had receiv'd. *a* **1745** SWIFT *Wks.* (1841) II. 72 That slight baffle it received at its first appearance in public.

4. The state of one who is baffled or bewildered.

1843 FOSTER in *Life & Corr.* (1846) II. 458, I remained in a kind of baffle between that perfectly preserved image, and his actual appearance.

5. = BAFFLER. Also, any shielding device or structure, in many technical uses (see quots.); *spec.* an acoustic screen.

1881 *Echo* 12 Dec. 6/1 There is a fire-brick 'baffle' above, on which the hot air is discharged. **1913** V. B. LEWIS *Oil Fuel* iv. 97 The top of the inlet tube for the sample of vapour is protected by a series of baffles. **1928** *Wireless World* 6 June 604/2 (*caption*) The baffle which greatly improves reproduction [of sound]..is incorporated in the cabinet. **1931** *B.B.C. Year-Bk.* 436/2 *Baffle*, a screen of non-resonant material, generally wood, largely used in conjunction with cone-type loud speakers instead of a horn, to ensure the radiation of the very low audible frequencies. **1939** in Henney & Dudley *Handbk. Photogr.* viii. 254 The use of baffles over the photoelectric cell [of an exposure meter]. **1951** *Gloss. Terms Plastics* (*B.S.I.*) 34 *Baffle*, a device used for the purpose of restricting the flow of hydraulic fluid in a high pressure line. It consists of a disc with a small central perforation. **1952** GRANVILLE *Dict. Theatr. Terms* 22 *Baffle*, any suitable sheet of material used to prevent a spill of light where not necessary. **1958** *Gloss. Terms High Vacuum Technol.* (*B.S.I.*) 12 *Baffle*, an obstruction placed near the mouth of a vapour pump to impede the entry of back-streaming vapour into the system. **1959** *Times* 31 July 14/4 The first earth baffle..has been built by Air India at London airport to suppress engine sounds during ground running.

attrib. and *Comb.*

1909 *Cent. Dict.* Suppl., Baffle-tube. **1926** *Chambers's Jrnl.* Apr. 270/1 The oil rises through a series of perforated baffle discs to the top of the tank. **1931** *Answers* 10 Oct. 36/2 Natural reproduction will be impoverished if a moving coil loud-speaker is used within a baffle board. **1933** *Archit. Rev.* LXXIII. 233 The six baffle-boards covering ventilation exhaust outlets. **1939** SAMUELY & HAMANN *Civil Protection* 167 Baffle wall. **1940** *Chambers's Techn. Dict.* 70/2 *Baffle tube*, a pipe of sufficient length to lower the temperature of hot gases before they enter a furnace. **1941** *New Statesman* 8 Mar. 235/1 Heavy baffle-walls have been built [in an air-raid shelter]. **1953** *Times* 10 Jan. (*headline*) Reducing Noise at Airport. Baffle Wall Nearing Completion.

†'**baffle**, *sb.*[2] *Obs.* [? for Sc. BAUCHLE.] ? A worn-out horse.

1639 T. DE GREY *Compl. Horsem.* 4 Iades and baffles, unusefull and unprofitable.

baffled ('bæf(ə)ld), *ppl. a.* [f. BAFFLE *v.* + -ED.]

†**1.** Disgraced, dishonoured. *Obs.*

1671 MILTON *Samson* 1237 Go, baffled coward. **1828** SCOTT *F.M. Perth* III. 202 Every worthy knight would hold you a baffled, forsworn caitiff.

2. Confounded, discomfited, checked or foiled.

a **1659** CLEVELAND *Gen. Poems* (1677) 14 Till baffled Poetry hangs down the head. **1693** *Apol. Clergy Scot.* 14 This baffled and hypocritical Sham. **1732** LEDIARD *Sethos* II. x. 440 To baffled reason love disdains to yield. **1860** ELLICOTT *Life our Lord* iii. 114 The baffled Tempter departs.

'**bafflegab.** orig. and chiefly *U.S.* [f. BAFFLE *v.* + GAB *sb.*[2]] Official or professional jargon which confuses more than it clarifies; gobbledegook.

1952 *Daily Tel.* 23 Jan. 4/6 A new word for lovers of officialese is bafflegab, invented by Mr. Milton A. Smith, assistant general counsel for the American Chamber of Commerce. He has won a prize for the word—and its definition: 'Multiloquence characterised by a consummate interfusion of circumlocution..and other familiar manifestations of abstruse expatiation commonly utilised for promulgations implementing procrustean determinations by governmental bodies.' **1958** I. BROWN *Words in our Time* 24 Here is a plain term used by Americans as an alternative to Gobbledygook; both describe the monstrous and mystifying language in which official documents are written... They do not speak bafflegab, perhaps, but, in the way of all politicians they must learn and practise the tricky evasive style now known as double-talk. **1969** Y. CARTER *Mr. Campion's Farthing* xii. 105 This is long-winded tripe dressed up in police court bafflegab. **1977** *It* June 2/3 Anarchism has got nothing to do with such bafflegab mystagoguery as'the common source of all energy'. **1984** *Listener* 2 Feb. 5/2 What I find incredibly naive is the critics' apparent belief that politicians will ever ..be completely frank while speaking 'on the record' about sensitive subjects... They inevitably descend publicly into quotable bafflegab.

bafflement ('bæf(ə)lmənt). [f. BAFFLE *v.* + -MENT.] The action of baffling or fact of being baffled; frustration, defeat in aim or endeavour.

1841 *Blackw. Mag.* XLIX. 462 The constant bafflement all their attempts meet with. **1874** BLACKIE *Self-Cult.* 77 Associated in his mind with bafflement and defeat.

baffle-plate. [BAFFLE *sb.*[1] 5.] A plate hindering or regulating the passage of fluid through an outlet or inlet, or the direction of sound. Hence **baffle-plated** *a.*, having a baffle-plate.

1882 *Nature* XXV. 220 A kind of baffle plate hung at the back of the grate. **1906** *Daily Chron.* 3 Mar. 3/6 A system of tubes or baffle-plates which break up the hot gas. **1908** *Westm. Gaz.* 31 Dec. 5/1 In this radiator the baffle plated hood replaces the frieze and trivet. **1920** *Chambers's Jrnl.* Nov. 767/1 [Gas] is passed upwards through water dripping from a series of baffle-plates in chambers known as scrubbers.

baffler ('bæflə(r)). [f. BAFFLE *v.* + -ER[1].] He who or that which baffles.

†**1.** A juggler, trickster; a trifler. *Obs.*

1606 HOLLAND *Sueton.* 72 Fortune tellers, iuglers, and Baflors. *a* **1677** BARROW *Serm.* (1687) I. xiv. 198 To deal seriously, were to yield too much respect to such a baffler.

2. He who or that which bewilders, confounds, defeats effort, or foils purposes.

1677 PLOT *Oxfordsh.* 42 Experience, that great baffler of speculation. **1702** BAYNARD *Cold Baths* II. (1709) 367 That Baffler of our Profession, the Gout. **1877** M. ARNOLD *Emped. on Etna* I. ii, Bafflers of our own prayers.

3. A contrivance used in stoves and furnaces, for interrupting the natural course of the heated air, and causing it to pass in another direction.

1861 RANKINE *Steam Eng.* 261 Large boiler flues are sometimes provided with bafflers; that is, projecting partitions which compel the hot gases to take a circuitous course.

'**baffling**, *vbl. sb.* [f. BAFFLE *v.* + -ING[1].]

†**1.** Treatment with insult or contumely. *Obs.*

1602 WARNER *Alb. Eng.* XIII. lxxvii. (1612) 320 The baffling of those Gods themselues, in those ribaldious plaies. **1620** DEKKER *Dreame* (1860) 14 That face..put vp spettings, baffulings, buffetings.

†**2.** Quibbling; trifling. *Obs.*

1653 S. FISHER *Baby Bapt.* To Rdr. 2 Absolute Absurdities, Babish Bafflings.

3. Discomfiture of endeavour, aim, purpose, etc.

1689 *Advant. Pres. Settlement* 13 The absolute baffling of that Dispensing Power. **1860** PUSEY *Min. Proph.* 489 A like baffling of hope.

'**baffling**, *ppl. a.* [f. as prec. + -ING[2].]

1. Bewildering; that defeats skill or endeavour.

1783 AINSWORTH *Lat. Dict.* (Morell), Baffling, *Decipiens, deludens*. **1817** MOORE *Lalla R.* (1824) 220 Baffling spells. **1875** WHITNEY *Life Lang.* ix. 166 His task..is..difficult and baffling.

2. *Naut.* Of winds: That blow about and make straight sailing impracticable; shifting, variable.

1772–84 COOK *Voy.* (1790) V. 1860 We had baffling light airs, but the wind soon settled at S. **1823** BYRON *Island* II. xxi, I saw her in the doldrums; for the wind Was light and baffling. **1854** G. RICHARDSON *Univ. Code* v, 798 = Have you had baffling winds?

'**bafflingly**, *adv.* [f. prec. + -LY[2].] In a baffling manner; confusingly.

1879 R. STEVENSON *Trav. Cevennes* 190 Objects..grew indistinct and melted bafflingly into each other.

'**bafflingness.** [f. as prec. + -NESS.] Baffling quality.

1864 in WEBSTER.

baffy ('bæfɪ). *Golf.* [f. BAFF *sb.* or *v.*[2]] A short wooden club used to hit the ball into the air. Also *baffy spoon*.

1888 *Daily News* 22 Sept. 5/1 The old 'Baffy', a funny little toy club, with a sloped face. **1890** H. G. HUTCHINSON et al. *Golf* 59 The 'baffy', very short and stiff and with face very much laid back. *Ibid.* 335 To Allan was due..the introduction of irons and cleeks for the approach to the hole, these shots having been previously played with baffy spoons.

baft. Also 6 boffeta, 6–8 bafta, 9 baftah [Prob. a. Pers. *baft*, wrought, woven.] A kind of coarse and cheap (generally cotton) fabric, originally of oriental manufacture, but now made in Great Britain for export, especially to Africa.

1598 W. PHILLIPS *Linschoten's Trav. Ind.* 18 Cotton Linnen of various sorts..Boffetas. **1612** PURCHAS *Pilgr.* I. 347 Baftas or white Callicos. **1722** *Lond. Gaz.* No. 6079/7 A Parcel of..Pelongs, Cuttanees, chequer'd Bafts, Nillaes, etc. **1779** FORREST *Voy. N. Guinea* 106 They purchase blue and red baftaes from the Chinese. **1845** STOCQUELER *Handbk. Brit. India* (1854) 195 Some silk manufactories here [Bhaugulpore]..produce a coarse stuff, called baftah. **1876** R. BURTON *Gorilla L.* I. 155 Blue baft from which the stiffening has been washed out.

baft (bɑːft, -æ-), *adv.* and *prep.* Forms: 1 **beæftan, bæftan, -on, -en, 1–3 bæfte, 2 bieften, befte, 3 biæften, biaften, (bafftenn), baften, bæfte, bafte, 4 bafft, 7 be-aft, 3–4, 7–9 baft.** [OE. *beæftan*, f. *be* by, at + *æftan* = Goth. *aftana* behind. Cf. AFT.]

A. *adv.*

1. Of place: Behind, in the rear; in later usage only *nautical*: Astern, aft, abaft. *arch.*

c **885** K. ÆLFRED *Oros.* I. x. §3 Micel ðæs heres ðe mid hiere beæftan wæs. **1205** LAY. 26927 þa weoren heo biuoren, and Bruttes biaften. *a* **1300** *E.E. Psalter* lxxviii. 66 He smate his faas in baft. *c* **1325** *E.E. Allit. P.* C. 148 þe bur ber to hit baft þat braste alle her gere. **1687** *Lond. Gaz.* No. 2272/4 Long Hatches from Fore and baft. **1759** *Lond. Mag.* XXVIII. 32 The powder room..was be-aft. **1837** MARRYAT *Dog-Fiend* xiii, 'Are they all forward?'..'Yes..not one soul baft.'

†2. Of time: After. *Obs. rare.*

1205 LAY. 31946 Hit ilomp inne frimdæȝen, feor her biæften.

†B. *prep.* [orig. only the adv. with dative of reference.] Behind, to the rear of. *Obs.*

a **800** *O.E. Chron.* an. 755 þæs cyninges þegnas þe him be æftan wærun [*Laud*, bæfton]..þa men þe he be æftan him læfde ær [*Laud*, be æfton]. *c* **1000** *Ags. Gosp.* Matt. xvi. 23 Gang bæftan me, Satanas! *c* **1160** *Hatton G.* ibid., Gange befte me. *c* **1200** ORMIN 14688 Tacc þær an shep bafftenn þin bacc. **1205** LAY. 26957 Richer and Beduer wenden heom bafte. *c* **1250** *Gen. & Ex.* 1333 Biaften bak he saȝ a s[c]ep. *c* **1400** *Beryn* 1576 Euery man..tofore the Shipp & bafft.

†**bafts**, *adv. Obs.* In 5 baftys. [f. BAFT *adv.*, with adverbial genitive *-s*, *-es*.] Behind.

c **1400** *Cov. Myst.* 180 Lete no barne beleve on bete baftys.

bag (bæg), *sb.* Forms: 3–7 **bagge**, 6–7 **bagg**, 4– **bag**. [Early ME. *bagge*: cf. ON. *baggi* 'bag, pack, bundle' (not elsewhere in Teutonic); also OF. *bague*, Pr. *bagua* baggage, med.L. *baga* chest, sack. The Eng. was possibly from the ON.; but the source of this, as well as of the Romanic words, is unknown; the Celtic derivation suggested by Diez is not tenable: Gaelic *bag* is from English. Of connexion with Teutonic **balgi-z*, Goth. *balgs*, OE. *belȝ*, *bælȝ*, *bæliȝ*, whence BELLY, BELLOWS, and the cogn. Celtic *bolg*, *balg*, there is no evidence.]

I. General sense.

1. a. A receptacle made of some flexible material closed in on all sides except at the top (where also it generally can be closed); a pouch, a small sack.

c **1230** *Ancr. R.* 168 Hit is beggares rihte uorte beren bagge on bac; & burgeises for to beren purses. *Ibid.*, Trusseaus, & purses, baggen, & packes. **1362** LANGL. *P. Pl.* A. Prol. 41 Til heor Bagges and heore Balies weren [bratful] I-crommet. *c* **1440** *Promp. Parv.* 21 Bagge, or poke: *Sacculus.* **1513** *Bk. Keruynge* in *Babees Bk.* 267 Haue fyue or syxe bagges for your ypocras to renne in, &..basyns to stande vnder your bagges. **1535** COVERDALE *1 Sam.* xvii. 40 And put them in the shepardes bagge which he had. **1622** R. HAWKINS *Voy. S. Sea* (1847) 80 Any man that putteth himself into the enemies port, had need of Argus eyes, and the wind in a bagge. **1626** BACON *Sylva* §6 Passing it through a woolen bagg. **1653** WALTON *Angler* 138 He would usually take three or four worms out of his bag. **1662** FULLER *Worthies* (1811) II. 579 (D.) Our English by-word to express such betwixt whom there is apparent odds of strength, 'He is able to put him up in a Bagge.' **1864** TENNYSON *En. Ard.* 63 The younger people..with bag and basket..went nutting.

b. ***green bag, blue bag***: a barrister's brief-bag.

1712 ARBUTHNOT *John Bull* (1755) 29 You will carry a green bag yourself, rather than we shall make an end of our law-suit. **1788** in G. Rose *Diaries* (1860) I. 96 Mr. Pitt had resolved..'to take his blue bag, and return to the bar.'

c. A base in baseball (see quot. 1857). *U.S.*

[**1857** *Spirit of Times* 28 Feb. 420/3 The first, second, and third bases shall be canvas bags, painted white, and filled with sand or saw-dust.] **1873** *Forest & Stream* 20 Nov. 231/1 In this inning, through error, the Princetons succeeded in getting the bags full, with no men out. **1917** C. MATHEWSON *Sec. Base Sloane* xiii. 177 Hunt was two yards from the bag when the ball reached third base.

d. *fig.* A preoccupation, mode of behaviour or experience; a distinctive style or category; esp. a characteristic manner of playing jazz or similar music. Cf. *bag of tricks* (sense 18 a below). *slang* (orig. *U.S.*).

1960 J. HENDRICKS in D. Cerulli et al. *Jazz Word* (1962) 140 Lack of acceptance is a drag... Man, that's really in another bag. **1962** *Jazz Jrnl.* Mar. 30 'Bag' is a current piece of trade jargon for hip musicians, and means something between a personal style and a body of work. **1966** *Sunday Times* (Colour Suppl.) 13 Feb. 35/4 'His bag is paper sculpture', 'she's in a folk-song bag right now'. **1966** *Crescendo* Dec. 16/1 Singing blues with Basie is another kind of bag.

2. With various substantives defining its purpose, the two words being hyphened, as *air-*, *bread-*, *cloak-*, *game-*, *mail-*, *money-*, *post-*, *soot-*, *travelling-*. See also CARPET-BAG *sb.*, NOSE-BAG, WIND-BAG.

1711 ADDISON *Spect.* No. 3 ¶8 The Hill of Mony Bags, and the Heaps of Mony. **1711** STEELE *ibid.* No. 132 ¶1 His Cloke-bag was fixed in the Seat of the Coach. **1716** in *Lond. Gaz.* No. 5411/4 Pistol-Bags of grey Cloth. **1782** A. MONRO *Compar. Anat.* 60 The construction and dilatation of the air-bag. **1814** MOORE *Post Bag* 284 The honour and delight of first ransacking the Post Bag. **1836** MARRYAT *Midsh. Easy* xii, There's nothing about bread bags in the articles of war, sir. **1837** CARLYLE *Fr. Rev.* III. IV. v. 234 Our 'redoubts of cotton-bags' are taken. **1862** GRIFFITHS *Artill. Man.* 220 Three feeds in the corn-bag. **1863** KINGSLEY *Water-Bab.* i. 18 Not if it's in the bottom of the soot-bag. **1883** *Fisheries Exhib. Catal.* 217 Travelling-bags..steamer bags, tourists' bags, railroad bags, pic-nic bags, dress-suit bags, hand bags, shopping bags, brief bags.

II. Specific uses.

3. = Money-bag, purse.

1393 GOWER *Conf.* II. 284 Be so the bagge and he [the avarous] accorden, Him reccheth nought what men recorden Of him. **1530** PALSGR. 196/2 Bagge, a purse. **1572** *Lament. Lady Scot.* in *Scot. Poems 16th C.* (1801) II. 249 Gif sum sect knaw that they haue geir or baggs. **1596** BP. BARLOW *Three Serm.* i. 120 Laying the payment..vpon their parentes bagges. **1611** BIBLE *John* xii. 6 Because he was a thief, and had the bag. **1633** BP. HALL *Hard Texts* 230 A wealthy foole doth in vain hope by all his bagges to purchase wisedome. **1765** TUCKER *Lt. Nat.* II. 519 The covetous man likes to count over his bags.

†4. *poet.* in *pl.* Bagpipes. *Obs.* Cf. *pipes*.

c **1275** MAPES *Body & Soul* 50 This pipers that this bagges blewen. **1790** *Scots Songs* II. 36 Then to his bags he flew wi' speed, About the drone he twisted.

5. A small silken pouch to contain the back-hair of a wig; cf. BAG-WIG.

1702 *Lond. Gaz.* No. 3864/4 A short man..wears a Peruke ty'd up in a Bag. **1793** T. JEFFERSON *Writ.* (1830) IV. 487 It was understood..that gentlemen should be dressed in bags. **1806** A. DUNCAN *Nelson's Fun.* 13 Two attendants..in full mourning dress, with black gowns, swords, and bags. **1865** CARLYLE *Fredk. Gt.* II. VI. vii. 213 He cannot..change the graceful French bag into the strict Prussian queue in a moment.

6. A measure of quantity for produce, varying according to the nature of the commodity.

1679 BEDLOE *Popish Plot* 15 Removing some Baggs of Hopps. **1751** CHAMBERS *Cycl.* s.v., A bag of almonds..is about 3 hundred weight. **1845** *Morn. Chron.* 22 Nov. 5/2 Potatoes..There are three bushels to the bag.

7. a. = Mail-bag, post-bag; mail.

1702 *Lond. Gaz.* No. 3814/4 Write by Ormskirk Bag. **1781** COWPER *Lett.* 23 May, The boy has lost the bag in which your letter must have been. **1814** MOORE *Post Bag* 283 The Bag from which the following Letters are selected.

b. A diplomatic bag.

1816 H. BROUGHAM *Let.* in H. Maxwell *Creevey Papers* (1903) I. xi. 252, I think it better to trust this to the post than to any of their d—d bags. **1852** THACKERAY *Let.* 15 Mar. (1946) III. 25 When Wm. Grey goes to Paris you'll have the use of the bag again. **1964** *Times* 6 July 11/3 It [*sc.* reciprocity] should mean..that embassies and bags are inviolate.

†8. *Med.* A kind of poultice. *Obs.*

1753 CHAMBERS *Cycl. Supp.*, *Bag*..a kind of fomentation ..of proper ingredients, inclosed in a bag.

9. *Sporting.* = Game-bag; *hence*, the contents of a game-bag, the quantity of fish or game however large (embracing *e.g.* elephants and buffaloes) killed at one time; the produce of a hunting, fishing, or shooting expedition. *fig.* Hence in *pl.* (*slang*), much, many, 'heaps'.

1486 *Bk. St. Albans* B iij, Ye most take a partrich in yowre bagge. **1530** PALSGR. 196/2 A fauconner's bagge, *gibissière*. **1858** W. H. RUSSELL *My Diary in India* 16 Mar. (1860) I. xxi. 348 The philanthropists who were cheering each other with the thought that there was sure 'to be a good bag at Lucknow', will be disappointed. **1863** SPEKE *Discov. Nile* 36 'The bags' we made counted two brindled gnu, four water-boc, one pallah-boc, and one pig. **1865** RUSKIN *Sesame* i. 84 The chance of a brace or two of game less in your own bag in a day's shooting. **1867** F. FRANCIS *Angling* i. (1880) 29 The artist in roach-fishing alone will make a fair bag on an indifferent day. **1900** *Daily News* 9 June 5/5 Our bag was 4 engines and 84 trucks, with a quantity of coal. **1917** P. H. GIBBS *Battles of Somme* 105 'We took bags of 'em [*sc.* Germans],' said an officer. **1919** W. H. DOWNING *Digger Dialects* 9 *Bags*, plenty; a large number. **1919** J. B. MORTON *Barber of Putney* xiii. 209 It's not gay, this life, but it might be bags worse. *Ibid.* xvii. 285 There's bags of good names, and yet blokes go an' call their kids Ermyntrude. **1930** BROPHY & PARTRIDGE *Songs & Slang Brit. Soldier 1914–18* 96 *Bags*, plenty, lots. E.g. 'Got any bully?'—'Yes, bags of it.' And especially *bags of room*. **1930** C. V. GRIMMETT *Getting Wickets* i. 32 It was with Prahran that I recorded my big successes in club cricket, my 'bags' in four seasons being 67, 39, 68 and 56 wickets respectively. **1940** I. HALSTEAD *Wings of Victory* i. ii. 56 What his personal 'bag' was I don't know —certainly it was over twenty. **1945** R. L. SEDDON *Whims of W.A.A.F.* 14 With 'bags' of ambition. **1955** *Times* 19 Aug. 2/5 A retrospective exhibition..an exhibition of drawings.. and now a film..this is Picasso's 'bag' for the summer of 1955. **1962** A. WESKER *Chips with Everything* I. i. 12 We 'ad bags o' fun, bags o' it.

fig. **1881** SIR W. HARCOURT *Sp. Glasgow* 26 Oct., Lord Salisbury and Sir S. Northcote..had a rattling day at Newcastle and Beverley—but I ask myself what is their bag?

III. Transferred senses; bag-like objects.

10. An udder, a dug.

1579 SPENSER *Sheph. Cal.* Feb. 81 Thy Ewes, that wont to haue blowen bags. **1642** H. MORE *Pre-exist. Soul* xlvii. (D.) Those wicked Hags..whose writhled bags Foul fiends oft suck. **1697** DRYDEN *Virg. Eclog.* ix. 41 So may thy Cows their burden'd Bags distend. **1784** TWAMLEY *Dairying* 97 Cows with good bags. **1856** EMERSON *Eng. Traits* v. 99 The cow is sacrificed to her bag, the ox to his surloin.

11. A sac (in the body of animal) containing honey, poison, etc. (Chiefly *fig.*)

1529 LATIMER *Serm.* (1844) 20 Yet there may remain a bag of rusty malice, 20 years old, in thy neighbour's bosom. **1590** SHAKS. *Mid. N.* III. i. 171 The honie-bags steale from the humble Bees. *a* **1700** DRYDEN (J.) The swelling poison of the several sects Shall burst its bag. **1818** BYRON *Juan* I. ccxiv, Hived in our bosoms like the bag o' the bee. **1837** CARLYLE *Fr. Rev.* II. I. iv. 33 While sting and poison-bag were left.

12. a. A baggy place, a fold.

1572 MASCAL *Govt. Cattle* (1627) 160 Bagge, is in the weekes of the horse mouth.

b. *spec.* in *Leather Industry* (see quot.).

1909 *Cent. Dict.* Suppl. 105 *Bag*, in *leather-manuf.*, fullness in the middle of a skin which prevents it from lying out flat and smooth.

c. A fold of loose skin beneath the (human) eyes. Usu. in *pl.*

1867 W. ALLINGHAM *Diary* 10 June in H. Gernsheim *J. M. Cameron* (1948) 25, I want to do a large photograph of Tennyson and he objects! Says I make bags under his eyes. **1894** SOMERVILLE & 'ROSS' *Real Charlotte* I. x. 147 The dark bags of skin under Julia Duffy's eyes became slowly red. **1910** J. BUCHAN *Prester John* xix. 316, I caught a glimpse of my face in it,..lined with blue bags below the eyes. **1938** H. G. WELLS *Apropos of Dolores* iv. 174 His large grey eyes had if anything got larger and the lower lids lower. He has bags under them.

13. *pl.* The stomach, entrails. (*North dial.* and *Sc.*)

14. *Coal-Min.* A cavity filled with gas or water.

a **1733** NORTH *Life Guilford* (1808) I. 286 (D.) An account of a bag of water, which was broke in his greatest colliery. **1851** *Coal-tr. Terms Northumbld. & Durh.*, *Bag of Gas*, a cavity found occasionally in fiery seams of coal, containing highly condensed gas.

15. *Naut.* '*Bag of the Head-rails*, the lowest part..or that part which forms the sweep of the rail.' Smyth *Sailor's Word-bk.* 1867.

16. *fig.* Clothes that hang loosely about the wearer; (*colloq.*) trousers. *pl.*

1853 'C. BEDE' *Verdant Green* vi. 51 Just jump into a pair of bags and Wellingtons. **1860** SMILES *Self-Help* vii. 180 He ..only appears stout because he puts himself into those bags (trousers). **1861** A. TROLLOPE in *Tales of all Countries* (ser. 2) 136 A pair of the loosest pantaloons—I might, perhaps, better describe them as bags. **1923** D. L. SAYERS *Whose Body?* iv. 82 I'll run round and change at the club. Can't feed with Freddie Arbuthnot in these bags. **1927** —— *Unnatural Death* vii. 84 Just brush my bags down, will you, old man?

17. A disparaging term for a woman, esp. one who is unattractive or elderly; = BAGGAGE 6. *slang* (orig. *U.S.*).

1924 P. MARKS *Plastic Age* xviii. 202, I don't..chase around with filthy bags or flunk my courses. **1928** *Amer. Speech* Feb. 218 Say, Cress, who was that bag I saw you with yesterday? **1949** T. RATTIGAN *Harlequinade* (1953) 61 That's enough from you, you old bag! **1950** *Penguin New Writing* XL. 45 'It's just like you, you dreary old bag,' he would say to a blowsy old pro. **1961** M. DICKENS *Heart of London* i. 77 I've never really known a pretty girl like you. At the training college they were all bags.

IV. Phrases.

18. a. ***bag of bones***: an emaciated living being. ***the whole bag of tricks***: every expedient, everything (in allusion to the fable of 'the Fox and the Cat'). Also ***bag of tricks***, stock of resources; sometimes with play on other senses of 'bag' (old woman, etc.). ***in the bottom of the bag***: remaining as a last resource or expedient.

1659 REYNOLDS in Burton *Diary* (1828) IV. 447 If this be done, which is in the bottom of the bag, and must be done, we shall..be able to buoy up our reputation. **1838** DICKENS *O. Twist* iv. 64 There, get down stairs, little bag o' bones. **1841** ELIZUR WRIGHT tr. *La Fontaine's Fables* (ed. 2) XII. xviii. 314 But fox, in arts of siege well versed, Ransacked his bag of tricks accursed. **1848** KINGSLEY *Saint's Trag.* IV. iii. 204, I am almost ashamed to punish A bag of skin and bones. **1874** HOTTEN *Slang Dict.* 76 *Bag of tricks*, refers to the whole of a means towards a result. 'That's the whole bag of tricks.' **1889** G. B. SHAW *Lond. Mus.* (1937) 129 She relied largely for her acting on the exploitation of what is nothing but a bag of tricks. **1898** A. BENNETT *Man from North* xvi. 152 I've had three 3 A.M. midwifery cases this week—forceps, chloroform, and the whole bag of tricks. **1909** H. G. WELLS *Tono-Bungay* III. ii. §3 301 Learn the whole bag of tricks in six months. **1922** JOYCE *Ulysses* 139 She was a nice old bag of tricks. **1924** GALSWORTHY *White Monkey* III. viii. 185 A being who completely robbed the world of its importance, 'snooped', as it were, the whole 'bag of tricks'. **1936** L. C. DOUGLAS *White Banners* xiii. 280 Men were all alike. A woman didn't have to carry a very big bag of tricks to achieve her purpose. **1942** 'P. WENTWORTH' *Danger Point* xl. 233 Fingerprints... A nice bag of tricks for our modern scientific police. You put 'em in a hat and shake 'em up, and then you put in your hand and pick your murderer. **1957** KEHOE *Technique Film & T.V. Make-Up* iii. 37 The make-up kit is the artist's tool box and bag of tricks.

b. ***bag of mystery*** (usu. in pl. *bags of m.*): a sausage or saveloy. *slang.*

1864 in HOTTEN *Slang Dict.* 69. **1879** W. J. BARRY *Up & Down* xvi. 163 A slice of bread was given with the 'bag of mystery', as some rowdies called the luscious saveloy. **1909** WARE *Passing Eng.* 15/2 If they're going to keep running-in polony fencers for putting rotten gee-gee into the bags of mystery, I hope they won't leave fried-fish-pushers alone. **1921** H. FOSTON *At the Front* xvi. 115[Have you] any bags of mysteries, otherwise sausages? **1962** *John O' London's* 14 June 571/1 The bags of mystery or links of love are sausages.

c. Colloq. phr. *in the bag* (i.e. game-bag; see sense 9): (*a*) *Austral.* and *N.Z.* (see quot. 1945); (*b*) (*to be put*) *in the bag*, (to be) taken prisoner; (*c*) (orig. *U.S.*) virtually assured or secured, as good as in one's possession.

1900 J. SCOTT *Tales of Colonial Turf* 33 The neddy was in the bag in the Cup; he was no trier. **1945** BAKER *Austral. Lang.* ix. 174 A horse set to lose a race is said to be *in the bag*. **1919** J. BUCHAN *Mr. Standfast* ii. 52 Unless I went out to the Front again and got put in the bag and sent to the same Boche prison. **1956** D. M. DAVIN *Sullen Bell* II. vii. 152 When you went in the bag the chaps probably said 'Too bad about old Gus'. **1922** *San Francisco Call & Post* 19 July 17 Yes, yes, yes, but listen to me—I get this from the jock himself—this is in the bag. **1926** *Emporia* (Kan.) *Gazette* 24 Sept. 1/2 After Tunney landed with that terrific right, the fight was in the bag. **1929** *Liverpool Daily Courier* 4 Sept. 9/1 If half the members of a Talkie audience shudder every time a character on the screen says..'It's in the bag', the other half make a mental note of the expression for future use. **1932** WODEHOUSE *Hot Water* i. 32 We're sitting pretty. The thing's in the bag. **1943** B. J. HURREN *Eastern Med.* v. 51 Crete was 'in the bag' for Jerry if he wished to take it. **1957** *Economist* 30 Nov. 765/1 The message..contains a frank warning that independence is not 'in the bag'.

19. † *to turn to bag and wallet*: to become a beggar. *to give* (*one*) *the bag to hold*: to engage any one while taking the opportunity to slip away, to leave in the lurch. *to give the bag to*: to leave without warning (*obs.*); also in mod. dial., to dismiss (a servant, etc.) Also *to get the bag*: to be dismissed; [Cf. to give the SACK]. *to let the cat out of the bag*: to disclose the secret. *to empty the bag* (Fr. *vider le sac*): to tell the whole story, finish the discussion.

1592 GREENE *Upst. Courtier* in *Harl. Misc.* (Malh.) II. 236 To giue your masters the bagge. **1599** HAKLUYT *Voy.* II. I. 161 The turning to bag and wallet of the infinite number of the poore people imploied in clothing. **1607** DEKKER & WEBSTER *Westw. Hoe* IV. ii. Wks. 1873 II. 340, I fear our oares haue giuen us the bag. **1647** *Speedy Hue & Crie* 1 He being sometime an Apprentice on London bridge..gave his Master the bag. **1760** *Lond. Mag.* XXIX. 224 We could have wished that the author..had not let the cat out of the bag. **1788** P. M. FRENEAU *Misc. Wks.* 414 He must give us the bag, Adhere to Old England, and sail with her flag. **1793** T. JEFFERSON *Writ.* (1859) IV. 7 She will leave Spain the bag to hold. **1806** T. G. FESSENDEN *Orig. Poems* 39 'To give the bag' is an expression common with the lower classes in New England, and indicates that Miss Delia will not honour Mr. Damon with her company in a tete-a-tete conversation. *Ibid.* 73 Jonathan..tumbled, sadly, all the way, Lest he should get the bag, sir. **1823** SCOTT *Peveril* vii, She gave me the bag to hold, and was smuggling in a corner with a rich old Puritan. **1825** J. NEAL *Bro. Jonathan* II. 277 Sent away, with a flea in your ear; some girl has given you the bag. **1849** C. BRONTË *Shirley* III. xiv. 300 This last epithet I choose to suppress, because it would let the cat out of the bag. **1870** etc. [see E.D.D.]. **1871** W. S. GILBERT *Palace of Truth* I. 13 While publishing the truth He's no idea that he is doing so; And..he let innumerable cats Out of unnumbered bags. **1913** 'IAN HAY' *Happy-go-lucky* i. 4 'Your fag, isn't he?' 'I gave him the bag two terms ago... Tiny has him now.'

20. bag and baggage: *orig.* a military phrase denoting all the property of an army collectively, and of the soldiers individually; hence the phrase, originally said to the credit of an army or general, *to march out* (*with*) *bag and baggage* (= Fr. *vie et bagues sauves*), i.e. with all belongings saved, without surrender of anything; to make an honourable retreat. Now used depreciatively to express the absolute character of any one's departure: to clear out completely, 'and a good riddance too!' *the bag and baggage policy*: see last two quots.

[**1422** RYMER *Fœdera* X. 206/2 (De salvo conductu) Cum armaturis..bonis..bogeis, baggagiis.] **1525** LD. BERNERS *Froiss.* II. xxiii. 59 We haue with vs all our bagges and baggages..that we haue wonne..by armes. *Ibid.* I. cccxx. 497 So all the men of warre within departed with bag and baggage. **1544** *Chron. Grey Friars* (1852) 47 The kynge gave them alle there lyffes and pardynd them to goo with bagge and bagges. **1580** NORTH *Plutarch* (1676) 922 To go safely with bag and baggage, never to return. **1600** SHAKS. *A. Y. L.* III. ii. 170 Let vs make an honorable retreit, though not with bagge and baggage, yet with scrip and scrippage. *c* **1620** MIDDLETON *Witch* (1778) 35 To kick this fellow..And send him downe stayres with his bag and baggage. **1667** *Lond. Gaz.* No. 163/2 Upon honorable conditions, marching off with Bag and Baggage, Drums beating, Colors flying. **1741** RICHARDSON *Pamela* II. 34 Bag and Baggage, said she, I'm glad you're going. **1870** SPURGEON *Treas. Dav.* Ps. cxix. 115 The king sent them packing bag and baggage. **1876** GLADSTONE *Bulgarian Horrors* 61 The Turks..their Zaptiehs and their Mudirs..their Kaimakams and their Pashas, one and all, bag and baggage, shall, I hope, clear out from the province they have desolated and profaned. **1882** *Daily News* 28 May 5/6 Cites the famous Bulgarian pamphlet, precognising the bag-and-baggage policy as evidence that Mr. Gladstone will never be a party to restoring Turkish authority.

V. *Comb.* and *attrib.*

21. General relations: **a.** attrib., as **bag-fox**; **b.** objective, as *bag-bearer*, *-bearing*, *-carrier*, *-maker*, *-making*, *-punching* (cf. PUNCH *sb.*²), *-snatcher*; **c.** similative and parasynthetic, as *bag-bedded*, *-cheeked*, *-like*, *-shaped*.

1598 ROWLANDS *Betray. Christ* 24 Apostle once, increasing Christ's eleuen, *Bagbearer, to the charge of purse assign'd. **1853** KANE *Grinnell Exp.* xxix. (1856) 254 A night upon the ice, tented and *bag-bedded. **1890** J. WATSON *Conf. Poacher* x. 137, I had arranged with a confederate to act as *bag-carrier. **1957** N. FRYE *Anat. Criticism* iii. 197 A dwarf who carries a bag of 'needments'. He is not a traitor, like the other bag-carrier Judas Iscariot. **1839** CARLYLE *Chartism* viii. 166 A plain, *bag-cheeked.. Lancashire Man. **1849** TODD *Cycl. Anat. & Phys.* IV. 1020/2 That skinny and *bag-like part of its mouth which is under the jaw. **1870** *Pall Mall G.* 15 Aug. 12 Flat moors.. on which *bagmaking becomes sheer business, and you have a tame monotony of sport. **1927** *Daily Express* 21 Sept. 1/2 Dempsey jogged some miles along the road yesterday, did *bag-punching, etc. **1950** J. DEMPSEY *Championship Fighting* xxiv. 180 Bag-punching is another exercise that conditions and sharpens. **1836** TODD *Cycl. Anat. & Phys.* II. 969/1 A dilated *bag-shaped crop. **1908** *Westm. Gaz.* 20 Aug. 8/2 Sentencing a *bag-snatcher..to three months with hard labour... Prisoner snatched away the satchel of..a nurse.

22. Special combinations: **bag-filter**, a filter made of a cloth bag; **bag-fox**, a fox brought alive in a bag to be turned out before the hounds; † **bag-granado**, a grenade enclosed in a bag; **bag job** *U.S. slang*, an illegal search of a suspect's property by agents of the Federal Bureau of Investigation, esp. for the purpose of copying or stealing incriminating documents, etc.; cf. *black bag* adj. phr. s.v. BLACK *a.* 19 a; **bag-muff**, a muff containing a pouch which serves as a bag; **bag-net**, a bag-shaped net for catching fish, insects, etc.; **bag-rod**, a fishing-rod which can be taken to pieces and carried in a case; **bag-sleeve**, a sleeve tight at the wrist and baggy above; **bag-wolf** (cf. *bag-fox*).

a **1877** KNIGHT *Dict. Mech.* I. 209/2 **Bag-filter*, (sugar refining) a device sometimes used in clearing saccharine solutions of feculencies and impurities mechanically suspended therein. **1910** *Encycl. Brit.* X. 346/2 A crude method [of filtration] consists of straining the liquid through cotton or other cloth..formed into long narrow bags ('bag-filters'). **1741** *Compl. Fam.-Piece* II. i. 296 Sometimes he is reserved alive, and hunted another Day, which is called a *Bag-Fox. **1814** C. MATHEWS *Mem.* II. 319 They turned out a *bag-fox and we had a good run of three miles. **1638-48** G. DANIEL *Eclog.* v. 238 These *Bag-Granadoes flie Still to Advantage Garrisons' Revolt. **1971** *Time* 11 Oct. 44/1 **Bag job*, in the U.S., an illegal search of a suspected spy's residence to obtain incriminating information. **1971** *Time* 25 Oct. 15/1 In the past, numerous spies..have been exposed by bag jobs. **1973** [see *black bag* adj. phr. s.v. BLACK *a.* 19 a]. **1980** *Christian Science Monitor* 19 Sept. 2/1 A US attorney told the jury to 'say no to bag jobs' during opening statements in the trial of two former FBI officials. **1884** *Girl's Own P.* 29 Nov. 138/2 The useful *bag muff appears in..great varieties. **1777** TRAVIS in Pennant *Zool.* IV. 12 Our fishermen use a *bag-net fixed to an iron hoop. **1848** HARDY in *Proc. Berw. Nat. Club* II. vi. 321 A *bag-net, which..secured the beetles. **1787** BEST *Angling* 11 These *bag-rods..go up in a small compass. **1844** R. HART *Antiq. Norfolk* xxii. 69 A sort of *bag-sleeve, tight at the wrist. **1862** M. NAPIER *Life Ld. Dundee* II. 151 No more *bag-wolves to afford such sport.

23. *bag and spoon*: used *attrib.* to designate a type of dredging apparatus (see quot. 1940).

1840 *Civ. Engin. & Archit. Jrnl.* III. 30/1 Dredging with the common bag and spoon apparatus. **1940** *Chambers's Techn. Dict.* 70/2 *Bag and spoon dredger*, an implement consisting of a leather bag laced to a steel hoop;..used to dredge soft material.

bag (bæg), *v.*¹ [f. the sb.]

1. *intr.* **a.** To swell out as a bag, to bulge; *Naut.* to drop away from the direct course, to sag.

c **1440** *Promp. Parv.* 21 Baggyn, or bocyn owte, *Tumeo*. **1650** FULLER *Pisgah* II. x. 211 A corner of Ephraim, which baggeth into the south. **1657** S. PURCHAS *Pol. Flying Ins.* 142 Sometimes one side of the ear is good corn, and the other bags..and..will be smutty. **1676** R. WISEMAN (J.) The skin ..bagged, and had a porringer full of matter in it. *a* **1848** MARRYAT *R. Reefer* xxxvi, He was bagging to leeward, like a..barge laden with a hay-stack.

b. To hang loosely like clothes that are too big. Said esp. of trousers which become out of shape at the knees.

1824 W. IRVING *T. Trav.* I. 265 Coat, which bagged loosely about him. **1859** I. TAYLOR *Logic in Theol.* 205 Dingy embroidered trappings..seen bagging upon the wooden effigies. **1893** *Scribner's Mag.* Sept. 293/1 A trouser-leg is more obstinate in its ugliness. If tight it bags at the knees. **1913** A. R. HOPE *Half & Half Tragedy* 32 The Captain of the school has a pair of new breeches..; but they bag at the knees.

† **2.** *intr.* To be pregnant. (Also *to be bagged.*)

a **1400** [see BAGGED]. **1530** PALSGR. 442/2, I bagge, as a doe dothe that is with faune..Se howe yonder doe is bagged. **1589** WARNER *Alb. Eng.* VI. xxx. (1597) 148 Wel, Venus shortly bagged, and ere long was Cupid bread. **1603** HOLLAND *Plutarch's Mor.* 597 (R.) The females, or does.. will conceive and be bagged. **1616** [see BAGGED].

3. *trans.* To cause to swell or bulge; to cram full.

1583 STANYHURST *Aeneis* II. (Arb.) 51 Thee mischeuus engyn, Ful bagd with weapons. **1620** *Eccl. Proc. Durh., Newcastle-on-T.*, The chest..was bagd up with monye. *a* **1656** BP. HALL *Fall of Pride* Wks. II. 408 (T.) How doth an unwelcome dropsie bagge up the eyes. **1757** SMEATON in *Phil. Trans.* L. 204 Almost all the lights [= windows] in the church, tho' not broke were bagged outward.

4. *trans.* To put into a bag or bags. *to bag up*: to put up in a bag; to shut or store up generally.

1573 TUSSER *Husb.* (1878) 139 Good husbandrie baggeth vp gold in his chest. **1577** HOLINSHED *England* III. viii. 54 They [saffron chives] are dried and pressed into cakes, and then bagged up. **1711** *Act* in *Lond. Gaz.* No. 4874/1 The precise Day..on which..they shall Bag..their Hops. **1798** W. HUTTON *Autobiog.* 12, I undressed, bagged up my things in decent order, and prepared for rest. **1870** LOWELL *Study Wind.* 1 Stopping..to bag a specimen.

5. To put game killed into a bag; *also*, to kill game (without reference to the bag). Also *absol.*

1814 *Month. Mag.* XXXVII. 238 To allow the royal sportsman to bag more birds than himself. **1844** HAWKER *Instr. Yng. Sportsmen* 148 To bag a dozen head of game without missing. **1859** JEPHSON *Brittany* ix. 150 My friend thus bagged two wolves. **1890** LD. LUGARD *Diaries* (1959) I. 135 In the evening I again hit several animals by the unanimous verdict of my men, but did not bag.

6. *colloq.* **a.** To seize, catch, take possession of, steal. To add to one's 'bag' (BAG *sb.* 9). *fig.*

1818 MOORE *Fudge Fam. Paris* vi, Who can help to bag a few, When Sidmouth wants a death or two. **1824** BYRON *Juan* XVI. lxii, The constable..Had bagg'd this poacher upon Nature's manor. **1857** HUGHES *Tom Brown* II. iii. 268 The idea of being led up to the Doctor..for bagging fowls. **1861** MAX MÜLLER *Chips* (1880) II. xxiv. 243 A stray story may thus be bagged in the West-end of London. **1879** *Bell's Life in London* 28 June 4/2 Whom Mr. Hornby very smartly 'bagged' at mid-on. **1936** J. DOS PASSOS *Big Money* 72 He was almost bagged by a taxicab crossing the street. **1940** I. HALSTEAD *Wings of Victory* I. ii. 59 Pilot Officer Elliott..has now bagged two. **1943** WARD-JACKSON *Piece of Cake* 11 *To bag, bagged*, to hit by aerial gunfire; shot down. **1945** *Finito! Po Valley Campaign* 17 They bagged 9,000 PWs and a battery of 15-inch guns.

b. To claim; reserve. Used esp. by children (see quot. 1914 and BAGS I). *colloq.*

1914 *Concise Oxf. Dict.* Add. 1045/2 *Bag*, (also, in school slang) claim on the ground of being the first to claim (*I b.*, but usu. *bags I* or *bags, first innings!*). **1923** J. MANCHON *Le Slang* 56, I'm going to bag the best chair. **1948** R. A. KNOX *Mass in Slow Motion* vii. 68 The other girl bagging the hot-water pipes first. **1968** *Listener* 29 Feb. 269, I bags be Anthony Wedgwood Benn.

7. To dismiss, discharge (a person). Cf. SACK *v.*¹ 5 a. Cf. BAG *sb.* 19.

1848 *Chaplain's Rep., Preston House of Correction* 61 The master told him if he did not mind his work he would 'bag' him. **1895** W. WESTALL *Sons of Belial* II. xxii. 83 'Not have me at th' shop!..You surely wouldn't bag me?.. Bagged, beggared, and disinherited!' he moaned. *Ibid.* 85 I'll work for nowt. Only don't bag me just like a common hand.

8. *to bag school*, to play truant. Also *to bag it*. *U.S.*

1934 J. O'HARA *Appointment in Samarra* (1935) vii. 203 She did not report him on Sunday afternoons when he 'bagged it' to go to a ball game. **1948** *Philadelphia Bulletin* 15 Jan. 14 Threatening him with castor oil, when he seemed set to bag school, never did any good.

bag, *v.*² Also 7 bagge, 9 badge. [Origin not ascertained: cf. BATCH.] To cut corn, pease, or beans, with a bagging or badging hook: see quot. 1865.

a **1697** AUBREY *Wilts, MS. R. Soc.* 123 (Halliw.) They cannot mowe it with a scythe, but they cutt it with such a hooke as they doe bagge pease with. **1830** *Edin. Encycl.* XIV. 234 They [beans] are bagged like wheat. **1865** *Gard. & Farmer's Vade M.* II. 123 The corn is either mown, or reaped, or bagged. In 'bagging,' as it is called, a heavy hook is used: a wisp of straw is cut first and doubled up, or a stick is used instead, held in the left hand, and with the right the heavy hook is driven against the corn close to the ground, and so, by successive strokes, the corn is cut, perhaps a foot deep, up against the standing crop; the wisp or stick in the left hand serving to guide it to a standing place. **1877** E. WARBURTON *Poems* 23 Sweet to see cornfields badged, and wheatsheaf bound.

Baganda (bəˈgændə), *sb.* and *a.* [Bantu name; cf. Swahili *Waganda*.] **A.** *sb.* A negroid Bantu-speaking people inhabiting Buganda, a province of Uganda on the N.W. shore of Lake Victoria. **B.** *adj.* Of or pertaining to this people.

[**1882** WILSON & FELKIN *Uganda & Egyptian Soudan* I. vii. 148 Several tribes are to be found in Uganda, living.. scattered through the country. The most important tribe, in every respect, is that of the Waganda.] **1889** R. P. ASHE *Two Kings of Uganda* vi. 47 Bloody raids for which the Baganda are infamously famous. *Ibid.* xviii. 215 (*heading*) Baganda converts and martyrs. **1902** *Encycl. Brit.* XXXIII. 541/2 The Bantu negroes..include the remarkable Baganda people. *Ibid.*, The Baganda are now mainly Christian. **1911** FRAZER *Golden Bough* (ed. 3) I. iii. 142 The Baganda believe that a barren wife infects her husband's garden with her own sterility. **1960** *Economist* 8 Oct. 136/2 The Uganda government must therefore press on with the February elections, despite the gyrations of the Baganda.

‖**bagarre** (bagɑːr). [F.] A scuffle, tumult. Also *fig.*

1897 CONRAD *Let.* 9 Aug. in G. Jean-Aubry *J.C.* (1927) I. 209 Posterity will be busy thieving, lying..and the half-dozen men lost in that *bagarre* are more likely to weep than to smile over those [*sc.* Kipling's] masterpieces. **1955** D. BARTON *Glorious Life* vi. 73 '*Fracas* with the twins?' '*Bagarre.* You saw?' **1963** *Punch* 6 Feb. 204/3 The subtle *bagarre* triggered off by a true conflict.

‖**bagasse** (bəˈgæs). [a. F. *bagasse*, ad. Sp. *bagazo*, husks of olives, grapes, etc., after pressing; perh. a variant of *bagage* 'lumber, trash' (Minsheu), with augmentative suffix *-azo*: cf. BAGGAGE 4.] **a.** The refuse products in sugar-making, whether from the cane or from beet. Also *attrib.* Cf. BEGASSE.

1833 B. SILLIMAN *Man. Sugar Cane* 15 Two boys at bagasse (ground cane) carts. **1835** J. H. INGRAHAM *South-West* I. 239 The *bagasse* or cane-trash (called in the West Indies *migass*) is..conveyed to a distance..to be burnt. **1854** in URE *Dict. Arts.* **1881** HEDGES *Sug. Canes* 23 On the opposite side of the mill is another apron, for conveying the Bagasse. **1882** *Contemp. Rev.* Sept. 360. **1960** *Times* 8 Jan. 7 Mauritius..solved the problems of a one-crop economy by burning 'bagasse', the fibre that remains after sugar cane is crushed. **1967** E. CHAMBERS *Photolitho-offset* xvi. 246 The fibres of straws, bamboos, sugar cane waste (bagasse) and palms can be used for paper-making.

b. = BAGASSOSIS.

1943 *New Orleans Med. & Surg. Jrnl.* XCV. 558 (*title*) Bagasse disease of the lung. **1944** *Newsweek* 26 June 80 A new industrial disease called bagasse was reported..among sugarcane workers who handled..the fibrous material.

ba'gasse-,burner, a furnace for consuming bagasse.

1883 *Century Mag.* Jan. 391 The huge, square, red brick bagasse-burner, into which the residuum of crushed sugar-cane passes.

bagassosis (bægə'səʊsɪs). *Path.* [mod.L., f. BAGASSE + -OSIS.] A disease of the lungs, due to inhalation of the dust of bagasse.

1941 JAMISON & HOPKINS in *New Orleans Med. & Surg. Jrnl.* XCIII. 580 (*title*) Bagassosis: A fungus disease of the lung. **1944** *Dorland's Med. Dict.* (ed. 20) 199/1 *Bagassosis*, a respiratory disorder due to the inhalation of the dust of bagasse, the waste of sugar cane after the sugar has been extracted. **1947** *Thorax* II. 99 The radiographic changes in the lungs in bagassosis are illustrated.

bagatelle (,bægə'tɛl). Forms: 7 **bagatell, baggatelle, bagatello, 7-8 bagatel, 8- bagatelle.** [a. F. *bagatelle*, ad. It. *bagatella*, a dim. form which Diez attaches to Parmesan *bagata* a little property, prob. from *baga*: see BAGGAGE. With *bagatello*, cf. -ADO *suff.* 2. Formerly quite naturalized in sense 1, now scarcely so; sense 2 is purely Eng. in origin and use.]

1. A trifle, a thing of no value or importance.

c **1645** HOWELL *Lett.* II. xxi, Your trifles and bagatels are ill bestowed upon me. **1658** J. ROBINSON *Eudoxa* i. 4 Every particular thing..even unto the smallest bagatello's. **1659** GAUDEN *Tears Ch.* 102 (D.) To please themselves with toyes and bagatelloes. **1679** MRS. BEHN *Feigned Court.* II. i, Ah Baggatelles, Seignior, Baggatelles. *a* **1733** NORTH *Exam.* II. v. ¶100 He makes a meer Bagatel of it. **1786** T. JEFFERSON *Writ.* 1859 I. 566 As to the satisfaction for slaves carried off, it is a bagatelle. **1872** BAKER *Nile Trib.* iv. 53 The bonâ fide tax is a bagatelle to the amounts squeezed from him by the ..soldiery.

b. A piece of verse or music in a light style.

1827 *Gent. Mag.* XCVII. II. 618 The best amatory and pastoral bagatelles in our language. **1880** GROVE *Dict. Mus.*, *Bagatelle*, a short piece of pianoforte music in a light style.

†**c.** *attrib.* or as *adj.* Trifling, trumpery. *Obs.*

1637 BASTWICK *Litany* I. 17 All which they haue..ouerthrowne with their baggatelle invention.

2. A game played on a table having a semi-circular end at which are nine holes. The balls used are struck from the opposite end of the board with a cue. The name is sometimes applied to a modified form of billiards known also as *semi-billiards*.

1819 *P.O. Lond. Direct.* 343 Thurston, John..Billiard Table and Bagatelle Manufacturer. **1854** MAYHEW *Lond. Labour* III. 298 They have cards and bagatelle to keep them.

b. *attrib.* as **bagatelle-ball, -board, -room.**

1837 DICKENS *Pickw.* xiv, A bagatelle-board on the first floor. **1854** MAYHEW *Lond. Labour* II. 19 The numbered sockets in a bagatelle-board. **1863** H. KINGSLEY *A. Elliot* II. xvii. 235 Austin went on knocking the bagatelle-balls about.

'bagaty, 'baggety. *Sc.* The lump-fish.

1710 R. SIBBALD *Fife & Kinross* II. ii. 52 *Lumpus alter*..which our Fishers call the Hush-Padle or Bagaty. **1794** in *Statist. Acc. Scotl.* XII. 521 The fish caught here are..mackerel, baggety, sand-eel [etc.]. **1810** [see PADDLE *sb.*[2]]. **1828** J. FLEMING *Hist. Brit. Anim.* 190 Lump-fish..Hush, Bagaty. **1867** SMYTH *Sailor's Word-bk.*, *Lump*..the trivial name of the baggety..*Cyclopterus lumpus*.

bage, bager, obs. forms of BADGE, BADGER.

bagel ('beɪg(ə)l). [ad. Yiddish *beygel*, app. (Webster) f. MHG. **böugel*, whence G. dial. *beugel*, *bäugl*, dim. of MHG. *boug-*, *bouc-* ring, bracelet:—OHG. *boug* = OE. *bēag* BEE[2].] A hard ring-shaped salty roll of bread. Also *attrib.* Cf. BEIGEL.

1932 L. GOLDING *Magnolia St.* x. 165 *Bagels* are like large wooden curtain-rings to look at... She cut them and buttered them. **1957** LUCILLE STERN *Midas Touch* III. xxiii. 174, I got lox and bagels. You hungry, Baruch? **1959** *Guardian* 3 Dec. 9/1 The 'Bronx Bagel-babies'—the middle class girls who leap feet first into the vie Bohême. *Ibid.*, Pursued by Bagel-babies..most of the genuine artists have moved East. **1961** *Encounter* XVI. No. 4. 22, I eat salty bagels in the sun. **1961** *Guardian* 25 Mar. 4/1 His haunts, like the bagel shop.

bagful ('bægfʊl). [f. BAG *sb.* + -FUL.] As much as a bag will contain.

c **1305** *St. Swithin* 57 in *E.E.P.* (1862) 45 Mid a bageful of eiren: a womman þer com. **1581** J. BELL *Haddon's Answ. Osor.* 7 Love us with a bagge full of love. **1856** KANE *Arct. Exp.* II. vii. 84 Six half-bushel bagfuls of frozen water.

baggage ('bægɪdʒ), *sb.* and *a.* Forms: 5-6 **bagage**, 6 **bagguage, baggadge, (badgage), bagige**, 5- **baggage.** [a. OF. *bagage* (15th c. in Littré) 'property packed up for carriage' (= Pr. *bagatge*, Sp. *bagage*), f. *baguer* 'to tie up, bind, truss up,' or f. the cogn. sb. *bagues*, i.e. 'bundles, packs' (used, much earlier, in the same sense as the collective *bagage*), pl. of *bague* = Pr. *bagua*, It. and late L *baga*; cf. BAG. Sense 4, not in Fr., is found in Sp. *bagage*; 6 and 7 have been referred by various etymologists to F. *bagasse* (= Pr. *baguassa*, Sp. *bagasa*, It. *bagascia*), with which they coincide in sense; but no formal connexion has been traced; they also arise naturally enough out of those that precede, and seem really to be senses of this word, at most influenced in use by the F. *bagasse*. The latter is itself of uncertain origin. See Littré.]

A. *sb.* Commonly *collective* in senses 1-4 (formerly occas. with *pl.*); in senses 5-7 an ordinary sb. with *pl.*

1. a. The collection of property in packages that one takes along with him on a journey; portable property; luggage. (Now rarely used in Great Britain for ordinary 'luggage' carried in the hand or taken with one by public conveyance; but the regular term in U.S.)

c **1430** *Pol. Rel. & L. Poems* (1866) 18 To gete hem Bagage, put hem sylffe in prees. *c* **1450** '*Chaucer's' Dreme* Wks. (Bell) 101 Was left not one, Horse, male, trusse, ne baggage. **1530** PALSGR. 196/2 Baggage, *baguaige*. **1578** T. N. tr. *Conq. W. India* 23 Indians..to serve and to cary baggage. **1703** MAUNDRELL *Journ. Jerus.* (1732) 11 Arrived with all our Baggage on the other side of the River. **1739** W. STEPHENS in *Colonial Rec. Georgia* (1906) IV. 410 The Captain..was carrying divers parcels of baggage to the water-side. **1766** GOLDSM. *Vic. W.* xx, Mrs. Arnold politely offered to send..for my son's baggage. **1842** J. S. BUCKINGHAM *Slave States* II. 173 The cart he was driving contained their baggage. **1852** C. A. BRISTED *Upper Ten Thousand* 81 An American never uses the conversational term luggage, but always speaks of his impediments as baggage. **1883** P. PEMBER in *Harper's Mag.* Dec. 110/1 Keep a sharp look out on your baggage.

b. *ellipt.* A baggage-car on a train. *U.S.*

1926 J. BLACK *You can't Win* vii. 82 It was a warm night, and riding the front end of the baggage was pleasant enough.

2. a. *spec.* The portable equipment of an army; = L. *impedimenta*.

1489 CAXTON *Faytes of A.* I. xiii. 34 Baggage and fardellages must be taken. **1523** LD. BERNER'S *Froiss.* I. xviii. 26 They of Heynaulte [sent back] their harneys and baggages by water. **1591** GARRARD *Art Warre* 13 Borne of the Boyes amongest other Baggage. **1650** FULLER *Pisgah* II. xi. 232 Two hundred..foot being faint stayed with the baggage. **1701** *Lond. Gaz.* No. 3711/1 Their Artillery and heavy Baggage have passed likewise. **1810** WELLINGTON in Gurw. *Disp.* V. 515 The baggage of the British army is always an embarrassment.

b. The baggage-train of an army, and the men guarding it.

1603 KNOLLES *Hist. Turkes*, Turning the head of their baggages toward the fort. **1611** BIBLE *Judith* vii. 2 Twelue thousand horsemen, beside the baggage, and other men that were afoot.

c. *bag and baggage*: see BAG 20.

†**3.** *fig.* Encumbrances, burdensome matters. *Obs.*

1607 BACON *Riches*, *Ess.* (Arb.) 230, I cannot call Riches better, then the Baggage of Vertue. **1757** SMOLLETT *Reprisal* I. viii. (1777) 160, I..never burden my brain with unnecessary baggage.

†**4. a.** Rubbish, refuse, dirt. *Obs.*

1549 CHALONER *Erasm. Moriæ Enc.* A iv, Nettles, Thistles ..or suche lyke baggage grow. **1576** GASCOIGNE *Steele Glas* (Arb.) 79 When brewers put no bagage in their beere. **1587** GOLDING *De Mornay* xviii. (1617) 318 Dust, Coales, Ashes and such other baggage. **1645** WARD *Serm. bef. Ho. Commons* 31 It runs out in weeds and baggage. **1661** HICKERINGILL *Jamaica* 88 A mere Glut, Like loathed Baggage to the nauseous Gut.

†**b.** Purulent or corrupt matter, pus. *Obs.*

1576 NEWTON *Lemnie's Complex.* 118 (D.) Naughty baggage and hurtfull phlegme. **1610** BARROUGH *Physick* V. vi. (1639) 278 The abscession being already come to suppuration..if the matter or any other baggage therein contained, be not discussed, etc.

†**c.** A trifle, a trashy article. *Obs.*

1579 TOMSON *Calvin's Serm. Tim.* 205/2 May decke her selfe simply..neither haue these little trifling bagages.

†**d.** *fig.* Spoken or written trash, rubbish, 'rot.'

1538 BALE *Thre Lawes* 1716 And shall thys baggage put by the word of God? **1545** ASCHAM *Toxoph.* (Arb.) 83 A Boke ..wherin he..settes oute much rifraffe, pelfery, trumpery, baggage, and beggerie ware. **1579** FULKE *Heskins's Parl.* 240 To read such beastly baggage.

†**e.** *fig.* Dregs, offscouring, riff-raff. *Obs.*

1603 H. CROSSE *Vertues Commw.* (1878) 117 The very scum, rascallitie, and baggage of the people.

†**f.** Contemptuously applied after the Reformation to the rites and accessories of Roman Catholic worship. *Obs.*

1549 OLDE *Erasm. Par. Eph.* Prol. C iiij, This Popyshe baggage of dumme ceremonies. **1566** KNOX *Hist. Ref.* Wks. 1846, I. 191 Pilgremage, pardonis, and otheris sic baggage. **1566** *Lincolnsh. Ch. Furn.* 88 Vestments, Copes, albes, Tunacles and all other such baggages were defaced. **1579** TOMSON *Calvin's Serm. Tim.* 85/1 They come with their deuotions, as to heare a masse, to do their baggage. **1587** FLEMING *Contn. Holinshed* III. 1368/1 With their hallowed baggages from Rome to poison the senses.

†**5.** A worthless or vile fellow. *Obs.*

1594 CAREW *Huarte's Exam. Wits* (1616) 209 They might soundly sleepe on his eyes, although by nature he were a baggage. **1601** HOLLAND *Pliny* I. 111 Catamites and shamefull baggages that king Alexander the Great left there.

6. A worthless good-for nothing woman; a woman of disreputable or immoral life, a strumpet.

1596 SHAKS. *Tam. Shr.* Induct. i. 3 Y'are a baggage, the Slies are no Rogues. **1601** R. JOHNSON *Kingd. & Commw.* 81 Every common soldior carrying with him his she-baggage. **1611** COTGR., *Bagasse*, a Baggage, Queane. **1693** W. ROBERTSON *Phraseol. Gen.* 197 A baggage, or Souldier's Punk, *Scortum Castrense*. **1712** STEELE *Spect.*, No. 450, ¶5 That Wife dying, I took another, but both proved to be idle Baggages. **1850** MRS. STOWE *Uncle Tom's C.* xii, He only swore the gal was a baggage, and that he was devilish unlucky. **1851** THACKERAY *Eng. Hum.* ii. (1858) 68 She was a disreputable, daring, laughing, painted French baggage, that Comic Muse.

7. Used familiarly or playfully of any young woman, especially in conjunction with *artful*, *cunning*, *sly*, *pert*, *saucy*, *silly*, etc. (Cf. *wench*, *minx*, *hussy*, *gipsy*, *rogue*, etc.)

1672 DAVENANT *Wits* (1673) 182 The Baggages About you are able to earn their own living. **1687** CONGREVE *Old Batch.* I. iii, I believe the Baggage loves me. **1715** ADDISON *Drummer* II. i, Here comes Abigal. I must teaze the baggage. **1766** GOLDSM. *Vic. W.* xxviii, Tell them they are two arrant little baggages. **1822** W. IRVING *Braceb. Hall* iii. 24 She has an orphan niece, a pretty, soft-hearted baggage.

†**B.** *adj.* (from attrib. use of the sb. in sense 4; cf. *trumpery*.) *Obs.*

†**1.** Rubbishy, refuse. *Obs.*

1548 UDALL *Erasm. Par. N.T.* Pref. 10 The trashe and bagguage stuf..this man hath sifted out. **1640** J. DYKE *Worthy Commun.* 203 Thistles, nettles, and such like baggage trash.

†**2.** Trashy, worthless, beggarly, trumpery, despicable; cf. A 4. *Obs.*

1553 BRENDE *Q. Curtius* B b vj, In respect wherof the spoiles of the Percians were but vile, and bagage. **1580** NORTH *Plutarch* (1676) 458 Hyccara, a baggage Village of the barbarous People. **1586** J. HOOKER *Girald. Irel.* in *Holinsh.* II., 157/1 So addicted to poperie and that baggage religion. **1605** A. WOTTON *Answ. Pop. Articles* 121 God..is crusht vp togeather into the compasse [of] a baggage wafer cake. *a* **1625** BOYS *Wks.* (1630) 183 We may not..breake God's net, because there are some baggage fish.

†**3.** Of persons: Morally worthless, good-for-nothing, vile, 'scurvy.' *Obs.*

1580 NORTH *Plutarch* (1676) 1003 This baggage fellow Burrus. **1592** WYRLEY *Armorie* 147 His baggage mind to craft was whole disposd. **1626** SHIRLEY *Maid's Rev.* IV. ii, That baggage Ambitious girl, Berinthia. **1668** ROLLE *Abridgm.* 56 Si home dit à..un Town-Clark..Thou art a..bribing Knave, a baggage Knave, a dissembling Knave..Action gist. *a* **1670** HACKET *Abp. Williams* II. 123 (D.) [He] had nothing to do with that baggage woman.

†**4.** Purulent, nasty, corrupt. *Obs.*

1576 NEWTON *Lemnie's Complex.* (1633) 177 Affected with this baggage phlegme and distilling humour. **1597** GERARD *Herbal* (1633) 665 [It] draweth forthe much baggage flegme.

C. *Comb.* and *Attrib.*

1. Obvious combinations, chiefly attrib., from the sb. in senses 1 and 2, as ***baggage-agent***, ***-animal***, ***-car***, ***-cart***, ***-elephant***, ***-hatch***, ***-horse***, ***-man***, ***-necessaries***, ***-tag***, ***-train***, ***-truck***, ***-wagon***. Also ***baggage-bound*** adj.

1858 W. P. SMITH *Railw. Celebr.* 2 (Advt.), On almost all the trains will be found Baggage or Express Agents. **1852** GROTE *Greece* II. lxix. IX. 44 Many baggage-animals perished of hunger. **1867** *Record* Supp. 7 Aug., The saddled donkeys, camels baggage-bound. **1833** *Amer. Railroad Jrnl.* II. 725/3 An agent is always stationed at the brake of the baggage car. **1878** B. F. TAYLOR *Between Gates* 26 A Babel of trunks is surging towards the baggage-cars. **1749** FIELDING *Tom Jones* VII. xi. (1840) 95 The portmanteau..being put up into the baggage-cart. **1842** J. S. BUCKINGHAM *Slave States* II. 173 A barouche..and a baggage-cart following with five trunks. **1824** *Edin. Rev.* XLI. 35, I amused myself with looking at a baggage-elephant. **1891** KIPLING *Light that Failed* xiv. 301 Cabin as close to the baggage-hatch as possible. **1640-1** *Kirkcudbr. War-Comm. Min. Bk.* (1855) 143 The Committie ordaines that Roger Oliver, baggage man of Ironegray, be answerable for the baggage horss thairof. **1820** SCOTT *Monast.* xxxv, The pedlar was..accommodated with the use of a baggage horse. **1791** BOSWELL *Johnson* (1831) III. 13 Intrusted to a fellow to be delivered to our baggage-man. **1879** F. R. STOCKTON *Rudder Grange* vii. 75, I went up-stairs and got a baggage tag. **1841** R. PARK *Pantology* 506 The baggage train should be placed either in the column, or so near it that it may be speedily defended. **1863** KINGLAKE *Crimea* II. 245 The baggage-train accompanying our forces. *a* **1861** T. WINTHROP *Life in Open Air* (1863) 228 The soldiers..shot overboard a heavy baggage-truck. **1936** L. C. DOUGLAS *White Banners* x. 223 Such chuff-chuffing of engines and clanging of bells and rattling of baggage-trucks. **1689** *Lond. Gaz.* No. 2423/4 A Train of Artillery and a good number of Baggage-Wagons. **1791** WASHINGTON *Diary* 21 Mar. (1925) IV. 149 My equipage and attendance consisted of a Chariot ..a light baggage Waggon and two horses. **1849** D. NASON *Jrnl.* 78 [I] got a ride in a baggage wagon, for which I paid 37½ cents.

2. Special comb.: **baggage-check**, a ticket for luggage on American railways; **baggage-man** or **-master**, one who has charge of the baggage of an army, or of the luggage on American railways; **baggage-room**, a luggage-office; **baggage-smasher**, American nickname for a railway-porter.

18.. Smith *Sup. Court Rep.* I. 522 A passenger having lost her *baggage check. **1848** *Hunt's Merch. Mag.* (U.S.) XVIII. 334 (*caption*) Railroad Baggage checks. **1948** *Sat. Even. Post* 25 Sept. 125 *One* ticket and *one* set of baggage checks takes you straight through to your overseas destination. **1858** *N.Y. Tribune* 14 Jan. 2/3 In the baggage car..the *baggage man..asked me what I wanted. **1904** *Westm. Gaz.* 4 May 5/1 A railway baggageman. **1815** WELLINGTON in Gurw. *Disp.* X. 349 An assistant *Baggage Master to each division. **1845** *Hunt's Merch. Mag.* (U.S.) XIII. 581 The conductor..is also called baggage-master. **1883** AGNES CRANE in *Leis. Ho.* 282/1 The baggage-masters leapt from their wide doors. *a* **1884** C. READE *Let.* in J. Hollingshead *Gaiety Chron.* (1898) iii. 144 He also does all utility business, and is baggage-master on tours, etc. An invaluable servant in a theatre with small pretensions. **1926** *Amer. Mercury* Mar. 340/2 The baggage-master at the college transfer remembered re-checking his trunks. **1819** P. WAKEFIELD *Excursions N. Amer.* (ed. 3) 25 On deck there are numerous conveniences, such as *baggage-rooms, smoking-rooms, &c. **1883** *Longman's Mag.* July 285 The wretched little booking-office, and the baggage-room. **1963** *P.M.L.A.* Dec. p. vii/2 (*list*) U.K. left luggage: U.S. baggage room. **1851** *San Francisco True Standard* 6 Mar. 2/2 *Baggage Smashers. **1880** *New Virginians* I. 37 Called 'baggage-smashers.' **1883** *Pall Mall G.* 14 June, The Saratoga trunks are hurled recklessly by the 'baggage-smashers' on to the deck.

baggaged ('bægɪdʒd), *ppl. a. nonce-wd.* [f. as though from a vb. *to baggage.*] Packed up.

1821 BYRON in Moore *Life* (1866) 528 They were all sealed and baggaged so as to have made it a month's work to get at them again.

'baggageless, *a.* Having no baggage; having lost one's baggage.

1891 *Daily News* 28 Nov. 3/6 On Sunday he wandered about alone and baggageless. **1905** *Westm. Gaz.* 6 Dec. 9/1 Drenched, weary, and baggageless travellers.

† **'baggagely**, *a. Obs.* [f. BAGGAGE + -LY[1].] Rubbishy, worthless.

1573 TUSSER *Husb.* (1878) 35 No storing of pasture with baggedglie tit. **1583** GOLDING *Calvin on Deut.* xcix. 613 The thinges..are baggagely trifles.

baggager ('bægɪdʒə(r)). [f. BAGGAGE + -ER[1].] One who carries or has charge of baggage. Also, a beast that carries baggage; a baggage horse, camel, etc.

1614 RALEIGH *Hist. World* III. (1736) 93 The Victuallers and baggagers [of the Army]. **1859** W. GREGORY *Egypt & Tunis* II. 214 Leaving the tents and baggagers to follow. **1859** *Blackw. Mag.* Apr. 459/2 Whack goes the long whip, aimed at the rearmost baggager. The aggrieved horse flies out with a bounce. **1908** *Animal Management* 279 The ordinary pace [is] two and a half miles an hour for 'baggagers', and up to twelve miles for riding camels.

† **'baggagery**. *Obs. rare*[-1]. [f. BAGGAGE (cf. the sb. (sense 4) and the adj.) + -RY: cf. *savagery.*] Worthless rabble; the offscourings of society.

1589 NASHE *Mart. Months Minde* 26 Men of the best sorte (an vnfit match for these of the basest baggagerie).

baggammon, obs. form of BACKGAMMON.

baggard, obs. form of BOGGART.

† **bagge**, *v. Obs. rare.* [Origin not ascertained: cf. BAGGINGLY. From the ambiguous value of ME. *gg*, we do not know whether to pronounce *badge* or *bag.*] To look askew, or obliquely; to leer, ogle, or glance aside; cf. ASQUINT 2 c.

1369 CHAUCER *Bk. Duchesse* 623 The trayteresse false and ful of gyle..That baggeth foule and loketh fayre. *c* **1380** WYCLIF *Serm.* Sel. Wks. 1869, I. 191 Men þat..reulen hem bi þe firste reule, þat þei baggen not þerfro.

bagge, obs. form of BAG and BADGE.

bagged (bægd), *ppl. a.* [f. BAG *v.* + -ED.]

†**1.** Big with young; pregnant. *Obs.*

a **1400** *Sir Perc.* 717 The mere was bagged with fole. **1520** WHITTINTON *Vulg.* (1527) 6 b, An hare bagged [*gravida*] maye not awaye. **1616** SURFL. & MARKH. *Countr. Farm* 697 The female being bagd.

2. Enclosed in, or as in, a bag; encysted.

1572 J. JONES *Bathes Buckstone* 15 a, Matter, cluddered, lomped or bagged, in any principall member. **1655** GURNALL *Chr. in Arm.* iv. §2 (1669) 425/1 The venom that is bagg'd in his heart. **1854** MRS. GASKELL *North & S.* xv, Right under the bagged-up chandelier.

3. Hanging in bags, hanging slack so as to drop in a curve.

1618 HOLYDAY *Juvenal* (1673) 188 Bagg'd cheeks, with wrinkles deep and wide. **1858** CARLYLE *Fredk. Gt.* I. III. v. 171 Cheeks somewhat bagged and wrinkly. **1867** F. FRANCIS *Angling* ii. (1880) 69 Without leaving any bagged or slack line.

4. Provided with bags.

1861 SALA *Tw. round Clock* 182 Here they come, bagged and bundled, and gesticulating and jabbering.

5. Having bags or udders.

1884 *Kendal Merc.* 26 Sept. 4/7 Their once famous..and well-bagged cows.

'bagger. [f. BAG *v.* + -ER[1].] **a.** One who encloses in bags; *spec.* a miser (*obs.*).

1740 *Collect. Sir T. Scot* 32 in Peck *Cromwell*, He spent, and lookt for no reward, He cold not play the bagger. **1763** *Museum Rusticum* I. 4 [The man who treads the hops into the bags] is called the bagger. **1844** H. STEPHENS *Bk. Farm* III. 1074 The best baggers use a wooden hook in the left hand to collect and bring together the cut wheat in a bundle-like shape to the ground.

b. A machine that encloses (something) in bags.

1896 *Daily News* 26 Sept. 3/5 A combined system of boring ships and baggers was invented [for canal building]. **1950** *N.Z. Jrnl. Agric.* Apr. 361/1 Mechanisation [for potato harvesting] in the form of mechanical planters, diggers, and in some cases baggers. **1960** *Farmer & Stockbreeder* 15 Mar. 104 The bagger model..has established its position as the best buy for the farmer.

baggety, var. BAGATY.

† **baggie** ('bægɪ). *Sc.* [f. BAG *sb.* + *-ie* = -Y[4].] A Scotch diminutive of BAG; the stomach.

1787 BURNS *To Auld Mare Maggie*, A guid New-year I wish thee Maggie! Hae, there's a ripp to thy auld baggie.

† **'baggier.** *Obs. Sc.* [a. F. *baguier*, f. *bague* ring.] A jewel-case.

1578 *Inventories* 265 (JAM.) A baggier contening xiii ringis.

baggily ('bægɪlɪ), *adv.* [f. BAGGY *a.* + -LY[2].] In a loose or baggy way.

1862 GRONOW *Remin.* I. 113 Black coats..baggily made.

bagginess ('bægɪnɪs). [f. as prec. + -NESS.] The state of being baggy, loose, or inflated.

1860 MASSON in *Macm. Mag.* May 3 What bagginess of phraseology round what slender shanks of meaning. **1882** *Nat. Baptist* XVIII. 6 A bagginess about the trousers.

bagging ('bægɪŋ), *vbl. sb.*[1] [f. BAG *v.*[1] + -ING[1].] The action of the verb *bag* in different senses.

† **a.** Becoming pregnant. *Obs.*

1611 in COTGR.

b. Bulging; hanging in slack folds.

1698 TYSON in *Phil. Trans.* XX. 130 The pouching or bagging out at both Extreams. **1879** RUTLEY *Stud. Rocks* iii. 13 Partial flexure or bagging down of strata.

c. Packing in bags or sacks. Also *concr.*, that which is bagged; and with *off*.

1711 *Act 9 Anne* in *Lond. Gaz.* No. 4874/2 Notice as to such Hops..twenty four Hours before every Days bagging of the same. **1737** MILLER *Gard. Dict.* s.v. *Lupulus*, The common Method of Bagging [Hops] is as follows. **1805** R. W. DICKSON *Pract. Agric.* II. 755 It is this..that induces the planter to make a distinction in the bagging of the article. **1900** *Daily News* 17 Sept. 2/7 *Hops*...At market to-day there was a fair supply of early baggings on offer. **1907** *Westm. Gaz.* 11 Sept. 5/1 Bagging and cartage are by no means the only charges that the merchant has to meet. **1958** *Farmer & Stockbreeder* 30 Sept. 74 Operators pick the potatoes off..the elevator-cum-picking table and throw them on the cross conveyor for discharge at the bagging-off point.

'bagging, *vbl. sb.*[2] Also **badging**. [f. BAG *v.*[2] + -ING[1].] A particular mode of reaping pease, beans, and sometimes wheat: see the quotations.

1677 PLOT *Oxfordsh.* 256 The Work-man taking a hook in each hand, cuts them with that in his right hand, and rolls them up..with that in his left, which they call bagging of Peas. **1830** *Edin. Encycl.* XIV. 234 Reaped..with a large toothless hook, in the manner called bagging. **1842** BRANDE *Dict. Art & Sc.*, *Bagging*, reaping corn or pulse with a hook ..separating the straw or haulm from the root by chopping instead of by a drawing cut. **1851** H. STEPHENS *Bk. of Farm* 4494 Reaping with the sickle is executed in England in a manner technically named bagging.

Comb. **bagging-hook**, **badging-hook**: the broad hook or sickle thus used; also called **bagging-bill**.

'bagging, *sb.*[1] *dial.* [? orig. a vbl. sb. expressing the act of carrying food in a bag, or transf. from a horse's feed carried in a bag.] Used in the northern counties of England for food eaten between regular meals; now, esp. in Lancashire, an afternoon meal, 'afternoon tea' in a substantial form.

1750 J. COLLIER in *Lanc. Gloss.* (E.D.S.), Hoo'll naw cum agen till baggin' time. **1850** BAMFORD *ibid.*, In the afternoon, oatcake and cheese or butter, or oatcake and buttermilk, sufficed for bagging. **1851** in *Cumberld. Gloss.* **1863** E. WAUGH *Lanc. Songs* 29 Th' baggin' were ready, an' o' lookin' sweet. **1879** in *Temple-Bar Mag.* Jan. 4 'Baggin' is not only lunch, but any accidental meal coming between two regular ones.

b. *Comb.*, as ***bagging-time***.

1835 URE *Philos. Manuf.* 387 Thirst must be quenched with tea at bagging-time. **1884** *Pall Mall G.* 11 Sept. 4/2.

bagging ('bægɪŋ), *sb.*[2] [f. BAG *sb.*[1] + -ING[1]; cf. *sacking*, *towelling*, *wrappering.*] Coarse woven fabric out of which bags are made.

1732 *Acc. Workhouses* 124 The spinning and weaving of hop bagging. **1834** HT. MARTINEAU *Demerara* vi. 78 Making the bagging and packages for our coffee at home. **1873** *Echo* 19 May 4/3 Paper made from old jute bagging.

b. *attrib.* or *adj.*; and in *comb.*, as ***bagging-factory***.

1732 *Acc. Workhouses* 165 The wool is sorted two ways, viz. into fine and baggin. **1850** MRS. STOWE *Uncle Tom's C.* ii. 10 Hired out by his master to work in a bagging-factory.

'bagging, *ppl. a.* [f. BAG *v.*[1] + -ING[2].] Bulging out, hanging in loose bag-like folds.

1598 FLORIO, *Sócchi*, a kind of socke..or bagging shooe vsed in old time. **1697** DRYDEN *Virg. Eclog.* ii. 53 They drein two bagging Udders every day. **1878** BOSW. SMITH *Carthage* 434 Jews with their bagging pantaloons.

† **'baggingly**, *adv. Obs.* [f. *bagging*, pr. pple. of BAGGE *v.*: the original Fr. so rendered in the quot. is *en lorgnoyant* 'leering, ogling, with a side glance': whence the explanation here given of this word and the vb.] With a side glance, with a leer or ogle.

c **1400** *Rom. Rose* 292 Envie..Hadde a wondirful lokyng; For she ne lokide but awrie, Or overthart, alle baggyngly.

baggit ('bægɪt). Also **baggot**. [? f. *baggit*, Sc. form of BAGGED (sense 1): cf. Holland *Pliny* (1634) I. 303, of conies.] An unbroken female salmon, one that has not shed its eggs when the spawning season is over (as distinct from a KELT or spent fish).

1848 W. & R. CHAMBERS *Information* I. 687 Adult fish having spawned..are then termed kelts; the male fish is sometimes also called a kipper, and the female a shedder or baggit. **1863** H. C. PENNELL *Angler-nat.* 267 Kippers, and.. Baggits—names by which they are frequently mentioned in Acts of Parliament. **1875** 'STONEHENGE' *Brit. Sports* I. v. iv. §9 Baggits generally descend the stream..when hooked. **1887** F. DAY *Brit. & Irish Salmonidæ* 98 The first decision respecting which is 'clean' or 'unclean' salmon was given in December, 1885, by Mr. Fowler, who considered that a 'baggit', or gravid but unspawned fish, comes under the term 'unclean'. **1931** W. J. M. MENZIES *Salmon* (ed. 2) ii. 39 A few female fish may be found very late in the season..full of unshed ova. Such fish are usually described as 'baggots' or 'rawners'. **1963** *Times* 26 Jan. 11/4 On Tweed they [*sc.* unspawned salmon] are called baggots and many hold that they are legal quarry for the spring angler... It is extraordinarily difficult to tell whether a baggot is in fact unbroken.

baggonet, obs. or vulgar form of BAYONET *sb.*

baggy ('bægɪ), *a.* and *sb. pl.* [f. BAG *sb.* + -Y.]

A. *adj.* **1. a.** Puffed or bulging out, hanging in loose folds.

1831 CARLYLE *Life* II. ix. 219 With wrinkly, even baggy, face. **1858** HAWTHORNE *Fr. & It. Jrnls.* (1872) I. 22 Red, baggy trousers. **1868** *Lessons Mid. Age* 123 A baggy cotton umbrella.

b. *Comb.*, as ***baggy-eyed***, ***-trousered*** adjs.

1955 *Astounding Sci. Fiction* Dec. 37 He was baggy-eyed from lack of slumber. **1958** U. BLOOM *Abiding City* viii. 144 Circuit is as dull as ditch-water, with that baggy-eyed old judge. **1928** BLUNDEN *Undertones of War* xv. 163 The substitute, a tall, baggy-trousered and agreeably boastful man.

2. *fig.* Of language: Inflated, verbose.

1866 *Pall Mall G.* 15 Dec., The Professor's diction was verbose, and—if we may use a homely figure—baggy.

3. ***baggy-minnow***, or simply ***baggie*** (in South of Scotland): the minnow.

1808 JAMIESON, *Baggie*, sometimes *bag-mennon*. **1827** J. WILSON *Noct. Ambr.* Wks. 1855 II. 388 Some had a' the appearance o' bein' baggy menons.

B. *sb. pl.* Baggy shorts (or trousers cut off above the knee) worn over swimming trunks by surfers; swimming trunks in this style. Also, such shorts as worn in regular use; baggy trousers. orig. *Austral.*

1962 *Australian Women's Weekly* 24 Oct. (Suppl.) 3/1 *Baggies*, baggy pants worn over swimsuits when riding a surfboard. **1963** *Time* 9 Aug. 49 To all, 'baggies' are the loose-legged boxer swim trunks worn by the boys. **1965** *S. Afr. Surfer* I. 38 Australian surfers..come bounding down the gangplank like kangaroos with boards under their arms and baggies in their pouches. **1967** *Britannica Bk. of Year* 802/1 *Baggies*, trousers (as denims or chinos) raggedly cut off for use as shorts or swim trunks. **1967** *Surfabout* IV. 14/2 Within a year Peter Troy was the 'gemmie king' of the group of young local surfers, all complete with bleached hair and baggies. **1969** *Sunday Mail* (Brisbane) 2 Feb. 20/5 The trousers ensemble of Sharyn Longton, of Corinda, stood out as top gear last night. Sharyn topped her putty baggies and white shirt with a sequined cotton bolero from Mexico. **1971** *Studies in English* (Univ. Cape Town) Feb. 29 Brilliant is of fairly wide application, e.g., a brilliant board, a brilliant ride, a brilliant pair of baggies. **1973** *To Our Returned Prisoners of War* (U.S. Office of Secretary of Defense) 1 *Baggies*, pants with cuff. Baggy. **1982** *Washington Post* 6 June H3/2 Among the more startling revelations: the basic black bikini..; drawstring 'baggies', which peel away to reveal spandex 'snuggies', and the 'advertiser'—swim shorts with a telephone number embroidered on the rear.

baghous, obs. form of BAKEHOUSE.

bagige-kite, obs. form of BAGGAGE-KITE.

baglap: see BALLUP.

† **'bagle.** *Obs.* Forms: 4 **bagelle, baghel**, 6 **bagle.** [a. ON. *bagall*, ad. L. *baculum*, *-us*, staff, rod.] The staff or crosier of a bishop.

1330 R. BRUNNE *Chron.* 282 A hard wele telle, þat bagelle & belle be filchid & fled. [in *Pol. Songs* (1839) 307 The baghel and the belle.] **1542** RECORDE *Gr. Artes* (1575) 314 Crooking in the little fynger, like the head of a bishops bagle. **1557** PHAER *Æneid.* VII. Tj, And held in hand his bagle rod (*Note*—A bagle staf whom prelats that time did use).

baglet ('bæglɪt). [See -LET.] A small bag.

1885 *Graphic* 3 Jan. 18/2 He has brought back in his baglet ..a dozen new-laid eggs, some milk, and a loaf of bread. **1926** *Chambers's Jrnl.* 101/2 She opened a black baglet she carried—a silken affair with an amber hoop.

bagman ('bægmən). Also **bagsman**. [f. BAG *sb.* + MAN.]

1. a. One who carries a bag.

1531 *Bursar's Bk. Durh.* (1844) 98 Willelmus Potter, bagman [a waged officer of the convent], per annum xiis.

b. A tramp (who carries his personal effects in a bag); a swagman (SWAG *sb.* 12). *Austral.*

1896 H. LAWSON *While Billy Boils* 51 'So you're a native of Australia?' said the bagman to the grey-beard. **1954** F. J. HARDY in *Coast to Coast* 76 I'd never been a real bagman... I'd taken work when it was offering. **1955** D. NILAND *Shiralee* 26 Macauley watched him approaching and recognized him at once for what he was, a flat country bagman. **1959** S. J. BAKER *Drum* 86 *Bagman's gazette*, a non-existent publication quoted as a source of rumour, esp. in the country.

2. a. *spec.* A commercial traveller, whose business it is to show samples and solicit orders on behalf of manufacturers, etc. (*Somewhat depreciatory.*)

1765 GOLDSM. *Ess.* i, The bag-man..was telling a better story. **1808** J. WOLCOTT (P. Pindar) *Peep R. Acad.* Wks. 1812 V. 360 The Bag-men as they travel by. **1815** T. PEACOCK *Headl. Hall* 2 In later days when commercial bagsmen began to scour the country. **1865** *Daily Tel.* 13 Dec. 5/4 A traveller—I mean a bagman, not a tourist—arriving with his samples at a provincial town.

b. One who collects or administers the collection of money obtained by racketeering and other dishonest means. *slang* (orig. and chiefly *U.S.*).

1928 *Funk's Stand. Dict.*, *Bagman* (slang, U.S.), one to whom graft is paid. **1952** *Sunday Times* 3 Feb. 5/3 The term 'bagman' has recently made a place for itself in New York crime. *Ibid.*, A bagman is one who administers the collection of graft money from either the underworld or the business world and its subsequent distribution among politicians and civil servants. **1954** MOCKRIDGE & PRALL *Big Fix* 234 Nobody believed, either, that Jim Moran kept all of the money he collected. For many years he had been known as a bagman, which in political jargon, is literally the man who carries the bag or boodle for somebody higher up. **1968** *Listener* 19 Sept. 376/2 Does all this simply mean that one of the Syndicate's bagmen has moved into the Master's Remsenburg NY neighbourhood. **1973** *National Times* (Austral.) 25-30 June 18/3 The money is always paid in cash, by personal contact in a pub or a car. The police 'bag man' will call once a month to collect. **1982** *Times* 19 June 5/1 Furino was known in gangland parlance as a 'bagman'. .. He used to make payments and pick up money on behalf of Mafia mobsters.

3. In sporting slang: A bag-fox.

1875 'STONEHENGE' *Brit. Sports* I. II. iv. §5 If..wild cubs cannot be found, a bagman or two must be obtained.

4. (See quot. 1921.)

1921 *Dict. Occup. Terms* (1927) §759 *Bagman* (Post Office); sorts and checks returned mail bags, and issues them as required. **1927** *Daily Express* 12 Aug. 9/5 Various classes of Post Office workers..Liftmen..London porters, bagmen, [etc.].

bagnard, obs. corrupt form of BAGNIO.

‖**bagne** (baɲ). [mod.F. adaptation of It. *bagno* or Sp. *baño* in this special sense, in which F. *bain* is not used.] = BAGNIO 2.

1863 KINGLAKE *Crimea* I. xiv. 314 They may be in the.. bagnes of Rochefort. **1866** *Stamford Merc.* 24 Aug., The Emperor..granted free pardons..to..prisoners..in the bagnes, houses of correction, or penal establishments.

bagnio ('bænjəʊ). Forms: 6 banio, 7 bagno, bagneo, bannia, -ier, -iard, bagnard, 7-9 bagnio. [a. It. *bagno*:—L. *balneum* bath. Cf. BALNEO.]

†**1.** A bath, a bathing-house; esp. one with hot baths, vapour-baths, and appliances for sweating, cupping, and other operations. (No longer applied to any such place in Britain, the nearest approach to which is the modern *Turkish Bath*; but applied as an alien word to the baths of Italian or Turkish cities.)

1615 G. SANDYS *Travels* 12 Upon the Castle Hill there is a Bannia..containing seueral roomes one hoter than another. **1624** MASSINGER *Renegado* I. ii, At the public bagnios or the mosques. **1653** GREAVES *Seraglio* 7 Dining rooms, Bagno's [*marginal note.* Bathes or hot-houses; it must be pronounced *Banios*]. **1682** *Lond. Gaz.* No. 1686/4 The Royal Bagnio is now in very good Order. **1683** TRYON *Way to Health* 324 Their Chambers are in the next degree to Bagneo's or Hot-Houses. **1695** CONGREVE *Love for Love* I. xiv, I have a Beau in a Bagnio, Cupping for a Complexion, and Sweating for a Shape. **1719** DE FOE *Crusoe* (1858) 601 Just as they heat the bagnios in England. **1774** GOLDSM. *Nat. Hist.* (1862) I. VI. v. 480 The beavers make two apertures..one is a passage to their bagnio. **1820** MAIR *Tyro's Dict.* 376 *Sudatorium*, a bagnio or hot house, to sweat in.

2. An oriental prison, a place of detention for slaves, a penal establishment.

(So in It. and Sp., and F. *bagne*. The origin of this use of the word is doubtful: see conjectures in Chambers *Cycl.* 1751 and Littré.)

1599 HAKLUYT *Voy.* II. I. 186 The king sent..to the Banio: (this Banio is the prison wheras all the captiues lay at night). *c* **1645** HOWELL *Lett.* (1650) I. 42 A slave in the bannier at Algier. **1660-1** PEPYS *Diary* 8 Feb., Stories of Algiers and the..slaves there..How they are all, at night, called into their master's Bagnard. **1687** RYCAUT *Hist. Turks* II. App. 5 A prison and Banniard of Slaves. **1728** MORGAN *Algiers* II. iv. 268 He sent him to his Bagnio, among the rest of his Slaves. **1847** DISRAELI *Tancred* VI. v, To be sent to the bagnio or the galleys.

3. A brothel, a house of prostitution. (Cf. similar application of STEW.)

1624 MASSINGER *Parl. Love* II. ii, To be sold to a brothel Or a common bagnio. **1747** HOADLEY *Susp. Husb.* II. iv. (1756) 27 Carry her to a Bagnio, and there you may lodge with her. **1851** THACKERAY *Eng. Hum.* v. (1858) 243 How the prodigal drinks and sports at the bagnio. **1862** WRIGHT *Dom. Mann.* 491 They were soon used to such an extent for illicit intrigues, that the name of a hothouse or bagnio became equivalent to that of a brothel.

†**4.** = BATH in *Chemistry*. Also *attrib.*

1696 E. SMITH in *Phil. Trans.* XIX. 229 Two hundred Drams Calcined at a Bagnio Fire.

Bag'nolians, *sb. pl. Eccl. Hist.* Also in L. form ‖**Bagnolenses**. [f. *Bagnoles* in Languedoc, where they originated.] A sect of heretics in the 8th century, who rejected the Old and part of the New Testament, and held generally the doctrines of the Manicheans.

1727-51 in CHAMBERS *Cycl.* **1847** in CRAIG; and mod. Dicts.

bagonet, obs. or vulgar form of BAYONET *sb.*

bagpipe ('bægpaɪp), *sb.* Forms: 4-7 **baggepipe**, 5-6 **-pype**, **bagpype**, 7 **bagg-pipe**, 6- **bag-pipe**, **bagpipe**. [f. BAG *sb.*[1] + PIPE.]

1. A musical instrument of great antiquity and wide diffusion, consisting of an air-tight wind-bag and one or more reed-pipes into which the air is pressed by the performer.

Formerly a favourite rural English musical instrument; now chiefly used in the Scottish Highlands and in Ireland. The modern Highland bagpipe consists of a greased leathern bag, covered with flannel, inflated by blowing into a valved mouth-tube, and having three *drones* or bass pipes, and a *chanter* for the tenor or treble.

c **1386** CHAUCER *Prol.* 565 A baggepipe wel coude he blowe and soune. **1483** *Cath. Angl.* 17 Bagpype, *panduca*. **1530** PALSGR. 196/2 Bagge pype, *cornemuse*. **1557** Tottell's *Misc.* (Arb.) 197 And bagpipe, solace of the rurall bride. **1579** SPENSER *Sheph. Cal.* Apr. 3 Or is thy Bagpype broke, that soundes so sweete? **1596** SHAKS. *1 Hen. IV*, I. ii. 86 As Melancholly as..a Louers Lute..or the Drone of a Lincolnshire Bagpipe. *c* **1625** *MS. Bodl.* No. 30. 16 b, If they heare the baggepipe then the beares are coming. **1638** HEYWOOD *Witches Lanc.* III. i. Wks. 1874 IV. 217 No Witchcraft can take hold of a Lancashire Bag-pipe. **1678** OTWAY *Friendship in F.* 30 A Scotch Song! I hate it worse then a Scotch Bagpipe. **1864** ENGEL *Mus. Anc. Nat.* 78 The bag-pipe is also very universal throughout Asia.

b. Now often used in *plural*, esp. in Scotland.

a **1613** OVERBURY *A Wife* (1638) 175 Don Quixotes Water-mills are still Scotch Bagpipes to him. **1683** TRYON *Way to Health* 654 Bag-Pipes are under the dominion of Venus & Mars..This sort of Musick is sometimes used in Wars. **1763-5** CHURCHILL *Proph. Famine* Poems I. 110 With mikle art, could on the bag pipes play. **1876** GRANT *Burgh Sch. Scot.* II. 380 Discoursing laments upon the Bagpipes.

†**2.** A retort shaped like a bagpipe. *Obs.*

1558 WARDE *Alexis' Secr.* (1568) 14 b, Put it into a croke necked viole of glasse which distillars call a Bagpipe.

3. Applied to the organ of sound of an insect.

1833 BREWSTER *Nat. Magic* ix. 233 The Cicadæ or locusts in North America appear..to be furnished with a bagpipe on which they play a variety of notes.

4. *fig.* **a.** An inflated and senseless talker, a windbag. **b.** A long-winded monotonous speaker.

1603 H. CROSSE *Vertues Commw.* (1878) 103 The Seruingman, the Image of sloath, the bagge-pipe of vanitie, like a windie Instrument, soundeth nothing but prophanenesse. **1850** CARLYLE *Latter-d. Pamph.* v. (1872) 169 Such parliamentary bagpipes I myself have heard play tunes. **1884** *Chr. World* 19 June 463/4 Two fresh sermons a week..from the one poor droning theological bagpipe.

5. *Comb.*, as **bagpipeless**, without bagpipes; **bagpipe-like**, like a bagpipe.

1618 D. BELCHIER *Hans Beere-pot* E iv, Or Bagge-pype-like, not speake before thou art full. **1812** W. TENNANT *Anster Fair* IV. lxvi, The poor pipers bagpipeless they saw.

'bagpipe, *v. Naut.* [f. the sb., in reference to the shape assumed by the sail.] (See quot.)

1769 FALCONER *Dict. Marine* (1789) s.v., To bagpipe the mizen is to lay it aback, by bringing the sheet to the mizen-shrouds.

bagpiper ('bægˌpaɪpə(r)). [f. prec. + -ER[1].] One who plays on a bagpipe; commonly called a *piper*.

c **1440** *Promp. Parv.* 21 Baggepypere, *panducarius*. *c* **1570** THYNNE *Pride & Lowl.* (1841) 53 Where nought else but a bagge piper is to see. **1596** SHAKS. *Merch. V.* I. i. 53 Laugh like Parrats at a bag-piper. **1800** WORDSW. *Michael* 52 Like the noise Of bagpipers on distant Highland hills.

'bagˌpiping, *vbl. sb.* [as from a vb. *to bagpipe* + -ING[1].] The action of playing on a bagpipe.

1594 MORLEY *Madrigalls* I. E iij b, Who comes heere: with bagpiping and drumming. **1882** MASSON in *Macm. Mag.* XLV. 238 That fortnight of feastings, processionings, huzzaings, and bagpipings.

†**'bagˌpudding.** *Obs.* [f. BAG *sb.*[1] + PUDDING.]

1. A pudding boiled in a bag.

1598 in FLORIO. **1600** HEYWOOD *1 Edw. IV*, Wks. 1874 I 47 Thou shalt be welcome to beef and bacon, and perhaps a bag-pudding. **1641** W. CARTWRIGHT *Ordinary* II. i, A solemn son of Bagpudding and Pottage. **1817** SCOTT *Rob Roy* vi, To make room for the beef and the bagpuddings.

†**2.** *fig.* ? Clown. *Obs.* (Cf. *jackpudding.*)

1608 DAY *Hum. out of Br.* II. i. (1881) 25 Farewell, sweet heart.—God a mercy, bagpudding.

bag-reef ('bægriːf). *Naut.* (See quot.)

1867 SMYTH *Sailor's Word-bk.*, *Bag-reef*, a fourth or lower reef of fore-and-aft sails, often used in the royal navy. *Bag-reef of topsails*, first reef (of five in American navy); a short reef, usually taken in to prevent a large sail from bagging when on a wind.

bags I. [BAG *v.*[1] 6 b; cf. the vulgar 'says I'.] A formula used (orig. by children) to assert a claim to an article, or the right to act in a certain way, on the ground that one is the first to speak up. Also simply *bags*, or with other extensions, as *bags not*, etc.

1866 A. DOBSON *Bob Trevor & I* II. in *Beeton's Ann.* 215 Deep in a hole..gleamed the clear water of a shallow well. 'Bags I first drink,' says Bob, according to the polite practice of schoolboys. **1886** R. HOLLAND *Gloss. County Chester*, *Bags I*,..an expression used by boys in claiming the first place in a game; or in laying claim to any treasure trove. **1899** KIPLING *Stalky* 35 There's a *Monte Cristo* in that lower shelf. I saw it. Bags I, next time we go to Aves! **1921** A. A. MILNE *Second Plays* 7 Bags I all the presents. **1926** 'R. CROMPTON' *William—the Conqueror* ix. 167 'Whose turn is it to get something next?' said Ginger. 'Bags me,' said William. **1937** J. B. PRIESTLEY *Time & Conways* I. 3 Bags I this one. **1940** M. MARPLES *Pub. School Slang* 9 Bags not.. establishes exemption from anything unpleasant. **1946** B. MARSHALL *George Brown's Schooldays* xxi. 89 'Bags I do not ask about the room,' Abinger said. 'What about you doing the gassing instead of me?' 'But I bagsed-I I didn't,' Abinger protested. **1950** B. SUTTON-SMITH *Our Street* i. 25 [They] would all sit.. 'bagzing'. I bagz we go to the Zoo. *Ibid.* 26 He always made this bagz... I don't bagz the Zoo.

†**bague.** *Obs.* [a. F. *bague*, in med.L. *baga*, of uncertain origin.] A ring, a brooch.

1475 CAXTON *Jason* 106 Medea toke alle the most richest Jewels and bagues portatif.

baguette (bəˈgɛt). [a. F. *baguette* (a small rod or wand; in *Arch.* (as in Eng.) ad. It. *bacchetta* little rod, dim. of *bacchio*:—L. *baculum* staff.] **1.** A small moulding of semicircular section, of the astragal species.

1727-51 CHAMBERS *Cycl.*, *Baguette*, in architecture, a little round moulding less than an astragal..According to M. le Clerc, when the baguette is enriched with ornaments, it changes its name, and is called *chaplet*. **1842** GWILT *Encycl. Archit.* III. i. 684 The astragal is also known by the names of bead and baguette.

2. *Mus.* (See quot. 1938.)

1876 STAINER & BARRETT *Dict. Mus. Terms* 43/2 Baguettes. **1938** *Oxf. Compan. Mus.* 63/2 *Baguette*, drumstick (also sometimes used for 'baton', and as the name for the stick of a fiddle bow).

3. A gem, usu. a diamond, cut in a long rectangular shape. Also *attrib.*

1926 *National Jeweler* Nov. 33 Rings in which.. baguettes, pentagons, hexagons or gems of other fancy shapes permit variety of design. **1935** *Times* 2 Dec. 19/4 In one paré and baguette diamonds form a design like two harps. The baguettes are used like a scroll. **1938** *Encycl. Brit. Bk. of Year* 276/1 Jewellers have made great use of the baguette or baton-cut diamond to produce pattern and variety in design.

4. A long, thin loaf of French bread, of various sizes in different regions, but usu. smaller than a *flûte*. Cf. *French stick* s.v. STICK *sb.*[1] 8 f.

1958 R. GODDEN *Greengage Summer* vi. 60 One of the long thin loaves called 'baguettes'. **1959** 'M. AINSWORTH' *Murder is Catching* xv. 165 He was carrying a string bag..with a thin baguette loaf poking out of one corner. **1966** G. GREENE *Comedians* I. iii. 66 Long *baguettes* of bread, three to a table, were set out with meagre portions of butter and jam. **1970** *Guardian* 22 Aug. 3/8 The baguette..is the classic French loaf. By law it must weigh 250 grammes. **1977** *Lancet* 24 and 31 Dec. 1346/2 The sandwich when it came was a quarter of a baguette generously filled with ham.

bagwash ('bægwɒʃ). [BAG *sb.*] The rough unfinished washing of clothes; a laundry that undertakes such rough washing; the 'bag' of clothes prepared for, or given, this type of washing. Also *attrib.*

1937 EVE GARNETT *Family from One End Street* i. 4 A blue board on which was painted..'The Ideal Laundry. Careful Hand Work', and underneath..'Bag-wash'. **1944** *Our Towns* (ed. 2) ii. 61 There is as yet no good answer to the difficulties of the townswoman in congested areas except municipal washhouses or the bag-wash. **1949** *Here & Now* (N.Z.) Oct. 17/3 The bag-wash service is certainly not cheap. **1950** *Ibid.* Dec. 10/1 Some send their clothes to the bagwash and do only occasional washing at home. **1952** *Economist* 20 Sept. 673 Self-service launderettes are shops where a woman 'posts' her washing into a machine which delivers it half an hour later, washed and semi-dried... It is basically the old 'bagwash' idea. **1966** *Times* 1 Dec. 15/3 If you are interested in finding a laundry offering bagwash, you should check with the Institute of British Launderers and Cleaners, who will tell you whether there is one within easy reach.

bag-wig ('bæg'wɪg). (Also as two words.) A wig fashionable in the 18th century, the back-hair of which was enclosed in an ornamental bag.

1717 MRS. CENTLIVRE *Bold Stroke* III. i, Now must Bag Wig and Bus'ness come in Play; A Thirty-Thousand-Pound Girl leads the Way. **1766** ANSTEY *Bath Guide* x. 60 Bag-wig, and lac'd Ruffles, and black Solitaire. **1850** W. IRVING *Goldsm.* xxv. 252 Walking the Strand in grand array with bag-wig and sword.

Hence **bag-wigged**, *a.*, wearing a bag-wig.

1775 SHERIDAN *St. Patr. Day* II. iv. (1883) 236 Pig-tailed lawyers and bag-wigged attorneys.

†**bag-wood.** *Obs.* [Apparently f. BAG *v.*[2] + WOOD.] Small branches of trees, twigs, etc. such

as could be lopped off with a bagging hook or bill, used for fuel.

1525 in *Bodmin Registers* (1827–38) 103 To have their burden wood to bear and carry away upon their backs, of lot, crop, hook, and bag wood. [See *N. & Q.* Ser. I. II. 204.]

'bag-worm. *U.S.* [BAG *sb.* 1.] The larva of American lepidoptera of the family Psychidæ (esp. *Thyridopteryx* and *Œceticus*), injurious to trees, which builds as a portable habitation a silken case or sac covered with little twigs and leaves. Called also ***basket-worm, drop-worm***.

1862 *Congress. Globe* Jan. 232 On the avenue and in the parks you will find the evergreen trees.. being destroyed by the bag-worm. **1871** H. B. STOWE *Oldtown Fireside Stories* 158 The young Hokums was jest like bag-worms, the more they growed the more they eat. **1884** H. C. MCCOOK *Tenants Old Farm* 384 Basket or bag-worms. **1897** J. H. COMSTOCK *Insect Life* 204 The Bag-worms, family *Psychidæ*. **1899** *Camb. Nat. Hist.* VI. II. vi. 394 One of the North American basket- or bag-worms *Thyridopteryx ephemeraeformis*.

bah (bɑː), *int.* [Prob. after mod.F. *bah!* in same sense.] An exclamation expressive of contempt.

[**1600** DEKKER *Gentle Craft* Wks. I. 40 Away she flung.. nor said bih nor bah.] **1817** BYRON *Beppo* xxxii, Dreading the deep damnation of his 'bah!' **1848** KINGSLEY *Saint's Trag.* III. iii, Bah! priest! What can this Marpurg-madness do for me?

2. Used as a vb. [Cf. *to pooh-pooh*, etc.]

1838 DICKENS *Old C. Shop* (C.D. ed.) 33 Mr. Richard.. is Bah!'d for his pains.

bahadur (bəˈhɔːdʊ(r)). *Anglo-Ind.* Also 8, 9 **behauder, baha(u)door, bahawder.** [Hindi *bahādur* hero, champion.] A great man, distinguished personage. Often affixed as a title to an officer's name.

'*Bahādur* and *Sirdār Bahādur* are also the official titles of members of the 2nd and 1st classes respectively of the Order of British India, established for native officers of the army in 1837' (Yule).

1776 *Trial of J. Fowke, F. Fowke, etc.* 1/1 Joseph Fowke of Calcutta, Gentleman,.. Maha Rajah Nundocomar, Bahader, late of the same place inhabitant. **1781** J. LINDSAY in A. W. C. Lindsay *Lives* (1849) III. 296 Sheikh Hussein.. tells me that our army has beat the Behauder [*sc.* Hyder Ali]. **1841** THACKERAY *Major Gahagan* iv. in *Comic Tales & Sk.* II. 80 The lips of the Bahawder are closed. *Ibid.*, Bobbachy Bahawder has seen the dreadful Feringhee. **1848** 'J. KIRKLAND' *Eerie Laird* x. 110 While he, a man of genius, must be content with the empty title of Bahadur (or knight). **1879** in T. H. S. Escott *Pillars Emp.* 275 There is nothing of the great *bahawder* about him; he is easy of access, civil, and obliging to all who approach him. **1922** *Blackw. Mag.* Oct. 519/2 He was a Bahadur, which is Indian for 'hell of a fellow'. **1957** P. KEMP *Mine were of Trouble* iii. 48, I fancied myself one of.. Tamerlaine's bahadurs.

Hence **bahadur** *v. intr.*, to play the bahadur.

1860 W. H. RUSSELL *Diary India* I. 272 They had been curvetting, prancing, and bahadooring with their swords in the air.

Baha'i (bæˈhɑːiː). Also **Bahai, Beha'i.** [Pers.] A follower of Baha-ullah (1817–92) and his son Abdul Baha (1844–1921), propagators of a religion based on BABISM; the doctrine and practice of this religion. Also *attrib.* Hence **Ba'haism, Ba'haist, Ba'haite.**

1889 E. G. BROWNE in *Jrnl. R. Asiatic Soc.* XXI. 518 The followers of Behá have been increasing in number and influence... Thus at the present day nearly all the Bábis are Behá'is. **1892** —— in *Relig. Syst. World* 351 So for these Behá'is, as they are now called, the writings of the Báb became an old testament. **1903** —— in M. H. Phelps *Abbas Effendi* p. xxix, The religion of Babism, or Beha'ism. *Ibid.* p. xxxiii, The Babis, who have since that time generally styled themselves.. 'Beha'is'. **1909** E. HAMMOND *Splendour of God* 10 Bahais.. claim that Bahaism has.. the Light of Love. **1909** H. DREYFUS *Univ. Religion* 26 The Bahai theology. *Ibid.* 72 When finally they left the neighbourhood of Baghdád,.. the Babis had become Bahais. **1914** T. K. CHEYNE *Reconcil. Races & Relig.* 132 The confinement of the Bahaites at Acre. **1924** *Expositor* Feb. 152 The Bahaists .. have been turning their attention to the Western world and its Christianity. **1959** *Times* 23 Mar. 9/4 Baha'i is a Persian sect founded early in the last century.

‖**bahar, barr(e** (bəˈhɑː(r)). [Arab., *bahār.*] A measure of weight used in parts of India and China, varying in value in different places from 223 to 625 lbs.

1753 in CHAMBERS *Cycl. Supp.*

Bahasa (baˈhɑːsə). [a. Mal. (*Bahasa Indonesia*, etc.), f. Skr. *bhāṣā* speech, language.] The variety of Malay used as the national language of the Republic of Indonesia (*Bahasa Indonesia*) or of Malaysia (*Bahasa Malaysia*). Also *ellipt.*

1952 *Amer. Jrnl. Sociol.* July 23/1 The Indonesian word for culture.. is.. a deliberate creation—as is much of the entire national Indonesian language (*Bahassa Indonesia*)—of contemporary nationalism. **1954** PEI & GAYNOR *Dict. Linguistics* 130 *Malay*... Now adopted, under the name *Bahasa Indonesia*, as the official tongue of Indonesia. **1955** D. WOODMAN *Republic of Indonesia* xiv. 297 In the local schools provincial languages will continue to be taught but Bahasa Indonesia is now compulsory for them all. **1958** [see INDONESIAN *a.* and *sb.*]. **1967** *Tenggara* (Univ. Malaya) I. 112 The making of Malay as the official language of Indonesia was solemnly pledged by Indonesian youths in the famous *Sumpah Pemuda* of 28th October, 1928. This pledge taken at the Youths' Congress was also responsible for the renaming of Malay as spoken in Indonesia as *Bahasa Indonesia*. **1969** *Malaysia Year Bk.* xiii. 268 It [*sc.* radio News Division] introduced master bulletins in Bahasa Malaysia progressively as from 1967. **1970** *Sruth* (Inverness) 16 Apr. 2/1 UNESCO has said this about the revival of Irish in Eire: 'It is clearly silly and a waste of time to scold the Irish, for instance, for reviving their ancient tongue, or the Indonesians for adopting Bahasa in preference to a European language of wide diffusion.' **1972** *Straits Times* (Malaysian ed.) 4 May 12/1 (Advt.), Working knowledge of Chinese and Bahasa Malaysia is essential. **1974** *Language Sciences* Aug. 17/2 Since 1928, when Malay was adopted as the national language and given the name of Bahasa Indonesia, regional languages with all their dialects have continued to survive. **1980** *English World-Wide* I. 1. 99 This is still used.. if at least one of the participants in a speech situation has not been educated in English or.. Bahasa Malaysia.

Bahiric, var. BOHAIRIC.

‖**baht** (bɑːt). Also **baat, bat.** [Thai *bāt.*] = TICAL; the basic monetary unit of Thailand.

1828 J. CRAWFURD *Jrnl. Embassy to Courts of Siam & Cochin China* xiii. 331 The bat, or tical, was assayed at the mint of Calcutta... The value.. is about 2*s.* 6*d.* **1872** *Coin Book* 81 Baat, Siamese, Silver, value 2*s.* 6*d.*, nut shaped. **1911** *Encycl. Brit.* XXV. 6/1 The tical (*baht*) is the unit of currency and also the unit of weight [in Siam]. *Ibid.* XXVIII. 491/1 Bat, or Tical.. 234 grains. **1962** R. A. G. CARSON *Coins* 551 Yet another category of silver currency in Siam is the bat or tical, a bullet-shaped piece with turned-in ends. **1963** *Whitaker's Almanack* 934/1 The exchange rate for the *Baht* is not officially fixed, but has for some time remained in the neighbourhood of *Baht* 59 = £1 sterling, with little fluctuation.

‖**ba'hut.** [a. F. *bahutte.*] **1.** A dress for masquerading, a domino. *Obs.*

1784 MISS BERRY *Jrnl. & Corr.* I. 76 Put on our bahuts and went.. to.. the Florentine Theatre.

2. [a. F. *bahut.*] An ornamented chest, esp. one having a rounded top; an ornamented cabinet.

1840 THACKERAY *Pict. Rhapsody* in *Fraser's Mag.* July 115/1 A chest of drawers, secrétaire, cabinet, or *bahut*. *a* **1916** H. JAMES *Ivory Tower* (1917) III. v. 207 A tall inlaid and brass-bound French *bahut*.

bahuvrihi (bæhuːˈvriːhɪ), *a.* (*sb.*) *Gram.* [Skr., lit. having much rice, f. *bahú* much + *vrīhí* rice.] Of a word: composed of an adjective and a substantive so as to form, principally, a possessive adjective, like the word *bahuvrihi* itself; also *gen.*, forming a compound that is a part of speech different from its head member; *absol.*, such a compound.

1846 MONIER-WILLIAMS *Elem. Gram. Sanscr.* ix. 157 Native grammarians class compound nouns under five heads:.. The 5th, *Bahuvríhi*, or those formed of any number of words associated to form an epithet to a noun. **1872** —— *Skr.-Eng. Dict.* p. xii, When a student is in doubt whether to translate compounds like *Indra-śatru* as Bahuvrīhis or Tatpurushas. **1914** JESPERSEN *Mod. Eng. Gram.* II. 148 In (bahuvrihi) compounds we have formal plurals denoting one single being and used as singulars, as in *a sly-boots*,.. *a lazybones*. **1939** L. H. GRAY *Found. Lang.* vi. 163 Possessive compounds (also called by the native Sanskrit grammatical term *bahuvrīhi*..) result, in the main, from the transformation of a compound noun into an adjective with the meaning 'possessing (or possessed of) so-and-so', e.g... Greek ῥοδο-δάκτυλος 'rose-fingered', ἄ-παις 'child-less'; Latin *magn-animus* 'great-minded',.. and such English words as those just given as translations. **1944** *Mod. Lang. Notes* LIX. 525 Today we are witnessing a rebirth of the Bahuvrīhi type in.. *high-potency vitamins*.

Baianism (ˈbeɪjənɪz(ə)m). [Cf. F. *baïanisme* (1738), *baïaniste* (1720).] The heretical teaching of the Flemish theologian Michel de Bay (latinized as Baius), 1513–89, a forerunner of the Jansenists. So **'Baianist**, a supporter of this teaching, a follower of Bay. Also *attrib.* or as *adj.*

1733 J. GORDON *Mem.* (title-p.), Wherein.. the History of Baianism, Jansenism, and the Constitution *Unigenitus*, [is] impartially related. *Ibid.* 33 The Bull.. did not meet with the same Reception from the Secular Clergy, who for a considerable time openly oppos'd it, and who for that Reason were called Baianists. **1928** J. BRODRICK *Card. Bellarmine* I. iv. 74 Heresies allied to Baianism. **1936** N. J. ABERCROMBIE *Origins of Jansenism* I. 90 Nothing more deplorable than the moral condition of fallen man, in the Baianist system, can be imagined. *Ibid.* 125 It may have been the influence of Jansson.. that determined the young Jansen to enter the Baianist camp. *Ibid.* II. 214 The Jansenist approach to the problems of grace was.. familiar inasmuch as it was Baianist.

†**baiardour.** *Obs.* [AF. = OF. *baïardeur*, a mason's labourer, who helps to carry the *baïard*, mod.F. *bayart*, *baïart*, or large hand-barrow with six handles on which building stones are carried. Erroneously connected in the Dictionaries with L. *bājulātor*, and explained from Phillips (1706) onward, as 'a carrier or bearer of any weight or burden.' Perhaps never used in Eng.: cf. BAYARD².]

P. BLESENSIS *Contin. Hist. Croyland* 120 Duos incisores.. et duos bajardours servituros ad cariagium petræ.

baid, north. f. BODE *sb.*; pa. t. of BIDE *v.*

baie, baies, obs. ff. BAY *sb.* and *a.*, BAIZE.

baight, baign(e, obs. forms of BAIT, BAIN.

‖**baignoire** (ˈbɛnwar, -wɔː(r)). [F.; lit. 'a vessel for bathing in,' f. *baigner* to bathe; also as in Eng.] A box at the theatre on the same level as the stalls.

1873 BROWNING *Red Cott. Night-C.* 984 Should one display One's robe a trifle o'er the baignoire-edge. **1883** *Harper's Mag.* Nov. 884/1 The twelve baignoirs.. are left at the disposal of the manager.

baik, obs. f. BAKE; var. BECK *v. Obs.*

baikalite (ˈbeɪkəlaɪt). *Min.* [f. *Baikal*, lake in Siberia + -ITE.] A dark dingy green variety of SAHLITE. (Dana.)

1794 KIRWAN *Min.* I. 509. **1843** HUMBLE *Dict. Geol.*

'baikerinite. *Min.* A viscid substance with balsamic odour and taste like that of wood-tar. (Dana.)

'baikerite. *Min.* A wax-like mixture found near Lake Baikal consisting chiefly of ozocerite and baikerinite. (Dana.)

'baikie. *Sc.* A piece of curved wood used in fastening cows to the stake; in some places (according to Jamieson) the stake itself.

1598 D. FERGUSON *Sc. Prov.* (1785) 8 (JAM.) Better haud loose, nor bound to an ill bakie. **1851** H. STEPHENS *Bk. of Farm* 1131 Cows are bound to a stake in the stall.. One method of binding is with the baikie.. flat to the neck of the cow.

bail (beɪl), *sb.*¹ Also 5 **bayll, baill,** 5–7 **bayle,** 6–7 **bayl, bale, baile.** [In senses 1 and 2, a. OF. *bail* 'power, custody, jurisdiction,' and 'delivery,' n. of action f. *baillier*, in its senses of 'take charge of, guard, control,' and 'hand over, deliver' (see BAIL *v.*¹). The remaining senses are peculiarly English, and their development not quite certain. But from the Latin phrase *tradere in ballium alicui*, found 1259, and the AF. *lesser en bail* (1331), it seems that *bail* was originally related to sense 1, and meant the 'custody or charge' (i.e. of the surety); cf. also the equivalent *mainprise, manucaptio*. But it must soon have been associated in meaning with sense 2, and the AF. *bailler* to deliver (chattels), since already in 16th c. it was explained as 'the *delivery* or handing over of the accused to his surety,' whence transferred to the *security* in consideration of which he was so delivered, and finally to the *surety* himself who became or gave security for his reappearance in court when called for judgement. There is nothing approaching these senses in Fr., while, on the other hand, the Fr. sense 'lease' is not in English.

Fr. *bail*, the n. of action, must be carefully distinguished from *bail* 'governor, ruler, tutor, guardian' (= Pr. *baile*, Sp. *bayle*, Pg. *bailio*, It. *bailo, balio*: —L. *bājulus*), never adopted in English (though sometimes erroneously stated to be the direct source of sense 6). *Bail* = *bājulus* was the primary word; thence the vb. *bailler* = *bājulāre*; thence again the n. of action *bail* formed in French, and adopted in English. (The word is discussed by COKE *4th. Inst.* 178.)]

†**1.** Charge, custody, jurisdiction, power. *Obs.*

a **1400** *Cov. Myst.* (1841) 292 His body is undyr your bayle. **1470** HARDING *Chron.* xxviii, In battaill greate hir tooke and putte in baill. **1489** CAXTON *Faytes of A.* I. xv. 39 So grete a thyng as is the bayll and charge of the noblesse. **1596** SPENSER *F.Q.* VII. vi. 49 Faunus, now within their baile.

†**2.** A handing over, delivery, giving. *Obs.* [perh. not in Eng.; but cf. 4.]

[**1292** BRITTON II. ix. §3 Cum acun bail de seysine deit estre fet. (When any livery of seisin is to be made.)]

†**3.** The charge or friendly custody of a person who otherwise might be kept in prison, upon security given that he shall be forthcoming at a time and place assigned. *Obs.* (But the phrase *admitted to bail*, formerly *let to bail*, originated in this sense, though subsequently otherwise analysed.)

[**1259** *Provisions of Barons* (Stubbs *Sel. Chart.* 396) Quod hii quibus traditur in ballium eum habeant coram justitiis. **1331** *Act 5 Edw. III*, viii, Et ont este par les ditz Marescaux lessez en bail. (*transl.* Pulton: And by the Marshalles of the Kings Bench have been let to baile.)] **1581** LAMBARDE *Eiren.* III. ii. (1602) 333 That no Iustice, nor Iustices of peace, should let to bayle any person contrary to the said statute. **1649** SELDEN *Laws of Eng.* I. xxxvi. (1739) 53 Admitted to Bail if the offences were bailable. **1809** TOMLINS *Law Dict.* s.v., To admit any to bail who ought not by law to be admitted is punishable by fine.

†**4.** Temporary delivery or release from imprisonment, on finding sureties or security to appear for trial; *also*, release, in a more general sense. *Obs.*

1466 *Mann. & Househ. Exp.* 169 Robard Henengham becam sewerte to my mastyr for the bayle of on Willyam Valenden of Manytre that was in the castell of Colchestre. **1509** BARCLAY *Ship of Fooles* (1570) 4 There shall be no bayle nor treating of mainprise. **1542** *Act 34 & 35 Hen. VIII*, xxvii. §50 The Prenotarie to haue.. for the bayle of euery person of felony, twelue pens. **1598** ROWLANDS *Betray. Christ* 16 More dead then Lazarus in his stincking graue, When he deaths vaut till fift daies baile indured. **1642**

Declar. Lords & Comm. 22 Dec. 6 To some common Goale, there to remaine without Bayle or Mainprize. **1768** Blackstone *Comm.* IV. 294 The nature of bail is..a delivery, or bailment, of a person to his sureties, upon their giving (together with himself) sufficient security for his appearance.

5. Security given for the release of a prisoner from imprisonment, pending his trail.

[**1331** *Act 5 Edw. III*, viii, Et ne les soeffrent nulle part aler walkerants ne par bail ne santz bail.] **1495** *Act 11 Hen. VII*, vii, They [shall]..be put to sufficient baill. **1580** Stow *Chron. Hen. VIII* an. 1540 (R.) Giuing liberty to..his prisoners to go under baill. **1605** Verstegan *Dec. Intell.* x. (1628) 328 Putting in bayl to be freed or protected for the time from prison. **1607** Heywood *Wom. Kilde* Wks. 1874 II. 130, I am not free, I go but under baile. **1671** F. Philipps *Reg. Necess.* 288 They ought not to be released until they..give Bayl to appear, and answer the action. **1691** Wood *Ath. Oxon.* II. 146 He had his liberty upon bayle of 40000*l.* **1713** Swift *Cadenus & V.* Wks. 1755 III. II. 30 That both parties Shou'd..appear, and save their bail. **1742** Middleton *Cicero* I. III. 193 A miserable, needy crew, who had..forfeited their bails. **1862** Trollope *Orley F.* xiii. 98 His client..was prepared with bail to any amount.

b. *fig.* Security, surety, guarantee.

a **1593** H. Smith *Serm.* (1637) 350 Death would take no baile, we are all tenants at will and we must leave..at a day's, at an houres warning. **1626** Bernard *Isle of Man* (1627) 81 None being sufficient to lay in bayle to answer God for the sin. **1645** Milton *Tetrach.* Wks. 1738 I. 251 Doubtless this man hath bail enough to be no Adulterer.

c. *to give leg bail* (jocular): to be beholden to one's own legs for escape, to run away.

1775 Adair *Amer. Ind.* 277, I had concluded to use no chivalry, but give them leg-bail instead of it, by..making for a deep swamp. **1841** Marryat *Poacher* xxii, Given them leg bail, I'll swear.

6. The person or persons who procure the release of a prisoner from the custody of the officer arresting him, or from prison, by becoming surety for his appearance in court for trial.

The bail now becomes answerable with his money, but formerly he might have to give his own person as security, whence the phrase *to be* or *become bail*, i.e. security, as opposed *to give* or *put in bail* of sense 5.

1593 Shaks. *2 Hen. VI.* v. i. 111 Sirrah, call in my sonne to be my bale. 120 The sonnes of Yorke shall be their Fathers baile. **1644** Milton *Areop.* (Arb.) 56 His bayl and surety. **1649** Selden *Laws of Eng.* I. xxxvi. (1739) 53 If the party bailed made default..his Bail suffered as Principal. **1676** D'Urfey *Mad. Fickle* v. iii. (1677) 65 Well, leave 'em with me, I'll be Bail for their appearance to morrow. **1869** J. Martineau *Ess.* II. 112 [He] must stand bail for himself in the court of truth.

fig. **1820** Byron *Juan* v. xcix, I won't be bail for anything beyond. **1850** Thackeray *Pendennis* xxx. (1884) 292 Ye'll spend it like a man of spirit—I'll go bail for that.

¶In consequence of the transition of meaning in senses 3–6, many phrases are current which are not easily analysed. 'To say that the magistrate *bails* the prisoner (see bail *v.*[1] 2) is now somewhat old-fashioned. Generally, the magistrate *accepts bail, admits to bail, allows bail*, or (occasionally) *holds to bail*, or *takes bail*. I have also seen *grants bail*. The regular phrase of the Statute-book is, I think, "the magistrate may *admit him to bail*." In 45 Geo. III, c. 92, the magistrate also *takes bail*, the prisoner *gives bail*. *Bail* is also *offered* by the prisoner, and may be *refused* by the magistrate; on the day appointed his bail *surrender, render, bring in*, or *produce him* in court, or the accused *surrenders to his bail*. In the latter phrase, there is a notion of his delivering himself up in discharge of the recognizances into which he himself, as well as his sureties, has entered, for his appearance. This idea also colours the later use of *hold to bail, admit to bail*.' (F. W. Maitland.)

7. *Comb.* **bail-bond**, the bond or security entered into by a bail; **bail-piece**: (see quot.).

1709 *Act 7 Anne* in *Lond. Gaz.* No. 4538/1 All Bail Bonds given by the said Ambassador..are utterly Null and Void. **1815** Scott *Guy M.* lii, Where shall we find one to draw the bail-bond? **1768** Blackstone *Comm.* III. 291 Which recognizance is transmitted to the court in a slip of parchment intitled a bail piece.

bail, *sb.*[2] Forms: 5 beyl, bayl, 5–7 bayle, 7 baile, 7– bail, (8–9 erron. bale). [ME. *beyl*, prob. a. ON. *beygla*, Da. *böile*, Sw. *bögel, bygel*, bending, ring, hoop, guard of a sword-handle, etc; cf. also ON. *beyla* hump, swelling (Vigf.); all from ON. *beygja* = OE. *bēȝan, býȝan*, to bend, bow. There may even have been an OE. **beȝel, byȝel*; cf. LG. *bögel* in same sense.]

1. A hoop or ring; a half-hoop for supporting the cover of a wagon or cradle, the tilt of a boat. etc.

1447 Bokenham *Seyntys* 120 My right hand arayid.. Wyth a precyous beyl of gold hath he. **1494** *Ord. R. Househ.* 127 Twoe cradlebands of crimsonne velvett and a bayle.. for the same. **1529** *Privy Purse Exp. Hen. VIII* (1827) 11 To the same watermen for fowre bayles for the saied barge. **1669** Worlidge *Syst. Agric.* (1681) 216 Two small round Hoops or Arches..like unto the two end-Hoops or Bails of a Carriers Waggon, or a Tilt-boat. **1748** (ed. 4) De Foe, etc. *Tour Gt. Brit.* I. 143 (D.) An act of Parliament passed in 1736–7..prohibits close Decks and Bails nailed down in the Wherries. **1884** *W. Sussex Gaz.* 25 Sept., A capital large rick cloth, with bail.

2. The hoop-handle of a kettle or similar vessel.

1463 *Bury Wills* (1850) 23 A litell chafour with a beyl and a lyd. **1607** Topsell *Serpents* 767 About the same vessel [caldron or kettle]..binde this..to the handle or bayl thereof. **1741** Payne *Phil. Trans.* XLI. 823 A Handle or Bale ..by which it may be hung or held up. **1865** E. Burritt *Walk* 460 The old-fashioned bails of our brass-kettles. **1866** Howells *Venet. Life* 36 A small pot of glazed earthenware having an earthen bale.

bail, bayle (beɪl), *sb.*[3] Forms: 3–6 baile, 4 baille, 4–6 bail, bayle, 6 bayl, bayll, 9 bayle (sense 2), bail, bale (sense 4). [ME., a. OF. *bail* and *baile, baille* in same sense, of doubtful origin; perh. verbal sbs. f. *baillier* to enclose, shut (1321 in Godef.), unless indeed they are the source of that word: see bail *v.*[3] Cf. also next, and bailey.

It is phonetically possible that *bail, baille*, represent L. *baculum*, pl. *bacula*, sticks, in the sense of 'stakes, palisade,' but historical evidence of such a development of sense is wanting.]

1. *pl.* Outer line of fortification, formed of stakes; palisades, barriers.

1523 Ld. Berners *Froiss.* I. xxxviii. 52 The heynows conquered by force the baylles. *Ibid.* xlvii. 66 A lytell skirmyssh before the bayles. *Ibid.* 67 They rode in good order, and came to the bayls. **1795** Southey *Joan of Arc* VIII. 156 O'er the bayle, The bayle now levell'd by victorious France, The assailants pass'd.

2. The wall of the outer court of a feudal castle; extended to each of the successive walls which separate the courts. *Hence*, sometimes used for the courts themselves. See bailey.

a **1300** *Cursor M.* 10023 þe baile midelmast o thre, Bitakens wel hir chastite..Nam o bail it hat for-þi For it hir heild als in baili. *c* **1320** *Cast. Loue* 687 Seþþe beoþ þre Bayles wiþ-alle So feir i-diht wt strong walle. *c* **1450** *Merlin* vii. 113 That thei wolde ley siege environ the baile. **1570–87** Holinshed *Scot. Chron.* (1806) II. 368 The lord Fleming.. fled out by the postern gate, at the neither baile. **1813** Hogg *Queen's Wake* 253 Both bayle and keep rang with the din.

†**3.** *pl.* The bulwarks of a boat. *Obs.*

1577 Holinshed *Chron.* III. 921/2 His barge..with yeomen standing vpon the bails. **1558–1603** Nichols *Progr. Q. Eliz.* II. 285 One of the watermen..being the second man next unto the bales of the said barge.

4. A bar or pole to separate horses standing in an open stable; a ***swinging bail*** is hung at one end from the manger, and at the other from the ceiling.

1844 *Regul. & Ord. Army* 351 When the horse is deposited in the hold..it is the duty of the ship's carpenter to fix the bails which are to secure him. **1851** *Ord. & Regul. R. Engineers* xix. 96 Battery Stables..70 Bail Stalls..9 ft. by 5½ ft. **1859** 'Stonehenge' *Rural Sports* 583 With bales horses can be stowed much more thickly than with travises. **1877** —— *Horse* xiii. 205 A Gangway-Bail is..a strong piece of oak which is dropped into a mortice in the stall-post at one end, and into another made in the wall opposite.

5. (In Australia and N.Z.): A framework for securing the head of a cow while she is milked.

1847 'A. Harris' *Settlers & Convicts* xiv. 287 Next get up a moderate sized stockyard... Let it contain milking bales. *Ibid.* xvi. 345, I..had seen my own cow in his bale, and the milk carried into his dairy. **1859** F. Fuller *5 Yrs. Residence in N.Z.* viii. 170 [The heifer] is secured by fastening the bails. **1861** *Newcastle Advertiser* (N.S.W.) 24 Apr. 1 Next day I was dragged by the neck to a bail, And milked by a hairy-faced man with a pail. **1874** W. M. Baines *Narr. Edw. Crewe* x. 225 The former bovine female..would have been impossible to milk without a 'bail'. **1885** E. A. Petherick *in letter*: The cows are taken to the bails, which may be in the open air, in a shed, or in stalls as in a stable. **1952** G. Wilson *Julien Ware* i. 5 In the yard outside the bail a second cow.. stumbled uncertainly.

6. Of a typewriter: a hinged bar which holds the paper against the platen. Also ***bail bar, roller***.

1931 M. Crooks *Bk. Underwood Typewriter* xii. 85 The paper is normally held by the Carriage Bail. **1950** —— & Dawson *Dict. Typewriting* (ed. 5) 23 Bail. The complete term, namely 'Paper Bail', is the name given to the swivelled arm which holds the paper down on to the paper cylinder. **1959** *Observer* 4 Oct. 15/4 Every typewriter has a 'bail-bar' to hold the paper down, and usually this has to be lifted up and down when inserting paper. **1962** *Which?* Dec. 353 (*caption*) Paper bail bar. *Ibid.* 354 The bail bar, which should hold the paper against the platen, was thin and bent easily... Bail rollers on the bail bar are an additional way of holding the paper on to the platen.

bail, *sb.*[4] [Godefroy says 'In the arrondissement of Vervains and of Avesnes *bail* is the name of a horizontal piece of wood fixed upon two stakes.' This is exactly the cricket bail of the last century: the origin of the Fr. is uncertain; perh. identical with the preceding word; scarcely an independent repr. of L. *baculum*.]

†**1.** A cross bar. *Obs.*

1575 Turbervile *Booke of Falconrie* 358 Set them uppon some pearche or bayle of wood that they maye by that meanes the better keepe their feathers unbroken, and eschue the dragging of their traines upon the ground.

2. In *Cricket*, name of each of the two pieces of wood laid across the tops of the three stumps which form the wicket. Also *attrib.*, as ***bail ball*** = bailer[2].

(The bails are at present made 4 inches long, turned and shaped on the lathe; but originally the wicket consisted of a single bail, two feet long, laid across two stumps.

c **1742** J. Love *Cricket* III. 20 To such impetuous Might compell'd to yield The Bail. **1770** J. Love *Cricket* 19 The *Bail*, and mangled *Stumps* bestrew the Field. **1799** in *Hoyle's Games* (1803) 301 The striker is out if the bail is bowled off. **1813** *Sports of Childhood* Cricket 22 The Wicket consists of two pieces of wood fixed upright, and kept together by another piece, which is laid across the top and is called a Bail. **1833** Strutt *Sports & Past.* (Hone) 106 Of late years the wicket consists of three stumps and two bails. **1833** J. Mitford in *Gentl. Mag.* Sept. 235/2 Tom Walker laid down a bail ball. **1861** Whyte-Melville *Tilb. Nogo* 167 My bails fly upwards; and..I am disagreeably conscious of being 'bowled out.'

†**bail**, *sb.*[5] *Naut. Obs.* Forms: 5 beyle, 7 baile, 8 bail. [In earlier form *baile*, a. F. *baille* (in nautical language) a bucket, a pail, prob.:—late L. *bacula*, dim. of *baca, bacca*, back *sb.*[2]] A bucket or shallow tub used on board ship, esp. for emptying out water; any small vessel used to bail the water out of a boat.

1466 *Mann. & Househ. Exp.* 211 My master paid to Perse berebrewer for vj beyles for the spynas vijd. **1772–84** Cook *Voy.* (1790) I. 157 The gentlemen likewise saw the bail of a canoe..made of a human skull. **1867** Smyth *Sailor's Word-bk.*, *Bayle*, an old term for *bucket*.

bail (beɪl), *v.*[1] Forms: 5–7 bayl(e, 6 bale, baal, 6–7 baile, 6– bail. [a. OF. *baillier, bailier, bailler* (= Pr. *bailar*):—L. *bājulāre* 'to bear a burden, to carry,' afterwards 'to carry on, manage, rule,' and 'to be guardian or tutor,' whence *baillier* ranged in OF. from 'bear, carry, handle, treat, manage, conduct, govern, control, rule, take charge of, guard,' to 'take hold of, receive, take, take away,' and 'hand over, deliver, give.' From the last of these arose the Anglo-French legal sense of 'deliver,' narrowed down in use to 'deliver on trust on certain conditions.' Sense 2 is probably immediately from bail *sb.*[1] 3, 4, as if short for 'let to bail, admit to bail,' but clearly influenced by AF. *bailler* in sense 1, so as to make 'deliver' or 'liberate' at length the leading idea. Hence extended from the act of the magistrate to that of the surety, and used in various transferred senses.]

I. Immediately from F. *baillier*.

1. 'To deliver (goods) in trust, upon a contract expressed or implied that the trust shall be faithfully executed on the part of the bailee.' Blackstone. [See bailment, bailor, bailee.]

[*c* **1320** *Year-bk. Edw. II*, 270 A tort luy detient viij escritz, les queux il luy bailla a rebailler a sa volounte.] **1768** Blackstone *Comm.* II. 452 If cloth be delivered, or (in our legal dialect) bailed, to a taylor to make a suit of cloaths.

II. Immediately from bail *sb.*[1]

2. To admit to bail, to liberate on bail; to release (a person) from immediate arrest or imprisonment, on security being given by one or more sureties that the person so released shall be duly presented for trial. Said of the magistrate. *arch.*

1548 Hall *Chron.* Hen. VIII an. 14 (R.) Al the other, if they would be bayled, to fynde sureties for their trueth and allegeaunce. **1555** *Act 2–3 Mary* x. § 1 (1632), Such Justices ..as haue authority to baile any prisoner brought before them. **1641** *Termes de la Ley* 35 b, Upon the Bonds of these Sureties..he is bailed, that is to say, set at liberty, untill the day appointed for his appearance. **1715** Burnet *Own Time* III. (R.) Jeffries was bolder, so he bailed him. **1771** *Junius Lett.* lxv. 328 You have bailed a man..whom the lord mayor of London had refused to bail. **1827** Hallam *Const. Hist.* (1876) II. viii. 3 Charles..told them he was content the prisoners should be bailed.

†**b.** *fig.* and *gen.* To liberate from imprisonment.

1581 Studley *Seneca's Herc. Œtæus* 216 b, Hath hell no power to hold thy sprite..Or else hath Pluto baalde thee out? **1592** Greene *Conny Catch.* II. 31 Sirra see if your pick-locks will serue the turne to bale you hence. **1600** S. Nicholson *Acolastus* (1876) 27 It's hard to bayle imprisoned thoughts againe.

3. To procure the liberation of (any one) from prison or arrest, by becoming bail or security for him. (*To bail out* implies that he is already in prison.) Also *fig.*

1587 Fleming *Contn. Holinshed* III. 353/1 A woman.. whome the same Bruistar had bailed out of Bridewell. **1588** Shaks. *Tit. A.* II. iii. 299 Thou shalt not baile them, see thou follow me. **1642** Fuller *Holy & Prof. St.* I. iv. 11 The dearest Husband cannot bail his wife when death awaits her. **1791** Boswell *Johnson* (1831) I. 233, I shall have my old friend to bail out of the round-house. *a* **1832** Mackintosh *Revol. of* 1688 Wks. 1846 II. 281 Twenty-eight peers were prepared to bail them, if bail should be required. **1859** Mrs. Gaskell *Round the Sofa* 58, I offer to bail the fellow out, and to be responsible for his appearance at the sessions.

4. *fig.* To be security or pledge for; to secure, guarantee, protect.

1587 *Myrr. Mag.*, *Madan* xii. 4 Grace and prudence bayles our carefull bandes. **1620** Sanderson *Serm.* I. 166 This stranger, this Lot..hath bayled you hitherto, and given you protection. *a* **1659** Osborn *Q. Eliz.* (1673) 464 Let the Proverb *As sure as Check* bayl me from the least suspicion of hyperboly.

bail, *v.*[2] ? *Obs.* [f. bail *sb.*[2]] To hoop, gird.

1548 [see bailed *ppl. a.*]. **1594** Nashe *Unfort. Trav.* 59 Close soldered, and baílde about with yron.

bail, *v.*[3] Also 6 bale. [App. ad. OF. *baillier* to enclose, shut, of doubtful source: immediately related to *bail, baille*, bail *sb.*[3], though it is not yet certain which is derived from the other; if the vb. be the source, it may be perh. only another sense of *baillier*, to have charge of, control, guard, etc.: see bail *v.*[1]]

1. To confine. *rare.*

c **1600** SHAKS. *Sonnets* No. 133 Prison my heart in thy steele bosomes warde, But then my friends heart let my poore heart bale, Who ere keepes me, let my heart be his garde. **1852** SIR W. HAMILTON *Disc.* 303 The infinite spirit does not bail itself under proportion and number.

2. To secure the head of a cow in a 'bail' while she is milked. (One leg is also usually secured.) Usu. with *up. Austral.* and *N.Z.*

1846 C. J. PHARAZYN *Jrnl.* 25 Aug. (MS.) 54 Helped George in bailing up Durham [a cow]. **1853** J. ROCHFORT *Adv. Surveyor N.Z.* iii. 24 We were just in time to see his men bailing up some cattle [at the station]; *i.e.* the cow is made to put her head between two posts, when a bar slides across the space and catches her by the neck, rendering it impossible to get her head back. **1860** R. DONALDSON *Bush Lays & Rhymes* 14 A young cow must be bailed. *a* **1885** *Mod.* (from E. A. Petherick) 'Have you bailed up the cows?' 'Yes, they're bailed up.' **1888** 'R. BOLDREWOOD' *Robbery under Arms* I. vii. 89 She could frighten a wildish cow, and bail up anything that would stay in a yard with her. **1906** E. W. ELKINGTON *Adrift in N.Z.* i. 16 The cows..refused to be bailed up. **1950** *N.Z. Jrnl. Agric.* Sept. 268 After the heifer has been bailed in the normal way the board is swung into position.

3. (Orig. said of Australian bushrangers.) To 'stick up' travellers in order to rob them; to 'corner' a wild boar (or other hunted animal); (in weakened sense) to detain (a person); also *transf.* Also *intr.*, to surrender (by throwing up the arms). Usu. with *up. Austral.* and *N.Z.*

1840 *Sydney Herald* 31 Jan. 2/4 Only think of one man [*sc.* a bushranger] bailing up the master and twelve men. **1853** MRS. C. CLACY *Lady's Visit to Gold Diggings* xvi. 235 But can picture their horror when ordered to 'bail up' by a party of Australian Turpins. **1855** W. HOWITT *Land, Labour, & Gold* II. xxxix. 309 So long as that is wrong, the whole community will be wrong, — in colonial phrase, 'bailed up' at the mercy of its own tenants. **1872** LADY BARKER in D. M. Davin *N.Z. Short Stories* (1953) 25 Our head shepherd recognized an old enemy in the dead boar, and declared that he and his dogs had bailed him up unsuccessfully 'many a time and oft'. **1879** W. J. BARRY *Up & Down* xii. 112 She bailed me up, and asked me if I was going to keep my promise and marry her? **1880** *Melbourne Argus* 22 July 1/7 We were bailed up by an armed man on horseback. —— in *Leisure Ho.* (1885) 197 'Bail up! Throw up your arms, I'm Ned Kelly!' **1885** H. FINCH-HATTON *Advance Australia!* vii. 105 A little further on the boar 'bailed up' on the top of a ridge. **1888** A. H. DUNCAN *Wakatipians* x. 105 We are bailed up by the snow, and look like frozen Esquimaux. **1894** J. K. ARTHUR *Kangaroo & Kauri* II. iii. 98 The pigs will oftentimes 'bale up', or stop, and with their back to a rock, tree, or other obstacle, keep two or more dogs at bay for a long time. **1894** H. NISBET *Bush Girl's Romance* 144 Reginald..acted like a wise man and 'bailed up', that is, he dropped his knife and threw up his hands as a sign of his submission. **1895** G. CHAMIER *South-Sea Siren* xiv. 205 He was immediately 'bailed up' [by the surveyors], and made to dismount against his will to partake of some refreshment. **1900** D. McK. WRIGHT *Wisps of Tussock* 50 He bailed me up straight for a shilling. **1904** M. CRADOCK *Sport in N.Z.* I. iii. 67 Unless he [*s.c.* the pig] is a peculiarly obstinate beast the dogs very soon 'bail him up' again. **1911** *Chambers's Jrnl.* 4 Mar. 222/2 The dogs have 'bailed' a fighting old boar in a rock-cleft. **1930** E. WALLACE *White Face* xiii. 213 'Bail up!' It was an expression of the old Australian bushrangers. It's still used by the hold-up men in Australia. **1943** F. DAVISON in *Coast to Coast 1942* 194, I didn't like the colour of those who had him bailed up. **1946** —— *Dusty* (1947) ix. 94 The border collie's shrill barking when he had a goanna bailed up always brought him to the scene. **1960** B. CRUMP *Good Keen Man* 84, I couldn't see eye-to-eye with Jim on the matter of going in on bailed boars with a slasher.

bail, *v.*[4] Also 5-7 baile, bayle, (7-9 bale). [f. BAIL *sb.*[5]]

1. Now often less correctly BALE, q.v. To lade or throw water out of a boat, etc., with buckets (formerly called bails), pails, basins, or other vessels. **a.** To bail *the water* (out).

1613 PURCHAS *Pilgr.* IX. xiv. 911 They bailed and pumped two thousand tuns and yet were ten foot deepe. **1622** R. HAWKINS *Voy. S. Sea* 226 In clearing and bayling the water. **1624** CAPT. SMITH *Virginia* v. 174 Buckets..to baile out the water. **1829** MARRYAT *F. Mildmay* xi, One [man] to bail the water out.

b. To bail *the boat* (out).

1840 R. DANA *Bef. Mast* xviii. 50 By the help of a small bucket and our hats we bailed her out. **1841** CATLIN *N. Amer. Ind.* (1844) II. xlviii. 111 Ladles to bail them out.

c. *absol.*

1624 CAPT. SMITH *Virginia* v. 174 Bailing and pumping three daies and three nights without intermission. **1682** SIR J. BERRY in *Lond. Gaz.* No. 1720/7 Still working with the Pumps and Bailing, but to no purpose.

2. *to bail out* (*Aeronaut.*): see BALE *v.*[2] 2.

†**'bailable**, *a.*[1] *Obs.* In 5-6 baleable. [a. OF. *baillable* f. *bailler* in sense of 'deliver.'] Capable of being delivered, deliverable.

1502 ARNOLD *Chron.* (1811) 121 If thes oure presentis lettres patentis..be not baleable.

bailable ('beɪləb(ə)l), *a.*[2] Also 6-7 baileable, bayl(e-. [f. BAIL *v.*[1] and *sb.*[1] + -ABLE.]

1. Of persons: Entitled to be released on bail.

1554 *Act 1-2 Mary* xiii. §3 Any person or persons..being bayleable by the law. **1626** BERNARD *Isle Of Man* (1627) 76 To send him to Gaole, if he be not baileable. **1796** MORSE *Amer. Geog.* I. 561 All persons shall be bailable, unless for capital offences.

2. Of an offence or process: Admitting of bail.

1649 SELDEN *Laws of Eng.* I. xxxvi. (1739) 53 He was.. admitted to Bail if the offences were bailable. **1817** JAS. MILL *Brit. India* II. v. vi. 572 A capias was granted, with a bailable clause. **1859** LD. J. CAMPBELL in Ellis *Law Rep.* II. 114 Directed only against bailable process.

bailage ('beɪlɪdʒ). Also 9 balliage, bailiage. [f. BAIL *v.*[1], or AF. *baillier* to deliver: perh. there was an AF. **bailliage* or med.L. **balliagium* in this sense.] A duty upon delivery of goods.

1753 CHAMBERS *Cycl. Supp.* s.v., Water *Bailiage* or *Bailage*, is an antient duty received by the city of London, for all goods and merchandises brought into or carried out of the port. **1800** COLQUHOUN *Comm. Thames* xi. 332 Of Balliage, or Delivery of Goods. **1809** R. LANGFORD *Introd. Trade* 129 *Bailage*, duty paid on goods to the City of London.

¶ See also BAILLIAGE.

'bail-dock, 'bale-dock. *Obs.* [? f. BAIL *sb.*[3] barrier: see DOCK.] At the Old Bailey, London, (formerly) 'a small room taken from one of the corners of the court, and left open at the top; in which, during the trials, are put some of the malefactors.' *Scots Mag.* 1753 XV. 42/1.

1624 HEYWOOD *Gunaik.* III. 159 The sessions is dissolved, the bench and bale-docke cleered. **1662** ELLWOOD *Autobiog.* (1767) 148 Away I was taken and thrust into the Bail-dock to my other Friends who had been called before me. **1670** PENN *Truth Rescued* 8, I was commanded to the Bale-Dock for Turbulency and Impertinency. **1716** *Lond. Gaz.* No. 5399/3 James Goodman..made his Escape..by leaping over the Spikes of the Bail-Dock and the Rails at the Sessions-House in the Old-Baily. **1823** LAMB *Elia* (1860) 72, I remember Penn before his accusers, and Fox in the bail-dock.

† **baile, bayle,** *int. Obs.* [Perh. imperative of Fr. *bailler* in sense 'Deliver (blows)!' But cf. *bailler sa foi*, in Littré.] A call to combatants to engage.

a **1529** SKELTON *Agst. Garnesche* 31 Baile, baile at you bothe, frantike folys! *c* **1530** LD. BERNERS *Arth. Lyt. Bryt.* 364 Than harodes began to crye: knightes, do your best! go togyder, bayle! bayle! Than began the tournay.

bailed (beɪld), *ppl. a.*[1] [f. BAIL *v.*[1] + -ED.] Released on bail.

1552 HULOET, Bayled, or lette to bayle, *Vadimonio obstrictus*. **1664** BUTLER *Hud.* II. iii. 73 Like a Bail'd and Main-priz'd Lover, Although at large I am bound over.

bailed (beɪld), *ppl. a.*[2] [f. BAIL *v.*[2] + -ED.] Hooped (and covered) as a wagon.

1548 HALL *Chron.* (1809) 801 Then came the Quene in a litter of white clothe of golde not covered nor Bayled. **1598** STOW *Survey* xli. (1603) 436 A close cart, bayled ouer.

bailee (ˌbeɪ'liː). *Law.* Also 6 baily, 7 baylee. [f. BAIL *v.*[1] + -EE.] One to whom goods are committed in trust for a specific purpose.

1528 PERKINS *Prof. Bk.* ii. §140 (1642) 62 If.. afterwards the Baily deliver the Obligation to whom it was made. **1613** SIR H. FINCH *Law* (1636) 180 The baylement of goods to imploy, is, when the Bailee hath the things themselues to vse to anothers profit. **1875** POSTE *Gaius* III. 423 These contracts ..all imply a delivery from the bailor to the bailee and a redelivery from the bailee to the bailor.

'bailer[1]. [f. BAIL *v.*[4] + -ER[1].] **1.** He who or that which bails water out; a man employed to bail out a ship; a utensil used for this purpose, a machine constructed to lift and throw out water from a pit, etc.

1883 KINGSTON *Paddy Finn* xv. 190 There was no bailer; but I had seized my hat. **1883** *Century Mag.* July 330/1 The 'sand-pump' and 'bailer,' employed to take up and hoist out the pulverized rock and water. **1883** *Daily News* 15 Sept. 2/7 (*Shipping*), [Ship] Hardwick..half full of water..Bailers have been employed.

2. *attrib.* **bailer shell**, the shell of a gastropod mollusc of the genus *Cymbium* found in the south-western Pacific, also called MELON-*shell*; also, the mollusc itself.

1908 E. J. BANFIELD *Confessions of Beachcomber* I. iv. 148 The bailer shell alive is like an egg, in the fact that it is full of meat. **1926** *Austral. Encycl.* II. 135/2 The most useful of all molluscs was the Melon or Bailer-shell (*Cymbium flammeum*), which served for a canoe-bailer. **1929** *Times* 2 Aug. 14/1 Several melon or bailer shells were as large as footballs. **1947** I. L. IDRIESS *Isles of Despair* viii. 56 Many a bailer shell filled with rich turtle soup. **1955** A. ROSS *Australia 55* 121 Beautiful bailer shells, so-called because the natives use them to bail from their canoes.

'bailer[2]. *Cricket.* [f. BAIL *sb.*[4] + -ER[1].] A ball so bowled as to hit the bails.

1833 J. MITFORD in *Gentl. Mag.* Sept. 236/1 [The practice of going out to meet the ball] saves alike the fingers and the wickets from a first-rate top-bailer. **1865** *Field* 9 Sept. 189/2 Mr. Sale..at length bowled Capt. Parnell with an irresistible bailer. **1881** *Daily News* 29 June 2/6 (*Cricket*), A fine bailer from Studd beat Peake when 246 had been made. **1882** *Daily Tel.* 27 May, A bailer from Jones just managed to destroy his chance.

bailey ('beɪlɪ). Forms: 3 baili, 4 bayly, -lie, -lye, bailye, bailly, baly, 4-5 baillie, 4-6 baily, bailie, 9 bailey. [a ME. variant of *bayle*, BAIL *sb.*[3]: possibly from the med.L. form *balium, ballium*; cf. *Vetus Ballium* = Old Bailey, Du Cange. Not in Fr. It coincides in its spellings with BAILLIE, with which it was probably confused.]

1. The external wall enclosing the outer court, and forming the first line of defence, of a feudal castle; and, in a wider sense, any of the circuits of walls or defences which surrounded the keep.

a **1300** *Cursor M.* 10023 þe midmast bailly of þe þre Bitokeneþ wel hir chastite..Name of baily hit haþ for-þi For hit [hir] helde euer in baily [*v.r.* bailey, bayly]. *Ibid.* 10034 þere stonden þre bailyes wiþoute þat wel kepen þat castel From arwe shet & quarel. *c* **1325** *E.E. Allit. P.* A. 1082 As quen I blusched vponþat baly, So ferly þer-of-watz þe falure. **1851** TURNER *Dom. Archit.* I. i. 16 The more recent habitation reared within its enclosures or baileys.

2. In later writers: The outer court or base court of a feudal castle; also, either of the two (or three courts) formed by the spaces between the circuits of walls or defences. Hence *outer bailey*, *inner bailey*.

1845 *Gloss. Goth. Archit.* I. 37 Bailey was a name given to the courts of a castle formed by the spaces between the circuits of walls or defences which surrounded the keep. **1851** TURNER *Dom. Archit.* I. i. 17 The royal apartments were not in the keep, but in the court-yard, or bailey. **1862** *Luck of Ladysmede* I. 93 The entrance-gate..led into a narrow outer bailey.

3. (Retained in proper names: e.g. the *Old Bailey* in London, the seat of the Central Criminal Court, so called from the ancient *bailey* or *ballium* of the city wall between Lud Gate and New Gate, within which it was situated.)

1570 *Piththy Note to Papists* (Collier) 15 The Draile, wheron he lay fast bound in midst olde baily street. **1587** FLEMING *Contn. Holinshed* III. 357/1 At a sessions holden in the justice hall in the old bailie of London. **1865** *Morn. Star* 5 July, The phrase, 'Old Bailey style,' is an ordinary *façon de parler*, and is well understood to mean..a certain license of vituperation which has been supposed, rightly or wrongly, to characterise its proceedings.

bailey, obs. variant of BAILIE.

Bailey bridge ('beɪlɪ). [f. name of Donald (later Sir D.) Coleman *Bailey* (1901-85), English engineer, its designer.] A bridge of lattice steel designed for rapid assembly from prefabricated standard parts, used esp. in military operations. Also *B. bridging* and *ellipt.*

1944 *Hutchinson's Pict. Hist. War* Apr.-Sept. 269 The story of the development of the Bailey bridging equipment ..has been revealed. **1944** *Times* 14 Dec. 3/3 A Bailey bridge more than 1,000 ft. long has been built over the Chindwin near Kalewa. **1945** *Finito! Po Valley Campaign* 7 The stuff for Bailey Bridges. *Ibid.* 23 Engineers toiled ceaselessly to span the river with Baileys. **1956** W. SLIM *Defeat into Victory* xvi. 366 On the 10th December [1944] our engineers completed a floating Bailey bridge over the Chindwin. Its length was 1,154 feet, then the longest Bailey bridge in the world.

bailiage, -iary, variants of BAILAGE, -IERY.

bailie ('beɪlɪ). Forms: 3 bailli, -ie, 3-4 baili, 3-7 bayly, 4 bayli, bayely, 4-5 baylle, 4-6 bayle, bailye, 4-8 bailly, 5 bailȝhey, 5-6 baly, 5-7 bayley, 6 baylay, bailȝie, 7 baylie, 7-8 baillie, bailey, 4-9 baily, 6- bailie. [ME. *bailli*, a. OF. *bailli* (13th c.), later form of *baillis, baillif*, BAILIFF, q.v.] Another form of the word BAILIFF, with which it was formerly interchangeable; now obsolete in England, but retained in a special sense in Scotland.

†**1.** = BAILIFF 1. *Obs.*

1297 R. GLOUC. 129 To þe baylys of þe toun hastiliche heo wende. *a* **1300** *Cursor M.* 5008 þar vs tok þe hei baili [*v.r.* bailly, bayli, baily]. *Ibid.* 9558 He ne had neuer sa gret envie, Als þis man for to be baillie [*v.r.* bayly]. **1483** CAXTON *Gold. Leg.* 306/1 Mayres, Shereues, baylles, and suche other lasse offyces. **1494** FABYAN *Hen. III*, an. 1266 (R.) Ye baylly of the castell of Wyndesore. **1501** *Plumpton Corr.* 159 The baylay of Byngham Vapentake. **1527** GARDINER in Pocock *Rec. Ref.* I. 75 Being advised by the baly of Dover so to do. **1530** *Proper Dyaloge* (1863) 39 Euery secular lorde..is Gods bayly. **1598** HAKLUYT *Voy.* I. 129 Sent to the Sherife of Sudsex, to the Maior and Communaltie of the Citie of Winchester, to the Baily of Southampton, the Baily of Lenne, the Baily of Kent. **1662** FULLER *Worthies* II. 129 At Ashby De La Zouch..where his Father under the Earl of Huntington, was Governour or Baly of the Town.

humorously. **1652** BROME *Jov. Crew* I. 364 Then up rise Randal, Bayley of the Beggars.

2. *In Scotland.* †**a.** *formerly*, The chief magistrate of a barony or part of a county, having functions equivalent to those of a sheriff. *Obs.*

1375 BARBOUR *Bruce* I. 190 Schyrreffys and bailȝheys maid he then. **1425** *Acts Jas. I* (1597) §63 The Kingis Baillie, or a Depute of the towne. **1634-46** ROW *Hist. Kirk* (1842) 87 For other civill and criminall jurisdictions, the heretable baillies might supplie that part. **1754** ERSKINE *Princ. Sc. Law* (1809) 38 Where lands, not erected into a regality, fell into the King's hands, he appointed a bailie over them, whose jurisdiction was equal to that of a sheriff.

b. *now.* A municipal magistrate corresponding to the English alderman.

1484 CAXTON *Chyualry* 23 Kynges and prynces which make prouostes and baillyes of other persones than of knyȝtes. **1558** *Instr. of Sasine* in *Annals of Hawick* 331 In the hands of Adam Cessfurde, ane of ye bailȝies of Hawick. **1609** SKENE *Reg. Mag.* 128 At the first head Court after Michaelmes, the Baillies sould be chosen. **1796** MORSE *Amer. Geog.* II. 162 Edinburgh is governed by a lord provost, four baillies. **1818** SCOTT *Rob Roy* xxix, I am a free burgess and a magistrate o' Glasgow; Nicol Jarvie is my name, I am a bailie, be praised for the honour.

†**3.** = BAILIFF 2. *Obs.* (or *dial.*)

c **1340** *Cursor M.* (Trin.) 12914 As baily [*Cott.* bedel] goþ bifore Iustise. *c* **1386** CHAUCER *Freres T.* 92 'Artow than a bayely?' 'Ye,' quod he. **1460** *Townley Myst.* 17 A mekille myschaunce And the bayles us take. **1542** BRINKLOW *Complaynt* vii. (1874) 21 Euery man is a bayly to attache a felon. *c* **1600** NORDEN *Spec. Brit.* Cornw. (1728) 73 A libertye when the Shirifes Baylye can not areste. **1668** SHADWELL *Sullen Lov.* III. Wks. 1720 I. 63 Worse than a Bayley, that arrests in the Inns of Court. [In Scotland, constables specially employed in carrying out the Tweed Fisheries' Acts are called Water-bailies.]

fig. **1621** QUARLES *Argalus & P.* (1678) 120 Natures pale-fac'd Bailey now distrains His blood.

†**4.** = BAILIFF 3. *Obs.*

c **1375** WYCLIF *Serm.* Sel. Wks. 1869 I. 24 þis bailly [*Luke* xvi. 1] was worldly wyse. **1483** CAXTON *Gold. Leg.* 41/3 That Eleazar the sone of my baily be myn heyr. **1523** FITZHERB. *Husb.* §134 If thou haue any wode to sell..cause thy bayly ..to do it for the. **1602** FULBECKE *2nd Pt. Parall.* 45 A bailie is he to whom a speciall charge of procuring a mans profite, and the valuable increase of his wealth is committed. **1661** PEPYS *Diary* 19 July, Agreeing with Hauker to have a care of my business in my absence..to be our bayly. **1688** SHADWELL *Sqr. Alsatia* II. i. 43 A very pretty fellow for a gentleman's bailey. **1730** SWIFT *Panegyr. Dean* Misc. (1735) V. 137 You merit new Employments daily: Our Thatcher, Ditcher, Gard'ner, Baily.

5. bailie-errant = bailiff-errant: see BAILIFF 4.

1528 TINDALE *Obed. Chr. Man* Wks. I. 204 The sheriffs, baily-errants, constables, and such like officers.

bailie, variant of BAILLIE, *Obs.*, jurisdiction, and of BAILEY, court-wall of a castle.

bailiery, -ary ('beɪlɪərɪ, 'beɪlɪrɪ). *Obs.* exc. *Hist.* Forms: 7–9 **baillerie, -ery, baylerie, baylairy,** 7–8 **bailiary,** 8 **bailliary, -ery,** 8–9 **bailiery** [In 17th c. *baillerie*, a. F. **baillerie* office of the *bailli* or BAILIE.] The jurisdiction of a bailie; *esp.*, in Scotland, before the abolition of hereditary jurisdictions, a district administered by a bailie instead of by a sheriff.

1425 *Acts Jas. I* (1597) §67 That ilke Schireffe giue open bidding to the people of his Bailliarie. **1609** SKENE *Reg. Maj.* 161 Within their houses, lands, bounds, or Bailleries. **1639** SPOTTISWOOD *Hist. Ch. Scot.* VI. (1677) 286 Proclamations sent to the Sheriffdoms of Edinburgh, Hadington, Linlithgow..and to the Bailiaries of Kyle and Cunningham. *a* **1649** DRUMM. OF HAWTH. *Jas. II*, Wks. (1711) 24 The baylerie of Aderbrothock. **1679** *Proclam. Edinb.* 4 May, Bayliffs of Regalities and Bayliaries. **1708** *Proclam.* 11 July in *Lond. Gaz.* No. 4456/1 We Require..Baillies of Bailliaries. **1754** ERSKINE *Princ. Sc. Law* (1809) 38 By the late jurisdiction act, 20 Geo. II. c. 43, all heritable regalities and bailieries, and all such heritable sheriff-ships and stewartries, as were only parts of a shire, are dissolved.

bailieship ('beɪlɪʃɪp). Forms: 4– **bailly-, baili-, bayely-, baili-, bealie-, bayly-, bailie-, -ship, -shyppe.** [f. BAILIE + -SHIP: see also BAILIFFSHIP.]

†**1.** Stewardship. *lit.* and *fig. Obs.*

c **1375** WYCLIF *Serm.* Sel. Wks. 1869 I. 22 A reckenynge of þi baillyship. **1532** HERVET *Xenophon's Househ.* (1768) 58 What profyte shulde we haue by his bayelyshyppe? **1582** N.T. (Rhem.) *Luke* xvi. 2 Render account of thy bailiship: for now thou canst no more be bailife.

2. The office of a bailie or (*obs.*) a bailiff.

c **1472** *Plumpton Corr.* 27 The office of the bailiship of Sesey. **1589** *Wills & Inv. N.C.* (1860) 166 With all my ryght of the bealieship of Carham. **1602** FULBECKE *2nd Pt. Parall.* 45 More agreable to our lawe especially in this matter of baileship.

3. The district under a bailie or bailiff.

1502 ARNOLD *Chron* (1811) 212 Them which out of his baylyship comen as marchauntis. **1681** *Lond. Gaz.* No. 1598/2 The Bayliship of Drenthe, which is a part of the Province of Groningen.

bailiff ('beɪlɪf). Forms: 3–5 **baillif,** 3–7 **bailif,** 4 **balyf,** 5 **baillyve,** 6 **bailliff, bailiffe, baliffe, balyfe, -yve, -ive, baylyff, bailiefe,** 6–7 **baylife, bayliffe,** 7 **bailife, bailive,** 7–8 **bayliff,** 6– **bailiff.** [ME. *baillif*, a. OF. *baillif*, obj. case of *baillis* (12th c.):—late L. *bājulīvus*, prop. an adj. f. *bājulus*, originally 'carrier,' afterwards 'carrier on, manager, administrator.' (See BAIL *sb.*[1] and cf. *bājulāre* under BAIL *v.*[1] *Bājulīvus* thus meant '(one) having the nature or character of a *bājulus*.' In med.L. *ballivus, baillivus, balivus*, from the F. and Eng. words.)]

1. One charged with public administrative authority in a certain district. **a.** In *England*, formerly applied to the king's officers generally, including sheriffs, mayors, etc. nominated by him, but *especially* to the chief officer of a hundred; still the title of the chief magistrate of various towns, as the *High-bailiff of Westminster*, and of the keeper of some of the royal castles, as the *Bailiff of Dover Castle*.

1297 R. GLOUC. 473 That ple solde be ibroȝt Biuore the king and is bailifs. *a* **1300** *Cursor M.* 6445 Ietro him gaf counsaile vnder baillifes [*v.r.* baillis, bayles, bailies] ham to sette. **1480** CAXTON *Chron. Eng.* ccxxi. 213 The quene sent in hast to the Baillifs of wynchestre. **1691** WOOD *Ath. Oxon.* II./290 His father..was then Bailive of Hemlingford hundred. **1757** BURKE *Abridgm. Eng. Hist.* Wks. X. 343 The bailiffs of hundreds, and tithings, and boroughs, with their people. **1835** *Penny Cycl.* III. 290/1 The sheriff is called the King's bailiff, and his county is his bailiwick. **1873** STUBBS *Const. Hist.* I. v. 102 The *gerefa*, who becomes after the Conquest the bailiff of the hundred. *Ibid.* III. xxi. 561 In those towns in which there was no mayor, the presidency of the local courts remained with the bailiffs.

fig. **1655** FULLER *Hist. Camb.* (1840) 105 Down comes the bailiff of Bedford (so the country-people commonly call the overflowing of the river Ouse), attended..with many servants..and breaks down all their paper-banks.

b. Used as the English form of the title of various foreign magistrates; e.g. the French *bailli*, and German *Landvogt*; also of the *bailly* or first civil officer in the Channel Islands, and formerly also of the Sc. BAILIE.

1681 *Act* (Scotl.), *Lond. Gaz.* No. 1649/2 Sheriffs, Stewards, Bailiffs of Royalty and Regality. **1693** *Apol. Clergy Scot.* 23 One of the Magistrates of Glasgow..made a Bailiff by the Archbishop. **1694** FALLE *Jersey* v. 129 Bailiff and Jurats of the said Isle for the time being. **1753** HANWAY *Trav.* (1762) II. I. iv. 22 The great bailiff of the district, of which there are..about twenty five in the hanoverian dominions. **1855** MILMAN *Lat. Chr.* (1864) V. IX. vii. 366 Henry while yet Bailiff of the Empire, during the captivity of Baldwin. **1860** MOTLEY *Netherl.* (1868) I. iii. 77 De Griyse formerly bailiff of Bruges. **1862** ANSTED *Channel Isl.* IV. xxiii. 524 The *Bailiff* or Judge, is the first civil officer in each island. **1864** KIRK *Chas. Bold* I. II. ii. 492 A royal envoy, the bailiff of Lyons.

2. An officer of justice under a sheriff, who executes writs and processes, distrains, and arrests; a warrant officer, pursuivant, or catchpoll.

1377 LANGL. *P. Pl.* B. II. 59 Shireues and here clerkes, Bedelles and Bailliues. **1538** BALE *Thre Lawes* 1613 Ther someners and ther scribes..With balyues and catchpolles. **1588** FRAUNCE *Lawiers Log.* I. xix. 67 Returned by the Shiriffe and warned by his bayliffe. **1611** SHAKS. *Wint. T.* IV. iii. 102 He hath bene since an Ape-bearer, then a Processe-seruer (a Bayliffe). **1712** STEELE *Spect.* No. 330 ¶3, I was arrested and conveyed..to a Bayliff's house. **1863** BURTON *Bk. Hunter* 326 A bailiff making an inventory of goods on which he has taken execution.

fig. *a* **1656** BP. HALL *Rem. Wks.* (1660) 22 The conscience is but God's Bayliff.

3. The agent of the lord of a manor, who collects his rents, etc.; the steward of a landholder, who manages his estate; one who superintends the husbandry of a farm for its owner or tenant.

1531 ELYOT *Gov.* III. xx. **1574** tr. *Littleton's Tenures* 17 a, Which they shall delyver unto the stewarde or baylife. **1617** *Janua Ling.* 526 The baliffe gathereth-in harvest into the barne. **1678** R. LESTRANGE *Seneca's Mor.* (1702) 420 My Bayliff told me 'twas none of his Fault. **1848** KINGSLEY *Saint's Trag.* III. ii. 156 Here's Father January taken a lease of March month, and put in Jack Frost for bailiff. **1866** GEO. ELIOT *F. Holt* (1868) 36 I'm going over one of the farms.. with the bailiff.

4. *Comb.*, as *bailiff-haunted*; †**bailiff-errant** (see quot.); **bailiff-peers**, assessors of the bailiff of a town. See also BUM-BAILIFF.

1612 DAVIES *Why Ireland, etc.* (1787) 201 The under-sheriffs and bayliffs errant are better guides and spies. **1641** *Termes de la Ley* 35 Baylifes Errant are those that the Sherife maketh and appointeth to go about the County to execute Writs, to summon the county, Sessions, assises and such like. **1707** *Lond. Gaz.* No. 4338/1 The humble Address of the Bailiff, Recorder..Bailiff-Peers, Town Clerk, and Burgesses of Wenlock. **1812** J. & H. SMITH *Rej. Addr., Cui bono* ix, The bailiff-haunted throng.

'bailiffry. *rare.* Also 7 **bailivery.** [f. prec. + -RY. Cf. BAILIERY.] The office or jurisdiction of a bailiff, or bailie; a BAILIERY.

1598 STOW *Surv.* (Strype 1754) II. v. xxvii. 474/1 The Sheriffs Aldermen and Serjeants by authority of their Bailivery. **1708** CHAMBERLAYNE *St. Gt. Brit.* II. I. ii. (1743) 306 Hereditary bailiffs of the king's Bailiffry [anglicized for *bailies* and *bailiery*].

bailiffship ('beɪlɪfʃɪp). [f. as prec. + -SHIP.] The office of bailiff.

1651 W. CARTWRIGHT *Ordinary* in Dodsl. *O.P.*X. 258 Let me now begin My bailiff-ship. **1863** CHEVRON in *N. & Q.* Ser. III. III. 185 The bailiff-ship or ministration of justice.

†**'bailiffwick.** *Obs.* [f. as prec. + -WICK.]

1. The district under the jurisdiction of a bailiff.

1709 STRYPE *Ann. Ref.* I. xxvi. 312 In case the sheriff.. return, that the party..could not be found within his bailiff-wick. **1766** in Entick *London* IV. 319 Proclaimed.. throughout the whole bailiffwick.

2. The office of a bailiff; = BAILIFFSHIP.

1509 *Act 1 Hen. VIII.* xix. §6 Baillifwikes or Baillyshyps of the Maners of Multon and Skirkebekys. **1570** *Act 13 Eliz.* IV. §13 His..office of Sheriffwicke, Escheatorship or Bayliffewike.

3. Stewardship.

1605 *Answ. Supp. Disc. Rom. Doctr.* 25 Popes and Princes must render account of their Bailifewicke.

'bailing, *vbl. sb.* [f. BAIL *v.*[1] + -ING[1].] A releasing on bail.

1542–3 *Act 34 & 35 Hen. VIII*, xxvii. §50 For the apparaunce and baylynge of common maynprise, two pens. **1628** in Rushw. *Hist. Coll.* (1659) I. 529 Bayling is a grace or favor of a Court of Justice.

'bailing, *vbl. sb.*[2] [f. BAIL *v.*[4] + -ING[1].] The lading or scooping of water out of a boat.

1682 SIR J. BERRY in *Lond. Gaz.* No. 1720/7 All our Pumps and Materials for bailing. **1748** ANSON *Voy.* I. iii. 24 With four pumps and bailing he could not free her.

†**bailiric.** *Obs.* [f. BAILIE + -RIC, OE. *ríc* rule, dominion.] = BAILIWICK.

1570 LEVINS *Manip.* 121 There be dyuers other that ende in *ricke* or *wicke*, signifying offices which have their latine in *atus*, or in *ura*: as..A Baylyrick *villicatus*, a Bayly-wick *villicatura*.

†**'bailivate.** *Obs.* [ad. med.L. *baillivātus*, *ballivātus*, f. *ballivus*, f. F. *baillif*; see -ATE[1].] The office of a bailiff, bailiffship.

1721 STRYPE *Eccl. Mem.* III. III. 30 With the bailivate of the town of Eltham.

bailive, -ry, obs. forms of BAILIFF, -RY.

bailiwick ('beɪlɪwɪk). Forms: 5–9 **bayly-, bally-, bayli-, baili-, bali-, baily-, bayl-, baylie-, baly-, bailly-, bailli-, -weke, -wyke, -wick(e, -wik(e** (more than 20 forms). [f. BAILIE + -WICK: see also BAILIFFWICK.]

1. a. A district or place under the jurisdiction of a bailie or bailiff. Used in *Eng. Hist.* as a general term including *sheriffdom*; and applied to foreign towns or districts under a *vogt* or *bailli*.

c **1460** FORTESCUE *Abs. & Lim. Mon.* (1714) 123 A mean Bayliff may do more in his Bayly-Weke. **1574** tr. *Littleton's Tenures* 51 a, By the othe of xii true men of hys bayliwike. **1596** SPENSER *State Irel.* Wks. (1862) 553/2 The sheriffe of the shire, whose peculiar office it is to walke up and downe his bayli-wicke. **1678** T. JONES *Heart & Right Sov.* 88 Our British Isles, which never were within the diocess or bayliwick of Rome. **1759** B. MARTIN *Nat. Hist. Eng.* II. 355 A fair Bailiwick and Town corporate. **1796** MORSE *Amer. Geog.* II. 305 Berne. This Canton contains 72 bailiwicks. **1862** ANSTED *Channel Isl.* IV. xxiii. 519 Guernsey, Alderney, and Sark, together with Herm..composing the Bailiwick of Guernsey. **1884** *Law Rep.* Chanc. Div. XXV. 341 The sheriff..made a return..that Mr. S. had no lay fee within his bailiwick.

b. *transf.* 'One's natural or proper place or sphere' (D.A.). Chiefly *U.S.*

1843 *Knickerbocker* XXI. 589 A friend..inside the southern division of Mason and Dixon's 'bailiwick'. **1892** *Outing* (U.S.) Apr. 16/1 The baggage-man stared a little when we piled our 'truck' into his bailiwick. **1911** R. D. SAUNDERS *Col. Todhunter* ix. 119 I'm skeered to the marrow, ..because I'm out o' my bailiwick. **1940** *S.P.E. Tract* LVI. 216 *Bailiwick*..has given rise to the common phrase 'out of one's bailiwick', i.e. outside of one's natural sphere or function.

2. The office or jurisdiction of a bailie or a bailiff. (Now only *Hist.*)

1494 FABYAN VII. 528 The offyce of ballywyke. *a* **1649** DRUMM. OF HAWTH. *Jas. V.* Wks. (1711) 88 A suit..about the ballywick of Jedburgh-forrest. **1687** N. JOHNSTON *Assur. Abbey Lands* 69 Other Ecclesiastical Benefices, Provost-ships, Baly-wicks, Commendams, Canon-ships, etc. **1875** STUBBS *Const. Hist.* II. xvii. 557 No gift of land, franchise..or bailiwick should be made.

†**3.** Stewardship. (Cf. BAILIESHIP.) *Obs.*

1550 CROWLEY *Epigr.* 1257 Christe shall saie at the laste daye, Geve accounts of your baliwickes. **1601** DENT *Pathw. Heaven* (1603) 171 To give an account of our bailywicke.

4. *Comb.* **bailiwick-town,** a town under the jurisdiction of a bailiff; the chief town of a hundred.

1675 OGILBY *Brit.* 172 Hexham..is at present a well-built Bailiwick Town. **1724** DE FOE, etc. *Tour Gt. Brit.* (1769) III. 241 The Bailiwick-town of Hexham.

baille, obs. form of BAIL in various senses.

baillery, obs. form of BAILIERY.

bailliage ('beɪlɪɪdʒ). Forms: 6 **bayly-,** 6–7 **bali-,** 7 **balli-, bayli-, baily-,** 8– **baill-, bail-, bailliage.** [a. F. *bailliage* (= Pr. *bailiatge*, Sp. *bailiage*), f. *bailli*: see BAILIFF and -AGE. Made in med.L. *baill(i)agium, baliaticum*, but answering to a L. type **bājulīvāticum*.]

1. The jurisdiction or district of a bailiff; formerly sometimes applied to an English bailiwick, but now only to that of a French or Swiss *bailli*, or other foreign prefecture.

1513 EARL WORC. in Strype *Eccl. Mem.* I. i. 5 This town ..and all the bayliage should have no resort..but to the Arch-bishop of Canterbury. **1525** LD. BERNERS *Froiss.* II. cci. [cxcvii.] 615 The hole duchy of Acquytayne.. baylyages, sygnories, and wasselages. **1599** HAKLUYT *Voy.* II. 80 The first bailiage or priorie that should be vacant. **1680** *Relig. Dutch* iv. 38 Divonne, in the Balliage of Gex. **1777** HOWARD *Prisons Eng.* (1780) 81 The other prison for the bailliage, contains nineteen chambers. **1791** BURKE *App. Whigs* Wks. VI. 231 The several orders, in their several baillages..were the 'people' of France. **1882** *Athenæum* 30 Dec. 896/2 The twelve peers of the castle had..appeal in some cases from the sovereign bailliage.

¶ See also BAILIAGE.

†**baillie, bailly.** *Obs.* Forms: 3–4 **baillie, bailye, balye,** 4 **baili, -y, balie, bayly(e, beylie,** 4–5 **baly, baillye,** 5 **bailly, bayllye,** 4–8 **baillie.** [ME. *baillie*, a. OF. *baillie* (= Pr. *bailia*, It. *balia*) :—late L. *bājulīa*, f. *bājulus* officer, bailiff (It. *bailo, balio*, Pr. *baile*, OF. *bail*), with Romanic *-'ia* of office. In med.L. *ballia, balia, baylia, bayllia*, from the modern langs. In Eng. the old spellings are mixed up confusedly with those of BAILIE (F. *bailli*) and BAILEY (F. *baille*).]

1. The jurisdiction, authority, charge, or office of a BAILIE or BAILIFF, in the original sense; jurisdiction or charge committed to an officer, delegated authority; stewardship.

c **1305** *Fall & Passion 22* in *E.E.P.* (1862) 13 God ȝaf him a gret maistre..of paradis al þe balye. **1330** R. BRUNNE *Chron.* 280 þise tuo had baly of þis londes tueye. **1388** WYCLIF *Luke* xvi. 2 ȝelde reckynyng of thi baili, for thou miȝte not now be baili. *c* **1400** *Gamelyn* 709 Now is thy brother scherreue, and hath the baillye. **1553-87** FOXE *A. & M.* I. 623/1 Then it shall be said to us..yeld reckoning of thy baily. **1738** *Hist. Crt. Excheq.* i. 3 There were two Sorts of Jurisdictions, the Fieffal and Bailie..This was the ordinary Jurisdiction which from the Bailees in Normandy was here delivered over to the Sheriff in every County which thence was called his Bailywick.

2. *gen.* Jurisdiction, authority, control, charge. *a* **1300** *Cursor M.* 9551 þis ilk king..A seruand had in his baili [*v.r.* bayly, baily]. *c* **1380** *Sir Ferumb.* 4335 He haueþ · on ys baylye x. þousant knyȝtes..To don al at ys wille. *c* **1400** *Rom. Rose* 4302 Whanne Jelousie Hadde Bealacoil in his baillie. *c* **1450** *Merlin* vii. 111 His seal, whiche that Vlfin hath yet in his kepynge in his bailly. *c* **1460** *Towneley Myst.* 207 Thou art here in our baly withoutten any grace of skap. **1475** CAXTON *Jason* 60 b, Whan the quene Ysiphile sawe that she had Jason in her bayllye.

3. The district under the jurisdiction of BAILIFF or BAILIE; a bailiwick.

[**1292** BRITTON I. ii. §9 Aylours qe en sa baillie (Elsewhere than in his bailiwick).] *c* **1314** *Guy Warw.* 249 Wold God.. That he were here in mi beylie. *c* **1325** *E.E. Allit. P.* A. 315 þou schal won in þis bayly. **1330** R. BRUNNE *Chron.* 61 þe duke Siward had taken in his balie Machog.

bailliwage, obs. form of BAILLIAGE.

1685 *Lond. Gaz.* No. 1996/3 Certain Bailliwages belonging to them that border upon the French Territories.

bailment (ˈbeɪlmənt). [a. OF. *baillement*, f. *bailler* to bail, give, deliver.]

1. Delivery, handing over, or giving for a specific purpose; according to Blackstone, delivery in trust, upon a contract expressed or implied, that the trust shall be faithfully executed on the part of the bailee.

1602 FULBECKE *1st Pt. Parall.* Introd. viij, To treat of borrowing and lending, and of the bailement or deliuery of goods and chattels. **1624** *Termes de la Ley* 39 Bailement is a diliuerie of things..to another, sometimes to be deliuered backe to the bailor..sometimes to the vse of the Bailee. **1768** BLACKSTONE *Comm.* II. 452. **1809** R. LANGFORD *Introd. Trade* 129 *Bailment*, goods delivered in trust for the fulfilment of an agreement. **1875** POSTE *Gaius* III. 423 Deposit, loan for use, pawn or pledge, letting and hiring, and mandate, are grouped together in English law under the head of Bailments.

2. The action of bailing a prisoner or person accused. Also the record of the same.

1554 *Act 1 & 2 Mary* xiii. §3 (An Act touching Bailment of Persons)..At the Time of the said Bailment or Mainprise. **1581** LAMBARDE *Eiren.* III. ii. (1588) 338 The booke of the *Norman Customes* calleth *Bailement* a liue prison. **1619** DALTON *Countr. Just.* cxiv, Bailment..is the saving or delivery of a man out of prison, before that he hath satisfied the law. **1628** *King's Letter* in Rushw. (1659) I. 560 Our Judges shall proceed to the Deliverance or Bailment of the Prisoner. **1772** *Junius Lett.* lxviii. 340 The business touching bailment of prisoners. **1826** *Act Geo. IV*, lxiv. §3 [The magistrate is to] subscribe all examinations, informations, bailments, and recognizances. **1876** FOX BOURNE *Locke* I. i. 5.

‖**bailo** (ˈbaɪlo). Rarely **baile**. [It. *bailo* (also *balio* = Pg. *bailio*, Sp. *bayle*, *baile*, Pr., F. *baile*, OF. *bail*):—L. *bājulus*, orig. 'carrier, bearer of burdens,' subseq. 'tutor, governor, administrator, magistrate, bailiff'; in med.L. also *bailus*, *balius*. See BAIL *sb.*[1] and BAILIFF.] The title of the Venetian 'Resident' at the Ottoman Porte.

1682 WHELER *Journ. Greece* I. 1 A Bailo, or Ambassador from the State of Venice, was to part for Constantinople. **1705** *Lond. Gaz.* No. 4139/4 Their Bailo or Resident at the Ottoman Porte. **1832** tr. *Sismondi's Ital. Rep.* xi. 254 A baile, who was to be..its ambassador there, and the judge of all the Venetian subjects in the Levant.

bailor (ˌbeɪˈlɔː(r)). *Law.* [f. BAIL *v.*[1] + -OR; cf. *bailee.*] One who delivers goods, etc. to another for a specific purpose.

1602 FULBECKE *2nd Pt. Parall.* 31 The bailor shall not anie way be charged by vertue of this bond. **1624** [see BAILMENT]. **1830** *Edin. Encycl.* III. 207 In bailment there is a special qualified property transferred from the bailor to the bailee, together with the possession. **1845** *Law Rep., Com. Bench* I. 672 (*marg.*) A bailee of goods for hire, by selling them, determines the bailment, and the bailor may maintain trover against the purchaser.

bailsman (ˈbeɪlzmən). [f. *bail's*, gen. of BAIL *sb.*[1] + MAN.] One who gives bail for another; a bail.

1862 TROLLOPE *Orley F.* xiii. 97 To act as one of the bailsmen for his mother's appearance at the trial. **1875** STUBBS *Const. Hist.* III. xx. 425 For each of them manucaptors or bailsmen were provided.

baily, obs. form of BAILIE, BAILEY, BAILLIE.

Baily's beads: see BEAD *sb.* 7.

†**bain** (beɪn), *a.* (*sb.*) and *adv. Obs.* exc. *dial.* Forms: 4-5 **bayn**, 5 **beyn**, 5-6 **bayne**, 6-9 **bane**, 6-7 **bain**. [a. ON. *beinn* straight, direct; also, ready to serve, hospitable.]

A. *adj.* **1.** Ready, willing, inclined.

c **1325** *E.E. Allit. P.* C. 136 So bayn wer þay boþe two, his bone for to wyrk. *c* **1440** *Morte Arth.* (Roxb.) 104 To batayle be ye bayne. **1513** DOUGLAS *Æneis* III. ii. 58 To seik ȝour ald modir mak ȝou bane. *c* **1550** *Turke & Gowin* 109 in Furniv. *Percy Folio* I. 94, I will be att thy bidding baine. **1674** RAY *N. Countr. Wds.* 4 *Bain*, Willing, Forward.

2. Supple, lithe, limber.

c **1440** *Promp. Parv.* 29 Beyn or plyaunte, *Flexibilis*. **1565** GOLDING *Ovid's Met.* III. (1593) 77 And wantonly they writh..among the waves their bodies baine and lyth. **1674** RAY *S. & E. Countr. Wds.* 59 *Bain*, Lithe, limber-joynted.

3. Direct; near, short. *north. dial.* [Cf. ON. '*beinstr vegr* straightest, shortest way,' Vigfusson.]

1864 ATKINSON *Whitby Gloss.*, *Banest*, nearest, 'That way 's the banest.' **1864** T. CLARKE in *Kendal Merc.* 30 Jan. (*Westm. dial.*), A swind mi ways t' banest geeat ower t' fell.

B. quasi-*sb.* A ready or willing one.

c **1460** *Towneley Myst.* 82 He has bene sene agane, The buxumnes of his bane [*respexit humilitatem ancillæ suæ*].

C. as *adv.* **1.** Readily, willingly.

c **1325** *E.E. Allit. P.* B. 1511 Ful bayn birlen þise oþer. *c* **1450** *Gaw. & Gologras* I. vi, The berne besely and bane blenkit hym about. **1513** DOUGLAS *Æneis* v. Prol. 58 Byand byssely, and bane [*v.r.* bayne], buge, beuir, & bice.

2. Conveniently near, 'handy.' *north. dial.*

? *a* **1700** *Anc. Poems, Ball., etc.* (1846) 215 Bane ta Claapan town-gate lived an oud Yorkshire tike. **1824** *Craven Dial.* I. 11 We're vara bane tot' beck.

†**bain**, *sb. Obs.* Forms: 5-6 **baygne**, 5-7 **bayne**, **baine**, 6-7 **bane**, **bain**. [a. F. *bain* (= Pr. *banh*, It. *bagno*, Sp. *baño*):—L. *balneum* bath.]

1. A quantity of water or other liquid placed in a suitable receptacle, in which one may bathe.

1475 CAXTON *Jason* 105 b, His lady..had made redy a right fayr baygne. **1594** CAREW *Huarte's Exam. Wits* xv. (1596) 284 The baigne must consist of water fresh and warme. **1614** CHAPMAN *Odyss.* x. 567 My men, In Circes house, were all, in several bain, Studiously sweeten'd. *a* **1641** BP. MOUNTAGU *Acts & Mon.* 306 [They] had caused a bane of warmed oyle to be provided for him.

fig. **1563** *Myrr. for Mag.* Induct. lxvii, And bathed him in the bayne Of his sonnes blud before the altare slayne.

b. The vessel in which this water is held.

1491 CAXTON *Vitas Patr.* (W. de W.) II. 273 a/1 He axed of hym yf he had ony bayne wherin he myghte wasshe hym. **1523** LD. BERNERS *Froiss.* I. ccccxiv. 702 The cradell wherein the erle was kept..and a fayre bayne wherein he was wont to be bayned. **1543** RECORDE *Gr. Arts* (1640) 400 He chanced to enter into a Baine full of water to wash him.

c. *abstractly*, An act of bathing, a bath.

1483 CAXTON *Esope* 2 b, Chargyng hym to kepe them tyl he..retourned fro his bayne. **1563** B. GOOGE *Eglogs* (Arb.) 116 Pryncely Nymphes accompanyed Diana in her Baynes.

2. A room or building fitted up for bathing, having hot baths, etc.; a public bath; = BAGNIO 1.

1494 FABYAN v. cxxv. 106 Whan he came out of his stewe or bayne. **1530** PALSGR. 182 *Vnes estevues*, a hote house or a bayne. **1540** HYRDE *Vives' Instr. Chr. Wom.* (1592) U iij, That rude and uncomly manner..that men and their wives shal wash both together in one bane. **1606** HOLLAND *Sueton.* 216 He passed through a crosse lane to the Baines for to bath. **1693** W. ROBERTSON *Phraseol. Gen.* 197 Bain or Bath, *Balneum*.

3. A spring of hot or medicinal water.

1538 LELAND *Itin.* II. 66 The Colour of the Water of the Baynes is as it were a depe Blew Se Water. **1610** HOLLAND *Camden's Brit.* I. 557 Buxton, that of great name shalt be for hote and holsome baine. **1655** DIGGES *Compl. Ambass.* 136 Gone to Arragon, to certain Baynes there, for her health.

4. in *pl.* Stews; = BAGNIO *sb.* 3.

1541 ELYOT *Image Gov.* (1549) 6 In common baines and bordell houses. **1599** BP. HALL *Sat.* VI. i. 27 As pure as olde Labulla from the baynes.

5. *Chem.* An apparatus for heating through the medium of water, sand, etc., more gradually than by direct exposure to fire. Cf. BATH.

1477 NORTON *Ord. Alch.* v. in Ashm. (1652) 62 Baines maie helpe and cause also destruction. **1657** W. COLES *Adam in Eden* xxxvi, It has been bathed well in the bain or stove.

6. *Comb.*, as ***bain keeper***.

1569 J. SANFORD *Agrippa's Van. Artes* 107 b, Likewise Barbars, Bainekepers, and Shepherdes. **1603** HOLLAND *Plutarch's Mor.* 174 (R.) Taking no pleasure nor delight in the world..no more than the bain-keeper's poor asse.

†**bain**, *v. Obs.* Forms: 5 **baygne**, 5-6 **bayn(e**, 7 **baigne**, 6-7 **bain(e**. [a. F. *baigne-r* (= Pr. *banhar*, Sp. *bañar*, It. *bagnare*):—L. *balneāre*, f. *balneum* bath.]

1. *trans.* and *refl.* To bathe or wash; to drench.

1398 TREVISA *Barth De P.R.* VI. x. (1495) 195 The mydwyfe..baynyth hym with salte and hony to comforte his lymmes. **1474** CAXTON *Chesse* II. iv. 32 Whan the knyhtes ben maad they ben bayned or bathed. **1577** HANMER *Anc. Eccl. Hist.* (1619) 50 John the Apostle..to baine himself, entred into a bath. **1602** CAREW *Cornwall* 108 b, To baigne them..with a worse perfume.

b. *fig.* or *rhetorically.*

1491 CAXTON *Vitas Patr.* (W. de W.) I. lxvi. 115 a/2 His body was alle bayned and bydewed in teres and water. **1557** EARL SURREY in Tottell's *Misc.* (Arb.) 5 Salt teares doe bayne my brest. *a* **1652** J. VICARS in Farr's *S.P.* (1848) 124 Haile-stones he rained, And with feirce flames of fire them bained.

2. *intr.* (for *refl.*) To bathe oneself. *lit.* and *fig.*

1483 CAXTON *Gold. Leg.* 164/4 Ne neuer rasour touched his heed ne he neuer baygned. *c* **1500** *Love Song* in Halliw. *Nugæ P.* 68 In gladnesse I swym and baine. **1573** TWYNE *Æneid.* XI. K k j b, The launce..in virgins blood doth bayne.

bain, obs. form of BANE; north. dial. f. BONE.

†**bained, baynyd**, *a. Obs.* [a. OF. *baien*, *bayen*, *bain*, *bayn*; altered to the form of an Eng. pa. pple.] Of peas and beans: Burst, split.

c **1440** *Promp. Parv.* 21/1 Baynyd, as benys or pesyn, *fresus*.

†**baiˈnilla.** *Obs. rare*⁻¹. [Early form of VANILLA; cf. Pg. *bainilha*.]

1691 WORLIDGE *Treat. Cider* 178 Some compound with it ..Orejuela, Bainilla, Sapoyall, Orange-flower-water.

†**ˈbaining**, *vbl. sb.* [f. BAIN *v.* + -ING[1].] Bathing.

1528 PAYNELL *Salerne Regim.* Y ij b, Eschewe..laborious baynynge.

bainite (ˈbeɪnaɪt). [f. Edgar C. *Bain*, U.S. metallurgist (*b.* 1891) + -ITE[1].] A constituent produced at a certain stage in the heat treatment of steel (see quot. 1939[1]).

1935 A. SAUVEUR *Metallogr. & Heat Treatm. Iron & Steel* (ed. 4) xv. 235 This..constituent microscopically resembles somewhat tempered martensite although its properties are distinctly different... The associates of Bain at the Laboratory at which he was formerly located designate it as 'Bainite'. **1939** E. C. BAIN *Alloying Elem. in Steel* ii. 41 These structures known as 'bainite' formed at temperatures roughly between 1000 and 380 degrees Fahr. (500 and 150 degrees Cent.) in carbon steel have interesting mechanical properties, being tougher for the same hardness than tempered martensite. **1939** *Jrnl. Iron & Steel Inst.* CXL. 107 The extreme types differ fairly considerably from each other, for which reason certain writers have separated them into 'upper bainite' and 'lower bainite'. **1954** *Gloss. Terms Iron & Steel* (*B.S.I.*) I. 6 *Bainite*, the constituent produced when austenite transforms at a temperature below that at which pearlite is produced and above that at which martensite is formed. **1956** *Nature* 3 Mar. 420/2 Bainite reactions..and the stabilization of austenite.

†**ˈbainly**, *adv. Obs.* [f. BAIN *a.* + -LY[2].] Readily, willingly; at once.

c **1400** *Destr. Troy* XIX. 8082 Then Breisaid, the bright, bainly onswart. *c* **1460** *Towneley Myst.* 164 And to thare bydyng bayn bowy.

‖**bain-marie** (bɛ̃mari). [F.; ad. L. *balneum Mariæ* (14th c.), lit. 'the bath of Mary,' so called, Littré thinks, from the gentleness of this method of heating.] (See quot.)

1822 KITCHENER *Cook's Oracle* 398 'Bain-Marie' is a flat vessel containing boiling water; you put all your stewpans into the water, and keep that water always very hot, but it must not boil. **1875** URE *Dict. Arts* I. 280 Bain-marie, a vessel of water in which saucepans, etc. are placed to warm food, or to prepare it and some pharmaceutical preparations.

bair, obs. form of BARE, BOAR, BORE.

‖**Bairam** (baɪˈrɑːm, ˈbaɪrəm). Forms: 6 **beyram**, 7 **bairan**, 8 **bajram**, **bayram**, 6- **bairam**. [Turk. *baïrām*, *beïram*, Pers. *bairām*.] The name of two Mohammedan festivals—the ***Lesser Bairam***, lasting three days, which follows the fast of Ramadan, and the ***Greater Bairam***, seventy days later, lasting four days.

1599 HAKLUYT *Voy.* II. I. 196 The Turkes Beyram..one of their chiefest feastes. **1687** *Lond. Gaz.* No. 2291/2 Their Lesser Bairam..falls out about the middle of October. **1813** BYRON *Giaour* viii, To-night the Bairam feast's begun.

bairn (bɛən, in Sc. bern). Forms: *α.* 1-3 **bearn**, 2-3 **bern**, **bærn**, (4 **byern**,) 7 **berne**, **bearn**. *β.* 1-9 **barn** (3 **barrn**, **barin**, 4 **baron**), 4-7 **barne**. *γ.* 5-9 **bairn**. [Common Teutonic: OE. *bearn* = OFris. *bern*, OS., OHG., MHG., Goth., ON., Da., Sw. *barn*, (MDu. *baren*):—OTeut. **barno-(m)*, f. *beran* to bear. Lost in G. and Du.; also in southern Eng., where the modern repr. of OE. *bearn* would have been *bern* (cf. *fern*) or *barn* (cf. *arm*, *warn*). In fact, *berne* survived in the south to 1300, *barn* still survives in northern English, and was used by Shakspere; *bairn* is the Scotch form (cf. *fairn*, *airm*, *wairn*), occasionally used in literary English since 1700. It is doubtful whether the *berne*, *bearn* of some 17th c. Eng. writers was a survival of the early southern form, or a variant spelling of *bairn*. The pl. *bærn* in Ormin is the ON. *börn*, hence it is probable that the northern singular *barn* is as much of ON. as of OE. origin.]

A child; a son or daughter. (Expressing relationship, rather than age.)

α. *Beowulf* 1063 Beowulf maþelode, bearn Ecȝþéowes. *c* **1000** *Ags. Gosp.* Matt. v. 35 Ðæt ȝe sín eowres Fæder bearn. *c* **1160** *Hatton G.* ibid., Eowres Fader bærn. *a* **1200** *Trin. Coll. Hom.* 131 Alle þe bernes . þe ben boren of wifes bosem. *c* **1230** *Ancr. R.* 272 Recabes sunen..helle bearnes. *c* **1300** Wright *Lyric P.* xviii. 58 Suete Ihesu, berne best. **1621** B. JONSON *Gipsies Metam.*, Have care of your bearns. **1621** BURTON *Anat. Mel.* III. ii. v. v, Many fair lovely bernes to you betide. *a* **1688** DK. BUCKHM. *Pump Parl.* Wks. 1705 II. 99 Our Bearns and Wives.

β. **830** in Thorpe *Diplom.* 465 His barna sue huelc sue lifes sie. *c* **1200** ORMIN 8039 Herode king let slæn þa little barrness. *Ibid.* 6808 þatt wærenn Noþess þrinne bærn. *a* **1275** *Prov. Alfred* 589 in *O.E. Misc.* 135 þu ard mi barin dere. **1330** R. BRUNNE *Chron.* 310 To se hir and hir barn. *c* **1340** *Cursor M.* 904 (Fairf.) In sorow þou sal þi barnys bere [*v.r.* berns, childer, children]. *a* **1400** *Cov. Myst.* (1841) 182 Alas, ywhy was my baron born. *c* **1420** *Anturs of Arth.* xviii.

6 That blisfulle barne in Bedelem was born. **1577** HARRISON *England* II. v. 108 To this daie, even the common sort doo call their male children *barnes* here in England, especiallie in the north countrie. **1611** SHAKS. *Wint. T.* III. ii. 70 Mercy on's, a Barne? A very pretty barne; A boy, or a Childe I wonder? **1687** DE LA PRYME *Diary* (1869) 11 No one scarce believes that she [the queen] is realy with barn. **1711** J. GREENWOOD *Eng. Gram.* 276 Bearn, Barn, a Son, or Off-spring (a Word common with the Scotch, and our North-Countreymen). **1864** TENNYSON *North. Farmer* 6 Bessy Marris's barne! tha knaws she laäid it to meä.

γ. **1513–75** *Diurn. Occurr.* (1833) 67 Efter them wes ane cart with certane bairnes. **1549** *Compl. Scot.* xv. 123 It is fors to me & vyf and bayrns to drynk vattir. *a* **1605** MONTGOMERIE *Poems* (1821) 18 Burnt bairn with fyre the danger dreidis. *a* **1626** BEAUM. & FL. *Love's Cure* III. i, Has he not well provided for the bairn? **1703** PENN in *Pa. Hist. Mem.* IX. 241, I wish.. I had it for one of my poor bairns. **1714** SWIFT *Corr.* Wks. 1841 II. 527, I wish I could return your compliments as to my wife and bairns. **1857** H. REED *Lect. Brit. Poets* x. II. 25 That deep dark-eyed Scottish bairn was Robert Burns. **1867** FREEMAN *Norm. Conq.* (1876) I. vi. 483 Harthacnut too.. was at least a kingly bairn.

Comb. (all *north. dial.*) **bairn-dole**, child's portion; **bairn-like** *a.*, child-like, *adv.* in child-like manner; †**bairn-part**, child's portion; **bairn(s)-bed**, womb; †**barn-site**, anxiety about children; **bairn's-play**, child's play; **bairn's-maid, -woman**, nurse-maid, nurse.

1858 TRENCH *Parables* xxiv. (1877) 393 The portion of goods that falleth to me; his '*bairndole,' as they would call it in Yorkshire. *c* **1425** WYNTOUN *Cron.* IX. xx. 111 That suld noucht han been done *barnelike. **1533** *Wills & Inv. N.C.* (1860) 112 That my sonne and.. my dowghter have their *barne partes of my goodes. **1549** *Compl. Scot.* 67 Ane vomans *bayrnis bed [*printed* hed]. **1863** *Provinc. Danby* s.v., She's got a swelling on the *bairn bed. *a* **1300** *Cursor M.* 11625 Ne haf yee for me na barn-site. **1863** *Reader* 8 Apr. 386 Who was *bairn's-maid to a daughter of the great philosopher. **1637** RUTHERFORD *Lett.* 88 (1862) I. 226 To make it a matter of *bairn's play. **1823** GALT *Entail* I. i. 2 Who, in her youth, was *bairnswoman to his son.

Hence (*north. dial.*) **'bairnie**, little child; **'bairnish** *a.*, childish; **'bairnishness**.

†**'bairnheid.** *Obs.* or *north. dial.* [f. BAIRN + HEAD, -HOOD.]

1. Childhood, infancy.

a **1300** *Cursor M.* 166 Mani a dede þat iesu did in his barnhede. **1393** LANGL. *P. Pl.* C. XIX. 136 Bold in hus barnhede. *c* **1425** WYNTOUN *Cron.* v. i. 119 Hys Barnehede Was passyd, and enteryde in Manhede. **1588** A. KING *Canisius' Catech.* 38 Euer from my bairnheid.

†**2.** Childishness. *Obs.*

c **1505** DUNBAR *To King* x, Sic barneheid biddis my brydill renye.

bairnhood. [BAIRN; cf. BAIRNHEID.] Childhood. *Sc.* or *affected.*

a **1835** JOSEPH GRANT in *Whistle-Binkie* (1890) II. 161 The broomy hill, Where we used to stray in bairnhood's day. **1894** R. FORD (*title*) Ballads of Bairnhood.

'bairnless, *a. Sc.* and *north. dial.* Childless.

a **1300** *Cursor M.* 7086 Barnles was his moder lang.

'bairnliness. *Sc.* and *north. dial.* [f. next + -NESS.] Childishness.

1838 *Blackw. Mag.* XLIII. 270 Driven to the bairnliness of supping peas with a spoon. **1863** GROSART *Small Sins* Pref. 9 Laborious ingenuity or childishness (*note*, perhaps our vernacular 'bairnliness' better expresses the thing).

'bairnly, *a. Sc.* & *north. dial.* [f. BAIRN + -LY[1].]

1. Childish.

1533 BELLENDENE *Livy* I. (1822) 100 Thair insolent and barnelie contencioun. **1663** BLAIR *Autobiog.* i. 1, I used my bairnly endeavour. **1837** R. NICOLL *Poems* (1843) 80, I hae left them now for ever, But, to greet would bairnly be.

2. Child-like, in childhood.

1603 *Philotus* xc, The las bot bairnlie is and ȝoung. *Ibid.*, A bairnelie lasse lyke me, Mair meit his oy nor wyfe to be.

†**'bairnly,** *adv. Obs.* [f. as prec. + -LY[2].]

1483 *Cath. Angl.* 22/2 Barnely, *infantuose, pueriliter.*

'bairn-team. *north. dial.* Forms: 1 bearn- 3 bern-, barn-team, -tem, beren-tem, 4 barn-, barne-teem, 4–5 barn(e-tem(e, 4–6 -tyme, 5 -teame, 7 bairn-teme, 8 -time, 9 -teem; see also BARM-TEAM. [f. BAIRN + TEAM.] Brood of children, offspring, family; posterity.

c **885** K. ÆLFRED *Oros.* I. xiv. 1 Fultumlease æt hiora bearn-teamum. *c* **1220** *Hali Meid.* 31 In breades wone brede ti barnteam. *c* **1250** *Gen. & Ex.* 3747 Chore was is bernteam. *c* **1300** *Cursor M.* 4828 We ar all a man barnteme [*Fairf. MS.* an monnes barneteme]. *a* **1400** *Relig. Pieces fr. Thornt. MS.* 57 þe firste of þis foule barnetyme. *c* **1460** *Towneley Myst.* 212 Wepe nothyng for me Bot forȝoure self and ȝoure barneteme. **1513** DOUGLAS *Æneis* XII. xiii. 134 Bair at a birth.. that barntyme miserabill. **1637** RUTHERFORD *Lett.* 105 (1862) I. 266 The fair flock and blessed bairn-teme of the first-born. **1786** BURNS *A Dream* xi, Thae bonnie bairntime, Heav'n has lent. **1855** *Whitby Gloss.*, *Bairn-teems*, troops of children.

‖**baisemain.** *Obs.* [Fr., f. *baise-r* to kiss + *main* hand.] A kiss of the hands: in *pl.* compliments, respects.

[**1596** SPENSER *F.Q.* III. i. 56 Every Knight.. Gan choose his dame with *basciomani* gay.] **1656** in BLOUNT *Glossogr.* **1707** FARQUHAR *Beaux' Strat.* III. ii. 25 Do my Baisemains to the gentleman, and tell him I will.. wait on him immediately. **1748** SMOLLETT *Rod. Rand.* xlvi. (1804) 318 Do the doctor's baise-mains to the lady, and squire her hither.

†**'baisement.** *Obs. rare*[−1]. [corrupt f. prec.; but cf. F. *baisement* (Cotgr.), f. *baiser.*] = prec.

c **1654** FLECKNOE *Trav.* 18 My most humble Baisements, I beseech you, to the Lady Marquesse.

†**'baisier.** *Obs.* [a. OF. *baisier* (mod. *baiser*) to kiss, inf. used subst.] A kiss, a kissing.

c **1450** *Merlin* xx. 323 Hit is the baisyers, yef to the lady it plese. **1475** CAXTON *Jason* 99 b, And their began there amorouse baisiers or kyssinges.

baisk, variant of BASK *a. Obs.* bitter.

baisse, variant of BASE *v.* and BASH *v.*

baister, baisting: var. ff. BASTER[1], BASTING *vbl. sb.*[1]

1881 *Instr. Census Clerks* (1885) 74 Braider,.. Stitcher, Baister, Button-hole Maker. **1890** *Daily News* 2 Jan. 5/3 Baisting cotton. **1902** *Daily Chron.* 5 Mar. 10/5 Coat Machinists.. wanted, baisters and finishers. **1906** *Ibid.* 28 May 11/7 Tailoresses wanted; must be good coat baisters.

bait (beɪt), *v.*[1] Forms: 3 beȝȝt-en, beyte-n, 4–6 bayt, baite, 4–7 bayte, 5–6 beyt, 6 baight, 6–7 bate, 4– bait. [ME. *beȝȝten, beyten*, a. ON. *beita* to cause to bite (= OE. *bǽtan*, OHG., MHG. *beizen*, Goth **baitjan*), causal of *bíta* to BITE; but in branch III prob. directly from BAIT *sb.*[1]: cf. OE. *bátian*, f. *bát* bait. With branch I cf. OF. *beter*, also from ON.]

I. To cause to bite other creatures.

†**1.** *trans.* To set on (a dog) to bite or worry. (Cf. the similar construction in BATE *v.*[1]).

c **1350** *Will. Palerne* 11 þe herd had wiþ him an hound.. For to bayte on his bestes wanne þai to brode went.

†**b.** *fig.* To set on, incite, exasperate. Cf. ABAIT.

c **1378** WYCLIF *De Off. Past.* Wks. (1880) 437 Prelatis.. baytiþ a pariȝshen aȝenus þe persoun.

2. To set on dogs to bite and worry (an animal, such as the bear, boar, bull, badger, etc., usually chained or confined for this purpose), to attack *with* dogs for sport; formerly, also, to hunt or chase with dogs.

a **1300** *Havelok* 1840 And shoten on him, so don on bere Dogges.. Thanne men doth the bere beyte. *c* **1325** *E.E. Allit. P.* B. 55 My boles & my borez arn bayted & slayne. *c* **1440** *Promp. Parv.* 29 Beyton wyth howndys, berys, bolys, or other lyke, *canibus agitare*. **1593** SHAKS. *2 Hen. VI*, v. i. 148 Are these thy Beares? Wee'l bate thy Bears to death. **1606** HOLLAND *Sueton.* 120 There was a wild bore put foorth into the open shew-place for to be baited. **1801** STRUTT *Sports & Past.* III. vi. 217 The cruel diversion of baiting a horse with dogs.

b. *fig.* To cause (a person) to be molested, harassed, or persecuted (*with*).

1642 FULLER *Holy & Prof. St.* I. iii. 9 Such husbands as bait the mistris with her maids. **1655** *Trial Col. Penruddock* in Howell *St. Trials* (1816) V. 775 Sir, you have put me in a bear's skin, and now you will bait me with a witness.

c. (in sense of 4, but retaining some idea of intermediate agency, as in prec.)

1555 *Fardle Facions* II. xi. 250 Thei reuile him, and baite him with shames and reproche. **1659** GODFREY in Burton's *Diary* (1828) IV. 347 It was a breach of privilege to bait you with those interrogations. **1778** JOHNSON in *Boswell* (1831) IV. 124, I will not be baited with *what* and *why*.

3. To attack with endeavour to bite and tear, as dogs attack a chained or confined animal (cf. 2).

1553–87 FOXE *A. & M.* (1596) 43/2 Attalus.. was baited of the beasts. **1596** SPENSER *F.Q.* I. xii. 35 As chained beare whom cruell dogs doe bait. *Mod.* They set on several dogs to bait the badger.

b. *absol.*

c **1430** *Hymns to Virg.* (1867) 77 Helle houndis berken and baite. **1547** BOORDE *Introd. Knowl.* 187 Kur dogges, For men shyns they wyl ly in wayte; It is a good sport to se them so to bayte. **1735** SOMERVILLE *Chase* IV. 332 Raving he foams, and howls, and barks, and bates.

4. *fig.* To persecute or harass with persistent attacks (a person more or less unable to escape); to worry or torment in an exasperating manner, esp. from a wanton or malicious desire to inflict pain.

c **1200** ORMIN 10171 Þise Puplicaness.. durrsten beȝȝtenn menn Forr æþelike gillte. *c* **1400** *Rom. Rose* 1612 Folk of grettist wit Ben soone caught heere & awayted; Withouten respite ben they baited. **1635** R. BOLTON *Comf. Affl. Consc.* 173 God must let loose his Lawe, Sinne, Conscience, and Satan to bate us. **1751** JOHNSON *Rambl.* No. 176 ¶4 The diversion of baiting an author has the sanction of all ages. **1834** MACAULAY *Pitt, Ess.* (1854) I. 301 The new Secretary of State had been so unmercifully baited by the Paymaster of the Forces.

†**b.** *intr.* with *at* (in same sense). *Obs.*

1579 TOMSON *Calvin's Serm. Tim.* 956/2 Why are they so alwayes bayting at me? **1607** DEKKER *Knt's. Conjur.* (1842) 38 Bayted at by whole kennels of yelping watermen. **1679** *Hist. Jetzer* 9 The Fathers all this while were baiting at him.

II. To cause a creature to bite for its own refreshment; to feed.

5. *trans.* To give food and drink to (a horse or other beast), *esp.* when upon a journey; to feed.

1375 BARBOUR *Bruce* XIII. 589 Than lichtit thai.. Till bayt thar horss. *c* **1400** MAUNDEV. xxii. 243 While that [he] reste him, And bayte his Dromedarie or his hors. **1596** SPENSER *F.Q.* I. i. 32 The sunne.. At night doth baite his steedes the ocean waves emong. **1697** *C'tess D'Aunoy's Trav.* (1706) 47 And stop at the Bank of some River, where the Mule-Drivers bate their Mules. **1799** J. ROBERTSON *Agric. Perth* 200 You have this second crop of clover.. to bait your cows. **1858** THACKERAY *Virginians* x. 79 Whilst their horses were baited, they entered the public room.

6. (*refl.* and) *intr.* Said of horses or other beasts: To take food, to feed, *esp.* at a stage of a journey.

c **1386** CHAUCER *Sir Thopas* 202 By him baytith his destrer Of herbes fyne and goode. **1394** *P. Pl. Crede* 375 Þey ben digne as dich water þat dogges in bayteþ. *c* **1435** *Torr. Portugal* 1566 Unbrydelid his stede And let hym bayte hym on the ground. **1523** FITZHERB. *Husb.* §22 In lodynge of hey or corne, the cattel is alwaye eatynge or beytynge. **1832** B'NESS BUNSEN in Hare *Life* I. ix. 384 An osteria.. at which our horses were to bait.

7. *intr.* Of travellers: To stop at an inn, orig. to feed the horses, but later also to rest and refresh themselves; *hence*, to make a brief stay or sojourn.

1375 BARBOUR *Bruce* XIII. 599 A litill quhile thai baitit thar. **1475** CAXTON *Jason* 37 b, They cam for to bayte in the logging wher her frende Jason had logged. **1577** HOLINSHED *Chron.* II. 16/2 The caue or den wherein saint Paule is said to haue baited or sojorned. **1659–60** PEPYS *Diary* 24 Feb., At Puckeridge we baited, where we had a loin of mutton fried. **1777** SHERIDAN *Trip Scarb.* I. ii, To bait here a few days longer, to recover the fatigue of his journey. **1874** MOTLEY *Barneveld* I. iv. 179 They set forth on their journey—stopping in the middle of the day to bait.

b. *fig.*

1639 FULLER *Holy War* III. xxix. (1840) 170 A prince.. only baiteth at learning, and maketh not his profession to lodge in. **1671** MILTON *Samson* 1538 For evil news rides post, while good news baits. **1823** LAMB *Elia* Ser. I. xxi. (1865) 165 Trace it [the sentiment] baiting at this town, stopping to refresh at t'other village.

†**8.** *intr.* (and *refl.*) To feed, take nourishment.

c **1386** CHAUCER *Man of L's T.* 368 On many a sory meel now may she bayte. *a* **1400** *Sir Perc.* 187 A tryppe of gayte [= goats], With mylke of thame for to bayte To hir lyves fode. **1633** P. FLETCHER *Purple Isl.* VIII. xlv, So fisher waits To bait himself with fish, his hook And fish with baits.

†**b.** *fig.* of the eyes: To feast.

c **1374** CHAUCER *Troylus* I. 193 If knyght or squyer.. lete his eyen bayte On eny woman. **1632** G. FLETCHER *Christs Vict.* II. v, If he stood still, their eyes upon him baited.

III. To provide with a bait, offer a bait to. [Prob. a later independent formation on the sb.]

9. *trans.* To furnish (a hook, trap) with a bait.

a **1300** *Cursor M.* 13285 Quiles þai þair lines war baitand. **1398** TREVISA *Barth. De P.R.* XVIII. cxv. (1495) 856 Fysshe hokys ben bayted wyth suche wormes in stede of bayte. **1556** J. HEYWOOD *Spider & F.* lxix. 43 This trap.. for spiders is baighted. **1663** BUTLER *Hud.* I. I. 384 Cheese or Bacon.. To bait a Mouse-trap. **1725** POPE *Odyss.* IV. 499 My absent mates.. Bait the barb'd steel.

fig. **1548** UDALL, etc. *Erasm. Par. Matt.* iv. 8 (R.) His hooke bayted with yͤ enticement of vayne glory. **1726** DE FOE *Hist. Devil* II. vi. (1840) 251 He baited his hook with the city of Milan. **1820** SCOTT *Monast.* xxii, Baited thy tongue with falsehood.

b. *absol.* (*lit.* and *fig.*)

1753 CHAMBERS *Cycl. Supp.* s.v., For cod they bait with herring. **1863** MRS. CLARKE *Shaks. Char.* ix. 218 She therefore baited for, and caught her prey.

10. To lay (a place) with bait, so as to attract the prey.

1623 *Althorp MS.* in Simpkinson *Washingtons* Introd. 44 The ratcatcher for a coter's wages for bating the house. **1665** BOYLE *Occas. Refl.* IV. xiv, He had liberally Baited the place over-night with Corn, as well as Worms. **1867** F. FRANCIS *Angling* i. (1880) 33 When once the place has been baited.

11. To offer bait to; to allure, entice, tempt.

1590 SHAKS. *Com. Err.* II. i. 94 Doe their gay vestments his affections baite? **1596** —— *Merch. V.* III. i. 55 His flesh, what's that good for? *Shy.* To baite fish withall. **1865** DIXON *Holy Land* I. 173 Just as the harvests of Kent and Mercia used to bait the Saxon vikings.

bait, *v.*[2] *Falconry.* See better spelling, BATE *v.*[1]

bait (beɪt), *sb.*[1] Forms: 4–6 **bayte**, 5 **beyt**, 5–6 **bayt**, 6 **beyte**, 6–7 **baight**, 6–8 **baite**, 5– **bait**. [Partly a. ON. *beit* (neut.) pasture, *beita* (fem.) food, esp. as used to entice a prey, cogn. w. OE. *bát* f. food, MHG. *beiz* n., *beize* f. hunting; in part directly f. BAIT *v.*[1]]

I. Food used to entice a prey.

1. a. An attractive morsel of food placed on a hook or in a trap, in order to allure fish or other animals to seize it and be thereby captured.

a **1300** *Cursor M.* 16931 þe bait apon þe hok. *a* **1325** *Metr. Hom.* 12 Als fisce es tan wit bait and hoc. **1444** *Pol. Poems* (1859) II. 219 Bosard with botirflyes makith beytis for a crane. *a* **1639** BRETON in Farr's *S.P.* (1845) I. 182 Wherein as hook within the Baight.. Some hidden poyson lurking lyes. **1653** WALTON *Angler* 53 Let your bait fall gently upon the water. **1836** HOR. SMITH *Tin Trump.* (1876) 49 Bait—one animal impaled upon a hook, in order to torture a second for the amusement of a third.

b. Worms, fish, etc., to be used for this purpose.

1496 *Bk. St. Albans* Fishing 7 How ye shall make your baytes brede where ye shall fynde them: and how ye shall kepe theym. **1653** WALTON *Angler* To Rdr. 7 With advise how to make the Fly, and keep the live baits. **1799** G. SMITH *Laboratory* II. 267 Some trouble.. to keep the bait alive.

2. *fig.* An enticement, allurement, temptation.

c **1400** *MS. Cantab.* Ff. II. 38. [46/2] 54/2 Thys worlde ys but the fendys beyte. **1460** *Pol. Rel. & L. Poems* (1866) 155 My body I made hyr hertys baite. **1573** TUSSER *Husb.* (1878) 179 A doore without locke, is a baite for a knaue. **1745** DE FOE *Eng. Tradesm.* I. vi. 36 The profits of trade are baits to the avaricious shopkeeper. **1849** MACAULAY *Hist. Eng.* I. 246 He considered titles and great offices as baits which could allure none but fools.

3. *Comb.* and *attrib.*, as **bait-can, -fish, -fisher, -fishing, -gatherer, -kettle, -tackle.**
1799 G. SMITH *Laboratory* II. 267 By frequently dipping your bait-kettle in the water. **1820** *Western Rev.* (Kentucky) II. 241 *Rutilus compressus*, a small fish..called Fall-fish, Bait-fish, Minny, etc. **1832** *Chambers's Edin. Jrnl.* 14 Apr. 44/1 The same observations apply..to bait fishing. **1835** *Ibid.* 3 Jan. 390/3 Some bait-fishers..use the smaller sorts [of hooks];..The bait-tackle ought to be loaded..with a pellet or two of lead. **1842** JOHNSTON in *Proc. Berw. Nat. Club* II. x. 36 The bait-gatherer, for picking them from the rocks..has 8*d.* per day. **1952** E. HEMINGWAY *Old Man & Sea* 35 No flying fish broke the surface and there was no scattering of bait fish.

II. Food generally.

†4. Food, refreshment; *esp.* a feed for horses, or slight repast for travellers, upon a journey. Still *dial.* light refreshment taken between meals.
1570 LEVINS *Manip.* /203 Bayt, *refrigerium, refectio.* **1573** TUSSER *Husb.* (1878) 203 O thou fit bait for wormes! **1661** LOVELL *Hist. Anim. Min.* Introd., When they [serpents] devoure any great baite, they contract themselves. **1706** E. WARD *Hud. Rediv.* I. XII. 24 Could (if she 'ad had her Will) have eat The Saddle Stuffing for a Bait. **1741** RICHARDSON *Pamela* (1824) I. xxxii. 56 Stopping for a little bait to the horses. **1851** *Coal-tr. Terms Northumbld. & Durh.*, Bait, provision taken by a pitman to his work. **1883** *Harper's Mag.* Apr. 655/1 Afternoon 'bait,' or lunch [in Sussex].

5. A halt for refreshment in the course of a journey; a stoppage for rest. *Welsh* or *Scotch bait*: allowing a horse to stand still a few minutes at the top of a hill (see Fuller *Worthies* IV. 7).
1579 LYLY *Euphues* (Arb.) 250 This merry winde will immediately bring vs to an easie bayte. **1594** NASHE *Unfort. Trav.* 12 To haue gone to heauen without a bait. **1633** P. FLETCHER *Elisa* I. xli, Heav'nly fires..Whose motion is their bait, whose rest is restlesse giring. **1809** PINKNEY *Trav. France* 80 They make a stage of thirty miles without a bait.

†6. *fig.* **a.** Refreshment; a lawyer's 'refresher.' **b.** A hasty meal like a traveller's, a snack. *Obs.*
a. **1579** LYLY *Euphues* (Arb.) 198 A pleasaunt companion is a bait in a journy. **1603** FLORIO *Montaigne* II. xii. (1632) 319 Have you paid him [the Lawyer] well, have you given him a good baite or fee?
b. **1662** FULLER *Worthies* (1840) II. 507 He rather took a bait than made a meal at the inns of court, whilst he studied the laws therein. **1666** EVELYN *Diary* (1827) IV. 175, I now and then get a baite at philosophy.

7. *Comb.* and *attrib.*, as **bait-land** (see quot.); **bait-poke**, a bag for holding a miner's 'bait.'
1725 DE FOE *Voy. round World* (1840) 122 A bait-land, or port of refreshment. **1863** Robson's *Bards of Tyne* 271 And queer things behint them like pitmen's bait pokes.

III. The act of setting dogs to worry other animals; baiting; also (*obs.*) chasing with dogs.
[*c* **1340** *Gaw. & Gr. Knt.* 1461 þen, brayn-wod for bate, on burnez he [the boar] rasez.] *c* **1450** HENRYSON *Mor. Fab.* 67 At the next bayte in faith yee shall bee slaine. **1570** LEVINS *Manip.* /203 Bayt of a beare, *ursi prelium.* Bayt of a bul, *tauri venatio.*

bait, *sb.*², **bate** (beɪt), *sb.*⁶ *slang.* [f. BAIT *v.*¹] A fit of bad temper; a rage. Hence **'baity** *a.*
1857 [A. L. MAYHEW in *Eng. Dial. Dict.* s.v. *Bate* sb.³ 'He was in an awful bait' was common in the Clapham Grammar School, 1857]. **1882** 'F. ANSTEY' *Vice Versâ* (ed. 4) iii. 48 It would put him in no end of a bait. **1899** E. PHILLPOTTS *Human Boy* 95 I've just left Milly, and she's in a frightful bate. **1899** KIPLING *Stalky & Co.* 152 'What a bait you're in!' said Stalky. *Ibid.* 205, I got in no end of a bait. **1921** S. THOMPSON *Rough Crossing* ii. 86 Jolly lucky the C.O. didn't notice it yesterday—he gets 'baity' on these occasions. **1925** *Chambers's Jrnl.* 838/1 Now I must be going, or else dad'll be baity with me. **1953** E. TAYLOR *Sleeping Beauty* vii. 134 Flying into a bate, as we used to say at school.

bait, variant of BATE, BEAT; obs. form of BOAT.

baitable ('beɪtəb(ə)l), *a.* [f. BAIT *v.*¹ + -ABLE.] Serviceable as cattle fodder.
1890 *Jrnl. R. Agric. Soc.* 756 At Meldon not only was there clover, but also a considerable quantity of baitable grasses. *Ibid.* 759 Grasses which are rejected when the stock has a sufficient supply of baitable food to permit of a choice.

baited ('beɪtɪd), *ppl. a.* [f. BAIT *v.*¹ + -ED.]
1. Worried by dogs; *fig.* harassed, tormented.
1720 SWIFT *Run on Bank.* Wks. 1755 IV. I. 24 A baited banker thus desponds. *Mod.* Furious as a baited bull.
2. Furnished with a bait; *fig.* rendered alluring or enticing, attractive.
c **1600** *Rob. Hood* (Ritson) xvi. 44 Others cast in their bated hooks. *a* **1650** CRASHAW *Delights Muses* (1858) 122 With baited smiles if he display His fawning cheeks. **1762–9** FALCONER *Shipwr.* II. 72 The crew..spread the baited snare. **1840** R. DANA *Bef. Mast* v. 12 We caught one or two with a baited hook.

baiter ('beɪtə(r)). [f. BAIT *v.*¹ + -ER¹.] One who baits or worries; *fig.* a tormenter, a 'tease.'
1611 COTGR., *Vanneur*..also a chider, schooler, bayter. *a* **1845** HOOD *Storm at Hastings* xxv, Jagged billows rearing up..Like ragged roaring bears against the baiter.

baith, northern form of BOTH.

†**baithe**, *v. Obs. rare.* [Cf. ON. *beiða* to ask, beg.] To grant; to agree, consent.
c **1300** in Wright *Lyric P.* 27 þat bayeþ me mi bone. *c* **1340** *Gaw. & Gr. Knt.* 327, I schal baiþen þy bone þat þou boden habbes. *Ibid.* 1404 þay bayþen in þe morn To fylle þe same forwardez þat þay byfore maden. *Ibid.* **1840** Lettez be your bisinesse, for I bayþe hit yow neuer to graunte.

baiting ('beɪtɪŋ), *vbl. sb.* [f. BAIT *v.*¹ + -ING¹.]
1. The action of setting on dogs to worry a chained or confined animal; formerly, also, the hunting or chasing of wild animals with dogs. Often in *comb.*: see BADGER, BEAR, BULL.
c **1300** *K. Alis.* 199 Of liouns chase, of beore baityng. *c* **1440** *Promp. Parv.* 29 Beytynge of bestys wyth howndys. *Exagitacio.* **1589** PUTTENHAM *Eng. Poesie* I. xvii, In those great Amphitheaters, were exhibited..their baitings of wild beasts. **1768** BOSWELL *Corsica* (ed. 2) 318, I have seen a Corsican in the very heat of a baiting..drive off the dogs.
b. *fig.* The action of worrying and harassing; persistent annoyance, persecution, torment.
1303 R. BRUNNE *Handl. Synne* 10895 He shal hem chastyse wyþ smert speche, Wyþ small baytinges ande nat wyþ wreche. *a* **1643** H. BURTON (*title*) The Baiting of the Pope's Bvll. *a* **1859** MACAULAY *Hist. Eng.* V. 243 Mortified and intimidated by the baiting of the last session.
c. *attrib.*, as in **baiting-house, -place, -stake.**
1593 SHAKS. *2 Hen. VI*, v. i. 150 Wee'l bate thy Bears to death..If thou dar'st bring them to the bayting place. **1689** *Pol. Ballads* (1860) II. 3 (*title*), Rome in an Uproar; or, the Pope's Bulls brought to the baiting-stake.
2. The action of giving food to horses, or of taking wayside refreshment, upon a journey.
c **1440** *Promp. Parv.* 29 Beytynge of horse, *Pabulacio.* **1513** MORE *Rich. III* (1641) 355 Never resting nor themselves refreshing, except the bayting of their horses. **1655** W. MEWE in Hartlib *Ref. Commw. Bees* 47 Travellers, that have benighted themselves by their frolick baitings. **1884** *Harper's Mag.* Oct. 728/2 Hay..for the baiting of the horses.
b. The place at which, or occasion when, a halt is made for refreshment on a journey.
1475 CAXTON *Jason* 37 b, Quene Myrro..taried than not longe at that bayting. **1753** RICHARDSON *Grandison* (1781) I. iv. 14 Mr. Fenwick attended us to our first baiting.
c. *attrib.*, as in **baiting-place, -season, -town.**
1514 BARCLAY *Cyt. & Uplondyshm.* Introd. (1847) 15 The Court is the bayting place of hell. **1610** HOLLAND *Camden's Brit.* I. 509 The next stations and baiting townes. *a* **1639** WHATELEY *Prototypes* I. iv. (1640) 47 This [world] is a baiting-place and not a place of habitation. **1872** JENKINSON *Guide Eng. Lakes* (1879) 55 The Wool-Pack Inn, a snug little baiting place.
3. The action of furnishing (a hook, trap, etc.), or of strewing a fishing-ground, with bait.
1653 WALTON *Angler* 153 This direction for the baiting your ledger hook. **1867** F. FRANCIS *Angling* ii. (1880) 71 To repeat the baitings..two or three times.
b. *attrib.*, as in **baiting-needle, -place.**
1708 *Proclam.* in *Lond. Gaz.* No. 4452/2 So as to Annoy the Haling of Sayns in the usual Baiting Places. **1875** 'STONEHENGE' *Brit. Sports* I. v. iii. §10 The gimp is passed under a good broad strip of skin with the baiting-needle.

†**'baiting**, *ppl. a. Obs. rare.* [f. BAIT *v.* + -ING².] That baits: worrying; enticing, attractive.
1585 Q. ELIZ. in *Four C. Eng. Lett.* 29 Some ennemis..shal loose muche travel, with making frustrat thar baiting stratagems. **1663** SIR G. MACKENZIE *Relig. Stoic.* xv. (1658) 137 Far more baiting, seeing it appeared with all the charms.

baitless ('beɪtlɪs), *a. rare.* [f. BAIT *sb.* + -LESS.]
1. Without food, without refreshment.
1600 ROWLANDS *Let. Humours Blood* i. 47 to trauaile so long baitlesse, sure 'tis much.
2. Not furnished with bait (for fish); unbaited.
1854 *Tait's Mag.* XXI. 275/1 Holding in his hand the listless line, whose baitless hook, three fathoms down, has become a jest and a laughing-stock to..the finny tribe.

baitylos: see BÆTYL.

‖**bai-u** ('baɪjuː). [Jap., f. *bai* plum + *u* rain.] (A season of) rainfall in Japan in early or midsummer (see quots.).
1910 *Bull. Central Meteor. Observ. Japan* I. v. 1 (*title*) On the Bai-u or Rainy Season in Japan. **1922** W. G. KENDREW *Climates of Cont.* III. xxii. 142 [In Japan] this rainy season is commonly called the 'Bai-u', meaning the plum-rains, as it comes when plums are getting ripe. **1945** G. T. TREWARTHA *Japan* (1947) I. ii. 42 Much cloudiness, abundant rain, high humidity, and high sensible temperatures make the so-called *bai-u* or plum rains a very..gloomy season.

baize (beɪz), *sb.* Forms: 6–8 **bayes**, 7 **baies, bease, bayz(e**, 7–9 **bays**, 7– **baize**. [a. F. *baies* (1570 in Godefroy,'les baies et sarges'), pl. fem. used subst. of adj. *bai*:—L. *badius* chestnut-coloured, BAY; so named probably from its original colour. The same material is called in It. *bajetta* (Florio 1598), Sp. *bayeta*, Du. *baai*, Da. *bai*, Sw. *boi*. The plural form of the adopted word was soon misunderstood, and treated as a collective sing. (occas. with pl. *bayses*), whence the spelling *bayze, baize*, rare bef. 1800, but now quite established; the etymological sing. BAY is, however, also found.]
1. **a.** A coarse woollen stuff, having a long nap, now used chiefly for linings, coverings, curtains, etc., in warmer countries for articles of clothing, e.g. shirts, petticoats, ponchos; it was formerly, when made of finer and lighter texture, used as a clothing material in Britain also.
1578 (in BECK *Drapers' Dict.* 17) Blewe and blacke bayse. **1586** HARRISON *England* I. II. v. 132 The wares they carrie out of the realme are..baies, bustian, mockadoes, etc. **1635** N. R. *Camden's Hist. Eliz.* I. 101 Those light stuffes which they call Bayes and Sayes. **1667** PEPYS *Diary* (1879) IV. 250 A cloak of Colchester bayze. **1712** ARBUTHNOT *John Bull* (1755) 9 The price of broad cloath, wool and bayses. **1732** *Acc. Workhouses* 51, 70 yards of red bays..for under petticoats. **1801** FELTON *Carriages* I. 220 The Well of a Carriage is lined with linen or baize. **1882** BECK *Drapers' Dict.* 14 Bays, bayze, baize..was first introduced here in 1561.
b. *attrib.*
1634 BRERETON *Trav.* (1844) 52 He sat up in bed, and was in a thin bease waistcoat. **1834** C. MATHEWS *Let.* 20 Jan. in Mrs. Mathews *Memoirs C.M.* (1839) IV. xiii. 256 He sat down contentedly before the green baize table. **1837** HAWTHORNE *Twice-told T.* (1851) II. vi. 90 Fishermen, in red baize shirts. **1853** DICKENS *Bleak H.* xli. 405 There is an inner baize door too.
2. A curtain, table-cover, etc. of baize.
1862 *Lond. Rev.* 30 Aug. 193 The great baize will soon fall down. **1880** BROWNING *Dram. Idylls, Clive* 103 Cocky fancied that a clerk must feel Quite sufficient honor in bending over one green baize.
3. *attrib.*, as in **baize-factor.**
1766 *Ann. Reg.* 53/2 A baize factor has presented the Mayor of Colchester..a rich gold chain. **1852** DICKENS *Bleak Ho.* xxvi. §1 Gentlemen of the green baize road, who could discourse from personal experience of foreign galleys and home treadmills.

baize, *v.* [f. prec. sb.] To cover or line with baize. Hence **baized** *ppl. a.*, **baizing** *vbl. sb.*
1830 MISS MITFORD *Village* Ser. IV. (1863) 250 Baizing the door of the library; and new painting the hall. **1882** J. BAKER *Hist. Scarboro'* 160 Pews..being baized or cushioned.

bajada (bə'hɑːdə). Also **bahada**. [a. Sp. *bajada* descent, slope.] In the south-west of N. America, a descent or slope; *spec.* that section of a piedmont slope formed by aggradation and composed of rock debris (detritus).
1866 *New Mexican* 17 Nov. 2/3 The road from here to Algodones by way of the Bajada is being worked. **1909** C. F. TOLMAN in *Jrnl. Geol.* XVII. 141 The *bajada*: Extending down from the rock surfaces are flanking detrital slopes, built up by terrestrial deposition. **1933** *Amer. Speech* Oct. 8/2 Special types of plant life..which can best be described as bahada inhabiting. **1937** WOOLDRIDGE & MORGAN *Physical Basis Geogr.* xx. 311 Gently sloping surfaces... The first type is the 'bajada', plainly due to aggradation by floods debouching from the mountain valleys. Bajada plains are underlain by thick accumulations of coarse alluvia. **1960** B. W. SPARKS *Geomorphology* xi. 256 The whole slope from the range to the infilled playa lake is usually termed a piedmont. The upper part is often, but not always, a rock-cut surface, normally termed a pediment, while the lower part is an aggradation feature formed of detritus from the ranges and termed a bahada.

Bajan, Bajun, var. BADIAN *sb.*² and *a.*

bajan-, -on, variants of BEJAN.

bajardour: see BAIARDOUR.

‖**bajocco** (ba'jɔkko). Pl. **bajocchi** (-'ɔkki). In 6 englished as **byok, baiock.** [It., f. *bajo* brown.] A small Italian copper coin (now obsolete) worth about a halfpenny.
1547 BOORDE *Introd. Knowl.* 179 In bras they haue kateryns and byokes, and denares. **1590** MUNDAY *Eng. Rom. Life* in *Harl. Misc.* (1809) II. 202 Supping so well as I coulde with..one quatrine bestowed in ricoct..a baiock in bread. **1860** *All Y. Round* No. 70. 475 Vellum-bound books, at five baiocchi—twopence halfpenny. **1864** *Leeds Merc.* 11 Mar., And left the priest without a single bajocco.

‖**bajri** ('bɑːdʒriː). Also **bajree, -eree, -uree, -ury, -ra.** The name in Indian vernaculars of various kinds of grain (e.g. *Penicillaria spicata, Panicum vulgare*) extensively grown in India.
1813 J. FORBES *Orient. Mem.* I. 194 Bajeree, natchee, and some inferior grains. **1864** *Daily Tel.* 15 Aug., A good crop of bajri. **1884** *Health Exhib. Catal.* Pref. 43 Samples of bajra and jowar, the chief grain foods.

‖**baju** ('bɑːdʒuː). Also **badju.** [Malay.] A short loose jacket worn in Malaya.
1820 J. CRAWFURD *Hist. Ind. Archipelago* I. II. ii. 210 The second great portion of dress is the *coat*, called by the Malays *baju*, and by the Javanese..*rasukan*. It..may generally be described as a frock with sleeves, longer or shorter, according to the sex..of the wearer. **1834** [see SARONG 1]. **1902** *Bulletin* (Sydney) 13 Dec. 16 A painted Mongolian person..with his baju buttoned awry. **1939** *Atlantic Monthly* 858 A layette of diminutive bright calico *bajus* and sarongs. **1939** A. KEITH *Land below Wind* ix. 150 A figured baju which fell naïvely from his slender shoulders. **1961** CONYN & MARTEN *Bali Ballet Murder* vii. 70 The gaily printed *badjus* of the women.

†**'bajulate**, *v. Obs. rare.* [f. *bājulāt-* ppl. stem of *bājulāre* to carry, f. *bājulus* porter.] To carry (a heavy burden); to carry as a BADGER *sb.*¹
1613 R. C. *Table Alph.*, *Baiulate* [printed *bainbate*], beare, or carry like a porter. **1662** FULLER *Worthies* III. 97 Which [roads], if mended, Higglers would mount, as bajulating them [*i.e.* provisions] to London.

bak-, obs. sp of BAC-, BACK-, q.v.

bak, earlier form of BAT *sb.* winged mammal.

bak(e, obs. form of BACK.

†**bakbred(e.** *north. dial.* Also 5 **bacbrede**, 7 **bagbread.** [f. BAKE *v.* + BRED, flat board.] A

board on which bread is made, a paste-board; = BAKEBOARD.
1483 *Cath. Ang.* 17 Bacbrede, *vbi* bakebrede. Bakbrede: *rotabulum et cetera; vbi* a muldyngborde. **1625–6** *Inv. R. Hay* in *Reg. Dean & Ch. Yrk.*, One kneidinge kitt, a bag-bread, and a spittle. [**1875** *Lanc. Gloss.* Bak-brede. In South of Scotl. *ba'brede bawbred, bawbret*: see Jamieson.]

bake (beɪk), *v.* Forms: 1 bacan, 3–5 bake(n, 5 -yn, 6 baake, 7 baque, 4– bake. *Pa. t.* 1–4 bóc, 4 booc, book, bakide, 5 boke, (6 *Sc.* buik, beuk,) 5– baked. *Pa. pple.* 1 bacen, 2–7 baken, 4 baake, 4–5 bacun, ybake, ibake, 4–6 bake, 5 bakun, (6 *Sc.* backin, baikin, baykin, ybaik), 6 bakt, 6– baked. [Common Teutonic: OE. *bac-an* = OHG. *bach-an, pach-an*, MHG. *bachen*, ON., Sw. *baka*, Da. *bage*; also, OHG *bacchan*, MHG. and G. *backen*, MDu. *backen*, Du. *bakken*, OS. *bakken*. OTeut. ? **bak-an* (perh., as Paul thinks, in present stem *bakka-*, by assimilation of a *Suff.*, ? from *bak-ná*), cogn. w. Gr. φώγ-ειν to roast, parch, toast, pointing to an Aryan *bhōg-*. Originally a strong vb.; the str. pa. t. survived to *c* 1400, and is still used dialectally; the str. pa. pple. *baken* occurs five times in the Bible of 1611 as against two examples of *baked*, and is still in reg. use in the north. The weak pa. t. *baked* appeared before 1400; the weak pa. pple. in 16th c., and is alone found in Shakspere.]

1. a. *trans.* To cook by dry heat acting by conduction, and not by radiation, hence either in a closed place (oven, ashes, etc.), or on a heated surface (bakestone, griddle, live coals); primarily used of preparing bread, then of potatoes, apples, the flesh of animals. (Thus, in the primary sense, distinguished from *roast*: but in transferred uses they are not sharply separated.) Often *absolutely*.
c **1000** *Ælfric Ex.* xii. 39 Hí bócon þæt melu. —— *Lev.* xxvi. 26 Fif bacaþ on ánum ofene. *c* **1200** ORMIN 992 Bulltedd bræd þatt bakenn wass in ofne. **1382** WYCLIF *1 Sam.* xxviii. 24 She..boke [booc, boc] therf looves. **1388** —— *Isa.* xliv. 15 He brente and bakide looues. **1393** GOWER *Conf.* II. 208 A capon in that one was bake. **1398** TREVISA *Barth. De P.R.* XVII. lxvii. (1495) 643 Some brede is bake vnder asshen. **1513** DOUGLAS *Æneis* I. iv. 40 The cornes..Thai grand, and syne buik at the fire. **1530** PALSGR. 442/1, I baake a batche of breed in an oven..Have you baken your breed yet. **1598** SHAKS. *Merry W.* I. iv. 101, I wash, ring, brew, bake, scowre ..make the beds, and doe all my selfe. **1611** BIBLE *Lev.* vi. 17 It shall not be baken with leauen. —— *Isa.* xliv. 19, I haue baked bread vpon the coales. **1768** SMOLLETT *Humph. Cl.* Let. 8 June, My bread is..baked in my own oven. **1836** DICKENS *Pickw.* xlv, We have half a leg of mutton, baked, at a quarter before three. **1855** ELIZA ACTON *Mod. Cookery* ii. 55 *To bake fish*, a gentle oven may be used.

b. *fig.* To ripen with heat.
1697 DRYDEN *Virg., Georg.* II. 754 The Vine her liquid Harvest yields, Bak'd in the Sun-shine.

†**c.** *fig.* To prepare, make ready. *Obs.*
1460 in *Pol. R. & L. Poems* (1866) 194 Whan þou doest thus, there bale þou bakeste.

2. *trans.* To harden by heat: **a.** in a (brick) kiln.
1388 WYCLIF *Gen.* xi. 3 Make we tiel stonys, and bake we tho with fier. **1868** J. MARRYAT *Pottery* Gloss. s.v. *Kiln*, The furnaces employed to fire or bake pottery.

b. as the sun hardens the ground.
1697 DRYDEN *Virg., Georg.* IV. 618 The Sun..bak'd the Mud. **1821** BYRON *Heav. & Earth* iii. 189 When the hot sun hath baked the reeking soil Into a world.

3. To harden as frost does.
1572 B. GOOGE *Heresbach's Husb.* (1586) 52b, The cold of the Winter doth bake and season the ground. **1610** SHAKS. *Temp.* I. ii. 256 Th' earth When it is bak'd with frost.

†**4.** To form into a cake or mass; to cake. *Obs.*
c **1460** *Bk. Curtasye* in *Babees Bk.* (1868) 303 An apys mow men sayne he makes, þat brede and flesshe in hys cheke bakes. **1592** SHAKS. *Rom. & Jul.* I. iv. 89 That very Mab that ..bakes the Elk-locks in foule sluttish haires. *a* **1631** DONNE *Serm.* xii. 117 The old dirt is still baked on my hands. **1684** tr. *Bonet's Merc. Compit.* I. 8 If the root of the Tongue and the Windpipe, have any glutinous stuff baked to them.

5. *intr.* (for *refl.*) **a.** To undergo the process of baking; to become firm or hard with heat. Of land.
1605 SHAKS. *Macb.* IV. i. 13 Fillet of a Fenny Snake, In the Cauldron boyle and bake. **1755** in JOHNSON. **1850** N. KINGSLEY *Diary* 12 Feb. (1914) 109 The soil looks as if it would bake hard. **1869** *Rep. U.S. Commissioner Agric.* 357 When the proportions of clay and sand are such that the soil will not bake,..it may properly be called loam. **1873** J. H. BEADLE *Undevel. West* xxxiii. 710 The land is never water-soaked, never 'bakes', and I never saw a clod as big as my fist. **1876** GREEN *Short Hist.* i. §5 The cakes which were baking on the hearth. *Mod.* These apples do not bake well. How the London Clay bakes in the sun!

b. To be made uncomfortably hot (by the sun, a fire, etc.). *colloq.*
1937 M. SHARP *Nutmeg Tree* x. 123 'I'm going to bake,' thought Julia..and indeed the plain..shimmered under a heat mist.

6. Phrases and proverbs: ***to bake one's bread***: to 'do for' one. ***as they brew, so let them bake***: as they begin, so let them proceed. ***only half-baked***: (*colloq.*) deficient in sense; half-witted.
c **1380** *Sir Ferumb.* 577 For euere my bred had be bake: myn lyf dawes had be tynt. **1599** PORTER *Angry Wom. Abingd.* (1841) 82 Euen as they brew, so let them bake. **1675** COTTON *Scoff. Scoft* 150, I should do very imprudently.. Either to meddle or to make: But as they brew, so let 'um bake. **1864** *N. & Q.* Ser. III. VI. 494/2 He is only half-baked, put in with the bread and taken out with the cakes.

7. *Comb.*, in which *bake*, in sense of vbl. sb. *baking*, is used attrib., as ***bake-kettle, -oven, -pan, -shop***; **bake office** *dial.*, (*a*) = BAKEHOUSE; (*b*) a baker's shop (*Eng. Dial. Dict.*). Also BAKE-BOARD, -HOUSE, -STONE, BAK-BRED, q.v.
c **1000** ÆLFRIC *Gloss.* (Zup.) 316 *Pistrinum*, bæcern. **1579** LANGHAM *Gard. Health* (1633) 529 Bake them vnder a bake-pan of earth. **1840** R. DANA *Bef. Mast* xxxv. 133 Tin bake-pans and other notions. **1874** in Thirsk & Imray *Suff. Farming 19th Cent.* (1958) 121 Bake office common to the 3 tenements. **1880** N. BISHOP *Sneak-Box* 317, I..built a fire in my bake-kettle. **1883** *Harper's Mag.* Mar. 504/2 A few old men trudge about their bake-ovens. **1872** MARK TWAIN *Innoc. Abr.* xxxi. 240 There are the bake-shops.

bake, *sb.* [f. the vb.] **1.** in *Sc.* A biscuit.
1787 BURNS *Holy Fair* xviii, Here's crying out for bakes and gills. **1823** GALT *Entail* xciii, We can divide the bakes.

2. a. 'The act, process, or result, of baking.' (Webster.)
1565 T. COOPER *Thes., Acapna thysia*, sacrifices without smoke: spoken of a simple feaste wherin is neyther bake, sodde, nor roste. **1851** *Knickerbocker* XXXVIII. 187 Saint Peter [in stained glass] is a little cracked..but I've got a first-rate bake on Paul. **1882** LEES & CLUTTERBUCK *Three in Norway* xvi. 126 After this Esau finished the oven, and accomplished a bake of bread therein. **1961** *Guardian* 27 Sept. 8/3 Many older housewives..find great satisfaction in a monster weekly 'bake'. **1963** *Listener* 21 Mar. 535/3 For *apple and pork bake* you will need..4 pork chops.

b. A social gathering at which a meal, esp. of baked food, is served; a clambake. *U.S.*
1846 *Spirit of Times* (N.Y.) 6 June 174/3 The grand 'bake' at the village hotel. **1935** STEINBECK *Tortilla Flat* viii. 148 He saw that it was a Girl Scout wienie bake.

bake, earlier form of BAKEN *ppl. a.*

bake-apple. *Canadian.* Also **baked-apple.** [BAKE *v.* 7.] The (dried) fruit of the cloudberry. Also *attrib.*
1775 G. CARTWRIGHT *Jrnl. Labrador* 3 Aug. (1792) II. 96, I saw the first baked apples. **1792** *Ibid.* I. p. ix, Baked Apple. The fruit of a plant so called, from the similarity of taste to that of the pulp of a roasted apple. **1829** T. C. HALIBURTON *Hist. & Stat. Acct. Nova Scotia* II. 216 The berry being nearly of the size and appearance of the yellow Antwerp raspberry,..is termed by the residents, 'bake-apple'. **1839** E. W. TUCKER *Five Months Labrador* 104 Several small shrubs are found in the country which bear fruit, the principal one of which is called the baked apple berry. **1895** *Outing* (U.S.) XXVII. 18/1 The outlying islands furnish the curlew-berry and bake-apple in profusion. **1938** *Geogr. Jrnl.* XCII. 155 On the marshes were bakeapple, pitcher plant, Labrador tea, and occasional groups of blueberry. **1950** A. P. HERBERT *Independent Member* 283 Bake-apples (little ground fruit the size of raspberries).

'bakeboard. Also 6 backbord, -boarde, 9 -buird (all in *north. dial.*, to which the word is confined.) [f. BAKE *v.* + BOARD.] A board on which dough is kneaded and rolled out in making bread; a paste-board.
1562 *Richmond. Wills* (1853) 156 Item iij chayres, stolles, and cardstocks, iij^{s}..backbords, xij^{d}. **1563** *Wills & Inv. N.C.* (1835) 169 A kneadinge bassyn, a knoppe, a gielfatte, a backbourde. **1808** *Cumbrian Ball.* liv. 122 As flat as a back-buird. **1878** in HALLIWELL.

baked (beɪkt), *ppl. a.* [pa. pple. of BAKE: see -ED; for earlier forms see BAKEN.]
1. a. Cooked by dry heat.
1611 BIBLE *1 Chron.* xxiii. 29 That which is baked in the panne. **1620** VENNER *Via Recta* vii. 111 Baked Peares are much wholesomer then raw. **1836** DICKENS in *Bell's Life in London* 17 Jan. 1/1 The baked-'tatur man has departed. **1875** *Chamb. Jrnl.* No. 133. 66 The baked-potato men are doing a good trade.

b. ***baked beans***, haricot beans so cooked (now a popular tinned food, prepared in tomato sauce).
1832 L. M. CHILD *Frugal Housewife* 51 Baked beans are a very simple dish, yet few cook them well. **1873** 'SUSAN COOLIDGE' *What Katy Did* iv. 42 A breakfast of baked beans. **1920** F. E. GREEN *Hist. Eng. Agric. Labourer* ii. 47 Farmers did not have recourse to..letting their fields..as advertising sites for Somebody's Pills or Baked Beans. **1933** *Punch* 15 Feb. 170/2 All you have to do to give your family a really new tasty meal is to take a tin-opener and one tin of baked beans.

2. Dried or fired in a (brick) kiln.
1545 JOYE *Exp. Daniel* ii. 31 Golde, syluer, latine, yerne and bakt potte erth. **1609** BIBLE (Douay) *Isa.* xvi. 7 Walles of baqued bricke. **1858** BIRCH *Anc. Pottery* Introd. 5 Remains of baked earthenware. **1869** RAWLINSON *Five Mon.* I. v, The sun-dried bricks have even more variety of size than the baked ones.

3. a. Hardened or caked by heat (or otherwise).
1615 LATHAM *Falconry* (1633) 64 Their grease..will lie baked blew to their sides. **1858** W. ELLIS *Vis. Madagascar* viii. 206 The soil..is hard-baked reddish earth.

b. *Typogr.* (See quot. 1688.)
1683 MOXON *Mech. Exerc., Printing* II. xxii. 257 Compositers in this Case say, The Letter is Bak'd. **1688** R. HOLME *Armory* III. iii. 119/1 *Bake*, is when Letters stick together in distributing.. This is called the *Letter is Baked*. **1963** KENNEISON & SPILMAN *Dict. Printing* 13 *Baked* (or *caked*), said of type which sticks together, thus making it difficult to distribute.

†**4. baked meat**, pastry: see BAKE-MEAT. *Obs.*

bakehouse ('beɪkhaʊs). Forms: 1 ? bæchús, 4–6 bakhows(e, 5 bakkehouse, 5–6 bachous, 6 backhous(e, backehouse, (*Sc.* baghous), 4– bakehouse. [OE. *bæc-*, from *bacan* to BAKE + *hús* HOUSE.] A building or apartment in which bread is made, having an oven for baking it. Also, one in which loaf-sugar is made.
a **1400** *Gloss.* in Wright's *Voc.* 178 Bakehouse, *pistrinum*. *c* **1420** *Pallad. on Husb.* I. 1144 Thi bakhouse therwith all thou maist avance. *c* **1440** *Promp. Parv.* 21/2 Bakhowse, or bakynge howse. **1502** ARNOLD *Chron.* 93 Ye shal kepe noo bachous. **1524** WRIOTHESLEY *Chron.* (1875) I. 14 One Pickeringe, sometyme of the Kings bakehowse. **1606** HOLLAND *Sueton.* 141 The uery jades which serued mils and backe-houses. **1624** MASSINGER *Parl. Love* IV. v, Live to be the talk Of the conduit and the bakehouse. **1697** *Lond. Gaz.* No. 3313/4 To be Lett, either for a Brew-house..or for a Sugar Bake House. **1862** *Lond. Rev.* 16 Aug. 140 The temperature of a bakehouse ranges from about 75 to upwards of 80 degrees.

bakelite ('beɪkəlaɪt). Also **Bakelite.** [ad. G. *bakelit* (*Chem. Zentralblatt*, 1909, 1478), f. the name of L. H. *Baekeland* (1863–1944) its inventor + -ITE[1].] A proprietary term for a condensation product of phenol or other phenolic bodies and formaldehyde used as a plastic and for insulating purposes. Also *attrib.*
1909 L. H. BAEKELAND in *Jrnl. Ind. & Engin. Chem.* I. 149/2 (*title*) The Synthesis, Constitution, and Uses of Bakelite. **1913** *Jrnl. Soc. Chem. Ind.* 16 June 563/2 Bakelite varnish has been suggested for use as an antiseptic in hospitals. **1921** THORPE *Dict. Applied Chem.* I. 501/1 There are..bakelite plants in Germany, France and England, and several factories where bakelite goods, such as buttons, are manufactured under licence. **1962** *Which?* Aug. 249/2 Bakelite Ltd now produce many different plastics, more than one of which is called Bakelite. **1964** N. G. CLARK *Mod. Org. Chem.* xvii. 363 A further example of thermo-setting polymers is provided by the Bakelite-type resins, from formaldehyde and phenol.

†**'bake-meat.** *Obs.* [f. *bake* = BAKEN *pa. pple.*; also *baken meat, baked meat.*] Pastry, a pie.
c **1386** CHAUCER *Prol.* 343 Withoute bake mete was never his hous. *c* **1420** *Liber Cocorum* (1862) 55 Bakyn mete..And most daynté, come byhynde. *c* **1460** J. RUSSELL *Bk. Nurture* in *Babees Bk.* (1868) 146 Almanere bakemetes þat byn good and hoot, Open hem aboue þe brym of þe coffyn cote. **1530** PALSGR. 196/2 Bake meate, *uiande en paste.* **1602** SHAKS. *Ham.* I. ii. 180 The Funerall Bakt-meats Did coldly furnish forth the Marriage Tables. **1611** BIBLE *Gen.* xl. 17 All manner of bakemeetes for Pharaoh. **1624** MASSINGER *Renegado* V. v, To carry This bake-meat to Vitelli. *a* **1700** *White Devil* in Dodsl. *O.P.* VI. 312 (N.) As if a man Should know what fowl is coffin'd in a bak'd meat Afore it is cut up.

baken ('beɪk(ə)n), *ppl. a. arch.* Earlier forms, **bake, ybake,** etc.: see under BAKE *v.* [strong pa. pple. of BAKE *v.*: see -EN. Now superseded by BAKED in literary Eng., but still in north. dial.]
1. Baked, as bread or meat.
c **1325** *Cœur de L.* 3613 Ne eete off flesch, baken ne brede. **1340** *Ayenb.* 112 Bread tuies ybake huermide he astoreþ his ssip. **1382** WYCLIF *Lev.* ii. 4 He shal offre baake sacrifice. *c* **1420** *Liber Cocorum* (1862) 54 Bakun turbut and sawmon ibake. **1562** J. HEYWOOD *Prov. & Epigr.* (1867) 37 Boylde beefe and bake mutton. **1611** BIBLE *1 Kings* xix. 6 A cake baken on the coales. *Mod. Sc.* New-baken bread.

2. Baked in a kiln; hardened, dried.
c **1385** CHAUCER *L.G.W.* 709 Wallis..of harde tilis wel I-bake. **1513** DOUGLAS *Æneis* XI. xi. 47 The schaft was sad and sound and weill ybaik. **1544** PHAËR *Regim.* (1560) I iij b, Baken or dryed as clay is in the fourneis. **1549** *Compl. Scot.* vi. 46 Ane of the tabilis vas of baikyn stane, and the tothir.. of onbaykyn stane.

†**3. baken meat**, pastry: see BAKE-MEAT. *Obs.*

baken, obs. form of BACON *sb.*

baker ('beɪkə(r)). Forms: 1 bæcere, 3–5 **bakere,** 4 **bachare,** 5–7 **backer,** 4– **baker.** [OE. *bæcere*, f. *bacan* to bake + -ER[1]; cogn. with ON. *bakari*, Sw. *bagare*, Da. *bagere*, OHG. *bacher*; OS. *bakkeri*, Du. *bakker*, G. *bäcker*:—OTeut. **bak(k)arjo-z.*]
1. One who bakes; *spec.* one whose business it is to make bread.
a **1000** ÆLFRIC *Colloquy* Q. 5, Sume cypmenn, sume scewyrhtan, sealteras, bæceras. *Ibid.* Q. 54, Hwæt segst þu, bæcere? *c* **1300** *Men Lif* 16 in *E.E.P.* (1862) 155 Hail be ȝe bakers wiþ ȝur louis smale. *c* **1300** *Relig. Songs* vii. 35 Alle theos false chepmen, the feond heom wule habbe, Bachares and brueres. **1466** *Mann. & Househ. Exp.* 211 To..the backers wyffe, for v. mennes borde. *c* **1500** ARNOLD *Chron.* (1811) 9 That backers or myllars stelying paste or mele be drawen vpon an hyrdel. **1598** STOW *Survey* (1633) 208 A Pillorie, for the punishment of Bakers, offending in the assise of bread. **1602** SHAKS. *Ham.* IV. v. 42 They say the Owle was a Bakers daughter. **1604** DEKKER *Honest Wh.* Wks. 1873 II. 122 Are not Bakers armes the skales of Iustice? yet is not their bread light? **1768** SMOLLETT *Humph. Cl.* Let. 8 June, The miller or the baker is obliged to poison them and their families, in order to live by his profession. **1847** KINGLAKE *Eothen* xvii, The very first baker of bread that ever lived must have done his work exactly as the Arab does at this day.

2. 'A small portable tin oven in which baking is performed.' In U.S. (Webster.)
1841 *Lowell* (Mass.) *Offering* I. 227 (Th.), A peep into the baker told that the potatoes were cooked. *a* **1862** THOREAU *Maine W.* (1864) 249 Somebody had left..on a deserted log ..a loaf of bread baked in a Yankee-baker. **1897** *Outing* (U.S.) XXIX. 489/1 The cooking utensils consisting of

three dripping pans, one patented baker and one large coffee-pot.

3. An artificial salmon fly in angling.

1867 F. Francis *Angling* x. (1880) 345 The Baker is another good general fly.

4. *Proverbs.* (As to the Pillory see 1598 in 1.)

1562 J. Heywood *Prov. & Epigr.* (1867) 47, I feare we parte not yéet, Quoth the baker to the pylorie. **1660** Howell *Eng. Prov.* 11 Ile take no leave of you, quoth the Baker to the Pillory. **1857** *N. & Q.* 21 Mar., Pull Devil, Pull Baker, in England's the cry.

5. *Comb.*, as **baker-feet, -legs, -knees, baker's knee**, names of deformities of the lower extremities incident to bakers; **baker-legged, -kneed,** *a.*, having these deformities; **baker's bread**, bread baked by a baker (opp. home-baked); **baker's itch**, a species of tetter or psoriasis to which the hands of bakers and cooks are liable; **baker's salt**, an appellation of commercial carbonate of ammonia, used instead of yeast in pastry and bread.

1611 Cotgr., *Iarretier*..Baker-legd, that goes in at the knees. **1652** Gaule *Magastrom.* 186 Baker-kneed signifies effeminate. **1656** Du Gard *Gate Lat. Unl.* §292 Hee that is baker-legged, rub's his knees against one another. **1656** *Artif. Handsom.* (1662) 79 The unhandsome warpings of bow Leggs and baker Feet. **1659** *Lady Alimony* v. v. in Hazl. *Dodsl.* XIV. 361 His puny baker-legs. **1784** J. Barry *Lect. Art* ii. (1848) 94 Knocked or baker knees. **1871** *Figure Training* 39 Baker's knee, as it is called, or an inclining inwards of the right knee-joint until it closely resembles the right side of a letter K, is the almost certain penalty of habitually bearing any burden of bulk in the right hand. **1813** Jane Austen *Let.* 3 Nov. (1932) II. 367, I suppose you will be going to Streatham, to see quiet Mr. Hill & eat very bad Baker's bread. **1860** F. Nightingale *Notes on Nursing* vii. 42, I have known patients..[who] could not eat baker's bread. **1964** M. Lochhead *Vict. Househ.* vii. 104 The women..were..good bakers... Baker's bread was..an extravagance.

6. *baker's dozen*: thirteen. (See last quot.)

1599 J. Cooke *Tu Quoque* in Dodsl. *O.P.* (1780) VII. 49 Mine's a baker's dozen: Master Bubble, tell your money. **1611** in Florio. **1733** Fielding *Quix.* III. vi, I dare swear there were a good round baker's dozen at least. **1859** Riley *Liber Albus* Pref. 68 These dealers..[Hucksters] on purchasing their bread from the bakers, were privileged by law to receive thirteen batches for twelve, and this would seem to have been the extent of their profits. Hence the expression, still in use, 'A baker's dozen.'

'bakerdom, condition of a baker. **'bakership,** skill as a baker.

1883 *Pall Mall G.* 28 Apr. 3/1 The first baker..was about to produce a card to prove his bakerdom and respectability.

bakeress ('beɪkərɪs). *rare.* [f. Baker + -ess; cf. *baxter* and *backstress*.] A female baker.

1837 Carlyle *Fr. Rev.* I. vii. xi. 352 The Baker, the Bakeress, and Baker's Boy. **1872** *Vagab. Jack* i. in *Casquet Lit.*, I have a perfect recollection of the pretty bakeress.

'bakerly, *a.* and *adv.* [f. Baker + -ly².] Baker-like; after the manner of a baker.

1593 *Pass. Morrice* 82 Spindle shankte, or bakerly kneed.

bakery ('beɪkərɪ). [f. Baker + -y: see -ery.]

1. Baker's work; the craft or business of the baker.

1545 Joye *Exp. Dan.* xii. (R.) Daniel saw his feet to be made and bakt but of britel bakkery. **1765** Smollett *Trav.* 186 The butchery and the bakery which they farm at so much a year.

2. A place for making bread; the whole establishment of a baker. Also, a shop where baked products are sold. *U.S.*

c **1820** *14th Rep. Hist. MSS. Comm.* App. iii (1894). 50 We marched a long forced march to the relief of Beaton, who had burnt the French backery at Marburgh. **1832** F. Trollope *Dom. Manners Amer.* I. 85 There are no..shops for eatables except *bakeries*, as they are called. **1842** Dickens *Amer. Notes* iv. 153 Every 'Bakery', 'Grocery', and 'Bookbindery', and other kind of store. **1857** Eliza Acton *Eng. Bread-Bk.* 40 Converting the small bakeries, conducted on the old system, into mechanical bakeries. **1872** Yeats *Techn. Hist. Comm.* 116 Public bakeries were established in 1276. **1923** K. D. Wiggin *Garden of Memory* 112, I bought my luncheon at a different bakery every day.

'bakestone. Commonly in dialect form 6- **bak-, backstone.** [f. Bake *v.* + Stone.] A flat stone or slate on which cakes are baked in the oven; a plate of iron used for the same purpose.

1531 *Lanc. Wills* (1857) I. 113 One backstoone and one spetil. **1575** *Richmond. Wills* (1853) 255, i backstone, iij^d. j. yron speite..j litle broile yron. **1741** Ellis *Mod. Husb.* II. ii. 31 In Shropshire they..make thin Cakes on a Back or Bake-stone. **1818** in *E. Burt's Lett. N. Scotl.* I. 246 Poured out upon the bake-stone like a pan-cake. **1865** Mrs. Stretton *Queen of C.* 150 A backstone cake out of the oven. **1869** Blackmore *Lorna D.* xxix. (D.) Here's to the oats with the backstone on the board! **1962** *Guardian* 9 Nov. 8/4 A Welsh bakestone or a Scottish girdle.

bakestre, obs. form of Baxter, female baker.

Bakewell ('beɪkwɛl). The name of a town in Derbyshire used *attrib.* to designate a baked sweet, consisting of a pastry case lined with a layer of jam and filled with a rich almond paste.

1845 E. Acton *Mod. Cookery* xviii. 467 Bakewell Pudding ..is famous not only in Derbyshire. **1861** Mrs. Beeton *Bk. Househ. Managem.* xxvii. 630 *Bakewell Pudding*..puff-paste ..eggs..sugar..butter..almonds, jam. **1883** [see Jam *sb.*² c]. **1906** Mrs. Beeton *Househ. Managem.* xxxii. 927 Bakewell Pudding (..Bakewell Tart). **1959** R. Postgate *Good Food Guide 1959–60* 32 Among the dishes tested and praised by members are..braised ham and Bakewell tart.

bakey, bakie ('beɪkɪ, 'bækɪ). *Sc.* Also **baikie.** [? dim. of Back *sb.*²; or ad. F. *baquet*: cf. Backet.] A square wooden vessel for carrying coals, etc. Hence **bakieful.**

1826 J. Wilson *Noct. Ambr.* Wks. 1855 I. 174 The bakiefu's o' ashes. **1837** *Blackw. Mag.* XLI. 414 The chamber-maid..swept them all away in her bakey.

bakhara, var. Buckaroo.

baking ('beɪkɪŋ), *vbl. sb.* [f. Bake *v.* + -ing¹.]

1. The action of the verb Bake; the process of preparing bread; the hardening or 'firing' of earthenware. Also *spec.* in *Typogr.* (see quot.). Cf. Baked *ppl. a.* 3 b.

1398 Trevisa *Barth. De P.R.* xvii. lxvii. (1495) 643 Brede is made of mele by medlynge of water and bakyng of fyre. **1477** Norton *Ord. Alch.* v. (Ashm. 1652) 55 In Bakinge, and Brewinge, and other Crafts all. **1622** Heylin *Cosmogr.* in Sir T. Blount *Nat Hist.* (1693) 138 The Boyling and Baking of Sugar. **1683** Moxon *Mech. Exerc., Printing* II. xxii. 257 This sticking together of the *Letter* is call'd *Baking* of the Letter. **1847** Kinglake *Eothen* xvii, Principles of bread-baking..sanctioned by the experience of ages. **1868** J. Marryat *Pottery* Gloss. s.v. *Kiln*, The only colours.. which will endure the extreme heat of the first baking.

2. The product of this action; the bread baked at a time, a batch.

c **1440** *Promp. Parv.* 21/2 Bakynge (or bahche), *pistura.* **1598** Florio, *Fornata*, an ouen full, or a batche of bread, a baking. **1860** Miss Yonge *Stokesley Secr.* xiii. (1880) 306 Susan with..her plate of bakings.

3. *Comb.* and *Attrib.*, as ***baking craft, -dish, hours, -house, -iron, -oven, -plate, -soda*** (cf. Soda¹ 1 b), ***-tin***; **baking-powder**, a powder used in baking as a substitute for yeast, through the effervescence of which carbonic acid is diffused through the dough., orig. *U.S.*

1398 Trevisa *Barth. De P.R.* xvii. lxvii. (1495) 643 By *bakynge crafte brede is made. **1856** Dickens *Dorrit* I. v. 39 Preparing a *baking-dish of beef and pudding. **1863** *Scotsman* 16 Mar., To enter bakehouses during *baking hours. *c* **1440** *Promp. Parv.* 21/2 *Bakynge howse, *panificium.* **1884** *Health Exhib. Catal.* 120/2 Patent Hot-Air Continuous Baking Oven, with Travelling Baking Plate. **1601** Holland *Pliny* I. 567 Plautus..maketh mention of.. a *baking pan. **1563** *Thersites* in *Old Plays* (1848) 41 The backster of Balockburye with her *baking pele. **1884** Baking plate [see *baking oven* above]. **1850** *Family Friend* III. App. 2/1 Chemical analyses of two of the *baking powders in most general use. **1861** Mrs. Beeton *Bk. Househ. Managem.* xxxv. 856, 2 teaspoonfuls of baking-powder. **1909** *Westm. Gaz.* 1 June 7/4 Baking-powder beer. **1845** E. Acton *Mod. Cookery* xvi. 425 When the mixture has simmered..pour it out upon a delicately clean baking-tin. **1959** A. Wesker *Roots* ii. i. 49 Mother, where's the bakin' tin?

'baking, *ppl. a.* [f. as prec. + -ing².] That bakes; hot enough to bake. Hence **bakingly** *adv.*

1786 Washington *Diaries* 9 May (1925) III. 58 The ground, by the heavy rains..and baking Winds since, had got immensely hard. **1865** F. Parkman *Champlain* ix. (1875) 302 The fierce sun fell on the bald, baking rock. **1882** Russell in *Macm. Mag.* XLVI. 331/1 Under the 'baking sun.' **1867** Miss Broughton *Not Wisely* I. 18 Too bakingly hot for a long walk. **1880** Miss Fothergill *Wellfields* I. iii, The sun shone bakingly upon the round stones. **1934** 'G. Orwell' *Burmese Days* xi. 170 It's getting beastly hot, isn't it?.. Isn't it simply *baking*!

bakken, bakker, -more: see Back-.

baklava ('baklava). Also **baclava.** [Turkish.] A dessert made from thin pieces of flaky pastry, honey, and nuts, usually cut into lozenge-shaped pieces.

1653 Bocklava [see Close *v.* 21 b]. **1824** J. J. Morier *Adv. Hajji Baba* I. xxiv. 258 Some rare sweetmeats, with *baklava* (sweet cake) made in the royal seraglio. **1936** M. H. Bradley *Five-Minute Girl* 37 People who like baklava and lamb go to Papadopoulos. **1960** *Times* 29 Oct. 9/6 Or have pilaff, kebab and baklava in an oil-lit tavern in the Turkish quarter. **1967** I. Marder *Paris Bit* i. 20 Natasha, who had an impressive appetite, finished with a slab of *baclava*.

bakoun, obs. form of Bacon *sb.*

‖**baksheesh, bakhshish** (bækʃiːʃ), *sb.* Forms: 7 **bacsheese,** 8 **buxie, backsishe, bacshish,** 9 **bach-, backshish, ba(c)ksheesh, bu(c)kshish, -sheesh, buxees, bakhshîsh.** [Pers. *bakhshīsh* present, f. *bakhshī-dan* to give; now used in Arabic, Turkish, and Urdu.] Oriental term for: A gratuity, present of money, 'tip.'

[**1625** Purchas *Pilgrimes* II. 1340 Who..would prostitute her selfe to any man Bacsheese (as they say in the Arabicke tonque) that is gratis freely.] **1755–60** Ives 51 (Col. Yule) Buxie money. **1775** R. Chandler *Trav. Asia Min.* viii. 1825 A demand of bac-shish, a reward or present; which term, from its frequent use, was already become very familiar to us. **1781** *Gentl. Mag.* 113 The Backsishe, or money to drink. **1814** Mrs. Sherwood *Henry & Bearer* 29 And gave Boosy ..four rupees, buckshish. **1854** W. Arnold *Oakfield* I. 239 The relieved bearers..most unceremoniously demanded buxees. **1863** Miss Whately *Ragged Life Egypt* x. 84 Asking loudly for backsheesh. **1876** *Times* 20 Apr., Fresh baksheesh to the unworthy minions of the harem.

'baksheesh, *v.* [f. prec.] To give a present of money to; to bribe, 'tip.' Also *absol.* quasi-*intr.*

1867 *Good Words* 1 Mar. 184/1 We backshished our caffagi, and left Aiasaluck at sunrise. **1882** *Macm. Mag.* XLVI. 167 The higher grades..were reserved for those who backsheeshed the highest. **1884** Gen. Gordon in *Pall Mall G.* 6 May 12/1 You would..make terms with Mahdi by making me backsheesh Mahdi.

bakster, obs. f. Baxter, female baker.

bakstone, obs. and dial. f. Bakestone.

bakt, obs. f. Baked.

baku ('beɪkʊ). Also **-ou.** [Native name in Philippines.] A fine kind of straw grown in the Philippines and woven in China.

1927 *Vogue* Mar. 40 Baku, a linen-like straw. **1928** *Ibid.* 4 Apr. 26 (Advt.), Natural Bakou Straw, trimmed with a feather cockade. **1929** *Ibid.* 20 Feb. 52 Toque of beige baku straw. **1929** *Chicago Tribune* 9 May, Bakus and balibuntals.

bal. Also 6–7 **ball.** [a. Cornish *bal* 'collection of mines.'] A mine. *Attrib.*, as in *bal-girl, -work.*

c **1600** Norden *Spec. Brit.* Cornw. (1728) 45 Godolphyn ball. **1678** *Phil. Trans.* XII. 951 Godolphin Ball is the most famous of all the Balls or Mines in Cornwall. **1812** *Ann. Reg.* 52/1 Bal girls, as the girls are called who work about the mines. **1851** Kingsley *Yeast* xiii. 252 He could not stand the bal work.

bal, obs. f. Ball and Bale *sb.* fire.

Balaam ('beɪləm).

1. Name of the prophet whose history is narrated in *Numbers* xxii–xxiv, used connotatively. Hence: **Balaam** *v.*, to make a Balaam of. **Balaamite,** one who follows religion for the sake of gain; whence **Balaamitical** *a.*

1648 Milton *Observ. Art. Peace* Wks. (1851) 571 God.. hath so dispos'd the mouth of these Balaams, that comming to Curse, they have stumbled into a kind of Blessing. **1598** T. Bastard *Chrestoleros* (1880) 87 Bala-ming his patron which did him this wrong, Am not I thine asse which haue seru'd thee thus long. **1559** *Hist. Est. Scot.* in *Wodr. Soc. Misc.* 73 The Bishopp of St. Andrewes, with his Balamites, came to St. Giles Kirk. **1561** Daus tr. *Bullinger on Apoc.* (1573) 36 b, Maintayning the Nicolaitan or Balaamiticall doctrine.

2. (In journalistic slang) Trumpery paragraphs reserved to fill up the columns of a newspaper or magazine. **Balaam-box** (or **-basket**), a receptacle for such matter (also *fig.*); in U.S. printing-offices, a place in which stereotype paragraphs are kept for similar use.

1826 Scott *Mal. Malagr.* iii. 3 How much Balaam (speaking technically) I have edged out of your valuable paper. **1827** *Blackw. Mag.* Mar. 340 Several dozen letters on the same subject now in our Balaam-box. **1839** Lockhart *Scott* lxx. (1842) 622 *Balaam* is the cant name for asinine paragraphs about monstrous productions of nature and the like, kept standing in type to be used whenever the real news of the day leave an awkward space that must be filled up somehow. **1861** A. K. H. B. *Recr. Country P.* Ser. ii. 59 Rubbishing articles which are at present consigned to the Balaam-box. **1866** *Harper's Mag.* May 816/1 There have been a number of anecdotes lying loose in the Balaam basket of memory. **1873** F. Hall *Mod. Eng.* 17 Consigned, by the editor, to his balaam-basket.

balace, obs. form of Balas (ruby).

‖**balachong** ('bælətʃɒŋ). Also 7 **balachaun,** 9 **balichung.** [a. Malay *bâlachân.*] A condiment for rice, much used in China, consisting of putrid shrimps or small fishes pounded up with salt and spices, and then dried.

1697 Dampier in Southey *Comm.-pl. Bk.* Ser. II. (1849) 602 Balachaun is a composition of a strong savour, yet a very delightsome dish to the Tonquinese. **1854** Stocqueler *Brit. India* 279 Rice..is rendered savoury by the addition of salt, ngapee, or balachoung. **1864** in Webster.

Balaclava (bæləˈklɑːvə). *Balaclava helmet* (also *cap*): a woollen covering for the head and neck worn esp. by soldiers on active service; named after the Crimean village of Balaclava near Sebastopol, the site of a battle fought in the Crimean war, 25 October 1854. Also *ellipt.*

1881 *Cliftonian* Feb. 376 Balaclava caps. **1892** C. T. Dent et al. *Mountaineering* 48 A knitted woollen Balaclava (Templar) cap is useful for sleeping out. **1900** *Queen* 10 Feb. 222/1 Balaclava Helmet in crochet. **1914** *Scotsman* 17 Sept. 8/5 The articles which at the moment will be most useful to officers and men in ships afloat are..Balaclava helmets, mufflers. **1926** *Blackw. Mag.* Mar. 398/1 Baa's balaclava helmet and woolly muffler were flaked with white.

balade, -adde, obs. ff. Ballad *sb.*, Ballade.

baladine ('bælədiːn). Also 6–7 **balladin(e,** 7 **baladyne.** [a. F. *baladin, -ine*, f. *ballade* dancing-song: see Ballad *sb.*]

†**1.** A theatrical dancer; a mountebank, buffoon.

1599 *Basilikon Doron* (1603) 127 Delight not to keepe..in your company, comœdians or balladines. **1605** Bacon *Adv. Learn.* ii. xv. §1 Trickes of Tumblers Funambuloes, Baladynes. **1676** Etherede *Man of Mode* ii. i. 19 (1684) Their best Balladins, who are Now practising a famous Ballat.

2. A female public dancer. *rare.*

1863 BROWNING *In Balcony* II, The first breathing woman's cheek, First dancer's, gipsy's, or street baladine's.

†**3.** A ballad-maker or -singer. Cf. BALLADIER.

1604 HIERON *Wks.* I. 551 D d d iij, Meeting with our common aduersary..in the fashion of a Rimer or Balladine.

balakhana (bælə'kɑːnə). Also **-khaneh, -hané.** [Pers. *bālā-khāna* upper room.] An upper room in a Persian house, in which travellers are lodged.

1840 J. B. FRASER *Trav. Koordistan* I. ii. 31 Desiring that this Khan should have such a suite of rooms..and another such a *dellân*, or *balakhaneh*. **1882** O'DONOVAN *Merv Oasis* I. xxii. 369 Above the arch was a square-topped room known as the *bala hané*, which served as quarters for the better class of travellers, as well as a kind of watch-tower. **1921** *Blackw. Mag.* Dec. 825/2 Very soon our horses were tethered, and champing good dry lucerne under the bala-khaneh of a two-storied guest-house.

balalaika (bælə'laɪkə) [Russ.] A musical instrument of the guitar kind, with a triangular body, popular in Russia and other Slav countries. Also *attrib.*

1788 tr. *Staehlin's Anecd. Peter Gt.* 319 In his youth he had never heard any [music] but that of drums, fifes, balalaïkas, and bagecs. **1864** ENGEL *Mus. Anc. Nat.* 55 The Russian *balalaika*, an instrument said to be of high antiquity. **1885** A. J. C. HARE *Stud. Russia* i. 27 Formerly the peasants used to dance the Barina..accompanied by the Balalaika. **1913** 'SAKI' *When William Came* iii. 43 The thrumming music of a balalaika orchestra coming up from the restaurant below. **1954** *Grove's Dict. Mus.* (ed. 5) I. 368/2 Balalaika bands have frequently visited Western Europe.

†**'balan.** *Obs.* [? a. OF. *balin, ballin*: see Godef.] A strong stuff made of tow.

1340 *Alexander* (Stev.) 4851 In bole and in balan buskes he his fotez. [L. *fecit sibi subtalares lineos.*]

balance ('bæləns), *sb.* Forms: 4–5 **balaunce,** 5 **belans, belauns, -nce,** 5–6 **ballaunce,** 6 **ballanis, -es,** 6–8 **ballance,** 7 **bilanz,** 3– **balance.** [a. Fr. *balance* (= Sp. *balanza*, Pr. *balansa*, It. *bilancia*):—late L. **bilancia* a pair of scales, f. cl. L. *bilanx, bilanc-em*, adj. (in *libra bilanx*) 'two-scaled,' f. *bi-* twice + *lanx* flat plate, scale.]

I. Literal senses.

1. An apparatus for weighing, consisting of a beam poised so as to move freely on a central pivot, with a scale pan at each end.

[*c* **1275** in *Liber Albus* I. 226 Deit estre peise par balaunce le Roy. **1297** *Lib. Custum.* 107 (Probatio Tronæ.) Silvester de Farnham custos balanciæ Domini Regis.]

c **1350** *Will. Palerne* 947 Wel y understande whider þe balaunce bowes. *c* **1386** CHAUCER *Monkes T.* 508 And in a balaunce weyen eche mountaine. *c* **1450** in Wright's *Voc.* 227 *Bilanx*, belans. **1494** *Act 11 Hen. VII*, iv, In every City ..should be a common Balance, with common Weights. **1573** BIBLE (Bishops') *Prov.* xvi. 11 A true weight and ballaunce are the Lordes iudgement. **1635** N. CARPENTER *Geog. Del.* I. ii. 31 The Bilanz or Ballance. **1771** *Junius Lett.* lii 266 We incline the balance..by lessening the weight in one scale. **1881** N.T. (Revised) *Rev.* vi. 5 He had a balance in his hand [**1611** a pair of balances].

†**2.** *sing.* One scale of a balance; *pl.* 'scales.' **a.** with pl. *balances. Obs.* or *dial.*

1388 WYCLIF *Ps.* lxii. 9 The sones of men ben liers in balauncis. *a* **1450** *Knt. de la Tour* (1868) 65 Alle her good dedes in the same balaunce..and alle her evelle dedes in that other balaunce. **1596** SPENSER *F.Q.* v. ii. 35 Weighed out in ballaunces. **1611** BIBLE *Rev.* vi. 5 A pair of balances in his hand. **1645** DIGBY *Nat. Bodies* iii. (1658) 19 Take a pinte of air; and weigh it against a pinte of water, and you will see the ballance of the last go down a main.

†**b.** The plural was sometimes *balance.* (Partly due to final *-s, -ce*, partly to confusion of sense.) *Obs.*

c **1430** LYDG. *Min. Poems* 141 Weyed in ballaunce. **1596** SHAKS. *Merch. V.* IV. i. 255 Are there balance heere to weigh the flesh? **1655** FULLER *Ch. Hist.* II. i. §6 I. 138 In one Hand ..a Red Rose, in the other a pair of Ballance.

†**3.** A flat dish resembling a scale; L. *lanx. Obs.*

1513 DOUGLAS *Æneis* XII. iv. 142 Syne furth of platis or ballancis belive, Wyth pasit flesch plenist the altaris.

4. a. One of the zodiacal constellations (more commonly called *Libra*). **b.** The seventh sign of the Zodiac ♎, into which the sun enters at the autumnal equinox.

In the time of Hipparchus, B.C. 130, the *sign* corresponded with the *constellation*, whence the name; but owing to the precession of the equinoxes, its first point is now far in the west of the constellation *Virgo.*

1488 CAXTON *Chast. Goddes Chyld.* 19 A planete that men call libra that is as moche to say as a balaunce. *c* **1500** *Almanak (for* 1386) 2 Saturn es exalted in þe 20 gre of þe Balaunce. **1697** DRYDEN *Virg. Georg.* I. 46 And seated near the Ballance, poise the Days. **1831** CARLYLE *Sart. Res.* II. i, The celestial Balance.

5. By recent extension: Any apparatus used in weighing, whether acting by leverage, or by the resistance of a spring.

1829 U.K.S. *Nat. Philos.* I. *Mech.* II. v. §45 The Danish balance is a steel-yard. **1832** —— II. *Electr.* iv. §74 The most perfect electrometer for measuring very small quantities of electricity, is..the torsion balance.

6. *Watchmaking.* **a.** A mechanical contrivance which regulates the speed of a clock or watch.

1660 BOYLE *New Exp. Phys.-Mech.* xxvii. 206 The noise made by the ballance. **1727** POPE *Bathos* 114 In clock-making one artist makes the balance, another the spring. **1884** F. BRITTEN *Watch & Clockm.* 15 Gold balances are preferable to steel.

†**b.** A pendulum. *Obs. rare.*

1647 H. MORE *Song of Soul* Notes 152/2 The nearer you place the lead to the centre, the swifter the balance moves.

7. *Naut.* The operation or result of reefing with a BALANCE-REEF: see 22.

1762–9 FALCONER *Shipwr.* II. 387 The head, with doubling canvas fenced around, In balance near the lofty peak they bound. **1769** —— *Dict. Marine* (1789) s.v., The balance of the mizen is thus performed.

¶ Confused with BALLAST. (Cf. also BALLACE.)

1548 UDALL, etc. *Erasm. Par. John* 5 No otherwyse than the balans dothe staye the shippes in tyme of tempest. **1656** BLOUNT *Glossogr.*, Balasse, ballast, or ballance.

II. Figurative senses.

8. a. The metaphorical balance of justice, reason, opinion, by which actions and principles are weighed or estimated.

c **1410** HOCCLEVE *Mother of God* 20 The fende..wil pluk at the balance To wey vs doun. **1573** *Scot. Poems 16th C.* (1801) II. 297 Beir equal ballanis baith to riche and puir. **1590** SHAKS. *Mids. N.* v. 324 A Moth wil turne the ballance, which Piramus which Thisby is the better. **1732** POPE *Ess. Man* I. 121 Snatch from his hands the balance and the rod, Rejudge his justice, be the God of God! **1852** TUPPER *Proverb. Philos.* 288 Who..poised in the balances of order the power to attract and to repel?

†**b.** One scale of the balance. *Obs.*

1593 SHAKS. *Rich. II*, III. iv. 87 But in the Ballance of great Bullingbrooke, Besides himselfe, are all the English Peeres. **1635** QUARLES *Embl.* I. iv. (1718) 17 Put in the triple crown Thy balance will not draw: thy balance will not down.

9. The wavering balance of Fortune or chance, in which issues hang in suspense.

c **1320** *Syr Bevis* 1559 Almest is lif was in balaunse. *a* **1420** OCCLEVE *De Reg. Princ.* 60 Best is I strive nat Ageyn the peys of fortunes balaunce. **1577** HOLINSHED *Chron.* I. 34/2 The victorie depended long in doubtfull balance. **1612** WOODALL *Surg. Mate* Wks. (1653) 24 Mens lives hang in the ballance. **1718** POPE *Iliad* XXII. 271 Jove lifts the golden balances, that show The fates of mortal men. **1881** [see HANG *v.* 17 a].

†**10.** Hence: **a.** Subjective uncertainty; hesitation, wavering, doubt. *Obs.*

1297 R. GLOUC. 200 Hii were syker al, wyþoute balance. **1340** *Ayenb.* 30 Hy byeth ine greate balance of hyre helþe of zaule. **1483** CAXTON *G. de la Tour* G viij b, As they were in suche balaunces theyr child deyde. **1683** TEMPLE *Mem.* Wks. 1731 I. 439 Our Counsels at Court were so in ballance, between the Desires of living at least fair with France, and the Fears of too much displeasing the Parliaments.

†**b.** Objective uncertainty or suspense; risk, hazard.

1330 R. BRUNNE *Chron.* 156 Ten þousand mark & mo, þat now er in balance. **1386** CHAUCER *Chan. Yem. Prol. & T.* 58, I dar lay in balaunce Al that I have in my possessioun. *a* **1450** *Knt. de la Tour* (1868) 56 A woman puttithe her worshipe in balance to ansuere and speke to moche. **1523** LD. BERNERS *Froiss.* I. cccxiii. 478 For the loue of me ye haue put in balance your landes. **1685** BURNET tr. *More's Utop.* 129 On whom..they cast the chief Balance of the War.

11. Power to decide or determine; authoritative control.

1393 GOWER *Conf.* III. 381 There is a state..Above all other on erthe here, Which hath the londe in his balaunce. **1579** FENTON *Guicciard.* (1599) Ep. Ded., God hath..put into your hands the ballance of power. **1760** ROBERTSON *Hist. Scot.* I. (1831) 75 Henry viii. of England held the balance with less delicacy, but with a stronger hand.

III. That which balances, or produces equilibrium.

12. A weight put into one scale to equal the preponderating weight in the other, and produce equilibrium; a counterpoise. Hence *fig.* a thing of equal influence, importance, or value; a counter-consideration, set-off, match.

1601 SHAKS. *All's Well* II. iii. 183 To whom I promise A counterpoize: If not to thy estate, A ballance more repleat. **1659** NEVILLE in Burton's *Diary* (1828) IV. 25 You give them salaries to be your balance. **1723** WODROW *Corr.* (1843) III. 75 A sweet balance, yea, an overbalance, in sweet communion with God. **1876** GREEN *Short Hist.* vii. §6 (1882) 404 If France..had ceased to be a balance to Spain, she found a new balance in Flanders.

IV. A balanced condition.

13. A condition in which two (or more) opposing forces balance each other; equilibrium: **a.** of things ponderable.

1713 DERHAM *Phys.-Theol.* 14 *note*, Such Alterations in the æquipoise or ballance of the Atmosphere. **1878** GEO. ELIOT *Coll. Breakf. P.* 283 The balance of the planets and the sun.

b. Of things imponderable.

1642 SIR T. BROWNE *Relig. Med.* II. §1. 136 Where I find their actions in ballance with my Country-men's, I honour ..them. *a* **1718** PENN *Tracts* Wks. 1726 I. 693 Two Degrees of Cold, to two of Heat, make a Poyze in Elements, and a Ballance in Nature. **1869** J. MARTINEAU *Ess.* II. 110 The perfect balance of the two elements of consciousness.

c. *balance of power* (*in Europe*): such an adjustment of power among sovereign states that no single state is in a position to interfere with the independence of the rest; international equilibrium.

[See **1579** in 11: ballance of power.]

1677 YARRANTON *Eng. Impr.* To Reader, Great danger might ensue in breaking the Ballance of Europe. **1701** in *Lond. Gaz.* No. 3758/7 Your Glorious Design of Re-establishing a just Ballance of Power in Europe. **1761** CHURCHILL *Night* Poems I. 88 Europe's balance hangs upon his tongue. **1862** STANLEY *Jew. Ch.* (1877) I. xi. 204 The battle of Lutzen which determined the balance of power between Roman Catholicism and Protestantism in Germany.

d. *balance of nature*, a state of equilibrium in nature produced by the interaction of living organisms; ecological balance.

1909 G. ABBEY (*title*) The balance of nature and modern conditions of cultivation. **1923** H. G. WELLS *Men like Gods* I. vi. 84 But presently he made it clear that there had been something very ancient and beautiful called the 'Balance of Nature' which the scientific methods of Utopia had destroyed. **1933** *Discovery* July 224/2 The interference of man with the balance of nature had almost always brought evil in its train. **1962** H. HANSON *Dict. Ecol.* 41 *Balance of nature*, (Ecological Balance), the state in an Ecosystem when the interrelationships of organisms..are harmonious or integrated to a considerable degree, e.g., a climax forest.

e. Phr. *balance of terror*, balance of power based on the possession of weapons of 'terror', esp. nuclear weapons.

1960 B. M. GOLDWATER *Conscience of Conservative* 91 If war is unthinkable to us but not to them, the famous 'balance of terror' is not a balance at all, but an instrument of blackmail. **1962** *Listener* 29 Mar. 548/1 There are other technical trends which seem to be contributing stability to the balance of terror between the Great Powers. **1962** *Observer* 13 May 15/4 The 'balance of terror' is always in danger of being upset by technical advance (e.g., in anti-missile missiles). **1965** H. KAHN *On Escalation* xiii. 246 A confusing thing about tactics..in a balance-of-terror situation is the great reliance on messages, symbols..and even 'spectacles'.

14. a. General harmony between the parts of anything, springing from the observance of just proportion and relation; esp. in the Arts of Design.

1732 POPE *Ess. Man* II. 120 These mix'd with art..Make and maintain the balance of the mind. **1856** RUSKIN *Mod. Paint.* III. I. viii, In all perfectly beautiful objects, there is found the opposition of one part to another, and a reciprocal balance. **1883** —— *Art of England* i. 11 Absolutely faithful balances of colour and shade. **1884** *Sat. Rev.* 14 June 778 1 She has in no way attempted to alter the balance of the characters [in a play].

b. *spec.* of the arrangement and adjustment of sources of sound; the sound thus produced.

1929 *B.B.C. Year-Bk. 1930* 312 For balance and control ..a volume control handle varies the input to the control amplifier, and consequently the strength passed to the transmitter. **1929** *Melody Maker* Jan. 61/2 Then again balance is bad all over the place; rhythm gets lost, saxophones are often overpowering. **1933** L. E. C. HUGHES *Elem. Engin. Acoustics* vii. 141 As the sensitivities of the two ears are generally different, the balance is again taken with the receivers interchanged. **1941** *B.B.C. Gloss. Broadc. Terms* 4 *Balance*, placing of artists, speakers, or other sources of sound in relation to a microphone or microphones, or vice versa. *Ibid.*, *Balance Test*, test to establish the best balance for a particular broadcast. **1946** *Penguin Music Mag.* Dec. 48 In a *tutti* passage..I am bound to hear the brass to the almost total exclusion of the 'cellos. .. Therefore..we can seldom hear what *you* hear in the matter of the all-important balance. **1962** A. NISBETT *Technique Sound Studio* i. 13 The man responsible for balance, mixing, and control may be a 'balance engineer' or 'programme engineer'.

15. Stability or steadiness due to the equilibrium prevailing between all the forces of any system. **a.** Physical equipoise, perfectly balanced action.

1667 MILTON *P.L.* I. 349 In even ballance down they light. **1840** DICKENS *Old C. Shop* xxiii, Swayed himself to and fro to preserve his balance. **1859** HELPS *Friends in C.* Ser. II. II. viii. 167 But lost his own balance and fell out of the boat.

b. Equipoise of mind, character, or feelings; equanimity, mental composure, sanity.

1856 KANE *Arct. Exp.* I. xvi. 198 If my mind had retained its balance. **1876** MOZLEY *Univ. Serm.* xvi. 266 A strong moral character..keeps its balance, and is not carried away by the love of human praise.

c. *off* or *out of balance.*

1881 G. W. CABLE *Mme Delphine* x. 52 As a banker, at least, he was certainly out of balance. **1954** F. C. AVIS *Boxing Ref. Dict.* 77 *Off balance*, with the weight not properly distributed over the legs, and thus in a dangerous position in regard to an opponent. **1960** E. P. C. COTTER *Tackle Croquet this Way* ix. 61 My opponent's tail was up so I decided to get him off balance if I could. **1962** *Which?* (Car Suppl.) Oct. 137/2 Two had wheels out of balance on delivery.

V. The turn of the balance.

16. The preponderating weight; the net result of estimating conflicting principles, forces, etc.

1747 CHESTERF. *Lett.* 121 I. 327 This pleasure will increase so that the balance will be greatly to your advantage. **1844** LD. BROUGHAM *Brit. Const.* xv. (1862) 219 The balance of evidence appears in favour of the due execution. **1856** FROUDE *Hist. Eng.* (1858) I. iii. 267 In Germany..the balance of unjust interference lay on the imperial side.

VI. The adjustment of accounts.

17. a. The process of finding the difference, if any, between the Dr. and Cr. sides of an account, or set of accounts; the exhibition of this process in a tabular form; the result so ascertained or exhibited.

1588 MELLIS *Briefe Instr.* F viij b, The ballance of your booke is to be vnderstoode, a leafe of paper disposed and made in length and crossed in the middes, etc... Yf the summes of money, of Debitor and Creditor bee like, than is your ballance well. **1662** PEPYS *Diary* 30 Sept., I have also made up..my monthly ballance and find that..I am worth £680. **1727** ARBUTHNOT *John Bull* 90 John..brought in Frog debtor to him upon the balance, £3382 12*s.* **1882** *Daily*

Tel. 4 May, £160,000 has been taken out on balance for export.

b. esp. ***to strike a balance***: to determine the exact difference, if any, between the two sides of an account or set of accounts. *lit.* and *fig.*

1638 Wilkins *New World* I Those rewards and punishments by which..the balance of good and evil in this life is to be struck. **1874** Blackie *Self-Cult.* 87 Not to run long accounts, but to strike clear balances at certain set seasons.

c. *gen.* A comparative reckoning. Phr. ***on balance*** (or ***upon the balance***): taking everything into consideration.

1719 W. Wood *Surv. Trade* 67 This Nation gained upon a Balance of the Ships taken from us, and the Captures we made of the Enemy. **1843** *Ainsworth's Mag.* IV. 308 Upon the 'balance', as the betting men say, women are quite as mercenary as men. **1861** Pycroft *Agony P.* xliii. 364 The blessings of the Langley Cottage, whether greater or less upon the balance, were of a kind not known at Langley Hall. **1928** *Britain's Industr. Future* II. vii. 89 We believe that these provisions would be, on balance, overwhelmingly in the interest of the investor. **1966** *Listener* 6 Jan. 14/2 The impression in India that Britain has tended, on balance, to take the Pakistan side in the Kashmir dispute.

d. ***balance of trade***: the estimation of the difference of value between the commercial exports and imports of a country; the difference itself, as it is in favour of, or against, the country.

1668 Child *Disc. Trade* (1694) 164 The Ballance of Trade ..is to be taken by a strict scrutiny of what proportion the value of the Commodities exported out of this Kingdom bear, to those imported. **1721** C. King *Brit. Merch.* II. 12 Portugal pays us a Million every Year upon the Ballance of Trade. **1830** *Edinb. Encycl.* IV. 370 The exploded doctrine of a balance of trade. **1879** Fawcett *Free Trade & Prot.* 18 Granting bounties on exports..with a view of creating a favourable balance of trade.

e. ***balance of payments***: the estimation of the difference of value between payments into and out of a country. (*Balance of trade* (17 d), i.e. of merchandise, covers the principal items on both sides, but *balance of payments* also includes the 'invisible' items, interest on loans, tourist expenditure, etc.) Also in *attrib.* use.

1844 Mill *Ess. Pol. Econ.* i. 43 The tribute..restores the balance of payments between the two countries. **1863** *New Englander* Jan. 63 The natural effect of all this was to create for the moment a heavy balance of payments against the North. **1931** *Economist* 12 Dec. 1110/2 Study our national balance of payments, in order to see whether..restriction of imports..might..save the pound from..depreciation. **1955** *Times* 10 Sept. 6/6 Mr. Butler,..said that he thought the balance of payments problem was on the whole being kept in hand. **1958** *Listener* 31 July 151/1 So far, pressures on the balance of payments have been met successfully by foreign loans.

18. An equality between the total of the two sides of an account, when added up, after making all entries on both sides. Cf. 13.

165. Pepys *Diary* (1879) IV. 139, I do bring my accounts to a very near balance. **1881** Gladstone in *Times* 8 Oct. 6/4 While we exported £8,860,000, we imported £8,509,000. That is very nearly a balance.

19. a. The difference between the Dr. and Cr. sides of an account, or set of accounts.

1622 Malynes *Anc. Law-Merch.* 370 Take all the remainders of the Accounts by Debitor and Creditor, which is the ballance of the Booke. **1819** J. Greig *Rep. Acc. Edin.* 7 The balance shews the increase of the City's debts. **1866** Crump *Banking* iii. 76 Such arrangements may continue for years without the balance ever being a credit-balance.

b. ***balance*** (***of indebtedness***): the difference between the total amounts which two persons, societies, or nations mutually owe each other.

1786 Burke *Art. agst. Hastings* xv. §1 The enormous balances and remissions on that settlement arose from a general collusion between the farmers and collectors. **1818** Byron *Juan* I. clxvii, We..draw the accompts of evil, And find a deuced balance with the devil. **1866** Crump *Banking* vii. 157 The fundamental principle, upon which the price of bills rests in the 'balance of indebtedness.'

20. a. ***balance*** (***in hand***): the sum of money remaining over after realizing all assets and discharging all liabilities. Also *fig.*, something to spare. **b.** ***balance*** (***due***): the sum still outstanding on an account.

1720 *Lond. Gaz.* No. 5842/4 A Bill for the Ballance of his Victualling Account. **1761** Hume *Hist. Eng.* I. viii. 175 He required him..to pay the balance due. **1768** Smollett *Humph. Cl.* Let. 3 Oct., Thou hast indeed paid me 'scot and lot': and even left a balance in my hands. **1828** Tytler *Hist. Scot.* (1864) I. 221 The large balance of the ransom which still remained unpaid. [**1847** in Thirsk & Imray *Suff. Farming 19th Cent.* (1958) 163, I have written to Mr. Woodley to ask him what amount he will require in his hands to save us from the interest. We have generally had a balance in his hands of £400 or £500.] **1865** [see fork *v.* 5]. **1876** Hamerton *Intell. Life* II. i. 44 A delightful balance at his bankers. **1876** *Coursing Calendar* 5 Wheatear..working with great smartness, won with a nice balance in hand. **1957** *Hampshire Chron.* 3 Aug., At the annual meeting of the Winchester and District Football League..a balance in hand of £1 17*s.* 9*d.* was reported.

21. *Comm. slang*: The remainder, the rest. orig. *U.S.*

1788 in *Pennsylv. Mag. Hist. & Biog.* (1894) XVIII. 62 Arose early and sent off the balance of our things. **1817** S. R. Brown *Western Gaz.* 167 The inhabitants are more than half French; the balance consists of emigrants..from various parts of Europe and America. **1845** S. Judd *Margaret* I. xiii. 96 Deacon Hadlock himself, hearing Obed's entreaties, consented to remit the balance of the penalty. **1875** *Blackw. Mag.* Apr. 443 Balance, long familiar to American ears, is becoming so to ours. In an account of a ship on fire we read 'Those saved remained the balance of the night watching the burning wreck.' **1883** P. Fitzgerald *Recr. Lit. Man* 170 Every one is away shooting or riding; a balance of the ladies is left.

22. *Comb.* **balance-beam**, the beam of a balance, *also* the beam keeping a drawbridge balanced aloft; **balance-bob** (see quot.); **balance-crane** (see quot. 1904); **balance-fish**, the hammer-headed shark (*Squalus zygæna*); **balance-frame** (see quot.); **balance-knife**, a table-knife of which the handle is made sufficiently heavy to keep the blade from touching the cloth; **balance-man**, one who acts as an equipoise and preserves the balance; **balance-master, -mistress**, a posture-maker, tumbler, 'equilibrist'; **balance-reef**, the closest reef of a lower fore-and-aft sail, making it nearly triangular, used to steady the ship in stormy weather, whence ***balance-reefed***; **balance-seat**, a mode of riding in which the body is balanced in the saddle without support from the stirrups; **balance-sheet**, a tabular statement of assets and liabilities, showing the character and amount of the balance; **balance-step** (= goose-step *sb.* b); **balance weight**, a counterpoise weight; **balance-wise** *adv.*, in the manner of a balance; **balance-yard**, the beam of a balance. Also ***balance-holder, -maker***, etc., and many attrib. combinations in *Watchmaking* (see 6), as ***balance-arc, -cock, -spring, -staff, -wheel*** (also *fig.*); also, a similar device on a sewing-machine.

1813 Scott *Triermain* I. xv, The *balance-beams obey'd the blast, And down the trembling drawbridge cast. *c* **1865** J. Wylde in *Circ. Sc.* I. 404/1 Excess of weight..may..damage the *balance-beam. **1838** *Civ. Engin. & Archit. Jrnl.* I. 409/1 The heavy pump rods, *balance bobs &c., attached to a mining engine. **1881** Raymond *Mining Gloss.*, *Balance-bob*, a heavy lever ballasted at one end, and attached at the other to the pump-rod, the weight of which it thus helps to carry. *a* **1877** Knight *Dict. Mech.* I. 212/1 The *balance-cock of a watch affords a bearing for the upper pivot of a watch-balance. **1962** E. Bruton *Dict. Clocks & Watches* 19 *Balance cock*, the cock that holds the bearing, normally a shock absorber, for one end of the balance. **1824** R. Stevenson *Bell Rock Lighthouse* 520 The *Balance-Crane, constructed for building the upper part of the Bell Rock Light-house. **1904** Goodchild & Tweney *Technol. & Sci. Dict.* 136/2 Some heavy weight is fixed..opposite to the point at which the jib is fixed... These arrangements constitute what is called a balance crane. **1683–4** Robinson in *Phil. Trans.* XXIX. 479 The Zygæna or *Ballance Fish, as large as the Saw Fish. **1815** *Encycl. Brit.* XI. 107 Hammer-headed shark, or *balance-fish. *c* **1850** *Rudim. Nav.* 9 *Balance frames, those frames, or bends of timber, of the same capacity or area, which are equally distant from the centre of gravity. **1880** Muirhead *Gaius* II. §107 What has been said about witnesses applies equally to the *balance-holder. **1833** J. Holland *Manuf. Metal* II. 14 The fabrication of what are called *balance knives. **1611** Cotgr., *Balancier*, a *ballance-maker. **1828** Steuart *Planter's G.* 251 Sending up a couple of *Balancemen to the top; who..serve as movable makeweights. **1753** Hogarth *Anal. Beauty* xv. 210 The *balance-master's attention to a single point, in order to preserve his balance. **1801** Strutt *Sp. & Past.* III. v. (1845) 231 Tymbesteres, or *balance-mistresses. **1782** P. Freneau *Misc. Works* (1788) 387 What he calls single, double, and *balance-reef *eyelet holes.* **1794** D. Steel *Rigging & Seamanship* I. 86 *Balance-reef*, a reef-band that crosses a sail diagonally, and is used to contract it in a storm. **1840** J. F. Cooper *Pathfinder* II. v. 184 By half-past two he had put a balance-reef in the sail. **1840** R. Dana *Bef. Mast* v. 10 Under close-reefed topsails, *balance-reefed trysail. **1873** *Daily News* 21 May 5/6 That patent hernia-producing institution, the *balance-seat. **1849** Cobden *Speeches* 4 The *balance-sheets of our merchants and manufacturers have been equally adverse. **1838** *U.S. Mag. & Democr. Rev.* I. 42 He becomes familiar..with trial balances, *balance sheets, [etc.]. **1853** (13 Oct.) Bright *Peace, Sp.* (1876) 462 If a balance-sheet could be shown of what Algeria has cost France. **1833** *Regul. Instr. Cavalry* I. 16 The *balance step in double time. **1884** F. Britten *Watch & Clockm.* 246 The *balance spring has then to be unpinned every time the *balance staff is removed. **1690** *Lond. Gaz.* No. 2550/4 A Silver *Ballance-Watch. **1824** R. Stevenson *Bell Rock Lighthouse* v. 296 The upright shaft of the new crane was to be kept in an erect position by a *balance-weight acting upon the opposite end of the loaded working-beam. **1862** *Catal. Internat. Exhib.* II. x. 21 The cage returning to the upper floor for a fresh load by means of a balance weight. **1960** J. G. Horner *Dict. Mech. Engin.* (ed. 8) 19 The weights placed in the driving-wheels of locomotives are termed balance weights. **1747** *Encycl. Brit.* XVIII. 806/1 The *balance-wheel obliges the balance to vibrate backwards and forwards like a pendulum. **1958** M. E. Burton *Lett. M. Wordsworth* p. xxviii, Mary often chooses to remain behind. She is the balance-wheel. **1961** *Which?* Nov. 277 (*diagram*) Balance wheel [of a sewing-machine]. **1655** Mrq. Worc. *Cent. Inv.* xx, How to bring up water *Balance-wise. **1669** *Phil. Trans.* IV. 937 Watches, which instead of a *Ballance-wheele are regulated by a Pendulum. **1863** Mrs. C. Clarke *Shaks. Char.* viii. 212 Fabian..is the *balance-wheel between the other two, to keep them in check. **1810** Coleridge *Friend* (1865) 35 The other scale..seemed full up to the very *balance-yard.

balance ('bæləns), *v.* [a. F. *balancer*, f. *balance* sb. (Like the sb., in certain senses confused with *ballast*.)]

I. To place or weigh in the scales. Chiefly *fig.*

1. *trans.* To weigh (a matter); to estimate the two aspects or sides of anything; to ponder.

1694 R. Lestrange *Fables* ccccv. 436 We Weigh and Ballance things before we pronounce them to be either Good or Evil. **1775** Sheridan *Rivals* III. i, Weighing and balancing what you were pleased to mention. **1847** Tennyson *Princ.* III. 149 She balanced this a little, And told me she would answer us to-day.

2. To weigh two things, considerations, etc., against each other, so as to ascertain which preponderates.

1596 Spenser *F.Q.* v. ii. 31 Then would he ballaunce heaven and hell together. **1629** R. Hill *Pathw. Piety* II. 137 Christ..is balanced with Barabbas, and thought lighter than a murderer. **1736** Butler *Anal.* I. iii. 47 To weigh and balance Pleasures and Uneasinesses. **1875** Grindon *Life* i. 1 Truth..is determined by balancing probabilities. **1883** Gilmour *Mongols* xviii. 216 His good and bad actions are balanced against each other.

3. To counterbalance or counterpoise one thing *by*, *with*, or *against* another.

1624 Ld. Kensington in Ellis *Orig. Lett.* I. 301 III. 173 That the honor of the Prince..might be deerer to her then to be balanced with that which, etc. **1625** Bacon *Ess.* (1862) 154 Another meanes to curbe them, is to Ballance them by others, as Proud as they. **1850** Ruskin *Mod. Paint.* III. §i. viii, A mass of subdued colour may be balanced by a point of a powerful one. **1860** Pusey *Min. Proph.* 47 The self-same wisdom which balanced Egypt against Assyria. **1884** *American* VII. 345 To balance asymmetrically-placed entrance-doors with lobsided windows.

4. To bring to or keep in equilibrium. *spec.* of sources of sound (cf. balance *sb.* 14 b).

1634 Habington *Castara* 47 That Kings, to ballance true content, shall say: Would they were great as we, we blest as they. **1738** Pope *Epil. Sat.* I. 60 Did not the sneer of more impartial men At sense and virtue balance all again. **1810** Coleridge *Friend* (1865) 81 On which it may fix its attention, and thus balance its own energies. **1853** Brimley *Ess.* 282 [The painter] may fail to balance his masses. **1928** *B.B.C. Handbk. 1929* 68 A..new design of control room has been decided upon, wherein effects, echoes, background music, etc. can be mixed together and so balanced by a specially-trained operator. **1933** L. E. C. Hughes *Elem. Engin. Acoustics* vii. 141 The..method is to accept the calibration curve of a moving-coil receiver, and to balance their output when supplied by a constant note. **1962** A. Nisbett *Technique Sound Studio* ii. 48 Completely dead sound is difficult to balance. *Ibid.* iii. 52 When balancing music there is..no clear-cut set of rules.

5. a. To steady (a body under the influence of opposing forces); to poise, keep steady or erect.

1840 Dickens *Old C. Shop* xiii, Strong men..balancing chests of drawers..upon their heads. **1875** Buckland *Log-Bk.* 54 Sculptors are sometimes obliged to use a species of tail in balancing their statues.

b. *refl.* and *intr.* To keep oneself in equilibrium.

1833 *Regul. Instr. Cavalry* I. 15 The Instructor will..make the recruit balance upon the left foot. **1866** Howells *Venet. Life* iv. 58 Balanced herself half over the balcony-rail.

6. To steady, give (mental) balance or ballast to.

1685 Baxter *Paraphr. N.T.* 1 Tim. iii. 6 Young, raw Christians..have had less time to learn the great things which should ballance them. [See balanced *ppl. a.* 3.]

II. To act as things in the opposite scales of a balance; *lit.* and *fig.*

7. *trans.* To equal in weight, counterpoise, neutralize the weight of. Also *absol.* to balance (each other).

a **1727** Newton (J.) The attraction of the glass is balanced ..by the contrary attraction of the liquor. **1878** Huxley *Physiogr.* 91 The column of water..balances the atmospheric pressure. *Mod.* Do these scales balance?

8. *Hence*: To compensate, neutralize the effect of, make up for.

a **1593** Marlowe *Dido* III. iv, I saw no King like thee, Whose golden crown might balance my content. **1655** Fuller *Ch. Hist.* VI. ii. §57 III. 292 Wherefore, to ballance the Protestants, the Jesuits were set on foot. **1726** Butler *Serm. Rolls Chap.* v. 90 So many things..balance the Sorrow of it. **1837** J. H. Newman *Par. Serm.* I. xxiv. 358 Our duties balance each other. **1870** Morris *Earthly Par.* I. I. 384 And weariness was balanced with delight.

9. *intr.* To act as a counterpoise, be equal (*with*).

1579 Beard *Theat. Gods Judgm.* (1612) 539 Could such a punishment ballance with his so..great offences?

III. To oscillate like the beam of a balance.

10. *intr.* To waver, deliberate, hesitate. Cf. 1.

1655 Earl Orrery *Parthen.* (1676) 628 Her great danger ..invited my assistance, which, without balancing, I ran to pay her. **1753** Richardson *Grandison* (1781) II. xxvi. 246 He had..no very strong aspirations after matrimony, and had balanced about it a good while. **1825** R. Ward *Tremaine* I. v. 37 Mrs. Belson balanced some time upon this, as any good mother would. **1850** Merivale *Rom. Emp.* (1865) I. ix. 373 The same disposition to balance and temporize.. wrecked his fortunes as a statesman.

11. Of partners in dancing: To move to and fro in converse directions like the arms of a balance, to *set to* a partner.

1775 Sheridan *Rivals* III. iv. (1883) 113, I must rub up my balancing, and chasing, and boring. **1859** in Worcester.

12. *trans.* To sway backwards and forwards.

1728 Pope *Dunc.* III. 200 Tuning his voice and balancing his hands.

IV. Of an account. *lit.* and *fig.*

13. *trans.* To add up the debit and credit sides of an account or set of accounts, and ascertain the difference, if any, between their respective amounts.

1588 Mellis *Briefe Instr.* E vij, At your viages returne.. ballance vp the bookes. **1724** Swift *Drapier's Lett.* Wks.

1755 V. II. 130 To compute and balance my gain and my loss. **1796** BURKE *Corr.* (1844) IV. 383 Thus we balance the account;—defeat and dishonour abroad; oppression at home. *a* **1842** TENNYSON *Audley Crt.* 43 'Oh! who would cast and balance at a desk?'

14. a. To make such entries in an account or set of accounts as make the two sides equal; to produce an equality in the total amounts of the debit and credit entries of a set of accounts.

b. In this sense, also, accounts are said (intr.) *to balance* (i.e. themselves); or an entry is said to *balance the account*, or *balance* an opposite entry.

1622 MALYNES *Anc. Law-Merch.* 371 And if he had beene a loser by the Account of profit and losse, then must he make his Capitall Debtor, and the said Account Creditor, to ballance the matter. **1675** GREGORY in Rigaud *Corr. Sci. Men* II. 276, I cannot perceive how the balance balanceth the book. **1748** ANSON *Voy.* III. viii. 373 The happy crisis which was to ballance the account of all their past calamities. **1878** JEVONS *Prin. Pol. Econ.* 52 To make the profits of the successful business balance the losses of the unfortunate ones.

15. *Hence*: To settle (an account) by paying an amount due, to clear off a liability

1740 CIBBER *Apol.* (1756) I. 142 The end of the season, when dues to ballance came too thick upon 'em. **1877** H. PAGE *De Quincey* II. xvi. 20 A cheque for £30, to balance his account.

V. 16. *Naut.* To reef with a balance-reef, so as to steady the ship in bad weather: see BALANCE *sb.* 22. Perhaps originally *ballast*.

[Cf. **1697** DAMPIER *Voy.* (1729) I. 414 We furl'd our Main-sail, and ballasted our Mizen.] **1762–9** FALCONER *Shipwr.* II. 460 The balanced mizen, rending to the head. **1769** —— *Dict. Marine* (1789), s.v., A boom main-sail is balanced, after all its reefs are taken in, by rolling up..the aftmost lower corner.

¶**17.** To ballast. *Obs. rare.* Cf. BALANCE *sb.* 7¶.

1583 STUBBES *Anat. Abus.* (1836) 202 There is no ship so balanced with massie matter as their heades are fraught with all kinde of baudie songes. [Cf. **1769** FALCONER *Dict. Marine* (1789) *Upper-work*..that part of a ship which is above the surface of the water when she is properly balanced for a sea-voyage.]

‖**balancé** (balɑ̃se). [Abbrev. of F. *pas balancé*, lit. 'balanced step'.] A dance step, now spec. in *Ballet*, comprising a swaying movement from one foot to the other; hence (see quot. 1847) the quality implicit in the step, sinuosity.

[**1728** J. ESSEX tr. *Rameau's Dancing Master* xxiv. 57, I have seen many Persons make Balances in dancing a Menuet.] *c* **1770** G.-A. GALLINI *Crit. Obs. Art Dancing* 5 Le Balancé. This is done by Sinking, then Rising as you Step forward or sideways with one foot. **1786** S. J. GARDINER *Def. Minuet-Dancing* 54 The steps generally made use of in Cotillions are Balancé, Rigodon. **1847** R. BARTON tr. *Blasis's Notes upon Dancing* I. 49 The steps are to be remarked for their *balancé*, lightness, grace, and elasticity. **1952** KERSLEY & SINCLAIR *Dict. Ballet Terms* 11 *Balancé*, a rocking step in waltz-rhythm..can also be done swaying backwards and forwards instead of from side to side.

balanceable ('bælənsəb(ə)l), *a.* [f. BALANCE *v.* + -ABLE.] Capable of being balanced.

1667 WATERHOUSE *Fire Lond.* 3 Great successes..which they judge no otherwise ballanceable than by this spoil.

balanced ('bælənst), *ppl. a.* [f. as prec. + -ED.]

1. *lit.* **a.** Poised; so arranged, placed, or adjusted with a counterpoise, as to remain in equilibrium.

1611 COTGR., *Balancé*, Ballanced, weighed, peised. **1667** MILTON *P.L.* IV. 1000 The pendulous round Earth with ballanc't Aire In counterpoise. **1814** SCOTT *Ld. of Isles* III. xv, Loose crags..chance-poised and balanced, lay.

b. *spec.* Of a rudder or of the control surface of an aeroplane: see quots.

1869 *Daily News* 12 June, The Cerberus has a balanced rudder. **1874** S. J. P. THEARLE *Naval Archit.* (Adv. Sci. ser.) IV. xx. 340 The balanced rudder revolves about an axis so situated that about two-thirds the area of the rudder is on the aft, and the remaining one-third on the fore side of the axis. **1920** *Flight* 5 Aug. 867/2 The aeronautical engineer needs some simple rule for the design of balanced control surfaces. **1922** *Flight* XIV. 344/1 Balanced ailerons are fitted to the top plane only. *Ibid.* The tail plains [*sic*]..consist of ..two balanced elevators hinged to the stabiliser, and a balanced rudder. **1950** *Gloss. Aeronaut. Terms (B.S.I.)* I. 34 *Balanced surface*, a control surface in which the aerodynamic hinge moment opposing rotation has been reduced by so shaping it that part of the surface is forward of the hinge, or by fitting it to a balance tab, or by other means.

2. Having the opposed parts or tendencies so adjusted as to produce equilibrium or equality.

1592 DANIEL *Compl. Rosam.* (1717) 47 Thus stood I ballanc'd equally precise, Till my frail Flesh did weigh me down to Sin. **1727** SWIFT *Balance Eur.* Wks. 1755 III. II. 128 Now Europe's balanc'd, neither side prevails. **1870** JEBB *Sophocles' Electra* Introd. 10 Contending and almost balanced claims. **1877** RUSKIN *Laws Fesole* I. ii, Every system is imperfect which pays more than a balanced and equitable attention to any one of the three skills.

3. a. Well arranged or disposed; stable in character by due proportion of parts.

1624 QUARLES *Sion's Sonn.* (1717) 349 The ruby portals of thy ballanc'd words Send forth a welcome relish. **1836** J. GILBERT *Chr. Atonem.* iii. (1852) 60 Neither can it..operate with any weight upon a justly balanced mind. **1878** T. SINCLAIR *Mount* 83 The birth of a balanced artist.

b. spec. *Dietetics.* Containing a suitable proportion of each type of nutriment required for adequate nutrition.

1908 *Sci. Amer.* Suppl. 24 Oct. 267/2 The early summer dinner..of lamb and peas with a salad, bread and butter, and a little fruit perhaps, makes a good example of a well-balanced meal. **1912** *Delineator* LXXX. 45 Problem of supplying a properly balanced menu. **1917** *Ladies' Home Jrnl.* Nov. 56/2 She can't understand what is meant by a 'balanced meal'. **1936** *Discovery* Apr. 98/2 A balanced diet, not merely a copious one is indicated.

4. *Logic.* (See quot.)

1849 ABP. THOMSON *Laws Th.* §71 The middle [term] is said to be balanced when it is distributed in both premisses alike. The extremes of the conclusion are balanced when both alike are distributed. **1870** BOWEN *Logic* viii. 258 Moods..balanced as respects both Terms and Propositions.

5. *Naut.* Reefed with a balance-reef (see BALANCE *v.* 16).

1750 in *Essex* (Salem, Mass.) *Inst. Hist. Coll.* (1910) XLVI. 96 We were obliged to hand the jibb and lay too under ballanced mainsail. **1762–9** [see BALANCE *v.* 16]. **1802** A. ELLICOTT *Jrnl.* 26 Nov. (1803) 256 We had to heave too under a balanced main-sail.

6. Other *techn.* uses.

1902 G. S. NEWTH *Text-Bk. Inorg. Chem.* (ed. 9) I. x. 88 Reactions of this order are known as reversible or balanced actions. **1904** GOODCHILD & TWENEY *Technol. & Sci. Dict.* 38/1 *Balanced Steps*, the method of arranging the steps of geometrical stairs to increase the going (width) at the small ends of the winders, and to give a better falling line to the handrail. **1918** W. H. ECCLES *Wireless Teleg.* (ed. 2) 489 *Balanced Detectors*, a term applied to an arrangement of opposed rectifying detectors for reducing the effects of strong Xs in receiving apparatus. **1924** ROGET *Dict. Electr. Terms* 17/1 *Balanced load*, a load in a three-wire system which is equally shared by the two sides, or in a polyphase system, where it is equally shared by the various phases. *Ibid.*, Balanced modulator. **1929** WILSON & WEBB *Mod. Gramophones & Electr. Reproducers* ix. 180 There is no permanent magnetic pull on the armature when no signal is passing through the coil. This type is therefore known as a 'balanced armature'. **1930** PHILLIPS & TUTT *Mod. Gas Fitting* xi. 341 The 'Balance' radiator is so called in that the air inlet and combustion products outlets are made continuous and 'balanced'. **1933** EDGCUMBE & OCKENDEN *Indust. Electr. Measuring Instr.* xiii. 279 A strictly 'balanced' circuit is one in which the currents, voltages, and phase displacements are the same for each phase. **1938** FRITSCH & SALISBURY *Plant Form & Function* v. 49 A mixture of ions in solution in such proportions that they exert no toxic effect is called a *balanced solution.* **1940** L. HARTSHORN *Radio Freq. Meas.* iii. 48 The potential of one terminal is always as much above that of the screen (earth) as that of the other is below it. This is known as the balanced condition. **1944** *Hackh's Chem. Dict.* (ed. 3) 96/1 *Balanced reaction*, a reaction which can be made to proceed in either direction by variation of either temperature, pressure or concentration of the reactants. **1955** *Archit. Rev.* CXVII. 93/2 Balanced-flue gas heaters are provided in the kitchens and serve the sink, lavatory basin and bath.

balancement ('bælənsmənt). *rare.* [f. as prec. + -MENT.] The action of balancing; a balanced condition; equilibrium, equipoise.

1862 R. PATTERSON *Ess. Hist. & A.* 332 Sacrificing a complete balancement of parts for the sake of obtaining variety.

balancer ('bælənsə(r)). [f. as prec. + -ER[1]; cf. AF. *balancer*, OF. *balancier*.]

†**1.** One who weighs with a balance. *Obs. rare.*

[**1309** *Hustings Rolls Lond.* No. 38. 102 Ralph le Balancer, Pepperer. **1320** *Ibid.* No. 49. 1 Le Balauncer.] **1413** LYDG. *Pylgr. Sowle* I. xxxiv. (1859) 37 Neyeng toward the balaunce ..she sayd to the balauncer; How is it in oure partye? **1611** COTGR., *Balanceur*, a ballancer; a weigher of things in a ballance.

2. One who balances himself in difficult positions; a tumbler, acrobat.

c **1510** *Cocke Lorelles B.* 10 Balancers, tynne casters, and skryueners. **1785** REID *Int. Powers* IV. iv, The feats of balancers and rope dancers. **1841** DE QUINCEY *Rhet.* (1860) 355 Posture-maker or balancer.

3. One who keeps things in equilibrium, or maintains the balance of power.

1731 A. HILL *Adv. Poets* xxxi, Ballancers of State. **1795** *Scots Mag.* LVII. 884/2 A republican balancer of Europe, which the new republic would be.

4. Something which helps to preserve the balance; *spec.* the knobbed filaments (*haltēres* or *poisers*), which in two-winged flies replace the posterior wings, a name given (in F.) by Réaumur from their resemblance to the *balancier* used in coining. In technical uses (see quots.).

1753 CHAMBERS *Cycl. Supp.*, *Ballancers*..under the wings of the two-winged flies. **1854** OWEN in *Circ. Sc.* Org. Nat. II. 56/1 In the long-bodied..abdominal fishes, the ventrals ..subserve the office of accessory balancers. **1863** WOOD *Illustr. Nat. Hist.* III. 554 The..halteres or balancers..are the only vestiges of the hinder pair of wings. **1904** S. P. THOMPSON *Dynamo-Electric Mach.* (ed. 7) I. 775 Uses of Motor-Generator Combinations... Equalization of voltages in a 3-wire or 5-wire system of distribution; in which case, the apparatus is termed a Balancer. **1923** *Daily Mail* 17 Feb. 4 The Lanchester balancer incorporated with the five-bearing crankshaft... The balancer consists of two weighted drums driven by a helical gear wheel fixed to a web of the crankshaft. They revolve at twice the crankshaft's speed and ensure its perfect balance and harmony.

5. balancer mash, meal, a supplementary food for poultry (see quot. 1951).

1950 A. CHRISTIE *Murder is Announced* i. 15 [She] was conscientiously stirring in handfuls of balancer meal to a.. basin full of cooked potato peelings. **1951** W. P. BLOUNT *Hen Batteries* viii. 122 *Balancer Meal* is not a complete feed in itself. It is intended to provide those main nutrients (proteins) deficient in ordinary household scraps. **1955** *Pract. Poultry Keeping* (ed. 5) viii. 61 A grain balancer mash should be used for this form of feeding and may be the same as for dry mash.

balancing ('bælənsɪŋ), *vbl. sb.* [f. BALANCE *v.* + -ING[1].] The action of the vb. BALANCE.

1. *lit.* Weighing, poising; acrobatic posturing.

1599 SANDYS *Europæ Spec.* (1632) 162 The Arts of Alchymy and Ballancing. **1674** N. FAIRFAX *Bulk & Selv.* 76 The wheels and springs or ballancings of Nature. **1801** STRUTT *Sports & Past.* III. v. 190 Tumbling, and balancing ..exhibited by the gleemen. **1883** PAYN *Thicker than W.* I. 181 Beginning to lose confidence in his balancing pole upon this very high rope.

2. *fig.* Pondering, consideration, critical comparison.

1666 TILLOTSON *Rule Faith* II. iii. §10 Exact balancing of every particular word. **1739** HUME *Hum. Nat.* II. ii. (1874) I. 339 Objections and replies, and ballancing of arguments.

3. Hesitation between opposing considerations; uncertainty.

1598 BACON *Faction, Ess.* (Arb.) 80 When Matters haue stucke long in ballancing. **1817** FOSTER *Life & Corr.* (1846) I. cv. 465, I am in a great state of doubt and balancing. **1884** *Harper's Mag.* Jan. 189/1 Balancings between Torquay and Madeira.

4. The placing of one thing over against another as in a balance, compensation; reduction to equilibrium, proportionate adjustment.

1612 TRAVERS *Supplic.* in Hooker *Eccl. Pol.* II. 656 So unequal a balancing of faults and punishments. **1647** W. BROWNE *Polex.* ¶iiij a, Knowing not how to reward an action that was beyond all ballancing. **1860** MILL *Repr. Govt.* (1865) 87/2 This balancing of evil by evil. **1884** *Pall Mall G.* 23 Feb. 4/1 There was [no] finer balancing of mental and moral gifts than in Mr. Cobden.

5. Comparison, or equalization, of the credit and debit totals of an account.

1668 WILKINS *Real Char.* II. i. §5. 41 Ballancing, Evening of Accounts. **1721** C. KING *Brit. Merch.* II. 10 By such a Ballancing of Accounts. **1803** *Edin. Rev.* II. 16 The balancing system.

6. Oscillation about a position of equilibrium.

1868 LOCKYER *Heavens* 457 A top..undergoes also a balancing of its axis of figure or rotation, analogous to the oscillations of the Earth.

'**balancing,** *ppl. a.* [f. as prec. + -ING[2].]

1. Weighing, pondering; hesitating.

1850 MAURICE *Mor. & Met. Phil.* vii. §5. 228 Cicero..had a singularly equitable, balancing, compromising nature.

2. Producing equilibrium, compensating.

1645 W. GOODE *Publ. Spir.* A ij b, That Ballancing providence of our most wise God. **1849** RUSKIN *Sev. Lamps* iv. §26 Buildings are generally bad which have large balancing features at the extremities. **1854** H. MILLER *Sch. & Schm.* iii. (1857) 42 Though there were..no trees, there were some balancing advantages.

3. Acrobatic.

1801 STRUTT *Sports & Past.* III. v. 190 Tumbling and balancing women.

‖**balandra** (bə'lændrə). [Sp.; cf. BILANDER.] A small coasting vessel.

1845 DARWIN *Voy. Nat.* vii. (1873) 134 A balandra, or one-masted vessel of about a hundred tons' burden.

balanid ('bælənɪd). *Zool.* [f. BALAN-US + -ID.] A member of the *Balanidæ* or Acorn-shells.

1836 TODD *Cycl. Anat. & Phys.* I. 685/1 The shells of the Balanids present several striking peculiarities of structure.

balaniferous (bælə'nɪfərəs), *a.* [f. L. *balanus* acorn + -(I)FEROUS; cf. F. *balanifère*.] Acorn-bearing.

1881 in *Syd. Soc. Lex.*

balanite ('bælənaɪt). [ad. L. *balanītes*, a. Gr. βαλανίτης acorn-shaped, f. βάλανος acorn.]

†**1.** A kind of precious stone. *Obs.*

1598 SYLVESTER *Du Bartas* (1608) 462 Beset with Bal'nites, rubies, chrysolites. [**1601** HOLLAND *Pliny* XXXVII. x. II. 625 As for the stone Balanites, there be two kinds..of a greenish colour, and resembling Corinth brasse. **1753** CHAMBERS *Cycl. Supp.*, Some think the *balanites* to have been the *lapis judaicus*.]

2. A fossil balanid.

1835 KIRBY *Hab. & Inst. Anim.* xiii, The second Order of Cirripedes consists of the Balanites or Acorn-barnacles.

balanitis (bælə'naɪtɪs). *Path.* and *Vet. Sci.* [mod.L., a. Gr. βάλανος acorn + -ITIS.] Inflammation of the glans penis in mammals.

1853 in MAYNE *Expos. Lex.* **1871** *Med. Times* (Philad.) *1870–71* I. 397 (*title*) Balanitis. **1879** *Syd. Soc. Lex.* I, *Balanitis*, inflammation of the surface of the glans penis, with purulent discharge. It may be simple or gonorrhœal. **1881** *Trans. Internat. Med. Congr. 1881* III. 142 Professor Kaposi, Vienna, mentioned that..diabetic patients are disposed to balanitis. **1922** R. LEIGHTON *Compl. Bk. Dog* xxii. 344 There are few troubles of the genital organs that need attention in either dog or bitch. What is called *Balanitis* is a slight running of pus from the organ of the male. **1955** GAIGER & DAVIES *Vet. Path. & Bacteriol.* (ed. 4) xxv. 684 Balanitis, or inflammation of the mucous membrane covering the glans penis and lining the prepuce, is not infrequently met with in animals.

balanoid ('bælənɔɪd), *a.* and *sb.* [ad. Gr. βαλανοειδής, f. βάλανος acorn: see -OID.] **A.** *adj.* Acorn-shaped. **B.** *sb.* An acorn-shell or balanid.

1869 NICHOLSON *Zool.* (1880) xxxi. 291 The Balanoids are shallow-water forms. **1881** in *Syd. Soc. Lex.*

†**'balant**, *a. Obs.* [ad. L. *bālāntem*, pr. pple. of *bālāre* to bleat.] Bleating, baaing.
1702 C. MATHER *Magn. Christi* VII. App. (1852) 620 The balant and latrant noises of that sort of people.

‖**balanus** ('bælənəs). [L., a. Gr. *βάλανος* acorn.] = ACORN-SHELL.
1727–41 in CHAMBERS *Cycl.* **1839** RIDDELL in *Proc. Berw. Nat. Club* I. VII. 197 May and June.. when the young Balani are most numerous.

balao (bə'laʊ, ‖balao). Also **ballaho(o**, etc. [Sp.] The half-beak.
1854–5 *Trans. Jamaica Soc. Arts* I. 144 Hæmirhamphus Braziliensis, Ballahoo. **1858** DE VERTEUIL *Trinidad* 448 *Hemiramphus.* 1 species (s).. (s) Balaou. *Ibid.* 451 The balaou and gar-fish are commonly caught at night by torch-light, or with the seine. **1867** T. F. DE VOE *Market Assistant* 199 There are likewise to be caught in the winter season, fish, by towing over this bank, if a person has suitable bait, such as the *ballaho*, which they have generally in the West Indies. **1893** *Funk's Stand. Dict.*, *Balahoo* (W. Ind.), a halfbeak. **1896** JORDAN & EVERMANN *Fishes N. Amer.* I. 723 *Hemirhamphus balao*... If a valid species, this must be the original *balaó*, which is said to have the caudal bluish, and the common species will stand as *H. brasiliensis.* **1898** MORRIS *Austral Eng.* 16/1 *Ballahoo*, a name applied to the *Garfish*.. by Sydney fishermen. The word is West Indian, and is applied there to a fast-sailing schooner; also spelled *Bullahoo* and *Ballahou.* **1922** *Outing* (U.S.) Mar. 253/1 For sail and other large fish they use a sardine-sized, sword-nosed minnow called a ballyhoo. **1949** *Esquire* Mar. 81/6 Bait—mullet, squid, balao, [etc.].

balas ('bæləs). Forms: 5– **balas**; also 5 **balace, -ase, -ess, -is, -eys,** 6 **bales, -ays, ballass, -ais,** 6–8 **balasse,** 6–9 **balass, ballas,** 7 **-ase, -eys, balais,** (**ballest**). [a. OF. *balais, balai*, cogn. with Pr. *balays, balach*, It. *balascio*, Sp. *balax*, med.L. *balascus* (Marco Polo), *balascius, -asius*, ad. Arab. *balakhsh*, f. Pers. *Badakhshān*, the district near Sarmacand where they are found.] A delicate rose-red variety of the spinel ruby.
1434 *Test. Ebor.* (1836) I. 363 Unum annulum de auro, cum uno balase. **1423** JAS. I. *King's Q.* II. xxvii, Grete balas lemyng as the fyre. **1439** *E.E. Wills* (1882) 118 My Noych with my Baleys. **1494** FABYAN VII. 540 Dyamantys, rubyes and balessys. **1577** HOLINSHED *Chron.* III. 801/1 A great bauderike about his necke of great balasses. **1877** W. JONES *Finger-ring L.* 247 Sapphires, balasses, diamonds.
b. Now usually ***balas-ruby***.
1596 DANETT *Comines Hist. Fr.* (1614) 279 Fowerteene Rubies ballais. **1611** COTGR., *Ballay*, a balleys Rubie. **1623** JAS. I. in *Four C. Eng. Lett.* 46 The collar of great ballest rubies. **1822** SCOTT *Nigel* v, A carcanet of large balas rubies. **1874** WESTROPP *Prec. Stones* 18 The balas ruby is of a delicate rose-pink colour, showing a blue tint when looked through.

balase, -ass, *sb.* and *v.*, intermediate forms due to confusion of BALANCE and BALLAST.
1609 BIBLE (Douay) *Ezek.* xlv. 11 According to the measure of a core shal be the equal balassing of them. **1656** BLOUNT *Glossogr.*, *Balasse, ballast* or *ballance*.. any thing of weight laid in the bottom of Ships to make them go upright.

balastre, balastriar: see BALIST-.

balata ('bælətə). Also 9 **ballata.** [S. Amer. Sp., prob. ad. a native word. So Fr. (1777).]
1. Any of several trees of Guiana and the W. Indies belonging to the family Sapotaceæ, esp. *Mimusops balata*. Also ***balata-tree***.
1858 DE VERTEUIL *Trinidad* 101 Balata (*Mimusops*). The Balata, or Bullet-wood, is one of our best and most useful timbers. **1860** *Jrnl. Soc. Arts* 24 Aug. 713/2 It appears also that the *Sapota Mulleri*, the tree producing the gutta percha of Surinam, is called Balata in French Guiana, Les Antilles, and elsewhere. **1864** GRISEBACH *Flora Brit. W. Ind. Isl.* 781 Ballata tree (Dominica): *Bumelia retusa.* **1871** KINGSLEY *At Last* I. vi. 223 A huge dark-headed Balata [*note* Mimusops Balata]. *Ibid.* vii. 257 (*page-heading*) The Balata Tree. **1922** W. SCHLICH *Man. Forestry* (ed. 4) I. II. 322 *Mimusops globosa*, the Balata, go to 120 feet high.
2. The dried juice or gum of *Mimusops balata*, used as a substitute for gutta-percha. Also *attrib.* and *Comb.*
1860 *Jrnl. Soc. Arts* 24 Aug. 713/2 A few months ago it was announced in the French journals that M. Serres, Pharmacien, at Paris, had been so fortunate as to prepare gutta percha from the Balatas of the sapotaceous plants in Guiana and Central America. **1862** *Catal. Contrib. Brit. Guiana to Internat. Exhib.* in R. Duff *Br. Guiana* (1866) 99 The leaves, branches, and trunk [of the bully tree] produce a whitish milk, forming the gum, now known as ballata. **1864** W. HOLMES in *Jrnl. Soc. Arts* 4 Mar. 245/2, I believe ..that *Balata*..will supply the great want of the day, as a good insulating medium for telegraphic purposes. **1867** W. T. VENESS *El Dorado* ix. 94 The ballata-gatherer..may thus bleed a great many trees in a single day. **1939** *Nature* 12 Aug. 300/2 Thus a polymerhomologous series of celluloses exists and the same holds also for starch, glycogen, caoutchouc and balata. **1958** J. CAREW *Wild Coast* iv. 51 He had left the balata fields. *Ibid.* 52 He was carrying a heavy balata-coated canvas bag. **1959** *B.S.I. News* June 10/2 Rubber-textile and balata-textile belting in many varieties..is extensively used for power transmission of all kinds.

†**'balatron, -oon.** *Obs. rare.* [ad. L. *balatrōnem* (= *blaterōnem*) babbler, prater, buffoon.] A buffoon, a contemptible fellow.
1623 COCKERAM, *Ballatron*, a rascally base knaue. **1678** MRS. BEHN *Sir P. Fancy* v. i. 303 The affront this Balatroon has offer'd me.

balatronic (bælə'trɒnɪk), *a.* [f. L. *balatrōnem* (see prec.) + -IC.] Of or pertaining to buffoons.
1883 SALA *Illust. Lond. News* 10 Nov. 451 Students of the Balatronic dialect who..keep..an interleaved copy of the Slang Dictionary.

‖**balausta** (bə'lɔːstə). *Bot.* [mod.L. (Linn.); cf. next.] The fruit of the pomegranate.
1842 in BRANDE *Dict. Art & Sc.* **1870** BENTLEY *Bot.* 315 The Balausta is an inferior, many-celled, many-seeded, indehiscent fruit, with a tough pericarp.

balaustine (bə'lɔːstɪn). Also 7 **balaustin,** 8 **-ian.** [ad. Gr. *βαλαύστιον* (in same sense), or subst. use of an adj. formed from it.] The red rose-like flower of the wild pomegranate, which, when dried, is used in medicine as an astringent.
1671 SALMON *Syn. Med.* III. lxxxii. 716 Decoction of Balaustins. **1728** LEWIS in *Phil. Trans.* XXXV 490 Astringent Drugs, as Galls, Oak-Leaves and Balaustians. **1757** WALKER *ibid.* L. 121 A tincture of balaustine-flowers. **1839** in HOOPER *Med. Dict.*

†**ba'lausty.** *Obs.* Also 6 **balastye.** [ad. L. *balaustium*, a. Gr. *βαλαίστιον*.] = prec.
1541 R. COPLAND *Guydon's Quest. Cyrurg.*, A playster of Bolarmynyke, galles, balastye, and other that staunche blode. **1612** WOODALL *Surg. Mate* Wks. (1653) 181 Balausties, which are flowers of Pomegranats.

‖**balayeuse** (balɛjøːz). *Dressmaking.* [Fr., fem. of *balayeur* sweeper.] (See quot. 1882.)
1882 CAULFEILD & SAWARD *Dict. Needlework*, *Balayeuse, or Sweeper.*—A French term to signify the frilling of material or lace which lines the extreme edge of a dress skirt to keep the train clean as it sweeps along the floor. The balayeuse is allowed to project beyond the edge of the dress, so as to form a decorative as well as a useful trimming. **1894** *Daily News* 20 Jan. 5/7 Three flounces of..silk forming a richly-rustling balayeuse beneath the hem.

balayne, balays, obs. ff. BALEEN, BALAS (ruby).

Balbriggan (bæl'brɪgən). The name of a town in Ireland, applied *attrib.* to a knitted cotton fabric manufactured there, used in hose, underwear, etc.; also to other products, and *ellipt.*
1859 G. A. SALA *Tw. round Clock* (1861) 128 A white hat with a black band, surmounting a rough coat, cord trousers, and Balbriggan boots. **1885** *Queen* 24 Oct. (Advt.), Ladies' Stockings... In Balbriggan (fourteen qualities). **1887** R. DENNIS *Industr. Irel.* ix. 104 Hosiery..is well described as having 'slipped away' from Ireland—save perhaps in the solitary instance of the Balbriggan hose, which is still in great demand. **1910** *Encycl. Brit.* III. 242/1 The town has considerable manufactures of cottons and hosiery, 'Balbriggan hose' being well known. **1922** JOYCE *Ulysses* 291 High Balbriggan buskins. **1928** A. CHRISTIE *Myst. Blue Train* xxx. 251 With a pair of good Balbriggan stockings on and sensible shoes. **1941** H. ASBURY *Underworld of Chicago* 272 Two suits of heavy underwear, one of wool and one of balbriggan.

balbutiate (bæl'bjuːʃɪeɪt), *v.* Also (badly) **balbucinate.** [f. L. *balbūtī-re* to stammer + -ATE[3]; cf. F. *balbutier*.] To stammer or stutter.
1731 in BAILEY; and in mod. Dicts.

balbutient (bæl'bjuːʃɪənt), *a.* [ad. L. *balbūtient-em*: see prec.] Stammering, stuttering.
1642 H. MORE *Song of Soul* III. III. xxiv, I have with tongue balbutient Prattled to th' weaker ear. **1678** CUDWORTH *Intell. Syst.* I. iv. §18. 316 Speech..that is but imperfect, balbutient and inarticulate.

‖**balbuties** (bæl'bjuːʃiːz). *Med.* [mod.L., f. *balbūtīre*.] Stammering, stuttering; lisping.
1655 CULPEPPER *Riverius* v. iv. 127 Balbuties, a kind of Stammering, which keepeth men from pronouncing of the Letter R. **1859** WORCESTER, *Balbuties*, stammering; vicious pronunciation, in which *b* and *l* are substituted for other consonants.

†**balcon.** *Obs. rare*[−1]. [f. F., Sp., or Pr. *balcon* = It. *balcone*: see BALCONY.] = BALCONY.
1635 J. HAYWARD *Banish'd Virg.* 142 Lights in all their balcons. **1665** PEPYS *Diary*, 1 June, We..stood in the balcon.

balconette (bælkə'nɛt). [f. BALCON-Y + -ETTE.] A miniature balcony.
1876 T. HARDY *Hand Ethelb.* II. xlviii. 273 A timber-built cottage, having ornamental barge-boards, balconettes, and porch.

balconied ('bælkənɪd), *ppl. a.* [f. next + -ED[2].] Furnished with a balcony or balconies.
a **1733** NORTH *Exam.* III. vii. 86 The House was double balconied in Front. **1869** MRS. WHITNEY *Hitherto* xliv, That pleasant, high, balconied room.

balcony ('bælkənɪ). Forms: 7 **balcone, -ona, -onia, -onie, -onee, belcony, -ey, bellcony, -ey,** 7– **balcony.** [a. It. *balcōne* (= F., Pr., Sp. *balcon*, Pg. *balcão*), formed with augmentative suffix *-one* from It. *balco, palco*, scaffold, a. OHG. *balcho, palcho* (= mod.G. *balken*, Eng. *balk*) a beam. Till *c* 1825 the pronunc. was regularly bæl'kəʊnɪ; but 'bælkənɪ (once in Swift), 'which,' said Samuel Rogers, 'makes me sick,' is now established.]
1. A kind of platform projecting from the wall of a house or room, supported by pillars, brackets, or consoles, and enclosed by a balustrade.
1618 HOLYDAY *Juvenal* 223 It was properly a balcone, and so the building it self did jetty out. **1633** G. HERBERT *World* ii. in *Temple* 76 Then Pleasure came, who liking not the fashion, Began to make Balcones, Terraces. **1640** BROME *Sparagus Gard.* III. iv. 159 Squinting up at Windowes and Belconies. **1727** SWIFT *Tom Clinch* Misc. (1735) V. 145 The Maids to the Doors and the Balconies ran, And said, lack-a-day! he's a proper young Man. **1783** COWPER *Gilpin* 142 At Edmonton his loving wife From the balcony spied Her tender husband. **1817** BYRON *Beppo* xi, And like so many Venuses of Titian's They look when leaning over the balcony, Or stepp'd from out a picture by Giorgione. **1832** TENNYSON *Mariana in S.* viii, Backward the lattice-blind she flung, and lean'd upon the balcony. **1845** BROWNING *Fl. Duchess* §15. 505 To breathe the fresh air from the Balcony.
fig. **1650** B. *Discollim.* 2 First to the Title..Next to the Belcony or Preamble.
2. The similar structure at the stern of large ships.
1666 PEPYS *Diary* (1879) IV. 143 A very good ship, but with galleries quite round the sterne like a balcone. *c* **1850** *Rudim. Nav.* (Weale) 94 *Balcony*, the gallery in the stern of large ships.
3. In theatres: †**a.** *formerly*, A stage-box. **b.** *now*, (generally) The open part above the dress circle, between that and the 'gallery.' In Music Halls and other public buildings, variously applied, according to structure.
1718 *Rem. Rochester* 106 Fairly in public he plays out his Game, Betimes bespeaks Balconies. **1883** *Harper's Mag.* Nov. 882/2 The three tiers of boxes and the balcony of which the auditorium consists.
4. *attrib.*, as in ***balcony-chamber, -door, -window.***
1635 *Althorp MS.* in Simpkinson *Washingtons* Introd. 70 Tymber for the balconia doores. **1636** LAUD in *4th Rep. Com. Hist. MSS.* (1874) 153/2 A balconee window and a stair-case. **1800** COLERIDGE *Piccolomini* I. vi, Why was the balcony-chamber countermanded?

‖**bal costumé** (bal kostyme). [Fr., lit. 'costumed ball'.] A fancy-dress ball.
1826 M. WILMOT *Let.* 29 Feb. (1935) 234 Our Ambassadrice had plann'd to give a ball costume early in the Carnival. **1848** G. E. JEWSBURY *Let.* 4 Oct. (1892) 256 Dandified 'Church-of-Englandism', which bears the same relation to 'the Church' that a polite assemblage of ladies and gentlemen at a 'bal costumé' bears to the countries after which they have dressed themselves. **1861** G. DU MAURIER *Let.* [Jan.] in D. du Maurier *Young G. du M.* (1951) 30 On the 14th there is going to be a grand bal costumé..—150 or 200 people. **1896** BEERBOHM *Dandies* in *Wks.* 20 The clinquant corslet of the Swiss girl just survives at *bals costumés*.

bald (bɔːld), *a.* Forms: 3–5 **ballede,** 4–5 **balled, -yd, -id, -it,** 5 **belde, bellyde,** 5–7 **balde,** 6 **baulde,** 7 **bal'd, ball'd,** 8–9 *Sc.* **beld,** 6– **bald.** [ME. *balled*, of uncertain origin; in sense 1, apparently a ppl. form from BALL *v.* or *sb.*, with the sense of 'protuberant or rounded like a ball,' whence possibly 'smooth,' and, as applied to the head, 'hairless.' But the analogy of many words for 'bald' in various langs., in which the sense arises out of that of 'shining, white,' or esp. that of 'having a white patch on the forehead,' as in 'bald-faced stag,' 'bald-coot,' with the actual appearance of this sense in BALL *sb.*[2], strongly favours the idea that ME. *ball-ed* was a derivative of the latter (cf. also BALLARD), which is with evident propriety referred to Welsh *bàl*, as explained under sense 5. The chief difficulty is the rarity of the simple *ball*, and lack of early instances to prove its Eng. use before the appearance of *ball-ed*. For the termination, Sievers compares OE. *-ede* (OS. *-odi*) used esp. of bodily defects, as in *heal-ede* ruptured, *hofer-ede* hunchbacked, etc.
Cf. the analogy of MDu. *blaer* 'bald' and *blare*, Du. *blaar* 'white patch on the forehead' of a horse, etc.; also of MHG. *blas* 'bald,' earlier 'shining,' and *blasse* 'white patch on the forehead'; also of Du. *bles* 'bald' and *blesse*; and see *blas* in Grimm; also Wedgwood and Skeat. Cf. also Gr. *φαλακρός* 'bald,' lit. 'white- or shining-pated.' There seems little ground for the suggestion of Kluge that *balled* represents a lost OE. **bællod* = **bærlod*, Goth. **bazloþs*, from OTeut. *baz-oz* BARE.]
I. Literal senses.
†**1.** ? Rotund, of full habit, corpulent. *Obs.*
1297 R. GLOUC. 377 Suyþe þycke man he was..Gret womede & ballede. *Ibid.* 429 Ballede he was, & þycke of breste, of body vat also. [Cf. also BOLLED.]
2. a. Having no hair on some part of the head where it would naturally grow; hairless.
c **1386** CHAUCER *Prol.* 198 His heed was ballid, and schon as eny glas. **1387** TREVISA *Higden* Rolls Ser. III. 285 A balled fortop [*recalva fronte*]. **1398** —— *Barth. De P.R.* v. iv. (1495) 108 The formeste partye of the heede wexyth soone balde. **1474** CAXTON *Chesse* 55 Julius Cesar was ballyd wherof he had displaisir. **1483** *Cath. Angl.* 27 To make belde (*v.r.* bellyde), *decaluere.* **1590** SHAKS. *Com. Err.* II. ii. 70 The plaine bald pate of Father time himselfe. **1691** *Lond. Gaz.* No. 2724/4 Wears his own Hair but ball'd on the fore part of his Head. **1794** BURNS *J. Anderson*, But now your brow is

beld, John. **1870** GEO. ELIOT *Middlem.* I. v, Dreadful to see the skin of his bald head moving about.

b. *fig.* esp. in reference to the necessity of 'seizing time *by the forelock*.'

c **1590** MARLOWE *Jew of M.* v. ii, Begin betimes; Occasion's bald behind; Slip not thine opportunity. **1606** DEKKER *Sev. Sins* VI. (Arb.) 40 Thy Inhabitants Shaue their Consciences so close, that in the ende they growe balde, and bring foorth no goodnesse. **1663** BP. PATRICK *Parab. Pilgr.* 259 They let those opportunities grow old..and suffer them to be bald before they mind to apprehend them.

3. Without hair (feathers, etc.) on other parts of the body than the head.

c **1340** *Cursor M.* (Fairf.) 3490 þe first was borne [Esau] was rughe of hare, þe toþer childe was ballede [*Cott.* smeth, *Gött.* sleyht, *Trin.* sleiȝte] and bare. **1607** TOPSELL *Four-f. Beasts* 407 Beavers..have been found bald on the back. **1640** W. HODGSON *Div. Cosmogr.* 97 Eagles moult off their feathers, and so become bald. **1771** BARRINGTON in *Phil. Trans.* LXII. 6, I..do not find that their [Rabbits'] ears are balder than those of a Hare.

4. *transf.* Without the usual or natural covering (in various senses): **a.** Of trees, mountains, etc.: Leafless, treeless, barren, bare. **b.** Of cloth: Napless. **c.** Of wheat, grain, etc.: Awnless, beardless. †**d.** Of persons: Bare-headed. **e.** Of eyes: Lidless, staring.

1600 SHAKS. *A.Y.L.* IV. iii. 106 An old Oake, whose bows were moss'd with age, And high top bald with drie antiquitie. **1607** —— *Cor.* IV. v. 206 The Senators..stand bald before him. **1610** —— *Temp.* IV. 238 Now Ierkin you are like to lose your haire, & proue a bald Ierkin. **1642** FULLER *Holy & Prof. St.* III. vii. 166 Where a place is bald of wood. *c* **1800** COLERIDGE *Chamouni*, Thy bald, awful head, O sovran Blanc! **1804** J. ROBERTS *Pennsylv. Farmer* 114 What kind is the most productive,..bearded or bald? **1809** J. BARLOW *Columb.* III. 414 The bald eyes [of a dead tiger] glare, the paws depend below. **1840** C. F. HOFFMAN *Greyslaer* I. x. 116 There's a ledge of bald rock to the left yonder. **1856** *Trans. Mich. Agric. Soc.* VII. 805 He..raises ..the old-fashioned bald or bearded wheat. **1872** E. EGGLESTON *End of World* xli. 257 A large bald hill overlooking the Ohio was to be the mount of ascension. **1878** TENNYSON *Q. Mary* I. i. 7 Fray'd i' the knees, and out at elbow, and bald o' the back. **1919** *Chambers's Jrnl.* Oct. 654/1 Egyptian cotton-seed..is devoid of these short fibres, and hence is commonly termed 'bald' seed. **1946** R. S. THOMAS *Stones of Field* 14 The bald Welsh hills.

f. Of a tyre: having a worn tread. *colloq.*

[**1938** *Amer. Speech* XIII. 308/1 [Bus drivers] *Bald-headed tires*, tires, the tread of which is worn off and the white fabric shows through.] **1958** *Motor* 1 Jan. 868/1 An elderly, thin, tyre that has grown bald in its master's service. **1962** *Observer* 21 Jan. 38/3 The insurance company would not pay for the damage because his tyres were bald. **1970** *Toronto Daily Star* 24 Sept. 39/1 The National Bureau of Standards [of U.S.A.]..defined 'bald' to mean a tire with one-sixteenth of an inch of tread or less. **1984** *Times* 20 Oct. 3/1 Basra was stopped by the police for a bald tyre while driving home from work.

5. Streaked or marked with white. [Cf. Welsh *ceffyl bàl* a horse with a white streak or mark on the face (F. *cheval belle-face*), where *bàl* may be an adj., or a sb. construed as a genitive.]

[**1594** BARNFIELD *Aff. Sheph.* I. xxviii, I haue a pie-bald Curre to hunt the Hare.] **1690** *Lond. Gaz.* No. 2575/4 A black Mare with 3 white Feet, and a bald Face. **1711** *Ibid.* No. 4848/4 Strayed..a black bald Gelding.

II. Figurative. (Cf. SLIGHT *a.* and G. *blasz.*)

6. Bare or destitute of meaning or force; lacking in pregnant import or vividness of description; meagre, trivial, paltry.

1362 LANGL. *P. Pl.* A. XI. 41 And Bringeþ forþ Ballede Resouns. **1581** J. BELL *Haddon's Answ. Osor.* 428 b, What a bald devise is this of the man? **1593** NASHE *Christ's T.* 63 b, Had rather heare a iarring black-sant, then one of theyr balde sermons. **1791** BOSWELL *Johnson* 8 Apr. 1775, Tom Davies repeated, in a very bald manner, the story of Dr. Johnson's first repartee to me. **1817** COLERIDGE *Biog. Lit.* 224 The meaning dwindles into some bald truism.

7. Bare or destitute of ornament and grace; unadorned, meagrely simple: **a.** of literary style.

1589 NASHE *Anat. Absurd.* 22 Bald affected eloquence. **1693** W. ROBERTSON *Phraseol. Gen.* 1365 Translated word for word..into bald Latine. **1851** BRIMLEY *Ess.* 123 To translate into bald prose those high-coloured and nobly musical passages of the Prelude.

b. of works of art, buildings, etc.

1825 LD. COCKBURN *Mem.* 286 In towns the great modern object has..been..to reduce everything to the dullest and baldest uniformity. **1850** TENNYSON *In Mem.* vii, Thro' the drizzling rain On the bald street breaks the blank day.

8. Undisguised, palpable, evident.

1854 G. ABBOTT *Napoleon* II. xviii. 343 Admitted, in all its bald baseness. **1870** LOWELL *Among Bks.* Ser. II. (1873) 314 A bald egotism which is quite above and beyond selfishness.

III. *Comb.*, chiefly parasynthetic deriv., as ***bald-crowned*** (sense 2), ***-nosed*** (sense 5). See also BALD-COOT, -FACED, EAGLE, -HEAD, -PATE, -RIB, and *bald* BUZZARD, KITE, LOCUST, etc.

1689 *Ibid.* 2503/4 A brown Gelding..bald Nosed. **1716** *Ibid.* 5494/4 A..well-set Man, bald-crowned.

†**bald** (bɔːld). *v. Obs.* [f. prec.] To make bald. deprive of hair. *lit.* and *fig.*

1602 FULBECKE *Pandects* 78 In Germany they vse to cut off the heare of an adultresse..I haue seene some of them balded here in Englande. **1628** FELTHAM *Resolves* I. iv. (1647) 9 While..Winter bald's the shag-hair'd wood.

bald, *sb.* [f. BALD *a.*] **1.** A mountain summit or region naturally bare of forest, esp. in the southern Appalachians. *U.S.*

1838 *Southern Lit. Messenger* IV. 231/2 We came to the top of the near Bald. **1885** 'C. E. CRADDOCK' *Prophet Gt. Smoky Mts.* i. 2 She paused often, and looked idly..at the great 'bald' of the mountain. **1943** R. PEATTIE et al. *Great Smokies* 154 Aboriginally, the Appalachian forests were vast in extent, clothing the mountains, except for the 'balds', from top to bottom.

2. A species of domestic pigeon; = BALD-HEAD (quot. 1867).

1854 *Poultry Chron.* I. 21/2 For the best pair of Balds or Beards. **1876** R. FULTON *Illustr. Bk. Pigeons* xi. 172 There are plenty of the pleasant-faced Balds which are all that could be desired in colour and marking. *Ibid.* 173 The Bald has so many white flights in each wing.

bald, early and north. form of BOLD.

baldachin, -quin (ˈbældəkɪn). Forms: 6-8 baldakin(e, 7 balduquino, 7-9 baldacchino, 8-9 baldachin, 9 -chine, -chino, baldaquin: see also BAUDEKIN. [a. F., Sp. *baldaquin*, It. *baldacchino*, in med.L. *baldakinus*, *-ekinus*, *baudaquinus*, *-ekinus*, f. *Baldacco*, It. form of *Bagdad*, the city in Asia where the material was made. Cf. the earlier BAUDEKIN, through OF. *baudekin, -quin*, usual in sense 1. The It. form *baldacchino* is also used.]

1. A rich embroidered stuff, originally woven with woof of silk and warp of gold thread; rich brocade.

1598 HAKLUYT *Voy.* I. 54 They weare Jackets..of buckeram, skarlet, or Baldakines. **1753** CHAMBERS *Cycl. Supp.*, *Baldachin*, or Baldakin, or Baldekin, popularly Baudekin..a rich kind of cloth. **1880** YULE in Birdwood *Ind. Arts* II. 71 Rich silk and gold brocades were called Baldachini, or in English, Baudekins.

2. A structure in the form of a canopy, either supported on columns, suspended from the roof, or projecting from the wall, placed above an altar, throne, or door-way; so called as having been originally of the material described in prec. sense.

1645 EVELYN *Mem.* (1857) I. 110 The room..having a state or balduquino of crimson velvet. *Ibid.* 145 An elevated throne, and a baldacchino, or canopy of state..over it. **1848** THACKERAY *Van. Fair* xlviii, The baldaquin of St. Peter's. **1850** BROWNING *Christm. Eve*, Heave loftier yet the baldachin. **1878** LADY HERBERT tr. *Hübner's Trav.* I. xii. 182 Heavy clouds shroud the tops of the mountains as with a baldachino.

ˈbaldachined, *a.* [f. BALDACHIN *sb.* 2 + -ED².] Canopied, covered with a baldachin.

1906 B'NESS VON HUTTEN *What became of Pam* vi. 150 In her baldachined bed with the bestarred silk curtains. **1914** T. HARDY *Satires of Circumstance* 157 The God with the baldachined altar overhead. **1966** AUDEN *About House* 42 An Emperor's baldachined..couch.

†**ˈbaldare.** *Obs. rare*⁻¹. [Cf. dial. *balder* vb. 'to use coarse language' Halliw., and Du. *balder-en* to roar, thunder: see also BALDERDASH.] Din, uproarious noise.

1583 STANYHURST *Æneis* IV. 108 Theire brayns vnquieted with this baldare be buzing [*ea cura quietos sollicitat*].

bald-coot. Also (*metri gratiâ*) baldicoot. Popular name for the Coot (*Fulica atra*), from its pure white wide frontal plate, destitute of feathers. Used fig. and contemptuously as = BALD-HEAD. Cf. COOT *sb.*¹ 2.

a **1300** W. DE BIBLESW. in Wright's *Voc.* 165 *Une blarye* (*glossed*) a balled cote. **1616** BEAUM. & FL. *Knt. Malta* I. i, Unfledge them of their..perriwigs, And they appear like bald-cootes, in the nest. **1802** in G. MONTAGU *Ornith. Dict.* **1823** BYRON *Juan* XIV. lxxxiii, The bald-coot bully, Alexander. **1848** KINGSLEY *Saint's Trag.* III. iv. 176 Your princesses, that..demean themselves to hob and nob with these black baldicoots [*i.e.* monks with shaven crowns]!

bald eagle, bald-eagle. *U.S.* [BALD *a.* 2.] The American eagle. (Cf. EAGLE *sb.* 1 b.)

1688 in *Phil. Trans. 1693* (1694) XVII. 989 The Second is the Bald Eagle, for the Body and part of the Neck being of a dark brown, the upper part of the Neck and Head is covered with a white sort of Down, whereby it looks very bald, whence it is so named. **1705** BEVERLEY *Virginia* II. 35 The Bald-Eagle no sooner perceives a Hawk that has taken his Prey, but he immediately pursues. **1803** [see EAGLE *sb.* 1 b]. **1868** *Amer. Naturalist* II. 194 So cautious is he lest the Bald-eagle (*Haliaetus leucocephalus*)..may approach. **1878** J. H. BEADLE *Western Wilds* xxx. 483 Small is the pleasure one can take..in the sweep of the bald eagle.

balden (ˈbɔːld(ə)n), *v.* [f. BALD *a.* + -EN.] **a.** *trans.* To make bald. **b.** *intr.* To become bald. Hence **baldening** *ppl. a.*

1883 MISS BROUGHTON *Belinda* II. III. iii. 7 Old, sparse, colourless hair, thriftily drawn across the baldening crown.

Balder, -ur. [ON. *Baldr*, cogn. w. OE. *baldor*, *bealdor* hero, prince, f. *bald*: see BOLD.] Name of a Scandinavian deity, occurring in certain plant-names:— **Balder-herb** (*Amaranthus hypochondriacus*); **Balder brae, Balder's brae, Baldeyebrow** [ON. *Baldrs-brá*] (*Anthemis Cotula*). See also BALDMONEY and BADDERLOCKS.

1552 HULOET, *Baldar herbe.* **1770** BP. PERCY *Mallet's N. Antiq.* (Bohn) 417 Thou may'st have some idea of the beauty of his hair when I tell thee that the whitest of all plants is called Baldur's brow.

balderdash (ˈbɔːldədæʃ), *sb.* [Etymology unknown: see below.]

†**1.** ? Froth or frothy liquid. *Obs.*

1596 NASHE *Saffron Walden* To Rdr. 11 Two blunderkins, hauing their braines stuft with nought but balder-dash. **1599** —— *Lent. Stuffe* 8 They would no more ..have their heads washed with his bubbly spume or barbers balderdash.

†**2.** A jumbled mixture of liquors, *e.g.* of milk and beer, beer and wine, brandy and mineral waters. *Obs.*

1611 CHAPMAN *May-day* III. Dram. Wks. 1873 II. 374 S'fut winesucker, what have you fild vs heere? baldre-dash? **1629** B. JONSON *New Inn* I. ii, Beer or butter-milk, mingled together..It is against my free-hold..To drink such balder-dash. **1637** J. TAYLOR (Water P.) *Drink & Welc.* (Worc.), Beer, by a mixture of wine hath lost both name and nature, and is called balderdash. **1693** W. ROBERTSON *Phraseol. Gen.* 198 Balderdash; of drink; *Mixta Potio.*

b. attrib. **1641** HEYWOOD *Reader, here you'll, etc.* 6 Where sope hath fayl'd without, Balderdash wines within will worke no doubt. **1680** *Revenge* v. 68 Ballderdash Wine.

3. *transf.* A senseless jumble of words; nonsense, trash, spoken or written.

1674 MARVELL *Reh. Transp.* II. 243 Did ever Divine rattle out such prophane Balderdash! **1721** AMHERST *Terræ Fil.* 257 Trap's second-brew'd balderdash runs thus: Pyrrhus tells you, etc. **1812** *Edin. Rev.* XX. 419 The balderdash which men must talk at popular meetings. **1849** MACAULAY *Hist. Eng.* I. 351, I am almost ashamed to quote such nauseous balderdash. **1854** THACKERAY *Newcomes* I. 10 To defile the ears of young boys with this wicked balderdash. **1865** CARLYLE *Fredk. Gt.* II. VII. v. 287 No end of florid inflated tautologic ornamental balderdash.

4. *dial.* Filthy, obscene language or writing.

[Cf. 1849 and 1854 in 3.]

[From the evidence at present, the inference is that the current sense was transferred from 1 or 2, either with the notion of 'frothy talk,' or of 'a senseless farrago' or 'jumble of words.' Most etymologists have however assumed 3 to be the original sense, and sought its explanation in the obvious similarity of *balder* to dial. *balder* 'to use coarse language,' Du. *balderen* 'to roar, thunder,' Norwegian *baldra*, Icel. *baldrast, ballrast* 'to make a clatter,' and of *-dash* to the vb. *dash* in various senses. The Welsh *baldorddus* adj., f. *baldordd* 'idle noisy talk, chatter,' has also been adduced. Malone conjectured a reference to 'the froth and foam made by barbers in *dashing* their *balls* backward and forward in hot water.' Other conjectures may be found in Wedgwood, Skeat, and E. Müller. Cf. also BALDUCTUM.]

ˈbalderdash, *v.* [f. prec. sb.] To make a jumbled mixture of (liquors); to mix *with* inferior ingredients, to adulterate.

1674 in D'URFEY *Pills* (1872) III. 304 When Thames was balderdashed with Tweed. **1730** MANDEVILLE *Hypochond. Dis.* 279 (L.) Wine or brandy..balderdashed with two or three sorts of simple waters. **1771** SMOLLETT *Humph. Cl.* (1815) 143 Wine..a vile, unpalatable, and pernicious sophistication, balderdashed with cider, corn-spirit, and the juice of sloes.

fig. **1714** MILBOURNE *Traitor's Rew.* Pref., Was ever God's word so balderdash'd? **1821** W. IRVING in Warner *Life* (1882) 136 A fostered growth of poetry and romance, and balderdashed with false sentiment.

bald-face. *U.S.* [BALD *a.* 2.] **1.** The widgeon (also called *bald-head, -pate*).

1709 J. LAWSON *New Voy. Carolina* 151 The bald or white Faces are a good Fowl. *Marg.* Bald-Faces. **1768** WASHINGTON *Diaries* (1925) I. 253 Went a ducking between breakfast and dinner and killd 2 Mallards and 5 bald faces.

2. A variety of whisky. *slang.*

1840 *Daily Pennant* (St. Louis) 28 Apr. (Th.), He called lustily for a horn of bald-face and molasses. **1848** *Knickerbocker* XXXII. 402 What is classically denominated 'bald-face', or old brown whiskey. **1872** SCHELE DE VERE *Americanisms* 581 *Bald-face*, one of the many slang terms under which bad whiskey passes in the West.

ˈbald-faced, *a.* [BALD *a.*] Having a bald face.

1648 in *Archives of Maryland* (1887) IV. 425 A Bawld-facd heighfer. **1677** *Lond. Gaz.* No. 1237/4 A sorrel Mare.. bald-faced, and but one eye. **1861** *Trans. Ill. Agric. Soc.* IV. 341 The nest of our bald-faced hornet is occasionally suspended in a house to kill off the house-flies. **1885** *Century Mag.* Nov. 60/2 He jogged along on his bald-faced bay in the bleak untempered light.

ˈbald-head. [f. BALD *a.*] One who has a bald head; also *attrib.*; *transf.* a kind of pigeon.

1535 COVERDALE *2 Kings* ii. 23 Come vp here thou balde heade [WYCLIF, ballard]. **1820** KEATS *Lamia* II. 245 The bald-head philosopher. **1821** BYRON *Foscari* III. i. 244 Held in the bondage of ten bald-heads. **1855** *Poultry Chron.* III. 491/2 Mr. Woodhouse will show his Crested Bald-head. **1867** TEGETMEIER *Pigeons* xi. 123 A pair of common Tumblers..such as Bald-heads.

bald-headed, *a.* **a.** = BALD *a.* ***bald-headed eagle***, the bald eagle.

1580 HOLLYBAND *Treas. Fr. Tong.*, *Chauve par devant*, baldheaded. **1632** MASSINGER *City Mad.* IV. ii, Thy proper and bald-headed coachman. **1829** J. MACTAGGART *Three Years in Canada* I. 22, I had seen a couple of bald-headed eagles the day before. **1836** M. A. HOLLEY *Texas* v. 100 The bald-headed eagle and the Mexican eagle..are very common. **1863** KEMBLE *Resid. Georgia* 68 A magnificent bald-headed eagle. **1935** *Times Lit. Suppl.* 28 Mar. 214/2 The subject..is the bald-headed eagle..the original of 'Uncle Sam's bird'.

b. colloq. phr. (orig. *U.S.*) ***to go bald-headed*** (*into, for, at*), to stake everything, to disregard consequences, to attack without care or thought; also ***to go it bald-headed***. Hence **bald-'headedly** *adv.* (in similar sense).
1848 LOWELL *Biglow P.* Ser. I. vi. 79 'Pious editor' x, I scent wich pays the best, an' then Go into it baldheaded. **1867** *Ibid.* Ser. II. Introd., 'To go it bald-headed': in great haste, as where one rushes out without his hat. **1888** *Pall Mall Gaz.* 22 June 4/2 The Chicago Republicans, to use an Americanism, have gone 'baldheaded' for Protection. **1915** W. J. GORDON *Flags of World* 77 Warburg, where the colonel of the Blues, the Marquis of Granby, after a high trot of five miles led them hatless in the charge, 'going bald-headed for the enemy', and thus originated the well-known phrase. **1920** W. J. LOCKE *House of Baltazar* v. 61 Quong Ho..tried..zealously, then desperately, then bald-headedly, but never a wild blow could pass the easy guard of his smiling master. **1942** R. G. COLLINGWOOD *New Leviathan* 116 A sensible man does not go bald-headed into a brain-twister. **1960** M. STEWART *My Brother Michael* xiv. 180 You went bald-headed for the poor chap.

balding, *a.* [f. BALD *a.* + -ING².] Going bald.
1938 *Time* 5 Dec. 12 He crams a golf cap on his balding grey head. **1941** *Time* 25 Aug. 43/1 Moonfaced, balding, bespectacled, Mort broods a great deal about his health. **1951** M. DICKENS *My Turn to make Tea* v. 91 A balding man in an evening suit. **1958** *Times* 8 Oct. 6/5 The quintessentially balding lodger in raincoat and bowler.

baldish ('bɔːldɪʃ), *a.* [f. BALD *a.* + -ISH.] Somewhat or a little bald.
1833 in *Byron's Wks.* (1846) 742/1 The Emperor Alexander was baldish. **1878** H. JAMES *Europeans* I. iii. 93 He has a baldish head.

baldly ('bɔːldlɪ), *adv.* [f. BALD *a.* + -LY².] In a bald manner; meagrely; nakedly.
1603 HOLLAND *Plutarch's Mor.* 1057 (R.) They do allegorize but very baldly. **1863** KINGLAKE *Crimea* (1877) II. xiv. 236 They did not state baldly what they had ascertained.

baldmoney ('bɔːldmʌnɪ). *Herb.* Forms: 4 **baldemoin**, 5 **-moyn**, 6 **baldmoyne**, 7 **baldimonie**, **-emony**, **baudmoney**, 8 **baldmonie**, 6– **baldmoney**. [Etymol. unknown; the early forms point to a Fr. **baudemoin(e*; with the termination cf. *agrimony*, F. *aigremoine*; but this hardly answers to L. *valde bona*, a plant mentioned in the Great Herbal: see Prior *Names of Plants*. The modern explanation *Balder's money* is a baseless conjecture.]
†**1.** Gentian, of various species. *Obs.*
1393 GOWER *Conf.* I. 99 Loke, how a seke man for his hele Taketh baldemoin with canele. *c* **1440** *Promp. Parv.* 22/1 Baldemoyn (*v.r.* baldmony, baldemonye), *Genciana*. **1597** GERARD *Herbal* II. c. §4 (1633) 352 Gentian is named in English Felwoort Gentian; Bitterwoort; Baldmoyne, and Baldmoney. **1863** MISS YONGE *Chr. Names* II. ii. 209.
2. An umbelliferous plant (*Meum athamanticum*), with yellowish flowers, the root of which is eaten in the Scottish Highlands as a carminative.
1598 FLORIO, *Meo*..the herbe spignell, mew, beare-woort or baldmoney. **1690** RAY *Synop. Stirp.*, Spignel or Mew. In Westmorland..it is known to all the Country People by the name of *Bald-Money*, or (as they pronounce it) *Bawd-Money*. **1861** MISS PRATT *Flower. Pl.* III. 49 Mew or Baldmoney..is pleasantly and powerfully aromatic.

'baldness. [f. BALD *a.* + -NESS.]
1. Absence or loss of hair, *esp.* from the head.
1382 WYCLIF *Deut.* xiv. 1 3e shulen not kut, ne make ballidnes [**1388** ballidnesse, **1535** COVERD. baldnesse.] **1398** TREVISA *Barth. De P.R.* VI. xxi, 3if mete is to skarse, it..bredeþ ffallynge of heer and ballidnesse. *a* **1448** *note to* R. GLOUC. 482 The harme of balledness. **1608** TOPSELL *Serpents* 674 The thinnesse, smoothnesse, and baldnesse, of the skin [of Chameleons]. **1705** SWIFT *Salamand.*, And there corrupting to a wound, Spreads leprosy and baldness round. **1850** THACKERAY *Pendennis* xlv. (1884) 443 Baldness is busy with his crown.
fig. **1382** WYCLIF *Jer.* xlvii. 5 Ther cam ballidnesse vp on Gasam. **1788** BURKE *Sp. W. Hastings* Wks. XIII. 221 Conquest may cover its baldness with its own laurels.
2. *transf.* Lack of natural covering; *e.g.* the bareness of an unwooded country.
1863 BARING-GOULD *Iceland* 103 The baldness of the land..made it impossible to get under cover.
3. *fig.* Meagre simplicity or poverty of style; lack of ornament; bareness, nakedness.
1774 WARTON *Eng. Poetry* (1840) III. xli. 5 Borde has all the baldness of allusion and barbarity of versification belonging to Skelton. **1844** STANLEY *Arnold* I. iv. 186 From the baldness of his earlier works to the vigorous English of his mature age. **1878** P. BAYNE *Purit. Rev.* iii. 87 The harshness and baldness of Puritan worship.

bald-pate. [f. BALD *a.*] **a.** One who has a bald head; *transf.* an American widgeon (*Anas americana* or *Mareca americana*), and a variety of pigeon.
1601 DENT *Pathw. Heaven* 131 Mocked Elisha..calling him bald-head, bald-pate. **1813** A. WILSON *Amer. Ornith.* VIII. 86 The..widgeons, or as they are called round the bay, bald pates. **1838** AUDUBON *Ornith. Biog.* IV. 337 In the Western Country, and in most parts of the Eastern and Middle States, it is called the *Bald Pate*. **1865** E. NOEL *Richter's Flower Pieces* (1871) I. v. 141 But had solicited the bald-pates in vain. **1883** *Century Mag.* XXVI. 925 Mallard, baldpate, and wood-duck. **1907** *Westm. Gaz.* 25 Nov. 8/3 The 'bald-pate', as it is familiarly called, is a gregarious bird, frequenting the North American estuaries.

b. *attrib.* quasi-*adj.* = BALD *a.* (in various senses).
1578 LYTE *Dodoens* 405 Osmunde baldepate or Pylde Osmunde. *c* **1590** MARLOWE *Faust.* vii. 48 A troop of Bald-pate friars. **1683** SOAME & DRYDEN *Art of Poetry* (T.) Nor perriwig with snow the baldpate woods. **1827** MONTGOMERY *Pelican Isl.* II. 244 Swarms..Cover'd the bald-pate reef.

bald-pated, *a.* = prec.; whence **bald-patedness**.
1603 SHAKS. *Meas. for M.* v. i. 357 You bald-pated lying rascall. **1606** DAY *Isle of Gulls* IV. v, This same baldpated oak. **1818** SCOTT *Rob Roy* xxxi, A forked, uncased, bald-pated, beggarly-looking scare-crow. **1611** COTGR., *Chauveté*, Bauldnesse, bauld-patednesse.

bald-rib ('bɔːldrɪb). [f. BALD *a.*] A joint of pork cut from nearer the rump than the spare-rib, so called 'because the bones thereof are made bald and bare of flesh' (Minsheu). Humorously used of: A lean bony person.
1598 FLORIO, *Pancetta*..a bald-rib of porke. **1621** MIDDLETON *Mayor of Q.* III. iii, Thou art such a spiny baldrib. **1674** in D'URFEY *Pills* (1872) III. 320 His trenchant Blade..ran thro' the monster's Bald-rib. **1828** SOUTHEY *To A. Cunningham* Wks. III. 316 Baldrib, griskin, chine, or chop.

baldric ('bɔːldrɪk). Forms: 3 **baudry**, 4 **bauderyk**, **bawdrik**, 5 **bawderyke**, 5–6 **-derick(e**, **-dryk(e**, 5–7 **baudrik(e**, 5–9 **bawdrick**, 6 **baudericke**, **-ike**, **bawdrikke**, **bauldrick(e**, **baldricke**, (**baldrege**), 6–7 **baudricke**, **bawdrike**, 7 **bautricke**, **balderiche**, **balledricke**, 7–9 **baldrick**, 9 **baudrick**, 8– **baldric**. [Identical in sense with old MHG. *balderich*, *palderich* (Schade); also with OF. *baldrei*, *baudrei* (in later F. *baudroy*), and with med.L. *baldringus*. The origin and history of the word are alike obscure: the first part is usually referred to L. *balteus* or its Teutonic adaptations (OHG. *balz*, Eng. *belt*); but none of these satisfactorily account for *bald-*. The mutual relations of the forms in the different langs. are also uncertain: the early Eng. *baudry* was evidently from OF.; for the relation in which *bauderyk*, *bawdrik*, stands to the MHG. forms, evidence is wanting.]
1. A belt or girdle, usually of leather and richly ornamented, worn pendent from one shoulder across the breast and under the opposite arm, and used to support the wearer's sword, bugle, etc.
c **1300** *K. Alis.* 4698 Y wolde..sette heom on hyghe hors, And yiuen stele and baudry, As men don the kynges amy. *c* **1340** *Gaw. & Gr. Knt.* 2486 As a bauderyk, bounden bi his syde. *c* **1386** CHAUCER *Prol.* 116 An horn he bar, the bawdrik was of grene. *c* **1440** *Promp. Parv.* 27 Bawderyke, *Strophius*. **1534** MORE *On the Passion* Wks. 1272/2 A beare-ward with his syluer buttened bawdrike. **1596** SPENSER *F.Q.* I. vii. 29 Athwart his brest a bauldrick brave he ware. **1718** POPE *Iliad* III. 415 A radiant baldric, o'er his shoulder ty'd, Sustained the sword. **1832** TENNYSON *L. Shalott* III. ii, And from his blazon'd baldric slung A mighty silver bugle hung. **1843** LYTTON *Last Bar.* II. i, Buckle my baldrick.
fig. **1879** FARRAR *St. Paul* II. 508 Let spiritual truth be their baldric or binding girdle (*Eph.* vi. 14).
b. The strap of a shield, by which it was hung round the neck.
c **1340** *Gaw. & Gr. Knt.* 621 He braydez hit [þe schelde] by þe bauderyk, aboute þe hals kestes.
2. *fig.* The zodiac, viewed as a gem-studded belt.
1596 SPENSER *F.Q.* v. i. 11 Those twelve signes which nightly we do see The heavens bright-shining baudricke to enchace. **1621** QUARLES *Esther* (1717) 128 Astrea..in the shining Baudrike takes her Seat.
†**3.** A chain for the neck, necklace. *Obs.*
1530 PALSGR. 196/2 Baldrike for a ladyes necke, *Carcan*. **1577** HOLINSHED *Chron.* III. 801/1 A great bauderike about his necke, of balasses. **1834** PLANCHÉ *Brit. Costume* 154 A baldrick of gold about his neck, trailing down behind him.
†**4.** The leather-gear with its appurtenances, by which the clapper of a church bell was suspended. *Obs.*
1428 *Eng. Ch. Furniture* (1866) 180 Pro j baudryk, vjd. **1520** in Nichols *Churchw. Acc.* (1797) 309 A Baldrege to the second bele. **1618** in *N. & Q.* I. (1851) III. 435/1 For mendine of yᵉ balderiche for yᵉ foore bell, *vid.* **1693** W. ROBERTSON *Phraseol. Gen.* 216 A Bawdricke of a Bell-clapper. **1742** in BAILEY. [Not in J.]
5. *Comb.* **baldric-wise** *adv.*
1590 PEELE *Polyhymn.* (1829) II. 202 Rich bandalier, That bauldrick-wise he ware. **1622** F. MARKHAM *Bk. War* I. ix. 34 About his body, Bautricke-wise, from the left shoulder and vnder the right arme.

†**bal'ductum**, **-ta.** *Obs.* Also 6 **balducktum**, **-ducketome.** [med.L. *balducta* 'pressed milk,' curd. Said in Du Cange to be '*quasi valde ducta*'; which looks like 'popular etymology.']
1. A posset, hot milk curdled with ale or wine.
c **1450** in Wright *Voc.* (W.) 567 *Balducta*, a crudde, a poshet. *Ibid.* 789 *Lactatum, balductum*, a poset. **1483** *Cath. Angl.* 288/1 A posset, *balducta*.
2. *fig.* A farrago of words; trash, balderdash.
1593 G. HARVEY *Pierce's Super.* 139 The stalest dudgen or absurdest balductum that they or their mates can invent. **1617** COLLINS *Def. Bp. Ely* II. viii. 295 Will this balductum neuer be left?

3. *attrib.* quasi-*adj.* Trashy, rubbishy.
1577 HOLINSHED *Chron.* II. 29/2 The Irish doubtlesse repose a great affiance in this balducktum dreame. **1583** STANYHURST *Æneis* Ded. (Arb.) 10 Their rude rythming and balducketome ballads. **1596** HARINGTON *Ulysses upon Ajax*, Besides, what balductum play is not full of them?

Baldwin ('bɔːldwɪn). *U.S.* [The personal name.] A common variety of eating apple; a tree bearing this variety of apple.
1826 *Catal. Fruits in Gard. Hortic. Soc. Lond.* 108 (Apples) Baldwin's. **1842** *Ibid.* (ed. 3) 5 Apples... Baldwin. **1848** LOWELL *Biglow P.* Ser. I. ix. 142 Looking out through my study window, I see Mr. Biglow..busy in gathering his Baldwins. **1860** *Trans. Mich. State Agric. Soc. 1858* X. 254 Baldwin is a very popular market fruit in New England. **1861** *Trans. Ill. Agric. Soc.* IV. 468 Our farmers set in the early orchards of Wisconsin a large proportion of Roxbury Russets, Baldwins,..and Spitzenbergs. **1887** M. E. WILKINS *Humble Romance* 238 On the right of the garden were two old apple-trees, a Baldwin and a Porter.

baldy ('bɔːldɪ). *colloq.* [f. BALD *a.* + -Y⁶.] A bald-headed person. Also *transf.* and as a nickname. Also as *adj.* and in *Comb.*, ***baldy-headed*** adj., *Sc.* and *dial.*
1863 *Rio Abajo Press* 28 Apr. 2/2 Within the perlieus [*sic*] of the Rio Chiquito and 'Old Baldy'. **1909** WEBSTER *Baldy*, somewhat bald. **1916** JOYCE *Portr. Artist* (1917) 59 He thought of the baldy head of the prefect of studies. **1925** *Scots Mag.* Dec. 196 A big, gauky stirk o' a bauldy-heided dominy! **1927** A. CLARKE *Son of Learning* III. 54 There is a baldy spot Lighting your crown. **1931** 'DEAN STIFF' *Milk & Honey Route* 199 *Baldy*, generally an old man 'with a high forehead'. **1936** F. CLUNE *Roaming the Darling* xvi. 143 A baldy and paunchy old cove, hosing down the footpath. **1936** I. L. IDRIESS *Cattle King* xi. 99 He's got a couple of good sorts of mares and a good-looking baldy chestnut. **1944** A. CLARKE *Viscount of Blarney* (1945) 35 I'll leave the lantern..for old baldy pate. **1952** B. MALAMUD *Natural* 89 Pop scratched his baldy. **1953** in WENTWORTH & FLEXNER *Dict. Amer. Slang* (1960) 15/2 Baldies are more romantic. **1959** I. & P. OPIE *Lore & Lang. Schoolch.* xvi. 359 The only thing I dinna like Is the baldy-headed master.

†**bale**, *a.* *Obs.* Forms: 1 **balu**, **bealu**, *def.* **balewe**, **bealwe**, 2–3 **bali**, 3 **balu**, **beali**, **bæl**, 3–5 **bale**. [Common Teut.; = Goth. *balws* (in compds., as *balwa-wesei* wickedness, *balwjan* to plague, torment, *balweins* torment):—OTeut. **balwoz*.]
1. Actively evil, deadly, dire, pernicious, destructive, fatal, cruel, tormenting.
Beowulf 1958 Nearwe befongen balwon bendum. *a* **1000** *Cædmon's Satan* (Gr.) 484 Swá inc se balewa hét. *c* **1175** *Cott. Hom.* 281 þa buffetes and ta bali duntes þat tu þoledest. **1205** LAY. 5943 To-brokene mid þeon balu fehte. *c* **1220** *St. Marher.* 13 Tu..me wið bale bondes bitterliche bindest. *c* **1325** *E.E. Allit. P.* B. 1243 So biten with þe bale hunger. *c* **1400** *Destr. Troy* IV. 1388 Bannet worthe the bale tyme þat ho borne was.
2. *subjectively*, Sorrowing, mournful, woeful.
c **1220** *Leg. St. Kath.* 2367 Nalde 3e nawt bringe me forð toward blisse wið se bale bere. *c* **1400** *Destr. Troy* VI. 2681 Ho brast out with a birre from hir bale hert.

bale (beɪl), *sb.*¹ Forms: 1 **balu**, **bealu**, **bealo**, *gen.* **beal(o)wes**, *pl.* **beal(e)wu**, 3 **balu**, **bælu**, **balw**, **ballu**, **baluw**, **balluw**, **baleu**, **balwe**, 3 – **bale**, (4 **bal**, **baal**, 5 **bael**, **bayle**, 5–6 *Sc.* **baill**, **bayle**, 7 **baile**). [Common Teut.: OE. *balu*, *bealu*, (gen. *bealwes*) = OS. and OFris. *balu*, OHG. *balo*, ON. *böl*:—OTeut. **balwo-(m)*, the neuter of the prec. adjective; cf. *evil*, *ill*, *good*, as sbs. Almost confined to poetry from OE. downwards; in ME. it seems to have derived fresh vitality from the ON. *böl*, pronounced (bɔl), whence also its alliterative use with *bote* 'remedy, relief,' and *bete* 'to relieve.' More of English origin, perhaps, is its alliterative opposition to *bliss*. Marked obsolete in dictionaries soon after 1600, and rare thence to the present century, when its undefined vague sense of evil has made it a favourite word with the poets.]
I. Senses.
1. Evil, especially considered in its active operation, as destroying, blasting, injuring, hurting, paining, tormenting; fatal, dire, or malign quality or influence; woe, mischief, harm, injury; in earlier use often = death, infliction of death.
a **1000** *Cædmon's Satan* (Gr.) 682 Bealowes gást [= the devil]. *a* **1000** *Ags. Ps.* lix. 2 Me wið blodhreowes weres bealuwe ʒehæle. **1076** *O.E. Chron.*, þær wæs þæt bryd ealo, þæt wæs manegra manna bealo. **1205** LAY. 1455 Balu com on ueste. *Ibid.* 5016 Whet wult þu balwe menge? **1330** R. BRUNNE *Chron.* 74 þe Komyn had his bale, his lif was lightly sold. **1340** HAMPOLE *Pr. Consc.* 6103 That day [of doom], þe day of bale and of bitternes. *c* **1340** *Alex. & Dind.* 163 þi bestus of bale · þat bi þe water ferde. *c* **1440** *Gesta Rom.* (1879) 188, I am worthi al this bale, for I tolde to the woman al my counseill. **1579** SPENSER *Sheph. Cal.* Nov. 84 The flouret..buryed long in Winters bale. **1647** CLEVELAND *Smectymn.*, Caligula, whose pride was Mankinds Baile. **1748** THOMSON *Cast. Indol.* I. i, Withouten that would come an heavyer bale. **1870** BRYANT *Homer* I. II. 75 Tidings of bale she brought.
b. Evil-speaking, abuse.
c **1220** *Leg. St. Kath.* 551 Ha tukeð ure godes to balewe & to bismere.

2. Evil in its passive aspect; physical suffering, torment, pain, woe.

c **1250** *Gen. & Ex.* 68 Deuel dwale, Đat made ilc sorȝe, and euerilc bale. *a* **1300** *Cursor M.* 19379 Þat neuer for na bale ne buud. *c* **1325** *E.E. Allit. P.* A. 477 & lyued in penance.. With bodyly bale hym blysse to byye. **1393** LANGL. *P. Pl.* C. XXI. 34 And bringe adoun · bale and deþ for euere. *c* **1460** *Frere & Boy* in Ritson *Anc. P.P.* 35 God that.. dranke both eysell and gall, Brynge vs out of bale. **1575** CHURCHYARD *Chippes* (1817) 211 Borne vnto bale, and subiect to debate. *c* **1824** CAMPBELL *Fragm. Oratorio* 37 The bitterness of my bale. **1834** SOUTHEY *Doctor* (1862) 35 Death.. calls up a soul from bale, to give an account of his own sufferings.

3. Mental suffering; misery, sorrow, grief.

c **1325** *E.E. Allit. P.* A. 18 My breste in bale bot bolne & bele. *c* **1400** *Melayne* 576 For bale hym thoght he brynt. *c* **1425** *Sev. Sages* (P.) 258 He that tolde hire that tale, Broght him in mykil bael. **1596** SPENSER *F.Q.* I. ix. 29 Our feeble harts Embost with bale, and bitter byting griefe. **1616** BULLOKAR, *Bale* (Now out of vse), Sorrow, great miserie. **1847** DISRAELI *Tancred* II. i. (1871) 55 Relieve my spirit from the bale that bows it down.

II. Phrases and locutions:

4. ***to work, bake, brew bale***: to make mischief, prepare woe or misery.

c **1200** *Trin. Coll. Hom.* 257 Bale to breówe. **1330** R. BRUNNE *Chron.* 55 How falsnes brewes bale with him, and many mo. *c* **1400** *Judicium* (1822) 11 Your baill now brewys. *c* **1460** in *Pol. Rel. & L. Poems* (1866) 144 Whan þou doest thus, there bale þou bakeste. *Ibid.* 100 Y am worsse than wode Myn owne bale for to brewe. **1594** NASHE *Unfort. Trav.* 37 To work hir bale.

5. Opposed alliteratively to *bliss, blithe*.

c **1325** *E.E. Allit. P.* A. 373 My blysse, my bale ȝe han ben boþe. *c* **1400** *St. Alexius* (Trin.) 140 Hire blesse turnde to Bale. *c* **1450** HENRYSON *Mor. Fables* 19 Be blith in baill, for that is best remead. *c* **1470** HENRY *Wallace* IV. 337 Now lycht, now sadd, now blissful, now in baill. **1576** GASCOIGNE *Princely Pleas.* (1821) 33 And turn your present bliss to after bales. **1598** YONG *Diana* 440 That still deducts my life in blisselesse bale. **1797** COLERIDGE *Christabel* I, Her face resigned to bliss or bale. **1876** LOWELL *Poet Wks.* (1879) 468/2 Was it a comet or star; Omen of blessing or bale?

6. Opposed to *boot* (ME. *bote*) 'relief, remedy,' and *bete* vb. 'to relieve, mend.' So in Icel., *böl og bót* 'bale and boot,' *bölva bætr* 'boots of bales.'

c **1275** *Luue Ron* 125 in *O.E. Misc.* 97 Þar-inne is vich balewes bóte. *a* **1300** *Cursor M.* 44 Quedur þai be worthi or bale or bote. *Ibid.* 105 All vr balis for to bete. **1393** LANGL. *P. Pl.* C. XXI. 208 Hit is a botles bale. *c* **1420** *Sir Amadace* iv, That myȝte not bete my bale! *c* **1460** J. RUSSELL *Bk. Nurture* in *Babees Bk.* (1863) 183 Than brynge hym to his bed, his bales there to bete. *c* **1460** *Towneley Myst.* 28 Thank we that fre, Beytter of baylle. **1488** *Chevy Chase* in Maidment *Scot. Bal.* (1861) I. 80 Ihesue Crist our ballys bete And to the blys us brynge. **1496** *Dives & Paup.* (W. de W.) II. xix. 157/2 The holy ghoost.. is bote of euery bale. **1562** J. HEYWOOD *Prov. & Epigr.* (1867) 52 This rather bryngeth bale then boote. **1565** J. HALL *Hist. Expost.* 34 Oure boote mixed wyth bale. **1867** G. MACDONALD *Poems* 144 Where he had found Boot for every bale

7. *Proverbs.* Cf. Icel. *þegar böl er hæst er bót næst* 'when bale is highest boot is nighest,' etc.

a **1250** *Owl & Night.* 687 Hwon þe bale is alre hecst þonne is þe bote alre necst. *a* **1300** *Cursor M.* 4775 Quen þe bal ys alder hext þen sum time ys bote next. *c* **1330** *Florice & Bl.* 858 After bale hem com bote. **1393** LANGL. *P. Pl.* C. v. 88 Betere ys þat bote · bale a-doun brynge, Than bale be ybete · and bote neuere þe betere. *c* **1400** *Test. Love* II. (1560) 288 b/1 When bale is greatest then is bote a nie bore. *c* **1430** *Syr Gener.* 3328 Aftre bale euer cometh bote. **1562** J. HEYWOOD *Prov. & Epigr.* (1867) 38 Comforte your selfe with this old text.. when bale is hekst, boote is next. *a* **1600** *Sir Aldingar* 177 in Furniv. *Percy Folio* I. 171 When Bale is att hyest, boote is att next. **1870** MORRIS *Earthly Par.* II. III. 524 Bettered is bale by bale that follows it, The saw saith.

8. *Comb.* †**bale-sithe** [OE. *bealu-síð*, f. *sið* expedition, adventure, fortune, lot], death, destruction; evil-doing, mischief; evil fortune, calamity. †**bale-stour** [*stour* tumult, battle], fatal struggle, death-throe. The OE. poetical compounds were very numerous, e.g. *bealu-cræft* magic art, *bealu dǽd* sin, *bealu-ráp* deadly rope, *bealu-spell* fatal news, *bealu-þanc* malicious thought.

a **1000** *Cædmon's Ex.* (Gr.) 5 Æfter bealusíðe. *c* **1175** *Lamb Hom.* 185 Al imengd wiþ balewsið and wiþ bitternesse. *c* **1200** *Saloman & Sat.* (1848) 236 þæt he ne solde þe upbreidin of þine balesiþes. **1205** LAY. 567 Iwenden toward Brutun to his bale-siðe. *Ibid.* 651 & abat his bale-siðes. *c* **1220** *St. Marher.* 23 Lif þat a lesteð buten balesið. *c* **1325** *E.E. Allit. P.* C. 426 Bed me bilyue my bale stour, & bryng me on ende.

bale (beɪl), *sb.*[2] Forms: 1 **bǽl**, 4– **bale**; (*Sc.* 4 **baile**, 5 **belle**, 6 **baill**, **bele**, 8 **beal**, 5– **bail**). [Comm. Teut., though known only in OE. *bǽl* and ON. *bál* great fire, blazing pile, funeral pyre:—OTeut. *bǣl-o(m)*, cogn. with Skr. *bhālas* lustre, Gr. *φαλός* shining, bright. In ME. and mod.E. almost exclusively northern, and app. from ON. *bál* rather than OE. *bǽl*, which would have given mod. *beal, beel.* By later writers much mixed up with the preceding word: see 3. Cf. also BALE-FIRE.]

†**1.** *gen.* A great consuming fire, a conflagration; a blazing pile, a bonfire. *Obs.*

[An immense bonfire of faggots and boughs, formerly (until *c* 1840) kindled annually in November on the village green of Denholm in Roxburghshire, was called the *Bale* or *Bowa-bale*.]

a **1000** *Beowulf* 4633 Befangen bæle and bronde. **1375** BARBOUR *Bruce* XVII. 619 Thai flaggatis byrnand in a baill. *c* **1420** *Anturs of Arth.* xv, I brenne as a belle. **1557** in Tottell's *Misc.* (Arb.) 266 Such heat.. As Priamus towne felt not more flame, when did the bale begin. *a* **1600** *Christis Kirk Gr.* xxiii, And brane-wode brynt in bailis.

2. *spec.* **a.** A funeral pile or pyre. (Long *obs.*, but used by W. Morris.)

a **1000** *Beowulf* 2223 Betst beado-rinca wæs on bæl ȝearu. *c* **1394** *P. Pl. Crede* 667 To brenne the body In a bale of fiir. **1876** MORRIS *Sigurd* III. 305 Far out in the people's meadows they raise a bale on high.. and thereon shall the mighty lie.

b. A signal- or beacon-fire. (*Scotch.*) *arch.*

1455 *Act. 12 Jas. II* (1597) §48 The quhilkis.. sal make taikenings be bailes burning & fire. Ane Baile, is warning of their cumminge.. twa bailes togidder at anis, they are cumming in deed. **1513** DOUGLAS *Æneis* II. vi. (v.) 13 The taknyng or the bail [*v.r.* bele] of fire. **1535** STEWART *Cron. Scot.* II. 151 Richt mony fyre and balis gart burne brycht; And mony blast gart blaw of buglis horne. **1805** SCOTT *Last Minstr.* III. xxvii, On Penchryst glows a bale of fire, And three are kindling on Priesthaughswire.

3. *fig.* Sometimes confused with BALE *sb.*[1]

1568 LAUDER *Lament.* 81 My breist in baill it dois combure. **1596** SPENSER *F.Q.* I. ix. 16 He strove to cloak his inward bale And hide the smoke that did his fire display.

bale (beɪl), *sb.*[3] Forms: 4– **bale** (6 **balle**, 6–8 **ball**), 7 **bayl**, 7–8 **bail**. [ME. *bale*, perh. a. OF. *bale*, *balle*, = Pr. and Sp. *bala*, It. *balla*, *palla*, med.L. *bala*, *balla*, 'ball' and 'rounded package,' generally taken to be an adoption of OHG. *balla*, *palla*, ball (BALL *sb.*[1]); though some refer it to Gr. *πάλλα* ball. But the Eng. may be immediately from Flemish *bale* (mod.Du. *baal*) 'bale,' itself adopted from F. or other Romanic lang. *Bale* and *ball* have from the first been distinct in Eng., though *ball* (for F. *balle*) is occasional in this sense in 17–18th c.]

1. A large bundle or package of merchandise, originally of more or less rounded shape; now, *spec.* a package closely pressed, done up in canvas or other wrapping, and tightly corded or hooped with copper or iron, for transportation.

c **1325** *E.E. Allit. P.* C. 57 Busy ouer-borde bale to kest. *c* **1380** *Sir Ferumb.* 4201 Þay fulde sakkes, & trossede males, To Charyotes þay drowen þe grete bales. *a* **1400** *Cov. Myst.* 210 Of spicery ther growyth many an C. balys. **1540** *Act. 32 Hen. VIII*, xiiii, A bale of saies of vi. fote high. **1695** W. LOWNDES *Amendm. Silv. Coins* 6 The Merchants.. concealed the Parcels in Bails of Cloth. **1755** *Mem. Capt. P. Drake* II. iii. 59 Putting the Bails on board. **1765** TUCKER *Lt. Nat.* II. 416 Known to put false marks upon their bales. **1850** TENNYSON *In Mem.* xiii, As tho' they brought but merchants' bales.

2. (Used with more or less precision as a measure of quantity.)

1502 ARNOLDS *Chron.* (1811) 206 A balle bokrom conteyneth lx. pecis.. a balle fustian conteyneth xlv. half peces. **1740** *Mem. Turkey* in Hanway *Trav.* (1762) I. I. viii. 40 A reduction of their Custom.. to thirty dollars the bale of twenty pieces. **1753** CHAMBERS *Cycl. Supp.* s.v., A bale or ballon of crown paper.. consists of 14 reams. **1863** (30 June) BRIGHT *Amer., Sp.* (1876) 138 To grow one thousand bales of cotton a year. **1880** W. WHITELEY *Diary & Alm.* 82 Bale of coffee (Mocha) = 2 to 2½ cwt.

3. *attrib.* and *Comb.* **bale-sack**; **bale-band** (see quot.); **bale-cloth** *U.S.*, cloth used for covering bales; **bale-goods**, merchandise in bales: as opposed to *case-goods*; **bale-sling** (see quot. 1891).

1891 H. PATTERSON *Naut. Dict.*, *Bale-band*, a big shackle-shaped iron at the mast-head, supported by the cap-band, and to which the standing part of the flying jib-stay is bent on. **1797** B. HAWKINS *Let.* in *Georgia Hist. Soc. Coll.* (1916) IX. 346, 8 yds. bale cloth to Harry Dergin, at 12½c., $1.00. **1865** *Trans. Ill. Agric. Soc.* V. 159 We have pressed the sirup from the sugar through fine bale-cloth. **1694** *Lond. Gaz.* No. 3032/3 Bound with Glass and Bale Goods.. for *Bourdeaux*. **1790** BEATSON *Nav. & Mil. Mem.* I. 217 Her cargo consisted of cordage and bale goods. **1800** *Asiatic Ann. Reg.* III. 41/2 One of the above ships had on board a very valuable cargo of bale goods. **1894** *Idler* Sept. 135 The original freight of the ship had been bale goods. **1883** *Century Mag.* Oct. 817/2 This man flung them into an enormous bale-sack, swinging wide-mouthed from a derrick. **1883** *Man. Seamanship for Boys* 93 There are several methods of slinging a cask, either with a pair of butt slings, bale slings, or a bowline knot. **1891** H. PATTERSON *Naut. Dict.*, *Bale-sling*, a simple strap passed round a bale or bag, the two ends meeting on top, one dipping under the other.

†**4.** The set of dice for any special game, formerly *usually three*. *Obs.*

1481–90 *Howard Househ. Bks.* 327 Paid to Jeffery for a bale of dysse iiiijd. **1577** HOLINSHED *Chron.* III. 848/2 Diuerse bales of dice, and.. certeine paires of cards. **1578** *Richmond. Wills* (1853) 277, Iij ball of dyce, ixd. **1614** J. COOKE *Tu Quoque* in Dodsl. VII. 50 (N.) A pox upon these dice! give's a fresh bale. **1632** ROWLEY *Woman never vexed* II. i. in Hazl. *Dodsl.* XXI. 121 Give's a bale of dice! [They play at 'Passage' and throw] Two treys and an ace, Two quatres and a trey. **1680** COTTON *Compl. Gamester* in Singer *Play. Cards* 336 They [loaded dice] are sold in many places about the town; price current.. eight shillings, whereas an ordinary bale is sold for sixpence. **1822** SCOTT *Nigel* xxiii, The Captain, taking a bale of dice from the sleeve of his coat.

†**5.** ? A bolus, a pill = BALL *sb.*[1] 11. *Obs.*

1576 BAKER *Gesner's Jewell Health* 183 b, I gave.. to a melancholy person.. five graynes.. in a bale or dose.

†**bale**, *v.*[1] *Obs. rare*[−1]. [a. OF. *baler* (since 16th c. *baller*) to dance (= Pr. *balar*, It. *ballare*, Sp., Pg. *bailar*):—late L. (Isidore) *ballāre* to dance. Some think the L. formed from Gr. *βαλλίζειν* to dance, some f. *balla* BALL *sb.*[1], on the alleged ground that, in the Middle Ages, tennis was accompanied with dancing and song.] To dance.

a **1300** *Cursor M.* 13138 His broþer doghter.. Com þaim be-for al for to bale, Baled wel and tumbel wit-al.

bale (beɪl). *v.*[2] [f. BALE *sb.*[3]] **1.** To make up into a bale or bales.

1760 GOLDSM. *Cit. W.* v, These goods are baled up and consigned to a factor abroad. **1879** T. ESCOTT *England* I. 224 The cotton itself has been.. baled, and sent down to the seaport.

2. ***to bale out.*** [Usually so spelt, as if the action were that of letting a bundle through a trapdoor; but also (esp. *U.S.*) as *bail*, as if a use of BAIL *v.*[4], to lade out.] *intr.* (Of an airman) to make an emergency descent by parachute from his machine. Hence also (rare) sb. ***bail-out.*** orig. *U.S.*

1930 C. J. V. MURPHY *Parachute* 272 Some say the pilot 'bailed out' the moment he went into the spin. **1932** *N.Y. Times* 11 Apr. 3/2 He successfully bailed out of an airplane at an elevation of 1,500 feet. **1939** F. D. TREDREY *Pilot's Summer* 28 If you bale out and land in water.. a smart rap will release the whole lot and you can swim free. **1940** *Times* 15 Aug. 4/2 He baled out before his machine crashed. **1955** *Sci. News Let.* 8 Jan. 23 The purpose.. was to explore human tolerances during a high speed bailout from jet planes.

bale (beɪl), *v.*[3] [Erroneous spelling of BAIL *v*[4], q.v.] To lade or throw water out of a boat or ship with buckets (formerly called *bails*) or other vessels. *Const.* to bale the water out, bale the boat (out). ***to bale up***: to scoop up. See BAIL *v.*[4]

[**1627** CAPT. SMITH *Seaman's Gram.* vi. 27 To baile or cast out the water.] **1692** *Ibid.* I. xvi. 75 *To Bale*, to lade Water out of the Ships Hold with Buckets, or the like. **1748** ANSON *Voy.* III. v. 342 In baling out the water. **1833** MARRYAT *Perc. Keene* xvi, Let's bale the boat out first. **1884** *Graphic* 23 Aug. 190/2 Herrings.. in such surprising quantities that they can be baled up with a basket.

bale, obs. spelling of BAIL *sb.* and *v.*; improperly for BAIL *sb.*[2] handle; and obs. f. BELLY.

†**Baleare**, *a. Obs.* [f. L *Baleāris.*] = BALEARIC. Hence **Bale'arian** *a.* and *sb.*, and **Balearic** (bæliːˈærɪk), *a.* [L. *Baleāric-us*], of or pertaining to, *sb.* a native of, the islands Majorca, Minorca, Iviça, etc. (called by the Romans *Baleares insulæ*), in the Mediterranean Sea. ***Balearic Crane***: the Crowned Crane.

1576 LAMBARDE *Peramb. Kent* (1862) 299 The Iles named Baleares. **1601** HOLLAND *Pliny* I. 60 The two Baleare Islands. **1618** BOLTON *Florus* III. vi. (1636) 191 The Tuscan Sea.. [and] the Balearian. **1661** LOVELL *Hist. Anim. & Min.* Introd., The Crane, balearick or japonian. **1807** ROBINSON *Archæol. Græca* IV. iv. 348 The Achaians.. are thought by some to have excelled the Balearians.

baled (beɪld), *ppl. a.* [f. BALE *v.*[2] + -ED.] Packed or made into bales.

1828 *Free Press* (Tarboro, N. Carolina) 7 Nov., Cotton in the seed and baled Cotton. **1865** *Morning Star* 24 Apr., The baled cotton. **1872** E. EGGLESTON *End of World* xxx. 197 [The steamer] took on a new cargo of baled hay and corn and flour. **1895** *Daily News* 19 Oct. 2/4 The market for baled jute is quieter. **1898** *Westm. Gaz.* 28 Oct. 5/3 Baled hay should be stored before the winter sets in. **1918** *Nation* (N.Y.) 7 Feb. 168/1 The baled straw for the mattresses.

baleen (bəˈliːn). Forms; 4–6 **baleyne**, 4–5 **balayn(e**, 4–6 **balene**, 5 **-ien**, 6 **ballane**, **ballen**, 7 **balæne**, 8– **baleen**. [ME. *baleyne*, *-ayne*, a. OF. *baleine*, *-aine* whale, whalebone:—L. *balæna* whale.]

†**1.** A whale. *Obs.*

1387 TREVISA *Higden* (Rolls Ser.) I. xli, Baleynes, grete fisches as hit were of whales kynde. *c* **1450** in Wright's *Voc.* (W.) /704 *Balena*, a balene. *c* **1480** CAXTON *Ovid's Met.* XII. xv, Balaynes or whales, dolphins, mermaydes.. and alle other fyshes. **1572** BOSSEWELL *Armorie* II. 65 Balene is a fishe greate and huge. **1601** HOLLAND *Pliny* I. 238 From the forehead, in the Balænes.

2. ? The fish called Sea-bream: 'perhaps from its supposed habit, mentioned by Pliny, of accompanying the *balæna* or whale' (Riley *Gloss.* to *Lib. Custum.* 785/1).

c **1185** NECKAM in Wright's *Voc.* 97 *Musculus*, baleyne. **1494** FABYAN VII. 586 For the firste course.—Brawne and mustarde. Dedellys in burneux. Frument with balien. Pyke in erbage. **1598** STOW *Survey* (Strype 1754) II. v. xxvi. 464/2 An hundred better Balenes of the same year salted for 16*s.*, that is 2*d.* per pound.

3. Whalebone. Also *attrib.* or as *adj.*, and: **baleen whale**, a whalebone-whale; any member of the suborder Mysticeti; also *ellipt.*

(The meaning is uncertain in some early quotations.)

c **1325** *Coeur de L.* 2982 Off balayn, both scheeld & targe. **1513** DOUGLAS *Æneis* VII. xiii. 68 A ballen [*v.r.* balen] pavis coueris thair left sydis. **1523** LD. BERNERS *Froiss.* I. ccccxix. 734 Gantlettes of steele and baleyne. **1535** STEWART *Cron. Scot.* III. 453 Cors-bowis of ballane that war gude. **1708** J. CHAMBERLAYNE *St. Gt. Brit.* II. I. iii. (1743) 331 Great whales of the Baleen, or whale bone kind. **1824** MEYRICK *Anc. Armour* Gloss. **1836** TODD *Cycl. Anat. & Phys.* 573/2 At each side of their [*i.e.* whales'] palate grow, transversely, horny plates, named baleen. *Ibid.* The base of each baleen-plate. **1874** WOOD *Nat. Hist.* 142 When first born, the young whale is without the baleen. **1874** C. M. SCAMMON *Marine*

Mammals vi. 66 This great northern baleen whale, in its principal proportions, resembles the *Balæna mysticetus*. **1878** *Cassell's Nat. Hist.* II. 257 Scammon says that three or four [killer-whales] do not hesitate to grapple with the largest Baleen Whales. **1958** *Times* 12 Nov. 11/6 There are two kinds of whale caught, the baleen and the sperm.

bale-fire ('beɪlfaɪə(r)). Forms: 1 **bǽl-fýr**, 5- **bale-**; also *Sc.* 5 **bayle-**, 6 **baill-**, **bald-**, 6–9 **bail-**, 8 **beal-**, 9 **bele- beal-**, **bael**, **baal-fire**. [Found in OE. poetry: then not till the 14th c.; and till lately confined to Scotch. Not in Johnson, nor in Todd 1818. Compd. of BALE *sb.*[2] + FIRE; the former part was apparently at times confused with BALE *sb.*[1]: cf. *balowe-fire* 'fatal or evil fire' already in 15th c., and the use of *bale-fire* by various modern writers as if = 'lurid, ghastly fire.' Antiquaries, with theories of Celtic or Canaanitish idolatry, have written *beal-*, *Baal-fire*: cf. BELTANE.]

1. A great fire in the open air, a blazing pile or heap kindled to consume anything. In OE. *spec.* the fire of a funeral pile.

a **1000** *Beowulf* 6278 Ongunnon þá on beorᵹe bǽl-fýra mæst..weccan. *c* **1400** *Melayne* 488 Thay tuke þe grete lordes with Ire, And brynte þam in þat bale fire. *c* **1470** HENRY *Wallace* IV. 718 Bot thou tell in bayle fire sall thou de. **1535** STEWART *Cron. Scot.* I. 355 In ane baill fyre thai brint it all in as. **1549** *Compl. Scot.* vi. 42 As plutois paleis hed been birnand in ane bald fyir. **1812** BYRON *Ch. Har.* I. xxxviii, The fires of death, The bale-fires flash on high. **1813** HOGG *Queen's Wake* 83 They set ane bele-fire him about, And they burnit him skin and bone. **1882** FARRAR *Early Chr.* II. 190 The horrible illumination flung by the bale-fires of martyrdom upon the palace and gardens of the Beast.

2. A great fire kindled as a signal; a beacon-fire. (Only 19th c.: apparently first used by Sir W. Scott. The contemporary name was simply *bale*.)

1805 SCOTT *Last Minstr.* IV. i, Sweet Teviot! on thy silver tide The glaring bale-fires blaze no more. **1852** MISS YONGE *Cameos* II. xx. 220 The bail fire announced the appearance of the enemy. **1861** *Black's Guide Sussex* 536 Crowborough was one of the beacon stations..where the bale-fire was lighted.

3. Any great fire, a bonfire, *feu de joie*.

1800–24 CAMPBELL *O'Connor's Child* vii, Beal-fires for your jubilee Upon a thousand mountains glow'd. **1850** MERIVALE *Rom. Emp.* (1865) III. xxiii. 62 He caused the city to be illuminated with torches and balefires. **1852** D. MOIR *Burns Fest.* Wks. II. 7 Stir the beal-fire, wave the banner, Bid the thundering cannon sound.

4. ? Associated with BALE *sb.*[1].

1855 MOTLEY *Dutch Rep.* VI. i. (1866) 774 The focus of discord..from whence radiated..the bale-fires of murderous licence and savage anarchy. **1872** SPURGEON *Treas. Dav.* Ps. lxxvii. 17 With blue bale-fires revealing the innermost caverns of the hungry sea.

baleful ('beɪlfʊl), *a.* Forms: 1 **bealu-**, **bealofull**, 2–3 **balufull**, 3 **baluhful**, 3–5 **balful(l**, 4 **ballefull**, 3- **baleful(l**. [OE. *bealu-full*, f. *bealu* BALE *sb.*[1] + -FULL. Until recent times almost exclusively poetic; still chiefly literary.]

1. Full of malign, deadly, or noxious influence; pernicious, destructive, noxious, injurious, mischievous, malignant: **a.** *physically* or *generally*.

a **1000** *Crist* (Grein) 259 Se bealofulla [= the devil] hyneþ heardlice. *c* **1220** *St. Marher.* 10 To beoren me into his balefule hole. **1230** *Ancr. R.* 114 So baluhful & so bitter! *c* **1400** *Destr. Troy* I. 167 These balfull bestes were..ffull flaumond of fyre. **1592** SHAKS. *Rom. & Jul.* II. iii. 8 Balefull weedes, and precious Iuiced flowers. **1676** *Black Prince* in *Harl. Misc.* (1793) 51 Great flocks of ravens, and other baleful birds of prey. **1712** SWIFT *Wond. Proph.* Wks. 1755 III. I. 173 This baleful dog-star. **1800–24** CAMPBELL *To Sir F. Burdett* v, His hate is baleful, but his love is worse. **1862** RAWLINSON *Anc. Mon.* I. i. 32 The baleful simoon sweeps across the entire tract.

b. *morally*.

c **1175** *Lamb. Hom.* 215 Tend mine heorte and uorbern alþat is baluful þer inne. *c* **1300** *Lay-Folks Mass-Bk.* B. 404 þat may lese alle baleful bandes. **1589** GREENE *Menaph.* (Arb.) 22 The baleful laborinth of despaire. **1597** LOK in Farr's *S.P.* (1845) I. 138 Through baleful lust of gold. **1751** SMOLLETT *Per. Pic.* (1779) III. lxxxi. 109 O baleful Envy! thou self-tormenting fiend. **1863** W. PHILLIPS *Speeches* xvi. 362 The potent and baleful prejudice of color.

2. *subjectively*: **a.** Full of pain or suffering, painful. *Obs.*

c **1200** *Trin. Coll. Hom.* 181 On þisse liue we beð on balfulle swinche for adames gulte. **1579** SPENSER *Sheph. Cal.* Jan., Such stormie stoures do breede my balefull smart.

b. Unhappy, wretched, miserable; distressed, sorrowful, mournful. *arch.*

c **1325** *E.E. Allit. P.* C. 979 þe balleful burde [Lot's wife], þat neuer bode keped. *c* **1420** *Anturs of Arth.* xlii, The balefulle birde blenked on his blode. **1535** STEWART *Cron. Scot.* I. 124 The ȝoutting, ȝouling, and the bailfull beir Tha maid. **1596** DRAYTON *Legends* iii. 14 That Baleful sounds immovably do'st breathe. **1812** J. WILSON *Isle of Palms* I. 533 Baleful spirits barr'd from realms of bliss.

balefully ('beɪlfʊlɪ), *adv.* [f. prec. + -LY[2].] In a baleful manner: **a.** Injuriously, hurtfully; **b.** Miserably, painfully, sadly.

c **1350** *Will. Palerne* 3959 I balfulli here-bi-fore was brout al bi-neþe. *Ibid.* 84 So balfully he grinneþ. *c* **1400** *Destr. Troy* XXIX. 11983 The burgh..baillfully distroyet. **1838** CARLYLE *Misc.* (1857) IV. 173 And hurry him balefully into Night! **1842** WHITTOCK *Compl. Bk. Trades* 438 Which laws..operated balefully upon the superiority of the articles.

'balefulness. [f. prec. + -NESS.] Baleful quality or condition: **a.** Hurtfulness; **b.** Distress, sadness.

1592 WYRLEY *Armorie* 145 Contenting ioy changd into balefulnes. **1596** SPENSER *F.Q.* II. xii. 83 Their blisse be turn'd to balefulnesse. **1866** *Lond. Rev.* 10 Mar. 276/1 Forms of balefulness which defy the most ingenious apologist of physical science.

'baleless, *a. arch.* [OE. *bealuléas*, f. *bealu* BALE *sb.*[1] + -LESS.] Harmless, innocent.

a **1000** *Gnom. V. Ex.* (Gr.) 39 Bealoléas heorte. **1065** *O.E. Chron.*, *Elegy Edw. Conf.* (MS. C.), Wæs á bliðe-mod bealuleas kyng [D. bealeleas]. *c* **1325** *E.E. Allit. P.* C. 227 þay in balelez blod þer blenden her handez. **1869** FREEMAN *Norm. Conq.* (1876) III. 30 Looked back to the happy days of the baleless king.

'baler[1]. He who or that which bales; a scoop for baling out water. See BAILER.

1875 BEDFORD *Sailor's Pocket Bk.* vi. 236 Any boat using propelling power, such as oars, balers..to be disqualified.

baler[2]. [f. BALE *v.*[2]] **a.** A machine or apparatus for baling hay, straw, metal, etc.

1888 *Voice* (N.Y.), Why are not balers as common as threshers? I believe it is owing to..manufacturers..not pushing the balers. **1926** *Glasgow Herald* 26 June 5/7 The baler seems a practical machine and might be tried in large nurseries. **1936** *Discovery* June 193/1 The installation of two large grass-driers and automatic balers on his Warwickshire farm. **1963** *Times* 10 Dec. 5/1 These men..with one movement of their giant balers can reduce [an old motor-car]..to a cube of metal the size of a biscuit tin.

b. One who makes up bales.

1889 in *Cent. Dict.* **1910** *Daily Chron.* 2 Feb. 5/4 One application was for three newspaper balers.

balery, obs. form of BAILIERY.

bales, -ess, obs. ff. BALAS (ruby) and BELLOWS.

balesse, -est, obs. ff. BALLAST.

balester, variant of BALISTER.

† **ba'let(te.** *Obs.* [a. OF. *balete*, *ballete*, *-ette*, dim. of *bale*, *balle*: see -ETTE.] A small bale.

1453 in Heath *Grocers' Comp.* (1869) 421 Greynes, 1 balet, yᵉ C xijd... Woode, yᵉ balett ijd. **1540** *Act. 32 Hen. VIII*, xiv, Accompting .viii. whole bales, or .xvi. demi balettes for a tunne.

baleu, erroneous form of BALAS (ruby).

1653 URQUHART *Rabelais* I. viii, A perfect baleu [ed. 1737 (Ozell) baleau] rubie. *Ibid.* I. lvi, Carbuncles, rubies, baleus.

† **baleys,** *sb. Obs.* Forms: 3–5 **baleis**, 4–5 **baleys**, 5 **ballys**, **baleese**, 6 **balys**. [a. OF. *baleis*, nom. sing. (or acc. pl.) of *balei* (mod. *balai*) besom, broom. As early OF. had sing. nom. *baleis*, while later OF. had sing. *balei*, pl. *baleis*, it is difficult to say from which of these the final *-s* in Eng. was derived. The quasi-collective sense of 'birch' points to the pl.] A rod; also a bundle of twigs used in flogging, a 'birch,' a scourge.

a **1259** MATT. PARIS *Chron.* (1880) v. 324 Ferens in manu virgam quam vulgariter baleis appellamus. *c* **1315** SHOREHAM 47 Ine the temple, sweete Ihesus..makede a baleys, And bet out..Tho that bouȝte and sealde. **1377** LANGL. *P. Pl.* B. XII. 12 With þise bitter baleyses God beteth his dere childeren. *c* **1440** *Promp. Parv.* 537 ȝerde, baleys, *virga*. **1475** *Bk. Noblesse* (1860) 54 To be betyn nakid withe baleese and sharpe roddis. *c* **1485** *Digby Myst.* (1882) III. 735 Thys hard balys on þi bottokkys xall byte! **1517** TORKINGTON *Pilgr.* (1884) 3 He had a balys in hys hond.

baleys, *v. Obs.* exc. *dial.* [f. the sb.] To birch, to flog.

1377 LANGL. *P. Pl.* B. v. 175 Baleised on þe bar ers · and no breche bitwene. **1879** *Shropsh. Gloss.*, *Baleise*, to beat, to flog, to whip; also *Bellise*.

baleys, obs. form of BALAS (ruby).

† **balgh,** *a. Obs.* Forms: 4 **balȝe**, **balowe**, 5 **balheu**, **balwe**. [Cf. OE. *belᵹ* bag, belly.]

1. Round, rounded; ? swelling.

c **1340** *Alexander* (Stev.) 4923 Balgh brade in þe brest. & on the bely sklendire. *c* **1340** *Gaw. & Gr. Knt.* 2172 A balȝe berȝ bi a bonke. *Ibid.* 2032 Vpon his balȝe haunchez. *c* **1430** *Chev. Assigne* 316 Balowe tymbre & bygge.

2. Smooth.

c **1440** *Promp. Parv.* 22 Balhew, or pleyn [**1499** balwe or playne], *Planus*.

baliage, balie, obs. ff. BAILLIAGE, BAILLIE.

balibuntal (bælɪ'bʌnt(ə)l). Also **balli-**, **bally-**, **-buntl(e** (as one word or as two); also shortened to **bal(l)i**. [Short for *Baliuag buntal*, a weave of BUNTAL originating from Baliuag in Bulacan, Philippine Islands.] A fine straw of a very close weave, used for hats. Also *attrib.*, and short for *balibuntal hat*.

[**1911** *Philippine Jrnl. Science* Sect. C. VI. 115 The Baliuag buntal hat is..more closely woven than that of Lucban, and is consequently stronger.] **1913** T. MULLER *Industr. Fiber Plants of Philippines*, (*Philippine Islands*) *Bur. Educ. Bull.* 49, 84 Only the best weavers can make the buntal-sawalis or bali-buntals as these Baliuag hats are called..usually known there [*sc.* in U.S.] as 'Manilas'. **1918** *N.Y. Times* 25 Apr. 5 (Advt.), The Bally Buntle is one of the strictly new, extremely modish Hats. **1925** *Ibid.* 1 Mar. (Advt.), Hats of Horse Hair, Balli Buntle, Bankok. **1927** *Observer* 12 June 11/4 A bali-buntal in mauve. **1928** *N.Y. Times* 1 Apr. 7 (Advt.), Baku and Balibuntal are favorite straws for Easter Wear. *Ibid.* 11 Apr. (Advt.), This Untrimmed Ballibuntl Needs Little Adornment. **1929** [see BAKU]. **1961** *Harper's Bazaar* Feb. 53 Hat of white balibuntal.

‖ **'balin.** *Obs.* [irregular a. L. *balin*, in Pliny, acc. of *balis*, a. Gr. *βάλλις*.] An unknown plant, supposed to have wonderful medicinal virtues.

1546 LANGLEY *Pol. Verg. De Invent.* I. xvii. 30 a, Slain by the virtue of an herbe called Balin. **1609** HEYWOOD *Bryt. Troy* IV. xi, Hauing th' herbe Balin in his wounds infusd, Restores his life.

Balinese (bɑːlɪ'niːz), *a.* and *sb.* [f. *Bali* + -ESE after Du. *Balinees*.] **A.** *adj.* Of or pertaining to the island of Bali in Indonesia, or to its inhabitants. **B.** *sb.* **1.** A native of Bali; as collect. sing., the people of Bali. **2.** The language spoken by this people.

1820 J. CRAWFURD *Hist. Ind. Archipelago* I. I. iv. 69 The diversion of cock-fighting is most especially in vogue among the Malays, the people of Celebes, and the Balinese. *Ibid.* II. v. i. 27 They..have been translated into the Balinese and Malay languages. *Ibid.* II. v. iv. 69 The Balinese is the sole language of the island of Bali. **1872** *Appleton's Jrnl.* Aug. 120/2 Many of the Balinese seem to possess *sarongs* of this description. **1935** *Times Lit. Suppl.* 15 Aug. 508/4 Another important class of Balinese antiquities is richly carved water-spouts. **1954** PEI & GAYNOR *Dict. Linguistics* 25 *Balinese*, a language spoken by about 1,000,000 persons on the island of Bali; a member of the Indonesian sub-family of the Malayo-Polynesian family of languages.

baling ('beɪlɪŋ), *vbl. sb.*[1] [f. BALE *v.*[2] + -ING[1].] The process of packing in bales. Also *attrib.*

1761 GOLDSM. *Cit. W.* cviii, The methods of baling them up. **1810** F. CUMING *Sk. Tour Western Country* xxvi. 165 There is [in Lexington, Ky.] one manufacturer of baling cloth. **1815** *Niles' Reg.* IX. 187/1 They are considered much superior to all other baling presses. **1879** T. ESCOTT *Engl.* I. 147 The baling and casing of goods. **1922** *Outing* (U.S.) June 110/2 The time was now come..to get out..rope and baling wire. **1959** *Engineering* 9 Jan. 58/1 A scrap yard adjoins the melting shop, the handling equipment including a..baling press.

baling, *vbl. sb.*[2] Also (properly) 6–8 **bailing**. The emptying of water from a boat or other vessel.

1856 KANE *Arct. Exp.* II. xxix. 286 So unseaworthy as to require constant baling.

† **balinger** ('bælɪndʒə(r)). *Obs.* exc. *Hist.* Forms: 4–6 **balynger**, **-ingar**, 5 **-gere**, **balangar**, **-yngar**, **-engere**, **ballenger**, **-unger**, **balyner**, 5–6 **ballynger**, 5–8 **balenger**, 6 **balengar**, **-anger**, **ballyngare**, **-ingere**, **-ingar**, 7 **-anger**, **-inger**, 6–9 **-enger**, 5- **balinger**. [a. AF. *balengier* (Froissart), *ballenjer* (in Du Cange), = OF. *baleinier*, a whale-ship, f. *baleine* whale; afterwards employed generically: so It. *baleniera* 'kind of light pinnace.']

A small and light sea-going vessel, apparently a kind of sloop, much used in the 15th and 16th centuries; according to Adm. Smyth, without forecastle. Its nature was already forgotten in 1670, when Blount could only infer the meaning of the word from old statutes; but the term is commonly used by modern historians in referring to the naval affairs of those times.

1391 in *MS. Reg. Test. Ebor.* I. 67 [Rob. de Rillington of Scarbro' leaves to Wm. Percy] dimidietatem nostri balingar. [**1400** HENRY IV. *Brief* in Rymer *Fœdera* VIII. 147 Aliquam Navem, Bargeam, sive Balingeram, de Guerra Armatam.] *c* **1400** *Petit. in Parl. 2 Hen. IV.* xxii, Pur faire certeines Barges & Balyngers. *a* **1422** HEN. V. in Ellis *Orig. Lett.* III. 31 I. 72 Our grete shippes, carrakes, barges and balyngers. **1475** CAXTON *Jason* 108 Foure litill shippes at facon of balingers. **1525** LD. BERNERS *Froiss.* II. xlvi. 158 They knewe by theyr balengers that the armye of Englande was comynge. **1531–2** *Act 23 Hen. VIII*, v. §2 The common passages of shyppes balengers and botes. **1598** STOW *Survey* (Strype 1754) I. I. xiii. 57/1 By means whereof Boats and Ballangers were hindered in their passages. **1622** CALLIS *Stat. Sewers* (1647) 34 A port is a harbor and safe arrival for ships, boats, and ballengers of burthen. **1670** BLOUNT *Law Dict.*, *Balenger*, Seems to have been a kind of Barge or Water-vessel, by the Statute 28H. 6, cap. 5. **1865** W. MILLER *Jott. Kent* 45 In the year 1401..the barges with eighty, and the balingers with forty men.

fig. *c* **1502** *Joseph Arim.* (Pynson) 425 Hayle! myghty balynger, charged with plenty!

b. *comb.* **balinger-master** (cf. *ship-master*).

1463 *Mann. & H. Exp.* 194 John More my balynger master.

balisier (bælɪːzjeɪ). [Fr.] The West Indian musaceous plant *Heliconia bihai*, with very large leaves and brilliant orange flowers.

1858 DE VERTEUIL *Trinidad* 95 Balizier (*Heliconia*). **1871** KINGSLEY *At Last* I. vi. 222 Under the shade of great Balisiers or wild plantains. [*note*] Heliconia. *Ibid.* vii. 266 Above these, again, the Balisiers bend their long leaves, eight or ten feet long apiece. **1953** P. L. FERMOR *Violins of St.-Jacques* 18 Punctilious flower-paintings of hibiscus and balisier.

balisse, -ist, obs. forms of BALLAST.

†**ba'lister**[1], **-ester.** *Obs.* [a. OF. *balestier*:—L. *ballistārius*, late L. *balestārius* arbalester; cf. BALLISTIER.] An arbalester, a crossbow-man.
1489 CAXTON *Faytes of A.* I. xxiii. 71 Gonners, balesters, and archers. **1613** T. GODWIN *Rom. Antiq.* (1658) 263 Near unto which standeth the cunning balister.

†**ba'lister**[2]. *Obs. rare*—[1]. [a. OF. *balestre*:—L. *ballistra* (late L. *balestra* arbalest), variant of BALLISTA.] An arbalest, a crossbow.
1697 BLOUNT *Anc. Tenures* 92 (T.) Thread, to make a false string for the king's balister or crossbow.

balistic, -ics, var. ff. BALLISTIC, -ICS.

‖**balistraria** (bælɪ'streərɪə). *Arch.* [med.L., properly fem. of adj. *ballistrārius*.; see next.]
a. A cruciform aperture in the walls of a fortress, through which arbalesters discharged their weapons. **b.** A room in which arbalests were kept.
1845 in *Gloss. Gothic Archit.* I. 38.

†**ba'listrier.** *Obs. rare.* In 6 **balastriar.** [a. OF. *balestrier*:—L. *ballistrārius*; cf. med.L. *balestrārius*.] An arbalester, a crossbow-man.
1440 SHIRLEY *Dethe K. James* (1818) 23 Ane heghe ynstrument of tymbire, upon which balastriars and bowyers usyn to hong thare..bowes.
¶ See also BALLIST- for modern derivatives from L.

balival ('bælɪvəl), *a.* [f. med.L. *balīv-us, ball-, baill-*, f. F. *baillif*:—late L. *bājulīvus* (see BAILIFF) + -AL[1].] Of or pertaining to a 'bailiff' or his office.
1854 LONGSTAFFE *Hist. Darlington* II. i. 93 Dickon-kists.. constituted an estate of the balival family of Barnes.

baliwick(e, obs. form of BAILIWICK.

‖**balize** (bə'li:z). [F. *balise* = Sp. *valiza*; of uncertain origin.] A kind of beacon erected at sea, consisting of a pole surmounted by some object, such as a small barrel.
1847 in CRAIG.

balk, baulk (bɔ:k), *sb.*[1] Forms: 1 **balca, balc,** 3–7 **balke,** 5–7 **baulke,** 6 **balcke,** 7–9 **baulk** (*north. dial.* **bauk, bawk**), 3– **balk.** [Common Teutonic, presenting several variant stems, with partial differentiation of sense: OE. *balca* ridge, bank = OFris. *balca*, OS. *balco*, MDu. *balke, balc*, Du. *balk*, OHG. *balcho, balco*, MHG. *balke*, G. *balken*, 'beam, *trabs*,' also OE. *bolca* 'gangway of a ship,' and ON. *bjalki* (Sw. *biælke, bielke*, Da. *bjelke*) 'beam,' corresponding respectively to an OTeut. ablaut-series **balkon-*, **bolkon-*, **belkon-*; also ON. *bálkr, bǫlkr*, 'beam, bar, partition, division', OSw. *balker, bolker*, Sw. *balk* 'beam, balk, partition, section of a law':—OTeut. **balku-z*. OE. *balc* '*porca*' (see 3), is either an error for *balca*, or = ON. *bálkr*. The relation of OE. *bælc* 'covering (? flooring)' is doubtful. The original sense was perh. 'bar'; cf. L. *suf-fla(g)men*, from Aryan **bhalg-, bhlag-*. The OE. *balca* (*balc*) and ON. *bálkr* appear to be combined in the ME.; whether the latter distinguished *balke* and *balk*, the evidence does not show. *Balk* is the analogous spelling: cf. *stalk, talk, walk*, etc.; but *baulk* is frequent, and in Billiards (sense 9) the prevailing spelling.]

I. A ridge generally, a dividing ridge; a bar.
†**1.** A ridge, heap, or mound upon the ground; *e.g.* a grave-mound. *Obs.*
c **885** K. ÆLFRED *Boeth.* xvi. §2 þa het he hí bindan, and on balcan leȝan. *c* **1325** *E.E. Allit. Poems* A. 62 My body on balke þer bod in sweuen.
†**2.** A dividing ridge (of land); an isthmus; a bar of sand, etc. *Obs.*
1538 LELAND *Itin.* V. 16 A litle Balk of Sand cast up, the wich at low waters prohibitih the Se to cum about. **1565** GOLDING *Ovid's Met.* VI. (1593) 140 The narrow balke at which two seas do meete at hand. *Ibid.* VII. 164 The balcke that makes the strait divorce Between the seas Ionian and Aegean. **1633** P. FLETCHER *Purple Isl.* IV. xi, A border-city these two coasts removing; Which, like a balk.. Disparts the terms of anger and of loving.

II. A ridge left in ploughing; a miss, slip.
3. A ridge between two furrows (L. *porca*), or a strip of ground left unploughed as a boundary line between two ploughed portions.
c **1000** *Ælfric Gloss.* in Wright *Voc.* (W.) 147 *Porca*, balc. *a* **1300** W. DE BIBLESW. in Wright *Voc.* 159 *Vert choral*, a grene balke. **1393** LANGL. *P. Pl.* C. IX. 114 Dykers and deluers diggeden vp þe balkes. **1483** *Cath. Angl.* 19/1 Balke betwyx twa furris; *creb(r)o, porca.* **1562** BULLEYN *Bk. Simples* 16 b, Euery mere and balke is full of it [Scabios] in June. **1563** *Homilies* II. *Rogat. Week* IV. (1859) 498 How covetous men nowe a dayes plow vp so nigh the common balkes and walkes. **1576** GASCOIGNE *Steele Glas* (Arb.) 78 Earing vp the balks that part their bounds. **1604** BRETON *Pass. Sheph.* 13 The merrie countrie lad, Who upon a faire greene balk May at pleasure sit and walke. **1725** A. RAMSAY *Gent. Sheph.* V. iii, Last night I met him on a bawk, Whare yellow corn was growing. **1799** J. ROBERTSON *Agric. Perth* 196 These earthern boundaries (baulks) are wearing fast out. **1821** CLARE *Vill. Minstr.* II. 104 He takes his rambles ..Down narrow balks that intersect the fields.
4. a. A ridge or piece left unploughed by accident or carelessness; a piece missed in ploughing. (Often in phrase *to make a balk* or *balks*.)
c **1420** *Pallad. on Husb.* II. 15 The balke, that that calle, unered lande And overheled, beholde that there be noon. *c* **1430** LYDG. *Bochas.* VII. viii b (1554) 172 Making no balkes, yᵉ plough was truely hold. **1523** FITZHERB. *Husb.* §7 If he goo to the ploughe, and loke backwarde, he seeth not, whether the plough..make a balke. **1647** FULLER *Good Th. in Worse T.* Observ. xvi, The husbandman may dart forth an ejaculation, and not make a balk the more. *a* **1703** BURKITT *On N.T.* Luke ix. 62 He that ploughs must keep on, and make no balks. **1840** *Penny Cycl.* XVIII. 277/2 The leaving of balks is a great fault, and is owing to..the ploughman not holding his plough upright.
b. Hence *fig.*, esp. in *to make a balk of good ground*: to waste or throw away a good chance.
1605 CAMDEN *Rem.* (1637) 302 Make hay while sunne shines. Make not a balke of good ground. **1640** FULLER *Joseph's Coat* (1867) 35 The rich Corinthians, in not inviting the poor, made balks of good ground. *a* **1652** BROME *New Acad.* III. i, Your plow makes vile baulkes of my money. **1857** Bohn's *Handbk. Prov.* 69 Make not balks of good ground.
5. †**a.** *fig.* A slip, mistake, a blunder. *to make a balk*: to blunder, go wrong. *Obs.*
c **1430** *Hymns to Virg.* (1867) 92 þouȝ a ȝong man make a balke, ȝit take to þi mynde *reuertere.* **1661** ANNAND *Panem Quotid.* 18 They..make such bawlks in their prayer. **1717** TUDWAY in Ellis *Orig. Lett.* II. 435 IV. 311 Bentley's baulks and blunders about the king's reception.
b. *U.S.* In baseball: (see quot. 1867). Also *attrib.*
1845 in *Appleton's Ann. Cycl.* (1886) X. 77/2 A runner can not be put out..when a balk is made by the pitcher. **1867** H. CHADWICK *Beadle's Dime Base-Ball Player* 53 A balked Ball. —Should the pitcher move his foot in delivery—thereby making a 'balk'—and the Umpire call a 'balk' until the ball is returned to the pitcher, [etc.]. **1913** *Amer. Mag.* Sept. 24/1 Kilroy caught seven by his balk motion.
†**6.** *fig.* An omission, an exception. *Obs.* or *dial.*
1596 SPENSER *F.Q.* VI. xi. 16 They fall to strokes..Not sparing wight, ne leaving any balke. **1666** BUNYAN *Grace Ab.* ⁋315 But then I have asked why they made baulks? why they did salute the most handsome and let the ill favoured go? **1775** J. COLLIER *Tim Bobbin* 60 I'r so keen bitt'n I made no bawks at o hay seed.

III. A ridge in one's path; A stumbling-block, check; a term in billiards.
†**7.** A ridge in the way, over which one may stumble; a stumbling-block, obstacle. *Obs.*
1549 LATIMER *Serm. bef. Edw. VI* (1869) 36 We wold not walke in by-walkes, where are many balkes. **1562** STERNHOLD & H. *Ps.* xviii. 35 So that my feete shall neuer slip, Nor stumble at a balke. **1747** HOOSON *Miner's Dict.* Nj, How many Baulks and Obstructions..happen by the way.
8. *fig.* **a.** A hindrance, check, or defeat.
1660 T. M. *Hist. Indep.* IV. 78 As a balk to which the Committee of safety declared..that they had transmitted a great part of a form of government, etc. *a* **1716** SOUTH *Serm.* VI. 311 (T.) There cannot be a greater balk to the tempter. **1725** DE FOE *Voy. round World* (1840) 341 This was a balk to them and put a damp to their new projects. **1823** LAMB *Elia* Ser. I. xxi. (1865) 162 It would be some balk to the spirit of conversation if you knew.
b. A disappointment.
1733 SWIFT *Wks.* (1745) VIII. 122 Poor Tom has got a plaguy baulk. **1741** RICHARDSON *Pamela* (1824) I. VIII. 244 It was a great baulk to her, that you did not comply with my request.
c. Of a horse: an instance of balking (cf. BALK *v.*[1] 3).
1866 E. KEYES *Diary* 28 Apr. in *Colorado Mag.* (1933) X. 72 The horses were not used to being driven together..we had balks innumerable..but in the end on we would go as merry as ever.
9. a. *transf.* The part of a billiard table behind a transverse line (the 'baulk-line') near one end, within the D or half-circle of which a player whose ball is in hand must place it to make his stroke. (As, in billiards, such player must play out from baulk, and can strike only indirectly at a ball lying within it, the original sense of the term was perhaps that of 'check.') In *U.S.*, *baulk-line* is also applied to one of four lines drawn parallel to the side of the table or diagonally across the corners; also designating a carom billiards game in which these lines restrict scoring (see quot. 1910). Also *attrib.*
1800 *Hoyle's Games* 250 When the striker's and the red ball are within the baulk, he is not obliged to pass the ball. **1839** E. KENTFIELD *Billiards* 3 At the lower end of the table ..is a line technically termed the Baulk Line. **1874** WHYTE-MELVILLE *Uncle John* ix, She strung to begin—won—and put her ball in balk. **1896** W. BROADFOOT et al. *Billiards* ix. 283 (*heading*) Safety and baulk play. *Ibid.* ix. 285 A few examples of safety and baulk strokes. **1906** *Daily Chron.* 19 Apr. 4/7 The 18.1 in. baulk-line champion. **1910** *Encycl. Brit.* III. 939/1 Various schemes have been devised to make the game more difficult. One of these is known as the 'continuous baulk-line'. Lines are drawn, 8, 14, 18 or even 22 in. from the rails, parallel to the side of the table... In the case of the *Triangular Baulk-line*, lines are drawn at the four corners. *Ibid.*, The 'anchor baulk-lines'..are drawn at the end of a baulk-line where it touches the rail.
b. *to make a baulk*: to bring one's own and the red ball within the baulk, when the opponent's ball is in hand.
1839 E. KENTFIELD *Billiards* 24 Directions for making what are termed baulks.

IV. A beam of wood.
10. A roughly squared beam of timber; sometimes used technically to designate Baltic timber, which is roughly dressed before shipment.
c **1300** *Cursor M.* 8783 þe balk þat mast þe werk suld bind þai soght, and noþer-quar cuth find. *c* **1386** CHAUCER *Reeves Prol.* 66 He can wel in myn eye see a stalke, But in his owne he can nought seen a balke. **1483** *Cath. Angl.* 19/1 Balke of a howse, *trabs.* **1662** PEPYS *Diary* 23 June, Deales, spars, and bulks. **1666** *Lond. Gaz.* No. 35/4 Laden with Oaken and Firr Balks. **1677** MOXON *Mech. Exerc.* (1703) 157 Bauk, a piece of Fir unslit, from four to ten inches square. **1734** *Builder's Dict., Balks*..so some call great pieces of Timber coming from beyond Seas by Floats. **1793** SMEATON *Edystone L.* §38 A course of squared oak balks. **1881** *Mechanic* §136 The strongest timber obtainable..is that which is sawn out of baulks. **1884** *Timber Tr. Jrnl.* 14 June 417/3 Danzig fir balks.
11. A tie-beam of a house, stretching from wall to wall. In old one-storey houses these were often exposed and used for hanging or placing articles on, or laid with boards so as to form a loft, called 'the balks.' Now chiefly *north.*
a **1300** W. DE BIBLESW. in Wright *Voc.* 170 *Les trayes* (*gloss* balkes). *c* **1386** CHAUCER *Miller's T.* 440 Laddres thre To clymben by the ronges..Unto the tubbes hangyng in the balkes. **1535** COVERDALE *Zeph.* ii. 14 Foules shal synge in the wyndowes and rauens shal syt vpon the balckes. **1565** GOLDING *Ovid's Met.* VIII. (1593) 202 A flitch of restie bacon from the balke made blacke with smoke. **1641** BEST *Farm Bks.* (1856) 53 When wee have brought up the farre roomestead as high as the balke. **1691** RAY *N. Countr. Wds.* 5 The Balk or Bawk, the Summer-beam or Dorman. *c* **1760** ? MICKLE *Nae Luck about the Hoose*, There's twa fat hens upon the bauk. **1837** CARLYLE *Fr. Rev.* II. I. xii. (D.) The stiffest balk bends more or less; all joists creak.
12. A cross-beam or bar in a chimney or kiln.
1432 *Test. Ebor.* (1855) II. 23 Unum instrumentum ferreum in camino aulæ, vocatum *balk.* ? *a* **1600** *Felon Sow of Rokeby*, The sew was in the kiln hole down As they were on the balke aboon.
13. The beam of a balance. *Obs.* exc. *dial.*
1399 *Fabric Rolls Yk. Minstr.* in *Linc. Gloss.* (E.D.S.), I balke ferri cum les scales et ponderibus. **1571** *Wills & Inv. N.C.* (1855) II. 364 Payre of great skales wᵗʰ yᵉ balk. **1671** FLAVEL *Fount. Life* iv. 10 The Balk of a Balance, to weigh Christ's excellency. **1854** H. MILLER *Sch. & Schm.* xxiii. (1858) 509 To give..his customers 'the cast of the baulk.' *Sc. Proverb*, The young lamb comes as often to the bauk as the auld ewe.
14. *Comb.* †**balk-line,** ? a line hanging from the cross-beams; †**balk-staff,** a quarter-staff; **balk-yard,** a timber-yard.
c **1400** *Beryn* 153 He berith a Bal[k]staff quod the toon, and els a rakis ende. **1506** in Blomefield *Norfolk* V. 1670 A new balk-line to the star, and rysing star, viijᵈ. **1664** COTTON *Scarron.* I. (1715) 10 Balk-Staves and Cudgels, Pikes and Truncheons. **1674** RAY *N. Countr. Wds.* 4 *Balk-staff*, a Quarter-staff, a great Staff like a Pole or Beam. **1823** *Let.* in Polwhele *Trad. & Recoll.* (1826) II. 770 Straying into a balk-yard fell over a beam of timber.

V. In fishing. [The connexion of 16 with the other senses is doubtful.]
15. *dial.* A set of stout stakes surrounded by netting or wicker work for catching fish.
1836 SIR G. HEAD *Home Tour* 430, I observed some fish 'balks' on the sands..The fish are taken on the sand within the balk at low water.
16. The stout rope at the top of fishing nets by which they are fastened one to another in a 'fleet.' (In Cornw. *balch.*)
1847 H. MILLER *First. Impr.* i. 3 Away from wave-top to wave-top, like the cork baulk of a fisherman's net afloat on the swell. **1880** *E. Cornw. Gloss.* (E.D.S.), *Balch*, a stout cord used for the head-line of a fishing net.

balk, *sb.*[2] [f. BALK *v.*[1] in the local sense of 'to leave unfinished'.] Of cloth: in the raw or unfinished state.
1841 R. W. HAMILTON *Nugæ Lit.* 357 (Yorks. Dial.) *Balk*, ..cloth in an unfinished state. **1860** S. JUBB *Hist. Shoddy-Trade* 40 Short Ends were sold to the merchants..in the grey raised (not balk) state. **1876** W. CUDWORTH *Bradford* 519 These clothiers attended the Leeds White Cloth Market ..selling their cloth in the 'balk', or raw state.

balk (bɔ:k), *v.*[1] Forms: 6 **balck,** 6–7 **balke,** 7 **baulke, bawk,** 8 **bauk,** 6–9 **baulk,** 4– **balk.** [f. BALK, BAULK *sb.*[1]]
I. †**1.** *trans.* (and *absol.*) To make balks in ploughing; to plough up in ridges. *Obs.*
1393 GOWER *Conf.* III. 296 But so well halt no man the plough, That he ne balketh other while. *c* **1420** *Pallad. on Husb.* I. 184 To tille a felde man must have diligence, And balk it not. **1583** STANYHURST *Æneis* I. (Arb.) 22 With forck King Neptun is ayding. He balcks thee quicksands, and fluds dooth mollefye. **1611** COTGR., *Assilloner*, to baulke, or plow up in baulkes. [*a* **1640** JACKSON *Creed* XI. cxxxix. Wks. XI. 203 Whilst we labour to plough up your hearts..we must not balk that saying of St. John.]
II. 2. *trans.* To miss or omit intentionally. †**a.** *lit.* To pass by (a place), to avoid in passing; to shun.
1484 *Paston Lett.* 859 III. 279 Mastyer Baley..woold not have balkyd this pore loggeyng to Norwyche wardes. **1612–5** BP. HALL *Contempl. N.T.* IV. iii. 173 Jericho was in his way from Galilee to Jerusalem: he baulks it not, though it were outwardly cursed. **1684** LADY R. RUSSELL *Lett.* I. xv. 43, I hope you will not balk Totteridge, if I am here. *a* **1733** NORTH *Exam.* II. iv. ⁋94 Going to Lord Clarendon..

baulking the Secretary. **1783** AINSWORTH *Lat. Dict.* (Morell) s.v. *Balk*, I will not balk your house.

b. *fig.* To pass over, overlook, refrain from noticing (what comes in one's way); to shirk, ignore.

c **1440** *Promp. Parv.* 22 Balkyn, or ouerskyppyn, *omitto.* **1582** FLEETWOOD in Ellis *Orig. Lett.* II. 216 III. 90 As for my Lo. Maior.. I am dryven every daie to bawk hym and his doynges. **1640** BP. HALL *Episc.* I. §11. 39, I may not baulke two pregnant testimonies of the Fathers. **1656** SANDERSON *Serm.* II. 160 The spying of motes in our brother's eye, and baulking of beams in our own. **1684** *Cont. Foxe's A. & M.* III. 900 The Bayliff would fain have baulked him, As if he had not seen him. **1742** RICHARDSON *Pamela* III. 42 Let me tell you, (nor will I balk it) my Brother.. will want one Apology for his Conduct. **1848** L. HUNT *Jar of Honey* Pref. 4 No topic is baulked if it come uppermost.

c. To refuse (anything offered or that comes in course, *e.g.* food or drink).

1587 TURBERV. *Trag. T.* (1837) 230 And balke your bed for shame. **1619** FLETCHER *M. Thomas* I. i. 386 A bait you cannot balk Sir. **1649** BLITH *Eng. Improv. Impr.* (1653) 183 If the stalk grow big, cattell will balk it. *a* **1784** JOHNSON in *Boswell* (1831) I. 236, I never.. balked an invitation out to dinner. **1810** CRABBE *Borough* xvi, He took them all and never balk'd his glass.

d. To avoid (a duty or responsibility).

1631 PRESTON *Effect. Faith* 146 Thou must not balke the way of Religion, because of the troubles thou meetest. *a* **1707** BEVERIDGE *Priv. Th.* II. 103 Not that we should run ourselves into danger, but that we should baulk no Duty to avoid it. **1785** COWPER *Tirocin.* 257 Such an age as ours baulks no expence.

e. To let slip, fail to use, seize, keep, reach, etc.

1601 SHAKS. *Twel. N.* III. ii. 26 This was look't for at your hand, and this was baulkt. **1697** DRYDEN *Virg. Georg.* Ded. If I balk'd this opportunity. **1724** A. RAMSAY *Tea-t. Misc.* (1733) I. 2 This point of a' his wishes He wadna with set speeches bauk. **1826** HOR. SMITH *Gai. & Grav.* in *Casquet of Lit.* I. 326/2 My adviser insisted upon my not baulking my luck.

3. a. *intr.* To stop short as at an obstacle, to pull up, swerve. *Esp.* of a horse: To jib, refuse to go on, or to leap, to shy; also of the rider, and of any one on foot, refusing a leap. Also *fig.* (*colloq.*) to shy or jib *at*.

1481 CAXTON *Reynard* (Arb.) 32 Isegrym balked and sayde, ye make moche a doo, sir Tybert. **1596** SPENSER *F.Q.* IV. x. 25 Ne ever ought but of their true loves talkt, Ne ever for rebuke or blame of any balkt. **1722** DE FOE *Moll. Fl.* (1840) 78 If he balked, I knew I was undone. **1756** C. LUCAS *Ess. Waters* III. 340 No man, that drinks water, baulks at a pint.. in the day. **1843** LEVER *J. Hinton* xxv, Burke.. suddenly swerved his horse round, and affecting to baulk, cantered back. **1862** *Melbourne Leader* 5 July, His horse balked at a leap, and threw him. **1908** J. M. DILLON *Motor Days Eng.* xx. 241 It was the only time I ever saw Maud balk at gooseberries.

†**b.** To lie out of the way. *Obs.*

1591 SPENSER *M. Hubberd* 268 Labour that did from his liking balke.

†**4.** *trans.* To miss by error or inadvertence. *Obs.*

1579 SPENSER *Sheph. Cal.* Sept. 93 They.. balk the right way, and strayen abroad. **1659** FELTHAM *Low Countr.* (1677) 46 You cannot baulk your Road without the hazard of drowning. **1710** PALMER *Proverbs* 6 Young dogs.. balk the true game to ply every scent.

III. 5. *trans.* To place a balk in the way of. **a.** To check, hinder, thwart (a person or his action).

1589 WARNER *Alb. Eng.* VI. xxxi. (1612) 153, I sometimes proffered kindnesse.. but.. was balked with a blush. **1635** SWAN *Spec. M.* v. §2 (1643) 105 The King.. must not be baulked in his late proceedings. **1726** DE FOE *Hist. Devil* I. xi. (1840) 155 An enemy who is baulked and defeated, but not overcome. **1821** BYRON *Two Fosc.* I. i, They shall not balk my entrance. **1855** PRESCOTT *Philip II*, I. II. xiii. 292 The sturdy cavalier was not to be balked in his purpose.

b. To check (feelings, or a person in his feelings).

1682 DRYDEN *Rel. Laici* 212 Nor doth it balk my charity to find The Egyptian Bishop of another mind. **1746** LD. MALMESBURY *Lett.* I. 37 Lord Talbot was not much baulked with this rebuke. **1855** HT. MARTINEAU *Autobiog.* I. 92 My home affections.. all the stronger for having been repressed and baulked.

c. To disappoint (expectations, or any one in his expectations).

1590 MARLOWE *Edw. II*, II. v, We.. must not come so near to balk their lips. **1652** BROME *Jov. Crew* II. 389 May your Store Never decay, nor baulk the Poor. **1725** POPE *Odyss.* x. 135 Balk'd of his prey, the yelling monster flies. **1854** THACKERAY *Newcomes* I. 286 Balk yourself of the pleasure of bullying. **1873** SPENSER *Stud. Sociol.* vii. 161 Time after time our hopes are balked.

d. To frustrate, foil, render unsuccessful.

1635 QUARLES *Emblems* III. xiv. (1718) 182 To baulk those ills which present joys bewray. **1727** SWIFT *Censure* Misc. (1735) V. 104 The most effectual Way to baulk Their Malice, is—— to let them talk. **1848** KINGSLEY *Saint's Trag.* II. v. 90 With which we try to balk the curse of Eve.

†**6.** *trans.* and *absol.* To meet arguments with objections; to quibble, chop logic, bandy words.

1596 SPENSER *F.Q.* III. ii. 12 Her list in stryfull termes with him to balke. **1596** SHAKS. *Tam. Shrew* I. i. 34 Balke Lodgicke with acquaintaince that you haue. **1653** MANTON *Exp. James* iii. 2 Wks. IV. 227 They do not divide and baulk with God.

balk, *v.*² ? *Obs.* [prob. a. Du. *balk-en* to bray, bawl, shout, cogn. with OE. *bælcan* to shout, vociferate (which would itself have given *balch*).] To signify to fishing-boats the direction taken by the shoals of herrings or pilchards, as seen from heights overlooking the sea; done at first by bawling or shouting, subsequently by signals. See BALKER².

1603 *Act 1 Jas. I*, xxiii, To wache for the saide Fishe, and to balke, hue, conde, direct, and guide the Fishermen which shall be vpon the saide Sea and Sea Coasts for the takinge of the saide Fishe.

Balkan (ˈbɔːlkən), *a.* Of or pertaining to the peninsula bounded by the Adriatic, Ægean, and Black Seas, or to the countries or peoples of this region; *spec.* with allusion to the relations (often characterized by threatened hostilities) of the Balkan states to each other or to the rest of Europe; so in the derivatives, **Balkanic** (bɔːlˈkænɪk), ˈ**Balkanoid** *adjs.*, ˈ**Balkanism**.

1835 *Penny Cycl.* III. 327/1 Balkan Mountains, or Great Balkan. **1854** *Jrnl. R. Geogr. Soc.* XXIV. 53 The plateau of the principal Balkan chain. **1876** W. FORSYTH *Slavonic Prov.* v. 131 Bulgaria.. is separated from Roumelia on the south by the lofty range of the Balkan Mountains. **1886** J. G. C. MINCHIN *Growth of Freedom in Balkan Peninsula* v. 92 The Russians dismembered the Ottoman Empire, while she succeeded in keeping the Balkan States weak and divided. **1891** *Fortn. Rev.* Sept. 365 A Balkan Federation.. a scheme for the confederation of the young States of the Balkan Peninsula. **1915** A. D. INNES *Hohenz.* vi. 88 The next episode presents itself with the great Balkan War. *Ibid.*, In dealing with the Balkan problem, the Powers ought not to regard themselves as two hostile groups. **1915** *Sphere* 28 Aug. 214/1 The unhappy war between the Balkanic allies after the defeat of Turkey. **1922** *Encycl. Brit.* XXX. 370/2 Balkanic Italy (country of Gorizia E. of the Isonzo, W. Carniola, Istria, Trieste and Zara). **1924** *Scribner's Mag.* Jan. 19/2 Patches of glaring 'Westernism'.. merely emphasize Belgrade's fundamental 'Balkanism'. **1925** *Public Opinion* 23 Jan. 86/2 His swarthy face with its cunning Balkanic eyes. **1925** *Contemp. Rev.* Apr. 476 Matters that, like everything Balkanic, lie very much on the knees of the gods. **1932** E. WEEKLEY *Words & Names* x. 152 Romances dealing with imaginary Balkanoid principalities of homicidal atmosphere. **1962** *Listener* 25 Jan. 157/1 There are all the makings of a 'Balkan situation' in West Africa.

b. *Balkan frame*: a frame, with weights and pulleys attached, used to provide support and traction for fractured limbs.

1929 F. A. POTTLE *Stretchers* (1930) 104 Many of the beds are fitted with elaborate frameworks of wood ('Balkan frames') for the proper treatment of fractures. **1936** J. DOS PASSOS *Big Money* 309 Charley was in the hospital three months with his leg in a Balkan frame.

Hence ˈ**Balkanize** *v.*, to divide (a region) into a number of smaller and often mutually hostile units, as was done in the Balkan Peninsula in the late 19th and early 20th centuries. So ˌ**Balkaniˈzation**, ˈ**Balkanized** *ppl. a.*, ˈ**Balkanizing** *vbl. sb.* and *ppl. a.*

1920 *19th Cent.* Mar. 536 Great Britain has been accused by French observers of pursuing a policy aimed at the Balkanisation of the Baltic provinces. *Ibid.* Nov. 801 They can see nothing in.. his Balkanising policy but a continual threat to European peace. **1920** *Public Opinion* 2 July 4/3 In this unhappy Balkanised world.. every state is at issue with its neighbours. **1921** S. GRAHAM *Europe—Whither Bound?* vii. 95 Hungary avers that a large stretch of Hungarian territory.. is being Balkanized. **1922** A. J. TOYNBEE *Western Question in Greece & Turkey* i. 25 The word 'Balkanisation'.. was coined by German socialists to describe what was done to the western fringe of the Russian Empire by the Peace of Brest-Litovsk. **1931** A. L. ROWSE *Polit. & Younger Gen.* x. 267 A war which began with the attempt to impose order in the Balkans has had the effect of balkanizing Europe. **1960** *Economist* 15 Oct. 216/1 The African leaders.. owe it to themselves.. to grasp what there is in the majority report for them before they opt for balkanisation. **1967** *Listener* 11 May 607/2 A great majority of senior states and leaders would consider such a new Balkanizing of the world disastrous.

balked (bɔːkt), *ppl. a.* [f. BALK *v.*¹ + -ED.]

†**1.** Ridged, ribbed. *Obs.*

1597 GERARDE *Herbal* II. cxc. (1633) 607 Streaked or balked as it were with sundry stiffe streakes or ribbes running along every leafe.

†**2.** ? Heaped up; piled in a heap. *Obs.*

1596 SHAKS. *1 Hen. IV.* I. i. 69 Two and twenty Knights Balk'd in their owne blood did Sir Walter see.

3. Checked, foiled; disappointed.

1704 STEELE *Tend. Husb.* I. v, I came up to be married, I don't care to go down and look baulk'd. **1848** THACKERAY *Van. Fair* xxxv. (1866) 294 Pang of balked affection.

4. *U.S.* In baseball: (see BALK *sb.*¹ 5 b).

†ˈ**balkening**, *ppl. a. Obs.* [as if pr. pple. of a verb *balken.*] Rising in a ridge.

1538 LELAND *Itin.* IV. 126 A Towne.. standing somewhat clyminge on the side of a small balkening Ground.

ˈ**balker**¹. [f. BALK *v.*¹ + -ER.¹.] One who balks; one who makes balks, or frequents them.

1549 LATIMER *Serm. bef. Edw. VI.* (Arb.) 30 They walke not directly and plainely, but delight in balkes, and stubble way. Let vs no more desyre to be baukers [*printed* bankers]. **1783** AINSWORTH *Lat. Dict.* (Morell), Balker, *imporcator.*

ˈ**balker**². [f. BALK *v.*² + -ER¹.] A man stationed on an eminence by the shore to signal to fishing-boats the direction taken by the shoals of herring or pilchards; a huer, hooer, or conder.

1602 CAREW *Cornwall* 32 b, Directed in theire worke by a Balker, or Huer who standeth on the Cliffe side, and from thence, best discerneth the quantitie and course of the Pilcherd. **1603** *Act 1 Jas. I*, xxiii, Diuers persons.. called Balcors, Huors, Condors, Directors or Guidors.. have vsed to watch and attend vpon the high Hilles and Grounds neere adioyning to the Sea Coasts for the giving Notice to the Fishermen. **1754** T. GARDNER *Hist. Dunwich* 163 A Conder.. whereon the Balkers stood to notify, by Signals of Boughs.. the Direction of the Herring Sholes. **1841** *Blackw. Mag.* L. 152 Let them be our quarry men, our falcons.. our balkers,—'herrings ahead, ho!'

ˈ**balkiness.** [f. BALKY *a.*] The quality of being balky.

1894 *Outing* (U.S.) XXIV. 349/1 The mules were the very embodiment of balkiness. **1909** J. C. LINCOLN *Keziah Coffin* x. 143, I, bein' a Hammond, with some of the Hammond balkiness in me, I set my foot down as hard as his.

ˈ**balking**, *vbl. sb.*¹ [f. BALK *v.*¹ + -ING¹.] The action of BALK *v.*¹ in various senses.

1549 LATIMER *Serm. bef. Edw. VI.* (Arb.) 36 Amongest many balkinges, is much stumbling. **1649** BLITH *Eng. Improv. Impr.* (1653) 182 It is my constant cry to my own Husbandmen to take heed of Ploough-balking and Harrow balking, but now I say in a more especial manner, take heed of Seed-balking. **1783** AINSWORTH *Lat. Dict.* (Morell), Balking, *imporcatio*, [also] *omissio, prætermissio.* **1875** B. TAYLOR *Faust* I. iv. 71 Fall to and show no timid balking.

†ˈ**balking**, *vbl. sb.*² ? *Obs.* [f. BALK *v.*² + -ING¹.] The guiding of fishing-boats by shouting or signalling from a height.

1603 *Act 1 Jas. I*, xxiii, For watching of the saide Fishe, or for balkinge, huinge, condinge, directinge or guidinge of the saide Fishermen in their Boates.

ˈ**balking**, *ppl. a.* [f. BALK *v.*¹ + -ING².] That balks; checking; shying.

Mod. Balking circumstances; a balking horse.

ˈ**balkingly**, *adv.* [f. prec. + -LY².] In such a manner as to balk.

1864 in WEBSTER.

†ˈ**balkish**, *a. Obs.* [f. BALK *sb.*¹ + -ISH¹.] Characterized by balks or ridges; uneven, rough.

1577 STANYHURST in *Æneis* (Arb.) Introd. 12 That my penne shoulde walke.. in that craggie and balkishe way.

balky (ˈbɔːkɪ), *a.* Also **baulky**. [f. BALK *sb.*¹ + -Y¹.] Given to balking (as a horse); reluctant to proceed; contrary, perverse.

1847 J. T. HUGHES *Doniphan's Exped.* (1907) 14/1 The mules and other animals.. often became refractory and balky. **1856** OLMSTED *Slave States* 197 Advice how to cure a balky horse: '*Sell* him, my lord.' **1857** *Quinland* II. xvi. II. 117 One of his horses is baulky, and he can't go any farther. **1873** W. MAYO *Never Again* xxiii. 291 Making a balky Crœsus step up to his collar. **1897** KIPLING *Capt. Cour.* vii. 147 Young Olley's gittin' kinder baulky an' excited. **1957** *Economist* 21 Dec. 1052/2 When federal officials hoped to proceed to more substantial matters such as public housing and public assistance, the states turned balky.

balky, obs. form of BULKY.

ball (bɔːl), *sb.*¹ Forms: 3-7 **bal**, 4-6 **balle**, 6 **baule, bawle**, 5- **ball**. [ME. *bal* (inflected *ball-e, -es*), a. ON. *böllr* (pron. bɔllr; cf. OSw. *baller*, Sw. *båll*):—OTeut. **ballu-z*, (whence probably MHG. *bal, ball-es*, MDu. *bal*). Cogn. with OHG. *ballo, pallo*, MHG. *balle*:—OTeut. **ballon* (wk. masc.), and OHG. *ballâ, pallâ*, MHG. *balle*:—OTeut. **ballôn* (wk. fem.). No OE. representative of any of these is known. (The answering forms in OE. would have been **beallu, -a, -e*: cf. *bealluc*, BALLOCK.) If *ball-* was native in Teutonic, it may have been cognate with L. *foll-is* in sense of a 'thing blown up or inflated.' In the later ME. spelling *balle*, the word coincided graphically with F. *balle* 'ball' and 'bale,' which has hence been erroneously assumed to be its source. Cf. BALE *sb.*³]

I. A globe or globular body.

1. a. *generally.*

a **1300** *Fragm.* 89 in Wright *Pop. Sc.* 134 As me mai bi a candle i-seo, that is bisides a balle, That ȝeveth liȝt on hire hal-vendel. *c* **1340** *Cursor M.* (Fairf.) 521 His heued ys rouned as a balle. **1340** *Ayenb.* 179 þe pyef.. þrauþ þane little bal in-to þe hondes þrote þet he ne ssel naȝt berke. *c* **1386** CHAUCER *Knts. T.* 1756 He rolleth vnder foot as dooth a bal. **1398** TREVISA *Barth. de P. R.* XVI. lxxx. (1495) 579 Wyth balles of leed men assaye depnesse. **1578** LYTE *Dodoens* 167 Turned into a round heauie baule. **1626** BACON *Sylva* §696 The Wormes with many feet which round themselves into Balls. **1716-8** LADY MONTAGUE *Lett.* 38 I. 150 The.. tents.. are adorned on the top with guilded balls. **1824** LANDOR *Imag. Conv.* xvii. Wks. 1846 I. 107 A ball must strike the earth before it can rebound. **1831** BLAKEY *Free Will* 151 To attend to them all at one time as jugglers do with their balls. **1878** MRS. H. WOOD *Pomeroy Ab.* 242 A short, stout ball of a woman.

b. *ball and chain*, a heavy metal ball secured by a chain to the leg of a prisoner or convict, to prevent escape. Also *chain and ball* (s.v. CHAIN *sb.* 2 a). *U.S.*

1835 J. H. INGRAHAM *South-West* II. 189 The threat of the Calaboose, or the 'ball and chain'. **1873** J. H. BEADLE *Undeveloped West* vii. 132 Those who had fined and imprisoned culprits, or sent them to work with ball and chain. **1902** W. N. HARBEN *Abner Daniel* 94 They put a ball an' chain to one of his ankles an' sent him out with the nigger gang.

2. *spec.* Any planetary or celestial body, *esp.* the earth, 'the globe.' Now always with qualification, 'terrestrial,' 'earthly,' etc.

a 1300 *Fragm.* 255 in Wright *Pop. Sc.* 137 Urthe is amidde the see a lute bal and round. 1548 UDALL, etc. *Erasm. Par. Acts* xvii. 24 (R.) The heauenly balles and circles aboue. 1593 SHAKS. *Rich. II*, III. ii. 41 From vnder this Terrestrial Ball. 1697 DRYDEN *Virg. Eclog.* vi. 52 This goodly Ball. 1712 ADDISON *Spect.* No. 465 What, though in solemn silence all Move round the dark terrestrial ball. 1717 POPE *Elegy Unfort. Lady* 35 If eternal Justice rules the ball. 1834 TENNYSON *Two Voices* 35 No compound of this earthly ball.

†3. The golden 'orb' borne together with the sceptre as the emblem of sovereignty. *Obs.*

c 1485 *Digby Myst.* (1882) (Mor. Wisd.) i. Argt., In his left hand a ball of gold with a crosse þer-vpon. 1599 SHAKS. *Hen. V*, IV. i 277 The Scepter, and the Ball, the Sword, the Mase, the Crowne Imperiall. 1622 BACON *Hen. VII.* 149 A young Man, that..ought to hold in his hand the Ball of a Kingdome. 1715 POPE *Ep. Miss Blount*, Thus vanish sceptres, coronets, and balls.

4. a. A globular body to play with, which is thrown, kicked, knocked, or batted about, in various games, as hand-ball, foot-ball, tennis, golf, cricket, croquet, billiards, etc. It varies greatly in size and material according to the game.

(This was perhaps the earliest sense in English.)

1205 LAY. 24703 Summe heo driuen balles wide ȝeond þa feldes. *c* 1320 *Seuyn Sag.* (W.) 2004 With that bal togider they plaid. *c* 1340 *Cursor M.* (Fairf.) 13139 His broþer doghter..come playand hir wiþ a balle. 1483 *Cath. Angl.* 19/1 Balle, *pila*. 1530 PALSGR. 196/2 Ball to play at tennes with—*estevf.* 1562 J. HEYWOOD *Prov. & Epigr.* (1867) 35 Thou hast striken the ball, vnder the lyne. 1599 SHAKS. *Hen. V*, I. ii. 261 When we haue matcht our Rackets to these Balles. 1611 BIBLE *Isa.* xxii. 18 He will surely..tosse thee like a ball. 1721 BAILEY, *Cricket*, a sort of Play with Bats and a Ball. 1807 CRABBE *Village* I. Wks. 1823 I. 16 The flying ball, The bat, the wicket, were his labours all. 1857 HUGHES *Tom Brown* II. 58/2 The ball flies off his bat to all parts of the field.

See also BILLIARD-, CRICKET-, FOOT-BALL, etc.

b. A game played with a ball (*spec.* in *U.S.*, baseball); also an annual contest at hand-ball, played on a holiday in most of the towns and villages on the Scottish Border.

c 1350 *Life of Cuthbert* in Strutt *Sports & Past.* II. iii, He pleyde atte balle with the Children that his fellowes were. 1598 STOW *Survey* 68 After dinner all the youthes goe into the fieldes to play at the ball. 1675 COTTON *Scoffer Scoft* 50 To play at Cat, at Trap, or Ball. 1831 *Proc. Berw. Nat. Club.* I. 45 (*Article*) The game of Ball as played in Dunse on Fastern's Eve. 1847 TENNYSON *Princess* III. 199 Quoit, tennis, ball—no games? 1868 H. CHADWICK *Base Ball* 162 The National Game of ball of Americans. 1896 KNOWLES & MORTON *Baseball* 71 He saw ball played by the American Students.

c. A throw, toss, or 'delivery' of the ball in certain games, *esp.* in *Cricket*, the particulars of its course and effect being included in the notion. ***no ball*** in *Cricket*, one unfairly bowled; ***wide ball***, one not properly within the batsman's reach; ***the balls are over***: cf. OVER *adv.* 5 c.

1483 *Cath. Angl.* 19 Balle *alipatus qui iaculatur pilam.* 1773 *Gentl. Mag.* Nov. 568 The modern way Of blocking every ball at play. 1819 MISS MITFORD *Village* (1848) I. 177 That brilliant hitter..gained eight from two successive balls. 1837 DICKENS *Pickw.* vii, He blocked the doubtful balls, missed the bad ones, took the good ones. 1850 *Cricket Manual* 54 The names of the bowlers who bowl 'wide balls' or 'no balls'..to be placed on the score. 1870 *New Sporting Mag.* LX. 271 'The Balls are over.' Some of the umpires of the present day corrupt the four words..into '*Ver*'. 1894 E. B. V. CHRISTIAN *At Sign of Wkt.* 75 For him who falls, His hundred made..There need no tears,..'the balls Are over' now.

5. a. A missile (originally always spherical, now also conical or cylindrical with convex top) projected from an engine of war, in early times from catapults and crossbows, and now from cannons, muskets, pistols, and other fire-arms. In artillery, a solid as distinguished from a hollow projectile; these are of iron, but formerly were often of stone; the balls fired from small-arms are also called *bullets*, and are made of lead.

1387 TREVISA *Higden* Rolls Ser. I. 297 þe men of þat lond ..vseþ balles and alblastres. 1588 *Ord. King's Fleet* in *Harl. Misc.* (1810) I. 118 The artillery..being all charged with their balls. 1599 SHAKS. *Hen. V*, v. ii. 17 The fatall Balls of murthering Basiliskes. *a* 1631 DONNE *Epigr.* (1652) 100 Threatening balls in showres of murther fly. 1667 MILTON *P.L.* VI. 518 Mineral and Stone..to found their Engins and their Balls Of missive ruin. 1692 *Diary Siege Lymerick* 28 March out with their Arms, Baggage, Drums beating, Ball in Mouth..Colours flying. 1718 LADY MONTAGU *Lett.* 49 II. 58 Tombs of fine marble..daily lessened by the prodigious balls that the Turks make from them for their cannon. 1812 *Examiner* 19 Oct. 659/1 More than 600,000 balls and shells. 1858 W. ELLIS *Vis. Madagascar* xii. 330 A round stone, like a large cannon-ball.

b. *collectively.*

1584 SANDERS in Arb. *Garner* II. 16 The King had discharged three shots without ball. 1710 *Lond. Gaz.* No. 4702/2 The Powder, small Ball, and small Arms remaining in the Garrisons. 1849 MACAULAY *Hist. Eng.* I. 479 A body of troops..was ordered to load with ball.

6. a. *Pyrotechny* and *Mil.* A globular case or shell filled with combustibles, intended to set buildings on fire, or to give light, smoke, etc.; e.g. ***fire-balls***, ***smoke-balls***, ***stink-balls***.

1753 CHAMBERS *Cycl. Supp.* s.v., Smoak, or dark Balls.. fill the air with smoak, and..prevent discoveries. Sky Balls ..bursting like rockets, afford a spectacle of decoration.

b. Phr. ***ball of fire***: (*a*) *slang*, a glass of brandy; (*b*) = FIRE-BALL; (*c*) *fig.*, a person of great liveliness or spirit (cf. FIRE *sb.* 13).

1821 J. BURROWES *Life in St. George's Fields* 25 *Ball of fire*, glass of brandy. 1889 BARRÈRE & LELAND *Dict. Slang* I. 70/2 A *ball* of fire in popular slang is a glass of brandy, in allusion to the fieriness and pungency of the wretchedly bad spirit sold as brandy to the lower classes. 1953 G. LAMMING *In Castle of Skin* ii. 21 The white gentl'man..run [*sic*] like a ball of fire all the way home. 1958 J. D. MACDONALD *Executioners* (1959) x. 159 You haven't been a ball of fire around here lately. 1960 N. MITFORD *Don't tell Alfred* ii. 26 Yes, I know her. Not a ball of fire, is she? 1964 M. M. GOWING *Brit. & Atomic Energy 1939–1945* ix. 265 Sir Geoffrey [Taylor] also stimulated serious theoretical investigation into the 'ball of fire' phenomena in the explosion.

7. A globular body of wood, ivory, or other substance, used in voting by BALLOT (q.v.), each voter being provided with one black and one white. Hence ***to black-ball***, q.v.

1580 NORTH *Plutarch* (1656) 927 The Judges..would never take their bals to ballot against him. 1620 *Reliq. Wotton.* (1672) 309 In the first Ballotation..the Balls were equal. *a* 1700 DRYDEN (J.) For ev'ry number'd captive put a ball Into an urn: three only black be there, The rest, all white, are safe. 1709 *Lond. Gaz.* No. 4543/1 They took a Boy to draw the Balls. 1884 C. DICKENS *Dict. Lond.* 25/1 One black ball in three excludes.

†8. In the phrase ***ball in the hood***, applied in grim humour to the head (partly *fig.* from 4). *Obs.*

c 1300 *K. Alis.* 6481 Mony of his knyghtis gode Loren theo balles in heore hode. *c* 1325 *Cœur de L.* 4523 Men of armes the swerdes outbreyde; Balles out of hoodes, soone they pleyde. *c* 1460 *Towneley Myst.* 17, I shrew thi balle under thi hode. *c* 1500 *Rob. Hood* (Ritson) i. 1454 He ne shall lese his hede, That is the best ball in his hode.

9. ***ball of the eye***: a. orig. the 'apple' or pupil; b. now, the eye itself within the lids and socket.

c 1440 *Promp. Parv.* 21 Balle of þe ye, *Pupilla.* 1530 PALSGR. 196/2 Ball, of the eye, *La prunelle de loyl.* 1577 tr. *Bullinger's Decades* (1592) 157 The balles of his eyes shall see nought but darknesse. 1596 SHAKS. *Merch. V*, III. ii. 117. 1671 MILTON *Samson* 94 Such a tender ball as the eye. 1709 STEELE *Tatler* No. 145 ¶2 The Balls of Sight are so form'd, that one Man's Eyes are Spectacles to another to read his Heart with. 1808 SCOTT *Marm.* II. xxii, Raising his sightless balls to heaven. 1870 BRYANT *Homer* XIV. II. 71 Him Peneleus smote..In the eye's socket, forcing out the ball.

II. A globular or rounded mass of material.

10. A globular or rounded mass of any substance. a. *gen.* (cf. SNOWBALL).

1205 LAY. 17443 Nu ȝe maȝen heom habben swulche veðerene balles. *c* 1385 CHAUCER *L.G.W.* 2003 Ballis..Of wex and tow. 1588 SHAKS. *L.L.L.* III. i. 199 With two pitch bals stucke in her face for eyes. 1648 HERRICK *Hesper.* Wks. 1869 II. 328 Balls of cowslips, daisie rings. 1783 AINSWORTH *Lat. Dict.*, A musk ball, or sweet ball, *Pastillus.* 1875 BUCKLAND *Log-Bk.* 204 A living ball of Crabs.

b. *spec.* A spherical piece of soap. (Not now used specifically).

1593 NASHE *Christ's T.* (1613) 25 As a Barber wasteth his Ball in the water. 1611 BIBLE *Susanna* i. 17 Then she said to her maids, bring me oil & washinge balls. 1624 FLETCHER *Rule a Wife* III. i. 286 Balls..to wash out your stains. 1783 AINSWORTH *Lat. Dict.* (Morell), *Mattiacæ pilæ*..soap-balls, washing-balls.

c. A globular mass formed by winding thread, a clew or clue. L. *glomus.*

1572 J. JONES *Bathe Buckstone* 12b, The wind baule, or yarne ball. 1841 MARRYAT *Poacher* xv, You had a ball of twine. 1884 BLACK in *Harper's Mag.* May 951/1 She got her knitting-needles and a ball of wool.

d. *Metallurgy.* A mass of puddled iron formed by the workman into a pasty lump, to be hammered and rolled when taken from the furnace.

1825 J. NICHOLSON *Oper. Mech.* 334 When the iron is deprived of the carbon..the furnaceman rolls it up into balls of one half or three quarters of a cwt. each. 1855 W. TRURAN *Iron Manuf.* 134/1 After 8 or 9 minutes raking of the iron, now in the condition of pasty lumps,..the puddler commences the formation of the puddle balls. 1875 [see BLOOM *sb.*[2]]. 1892 F. JOYNSON *Iron & Steel Maker* 89 The worker of the puddler is..confined to..the production of the lumps or masses of metal technically called 'balls', and sometimes, though rarely in this country, 'blooms'.

e. = CLOD *sb.* 3 c.

1881 *Encycl. Brit.* XII. 239/1 The tree will then be ready to lift if carefully prized up from beneath the ball. 1885 G. NICHOLSON *Dict. Gardening* I. 153/2 *Ball.* This term is used in reference to the roots and mass of earth as they are moulded into form... The masses of roots and earth which ..must be taken intact when removing the plants, are also termed Balls. 1924 H. H. THOMAS *Compl. Amat. Gardener* iii. 18 The larger the 'ball' the more quickly will a tree or plant recover after having been transplanted.

11. *Med.* A bolus; medicine in the form of a ball or large pill. Now only in *Veterinary Medicine.*

1576 EARL OXFORD *Love Quest.* in Fuller *Worthies* IV. (1872) 58 His bitter ball is sugred blisse. 1720 *Lond. Gaz.* No. 5831/4 The Cordial Horse-Balls, at 4*s.* per Pound. 1753 CHAMBERS *Cycl. Supp.*, s.v., We meet with balls for the tooth-ach. 1877 STONEHENGE *Horse* xxxii. 581 Medicine may be given to the horse..in the solid form as a ball.

12. (from F. *balle*) A rounded package, a BALE.

1583 J. NEWBERY in Arb. *Garner* III. 172 Hath sent you in the Emanuel a ball of Nutmegs. 1653 URQUHART *Rabelais* I. xxxvii, Seven balls of bullets [*sept balles de boullets*] at a dozen the ball. 1796 MORSE *Amer. Geog.* II. 389 Fifteen balls of rosemary, the ball weighing 750 pounds.

III. Objects or parts with rounded outline.

13. A kind of small cushion, leather-covered or formed of composition, used by printers for inking the type. Now superseded by the roller.

1611 COTGR., *Pompette d' imprimeur*, a Printers Pumpet-ball..wherewith hee beates, or layes Inke on, the Formes. 1753 CHAMBERS *Cycl. Supp.*, *Ball* among *Printers* a kind of wooden tunnel stuffed with wool, contained in a cover of sheep's skin..with which the ink is applied. 1824 J. JOHNSON *Typogr.* II. 531 About the year 1815, composition balls were introduced at Weybridge. 1830 *Edin. Encycl.* XIII. 46 When the printing balls are applied, the ink is received by the oiled parts of the stone.

14. A spherical or rounded part of various machines; e.g. *the ball of a harrow*; *of a cart-wheel* (the nave or hub); *of a pendulum* (the bob).

1641 BEST *Farm. Bks.* (1856) 107 These rammers are made of old everinges, harrowe balls, or such like things as have holes. 1693 W. ROBERTSON *Phraseol. Gen.* 199 The ball of a Cart-wheel; *arbuscula.*

15. a. Any rounded protuberant part of the body; now chiefly applied to those at the base of the thumb and great toe; *formerly*, also a callosity on the hand or foot.

1483 *Cath. Angl.* 19/1 A Balle of þ[e] hand or of fote, *callus.* 1530 PALSGR. 196/2 Ball of the cheke, *pommeav de la jove.* 1547 *Act. 1 Ed. VI*, iii, §2 Such Slaue, or loiterer to bee marked on the..ball of the cheeke with an hot iron. 1586 WARNER *Alb. Eng.* IV. xx. 97 Beating Balles, her vained breasts. 1752 CARTE *Hist. Eng.* III. 542 The women painted about the eyes and the Balls of the cheeks with an azure colour. 1833 *Regul. Instr. Cavalry* I. 14 The recruit brings the ball of the right foot to the left heel. 1875 BUCKLAND *Log-Bk.* 22 Large muscle which forms the ball of the thumb.

b. Pl. *vulg.* The testicles; *fig.* nonsense, freq. as *int.*; hence *vbl. phr.*, ***to make a balls of***, to muddle, to do badly, to make a mess of. Cf. *to ball up* (BALL *v.*[1] 6 b).

a 1325, *a* 1456 in M.E.D. 1889 BARRÈRE & LELAND *Dict. Slang*, s.v. *Balls*: 'To make *balls* of it', to make a mistake, to get into trouble. *Balls, all* (popular), all rubbish. 1890 FARMER *Slang* I. 109/2 *All balls*, all rubbish; nonsense. 1903 O. WISTER *Philosophy 4: A Story of Harvard Univ.* i. 10 'If I were to stop thinking about you, you'd evaporate.' 'Which is balls,' observed the second boy judicially, again in the slang of his period, 'and can be proved so. For you're not always thinking about me, and I've never evaporated once.' 1922 JOYCE *Ulysses* 134 All balls! Bulldosing the public! 1928 D. H. LAWRENCE *Lady Chatterley* xv. 263 She.. gathered his balls in her hand. 1934 'G. ORWELL' *Burmese Days* ii. 34 'We all think this idea of electing a native to the Club is absolute ——' Ellis was going to have said 'absolute balls'. 1945 *Penguin New Writing* XXVI. 59 They are all of the opinion you can't write and be a soldier same time. Myself I think that's all balls. 1946 B. MARSHALL *George Brown's Schooldays* 79 What do you mean by talking all that unpatriotic balls to the Old Man yesterday? 1956 A. WILSON *Anglo-Saxon Attitudes* II. ii. 346 'Look here! this is awful balls,' said John. 1958 S. BECKETT *Endgame* 21 I've made a balls of the fly. 1960 LEONARD COOPER *Accomplices* IV. v. 243 Fanciful? Balls! It's what happens.

c. ***balls-up***, a confusion, a muddle, a mess. Hence ***to balls up*** = ***to ball up*** (BALL *v.*[1] 6 b). *vulg.*

1939 'G. ORWELL' *Coming up for Air* II. viii. 150 You couldn't go on regarding society as something eternal and unquestionable, like a pyramid. You knew it was just a balls-up. 1945 *Penguin New Writing* XXVI. 51 'What d'you make of this case, corporal?' 'Bleeding balls-up, between you and me.' 1956 R. FULLER *Image of Society* viii. 197 Stuart Blackledge made a ballsup of the valuation.

1947 E. TAYLOR *View of Harbour* v. 76 You will balls everything up with your indifference. 1961 S. PRICE *Just for Record* viii. 72 The public would laugh fit to bust if someone really ballsed-up the Civil Service.

d. *pl.* Courage, determination; (manly) power or strength; masculinity. Cf. BALLSY *a.* and COJONES. *slang* (chiefly *U.S.*).

[1928 D. H. LAWRENCE *Lady Chatterley's Lover* xiv. 236 You say a man's got no brain, when he's a fool... And when he's got none of that spunky wild bit of a man in him, you say he's got no balls. When he's sort of tame.] 1958 in Wentworth & Flexner *Dict. Amer. Slang* (1960) 17/1 (*oral*) That copy is too weak. Rewrite it and put balls on it! 1968 *Internat. Times* 5 Jan. 5/1 The castrated version of Olympia Press which was for a time published in England has gone.. sadly..for even that watered down stuff, all promise and no balls..was better than..third rate mimeographed merde. 1970 *Daily Tel.* (Colour Suppl.) 15 May 35/4 [American loq.] Maggie's no mop..she's got more balls than a Christmas tree. 1979 *Tucson Mag.* Jan. 29/3, I told him I just can't do it that way... I suppose it took balls, but it is no more balls than anyone should have for themselves. 1984 M. AMIS *Money* 315 Just keeping a handhold and staying where you are,..even that takes tons of balls.

16. The central hollow of the palm of the hand or sole of the foot (*obs.*); the central part of an animal's foot.

1601 DENT *Path-w. Heaven* 242 Some men..will easilie feele the lightest feather..laide vpon the ball of their hands. 1615 LATHAM *Falconry* (1633) 133 The pinne groweth in the bales of the feet of vnquiet Hawkes. 1677 MOXON *Mech. Exerc.* (1703) 120 They..hold one end of it down with the Ball of the Foot. 1753 CHAMBERS *Cycl. Supp.* s.v., Ball of the foot of a dog is the prominent part of the middle of the foot. 1783 AINSWORTH *Lat. Dict.* (Morell), Ball of the hand, *Palma.* Ball of the foot, *Planta pedis.*

17. ***ball of a pillar*** in *Arch.*: the scotia, a hollow moulding between the fillets in the base of a pillar or column.

1783 AINSWORTH *Lat. Dict.*, Ball of a pillar, *scotia.*

IV. Phrases and phraseological combinations.

18. a. *fig.* from games, *football, tennis*, etc.:—***to catch*** or ***take the ball before the bound***: to anticipate an opportunity; ***to have the ball at one's foot (feet)*** or ***before one***: to have a thing in one's power; ***to have*** or ***keep one's eye on the ball***: to be, or to remain, alert; ***to keep the ball up*** or ***rolling***: to keep the conversation or an undertaking from flagging; also ***to set*** (or ***start***) ***the ball rolling***: to begin a conversation, undertaking, etc.; ***to play ball*** (***with***): to act fairly (with), to co-operate (with); ***to take up the ball***: to take one's turn in conversation, etc.; ***the ball is with you***: it is your turn; similarly, ***the ball is in one's*** (or ***another's***) ***court*** [COURT *sb.*[1] 4], etc.

1589 PUTTENHAM *Eng. Poesie* III. xix, We do preuent them ..and do catch the ball (as they are wont to say) before it come to the ground. *a* **1641** in E. Beveridge *Fergusson's Scot. Proverbs* (1924) MS. No. 588 He has the ball at his foot. *c* **1645** HOWELL *Lett.* IV. ix, It concerns you not to be over-hasty herein, not to take the Ball before the Bound. *c* **1661** *Papers on Alterat. Prayer-bk.* 24 You have the ball before you, and have the wind and sun, and the power of contending without controll. **1693** J. HOWE *Carnality Relig. Contention* ii. 75 A mighty pleasure is taken to see the *Saw drawn*, and the *Ball kept up*. **1781** BENTHAM *To G. Wilson* Wks. 1843 X. 104, I put a word in now and then to keep the ball up. *c* **1800** LD. AUCKLAND *Corr.* (1862) III. 416 We have the ball at our feet, and if the Government will allow us .. the rebellion will be crushed. **1809** WELLINGTON in Gurw. *Disp.* V. 365 If the Spaniards had not lost two armies lately, we should keep up the ball for another year. **1840** *Log Cabin & Hard Cider Melodies* 58 Virginia will keep her ball rolling. **1850** W. COLTON *Deck & Port* xiv. 390 That courageous organisation which set the ball of Anglo-Saxon supremacy rolling in California. **1857** TROLLOPE *Three Clerks* I. ix. 183 The ball is at your foot now, but it won't remain there. **1873** LYTTON *Parisians* II. v. iii. 142 The Duchesse .. took up the ball of the conversation. **1878** GEO. ELIOT *Coll. Breakf. P.* 345 Louder Rosencranz Took up the ball. **1884** MRS. H. WARD *Miss Bretherton* iv. 84 She has a dry original way of judging a novel which is stimulating and keeps the ball rolling. **1903** 'H. MCHUGH' *Back to Woods* vii. 100 Well, if Bunch should refuse to play ball I could send the check back to Uncle Peter. **1906** A. T. QUILLER-COUCH *Cornish Window* 127 Relief..came with his election as Fellow of Oriel .. and the brilliant young scholar had .. the ball at his feet. **1907** in *Screen Bk.* (1937) 102 We were forever being told 'Keep your eye on the ball'. **1911** P. V. COHN tr. *Nietzsche's Human, All too Human* II. 323 Such persons are in a position to start the ball of slander rolling. **1913** A. R. HOPE *Half & Half Trag.* 250 These amateurs failed to keep the ball rolling. **1930** C. TERRETT *Only Saps Work* 149 The police of Buffalo are too dumb—it would be redundant, I suppose, to say 'and honest'—to play ball with the hold-up mobs. **1932** *Times Lit. Suppl.* 28 Jan. 54/2 Since Malthus set the ball rolling, public opinion has undergone profound metamorphoses. **1944** L. A. G. STRONG *Director* 31 You play ball with me, and I'll see you don't regret it. **1958** *Spectator* 15 Aug. 230/2 This is an admirably professional book ..; its authors keep their eyes on the ball. **1963** *Brewer's Dict. Phr. & Fable* (ed. 8) 68/1 *The ball is with you*, or *in your court*. It is your turn now. **1967** A. NEWMAN *Three into Two* i. 5 No doubt she would play safe and .. the ball would be back in his court. **1984** *Financial Times* 28 Apr. 4/4 'The ball is in his court,' said Mr Ken Ashton .. after a meeting of the union's executive yesterday. **1985** R. C. A. WHITE *Admin. of Justice* viii. 131 The ball is now back in the plaintiff's court. The plaintiff may .. seek further .. but, sooner or later, must file a defence to any counterclaim.

b. ***to have*** (something), or ***to be, on the ball***: to have special merit, to be alert. *U.S. colloq.*

to be on the ball is now also U.K.

1912 *Collier's* 13 Apr. 19/1 He's got nothing on the ball—nothing at all. **1935** *Mademoiselle* Sept. 61/3 The lass has much on the ball. **1947** A. MILLER *All my Sons* (1958) I. 65 Now you're talkin', Bert. Now you're on the ball. **1961** *Listener* 28 Dec. 1136/2 The B.B.C. are 'on the ball' as the Americans would say. **1968** *Times* 19 Apr. 13/4 Kenneth Loach's direction [of a television play] was nothing if not on the ball.

19. a. ball and socket (joint): a joint formed of a ball or rounded extremity partly enclosed in a cup or socket, which thus has great freedom of play combined with strength.

1669 BOYLE *Cont. New Exper.* I. xxii. 74 This travailing Baroscope being furnished at its upper end with a very good Ball and Socket. **1741** MONRO *Anat.* 42 *Enarthrosis*, or the Ball and Socket .. when a large Head is received into a deep Cavity. **1809** HOME in *Phil. Trans.* XCIX. 182 There is a regular ball and socket joint between every two vertebræ. **1863** MRS. C. CLARKE *Shaks. Char.* 159 By .. impenetrable assurance, and a ball-and-socket morality. **1870** ROLLESTON *Anim. Life* 33 Ball and socket articulation.

b. ball-and-claw *attrib.* = claw-and-ball (see CLAW *sb.* 8).

1904 E. SINGLETON *French & Eng. Furniture* 237 In not one of Chippendale's drawings of chairs does the simple ball-and-claw foot occur. **1960** H. HAYWARD *Antique Coll.* 23/1 *Ball and claw foot* (*or claw and ball*), terminal to a cabriole leg... In use on English furniture from the early until the late years of the 18th cent.

20. ***three*** (***golden***) ***balls***: the sign of a pawnbroker; supposed by some to be derived from the ensign of the wealthy Medici family. Also formerly ***three blue balls***.

1748 SMOLLETT *Rod. Rand.* xvi. 123 He .. unbuckled his hanger, and shewing me the sign of three blue balls, desired me to .. pawn it. **1788** V. KNOX *Winter Evenings* II. v. iv. 129 Pawn at some distant house, known by the sign of the three blue [ed. 2, 1790 golden] balls. *a* **1845** HOOD *Pawning Watch* ix, I've gone to a dance for my supper; And now I must go to Three Balls! **1861** SALA *Tw. round Clock* 180 The brethren of the three golden balls.

V. *Comb.* **21.** General combinations, mostly *attrib.* (in various senses, but esp. football and baseball), as ***ball-alley***, ***-club*** (N. Amer.), ***-control***, ***-field***, ***-firing***, ***game***, ***-green***, ***ground***, ***-play***, ***-player***, ***-playing***, ***-practice***, ***-stick***, ***-team***; also the adjs. ***ball-proof***, ***-piled***, ***-shaped***.

1865 *Englishm. Mag.* Oct. 313 *Ball-alleys and racquet-courts were the exception. **1845** *Brooklyn Even. Star* 23 Oct. 2/3 A match of base ball was played on Tuesday at the Elysian Fields, Hoboken, between eight members of the New York *Ball Club and the same number of players from Brooklyn. **1985** *Globe & Mail* (Toronto) 10 Oct. A24/6 Most of the new tickets .. were returned to the ballclub by out-of-town baseball organizations this week. **1928** *Sunday Dispatch* 2 Sept. 1/1 Clever *ball control is returning to our football enclosures. **1951** *Swimming* (E.S.S.A.) vi. 113 You are mastering ball-control, one of the most important phases of the game [*sc.* water polo]. **1867** *Ball Players' Chron.* 13 June 4/2 Let us train up assemblages to good behavior on *ball-fields. **1833** *Regul. Instr. Cavalry* I. 31 **Ball Firing* .. at a target. **1848** *Knickerbocker* XVIII. 216 The boys suspend their *ball game while he drives over the green. **1898** S. HALE *Lett.* (1919) 335 These men were just like .. Harvard men, after the ball game has gone right for us. **1944** E. BLUNDEN *Cricket Country* xii. 126 His ball-game tendencies alarmed some of the authorities. **1961** *New Left Review* July/Aug. 57/2 Another ball-games court for older boys. **1657** COLVIL *Whigs Supplic.* (1751) 19 Making a *ball-green on his chin; As trees do sometime in a wood. **1772** D. TAITT in N. D. Mereness *Trav. Amer. Colonies* (1916) 546 [I] then went to a *Ball ground .. where the Eutchie and Geehaw people were playing Ball. **1856** *Spirit of Times* 13 Dec. 245/1 The Club presented their President with an elegant silver Pitcher, with a view of the ball ground carved out upon it. **1884** *Harper's Mag.* Jan. 297/2 Sites for ball-grounds and race-tracks. **1812** BYRON *Ch. Har.* I. li, The *ball-piled pyramid. *c* **1230** *Ancr. R.* 218 Iðe uorme ȝeres nis hit bute *bal-pleouwe. **1765** H. TIMBERLAKE *Mem.* 79, I was not a little pleased likewise with their ball-plays. **1855** LONGF. *Hiaw.* xi. 62 Skilled .. in the play of quoits and ball-play. **1619** SANDERSON *Serm.* I. 7 As *ball-players with the ball. When the ball is once up, they labour to keep it up. **1837** J. D. WHITNEY in E. T. Brewster *Life & Lett. J.D.W.* (1909) 20 For my part, I could never make a ball player. **1827** T. L. MCKENNEY *Tour to Lakes* 181 The little naked Indian boys .. were .. playing ball... This *ball-playing is not unlike our game of bandy. **1818** SCOTT *Rob. Roy* xxxi, A regimental target set up for *ball practice. **1854** OWEN in *Circ. Sc.* II. 45/2 The *ball-proof character of the skin. **1884** J. COLBORNE *With Hicks Pasha* 241 Round *ball-shaped boxes. **1775** J. ADAIR *Hist. Amer. Indians* 400 The *ball-sticks are about two feet long, the lower end somewhat resembling the palm of the hand, and .. worked with deerskin thongs. Between these, they catch the ball, and throw it a great distance. **1846** J. J. HOOPER *Adv. Simon Suggs* ix. 113 They .. knock down their antagonists with their ball-sticks. **1888** *Outing* (U.S.) July 356/1 The *personnel* of the average professional *ball team .. has improved. **1936** J. DOS PASSOS *Big Money* 17 At Exeter he was head of his class and captain of the ballteam.

22. Special combinations: **ball-'bearing(s)**, a mechanical contrivance for lessening friction by means of small loose metal balls, used for the bearings of axles; † **ball-bellows**, a hollow metal ball formerly used for producing a steam blast; **ball boy**, one who fields balls for the players at a lawn tennis tournament; **ball-cartridge**, a gun-cartridge, or pistol-cartridge containing a bullet; **ball clay**, very adhesive clay, as that brought up in lumps sticking to a ship's anchor; esp. a fine-textured clay, found mainly in south-western England, which is used in the manufacture of earthenware; **ball-cock**, a self-regulating cistern-tap turned off and on by the rising or falling of a hollow ball floating on the surface of the liquid; **ball-court**, an area (such as a paved yard) for the playing of ball games; *spec.* in *Archæol.*, a feature of the remains of the Maya civilization in Central America; **ball-drawer**, an instrument for extracting balls from fire-arms; **ball-flower** (*Arch.*), an ornament like a ball enclosed within three or four petals of a flower, often inserted in a hollow moulding; **ball-fringe**, a decorative fringe (for a mantelpiece, etc.) consisting of ball-shaped materials hung at intervals; **ball game**, (*a*) (see sense 21); (*b*) *fig.* (chiefly *U.S.*), a state of affairs, a continuing activity, contest, etc.; freq. in colloq. phr. ***a different*** (***new***, etc.) ***ball game***, one in which new factors come into play; **ball-headed** *a.*, with the head shaped like a ball; **ball joint**, a ball-and-socket joint; **ball-lightning**, lightning in a globular form; = *globe-lightning*; **ball mill** (see quot. 1911); **ball-mine**, a kind of iron-ore found in rounded lumps or nodules; **ball-peen, -pome** (see PEEN *sb.*, POME *sb.*[1] 3); **ball-planting**, a method of transplanting trees (see quot.; cf. 10 e); **ball-pointed** *a.*, having a (minute) ball-shaped point; **ball(-point) pen**, one of which the writing point is a minute ball which is inked from an inner reservoir; also *ellipt.* **ball-point**; **ball-race** (see RACE *sb.*[1] 8 g); **ball smut** = BUNT *sb.*[2] 2 (see SMUT-BALL); **ball-stamp**, an American ore-crushing machine; **ball-stock**, the stock or handle of a printer's ball; **ball-stone**, a rounded lump of ironstone or limestone; **ball-tap** (= *ball-cock*); **ball-thistle**, the Globe Thistle, also a species of Echinops; **ball-trap** (see TRAP *sb.*[1] 8 and cf. *ball-valve*); **ball turret** *Aeronaut.* (see quot. 1956); **ball-valve**, a valve opened or closed by the rising or falling of a ball which exactly fits a cup-shaped opening in the seat; † **ball-vein**, a kind of iron ore in nodules formerly worked in Sussex; **ball-weed**, knapweed (*Centaurea nigra*).

1883 *Knowledge* 3 Aug. 76/1 Three machines .. with *ball-bearings. **1634** T. JOHNSON tr. *Parey's Chirurg.* XI. (1678) 276 *Ball-bellows .. made of Brass in form of a Pear, with a very small hole in their lesser ends. **1903** *Westm. Gaz.* 29 Aug. 6/1 A black moving surface, over which red-coated *ball boys dart. **1968** *Observer* 28 Apr. 22/2 The tall, dark Gonzales .. telling an industrious ball-boy to calm down. **1803** LD. COLCHESTER *Diary & Corr.* I. 451 A quantity of pikes, of *ball-cartridges and of combustibles. **1833** MARRYAT *P. Simple* (1863) 399 The captain .. ordered the marines to load with *ball-cartridge. **1811** *Agric. Surv. Ayrsh.* 4 (JAM.) If steril and adhesive, it is sometimes termed strong as *ball-clay. **1865** E. METEYARD *Life J. Wedgwood* iv. 140 The imported clay was used as a wash, previously to firing. This was called 'Ball clay' .. from being made up in heaps weighing sixty or seventy pounds each. **1903** *Daily Mail* 7 Sept. 5/5 They are the only mines in the world that produce the 'ball clay', without which the manufacture of earthenware is impossible. **1957** Ball clay [see BLUE *a.* 12 c]. **1968** *Radio Times* 2 May 17/2 Digging for valuable ball clay makes ugly scars across the Devon countryside. **1790** J. DRING *Brit. Pat.* No. 1725 A certain improvement on all cocks, which from the nature of such improvement are termed *ball cocks. *c* **1850** *Knight's Pract. Dict. Mech.* I. 558 A house-service pipe provided with a ball-cock, etc. **1677** PLOT *Oxfordsh.* 17 The *Ball-Court at Corpus Christi Coll. **1721** AMHERST *Terræ Fil.* 179 The old ball-court, where I have had many a game at fives. **1867** G. M. HOPKINS in *Lett. & Jrnls.* (1959) I. 159 The boys flooded the ball-court and slid and skated on it. **1912** J. W. FEWKES in *Ann. Rep. Bureau Amer. Ethnol.* XXVIII. 93 A long court extends across the whole south end of the compound. Its form suggests a ball court or course for foot races. **1959** *Listener* 12 Mar. 447/2 Huge pyramids, temples, and sacred ball courts are scattered over an area half a mile square [at Chichen Itza, Yucatan, Mexico]. **1844** *Regul. & Ord. Army* 96 One *Ball-drawer to each Rifle. **1845** *Archæol. Jrnl.* I. 100 The Chapel in Marten's tower with its *ball-flower moulding. **1862** *Archæol.* XXXIX. 182 The *ball-flower pattern .. carries down the building so late as 1340. **1909** H. G. WELLS *Tono-Bungay* I. ii. 64 Stuff with *ball fringe along the mantel. **1968** *Globe & Mail* (Toronto) 3 Feb. 9/4 'Then it will look like a different *ball game,' he said. 'We might see these recent attacks as a kind of last gasp.' **1969** *Outdoor Life* Mar. 134/2 As the trite saying goes, the Mark V made the use of buckshot a new ball game. **1969** *N.Y. Times* 12 Apr. 1 One key adviser called the Liberal party nomination 'the ball game, in many ways'. **1970** *TV Guide* (U.S.) 3 Jan. A-1 At the half time it's NBC ahead in the network ratings ball game on every count—NBC says. **1971** *New Yorker* 13 Mar. 30 If an invasion took place the Chinese might enter the war. If this were to happen, some official .. would no doubt announce that we were in a 'whole new ballgame'. **1977** I. SHAW *Beggarman, Thief* I. viii. 101 This mother was another ball game. **1982** S. BELLOW *Dean's December* xii. 221 'But the antagonism of people in Chicago is insignificant. He has another ball game in mind altogether.' (Corde enjoyed hearing slang.) **1984** *Times* 23 Nov. 13/6 With the proposed parental contribution to the tuition fees of students in higher education the parents enter an entirely new ball-game. **1902** *How to make useful Things* 48/2 With a *ball-headed hammer strike the petals of the discs. **1957** R. LISTER *Decorative Wrought Ironwork* ii. 48 *Ball-headed set pins* (that is ball-headed bolts) can give a decorative appearance to a bolted joint. *a* **1884** KNIGHT *Dict. Mech.* Suppl. 70/2 **Ball-joint hinge*, one having a flexible knuckle. **1930** *Engineering* 7 Feb. 177/2 The connections with the headers made with ball joints. **1962** *Which?* (Car Suppl.) Oct. 139/2 Grease from lower front suspension ball joints. **1857** J. P. NICHOL *Cycl. Physical Sci.* 431/2 **Ball lightnings* or *globes of fire* .. move slowly from the clouds to the Earth. **1930** *Discovery* Dec. 391/2 Ball lightning is probably the most interesting form of lightning discharge. **1903** R. H. RICHARDS *Ore Dressing* I. vi. 260 The Bruckner *Ball Mill was the parent form .. and consisted of a cylinder revolving on a horizontal axis with die plates around the circumference. The ore ground by balls, passed out through the spaces between the die plates. **1911** *Encycl. Brit.* XX. 239/1 The ball mill is a horizontal revolving cylinder with iron balls in it which do the grinding. **1930** *Engineering* 16 May 633/3 The contents of the weighing machine are discharged directly into one of four ball mills. **1963** J. OSBORNE *Dental Mechanics* (ed. 5) xi. 242 The pigments are usually impregnated to the surface of the polymer particles by means of a ball mill. **1702** in *Phil. Trans.* XXIII. 1072 A sort of Iron Stone, akin to that which they call in Staffordshire *Ballmine. *a* **1877** KNIGHT *Dict. Mech.* I. 224/2 **Ball-peen Hammer*, a metal-worker's hammer with a spherical peen. *a* **1884** *Ibid.* Suppl. 71/1 *Ball-peen Hammer*, one whose peen is round, or ball-shaped. **1946** *Esquire* (Chicago) Nov. 155 Biro who introduced the first *ball-pen presents .. a sensational new invention. **1958** *Times* 2 June p. vi/3 Gas is used .. in the manufacture of familiar articles such as ball pens, aircraft engines, [etc.]. **1905** *Terms Forestry & Logging* (*U.S. Dept. Agric.*) 6 **Ball planting*, a method of transplanting young trees with balls or lumps of earth around the roots. **1948** *Specifications of Inventions, Pat. Spec.* 617/176 A *ball point pen of new and improved construction. **1958** *Times Rev. Industry* June 22/2 The ball-point pen has a universally inimical effect upon .. handwriting. **1959** R. GANT *World in Jug* 124, I .. looked at him, sitting there .. holding a ball-point. **1935** *Jrnl. R. Aeronaut. Soc.* XXXIX. 1054 A few specimens of brass were measured .. using a *ball-pointed micrometer. **1952** 'C. BRAND' *London Particular* xvi. 217 Sergeant Bedd licked the end of his ball-pointed pen. **1922** *Weekly Dispatch* 17 Dec. 15, 1-lb. *Ball-pome Hammer. **1907** *Westm. Gaz.* 18 Nov. 7/2 The *ball-races fitted between the springs and the axle on which the long semi-elliptical springs are carried. **1908** *Ibid.* 30 June 4/2 Of the three Ariels [one] had the misfortune to break a ball-race in the hub. **1934** WEBSTER, *Ball smut. **1950** *N.Z. Jrnl. Agric.* Dec. 508/1 The need for some type of seed treatment to control ball smut was soon recognised. **1881** RAYMOND *Mining Gloss.*, **Ball-Stamp*, a stamp for crushing rock, operated directly by steam power. **1803** J. PLYMLEY *Agric. Shropsh.* i. 56 *Ballstone and earth. **1849** MURCHISON *Siluria* vi. 116 The ballstones..being more crystalline than the nodules. **1597** GERARD *Herbal* II. ccccclxxviii. (1633) 1152 *Carduus eriocephalus*..is called in English, Globe Thistle, and *Ball-Thistle. **1873** PARKES *Pract. Hygiene* (ed. 4) 344 The *ball-trap is used in some special cases only; a ball is lifted up as the water rises, until it impinges on and closes an orifice. **1945** *Aeronautics* Feb. 43/3 Nose turrets are supplied..and the retractable Sperry-designed *ball turrets. **1956** W. A. HEFLIN *U.S. Air Force Dict.* 71/1 *Ball turret*, a turret in the shape of a ball, designed to project or to be let down from the belly of an airplane, and to house the gunner. **1839** TODD *Cycl. Anat. & Phys.* III. 631/2 A mechanical office somewhat on the principle of the *ball-valve. **1753** CHAMBERS *Cycl. Supp.*, **Ball-vein*..a name given by the miners in Sussex to a sort of iron ore.

ball (bɔːl), *sb.*[2] [a. F. *bal* (= Pr. *bal*, It. *ballo* dancing), f. *bal-er*, *ball-er* to dance: see BALE *v*.[1] (In Chapman and Shirley's *Ball* (see sense 2) there was some punning reference to a golden ball worn by the presiding lady: see Gifford's note.)]

†**1.** A dance or dancing. *Obs.*

1633 H. COGAN *Pinto's Voy.* lxxix. 321 All of them together..danced a Ball to the tune of two Harps and a Viol.

2. a. A social assembly for dancing, often of people belonging to the same or a connected establishment, society, profession, etc., with an organized programme and often accompanied by special entertainment; phrases, ***to give a ball***, ***go to a ball***; also, ***to open the ball***, (*fig.*) to commence operations.

1632–9 CHAPMAN & SHIRLEY *Ball* IV. iii, *L.* Some malice has corrupted your opinion of what we call the Ball. *W.* Your dancing business? **1649** JER. TAYLOR *Gt. Exemp.* II. Add. xii. 93 Avoid carnivals and balls..the perdition of precious houres. **1679** PENN *Addr. Prot.* 19 They had got a Calf of Gold, and were Dancing about it. But it was a Dismal Ball, and they paid dear for their Junket. **1712** STEELE *Spect.* No. 466 ⁋3 On Thursday next, I make a Ball for my Daughter. **1779** J. MOORE *View Soc. Fr.* 175 Count Finkenstein gave a great dinner and ball. **1812** BYRON *Waltz* xiii. *note*, Waltz and the battle of Austerlitz are..said to have opened the ball together. **1841** ORDERSON *Creol.* vi. 63 Miss Fairfield..was the first lady handed out to 'open the ball.' **1863** MARY HOWITT *F. Bremer's Greece* I. v. 146, I was very willing to see a royal ball at Athens.

b. A very enjoyable time; a period of uninhibited amusement; esp. in phr. ***to have a ball***. *slang* (orig. *U.S.*).

1945 L. SHELLY *Hepcats Jive Talk Dict.* 25/2 *Having a ball*, having a hectic time. **1946** MEZZROW & WOLFE *Really Blues* v. 75 An entertainer..was having a ball all to herself. **1959** C. MACINNES *Absolute Beginners* 126 My poor old battered parent was really having a tremendous ball. **1955** TENNESSEE WILLIAMS *Cat on Hot Tin Roof* (1956) II. 77 What is it they call it, have me a —— ball! **1956** 'E. S. AARONS' *Assignment Treason* v. 40 Quenton has himself a ball. **1967** J. PORTER *Dover & Unkindest Cut of All* xii. 132 Have yourself a ball! Go gay!

3. With limiting attribute, **a.** descriptive, as †***ball-mask*** (= F. *bal-masqué*), ***ball-royal***, ***calico-***, ***dignity-***, ***fancy-***, ***masking-ball***; **b.** indicating the object or occasion, as ***archery-***, ***charity-***, ***race-ball***.

1672 DRYDEN *Marr. à la Mode* Prol., A masking ball, to recommend our play. **1770** WILKES *corr.* (1805) IV. 36 You did not mention particularly about the ball-mask. **1833** MARRYAT *P. Simple* (1863) 228 A dignity ball is a ball given by the most consequential of their coloured people. *a* **1847** MRS. SHERWOOD *Lady of Manor* V. xxix. 70 It was the first dress-ball I had attended. **1849** SOUTHEY *Common-pl. Bk.* Ser. II. 327 As great a performer in a ball-royal as himself. **1876** GEO. ELIOT *Dan. Der.* II. xi, The archery ball..was not an escapement for youthful high spirits.

4. *attrib.*, as ***ball-dancing***, ***-day***, ***-dress***, ***-night***, ***-room***, ***supper***; **ball-book** *U.S.*, a dance-card. Also BALL-ROOM.

1868 L. M. ALCOTT *Little Women* (1871) II. xiv. 363 She showed him her ball-book with demure satisfaction. **1728** J. ESSEX (*title*) Dancing-Master..the manner of performing all steps in Ball Dancing. **1751** SMOLLETT *Per. Pic.* (1779) III. lxxvi. 26 The careful matron..on the ball-day feigned herself extremely ill. **1789** BETSY SHERIDAN *Jrnl.* (1960) 154, I was interrupted by Miss Bouverie coming up to shew me her Ball dress. **1848** DICKENS *Dombey* xiv. 140 She came: looking so beautiful in her simple ball dress. **1875** HELEN MATHERS *Comin' thro' Rye* II. vii, How many yards of stuff an orthodox ample ball dress requires. **1771** SMOLLETT *H. Clinker* II. 4 July 141 The company, on a ball-night, must look like an assembly of..fairies. **1837** DICKENS *Pickw.* xxxiv. 377 The ball-nights in Ba—ath are moments snatched from Paradise. **1848** THACKERAY *Van. Fair* iii. 17 What causes respectable parents to..spend a fifth of their year's income in ball suppers and iced champagne? **1712** STEELE *Spect.* No. 431 ⁋3, I then nibbled all the red Wax of our last Ball-Tickets.

†**ball**, *sb.*[3] *Obs.* [prob. f. Celtic: cf. Welsh *bàl* sb. or ? adj., in *ceffyl bàl* 'a horse having a white streak on the forehead,' Breton *bal* 'a white mark on an animal's face,' Ir. and Gael. *bal* spot, mark.]

1. A white streak or spot; ? a bald place.

1523 FITZHERB. *Husb.* §73 The .ii . propertyes of a bauson [*i.e.* badger]. The fyrste is, to haue a whyte rase or a ball in the foreheed; the seconde, to haue a whyte fote.

2. ? A white-faced horse; hence a horse's name.

1573 TUSSER *Husb.* 185 Be wise who first doth teach thy childe that Art, Least homelie breaker mar fine ambling ball.

ball, *sb.*[4] Chiefly *Irish*. [Of obscure origin.] Usu. in phr. ***ball of malt***, a glass of (Irish) malt whiskey.

Connection with the slang phr. *ball of fire* 'a glass of brandy' (BALL *sb.*[1] 6 b) and with the slang use of *ball* in the sense 'prison ration of food' (recorded in H. Brandon, 1839, and in slang dicts.) has been suggested but cannot be substantiated. Connection with BOLL *sb.*[2] or BOWL *sb.*[1] is ruled out on phonological grounds.

1925 O'CASEY *Juno & Paycock* II. 63 There's nothing like a ball o' malt occasional like. **1941** L. A. G. STRONG *Bay* iv. 89 'Will you take a ball of malt?' I realized he was offering me the whiskey. **1962** *Spectator* 5 Oct. 528 Some foolish administrator had let him loose on innumerable balls of malt. **1966** H. KANE *Devil to Pay* vi. 31, I..went behind the bar and made myself a new ball of Scotch and water.

ball (bɔːl), *v.*[1] [f. BALL *sb.*[1]]

1. *trans.* To round or swell out (the cheeks, etc.).

1593 NASHE *Christ's T.* (1613) 41 The mayden-Moone.. shall haue her crimson cheeks (as they wold burst) round balled out with blood.

2. a. To make (snow, etc.) into a ball; to wind (thread) into a ball.

1658 A Fox tr. *Wurtz' Surg.* II. xxv. 157 Ball the bones together with your hands, as a snow-ball is made. **1849** *Blackw. Mag.* Aug. 199/1 She..asked me to hold her woollen yarns for her as she balled them off. **1856** KANE *Arct. Ex.* II. ix. 95 Brooks balls off twine.

b. To clench (the fist) tightly. Also with *up*: to roll up in a ball-like lump or mass.

1823 *New Monthly Mag.* VII. 542 Ball'd up to a mass, in a moment uncoil'd They rose, and again disappear'd in the dark. **1889** W. C. RUSSELL *Marooned* I. xvi. 308 A spun-yarn winch was rattling on the forecastle; and the half-blood Charles..was balling up the stuff as it was manufactured. **1890** BARING-GOULD *Arminell* I. vi. 99 With teeth clenched, and fists balled in his breeches pocket. **1925** *Chambers's Jrnl.* 581/1 No one had ever seen a balled-up swallow.

c. Metallurgy. ***to ball up***: to form (molten iron) into balls in the puddling furnace, for hammering or rolling. Also **balling up** *vbl. sb.* Cf. BALL *sb.*[1] 10 d.

1855 W. TRURAN *Iron Manuf.* 134/1 The period for balling-up arrives. **1868** F. H. JOYNSON *Metals* 62 The metallic matter is..balled up and shingled. **1887** PHILLIPS & BAUERMAN *Elem. Metallurgy* (ed. 2) 294 When the whole charge has been balled up. **1895** T. TURNER *Metall. Iron & Steel* 291 *Balling up stage*, which occupies some twenty minutes.

3. *intr.* To gather (itself) into a ball. Also *fig.*

1713 *Lond. & Country Brew.* I. (1742) 26 Stirring it [malt] all the while..that it may not ball. **1814** SOUTHEY *Lett.* (1856) II. 342 In clogs..snow balls under the wooden sole. **1880** BLACKMORE *M. Anerley* xl, The snow would..ball wherever any softness was. **1921** GALSWORTHY *To Let* III. vii. 271 All the old car-wise feelings..balled within him.

4. a. *trans.* To clog. **b.** *intr.* To become clogged, with balls (of snow, etc.).

1760 *New Eng. Hist. & Geneal. Reg.* XXXVI. 31 A thaw, heavy travelling, the Snow shoes balling. **1828** WEBSTER s.v., We say, the horse balls. **1848** A. BRONTË *Tenant of Wildfell Hall* III. xiv. 284 The snow..clogged the wheels and balled the horses' feet. **1863** J. BROWN *Horæ Subs.* 74 The pony stumbled through the..snow..getting its feet balled.

5. *trans.* Of bees: to surround (the queen) in a dense cluster, often with the result that she is suffocated or crushed to death.

1888 F. R. CHESHIRE *Bees* II. 426 If very many pass the guards [of a strange hive] unchallenged, they are likely to ball the queen, and possibly destroy her. **1919** T. W. COWAN *Bee-keeper's Guide Bk.* (ed. 23) 141 It is sometimes very difficult to introduce queens into hives having no young bees, as the old bees frequently 'ball' the queen and hug her to death unless she be released.

6. ***to ball up***: **a.** *intr.* To become clogged. (Cf. 4 b.) Also *fig.* (see quot. 1856). *U.S.*

1856 B. H. HALL *College Words* (ed. 2) 19 *Ball up*, at Middlebury College, to fail at recitation or examination. **1903** CLAPIN *Dict. Amer.* 35 It probably comes from the 'balling up' of a horse in soft, new fallen snow, when a snow-ball forms within each shoe.

b. *trans.* To clog; to bring into a state of entanglement, confusion, or difficulty. (Freq. in form ***balled up***.) *slang* (orig *U.S.*).

1885 'MARK TWAIN' *Lett.* (1917) II. xxv. 465 It will 'ball up' the binderies again. **1887** *Harper's Mag.* Sept. 605/2 'You seem balled up about something.'..'Balled up!..I'm done for.' **1896** ADE *Artie* xi. 98 She had him balled up till he couldn't say a word. **1911** H. QUICK *Yellowstone Nights* ix. 238 Every time old Hen stepped, he balled things up worse. **1930** D. PARKER *Laments for Living* 6, I didn't mean to say that. You get me so balled up. **1932** J. DOS PASSOS *1919* (1937) 279 Bud..had gotten balled up with a girl in Galveston who was trying to blackmail him. **1934** E. LINKLATER *Magnus Merriman* xi. 128 Gee, I'm sorry I was late! I got all balled-up over the time. **1936** N. COWARD '*Red Peppers*' in *To-night at 8.30* I. 90 You can't even do a straight walk off without balling it up. **1959** J. DRUMMOND *Black Unicorn* xiv. 100 These electrical devices are always getting balled up.

7. *intr.* Of roses: to fail to open properly, decaying in the half-open bud.

1930 H. H. THOMAS *Amateur's Rose Book* iii. 11 A rose is said to 'ball' when the petals stick together and fail to open.

8. ***to ball the jack***, to travel fast, to hurry; also in extended use. *U.S. slang.*

c **1925** in H. Wentworth *Amer. Dial. Dict.* 41/1 The car certainly did ball the jack. **1941** J. H. STREET *In my Father's House* 67 (Wentworth & Flexner), Mr. Murdo balled the jack. *Ibid.* 268 They think as soon as you die you go balling-the-jack to God. **1942** BERREY & VAN DEN BARK *Amer. Thes. Slang* §156/4 *Be reckless; hasten or strive recklessly*, ball the jack. **1957** KEROUAC *On Road* (1958) iii. 16 He balled the jack and told stories for a couple of hours.

ball, *v.*[2] ? *Obs. rare*[−1]. [f. BALL *sb.*[1], sense 4.] To play at ball.

1681 *Trial S. Colledge* 37 When I came, he was balling.

†**ball**, *v.*[3] *Obs.* [? f. BALL *sb.*] *intr.* ? To strike, thump, shower blows.

c **1400** *Beryn* 1026 And stert up in a wood rage, and ballid on his croun.

ball (bɔːl), *v.*[4] [f. BALL *sb.*[2]; cf. BALE *v.*[1]] **1.** *intr.* To take part in a ball.

1782 LORD FIFE *Let.* 8 June in *Lord Fife & his Factor* (1925) vi. 143 Dined, visited and balled at all the great houses. **1855** *Harper's Mag.* April 821/1 It is the temperature that sets people dancing and balling.

2. To enjoy oneself; to 'have a ball' (see BALL *sb.*[2] 2 b); also ***to ball it up***. So **balling** *vbl. sb. N. Amer. slang.*

1942 *Amer. Mercury* July 94/1 *Balling*, having fun. **1946** MEZZROW & WOLFE *Really Blues* iii. 32 Joe Tuckman felt like balling that night cause he beat Big Izzy..in the crap game. **1961** R. BLOCH *Blood runs Cold* (1963) 156 Balling for kicks was enough. **1962** K. ORVIS *Damned & Destroyed* x. 70 A so-called friend invites you..to a coloured joint—to ball it up for a night.

ball (bɔːl), *v.*[5] [Erron. form of BAWL *v.*] With *out* (see BAWL *v.* 3 c). Hence ***balling-out***, a vehement reprimand.

1959 A. CHRISTIE *Cat among Pigeons* xix. 199 She picked it up and forgot to replace it—walked out with it and Springer balled her out. **1959** P. MCCUTCHAN *Storm South* vii. 94 He gave me quite the worst balling out I'll ever live to tell of.

ball (bɔːl), *v.*[6] *coarse slang* (orig. *U.S.*). [Perh. an extension of BALL *v.*[4] 2, infl. by BALL *sb.*[1] 15 b.] *trans.* To copulate or have sexual intercourse with (usu. with man as subj.). Also *intr.*

1955 W. GADDIS *Recognitions* II. i. 308 He used to bring her down here to shock her, and then take her home and ball her...—*Edna?* said Otto, unable to swallow.—With *him?* **1962** J. BALDWIN *Another Country* I. i. 76 Next to him..sat a girl he had balled once or twice. **1963** *Realist* June 29 Is it bizarre that married guys have to jerk off more than anyone else, because your old ladies won't ball you and you can't chippie? **1966** T. LEARY *Politics of Ecstasy* xii. 189 The way you ball (or avoid balling) is your central sacramental activity. **1974** G. PALEY *Enormous Changes at Last Minute* 154 You like to ball?.. Then he put up her dress and take down her panties. **1978** G. VIDAL *Kalki* i. 9 And you can tell the world all about those chicks that you ball.

‖**ballabile** (bal'labile). Pl. **ballabili**. [It., f. *ballare* to dance: see BALE *v.*[1]] (See quot. 1847[1].)

1847 R. BARTON *Blasis's Notes upon Dancing* III. 111 We shall consider the celebrated *Maestro*, first as a composer of Ballets, *pas*, *ballabile*, and other chorographic matters... The word *ballabile* signifies a dance executed by a large number of persons; that is, the general *corps* of the Ballet; the term was introduced into France, and other countries, by Blasis. *Ibid.* 112 These *ballabili* were all of them esteemed as master-pieces in the art. **1953** *Ballet Ann.* VII. 66/1 The *ballabile* of the last movement with the soloists in the centre and the *corps* in a wide arc on the three sides doing simple *battements tendus*. **1959** *Times* 7 Mar. 9/6 A thoroughly lilting and *ballabile* tempo.

ballace, obs. form of BALLAST.

ballad ('bæləd), *sb.* Forms: 4–6 **balade**, 5 **balaade**, **-adde**, 6 **balat(e**, **-ette**, **ballat**, **-att**, **-ed**, **-ete**, **-ette**, **-ytte**, 6–7 **ballet**, **ballade**, 7– (*Sc.*) **ballant**, 6– **ballad**. [ME. *balade*, a. OF. *balade* (mod. *ballade*) dancing-song, ad. Pr. *balada* dance, dancing-song, f. *balar*:—late L. *ballāre* to dance: cf. BALE *v.*[1] In 16th and 17th c. the termination *-ad* was commonly changed into the more familiar *-at(e*, *-et* (cf. *salad*, *sallet*), and this in Sc. further corrupted to *-ant*. Cf. BALLET *sb.*[1], the adoption of which has probably tended to restore the spelling *ballad*, and the revived form BALLET *sb.*[3] The primitive meaning of *dance* was in Pr. and It., but the word was adopted in Fr. and Eng. only in transferred senses. See also BALLADE.]

†**1.** A song intended as the accompaniment to a dance; the tune to which the song is sung. *Obs.*

c **1500** DUNBAR *Gold. Targe* 129 And sang ballettis with michty notis clere: Ladyes to dance full sobirly assayit. **1545** ASCHAM *Toxoph.* (Arb.) 39 These balades and roundes, these galiardes, pauanes and daunces. **1549** OLDE *Erasm. Par. Eph.* v. 19 That can stirre vs, not to wanton dauncynges or folyshe ballettes. *a* **1616** B. JONSON *Love Rest.* 12 Unlesse we should come in like a Morrice-dance, and whistle our ballat our selves.

2. A light, simple song of any kind; now *spec.* a sentimental or romantic composition of two or more verses, each of which is sung to the same melody, the musical accompaniment being strictly subordinate to the air.

1492 in Michelet *Scot. Lang.* 218 For the singyn of a ballat to the King. *c* **1500** *Mayd Emlyn* in *Poet. Tracts* (1842) 16 We do nought togyder, But prycked balades synge. **1521** *State Papers Hen. VIII*, I. 10 Mr. Almoner, in hys sermone, broght in the balates off 'Passe tyme with goodde cumpanye,' and 'I love unlovydde.' **1568** BIBLE (Bishops') *title*, The Ballet of Ballets of Solomon. **1589** PUTTENHAM *Eng. Poesie* I. xx, Ballades of praise called *Encomia*. **1664–5** PEPYS *Diary* 2 Jan., I occasioned much mirth by a ballet I brought with me, made from the seamen at sea to their ladies in town [*i.e.* Ld. Dorset's 'To all you Ladies']. **1770** GOLDSM. *Des. Vil.* 244 No more the woodman's ballad shall prevail. **1855** TENNYSON *Maud.* I. v. i, She is singing an air that is known to me, A passionate ballad gallant and gay. **1879** GROVE *Dict. Mus.* I. 129/2 At the present time a ballad in music is generally understood to be a sentimental or romantic composition of a simple and unpretentious character, having two or more verses of poetry, but with the melody or tune complete in the first, and repeated for each succeeding verse. **1898** A. BENNETT *Man from North* xxi. 191 The song was a mediocre drawing-room ballad. **1906** —— *Whom God hath Joined* x. 367 The power of the drawing-room ballad rendered by a few fiddlers in the warm obscurity of an August evening. **1927** *Melody Maker* Aug. 768 (Advt.), 'Morning', Fox-trot Ballad by Pat Thayer. **1965** *New Statesman* 9 Apr. 586/1 Miss Staton has no special gift for the pocket one-woman song-drama which is (under the name 'ballad') the basis of the night-club repertoire.

†**3.** A popular song; often *spec.* one celebrating or scurrilously attacking persons or institutions. (The 'ballad' in this and prec. sense was often printed as a broadsheet.) *Obs.*

1556 *Chron. Grey Friars* (1852) 57 Many ballyttes made of dyvers partys agayne the blyssyd sacrament. **1597** SHAKS. *2 Hen. IV*, IV. iii. 52, I will haue it in a particular Ballad, with my owne Picture on the top of it. **1602** *Ret. fr. Parnass.* I. ii. (Arb.) 10 Who makes a ballet for an ale-house doore. **1704** A. FLETCHER (of Saltoun) *Acct. Conversation* 9 Tempted to all manner of Lewdness by infamous Ballads sung in every corner of the Streets.. I know a very wise man that believed that if a man were permitted to make all the Ballads, he need not care who should make the Laws of a Nation. **1727** SWIFT *Furth. Acct. Curll* Wks. 1755 III. I. 160 Resolved, That a ballad be made against Mr. Pope. **1782** BURNEY *Hist. Mus.* II. iv. 343 *note*, The English Ballad has long been.. confined to a low species of Song. **1825** J. WILSON *Noct. Ambr.* Wks. I. 2 A beuk of old ballants as yellow as the cowslips.

†**4.** A proverbial saying, usually in form of a couplet; a posy. (Cf. L. *cantilena*.) *Obs.*

1528 MORE *Heresyes* I. Wks. 177/1 Than haue we well walked after the balade: The further I goo the more behynde. **1562** J. HEYWOOD *Prov. & Epigr.* (1867) 54 Spend, and god shall send.. saith tholde ballet. **1601** SHAKS. *All's Well* I. iii. 63 For I the Ballad will repeate, which men full true shall finde, your marriage comes by destinie, your Cuckow sings by kinde.

5. A simple spirited poem in short stanzas, originally a 'ballad' in sense 3, in which some popular story is graphically narrated. (This sense is esentially modern: with Milton, Addison, and even Johnson, the idea of *song* was present.)

[**1670** MILTON *Hist. Eng.* v. Wks. (1851) 226 The song ..(for.. he refus'd not the autority of Ballats for want of better). **1712** ADDISON *Spect.* No. 70 ⁋3 The old Song of Chevy-Chase is the favourite Ballad of the common People of England.] **1751** JOHNSON *Rambl.* No. 177 ⁋9 Cantilenus turned all his thoughts upon old ballads.. He offered to shew me a copy of the Children in the Wood. **1783** COWPER *Lett.* 3 Aug., The ballad is a species of poetry, I believe, peculiar to this country.. simplicity and ease are its proper characteristics. **1817** COLERIDGE *Sibyl. Leaves*, The Bard.. who made The grand old ballad of Sir Patrick Spence. **1858** LONGF. *Children*, Ye are better than all the ballads That ever were sung or said; For ye are our living poems, And all the rest are dead. **1870** SWINBURNE *Ess. & Stud.* (1875) 85 The highest form of ballad requires from a poet at once narrative power, lyrical, and dramatic. **1872** BUCKLE *Misc. Wks.* I. 161 All history is at first poetry, i.e. ballads.

6. *Comb.* **a.** attrib., as ***ballad-form, -lore, -measure, -poetry, -rime*** (1447), ***-stanza, -stuff, -tune***; **b.** objective gen. with vbl. or agent-noun, as ***ballad-making*** (1505), ***-singing, ballad-composer, -maker*** (1586), ***-reciter, -singer, -writer***, BALLAD-MONGER. Also **ballad concert**, a concert devoted mainly to ballads (sense 2); **ballad-farce, -opera**, a play into which popular songs are introduced; **ballad-wise** *adv.*, in the manner of a ballad, in song.

1947 A. EINSTEIN *Mus. in Romantic Era* vi. 58 Carl Loewe, Schubert's rival as a *ballad-composer. **1868** *Times* 23 Mar. 12/6 The admirable London *Ballad Concerts of Mr. John Boosey are still drawing crowds. **1879** GROVE *Dict. Mus.* I. 129/2 'Ballad concerts'.. often contain songs of all kinds. **1903** *Daily Chron.* 21 Mar. 8/4 A Concert Diary. Mar. 21. —London Ballad Concert, Queen's Hall. **1747** T. WHINCOP *Scanderbeg* 185/1 Betty, or The Country Bumpkins, a *Ballad-Farce, acted.. at the Theatre in Drury-lane, 1738. **1787** SIR J. HAWKINS *Johnson* 198 (Jod.) An impatience for pantomimes and ballad-farces. **1865** M. ARNOLD *Ess. Crit.* (1875) 210 A *ballad-form which has more rapidity and grace. **1902** *Q. Rev.* Oct. 478 The wind-riding Erlking of German *ballad-lore. **1586** WEBBE *Eng. Poetrie* (Arb.) 36 The vncountable rabble of ryming *Ballet-makers. **1667** DRYDEN & DUKE OF NEWCASTLE *Martin Mar-all* (1668) v. 55 You mistake me for Martin Parker, the Ballad-Maker. **1815** SCOTT *Guy M.* xli, The devil take all ballads, and ballad-makers, and ballad-singers! *c* **1505** DUNBAR *Lament for Makaris* 60 Fra *balat making et trigide. **1775** *Ann. Reg.* 40/2 He wrote it in *ballad measure. **1779** JOHNSON *L.P.* Wks. 1816 X. 218 We owe to Gay the *Ballad-Opera. **1863** BURTON *Bk. Hunter* 300 That delightful department of literature, our *ballad poetry. **1447** BOKENHAM *Seyntys* 60, What best plesyth me I have as I can declaryd in latyn In *balaade ryme. **1598** FLORIO *Worlde of Wordes* 57/3 *Cantinbanco*, a mountibanke, a *ballad-singer. **1682** *London Gaz.* No. 1712, 13–17 Apr., Mr. John Clarke.. did rent of Charles Killigrew Esq; the Licencing of all Ballad-Singers. **1707** *Lond. Gaz.* No. 4370/4 Israel Sewell.. a professyd Ballad-singer. **1831** CARLYLE *Sart. Res.* II. ii, Ballad-singers brayed, Auctioneers grew hoarse. **1934** *Ess. & Stud.* XIX. 102 The stanza, not itself a *ballad-stanza, of *The Dark Ladie*. **1599** MARSTON *Sco. Villanie* 194 Then hence base *ballad stuffe. **1589** PUTTENHAM *Eng. Poesie* (Arb.) 65 This was done in *ballade wise.. and was song very sweetely. **1846** WRIGHT *Ess. Mid. Ages* II. xvii. 200 The *ballad-writers of after-times.

ˈballad, *v.* ? *Obs.* Forms: 6–7 **ballat**, 7 **balett**, 8 **ballet**, 7– **ballad**. [f. prec. sb.; cf. OF. *balader*.]

1. *intr.* To write or compose ballads.

1592 G. HARVEY *Four Lett.* 5 But who.. like Elderton for ballating, Greene for pamfletting? *c* **1600** DONNE *Juvenilia* i. (1633) B, Enuious Libellers ballad against them [women].

2. *trans.* To make (a person) the subject of ballads, or popular songs, especially scurrilous ones.

1606 SHAKS. *Ant. & Cl.* v. ii. 216 And scald Rimers [will] Ballad vs out a Tune. **1636** HEYWOOD *Challenge* II. i. Wks. 1874 V. 23, I shall be Ballated, Sung up and downe by minstrills. **1721** SOUTHERN *Disappointm.* III. i. 107 Stag'd to the crowd.. Nay, balleted about the streets in rhime.

ballade (bəˈlɑːd). Also 4–6 **balade**. [An earlier (also mod.F.) spelling and pronunciation of BALLAD *sb.*, now used as a technical term. (In 14–15th c. *baˈlade*; in 16th also *ballade*, but then pronounced *ˈballad*); see above.]

1. a. *strictly*, A poem consisting of one or more terns, or triplets of seven- or (afterwards) eight-lined stanzas each ending with the same line as refrain, and (usually) an envoy; *e.g.* Chaucer's *Compleynt of Venus, To his Purse*, etc. **b.** A poem divided into stanzas of equal length, usually of seven or eight lines. †**c.** *occas.* One of these stanzas (*obs.*).

c **1385** CHAUCER *L.G.W.* 270 This balade [of 3 seven-lined stanzas] may ful wel y-sungen be.. by my lady free. *c* **1430** LYDG. *Chichev. & Byc.* in Dodsl. XII. 333 An ymage in poete wise seyeng these iii balades [7-lined stanzas]. *c* **1430** SHIRLEY in *Chaucer's Min. P.* 412 A balade [*Compleynt of Venus*] translated out of frenshe in to englishe by Chaucier Geffrey. **1509** BARCLAY *Ship of Fooles* (1871) II. 2 My balade bare of frute and eloquence. **1882** *Ch. Q. Rev.* 374 Where Mr. Swinburne chooses to bind himself by the strict laws of.. the ballade.

2. *abstr.* or *collect.* Poetry of this form.

c **1385** CHAUCER *L.G.W.* 539 That ilke tyme thou made 'hid Absolon thy tresses' in balade. **1470** HARDING *Chron.* Proem iv, Into balade I wyll it nowe translate. **1555** *Fardle Facions* II. xi. 248 The victories of their forefathers and eldres, thei put into Balade. **1587** GASCOIGNE *Instr. making Verse* §14 A man may write Ballade in a staffe of five lines every line contayning eight or six sillables.

3. ***ballade royal***: stanzas of seven or (afterwards) eight lines of ten syllables; called also *rime* or *rhythm royal*.

The name originated in the fact that King James I of Scotland composed the *King's Quair* 1423, in 7-line stanzas of structure *a b a b b c c*. The *Ballat Royal* of James I of England had an additional *b* line between the two in *c*.

1483 CAXTON *Cato* 2 Ful craftyly hath made it in balade ryal. **1494** FABYAN VII. 406, I haue therfore set them out in baladde royall. **1585** JAMES I. *Ess. Poesie* (Arb.) 67 This kynde of verse following, callit Ballat Royal.

4. A piece of instrumental music, usually of a lyrical or romantic character (see quots.).

1863 F. CHOPIN (*title*) 3d. Ballade in A Flat. **1879** GROVE *Dict. Mus.* I. 129/2 *Ballade*, a name adopted by Chopin for four pieces of pianoforte music (op. 23, 38, 47, 52) which, however brilliant or beautiful, have no peculiar form or character of their own, beyond being written in triple time. **1938** *Oxf. Compan. Mus.* 68/1 No particular one form is associated with the instrumental ballade.

balladeer (bæləˈdɪə(r)). [f. BALLAD *sb.* + -EER.] One who sings or composes ballads. Cf. BALLADER.

1830 SCOTT *Auchindrane* II. i. 172 The balladeer, whose voice has still two notes left. **1952** B. ULANOV *Hist. Jazz* (1958) xxi. 276 The band had.. a good balladeer (Al Hibbler). **1958** O. W. BURT *Amer. Murder Ballads* p. xii, Songs and poems and jingles written by humble balladeers about true murders.

ballader (ˈbælədə(r)). Also 6 **balletter**, 7 **-ater, -adder**. [f. BALLAD *v.* or *sb.* + -ER¹.] A writer of ballads or (*obs.*) of scurrilous verses.

1589 NASHE *Almond for P.* Ded. 3 A man cannot haue a bout with a Balletter.. but hee shall be in daunger of a further displeasure. **1637** HEYWOOD *Pleas. Dial.* 283 A base and infamous Balladder, who disperst a scandalous riming Libell. **1878** SIMPSON *Sch. Shaks.* I. 134 As balladers and dramatists agree in representing his case.

balladic (bəˈlædɪk), *a.* [f. BALLAD *sb.* + -IC.] Of the nature of, or pertaining to, ballads. So †**baˈlladical** *a. Obs.*

1615 A. STAFFORD *Heav. Dogge* To Rdr. 18 To read Ballads, and books Balladicall. **1865** *Sat. Rev.* 19 Aug. 245/1 Spirit-stirring verse, lyric or balladic. **1881** *Blackw. Mag.* Mar., The Spenserian blank verse and balladic aspirants.

†**ballaˈdier.** *Obs.* [f. BALLAD *sb.* + -IER. App. not in Fr.] A street ballad-singer.

1637 *Dedic. V.* in *Randolph's Poems* (1875) 504 They had tried the balladier's or fiddler's trade. **1651** BIGGS *New Disp.* §256 Loose stage-player, Balladier, or blind harper.

balladin(e, variant of BALADINE.

balladingr (ˈbælədɪŋ), *vbl. sb.* [f. BALLAD *v.* + -ING¹.] The writing or composition of ballads.

1600 ROWLANDS *Let. Humours Blood* xv. 21 Amorous Austin spendes much Balleting, In rimeing Letters. **1670** F. BUSHBY *Marcelia* Prol. A iij b, With Ballading I think she mad is grown.

ˈballading, *ppl. a.* [f. as prec. + -ING².] That writes or composes ballads.

1599 NASHE *Saffron Walden* 99 Deloney, the balletting Silke-weaver. *a* **1637** B. JONSON *Masques* (T.) A whining, ballading lover.

balladism (ˈbælədɪz(ə)m). [f. BALLAD *sb.* + -ISM.] The characteristic quality of ballads.

1866 PALGRAVE in *Fortn. Rev.* 15 June 301 The more complete balladism, if I may use the word, of Lady A. Lindsay's 'Auld Robin Gray.'

balladist (ˈbælədɪst). [f. as prec. + -IST.] A maker of ballads; a ballader.

1858 BAILLY *Age* 193 Whereon for rollicking balladist to declaim. **1883** *St. James's Gaz.* 9 Feb. 6 Such are the epithets which the balladists love to heap upon him.

balladize (ˈbælədaɪz), *v.* [f. as prec. + -IZE.] **a.** *intr.* To make ballads. **b.** *trans.* To make into a ballad, turn into ballad form. Hence **balladized**, **balladizing** *ppl. a.*

1598 MUNDAY & CHETTLE *Earl Huntingdon* in Hazl. *Dodsl.* (1874) VIII. 258 Muddy slaves, whose balladising rhymes With words unpolish'd show their brutish thoughts. **1834** SOUTHEY *Lett.* (1856) IV. 384 If I can succeed in balladising this exploit, you shall have the song. **1879** J. P. COLLIER *Hist. Dram. Poetry* I. 107 *note*, A balladised Eskdale tradition.

ˈballadling. *nonce-wd.* A little ballad.

1798 SOUTHEY in Robberds' *Mem. W. Taylor* I. 240 Some tolerable balladlings, and some tolerable stories.

ballad-monger (ˈbæləd,mʌŋgə(r)). [See -MONGER.] One who deals in ballads: **a.** used contemptuously by Shakspere, and by others in imitation, for: Ballad-maker.

1596 SHAKS. *1 Hen IV*, III. i. 130, I had rather be a Kitten, and cry mew, Then one of these same Meeter Ballad-mongers. **1756** J. WARTON *Ess. Pope* (1782) I. vii. 356 Villon was merely a pert and insipid ballad monger. **1809** BYRON *Bards & Rev.* xii, Behold the ballad-monger Southey rise!

b. A seller of ballads.

1653 URQUHART *Rabelais* I. ix, An old paultry book.. sold by the hawking Pedlars and Balladmongers. **1874** MOTLEY *Barneveld* II. xviii. 252 All the ballad-mongers and broad-sheet vendors of the town.

Hence **ballad-mongering** *vbl. sb.*

1809 BYRON *Bards & Rev.* Argt. (MS.), The poet.. reviléth Walter Scott for.. ballad-mongering.

balladry (ˈbælədrɪ). Also 6 **balletry, -adrie**, 7 **-atry**. [f. BALLAD *sb.* + -RY.] Ballad poetry; composition in the ballad style. (Formerly often *depreciative*; cf. BALLAD *sb.* 3.)

1598 E. GILPIN *Skial.* (1878) 6 Such massacre's made of thy balladry. **1631** BRATHWAIT *Whimzies* 138 An obscene veine of ballatry which makes the wenches of the greene laugh. *a* **1695** PURCELL *Anthems* Pref. (T.) The levity and balladry of our neighbours. **1849** *Blackw. Mag.* LXV. 455 Torturing himself to unite old balladry with modern sentiment.

ballaho(o): see BALAO.

ballahou, ballahoo (,bæləˈhuː). *Naut.* and *West Ind.* [ad. Sp. *balahú* schooner.] See quots. 1867 and 1958; also, applied contemptuously to a lubberly or ungainly vessel. Cf. BALLYHOO OF BLAZES.

1867 SMYTH *Sailor's Word-Bk.* 71 *Ballahou*, a sharp-floored fast-sailing schooner, with taunt fore-and-aft sails, and no topsails, common in Bermuda and the West Indies. The foremast of the ballahou rakes forward, the mainmast aft. **1889** *Cent. Dict.*, *Ballahou*, a fast-sailing two-masted vessel [etc.]. 2. A term of derision applied to an ill-conditioned, slovenly ship. **1923** CONRAD *Rover* iii. 39 What made for him the life of any strange shore were the craft that belonged to it: canoes, catamarans, ballahous, praus [etc.]. **1958** J. CAREW *Wild Coast* xx. 241 Doorne.. rented out a fleet of ballahoos.. so that those who did not own these flat-bottomed punts could ply up and down.

ballan (ˈbælən). *Zool.* A fish: a variety of Wrasse (*Labrus maculatus*).

1769 PENNANT *Brit. Zool.* III. 343 Ballan.. is a kind of Wrasse, sent from Scarborough. **1839** *Penny Cycl.* XIII. 261/1 The Ballan Wrasse.. is about eighteen inches long, of a red colour above, pale orange beneath.

ballarag, obs. form of BULLYRAG.

†**ˈballard¹**. *Obs.* [app. f. BALL *sb.³* + -ARD. Cf. BALD.] A bald-headed person.

1382 WYCLIF *2 Kings* ii. 23 And scorneden to hym seying, Stye up, ballard! **1485** CAXTON *Trevisa's Higden* I. xxv. 25 One sayde to Julius.. *Salue calue*, that is hayll balard.

†**ballard²**. *Obs.* A kind of musical instrument.

1625 PURCHAS *Pilgrims* II. 1573 Their ballards are a foot aboue ground, hollow vnder, with some seventeen Keyes on the top, on which the Player strikes.. with two strikes a foot long, with balls fastned on the end.

†**ˈballart.** *rare*⁻¹. Obs. appellation of the hare; of unknown meaning and origin.

c **1300** *Names of Hare* in *Rel. Ant.* I. 133 The wei-betere, the ballart The go-bi-dish, the soillart.

ballast ('bæləst), *sb.* Forms: 6–8 **balast**, 6–7 **ballace**, 6 **ballass**, **-esse**, **balest**, **-ist**, 7 **balasse**, **-ase**, **ballasse**, **-ais**, 7 **ballast**. [Now found in most of the European langs.; Sw. Da., Fris., Du., LG. (whence Ger., Russ., Fr.) *ballast*. Origin doubtful: the oldest form is possibly OSw. and ODa. *barlast* (before 1400, and regularly in 15th c.), f. *bar* bare + *last* load, with the sense of '*bare*, naked, or mere *load* or weight,' i.e. lading which is mere load, lading for the sake of weight merely. Thence *ballast*, with *ll* for *rl* by assimilation, already in 15th c. Sw. and Da., whence in Eng. soon after 1500. The later Da. *bag-last* 'back-load,' Du. (17th c.) *balg-last* 'belly-load,' were corrupted by 'popular etymology.' The final *t* was lost in Flem. *ballas*, and the 16–17th c. Eng. *ballace*, *-as* (first in the vb, where *ballast* was plausibly analysed as *ballass-ed*.) Contact of sense further often confused *ballace* and BALLANCE.

(The form *ballast* also occurs before 1400 in LG., and is taken as the original by Schiller and Lübben, who explain it from *bal* bad (= BALE *a.*) as *bad lading* 'schlechte Schiffsfracht, die man nur ladet um dem Schiffe den nöthigen Tiefgang zu geben.' If this is well founded, *barlast* would rank with *bag-*, *balg-last*, as a popular perversion.)]

1. a. Gravel, sand, stones, iron, lead, or any heavy material, placed in the hold of a ship, in order to sink her to such a depth as to prevent her from capsizing when under sail or in motion.

1530 PALSGR. 196/2 Balast of a shyppe, *lestage*. **1536** *Act 27 Hen. VIII*, xviii, Balest for shippes. **1568** C. WATSON *Polyb.* 49b, And cast their ballesse over borde. **1610** HOLLAND *Camden's Brit.* I. 712 Coblestones for ballais. **1697** DRYDEN *Virg. Georg.* IV. 285 With sandy Ballast Sailors trim the Boat. **1718** STEELE *Fish-pool* 180 Ballast must be used to sink her down to the center of motion. **1855** MACAULAY *Hist. Eng.* III. 727 The gravel which was the ballast of their smack.

b. A substance, usu. sand or water, carried in the car of a balloon or airship to steady it in flight, and jettisoned when it is desired to ascend to a higher level. Also *attrib.*

1784 FRANKLIN *Let.* 16 Jan. (1907) IX. 156 They discharged some of their Ballast of Sand when they would rise again. **1785** CAVALLO *Aerostation* 288 The ballast hitherto used for aerostatic machines has been generally sand. **1908** H. G. WELLS *War in Air* i. 9 The descent of ballast upon his potatoes. **1916** *Sphere* 18 Mar. 292/1 This Zeppelin..must have got rid of 5 tons of fuel and ballast (i.e., water or ammunition). **1917** *Ibid.* 3 Nov. 103/1 The water ballast [in a zeppelin] froze. **1927** V. W. PAGÉ *Modern Aircraft* (1928) ii. 50 Ballast must be carried on an airship for use in possible emergencies in landing the ship.

2. *in ballast*: **a.** (also *on the ballast*) in the hold. **b.** Of ships: Laden with ballast only. **c.** Of materials: In the capacity of ballast.

1592 NASHE *P. Penilesse* (ed. 2) 9 Hee will to the sea..and ..lyes in brine in Balist, and is lamentable sicke. *c* **1630** RISDON *Surv. Devon* §272 Ninety were sick on the ballast. **1691** *Lond. Gaz.* No. 2637/3 Merchant-men bound in Ballast from Havre de Grace. **1815** SCOTT *Guy M.* v, Smuggler, when his guns are in ballast..pirate, when he gets them mounted. **1866** ROGERS *Agric. & Prices* I. xviii. 423 Sea-coal was taken in ballast. **1878** in *Daily News* 26 Sept. 2/3 When in ballast the Bywell Castle draws 12 feet aft.

3. *fig.* That which tends to give stability in morals or politics, to steady the mind or feelings, etc.

1612 BACON *Vain-glory, Ess.* (Arb.) 464 Solid and sober natures, have more of the ballast, then of the saile. **1670** WALTON *Lives* II. 100 Having to his great Wit added the ballast of Learning. **1720** SWIFT *Fates Clergym.* Wks. 1755 II. II. 25 It wants the ballast of those, whom the world calls moderate men. **1852** LD. COCKBURN *Jeffrey* I. 342 Delay is often the ballast of sound legislation.

†**4.** *transf.* Load, burden, freight. *Obs.*

1620 QUARLES *Jonah* Poems (1717) 54 Go to Niniveh.. behold the Ballace And burthen of her bulk, is nought but sin. **1631** MASSINGER *Beleeve as* IV. iii, What woulde you have, sir? *Ber.* My ballace [*i.e.* some food] about me; I shall nere sayle well els. **1646** J. HALL *Poems* I. 15 Shall not I congeal to see Doris the Ballast of thine arms?

5. Gravel, broken stone, slag, or other material, similar to that employed as ballast in ships, used to form the bed of a railroad, in which the sleepers are fixed. Also recently applied to burnt clay used for the same purpose, or as a substratum for new roads, etc.

1837 [see BALLASTING *vbl. sb.*] **1847** in CRAIG. **1860** *Engineer* 30 Mar. 207/2 A joint sleeper..laid in the ballast beneath the rail joints. **1876** ROUTLEDGE *Discov.* 63 The permanent way is formed first of ballast. **1881** *Mechanic* §1098 When the soil is clayey it may be converted into balast ..a useful material for making roads. *Mod.* A path made with 'burnt ballast.'

6. *Comb.* **a.** objective with vbl. sb. or agent-noun, as *ballast-getter*, *-heaver*; **b.** attrib., as *ballast-bag*, *-boat*, *-engine*, *-lighter*, *-train*, *-wagon*. Also **ballast-fin** *U.S.*, a fin-shaped metal extension of the keel of a yacht serving to ballast her and to enable her to sail close to the wind, **ballast-man**, one employed in supplying ballast to ships; **ballast-office**, one controlling the supply of ballast to ships; **ballast-ports**, square holes cut in the sides of merchantmen for taking in ballast; **ballast-shovel**, 'a round-mouthed shovel' (Raymond *Mining Gloss.* 1881).

1890 A. GIBERNE *Ocean of Air* xvii. 151 At 23,000 feet, Mr. Coxwell,..examining his *ballast-bags, decided that we must..descend. **1755** *Gentl. Mag.* XXV. 445 *Ballast-boats and lighters. **1865** *Times* 13 Jan., A load was attached to the *ballast-engine. **1894** *Outing* (U.S.) XXIV. 194/2, I have not a word to say against the *ballast-fin so far as racing is concerned. **1839** DICKENS *O. Twist* (1850) 267/1 Labourers of the lowest class, *ballast-heavers, coal-whippers. **1803** *Ann. Reg.* 399/1 A *ballast-lighter..struck the side of the ship. **1715** *Lond. Gaz.* No. 5347/3 Abuses committed by the *Ballastmen upon the..Thames. **1598** STOW *Survey* (1754) II. v. xviii. 389/2 Deptford strand..where their *Ballast office is also kept. **1835** *Penny Cycl.* III. 330/2 Ballast-office Corporation, Dublin, or, more correctly, the Corporation for Preserving and Improving the Port of Dublin. **1864** *Times* 24 Dec., He was in the hinder portion of the *ballast train. **1848** *Athenæum* 5 Aug. 773 A train of huge iron shovels or *ballast-waggons, as they are called.

7. *Electr.* A device used in an electrical circuit to stabilize the current under changing conditions; esp. in *Comb.*

1924 ROGET *Dict. Electr. Terms* 17/2 *Ballast resistance*, (1) A steadying resistance used to limit variations of current in a circuit. (2) In *Track Circuit Signalling*, the leakage resistance across the ballast between the two track rails. **1931** L. B. TURNER *Wireless* v. 121 It is on account of the negative slope resistance that arc lamps are always run with a ballast resistance in series. **1939** *Electr. Communication* XVIII. 115/1 The iron wire ballast lamp, ballast resistor or barretter, as it is sometimes called, is a device..for maintaining between very narrow limits the electric current flowing in a circuit, in spite of considerable voltage fluctuations. **1962** M. G. SAY *Conc. Encycl. Electr. Engin.* 80/2 A resistor is used as a ballast in a rectifier battery-charging circuit to prevent excessive current in the event of variation in supply voltage.

ballast ('bæləst), *v.* Forms: 6 **balase**, **-esse**, **-isse**, 6–7 **balasse**, **ballasse**, **-ace**, **-ase**, 7 **balast**, **ballise**, **-ize**, **-aise**, 7– **ballast**. [f. prec. sb.]

1. a. *trans.* To furnish (a ship) with ballast; to render (her) steady under sail by a sufficient weight in the hold.

1538 LELAND *Itin.* I. 52 The Shipes were balissed with great coble stone. **1604** DRAYTON *Owle* 78 To ballast Ships for steddinesse in winde. **1655** TUCKNEY *Good Day Impr.* 34 So much burden would serve to ballast the ship, more would sink it. **1866** KINGSLEY *Herew.* v. 114 They ballasted their ship with pebbles.

b. *trans.* Also used of balloons and other airships.

1784 *Boston Mag.* June 323/1 The car was ballasted with sand bags. **1786** JOHN JEFFRIES *Narr. Two Aerial Voyages* 20 Those who wish to go a great distance..with a Balloon, should..ballast their Balloon so that it will not rise above a certain height.

2. *transf.* To steady (generally).

1596 FITZ-GEFFREY *Sir F. Drake* (1881) 54 Constant stabilitie ballassed her [*i.e.* Fortune's] feete. **1601** HOLLAND *Pliny* x. xxiii, Cranes..ballaise themselves with stones in their feet, that they flie more steadie.

3. *fig.* To steady mentally or morally.

c **1600** *Pharisaisme & Chr.* 35 Ballace your wavering hearts with the sound truth of godlinesse. **1655** GURNALL *Chr. in Arm.* xi. §1. (1669) 113 If he be not well ballast with humility, a little gust..will tople him into this sin. **1792** A. YOUNG *Trav. France* 547 Mature deliberation is wanted to ballast the impetuosity of the people.

†**4.** To freight, load (*with* cargo). *Obs.*

1590 SHAKS. *Com. Err.* III. ii. 140 Who sent whole Armadoes of Carrects to be ballast at her nose. **1622** CALLIS *Stat. Sewers* I, I lanched forth my Ship..furnish'd and ballist with Merchandize. **1666** *Lond. Gaz.* No. 93/1 Four ships well laden and ballasted with Goods.

5. *transf.* and *fig.* To load, burden, weight, weigh down. *arch.*

1566 DRANT *Wail Jerem.* Kvj, He ballasde me with balefull bitternes. **1592** NASHE *P. Penilesse* 14 A wolfe being about to deuoure a horse doth balist his belly with earth, that he may hang the heauier vpon him. **1630** BRATHWAIT *Eng. Gentl.* (1641) 299 Their conceits are ever ballased with harshnesse. **1816** SCOTT *Old Mort.* ix, These yellow rascals must serve to ballast my purse a little longer.

6. To fill in or form with ballast (the bed of a railroad, etc.); cf. BALLAST *sb.* 5.

1864 in WEBSTER. **1881** *Chicago Times* 4 June, Laying down steel rails and liberally ballasting the whole line.

¶ Confused with BALANCE *v.* See BALANCE *sb.* 7.

1611 SPEED *Hist. Gt. Brit.* VI. iv. 55 The cause for Tribute was ballized betwixt them. **1697** DAMPIER *Voy.* (1729) I. 414 We furl'd our Main-sail, and ballasted our Mizen.

ballastage ('bæləstɪdʒ). [f. BALLAST *sb.* + -AGE.] Toll paid for the privilege of taking ballast.

1691 T. H[ALE] *Acc. New Invent.* 95 The Right of the Ballastage..belongs to the Admiral. **1759** *Ann. Reg.* 97/2 Better regulation of lastage and Ballastage in the Thames.

ballasted ('bæləstɪd), *ppl. a.* [f. BALLAST *v.* + -ED.] Furnished with ballast; rendered steady or stable.

1552 HULOET, Balessed, *saburratus*. **1586** BRIGHT *Melanch.* xxxv. 195 They be well ballaced with knowledge of the Scriptures. *c* **1645** HOWELL *Lett.* (1650) II. 32 Those that have their heads lightly ballasted. *a* **1797** H. WALPOLE *Mem. Geo. III* (1845) I. xxi. 305 The poor young man's head ..was by no means ballasted by a good heart.

'**ballaster.** [f. as prec. + -ER[1].] One who supplies ships with ballast.

1659 *Commons Jrnls.* VII. 740 (D.) The office of ballaster, and of Lading..and Ballasting of ships and vessels.

ballasting ('bæləstɪŋ), *vbl. sb.* [f. BALLAST *v.* + -ING[1].] The action or process of supplying with ballast; *concr.* and *fig.* = BALLAST *sb.* Also with *up*: used of balloons and other airships.

1536 *Act 27 Hen. VIII*, xviii, The office and ordering of and for balasting for shippes. **1769** FALCONER *Dict. Marine* (1789), *Lestage*, the ballasting of a ship, or furnishing her with ballast. **1837** *Athenæum* 21 Jan. 52/1 Fir planks.. bedded on ballasting, which is loose gravel. **1882** *Daily Tel.* 8 Apr., If he have the smallest possible ballasting of common sense. **1918** W. E. DOMMETT *Dict. Aircraft* 9 *Ballasting up*. In an airship, the process of adjusting the weights in the car until the ship is slightly lighter than air. **1950** *Gloss. Aeronaut. Terms (B.S.I.)* I. 46 *Ballasting-up*, the operation of adjusting the buoyancy or trim by releasing ballast or gas.

'**ballastless**, *a.* [BALLAST *sb.*] Without ballast; *fig.* unsteady.

1885 L. A. WINGFIELD *Barbara Philpot* III. ii. 34 She was unstable and ballastless, subject to delusions. **1886** *Bedfordsh. Times* 30 Oct. 5 They serve the purpose of ballast to a ballast-less leader.

ballat, **-ry**, obs. forms of BALLAD *sb.*, -RY.

‖**ballata** (bə'lɑːtə). Pl. **ballate**. [It., f. Pr. *balada*: see BALLAD *sb.*] (See quot. 1959.)

1762 G.-A. GALLINI *Treat. Art Dancing* 196 Ballads, which is a true word for a song at once sung and danced: *ballare* signifying to dance; and *ballata*, a song, composed to be danced. **1782** C. BURNEY *Hist. Music.* II. 343 *Ballata*, whence the French had their word *Balade*, and the English *Ballad*, has long been detached from dancing, and indeed confined to a low species of song. **1912** E. POUND tr. *Sonnets & Ballate of Guido Cavalcanti* 91 This is not really a ballatta but is the first stanza of a lost canzone. **1939** L. ELLINWOOD *Wks. F. Landini* p. xxvii, The verses of the madrigals, as contrasted with the more frivolous texts of the *ballate*, are serious and expressive. **1959** WESTRUP & HARRISON *Collins Mus. Encycl.* 49/2 *Ballata*, a 14th-cent. Italian verse-form, in which the refrain occurs at the beginning and end of the stanza.

ballatoon (bælə'tuːn). A heavy luggage-boat used on Russian rivers for the transport of timber.

1828 in WEBSTER.

ball-breaker. *slang* (orig. *U.S.*). [BALL *sb.*[1] 15 b.] **a.** A difficult, boring, or exasperating job, problem, or situation. **b.** A person who sets difficult work or problems; a hard taskmaster. **c.** A dominating woman, one who destroys the self-confidence of a man.

1954 J. A. WEINGARTEN *Amer. Dict. Slang* 15/1. **1970** N. ARMSTRONG et al. *First on Moon* iii. 57 The quality control inspector is a sort of nitpicker. We're the ball breakers, in plain English. We're the most unwanted people. **1975** D. LODGE *Changing Places* v. 213 Désirée is a ball-breaker. She eats men like your husband for breakfast. **1975** *Observer* 21 Dec. 21/8 A meticulously groomed, flint-profiled ball breaker with a taste for leopard-skin prints, Margo is the repository of every known prejudice common among the landless landed gentry. **1977** I. SHAW *Beggarman, Thief* I. vii. 94 Tom told me about that wife of his. A real ball-breaker, isn't she? **1985** *Company* Dec. 60/2 They [*sc.* women] are now reaching senior positions..where their arrival is creating new male horror stories about aggressive ball-breakers.

Hence **ball-breaking** *ppl. a.*

1976 *Weekend Mag.* (Montreal) 3 Jan. 2/2 The women's movement is a bunch of ball-breaking bitches.

ball-buster. *slang* (orig. *U.S.*). [BALL *sb.*[1] 15 b.] = prec.

1954 J. A. WEINGARTEN *Amer. Dict. Slang* 15/2. **1975** *Verbatim* Feb. 5/2 The term *ballbuster*..is a graphic, forceful expletive, typically applied to a domineering female. **1980** M. FRENCH *Bleeding Heart* vii. 258 A woman who blames men or male society for anything, who complains, is seen as a..castrator, an Amazon, a ballbuster.

So **ball-busting** *ppl. a.*

1944 W. L. MOORE in L. Warfield *Fighting Words* 92 Connelly was coming to look upon shore patrol as merely a time-killer, a ball-busting detail, something a little less foolish than continual close order drill. **1974** *Black World* Aug. 11/2 We can begin by seeing what Black women have done with the legendary and romanticized image of the Black woman as Superwoman—bad-talking and ball-busting, strong enough to sustain her family and herself through the hardest conditions. **1978** J. WAMBAUGH *Black Marble* xv. 346 Couple a real ball-bustin cops! How bout that!

†**balle**, *sb. Obs.* [perh. f. the L. *bal-āre* to bleat; cf. BAA. But cf. also BALL *sb.*[3]] A name formerly applied to a sheep.

c **1440** *Promp. Parv.* 22/1 Balle, schepys name, ballator.

balled (bɔːld), *ppl. a.* [f. BALL *v.*[1] and *sb.*[1] + -ED.] **a.** Formed into a ball. †**b.** Cleared of balls or lumps; cf. *shelled peas*.

1591 PERCIVALL *Sp. Dict.*, *Desterronada tierra*, clods of earth broken, balled ground, or rolled ground. **1759** MARTIN *Nat. Hist.* II. 112 When ball'd it is laid on Hurdles to dry. **1851** L. GORDON *in Art Jrnl. Illust. Cat.* vii * */1 After the yarn had been made into a balled warp. **1875** BROWNING *Aristoph. Apol.* 103 The balled fist broke brow like thunderbolt.

balled, obs. form of BALD.

ballenger, **-inger**, variants of BALINGER.

baller ('bɔːlə(r)). [f. BALL *v.*[1] and *sb.*[2] + -ER[1].]

1. One who forms anything into balls. Also *spec.* a workman who charges puddled bars into a balling or reheating furnace.

1825 J. NICHOLSON *Oper. Mech.* 461 If china is to be made, the baller, previously to forming the clay into a ball, breaks it in two. **1865** ELIZA METEYARD *Wedgwood* I. 232 The weighing of clay at the baller's scales. **1881** *Instr. Census Clerks* (1885) 104 Baller (Tin Plate).

†**2.** One who takes part in a ball for dancing.

1668 PEPYS *Diary* 30 May, Here I first understood..the meaning of the Company that lately were called 'Ballers.'

3. a. One who makes yarn, etc., into balls; one who attends to a balling machine. **b.** A balling machine.

1881 *Instr. Census Clerks* (1885) 104 Baller (Carpet). **1884** McLAREN *Spinning* 216 The balling head and creel motion ranks along with Blamire's as the best... The sliver before going into the baller can be drawn off the doffer in two ways. *Ibid.* 220 This is a side-drawing system, and, on our former supposition of speeds, would have the same number of doublings per sliver as in the baller.

ballerina (bælə'riːnə). Pl. **ballerinas**; formerly also **ballerine** (as It.). [It., fem. of *ballerino.*] **a.** A female dancer, a ballet-girl. In mod. use almost exclusively a dancer taking one of the five leading classical female roles in ballet.

1792 A. YOUNG *Trav. France* 216 The *ballarini*, or female dancers, have the same fury of motion. **1815** BYRON in Moore *Life* 289 A row among our ballerinas. **1878** in Grove *Dict. Music* I. 131 The first professional ballerina of note.. was Mlle. Lafontaine. *Ibid.* 132 These eminent ballerine. **1911** J. E. CRAWFORD FLITCH *Mod. Dancing* ix. 127 At seventeen they [*sc.* pupils at the Imperial (Russian) Ballet School] begin their career as members of the *corps de ballet*, from which the most prominent rise upwards..through the various grades of..*premier sujet*, *première danseuse* or *ballerina*, and *ballerina assoluta*. **1934** A. L. HASKELL *Balletomania* iii. 57 Actually, even in Russia, the home of ballet, the *ballerina* was a rarity. It was as definite and as official a rank as that of General... There were only five *ballerinas* of the Maryinsky at any one time. **1936** 'C. BRAHMS' *Footnotes to Ballet* II. 70 But whatever her position (whether she be ballerina or chorina), the dancer is extended at her best in this work. **1952** *Even. News* 5 Jan. 4/3 A young dancer not yet accorded ballerina status. **1962** *Times* 14 Dec. 16/4 Madame Catherine Geltzer, the Russian ballerina assoluta.

b. ballerina shoe, a light, pliable shoe of the shape worn by ballerinas; also *ellipt.*

1950 *Leader* 1 Apr. 34/2 Flat 'ballerina' shoes with criss-cross straps. **1959** *Housewife* June 26 We show the Ladies 38 slip on Ballerina.

ballet ('bæleɪ, 'bale; rarely 'bælɪt), *sb.*[1] Forms: **balette, -et, -at,** 7–9 **ballette,** 8– **ballet.** [a. F. *ballet*, dim. of *bal* dance: see BALL *sb.*[2] In 17th c. the forms were confused with those of BALLAD *sb.*]

1. a. A theatrical representation, consisting of dancing and pantomime, orginally employed to illustrate dramatically the costumes and manners of other nations, but now for the most part regarded as an artistic exhibition of skill in dancing.

1667 DRYDEN *Ess. Dram. Poesie* Wks. 1725 I. 54 Not a Balette or Masque, but a play. **1676** ETHERIDGE *Man of Mode* II. i. (1684) 19 [The Russian] Balladins..are Now practising a famous Ballat, which will Be suddenly danc'd at the Bear-Garden. **1773** *Gentl. Mag.* XLIII. 479 One of the ballets of the opera at Palermo, is a representation of Vauxhall Gardens. *a* **1845** HOOD *Vauxhall* vii, Time's ripe for the Ballet, Like bees they all rally. **1865** *Law Times Rep.* 371 A ballet of action has a plot, a ballet of divertissement has none.

b. *transf.*

1926 C. DAY LEWIS in *Oxford Poetry* 15 The ballet of minnows Moving together In lithe sarabande.

c. In various French phrases, as ***ballet blanc*** [lit. 'white ballet']: a ballet in which the ballerinas are dressed in white; ***ballet bouffe, bouffon***: a comic ballet; ***ballet d'action*** [lit. 'ballet of action']: a ballet in which the dancing is used to convey a plot or theme; a dramatic ballet.

1797 *Encycl. Brit.* V. 664/2 Such figures must give way to nature in what we term *ballets d'action*. **1849** A. B. REACH *Cl. Lorimer* i. 29 The new ballet d'action, called 'La Reine des Feu Follets'. **1947** *Horizon* Nov. 293 There is nothing to show whether these *Scènes* were composed to any preconceived plan of action; but as they stand, they seem to imply a *ballet blanc*. **1947** *Ballet Ann.* I. 28 *Helen of Troy*, another Offenbach *ballet-bouffe*..a light and not very original frolic. **1950** *Ibid.* IV. 53 The magnificent costume billowing around her in an ectoplasmic ecstasy that would have delighted Gautier, father of *le ballet blanc*. **1958** *Listener* 5 June 955/3 Rameau's *ballet bouffon* enters the category under false colours. **1962** *Times* 4 Jan. 12/5 The *noble* stately measures of the eighteenth-century *ballet d'action*.

†**2.** *gen.* A dance. *Obs.*

1782 S. ROGERS *Ital. Song* 14 The ballet danced in twilight glade. **1829** SCOTT *Demonol.* i. 20 The daily persecution of this domestic ballet.

3. *attrib.*, as ***ballet-dance, -dancer, -drama, -girl, -goer, -lover, -music, -romance, -shoe, -skirt***; **ballet-master, -mistress**, one who arranges and directs the dancing of the ballet.

1796 Ballet dance [see *back-countryman*]. **1912** W. OWEN *Let.* 28 Oct. (1967) 165 A lesson in the ballet-dance. **1836** *Q. Rev.* No. 111. 87 Daughter of a worn-out ballet-dancer. **1915** R. LANKESTER *Divers. Nat.* 176 The great traditions of fine stage-dancing and ballet-drama. **1848** THACKERAY *Van. Fair* liii. (1853) 443 Your mother, the ballet girl. **1938** *New Statesman* 23 July 152/2 When the ordinary ballet-goer is confronted with a new ballet..he is likely first of all to be taken with the story. **1962** *Times* 25 Apr. 16/5 Everything that the orthodox ballet critic and ballet-lover hold dear. **1762** G.-A. GALLINI *Treat. Art Dancing* 122 A good ballet-master must especially have regard to both poetical and picturesque invention. **1797** *Monthly Mirror* Aug. 115 Byrne is the ballet master. **1823** BYRON *Juan* XIV. xxxviii, Danced..Not like a ballet-master in the van Of his drill'd nymphs. **1843** W. H. OXBERRY *Budget of Plays* (1844) I. 216/2 Astley's..Ballet Mistress, Miss Cushnie. **1871** *Echo* 4 Nov., Ballet-mistress at the Grand Opera. **1835** *Penny Cycl.* III. 331/2 A composer of good ballet-music is carefully attentive to locality and to nationality. **1801** *Monthly Mirror* Aug. 131 *The Corsair*..A grand ballet romance, under this title, was performed for the first time. **1867** T. W. ROBERTSON *Caste* I. 5 (*stage direction*) A small table..with ballet-shoe and skirt on it. *Ibid.* III. 34 (*stage direction*) Jug ..on table, bandbox and ballet skirt on table. **1901** 'L. MALET' *Hist. Sir R. Calmady* I. v. 37 The sustaining power of costume, whether it take the form of ballet-skirt or monk's frock.

Hence **balletic** (bæ'lɛtɪk) *a.*, of or pertaining to the ballet; **ba'lletically** *adv.*, in relation to the ballet.

1930 T. KARSAVINA *Theatre Street* II. xvi. 212 A 'balletic' form of dance was termed classical from time immemorial. **1936** 'C. BRAHMS' *Footnotes to Ballet* II. §6. 112 Balletically the symphonies evade him. **1958** *Times* 16 Sept. 3/2 Two familiar balletic motifs are thus involved—the eternal triangle, and the opposition between mob and individual.

ballet ('bælɪt), *sb.*[2] [f. BALL *sb.*[1] + -ET[1], dim. suffix; cf. OF. *balette.*] A little ball, esp. in *Her.*

1727–51 CHAMBERS *Cycl.*, *Balls* or *Ballets*..make a frequent bearing in coats of arms..[they are called] *pomeis* when vert, *pellets* or *agresses* when sable, *oranges* when tanne.

ballet ('bælɪt), *sb.*[3] *Hist.* [16–17th-c. spelling of BALLAD *sb.*] A form of madrigal in dance-rhythm.

1595 T. MORLEY (*title*) The first booke of balletts to fiue voyces. **1597** T. MORLEY *Introd. Mus.* 180 An other kind.. of Ballets, commonlie called *fa las*..deuised to be daunced to voices. **1598** T. WEELKES (*title*) Balletts and madrigals to fiue voyces. **1789** BURNEY *Hist. Mus.* III. 101 *Ballets*, or *Fa las*, to five voices. **1867** [see FA-LA b]. **1879** GROVE *Dict. Mus.* I. 132/2 *Ballets*, compositions of a light character, but somewhat in the madrigal style, frequently with a 'Fa la' burden which could be both sung and danced to. **1921** E. H. FELLOWES *Eng. Madrigal Composers* 57 An essential feature of the Ballet..was the introduction, at the end of each section, of a florid and rhythmical passage vocalized to the syllables *Fa la la*. **1942** E. BLOM *Music in Engl.* vii. 111 The canzonets and ballets, the lightest pieces for combined voices written by the Elizabethan and Jacobean masters.

'ballet, *v.* [f. BALLET *sb.*[1]] To express by ballet-action or pantomime.

1851 MAYHEW *Lond. Labour* III. 155 (Hoppe) Old man picks up Simpkin, and ballets to him that he's very sorry.. He ballets to her: 'Will you come down here and dance?'

ballet, -ette, obs. forms of BALLAD.

balletomane (bælɛtə'meɪn). [f. BALLET *sb.*[1] + -O + -MANE.] An enthusiast for ballet performances. Hence **balleto'mania**, passionate addiction to ballet.

1930 *Time & Tide* 28 Mar. 410 The *balletomanes* of the Marinsky Theatre, an audience 'very knowledgeable, exacting, somewhat dogmatic and conservative', but.. enthusiastic. **1934** A. L. HASKELL *Balletomania* 34 The *balletomane* has always been a thoroughly Russian product, and from what I hear, is to this day, in spite of all the material hardships... Ballet originated at a Court, flourished under an Emperor, but *balletomania* is the privilege of no one class. **1937** *Times* 10 Sept. 13/4 There is every sign that the period of balletomania is over, that the art can now bear rational discussion and criticism. **1947** *Ballet Ann.* I. 22 *Giselle* inspires more passionate enthusiasm among *balletomanes* than any other work.

Balling ('bɔːlɪŋ), *sb.* The name of Carl J. N. *Balling* (1805–68), Bohemian chemist, used *attrib.* to designate a scale of densities marked on hydrometers or a hydrometer marked with this scale.

[**1912** C. A. BROWNE *Handbk. Sugar Analysis* iii. 29 One of the best-known tables for the specific gravity of sugar solutions is that of Balling, published in 1854, and which served as a basis for the better-known..table of Brix. *Ibid.* p. xviii, Balling's specific gravity table.] **1935** *Soc. Chem. Ind.* (*Chem. Engin. Group*) *Data Sheet* X, *Hydrometer Scales* 8 The relationship between the Barkometer, Brix (sugar) and Balling scales and specific gravity. **1941** BROWNE & ZERBAN *Physical & Chem. Methods Sugar Analysis* (ed. 3) iii. 74 The construction of a hydrometer to read direct percentages of sucrose is first due to Balling... The divisions of the scale are usually called degrees Balling or degrees Brix. *Ibid.* 1310/1 Balling hydrometer.

balling ('bɔːlɪŋ), *vbl. sb.*[1] [f. BALL *v.*[1] + -ING[1].]

1. Formation into a ball or balls; occas. *attrib.*, as in ***balling-machine*** (for winding twine), ***-furnace***.

1713 *Lond. & Country Brew.* II. (1743) 135 This Mixing of the Malt..will prevent its Balling, or Gathering together in Heaps. **1869** *Eng. Mech.* 31 Dec. 387/2 Engravings of a ½ lb. and 1 lb. balling machine. **1881** RAYMOND *Mining Gloss.*, *Balling*, the aggregation of iron in the puddling..process into balls or loups. **1884** W. S. B. McLAREN *Spinning* 116 Balling, or making into 'tops'. *Ibid.* 117 As this balling head moves from side to side quickly, the ball is made by the sliver constantly passing from side to side. *Ibid.* 221 With the Blamire and balling systems one card can run while the other is standing.

2. The throwing of (snow-) balls.

1865 G. MACDONALD *A. Forbes* xvi. 64 The balling ceased, that Annie..might pass in safety.

3. *Veterinary Med.* The administration of medicine to a horse in the form of a ball (see BALL *sb.*[1] 11); ***balling gun, iron, pistol***, instruments sometimes used for this purpose.

1805 T. BOARDMAN *Dict. Veterinary Art* s.v. *Ball*, In order to prevent the fingers, &c. from being hurt by the teeth, an iron instrument covered with cloth (which is known to most grooms under the denomination of *a balling iron*) is put into the fore part of the horse's mouth, which keeps it at a proper wideness. **1831** YOUATT *Horse* 385 The balling iron, while it often wounds and permanently injures the bars, occasions the horse to struggle more than he otherwise would against the administration of the ball. *a* **1877** KNIGHT *Dict. Mech.* I. 220/2 Balling-gun. **1884** M. H. HAYES *Veterin. Notes* (ed. 3) 456 The *balling iron* is an instrument for keeping the mouth open. *Ibid.* 457 A *balling pistol* is useful for giving balls to fractious animals. **1908** *Animal Managem.* 308 *Balling.*—Take the tongue in the left hand..and push the ball as far as possible over the root of the tongue. **1960** *Farmer & Stockbreeder* 22 Mar. 43/2 Applied by balling gun directly into the gullet.

4. Of bees: see BALL *v.*[1] 5.

1926 *Chambers's Jrnl.* July 434/2 In the 'balling' of their queens, bees give an outstanding illustration of their tendency to do foolish things.

†**'balling,** *vbl. sb.*[2] [f. BALL *v.*[2] + -ING[1].] Frequenting of balls, dancing.

1634–46 ROW *Hist. Kirk.* (1842) 172 She..is to be admonished for night-waking, balling, etc. **1676** W. ROW *Suppl. Blair's Autobiog.* x. (1848) 226 There was balling and dancing till near day.

†**'ballised,** *ppl. a.* [? for *pallised* (cf. *palysyd*, 15th c., = *palisadoed*), ad. F. *palissé* surrounded with pales.] Enclosed with a railing or balustrade.

1624 WOTTON *Archit.* (1672) 46 Palladio..leaveth this Tarrace uncovered in the middle, and ballised about. —— in *Reliq. Wotton.* (1651) 245 Certain *ballised* out-standings to satisfie curiosity of sight.

ballist ('bælɪst). *rare.* Also 4–7 **balist.** [ad. L. *ballista*: see next.] = next.

1382 WYCLIF *1 Macc.* vi. 20 Thei maden balistis, *an instrument for to cast shaftis and stoonys* [**1388** arblastis; **1609** *Douay*, balists]. **1600** HOLLAND *Livy* XXIV. xl. 537 Catapults and Balists..provided for the assault of the cittie. **1861** LEWIN *Jerus.* 87 On the side of Judas were mines and ballists and desperate sallies.

‖**ballista** (bə'lɪstə). Also 6–9 **balista.** Pl. **ballistæ**, occas. **ballistas.** [L., f. (ultimately) Gr. βάλλειν to throw. The spelling with *ll* is etymologically preferable.] An ancient military engine, resembling a bow stretched with cords and thongs, used to hurl stones and other missiles; in med.L. also loosely for: Arbalest.

1598 GRENEWEY *Tacitus' Ann.* XV. ii. 224 Beating off the Barbarians with stones and speares out of Balistas and other engines. **1765** TUCKER *Lt. Nat.* II. 673 Who batters not with the balistæ and catapultæ. **1828** LANDOR *Imag. Conv.* (1846) 460 The sublimity which he attains who is hurled into the air from a ballista. **1852** MISS YONGE *Cameos* XXIV. 185 Often himself aiming a balista at the walls.

ballistic (bə'lɪstɪk), *a.* Also **balistic.** [f. prec. + -IC.] **a.** Of or pertaining to the throwing of missiles; projectile.

1775 in ASH. **1854** *Blackw. Mag.* LXXV. 530 The term ..*mangonel* was generally applicable to balistic engines. **1879** *Cassell's Techn. Educ.* I. 194 Increasing the ballistic power of our weapons.

b. ***ballistic pendulum***: an instrument for determining the relative velocity of projectiles.

1778 HUTTON in *Phil. Trans.* LXVIII. 54 This large ballistic pendulum, after being struck by the ball. **1879** THOMSON & TAIT *Nat. Phil.* I. I. §298 Robins' Ballistic Pendulum, a massive cylindrical block of wood cased in a cylindrical sheath of iron closed at one end and moveable about a horizontal axis.

c. ***ballistic galvanometer***, one in which damping is minimized, used to measure transient currents.

1878 AYRTON & PERRY in *Rep. Brit. Assoc.* 487 To obtain a galvanometric arrangement of sufficient sensibility to measure the small capacity of such an air condenser, and sufficiently ballistic that the air damping should be almost inappreciable... The arrangement of a ballistic galvanometer to fulfil the two conditions mentioned..was very troublesome. **1879** —— in *Phil. Mag.* Apr. 287 There was always some slight damping even in our ballistic galvanometer. **1880** J. E. H. GORDON *Phys. Treat. Electr. & Magn.* I. 240 In order to diminish the resistance of the air as much as possible, a 'balistic galvanometer' has been used.

d. ***ballistic missile, rocket***, a guided missile or rocket in which the guidance is effective only during the phase of propulsion; one that is powered only when ascending and then falls freely.

1949 *Jrnl. Amer. Rocket Soc.* Dec. 165 We have traced the path from the unguided small rocket to the huge ballistic rocket. **1954** *Commonw.* 1 Oct. 621/2 The so-called IBM, or intercontinental ballistic missile with nuclear warhead, is the ugly development next to be expected. **1958** *Engineering* 14 Mar. 331/1 To put a ballistic missile on the right course ..the guidance has to be accomplished while the engines are still firing. **1959** A. E. PUCKETT *Guided Missile Engin.* ii. 7

Ballistic missiles..follow trajectories determined primarily by initial velocity and gravity.

e. ***ballistic camera***, a camera used to photograph the phenomena of high velocity flight, esp. of ballistic missiles, etc.

1956 W. von Braun in *Jrnl. Brit. Interplan. Soc.* XV. 129 An isolated spot on the artillery firing range where were set up a formidable array of..ballistic cameras and chronographs. **1959** G. Merrill *Dict. Guided Missiles & Space Flight* 76/1 *Ballistic camera*, a camera used to photograph high velocity flight phenomena... Ballistic cameras are usually used to cover the terminal or launch phases of flight.

ba'llistically, *adv.* **a.** As regards ballistics. **b.** By force of gravity and momentum alone.

1879 Ayrton & Perry in *Phil. Mag.* Apr. 284 But this arrangement [of the galvanometer]..had far too much damping for being used ballistically. **1889** J. A. Longridge *Internal Ballistics* 16 Although there is no positive evidence of 'Dissociation' in a gun, it may be well to examine what would be the effect ballistically, if it did take place. **1969** *Sci. Jrnl.* July 70/3 A single warhead..fell ballistically on to its target.

ballistician (bælɪ'stɪʃən). [f. ballistic *a.* + -ian.] One who studies, or is skilled in, the science of ballistics.

1909 in Webster. **1936** J. E. Hoover *Sci. Meth. Crime Det.* 17 The forensic ballistician is often very helpful to the courts in furnishing opinions as to the effective range at which powder burns occur. **1936** *Discovery* Apr. 125/2 The war-rocket, with a minimum range of 500 miles..is a disconcerting revelation in these restless times, but a ballistician would doubtless regard its possibilities unfavourably. **1948** *Sci. News* VII. 23 Hitherto the behaviour of bodies moving at very high speeds through the air has been mainly the concern of the ballistician.

ba'llistics, *sb. pl.* Also balist-. [f. ballistic *a.*; cf. *athletics*, *acoustics*, etc., and F. *balistique*.] 'The art of throwing heavy bodies' (Chambers); the science of projectiles.

exterior ballistics, that branch of ballistics which deals with the flight of the projectile after leaving the gun; ***interior*** (or ***internal***) ***ballistics***, that branch which deals with the propulsive effect of a charge and the motion of the projectile in the bore of the gun. For *terminal ballistics* see terminal A. *adj.*

1753 Chambers *Cycl. Supp.* **1840** *Civil Eng. & Arch. Jrnl.* III. 21/2 They afford positive data, and the bases of experimental balistics, so necessary for artillery practice. **1873** F. Bashforth *Motion of Projectiles* p. viii, On the institution of the Advanced Class for Officers of the Royal Artillery in 1864, there was no satisfactory work on ballistics. **1886** J. M. Ingalls *Exterior Ballistics in Plane of Fire* 5 The motion of a projectile may be studied under three different aspects..called respectively *Interior Ballistics*, *Exterior Ballistics*, and *Ballistics of Penetration*. 1. *Interior Ballistics.*—Interior Ballistics treats of the motion of a projectile within the bore of the gun while it is acted upon by the highly elastic gases into which the powder is converted by combustion... 2. *Exterior Ballistics.*—Exterior Ballistics considers the circumstances of motion of a projectile from the time it emerges from the gun until it strikes the object aimed at. **1889** J. A. Longridge (*title*) Internal Ballistics. **1917** W. H. Tschappat *Ordnance & Gunnery* iv. 108 Interior ballistics treats of the motion of the projectile while still in the bore of the gun. *Ibid.* ix. 424 Exterior ballistics treats of the motion of a projectile after it has left the piece.

†**ballistier**. *Obs. rare.* In 7 balistier. [ad. L. *ballistārius*, f. ballista.] A soldier who worked or discharged a ballista.

1609 Holland *Amm. Marcel.* xvi. ii. 53 Men of armes and balistiers [*Ballistariis*], unmeet souldiers to protect..their ruler. *Ibid.* 221 The balistier himselfe.

¶ See also balister, etc.

ballistite ('bælɪstaɪt). [f. ballist(a + -ite[1].] A smokeless powder invented by A. Nobel, consisting of gun-cotton and nitroglycerine in about equal parts.

1892 *Arms & Explosives* Oct. 11/1 The new explosive 'Ballistite', which the Italian War Office has lately been experimenting with. **1895** O. Guttmann *Manuf. Explosives* II. 254 Nobel's ballistite, which has soluble gun-cotton as its base. **1912** J. M. Ingalls *Interior Ballistics* (ed. 3) 140 The ballistite..was in the form of cubes 0·3 of an inch on a side.

ballistocardiograph (bə,lɪstəʊ'kɑːdɪəʊgrɑːf, -græf). [f. ballist(ic *a.* + -o + cardiograph.] An instrument for recording the movements of the body caused by ejection of blood from the ventricles at each beat of the heart. Hence **ba,llisto'cardiogram**, the record made by such an instrument; **ba,llistocardio'graphic** *a.*, of or pertaining to a ballistocardiograph or ballistocardiography; **ba,llistocardi'ography**, the use of a ballistocardiograph.

1938 I. Starr et al. in *Amer. Jrnl. Physiol.* CXXIII. 195 (*title*) Apparatus for recording the heart's recoil and the blood's impacts in man (ballistocardiograph). **1938** —— in *Jrnl. Clinical Investigation* XVII. 507/1 The ballistocardiogram makes a new kind of information easily available to clinicians in the routine examination of patients with cardiac and circulatory disease. **1939** —— in *Amer. Jrnl. Physiol.* CXXVII. 21 To avoid unconscious bias the ballistocardiograph film was never developed until the result obtained by the ethyl iodide method was written in the record book. Then the ballistocardiograms were inspected. *Ibid.* 22 The dog and dog board were placed on the ballistocardiographic table. **1945** *Amer. Jrnl. Physiol.* CXLIV. 557 (*title*) The relationship between the cardiac ejection curve and the ballistocardiographic forces. **1951** *Ibid.* CLXV. 497 (*title*) Ballistocardiography in Experimental Mitral Insufficiency. **1956** *Nature* 17 Mar. 513/2 The use of the ballistocardiogram in assessing the functioning of the heart. **1968** *New Scientist* 9 May 269/2 Ballistocardiography, by which the mechanical performance of the heart as a pump can be assessed.

‖**ballium** ('bælɪəm). [med.L., app. f. F. *bail*.] = bail *sb.*[3] 2, and bailey.

1798 N. Drake *Lit. Hours* (1820) III. lix. 323 And where the ballium rear'd its strength, And where its turrets rose. **1810** Miss Porter *Scot. Chiefs* 121 Just as the whole of Wallace's men had leaped the wall, the inner ballium gate burst open. **1813** Scott *Trierm.* iii. ix, A banner'd Castle, keep and tower..And barbican and ballium vast.

ballock ('bɒlək). Not in polite use. Forms: 1 bealluc, 4 ballok, 4–5 ballokke, -oke, 5 balluk, -uc, balok, -ock, 6 ballocke, 6– ballock. [Prob. a deriv. of Teut. *ball-* (see ball *sb.*[1]), of which the OE. repr. would be **beall-u*, *-a*, or *-e*.]

1. a. A testicle.

c **1000** *Gloss.* in Wright *Voc.* (W.) /265 *Testiculi*, beallucas. **1382** Wyclif *Lev.* xxii. 24 Al beeste that..kitt and taken awey the ballokes is. **1486** *Bk. St. Albans, Hawking* C viij, Geue hir the ballockye [**1496** balockes] of a Buc. **1579** Baker *Guydon's Quest. Cyrurg.* 33. **1721–1800** in Bailey. Not in J. **1966** J. K. Baxter *Pig Island Lett.* 35 I'd give my ballocks now For a bucket of steam.

†**b.** *Comb.* (all obs.): **ballock-cod**, the scrotum; **ballock('s)-grass** (also ***hare's*** and ***sweet ballocks***), popular name of several species of orchis, from the shape of the tubers; **ballock-hafted** *a.*, with a ball(ock)-shaped handle; **ballock-knife**, ? one worn at the girdle (cf. L. *clūnāculum*, f. *clūnis*); **ballock-stone** = ballock; **ballock-wort**, orchis.

c **1450** in Wright *Voc.* (W.) /599 *Omembrana*, balluc cod. *Ibid.* /677 *Piga*, balloke code. **1562** Turner *Herbal* ii. 128 b, Whyt satyrion..or in other more vnmanerly speche, hares ballockes. **1578** Lyte *Dodoens* 222 Some cal it also Orchis.. Ballock grasse..and Bastard Satyrion. **1597** Gerard *Herbal* i. cii. §4. 169 *Orchis spiralis*..some call them Sweet Ballocks. **1655** Mouff. & Benn. *Health's Impr.* (1746) 313 Ballock's-grass, or Satyrium. **1438** *Test. Ebor.* (1855) 63 Unum dagar ballokhefted. **1377** Langl. *P. Pl.* B. xv. 121 A ballok-knyf With botones ouergylte. *c* **1460** *Towneley Myst.* 236, I have brysten both my balok stones, So fast hyed I hedyr. *c* **1450** in Wright *Voc.* (W.) /609 *Saturia*, ballokwort.

2. *pl. fig.* **a.** A person (in a state of entanglement or confusion). Cf. bollock 3.

1916 Joyce *Portr. Artist* 272 I'm a ballocks, he said, shaking his head in despair. **1922** —— *Ulysses* 287 Who's the old ballocks you were talking to?

b. Nonsense. Cf. ball *sb.*[1] 15 b.

1939 J. Cary *Mister Johnson* 193 For God's sake, don't talk ballocks, Johnson.

3. Comb. ***ballock-naked*** adj., completely naked.

1922 Joyce *Ulysses* 610 See them there stark ballock-naked.

'ballock, *v. slang.* Also bollock. [f. the sb.; cf. bollock.] *trans.* To reprimand or tell off severely. Freq. **'ballocking** *vbl. sb.*, a severe reprimand; cf. rollicking *vbl. sb.* 2.

1938 Partridge *Dict. Slang* (ed. 2) Add. 978/1. **1948** — *Dict. Forces' Slang* 9 Ballocking, bollocking. **1950** C. MacInnes *To Victors* ii. 211 I'm going to give Frau Dieckhoff a good bollocking. **1959** I. Jefferies *Thirteen Days* v. 63 He had been bollocking a sick man. **1967** D. Pinner *Ritual* xviii. 176 He knew he would get a bollocking from his super. **1973** M. Amis *Rachel Papers* 19 Jenny gave me a formulaic ballocking for not alerting her of my premature arrival. **1974** P. Wright *Lang. Brit. Industry* xi. 95, I got ballocked left, right and centre. **1978** *Times Lit. Suppl.* 17 Feb. 199/1 Sir John French, CIGS, came down for open day at 'The Shop', gave everyone a bollocking for slackness and indiscipline, and shortly afterwards retired the Commandant.

balloen, ballong, var. of balloon *sb.*[2]

†**ballon**[1]. *Obs. rare*[−1]. [a. F. *balon* 'a little ball or packe' (Cotgr.), f. *bale*, *balle*, bale *sb*[3].]

1753 Chambers *Cycl. Supp.* s.v. *Bale*, A bale or ballon of paper..consists of 14 reams.

‖**ballon**[2] (balɔ̃). [Fr., balloon.] **1.** Elasticity or buoyancy in dancing; the smooth falling and rising of the feet in the passage from step to step.

1830 R. Barton tr. *Blasis's Code of Terpsichore* ii. i. 53 Observe the *ballon*; nothing can be more delightful than to see you bounding with graceful elasticity in your steps, scarcely touching the ground, and seeming at every movement on the point of flying into the air. **1922** Beauclerk & Evrenov tr. *Svetlov's Thamar Karsavina* 32 When he [*sc.* Nijinsky] was rehearsing it was customary for other artists to..ask him to show them his great step (ballon). **1936** A. L. Haskell *Prelude to Ballet* 111 *Ballon*, referring not to the height of a jump but to the correct manner of landing in order to take off again (i.e. bounce). **1958** *Times* 11 Dec. 3/2 As he [*sc.* Stravinsky] came on to the platform he stumbled and regained his balance with a dancer's *ballon*.

2. A balloon glass (see balloon *sb.*[1] 10).

1934 E. Waugh *Handful of Dust* ii. 75 A ballon of liqueur brandy. **1939** J. Dell *Nobody ordered Wolves* xvii. 296 'I've just been thinking,' he declared, turning a *ballon* slowly by the stem.

‖**ballon d'essai** (balɔ̃ desɛ). [Fr., trial balloon.] An experimental project or piece of policy put forward to test the feeling or attitude of a person or body of persons; a feeler.

1883 *Standard* 24 Jan. 5 (Stanf.), The contents [of the letter] would make it appear a sort of *ballon d'essai*, designed to throw light on the prospects of an Orleanist Restoration in France. **1905** Mrs. H. Ward *Marriage W. Ashe* xiii. 259 In the early morning she had sent her note to Kitty—a *ballon d'essai*, despatched in a horror of great fear. **1928** *Daily Tel.* 18 Sept. 11/5 The rumours about Mlle. Lenglen's future plans have recently died down. This one may be in the nature of a ballon d'essai. **1942** *Mind* LI. 71 A good deal of Hume's theory of belief is rather a *ballon d'essai* than meant altogether seriously.

‖**ballonné** (balɔne). Also erron. **ballone, balloné.** [Fr., pa. pple. of *ballonner* to swell or puff out, distend.] (See quot. 1957.)

1778 *English Mag.* Feb. 59/2, I would not have a man enter a room *en petit maitre*, and present himself with a *pas grave* or a *balloné*. **1890** *All Year Round* 4 Oct. 321/1 Caroline Rosati..was a most fascinating representative of —to use a technical term—the 'ballonné' school of dancing. **1911** J. E. Crawford Flitch *Mod. Dancing* ii. 30 Its [*sc.* the ballet's] technique was developed by the introduction of pirouettes,..ballones. **1922** Beauclerk & Evrenov tr. *Svetlov's Thamar Karsavina* 30 accomplishing various brilliant steps (*ballonés*) in the *Nereids*. **1957** G. B. Wilson *Dict. Ballet* 46 *Ballonné*..lit. a ball-like or bouncing step. Any broad bounding movement and especially a movement in which the dancer springs upwards, opening one leg at hip height to the front, side, or back, and alights on the other foot, closing the first on the cou-de-pied.

ballonnet, ballonet ('bælənɛt). Also **-ette**. [ad. F. *ballonnet*, dim. of *ballon* balloon.] A balloon capable of being inflated with air, placed inside a balloon or airship to enable it to keep its shape during deflation. Also, one of the sections, filled with hydrogen, of the envelope of an airship.

1902 E. P. Lyle in *Ann. Rep. Smithsonian 1901* 583 The ballonet fills with air automatically from a pump worked by the motor. **1903** *Daily Chron.* 21 Sept. 3/6 In the central compartment is an internal air balloon, or *ballonnette*. **1907** *Cornh. Mag.* May 609 An internal balloon or 'ballonet'. **1915** *Sphere* 6 Feb. 152/1 At high altitudes the ballonettes [of the zeppelin] leak, and the covering does not by any means wholly retain the hydrogen. **1916** *Ibid.* 1 Jan. 24 (*caption*) Sectional view of a zeppelin airship, showing the arrangement of the hydrogen and air ballonets which control the weight of the airship. *Ibid.* 5 Feb. 143 The balloon is composed of one main elongated ballonet inflated with hydrogen or some other very light gas; a second internal ballonet is inflated with air as required in order to maintain the shape of the balloon. **1916** C. C. Turner *Aircraft of To-day* xiii. 203 All non-rigid and semi-rigid airships are provided with ballonnets.

ballon-sonde (balɔ̃sɔ̃d). *Meteorol.* [Fr., in same sense.] A small balloon, also called a ***sounding balloon*** or ***registering balloon***, used for recording atmospheric conditions.

1901 *Aeronaut. Jrnl.* Jan. 3/2 In another part of this journal will be seen the record of the first ascent of a'ballon sonde' in England. [**1902** *Encycl. Brit.* XXX. 708/2 As these ascensions are made with great velocity, and therefore as nearly vertical as possible, they are called 'soundings', because of their analogy to the mariner's usage at sea, and the balloon is called a 'sounding balloon'.] **1924** J. E. Hodgson *Hist. Aeronautics Gt. Brit.* i. 22 The use of pilot balloons, or *ballons-sondes*, capable of carrying recording instruments to immense heights. **1951** *Gloss. Aeronaut. Terms (B.S.I.)* III. 41 *Registering balloon, Ballon sonde.* A small free balloon carrying self-recording instruments for obtaining information on upper-air conditions. [B.S.I. prefers *registering balloon*.]

balloon (bə'luːn), *sb.*[1] Forms: 6 **ballone, balonne, 6–7 baloun(e, 7 balone, -oone, balloone, 8–9 ballon, 8– balloon.** [ad. It. *ballone* 'great ball, football' (Florio 1598), augmentative of *balla* ball *sb.*[1] Cf. F. *ballon* (16th c.), which *balloon* subseq. followed in its senses.]

†**1.** A large inflated ball of strong double leather, struck to and fro by the arm defended by a bracer of wood. *Obs.*

1592 Sylvester tr. *Du Bartas's Ship-Wracke of Jonas* in *Triumph of Faith* 19 One ship that skips from stars to ground, From waue to waue (like windy *Balloones* bound). **1598** Florio, *Ballone*, a great ball, a ballone to play at with braces, a footeball. **1626** T. H. *Caussin's Holy Crt.* 234 Windblowne Balones..tossed this way and that way, sometyme with the foote, sometyme with the hand. **1801** Strutt *Sports & Past.* ii. iii. 88 The balloon or wind-ball resembled the follis of the Romans.

†**2.** The game played with this ball. *Obs.*

1580 North *Plutarch* (1656) 960 He would play at Tennis, and at the Ballone. **1636** Randolph in *Ann. Dubrensia* (1877) 19 Foote-ball with vs, may be with them Baloone. **1662** Fuller *Worthies* ii. 137 Being challenged by an Italian Gentleman to play at Baloun. **1820** Scott *Monast.* xxi, The winning party at that wondrous match at ballon.

†**3.** *Pyrotechny.* 'A ball of pasteboard, stuffed with combustible matter, which, when fired [from a mortar], mounts to a considerable height in the air, and then bursts into bright sparks of fire resembling stars.' J. Also *attrib.* in ***balloon-wheel***. *Obs.* (Now called *shell* or *bomb*.)

1634 J. B[ate] *Myst. Nat. & Art.* ii. 83 How to make Balloones, also the Morter Peece to discharge them..Into this Balloone you may put Rockets, Serpents, Starres, Fiends, Petards. **1688** in Ellis *Orig. Lett.* ii. 344 IV. 112 Several thousands of Baloons that are to be shot into the air. **1753** *Publ. Advertiser* 24 Sept. 3/2 Order of Firing..(2) Sky-rockets..(4) Two Air-Balloons..(13) Two Balloons..(19)

A large Balloon Wheel which throws out of eight Boxes, Stars and Serpents.

4. *Arch.* A round ball or globe placed on the top of a pillar, pier, etc., to crown it.

1656 in BLOUNT *Glossogr.* **1753** CHAMBERS *Cycl. Supp.* s.v., A balloon is to be proportioned to the magnitude, and altitude of the body. **1875** GWILT *Archit., Balloon*..the same name is given to the balls on the top of cathedrals, as at..St. Paul's in London.

5. *Chem.* A large globose glass vessel, with one or more short necks, used to receive the products of distillation, etc.

1727–51 CHAMBERS *Cycl., Balloon* or *Ballon.* **1783** PRIESTLEY in *Phil. Trans.* LXXIII. 417 Interposing a large glass balloon between the retort and the recipient for the air. **1854** SCOFFERN in *Orr's Circ. Sc.* Chem. 160 Let it pass through a glass balloon.

6. a. An air-tight envelope of paper, silk, or similar material, usually globose or pear-shaped, which, when inflated with light gas, rises in the air, and will carry with it a considerable weight; to large balloons a *car* strong enough to carry human beings can be attached, and hence they are used for observing atmospheric phenomena, for military reconnoitring, and, though with little success at present, as a means of travelling through the air.

1783 *Europ. Mag.* IV. 272 Monsieur de Montgolfiers Air Balloon. **1783** COWPER *Lett.* 29 Sept., What is your opinion of these air balloons? I am quite charmed with the discovery. **1785** PRIESTLEY in *Phil. Trans.* LXXV. 297 Filling balloons with the lightest inflammable air. **1803** WORDSW. *Blind Highl. Boy* xxxiv, The bravest traveller in balloon Mounting as if to reach the Moon. **1831** LARDNER *Pneumat.* vii. 339 The step from fire balloons to balloons filled with gas..was now easy and obvious.

b. Similar to that described in sense 6 a, but of miniature size, usu. inflated with air, and designed as a child's toy.

Quot. 1848 may be sense 6 a.

1848 LOWELL *Biglow Papers* v. 69 'Yes, the North,' sez Colquitt, 'Ef we Southerners all quit, Would go down like a busted balloon.' **1858** *Househ. Words* CCCCX. 168/2 Amateurs were able to supply themselves with toy balloons made of goldbeaters' leaf, and bearing the name of Minimum. **1865** A. MEGSON *Recollections of Lupset* 7 Then come the balloons,..those aerial toys which ever and anon drop short in the sheep pasture. **1877** *Punch* 10 Nov. 210 And those lovely Balloons they give one, with 'Louvre' printed on them. **1902** J. M. BARRIE *Little White Bird* xiii. 128 You speak to the lady with the balloons, who sits just outside [Kensington Gardens]... She sits very squat, for the balloons are always tugging at her. **1908** H. G. WELLS *War in Air* vi. 181 Small children's air-balloons of the latest model attached to a string became a serious check to the pedestrian in Central Park. **1926** A. A. MILNE *Winnie-the-Pooh* i. 10 You had balloons at the party. **1937** N. STREATFEILD *Caroline England* xii. 186 I'm blown up like a penny balloon.

c. Colloq. phr. (***when***) ***the balloon goes up***, the operation, action, battle, affair, excitement, etc., begins (now or at some specified time).

1924 P. MACDONALD *Rasp* xv. 210 'When's the magistrate's court?'..'The balloon, I believe, goes up at 10 a.m.' **1925** FRASER & GIBBONS *Soldier & Sailor Words* 15 *The balloon*, a colloquial term used of any event, e.g. 'What time does the balloon go up?' the speaker meaning, 'What time is the parade?' **1932** WODEHOUSE *Hot Water* xiii. 222 This was the moment when he must put his fortune to the test, to win or lose it all. Now or never must the balloon go up. **1943** H. BOLITHO *Combat Report* xxx. 79 Suddenly the balloon went up. There were 110's and 87's all around us, and the 87's started dive-bombing a jetty. **1957** J. BRAINE *Room at Top* v. 50 Merely because I let you give me a beery kiss in the Props Room, you think the balloon's going up. **1959** *Punch* 21 Oct. 322/1 The international rules of war [are] apt to be waived when the balloon goes up.

7. a. *fig.* Anything inflated, empty, and hollow.

1812 BYRON *Parenthet. Address*, Borne in the vast balloon of Busby's song. **1829** CARLYLE *Misc.* (1857) I. 272 The hollow balloon of popular applause.

b. A lofty hit or kick given to a cricket-ball, base-ball, or football. *colloq.*

1904 *Daily Chron.* 8 June 5/3 With his score at 45 Jackson was missed off a 'balloon' in the long field by Gooder. **1922** *Daily Mail* 8 Dec. 11 For the most part the ball was kicked anywhere—for choice high in the air. 'There's no one up there,' shouted an ironical spectator after one of many balloons.

c. *Cricket.* = DUCK *sb.*[1] 7. *colloq.*

1906 A. E. KNIGHT *Complete Cr.* 341 A batsman who has failed to score gets a 'blob', a 'balloon', a 'duck', or a 'duck's egg'.

8. *Horticulture* : **a.** A method of training fruit-trees in which the branches are curved from a height of six or seven feet down to the ground, forming the shape of a balloon. **b.** A balloon-shaped trellis for training plants upon.

1834 *Penny Cycl.* II. 191/1 A mode of managing apple-trees called Balloon training. **1881** *Gard. Chron.* XVI. 336 Plants that have been trained on balloons twenty years ago, are treated in the same way still.

9. a. The balloon-shaped outline containing words represented in comic engravings as issuing from the mouth of a person. Also one containing thoughts represented as issuing from a person's head.

1844 DICKENS *Mart. Chuz.* xxxi. 376 Diabolical sentiments..were represented as issuing from his mouth in fat balloons. **1868** L. M. ALCOTT *Little Women* (1871) iv. 66 She drew a picture of Mr. Davis, with..the words 'Young ladies, my eye is upon you!' coming out of his mouth in a balloon thing. **1947** N. MARSH *Final Curtain* xii. 190 One almost expected some dubious caption to issue in a balloon from her lips. **1963** *Listener* 7 Feb. 252/2 The device found in comics where a balloon is shown coming out of a character's head with 'thinks' written over it.

b. A balloon-shaped outline containing words, etc., to be added to matter set up in proof, typed, or the like.

1935 D. L. SAYERS *Gaudy Night* iii. 45 I'm afraid it's rather full of marginal balloons and interlineations. **1956** F. SWINNERTON *Background w. Chorus* II. xvii. 194 Balloons thereafter adorned the galley proofs.

10. *Comb.* **a.** objective with vbl. sb. or agent-noun, as ***balloon-corps***, ***-driver***, ***-flying***, ***-navigation***, ***-shed***, ***-squadron***; **b.** similative, as ***balloon-cap*** (so ***balloon*** ellipt.), ***-foresail***, ***-hat***, ***-sail***, ***-sleeve***; **c.** para-synthetic, as ***balloon-shaped*** adj. Also **balloon barrage**, a defence against hostile aircraft consisting of a connected system of balloons carrying wire cables reaching to the ground; also called ***balloon apron***; **balloon-brasser** (cf. F. *brassart* 'the woodden cuffe or bracer worne by Balloone-players,' Cotgr. 1611); **balloon cloth**, **fabric**, a very strong, fine, closely-woven fabric orig. used for the envelopes of aerial balloons; **balloon-fish** (see quot.); **balloon flower**, a popular name for the Chinese bell-flower, *Platycodon grandiflorus*, an erect herbaceous perennial having large bell-shaped flowers which in bud resemble balloons; **balloon frame**, **framing**, a structure of light timbers fitted together to form the skeleton of a building (chiefly *U.S.*); **balloonful**, as much as a balloon will hold; **balloon glass**, **goblet**, a large globular drinking-glass (also ***balloon*** ellipt.; cf. BALLON 2); †**balloon-letter**, a letter sent by balloon; so †***balloon post***, †***postman***; **balloon-like** *a.*, like a balloon, immoderately swollen or puffed up; **balloon-satellite**, a balloon-shaped communications satellite; **balloon silk** (see quot. 1940[1]); **balloon tyre**, a low-pressure pneumatic tyre of large section; also **balloon-tyred** *a.*; **balloon vine** *U.S.*, a tropical American vine, *Cardiospermum halicacabum*, which bears large balloon-like pods.

1917 in H. A. JONES *War in Air* (1935) V. i. 68 On the 22nd of September [1917], in orders issued to home defence pilots, it was stated: '*Balloon Aprons and other obstructions will be established.' **1925** J. MORRIS *German Air Raids on Gt. Brit.* II. iv. 253 The balloon apron..consisted of steel cables suspended from a line held in the air by means of captive balloons. **1929** E. B. ASHMORE *Air Defence* v. 55, I produced my idea for a balloon apron barrage to be put up just outside London and inside the aeroplane patrol lines. **1919** R. H. REECE *Night Bombing with Bedouins* iii. 45 Small blue crosses represent the position of enemy *balloon barrages and their height. **1937** *Flight* 16 Dec. 609/2 A balloon barrage, as part of the air defences of London, is almost an accomplished fact. **1939** *Guardian* 20 Oct. 642/2 In my own garden at Lambeth Palace..are men who supply the balloon barrage... The men are good enough to call it the 'archblimp'. **1650** WELDON *Crt. K. James* (1817) 47 Lifting up his hand over his head with a *Ballon brasser. **1780–6** J. WOLCOTT (P. Pindar) *Odes R. Acad.* Wks. 1794 I. 116 A *balloon cap, a shawl, a muff. **1784** BETSY SHERIDAN *Jrnl.* (1960) 26 Even silk Balloons are almost out—I have not seen a Cap since I came. **1912** C. B. HAYWARD *Pract. Aeronaut.* I. iii. 14 Three layers of this rubberized fabric are cemented together to form what is known as '*balloon cloth', which is about as impermeable a material as can be made without involving undue weight. **1917** *Illustr. London News* 17 Nov. 601/2, I walked inside the envelope [of a Zeppelin]... On the way I passed a tube of balloon cloth. **1865** *Mechanics' Mag.* 4 Aug. 64/2 A *balloon corps should..assist in the operations of our own forces. **1838** *Let.* in H. Turner *Astra Castra* 403 That..safest *balloon-driver in the world..Mr. Green. **1919** *U.S. Navy Dept.: Type 'M' Kite Balloon Handbk.* iv. 37 All cloth used for *balloon fabric..is inspected for flaws... The raw cloth is then coated with rubber. **1834** GRIFFITH *Cuvier's Anim. K.* X. 579 From the faculty they [the Diodontes] possess of distending their bodies with air, these fishes have received the vulgar name of..*balloon-fish. **1867** SMYTH *Sailor's Wd.-bk., Balloon-fish*, a plecto-gnathous fish, covered with spines. **1901** G. NICHOLSON *Dict. Gardening Cent. Suppl.* 607/2 *Platycodon.* Chinese *Balloon Flower. **1962** *Amat. Gardening* 31 Mar. 5/1 The platycodons are called balloon flowers because the buds before they open resemble a balloon. **1837** CARLYLE *Fr. Rev.* I. III. viii. 130 A Golden or Paper Age of Hope; with its horse-racings, *balloon flyings, etc. **1883** *Times* 27 Aug. 8/2 With *balloon foresails and flying jibs. **1853** J. W. BOND *Minnesota* 122 A little clump of shanties and *balloon-frames. **1873** E. EGGLESTON *Myst. Metrop.* xxxv. 302 When at last he saw the familiar balloon-frame houses. **1945** *Archit. Rev.* XCVIII. 40/2 The great cities could never have arisen as quickly as they did if it were not for the invention of the balloon frame, which substituted a simple construction of nails and plates for the old craft of mortised and tenoned joints in wooden house construction. **1855** *Trans. Amer. Inst. N.Y.* 394 The *balloon framing used in the Western States and California. **1940** *Chambers's Techn. Dict.* 73/2 *Balloon framing*, a cheap and rapid method of construction in which all timbers are of light scantling, and are held together entirely by nails and spikes, only the corner posts being tenoned: used in place of braced framing. **1883** *St. James's Gaz.* 5 May, A *balloonful of lofty aims..and soaring ideas. **1940** A. HOCKING *Wicked Flee* x. 233 Austen slowly turned his *balloon glass of cognac between the palms of his hands. **1951** 'J. WYNDHAM' *Day of Triffids* v. 101 The plutocratic-looking balloon with the puddle of unpriceable brandy was mine. **1931** R. ALDINGTON *Colonel's Daughter* III. 166 A large *balloon goblet of very thin glass with a shallow gold deposit of brandy still in it. **1803** *Lett. Miss Riversdale* III. 202 She kept..running her *balloon hat into every eye. **1870** L. RUSSELL *Let.* 7 Nov. in *Amberley Papers* (1937) II. xvi. 454, I have had three *balloon letters quite lately [from her parents in Paris]. **1861** A. WYNTER *Soc. Bees* 120 The dominant *balloon-like tumour. **1879** GEO. ELIOT *Theo. Such* 96 His addled originalities..and balloon-like conclusions. **1816** G. CAYLEY in *Phil. Mag.* XLVII. 328 *Balloon navigation does hold out the capabilities I have so daringly ventured to investigate. **1870** *Food Jrnl.* 1 Nov. 539 By *balloon post. Oct. 19. **1885** *Encycl. Brit.* XIX. 581/2 The heroism displayed by French *balloon postmen. **1899** *Cent. Dict.*, *Balloon sail. **1948** R. DE KERCHOVE *Internat. Maritime Dict.* 34/2 *Balloon sail*, a general term used for light racing and cruising sails found on yachts, such as balloon jib, balloon topsail and foresail. **1961** F. H. BURGESS *Dict. Sailing* 19 *Balloon sails*, extra large sails of light material used as large jibs or spinnakers in yacht racing. **1960** *Aeroplane* XCIX. 270/3 The minute pressure of sunlight is forcing the 80-lb., 100-ft.-dia. *balloon-satellite Echo steadily towards the Earth's atmosphere and ultimate destruction. **1962** *Ibid.* CII. 58/2 After being launched successfully from the Thor booster on Jan. 15, the first of the rigidized balloon-satellites on sub-orbital test..began to inflate according to programme but disrupted before reaching its full diameter of 135 ft. **1964** *Yearbook Astr. 1965* 141 Transmissions from the United States were being sent by conventional means to Jodrell Bank for reflection to Gorky via the polar-orbiting balloon-satellite. *c* **1900** in M. Johnson *Amer. Advertising* (*a* 1960), Long sleeves, *balloon shaped bottom with wide lace trimming. **1936** T. ROHAN *Conf. of Dealer* (ed. 4) 8 A large 18th century English balloon-shaped bracket clock. **1907** *Westm. Gaz.* 11 Sept. 8/3 The great doors of the *balloon-shed were slowly opened. **1940** G. W. MARTIN *Modern Camping Guide* v. 69 Terms used in connection with tent materials... **Balloon Silk*..a fine cloth made of Sea Island or Egyptian cotton. The term is misleading, as no silk is used in its manufacture. **1940** HEMINGWAY *For whom Bell Tolls* viii. 74 The worn, spotted green balloon silk outer covering of the five-year-old down robe. **1837** *Southern Lit. Messenger* III. 3 Women come to the spring for water in great *balloon sleeves and prunella shoes. **1857** GEO. ELIOT *Amos Barton* iii. in *Blackw. Mag.* Jan. 17/1 Very stiff balloon sleeves..without which a woman's dress was nought in those days. **1860** *All Y. Round* 477 By the help of balloon sleeves and peg-tops. **1940** *Ann. Reg. 1939* 23 The *balloon squadrons in London were now practically up to establishment. **1924** *Motor* 27 May 715/1 The low-pressure or *balloon tyre manufacturers in the United States have adopted the straight-sided type of rim exclusively. **1933** *Jrnl. R. Aeronaut. Soc.* XXXVII. 795 Two types of aeroplane balloon tyres are shown. **1895** *Daily News* 1 June 3/1 The Princess Maud..here mounted on a *balloon-tired 'safety'. **1836** MRS. LINCOLN *Botany* (1837) App. 84 *Balloon vine, East Indies. **1901** C. T. MOHR *Plant Life Alabama*, Balloon Vine..Louisianian area, South Carolina, [etc.].

Hence **balloo'nation**, **ballooning**, **ba'lloonism**, **balloono'mania** (all used by Horace Walpole). Also the nonce-words: **ba'lloonacy** (with word-play on *lunacy*), mania for ballooning. **ba'lloonatic** *a.* and *sb.* (cf. *lunatic*), (one who is) balloon-mad. **ba'lloo nical** *a.*, connected with balloons, aeronautical. **ba'lloonicism**, a technical phrase in ballooning.

1864 *Daily Tel.* 19 Feb., We live in an age of balloonacy. **1882** *West. Daily Press* 27 Mar. 3/1 A sharp epidemic of balloonacy. **1865** *Daily Tel.* 22 Nov. 5/3 That Nadar, the balloonatic, has sold his balloon. **1882** *Moonshine* V. 163 Another balloonatic attempt to cross the Channel. **1784** in *Athenæum* (1865) No. 1968. 78/3 'Balloonation,' as it was called. **1851** *Househ. Wds.* 25 Oct. 103 The four hundred and eighty-ninth year of his balloonical age; having made that number of ascents. **1838** *Let.* in H. Turner *Astra C.* 399 How could I have avoided the perpetration of a few balloonicisms?

‖**ba'lloon, balloen**, *sb.*[2] Also 7 balon, 8 ballong, baloen. A Siamese state-barge, upwards of a hundred feet long, and richly decorated.

1633 H. COGAN *Pinto's Voy.* xi. (1663) 35 With a Galley, five Foists, two Catures, 20 Balons and 300 men. **1753** CHAMBERS *Cycl. Supp., Balloon*, or *Baloen*..The balloons are a kind of brigantine, managed with oars. **1755** CAPT. R. JACKSON in Dalrymple *Orient. Repert.* I. 195 The Burmas has now Eighty Ballongs, none of which [h]as great Guns. **1867** SMYTH *Sailor's Word-bk., Balloen.*

balloon (bəˈluːn), *v.* [f. BALLOON *sb.*[1]]

1. *trans.* To carry up in, or as in, a balloon.

1792 T. TWINING in *Country Clergym. 18th C.* (1882) 163 I..never yet seemed so ballooned and above the globe as in ascending this great hill. **1802** G. COLMAN *Br. Grins, Reckoning with Time* vi, Thy pinions next Ballooned me from the schools to town.

2. *intr.* To ascend in a balloon. (*trans.*; cf. *race.*)

1821 [see BALLOONING *vbl. sb.* 1 a] **1881** *Echo* 3/4 An American balloonist has offered to 'balloon' anybody in the United States. **1882** *Standard* 2 Feb. 5/7 Whose wife was afterwards killed whilst Ballooning.

3. a. *intr.* To swell or puff out like a balloon.

1841 ORDERSON *Creol.* ix. 99 *En bon point* that..ballooned to dimensions which..filled her arm chair. **1872** *Cornh. Mag.* June 708 His red gown ballooning behind him.

b. *trans.* To puff out or cause to be inflated like a balloon; *spec.* to distend with air, gas, or water, as the abdomen in tympanites, or the rectum or vagina with specially constructed apparatus.

1889 [see BALLOONING *vbl. sb.* 2]. **1906** *Macm. Mag.* Dec. 119 The wind..ballooned his cassock and carried his hat into the ditch. **1909** *Practitioner* Dec. 807 Several equal lengths of rubber tubing..were obtained, and at about the centre of some of them aneurysms..were ballooned.

4. To hit (a cricket-ball) or kick (a football) high in the air. *colloq.*

1904 *Daily Chron.* 20 July 7/2 As he did not quite get to the ball, he ballooned it to Garnett in the out-field, who brought off a well-judged catch. **1927** *Daily Tel.* 8 Feb. 16/3 As for the half-backs, they lacked method; it was not a light or flighty ball, but they were for ever ballooning it.

5. *intr.* Of an aeroplane: to rise up in the air, esp. as the result of a hard bounce on landing.
1931 P. W. F. MILLS *Angles on Pract. Flying* vi. 54 Certain types of aeroplane..retain [in landing] a degree of buoyancy sufficient to cause an uncomfortable tendency to 'balloon'. **1949** J. R. COLE *It was so Late* 87 The aircraft ballooned when the wheels hit; it shot up thirty feet and seemed to hang suspended.

ballooned (bəˈluːnd), *ppl. a.* [f. BALLOON *v.* + -ED[1].] Swollen or puffed out like a balloon.
1889 in *Cent. Dict.* **1925** W. DEEPING *Sorrell & Son* ii. 20 Sorrell saw the labouring of the ballooned waistcoat. **1930** R. CAMPBELL *Adamastor* 80 Their breasts ballooned with lust and song, The fat sopranos kick.

ballooner (bəˈluːnə(r)). [f. BALLOON + -ER[1].]
1. One who makes balloon ascents; an aeronaut.
1783 *Morning Herald* 15 Dec. 2/3 The sagacious King of Spain..will out-balloon all former ballooners. **1864** *Athenæum* No. 1933. 631/3 The Godards, practised ballooners. **1882** MATT. WILLIAMS *Sc. in Short Chap.* xxvi. 219 Not a mere sensational ballooner.
2. *Naut.* A balloon-like sail.
1883 *Times* 27 Aug. 8/2 The Marjorie [had] her ballooner aloft. **1884** *Field* 24 May 722 Tara put up her ballooner.

baˈlloonery, -nry. [f. as prec. + -RY.] The management of balloons; aeronautics.
1859 WORCESTER cites *Q. Rev.*

balloonet (bəˈluːnɛt). Also **-ette.** = BALLONNET.
1902 *Westm. Gaz.* 11 Apr. 8/1 Within the main balloon there is to be a smaller balloon. This can be filled with air. If, therefore, the balloon becomes slack, it can immediately be made taut by pumping air into the balloonet. **1908** H. G. WELLS *War in Air* iii. 93 A long internal balloonette of oiled and toughened silk canvas.

†**ballooˈnier.** *Obs. rare*$^{-1}$. [ad. It. *balloniere.*] A maker of balloons (*i.e.* those used for arm-play).
1598 FLORIO, *Gonfiatoio*, a squirt of brasse that Balloniers vse to blowe their ballones full of winde.

ballooning (bəˈluːnɪŋ), *vbl. sb.* [f. BALLOON *v.* + -ING[1].] **1. a.** The science and practice of ascending in and making use of balloons; aeronautics. Also *attrib.*
1784 H. SMEATHMAN *Let.* 16 July in Pettigrew *Mem. of Lettsom* (1817) II. 275 This I thought might have been done by ballooning. **1821** C. MATHEWS *Mem.* III. viii. 178 A very learned dissertation on ballooning. **1870** *Pall Mall G.* 7 Sept. 4 Military ballooning. **1877** BLACKIE *Wise Men* 343 Helmless balloonings in the pathless air. **1961** *Daily Tel.* 1 May 13/1 President of the ballooning club in Holland.
b. *Aeronaut.* (See BALLOON *v.* 5.)
1922 *Flight* 1 June 317/2 Some serious porpoising or 'ballooning'..may occur. **1935** P. W. F. MILLS *Elem. Pract. Flying* vii. 103 The underlying cause of ballooning is usually too fast a gliding speed.
2. a. Dilatation of the walls of a cavity of the body as a symptom or for therapeutic purposes.
1889 T. BRYANT in *Lancet* 5 Jan. 8/1 On the diagnostic value of 'ballooning of the rectum' in cases of stricture of the bowel... The surgeon will often find..that he has entered a cavity, the walls of which are expanded or 'ballooned'... The extent of ballooning will be found to vary in every case. **1890** BILLINGS *Med. Dict., Ballooning, vaginal*, distension of vagina as by tampons, water- or air-bags, etc. **1893** A. S. ECCLES *Sciatica* 3 In the remaining nine cases there was more or less ballooning of the rectum.
b. *Path.* Distension of cells, etc. (see quot. 1913).
1913 E. M. BROCKBANK in *Med. Chron.* Sept. 292 When the acidity of the gastric juice reaches a certain degree..the red corpuscles are seen to distend in a most peculiar manner which for descriptive convenience I describe as 'ballooning'. **1962** *Lancet* 28 Apr. 885/2 Severe fatty change of the fine droplet type, without 'ballooning' of the cells.
3. *Spinning.* (See quots.)
1904 GOODCHILD & TWENEY *Technol. & Sci. Dict.* 39/1 *Ballooning* (Cotton Spinning), a defect in ring spinning caused by the high velocity of the ring traveller. This has the effect of causing the spun thread to fly outwards as it winds round the bobbin. **1924** T. LAWSON *Woollen Yarn Production* p. ix, *Ballooning*, extension of the arc of the axis of the spinning thread. **1963** A. J. HALL *Textile Sci.* v. 261 (*caption*) Showing how the accumulation of static electricity on a thread..can cause the individual fibres of which the thread is composed to repel each other and so cause 'ballooning' sufficient to make the manipulation of the thread difficult.

baˈllooning, *ppl. a.* [f. as prec. + -ING[2].] Soaring, swelling, or puffed out, like a balloon.
1875 EMERSON *Lett. & Soc. Aims* i. 16 A grand pair of ballooning wings. **1878** T. SINCLAIR *Mount* 33 Gas-brained, ballooning, wandering men.

baˈlloonist. [f. as prec. + -IST.] An aeronaut. Also *fig.*
1784 *Morning Herald* 10 Aug. 3/1 Mr. Smeathman, an active and distinguished Balloonist. **1828** [see AIR-BALLOONIST]. **1870** *Standard* 7 Dec., The balloonists had a narrow escape of being carried out into the Atlantic. **1906** *Daily Chron.* 28 Aug. 4/4 If you are a balloonist in the social world, you may find a difficulty with the soup.

balloony (bəˈluːnɪ), *a.* [f. BALLOON *sb.*[1] + -Y[1].] Resembling a balloon or balloons.
1908 *Daily Chron.* 9 Oct. 7/1 Great balloony skirts called crinolines. **1936** 'A. BRIDGE' *Song in House* 76 The long balloony line of the lime avenue.

ballot (ˈbælət), *sb.*[1] [ad. It. *ballotta* 'a rounde bullet..a voice or lot' (Florio 1598), dim. of *balla* BALL *sb.*[1]: see -OT. Cf. F. *ballotte*, 16th c. (now *arch.*). The early instances refer to Venice.]
1. A small ball used for secret voting; hence, by extension, a ticket, paper, etc. so used.
1549 THOMAS *Hist. Italie* (1561) 79 Boxes, into whiche, if he wyll, he may let fall his ballot, that no man can perceiue hym. **1660** MILTON *Free Commw.* Wks. (1851) 438 To convey each Man his bean or ballot into the Box. **1710** *Lond. Gaz.* No. 4646/1 Elected by a great Majority of the Ballots. **1864** *Even. Standard* 2 Nov., The voting was not very general, only 25,000 ballots being polled altogether.
2. The method or system of secret voting, originally by means of small balls placed in an urn or box; an application of this mode of voting; also the whole number of votes thus recorded.
1549 THOMAS *Hist. Italie* 77 A triall of theyr sentences by Ballot. **1681** NEVILE *Plato Rediv.* 78 The Doctrine of the Ballot which is our [the Venetians'] chief excellency. **1742** MIDDLETON *Cicero* I. II. 153 Not by an open vote, but by a kind of ballot, or little tickets of wood distributed to the Citizens. **1781** GIBBON *Decl. & F.* III. lxx. 793 The sense of the majority was decided by a secret ballot. **1840** MACAULAY *Clive, Ess.* (1854) II. 529 Sulivan wished to try the result of a ballot. **1880** MCCARTHY *Own Times* IV. lix. 309 No reform had seemed more unlikely than the adoption of the ballot.
3. A method of drawing lots by taking out small balls, etc., from a box; hence *gen.* lot-drawing.
a **1680** BUTLER *Rem.* (1759) I. 81 To put it to the Chance, and try, I' th' Ballot of a Box and Dye, Whether his Money be his own. **1757** LIND *Lett. Navy* ii. 98 Where there are more officers qualified to sit at a court martial, that they may be chose by ballot. **1786** *Act 26 Geo. III*, cvii. §24 The Number of Men..to be chosen by Ballot out of the List returned. **1815** WELLINGTON in Gurw. *Disp.* XII. 430 Difficulties..in consequence of the ballot for the militia.
4. *Comb.* **ballot-box**, a box in which voting ballots are deposited, or from which, in drawing lots, small balls are taken out; also *fig.* the ballot, secret voting; **ballot-man**, an advocate of secret voting; **ballot-paper**, the voting-paper used in secret voting; **ballot-rigging** [RIG *v.*[6] 2], the fraudulent manipulation of a ballot.
a **1680** BUTLER *Rem.* (1759) I. 23 Some held no Way so orthodox To try it, as the Ballot-Box. **1851** DIXON *W. Penn* xvii. (1872) 146 Representatives were to be elected..by the ballot-box. **1859** GEN. P. THOMPSON *Audi Alt.* II. c. 91 To hunt a Chartist or a Ballot-man. **1865** *Cornh. Mag.* XI. 115 The ballot-papers of the electors were collected in a bucket. **1959** *Daily Tel.* 1 Dec. 1/8 Ballot rigging in the union. **1961** *Times* 2 June 10/4 Newspaper charges of ballot-rigging.

ˈballot, *sb.*[2] [a. F. *ballot*, dim. of *balle* BALE *sb.*[2] Cf. BALET.] A small bale, of 70 to 120 lbs.
1865 *Times* 13 Feb., The bulk of the..bales and ballots brought forward had to be withdrawn. *Mod.* Alpaca and Peruvian wools come in ballots.

ballot (ˈbælət), *v.*[1] Also 7 **ballat, -et, balet,** 7–8 **balot:** see BALLOTING *vbl. sb.* Pples. **balloted, -ing.** [a. It. *ballott-are* 'to choose, to cast or draw lots with bullets' (Florio 1598), f. *ballotta*: see BALLOT *sb.*[1] Cf. F. *ballotter*, 16th c.]
†**1.** *trans.* To vote, for approval, selection or rejection, upon (a proposed resolution, candidate, etc.), by depositing small balls in an urn or box, or by some other secret method. *Obs.*
1549 THOMAS *Hist. Italie* (1561) 77 This priuilege, to haue his onely oppinion ballotted, no man hath but he [the Doge]. **1618** WOTTON in *Reliq.* (1685) 262 None of the Competitors arriving to a sufficient number of Balls, they fell to ballote some others. **1691** WOOD *Ath. Oxon.* II./439 This Gang had a Balloting-box and balloted how things should be carried.
2. a. *intr.* To give a secret vote (*for, against*).
1580 NORTH *Plutarch* (1656) 927 The Judges..would never take their bals to ballot against him. *a* **1797** BURKE *Sp. Short. Parl.* Wks. X. 89 The Electors shall ballot; the Members of Parliament also shall decide by ballot. *c* **1810** ROSE in *Byron's Wks.* (1846) 230/2 Balloting now for merit, now for hunger.
b. *to ballot for*: to select (a body of officials, etc.), elect or reject (an individual candidate), by secret voting. Often with *indirect passive*; cf. 4.
1695 LUTTRELL *Brief Rel.* III. 464 The two houses ballotted for a committee..to take Sir Thomas Cooks examination. **1773** JOHNSON in *Boswell* 30 Apr., I was this evening to be ballotted for as candidate for admission into that society. **1869** *Daily News* 17 Dec., Twelve candidates for the fellowship were proposed and ordered to be balloted for.
3. *trans.* To select by the drawing of lots (*e.g.* conscripts *for* military service).
1785 COWPER *Task* IV. 623 The clown..Is balloted, and trembles at the news. **1837** CARLYLE *Fr. Rev.* III. I. i. 15 Peasants..who will not be balloted for Soldiers.
4. *to ballot for*: to select by lot, draw lots for.
1786 *Act 26 Geo. III*, cvii. §24 *marg.*, To appoint what Number of Men shall serve..who are to be ballotted for.
1884 *Manch. Exam.* 21 Mar. 5/4 Mr. Slagg intends to ballot for another day for his resolution.
5. *trans.* To procure the vote by ballot of (a body of voters) on a specific motion.
1898 *Daily News* 25 June 6/6 The Llwynpia colliers to-day rejected a motion to ballot the men for or against a sliding scale. **1899** *Ibid.* 9 Jan. 7/3 If the textile unions are to be balloted on the question of raising the age.

†**baˈllot,** *v.*[2] *Obs. rare.* In 7 **balot.** [a. F. *ballotte-r*, f. *ballotte* small ball.] To toss about like a ball, drive hither and thither.
1680 *Nation's Int. Pretensions Dk. York* 4 That we be not again Balotted into a Field of Blood.

ballotade (bæləˈteɪd, -ˈɑːd). [a. F. *ballottade*, f. *ballotter*: see prec. and -ADE.] A kind of leap in which a managed horse bends his four legs without jerking out the hind ones.
1727–51 in CHAMBERS. **1815** *Encycl. Brit.* III. 355.

ˈballotage. [a. F. *ballottage*, f. *ballotter*: see -AGE.] In France, the second ballot, to decide between the two candidates who have come nearest to obtaining the legal majority.
1869 *Daily News* 9 Dec., M. Glais-Bizoin at the ballotage of yesterday was elected. **1883** *Leeds Merc.* 26 Sept. 2 He was absolutely nowhere on the ballotage.

†**ˈballotant.** *Obs. rare*$^{-1}$. [a. F. *ballottant*, pr. pple. of *ballotter.*] A voter by ballot.
1656 J. HARRINGTON *Oceana* (1700) 93 The number of the Ballotants at either Urn.

†**balloˈtation.** *Obs.* [f. BALLOT *v.* (or its F. or It. equivalent) + -ATION.] Voting by ballot.
1620 *Reliq. Wotton.* (1672) 309 In the first Ballotation, the Balls were equal. **1677** *Govt. Venice* 39 Every man speaks *pro* or *con* as he thinks fit; and afterwards they proceed to Balotation.

†**baˈllote.** *Herb. Obs.* [a. F. *ballote* or It. *ballotte*, ad. L. *ballōtē*, a. Gr. βαλλωτή.] The Black Stinking Horehound (*Ballota nigra*).
1551 TURNER *Herbal* F j b, Ballote hath foursquare stalkes. **1700** PETIVER in *Phil. Trans.* XXII. 607 The leaves of this plant..resemble our Ballote or stinking Horehound.

ˈballoted, *ppl. a.* [BALLOT *v.* + -ED.] Selected by ballot or lot.
1843 CARLYLE *Past & Pr.* 298 Plainly a ballotted soldier.

balloteer (bæləˈtɪə(r)). [f. BALLOT *sb.*[1] + -EER[1].] An advocate of the ballot.
1867 *Examiner* 19 Jan. 36 We are balloteers, but we cannot countenance a charge so unjust.

balloter (ˈbælətə(r)). [f. BALLOT *v.*[1] + -ER[1].] A voter by ballot.
1757 FORSTER in *Phil. Trans.* L. 460 The number of ballotters. **1758** BRAKENRIDGE *ibid.* 471 The electors or balloters are the fencible men.

baˈllotically, *adv. nonce-wd.* In reference to the ballot.
c **1842** SYD. SMITH *Ballot* Wks. 1859 II. 316/1 How has any father, ballotically speaking, a right to control the votes of his family?

†**ˈballotin.** *Obs. nonce-wd.* [f. BALLOT.] An officer in charge of a ballot-box.
1656 J. HARRINGTON *Oceana* (1700) 116 Wherupon eight Ballotins or Pages..take eight of the Boxes. *Ibid.* The Ballotins having thus gather'd the Suffrages.

balloting (ˈbælətɪŋ), *vbl. sb.* [f. BALLOT *v.*[1]]
1. Voting by ballot or by some secret method.
1549 THOMAS *Hist. Italie* (1561) 77 Many have reported, that the Duke in ballottyng should haue two voices. **1704** ADDISON *Italy* (1733) 87 They decide all by Baloting. **1870** *Daily News* 23 Nov., In 182 electoral colleges a second balloting will be necessary.
2. Selection by lot, drawing of lots.
a **1618** RALEIGH *Remains* (1644) 56 To elect Magistrates..by Lot or Ballating. **1699** *Def. Vind. Chas. I*, 25 We must go to balleting for the Controversie, and take the Papers as they arise. **1773** *Gentl. Mag.* XLIII. 51 That no constable..should have any authority in balloting of soldiers. **1873** *Daily News* 25 Aug., At the close of balloting for places.
3. *attrib.*, as in ***balloting-book, -box, -glass.***
1622 in Heath *Grocers' Comp.* (1869) 100 To trie the sayde election by the ballotynge box. **1677** YARRANTON *Eng. Impr.* 34 Each Freeholder drops into the Baletting Box one Bowle ..And for chusing of Parliamentmen and all publick Votes in Corporations, it were happy it were so. **1700** LUTTRELL *Brief Rel.* IV. 628 Each member put into the balloting glasse [a] list of 13 commissioners. **1797** *Ann. Reg.* 2/1 The balloting books..they carried away in triumph.

ballotist (ˈbælətɪst). [f. BALLOT *sb.*[1] + -IST.] A professed advocate of the ballot.
1837 SYD. SMITH *Wks.* 771 Votes, sheltered (as the ballotists suppose) from intimidation.

‖**ballotté** (balɔte). *Ballet.* [F., f. pa. pple. of *ballotter* to toss or shake about.] (See quot. 1957.)
1894 E. SCOTT *Dancing* vi. 60 *Ballotté*, 'throwing here and there step'. A movement in which the feet are crossed alternately one before or behind the other. **1913** C. D'ALBERT *Encycl. Dancing* 5 *Balloté* or *Ballottés*, to toss about. When the feet are crossed alternately one before or behind the other. **1957** G. B. L. WILSON *Dict. Ballet* 46 *Ballotté*, lit. a tossing movement. A movement in which the dancer raises the left foot behind the knee of the supporting

leg, and, with a slight plié, springs upwards, crossing one foot in front of the other at the cou-de-pied, alighting on the left foot, whilst extending the right in a developpé to the front..then bringing it in to the knee.

‖**ballottement** (bəˈlɒtmənt). *Med.* [Fr., f. *ballotter*: see BALLOT *v.*[2]] A mode of diagnosing pregnancy, in which, upon a sudden push with the finger on the front of the uterus, the fœtus is felt to move away and return again.

1839 HOOPER *Med. Dict.* 242. **1861** TANNER *Pregn.* ii. 43.

†ˈ**ballow**, *sb.*[1] [Only in the Shaksp. Folio of 1623, and subseq. editions, in loc. cit., where the Quartos have *battero*, and *bat* (stick, rough walking-stick); besides which, *batton*, *battoun*, 'stick, cudgel' obs. f. BATON *sb.* (q.v.) is a probable emendation. Bailey (1742) has '*Ballow*, a pole, a long stick, quarter-staff, etc. *Shakesp.*' (quoted by Halliwell as '*Northern*'): but no such word seems to exist, or to have any etymological justification.]

1605 SHAKS. *Lear* IV. vi. 247 Ice try whither your Costard, or my Ballow be the harder. [Cf. **1675** COTTON *Scoffer Scoft* 44 With my Battoon I'le bang his sconce.]

ballow (ˈbæləʊ), *sb.*[2] 'Deep water inside a shoal or bar.' Smyth *Sailor's Word-bk.* 1867.

†ˈ**ballow**, *a. Obs. rare*⁻¹. Etymol. and meaning uncertain. A marginal note to Drayton says 'Gaunt.' But cf. BALGH *a.*

1612 DRAYTON *Poly-olb.* Song iii. 40 The ballow Nag outstrips the winds in chase.

ˈ**ballpark**. orig. and chiefly *U.S.* Also **ball park**, **ball-park**. [f. BALL *sb.*[1] + PARK *sb.*]

1. A baseball stadium.

1899 *Chicago Daily News* 4 Aug. 6/1 Billy Phyle..went out to the ball park. **1957** *Economist* 23 Nov. 687/1 Shortly after the war..attendance at the ball parks began to slump as a result of television.

2. *transf.* and *fig.* **a.** A broad area of approximation, similarity, etc.; a range within which comparison is possible. *spec.* in *Astronautics*, the area within which a spacecraft is expected to return to earth. Also *attrib.*

1960 *San Francisco Examiner* 21 Aug. I. 10/3 The Discoverer XIV capsule..came down 200 miles from the center of its predicted impact area, but still within the designated 'ballpark' area. **1961** *Times* (Seattle, Washington) 15 Oct. 1 The aerial recovery in an area called the 'ballpark' was the sixth in the Discoverer series. **1962** *Wall St. Jrnl.* 19 June 8/6 (Advt.), Its speed, range, and over-the-weather altitude put it in the same ballpark with the big airline jets. **1970** *Observer* 24 May 40/6 You guys all belong in the same ballpark. **1978** *New Scientist* 4 May 277/2 The volume of carbon dioxide required to produce surface carbon..would have created an atmosphere 'in the ballpark of Venus'. **1985** *Dirt Bike* Mar. 29/2 You really can't buy a better out-of-the-box suspension than this, and on that basis, the KTM is hardly out of the ballpark.

b. A sphere of activity, influence, etc.

1963 *San Francisco News Call-Bull.* 6 Nov. 51/1 They might find 'pockets of overbuilding in their own ball park'. **1968** *Globe & Mail* (Toronto) 3 Feb. B2/7 Exemption from any marketing plans..'pretty well would have given them the ball park to themselves'. **1971** *San Francisco Examiner* 10 Aug. 18/2 Perhaps your mother-in-law 'took over' because she is an R.N. and the hospital is her ballpark. **1982** *Daily Tel.* 2 Aug. 20/7 They were re-stating the management's objectives or 'redefining the ball-park', according to Mr Merryweather. **1986** *Marketing* 11 Sept. 26/1 It is difficult to know how the new Chinese masters will regard the activities of the colony...So the ball park still isn't clearly defined.

c. In colloq. phr. ***in the (right) ballpark***, plausibly accurate, within reasonable bounds.

1968 *San Francisco Examiner* 8 Oct. 58/7 The figures I have indicate this pay-out is 'in the ball park'. **1972** *Sat. Rev. Sci.* (U.S.) 13 May 59/2 We *can* save lives with adequately equipped ambulances and properly trained personnel. It may be 50,000 or 75,000, but a figure of 60,000 is in the right ball park. **1977** R. E. MEGILL *Introd. Risk Analysis* xiv. 154 The Delphi technique of brainstorming can often produce answers surprisingly close to reality, but it may also produce one not even in the 'ball park'. **1978** *SLR Camera* Dec. 61/3 This basic filtration, though, has very often saved me a test strip because it's got me into the right ball park filter-wise. **1985** *Aviation Week & Space Technol.* 23 Sept. 14/2 A previously established gross takeoff weight target of 50,000 lb. remains in effect... 'We're confident we're in the right ballpark now,' Russ said.

3. *attrib.*, approximate, within a reasonable range of accuracy, as ***ballpark estimate***, ***figure***, etc.

1967 *Wall St. Jrnl.* 7 June 4, I gave them a guess of somewhere around £1.5 billion... I thought it was a ball-park figure. **1969** *San Francisco Examiner* 23 June 2/6 A 'ballpark estimate' put the cost of such a plan at possibly £20 billion the first year. **1976** *Offshore Platforms & Pipelining* 72/2 This technique..gives only 'ball park' types of answers. **1984** *New Yorker* 14 May 42/2 How many times per week do you have sexual relations? On the average—just a ballpark figure.

ball-room (ˈbɔːlruːm). [BALL *sb.*[2] 4.] A room designed or suitable for dancing. Also *attrib.*, esp. in ***ball-room dancing***, social dancing in a ball-room as a recreation.

1736 FOG *Jrnl.* 30 Nov. in *London Mag.* (1737) Apr. 190/2 The Conspirators..were first to blow up the Ball-Room. **1752** JOHNSON *Rambl.* 201 ⁋8 The play-house, the ball-room, or the card-table. **1875** HELEN MATHERS *Comin' thro' Rye* II. ix, Ball-room conversation is never expected to be very wise, is it? **1894** E. SCOTT *Dancing* iv. 24 Not..half the people who professed to teach ball-room dancing really knew the difference. **1911** KIPLING *Big Steamers* in Fletcher & Kipling *Hist. England* xii. 236 Oh, the Channel's as bright as a ball-room already. **1923** WODEHOUSE *Adv. Sally* ii. 54 The only thing I could do..was ball-room dancing, so I ball-room danced. **1929** *Melody Maker* Jan. 10/1, I was given the opportunity of seeing the New Playhouse ballroom opened by the Green Brothers. *Ibid.* 10/3 Ballroom dancing has been slumping steadily.

ballsy (ˈbɒlzɪ), *a. slang* (chiefly *U.S.*). [f. *balls*, pl. of BALL *sb.*[1] (senses 15 b, c, d) + -Y[1].] **a.** Nonsensical, ridiculous. *rare.* **b.** Courageous, plucky; determined, spirited; also, powerful, aggressive, masculine. Cf. BALL *sb.*[1] 15 d.

1942 S. SMITH 'Girls!' in *Mother, What is Man?* 15 Oh the awful balsy nonsense that this woman cried. **1959** N. MAILER *Advts. for Myself* (1961) 401 Truman Capote..is tart as a grand aunt, but in his way he is a ballsy little guy. **1967** *True* Feb. 54/2 You need balls to slap a bug on someone. It's a very ballsy thing to do. **1970** *Daily Tel.* (Colour Suppl.) 15 May 34/2 It's the only Western I know that has a great part for a woman—not a dance hall, ballsy broad, but a *woman*. **1971** *Melody Maker* 9 Oct. 11/7, I suppose one could say that rock should be heavy and ballsy. **1978** J. HYAMS *Pool* xvi. 245 He had become a ballsy man, everything her husband was not. **1983** E. LEONARD *LaBrava* (1985) viii. 69 The old man was showing off..he knew his way around. Ballsy little eighty-year-old guy.

†ˈ**ballup**. *Obs.* exc. *dial.* [prob. the same as *bag lap*, in *Compl. Scotl.* vi. 66.] 'The front or flap of the small-clothes.' Halliwell. (Common in north. dial.)

c **1600** *Rob. Hood* (Ritson) xxiii. 58 Then he put on the old mans breeks, Was patch'd from ballup to side.

balluster, obs. form of BALUSTER.

bally (ˈbælɪ), *a.* and *adv. slang.* A euphemism for *bloody* (see BLOODY *a.* 10), used as a vague intensive of general application; 'jolly', 'confounded'. Cf. *absoballylutely* (s.v. ABSOLUTELY *adv.*).

[**1847** THACKERAY in *Fraser's Mag.* Jan. 126/2 Ha! What have we here? *M. A. Titmarsh's Christmas-Book—Mrs. Perkins's Ball.* Dedicated to the Mulligan of Ballymulligan. Ballymulligan! Ballyfiddlestick!] **1885** *Sporting Times* 11 Apr. 1/4 Too bad, too bad! after getting fourteen days or forty bob, the bally rag don't even mention it. *Ibid.* 3/4 Has that bally Ptolemy won, d'ye know? **1887** S. BUTLER in H. F. Jones *Memoir* (1919) II. xxvi. 54 No one in those days gave him or herself any bally airs about it. **1898** STEEVENS *With Kitchener to Khartum* 112 I've been in this bally country five years. **1919** C. ORR *Glorious Thing* v. 56, I..talked gaily about the bally old war. **1922** H. WALPOLE *Cathedral* I. vi. 103 All the time behind you and them some force was insisting on places being taken, connections being formed. One was simply a bally pawn..a bally pawn. **1939** G. B. SHAW *Geneva* IV. 54 The staggering, paralyzing, jolly bally breath-bereaving point..is that the dictators have been summoned.

ballyhoo (bælɪˈhuː), *sb.* orig. *U.S.* [Etym. unknown.] A barker's touting speech; hence, blarney, bombastic nonsense; extravagant advertisement of any kind.

1901 *World's Work* Aug. 1100/2 First there is the ballyhoo—any sort of a performance outside the show, from the coon songs of the pickaninnies in front of the Old Plantation, to the tinkling tamborines of the dancers on the stage of 'Around the World'. **1914** JACKSON & HELLYER *Vocab. Criminal Slang* 16 *Bally hoo*, noun. Current amongst exhibition and 'flat-joint' grafters. A free entertainment used for a decoy to attract customers. **1914** *Philad. Even. Post* 9 May, A live, little park full of side show tents..with..barkers spieling before the entrances and all the ballyhoos going at full blast. **1925** H. L. FOSTER *Trop. Tramp Tourists* 36 Above all, don't let them use a megaphone. It's too much like a ballyhoo. **1927** *Daily Express* 21 Sept. 1/2 Mr. Wiener, chairman of the Pennsylvania State Athletic Commission..calls Dempsey's letter 'mere ballyhoo'. **1928** *Ibid.* 3 Mar. 9/3 Mr. McAndrew characterised Mr. Thompson's charges as 'lies and ballyhoo'. **1932** D. B. WYNDHAM LEWIS *Emperor of West* i. 9 Mr. Christopher Hollis has dealt fittingly with some of this popular pro-Elizabethan rhetoric or ballyhoo.

Hence **bally**ˈ**hoo** *v. trans.*, to cajole by extravagant advertisement or praise (after the manner of a barker); to advertise or praise extravagantly. Also **bally**ˈ**hooer**, **bally**ˈ**hooist**, one indulging in ballyhooing.

1901 *World's Work* Aug. 1100/2 Last of the professions on the Midway are those of the 'barker', 'ballyhooer' and 'spieler'. **1922** *Collier's* 4 Mar. 7/2, I don't like to ballyhoo myself..but here's a picture which will make you..bite your nails. **1927** *Scots Observer* 28 May, Our people will not be bullied and bally-hoed into churchgoing or anything else. **1928** *Weekly Dispatch* 6 May 15/2 How the late P. T. Barnum would have enjoyed ballyhoo-ing this new Drury Lane spectacle! **1941** *Manch. Guardian* 18 Apr. 8/5 War Weapons Week not Ballyhoo... 'That, I think,' he said, 'is the complete answer to what I term the ballyhooists.' **1948** *Atlantic Monthly* Mar. 24/1 They are ballyhooed, pushed, yelled, screamed, and in every way propagandized into the consciousness of the voters. **1950** 'S. RANSOME' *Deadly Miss Ashley* ii. 17 The fortunes paid to ballyhooers of phony antiseptics. **1966** *Economist* 20 Aug. 748/1 British Rail is ballyhooing the pleasures of its electrified services a bit loudly.

ballyhoo of blazes. *Nautical slang.* Also **ballyhoo.** [Etym. of first element uncertain, but perh. same word as BALLAHOU (see *Amer. Speech* (1945) XX. 184 ff.).] Sailors' term of contempt for a vessel which they dislike for any reason.

1836 *Knickerbocker* Aug. 203 Jack Marlinspike..couldn't get a situation afore the mast of a Ballyhoo coasting-brig. **1847** H. MELVILLE *Omoo* lxxvi. 295 Steer clear of the likes of this ballyhoo of blazes as long as ye live. **1897** KIPLING *Capt. Cour.* iii. 69 Tom Platt, this bally-hoo's not the *Ohio*. *Ibid.* ix. 205 Oh, ef it had bin even the Fish C'mmission boat instid o' this bally-hoo o'blazes. **1929** F. C. BOWEN *Sea Slang* 6 *Ballyhoo of blazes*..the last word of contempt for a slovenly ship.

ballyrag, **ballyragging**, etc., varr. BULLYRAG, -RAGGING.

ballytte, obs. form of BALLAD.

balm (bɑːm), *sb.* Forms: 3 **basme**, 3–5 **bame**, (4 **balsme**), 4–7 **bawm(e**, 4–8 **baume**, 4–9 **baum**, 5 **bavme**, 5–6 **bawlme**, 5–7 **baulme**, **balme**, 7 **baulm**, 6– **balm**. [ME. *basme*, *bame*, a. OF. *basme*, later *bâme* (= Pr. *basme*, It. *balsamo*):—L. *balsamum*: see BALSAM, -UM. Also ME. *baume*, *bawme*, a. OF. (13th c.) *bausme*, *baume*, literary or semi-literary refashionings of *basme*, *bâme*, influenced by L. *bal-*; whence also come the Eng. spellings *balsme*, *baulm(e*, *bawlm(e*, through which the ME. *baum(e*, *bawm(e*, has been gradually altered to *balm*.]

I. The aromatic resinous product.

1. An aromatic substance, consisting of resin mixed with volatile oils, exuding naturally from various trees of the genus *Balsamodendron*, and much prized for its fragrance and medicinal properties. (Cf. BALSAM 1 b.)

c **1220** *Hali Meid.* 13 Swote smirles..þ at is icleopet basme. **1340** HAMPOLE *Pr. Consc.* 652 Of herbes and tres, springes baum ful gude. *c* **1400** MAUNDEV. v. 52 Fyn Bawme is more hevy twyes, than is the Bawme that is sophisticate. *Ibid.* xxvii. 276 Brennethe a vesselle..fulle of Bawme, for to ȝeven gode smelle. **1494** FABYAN VI. clvi. 145 He sent to hym also tentis of ryche sylke & baulme naturall. **1563** T. GALE *Antidot.* II. 35 This oile hath al the vertues of true Balme. **1697** DRYDEN *Virg. Georg.* II. 165 Balm slowly trickles through the bleeding Veins Of happy Shrubs, in Idumæan Plains. *a* **1842** TENNYSON *St. S. Stylites* 208 Spikenard, and balm, and frankincense.

†**2.** An aromatic preparation for embalming the dead. *Obs.*

c **1340** *Cursor M.* (Laud MS.) 11503 A bawme of wonder bytternes That dedmen with anoynted is. **1480** CAXTON *Chron. Eng.* ccxliii. 284 Kyng Henry..closed it [the body of King Richard] in a fayre cheste with dyuerse speceryes and baumes. **1618** [See BALMER[1].]

3. Fragrant oil or ointment used for anointing.

1447 BOKENHAM *Seyntys* 138 Wyth swete bawm she anoyntyd had be. **1593** SHAKS. *Rich. II*, III. ii. 55 Not all the water in the rough rude Sea Can wash the Balme from an anoynted King. **1623** FAVINE *Theat. Hon.* II. xiii. 254 The holy Viole or Bottell, full of Baulme.

4. *fig.* Aromatic fragrance, agreeable perfume.

1483 CAXTON *Gold. Leg.* 220/3 She had sothly the bame of good odour..in conuersacion. **1570** HOLINSHED *Scot. Chron.* I. 26 The proverbe..that the sow recks not of balme. **1728** THOMSON *Spring* 733 When nought but balm is breathing thro' the woods. **1866** B. TAYLOR *Poems of Orient* 158, I love the palm, With his leaves of beauty, his fruit of balm.

5. Aromatic ointment used for soothing pain or healing wounds; = BALSAM *sb.* 2. *arch.*

1393 GOWER *Conf.* III. 315 This maister hath her every jointe With..balsme anointe. **1486** *Bk. St. Albans, Hawking* A iiij, Anoynt the soore with bawme. **1563** T. GALE *Antidot.* II. 34 The Baulme wherewyth greene and freshe woundes are spedilye cured. **1671** MILTON *Samson* 186 As Balm to fester'd wounds.

6. *transf.* or *fig.* A healing, soothing, or softly restorative, agency or influence.

1549 *Bk. Com. Prayer* Ps. cxli. 5 Let not their precious balms break my head. **1594** SHAKS. *Rich. III*, I. ii. 13 Loe, in these windowes..I powre the helplesse Balme of my poore eyes. **1643** N. LOCKYER (*title*) Baulme for Bleeding England and Ireland. **1667** MILTON *P.L.* II. 402 The soft delicious Air..Shall breath her balme. **1755** YOUNG *Centaur* iv. Wks. 1757 IV. 208 There is a sovereign balm in prayer. **1807** CRABBE *Library* 57 See here the balms that passion's wounds assuage. **1870** BRYANT *Homer* VII. I. 235 They laid them down to rest, And so received the balm of sleep.

7. *Comb.* and *Attrib.*, as ***balm-breathing***, ***-dew***, ***-liquor***, ***-shrub***, ***-tree***, ***-word***; also ***balm-like*** adj.; **balm-shed**, the season when balm is distilled.

1595 LODGE *Fig for Momus* v, To guide the Sages of *balme-breathing East. **1830** TENNYSON *Talking Oak* 268 Balm-dews to bathe thy feet. **1569** SPENSER *Sonn.* ix, With *Balmlike odor did perfume the aire. *c* **1570** *Scot. Poems 16th C.* (1801) II. 304 In rottin bosses no *balme liquor lyes. **1840** BROWNING *Sordello* VI. 445 Why grudge your having gained..The brakes at *balm-shed. **1840** CARLYLE *Heroes* ii. 74 Odoriferous *balm-shrubs. **1601** HOLLAND *Pliny* XVI. xxxii, The *balm tree can abide no other place but Iury. **1871** MACDUFF *Mem. Patmos* vi. 75 What *balm-words for the martyred disciples.

II. 8. A tree yielding balm; these trees belong to the genus *Balsamodendron*, N.O. *Amyridaceæ*, and are found in Asia and northern Africa.

1387 TREVISA *Higden* Rolls Ser. I. 107 Iudea is riche..of baume [L. *balsamis*], of olyues, of pomgarnet. *c* **1440** *Promp. Parv.* 27/1 Bawme, tre, *balsamus*. *a* **1520** *Myrr. Our Ladye* 285 Bawlme ys a tree and all that ys therein ys vertuous. **1626** BACON *New Atl.* (1658) 25 The Crosier of Balm-wood, the Pastoral Staff of Cedar. **1835** *Penny Cycl.* III. 345/1 The bark of the above-mentioned species of balm.

III. 9. a. Name of some fragrant garden herbs (N.O. *Labiatæ*); the chief are Balm Gentle or Balm-mint (*Melissa officinalis*) and Bastard Balm (*Melittis melissophyllum*). Also Field Balm (*Calamintha Nepeta*).

c **1440** *Promp. Parv.* 27 Bawme, herbe..*melissa.* **1551** TURNER *Herbal* D iiij, The comon baume..is but a bastard kynde, and the true bawme..may be called in English, bawme gentle. **1600** CHAPMAN *Odyss.* v. 97 With sweet balm-gentle, and blue violets hid. **1713** PETIVER in *Phil. Trans.* XXVIII. 195 Our common Garden Baulm. **1813** C. MARSHALL *Garden.* xvi. (ed. 5) 263 Balm is either plain or variegated.

b. *attrib.* in domestic or medicinal preparations, as ***balm-tea, -water, -wine***; and parasynthetic deriv., as ***balm-leaved***. **balm-mint** = BALSAM-MINT.

1752 MRS. DELANY *Autobiog.* (1861) III. 131 Whey at 7 this morning and baume tea at 10. *a* **1811** MARJORY FLEMING *Jrnl.* (1934) II. 54 Ravelston is a fine pla[ce] because I got balm win[e] and many other dain[ties]. **1861** DELAMER *Kitch. Gard.* 122 Balm-tea is a sudorific and febrifuge in high repute amongst village doctresses. **1712** tr. *Pomet's Hist. Drugs* I. 73 Distill'd from White-Wine, Rose or Balm-Water. **1816** SCOTT *Antiq.* vi, 'Would you take ony thing?—a glass of balm wine?' **1861** MISS PRATT *Flower. Pl.* IV. 118 Balm-leaved Figwort. **1562** TURNER *Herbal* II. 140 a, A kinde of mint that is called in English baum mynte.

IV. Balm of Gilead: see also BALSAM.

10. a. (Also ***balm of Mecca***.) A gold-coloured oleo-resin exuded from the tree *Balsamodendron Gileadense*, or perhaps *B. Opobalsamum*, formerly much esteemed as an antiseptic and vulnerary. **b.** A factitious or 'quack' imitation of this. **c.** ***American B. of G.***: a resin obtained from the *Icica carana*.

(*Balsamodendron* probably yields the *βάλσαμον*, *balsamum*, of the ancients. The term 'balm *of Gilead*' is modern, and like the botanical specific name *Gileadense*, originated in the assumption that this is the substance mentioned in the Bible as found in Gilead, and called in the English translation 'balm.' But the Heb. word *tsŏri* rendered 'balm' was not identified with *βάλσαμον*, *balsamum* by the LXX or Vulgate, which render it *ῥητίνη*, *resina*, resin. 'Balm' began with Coverdale.)

1535 COVERDALE *Gen.* xxxvii. 25 Ismaelites comyng from Gilead with..spyces, balme [WYCL. swete gumme, PURVEY rosyn], and myrre. **1560** BIBLE (Geneva) *Jer.* viii. 22 Is there no balme [WYCLIF, gumme, resyn; COVERDALE, triacle] at Gilead? is there no Physition there? **1703** MAUNDRELL *Journ. Jerus.* (1721) 86 This Oyl they take inwardly.. preferring it before Balm of Gilead. **1717** LADY MONTAGUE *Lett.* 42 II. 9 As to the balm of Mecca, I will certainly send you some. **1812** *Examiner* 30 Nov. 765/1 The sale of the Balm of Gilead has not been quite so extensive.

11. The evergreen shrub *Dracocephalum canariense* (*Treas. Bot.*); in quot. perhaps common Balm.

1767 WATSON in *Phil. Trans.* LVII. 443, I saw even the plant, usually called Balm of Gilead..flourishing without shelter [in or near London].

12. *attrib.* in ***Balm of Gilead shrub***. **Balm of Gilead fir**: the N. American species yielding Canada Balsam.

1769 SIR J. HILL *Fam. Herbal, Balm of Gilead Shrub*.. grows to five or six feet high. **1833** *Penny Cycl.* I. 30/1 The Balm of Gilead Fir..found..in the coldest parts of North America.

balm (bɑːm), *v. arch.* Forms: 4–5 **bame**, 4–6 **bawme**, (5 **boum**), 5–6 **balme**, (**balmbe**), 6 **baum**, 7– **balm**. [app. f. BALM *sb.*; but cf. OF. *enbasmer* (12th c.), also *balsamer* to embalm, *bausmer* ? to breathe perfume.]

1. *trans.* To embalm. *arch.*

c **1300** *K. Alis.* 4671 Theo body was bawmed, and leyd in a schryne. *c* **1420** *Anturs Arth.* xiv, Quyl the body be boumet and broȝte on a bere. **1611** SPEED *Hist. Gt. Brit.* IX. xxiv. (1632) 1161 Shee balming it [the head], sent it to her Holy Father. **1845** KINGLAKE *Eothen* vi. 95 May have been a live king just after the Flood, but has since lain balmed in spice.

†**2.** To anoint with fragrant, soothing, or cleansing oil or other liquid. *Obs.*

1398 TREVISA *Barth. De P.R.* VII. xxi. (1495) 238 The sore place shall be bamyd wyth oylle of roses. **1486** *Bk. St. Albans, Hawking*, A vj, [The hawk] fetchith moysture lyk oyle at her tayle, and bamyth her fete. **1596** SHAKS. *Tam. Shr.* Induct. 48 Balme his foule head in warme distilled waters. **1600** CHAPMAN *Odyss.* IV. 60 Where handmaids.. Bath'd, balm'd them.

†**b.** To mix or impregnate with balm. *Obs.*

1530 PALSGR. 444/2 When a medicyn is bawmed it hath a stronge savour.

†**c.** To smear with something resinous or sticky; also *rarely*, to smear on (the sticky material). *Obs.* or *dial.*

1382 WYCLIF *John* ix. 6 He..leyde, or bawmede, the cley on his yȝen. **1388** —— *Ex.* ii. 3 Sche bawmede [**1382** glewide] it with tar and pitch. **1398** TREVISA *Barth. De P.R.* XII. iv. Some [bees] bryngeþ..þinges þat ben sumdel gleymy and glewy, and bawmeþ þerwith þe hyue. **1857** WRIGHT *Provinc. Dict.*, He bawmed and slawmed it all over mortar and wash.

3. To soothe, alleviate (pain, sorrow, etc.). *arch.*

a **1400** *Chester Pl.* 165 Myrre..is beste to balmbe his thoo. **1605** SHAKS. *Lear* III. vi. 105 This rest might yet have balm'd thy broken senses. **1877** M. ARNOLD *Poems* I. 203 Only death can balm thy woe.

balm-apple: see *balsam-apple* in BALSAM *sb.* 10.

‖**bal masqué** (bal maske). [F.] A masked ball (see MASKED *ppl. a.*[2] 1 b).

1768 EARL OF CARLISLE *Let.* 31 May in J. H. Jesse *G. Selwyn & Contemp.* (1843) II. 303, I am going to a great dinner to-day..and after that to a *bal masqué* at court. **1775** H. WALPOLE *Let.* 23 Aug. (1904) IX. 239 On Friday he gives a *bal masqué* to the universe. **1817** H. C. CAMPBELL *Journey to Florence* 4 Oct. (1951) 101 Afterwards there was a Bal masqué at the Pergola. **1902** G. K. CHESTERTON *12 Types* 4 A disguise as tawdry and deceptive as the costume of a 'bal masqué'.

'balm-ˌcricket. [earlier *baum-cricket*, app. a mistranslation of G. *baum-grille*, 'tree-cricket,' by confusion with ME. *baum* BALM. (Taken by Tennyson, he tells us, from Dalzel.)] The cicada.

1783 BAILEY, *Cicada*, the Baum-cricket, a genus of four-winged insects. **1783** AINSWORTH *Lat. Dict.* II, *Cicada*, a sauterelle, or, according to others, a balm-cricket. **1797** DALZEL *Analec. Maj.* II. 187 (note on Theocr. *Idyll* I. 148) *Τέττιξ*, *Cicada* veterum..*Cicada orni* Linn., Angl. the Balm Cricket. **1833** TENNYSON *Dirge* vii, The balm-cricket carols clear In the green that folds thy grave.

†**'balmer**[1]. *Obs. rare*$^{-1}$. [f. BALM + -ER[1].] (He who or) that which embalms.

a **1618** RALEIGH *Rem.* (1644) 256 Bloud must be my Bodies only Balmer..No other Balm will there be given.

†**'balmer**[2]. *Obs. rare*$^{-1}$. 'Apparently some kind of coloured cloth.' Halliwell.

a **1400** *Chester Plays* 172 Princes, prelates of price Barrones in balmer and byse.

balmify ('bɑːmɪfaɪ), *v.* [f. BALMY *a.* + -FY = L. *-ficāre* to make.] To render balmy.

1733 CHEYNE *Eng. Malady* 306 (L.) The fluids have been entirely sweetened and balmified.

balmily ('bɑːmɪlɪ), *adv.* [f. BALMY *a.* + -LY[2].] In a balmy manner.

1819 J. H. WIFFEN *Aspley Wood* II. lxxii in *Aonian Hours* 107 How balmily the breeze Breathes from the sky-aspiring larch! **1861** *Temple Bar* II. 476 The wind..was breathing balmily.

'balminess. [f. as prec. + -NESS.] The state or quality of being balmy.

1733 CHEYNE *Eng. Malady* I. ii. §2 The Blood declines from its due Fluidity and Balmyness [cf. BALSAM 4]. **1862** GOULBURN *Pers. Relig.* III. (1873) 199 A delicious balminess in the air.

balming ('bɑːmɪŋ), *vbl. sb.* [f. BALM *v.* + -ING[1].] The action **a.** of embalming, **b.** of anointing with balm, **c.** of soothing.

1582 N. T. (Rhem.) *John* xii. *marg.*, The deuout offices of balming and anointing the dead bodies. **1600** CHAPMAN *Odyss.* XVIII. (R.) Forbeare to speake Of baths, or balmings. **1844** DICKENS *Mar. Chuz.* (C.D. ed.) 202 Hearts want binding and spirits want balming when people die.

Balmoral (bæl'mɒrəl). [name of Queen Victoria's residence in Scotland.] Used as a specific name of: **a.** A variety of Scotch cap. **b.** A kind of figured woollen petticoat. **c.** A kind of boot lacing in front.

1857 J. E. RITCHIE *Night Side London* 160 Smith with his Balmoral boots, Brown with his all-round collar. **1859** H. J. BYRON *Nymph of Lurleyburg* iv, Whose *morals* are not tight laced—oh dear, no—Though their *bal-morals* are extremely so. **1859** *Habits of Good Society* iv. 177 Victoria has assumed the Balmoral petticoat. *Ibid.* 178 She has courageously accompanied it with the Balmoral boot. **1864** LOCKER *Lond. Lyrics* (1876) 43, I know that when they walk in grass, she wears Balmorals. **1867** F. LUDLOW *Brace of Boys* 263 A skirt of garnet silk looped up over a pretty Balmoral. **1867** *Summer L. Goldthwaite's Life* 77 Rosetted slippers instead of heavy Balmoral Boots.

‖**bal musette** (balmyzɛt). [F.] In France, a popular dance-hall (with an accordion band). Also *attrib.*

1926 HEMINGWAY *Fiesta* (1927) I. iii. 25 The dancing-club was a *bal musette.* **1934** H. MILLER *Tropic of Cancer* (1961) 295 They were urging me to accompany them to a *bal musette.* **1934** C. LAMBERT *Music Ho!* II. 94 The bal-musette sentimentality of the valses of Auric. **1959** 'F. NEWTON' *Jazz Scene* xiii. 235 Such native European forms of light entertainment as..accordion and *bal musette* music.

balmy ('bɑːmɪ), *a.* [f. BALM *sb.* + -Y[1].]

1. Yielding or producing balm.

1667 MILTON *P.L.* v. 24 What drops the Myrrhe, and what the balmie Reed. **1742** COLLINS *Eclog.* i. 49 The balmy shrub for you shall love our shore.

†**2.** Of the consistency of balm; resinous. *Obs.*

1782 MONRO *Anat.* 14 The marrow is..oily and balmy in middle age.

3. Delicately and deliciously fragrant.

c **1500** DUNBAR *Gold. Targe* 97 Ewiry blome..Opnyt & spred thair balmy leves. **1604** SHAKS. *Oth.* v. ii. 16 Ile smell thee on the Tree. Oh Balmy breath. **1794** BURNS *Wks.* IV. 313 Like a baumy kiss. **1824** MISS MITFORD *Village* Ser. I. (1863) 85 Under the shade of those balmy firs.

4. *fig.* Deliciously soft and soothing.

1604 SHAKS. *Oth.* II. ii. 259 To haue their Balmy slumbers wak'd with strife. **1742** YOUNG *Nt. Th.* I. 1 Tir'd Nature's sweet restorer, balmy Sleep! **1857** HEAVYSEGE *Saul* (1869) 161 The balmy sense of fault forgiven.

5. Of wind, air, weather, etc. (combining senses 3 and 4): Deliciously mild, fragrant, and soothing.

1704 POPE *Winter* 48 The balmy zephyrs. **1850** TENNYSON *In Mem.* xvii, And balmy drops..Slide from the bosom of the stars. **1867** MISS BRADDON *R. Godwin* II. v. 73 When the August weather was brightest and balmiest.

6. Of healing virtue, medicinally soothing.

1746 COLLINS *Ode to Pity* i, With balmy hands his wounds to bind. **1796** BURKE *Regic. Peace* Wks. 1842 II. 318 To assuage his bruised dignity with half a yard square of balmy diplomatick diachylon. **1826** E. IRVING *Babylon* II. 391 The cure for a disease, is to send..balmy medicines.

7. 'Soft', weak-minded, idiotic. Also as *sb.* (see quot. 1903). See also BARMY *a. slang.*

1851 MAYHEW *Lond. Labour* I. 217/2 (Street-patterers' slang) *Balmy*, insane. **1859** HOTTEN *Slang Dict.*, *Balmy*, insane. **1891** FARMER *Slang* II. 224/1 Balmy in one's crumpet. **1892** *Daily News* 17 Nov. 6/6 Regarding the old 'balmy' criminals, they are poor creatures, far more to be pitied than condemned. **1903** LD. W. NEVILL *Penal Servitude* 150 These are officially classed as 'W. M.'—that is, weak-minded—but are invariably known colloquially as 'balmies'. *Ibid.* 151 A man who appears to be playing 'balmy'. **1912** MASEFIELD *Dauber* II. in *English Rev.* Oct. 350 Painting's a balmy's job [*ed.* 1913, p. 21 a balmy job] not worth a nail. **1922** 'R. CROMPTON' *Just—William* xi. §1. 206 'I s'pose you're balmy on her,' he said resignedly. **1929** J. B. PRIESTLEY *Good Companions* III. i. 460 People here must have gone balmy.

8. *absol.* Sleep. (Cf. sense 4.) *slang.*

1840 DICKENS *Old C. Shop* viii, As it's rather late, I'll try and get a wink or two of the balmy.

†**balne.** *Obs.* 5–7; also 6 **bawne.** [ad. L. *balneum* bath.] A (warm) bath: see BALNEUM.

1471 RIPLEY *Comp. Alch.* in Ashm. (1652) v. 149 Wyth hete of Balne, or ells of our Dounghyll. **1570** LEVINS *Manip.* /44 Bawne, bath. **1605** TIMME *Quersit.* III. 168 Conuenient digestions in the heate of balne Mary.

balneal ('bælnɪːəl), *a.* [f. L. *balne-um* + -AL[1].] Of or pertaining to a (warm) bath, or to bathing.

c **1645** HOWELL *Lett.* (1650) I. 292 Others attribute this balneal heat unto the sun. **1883** *Athenæum* 22 Sept. 363/1 The balneal usages of the local Romans.

balneary ('bælnɪːərɪ), *sb.* and *a.* [ad. L. *balneārium* in cl. L. only in pl. *balneāria*, from adj. *balneārius* belonging to the *balneum* bath.] **A.** *sb.* A bath or bathing-place; a medicinal spring.

1646 SIR T. BROWNE *Pseud. Ep.* VI. vii. 309 The Balnearies or bathing places. **1864** R. BURTON *Dahome* II. 298 A raised earth rim for a balneary.

B. *adj.* Of or pertaining to the bath or bathing.

1883 H. JAMES *Portr. Places* vii. 142 The French do not treat their beaches as we do ours—as..places animated simply during the balneary hours. **1924** *Weekly Westm.* 29 Aug. 530/3 In fantasy I view and loathe each balneary station—I have been down at Pebbleton-on-Sea.

balneation (bælnɪː'eɪʃən). ? *Obs.* [n. of action f. med.L. *balneāre* to bathe: see -ATION.] Bathing.

1646 SIR T. BROWNE *Pseud. Ep.* II. vi. 101 Balneations, washings, and fomentations. **1656** in Blount *Glossogr.*; and in mod. Dicts.

†**'balneatory,** *a. Obs.*$^{-0}$ [ad. L. *balneātōrius*, f. *balneātor* bath-keeper: see -ORY.] 'Of or pertaining to a bath' Bailey 1731.

†**'balneo.** *Obs.* Latinized spelling of BAGNIO 1, 2. See also BALNEUM.

1659 GAUDEN *Tears Ch.* 351 The Balneos and Theatres of free Cities. **1702** W. J. *Bruyn's Voy. Levant* x. 36 The Balneo of the Slaves belonging to the Grand Signior.

balneography (bælnɪː'ɒgrəfɪ). [f. L. *balneum* bath + Gr. *-γραφία* writing.] A description of, or treatise upon, baths. **balne'ology** [see -LOGY], scientific medical study of bathing and medicinal springs. **balneological** (ˌbælnɪːəʊ'lɒdʒɪkəl), *a.* of or pertaining to balneology. **balneotherapy** (-'θɛrəpɪ) [Gr. *θεραπεία* medical treatment], treatment of disease by baths or medicinal springs; hence **ˌbalneothera'peutic** *a.*

1879 *Nature* 9 Oct. 551/2 Balneological works, treating of the European mineral springs. **1883** *Harper's Mag.* June 122/1 The physician who has..experience in balneology. **1881** J. N. HYDE in *von Ziemssen's Cycl. Med.* Suppl. 184 Balneotherapy, when there was no mercury used, has proved of no greater worth. **1906** *Practitioner* Dec. 764 The initiation of balneo-therapeutic measures. **1907** H. & F. P. WEBER (*title*) Climatotherapy and Balneotherapy.

balneologist (bælnɪː'ɒlədʒɪst). [f. L. *balneum* bath + -OLOGIST.] An expert in balneology.

1872 *Lancet* 20 Apr. 532/1 At Aix is to be found the most learned of living balneologists, Dr. Lerschet. **1902** *Times* 22 Jan. 2/4 Applications are invited for the appointment of balneologist under the New Zealand Government in connexion with the Thermal Springs of the Colony. **1921** *Times Lit. Suppl.* 6 Oct. 646/3 Dr. Herbert..in 1902 was appointed as Government balneologist to advise on the development of the health resorts of New Zealand.

‖**balneum** ('bælnɪəm). [L.; = bath.]

1. A bath or bathing.

1652 FRENCH *Yorksh. Spa* iv. 45 Water is used..first by way of *Balneum*, or bathing the whole body. *Ibid.* 49 A cold *Balneum*.

2. *Alch.*, *Chem.*, and *Cookery*. (Short for the fuller *Balneum Mariæ*, erron. *Maris*): = BAIN MARIE. (The L. ablative *balneo*, occurring after 'in,' was occas. taken as the name of the vessel.)

1471 RIPLEY *Comp. Alch.* in Ashm. (1652) Ep. 116 Then in Balneo of Mary togeather let them be circulat. **1594** PLAT *Jewell-Ho.* II. 23 You must have a large Balneo wherein you may place sixe or eight glasse bodies at once. **1641** FRENCH *Distill.* i. (1651) 14 A Balneum as hot as ashes. *Ibid.* iv. 96 Digest them in a temperate *Balneo*. **1796** MRS. GLASSE *Cookery* xxv. 378 Distil them in a glass still, *balneum Mariæ*. **1811** HOOPER *Med. Dict.*, *Balneum Mariæ, Balneum Maris*, a warm water bath.

balon(e, -oone, -oune, obs. ff. BALLOON.

baloney, boloney (bəˈləʊnɪ, bə-), *sb.* and *int. slang* (orig. *U.S.*). [Commonly regarded as f. BOLOGNA (*sausage*) but the connection remains conjectural.] Humbug: nonsense.

1928 *Sat. Even. Post* 28 Nov. 21 Gee, that's a long shot. Boloney! That's not the ball—it's the divot. **1935** *Discovery* Dec. 378/2 He even suggests that much of modern psychiatry is 'hooey' and 'baloney'. **1935** E. WEEKLEY *Something about Words* 64 *Boloney* must surely be for *Bologna* sausage (whence also the English *polony*, dating from the 18th century), influenced perhaps by the contemptuous sense associated with the German *wurst*. **1958** *Times* 15 Nov. 5/3 That nick-name was absolute baloney. **1959** J. BRAINE *Vodi* vi. 93 All that baloney about going upstairs to play a harp or downstairs to roast. **1959** *Daily Mail* 15 Jan. 1/5 This is the official baloney that her family life would suffer if she were to live on a Commonwealth scale.

balotted: see BALLOT *v.*[2].

† **baˈlow, baˈloo**, *int.* and *sb. Obs.* [Apparently a nursery utterance, and probably without derivation: it varied with *balililow*, and *baw lu la law*. According to Jamieson 'supposed to be part of an old Fr. lullaby, *Bas le loup!*, or *bas, là le loup!*' (*down! there the wolf*), but this is a mere conjecture without any known historical basis.]

A. *interj.* An utterance used in lulling to sleep.

a **1724** *Lady A. Bothwell's Lament* in *Tea-t. Misc.* (1733) II. 130 Balow my boy, ly still and sleep. It grieves me sore to hear thee weep.

B. *sb.* **a.** A lullaby. **b.** A song and tune containing this word.

1611 BEAUM. & FL. *Knt. of Burning Pestle* ii. (Boucher) You musicians play Baloo. **1619** Z. BOYD *L. Battell* 308 (JAM.) Lulled with Sathan's 'balowes.' **1794** RITSON *Scot. Songs, Ess.* 109 (JAM.) The editor.. pretends that.. there are two 'balowes,' as they are stiled, the first, 'The balow Allan,' the second 'Palmer's Balow'.. commonly called Lady Bothwell's Lament.

† **ˈbalowe-fire.** *Obs.* In form = 'Fatal or destroying fire,' f. BALE *a.* or BALE *sb.*[1]; but used in the sense of BALE-FIRE 1, q.v.

c **1430** *Chev. Assigne* 233 Þe ȝondere is my qwene· betrice she hette, In þe ȝondere balowe fyre · is buskedde to brenne. *Ibid.* 344 Brente here in þe balowe fyer alle to browne askes. [cf. **1855** *Whitby Gloss.*, *Bally-bleeze* [Balow-blaze], a bonfire.]

balrag, obs. form of BULLYRAG.

‖ **balsa** (ˈbɔːlsə, ˈbælsə). Also 8 **balza**. [Sp. 'a boat.' Minsheu 1623.] **1.** A raft, or fishing-float, used chiefly on the Pacific coasts of South America. Also, *balsa raft*.

1777 ROBERTSON *Hist. Amer.* II. VII. 320 Where the rivers became deep.. they are passed in Balzas, or floats. **1850** PRESCOTT *Peru* II. 3 To transport the commander's baggage and the military stores on some of the Indian balsas. **1915** 'BARTIMEUS' *Tall Ship* i. 15 The Commander.. was standing on the balsa raft.

2. A bombaceous tree of tropical America, *Ochroma lagopus*; also, the wood of this tree, used for its extreme lightness. Also *balsa tree, wood*. Cf. CORKWOOD 2.

1866 LINDLEY & MOORE *Treas. Bot.* s.v. *Ochroma*, The very buoyant rafts or balsas, the unsinkable properties of which caused such surprise among the discoverers of America, are likewise made of it, whence the tree is called Balsa in some parts of America. **1917** *Sci. Amer.* Nov. 345/3 A new wood, apparently little known and called balsa wood, is exceedingly light. **1920** *Flight* XII. 1301/2 Balsa wood.. is so extremely light that it can be recommended for making aerofoils. **1924** *Contemp. Rev.* Jan. 95 The balsa tree, a wood which, from its extreme lightness, is specially suitable in the construction of aeroplanes. **1933** *Discovery* June 194/1 Advance scouts had drifted on a balsa-wood raft. **1951** *Oxf. Jun. Encycl.* VII. 223/2 Balsa is only half the weight of cork, and is the lightest and softest of commercial woods.

balsam (ˈbɔːlsəm), *sb.* (and *a.*) Forms: 1 **balsam, balzam, balzama**; 6–7 **balsome**, 7 **-um, -ame**, 7–8 **-om**, 7– **balsam**. [ad. L. *balsam-um*: see below. Found already in OE. as *balsam, balzam* (neut.), and *balzama, -e*, wk. ? m. or f.; then not till *c* 1600, the general popular sense having been meanwhile supplied by *basme, baume* from F. (see BALM), and the more specific sense, from the Renascence, by the L. *balsamum* unchanged, and occasionally by It. *balsamo*: see these words.]

A. *sb.* **I.** The aromatic resinous product.

1. An aromatic vegetable juice; = BALM *sb.* 1.

c **1000** *Sax. Leechd.* II. lxiv, Þis is balzaman smyring wiþ eallum untrumnessum. *Ibid.* Cruc on þam heafde.. sceal on balzame beon. **1624** CAPT. SMITH *Virginia* II. 26 A very cleare and odoriferous Gumme.. which some called Balsom. *a* **1711** KEN *Blandina* Wks. 1721 IV. 526 The Trees .. In od'rous Balsam bleed away. **1872** YEATS *Growth Comm.* 16 Gems, spices, and balsams brought from India and Arabia.

b. specifically: ***true balsam***, or ***balsam of Mecca***, the earliest known sort, is BALM OF GILEAD, q.v. The discovery of America brought knowledge of many other natural balsams or oleo-resins, e.g. ***balsam of Acouchi, of Copaiba, of Peru, of Tolu***, all used medicinally, and ***Canada Balsam***, from the Balm of Gilead Fir, used also in mounting objects for the microscope.

1671 SALMON *Syn. Med.* III. xxiii. 444 Balsamum verum, the true Balsam.. is the chief of the Oyls and Balsams in the world. *Ibid.* Balsam of Tolu.. hath the same virtue with the former. **1721** *Lond. Gaz.* No. 5939/2 Six Pots of Balsam of Mecca. **1771** J. S. *Le Dran's Observ. Surg.* 43 Slips of.. Linen, moistened with Balsam of Peru. **1830** LINDLEY *Nat. Syst. Bot.* 127 Balsam of Acouchi is produced by *Icica acuchina*. **1831** BREWSTER *Optics* xxi. 191 Cementing upon it a plate of glass with Canada balsam.

2. An aromatic oily or resinous medicinal preparation, usually for external application, for healing wounds or soothing pain.

1579 LANGHAM *Gard. Health* (1633) 582 A balsam, take oile oliue one pint, S. Iohns wort, Betony, Centory, & Selfeheale, ana one handfull. **1612** WOODALL *Surg. Mate* Wks. (1653) 34 This unguent is a sure Balsame for wounds of any sort. **1671** SALMON *Syn. Med.* III. xxix. 490 Balsams .. are made of Oyl, Butter, Fat, Suet, Gums, Rosins, and other things which will mix or melt. **1720** GAY *Poems* (1745) I. 120 His pills, his balsams and his Ague-spells. **1864** SKEAT *Uhland's Poems* 236 Ah! no balsam e'er shall heal him.

b. specifically, of various substances dissolved in oil or turpentine, as ***balsam of aniseed, of saturn*** (see quot.), ***of steel, of sulphur***.

1694 *Phil. Trans.* XVIII. 200 Balsam of Sulphur.. made with Oyl of Turpentine and Brimstone. **1727–51** CHAMBERS *Cycl.*, *Balsam of Saturn* is a salt, or sugar of lead, dissolved in oil or spirit of turpentine. **1822** IMISON *Sc. & Art.* II. 128 Fixed oils dissolve sulphur and then form Balsams.

3. *fig.* A healing, soothing agent or agency.

1607 SHAKS. *Timon* III. v. 10 Is this the Balsome, that the vsuring Senat Powres into Captaines wounds? **1621** BURTON *Anat. Mel.* III. iv. II. iii. (1651) 698 No salvation, no balsome for their diseased souls. *a* **1764** LLOYD *To G. Colman* Poet. Wks. 1774 I. 109 From friendship's source the balsam flows. **1884** TENNYSON *Becket* 24 Was not the people's blessing.. a balsam to thy blood?

† **4.** *transf.* in *Alch.* A healthful preservative essence, of oily and softly penetrative nature, conceived by Paracelsus to exist in all organic bodies. Cf. BALSAMUM 3. *Obs.*

1643 SIR T. BROWNE *Relig. Med.* I. §43 Radicall balsome, or vitall sulphur of the parts. **1658** A. FOX *Wurtz' Surg.* I. vi. 25 The humidity of the naturall balsum, which alwayes like a chrystal lyeth on the wound. **1733** CHEYNE *Eng. Malady* II. iii. §1. 137 The Blood is return'd to its due Degree of Thinness, Fluidity, and Balsam. **1753** CHAMBERS *Cycl. Supp.* s.v., Internal balsam.. called also *gluten naturæ*.

† **5.** = BALM *sb.* 2; *fig.* a preservative. *Obs.*

1658 SIR T. BROWNE *Hydriot.* iv. (1736) 43 Noble Acts which are the Balsom of our Memories. **1753** CHAMBERS *Cycl. Supp.* s.v., Dead Balsam.. of myrrh and aloes.. for drying and absorbing the humours of dead bodies.

6. *Chem.* Compounds, insoluble in water, consisting of resins mixed with volatile oils. Formerly only those oleo-resinous compounds which contained benzoic acid were called balsams: the Fr. *baume* has this limited meaning.

1673 GREW *Anat. Roots* iii. §21 A curious Balsame of a Citrine Colour.. I call it a Balsame; because it will not dissolve in water. **1819** CHILDREN *Chem. Anal.* 296 Resinous matters which afford benzoic acid when heated.. one of the chief characteristics by which balsams are distinguished from resins.

7. *attrib.*, as in ***balsam-fir, -oil, -poplar, -tree***.

1601 HOLLAND *Pliny* XXIII. iv, The Balsame oile, called Balm, is of all others most pretious. **1695** BLACKMORE *Pr. Arth.* II. 147 The fragrant Balsom-Tree distills around Her healing Riches. **1865** PARKMAN *Champlain* xii. (1875) 342 The spruce, hemlock, balsam-fir, or pine. **1882** *Garden* 14 Jan. 15/2 The Balsam Poplar and the Lombardy grow rapidly near water.

II. 8. A tree yielding balsam: see BALM *sb.* 8.

c **1000** ÆLFRIC *Gloss.* in Wright *Voc.* (W.) /139 *Carpo balsami*, balsames blæd. *Opobalsamum*, balsames tear. **1651** JER. TAYLOR *Course Serm.* I. i. 7 Falling like the tears of the balsam of Iudea. **1876** HARLEY *Mat. Med.* 629 Balsam of Tolu, a lofty evergreen tree.

III. 9. A flowering plant, of the genus *Impatiens*, distinguished by its hooded and spurred coloured sepals, and thick succulent stem. Usually applied to *Impatiens Balsamina*, an ornamental garden flower producing under culture variegated double blossoms; sometimes also to the yellow-flowered *I. Noli-tangere*, found wild in Britain.

1741 *Compl. Fam.-Piece* II. iii. 379 Female Balsams, Larkspurs, Convolvulus. **1794** MARTYN *Rousseau's Bot.* xxvi. 407 A wild species called Yellow Balsam and also by the familiar names of Quick-in-hand and Touch-me-not. **1884** *U.P. Mag.* Apr. 149 The stand of balsams in the windows.

10. balsam apple (or **balm apple**): **a.** properly, name of species of *Momordica* (*M. Balsamina, M. Charantia*), gourd-like plants with highly coloured fruits or 'apples,' also called *Apple of Jerusalem*, and 'Male' Balsam Apple; **b.** absurdly, given also to the common garden Balsam ('Female' Balsam Apple) because both were called by early herbalists *Balsamina*: see BALSAMINE; **balsam-mint, balsamint** (or **balsam-tansy**): ALECOST or Costmary (*Tanacetum Balsamita*).

1578 LYTE *Dodoens* 441 The one is called the Male *Balsem, or Balme apple. The other is called the female Balsem apple. **1597** GERARDE *Herbal* II. lxx. (1633) 362 Balme apple or apple of Hierusalem grows but in hot countries. **1598** FLORIO, *Caranza*, the herb called the Balsam apple. **1611** COTGR., *Balsamine*, the balsam apple (whose oyle doth close up wounds like Balme). **1725** BRADLEY *Fam. Dict.* s.v., Balm, or Balsam-Apple (Female), a Plant.. a Foot and a half high, of a reddish Colour at the Bottom, etc. *c* **1000** ÆLFRIC *Gloss.* in Wright *Voc.* (W.) /136 *Sisimbrium*, *balsminte. **1578** LYTE *Dodoens* 250 Balsamynte floureth in July and August. **1607** TOPSELL *Four-f. Beasts* 419 The herb called Baltsamint or Costmary. **1865** *Intell. Observ.* No. 36. 466 *Balsam-tansy acted still more powerfully.

† **B.** as *adj.* Balmy, deliciously fragrant.

1621 BURTON *Anat. Mel.* III. ii. IV. i. 530 She will adventure all her estate.. for a Nectarean, a balsome kiss alone.

balsam (ˈbɔːlsəm), *v.* [f. BALSAM *sb.*]

1. To anoint or impregnate with balsam; to perfume; to heal, salve.

a **1666** WHARTON *Wks.* (1683) 398 Tranquillity succeeds our Brutish Wars, Balsoms our Wounds. *a* **1670** HACKET *Abp. Williams* I. (1693) 57 The Gifts of our young.. Age are very sweet, when they are Balsam'd with Discretion. **1800** MOORE *Anacreon* lvi. 18 To balsam every mortal woe!

2. *intr.* (for *refl.*) To anoint oneself with balsam.

1846 *Sismondi's Lit. Europe* II. xxxviii. 520 To bathe and balsam in the streams of joy.

3. *trans.* To embalm. *rare.*

1855 MOTLEY *Dutch Rep.* (1861) I. 222 [He] fell down dead.. We have had him balsamed and sent home.

† **ˈbalsamate**, *a. Obs. rare*[−1]. [ad. med.L. *balsamātus*, pa. pple. of *balsamāre*; cf. late OF. *balsamé*.] Embalmed.

1470 HARDING *Chron.* XCV. xvii, He made his ymage of laton.. In whiche he put his body balsomate.

balsamation (bɔːlsəˈmeɪʃən, bæl-). [n. of action f. med.L. *balsamāre*: see prec.] The process of embalming or preserving from putrefaction.

1681 *Phil. Collect.* XII. 104 An Universal Balsamation, or Conservation of all things Animal, or Vegetable. **1753** CHAMBERS *Cycl. Supp.*, *Balsamation*.. the act or art of embalming dead bodies.

balsamed (ˈbɔːlsəmd), *ppl. a.* [f. BALSAM + -ED.] Covered with balsam.

1854 J. HOGG *Microsc.* I. iii. (1867) 212 The specimen being placed on the balsamed surface.

balsamic (bɔːlˈsæmɪk, bæl-), *a.* and *sb.* [f. Gr. βάλσαμ-ον BALSAM + -IC.] **A.** *adj.*

1. Of the nature of, or yielding, balsam.

1676 GREW *Anat. Flowers* II. ii. §10 A Gummy or Balsamick Juyce. *a* **1711** KEN *Hymnotheo* Wks. 1721 III. 228 Gilead, on whose od'rous Top, Balsamick Gums, like liquid Amber, drop. **1805** *Edin. Rev.* VI. 411 Some balsamic pine.

2. Having the delicate aromatic fragrance of balsam; deliciously fragrant, balmy.

1714 STEELE *Solomon's Song*, Breathes thro' the Air a soft Balsamic Scent. **1873** LONGF. *Monk. Casal. Mag.* xxiii, The sweet Balsamic exhalations of the pine.

3. Having the healing properties of balsam; soothing, restorative, health-giving.

1605 TIMME *Quersit.* I. xi. 48 The uniuersall balsamick medicine. **1717** LADY MONTAGU *Lett.* 47 II. 39 Very balsamic for disordered heads. **1793** T. BEDDOES *Let. Darwin* 72 The supposition that the sweet breath of the cow is healing and balsamic. **1855** MACAULAY *Hist. Eng.* III. 479 The balsamic virtues of the royal hand.

4. Of, pertaining to, or full of, the subtle healthful influence or 'radical balsam' conceived of by alchemists; cf. BALSAM *sb.* 4.

1644 DIGBY *Nat. Bodies* xxiii. §8. 212 With three sortes of riuers or brookes, to runne through him.. the one of a gentle balsamike oyle. **1686** GOAD *Celest. Bod.* II. ix. 284 The proper Preservative, some would call it the Balsamick Spirit, of the Fruit is dislodged by the Cold. **1733** CHEYNE *Eng. Malady* II. i. §2. 113 To make the Iuices [of the Body] soft, sweet, and balsamick.

5. *fig.* Soothing, healing, gently restorative, balmy.

1667 *Decay Chr. Piety* xvii. §15. 357 Nor are those wounds ever like to close, till our zeal grow more balsamick. **1752** JOHNSON *Rambl.* No. 202 ⁋3 Sleep that sheds his balsamick anodynes only on the cottage. **1870** DELITZSCH in Spurgeon *Treas. Dav.* Ps. c. 3 Balsamic consolation.

6. Intended to hold balsam.

1818 J. HOBHOUSE *Hist. Illustr.* 557 The little balsamic vase called 'Lecythus,' an unknown utensil of clay.

B. *sb.* A soothing or healing medicine or application. Cf. BALM *sb.* 5, BALSAM *sb.* 2.

1713 *Lond. & Country Brew.* I. (1742) 68 Harvest-Men.. stand most in Need of the greatest Balsamics. **1756** NUGENT *Gr. Tour* II. 423 This herb is reckoned such a sovereign balsamic, as to cure wounds almost with a touch. **1881** *Philadelphia Record* No. 3443. 3 This balsamic had been brought before the Therapeutical Society.

† **bal'samical**, *a.* *Obs.* [f. prec. + -AL¹.] = prec.
1605 TIMME *Quersit.* II. vi. 129 His balsamical vertue, or radical balsam. **1677** HALE *Prim. Orig. Man.* I. i. 30 The Balsamical humour of my Blood. **1695** WESTMACOTT *Script. Herb.* 147 The Tops and Twigs of these resinous Plants.. emit Balsamical Effluviums.

bal'samically, *adv.* [f. prec. + -LY².] After the manner of a balsam.

† **bal'samicness.** *Obs. rare.* [f. BALSAMIC + -NESS.] The quality of being balsamic; fragrancy.
1737 MILLER *Gard. Dict.* s.v. *Vitis*, This Wine has a Body, a Tartness, a Headiness, a Balsamickness or Perfume.

balsamiferous (bɔːlsə'mɪfərəs, bæl-), *a.* [f. L. *balsam-um* BALSAM + -(I)FEROUS.] Yielding or producing balsam.
1683-4 ROBINSON in *Phil. Trans.* XXIX. 475 Balsamiferous, Gummiferous, and Saccharine Plants. **1864** WEBSTER, *Balsamodendron*, a genus of balsamiferous plants.

† **'balsamine.** *Bot. Obs.* [a. F. *balsamine*, ad. Gr. *βαλσαμίνη* balsam-plant, f. *βάλσαμον*: see BALSAM *sb.* and -INE.] Book name for: **a.** BALSAM APPLE; **b.** the plant Balsam (*Impatiens Balsamina*). Fuchsius had distinguished these as *Balsamine mas*, and *B. femina.*
[**1542** FUCHSIUS *Hist. Stirpium*, Duo Balsamines genera damus. Primam, quam nos certioris discriminis gratia marem fecimus.. Alteram, quam feminam nominauimus.] **1578** LYTE *Dodoens* 441 By the name of Balsamine, you must now understand two sorts of apples.. The one is called the Male Balsem, or Balme apple. **1794** MARTYN *Rousseau's Bot.* xxvi. 407 True Balsam, or more properly Balsamine.

Balsamint, -mynt: see BALSAM *sb.* 10.

† **balsa'mitic**, *a. Obs. rare.* In 7 **balsamittique**. [ad. med.L. *balsamitic-us*, f. *balsamum*: see -ITIC.] = BALSAMIC. Hence **balsamiticness**.
1667 WATERHOUSE *Fire Lond.* 39 Corrosion coming into the room of Balsamittiqueness.

'balsamize, *v.* ? *Obs.* [ad. med.L. *balsamizā-re*, f. *balsamum*: see -IZE.] To render balsamic.
1748 *Lond. Mag.* 362 To balsamize the blood.

† **'balsamo.** *Obs.* [a. It. *balsamo*:—L. *balsamum*] = BALSAM, BALSAMUM.
1594 GREENE *Look. Glasse* (1861) 124 Fetch balsamo, the kind preserver of life.

'balsamous, *a.* ? *Obs.* [f. L. *balsam-um* + -OUS.] = BALSAMIC.
1684 tr. *Bonet's Merc. Compit.* III. 76 A Cephalick balsamous liniment. **1762** STERNE *Tr. Shandy* V. xxxvi. 125 The radical moisture is.. an oily and balsamous substance.

‖ **'balsamum.** *Obs.* [a. L. *balsamum*, a. Gr. *βάλσαμον* the balsam-tree, and its resin (prob. f. Semitic: cf. Heb. *besem*, *bāsām*, 'spice'; though the LXX never render this word by *βάλσαμον*, nor the Vulg. by *balsamum*, words which do not occur in these versions. Occas. used in OE. in the general sense of BALM, and in regular use from *c* 1400 to 17th c., in the specific senses, in which BALSAM is now substituted.]
1. An aromatic resinous vegetable juice; = BALM *sb.* 1, BALSAM *sb.* 1.
c **885** K. ÆLFRED *Bæda* III. viii. (Bosw.), Héddern ða balsamum on wære. **1590** MARLOWE *2nd Pt. Tamburl.* IV. ii, An ointment.. distilled from the purest balsamum. **1636** FEATLY *Clavis Myst.* viii. 100 To discerne a sented poyson from Balsamum.
2. = BALM *sb.* 2-5.
c **1400** *Destr. Troy* XXI. 8776 A prise oyntment of bavme and of balsamom. **1590** SHAKS. *Com. Err.* IV. i. 89, I haue bought The Oyle, the Balsamum, and Aqua-vitæ. *a* **1653** G. DANIEL *Idyll* iii. 113 To plaister o're These Vlcers with a Balsamum.
fig. **1601** CHESTER. *Love's Mart.* lxxxviii, Heart-curing Balsamum. *a* **1631** DONNE *Serm.* xli. 410 The Balsamum of this kisse.
3. *Alch.* = BALSAM *sb.* 4.
a **1631** DONNE *Serm.* xxxii. 313 Everything hath in it.. a naturall Balsamum; which if any wound or hurt which that Creature hath received be kept clean from Extrinsique putrefaction, will heal of itself. **1650** FRENCH *Chym. Dict.*, *Balsamum* is a substance of bodies preserving things from putrefaction.
4. A tree yielding balm or balsam; = BALSAM *sb.* 8.
1398 TREVISA *Barth. De P.R.* XVII. xviii. (1495) 614 The bowes of Balsamum ben softly kytte wyth a knyfe of boon.
5. *attrib.*, as in ***balsamum-tree*** (= prec.).
1603 SIR C. HEYDON *Jud. Astrol.* xxii. 485 The Viper delighteth in the shadow of the Balsamum tree.

balsamy ('bɔːlsəmɪ), *a.* [f. BALSAM *sb.* + -Y¹.] Balsam-like in aromatic fragrance, balmy.
1687 FLOYER *Touch-st. Med.* I 267 The Herb smells Balsamy. **1880** MISS BIRD *Japan* I. 357 The trees flung their balsamy aromatic scent.. upon the air.

balsome, -um, obs. forms of BALSAM.

balstone, corrupt form of BAUSON.

Balt (bɔːlt), *sb.* and *a.* [ad. late L. (Jordanes) *Balthæ.*] **A.** *sb.* A native or inhabitant of one of the Baltic states of Lithuania, Latvia and Estonia; *spec.* a German inhabitant of any of these states (see quot. 1937). **B.** *adj.* Of or pertaining to (a person from one of) these states.
1878 R. G. LATHAM in W. Smith *Dict. Gr. & Rom. Geogr.* 375/2 For a *Balt*, or an *Amal*, as real personages, we look in vain. Populations, however, to which they were *Eponymi*, we find in the two localities Baltia [Baltic] and Abalus. **1909** WEBSTER, *Balts*, Lithuanians, who, together with the Letts, were probably the Æstii of Tacitus. **1922** E. J. HARRISON *Lithuania* iii. 37 The Lithuanians together with the Letts and Old Prussians form a family of Aestians or Balts. *Ibid.* iii. 39 To-day the ancient Balts are represented only by the Lithuanians and the Letts or Latvians. **1937** *Discovery* Aug. 234/2 In 1918 the German baronial families were deprived of their estates... As late as 1918 the Baltic barons or 'balts' as they are always called, were planning to colonise Estonia with two and a half million small farmers from Germany. **1939** *Times* 1 Nov. 7/1 The exchange of documents ratifying the repatriation of Balts from Latvia is expected to take place in Berlin to-morrow. **1954** J. B. PRIESTLEY *Magicians* iii. 60 Wayland, it appeared, was part English, part Balt.

'balter, *v. Obs.* exc. *dial.* Also 7 **baulter**, 8-9 *dial.* **bauter**. [prob. from ON; cf. Da. *baltre*, *boltre* to wallow, welter, tumble. See also BOULTER. The connexion between senses 1 and 2 and the others is not clear, but it may be either through the notion of *tumbling* (the hair), or of *weltering*.]
† **1.** *intr.* To tumble about, to dance clumsily. (Isolated later example of *baltering*.)
c **1325** *E.E. Allit. P.* B. 103 Þay ben boþe blynde & balterande cruppelez. *Ibid.* C. 459 Blyþe of his wodbynde he balteres þer vnde[r]. *c* **1440** *Morte Arth.* (Roxb.) 66 He [the bear] baltyrde, he bleryde, He braundyschte thereafter. *a* **1500** *Colkelbie Sow* I. 302 (JAM.) Sum trottit.. Sum balterit. **1952** AUDEN *Nones* 39 The baltering torrent Shrunk to a soodling thread.
2. *trans.* (See quot.) *dial.*
1873 *Whitby Gloss.* (E.D.S.), *Bauter*, to tread in a clownish manner, as an ox does the grass.
3. *trans.* To tangle, 'mat' (the hair).
1693 W. ROBERTSON *Phraseol. Gen.* 216 To baulter one's hair, *complicare crines.* **1879** *Shropsh. Gloss.* (E.D.S.), *Bautered*, tangled, unkempt; said of hair.
4. *trans.* To clot or clog with anything sticky.
1601 HOLLAND *Pliny* XXIX. ii, Filthy excrements hanging to sheeps tailes.. baltered together into round pils or bals. [See BALTER *sb.*]
5. *intr.* (for *refl.*) To form tangled knots or clots, to stick together by coagulation.
1601 HOLLAND *Pliny* XII. xvii, It [a goat's beard] baltereth and cluttereth into knots and balls.

'balter, *sb. dial.* [f. prec. vb.] A clot, a coagulated lump.
Mod. Northampton dial. Batter is said to be baltered when the flour is not all mixed, but hangs together in small dry lumps which are called balters.

Balthazar (bæl'θæzə(r), 'bælθəˌzɑː(r)). Also **Balthasar, Belshazzar.** [So called in allusion to *Balthazar* (Belshazzar), 'king of Babylon', who 'made a great feast.. and drank wine before the thousand' (Daniel v. 1).] A very large wine-bottle (see quots.).
1935 A. L. SIMON *Dict. Wine* 22 *Balthasar*, a fancy name for a fancy bottle to hold some 16 ordinary bottles, or 12·80 litres, equal to about 2·75 gallons. **1959** *Gloss. Packaging Terms* (*B.S.I.*) 28 *Belshazzar*, a wine bottle—capacity 16 reputed quarts. **1962** *Times* 25 May 13/4 Methuselah.., Salmanasar, Balthasar, Nebuchadnezzar—'usually applied respectively to eight, twelve, sixteen, and twenty bottle containers'.

Baltic ('bɔːltɪk), *a.* and *sb.* [f. med.L. *Balticus*; cf. BALT.] **A.** *adj.* **1.** Of, pertaining to, designating or bordering upon an almost landlocked sea in N. Europe (Russ. *Baltiĭskoe Móre*), called by the neighbouring Germanic countries 'East Sea' (G. *Ostsee*, etc.); *spec.* of or belonging to the states of Lithuania, Latvia, and Estonia and their inhabitants.
c **1590** A. ASHLEY (*title*) The Second Part of the Mariners Mirrour.. with all the sounds of Denmark, & the Baltick sea. **1608** TOPSELL *Serpents* 236 There be also in the Sueuian-Ocean or Balthicke-sea, Serpents of thirty or forty foote in length. **1845** *Ainsworth's Mag.* VIII. 161 The failure of a long established Baltic house at Kingston upon Hull. **1920** *19th Cent.* Mar. 536 A policy aimed at the Balkanisation of the Baltic provinces. **1937** [see BALT *sb.* and *a.*].
2. Applied to a branch of the Indo-European languages comprising Lithuanian, Lettish, and Old Prussian, usu. classified with the Slavic group (see BALTO-).
1887 SKEAT *Princ. Eng. Etym.* vii. 102 Of the *Lettic* or *Baltic* group, the most interesting is the Lithuanian, spoken in parts of Eastern Prussia. **1888** [see LETTISH]. **1891** A. L. MAYHEW *O.E. Phonol.* p. xii, Baltic-Slavonic, including Old Prussian, Lithuanian, Lettish, and Old Bulgarian.
3. In specific combinations with sbs., as ***Baltic pine*** (see PINE *sb.*² 2); ***Baltic shield***, the Archæan platform of Finland and E. Scandinavia.
1866 Baltic pine [see PINE *sb.*² 2]. **1891** W. SCHLICH *Man. Forestry* II. iv. 290 The timber of the Spruce.. is known in Britian as white Baltic pine. **1906** B. C. SOLLAS tr. *Suess's Face of Earth* II. III. ii. 76 East of the glint lies the Archaean table-land of the gulf of Bothnia; that is, the Baltic shield.

B. *sb.* The Baltic Sea; the lands bordering upon it.
1720 *Phil. Trans.* Abr. VI. 498 Observations on the variations of the needle in the Baltic. **1776** GIBBON *Decl. & F.* (1782) I. ix. 272 Some tribes.. on the coast of the Baltic, acknowledged the authority of kings, though without relinquishing the rights of men. **1935** HUXLEY & HADDON *We Europeans* vii. 237 The 'Windmill Hill'.. type of pottery .. was brought from the Baltic by long-headed people who buried their dead in long barrows.

Baltimore ('bɔːltɪmɔə(r)). Also **Baltimore-bird, -oriole.** [See quot.; Lord Baltimore was formerly proprietor of Maryland.] A bird (*Icterus Baltimorii*) of the Starling family, found throughout North America.
1669 N. SHRIGLEY *True Rel. Virginia & Mary-land* 4 Fowle naturally to the Land are.. Redbirds, the Baltenore [*sic*] bird, being black and yellow, [etc.]. **1676** J. SPEED *Theatre of Empire* II. 44 That which is black and yellow is called the *Baltemore*-bird, from the colours of his Lordships Coat of Arms. **1730** MORTIMER in *Phil. Trans.* XXVI. 432 The Baltimore Bird hath its Name from being of the same Colour with Lord Baltimore's Coat of Arms. **1813** A. WILSON *Baltimore Bird* Wks. 279 The orange, black-capped Baltimore is seen. **1868** WOOD *Homes without H.* xiii. 239 The Baltimore Oriole.. coloured with orange and black in bold contrast.

Balto- ('bɔːltəʊ), comb. form of *Baltic*, as in ***Balto-Lithuanian***; **ˌBalto-'Slavic, -Sla'vonic** *a.* and *sb.*, the designation of the group of Indo-European languages which comprises the Baltic branch and the Slavonic branch (Russian, Polish, Czech, Serbian, Bulgarian, etc.).
1896 O. F. EMERSON *Brief Hist. Eng. Lang.* i. 8 The Balto-Slavic branch consists of two divisions. **1909** WEBSTER, Balto-Slavonic, adj. **1910** *Encycl. Brit.* XIV. 495/1 North of the Black Sea.. comes the great Balto-Slavonic group. *Ibid.* XVI. 246/1 The words *mentīri*, *rōs*, *ignis* have close equivalents in Balto-Slavonic. **1922** E. J. HARRISON *Lithuania* ii. 32 In 1654 the Old Prussians.. renounced their Balto-Lithuanian idiom in favour of German. **1948** D. DIRINGER *Alphabet* II. v. 347 The new language may hold an intermediate position between.. Balto-Slavonic and Greek.

Baluch (bə'luːtʃ), **Baluchi** (bə'luːtʃɪ), *sb.* and *a.* Also 7 **Bolloch, Balloch, Buluch, Boloch,** 8 **Ballowch,** 9 **Belooch(e, -ee, Bloach, Bilochee, Baloochi,** etc. [Pers. *Balūchī*.] **A.** *sb.* **1.** An inhabitant or native of Baluchistan, a region lying between the lower Indus and south-east Persia. **2.** The Iranian language of Baluchistan. **B.** *adj.* Of or pertaining to this people or their language.
1616 T. ROE *Let.* 27 Nov. (1899) II. 353 Subiect to the robberyes of the Baloochs. **1617** PURCHAS *Pilgrimage* (ed. 3) 550 The Persian Gulfe hath beene awed, and the Arabike or Red Sea tamed, in requitall of the Turkes and Buluches Trecheries. **1619** in W. Foster *Eng. Factories India* (1906) 84 [They blame the] 'Bolloches' [for the disaster]. **1727** A. HAMILTON *New Acc. E. Indies* I. 107 They were lodged in a Caravanseray, where the Ballowches came with about 300 to attack them. **1816** H. POTTINGER *Trav. Beloochistan* 53 The Belooches, who form.. the whole of the population throughout Beloochistan, are a people whose origin is so obscure [etc.]. **1848** L. R. STACY *Narr. Beloochistan & Affghanistan* 72 The Brahooe and Belooche tribes. **1875** R. CALDWELL *Languages of India* 4 The languages spoken on the further side of the Indian frontier, such as Belūchi, on the north-west. **1875** *Encycl. Brit.* III. 300/1 (*Baluchistan*) The country derives its name from the Baluches, but the Brahoes are considered the dominant race. **1882** FLOYER *Unexpl. Baluchistan* 158 One tribe of Balūchis will 'chapao', or plunder, another tribe directly they get a chance. **1885** *Encycl. Brit.* XVIII. 655/2 Baluch, the language of Baluchistan.. very closely akin to New Persian. **1886** *Ibid.* XX. 109/2 Baluchi is spoken on the same frontier, farther south, adjacent to Baluchistan. **1920** *Blackw. Mag.* Aug. 185/2 He spoke only Baluchi and indifferent Persian. **1925** *Ibid.* Apr. 490/2 He knew exactly the line of conduct which would most effectively appeal to the Baluch nature.

baluchitherium (bəluːtʃɪ'θɪərɪəm). *Palæont.* [mod.L., f. prec. + Gr. *θηρίον* beast.] A gigantic extinct land mammal of which remains have been found in the upper Oligocene deposits of the Bugti hills of Baluchistan.
1913 C. FORSTER-COOPER in *Ann. & Mag. Nat. Hist.* XII. 504, I learn that the generic name *Thaumastotherium* proposed.. is preoccupied. The generic name *Baluchitherium* is therefore proposed as a substitute. **1925** *Chambers's Jrnl.* 217/2 It was a baluchitherium, the greatest of all varieties of rhinoceros. It stood thirteen feet at the shoulder, and its neck, relatively as long as a horse's, gave it an additional reach of four or five feet. **1966** C. A. W. GUGGISBERG *S.O.S. Rhino* ii. 26 With a length of twenty-eight feet and standing seventeen to eighteen feet at the shoulder, Baluchitherium equalled or exceeded the imperial mammoth.

baluster ('bæləstə(r)). Forms: 7- **baluster**; also 7 **ballester, 7-8 balluster, -aster, -ister, balister.** See also BANISTER. [a. F. *balustre* masc. 'baluster,' 16th c. ad. It. *balaustro* in same sense; so named from It. *balausta*, *balaustra* (F. *balauste*, *balustre* fem., in Cotgrave 1611), in Florio *balausto* 'the blossom of the wild pomegranate' (L. *balaustium*, a. Gr. *βαλαύστιον* in same sense), on account of the resemblance of a baluster to the double-curving calyx-tube of this flower. In English, corrupted already in 17th c. to *barrester*, *-ister*, *bannister*, BANISTER, which last is now, in sense 3, the prevailing form.]

1. a. A short pillar or column, of circular section, and curving outline (properly, double-curved), slender above and swelling below into an elliptical or pear-shaped bulge; usually applied in a series called a *balustrade*.

1602 CAREW *Cornwall* 107 a, Planched ouer and rayled about with ballisters. **1611** COTGR., *Balustres*, Ballisters; little, round, and short pillars, ranked on the outside of Cloisters, Terraces, Galleries, etc. **1697** *C'tess D'Aunoy's Trav. Spain* (1706) 125 Her Bed-Head was adorned with four Rows of little Copper Ballisters. **1716–8** LADY MONTAGUE *Lett.* 37 I. 153 Marble galleries..with marble balusters. **1879** SIR G. SCOTT *Lect. Archit.* II. 37 What are called baluster columns, or short pillars, turned in a lathe, not unlike Elizabethan balusters, bulging in the middle.

b. A similar pillar used in a window.

1844 F. PALEY *Ch. Restorers* 5 Belfry windows, each of two lights, separated by a baluster shaft. **1861** PARKER *Goth. Archit.* (1874) 319 *Baluster*, in windows, a small pillar swelling in the middle.

2. A slender upright post or pillar of any shape supporting a rail; in *pl.* a railing or balustrade.

1663 *Flagellum or O. Cromwell* (1672) 189 Environed with Rails and Ballasters four square covered with Velvet. **1682** WHELER *Journ. Greece* II. 204 An Area..with Balusters or Rails about it. **1725** tr. *Dupin's Eccl. Hist. 17th c.* I. v. 101 The Sanctuary was a Place in the Choir..separated by Balusters. **1787** BECKFORD *Italy* (1834) II. 326 Enriched with balusters of rich bronze.

3. (Usually in *pl.*) The upright posts or rails which support the handrail, and guard the side, of a staircase; often applied to the whole structure of uprights and handrail. Now more usually BANISTER(S, q.v.

1753 *World* 22 Nov., The Bedlamites leap'd over the Balisters of the Staircase. **1823** P. NICHOLSON *Pract. Build.* 200 Balusters are vertical pieces fixed on the steps for supporting the hand-rail. **1853** *Ch. Auchester* I. 42 A staircase..of a rich brown colour..so also were the balusters.

4. *collect. sing.* A balustrade, or protective railing. *arch.*

1644 EVELYN *Mem.* (1857) I. 67 A border of freestone.. with a rail and baluster of pure white marble. **1670** LASSELS *Voy. Italy* II. 29 A continual baluster, or row of rayles. *a* **1720** SHEFFIELD (Dk. Buckhm.) *Wks.* (1753) II. 221 These stairs..are so very easy, there is no need of leaning on the iron balluster. **1756** NUGENT *Gr. Tour* I. 116 The choir is separated from the body of the church by a ballister.

5. *Class. Arch.* 'The lateral part of the volute of an Ionic capital.' Gwilt.

6. *attrib.* and *Comb.*: ***baluster column*** or ***shaft*** (see quot. 1853); ***baluster-rail***. Esp. in sense 'having the shape of a baluster', as ***baluster handle, jug, pitcher, stem, vase***; so ***baluster-shaped*** adj.

1844 Baluster shaft [see BALUSTER 1 b]. **1853** *Archit. Publ. Soc. Dict.*, *Baluster column*, the name given to a pillar used in the so-called Saxon architecture of England for a divisional support in windows. **1871** FRANKS *Catal. Slade Coll. Glass* 120 Goblet, with a..baluster stem. **1878** W. J. CRIPPS *O. Eng. Plate* x. 292 The foot is much like those of earlier cups, but the stem is different, being formed as acanthus or other leaves, the upper part of it baluster-shaped. **1906** *Daily Chron.* 28 Sept. 7/5 Going downstairs, his brother wrenched a baluster-rail out of the staircase. **1912** *Eng. Hist. Rev.* Oct. 832 A rather early baluster-stem cup. **1933** *Burlington Mag.* July 36/2 A baluster vase.. illustrates in its lotus design the type with ornament painted in outline. **1938** *Oxoniensia* III. 11 The so-called 'baluster' pitchers from London, Oxford or York. **1939** *Ibid.* IV. 122 The baluster jug from Well 9..supplies a clue to the upper limit of the group. **1956** G. TAYLOR *Silver* vii. 149 Saucepans..with everted lips, and a turned wooden baluster handle.

'balustered, *ppl. a.* Also 7 ballis-, balustred. [f. prec. + -ED².] Furnished with, or enclosed by, balusters.

1644 EVELYN *Mem.* (1819) I. 45 The upper terrace..with double declivities, arched and baluster'd. **1655** F. G. *Scudery's Artamenes* VIII. II. 106 We passed through a long ascent rayled and ballistred. **1691** WOOD *Ath. Oxon.* I./859 A black Marble ballastred.

balustrade (ˌbælə'streɪd). [a. F. *balustrade*, f. *balustre* BALUSTER, after It. *balaustrata*, Sp. *balaustrada*.] A row of balusters, surmounted by a rail or coping, forming an ornamental parapet or barrier along the edge of a terrace, balcony, etc.

1644 EVELYN *Mem.* (1857) I. 96 A terrace at each side having rustic uncut balustrades. **1749** LADY MONTAGUE *Lett.* 48 III. 82 The magnificent bath..circled by a marble balustrade. **1820** KEATS *St. Agnes* xxii, Her faltering hand upon the balustrade, Old Angela was feeling for the stair. **1870** F. WILSON *Ch. Lindisf.* 102 The altar rail is a turned balustrade.

fig. **1829** SCOTT *Anne of G.* ii, 'My arm,' she said, 'is but a slight balustrade.'

balustraded (ˌbælə'streɪdɪd), *ppl. a.* Also 8 -ated. [f. prec. + -ED².] Furnished with a balustrade.

1774 PENNANT *Tour Scot.* 1 Galleries..open and balustrated in front. **1876** BLACKMORE *Cripps* II. viii. 130 The balustraded gallery.

ˌbalu'strading. [f. as prec. + -ING¹; cf. *railing*.] Balustrade-work.

1880 L. WALLACE *Ben-hur* IV. v, The lines of division were guarded by low balustrading, broken by massive pedestals.

baly(e, balyf(e, -yve, obs. forms of BAILEY, BAILIE, BAILIFF.

balyngar, obs. form of BALINGER.

balza, variant of BALSA.

Balzacian (bæl'zækɪən), *a.* and *sb.* [f. the name of the French novelist H. de *Balzac* (1799–1850) + -IAN.] **A.** *adj.* Of or pertaining to or characteristic of Balzac or his style.

1874 GEO. ELIOT *Let.* 16 June (1956) VI. 57 The Balzacian view of Paris. **1892** W. JAMES *Let.* 11 Apr. (1920) I. 318 He is a real Balzackian figure—a regular porker, coarse, vulgar, vain, cunning, mendacious. **1927** *Observer* 1 May 6 There might seem a Balzacian pathos about it. **1958** *Spectator* 4 July 33/1 Balzacian characters set against a Boudin coast-scape.

B. *sb.* An authority on or student of the writings of Balzac.

1905 *Daily Chron.* 10 May 3/3 Mr. Helm is a discriminating Balzacian. **1923** A. HUXLEY *On Margin* xviii. 131 Balzacians will remember the advertisements composed by Finot and the Illustrious Gaudissard.

‖**balzan.** *Obs.* [Fr.; cf. BAUSON.] (See quot.)

1660 HOWELL *Dict.*, Balzan, or a horse that hath four white feet, [It.] *cavallo balzano*, [Fr.] *cheval balzan*.

balzarine ('bælzəˌriːn). A light dress-fabric of mixed cotton and wool.

1849 *The Trelawny* (Jamaica) 24 Apr. 1/2 Muslin De' Laines and Balzareens. **1854** *Chambers's Jrnl.* II. 50 Four matrons in balzarine. **1927** E. SITWELL *Rustic Elegies* 78 The Amazons wear balzarine of jonquille.

bam (bæm), *v. slang.* Also 8 **bamb.** [Of the same age as BAMBOOZLE, of which it appears to be either an abbreviation (cf. the *Tatler* No. 230 on *phizz., hipps., mobb., pozz., rep.*, 'and many more' 'Refinements of Twenty Years past'), or else the source of its first syllable.]

trans. To hoax, practise on the credulity of, deceive, impose upon, cozen.

1738 SWIFT *Polite Conv.* i. Wks. (1755) XI. 214 Her ladyship was plaguily bamb'd. **1747** GARRICK *Miss in Teens* II. i, I'll break a lamp, bully a constable, bam a justice, or bilk a box-keeper, with any man. *a* **1777** FOOTE (in Webster), Some conspiracy..to bam, to chouse me out of my money. **1830** MARRYAT *King's Own* xlix, Now you're bamming me —don't attempt to put such stories off on your old granny.

b. *absol.* or *intr.* To hoax, impose upon the credulous.

1707 CIBBER *Double Gallant* I. ii. (1736) 19 'Pray, Sir, what is't you do understand?' *Sound.* 'Bite, Bam, and the best of the Lay, old Boy.' **1825** R. WARD *Tremaine* III. xxi. 379, I should say Rector was bamming. **1859** G. MASSEY in *Sat. Rev.* 5 Mar., Our greatest of men is Harlequin Pam, 'The Times' says so, and 'the Times' cannot bam!

bam, *sb. slang.* [f. prec. vb.] A story intended to impose upon the credulous; a hoax or imposition.

1728 *Life & Char. Harvey the Conjuror* 21 He called the Profession of a Doctorship, in Physic, a *Bamm*, upon the World, which is a *Bite*, in modern Language. **1762** FOOTE *Orators* I. i, He is all upon his fun; he lecture! why, 'tis all but a bam. **1815** SCOTT *Guy M.* iii, Humble efforts at jocularity chiefly confined to what were then called bites and bams, since denominated hoaxes and quizzes.

bam (bæm), *int.* [Echoic.] An interjection imitating the sound of a hard blow.

1922 JOYCE *Ulysses* 109 Bam! expires. Gone at last. **1962** *Spectator* 25 May 674/2 Think of the United States as a 3,000-mile-broad comic strip where significant occasions go bam, pop and zowie.

‖**bambino** (bam'bino). [It., dim. of *bambo* silly; the same root is found in L. *bambalio* dolt, blockhead, Gr. βαμβαίνειν, βαμβαλίζειν to stammer.] A child, a baby; *spec.* an image of the infant Jesus in swaddling-clothes, exhibited at Christmas in churches in Italy.

1761 STERNE *Tr. Shandy* (1802) III. xiv. 302 When a state-orator has..hid his bambino in his mantle so cunningly. **1863** GEO. ELIOT *Romola* xxxiii, I'll bring you some breakfast, and show you the bambino. **1866** HOWELLS *Venet. Life* xvii. 258 A hideous Bambino, and a Madonna in crinoline.

bambocciade. Also **bambochade.** [ad. F. *bambochade*, It. *bambocciata*, f. *bamboccio* child, simpleton, puppet (f. *bambo*, see prec.), given as nickname to the painter Peter de Laer.] A painting of rustic and grotesque scenes, especially from low life.

1816 M. BRYAN *Biog. & Crit. Dict. Painters* I. 317 He quitted historical subjects to paint bambochades. **1868** in CHAMBERS *Encycl.*

bamboo (bæm'buː), *sb.* Forms: 6 bambus, 6–7 bambo (? -os), 7 pambou, bambou, bambouse, bambow, 7–8 bamboe, 7–9 bambu, 8– bamboo. [Original source doubtful: now in Malay (Central Sumatra), Sundanese, and Javanese (W. and Central Java) *bambu*; but some consider it an introduced word there, and take the original to be Canarese *bănbŭ* or *banwu*. The native word in the Concan, in 16th c., was represented by the Portuguese as *mambu*, still found after 1600. Cf. Du. *bamboes* (= -ūs), G. *bambus*, Fr. *bambou*, It., Sp. and Pg. *bambu*, mod.L. *bambūsa*; the forms *bambus, -bous, -bouse*, come through Du., which seems to have been the European lang. in which the word first appeared with initial *b*; the final *s* in Du., etc. is not explained.]

1. a. A genus of giant-grasses (genus *Bambusa*), numerous species of which are common throughout the tropics. Also the stem of any of these used as a stick, or as material.

[**1563** GARCIA DE ORTA *Simples e Drogues* 194 Aquellas canas daquella arvore chamam os Indios, onde nasce, *mambu*. (The canes of that tree the Indians where it grows call *mambu*.)] **1598** W. PHILLIPS *Linschoten's Trav. Ind.* (1864) 174 A thicke Reed, as big as a mans legge, which is called *Bambus*. **1599** HAKLUYT *Voy.* II. I. 258 The houses are made of Canes which they call Bambos. **1662** GERBIER *Princ.* 3 Bambouses, as they call the Poles to which they tye a Woollen Hammac to lye in. **1671** *Phil. Trans.* VI. 3010 Very artificial boats..made of large Canes, called Bambu. **1681** R. KNOX *Hist. Ceylon* 37 The ends of the Bambou..are largely tipped with silver. **1687** A. LOVELL *Thevenot's Trav.* III. I. xxxi. 54 The pambous that serve for palanquins. **1697** DAMPIER *Voy.* (1729) III. I. 324 Bamboes grow here but too plentifully. **1748** ANSON *Voy.* III. v. 341 Mast, yard, boom and outriggers, are all made of bamboo. *a* **1826** HEBER *Even. Walk Bengal*, Beneath the bamboo's arched bough. **1872** OLIVER *Elem. Bot.* II. 281 The light, hollow, jointed stems of the Bamboo. [**1884** *Athenæum* 26 Apr. 539/1 The palms and bambusas of a sub-tropical garden.]

b. Cane-coloured porcelain biscuit, invented by Wedgwood. Also ***bamboo ware***.

1787 JOS. WEDGWOOD in L. Jewitt *Wedgwoods* (1865) 310 *Bamboo*, or cane-coloured bisqué porcelain, of the same nature with the porcelain No. 3 [*i.e.* a fine white biscuit ware]. **1865** L. JEWITT *Wedgwoods* 410 An open basket of bamboo. **1904** W. BURTON *Hist. Eng. Earthenware* 162 The simple patterns of lines and foliage in blue and green enamel which he [*sc.* Elijah Mayer] used on his bamboo wares.

2. *attrib.*, as ***bamboo cane, reed***; esp. when used as a material, as ***bamboo-basket, -book, -cane***; also parasynthetic deriv., as ***bamboo-coloured, -walled***. **bamboo-coolie**, one that carries loads suspended on bamboos; **bamboo curtain** [after IRON CURTAIN; cf. CHICK *sb.*²], a political and economic 'curtain' or barrier between territories under the control of the Communist régime in China and non-Communist countries; also *transf.*; **bamboo fern**, a fern, *Coniogramme japonica*, native to Japan; **bamboo-fish** *S. Afr.*, the sea-fish *Sarpa salpa* (family Sparidæ); also called (*striped*) KARANTEEN; **bamboo-grass**, bamboo, or a grass that resembles it; **bamboo joint**, an internode of bamboo (with its nodes) cut and fashioned into a vessel for carrying water, cooking rice, etc.; **bamboo palm** (see quot. 1891); **bamboo rat**, a rodent belonging to the genus *Rhizomys*, found in Malacca; **bamboo shoot**, a young, edible shoot of the bamboo; **bamboo ware** (see 1 b above).

1877 TIELE *Hist. Relig.* 36 The Bamboo-books supply many details about him. **1685** *Lond. Gaz.* No. 2099/4 A small Bambow Cane, with a black Head. **1737** G. SMITH *Cur. Relat.* I. iii. 390 A Bamboe Cane, which was about 18 or 20 Foot long. **1800** WELLINGTON in Gurw. *Disp.* I. 79 Carriage for the tents [will not be required] excepting a few bamboo coolies. **1949** *Time* 14 Mar. 55 The Communist bosses of Peiping dropped a bamboo curtain, cutting off Peiping from the world. **1955** *Sc. Jrnl. Theol.* VIII. 422 'One Body in Christ' is written by a man who stands on the Reformed side of the theological bamboo curtain. **1957** *Listener* 6 June 903/2 We can't keep 400,000,000 people behind an economic bamboo curtain for ever. **1930** L. H. & E. Z. BAILEY *Hortus* 170/2 Coniogramme..japonica (*Gymnogramma japonica*). Bamboo-Fern..Japan, Formosa. **1913** W. W. THOMPSON *Sea Fisheries Cape Col.* ii. 61 The pretty little bamboo-fish of the Cape is also known as stink-fish, and is the mooi nooitje of Hermanus and Struys Bay, the streepje of the Knysna and the silver karanteen of Natal. **1930** Bamboo-fish [see KARANTEEN]. **1862** MAYHEW *Crim. Prisons* 62 The player on the bamboo-flute. **1909** *Cent. Dict.* Suppl., Bamboo-grass. **1920** *Blackw. Mag.* June 822/1 Coarse bamboo-grass began to fringe the banks. **1924** M. L. MILNE *Home of Eastern Clan* iii. 47 Water is carried in large bamboo joints. These are pierced near the top, a string is passed through the holes, and the joints are hung on one end of a pole, which rests on the shoulders. **1866** Bamboo palm [see PALM *sb.*¹ 1 c]. **1891** *Kew Bulletin* Jan. 3 The 'Bamboo' palm, or *Raphia vinifera*, is perhaps the commonest tree in the swamps [of Lagos]. **1881** R. HUNTER et al. *Encycl. Dict.*, *Bamboo-rat*, a rodent mammal belonging to Gray's genus Rhizomys. **1914** *Brit. Mus. Return* 135 An Ashy Bamboo Rat (*Rhizomys canescens*) from the Shan States. **1796** STEDMAN *Surinam.* I. ix. Another followed behind with a bamboo-rattan. **1737** G. SMITH *Cur. Relat.* I. i. 66 Twisted together with Bambo's Reeds. **1858** W. ELLIS *Vis. Madagascar* iv. 108 Low cane or bamboo-walled cottages. **1889** KIPLING *From Sea to Sea* (1899) I. xi. 303 After the bamboo-shoots came..white beans in sweet sauce. **1940** A. SIMON *Conc. Encycl. Gastron.* II. 55/2, 1 small tin bamboo shoots.

bam'boo, *v.* [f. prec. sb.] **1.** To beat or 'cane' with a bamboo. Hence **bam'booing** *vbl. sb.*

1816 'QUIZ' *Grand Master* VIII. 213 Or else they wou'd Get most confoundedly bamboo'd. **1818** J. M'LEOD *Voy. Alceste* ii. (1820) 42 One [Chinese] pickpocket.. received a very severe bambooing. *a* **1845** SYD. SMITH quoted in *Non-conf.* V. 266 Wellington bamboos his followers, and Peel bamboozles them.

2. *trans.* To furnish with bamboo or bamboo laths.

1925 *Blackw. Mag.* Apr. 537/2 The roof was bambooed and ready to be thatched.

bamboos (bæm'bu:s). *S. Afr.* Also **-ous**. [ad. Du. *bamboes* BAMBOO.] A wooden vessel for milk, water, etc. Cf. *bamboo joint* s.v. BAMBOO *sb.* 2.

1822 J. CAMPBELL *Trav. S. Africa* I. iii. 46 They brought us three bambooses... A bamboos is a deep wooden vessel ..cut out of a block of wood. **1842** R. MOFFAT *Missionary Labours S. Africa* x. 144 A kind housewife would hang a bamboos, or wooden vessel filled with milk..near my head. **1844** J. BACKHOUSE *Narr. Visit Mauritius & S. Afr.* 565 Bambouses..are a sort of jars made of willow-wood.

bamboozle (bæm'bu:z(ə)l), *v.* Also 8 bambouzle. [Appears about 1700; mentioned in the *Tatler* No. 230 (on 'the continual Corruption of our English Tongue') among other slang terms (*banter*, *put*, *kidney*, *sham*, *mob*, *bubble*, *bully*, etc.) recently invented or brought into vogue. Prob. therefore of cant origin; the statement that it is a Gipsy word wants proof. Cf. the similar *bom-*, *bumbaze*, in Sc. writers since *c* 1725, and BAM.]

1. *trans.* To deceive by trickery, hoax, cozen, impose upon.

1703 CIBBER *She wou'd, etc.* II. i. (1736) 34 Sham Proofs, that they propos'd to bamboozle me with. **1710** SWIFT *Tatler* No. 230 ¶7 Certain Words invented by some pretty Fellows, such as Banter, Bamboozle, Country Put..some of which are now struggling for the vogue. **1847** BARHAM *St. Cuthb.* in *Ingol. Leg.* (1877) 217 It's supposed by this trick he bamboozled Old Nick.

b. *absol.* or *intr.* To practise trickery.

1703 CIBBER *She wou'd, etc.* IV. i, The old Rogue..knows how to Bamboozle. **1866** G. MACDONALD *Ann. Q. Neighb.* ix. 143 You wouldn't even bamboozle a little at a bazaar.

2. To mystify, perplex, confound.

1712 ARBUTHNOT *John Bull* (1755) 89 After Nic. had bambouzled John a while about the 18,000 and the 28,000. **1854** MRS. GASKELL *North & S.* xl, He fairly bamboozles me. He is two chaps.

3. *to bamboozle away*: to get rid of by bamboozling. *to bamboozle into*: to persuade to a belief or course of action by bamboozling. *to bamboozle out of*: to take away (something) trickily from (a person). Cf. ARGUE *v.* 8, 9.

1716 ROWE *Biter* I. i. 19 You intend to bambouzle me out of a Beef Stake. **1728** EARBERY tr. *Burnet's St. Dead* I. 89 The Gnosticks bambouzled away all the Corporeal resurrection. **1878** BLACK *Green Past.* xli. 326 Who has bamboozled himself into the erroneous belief that, etc.

bam'boozle, *sb.* [f. prec.] Bamboozling.

1703 CIBBER *She wou'd, etc.* IV. i. (1736) 53 I'll have a touch of the Bamboozle with him. **1861** *Sat. Rev.* 16 Feb. 6/2 Government by bamboozle always presents considerable advantages at first sight.

bam'boozled, *ppl. a.* [f. prec. vb. + -ED.] Deceived or mystified by trickery, hoaxed, cozened.

1866 *Sixpenny Mag.* Jan. 372/2 His daughter..fled back to her bamboozled parent.

bamboozlement (bæm'bu:z(ə)lmənt). [f. as prec. + -MENT.] The action or process of bamboozling; tricky deception or mystification.

1855 *Scot. Rev.* 188 Washington Irving..exercises..his rare powers of bamboozlement and laughter-stirring. **1865** *Morn. Star* 19 June, Attempting our bamboozlement when the facts are patent to everybody.

bamboozler (bæm'bu:zlə(r)). [f. as prec. + -ER[1].] One who hoaxes or mystifies by trickery.

1712 ARBUTHNOT *John Bull* (1755) 58 Fellows, they call banterers and bamboozlers, that play such tricks.

bam'boozling, *vbl. sb.* = BAMBOOZLEMENT.

1709 STEELE *Tatler* No. 31 ¶7 Sir, I perceive this is to you all *bamboozling*..All this good language was lost upon him. **1812** J. & H. SMITH *Reject. Addr.* v. (1873) 35 The dramatic bamboozling they have hitherto laboured under.

bambosh. *slang.* [App. f. BAM + BOSH.] Deceptive humbug.

1865 *Day of Rest* Oct. 585 I was deaf to all that bambosh.

bamboula (bæm'bu:lə). [Creole Fr.] (See quot. 1938.)

1883 *Cent. Mag.* Nov. 45/2 In New Orleans..a minute's walk..will bring you to Congo square..where the negro slaves once held their bamboulas. *Ibid.*, Every Sunday afternoon the bamboula dancers were summoned to a wood-yard. **1938** *Oxf. Compan. Mus.* 73/1 *Bamboula*, (1) a primitive negro tambourine, formerly in use in Louisiana and still in use in the West Indies. (2) A dance to which this instrument is the accompaniment. **1956** M. STEARNS *Story of Jazz* (1957) iii. 26 The Congo, as such, is no longer danced in New Orleans, but it is still danced in Haiti, along with the Bamboula.

bambusa: see BAMBOO.

bame, obs. form of BALM.

ban (bæn), *v.* Forms: 1 banna-n, bonna-n, 3 banni-en, bonni-en, banni, 3–5 banne-n, -yn, 3–7 banne, 4–5 bann, (6 bawn), 4– ban. Inflexions: see below. [OE. *bannan*, pa. t. *béonn*, pa. pple. *bannen*, to summon (also *abannan* and *ȝebannan* to proclaim, summon) = OFris. *banna*, *bonna* (pa. t. *bén*, *bante*) to proclaim, command, OHG. *bannan*, MHG. and MDu. *bannen*, ON. *banna* (pa. t. *bannaða*) to prohibit, interdict, curse, Sw. *banna* to reprove, chide, *bannas* to curse, Da. *bande* to curse, execrate:—OTeut. **bannan* 'to proclaim under penalty, or with a threat,' perhaps orig. merely 'to proclaim, publicly announce', f. root *ba-*, cogn. w. Gr. φα-, L. *fa-*, speak. In OE. (as in OHG., OS., and MHG.) a strong verb; but with weak pa. t. and pple. *banned*, already in Layamon. Sense 1 is from OE.; the other senses, first in north. dial., are probably from ON. Cf. BAN *sb.*, which may also have re-acted on the verb.]

I. To summon. [from OE].

†**1. a.** *trans.* To summon by proclamation. (Chiefly, in early use, to arms.) *Obs.*

a **1000** CYNEWULF *Riddles* ii. in Sweet *Reader* 180 Hwílum ic to hilde hléoðre bonne wilȝehléðan. **1048** *O.E. Chron.*, Hét se cyning bannan út here. **1205** LAY. 8054 Þe king lette blawen & bonnien [**1250** banni] his ferden. *c* **1250** *Gen. & Ex.* 3213 Pharaon bannede vt his here. *c* **1380** *Sir Ferumb.* 5424 Aȝen ys broþer wende he faste..Wiþ oþre þat he gan banne.

†**b.** To call forth, call for (things). *Obs.*

1205 LAY. 22288 Heo ruokeden burnen, bonneden helmes. *Ibid.* 27132 Summe bonneden wepnen. *c* **1325** *E.E. Allit. P.* B. 629, I shall..brynge a morsel of bred to banne your herte.

II. To curse, anathematize, interdict. [from ON., ? and med.L. *bannum*.]

2. a. To curse, imprecate damnation upon. *arch.*

a **1275** *Prov. Alfred* 441 in *O.E. Misc.* 129 He sal banne þat wiȝt þat him first taȝte. **1375** BARBOUR *Bruce* xv. 536 Quhen wiffis vald thar childir ban, Thai wald..Beteche thame to the blak dowglass. **1460** *Pol. Rel. & L. Poems* 180 And some men ban the, & some men blesse. *a* **1555** LATIMER *Serm. & Rem.* (1845) 302 They will curse and ban..even into the deep pit of hell, all that gainsay their appetite. **1607** HEYWOOD *Fayre Mayde* Wks. II. 72 Banne my starres. **1621** QUARLES *Div. Poems, Esther* xvii, Another bannes the night his sonnes were borne. **1718** MOTTEUX *Quix.* (1733) I. 165 Sancho..bann'd his Master to the bottomless Pit. **1827** HOOD *Hero & L.* xxi, And bans his labour like a hopeless slave. **1868** MORRIS *Jason* II. 110 Ever she blessed the old and banned the new.

†**b.** with *subord. cl. Obs.*

c **1350** *Will. Palerne* 1644, I may banne þat I was born. **1393** GOWER *Conf.* II. 96, I curse and banne That ever slepe was made for eye. **1557** Tottell's *Misc.* (Arb.) 191 And now they banne that they were borne.

3. *intr.* To curse, utter curses. *arch.*

a **1300** *Cursor M.* 12050 To teche him..not to bann. **1583** STUBBES *Anat. Abus.* 72 Then fell she to sweare..and banne. **1609** DAVIES in Farr's *S.P.* (1848) 183 Like a fiend, he banned with his breath. **1673** SHADWELL *Epsom Wells* II. Wks. 1720 II. 221 Ay, now you ban and curse, you wretch. **1762** CHURCHILL *Ghost* II. Poems I. 209 Then shall He ban at Heaven's decrees. **1820** BYRON *Morg. Mag.* xxxv, Yet harsh and haughty, as he lay he bann'd.

4. *trans.* and *absol.* To chide, address with angry and maledictory language. *dial.*

1340 HAMPOLE *Pr. Consc.* 3485 When þou bannes any man, In wham þou fyndes na gilt to ban. *c* **1400** *Destr. Troy* XII. 4935 Neuer buerne will vs blame, ne ban for our dede. **1577** tr. *Bullinger's Decades* (1592) 132 Bitter speeches, wherewith we vse to curse and ban our neighbors. **1794** in Burns *Wks.* IV. 176 Even though she bans and scaulds a wee. **1816** SCOTT *Antiq.* xxvi, And scauld and ban wi' ilka wife that will scauld and ban wi' her.

5. To pronounce an ecclesiastical curse upon, to anathematize. *arch.*

1303 R. BRUNNE *Handl. Synne* 9176 Þe prest hem bannede. *c* **1400** *Apol. Loll.* 26 Þei..bannun him, or puttun him out of comyn, or haldun him cursid. **1470** HARDING *Chron.* lxxxvii, The Church also may banne full sore those striues. **1483** *Cath. Angl.* 20 Banne, *annathematizare*. **1814** SCOTT *Ld. Isles* II. xxviii, Bans all who aid thee in the strife. **1874** HOLLAND *Mistr. Manse* ix. 155 As rose the priest With power to bless and right to ban.

6. To interdict, proscribe, prohibit: **a.** a thing.

1816 BYRON *Pris. Chillon* i, To whom the goodly earth and air Are bann'd and barr'd. **1832** LYTTON *Eug. Aram* v. vii, The sublime and shaded mysteries that are banned mortality. **1865** LECKY *Ration.* (1878) II. 41 The religion of the immense majority..was banned and proscribed.

b. a person.

1848 KINGSLEY *Saint's Trag.* III. ii. 185 No foe Can ban us from that rest. **1863** W. STORY *Roba di Roma* xv. 320 He banned them from the city. **1874** BLACKIE *Self-Cult.* 86 You may..ban yourself from voluntarily marching into it.

7. *ban the bomb*: the slogan of those advocating nuclear disarmament, used (with hyphens) as attrib. phr.

1960 *News Chron.* 22 Apr. 6/3 The ban-the-bomb campaigners are well advanced with their arrangements to make a new challenge.

ban (bæn), *sb.*[1] Forms: 3– ban; 3–7 **banne**, 4–6 **bane**, 9 **bann**. [Partly a. OF. *ban*, with influence of med.L. *bannum*; partly from BAN *v.* Ultimately all these go back to the same source; F. *ban* 'proclamation, publication, summons, proscription, outlawry, banishment, assemblage of military vassals' was:—late L. *bannum*, ad. Teut. (OHG., MHG., OS., OFris., MDu.) *bann*, *ban*, sb. 'proclamation commanding or forbidding under threat or penalty,' f. *bann-an* to BAN. The simple sb. *bann* does not appear in OE., which had however *ȝebann*, rare ME. IBAN 'proclamation, edict, f. the deriv. *ȝebannan*. The ON. *bann* 'excommunication, interdict, prohibition, curse,' seems too late to have been the source of the Eng. But, as OE. had the vb. *bannan*, *ban* from OF. easily assumed the position of its vbl. sb., and the two words, with the med.L. *bannum*, *-us*, in its various legal and ecclesiastical uses, subseq. re-acted upon each other, so that the development of sense is complicated.]

I. Authoritative proclamation, and attached senses, from Fr.

1. A public proclamation or edict; a summons by public proclamation. Chiefly, in early use, a summons to arms.

1297 R. GLOUC. 188 Þer come to þys rounde table, as he sende ys ban, Aunsel kyng of Scotlond, and al so Vryan. *c* **1325** *E.E. Allit. P.* B. 1361 Baltazar þurȝ Babiloyn his banne gart crye. *c* **1350** *Will. Palerne* 2252 Þe bane is so maked. *a* **1400** in *Eng. Gilds.* 359 To w[h]eche selynge lat crye þe ban þorghe þe town. *c* **1450** LONELICH *Grail* lii. 761 That ȝe a bane dyde crye thorwh-owt ȝoure lond..Atte the brigge to iusten with a knyht. [**1641** *Termes de la Ley* 37 b, Bans is common and ordinary amongst the Feudists, and signifies a proclamation, or any publike notice.]

‖**2. a.** In feudal usage: The gathering of the (French) king's vassals for war; the whole body of vassals so assembled, or liable to be summoned; originally, the same as *arrière-ban*: in the 16th c., French usage created a distinction between *ban* and *arrière-ban*, for which see the latter word.

b. In actual use: In the French military system, the *ban* is the younger and more effective part of the population liable to serve in the militia or national guard, the *arrière-ban* the reserve, consisting of the older citizens; in the Prussian system, the first and second *bans* are the two divisions of the Landwehr.

a. *a* **1250** *Owl & Night.* 390 Ich folȝi than aȝte manne, An flo bi niȝt in hore banne. **1591** UNTON *Corr.* (1847) 54 He hath sente abroad to assemble his van and arriere van. **1671** CROWNE *Juliana* I. 8 The Ban and the Arrierban are met arm'd in the field to choose a king. **1683** TEMPLE *Mem.* Wks. 1731 I. 392 France was at such a Pinch..that they call'd their Ban and Arriere Ban, the assembling whereof had been long disus'd, and in a manner antiquated. **1818** HALLAM *Mid. Ages* II. ii, The ban was sometimes convoked, that is, the possessors of the fiefs were called upon for military services. **1874** BOUTELL *Arms & Arm.* vii. 98 The act of calling together the vassals in armed array, was entitled 'convoking the ban.'

b. 1813 *Examiner* 18 Jan. 38/1 The 100 cohorts of the first Ban of the National Guards. **1866** *Cornh. Mag.* Nov. 555 The term of service [in Prussian Army] was fixed at twenty years, three of which were to be passed in the ranks of the regular army, two in the reserve, eight in the Land-wehr of the first ban, and seven in that of the second ban.

‖**3.** Sentence of banishment; whence 'to keep,' or 'break his ban.' (A Gallicism.)

1873 BURTON *Hist. Scot.* V. lviii. 236 Arran, hearing alarming rumours, broke his ban at Kinniel and hurried to Court.

II. Proclamation of marriage: in this sense always in *pl.*, now spelt BANNS, q.v.

III. Anathematization, curse.

4. A formal ecclesiastical denunciation; anathema, interdict, excommunication.

1481 CAXTON *Reynard* (Arb.) 43, I stonde a cursed and am in the popes banne. **1638** *Penit. Conf.* vii. (1657) 115 The third Ban is upon those that affirm the Confession of all sins ..to be impossible. **1814** SCOTT *Ld. Isles* II. xxiv, A wretch, beneath the ban Of Pope and Church. **1860** R. VAUGHAN *Mystics* I. 164 Strasburg, and all the states which adhere to Louis, are placed under the bann.

b. *fig.* or *transf.*

1790 BURKE *Fr. Rev.* Wks. V. 45 All of whom this arch-pontiff of the 'rights of men' puts into the sweeping clause of ban and anathema.

5. *gen.* A curse, having, or supposed to have, supernatural sanction, and baleful influence.

1602 SHAKS. *Ham.* III. ii. 269 With Hecats Ban, thrice blasted, thrice infected. **1822** BYRON *Werner* II. i. 84 A prodigal son, beneath his father's ban. **1829** SCOTT *Demonol.* i. 41 The negro pines to death who is laid under the ban of an Obi woman. **1874** H. REYNOLDS *John Bapt.* iii.§4. 221 The land might be smitten by the ban which once fell upon the Canaanites.

6. An imprecation of a curse, an execration or malediction expressing anger.

1596 SPENSER *F.Q.* III. vii. 39 With blasphemous bannes. **1605** SHAKS. *Lear* II. iii. 19 Sometimes with Lunaticke bans, sometime with Praiers. **1783–94** W. BLAKE *Songs of Exp.*, *London* 7 In every ban, The mind-forged manacles I hear. **1879** LOWELL *Poet. Wks.* 381/2 With many a ban the fisherman Had stumbled o'er and spurned it.

IV. Denunciation, prohibition.

7. A formal and authoritative prohibition; a prohibitory command or edict, an interdict.

1667 MILTON *P.L.* IX. 925 To taste it under banne to touch. **1845** R. HAMILTON *Pop. Educ.* vi. 126 Bring back the age when Revelation was proscribed. Once more set the ban upon it. **1872** FREEMAN *Norm. Conq.* (1876) IV. xviii. 291 The teaching which put a ban on the flesh of the horse as the food of Christian men. *Ibid.* V. xxiv. 489 The ban against the tournament was fruitless.

8. A proclamation issued against any one by the civil power; sentence of outlawry; esp. 'Ban of the (Holy Roman) Empire.'

a **1674** CLARENDON *Hist. Reb.* I. I. (1702) 14 The Prince Electour..had..incurred the Ban of the Empire in an Imperial Dyet. **1708** *Lond. Gaz.* No. 4451/1 To Day the Duke of Mantua was put to the Ban of the Empire. **1810** COLERIDGE *Friend* (1865) 82 Charles V had pronounced the ban upon him [Luther] and limited his safe convoy to one and twenty days. **1827** HALLAM *Const. Hist.* (1876) III. xviii. 403 The Presbyterians..were under the ban of the law. **1832** HT. MARTINEAU *Ireland* v. 80 Under ban for burning his late dwelling.

9. *fig.* Practical denunciation, prohibition, or outlawry, not formally pronounced, as that of society or public opinion.

1839 HALLAM *Hist. Lit.* IV. IV. ii. §21 Still under the ban of an orthodox clergy. **1859** MILL *Liberty* ii. 58 Opinions which are under the ban of society. **1863** KEMBLE *Resid. Georgia* 11 Free from the chain..of slavery; but they are not the less under a ban. **1869** J. MARTINEAU *Ess.* II. 77 What are the objects upon which..the ban of morality is set?

‖**ban** (bæn), *sb.*[2] [Pers. *bān* lord, master, keeper; brought into Europe by the Avars who ruled in Slavonic countries subject to Hungary.] The name given to the governor or viceroy of certain military districts in Hungary, Slavonia, and Croatia, who takes the command in time of war.

Hence: **banate, bannat**, the district under the jurisdiction of a ban, as the Hungarian Banate, the Banate of Croatia; **banal** *a.*, of or pertaining to a ban; *sb.* a Banate.

1614 SELDEN *Titles Hon.* 381 The Hungarian Bans..are Presidents or Gouernors of some Kingdomes belonging to that Kingdom, as Dalmatia, Croatia, Slauonia, Seruia and others. **1687** *Lond. Gaz.* No. 2224/3 The Ban of Croatia had ..drawn together the Imperial Troops..to oppose their design. **1804** CAMPBELL *Turk. Lady*, On Transylvania's Bannat When the Crescent shone afar. **1832** tr. *Sismondi's Ital. Repub.* xi. 255 The kingdom of Bosnia, and the bannat of Sclavonia. **1835** *Penny Cycl.* III. 359/2 The Banal Frontier was formed in the course of the year 1696. **1860** R. D. in *Vac. Tour* 107 Numerous dukes, princes, and bans.. exercised sway in the country now called Servia.

‖**ban** (bɑ̃), *sb.*[3] [Fr.] (See quot. 1900.)

1900 *Daily News* 14 Aug. 8/2 On the falling of the curtain, however, when a 'ban' was called for, the ice was broken. The 'ban' is the characteristic ovation of the French student. **1906** *Daily Chron.* 20 Aug. 6/5 At the end it was 'Vive' everybody, and a perfect salvo of 'triple bans' was given.

Banagher ('bænəgə(r)). [Name of a town in Ireland, which is said to have become proverbial as a 'rotten borough'.] Phr. *to beat* (or *bang*) *Banagher*: to surpass everything. (Cf. BANG *v.* 6.)

1830 W. CARLETON *Traits & Stories* I. 50 'O, by this and by that,' says he, 'but that bates Bannagher!' *a* **1845** BARHAM *Ingol. Leg.* (1847) Ser. III. 300 *House-warming*, Whose name ..in the records of fame..beats Banagher. **1855** T. C. HALIBURTON *Nature & Human Nature* II. vii. 226 That would bang Banaghar. **1890** FARMER *Slang* s.v., *He beats Banaghan*, an Irish saying of one who tells wonderful stories. **1928** *Weekly Disp.* 24 June 2 'You beat Banagher Pat,' said Willie, admiringly, 'and Banagher beat the Divil.'

banak ('bænək). [Native name in Honduras.] A hardwood tree of the genus *Virola* grown esp. in central America; also its timber.

1921 C. HUMMEL *Rep. Forests Brit. Honduras* 59 Name of tree. Banak..Fairly large quantity in the south of the Colony..stems of large size, good shape and free of knots. **1948** A. L. HOWARD *Timbers of World* (ed. 3) 54 *Banak, Virola merendonia* Pittier..British Honduras and South America. A very light mahogany-coloured wood, with a straight, even, regular grain.

banal ('beɪnəl, bə'nɑːl), *a.* Also 8–9 **bannal**. [a. F. *banal*, in Cotgr. *bannal*, f. *ban*:—med.L. *bannum*: see BAN *sb.*[1], and -AL[1].]

1. Of or belonging to compulsory feudal service.

1753 CHAMBERS *Cycl. Supp.*, *Bannal-Mill*, a kind of feudal service, whereby the tenants of a certain district are obliged to carry their corn to be ground at a certain mill, and to be baked at a certain oven for the benefit of the lord. **1864** SIR F. PALGRAVE *Norm. & Eng.* IV. 281 A bannal-oven of which the lord enjoyed the monopoly.

2. (From the intermediate sense of, Open to the use of all the community): Commonplace, common, trite; trivial, petty.

[**1837** *Athenæum* No. 504. 453 These *bannales* personages are 'much of a muchness.'] **1840** *New Monthly Mag.* LIX. 458 All that her late companions can draw from her is the *banal* declaration, that she 'never knew what happiness was before'. **1864** *N. & Q.* Ser. III. VI. 480 Facetious fools..set up the banal laugh. **1868** BROWNING *Ring & Bk.* x. 820 You must show the warrant, just The banal scrap, clerk's scribble. **1883** R. BURTON & CAM. *Gold Coast* I. iii. 54 Prizes were banal as medals after a modern war.

banality (bə'nælɪtɪ). [ad. F. *banalité*, f. *banal*: see prec. and -ALITY.]

1. Anything trite or trivial; a commonplace.

1861 SALA *Tw. round Clock* 244 That he is getting old, or that he looks remarkably young, or some equally relevant banalities. **1871** BROWNING *Balaust.* 1514 The decent praise, the due regret, And each banality prescribed of old.

2. Commonplace character, triteness, triviality.

1878 DOWDEN *Stud. Lit.* 394 The banality of these poetic sorrows and aspirations. **1881** SAINTSBURY in *Academy* 5 Feb. 92/3 Bewitched by the absence of banality in his work.

banalize (bə'nɑːlaɪz), *v.* [f. BANAL *a.* + -IZE.] *trans.* To render banal; to make commonplace.

1949 KOESTLER *Insight & Outlook* xxviii. 380 But the great majority found a solution..in conventionalizing and banalizing Death itself. **1958** L. FORSTER in *Aspects of Translation* 25 The girl has lost her heart, and this banal idea banalizes what follows. **1964** *Sci. Amer.* May 140 The great and good traditional virtues have been eroded: love, generosity, self-denial, truthfulness, honesty, loyalty, friendship, kindness to children. That many of these traits have been banalized by advertising seems incidental. **1985** *N.Y. Times* 8 Nov. C1/4 Many of the images that resulted are now classics in their kind. Endlessly travestied and banalized, they long ago lost their initial freshness.

Hence **banali'zation; ba'nalized, ba'nalizing** *ppl. adjs.*

1964 S. BELLOW *Herzog* 76 Reaching at last the point of denying the humanity of the industrialized, 'banalized' masses. **1968** *Sat. Rev.* (U.S.) 21 Sept. 77/1 It is possible that the affluence..of our society has allowed a Deweyian commitment to survive its..banalization at the hands of professional educators. **1973** MATIAS & WILLEMEN tr. M. Cegarra in *Screen* Spring/Summer 143 Criticism..of simplified, simplifying and banalizing 'examples'. **1985** C. RYCROFT *Psychoanalysis & Beyond* v. 83 The kind of background information which would enable one to decide whether the slips he quotes are interferences by repressed thoughts or merely banalisations.

banally, *adv.* [f. BANAL *a.* 2 + -LY[2].] In a banal manner.

1934 in WEBSTER. **1944** *Mind* LIII. 151 If we say, somewhat banally, that it leads from arbitrary taboo and tribalism to the reasoned pursuit of what is genuinely best for everyone, [etc.].

banana (bə'nɑːnə). Also 7 **bonana, bonano**. [a. Pg. or Sp. *banana* (the fruit), *banano* (the tree), given by De Orta (1563) and Pigafetta, as the native name in Guinea (Congo).]

1. A tree (*Musa sapientum*) cultivated largely in tropical and subtropical climates, especially in the islands of the Atlantic and Pacific; it grows to a height of 20 feet, and has its stem marked with purple spots and streaks.

1697 DAMPIER *Voy.* (1729) I. 316 The Bonano Tree is exactly like the Plantain. **1810** SOUTHEY *Kehama* XVI. v, That, like the broad banana growing, Raised their long wrinkled leaves of purple hue. **1830** LINDLEY *Nat. Syst. Bot.* 270 The young shoots of the Banana are eaten as a delicate vegetable.

2. a. The fruit of this tree, growing in clusters of angular, finger-like berries, containing within their rind a luscious and highly nutritious pulp.

[**1563** GARCIA DE ORTA *Simples e Drogues* 93 b, Tambem ha estes figos em Guiné, chamam lhe bananas.] **1597** HARTWELL *Pigafetta's Congo* in *Coll. Trav.* (1745) II. 553 Other fruits there are, termed Banana, which we verily think to be the Muses of Egypt and Soria. **1613** PURCHAS *Pilgr.* I. v. xvi. 452 Amboyna bringeth forth..Coquos, Bonana's.. and other fruits. **1796** STEDMAN *Surinam* I. ix. 205 Refreshed with..plaintains, bananas, oranges. **1823** BYRON *Island* IV. viii, The ripe banana from the mellow hill.

b. The yellow colour of a ripe banana. Also *banan* (= F. *banane*).

1923 *Daily Mail* 3 Apr. 10 In shades of..Banana and Cream. *Ibid.* 7 May 1 In Pale Jade, Banan, Tuscan.

3. *pl.* Crazy, mad, wild (with excitement, anger, frustration, etc.), esp. in phr. *to go* (also *drive*) *bananas*. *colloq.*

[**1935** A. J. POLLOCK *Underworld Speaks* 53/1 *He's bananas*, he's sexually perverted; a degenerate.] **1968–70** *Current Slang* (Univ. S. Dakota) III.–IV. 6 *Bananas*, adj., excited and upset; 'wild'.—College students, both sexes, Kentucky.—I'd say it, but everyone would just go *bananas*. **1970** *Times* 9 Mar. 43 Liza [Minnelli] moved into the sheltered regimented Barbizon Hotel for Women. Liza says: 'I went bananas!' **1974** *Sunday Sun* (Brisbane) 3 Feb. 38/3 He just went bananas. My husband tried to take the bottle from him and he wouldn't let go... He jumped onto the television and then onto the china cabinet. **1974** *TV Times* (Brisbane) 28 Sept. 17/1 'I admit I'm half-bananas—not completely bananas,' he said, 'and the part I play in Dirty Mary, Crazy Larry is a lot like me. Larry is a stock-car racer who goes ape behind the wheel.' **1974** K. MILLET *Flying* (1975) II. 194 It was driving me bananas, with my sainted mother at the wheel. **1976** *Observer* 11 Jan. 3/5 She says with her usual verve: 'The Government have gone bananas over a woman tortured in Chile.' **1978** J. KRANTZ *Scruples* xiv. 412 Jesus, thought Lester, his first movie star and she turns out to be a bit bananas. **1980** *Times* 1 Oct. 4/1 When the left wing of the Labour Party looks as if it is going to lose, it is described as bananas. **1985** *Sunday Times* 13 Jan. 5/2 Before we all go bananas about electric cars let me remind you that this is nothing new.

4. *attrib.*, as in ***banana-leaf, -tree*** (see sense 1); ***banana-skin*** (also *fig.*) (sense 2); **banana bird**, a gregarious West Indian bird (*Xanthornus icterus*), belonging to the Starling family; also, a name applied to certain South American and West Indian species now included in the genus *Icterus*; also = *banana quit*; **banana boat**, a boat carrying bananas; also *Mil. slang* (see quot. 1945); **banana flour**, a flour made from dried bananas; **banana fly** (see quot.); **banana liquid** (see quot.); **banana-oil**, (*a*) = *banana liquid*; (*b*) *slang*, nonsense; insincere or insane talk or behaviour; cf. *apple-sauce*; **banana quit**: see QUIT *sb.*[1]; **banana republic**, *colloq.* applied to a small state, esp. in central America, whose economy is almost entirely dependent on its fruit-exporting trade; **banana solution**, a solution, having the odour of bananas, used as a vehicle in applying bronze pigments; **banana split** (orig. *U.S.*), a popular concoction of ice-cream and a split banana.

1713 SLOANE in Ray *Synopsis Avium* 187 *Passer coeruleofuscus*. The Bonana Bird..Arbores Bonanas dictas frequentat, unde nomen. **1734** ALBIN *Nat. Hist. Birds* II. 37 The Banana Bird from Jamaica..of the Bigness of our English Starling. **1756** P. BROWNE *Jamaica* (1789) 477 *Icterus major*..The large Banana Bird. **1847** GOSSE & HILL *Birds of Jamaica* 226 Banana-bird. *Icterus leucopteryx*... Fruit is his principal diet; a ripe banana, or orange. **1916** W. A. DU PUY *Uncle Sam* 119 The skipper of the banana boat. **1943** HUNT & PRINGLE *Service Slang* 12 *Banana boat*, an invasion barge. **1945** PARTRIDGE *Dict. R.A.F. Slang* 14 *Banana boat*, an aircraft-carrier, according to the R.A.F. To soldiers it means an invasion barge. **1962** *Guardian* 12 Oct. 15/4 They travel by any convenient method, from..luxury liners to banana boats. **1890** LD. LUGARD *Diaries* 6 Dec. (1959) I. 409 The flour of the country is almost solely banana flour. **1951** *Gd. Housek. Home Encycl.* 345/2 Banana Flour.. is ideal for flavoring cakes, buns and biscuits. **1921** *Conquest* Sept. 493/2 The common Banana Fly (*Drosophila ampelophila*). **1809** SHAW *Gen. Zool.* VII. 431 The under side of a Banana-leaf. **1845** DARWIN *Voy. Nat.* xviii, It rained very heavily, but the good thatch of banana-leaves kept us dry. **1916** L. A. FLEMMING *Practical Tanning* (ed. 3) 474 Because of its characteristic odor the amyl acetate solution is frequently called banana liquid. **1927** WODEHOUSE in *Sunday Express* 16 Oct. 9/5 This is pure banana oil. It is not like you to..gibber. **1934** H. HILER *Notes Technique Painting* i. 44 The watercolour fixative..is usually known as 'banana oil' or 'banana solution'. **1960** WODEHOUSE *Jeeves in Offing* ix. 95 The sort of banana oil that passes between statesmen at conferences..before they tear their whiskers off and get down to cases. **1935** *Esquire* July 70/1 We strung along with Major Brown on the inhuman aspects of war in the banana republics. **1949** KOESTLER *Promise & Fulfilment* xiii. 143 The somewhat jerky behaviour displayed by the Central American banana republics. **1907** *Westm. Gaz.* 19 Sept. 2/3 The banana-skin trouble in this direction had seemed to be sufficient of a fresh nuisance. **1934** WODEHOUSE *Right Ho, Jeeves!* i. 17 Treading upon Life's banana skins. **1961** H. R. TREVOR-ROPER in *Encounter* July 96 The love of..laying banana-skins to disconcert the gravity and upset the balance of the orthodox. **1920** ADE *Hand-made Fables* 151, I recall many useful and interesting citizens who would walk around a banana split to get to a rickey. **1931** E. LINKLATER *Juan in Amer.* II. ix. 117 Brighter lights and larger jazz-bands and stronger gin and sweeter banana-splits. **1938** E. BOWEN *Death of Heart* II. v. 257 They ate poached eggs on haddock and banana splits.

Ba'nanaland. [See quot. 1898.] A colloquial Australian name for Queensland. Hence **Ba'nanalander.**

1898 MORRIS *Austral English*, *Banana-land*, slang name for Queensland, where bananas grow in abundance. *Bananalander*, slang for a Queenslander. **1901** *Westm. Gaz.* 2 Apr. 1/3 The Bananaland capital. **1901** *Daily Chron.* 4 Apr. 5/1 [He] was born in 'Bananaland'. *Ibid.* 18 Nov. 5/1 The Bananaland statesman. **1933** *Bulletin* (Sydney) 11 Jan. 10 Bananaland has had a fruit marketing organisation for years. **1934** T. WOOD *Cobbers* 144 So let this mob of Cornstalks, Croweaters, Sandgropers, and Bananalanders go on yapping, say Victorians.

banar, obsolete form of BANNER.

banausian (bə'nɔːsɪən), *a.* [f. as BANAUSIC *a.* + -IAN.] = BANAUSIC *a.*

1901 LAURIE *Training of Teachers* 235 The occupations which to the Greek sages were banausian, if not degrading.

banausic (bə'nɔːsɪk), *a.* [ad. Gr. βαναυσικός of or for mechanics, f. βάναυσος working by fire, mechanical, f. βαῦνος furnace, forge.] Merely mechanical, proper to a mechanic.

1845 G. SMYTHE in *Oxf. & Camb. Rev.* Aug. 206 When the Banausic principle (we must coin a word from the most expressive of languages to express all its intense vulgarity) began to obtain. **1876** GROTE *Eth. Fragm.* vi. 227 Alleged that the teaching music as a manual art was banausic and degrading. **1901** J. C. COLLINS *Ephemera Critica* 68 The one instinct in them which is not quite banausic being the conscientious thoroughness with which they impart what they have been taught. **1957** *London Mag.* July 57 A sensitive, self conscious creature..in sad revolt against uncongenially banausic employment.

Banbury. A town in Oxfordshire, England, formerly noted for the number and zeal of its Puritan inhabitants, still for its cakes.

a **1535** LATIMER *Serm. & Rem.* (1845) II. 299 (D.) Their laws, customs, ceremonies, and Banbury glosses. **1598** SHAKS. *Merry W.* I. i. 130 *Bar. (to Slender)* You Banbery Cheese. **1601** *Pasquil & Kath.* III. 178 Put off your clothes, and you are like a Banbery cheese, Nothing but paring. **1614** B. JONSON *Barth. Fair* I, The reverend elder, you told me of, your Banbury man. **1615** MARKHAM *Eng. Housew.* II. ii. (1668) 100 To make Banbury Cakes. *a* **1848** MARRYAT *R. Reefer* xiii, Had they not trustingly eschewed banbury-cakes. **1863** Sala *Capt. Dang.* I. i. 15, I did ever hate your sanctimonious Banbury-man.

‖**banc** (bæŋk). *Law.* [AF. *banc*, 'bench': see BANK *sb.*] Bench; in phrase *in banc* = in BANCO.

1727–51 Chambers *Cycl.* s.v., King's Banc, or Bench. **1863** Cox *Inst. Eng. Govt.* II. ix. 526 Disposed of in each court when sitting in banc (in banco) that is, by several of the justices sitting together.

banche, 'to snatch' (Levins *Manip.*/22).

banck, -ier, obs. forms of BANK, BANKER.

bancket, -cquet, obs. forms of BANQUET.

‖**banco** ('bæŋkəʊ), *a.* [It.; = bank.] A term used to indicate the bank money of account in certain places, as distinguished from the current money or *currency*, when the latter had been depreciated from the earlier value retained by bankers in calculating exchanges with foreign countries. Thus at Hamburg, while the current mark was worth 1*s.* $1\frac{1}{16}$*d.*, the mark *banco* was valued at 1*s.* $5\frac{1}{4}$*d.* sterling.

1753 Hanway *Trav.* (1762) I. VII. lxxxviii. 407 Exchange .. 290 grosch per pound flemish banco. **1759** Chesterf. *Lett.* 350 IV. 158 The Specie, Banco, Usances, Agio. **1809** R. Langford *Introd. Trade* 28 Three Thousand Banco Marks [at Hamburgh].

‖**banco** ('bæŋkəʊ), *sb. Law.* [L., abl. of *bancus* bench: see BANK *sb.*[2], and cf. BANC.] In L. phr. *in banco* = on the bench: applied to sittings of a Superior Court of Common Law as a full court, as distinguished from the sittings of the judges at Nisi Prius, or on circuit.

1768 [see BANK *sb.*[2] 2]. **1863** [see BANC].

‖**banco** ('bæŋkəʊ), *int.* [Fr., a. It. *banco* (see BANK *sb.*[3]).] In games of hazard such as baccarat and chemin-de-fer, a player's proposal to the banker to stake his capital on a single coup.

1789 J. Moore *Zeluco* I. viii. 38 As he shook the box, being about to throw, the Hussar officer cried, Banco; and the others took up what they had staked. **1910** *Encycl. Brit.* III. 121/1 The banker places before him the sum he wishes to stake and the punters do likewise, unless a punter desires to *go bank*, signifying his intention by saying, *Banco*! In this case he plays against the entire stake of the banker. **1964** A. Wykes *Gambling* vii. 178 Any player may bet against the whole of the banker's stake by calling 'banco'.

banco, var. BUNCO *sb.*

bancour, bancqwer, variants of BANKER[1].

band (bænd), *sb.*[1] Also 4–5 **bande**. [ME. *band*, *bond*, a. ON. *band* neut. (Da. *baand*, Sw. *band*) = OS., OFris. *band*, OHG. *bant*, *pant*:—OTeut. **bando-(m)*, f. *band-* stem of *bind-an* to BIND. Not in Gothic, nor in OE., which had only the cogn. *bęnd* fem.:—OTeut. **bandjâ-*: see BEND *sb.*[1] which survived in ME. alongside of *band*, *bond*. *Band* and *bond* were at first merely phonetic variants (cf. *land*, *lond*, *stand*, *stond*, *man*, *mon*, etc.), but are now largely differentiated in use, *bond* being usual in branch II, in which *band* is archaic or obsolete. Cf. BAND[2], which in mod. use is treated as identical with this.]

I. *literally*, That with or by which a person or thing is bound.

1. Anything with which one's body or limbs are bound, in restraint of personal liberty; a shackle, chain, fetter, manacle. *arch.*

c **1200** Ormin 19821 Herode .. band himm wiþþ irrene band. *a* **1300** *Cursor M.* 7170 Sampson .. gaf a braide .. þat alle þe bandis of him brast. *c* **1460** *Towneley Myst.* 217 A bande .. to bynde his hande. **1551** Robinson tr. *More's Utop.* 121 These sortes of bondemen they kepe .. in bandes. **1590** Marlowe *Edw. II*, III. i, Must I fall, and die in bands? **1611** Bible *Acts* xvi. 26 The doores were opened, and euery ones bands were loosed. **1833** Tennyson *Poems* 5 To chain with chains, and bind with bands That island queen.

†**b.** *abstr.* Confinement, imprisonment, custody.

a **1300** *Cursor M.* 4437 þat oþer in prisun war or band. *Ibid.* 5802, I wil þaim bring vte of his band. *c* **1430** *Hymns Virg.* (1867) 52 þat sauede my sone fro bittir bande!

†**c.** ***Our Lady's bands***: 'confinement' at childbirth, accouchement. *Obs.* (Cf. BEND.)

1495 *Festival* in Strype *Eccl. Mem.* I. II. App. xxxvii. 99. Pray .. for al women which be in our Ladyes bandes.

2. A string with which any loose thing is bound. **a.** The tie of straw with which sheaves are bound, a rope of hay used by the hay-binder, and *gen.* a rope or string of straw, rushes, or similar material.

c **1325** *Metr. Hom.* 146 Gaderes the darnel first in bande. **1523** Fitzherb. *Husb.* §28 And with his rake and his syckle, taketh vp the barley or otes, and layth them vppon the bande. **1592** Shaks. *Ven. & Ad.* xxxviii, Her armes infold him like a band. **1832** Ht. Martineau *Life in Wilds* iii. 38 She tied the twigs .. with bands of rushes. **1864** Atkinson *Whitby Gloss.*, *Band*, a rope or string. 'It is not worth a band's end.'

b. *Book-binding.* Name of the cords or straps crossing the back of a book, by attachment to which the quires or sheets are 'bound' together.

1759 Boyer *Fr. Dict.*, A band (for a Book), *nerf ficelle cousue au dos d'un Livre.* **1879** *Cassell's Techn. Educ.* IV. 40 The bands are pieces of strongish string or cord, which are fastened perpendicularly at fixed distances on a frame rising at the edge of a board, on which the sheets of paper are placed one by one.

3. The hinges of a door or gate; *esp.* long strips of iron extending across the surface by which it is hung on the crooks.

a **1300** *Cursor M.* 19306 þe prisun dors [he] left als he fand, Noiþer he brak ne barr ne band. **1483** *Cath. Angl.* 19 Bande of a dure, *vertebra.* **1565** *Richmond. Wills* (1853) 178, Iiij iron bandes for a doore. **1571** in *Mem. Rip.* (1882) I. 309 Lockes, keyes, and bandes of yron. **1864** Atkinson *Whitby Gloss.*, *Bands*, 'a pair o' bands,' a couple of hinges.

4. A connecting piece, by which the parts of a complex thing are held firmly together.

a **1300** *Cursor M.* 1671 First binde wele wiþ balk and bandes. **1483** *Cath. Angl.* 19 Bande of a howse; *lacunar .. loramentum.* **1523** Fitzherb. *Husb.* §3 The sharebeame, the which is the keye and the chiefe bande of all the plough. **1593** Shaks. *Rich. II.* II. ii. 71 Who gently would dissolue the bands of life. **1611** Bible *Col.* xi. 19 All the body by ioynts and bands .. knit together. **1627** Capt. Smith *Seaman's Gram.* ii. 14 Clamps, middle bands and sleepers .. for binding within. **1881** C. Edwards *Organs* 41 The use of this band is for the insertion of the wind trunk or trunks.

5. A string, strap, or chain, by which a child or animal is held in hand, led, or tied up. *lit.* and *fig.*

a **1300** *Cursor M.* 14969 A moder ass yee sal þar find, And yee hir sal vn-do vte of hir band. **1413** Lydg. *Pylgr. Sowle* v. ix. (1483) 100 As an hound that tyed is with a band. **1690** W. Walker *Idiom. Anglo-Lat.* 519 He hath the world in a band. **1738** C. Wesley *Hymn*, '*When to the Temple*' iii, And lead with Bands of Love.

†**6.** *Logic.* The copula. *Obs. rare.*

1588 Fraunce *Lawiers Log.* II. i. 86 b, An axiome [i.e. proposition] hath two partes, the bande, and the partes bound. **1628** T. Spencer *Logick* 160 A simple Axiome is that, the band whereof is a Verbe.

II. *figuratively*, A moral, spiritual, or legal bond of restraint or union: a BOND.

7. *fig.* (from 1): The 'shackles' of sin or vice, the 'chains' of sleep, the 'fetters' of formula, etc.

c **1200** Ormin 14778 He wollde lesenn hemm ut off þewwdo-mess bandess. *a* **1300** *E.E. Psalter* lvii. 3 He sent fra heven, lesed me of band. **1340** Hampole *Pr. Consc.* 3207 Bunden faste With bandes of syn. **1549** *Bk. Com. Prayer*, 24 Sund. Trin., Delyuered from the bandes of all those sinnes which by our frayltie we haue committed. **1725** Pope *Odyss.* xx. 68 The downy bands of sleep. **1881** *Daily News* 21 Jan. 5/1 Loosening himself from the bands of formula.

8. An obligation by which action is checked or restrained, or persons reciprocally bound to each other; a tie, restraint, bond.

a **1300** *Cursor M.* 13710 þis womman þe band [*v.r.* bond] has broken of hir sposail. **1375** Barbour *Bruce* I. 267 Wedding is the hardest band That ony man may tak on hand. **1591** Spenser *Ruins of Time* Ded., With howe straight bandes of duetie I was tied to him. **1600** Shaks. *A.Y.L.* v. iv. 136 To ioyne in Hymens bands. **1725** Pope *Odyss.* IX. 563 Thy barb'rous breach of hospitable bands. **1762** Hume *Hist. Eng.* (1806) IV. lxv. 774 Few .. were attached .. by any other band than that of inclination. **1823** Lamb *Elia* Ser. II. xix. (1865) 369 Having worn the nuptial bands .. longer than her friend. **1856** Dove *Logic Chr. Faith* v. i. §2. 293 The immortal bands of obligation to himself.

9. A uniting or cementing force or influence by which a union of any kind is maintained; a pledge. *arch.*; now BOND.

1483 *Cath. Angl.* 19 Bande of luffe, *fedus, pignus.* **1569** J. Rogers *Gl. Godly Love* 186 Children is the very sure band of love. **1625** Bacon *Unity in Relig.*, *Ess.* (Arb.) 423 Religion being the chiefe Band of humane Society. **1796** Morse *Amer. Geog.* I. 318 Fear .. continued to operate as a band of political union.

10. An agreement, or promise, binding on him who makes it. *arch.*; now BOND.

a **1440** *Sir Degrev.* 957 He hath gyf us by band An c pownd worth of land. **1470** Harding *Chron.* CXX. i, False .. of his band Whiche to the kynge he made. **1535** Stewart *Cron. Scot.* II. 253 How Arthure his aith and band hed brokin. *c* **1605** G. Wilkins *Mis. Enf. Marriage* v. in *Dodsl.* (1780) V. 106 From this your oath and band .. you have run. **1752** Carte *Hist. Eng.* III. 436 He signed a Band, that .. he would bear all concerned in it harmless. **1814** Scott *Ld. of Isles* IV. xiv, To fulfil our father's band, I proffer'd all I could.

11. Security given; a deed legally executed, binding on him who delivers it. *arch.*; now BOND.

1521 *State Papers Hen. VIII*, I. 27 The provision and bande to be made for your indempnitie. **1580** Lyly *Euphues* (Arb.) 229 Enter not into bands, no not for thy best friends. **1596** Shaks. *1 Hen. IV*, III. ii. 157 The end of Life cancells all Bands. **1642** Fuller *Holy & Prof. St.* v. xiii. 409 This property of an honest man, that his word is as good as his band. **1724** A. Ramsay *Tea-t. Misc.* (1733) II. 122 There's meikle good love in bands and bags. **1818** Scott *Hrt. Midl.* xxvi, Deil a wadset, heritable band, or burden.

†**b.** Security, pledge. *Obs.*

1596 Spenser *F.Q.* VI. i. 31 He sent to her his basenet as a faithfull band.

†**12.** A covenant, a league. *Sc. Obs.*

1452 Earl Douglas in Tytler *Hist. Scot.* (1864) II. 387 That I shall make na band na ligg in tyme coming. **1513–75** *Diurn. Occurr.* (1833) 273 To mak ane band and confideratioun with the Quene of Ingland. **1649** Bp. Guthry *Mem.* (1702) 76 A Band found to be amongst a Number of Noblemen, wherein they had combin'd to oppose, etc. **1873** Burton *Hist. Scot.* V. lvii. 178 The 'band' for the murder produced by Balfour in a green box.

III. *abstractly*, Binding quality, or bound state.

†**13.** Binding quality or power. *Obs.*

1616 Surfl. & Markh. *Countr. Farm* 576 The meale hath not so good a band, neither yet is it altogether so clammie. *a* **1619** Donne *Biathan.* (1644) 143 This obligation .. is of stronger hold, and of straighter band.

†**14.** A state of union or connexion. *Obs.*

1631 Rutherford *Lett.* 18 (1862) I. 77 Give them grace .. to take band with the fair chief Cornerstone. *Ibid.* 131 Keep band with the cornerstone.

IV. 15. *Comb.* **band-stone**, a stone that passes through a wall from side to side, and thus binds the structure together, used especially in dry-stone walls in the north.

band (bænd) *sb.*[2] In 4–7 **bande** [Late ME. *bande*, a. F. *bande* 'flat strip or strap, fascia, edge, side'; in OF. also *bende* = Pr. and It. *benda*, Lomb. *binda*, a. OHG. *bindâ*:—OTeut. **bindôn*, from *bindan* to bind: thus ultimately cognate with BAND *sb.*[1], with which, since the loss of final *-e*, it has been formally identical in English. The variant BEND, from the earlier OF. *bende*, is retained in Heraldry.

(Although OF. *bende* would of itself give a later *bande*, the F. and It. forms suggest that both *banda* and *benda* may have existed from the first in Romanic: see next word.)]

I. *Of shape and function.*

1. A strip of any material flat and thin, used to bind together, clasp, or gird.

a. A hoop or fillet for putting round anything.

1483 *Cath. Angl.* 19 Bande of a carte, *crusta, crustola.* **1753** Chambers *Cycl. Supp.*, *Band*, in matters of artillery .. a hoop of iron used about the carriage of a gun.

b. ***bands of a saddle***: two pieces of iron nailed upon the bows to hold them in their proper place.

1753 Chambers *Cycl. Supp.* s.v., Besides the two great bands, the fore-bow has a small one, called the wither-band.

2. *esp.* A flat strip of a flexible substance (*e.g.* any fabric, leather, india-rubber, paper), used to bind round an object. Various *spec.* uses: an identifying strip placed round the leg of a bird (cf. *bird-band*); an advertising strip round a book; a strip of paper round a cigar.

1611 Cotgr., *Bande*, a band: properly a long and narrow peece of any stuffe. *c* **1800** Mrs. Hunter in *1001 Gems of Song* (1883) 87 My mother bids me bind my hair With bands of rosy hue. *a* **1885** *Mod.* A roll of paper secured by an elastic band.

1914 *Country Life* July 36/2 These up-to-date bands are made in eight different sizes, some one of which is sure to fit the bird you wish to tag. **1937** *Brit. Birds* XXXI. 239 Any observer chancing to meet a straggler on this side of the Atlantic can learn the origin of the bird by reporting the exact order of the various bands.

1932 Q. D. Leavis *Fiction & Reading Public* I. ii. 22 An enterprising publisher will reissue the novel with a band or new dust-jacket exhibiting the caption. **1958** *Bookseller* 12 Apr. 1369/1 'Royal Ballet' Bands .. —have prepared bands for the jackets of *The Sadler's Wells Ballet.*

1923 W. J. Locke *Moordius & Co.* vii. 96 He selected a cigar, .. removed the band and clipped the point. **1935** A. E. W. Mason *They wouldn't be Chessmen* ix. 115 What's the use of me paying fourpence for a 'Avana cigar if I've got to take the band off before I smoke it?

3. A flat strip or strap of the above description, forming part of, or used to confine, a dress at the waist, neck, wrists, etc., or to encircle and confine a cap, hat, or other article of apparel.

1552 Huloet, Bande or lace of a cappe or hatte, *spira.* **1562** J. Heywood *Prov. & Epigr.* (1867) 207 Headband, smockbande. **1599** Thynne *Animadv.* (1865) 21 A bande aboute oure cappes, sette with golde Buttons. **1611** Bible *Ecclus.* vi. 30 Her bands are purple lace. **1841** Catlin *N. Amer. Ind.* II. lv. 198 His hat-band of silver lace. **1843** Hood *Shirt* iii, Seam and gusset, and band, Band, and gusset, and seam. **1882** *Mag. Art* V. 339 Full bodices with bands high up round the waists.

4. *spec.* **a.** The neck-band or collar of a shirt, orig. used to make it fit closely round the neck, afterwards expanded ornamentally. Hence, in 16th and 17th century, a collar or ruff worn round the neck by man or woman.

1568 Bible (Bishops') *Ex.* xxxix. 23 With a band round about the coller that it should not rent. **1591** Florio *Sec. Fruites* 5 With what band will you have it? With a falling band. **1620** H. Fitzgeffery *Notes fr. Blackfryers*, Hee is of England by his yellow Band. *c* **1625** *Poems on Costume* (1849) 112 With laces long and broad, As now are women's bands. **1632** Sherwood *Eng. Fr. Dict.*, Band (for the necke), *Collet.* A falling band, *Rabat.* A ruffe band, *Fraize.* **1635** Brereton *Trav.* (1844) 103 Young maids .. some with broad thin shag ruffs .. others with half bands. **1712** Steele *Spect.* No. 264 ¶2 A Taylor's Widow, who washes and can clear-starch his Bands. **1755** Smollett *Quix.* II. II. i, His band was collegian, neither starched nor laced.

b. The development of a falling collar into a pair of strips (now called *bands*) hanging down in front, as part of a conventional dress, clerical, legal, or academical.

a **1700** Sedley *Sonn.* Wks. 1722 I. 12 That fix Salvation to Short Band and Hair. *c* **1760** Gray *Candidate*, Divinity heard .. She stroked up her belly, and stroked down her band. **1779** Johnson *Pope*, *L.P.* (1787) IV. 60 In a clergyman's gown, but with a lawyer's band. **1807** Crabbe *Par. Reg.* III. 867 Careless was he of surplice, hood, and band. **1822** NARES s.v., What was within these forty years called *a band* at the Universities, is now called *a pair of bands*. **1866** G. MACDONALD *Ann. Q. Neighb.* viii. (1878) 131 With my surplice and bands.

5. A strip of linen, or the like, to swathe the body or any part of it; a bandage.

1568 BIBLE (Bishops') *Job* xxxviii. 9, I made darknesse as his swadlyng band. **1582** N. T. (Rhem.) *John* xi. 44 Dead, bound feete and handes with winding bandes. **1599** SHAKS. *Hen. V*, v. ii. Cho., Henry the Sixt, in Infant Bands. **1703** TATE *Paraphr. Luke* ii, All meanly wrapt in swathing bands And in a manger laid. **1751** CHAMBERS *Cycl.* s.v., A band, or roller, when applied, becomes a bandage.

6. *Naut.* 'A slip of canvas stitched across a sail to strengthen the parts most liable to pressure.'

1769 FALCONER *Dict. Marine* (1789), *Reef-band*, a piece of canvas, sewed across the sail, to strengthen it in the place where the eylet-holes of the reefs are formed. **1860** *Merc. Mar. Mag.* VII. 114 Whip up the sail to the reef band.

7. *Mech.* A flat strap, belt, or other connexion, passing round two wheels or shafts, by which motion is communicated from the one to the other.

1705 HAUKSBEE in *Phil. Trans.* XXV. 2166 The small Wheel which the Band surrounds from the great one. **1801** BLOOMFIELD *Rural T.* (1802) 3 She straight slipp'd off the Wall, and Band. **1860** *All Y. Round* No. 57. 162 The flying bands, the rattle of two hundred looms.

II. *Of shape only, without any binding function.*

†**8.** A side or flitch (of bacon). [The earliest use in Eng., f. OF. *bande* side.]

c **1394** *P. Pl. Crede* 763 And wiþ þe bandes [*v.r.* randes] of bakun his baly for to fillen. [**1611** COTGR., *Bande de larde*, a flitch or side of bacon.]

9. a. Anything having the shape or appearance of a band in sense 1; esp. a flat surface with parallel sides, and of more or less breadth, running across or around an object.

1823 P. NICHOLSON *Pract. Build.* 581 Bande or Band; a narrow flat surface, having its face in a vertical plane. **1836–9** TODD *Cycl. Anat. & Phys.* II. 621/1 The bands spring from ..the apicial part of the left ventricle. **1861** PARKER *Introd. Goth. Archit.* (1874) 319 *Band*, a ring round a shaft, as if to bind it to the larger pillar. **1879** H. PHILLIPS *Add. Notes Coins* 3 Upon a band in centre extending from side to side of the medal is the sign Aquarius. **1881** *Syd. Soc. Lex.*, *Band, flattened*, the cylinder-axis of white nerve fibre.

b. *Recording.* (See quot. 1962.)

1953 *His Master's Voice Record No. ALP 1052, Elgar Symphony No. 1* (cover), Side 1. Band 1—First movement. .. Band 2—Second movement. **1957** *Records & Recording* Oct. 35/3 It looks like a normal LP, but..it plays for only half the time—the first track is on the outside, separated by a blank band from the second inner track. **1962** A. NISBETT *Technique Sound Studio* 242 *Band*, separately recorded section of a disc, of which there may be several on a side. By extension, the term may also mean an individual section of a tape recording which is bounded by spacers.

10. a. A more or less broad stripe, distinguished by colour or aspect from the surface which it crosses; *hence*, a particular portion, space, or region of a certain breadth crossing a surface.

1470–85 MALORY *Arthur* I. xiv, With bandys of grene, and therupon gold. **1494** FABYAN VII. 423 Iakettys or cotys of demy partye of yolowe and grene, with a bande of whyte caste ouerthwarte. **1833** LYELL *Princ. Geol.* III. 228 The arenaceous strata do not form one continuous band around the margin of the basin. **1857** LIVINGSTONE *Trav.* xxiv. 472 We came upon another broad band of the same flower. **1865** GEIKIE *Scen. & Geol. Scot.* xi. 297 Successive bands of dark rock and grassy slope. **1876** GEO. ELIOT *Dan. Der.* II. xxiii. 89 The..sunshine..came..through the windows in slanting bands of brightness.

b. *bands*: a fault in flannel and serge cloth, when, from the uneven shrinking of defective weft, tight inelastic stripes occur here and there across the piece.

c. *fig.* = RANGE *sb.*[1] 10 b. (Cf. BAND *sb.*[3] 5.)

1929 A. LLOYD JAMES in *S.P.E. Tract* XXXII. 6 We now have a certain type, or rather a carefully chosen band of types of English. *Ibid.* 9 Those who speak any one variety of the narrow band are recognised as educated speakers. **1959** *Listener* 19 Feb. 331/1 The standard of play.. is at a fairly level band of skill and teamwork throughout, at least in Division One.

11. a. *Ent.* A transverse stripe of any colour, also called *fascia*; **b.** *Bot.* A space between any two elevated lines or ribs on the fruit of umbelliferous plants; also called *vitta*.

1841 E. NEWMAN *Hist. Brit. Ins.* III. ii. 175 A fillet is a longitudinal stripe, and a band or fascia is a transverse one. **1845** *Florist's Jrnl.* Aug. 175 Bands, or Vittæ, the flattened or hollow spaces between the elevated ribs of the fruit of umbelliferous plants.

12. *Geol.* A stratum with a band-like section.

1837 *Penny Cycl.* VII. 285/2 Layers of what the miners call *band*..very thin beds of clay-slate. **1839** MURCHISON *Silur. Syst.* I. xxxv. 472 A band of iron ore. **1858** GEIKIE *Hist. Boulder* x. 198 A mass of hard yellow calcareous shale, known to the workmen as 'bands.'

13. *Physics.* A group of closely-spaced lines, esp. in a molecular spectrum; **band spectrum**, a spectrum characterized by such bands.

1831 BREWSTER *Optics* x. 86 Halfway between A and B is a group of seven or eight [lines], forming together a dark band. **1869** H. E. ROSCOE *Spectrum Analysis* iv. 146 In the case of bodies whose spectra change from bands to lines on increase of temperature, a recombination of the elements occurs on cooling, and the band spectrum of the compound reappears. **1885** —— *Ibid.* (ed. 4) iii. 130 Nearly all bodies.. have been found to exhibit both a band and a line spectrum, the band spectrum always belonging to the lower temperature. **1903** A. M. CLERKE *Problems in Astrophysics* iii. 39 Band-spectra..display no sensitiveness to pressure. **1923** GLAZEBROOK *Dict. Appl. Physics* IV. 786/1 Bands, which are usually associated with the spectra of compounds of molecules, consist of groups of lines which converge to definite heads. **1957** *Encycl. Brit.* III. 25/2 A spectrum consists of lines showing certain definite regularities of arrangement. The so-called 'line spectra' are attributable to atoms, and band spectra are due to molecules... Such a series [of lines] appears to terminate abruptly at the point where the separation of the lines is least; this is called the head of the band, and is a prominent feature of most band spectra.

14. *Electr.* A range of frequencies or wavelengths that falls between two given limits; = *wave-band*. Also in *Comb.*, as **band-pass filter**, an electrical filter with a very low attenuation for currents within given limits of frequency; **band width, bandwidth**, the interval separating the limits of a band.

1922 A. F. COLLINS *Radio Amat. Handbk.* 321 When continuous waves are being sent out and..modulated by a microphone transmitter the different audio frequencies set up corresponding radio frequencies and the energy of these are emitted by the aerial; this results in waves of different lengths, or a band of waves as it is called. **1922** *Encycl. Brit.* XXXII. 712/2 The appurtenances specially developed for accomplishing this selection [of frequencies] in carrier current telephony are known as 'band-pass electrical filters'. **1929** T. E. SHEA *Transmission Networks & Wave Filters* II. vii. 235 This type of filter excludes, or attenuates, all frequencies lying between its two cut-off frequencies, but.. transmits..frequencies above and below this band. It is therefore commonly called a 'band elimination' filter. **1930** *Discovery* Dec. 398/2 The band-pass filter, which follows the low frequency modulator, allows the lower side-band to pass with an attenuation of six decibels. **1930** *Proc. Inst. Radio Engin.* XVIII. 168 The greater band width being required as the standard of quality [*sc.* in broadcast speech or music] becomes higher. **1931** *Daily Express* 21 Sept. 7/4 An advanced form of band-pass tuning. **1933** K. HENNEY *Radio Engin. Handbk.* XVII. 444 Television..requires a very wide band; high-grade program broadcasting, a fairly wide band; satisfactory speech, a somewhat narrower band. **1935** *Ibid.* (ed. 2) 171 Filters are divided into four classes, according to the frequency bands which they are intended to transmit, namely, low pass, high pass, band pass, band elimination. **1940** *Amat. Radio Handbk.* (ed. 2) 59/2 The main inductance L_2 is tuned by C_2 and C_3..the latter of smaller capacity for band-spread purposes. **1940** *Wireless Engineer* XVII. 394/1 Band-spreading may be defined as the deliberate limitation of the frequency range covered by a tuning unit, in order to facilitate the process of tuning. **1944** *Electronic Engin.* XVI. 322 Both colour reproduction and definition would require a very much greater band-width. **1951** *Good Housek. Home Encycl.* 230/1 If the set is required for short-wave reception as well as for the long and medium bands. **1959** *Times* 16 Jan. 10/1 The most important decision the C.C.I.R. will have to make..refers to the bandwidth of television transmissions in Bands IV and V. **1969** *Ibid.* 27 Mar. 12/8 Measurements giving the energy emitted in selected wavelength bands have been made on 300 stars.

III. *Comb.*, as ***band-maker, -reel, -wimble***; also ***band-like, -shaped*** adj. **band-brake**, a brake consisting of a band operating on a spindle; **band-case** = BAND-BOX; **band ceramic** (see BANDKERAMIK); **band clutch**, a clutch consisting of a band operating on a spindle or drum; **band-collar** (cf. 4 above); **band-fish**, a fish of the genus *Cepola*, belonging to the ribbon-shaped family of the order *Acanthopteri*; **band-knife**, an 'endless' knife; **band-pulley**, a flat-faced wheel, fixed on a shaft and driven by a band; **band-saw**, an endless saw, consisting of a steel belt with a serrated edge running with great speed over wheels; **band-sawyer**, an operative who uses a band-saw; **band-string**, a string for fastening bands (see above,[3] 4), in the 17th c. ornamented with tassels, etc (see Fairholt *Costume* 423); **band-wheel**, a wheel to which motion is communicated by a band running over it. Also BANDBOX, q.v.

1889 *Cent. Dict.*, *Band-brake. **1908** *Daily Chron.* 21 Nov 9/4 A band-brake operates on the balance gear. **1635** T. CRANLEY *Amanda* xliii, Within a *Band-case lies thy Ruffe. **1910** *Cycl. Automobile Engin.* I. 210 The most usual place in which the *band clutch is found is in connection with a planetary transmission. **1957** *Encycl. Brit.* V. 864/1 Band clutches are usually installed when it is necessary to transmit heavy loads accompanied by shocks. **1820** SCOTT *Abbot* iv, A speck of soot upon his *band-collar. **1836** YARRELL *Brit. Fishes* I. 224 Red *Band-fish, Snakefish, Ribandfish = *Cepola rubescens*. **1926** *Glasgow Herald* 12 July 8 Following the sewing machine come[s] the *band-knife. **1839** TODD *Cycl. Anat. & Phys.* III. 769/2 A *band-like commissure. **1864** WEBSTER s.v. *Saw*, *Band-saw. **1890** W. J. GORDON *Foundry* i. 30 A band-saw..which cuts through iron like cheese. **1916** *Daily Colonist* (Victoria, B.C.) 9 July 13/4 The machinery is already partly installed in the bandsaw mill. **1909** *Daily Chron.* 25 Sept. 7/6 *Band Sawyer wanted. **1599** B. JONSON *Cynthia's Rev.* v. iv, This is called the solemn *band-string. **1689** SELDEN *Table T.* 85 If a man..twirls his Bandstrings. **1691** WOOD *Ath. Oxon.* II. 556 He [wore] snakebone bandstrings (or bandstrings with very large tassels). **1816** SCOTT *Antiq.* ix, Wi' mony a button and a bandstring about it. **1407** *Test. Ebor* (1836) I. 347, j. mortas-wymbyll, j. *band-wymbyll, j. hoke, ii. planes.

band (bænd), *sb.*[3] Also 5–6 **bande**. [Late 15th c. *bande*, a. F. *bande* = Pr., Sp., It. *banda*, app. adopted from Teutonic (cf. OHG. *bant*, OS., ON. *band*: see BAND *sb.*[1]; also Goth. *bandi*: see BEND *sb.*[1]). The word received in Romanic a new development of sense, not found in Teutonic, with which it has since been taken back, not only into Eng., but also into Ger. (*bande*) and Du. (*bende*, formerly *bande*); the adoption being facilitated by its obvious connexion with the native words. In Eng., where the pre-existing BAND *sb.*[1], was synonymous with *bend*, the present word was, by confusion with these, also often written *bend*. So also in mod.Du. *bende* for *bande*, by assoc. with a native *bende*: see BEND *sb.*[1]

The actual history of *banda* in this sense, and its relation to the Teutonic forms, are not without uncertainty, owing to our ignorance at present of its age, and to the fact that It., Sp., Pg. *banda*, F. *bande*, are found also as synonyms of *benda*, *bende* 'fascia' (which, except in It., they have now indeed superseded), while conversely Littré's earliest example of *bande* 'troop' is spelt *bende*, thus showing at least form-association between the two words. And some actually identify them: Du Cange says that the company of soldiers formed by Alfonso of Castille was called a *banda*, from the red *banda* or ribbon worn by them as a sash; and the new ed. of the *Vocab. della Crusca* explains *banda* as 'Company of soldiers, because originally distinguished by a *banda* or band of cloth of a certain colour.' But Littré refers *banda, bande* 'troop' to late L. *bandum* BANNER; and Du Cange shows med.L. *bandus* in sense both of 'fascia,' and of 'company of men collected under a certain leader or *banner*,' thus associating all three notions. Whatever the original source, it is evident that the popular feeling associated *benda, banda*, 'fascia, stripe, sash, scarf, ribbon,' *banda*, 'company, troop,' and *bandum* 'banner.']

1. a. An organized company; a troop. Said of armed men, also of robbers, assassins, etc.

1490 CAXTON *Eneydos* lv. 152 Mesapus wyth a goode bande of folke. **1568** BIBLE (Bishops') *2 Kings* xxiv. 2 Bandes of the Chaldees, and bandes of the Syrians. **1598** BARRET *Theor. Warres* I. i. 5 Trayned companies, and selected bandes. **1667** MILTON *P.L.* II. 997 Her victorious Bands. **1822** BYRON *Werner* IV. i. 301 The 'black bands' who still Ravage the frontier. **1826** SOUTHEY *Lett. C. Butler* 499 A whole band of robbers were converted. **1860** PUSEY *Min. Proph.* 330 Small bands, unable to resist in the open field.

b. *trained* or *train-band*: see TRAIN-BAND.

2. A confederation of persons having a common purpose.

1557 N. T. (Genev.) *Ep.* *iii, The traiterous bande. **1738** WESLEY *Wks.* (1872) I. 92 That the persons so meeting be divided into several bands, or little companies. **1879** FURNIVALL in *New Shaks. Soc. Rep.* 11. The band of English men and women whose bond of oneness is 'to do honour to Shakspere.'

3. a. A company of persons or animals in movement.

1601 SHAKS. *All's Well* IV. i. 16 He must thinke vs some band of strangers. **1611** BIBLE *Gen.* xxxii. 7 Hee diuided the ..camels into two bands. **1725** POPE *Odyss.* XXII. 521 The matron-train with all the virgin-band. **1770** GOLDSM. *Des. Vill.* 401 Downward they move, a melancholy band. **1876** GREEN *Short Hist.* iv. §6 The little band of fugitives.

b. A herd or flock. *N. Amer.*

1824 S. BLACK *Jrnl. Voy. fr. Rocky Mt.* (1955) 73 The band of Carribou is gone farther. **1824** W. H. KEATING *Narr. Exped. St. Peter's River* I. viii. 379 The term *band*, as applied to a herd of buffalo, has almost become technical, being the one in use in the west. *a* **1861** T. WINTHROP *John Brent* (1883) ii. 11, I had come upon a band of horses feeding on the prairie. **1872** SCHELE DE VERE *Americanisms* 210 California for instance, forms its vast flocks of sheep into *bands*, of about a thousand each. **1920** J. M. HUNTER *Trail Drivers of Texas* 319 How many of the 'band' (meaning the herd) are gone? **1953** *Canad. Geogr. Jrnl.* XLVI. 246/2 Herder and 'band' (not flock) have lost their lives in blizzards year after year.

4. a. A company of musicians; the company of musicians attached to a regiment of the Army.

1660–3 *Warrant Bk.* iv. 316 George Hudson and Davies Mell to give orders for the band of Music^ns^. *Ibid.* 384 His Maties Band of Violins. **1766** ENTICK *London* IV. 446 The entertainment consists of a fine band of music. **1812** J. WILSON *Isle of Palms* IV. 442 The music bands both near and far Are playing. **1832** *Regul. Instr. Cavalry* III. 58 The Band ..plays whilst the Regiment is passing. **1845** E. HOLMES *Mozart* 6 Pieces which it seems were daily performed..by a band on the fortifications.

b. Colloq. phrases: ***when the band begins to play***, when matters become serious; ***to beat the band***, lit. so as to drown the noise made by the band; hence, to exceed, surpass, or beat everything.

1890 KIPLING *Barrack-r. Ballads* (1892) 6 It's 'Thank you, Mister Atkins', when the band begins to play. **1897** C. M. FLANDRAU *Harvard Episodes* 223, I was on the box-seat driving, you know,—lickety-split, to beat the band. **1900** G. BONNER *Hard-Pan* iii. 81 Doesn't that beat the band? **1910** W. M. RAINE *B. O'Connor* ii. 24 It's send for Bucky quick when the band begins to play. *Ibid.* 236 Eating together like brothers and laughing to beat the band. **1920** WODEHOUSE *Coming of Bill* II. vi. 167 You certainly are working to beat the band just now. **1923** A. CHRISTIE *Murder on Links* viii. 101 Well, if that doesn't beat the band!

†**5.** *fig.* A group of things. *Obs.*

1690 LOCKE *Hum. Und.* III. iii, Those Things we..have ranked into Bands, under distinct Names or Ensigns.

6. Band of Hope, a name given (first about 1847) to associations of young people who pledge themselves to total abstinence from the use of intoxicating liquors.

1847 J. TUNNICLIFF *Temperance song*, '*Come, all dear children*,' The Band of Hope shall be our name, the Temperance star our guide. **1878** *Temp. Record* 17 Jan. 33/2 Thus we find, in every city, town, and hamlet, Bands of Hope, and Senior Bands of Hope.

7. *Comb.*, as **band-brother**, **-leader**, **-leading**, **-playing**, **-roll**, **-room**, **-society**. **band-master**, the leader of a band of musicians, whence **band-mastered** *ppl. a.*; **band parts**, written or printed pieces of music (see PART *sb.* 10) for each member of a band of musicians; **band shell** *U.S.*, a bandstand in the form of a large concave shell with special acoustical properties; see SHELL *sb.* 12 c; **band-stand**, a platform or other structure for the use of a band of musicians.

1742 *Observ. Methodists* 20 Give my dear Love to my dear *Band Brethren. **1894** *Munsey's Mag.* XII. 411 (*heading*) Famous American *band leaders. **1927** *Melody Maker* Aug. 813/1 All band leaders still find it very difficult to obtain good instrumentalists. **1961** *Times* 20 May 11/4 Another bandleader-composer in search of his youth is Count Basie. **1955** L. FEATHER *Encycl. Jazz* (1956) i. 18 The *bandleading career that was to take many great Negro jazzmen.. North. **1858** W. ELLIS *Vis. Madagascar* xiii. 369 The *bandmaster of one of the English regiments. **1865** RUSKIN *Sesame* 110 A large species of marsh mosquito..melodious, *band-mastered, trumpeting in the summer air. **1895** A. ROBERTS *Adv. by Rail* iii. 45, I had a box stolen. Amongst other things, it contained my *band-parts. **1909** *Daily Chron.* 5 Oct. 1/3 An evening of excellent American *band-playing. **1693** W. ROBERTSON *Phraseol. Gen.* 200 A *bandroll or Muster-roll. **1909** *Cent. Dict.* Suppl., *Band-room, a store-room on a flag-ship in which the bandsmen keep their instruments and music. **1929** *Melody Maker* Jan. 59/1 A suite comprising waiting-room, band-room, engineers' room, announcer's room. **1933** P. GODFREY *Back-Stage* i. 15 The stage-manager looks at his watch: it is time to warn the 'band-room'. **1928** *Amer. City* Sept. 115/3 A *band-shell of good design was erected a few years ago in Spaulding Park, Muskogee, Okla. **1938** *Sun* (Baltimore) 2 Aug. 18/4 The Musical Union of Baltimore..had requested the Board of Park Commissioners to build a band shell below the mansion house in Druid Hill Park. **1964** MRS. L. B. JOHNSON *White House Diary* 6 May (1970) 132 The service band was playing merrily in front of the bandshell. **1984** *N. Florida Activities Guide* Spring 30/1 Free concerts in the beach-front bandshell. **1742** *Observ. Methodists* 20 Forming them into *Band Societies. **1859** J. LANG *Wand. India* 256 On the parade ground and at the *band stand. **1879** *Spectator* 7 June 719 Co-operating in labour, which the late Prof. Clifford used to speak of..as *band-work.

band (bænd), *sb.*[4] [Of uncertain origin: it may be conjecturally connected either with BAND *sb.*[2], or with BANDE = bound, bourne, as separating two valleys or gills; the Welsh *bant* 'height' has also been compared.]

A ridge of a hill; commonly applied in the English Lake district to a long ridge-like hill of minor height, or to a long narrow sloping offshoot from a higher hill or mountain.

1513 DOUGLAS *Æneis* XI. x. 63 Him self ascendis the hie band of the hyll. **1869** PEACOCK *Gloss. Lonsdale Dial.*, *Band*, the summit of a minor hill, as 'Swirl band,' Tilberthwaite fell. **1872** JENKINSON *Eng. Lakes* (1879) 23 The vale head of Langdale is divided by the Band into the Mickleden and Oxendale glens.

†**band(e**, *sb.*[5] *Obs.* [var. of *bonde*, a ME. form of BOUND *sb.*] = BOUND, limit.

c **1420** *Avow. Arth.* iii, None so hardi Durste bide in his bandus. **1470** HARDING *Chron.* x. vii, To let hym passe and ride Frely, where so they would withouten bande. **1470–85** MALORY *Arthur* II. xvii, Thow passyst thy bandes to come this waye. **1523** LD. BERNERS *Froiss.* I. ccxxxii. 321 They haue..done many an yuell dede in the bandes of Tholous.

band (bænd), *v.*[1] [a. F. *bande-r*, f. *bande* BAND *sb.*[1] and [2], the senses of which run together in the verb. Perh. partly derived from the Eng. sbs.]

1. *trans.* To bind or fasten with a band or bands.

1488–1852 [see BANDED 1.]

2. †**a.** To furnish with a band, to bind (a garment). **b.** To cover with a band or bandage. *Obs.*

1530 PALSGR. 443/1, I bande a garment or a maser, or any suche lyke..Bande your jacket, it shall be strongar. *a* **1700** DRYDEN (J.) His eyes were banded over. **1855** *Bookseller* 5 Mar. (*Advt.*) Prospectuses folded, banded, and stamped for Post.

c. To furnish (a bird) with an identifying band. So *banded* ppl. adj., *banding* vbl. sb. and ppl. adj. (See also *bird-banding*.) orig. *U.S.*

1914 *Lit. Digest* 17 Jan. 102/2 Last year over 150 young American and snowy egrets were banded. **1930** E. W. HENDY *Wild Exmoor* xviii. 275 The promiscuous habits of house wrens banded (i.e. ringed) in Ohio. **1930** J. S. HUXLEY *Bird-Watching* iii. 47 The practice of banding birds—attaching a light numbered and dated ring of metal to their legs, either when still in the nest, or after being caught in a special and harmless trap and subsequently set free again. *Ibid.*, This banding method has..been used to shed light upon other sides of bird-life. **1934** *Discovery* Apr. 111/1 It was natural that those species to be banded..should be the common frequenters of our gardens. *Ibid.* 112/2 The banding records indicate that..those that migrate through and winter in the east would be very slow to re-populate the devastated areas in the west.

3. To mark with bands or stripes.

1853 KANE *Grinnell Exp.* xxviii. (1856) 230 An opalescent purple, that banded the entire horizon. **1878** HUXLEY *Physiogr.* xix. 328 Each of these halves is banded round by a number of circles.

4. To join or form into a band or company; to unite, confederate, league: **a.** *trans.* and *refl.* Also, to form (cattle or sheep) into a herd or flock (*U.S.*).

1530 PALSGR. 443/1 He bandeth hymselfe with your enemyes. **1581** J. BELL *Haddon's Answ. Osor.* A ij, Bandyng ..all his knowledge and skill agaynst the professed doctrine of our Religion. *a* **1593** H. SMITH *Wks.* (1867) II. 184 The rulers band themselves against him. **1667** MILTON *P.L.* v. 714 What multitudes Were banded to oppose his high Decree. **1876** GREEN *Short Hist.* ii. §6. 91 Everywhere.. men banded themselves together for prayer. **1878** B. F. TAYLOR *Between Gates* 266 Leave him to 'band' his sheep and herd his bees as he pleases.

b. *intr.*

1530 PALSGR. 443/1 He bandeth with them that wyll forsake hym, whan he hath most nede. **1596** SPENSER *F.Q.* I. iv. 36 Huge routs of people did about them band. **1611** BIBLE *Acts* xxiii. 12 Certaine of the Iewes banded together. **1845** R. HAMILTON *Pop. Educ.* vi. 118 The enemies of Sabbath school Instruction are too scattered to band, too imbecile to argue.

†**band**, *v.*[2] *Obs.* [either a. F. *bander*, or shortened form of BANDY *v.*; cf. the pa. pples. *banded*, *bandied*, of similar sound.] = BANDY *v.* in various senses.

1580 HOLLYBAND *Treas. Fr. Tong.*, *Prebender en vn tripot*, to band in the tennice. **1596** SPENSER *F.Q.* III. ii. 41 Swete love such lewdnes bands from his faire companee. **1613** W. BROWNE *Brit. Past.* I. iv, He..Had heapes of fire-brands banded at his face. **1616** BEAUM. & FL. *Cust. Countr.* vi, Adverse fortune Banding us from one hazard to another. **1641** SHIRLEY *Cardinal* v. iii, Thus banded out o' the world by a woman's plot! **1672** DRYDEN *Conq. Granada* I. i. (1725) 36 Though they band and jar.

‖**banda** ('bændə). [Swahili.] A thatched house in parts of Africa.

1920 *Blackw. Mag.* CCVII. 651/2 Opposite some tumble-down bandas, a motor-lorry is waiting. **1951** R. CAMPBELL *Light on Dark Horse* x. 137 This banda or hut was made entirely of coconut palms.

bandabast, bandabust, varr. BUNDOBUST.

bandage ('bændɪdʒ), *sb.* [a. F. *bandage*, f. *bande* BAND *sb.*[2]: see -AGE. Orig. a term of surgery.]

1. *Surg.* A strip or band of woven material used to bind up a wound, sore, or fractured limb.

1599 A. M. *Gabelhouer's Bk. Physic* 185/2 On the syde of the Rupture, ther must be sowede a little bandage. **1725** POPE *Odyss.* XIX. 535 With bandage firm Ulysses' knee they bound. **1748** SMOLLETT *Rod. Rand.* xxviii, We reduced the fracture, dressed the wound, applied the eighteen-tailed bandage. **1850** MRS. STOWE *Uncle Tom's C.* xvii, There, there—let me fix this bandage.

b. *abst.* = BANDAGING *vbl. sb.* 1.

1720 *Lond. Gaz.* No. 5901/3 Lectures in Osteology, Bandage, etc.

2. A strip of any flexible material used for binding or covering up, *esp.* for blindfolding the eyes.

1715 GARTH *Claremont* (R.) Justice [shall] need no bandage for her eyes. **1799** G. SMITH *Laborat.* I. 15 Glue them together with a bandage of paper. **1813** SHELLEY *Q. Mab.* 190 Like bandages of straw Beneath a wakened giant's strength.

fig. **1750** SHENSTONE *Ode Indol.* 12 Ah! gentle Sloth! indulgent spread The same soft bandage o'er my mind. **1862** MAURICE *Mor. & Met. Phil.* IV. v. §66 Tie the controversy with bandages of argument.

3. A band or strip of material used to bind together and strengthen any structure. *arch.*

1766 ENTICK *London* IV. 205 A channel cut into the bandage of Portland-stone. **1842** GWILT *Encycl. Archit.* Gloss., *Bandages*, the rings or chains of iron inserted in the corners of a stone wall..which act as a tie on the walls to keep them together.

bandage ('bændɪdʒ), *v.* [f. prec. sb.] To tie or bind up with a bandage. *lit.* and *fig.*

1774 GOLDSM. *Nat. Hist.* II. xi. (JOD.) Their artificial deformities of..bandaging the feet. **1831** CARLYLE *Sart. Res.* III. i, So bandaged, and hampered, and hemmed in.. with thousand requisitions. **1873** Æ. MUNRO *Nursing* iv. 159 To bandage a part well.

'**bandaged**, *ppl. a.* [f. prec. + -ED.] Bound or tied up with a bandage.

1855 MACAULAY *Hist. Eng.* III. 636 Managing the bridle with a bandaged arm. **1879** BARING-GOULD *Germ.* I. 391 The bandaged boy in blind-man's-buff.

bandager ('bændɪdʒə(r)). [f. as prec. + -ER[1].] One who bandages (wounds).

1851 H. C. ROBINSON *Diary* II. 295 His skill as a bandager.

'**bandaging**, *vbl. sb.* [f. as prec. + -ING[1].]

1. The action or art of applying bandages.

1835 *Penny Cycl.* III. 365/1 Courses of lectures on bandaging. **1838** HT. MARTINEAU *West. Trav.* I. 206 Whether the bandaging of his ancle gave him pain.

2. *concr.* Material for bandages.

1819 *Pantolog.* s.v. *Surgery*, Adhesive plaster with proper bandaging is to be used.

bandagist ('bændɪdʒɪst). [f. BANDAGE *sb.* + -IST; cf. F. *bandagiste.*] A maker of bandages.

1859 WORCESTER cites DUNGLISON. **1871** T. SMITH in *Syst. Surg.* V. 506 The instrument-maker or bandagist.

'**Band-Aid**, *sb.* and *a.* orig. *U.S.* Also with small initials or as one word. **A.** *sb.* **1.** A proprietary name for a type of sticking-plaster with a gauze pad. Also, a strip of Band-Aid.

1924 *Official Gaz.* (U.S. Patent Office) 4 Nov. TM27/1 Johnson & Johnson, New Brunswick, N.J...*Band-Aid*.. protective surgical dressing in the form of a bandage. Claims use since November, 1920. **1926–7** *Army & Navy Stores Catal.* 461/1 Band Aid..'a protective dressing for cuts and wounds'..tin 1/-. **1933** *Trade Marks Jrnl.* 22 Feb. 213 Band-Aid... Medicated dressings for human use. Johnson & Johnson (Great Britain) Limited,..Slough, Buckinghamshire; Manufacturers. **1948** 'P. QUENTIN' *Run to Death* xx. 147, I..found a band aid. I applied it neatly over the burn. **1958** R. CHANDLER *Playback* xix. 157 He was as adhesive as a band-aid. **1964** *Trade Marks Jrnl.* 23 Sept. 1532/2 Band-aid... Pharmaceutical and sanitary substances;..medical and surgical plasters, materials prepared for bandaging;..first aid boxes sold complete. Johnson & Johnson,..New Brunswick, State of Jersey, United States of America; manufacturers and merchants. **1976** N. THORNBURG *Cutter & Bone* xi. 267 Why not aspirin? Or a Band-Aid? **1983** *Listener* 30 June 31/3 There was some marvellous singing and playing, including footage of Alfred Brendel playing ineffable Liszt with Band-Aids on most of his fingers.

2. *fig.* A temporary or makeshift solution to a problem, etc.; a palliative.

1968 *United Church Observer* 15 Mar. 36/1 It was another of those political band-aids patted over a minor sore. **1974** R. M. PIRSIG *Zen & Art of Motorcycle Maintenance* (1976) I. v. 61 Consoling words are more for strangers, for hospitals, not kin. Little emotional Band-Aids like that aren't what he needs. **1981** *Sunday Times* 12 July 17/4 So much social work is just Band-Aid. **1985** *Nat. Westminster Bank Q. Rev.* May 4 Successive applications of bandaids of differing descriptions is to be preferred to the application of mere common sense.

B. *adj.* Makeshift or temporary; palliative.

1970 *Times* 20 Apr. 19 Better and better economic coordination might prevent the need for such heavy reliance on financial 'band-aid' solutions. **1974** *Kingston* (Ont.) *Whig-Standard* 26 Jan. 7/5 Band-aid measures like tinkering with traffic will not revitalize the downtown area. **1976** *Sydney Morning Herald* 23 Sept. 14/5 Two Sydney Harbour ferries ordered from the Newcastle Shipyards by the State Government were only a 'band-aid arrangement' to help the industry. **1984** *Gainesville* (Florida) *Sun* 4 Apr. 4A/1 The alternatives you propose are just 'Band-Aid' solutions.

Hence as *v. trans.*, to apply a makeshift or temporary solution to (a problem, etc.); also with *over*.

1972 *N.Y. Times Mag.* 29 Oct. 21 A problem of this dimension cannot be ignored or Band-aided over. **1975** *Daily Colonist* (Victoria, B.C.) 19 Nov. 19/1 The courts of Victoria..will probably be bandaided through their present time and space crisis. **1976** *National Observer* (U.S.) 18 Sept. 18/2 This is just Band-Aiding the cancer. **1983** *N.Y. Times* 23 June A15 Buy it now, Band-Aid it later.

†**bandalore.** A toy containing a coiled spring, which caused it, when thrown down, to rise again to the hand, by the winding up of the string by which it was held.

1824 MISS MITFORD *Village* Ser. I. (1863) 198 A gone-by toy, called a bandalore. **1864** *Athenæum* 10 Sept. 330/2 Our Iron Duke..in Dublin playing with a Bandalore, now an obsolete toy.

bandanna, -ana (bæn'dænə). Also 8 **bandanno.** [cf. Hindustani *bāndhnū* 'a mode of dyeing in which the cloth is tied in different places, to prevent the parts from receiving the dye' (Shakspear *Dict.*); prob. adopted first in Pg.] A richly coloured silk handkerchief, with spots left white or yellow by the process described above. The name is now applied to cotton handkerchiefs also, and the pattern is produced by chemical agency.

1752 in J. Long *Bengal* (1870) 31 Plain taffaties, ordinary bandannoes, and chappas. **1854** THACKERAY *Newcomes* I. 39 Waving his yellow bandanna. **1875** MISS BIRD *Hawaii* 134 Many had tied bandanas in a graceful knot over the left shoulder.

attrib. **1824** *Ann. Reg.* 140/2 Bandana handkerchiefs. **1843** CARLYLE *Past & Pr.* (1858) 285 Beautiful bandana webs.

bandar ('bʌndə(r)). Also **bander, bunder.** [Hind.] The Rhesus monkey, *Macaca mulatta.* Also in ***Bandar-log*** [Hind. *log* people], Kipling's nation of monkeys (see quot. 1894); hence *fig.*, any body of irresponsible chatterers.

1885 KIPLING *Dep. Ditties* (1899) 54 It was an artless *Bandar*, and he danced upon a pine. **1894** —— *2nd Jungle Bk.* (1895) 63 Men are blood-brothers of the *Bandar-log*. **1917** 'IAN HAY' *Carrying On* xiii. 313 That is just what the *Bandar Log* overlook, when they jabber about the dreadful industrial upheaval that is coming with peace. **1922** *Chambers's Jrnl.* June 353/1 He was too used to the wordy clatter of the *bunderlogue* to notice it. *Ibid.*, Their attentions the unhappy *bunder* would gladly dispense with. **1961** *Times* 23 Nov. 17/3 He castigates the *banderlog* at all levels.

bandbox ('bændbɒks). Also 7–8 **ban-box.** [f. BAND *sb.*[2] + BOX.] **a.** A slight box of card-board or very thin chip covered with paper, for collars, caps, hats, and millinery; originally made for the 'bands' or ruffs of the 17th c. Also *fig.*, a fragile or flimsy structure or one in which the accommodation is restricted.

1631 T. POWELL *Tom All Trades* 173 Carrying the Bandbox under their apron. **1633** ROWLEY *Match at Midn.* IV. in *Dodsl.* (1780) VII. 413 Enter Maid with a band-box. *Constable.* How, now! where ha' you been?.. *Maid.* For my mistress's ruff, at her sempstress'. **1712** ADDISON *Spect.* No. 311 ¶1, I..do not suffer a Ban-box to be carried into her Room before it has been searched. **1720** GAY *Poems* (1745) I. 189 With empty ban-box she delights to range. **1758** J. S. *Le Dran's Observ. Surg.* (1771) 340 Such Wood as they make

Bandboxes..with. **1859** HELPS *Friends in C.* Ser. II. II. viii. 148 A thing..to be chiefly kept in a bandbox. **1875** H. LEE *Octopus* viii. 81 The vessel was lightly built—a mere bandbox of a craft.

b. ***to look as if one came out of a bandbox*** (and similar phrases): to look extremely smart and neat. orig. *U.S.*

1825 S. WOODWORTH *Forest Rose* I. i, He is a genteel, delightful looking fellow, neat as a starched tucker fresh from a banbox [*sic*]. **1833** *Knickerbocker* I. 198 The old gentleman..popped into the room, looking as if he had stepped out of a bandbox. **1869** 'MARK TWAIN' *Innoc. Abroad* xxxviii. 410 They are all.. exceedingly neat and cleanly..as if they were just out of a band-box. **1888** 'R. BOLDREWOOD' *Robb. under Arms* III. vii. 94 Starlight.. looked as if he'd just come out of a band-box. **1941** M. MARLETT *Death has Thousand Doors* (1950) iv. 32 She invariably looked as though she had stepped out of the proverbial bandbox.

c. attrib. and Comb. ***bandbox thing***: (cf. sense a, quot. 1859.). Also in senses: (*a*) resembling a bandbox; flimsy, fragile; (*b*) conspicuously neat and clean; dressed-up.

1727 SWIFT *Let.* 9 July (1912) III. 405 Letters..which.. I can sell at good advantage to the band-box and trunk-maker. **1774** *Westm. Mag.* II. 454 The good man..turned the eye of contempt upon the Band-box *Thing*, and..said, 'I believe 'tis a Doll.' **1838** *S. Lit. Messenger* IV. 638/2 To render fur caps and bandbox hats for winter..articles of vital necessity. **1844** THACKERAY *May Gambols* in *Fraser's Mag.* June 707/2 Spick and span *bandbox* churches of the pointed Norman style. *a* **1852** MOORE *Country Dance & Quad.* xiii. 51 A band-box thing, all art and lace, Down from her nose-tip to her shoe-tie. **1894** *Sketch* 13 June 355/1 The best stage-management in the world could not have made the thing lifelike..on that bandbox stage. **1916** J. BUCHAN *Greenmantle* xi. 143 Better a bloody end in a street scrap than the tender mercies of that bandbox bravo. **1939** AUDEN & ISHERWOOD *Journey to War* v. 130 Little band-box officers, slim and smart. **1967** V. H. GIELGUD *Conduct of Member* xx. 160 She was wearing a dressing-gown..but preserved her usual band-box quality of neat fastidiousness.

bandboxical (bænd'bɒksɪkəl), *a.* *colloq.* [f. prec., after words from Gr., as *paradoxical.*] Having the appearance or size of a bandbox.

1787 BECKFORD *Italy* (1834) II. 175 Cooped up in a close, bandboxical apartment. **1873** MISS BRADDON *Str. & Pilgr.* III. i. 240 Square bandboxical rooms.

bandboxy ('bændbɒksɪ), *a.* [f. BANDBOX + -Y[1].] Resembling a bandbox in shape, the fragility of its structure, or its restricted accommodation. (Cf. BANDBOXICAL *a.*)

1855 B. TAYLOR *Pictures of Palestine* xxxvi. 428 Those bandboxy sombreros which I at first thought so ungainly. **1891** *Cornh. Mag.* Feb. 160 Houses,..light and small and bandboxy. **1896** C. ALLEN *Papier Mâché* 80 Sheds, and bandboxy houses all tilted up on stumps.

b. Extremely neat. *U.S.*

1870 L. M. ALCOTT *Old-Fash. Girl* xii. 195 The dance and the race had taken the 'band-boxy' air out of Tom's elegant array.

‖**bandeau** (bɑ̃'do). Pl. **-eaux.** [Fr.:—OF. *bandel*, dim. form from *bande* BAND *sb.*[2]; cf. BANDORE[2].] **a.** A narrow band or fillet worn by women to bind the hair, or as part of a head-dress. **b.** A bandage for the eyes.

1706 T. BETTERTON *Amorous Widow* I. 4 The fairest Hair, the beautiful'st Curls do not become your Forehead, so well as a *Bando* did. *c* **1790** MISS BURNEY *Diary* (1842) I. 98 (D.) That bandeau..was worn by every woman at court. *a* **1847** MRS. SHERWOOD *Lady of Manor* III. xxi. 277 Just make up this bandeau for my hair. ? **1858** C. MATHEWS *Autobiog.* (1879) I, In a laced night-cap with sky-blue bandeau. **1861** GEN. P. THOMPSON *Audi Alt.* III. clxi. 175 The Chancellor of the Exchequer, as Paul Louis said of fortune, sees under his bandeau. **1908** [see BARRETTE 2]. **1959** *Sunday Times* 5 Apr. 22/5 As small as it is possible to be and still be called a hat, a bandeau and bow are caught in a cage of veiling.

c. A strip of velvet or other material generally made up in a circular form to be stitched inside the lower part of the crown of a hat that is too large for the head.

1908 *Daily Chron.* 29 Jan. 4/7 With the right sort of 'bandeau'..you need not wear a hatpin at all.

banded ('bændɪd). *ppl. a.* [f. BAND *v.* + -ED]

1. Bound or fastened with, or as if with, a band.

1488 *Invent.* in Tytler *Hist. Scot.* (1864) II. 391 A bandit kist like a gardeviant. **1813** SCOTT *Rokeby* III. xxiv, These iron-banded chests to gain. **1852** TUPPER *Prov. Philos.* 409 One fortuitous grain might dislocate the banded universe.

2. Furnished with a band (or bands); in *Her.* with a band differing in colour from the garb.

1787 PORNY *Heraldry* 151 Three Blackamoors' Heads in Profile..banded Argent and Gules. **1823** P. NICHOLSON *Pract. Build.* 581 Banded column, a column encircled with Bands, or annular rustics. **1837** MARRYAT *Dog-Fiend* vii, A ..gold-banded cocked hat. **1855** TENNYSON *Maud* I. viii, The snowy-banded..Delicate-handed priest.

3. a. Marked with bands or stripes; esp. in specific zoological and botanical names.

1814 MITCHILL *Fishes N.Y.* 427 Banded Mackerel. *Scomber zonatus.* **1823** E. JAMES *Exped. Rocky Mts.* I. 267 *Crotalus horridus*, Banded rattlesnake. **1836** [see KANGAROO *sb.* 2]. *a* **1842** TENNYSON *Eleanore*, The yellow-banded bees. **1848** BARTLETT *Dict. Amer.* 165 *Grunter*, one of the popular names of the fish called by naturalists the *Banded Drum.* **1870** *Amer. Naturalist* IV. 102 The banded Sunfish (*Bryttus Chaetodon*). **1921** H. GUTHRIE-SMITH *Tutira* xxiii. 207 The Banded Dottrel (*Charadrius bicinctus*). **1949** C. LONGFIELD *Dragonflies* (ed. 2) 43 *Agrion splendens*, the Banded Agrion.

b. *Geol.* (See quots.)

1859 *Q. Jrnl. Geol. Soc.* XV. 193 Peculiar banded flints in the chalk..exhibit a central longitudinal axis or narrow stem, crossed on its middle third by numerous short parallel stripes of alternately light and dark flint. **1876** PAGE *Advd. Text-bk. Geol.* xvii. 310 This banded appearance of a lias cliff. **1889** *Cent. Dict.*, *Banded structure*, the structure of a rock which is..divided into layers... The structure of a mineral made up of a series of layers.., as onyx. **1904** GOODCHILD & TWENEY *Technol. & Sci. Dict.* 39/2 *Banded Structure.* This term is..coming into use in a more restricted sense, as descriptive of the parallel structures observable in gneisses.

4. Confederated, leagued, allied.

1601 BP. BARLOW *Serm. Paules Crosse* 61 This conspiracie thus banded. **1667** MILTON *P.L.* VI. 85 The banded Powers of Satan. **1855** MACAULAY *Hist. Eng.* IV. 274 The poet addressed himself to the banded enemies of France.

†'**bandel, bandle.** *Obs.* [a. OF. *bandele, -elle*, dim. of *bande* BAND *sb.*[2]] A swaddling-band.

1598 FLORIO, *Fasciola*, a little bandle, a little swadling clout. **1603** —— *Montaigne* II. xii. (1632) 253 The bandles and swathes about our children. *Ibid.* 299 Foure [gods] to a childe, as protectors of his bandels, of his drinke, etc.

bandelet ('bændəlɪt). Also 7 **bandelette.** [a. F. *bandelette*, dim. of OF. *bandele* little band. Cf. BANDLET.] A small band, streak, or fillet; in *Arch.* a small flat moulding encompassing a column.

1647 W. BROWNE *Polex.* 99 The fairest Princesse that hath ever worne the sacred Bandelette of the Incas. **1696** in PHILLIPS. **1751** EARL ORRERY *On Swift* 89 (T.) The longer he wore the diadem, the bandelet still became more tight and irksome. **1863** R. HILL *Jamaica Seas. Notes* 194 The fish ..is roseate in colour, varied with bandelets.

bander ('bændə(r)). *arch.* [f. BAND *v.* + -ER[1].] One who bands or leagues; a confederate.

1563 *Myrr. Mag.*, *Somerset* xxiv, Theyr banders to elect. **1591** PERCIVALL *Span. Dict.*, *Vandolero*, a bander, he that followeth a faction. **1649** BP. GUTHRY *Mem.* (1702) 77 So many of the Banders as happen'd to be at home..were cited to appear. **1820** SCOTT *Abbot* xx, The lords who have become banders in the west.

‖**banderilla** (bande'riʎa). Also **banderillo.** [Sp., dim. of *bandera* BANNER.] A little dart, ornamented with a banderole, which dexterous bull-fighters stick into the neck and shoulders of the bull; also *fig.*

1797 [see next]. **1865** *Pall Mall G.* 23 Nov. 3 He will begin to see the barb of the banderilla under its paper disguise. **1882** H. DE WINDT *On Equator* ix. 138 Each was armed with the *banderillo*, small barbed darts, about a foot long. **1927** HEMINGWAY *Men without Women* 44 Fuentes..sank the banderillos straight down. **1939** SPENDER & GILI tr. *Lorca's Poems* 123 How tremendous with the final Banderillas of darkness. **1948** L. MACNEICE *Holes in Sky* 61 Gaudy banderillas May quiver in our flanks.

Hence as *v. trans.* and *intr.* (also in Sp. form **banderillear**), to stick a banderilla into (a bull). So **bande'rilling** *vbl. sb.*

1932 HEMINGWAY *Death in Aft.* xvii. 197 Bulls which will not charge..are banderilla-ed by..the media-vuelta or half-turn. *Ibid.* 198 Very rarely..a man is able to banderillear properly from both sides. **1932** R. CAMPBELL *Taurine Provence* iii. 70 The art of banderilling is not only a matter of speed.

banderillero (ˌbanderi'ʎero) [f. BANDERILLA, with agential suffix *-ero*]. The bull-fighter who uses banderillas.Also *fig.*

1797 *Encycl. Brit.* III. 772/1 The..*banderilleros*..plunge into his neck..a kind of darts called *banderillas.* **1845** R. FORD *Trav. Spain* I. II. 182 The *banderilleros* go right up to him, holding the arrows at the shaft, and pointing the barbs at the bull. **1864** DK. MANCH. *Crt. & Soc. Eliz. to Anne* I. 24 The ladies danced with picadors and banderilleros. **1932** HEMINGWAY *Death in Aft.* iii. 26 Men who..place the banderillas..are called peones or banderilleros. **1934** R. CAMPBELL *Broken Record* ii. 48, I am only a banderillero in the cuadrilla of that great matador [Wyndham Lewis].

banderol(e, bandrol, bannerol ('bændərəl, -əʊl, 'bænərəl). Forms: 6 **banerol, banaroll, bannerall,** 7 **bandroul(e, -role, -roll, banrol, bannerolle,** 7–9 **banneroll,** 8 **banner-roll,** 6– **banderol, bannerol,** 9 **bannerole, banderole, (bandarole), bandrol.** [a. F. *banderole* (15th c. *banerolle*, 16th c. *banderolle*), dim. of *bandière, bannière*, BANNER, probably after It. *banderuola*, dim. of *bandiera* BANNER.]

1. A long narrow flag, with cleft end, flying from the mast-heads of ships, carried in battle, etc.

1562 LEIGH *Armory* 189 Any Banner, Standard, Banaroll. **1612** DRAYTON *Poly-olb.* xxii. (1748) 342 Let them in the field be by their band-rouls known. **1681** *Disc. Tanger* 16 Gayland..sent his Treasurer with a White Bandrol, offering terms of Peace. **1808** SCOTT *Marm.* IV. xxxviii, Scroll, pennon, pensil, bandrol, there O'er the pavilions flew. **1870** *Standard* 5 Dec., Disarmed a colour serjeant.. and seized on the bannerol he carried.

2. A small ornamental streamer, *e.g.* that attached to the lance of a knight; in *Her.* one hanging down from the crook of a crosier, and folding over the staff.

1596 SPENSER *F.Q.* VI. vii. 26 To despoyle of knightly bannerall. **1615** G. SANDYS *Trav.* 124 Thousands of Pilgrims..euery one with his banrol in his hand. **1829** W. IRVING *Granada* (1850) 21 The..lances bore gay bandaroles. **1848** LYTTON *Harold* iii. 212 The lance with its pointed banderol. **1851** S. JUDD *Margaret* xvii. (1871) 149 Her hair streamed bandrols in the wind.

b. 'The little fringed silk flag that hangs on a trumpet' J.

1587 FLEMING *Contn. Holinshed* III. 490/1 Trumpeters.. sounding their trumpets most roiallie, their bannerols displaied.

3. A ribbon-like scroll bearing a device or inscription.

1622 F. MARKHAM *Bk. Warre* II. ix. 74 His Colors..are euermore contained in the Band-role vpon which his Crest standeth. **1875** FORTNUM *Maiolica* iii. 30 Portraits of ladies with a ribbon or banderole on which the name is inscribed.

4. *Arch.* A flat band with an inscription, used in decorating buildings of the Renascence period.

5. A banner about a yard square, borne at the funerals of great men, and placed over the tomb. [See BANNEROL.]

bandersnatch ('bændəsnætʃ). [Invented by 'L. Carroll' (C. L. Dodgson); presumably a portmanteau word like its stock epithet *frumious.*] A fleet, furious, fuming, fabulous creature, of dangerous propensities, immune to bribery and too fast to flee from; later, used vaguely to suggest any creature with such qualities.

1871 'L. CARROLL' *Through Looking-Glass* i. 22 Beware the Jubjub bird, and shun The frumious Bandersnatch! **1876** —— *Hunting of Snark* vii, But the Bandersnatch merely extended its neck And grabbed at the Banker again. **1908** *Daily Chron.* 19 Aug. 7/4 'There may be a bandersnatch,' he said doubtfully, dusting the ground with his palmetto fan. **1936** C. S. LEWIS *Alleg. Love* vii. 301 Always, at the critical moment, a strange knight, a swift ship, a bandersnatch or a boojum, breaks in. **1959** —— *Let.* 15 May (1966) 287 No one ever influenced Tolkien—you might as well try to influence a bandersnatch.

bandicoot ('bændɪkuːt). Also 9 **-icoote, -ycoot.** [corruption of Telugu *pandi-kokku*, lit. 'pig-rat' (Col. Yule).]

1. A large Indian rat (*Mus malabaricus* or *giganteus*), as big as a cat, and very destructive. (Wrongly used in quot. 1789 for the Musk-rat.)

1789 MUNRO *Narrat.* 32 The Bandicoot, or musk rat, is another troublesome animal..from its offensive smell. **1813** J. FORBES *Orient. Mem.* III. 41 Bandicoote rat[s] frequently undermine ware houses and destroy every kind of merchandise. **1860** TENNENT *Ceylon* I. 150 Another favourite article of food with the coolies is the pig-rat or Bandicoot.

2. A genus of insectivorous Australian marsupials (*Perameles*), somewhat resembling the above.

1827 P. CUNNINGHAM *Two Years N. S. Wales* I. xvii. 316 The *bandicoot* is about four times the size of a rat, without a tail, and burrows in the ground or in hollow trees. **1831** TYERMAN & BENN. *Voy. & Trav.* II. xxxvi. 149 The dogs also worried a bandy-coot..an animal..with a head and tail resembling those of a rat, and a pouch under the belly for the reception of its young. **1839** TODD *Cycl. Anat. & Phys.* III. 260/2 Marsupials commonly known in Australia by the name of Bandicoots. **1865** J. G. WOOD *Homes without Hands* 307 The second Building Mammal on our list is..the.. Rabbit-eared Bandicoot. **1888** 'R. BOLDREWOOD' *Robb. under Arms* I. i. 7 I'd be as miserable as a bandicoot. **1936** I. L. IDRIESS *Cattle King* xxiii. 203 Country that was tiptop a few years ago now wouldn't feed a bandicoot.

bandie ('bændɪ). *Sc.* and *north.* Also **bandy.** [perh. derived from BANSTICKLE.] The stickleback, *Gasterosteus aculeatus.*

1825 in JAMIESON. **1854** in A. E. BAKER *Gloss. Northampt. Words.* **1876** SMILES *Sc. Natur.* i. 14 'Mother,' said he, 'where are my crabs and bandies?' **1921** *Glasgow Herald* 25 Mar. 7/2 Little boys poking in their depths for bandies.

bandied ('bændɪd), *ppl. a.* [f. BANDY *v.* + -ED.] Tossed to and fro. *lit.* and *fig.*

1663 BUTLER *Hud.* I. II. 55 Whipp'd Tops and bandy'd Balls, The learned hold are Animals. **1851** SIR F. PALGRAVE *Norm. & Eng.* I. 202 How cruel then, such bandied terms as 'base servility.'

bandiness ('bændɪnɪs). [f. BANDY *a.* + -NESS.] The quality of being bandy-legged or crooked.

1840 DICKENS *Old C. Shop* xxxvi, If..any moral twist or bandiness could be found, Miss Sally Brass's nurse was alone to blame.

banding ('bændɪŋ), *vbl. sb.*[1] [f. BAND *v.*[1]]

1. Combining, joining in parties or factions; leaguing, confederation.

1575 CHURCHYARD *Chippes* (1817) 190 Great banding then, began in Borough towne. *c* **1645** HOWELL *Lett.* (1650). I. 316 There being divers bandings, and factions at court. **1792** BURKE *Let. Langrishe* Wks. VI. 358 As little do I relish any bandings or associations for procuring it. **1860** GEN. P. THOMPSON *Audi Alt.* III. cvii. 20 The banding of man with man keeps down felonious action.

2. Formation of, or marking with, bands or stripes. ***banding-plane***: a plane used for cutting out grooves and inlaying strings and bands in straight and circular work.

1739 LABELYE *Piers Westm. Br.* 41 Each of the Piers of the intended Bridge will be built..with the same Bandings, the same Cementing and Crampings, as if built upon dry Ground. **1859** in WORCESTER. **1862** DANA *Man. Geol.* 651 Its banding the stream with colder and warmer waters.

3. = BAND *sb.*² 3.
1892 *Daily News* 2 July 6/7 White sailor hat, with blue ribbon banding.

† **'banding,** *vbl. sb.*² *Obs.* [f. BAND *v.*² + -ING¹.] = BANDYING.
1589 GREENE *Menaphon* (Arb.) 45 There was a banding of such lookes. **1611** SPEED *Hist. Gt. Brit.* IX. xxiv. 138 Fortune ..made him a Ball for her banding. *c* **1645** HOWELL *Lett.* (1650) I. 327 The..bandings of opinions we had lately at Gresham college.

'banding, *ppl. a.* [f. BAND *v.*¹ + -ING².] Confederate, leaguing.
1602 W. WATSON *Decacord.* 62 This banding impudencie of the Jesuits.

bandit ('bændɪt). Pl. ban'ditti, 'bandits. Forms: 6-7 **bandetto, 7 bandite, -ditto, -dyto, -diti, 7-8 -ditty, -dito, 7- bandit.** *Pl. α.* 6 **-deti, 7 -ditie, 7-8 -diti, -ditty, -dity, 7- ditti;** *β.* **6-7 -dettos, 7 -ditos, -ditoes, -detties, -dities, 7-8 -ditties, 7- dits.** [a. It. *bandito* 'proclaimed, proscribed,' in pl. *banditi* sb. 'outlaws,' pa. pple. of *bandire* = med.L. *bannīre* to proclaim, proscribe: see BAN *sb.* and *v.*, and cf. BANISH. Early spellings, as well as the current pl. *banditti*, were apparently corrupted by form-assoc. with DITTO *sb.*, It. *detto*, pl. *detti*. The It. sing. *bandito* is not now used in Eng.: *bandit* is also mod.F. But the pl. *banditti* (for It. *banditi*) is more used than *bandits*, esp. in reference to an organized band of robbers; in which sense it has also been used as a collective sing.; in 17th c. this was taken as an individual sing., with pl. *-is*, *-ies*.]

a. *lit.* One who is proscribed or outlawed; *hence*, a lawless desperate marauder, a brigand: usually applied to members of the organized gangs which infest the mountainous districts of Italy, Sicily, Spain, Greece, and Turkey. Also, in modern use, = GANGSTER I. See also *one-armed bandit*.
(*Bandetto* in first quot. may be attrib. sb. or ppl. adj.)
1593 SHAKS. *2 Hen. VI*, IV. i. 135 A Romane Sworder, and Bandetto slaue. **1594** NASHE *Unfort. Trav.* 57 The Bandettos..are certayne outlawes that lie betwixt Rome and Naples. **1602** *Life T. Cromwell* II. i. 95 The banditti do you call them?.. I am sure we call them plain thieves in England. **1611** CORYAT *Crudities* 117 The Bandits..are the murdering robbers upon the Alpes. **1688** *Lond. Gaz.* No. 2310/3 He had lived as a Banditti in Anatolia. **1713** STEELE *Englishm.* No. 13. 84 The Examiner is no more a Tory.. than a Bandito is a Soldier. **1719** D'URFEY *Pills* (1872) II. 292 Each conquering great Commander, And mighty Alexander, Were Bandittics too. **1800** COLQUHOUN *Comm. Thames* vi. 240 A set of lawless Banditti infested the River. **1840** HOOD *Up Rhine* 191 Why, every Baron in the land was a bandit. **1876** GREEN *Short Hist.* v. §1. 224 The routed soldiery turned into free companies of bandits. **1935** E. WEEKLEY *Something about Words* ii. 44 *Bandits* were formerly Italians, picturesque in costume and impressive in armament; now that they are revived, they ride in motor-cars. **1935** *Amer. Speech* Apr. 120/1 The world of crime has its significant distinctions: *hijacker, car bandit,* [etc.]. **1944** AUDEN *For Time Being* (1945) 116 The bandit who is good to his mother.

b. *collective sing.* A company of bandits.
1706 DE FOE *Jure Div.* II. 15 He form'd the First Banditty of the Age. **1799** WELLINGTON in Owen *Disp.* 146 In which province an adventurer had assembled a banditti. **1826** SCOTT *Woodst.* v. 195 Deer-stealers..are ever a desperate banditti.

c. *attrib.*; and in *comb.*, as ***bandit-haunted***.
[Cf. **1593** in 1.] **1854** J. ABBOTT *Napoleon* I. xii. 208 Fierce banditti bands. **1855** MILMAN *Lat. Chr.* (1864) V. IX. ii. 229 Wild Bohemians and bandit soldiers. **1859** TENNYSON *Enid* 879 Bandit-haunted holds.

d. *transf.* A hostile aircraft (see quot. 1943).
1942 I. GLEED *Arise to Conquer* xii. 111 One bandit shot down in sea about ten miles out. **1943** C. H. WARD-JACKSON *Piece of Cake* 12 Bandit, enemy aircraft. It is used throughout Fighter Command, and elsewhere... The term was orginally a code word.

† **'bandit,** *v. Obs.* [f. It. *bandito* proscribed: see prec.] To proscribe, banish, outlaw.
1611 CORYAT *Crudities* 287 All light gold is bandited, that is, banished out of the Citie [Venice]. **1652** S. S. *Secretaries Stud.* 264 A Noble man..long since Bandited by the State, for murthering a Gentleman.

banditism ('bændɪtɪz(ə)m). [f. BANDIT + -ISM. Cf. F. *banditisme* (Flaubert, 1853).] The practices of bandits.
1885 *Manch. Guardian* 25 May 8 In England they reestablish the fusillade, in Russia torture, in Germany banditism. **1921** *19th Cent.* Sept. 407 The resistance of the peasantry to the Communist system of food supply is one of the causes of the development of banditism. **1941** KOESTLER *Scum of Earth* 116 Cyrano's régime had been old-fashioned, nineteenth-century banditism.

banditry ('bændɪtrɪ). [f. BANDIT + -RY.] The practices of bandits.
1922 *Q. Rev.* July 157 Already they have made short work of banditry. **1924** *Glasgow Herald* 29 Oct. 8 The ponderous banditry which the Chinese dignify by the name of war.

‖**Bandkeramik** ('bantkɛˌramɪk). *Archæol.* Also band ceramic. [G. (F. Klopfleisch 1883, in *Vorgeschichtliche Alterthümer der Provinz Sachsen* I. 92).] A type of neolithic pottery with banded decoration. Also *attrib.*
1921 J. M. TYLER *New Stone Age North. Europe* vii. 155 The pottery of northern Europe can be distributed into a few groups or general types..I. Banded pottery ..*Bandkeramik*. **1936** *Discovery* Sept. 289/1 The pottery is similar to the 'band ceramic' of central Europe. **1940** C. F. C. HAWKES *Prehist. Found. Europe* iv. 117 The great settlement of Lindenthal near Cologne, in which the whole history of the *Bandkeramik* culture in this far north-western region has been exposed in detail. **1953** J. PROCHÁZKA tr. *Hrozný's Anc. Hist. W. Asia, India & Crete* xvii. 220 The Illyrian and Thracian peoples are responsible for the band ceramics.

bandle ('bænd(ə)l). [ad. Irish *bannlamh* cubit, f. *bann* measure + *lamh* hand, arm.] An Irish measure of two feet in length.
1623 in COCKERAM. **1672** PETTY *Pol. Anat.* (1691) 98 Seventeen Bandles make a Man's Suit, and twelve make a Cloak. [Still in 1865 used in Bandon, co. Cork.]

bandle, var. BANDEL, *Obs.*, swaddling-band.

bandless ('bændlɪs), *a.* [f. BAND *sb.* + -LESS.] Without a band (in various senses); whence **bandlessly** *adv.*, **bandlessness**.
1660 HEXHAM *Dutch Dict.*, *Bondeloos*, Bandlesse or Unbound. **1862** *Times*, Epsom Downs..bandless, niggerless.

bandlet ('bændlɪt). [f. BAND *sb.*² + -LET; or syncopated from BANDELET.] A small band, fillet, or streak; in *Arch.* = BANDELET.
1727-51 in CHAMBERS *Cycl.* **1850** MRS. JAMESON *Leg. Monast. Ord.* (1863) 110 Two bars or bandlets gules. **1883** PIAZZI SMYTH in *Observat.* No. 83. 81 The bandlets of lines in this mysterious *a* band. **1883** BIRCH *Assyr. Antiq.* 50 His hair is covered with a broad bandlet.

‖**'bando.** *Obs.* [a. It. (and Sp.) *bando* = med.L. *bannum* BAN.] A public proclamation.
1598 BARRET *Theor. Warres* IV. i. 118 The Commaunds, lawes, and bandos of the high Generall. **1642** SHIRLEY *Sisters* v. ii, The last bando—'He that can bring Frapolo, the chief bandit..Shall have free pardon.'

bandobast, bandobust, var. BUNDOBUST.

bandog ('bændɒg). Forms: 5-7 **band-dogge, 5 bande doge, bon-, bonde dogge, 6 band-dogg, 6-7 band-dog, bandogge, 7 ban-dogg, 6- ban-dog, bandog.** [f. BAND *sb.*¹ 6 = fastening + DOG.] *orig.* A dog tied or chained up, either to guard a house, or on account of its ferocity; hence *gen.* a mastiff, bloodhound.
c **1425** in Wright's *Voc.* 187 *Molosus*, band-dogge. *c* **1440** *Promp. Parv.* 43 Bondogge (**1499** bonde dogge), *Molosus*. *c* **1560** *Thersites* in Hazl. *Dodsl.* I. 399 The bandog Cerberus from hell he bare away. **1577** HARRISON *England* III. vii. 44 The mastiffe, tie dog, or banddog, so called bicause manie of them are tied up in chaines..for dooing hurt abroad. **1669** ETHEREDGE *Love in Tub* IV. iii, As fierce as a Ban-dog that has newly broke his chain. **1813** SCOTT *Rokeby* v. xxxvi, As the bull, at bay, Tosses the ban-dogs from his way.

b. *fig.*; also in phr. ***to speak bandog and Bedlam***: i.e. furiously and madly.
1600 DEKKER *Gentle Craft* Wks. 1873 I. 19 O master, is it you that speak bandog and Bedlam this morning? **1610** *Chester's Tri., Envie* 12 Thou envious Bandogge, speake and doe thy worst. **1645** USSHER *Body of Div.* (1647) 376 Letting loose Satan, his band-dog, to..molest the godly. **1829** SCOTT *Anne of G.* (1833) I. 133 He was usually spoken of as the bandog of Burgundy, or the Alsatian mastiff.

c. *attributive* or *appositive*.
1616 BEAUM. & FL. *Wit without M.* v. i, Bitten with bandog-fleas. **1629** H. BURTON *Babel no Beth.* Ep. Ded. 9 All the band-dog heresies of hell were let loose.

bandoleer, -ier (bændə'lɪə(r)). Forms: 6 **bandollier, -dileare, 6-7 bande-, 7 bandileer(e, -leir, -lier, bandier, bandooleer(e, -leir, -lier, 8 bandaleer, 6-9 bandalier, 7-9 bandelier, 7- bandoleer, -ier,** Also, **7 bandileero, -iliero, -aliero.** [a. F. *bandouillere* (Cotgr. 1611), mod. *bandoulière*; from It. *bandoliera*, or Sp. *bandolera*, f. *bandola*, dim. of *banda* BAND. With the forms in *-ero*, cf. -ADO².]

†1. A broad belt, worn over the shoulder and across the breast, by which a wallet might be suspended at the side. *Obs.*
a **1577** GASCOIGNE *Flowers, Herbs, etc.* (1587) 186 As Bandolliers for who in mountains dwelles. *a* **1626** MIDDLETON *Black Bk.* Wks. V. 517, I threw mine arms, like a scarf or bandileer, cross the lieutenants melancholy bosom. **1634** HEYWOOD *Witches of Lanc.* II. Wks. 1874 IV. 201, I have..this my bandileer of bottles, to fill to night. **1767** DUCAREL *Anglo-Norm. Antiq.* 47 Their surplices covered with Bandaleer's of flowers.
transf. or *fig.* **1598** SYLVESTER *Du Bartas* (1608) 370 Three thousand times the sun Hath gallopt round Heaven's golden bandeleer.

2. *esp.* A belt of this kind worn by soldiers; orig. it helped to support the musket, and had also attached twelve little cases, each containing a charge for the musket; *later*, a shoulder-belt fitted with little loops, in which cartridges are suspended.
1596 *Unton Invent.* 3 Six musketts with bandileares. **1622** F. MARKHAM *Bk. Warre* I. ix. 3 To this Bandiliere shall bee fastened by long double strings, that they may with more ease be brought to the mouth of the musquet, one large priming charge..and at least twelve other charges. **1672** CHAS. II. *Warrant* 2 Apr., One matchlocke musquet, with a collar of bandaliero. **1768** STERNE *Sent. Journ.* (1774) I. 321 A rusty old sword, and a bandoleer. **1818** SCOTT *Leg. Montrose* ii, A bandelier containing his charges of ammunition. **1885** *Daily News* 20 Feb. 5/6 Mounted infantry..in..Khaki helmets, puggarees, bandoliers.

3. By transference: in *sing.* One of the cases or boxes containing a charge for the musket; hence used in *pl.* as = prec.
1611 COTGR., *Bandovilleres*, a musketiers bandooleers; or charges like little boxes, hanging at a belt about his necke. **1624** CAPT. SMITH *Virginia* IV. 160 Master Argent had put his Bandileir of powder in his hat. *a* **1659** CLEVELAND *Wks.* 30 Like Cartrages, or Linnen Bandileers Exhausted of their Sulphurous Contents. **1728** FIELDING *Love in Masques* Wks. 1775 I. 76 Get down my broad-sword and bandaliers. **1818** SCOTT *Hrt. Midl.* xii, 'He was in his bandaliers to hae joined the ungracious Highlanders in 1715.'

bandolero (bændəʊ'lɛərəʊ). [Sp.] A highwayman or robber. Also *attrib.*
[**1645** J. HOWELL *Ep. Ho-Elianæ* I. xxiii. 43 These parts of the Pyreneys that border upon the Mediterranean, are never without Theeves by Land (call'd *Bandoleros*).] **1832** W. IRVING *Alhambra* (1896) 9 The solitary *bandolero*, armed to the teeth..hovers about them. **1927** *Chambers's Jrnl.* 733/2, I was soon rigged out in the costume of a Spanish villager; that is, rope-soled shoes, white woollen stockings, bright yellow knickerbockers, a frilled shirt, and a bandolero hat.

bandoliered (bændə'lɪəd), *a.* [f. BANDOLEER, -IER + -ED².] Wearing a bandolier.
1900 *Daily News* 29 Jan. 7/5 The dashing bandoliered invader. **1921** *Blackw. Mag.* Oct. 458/1 A bandoliered and sheep-skin cloaked policeman.

bandoline ('bændəlɪn), *sb.* [? f. *band* or *bandeau*.] A gummy preparation for fixing the hair.
1846 'A LADY' *Jewish Manual* 206 As a bandoline to make the hair set close..linseed..boiling water..rose-water. **1861** DELAMER *Kitch. Gard.* 162 The boiled pips [of Quince] make the glutinous preparation called bandoline. **1876** HARLEY *Mat. Med.* 361 Used for jellies and soups..and as bandoline for keeping the hair in form. **1957** V. J. KEHOE *Technique Film & T.V. Make-Up* iii. 31 *Bandoline*, a viscous liquid used for setting hair stiffly in place.

bandoline ('bændəlɪn), *v.* [f. the sb.] To dress (the hair) with bandoline. Hence **'bandolined** *ppl. a.*, **'bandolining** *vbl. sb.*
1856 *Scot. Rev.* IV. 119 A moustache—turning up at the ends in two points well bandolined together. **1866** DICKENS *Rugby Junction* iii, in *Christmas Stories* (1956) 516 You should see our Bandolining Room..where Our Missis and our young ladies Bandolines their hair... You should see 'em at it,..Bandolining away, as if they was anointing themselves for the combat. **1876** *Tinsley's Mag.* XIX. 401 Moustaches..carefully bandolined into a ring at each end. **1933** MRS. C. S. PEEL *Life's Enchanted Cup* i. 6, I remember, too, that the smooth, parted front hair was 'bandolined' with a stick of some white greasy composition.

† **'bandon, -oun,** *sb. Obs.* Forms: **3 bandun, baundune, 3-5 bandom, 3-7 bandon, 4 baoundoun, 4-5 baundon, 4-6 bandoun(e, 5 bandum, 5-6 bandone.** [a. OF. *bandon*, *bandun*, 'public proclamation, ban, jurisdiction, authority, disposal, discretion, license' = Pr. *bandon*, f. (through a deriv. form **bando -ōnem*) late L. *band-um* = *bann-um* 'public proclamation, edict, interdict,' ad. Teut. *bann*: see BAN *sb.*¹ There was a confusion in Romanic between *bannum* and *bandum*: Du Cange shows *bannum* for *bandum*, BANNER, as well as *bandum* for *bannum* 'edict'; cf. BANISH, BANDIT, BANNER, BANDEROLE. (There is no etymological connexion in Teutonic between *bann*, *bann-an*, and *bandwa* token, *bandwjan* to signify.)]

Jurisdiction, authority, dominion, control; power of disposal, full discretion, or authority to deal with. ***to be in*** or ***at any one's bandon***: to be under his control, at his disposal, will, or pleasure. To have a thing ***in one's bandon***: at one's full or free disposal.
c **1230** *Ancr. R.* 338 þe terme is ine Godes honden: and nout i þine baundune [*earlier MS.* bandun]. *a* **1300** *Cursor M.* 9013 þe man sco has in hir bandom. *c* **1300** *K. Alis.* 3180 The emperour, and his barouns, Yeildith heom to thy baundouns. *c* **1470** HENRY *Wallace* XI. 1376, I thocht haiff maid Ingland at his bandoun. **1483** CAXTON *G. de la Tour* E vij, The kyng..gafe hym baundon ouer all the goodes. **1535** STEWART *Cron. Scot.* III. 181 Wnder his bandoun think I neuir to be. **1611** COTGR., *Abandon*, bandon..full libertie for others to use a thing.

Hence the F. and ME. phr. ***a bando(u)n***, in control, at one's disposal; *also*, at one's own free will, freely, unrestraindly; whence the vb. *abandonn-er* = *mettre à bandon*: see ABANDON.

† **'bandon,** *v.*¹ *Obs.* [aphetic f. ABANDON *v.*]
1. To have under control, subdue; = ABANDON *v.* 1.
c **1450** HENRYSON *Mor. Fab.* 80 For all the beastes before that bandoned beene Will shute vpon my beastes with yre.
2. *refl.* To give oneself up; = ABANDON *v.* 4.
a **1300** *Cursor M.* 14906 He wil him bandun [*v.r.* baundoun] nu þar-till [to death] Ful freli wit his aun wil.
3. To forsake; = ABANDON *v.* 8.

1587 Turberv. *Trag. T.* (1837) 53 Forgo thy solenne walks, bandon Classic wood.

4. To banish; = ABANDON *v.* 11.

1592 Wyrley *Armorie* 108 Thoughts, griefes, sad cares, are bandon[ed] then away.

† **'bandon,** *v.*² *Obs. rare*⁻¹. [? for *banden*; cf. BAND *sb.*² 10 b, BANDY *a.* 1.] Of cloth: To shrink unevenly, so that tight inelastic 'bands' occur here and there across the piece.

1552 *Act 5 & 6 Edw. VI*, 6 §1 (Ruffhead) When the clothes so made, be put in the water to try them, they rise out .. in some place narrower than some, beside such cockeling, bandoning, and divers .. notable Faults.

bandoneon (bæn'dɒnɪən, bæn'dəʊniːən). *Mus.* Also **bandoleon, bandonion.** [a. Ger., f. the name of Heinrich *Band* (see below) + *-on-* + *-eón* (as in G. *Akkordeon*); cf. F. *bandonéon* (Trésor, 1928), *bandoléon*, S. Amer. Sp. *bandoneón*.] A kind of button accordion invented by Band *c* 1840, and typical of Argentine tango orchestras.

1925 *Daily News* 1 Oct. 7/6 The Tango band consists of piano, harmonium, guitar, symphonic mandoline, concertina and bandoleons. **1934** Webster, Bandonion. **1938** *Oxf. Compan. Mus.* 788/1 The Bandonion is an Argentine type of accordion. There is no keyboard—merely buttons. **1961** A. Baines *Mus. Instruments* xiii. 325 The Bandoneon, a solo instrument in Argentine tango orchestras, is itself a square-built button accordion invented by Band of Kleefeld, *c.* 1840. **1982** *Daily Tel.* 7 Sept. 9/1 In '5 Tango's', [set] to music by the Argentinian composer Astor Piazzolla for the bandoneon, .. van Maneu shows a .. flair for tango rhythms.

† **'bandonly,** *adv. Obs. rare*⁻¹. [aphetic f. ABANDONLY.] Recklessly, daringly.

c **1470** Henry *Wallace* v. 886 How that so bandounly, Wallace abaid ner hand thar chewalry.

bandore¹ (bæn'dɔə(r), 'bændɔə(r)). Also 6 **bandurion,** 6–7 **-dora.** [ad. Sp. or Pg.; the Romanic forms show much phonetic perversion: Sp. *ban'durria, ban'dola*, Pg. *bandurra*, Fr. *mandore*, formerly *mandole*, It. *man'dola, pan'dora, pan'dura*; all repr. L. *pandūra, pandūrium*, a. Gr. πανδοῦρα, πανδυρίς, a musical instrument. Hence also, by further corruption, BANJO.] A musical instrument resembling a guitar or lute, with three, four, or six wire strings, used as a bass to the cittern.

1566 Gascoigne *Jocasta* (1848) 133 A dolefull and straunge noyse of violles, Cythren, Bandurion. **1591** Percivall *Span. Dict.*, *Vihuela*, a bandore. **1626** Bacon *Sylva* §146 A Bandora, Orpharion, or Cittern, which have likewise Wire-strings. **1689** Shadwell *Bury-Fair* iii. Wks. 1720 IV. 161 The best musick in England .. shawm and bandore. **1883** J. Hawthorne in *Harper's Mag.* Nov. 933/2, I would lightly touch the strings of my bandore.

attrib. **1607** Heywood *Fayre Mayde Exch.* Wks. 1874 II. 20 What's her haire? faith two Bandora wiars.

† **ban'dore**². *Obs.* [corruption of F. *bandeau* 'anciennement, coiffure des veuves' (Littré).] A widow's head-dress.

a **1712** W. King *Ovid's Ars Am.* 142 Our grandmothers, they tell us, wore Their fardingale and their Bandore. **1719** D'Urfey *Pills* (1872) II. 11 The buxom Widow, with Bandore and Peak.

bandrol(e, -roll, var. BANDEROLE.

bandsman ('bændzmən). **a.** A member of a band or company; *esp.* of a band of musicians. **b.** (see quot.)

a **1842** Cunningham *My Native Vale* vi, I .. joy'd to see the bandsmen smile. **1864** *Even. Standard* 29 Oct., The colours having to be given into the custody of the bandsmen alone. **1884** *Weekly Times* 5 Sept. 3/3 Along with them a bandsman from the steamer.

b. **1852** Tomlinson *Encycl.* I. 392/2 The next class of miners .. are the .. bandsmen or bondsmen, from the circumstance of their working in connexion with the *band* or flat rope by which the coal, etc. is hoisted.

bandster ('bændstə(r)). [f. BAND *sb.*¹ + -STER; cf. *maltster*.] One who binds sheaves after reapers.

a **1794** in Ritson *Scot. Songs* II. 3 (Jam.) The bansters are runkled, lyart, and grey. **1863** Tom Taylor *Pict. in Wds.* ix, Onward press the shearers, The bandsters come behind.

‖ **ban'durria.** [Sp.] = BANDORE¹.

1842 Longf. *Sp. Stud.* i. ii, We play the bandurria.

'band-wagon. orig. *U.S.* Also **-waggon.** [BAND *sb.*³] A large wagon, capable of carrying the band in a procession. Freq. *fig.*, as of one conveying a 'band' of usu. successful (political) leaders. Hence *to climb, hop, jump*, etc., *on the band-wagon*, to join in what seems likely to be a successful enterprise, to strive to join the winning side.

1855 Barnum *Life* 205 At Vicksburg we sold all our land conveyances excepting four horses and the 'band wagon'. **1893** *Congress. Rec.* 25 Aug. 897/1 It is a lamentable fact that .. our commercial enemy .. should come along with a band wagon loaded with hobgoblins. **1899** T. Roosevelt *Let.* 28 Apr. (1951) II. 999 When I once became sure of one majority they tumbled over each other to get aboard the band wagon. **1905** *N.Y. Even. Post* 21 Oct. 1 Jerome's band wagon began to move over the town to-day. It bears on its sides announcements of these mass meetings on Monday night. **1906** *Ibid.* 5 Sept. 4 Many of those Democrats .. who rushed into the Bryan band-wagon .. will now be seen crawling out over the tailboard. **1927** J. Needham *Man a Machine* iii. 67 Neo-Lamarckism, whose 'band-wagon' has been so kindly thrown open to all by an eminent English friend of Sig. Rignano's. **1933** *Amer. Speech* VIII. i. 22/2 The socialists climbed on the alliteration band-wagon with *Sail safely and surely with Socialism.* **1940** H. G. Wells *New World Order* §7. 104, I find most of these United States of Europe movements are now jumping on to the Federation band-waggon. **1941** A. L. Rowse *Tudor Cornwall* iv. 86 A few who were forward Protestants .. may be said to have jumped on the band-waggon. **1950** *Hansard Commons* CDLXXII. 970 The Tory party are now trying to climb on to the band wagon. **1959** *Observer* 1 Feb. 10/4 He is surrounded by yes-men who have jumped on the bandwagon.

attrib. **1908** *Nation* 16 Apr. 343/1 We shall now hear the 'band-wagon' argument for Taft more confidently than ever. **1958** *Times Lit. Suppl.* 15 Aug. p. xxxii/1, The whipping-up of public emotions has been made the excuse for the cult of band-waggon personalities.

Hence **band-wagoner, band-wagoning.**

1949 *Here & Now* (N.Z.) Oct. 13/1 Not having had the wit to see that Labour never amounted to anything in terms of real power, he is paying the penalty now for his band-waggoning. **1958** C. S. Lewis *Reflections on Psalms* vii. 70 Here is the perfect band-wagoner. Immediately on the decision 'This is a revolting tyranny', follows the question 'How can I as quickly as possible cease to be one of the victims and become one of the tyrants?' *Ibid.* 71 There are subtler, more social or intellectual forms of band-wagoning which might deceive us. **1958** *Times* 1 Dec. 10/2 The bandwagoners—latter-day 'Gaullists' .. who have found it convenient for electoral and other purposes to fight under U.N.R. colours.

bandwidth: see BAND *sb.*² 15.

bandy ('bændɪ), *v.* Also 6–7 **bandie.** [The origin of this and of BANDY *sb.*¹ is very obscure. Cf. F. *bander* 'to bandie at Tennis' Cotgr.; perhaps f. *bande* side. With Branch II. cf. F. *bander*, in *se bander contre*, 'to bandy or oppose himself against, with his whole power; or to joyne in league with others against' (Cotgr.), also Sp. *bandear* 'to bandy, to follow a faction, to help a side, to become factious' (Minsheu), It. *bandare* 'to side or bandy' (Florio). Cf. also BAND *v.*¹: but while these answer in sense, no satisfactory explanation of the terminal *-ie, -y* presents itself.]

I.

1. *trans.* To throw or strike (a ball) to and fro, as in the games of tennis and bandy. (Mostly with figurative reference.)

1577 Holinshed *Chron.* III. 1077/2 Kingdoms .. be no balles for me to bandie. **1592** Nashe *P. Penilesse* 15 b, They may make Ruffians hall of Hell: and there bandy balles of Brimstone at one anothers head. **1678** Cudworth *Intell. Syst.* 845 Had we no Mastery at all over our Thoughts, but they were all like Tennis Balls, Bandied, and Struck upon us, as it were by Rackets from without. **1842** W. Grove *Corr. Phys. Forces* 20 A ball of caoutchouc, bandied about. **1860** Tennyson *Vis. Sin* iv, xi, To be the ball of Time, Bandied by the hands of fools.

b. *absol.*

1612 Webster *Vittoria Cor.* (N.) While he had been bandying at tennis He might have .. struck His soul into the hazard. **1699** Coles *Eng. Lat. Dict.*, To bandy at Tennis, *reticulo pellere.*

c. *intr.* To bound like a ball struck or driven.

1658 R. White tr. *Digby's Powd. Symp.* (1660) 20 Untill she bandies .. upon another solid body, and so she continueth to make new boundings here and there.

† 2. To toss, drive, or throw aside or away. *Obs.*

1591 *Troub. Raigne K. John* (1611) 69 If Arthurs death be dismall to be heard, Bandie the newes for rumors of untruth: He liues my Lord. *a* **1593** Marlowe *Lust's Dom.* i. iv, The Cardinal, would bandy me away from Spain. **1667** H. More *Div. Dial.* i. §8 (1713) 17 If the Earth had been bandied out of one Vortex into another.

3. To toss from side to side, like a tennis-ball.

1596 Spenser *State Irel.* Wks. (1862) 531/2 And from one hand to another doe bandie the service like a tennis-ball. **1650** Fuller *Pisgah* ii. ix. 190 Those Lepers .. bandied betwixt two deaths of the famine and the sword. **1712** Blackmore *Creation* ii. (1736) 47 What vig'rous arm .. Bandies the mighty globe still to and fro? **1864** Gilbert & Churchill *Dolom. Mts.*, The path .. was bandied from side to side on rough bridges.

4. To toss or pass from one to another, in a circle or group; to toss about.

1600 Dekker *Fortun.* Wks. I. 143 Now he's bandyed by the seas in scorne, From wave to wave. **1675** Crowne *Calisto* i. i. 8 Hark, how they bandy praise and flattery round! **1838** Dickens *Nich. Nick.* xxx, The stories they invent .. and bandy from mouth to mouth!

b. (Often emphasized by *about*.)

1597 Drayton *Mortimer.* 17 But fortune .. straight begins to bandy him about. **1748** Anson *Voy.* ii. ii. 130 Thus was this unhappy vessel bandied about within a few leagues of her intended harbour. **1847** Barham *Ingol. Leg.* (1877) 234 Bandied about thus from pillar to post. **1872** Black *Adv. Phaeton* xxxi. 416 Sharp words were being bandied about. **1885** Sir J. Pearson *Law Times Rep.* LII. (N.S.) 183/1 Suitors being bandied about from one court to another.

5. To discuss from mouth to mouth. Cf. 4 b.

1642 *View of Print. Book int. Observ.* 40 To debate and bandy the principles of Government. **1692** Wagstaffe *Vind. Carol.* i. 18 A Bill was preferr'd .. touching Monopolies, and was strongly bandied on both sides. **1768** H. Walpole *Hist. Doubts* 40 His own legitimacy, which was too much connected with that of his brothers to be tossed and bandied about before the multitude. **1850** W. Irving *Goldsm.* xxix. 289 Your name is .. frequently bandied at table among us.

b. *absol.* or *intr.*

1603 Florio *Montaigne* (1634) 191 Lucretius, may Philosophie and bandie at his pleasure.

6. To give and take (blows, words, reproaches, compliments, etc.); to exchange. ***to bandy words*** = to argue pertinaciously, wrangle.

1589 Greene *Menaph.* (Arb.) 45 It little fits in this companie to bandie taunts of love. **1598** Greenwey *Tacitus' Ann.* vi. viii. 134 Rushing in couragiously to bandy stroakes. **1677** *Govt. Venice* 271 When they had bandied Arguments at home, they went to fight their Enemies abroad. **1828** Scott *F.M. Perth* iv, Bandy not words, but begone. **1855** Motley *Dutch Rep.* I. 27 Bandying blows in the thickest of the fight.

b. *with* (and recently *against*) a person.

1593 Nashe *Christ's T.* (1613) 79 His Backe bandieth colours with the Sunne. **1605** Shaks. *Lear* i. iv. 92 Do you bandy lookes with me, you Rascall? **1767** Johnson in *Boswell* (1831) II. 36 It was not for me to bandy civilities with my sovereign. **1847** L. Hunt *Men, Wom. & Bks.* II. xi. 280 The leaders .. bandied against one another the foulest charges. **1880** Dixon *Windsor* III. vii. 69 She could not bandy words with insolent pages.

c. one thing *for* another.

1593 Shaks. *3 Hen. VI*, i. iv. 49, I will not bandie with thee word for word, But buckler with thee blowes. **1603** Drayton *Heroic. Ep.* xiv. 45 To bandy Woe for Woe and Teare for Teare.

II.

† 7. To band together, league, confederate: **a.** *trans.* and *refl.* (cf. F. *se bander*.)

1597 *Prayers* in *Liturg. Q. Eliz.* (1847) 676 Our enemies .. conspire and bandy themselves against us. **1632** C. Hughes *Saints Losse* 38 All the kings of the earth bandy themselves to fight with him. **1656** Trapp *Exp. Rev.* ix. 5 Antichrist and his actuaries bandy and bend all their forces to destroy souls. **1659** J. Harrington *Lawgiving* (1700) 397 Korah, Dathan, and Abiram .. bandy'd themselves against Moses. **1818** Scott *Br. Lamm.* iii, Here is his son already bandying and making a faction.

b. *intr.*

1633 G. Herbert *Humil.* iv. in *Temple* 62 Joyntly bandying, They drive them soon away. **1673** *Lady's Call.* ii. iii. §18 The servants .. bandy into leagues and parties. **1755** Carte *Hist. Eng.* IV. 116 If he bandied to remove his father's servants. **1758** Jortin *Erasm.* I. 192 Giddy and ignorant young men .. had bandied together in a body, calling themselves Trojans.

8. *intr.* To contend, strive, fight. (Cf. Cotgr. '*Se bander contre*, to bandie, or oppose himselfe against.')

1588 Shaks. *Tit. A.* i. i. 313 A Valliant sonne in-law .. One, fit to bandy with thy lawlesse Sonnes. **1643** Milton *Divorce* ii. xxi. Wks. (1851) 122 That Law may bandy with nature, and traverse her sage motions, was an error. **1660** —— *Free Commw.* Wks. 1738 I. 594 Neither did the People of Rome bandy with their Senate while any of the Tarquins liv'd. **1705** Hickeringill *Priest-cr.* i. (1721) 55 Let them bandy against one another till I part them.

bandy ('bændɪ), *sb.*¹ [App. f. the vb.; but the origin of sense 5, and the order of the senses are quite uncertain.]

I. † 1. A particular way of playing at tennis, the nature of which is not now known. It does not appear from the quotations whether *bandy* was the same as *check*, i.e. the modern 'cramped game' of 'touch no walls.' *Obs.*

1578 T. N. tr. *Conq. W. India* 179 They play not at chases, but at bandie or at Check, that is, if the ball touch the wall, it looseth. **1607** *Lingua* ii. v. in Hazl. *Dodsl.* IX. 381 The shooting stars .. Are nothing but the balls they lose at bandy.

† 2. A stroke with a racket, a ball so struck; a 'return' at tennis. *Obs.*

1598 Marston *Met. Pigmal. Im.* i. 141 Straight with loud mouth (a bandy Sir) he cries. **1627** Drayton *Agincourt* (1748) 4 They such racket shall in Paris see When over line such bandies I shall drive, As that, before the set be fully done, France may perhaps into the hazard run. **1655** J. Cotgrave *Wit's Interpr.* 7 A bandie ho! the people crie, And so the ball takes flight.

† 3. *fig. Obs.*

1602 Dekker *Satirom.* Wks. I. 243 Take this bandy with the racket of patience. **1604** Edmonds *Observ. Cæsar's Comm.* 21 Their factions .. caused one partie to bring in Ariouistus .. and the other partie, the Romaines to make good their bandy. **1638** Ford *Fancies* v. iii. (1811) 210 Not wronged me? .. this is the bandy of a patience Beyond all sufferance.

II. 4. A game, also called **bandy-ball,** in which a small ball is driven to and fro over the ground, with bent club sticks, by two sides of players; the same as HOCKEY.

1693 D'Urfey *Yorksh. Heiress*, The prettiest fellow At bandy once and cricket. **1796** Southey *Lett. Spain* (1799) 133 A royal recreation similar to what boys call Bandy in England. **1822** W. Irving *Braceb. Hall* II. 64 Bandy-ball, trapball, wrestling, leaping. **1860** Geo. Eliot *Mill on Floss* I. 77 She's only a girl—she can't play at bandy.

5. A club bent or curved at its lower end, used for striking the ball in this game.

1629 T. Adams *Medit. Creed* Wks. 1861 III. 122 The mathematician [will not] lend his engines for wasters and bandies. **1681** R. Knox *Hist. Ceylon* 50 All which .. carry staves in their hands like to Bandyes, the crooked end uppermost. **1850** *Cricketer's Man*, 24 Sending it with blows of their bandies, whizzing through the air.

6. *bandy-wicket* (see quots.). *dial.*

1749 Ellis *Syst. Improvem. Sheep* ii. iv. 199 The bad Example of others, who .. play at Bandy-wicket .. on the Sabbath-Day. **1823** E. Moor *Suffolk Words* 14 *Bandy-*

wicket, a game with bats, or sticks, and ball, like cricket—but with bricks..or..hats, instead of bales and stumps, for wickets. *a* **1825** Forby *Vocab. E. Anglia* (1830) I. 14 *Bandy-wicket*, the game of cricket. Of the several games at ball played with a bandy, that in which a ball is aimed by one player at a wicket, defended by the adversary with his bandy, must be allowed to be very appropriately called *bandy-wicket*.

bandy (ˈbændɪ), *sb.*² [a. Telugu *baṇḍi*, Tamil *vaṇḍi*.] A carriage, bullock-carriage, buggy, or cart, used in India.

1761 *Madras Courier* 29 Sept., To be sold, an elegant new and fashionable Bandy, with copper pannels, lined with Morocco leather. **1800** Sir T. Munro *Life* I. 243 No wheel carriages..not even a buffalo-bandy. **1854** Stocqueler *Handbk. Brit. India* 109 A buggy being a one-horse vehicle ..(at Madras they call it a bandy).

bandy (ˈbændɪ), *a.* [see the senses.]

1. Of legs: Curved laterally with the concavity inward. [perh. attrib. use of bandy *sb.*¹ 'hockey-stick.'] Also used briefly for *bandy-legged*.

1687 Shadwell *Juvenal* x. 441 No Noble Youth with Bandy-leggs. **1727** Swift *Wom. Mind* Wks. 1755 IV. i. 85 Nor makes a scruple to expose Your bandy leg, or crooked nose. **1783–94** Blake *Songs Innoc. Little Vagab.* 12 Dame Lurch.. Would not have bandy children. **1815** Scott *Guy M.* xxix, A little mongrel cur, with bandy legs.

Hence **bandy-legged**, *a.*

1688 *Lond. Gaz.* No. 2392/4 A bandy-leged splafooted elderly Man. **1849** W. Irving *Crayon Misc.* 233 Short and bandy-legged..his little legs curving like a pair of parentheses below his kilt.

2. Marked with bands; cf. band *sb.*² 10 b. [f. band *sb.*² + -y¹.]

1552 *Act 5–6 Ed. VI*, vi. §27 Cloth..either pursie, bandie, squally by warpe or woufe. **1601** *Act 43 Eliz.* x. §1 Clothes ..squally, cockling, bandy, light and notably faulty.

3. Full of bands. [f. band *sb.*³ 4 + -y¹.]

1852 Dickens *Lett.* I. 279 Not quite a place to my taste, being too bandy (I mean musical, no reference to its legs).

bandy, var. bandie.

bandy-bandy (ˈbændɪ ˌbændɪ). The native name in Australia of a nocturnal snake, *Furina annulata*, marked with black and white bands; also called *bandy-snake*.

1926 *Austral. Encycl.* II. 473/2 *Furina annulata* (Bandy-bandy, Black-and-white-ringed Snake), another common venomous kind, sometimes grows to 30 inches... This species is better known as *F. occipitalis*, but the specific name *annulata* has priority. **1958** *Ibid.* VIII. 167/1 The black-and-white ringed snake, or bandy-bandy,..is very widely known and is often referred to as being deadly. **1959** J. Wright *Generations of Men* 19 The curious pink bandy-snakes that scuttled in and out of the bushes in the garden.

bandying (ˈbændiɪŋ), *vbl. sb.* [f. bandy *v.* + -ing¹.] The action of the vb. bandy: **a.** Tossing to and fro, exchange (of blows, words, etc.). **b.** Contentious argument, disputation. **c.** Contention, strife. †**d.** Confederation, league.

1591 Shaks. *Rom. & Jul.* iii. i. 92 The prince expresly hath Forbidden bandying in Verona streetes. **1662** Stillingfleet *Orig. Sacr.* iii. iv. §15 (L.) The bandyings of this controversie. **1689** Hickeringill *Modest Inq.* ii. 17 What Combination? What Bandying against it? **1719** Swift *To Yng. Clergym.* Wks. 1755 II. ii. 19 The perpetual bandying of factions among us. **1822** Scott *Nigel* xi, Where there is such bandying of private feuds and public factions.

ˈ**bandying**, *ppl. a.* [f. as prec. + -ing².] That bandies, tosses to and fro, disputes, etc.: see the vb.

1665 Glanvill *Sceps. Sci.* i. 14 All the bandying attempts of resolution. **1677** Marvell *Growth Popery* 6 The crew of bandying Cardinals.

bandyman (ˈbændɪmən). [f. bandy *sb.*² + man *sb.*¹] The driver of a bandy (see bandy *sb.*²).

a **1881** Caldwell (Ogilvie), When also, as all over India, our white kinsmen speak of bandymen and bandies, the word thus anglicized is simply the old Tamilian one. **1922** *Other Lands* Apr. 76/2 The shout of 'Ho, Bandyman'.

bane (beɪn), *sb.*¹ Forms: 1 bana, bona, 2–4 bone, (4 ban, bon, 5 boyn, 6 baene), 3– bane; 5–6 bayn(e, 6–7 bain(e. [Common Teut.: OE. *bana*, *bona* = OFris. *bona*, OS., OHG. *bano*, MHG. *bane*, *ban*, ON. *bani*, Sw., Da. *bane*, 'death, murder':—*OTeut. *banon-* wk. masc. Cogn. w. Goth. *banja*, ON., OE. *ben*:—OTeut. **banjâ-* (str. fem.) wound.]

†**1.** A slayer or murderer; one who causes the death or destruction of another. *Obs.*

Beowulf 3491 Bona swiðe neah..fyrenum sceoteð. *a* **800** *O.E. Chron.* an. 755 Hie næfre his banan folʒian noldon. **1205** Lay. 5806 ʒe beoð ure bernenne bone. *a* **1300** *Cursor M.* 7634 Philistiens sal be his ban. *c* **1385** Chaucer *L.G.W.* 2147 He overcom this beste & was his ban. *a* **1400** *Sir Perc.* 1338 Who that may his bon be, Salle hafe this kyngdome and me. *c* **1460** *Towneley Myst.* 17 *Caym*, I sloghe my brother.. I pray the..To ryn away with the bayn. **1513** More *Rich. III.* Wks. 51/2 The brother hath bene the brothers bane. **1588** Shaks. *Tit. A.* v. iii. 73 Let Rome herselfe be bane vnto herselfe. **1682** *Yorksh. Diaries* (Surtees) II. 303 The Jury found the horse the bane. **1691** Blount *Law Dict.* s.v., I will be the Bane of him, is a common saying. [**1861** H. Riley tr. *Liber Alb.* 86 The horse aforesaid, which had been the bane of the said boy.]

†**2.** That which causes death, or destroys life.

a **1000** *Beowulf* 4413 Hilde mecas..tó bonan wurdon. *c* **1230** *Ancr. R.* 222 One þinge þet..is þauh soule bone, & wei to deadlich sunne. *c* **1386** Chaucer *Knts. T.* 239, I was hurt right now thurgh myn yhe Into myn herte, that wol my bane be. *c* **1400** *Ywaine & Gaw.* 1854 The water sone had bene my bane. **1647** H. More *Song of Soul* ii. App. xcvii, Brimstone thick and clouds of fiery bain.

b. *esp.* Poison. Now only *fig.*, and referred to 4. Also in *comb.*, in names of poisonous plants or substances, as dogbane, henbane, leopard's bane, rat's bane, wolf's bane, etc., q.v.

1398 Trevisa *Barth. De P.R.* v. xx. (1495) 208 Henbane is mannis bane. *c* **1440** *Promp. Parv.* 22 Bane, or poyson. **1573** Tusser *Husb.* (1878) 172 Bane for the rats. **1586** Warner *Alb. Eng.* ii. viii. 33 To the baene therein He mixed somewhat of his bloud. **1614** Chapman *Odyss.* i. 404 Bane to poison his sharp arrows heads. **1684** tr. *Bonet's Merc. Compit.* iii. 111 Medicines..taken inwardly against Banes and Poisons. **1713** Addison *Cato* v. i, My bane and antidote are both before me. **1735** Somerville *Chase* iv. 331 The Dog whose fatal Bite convey'd th' infectious Bane. **1862** Maurice *Mor. & Met. Phil.* IV. vii. §87 In which Spinoza offers at once the bane and the antidote.

†**3.** Murder, death, destruction: in later usage chiefly in phrases, ***catch, fetch, get, receive, take one's bane*** = 'catch one's death,' in which it passes into 2. (See esp. quot. 1655). *Obs.*

c **1175** *Cott. Hom.* 243 Ne cepeð hi of hus gold ne selfer but ure bane. *c* **1374** Chaucer *Troylus* v. 602 For which the folk of Thebes caught hire bane. *c* **1400** *Ywaine & Gaw.* 816 Thai ne myght wreke thair lord bane. **1594** Greene *Look. Glasse* (1861) 131 'Twere best you did, for fear you catch your bane. **1605** Shaks. *Macb.* v. iii. 60 I will not be affraid of Death and Bane, Till Birname Forrest come to Dunsinane. **1655** Fuller *Ch. Hist.* ix. IV. 402 The two Iudges..getting their banes there, died few dayes after.

4. That which causes ruin, or is pernicious to well-being; the agent or instrument of ruin or woe, the 'curse.' (Now the ordinary sense.)

1577 Harrison *England* ii. xxi. 333 Inconstancie..a bane unto all natures. **1596** Bp. Barlow *Three Serm.* i. 117 Cardes and Dice, the verie baine of any familie. **1655** Fuller *Ch. Hist.* ii. iii. §37 I. 275 Bold Beggars are the Bane of the best Bounty. **1674** Marvell *Reh. Transp.* ii. 135 The great bane and scandal of the Church. **1709** Steele *Tatler* No. 9 ⁋2 Those Rogues, the Bane to all excellent Performances, the Imitators. **1791** Burke *Corr.* (1844) III. 186 Theoretic plans of constitution have been the bane of France. **1853** C. Brontë *Villette* xxxiv. (1876) 378 She who had been the bane of his life. **1858** Holland *Titcomb's Lett.* vii. 132 Selfishness is the bane of all life.

5. Ruin, fatal mischief; woful or hapless fate; harm, woe. Chiefly *poetical*.

c **1400** *Judicium* (1822) 2 For deds that I haue done..I must abide my boyn. **1594** Greene *Look. Glasse* (1861) 117 That sweet boy that wrought bright Venus bane. **1633** G. Herbert *Forerunners* iv. in *Temple* 171 Hath some fond lover tic'd thee to thy bane? **1866** Kingsley *Herew.* Prel. 3 He finds out..for his weal and his bane that, etc.

6. A disease in sheep, the 'rot.'

1859 in Worcester.

7. *Comb.*, as *bane-touch*.

1649 Selden *Laws of Eng.* i. xxxvii. (1739) 56 Men being weary of such bane-touches, the Clergy that cried it up, their successors cried it down.

†**bane**, *sb.*² *Obs.* [See ban, banns.] A proclamation of a marriage; a prelude of a play. In the latter sense more freq. in pl. *banes*, now banns.

c **1440** *Promp. Parv.* 22 Bane of a pley (**1499** or mariage), *Banna, coragium* (**1499** *preludium*). **1483** *Cath. Angl.* 20 Bane (*v.r.* Bayne) of a play; *preludium, proludium*.

bane, *v. arch.* Also 7 bain, (baen). [f. bane *sb.*¹]

†**1.** *trans.* To kill: said esp. of poison. *Obs.*

1578 Lyte *Dodoens* 426 Aconit that baneth, or killeth Panthers. **1589** Warner *Alb. Eng.* v. xxv. (1612) 119 Poysned by a Monke, that baend himselfe, that Iohn might dye. **1596** Shaks. *Merch. V.* iv. i. 46 If my house be troubled with a Rat, And I..giue ten thousand Ducates To haue it bain'd?

2. To harm, hurt, injure, poison: **a.** physically.

1587 Turberv. *Disprayse Wom.* (R.) Hidden hookes..To bane thee when thou bite. **1615** Latham *Falconry* (1633) 102 Surfeited in their bodies, and also baned in their liuers. *a* **1632** G. Herbert *Country Parson* v. (T.) If a shepherd knew not which grass will bane, or which not. **1667** *Phil. Trans.* II. 526 The Smoak..will bane them. **1827** Keble *Chr. Year* 5th Sund. Easter, For what shall heal, when holy water banes?

b. morally or socially.

1601 Dent *Pathw. Heaven* 71 Couetousnesse..baneth our Gentlemen. **1643** Burroughes *Exp. Hosea* iv. (1652) 61 To be poison to them to have baned their soules.

bane, obs. form of bain *adv.* readily, and bone.

baneberry (ˈbeɪnbɛrɪ). [f. bane, poison + berry.] The fruit of a plant *Actæa spicata* (N.O. *Ranunculaceæ*); also the plant itself, otherwise called Herb Christopher.

1755 *Gentl. Mag.* XXV. 492 Bane-berries, are poisonous in a very high degree. **1853** Lindley *Veg. K.* 427 The black berries of the *Bane-Berry*..are poisonous.

†**baned**, *ppl. a. Obs.* [f. bane *v.* + -ed.] Ruined, destroyed; injured, hurt.

1568 T. Howell *Arb. Amitie* (1879) 67 To bruse my baned bones. **1578** T. Procter *Gorg. Gallery* I. 4 My Baned limmes. **1639** Fuller *Holy War* iii. xii, The voyage of these two kings..baned with mutual discord and emulation.

baneful (ˈbeɪnfʊl), *a.* [f. bane *sb.*¹ + -ful.]

1. Life-destroying; poisonous.

a **1593** H. Smith *Wks.* (1867) II. 475 The old serpent's baneful breath. **1598** Sylvester *Du Bartas* i. iii. (1641) 27 The banefull Aconite. **1697** Dryden *Virg. Eclog.* iii. 124 The Nightly Wolf is baneful to the Fold. **1791** Cowper *Iliad* xxii. 107 Herbs Of baneful juice. *c* **1854** Stanley *Sinai & Pal.* vii. (1858) 290 No living creature could survive the baneful atmosphere which hung upon its waters.

2. Destructive to well-being, pernicious, injurious.

1579 Spenser *Sheph. Cal.* Aug. 173 Helpe me ye banefull byrds. **1586** Marlowe *1st Pt. Tamburl.* v. ii, A sight.. baneful to their souls. **1770** Goldsm. *Des. Vill.* 311 To see ten thousand baneful arts combined. **1832** Ht. Martineau *Ireland* i. 4 Very baneful superstition. **1868** Freeman *Norm. Conq.* (1876) II. x. 503 Whose results..would prove most baneful, if not ruinous, to the country.

ˈ**banefully**, *adv.* [f. prec. + -ly².] In a hurtful or pernicious manner.

1865 *Reader* 2 Sept. 253/2 Which..influenced banefully ..the fortunes of Prince Charlie.

ˈ**banefulness.** [f. as prec. + -ness.] The quality of being baneful; hurtfulness.

ˈ**baner.** *rare*⁻¹. [f. bane *v.* + -er¹.] He who or that which kills, poisons, destroys, or ruins.

1598 Sylvester *Du Bartas* i. vi. 259 Dying himself, kils with his bane his Baner.

banesman (ˈbeɪnzmən). *pseudo-arch.* Also **baneman.** [Rendering of ON. *banamaðr*, f. *bana*, gen. of *bani* bane *sb.*¹ + *maðr* man *sb.*¹] A murderer.

1870 Magnússon & Morris tr. *Völsunga Saga* ii. 3 He had slain all his father's banesmen. **1926** *Trans. Scott. Ecclesiol. Soc.* 74 He prayed, not only for himself and his friends, but still more for 'his foes and banemen'.

banewort (ˈbeɪnwɜːt). [f. bane poison + wort, OE. *wyrt*, plant, herb.] **a.** *gen.* Any poisonous plant (*dial.*). **b.** *spec.* The Lesser Spearwort (*Ranunculus Flammula*), reputed to poison sheep. **c.** The Deadly Nightshade.

a. 1864 *Whitby Gloss.* s.v., It's some mak o' banewort. **b. 1578** Lyte *Dodoens* 425 Called in some places of Englande Sperworte, it may be also called Banewort. **1597** Gerarde *Herbal* ii. ccclxx. (1633) 962 Speare, Crowfoot, and Bane woort because it is dangerous and deadly for sheep. **1635** Swan *Spec. M.* (1670) 219 Spear-wort, or Bane-wort, is an herb which if it be taken inwardly is deadly. **c.** [Halliwell cites Skinner.] **1861** Miss Pratt *Flower. Pl.* IV. 72 Dwale, or Deadly Nightshade..Early English botanists called it Bane-wort.

bang (bæŋ), *v.*¹ Also 6 bangue. [First in 16th c.; perh. previously in north. dial. from Scand. Cf. ON. *banga*, OSw. *bånga*, to hammer; also LG. *bangen*, *bangeln* to strike, beat, Ger. *bengel* cudgel.]

I. 1. *trans.* To strike violently with a resounding blow; to thump, thrash.

? *c* **1550** *Rob. Hood* (Ritson) ix. 95 Either yield to me the daie, Or I will bang thy back and sides. **1570** Levins *Manip.* /23 To bangue, *fustigare*. **1593** Nashe 4 *Lett. Confut.* 37 A bigge fat lusty wench it is, and hath an arme like an Amazon, and will bang the abhominationly if euer she catch thee. **1675** Cotton *Scoffer Scoft* 44 With my Battoon I'le bang his sconce. **1794** Burns *Wks.* 133 Oh aye my wife she dang me, And aft my wife did bang me. **1847** Tennyson *Princ.* v. 494 Like an iron-clanging anvil bang'd With hammers.

2. Hence, in various const., expressing: **a.** violent action producing loud noise, as ***to bang off*** (a gun, music on a piano, etc.), and esp. ***to bang*** (a door) = to shut it violently, to slam; or **b.** to drive or knock with violence.

a. 1787 Beckford *Italy* II. 136 A most complicated sonata, banged off on the chimes. **1814** Scott *Wav.* III. 238 Twa unlucky red-coats..banged off a gun at him. **1816** Miss Austen *Emma* I. i. 5 She always turns the lock of the door the right way and never bangs it. **1878** Black *Green Past.* xxxiv. 277 The door was banged to. **1894** G. Du Maurier *Trilby* I. 31 He strummed: 'Messieurs les étudiants'..striking wrong notes, and banging out a bass in a different key.

b. 1877 *Daily News* 1 Nov. 6/1 This is now being banged into the heads that have planned..this campaign.

3. *intr.* To strike violently or noisily; to bump or thump. Of a door: To close with a loud report, to slam.

1713 *Guardian* No. 143 (1756) II. 234 It banged against his calf and jarred upon his right heel. **1860** W. Collins *Wom. White* i. vii. 31 Taking great pains not to let the doors bang. **1883** V. Stuart *Egypt* 302 Our boats were banging against the sides of the Era, making sleep impossible.

4. Hence: To make a violent noise, *e.g.* by the discharge of fire-arms.

1840 R. Dana *Bef. Mast* xxxvi. 136 The watch on deck were banging away at the guns every few minutes.

II. 5. a. *trans.* To beat violently, knock about; to thrash or drub, defeat, worst. *lit.* and *fig.* Hence ***banged up*** ppl. adj., knocked about (*U.S. colloq.*).

1604 Shaks. *Oth.* ii. i. 21 The desperate Tempest hath so bang'd the Turkes, That their designement halts. **1651** Lilly *Chas. I* (1774) 246 He was presently after well banged by Essex. **1784** Cowper *Wks.* (1876) 183 You are a clergyman, and I have banged your order. **1816** Scott *Old Mort.* 80 It's not easy to bang the soldier with his bandoleers. **1886** E. L. Dorsey *Midshipman Bob* ii. vii. 172 Then Young dragged himself on those banged up legs ever so far..to the Life-Saving Station. **1886** *Harper's Mag.* June 107 Even the trig, irreproachable commercial drummer actually looks banged up and nothing of a man. **1934** J. M. CAIN *Postman always rings Twice* viii. 76, I began to fool with her blouse, to bust the buttons, so that she would look banged up.

†**b.** *to bang it out* or *about*: to come to blows, fight it out. *Obs.*

c **1600** *Rob. Hood* (Ritson) xvii. 85 With a but of sack we will bang it about, To see who wins the day. **1622** HEYLIN *Cosmogr.* I. (1682) 282 If any two were displeased, they expected no law, but bang'd it out bravely.

c. *Comm.* To beat down, overwhelm. Also *Stock Exchange*, to depress (prices, the market). Cf. HAMMER *v.* 2 d (*b*).

1884 *Marten & Christoph. Monthly Circ.* 31 Mar., Speculators for the fall are as usual taking the opportunity to bang the market by heavy sales. **1907** *Daily Chron.* 10 Dec. 5/4 What prompted the selling is unknown. It appears like an attempt to bang the price. **1927** *Sunday Times* 13 Feb. 2 Attempts to bang prices failed to induce much selling. **1938** *New Statesman* 30 Apr. 750/1 Oil shares were banged in the 'Street' on Tuesday night, the leaders falling by about 5*s*.

6. *colloq.* To 'beat,' surpass, excel, outdo.

1808 *Cumbrian Ball.* iv. 13 Cocker Wully lap bawk-heet.. But Tamer in her stockin feet, She bang'd him out and out. **1837** DICKENS in *Life* II. i. 34 The next Pickwick will bang all the others. *Mod. Sc.* That bangs a' I e'er met wi'. *Irish Provb.* This bangs Bannagher.

III. 7. a. *intr.* (*dial.*) To throw oneself or spring with a sudden impetuous movement, to dash, to bounce.

1795 H. MACNEILL *Will & Jean*, Up he bang'd; and, sair afflicted, Sad and silent took the road. **1813** *Examiner* 18 Jan. 43/1 The mob.. called out, 'Bang up lads, in with you.' **1813** MAR. EDGEWORTH *Patron.* II. xxx. 257 English Clay left his D.T.O... and banged down to Clay-hall.

b. *trans.* To throw with sudden violence.

1768 Ross *Helenore* 143 (JAM.) Then I'll bang out my beggar dish.

IV. 8. The verb stem is used adverbially with other verbs, esp. *come*, *go*, in the senses of: **a.** with a violent blow or shock; **b.** with a sudden and violent clap or explosive noise; **c.** all of a sudden (*tout d'un coup*), suddenly and abruptly, all at once, as in 'to cut a thing bang off.' **d.** *bang off*, immediately, without delay. Cf. BANG *adv.*

a. **1832** *Blackw. Mag.* XXXII. 31 A 32 lb. shot struck us bang on the quarter. **1841** MARRYAT *Poacher* xxviii, We came bang against one another. **1842** SIR T. MARTIN in *Fraser's Mag.* Dec., Bang went my haunch against an.. angle of my bed. **1912** D. H. LAWRENCE *Let.* 2 Sept. (1932) 55 Then bang-slap went my heart.

b. **1855** O. W. HOLMES *Poems* 139 Bang went the magazine! **1855** BROWNING *Up in Villa* Wks. 1863 I. 53 Bang, whang, whang goes the drum. **1882** O'DONOVAN *Merv.* I. 311 Bang, came another blank shot.

c. **1795** H. MACNEILL *Will & Jean* I, Bang! cam in Mat Smith and's brither. **1868** *Punch* 5 Dec. 235/1 Mun, a had na' been the-erre abune Twa Hoours when—Bang—went Saxpence! **1886** W. JAMES *Let.* 29 Aug. in R. B. Perry *Thought & Char. W. J.* (1935) I. 602 The moment I get interested in anything, bang goes my sleep. **1895** G. B. SHAW *Let.* 28 Nov. in *E. Terry & Shaw* (1931) 20 Somebody will give a surreptitious performance of it: and then bang goes my copyright. **1909** T. E. LAWRENCE *Lett.* (1938) 79, I am afraid I have to drive from here to Urfa (Edessa) which is going to cost me about £7: so bang go my proposed purchases in Damascus.

d. **1886** BAUMANN *Londinismen* 7/1 *Bang-off*.. he wrote it ~ *er schrieb's in einem Zuge.* **1895** H. JAMES *Notebks.* 14 Feb. (1947) 188 This thing has for my bang-off purpose the immense merit of having no prescribed or imposed length. **1896** —— *Spoils Poynton* (1897) viii, She may.. think I may want to make her reply bang off?

e. *humorous* (with allusion to 'bang goes saxpence' as in 8 c): to spend ('saxpence') all at once in a fit of extravagance. Hence '**banging** *vbl. sb.*

1897 *Westm. Gaz.* 17 May 10/1 The desirability of avoiding any unnecessary banging of saxpences. **1901** *Daily Chron.* 11 Nov. 3/7 Our Northern friends look twice before they 'bang' their 'saxpences'.

9. a. *Comb.* with sb. as obj., **bang-beggar**, a strong staff (*Sc.*), a constable or beadle (*dial.*); †**bang-pitcher**, a drunkard; **bang-straw** (*dial.*), a thresher.

1865 E. WAUGH *Barrel Org.* 29 Owd Pudge, th' bang-beggar, coom runnin' into th' pew. **1639** J. CLARKE *Parœmiol.* 102 A notable bang-pitcher, *Silenus alter.*

b. **bang-about** *a.* (cf. KNOCK-ABOUT *a.*), rough, boisterous.

1933 E. A. ROBERTSON *Ordinary Families* ix. 199 Dru, that devilish sailor and bang-about good sort! **1960** V. GIELGUD *To Bed at Noon* III. ix. 222 She keeps the wild-bull bang-about side of Rupert in hand.

10. Slang phr. *bang to rights*, of a criminal: (caught) red-handed. Also *banged to rights*.

1904 'No. 1500' *Life in Sing Sing* 255/1 *Bang to Rights*, caught in the act. **1932** A. R. L. GARDNER *Tinker's Kitchen* (Gloss.) 281 *Banged to rights*, found in possession of stolen property. **1958** F. NORMAN *Bang to Rights* I. 33 One night a screw looked through his spie hole and captured him bang to rights. **1962** *New Statesman* 21 Dec. 897/2 If I was making a book on the chances of my being banged to rights, you or any other punter could have 100 to eight to any amount.

V. Misc. use. **11.** *trans.* and *intr.* To copulate (with), to have sexual intercourse (with). *slang.*

1937 in PARTRIDGE *Dict. Slang.* **1957** J. KEROUAC *On Road* (1958) vii. 42 He rushes from Marylou to Camille.. and bangs her once. *Ibid.* 43 Marylou's all for it [*sc.* divorce], but she insists on banging in the interim. **1962** K. ORVIS *Damned & Destroyed* xiv. 90 We banged twice more after you left.

bang, *v.*² [f. BANG *sb.*²] To cut (the front hair) square across, so that it ends abruptly.

1882 *Century Mag.* XXV. 192 He was bareheaded, his hair banged even with his eyebrows in front. **1883** *Harper's Mag.* Mar. 492/2 They wear their.. hair 'banged' low over their foreheads.

bang (bæŋ), *sb.*¹ [f. BANG *v.*¹; cf. ON. *bang*, OSw. *bång* a hammering, Da. *bank* a beating.]

1. a. A heavy resounding blow, a thump.

?*c* **1550** *Rob. Hood* (Ritson) vi. 79 All the wood rang at every bang. [**1570** LEVINS *Manip.* /23 Bangue, *fustis*]. **1598** FLORIO, *Sergozzone*, a bang or rap giuen upon the necke. **1601** SHAKS. *Jul. C.* III. iii. 20 You'l beare me a bang for that I feare. **1663** BUTLER *Hud.* I. ii. 831 With many a stiff thwack, many a bang, Hard Crab-tree and old Iron rang. *a* **1845** HOOD *Lay Real Life* vii, Many a bitter bang I bore.

†**b.** A drubbing, defeat. *Obs. rare.*

1644 SIR G. RADCLIFFE in Carte's *Collect.* (1735) 329 After a shrewd bang Prince Rupert is recruiting gallantly.

2. a. A sudden, violent or explosive noise; *e.g.* the report of fire-arms.

1855 THACKERAY *Newcomes* II. 58 (L.) The steps of a fine belozenged carriage were let down with a bang. **1884** J. COLBORNE *Hicks Pasha* 160 The sharp bang of a section of howitzers.

b. With allusion to T. S. Eliot's line (see quot. 1925).

1925 T. S. ELIOT *Hollow Men* v. 31 in *Poems* 99 This is the way the world ends Not with a bang but a whimper. **1931** R. ALDINGTON *Colonel's Daughter* I. 56, I wish you'd all shoot yourselves with a bang, instead of continuing to whimper. **1953** 'M. INNES' *Christmas at Candleshoe* i. 16 Benison is going to end not with a bang but a whimper. **1959** *Times* 16 Dec. 3/2 Here the world ends neither with a bang nor a whimper, but with a slow, resigned sigh at its own criminal imbecility.

c. *spec.* A nuclear explosion.

[**1951** *Time* 16 Apr. 17/1 (*title*) Bang! The Day when A-Bomb hit Hiroshima... The old woman neither heard bang nor felt shock, but both ceiling and roof fell down.] **1955** *Times* 17 May 11/3 Even if these bangs are let off with disgust, not gusto, they can rock international friendship and confidence. **1957** J. OSBORNE *Look back in Anger* III. i, If the big bang does come, and we all get killed off, it won't be in aid of the old-fashioned grand design.

d. Short for *sonic bang* (see SONIC *a.*). Also *attrib.*

1955 *Britannica Bk. of Year* 489/2 A new piece of R.A.F. slang emerged in *Bang-Book*, a register that pilots were required to sign in the event of their having broken through the sound-barrier. **1955** *Times* 12 July 8/6 If the pilot produces a 'bang' accidentally.. he must report this immediately to flying control, who notify the command head-quarters. **1963** *Aeroplane* CV. 5/3 He described the strip of country subjected to sonic bangs from aircraft as the 'bang swath', whose boundary of area was the envelope of the bang rays.

3. A sudden impetuous movement; impetus, go.

c **1774** C. KEITH *Farmer's Ha'*, As he was working lang and strang, And fallowin wi' pith and bang. **1870** J. KAYE *Sepoy War* II. VI. iv. 554 An unwonted amount of confidence and bang.

4. *colloq.* A 'thumping' lie, a banger; ***bang-words***: explosive epithets, 'swear' words.

1879 MEREDITH *Egoist* xxix, Every crack and bang in a boy's vocabulary. **1906** *Westm. Gaz.* 20 Jan. 2/1 When the recipient of a letter has to.. go in for a comparative analysis of the different letters.. he is justified in using bang words.

5. [Cf. BANG *sb.*³] Excitement, pleasure; a 'kick'. *U.S. slang.*

1931 D. RUNYON *Guys & Dolls* (1932) vi. 129 He seems to be getting a great bang out of the doings. **1951** J. D. SALINGER *Catcher in Rye* iv. 37, I hate the movies like poison, but I get a bang imitating them.

6. [Cf. BANG *v.*¹ 11.] An act of sexual intercourse. *slang.*

1937 in PARTRIDGE *Dict. Slang.* **1965** A. PRIOR *Interrogators* xii. 239 Isn't it amazing.. what a quick bang does for old Lance. **1968** J. UPDIKE *Couples* i. 35, I bet she even gives him a bang now and then.

bang (bæŋ), *sb.*² [= hair cut 'bang' off; cf. BANG-TAIL.] The front hair cut square across the forehead. (Orig. in U.S.) Hence **banged** *ppl. a.*

1878 F. M. A. ROE *Army Lett.* (1909) 186 It had a heavy bang of fiery red hair. **1880** HOWELLS *Undisc. Country* viii. 113 His hair cut in front like a young lady's bang. **1880** *Even. Stand.* 3 Apr. 4/4 The present style of banged girl. **1936** M. H. BRADLEY *Five-Minute Girl* ii. 23 The straight dark hair, with its heavy bang across her childish forehead.

bang *sb.*³ **a.** obs. form of BHANG, Indian hemp.

b. Revived (*U.S. slang*) and often treated as if a slang sense of BANG *sb.*¹ Also, a 'shot' (of cocaine, etc.).

[**1922** E. F. MURPHY *Black Candle* (1926) I. vi. 61 He resorts to 'a shot' of morphine, or 'a bhang' of cocaine.] **1929** C. G. GIVENS in *Sat. Even. Post* 13 Apr. 54/4 An addict is.. a bangster, and a bang is a load, a charge or a hyp of the drug he uses. **1933** *Amer. Speech* Apr. 27/2 The injection of dope is referred to as *a bang in the arm* or *a shot in the arm.* **1962** K. ORVIS *Damned & Destroyed* xii. 82 He.. talked me into sampling a bang.

bang, *adv.* [See BANG *v.*¹ 8, and cf. SLAM-BANG.] Thoroughly, completely; exactly. orig. *dial.* and *U.S.*, now *colloq.*

1828 *Night Watch* II. 17, I fetched way bang overboard into the trawl. **1885** TENNYSON *Tiresias* 109 Steevie be right good manners bang thruf to the tip o' the taail. **1907** G. B. SHAW *How he Lied* in *Works* (1930) XI. 192 Do.. you propose that we should walk right bang up to Teddy and tell him we're going away together? **1924** A. J. SMALL *Frozen Gold* i. 28 Here they were right bang on hand—and.. they might as well be a thousand miles away. **1931** L. A. G. STRONG *Garden* xix. 170 Bang opposite him.. hung a.. blue cylinder. **1938** G. GREENE *Brighton Rock* II. i. 74 He.. led the way bang straight down Frank's stairs.

b. *bang on*, exactly on. (Cf. quot. 1832 s.v. BANG *v.*¹ 8.) Used as *adj.*, exactly right, extremely apposite, excellent.

1936 *Punch* 22 Apr. 461/3 'Quiet garden square near Hyde Park. Real hot water. Bang on Tubes.' *Newspaper Advt.* **1943** HUNT & PRINGLE *Service Slang* 12 *Bang on*, bomber slang for 'O.K.' or 'Everything's all right'. **1945** PARTRIDGE *Dict. R.A.F. Slang* 14 *Bang on*!, All right! Correct! In Bomber Command: from a bomb dropped *bang on* (exactly on) the target. **1945** C. H. WARD-JACKSON *Piece of Cake* (ed. 2) 12 *Bang-on*, perfect, excellent. **1949** E. POUND *Pisan Cantos* lxxx. 94 And he dumped all his old stock of calicos plumb bang on the germans. **1958** *Times* 4 Jan. 6/1 'Steering by the sun from earlier fixes we came bang on the base,' Sir Edmund Hillary reported. **1958** *Spectator* 14 Feb. 210/3 As a realistic tale of low life in London, it is bang on. **1958** *Oxf. Mag.* 27 Feb. 324/2 It [*sc.* a play] has enough quality and sense of the theatre to suggest that before long he will land one bang on the target. **1958** J. WAIN *Contenders* 6 I'd been to Brighton for a holiday, and I thought it was bang-on.

bangalay (bæˈŋælɪ). *Austral.* Also (*slang*) **bang alley.** [Native name.] Bastard mahogany.

1884 A. NILSON *Timber Trees N.S.W.* 133 Bangalay. Eucalyptus botryoides. Myrtaceæ. **1898** MORRIS *Austral English* 18/1 *Bangalay*, a Sydney workmen's name for the timber of *Eucalyptus botrioides*, Smith... The name is aboriginal, and by workmen is always pronounced Bang Alley. **1935** *Bulletin* (Sydney) 2 Jan. 21/4 Here in the Waikato (M.L.) district, *E. botryoides* (bangalay) has grown from a seedling to 15 ft. 2 in. in 18 months.

Bangalore torpedo (ˈbæŋgəˌlɔː tɔːˈpiːdəʊ). *Mil.* [f. *Bangalore*, south Indian city.] A tube containing explosive used by troops for blowing up wire entanglements.

1913 R. L. MCCLINTOCK in *R.E. Jrnl.* Mar. 135 (*caption*) The Bangalore 'Torpedo' for destroying wire entanglements. *Ibid.* 137 The 'Bangalore Torpedo' system is both quick to load and easy to carry up and place. **1925** FRASER & GIBBONS *Soldier & Sailor Words*, *Bangalore torpedo*, a device for clearing a pathway through a barbed wire entanglement... Introduced on the Western Front early in 1915. **1941** *Illustr. London News* CXCVIII. 80/2 The Bangalore Torpedo, first used by an inventive R.E. officer at Bangalore, consists of sectional tubes, each packed with explosive, having a pointed nose and a hollow cone at the base, into which fits the nose of the next section.

bangalow (ˈbæŋgələʊ). Also **-alo.** [Native name.] Either of two Australian palms of the genus *Archontophœnix*, esp. *A. cunninghamiana*, having feathery leaves. Also *attrib.*

[**1826** J. ATKINSON *Agric. & Grazing N.S.W.* 4 The bangally, much resembling the cabbage tree in appearance, but having some long and wide leaves of a thick and tenacious texture; these the natives tie up at each end in the form of a boat, and use them for carrying water.] **1851** J. HENDERSON *Excurs. N.S.W.* II. ix. 229 The Bangalo.. is a palm, and a native of the brushes... Its bunch of large leaves, surmounting a fine, straight stem, has a very beautiful effect. **1878** W. R. GUILFOYLE *Austral. Bot.* 18 The Aborigines of New South Wales and Queensland.. eat the young leaves of the cabbage and bangalow palms. *a* **1882** H. C. KENDALL *Poems* (1886) 193 You see, he was bred in a bangalow wood, And bangalow pith was the principal food. **1905** *Westm. Gaz.* 22 Mar. 2/1 The forest of lofty gums and iron-barks, and clumps of graceful bangalow palms.

banger (ˈbæŋə(r)), *sb.*¹ [f. BANG *v.*¹ + -ER¹.]

1. He who or that which bangs; *slang*, an astounding lie, a 'thumper.'

1657 A. C[ROWTHER] & T. V[INCENT SADLER] *Daily Exercise, of the Devout Rosarists* 374 To omit any necessary Ceremonie, or commit any notorious banger, in saying Mass, or administering any Sacrament. **1814** G. HANGER *Sporting* (on fly-leaf), A Sportsman entire—who says nay, tells a banger. **1899** *Daily News* 23 Sept. 6/3 In London the unfortunate lady banger would have been run in as a nuisance. **1959** I. & P. OPIE *Lore & Lang. Schoolchildren* xii. 283 They classify their fireworks as 'bangers', 'pretty ones', 'hoppers', and rockets.

2. A bludgeon. *U.S. slang* (at Yale).

1849 (*title*) The Yale Banger (Th.). **1856** *Yale Lit. Mag.* XXI. 282 (Th.), Brandishing a banger above my head, I came on to the stage with a yell. **1906** *Springfield Weekly Republ.* 10 May 1 He.. has rescued from some museum of Yale antiquities.. his old 'banger' of student days.

3. A kiss, esp. a violent one. *slang.*

1898 *Daily News* 25 Jan. 7/3 There were hieroglyphics in the form of crosses for kisses; in one case the cross occupying a very large space.. having written against it 'Oh, what a banger'. **1959** H. HOBSON *Mission House Murder* ii. 19 'Here —give us a banger first.' Honeypuss.. obediently offered him her lips.

4. A sausage. *slang.*

1919 W. H. DOWNING *Digger Dialects* 10 *Banger*, a sausage. **1928** *Weekly Dispatch* 27 May 14 Away they [*sc.* the boats] go fully laden with men and tea—not forgetting bangers (sausages) to cook after bathing. **1949** M. DICKENS *Flowers on Grass* vii. 182 The chap had bought him tea and bangers and mash. **1959** *Times* 5 Nov. 13/6 There is.. nothing exclusive about the childish use of 'banger' for sausage.

5. An old motor vehicle, esp. one which runs noisily. Usu. *old banger*. *slang.*

1962 B. KNOX *Little Drops of Blood* iii. 82 When we sell a car we've got to take in some old banger in part exchange. **1963** BIRD & HUTTON-STOTT *Veteran Motor Car* 129 Such cars were thought of insignificant historical interest by comparison with the pre-1905 Brighton Bangers. **1970**

Oxford Mail (Motoring Suppl.) 24 June 5/1 The paintwork may gleam, the highly-polished chromium may sparkle, but beware: the outward appearance may cloak a banger which could prove an embarrassment and a drain on the pocket for the rest of its life. **1976** *Southern Even. Echo* (Southampton) 2 Nov. 5/8 Banger racing driver 'Dopey' Don Stevens, who recently won the Dutch Championship, was convicted at Lymington Court yesterday of driving carelessly. **1985** *Times* 11 Feb. 13/7 It is true though that one misses out on one's husband's early years of struggle: the rented flats, .. the third-hand old bangers, the terrifying overdraft.

† **banger**, *sb.*^{2} *U.S.* var. BANJO. *Obs.*

1775 J. ADAIR *Hist. Amer. Indians* 175 One of their old sacred musical instruments .. resembled the Negroe-Banger in shape. **1803** J. DAVIS *Travels in U.S.A.* 379 My young master .. made me learn to play the Banger. **1849** in *Amer. Speech* (1951) XXVI. 182 About a douzen [*sic*] negroes .. enjoying the innocent amusement of playing the banger.

banghy, var. BANGY.

banging (ˈbæŋɪŋ), *vbl. sb.*^{1} [f. BANG *v.*^{1} + -ING^{1}.] The action of striking violently and noisily.

1647 WHARTON *Irel. War* Wks. (1683) 256 There shall be much banging and slashing amongst Men. **1709** STEELE *Tatler* No. 70 ¶4 So neither is banging a Cushion Oratory. **1853** KANE *Grinnell Exp.* xliii. (1856) 402 We have been nearly three hours subjected to this banging.

banging (ˈbæŋɪŋ), *vbl. sb.*^{2} [f. BANG *v.*^{2} + -ING^{1}.] The action of BANG *v.*^{2}

1877 F. H. BURNETT *Pretty Polly Pemberton* (1878) i. 12 Her hair is cut, on her round white forehead, Sir Peter Lely fashion, (they call it banging, I believe).

ˈ**banging**, *ppl. a.* [f. BANG *v.*^{1} + -ING^{2}.] Dealing violent blows, striking violently and noisily; *fig.* (*colloq.*) overwhelming, 'thumping.'

1560 *Disob. Child* in Hazl. *Dodsl.* II. 282 What banging, what cursing, Long-tongue, is with thee. **1596** NASHE *Saffron Walden* X ij b, The bangingest things .. which I can picke out .. are these. **1616** HOLYDAY *Juvenal* 185 Then th' axe their chariot-wheels with banging stroak Splits out. **1864** ARCHD. DENISON in *Daily Tel.* 31 Aug., They could win it with a great banging majority.

Bangkok (bæŋkɒk). (Stress variable.) [Name of the capital of Thailand.] A kind of woven straw for hats.

1920 *Tatler* 16 June p. xxv (Advt.), Becoming Hat for Country Wear. In Bangkok, crown and edge of printed union. **1924** *Sketch* 9 Apr. p. xii, Charming Hat in Chinese bangkok. **1927** *Observer* 28 Aug. 17/2 It matters little whether it [*sc.* a hat-shape] be carried out in felt or bangkok or manilla.

bangla, obs. form of BUNGALOW.

Bangladeshi (ˌbæŋgləˈdɛʃɪ, ˌbʌŋg-), *sb.* and *a.* [f. the name *Bangladesh* 'Land of Bengal' + -I.] **A.** *sb.* Pl. **Bangladeshi, -s.** A native or inhabitant of the People's Republic of Bangladesh, formed in 1971 (formerly the province of East Pakistan). **B.** *adj.* Of or pertaining to Bangladesh, its natives, or its inhabitants.

1971 *Guardian* 17 Dec. 13/4 What .. do you call a citizen of Bangladesh and what is the adjectival form? .. Four Professors of Bengali gathered in London and .. coined the form: 'Bangladeshiya' ... At the Bangladesh mission .. this was amended .. to 'Bangladeshi.' **1972** *Ibid.* 22 Aug. 10/3 Nine out of 10 Bangladeshi are peasants. **1975** *Ann. Reg. 1974* 296 Pakistan returned the Bangladeshi civilians who had been detained in Pakistan after the war. **1976** *Listener* 20 May 636/3 Different sections of the Asian community: Indians, Pakistanis and Bangladeshis. **1984** *Observer* 4 Mar. 2/7 He is one of only two Bangladeshi councillors in a borough which is home for an estimated 30,000 Bangladeshis.

† ˈ**bangle**, *v. Obs.* or *dial.* [Etymol. unknown.]

1. Orig. of hawks: To beat about, flutter aimlessly, in the air, instead of making direct for the quarry. See BANGLING *ppl. a.*

2. *to bangle* (*away*): to fritter away, squander.

1621 BURTON *Anat. Mel.* I. ii. III. x. (1651) 107 We bangle away our best days, befool out our times. **1636** W. SAMPSON *Vow Breaker* (N.) Thy titles are so bangld with thy debts. **1658** *Whole Duty Man* xvi. §18 (1684) 134 If we wilfully bangle away this so precious a Legacy. [In *Lanc.* (Halliwell).]

3. *intr.* To flap, hang loosely.

1622 T. STOUGHTON *Chr. Sacr.* xii. 166 Hats .. broad brimmed .. bangling about the eares of men, and hiding their faces. **1878** HALLIWELL s.v., A bangled hat means one bent down or slouched.

4. *dial.* To beat down (*e.g.* corn by wind or rain).

5. bangle(d) ear, one hanging loosely or flapping, like a spaniel's; hence ***bangle-eared*** ppl. adj.

1567 DRANT *Horace Epist.* I. xviii. F iiij, A sight of bangle eared houndes. **1647** WARD *Simp. Cobler* (1843) 90, I hold him prudent that in these fastidious times will helpe .. bangled ears, with pretty quicke pluckes. **1725** BRADLEY *Fam. Dict.*, *Bangle-Ears*, an Imperfection in a Horse. [In mod. Dicts.]

bangle (bæŋg(ə)l). [a. Hind. *bangṛī*, *bangrī*, orig. a coloured glass ring worn on the wrist by women.] A ring-bracelet or anklet.

1787 *Archaeol.* VIII. 256 (D.) The ankles and wrists ornamented with large rings or bangles. **1798** GREVILLE in *Phil. Trans.* LXXXVIII. 405 The venders of glass bangles. **1830** MARRYAT *King's Own* xlii, The women .. wear .. gold bangles upon their arms and legs.

bangled (ˈbæŋg(ə)ld), *ppl. a.* [f. prec. + -ED^{2}.] Wearing or adorned with bangles.

1864 SALA in *Daily Tel.* 10 June, Clad in Tyrian purple, bangled and braided. **1884** *Harper's Mag.* Sept. 530/2 Gold-bangled sleeve.

† ˈ**bangling**, *vbl. sb. Obs.* [f. BANGLE *v.* + -ING^{1}.] Petty, frivolous contention; squabbling.

1612 T. JAMES *Jesuits Downef.* 68 What banglings had he with Creswell. **1621** MOLLE *Camerar. Liv. Libr.* III. xi. 186 Hauing liued in marriage without .. bangling and strife.

† ˈ**bangling**, *ppl. a. Obs.* [f. as prec. + -ING^{2}.] That bangles: see BANGLE *v.*, and prec. word.

1615 *Curry-c. for Coxe-c.* i. 46 My Master .. hath met with a bangling Sophister. **1633** T. NASH *Quaternio* 19 One good hawke [is to be preferred] before ten bangling buzzards. *a* **1639** S. WARD *Serm.* 83 (D.) No bangling hawk, but with a high flier will mend her pitch.

bango (ˈbæŋgəʊ). An East African reed.

1899 WERNER *Captain of Locusts* 15 His dug-out canoe .. was found .. among the *bango* in a sheltered backwater. *Ibid.* 66 Sleepy natives .. were turning over on their *bango* mats. **1907** *Macm. Mag.* May 525 All the bango reed was dead and burnt.

Bangorian (bæŋˈgɔərɪən), *a.* [f. *Bangor* + -IAN.] Of or pertaining to Bangor, N. Wales, in ***Bangorian controversy***, a religious controversy raised by a sermon preached before the king in 1717 by Benjamin Hoadly, Bishop of Bangor, directed against the non-jurors.

1718 C. NORRIS (*title*) The Reconciler, or the *Bangorian Controversy*, abridg'd. **1759** GOLDSMITH *Bee* VII. 201 They are informed of the excellence of the Bangorian controversy. **1875** *Encycl. Brit.* III. 280/2 It was the year [1717] in which Bishop Hoadley preached that famous sermon on *The Kingdom of Christ*, which gave rise to the .. theological war known as the 'Bangorian controversy'. **1881** *Ibid.* XII. 29/1 A war of pamphlets known as the Bangorian controversy.

Hence as *sb.*, a supporter of Benjamin Hoadly.

1721 [see CONSTITUTIONER 2].

† ˈ**bangster.** *Obs.* or *dial.* Also 6 **bangister, -eister, 7 -ester.** [f. BANG *v.* + -STER: cf. *banger.*]

1. A burly violent fellow; a bully, a braggart.

c **1570** *Leg. Bp. St. Andrews* in *Scot. Poems 16th C.* (1801) II. 326 Proude ambitious bangsters. **1651** CALDERWOOD *Hist. Kirk* (1843) II. 516 My lord, mak us quite of thir Matchiavelian and bangester lords. **1766** ROSS *Helenore* 89 (JAM.) That yet have bangsters on their boddom set.

2. One who beats his opponents; a victor, winner.

1820 SCOTT *Abbot* xix, If the Pope's champions are to be bangsters in our very changehouses. **1824** —— *St. Ronan's* I. 183 (D.) You are so certain of being the bangster, so very certain I mean of sweeping stakes.

† ˈ**bangstry.** *Obs. rare*$^{-1}$. [f. prec. + -Y.] The action of a bangster; masterful violence.

1594 *Acts James VI* (1597) §217 Persones wrangouslie intrusing themselues in the rowmes and possessiones of vtheris be bangstrie and force.

ˈ**bang-**ˈ**tail.** [cf. BANG *v.* 8 c.] A (horse's) tail, of which the hair is allowed to grow to a considerable length and then cut horizontally across so as to form a flat even tassel-like end. Also, a horse or other animal (in Australia, esp. cattle) whose tail has been cut in this way; in *U.S. slang*, any horse, esp. a race-horse; ***bang-tail muster***: in Australia, a round-up of cattle during which the tuft at the end of the tail is cut straight across as the cattle are counted. Hence **bang-tailed** *ppl. a.*

1861 HUGHES *Tom Brown at Oxf.* vi. (D.) 'These bang-tailed little sinners any good?' said Drysdale, throwing some cock-a-bondies across the table. **1870** *Daily News* 19 July 6 A good mare with a bang tail. **1887** W. S. S. TYRWHITT *New Chum in Queensland Bush* iii. 61 Every third or fourth year on a cattle station, they have what is called a 'bang tail muster'; that is to say, all the cattle are brought into the yards, and have the long hairs at the end of the tail cut off square, with knives or sheep-shears... The object of it is, to .. find out the actual number of cattle on the run. **1921** *Collier's* 27 Aug. 20/2 If by some miracle the bangtail wins —beat it! **1927** M. M. BENNETT *Christison* xxv. 223 In a bang-tail muster each animal was put through the yards and counted, the tip of hair on its tail being cut off square.

bangue, variant of BHANG; obs. f. BANG.

ˈ**bang-up**, *adj. phr.*, (*advb. phr.*), and *sb. slang.* Also **banged-up.** [? as if *bang* or *close up* to a line. Cf. *slap-up*.] **A.** *adj.* Quite up to the mark, stylish, in the pink of fashion. See also quot. 1811.

1810 C. I. M. DIBDIN *Bang Up!* 6 'Bang-up' seems the watchword to be, From one tip-top driver to t'other. **1811** *Lex. Balatronicum, Bang Up, (Whip)* quite the thing, hellish fine... A bang-up cove; a dashing fellow who spends his money freely. To bang up prime: to bring your horses up in a dashing or fine style: as the swell's rattler and prads are bang up prime; the gentleman sports an elegant carriage and fine horses. **1812** H. & J. SMITH *Rej. Addr.* (1833) 163 Dance a bang-up theatrical cotillion. **1821** COMBE (Dr. Syntax) *Wife* v. (D.) Thus banged-up, sweeten'd, and clean shav'd. **1843** LEVER *J. Hinton* vii. 43 His spotted neckcloth knotted in bang-up mode. **1865** DICKENS *Mut. Fr.* I. II. viii. 239 A slap-up gal in a bang-up chariot. **1923** R. D. PAINE *Comr. Rolling Ocean* vii. 118 The salaries are bang-up nowadays. **1938** I. KUHN *Assigned to Adv.* iv. 39 There'd be a bang-up dinner, then a drive to some place outside the city where they could dance.

B. *advb. phr.* ***bang up*** = quite close up (to), right up (to). In modern use, freq. in *attrib.* phrases.

1819 J. H. VAUX *Mem.* II. 154 A person, whose dress .. is in the first style of perfection, is declared to be *bang up to the mark.* A man who has behaved with extraordinary spirit .. is also said to have come *bang up to the mark.* **1858** LYTTON *What will he do with it?* I. i, Smart and sharp, bang up to the day. **1907** [see BANG *adv.*]. **1914** JOYCE *Dubliners* 260 Drive bang up against Trinity College gates. **1963** *Times Lit. Suppl.* 8 Feb. 92/5 Bang-up-to-date neutron know-how. **1963** *Listener* 21 Feb. 353/2 They had a bang-up-to-the-minute subject in Mr. Harold Wilson's election to the Labour Party leadership.

C. *sb.* **a.** A man of fashion; a dandy. *Obs.*

1811 *Lex. Balatronicum* Pref., We trust .. that the whole tribe of second-rate Bang ups will feel grateful [etc.]. **1824** *Examiner* 613/1 Our Corinthians, *Roués* and Bang-ups. **1882** *Punch* 22 Apr. 185/1 The Trio turned into the Arcade and saw a number of gay sparks and fair ones promenading... These then are the dandies, the fops, the goes, and the bang-ups, these the Corinthians of to-day.

b. A heavy overcoat (see quot. 1903). *U.S.*

[**1810** *Sporting Mag.* Dec. 127/1 One article was .. a *bang-up* great coat.] **1835** *Fraser's Mag.* XI. 298 Dames in bang-ups, Shawls swath'd round men. **1842** *Spirit of Times* (Philad.) 13 Jan. (Th.), A gentleman dressed in a dark coloured fashionable bang-up. **1843** LEVER *J. Hinton* xxi, A green coat .. over which he wore .. a white 'bang-up', as it was called. **1846** J. KEEGAN *Leg. & Poems* (1907) 396 His old grey frieze bang-up. **1853** *Public Ledger* (Philad.) 11 June (De Vere), He was attired in an old bang-up, black vest, grey pants, and straw hat. **1903** CLAPIN *Dict. Amer.* 36 *Bang-up*, an old word for a heavy overcoat, still surviving in some parts of the Union.

bangy, banghy (ˈbaŋgɪ). *India.* [ad. Hind. *bahangī*, Marathi *bangī* (Skr. *vihaṃgikā*).] A yoke for carrying loads; such a yoke with its pair of baskets or boxes; hence, parcel post.

1789 R. BROOME *Lett. Simpkin the Second* 21 I'll give them Two Thousand, with Bangies and Coolies. **1809** VISCT. VALENTIA *Voy. & Trav. India* I. 67 We take .., in six bangys, sufficient changes of linen. **1810** T. WILLIAMSON *E. India Vade-Mecum* I. 325 The bangy-wollah, that is, the bearer who carries the bangy. **1837** T. BACON *First Impr. Hindostan* II. vii. 218 A weighty banghi-load of provisions. **1840** *Narr. Three Months' March India* vii. 200 Hindoos carrying small baskets .. in bangy-fashion. **1842** G. ARTHUR *Let.* 27 Oct. in Ld. Ellenborough *Ind. Adminstr.* (1874) 221, I will forward with this, by bhangy dâk, a copy of [a book].

banian (ˈbænɪən). Forms: 6 **baniane,** 7 **bannyan,** 7–8 **bannian,** 8–9 **banyan,** 7– **banian.** [a. Pg. *banian*, prob. a. Arab. *banyān* (16th c.), ad. Gujarātī *vāṇiyo* man of the trading caste, f. Skr. *vaṇij* merchant. 'The terminal nasal may be taken from the plural form *vāṇiyān*' (Col. Yule).]

1. A Hindoo trader, especially one from the province of Guzerat ('many of which have for ages been settled in Arabian ports, and known by this name' —Col. Yule); sometimes applied by early writers to all Hindoos in Western India.

1599 HAKLUYT *Voy.* II. I. 310 A Baniane .. one of the Indians inhabiting the countrey of Cambaia. **1634** SIR T. HERBERT *Trav.* 37 The Bannyans are tawny in complexion, are craftie, faire spoken, exquisite Merchants and superstitious. **1676** *Phil. Trans.* XI. 752 The religion of the Banians not permitting them to eat any thing that hath had life. **1845** STOCQUELER *Handbk. Brit. Ind.* (1854) 23 Bhyses, or Banians, are the trading class.

2. In Bengal applied to: A native broker attached to a house of business, or a person similarly employed by a private gentleman; now usually called *sircar*.

1687 A. LOVELL *Thevenot's Trav.* III. I. xxxii. 55 Every one hath his banian in the Indies. **1783** BURKE *Sp. E. Ind. Bill* Wks. 1842 I. 293 Mr. Hastings's bannian was, after this auction, found possessed of territories, etc. **1845** STOCQUELER *Handbk. Brit. Ind.* (1854) 40 Banians or dubashes (a species of broker to the European houses).

3. A loose gown, jacket, or shirt of flannel, worn in India. (Originally *attrib.* from sense 1.)

1725 in *Harl. Misc.* VIII. 297 (D.) I have lost nothing by it but a banyan shirt, a corner of my quilt, and my bible singed. **1772** GRAVES *Spir. Quix.* XI. iv. (D.) His banyan with silver clasp wrapt round His shrinking paunch. **1845** STOCQUELER *Handbk. Brit. Ind.* (1854) 315 Even in the low country a light flannel banian (jacket or shirt) is of service.

4. *attrib.* (in reference to the Banians' abstinence from flesh and sacred estimation of animal life): **banian-day** (*Naut.*), one on which no meat is served out; **banian-hospital**, one for animals.

1748 SMOLLETT *Rod. Rand.* xxv. (D.) On Mondays, Wednesdays, and Fridays the ship's company had no allowance of meat, and .. these meagre days were called banyan days. **1823** LAMB *Elia* Ser. I. iii. (1865) 19 We had three banyan to four meat days in the week. **1813** J. FORBES *Orient. Mem.* III. 129 A banian-hospital .. where he saw a number of sick oxen, camels, and horses.

5. banian- or **banyan-tree**, now often simply **banyan**: the Indian Fig Tree (*Ficus religiosa* or *indica*) a remarkable East Indian tree, the branches of which drop shoots to the ground, that take root and support their parent branches; extending in this way, one tree will often cover a large expanse of ground. [*Banian Tree, Banians' Tree, Tree of the Banians*, was originally a local appellation given by Europeans to an individual tree of this species growing near Gombroon on the Persian Gulf, under which the *Banians*, or Hindu traders settled in that port, had built a little pagoda; thence it was extended to others, and finally taken as the English name of the species. It is not so called in any Indian language.]

1634 SIR T. HERBERT *Trav.* II. (1638) 122 A Tree (or rather twenty Trees, the boughs rooting and springing up a whole aker together)..named by us the Bannyan Tree, from their adorning and adoring it with ribbons and streamers of varicoloured Taffata. *c* **1650** tr. *Tavernier* I. 255 Near to the city of Ormus was a Bannians tree. [**1687** A. LOVELL *Thevenot's Trav.* III. I. xiv. 25 The war-tree..called the tree of banians.] **1791** NEWTE *Tour Eng. & Scot.* 416 The Banian tree of India, the most stupendous effort of vegetable nature. **1857** LIVINGSTONE *Trav.* xii. 212 Most..send down roots from their branches like the banian. **1860** GOSSE *Rom. Nat. Hist.* 133 The banyan, or sacred fig of India.

baning ('beɪnɪŋ), *vbl. sb.* [f. BANE *v.* + -ING[1].] Poisoning.

1530 TINDALE *Exod.* Prol., Then God sendeth his curses among them, as hunger, dearth, murrain, baning, pestilence.

banio, obs. form of BAGNIO.

banish ('bænɪʃ), *v.* Forms: 4 **banyse, -isshe**, 4–6 **-ysshe**, 5 **bannysshe**, 6 **-ysche, -ish, banysh(e, -ych**, 4– **banish**. [a. OF. *baniss-* lengthened stem of *banir* (mod. *bannir*):—late L. *bannīre*, f. *bannum* proclamation: see BAN.]

†**1.** *orig.* To put to the ban, 'proclaim' as an outlaw, to outlaw. *Obs.*

c **1320–1617** [See BANISHED.]

2. To condemn (a person) by public edict or sentence to leave the country; to exile, expatriate: **a.** with *from, out of.*

1375 BARBOUR *Bruce* IV. 522 We are out of our cuntre Banyst. **1485** CAXTON *Chas. Gt.* 13 Whom..her uncle bannysshed fro hys contrey. **1530** PALSGR. 443/2 The kyng hath banysshed hym out of his realme. **1610** SHAKS. *Temp.* I. ii. 266 Sycorax..from Argier Thou know'st was banish'd. **1848** tr. *Gieseler's Ch. Hist.* II. ii. 109 They had been banished from Rome.

b. with *double obj.* (of person and place).

1494 FABYAN I. ii. 9 He was banysshed the Countre. **1674** HICKMAN *Hist. Quinquart.* 36 Godescalk was banished Germany. **1796** MORSE *Amer. Geog.* II. 295 He that shall be convicted there of is to be banished the kingdom.

c. *simply.*

c **1385** CHAUCER *L.G.W.* 1863 That Tarquyny shulde ybanysshed be there-fore. **1651** HOBBES *Leviath.* II. xxi. 110 Banished an Aristides, for his reputation of Justice. **1879** FROUDE *Cæsar* xv. 227 Clodius had banished Cicero.

3. *gen.* To send or drive away, expel, dismiss imperatively (a person). Const. as in prec.

c **1450** *Compl. Loveres Lyfe* xlvi, Though I be banysshed out of her syght. **1548** UDALL, etc. *Erasm. Par. Matt.* xii. 43 (R.) Beyng banyshed from his olde hospitall, he walketh in dry and baren places. **1591** SHAKS. *Two Gent.* III. i. 171 To die, is to be banisht from my selfe. **1593** —— *2 Hen. VI*, II. i. 197, I banish her my Bed. **1732** POPE *Mor. Ess.* III. 330 Banish'd the doctor, and expell'd the friend. **1826** DISRAELI *Viv. Grey* VII. ix. 438 Who had they dared to imitate him.. would have been banished society.

4. To drive away, expel, dismiss (a thing).

1460 *Pol. Rel. & L. Poems* (1866) 78 Sithe al manere of Iustice and pyte is banshid out of a ladies entente. **1596** SHAKS. *Tam. Shr.* Induct. ii. 34 Banish hence these abiect lowlie dreames. **1637** MILTON *Comus* 413 And gladly banish squint suspicion. **1742** RICHARDSON *Pamela* III. 263 Industry would have been banish'd the Earth. **1871** MARKBY *Elem. Law* §202 Try to recall an absent thought or to banish a present one.

†**5.** To clear out, empty. Cf. AVOID *v. Obs.*

1494 FABYAN VI. clxvii. 133 [They] banysshed that cytie as they had doon the other. **1573** TUSSER *Husb.* (1878) 17 To banish house of blasphemie, least crosses crosse vnluckelie.

banished ('bænɪʃt), *ppl. a.* Also 4 (*Sc.*) **banyst**, 6 **-eist**. [f. prec. + -ED.]

†**1.** Outlawed, put to the ban. ***banished man***: an outlaw, a bandit. *Obs.*

[*c* **1320** *Sir Beues* 4129 This forbannuste man Is come the land agan.] **1398** TREVISA *Barth. De P.R.* XIV. li. (1495) A deserte is the lodges of banyssht men and of theues. **1591** SHAKS. *Two Gent.* V. iv. 152 These banish'd men, that I haue kept withall. **1617** MORYSON *Itin.* I. II. ii. 104 These banished men lurking upon the confines of the Popes state.. make excursions..to doe robberies.

2. Exiled, expatriated; driven away, dismissed.

1578 *Chr. Prayers* in *Priv. Prayers* (1851) 514 Whensoever this banished and wayfaring soul of mine shall depart hence. **1582–8** *Hist. Jas. VI* (1804) 274 The uther twa cheefe baneist lords. **1611** BIBLE *2 Sam.* xiv. 13 The King doeth not fetch home againe his banished. **1717** POPE *Eloïsa* 52 Some banish'd lover, or some captive maid. **1855** MACAULAY *Hist. Eng.* IV. 421 Who had heroically laid down his life for the banished King.

banisher ('bænɪʃə(r)). [f. as prec. + -ER[1].] He who or that which banishes or drives away.

c **1450** HENRYSON *Test. Cres.* (R.) Faire Phebus..banisher of night. **1607** SHAKS. *Cor.* IV. v. 89 To be full quit of those my Banishers. **1729** M. BROWNE *Piscat. Eclog.* Ded. (1773) 10 Solitude, soft Banisher of care. **1834** CARLYLE *Fr. Rev.* I. i. I. 6 Maupeon, the banisher of Parlements.

'**banishing**, *vbl. sb.* [f. as prec.] = next.

1523 LD. BERNERS *Froiss.* I. viii. 7 The kynge..defended euery parsone, on payne of banysshyng..that none shulde ..go. **1641** PRYNNE *Prelates Tyrrany* 177 The banishing and exiling of Freemen out of their native country.

banishment ('bænɪʃmənt). [f. as prec. + -MENT.]

1. The action of authoritatively expelling from the country; a state of exile; expatriation.

1507 *Bk. Gd. Mann.* (W. de W.) Biij, For he..hadde kepte hym from banysshement. **1607** SHAKS. *Cor.* IV. iii. 22 The Nobles receyue so to heart, the Banishment of that worthy Coriolanus. **1776** GIBBON *Decl. & F.* I. xvi. 402 A sentence of banishment was pronounced. **1855** MERIVALE *Rom. Emp.* (1875) IV. xxxviii. 333 Some exiles contrived to avoid going to their places of banishment.

2. *gen.* The action of peremptorily sending away; a state of enforced absence; dismissal.

1535 COVERDALE *Ps.* cxx. 5 Wo is me yͭ my banishment endureth so longe. *a* **1744** POPE in *Lady Montague's Lett.* 23 I. 70, I wish..you might pass to your banishment by the most pleasant way. **1832** HT. MARTINEAU *Ella of Gar.* ii. 23 Their banishment was a sign that dinner was ready.

banister ('bænɪstə(r)). Also **bannister**. [corruption of BALUSTER, q.v.; though condemned by Nicholson as 'improper,' by Stuart (*Dict. Archit.* 1830) and Gwilt as 'vulgar,' the term had already taken literary rank, and has now acquired general acceptance.] Usually in *pl.*: Slender upright posts or rails, *esp.* those guarding the side of a staircase, and supporting the handrail; often applied to the whole structure of uprights and handrail.

1667 PRIMATT *City & C. Build.* 66 Posts, Rails, Bannisters. **1677** MOXON *Mech. Exerc.* (1703) 165 A pair of Stairs..with Walls and Railes and Bannisters. **1765** H. WALPOLE *Otranto* v. (1798) 81 The uppermost bannister of the great stairs. **1766** ENTICK *London* IV. 63 A neat altar-piece, inclosed with rails and banisters. **1775** SHERIDAN *Rivals* II. i, He comes down stairs..thumping the banisters all the way. **1860** W. COLLINS *Wom. White* 490 He held fast by the banisters, as he descended the stairs.

b. *collect. sing.* = Banisters; cf. BALUSTER 4.

1851 MAYHEW *Lond. Labour* 344 Going down your staircase, I should be all right so long as I touched the bannister.

bani(y)a, var. BUNNIA.

banjax ('bændʒæks), *v. Anglo-Ir. slang.* [Etym. unknown; perh. orig. Dublin slang.] *trans.* To batter or destroy (a person or thing); to ruin; to confound, stymie. So '**banjaxed** *ppl. a.*, ruined, stymied.

1939 'F. O'BRIEN' *At Swim-two-Birds* 240 Here is his black heart sitting there as large as life in the middle of the pulp of his banjaxed corpse. **1956** S. BECKETT *Waiting for Godot* (rev. ed.) 79 Lucky might get going all of a sudden. Then we'd be banjaxed [1954: ballocksed]. **1959** D. O'NEILL *Life has no Price* ix. 169, I had the right to leave him talk, I suppose, and banjax us altogether? **1968** *Observer* 29 Dec. 19/1 You completely banjax the whole psychological impact. **1969** G. LYALL *Venus with Pistol* viii. 48 The man *is* a twit. I mean, he banjaxed that Zurich trip. **1972** *New Yorker* 28 Oct. 40/1 Ha-ha, so she ups and banjaxed the old man one night with a broken spade handle. **1974** *Nature* 22 Nov. 334/1 My sense of enlightenment was somewhat tempered by the banjaxed mood in which I found myself. **1976** U. HOLDEN *String Horses* viii. 102 The dawn suicide the day before had made a lot of work and worry, had banjaxed things for a while. **1979** T. WOGAN *Banjaxed* (1980) 78, I am out to banjax the bookies.

banjo ('bændʒəʊ). Also (earlier) **banjore, banjer.** [A corruption of BANDORE, through Negro slave pronunciation, *ban'jōre, ban'jō.*] **1. a.** A stringed musical instrument, played with the fingers, having a head and neck like a guitar, and a body like a tambourine; a modification of the bandore.

[**1764** GRAINGER *Sugar-Cane* IV, To the wild banshaw's melancholy sound.] **1774** P. V. FITHIAN *Jrnl.* (1900) 103 In the School-Room,..several Negroes & Ben & Harry are playing on a Banjo & dancing. *c* **1790** DIBDIN *Sea-songs* (title), The Negro and his Banjer. **1801** MAR. EDGEWORTH *Belinda* II. xviii. 7 'What is this, mamma?—It is not a guitar, is it?' 'No, my dear, it is called a banjore; it is an African instrument, of which the negroes are particularly fond.' **1801** *Port Folio* (Philad.) I. 270 (Th.), The sound of Banneker's banjo would be as tuneable as Gallatin's spoken French. **1836** *Southern Lit. Messenger* II. 162, I found a crowd of negroes..dancing..to the music of a banjo. *a* **1845** *Negro Melodies* (in Bartlett), Dey dance all night to de ole banjo, Wid a cornstalk fiddle, and a shoe-string bow. **1846** *Punch* 26 Sept. 126 The music-master of the regiment has been sent with a cornet-a-piston and a banjo to play to Queen Pomare. **1847** *Ibid.* 27 Feb. 94 The present is the age of bones and banjos.

b. With distinguishing term.

1934 S. R. NELSON *All about Jazz* ii. 53 The banjolin was ..soon discarded in favour of the Tenor Banjo. **1961** A. BIRCH in A. Baines *Mus. Instruments* vii. 182 For the violinist who wished to play some more suitable instrument in the dance-band of the twenties there was the 'tenor-banjo' tuned in fifths.

2. a. *transf.* Applied to contrivances of the shape of a banjo: see quots.

1867 SMYTH *Sailor's Word-bk.*, *Banjo*, the brass frame in which the screw-propeller of a steamer works, and is hung for hoisting the screw on deck... The banjo is essential to lifting the screw. **1902** *Encycl. Brit.* XXXII. 147/2 (*Railways*) The enclosed disc signal, commonly called a 'banjo', is a circular box..with a glass-covered opening, behind which a red disc is shown to indicate stop. **1964** *Gloss. Letterpress Rotary Print. Terms* (*B.S.I.*) 9 *Banjo*, the end adjusting duct screw.

b. *spec.* A shovel; an entrenching tool. Chiefly *Austral.* and *N.Z.*

1918 *N.Z. Exped. Force Chron.* 30 Aug. 57/1 We are still wielding the old 'Banjo' in good style. **1925** in FRASER & GIBBONS *Soldier & Sailor Words.* **1931** 'DEAN STIFF' *Milk & Honey Route* 199 *Banjo*, a short-handled shovel. **1933** *Bulletin* (Sydney) 22 Nov. 21/1 With banjo, pick and barrow I toil. **1954** *Coast to Coast* 67 All swung their banjos so hard that production costs dropped. **1960** *N.Z. Listener* 21 Oct. 7/3 'It's interesting work—anything's better than the banjo.' 'The banjo?' 'A shovel. Some people call it a Mexican side-loader.' **1966** T. H. SHEPPARD *Dict. Railway Slang* (ed. 2) 3 *Banjo*, fireman's shovel.

3. *attrib.*, as in ***banjo-player, -playing***; with the meaning 'banjo-shaped', as ***banjo axle, union***; **banjo-clock** *U.S.*, a clock in a case shaped like a banjo; **banjo-frame** (see quot. 1888).

1847 *Punch* 27 Feb. 94 Bone and banjo minstrels. **1865** *Sat. Rev.* 4 Feb. 134/1 A converted banjo-player. *Ibid.*, Banjo-playing being..a negro form of fetish-worship. **1888** *Lockwood's Dict. Mech. Engin.*, *Bow Connecting-Rod*..or *Banjo Frame*, a form of connecting-rod employed in steam pumps. **1903** F. C. MORSE *Furniture of Olden Time* xi. 328 Simon Willard patented in 1802 an 'improved time-piece' which Mr. Howard says is the clock now known as the 'banjo' clock from its shape. **1922** *Autocar* 10 Nov. 962 A vertical banjo type of back axle. *Ibid.* 982 A neat banjo axle. **1958** *Times* 10 Oct. 8/3 He had found a leak in the banjo union of the cylinder [*sc.* of a car]. *Ibid.*, He had tightened the banjo union nut one-sixth of a turn. **1959** *Engineering* 6 Feb. 187/3 The air from the compressor..then passes through a banjo type junction.

banjoist ('bændʒəʊɪst). [f. prec. + -IST.] One who plays a banjo.

1880 *Daily Tel.* 23 Dec., Songs sentimental and comic.. arranged by Ballantine (banjoist). **1884** *Sat. Rev.* 7 June 740/2 The place of the stately Interlocutor..was filled by the banjoist.

banjolin ('bændʒəlɪn). Also **-ine**. [f. BANJO + *-lin* of MANDOLIN.] A musical instrument combining the characteristics of the banjo and mandolin.

1889 *Pall Mall Gaz.* 4 July 5/1 An instrument that appeared to be a cross between a banjo and a mandolin—dubbed on the spot a 'banjolin'. **1923** *Ashore & Afloat* Aug. (Advt.), Banjolins or Jazz Banjos. **1950** J. VEDEY *Band Leaders* 39 One playing drums and the other the banjoline, an instrument which was enjoying popularity in dance bands but which is now obsolete. **1961** A. BIRCH in A. Baines *Mus. Instruments* vii. 182 The mandolinist could play the double-strung 'banjo-mandoline' or the single strings of the 'banjoline'.

banjulele (bændʒə'leɪliː). Also **banjo-**. [f. BANJ(O + *-ulele* of UKULELE.] A stringed musical instrument of a type between a banjo and a ukulele.

1925 *Glasgow Herald* 7 Apr. 8 A native band playing on banjoleles, a sort of zither, from which the tones are provided by gourds filled with varying amounts of water. **1926** *Bulletin* 27 Feb. 10 Alvin D. Keech, from Hawaii, has secured a British patent for his invention, the banjulele. **1926** *Westm. Gaz.* 1 July, A youth..strumming on a banjulele. **1937** *Sunday Times* 21 Feb. 4/4 Driven to try to pawn his precious banjolele.

bank (bæŋk), *sb.*[1] Forms: (1 ? **banca**), 3–7 **banke**, (3 *Orm.* **bannke**), 4 **bonc, bonkk(e**, 4–5 **bonke**, (5 **bunk(e,)** 4–6 **bonk**, 6 **banc, banck(e**, 3– **bank**. [ME. *banke*, prob. a. Old Norse **banke*, **banki* = OIcelandic *bakki* ridge, eminence, bank of clouds, of a river, chasm, etc. (whence Da. *bakke*, Sw. *backe*, hillock, hill, rising ground, ascent, acclivity):—OTeut. **bankon-*; cogn. with OTeut. **banki-z*, see BANK[2] and BENCH; the primary sense of *bank-* being probably 'shelf,' natural or artificial, of earth, rock, sand, or wood. The OE. repr. of *banki, bakki*, would be **banca*, **bǫnca*: a compound *hó(h)banca* in sense of 'heel-bench, couch' actually occurs once in a vocabulary, but this may be, as the sense suggests, one of the class of weak compounds from strong sbs. (cf. *ándaga* from *dæg*); in any case the senses of ME. *banke*, as well as its first appearance in the northern dialect, point to its Scandinavian source.]

I. A raised shelf or ridge of ground, etc.

1. A portion of the surface of the ground raised or thrown up into a ridge or shelf; a lengthened mound with steeply sloping sides. *Hence*, One side or slope of such a ridge or mound. Now chiefly in *hedge-bank.*

c **1200** ORMIN 9210 Whærse iss all unnsmeþe get þurrh bannkess & þurrh græfess. **1377** LANGL. *P. Pl.* B. v. 521 But flustreden forth as bestes ouer bankes and hilles. *a* **1400** *Cov. Myst.* 170 Downe I ley me upone this banke. **1590** SHAKS. *Mids. N.* II. i. 249, I know a banke where the wilde time blowes. *Ibid.* II. ii. 40 Finde you out a bed, For I vpon this banke will rest my head. **1596** SPENSER *F.Q.* II. iii. 6 Sitting ydle on a sunny banck. **1807** CRABBE *Par. Reg.* II. 170 Toyed by each bank and trifled at each stile. **1862** BARNES *Rhymes Dorset Dial.* I. 22 Yellow cowslip-banks.

†**2. a.** A high ground, height, hill, fell. *Obs.* exc. in *north. dial.*

c **1325** *E.E. Allit. P.* A. 906 Bydez here by þys blysful bonc. *c* **1340** *Gaw. & Gr. Knt.* 14 On mony bonkkes ful brode Bretayn he settez. *c* **1420** *Anturs Arth.* iv, To beker at the barrens, in bonkes so bare.

b. *Hence*: The slope or acclivity of a hill, a hillside, a brae; a 'hanger'. *spec.* on a railway track. Still common in the north; cf. *up-bank* = up-hill.

1362 LANGL. *P. Pl.* A. Prol. 8 To reste Vnder a brod banke bi a bourne syde. *a* **1400** *Death & Life* (Warton) x, And as she came by the bankes, the boughes.. lowted to that ladye, and layd forth their branches. **1549** *Compl. Scot.* vi. 37 There vas ane grene banc ful of rammel grene treis. **1570** LEVINS *Manip.* /24 Banke of an hill, *procliuitas*. **1631** STOW *Chron.* 1088 Two hills their euen Bankes doe somewhat seeme to stretch. **1808** ANDERSON *Borrowdale Johnnie*, It tuik me nine days and six hours comin up-bank. **1816** MISS AUSTEN *Emma* III. vi. 309 A bank of considerable abruptness & grandeur. **1875** J. A. H. MURRAY *Thos. of Erceldoune* 2 Thomas, lying on Huntley Banks, sees the lady riding by. **1879** *Shropsh. Gloss.* (E.D.S.), *Bonk*, a sloping height. **1893** in *Funk's Stand. Dict.* **1908** *Railway Mag.* Feb. 111/1 The fastest work I ever recorded with the same loads up the Hemerdon and Burlescombe banks.

†**3.** An artificial earthwork, an embankment, *esp.* for military use. *Obs.*

1535 COVERDALE *2 Sam.* xx. 15 Beseged him.. and made a banke aboute the cite. **1552** HULOET, *Banckes* defensyue againste subundation called Seabanckes or Sea-dickes. **1601** HOLLAND *Pliny* (1634) I. 59 Fenced on the East-side with the bank or rampier of Tarquinius. **1611** BIBLE *2 Sam.* xx. 15 They cast vp a banke against the city.

†**4.** An ant-hill. *Obs.*

1667 E. KING in *Phil. Trans.* II. 425 If either of the other two sorts be put into the black Ants Bank. **1747** GOULD *Eng. Ants* 76 We suppose a Bank of Hill Ants to amount.. to six Thousand.

5. A shelving elevation in the sea or the bed of a river, rising to or near the surface, composed of sand, mud, gravel, etc. Also a bed of oysters, mussels, or the like.

1605 SHAKS. *Macb.* I. vii. 7 But here, vpon this Banke and Schoole of time, Wee'ld iumpe the life to come. **1696** *Lond. Gaz.* No. 3221/4 Near the Banks of Dunkirk. **1702** *Ibid.* No. 3842/4 Fish from the Bank of Newfoundland. **1719** DE FOE *Crusoe* (1858) 437 The Banks (so they call the place where they catch the fish). **1851** LONGF. *Gold. Leg.* v. ad fin., No danger of bank or breaker. **1861** HULME tr. *Moquin-Tandon* II. III. ii. 86 Oysters.. in vast numbers, forming what are termed Oyster banks.

6. A long flat-topped mass: e.g. of cloud or mist stretching above the horizon, of piled-up ice or snow, etc.

? *a* **1626** BACON *Charge* 4 (T.) A bank of clouds in the north or west. **1840** R. DANA *Bef. Mast* xxxi. 113 On the starboard bow was a bank of mist. **1848** KINGSLEY *Saint's Trag.* IV. 201 A long dim formless fog-bank creeping low. **1860** FITZ-ROY in *Merc. Mar. Mag.* VII. 342 The first indications of daylight are seen above a bank of clouds.

7. *Mining.* **a.** 'The face of the coal at which miners are working.' **b.** 'An ore-deposit or coal-bed worked by surface excavations or drifts above water-level.' Raymond *Mining Gloss.* 1881.

1862 *Chamb. Jrnl.* Apr. 216 The work is continued in one set until the bank is pierced through, and the next strait set is reached.

II. A bordering slope.

8. a. The shelving or sloping margin of a river or stream; the ground bordering upon a river.

c **1300** *K. Alis.* 3495 That he no sank, Til he com to the water bank. **1330** R. BRUNNE *Chron.* 241 Ouer þe water.. fro bank to bank. *c* **1440** *Promp. Parv.* 23 Banke of watyr, *Ripa.* **1601** SHAKS. *Jul. C.* I. i. 50 Tyber trembled vnderneath her bankes. **1635** N. CARPENTER *Geog. Del.* II. ix. 160 Some riuers ouerflow their bankes at some certaine times. **1703** MAUNDRELL *Journ. Jerus.* (1732) 82 This second bank [of the Jordan] is beset with Bushes and Trees. **1860** TYNDALL *Glac.* I. §17. 120 The left bank of the glacier. **1878** HUXLEY *Physiogr.* 5 Geographers have agreed to call that bank which lies upon your right side as you go down towards the sea the right bank.

b. *fig.*

1576 FLEMING tr. *Caius' Dogs* in Arb. *Garner* III. 257 Within the banks of his remembrance. **1642** FULLER *Holy & Prof. St.* I. xi. 33 Liberality should as well have banks as a stream. **1665** GLANVILL *Sceps. Sci.* Addr. 13 Like a mighty deluge.. beat down all the Banks of Laws, Vertue, and Sobriety.

c. Phr. ***bank and bank*** (see quot. 1933). *N.Z.*

1863 S. BUTLER *First Year in Canterbury Settlement* vi. 79 Half a dozen times in a year, the river is what is called bank and bank, that is to say, one mass of water from one side to the other. **1933** L. G. D. ACLAND in *Press* (Christchurch) 9 Sept. 15/7 *Bank and bank.* A river runs b. and b. when all the streams join into one; i.e., when in high flood.

†**9.** The sea-coast or shore. *Obs.*

c **1350** *Will. Palerne* 2717 þe riche cite.. vpon þe see bonke. **1387** TREVISA *Higden* Rolls Ser. VII. 135 He sette ones.. his chaier in þe banke of þe see. *c* **1400** *Destr. Troy* VII. 2870 Brode sailes vp braid; bonkis pai leuyt. *a* **1470** TIPTOFT *Caesar* iii. (1530) 4 The open playne banke of Brytayne. **1535** STEWART *Cron. Scot.* II. 437 Fra the West se bank. **1592** SHAKS. *2 Hen. VI*, III. ii. 83 And twice by aukward winde from Englands banke Droue backe againe.

10. A raised or rising edge or margin of a pond, lake, pit, road, railway cutting, or other hollow place; in *Mining*, the surface of the ground at the pit-mouth, or top of the shaft.

1330 R. BRUNNE *Chron.* 182 The dikes were fulle wide with bankis hie without. *c* **1400** *Destr. Troy* XXXII. 12664 When þe prinse was past to þe pit bothum, þe buernes on þe bonk bet hym with stonys. **1667** MILTON *P.L.* IV. 262 The fringed Bank [of a lake]. **1708** J. C. *Compl. Collier* (1845) 32 Horses to draw your Coals to Bank (or Day) out of the Pit. **1722** WOLLASTON *Relig. Nat.* ix. 206 Daisies on the banks of the road. **1881** RAYMOND *Mining Gloss.*, *Bank*, the ground at the top of a shaft. Ores are brought 'to bank,' *i.e.* 'to grass.' **1892** *Daily News* 11 Mar. 5/7 The preparations which are made at many pits to bring horses and ponies 'to bank'.

†**11.** *spec.* (from 8) The south side of the Thames opposite London [also called *Bankside*], and the brothel-quarter located there (suppressed in 1546).

1536 *Remed. Sedition* 21 As moche shame for an honest man to come out of a tauerne.. as it is here to come from the banke. **1548** CROWLEY in Strype *Eccl. Mem.* II. I. xvii. 142 Sisters of the Bank, the stumbling-blocks of all frail youth. **1598** STOW *Survey* (1633) 448 On this Banke was sometime the *Bordello* or Stewes.

12. *Aeronaut.* The lateral inclination of an aeroplane when turning or rounding a curve.

1913 C. MELLOR *Airman* vi. Illustration 29 A left-handed turn with plenty of bank. **1928** C. F. S. GAMBLE *North Sea Air Station* xiii. 225 When turning with a heavy bank. **1955** *Times* 13 July 4/6 The maximum of the bank was about 40 deg. When the bank was jerked off there was a crash and he saw the port wing was gone.

III. 13. *Comb.*, chiefly *attrib.*, as **bank-bait**, the may-fly; **bank-barn** *N. Amer.* (see quot. 1909); **bank beaver** (see BEAVER[1] 1 b); **bank cress** (*Herb.*), the Hedge-mustard (*Sisymbrium officinale*); **bank-engine**, (*a*) the engine at a pit's mouth; (*b*) a locomotive used to assist in taking a heavy load up a steep incline (= BANKER[3] 5); **bank-fence**, one consisting of a bank of earth; **bank-fish**, cod from Newfoundland-bank, whence ***bank-fisherman***, ***-fishing***, ***-fishery***; **bank-harbour**, one protected by banks of mud, sand, etc.; **bank-head**, a pit's mouth (see 10); **bank-high** *a.*, swollen up to the banks; **bank-hook**, a large fishing-hook, baited, and attached by a line to the bank of a stream; **bank-jug**, the Willow Warbler, or Willow Wren; **bank-manager**, the superintendent at a pit's mouth; **bank-martin**, **-swallow**, the Sand-martin; **bank-smack**, a Newfoundland fishing smack.

1879 E. P. WRIGHT *Animal Life* 485 A great many [may-flies] fall into the water a prey to fishes... Hence the name *bank-bait. **1894** *Congress. Rec.* Jan. 1036/1 On my father's farm, when I was a boy, there stood a *big bank-barn. **1906** 'R. CONNOR' *Doctor* 26 The foundation of the bank-barn. **1909** *Cent. Dict.* Suppl., *Bank-barn*, a barn built on a hill-side or sloping ground, so that three sides of the lower story are surrounded by earth, the fourth being unbanked. **1968** *Globe & Mail* (Toronto) 13 Feb. 31/6 (Advt.), New bank barn 36 × 80, equipped for 38 cows. **1863** PRIOR *Plant-n.* 14 **Bank cress*, from its growth in hedge banks. **1893** *Funk's Stand. Dict.*, *Bank-engine. **1707** MORTIMER *Husb.* 231 The *Bank-fence is likewise a good shelter for the Land and the Cattle. **1666** *Lond. Gaz.* No. 79/1 Three prizes, one with *Bankfish. **1705** *Ibid.* No. 4103/4 Newfoundland *Bank-Fish.. equal to the North-Sea Cod. **1782** ST. J. DE CRÈVECŒUR *Lett. Amer. Farmer* iv. 146 Nantucket is a great nursery of seamen, pilots, coasters, and *bank-fishermen. **1777** in *9th Rep. Hist. MSS. Comm.* App. III. II. (1910) 69 Without a large force is sent out to me the *bank fishery is at a stand. **1861** *New Amer. Cycl.* XII. 302/1 About.. 80 [vessels are employed] in the coast and bank fisheries. **1797** *Encycl. Brit.* XIII. 27/1 The *bank fishing season, begins the 10th of May. **1955** *Bulletin* (Bridgewater, N.S.) 9 Mar. 9/2 A number of fishermen.. have gone sealing out of Halifax, or engaged in bank fishing. **1882** *Standard* 5 Sept. 4/6 The accumulations on the '*bank head' are lower than is usual, and all the collieries are full of orders. **1882** *Daily Tel.* 28 Oct. 2/4 Streams everywhere are *bank high, and flooded. **1884** *Yorksh. Post* 9 Jan., A bank manager in London or Liverpool was a very different personage from a *bank manager in Staffordshire or the mining regions generally, where he has to superintend the operations at the pit's mouth. **1774** G. WHITE *Selborne* lix, The *bank-martin terebrates a round and regular hole in the sand or earth. **1883** *Fisheries Exhib. Catal.* 355 The fishery is carried on.. in larger vessels, called *bank-smacks. **1655** MOUFFET & BENN. *Health's Impr.* (1746) 188 Be they either House-Swallows, or *Bank-Swallows.

bank (bæŋk), *sb.*[2] Forms: (1 banca), 3 bonck, baunk, 5–6 banck(e, 6–7 banke, 6– bank. [ME. *baunk*, *banck*, apparently a. OF. *banc* 'bench' (= Pr. *banc*, It., Sp., Pg. *banco*):—late L. *bancus* bench, 'scamnum,' ad. Teut. *bank*, *banc* (OS., MHG., MDu. *banc*, OHG. *banch*, G., Du. *bank*):—OTeut. **banki-z* BENCH; cognate with BANK *sb.*[1]:—OTeut. **bankon-*. If however OE. *hó(h)banca* 'heel-bench, couch, sofa,' was really a compound of an OE. **banca* (see prec.), the ME. word might be the lineal descendant of that, subsequently identified with the Fr. *banc*. The true native equivalent is BENCH:—OE. *bęnc*.]

†**1.** A long seat for several to sit on, a bench, or form; a platform or stage to speak from. *Obs.* (Cf. *mountebank.*)

[*a* **1050** in Wright *Voc.* (W.) /280 *Sponda*, hobanca.] **1205** LAY. 25185 þa spæc Angel þe king.. And stod uppen ane boncke [**1250** vp on benche]. **1527** in Pocock *Rec. Ref.* I. xxvi. 54 Where was prepared a bancke with quyssons and carpets. **1605** B. JONSON *Volp.* II. ii. (1616) 467 Fellowes, to mount a banke! Did your instructor.. neer discourse to you Of the Italian mountebankes? **1661** HEYLIN *Hist. Ref.* II. iii. 69 Twelve Levites standing on the bank or stage. *a* **1680** BUTLER *Rem.* (1759) II. 59 A State-Quack, that mounts his Bank in some obscure Nook, and vapours what Cures he could do on the Body politic.

2. A seat of justice; = BENCH. ***Bank Royal***: King's Bench. ***Common Bank***: Common Pleas. (Cf. also BANCO *sb.*) *arch.* or *Obs.*

1275 *Act 3 Edw. I*, xlvi, Les Justices al Baunk le Roi & Justices de Baunk a Westm. *c* **1450** *Pol. Poems* (1859) II. 228 Fewe can ascape hit of the banck rialle. **1649** SELDEN *Laws of Eng.* I. lxvii. (1739) 163 Tryals in the common Bank, or other Courts at Westminster. **1657** HOWELL *Londinop.* 368 The Courts and Benches, or Banks of Justices. **1700** TYRRELL *Hist. Eng.* II. 1109 General days in Bank in real Actions. **1768** BLACKSTONE *Comm.* III. 277 Days in bank, *dies in banco*, days of appearance in the court of common pleas.

3. The bench occupied by the rowers of each oar in a galley. (So in Fr., It., Ger.)

1599 HAKLUYT *Voy.* II. I. 169 The gally had.. at euery banke or oare seuen men to rowe. **1687** B. RANDOLPH *Archipel.* 54 Every time that they tugg the oar they rise with their bodys, and fall back on the banks. **1728** MORGAN *Algiers* II. ii. 224 Their Galeot (which had but eighteen Banks on a side). **1855** SINGLETON *Virgil* I. 384 Awake, My men, and take your seats upon the banks.

4. *catachr.* A rank or tier of oars; used chiefly in reference to the ancient galleys, which had several tiers one above another.

1614 RALEIGH *Hist. World* II. v. i. §6. 296 One of the Carthaginian Gallies, of fiue bankes. **1622** HEYLIN *Cosmogr.* IV. (1682) 86 Gallies, with two banks of Oars upon a side. **1797** HOLCROFT *Stolberg's Trav.* IV. xci. 67 Dionysius supplied his gallies with five banks of rowers. **1807** ROBINSON *Archæol. Græca* IV. xiii. 387 Several orders or banks of oars, which.. being fixed at the back of each other, ascended gradually in the manner of stairs. **1866** KINGSLEY *Herew.* v. 114 Each ship had double banks for twelve oars a side.

5. a. A row of keys on an organ.

1884 *Harper's Mag.* July 272/1 What an organist would call a 'bank' of ivory keys.

b. A row of keys on a typewriter.

1875 [see TYPEWRITER 1]. **1959** *Chambers's Encycl.* XIV. 66/2 The keyboard had four straight rows, or 'banks', of eleven keys each.

†**6.** A shelf. (Cf. G. *bücherbank*, etc.) *Obs. rare.*

1577 HELLOWES *Gueuara's Ep.* 125 A banke of olde bookes.

7. a. A bench or table used in various trades; *esp.* in *Printing*, the table on which the sheets are laid before or after printing. (Cf. It. *banco.*)

1565 *Act 8 Eliz.* xi. §4 The same Cap [shall] be first well scoured and closed, upon the Bank. **1867** *N. & Q.* 30 Nov. 432 When a man is about to work a block of stone, he places it upon a stool or stout table.. termed a 'bank.'

b. ***optical bank***: an optical bench; a graduated bench, usually of steel, on which the holders of lenses, prisms, etc., may be set up in alignment.

1888 *Electrician* 21 Sept., To order expensive and highly polished optical banks and other apparatus from an instrument maker.

8. a. The floor of a glass-melting furnace. **b.** A pottery. Cf. *pot-bank* (POT *sb.*[1] 14).

1880 CH. MASON *Forty Shires* 156 Each manufactory [of pottery] is called a 'bank.' **1902** A. BENNETT *Anna of Five Towns* iii. 61 What's amiss with this bank is that it wants pullin' down. **1903** —— *Leonora* iii. 91 He's somewhere on the bank, sir—speaking to the mouldmaker.

9. A creel for holding rows of bobbins of cotton.

10. A set of similar pieces of apparatus or units of equipment grouped together. In various spec. uses: **a.** *Electr.* Lights arranged in rows or tiers.

1902 WEBSTER Add., *Bank*, a group or series of objects arranged near together; as, a *bank* of electric lamps, etc. **1911** D. S. HULFISH *Cycl. Motion-Pict. Work* II. 102 A bank of mercury-vapor lamps is suspended from the ceiling. **1935** *Discovery* Apr. 111/1 'Drifting' news signs, in which a series of letters is caused to drift across the face of a bank of lamps. **1958** *Times* 24 Sept. 13/4 A huge bank of lights dominates this rebuilt sound stage.

b. In *Automatic Telephony*: a series of fixed contacts in a selector or switch.

1904 M. M. KIRKMAN *Telegraph & Telephone* II. iii. 50 The contact banks consist of ten layers of contacts... The top bank is known as the 'private' bank, while the two lower banks are called 'line' banks. **1922** *Encycl. Brit.* XXXII. 708/2 Banks of contacts for 200 and 500 [telephone] lines respectively are employed. **1926** *Gloss. Electr. Terms* (Brit. Engin. Stand.) 174 *Wiper*, that portion of the moving member of a selector or other similar device which engages with the contacts of a bank.

bank (bæŋk), *sb.*[3] Forms: 5–7 **banke**, 6 **bancke**, 7 **banque**, **banck**, 7– **bank**. [Early mod.E. *banke*, a. F. *banque*, ad. It. *banca* fem., used side by side, and in same sense, with *banco* masc.; ad. Teut. *bank*, *banc*, bench: see prec. word. The double form and gender in Romanic, cf. It., Sp., Pg. *banco*, *banca*, Pr. *banc*, *banca*, F. *banc*, *banche*, are apparently original (see med.L. *bancus*, *banca*, in Du Cange), and due to the double gender of the German: OHG. *der*, *diu banch*, MHG. *der*, *die banc*, early mod. and dial. G. *der*, *die bank*. The original meaning 'shelf, bench' (see BANK[1] and [2], and BENCH) was extended in It. to that of 'tradesman's stall, counter, money-changer's table, *mensa argentaria*, τράπεζα,' whence 'money-shop, bank,' a use of the word which passed, with the trade of banking, from Italy into other countries. In this sense, It. uses both *banco* and *banca*, Sp. and Pg. the masc. *banco*; but in F. the It. fem. *banca* was adapted as *banque*, whence Eng. *banke*, *bank*. The word is thus ultimately identical with BENCH and BANK[2], and cognate with BANK[1].

(Although, in It., *monte* 'mount, heap, amount, stock,' was used in some of the senses of 'bank,' the notion that the name *banco, banca*, originated in a German rendering of *monte* is erroneous: G. *bank* had no such sense as 'mount, heap,' only that of 'bench, shelf.' Rather is it the fact, that in the development of banking, the *banco* of the money-changer, and the *monte* or 'joint-stock capital' were at length combined, and *bank* applied in Eng. to both.)]

I. A money-dealer's table, counter, or shop.

†**1.** The table or counter of a money-changer or dealer in money. *Obs.* exc. *Hist.*

1567 JEWEL *Def. Apol.* (1611) 462 Christ overthrew the Exchangers bankes, meaning thereby, that there may be no coine in the Church, but only Spirituall. **1584** FENNER *Def. Ministers* (1587) 98 Christ ouerthrew the exchaungers banckes. **1598** FLORIO, *Banco*, a bench, a marchants banke, or counting house, a counter. **1611** COTGR., *Banque*, a banke, where money is let out to use: or lent, or returned by exchange: also, the table whereon such money is told. **1846** ARNOLD *Hist. Rome* II. xxvii. 72 These established their banks or tables in the forum, like ordinary bankers.

†**2.** The shop, office, or place of business of a money-dealer. (Cf. BANKER[2] 1 a, b.) Now merged in 7 a.

1474 CAXTON *Chesse* III. iv, There was a..chaungeour.. A man cam to hym and sayd and affermyd that he had delyueryd in to his banke v hondred floryns of gold to kepe. **1526** TINDALE *Luke* xix. 23 Wherfore then gavest not thou my money into the banke [Gr. τράπεζα; WYCLIF, borde; COVERDALE, exchaunge Banke]? **1552** HULOET, Bancke of exchaunge, *Argentaria*. **1649** JER. TAYLOR *Gt. Exemp.* II. xi. 21 Exchangers of Money made the temple to be the market and the banke.

II. An amount or stock of money.

†**3. a.** A sum of money, an amount (It. *monte*); a 'pile.' (Cf. 'mounts of coin' in last quot.) *Obs.*

1515 BARCLAY *Eglogs* i. (1570) A v/3 Where shall I..some little banke procure, That from the bagge and staffe mine age may be sure. **1652** BROME *Jov. Crew* I. Wks. 358 Cash; which added Unto your former Banck, makes up in all Twelve thousand and odd pounds. **1715** BURNET *Own Time* (1766) II. 146 He had got a great bank of money to be prepared. **1758** J. BLAKE *Mar. Syst.* 68 The..payments will constitute a bank, or nest egg. [Cf. *c* **1645** HOWELL *Lett.* (1753) 128 And bring in Mounts of Coin His Mints to feed, And Banquers (trafics chief suporters) breed.]

†**b.** *esp.* A sum to draw upon. *Obs.*

1642 FULLER *Holy & Prof. St.* III. xxiv. 225 S. Paul finds a constant bank for Ministers Maintenance lockt up in a Ceremoniall Law. **1665** S. BING in Ellis *Orig. Lett.* II. 310 IV. 24 To extend your charity to the outrunning the bank you honoured me with.

†**c.** A batch of paper-money. *Obs.* (exc. *Hist.*)

1878 F. WALKER *Money* xv. 319 In 1738 a Bank of £100,000 was issued with new provisions for securing the interest of the mortgages.

4. In games of hazard, the amount or pile of money which the player who plays against all the others, *e.g.* the proprietor of the gaming-table, has before him.

c **1720** POPE *Basset-T.* 78 When Kings, Queens, Knaves, are set in decent rank: Expos'd in glorious heaps the tempting Bank. *c* **1750** H. WALPOLE in *Harper's Mag.* July (1884) 258/1 He saw neither the bank nor his own cards. **1850** THACKERAY *Pendennis* lvi. (1884) 548 He had seen his friend..lose eighteen thousand at a sitting, and break the bank three nights running at Paris. **1865** TYLOR *Early Hist. Man.* vii. 175 It is certainly playing against the bank.

†**5.** An amount made up by the contributions of many; a joint stock or capital. *Obs.*

1625 BACON *Usury, Ess.* (Arb.) 545 Let it be no Banke or Common Stocke, but euery Man be Master of his owne Money. *c* **1645** HOWELL *Lett.* (1650) II. 11 They advance trade whersoever they com; with the banks of mony. **1790** BURKE *Fr. Rev.* 129 The stock in each man is small, and.. individuals would do better to avail themselves of the general bank and capital of nations and of ages.

†**6.** An amount so contributed for lending to the poor; a loan-bank; whence the modern pawn-broker's establishment (Fr. *mont de piété*). *Obs.*

1622 MALYNES *Anc. Law Merch.* II. xiii. 335 In Italie there are *Montes pietatis*, that is to say, Mounts or Bankes of Charitie, places where great summes of money are by legacies given for reliefe of the poore, to borrow vpon pawnes. **1646** BENBRIGGE *Vsura Accom.* 3 For their [the poor's] rescue may be collected *Mons pietatis, sive charitatis*, a Banke of piety or charity..a certaine summe of money, or things..which is laid up for the reliefe of the poore, either by one rich man, or by many. **1659** TORRIANO *Dict., Monte di pietà*, a publick stock or bank maintained for the relief of the poor, where pawns may be taken. **1663** GERBIER *Counsel* Ej a, A Bank of Loane in that part of the Suburbs of this great City.

fig. **1649** JER. TAYLOR *Gt. Exemp.* II. ix. 110 The talent which God hath intrusted to us in the banks of nature and grace. **1704** E. ARWAKER *Embass. Heav.* ix, Is not thy Bank of Blessings yet dismay'd, To Lend, where so unthankfully Repaid?

III. (Ordinary modern sense.)

7. An establishment for the custody of money received from, or on behalf of, its customers. Its essential duty is the payment of the orders given on it by the customers; its profits arise mainly from the investment of the money left unused by them.

a. Banks (in England) may be divided into—

a. Private Banks, carried on by one or more (in Great Britain not exceeding *ten*) persons in partnership. Cf. sense 2 above.

b. Joint-Stock Banks, of which the capital is subscribed by a large number of shareholders. (Cf. sense 5 above). Of these the greatest is..

c. The Bank of England, shortly 'The Bank,' a corporation of subscribers and contributors to a capital sum of £1,200,000, to whom a charter was granted in 1694 (by the name or style of ' the Governor and Company of the B. of E.'), on condition of their lending that sum to the Government, with certain privileges now no longer existing, or maintained only for the benefit of the State. Its duties are to manage the service of the public debt, to receive and account for the revenue when collected, and to provide and attend to the automatically regulated issue of legal tender notes. Its banking business is of the same nature as that of the other joint-stock or private banks, its chief customer being the Government.

[Cf. **1526** in 2. **1548** UDALL, etc. *Erasm. Par. Luke* xix. 23 Haue deliuered foorth my money to the kepers of the banke. *c* **1590** MARLOWE *Jew of M.* IV. i, In Florence, Venice, Antwerp..Have I debts owing; and..Great sums of money lying in the banco.] **1622** MALYNES *Anc. Law Merch.* I. xx. 131 A Banke is properly a collection of all the readie money of some Kingdome, into the hands of some persons licensed thereunto by publicke authoritie. **1734** tr. *Rollin's Anc. Hist.* (1827) III. VII. §10. 344 The bank of all Greece which he had sent for from Delos. **1849** SAXE *Poems, Times* 373 Always abundance of gold in the Banks. **1850** MERIVALE *Rom. Emp.* (1865) III. xxx. 397 The temples of the ancient world were the banks in which private possessors deposited their most precious effects. **1876** B. PRICE *Currency & B.* 102, I defined a bank to be an institution for the transfer of debts.

a. 1694 (*title*) Brief account of the intended Bank of England. **1720** SWIFT *Irish Manuf.* Wks. 1761 III. 14, I cannot forbear saying one word upon a thing they call a *bank*, which I hear is projecting in this town. **1828** TAYLOR *Money Syst. Eng.* 138 The Bank of England had parted with six or eight millions of gold at the current mint price. **1834** GILBART *Hist. Bank.* 95 The number of private country banks, and branches of private banks, in England and Wales is 638. **1881** H. H. GIBBS *Double Standard* 69 The result would really be..that the Bank would always hold both Silver and Gold bullion.

b. bank of deposit, a bank that receives lodgements of money. **bank of issue** or **circulation**, a bank which issues its own notes or promises to pay; in Great Britain a bank to which the right of issue was continued by the Acts of 1844–45. **branch bank**, a branch-office of a bank, established to give banking facilities to a locality at a distance from the head-office. **savings-bank**, a bank of which the express object is to take charge of the savings of the poorer classes, or of small sums of money.

1834 GILBART *Hist. Bank.* 109 The establishment of branch banks may be considered as the effect of the formation of joint-stock banks. *Ibid.* 133 Similar accusations may be as justly advanced against banks of deposit as against banks of circulation. **1863** HAYDN *Dict. Dates* 67 The branch banks of the Bank of England in the chief towns of the kingdom..have all been formed since 1828.

c. *fig.*

1642 ROGERS *Naaman* 543 As affliction is a furnace, so is it a banque: Job had twice as much after he had lost all as before. *a* **1716** LOUTH (J.) Pardons and indulgences..out of the common bank and treasury of the church.

d. *in bank*: in a bank or the bank, at one's bankers'. Also *fig.*: in store.

1563 *Homilies* II. xi. I. (1850) 387 He which sheweth mercy to the poore doth lay his money in banke to the Lord. **1622** MALYNES *Anc. Law Merch.* II. xi. 335 The paiments by Assignement in Banke without handling of moneys. **1646** EVANCE *Noble Order* 13 The benefits..in hand, besides the blessings that are in banck. *a* **1747** S. CIBBER *Let.* in D. Garrick *Private Corresp.* (1831) I. 50 She is the greatest coquet in England, and has half-a-dozen husbands in bank, in case of your death. **1753** WHITEFIELD in *Scots Mag.* May 214/1 The young man has the balance in bank. **1844** *Knickerbocker* XXIII. 14 [She] claimed..among her chattels sundry shares in bank. **1902** O. WISTER *Virginian* xxiii. 273 Take my land away to-morrow, and I'd still have my savings in bank.

e. Phr. *in the Bank* (see quot. 1930).

1930 M. CLARK *Home Trade* xxix. 234 In the language of the Money Market, money becomes tight and, maybe, the loans available from the banks are insufficient to go round. Then the assistance of the Bank of England is sought and the Money Market is said to be 'in the Bank'. **1955** *Times* 30 June 16/7 Credit was tighter in Lombard Street yesterday, and one or two houses were 'in the Bank' for a very small amount.

f. *transf.* A store of things for future use, a reserve supply: *spec.* of blood for transfusion, tissue for grafting, or the like. Cf. *blood-bank* (s.v. BLOOD *sb.* 21), *eye bank* (s.v. EYE *sb.*[1] 28). orig. *U.S.*

1938 *Life* 28 Feb. 33/2 The bank maintains a postive balance of blood. **1944** *Reader's Digest* XLV. 25 (*title*) Banks for Human 'Spare Parts'. **1945** *Ann. Reg. 1944* 379 Nerve 'banks' for the supply of quick frozen and dried nerve fragments for nerve grafts were developed. **1947** *Lancet* 12 Apr. 493/2 The value of a bone bank. **1959** *Times* 13 Mar. 15/2 A foetal tissue bank is being established at the Royal Marsden Hospital, comparable to the eye banks. **1963** *Times* 16 Feb. 9/2 We must be prepared for the day when 'banks' of different organs..will be integral parts of all major hospitals.

g. Catch-phr. ***to laugh***, etc., (orig. ***to cry***) ***all the way to the bank***: to relish (orig. *iron.*, to deplore) the fact that one is making money, esp. undeservedly or at the expense of others.

1956 *Daily Mirror* 26 Sept. 6/4 On the occasion in New York at a concert in Madison Square Garden when he had the greatest reception of his life and the critics slayed him mercilessly, Liberace said: 'The take was terrific but the critics killed me. My brother George cried all the way to the bank.' **1959** *Times* 9 June 14/7 He [*sc.* Liberace] agreed that the expression: 'I cried all the way to the Bank' had become a standard gag of his. He used it to reply to critics who did not like his performances. **1969** *Listener* 2 Jan. 17/3, I thought: ah no, this isn't right at all people will laugh at me. Then I said: better laugh all the way to the bank than just be laughed at. **1973** W. V. LIBERACE *Autobiogr.* ii. 28 When the reviews are bad I tell my staff that they can join me as I cry all the way to the bank. All this crying 'all the way to the bank' is not intended to give the idea that I'm just in this business to make a living. **1977** *Zigzag* Aug. 22/2 Look at Screaming Lord Sutch for example, or Alice Cooper gibbering all the way to the bank. **1985** *National Trust* Midsummer 22/2 The taxpayer may be called in to 'save' it [*sc.* a great house] for the nation. Then the owner laughs all the way to the bank, and the devil can take his conscience.

8. *Comb.*: **a.** attrib. or obj. genitive, as ***bank-account***, ***-accountant***, ***-building***, ***-charter***, ***-clerk***, ***-coffer***, ***-counter***, ***-deposit***, ***-depositor***, ***-director***, ***-manager***, ***-master*** (obs.), ***-monger***, ***-president***, ***-robber***, ***-robbery***, ***-snatcher***.

1799 C. B. BROWN *A. Mervyn* iv. 39 Have I not seen his bank account. His deposits..amount to not less than half a million. **1929** D. H. LAWRENCE *Pansies* 33 With bank accounts and insurance policies Don't sympathise. **1834** GILBART *Hist. Bank.* 30 In 1708 the Bank charter was extended or renewed until the expiration of twelve months. **1803** *Edin. Rev.* II. 103 The bank-coffers are drained of gold. **1854** H. MILLER *Sch. & Schm.* (1858) 526 Behind the bank-counter. **1832** *Chambers's Edinb. Jrnl.* I. 186/1 After exhausting his bank deposits, he still felt himself in difficulties. **1940** G. CROWTHER *Outl. Money* ii. 40 The ordinary bank depositor keeps all his money in the bank and makes his daily payments out of it. **1828** TAYLOR *Money Syst. Eng.* 193 That the bank directors be required to pay their notes on demand in gold at the market price. **1860** TROLLOPE *Framley P.* xlii. 151 The bank manager from Barchester. *c* **1618** FLETCHER *Pilgr.* I. 51 Rogues and Beggars have got the trick now to become Banckmasters. **1814** JEFFERSON *Let.* 24 Jan. in *Writings* (1854) VI. 305, I was derided as a maniac by the tribe of bank-mongers. **1853** *Harper's Mag.* Jan. 193 As if some invalid clergyman or bank-president, in white cravat, wished sedately to have his carriage called. **1799** *Aurora* (Philad.) 15 Mar. (Th.), Groups of pickpockets, bank-robbers, and hen-pecked dotards. **1894** NISBET *Bush Girl's Rom.* 277 Wildrake was the real criminal and bank-robber. **1854** DICKENS *Hard T.* III. viii. 339, I have suspected young Mr. Tom of this bank-robbery from the first. **1890** *Harper's Mag.* Feb. 472 One of the most daring bank snatchers in the city effected two robberies in the course of a single day.

b. Special combinations: **bank annuities**, a technical term for certain British government funds; usually, the Consolidated 3 per cent. Annuities, or 'consols'; **bank balance**, the net amount held by a depositor in a bank account; **bank card, bankcard**, a cheque card or credit card issued by a bank (cf. *banker's card* s.v. BANKER[2] 1 c); also, a cashpoint card; **bank charge**, a fee debited by a bank to a customer's current account for each transaction it carries out on the customer's behalf, and for certain other services; usu. in *pl.*; **bank-cheque**, a cheque or order to pay issued upon a bank; **bank-circulation**, a name applied to receipts given by the Bank of England to contributors to the loan made to the Government in 1751, which circulated as paper currency; **bank-clerk**, a clerk (see CLERK *sb.* 6 b) in a bank; hence ***bank-clerkly*** adj.; **bank-court**, the weekly meeting of the Governor and Directors of the Bank of England, or other joint-stock bank; *also*, the general court of proprietors; **bank-credit**, a credit opened for any person by a correspondent of a bank, to enable the former to draw for the amount; **bank-money** (cf. BANCO *a.*); *also*, money in the bank; **bank-paper**, (*a*) bank-notes in circulation; bills of exchange accepted by a banker; (*b*) (see quot. 1888); **bank-parlour**, the court-room of the Bank of England; the room in which a banker or bank-manager does business with borrowers; **bank-post**, a kind of writing-paper used for foreign correspondence; **bank-rate**, (*a*) the rate per cent. per annum fixed from time to time by the Bank of England, at which the company is prepared to discount bills of exchange having not more than 95 days to run; replaced in October 1972 by *minimum lending rate* (see MINIMUM *a.* b); (*b*) *loosely*, any rate of interest charged by a bank; **bank-receipt**, *formerly*, a receipt given by the Bank of England on its formation, for money deposited to be drawn against; *now*, an acknowledgement given by a banker for money deposited on a current account; **bank-roll** *U.S.*, a roll of bank-notes; hence as *v. trans. colloq.*, to support financially; **bank statement**, a record supplied periodically or on request by a bank to an account-holder, showing all credits and debits over a given period, and the current balance of the account; **bank-stock**, the capital stock of the Bank of England, being the aggregate of the shares therein owned by the various proprietors; its original amount was £1,200,000; it is now £14,553,000; **bank-token**, a token issued by a bank to serve for payments, on its responsibility, during a scarcity of silver coin; **bankward** *a.* and *adv.*, towards the bank. See also BANK-BILL, -BOOK, -HOLIDAY, -NOTE.

1931 H. CRANE *Let.* 10 Jan. (1965) 363 A *bank balance sufficient at least to my carfare east again. **1986** *Los Angeles Times* 8 Aug. VI. 28/3 'We started January, 1984, with no bank balance, some assets, some experience, a small, dedicated staff and 1,000 subscribers,' Thoman said. **1970** *New Scientist* 23 July 181/1 Development of existing *bank cards—including both cheque guarantee cards and credit cards..—will play a major role in the advance towards a 'cashless and chequeless society'. **1973** *Courier-Mail* (Brisbane) 14 Nov. 19/7 Each bank participating in the scheme will issue the same uniformly designed 'bankcard' with its own bank name appearing on the back. **1980** *N.Y. Times Mag.* 13 July 27 He..sticks his plastic bank card in the slot... And..a series of bills slides out. **1983** *Truckin' Life* Oct. 45/1 The drivers can obtain fuel by using a special plastic credit card..issued by Amoco. These cards..are similar to any bankcards..and work on the same principle. **1885** G. RAE *Country Banker* xix. 138 (*heading*) *Bank charges. **1923** *Jrnl. Inst. Bankers* XLIV. 113 If a profit and loss account is to show a correct view of a trader's or manufacturer's affairs, it should include the bank charges and allowances which have accrued up to the date of the account. **1986** *Economist* 3 May 94/1 As interest rates decline, watch out for more redundancies among bank staff and more automated tellers. Bank charges will also go up. **1803** JEFFERSON in *Harper's Mag.* Mar. (1885) 541/2, I enclose you a *bank-check for twenty-two and a half dollars. **1753** *Scots Mag.* May 262/1 *Bank-circulation 2*l.* 15*s.* prem. **1834** GILBART *Hist. Bank.* 38 In 1751, in order to raise the sum promised to be lent to the Government, the bank established what was called 'Bank Circulation.' **1829** *Harlequin* 13 June 35 This burlesque was written by Mr. Rhodes, who was 'only a *bank-clerk'. **1859** SALA *Tw. round Clock* 42 From sober Hackney, and Dalston, and Kingsland, bank-clerk beloved. **1920** E. POUND *H. S. Mauberley* 19 But in Ealing With the most bank-clerkly of Englishmen? **1959** *Listener* 23 July 153/3 The same sort of boyish fun—or bank-clerkly humour—induced inordinate pleasure [etc.]. **1752** HUME *Balance of Trade, Ess.* (1817) I. 318 An invention of this kind, which was fallen upon some years ago by the banks of Edinburgh..called a *Bank-Credit. **1636** HEALEY *Theophrast.* 79 He, that boastes upon the Exchange, that he hath store of *banke mony. **1753** HANWAY *Trav.* (1762) II. I. iii. 17 A ducat which passes for seven marks current, is worth but six bank money. *Ibid.* vii. 35 He sells his bank-money for current money. **1790** BURKE *Fr. Rev.* Wks. V. 411 They imagine that our flourishing state in England is owing to that *bank-paper, and not the bank-paper to the flourishing condition of our commerce. **1888** C. T. JACOBI *Printers' Vocab.* 6 *Bank paper*, a thin paper mostly used for foreign letter or note paper to save cost of postage. **1859** SALA *Tw. round Clock* 160 Tremendous bank-partners ..pay a farewell visit to the *bank parlour. **1884** *Lisbon* (Dakota) *Clipper* 30 Oct. /3 The caution which has prevailed ..in bank parlors is not at all relaxed. **1854** C. TOMLINSON *Cycl. Useful Arts* II. 369/1 *Names, dimensions,* and *weight per ream* of Writing and Drawing Papers... *Bank post 19 by 15½ [inches] 7 [lb.]. **1879** *Cassell's Techn. Educ.* III. 397 The ordinary Saxe paper will answer very well, as will also.. Bank-post. **1876** FAWCETT *Pol. Econ.* III. vi. 361 The *Bank-rate of discount, is the measure, at any particular time, of the value of money. **1972** *Daily Tel.* 10 Oct. 17/2 Bank rate is no more. As from Friday..[it] will be superseded by a new rate linked by a direct formula to market rates. **1974** *Latin Amer.* 1 Mar. 67/1 Colombia: The government has raised bank rates from 14 to 16 per cent in an effort to control the rate of inflation. **1986** *Today* 23 Aug. 27 Base rate 10.0%. Bank overdraft rate Authorised 15.0–17%... All Bank rates supplied by Midland Bank. **1703** *Lond. Gaz.* No. 3902/4 A *Bank Receipt..promising to be accountable to John Radhams for 4 Notes for 50*l.* each. **1887** *Courier-Jrnl.* (U.S.) 23 Jan. 5/3 One night a well-dressed stranger went over and won the *bank roll. **1928** J. P. MCEVOY *Showgirl* vii. 106 That's the one Milton wants to bankroll, isn't it? **1938** *Amer. Speech* XIII. 196 Bank-rolling. **1944** D. RUNYON *R. à la Carte* (1946) vi. 92, I am not able to bank-roll you to a very large start. **1959** *Times Lit. Suppl.* 30 Oct. 628/4 He was the big banker of New York crime; he kept the bankroll. **1959** J. R. MACDONALD *Galton Case* (1960) xxi. 165 Who's bankrolling you? Dr. Howell? **1967** *Boston Sunday Herald* 26 Mar. IV. 5/4 The network has.. bankrolled the Broadway production of 'My Fair Lady'. **1968** *Globe & Mail* (Toronto) Mag. 17 Feb. 9/2 An angry Texan is said to have bet his $45,000 bank roll that Jowett couldn't do it. **1916** W. H. KNIFFIN *Pract. Work of Bank* (ed. 2) x. 318d The bookkeeping machine for *bank statements. **1959** *Which?* VI. 58/2 At the end of the report, we give the analysis of thirty-four bank statements generously sent us by our members. **1986** *Economist* 29 Mar. 67/3 Brazilian banks offer..such perks (to their bigger customers) as bank statements delivered daily to their offices. **1705** HICKERINGILL *Priest-cr.* I. (1721) 9 The Market Price varies as does the *Bank Stock. **1710** ADDISON *Tatler* No. 243 ¶6 How went Bank-Stock to Day at 'Change? **1812** *Examiner* 21 Sept. 607/2 Convicted of uttering 3*s.* *Bank-tokens, knowing them to be false. **1865** *Pall Mall G.* 13 Nov. 3 In the full tide of one's *bank-ward voyage.

bank (bæŋk), *v.*[1] [f. BANK *sb.*[1]]

I. 1. *trans.* To form a bank to; to border, edge, hem in as a bank.

1590 GREENE *Neuer too Late* (1600) 23 A silent streame.. Banckt about with choyce of flowers. **1727** THOMSON *Summer* 660 Burning sands, that bank the shrubby vales. **1801** SOUTHEY *Thalaba* v. xxii, A ridge of rocks that bank'd its side.

†**2.** *intr.* To border *upon*. *Obs.*

1598 STOW *Surv.* vii. (1603) 68 The next Tower or Castle, banckiting [*sic*] also on the riuer of Thames. *Ibid.* xxxviii. (1603) 336 This Castle banketh on the River Thames.

3. *trans.* To confine within a bank. Also *fig.*

1622 CALLIS *Stat. Sewers* (1647) 70 Kept and preserved by banking and new fencing in. **1662** FULLER *Worthies* (1840) III. 388 The prince and people..Both being bank'd in their respective station. **1883** *Eng. Illust. Mag.* Nov. 75/1 The river is banked high on either side.

4. *Watchmaking*: **a.** *trans.* To confine the movements of the escapement, which is the function of the two banking-pins in a watch. **b.** *intr.* To impinge against the banking-pins; said of the escapement (or of the watch).

1765 LUDLAM in *Phil. Trans.* LV. 207 The brass pin..is for the other arm of the beam to bank against. **1884** F. BRITTEN *Watch & Clockm.* 20 The escapement may be banked through the spring. *Ibid.* 74 If the watch persistently banks, it is an indication that the balance is too light.

II. †**5.** To coast, to skirt. *Obs.*

1595 SHAKS. *John* v. ii. 104, I haue bank'd their Townes?

6. To bring ashore, to land.

1873 G. DAVIES *Mount. & Mere* ii. 11 Scarcely giving a flap of the tail till they were banked.

7. To shelter under a bank.

1865 W. WHITE *E. Eng.* I. 110 As decoy men say, they are then comfortably banked.

III. 8. a. *trans.* To heap or pile *up*. Also *fig.*

1712 J. JAMES tr. *Dézallier d'Argenville's Gardening* II. ii. 111 You bank it up by causing Earth to be laid about the Foot of it. **1833** HT. MARTINEAU *Charmed Sea* iv. 59 They had banked up the snow. **1872** BLACK *Adv. Phaeton* xxiii. 317 The clouds had got banked up in great billows of vapour. **1920** *Round Table* Dec. 88 The steady march of Russia eastwards, and her threat to..the independence and future of Japan was rapidly banking up the clouds of war.

b. *spec.* To pile up (logs) at a landing, etc., for transport by water or rail. *U.S.* and *Canada.*

1856 *Trans. Mich. Agric. Soc.* VII. 828 There will be logs enough cut and 'banked' for 100,000,000 feet of lumber. We are informed that the amount now banked daily, will amount to 2,500,000 feet. **1888** *B.C. Moon* 21 Apr., Wright & Davis..have purchased the logs banked at West Superior. **1904** S. E. WHITE *Blazed Trail Stories* iii. 40 The firm agreed to pay..for all saw-logs banked at a rollway.

9. *intr.* (for *refl.*) To rise *up* into banks. Also, to pile *up*, accumulate. Also *absol.*

1870 *Daily News* 28 Dec., The smoke..was still banking up in large clouds. **1883** BLACK in *Harper's Mag.* Dec. 69/2 Clouds begin to bank up. **1889** *Good Words* Mar. 154/1 The driven snow was now banking itself up in wreaths. **1889** E. RANDOLPH *New Eve* I. i. 40 The fleecy clouds..are already banking to prepare the sun his couch. **1922** *Glasgow Herald* 24 Nov. 9 Imagine..a gravelled roadway flanked by redcoats, and a crowd banking and shelving on both sides. **1955** *Times* 24 May 19/4 The six months' gap..had allowed the traffic to bank up.

10. To make up a fire, by covering it with a heap of fuel so pressed down that it will remain a long time burning slowly. Also *to bank down* (example is *fig.*).

1860 *Merc. Mar. Mag.* VII. 330 The fires had been banked. **1865** DICKENS *Mut. Fr.* ii. 277 Fire carefully banked up with damp cinders. **1923** D. H. LAWRENCE *Birds, Beasts & Flowers* 82 His fires of wrath are banked down.

11. *to bank out*: to empty out (coal as drawn from the pit) into a heap.

1851 in *Coal-tr. Terms Northumbld. & Durh.* 6.

12. *trans.* **a.** To ascend (an inclined surface). **b.** To cause to travel an ascending track; also in *vbl. sb.* (attrib. in *banking engine* = *bank-engine*, BANK *sb.*[1] 13).

1892 *Livestock Jrnl. Alm.* 34 They ascended a steep hill, banking field after field to a flag-post at the top. **1908** *Model Engineer & Electr.* 11 June 570 Where banking engines are employed for assisting trains on inclines. *Ibid.*, Wherever banking assistance is taken. *Ibid.*, The practice of banking trains out of Euston, up the Camden incline.

13. *trans.* In *Aeronautics*, to tilt (an aeroplane) sideways in turning. Also *intr.*, to incline sideways in turning. Also with *up*.

1911 GRAHAME-WHITE & HARPER *Aeroplane* 133 He 'banked' his biplane over too sharply. **1913** C. MELLOR *Airman* vi. 29 We swung round left-handed and the machine 'banked' up to the right. **1920** *Blackw. Mag.* July 72/2 Adam Smythe..then banked left-handed towards Delhi Fort.

bank, *v.*[2] [f. BANK *sb.*[3]]

1. *intr.* To keep a bank, act as a banker. (Chiefly in ppl. adj. and vbl. sb., as in *banking-house*, etc.)

1727–51 CHAMBERS *Cycl.*, *Banker*, a person who banks, that is, negotiates and trafficks in money. **1912** E. V. LUCAS *Wand. in Florence* v. 60 Giovanni [de' Medici] had been a banker before everything, Cosimo an administrator... Lorenzo continued to bank but mismanaged the work and lost heavily.

2. *intr.* To deposit money or keep an account with a banker.

1833 HT. MARTINEAU *Berkeley* I. i. 4 A man who brings a splendid capital, and will, no doubt, bank with us at D——. **1880** HOWELLS *Undisc. Country* vi. 103 You'll have to bank with me to the extent of tickets home.

3. *trans.* To deposit in a bank. Also, to convert into current money, 'realize.'

1838 *Actors by Daylight* I. 55 After having 'banked' their cash. **1864** SALA in *Daily Tel.* 11 Oct., Those who have.. banked their greenbacks. **1868** *Daily News* 2 Sept., If parliament were to bank this whole estate.

4. a. *intr.* To form a 'bank' at a gaming-table; to play against all comers.

1826 DISRAELI *Viv. Grey* v. xiii. 239 The plan will be for two to bank against the table.

b. To 'put one's money' *upon*; to count or rely *on* with confidence or assurance. Also const. *that. colloq.* (orig. *U.S.*).

1884 NYE *Baled Hay* 127 The man who ranks as a dignified snoozer, and banks on winning wealth and a deathless name. **1892** *Congress. Rec.* Apr., App. 249/2, I am not banking heavily on [him]..as an honest man. **1898** *Sun* (N.Y.) 14 Sept., The Democrats are banking upon this movement to help them out this fall. **1903** A. ADAMS *Log Cowboy* vi. 79, I was banking plenty strong, that next year.. I'd take her home with me. **1910** W. M. RAINE *B. O'Connor* 58 The one friend you would have banked on to a finish. **1949** DODIE SMITH *I capture Castle* I. ix. 152 'Don't bank on things too much,' I begged. 'Simon may not have the faintest idea of proposing.'

5. *trans.* To store (blood, tissue, or the like) for future use. orig. *U.S.* Cf. BANK *sb.*[3] 7 f.

1938 *Life* 28 Feb. 33/2 Here you see how blood is taken in, banked and given out. **1963** *Guardian* 17 July 1/1 Aortic heart valves from young victims of road crashes are being 'banked' by a team of doctors to replace those of older people.

ˈ**bankable**, *a.* Orig. *U.S.* [f. BANK *sb.*[3] or *v.*[2]]

a. Receivable at a bank, as in 'bankable securities'. Also *fig.*

1818 M. & S. C. AUSTIN *Austin Papers* (1924) 329 The money must be *Bankable*, as none other will do. **1832** *Register Deb. Congress* 7 Mar. 204 A currency..perhaps not bankable at all places. *Ibid.*, Any broker..would make it bankable any where in the Union. **1848** BARTLETT *Dict. Amer.* 22 In New York, at auction sales, the auctioneer.. invariably states, that the money must be bankable. **1921** *Collier's* 19 Feb. 17/1 (*heading*) Good will a bankable asset. **1973** *Times* 2 Mar. 18/6 This promise has been described as a 'bankable assurance'. **1984** *Daily Tel.* 7 Sept. 18/1 Mr Reid..tried, earlier this year, to insist on some bankable commitments to phase out surplus manning. **1985** *Globe & Mail* (Toronto) 10 Oct. D4/5 It is undeniable that after 17 years in England, there is something to be said for bankable sunshine.

b. *spec.* Of a business venture: certain to yield a profit; of a show-business personality: sufficiently famous to ensure the funding and ultimate success of a production.

1958 A. O. HIRSCHMAN *Strategy of Econ. Devel.* x. 191 Entirely too much has been made of the argument that development is held back not by the scarcity of funds, but by a scarcity of 'bankable', i.e., well-conceived and engineered, projects. **1964** *Maclean's Mag.* 2 Dec. 54/1 Julie Andrews.. didn't have a bankable name at the time. **1968** *Look* 6 Aug. 68/1 A bankable actor is one with whose name a producer can raise enough money to make a film. **1978** *Times* 1 Sept. 6/1 Co-authored by Joe Eszterhas and its star, the bankable Sylvester Stallone, the film opens with a charged orchestral overture. **1979** *Economist* 7 July 115 Sir Keith Joseph, as chief banker to BSC, will not bring forward proposals to parliament for a capital restructuring until the thing is bankable. **1985** *New Yorker* 29 Apr. 61/3 Becoming highly bankable, Allen discovered, meant becoming instantly popular with incipient entrepreneurs. **1986** *Sight & Sound Q.* Winter 26/2 With the success of darts on television, surely there's a bankable film here.

†ˈ**bankage.** *Obs.* [? f. BANK *sb.*[1] + -AGE.] ? A landing duty.

1577 HARRISON *England* II. v. 113 His Prædia..were tributes, tolles, portage, bankage, stackage..and such like.

bank-bill. [See BANK *sb.*[3] and BILL.] **a.** Formerly, and still sometimes in the provinces, and in U.S., synonymous with BANK-NOTE. **b.** A bill drawn by one bank upon another, payable at a future date, or on demand; synonymous with *banker's draft.* †**c.** (*sealed*) *bank bill*: a form of bill or note, bearing interest, issued by the Bank of England at its foundation, but long since discontinued. **d.** *bank post bill*: a bill, usually at seven days' sight, issued by the Bank of England for convenience of transmission through the post.

1696 *Lond. Gaz.* No. 3166/4 A Bank Bill for 100*l.* with Interest at 2*d.* a day. *Ibid.* No. 3234/4 Bank Seal Bills, payable with Interest at the Rate of 6 per Cent. per Annum. **1709** STEELE *Tatler* No. 26 ¶9 If I have not left..Bank Bills for 200*l.* **1711** *Lond. Gaz.* No. 4875/4 Lost..a Sealed Bank Bill of 100*l.* at 6 per Cent. **1752** HUME *Ess. & Treat.* (1777) I. 336 To stuff the nation with this fine commodity of bank-bills and chequer-notes. **1809** R. LANGFORD *Introd. Trade* 130 Bank bill, a note on the bank, which being accepted by a cashier, will be paid when due. **1812** *Examiner* 28 Dec. 820/2 The amount of Bank of England Notes and Bank Post Bills now in circulation. **1863** HAYDN *Dict. Dates* 67 Bank bills were paid in silver, 1745. The first bank post-bills were issued 1754. **1878** SYMONDS *Shelley* 85 The..story of his having once constructed a boat out of a bank-post bill.

bank-book. [See BANK *sb.*[3]] **a.** One of the books in which the transactions of a bank are entered. **b.** A book furnished by a banker to each customer, containing a transcript of his account in the Bank Ledger, also called *pass-book.* (In both senses *banker's book* is also used.)

1714 in *Lond. Gaz.* No. 5266/10 Lost..Mr. Salamon of Moses Pereira's Bank Book. **1753** HANWAY *Trav.* (1762) II. I. vii. 35 To see that his accounts agree with those of the bank books. **1884** *Harper's Mag.* June 28/2 I've left you my bank-book.

banked (bæŋkt), *ppl. a.* [f. BANK *sb.*[1] or *v.*[1]]

1. Having a bank or banks.

1623 BINGHAM *Xenophon* 108 A hollow-bank'd brooke. **1649** BLITH *Eng. Improv. Impr.* (1652) 11 One acre plain or bancked. **1881** EDITH COXON *Basil Plant* II. 24 The banked hedge skirting the field.

2. Heaped, piled up; esp. in ***banked up***, said also of a fire when covered up with fresh fuel so as to burn away but slowly.

1567 DRANT *Horace' Epist.* B vj, Ritche in banqued golde. **1868** H. LEE *B. Godfrey* lvii. 327 Banked-up..clouds.

'banker[1]. Now *arch.* or *dial.* Also 3 **bancour, banquer(e, bankewere, bankqwer, banwher,** 6 **banckwarre, bankard, bynker.** [a. AF. **banquer*, **banker* = ONF. *bankier, banquier, bancquier*, f. *banc* bench.] A covering, generally of tapestry, for a bench or chair.

1311 *Chart. Finchall* (1837) App. 4, Iiij banker. **1395** *E.E. Wills* (1882) 5 An Halle, with docere, costers and bankers. *c* **1410** LOVE *Bonavent. Mirr.* xv. (Gibbs MS.) 38 On þe bare grounde, ffor þare hadde he neyther banker ne cuschyne. *c* **1420** *Anturs Arth.* xxxv. 2 With beddus brauderit o brode, and bankers y-dyȝte. *c* **1450** HOLLAND *Houlat* xix. 9 Braid burdis and benkis, ourbeld vith bancouris of gold. **1483** *Cath. Angl.* 20 Bankqwer, Bankewere, *bancarium, dorsorium*. *c* **1485** *E.E. Misc.* (1855) 4 The dosers alle of camaca, The bankers alle of taffeta. **1502** ARNOLD *Chron.* (1811) 244 The hangyng bankers and cussyons in my halle. **1534** *Lincolnsh. Ch. Furn.* 186 A olde bankard made of an olde carpett. **1541** *Lanc. Wills* (1857) I. 106, Ij fforrnes with ij bankers. **1574** *Richmond. Wills* (1853) 248 A hawlinge, a bynker of wannes, and ij fox skynnes. **1660** *Act 12 Chas. II*, iv. Sched., Bankers of Verdure, the dozen pieces, iv*l.* **1870** BOTTRELL *Trad. W. Cornwall* 257 The cosy, old, panelled settle, but now without the bankers and dorsars, or the cushions, for the seats and back. **1890** W. MORRIS in *Eng. Illustr. Mag.* July 755 Some went to the chests and brought out the rich hangings, the goodly bankers and dorsars.

banker[2] ('bæŋkə(r)). Also 6 **bankor,** 7 **bancker, banquer,** 7–8 **banquier.** [f. BANK *sb.*[3] + -ER, after F. *banquier*, freq. used in Eng. in 17th c.]

1. The keeper or manager of a BANK *sb.*[3]

†**a.** *orig.* A money-changer; *then*, one who dealt in bills of exchange, giving drafts and making remittances. *Obs.*

1534 MORE *On the Passion* Wks. 1385/2 In the temple, he had ouerthrowen the bankers tables. **1591** PERCIVALL *Span. Dict.*, *Banquero*, a bankor, an exchanger of money, *Argentarius*. **1624** HEYWOOD *Gunaik.* VI. 271 One Philippus, a bancker, or one that dealt in the exchange of money. *c* **1654** FLECKNOE *Trav.* 103 in Southey *Comm.-pl. Bk.* Ser. II. (1849) 328 Our English money, current with much adoe in neighbouring countries..but farther off you must go to Banquiers of your own nation, or none will take it of your hands. **1683** PETTUS *Fleta Min.* II. 91 Monyers..lately called Bankers.

†**b.** *subseq.* One who also received money in deposit, and lent it upon interest, acting as an intermediary between borrowers and lenders. *Obs.*

1553 UDALL *Roister D.* I. i. (Arb.) 11 Truely of all men he is my chiefe banker, Both for meate and money. **1611** COTGR., *Argentier*..a Banker, one that lendeth, or exchangeth, money for gaine. **1611** SPEED *Hist. Gt. Brit.* IX. xii. §64 To embogge himselfe in the Bankers and Usurers Bookes. **1660** STANLEY *Hist. Philos.* (1701) 291/1 He deposited some Money in the hands of a Banquier. **1670** MARVELL *Corr.* 166 (1875) II. 356 Voted that..all money in the hand of banquiers shall pay 15*s.* per 100*l.* **1757** BURKE *Abridgm. Eng. Hist.* Wks. X. 232 The provinces [of Rome] were overrun by publicans..confiscators, usurers, bankers.

Hence (in its beginnings not separable from the prec): **c.** *mod.* The proprietor or one of the proprietors of a private bank; the manager or one of the managing body of a joint-stock bank; in *pl.* a joint-stock banking company.

bankers' books, Books of Account, etc., extracts from which are admissible as evidence in a British Court of Law under 'The Bankers' Books Evidence Act, 1876.' ***banker's book*** also = *bank pass-book*. Also, ***banker's card*** = *cheque card* s.v. CHEQUE, CHECK 4.

1670–1 *Act 22 Chas. II.* in Blount *Law Dict.* s.v., Whereas several persons, Goldsmiths and others, by taking or borrowing great sums of mony, and lending out the same again, for extraordinary hire and profit, have gained and acquired to themselves the reputation and name of Bankers. **1671** DRYDEN *Even. Love* Epil., And Banquier-like, each day Accept new Bills, and he must break, or pay. **1727** SWIFT *State Irel.* Wks. 1761 III. 174 The daily increase of bankers, who may be a necessary evil in a trading country, but so ruinous in ours. **1761** *Gentl. Mag.* XXXI. 601 Imposed on a young man, a banker's-clerk. **1796** BURKE *Regic. Peace* i. Wks. VIII. 153 There were not..twelve bankers shops at that time out of London. **1843** DICKENS *Chr. Carol* 18 Scrooge took his melancholy dinner..and beguiled the rest of the evening with his banker's-book. **1858** LD. ST. LEONARDS *Handy-bk. Prop. Law* VII. 42 You..deposit your money at a private banker's, or in the Bank of England. **1866** CRUMP *Banking* 79 As money rises in value, the balances in the hands of bankers decrease. **1967** *Banker* July 628/2 Belgium's largest bank, the Société Générale de Banque, has followed the British banks and introduced a cheque card on the lines of the bankers card. **1976** *Economist* 9 Oct. 94/2 Even if your cheque is backed by a bankers' card ..you will usually be charged 4p in the £. **1984** *Which?* Apr. 147/2 Pay..by cash or a cheque supported by a banker's card.

2. Applied to a contributor to a *Mons Pietatis*: see BANK *sb.*[3] 6.

1646 BENBRIGGE *Usura Accom.* 11 Neither Banke nor Bankers (as I may call the Contributors) can conceive they suffer any losse by..lending to the poor freely: because what they even give..is lent in Usury to the Lord.

3. One who keeps the 'bank' in a gambling house: the dealer, in some games of chance.

1826 HOR. SMITH *Gai. & Grav.* in *Casquet Lit.* 1877 I. 325/1 Each banker was provided with a *rateau*, or rake. **1850** BOHN *Handbk. Games* 328 *Commerce*..After determining the deal, the dealer, styled also the banker, shuffles the pack. *Ibid.* 342 *Rouge et noir*..To form the game, it is necessary that there should be a banker, or *tailleur* (Dealer), who represents him, and players, the number of whom is unlimited. **1884** *Law Times Rep.* 30 Aug. 809/2 Each banker pays 1 per cent. and the punters 5*s.* each.

4. A card game in which the banker divides the pack into a number of piles placed face downward, and each punter bets on the chance that the bottom card of the pile chosen by him is higher than the bottom card of the pile left to the banker.

1891 *Daily News* 3 Dec. 7/6 A boy..was charged with gambling with cards at 'banker'. **1903** *Daily Chron.* 14 Mar. 7/5 He got £150 during the voyage home on the troopship by playing 'banker' and 'the crown and anchor'.

5. In *Football Pools*: a result which one forecasts consistently in a series of entries. Cf. BANK *v.*[2] 4 b.

1947 *Answers* 30 Aug. 9/3 This is the method of entry for a 14-match pool, allowing for six permutated matches with eight bankers. In 12- and 13-match pools, the bankers required will be six and seven respectively. **1958** *Punch* 27 Aug. 265/3 No pools investor of quality would seek advice from hacks who write: Wolves have banker look.

banker[3] ('bæŋkə(r)). [f. BANK *sb.*[1] + -ER[1].]

1. a. [Cf. F. *banquier* in same sense.] A ship employed in cod-fishing on the Bank of Newfoundland.

1666 *Lond. Gaz.* No. 107/1 Who in Crusing, lighted upon a French Banker which he took. **1710** *Ibid.* No. 4712/3 A French Banker of fourteen Guns, laden with Fish, arrived there from Newfoundland. **1769** in FALCONER *Dict. Marine.* **1815** in J. Q. Adams *Duplicate Lett.* (1822) 219 Those descriptions of vessels are not so valuable as the bankers, more particularly those that go from the District of Maine, Connecticut, and Rhode Island. **1880** *Harper's Mag.* Aug. 350/1 The long voyages of the bankers. **1960** *Atlantic Advocate* Nov. 30 New vessels—craft of fifty tons or less, and less than half the size of latter-day bankers.

b. A fisherman on the Bank of Newfoundland.

1861 *Harper's Mag.* Mar. 461/2 On the banks of Newfoundland..some of the old bankers predicted a gale. **1907** J. G. MILLAIS *Newfoundland* vii. 154 The fishermen of all lands have to encounter the perils of the deep, but none have to face the risks that the 'bankers' do.

2. A labourer who makes banks of earth, ditches, etc. (Chiefly used in the eastern counties of England.)

1795 *Gentl. Mag.* 632 In the fen countries the labourers are denominated bankers. *a* **1821** in *Times* 25 Aug. (1870) 4/6 A poor man, a witness in court, said in answer to the same question [What he was?] 'a banker.' The Judge.. remarked, 'We cannot have any absurdity.' **1873** PEACOCK in *N. & Q.* Ser. IV. XII. 274 Some 'bankers' who were engaged in widening a drain.

3. *Hunting.* A horse which can jump on and off field banks too large to be cleared. (Cf. *fencer*.)

Generally with qualification, as 'In following the hounds in Devonshire, you must ride a good banker.'

4. (*in Australia*). A river full to the brim.

1890 *Cassell's Picturesque Australasia* III. 175 The Murrumbidgee was running a 'banker'—water right up to the banks. **1936** M. FRANKLIN *All that Swagger* x. 88 Every stream Delacy..met was a banker. **1936** I. L. IDRIESS *Cattle King* xvi. 162 Occasionally a river or creek in a raging banker would defeat the little time-tables of man.

5. ***banker*** (***engine***), a locomotive used to assist in taking a heavy load up a steep slope. (Cf. *bank-engine*, BANK *sb.*[1] 13.)

1907 *Westm. Gaz.* 3 Dec. 7/2 A 'banker' engine had been fixed to the rear of the mineral train to help to take the load up a steep incline. After going some 300 yards the 'banker' was cast off.

'banker[4]. [f. BANK *sb.*[2] bench; in senses a, b. perh. a perversion of It. *banco* a (statuary's) bench.]

a. A wooden bench used in bricklaying for dressing bricks. **b.** A stone bench used by masons for hewing on. **banker-mark** (see quots. 1888 and 1928). **c.** A local name for a pile of Purbeck stone from the quarry.

1677 MOXON *Mech. Exerc.* (1703) 246 A Banker, to cut the Bricks upon, which is a piece of Timber about six foot long ..fixt..about three foot high from the Floor. **1793** SMEATON *Edystone L.* §167 *note*, A Banker in a mason's yard is a square stone of a suitable size, made use of as a work bench. **1832** CARLYLE *Remin.* (1881) I. 46 The Master-builder..once laid a shilling on his 'banker.' **1881** *Daily News* 5 Sept. 6/3 The immense masses of stone called 'bankers' that line Swanage shore. **1885** *Harper's Mag.* Jan. 244/1 The stone..has to be removed from the 'bankers' in carts. **1888** T. W. WHITLEY in *Leamington Spa Courier* 11 Aug. 7/6 Each man as he finishes his work at the banker, places his mark upon the stone before it leaves the shed. The banker is the stone bed or bench upon which a mason works. .. These marks have hence been called banker marks, and perhaps the name is more appropriate than that of masons marks. **1910** *Encycl. Brit.* III. 319/2 Banker-marks are..to be found on all old buildings of consequence, ecclesiastical or otherwise. **1928** G. G. COULTON *Art & Reformation* viii. 143 'Banker-marks', that is, the mason's sign-manual which he set on his finished stone before it left the banker, or working-bench.

bankerdom ('bæŋkədəm). [see -DOM.] The class or body of bankers; the banking interest.

1863 DICEY *Federal St.* I. 170 The *Herald*, supported by the bankerdom of the North.

bankeress ('bæŋkərɪs). *nonce-wd.* [see -ESS.] A female banker; a banker's wife.

1854 THACKERAY *Newcomes* I. xxiv. 229, I dined there a couple of months ago, and the bankeress said something about you. **1883** *American* V. 200 The late Countess of Jersey was only received on sufferance in some houses in Vienna, because she was a bankeress.

†**'bankering,** *vbl. sb. Obs.* [f. BANKER[2]; cf. *carpentering*.] Occupation as a banker, banking.

1668 CHILD *Disc. Trade* (1694) 51 Before this way of private bankering came up.

bankerly ('bæŋkəlɪ), *a.* orig. *U.S.* [f. BANKER[2] + -LY[1].] Of or relating to bankers; characteristic of or resembling a banker.

1974 *Time* 21 Jan. 55/1 The bank's president..seemed particularly interested in bankerly decorum. **1976** *Ibid.* 27 Sept. 65/2 Balding, bankerly Mike Levy went East to college. **1980** L. BIRNBACH et al. *Official Preppy Handbk.* 149/3 (*caption*) The most bankerly of coats. **1982** *Economist* 8 May 101/3 Those firms that offer anonymous money-market funds..hope to profit from this bankerly desire for independence. **1985** *Times* 1 Nov. 15/2 It does..caution governments to take a bankerly line.

banket (bæŋ'kɛt), *sb.*[1] [Du., a confection resembling almond hardbake (see quot. 1887).] The name given by the early gold-diggers of the Transvaal to the gold-bearing conglomerates of the Witwatersrand, later extended to similar conglomerates elsewhere.

1887 *Chambers's Jrnl.* Apr. 284 The conglomerate..is a peculiar formation of almond-shaped pebbles, pressed into a solid mass in a bed of rock of an igneous nature, and is called 'Banket' on account of its resemblance to a favourite Dutch sweetmeat known in England as almond rock. The 'Banket' is also rich in gold. **1897** BRYCE *Impressions S. Africa* 217 In 1885 the conglomerate or *banket* beds of the Witwatersrand were discovered. **1900** *Times* 13 Feb. 13/3 The banket formation of the Witwatersrand. **1902** *Encycl. Brit.* XXIX. 17/2 Deposits similar to the Witwatersrand banket occur in Zululand, and also on the Gold Coast of Africa. **1932** WATERMEYER & HOFFENBERG *Witwatersrand Mining Practice* ii. 28 The world-wide fame of the gold deposits of the Witwatersrand has resulted in the term 'banket' or 'banket reef' being adopted for gold-bearing conglomerates in several other parts of the world. **1954** D. DIVINE *Golden Fool* vi. 57 Another smaller outcrop of the same stone—banket, he called it—a sort of fruit cake of pebbles and small pieces in a conglomerate.

[**banket,** *sb.*[2] Error for BANKER[4] a.

1846 W. M. BUCHANAN *Technol. Dict.*, *Banket*, in *bricklaying*, a piece of wood of about eight inches square, and nine feet in length, on which to cut the bricks. Hence in **1864** WEBSTER, **1889** *Century Dict.*]

banket, -etter, etc.: see BANQUET.

'bank-'full, *a.* Full to the bank or brink.

c **1581** J. FALKNER in *Eng. Mech.* 4 Feb. (1870) 500/2 The same water in the morning before was bankefull. **1637** RUTHERFORD *Lett.* 169 (1862) I. 397 A little of God would make my soul bankfull. **1865** MILTON & CHEADLE *N.-W. Passage* 275 This river was..bank full with glacier water.

bank 'holiday. [See BANK *sb.*[3] and HOLIDAY.] A day on which banks are legally closed, so as to afford a holiday to those employed in them. (Bills payable on these days are paid on the following day.) Also *attrib.*; and as *adj.*, (as if) enjoying a bank holiday; festive. Hence **bank-'holidayish** *a.*

Certain Saints' days and anniversaries, to the number in all of about 33 days per annum, were kept as Holidays at the Bank of England. In 1834 these holidays were reduced to Good Friday, the 1st of May, 1st of November, and Christmas Day. By Sir John Lubbock's Act, passed in 1871, the following bank-holidays were constituted in Great Britain: *In England and Ireland*, Easter Monday, Whit Monday, the first Monday in August, the 26th of December (Boxing Day); *in Scotland*, New Year's Day, the first Monday in May, the first Monday in August, Christmas Day. When any of these days falls on Sunday, the Monday following is the bank-holiday.

1871 *Act 34 Vict.* xvii. (*title*) An Act to make provision for Bank Holidays. *Ibid.* 7 This act may be cited for all purposes as the Bank Holidays Act, 1871. **1879** JEFFERIES *Wild Life in S.C.* 103 These two main fairs are the Bank Holidays of rural life. **1897** *Westm. Gaz.* 7 Aug. (Advt.), Bank holiday attractions. *Ibid.*, Bank holiday programme. **1899** CONAN DOYLE *Duet* (1909) 9/2 If he had to travel all the way from Edinburgh with a Bank-holiday crowd. **1926** S. T. WARNER *Lolly Willowes* III. 244 Grass that has been laid upon has always a rather bank-holidayish look. **1930** R. LEHMANN *Note in Music* vii. 294 'We look very bank-holiday,' she said. **1938** L. MACNEICE *Zoo* xiv. 227 We felt pleasantly Bank Holidayish.

banking ('bæŋkɪŋ), *vbl. sb.* [Several distinct formations, from BANK in various senses.]

1. a. The business of a banker; the keeping or management of a bank.

1735 BERKELEY *Querist* (L.) Banking brings no treasure into the kingdom. **1834** GILBART *Hist. Banking* 9 So early as the year 1349..banking was carried on by the drapers of Barcelona. **1883** H. MACLEOD *Banking* vi. §3 The very essence of 'Banking' is to receive money as a Mutuum.

b. *attrib.*

1779 ARNOT *Hist. Edin.* IV. iv. (1816) 411 Those abuses which had crept into the banking business. **1809** R. LANGFORD *Introd. Trade* 20 Without regard to banking hours. **1861** GOSCHEN *For. Exch.* 33 The primary cause which makes England the great banking centre of the world. **1881** *Builder* 8 Oct. (*Advt.*), Solid Mahogany Banking Counter.

2. The construction of banks or embankments.
1610 FOLKINGHAM *Art of Survey* II. ii. 50 Sometimes this Compound Boundage implies a mutuall propertie or duty participable to the Conterminants, as bancking, balking, [etc.]. **1712** J. JAMES tr. *Dézallier d'Argenville's Gardening* II. ii. 106 It is call'd Earthing or Banking up a Stake, when you cause Earth to be brought, and make a Bank about the foot of it. **1753** CHAMBERS *Cycl. Supp.* s.v., With respect to the water which is to be kept out, this is called banking. **1818** COBBETT *Resid. U.S.* (1822) 181 Banking, hedging, they know nothing about. They have no idea of the use of a bill-hook. **1845** C. M. KIRKLAND *Western Clearings* 103 'Banking up'..consists in piling earth round the foundations. **1865** *Nation* (U.S.) I. 683 He has so much a task for banking.

3. Embankment.
1776 G. SEMPLE *Building in Water* xv. 101 The banking.. is to extend from Pier to Pier. *Ibid.* 107 The banking or artificial Bed of the River. **1853** KANE *Grinnell Exp.* xxxv. (1856) 321, I observed one spot where the banking remained.

4. Fishing on the Newfoundland (or other) Bank.
1842 SIR J. PARK *Mar. Insur.* I. ii. 100 §2 Upon their arrival, ships are..employed in banking. **1848** ARNOULD *Mar. Insur.* (1866) I. I. v. 273 After their arrival at Newfoundland, engaged for some time in fishing (called banking).

5. In *Watchmaking*: Limitation of the motion of the balance, by the ***banking-pins*** or ***-screw***.
1870 *Eng. Mech.* 7 Jan. 403/1 It consists in placing the banking pins at the tail of the lever. **1879** *Cassell's Techn. Educ.* IV. 386/2 In this escapement it is necessary to limit the motion of the balance to one half turn, measured from its repose, which is technically called 'banking.' **1884** F. BRITTEN *Watch and Clockm.* 29 [The] Banking Screw [is].. an adjustable screw in the chronometer escapement.

6. ***banking-ground*** (in *U.S. lumber-trade*): a place where logs are brought to a river bank.
1880 *Lumberman's Gaz.* 28 Jan., The banking ground is about 125 feet above the bed of the river.

7. On a road or track: see quot. 1904.
1904 GOODCHILD & TWENEY *Technol. & Sci. Dict.* 40/1 *Banking of cycle tracks*, the raising of the outer edge of a bend in the track to counteract the centrifugal force. **1905** *Cycling* 26 Apr. 362/1 Herne Hill track is now in very good condition. The banking is not so steep as the Palace track. **1937** *Times* 13 Apr. p. viii/2 The danger of vehicles leaving the road at bends..has during recent years been counter-balanced..by the process known as 'banking' or super-elevating.

'banking, *ppl. a.*[1] [f. BANK *v.* + -ING[2].] That keeps a bank or follows the profession of a banker.
1641 MILTON *Ch. Discip.* II. Wks. (1851) 65 That banking den of theeves. **1677** YARRANTON *Eng. Impr.* 18 Any of the banking Goldsmiths or Merchants.

'banking, *ppl. a.*[2] [f. BANK *v.*[1] 9.] Forming into banks.
c **1867** 'MARK TWAIN' *Sketches* in *Wks.* XIX. 372 A weird picture, that small company of frantic men fighting the banking snows.

'banking-house. A house in which banking operations are carried on; a mercantile firm engaged in banking or some branch of it.
1809 R. LANGFORD *Introd. Trade* 129, *Banking-house*, a receptacle for people's money for commercial purposes. **1816** *Gentl. Mag.* LXXXVI. I. 97 Became a partner in the banking-house of Down, Thornton, and Free. **1855** MACAULAY *Hist. Eng.* IV. 490 The days when there was not a single banking house in the city of London. **1879** ESCOTT *England* I. 233 The difference existing between the two classes of business—a banking house and a bank.

bankless ('bæŋklɪs), *a.* [f. BANK *sb.*[1] + -LESS.] Having no banks or borders.
1612 J. DAVIES *Muse's Sacr.* 15 (D.) For thou of beauty art the banckless Sea. **1869** RUSKIN *Q. of Air* §143 Lost.. amidst bankless, boundless marsh.

bankman, obs. form of BANKSMAN.

bank-note. [See BANK *sb.*[3], and NOTE.] A promissory note given by a banker: *formerly*, one payable at a fixed date and to a specified person; *now*, one payable to bearer on demand, and intended to circulate as money.
(Their issue is now regulated by Act 7 & 8 Vict. cap. 32.)
1695 *Lond. Gaz.* No. 3046/4 A Bank Note for 17*l.* 2*s.* 4*d.* payable to Philip Wheake. **1714** *Ibid.* No. 5239/3 Lost..10 Bank Circulation Notes..none of them payable for several Months. *Ibid.* No. 5271/4 Four Circular Bank Notes for 100*l.* each all payable to Mr. Pope..or Bearer, with Interest. **1789** WOLCOTT (P. Pindar) *Wks.* (1812) II. 116 So prudent, numbers each bank-note and jewel. **1812** *Examiner* 28 Sept. 622/2 What is a bank note but a promise to pay the bearer a certain quantity of gold? **1870** BOWEN *Logic* ix. 274 Money may mean either specie, or bank-notes, or currency consisting of a mixture of these two.
fig. **1850** CARLYLE *Latter-d. Pamph.* v. 9 If speech is the banknote for an inward capital of culture.

bankrupt ('bæŋkrʌpt), *sb.* Forms: 6 **banke rota, banckroupt(e, banckerout, banquerowpte, banqwerooute,** 6–7 **banckrout, banque-, banqrout(e, banke-, bankrout(e, bankerupt,** 7 **bankcrout, banck-, banquerupt, (bankrup, banker-up),** 6– **bankrupt.** [In 16th c. *banke rota*, *banqueroute*, a. It. *banca rotta* (Florio), and its F. adaptation *banqueroute* (in Cotgr. *banqueroutte*), with the second part subsequently assimilated to the equivalent L. *ruptus*, as in *abrupt*, etc. The It. *banca rotta* is literally 'bank broken,' or 'bench broken.' The transference of sense from the fact to the agent (in sense 2) is peculiar to Eng.: cf. BANKRUPT *a.* and med.L. *ruptus*.
According to Johnson 'it is said' that when an Italian money-changer became insolvent, 'his bench was broke.' But *rotto, rotta* is also 'wrecked' (used of a ship); and fig. 'discomfited, defeated, interrupted, stopped.' Cf. the familiar use of *break* = become insolvent, *broken* insolvent; also med.L. *ruptura* failure, *ruptus* broken man, bankrupt, 'creditorum fraudator, aut decoctor, qui dissolvit argentariam et foro cedit' in Du Cange, who has an example dated 1334.]

†**1.** The wreck or break-up of a trader's business in consequence of his failure to pay his creditors; or (in early use) his shutting up or desertion of his place of business without payment of his liabilities. Chiefly in the phrase 'to make bankeroute' or 'bankrupt' (Fr. *faire banqueroute*, 1536). Afterwards called *bankrupting*, *bankruptism*, *bankrupture*, *bankruptship*, and now BANKRUPTCY, q.v. *Obs.*
1539 *State Papers Hen. VIII*, I. 609 With danger to make banke rota. **1543** *Act 34 Hen. VIII*, iv. (*title*) An Act against suche parsons as do make bankrupt. **1562** BULLEYN *Bk. Simples* in *Babees Bk.* (1868) 241 Vtterly vndone, and cast either into miserable pouertie, prisonment, bankeroute, &c. **1663** GERBIER *Counsel* E j b, Trade strengthned, encreased, and many Bankrouts prevented. **1684** *Lond. Gaz.* No. 1980/4 Empowered by the Commissioners of Bankrupt. **1712** ARBUTHNOT *John Bull* (1755) 35 A statute of bankrupt.

2. A merchant, trader, or other person, whose property and effects, on his becoming insolvent, are administered and distributed for the benefit of all his creditors, under that system of statutory regulations called the Bankrupt or Bankruptcy Laws. As these laws (which began in England with Acts 34 and 35 Henry VIII, c. 4) were originally directed against fraudulent traders, who absconded with the property of their creditors, or eluded the attempts of creditors to get at them, the earlier senses were:

†**a.** in *Law*. 'A trader who secretes himself, or does certain other acts tending to defraud his creditors.' Blackstone.

†**b.** *popularly*. One who has brought himself into debt by reckless expenditure or riotous living; a fugitive from his creditors, a broken man in sanctuary or outlawry. (In these senses the bankrupt was a *criminal*.)
1533 MORE *Apol.* xxi. Wks. 881/2 Suche bancke rouptes.. which whan they haue wasted and missespent their own, woulde than be very faine..robbe spirituall and temporall to. **1548** HALL *Chron. Hen. VII* an. 11. 37 Some Banqueroutes, some false Englyshe sanctuary men, some Theues. **1580** BARET *Alv.* B 140 One that hath riotously wasted his substance, a banqueroute, *Decoctor*. **1593** R. HARVEY *Philad.*, By gathering more bankrupts & ruffians to his side. **1613** R. C. *Table Alph.*, *Bankerupt*, bankrout, waster. **1614** RALEIGH *Hist. World* IV. vii. §1. 533 Upon instigation of some desperate bankrouts..they made an uproar. **1678** MARVELL *Corr.* 358 Wks. II. 628 A Generall Bill..to find a more effectuall way for discovering of the Estates of Bankroutes. **1709** STEELE *Tatler* No. 44 ¶6 He can no more live here than if he were a downright Bankrupt.

By gradual extension of sense, and modifications of the statutes of bankruptcy:

†**c.** in *Law*. Also, a trader, who did certain acts which had the effect of defeating his creditors of their property, without reference to any intention on his part.

d. in *Mod. Law*. Any trader or other person insolvent, who, on the petition of a creditor or creditors, or on his own petition, to the Bankruptcy Court, is declared or adjudged bankrupt, and his estates administered as stated above.
Formerly only a trader could be made a *bankrupt*; other persons became *insolvent*; in U.S. the legal distinction between the two was abolished in 1841, and in England in 1869; it had long before disappeared in popular use.
1707 *Lond. Gaz.* No. 4335/4 A Commission of Bankrupt being awarded against John Oliver..and he being declared a Bankrupt. **1718** *Free-thinker* No. 86. 215 A Friend of mine ..had lately the Misfortune to become a Bankrupt. **1869** *Act 32–3 Victoria* lxxi. 76 A single creditor..of not less than fifty pounds, may present a petition to the Court, praying that the debtor be adjudged a bankrupt.

e. *popularly*. An insolvent debtor; one who is unable to meet his liabilities, whether he is in the Bankruptcy Court or not.
1580 SIDNEY *Arcadia* VI. 503 Shall my meanes help to make up a bankrout in his estate. **1596** SHAKS. *Merch. V.* IV. i. 122 To cut the forfeiture from that bankrout there.

†**f.** ***to play the bankrupt***: to become insolvent, to fail to pay one's debts; *often*, to play false with the money of others, and *fig.* to prove false to a trust of any kind. *Obs.*
1577 HOLINSHED *Chron.* III. 812/2 Jerome Bonuise, which had plaied bankerupt, and was conueied out of the realme for debt. **1580** *Ord. Prayer* in *Liturg. Serv. Q. Eliz.* (1847) 573 Till he have gotten great sums of money in his hand, that he may play the Bankeroute, to the undoing of such as trust him. **1614** SYLVESTER *Bethulia* III. 70 And with th' Almighty playing banque-rout, With greater Rage his law they persecute. **1623** BACON *Wks.* (1834) XII. 448 These modern languages will, at one time or other, play the bank-rupts with books. **1643** HORN & ROB. *Gate Lang. Unl.* §865 Hee is constrained to breake (play the bankrout), and to borrow of one and pay another. *c* **1660** J. HARINGTON *Epigr.* in Singer *Playing Cards* 254 The last game now in use is *Bankerout*, Which will be plaid at still, I stand in doubt, Until *Lavolta* turn the wheel of time.

3. *transf.* One hopelessly in debt; one who has lost all his means, and is without resources.
1586 T. B. *La Primaud. Fr. Acad.* (1594) 206 Perceiving themselves to be brought to the estate of bankerupts, as we commonly saie. **1594** DRAYTON *Idea* 41 All is Thine which hath been due to Me, And I a Bankrupt, quite undone by Thee. **1600** C'TESS. ESSEX in Ellis *Orig. Lett.* I. 237 III. 57 To recken my self a bankcrout till I have yeelded you some demonstrative testimonie. *c* **1620** Z. BOYD *Zion's Flowers* (1855) 49 He who in sloath doth like a Dor-Mouse sleepe, Shall at the last sure prove a Banker-up.

b. *fig.* (Cf. BANKRUPT *a.* 2.)
1579 LYLY *Euphues* (Arb.) 141 Not onely unthrifts of their money but banckerouts of good manners.

4. *attrib.*, as in ***bankrupt laws***, ***system***; also ***bankruptlike*** adj.
1668 ROLLE *Abridgem.* I. 47 Thou art a bankruptlike knave. **1809** R. LANGFORD *Introd. Trade* 116 The bankrupt laws in England do not extend to Scotland.

'bankrupt, *v.* Forms: 6 **banckerowt-en,** 6–7 **banke-, bankrout(e, banquerout,** 7 **banckroute, bankerupt, -rumpt.** [App. f. the sb. (in sense 1); orig. short for 'to make bankrupt': the trans. sense is later, and perh. favoured by the analogy of *disrupt*, etc. Not in It. or Fr.]

†**1.** To become bankrupt, to fail, to 'break'; = the early phrase 'to make bankrupt.' (Often in the sense of fraudulent failure: see BANKRUPT *sb.* 1.)
1552 HULOET, Banckerowten, or make banckerowte, or banckrupte. **1570** LEVINS *Manip.* /229 To bankerout, *fidem fallere*. **1608** CHAPMAN *Bryon's Conspir.* Plays 1873 II. 234 He that winnes Empire with the losse of faith, Out-buies it: and will banck-route. **1689** [see BANKRUPTING *vbl. sb.*].

2. *trans.* To make or render (any one) bankrupt; to make insolvent.
1616 BEAUM. & FL. *Laws Candy* III. i, He..will be bankrupted so much the sooner. **1650** WELDON *Crt. & Char. Jas. I*, 58 If they had already impoverished the Kingdome; by the union, they would bankerupt it. **1865** *Times* 31 July, There is some fear of bankrupting the Treasury. **1881** *Daily News* 17 Sept. 20/7 A bad season or two inevitably bankrupts the tenant.

†**3.** To reduce to beggary, beggar, exhaust the resources of. *lit.* and *fig.* *Obs.*
1588 SHAKS. *L.L.L.* I. i. 27 Make rich the ribs, but bankerout the wits. **1593** NASHE *Christ's T.* (1613) 64, I should bankroute them all in description. **1650** FULLER *Pisgah* II. ix. §44 Seven hundred Queens..were able to bankrupt the Land of Ophir. *a* **1659** CLEVELAND *On a Fly* 16 In this single Death of thee Th' hast bankrupt all *Antiquity*. *c* **1700** *Gentl. Instruct.* (1732) 480 He is bankrupted of Patience, Money and Grace. **1748** RICHARDSON *Clarissa* (1811) VII. 258 Art thou sure that the making good of such a vow will not totally bankrupt thee?

'bankrupt, *a.* Forms: 6–7 **bankerupt, bancke-, banquerout(e, banke-, bankrout,** 7 **banckrowt, -rout, -rupt, banquerupt,** 6– **bankrupt.** [Connected in origin with the sb. in sense 2, and, like that, peculiar to Eng. It may be the short pa. pple. of the vb. *to* BANKRUPT, influenced also by L. *rupt-us* broken.]

1. Under legal process because of insolvency; unable to pay debts; insolvent. For the historical development of the senses, see BANKRUPT *sb.* 2.
1570 LEVINS *Manip.* /228 Bankerout, *fidifragus, ære alieno oppressus*. **1580** BARET *Alv.* B 139 He is banquerout, *Il est faict banqueroupte*. **1592** *No-body & Some-b.* (1878) 283 To make that Nobody bankrout, make him flie His Country, and be never heard of more. **1631** R. KNEVET *Rhodon & I.* II. iii, A bankrupt Tenant..That flyes by night from an unprofitable Farme. **1710** *Pol. Ballads* (1860) 73 The bankrupt nation to restore, And pay the millions lent. **1848** THACKERAY *Van. Fair* xviii, Breaking the heart of that ruined bankrupt man.

2. *fig.* (various aspects of the bankrupt.)

†**a.** Discredited, having forfeited all credit. *Obs.*
1566 T. STAPLETON *Ret. Untr. Jewel*, For farder Credit off your Worde, you will stande (I feare) for banckeroute. **1601** CORNWALLYES *Ess.* II. xliii. (1631) 208 To be out of fashion, is to bee banquerupt. **1612** W. PARKES *Curtaine-Dr.* (1876) 3 Vertue is bankerout, dares not shew his face.

b. At the end of one's resources, exhausted.
1589 NASHE *Almond for P.* 9a, Your banquerout inuention, cleane out at the elbowes. **1591** SHAKS. *Two Gent.* II. iv. 42, I shall make your wit bankrupt. **1623** L. DYGES in *Shaks. C. Praise*, Untill our bankrout Stage be sped. **1749** SMOLLETT *Regicide* II. v. (1777) 35 What recompence (thus bankrupt as I am!) Shall speak my grateful soul! **1775** SHERIDAN *Rivals* v. i. 147, I am bankrupt in gratitude!

c. Stript bare, bereft, destitute *of*, or now wanting *in* (a property or quality formerly present, or that ought to be present).
1589 NASHE in Greene *Menaph.* (Arb.) 17 Those idiots.. that have made Art bankerout of her ornaments. **1651** *Reliq. Wotton.* 474 Yet am I not so bank-rupt of intelligence, but that I have heard of those rural passages. **1681** DRYDEN *Abs. & Achit.* I. 168 Bankrupt of life, yet prodigal of ease. **1848** H. ROGERS *Ess.* I. vi. 318 A man intellectually poverty-stricken, bank-rupt in all science and argument.

bankruptcy ('bæŋkrəpsɪ). Also 8 -sie. [f. BANKRUPT + -CY, prob. on the analogy of *insolvency*, but with *-t* erroneously retained in spelling, instead of being merged in the suffix *-cy* = *-tie*, *-tia*. The sense was orig. expressed by the simple *bankrupt* (F. *la banqueroute*): on the application of this to the person involved (F. *le banqueroutier*), the fact was successively termed *bankrupting*, *bankruptism*, *bankrupture*, *bankruptship*, and finally, *c* 1700, *bankruptcy*.]

1. The state of being bankrupt; the fact of becoming bankrupt.

1700 J. LAW *Counc. Trade* (1751) Introd. 14 By wilful fraud or bankruptsie of councellors of trade. **1712** STEELE *Spect.* No. 428 ¶2 That most dreadful of all human Conditions, the Case of Bankruptcy. **1753** HANWAY *Trav.* (1762) II. I. viii. 39 The state might thus be reduced to bankruptcy. **1776** ADAM SMITH *W.N.* I. I. I. x. 116 Bankruptcies are most frequent in the most hazardous trades. **1848** THACKERAY *Van. Fair* xviii, His bills were protested: his act of bankruptcy formal. **1875** POSTE *Gaius* III. 342 Roman law never established any distinction between traders and non-traders, in other words, between bankruptcy and insolvency.

b. *attrib.*, as ***Bankruptcy Court, laws***, etc.

1864 *Derby Merc.* 7 Dec., The Bankruptcy Court officials. **1883** *Law Times* 20 Oct. 408/1 The object of a bankruptcy law.. should be the economical and honest distribution of a bankrupt's estate.

2. *fig.* Utter wreck, ruin, or loss of (any good quality).

1761 *Brit. Mag.* II. 441 They dread a bankruptcy of head and sense. **1797** BURKE *Corr.* IV. 433 A general bankruptcy of reputation in both parties. **1853** A. MORRIS *Business* v. 104 The greatest bankruptcy is not of fortune but of faith.

'bankrupted, *ppl. a.* [f. BANKRUPT *v.* + -ED.] Rendered bankrupt, reduced to bankruptcy.

1668 *Lond. Gaz.* No. 273/2 The Sieur Tillier.. being lately bankrupted, and fled. **1882** *Century Mag.* 379/1 Property.. bought of a bankrupted owner.

†**'bankrupting**, *vbl. sb.* [f. BANKRUPT *v.* + -ING[1].] The becoming or being bankrupt; an earlier term for BANKRUPTCY.

1577 NORTHBROOKE *Dicing* (1843) 119 It is a doore and windowe into—pouertie, bankrupting. **1689** *Def. Liberty agst. Tyrants* 144 Can the bankrumpting of one of the Obligees quit the rest of their ingagement?

†**'bankruptism.** *Obs.* [see -ISM.] An earlier term for BANKRUPTCY.

1606 DEKKER *Sev. Sins* I. (Arb.) 18 How deadly.. an enemy to the State this Politick Bankruptisme hath bin. **1630** J. TAYLOR (Water P.) *Wks.* III. 66/1 He is in danger of breaking or bankruptisme.

†**'bankruptly**, *a.* *Obs.* [f. BANKRUPT *sb.* + -LY[1].] Like or befitting a bankrupt.

1613 PURCHAS *Pilgr.* I. IV. vii. 330 Bankruptly shifts, beseeming only the Merchants of Babylon. **1668** ROLLE *Abridgem.* I. 47 Thou art a bankruptly Knave.

†**'bankruptship.** *Obs. rare*[−1]. [see -SHIP.] An earlier term for BANKRUPTCY.

1656 EARL MONM. *Advt. Parnass.* 359 The most important Bankruptship.. that ever hapned in the memory of man.

†**'bankrupture.** *Obs. rare.* [f. BANKRUPT *v.* + -URE.] An earlier term for BANKRUPTCY.

1617 COLLINS *Def. Bp. Ely* II. ix. 367 Bankruptures of religion. **1622** MABBE *Aleman's Guzman D' Alf.* I. 7 In what Consistory.. hath Bankrupture beene.. condemned for a Sinne?

‖**'bankshall.** Forms: 7 bancksall, 7–8 banksall, 7–9 banksoll, 8 bancshall, 8– banksaul, 7– bankshall. [A word now common from India to China: in Malay *bāngsal* shed, storehouse, porch, but prob. orig. Bengali *bankaśālā* 'hall of trade,' or perh. Skr. *bhāṇḍaśālā* storehouse or magazine. (Col. Yule.)] **a.** A warehouse. **b.** The office of a Harbour Master or other port authority.

1673 FRYER *E. Ind. & Persia* 27 (Y.) Their Bank Solls, or Custom House Keys, where they land. **1688** *Camd. Soc. Misc.* (1881) 38 Who was come down to the bancksall, or point of sand goeing into the river [Hooghly]. **1727** A. HAMILTON *Acc. E. Indies* II. 6 (Y.) Above it is the Dutch Bankshall, a Place where their ships ride. **1813** J. FORBES *Orient. Mem.* IV. 109 (Y.) A large banksaul or warehouse at Mirzapore for the reception of pepper and sandalwood. **1850** *Jrnl. Ind. Archipelago* IV. 182 *Bankshall*, the name given by Europeans to the office of the Master Attendant, or Intendant of a Port. It is most probably taken from the Malay word *Bañgsal*, a shed, an outhouse.

banksia ('bæŋksɪə). [Named after Sir Joseph Banks.] **1.** A genus of Australian shrubs, with umbellate flowers, cultivated as ornamental shrubs in Europe.

1803 MALTHUS *Popul.* I. iii. (1806) I. 34 The flowers of the different banksias. **1873** DAWSON *Earth & Man* viii. 200 Trees now confined to Australia.. as the banksias. **1881** BLACKMORE *Christowell* v, Bars of sunshine chequered by some Banksian sprays.

2. ***Banksia rose***: the Banksian rose (see next).

1890 [see TIME *sb.* 15b]. **1905** 'Q' *Shining Ferry* i. 2 A climbing Banksia rose overgrew the sill and ran up the mullions. **1934** *Bulletin* (Sydney) 21 Feb. 21/3 A Banksia-rose bush planted as a cutting 50 years ago last August.

Banksian ('bæŋksɪən), *a.* [f. the name *Banks*: see below and -IAN.] Epithet of: (*a*) a Chinese species of climbing rose, bearing small white or yellow flowers in clusters, named after Lady Banks; (*b*) the Labrador, Grey, or Jack Pine, *Pinus banksiana*, named after Sir Joseph Banks.

1837 [see ROSE *sb.* 3a]. **1841** MRS. LOUDON *Ladies' Comp. Fl. Gard.* 252/1 The Banksian Roses.. which are of two kinds. **1864** S. HIBBERD *Rose Bk.* 31 The Double White Banksian was introduced in 1807, and was so named in honour of Lady Banks. **1872** W. F. BUTLER *Great Lone Land* (ed. 2) xxii. 346 The juniper, the banksian pine, and the black spruce. **1886** *Encycl. Brit.* XX. 851 The Banksian Rose is a Chinese climbing species, with small white or fawn-coloured flowers of great beauty. **1920** *19th Cent.* July 175 The little yellow Banksian is still incomparable.

'bank-'side. [f. BANK *sb.*[1]]

1. The sloping side of a bank.

1596 SPENSER *State Irel.* Wks. 1805 VIII. 367 They can prettily shroud themselves under a bush or bankside. **1834** *Infant Hymnings* 20 They are nestling together.. In the hedge-row, the bank-side, or under the eaves.

2. The margin of sea (*obs.*), lake, or river.

a **1618** RALEIGH *Lett.* in *Rem.* (1661) 238 When he came to the bank-side to Land. **1625** K. LONG tr. *Barclay's Argenis* IV. xx. 313 Being landed at the bank-side of the Lake. **1669** WORLIDGE *Syst. Agric.* (1681) 254 This Net is either thrown off from the Bank-side, or from a Boat. **1867** *Times* 7 Oct., Puts his hand into the water by the bankside.

†**b.** Name of the side of the Thames at Southwark opposite to London. (Cf. BANK *sb.*[1] 11.) *Obs.*

1599 B. JONSON *Ev. Man out of Hum.* v. v, Some cunning woman here o' the *Banke-side*. **1633** MASSINGER *New Way* IV. ii, You lodged upon the Bankside. **1721** STRYPE *Eccl. Mem.* II. I. xvii. 142 The Bank-side where the Stews were.

banksman ('bænksmən). Also 6–7 **bankman.** [f. BANK *sb.*[1] + MAN.] An over-looker above ground at a coal-mine, a 'bank-manager.'

1598 *Wills & Inv. N.C.* II. (1860) 335 Who haith served me as a banckman, at those pittes. **1604** *MS. Eccl. Proc. Durh.*, James Carre, then bankeman of the said cole pittes. **1851** *Coal-tr. Terms Northumbld. & Durh.* 6 The banksman's wages are about 4*s.* per day. **1862** *Chamb. Jrnl.* 215 Repulsed by the banksman of the nearest pit.

bankvar, obs. form of BANKER[1].

1498 *Acc.* in C. Innes *Scot. Mid. Ages* viii. (1860) 244 A bankvar cost 18*d.* the ell, 16 ells long.

'banky, *a.* [f. BANK *sb.*[1] + -Y[1].] Full of banks, ridgy; of or pertaining to a bank; inclined like a bank or hill side; hilly.

1610 MARKHAM *Masterp.* II. liii. 304 Vpon a hard and stony ground, and after vpon a bancky ground. **1649** BLITH *Eng. Improv. Impr.* (1653) Ded., Old mossy, rushy, bankie pasture Lands. **1710** PHILIPS *Pastorals* vi. 5 And here below, the Banky Shore along, Your Heifers graze. **1729** M. BROWNE *Piscat. Eclog.* ix. (1773) 134 The banky shelter. **1863** ATKINSON *Provinc. Danby*, There's a vast o' banky land iv it. T' rooad to Whitby's sair an' banky. **1868** *Jrnl. R. Agric. Soc.* IV. 266, 120 acres of banky grass land. **1931** *Observer* 4 Oct. 26/5 The banky marge of a woodland.. will be a good site for a large colony.

bannat(e: see BAN *sb.*[2]

banne, obs. form of BAWN.

banned (bænd), *ppl. a.* [f. BAN *v.* + -ED.] **a.** Cursed. **b.** Prohibited, forbidden.

1340 *Alex. & Dind.* 808 To bale were ȝe.. bore for bannede werkus. **1592** CHETTLE *Kind-Harts Dr.* (1841) 46 You fare as the fox, the more band the better hap. **1596** SPENSER *Hymne Heav. Love* 184 Free that was thrall, and blessed that was band. **1860** *All Y. Round* No. 68. 421 The banned languages waxed stronger.

†**banneour.** *Obs.* Forms: α. 3 **baneur**, 4 **baneour(e**, **baniour**, 5 **banneoure**, 4–5 **banyour(e**, **banyer(e**; β. 5–6 **baner(e**, 5 **baneer.** [(α) ME. *baneur*, *-eour*, a. AF. *banëour* = OF. *baneor*:—late L. **bannātōr-em*; also (β) ME. *banere*, a. OF. *banère*, nom. case of the same word:—late L. **bannātor*; f. *bannum*, *bandum* standard: see BANNER.] A banner-bearer, a standard-bearer.

α. **1297** R. GLOUC. 361 And slou anon a Englysse man, þat a baner bere, And efsone anoþer baneur, & þe þrydde almest al so. *a* **1300** *Cursor M.* 12723 Sant iohn com als baneur [*v.r.* baniour, banerere]. **1377** LANGL. *P. Pl.* B. xv. 428 Go bifore As a good baneoure. *c* **1440** *Promp. Parv.* 23 Banyowre or bannerberere, *Vexillarius*.

β. **1403** in *Eulogium Hist.* (1863) III. 397 Procede, signifer; quod est dictu: 'anauant baner.' *c* **1440** *Generydes* 2055 His sonne ser Abell he was baneer. *Ibid.* 2128 Of his batell he made hym Banere. **1513** DOUGLAS *Æneis* (1710) IV. Prol. 180 Ware na baneris for to perys mo.

¶In OF. or AF. sometimes used in sense of *banneret*, with fem. *baneresse* banneret's wife; so in Anglo-Lat. *banerus*; whence later writers occasionally put *banneret* for *baneour*: see BANNERET 3.

1297 [see BANNERET 1a.] *a* **1300** LANGTOFT in *Excerpta Hist.* (1830) I. (Godef.) Li count, et li baneour, et ses bachelers. CHRIST. DE PIZ. (Godef.) Plusieurs autres contesses, baneresses, dames, et damoiselles. **1485** *Instrum. conv. Ord. Brit.* in Du Cange s.v. *Bannerettus*, Comites, Barones, Banerii, Baccalarii.

banner ('bænə(r)), *sb.*[1] Forms: 3–5 **baner(e**, 5–6 **banor**, 6 **bannar**, 4– **banner.** [a. OF. *banere*, *baniere* (= Pr. *banieira*, *bandieira*, Sp. *bandera*, Pg. *bandeira*, It. *bandiera*), on L. type **bandāria*, f. late L. *bandum*, *bannum* standard, 'vexillum quod *bandum* appellant' (Paul. Diac. *c* 775), f. Goth. *bandwa*, *bandwô* 'signum,' sign, token, perh. from same root as *band* and *bind*. In Romanic confused with *bannum* BAN.]

1. a. *prop.* A piece of stout taffeta, or other cloth, attached by one side to the upper part of a long pole or staff, and used as the standard of an emperor, king, lord, or knight, under (or after) which he and his men marched to war, and which served as their rallying-point in battle; *hence*, that of a country, nation, army, or company. Phrases: ***to join the banner of***, ***follow the banner of***. In the literal sense, now chiefly historical; in poetry and elevated prose, applied to the *standard* or *flag* of a country; common in figurative expressions.

Heraldically, a *banner* means a square or quadrangular flag, displaying the arms of the person in whose honour it is borne, and varying in size from that of an emperor, six feet square, to that of a knight banneret, three feet square. In this sense we still commonly speak of the banners of the Knights of the Garter, in St. George's Chapel, Windsor.

c **1230** *Ancr. R.* 300 Schrift.. is gunfaneur, & bereð her þe banere biuoren alle Godes ferde. **1297** R. GLOUC. 541 The burgeis.. arerde tueie baners, & wende hom vorth iarmed. *c* **1340** *Cursor M.* (Fairf.) 12913 As baner borne be-forþe king. **1386** CHAUCER *Knts. T.* 1552 In thy temple I wol my baner honge. **1574** tr. *Littleton's Tenures* 33b, To beare the kynges bannar. **1605** SHAKS. *Macb.* v. v. 1 Hang out our Banners on the outward walls, The Cry is still, they come. **1611** BIBLE *Sol. Song* vi. 4 Terrible as an armie with banners. **1769** *Junius Lett.* xxxv. 163 To fight under the banners of their enemies. **1809** J. BARLOW *Columb.* I. 2, I sing the Mariner who first unfurl'd An eastern banner o'er the western world. *a* **1842** MACAULAY *Armada*, Our glorious *semper eadem*, the banner of our pride! The freshening breeze of eve unfurled that banner's massy fold. **18..** KEY, 'Tis the star-spangled banner! Oh long may it wave O'er the land of the free, and the home of the brave! **1864** CURTIS *Sch. Hist. Eng.* 121 A number joined the banner of a Scotch knight named Wallace. **1864** BOUTELL *Heraldry Hist. & Pop.* xviii. 288 Banners were in use in the middle ages at sea, as well as on land.

b. in fig. expressions referring to moral struggles.

c **1380** WYCLIF *Sel. Wks.* 1871 III. 308 Þe baner of Crist on þe croos. **1552** *Bapt. Infants* in *Bk. Com. Prayer*, Manfully to fight vnder his banner agaynste sinne, the world, and the deuil. **1847** YEOWELL *Anc. Brit. Ch.* ii. 12 Planted the banner of the cross upon the ruins of heathenism.

c. in fig. reference to the protection symbolized by a national flag floating over a place.

c **1400** MAUNDEV. xxv. 26 The Banere of Jesu Christ is alle weyes displayed.. to the help of his trewe lovynge servauntes. **1564** HAWARD *Eutrop.* To Rdr., The boldlyer, under the banner of hys protectyon. **1722** SEWEL *Hist. Quakers* (1795) I. IV. 272 Thy.. banner was over my head.

d. (Attributed *fig.* to things.)

a **1822** B. CORNWALL *Sicil. Story, Autumn* iv, Already have the elements unfurled Their banners. *a* **1859** J. PERCIVAL *Eagle*, Where wide the storms their banners fling.

e. A flag awarded as a distinction. (See quot. 1840 and cf. 6b.) *U.S.*

1840 *Log Cabin* (N.Y.) 5 Dec. 2/3 It is known that the Ladies of New Orleans early in the late contest offered a splendid Banner to the State which should give the largest relative majority for Harrison and Tyler in its popular vote for Presidential Electors. **1900** *Century Mag.* LIX. 636/1 Local authorities.. united in the belief that.. Ashtabula County might be accorded the banner.

2. a. An ensign or flag bearing some device, borne in a procession, religious, civic, or political, for purposes of symbolism or display. (Sometimes specifically restricted to an ensign other than an ordinary flag, *e.g.* one extended in a frame, one attached by its upper edge or supported by two staves, so as to remain open.)

Of these the earliest were the religious banners, usually those of patron saints, which were often carried to battle, and there served as banners in sense 1. The banners of guilds and city companies, also partook of both characters.

c **1305** *St. Edmund* 351 in *E.E.P.* (1862) 80 Þis holi man also Prechede a dai at Oxenford.. In alle halewe church ȝerd: in þe norþ side Mid þe baners at vnderne. **1552–66** [see BANNER-CLOTH below in 6]. **1726** TINDAL *Rapin's Engl.* (1757) II. 207 A mast, on the top of which they placed a silver pix with a consecrated host, and the banners of St. Peter and St. John of Beverly, to serve as an ensign. [**1751** CHAMBERS *Cycl.* s.v., The French retain the denomination banner, in speaking of ecclesiastical processions; where the people, having each a cross on, march under a banner, representing the church militant.] *c* **1850** LONGF. *Excelsior*, A banner with the strange device, Excelsior. **1856** KANE *Arct. Expl.* I. xvi. 191 A little Masonic banner hanging from a tent-pole. **1878** C. DICKENS *Dict. Lond.* 154/1 [Lord Mayor's Show] The streaming flags and banners give unwonted life and colour to the dingy scene.

b. *fig.* Anything displayed as a profession of principles.

1581 HANMER (*title*) The Jesuites Banner, Displaying their original and successe. **1611** BIBLE *Ps.* lx. 4 Thou hast giuen a banner to them that feare thee; that it may be displayed. **1884** *Contemp. Rev.* Mar. 325 Dynamite has become.. the banner of the extreme revolutionary party.

c. A headline in large type, esp. one running across a whole page in a newspaper. Also *attrib.*, esp. ***banner headline***. orig. *U.S.*

1913 W. G. BLEYER *Newsp. Writing & Editing* xi. 305 Important news may be given as a head of one, two, or three parts extending across the whole front page. Such a head is often called a 'banner'. **1915** G. M. HYDE *Newspaper Editing* I. v. 167 Banner headlines have undergone a strange evolution. They were invented to assist in street sales by advertising the news. **1952** V. GOLLANCZ *My Dear Timothy* xx. 275 The *Daily Herald* came out with a huge banner headline, in letters half an inch high, on its opening page. **1957** *Listener* 1 Aug. 165/1 A five-column streamer in looming Gothic, followed by a banner line in some sort of spidery italic. **1965** *Ibid.* 9 Sept. 374/2 There is no longer a morning newspaper bravely bearing the name of Manchester on its banner-head.

3. †**a.** *transf.* The company or 'side' ranged under a particular banner. *Obs.* exc. *Hist.*

1330 R. BRUNNE *Chron.* 242 He went to play a wile with fo of his banere. *Ibid.* 306 þei were euer in wehere.. Whilk was best banere, with þat side forto hold. **1818** J. HOBHOUSE *Hist. Illustr.* (ed. 2) 543 The Count of Campania..has contrived that three banners of horse should leave his party by stealth.

b. (*a*) Each of the eight divisions, with distinguishing flags or banners, into which the Manchu army was divided. (*b*) A military subdivision of Mongolian tribes. Cf. BANNERMAN 2.

1842 K. S. MACKENZIE *Narr. Second Campaign in China* ix. 140 The army is divided into eight divisions, distinguished by the colour of their respective flag; the yellow or Imperial..being the highest, next the white banner, red and blue banners. **1848** S. W. WILLIAMS *Middle Kingd.* I. vii. 333 The Manchu army..was assisted by Mongols and Chinese, the three nations were divided into eight corps or 'banners'. **1880** J. ROSS *Manchus* xvi. 610 Up till 1613 the Manchus were divided into four banners—yellow, red, blue and white; but they had become so large an army, that for efficiency in manoeuvring they were subdivided into as many more—bordered yellow, bordered red, bordered blue, and bordered white. *Ibid.* 611 In 1635, the Mongols were separated from the Manchu banners, under eight banners of their own. **1894** *New Review* Nov. 528 The Banner troops received donations from the Emperor.

†**4.** = BANDEROLE 2 b. *Obs. rare.*

1599 SHAKS. *Hen. V*, IV. ii. 60, I will the Banner from a Trumpet take, And vse it for my haste.

5. *Bot.* The *vexillum* of a papilionaceous flower.

1794 MARTYN *Rousseau's Bot.* iii. 35 A large petal, covering the others and occupying the upper part of the corolla..the standard or banner. **1880** GRAY *Bot. Text-bk.* 398.

6. a. *Comb.*, as ***banner-flying***, ***-cloth***, ***-pole***, ***-rag***, ***-staff***, ***-towing*** (in aerial advertising); also ***banner-like***, ***-shaped***, ***-fashioned***, adjs. **banner-bearer**, standard-bearer, ensign; **banner cloud**, a cloud that streams outwards from the lee side of a mountain peak; **banner-cry**, a cry summoning men to join a banner, a slogan; **banner headline** (see sense 2 c); **banner-screen**, a fire-screen hung by its upper edge (cf. 2); **bannerless** *a.*, without a banner; **bannerwise** *adv.*, after the manner of a banner.

c **1440** *Promp. Parv.* 23 Banyowre, or *bannerberere, *Vexillarius.* **1603-5** SIR J. MELVIL *Mem.* (1735) 31 Eleven Banner-bearers went up to the Breach. **1847** *Nation. Cycl.* II. 819 Distinguished persons were..attended by a banner-bearer. **1552** *Invent. Ch. Goods* in *Norf. Archæol.* (1865) VII. 52 Item twoo lenten *Banner clothes valued at viiijs. **1566** *Eng. Ch. Furniture* (1866) 33 Item iij banner clothes sold to Gilbert Grene one of the churchwardens..who defacid theim. **1835** *Penny Cycl.* III. 407 The banner-cloth [of St. Cuthbert, at Durham] was a yard broad and five quarters deep..of red velvet, on both sides most sumptuously embroidered and wrought with flowers of green silk and gold. **1909** *Cent. Dict.* Suppl., *Banner-cloud. **1957** *Meteorol. Gloss.* (*Air Ministry*) (ed. 3) 32 The Helm Cloud over Crossfell Range, the Table Cloth over Table Mountain..are..well-known examples of banner cloud. **1810** SCOTT *Lady of L.* VI. xvii, The *banner-cry of hell. **1631** WEEVER *Anc. Fun. Mon.* 847 The *Banner-fashioned Shield. **1930** *Flight* 7 Feb. 195/1 Another profitable use to which N.A.L. have been putting their machines is *banner-flying. *c* **1850** J. JESSE *Last of Roses* III. 5 (L.) Your heir Rides forth alone, and *bannerless. **1566** *Eng. Ch. Furniture* (1866) 110 Item, a crose, a stafe, and ij *banner pooles.. defaced by the..churchwardens. **1880** BROWNING *Dram. Idyls, Clive* 58 Sockets made for banner-poles. **1875** B. TAYLOR *Faust* IV. ii. II. 249 The *banner-rags of standards flutter. **1566** *Eng. Ch. Furniture* (1866) 65 Item, banners, *banner staves, and crosse staves. **1815** WORDSW. *Wh. Doe* VI, The banner-staff was in his hand. **1864** *Soc. Sc. Rev.* 84 Able to execute a *banner screen with any lady in the land. **1960** *Guardian* 29 Dec. 3/1 The rates for *banner-towing are between £25 and £30 an hour. **1884** O'DONOVAN *Merv* xx. 221 A piece of tattered linen, floating *bannerwise at its extremity.

b. *attrib.* or quasi-*adj.* Entitled to a banner as a distinction (orig. in ***banner state***, ***county***); hence, pre-eminent, supreme. *U.S.*

1840 *Niles' Reg.* 5 Dec. 210/1 Which is the Banner State? —The Whigs..proposed to designate whichever state should give the Harrison ticket the largest majority, as the banner state. *Ibid.*, The banner county. Designation is claimed by Worcester, Massachusetts. **1843** *Knickerbocker* XXII. 431 He who was for many years the banner-veteran of our worthies. **1886** *Harper's Mag.* June 78/2 The Magnolia Plantation..which claims to be one of the banner plantations of the State. **1887** *Ibid.* July 237/2 She had the banner crop of tobacco in that county last year. **1903** *N. Y. Even. Post* 21 Sept., The earnings of all Vanderbilt lines had a banner month in August. **1911** S. E. WHITE *Bobby Orde* (1916) x. 128 On his banner day he brought down two fox-squirrels. **1931** G. T. CLARK *Leland Stanford* x. 361 That was the farm's banner year, for at the close of the season it held world trotting records for yearlings..and stallions. **1967** *Boston Sunday Herald* 26 Mar. III. 3/2 Next season will be a banner year for the browns, reports the American Wool Council.

banner ('bænə(r)), *sb.*² [f. BAN *v.* + -ER¹.] One who bans or curses.

c **1440** *Promp. Parv.* 22 Bannare or cursere, *Imprecator.* **1483** *Cath. Angl.* 20 Banner, *deuotator.* **1548** CRANMER *Catech.* 23 Deuylish swerers, banners and cursers. **1627** *Guide Agst. Witches* II. ii. 95 Bitter banners and cursers.

'**banner**, *v.* [f. BANNER *sb.*¹]

1. To furnish with a banner, decorate with banners.

1809 J. BARLOW *Columb.* v. 269 High bannering bright the air. **1870** *Daily News* 10 Oct., The city..is thickly bannered. **1874** HOLLAND *Mistr. Manse* ii. 119 Who with silken parasol, Bannered the army that she led.

†**2.** *intr.* To raise a banner or standard (*against*).

1588 J. HARVEY *Discours. Probl.* 46 That the Turk should adventure, or dare to banner, against them who, etc.

3. *trans.* To announce in a banner headline (see BANNER *sb.*¹ 2 c).

1951 *Manch. Guardian Weekly* 15 Mar. 10/4 It prominently reported what the Miami 'Daily News' had bannered the night before. **1959** D. BEATY *Cone of Silence* xix. 209 The name of the aircraft that for years they strove to perfect has been bannered across the papers of the world with the most tragic connotations.

bannered ('bænəd), *ppl. a.* [f. BANNER *sb.*¹ or *v.* + -ED.]

1. Furnished with a banner or banners. Also *fig.*

1667 MILTON *P.L.* II. 885 A Bannerd Host, Under spread Ensigns marching. **1810** SCOTT *Lady of L.* II. viii, Bothwell's bannered hall. **1869** 'MARK TWAIN' *Innoc. Abroad* xxx. 317 Clothes-lines..waving their bannered raggedness over the swarms of people below. **1897** *Westm. Gaz.* 9 Dec. 2/1 Through arched and bannered woodlands. **1908** *Daily Chron.* 2 June 3/2 The English Prince daily contemplated the bannered lines which he had been born to lead. **1952** R. CAMPBELL tr. *Poems of Baudelaire* 166 Our torch-like hearts their bannered flames unroll.

2. Borne or blazoned on a banner.

1796 SOUTHEY *Joan of Arc* v. 130 The banner'd Lion waved on Gergeau's wall. **1810** SCOTT *Lady of L.* II. xvi, Sir Roderick's bannered pine. **1816** W. TAYLOR in *Month. Mag.* XLI. 526 Three lions passant banner'd they expand.

† '**bannerer.** *Obs.* exc. *Hist.* Also 4-6 banerer(e, 5-6 banarer, 5 banerrere. [a. AF. *banerer* = OF. *banerier*, f. *banière* BANNER.]

1. One who carries a banner, a standard-bearer.

c **1340** *Cursor M.* (Trin.) 12723 Ion as banerere of honour Coom þo bifore oure saueour. *a* **1400** *Octouian* 1604 Yonge Octouian..Was banerrere of that batayle. **1483** CAXTON *Gold. Leg.* 300/2 One of the Baneres..tooke the Banere and stode amonge them. **1598** STOW *Surv.* vii. (1603) 63 His heires..are chiefe Banerers of London. **1881** A. MACGEORGE *Flags* 34 The bearer of a banner, or bannerer as he was called.

fig. **1387** TREVISA *Higden* Rolls Ser. VII. 93 He þat was i-made chief banerer of þis doynge deied in þe myddes of þe drynkynge.

2. = BANNERET. (Cf. BANNEOUR 2, BANNERET 3.)

1484 CAXTON *Chyualry* 69 A kniȝt banerere whiche has under hym many knyghtes.

banneret ('bænərɪt). Forms: 3-6 **baneret**, 5-6 **banret**, 4-6 (*Sc.*) **banrent**, (7 **bannerent**, **bannarite**), 4- **banneret**; *pl.* 4-6 **-ettis**, **-ettes**. [ME. *baneret*, a. OF. *baneret*, f. *banière*, with early ending of pa. pple.:—L. *-ātus*; *lit.* 'bannered.']

1. a. Originally, a knight able and entitled to bring a company of vassals into the field under his own banner, and who ranked next to a baron and above other knights: in this sense commonly used substantively, as a title of rank or dignity, and contrasted with *knight*, though sometimes with *bachelor*. **b.** Subsequently, the title and rank were conferred for valiant deeds done in the king's presence on the field of battle (perhaps, also, on other occasions or for other grounds), and, with the decay of the feudal system, came to constitute merely a rank or order of knighthood: in this use occur both *banneret* and *knight-banneret*, the latter opposed to *knight-bachelor*. On the institution of the order of baronets in 1611, precedence was given to these over all bannerets 'except such as were made in the field, under the banner, the king being present,' and after this the order of knights-bannerets was allowed to die out.

Note. The original sense was mainly French; 'in England there were few tenants bringing any considerable number of men who were not of the rank of the barons' (*Penny Cycl.*); the first recorded instance of use b. is in the 15th year of Edward III, when John de Copeland was made a banneret for his capture of King David Bruce at Neville's Cross. In the claim of Baronets to precedency (in 1612) it is said 'there are not *Bannerets* now in being and peradventure never shall be'; and although the title has been claimed for certain persons knighted since that day, heraldic authorities do not admit the validity of the claim. See the matter discussed in Nicolas' *Hist. Knighthood* (1842) I. pp. xxxii-xliii. In later times an explanation of the name was sought either in its being conferred on the field 'under the banner,' or in the alleged fact that at its bestowal the knight's pennon was symbolically cut square to banner shape.

a. 1297 R. GLOUC. 551 Seue baners also, that aȝe Sir Simond were..& þe oþer banerets, & kniȝtes mani oþer. **1375** BARBOUR *Bruce* XI 529 Thre banrentis of full mekill mycht War capitanys of all that rout. [**1382** *Act 5 Rich. II*, ii. §4 (Berthelet) Duke, erle, baron, baneret, knyght of the shyre.] *c* **1440** *Morte Arth.* 1424 The banerettes bolde, and bachelleres noble. **1480** CAXTON *Chron. Eng.* cxcvii. 176 Many other barons and banrettes. *c* **1538** LYNDESAY *Justing Watson & B.* 7 Monie ane knicht, barroun and banrent. **1611** GWILLIM *Heraldry* VI. vi. 270 Nobles..of which rancke a Banneret or (as some call them) a Baronet is the lowest. **1641** *Termes de la Ley* 37 Bannerets were anciently called by Summons to the Court of Parliament.

b. 1548 W. PATTEN *Exp. Scotl.* in Arb. *Garner* III. 147 Sir Ralph Sadler, Sir Francis Byran, Sir Ralph Vane..These Knights were made Bannerets. **1602** SEGAR *Hon. Mil. & Civ.* II. x. § 3, I suppose the Scots doe call a Knight of this creation a Bannerent, for having his Banner rent. **1605** CAMDEN *Rem.* (1637) 271 Sir Richard Croftes, who was made Banneret at the battell of Stoke. **1611** COTGR. s.v., A Banneret or Knight bannerett..a title (the priuiledge whereof was to haue a banner of his own for his people to march and serue under) giuen by the Kings of France to such as had ten vassals, and means to maintaine a troupe of horse; or vnto any gentleman that had valiantly carryed himselfe in two royall battels. **1655** GURNALL *Chr. in Arm.* I. 5 For which he came out of the Field God's Bannarite. **1863** HAYDN *Dict. Dates* 69 A Banneret, a dignity..disused from the reign of Charles I., but revived by George III. in the person of Sir William Erskine in 1764.

c. knight banneret.

1475 *Bk. Noblesse* 14 And many other knightis and gentiles..of whiche were taken and sleine .lij. knightis banerettis. **1523** LD. BERNERS *Froiss.* I. xx. 29 A knyght baneret, and vii. other knyghtis, of the realme of Scotland. **1577** HARRISON *England* II. v. 127 An order of knights called knights Bannerets, who are made in the field with the ceremonie of cutting awaie the point of his penant of armes, and making it as it were a banner. **1635** tr. *Camden's Hist. Eliz.* III. (1688) 401 Sir Ralph Sadleir..the last Knyht Banneret of England. **1768** BLACKSTONE *Comm.* I. 404 Next follows a knight banneret; who indeed by statutes 5 Ric. II. st. 2. c. 4..is ranked next after barons. **1834** *Penny Cycl.* III. 409 The dignity conferred on Captain, now Sir Henry Trollope, was understood to be that of a knight banneret.

2. A title borne by certain officers in some of the Swiss cantons and Italian republics.

1689 BURNET *Tracts* (1689) I. 14 The Chief Magistrates are two Advoyers..After them, there are the four Bannerets, who answer to the Tribunes of the People in Rome. **1708** *Lond. Gaz.* No. 4428/14 Banneret Willading is chosen Avoyer. **1832** *Sismondi's Ital. Rep.* viii. 176 The senators and bannerets of Rome.

3. Confused with BANNERER. (See BANNEOUR.)

1494 FABYAN VI. ccxvii. 236 A baner, or baneret, called Thilfer, a Norman. **1829** HEATH *Grocers' Comp.* (1869) 3 The Lord Fitzwalter hereditary chastellain banneret or standard-bearer of London.

'**banneret**, *v. rare*⁻¹. [f. the sb.] *trans.* To create a banneret.

1662 FULLER *Worthies* I. 464 (D.) Amongst the thirteen then bannerretted in the King's Army.

bannerette (,bænə'rɛt). Also 3 **banerett**, 4- **banneret**. [a. OF. *banerete*, *banerette*, dim. of *banière* BANNER: see -ETTE.] A small banner.

c **1300** *K. Alis.* 5236 Many banere and banerett Was on pauyloun y-sett. **1601** SHAKS. *All's Well* II. iii. 213 The scarffes, and the bannerets, about thee. **1865** *Morn. Star* 24 Feb., Over the pulpit was suspended a bannerett with the arms of the Cardinal. **1884** *Daily News* 13 Oct. 2/2 A bannerette having on one side a portrait of the Prime Minister. **1914** YEATS *Responsibilities* 38 Packed his marriage day With banneret and pennon. **1916** E. POUND *Lustra* 101 The crackling of small fires, the bannerets, The lazy leopards on the largest banner.

'**bannerman.** [f. BANNER *sb.*¹ + MAN.] **1.** *Sc. arch.* A standard-bearer, an ensign.

? *a* **1500** *Batt. Harlaw* xxvii, The kingis cheif bannerman was he. **1536** BELLENDENE *Cron. Scot.* (1821) II. 283 He espyit his banerman..trimbland. **1818** SCOTT *Hrt. Midl.* xxx, The renowned Daniel Cameron, our last blessed bannerman.

2. A soldier belonging to any of the eight banners of the Manchu army.

1899 MRS. H. FRASER *Dipl. Wife in Japan* II. 133 Shinno-Shiko nodded to his green bannermen to slay them. **1908** *Westm. Gaz.* 17 Dec. 7/3 The Manchu 'Bannermen' (soldiery) of Pekin.

bannerol ('bænərəʊl, -əl). A variant form of BANDEROLE (q.v.), found in all senses, and regularly used in that of: A banner about a yard square, borne at the funerals of great men, and placed over the tomb.

1548 HALL *Chron. Hen. V.* an. 10, CCC persons holdyng long torches, and lordes bearyng baners, banerols and penons. **1605** CAMDEN *Rem.* (1637) 206 King Oswald had a banneroll of gold and purple..set over his tombe. **1670** F. SANDFORD *Funeral Dk. Albemarle* (1722) 28 The ten Bannerols were offered by Pairs. **1721** *Lond. Gaz.* No. 5930/2 Six Banner-Rolls being carried on the Sides of the Herse by six Gentlemen. **1852** *Gentl. Mag.* CXXII. II. 592 Bannerols are banners of increased width, so made in order to display..the most distinguished alliances from which the deceased was descended.

‖**ba'nnimus.** *Obs.* [L.; = 'We banish': 1st pers. pl. pres. ind. of *bannire*; cf. *mittimus.*] = BANNITION.

1654 GAYTON *Fest. Notes* II. vi. 61 The Neglect, the Goby, the Bannimus from the Table. **1727–51** CHAMBERS *Cycl., Bannimus,* the form of expulsion of any member from the university of Oxford by affixing the sentence up in some public place, as a denunciation or promulgation of it.

banning ('bænɪŋ), *vbl. sb.* [f. BAN *v.* + -ING^1.] **a.** Cursing. **b.** Prohibition.

a **1300** *Cursor M.* 11954 Yur sun.. Wit his banning has slan vr child. **1566** STUDLEY *Seneca's Medea, Trag.* (1581) 120 That my bitter bannings may with mischiefe most abounde. **1818** SCOTT *Rob Roy* xxxix, Ower bad for blessing, and ower gude for banning.

'banning, *ppl. a.* That bans, cursing.

1586 WARNER *Alb. Eng.* III. xviii. (1597) 82 Whome the Priests the Druides inuade With banning words. **1591** SHAKS. *1 Hen. VI,* v. iii. 42 Fell banning Hagge!

†**bannition** (bə'nɪʃən). *Obs.* [ad. med.L. *bannītiōnem*, n. of action f. *bannīre* to BAN, BANISH.] Banishment, expulsion, *esp.* from a university.

a **1644** LAUD *Rem.* II. 191 (T.) To send him out of the university too by bannition. **1758** *Vinerian Stat.* in Blackstone *Comm.* I. 29 Such misbehaviour as shall amount to bannition by the university statutes.

bannock ('bænək). Forms: 1 bannuc, 5 -ok, 7 -ack, 6- -ock, (9 *Sc.* banno', banna, dim. bannockie). [a Gael. *bannach*, ? ad. L. *pānicium* f. *pānis* bread.]

1. The name, in Scotland and north of England, of a form in which home-made bread is made; usually unleavened, of large size, round or oval form, and flattish, without being as thin as 'scon' or oat-cake. In Scotland, bannocks are usually of barley- or pease-meal, but may be of wheaten flour; in some parts a large fruit cake or bun of the same shape is called a *currant-bannock.* In north of England the name is sometimes given to oat- or haver-bread, when made thicker and softer than an oat-cake; but local usage varies. (Cf. the dialect glossaries).

a **1000** *Gloss* in Haupt *Zeitsch.* IX. 463 *Bucellam semiplenam,* healfne bannuc. **1483** *Cath. Angl.* 20 Bannok, *focacius, panis subcinericius.* **1562** TURNER *Herbal* II. 33 a, Somthyng rysyng in bignes toward the middes, as a litle cake or bannock.. which is hastely baked upon ye harth. **1630** J. TAYLOR (Water P.) *Wks.* I. 78/2 Or Oaten cakes or Bannacks, as in North Britaine. **1663** in Spalding *Troub. Chas. I* (1829) 114 Baked good bannocks at the fire. **1674** RAY *N. Countr. Wds.* 5 Tharcakes, the same with Bannocks, viz. Cakes made of Oat-meal.. without Yeast or Leaven. **1724** A. RAMSAY *Tea-t. Misc.* (1733) II. 167 She gi'es us white bannocks. **1818** SCOTT *Hrt. Midl.* viii, To procure butter-milk and pease-bannocks. **1860** *All Y. Round* No. 45. 440 Barley bannocks and oat cake long remained the staff of life in villages in Scotland. [**1870** R. CHAMBERS *Pop. Rhymes Scotl.* 86 'Welcome, welcome, wee bannockie!' *Ibid.* 87 And that was the end o' the banna.]

†**2.** 'A small quantity of meal [sufficient to make a bannock] due to the servants of a mill by those grinding their corns or thirled thereto, ordinarily termed in charters of mills the sequels.' Spottiswoode's *MS. Law Dict.* in Jamieson. *Obs.*

1773 ERSKINE *Inst. Sc. Law* II. ix. §19 (JAM.) The sequels.. pass by the name of knaveship.. bannock, and lock.

3. *Comb.* (all *Sc.*), as ***bannock-fed, -shaped*; bannock-fluke** (also *bannet-*), the turbot; **bannock-stick,** a wooden roller for rolling out bannocks; **bannock-stone** = BAKESTONE.

1844 in *Proc. Berw. Nat. Club* II. xii. 102 The folk are bannock-fed. **1816** SCOTT *Antiq.* xi, Caller haddocks and whitings—a bannock-fluke and a cock-paddle. **1724** A. RAMSAY *Tea-t. Misc.* (1733) II. 181 Bakbread and a bannock-stane. *a* **1800** HOGG *Jacobite Relics* (1819) I. 118 (JAM.) A bassie and a bannock-stick.

banns (bænz), *sb. pl.* Forms: 5 bane (*sing.*), 5–7 banes, (6 baynes, 6–7 baines), 6 bannes, 6- bans, banns. [The same word as BAN *sb.*^{1} 'proclamation,' in a specific use, in which it was from some cause regularly pronounced with long *ā* from 15th to 17th c. The Prayer-book of 1549 has exceptionally *bannes*, that of 1552 *bannes* and *banes*, all edd. from 1559 to 1661 *banes*, from 1662 onward *banns*, after med.L. *bannum*, used, as well as F. *ban*, in same sense. The singular occurs in 15th c.; the plural only is found after.]

1. Proclamation or public notice given in church of an intended marriage, in order that those who know of any impediment thereto may have opportunity of lodging objections. Phrases: to *bid* (obs.), ***ask, publish, put up the banns.***

[**1198–1216** *Decret. Gregorii* IV. xviii. vi, Quando banna secundum consuetudinem in ecclesiis edebantur. *a* **1328** *Concil. Provinc. Cantuar.* (Wilkins) II. 554 Contractibus matrimonialibus absque bannorum editione prehabita initis.] *c* **1440** *Promp. Parv.* 22 Bane of a pley (**1499** or mariage), *Banna, preludium.* *c* **1530** LD. BERNERS *Arth. Lyt. Bryt.* (1814) 402 The byshop.. there dydde axe the banes betwene them. **1549** *Bk. Com. Prayer* Matrim., The bannes must be asked three seueral Soondaies. **1596** SHAKS. *Tam. Shr.* II. i. 181 Ile craue the day When I shall aske the banes, and when be married. **1599** BP. HALL *Sat.* IV. i. 124 Go bid the baines and point the bridall day. **1642** FULLER *Holy & Prof. St.* I. ix. 24 Seeing that heaven did ask the banes, why should earth forbid them? **1662** *Bk. Com. Prayer* Matrim., The Banns of all that are to be married together must be published. [So in 1885.] **1694** FALLE *Jersey* v. 142 The Banes shall be asked three Sundays successively. **1720** GAY *Poems* (1745) I. 252 Our bans thrice bid! **1863** HAYDN *Dict. Dates* 69 The present custom of asking banns.. introduced into the Gallican church about A.D. 1210.

b. ***to forbid the banns***: to make a formal objection to the intended marriage. Also *fig.*

1579 LYLY *Euphues* (Arb.) 51 Had not Euphues.. forbidden the banes of Matrimony. **1596** SPENSER *F.Q.* I. xii. 36 The late forbidden bains. *a* **1617** HIERON *Wks.* II. 472 If any man can forbid this Banes. **1709** STEELE *Tatler* No. 105 ¶4 The Parents of his Mistress forbad the Banes. *a* **1778** PITT (*on coalition of Fox and North*), I know of a just and lawful impediment; and in the name of the public weal, I forbid the banns. **1829** SOUTHEY *O. Newman* ii. Wks. X. 286 Should loyalty Forbid the banns.

†**2.** Proclamation or prologue of a play.

1440 [see 1]. **1483** *Cath. Angl.* 20 Bane (Bayn) of a play, *preludium, proludium.* **1600** *Chester Plays,* The Banes which are reade beefore the beginninge of the playes. *c* **1609** D. ROGERS in *Digby Myst.* Introd. (1882) 19 A man.. published the tyme and the matter of ye playes in breife, which was called 'ye readinge of the banes.' **1884** SYMONDS *Shaks. Predecess.* iii. 105 The Banes, or proclamation which introduced them to the public.

'bannut. *dial.* Forms: 5 bannenote, 6 banocke, 9 bannet, 7- bannut. [f. *ban, banne*, of unknown meaning + *nut.*] A walnut; but in an early vocabulary applied to the filbert.

c **1450** in Wülcker *Voc.* /629 *Auelana,* bannenote-tre. **1542** BOORDE *Dyetary* xxi. 283 The walnut and the banocke be of one operacyon. **1821** SOUTHEY *Life & Corr.* (1849) I. 54 The boys were employed also to squail at the bannets, that is, to throw at his walnuts. **1879** in *Shropsh. Gloss.* (E.D.S.), Bannut.

banquet ('bæŋkwɪt), *sb.*^{1} Forms: 5 bankat, 5–6 -ett(e, 6 bancket, -ette, -it, bancquet, -ett, 6–7 banket, 6- banquet. [a. F. *banquet* (15th c. in Littré), dim. of *banc* bench, corresponding to It. *banchetto*, dim. of *banco* 'table'; cf. *table, board*, in sense of 'meals.' The development of sense in It. has yet to be investigated: possibly sense 2, or 3, will prove to have preceded 1.]

1. A feast, a sumptuous entertainment of food and drink; now usually a ceremonial or state feast, followed by speeches.

1483 CAXTON *Gold. Leg.* 246/2 He there bayned and made bankettis in etyng and drynkyng. **1502** ARNOLD *Chron.* (1811) Introd. 41 There the Kinge helde ryal iustis, turnais, and bankettis. **1555** *Fardle Facions* I. iv. 48 In bancquettes of honour.. they serue in rawe flesh very finely minced. **1604** T. WRIGHT *Passions* v. §2. 163 Depriue great bankets of musicke, and the feast is not intire. **1711** POPE *Temp. Fame* 382 Ours is the place at banquets, balls and plays. **1849** MACAULAY *Hist. Eng.* iii, The halls of the great companies were enlivened by many sumptuous banquets. **1885** *Daily News* 4 June 6/8 Last evening the Lord Mayor.. gave a banquet to her Majesty's Judges.

b. *transf.* and *fig.*; sometimes *ironical.*

c **1495** DUNBAR *Twa Mariit Wom.* 430 To furnyse a bancat [*v.r.* bankat] In Venus chalmer. **1542** ELYOT (*title*) The Bankette of Sapience. **1580** SIDNEY *Arcadia* III. 280 Had trayned out the Princesses to their banket of miserie. **1613** R. C. *Table Alph., Pittance,* short banquet. **1791–1824** D'ISRAELI *Cur. Lit.* (1866) 16 Thus a single point, by the hand of a skilful artist, may become a varied banquet.

c. Applied to the Eucharist or Lord's Supper.

1563 *Homilies* II. *Sacram.* II. (1859) 449 O heavenly banquet, then so used. **1597** HOOKER *Eccl. Pol.* v. lxvii. §11 Christ assisting this heavenly banquet with his personal presence.

†**2.** A slight repast between meals. Sometimes called *running banquet.* (Often *transf.* and *fig.*, as in prec. sense.) *Obs.*

1509 FISHER *Wks.* I. 294 Eschewynge bankettes, rere-soupers, joncryes betwyxe meles. **1552** HULOET, Banquet before supper, *Antecœnium.* **1613** SHAKS. *Hen. VIII,* III. iv. 69 Besides the running Banquet of two Beadles [*i.e.* a whipping] that is to come. **1620** VENNER *Via Recta* v. 91 At banquets betweene meales, when the stomache is empty. **1657** JORDAN *Walks Isling.* Prol., A Play of Walks, or you may please to rank it, With that which Ladies love, A running Banquet.

3. A course of sweetmeats, fruit, and wine, served either as a separate entertainment, or as a continuation of the principal meal, but in the latter case usually in a different room; a dessert. *Obs.* in gen. use; but cf. 'cake and wine banquet' in Scotland, 'fruit banquet' in northern counties.

1523 LD. BERNERS *Froiss.* I. cccciii, He gaue dyners, suppers, and banketes to ladyes and damosels. **1588** COGAN *Haven Health* ccxii. (1612) 191 Yea, and after supper for feare lest they bee not full gorged, to haue a delicate banquet, with abundance of wine. **1610** BARROUGH *Physick* III. xxx. (1639) 151 Let his banket be Almonds. **1703** *Lond. Gaz.* No. 3943/4 A Ball, which.. ended in a very handsome Banquet of Sweetmeats.

†**b.** A sweetmeat, a dainty dish; *collect.* sweetmeats, dessert.

1534 LD. BERNERS *Gold. Bk. M. Aurel* (1546) D iiij, To inuent newe maner of meates and bankettes. **1681** *Lond. Gaz.* No. 1623/4 Four Tables, covered with high Piramids of all sorts of Banquet. *a* **1700** SEDLEY *Poems* Wks. 1722 I. 36 Some with full Cups, with Banquets some attend.

†**4.** A wine-drinking carousal. *Obs.*

1535 COVERDALE *1 Macc.* xvi. 15 Where he made them a bancket [Gr. πότον]. **1552** HULOET, Banquet called a rere banquet or drynkynge, *repotium.* **1603** HOLLAND *Plutarch's Mor.* 612 A banket, where they shall be put to quaffe and carrouse in their turne. **1719** YOUNG *Busiris* I. i. (1757) 19 The drunken banquet.

5. *attrib.*, as in ***banquet-beagle, -chamber, -hall,*** etc.

1535 COVERDALE *Eccles.* vii. 2 It is better to go into a house of mournynge, then into a bancket house. **1599** B. JONSON *Ev. Man out of Hum.* Dram. Pers., A good feast-hound, or banquet-beagle, that will scent you out a supper some three miles off. **1837** LYTTON *E. Maltrav.* v. viii, The lamps are dead in the banquet-room of yesterday. **1852** TUPPER *Prov. Philos.* 385 The grave, that dismal banquet-hall.

See also BANQUETTE.

banquet, *sb.*^{2} *Horsemanship.* [a. F. *banquet* in same sense: see Littré.] See quot.

1753 CHAMBERS *Cycl. Supp.* s.v., Banquet in the manege, denotes that small part of the branch of a bridle under the eye. *Ibid. Banquet-line,* an imaginary line drawn by the bit-makers along the banquet, in forging a bit.

banquet ('bæŋkwɪt), *v.* Also 6–7 **banket.** *Pples.* **banqueted, -ing.** [a. F. *banquete-r*, f. *banquet*; see prec.]

1. *trans.* To entertain at a banquet or banquets; to provide a banquet for, to feast, regale.

c **1538** LYNDESAY *Sqr. Meldrum* 854 They banketted him fra hand to hand. **1594** NASHE *Unfort. Trav.* 32 Not a dogge .. but shall bee banketted with Rhenish wine and sturgion. *a* **1797** H. WALPOLE *Mem. Geo. II,* I. 370 Being banqueted much on the road. *c* **1840** LYTTON *Devereux* VI. ii, As an oak banqueteth the destroying worm.

fig. **1676** D'URFEY *Mad. Fickle* v. i. (1677) 52 Happy the Man that takes delight In Banquetting the Sences.

2. *intr.* To take part in a banquet or banquets; to regale oneself; to feast, carouse. Const. *on.*

1514 BARCLAY *Cyt. & Uplondyshm.* 30 To Baccus they banket. **1573** TUSSER *Husb.* (1878) 68 At Christmas we banket, the rich with the poore. **1725** POPE *Odyss.* x. 662 A vulgar soul Born but to banquet, and to drain the bowl. **1855** SINGLETON *Virgil* I. 144 Ere that banquetted a godless race On butchered steers.

fig. **1588** SHAKS. *L.L.L.* I. i. 25 The minde shall banquet, though the body pine. **1751** JOHNSON *Rambl.* No. 162 ¶11 Thrasybulus had banqueted on flattery. **1857** HEAVYSEGE *Saul* (1869) 172 To banquet on the sounds.

†**3.** To take a BANQUET (in senses 2 and 3). *Obs.*

1564 P. MOORE *Hope Health* II. ii. 22 Let them eschue.. drinking or banquetting betwene meales. *c* **1800** GIFFORD in Southey *Comm.-pl. Bk.* Ser. II. (1849) 323 The common place of banqueting, or of eating the dessert.

†**'banquetant.** *Obs. rare*$^{-1}$. [a. F. *banquetant*, pr. pple. of *banqueter.*] = BANQUETER 1.

1615 CHAPMAN *Odyss.* xx. 280 Are there not beside Other great banquetants?

banqueteer (bæŋkwɪ'tɪə(r)). = BANQUETER 2.

1821 *Blackw. Mag.* IX. 322 Then canst thou image forth each banqueteer. **1824** BYRON *Juan* XVI. viii, The banqueteers had dropp'd off one by one.

banqueter ('bæŋkwɪtə(r)). [f. BANQUET *v.* + -ER^1; cf. F. *banqueteur.*]

†**1.** The giver of a banquet; a host, entertainer.

1542 UDALL *Erasm. Apoph.* 189 a, The feaster or banquetter plaied.. the niggarde. **1637** GILLESPIE *Eng.-Pop. Cerem.* III. v. 86 He is our loving and kinde Banqueter.

2. A guest at a banquet, a feaster; a reveller.

1549 LATIMER *Serm. bef. Edw. VI*, ii. (Arb.) 62 Blessed is the Lande where.. Kynges be no banketers. **1617** *Janua Ling.* 506 Inordinate banquetters cram themselves in cellars. **1624** HEYWOOD *Gunaik.* II. 65 All such banquetters be either musicall or learned. **1801** SOUTHEY *Thalaba* VI. xxvii, With earnest eyes the banqueters Fed on the sight impure.

¶ Used for: Broker, trafficker, BANKER^2.

1534 WHITTINTON *Tullyes Offyces* I. 18, I aske no golde.. nor gyue me no banketters in warre, but men of armes. **1552** HULOET, Banqueter, or he that kepeth a banck of mony.

'banqueting, *vbl. sb.* [f. as prec. + -ING^1.]

1. Giving of banquets (*obs.*); indulgence in luxurious entertainment, feasting, carousal.

1535 COVERDALE *Job* i. 5 When they had passed ouer the tyme of their banckettinge rounde aboute. **1582** N. T. (Rhem.) *1 Pet.* iv. 3 Excesse of wine, banketings, potations. **1611** *ibid.*, Excesse of wine, reuellings, banquettings [Gr. πότοις]. **1801** SOUTHEY *Thalaba* IX. xxxi, I have seen the Gouls Fight for the dainty at their banqueting.

2. *attrib.* **a.** in general sense.

1563 *Homilies* II. viii. II. (1859) 350 This feast is now prepared in God's banqueting-house, the church. **1570–87** HOLINSHED *Scot. Chron.* I. 365 Such banketting cheare as was used amongst his people. **1656** COWLEY *Davideis* III. (1669) 112 Citron.. was most used for banquetting Beds and Tables. **1814** SCOTT *Wav.* xx, Ere Waverley entered the banqueting hall. **1852** GROTE *Greece* II. lxxvii. X. 117 Phyllidas now conducted the pretended women into the banqueting-room.

†**b.** in reference to BANQUET *v.* 3, *sb.* 2, 3. *Obs.*

1586 COGAN *Haven Health* cxv. (1636) 116 To preserve Berberries whole, for a banqueting dish. **1610** BARROUGH *Physick* III. vii. (1639) 109 Let their banketting meetes be Pistacium, Almonds. *c* **1645** HOWELL *Lett.* I. v. ix, Philosophy should be your substantial food, Poetry your banqueting-stuff. *a* **1699** LADY HALKETT *Autobiog.* (1875) 12, I must come out by the Banketting howse in the garden.

‖**banquette** (bɑ̃'kɛt). [Fr., ad. It. *banchetta*, dim. of *banca* 'bench, shelf.' Formerly anglicized as *banket*, *-quet*.]

1. A raised way running along the inside of a rampart or parapet, or bottom of a trench, on which soldiers stand to fire at the enemy.

1629 *S'hertogenbosh* 19 We began to make.. Trenches with double bankets or feet benches. **1782** P. BRUCE *Mem.* I. 28 Six officers.. sitting in a row on the banquet, had their legs all shot off. **1877** KINGLAKE *Crimea* IV. xiii. 311 Korniloff mounted the banquette at the projecting angle of the bastion.

2. The footway of a bridge, or other thoroughfare, when raised above the carriage-way.

1772 C. HUTTON *Bridges* v. 83 The banquet or raised foot way on each side, leaving a sufficient breadth in the middle for horses and carriages. **1842** in GWILT. **1848** BARTLETT *Dict. Amer.*, *Banquette*, the name for a side-walk in some of our Southern cities.

3. The long low bench behind the driver in a French 'diligence' or omnibus.

1859 *All Y. Round* No. 33. 151 A peasant in blue blouse, who was in the banquette with me.

4. An upholstered bench-like seat.

1851 [see SALA[1]]. **1933** *Archit. Rev.* LXXIV. 242 (*caption*) A view across the counter from the serving side shows the wide recess round which runs a long low banquette covered in a brilliant red tartan. **1953** *Ibid.* CXIII. 168/1 (*caption*) Banquette seating in the staff cafeteria. **1958** E. DUNDY *Dud Avocado* I. vi. 92 Along the walls [of the café] ran a banquette upholstered in very old red plush.

† **'banrent.** *Obs.* Scotch form of BANNERET.

bansel, dial. variant of BENSEL.

banshee ('bænʃiː). Forms: 8 **benshi, -shea,** 9 **-shie, banshie, -shee.** [A phonetic spelling of Ir. *bean sidhe*:—OIr. *ben síde* 'female, or woman, of the fairies or elves.'] A supernatural being supposed by the peasantry of Ireland and the Scottish Highlands to wail under the windows of a house where one of the inmates is about to die. Certain families of rank were reputed to have a special 'family spirit' of this kind.

1771 PENNANT *Tour Scot.* 24 Aug. (1769), The cries and shrieks of Benshi, or the Fairies wife. **1810** SCOTT *Lady of L.* III. vii, The fatal Ben-shie's boading scream. **1829** —— *Demonol.* x. 348 The distinction of a banshie is only allowed to families of the pure Milesian stock. **1876** MISS BRADDON *J. Haggard's D.* II. 67 As if she had heard the family banshee shrieking at her.

banskin (= *barm-skin*); see BARM *sb.*[1] 3.

banstickle ('bænstɪk(ə)l). 5–; also 5 **baynstikille, (bafynstylkylle), beynstekle, banstykyll,** 6–8 **bansticle.** [prob. repr. an OE. **bánsticels*, f. *bán* bone + *sticels* prick, sting; cf. G. *stachelfisch*.] Name of the Three-spined Stickleback.

c **1450** HENRYSON *Mor. Fab.* 65, I can neither fish with huke nor net, To take ane banstickle. **1483** *Cath. Angl.* 17 Bafynstylkylle (*v.r.* Baynstikille); *gamerus, asparagus*. **1552** HULOET, Bansticle, *trachida*. **1611** COTGR., *Espinoche*, banstickle, or stickleback. **1787** BEST *Angling* 61 The common Prickleback, Sharpling or Banstickle. **1857** WRIGHT *Provinc. Dict.*, *Banstickle*, the Stickleback.. In Wiltshire it is called a *banticle*.

bant *v.*: see BANTING.

bantam ('bæntəm). [Supposed to be named from Bantam in the north-west of Java, whence perhaps the fowls were imported to Europe, though, according to Crawford, originally from Japan.]

1. a. A small variety of the domestic fowl, most breeds of which have feathered legs: the cocks are spirited fighters.

1749 MRS. DELANY *Autobiog.* (1861) II. 518 We fed all the bantams, guinea-fowl, pheasants. **1862** BARNES *Rhymes Dorset Dial.* I. 184 Knock'd the bantam cock right down.

b. *fig.* in reference to small size or 'cockiness.'

1782 WOLCOTT (P. Pindar) *Ode R. Acad.* Wks. 1812 I. 21 And struts the veriest Bantam-cock of paint. **1837** DICKENS *Pickw.* 469 'Do you always smoke arter you goes to bed, old cock?'.. 'Yes, I does, young bantam.' **1863** BURTON *Bk. Hunter* 59 Those pretty little pets, the Elzevir classics, a sort of literary bantams.

c. ***bantam weight*** (Boxing): see quot. 1954.

1884 *Times* 10 Apr. 6/4 The competitions were this year five in number, or one more than usual, a cup having been instituted for 'bantam weights', or men not exceeding 8 st. 4 lb. **1894** *Outing* (U.S.) XXIV. 71/2 An attempt to match the coxswains for a bantam-weight contest. **1897** *Encycl. Sport* May 139/2 Boxers are divided by the Amateur Boxing Association into five classes, according to their weights, as follows:—Bantam Weight, not exceeding 8 st. 4 lb. **1903**, **1910** [see WELTER WEIGHT 2]. **1954** F. C. AVIS *Boxing Ref. Dict.* 8 *Bantamweight*, a standard weight division for professional boxers weighing more than 8 st. but not more than 8 st. 6 lb.; amateurs 8 st. and 8 st. 7 lb. respectively.

d. Applied to battalions, etc., of small-sized soldiers.

1914 *Daily Express* 20 Nov. 5/5 'Bigland's Bantams' will probably be the pet name of a battalion which is being raised of men who are just too short to enlist under the ordinary conditions... The Bantams Battalion has been recognised by the War Office. **1914** *Scotsman* 11 Dec. 7/4 The Edinburgh Rotary Club.. has now completed arrangements for the raising of a 'Bantam Battalion'. **1927** *Observer* 30 Oct. 7 The 35th was a bantam division which went out to France very early in 1916.

2. ***bantam-work***: 'a kind of Indian painting, and carving on wood, resembling Japan-work, only more gay.' Chambers *Cycl. Supp.* 1753.

† **bantel, -ele, elle.** *Obs.* ? 'A post, pillar.'

c **1325** *E.E. Allit. P.* A. 991 With bantelez twelue on basyng boun. *Ibid.* 1016 þe wal abof þe bantels bent. *Ibid.* B. 1459 Enbaned vnder batelment with bantelles quoynt.

banteng, banting ('bæntɛŋ, 'bæntɪŋ). [Malay.] A species of wild ox; = TSINE.

1817 T. S. RAFFLES *Hist. Java* I. i. 49 Wild quadrupeds, the rhinoceros, and *bánteng*, or wild Javan ox. **1860** *Chambers's Encycl.* I. 674/2 *Banteng*.. a native of Java and Borneo.. black, with white legs. **1880** *Encycl. Brit.* XII. 742/2 The *tsine* or *banting* (*Bibos sondaicus*), found in Burmah. **1894** *Field* 9 June 815/3 Blood-curdling tales are told in Batavia of the ferocity of the rhinoceros and banteng. **1900**, **1903** [see TSINE]. **1961** *Times* 20 May 6/3 Whipsnade Zoo today announced the birth of a female banteng calf.

banter ('bæntə(r)), *sb.* [Of unknown etymology: it is doubtful whether the vb. or sb. was the earlier; existing evidence is in favour of the vb. The sb. was treated as slang in 1688: Swift, in the *Apology* to his *Tale of a Tub* (1710), says that it 'was first borrowed from the bullies in White Friars, then fell among the footmen, and at last retired to the pedants'; in *Tatler* No. 230, he classes it with *bamboozle*, *country put*, and *kidney*, as a word 'invented by some pretty Fellows' and 'now struggling for the Vogue.' But the vb. was then nearly 40 years old.

1690 LOCKE *Hum. Und.* III. ix. §7 He that first brought the word.. *Banter* in use, put together as he thought fit, those Ideas he made it stand for. **1710** SWIFT *Tatler* No. 230 ¶7, I have done my utmost for some years past to stop the Progress of *Mobb* and *Banter*. **1722** WODROW *Corr.* (1843) II. 659 Such plain raillery, that unless I should learn banter and Billingsgate, which I still thought below a historian, there is no answering it.]

1. Wanton nonsense talked in ridicule of a subject or person; *hence*, humorous ridicule generally; *now usually*, good-humoured raillery, pleasantry.

1702 *Eng. Theophrast.* 232 The ordinary reasons of War and Peace, are very little better than Banter and Paradox. **1705** S. WHATELY in Perry *Hist. Coll. Amer. Col. Ch.* I. 172, I know no better way of answering bombast, than by banter. **1710** SWIFT *T. Tub* (1760) Apol. 11 Peter's Banter (as he calls it in his Alsatia phrase) upon transubstantiation. **1844** DICKENS *Mar. Chuz.* (C.D. ed.) 249 She took it for banter, and giggled excessively. **1880** L. STEPHEN *Pope* v. 113 Gay .. had an illimitable flow of good-tempered banter.

2. An instance of such ridicule, a merry jest. *arch.*

1700 *Ch. Eng. Loyalty* in Somers *Tracts* II. 562 'Tis such a Jest, such a Banter, to say, we did take up Arms, but we did not kill him: Bless us, kill our King, we wou'd not have hurt a Hair of his Head! **1759** DILWORTH *Pope* 80 Satires on the nobility of both sexes, banters upon good authors. **1822** W. IRVING *Braceb. Hall* xvii. 147 The general had received all her approaches with a banter.

†**3.** A matter of ridicule or jest. *Obs.*

1719 D'URFEY *Pills* (1872) I. 167 Your zeal's a Banter to all men of Sense.

4. (*U.S.*) A challenge to a race, shooting-match, etc.

1835 LONGSTREET *Georgia Scenes* 26 No, said Peter, you made the banter, now make your pass. **1848** in BARTLETT *Dict. Amer.* *a* **1861** WINTHROP *John Brent* (1883) ii. 16 I'm goan to make yer a fair banter. **1872** SCHELE DE VERE *Americanisms* 439 We had a fine banter, but the match was postponed till spring.

banter ('bæntə(r)), *v.* [See prec.]

1. *trans.* To make fun of (a person); to hold up to ridicule, 'roast'; to jest at, rally, 'chaff.' Now usually of good-humoured raillery.

1676 D'URFEY *Mad. Fickle* v. i. (1677) 50 Banter him, banter him, Toby. 'Tis a conceited old Scarab, and will yield us excellent sport. **1741** RICHARDSON *Pamela* (1824) I. 112 You delight to banter your poor servant, said I. **1824** W. IRVING *T. Trav.* I. 91 Hag-ridden by my own fancy all night, and then bantered on my haggard looks the next day. **1865** CARLYLE *Fredk. Gt.* IX. xx. vi. 116 Poor Quintus was bantered about it, all his life after, by this merciless King.

†**2.** To ridicule, make a jest of (a thing). *Obs.*

1704 W. PERRY *Hist. Coll. Amer. Col. Ch.* I. 180 Turns his Pulpit to a Stage, And banters reformation. **1754** CHATHAM *Lett. Nephew* iv. 24 If they banter your regularity, order, and love of study, banter in return their neglect of them.

3. To impose upon (a person), originally in jest; to delude, cheat, trick, bamboozle. *arch.*

a **1688** VILLIERS (Dk. Buckhm.) *Confer.* (1775) 174 'Tis impossible, that all my senses should be banter'd and cheated. **1710** *Select. Harl. Misc.* (1793) 561 There was no bantering the commissioners named in the bill, because they knew them to be men of sense, honour, and courage. **1722** DE FOE *Moll. Fl.* (1840) 60 We diverted ourselves with bantering several poor scholars, with hopes of being at least his lordship's chaplain. **1815** SCOTT *Guy M.* li, Somebody had been bantering him with an imposition.

4. ***to banter out of***: to do out of by banter.

1687 T. BROWN *Saints in Upr.* Wks. 1730 I. 74 To banter folks out of their senses. **1721** AMHERST *Terræ Fil.* xxxvii. 195 We will not be banter'd out of it by false parallels.

5. *absol.* or *intr.* (in prec. senses.)

1688 SHADWELL *Sqr. Alsatia* I. i. 15 He shall cut a sham, or banter with the best wit or poet of em all. **1707** FARQUHAR *Beaux' Strat.* v. iii. 63 He fights, loves, and banters, all in a Breath. **1865** GROTE *Plato* I. vii. 291 His.. homely vein of illustration seemed to favour the supposition that he was bantering.

6. (*U.S.*) To challenge, defy, to a race, match, etc.

1810 F. CUMING *Sk. Tour Western Country* 135 Two hunters.. bantered each other to go out and kill a deer. **1834** CARRUTHERS *Kentuckian in N.Y.* I. 183, I was thinking of walking out into the country and bantering somebody for a footrace. **1836** D. CROCKETT *Exploits in Texas* 83 The black-leg set to work with his thimble again, and bantered me to bet. **1848** in BARTLETT *Dict. Amer.* **1860** *Knickerbocker* Aug. LVI. 221 The farmer again bantered him to buy his berries. **1872** E. EGGLESTON *End of World* xxvi. 177 The cards were put face down, and the company was bantered to bet the wine. **1902** HARBEN *Abner Daniel* 163 Colonel Barclay has.. bantered me for a trade time an' again.

banteree (ˌbæntə'riː). [f. prec. + -EE.] One who is bantered.

1823 *Blackw. Mag.* XIII. 269 Fixing the attention of the banteree.. and amusing the company with his perplexity.

banterer ('bæntərə(r)). [f. as prec. + -ER[1].]

1. One who turns things into ridicule; *later*, one who indulges in good-humoured jest or raillery.

1678 WOOD *Life* 6 Sept. (D.) The banterers of Oxford (a set of scholars so called, some M.A.), who make it their employment to talk at a venture, lye and prate what nonsense they please; if they see a man talk seriously, they talk floridly nonsense, and care not what he says. **1691** —— *Ath. Oxon.* I./834 He being a reputed Banterer, I could never believe him. **1692** E. WALKER *Epictetus' Mor.* lxvii, Amongst rude Ignorants.. To talk of Precepts, Maxims, and of Rules, Is to be laugh'd at, thought a Banterer. **1706** COLLIER *Refl. Ridic.* 130 Profess'd Banterers chuse rather to disoblige their best Friends, than to lose the opportunity of speaking their Jest. **1847** H. GREVILLE *Leaves fr. Diary* 205 Amusing, but too much of a banterer to please me.

2. One who imposes on, or bamboozles. *arch.*

1709 STEELE *Tatler* No. 12 ¶1 Gamesters, banterers, biters.. are, in their several species, the modern men of wit. **1712** ARBUTHNOT *John Bull* (1727) 58 A sort of fellows, they call banterers and bamboozlers, that play such tricks. **1849** MACAULAY *Hist. Eng.* I. iii. 369 An excellent subject for the operations of swindlers and banterers.

bantering ('bæntərɪŋ), *vbl. sb.* [f. as prec. + -ING[1].] Raillery, jesting, banter, 'chaff.'

1710 SWIFT *T. Tub* Apol. (R.), If this bantering, as they call it, be so despicable. **1857** LIVINGSTONE *Trav.* ix. 183 The audience acquiesce in this bantering and enforce silence.

'bantering, *ppl. a.* [f. as prec. + -ING[2].] Jesting, chaffing; bamboozling (*arch.*).

1691 WOOD *Ath. Oxon.* I./893 He.. delighted to please himself in a juvenile and bantring way. **1709** BERKELEY *The. Vision* §135 A question downright bantering and unintelligible. **1879** FARRAR *St. Paul* 703 His bantering answer to St. Paul's appeal.

'banteringly, *adv.* [f. prec. + -LY[2].] In a bantering, jesting manner.

1863 MRS. C. CLARKE *Shaks. Char.* x. 258 Lavatch banteringly replies to his lady. **1883** *Harper's Mag.* Oct. 702/1 'Perhaps you intend to embark for Australia?' she added, banteringly.

bantery ('bæntərɪ), *a.* [f. BANTER *sb.* + -Y[1].] Full of banter or 'chaff.'

1865 CARLYLE *Fredk. Gt.* IV. II. iii. 54 Its wit is very copious, but slashy, bantery. **1867** —— *Remin.* II. 51 Cooing, bantery, lovingly quizzical.

banting, var. BANTENG.

Banting ('bæntɪŋ). Name of a London cabinet-maker, whose method of reducing corpulence by avoiding fat, starch, and sugar in food, was published and much discussed in the year 1864. Hence **Bantingism**, **Bantingize** *v.*, and, **Banting** being humorously treated as a vbl. sb., the vb. *to* **bant**.

1864 *Reader* No. 91. 392/1 A few observations on Bantingism. **1864** *Times* 12 Aug. 4 The Classics seemed to have undergone a successful course of Banting. **1865** *Pall Mall G.* 12 June 9 If he is.. gouty, obese, and nervous, we strongly recommend him to 'bant.' **1881** *Echo* 24 June, There are fewer persons 'Bantingised' in America than in England. **1883** *Knowledge* 27 July 49/2 Bantingism excludes beer, butter, and sugar.

bantling ('bæntlɪŋ). [possibly f. BAND, swathe + -LING; but considered by Mahn, with greater probability, a corruption of Ger. *bänkling* bastard f. *bank* bench, i.e. 'a child begotten on a bench, and not in the marriage-bed'; cf. BASTARD.] A young or small child, a brat. (Often used depreciatively, and formerly as a synonym of *bastard*.)

1593 DRAYTON *Eclog.* vii. 102 Lovely Venus.. Smiling to see her wanton Bantlings game. **1635** QUARLES *Emblems* II. viii. (1718) 93 See how the dancing bells turn round.. To please my bantling! **1756** *Connoisseur* No. 123 (1774) IV. 142 Their base-born bantlings. **1791** WOLCOTT (P. Pindar) *Rights Kings* Wks. 1812 II. 389 We whip a bantling when it kicks and cries. **1809** W. IRVING *Knickerb.* (1861) 48 A tender virgin, accidentally and unaccountably enriched with a bantling. **1831** COLERIDGE *Table T.* 24 July, Some real new-born bantling.

fig. **1679** R. W. *O. Cromwell's Ghost* 1 Vices like these, you know were heretofore The only grateful Bantlings. **1808** BYRON *Let. Becher* Wks. (1846) 402/1 The interest you have taken in me and my poetical bantlings. **1864** TENNYSON

Boadicea, Lo their precious Roman bantling, lo the colony Camulodune.

Bantu (ˈbæntuː, bænˈtuː, -ɑː-), *a.* and *sb.* [In certain Bantu dialects, pl. (also *abantu*, etc.) of *-ntu* man.] **A.** *adj.* Of or pertaining to an extensive group of negroid peoples inhabiting the equatorial and southern regions of Africa, and of the languages spoken by them; originally given to the family of languages by W. H. I. Bleek. **B.** *sb.* **1.** *ellipt.* as *pl.* Bantu people. **2.** Any of the languages spoken by them.

1862 BLEEK *Compar. Gram. S. Afr. Lang.* I. 4 The South African division of the Bâ-ntu family of languages consists of one large middle body, occupying almost the whole known territory between the tropic of Capricorn and the equator. *Ibid.* 11 The abandonment in the Bâ-ntu languages of such syllabic elements as are more difficult of pronunciation. **1880** *Encycl. Brit.* XIII. 820/2. **1884** *Ibid.* XVII. 319/1. **1926** *Contemp. Rev.* Mar. 298 The Bantu, or Native races, numbering 4,698,000. **1948** M. GUTHRIE *Classif. Bantu Lang.* 19 Although languages of this kind cannot be called Bantu owing to their not having the complete prefix system we have described as a criterion, their relationship to the Bantu languages is sufficiently close for them to be taken into account. We shall therefore call them 'Sub-Bantu'. **1951** R. FIRTH *Elem. Social Organization* i. 8 In parts of Bantu Africa, to give a person an ancestor's name means that he is believed to reincarnate that ancestor's spirit.

Bantustan (bæntuːˈstɑːn, -æn, ˈbɑːntuːstɑːn). Also **bantustan**. [f. BANTU *a.* and *sb.* + *-stan*, terminal element meaning 'place' or 'home' in various Indo-Aryan languages, after *Hindustan*, *Pakistan*, etc.] An unofficial name for any of the separate homelands set aside for occupation by Black Africans in the Republic of South Africa. Also *attrib.*, designating the policy of establishing separate territories for Black citizens.

1949 *Round Table* June 208 A great Bantu State or group of States to which at least one ingenious thinker has affixed the term 'Bantustan'. **1951** J. D. L. KRUGER *Bantustan: Study in Pract. Apartheid* iv. 19 The proposed area which is contemplated as the non-white State.. will be referred to as Bantustan. **1954** *Observer* 20 June 4/5 The 'Bantustan' conception of the Nationalist intellectuals and the Dutch Reformed Church.. means the absolute division of South Africa into Black and White territories. **1968** *Economist* 20 Apr. 41 The government has found it cannot consolidate the scattered tribal areas into the eight coherent Bantustans which the original scheme envisaged. **1969** *Reporter* (Nairobi) 16 May 14/2 The 'bantustans' are to be situated in regions without natural resources. *Ibid.*, Another aspect of South Africa's 'bantustan' policy is the undue emphasis on the uniqueness of customs and traditions in individual tribes. **1977** *Times Lit. Suppl.* 20 May 630/1 The Homelands or Bantustans, as they used to be nicknamed. **1982** *Drum* Mar. 28 Mphephu.. believes that a sucker is born everyday—especially in the bantustans. **1985** *African Communist* c. 89 Some leaders of the Bantustans have protested to the S.A. government against its constitutional reforms.

banwurt, -wyrt, obs. ff. BONE-WORT.

banxring (ˈbæŋksrɪŋ). [a. Javanese *bangsring* (Horsfield), native name of the species.] A genus of small insectivorous animals (*Tupaia*) approaching the squirrel in appearance and arboreal habits, found in Java, Sumatra, and adjoining islands; properly the name belongs only to the Javanese species (*T. Javanica*) discovered by Horsfield about 1806, the Sumatran species being called *tupai*.

1824 HORSFIELD *Zool. Res. Java* s.v. *Tupaia*, The Bangsring fell under my observation during an early period of my researches in Java. **1847** CARPENTER *Zool.* §179 The *banxring*, a remarkable animal of which only three species are known. **1869** NICHOLSON *Zool.* (1880) 770 'Banxrings' or 'squirrel-shrews' of.. the Malay Archipelago.

banya, var. BUNNIA.

banyan (ˈbænɪən). A variant of BANIAN; now the prevailing spelling used for the *Banian* or *Banyan tree*. See BANIAN 5.

banzai (bænˈzaɪ), *int.* [Jap., literally, ten thousand years.] **1.** A shout or cheer used by the Japanese in greeting the emperor or in battle. Also as *sb.*

1893 E. ARNOLD *Adzuma* II. i, At the departure of the Imperial train, the citizens raise loyal cries of 'banzai! banzai!' **1904** *Daily Chron.* 12 Feb. 5/5 The crowd sang national songs, and shouted 'Banzai' continuously. **1905** *Times* 7 Oct., Enthusiastic banzais were given for King Edward and the Emperor of Japan.

2. *attrib.* or as *adj.* = (as if) shouting 'banzai', uproarious, jollificatory. *slang.*

1929 F. BOWEN *Sea Slang* 7 *Banzai Party*, a party of naval men going ashore for a spree. **1932** KIPLING *Limits & Renewals* 199 That's how it was till the Squadron returned. .. The *banzai*-parties came ashore, all hats and hosannas like a tax-payers' treat.

b. Applied to a reckless attack by Japanese servicemen.

1945 *Coast to Coast 1944* 106 Out in the glaring sky a Zero started its Banzai run. **1945** *San Francisco News* 13 June 1/5 Smashed desperate 'banzai' charges by doomed enemy survivors.

baobab (ˈbɑːəʊbæb). Also 7 **bahobab, boabab.** [First mentioned by Prosper Alpinus *Hist. Nat. Ægypti* (Venice 1592), ch. xvii, *De Bahobab*, who speaks of the use of its fruit 'in Æthiopia': apparently, therefore, the name belongs to some central African lang.] A tree (*Adansonia digitata*), also called 'Monkey-bread,' and Ethiopian Sour Gourd, with a stem of enormous thickness, found from Senegambia and Abyssinia to Lake Ngami, and long naturalized in Ceylon and some parts of India; considered by Humboldt to be 'the oldest organic monument of our planet.' The fibres of the bark are used for ropes and cloth.

1640 PARKINSON *Theat. Bot.* 1632 This [Ethiopian Sowre Gourd] is very like to be.. the Bahobab of Alpinus. **1681** R. KNOX *Ceylon* in Arb. *Garner* I. 441 There was also a baobab tree growing just by the fort. **1797** HOLCROFT *Stolberg's Trav.* IV. xciv. 310 The African tree called *Barbab* [sic], described.. by Adanson. **1857** LIVINGSTONE *Trav.* xxviii. 573 We spent a night at a baobab, which was hollow and would hold twenty men inside. **1866** A. BROWN in *Treas. Bot.* 18 The fibre [of the bark] is so strong as to give rise to a common saying in Bengal: 'As secure as an elephant bound with a baobab rope.'

baon, obs. form of BAWN.

bap (bæp). *Sc.* [Etymol. unknown.] A small loaf or 'roll' of bakers' bread, made of various sizes and shapes in different parts of Scotland.

1513–75 *Diurn. Occurr.* (1833) 301 Bappis of nyne for xij*d.* **1724** A. RAMSAY *Tea-t. Misc.* I. 91 Sowens and farles and Baps. *c* **1800** MRS. LYON in Ramsay *Remin.* (1870) Introd. 13 Are ye for your burial baps round or square?

Baphomet (ˈbæfəʊmɛt). [a. F. *Baphomet*; cf. Pr. *Bafomet*, OSp. *Mafomat*.] **a.** A form of the name Mahomet used by mediæval writers. **b.** Alleged name of the idol which the Templars were accused of worshipping. (According to l'Abbé Constant, quoted by Littré, this word was cabalistically formed by writing backward *tem. o. h .p. ab.*, abbreviation of *templi omnium hominum pacis abbas*, 'abbot' or 'father of the temple of peace of all men.') Hence **Bapho'metic** *a.*

1818 HALLAM *Mid. Ages* (1872) I. 140 Baphomet is a secret word ascribed to the Templars. **1855** MILMAN *Lat. Chr.* VII. XII. ii. 278 The great stress.. in the condemnation of the templars is laid on the worship of Baphomet. The talismans, bowls, symbols, are even called Baphometic. **1831** CARLYLE *Sart. Res.* II. vii, My Spiritual New-birth, or Baphometic Fire-baptism.

baptism (ˈbæptɪz(ə)m). Forms: *α.* 3–5 **bapteme,** 3–6 **baptem, -im,** 3–7 **-ime,** 4–6 **baptym(e,** (6 **babtym);** *β.* 4–7 **baptisme,** (5 **baptesme, batesme),** 6–7 **baptysme,** 7– **baptism.** [ME. *bapteme*, a. OF. *baptesme*, *baptême* (also *batesme*, *batême*), semi-popular adaptations of L. *baptismus*, a. Gr. βαπτισμός, n. of action f. βαπτίζ-ειν to BAPTIZE. In 16th c. assimilated to the L. and Gr.]

1. The action or ceremony of baptizing; immersion of a person in water, or application of water by pouring or sprinkling, as a religious rite, symbolical of moral or spiritual purification or regeneration, and, as a Christian ordinance, betokening initiation into the Church. ***name of baptism***: see BAPTISMAL name.

(With possessive and objective genitive; *e.g.* 'John's baptism,' that administered by John, 'the jailer's baptism,' that received by the jailer.)

α. *a* **1300** *Cursor M.* 12726 In þis hali Ion time Was lagh bigun neu of baptim. *c* **1325** *E.E. Allit. P.* A. 626 In þe water of baptem þay dyssente. **1382** WYCLIF *Matt.* iii. 7 Seeynge many of Pharisees.. commynge to his bapteme. **1494** FABYAN VI. clv. 143 After he had clothyd them with the mantell of baptym. **1521** FISHER *Wks.* I. 334 The sacramente of baptyme. **1589** *Marprel. Epit.* (1843) 28 For baptim doth not contain the perfection of religion.

β. **1377** LANGL. *P. Pl.* B. XVIII. 375 Bretheren in blode & in baptesme. **1489** CAXTON *Faytes of A.* III. xxi. 219 A madde man.. may not receyue batesme. **1528** MORE *Heresyes* I. Wks. 167/1 *Ipsum audite* saide the father at the tyme of his baptisme. **1628** COKE *On Litt.* 3 a, The purchaser be named by the name of baptism and his surname. **1651** HOBBES *Leviath.* (1839) 499 Baptism is the sacrament of allegiance of them that are to be received into the kingdom of God. **1851** ROBERTSON *Serm.* Ser. IV. (1863) I. 25 Christian Baptism.. on God's part is an authoritative revelation of his Paternity; on man's part it is an acceptance of God's covenant.

2. *fig.* **a.** (in various senses; cf. BAPTIZE *v.* 2.) Also applied to the death by violence, or 'baptism of blood,' of unbaptized martyrs, and to the ceremony of blessing and naming church bells and ships. (Cf. Du Cange *Campanas Baptizari*.)

1382 WYCLIF *Luke* xii. 50 Sothli I haue to be baptisid with baptym. **1585** ABP. SANDYS *Serm.* (1841) 19 They upon their foundation have builded the baptism of bells and ships. **1648** HERRICK *Hesper.* (1869) 100 Those maiden showers Which by the peep of day do strew A baptime o'er the flowers. **1860** EDERSHEIM *Kurtz' Ch. Hist.* I. §54 The baptism of blood in martyrdom. *Mod.* A severe baptism of suffering.

b. ***baptism of fire***: after eccl. Gr. βάπτισμα πυρός (e.g. Macarius Ægyptius *Hom.* xxvii. 17; cf. Matt. iii. 11), (*a*) the grace of the Holy Spirit imparted through baptism, as distinguished from the sacrament or rite; (*b*) martyrdom, esp. by fire; (*c*) the undergoing of any severe ordeal or painful experience; (*d*) a soldier's first experience 'under fire' in battle (so F. *baptême de feu*). Cf. *fire-baptism* s.v. FIRE *sb.* B. 3 a.

[**1822** B. E. O'MEARA *Napoleon in Exile* I. 107, I love a brave soldier who has undergone, *le baptême du fer*, whatever nation he may belong to.] **1857** G. LAWRENCE *Guy Liv.* xiii, It's only in their baptism of fire that the young ones shrink and start. **1881** R. HUNTER et al. *Encycl. Dict.* s.v., When during the Franco-German war of 1870, Prince Louis Napoleon.. was first exposed, by direction of his father, Napoleon III, and with his own consent, to the fire of the enemy at Saarbrück, the event was called a 'baptism of fire'.

baptismal (bæpˈtɪzməl), *a.* [ad. med.L. *baptismāl-is*: see BAPTISM and -AL[1].] Of, pertaining to, or connected with baptism. Also *ellipt.* = *baptismal name*, the personal or 'Christian' name given at baptism.

1641 J. JACKSON *True Evang. T.* iii. 175 His Baptismall Laver [was] awaited by a Dove. **1651** BAXTER *Inft. Bapt.* 293 This Doctrine of Baptismal Regeneration. *a* **1711** KEN *Hymnotheo* Wks. 1721 III. 106 Thy Mercy I invoke, For my Baptismal Vow so often broke. **1869** FREEMAN *Norm. Conq.* (1876) III. xii. 138 Geoffrey also changed his baptismal name. **1872** DE MORGAN *Budg. Parad.* 120 Mr. Andrew Theophilus Smith, or some such unlikely pair of baptismals.

bap'tismally, *adv.* [f. prec. + -LY[2].] In a baptismal manner, by baptism.

1850 MRS. BROWNING *Pet Name* Poems II. 384 Names acquired baptismally. **1861** R. MONTGOMERY *Gleams on Font* 30 Vital.. is the germ Baptismally by grace implanted there.

baptist (ˈbæptɪst). [a. OF. *baptiste*, ad. L. *baptista*, ad. Gr. βαπτιστής, n. of agent f. βαπτίζειν to BAPTIZE.]

1. One who baptizes; *esp.* as applied to John, the forerunner of Jesus Christ. ***Baptist's day***: the 24th of June.

c **1200** *Trin. Coll. Hom.* 131 Seint iohan baptiste was bihaueded. *c* **1230** *Ancr. R.* 160 Sein Johan.. was Godes baptiste. *c* **1400** *Rom. Rose* 7000 Gret wodes everichon, I lete hem to the Baptist Johan. **1589** WARNER *Alb. Eng.* v. xxiv. (1597) 121 At Baptis-day with Ale and cakes bout bon-fires neighbors stood. **1815** SCOTT *Ld. Isles* VI. iv, Ere John the Baptist's eve. **1871** [see BAPTIZEE]. **1879** FARRAR *St. Paul* 463 Disciples of the Baptist.

2. One who immerses himself, or is immersed. *rare.*

1775 ADAIR *Amer. Ind.* 296 The Baptist, or dipped person, came out.. good-humoured after his purification. *c* **1811** FUSELI *Lect. Art* iv. (1848) 457 Varied groups of baptists, immersing themselves.

3. A member of that Protestant religious body which holds that baptism ought to be administered only to believers, and by immersion; at first and till present century, called, by opponents ANABAPTISTS. [Perhaps this use originated in the early names, *Baptized* Believers, Churches, etc. Cf. *baptist(e* early pa. pple. of BAPTIZE.]

[**1654** (*title*) The Humble.. Vindication.. [of] severall of the Baptized Churches in this Nation.] **1654** W. BRITTEN (*title*) The Moderate Baptist. **1674** J. MEAD (*title*) A brief account of passages between Quakers and Baptists. **1852** MOORE *Cherries*, Methodists, of birds the aptest.. And that water-fowl the Baptist. **1860** EADIE *Eccl. Cycl.* s.v., A conspiracy.. in 1661.. brought forth from the Baptists another disavowal of Anabaptist principles. [See ANABAPTIST 3.]

b. *attrib.* quasi-*adj.*

1717 (*title*) Rules of the Particular Baptist Fund. **1766** ENTICK *London* IV. 309 At the Boar's-head.. is a Baptist meeting. **1847** *Nation. Cycl.* II. 827 Persons who do not embrace the Baptist tenet.

baptist(e, earlier form of BATISTE.

† **bap'tiste.** *Obs. rare*$^{-1}$. Baptism.

1460 *Lybeaus Disc.* 212 Thorgh helpe of Cryst, That in the flome tok baptyste.

baptistery, baptistry (ˈbæptɪstərɪ, ˈbæptɪstrɪ). Also 5 **bapetystore, baptyzatorye,** 7 **baptistory.** [a. OF. *baptisterie*, mod. *baptistère*, ad. L. *baptistērium*, a. Gr. βαπτιστήριον bathing-place, baptistery, f. βαπτίζειν to BAPTIZE. *Baptizatorye* represented a med.L. modification, *baptizātōrium*.]

1. That part of a church (or, in early times, a separate building contiguous to the church), in which the rite of baptism is administered.

1460 in *Pol. Rel. & L. Poems* (1866) 138 The bapetystore there he founde. **1485** CAXTON *Chas. Gt.* 19 He dyd do.. compose baptyzatoryes & frentes convenably. **1579** FULKE *Confut. Sanders* 675 The image.. painted in the Baptistery. **1636** PRYNNE *Unbish. Tim. & Tit.* (1661) 54 To enter into the Baptistory. **1840** BARHAM *Ingol. Leg.* 308 They've searched the aisles and Baptistry. **1849** FREEMAN *Archit.* 161 The round sepulchral chapel and the polygonal baptistery.

2. In modern Baptist places of worship, a receptacle containing water for the baptismal rite.

1835 *Penny Cycl.* III. 416/1. 1853 WAYLAND *Mem. Judson* II. v. 187 Leading into the Maulmain baptistery the pious captain of the Ramsay.

3. = BAPTISM. (So OF. *baptisterie*, and med.L.)

1851 MRS. BROWNING *Casa Guidi* 19 Having tried the tank Of the church-waters used for baptistry.

Baptistic (bæp'tɪstɪk), *a.* [ad. Gr. βαπτιστικός, f. βαπτίζειν to BAPTIZE.] = BAPTIST 3 b.

1884 *Ch. Times* 413/1 The Baptistic craze of immersionism. *Ibid.* The Baptistic organs.

†**bap'tistical,** *a. Obs. rare.* [f. as prec. + -AL[1].] Of or belonging to baptism.

1658 BRAMHALL *Schism Guarded* 205, *Abrenuncio, Credo*, this baptisticall profession, which he ignorantly laugheth at.

baptizable (bæp'taɪzəb(ə)l), *a.* [f. BAPTIZE *v.* + -ABLE.] Capable of, or fit for, baptism.

1659 GAUDEN *Tears of Ch.* 284 (D.) The condition limiting persons baptizable, which is actual believing. 1685 BAXTER *Paraphr. N.T.* Matt. xxviii, Meerly to consent to learn of Christ, makes one a baptizable disciple.

†**bapti'zation.** *Obs.* [ad. L. *baptīzātiōn-em*, n. of action f. *baptīzāre* to BAPTIZE] = BAPTISM.

1470 HARDING *Chron.* li. vii, By his baptizacion Whiche Ioseph gaue vnto Aruigarus. 1651 JER. TAYLOR *Clerus Dom.* 23 Their baptizations were null. 1704 HEARNE *Duct. Hist.* I. 229 A Baptization or Washing away of all Pollution.

baptizatory: see BAPTISTERY.

baptize (bæp'taɪz), *v.* Forms: 3-4 **baptis,** 4 **-iz,** 4-5 **baptyse,** 6 **baptyze,** 3-9 **baptise,** 3- **baptize.** *Obs. pa. pple.* 3-6 **baptist(e,** 4 **-este.** [a. F. *baptise-r, -izer* (11th c.), ad. L. *baptīzā-re*, ad. Gr. βαπτίζειν 'to immerse, bathe, wash, drench,' in Christian use appropriated to the religious rite, f. βάπτειν to dip, plunge, bathe.]

1. *trans.* To immerse in water, or pour or sprinkle water upon, as a means of ceremonial purification, or in token of initiation into a religious society, especially into the Christian Church; to christen.

1297 R. GLOUC. 86 He was ybaptized þere. *a* 1300 *Cursor M.* 12654 Þe time þat he on cristen lai suld baptist be. *Ibid.* 12897 Selcut was to thinc.. þe clerc to baptis þe prist. 1480 CAXTON *Chron. Eng.* IV. (1520) 28/2 Oure lorde Jhesu cryst at 30 yere of age was baptysed. 1561 T. NORTON *Calvin's Inst.* IV. 105 The very worde of Baptizing signifieth to dippe. 1667 MILTON *P.L.* XII. 442 Them who shall beleeve, Baptizing in the profluent streame. 1833 CRUSE *Eusebius* VI. xliii. 266 Baptised by aspersion.

b. *absol.* To administer the rite of baptism.

c 1325 *E.E. Allit. P.* A. 817 Þer as baptysed þe goude saynt Ion. 1670 G. H. *Hist. Cardinals* I. III. 68 The Bishop Ordains, the Priest Baptizes.

2. *fig.* (in various shades of meaning, in reference to initiation, spiritual agency, etc.) Cf. BAPTISM 2.

1382 WYCLIF *Acts* i. 5 3e schulen be baptysid in the Hooly Gost. 1651 C. CARTWRIGHT *Cert. Relig.* II. 62 Is not God able to baptize Infants with his Spirit? 1655 BAXTER *Quakers' Catech.* 23 You would have us baptize our Bels to make them spirituall. 1858 O. W. HOLMES *Aut. Breakf. T.* xi, Sorrow had baptised her. 1861 EMMA TOKE *Innoc. Day* in *Hymns A. & M.* No. 54, Baptized in their own blood. 1865 *Cornh. Mag.* Oct. 451 A view which every day baptizes into fresh beauty.

3. With allusion to an important part of the ceremony of baptizing or christening infants or heathens: To give a name to, name, denominate.

[*c* 1450 *Merlin* v. 91 Antor made the childe to be baptised, and cleped hym Arthur.] 1549 *Compl. Scot.* 4 Historiagrephours hes baptist hym to be ane of the principal of al the nyne noblis. 1592 SHAKS. *Rom. & Jul.* II. ii. 50 Ile be new baptiz'd; Hence foorth I neuer will be Romeo. 1604 T. WRIGHT *Passions* Pref., This..honestie, other Nations baptize with the Name of Simplicitie. 1838 J. GRANT *Sk. in Lond.* (1860) 306 Chalk-and-water, which, for the purpose of sale, was baptised milk.

†**bap'tize, -ise, -is,** *sb. Obs. rare.* [f. prec. vb.] Baptism.

a 1300 *Cursor M.* 12754 In water baptised he al þaa þat com til him baptis [*v.r.* baptize] to ta. 1460 *Lybeaus Disc.* 1360 I schall for thys baptyse Ryght well quyte thy servyse.

bap'tized, *ppl. a.* [f. as prec. + -ED.] Subjected to the rite of baptism; †*vulgarly*, watered, diluted (*obs.*).

1636 HEALEY *Theophrast.* 46 He wil give his best friends his baptised wine. 1687 *Lond. Gaz.* No. 2252/4 The Congregations of Baptized Believers. 1831 CARLYLE *Sart. Res.* II. viii, The fire-baptised soul.

baptizee (bæptaɪ'ziː). *rare.* [f. as prec. + -EE.] A recipient of baptism, a baptized person.

1871 E. NOEL tr. *Richter's Flower Pieces* II. 68 For the baptist to touch the head of the baptisee with the water.

baptizement (bæp'taɪzmənt) *rare.* [f. as prec. + -MENT; cf. OF. *baptisement.*] The action of baptizing; baptism.

1818 J. HOBHOUSE *Hist. Illustr.* 90 The fountain springing up for the baptizement of his jailer.

baptizer (bæp'taɪzə(r)). [f. as prec. + -ER[1].] One who baptizes; occas. used of John the Baptist.

1483 *Cath. Angl.* 20/1 A baptizer, *baptista.* 1548 UDALL, etc. *Erasm. Par. Matt.* iii. 14 Did refuse the office of a baptiser. 1645 PAGITT *Heresiogr.* (1661) 40 The Baptizer and the party baptized go both into the Rivers. 1865 *Gentl. Mag.* CCXVIII. 84 The Baptizer signified that he was not worthy to have been even the forerunner of the Saviour.

bap'tizing, *vbl. sb.* [f. as prec. + -ING[1].] The action or ceremony of baptism.

1297 R. GLOUC. 86 He bi com in hys baptizing hol of ys wo. *a* 1300 *Cursor M.* 171 Þere shul 3e here.. Siþen of Iones baptizyng. 1653 MILTON *Hirelings* Wks. (1851) 362 How ill had it becom'd John the Baptist to demand Fees for his baptizing. 1880 *New Virginians* II. 234 The nigger baptisings have been always held at such distances.

bap'tizing, *ppl. a.* That baptizes.

1671 MILTON *P.R.* I. 328 Our new baptizing Prophet. 1675 BAXTER *Cath. Theol.* II. XI. 249 Every Baptising Minister prerequireth the profession of it.

baque, obsolete form of BAKE.

‖**baquet** (bake). [Fr., dim. of *bac* BACK *sb.*[2]; cf. BACKET.] A small tub or trough.

1786 *Lounger* No. 99. 417 From the baquet rise those enchanted rods by which the magnetic virtue..is transmitted. [Mesmer employed a baquet filled with water in his magnetic experiments.]

bar (bɑː(r)), *sb.*[1] Forms: 2-7 **barre,** 3-7 **barr,** 5- **bar.** [ME. *barre*, a. OF. *barre* (= Pr., It., Sp., Pg. *barra*):—late L. *barra* of unknown origin. The Celtic derivation accepted by Diez is now discredited: OIr. *barr* 'bushy top,' and its cognates, in no way suit the sense; Welsh *bar* 'bar' is from Eng., and Breton *barren* 'bar' from Fr. (The development of sense had to a great extent taken place before the word was adopted in English.)]

I. A piece of any material long in proportion to its thickness or width.

* *Of shape only.*

1. *gen.* A straight piece of wood, metal, or other rigid material, long in proportion to its thickness.

1388 WYCLIF *Num.* iv. 10 Thei schulen putte in barris [1382 beryng staues]. 1690 W. WALKER *Idiom. Anglo-Lat.* 38 To beat down the statute [? statue] with bars. 1753 CHAMBERS *Cycl. Supp., Bar*, among printers, denotes a piece of iron..whereby the screw of the press is turned in printing. 1815 SCOTT *Guy M.* lvii, A pallet-bed was placed close to the bar of iron. 1860 H. STUART *Seaman's Catech.* 11 On the barrel [of a rifle] is the..sliding bar. 1881 C. EDWARDS *Organs* 50 The sound-bars are glued in place. 1881 RAYMOND *Mining Gloss., Bar*, a drilling or tamping-rod.

fig. 1388 WYCLIF *Isa.* xxvii. 1 The Lord schal visite in his hard swerd..on leuyathan, serpent, a barre [1382 a leuour.] 1684 CHARNOCK *Attrib. God* II. 6 Leviathan is here called a bar-serpent..as mighty men are called bars in Scripture.

2. *spec.* **a.** A thick rod of iron or wood used in a trial of strength, the players contending which of them could throw or pitch it farthest; the distance thrown was measured in lengths of the bar. Hence in obs. fig. phrases.

1531 ELYOT *Gov.* I. xvi, Throwyng the heuy stone or barre playing at tenyse. 1600 ROWLANDS *Let. Humours Blood* iv. 64 To pitch the barre, or to shoote off a gunne. 1715 PRIOR *Alma* I. 311 While John for ninepins does declare, And Roger loves to pitch the bar. 1801 STRUTT *Sports & Past.* Introd. 13 To amuse himself in archery, casting of the bar, wrestling.

fig. 1647 CLEVELAND *Char. Lond.-Diurn.* 5 First, Stamford slew him: then Waller outkilled that halfe a Barre. 1712 ADDISON *Spect.* No. 538 ¶5, I did not disbelieve..but yet I thought some in the company had been endeavouring who should pitch the bar farthest. *a* 1733 NORTH *Lives* II. 37 The objectors..outdo, many bars, all that themselves found fault with. 1742 RICHARDSON *Pamela* III. 324 Here's a mere Baby..outdoes 'em by a Bar's Length.

†**b.** An iron bar used in breaking criminals on the wheel. *Obs.*

1577 HARRISON *England* II. xi. 223 We have use neither of the wheele nor of the barre.

c. A rod-shaped heating element used in certain types of electric fire. Cf. ELEMENT *sb.* 4 c and *one-bar* adj. s.v. ONE *numeral a.* 33, etc.

1926-7 *Army & Navy Stores Catal.* 344/1 Electric radiators..Two bars (1,000 watts each). 1949 E. BOWEN *Heat of Day* vii. 131 She switched on one more bar of the electric fire. 1970 M. KENYON *100,000 Welcomes* v. 32 One bar of a puny electric fire glowed in the hearth.

3. a. A narrow four-sided block of metal or material as manufactured, *e.g.* of iron, or soap, chocolate, etc.; an ingot of precious metal. Cf. *bar-iron* in IV.

1595 T. MAYNARDE *Drake's Voy.* (1849) 18 We got here twenty barres of silver. 1753 CHAMBERS *Cycl. Supp., Bars* of Iron are made of the metal of the sows and pigs, as they come from the furnaces. 1833 MARRYAT *P. Simple* iv, Four cakes of Windsor, and two bars of yellow for washing. 1876 HUMPHREY *Coin Collect. Man.* ii. 9 Bars form a sort of transition stage between the weighed money and true coins. 1906 *Daily Chron.* 25 July 6/4 A shop-worn chocolate-cream bar. 1959 *Elizabethan* Apr. 10/1, I gave you a bar of chocolate on the train from London.

b. Used as a standard of weight or a denomination of currency. Cf. BAHAR, BARR(E.

1732 *Abstr. of Voy. to New Calabar River, 1699, taken from Jrnl. of James Barbot* in *Coll. Voy. & Trav.* V. 460/1 We adjusted with them the reduction of our merchandize into bars of iron, as the standard coin, viz. One bunch of beads, one bar... One piece broad Hamborough, one *ditto.* One piece Nicanees, three *ditto*... And so *pro rata*, for every other sort of goods. 1732 in F. MOORE *Trav. Inland Afr.* (1738) App. II. 9 Barr, or Sixteenth Part of an Ounce of Gold. 1738 *Ibid.* 45 A Barr is a Denomination given to a certain Quantity of Goods of any kind, which Quantity was of equal Value among the Natives to a Barr of Iron, when this River was first traded to. Thus..an Ounce of Silver is but a Barr. 1737 J. ATKINS *Voy. to Guinea* (ed. 2) 40 They all keep Grometta s (Negro Servants) which they hire from Sherbro River, at two Accys or Bars a Month. 1755 JOHNSON, *Bar*, in African traffick, is used for a denomination of price; payment being formerly made to the Negroes almost wholly in iron bars.

c. A pound; esp. in ***half a bar***, ten shillings. *slang.*

1911 J. W. HORSLEY *I Remember* xi. 254 Others [slang words] were new to me, such as..'bar' for a sovereign. 1938 F. D. SHARPE *S. of Flying Squad* 331 *Half a bar*, ten shillings. 1939 J. B. PRIESTLEY *Let People Sing* x. 256 Knocker brought out some money and examined it. '..A nicker, half a bar, a caser an' a hole.' 1958 M. PUGH *Wilderness of Monkeys* 77 Half a bar, or what you call ten bob?

†**4. a.** An ornamental transverse band on a girdle, saddle, etc.; *subseq.* an ornamental boss of any shape. Also, a girdle or band. *Obs.*

c 1340 *Gaw. & Gr. Knt.* 162 Boþe þe barres of his belt & oþer blyþe stones. *c* 1385 CHAUCER *L.G.W.* 1200 With sadyll rede enbrowderyd with delyte, Of gold the barres vpp enbosid high. *c* 1400 *Rom. Rose* 1103 The barres were of gold ful fyne, Upon a tyssu of satyne. *c* 1400 *Destr. Troy* XXXIII. 13019 Orestes..comaundet, Bare to the barre bryng him his moder. 1433 *Test. Ebor.* (1855) II. 48 Unam zonam ornatam cum octo barres. *c* 1440 *Promp. Parv.* 24 Barre of a gyrdylle, or oþer harneys, *stipa.* 1562 J. HEYWOOD *Prov. & Epigr.* (1867) 179 The barres of mens breeches haue such strong stitching.

b. A small slip of silver fixed transversely below the clasp of a medal, as an additional mark of distinction.

1864 BOUTELL *Heraldry Hist. & Pop.* xx. 353 A Bar is attached to the ribbon for every act of such gallantry as would have won the Cross. 1885 *Standard* 2 Mar. 3/5 He affixed the medals and bars to the breasts of the..recipients.

5. a. A straight strip or stripe, narrow in proportion to its length, a broad line; *e.g.* of colour. ***stars and bars***: see STAR *sb.*[1] 6 b.

c 1440 in *Househ. Ord.* (1790) 460 Lay orethwart him [a roast pig] one barre of silver foile, and another of golde. 1609 C. BUTLER *Fem. Mon.* i. (1623) Biij, In each joynt a golden Barre in stead of those three whitish rings which other Bees haue. 1806 WORDSW. *Sonn. Liberty, Ode* 28 A blue bar of solid cloud Across the setting sun. 1878 GURNEY *Crystallog.* 10 The bar or line drawn over the 2 denotes, etc.

fig. 1865 CARLYLE *Fredk. Gt.* VII. XVIII. ii. 122 The brightest triumph has a bar of black in it.

b. ***bar of Michael Angelo***, the superciliary ridge or prominence of the frontal bone at the base of the forehead, characteristic of the heads of Michael Angelo's statues.

1850 TENNYSON *In Mem.* lxxxv. 127 And over those ethereal eyes The bar of Michael Angelo.

6. *Her.* An honourable ordinary, formed (like the fess) by two parallel lines drawn horizontally across the shield, and including not more than its fifth part. ***bar sinister***: in popular, but erroneous phrase, the heraldic sign of illegitimacy; see BATON, BEND, (*sinister*). ***bar-gemel***: a double bar, or small bars placed in couplets.

1592 WYRLEY *Armorie* 97 Sir Lewis Harcourt came, Two golden bars that bare in field of guls. 1610 GWILLIM *Heraldry* II. vi. (1660) 70 A Barre is..drawne overthwart the Escocheon..it containeth the fifth part of the Field. *Ibid.* 91 Termed in Blazon Barres Gemelles of the Latine word *Gemellus*, which signifieth a *Twin.* 1727-51 CHAMBERS *Cycl.* s.v., The bar may be placed in any part of the field. 1823 SCOTT *Quentin D.* II. xviii. 358 My bar sinister may never be surmounted by the coronet of Croye.

7. *Farriery.* **a.** (usually *pl.*) The transverse ridged divisions of a horse's palate: below those which lie between the molar and canine teeth the bar of the bit is inserted. **b.** The recurved ends of the wall or crust of a horse's hoof, meeting at an acute angle in the centre of the sole.

1617 MARKHAM *Caval.* II. 52 It giueth libertie to the tongue, offendeth not the barres, and keepeth the mouth in tendernesse. 1725 BRADLEY *Fam. Dict.* s.v. *Yellows*, After they have blooded the Horse..in the third Bar, on the pallate of the Mouth. 1831 YOUATT *Horse* xviii. (1872) 398 Smiths..too often habitually pursue..the injurious practice of removing the bars [of the hoof]. 1884 E. ANDERSON *Horsemanship* I. v. 17 The curb bit should..take a bearing upon the bare bars of the mouth.

** *Of shape and confining purpose.*

8. *esp.* A stake or rod of iron or wood used to fasten a gate, door, hatch, etc.

c 1175 *Lamb. Hom.* 131 He..tobrec þa irene barren of helle. *c* 1325 *E.E. Allit. P.* B. 884 Steken þe 3ates ston-harde wyth stalworth barrez. 1388 WYCLIF *Ex.* xxvi. 26 Fyve barris of trees..to holde togidere the tablis. *a* 1420 OCCLEVE *De Reg. Princ.* 1104 And up is broke lok, haspe, barre, and pynne. 1535 COVERDALE *Judg.* xvi. 3 Toke holde on both yͤ syde portes of yͤ gate..and lifte them out with the barres. 1667 MILTON *P.L.* II. 877 And every Bolt and Bar..with ease Unfast'ns. 1867 SMYTH *Sailor's Word-bk., Hatch-bars*, flat iron bars to lock over the hatches.

9. a. A straight, strong rod of iron or wood fixed across any way of ingress or egress, or forming part of a fence, gate, grating, or the like.

c **1386** CHAUCER *Knts. T.* 219 Thurgh a wyndow thikke of many a barre Of Iren. *c* **1440** *Promp. Parv.* 24 Barre abowte a graue or awter. *a* **1658** LOVELACE *To Althea*, Stone walls do not a prison make, Nor iron bars a cage. **1711** ADDISON *Spect.* No. 57 ¶3 She..makes nothing of leaping over a six-bar gate. **1818** SCOTT *Rob Roy* xxii, Like a fine horse brought up to the leaping-bar. **1883** *Harper's Mag.* Sept. 491/1 The cows lowing at the pasture bars.

b. *spec.* in *pl.* A set of wooden rails which may be withdrawn to afford an opening through a fence or wall. (Cf. DRAW-BAR.) *U.S.*

1639 in *Conn. Hist. Soc. Coll.* (1897) VI. 5 All the fences & gates..to the bares shall be sufitiently mad up. **1660** in *Rec. Providence, R.I.* II. 139 Provided that they Keepe a Sufficient inlett of Barres at Each End of the highway for A cart to passe through. **1703** *Ibid.* V. 109 [He] shall set up a Gate, or inlet of Barrs in said fence. **1887** M. E. WILKINS *Humble Romance* 315 The younger of the two old women let down the bars which separated the blooming field..from the road, and they passed through.

c. *Football*, etc. = CROSS-BAR 1 a.

1882 *Blackburn Times* 1 Apr. 3/3 Ashton, M'Guire, and Towers completely baffled the backs, a good centre giving Ashton a rare opportunity of scoring, but he sent the ball over the bar. **1894** *N. Brit. Daily Mail* (Glasgow) 9 Apr. 3/6 The ball hit the bar, and after bounding back, went over Haddow's head and right into the net. **1986** *Football Monthly* June 34/2 Rush gave another indication of what was to come later when he headed over the bar.

d. In colloq. phr. ***behind bars***, of a person: in prison, locked away.

[**1914** W. L. TAYLOR *Man behind the Bars* i. 13 A short story read aloud was always a pleasure to the men behind the bars.] **1951** M. MCLUHAN *Mech. Bride* (1967) 151/2 The crimes for which the professionals are behind bars. **1966** A. SACHS *Jail Diary* xxvi. 232 He must know that the career he has chosen will inevitably involve him in spending a large portion of his life behind bars. **1977** *Borneo Bull.* 7 May 10/3 Now Hassan.., who got $50 out of the deal, is behind bars for six months.

10. One of the series of iron rods fixed in the front of a grate or bottom of a boiler furnace to prevent the fuel from falling out.

1677 MOXON *Mech. Exerc.* (1703) 13 A course sort of Iron ..fit for Fire-bars. **1866** G. MACDONALD *Ann. Q. Neighb.* xxxi. (1878) 541 Thrust it between the bars, pushing it in fiercely with the poker.

11. A transverse piece of wood making fast the head of a wine-cask. (If a cask is lying horizontal, wine is drawn from 'below the bar,' when it is more than half empty.)

1520 WHITTINTON *Vulg.* 13 b, This wyne drynketh lowe or under the barre, *Hoc vinum languescit.* **1576** LAMBARDE *Peramb. Kent* (1826) 385 All the emptie hogsheads..and (for sixe tunne of wine) so many as should be drunke under the barre. **1611** COTGR., *Empeigner le bout d'vne douve*, to pin the barre of a peece of caske.

II. That which confines, encloses, limits, or obstructs, with no special reference to shape.

* *A material barrier.*

12. *gen.* A material structure, forming a secure enclosure, or obstructing entry or egress; a barrier.

c **1325** *E.E. Allit. P.* B. 963 Þe grete barrez of þe abyme he barst vp. **1388** WYCLIF *Jonah* ii. 7 The barris of erthe closiden me togidere. **1667** MILTON *P.L.* x. 417 With rebounding surge the barrs assaild. **1700** DRYDEN *Pal. & Arc.* 1024 In equal fight From out the bars to force his opposite. **1867** SMYTH *Sailor's Wd.-bk.*, *Bar*, a boom formed of huge trees or spars lashed together, moored transversely across a port. **1872** BROWNING *Fifine* cxxii, That caverned passage..a grim Bar-sinister, soon blocks abrupt your path.

13. a. *spec.* A barrier closing the entrance into a city, formed originally of 'posts, rails, and a chain.' Afterwards applied to the gate by which these were replaced, as in *Temple-bar*, and the Bars or gates of York, etc.

c **1220** *Leg. St. Kath.* 2348 Bihefden hire utewið þe barren of þe burhe. **1410** *E.E. Wills* (1882) 16 The Cherch of seynt Clementis wythowtyn Templebarr. **1490** CAXTON *Eneydos* lvi. 153 Slawghter made bothe of men and of horses by fore the barres of the towne. **1645** PAGITT *Heresiogr.* (1647) 35 A house without the Barres at Algate. **1691** RAY *N. Countr. Wds.* 6 *Barr*, a Gate of a City, as Bootham Bar, Monkbar.. in the City of York. **1843** *Penny Cycl.* s.v. *York*, There are four principal gates, or bars, as they are usually called.

b. A toll-house gate or barrier; cf. TOLL-BAR.

1540 *Act 32 Hen. VIII*, xvii. §1 The said lane called Graies Inne Lane, from Holborne bars northward. **1813** *Examiner* 19 Apr. 243/1 The only light..was that shed by the toll-bar lamp, and..the bar is at a distance of about 150 yards.

†**c.** A hurdle. *Obs.*

1641 H. BEST *Farm. Bks.* (1856) 15 The seconde thinge belonginge to a barre is spelles..the third thinge belonginge to a barre is a dagger.

d. (Also in Fr. form *barre*.) A horizontal bar fixed to the wall at waist level, serving as a support for dancers in certain of their exercises.

1883 DUTTON COOK *On Stage* II. i. 4 Then the pupil is taught to stand on one leg while extending the other until the foot rests upon a horizontal bar raised some four or five feet above the floor. **1922** BEAUMONT & IDZIKOWSKI *Manual Class. Theatr. Dancing* II. i. 33 Generally the bar is of wood, and is fixed to the walls of the practice room in a horizontal position. **1936** A. L. HASKELL *Prelude to Ballet* ii. 7 She performs her complicated routine, first hanging on to the *barre*, wooden counterpart to the hands of a partner. **1968** J. WINEARLS *Mod. Dance* (ed. 2) ii. 77 Exercises at the barre should be done daily in the same order.

†**14.** A defensive barrier, a bulwark. *Obs.*

1603 FLORIO *Montaigne* I. xlvii. (1632) 154 Having so many Cities, Townes, Holds, Castles, and Barres for his securitie. **1618** BOLTON *Florus* IV. ii. (1636) 284 Utica..the other maine fort or barre of Africa.

15. a. A bank of sand, silt, etc., across the mouth of a river or harbour, which obstructs navigation.

1586 J. HOOKER *Girald. Irel.* in *Holinsh.* II. 16/2 The port or hauen of Dublin is a barred hauen, and great ships..doo lie in a certeine rode without the barre. **1621** QUARLES *Argalus & P.* (1678) 81 Our Pinnace is past o'er The Bar, and rides before the Maiden-tower. **1720** *Lond. Gaz.* No. 5821/1 Three Ships were lost upon the Bar. **1868** G. DUFF *Pol. Surv.* 100 Rivers which are, as usual in Japan, obstructed by a dangerous bar.

b. See *bar-diggings* in 30.

1862 R. MAYNE *Brit. Columbia* 65 Bars..all those places where gold is found and worked, on a river's bank, are called by that name.

16. *Mus.* 'A vertical line drawn across the stave to divide a musical composition into portions of equal duration, and to indicate the periodical recurrence of the accent' (F. Taylor in Grove *Dict. Mus.*); *also*, the portion contained between two such lines, technically called the 'measure.' ***double bar***: two parallel vertical lines, marking the close of a strain or section. *attrib.* in ***bar-line***.

1665 C. SIMPSON *Princ. Mus.* 25 Distinguished by Strokes crossing the Lines, which..are called Bars. **1674** PLAYFORD *Skill Mus.* I. xi. 35 Bars are of two sorts, single and double. The single Bars serve to divide the Time, according to the Measure of the Semibreve. The double Bars are set to divide the several Strains or Stanzaes of the Songs and Lessons. **1779** SHERIDAN *Critic* II. i, Will you play a few bars? **1795** MASON *Ch. Music* i. 13 One note in every bar should be accented. **1881** MACFARREN *Counterp.* 19 To continue a note for two bars or more is not melody. **1927** GROVE *Dict. Mus.* (ed. 3) I. 219/1 A bar..is, literally, the straight line drawn across the stave to mark the metrical accent... In ordinary parlance that is now called the 'bar-line'. **1959** WIMSATT & BEARDSLEY in *P.M.L.A.* Dec. 589 Music—or at least music with bar-lines..—is precisely a time-measuring notation.

17. in pl. *bars*: the game of 'prisoner's base' or 'chevy.' The players, after choosing sides, occupy two camps or enclosures, and any player leaving his enclosure is chased by one of the opposite side, and, if caught, made a prisoner. Still in *north. dial.*

c **1400** *MS. Cott. Cleop.* D. ix. 156 b, Þe children ournen at þe bars. **1450** MYRC 336 Bal and bares and suche play Out of chyrcheȝorde put away. **1611** COTGR., *Barres*, the play at Bace or Prison Bars. *a* **1795** AIKIN *Evenings at H.* xvii. 276 At cricket, taw, and prison-bars, He bore away the bell. **1801** STRUTT *Sports & Past.* II. ii. 71 A rustic game called base or bars, and in some places prisoners' bars.

** *An immaterial barrier.*

18. *Law.* A plea or objection of force sufficient to arrest entirely an action or claim at law.

1495 *Act 2 Hen. VII*, xxiv. §1 A sufficient barre of the seid atteynte. **1528** PERKINS *Prof. Bk.* v. §410 Such assignment shall not be a barre in a 'Scire Facias.' **1599** SHAKS. *Hen. V*, I. ii. 42 Pharamond, The founder of this Law and Female Barre. **1641** *Termes de la Ley* 37 b, Barre is when the defendant in any action pleadeth a plea which is a sufficient answer, and that destroyeth the action of the plaintife for ever. **1879** *Cassell's Techn. Educ.* IV. 91/1 It is no bar to the validity of a patent.

19. *fig.* An obstruction, obstacle; a barrier.

1531 *Dial. Laws Eng.* II. xlix. (1638) 153 This warranty is no barre in conscience, though it be a barre in the law. **1649** BP. REYNOLDS *Serm. Hosea* iii. 40 The special barre and obstacle that keeps men from Christ. **1713** ADDISON *Cato* I. ii, His baffled arms, and ruined cause, Are bars to my ambition. **1782** BURKE *Penal Laws* Wks. VI. 272 Thereby fixing a permanent bar against any relief. **1877** L. MORRIS *Epic of Hades* II. 92 Nature..has set this bar Betwixt success and failure.

20. Phrases: †***to make bar of***: to stop short at. †***by the bar***: by means of the very obstacle interposed. ***in bar*** (***of***, rarely ***to***): as a sufficient reason or plea (against), to prevent.

c **1590** MARLOWE *Jew of M.* I. ii, In extremity We ought to make bar of no policy. **1609** HOLLAND *Amm. Marcel.* xxv. ix. 279 By the barre, as one would say, whereof they continued ..without taking any harme. **1715** BURNET *Own Time* (1766) II. 92 Their protestation was only in barr to the Lords doing anything besides the trial. **1827** HALLAM *Const. Hist.* (1876) II. xii. 414 Danby..pleaded a pardon secretly obtained from the King, in bar of the prosecution. **1842** H. E. MANNING *Serm.* (1848) I. xiv. 205 These are the habits of life which are pleaded in bar of the daily worship of God.

†**21.** A kind of false die, on which certain numbers are prevented from turning up. See BARRED (*dice*).

1545 ASCHAM *Toxoph.* (Arb.) 55 Certayne termes.. appropriate to theyr playing; wherby they wyl drawe a mannes money, but paye none, whiche they cal barres. **1592** *No-body & Some-b.* 1517 Those Demi-bars..Those bar Sizeaces. **1753** CHAMBERS *Cycl. Supp.*, *Barr Dice*, a species of false dice, so formed that they will not easily lie on certain sides.

III. A rail or barrier acquiring from its use special technical significance; the space it encloses.

* *In a court of justice.*

22. a. The barrier or wooden rail marking off the immediate precinct of the judge's seat, at which prisoners are stationed for arraignment, trial, or sentence.

a **1400** *Cov. Myst.* 314 Brynge forthe to the barre that arn to be dempt. **1480** CAXTON *Chron. Eng.* VII. (1520) 102/2 He was ledde to barre before the kinges justyces. **1613** SHAKS. *Hen. VIII*, II. i. 12 The great Duke Came to the Bar; where, to his accusations He pleaded still not guilty. **1845** DISRAELI *Sybil* 266 Hurried like a criminal to the bar of a police-office.

b. *fig.* A tribunal, *e.g.* that of reason, public opinion, conscience.

c **1375** WYCLIF *Serm.* Sel. Wks. 1871 II. 186 Ech man mote nedis stonde at þe barre bifore Crist. **1594** SHAKS. *Rich. III*, V. iii. 199 All seuerall sinnes, all vs'd in each degree, Throng all to' th' Barre, crying all, Guilty, Guilty. **1665** GLANVILL *Sceps. Sci.* xiv. 88 When self is at the bar, the sentence is not like to be impartial. **1724** WATTS *Logic* II. iii. §4 (1822) 236 Calling all the principles of our younger years to the bar of maturer reason. **1837** CARLYLE *Fr. Rev.* I. I. iv. 24 The Judgment-bar of the Most High God.

23. a. This barrier, as the place at which all the business of the court was transacted, soon became synonymous with: Court; *esp.* in phr. ***at*** (***the***) ***bar***: in court, in open court. ***trial at bar***: a trial before the full court in which the action or indictment is brought; in England, the Queen's Bench Division.

c **1330** in *Pol. Songs* 339 Countours in benche that stondeth at the barre, Theih wolen bigile the. **1393** LANGL. *P. Pl.* C. I. 160 Seriauntes hij semede · þat seruen atte barre. **1460** CAPGRAVE *Chron.* 222 This ȝere [1362] was ordeyned that alle plees at the barre schuld be in Englisch tunge. **1550** CROWLEY *Last Trump.* 911 Thou wilt stand at a barre ballyng. **1656** COWLEY *Pind. Odes* Wks. I. 228 Thou neither great..at th' Exchange shalt be, nor at the wrangling Bar. **1689** *Tryal Bps.*, We are very desirous it should be tryed at Bar. **1803** J. MARSHALL *Const. Opin.* (1839) 2 These principles have been very ably argued at the bar. **1866** *N. & Q.* Ser. III. IX. 449/2 The first instance of a trial at bar has just occurred at Melbourne.

b. A (particular) court of law, *esp.* in the phr. ***to practise at*** (***such a***) ***bar***. [Compare 25–26.]

1559 [see 25]. **1583** STUBBES *Anat. Abus.* II. 16 Notwithstanding that they [lawiers] can be present but at one barre at once, yet will they take diuers fees of sundry clients to speake for them at three or foure places in one day. **1723** *Lond. Gaz.* No. 6211/2 They went to the Exchequer Bar. **1841** ORDERSON *Creol.* xiv. 152 Who was..expected out to practise at the Barbados bar. **1844** LD. BROUGHAM *Brit. Const.* xix. §6 (1862) 360, I have practised at the bar of the House of Lords.

** *In the Inns of Court.*

†**24.** A barrier or partition separating the seats of the benchers or readers from the rest of the hall, to which students, after they had attained a certain standing, were 'called' from the body of the hall, for the purpose of taking a principal part in the mootings or exercises of the house. *Obs.* See BARRISTER. Hence the phrases:—***to be called to the bar***: to be admitted a barrister. †***to cast over the bar***: to deprive of the status of a barrister, to disbar; *gen.* to reject.

After 1600, when utter-barristers, as well as sergeants and apprentices-at-law were allowed to plead in the law-courts, *bar* in these phrases seems to have been popularly assumed to mean the bar in a court of justice, outside of which ordinary barristers appear to plead, while King's Counsel and Sergeants-at-Law have places within it. Hence the mod. phrase ***to be called within the bar***: to be appointed King's (or Queen's) Counsel.

c **1545** [See BARRISTER]. **1574** N. BACON *Order of Council* [regulating proc. of Inns of Court] in *Penny Cycl.* III. 504 That none be called to the utter bar but by the ordinary council of the House..in term time. **1608** *2nd Pt. Def. Reas. Refus. Subscr.* 160 His note that Zanchy maketh no doubt.. maie be caste over the barre. **1625** K. LONG tr. *Barclay's Argenis* III. xxii. 221 If any Clyent bribeth..the Lawier that receiveth, shall be cast over the Barre. **1650** B. *Discollim.* 48, I was call'd to the Barre six yeares agoe. **1701** LUTTRELL *Brief Rel.* (1857) V. 69 A Yorkshire attorney..had his gown pulled off, and he thrown over the bar, for disobeying the rules of that court. **1768** BLACKSTONE *Comm.* III. xxviii, These [barristers having patents of precedence]..rank promiscuously with the king's counsel, and together with them sit within the bar of the respective courts. **1864** TENNYSON *Aylmer's F.* 59 A year or two before Call'd to the bar. **1885** *Law Jrnl.* 13 June 364/1 That his Royal Highness Prince Albert Victor of Wales be called to the degree of the Utter Bar.

25. a. The whole body of barristers, or *spec.* the barristers practising in a particular court, circuit, or country. (Cf. 23 b.)

1559 *Ord. Judges* in Dugdale *Orig. Jurid.* (1671) 310 That an exhortation should be given to the utter Barr that none should come to any Barr at Westminster..under ten years continuance. **1695** *Pol. Ballads* (1860) II. 50 The Bar, the Pulpit and the Press Nefariously combine. **1864** *Times* 4 Nov., The dinner to be given by the English Bar to M. Berryer.

b. The counsel retained in a particular case.

1891 E. KINGLAKE *Australian at Home* 36 He had as strong a Bar as could be retained on his side. **1892** *Daily News* 25 Mar. 5/2 There has rarely been such a Bar in any modern case, either for quantity or for quality. Sir Charles Russell, the Attorney-General, the Solicitor-General, Sir Henry James, Mr. Inderwick, and Mr. Tindal Atkinson were but a few of them.

26. *abstractly* (combining 23 and 24): Occupation as counsel in a court of justice; the profession of a barrister.

1632 MASS. & FIELD *Fatal Dowry* I. ii, Your fees are boundless at the bar. **1709** STEELE & ADD. *Tatler* No. 101 ¶1

A Lawyer, who leaves the Bar for Chamber-Practice. **1770** LANGHORNE *Plutarch* (1879) II. 586/2 He cultivated oratory, most particularly that of the bar. **1879** FROUDE *Cæsar* viii. 84 He chose the bar for his profession.

*** *In legislative assemblies.*

27. The rail or barrier dividing from the body of the house a space near the door, to which non-members may be admitted for business purposes.

*a***1577** SIR T. SMITH *Commw. Eng.* II. ii, They [the Commons] coming all with him [the Speaker] to a bar which is at the nether end of the upper house. **1790** BURKE *Fr. Rev.* 349 Giving an account of his government at the bar of the same assembly. **1849** MACAULAY *Hist. Eng.* I. 520 The people of Bristol..sent up a deputation which was heard at the bar of the Commons.

**** *In an inn, or other place of refreshment.*

28. a. A barrier or counter, over which drink (or food) is served out to customers, in an inn, hotel, or tavern, and hence, in a coffee-house, at a railway-station, etc.; *also*, the space behind this barrier, and sometimes the whole apartment containing it.

1592 GREENE *Art Conny Catch.* III. 20 He was acquainted with one of the seruants..of whom he could haue two pennyworth of Rose-water for a peny..wherefore he would step to the barre vnto him. **1601** SHAKS. *Twel. N.* I. iii. 74 Bring your hand to'th Buttry barre, and let it drinke. **1712** ADDISON *Spect.* No. 403 ¶9, [I] laid down my Penny at the Barr..and made the best of my way to Cheapside. **1835** MARRYAT *Jac. Faith.* xii, He sees the girl in the bar. **1837** HAWTHORNE *Amer. Note-bks.* (1871) I. 42 A bottle of champagne was quaffed at the bar.

b. With defining word: a shop counter at which a particular item or group of items is sold. orig. *U.S.*

1954 *Word Study* Feb. 4/1 In a New Jersey suburban town someone has opened what she calls 'Mi-Lady's Corset Bar'. From its wares mi-lady probably gets food for thought. **1965** *Harper's Bazaar* May 27 The..stocking bar.

IV. *Comb.* and *Attrib.*

29. General relations, chiefly attrib.; **a.** In sense 1, as ***bar-lock, -magnet.*** **b.** In senses 23–26, as ***bar-anecdote, -oratory.***

a. 1828 F. WATKINS *Electro-Magnetism* 18 A fundamental principle of magnetism may be shown by freely suspending on its centre of gravity an artificial bar magnet. **1831** J. HOLLAND *Manuf. Metal* I. 118 The new bar-suspension-bridge. **1860** TYNDALL *Glac.* I. §40. 141 The exact polar arrangement of an ordinary bar-magnet. **1875** 'STONEHENGE' *Brit. Sports* I. I. xi. §1 The back-actioned lock does not speak so well as the old bar-lock.

b. 1755 CARTE *Hist. Eng.* IV. 330 The habitual chicanes of bar-oratory. **1820** (*title*) Cut and Come again, or Humorous Bar Anecdotes.

c. In sense 28, as ***bar-board, -boy, -counter, -girl, -loafer*** (hence ***-loafing*** adj.), ***-person, -snack, -staff, -stool, -window***; **bar-room, -parlour,** BARMAID, -MAN.

1723 MRS. CENTLIVRE *Gotham Elect.* I. 158 Zome that like your Port Wines still, but very few..as my Bar-board can witness. **1631** HEYWOOD *Maid of West* Wks. 1874 II. 276 The next Vintage I hope to be Barre-boy. **1842** DICKENS *Amer. Notes* I. vi. 218 He finishes by leaping gloriously upon the bar-counter, and calling for something to drink. **1945** KOESTLER *Twilight Bar* I (*stage direction*) At front, left, semicircular bar counter with high bar-stools. **1857** C. KINGSLEY *Two Y. Ago* III. vi. 165 The bar girl, who knew his humour, came forward. **1870** D. J. KIRWAN *Palace & Hovel* (1963) viii. 82 A little girl, with a bold face..acted as a bar-girl. **1963** *Times Lit. Suppl.* 19 Apr. 262/4 Changes in postwar Japan: the popularity of 'bar-girls', the modern substitute for geisha. **1968** *Listener* 23 May 657/1 Few Americans now are seen in central Saigon;..respectable girls will now venture down Tu Do Street, which the bar girls have abandoned. **1889** G. B. SHAW in *Star* 30 Aug. 2/3 The mere bar loafers at these concerts. *Ibid.* 20 Sept. 2/5 The horse-collar bar-loafing buffoonery. **1976** *Evening Standard* 14 June 25/8 (Advt.), Bar person, experienced, required... Barperson required. **1982** *Financial Times* 8 May 9/1 Shop assistants seem more inclined to perform their function, bar persons and patrons more disposed to know you, and at petrol pumps your number plate..attracts suitable comment. **1959** in W. R. Bawden *Tankard Trails* (Charles Wells Ltd.) 96 (Advt.), The Peacock Hotel Mill Street Bedford Bar lunches & snacks. **1969** in *Ibid.* 93 (Advt.), The Duke Inn Kempston... Bar snacks at all times. **1978** *Morecambe Guardian* 14 Mar. 14 (Advt.), Bar snacks and basket meals available. **1986** *N.Y. Times* 29 June X17/6 Lattice House is a recently restored timber-framed pub... Serves real ale, a lunch menu and bar snacks in the evening. **1965** J. H. COOMBS *Bar Service* p. ix, Although primarily written for learner bar-staff this manual can be equally valuable to prospective brewery Tenants. **1986** *Financial Times* 24 Sept. I. 17/4 About 100,000 club stewards and bar staff in public houses and clubs learnt yesterday that they face a pay cut before Christmas. **1922** JOYCE *Ulysses* 446 Bob Doran, toppling from a high bar-stool, sways over the munching spaniel. **1857** HUGHES *Tom Brown* I. iv, The red curtains of the bar-window.

30. Special combinations: **bar-armature** *Electr. Engin.*, a bar-wound armature; **bar-bell,** a steel bar weighted with a ball of iron at each end, used as a dumb-bell; **bar billiards,** a variation of billiards popular in bars and public houses, in which points are scored by striking the object balls into holes in the table, and penalties incurred if the wooden pegs that stand near the holes are knocked over; **bar-boat,** (*a*) one marking the position of a bar (sense 15); (*b*) a boat adapted for carrying goods across the bar of a river; **bar-boy,** a boy employed to fix and clean the fire-bars of a locomotive engine; **bar-button,** one in the shape of a bar; **bar chart** = *bar diagram* below; **bar-code,** a machine-readable code consisting of a series of alternating lines and spaces of varying width, used esp. for stock control; cf. *Universal Product Code* s.v. UNIVERSAL *a.* 14; hence as *v. trans.*, to mark or provide with a bar-code; also **bar-coded,** *ppl. a.*, **bar-coding** *vbl. sb.*; **bar-cutter,** a shearing machine for cutting metallic bars into lengths; a shearing-machine for cutting metallic bars into lengths; a workman who passes the metal through the machine; **bar diagram,** a statistical diagram in which numerical quantities are represented by the height or length of rectangles of equal width, drawn usu. side by side along an axis; **bar-diggings** (see quot.); **bar-fee** (see quot.); **bar-fly,** a frequenter of bars; **bar-frame,** the frame which supports the metallic bars of a furnace; **bar-frame** (or **-framed**) *a.*, of a bee-hive: fitted with bars instead of sections; †**bar-gate,** a barrier-gate; also *fig.* (cf. sense 14); **bar-gemel** (see 6); **bar-gown,** a lawyer's gown, *fig.* a lawyer; **bar graph** = *bar diagram* above; **bar-head(ed goose,** a goose found in India and Central Asia, *Anser indicus*; **bar-hive,** a bar-framed beehive; **bar-iron,** iron wrought into malleable bars; **bar-keel,** one composed of rectangular bars of iron or steel; **bar-keep** *U.S.*, a bar-keeper (for refreshments); **bar-keeper,** one who keeps or manages a bar for refreshments, who keeps a toll-bar, or keeps guard at a barrier; **bar-movement,** a type of watch movement in which the upper pivots are carried in bars; **bar-parlour,** a small room adjoining the bar of a public-house; **bar-pin** (see sense 11); **bar-point,** the point or division nearest the bar in the outer 'table' of a backgammon board; **bar-post,** the post which receives the ends of movable bars used instead of a gate; **bar-room,** the public room containing the bar in a tavern or hotel, a tap-room; also *attrib.*; **bar-share plough,** one with a bar extending backward from the point of the share; **bar-shear** (= *bar-cutter*); **bar-shoe,** a horse-shoe with a bar across the hinder part to protect the tender frog of the heel; **bar-shot,** a double shot consisting of two half cannon-balls joined by an iron bar, used in sea-warfare to injure masts and rigging; **bar-silver,** silver in bars (cf. 3); so **bar-tin**; **bar-soap,** soap made up into bars as distinguished from soap in cakes or tablets; also *attrib.*; **bar-super** (see quot.); **bar tacker** (see quot.); so *bar tack, -tacking*; **bar-tailed godwit**: see GODWIT; **bar-tracery** (see quot.); **bar-way,** a passage into a field, closed by movable horizontal bars fitted into vertical posts; **bar-ways, -wise** *adv.*, in the manner of a bar; **bar winding** *Electr. Engin.*, an armature-winding consisting of metal bars; **bar-wound** *a.*, of an armature: fitted with bars instead of wires.

1888 S. P. THOMPSON *Dynamo-Electric Machinery* (ed. 3) 646 (*Index*) *Bar Armatures. **1904** GOODCHILD & TWENEY *Technol. & Sci. Dict.* 40/1 *Bar armature*, a large armature in which the windings are built up of copper bars instead of continuous wire. **1887** *Hour Glass* I. 17 A complete set of dumb-bell, *bar-bell, marching and running exercises. **1895** *Cal. Univ. Nebraska 1895–6* 252 The gymnasium..is well equipped with clubs, wands, bar bells, and dumb bells. **1966** T. FINN *Watney Bk. Pub Games* iii. 21 *Bar billiards is of French origin, reaching this country some years ago, and spreading steadily from urban to rural areas. **1969** J. WAINWRIGHT *Take-over Men* viii. 136 Doing!.. What the hell d'you think I'm doing? Playing bar-billiards? **1982** *Financial Times* 3 Apr. I. 15/2 It is hard to imagine some of the other games—bar billiards, eight-ball pool, shove-ha'penny—working very well on the small screen. **1857** C. GRIBBLE in *Merc. Mar. Mag.* (1858) V. 4 The *Bar-boat on he C. W. Bar. **1883** MOLONEY *W. African Fisheries* 17 (Fish. Exhib. Publ.) Bar-boats of seven to eight tons have been used at Lagos. **1897** M. KINGSLEY *W. Africa* 635 [It is] too bad a bar for boats to cross; but a steamer on the Lagos bar boat plan might manage it. **1881** M. REYNOLDS *Engine Driv.* 7 A *bar-boy..has to creep through the fire-hole door of the engine..to arrange the fire-bars, etc. **1685** *Lond. Gaz.* No. 2072/4 And *bar Buttons on the Coat sleeves. **1914** *Engin. Mag.* Nov. 229/2 The horizontal scale for this curve is exactly the same as for the *bar chart above. **1935** *N.Y. Times* 15 Sept. x. 6/4 Curves and bar charts are not easily remembered because the reader has seen other curves and bars..showing totally different facts. **1962** A. BATTERSBY *Guide to Stock Control* iii. 26 We can draw a conventional 'bar-chart' or 'histogram' as in Fig. 9 by first grouping the figures into classes or 'slices' of the same range. **1985** *Which Computer?* Apr. 53/3 The word processor, for example, can leave space in a document for a bar chart produced by the spreadsheet. **1963** W. J. BIJLEVELD *Automatic Reading of Digits* vi. 47 Addressograph-Multigraph suggests the use of digits with an external *bar code... The digits with their bar-code to match are shown in fig. 67. **1970** O. DOPPING *Computers & Data Processing* iii. 62 Certain cash registers can record a machine-readable bar code on the internal control tape with ink. **1978** *Publishers Weekly* 10 Apr. 36 The Council of Periodical Distributors has asked mass market publishers to..'bar-code' their books, so that distributors will be able to provide sales and returns information to publishers with greater speed. **1980** C. S. FRENCH *Computer Sci.* xv. 85 Optical reading is done by using printed 'bar-codes'; ie alternating lines and spaces which represent data in binary. **1982** *Times* 23 Apr. 23/2 Manufacturers are bar-coding enough goods to make laser scanning an attractive commercial proposition. **1984** *Listener* 5 July 20/1 Have you ever tried to..talk to Ms. E. Budworth..about ISBN numbers and barcodes? **1973** *Bar-coded [see *light pen* s.v. LIGHT *sb.* 16]. **1983** *Listener* 29 Sept. 38/4 With your special receiver and bar-coded *Radio Times*, you move a light-pen over the code for a selected programme. **1977** *Grocer* 3 Sept. 75/3 Article numbering and *bar coding will offer..important benefits in terms of more efficient stock control. **1980** *Daily Tel.* 14 July 18/4 Bar-coding does away with the costly business of pricing each individual item and provides the customer with a print-out at the till of what was purchased. *a***1877** KNIGHT *Dict. Mech.* II. 229/2 **Bar-cutter* (Metal-working), a shearing-machine which cuts metallic bars into lengths. **1904** *Westm. Gaz.* 13 June 7/2 He gives bar-cutters an advance of a halfpenny per ton. **1923** R. PEARL *Med. Biometry & Statistics* vi. 109 *Bar diagrams find perhaps their most appropriate field of usefulness in the graphic representation of *discontinuous* variates. **1956** *Biometrika* XXXXIII. 245 He illustrated his *British Family Antiquity* with several beautifully executed bar diagrams... This type of diagram, Playfair conceded, had long been used in chronology. **1881** RAYMOND *Mining Gloss.*, **Bar-diggings*, gold-washing claims located on the bars (shallows) of a stream. **1641** *Termes de la Ley* 38 **Barre fee* is a fee of twenty pence, which every prisoner acquitted of Felony payes to the Gaoler. **1910** *Sat. Even. Post* 16 July 5/2 Then, after having confessed to so much money, he hastened out, for he wud not be stung by *bar-flies. **1932** C. ISHERWOOD *Memorial* III. ii. 201 A small market-town, inhabited by commercial travellers,..and other bar-flies. **1944** AUDEN *For Time Being* (1945) 80 The pay-off lines of limericks in which The weak resentful bar-fly shows his sting. **1881** *Gardening Illustr.* 7 May 123/3 There would be no difficulty whatever in putting swarms of bees into a *bar-frame hive, provided it has a movable top and floor-board. **1892** Bar frame [see SUPER *sb.* 4]. **1906** *Daily Chron.* 18 June 6/6 Bar-frame beehives. *Ibid.* 1 Sept. 6/4 Bar-framed hives. **1600** HOLLAND *Livy* VI. ix. 222 Those two townes stood even against Hetruria, as it were the very keies and *bar-gates [*claustra*] from thence. **1631** WEEVER *Anc. Fun. Mon.* 574 Valiantly defending..the Barre-yates and entrance into the Towne. **1664** BUTLER *Hud.* II. III. 16 Others believe no Voice t' an Organ; So sweet as Lawyer's in his *Bar-gown. **1682** N. O. *Boileau's Lutrin* I. 4 Troops of Barr-gowns rang'd under her Banner. **1925** B. F. YOUNG *Statistics in Business* xxx. 316 *Bar-graphs in the form of progress charts are used to represent a changing condition such as the output of a factory. **1952** MONKHOUSE & WILKINSON *Maps & Diagrams* i. 27 *Columnar diagrams*, sometimes known as bar-graphs, consist of a series of columns or bars proportional in length to the quantities they represent. **1978** *Gramophone* June 122/3 This makes it possible to produce a real-time bar-graph frequency analysis in octave bands displayed on an ordinary television set. **1924** *Glasgow Herald* 29 July 8 The *barhead goose and the ruddy sheldrak collect in flocks on the Tibetan swamps. **1879** *Encycl. Brit.* X. 777/2 The *Bar-headed Goose (*Anser indicus*). **1884** PHIN *Dict. Apiculture* 70 *Bars*, strips of wood to which combs are attached, and from which they hang in *bar-hives. **1677** YARRANTON *Eng. Improv.* 57 Infinite quantities of Raw Iron..with *Bar Iron and Wire. **1860** H. STUART *Seaman's Catech.* 59 The best bar-iron is obtained from Sweden. **1874** THEARLE *Naval Archit.* (Adv. Sc. ser.) IV. xvii. 268 The *Bar Keel..is generally of hammered iron, made in pieces as long as can be conveniently forged. **1846** *Spirit of Times* (N.Y.) 4 July 218/2 We embarked..in company with..a **barkeep* to mix the l-q-rs. **1902** KIPLING *Captive* in *Traffics & Discoveries* (1904) 8 Take away his hair and his gun and he'd make a first-class Schenectady bar-keep. **1918** H. A. VACHELL *Some Happenings* i. 2 Hobo listened attentively to the bar-keep. **1712** STEELE *Spect.* No. 534 ¶5, I am..*bar-keeper of a coffee-house. **1748** SMOLLETT *Rod. Rand.* xxiv. (1804) 160 She..was hired in the quality of bar-keeper. **1818** SCOTT *Hrt. Midl.* xxi, Securing, through his interest with the bar-keepers and macers, a seat for Deans. **1883** *Harper's Mag.* 820/2 The firm of barkeepers. **1903** F. J. GARRARD *Watch Repairing* i. 1 To describe, in general terms, the mechanism of a watch ..a Geneva '*bar' movement will be used as an illustration ..as its 'bar' construction enables all the wheelwork to be seen. **1962** E. BRUTON *Dict. Clocks & Watches* 21 *Bar movement*, early form of partly machine-made watch movement in which bars, or bridges and cocks, are used to hold bearings for one pivot of each wheel, for easy dismantling. **1876** E. JENKINS *Queen's H.* 4 To hold meetings in the *bar-parlour and the coffee-room. **1611** COTGR., *Empeigne*, the *barre-pinnes of a peece of caske. **1743** HOYLE *Back-gammon* ii. 10 The next best Point (after you have gained your *Cinq.* Point) is to make your **Barr* Point. **1870** Bar-point [see POINT *sb.*[1] B. 3g]. **1797** J. HILTZHEIMER *Diary* 28 July (1893) 245 Seider's contrivance for bringing water from a spring in his garden, through pipes into his *bar-room. **1809** KENDALL *Trav.* III. lxxx. 231 The bar-room of a public-house is what in England is called a tap-room. **1839** 'MRS. MARY CLAVERS' *New Home* i. 9 When my husband..drew with a piece of chalk on the bar-room table at Danforth's the plan of a village. **1844** DICKENS *Mar. Chuz.* xvi, Major Pawkins proposed an adjournment to a neighbouring bar-room. **1946** AUDEN *Introd.* in H. James *Amer. Scene* p. v, One can easily imagine Stendhal or Tolstoi or Dostoievsky becoming involved in a bar-room fight, but James, never. **1954** *Encounter* Mar. 19/1 Those women in Western movies who share the hero's understanding of life are prostitutes (or, as they are usually presented, bar-room entertainers). **1831** YOUATT *Horse* xx. (1872) 437 A *bar-shoe is the common shoe with the heels carried round to meet each other, thus forming a bar. **1832** MISS MITFORD *Village* Ser. v. (1863) 343 Colman thinks it's only a prick..and advises one of his bar shoes. **1756** *Gentl. Mag.* XXVI. 506 The great quantity of *bar-shot..which the French fired in upon us, tore our sails. **1824** *Catawba Jrnl.* (N.C.) 26 Oct. 10 [dozen] *Bar Soap. **1872** 'MARK TWAIN' *Roughing It* iv. 41 A piece of yellow bar-soap. **1893** EARL DUNMORE *Pamirs* I. 64 Some common yellow bar-soap. **1906** *Westm. Gaz.* 25 Oct. 7/2 Bar-soap sellers. **1884**

PHIN *Dict. Apiculture* 70 A *bar super is simply a case or crate in which the honeycomb is hung from bars. **1921** *Dict. Occup. Terms* (1927) §419 **Bar tacker*, baists or tacks round button-holes of tailored garments, to keep parts together before holes are cut. **1955** J. E. LIBERTY *Pract. Tailoring* (ed. 2) xi. 204 The Bar Tack is usually done with buttonhole twist. A bar of two or three stitches is formed... It is then worked with a small over stitching from end to end. **1959** J. YATES-BENYOW *Weak & Wicked* x. 151 Other unfamiliar-sounding occupations necessary for the output of up-to-date off-the-peg clothing—..bar-tacking. **1828** J. FLEMING *Hist. Brit. Animals* 107 L. *rufa*. *Bar-tailed Godwit.—All the tail-feathers with black and white bands. **1981** J. GOODERS *Bird Seekers' Guide* 106 About 40,000 bar-tailed godwits winter in Britain, mostly in the north-west and east on the larger estuaries. **1746** HANWAY *Trav.* (1762) I. v. lxxiii. 336 A quantity of *bar tin. **1861** PARKER *Goth. Archit.* (1874) 319 **Bar-tracery*, window-tracery which distinguishes Gothic work, resembling more a bar of iron twisted into various forms than stone. **1572** BOSSEWELL *Armorie* II. 130 A Bores head..betwene two dartes *barwaies. **1903** F. B. DE GRESS tr. *Arnold's Armature Windings* 86 The author uses this kind of *bar winding for 4-pole and other multipolar lighting generators using notched armatures. **1907** HOBART & ELLIS *Armature Construction* ix. 227 In such cases it is more usual to carry out the winding as a 'bar winding', where the conductors or bars are slipped into the slots from the end, and then connected up into coils by means of separate V-end connectors all the same size and shape. **1864** BOUTELL *Heraldry Hist. & Pop.* vii. 33 A Riband crossing the shield *bar-wise. **1902** *Encycl. Brit.* XXVII. 583/2 If, however, the current in each conductor is large, the drum armature must be *bar-wound. **1940** *Chambers's Techn. Dict.* 76/1 *Bar-wound armature*, an armature with large sectioned conductors which are insulated and fixed in position and connected, in contrast with former-wound conductors which are sufficiently thin to be inserted, after shaping in a suitable jig.

†**bar**, *sb.*² *Obs. rare.* [a. OF. *bar*, *ber* (also *bars*, *bers*):—late L. *bāro* (also *bārus*), from the acc. of which, *bārōnem*, came OF. *baron* BARON.] By-form of BARON.

1297 R. GLOUC. 544 Ech bar him..out of toune drou.

bar, *sb.*³ [a. F. *bar* 'the fish called a Base' (Cotgr.)] A large acanthopterygious European fish (*Sciæna aquila*), also known as the *maigre*.

1724 DE FOE, etc. *Tour Gt. Brit.* (1769) III. 341 [In Jersey is found] the Bar, an exquisite Fish, sometimes two feet in length. **1863** *Life in Norm.* I. 166, I sold them all, except one nice bar and a brill.

bar *sb.*⁴ (= G. *berg*): see BARMASTER, BARMOTE.

bar *sb.*⁵ *U.S.* Short for *mosquito bar.* (Cf. MOSQUITO 2 b.) Cf. BEAR *sb.*⁶

1847 C. LANMAN *Summer in Wilderness* xxiv. 143 Had I not taken with me..bar netting..the creatures would have eaten me. **1866** J. C. GREGG *Life in Army* xv. 140 Nothing can exceed the luxury of lying down inside your 'bars' of a midsummer night, and feeling secure from their voracious bills. **1894** 'MARK TWAIN' *Those Twins* 415 Get their bed ready..and see that you drive all the mosquitoes out of their bar.

bar (bɑː(r)), *sb.*⁶ [f. Gr. βάρος weight; cf. ISOBAR.]

1. A unit of pressure equivalent to one dyne per square centimetre.

1903 RICHARDS & STULL *New Method determining Compressibility* 43 Might not the pressure of a dyne per square centimeter be suitably called a *bar*?

2. A unit of barometric pressure equivalent to a pressure of 29·53 inches or 750·1 mm. of mercury at 0° C. in latitude 45°. (See also quot. 1918.)

1910 V. BJERKNES et al. *Dynamic Meteorol. & Hydrography* I. i. 7 It will be necessary for us to have names for the employed units of pressure..some name derived from the word 'barometer'. We shall choose the name *bar* as being the shortest, and designate the decimal parts of it as the decibar, centibar, and millibar. *Ibid.*, We find that 1 meter of mercury at 0° C. at a place where gravity has this standard value exerts the pressure of 1·333193 bars. **1914** *Q. Jrnl. R. Meteorol. Soc.* Apr. 160, I [*sc.* Bjerknes] therefore coined the terms 'bar', 'decibar', 'centibar', and 'millibar', as names for the units of pressure... I employed these expressions for the first time in a paper published in 1906 [in *Beiträge zur Physik der freien Atmosphäre*, Strassburg]. **1917** A. MCADIE in *Ann. Astron. Observ. Harvard* LXXXIII. 47 The term millibar was unfortunately used by Bjerknes in his 'Dynamic Meteorology and Hydrography'. He defined the *bar* as a megadyne atmosphere, seemingly unaware of a prior use of the word by Richards and others in its proper sense. **1918** *Meteorol. Gloss.* 43 *Bar*..was introduced into practical meteorology by V. Bjerknes, and objection has been raised by McAdie..on the ground that the name had been previously appropriated by chemists to the C.G.S. unit of pressure, the dyne per square centimetre. The meteorological bar is thus one million chemical bars, and what chemists call a *bar* we should call a *microbar*.

bar (bɑː(r)), *v.* Forms: 4-7 **bare**, **barre**, 7 **barr**, 4- **bar**. Pa. t. and pple. **barred** (bɑːd), 5-6 **bard**. [ME. *barre-n*, a. OF. *barre-r* (12th c. in Littré), f. *barre* BAR *sb.*¹]

I. To make fast, fasten in, or out, with bars.

1. *trans.* **a.** To make fast (a door, etc.) by a bar or bars fixed across it; to fasten up or close (a place) with bars.

a **1300** *Cursor M.* 2788 Faste þe dores gon he bare. *c* **1400** *Destr. Troy* XIV. 6018 The Troiens..tyrnyt the ȝates, Barret hom bigly with barres of yrne. **1530** PALSGR. 444/1 He hath barred his wyndowes with yron in stede of lattesses. **1593** SHAKS. *Rich. II*, I. i. 180 A Iewell in a ten times barr'd vp Chest. **1611** BIBLE *Neh.* vii. 3 Shut the doores and barre them. **1769** FALCONER *Dict. Marine* (1789) *Bacler les ports*..to bar-in the gun-ports of a ship. **1876** GRANT *Burgh Sch.* II. v. 187 The scholars..barred the School against the master.

fig. **1633** P. FLETCHER *Purple Isl.* I. xvii, Their hearts with lead, with steel their sense is barr'd. *c* **1750** SHENSTONE *Ruin'd Ab.* 169 Heard..Heavn's decree With unremitting vengeance bar the skies. **1813** SCOTT *Rokeby* II. xi, Hearts..as marble hard, 'Gainst faith, and love, and pity barred.

†**b.** To surround with a barrier or fence. *Obs.*

c **1430** *Syr Tryam.* 1188 To the felde they farde, The place was barryd and dyght.

2. a. To fasten in, shut up, or confine securely (a person or thing) by means of bars. Also *transf.* and *fig.*

c **1460** *Towneley Myst.* 28, I was never bard ere..In sich an oostre as this. **1586** WARNER *Alb. Eng.* IV. xxii. (1597) 100 And bar him vp in walles. **1661** R. DAVENPORT *City Nt.-Cap* II. in Dodsl. *O.P.* (1780) XI. 297, I lock'd him Into my heart, and double-barr'd him there With reason and opinion. **1851** HT. MARTINEAU *Hist. Peace* (1877) III. IV. xii. 100 Some peasants barred themselves into the yard of a cottage. **1875** B. TAYLOR *Faust* II. iii. II. 127 Efficient bolts they are; The greatest wealth they safely bar!

b. *to bar out*: to shut out with a bar or bars.

c **1620** Z. BOYD *Zion's Flowers* (1855) 32 Yee grace barre out, and vanitie bolt in. **1680** ALLEN *Peace & Unity* 73 Sins..for which the Scripture doth expresly bar Men out of the Kingdom of Heaven. **1878** G. MACDONALD *Phantastes* iii. 17 Their crowded stems barred the sunlight out. [See BARRING *vbl. sb.*]

3. To close or obstruct (a way of approach) by some barrier; to block up, make impassable.

1596 SPENSER *F.Q.* I. viii. 13 With his bodie bard the way atwixt them twaine. **1673** TEMPLE *Ess. Irel.* Wks. 1731 I. 120 The Haven of Dublin is barr'd to that degree, as very much to obstruct the Trade of the City. **1855** KINGSLEY *Heroes* II. 213 Sciron..had barred the path with stones. **1876** GREEN *Short Hist.* i. §6 (1882) 49 The two forts with which the king barred the river.

fig. **1751** JOHNSON *Rambl.* No. 165 ¶2 The passes of the intellect are barred against her by prejudice and passion.

4. To obstruct, stop, or prevent (a person's progress, or a person in his progress).

1578 THYNNE *Let.* in *Animadv.* Introd. 59 Since I ame..barred bodely to approche your presence. **1588** SHAKS. *Tit. A.* I. i. 291 What villaine Boy, bar'st me my way in Rome? **1613** —— *Hen. VIII*, III. ii. 17 If you cannot Barre his accesse to th' king **1634** PRESTON *New Covt.* 25 Moses..[was] barred from coming into the land of Canaan. **1812** BYRON *Ch. Har.* II. lxix, Combined marauders half-way barred egress. **1878** B. TAYLOR *Deukalion* II. iv. 82 Bar with fire and steel her entrance.

5. *Law.* **a.** To arrest or stop (a person) by ground of legal objection from enforcing some claim.

1531 *Dial. Laws Eng.* II. xlix. (1638) 153 Such a warranty shall barre the heire. **1677** YARRANTON *Eng. Improv.* 15 Shall be a good Title to the Party Registring..and shall Barre all persons whatsoever. **1726** AYLIFFE *Parerg.* 158 Such Excommunication..shall not disable or bar his Adversary from his action. **1858** LD. ST. LEONARDS *Handy-bk. Prop. Law* XXIII. 182 For 20 years' possession by a third person will bar both you and them.

b. To stay or arrest (an action); to exclude or prevent the advancement of (a plea, claim, right.)

1552 HULOET, Barre an accion, *eximere actionem.* **1595** SHAKS. *John* II. i. 192 A Will, that barres the title of thy sonne. **1628** COKE *On Litt.* 372 b, If Tenant in taile..bee attainted of high treason, the estate taile is barred, and the Land is forfeited to the King. **1854** LADY LYTTON *Beh. Scenes* II. II. §12. 222 Settling a nominal sum on her to bar dower. **1884** *Law Rep.* Chanc. Div. XXVII. 530 The Plaintiff's right to set [the deed] aside is barred by laches.

6. a. To hinder, exclude, keep back, prevent, prohibit (a person) *from*; to deprive or debar *of.*

1551 WILSON *Logike* Ep. A ij b, From the which they have beene heretofore barred by tongues unacquainted. **1579** A. M[UNDAY] in Arb. *Garner* I. 207 Not to be barred of his enterprise. **1668** CHILD *Disc. Trade* (1694) 118, I know not why any should be barred from trading to those places. **1678** R. LESTRANGE *Seneca's Mor.* (1702) 275 A Disease..barrs us of some Pleasures, but procures us others. **1864** TENNYSON *Aylmer's F.* 505 Last from her own home-circle of the poor They barr'd her. **1870** BRYANT *Homer* XVI. II. 120 Lest the enemy seize our ships, and we Be barred of our return.

b. with *double object. arch.*

1577 HANMER *Anc. Eccl. Hist.* (1619) 174 He goeth about to barre us our liberty of meeting. **1597** SHAKS. *2 Hen. IV*, II. iv. 110, I will barre no honest man my house. **1692** R. LESTRANGE *Josephus' Answ. Apion* II. (1733) 867 If they had, they would never have barr'd themselves the Comfort. **1855** SINGLETON *Virgil* I. 328 For Fates Bar Helenus the knowledge of the rest.

†**c.** with *inf. phrase. Obs.*

c **1555** HARPSFIELD *Divorce Hen. VIII* (1878) 224 Is there anything here that barreth those that be under the patriarch of Alexandria..to appeal to the see apostolic? **1622** DEKKER *Virg. Mart.* II. i. Wks. 1873 IV. 25 She will not bar yeomen sprats to have their swinge.

d. *absolutely*

1583 STANYHURST *Aeneis* I. (Arb.) 34 For to shakhands freendly fear bars. **1624** BEDELL *Lett.* iv. 73 Errours..deadly, and such as barre from saluation.

7. To stop, hinder, prevent, prohibit (an action or event).

1559 *Myrr. Mag.*, *Dk. Clarence* lvi. 7 Yll dedes our destinies may barre. **1595** SPENSER *Sonn.* xliv, Orpheus with his harp theyr strife did bar. **1697** DRYDEN *Virg. Georg* I. 600 Ridgy Roofs..can scarce avail To barr the Ruin of the rattling Hail. **1822** T. TAYLOR *Apuleius' Gold. Ass* VI. 132 Having barred the barking of the dog by..the remaining sop. **1865** TYLOR *Early Hist. Man.* xiii. 363 They bar marriage in the female line.

8. To exclude from consideration, set aside.

1481–90 [see BARRING *prep.*]. **1596** SHAKS. *Merch. V.* II. ii. 208 Nay but I barre to night, you shall not gage me By what we doe to night. **1648** HERRICK *Hesper.* I. 225 When next thou do'st invite, barre state, And give me meate. **1718** *Free-thinker* No. 95. 287, I once more bar all Widowers. **1809** SYD. SMITH *Wks.* (1859) I. 176/1 We bar, in this discussion, any objection which proceeds, etc.

9. a. To take exception to, object to.

1611 BEAUM & FL. *Philaster* II. 25 Good Prince, be not bawdy, nor do not brag; these two I bar. **1808** WOLCOTT (P. Pindar) *One more Peep* Wks. 1812 V. 355 They call thee a fine China jar: But this I humbly beg to bar. **1903** WODEHOUSE *Prefect's Uncle* i. 11, I bar the man. He's slimy. **1913** C. MACKENZIE *Sinister St.* I. II. xvii. 435 Why, my dear girl, he's absolutely barred. He's as unpopular as anybody I know.

†**b.** *to bar the dice*: to declare the throw void. Cf. F. *barrer* 'annoncer, quand les dés sortent du cornet, qu'on annule le coup' (Littré). *Obs.* See also BARRED (*dice*).

1673 DRYDEN *Amboyna* II. i, He would have whip'd it up, as his own Fees..but that his Lord bar'd the Dice, and reckon'd it to him for a part of his Board Wages.

II. To mark with or make into bars.

10. To mark with a bar or bars, *e.g.* with stripes of colour, the 'bar' in music, etc. Cf. BARRED.

c **1340** [see BARRED]. *c* **1430** *Syr Gener.* 5636 His shelde was..Barred of asure and of sable. *c* **1440** *Promp. Parv.* 24 Barren harnes, *stipo.* **1789** BURNEY *Hist. Mus.* I. i. 7 Some of the letters were also barred..in order to change their symbolical import. **1821** KEATS *Lamia* 50 Eyed like a peacock, and all crimson barr'd. **1878** GURNEY *Crystallog.* 12 When either *h* or *l* is barred.

11. To make into bars.

1712 *Act 10 Anne* in *Lond. Gaz.* No. 5022/2 All gilt and silver Wire, and Bars..and all..Utensils for barring or drawing such Wire.

12. *to bar a vein* in *Farriery*: to disengage the vein of a horse, and tie it above and below a portion which is to be operated upon.

1753 CHAMBERS *Cycl. Supp.* App. s.v., When horses have got traverse mules, or kibed heels..it is common to barr a vein.

bar (bɑː(r)), *prep.* [f. BAR *v.*, either in imperative, or simple stem; prob. after *except*, *save*: cf. BARRING, *excepting*, *saving*.] **a.** Excluding from consideration, excepting, except, save, but for. ***bar none***, with no exceptions.

[Cf. **1648** in BAR *v.* 8.] **1714** MANDEVILLE *Fab. Bees* (1725) I. 306 Charity-boys..that swear and curse..and, bar the cloaths, are as much blackguard as ever Tower-hill..produc'd. **1727** SWIFT *To Sheridan* Wks. 1745 VIII. 348, I intended to be with you at Michaelmas, bar impossibilities. **1866** M. E. BRADDON *Lady's Mile* (ed. 4) II. vi. 192 Your 'Aspasia' is the greatest picture that ever was painted—'bar none', as Mr. Lobyer would say. **1870** *Standard* 14 Dec., This sortie, bar miracles, has decided the fate of Paris.

b. Esp. in *Betting*, indicating the number of horses excluded from odds being offered.

1860 HOTTEN *Slang Dict.* (ed. 2), *Bar*,..in common use in the betting-ring; 'I bet against the field bar two'. **1874** *Ibid.* (ed. 3) s.v., 'Two to one bar one', *i.e.*, two to one against any horse with the exception of one.

Bar, obs. abbreviation of BARONET; now *Bart.*

1720 *Lond. Gaz.* No. 5906/8 Sir Joseph Hodges, Bar.

bar, obs. or dial. f. BEAR barley, and of BOAR.

bar, obs. pa. t. of BEAR *v.* and BORE *v.*

baracan, -couta, var. BARRACAN, -CUDA.

baræsthesiometer (ˌbærɛsθiːsɪˈɒmɪtə(r)). Also bares-. [f. Gr. βάρος weight + αἴσθησις perception + -OMETER.] An instrument for measuring the sense of pressure. Hence **ˌbaræsthesioˈmetric** *a.*

1876 H. POWER tr. *von Ziemssen's Cycl. Med.* XI. 213 Eulenburg has materially facilitated the testing of the sense of pressure by constructing a baræsthesiometer.., on which, by varying pressure upon a string, different degrees of pressure may be read off on a dial. **1885** STIRLING tr. *Landois' Human Physiol.* 1092 In order to avoid the necessity of changing the weights, A. Eulenburg invented his baraesthesiometer, which is constructed on the same principle as a spiral spring paper-clip or balance. **1900** DORLAND *Med. Dict.* 102/2 Baresthesiometer.

‖**baragouin** (ˌbaraˈgwɛ̃, -gwɪn). Also 7-9 barr-. [a. F. *baragouin*, f. Breton *bara* bread + *gwîn* wine (Littré), or *gwenn* white, in reference to the astonishment of Breton soldiers at the sight of white bread (Roulin in Littré *Supp.*); used by the French of any outlandish language or unintelligible speech.] Language so altered in sound or sense as to become generally unintelligible; jargon, 'double-Dutch.' Hence **baraˈgouinish** *a.*

a **1613** OVERBURY *Charac. Lawyer* Wks. (1856) 84 He thinks no language worth knowing but his Barragouin. **1801** W. TAYLOR in *Month. Mag.* XI. 646 The barragouin of a professional lawyer. —— *ibid.* XII. 99 The parliamentary use of the word [*committee*] is anomalous; it there means the collective body of persons..and, in that baragouinish sense, is accented on the second syllable. **1860** *All Y. Round* No. 46. 461 Some horrible patois and baragouin of his own.

baraigne, -ane, barail, obs. ff. BARREN, -EL.

baralipton (bærəˈlɪptən). *Logic.* [A mnemonic vocable invented by the Scholastic philosophers, and used first in med.L.] A term constructed to represent by its first three vowels, etc. the first indirect mood of the first figure of syllogisms, in which the two premisses are universal affirmatives, and the conclusion a particular affirmative.

1653 URQUHART *Rabelais* I. xvii, After they had well argued pro and con, they concluded in Baralipton, that they should send the oldest. **1660** EARL ROSCOM. *Poems* 36 Apollo starts..At the rude rumbling Baralipton makes.

†**barane.** *Obs.* [f. BAR-IUM + -ANE 2 a.] Davy's proposed systematic name for chloride of barium.

1812 SIR H. DAVY *Chem. Philos.* 342.

†**bara-picklet.** *Obs.* In 7 barrapyclid. [ad. Welsh *bara pyglyd* 'pitchy bread,' perh. in reference to its colour.] (See quot.)

1611 COTGR., *Popelins*, soft cakes made of fine flower, kneaded with milke, etc...like our Welsh Barrapyclids. **1687** HOLME *Armorie* III. iii. 86 Barra Pickled, a light Bread made in round Cakes. **1704** *Dict. Rust. et Urb., Bara-picklet*, is Bread made of fine Flower, and knead up with Barm. [So **1852** in BRANDE.]

baraque, obs. form of BARRACK.

†**bara'rag.** *Obs.* A vocable invented to represent the sound of a trumpet; cf. *tantara*.

1523 SKELTON *Garl. Laurel*, Eolus, your trumpet..That bararag bloweth in every martial war. *Ibid.* To blow bararag till beth his eyen stare.

Bara Sahib: See BURRA SAHIB.

barasingha (baraˈsɪŋgə). Also barasinga, barasingh. [Hind. *bārah singā* lit. twelve-horn.] The east Indian deer *Cervus wallichii*; also, *C. duvauceli*, the Swamp Deer.

1862 *Proc. Zool. Soc.* IX. 136 Persian Deer..Barbary Deer..and Barasinga Deer (*C. duvaucellii*). **1863** *Ibid.* XV. 230 Fam. Cervidæ..Barasingha Deer (*C. duvaucelii*). **1880** *Encycl. Brit.* XII. 742/2 The swamp deer or *barasingha*.. which is common in Lower Bengal and Assam. **1894** KIPLING *2nd Jungle Bk.* (1895) 37 The *barasingh*, that big deer which is like our red deer, but stronger. **1902** [see *swamp deer*, s.v. SWAMP *sb.* 3 b]. **1921** *Brit. Mus. Return* 98 A Kashmir Barasingha (*Cervus cashmiriensis*). **1964** R. PERRY *World of Tiger* iv. 56 The wapiti, a red deer,..is represented in Indian forests by the Kashmir stag or barasingh, not to be confused with the barasingha or swamp-deer of the Terai. **1968** *Times* (Pakistan Suppl.) 6 Apr. p. viii/5 The tiger's principal prey, the gaur (jungle bison) and barasingha (marsh deer) were soon wiped out.

barat, -er, etc., obs. ff. BARRAT, -ER, etc.

barathea (bærəˈθiːə). [Origin unknown.] A cloth of a fine texture composed of a silk warp and woollen weft, also of cotton and wool and entirely of wool.

1862 *Internat. Exhib., Catal. Industr. Dept.* II. No. 3958, Cobourg, paramatta, barathea, reps, cords, cloths. **1897** *Daily News* 30 Oct. 6/5 Venetian crape..has taken the place of the old baratheas, Balmorals, bombazines, &c. **1953** K. AMIS *Lucky Jim* ix. 98 His lavender barathea trousers swayed gracefully with his walk. **1963** *Guardian* 15 Mar. 1/4 All ranks will receive a second suit of the No. 2 khaki service dress, of 22 oz. barathea.

‖**barathrum** (ˈbærəθrəm). [L., a. Gr. βάραθρον.] A pit, gulf. Hence: **a.** A deep pit at Athens, into which criminals condemned to death were thrown. **b.** (earlier in Eng.) The abyss, hell. **c.** An insatiable extortioner or glutton (so in It.).

a. 1849 GROTE *Greece* II. xxxix. V. 69 Aristeides himself is reported to have said, 'If the Athenians were wise, they would cast both of us into the barathrum.' **1874** MAHAFFY *Soc. Life Greece* viii. 251 Had the body been..cast into the barathrum.

b. 1520 *Treat. Galaunt* in Furniv. *Ballads* I. 449 Trysed to baratrum, tossed in fere. **1607** DEKKER *Knts. Conjur.* 19 Hee flung away in a furie, and leapt into Barathrum.

c. 1609 *Man in Moone* (1849) 27 A bottomlesse Barathrum, a mercilesse mony-monger. **1633** MASSINGER *New Way* III. ii, You barathrum of the shambles!

‖**ba'rato.** *Obs.* [Sp., adj. 'cheap'; sb. as in Eng.] A portion of a gamester's winnings given 'for luck' to the by-standers.

1622 MABBE *Aleman's Guzman D' Alf.* I. 147 And, though I were no Gamester, yet I might receiue *Barato* as a stander by. *Ibid.* II. 175, I get the money, but gaue it almost all away in *barato* to the standers by.

‖**baraza** (bəˈrɑːzə). [Swahili.] A place of public audience or reception; hence also a meeting, reception, palaver.

1892 LD. LUGARD *Diary* 17 Mar. (1959) III. 98 Big Baraza, most of the big chiefs present. **1926** *Blackw. Mag.* Apr. 549/1 In the big baraza or native council-house we noticed a native weaving cloth. **1928** *Daily Express* 2 Oct. 11/4 Hundreds of native tribal chiefs..have come here from all parts of the East African fastnesses to participate in the great Baraza (pow-wow) for the Prince to-morrow. **1959** *Times* 23 Feb. 12/7 The three native rulers of Uganda's western province will be among those who will greet her to-morrow at a *baraza*.

barb (bɑːb), *sb.*[1] Also 4–7 barbe. [a. F. *barbe*:—L. *barba* beard. Sense 8 is not cited in Fr.; cf. however OF. '*seetes barbees*' in Godef., and mod.F. *barbillon*. The appearance of the senses in Eng. did not correspond with their original development in Fr.]

I. A beard, or analogous appendage.

†‖**1.** The beard of a man. *Obs. rare.*

c **1450** *Merlin* vii. 117 A gode knyght and yonge, of prime barbe. **1688** HOLME *Armorie* II. xvii. 392 The Barbe, or Beard, is all the hair of the higher and lower lips, with Cheeks and Chin.

2. A similar appendage in various animals; *e.g.* feathers under the beak of a hawk (*obs.*), the wattles of a cock (*obs.*), a slender fleshy appendage hanging from the corners of the mouth of some fishes, such as the barbel and fishing-frog.

1486 *Bk. St. Albans* B j a, The federis vnder the beke be calde the barbe federis. **1601** HOLLAND *Pliny* II. 389 The nailes, and clawes of cocks..their barbs & spurs. **1688** HOLME *Armorie* II. xiv. 384 The Barb, Lobb, or Beard, is any long skinny substance that proceeds from the Fish Snout or Nose. **1863** H. PENNELL *Angler-nat.* 119 The barbs or beards..are given to the fish to assist it in feeling its way in deep, and..dark waters.

3. Part of a woman's head-dress, still sometimes worn by nuns, consisting of a piece of white plaited linen, passed over or under the chin, and reaching midway to the waist.

c **1374** CHAUCER *Troylus* II. 61 Do wey your barbe, and shew your face bare. *c* **1450** *E.E. Poems* (1862) 147 Yowre barbe, your wymppylle and your vayle. **1509–47** in Planché *Brit. Costume* (1832) 232 These estates are to wear the barbe under their throats. **1752** BALLARD *Mem. Learned Ladies* 16 Wearing of barbes at funerals over the chin and under the same. **1851** AGN. STRICKLAND *Queens Scot.* II. 10 Wearing white weeds and barbe.

4. *Veter. Surg.* in *pl.* Folds of the mucous membrane under the tongue of horses and cattle, protecting the orifices of the ducts of the submaxillary glands; the disease caused by their inflammation.

1523 FITZHERB. *Husb.* §82 The barbes be lyttell pappes in a horse mouth, and lette hym to byte. **1572** MASCALL *Govt. Cattle* (1627) 73. **1610** MARKHAM *Masterp.* II. xxxi. 265. **1721** BAILEY, *Barbes*, a Disease in black Cattle and Horses, known by two Paps under their Tongue. **1831** YOUATT *Horse* x. (1872) 233 The farriers call these swellings *barbs* or *paps*; and as soon as they discover them, mistaking the effect of disease for the cause of it, they set to work to cut them close off.

5. *Her.* A sepal (*pl.* the calyx) of a flower.

1572 BOSSEWELL *Armorie* II. 127 The Barbes of thys floure ..abide alwaies of theire proper colour, which is greene.

6. One of the lateral filaments or processes from the shaft of a feather, which bear the barbules.

1836 TODD *Cycl. Anat. & Phys.* I. 350 The vane [of the feather] consists of barbs and barbules. **1870** ROLLESTON *Anim. Life* Introd. 55 The *Ratitæ* have the barbs of their feathers disconnected.

7. Little roughnesses or ridges produced in the course of metal-working, *e.g.* by coiners and engravers; bur.

1842 WHITTOCK *Bk. Trades* 214 The scraper..for rubbing off the burr or 'barb' raised by the graver on the copper plate.

II. A recurved process. (The earliest sense in Eng.)

8. A sharp process curving back from the point of a piercing weapon (*e.g.* an arrow or spear, which have two, a fish-hook, which has one), rendering its extraction from a wound, etc. more difficult.

c **1340** *Gaw. & Gr. Knt.* 1457 Haled to hym of her arewez, hitten hym oft; Bot..þe barbez of his browe bite non wolde. **1544** ASCHAM *Toxoph.* (Arb.) 135 Two maner of arrowe heades..The one..hauyng two poyntes or barbes lookyng backewarde. **1769** FALCONER *Dict. Marine* (1789) G j b, A rag-bolt is retained in it's situation by..barbs. **1791** COWPER *Iliad* XI. 624 Skill'd in medicine, and to free The inherent barb. **1867** F. FRANCIS *Angling* iv. (1880) 112 Give it a pull so as to embed the barb.

fig. **1777** SHERIDAN *Sch. Scandal* I. i. 238 The malice of a good thing is the barb that makes it stick. **1875** B. TAYLOR *Faust* I. i. II. 3 Remove the burning barbs of his remorses.

9. *Bot.* A hooked hair.

1864 in WEBSTER. **1880** GRAY *Bot. Text-bk.* 398 *Barb*, a bristle or stout hair, which is hooked or double-hooked, or retrorsely appendaged at the tip.

III. [Cf. OF. *barde* ax, Ger. *barte* ax, ON. *barða*.]

†**10.** The edge of an ax. *Obs. rare.*

c **1340** *Gaw. & Gr. Knt.* 2310 He lyftes ly3tly his lome, & let hit doun fayre, With þe barbe of þe bitte bi þe bare nek.

†**barb**, *sb.*[2] *Obs.* [Corrupted from BARD[2]; perhaps confused with prec.] A covering for the breast and flanks of a war-horse, originally protective, but sometimes merely ornamental.

1566 PAINTER *Pal. Pleas.* I. 50 Had furnished the horses of the chariot with brasen barbes. **1596** SPENSER *F.Q.* II. ii. 11 His loftie steed with golden sell And goodly gorgeous barbes. **1611** SPEED *Hist. Gt. Brit.* IX. vii. 64 Great horse, whereof seauen-score had barbes, and caparisons armed with yron. **1630** HAYWARD *Edw. VI*, 32 Their horses were naked without any barbs.

barb (bɑːb), *sb.*[3] [a. F. *barbe*, f. *Barbarie*. (Also called a BARBARY.)] Occas. *attrib.*

1. A horse of the breed imported from Barbary and Morocco, noted for great speed and endurance.

1636 HEALEY *Theophrast.* xxiii. 82 Barbes, Jennets, and other horses of price. **1735** SOMERVILLE *Chase* III. 387 He reins his docile Barb with manly Grace. **1796** SCOTT *Will. & Helen* xxxii, Upon my black barb steed. **1823** LOCKHART *Sp. Ball., Calaynos* xxi, Loudly..his mailed barb did neigh.

2. A fancy variety of pigeon, of black or dun colour, originally introduced from Barbary.

1725 BRADLEY *Fam. Dict.* s.v. *Pigeon*, Many sorts of pigeons, such as..nuns, tumblers, Barbs. **1859** DARWIN *Orig. Spec.* i. 16 The barb..instead of a long beak, has a very short and broad one. *Ibid.* 19 Mongrel barb-fantails.

3. A black kelpie (see KELPIE[2]). *Austral.*

1926 K. S. PRICHARD *Working Bullocks* 209 The barb had never fought in a ring before. **1946** F. D. DAVISON *Dusty* (1947) iii. 33 Fine dogs,..black kelpies and red, barbs and border collies.

barb (bɑːb), *v.* [a. F. *barbe-r* (Cotgr.); cf. OF. *barbier*; f. *barbe* beard.]

1. a. To shave or trim the beard of (a person). *Obs.* in general use.

1587 TURBERV. *Trag. T.* (1837) 53 Doe barbe that boysterous beard. **1615** A. STAFFORD *Heav. Dogge* 64, I will stare my headsman in the face with as much confidendce as if he came to barbe mee. **1663** COWLEY *Cutter Coleman St.* II. v. II. 824 Neat Gentlemen..tho' never wash'd nor barb'd. **1693** W. ROBERTSON *Phraseol. Gen.* 206 To Barb.. *Tondere.* **1864** *Daily Tel.* 15 Feb., Where you can be shaved, or 'barbed,' as the locution is, shampooed, tittivated, curled.

b. *absol.* or *intr.* (for *refl.*)

1583 STUBBES *Anat. Abus.* II. 50 Their noble science of barbing. **1665** PEPYS *Diary* 27 Nov., Sat talking, and I barbing against to-morrow.

2. *transf.* in various senses: **a.** To clip (wool, cloth, coin, etc.). **b.** To mow (grass, etc.). **c.** To file off the bur or rough edges of metal-work. †**d.** The specific term for carving a lobster.

1483 *Act 1 Rich. III*, viii. Pream., Great quantitie of Wolls ..which ben..barbed and clakked. **1508** *Bk. Kerving* in *Babees Bk.* (1868) 265 Barbe that lopster. **1535** *Act 27 Hen. VIII.* xiii. §1 They [cloths] must be newly dressed, barbed, shorne. **1601** HOLLAND *Pliny* XVII. xxiii, The small sprigs must eftsoons be barbed (as it were) and shaven clean off. **1610** B. JONSON *Alch.* I. i. (1616) 608 I'll bring..thy necke Within a nooze, for laundering gold, and barbing it. **1652** BENLOWES *Theoph.* XII. ii. 236 The Mower, who..Wieldeth the crooked Sythe..To barb the flowrie Tresses of the verdant plains. **1863** SALA *Capt. Dang.* II. vii. 226 Gambling bullies..throwing their Highmen, or barbing gold.

†**3.** *fig.* **a.** To give a trimming or dressing to. **b.** To clip, cut back. *Obs.*

1614 RALEIGH *Hist. World* V. vi. §2 Justine having recovered forces lighted on Tiberius and barbed him after the same fashion. **1657** TRAPP *Comm. Esther* ii. 1 Vices may be barbed or benumbed, not mastered.

4. To furnish (an arrow, hook, etc.) with barbs.

1611 [see BARBED 4]. **1667** MILTON *P.L.* VI. 546 Ratling storm of Arrows barbd with fire. **1759** MASON *Caractacus* (R.) Haste, Evelina, barb my knotty spear. **1832** HT. MARTINEAU *Life in Wilds* v. 68, I will shew you how the natives barb them [arrows].

fig. **1777** SHERIDAN *Sch. Scandal* Portr. 232 She barbs with wit those darts too keen before. **1810** SOUTHEY *Kehama* x. xx, Flowers..With their petals barb'd the dart.

5. To pierce with, or as with, a barb. *rare.*

1803 MISS PORTER *Thaddeus* ix, It is your wretchedness that barbs me to the heart.

6. To bend into hook form the points of wire teeth used in carding textile fibres.

1890 NASMITH *Mod. Cotton Spinning Mach.* 94 There are two evils to be guarded against—the barbing or hooking of the wire points and the striation of the sides of the teeth. *Ibid.* 95 Striated sides and barbed points are common in this series.

†**'barbable**, *a.* *Obs.*$^{-0}$ [f. BARB *sb*[2] + -ABLE.]

1611 COTGR., *Bardable*, barbable; fit, or able to beare a barbed furniture, or armor.

barbacan, variant of BARBICAN.

barbacue, obs. form of BARBECUE.

Barbadian (bɑːˈbeɪdɪən), *a.* and *sb.* [f. BARBAD(OS + -IAN.] **A.** *adj.* Of or pertaining to Barbados or its inhabitants. **B.** *sb.* An inhabitant of Barbados. Cf. BADIAN *sb.*[2] and *a.*

1732 *Cal. State Papers, Col. Ser., Amer. & W. Indies* (1939) 6 'Tis noe more than a feather in the cap, but 'tis what the Barbadians like. **1741** *Caribbeana* I. 56 To our Lovely Country-Women, who are single, the Barbadian Batchelors, and Widowers, send lovingly Greeting. **1875** *Encycl. Brit.* III. 361/1 In the meantime Barbadian affairs had attracted notice in Parliament. *Ibid.*, Nor were the Barbadians themselves backward in stating their grievances. **1960** *Times* 11 Jan. 16/6 Not for nothing is Worrell known as the prince of Barbadian batsmen.

Barbados (bɑːˈbeɪdəʊz, -dɒs). Also **Barbadoes**. Name of an island (formerly a British colony) in the West Indies, believed to be derived from Pg. *las barbadas* 'bearded,' epithet applied by the Portuguese to the Indian fig-trees growing there; whence formerly 'the Barbadoes'. Hence: **Barbados-cherry**, the tart fruit, resembling a cherry, of the *Malpighia urens*. **Barbados**

gooseberry (see quot. 1876). **Barbados leg**, a form of elephantiasis incident to hot climates. **Barbados nuts**, the seeds or fruit, used as a purgative, of the *Jatropha Curcas*, or *Curcas purgans*, growing in S. America. **Barbados pride**, a beautiful plant (*Poinciana pulcherrima*) used for fences in tropical lands. **Barbados tar**, a kind of greenish petroleum. **Barbados-water**, a cordial flavoured with orange- and lemon-peel. Also † **barbados** *v.*, to transport (convicts) to Barbados (*obs.*).

1902 *Daily Chron.* 15 May 5/1 Attention is again called.. to the want of uniformity in the spelling of Barbados, many papers spelling it Barbadoes... All official documents emanating from the Colony, and all the stamps for upwards of half a century, have the word Barbados. **1858** W. Ellis *Vis. Madagascar* iv. 95 The greatest rarity to me was a fruit called Barbadoes cherry. **1756** P. Browne *Civil & Nat. Hist. Jamaica* 237 Cactus 1.. The Gooseberry, or Barbadoes Gooseberry Bush. **1876** *Encycl. Brit.* IV. 626/2 *Pereskia aculeata*, or Barbados Gooseberry, the *Cactus Pereskia* of Linnæus. **1849** Todd *Cycl. Anat. & Phys.* IV. 1097/1 The enlargement of the extremities commonly known by the name of Barbadoes leg. **1885** Lady Brassey *In Trades* 323 Among the flowers may be mentioned.. acacias, Barbadoes pride. **1698** Congreve *Way of World* iv. v, I banish.. all aniseed, cinnamon, citron and Barbadoes-waters. **1655** W. Gouge in Thurloe *State Papers* (1742) III. 495 The prisoners of the Tower shall, 'tis sayd, be Barbadozz'd. **1845** Carlyle *Cromwell* (1871) IV. 115 Be barbadoesed or worse.

barbal (ˈbɑːbəl), *a.* [f. L. *barb-a* beard + -al[1].] Of or belonging to the beard.

1650 Bulwer *Anthropomet.* Pref., 'Tis the neather lip's especial grace To fall down to the lowest barbal place. **1828** *Blackw. Mag.* XXIV. 615 Hoarifying my barbal extremity.

† **ˈbarbar**, *a.* and *sb. Obs.* Forms: 4–8 **barbar**, 6 **-our, -ir**, 8 **-are**. [a. F. *barbare* (14th c. in Littré), ad. L. *barbarus* barbarous. In 16th c. occasionally in L. form; now superseded by *barbarian* and *barbarous*.]

A. *sb.* = barbarian. (In later use Scotch.)

1382 Wyclif *1 Cor.* xiv. 11, I schal be to him, to whom I schal speke, a barbar. *c* **1590** A. Hume *Epist. G. Moncrief*, The Barbar rude of Thrace or Tartarie. *a* **1639** Spottiswood *Hist. Ch. Scot.* i. (1677) 5 Goths, Vandals, Franks, and other Barbars. **1723** M'Ward *Contend. Faith* 349 (Jam.) Blood shed by these barbars and burriers.

β. in Latin form *barbarus*.

1530 *Compend. olde Treat.* (1863) 52 Barbarus is he that vnderstondyth not yt he readeth in his mother tonge. **1549** Coverdale *Erasm. Par. Col.* iii. 11 Neither Gentile nor Jewe .. Barbarus or Sithian, bonde or free.

B. *adj.* = barbarous.

1535 Stewart *Cron. Scot.* II. 10 To execute sic barbour lawes agane. **1549** *Compl. Scot.* Prol. 16 Til excuse my barbir agrest termis. **1584** Hudson *Judith* ii. (1613) 354 (D.) The barbare yock of Moab. *a* **1726** Vanbrugh *False Fr.* iii. i. (1730) 125 Barbare Jacinta cast your eyes On your poor Lopez e'er he dies.

barbara (ˈbɑːbərə). *Logic.* [A Latin word (= barbarous things), taken as a mnemonic term, for its three *a*'s: 'A' indicating a universal affirmative proposition.] A term designating the first mood of the first figure of syllogisms. A syllogism in *Barbara* is one of which both the major and minor premisses, and the conclusion, are universal affirmatives: thus, all animals are mortal; all men are animals; ∴ all men are mortal.

1589 *Marprel. Epit.* E iij b, The moode answereth unto *Celarent*, elder daughter to *Barbara*. **1837–8** Sir W. Hamilton *Logic* xxii. (1866) I. 444 The unsatisfactory reduction by the logicians of Bocardo to Barbara by an apagogical exposition. **1880** Vern. Lee *Stud. 18th C. Italy* vi. 247 Attempts to turn him into an.. ordinary youth by means of teachers, colleges, logical barbaras and baraliptons.

Barbaresque (bɑːbəˈrɛsk), *a.* and *sb.* [modern a. F. *barbaresque* (= It. *barbaresco*) belonging to Barbary; cf. also Pg. *barbarisco* barbarous. See barbar and -esque, and cf. Barbary.]

A. *adj.* **1.** Of or pertaining to Barbary in Africa.

1824 Galt *Rothelan* III. 158 A red Barbaresque night-cap. **1881** *Times* 18 Apr. 4/1 That France should not be permitted to increase her Barbaresque possessions.

2. Barbarous in style, *esp.* in reference to art. [Cf. *picturesque*.]

1823 De Quincey *Language* (1860) 124 Barbarism.. generates its own barbaresque standards of taste. **1857** —— *Sketches* Wks. VI. 159 Architecture.. barbaresque—rich in decoration, at times colossal in proportions, but unsymmetrical. **1859** Masson *Brit. Novelists* iv. 220 The.. outstanding barbaresque and primitive in English society.

B. *sb.* A native of Barbary.

1804 T. Jefferson *Writ.* (1830) IV. 21 Our interests against the Barbaresques. **1862** Ludlow *Hist. U.S.* 74 Any [peace] concluded.. by a Christian power with the Barbaresques.

barbarian (bɑːˈbɛərɪən), *sb.* and *a.* Also 6 **-ien**. [a. F. *barbarien* (16th c.), f. F. *barbarie* or L. *barbaria* (see Barbary), on L. type *arbariānus*; cf. OF. *chrestien*:—L. *christiānus*. See -an, -ian. For sense-development see barbarous.]

A. *sb.*

1. *etymologically*, A foreigner, one whose language and customs differ from the speaker's.

1549 *Compl. Scot.* xiii. 106 Euere nation reputis vthers nations to be barbariens, quhen there tua natours and complexions ar contrar til vtheris [i.e. each other]. **1611** Bible *1 Cor.* xiv. 11, I shall be vnto him that speaketh, a Barbarian, and he that speaketh shal be a Barbarian vnto me. **1827** Hare *Guesses* (1859) 325 A barbarian is a person who does not talk as we talk, or dress as we dress, or eat as we eat; in short, who is so audacious as not to follow our practice in all the trivialities of manners. **1862** *Macm. Mag.* Nov. 58 Ovid.. laments that in his exile at Tomi he, the polished citizen, is a barbarian to all his neighbours.

2. *Hist.* **a.** One not a Greek. **b.** One living outside the pale of the Roman empire and its civilization, applied especially to the northern nations that overthrew them. **c.** One outside the pale of Christian civilization. **d.** With the Italians of the Renascence: One of a nation outside of Italy.

1604 Shaks. *Oth.* i. iii. 363 A fraile vow, betwixt an erring Barbarian [cf. sense 5] and a super-subtle Venetian. **1607** *Cor.* iii. i. 238, I would they were Barbarians.. not Romans. **1628** Hobbes *Thucyd.* 9 The Athenians.. expecting the coming of the Barbarian. **1660** Stanley *Hist. Philos.* (1701) 307/2 Of Men some are Grecians, some Barbarians. **1846** Arnold *Hist. Rome* II. xi. 364 The inhabitants of the left or eastern bank of the Rhone were.. no longer to be considered barbarians, but were become Romans both in their customs and in their language. **1863** Mayor in *Ascham's Scholem.* 242 Christoph. Longueil of Malines, the one 'barbarian' to whom the Italians allowed the title of 'Ciceronian.'

3. A rude, wild, uncivilized person.

1613 R. C. *Table Alph.*, *Barbarian*, a rude person. **1697** Dryden *Virg. Georg.* iii. 588 Skins of Beasts, the rude Barbarians wear. **1730** Thomson *Autumn* 57 The sad barbarian, roving, mixed With beasts of prey. **1861** Stanley *East. Ch.* xii. (1869) 381 The strange barbarian [Peter the Great] sought to evade the eagerness of our national curiosity. **1876** J. H. Newman *Hist. Sk.* I. i. i. 12 Nature herself fights, and conquers for the barbarian.

b. Sometimes distinguished from *savage* (perh. with a glance at 2).

1835 Arnold *Life & Corr.* (1844) I. vii. 408, I believe with you that savages could never civilize themselves, but barbarians I think might. **1851** D. Wilson *Preh. Ann.* II. iii. viii. 487 Still a barbarian, but had ceased to be a savage.

c. Applied by the Chinese contemptuously to foreigners.

1858 in *Merc. Mar. Mag.* V. 302 The character 'I' ('barbarian') not to be applied to the British Government, or to British subjects, in any Chinese official document.

4. An uncultured person, or one who has no sympathy with literary culture.

1762 Hume *Hist. Eng.* (1806) IV. lxii. 664 Cromwell, though himself a barbarian, was not insensible to literary merit. **1863** tr. *Let. Erasmus* in Ascham's *Scholem.* 245 At Oxford.. when a young scholar.. lectured in Greek with much success, a barbarian began in an address to the people to rave against Greek learning. **1873** M. Arnold *Lit. & Dogma* 1, I have myself called our aristocratic class Barbarians which is the contrary of Hellenes.. because.. for reading and thinking they have in general no great turn.

† **5.** A native of Barbary. [See Barbary.] *Obs.*

1578 Mascall *Plant. & Graff.* Ep., The Greeks for Greeke, the Barbarians for Barbarie, the Italian for Italie. **1583** Plat *New Exper.* (1594) 22 The Barbarians doe make a bright and orient crimosin colour therewith uppon leather. **1709** *Lond. Gaz.* No. 4571/2 The Governor of Otranto marched.. against the Barbarians.

† **b.** A Barbary horse. *Obs.*

1580 Blundeville *Horsemanship* i. (1609) 4 Those horses which we commonly call Barbarians, do come out of the king of Tunis land.

B. *adj.*

1. Applied by nations, generally depreciatively, to foreigners; thus at various times and with various speakers or writers: non-Hellenic, non-Roman (*most usual*), non-Christian.

1549 *Compl. Scot.* (1801) 259 Mair lyik til barbarien pepil, nor.. to cristyn pepil. **1606** Shaks. *Tr. & Cr.* ii. i. 51 Bought and solde.. like a Barbarian slaue. **1715** Pope *Mor. Ess.* v. 13 Barbarian blindness, Christian zeal conspire. **1817** Colebrooke *Algebra* Introd. 82 Several other terms of the art.. are not Sanscrit, but, apparently, barbarian. **1847** Hallam *Hist. Lit.* I. i. §1. 2 Establishment of the barbarian nations on the ruins of the Roman empire. **1862** *Macm. Mag.* Nov. 58 The announcement to one of the comedies of Plautus taken from the Greek, that 'Philemo wrote what Plautus has adapted to the barbarian tongue'—i.e. Latin.

2. Uncivilized, rude, savage, barbarous.

1591 Spenser *Ruins Rome* 416 Till that Barbarian hands it quite did spill. **1700** Dryden *Cymon & Iph.* 125 His broad barbarian sound. **1782** Paine *Let. Abbé Raynel* (1791) 45 This was not the condition of the barbarian world. Then the wants of men were few. **1859** Darwin *Orig. Spec.* i. (1873) 13 Geologists believe that barbarian man existed at an enormously remote period.

† **3.** Of or belonging to Barbary. *Obs.*

1577 Harrison *England* ii. vii. (1877) 168 The Morisco gowns, the Barbarian sleves. **1605** *Play Stucley* in *Sch. Shaks.* (1878) 254 We mount her back.. As we do use to serve Barbarian horse. **1699** in *Misc. Cur.* (1708) III. 381 The Mauritanian or Barbarian Moor.

barbarianess (bɑːˈbɛərɪənɪs). [f. barbarian *sb.* + -ess[1].] A female barbarian.

1868 M. Arnold *Let.* 5 Feb. (1895) I. 387 As a very charming Barbarianess, Lady Portsmouth, expresses a great desire to make my acquaintance, I daresay the race will bear no malice. **1885** *Nation* (N.Y.) 4 June 466 This perilous feat [*sc.* that of eating peas with a knife] he has, in person, contemplated as performed by a charming Viennese barbarianess.

barˈbarianism. [f. barbarian *sb.* + -ism.] The state or condition of a barbarian (in various senses).

1855 Milman *Lat. Chr.* (1864) II. iv. §1. 169 Adapted to the youthful barbarianism of the state of society, and to the Oriental character. **1864** *Reader* No. 87. 255/1 A very paragon of prosy barbarianism.

barˈbarianize, *v.* [f. as prec. + -ize.] To make barbarian, barbarize. Hence **barbarianized** *ppl. a.*

1856 Olmsted *Slave States* 523 South Carolina must.. either be democratized or barbarianized. **1885** *Pall Mall G.* 11 Apr. 5/1 Fanciful chronicle of a barbarianized England.

barbaric (bɑːˈbærɪk), *a.* and *sb.* Forms: 4 **barbarik**, 5 **-yke**, 6 **-ike**. [a. OF. *barbarique* (15th c.) of barbarous kind, in Wyclif perh. direct ad. L. *barbaric-us*, a. Gr. βαρβαρικός like a foreigner, f. βάρβαρος foreign, rude. See barbarous and -ic.]

A. *adj.*

1. = barbarous 3, barbarian *a.* 2.

1490 Caxton *Eneydos* viii. 36 The peple barbaryke in whom they were subcombed. *c* **1510** Barclay *Mirr. Gd. Mann.* (1570) F iij, A barbarike vilayne to play the oratour. **1513** *St. Werburge* (1848) 198 Barbarike nacions full of crudelite. *a* **1837** Colebrooke *Relig. & Philos. Hindus* (1858) 201 Correct language and barbaric dialects. **1855** Prescott *Philip II* (1857) I. i. i. 2 The barbaric empires of Mexico and Peru.

2. Pertaining or proper to barbarians or their art; in the characteristic style of barbarians, as opposed to that of civilized countries or ages.

1667 Milton *P.L.* ii. 1 Barbaric Pearl and Gold. **1711** Pope *Temp. Fame* 94 With diamond flaming, and Barbaric gold. **1813** Scott *Trierm.* iii. xx, Each maiden's short barbaric vest. **1857** S. Osborn *Quedah* xvi. 212 Heavy guns, mounted on very barbaric carriages. **1873** Black *Pr. Thule* xviii. 284 Barbaric splendour of decoration.

3. = barbarous 1, 2; barbarian *a.* 1.

1849 Grote *Greece* ii. xlxviii. VI. 167 Sending envoys to the Persian King and not to other barbaric powers. **1855** Milman *Lat. Chr.* (1864) II. iii. vii. 154 An inestimable present to a patrician, or an ex-consul, or a barbaric king.

† **B.** *sb.* A barbarian. *Obs. rare.*

1388 Wyclif *1 Cor.* xiv. 11 Y schal be to hym, to whom Y schal speke, a barbarik; and he.. to me, schal be a barbarik.

C. *Comb.*, as ***barbaric-speaking***.

1849 Grote *Greece* ii. ii. II. 354 Those many barbaric-speaking nations whom Herodotus believed to have changed their language and passed into Hellens.

† **barˈbarical**, *a. Obs.* [f. L. *barbaric-us* (see prec.) + -al[1].] = prec. in sense 2.

1553 T. Watson in Crowley *Sophistr. Watson* i. (1569) 179 This barbaricall violence.

barˈbarically, *adv.* [f. prec. + -ly[2].] In barbaric fashion or style; after the fashion of the uncivilized, illiterate, or unpolished.

1832 *Tour Germ. Prince* II. iii. 36 Nothing can be.. more barbarically elegant than these grotesque.. ornaments. **1862** Thornbury *Turner* I. 29 Barbarically ignorant of any art but that of portraiture. **1878** P. Bayne *Purit. Rev.* v. 183 Barbarically unclean in their persons.

Barbarie, obs. form of Barbary.

† **barˈbarious**, *a. Obs.* [f. Barbary, F. *barbarie*, or L. *barbar, -ia, -ies* + -ous.] = barbarous.

1570 Holinshed *Scot. Chron.* I. 25 Barbarious and miserable creatures. **1633** T. Stafford *Pac. Hib.* xvii. (1821) 663 The barbarious tyranny hee exercised upon his owne Countriemen. **1762** Goldsm. *Cit. W.* xi, Barbarious nations.

† **barˈbariousness.** *Obs.* [f. prec. + -ness.] = barbarousness.

1570 Ascham *Scholem.* i. (Arb.) 28 In the best Scholes of England barbariousnesse is bred up so in yong wittes. *Ibid.* 149 To rayle vpon poore England, objecting both extreme beggerie and mere barbariousnes unto it. **1599** Sandys *Europæ Spec.* (1637) 243 Who striveth by all means to plant barbariousnesse among them [the Muscovites].

barbarism (ˈbɑːbərɪz(ə)m). [a. F. *barbarisme* 13th c., ad. L. *barbarismus*, a. Gr. βαρβαρισμός 'foreign mode of speech,' f. βαρβαρίζ-ειν to (behave or) speak like a foreigner. The extension from language to social condition (= F. *barbarie*, L. *barbaria, -ies*) is exclusively English.]

1. The use of words or expressions not in accordance with the classical standard of a language, especially such as are of foreign origin; *orig.* the mixing of foreign words or phrases in Latin or Greek; *hence*, rudeness or unpolished condition of language.

1579 Lyly *Euphues* (Arb.) 131 Affected with their barbarisme. **1613** R. C. *Table Alph.*, *Barbarisme*, rudenesse, a corrupt forme of writing or speaking. **1660** Stanley *Hist. Philos.* (1701) 307/1 Amongst the faults of Speech is Barbarism. **1670** Cotton *Espernon* i. i. 16 The French Tongue, which then first began to purge it self from the Barbarism of past Ages.

b. A foreign or non-classical word or idiom.

1589 *Marprel Epit.* G j b, I would not haue you claime all the skill, in Barbarismes and Solecismes vnto your self. **1638** Baker *Balzac's Lett.* (1654) III. 135 He smells a Barbarisme, or an incongruity seven miles off. **1752**

Johnson *Rambl.* No. 194 ¶7 Every fashionable barbarism of the present winter. **1801** W. Taylor in *Month. Mag.* XII. 223 A barbarism, then, is a fault of style originating in rudeness and ignorance; but a solecism is a fault of style originating in affectation and over-refinement.

2. Barbarous social or intellectual condition; absence of culture; uncivilized ignorance and rudeness. (The proper opposite of *civilization*.)

1584 Powel *Lloyd's Cambria* 388 Withdraw any people from ciuility to Barbarisme. **1612** Davies *Why Ireland, etc.* (1787) 2 Have risen from barbarism to civility. **1665** Glanvill *Sceps. Sci.* 79 After Barbarism had overrun Rome and Athens. *c* **1854** Stanley *Sinai & Pal.* iii. (1858) 161 The imperceptible boundary between civilisation and barbarism.

b. A trait or characteristic of such a condition.

c **1645** Howell *Lett.* (1650) II. 52 Plundering and other barbarismes that reign now abroad. **1860** Gen. P. Thompson *Audi Alt.* III. cxiv. 45 All obsolete barbarisms are coming back upon us. **1871** *Daily News* 15 Dec., The open gas flames..are as much a barbarism in the view of sanitary science.

†**3.** Barbarous cruelty; barbarity. *Obs.*

1603 Florio *Montaigne* (1634) 393 Some spice of that barbarisme [death by torture]. **1611** Speed *Hist. Gt. Brit.* ix. xiv. (1632) 767 So exquisite a barbarisme, as Richards enfamishment. **1665** Manley *Grotius Low-C. Warrs* 715 Ignominously tormented and murthered, which in the Salvages, was but ignorance; but in the Spaniards, perfect Barbarisme.

barbarity (bɑːˈbærɪtɪ). In 6 -itie. [f. L. *barbar-us* barbarous + -ity: not in L. or F.]

†**1.** = barbarism 2. *Obs.* or *arch.* (The earliest sense, taking place of the earlier *barbarie*, and now in its turn superseded by *barbarism*.)

1570 Levins *Manip.* /109 Barbarite, *barbaries*. **1604** Jas. I. *Counterbl.* (Arb.) 99 From base corruption and barbarity. **1698** Sidney *On Govt.* iii. §13 (1704) 279 That wretched Barbarity in which the Romans found our Ancestors. **1773** Johnson *Lett.* 81 I. 161 A nation just rising from barbarity. **1819** R. Chapman *Jas. V.* 89 At this time..barbarity and ignorance had not overspread Scotland.

2. Barbarous or savage cruelty, such as is alien to civilization; inhumanity. (The usual sense.)

1685 *Gracian's Courtier's Oracle* 197 The barbarity whereof will be more supportable than the fierce and haughty humour of these men. **1725** De Foe *Voy. round World* (1840) 183 With breach of faith, with cruelty and barbarity. **1796** Morse *Amer. Geog.* I. 95 When defenceless women..and even babes, are made the victims of their shocking barbarity. **1884** *Pall Mall G.* 16 Aug. 2/1, I have seen some cases of horrible barbarity.

b. with *pl.* An act of barbarous cruelty.

1718 Pope *Iliad* xxiv. 263 Oh! might I..these barbarities repay! *a* **1731** Atterbury *Serm. Martyrd. Chas. I.* (R.) He had borne lesser barbarities. **1876** J. H. Newman *Hist. Sk.* I. i. 3 These two extraordinary men rivalled or exceeded Attila in their wholesale barbarities.

3. Of language: = barbarism 1, and 1 b. ? *Obs.*

1706 tr. *Dupin's Eccl. Hist. 16th C.* II. v. 39 He always uses Latine Terms and avoids Barbarity. **1727** Swift *Eng. Tongue* Wks. 1755 II. i. 129 To quit their simplicity of style for affected refinements..which ended by degrees in many barbarities. **1796** Pegge *Anonym.* (1809) 471 We have our *monstrous, prodigious, vast, shocking, devilish*, at every turn: are we not driving towards Barbarity?

4. Barbarism of style in art. **b.** with *pl.* An instance of want of artistic culture.

1644 Evelyn *Mem.* (1857) I. 107 When architecture was but newly recovered from the Gothic barbarity. **1860** Tyndall *Glac.* i. §27. 215 To shame by the beauty of her structures the comparative barbarities of Art. **1879** Miss Braddon *Vixen* I. i. 21 The oak panelling was painted white, a barbarity on the part of..the West End decorators.

barbarization (ˌbɑːbəraɪˈzeɪʃən). [f. next + -ation: cf. *civilization*.] **a.** The action of making barbarous. **b.** Barbarized state.

1822 W. Taylor in *Month. Mag.* LIII. 103 The misery..and barbarization of the boorish classes. **1854** *Blackw. Mag.* LXXVI. 143 The..barbarisation of the academic Latin. **1866** Howells *Venet. Life* (1883) II. xvi. 36 The barbarisation of the Italian continent by..civil wars.

barbarize (ˈbɑːbəraɪz), *v.* Also -ise. [In Milton's use (sense 1), ad. Gr. βαρβαρίζ-ειν to (behave or) speak like a barbarian, but in the other senses, the suffix has its modern transitive force as in *civil-ize*, as if f. L. *barbar-us* + -ize.]

1. *intr.* To speak or write like a barbarian; to violate the laws of Latin or Greek grammar.

1644 Milton *Educ.* (1883) 5 The ill habit..of wretched barbarizing against the Latin and Greek idiom. **1651** Barksdale *Nympha Lib.* (1816) 2 If she barbarise, like boys at school. **1801** W. Taylor in *Month. Mag.* XII. 223 To barbarize in language.

2. *trans.* To render barbarous.

1648 Jos. Beaumont *Psyche* xv. xlix. (T.) Barbarized by a mutual war. **1796** Burke *Let. Noble Lord* Wks. VIII. 18 The hideous changes which have since barbarized France. **1807** G. Chalmers *Caledonia* I. ii. vi. 307 To distract, and barbarize the Irish. **1868** Bushnell *Serm. living Subj.* 33 If we choose to let our hearts be barbarized.

b. To corrupt or alter (language) from any classical standard or type (or what is so considered).

1728 Morgan *Algiers* I. iv. 144 Darje was no other than Gregorio, tho' somewhat Barbarized. **1791–1824** D'Israeli *Cur. Lit.* (1858) III. 30 The French revolutionists..almost barbarised the pure French of the Augustan age of their literature. **1871** Freeman *Hist. Ess.* Ser. i. vi. 130 The names of the most famous European cities are mutilated or barbarized.

3. *intr.* To grow barbarous, fall into barbarism.

1824 *Blackw. Mag.* XV. 594 The Irish character..appears to be rapidly barbarizing. **1871** Lowell *Study Wind.* in *Casquet Lit.* I. 394/1, I felt myself sensibly barbarizing.

ˈbarbarized, *ppl. a.* [f. prec. + -ed.] Made barbarous; reduced to barbarism.

1602 Campion *Art Eng. Poesie* in *Ascham's Scholem.* (1863) 261 In those lack-learning times, and in barbarized Italy, began that vulgar and easie kind of Poesie..which we abusively call Rime and Meeter. **1839** Thirlwall *Greece* VI. xlix. 169 A barbarised colony of Cumæ.

ˈbarbarizing, *vbl. sb.* [f. as prec. + -ing[1].] The action or process of making barbarous.

1861 Max Müller *Lect. Sc. Lang.* Ser. i. v. (1864) 202 The same barbarising has affected all other Roman dialects.

ˈbarbarizing, *ppl. a.* [f. as prec. + -ing[2].] **a.** Acting or speaking as barbarians. **b.** Reducing to barbarism. **c.** Becoming barbarous.

1662 Fuller *Worthies* (1840) I. 203 These barbarizing English were..endeared to the interest of Ireland. **1809** Southey in *Q. Rev.* I. 288 Barbarous and barbarizing warfare. **1855** Milman *Lat. Chr.* (1864) IX. xiv. iii. 99 The barbarising Augustan historian. **1859** Kingsley *Misc.* II. 194 A stationary, if not a barbarizing system of society. **1874** Mahaffy *Soc. Life Greece* i. 5 Disintegrating and barbarising forces.

barbaˈrocracy. [f. Gr. βάρβαρος + -κρατία: see -cracy.] Government or rule by barbarians, as that of Italy by the German emperors.

1866 Felton *Anc. & Mod. Greece* II. xi. 486 Better fitted to live under a constitution than under a barbarocracy.

barbarous (ˈbɑːbərəs), *a.* [f. L. *barbar-us*, a. Gr. βάρβαρος + -ous: preceded in use by the simple barbar(e, without suffix. The Gr. word had probably a primary reference to speech, and is compared with L. *balbus* stammering. The sense-development in ancient times was (with the Greeks) 'foreign, non-Hellenic,' later 'outlandish, rude, brutal'; (with the Romans) 'not Latin nor Greek,' then 'pertaining to those outside the Roman empire'; hence 'uncivilized, uncultured,' and later 'non-Christian,' whence 'Saracen, heathen'; and generally 'savage, rude, savagely cruel, inhuman.' The later uses occur first in Eng., the L. and Gr. senses appearing only in translators or historians.]

1. Of language: **a.** *orig.* Not Greek; *subseq.* not Greek nor Latin; *hence*, not classical or pure (Latin or Greek), abounding in 'barbarisms.' Hence, **b.** Unpolished, without literary culture; pertaining to an illiterate people.

1526 *Pilgr. Perf.* (W. de W. 1531) 2 My wytte is grosse..and my tonge very barbarouse. **1538** Starkey *England* 193 To see al our law..wryten in thys barbarouse langage [i.e. old French]. **1547** Boorde *Introd. Knowl.* 221 Barbarouse Latin doth alter from trew Latins. **1570** Ascham *Scholem.* (1863) 71 Avoidyng barbarous ryming. **1600** Dymmok *Treat. Irel.* (1843) 47 Barbarous for the Latyn but cyuill for the sence. **1611** Cotgr., *Narquois*, the gibbridge, or barbarous language used among them [Gipsies]. **1612** Brinsley *Lud. Lit.* x. (1627) 147 Will still write false Latine, barbarous phrase. **1751** Johnson *Rambl.* No. 169 ¶6 From which [Latin]..the present European tongues are nothing more than barbarous degenerations. **1788** Reid *Aristot. Log.* iv. ii. 74 The mystery contained in the vowels of those barbarous words [*Barbara, Celarent*, etc.]. **1791** Cowper *Iliad* ii. 1063 The Carians, people of a barbarous speech. **1857** Ruskin *Pol. Econ. Art* 9 A wholly barbarous use of the word, barbarous in a double sense, for it is not English, and it is bad Greek.

2. Of people: Speaking a foreign language, foreign, outlandish; *orig.* non-Hellenic; *then*, not Roman, living outside the Roman Empire; *sometimes*, not Christian, heathen. (Often with a glance at sense 3.)

1542 Udall *Apoph.* 285 a, Bearyng rewle emong the Barbarous, that is to weete, the Portugalles. **1543** Traheron *Vigo's Wks.* Gloss., The barbarous auctours vse *alcohol*..for moost fyne poudre. **1611** Bible *Transl. Pref.* 4 The Scythian counted the Athenian, whom he did not vnderstand, barbarous. —— *Acts* xxviii. 2 The barbarous people shewed vs no little kindnesse. **1713** Pope *Windsor For.* 365 Let barb'rous Ganges arm a servile train.

3. Uncultured, uncivilized, unpolished; rude, rough, wild, savage. (Said of men, their manners, customs, products.) The usual opposite of *civilized*.

1538 Starkey *England* 117 A gret rudenes and a barbarouse custume usyd wyth us. **1587** Golding *De Mornay* viii. 96 Let vs come to Lawes, for euen the barbarousest people had of them. **1601** Shaks. *Twel. N.* iv. i. 52 Barbarous Caues, Where manners nere were preach'd. **1635** N. Carpenter *Geog. Del.* ii. xiii. 214 A barbarous and vnciuil place. **1658** Flecknoe *Epigr.* 67 Would tame fierce lions, and civilize barbarousest savages. **1780** Harris *Philol. Eng.* (1841) 514 Italy at the beginning of her history was barbarous. **1840** Carlyle *Heroes* ii. 105 An uncultured semi-barbarous son of Nature.

4. Savage in infliction of cruelty, cruelly harsh.

[**1538** Starkey *England* iv. 107 Tyrannys and Barbarus pryncys.] **1588** Shaks. *Tit. A.* i. i. 378 Thou art a Romaine, be not barbarous. *c* **1620** Z. Boyd *Zion's Flowers* (1855) 154 This barbarous villaine did no mercy show. *c* **1660** *Bk. Com. Prayer* K. Chas. Mart., A constant meek suffering of all barbarous indignities. **1749** Fielding *Tom Jones* xviii. xii, It would be barbarous to part Tom and the girl. **1876** Mozley *Univ. Serm.* v. 111 The barbarous aspect of war.

5. Like the speech of barbarians; harsh-sounding, rudely or coarsely noisy.

1645 Milton *Sonn.* xii, A barbarous noise environs me Of owls and cuckoos, asses, apes, and dogs. **1667** —— *P.L.* vii. 32 The barbarous dissonance Of Bacchus and his Revellers. **1725** De Foe *Voy. round World* (1840) 253 Innumerable rills..making a barbarous and unpleasant sound. **1856** Olmsted *Slave States* 24 The music was wild and barbarous.

†**6.** = barbaric 2. *Obs.*

1700 Dryden *Pal. & Arc.* iii. 65 The trappings of his horse emboss'd with barbarous gold.

barbarously (ˈbɑːbərəslɪ), *adv.* [f. prec. + -ly[2].] In a barbarous manner: **a.** as to speech.

1531 Elyot *Gov.* i. xiii, Whiche..speake the most barberously that they can imagine. **1589** Puttenham *Eng. Poesie* (Arb.) 257 The foulest vice in language is to speake barbarously. **1667** Dryden *Ess. Dram. Poesy* in Arb. *Garner* III. 563 New languages..barbarously mingled with the Latin. **1855** Liddell & Scott *Gr. Lex.*, Βαρβαροφωνέω, to speak Greek barbarously.

b. as to social or intellectual condition, culture, or art.

1552 Huloet, Barbarouslye or rudelye. **1657** Davenant *Rutland Ho.* (1673) 348 Loving so barbarously the uncleanly ease of his own life. *a* **1761** Mrs. Delany *Life & Corr.* (1861) III. 28 In the afternoon, went to hear 'Samson' murdered most barbarously.

c. as to cruelty.

1611 Bible 2 *Macc.* xv. 2 O destroy not so cruelly and barbarously. **1712** Addison *Spect.* No. 483 ¶2 Her mother used one of her nieces very barbarously. **1800** Coleridge *To Wedgewood* Jan., It is most barbarously cold.

barbarousness (ˈbɑːbərəsnɪs). [f. as prec. + -ness.] The quality of being barbarous; the degree of barbarism or barbarity: **a.** in language.

1548 Coverdale *Erasm. Par.* 2 *Cor.* xi. 6 He confesseth his rudenes and barbarousnes in language. **1564** Haward *Eutrop.* To Rdr., The barbarousnesse..of thys our Englyshe tounge. **1861** Wright *Ess. Archæol.* II. xxiii. 257 The barbarousness of monkish Latin.

b. in behaviour, condition, culture, or art.

1549 Latimer *Serm. bef. Edw. VI*, v. (Arb.) 140 That wyl brynge the Realme into a verye barbarousnes and vtter decaye of learnynge. **1761** Hume *Hist. Eng.* I. vi. 147 From the barbarousness of the country. **1866** *Sat. Rev.* 3 Mar. 256/1 A substantial resemblance..between the barbarousness of different periods.

c. in cruelty; = barbarity 2.

1548 Udall, etc., *Erasm. Par. Mark* v. 4 Cruell barbarousnesse of certain nations. **1680** Morden *Geog. Rect.* 460 Its Piracies..and its Barbarousness to its captives.

Barbary (ˈbɑːbərɪ). Forms: 4 **barberie**, 5 **barbre**, **barbarie**, **-ye**, 6 **barbery**, 5– **barbary**. [I. a. OF. *barbarie*, ad. L. *barbaria*, *barbariēs*, 'land of barbarians, barbarism,' f. *barbar-us* barbarous. In II. ult f. Arab. *Barbar*, *Berber*, applied by the Arab geographers from ancient times to the natives of N. Africa, west and south of Egypt. According to some native lexicographers, of native origin, f. Arab. *barbara* 'to talk noisily and confusedly' (which is not derived from Gr. βάρβαρος); according to others, a foreign word, African, Egyptian, or perh. from Greek. The actual relations (if any) of the Arabic and Gr. words cannot be settled; but in European langs. *Barbaria, Barbarie, Barbary*, have from the first been treated as identical with L. *barbaria*, Byzantine Gr. βαρβαρία land of barbarians: see sense 1.]

I. Barbarous nationality, state, or speech.

†**1.** Foreign nationality; *esp.* non-Christian, *i.e.* Saracen or pagan nationality; heathenism. *concr.* Non-Christian lands. Also *attrib.* = Paynim. *Obs.*

a **1300** *E.E. Psalter* cxiv. 1 In oute-gate of Iraele, Oute of Egipt..Of the folke of barberie. *c* **1386** Chaucer *Man of L.T.* 183 Allas, vnto the Barbre nacion I moste goon. **1432–50** tr. *Higden* (1865) I. 323 Wytlandia is..inhabite with peple of barbre worschippenge ydoles. **1480** Caxton *Chron. Eng.* ccxxxviii. 263 His fame..come in to hethnes and barbarye. **1513** Douglas *Æneis* xi. xv. 23 Hys hosing schane of wark of Barbary. **1629** Gaule *Pract. The.* 39 Not in the Barbary onely of a barbarous World, but in the Greece also of a gracious Church.

†**2.** Barbarity, barbarism, barbarousness. *Obs.*

1564 Becon *Flower Godly Pr.* (1844) 42 Nothing but cruel barbary and lion-like fierceness. *a* **1571** Jewell *Serm. bef. Queen* (1583), Come to such ignorance and barbarie. **1635** Skidmore in F. Lee *Valid. Anglic. Ord.* (1869) 84 Through tyrannical subjection and mere barbary of their inhabitants.

†**3.** Uncultivated speech, as opposed to a classical language or classic diction. Also *attrib.* *Obs.*

1509 Hawes *Past. Pleas.* 38 The langage rude..The barbary tongue. *Ibid.* 48 Tolde wyth tongue of barbary, In rude maner. **1608** Tourneur *Rev. Trag.* iv. ii. 107 Their common talke is nothing but Barbery Latin.

II. as proper name.

4. The Saracen countries along the north coast of Africa. (The only surviving sense.)

1596 Shaks. *Merch. V.* iii. ii. 272 From Lisbon, Barbary, and India. **1781** Gibbon *Decl. & F.* li, Has justly settled as a local denomination (Barbary) along the northern coast of Africa. **1843** Macaulay *Addison, Ess.* (1874) 701 The Polity and Religion of Barbary.

b. *attrib.*, esp. **Barbary ape, gum, hen, horse.**
1597 SHAKS. *2 Hen. IV*, II. iv. 108 Hee will not swagger with a Barbarie Henne. **1607** TOPSELL *Four-f. Beasts* 227 Which the common people call Barbary Horses. **1611** MARKHAM *Countr. Content* I. v, The Barbary Faulcon, the Merlin and the Hobby. **1774** GOLDSM. *Nat. Hist.* (1862) II. III. vi. 75 They [the Guinea-hen] are by some called the Barbary-hen. **1849** BROWNING *Solil. Sp. Cloister* Poems II. 269 As 'twere a Barbary Corsair's. **1875** URE *Dict. Arts* I. 289 Barbary Gum, sometimes called *Morocco gum*, the product of the *Acacia gummifera*, imported from Tripoli, etc. *Mod.* The only quadrumanous animal found in Europe is the Barbary Ape, of which a colony exists on the rock of Gibraltar.

c. *ellipt.* †A Barbary horse, a barb. *Obs.* Also, A kind of fancy pigeon. Cf. BARB *sb.*[3]
1609 B. JONSON *Sil. Wom.* IV. i, Be seen o' your Barbary often. **1653** J. HALL *Paradoxes* 145 That could outrun a Hart or a Barbary. **1834** R. MUDIE *Feath. Tribes Brit.* I. 74.

† **barbaryn**[1]. [a. OF. *barbarin, -ine*, ad. late L. **barbarīn-us*, f. *barbar-us* (taken substantively). Displaced in Eng. by *barbarian*.] = BARBARIAN.
1382 WYCLIF *Rom.* i. 14 To Grekis and barbaryns, *or hethene men*..I am dettour. **1483** *Leg. Rood* (1871) 155 Constantyn came wyth a grete multytude of barbaryns.

† **'barbaryn(e**[2]. *Obs. rare.* [f. med.L. *barbar-is* BARBERRY + -INE.] = BARBERRY.
c **1400** MAUNDEV. ii. 14 Oure Lord [was]..crouned eft with a whyte Thorn, that men clepeth Barbarynes [Fr. *berberis*]. *c* **1440** *Promp. Parv.* 21 Barbaryn frute, *Barbeum*. Barbaryn tre, *Barbaris*.

‖ **barbasco** (bɑːˈbæskəʊ). [Amer. Sp., app. alt. of Sp. *verbasco*, ad. L. *verbascum* mullein.] The popular name of a variety of S. American plants, chiefly of the family *Lonchocarpus*, the roots of which yield a poison; hence, the poison obtained from such a plant.
1860 MAYNE REID *Odd People* 53 They [*sc.* the Amazonian Indians]..fish with a harpoon spear..and sometimes by poisoning the water with the juice of a vine called barbasco. *Ibid.* 61 The deadly poisons of *barbasco* and mavacure. **1934** *Discovery* Sept. 251/1 Whereas such insect controls as Derris root..and Barbasco (*Lonchocarpus nicon*) are definitely exotic, pyrethrum is at home almost anywhere in the temperate zone. **1957** DORLAND *Med. Dict.* (ed. 23) 166/2 *Barbasco*, tropical plants, *Jacquinia paramensis* and *Paullinia pinnata*: used as fish poisons.

barbastel(le (bɑːbəˈstɛl, ˈbɑːbəstɛl). [a. F. *barbastelle*, It. *barbastrello* (Florio 1611).] A bat of a dark brown colour (*Plecotus barbastellus*), found in France and Germany.
1791 SMELLIE *Buffon's Nat. Hist.* IV. 323 The sixth species I call Barbastelle, from the Italian word *barbastello*, which also signifies a bat. **1813** BINGLEY *Anim. Biog.* I. 110 The Barbastelle Bat is somewhat larger than the two first species. **1847** CRAIG, *Barbastel Bat.*

barbate (ˈbɑːbeɪt), *a.* [ad. L. *barbātus* bearded, f. *barba* beard.] Bearded; in *Bot.* and *Zool.* furnished with a small hairy tuft or tufts.
1853 E. HAMILTON *Flora Homœop.* 217 Common Mullein ..The filaments..barbate. **1856-8** W. CLARK *Van der Hoeven's Zool.* I. 318 *Scatophaga*—Head barbate beneath.

† **'barbated,** *a. Obs. rare.* [f. as prec. + -ED.] **a.** Barbed, as an arrow. **b.** Bearded, barbate.
1782 T. WARTON *Hist. Kiddington* 63 (T.), A dart uncommonly barbated. **1802** REES *Cycl.*, *Barbated Leaf*, is a leaf terminated by a bunch of strong hairs.

† **bar'batulous,** *a. Obs.* [f. L. *barbātul-us*, dim. of *barbātus*.] Having but a small beard.
c **1600** *Timon* I. ii. (1842) 9 Old men wil be ashamed to be ouercome in counsayle..by one that is barbatulous.

‖ **Barbe.** [Fr., ad. It. and Rumansch *barba* (= med.L. *barba*, also *barbas, barbanus*) uncle, lit. 'the bearded.'] Respectful title given by the Vaudois to their teachers.
1710 in *Dupin's Eccl. Hist. 16th C.* I. III. 367 The Barbes ..have not the courage to own their Doctrine avowedly. **1838** G. FABER *Inquiry* 530 The Barbs who visited them from Apulia. *Ibid.* 338 Barbes.

barbecue (ˈbɑːbɪkjuː), *sb.* Forms: 7 barbecu, 7-8 borbecu, 8 barbicue, 7-9 barbacue, 8- barbecue, (9 babracot). [ad. Sp. *barbacoa*, a. Haitian *barbacòa* (E. B. Tylor) 'a framework of sticks set upon posts'; evidently the same as the *babracot* (? a French spelling) of the Indians of Guiana, mentioned by Im Thurn. (The alleged Fr. *barbe à queue* 'beard to tail,' is an absurd conjecture suggested merely by the sound of the word.)]

1. A rude wooden framework, used in America for sleeping on, and for supporting above a fire meat that is to be smoked or dried.
1697 DAMPIER *Voy.* (1699) I. 20 And lay there all night, upon our Borbecu's, or frames of Sticks, raised about 3 foot from the Ground. *Ibid.* I. 86 His Couch or Barbecu of Sticks. **1879** BODDAM-WHETHAM *Roraima* xiv. 155 For preservation, a barbecue is erected, and the fish are smoked over a fire. **1883** IM THURN *Indians of Guiana* ii. 47 Fires, above which were babracots loaded with beef. —— xi. 248 A babracot is a stage of green sticks built over a fire on which the meat is laid.

2. An iron frame for broiling very large joints.
1736 BAILEY *Househ. Dict.* 347 When the belly side is.. steady upon the gridiron or barbecue, pour into the belly of the hog, etc.

3. A hog, ox, or other animal broiled or roasted whole; see also quot. 1861, and BARBECUE *v.* 2.
1764 FOOTE *Patron* I. i. (1774) 6, I am invited to dinner on a barbicu. **1825** *Schuylkill Fishing Co.* in *Bibliographer* Dec. (1881) 25/1 A fine barbacue with spiced sauce. **1861** TYLOR *Anahuac* iv. 95 A kid that had been cooked in a hole in the ground, with embers upon it... This is called a 'barbacoa' —a barbecue.

4. a. A large social entertainment, usually in the open air, at which animals are roasted whole, and other provisions liberally supplied. Also *attrib. orig. U. S.*
1733 B. LYNDE *Diary* (1880) 138 Fair and hot; Browne, barbacue; hack overset. **1809** W. IRVING *Knickerb.* IV. ix. (1849) 240 Engaged in a great 'barbecue,' a kind of festivity or carouse much practised in Merryland. **1815** *Salem* (Mass.) *Gaz.* 30 June 3/2 An elegant Barbacue Dinner. **1881** H. PIERSON *In Brush* 90 On any occasion when the barbecue feast was to be the agreeable conclusion. **1884** *Boston* (Mass.) *Jrnl.* 27 Oct. 2/3 At the Brooklyn barbecue, which Governor Cleveland recently attended, 5000 kegs of beer were dispensed. **1935** *Words* Mar. 6/2 Today the American countryside is heavily sprinkled with barbecue stands. **1938** D. RUNYON *Take it Easy* 302 They are down in Florida running a barbecue stand. **1957** *Daily Mail* 5 Sept. 11/5 Anywhere they [*sc.* Americans] can find a clearing with a barbecue-pit set up, they bring out masses of steaks..and the bag of charcoal to make the fire. **1968** *Globe & Mail* (Toronto) 3 Feb. 41/3 (Advt.), Lovely covered patio with built-in barbecue. **1968** *Peace News* 21 June 7/4 (Advt.), London WC 1. 7.30 p.m. 29 Great James Street. Summer Peace Party and Barbecue.

b. A structure for cooking food over an open fire of wood or charcoal, usu. out of doors, and freq. as part of a party or other social entertainment.
1931 *Sunset* June 10 (*heading*) How to build a barbecue. **1933** C. MCKAY *Banana Bottom* vii. 88 Her husband..had been the best barbecue-builder of Banana Bottom. **1965** *Courier-Mail* (Brisbane) 9 Oct. 17/9 To make a flowerpot barbecue get a clay flowerpot... When all the charcoal is red start cooking. **1975** *Islander* (Victoria, B.C.) 17 Aug. 8/2 We all know the taste of corn roasted on the barbecue. **1980** *Daily Tel.* 26 June 3/1 A 10 ft high 8 ft wide barbecue with two chimneys..in the garden..has got to be pulled down. **1986** *Pract. Householder* July 15/1 The delicious aroma drifting across a neighbour's fence of food cooking over charcoal is enough to make anyone yearn for a barbecue of their own.

5. An open floor on which coffee-beans, etc. may be spread out to dry.
1855 KINGSLEY *Westw. Ho!* xix. (D.), The barbecu or terrace of white plaster, which ran all round the front. **1883** *Cassell's Mag.* Aug. 528/1 The [coffee-]beans..are carried to the 'barbacue,' an open space paved with cement or asphalte, where they are spread on matting..to dry. **1885** LADY BRASSEY *In Trades* 235 A barbecue is the name given, in Jamaica, to the house which contains the threshing-floor and apparatus for drying the coffee.

barbecue (ˈbɑːbɪkjuː), *v.* Forms: 7-9 barbacue, -icu(e, 8- ikew, 8- barbecue. [f. prec. sb.]

1. To dry or cure (flesh, etc.) by exposure upon a barbecue; see the sb. (senses 1 and 5).
1661 HICKERINGILL *Jamaica* 76 Some are slain, And their flesh forthwith Barbacu'd and eat. **1775** ADAIR *Amer. Ind.* 408 They cut them [pompions] into..slices, which they barbacue, or dry with a slow heat. **1794** STEDMAN *Surinam* (1813) I. xv. 406 They use little or no salt, but barbacue their game and fish in the smoke. **1839** [see BARBECUED 1].

2. To broil or roast (an animal) whole; *e.g.* to split a hog to the backbone, fill the belly with wine and stuffing, and cook it on a huge gridiron, basting with wine. Sometimes, to cook (a joint) with the same accessories. See also BARBECUE *sb.* 3.
1690 MRS. BEHN *Widow R.* II. iv. 356 Let's barbicu this fat rogue. **1702** C. MATHER *Magn. Christi* VII. vi. (1852) 556 When they came to see the bodies of so many of their countrymen terribly barbikew'd. **1769** MRS. RAFFALD *Eng. Housekpr.* (1778) 111 To barbecue a Leg of Pork. **1823** LAMB *Roast Pig, Elia* (1867) 163 Barbecue your whole hogs to your palate. **1920** J. M. HUNTER *Trail Drivers of Texas* 82 We killed and barbecued a beef.

barbecued (ˈbɑːbɪkjuːd), *ppl. a.* [f. prec. + -ED.]

1. Dried or cured by exposure on a barbecue.
1737 WESLEY *Wks.* (1872) I. 44 A little barbecued bear's flesh, (that is, dried in the sun). **1839** W. IRVING *Wolfert's R.* (1855) 221 Loaded with barbacued meat.

2. Broiled or roasted whole.
1732 POPE *Horace' Sat.* II. ii. 26 Send me, Gods! a whole Hog barbecu'd! **1807** MRS. DORSET *Peacock at H.*, A barbecued mouse was prepared for the owl. **1847** BARHAM *Ingol. Leg.* (1877) 209 The barbecu'd sucking-pig's crisp'd to a turn.

'barbecuing, *vbl. sb.* [f. as prec. + -ING[1].] The action or process of the vb. BARBECUE.
1705 R. BEVERLEY *Virginia* III. iv. 13 They [the Indians] have two ways of Broyling, *viz.* one by laying the Meat.. upon Sticks rais'd upon Forks at some distance above the live Coals..this they, and we also from them, call Barbacueing. **1716** *Wodrow Corr.* (1843) II. 150 When these diabolical operations were gone through, they finished all by barbikewing of the gentleman! **1794** STEDMAN *Surinam* (1813) I. 261 The barbacuing consists in laying the fish upon twigs of wood above the fire, where, by the smoke, they dry. **1968** *Globe & Mail* (Toronto) 17 Feb. 45 (Advt.), Tree shaded patio for summer barbecueing.

barbecute, *v.* and *ppl. a.* Also 9 babracot, -ed. Variants of BARBECUE, -D.
1687 CLAYTON in *Phil. Trans.* XLI. 160 A Piece of Venison barbecuted, that is, wrapped up in leaves, and roasted in the Embers. **1743** DK. RICHMOND *ibid.* XLII. 511 He then laid it quite open like..a Barbacute Pig to be broiled. **1883** IM THURN *Indians of Guiana* xi. 248 The meat and most of the fish is smoked or babracoted.

barbed (bɑːbd), *ppl. a.*[1] [f. BARB *v.*, *sb.*[1] + -ED.]

† **1.** Bearded. *Obs. rare.*
1693 W. ROBERTSON *Phraseol. Gen.* 206 Barbed (i.e. *Barbam habens*), *Barbatus*.

† **2.** Wearing a BARB (sense 3). *Obs.*
1526 SKELTON *Magnyf.* 1000 Barbyd lyke a nonne. **1601** W. PARRY *Sherley's Trav.* (1863) 16 Their women are..very faire, barbed every where.

3. *Her.* Having a calyx 'coloured proper.'
1611 GWILLIM *Heraldry* III. ix. 110 A rose gules Barbed and Seeded. **1864** BOUTELL *Heraldry Hist. & Pop.* xi. 70 The term *barbed* denotes the small green leaves, the points of which appear about an heraldic rose.

4. a. Furnished with a barb or barbs.
1611 BIBLE *Job* xli. 7 Canst thou fill his skinne with barbed yrons? **1718** POPE *Odyss.* IV. 499 Bait the barb'd steel. **1870** BRYANT *Homer* I. VIII. 251 Eight barbèd shafts I sent.

b. *barbed wire*: see WIRE *sb.* 1 e.

barbed (bɑːbd, ˈbɑːbɪd), *ppl. a.*[2] [f. BARB *sb.*[2] + -ED.] Of a horse: Armed or caparisoned with a *barb* or bard; properly BARDED.
1509 HAWES *Past. Pleas.* XXVII. lvii, My fayre barbed stede. *a* **1618** RALEIGH *Prerog. Parl.* (1628) 27 Many Earles could bring into the field a thousand Barbed horses. *a* **1711** KEN *Edmund* Wks. 1721 II. 84 As a barb'd Steed in Fight, who nothing fears. **1814** SCOTT *Ld. Isles* VI. xxiii, Or what may their short swords avail, 'Gainst barbed horse and shirts of mail?

† **barbed-cat.** *Obs.* A military engine; see quot.
1489 CAXTON *Faytes of A.* II. xxix. I vj b, For to make a werrely holde that men calle a barbed catte, and a bewfray that shal have ix. fadome of lengthe and two of brede, and the said catte six fadome of lengthe and two of brede.

barbel (ˈbɑːbəl). Forms: 4-5 barbell(e, 5-6 -byl(l, 6-7 -bil(l, 6-8 -ble, 7 -bell, 6- barbel. [a. OF. *barbel* (13th c. in Littré), mod. *barbeau* 'barbel,' and 'little beard':—late L. *barbellus*, dim. of *barbus* barbel (the fish), f. *barba* beard. Cf. It. *barbolo* the fish.]

1. A large European fresh-water fish (*Barbus vulgaris*) of the Carp tribe, deriving its name from the fleshy filaments which hang from its mouth.
c **1380** CHAUCER *Balade* Add. MS. 16156 B.M., þat Barbell had swolowed boþe hooke and lace. **1496** *Bk. St. Albans, Fysshynge* (1810) 26 The barbyll is a swete fysshe, but it is a greasy meete and a peryllous for mannys body. **1558** *Act 1 Eliz.* xvii § 1 No person..shall take..any Barbel not being in Length twelve Inches. **1570** LEVINS *Manip.* /29 A barble, fish, *barbo, -onis*. **1611** CORYAT *Crudities* 477 Great abundance of good fishes..especially the delicate barbils. **1867** F. FRANCIS *Angling* i. (1880) 50 The barbel, so named from the barbs or wattles that depend from the side of the mouth.

2. A fleshy filament hanging from the corners of the mouth of some fishes, e.g. of the barbel.
1601 HOLLAND *Pliny* I. 261 Her little hornes or Barbils which she [the sea-Frog] hath bearing forth vnder her eies. **1698** *Phil. Trans.* XX. 91 Those Barbles which..the Conger is never without. **1880** GUNTHER *Fishes* 37 Barbels..if developed and movable, are sensitive organs of touch.

3. A variety of house-pigeon. ? *Obs. rare.*
1741 *Compl. Fam. Piece* III. 512 The Barbel has a red Eye, a short Tail, and a Bill like a Bulfinch.

† **4.** Part of a helmet protecting the chin (= OF. *barbier, -iere.*)
c **1314** *Guy Warw.* (1840) 160 His barbel first adoun he deth, Withouten colour his neb he seth.

† **'barbeled, -bled,** *ppl. a. Obs.* [f. OF. *barbelé* barbed + -ED.] Barbed, having recurved points.
1375 BARBOUR *Bruce* VIII. 57 Vith arrowes barblyt braid. *c* **1480** CAXTON *Ovid's Met.* XII. xii, He smote hym fleynge with an arowe barbeled.

barbellate (ˈbɑːbəleɪt), *a.* [f. mod.L. *barbell-a*, dim. of *barbula* little beard + -ATE[2].] Furnished with *barbellæ* or short stiff hairs: specific epithet of the pappus in some Composite plants.
1847 in CRAIG.

barbelled, -eled (ˈbɑːbəld), *ppl. a.* [f. BARBEL + -ED[2].] Furnished with barbels.
1883 *Harper's Mag.* Dec. 106/2 The tall and barbeled dorsal fins were out of water.

barbelling, -eling (ˈbɑːbəlɪŋ), *vbl. sb.* [f. as prec. + -ING[1]; cf. *shrimping*.] Fishing for barbel.
1867 F. FRANCIS *Angling* iii. 76 As set forth in barbelling.

barbellulate (bɑːˈbɛljʊleɪt), *a.* [f. mod.L. *barbellula*, dim. of *barbella*: see BARBELLATE.] Furnished with *barbellulæ* or minute conical spines; specific epithet of the pappus in some Composite plants.
1847 in CRAIG.

barber (ˈbɑːbə(r)), *sb.* Forms: 4-7 barbour, -or, 5 -ore, -ur, 6 -oure, 6-7 -ar, 4- barber. [ME. *barbour*, a. AF. *barbour*, OF. *barbeor*:—L. type *barbātōr-em*. *Barber*, rare bef. 1500, is partly due to substitution of *-er* for earlier *our*, partly to F. *barbier* (= It. *barbiere*):—L. type **barbārius*; both f. *barba* beard.]

1. a. A man, or more rarely a woman, whose business it is to shave or trim the beards, and cut and dress the hair, of customers. (Now largely replaced by ***hairdresser***.)

Formerly the barber was also a regular practitioner in surgery and dentistry. The Company of Barber-surgeons was incorporated by Edward IV. in 1461; under Henry VIII. the title was altered to 'Company of Barbers and Surgeons,' and barbers were restricted to the practice of dentistry; in 1745 they were divided into two distinct corporations.

c **1320** *Sir Tristr.* I. lxiii, A barbour was redi thare. *c* **1370** *Robt. Sicily* 54 They broght a barber hym beforne. **1382** Wyclif *Judg.* xvi. 19 She clepide the barbour, and he shoofe seven heeris of hym. *c* **1450** in Wright *Voc.* (W.) /692 *Hec tonstrix*, a barbor. **1474** Caxton *Chesse* 74 For fere and doubte of the barbours he made his doughters to lerne shaue. **1594** Plat *Jewell-ho.* III. 74 If your teeth be verie scalie, let som expert Barber first take off the scales. **1624** Capt. Smith *Virginia* II. 30 For Barbers they vse their women. *a* **1625** Boys *Wks.* (1629) 59 Like Barbars, who cut all other except themselves. **1722** De Foe *Mem. Cavalier* (1840) 14 No surgeon to be had but a sorry country barber. **1837** Thirlwall *Greece* IV. xxvii. 1 He took his seat in a barber's shop. **1841** Dickens *Humph. Clock* 295, I would suggest that *barbers* is not exactly the kind of language which is agreeable and soothing to our feelings.. I believe there *is* such a word in the dictionary as *hairdressers*.

b. *fig.* One who clips or cuts short; a curtailer.

1609 B. Jonson *Sil. Wom.* III. ii. Wks. (1616) 554 An excellent barber of prayers.

c. *transf.* Applied *colloq.* to a bitterly cold wind which seems to 'cut' the face. Chiefly *Canada* and *N.Z.* Also, = ***frost-smoke*** (see FROST *sb.* 7 c).

1830 W. S. Moorsom *Lett. fr. Nova Scotia* 151 Frozen particles of the atmosphere, aptly termed by the natives 'the barber', sweep the surface of the water. **1832** J. M'Gregor *British Amer.* I. 133 The keen north-west wind, during winter, is often called the 'Barber' in America. **1867** Smyth *Sailor's Word-Bk.* 78 In meteorology, *barber* is a singular vapour rising in streams from the sea surface—owing probably to exhalations being condensed into a visible form, on entering a cold atmosphere. It is well known on the shores of Nova Scotia. **1899** *Westm. Gaz.* 1 Mar. 10/1 Our searching east winds are nothing in comparison with the Canadian 'barber'. **1914** J. S. Angus *Gloss. Shetland Dial.*, *Barber*, a haze which rises from the surface of water with a very keen freezing. **1933** L. Acland in *Press* (Christchurch) 16 Sept. 15/7 *The barber*, a very bitter cold wind which blows down the gorge of the Mawhera and afflicts.. Greymouth. The miners and drovers used the word in the 'sixties, and it is still in use. **1937** J. Elliott *Firth of Wellington* i. 22 Here [Grey Gorge] in winter raged an icy blast known as 'the barber', for it was as keen as the sharpest razor.

2. *attrib.*, as in ***barber fee***, ***-surgeon*** (see prec.), ***-surgery***; †**barber-monger**, a constant frequenter of the barber's shop, a fop.

c **1380** Wyclif *Sel. Wks.* (1871) III. 282 Money for barbour fees. **1605** Shaks. *Lear* II. ii. 36 You whoreson Cullyenly Barber-monger, draw. **1627** Capt. Smith *Seaman's Gram.* viii. 34 A certificate from Barber Chirurgions Hall of his sufficiency. **1645** Milton *Colast.* Wks. (1851) 358 And like an able text man slits it into fowr, that hee may the better come at it with his Barbar Surgery. **1684** tr. *Bonet's Merc. Compit.* III. 62 Eased by this common Barber-Surgeon's remedy.

3. Special combinations and locutions: ***barber's basin***, a round metal dish with a broad edge having a semicircular opening for the neck, so as to allow the chin to reach into the bowl (still sometimes used as a barber's sign). ***barber's block***, a rounded block on which wigs are made and displayed. ***barber's chair***, the chair common to all his customers, *fig.* a drab, strumpet (*obs.*). ***barber's itch*** or ***rash***: a disease affecting the face and neck, caused by a fungoid organism resulting from the use of insanitary shaving apparatus. ***barber's knife***, a razor (*obs.*). ***barber's music***, harsh discordant music, like that formerly produced by customers waiting their turn in a barber's shop, where a musical instrument was provided for their amusement. ***barber's pole***, a pole painted spirally with red and white stripes, used as a barber's sign.

1755 Smollett *Quix.* I. 191 That helmet.. which looks for all the world like a barber's basin. **1836** Hor. Smith *Tin Trump.* (1876) 192 A barber's block for supporting wigs. **1601** Shaks. *All's Well* II. ii. 16 Like a Barbers chaire that fits all buttockes. **1621** Burton *Anat. Mel.* III. iv. I. iii. (1651) 665 A notorious strumpet as common as a barbars chair. **1708** Motteux *Rabelais' Pantagr. Prognost.* v, Bonarobaes, Barbers chairs, Hedge-whores. **1890** Billings *Med. Dict.*, *Barber's itch*, tinea barbæ. **1660** Pepys *Diary* 5 June My Lord called for the lieutenant's cittern, and with two candlesticks, with money in them, for symbols, we made barber's music. **1849** Ld. Braybrooke *Pepys* V. 221 Decker also mentions a 'barber's cittern' for every servingman to play upon. **1684** *Lond. Gaz.* No. 1977/4 To be sold in York Building.. over against the Barbers Pole. **1906** *Daily Chron.* 2 Jan. 6/2 A skin complaint known as 'barber's rash'.

barber ('bɑːbə(r)), *v.* [f. prec. sb.] *trans.* To dress the beard and hair of, to trim. Also *fig.*

1606 Shaks. *Ant. & Cl.* II. ii. 229 Our Courteous Anthony .. Being barber'd ten times o're goes to the Feast. **1816** J. Gilchrist *Philos. Etym.* 145 Great grammarians.. capable of mending our standard compositions, and of *barbering* them into the fashion. **1877** E. Peacock *Gloss. Manley & Corringham, Linc.* 15/1, I alus barber my son o' Setterda' neet. **1904** *Windsor Mag.* Jan. 288/2 These latter [*sc. tondeurs*] will 'barber' a dog for a couple of francs. **1948** *Penguin New Writing* XXXIV. 29 He advised Father Eudex to barber his armpits. **1963** *Times* 12 Mar. p. vi/4 Light's noble belt of parklands around the capital has been so barbered and coiffured that rose gardens and ornamental ponds begin to replace gum-trees and native grasses.

Hence '**barbered** *ppl. a.*, trimmed or groomed by or as by a barber; also in extended use, of grass, etc.: cut closely.

1910 *Daily Chron.* 29 Jan. 6/1 Arnold.. dismissed him [Emerson].. as a barbered and eupeptic Carlyle. **1922** *Glasgow Herald* 22 Apr. 4 Bijou villas in barbered demesnes. **1947** W. de la Mare *Coll. Stories Childr.* 166 The trim barbered lawns.

barberess ('bɑːbərɪs). ? *Obs. rare.* [f. BARBER *sb.* + -ESS.] A female barber.

1611 Cotgr., *Barbiere*, a barbaresse; a woman, or she Barber. **1660** Hexham *Dutch Dict.*, *Barbierster*, a Woman barber, or a Barberesse. [In mod. Dicts.]

'**barbering**, *vbl. sb.* [f. BARBER *v.* + -ING[1].] The art or work of a barber; shaving, hairdressing.

1660 in *Select. Harl. Misc.* (1793) 380 The King was pleased to take notice of Richard's good barbering. **1860** Smiles *Self-Help* ii. 29 Wigs were worn.. an important part of the barbering business.

barberish ('bɑːbərɪʃ), *a.* In 5 barborysh. [f. BARBER + -ISH.] Of or belonging to a barber.

c **1440** *Promp. Parv.* 24/1 Barborysh hous, *barbitondium*.

†'**barberly**, *adv. Obs. rare*[−1]. [f. BARBER *sb.* + -LY[2].] With a barber's methods, by shaving.

1573 Tusser *Husb.* (1878) 111 That barberlie handled.. thou hast finisht thy cure.

barberry, berberry ('bɑːbərɪ, 'bɜːbərɪ). Forms: 5 barbere, 6–7 **barbery**, **-berie**, **-berrie**, 6–8 **berbery**, 6–9 **barbary**, 9 **berberry**, 8– **barberry**. [ad. med.L. *barbaris* (in Promp. Parv.), *berberis*, F. *berberis*, 16th c. *berbere*, Sp. *berberis*, It. *berberi*, of unknown origin and history. (An Arabic *barbāris*, sometimes cited, is a transcription of the Latin employed by Arabian botanists; there is no such word in native dictionaries, Arabic or Persian. Cf. the earlier BARBARYNE.]

1. A shrub (*Berberis vulgaris*) found native in Europe and N. America, with spiny shoots, and pendulous racemes of small yellow flowers, succeeded by oblong, red, sharply acid berries; the bark yields a bright yellow dye. Also the genus *Berberis*, of which several American species are cultivated as ornamental shrubs in Europe.

c **1420** *Anturs Arth.* vi, Vndur a lefe sale Of box and of barbere. **1578** Lyte *Dodoens* 684 The leaues and fruite of Barberies are of complexion colde. **1725** Bradley *Fam. Dict.*, *Berbery*, or Barberry-Bush. **1830** Lindley *Nat. Syst. Bot.* 31 The spines of the common Berberry are a curious state of leaf, in which the parenchyma is displaced, and the ribs have become indurated. **1872** Oliver *Elem. Bot.* II. 131 In most of the species of Barberry the terminal leaflet only is developed.

2. The berry of this tree.

1533 Elyot *Cast. Helth* (1541) 58 Digestyves of Choler: Endyve, Lettyse.. Berberyes. **1625** *Althorp MS.* in Simpkinson *Washingtons* Introd. 62 Lumpe sugar for conserve of barbaries. **1796** Mrs. Glasse *Cookery* v. 79 Garnish with barberries and lemon. **1864** H. Ainsworth *Tower Lond.* 85 A piquant sauce of oiled butter and barberries.

3. *attrib.*, as in ***barberry-bush***, ***-tree***, etc.

1578 Lyte *Dodoens* 684 With the greene leaues of the Barberie bush they make sawce to eate with meates. **1814** Sir H. Davy *Agric. Chem.* 266 The popular notion amongst farmers, that a barberry tree in the neighbourhood of a field of wheat often produces the mildew. **1839** Stonehouse *Axholme* 353 An old barbary tree. **1855** Longf. *Hiaw.* Introd. 103 The tangled barberry-bushes hang their tufts of crimson berries.

'**barberrying**, *vbl. sb.* Gathering barberries.

1859 Thoreau *Lett.* (1865) 182, I am off a-barberrying.

barber-shop. [BARBER *sb.* 2.]

1. A shop where a barber's services may be had. Now chiefly *N. Amer.*

1579 Fulke *Heskins' Parl.* 30 Alehouses and Barbar-shops. **1872** Mark Twain *Innoc. Abr.* xii. 82 We hunted for a barber-shop. **1916** W. A. Du Puy *Uncle Sam* 55 His dark locks breathed forth odors of the lotions of cheap barber shops. **1968** *Globe & Mail* (Toronto) 5 Feb. 26/9 (Advt.), Barber shop wanted to buy.

2. *attrib.*

1905 *Daily Chron.* 25 Jan. 3/3 The portrait [*sc.* of Hawthorne] with which we are all familiar—a curled barber-shop head—gives no idea of the.. charm of his face. **1931** W. Faulkner *Sanctuary* iv. 36 Don't think I spent last night with a couple of your barber-shop jellies for nothing.

b. Designating music of simple or 'close' harmony, esp. for a male vocal quartet, or a musical ensemble playing or singing such music. Cf. *barber's music* (see BARBER *sb.* 3). *colloq.* (orig. *U.S.*).

1910 William Tracey (*title*) Play that barber shop chord. **1912** W. Stevens *Let.* 26 Aug. (1967) 177 It was a chorus of barber-shop harmonies. **1926** H. C. Witwer *Roughly Speaking* 302 The barber shop quartette harmonizers and moonlight necking parties on the boat deck. **1934** C. Lambert *Music Ho!* III. 205 The phrase 'barber-shop chord' .. denotes a chord of unusual succulence. **1947** *Penguin Music Mag.* May 28 In his own work he [Tippett] has.. taken away the barber-shop harmonies and substituted pure harmonies. **1956** A. Huxley *Adonis & Alphabet* 90 That brass band, those mandolins and barber-shop ensembles. **1966** *Crescendo* Nov. 13/2 Those guys play what they call a barbershop harmony.

Barberton ('bɑːbətən). [The name of a town in the Transvaal, S. Africa.] ***Barberton daisy***: the Transvaal daisy (see TRANSVAAL). Also *ellipt.*

1906 B. Stoneman *Plants S. Afr.* 115 When several bracts surround a head of flowers, as in *Protea*, the Barberton daisy, and others of their tribe, they form an involucre. **1932** R. Marloth *Flora S. Afr.* III. II. 282 The best known species is *Gerbera Jamesoni* from the Eastern Transvaal, commonly called Barberton daisy, now cultivated in many varieties of colour and foliage. **1956** *R. Hort. Soc. Dict. Gardening* (ed. 2) II. 886/1 *Gerbera.. G. Jamesonii*. Barberton Daisy. **1960** C. Lighton *Cape Floral Kingdom* viii. 61 The Barberton daisy is known.. as the daisy from the Barberton district of the Transvaal, but outside the Union our Barbertons are commonly called gerberas.

barbery ('bɑːbərɪ). Also 5 (**barborery**), 6 **barbary**. [a. F. *barberie* (15th c. in Godefroy), f. *barbier* barber.]

†**1.** A barber's shop. *Obs.*

[*c* **1440** *Promp. Parv.* 24/1 Barborery, or barbours hous.]

2. The barber's art or craft; shaving.

1540 *Act 32 Hen. VIII*, xlii. §1 Offences.. against the good order of barbary or surgery. **1697** *View Penal Laws* 28 Neither shall any Chirurgeon there use Barbery or Shaving. **1867** *Pall Mall G.* 21 Feb. 4 Tonsor.. was a master in barbery.

†**barbet**[1]. *Obs.* [a. F. *barbette*, OF. *barbete*, dim. of *barbe* beard.]

1. A small beard or (?) barbel. *rare.*

1606 Holland *Sueton.* 114 *marg.*, Being skaly and having a couple of barbets.

2. = BARB *sb.*[1] 3.

c **1320** *Pol. Songs.* 154 The bout and the barbet wyth frountel shule feȝe.

barbet[2] ('bɑːbɪt). [a. F. *barbet*, prob. OF. *barbet* ppl. adj. = *barbu* 'bearded.']

1. A little dog with long curly hair, a poodle.

1780 Coxe *Russ. Disc.* 236 Hounds, grey-hounds, barbets. **1787** Beckford *Italy* (1834) II. 297 Fleeces.. as silky as the hair of a barbet. **1801** Hel. Williams *Sk. Fr. Rep.* II. xxxvi, Amidst those piles of corpses.. was a little barbet-dog.

†**2.** A name given by Reaumur and others to a worm covered with tufts of white filaments, which feeds on aphides. *Obs.*

1753 in Chambers *Cycl. Supp.*

3. A family of birds, found in warm countries, distinguished by a short conical bill, with tufts of bristles at its base. (In F., *barbu*.)

1824 Burchell *Trav.* I. 318 Little noisy barbet, which the Hottentots call *Hout Kapper* (wood cutter). **1880** Wallace *Isl. Life* ii. 27 Barbets are gaily-coloured fruit-eating birds.

‖**barbette** (bɑː'bɛt), *sb.* [Fr., dim. of *barbe* beard: see -ETTE.] A platform or mound of earth within a fortification, on which guns are raised so that they can be fired over the parapet. ***guns en barbette***, ***barbette gun*** or ***battery***: those so mounted as to fire over the parapet; similarly in ironclad ships (see quot. 1876). Hence, *attrib.*, as in ***barbette-cruiser***, ***-turret***.

1772 Simes *Mil. Guide*, When the parapet of a work is only of such a height that the guns may fire over it without being obliged to make embrasures, it is said the guns fire en Barbet. **1822** Byron *Juan* VII. xii, Two batteries.. Casemated one, and t'other 'a barbette.' **1872** C. King *Sierra Nev.* vii. 151 A huge slab pointed out like a barbette gun. **1876** *Daily News* 5 May 6/1 A 'barbette' battery.. is a battery of guns exposed on the upper deck, but enclosed in a fixed turret, which only partially.. protects the guns and the gunners. **1884** *Pall Mall G.* 2 Dec. 2/2 A twin-screw barbette cruiser.

†**barbette**, *v. Obs. rare*[−1]. [a. OF. *barbete-r*, *-etter* (= mod.F. *barboter*). Cf. It. *barbottare* to stammer, mumble, *balbottevole* stammering, L. *balbūtīre* to stammer.] To make inarticulate sounds, to mutter.

c **1480** Caxton *Ovid's Met.* XIV. iii, Whan they wene to speke they barbette wt gronyng voys.

barbican ('bɑːbɪkən). Forms: 3– **barbican**; 3 **barbycon**, **berbikan**, 4 **-can**, **barbygan**, 4–6 **-can(e**, 5 **barbakane**, 5–7 **-cane**, 6 **barbicane**, 7 **-con**. [a. F. *barbacane*, in 12th c. *barbaquenne* (= Pr., Sp. *barbacana*, Pg. *barbacão*, It. *barbacane*), of uncertain origin, perh. from Arab. or Pers.: *barbār khānah* is a possible Pers. combination, meaning 'house on the wall,' but examples of its actual use are wanting. Devic suggests Arab. *barbakh* canal or channel through which water flows, whence the sense 'loop-hole' might come. Littré gives as one sense in F., 'ouverture longue et étroite pour l'écoulement des eaux,' but sense 1 seems to be the earliest in OF. also. Col. Yule suggests Arab.-Pers. *bāb-khānah* 'gate-house,' the regular name in the east for a towered gateway; but it is not easy to derive from this the Romanic forms in *bar-*.]

1. An outer fortification or defence to a city or castle, *esp.* a double tower erected over a gate or bridge; often made strong and lofty, and serving as a watch-tower.

a **1300** W. DE BIBLESW. in Wright *Voc.* 130 Barbycons, *antemuralia.* *a* **1300** *Cursor M.* 10033 þe berbikans [*v.r.* barbycans, -icans] seuen þat es a-bute, þat standes thre bailles wit-vte..er þe seuen virtus. *c* **1320** *Cast. Loue* 697 Seue berbicans þer beoþ i-wrouht..And euerichon haþ ȝat and tour. **1494** FABYAN VII. 363 The Erle..made bulwerkes and barbycanys atwene the Toure and the cytie. **1596** SPENSER *F.Q.* II. ix. 25 Within the barbican a porter sate. **1633** T. STAFFORD *Pac. Hib.* ii. (1821) 520 The Barbican whereof being a stone wall of sixteene foot in height. **1821** SCOTT *Kenilw.* xxv, The usual entrance..over which he had erected a gate-house, or barbican.

fig. **1828** SCOTT *F.M. Perth* iv, Dawn seemed to abstain longer than usual from occupying her eastern barbican.

b. Retained as name of a street in London.

1632 MASSINGER *City Mad.* II. i, A Barbican broker will furnish me with outside. **1656** BLOUNT *Glossogr.* s.v., Hence *Barbican* by Red-cross-street in London.

†**2.** A temporary wooden tower or bulwark.

1489 CAXTON *Faytes of A.* II. xiv. 118 Barbakanes of tymbre shal be made fast to the batelmentes. *Ibid.* xxxviii. 161 In the grettest vesselles of werre men make towris and barbacanes.

†**3.** A loophole in the wall of a castle or city, through which missiles might be discharged. *Obs.*

1600 HOLLAND *Livy* XXIV. xxxiv. 532 He caused certaine barbacanes or loopeholes, almost a cubit deep..to be pierced through the wals.

'barbicanage. [ad. med.L. *barbicanāgium*, f. prec.: see -AGE.] Tribute paid for the construction and maintenance of barbicans.

c **1415** in Dodsworth & Dugdale *Monasticon* (1655) I. 976/2 De kaagio, muragio, paagio, barbicanagio. **1691** BLOUNT *Law Dict.*, *Barbicanage*, Money given to the maintenance of a Barbican, or Watch-Tower. Carta 17 Ed. 3. **1749** *Hist. Windsor* 120 Free from payment of Toll..Paviage Barbicanage.

barbicel ('bɑːbɪsəl). [ad. It. and mod.L. *barbicella*, dim. of *barba* beard; cf. L. *pedicellus* PEDICEL, dim. of *pediculus*, f. *pes* foot.] One of the minute hooked filaments which serve to interlock the barbules of a bird's feathers.

1869 GILLMORE *Rept. & Birds* Introd. 186 The barbules themselves frequently throw out filaments..called barbicels. **1874** COUES *Birds N.W.* 270 The fine barbules and barbicels.

barbierite ('bɑːbɪəraɪt). *Min.* [f. the name of P. *Barbier*, French chemist: see -ITE. Cf. Fr. *barbiérite*.] (See quots.)

1910 W. T. SCHALLER in *Amer. Jrnl. Sci.* XXX. 358, I propose to call this particular monoclinic soda feldspar *barbierite*, in honour of Prof. Ph. Barbier, of the University of Lyons, France. **1913** *Min. Mag.* XVI. 354 Barbierite..Monoclinic soda-feldspar ($NaAlSi_3O_8$) isomorphous with orthoclase and dimorphous with albite. **1957** *Encycl. Brit.* IX. 152/1 Such a [monoclinic] modification was earlier proposed..and given the name barbierite, but its reality as a mineral has been disputed.

barbiers ('bɑːbɪəz). [Fr. alteration of BERIBERI.] A paralytic disease common in India.

1698 FRYER *Acc. E. India & P.* 68 Whence follows Fluxes, Dropsy, Scurvy, Barbiers. **1768** LIND *Ess. Dis. Hot Climates* 260 The barbiers, a species of the palsy... Its attack is generally sudden, and entirely deprives the limbs of their motion. **1822** GOOD *Study Med.* III. 451 (*heading*) Beribery. Barbiers. **1833** *Cycl. Pract. Med.* I. 243 Barbiers is generally a chronic disease.

barbigerous (bɑː'bɪdʒərəs), *a.* [f. L. *barbiger* (f. *barba* beard + *-ger* bearing) + -OUS.] Bearded.

1731 in BAILEY. **1881** *Syd. Soc. Lex.*, *Barbigerous*..applied to petals that are hairy all over.

barbing ('bɑːbɪŋ), *vbl. sb.*[1] [f. BARB *v.* + -ING[1].]

†**1.** Shaving, hairdressing; clipping. *Obs.*

1485 *Act. 1 Hen. VII*, x. §7 The Wolle shuld be as it was shorne..withoute any sortyng, barbyng or clakkyng. **1581** SAVILE *Tacitus' Hist.* (1591) 215 Suffred his yellow haire to growe long without barbing. **1650** BULWER *Anthropomet.* ii. 49 The Abantes..were the first that used this kind of barbing. **1727-51** CHAMBERS *Cycl.*, *Barbing* is sometimes used in antient statutes for shearing.

attrib. **1639** DENTON in *Verney Papers* (1853) 236 Untill you send me a paire of barbinge sissers.

2. Furnishing with barbs.

'barbing, *vbl. sb.*[2] [f. BARB *sb.*[2] + -ING[1].] = BARDING.

1799 SCOTT *Sheph. T.* in *Lockhart* (1839) II. 35 In every stall..Stood a steed in barbing bright.

'barbing, *ppl. a.* [f. BARB *v.* + -ING[2].] **a.** Shaving; stripping bare. **b.** Furnishing with barbs.

1630 J. TAYLOR (Water P.) *Wks.* III. 28 As barbing Autumne robs the trees of leaues.

barbirousa, obsolete form of BABIROUSSA.

†**'barbit.** *Obs. rare*[−1]. [ad. L. *barbitos*, Gr. βάρβιτος lyre.] = BARBITON. (In quot. *attrib.*)

1624 HEYWOOD *Gunaik.* 389 No Barbit number suits this tragicke season.

barbital ('bɑːbɪtəl). The equivalent in the U.S. Pharmacopœia of BARBITONE.

1919 *Ann. Rep. Chem. Lab. Amer. Med. Assoc. 1918* XI. 54 During the year 1918, the laboratory examined several specimens of barbital... Barbital was introduced into medicine under the proprietary name 'Veronal'. *Ibid.* 54 Barbital is described..as diethylbarbituric acid. **1922** E. PHILLPOTTS *Grey Room* viii. 183 A woman, who had taken morphine and barbital, was found apparently dead. **1926** T. SOLLMANN *Man. Pharmacol.* (ed. 3) 757 Barbital (veronal; diethyl-barbituric acid). This was introduced by E. Fischer and Mering, 1903 and 1905... Barbital is used in nervous insomnia, mania and delirium.

†**'barbitist.** *Obs.* Also 7 **barbatist.** [ad. L. *barbitista*, ad. Gr. βαρβιτιστής, f. βάρβιτος: see -IST.] A player on the barbiton.

1656 BLOUNT *Glossogr.*, *Barbitist*, a Lutinist. **1693** W. ROBERTSON *Phraseol. Gen.* 207 A Barbatist or player on the Lute.

‖**barbiton, -os** ('bɑːbɪtən, -əs). [L. *barbiton, -os*, a Gr. βάρβιτον, *-ος*.] A many-stringed musical instrument; a kind of lyre or lute.

1545 ASCHAM *Toxoph.* (Arb.) 39 All maner of pypes, barbitons, sambukes..be condemned of Aristotle. **1753** CHAMBERS *Cycl. Supp.* s.v., The barbitos is said to have differed from the lyre and cithara. **1842** LYTTON *Zanoni* I. i, His barbiton, as the learned Mersennus tells us to call all the varieties of the great viol family.

barbitone ('bɑːbɪtəʊn). [f. as next + -ONE.] A hypnotic drug, diethyl barbituric acid, often known by the trade name VERONAL.

1914 *Brit. Pharmacopœia* 62 Barbitonum. Barbitone. Synonyms—Diethyl-barbituric Acid: Malonurea: Diethylmalonyl-urea..$C_8H_{12}N_2O_3$. **1918** *Nomencl. Dis.* (ed. 5), Chloral and other Hypnotic Drugs. Sulphonal, Trional, Tetronal, Barbitone, Proponal. **1923** *Brit. Pharmac. Codex* 175 Barbitone was introduced and first tested, pharmacologically and in clinical practice, under the trade-name Veronal. **1927** *Daily Express* 30 Dec. 7/7 The chemist..supplied a bottle containing twenty-five tablets of barbitone, which was the equivalent of veronal. **1957** J. BRAINE *Room at Top* xxii. 187 Its silence as different from real silence as a barbitone trance from natural sleep.

barbiturate (bɑː'bɪtjʊərət, -eɪt, bɑːbɪ'tjʊərət). *Chem.* [f. BARBITUR(IC *a.* + -ATE[1] 1 c.] A salt of barbituric acid; one of the group of hypnotic and sedative substances derived from barbituric acid. Also *attrib.* or as *adj.*

1928 *Biol. Abstr.* 17323 (*title*) Anesthesia in the dog of allyl-isopropyl-diethylamine barbiturate. **1930** *Lancet* 1 Mar. 473/2 G. Link, who has used isoamylethyl barbiturate in goitre surgery. *Ibid.* 15 Nov. 1086/1 (*title*) The Barbiturates in Labour Cases. **1931** *Ibid.* 14 Mar. 586/1 A symposium on the *Barbiturates in Anæsthesia* was opened by Dr. M. Nierenstein, who described in detail the chemistry of barbituric acid and its derivatives. **1955** *Sci. News Let.* 9 July 19/2 The barbiturate family of sleeping medicines. **1957** *N.Z. Listener* 26 July 15/3 Some of you must already be addicts to barbiturates... Ultimately not only physical but moral health deteriorates if you become a barbiturate habitue. **1963** *Times* 21 Dec. 6/2 The pathologist's view was that the overdose of barbiturate she had taken would have proved fatal. **1967** *Spectator* 7 July 10/1 As regards addiction, it is now definitely established that people can become dependent on barbiturates.

barbituric (bɑːbɪ'tjʊərɪk), *a. Chem.* [ad. F. *barbiturique* (Ann. de Chimie et de Physique, 1865), f. G. *barbitur* in *barbitursäure* (Baeyer 1863, in *Ann. d. Chemie und Pharm.*), f. *Barbara*, a woman's name.] ***barbituric acid***, an acid ($C_4H_4O_3N_2$) from which various hypnotic and sedative drugs are derived; malonyl urea.

1866 ODLING *Anim. Chem.* 128 Baeyer has increased the list of compounds by his discovery of..the violuric and barbituric acids. **1885** REMSEN *Org. Chem.* xii. 204 Barbituric acid..is a product obtained from uric acid. **1927** *Proc. R. Soc. Med.* 20 (*title*) The Clinical and Pathological Effects of Hypnotic Drugs of the Barbituric Acid and Sulphonal Groups. **1941** T. S. ELIOT *Dry Salvages* v. 14 To ..fiddle with pentagrams Or barbituric acids.

Barbizon ('bɑːbɪzən), *a.* [The name of a village near the forest of Fontainebleau, France.] Epithet of a French school of painting of the middle of the 19th century associated with the village of Barbizon.

1890 D. C. THOMSON (*title*) The Barbizon School of Painters. **1896** *McClure's Mag.* VI. 471/2 Corot, Daubigny, Dupré, Troyon, Diaz, Jacque, and others who, with our mania for classification, we call the 'Barbizon school'. **1967** *Listener* 12 Jan. 51/2 At the time he painted this picture the Impressionists were still..followers of the Barbizon painters, Courbet or Boudin.

barble ('bɑːb(ə)l). Also 5 **barbul, -ulle.** [ad. It. *barbola*:—L. *barbula*, dim. of *barba* beard.] = BARB *sb.*[1] 4.

c **1440** *Promp. Parv.* 24/1 Barbulle, sekenes of the mowthe. *c* **1595** MONTGOMERIE in Watson's *Coll.* III. 13 (Jam.) The Botch, and the Barbles. **1607** TOPSELL *Four-f. Beasts* 283 The Barbles or paps underneath the tongue. **1753** CHAMBERS *Cycl. Supp.*, *Barbles* in the manege, knots of superfluous flesh growing in the channels of a horse's mouth.

barble, obsolete form of BARBEL.

barbless ('bɑːblɪs), *a.* Unbarbed.

1882 *Daily News* 9 Feb. 5/2 Varieties of fish hooks..the flint and barbless bone articles of Esquimaux.

barbola (bɑː'bəʊlə). [Proprietary term, arbitrarily f. BARBOTINE.] In full ***barbola work***, decorative work composed chiefly of flowers and fruit modelled in a plastic paste and coloured, used to embellish small articles of wood, glass, pulp, etc.

1927 *Daily Express* 26 Sept. 5/5 Tiny porcelain-looking flowers..for the newest buttonholes..which are really a form of barbola work, are arranged in small round posies. **1928** *Ibid.* 22 Feb. 5/3 The latest designs in barbola work mirrors... The barbola or other wood-carving decoration is sparingly used—just a cluster of the painted raised flowers.

barbone (bɑː'bəʊnɪ). *Veterinary Path.* [It., lit. 'thick or long beard', augmentative form of *barba* (see BEARD *sb.*).] An infectious disease of buffaloes and cattle; hæmorrhagic septicæmia.

1907 F. S. H. BALDREY in *Jrnl. Trop. Vet. Sci.* II. 287, I obtained a culture of 'Barbone' or 'Hemorrhagic Septicæmia'... Nomenclature. Hemorrhagic Septicæmia, Pasturella des Bouffles (France), Barbone (Italy)..Ghotu, Golghotu or Ghotina (India). *Ibid.* 304 A peculiarity of Barbone, as it occurs in India, is that it seldom occurs in a violently epidemic form. **1929** *Veterinary Record* 24 Aug. 709/1 Hæmorrhagic septicæmia... The more common alternative terms applied to the condition are Barbone, Buffalo Disease, Buffalo Cholera, Pasteurellosis and, in Malaya..Hawa Kerbau.

barborery, -orysh: see BARBERY, BARBERISH.

†**bar'bose,** *a. Obs. rare*[−1]. [? f. L. *barba*: see -OSE.] ? Bearded.

1716 M. DAVIES *Ath. Brit.* III. 7 More like Verbose and Barbose or Morose Catechists..than well educated Scholars.

†**'barbot.** *Obs. rare*[−1]. [a. OF. *barbote, -oute, -ouste* (= It. *balbotta, barbotta*, med.L. *barbota*), considered by Jal a contraction of *barca-botta, barque-botte*, barrel-boat, from its appearance; Du Cange compares med.L. *barbuta* a kind of helmet.] A small vessel or sloop, having its deck protected by an arched covering of leather.

1579 FENTON *Guicciard.* IX. (1599) 397 With the losse of two fustes, two barbots, and..fourtie smaller vessels.

barbotine ('bɑːbətɪn). [a. F. *barbotine*, f. *barboter* to work noisily with the bill in water or mud (as a duck, etc.).] A thin creamy mixture of kaolin clay used to ornament pottery; pottery ornamented with barbotine. Also *attrib.*

1865 ELIZA METEYARD *Wedgwood* II. 122 The edging and letters in relief..being formed in yellow barbotine or slip. **1883** *Standard* 15 May 1/2 (*Advt.*) Lessons daily in Painting on glass, china, and barbotine. **1888** *Atalanta* Sept. 692/2 'Barbotine' work is like very rough painting with thick *impasto.* **1891** *Mag. Art* 353/1 There is 'barbotine' for those who like it—rich in colour. **1914** *Oxf. Univ. Gaz.* 573/1 (Rep. Ashmolean Mus.) Fragments of barbotine ware, showing that this type of pottery was popular in Memphis as well as in the Sudan.

barbott (cf. F. *barbotte*), variant of BURBOT.

Barbre, obsolete form of BARBARY.

‖**barbula** ('bɑːbjʊlə). [L., dim. *barba* beard.]

1. A small beard; see quot. ? *Obs.*

1688 HOLME *Armory* II. xvii. 392 The Barbula or pick-a-divant, or the little tuft of hair just under the middle of the lower Lip.

2. 'The inner row of fringes or teeth in the peristome of such mosses as *Tortula.*' *Treas. Bot.* 1866.

barbule ('bɑːbjuːl). [ad. L. *barbula*; see prec.]

1. = BARBEL 2. (So in med.L.)

1848 S. MAUNDER *Treas. Nat. Hist.* Gloss., Barbules, filamentous appendages..attached to the mouths of certain fishes. **1872** BAKER *Nile Tribut.* ix. 146 This fish has four long barbules in the upper jaw.

2. One of the series of pointed, and sometimes serrated or hooked, processes, fringing the barbs of a feather, and filling up the space between them.

1835 TODD *Cycl. Anat. & Phys.* I. 350/2 The barbules are given off from either side of the barbs. **1869** GILLMORE *Rept. & Birds* Introd. 185 These smaller filaments are the barbules, by means of which the barbs are retained in position.

3. *Bot.* = BARBULA 2.

1881 in *Syd. Soc. Lex.*

bar'bulye, *v. Sc. arch.* In 6 **barboulle, barbulȝie.** [a. F. *barbouille-r* (= Sp. *barbullar*, It. *barbugliare*) to besmear, speak confusedly; see Littré and Scheler.] To confuse, muddle, disorder.

c **1572** MONTGOMERIE *Cherry & Slae*, Everything apperit twae To my barbulyeit brain. **1588** A. KING *Canisius' Catech.* 113 Gif yᵉ sacrament of order by ouerthrauin yᵉ ecclesiasticall offices wald be barboulled and confused.

bar'bulye, *sb. Sc. arch.* [f. prec. vb.] Confusion, perplexity, quandary.

1820 HOGG *Winter T.* II. 41 (JAM.), I—stude—swutheryng what it avysit me neiste to doo in thilke barbulye.

barb wire: see WIRE *sb.* 1 e.

‖**barca** ('bɑːrka). [It.; see BARK *sb.*^{2}] A boat, skiff, barge.

1866 HOWELLS *Venet. Life* iv. 54 Drift along in the scarcely moving barcas. **1883** F. PEARD *Contradictions* I. 29 A barca with serenaders was slowly approaching.

‖**barca-longa.** *Obs.* Also 7 barqua-, 7–8 barco-longo. [Pg. or OSp.; lit. 'long barge.'] 'A large Spanish fishing-boat, navigated with lug-sails, and having two or three masts.. common in the Mediterranean.' Falconer *Dict. Marine* 1789.

1681 *Lond. Gaz.* 1608/1 With a Sloop and a Barqua-Longa. **1691** *Ibid.* No. 2708/1 The French.. have only one Barco Longo.. left. **1762** MORE in *Phil. Trans.* LII. 451 The selfsame barcalonga, or xebeck. **1790** BEATSON *Nav. & Mil. Mem.* I. 335 Sent Captain Veale in a barcolongo, attended by two feluccas, to attempt to destroy them.

barcarole, -olle ('bɑːkərəʊl). [In sense 1 ad. It. *barcaruolo* boatman; in sense 2 a. F. *barcarolle*, It. *barcaruola*, boatman's song; f. BARCA.]

‖**1.** An Italian boatman.

[**1611** *Panegyr. V.* in *Coryat's Crudities*, The Barcaruolo appetite His Gondola directed right Unto a female Elfe.] **1854** BADHAM *Halieut.* 200 We.. ordered our barcaroles to pull for the tonnaro.

2. A song sung by Venetian *barcaruoli* as they row their gondolas; a song or piece of music composed in imitation or reminiscence of such songs.

1779 in WARING *Dict. Mus.* **1819** MOORE *Venet. Air* ii, When maidens sing sweet barcarolles. **1850** MRS. BROWNING *Work & Cont.* Poems I. 336 The woman singeth.. A pleasant chant, ballad or barcarolle. **1866** *Cornh. Mag.* Nov. 564 With a song full of dole, A forlorn barcarole, As my gondola glides.

barcary, another form of BARKARY.

†**Barce'lona.** [Name of a town in Spain, with manufacture of silk.] **1.** A handkerchief or neckerchief of soft twilled silk. *Obs.*

1761 in E. Singleton *Social New York* (1902) 236 Black Barcelona handkerchiefs. **1795** WOLCOTT (P. Pindar) *Dinah* Wks. 1812 IV. 187 Now on this handkerchief, so starch and white, Was pinn'd a Barcelona, black and tight. *c* **1816** MRS. SHERWOOD *Stories Ch. Catech.* xiv. 117 She pulled out a Barcelona handkerchief. **1833** *The Amulet* 224 With.. a silk Barcelona round his neck, like any gentleman.

2. Used *attrib.* in ***Barcelona nut*** or as short for this.

1851 MAYHEW *Lond. Labour* I. 89/1 The 'Barcelonas' are from 4½*d.* to 6*d.* a quart to the street-sellers. **1880** *Encycl. Brit.* XI. 549/1 Hazel-nuts, under the name of Barcelona or Spanish nuts, are largely exported from France and Portugal, and especially Tarragona. **1899** [see PETROUS *a.* 1]. **1951** *Good Housek. Home Encycl.* 346/2 *Barcelona Nut*.. usually kiln-dried to make it keep well. *Ibid.* 505/1 Cultivated varieties include the Filbert, Cob and Barcelona.

barchan (bɑː'kɑːn). Also **barchane, barkhan.** [Native word.] A crescent-shaped dune of shifting sand such as occur in the deserts of Turkestan. Also *attrib.*

1888 *Encycl. Brit.* XXIII. 511/2 Shifting sands blown into *barkhans*, or elongated hills, sometimes 50 and 60 feet in height. **1897** [see MEDANO]. **1900** *Geogr. Jrnl.* XV. 24 On the higher portions of the foreland, to leeward and further from the river barchans (or medanos) occur. **1953** *Sci. News* XXVII. 14 The *barchan types* [of dune].. found only where the wind is predominantly from a single direction.

Barclaycard ('bɑːklɪkɑːd). Also **Barclay card.** [f. the name of *Barclay(s Bank* + CARD *sb.*^{2}] The name of a combined cheque guarantee card and credit card issued by Barclays Bank.

1966 *Times* 11 Jan. 13/3 The Barclay cards are to be available to non-customers. **1966** *Banker* Feb. 72/1 The aim is to cut down the use of cash.. by making 'Barclaycard' a customary method of making purchases. **1968** *Business Week* 13 Jan. 64/2 Bank of America, the world's largest bank, seems to have gotten a jump by franchising its BankAmericard to other banks... Its card is now interchangeable with Britain's Barclaycard. **1975** 'A. HALL' *Mandarin Cypher* ii. 33 TC's for five hundred pounds, a Barclaycard, two hundred in cash, it seemed a lot. **1981** *Daily Tel.* 31 Mar. 21 Perhaps the only major original package that has emerged in the last fifteen years has been the birth of Barclaycard in 1966. **1983** 'J. LE CARRÉ' *Little Drummer Girl* iii. 58 He had lost his passport and his wallet, and his Barclaycard, and his air ticket.

‖**bar'cone.** [It., augmentative of BARCA.] A vessel used for freight in the Mediterranean. (Webster has an anglicized form *barcon.*)

1847 CRAIG, *Barcone.*

Barcoo (bɑː'kuː). The name of a river in Queensland, Australia, used *attrib.* and *ellipt.* to designate certain local conditions, phenomena, etc. (see quots.).

1889 J. H. MAIDEN *Useful Native Plants Australia* 76 *Anthistiria membranacea*, Lindl... 'Barcoo Grass' of Queensland; also called 'Landsborough Grass'. One of the best pasture grasses in Queensland. **1898** MORRIS *Austral Engl.* 19 *Barcoo Rot*,.. persistent ulceration of the skin, chiefly on the back of the hands, and often originating in abrasions. *Ibid.* 20 *Barcoo Vomit*, a sickness occurring in inhabitants of various parts of the high land of the interior of Australia. **1903** 'T. COLLINS' *Such is Life* 30 Grand remedy for scurvy, and Barcoo rot, and the hundreds of natural diseases that flesh is subject to. **1934** *Bulletin* (Sydney) 21 Nov. 21/1 The electrical storms there [*sc.* Longreach, Queensland]—called Barcoos—are terrific and take toll of both human and stock life. **1945** BAKER *Austral. Lang.* iii. 62 *Barcoo spew, Barcoo vomit*.. a sickness characterized by vomiting after food is taken. **1958** D. NILAND *Call me when Cross turns over* 52 Don't try the Barcoo spews. A cow of a thing. **1967** *Sunday Mail Mag.* (Brisbane) 10 Sept. 3/2 Young Arthur, fortunately dodged the typhoid, but did collect a man-sized dose of what was popularly called Barcoo rot.

bard (bɑːd), *sb.*^{1} 5–; also 6–7 (*Sc.*) baird, 6 barth, 6–7 bardh. [a. Gael. and Ir. *bàrd*:—OCelt. **bardo-s* poet-singer, minstrel (whence Gr. βάρδος, L. *bardus*, as alien words, '*bardus* Gallice cantor appellatur, qui virorum fortium laudes canit,' Festus). In Eng. originally only an alien word from the mod. Celtic vernaculars, i.e. in Scotland *bard, baird* from Gaelic, in England *barth, bardh* from Welsh *bardd*, and *bard* from Irish, employed as in contemporary Celtic usage; first naturalized in Scotland, and then by no means appreciative in its use (see sense 2); afterwards, under the influence of the βάρδος, *bardus* of the classical writers, adopted in Eng. literature as a historical and poetic term.]

1. An ancient Celtic order of minstrel-poets, whose primary function appears to have been to compose and sing (usually to the harp) verses celebrating the achievements of chiefs and warriors, and who committed to verse historical and traditional facts, religious precepts, laws, genealogies, etc. Still the word for 'poet' in modern Celtic languages; and in Welsh *spec.* A poet or versifier who has been recognized at the Eisteddfod.

c **1450** HOLLAND *Houlate*, Sa come the Ruke with a rerd, and a rane roch, A bard out of Irland, with Banachadee! **1538** LELAND *Itin.* V. 15 Peraventure Lleuys Morganne the Barth was deceivid in this. **1584** POWEL *Lloyd's Cambria* 15 This word *Bardh* signified such as had knowledge of things to come. **1594** SHAKS. *Rich. III*, IV. ii. 109 A bard of Ireland told me once, I should not liue long after I saw Richmond. **1596** SPENSER *St. Irel.* (J.), There is amongst the Irish a kind of people called *bards*, which are to them instead of poets: whose profession is to set forth the praises or dispraises of men in their poems or rhime. **1610** HOLLAND *Camden's Brit.* I. 421 The funerall song or Dump of a most ancient British Bard. [*Note*, Poet]. **1615** *Val. Welshm.* (1663) A iv b, Call with your silver tones, that reverend Bardh. **1627** MAY *Lucan* I. (R.) You bards securely sung your elegyes [*fudistis carmina Bardi*]. **1780** BURKE *Sp. Econ. Ref.* Wks. III. 261 The invasion of King Edward and the massacre of the bards. **1879** MACLEAR *Celts* ii. 18 The Druidic order included.. the Bards or 'Glee-men.'

2. In early Lowland Scotch used for: A strolling musician or minstrel (into which the Celtic *bard* had degenerated, and against whom many laws were enacted); in 16th c. a term of contempt, but idealized by Scott by association with 4.

1449 *Act 6 Jas. II* (1597) §22 Gif there be onie that makis them fuilis and are bairdes, or vthers sic like rinnares about. **1457** *Ibid.* §80 Sornares, bairdes, maister-full beggers, or feinȝiet fuiles. ? *a* **1500** *Kenneth's Stat.* in Sir J. Balfour's *Patricks* 680 All vagabundis, fulis, bardis, scudlaris, and siclike idill pepill, sall be brint on the cheek. *c* **1505** DUNBAR *Flyting* 49 Irsche brybour baird, wyle beggar with thy brattis! **1609** SKENE *Rej. Mag.* 135 Feinzied fooles, bairdes, rynners about.. after sundrie punishments, may be hanged. **1805** SCOTT *Last Minstr.* Introd., The last of all the bards was he Who sung of Border chivalry.

3. Applied to the early versifying minstrels or poets of other nations, before the use of writing, as the Old English *gleeman*, Scandinavian *scald*, etc.

1623 COCKERAM, *Bardes*, ancient Poets. **1763** J. BROWN *Poetry & Mus.* iv. 41 After a certain Period of Civilization, the complex Character of Legislator and Bard would separate. **1775** T. WARTON *Eng. Poetry* I. Diss. i. 34 Various Islandic odes.. which were sung by the Scandinavian bards. **1855** MILMAN *Lat. Chr.* II. IV. iv. 283 A Teutonic literature has begun; the German bards have become Christian poets.

4. *poet.* A lyric or epic poet, a 'singer'; a poet generally. [Chiefly after Lucan; quot. 1627 in 1.]

[**1606** SHAKS. *Ant. & Cl.* III. ii. 16 Hoo, Hearts, Tongues, Figure, Scribes, Bards, Poets, cannot Thinke speake, cast write sing, number: hoo, His loue to Anthony.] **1667** MILTON *P.L.* VII. 34 That wild rout that tore the Thracian bard In Rhodopè. **1704** POPE *Messiah* 37 The Saviour comes, by ancient bards foretold. **1769** GARRICK *Song* Wks. 1785 II. 427 For the bard of all bards was a Warwickshire Bard. **1809** BYRON (*title*) English Bards and Scotch Reviewers. **1834** CUNNINGHAM *Burns* (1850) 154/2 The character of the Ayrshire bard. **1881** (*title*) The Bard of Avon Birthday Text-book compiled from Shakespeare's Plays and Poems.

5. *Comb.*, as *bard-craft*; *bard-like* adj.

1763 J. BROWN *Poetry & Mus.* ix. 168 The first great Bard-like Character we meet with [in China] is Confucius. **1808** SCOTT *Marm.* Introd. 213 The keener rush of blood That throbs through bard in bard-like mood. **1820** T. MITCHELL *Aristoph.* I. 205 Ye verse-smiths and bard-mechanicians. **1840** BROWNING *Sordello* II, 312 Forswearing bard-craft.

bard, *sb.*^{2} *Obs.* exc. *Hist.* Also 5–6 barde. [a. F. *barde* horse-armour, also 'a long saddle for an ass or mule of canvas' (Cotgr.); cf. It. *barda* horse-armour, also pack-saddle, and F. *bardelle* pack-saddle. These, and the existence of a dial. F. *aubarde*, seem to identify the word with Sp. and Pg. *albarda* pack-saddle, referred by Devic to Arab. *al-bardaʿah*, i.e. *al* the + *bardaʿah* 'stuffed pack-saddle for ass or mule' (Bocthor), 'covering placed over the back of a beast to alleviate the pressure of a pack-saddle' (Freytag). Whether the Fr. sense 'defensive armour for a horse' arose out of this is doubtful. Diez has compared ON. *bard* the beak of a ship, *barði* a beaked ship, a 'ram,' also (poet.) a shield. Also erroneously called BARB, q.v.]

1. (Usually *pl.*) A protective covering for the breast and flanks of a war-horse, made of metal plates, or of leather set with metal spikes or bosses, but sometimes (*e.g.* in tournaments) merely ornamental, and made of velvet or other rich stuff.

1480 CAXTON *Chron. Eng.* VII. (1520) 82/2 Stedes.. trapped with yron bardes. **1577** HOLINSHED *Chron.* III. 803/1 [The] bards of their horsses white veluet. **1611** GWILLIM *Heraldry* IV. xv. 232 The Shafron, the Cranet, and the Bard. **1727–51** CHAMBERS *Cycl.* s.v., The barde is an armour of iron or leather, wherewith the neck, breast, and shoulders of the horse are covered. **1830** JAMES *Darnley* xix, We shall find bards, if we want them.

2. *pl.* Armour composed of metal plates, formerly worn by men-at-arms.

1551 EDWARD VI. *Lit. Rem.* (1858) II. 375 Men of armes.. some with sleves and hauf cotes, some with bards and staves. **1570** HOLINSHED *Scot. Chron.* II. 129 A gentleman trimlie trapped with bards of steele. **1603** FLORIO *Montaigne* II. ix. (1632) 225 A compleat French man at armes, with all his bards.

3. *Comb.* **bard-wise** *adv.*, as if with bards.

1577 HOLINSHED *Chron.* III. 801/2 The kings spare horsse trapped bardwise, with harnesse brodred with bullion gold.

¶ By confusion (or misprint) for BARB *sb.*^{1} 4.

1653 *Consid. Dissolv. Crt. Chancery* 24 To cure the Mallender, Farses, Trunchions, Bards.. in a horse.

bard (bɑːd), *sb.*^{3} [a. F. *barde*, in same sense, transferred from the armour *barde*; see prec.] A thin slice of bacon used to cover a fowl, etc.

1706 PHILLIPS *New World Words* (ed. 6), *Menehout*.. a peculiar manner of baking Meat, cover'd with Bards, or thin Slices of Bacon, in an Oven between two Fires. **1725** BRADLEY *Fam. Dict.* s.v. *Neats Tongue*, Bards or thin Slices of Bacon.. Having covered the Tongues with other Beef-Stakes and Bacon Bards. **1736** BAILEY *Househ. Dict.*, *Bards*, broad slices of Bacon, with which pullets, capons, etc.. are sometimes covered before they are roasted. **1960** *Times* 1 Aug. 9/3 Barding. Covering with thin slices of fat bacon or pork (bards), poultry, game or meat that is deficient in natural fat and is to be either oven or pot roasted. Bards are also used to line.. a *terrine*.

bard (bɑːd), *v.*^{1} Also 6 baird, bayrd. [a. F. *barde-r* (15th c.), f. *barde* BARD *sb.*^{2} and ^{3}.]

1. To arm or caparison (a horse or man) with bards. (Chiefly in pa. pple.: cf. BARDED.)

a **1521** *Helyas* in Thoms *E.E. Pr. Rom.* (1858) III. 83 A good and mighty courser well barded and trapped. **1629** HOLLAND *Xenoph. Cyrop.* (1632) 71 To unloose the horses.. to bridle them.. also to bard them. **1805** SCOTT *Last. Minstr.* I. xxix, Scarce half the charger's neck was seen; For he was barded from counter to tail. **1845** *Blackw. Mag.* LVIII. 775 The gallant bay charger barded with steel.

2. To cover (a fowl, etc.) with slices of bacon.

1665 MOUFFET & BENN. *Health's Impr.* (1746) 117 Whether roast Meat be best.. larded, barded, scorch'd or basted. **1884** PHILLIS BROWNE in *Girl's Own P.* June 491/2 Cooks who are afraid to lard the breasts of game or poultry frequently content themselves with barding the same.

†**bard,** *v.*^{2} *Obs.* [app. due to confusion of BARB *v.* and BEARD.] To clip; = BARB *v.* 2.

1641 *Termes de la Ley* 61 To *bard* or *beard* wooll, is to cut the head and neck from the other part of the Fleece. **1693** W. ROBERTSON *Phraseol. Gen.* 207 To Bard, or beard wool, *extremitates vellerum tondere*.

†**bard,** *ppl. a. Obs.* [short for BARDED; perh. influenced by BARRED.] = BARDED 1, 2, BARBED^{2}.

1581 STYWARD *Martial Discip.* II. 127 The armed men, as well bard as light. **1609** HOLLAND *Amm. Marcel* XVI. x. 63 On bard horses [*cataphracti equites*].. harnessed all over with good corselets, and bard about [*cincti*] with guards of steele. **1627** DRAYTON *Agincourt* (1631) 11 Rich Sadles for the Light-horse and the Bard.

†'**bardan(e.** *Obs. rare.* [a. F. *bardane* 'the Clote, burre-docke, or great burre; the noisome, and stinking vermine, called, a Punie' (Cotgr.).]

1. The burdock.

c **1250** in Wright *Voc.* (W.) /557 *Lappa*, bardane, clote.

2. A bug.

1572 BOSSEWELL *Armorie* II. 52 All his body is roughe and sharpe, as the bodie of a Bardan.

†**bar'dash.** *Obs.* Also 6 bardass 6–7 bardasso, 7 -assa, -achio. [a. F. *bardache*, cogn. with It. *bardascia*, Sp. *bardajo, -axo*; perh. ad. Arab. *bardaj* slave.] A catamite, 'cinædus.'

1548 THOMAS *Ital. Dict.*, *Zanzeri*, bardasses. **1600** O. E. *Repl. Libel* I. ii. 43 Publikely maintaining bardassaes and concubines. **1653** URQUHART *Rabelais* III. xxv, Bardachio that thou art! **1721** MRS. CENTLIVRE *Plat. Lady* Epil. 190 With your false Calves, Bardash, and Fav'rites.

Hence **bardashing,** *vbl. sb. Obs.*

1678 BUTLER *Hud.* III. I. 278 Raptures of Platonick Lashing, And chast Contemplative Bardashing.

barded ('bɑːdɪd), *ppl. a.* [f. BARD *v.* + -ED.] Armed, caparisoned, or covered with bards.
1501 DOUGLAS *Pal. Hon.* I. xlvii, A bardit curser stout and bald. **1535** COVERDALE *Joel* ii. 4 They are to loke vpon like bayrded horses. **1596** DANETT *Comines' Hist. Fr.* (1614) 298 Two thousand men of armes barded. **1795** SOUTHEY *Joan of Arc* VI. 300 A man-at-arms upon a barded steed. **1880** DISRAELI *Endym.* lix. 267 The bells of a barded mule announced the Jester.

¶ By confusion or misprint for BARBED.
1598 SYLVESTER *Du Bartas* I. v. 41/3 If the Scolopendra have suckt-in The sowr-sweet morsell with the barded Pin.

†**bar'del(le.** *Obs. rare.* [a. F. *bardelle* (= It. *bardella*): see BARD *sb.*[2]] A pack-saddle.
1603 FLORIO *Montaigne* I. xlviii. (1632) 158 There is nothing accounted more base..than to use saddles or bardels. **1753** CHAMBERS *Cycl. Supp.*, *Bardelle*..denotes a saddle made in form of a great saddle, but only of cloth stuffed with straw, and tied tight down with packthread, without either leather, wood or iron.

Bardesanist (bɑː'dɛsənɪst). [ad. med.L. *Bardesanista.*] A member of the heretical sect founded in the 2nd century by Bardesanes, of Edessa in Mesopotamia, who, in addition to Manichæan views of good and evil, held that primeval man had an ethereal body, which was through sin enclosed in a gross carnal one, and that redemption consists in being divested of the latter and restored to the former. Hence **Bar'desanism**.
1674 HICKMAN *Hist. Quinquart.* 18 This matter of Manicheism and Bardesanism. **1751** in CHAMBERS *Cycl.*

bardess ('bɑːdɪs). *rare.* [f. BARD *sb.*[1] + -ESS.] A female bard, a poetess.
1822 *Blackw. Mag.* XII. 657 'The Living Bardesses of Britain.' **1879** *Fam. Her.* 22 Nov. 55/1 Her daughter was a 'Bardess.'

bardian ('bɑːdɪən), *a.* [f. BARD *sb.*[1] + -IAN.] Of or belonging to bards.
1652 GAULE *Magastrom.* 338 Their bardian odes.

bardic ('bɑːdɪk), *a.* [f. as prec. + -IC.] Of, pertaining to, or of the character of, bards.
1775 T. WARTON *Eng. Poetry* I. Diss. i. 51 *note*, An argument of the bardic institution being fetched from the east. **1803** W. TAYLOR in *Ann. Rev.* I. 261 The druidic or bardic order among the Cimbri. **1876** GREEN *Short Hist.* iv. §1 160 The court of Llewelyn was crowded with bardic singers.

barding ('bɑːdɪŋ), *vbl. sb.* [f. BARD *v.*[1] or *sb.*[2] + -ING[1].] Warlike or ornamental covering of a horse.
1536 BELLENDENE *Cron. Scot.* 25 (JAM.) Bellis that hang on thair bardyngis. **1834** PLANCHÉ *Brit. Costume* 144 The bardings of his horse..are similarly blazoned.

bardish ('bɑːdɪʃ), *a.* [f. BARD *sb.*[1] + -ISH.]
1. Of or belonging to bards. (*Rather depreciatory.*)
1612 SELDEN in Drayton *Poly-olb.* A ij, Incredible reports, and Bardish impostures. *a* **1790** T. WARTON *Poems* 78 (JOD.) One of the bardish traditions about Stonehenge.
†**2.** *Sc.* Rude, insolent; cf. BARDY. *Obs.*
a **1662** R. BAILLIE *Lett.* (1775) I. 311 (JAM.) The rest of that day [was]..mispent with the altercation of that bardish man Mr. D. Dogleish.

bardism ('bɑːdɪz(ə)m). [f. as prec. + -ISM.] The system, doctrine, or principles of bards.
1716 M. DAVIES *Ath. Brit.* II. 191 Welsh poetick Bardism is best cultivated in the Ionicks of Merionethshire. **1863** *Reader* No. 30. 75 That native Bardism which had been part and parcel of the aboriginal Druidism.

†**bardist.** *Obs. rare*[−1]. [f. as prec. + -IST.] An adherent or follower of the bards.
1588 J. HARVEY *Discours. Probl.* 84 Neither Persian Magician..nor French Druyde or Bardist.

bardlet ('bɑːdlɪt). [See -LET.] = next.
1867 *Athenæum* No. 2062. 587/2 The gossamer conceits of our bardlet. **1883** R. NOEL in *Contemp. Rev.* Nov. 716 That the Universe is..'a suck and a sell'..is..the encouraging strain of our latest bardlets.

bardling ('bɑːdlɪŋ). [f. as prec. + -LING.] A young or inexperienced poet; a poetaster.
1813 G. COLMAN *Br. Grins, Vagaries Vind.* liv, The bardling who in afternoons Warbles his published lays to melting tunes. **1858** BAILEY *Age* 64 So woe to you young bardlings scant of brains.

‖**bardocu'cullus.** *Obs.* [L.] A Gallic peasant's woollen cloak, with a hood or cowl, worn also by monks. Hence **bardocucullated** (= F. *bardococullé*), wearing a cowled cloak.
1611 CORYAT *Crudities* 225 A Bardocullus, that is, a Shepheard's ragged and weather-beaten cloake. **1708** MOTTEUX *Rabelais* v. iii, These monkhawks whom you see bardocucullated with a Bag.

bardolatry (bɑː'dɒlətrɪ). [f. BARD *sb.*[1] (sense 4) + -OLATRY.] Worship of the 'Bard of Avon', i.e. Shakespeare. (Occas. used of other writers.) So **bardolater** (-'ɒlətə(r)) [-OLATER], a worshipper of the Bard, a Shakespearolater; **bar'dolatrous** *a.*, tending to or characterized by bardolatry.
1901 G. B. SHAW *Plays for Puritans* Pref. p. xxxi, So much for Bardolatry! **1903** —— *Man & Superman* Ep. Ded. 30 Foolish Bardolaters make a virtue of this after their fashion. **1905** —— in *Sat. Rev.* 11 Feb. 170/2 The word 'pity' does not reach even the third row of the stalls, much less the gaping bardolatrous pit. **1911** *Times Lit. Suppl.* 9 Nov. 440/3 Playing for the sympathy of the 'bardolaters'. **1914** G. B. SHAW *Dark Lady* Pref. 112 The familiar plea of the Bardolatrous ignoramus, that Shakespear's coarseness was part of the manners of his time. **1952** *Scrutiny* XIX. 13 The writer who found it 'extremely salutary' that Milton's eminence should be questioned appears now..a resolute bardolater. **1958** *Listener* 19 June 1031/1 Could this bud of Bardolatrous love be proved a flower? **1963** *Punch* 26 June 934/3 Those whose Bardolatry..falls this side the '*Dream*'.

Bardolphian (bɑː'dɒlfɪən), *a.* [f. *Bardolph* (see below) + -IAN.] Resembling or characteristic of Bardolph, a character in Shakespeare's *Henry IV*, *Henry V*, and *Merry Wives of Windsor*, noted for his red nose.
1756 TOLDERVY *Hist. 2 Orphans* I. x. 81 The tears very seasonably rolled over his Bardolphian cheeks. *Ibid.* IV. xxiv. 134 His Bardolphian nose. **1827** J. WIGHT *More Mornings at Bow St.* 19 His face did bear certain *Bardolphian* tokens of late hours, and 'healths five fathoms deep'. **1899** *Manch. Guardian* 22 June 8/2 We do not agree with those who think that M. Coquelin has made too much of his nose [in 'Cyrano de Bergerac']. It is not Bardolphian or acquired. **1950** G. WILSON *Brave Comp.* iii. 30 That red face and large, pitted Bardolphian nose.

'bardship. [f. BARD *sb.*[1] + -SHIP.] The office, dignity, or personality of a bard; cf. *lordship*.
1787 BURNS *Border Tour* (Globe) 569 The Captain..showed a particular respect to my bardship. **1811** BYRON *Hints from Hor.* 478 Boys shall hunt your bardship up and down.

bardy ('bɑːdɪ), *a. Sc.* [Origin uncertain: perh. f. BARD *sb.*[1] sense 2.] Bold-faced, defiant; audacious, pert. Hence **'bardily** *adv.*, **'bardiness**.
1788 R. GALLOWAY *Poems* 202 (JAM.) Shun the pert and bardy dame, Whose words run swiftly void of sense. *Ibid.* 64 They, bardily, and hardily, Fac'd home or foreign foe. **1826** J. WILSON *Noct. Ambr.* Wks. 1855 I. 118 Haudin up the..chin o' him in a maist bardy and impertinent manner.

bardy ('bɑːdɪ), *sb. Austral.* Also **bardee, bardi.** [Aboriginal.] An edible Australian wood-boring grub (*Bardistus cibarius*) or its larvæ. Used locally in ***starve the bardies!***, an exclamatory phr. of surprise or disgust.
1926 R. J. TILLYARD *Insects Austral. & N.Z.* xx. 233 Coleoptera..The 'bardee' of Western Australia, *Bardistus cibarius* Newm., ranges right across to New South Wales; its larvae are found in the stems of grass-trees and 'black-boys' (*Xanthorrhoea*) and are eaten both by aborigines and white people. **1941** BAKER *Dict. Austral. Slang* 8 *Starve the bardies!*, a popular W.A.. ejaculation, synonymous with 'Stone the crows!' *a* **1951** X. HERBERT in Murdoch & Drake-Brockman *Austral. Short Stories* 299 Kaijek paused to look among the broken roots for bardies. **1959** A. UPFIELD *Bony & Black Virgin* xvii. 150 The bardee grubs came up from tree-trunks and..tree-roots to split their skins and emerge as great winged moths the size of a man's hand. *a* **1963** J. FOUNTAIN in B. James *Austral. Short Stories* (1963) 270 Fisher..sneaking round the corner..with a jar of bardi grubs under his arm.

bare (bɛə(r)), *a.*, *adv.*, *sb.* Forms: 1 **bær**, 3 **bar**, 4-5 **baar** (5-8 *Sc.* **bair**), 2- **bare.** [Common Teut.: OE. *bær* (= OS., OHG., MHG. *bar*, MDu. *baer*, G. and Du. *baar*, ON. *berr*, Da., Sw. *bar*):—OTeut. **baz-oz*, cogn. w. Lith. *basas*, OSlav. *bosŭ* barefoot; Aryan **bhos-ós*. The original short vowel is lengthened in mod.Eng., Du., and Ger.]
A. *adj.* **I.** Without covering.
1. a. Of the body or its parts: Unclothed, naked, nude.
a **1000** *Cædmon's Gen.* (Grein) 783 Bare hie ʒesáwon heora lichoman. **1297** R. GLOUC. 514 Manie in hor bare fless hom late croici vaste. *c* **1386** CHAUCER *Knts. T.* 900 On hir bare knees adoun they falle. *c* **1400** *Destr. Troy* xxx. 12269 Founden bare in his bed. **1596** SHAKS. *Merch. V.* IV. i. 252 Lay bare your bosome. **1611** BIBLE *Isa.* xlvii. 2 Make bare the legge, vncouer the thigh. **1713** STEELE *Englishm.* No. 1. 2 He filled my Hat..and then put it upon my bare Head. **1853** *Arab. Nts.* (Rtldg.) 229 Robbers, who stripped him as bare as my hand.
b. Stripped to the shirt or other under-garment; cf. *naked*, Gr. γυμνός.
1330 R. BRUNNE *Chron.* 161 Bare in serke and breke Isaac oway fled. **1866** KINGSLEY *Herew.* xiv. 181 You bid him go and fight in his bare shirt.
†**c.** *bare eye*: cf. 'naked eye.' *Obs.*
1664 POWER *Exp. Philos.* I. 18 Whose whole bulk to the bare eye is quite indiscernable. **1790** IMISON *Sch. Art.* I. 263 Holds his finger..between his bare eye and an object.
2. With the head uncovered. *arch.* = BARE-HEADED.
c **1386** CHAUCER *Prol.* 685 Dischevele, sauf his cappe, he rood al bare. **1596** SHAKS. *Merch. V.* II. ix. 44 How many then should couer that stand bare? **1633** G. HERBERT *Ch. Porch.* lxviii, When once thy foot enters the church, be bare. *a* **1674** CLARENDON *Hist. Reb.* III. XVI. 594 They all stood bare, whilst the Herаulds proclaim'd the King.
3. *fig.* Unconcealed, undisguised, open to view.
c **950** *Lindisf. Gosp.* Matt. v. 46 Ah ne & bær-suinniȝo ðis doas? **1526** TINDALE *Heb.* iv. 13 All thynges are naked and bare unto the eyes off hym. **1671** MILTON *Samson* 902 Bare in thy guilt how foul must thou appear! **1781** COWPER *Charity* 494 He hides behind a magisterial air His own offences, and strips others bare. **1827** KEBLE *Chr. Y.* 4 S. Lent xii, Bare to the rude world's withering view.
4. Of natural objects, as earth, heavens, trees: Without such covering as they have at other times, *e.g.* without vegetation, clouds, bark, foliage, etc.
c **885** K. ÆLFRED *Boeth.* xxxiv. §10 Sumna on cluðum, sumne on barum sondum. *c* **1175** *Lamb. Hom.* 181 Þurh ane godliese wude in-to ane bare felde. *a* **1300** *Cursor M.* 1321 Braunches..o bark al bare. **1523** FITZHERB. *Surv.* xxxv. (1539) 54 They wylle eate the grounde moste barest. **1611** BIBLE *Joel* i. 7 He hath..barked my figge tree: he hath made it cleane bare. **1720** *Lond. Gaz.* No. 5827/1 The Country between the two Armies being eaten bare. **1806** WORDSW. *Ode Immort.* 13 The Moon doth with delight Look round her when the heavens are bare. **1862** STANLEY *Jew. Ch.* (1877) I. ii. 22 Hills which are now bare were then covered with forest.
5. Of persons and animals: Stripped of a natural covering; deprived of hair, wool, flesh, etc.; bald.
a **1300** *Cursor M.* 5165 His heued it was all bar for eild. **1387** TREVISA *Higden* I. 115 Golgotha is to menynge a baar scolle. *c* **1450** HENRYSON *Tale of Dog* 112 The Scheip..Nakit and bair, syne to the feild couth pas. **1591** SHAKS. *Two Gent.* IV. i. 36 The bare scalpe of Robin Hoods fat Fryer. **1783-94** BLAKE *Chimney-sw.* 7 When your head's bare, You know that the soot cannot spoil your white hair.
6. a. Wanting appropriate covering, equipment, or array; unfurnished, uncovered.
c **1200** *Trin. Coll. Hom.* 139 Bare eorð to bedde, and hard ston to bolstre. *c* **1420** *Sir Amadace* xiv, For his mete he wold not spare, Burdes in the halle were neuyr bare. *c* **1600** *Rob. Hood* (Ritson) xvi. 44 When others cast in their bated hooks, The bare lines into the sea cast he. **1607** TOPSELL *Four-f. Beasts* 240 It is good to use your horse to backing both saddled and bare. **1722** SEWEL *Hist. Quakers* (1795) I. IV. 254 Fain to lie upon the bare boards. **1810** SCOTT *Lady of L.* I. xi, Nor were these earth-born Castles bare, Nor lacked they many a banner fair.
b. Without armour or weapons, unarmed. ? *Obs.*
1205 LAY. 17346 Þa Irisce weoren bare. *c* **1340** *Gaw. & Gr. Knt.* 277 If þou craue batayl bare, Here faylez þou not to fyȝt. **1549** CHEKE *Hurt. Sedit.* (1641) 25 Yee..hewed him bare, whom yee could not hurt armed. **1604** SHAKS. *Oth.* I. iii. 175 Men do their broken Weapons rather vse, Then their bare hands.
c. Of cloth: Napless, threadbare. Of weapons: Unsheathed. ***bare poles*** in *Naut.*: masts with no sails set; also ***bare-poled*** adj., having bare poles; also *transf.*, of trees lacking leaves or branches.
[*c* **1386** CHAUCER *Prol.* 260 With thredbare cope, as is a poure scolere.] **1483** *Act 1 Rich. III*, viii. Pream., Course Clothes..bare of Threde. **1591** SHAKS. *Two Gent.* II. iv. 45 Their bare Liueries. **1604** —— *Oth.* v. i. 3 Weare thy good Rapier bare. **1753** CHAMBERS *Cycl. Supp.* s.v., A cloth is said to be bare or naked, when the nap is too short. **1762** *Let.* 11 Nov. in *Ann. Reg. 1762* (ed. 5, 1787) 117/2 The ship sprung a leak, and we were obliged to lie to under bare poles. **1774** N. CRESSWELL *Jrnl.* 5 Aug. (1925) iii. 31 To furl the F.S. [*i.e.* fore-sail] and scud under bare pole. **1780** COXE *Russ. Disc.* 130 Drove 24 hours under bare poles. **1851** MELVILLE *Moby Dick* III. xxxiii. 197 The *Pequod*..bare-poled was left to fight a Typhoon. **1855** TENNYSON *Lt. Brigade*, Flash'd all their sabres bare. **1864** J. A. GRANT *Walk across Africa* 33 Open forests of bare-poled trees.
II. Stripped of surroundings, contents, property.
†**7.** Defenceless, unprotected, deserted. *Obs.*
1297 R. GLOUC. 388 Þe wule hii were in Normandye & Engelond so bare. *c* **1400** *Destr. Troy* IV. 1320 So bare leuyt, Vmfoldyng with his fos þat he ne fle might. **1551** EDW. VI. *Lit. Rem.* (1858) II. 353 If he found a bare company..to set upon them.
†**8.** Laid waste, desolate. *Obs.*
c **1305** *St. Edm. King* 20 in *E.E.P.* (1862) 87 Robbede al þat he fond & makede þane toun bar. *c* **1374** CHAUCER *Anel. & Arc.* 62 So desolate stode Thebes and so bare. **1593** SHAKS. *Lucr.* 1741 Like a late-sack'd island..Bare and unpeopled. **1642** MILTON *Sonn.* viii, To save the Athenian walls from ruin bare.
9. Without possessions, destitute, indigent, needy; scantily furnished. Const. *of*, rarely *in*: see b.
1205 LAY. 3420 Þat ich bare sitte, wunnen biræued. *c* **1280** *Sarmun* 44 in *E.E.P.* (1862) 5 He nel noȝt leue his eir al bare. *c* **1480** *Childe Bristowe* 554 in Hazl. *E.P.P.* (1864) 131 First was riche and sitthen bare. **1538** BALE *Thre Lawes* 1084 As bare as Job. **1755** SMOLLETT *Quix.* (1803) I. 233 Bare I was born, and bare I remain. **1827** KEBLE *Chr. Y.* Sexages. ix, Yet mercy hath not left us bare.
b. *c* **1220** *Bestiary* 144 in *O.E. Misc.* 5 Ðanne ðe neddre is..bare of his brest atter. *c* **1380** *Sir Ferumb.* 1641 Of blisse y am al bare. **1658** SIR T. BROWNE *Hydriot.* i. (1736) 16 We are bare in Historical Particulars. **1865** CARLYLE *Fredk. Gt.* III. IX. vii. 127 Old Father Margraf..does always keep us frightfully bare in money. **1883** *Ch. Times* 9 Nov. 813/2 Lutheranism is more bare of the attribute of saintliness than any other creed held by a large body of Christians.
10. Destitute or defective in various other respects: **a.** Without contents, empty.
1399 LANGL. *Rich. Redeless* IV. 21 No þing y-lafte but the bare baggis. *a* **1700** DRYDEN (J.) A bare treasury. *Nursery Rime, Mother Hubbard*, When she got there the cupboard was bare.
†**b.** Poor in quality, paltry, worthless. *Obs.*
1399 LANGL. *Rich. Redeless* IV. 70 So blynde and so ballid and bare was þe reson. *c* **1400** *Destr. Troy* VI. 2502 Soche bargens are bytter, þat hafe a bare end. **1592** SHAKS. *Ven. &*

Ad. 188 What bare excuses makest thou to be gone. **1596** —— *1 Hen. IV*, III. ii. 13 Such poore, such bare.. attempts.

c. Without literary or artistic effect; bald, meagre, unadorned.

c **1400** *Destr. Troy* Prol. 74 Cornelius translated it.. but he brought it so breff, and so bare leuyt, þat no lede might have likyng to loke þerappon. **1597** MORLEY *Introd. Mus.* 84 In long resting the harmonie seemeth bare. **1798** FERRIAR *Eng. Histor.* in *Illustr. Sterne* 248 The bare line of general narration is so happily ornamented.

†**d.** Simple, without luxury; unpolished, rude.

1583 STUBBES *Anat. Abus.* II. 72 Better it is to haue bare feeding than none at all. *c* **1596** SPENSER (J.) Yet was their manners then but bare and plain. **1603** KNOLLES *Hist. Turks* (1621) 76 This bare Northren people [the Tartars].

†**e.** *bare wind* in *Naut.*: one too much ahead to fill the sails well; scant. *Obs.*

1682 *Lond. Gaz.* No. 1744/4 This morning sailed the whole Fleet.. with a bare Wind at N.W. and by N. **1691** *Ibid.* No. 2671/4 Having but a bare Wind, and little of it. **1694** LUTTRELL *Brief Rel.* III. 320 The whole fleet was out of sight, with a bare wind at North.

III. Without anything of the nature of addition.

11. Without addition, mere, simple; —— and nothing else, —— only. *bare contract* in *Law*: an unconditional promise or surrender.

c **1200** *Moral Ode* 137 in *Lamb. Hom.* 167 Hefde he bon þer enne dei oðer twa bare tide. *c* **1315** SHOREHAM 35 Man moȝe lauede be Thorȝ bare repentaunce. **1393** GOWER *Conf.* II. 286, I set it at no more accompt, Than wolde a bare straw amount. **1577** HANMER *Anc. Eccl. Hist.* (1619) 104 They taught Christ to be.. but a bare Man. **1633** G. HERBERT *Love Unkn.* 40 in *Temple* 122 Many drunk bare wine. **1641** *Termes de la Ley* 211 Bare contract, or naked promise, is where a man bargaineth or selleth his lands, or goods.. and there is no recompence appointed to him for the doing thereof.. This is a naked contract, and voyd in Law. **1697** *C'tess D'Aunoy's Trav.* (1706) 109 Who can do you hurt by bare looking on you. **1711** ADDISON *Spect.* No. 69. 5 Nature indeed furnishes us with the bare Necessaries of Life. **1769** *Junius Lett.* xiii. 56 A bare contradiction will have no weight. **1844** LD. BROUGHAM *Brit. Const.* xix. §6 (1862) 373 A bare majority of seven to five.

†**12.** From the idea of completeness in itself; Sheer, absolute, very, actual. *Obs.*

1205 LAY. 20876 Ich habbe hine idriuen: to þan bare dæðe. *a* **1330** *Sire Degarré* 561 Thei he be the bare qued, He schal a-doune. *c* **1400** *Destr. Troy* XXIV. 9682 With strong batell & brem till the bare night. *Ibid.* 10805 Born to þe burghe in the bare tyme, Honerable Ector in armes to helpe.

IV. *Comb.* **a.** specially **bare-arse**, dial. name of the Little Grebe; **bare-belly** *Austral.* and *N.Z.*, a sheep with no wool on the belly; so ***bare-bellied*** adj.; **bare-board**: in phr. ***to go on bare-board***, to play without a stake on the gaming-table; **bare-bone**, a lean, skinny person; **bare-fallow**, land left fallow for a whole year; = *naked fallow* (see NAKED *a.* 9 d); hence as *v.*, to leave land fallow for a whole year; **bare-fallowing** *vbl. sb.*; **bare-man**, obs. term in *Sc. Law* for a bankrupt or 'broken' man.

c **1875** G. L. MEREDITH in A. J. Harrop *Adventuring in Maoriland* (1935) xiii. 143 Naturally, the easiest-shorn sheep—'bare-bellies' and 'bare-points'—are selected first. **1878** E. S. ELWELL *Boy Colonists* 109 The ewes have many of them at shearing-time no wool on the legs or under the belly, and hence are called 'bare-bellies'. Of course, these 'bare-bellied' ewes.. are very quickly shorn. **1956** G. BOWEN *Wool Away!* (ed. 2) 155 *Bare-belly*, a sheep with all the wool scraped or dropped off its belly. **1965** J. S. GUNN *Terminol. Shearing Industry* I. 6 *Barebelly*, a sheep with defective wool growth caused by a break in the fibre structure. This causes the wool to fall off the belly and legs, and the rest of the wool can be removed with a few blows or even with the hands. **1831** J. C. LOUDON *Encycl. Agric.* (ed. 2) III. vi. 801 The expediency or inexpediency of pulverising and cleaning the soil by a bare fallow, is a question that can be determined only by experience, and not by argument. **1831** *Q. Jrnl. Agric.* II. 101 Some writers maintain, that bare fallowing is not necessary on any kind of soil, as judicious management will prevent an influx of weeds. **1891** R. WALLACE *Rural Econ. Austral. & N.Z.* ix. 161 Bare-fallowing of land in place of manuring was too much practised as a means of restoration. **1961** *Agric. Hist. Rev.* IX. 3 A larger proportion of land was bare-fallowed.

b. adjs. formed by *bare* qualifying a sb., as ***bare-breech, -leg, -limb, -weight*** (also *adv.*: see 11), BARE-FOOT, -HEAD, equivalent in sense to: **c.** parasynthetic adjs. formed on prec. + -ED, as ***bare-armed***, (having the arms bare), ***-arsed, -bosomed, -breasted, -breeched, -chested, -knuckled, legged, -throated, -walled.*** **d.** ppl. adjs. in which *bare* acts as a verbal complement, as ***bare-bitten, -eaten, -gnawn, -worn.***

a. **1655** FULLER *Ch. Hist.* VI. vii. §3 III. 493 To vye ready silver with the King of Spaine, when he.. was fain to go on bare-board. **1596** SHAKS. *1 Hen. IV*, II. iv. 358 Heere comes leane Jacke, heere comes bare-bone. **1581** *Acts Jas. VI* (1597) §110 To hound out bair-men and vagabounds, to the attempting of sik foull.. enormities. **1609** SKENE *Reg. Maj.* Table 66 Bairman.. is he quha makes cession of his gudes and geir to his creditours. *a* **1763** SHENSTONE *Ess.* Wks. (1765) 172 A Miser, if honest, can be only honest bare-weight. **1801** HAN. MORE *Wks.* VIII. 248 Such bare-weight protestants prudently condition for retaining the Popish doctrine of indulgences.

b. **1205** [see BAREFOOT]. **1483** *Cath. Angl.* 21/1 Barlege, *incaligatus*. **1577** STANYHURST *Descr. Irel.* in *Holinsh.* VI. 51 Such barebreech brats as swarme in the English pale. **1583** —— *Æneid* 137 Baerlym swartye Pyracmon. **1587** *Cens. Loyall Subj.* (Collier) 25 Bareleg and barefoot they wandred.

c. *c* **1350** *Will. Palerne* 2767 A barlegged bold boie. **1562** J. HEYWOOD *Prov. & Epigr.* (1867) 16 To beg a breeche of a bare arst man. **1580** NORTH *Plutarch* (1676) 289 He would go out bare-necked to the waste. **1595** SHAKS. *John* V. ii. 177 In his fore-head sits A bare-rib'd death. **1647** R. STAPYLTON *Juvenal* 209 Then must bare-finger'd [= ringless] Pollio beg or fast. **1809** M. BERRY *Jrnl.* 31 May in 'Lewis Melville' *Berry Papers* (1914) VI. 291 Such an over-dressed, bare-bosomed, painted eye-browed figure one never saw! **1814** SCOTT *Wav.* xv, Four bare-legged dairy-maids. **1828** —— *F.M. Perth* vi, These bare-breeched Dunniewassals. **1855** WHITMAN *Leaves of Grass* 27 Press close barebosomed night! **1873** SYMONDS *Grk. Poets* xii. 403 Stately maidens and bare-chested youths. **1924** MASEFIELD *Sard Harker* I. 5 The truth man learns Fighting bare-knuckled Nature in the ring. **1927** D. H. LAWRENCE *Morn. in Mex.* 43 A bare-bosom, black-browed girl. **1928** D. H. LAWRENCE *Lady Chatt.* xv. 276 Nowt but a bare-arsed lass. **1950** HEMINGWAY *Across River* v. 29 Beyond the Sile there was nothing but bare-assed plain. **1975** *Forbes* (N.Y.) 1 July 34/1 As bare-breasted dancers bounced and the orchestra blared, Jim Walter, stone sober, fell sound asleep. **1986** *Los Angeles Times* 20 July v. 4/4, I was surprised that he didn't require that the bare-breasted statue be fitted with a brassiere.

d. **1577** tr. *Bullinger's Decades* Pref., Ministers.. bare bitten of their Patrons. **1603** FLORIO *Montaigne* I. xxvii. (1632) 96 A subject, common, bare-worne, and wyer-drawne. **1605** SHAKS. *Lear* V. iii. 122 By Treasons tooth bare-gnawne. **1627** MAY *Lucan* IX. 7 On their bare-eaten ground. **1770** GOLDSM. *Des. Vill.* 308 Ev'n the bareworn common is denied.

B. *adv.* [cf. Sw. *bara* only, Ger. *baar.*]

†**1.** Thoroughly, completely. (Cf. A 12). *Obs. rare.*

c **1340** *Gaw. & Gr. Knt.* 465 Ȝet breued watz hit ful bare, A meruayl among þo menne.

2. With numeral adjs.: No more than, at most; scarcely, BARELY. *arch.* or *Obs.*

c **1325** *E.E. Allit. P.* B. 1573 Out-taken bare two & þenne he þe þrydde. **1597** J. PAYNE *Royal Exch.* 46 Errors.. of bare 80 yeres continuans. **1678** OTWAY *Friendsh. in F.* 24 As hot-headed with my bare two Bottles, as a drunken Prentice. **1716** *Lond. Gaz.* 5410/4 Weighs bare ten Grains.

C. *sb.* [the adj. used *absol.*]

1. A naked part of the body; the bare skin.

c **1300** *St. Brandan* 612 And helede al aboute his bodi, nas ther no bar on him bileved. *c* **1400** *Destr. Troy* XIV. 5821 Hit shot þrough.. þe shire maile, to þe bare of þe body. **1526** TINDALE *Mark* xiv. 51 Cloothed in linnen apon the bare. **1611** BEAUM & FL. *King & No K.* II. 45 If ever I touch'd any bare of her. **1906** *Westm. Gaz.* 29 Dec. 16/1 The downtrodden slippers tied on with string, toes out, and hardly any sole: the child is walking 'on the bare', as the saying is.

fig. *c* **1600** MARSTON (in Webster), You have touched the very bare of truth.

†**2.** A bare space or place. *Obs.*

1683-4 *Gt. Frost* (1844) Introd. 19 Her [Thames'] watry green [shou'd] be turn'd into a bare. **1706** PHILLIPS, *Bare*, a Place without Grass, made smooth to Bowl in.

bare (bɛə(r)), *v.* [OE. **barian* (in *abarian*), f. *bær* BARE *a.*; cf. also *bęrian*, ON. *bera*, OHG. *barôn.*]

1. *trans.* To make or lay bare, uncover, open to view; to unsheathe (a weapon).

a **1000** *Beowulf* 2482 Benc-þelu beredon. *a* **1300** *Cursor M.* 1878 þorow a fowle.. may we knaw if þe erþ barid be. *c* **1420** *Pallad. on Husb.* IV. 14 The pith to bare is not thaire kynde. **1601** SHAKS. *Jul. C.* I. iii. 49 And thus vnbraced.. Haue bar'd my Bosome to the Thunder-stone. *a* **1725** POPE *Odyss.* XIX. 526 His tusks.. the sinewy fibres tore, And bared the bone. **1876** GREEN *Short Hist.* iv. §5 (1882) 197 Earl Warrenne bared a rusty sword. **1884** TENNYSON *Becket* 133 He bows, he bares his head.

2. *fig.* To disclose, reveal, make manifest.

[*c* **1000** ÆLFRIC *Joshua* ii. 20 Gif ðú abarast úre spræce.] *c* **1250** *Gen. & Ex.* 1912 His fader he it gan vn-hillen & baren. *c* **1325** *E.E. Allit. P.* B. 1149 þat watz bared in Babyloyn. *a* **1652** BROME *City Wit* IV. ii, To fall out and bare one anothers secrets. **1764** GOLDSM. *Trav.* 390 Tear off reserve, and bare my swelling heart. **1822** B. CORNWALL *Julian Apost.*, They did bare the secrets of the grave.

3. To strip, divest. Const. *of*, *from.*

c **1440** HYLTON *Scala Perf.* (W. de W. 1494) II. xx, Vntyll a soule can.. baren [bareyn 1533] hym from all the good dedes that he dooth. **1443** HEN. VI in Ellis *Orig. Lett.* III. 34 I. 80 Werres.. haue bared vs gretely of tresore. **1563** SACKVILLE *Myrr. Mag.* Induct. 2 With blustring blastes had al ybared the treen. **1857** LIVINGSTONE *Trav.* xix. 367 He quite bared his garden in feeding us. **1858** J. MARTINEAU *Stud. Chr.* 42 Stripped of every disguise, and bared of all that is conventional.

bare, obs. form of BOAR, BEAR.

bareback ('bɛəbæk), *a.*, *adv.* **a.** = BARE-BACKED 2. **b.** As *adj.* with noun of action.

1562 J. HEYWOOD *Prov. & Epigr.* (1867) 24 Where saddles lacke Better ride on a pad, than on the horse bare backe. **1768** in *Essex Inst. Hist. Coll.* (Salem, Mass.) XIV. 262 Went to Boston in sley..; came home bare back. **1870** O. LOGAN *Before Footlights* 369 When the 'bare-back rider' returns from the ring. **1880** 'MARK TWAIN' *Tramp Abroad* xxvi. 269 He could ride bareback and know and feel that he was safe. **1923** J. H. COOK *50 Years on Old Frontier* 48 Bareback riding was the order of the day.

bare-backed ('bɛəbækt), *a.* [see BARE *a.* 6.]

1. With the back bare.

1831 CARLYLE *Sart. Res.* III. vii, Some barefooted, some almost bare-backed.

2. *esp.* Of a horse: Without saddle, unsaddled; also with *ride* as *adv.*

1628 LE GRYS tr. *Barclay's Argenis.* 123 A Horse.. not bare-backt.. but with those trappings which the kings there did vse. **1854** J. STEPHENS *Centr. Amer.* 277 Mounted on a bare-backed horse.

‖**bareca, -ka** (ba'reka). [a. Sp. *bareca*, *barrica*; cf. BARRICO.] A small cask or keg, a BREAKER.

1773 in Hawkesworth *Voy.* X. 439 Barecas, or small casks which are filled at the head. **1867** SMYTH *Sailor's Word-bk.*, *Bareka.* **1875** BEDFORD *Sailor's Pocket-bk.* v. 155 A Bareca for Beacon should be fitted as a buoy.

bared (bɛəd). *ppl. a.* [f. BARE *v.* + -ED.]

1. Made bare, exposed to view, naked, nude.

a **1300** [see BARE *v.* 1.] **1552** HULOET, Bared, *nudatus*. **1583** BABINGTON *Commandm.* (1590) 432 As good Sem and Japheth did to their bared father. **1842** TENNYSON *Œnone* 137 Her clear and bared limbs.

2. Stripped, denuded, cleared of covering.

1382 WYCLIF *Num.* xx. 19 Bi the beryd weye [Vulg. *via trita*] we shulen goon. **1579** SPENSER *Sheph. Cal.* Feb. 112 His bared boughes were beaten with stormes. **1825** WATERTON *Wander.* I. i. 88 A rood or two of bared ground.

barefaced ('bɛəfeɪst), *a.* (in use sometimes approaching an *adv.*; cf. BAREFOOT, -ED).

1. With the face uncovered: *hence* **a.** with no hair on the face, beardless, whiskerless, also *fig.*; **b.** without mask or vizard.

1590 SHAKS. *Mids. N.* I. ii. 100 Some of your French Crownes haue no haire at all, and then you will play bare-fac'd. **1602** —— *Ham.* IV. v. 164 They bore him bare fac'd on the Beer. *a* **1762** LADY MONTAGUE *Lett.* xcii. 151 The.. ball, to which he has invited a few bare-faced, and the whole town en masque. **1869** BLACKMORE *Lorna D.* vii. 37 Under the foot of a barefaced hill. **1883** *Harper's Mag.* Feb. 485/2 Though others be by whiskers graced, A lawyer can't be too barefaced [cf. 3 a].

2. Unconcealed, undisguised, avowed, open. *arch.*

1605 SHAKS. *Macb.* III. i. 119 Though I could With bare-fac'd power sweepe him from my sight. **1687** R. LESTRANGE *Answ. Diss.* 1, I have liv'd Open and Barefac'd.. I will not Dye in a Disguise. **1766** tr. *Beccaria's Ess. Crimes* xx. (1793) 77 The assaults of barefaced and open tyranny.

3. Hence by gradual pejoration: Audacious, impudent, shameless: **a.** of persons, **b.** of actions, etc.

a. *a* **1674** CLARENDON *Hist. Reb.* (1704) III. XIII. 365 They barefaced own'd all that the Commissioners had propounded. **1720** OZELL *Vertot's Rom. Rep.* II. xiii. 260 That Cæsar was invading the Public Liberty, barefac'd. **1838** DICKENS *O. Twist* iii, 'Of all the artful and designing orphans.. you are one of the most bare-facedest.'

b. **1712** ADDISON *Spect.* No. 458 ¶7 Hypocrisy is not so pernicious as bare-faced Irreligion. **1850** MRS. STOWE *Uncle Tom's C.* xx. 207 Indignant at the barefaced lie.

'**barefacedly**, *adv.* [f. prec. + -LY[2].] In a barefaced manner; openly, shamelessly.

1684 BURNET tr. *More's Utop.* 56 In Courts.. a man must bare-facedly approve of the worst Councils. **1865** CARLYLE *Fredk. Gt.* IV. XII. xi. 244 Barefacedly unjust.

'**barefacedness.** [f. as prec. + -NESS.] Openness, effrontery, shamelessness.

a **1674** CLARENDON *Hist. Reb.* I. II. 117 They resorted.. to Mass.. with the same Barefacedness. **1825** COBBETT *Rur. Rides* 427 The barefacedness of the lie.

barefoot ('bɛəfʊt), *a.* and *adv.* Rarely 5-6 barefeet (*pl.*). [OE. *bærfót*, early ME. *barfot*; cf. ON. *berfœttr* adj., LG. *barfet*, G. *barfusz*. See BARE *a.* IV.] With the feet bare or naked, without shoes or stockings on: **a.** as *adj.*, passing (with verbs of motion) into **b.** *adv.* Also *U.S.* in fig. use (see quots. and cf. BARE-FOOTED *a.* c).

a. *c* **1000** *Peccat. Med.* (Bosw.) Bærfót, *nudipes*. **1205** LAY. 8843 Sone he dude hine bar-fot [**1250** bareuot]. *a* **1300** *Cursor M.* 6072 Lok þat þai be scod ilkan.. and barfote nan. **1592** SHAKS. *Rom. & Jul.* v. ii. 5 Going to find a bare-foote Brother out. **1679** *Hist. Jetzer* 38 The Covent of the Bare-foot Friers. **1818** J. HOBHOUSE *Hist. Illustr.* 253 The Emperor.. undertook a barefoot pilgrimage to Mount Garganus. **1870** LOWELL *Study Wind.* 43 Burns, whose bare-foot Muse got the color in her cheeks by vigorous exercise in all weathers.

b. *c* **1230** *Ancr. R.* 420 Ine sumer.. to gon and sitten baruot. *c* **1386** CHAUCER *Frankl. T.* 349 Thy Temple in Delphos wol I barefoot seke. **1483** CAXTON *Gold. Leg.* 249/2 Blessid chyldren.. haue gone upon the coles brennyng bar-feet. **1562** J. HEYWOOD *Prov. & Epigr.* (1867) 37 Who waitth for dead men shoen, shall go long barefoote. **1692** SOUTH 12 *Serm.* (1697) I. 40 He that thinks to expiate a sin by going barefoot, does the Penance of a Goose. **1856** FROUDE *Hist. Eng.* I. 81 Henry walked barefoot through the streets.

fig. **1866** LOWELL *Biglow P.* Ser. II. Introd., 'I take my tea barfoot,' said a backwoodsman when asked if he would have cream and sugar. **1888** *Chicago Herald* (Farmer), Never touch coffee unless you like it barefoot, that is, without sugar or milk.

c. spec. ***barefoot doctor*** [tr. Chinese *chìjiǎoyīshēng*, f. *chì* bare + *jiǎo* foot + *yīshēng* physician], a paramedical worker with basic medical training, esp. one working in rural China.

1971 *China Q.* Jan.–Mar. 185 Dr. Horn.. gives by far the most detailed account I have seen in English of the training, role, and supervision of the peasant-doctors (or 'barefoot doctors'), and their relationship to the mobile medical teams. **1972** J. S. AIRD in D. J. Dwyer *China Now* (1974) ix. 186 In a rural area near Peking in 1971, the *hsien* revolutionary committee mobilized sanitation workers and 'barefoot doctors'—youthful paramedics with a few months' basic training—to conduct birth control propaganda. **1974** *China Reconstructs* July 41/2 The term 'barefoot doctors' refers to medical workers trained from among commune members who continue to engage in farm work. As they first appeared in south China where the commune members work barefoot in the paddy fields, these new-type medical workers are called 'barefoot doctors'. **1975** *Nature* 21 Aug. 610/2 The term 'barefoot doctor' is now known the world over. It seems that it was first used in the Chiangchen People's Commune on the outskirts of Shanghai in 1965, where a medical team started teaching young farmers to perform some medical tasks. **1976** *Times* 31 Aug. (Malaysia Suppl.) p. vi/5 Sarawak's own 'barefoot doctors'.. are given up to three years paramedical training. **1979** D. Barlow *Sexually Transmitted Dis.* iii. 21 Any hopes of eventually controlling levels of infection will almost certainly depend on paramedical or 'barefoot' doctors playing a larger role. **1983** S. Naipaul *Hot Country* v. 70 The Government has worked out a plan for training barefoot doctors, an idea the President got when he went to China last year.

'bare-ˌfooted, *a.* [f. barefoot *a.* + -ed.] **a.** = prec., and more frequently used by recent writers. Of a horse: having a shoeless foot. **b.** quasi-*adv.*

a. *c* **1530** Ld. Berners *Arth. Lyt. Bryt.* (1814) 268 Chanons, preestes, and clarkes.. all barefoted. **1598** Hakluyt *Voy.* I. 109 Wee stoode.. bare-footed and bare-headed. **1670** G. H. *Hist. Cardinals* I. II. 46 The Preacher was a bare-footed Franciscan. **1884** Q. Victoria *More Leaves* 123 Picturesque barefooted lasses. **1906** Somerville & 'Ross' *Some Irish Yesterdays* 88 'Ye're barefooted,' he said. I found that I [*i.e.* my hunter] had indeed lost a foreshoe.

b. **1780** Coxe *Russ. Disc.* 104 The greatest part go barefooted. **1847** Longf. *Ev.* II. i, Thus did that poor soul wander.. Bleeding, barefooted over the shards and thorns.

c. *U.S.* (See quots. and cf. barefoot *a.*)

1847 Paulding *Amer. Comedies* 194, I thought even a Yankee knew that 'stone fence barefooted' is the polite English for whisky uncontaminated,—pure, sir! **1878** J. H. Beadle *Western Wilds* xii. 183 It was sod corn [*sc.* whisky] barefooted.

Hence **bare'footedness**.

1756 Toldervy *Hist. 2 Orphans* I. 74 Many worthy gentlemen are become egregious sufferers, both by the barefootedness of their horses and the loss of their hares. **1891** *Athenæum* 28 Nov. 714/1 The barefootedness of the women and children.

‖**barége** (ba'rɛʒ). Also barege, barège. [Fr.; from *Baréges* or *Barrége*, a village in the Hautes Pyrénées, France.]

1. A light, silky dress-fabric, resembling gauze, originally made at Baréges.

1828 Disraeli *Voyage Capt. Popanilla* xiv. 176 He had no doubt his mistress would look most charmingly in a barege. **1845** C. Ridley *Lett.* (1958) 192, I have got.. a sort of *barège* for evening, which I shall make very warm by lining with silk. **1848** Mrs. Gaskell *M. Barton* I. x. 191 The gay-coloured barège shawl. **1851** *Times* 4 Apr. 11/2 Barege shawls and silks. **1864** *Linnet's Trial* I. III. iv. 258 Miss Carr wore a slate-coloured barège. **1901** C. Morris *Life on Stage* (1902) 3, I had a tormenting barège veil over my face. **1927** E. Sitwell *Rustic Elegies* 79 On their deep barouche pillows In cashmere Alvandar, barège Isabelle.

2. A mineral water obtained at Baréges. Hence **barégin(e**, a glairy organic substance found in many mineral waters after exposure to the air.

1811 Hooper *Med. Dict.*, *Barege* waters are remarkable for a very smooth soapy feel. **1863** Watts *Dict. Chem.* I. 500 Baregin is in the moist state a transparent, gelatinous, nearly colourless substance.. When dried, it forms a horny mass.

'barehanded, *a.* and *adv.* [see bare *a.* 6.] Having nothing in or covering the hands, esp. carrying no weapon.

c **1440** *Lyfe of Ipom.* 2057 They hewyd the gloves of his hand; All bare-handyd faught þis knyght. **1874** Cleasby & Vigfusson *Icelandic-Eng. Dict.* 60/2 *Ber-hendr*, adj. bare-handed. **1895** *Educ. Rev.* Sept. 125 The civilized man has no superiority over the savage in bare-handed strength. **1919** F. Hurst *Humoresque* 142 I'll go barehanded to a snowball feast rather than wear your duds. **1930** G. Surrey *Shack in Coulee* xi. 93 His revolver was still in its holster. He was barehanded. **1949** N. Lloyd *Young Liberators* ii. 32 There are lots of tricks for fighting barehanded. **1958** *Times* 3 Dec. 5/1 Lilani Daka, a villager, went to the hut with a gun, but finding that it was not loaded he attacked the lion barehanded.

barehead ('bɛəhɛd), *a.* and *adv.* *arch.* = next.

c **1320** *Song Merci* 75 in *E.E.P.* (1862) 120 Barehed and barefot gan I go. *c* **1485** *Digby Myst.* (1882) III. 147 Stond bare hed, ye beggars! **1622** Rowlands *Good News* 25 Barehead curtesie doth entertaine My worship with What lacke you. **1854** *Blackw. Mag.* LXXVI. 424 He was obliged, barehead, to seek pardon from the injured party.

bare-headed ('bɛəˌhɛdɪd), *a.* and *adv.* [f. prec.: see bare *a.* IV; cf. *barefoot(ed.*] With the head uncovered, *esp.* as a token of respect. Hence **bare-headedness**.

c **1530** Ld. Berners *Arth. Lyt. Bryt.* (1814) 288 He was fayre & gracyous, and he was bare heded. **1601** Weever *Mirr. Mart.*, *Sir J. Oldcastle* Ded., I was contented he should stand bare-headed to these churlish times. **1709** Steele *Tatler* No. 39 ¶1 You shall see an Earl walk bare-headed to the Son of the meanest Artificer. **1822** Scott *Nigel* iii, I was a bare-headed girl at the time. *a* **1656** Bp. Hall *Rem.* 237 (L.) Bareheadedness was in Corinth.. a token of honour.

†**barehide.** *Obs.* Also 5–6 barhide, 7 bearehide. ? A hide with the hair removed, or one undressed.

c **1450** in Wülcker *Voc.* /567 *Barusia*, barhyde. *Ibid.* /575 *Coristerium*, barhyde. **1552** *Act 5 & 6 Edw. VI*, xv. §2 Leather Pots, Tankards, Barhides, or any other Wares of Leather. **1611** Florio, *Spazzacouerta*, a great hide to couer cartes, in Court we call them beare-hides. **1687** *Ord. R. Househ.* 394 For trunks, chests, hampers, barehides.. and also for little carts.

bareish, variant spelling of barish *a.*

barel, obs. form of barrel.

barely ('bɛəlɪ), *adv.* [f. bare *a.* + -ly².]

1. Nakedly, without covering, nudely.

1483 *Cath. Angl.* 21/1 Barely, *vbi* nakydly. **1570** Levins *Manip.* /101 Barely, *nude.* **1601** Shaks. *All's Well* IV. ii. 18 You barely leaue our thornes to pricke our selues.

2. Openly, without disguise or concealment, clearly, plainly.

c **950** *Lindisf. Gosp.* John xvi. 29 Nu.. bærlice ðu spreces. **1352** Minot *Poems* iii. (1795) 38 Thaire leders may thai barely ban. *a* **1670** Hacket *Cent. Serm.* (1675) 549 Here is the Resurrection of our Saviour barely and positively affirmed. **1875** Stubbs *Const. Hist.* II. xvii. 604 When the question is put barely before them they avoid committing themselves.

†**3.** Without qualification or reserve, unconditionally; wholly, completely; absolutely, positively. *Obs.*

c **1340** *Gaw. & Gr. Knt.* 548, I am boun to þe bur barely to morne, To seche þe gome of þe grene. *c* **1400** *Destr. Troy* XXIX. 12090 He besit hym barly þe burde forto seche. *Ibid.* XXV. 10132 A space for his spilt men spedely to graue, And bryng hom to berynes, barly no more. *c* **1425** Wyntoun *Cron.* VII. v. 125 Bot [= unless] barly þat þe Patrowne Suld gyve. hys Presentatyowne.

4. Merely, simply, only. *arch.*

1577 Hanmer *Anc. Eccl. Hist.* (1619) 526 Not barely in word, but truly in deed. **1682** Norris *Hierocles* 89 Goodness of action does not consist barely in not sinning. **1712** Hughes *Spect.* No. 467 ¶8 Instructive, as well as barely agreeable. **1817** Jas. Mill *Brit. India* II. v. ix. 717 The only objection.. might have been easily removed, by barely prescribing what sort of evidence they ought to receive.

5. Only just; *hence*, not quite, hardly, scarcely, with difficulty.

1494 Fabyan *Edw. I*, an. 1298 (R.) Barely xxviii. persons. **1562** J. Heywood *Prov. & Epigr.* (1867) 111 Thou fleest that vice not meanly nor barely, But mainely. **1697** Dryden *Virg. Eclog.* iii. 157 Their Bones are barely cover'd with their Skin. **1768** Ellis in *Phil. Trans.* LVIII. 77 Some wax that was barely fluid. **1805** T. Jefferson *Writ.* (1830) IV. 42 The Speakers.. had barely time to get out of his way. **1855** Bain *Senses & Int.* III. ii. §9 Sounds.. so faint as to be barely recognizable.

6. Scantily, poorly; baldly.

a **1535** More *Wks.* 255 (R.) Rehersing the tother syde nakedly and barely.. to make it seeme the more slender. *c* **1620** Z. Boyd *Zion's Flowers* (1855) 99 Let him.. be barely fed, With.. barly-bread. **1807** Crabbe *Par. Reg.* III. 848 Thy coat is thin; why, man, thou'rt barely drest.

baren ('bærɛn). [Jap.] A pad used in wood-block printing.

1895 W. Anderson *Jap. Wood Engr.* 63 Impressions are taken upon specially prepared paper by rubbing with a flat disc. (*baren*) worked by hand pressure. **1916** F. M. Fletcher *Wood-block Printing* ii. 12 Pressure is then applied to the back of the paper as it lies on the wet block. This is done by a round pad called the *baren* by the Japanese. It is made of a coil of cord covered by bamboo sheath. **1924** H. Furst *Mod. Woodcut* 94 The Japanese manner of designing in map-like spaces and printing from the plank by rubbing with the 'baren'.. became general.

bareness ('bɛənɪs). [f. bare *a.* + -ness.]

1. Nakedness, lack of covering.

1552 Huloet, Barenes, *nuditas.* *c* **1600** Shaks. *Sonn.* v, Beauty ore-snow'd and barenes euery where. **1810** Coleridge *Friend* (1865) 26 A clothing even of withered leaves is better than bareness.

2. Destitution, scantiness; baldness. *lit.* and *fig.*

1580 Hollyband *Treas. Fr. Tong.*, *Pouvreté*.. barenesse, want. **1590** *Pasquil's Apol.* I. B iij b, Compare the exposition.. with the barenesse of reading. **1666** South 12 *Serm.* (1697) I. 229 Stript of.. its Privileges, and made like the primitive Church for its Bareness. **1870** Emerson *Soc. & Solit.* i. 14 A man must be clothed with society, or we shall feel a certain bareness or poverty.

†**b.** Leanness. *Obs.*

1552 Huloet, Barenes or leannes of the bodye, *macies.* **1596** Shaks. *1 Hen. IV*, IV. ii. 77 For their barenesse.. they neuer learn'd that of me.

†**3.** Mere or simple quality; mereness. *Obs.*

1607 Dekker *Northw. Hoe* II. Wks. III. 25 My father could take vp, vpon the barenesse of his word fiue hundred pound.

baresark ('bɛəsɑːk), *sb.* and *adv.* [lit. = 'bare shirt,' in reference to a current etymology of berserker, q.v.] **A.** *sb.* (also *attrib.*) A berserker, or wild Norse warrior; sometimes explained as a warrior fighting in his 'bare shirt.' **B.** *adv.* In a shirt only, without armour.

1840 Carlyle *Heroes* vi, The great savage Baresark. **1857** Emerson *Poems* 187 Thy sires.. Failed to bequeath.. The Baresark marrow to thy bones. **1866** Kingsley *Herew.* xii. 169, I will go baresark to-morrow to the war.

baret, obs. f. barret, a kind of cap.

baret, -ette, -ettor, obs. ff. barrat, etc.

†**'barevis**, *a.* *Obs.* *rare*⁻¹. [f. bare *a.* IV. + ME. *vis* = OF. *vis* face:—L. *visus* sight, eyes.] = barefaced 1.

1330 R. Brunne *Chron.* 122 Scho ȝede out in hir smok.. Withouten kirtelle or kemse, saue kouerchef alle barevis.

barf, barfan, dial. ff. bargh, bargham.

barf (bɑːf), *v.* *slang* (orig. and chiefly *U.S.*). [Orig. unknown; perh. echoic.] *intr.* To vomit or retch. Occas. *trans.* (also with *up*).

1960 in Wentworth & Flexner *Dict. Amer. Slang.* **1963** T. Pynchon *V* i. 10 Here were your underage Marine barfing in the street, barmaid with a ship's propeller tattooed on each buttock. **1964** *Amer. Speech* XXXIX. 117 *Barf*, a verb meaning 'to vomit', assignable.. to approximately the fall of 1957 or summer of 1958. **1971** D. Heffron *Nice Fire & Some Moonpennies* vi. 51 He barfed all over shiny Ted's shiny old suit! All this dog-puke all over his shiny lap. **1976** *Whig-Standard* (Kingston, Ontario) 20 Feb. 6/5 It is a pity that it is necessary to intimidate.. people that we Canadians can imagine as prime minister, without barfing our bickies. **1982** *Chicago Sun-Times* 21 June 31 If you are Princess Diana, you have to stay home and do needlepoint until all danger of barfing in public is past. **1986** *Los Angeles Times* 29 June v. 5/1 If I go for 10, I'm probably going to have to barf up a lung.

barf (bɑːf), *sb.* *slang* (orig. and chiefly *U.S.*). [f. the vb.] An attack of vomiting; vomit, sick; also *int.*, a coarse exclamation of disgust.

1966 in *Dict. Amer. Regional Eng.* I. 153/2 *Barf bag*, one of those 'discreet' little bags tucked into a pouch on the back of an airplane seat. Used in case of air sickness. **1978** J. Wambaugh *Black Marble* viii. 111 I'd rather be gangbanged by a pack of Dobermans! Oh, barf! **1981** *N.Y. Times* 6 Sept. 51/1 Whereas the horror film was once spooky, now it is nauseating, measured by the barf, rather than the shiver. **1985** *Dirt Bike* Mar. 44/3 A word about the stock chain: barf. **1986** *Time* 26 May 67/3 The locker-room sadists, lubricious cheerleaders and barons of barf who populate the *Porky's* films.

Barff (bɑːf). *Metallurgy.* [The name of F. S. *Barff*, an American engineer.] A process for protecting iron and steel from rust by means of a coating of iron oxide produced by the application of steam to the heated surface. Hence **Barff** *v. trans.*, to treat by this process (Webster, 1934). See Bower-Barff.

1880 *Sci. Amer.* Suppl. 31 Jan. 3393/2 (*title*) The Barff Process for Preserving Iron. **1884** [see Bower-Barff]. **1951** *Good Housek. Home Encycl.* 41/1 In districts where the water is acid in reaction.., the metal is usually specially processed or 'Barffed'.

barfray; see berfray.

†**'barful**, *a.* [f. bar *sb.*¹ + -ful.] Full of bars or hindrances.

1601 Shaks. *Twel. N.* I. iv. 41 Yet a barrefull strife, Whoere I woe, my selfe would be his wife.

bargain ('bɑːgɪn), *sb.*¹ Forms: 4 **bargayn, -geyne**, 4–6 **-gan(e, -gayn(e**, 4–7 **gaine**, 5 **bergayne, bargen, -geyn**, 6 **bergan, bargyn, -gin**, 6– **bargain**. [a. OF. *bargaine*, also *bargaigne*, *-gagne*, *-caigne* = Pr., Pg. *barganha* (cf. Pr. *barganh*, It. *bargagno*), pointing to a late L. form **barcāne-um*, *-a*: see bargain *v.* The etymology being obscure, the development of meaning is also doubtful.]

†**1. a.** Discussion between two parties of the terms on which one is to give or do something to or for the other; chaffering; bargaining. *Obs.*

1330 R. Brunne *Chorn.* 270 Þe cardinals.. Oft for þe pes with Philip mad bergayn. **1362** Langl. *P. Pl.* A. v. 189 Bargeyns [C. bargeynes] and beuerages bi-gonne to aryse. *c* **1440** *Promp. Parv.* 24 Bargayne, *licitacio, stipulacio.* **1596** Shaks. *1 Hen. IV*, III. i. 139 In the way of Bargaine.. Ile cauill on the ninth part of a hayre.

†**b.** *to beat a* (*the*) *bargain*: to bargain, haggle.

1664 Killigrew *Parson's Wed.* III. v, To beat a bargain for a score of sheep. **1667** Pepys *Diary* 14 Aug., With a little beating the bargain, we come to a perfect agreement.

2. a. An agreement between two parties settling how much each gives and takes, or what each performs and receives, in a transaction between them; a compact.

c **1340** *Cursor M.* (Trin.) 16490 Al for nouȝt.. þe bargan made hit is. *c* **1386** Chaucer *Frankl. T.* 502 This bargaine is ful-drive.. Ye shul be paied trewely. **1464** *Mann. & Househ. Exp.* 261 In party of payment off theyr bargeyn.. v. *marc.* xxd. **1553** T. Wilson *Rhet.* 19 A bargain is a bargain, and must stand without all excepcion. **1597** Bacon *Good & Evil* (1862) 266 The second blow makes the fray, The second word makes the bargaine. **1599** Shaks. *Hen. V*, v. ii. 134, I loue you.. so clap hands, and a bargaine. **1674** Owen *Holy Spirit* (1693) 93 An Earnest is the Confirmation of a Bargain and Contract made. **1833** Ht. Martineau *Cinnamon & P.* v. 92 The colony will not long fulfil its part in this unequal bargain.

b. Sometimes applied to what one of the parties has contracted or stipulated to do or receive; or to the aspect of the compact towards one of the parties, *e.g.* a 'bad bargain.'

1502 *Ord. Crysten Men* (W. de W. 1506) IV. xxi. 224 The seller putteth in his bargayne that he may bye agayn his herytage. **1593** *Tell-trothe's N.Y. Gift* 33 Whosoever.. is bound to a bad bargain. **1603** Knolles *Hist. Turkes* (1638) 221 The best bargaine they could make therein. **1607** Topsell *Four-f. Beasts* 473 The buyer may condemn the seller if the cattel be not so good as his bargain. **1769** *Junius Lett.* v. 28 This is the losing bargain.

3. a. That which is acquired by bargaining; a purchase regarded in the light of its proving advantageous or the reverse; *without qualification*, an advantageous purchase.

1352 [see 7.] **1516** *Churchw. Acc. St. Marg.* (Nicholls) 8 Given to the broker that did help us to the bargain of the barneston, 4*d.* **a1619** FLETCHER *Wit without M.* v. 163 Before I buy a bargain of such Runts, I'le buy a Colledge for Bears. **a1656** BP. HALL *Rem. Wks.* (1660) 144 How may I get a good bargain? **1766** GOLDSM. *Vic. W.* xii, I had them a dead bargain, or I should not have bought them. **1812** *Examiner* 14 Sept. 591/2 They should not trust.. to buying *bargains*, as they will often meet.. with.. blind ones. **1882** PEBODY *Eng. Journalism* xv. 110 A couple of books.. which he had picked up as a bargain.

b. In certain coalfields in England, a piece of work let to the workmen making the lowest offer. Also Comb., as ***bargain-letting, -man, -taker, -work*** (see quot. 1851 in sense 8).

1825 E. MACKENZIE *Hist. Northumb.* (ed. 2) I. 100 These bargains are taken in partnerships, consisting of from two to eight men. **1858** SIMMONDS *Dict. Trade*, Bargain-men. **1881** *Instr. Census Clerks* (1885) 84 Copper Miner... Bargain Man. **1897** *Daily News* 18 Mar. 3/4 They cannot take special bits of work, known as bargains, but must go to the bargain-takers and ask them for rock to cut up. **1897** *Westm. Gaz.* 1 Sept. 7/1 Bargain-letting recommenced to-day at Lord Penrhyn's Carnarvonshire slate quarries.

c. *esp.* An article of which the price is professedly reduced for the purpose of a special sale in a shop or stores; also *attrib.* and *Comb.* designating persons and things associated with the practice of offering goods for sale in this way, e.g. ***bargain counter, -day, -hunt*** (also as *v. intr.*), ***-hunter, -hunting, -price, -sale, -seeker***; **bargain basement**, a basement floor where bargains are displayed; also *transf.* and *fig.*

1899 *Chicago Daily News* 25 May 19/6 There is not room in our Bargain Basement for all the bargains we have created for to-morrow. **1927** *Star* 1 June 6/1 Selfridge's Bargain Basement. **1932** *Daily Express* 27 June 11/3 Every railway company, every travel bureau, every steamship line has its own 'bargain basement'. **1935** *Brit. Jrnl. Psychol.* Oct. 190 Ghostly raiment which to them is none the less resplendent through being acquired in the bargain basement of compromise and expediency. **1959** *Economist* 10 Jan. 100/1 Any such bargain-basement nuclear deterrent as we could hope to produce and mount in this country will be minimally effective. **1888** *Scribner's Mag.* Jan. 65/2 Ladies .. in all the finery that the 'bargain counters' of Fourteenth Street could furnish. **1904** *Post Express* (Rochester, N.Y.) 22 July 4 The bargain counter rates for steerage traffic. **1908** G. BURGESS *Maxims of Methus.* xvi. 14 From the bargain counter she selecteth her gloves. **1887** *Puck* 23 Nov. 210/2 Football's too tame... You've never seen the women at Macy's on bargain-day. **1902** A. BENNETT *Anna of 5 Towns* xiii. 350 The bargain-hunt was up.., always second-hand, but always good. **1937** M. HILLIS *Orchids on Budget* (1938) iii. 39 If you *must* bargain-hunt, do it late in the season at a good shop. **1791** J. LACKINGTON *Memoirs* xix. 143 These very bargain hunters have given me double the price that I now charge. **1838** *Mag. Domestic Econ.* III. 201 If you leave it to their integrity.. you will generally be supplied with better provisions.. than by becoming a 'bargain hunter'. **1886** *Longm. Mag.* VII. 447 Last month was a lucky one for bargain-hunters. **1792** MARY WOLLSTONECR. *Rights Wom.* iv. 166 Those English women whose time is spent in.. shopping, bargain-hunting. **1884** C. DICKENS *Dict. Lond.* 82/1 People bargain-hunting in this market. **1938** *Encycl. Brit. Bk. of Yr. 1938* 423/1 Endeavours to lure the impoverished, bargain hunting public of the United States to the box office. **1904** *Westm. Gaz.* 7 Jan. 8/1 Jewellery and chiffons and laces are there, going at bargain prices. **1898** C. A. BATES *Clothing Bk.* No. 5211 Garments for which you pay the additional price at widely advertised 'bargain' sales. **1907** 'O. HENRY' *Trimmed Lamp* (1916) 114 'Have I ever chucked any bargain sale stuff at you, Moll?' asked the Kid, with calm dignity. **1834** *Chambers's Edin. Jrnl.* III. 145/3 The unrespective hands of brokers and bargain-seekers.

4. *transf.* A transaction that entails consequences, especially unpleasant ones; a (bad or unfortunate) 'business.' *arch.* or *Obs.*

*c***1400** *Rom. Rose* 4932 Youthe gynneth ofte siche bargeyne, That may not eende withouten peyne. **1413** LYDG. *Pylgr. Sowle* IV. xv. (1483) 63 One of vs thre must abye this bargeyn. *c***1460** *Towneley Myst.* 22 That bargan may they ban, That ille has done. **1690** LOCKE *Hum. Und.* I. iii. (1695) 20 God.. would certainly make it a very ill Bargain to the Transgressor.

†**5. a.** Contention or contest for the mastery; struggle, combat, fight, battle. *north. Obs.*

1375 BARBOUR *Bruce* VII. 221 He helpit hym swa in that bargane, That thai thre tratouris he has slane. *c***1400** *Destr. Troy* VI. 2502 Soche bargens are bytter, þat hafe a bare ende. **1513** DOUGLAS *Æneis* IV. Prol. 69 The meik hartis in belling .. Mak fers bargane. **1556** LAUDER *Tractate* 458 Thay suld be fre.. Frome toulȝe, bergane, and debait. **1606** WARNER *Alb. Eng.* XIV. xc. (1612) 365 On Brudus side the better of that bloudie bargaine went.

†**b.** *fig.* Bout, struggle, stour. *Obs.*

1615 CROOKE *Body of Man* 225 As in hard bargaines of trauell it often hapneth.. to Women.

6. *Law.* **bargain and sale.** (See quots.)

1602 FULBECKE *1st. Pt. Parall.* 13 When an imperfect bargaine and sale is to bee perfited, the bargainee dooth not take the profites. **1641** *Termes de la Ley* 37 By such a bargaine and sale lands may passe without livery of seisin, if the bargaine and sale bee by deed indented, sealed, and inrolled. **1876** DIGBY *Real Prop.* vi. 293 A bargain and sale was where the legal owner entered into an agreement with a purchaser for the sale to him of his interest, and the purchaser paid, or promised to pay, the money for the land.

7. Phrases. ***Dutch or wet bargain***: one concluded by the parties drinking together. ***into*** (*to* obs.) ***the bargain***: over and above what is stipulated or expected; moreover, besides. †***to buy the bargain dear***, (ellipt.) ***to buy the bargain***: to pay dearly for a thing. †***to sell any one a bargain***: to make a fool of him, to 'sell' him. ***to strike*** (*up* obs.) ***a bargain***: to come to terms over a purchase. ***to be off one's bargain***: to be released from an engagement. ***to make the best of a bad bargain***: to make the best of adverse circumstances.

1352 MINOT *Poems* vi. (1795) 28 Fro thai met with Inglismen, All thaire bargan dere thai boght. **1530** PALSGR. 455/1, I bye the bargayne, or I fele the hurte.. *Le marché me cuit.* **1588** SHAKS. *L.L.L.* III. i. 102 The Boy hath sold him a bargaine. **1607** TOPSELL *Four-f. Beasts* 473 If these things be true, then I will strike up the bargain. **1636** *Ariana* 55 An excellent meanes to revenge him on.. Palamede, and to have Ariana to the bargaine. **1640** BRATHWAIT *Boulster Lect.* 81 You may suspect mee that I relate these purposely to sell you a Bargaine. **1650** BP. HALL *Cases Consc.* 21 Before the bargaine be stricken. **1670** RAY *Prov.* 61 Make the *best* of a bad bargain. *a***1674** CLARENDON *Hist. Reb.* I. i. 45 He paid much too dear for his Wife's Fortune, by taking her Person into the bargain. **1678** OTWAY *Friendship in F.* 16, I hate a Dutch Bargain that's made in heat of Wine. **1712** ARBUTHNOT *John Bull* ii. 11 Matters have not been carried on with due secrecy; however, we must make the best of a bad Bargain. **1727** POPE *Bathos* 111 The principal branch of the *alamode* is the Prurient.. It consists.. of.. selling of bargains, and *double entendre.* **1729** FRANKLIN *Ess.* Wks. 1840 II. 31 What baser wretch first corrupted him, and then bought the bargain. **1753** *Scots Mag.* July 359/1 The bargain is to be struck at 700,000 florins. **1767** GRAY in *Corr. Nicholls* (1843) 68, I should have been glad to hear your uncles were off their bargain. **1790** BOSWELL *Johnson* (1811) II. 341 Mrs. Thrale was all for.. according to the vulgar phrase, 'making the best of a bad bargain.' **1805** WINDHAM *Speeches* (1812) II. 271 The recruit took the condition of a soldier, with a guinea to make it a wet bargain. **1876** FREEMAN *Norm. Conq.* IV. xvii. 7 Men had made up their minds to submit to what they could not help, and to make the best of a bad bargain. **1885** J. WRAY in *Chr. Herald* 22 Apr. 224/2 To give her view of things with her usual perspicacity, and with a striking emphasis into the bargain.

8. *Comb.*, as ***bargain-driving***. †**bargain-penny**, money paid 'on account,' by way of ratification of a bargain; † **Bargain-Saturday**, a hiring-day for servants; **bargain-wise** *adv.*, in the manner of a bargain; **bargain-work** (*dial.*), see quot.

1902 *Spectator* 27 Dec. 1023/2 Some men are, it might almost be said, victims of the habit of bargain-driving. **1930** T. S. ELIOT tr. *St.-J. Perse's Anabasis* 69 Manœuvres over field to ravish a woman, bargain-driving and plots. **1490** *Churchw. Acc. St. Dunstan's Canterb.*, Payde.. a bargayn peny for the whyte lymyng of owr Churche. **1796** PEGGE *Anonym.* (1809) 266 Earnest money, earnest penny, or bargain penny. **1860** E. VENABLES *Isle of Wight* 61 Three 'Bargain Saturdays' were held at Michaelmas for hiring servants. *a***1679** T. GOODWIN *Wks.* (1863) V. 28 We find this very covenant bargain-wise. **1851** *Coal-tr. Terms Northumbld. & Durh.* 8 Bargain-work, work.. let by proposal, amongst the workmen at a colliery, to the lowest offer.

†**'bargain**, *sb.*[2] *Obs.* exc. *dial.* [? same word as prec.] A small farm-holding.

1602 CAREW *Cornwall* 37 a, A farme, or (as wee call it) a bargaine can no sooner fall in hand, then the Survey Court shall be waited on. **1824** MISS MITFORD *Village* Ser. I. (1863) 81 What used to be called in this part of the country 'a little bargain': thirty or forty acres, perhaps, of arable land, which the owner and his sons cultivated themselves. **1881** *I. Wight Gloss.* Bargun.. a farm of small holding.

bargain ('bɑːgɪn), *v.* Forms: 4 bargeyne, 4–5 -gane, 4–6 -gayne, 5 -gan, -geyn, 7 -gaine, 6– **bargain.** [a. OF. *bargaigne-r* = Pr. *barganhar*, It. *bargagnare*:—late L. *barcāneāre, barcāniāre* (in Capit. Charles the Bald), which Diez proposes to refer (through **barcāne-us*: see BARGAIN *sb.*[1]) to *barca* 'a bark or barge, which,' according to the definition of Isidore, 'carries goods to and fro'; thence might arise the sense either of 'go backwards and forwards, come and go as to a matter, be off and on' (cf. mod.F. *barguigner* to hesitate, have difficulty in making up one's mind), or of 'trade, traffic, deal.' But difficulties attend both form- and sense-development; and the order of senses here followed is purely empirical.]

1. *intr.* To treat *with* any one as to the terms which one party is to give, and the other to accept, in a transaction between them; to try to secure the best possible terms; to haggle over terms.

*c***1375** WYCLIF *Serm.* Sel. Wks. 1871 II. 213 It is an open foly to bargayne wiþ preestis for siche preier. *c***1380** —— *Wks.* (1880) 472 Cardenals ben brouȝt yn bi antichrist to bargeyne bi symonye. **1525** LD. BERNERS *Froiss.* II. cxviii. [cxiv.] 339 We cannot both bargayne and bye all in one daye. **1611** COTGR., *Barguigner*, to chaffer; to bargaine; or (more properly) to wrangle, dodge, haggle.. in the making of a bargaine. **1634** PRESTON *New Covt.* 89 They will bargaine with the Lord, he will give thee this particular, thou shalt have this. **1701** PENN in *Pa. Hist. Soc. Mem.* IX. 56 No man living can defend us or bargain for us better than myself. **1859** JEPHSON *Brittany* ix. 136 Judas bargaining with the priests.

2. a. To agree to terms asked and offered; to arrange terms, come to terms; to stipulate; to make or strike a bargain, *with* a person, *for* a thing.

1483 *Cath. Angl.* 21/1 To bargan, *pacisci.* **1536** *MS.* in Thynne *Animadv.* Introd. 28 John Wylkynson.. hath convenanted and bargayned with Edmunde Pekham. **1578** T. N. tr. *Conq. W. India* 20 He.. bargained with one Fernando Alfonso, for certaine Hogges. **1593** SHAKS *2 Hen. VI*, I. i. 231 While his owne Lands are bargain'd for, and sold. **1712** ADDISON *Spect.* No. 511 ¶3 A merchant.. bargained for it, and carried it off. **1751** LADY MONTAGUE *Lett.* 56 III. 101 The marble was bespoke and the sculptor [was] bargained with. **1876** J. H. NEWMAN *Hist. Sk.* I. I. ii. 100 The Bishop.. acted for the Christians, and bargained for nothing more than their lives.

b. with *inf.* or *subord. cl.*

1596 SHAKS. *Tam. Shr.* II. i. 307 'Tis bargain'd.. That she shall still be curst in company. **1787** P. JONES in Sparks *Corr. Amer. Rev.* (1853) IV. 192, I.. have bargained to be landed in France. **1878** SIMPSON *School Shaks.* I. 46 Bagnall.. bargained to sell his estates.

3. fig. ***to bargain for***: to arrange for beforehand, to include in one's reckoning, arrangements, expectations, or forecast; to count on, expect.

1801 JANE AUSTEN *Let.* 3 Jan. (1952) 103 My Mother bargains for having no trouble at all in furnishing our house in Bath. **1840** MARRYAT *Olla Podr.* (Rtldg.) 330 More wind than we bargained for. **1856** LEVER *Martins Cro' M.* 277, I never bargained to dispute against such odds as this. **1883** FROUDE *Short Stud.* IV. I. vii. 79 In accepting Henry's money they had not bargained for exposure.

†**4. a.** *trans.* To agree to buy or sell; to contract for. *Obs.* exc. in legal phr. ***to bargain and sell.***

1488–9 *Act. 4 Hen. VII*, xl, No.. person.. [shall] bye or bargeyn.. any wollez than unshorne. *a***1716** SOUTH in Spurgeon *Treas. Dav.* Ps. ix. 16 The wages that sin bargains with the sinner are life, pleasure, and profit. **1768** [see BARGAINOR]. **1876** [see BARGAINEE].

b. ***to bargain away***: to part with, or lose, as the result of a bargain.

1868 GEO. ELIOT *F. Holt* 7 The heir.. had somehow bargained away the estate.

†**5.** (*Sc.*) To contend, strive, struggle, fight. *Obs.*

1375 BARBOUR *Bruce* IX. 224 To bargane with his Enymyss. *c***1470** HENRY *Wallace* x. 516 We sall bargane be nyne houris to morn. **1513** DOUGLAS *Æneis* III. iv. 52 Tak thair wapnis, and bargane every man Agane thai cruell peple.

†**'bargained**, *ppl. a. Obs.* [f. BARGAIN *v.* + -ED.] Agreed to, stipulated; engaged.

1552 HULOET, Bargayned, *contractus, sponsus.* Bargayned or promised to be performed, *stipulatus.* *c***1661** *Argyle's Last Will* in *Harl. Misc.* (1746) VIII. 26/1 My prefixed bargained Term of Years is even expired.

bargainee (ˌbɑːgɪ'niː). [f. as prec. + -EE.] The party with whom an agreement of bargain and sale is made; the purchaser.

1598 KITCHIN *Courts Leet* (1675) 203 The Bargainee shall make Oath in Court. **1691** BLOUNT *Law. Dict.* s.v. *Bargain*, Transferring the property thereof from the Bargainor to the Bargainee. **1876** DIGBY *Real Prop.* vii. §2. 323 A man bargained and sold in fee part of his estate and covenanted to give the bargainee the offer of the residue.

bargainer ('bɑːgɪnə(r)). [f. BARGAIN *v.* + -ER[1].]

1. One who is treating as to sale or purchase, a dealer, a trafficker; a chafferer, a haggler.

*c***1460** *Towneley Myst.* 313 Of thise kyrkchaterars here ar a menee, Of barganars and okerars and lufars of symonee. **1552** HULOET, Bargayner, or bargayne maker. **1632** SHERWOOD, A bargainer, *barguignard.* **1658** in Burton *Diary* (1828) III. 221 It would come better from another House, than from us, that are bargainers for the people. **1848** THACKERAY *Van. Fair* xvii, The sight of the comfortable old house.. ransacked by brokers and bargainers. **1857** MISS WINKWORTH *Tauler's Life* 123 Knowing how full the world is of such bargainers with God, among monks and nuns.

†**2.** = BARGAINOR. *Obs.*

1628 COKE *On Litt.* 218 a, The state is not reuested in the Bargainer before a re-entry.

†**3.** (*Sc.*) A quarreller, wrangler, bully. *Obs.*

*c***1500** DUNBAR *Dance* 34 Bostaris, braggaris, and barganeris.. All bodin in feir of weir.

'bargaining, *vbl. sb.* [f. BARGAIN *v.* + -ING[1].]

1. Trafficking, trading, buying and selling.

1401 *Pol. Poems* (1859) II. 77 Ȝe built your house with beggery, bargenyng and robberye **1526** TINDALE *1 Thess.* iii. 6 And defraude his brother in bargaynynge. **1727** W. MATHER *Yng. Man's Comp.* 396 By Bartering, is meant Goods for Goods. By Bargaining, is understood Money for Goods. **1788** BURNS *Lett.* 26 May, Extremely fortunate in all my buyings and bargainings.

2. Discussion of the terms of a purchase or contract; chaffering, haggling; negotiation.

1669 MARVELL *To Mayor of Hull* Wks. I. 122 A Bill.. against.. barganing for elections to Parliament. **1787** T. JEFFERSON *Writ.* (1859) II. 154, I do not understand bargaining, nor possess the dexterity requisite for the purpose. **1876** FAWCETT *Pol. Econ.* II. ix. 249 The word bargaining implies an antagonism of interest.

†**3.** (*Sc.*) Wrangling, contest, struggle, fighting.

1375 BARBOUR *Bruce* I. 306 Hard trawalys, and barganyngis. **1513** DOUGLAS *Æneis* I. v. 61 Eneas with hidous barganyng, In Itale thrawart peple sall doun thryng.

4. Special Comb. **bargaining chip**, an asset or advantage possessed by one side in negotiations, esp. one that can be surrendered in return for a corresponding concession; cf. CHIP *sb.*[1] 2 d.

1965 *Boston Daily Globe* 19 Nov. 13/8 Mr. Johnson.. had just ordered the first bombing of North Viet Nam in an effort to bring Hanoi to a conference table where the bargaining chips on both sides would be more closely matched. **1973** *Times* 26 Feb. (Arms for Peace Suppl.) p. ii/8 The Pentagon.. sets high value on the 'bargaining chip' principle which requires a nation to negotiate on level, or preferably superior, terms if it is not to lose out. **1979** *Economist* 16 June 43/2 The administration defends the M-

X decision by saying that it now has a bargaining chip to use with the Russians.

bargainor (ˌbɑːgɪˈnɔː(r)). *Law.* [f. as prec. + -OR.] The person making an agreement of bargain and sale of real property; the seller.

1602 FULBECKE *1st Pt. Parall.* 13 The bargainor should leuie a fine to the bargainee. **1768** BLACKSTONE *Comm.* II. 338 A real contract, whereby the bargainor for some pecuniary consideration bargains and sells, that is, contracts to convey, the land to the bargainee. **1876** DIGBY *Real. Prop.* vi. 294 The bargainor was in the view of the Chancellor the bare legal owner.

bargander, obs. form of BERGANDER.

bargaret, variant of BARGERET.

barge (bɑːdʒ), *sb.*[1] Forms: 4- barge, 4-7 berge, (7 barg). [a. OF. *barge* (= Pr. *barga*, *c* 1180, med.L. *barga*), of which the L. type might be either *barga* or **bārica*. Diez favours the latter, taking it as a possible derivative of L. *bāris*, Gr. *βᾶρις*, a kind of boat used on the Nile, an Egyptian word (Coptic *barí* a little pleasure-boat); but there is no evidence that this word was ever used in the West. As to *barga* see BARK *sb.*[2]

If *barge* was, as seems certain, the same as *barca*, BARK *sb.*[2], it was originally a ship's boat, used as a lighter, etc.; in OF., 13th c., we still find 'la barge de la nef' (Littré): cf. senses 2-4. But, as with *barca*, the name was extended to a boat or small ship with sails; and this was the first use in English: see sense 1. After the introduction (by Caxton) of *barque, barke* from 15th c. Fr., that word took the place of *barge*, which, after 1600, is found in the sense of 'ship' only in translators or historians. The modern senses revert more nearly to that of the original *barca*.]

†**1. a.** A small sea-going vessel with sails: used *specifically* for one next in size above the BALINGER, and *generally* as = Ship, vessel (in which use it is now superseded by BARK.) *Obs.* (except when historians reproduce it in the specific sense.)

a **1300** *Cursor M.* 24840 Þat ilke waw til oþir it weft, And bremli to þa bargis beft. *c* **1300** *K. Alis.* 852 Mid heore atire, schipes and barge They gan mony for to charge. *c* **1386** CHAUCER *Prol.* 410 His barge ycleped was the Maudelayne. *c* **1400** *Destr. Troy* xxx. 12406 Relikes of troy, þat he [Antenor] broght in his barge to the bare yle. *a* **1422** HEN. V in Ellis *Orig. Lett.* III. 31 I. 72 Owr grete shippes, carrakes, barges, and balyngers. *c* **1440** LONELICH *Grail* xxxv. 112 Alle the sees..that schepis or barges inne mown go. **1568** LD. SEMPLE *Fleming Bark*, I have a little Fleming Berge. **1652** NEEDHAM tr. *Selden's Mare Cl.* 301 Two Ships, two Barges and two Ballingers armed and fitted for war. **1875** STUBBS *Const. Hist.* III. 128 (transl. *Rot. Parl.* an. 1442) Each ship attended by a barge of eighty men, and a balynger of forty; also four 'spynes' of twenty-five men.

†**b.** *fig.* (cf. *bark, ship.*) *Obs.*

1526 SKELTON *Magnyf.* 38 But yf reason be regent and ruler of your barge. *c* **1550** *New Notbroune Mayd* 166 in Hazl. *E.P.P.* III. 8 In Sathans barge, Emparynge his good name. *a* **1577** GASCOIGNE *Wks.* (1587) 181, I seemed to swim in goodlucks barge. **1663** SIR G. MACKENZIE *Relig. Stoic* xx. (1685) 160 To stay still in the barge of the Church.

2. A flat-bottomed freight-boat, chiefly for canal- and river-navigation, either with or without sails: in the latter case also called a *lighter*; in the former, as in the Thames barges, generally dandy-rigged, having one important mast.

1480 CAXTON *Chron. Eng.* VII. (1520) 91 b/1 Bargees and botes and great plankes. **1494** FABYAN VII. 388 A brydge made of bargis [and] plankys to haue passed a water. **1570** LEVINS *Manip.* /31 Barge, *cimba, remulcus.* **1627** CAPT. SMITH *Seaman's Gram.* A ij, The Barge by graue Amocles was compos'd. **1725** DE FOE *Voy. round World* (1840) 324 Floats, like flat-bottomed barges. **1769** FALCONER *Dict. Marine* (1789), *Barge*, is also the name of a flat-bottomed vessel of burthen, for lading and discharging ships. **1842** TENNYSON *Lady of Shalott* iii, By the margin, willow-veil'd, Slide the heavy barges trail'd. **1846** GROTE *Greece* (1862) II. xx. 504 The merchandise was put into barges.

†**3.** *vaguely*, A rowing boat; esp. a ferry-boat. (Used to render L. *linter.*) *Obs.*

1470-85 MALORY *Arthur* I. xxv, Go ye into yonder barge, and row your self unto the swerd. **1567** DRANT *Horace' Epist.* I. xviii. F v, The Oste deuydes their bargies [*lintres*]. **1601** HOLLAND *Pliny* I. 74 Vpon the riuer Alpheus, there is passage by water in barges.

4. *spec.* The second boat of a man of war; a long narrow boat, generally with not less than ten oars, for the use of the chief officers.

1530 PALSGR. 460/1, I dare borde hym with my rowe barge. *a* **1618** RALEIGH *Apol.* 5, I had taken my Barge and gone a shoare. **1769** FALCONER *Dict. Marine* (1789) F iv, A barge properly never rows less than ten [oars]. **1773** BROWNRIGG in *Phil. Trans.* LXIV. 457 We went from the Centaur with the long-boat and barge. **1860** H. STUART *Seaman's Catech.* 9 Barges are..kept in order to carry distinguished persons when embarking or disembarking. **1863** *Cornh. Mag.* Feb., One of the larger boats, i.e. launch, barge, or pinnace.

5. A large vessel propelled by oars (or towed), generally much ornamented, and used on state occasions; an ornamental house-boat.

(The College 'Barges' at Oxford are ornamental house-boats, now permenently moored, and used as dressing- and sitting-rooms for university men on the river.)

1586 COGAN *Haven Health* i. (1612) 3 Sitting in a boate or barge which is rowed. **1606** SHAKS. *Ant. & Cl.* II. ii. 196 The Barge she sat in, like a burnisht Throne, Burnt on the water. **1682** *Lond. Gaz.* No. 1724/4 His Majesty passed by here in his barge. **1722** *Lond. Gaz.* No. 6107/3 The..Lord Mayor ..proceeded in the City Barge. **1849** MACAULAY *Hist. Eng.* I. 303 Who knew no more of winds and waves than could be learned in a gilded barge between Whitehall Stairs and Hampton Court. **1882** MURRAY *Berks* etc. 196 The walk by the Isis is bordered by the College barges.

6. a. (in *U.S.*) 'A double-decked passenger and freight vessel, without sails or power, and towed by a steamboat.' Webster.

b. A large carriage. *U.S.*

1882 HOWELLS *Modern Instance* xxvii. 328 Marcia watched him drive off toward the station in the hotel barge. **1903** *Boston Herald* 19 Aug., The visitors were conveyed in barges to the crest of High Pole hill. **1907** *Springfield Weekly Republ.* 21 Feb. 16 [A sleigh-ride] which required every four-horse barge in the north half of the county.

7. *Comb.*, chiefly attrib., as ***barge-builder, -cushion, -house, -load, -walk, -woman***; and the adjs. ***barge-like, laden***. See also BARGEMAN, -MASTER.

1609 *Act 7 James I* xviii, The..landing of every Barge-load..of the said Sand. **1685** *Lond. Gaz.* No. 2023/4 They lie now in a Barge-House..at Lambeth. **1773** *Gentl. Mag.* XLIII. 144 Who loll'd on barge-cushions at ease. **1850** MERIVALE *Rom. Emp.* (1865) III. xxviii. 322 His bargelike vessels thronged..the mouth of the inlet. **1864** *Daily Tel.* 6 Aug., A barge woman..seized the prisoner by the collar. **1880** BLACKMORE *M. Anerley* II. vii. 121 A jetty, a quay, and a barge-walk. **1960** *Times* 30 Apr. 9/1 A small party of Dutch soldiers was smuggled through the water-gate, concealed in a bargeload of peat.

barge, *sb.*[2] (See quot. 1908.)

1908 *Animal Management* 206 A piece of leather.. running from the fore-wale *beneath* the after-wale [of a horse's collar] is known as the 'barge'. **1946** N. WYMER *Eng. Country Crafts* v. 48 For the body he will make a leather throat-piece and stitch it..together with one edge of a piece of woollen cloth, to his barge.

barge, *sb.*[3] *slang.* [f. BARGE *v.*[2]] An argument, dispute.

1934 *Bulletin* (Sydney) 5 Dec. 36/2 The player-writer business has been causing a lot of barge in Brisbane. **1948** *Punch* 24 Nov. 491/3 Mr. Attlee and Mr. Churchill had a 'barge' on the subject of European Federation.

barge, *v.*[1] [f. BARGE *sb.*[1]]

†**1. a.** phr. ***to barge it***: to journey by barge. *Obs.*

1599 NASHE *Lent. Stuffe* in *Harl. Misc.* VI. 151 (D.) Whole tribes of males and females trotted, bargd it thither.

b. *intr.* To travel by barge.

1909 in WEBSTER. **1962** N. MAXWELL *Witch-Doctor's Appr.* ix. 111 Stretched on soft blankets in the shade of the pamacari..I was as comfortable as Cleopatra barging down the Nile.

2. *trans.* To carry by barge.

1649 BLITH *Eng. Improv. Impr.* (1653) 88 Were there a River to Barge it [soil] up and down. **1885** *Harper's Mag.* May 873/2 Of coals..750,000 tons are..annually..barged.

3. a. *intr.* To bump heavily *into* (a person), to knock roughly *against*; to go roughly and heavily *through, into, along, about*, or *against* (a place, etc.); also with advs. *about, around*. Also ***to barge one's way***.

1888 *Boy's Own Paper* Christmas No. 56/2 Dig your heels in, old chap,..and barge into the bank! **1890** FARMER *Slang* I. 124/1 *Barge*..(Uppingham School.)—To knock against a person; to come into collision with. **1899** *Daily News* 10 July 9/2 Defendant denied that the cocks were fighting. They were merely 'barging' as it was called in Lancashire. **1904** KIPLING *Traffics & Discov.* 318 You ought to have summoned me for trespass when I barged through your woods. **1904** —— in *Windsor Mag.* Jan. 234/2, I remember ..the dropped jaw of the midshipman in her whaler when we barged fairly into him. **1911** C. E. W. BEAN *'Dreadnought' of Darling* xxxviii. 339 A crowd of men came barging into the hut. **1915** W. J. LOCKE *Jaffery* xvii. 232 He ..barged mightily down Fleet Street. **1919** C. ORR *Glorious Thing* vi. 63 His first mishap was to barge into Isabel's fiancé, his second to be barged into by Isabel. **1924** *Blackw. Mag.* June 751/2 The camel..is an awkward and troublesome creature on a narrow road, especially if he takes fright, barging about to the danger of everybody. **1924** *Chambers's Jrnl.* 294/2 Pattering donkeys barge their way through the crowded alleys. **1961** *Times* 13 Feb. 4/2 Place kick..given for barging in the line-out.

b. *transf.* and *fig.*

1923 *Chambers's Jrnl.* 718/2, I hadn't barged about the world then. **1928** *Observer* 11 Mar. 14/5 There is a sort of masterful way in which a theme is made to barge its way through its surroundings. **1930** W. S. MAUGHAM *Cakes & Ale* iv. 50 He'll hate having a lot of strangers barging in on him.

c. *trans.* To cause to move forcibly or heavily.

1903 WODEHOUSE *Tales St. Austin's* 4 There was something wonderfully entertaining in the process of 'bargeing' the end man off the edge of the form into space. **1923** *Public Opinion* 19 Jan. 61/2 Heaven knows I'm always trying to barge it at you. **1924** W. J. LOCKE *Coming of Amos* viii. 93 By degrees he edged (or barged) his huge frame to the front rank. **1927** *Observer* 3 Apr. 27/6 Scotland bore down in a body, and Morton barged the ball past Brown.

barge (bɑːdʒ), *v.*[2] *slang.* ? *dial.* [? Back-formation f. BARGEE, as if 'to use the language of a bargee'.] *trans.* To abuse or 'slang' (a person).

a **1860** ALB. SMITH *Med. Student* (1861) 102 Whereupon they all began to barge the master at once; one saying 'his coffee was all snuff and chickweed.' **1881** J. F. T. KEANE *Six Months in Meccah* iv. 98 My informer..blaming those 'Shaitan' English, and barging them in choice Arabic.

barge-board (ˈbɑːdʒbɔəd). [See next.] A board, often ornamental, running along the edge of the gable of a house, to conceal the barge-couples, and prevent rain from driving in under the projecting barge-course.

1833 LOUDON *Cottage Archit.* 212 The roof..having barge boards against the west gable. *Ibid.* 422 Pierced openings in the verge board. **1845** *Gloss. Gothic Archit.* I. 42 Barge-board, Berge-board, Verge-board, or Parge-board. **1876** T. HARDY *Hand Ethelb.* II. xlviii. 273 A timber-built cottage, having ornamental barge-boards, balconettes, and porch.

ˈbarge-ˈcouple. [With *barge-* in this, the prec., and next, cf. med.L. *bargus*, a kind of gallows = cl. L. *furca*: Du Cange. The modern conjecture that it is a corruption of *verge* seems to be without any historical ground.] (See quotations.)

1562 LEIGH *Armory* 115 A Cheuron is made of Carpenters and is the highest part of y^e house..Carpenters call it at this day, the barge couples. **1611** GWILLIM *Heraldry* II. vi. (1660) 68 A paire of Barge couples or Rafters, such as Carpenters doe set on the highest part of the house, for bearing of the roof there of. **1842** GWILT *Archit.*, *Barge couples*, two beams mortised and tenoned together for the purpose of increasing the strength of a building.

barge-course (ˈbɑːdʒkɔəs). [See prec.] A portion of the roof of a house carried slightly beyond the wall at the gable-end, and made up underneath with mortar, to keep out rain, etc.

1668 LEYBOURN *Platf. Purch.* 109 The Barge Courses.. must be struck with Lime and hair Mortar. **1727** BRADLEY *Fam. Dict.*, *Barge-Course.* **1835** *Penny Cycl.* III. 450/1 Barge-boards..are often attached to the gables of old English houses, fixed near the extremity of the barge-course.

bargee (bɑːˈdʒiː). [f. BARGE *sb.*[1] + -EE. (The suffix is used irregularly.)] A bargeman.

1666 PEPYS *Diary* (1879) VI. 89 Spent the evening on the water, making sport with the Westerne bargees. **1831** HONE *Year Bk.* 672 A great sum is gained by the 'bargees' (bargemen, Eton phraseology). **1861** HUGHES *T. Brown Oxf.* xxxiii, A man who sets up for a country gentleman with the tongue of a Thames bargee. **1873** G. DAVIES *Mount. & Mere* xviii. 155 The bargees, who navigate barges laden with fragant hay or corn up the stream.

bargeman (ˈbɑːdʒmən). [f. BARGE *sb.*[1] + MAN.] A man who has charge of a barge; one of the crew or rowers of a barge.

1465 *Mann. & Househ. Exp.* 297 Gaff to the Kenges bargeman, xx *d.* *c* **1510** *Cocke Lorelles B.* 11 Bargemen, whery rowers, and dysers. **1596** SPENSER *F.Q.* VII. vii. 35 And backward yode as bargemen wont to fare. **1681** R. LESTRANGE (*title*) Dialogue between Sam the Ferriman of Dachet; Will, Waterman of London, and Tom, a Bargeman of Oxford. **1797** NELSON in Duncan *Life* (1806) 43 William Fearney, one of my bargemen. **1810** SCOTT *Lady of L.* III. xii, So rapidly the bargemen row.

bargemaster (ˈbɑːdʒˌmɑːstə(r)). The master or owner of a barge.

1648 *Clarendon St. Papers* II. App. 47 The bargemaster looking down into the barge. **1664-5** in C. Welch *Hist. Company of Pewterers* (1902) II. 132 The salary of Mr. Pike, barge master, was fixed on 16th March at 3*l.* yearly. **1710** *Lond. Gaz.* No. 4742/4 William Burley, of Oxford, Bargemaster. **1768** BLACKSTONE *Comm.* III. 164 There is also in law an implied contract with..a common carrier or bargemaster, to be answerable for the goods he carries. **1892** W. C. HAZLITT *Livery Companies* 475 The duties of the Bargemaster, which, after the discontinuance of water-pageants, have been confined to the supervision of the swans on the Thames. **1898** *Daily News* 21 Apr. 2/2 The Fishmongers' Company's late Bargemaster.—The office of bargemaster is one of the most ancient in the annals of the City Companies.

†**ˈbargenet(te.** Also 6 bargynet, -inet. [? erron. form.] = BARGERET.

1531 ELYOT *Gov.* I. xx. (1883) I. 230 We haue nowe base daunses bargenettes. **1572** GASCOIGNE *100 Flowres* (1576) 223 Mistresse, and I (because I haue seene the French maner of dauncing) will eftsones entreat you to daunce a Bargynet. **1600** *England's Helicon* (*title*) The Barginet of Antimachus.

barge-pole. A long pole with which a barge is propelled (see also quot. 1890); frequent in colloq. phr. (and variants) ***I wouldn't touch him*** (or ***it***) ***with*** (***the end of***) ***a barge-pole***, I refuse to have anything to do with him (or it).

1890 FARMER *Slang* I. 124 *Barge-Pole.* (Winchester College.) A large stick or thick bough, of which there was one in each fagot. Also generally used for any large piece of wood. **1893** LADY MONKSWELL *Diary* Dec. (1944) 239 It will be a long while before any political party touches Home Rule again with the end of a barge pole. **1914** H. A. VACHELL *Quinneys'* II. xvi. 229 If he was a fool I wouldn't touch him with a barge-pole. **1915** A. H. GIBBS *Persistent Lovers* li, Hideous little beast! I wouldn't touch him with the end of a barge pole. **1918** MRS. H. WARD *War & Elizabeth* v. 86 If he tries to leave me this funny old place..there are two can play at that game. I wouldn't touch it with a barge-pole.

†**ˈbarger.** *Obs. rare*[−1]. [f. BARGE *sb.*[1] + -ER[1].] A bargeman or bargemaster.

1602 CAREW *Cornwall* 108 b, Who..(like the Campellians in the North, and the London Bargers) forslow not to baigne them..with a worse perfume than Jugurth found fault with in the dungeon.

† **'bargeret.** *Obs.* Also 5–7 bargaret. [a. F. *bergerette*, f. *berger* shepherd.] A pastoral or rustic song and dance.

c **1400** *Floure & Leafe* 348 Sing right womanly A bargaret in praising the daisie. **1566** PAINTER *Pal. Pleas.* 154 b, I will make ye daunce sutch a bloudy bargeret. **1616** BULLOKAR, *Bargaret*, a kind of dance.

'barge-stone. [see BARGE-COUPLE.] In *plural*: Stones forming the sloping or stepped line of a gable.

1833 LOUDON *Cottage Archit.* 101 Stones placed on a wall .. as an abutment of the barge stones.

† **barget.** *Obs. rare.* [a. OF. *bargette*, dim. of *barge*: see BARGE and -ET[1].] A small barge.

1470–85 MALORY *Arthur* XVIII. xix, Let me be putte within a barget .. and that my barget be couerd with blak samyte. **1486** *Bk. St. Albans, Her.* A ij, Iafeth made first Barget and ther in he made a balle. [**1867** in SMYTH *Sailor's Word-bk.*]

† **bargh** (bɑːf). *dial.* Also barf, baurgh, barugh. [mod. northern form of BARROW, ME. *bergh*, OE. *beorh*, *beorȝ-*, mount, hill; perh. influenced by ON. *bjarg* rock-face, precipice. In sense 3 app. influenced by Ger. *berg-* mining-.]

1. A detached low ridge or hill.

1823 W. BUCKLAND *Reliq. Diluv.* 209 Similar ridges, known locally [in Yorkshire] by the name of barfs. **1855** *Whitby Gloss.* s.v., Langbarugh in Cleveland.

2. The steep face of a hill; a road up it.

1674 RAY *N. Countr. Wds.*, *Bargh*, a Horseway up a steep hill. *Yorkshire.*

† **3.** A mine. *Obs.* Cf. BARMASTER, BARMOTE.

1693 W. ROBERTSON *Phraseol. Gen.* 207 A Bargh, i.e. a mine, whereout of metalls are digged.

† **'bargham.** *Obs.* exc. *dial.* Forms: 5 **bargham, barwam, berhom**; also in mod. dial., **barfhame** (*Durh.*), **barfan** (*Yorksh.*), **bariham, barkham** (*Lanc.*), **baurghwan** (*north*, Grose), **brauchin** (*Cumberld.*), **brecham** (*Scotch*), **barkum** (*Craven*). [? f. OE. *beorȝ-an* to protect + HAME, q.v.] The collar of a working horse.

c **1475** in Wülcker *Voc.* /811 *Epicia*, berhom. **1483** *Cath. Angl.*, Bargham, Barwam, *epiphium*. **1824** *Craven Dial.* i. 6 They welted cart ower .. an brack th' barkum.

barghest ('bɑːˌgest). Also **barghaist, -guest, -ghost, -gest, -gaist.** [perh. ad. Ger. *berg-geist* mountain-demon, gnome; but by Scott referred to Ger. *bahre* bier, hearse, and by others to Ger. *bär* bear, with reference to its alleged form.] A goblin, fabled to appear in the form of a large dog, with various horrible characteristics, and to portend imminent death or misfortune.

1732 *Gentl. Mag.* Oct., The dæmon of Tidworth, the black dog of Winchester, and the bar-guest of York. **1818** SCOTT *Rob Roy* I. 223 (D.) He .. needed not to care 'for ghaist or barghaist, devil or dobbie.' **1849** W. IRVING *Braceb. Hall* 359 The village had its barguest, or bar-ghost. **1871** E. PEACOCK *Ralf Skirlaugh* II. 111 Tales about bargests.

barging ('bɑːdʒɪŋ), *vbl. sb.* [f. BARGE *sb.*[1] + -ING[1]. Cf. BARGE *v.*[1]] Transport by barge.

1901 *Fielden's Mag.* IV. 433/2 The cartage or barging of the material to sites. **1904** *Daily Chron.* 29 Jan. 3/6 The barging is done by contract. **1905** *Westm. Gaz.* 9 Mar. 9/2 The cost of 'barging' and transport.

† **'bar-goose.** *Obs.* [App. a contraction of *barnacle-goose*.] The barnacle-goose: see BARNACLE 2.

1598 SYLVESTER *Du Bartas* II. iv. I. (1633) 201/2 The (Trees-brood) Bar-geese, mid th' Hebridian wave .. their farflown wings do wave. **1647** N. WARD *Simp. Cobler* 25 Such garbes, as .. transclout them into gant bar-geese, ill-shapen shotten shell-fish, Egyptian Hieroglyphicks.

barhal, var. BHARAL.

bari- ('bɛərɪ), comb. form of BARIUM; = Having barium in chemical composition.

1880 *Athenæum* 13 Nov. 645/2 The Bari-Sulphates of Iron.

† **'baria.** *Chem. Obs.* Also **barya.** [f. BARIUM; cf. *strontia*, f. *strontium*.] = BARYTA.

1812 SIR H. DAVY *Chem. Philos.* 340 The only well known combination of barium, with oxygene, is baryta or baria. **1819** CHILDREN *Chem. Anal.* 443 One atom of baryum + one atom of oxygen, forms one atom of barya.

baric ('bɛərɪk), *a.*[1] *Chem.* [f. BAR-IUM + -IC.] Of barium; containing barium in composition.

1869 *Eng. Mech.* 12 Nov. 213/3 Preparing baric cyanide.

baric ('bærɪk), *a.*[2] [f. Gr. βάρ-ος weight + -IC.] Of or pertaining to weight, *esp.* that of the air as indicated by the barometer; barometric.

1881 *Times* 11 Mar., A continuation of the baric rise in most parts of our islands.

baricado, barico; see BARR-.

barilla (bəˈrɪlə, baˈriʎa). Forms: 7 **bariglia, barrilla,** 8 **berilla, barillia, barrilla, -ilha,** 8– **barilla.** [a. Sp. *barrilla*.]

1. A maritime plant (*Salsola Soda*) which grows extensively in Spain, Sicily, and the Canary Islands.

[Cf. **1748** in 2.] **1764** HEBERDEN in *Phil. Trans.* LV. 58 The fossil alkali .. which is procured from the Spanish barilla. **1884** *Pall Mall G.* 10 Oct. 11/2 Precipitous sides .. clothed with barilla and scattered pines.

2. a. An impure alkali produced by burning the dried plants of the preceding and allied species; formerly imported in large quantities, and used in the manufacture of soda, soap, and glass. **b.** Also applied to impure alkali made from kelp.

1622 MALYNES *Anc. Law-Merch.* 81 The Commodities of Spaine and Portugall, are .. Anchoues, Bay-berries, Bariglia. **1705** *Lond. Gaz.* No. 4096/2 Laden with Wine, Malaga-Soap, and Berilla. **1742** *Phil. Trans.* XLII. 71 The Salt of Glass-wort (called in England Barillia). **1748** *Ibid.* XLV. 561 This kind of Pot-ash is commonly called Barrilha, from an Herb of the same Name in Spain that produces it. **1863** WATTS *Dict. Chem.* I. 500 Kelp, a still more impure alkali .. is sometimes called *British barilla*.

barillet ('bærɪlɛt). [a. F. *barillet*, dim. of *baril* BARREL: see -ET[1].] A little barrel or cask; 'the barrel of a watch; the funnel of a sucking-pump' (Crabb in Worcester).

barin, obs. form of BAIRN.

baring ('bɛərɪŋ), *vbl. sb.* [f. BARE *v.* + -ING[1].]

1. The action of laying bare or uncovering; the removal of something so as to leave a bare place.

1601 SHAKS. *All's Well* IV. i. 53 Or the baring of my beard. **1753** CHAMBERS *Cycl. Supp.*, *Baring of trees* .. the taking away some of the earth over the roots. **1847** JEFFREY in Ld. Cockburn *Life* II. Let. 187 These barings of the heart should not be shown except to one's other self.

2. *concr.* That which is removed in this process; the superficial covering, the top soil.

1871 S. SHARP in *Archæol.* XLIII. 120 (D.) The baring, as it is called by the quarrymen, consists not only of the natural surface soil, but also of the upper soft bed of ferruginous rock. **1873** *Archæol.* XLV. 466 Bodies .. buried .. in pits sunk in the baring.

bar-iron: see BAR *sb.*[1] 30.

Barisal (bærɪˈsɑːl). [The name of a town in East Bengal.] ***Barisal guns***, booming sounds heard in Barisal and certain other regions, esp. on or near water.

1896 *Nature* 2 Jan. 197, I first heard the Barisal Guns in December 1871, on my way to Assam from Calcutta through the Sunderbans. **1902** *Encycl. Brit.* XXVI. 147/2 Barisal has given its name to a curious physical phenomenon, known as the 'Barisal guns', the cause of which has not yet been satisfactorily explained. These are noises, like the report of cannon, frequently heard in the channels of the delta of the Brahmaputra. **1936** *Discovery* Aug. 252/2 Mysterious booming sounds, like distant gunfire, which may be heard in the Australian desert and suitable places all over the world. In Australia they are known as Barisal guns, probably because so many white men from India retire over here.

barish ('bɛərɪʃ), *a.*; also 7–9 **bareish.** [f. BARE *a.* + -ISH[1].] Somewhat bare; thinly covered.

1661 LOVELL *Hist. Anim. & Min.* Introd., The taile is .. bareish in those that are rough. **1865** CARLYLE *Fredk. Gt.* VIII. iii, River Elbe sweeping through it, banks barish.

barita, earlier form of BARYTA.

barite ('bɛəraɪt). *Min.* [f. BAR-IUM + -ITE.] Dana's systematic name for the mineral BARYTES.

bariter, obs. form of BARRATER, -OR.

baritone ('bærɪtəʊn), *sb.* and *a.* Forms: 7 **bariton, barritone,** 9– **baritone, baryton,** 8–9 **barytone.** [a. F. *barytone*, or It. *baritono*, ad. Gr. βαρύτονος deep-sounding, f. βαρύ-ς heavy, deep + τόνος pitch, TONE.]

A. *sb.*

1. The male voice of compass intermediate between tenor and bass, ranging from lower A in the bass clef to lower F in the treble clef.

1609 DOULAND *Ornithop. Microl.* 84 Of the Baritone. The Bassus .. is the lowest part of each Song. Or it is an Harmony to be sung with a deepe voyce, which is called Baritonus. **1859** GEO. ELIOT *A. Bede* I The strong barytone .. which was heard above the sound of plane and hammer, singing—Awake, my soul.

fig. **1870** LOWELL *Among my Bks.* II. 240 Harmonies .. deep and eternal, like the undying barytone of the sea.

2. A singer possessing a baritone voice.

1821 BYRON *Juan* IV. lxxxix, Our baritone .. A pretty lad, but bursting with conceit. **1878** GROVE *Dict. Music* I. 127 Offered him an engagement as principal barytone.

3. A musical instrument of deep sound: † **a.** a kind of bass viol now obsolete; **b.** see quot. 1880; **c.** a baritone saxophone.

1685 *Lond. Gaz.* No. 2088/4 Some performance upon the Barritone. *c* **1790** HAYDN (*title*) Concertos for baryton with accompaniment of two violins and bass. **1880** GROVE *Dict. Mus.* I. 139 Baritone, the name usually applied to the smaller bass saxhorn in B♭ or C. **1952** B. ULANOV *Hist. Jazz* (1958) vi. 52 The scoring of two altos, two tenors, and a baritone in the present-day dance band.

B. *adj.*

a. Of the voice: Having a compass intermediate between bass and tenor. **b.** Of music: Suited for a baritone voice. **c.** Of a singer: Possessing a baritone voice.

1729 SWIFT *Corr.* (1841) II. 628, I recommend one Mr. Mason .. a barytone voice, for the vacancy. **1861** *Sat. Rev.* 16 Dec. 611 The present fashion of writing at the extreme end of the baritone register. **1871** PALGRAVE *Lyr. Poems* 50 And the deep rich oily Te Deum By the barytone canon sung.

d. Of an instrument: occurring in a 'family' of instruments between the tenor and the bass. So **baritone horn** (*a*) = A. 3 b; (*b*) *U.S.*, a baritone saxophone.

1876 STAINER & BARRETT *Dict. Mus. Terms* 385/2 s.v. *Saxophones*, Brass wind instruments, the invention of M. Sax... They are six in number, the high, soprano, alto, tenor, baritone and bass. **1883** GROVE *Dict. Mus.* III. 233/2 It [*sc.* the saxophone] is made in a number of sizes .. the contralto in F and E♭; the barytone in C and E♭; the bass in F and E♭, [etc.]. *Ibid.*, Those most used are the contralto and barytone varieties [of saxophone]. **1926** WHITEMAN & MCBRIDE *Jazz* ix. 193 One baritone saxophone is equal in sonorousness to a section of nine or ten cellos. **1938** *Oxf. Compan. Mus.* 626/2 *Heckelphone*, baritone oboe, basset oboe. **1949** L. FEATHER *Inside Be-Bop* ii. 11 He played baritone horn in the school band.

Hence **'baritonist**, a baritone-saxophone player.

1958 K. GOODWIN in P. Gammond *Decca Bk. of Jazz* xiii. 157 He has .. transferred his .. technique .. to the baritone-saxophone, and .. rates as the most important baritonist on the coast.

barium ('bɛərɪəm). *Chem.* Rarely (and obs.) **baryum.** [f. BAR-YTA, -YTES + -IUM; cf. *soda*, *sodium*. Davy purposely discarded the second syllable of *baryta*, as in his proposed *alumium* from *alumina*, and *magnium* from *magnesia*.] **a.** A white metallic element, not found native, but as the basis of the alkaline earth baryta. First separated by Sir H. Davy in 1808.

1808 SIR H. DAVY in *Phil. Trans.* XCVIII. 346, I shall venture to denominate the metals from the alkaline earths, barium, strontium, calcium, and magnium. **1819** [See BARIA]. **1873** WATTS *Fownes' Chem.* 357 Barium occurs as sulphate and carbonate, forming the veinstone in many lead mines.

attrib. **1869** ROSCOE *Chem* 221 Barium compounds occur somewhat more widely dispersed than those of strontium.

b. Special comb. **barium meal**, a mixture containing barium sulphate, a white compound that is opaque to X-rays, used in radiological examination of the alimentary tract. So also ***barium enema, swallow***.

1913 *Lancet* 31 May 1529/2 Dr. J. Delpratt Harris gave a demonstration of a Barium Meal in a case of Gastroenterostomy. **1930** D. A. RHINEHART *Roentgenographic Technique* xviii. 346 Postero-anterior views of the colon filled with a barium enema. **1940** *Med. Ann.* 507 A patient .. was submitted .. for a barium enema examination of the colon. **1946** *Brit. Jrnl. Radiology* Mar. 114/2 On examination with a barium swallow and meal it was seen that there was .. dilatation .. of the œsophagus. **1962** *Lancet* 13 Jan. 67/1 Barium-swallow examinations may fail to demonstrate œsophageal varices. **1966** *Listener* 24 Feb. 273/1 They performed all sorts of tests on me with barium meals.

bark (bɑːk), *sb.*[1] Forms: 4– **bark**; also 4 **barc,** 4–7 **barke,** 6 **barcke,** 7 **barque.** [a. Scand. *bark-* (ON. *börkr*, Sw., Da. *bark*):—OTeut. **barku-z*.]

1. a. The rind or outer sheath of the trunk and branches of trees, formed of tissue parallel with the wood. See quot. 1866.

a **1300** *Cursor M.* 1321 Braunches .. o bark al bare. *c* **1400** MAUNDEV. xvii. 189 Men hewen the Trees .. tille that the Bark be parted. **1535** COVERDALE *Joel* i. 7 They shal pyll of the barckes of my fygetrees. **1642** FULLER *Holy & Prof. St.* IV. xiii. 304 He is no friend to the tree, that strips it of the bark. **1675** GREW *Anat. Trunks* I. ii. §1 The Trunk .. hath Three general Parts .. the Barque, the Wood, and the Pith. **1866** *Treas. Bot.* 123 The only true bark is that of Exogens. In Endogens, False Bark, also called Cortical Integument, stands in place of bark.

b. That used as a material in dyeing, tanning, etc., or its bruised residue, 'spent bark,' 'tan.'

1565 *Act 8 Eliz.* xi. §3 No Person .. shall dye .. black, any Cap, with Bark or Swarf. **1594** PLAT *Jewell-ho.* I. 12 Men which tan the hides of beasts .. take yᵉ barkes of Oake. **1716** *Lond Gaz.* No. 5393/4 Bark is worth 2*s.* a Cart-Load. *Mod.* The street opposite the sick man's house was laid with bark.

c. A sort or piece of bark.

1647 W. BROWNE *Polex.* II. 116 Two great chaines of rootes and black barks he had about his neck.

† **2.** The rind, husk, or shell of fruit and grains.

1377 LANGL. *P. Pl.* B. XI. 251 On a walnot with-oute is a bitter barke. *c* **1440** *Gesta Rom.* lvi. 419 The ape wil gladly ete the kyrnelle of the note .. but when he sauours the soure barke, etc. **1586** COGAN *Haven Health* (1636) 34 A good handfull of Oaten barke. **1661** LOVELL *Hist. Anim. & Min.* 22 Wine in which the barks of a sweet pomegranat are.

† **3.** *gen.* An outer covering or husk; *esp.* a superficial crust or incrustation. *Obs.* exc. *dial.*

1601 HOLLAND *Pliny* I. 45 In the lake Velinus .. if wood be thrown in, it is couered ouer with a stony barke. **1725** POPE *Odyss.* XIII. 457 O'er thy smooth skin a bark of wrinkles spread. **1878** HALLIWELL *Dict.*, *Bark*, the tartar deposited by bottled wine or other liquor encrusting the bottle.

4. *dial.* and *slang.* The (human) skin.

a **1758** A. Ramsay *Poems* (1844) 88 And dang the bark Aff's shin. **1876** *Fam. Herald* 2 Dec. 80/1 With the 'bark' all off his shins from a blow with a hockey stick.

5. *fig.* Envelopment; outer covering; outside, external part. *arch.*

c **1374** Chaucer *Troylus* iv. 201 Yboundyn in the blakke barke of care. *c* **1400** *Rom. Rose* 7173 The bark and rynde, That makith the entencious blynde. **1587** Golding *De Mornay* xxv. 379 Such a Lawgiuer, as not onely had power ouer the barke of man. **1641** J. Jackson *True Evang. T.* i. 68 The Jews..stick in the barke, and expound the text to be fulfilled to the very letter of it.

6. phr. *to go* (etc.) ***between the bark and the tree.***

1562 J. Heywood *Prov. & Epigr.* (1867) 47 It were a foly for mee, To put my hande betweene the barke and the tree ..Betweene you. **1600** Holland *Livy* xxxvi. v. 921 To deale roundly and simply with no side, but to go betweene the bark and the tree. **1642** Rogers *Naaman* 303 So audacious as to go betweene barke and tree, breeding suspitions.. betweene man and wife. **1804** Mar. Edgeworth *Mod. Griselda* Wks. 1832 V. 299 An instigator of quarrels between man and wife, or, according to the plebeian but expressive apophthegm, one who would come between the bark and the tree. [Cf. Halliwell *Dict.* s.v., 'Between the bark and the wood,' a well-adjusted bargain, where neither party has the advantage.]

7. *specifically* in *Med.* (also ***Jesuits'*** or ***Peruvian Bark***): The bark of various species of the Cinchona tree, from which quinine is procured, formerly ground into powder and taken as a febrifuge.

1704 Watts *Life of Souls*, When bark and steel play well their game To save our sinking breath. **1719** D'Urfey *Pills* (1872) II. 344 Your Jesuits' Bark had proved a golden Bough. **1790** *Cook's Voy.* VI. 2241 That excellent medicine, Peruvian bark. **1852** Thackeray *Esmond* iii. viii. (1876) 393, I have known a woman preach Jesuit's bark.

fig. **1790** Boswell *Johnson* (1811) I. 195 In no writings whatever can be found more bark and steel for the mind.

8. *north. dial.* A candle-box. (See quot.)

1878 Halliwell *Dict.*, *Bark*, a cylindrical receptacle for candles; a candle-box. *North.* At first it was only a piece of bark nailed up against the wall.

9. *Comb.* General relations: **a.** attrib. or objective, as in ***bark-cloth***, ***-dust***, ***-mill***, ***-puller***, ***-string***, ***-vat***, ***-water***, ***-wose***. **b.** instrumental or limitative, as in ***bark-bared***, ***-feeder***, ***-formed***, ***-tanned***, ***-tanning***.

a. *c* **1440** *Promp. Parv.* 24 Barkarys barkewatyr, *naucea.* **1483** *Cath. Angl.* 22/1 Barke duste or wose, *frunium, ptipsana.* **1569** *Wills & Inv. N.C.* (1835) 307, Xl barke fatts xiijl. vjs. viijd. **1773** Barnard in *Phil. Trans.* LXIII. 218 The bark-pullers..were..alarmed by the shaking. **1854** J. Stephens *Centr. Amer.* 13 Tied together with bark-strings. **1864** J. A. Grant *Walk across Africa* 138 Or an Arab cloak or shawl of bark-cloth hung from his shoulder, reaching below the knee. **1880** Miss Bird *Japan* II. 82 A skin or bark-cloth vest. **1885** *Harper's Mag.* Jan. 276/1 Most tanners.. grind it in a bark-mill. **1951** R. Firth *Elements of Social Organization* ii. 51 The people still wear their traditional bark-cloth, made from the fibrous inner bark of the paper-mulberry tree.

b. ? **1712** J. Mortimer (J.) Excorticated and bark-bared trees. **1818** *Art Preserv. Feet* 112 The ancient system of bark tanning. **1858** W. Ellis *Vis. Madagascar* ii. 25 These bark-formed boards were laid side by side. **1859** Darwin *Orig. Spec.* iv. (1878) 66 We see leaf-eating insects green, and bark-feeders mottled grey. **1883** *Pall Mall G.* 5 July 5/2 Bark-tanned goods.

10. Special combinations: **bark-bed**, a hot-bed made of spent bark from a tannery; **bark-beetle**, any beetle of the family *Scolytidæ*, the members of which burrow beneath the bark of woody plants; **bark-borer** *U.S.*, a species of bark-beetle; **bark-bound** *a.*, hindered in growth by excessive tightness of the bark; **bark canoe** *U.S.*, a canoe made of birch-bark; † **bark-cobill** (Ger. *kubel*), a bark-vat; **bark-galling** (see quot.); **bark-heat**, that of a bark-bed; **bark-house**, one in which bark is stored, a tan-house; **bark-hut**, a hut built with the bark of trees; **bark-louse** *U.S.*, any one of a number of aphids infesting the bark of trees; **bark-mill** *U.S.*, a mill in which tanning bark is ground; **bark-peeler**, (*a*) a person who peels bark from a tree; (*b*) an implement for peeling bark; **bark-pit**, a pit filled with bark and water in which hides are steeped in tanning; **bark-stone** = castor[1] 2; **bark-stove**, a glazed structure placed over a bark-bed; **bark-tree**, English name of the Cinchonas; **bark-worm** (= *bark-louse*).

1732 Miller *Gard. Kal.* (1775) 70 The Coffee-trees..are placed in the *bark-bed. **1862** T. W. Harris *Insects Injur. Veget.* 85 Though these cylindrical *bark-beetles are of small size, they multiply very fast. **1953** H. L. Edlin *Forester's Handbk.* xvi. 264 A very large group known as bark beetles, because they feed and breed in and beneath the bark of living or dead trees. **1859** *Trans. Ill. Agric. Soc.* *1857–8* III. 345 Another species is that sometimes called the *bark borer, from its feeding exclusively upon the cambium immediately beneath the bark. **1615** W. Lawson *Orch. & Gard.* iii. xiii. (1668) 42 *Bark-bound, a disease in trees. **1673** Grew *Anat. Roots* ii. §2 Therefore are the Roots of many Herbs, Barque-bound, as well as the Trunks of Trees. **1831** *On Planting* ii. vi. 63 in *Libr. Useful Knowl.*, To secure against any chill or sudden effect of cold, so as to bring about ..the injury of being bark-bound, the most effectual impediment to growth either in height or thickness. **1725** in *Lancaster* (Mass.) *Rec.* (1884) 232, 27 day we traveld down the river and found a *bark cannow. **1888** *Harper's Mag.* Mar. 537/1 But only a bark canoe now and then comes along from one of the thirteen rivers. *c* **1550** Sir J. Balfour *Practicks* 588 The sype of thair *bark cobill. **1742** Bailey, **Bark-galling* is when trees are galled by being bound to stakes. **1781** Cowper *To Mrs. Hill* 19 Feb., I shall..keep them [seeds]..in a *bark heat. **1483** *Cath. Angl.* 22/1 *Barkhowse, *frunitorium.* **1541** *Lanc. Wills* I. 81 In ye barkhouse fyve dikar..tanned. **1660** *Boston Rec.* 155 Henry Bridgam..sett part of his barke house upon part of the townes land. **1721** *Boston Selectmen* 83 Liberty..to erect a bark house near Snow Hill. **1824** in Thornton *Amer. Gloss.* Suppl., A bark-house, and a good iron bark-mill. **1744** F. Moore *Voy. Georgia* 123 Some *bark-huts, which our friendly Indians had some time since built for their lodging. **1843** 'R. Carlton' *New Purchase* i. 2 We..talked of bark huts and bows and arrows. **1890** 'R. Boldrewood' *Miner's Right* vi. 61 Bark-huts, of which both sides, and sometimes doors are composed of sheets of the flattened eucalyptus bark. **1841** in Johnson *Farm Encycl.* (1868) 137/2 (D.A.E.), The *bark lice are found apparently torpid..sticking.. closely to the bark. **1959** Southwood & Leston *Land & Water Bugs* vi. 153 They [*sc.* Emesinæ] may also feed on insects already trapped in spiders' webs and they can attack bark-lice (Psocids) through their web. **1749** J. Eliot *Field-Husb.* (1934) ii. 37 Take your Clover Hay to a Tanners *Bark-mill, where they use a Stone Wheel, grind it. **1885** Bark-mill [see sense 9a]. **1862** *Rep. Comm. Patents: Agric.* (U.S.) 414 Tanneries sprang into existence..and the *bark-peelers and teamsters..made the whole region one of active and prosperous industry. **1902** *Encycl. Brit.* XXV. 376/1 All textile work [of American Indians] was done by hand; the only devices known were the bark-peeler, the shredder [etc.]. **1925** Hemingway *In our Time* (1926) i. 18 The shanties where the Indian bark-peelers lived. **1961** M. W. Barley *Eng. Farmhouse & Cottage* i. ii. 36 In Cumberland some sixty years ago barkpeelers built themselves huts which consisted of four poles lashed in pairs to support a ridge piece. **1805** M. Lewis in *Jrnls. Lewis & Clark Exped.* (1904) III. 319 The male beaver has six stones, two of which ..are called the *bark stones or castors. **1817** *Ann. Reg. 1816* 551/2 To prepare beaver-bait, the castor or bark stone is first gently pressed from the bladder-like bag which contains it. *Ibid.* 552/1 The bark stones are two inches in length. **1732** Miller *Gard. Kal.* (1775) 159 Exotic plants..especially those in the *bark-stove. **1783** Davidson in *Phil. Trans.* LXXIV. 455 (*article*) *Bark-Tree. **1852** Th. Ross *Humboldt's Trav.* I. ii. 59 *note*, The orange bark-tree (*Cinchona lancifolia*)..the red bark-tree (*C. oblongifolia*). **1655** Mouff. & Benn. *Health's Impr.* (1746) 188 Titmice feed..upon Caterpillars, *Bark-Worms and Flies. **1787** Best *Angling* 19 Bark-worm or Ashgrub, found under the bark of an oak, ash, or beech.

bark, barque (bɑːk), *sb.*[2] Forms: 5–7 **barke**, 5– **barque**, 6– **bark.** [a. F. *barque*, 15th c. ad. Pr., Sp., or It. *barca*:—L. *barca* (in Paulinus Nolanus *c* 400). Not in OFr., where the word used was *barge*.

Barge and *bark* are probably identical in origin, and possibly from Celtic; Thurneysen shows that OIr. *barc* (a fem. *a*-stem) may, if native, represent an original **barga*, with dialectal by-form **barca*, which would satisfactorily account at once for OF. *barge*, and the common Romanic *barca*. Diez takes *barca* as an early syncopated variant of the conjectural **bărica*, mentioned under barge, but as *barca* occurs *c* 400 and **bărica* not at all, this is improbable. As to the original meaning, Isidore, *c* 640, says '*Barca* est, quae cuncta navis commercia ad litus portat. Hanc navis in pelago propter nimias undas suo suscipit gremio.' So Florio (1598) explains It. *barca* as 'a barke, bote, wherrie, or lighter'; ed. 1611 has 'any kinde of Barke, Barge, or Boate'; Minsheu (1623) explains Sp. *barca* as 'a great boat, a barke, a skiffe, a hoarse boat'; and Cotgr. (1611) has Fr. *barque* 'a barque, little ship, great boat.' Cf. barge *sb.*[1] 2–4. The *barca* was thus apparently, originally, a large ship's boat, used as a lighter; on the Mediterranean, the name continued to be applied to an open boat, even while extended to a small vessel with sails; the latter was the sense with which the word was taken from French into English, and which it still retains both in general and specific use; but in the end of 16th c., the more primitive sense of 'large rowing boat, barge' was reintroduced from the languages of the Mediterranean.]

1. A small ship; in earlier times, a general term for all sailing vessels of small size, *e.g.* fishing-smacks, xebecs, pinnaces; in modern use, applied poetically or rhetorically to any sailing vessel, 'our gallant bark'; = barge 1.

1475 Caxton *Jason* 104 Some sayd that Iason was rentred in to the barque. **1494** Fabyan vii. ccxliv. 286 Flemynges: the whiche shyppyd them in smalle caruyles and barkys. **1552** Huloet, Barke or little shyppe, *lembus.* **1585** *Act 27 Eliz.* ii. §9 Every Owner and Master of any Ship, Bark or Boat. **1596** Shaks. *Merch. V.* ii. vi. 15 The skarfed barke puts from her natiue bay. **1625** K. Long tr. *Barclay's Argenis* ii. x. 93 A Pirate's Bark, well trimmed and rigged against stormes. **1667** Milton *P.L.* ii. 288 Whose Bark.. Or Pinnace, anchors in a craggy Bay. *a* **1687** Petty *Pol. Arith.* iii. (1691) 59 Seamen..do sometimes Sail in small Barks, sometimes in midling Ships, and sometimes in great Vessels of Defence. **1718** Pope *Iliad* i. 182 We launch a bark to plough the watery plains. **1769** Falconer *Dict. Marine* (1789), *Bark*, a general name given to small ships. **1851** Dixon *W. Penn* xvii. (1872) 142 Who had crossed the Atlantic in their barks.

b. *fig.* (Cf. *ship*, *vessel*.)

1605 Bacon *Adv. Learn.* ii. 70 Many other barques of knowledge haue beene cast away. *c* **1800** K. White *Lett.* (1837) 323 The poor bark of mortality. **1821** Shelley *Adonais* lv, My spirit's bark is driven, Far from the shore.

2. A rowing boat; formerly a large flat boat, a barge; now only poetically and vaguely; cf. sense 1.

1598 Barret *Theor. Warres* v. iv. 136 One cart to cary a bridge bark [*i.e.* for constructing a bridge]. **1611** Cotgr., *Barque*, a barke, little ship, great boat. **1715** *Lond. Gaz.* No. 5384/7 A Distribution was made among the Fleet of the Barks for landing the Infantry and the Shallops for towing those Barks. **1756** C. Lucas *Ess. Waters* II. 63 Let him not send us to sea..in an open barque, and without a pilot. **1790** Cowper *Iliad* i. 174 A bark with lusty rowers well supplied. **1813** Scott *Rokeby* ii. xxxi, The..swain May lightly row his bark to shore.

3. *spec.* A sailing vessel of particular rig; in 17th c. sometimes applied to the *barca-longa* of the Mediterranean; *now* to a three-masted vessel with fore- and main-masts square-rigged, and mizenmast 'fore-and-aft' rigged: till recent times a comparatively small vessel; now there are many of 3,000 to 5,000 tons, nearly all the larger steamers being *barks*. (In this sense frequently spelt *barque* by way of distinction.)

1601 Holland *Pliny* I. 190 The Cyrenians made fregates; the Phœnicians the bark, the Rhodians the Pinace and Brigantine. **1628** Hobbes *Thucyd.* (1822) 23 You had want of long barks against the Æginetæ. **1687** *Lond. Gaz.* No. 2228/1 Four Gallies, 4 Galiots, 2 Barques, and some other Vessels are fitting here. *Ibid.* No. 2248/1 The Bark that attends these Gallies is laden with Ammunition..and has likewise on board 30 Soldiers. **1722** *Ibid.* No. 6096/1 A French Snow or Bark..The said Snow had two Masts, and is of the Burthen of 50 or 60 Tons. **1769** Falconer *Dict. Marine* (1789), *Bark*..is peculiarly appropriated by seamen to those which carry three masts without a mizen top-sail. *Ibid.*, *Pinasse*, a square-sterned vessel, called in England a bark. **1771** *Phil. Trans.* LXI. 422 On board the *Endeavour* Bark, in a Voyage round the World. **1840** Marryat *Olla Podr.* (Rtldg.) 331 It was not the brig, but a bark. **1856** Kane *Arct. Exp.* II. xxix. 292 A steamer and a barque passed up.

4. *Comb.*, as † **bark-man**, a bargeman, a lighterman; **bark-rigged** *a.*, rigged like a barque.

1599 Hakluyt *Voy.* II. i. 227 When they are laden, the Barke-Men thrust the boate with her lading into the streame. **1858** *Merc. Mar. Mag.* V. 243 The Ava was.. barque-rigged.

bark (bɑːk), *sb.*[3] [f. bark *v.*[1]]

1. The sharp explosive cry uttered by dogs; the similar sound made by other animals, *e.g.* foxes and squirrels.

1562 J. Heywood *Prov. & Epigr.* (1867) 56 At euery dogs barke, seeme not to awake. **1796** Southey *Occas. Pieces* vii. Wks. II. 231 From many a day-dream has thy short quick bark Recall'd my wandering soul. **1875** Whitney *Life Lang.* i. 3 The dog's bark and howl signify..very different things.

2. **a.** *transf.* or *fig.*; *e.g.* the sound of cannon-firing; *colloq.* a cough.

1871 *Echo* 9 Jan. 5/1 The deep bark of our monster war-dogs. *Mod.* What a desperate bark you have! Try some jujubes.

b. contrasted with *bite*, esp. in phr. ***his bark is worse than his bite***: his angry words, threats, etc. are worse than the actual performance.

1663 *Lauderd. Papers* (1884) I. 131 It..is intended that that letter shall be a great bark if not a byt. **1816** Scott *Antiq.* II. vii. 186 'Monkbarns's bark,' said Miss Griselda Oldbuck..'is muckle waur than his bite.' **1842** De Quincey *Cicero* Wks. VI. 184 The bark of electioneering mobs is worse than their bite.

bark (bɑːk), *v.*[1] Forms: 1 **beorc-an**, 3 **beorken**, **borke-n**, **berke-n**, 3–5 **berke**, 4 (? **breke**), 5–7 **barke**, 6 **bercke**, 5– **bark.** *Pa. t.* 1? **bearc**, *pl.* **burcon**, 4–5 **burke**, **borke**; **berkyd**, 5– **barked.** *Pa. pple.* 1 **borcen**, 5– **barked.** [OE *beorcan*, str. vb., repr. an earlier *berc-an*, **berk-an*; cogn. w. OE. *borcian* 'to bark,' and ON. *berkja*, weak vb. 'to bark, to bluster.' Believed by some to be, in its origin, a variant of break, OE. *brecan*:—OTeut. **brek-an*; but if so, the differentiation must have taken place in prehistoric times. Cf. relation of L. *fragor* crackling noise, clamour, with *frag-*, *frang-ere* to break.]

1. *intr.* To utter a sharp explosive cry. (Orig. of dogs, hence of other animals, and *spec.* of foxes at rutting-time.) Const. *at* (*on*, *upon*, *against*, obs.).

c **885** K. Ælfred *Gregory's Past.* xv. 89 Dumbe hundas ne mágon beorcan. *c* **1000** Ælfric *Gram.* xxii. (Zup.) 129 Hund byrcþ. **1205** Lay. 21340 Beorkeð [**1250** borkeþ] his hundes. *c* **1330** *Kyng of Tars* 398 Ther stod hir bifore An hundred houndes blake, And borken on hire lasse and more. *c* **1350** *Will. Palerne* 47 He koured lowe, to bi-hold..whi his hound berkyd. *c* **1420** *Chron. Vilod.* 222 þe whelpus..Burke fast at þe kyng. **1596** Spenser *Astrophel* Ægl. 76 Wolues do howle and barke. **1610** Shaks. *Temp.* i. ii. 383 Harke, harke, bowgh wawgh: the watch-Dogges barke. **1611** Gwillim *Heraldry* iii. xiv. (1660) 166 You shall say a Fox Barketh. **1709** Steele *Tatler* No. 115 ⁋9 All the little Dogs in the Street..barked at him. **1877** Bryant *Among Trees* 76 And the brisk squirrel..barks with childish glee.

2. **a.** *fig.* To speak or cry out in a tone or temper that suggests the bark of a dog. ***to bark against*** (***or at***) ***the moon***: to clamour or agitate to no effect. ***to bark up the wrong tree*** (orig. U.S.): to make a mistake in one's object of pursuit or the means taken to attain it.

c **1230** *Ancr. R.* 122 Gif þu berkest aȝein þu ert hundes kunnes. **1387** Trevisa *Higden* (Rolls Ser.) VII. 443 þey.. dorste nouȝt berke [*v.r.* breke] for drede of oon man. **1549** *Compl. Scot.* xvi. 139 ȝe cry & berkis ilk ane contrar vthirs. *a* **1555** Latimer *Serm. & Rem.* (1845) 320 It is the scripture and not the translation, that ye bark against. **1655** Heywood *Fort. by Land* i. i. Wks. 1874 VI. 370 He hath such honourable friends to guard him, We should in that but bark against the moon. **1763** Churchill *Apol.* Poems I. 68

Though Mimics bark, and Envy split her cheek. **1832** J. Hall *Leg. West* 46 You are barking up the wrong tree, Johnson. **1855** Haliburton *Hum. Nat.* 124 in Bartlett *Dict. Amer.*, If you think to run a rig on me, you have made a mistake in the child, and barked up the wrong tree. **1887** *N. & Q.* 17 Sept. 221 Mr. Rye is barking up the wrong tree. **1899** [see lumber *v.*^{1} 1]. **1961** *Technology* Feb. 31/1 Her researches show the Government to be barking up the wrong tree.

b. To call out or 'spiel' at the entrance of a cheap shop or show to attract customers. (Cf. barker^1 2.) *U.S.*

1904 G. V. Hobart *Jim Hickey* v. 84 We could make sandwich money in front of a hootchy-kooch palace, barking at the Rubes. **1908** K. McGaffey *Sorrows of Show-Girl* 16 By gum, I'd take a job barking for a snake race. **1917** D. G. Phillips *Susan Lenox* I. xiii. 224 Pat, ready to take tickets, was 'barking' vigorously...addressing crowd. **1948** *Time* 19 July 90/2 [It] was another triumph for Liberty's brand of mass production plus carnival barking.

3. *mod. colloq.* **a.** To cough.

b. To emit an explosive sound, esp. of a fire-arm.

1853 F. W. Thomas *J. Randolph* 132 These boats bark so you can hardly hear yourself talk. **1907** S. E. White *Arizona Nights* III. xiii. 342 The Colt's forty-five barked once, and then again.

†**4.** *trans.* To bark at. *Obs. rare.*

c **1000** *Sax. Leechd.* I. 170 Gyf hwa þas wyrte mid him hafað..ne mæȝ he fram hundum beon borcen.

5. *trans.* or with *subord. cl.* (also ***bark out, forth***): To utter or give forth with a bark; to break out with, burst forth with.

c **1440** *Morte Arth.* 1351 He berkes myche boste. **1553–87** Foxe *A. & M.* 403 The abominable heresie..which impudently barketh that the ministers of the holy altars may and ought to use wives lawfully. **1586** T. B. *La Primaud. Fr. Acad.* (1594) 212 New imaginations and conceits..which they continually barke foorth. **1591** Spenser *Virg. Gnat* 346 Cerberus, whose many mouthes doo bay And barke out flames. **1644** Sir E. Dering *Prop. Sacr.* C iij, Others bark the Counter-tenour. **1821** Clare *Vill. Minstr.* II. 33 The dog bark'd a welcome. **1864** Tennyson *Enoch Arden &c.* 170 Bark an answer, Britain's raven! **1916** 'Boyd Cable' *Action Front* 131 Both the muzzles tilted a little and barked off another flight of shells. **1922** *N. & Q.* 12th Ser. XI. 206/2 A stable secret which has leaked out and is common property is referred to as 'the dogs are barking it'.

6. To drive *away* or *back* by barking.

1829 M. Mitford in *The Gem* 195 Frisk's own doggish exploit in barking away a set of pilferers. **1891** Meredith *One of our Conq.* II. iii. 42 The Dog..would have barked the breathing intruder an hundredfold back to earth.

bark (bɑːk), *v.*^{2} [f. bark *sb.*^{1}; cf. Sw. *barka*, Da. *berke*, to tan.]

1. *intr.* (with *over*) To form a bark.

c **1340** *Cursor M.* (Fairf.) 11824 And wiþ skratting he toke þe skurf, he barked ouer as a turfe.

2. *trans.* To treat with bark, steep in an infusion of bark; to tan.

1430 [See barked 2]. *c* **1440** *Promp. Parv.* 25 Barkyn lethyr, *frunio, tanno.* **1503–4** *Act 19 Hen. VII*, xix. Pream., Whedder the ledder be sufficiantly tanned and barked. **1565** *Wills & Inv. N.C.* (1835) 244 One hyde yt he had to barke for me. **1609** Skene *Reg. Maj.* 152 They buy leather & barks it. **1865** *Routledge's Mag. Boys* Nov. 687 A cellar..used for the purpose of barking the nets of the fishermen.

3. To strip off the bark from (a tree); to cut off a complete circle of bark from it, so as to kill it.

1545 *Act 37 Hen. VIII*, vi. §4 If any Person..unlawfully bark any Apple-trees. **1601** Holland *Pliny* I. 541 If trees be barked round about, they will die. **1796** C. Marshall *Garden.* (1813) 429 Mice..are apt to bark and to kill young trees. **1877** Browning *La Saisiaz* 373 Barked the bole, and broke the bough.

b. *fig.*

1603 Shaks. *Meas. for M.* III. i. 72 Would barke your honor from that trunke you beare, And leaue you naked.

c. *transf.* To scrape or rub off the skin (*esp.* from the shins and joints); to graze, abrade.

1850 B. Taylor *Eldorado* xvii. (1862) 171 Barking my hand on the rough bark of a branchless pine. **1880** Besant & Rice *Seamy Side* xxvii. 227 He had barked his elbows, broken his shins.

4. To enclose with or as with bark; to encrust.

1633 T. Adams *Exp. 2 Pet.* ii. 19 (1865) 544/2 Those anchorites that have barked up themselves in hollow trees. **1814** Cary *Dante* 90 From head to foot A tetter bark'd them round. **1840** De Quincey *Style* Wks. XI. 177 Some scaly leprosy..barking and hide-binding..the elastic flesh.

5. ***to bark*** (a squirrel, etc.): see quot.

[**1828** Audubon *Ornithol.* I. 294 A common way of killing squirrels is..to strike with the ball the bark of the tree immediately beneath the squirrel; the concussion produced by which kills the animal instantly without mutilating it.] **1865** Sala in *Daily Tel.* 29 May, Fellows that with their heavy barrels and small-bores can 'bark a squirrel.'

†**bark**, *v.*^{3} *Obs. rare.* [f. bark *sb.*^{2}; cf. OF. *barquer* to convey in a barge or bark.] To embark.

1592 Wyrley *Armorie* 36 Which valiant Earle Plantagenet namde At Hampton barkt, at Burdeux doth arive.

†**ˈbarkary.** *Obs.* Also **barcary.** [ad. med.L. *barcarium*, *bercarium*, *berquarium* (Spelman), *bercaria*, *berquaria* (Du Cange), for *berbicaria* sheepfold, f. *berbica* sheep = cl. L. *berbex*, *vervex* wether; hence cogn. with F. *bergerie*.] A 'sheep-cote,' a 'sheep-fold' (Spelman). (By some erron. referred to bark *sb.*^{1}, and said to be 'a tan-house.')

1594 Crompton *Jurisd.* 192 Houses or barcaryes. **1598** Manwood *Lawes Forest* §2 (1615) 75 Within the Regard of any Forest, no man may build any houses or barkaries. **1607** Cowell *Interpr.*, *Barkarie* is a heath house. 2. Some call it a Tanne-house. **1641** *Termes de la Ley* (1708) 74 Barcary signifies a farm-house as it seems.

barked (bɑːkt), *ppl. a.* [f. bark *v.*^{2} or *sb.*^{1}]

1. Covered with, or having, a bark; encrusted.

c **1505** Dunbar *Flyting* 202 Ane caprowsy barkit all with sweit. **1552** Huloet, Barked or rynded, *corticatus.* **1568** T. Howell *Arb. Amitie* (1879) 32 Flinted stones and barked tree. **1868** Geo. Eliot *F. Holt* 8 The thick-barked stems.

†**2.** Tanned. *Obs.*

c **1430** Lydg. *Min. Poems* 53 As barkid ledir his face is shynyng. **1569** *Wills & Inv. N.C.* (1835) 308 For a barked hide ijs. vjd. ? *a* **1800** in Aytoun *Ballads Scot.* (1858) II. 376 Auld she is..And tough like barked leather.

3. Stripped of its bark; *transf.* having the skin grazed or scraped off.

1611 Cotgr., *Pelard*, a round, and pilled, or barked sticke. **1854** *Gard. Chron.* 660 Leaving barked trees standing. **1884** *Harper's Mag.* Jan. 305/2 A 'barked' shin.

barken (ˈbɑːk(ə)n), *v. Sc.* [f. bark *sb.*^{1} + -en^2.]

1. *trans.* To dry up (any sticky daubing) into a hardened crust or bark; to cover or stiffen by this process.

1513–1827 [see barkened]. **1852** *Blackw. Mag.* LXXI. 739 Even at breakfast your trout are spoiled. They are barkened with oatmeal. **1861** Reade *Cloister & H.* xxiv. (D.) A shrewd frost that barkened the blood on my wounds.

2. *intr.* To dry and become a hardened crust.

1826 *Blackw. Mag.* XIX. 400 He will barken into bedimmed and shrivelled scaliness. **1829** Scott *Guy M.* xxiii, Let the blood barken upon the cut—that saves plaster.

ˈbarken, *a.* Chiefly *poet.* [f. bark *sb.*^{1} + -en^4.] Made or consisting of bark.

1755 T. Forbes in C. Gist *Jrnls.* (1893) 148 Easter Tuesday we embarked..in about 300 Batteaus or Canoes (not barken). **1835** R. M. Bird *Hawks of Hawk-h.* I. v. 61 Perhaps some tall and tawny hunter..may yet..urge his barken canoe over some cypress-fringed pool. **1864** G. M. Hopkins *Pilate* in *Note-Books* (1937) 15 Then knot a barken band To hold me quite fix'd in the selfsame plight. **1890** *Harper's Mag.* Aug. 365 A sword-lunge of assailant thunder Slashed down thy barken mail.

ˈbarkened, *ppl. a.* [f. barken *v.* + -ed.]

1. Dried into a hardened incrustation, encrusted with a sticky daubing which has dried on.

1513 Douglas *Æneis* II. vi. (v) 41 Witht barknit bluide, and puldir. **1827** Wilson *Noct. Ambr.* Wks. 1855 I. 305 Lyin a' barkened wi' blood in his coffin.

2. Tanned. Cf. barked 2.

1818 Scott *Hrt. Midl.* v, Effie used to help me to tumble the bundles o' barkened leather up and down.

barkentine, variant of barquentine.

barker (ˈbɑːkə(r)), *sb.*^{1} Also 4 **berkere,** 5 **-ar.** [f. bark *v.*^{1} + -er^1.]

1. One who or that which barks; a dog.

1393 Langl. *P. Pl.* C. x. 260 Thyne berkeres ben al blynde. *c* **1440** *Promp. Parv.* 32 Berkar, as a dogge, *latrator.* **1855** Singleton *Virgil* II. 276 Monster gods of every creed, Barker Anubis, too, 'gainst Neptune..ranged.

2. *fig.* A noisy assailant; an auction-room or shop tout; one who 'barks' at a cheap shop or show: see bark *v.*^{1} 2b. Chiefly *U.S.*

1483 Caxton *Gold. Leg.* 273/4 Whiche sometyme had ben a barker, bytter and blynde, ayenst the lettres. **1581** J. Bell *Haddon's Answ. Osor.* 81 b, Neither Jerome Osorius nor any other braulyng barker can..molest him. **1617** Collins *Def. Bp. Ely* Ep. Ded. 8 The aduersaries and barkers against Soueraignty. **1699** B. E. *Dict. Cant. Crew*, *Barker*, a Salesman's Servant that walks before the Shop, and cries, Cloaks, Coats, or Gowns, what d'ye lack, Sir. **1822** Hazlitt *Men & Mann.* Ser. II. xi. (1869) 232 As shopmen and barkers tease you to buy goods. **1859** Hotten *Slang Dict.*, *Barker*, a man employed to cry at the doors of gaffs, shows, and puffing shops, to entice people inside. **1862** Helps *Organiz. Daily Life* 123 A review which I delight in..because it always barks on the other side to the great barker. **1897** Howells *Landlord at Lion's Head* 247 The barker began to fill the night with hoarse cries of 'Miss Lynde's carriage; carriage for Miss Lynde!' **1903** *N.Y. Times* 28 Aug., Conditions were so dull that barkers had to be enlisted to call the public's attention to the boats. **1910** H. A. Franck *Vagabond Journ.* 276 The secretary was a man..with the voice of a side-show barker.

3. The Spotted Redshank (*Totanus fuscus*).

1802 G. Montagu *Ornith. Dict.* 21 [In Leicestershire.]

4. *slang.* A pistol; *occas.* a cannon.

1815 Scott *Guy M.* xxxiii, They are never without barkers and slashers. **1842** F. Cooper *Jack o' Lant.* I. 151 Four more carronades, with two barkers for'ard.

barker (ˈbɑːkə(r)), *sb.*^{2} Forms: 5 **barkere, barkar, bercar,** 5– **barker.** [f. bark *v.*^{2} + -er^1.]

†**1.** A tanner. *Obs.*

1402 *Test. Ebor.* (1836) I. 289 Lego uxori Ricardi Skyrtyn-bek, barkar, j. togam. *c* **1470** *King & Barker* 127 in Ritson's *Anc. P.P.* 65 Ther owr kyng and the barker partyd feyr a twyn. **1479** *Paston Lett.* 839 III. 253 An endenture of the bercars. **1503–4** *Act 19 Hen. VII*, xix, That no Tanner nor Barker put no maner of hyde nor Lether to sale. **1609** Skene *Reg. Maj.* 131 Of Barkers within Bvrgh.

2. One who strips off bark from trees.

1611 Cotgr., *Escorceur*, a barker of trees. **1829** E. Jesse *Jrnl. Natur.* 56 Our barkers go on rapidly with their work. *transf.* **1645** Milton *Colast.* Wks. (1847) 230/1 Infested..with bawling whippets and shin barkers.

Barker's mill. [Named from the inventor Dr. Barker, about the end of the 17th cent.] A mechanical contrivance for producing rotary motion, consisting of a hollow vertical revolving axis with two (or more) horizontal arms fitted into its lower end; water, admitted at the top of the central tube, fills that and the arms, and by its discharge through lateral apertures near the ends of the latter causes the whole machine to revolve in the direction opposite to that of the discharge, the moving power being the excess of hydrostatic pressure on the sides of the arms opposite to the openings, aided by centrifugal force.

barkey (ˈbɑːkɪ). Also **barkie, barky.** [f. bark *sb.*^{2} + -ey = -y^4.] *colloq.* A little bark.

1703 J. Campbell *Jrnl.* 27 Apr. in *Proc. Mass. Hist. Soc.* (1867) IX. 487 The Lark..In her Passage home meett 3 french Barkies. **1805** W. Hunter in *Naval Chron.* XIII. 36 Had we been acquainted with the real state of our Barkie's Bows. **1832** *Fraser's Mag.* IV. 464 Fears for the safety of his barky. **1847** Barham *Ingol. Leg.* (1877) 87 'Hookers,' barkeys and craft. **1867** in Smyth *Sailor's Word-bk.* **1930** *Sea Breezes* 73 This proved the old 'barkie's' undoing, as..she was..sunk off Picton by the Germans.

Barkhausen (ˈbɑːkaʊz(ə)n, -haʊz(ə)n). [The name of the German scientist H. *Barkhausen* (1881–1956).] **Barkhausen effect**: the name given to the series of sudden changes in the magnetization of a substance when the magnetizing force is gradually altered. **Barkhausen oscillation, oscillator** (see quots.).

1924 E. P. T. Tyndall in *Physical Rev.* XXIV. 439 Barkhausen effect for silicon steel... Barkhausen and Van der Pol consider the effect as due to the sudden re-orientation of groups or chains of molecular magnets. **1925** *Chem. Abstr.* XIX. 1659 Occurrence of Barkhausen oscillations in triodes. **1936** R. S. Glasgow *Radio Engin.* x. 310 (*caption*) Circuit for generating Barkhausen oscillations. **1940** *Chambers's Techn. Dict.* 76/2 *Barkhausen oscillator*, a generator of very high frequency oscillation (above 10^8 cps.), whose action depends on the transit time of the electrons from cathode to anode of a three-electrode valve. *Barkhausen-Kurz oscillations*, oscillations of very high frequency generated in a triode valve with a positive grid, the anode potential being approximately the same as the cathode. The oscillations are those of electrons passing to and fro through the grid. **1944** W. L. Emery *Radio Engin.* 284/1 (*Index*) Barkhausen-Kurz oscillator. **1957** *Encycl. Brit.* XIV. 646/1 *Barkhausen Effect.* In 1919 H. Barkhausen discovered the effect known by his name, and interpreted it as demonstrating that the magnetization of iron proceeds by steps and not in a continuous manner.

barking (ˈbɑːkɪŋ), *vbl. sb.*^{1} [f. bark *v.*^{1}]

1. The utterance of a dog's sharp explosive cry.

c **1300** *K. Alis.* 4966 From the brest to the grounde Men hy ben, abouen houndes. Berkyng of houndes hy habbe. **1684** Burnet tr. *More's Utop.* 122 What pleasure..in hearing the barking and howling of Dogs? **1795** Southey *Occas. Pieces* iii. Wks. II. 222 His barkings loud and quick.

b. *transf.* Harsh coughing.

1813 *Examiner* 1 Feb. 75/1 The play went on, amidst croaking, squeaking, barking.

2. *fig.* Angry or assailing outcry.

1549 Olde *Erasm. Par. 1st Tim.* iv. 11 Feare not any mens barkinges. **1857** Ruskin *Pol. Econ. Art* 35 To launch out into sudden barking at the first faults you see.

ˈbarking, *vbl. sb.*^{2} [f. bark *v.*^{2} + -ing^1.]

1. Steeping in an infusion of bark; tanning.

c **1440** *Promp. Parv.* 25 Barkynge of lethyr, *frunicio.* **1865** *Intell. Observ.* No. 38. 107 [The] Barking the nets of the fishermen.

2. The action of stripping off bark from trees; the cutting away of a ring of bark, so as to kill the tree, otherwise called ***ring-barking***. ***barking-irons***: tools used for this purpose.

1545 *Act 37 Hen. VIII*, vi. §1 Barking of Apple-trees. **1773** Barnard in *Phil. Trans.* LXIII. 218 Directing the falling and barking of a large quantity of timber. **1845** S. Judd *Margaret* I. iii. 12 Here were a draw-shave, a cross-cut saw..barking irons, a scythe. **1878** P. Bayne *Purit. Rev.* iii. 71 In order to blight and kill a whole forest..it is not necessary to fell every tree, but only..to perform the operation of barking. **1884** *Australasian* 8 Nov. 875/1 In ring-barking a belt of bark about a foot in width is taken off the tree.

ˈbarking, *ppl. a.*^{1} [f. bark *v.*^{1} + -ing^2.]

1. Uttering barks; 'giving tongue,' yelping.

1552 Huloet s.v. *Addition*, A barking dogge. **1842** Tennyson *Day Dream* 136 Barking dogs and crowing cocks.

2. a. *transf.* Uttering harsh, rough, or angry sounds, like a dog's barking; harsh-sounding.

1589 Puttenham *Eng. Poesie* (1869) 258 The rude and barking language of the Affricans. *c* **1800** Kirke White *Christm.-Day* 36 He had words To soothe the barking waves.

b. barking-bird, the *Pteroptochus Tarnu*, of Chiloe, so named from its voice; **barking deer,** the Indian muntjac, *Cervulus muntjac*, found in India, Burma, and Tibet; so named from its call;

barking iron (*slang*), a pistol; **barking spider** (see quot. 1952); **barking wolf** *U.S.* = COYOTE.
1845 DARWIN *Voy. Nat.* xiii. (1873) 288 An allied species is called by the natives 'Guidguid,' and by the English the barking-bird. **1880** *Encycl. Brit.* XII. 742/2 The barking deer or muntjac (*Cervulus vaginalis*). **1898** *Geogr. Jrnl.* XI. 502 The small barking deer, called 'pause' by the natives. **1939** A. KEITH *Land below Wind* xiv. 259 There is no meat as sweet as barking deer. **1785** GROSE *Dict. Vulgar T.*, *Barking Irons*, pistols, from their explosion resembling the bow-wow or barking of a dog. (*Irish*). **1825** PAULDING *John Bull in Amer.* 56 Seeing the barking iron [he] shrunk back. **1847** LE FANU *T. O'Brien* 63 Put up your barking-iron, and no more noise. **1934** *Bulletin* (Sydney) 24 Jan. 21/4 The barking spider of Central Australia and other stridulating species can probably hear quite well. **1952** A. G. MITCHELL in *Chambers's Shorter Eng. Dict.* Suppl. 790/1 *Barking spider*, a large reddish-brown spider of Central Australia, said to produce a barking or whistling sound. **1826** J. D. GODMAN *Amer. Nat. Hist.* I. 260 The Prairie or Barking Wolf..frequents the prairies..of the west. **1867** *Amer. Naturalist* I. 289 The Prairie or Barking Wolf (*Canis latrans*, Say), is by far the most abundant carnivorous animal in Arizona, as it is also in almost every part of the West.

3. *fig.* Raising clamorous outcry, noisily aggressive.
1599 MARSTON *Sco. Villanie* II. vii. 205, I stop thy currish barking chops. **1641** MILTON *Ch. Discip.* II. Wks. (1851) 40 His barking curses, and Excommunications. **1845** FORD *Handbk. Spain* i. 21 Bread and salt can appease the wayfarer's barking stomach.

ˈbarking, *ppl. a.*[2] [f. BARK *v.*[2] + -ING[2].] That 'barks'; following the trade of a tanner.
c **1600** *Rob. Hood* (Ritson) xxxv. 39 Barking tanner's sons.

ˈbarkingly, *adv.* [f. BARKING *ppl. a.*[1] + -LY[2].] In a barking manner.
1606 SYLVESTER *Imposture* 248 From the Pulpit barkingly he rings Bold blasphemies against the King of Kings. **1624** HEYWOOD *Gunaik.* 361 A woman barkingly clamorous.

barkle (ˈbɑːk(ə)l), *v. dial.* [f. BARK *v.*[2] (see sense 4) + -LE 3.] To cake, encrust (with dirt, etc.). So **ˈbarkled** *ppl. a.*
1819, etc. in *Eng. Dial. Dict.* **1913** D. H. LAWRENCE *Sons & Lovers* ii. 34 'Aven't you got a drink, Missis, for a man when he comes home barkled up from the pit? *Ibid.* xii. 311 Their barkled shoes hung heavy on their steps.

barkless (ˈbɑːklɪs), *a.*[1] [f. BARK *sb.*[1] + -LESS.] Devoid or stripped of bark.
1604 DRAYTON *Moses* (R.) The trees all barkless nakedly are left. **1817** BYRON *Manfred* I. ii. 67 Blasted pines.. barkless, branchless.

barkless (ˈbɑːklɪs), *a.*[2] [f. BARK *sb.*[3] + -LESS.] Having no bark: applied to a dog which rarely or never barks.
1938 *Tail-Wagger* May 172/1 About four years ago the Basenji or Congo Dog was introduced into England... The breed is barkless, being mute. **1950** A. C. SMITH *About our Dogs* xxiii. 353 The interest aroused by the 'Barkless Dogs' revealed the fact that one was exhibited at Crufts in 1895. **1957** B. VESEY-FITZGERALD *Domestic Dog* ix. 181 *The Basenji*. First introduced..in 1934, and widely known as the 'barkless dog'.

barkometer (bɑːˈkɒmɪtə(r)). [f. BARK *sb.*[1] + -OMETER.] A tanner's hydrometer for testing the strength of bark infusions.
1821 J. SWAN (*title*) Explanation of improved mode of Tanning;..intended to accompany the New Invented Barktrometer [*sic*]. *Ibid.* 40 Though you show us, by the assistance of your new Barktrometer that there is a something derived from the bark of which it shows the quantity. **1852** MORFIT *Tanning & Currying* (1853) 329 A barkometer..is specially adapted to testing the strength of bark lyes. **1882** [see *tan-liquor* s.v. TAN *sb.*[1] C. 1].

barkum, dial. form of BARGHAM, horse-collar.

barky (ˈbɑːkɪ), *a.* [f. BARK *sb.*[1] + -Y[1].]
1. Covered with bark.
1590 SHAKS. *Mids. N.* IV. i. 48 The female Iuy so Enrings the barky fingers of the Elme. **1656** DU GARD *Gate Lat. Unl.* §83 A stringgie root, a barkie stock. **1870** BRYANT *Homer* II. XVI. 153 Woods of beech and ash and barky cornel.
fig. **1604** BRETON *Pass. Sheph.* (1876) 6 Trees their barky silence breake, Cracke yet though they can not speake.
2. Of the nature of bark.
1835 BROWNING *Parac.* IV. 141 The barky scurf of leprosy.

barlady: see BYRLADY: By our Lady!

†**barla-ˈfumble.** *Sc. Obs.* Also -fummil. [cf. BARLEY *interj. phr.*; the second element is doubtful.] A call for a truce by one who has fallen in wrestling or play; improperly for: Fall, tumble.
a **1550** *Christis Kirk Gr.* xvi, Quhile he cryed barlafummil, I am slane. **1657** COLVIL *Whigs Supplic.* (1751) 110 When coach-men drinks and horses stumble, It's hard to miss a barla-fumble.

barley (ˈbɑːlɪ). Forms: 1–2 bærlíc, 3 barlic, barrliȝ, 4 barlykke, barlich(e, barli, 4–8 barly, 5 berley, berlik, 6–7 barlie, -lye, 8 *Sc.* barlic(k, 4– barley. [OE. *bærlíc*, of doubtful composition: *bær-* seems to point to OTeut. **baroz-*, **bariz-*, 'barley,' the latter of which gave OE. *bere* (see BEAR *sb.*[2]) with *ę* as proper umlaut of *a*; the suffix is evidently *-líc* (see -LY[1]), as if *bærlíc* meant at first, not *hordeum*, but *hordeāceus*.

Bærlíc first appears *attrib.* or as *adj.* in the name *Bærlícecroft*; cf. also BARLEY-CORN. The notion that *líc* is the word *léac* 'leek,' as in OE. *gárléac*, ME. *garleek*, *garleke*, now *garlic*, is phonetically out of the question. In *bær-*, can the vowel *æ* (for earlier *a*), instead of *ę*, be due to early syncopation, *bærr-*:—*barr-*, *barz-*, from *baroz-*, *bariz-*? Cf. ON. *barr*, North Fris. *bar*, *bær*. (But ON. *barlak*, in an Orcadian document, is prob. adopted from OE.) The *Rushw. Gloss.* has also *bæreflór* for *bereflór*, and late charters *bærtún* for *beretún*.

966 *Cod. Dipl.* VI. 79 Bærlíce croft. *c* **1200** ORMIN 15511 He fedde fif þusennde menn Wiþþ fife *barrliȝ lafess. (Cf. other attrib. instances under B.)]

A. 1. A hardy awned cereal (genus *Hordeum*), cultivated in all parts of the world; used partly as food, and largely (in Britain and the United States, mainly) in the preparation of malt liquors and spirits. **a.** The plant.
1303 R. BRUNNE *Handl. Synne* 10111 Whete corne wyl nat prykke, As otes dowun, or barlykke. **1382** WYCLIF *Ex.* ix. 31 The flax thanne and barlich [**1388** barli] was hurt. **1398** TREVISA *Barth. De P.R.* XVII. cxv, Boþe barley and bere is calde Ordeum. **1483** *Cath. Angl.* 22 Barly, *ordeum*. **1523** FITZHERB. *Husb.* §28 Barley and otes be moste commonly mowen. **1610** SHAKS. *Temp.* IV. i. 61 Thy rich Leas Of Wheate, Rye, Barley. **1795** *Scots Mag.* LVII. 544/1 The barleys are universally a great crop. **1872** OLIVER *Elem. Bot.* II. 279 Barley is considered to have been the first Cereal brought under cultivation.

b. The grain. *French*, *pearl*, *pot barley*; see quot.
1124 *O.E. Chron.*, Man sælde..þæt bærlic þæt is þre sed læpas to six scillingas. *c* **1220** *Bestiary* 291 in *O.E. Misc.* 10 Ðe mire suneð ðe barlic, ðanne ȝe fint te wete. **1362** LANGL. *P. Pl.* A. v. 133, I bouhte hire Barly [*v.r.* barliche]; heo breuh hit to sulle. *c* **1440** *Partonope* 3760 Brede made of berley or ellis of ote. **1523** FITZHERB. *Husb.* §13 That is the worste barley, and foure London bushels are suffycient for an acre. **1769** SIR J. HILL *Fam. Herb.* (1789) 72 French barley is skinned, and has the ends ground off; the pearl barley is reduced by a longer grinding to a little round white lump. **1857** ELIZA ACTON *Eng. Bread-Bk.* 73 Pot barley is barley of which the outer husk has been removed by millstones; it is used for making broth.

2. *transf.*
1884 F. BRITTEN *Watch & Clockm.* 29 Barleys..[are] the little projections formed by the operation of engine-turning.

B. *Comb.* and *Attrib.* (In 14–17th c. commonly *barli-*, *barly-*.)
1. General relations: **a.** objective with vbl. or agent-noun, as ***barley-buyer***, ***-sower***, ***-sowing***; **b.** instrumental with passive pple., as ***barley-fed*** (1851); **c.** simple attrib. as, (of the plant) ***barley-crop***, ***-earth***, ***-eddish***, ***-field***, ***-ground*** (1523), ***-harvest***, ***-mill***, ***-rick***, ***-seed***, ***-straw***, ***-stubble***; (of the grain) ***barley-bran***, ***-chaff***, ***-flour***, ***-groats***, ***-meal*** (1388); **d.** attrib. of material (= made of or with), as ***barley-beer***, ***-bread***, ***-broth***, ***-bun***, ***-cake***, ***-crust***, ***-gruel***, ***-loaf*** (1200), ***-pudding***, ***-scon***, ***-soup***.
1901 KIPLING *Kim* xiv. 367 A drink of *chang*—the *barley-beer that comes from Ladakh-way. **1906** *Daily Chron.* 16 Mar. 7/7 Not less than 85 per cent. of the total saccharine yielding materials shall be barley malt. This beer is to be known as 'barley beer'. **1599** HAKLUYT *Voy.* II. II. 80 *Barley-branne the Ilanders doe vse in stead of salt. *c* **1320** *Seuyn Sag.* 1573 *Barli-bred he et for gode. **1840** CARLYLE *Heroes* ii. 111 His [Mahomet's]..common diet was barley-bread and water. **1723** J. NOTT *Cook's & Confectioner's Dict.* BA 26, **Barley Broth.* Boil a Pound of French Barley in three Quarts of Water, with some whole Spice..put in Raisins..Butter, Rose-water, and Sugar, and so eat it. *c* **1806** D. WORDSWORTH *Tour Scotland* in *Jrnls.* (1941) I. 281 A fowl stewing in barley-broth. **1552** HULOET, *Barley bunne gentleman..suche ryche niggardes as lyue wyth barley breade, or otherwise hardlye. **1393** GOWER *Conf.* III. 216 Me thought I sigh a *barly-cake. **1846** GROTE *Greece* II. i. II. 297 His diet of sweet chestnuts, barley-cakes and pork. **1865** *Derby Merc.* 25 Jan., The straw of a *barley crop. **1669** WORLIDGE *Syst. Agric.* (1681) 247 Places for this sport, especially on the *Barley-edishes. **1851** KINGSLEY *Yeast* xi. 202 Your *barley-fed hares. **1863** MISS WHATELY *Ragged Life Egypt* xix. 187 *Barley-fields irrigated by a sacchia. **1620** VENNER *Via Recta* i. 18 If..*Barley flower and Rie flower..be added. **1523** FITZHERB. *Husb.* §10 Thou shalt sowe..thy beanes vpon the *barley grounde. **1769** MRS. RAFFALD *Eng. Housekpr.* (1778) 315 To make *Barley Gruel. **1611** BIBLE *Ruth* i. 22 The beginning of *barley haruest. **1930** T. S. ELIOT tr. *St.-J. Perse's Anabasis* 27 Man goes out at barley harvest. **1535** COVERDALE *Judg.* vii. 13 A baken *barlye lofe came rollinge downe. **1488** *Act. Audit.* 147 (JAM.) Fifty quarters of *berlik-malt. **1620** VENNER *Via Recta* ii. 39 Beere..made of Barly malt alone. **1382** WYCLIF *Num.* v. 15 A mesure..of *barli meele. **1599** HAKLUYT *Voy.* II. II. 4 Their bread was made of barley meale and goates milke. **1832** *Scoreby Farm Rep.* in *Brit. Husb.* (1840) III. 19 They have for the first fortnight boiled potatoes only, then a little barley-meal is added. **1797** JOHNSTON tr. *Beckmann's Inventions* I. 266 Mills by which grain is only freed from the husk and rounded, are called *barley-mills... The first kind of barley-mills is a German invention. **1840** J. C. LOUDON *Cottager's Manual Husb.* i. 9 The husking can only be well done at a barley-mill. **1820** SCOTT *Monast.* viii, The *barley-scones, which..were so good. **1831** *Sutherland Farm Rep.* in *Brit. Husb.* (1840) III. 72 The gates are again shut, until the completion of the *barley-seed. **1747** MRS. H. GLASSE *Art of Cookery* ix. 78 (*heading*) A *Barley Soup. **1935** BROWNE & WILLIAMS *World's Best Recipes* 22 (*heading*) Barley Soup. **1678** RAY *Prov.* 51 *Barly-straw's good fodder when the cow gives water. **1794** *Trans. Soc. Promotion Agric.* (U.S.) I. 145 Barley-straw is hearty fodder for horned cattle in the winter. **1837** *Flemish Husb.* in *Brit. Husb.* (1840) 59 This is their food during the whole winter with a little wheat or barley-straw. **1922** JOYCE *Ulysses* 263 We'll put a barleystraw in that Judas Iscariot's ear this time. **1733** TULL *Horse-Hoing Husb.* xi. 50 It has brought as good a Crop of Wheat on *Barley Stubble. **1913** MASEFIELD *Daffodil Fields* 67 Westward was barley-stubble not yet cleared.

2. Special combinations: **barley-bigg**, bigg or bear, a coarse variety of barley; **barley-bird**, name given locally to various birds appearing about the time of barley-sowing, as the wryneck, siskin, greenfinch, and sometimes the nightingale; **barley-bree**, **-broth**, strong ale; **barley-candy** (= *barley-sugar*); **barley-cracker**, a machine or appliance for cracking barley; †**barley-cream** (= *barley-milk*); **barley-grass**, meadow barley; †**barley-hat** (cf. BARLEY-CAP, -HOOD); **barley-hummeller**, a machine for separating barley from the awns; †**barley-island**, an ale-house; **barley-itch** (see quots.); †**barly-lepe**, a leap or basket for holding barley; †**barley-man**, one who received an allowance in barley, *hordearius*; **barley-milk**, a decoction or gruel of barley or barley-meal; **barley-mood** = BARLEY-HOOD; **barley-mow**, a stack of barley; †**barley-sele** (*obs.* or *dial.*), the season for sowing barley; †**barley-sick**, *a.*, intoxicated; **barley-straw**, (*fig.*) a trifle; **barley-sugar**, a confection, usually in twisted sticks, made from sugar, formerly by boiling in a decoction of barley; also *attrib.*, as ***barley-sugar drop***, ***stick***; *spec.* used to designate features of architecture, furniture, etc., which in shape resemble a twisted barley-sugar stick; **barley-wine**, a Greek wine or beer prepared from barley; also, a strong English ale. Also BARLEY-CAP, -CORN, -HOOD, -WATER, q.v.
1552 HULOET, *Barley bygge. *Vide* beerecorne. **1625** MARKHAM *Farew. Husb.* 135 Barley-big, or beare Barley. **1768** PENNANT *Zool.* II. 310 In Sussex it [the Siskin] is called the *barly-bird. **1863** *Yng. England* Aug. 127 In the Isle of Wight the bird commonly called the barley-bird is the wryneck. **1786** BURNS *Scotch Drink* xiii, How easy can the *barley-bree Cement the quarrel! **1593** *Bacchus Bountie* in *Harl. Misc.* (1809) II. 273 The *barley-broath aboue all other, did beare away the bell, and..neither grape nor berry might be compared to the maiestie of the mault. **1884** BLACK *Jud. Shaks.* xxxi, A cupful of barley-broth will do thee no harm. **1883** *Harper's Mag.*, Jan. 277/1 *Barley-candy statuettes. **1813** VANCOUVER *Agric. Devon* 131 The motion is communicated by a belt to the *barley-cracker. **1694** WESTMACOTT *Script. Herb.* 17 Ptisan was a meat of the Antients which we now call *Barly-Cream. **1795** W. WINTERBOTHAM *Hist. View U.S.* III. 401 Those which are found most common are..*Barley grass, *Hordeum pratense*. **1891** R. WALLACE *Rural Econ. Austral. & N.Z.* xxii. 294 Barley grass..Throughout Colonies, except Tasmania. *c* **1500** *Blowbols Test.* in Hazl. *E.P.P.* I. 105 They that be manly in dronkenesse for to fyte, Whan one ther hede is sett a *barly-hate. **1851** *Househ. Wds.* III. 358 The chaff-cutter, the *barley-hummeller. *a* **1640** DAY *Peregr. Schol.* (1881) 72 Goeing to take in fresh water at the *Barlie Iland. **1928** *Daily Express* 28 Nov. 4 It [*sc.* baker's itch] is similar to the affection from which millers suffer under the name of *barley itch', due to a small parasite which preys on the larvae of small moths which infest the grain. **1961** *Brit. Med. Dict.* 772 *Barley itch*, 1. Grain itch..2. A sensitivity to the plant *Mucuna pruriens*, which grows among the barley, and sheds irritant hairs. *c* **1440** *Promp. Parv.* 25 *Barly lepe, to kepe yn corne, *cumera*. **1601** HOLLAND *Pliny* I. 561 Sword-fencers, who vpon their allowance or pension giuen them in barly, were called Hordearij, (*i.* *Barley-men). **1607** TOPSELL *Four-f. Beasts* 303 *Barly milk, or juyce called of the old Writers..Cremor Ptisanæ. **1846** 'A LADY' *Jewish Manual* 178 *Barley Milk.* Boil..pearl barley..in new milk ..sweeten. **1790** MORRISON *Poems* 151 (JAM.) Hame the husband comes just roarin' fu'; Nor can she please him in his *barlic mood. **1714** GAY *Sheph. Week* Pastoral v. 75 Whenever by yon *Barley Mow I pass. *c* **1440** *Promp. Parv.* 25 *Barly-sele, *tempus ordeacium*. *a* **1721** PRIOR *Turtle & Sp.* (R.) She..could plead the law, And quarrel for a *barley-straw. **1830** LINDLEY *Nat. Syst. Bot.* 303 Barley-straw melts into a glass of a topaz yellow colour. **1712** tr. *Pomet's Hist. Drugs* I. 55 *Barley-Sugar is made either of white Sugar or brown. **1819** KEATS *Let.* 12 Apr. (1958) II. 52 As fine as barley sugar drops are to a schoolboy's tongue. **1859** L. WRAXALL tr. *Robert-Houdin's Mem.* II. xii. 257 The confectioner had exchanged the barley-sugar stick for the magician's wand. **1883** *Knowledge* 6 July 3/2 'Barley-sugar' ..was prepared by boiling down ordinary sugar in a decoction of pearl barley. **1936** W. DE LA MARE *Wind Blows Over* 239 The barley-sugar-legged walnut prie-dieu at her bedside. **1937** *Archit. Rev.* LXXXII. 63/2 The altars and chapels are there in both cases, but in Lecce the 'barley sugar' columns are of stone. **1939** G. GREENE *Lawless Roads* x. 233 Barley-sugar pillars up the façade. **1728** E. SMITH *Compleat Housewife* (ed. 2) 208 To make *Barley-Wine. Take..Barley..boil it..mix it with..White Wine..Borage water..Cluny-water..Lemons..Sugar..bottle it up. **1820** F. ACCUM *Art of Brewing* 1 The ancient Greek writers gave the name of barley wine to malt liquors. **1852** GROTE *Greece* II. lxx. IX. 144 A sort of barley-wine or beer in tubs, with the grains of barley on the surface. **1940** *Chambers's Techn. Dict.* 21/1 Burton and barley-wine are strong ales. **1953** *Word for Word* (Whitbread & Co.) 11/2 *Barley broth*, a form of strong ale (also barley wine..).

ˈbarley, *int. Sc.* and *north. dial.* [perh. a corruption of F. *parlez*, Eng. *parley*.] Parley, truce, quarter; 'a term used in the games of children, when a truce is demanded' (Jamieson).
1814 SCOTT *Wav.* xlii, A proper lad o' his quarters, that will not cry barley in a brulzie.

barley-break (ˈbɑːlɪbreɪk). Forms: 6 barle-breyke, barla-breik, 7 barly-breake, -brake, barley-, barlibreake, 7-8 barlibreak, barley-brake, -break, 9 *Sc.* barley-brack. [Of uncertain etymology; the first part has been explained from the prec. word, also from the grain *barley*, because played in a corn-field, or in a stack-yard (Jam.); the second from *break* as explained below.] An old country game, varying in different parts, but somewhat resembling *Prisoner's Bars*, originally played by six persons (three of each sex) in couples; one couple, being left in a middle den termed 'hell,' had to catch the others, who were allowed to separate or 'break' when hard pressed, and thus to change partners, but had when caught to take their turn as catchers. (See poetical description by Sidney in *Arcadia* I. *Lamon's song*, and Suckling in *Poems* (1646) 24.) In Scotland, according to Jamieson, one person had to catch the rest of the company, each of these as taken assisting their captor.

1557 MACHYN *Diary* (1848) 132 Master parsun..entryd into helle, and ther ded at the barle breyke with alle the wyffe of the sam parryche. *a* **1581** A. SCOTT *On May*, Sum rynnis at barla breikis lyk rammis. **1608** ARMIN *Nest Ninn.* (1842) 56 Like a girle at barley brake, leauing the last couple in hell, away she gads, and neuer lookes behinde her. **1794** SOUTHEY *Wat Tyler* I. Wks. II. 24 Since we were boys together And play'd at barley-brake. **1837** NICOLL *Poems* (1843) 81 At barley-bracks, we laughin' chased ilk kimmer we could see.

†'barley-,cap. *Obs.* [f. BARLEY, as source of malt liquor: cf. BARLEY-HOOD.] In phr. ***to have on*** or ***wear a barley-cap***: to be tipsy; hence ***barley-cap*** = tippler.

1598 E. GILPIN *Skial.* (1878) 67 Some weeuil, maultworme, barly-cap. **1611** COTGR., *Forbeu*..pot-shotten, whose fudling or barley Cap is on. **1679** O. HEYWOOD in *Yorksh. Diaries* (Surt.) II. 262 He never wore a cap, unlesse it was a barley-cap.

barley-corn ('bɑːlɪ,kɔːn). [See CORN.]

1. a. = BARLEY (the plant or grain).

1382 WYCLIF *2 Sam.* xiv. 30 The feelde of Ioab biside my feelde hauynge barli corn [**1388** ripe barli]. *c* **1440** *Promp. Parv.* 25/1 Barly corne, *ordeum.* **1836** THIRLWALL *Greece* II. xiv. 196 The juice of the vine or the barleycorn.

b. Personified as ***John Barleycorn***: esp. as the grain from which malt liquor is made.

c **1620** (*title*) in Pepysian Library, A pleasant new ballad.. of the bloody murther of Sir John Barleycorn. **17..** *John Barleycorn* in Percy's *Reliques*, John Barleycorn has got a beard Like any other man. **1786** BURNS *Scotch Drink* iii, John Barleycorn, Thou king o' grain.

2. A grain of barley.

1588 GREENE *Perimedes* 15 Preferre not a Barly-corne before a precious Iewell. **1612** WOODALL *Surg. Mate* Wks. (1653) 25 A full barley corne will well serve, or a good wheat corne. **1824** MISS MITFORD *Village* Ser. I. (1863) 83 A bantam-cock..turning so scornfully from the barley-corns which Annie is flinging towards him.

3. The length of a grain of barley taken as a measure, $\frac{1}{3}$ of an inch; formerly also $\frac{1}{4}$ of an inch.

1607 RECORDE *Gr. Arts* 326 It is ordained that 3 Barly Cornes dry and round, shall make vp the measure of an inch. **1611** COTGR., *Grain*..a Barlie-corne, or the fourth part of an ynch. **1688** HOLME *Armory* III. iii. 136 Barly Corn, is the length of 4 Poppy seeds, and 3 Corns make an Inch. **1729** SHELVOCKE *Artillery* I. 76 The Barley-corn (the fourth part of an Inch) is subdivided into 5 Poppy Seeds. **1873** MISS BROUGHTON *Nancy* I. 21 If father..move his head one barley-corn, we are all dead men.

4. *Building.* 'A little cavity between the mouldings of joiners' work..made with a kind of plane of the same name.' Chambers *Cycl. Supp.* 1753.

5. A gun-sight shaped like an inverted V.

1896 W. W. GREENER *Gun & its Devel.* (ed. 6) xxxi. 736 Military Match Rifles..The fore-sight must be the simple reversed V, or barley-corn military pattern. **1901** *Kynoch Jrnl.* Apr.–May 76/2 In our opinion the best sights for target purposes are the barleycorn foresight and tangent backsight. **1904** *Daily Chron.* 10 Dec. 7/6 The Small Arms Committee ..were of opinion that the barley-corn should be adhered to pending further trials with the other patterns of foresight.

'barley-,hood. [f. BARLEY (used for 'malt liquor') + -HOOD, suffix of condition; perh. with some reference to *hood* 'covering for the head': cf. *barley-hat* in BARLEY B 2.] A fit of drunkenness, or of ill humour or temper, brought on by drinking.

a **1529** SKELTON *El. Rummyng* 372 And as she was drynkynge, She fyll in a wrynkynge Wyth a barlyhood. **1725** A. RAMSAY *Gent. Sheph.* I. ii, In his barlickhoods, ne'er stick To lend his loving wife a loundering lick. **1805** A. SCOTT *Poems* 51 (JAM.) Whan e'er they take their barley-hoods, And heat of fancy fires their bludes.

'barley-,water. [f. BARLEY.] A drink, made by the decoction of pearl barley, used as a demulcent. † ***strong barley-water***: ale.

c **1320** *Seuyn Sag.* 1574 Barli-water, that was . i-sode. **1580** HOLLYBAND *Treas. Fr. Tong, Orgemonde*, Barlye water, *Tysante.* **1625** HART *Anat. Ur.* I. v. 46 The women..are not so busie..with the strong barley water as our British women. **1684** OTWAY *Atheist* Prol., And Barley-water Whey-fac'd Beau's write Satyrs. **1875** H. WOOD *Therap.* (1879) 581 Barley-water is used as a nutritious, demulcent drink in fevers.

†barling ('bɑːlɪŋ). *Obs.* [a. Sw. *bärling* pole, f. *bära* to bear.] A pole.

1611 *Rates* 2 (JAM.) Barlings, or fire-poles the hundreth —*xxl.* **1732** DE FOE, etc. *Tour Gt. Brit.* (1769) I. 64 Fir-Timber, Oaken Planks, Baulks, Barlings, Spars, Oars.

barlow knife. *U.S.* [From the name of the maker.] A large single-bladed pocket-knife.

1779 in *Documents Revol. Hist. New Jersey* (1906) III. 676 Barlow penknives. **1819** *Massachusetts Spy* 29 Dec. 3/2 A barlow knife, bloody, and another knife, rusty, lay along side of him. **1876** 'MARK TWAIN' *Tom Sawyer* iv. 30 Mary gave him a brand-new 'Barlow' knife. **1896** J. C. HARRIS *Sister Jane* 229 There on the side of the pew were the letters W. W. which many years ago I had carved with my barlow knife. *ellipt.* **1890** *Congress. Rec.* Aug. 8818/2 He did not want to carry a cheap and nasty knife, but the little fellow has to carry a ten cent Barlow.

†barm, *sb.*[1] *Obs.* exc. in *comb.* Forms: 1-2 **bearm**, 3 **bærm, berm**, 4-5 **barme**, 1- **barm.** [Common Teut.; with OE. *barm* (WSax. *bearm*) cf. OS., OFris., OHG., Sw., Da. *barm*, ON. *barmr*, Goth. *barms*:—OTeut. **barmo-z*, f. *ber-an* to bear. The early southern ME. *berm* represented the Saxon *bearm*; *barm* was the Anglian form.]

1. A bosom, a lap.

c **950** *Lindisf. Gosp.* Luke vi. 38 Hia sellað on barm iuer. *c* **1000** *Ags. Gosp.* ibid., Hiȝ syllað on eowerne bearm. *c* **1160** *Hatton Gosp.* John i. 18 On hys fader bearme. **1205** LAY. 30261 He nom his lauerdes hefd..in his bærm he hit læide. *c* **1230** *Ancr. R.* 212 þe slowe lið and slepeð iðe deofles berme, ase his deore deorling. *a* **1325** *Lay le Freine* 201 Sche yaf it souke opon hir barm. *c* **1410** LOVE *Bonavent. Mirr.* vi. (Gibbs MS.) Swetly klyppynge and kyssynge leyde hym in hier barme [**1510** (Pynson) barme; **1530** (W. de W.) lappe.] *c* **1460** *Towneley Myst.* 59 Hald thy hand soyn in thy barme, And as a lepre it shal be lyke. **1513** DOUGLAS *Æneis* XII. Prol. 76 Zephyrus comfortabill inspiratioun For till ressaue law in hyr barm adoun.

2. Edge, brim, 'breast,' 'brow.' *rare.* (So in ON.)

c **1340** *Alexander* (Stev.) 4811 þan come þai blesnand till a barme · of a brent lawe.

3. *Comb.* **barm-cloth, †barm-hatre** (*obs.*), an apron; **barm-fel, barm-skin** (*dial.*), a leather apron. Cf. BARVEL.

c **1000** ÆLFRIC *Gloss.* in Wright *Voc.* (W.) /127 *Mappula*, bearmclað. *c* **1300** *Men Lif* xv. in *E.E.P.* (1862) 155 Fair beþ ȝur barmhatres. *c* **1350** *Sat. Blacksmiths* in *Rel. Ant.* I. 240 Of a bole hyde ben here barmfellys. *c* **1386** CHAUCER *Milleres T.* 50 A barm-cloth eek as whit as morne mylk. *c* **1440** *Promp. Parv.* 25/1 Barnyskyn (**1499** barme skyn), *melotes.* **1594** NASHE *Unfort. Trav.* 16 An Elephantes eares that hanges on his shoulders like a countrie huswiues banskin [*sic*]. **1775** J. COLLIER *Tim Bobbin* 20 Hal..had his knockus lapt in his Barm-skin. **1857** WRIGHT *Provinc. Dict.* s.v., Her smock's as dirty and greasy as a barmskin. **1870** MORRIS *Earthly Par.* II. iii. 80 His mother o'er her barm-cloth wide Gazed forward.

barm (bɑːm), *sb.*[2] Forms: 1 **beorma**, 3 **beorme, berrme**, 4-5 **berm(e**, 5-7 **barme**, (7 **birme**), 7- **barm.** [OE. *beorma*; prob. common Teut. (:—**bermon-*), though early cognates are wanting; cf. Da. *bärme*, Sw. *barma*, Fris. *berme*, *barm*, LG. *borme*, *barme*, *barm*, mod.G. *bärme*.]

1. a. The froth that forms on the top of fermenting malt liquors, which is used to leaven bread, and to cause fermentation in other liquors; yeast, leaven.

c **1000** *Ags. Gosp.* Matt. xiii. 33 Heofena rice is ȝelic beor man. *c* **1200** ORMIN 996 Bræd All þeorrf wiþþutenn berrme. *c* **1386** CHAUCER *Chan. Yem. Prol. & T.* 260 Alum, glas, berme, wort. *c* **1420** *Liber Cocorum* 39 With egges and floure in batere þou make, Put berme þer to. **1601** HOLLAND *Pliny* II. 145 The froth or barme..[has] a property to keepe the skin faire and cleare in womens faces. **1688** in *Phil. Trans.* XVIII. 130 His Brains worked like Birme in an Ale-Fat. **1816** SCOTT *Antiq.* xi, The sea was working like barm.

b. *transf.* or *fig.* Ferment, fermenting agent.

c **1580** MONTGOMERIE *To R. Hudson*, This barme and blaidry buists up all my bees. **1666** G. HARVEY *Morb. Angl.* iv. 48, I assert the gall to be the barm or ferment of the venal blood. **1828** LANDOR *Imag. Conv.* (1846) II. 174 Milton's dough..is never the lighter for the barm he kneads up with it.

†2. The froth or 'head' of beer when poured out.

c **1275** *Sermun* in *O.E. Misc.* 188 Loȝe heo holdet hore galun, mid berme [*v.r.* beorme] heo hine fulleþ. *c* **1440** *Promp. Parv.* 32 Berme of ale or other lyke, *spuma.* **1483** *Cath. Angl.* 22/1 Barme, *spuma.*

3. *attrib.*, as in ***barm-fly, -froth, -man, -pot*** (also *fig.*); **barm-stick** *fig.*, a feeble-minded person (E.D.D.); also *attrib.*

1606 *Wily Beguiled* Prol. in Hazl. *Dodsl.* IX. 223 That barm-froth poet. **1676** COTTON *Angler* II. 335 Another Dun called the Barm-fly from its yeasty colour. **1913** D. H. LAWRENCE *Sons & Lovers* iii. 49 She was looking down the alley..for the barm-man. **1924** —— & SKINNER *Boy in Bush* 278 We've heard that barm-stick yarn before. **1925** *British Wkly.* 5 Mar. 557/1 The man who sold 'barm' (brewers' yeast) drove round the district..one saw women hastening over the heath, jug in hand, to catch the 'barm-man'. **1951** J. B. PRIESTLEY *Fest. Farbridge* I. i. 34 Lady Barth, a rich old barmpot. **1957** MANKOWITZ & HAGGAR *Encycl. Eng. Pott. & Porc.* 16/2 *Barm pot*, a pot for storing barm or yeast. **1963** T. & P. MORRIS *Pentonville* ix. 196 Thus a harmless schizophrenic will be classified by the staff as a 'barmpot' and by the prisoners as a 'nutter'.

barm, *v. Obs.* or *arch.* [f. prec. sb.]

1. To mix with yeast; to leaven, ferment.

[*c* **975** *Rushw. Gosp.* Matt. xiii. 33 Oþþæt ȝebeormad wæs all.] **1615** CROOKE *Body of Man* 245 The seed it selfe..is so houen and barmed as it were with spirits. **1616** SURFL. & MARKH. *Countr. Farm* 589 Your best ale must be barmed as soone as it is coold.

2. To rise in froth or fermentation.

c **1440** *Promp. Parv.* 32/2 Bermyn, or spurgyn as ale, *spumo.* **1822** *Provost* ii. 16 It set men's minds a barming and working.

barmaid ('bɑːmeɪd). [f. BAR *sb.*[1] 28.] A female who sells food and drink at the bar of a tavern or hotel. Also *attrib.* and *fig.*

a **1658** [see STROKE *v.*[1] 4]. **1772** GOLDSM. *Stoops to Conq.* Epil., Th' unblushing Bar-maid at a country inn. **1837** DICKENS *Pickw.* (1847) 9/2 The bar-maid had positively refused to draw him any more liquor. **1880** LADY JEBB *Let.* 3 June (1960) 159 She is lovelier than ever, in an exquisite highbred way, which throws such a barmaid beauty as Mrs. Fred. Myers completely in the shade. **1911** MASEFIELD *Everl. Mercy* 24 And then men ask, Are Barmaids chaste?

Hence **barmaidenly** *a.*

1881 *Daily News* 8 June 5 Bar-maidenly in their conception of polished badinage. **1905** G. B. SHAW in *Sat. Rev.* 11 Feb. 170/2 The merry lady with her barmaidenly repartees. **1932** *Times Lit. Suppl.* 27 Oct. 776/4 She was what some one once styled a 'barmaidenly maiden'.

barman ('bɑːmən). [f. BAR *sb.*[1]]

†1. A pleader at the bar; a barrister. *Obs.*

1657 REEVE *God's Plea* 8 Oh rare Pleader! there is not such a Barre-man to be found.

2. One who prepares bars, *e.g.* of metal for the manufacture of wire.

1714 MANDEVILLE *Fab. Bees* (1725) I. 249 The silver-spinner, the flatter, the wire-drawer, the bar-man, and the refiner.

3. A man who serves at the bar of a public-house, etc. Cf. BAR *sb.*[1] 28.

1837 DUNCUMB *Brit. Emigrant's Adv.* 76 He instantly called for the bar-man and taxed him with the imposition. **1865** E. CLAYTON *Cruel Fort.* II. 165 Two barmaids commenced a most vigorous flirtation with the young barman.

barmaster ('bɑː,mɑːstə(r)). Also 7 **barge-**, 7-8 **bergh-**, 8 **bargh-**. [Formerly *barghmaster*, ad. Ger. *bergmeister*, f. *berg-* mining.] A local judge amongst miners: see quot.

1662 FULLER *Worthies* I. 229 The Barge-Master keeps his two great Courts twice a year in Barge-Moot Hall..to decide Controversies, and punish offences betwixt Miners. **1721** BAILEY, *Bargh-master*, the Surveyor of a Mine. **1747** HOOSON *Miner's Dict.* s.v. *Bill*, By the Assistance of the Barmaster. **1875** URE *Dict. Arts* I. 292 *Bar-master*, in Derbyshire, the authority to whom all disputes in lead-mining are referred. He has charge of the standard 'dish' or measure used in measuring the ore.

barmbrack ('bɑːmbræk). *Anglo-Irish.* [corruption of Ir. *bairigen breac* speckled cake (Wh. Stokes).] A currant-bun.

1878 MISS YONGE *Yng. Stepmother* 317 A great barmbrack from Biddy. **1882** FLORA SHAW *Cast. Blair* 189 The number of buns and barm-bracks had to be calculated.

barmecidal (bɑːmɪ'saɪdəl), *a.* [f. next + -AL[1].] Like the Barmecide's feast; imaginarily satisfying or sumptuous; unreal, illusory.

a **1845** HOOD *Turtles* xiv, Having thro' one delighted sense, at least, Enjoy'd a sort of Barmecidal feast. **1845** MOZLEY *Blanco White, Ess.* (1878) II. 115 To reason simply on the superficies is a Barmecidal proceeding.

Barmecide ('bɑːmɪsaɪd). Patronymic of a family of princes ruling at Bagdad just before Haroun-al-Raschid, concerning one of whom the story is told in the Arabian Nights, that he put a succession of empty dishes before a beggar, pretending that they contained a sumptuous repast—a fiction which the beggar humorously accepted. Hence, one who offers imaginary food or illusory benefits. Often *attrib.*

1713 *Guardian* No. 162 The Barmecide was sitting at his table that seemed ready covered for an entertainment. **1842** DICKENS *Amer. Notes* (1850) 81/1 It is a Barmecide Feast; a pleasant field for the imagination to rove in. **1854** THACKERAY *Newcomes* II. 103 My dear Barmecide friend. **1863** *Reader* II. 506 Sharing the boundless hospitality of a Barmecide.

barminess ('bɑːmɪnɪs). [f. BARMY *a.* 2b + -NESS.] Weakness of intellect.

1896 [see BARMY *a.* 2b]. **1908** E. V. LUCAS *Over Bemerton's* vi. 60, I heard what sounded like a sarcastic sniff deprecative of her uncle's barminess.

barming ('bɑːmɪŋ). *Sc. rare.* [? f. BARM *v.*] The formation of barm on a fermenting liquor; *fig.* the accruing of interest upon money.

1823 GALT *Entail* I. xx. 169 Father..ordained me to hae a hundred a year out o' the barming o' his lying money.

Bar-Mitzvah (bɑː'mɪtsvɑː). *Judaism.* Also **-mitsvah, -mitzva.** [Heb., lit. 'son of commandment, man of duty'.] **a.** A Jewish boy who has reached the age of thirteen, regarded as the age of religious responsibility. **b.** The 'confirmation' ceremony in a synagogue on this occasion. Also *attrib.*

1861 *Children's Jewish Advocate* VII. 84 You look like my Samuel, whom I have not seen since he was *Barmitsva.* **1877** *Encycl. Brit.* VII. 134/1 This dull routine..continued till Emanuel was thirteen years old, when he returned to Neisse, to solemnize his religious majority (Bar-mitzva). **1891** M. FRIEDLÄNDER *Jewish Rel.* 481 The boy when thirteen years old is *bar-mitsvah*..bound to obey the Law, and responsible for his deeds. **1892** I. ZANGWILL *Childr. Ghetto* (1893) I. x. 97 My Ebenezer is *Bar-mitzvah* next Shabbos week. **1941** B. SCHULBERG *What makes Sammy Run?* ix. 181 *Bar-mitzvah* is the Hebrew ceremony celebrating a boy's reaching the state of manhood at the age of thirteen. **1960** *Commentary* June 493/2 Its willingness to accept boys over eleven for Bar Mitzvah preparation.

barmkin ('bɑːmkɪn). *north. arch.* Forms: 4 **barmeken,** (5 **barnekynch**), 6 **barmekyn, -kin, barnekine,** 5- **barmkin.** [Perh. f. Teut. *barm* (ON. *barmr* brim, border, edge, wing of castle; cf. BERM). The second syllable may be the dim. suffix -KIN, though the meaning hardly suits. Possibly a corruption of, or confused with, BARBICAN.]

The battlement of the outer fortification of a castle; the outer fortification, or barbican; a turret or watch tower on the outer wall.

c **1340** *Alexander* (Stev.) 1301 Balaan in þe barmeken · sa bitterly fiȝtis. *a* **1440** *Sir Degrev.* 375 At the barnekynch he abad, And lordelych doune lyght. *c* **1470** HENRY *Wallace* VIII. 1067 Fehew him self.. Throuch all the fyr can on the barmkyn lycht. **1513** DOUGLAS *Æneis* XII. x. 64 Thame quhilkis on the barmkin heid remanis. **1577** HOLINSHED *Chron.* III. 874/2 Ouerthrew eighteene towers of stone, with all their barnekines. *a* **1811** J. LEYDEN *Ld. Soulis* v, And he call'd on a page, who was witty and sage, To go to the barmkin high.

barmote ('bɑːməʊt). Also 7 **barge-,** 7-8 **bargh-,** 8 **barmoot,** 7-8 **berghmote.** [Earlier *barghmote*, f. Ger. *berg-* mining + MOTE, assembly, court; cf. *barmaster.*] A local court amongst miners: see quot.

1653 MANLOVE *Lead Mines* 14 Sute for oar must be in Barghmoot Court. **1732** DE FOE, &c. *Tour Gt. Brit.* (1769) III. 78 The Barmoot Court, kept at Wirksworth, to judge Controversies among the Miners, and adjust subterranean Quarrels and Disputes. **1747** HOOSON *Miner's Dict.* s.v. *Bill,* The meanest Labourer may recover his due Wages at the Barmote-court. **1881** RAYMOND *Mining Gloss., Barmote* (Derb.), a mining court.

†**barm-team.** *Obs.* Also **berem-tem, barmeteme.** A corruption of BAIRN-TEAM. (Perh. due to confusion with BARM *sb.*[1], bosom, lap.)

c **1250** *Gen. & Ex.* 3903 Al ðat berem-tem. *c* **1315** SHOREHAM 58 He hedde y-brout forthe his bearm-team Wythoute senne i-smaked. *c* **1430** *Chev. Assigne* v. 103 And hadde moche rewthe That swyche a barmeteme as yᵗ shulde so betyde. *c* **1440** *Bone Flor.* 10 Antenowre was of that barme-teme.

barmy ('bɑːmɪ), *a.* [f. BARM *sb.*[2] + Y[1].]

1. Of, full of, or covered with barm; frothing.

1535 LYNDESAY *Sat. Three Estates,* Gud barmie aill. **1601** B. JONSON *Poetast.* v. iii, That puft-up lump of barmy froth. *c* **1817** HOGG *Tales* II. 256 Like barmy beer in corked bottles.

2. a. *fig.* Full of ferment, excitedly active, flighty.

1602 *Ret. fr. Parnass.* I. ii. (Arb.) 9 Such barmy heads wil alwaies be working. *a* **1605** MONTGOMERIE *Poems* (1821) 49 Hope puts that hast into ȝour heid, Quhilk boyl's ȝour barmy brain. **1785** BURNS *Wks.* III. 85 Just now I've taen the fit o' rhyme, My barmie noddle's working prime.

b. = BALMY *a.* 7 (of which it is an altered form, after BARM *sb.*[2]). *slang.*

1892 *Answers* 27 Feb. 242/1 One plan is..to give foolish answers when asked questions. By this means the shammer gets known as being 'barmy' (weak-minded) among his shipmates. **1896** *Westm. Gaz.* 30 May 8/1 Should not 'balmy' be 'barmy'? I have known a person of weak intellect called 'Barmy Billy'... The prisoner..meant to simulate semi-idiocy, or 'barminess', not 'balminess'. **1902** *Ibid.* 8 Nov. 2/1 All the boys think him barmy.

3. *Comb.* **barmy-brained** *a.*, flighty; **barmy-froth,** (*fig.*) a flighty, empty-headed fellow.

1599 MARSTON *Sco. Villanie* 166 Each odde puisne of the Lawyers Inne, Each barmy-froth, that last day did beginne To read his little. **1824** SCOTT *St. Ronan's* xxxii, Cork-headed barmy-brained gowks!

barn (bɑːn), *sb.* Forms: 1 **bere-ern (bæren),** 1-2 **berern,** 1-4 **beren,** 1-6 **bern,** 3 **berrn,** 4-6 **berne,** (5 **beern, beyrne, baerne**), 5-7 **barne,** 7- **barn.** [OE. *bęre-ern* lit. 'barley-place,' f. *bęre* barley + *ærn, ern,* place, closet, store-room; reduced already in OE. to *bęrern, bęren, bęrn,* whence ME. *bern,* mod. *barn.*]

1. a. A covered building for the storage of grain; and, in wider usage, of hay, straw, flax, and other produce of the earth.

c **950** *Lindisf. Gosp.* Luke xii. 24 Ðæm ne is hordern ne ber-ern. *c* **975** *Rushw. G.* ibid., Bere-ern. *c* **1000** *Ags. G.* ibid., Nabbað hiȝ heddern ne bern. *c* **1200** ORMIN 10486 Sammenn alle þe clene corn & don itt inn hiss berrne. *c* **1220** *Bestiary* 263 *O.E. Misc.* 9 Ne bit ȝe (= she) nowt de barlic beren abuten. *c* **1386** CHAUCER *Wyfs T.* 15 Thropes and bernes, shepnes and dayeries. *c* **1475** in Wright *Voc.* 274 *Orium,* beyrne. **1489** CAXTON *Faytes of A.* II. xxiv. 138 A grete baerne within the said forest. **1523** FITZHERB. *Husb.* §26 [Rye] mowen..taketh more rowme in the barne than shorne corne dothe. **1551** ROBINSON tr. *More's Utop.* 160 Corne or graine..in the rich men's bernes. **1610** SHAKS. *Temp.* IV. i. 111 Barnes, and Garners, neuer empty. **1697** DRYDEN *Virg. Georg.* I. 74 And bursts the crowded Barns, with more than promis'd Gains. **1820** WORDSW. *Sonn. Duddon* xiii, One small hamlet.. Clustering with barn and byre, and spouting mill. **1872** JENKINSON *Eng. Lakes* 24 The [Grasmere] island has a clump of firs and a grey barn upon it.

fig. *a* **1520** *Myrr. Our Ladye* 211 Aungels myghte gather them in to euerlastynge barnes.

b. Applied to: A barn-like building for worship.

a **1721** PRIOR *To F. Shepherd,* So at pure barn of Loud Non-con, Where with my grannam I have gone.

c. A stable or cattle-house. *U.S.*

1770 J. R. FORSTER tr. *P. Kalm's Trav. N. America* I. 223 The *barns* had a peculiar kind of construction... In the middle was the threshing floor..on one side were stables for the horses, and on the other for the cows. **1828** MRS. ROYALL *Black Bk.* II. 71 Every farmer has his small wooden barn, under which name they include stables. **1901** M. D. BABCOCK *Thoughts* 17 Locking a barn seems no longer commonplace when the horse is stolen. **1904** *N.Y. Even. Post* 28 Jan. 1 Cattle were found frozen stiff in the barns by farmers this morning.

d. [Said to have originated in the phrase 'as big as a barn'.] In nuclear physics, 10^{-24} sq. cm., a unit of area used in the measurement of the cross-section of a nucleus.

1947 R. D. EVANS in C. Goodman *Sci. & Engin. Nucl. Power* i. 15 This area has been dubbed the 'barn', 1 barn = 10^{-24} cm^2 /nucleus. **1947** C. GOODMAN *Ibid.* ix. 290 The nuclear cross section, σ, in barns. **1950** S. GLASSTONE *Sourcebk. Atomic Energy* x. 264/2 A unit, called a *barn,* equal to 10^{-24} sq. cm. per nucleus, has been adopted. *note.* The term 'barn' was proposed in 1942 by the American physicists M. G. Holloway and C. P. Baker, as a result of a broadly humorous association of ideas. It served the purpose of a code word..and seemed appropriate because 'a cross section of 10^{-24} sq. cm. for nuclear processes was really as big as a barn'. **1957** *Sci. News* XLV. 106 The cross sections of gadolinium, samarium, and europium are 30,000, 4,250, and 2,500 barns respectively.

2. *Comb.* and *Attrib.*, as ***barn barley, -builder, form, -loft, -sweepings***; also **barn-ball,** a children's game of the United States (see quot. 1879); **barn-boss** *U.S.*, a horse-keeper; **barn-burner,** nick-name of the radical section of the Democratic party in U.S.; **barn-cellar,** a room under a barn, generally used as a cow-house; **barn chamber** *U.S.*, a loft above a barn; **barn-floor,** the floor of a barn, *hence* what is there stored; **barnful,** as much as a barn will contain; **barn-gallon,** a measure containing two imperial gallons, used in the milk-trade; **barn-like,** *a.*, like, or like that of, a barn; **barn-lot** *U.S.*, a piece of ground for or about a barn (see LOT *sb.* 6 a); **barn-raising** *U.S.*, 'the erection of the frame of a barn with the help of neighbours; a social gathering on this occasion' (*D.A.*); **barn(s)man,** a labourer in a barn, a thresher; **barn-owl,** a British bird of prey (*Strix flammea*), also called White, Church, and Screech Owl; **barn-shovel,** one used for corn; **barnstormer,** (*a*) applied depreciatively to a strolling player; whence ***barn-storming***; (*b*) *U. S. Aeronaut.* (see quot. 1928 and BARNSTORM *v.* 3); **barn-swallow,** the common house-swallow; **barnward** *adv.*, towards the barn; **barn-yard,** (*a*) the enclosure round a barn, a farm-yard; (*b*) *attrib.* of behaviour, language, etc.: characterized by lack of morality or propriety; coarse, indecent, earthy (orig. *U.S.*).

1841 *New Orl. Picayune* 25 May 2/2 Who has not played '*barn ball' in his boyhood? **1879** B. F. TAYLOR *Summer-Savoury* 122 The writer knew a boy..who never got farther than 'barn-ball', which means throwing a ball at the gable and catching it when it returns. **1901** W. CHURCHILL *Crisis* ix. 196 A tall man in his shirt sleeves was playing barn-ball with some boys. **1880** JEFFERIES *Gt. Estate* 152 *Barn barley ..i.e. that which had been stored in a barn. **1902** S. E. WHITE *Blazed Trail* xxix. 201 So Shearer had picked out a *barn-boss of his own. *a* **1610** BABINGTON *Wks.* (1622) 218 That rich *Barne-builder in the Gospell. *a* **1848** *N.Y. Tribune* in Bartlett *Dict. Amer.* 23 This school of Democrats was termed *Barnburners, in allusion to the story of an old Dutchman, who relieved himself of rats by burning down his barns which they infested,—just like exterminating all banks and corporations, to root out the abuses connected therewith. **1842** T. PARKER in Weiss *Life & Corr.* I. 184 A bull..tied up in the corner of the *barn-cellar. **1838** H. COLMAN *Mass. Agric. Surv. Rep.* 16 The best method of curing it [*sc.* herds grass]..is to..tie it in bundles; and set it upright in a *barn chamber. **1611** BIBLE *2 Kings* vi. 27 Whence shall I helpe thee? out of the *barne floore? **1863** KINGSLEY *Water-Bab.* vii. 272 Her decks were swept as clean as a barn floor. **1847** YEOWELL *Anc. Brit. Ch.* xii. 129 Very old Welsh Churches are of the *barn form. *a* **1619** FOTHERBY *Atheom.* II. viii. §4 Not by the bushell..but by the whole *Barnefull. **1858** SIMMONDS *Dict. Trade* 27/2 **Barn-gallon,* a double gallon of milk. **1865** W. WHITE *East. England* II. xv. 217 The gallon being a 'barn-gallon' of seventeen pints. **1662** GERBIER *Princ.* (1665) 36 Those *Barn-like Roofs of many Noble Persons Palaces. **1835** BECKFORD *Recoll.* 174 The barn-like saloon on their ground-floor. **1837** CARLYLE *Fr. Rev.* III. IV. v. 235 In cellars, *barn-lofts, in caves. **1724** *New Hampsh. Prob. Rec.* II. 250, I give to my Daughters..the other half part of my afores[aid] *barn Lott in Salsbury. **1932** W. FAULKNER *Light in Aug.* (1933) i. 12 When the wagon passes the house, goes on toward the barnlot. *c* **1800** A. CARLYLE *Autobiog.* (1860) 25, I took him for a grieve or *barnman. **1861** SMILES *Engineers* II. 112 A sufficient number of barnsmen for thrashing straw. **1674** RAY *Eng. Birds* 83 The common *Barn-owl or White Owl, *Aluco minor.* **1845** DARWIN *Voy. Nat.* xvii. (1852) 378 The short-eared and white barn-owls of Europe. **1856** T. D. PRICE *MS. Diary* 28 Apr. (D.A.), Went to D. D. Keller's *barn raising. **1952** *Economist* 9 Aug. 340/1 The old custom of 'barn-raising', at which neighbours and friends volunteered their services, is coming back into fashion [in the U.S.A.]. **1446** *Wills & Inv. N.C.* I. (1835) 95 Whetridell..hopper, *barnshoile. **1859** HOTTEN *Dict. Mod. Slang* 3 **Barn stormers,* theatrical performers who travel the country and act in barns, selecting short and frantic pieces to suit the rustic taste. **1884** *Pall Mall G.* 6 June 5/1 If this be barn-storming, Betterton and Garrick were barn-stormers. **1928** *Daily Mail* 7 May 6/4 *Barnstormers,* itinerant flyers, appearing at fairs and race tracks, like Lindbergh in his earlier years. **1930** *Punch* 19 Mar. 330/1 Those barn-stormers who tore the play's passions and the spectators' heart-strings to shreds. **1851** D. WILSON *Preh. Ann. Scot.* (1863) I. 416 Less skill than..the common *barn-swallow displays in the construction of its nest. **1840** CARLYLE *Heroes* ii. 96 Chaff, chopped straw, *barn-sweepings. **1884** ROE in *Harper's Mag.* July 247/2 The horses' heads were turned *barnward. **1513-75** *Diurn. Occurr.* (1833) 49 Thay brunt tua *barny-yairdis in Nether Keith. **1850** MRS. STOWE *Uncle Tom's C.* vii. 49 A barn-yard belonging to a large farming establishment. **1938** O. NASH *I'm a Stranger here Myself* 280 Some people calmly live a barnyard life because they find monogamy dull and arid. **1967** R. K. MASSIE *Nicholas & Alexandra* xvi. 195 In polite conversation, Rasputin used coarse barnyard expressions. **1977** *Time* 21 Nov. 70/2 A life that is full of the barnyard morality. **1981** W. SAFIRE in *N.Y. Times Mag.* 13 Dec. 16 What copy editors like to call 'a barnyard epithet'.

†**barn,** *v. Obs.* [f. the sb.] To house or store in a barn; to garner. Often *fig.*

1593 SHAKS. *Lucr.* cxxiii, And useless barns the harvest of his wits. **1647** FULLER *Good Th. in Worse T.* (1841) 110 Whose censures often barn up the chaff, and burn up the grain. **1702** C. MATHER *Magn. Chr.* III. III. (1852) 559 To plant and dress, and barn and beat their corn.

barn(e, obsolete form of BAIRN.

Barnabite ('bɑːnəbaɪt). [f. *Barnab-as* name of the apostle: see -ITE.] A member of the religious order 'thus called from the church of St. Barnabas at Milan' (Chambers *Cycl.* 1751).

1706 *Dupin's Eccl. Hist. 16th C.* II. IV. xi. 450 The Founders of the Order of Barnabites..were instructed by a Famous Preacher, one Serasino, who advised them to read St. Paul constantly, from whence they were called *Clerks of St. Paul.*

Barnaby ('bɑːnəbɪ). [a. F. *Barnabé,* ad. L. *Barnabas.*] By-form of the name Barnabas; whence **Barnaby-day, Barnaby bright,** or **long Barnaby,** St. Barnabas' Day, the 11th of June, in Old Style reckoned the 'longest day'; **Barnaby-thistle,** the *Centaurea solstitialis,* so named from its flowering about the 11th of June.

1595 SPENSER *Epithal.* 266 This day the sunne is in his chiefest hight, With Barnaby the bright. **1645** G. DANIEL *Poems* Wks. 1878 II. 49 This short December day, It would spin out, to make my Readers say, Long Barnabie was never halfe so gay. **1650** FULLER *Pisgah* II. xii. 255 Staying the Sun in Gibeon.. This was the Barnaby day of the whole world. **1670** EACHARD *Cont. Clergy* 32 Barnaby-bright would be much too short for him to tell you all that he could say. **1805** SCOTT *Last Minstr.* IV. iv, It was but last St. Barnabright They sieged him a whole summer night. **1598** FLORIO, *Calcatrippa,* Star-thistle, or Saint Barnabaes thistle.

barnacle ('bɑːnək(ə)l), *sb.*[1] Forms: *α.* 2 **bernac,** 5 **bernak(e, bernag.** *β.* 4-6 **bernacle,** 5 **barnakylle, -alle, byrnacle,** (6 **barneckle, burnacle**), 7-8 **barnicle,** 9 **bernicle,** 4- **barnacle.** [ME. *bernak,* a. OF. *bernac* 'camus'; of which *bernacle* seems to be a dim. form: cf. OF. *bernicles* in Joinville *c* 1275, in sense of the instrument of torture (sense 2) as used by the Saracens, for which Marsh has suggested an oriental origin, comparing Pers. *baran-dan* to compress, squeeze, *baranjah kar-dan* to inflict torture. But, so far as evidence goes, 1 was the earliest sense, and of western origin. The sense of 'spectacles' seems to arise naturally enough from the others, but has been treated by some as distinct, and referred to OF. *béricle* (since 15th c. *bésicle*) 'eye glass,' originally 'beryl':—late L. **bericulus,* dim. of *berillus, beryllus*: it is not easy to trace any phonetic connexion between this and *barnacles,* even though the mod.F. dialect of Berry has *berniques* 'spectacles.']

1. A kind of powerful bit or twitch for the mouth of horse or ass, used to restrain a restive animal; later, *spec.* an instrument consisting of two branches joined by a hinge, placed on the nose of a horse, if he has to be coerced into quietness when being shoed or surgically operated upon.

α. [*c* **1200** NECKAM *De Utensilibus* in Wright *Voc.* 100 Camum (*bernac*) vel capistrum (*chevestre*) sponte preterea.] *c* **1440** *Promp. Parv.* 33 Bernak for horse [**1499** bernakill], *chamus.* **1468** *Medulla Gram.* in *Cath. Angl.* 22 *Chamus,* a bernag for a hors. *a* **1500** in Wülcker *Voc.*/572 *Chamus,* a bernake.

β. **1382** Wyclif *Prov.* xxvi. 3 A scourge to an hors, and a bernacle to an asse. **1387** Trevisa *Higden* Rolls Ser. I. 353 þey dryueþ hir hors wiþ a chambre ȝerde [*virgam cameratam*] in þe ouer ende in stede of barnacles. **1483** *Cath. Angl.* 22/1 Barnakylle, Byrnacle, Barnakalle, *camus.* **1562** Leigh *Armorie* (1597) 104 Barnacle..is the chiefest instrument that the smith hath, to make the vntamed horsse gentile. **1607** Topsell *Four-f. Beasts* 251 Barnacles..put upon the Horses nose, to restrain his tenacious fury from biting, and kicking. **1774** Goldsm. *Nat. Hist.* I. i. (1862) I. 245 *note* The horse..being caught by the nose in barnacles. **1831** Youatt *Horse* xxii. (1872) 457 The barnacles are the handles of the pincers placed over and enclosing the muzzle.

2. An instrument of torture applied in a similar way. Also *fig.*

[**1382** Wyclif *2 Kings* xix. 28, I schal putten a cercle in thyn noos thrillis and a bernacle [Coverdale, brydle bitt; **1611** bridle] in thi lippis.] **1625** tr. *Gonsalvio's Sp. Inquis.* 145 Clapped a Barnacle vpon his tongue, which remained there vntill the fire had consumed it. **1679** *Hist. Jetzer* Pref., Magistrates may flatter themselves, that with the Barnacles of a strict and well-worded Oath they can hold a Jesuites Nose to the Grind-stone. **1870** Edgar *Runnymede* 109 To save my body from the bernicles.

3. *colloq.* in *pl.* = spectacles. [Probably from their bestriding and pinching the nose.]

1571 *Damon & P.* in Hazl. *Dodsl.* IV. 81 These spectacles put on. *Grim,* They be gay barnacles, yet I see never the better. **1593** Munday *Def. Contraries* 39 Eye glasses, otherwise called Bernacles. **1693** Motteux *Rabelais* v. xxvii, They had barnicles on the handles of their faces, or spectacles at most. **1823** Scott *Peveril* viii, No woman above sixteen ever did white-seam without barnacles.

barnacle (ˈbɑːnək(ə)l), *sb.*[2] Forms: *α.* 3 **bernekke**, 4–5 **bernake**, 5 **bernak, -ack**, (? **barnagge**). *β.* 5 **bernakill, barnakylle**, 5– **bernacle**, 6– **barnacle**, (7 **barnicle**, 9 **bernicle**). [ME. *bernekke, bernake*, identical with OF. *bernaque*, med.L. *bernaca, berneka.* (Other F. forms *bernache, barnache*; Pg. *bernaca, -acha, -icha*, Sp. *bernache*; med.L. also *barnaces, bernesta, barneta*, perhaps bad spellings). With the *β* forms cf. med. or mod.L. *bernicla, -ecela, -acula*, and mod.F. *bernicle, barnacle.* Ulterior history unknown.

The earliest attainable forms (omitting *barbates* in Albertus Magnus and *barliates* in Vincentius Bellovacensis, which seem too far off) are the Eng. *bernekke*, Anglo-Lat. *bernaca* (Giraldus Cambr. *c* 1175), *barneta*, ? *barneca* (Gervase of Tilbury *c* 1211), *berneka* (Vincent. Bellovac. 1200–1250). If English, this could only be *bare-neck* or *bear-neck*, of which the application is not evident. The history of this word is involved in an extraordinary growth of popular mythology, traced back as far as the 11th or 12th c. by Prof. Max Müller, *Lect. Sc. Lang.* (ed. 7) II. 583–604. It is there suggested that *bernacula* might be a variant of **pernacula*, a possible dim. of *perna* 'a kind of shell-fish,' afterwards confused with **bernicula*, a supposed aphetic form of **hibernicula*, which might be applied to the barnacle-goose from its being found in *Hibernia.* Others seek the source of the primitive *bernaca* in Celtic, comparing Gaelic *bairneach*, Welsh *brenig*, limpets. But as all the evidence shows that the name was originally applied to the *bird* which had the marvellous origin, not to the *shell* which, according to some, produced it, conjectures assuming the contrary seem to be beside the mark. The form *bernacle*, it will be seen, is not found before 15th c., and *bernacula* seems to be only its modern Lat. adaptation. If med.L. *bernecla, bernicla*, are earlier, they are suspiciously like erroneous forms of *bernecha, bernicha.* No connexion with barnacle *sb.*[1] can be traced: *bernac* was masc., *bernaque, -ache* fem., in Fr.]

1. A species of wild goose (*Anas leucopsis*) nearly allied to the Brent Goose, found in the arctic seas (where alone it breeds), and visiting the British coasts in winter.

This bird, of which the breeding-place was long unknown, was formerly believed to be produced out of the fruit of a tree growing by the sea-shore, or itself to grow upon the tree attached by its bill (whence also called *Tree Goose*), or to be produced out of a shell which grew upon this tree, or was engendered as a kind of 'mushroom' or spume from the corruption or rotting of timber in the water.

α. *a* **1227** Neckam in *Promp. Parv.* 32 De ave que vulgo dicitur bernekke. **1387** Trevisa *Higden* Rolls Ser. I. 335 þere beeþ bernakes foules liche to wylde gees; kynde bryngeþ hem forþ wonderliche out of trees. *c* **1400** Maundev. xxvi. 264 Of the Bernakes..In oure Contree weren Trees that beren a Fruyt, that becomen Briddes fleeynge. *c* **1440** [see *β*].

β. *c* **1440** *Promp. Parv.* 32 Barnakylle byrde [*v.r.* bernack, bernak], *barnacus, bernita, barnites.* **1480** Caxton *Trevisa's Descr. Brit.* 48 Ther ben bernacles, fowles lyke to wylde ghees, whiche growen wonderly vpon trees. *Ibid.* (1520) 2/2 Men of relygyon eet barnacles upon fastynge dayes bycause they ben not engendred with flesshe. **1598** Sylvester *Du Bartas* I. vi. (1641) 58/2 So rotten planks of broken ships do change To Barnacles..'Twas first a green tree, then a broken hull, Lately a Mushroom, now a flying Gull. **1599** Hakluyt *Voy.* II. I. 63 There stand certaine trees vpon the shore of the Irish sea, bearing fruit like unto a gourd, which ..doe fall into the water, and become birds called Bernacles. **1653** Walton *Angler* 189 The Barnacles and young Goslings bred by the Sun's heat and the rotten planks of an old Ship, and hatched of trees. **1674** Ray *Water Fowl* 95 The Bernacle, *Bernicla.* **1678** Sir R. Murray in *Phil. Trans.* XII. 926 Multitudes of little Shells; having within them little Birds perfectly shap'd, supposed to be Barnacles. **1694** Falle *Jersey* ii. 74 Bernacles..are only seen about the Sea, and in very cold Weather. **1774** Goldsm. *Nat. Hist.* III. 279 The Barnacle not..bred from a shell sticking to ships' bottoms. **1863** *Spring in Lapland* 362 The brent goose and the bernicle..breed either in Spitzbergen or East Finland. **1870** *Pall Mall G.* 12 Oct. 12 The barnacle is supposed by simple people to be developed out of the fishy parasite of the same name.

b. In this sense now often *Bernacle Goose*, to distinguish it from sense 2.

1768 Pennant *Zool.* (1812) II. 237 The Bernacle Goose. **1848** C. Johns *Week at Lizard* 333 Bernicle Goose. **1882** *Proc. Berw. Nat. Club* IX. 552 Bernacle Geese have been very abundant.

2. English name of the pedunculate genus of Cirripedes, which attach themselves to objects floating in the water, especially to the bottoms of ships, by a long fleshy foot-stalk. Sometimes used to include sessile Cirripedes: see acorn-shell.

(This was the 'shell-fish' out of which the Barnacle Goose was supposed to be produced, the long feathery cirri protruded from the valves suggesting the notion of plumage. Giraldus Cambrensis had himself seen more than a thousand of them 'conchylibus testis inclusæ,' hanging from one piece of timber on the shore.)

a **1581** Campion *Hist. Irel.* iii. (1633) 10 Barnacles, thousands at once, are noted along the shoares to hang by the beakes about the edges of putrified timber..which in processe taking lively heate of the Sunne, become water-foules. **1598** Florio, *Anitra*..the birde that breedes of a barnikle hanging vpon old ships. **1673** Ray *Journ. Low C.* 290 These Tortoises..had two great bunches of those they call Bernacle-shells sticking..to his back. **1678** Butler *Hud.* III. ii. 655 As barnacles turn Soland geese In th' islands of the Orcades. **1769** Falconer *Dict. Marine* (1789) *Cravan*, a barnacle, a small shell-fish..which fastens to a ship's bottom in a long voyage. **1859** Darwin *Orig. Spec.* xiv. (1873) 389 Cuvier did not perceive that a barnacle was a crustacean.

3. *fig.* A companion or follower that sticks close, and will not be dismissed; a constant attendant.

1607 Dekker *Northw. Hoe* III. Wks. 1873 III. 39 Ile cashiere all my yong barnicles. **1868** Miss Braddon *Trail Serp.* I. i. 7 Slopper found him a species of barnacle rather difficult to shake off.

†**b.** Perhaps in this sense used as the cant term for a decoy swindler: see quots., and cf. barnard.

1591 Greene *Disc. Cozenage* (1859) 23 Thus doth the Verser and the Setter feign a kind friendship to the Cony.. As thus they sit tipling, coms the Barnackle and thrusts open the doore..steps backe again: and very mannerly saith I cry you mercy Gentlemen, I thoght a frend of mine had bin heere. [See the whole passage.] **1608** Dekker *Belman Lond.* Wks. 1885 III. 131 He that..before counterfetted the dronken Bernard is now sober and called the Barnacle.

†**4.** One who speaks through his nose. *Obs. rare.*

1591 Percivall *Sp. Dict.*, *Gango*, a barnacle, one that speaketh through the nose, *Chenolopex.* [*Chenalopex* in Pliny, a species of goose.]

ˈbarnacle, *v.*[1] [f. barnacle *sb.*[1]] *trans.* To apply a barnacle to (a horse).

1861 S. Judd *Margaret* II. viii. (1871) 281 They banged him and barnacled him..and the more they did, the more he wouldn't stir.

ˈbarnacle (ˈbɑːnək(ə)l), *v.*[2] [f. barnacle *sb.*[2]] *trans.* To affix with persistent attachment.

1863 W. Story *Roba di R.* II. 34 This uncouth structure ..is barnacled upon the ruins of the once splendid portico. **1865** Mrs. Whitney *Gayworthys* xxiv. 236 He barnacled himself to Gershom, now, and shipped with him always.

barnacled (ˈbɑːnək(ə)ld), *ppl. a.* **a.** Covered with barnacles. Also *fig.* **b.** *colloq.* Wearing spectacles.

1691 T. H[ale] *Acc. New Invent.* 80 Cleaned with.. Scrapers, if barnicled. **1725** *New Canting Dict.* s.v. *Barnacles, The Cuffin Quire with his Nose Barnacled*..the Justice of Peace with his Spectacles on. **1829** *Olio* III. 55/2 The general reader and spokesman was ready barnacled for his office. **1878** R. Stevenson *Inland Voy.* 6 A gleam of spectacles. For though handsome lads, they were all (in the Scotch phrase) barnacled. **1884** *Blackw. Mag.* Oct. 523 My barnacled barque Drags..heavily on. **1890** *Jrnl. Educ.* 1 Mar. 149/2 With their brains barnacled over with shellfish facts. **1900** J. L. Allen *Incr. Purpose* xvi. 222 There might have been..fewer creeds barnacled in the World's Ship of Souls.

†**ˈbarnage.** *Obs.* [f. *barn*, variant of bairn + -age.] Childhood, infancy.

c **1325** *E.E. Allit. P.* B. 517 Ay hatz ben & wyl be ȝet fro her barnage. *c* **1375** Barbour *Troy-bk.* II. 2405 Norysede hime ine his barnage. **1513** Douglas *Æneis* v. Prol. 25 Quha lauchis nocht..in his barnage.

barnage, obs. f. baronage.

†**ˈbarnard.** *Obs.* Also 7 **bernard**. [app. a. variant of berner, one who waited with a relay of hounds to intercept a hunted animal.] The member of a gang of swindlers who acts as a decoy; a lurking scoundrel, a sharper. Cf. barnacle *sb*[2] 3 b.

1532 *Dice Play* (1850) 37 Another oily theft..is the barnards law: which, to be exactly practised asketh four persons at least, each of them to play a long several part by himself. **1562** Bulleyn in *Babees Bk.* (1868) 242 With a Barnards blowe, lurkyng in some lane, wodde, or hill top. **1591** Greene *Disc. Cozenage* (1859) 8 Foure persons were required..the Taker up, the Verser, the Barnard, and the Rutter. *Ibid.* Wks. 1885 X. 10 Comes in the Barnard stumbling into your companie, like some aged Farmer of the Countrey..and is so carelesse of his money, that out he throweth some fortie Angels on the boords end. **1608** Dekker *Belman Lond.* Wks. 1885 III. 126 The Bernard.. counterfets many parts in one, and is now a drunken man, anon in another humour..onely to blind the Cozen..the more easily to beguile him. [See the whole of the interesting descriptions in these works.]

barnbrack (ˈbɑːnbræk). *Ir.* [f. Ir. *bairghean* cake of bread + *breac* speckled.] A cake or loaf of bread containing currants. Cf. var. barmbrack.

[**1772** Vallancey *Ess. Antiq. Irish Lang.* 22 On St. Briget's Eve every Farmer's Wife in Ireland makes a Cake called bairin-breac.] **1867** P. Kennedy *Banks of Boro* xlii. 349 Piles of hot griddle-baked wheaten cakes.., barn-bracks, and other varieties of the staff of life. **1901** G. B. Shaw *Devil's Disciple* I. 12 Two green ware plates, on one of which she puts a barnbrack. **1928** *Universe* 3 Feb., A loaf of curious, very sweet currant bread is made and sold for All Souls Day. Even the poorest household manages to secure one of these Barn-bracks.

ˈbarn dance. orig. *U.S.* [barn *sb.*] A dance danced in a barn; applied *spec.* to a kind of schottische in which the partners advance side by side for a few steps and then dance a waltz or schottische step.

1892 *Daily News* 28 Sept. 5/5 The now inevitable barn dance figured once on the programme. **1895** L. Grove et al. *Dancing* 424 'Barn dance' is an American designation; but as many other dances take place in barns out West, it is difficult to see why the title is specially applied to this Scotch lilt and schottische hops. **1900** C. C. Munn *Uncle Terry* 20 If it was a barn dance she was always there and never lacked partners. *allusively.* **1898** Kipling *Fleet in Being* 7 We of the light horse did barn-dances about the windy floors.

barn-door. [f. barn *sb.*] **1.** The large door of a barn. (Applied humorously to a target too large to be easily missed, and, in *Cricket*, to a player that blocks every ball.)

1547 J. Heywood *Four P's* in Dodsl. *O.P.* (1780) I. 87 Bendynge his browes as brode as barne-durres. **1632** Milton *L'Allegro* 51 While the cock..to the stack or the barn-door, Stoutly struts his dames before. **1679** 'Tom Ticklefoot' *Trials of Wakeman* 9 My Old Master Clodpate would have been hanged before he would have missed such a Barn-dore. **1847** Longf. *Ev.* I. ii. 50 Heavily closed, with a jarring sound, the valves of the barn-doors.

2. *transf.* A door-like shutter in front of a lamp used for photographic purposes.

1942 Berrey & Van den Bark *Amer. Thes. Slang* 600 *Barn door*, a doorlike attachment on a lens to control the light. **1959** W. S. Sharps *Dict. Cinématogr.* 79/1 *Barn-doors*, adjustable flaps fitted to the front of a lighting unit, in order to control the spread of the light beam. **1960** O. Skilbeck *ABC Film & TV Terms* 16 *Barn door*, a variable mask designed to be used in front of studio lamps..and consisting of 'doors' opening longitudinally and/or vertically.

3. *attrib.* **a.** Reared at the barn-door.

c **1685** in *Dk. Buckhm's. Wks.* 1705 II. 48 She..slew a Barn-door Fowl with her own Hands. **1783** Wolcott (P. Pindar) *Ode to R. Acad.* i. Wks. I. 50 Plump as barn-door chicken. **1815** Scott *Guy M.* xlv, Our barn-door chuckies.

b. As large as, or resembling, a barn-door; often in humorous application (cf. sense 1 above). Also in *Comb.*

1829 *Blackw. Mag.* Dec. 856 Such is the birthright of Britons—to open their mouths barn-door wide... The aforesaid barn-door-wide mouths. **1865** Mrs. Whitney *Gayworthys* xxvi. 256 Skirts were trodden on..and there was more than one 'barn-door' rent. **1868** C. Box *Theory & Pract. Cricket* 91 The Gentlemen's wickets were 27 in. by 8; the Players' 36 in. by 12 in. This was called the Barn-Door Match. **1898** G. Giffen *With Bat & Ball* v. 64 It was almost painful to watch a giant of six feet and a half playing the barndoor game. **1932** Blunden *Face of Eng.* 76 He met each ball with a barn-door bat.

†**barné.** *Sc. Obs.* [a. OF. *barné*, (earlier *barnes, barnet*):—late L. *bārōnātus*, f. *bārōn-em*: see baron and -ate.] Assembly or body of barons, baronage.

1375 Barbour *Bruce* II. 50 The king..with his barne, Sat in till his parleament. *c* **1375** —— *St. Baptista* 499 Scho gert þe kinge Assemble hale his barne, þat landis held of hyme.

†**barne.** *Obs.* A kind of fish.

1602 Carew *Cornwall* 30 a, Of round fish there are Brit, Barne, &c. *Ibid.* 34 b, For bait they use Barne, Pilcherd, and Lugges.

barne, obs. f. bairn, barn, burn.

barnekin, -kynch: see barmkin.

barnet (ˈbɑːnɪt). *Rhyming slang.* Also **Barnet.** [The name of the London borough of *Barnet.*] In full ***Barnet fair***, the hair; hence, the head.

1857 'Ducange Anglicus' *Vulgar Tongue* 1 Barnet-Fair, hair. **1877** [see rogue *sb.* 2 d]. **1887** *Referee* 6 Nov. 7/3 As she walked along the street With her little 'plates of meat', And the summer sunshine falling On her golden 'Barnet Fair'. **1931** *Amer. Speech* VI. 392 *My barnett*, my head. **1946** *Ibid.* XXI. 46 *Bonny Fair.* Hair... This is certainly a mistake. The word in rhyming slang is *Barnet Fair*, named after the most famous horse fair in England, held at Barnet, in Hertfordshire, for four hundred years. **1962** F. Norman *Guntz* i. 7 They send you to a doss house, so that you can get lice in your barnet. **1967** J. Burke *Till Death us do Part* ii. 33 'You know I had hair. I'd still have it, too, if it hadn't been for the war. I saw service.'.. 'A lot of people saw service,' said Mike, 'but they didn't lose their barnets over it.' **1969** G. Sims *Sand Dollar* xi. 146 'Use your barnet!' Domino said.

'barney, *sb.* **1.** In various *dial.* and *slang* uses. **a.** A lark or spree.
1859 HOTTEN *Slang Dict.* 3 *Barney*, a lark, spree, rough enjoyment; 'get up a *barney*', to have a lark. *Barney*, a mob, a crowd.

b. Humbug, cheating; *spec.* an unfair sporting contest.
1865 B. BRIERLEY *Irkdale* II. 19, I won thee i' fair powell one toss an' no barney. **1882** *Even. News* 2 Sept. 1/6 Blackguardly barneys called Boxing Competitions. **1885** *Bell's Life* 3 Jan. 3/4 Few genuine matches have taken place this season,..though exhibitions and barney contests have been plentiful.

c. A noisy dispute or altercation. Also *Austral.* and *N.Z.*
1864 C. R. THATCHER *Colonial Songster* 86 A barney first commenced, in one of their *Celestial* revels. **1885** in Elworthy *W. Somerset Word-bk.* (1886) 45 I'll warn't there'll be a barney over thick job. **1888** 'R. BOLDREWOOD' *Robbery under Arms* II. xiii. 216 We had long talks and barneys over the whole thing. **1895** *Daily News* 4 Jan. 3/7 (E.D.D.), Selby runs out, and goes to get another knife, but I stops him, and the barney was all over. **1916** *Bulletin* (Sydney) 17 Feb. 48/4 We did 'ave a bit of a barney. She tole me I'd better be goin'. **1929** J. B. PRIESTLEY *Good Companions* I. iv. 112 He has a bit of a barney with the other two partners, decides to have a split. **1958** *Encounter* May 12/2 There was a right barney at the other end of the shop. **1958** D. NILAND *Call me when Cross turns over* 200 There should never have been a barney between them in the first place. **1959** *Spectator* 29 May 752/3 That a team will go forward without Maori players..is the only positive conclusion that can be drawn from the barney. **1964** J. BURKE *Hard Day's Night* i. 20 'If you're going to have a barney,' said John, 'I'll hold your coats.'

2. *Mining.* (See quot.)
1881 RAYMOND *Mining Gloss.*, *Barney*, a small car attached to a rope and used to push cars up a slope or inclined plane.

3. Phr. ***Barney's bull***, a worthless person or thing. Also *Austral.* (see quot. 1945).
1908 MASEFIELD *Capt. Margaret* iv. 98 Your trading lay.. is all Barney's bull. It's got more bugs than brains, as you might say. **1929** —— *Hawbucks* 76 Those girls, without any mother, only that old Barney's bull of a da. **1945** BAKER *Austral. Lang.* iv. 88 *All behind like Barney's bull*, delayed, backward (a play on the word *behind*, although the expression is probably as alliterative as it is biological).

barney ('bɑːnɪ), *v.* [f. prec.] **1.** *intr.* To argue, dispute. *dial.*, *Austral.* and *N.Z.*
1880 *Evening Post* (N.Z.) 7 Jan. 13/2 He saw the prisoner and prosecutor 'barneying' in the middle of some strangers. **1890** 'R. BOLDREWOOD' *Col. Reformer* II. xvi. 42 If you go barneying about calves..he'll best ye. **1913** A. BATHGATE *Sodger Sandy's Bairn* x. 77 But I can't barney with you all day.

2. To act or play unfairly; to cheat.
1905 *Daily Chron.* 17 Aug. 4/4 The thirst for money prizes and the gambling craze has brought in 'barneying' and the buying and selling of falls in professional [wrestling] rings. **1908** *Westmorld. Gaz.* 22 Aug. 8/3 Heavyweight wrestling.. Third round..T. T. and G. M. were both blown out for barneying.

barngun ('bɑːngʌn). *dial.* [f. *barn*, dial. var. BURN *v.*[1] + *gun*, dial. var. GOUND (OE. *gund* matter, pus).] An eruption of the skin; shingles.
1746 *Exmoor Courtship* in *Gentl. Mag.* XVI. 300/1 Vorewey struck out and came to a barngun. **1746** 'DEVONIENSIS' *Vocab. Exmoor*, *Ibid.* 405/2 *Barngun*, a breaking out in small pimples, or pustles in the skin. **1869** R. D. BLACKMORE *Lorna Doone* I. xviii. 206 'Thou art not come to me,' she said..'to be struck for bone-shave, nor to be blessed for barn-gun.' **1892** H. C. O'NEILL *Devon. Idyls* 87 When I were bad with the barngun.

barnhardtite ('bɑːnhɑːtaɪt). *Min.* [named from Barnhardt's Land, N. Carolina, where found: see -ITE.] A sulphide of iron and copper, of bronze-yellow colour with grayish-black streak.
1837–68 DANA *Min.* 67.

barnhede, -less, obs. ff. BAIRNHOOD, -LESS.

barnisch, -ish, -ysh, obs. ff. BURNISH.

barnless ('bɑːnlɪs), *a.* Void of barns.
1883 *American* VI. 317 The barnless plains of Montana.

barnnecks: see BEVERNEX.

barnstorm ('bɑːnstɔːm), *v.* [f. BARN *sb.* + STORM *v.* 7.] *intr.* **1.** *Theatr.* To tour (rural districts), giving theatrical performances of a popular kind (formerly often in barns).
1883 *Mercury* (N.Y.) in Ware *Passing Eng.* (1909) 20/1 Miss Helen Bancroft, who recently played in this city, was announced as with a barn-storming company. **1883** *Sporting Life* 29 Apr. 5/3 Footlight Flickerings. Owen Fawcett will go barn-storming through Michigan this summer. **1884** [see BARN *sb.* 2]. **1936** AUDEN & ISHERWOOD *Ascent of F6* II. 79, I have dreamed of a threadbare barnstorming actor, and he was a national symbol. **1949** *Here & Now* (N.Z.) Oct. 30/1 The National Orchestra..has this year been barnstorming with opera, and latterly with concert programmes, taking in provincial centres.

2. To make a rapid tour holding meetings for propaganda or election purposes. *U.S.*
1896 *Congress. Rec.* 7 Apr. 3661/1 [He] was barnstorming down in Georgia in favor of a gold monometallism. **1944** *Chicago Daily News* 27 Oct. 16/2 President Roosevelt indignantly denies that his New York and Chicago barnstorming trips violate his pledge not to campaign in the usual sense. **1947** *Time* 10 Mar. 21/1 Barnstorming Presidential Candidate Harold Stassen whirled through Belgium in one day.

3. *Aeronaut.* To give informal exhibition and sightseeing flights; to perform stunts at local functions. Chiefly *N. Amer.*
1928 L. GRAVATT *Pioneers of Air* 210 He gave exhibitions at county fairs, or barnstormed as the pilots say. **1933** F. B. WILLOUGHBY *Alaskans All* 90, I had an old army plane, and as a gypsy flyer I barnstormed thirty-seven states. **1936** *Christian Sci. Monitor* 20 Aug. 3/4 *Barnstorm*, to fly about from town to town taking passengers up for a small sum. **1936** F. CLUNE *Roaming round Darling* xiii. 116 They were flying from town to town, barnstorming as they called it. **1938** *Times* 19 July 14/5 Mr. Steve Reich, who had barnstormed with him in 1931, was as surprised as everybody else to hear he had flown to Ireland.

Barnum ('bɑːnəm). [The name of Phineas Taylor *Barnum* (1810–91), a pushing American show-proprietor.]
1. Humbug, nonsense; showmanship.
1856 G. D. BREWERTON *War in Kansas* 17 He believed the whole affair to be a 'Barnum'—*alias* humbug, of the most unmitigated kind. *a* **1914** JOYCE *Stephen Hero* (1944) xxi. 117 It's absurd: it's Barnum. He comes into the world God knows how, walks on the water. **1937** *Daily Express* 7 Jan. 10/5 There is a touch of Barnum about scientists which sets them whooping when any one of them has found something new.

2. *Comb.*
1874 W. JAMES *Let.* 8 Aug. (1920) I. vii. 182 The dreadful feeling of wounded pride and Barnum-born resentment may with time fade away. **1899** *Westm. Gaz.* 28 June 2/2 Was there ever a more Barnum-like sort of exhibition?

Hence **Barnumese** [see -ESE]; **Barnumesque** *a.* [see -ESQUE]. Cf. BARNUMIZE *v.*, BARNUMISM.
1888 FARMER *Americanisms* 40/1 We get words like *barnumese* and *telegraphese*, to signify exaggeration of style. **1890** W. J. GORDON *Foundry* 189 A florid prospectus in the best Barnumese. **1890** *Cornh. Mag.* Dec. 629 A perfectly Barnumesque profusion of quaint monstrosities.

Barnumize ('bɑːnəmaɪz), *v.* [f. BARNUM + -IZE.] To exhibit with a lavish display of puffing advertisements. **Barnumism**, exaggerated advertising or display, boastful 'tall talk.'
1851 W. B. HODGSON in *Life* vi. (1883) 87 Barnumised and puffed as Napoleon has been, he is not popular. **1852** *Blackw. Mag.* LXXII. 307 Barnumizing the prodigy through Europe. **1862** *Daily Tel.* 20 Oct., It is Barnumism that prompts clergymen to tell their flocks that they must fight the Confederates till Hell freezes, and then fight them on the ice.

barocco (bə'rɒkəʊ), *a.* and *sb.* [It.] = BAROQUE.
1877 SYMONDS *Renaiss. in Italy* III. ii. 99 Palladio was followed by the violent reactionaries of the *barocco* mannerism. *Ibid.* x. 503 Stucco, fresco, and gilding in a style only just removed from the *barocco*. **1881** S. BUTLER *Alps & Sanct. Piedmont* 332 The architecture is late, and *barocco*, not to say *rococo*, reigns everywhere. *a* **1902** —— *Note-Bks.* (1912) 260 The band played the barocco music on the barocco little piazza and we were all barocco together. **1923** L. PULLAN *Religion Since Reform.* vii. 221 Peter the Great.. pronounced the name of his new capital as if it were Dutch, and his architects built it after the manner of the Dutch and German barocco cities. **1955** E. POUND *Section: Rock-Drill* lxxxvii. 33 Then false fronts, barocco.

baroceptor (bærəʊ'sɛptə(r)). *Physiol.* [f. Gr. βάρο-ς weight + RE)CEPTOR.] A receptor sensitive to changes in pressure. Also *attrib.* Cf. BARORECEPTOR.
1949 C. L. EVANS *Princ. Human Physiol.* (ed. 10) V. xxxii. 595 The nerves originating in the carotid sinus are stimulated by stretch, i.e. they originate from special stretch receptors (baroceptors) in its walls. **1961** *Brit. Med. Dict.* 1218/1 *Pressure receptor*, often called pressoreceptor or baroceptor. **1961** *Lancet* 19 Aug. 439/2 A local modulator of baroceptor response.

barocyclonometer (ˌbærəʊsaɪkləʊ'nɒmɪtə(r)). [f. Gr. βάρο-ς weight + CYCLONE + -METER.] An aneroid barometer with diagrams and directions for detecting the existence of a storm at a distance of several hundred miles.
1906 *Month* Dec. 562 The ships that sail the seas of the Far East are equipped with the Barocyclonometer.

barogram ('bærəgræm). [f. next, after *telegram*.] The record traced by a barograph.
1884 *Leeds Merc.* 24 Mar. 8/5 The barograms obtained from some sixteen observatories.

barograph ('bærəgrɑːf, -æ-). [f. Gr. βάρο-ς weight + -γραφος -writing, -writer; cf. *telegraph*.] A barometer constructed on the aneroid principle, actuating mechanism which records automatically the variations in atmospheric pressure.
1865 *Reader* 9 Sept. 291/3 The self-recording barograph continues in operation. **1884** *Weekly Scotsman* 9 Feb. 4/1 A barometric chart—secured by means of the barograph.

baroko, -oco (bə'rəʊkəʊ). *Logic.* A mnemonic word, representing by its vowels the fourth mood of the second figure of syllogisms, in which the premisses are a universal affirmative and particular negative, and the conclusion a particular negative.
1581 FULKE in *Confer.* III. (1584) Pij b, It is neither in mode nor figure. *Fulke.* It is in Baroco. **1838** SIR W. HAMILTON *Logic* xxii. I. 443 Bocardo, which..with Baroco ..was the opprobrium of the scholastic system of reduction. **1870** BOWEN *Logic* 204 Baroko and Bokardo have been stumbling-blocks to the logicians.

†**'barolite.** [f. Gr. βάρο-ς weight + λίθος stone: see -LITE.] Obs. synonym of WITHERITE.
1794 KIRWAN *Min.* I. 134 Barolite, or aerated Barytes.

Barolo (bə'rəʊləʊ). [Named from *Barolo*, Piedmont, the region of its production.] A full-bodied red wine of Piedmont.
1875 H. VIZETELLY *Wines of World* IX. i. 136 The popular Barolo, a red wine produced from the Nebiolo grape. **1877** *Encycl. Brit.* VI. 272/2 In the vicinity [of Cuneo] a good wine is made called Barolo. **1902** A. BENNETT *Grand Babylon Hotel* xxii. 251 He proceeded to the Italian cellar, and descanted upon the excellence of Barolo from Piedmont. **1959** W. JAMES *Word-bk. Wines* 17 *Barolo*,..is high in alcohol (some 14 degrees or 24·5 proof).

barology (bə'rɒlədʒɪ). [f. Gr. βάρο-ς weight + -λογία discourse.] The scientific study of weight.
1859 in WORCESTER. **1863** MILL *Comte* 39 Physics.. divided by M. Comte into five departments: Barology, or the science of weights; Thermology, etc.

baromacrometer (ˌbærəʊmæ'krɒmɪtə(r)). [f. Gr. βάρο-ς weight + μακρό-ς length + μέτρον measure.] An instrument for ascertaining the weight and length of new-born infants.
1847 in CRAIG.

barometer (bə'rɒmɪtə(r)). Also 7 barrim-. [f. Gr. βάρο-ς weight + μέτρον measure.]
An instrument for determining the weight or pressure of the atmosphere, and hence for judging of probable changes in the weather, ascertaining the height of an ascent, etc.
(The common barometer is a straight glass tube, 34 inches long and closed at the top, filled with mercury, and inverted in an open cup of the same liquid. The ***siphon barometer*** is a curved tube, with the mercury in the shorter limb exposed to the air; it is adapted as the ***wheel barometer*** found in ordinary weather-glasses by putting on the mercury in the shorter limb a float with a cord attached, which passes over a pulley, and as the float rises or falls, moves the indicating hand. For very exact readings a lofty tube filled with glycerine is sometimes used. See also ANEROID.)
1665–6 *Phil. Trans.* I. 153 A Barometer or Baroscope first made publick by that Noble Searcher of Nature, Mr. Boyle. **1672** PETTY *Pol. Anat.* (1691) 48 Changes in the Air.. known by the Instrument call'd the Barrimeter. **1723** MRS. CENTLIVRE *Gamester* I. i, Your fob, like a Barometer, shews the temper of your heart, as that does the weather. **1813** SIR R. WILSON *Diary* II. 278 The Lutzen impression has made the bone of my left leg quite a barometer. [See ANEROID.] *fig.* **1752** HUME *Pol. Disc.* iv. 73 Interest is the true barometer of the State. **1827** HARE *Guesses* Ser. I. (1873) 154 Languages are the barometers of national thought and character. **1870** MISS BRIDGMAN *R. Lynne* I. xi. 173 The barometer of Mr. Selwyn's temper stood at stormy.

b. ***barometer-gauge***: an appliance resembling a barometer, attached to the receiver of an air-pump to indicate the rarity of the air within.
1783 CAVALLO in *Phil. Trans.* LXXIII. 449 A long barometer-gage was adapted to the pump by means of a bent brass tube.

barometric (bærəʊ'mɛtrɪk), *a.* [f. prec. + -IC; cf. Gr. μετρικός of measuring.] **a.** Of the nature of, pertaining to, or indicated by a barometer.
1802 REES *Cycl.* s.v. *Barometer*, The difference of the barometric heights. **1827** FARADAY *Chem. Manip.* xv. 378 The mean height or barometric pressure. **1831** LARDNER *Pneumat.* iv. 253 The column of mercury sustained in the barometric tube. **1854** SCOFFERN in *Orr's Circ. Sc.* Chem. 313 The barometric weather-glass is supplied with a dial index. **1884** F. BRITTEN *Watch & Clockm.* 29 Barometric Error..the alteration in the timekeeping of a clock due to changes in the density of the atmosphere.

b. ***barometric altimeter*** = ALTIMETER 2; ***barometric tendency*** (see quot.).
1930 *Proc. Inst. Radio Engin.* XVIII. 832 The barometric altimeter is adjusted to read altitude above the [landing] field. **1962** *Gloss. Aeronaut. Terms* (*B.S.I.*) v. 11 *Barometric altimeter*, an aneroid barometer graduated to indicate altitude according to a standard atmosphere. **1916** *Weather Map* (*Meteorol. Office*) 36 Barometric tendency..is the change in the pressure..within the three hours immediately preceding the fixed hours of observation.

baro'metrical, *a.* [f. as prec. + -ICAL.] = prec.
1665–6 BOYLE in *Phil. Trans.* I. 181 Barometrical Observations (as for brevities sake I use to call them). **1713** DERHAM *Phys. Theol.* 17 *note*, Barometrical and Thermometrical Instruments. **1751** JOHNSON *Rambl.* No. 117 ⁋9 A complete treatise of barometrical pneumatology. **1874** HARTWIG *Aerial W.* i. 5 The range of barometrical variations.

baro'metrically, *adv.* [f. prec. + -LY[2].] By means of a barometric observation.
1777 SHUCKBURGH in *Phil. Trans.* LXVII. 554 This gives for the height barometrically, 2748·9 ft. **1817** *Edin. Rev.* XXVIII. 180 Heights barometrically ascertained.

barometrograph (ˌbærəʊ'mɛtrəgrɑːf, -æ-). [f. Gr. βάρο-ς weight + μέτρο-ν measure + -γραφος -writing, -writer.] = BAROGRAPH.
1847 in CRAIG.

barometrography (-miː'trɒgrəfɪ). [f. as prec. + Gr. -γραφία description.] The department of science which treats of the barometer.

barometry (bə'rɒmɛtrɪ). [f. BAROMETER; cf. Gr. -μετρία measurement.] The art or science of barometric observation.

1713 SWIFT *Eleg. Partridge* Wks. 1755 III. II. 81 A scrap of parchment hung by geometry (A great refinement in barometry) Can, like the stars, foretel the weather. **1884** GURNEY & MYERS in *19th Cent.* 85 Further light on.. the path and barometry of the psychical storms.

barometz ('bærəmɛts). [App. an erroneous adaptation of Russ. *baranets* (dimin. of *baran* ram') applied to species of Club-moss, *Lycopodium*.] A spurious natural-history specimen, consisting of the creeping root-stock and frond-stalks of a woolly fern (*Cibotium barometz*) turned upside down; formerly represented as a creature half-animal and half-plant, and called the Scythian Lamb (already referred to by Maundevile, ch. xxvi. p. 264).

1791 E. DARWIN *Bot. Gard.* I. 279 Waves, gentle Barometz, thy golden hair. **1835** *Penny Cycl.* III. 485/2.

baron ('bærən). Forms: 2-4 **barun**, 4 **barune, baroune**, 4-6 **baroun, -own**, 5 **baroone, barrown**, 6 **barroun, barne**, 7 **barron**, 3- **baron**. [Early ME. *barun, -oun*, a. OF. *barun, -on*, acc. of *ber* (= Pr. *bar*, acc. *barón, baró*, Sp. *varon*, Pg. *varão*, It. *barone*):—late L. *baro, -ōnem*, of which the ordinary sense was 'man' (interchanging in Salic Law with *homo*), esp. in relation to some one else, as when we say 'the king's man,' passing on one side into 'servant, vassal,' on another into 'man as opposed to *slave*, freeman,' also as opposed to *wife* 'husband,' as opposed to *female* 'male.' Isidore explains *Mercenarii*, as 'qui serviunt accepta mercede, iidem et *barones* Graeco nomine, quod sint fortes in laboribus,' (connecting it with βαρύς); Cornutus (on Persius *Sat.* v.) explains *barones* (to which he attributes a Gaulish origin) as 'servos militum, qui utique stultissimi sunt, servos videlicet stultorum.' This seems to point to the cl. L. *bāro, -ōnem* 'simpleton, blockhead, dunce'; but there is nothing else to show whether this is the same word as *baro* 'man.' The laws of the Alemanns have in the same sense *barus*: if this were the original form, *baro* would be an augmentative.

The ulterior origin is unknown. It has been conjecturally referred to a Celtic **bar* 'hero' (which seems a figment); OHG. *bero*:—OTeut. **beron-* 'bearer, carrier'; a hypothetical Teut. **bar-*, with same sense; OE. *beorn*, 'warrior, brave, hero'; and Teut. *barn* 'bairn, child'; of which some are purely hypothetical, and others fail to explain the form or sense, or both.]

1. *Hist.* Originally, one who held, by military or other honourable service, from the king or other superior; afterwards restricted to the former or *king's barons*, and at length mostly applied to the greater of these (the *Great Barons*) who personally attended the Great Council, or, from the time of Henry III, were summoned by writ to Parliament; *hence*, a lord of Parliament, a noble, a peer.

Historically, all who held directly from the king were ***barons by tenure***, such of these as were summoned to Parliament were ***barons by writ***.

c **1200** *Trin. Coll. Hom.* 177 Þe wraððe of kinges and of barones bringen on þe folkes heorte grete stormes. **1205** LAY. 5319 Ælcches barunes sune. *c* **1275** in *O.E. Misc.* 92 Seynt Thomas wes biscop and barunes him quolde. **1297** R. GLOUC. 511 The barons sende to the king Philip of France, That he hom sende socour. *a* **1300** *Cursor M.* 13028 Iohn.. come right to herods hame Bifor his barounes euerilkane. **1393** LANGL. *P. Pl.* C. VII. 123 Thus beggers and barouns at debat aren ofte. **1485** CAXTON *Chas. Gt.* 144 The Admyral is wyth hys pryncypal barons at souper. **1577** HARRISON *England* II. v. (1877) 107 The baron is such a free lord as hath a lordship or baronie, whereof he beareth his name. **1596** SHAKS. *1 Hen. IV*, IV. iii. 66 The Lords and Barons of the Realme. **1603** DRAYTON (*title*) The Barrons War. **1614** SELDEN *Titles Hon.* 274 Which makes me think that, before Henry III., as well Barons of Earls as the King's Barons came to Parliament. **1641** MILTON *Ch. Govt.* Wks. (1851) 131 Cling fast to your Pontificall Sees.. quit yourselves like Barons. **1768** BLACKSTONE *Comm.* I. I. xii. 310 A baron's is the most general and universal title of nobility. **1782** PRIESTLEY *Corrupt. Chr.* II. x. 259 [Bishops] though churchmen.. actually were barons. **1799** J. ROBERTSON *Agric. Perth.* 40 A proprietor holding immediately of the crown, and having his lands either erected or confirmed by the king into a free barony.. is the only person, in strict law, denominated a baron. **1835** *Penny Cycl.* III. 487/1 Lesser Barons, or Barons of the Barons. *Ibid.* 489/2 Burford in Shropshire is also called a barony, and its former lords.. were called, in instruments of authority, barons of Burford, but had never summons to parliament nor privileges of peerage. **1863** COX *Inst. Eng. Govt.* I. vii. 65 The council of the king was a council of barons. **1876** FREEMAN *Norm. Conq.* V. xxiv. 412 The Barons of England, a name made dear to us by the great struggle of the thirteenth century.

2. a. A specific order or rank, being the lowest grade of nobility.

From the earliest period we find *baron* distinguished from *earl*, as the designation of an *untitled* military tenant; the name may be considered to have itself become a title, as distinct from a description of feudal relationship or of parliamentary privilege, with the creation of barons by patent, which began in the reign of Richard II.

a **1200** *Trin. Coll. Hom.* 35 Ne to kinge.ne to eorle.ne to barun. **1280** *Signs bef. Judgm.* in *E.E.P.* (1862) 10 Boþe kniȝt and barun.erl.and king. **1377** LANGL. *P. Pl.* B. XIII. 165 Neyther emperour ne emperesse, erl, kynge, ne baroun. *c* **1500** *Lancelot* 1684 Thi dukis, erlis, and thi gret baronis, Thi pur knychtis, and thi bachleris. *a* **1674** CLARENDON *Hist. Reb.* I. I. 10 In a short time.. he was made a Baron. **1690** TEMPLE *Heroic Virt.* Wks. 1731 I. 218 By Barons are now meant in England, such as are created by Patent, and thereby called to the House of Lords. **1790** BURKE *Fr. Rev.* Wks. V. 44 A sermon from.. a noble earl, or baron bold. **1884** *Lond. Gaz.* 4 Nov., The Queen has been pleased to direct letters patent to be passed under the Great Seal, granting the dignity of a Baron of the United Kingdom and Ireland unto the undermentioned persons.

b. A magnate in commerce, finance, or the like; a great merchant in a certain commodity, usu. defined by a qualifying word, as ***beef baron, coal baron***. (Cf. KING *sb.* 6 a.) orig. *U.S.*

[**1776** J. ADAMS *Familiar Lett.* (1876) 154 But the spirit of these Barons [*sc.* North Carolina gentry] is coming down, and it must submit.] **1818** *Niles' Reg.* XIV. 226/1 The name of a *Jew* and '*rag-baron*' is synonimous. **1885** *Century Mag.* Sept. 804 Who is responsible for [the depression]?.. Is it the 'silver barons' or the 'gold bugs'? **1887** *Harper's Mag.* Apr. 822/1 When the great 'coal barons'.. deliberately combine to put up the price of coal. **1894** J. L. FORD *Lit. Shop* (1896) iv. 46 Magazine barons. **1902** *Westm. Gaz.* 17 May 5/2 Nearly 150,000 coalminers are on strike in the anthracite region of Pennsylvania... The coal barons have built barricades and barbed wire fences around the shafts. **1904** 'O. HENRY' *Cabbages & Kings* 4 A rubber prince, a sarsaparilla, indigo, and mahogany baron. **1907** *Westm. Gaz.* 20 Dec. 9/4 The American beef barons, Armour's, Swift's, and Morris, are.. the greatest captains of commerce in any market. **1932** *Ann. Reg. 1931* 15 The 'money barons' were using the whole of their influence to restrict the raising of money for national development. **1932** WODEHOUSE *Louder & Funnier* 24 A couple of great film barons. **1947** J. HAYWARD *Prose Lit. since 1939* 47 Newspaper barons and film magnates have shown that it is not difficult to bend authors to their own desires. **1958** *Listener* 18 Dec. 1030/2 He became one of those barons who advance their fortunes under the slogan of National Trade.

c. Applied *gen.* to a person having power or influence in any sphere; in *Prison slang*: see quot. 1950.

1876 R. L. STEVENSON *Walking Tours* in *Cornh. Mag.* June 687 The great barons of the mind will not rally to the standard. **1919** *Athenæum* 15 Aug. 759/1 Slang in War-time... Baron, army commander. **1950** P. TEMPEST *Lag's Lexicon* 10 A baron is one who always has plenty of money and/or tobacco. **1958** F. NORMAN *Bang to Rights* I. 23 If people can't be barons with out going around punching little geezers up in the air. **1959** *Listener* 10 Dec. 1050/1 A round dozen barons of the microscope, from Cambridge, London, Edinburgh, Paris, Pennsylvania, Wisconsin, California, Moscow.

†**3.** Anciently applied to the freemen of London, York, and some other places, who were homagers of the king, bound to suit and service; applied till the 18th c. to the freemen of the Cinque Ports, who had the feudal service of bearing the canopy over the head of the sovereign on the day of coronation; and, till the Reform Bill of 1832, to the burgesses returned by these ports to Parliament. *Obs.*

[*a* **1259** MATT. PARIS (in Spelman) Londonienses quos.. Barones consuevimus appellare.] **1598** HAKLUYT *Voy.* I. 17 Writs.. directed.. to the Bailifes of Hastings, Hithe, Rumney, Douer, and Sandwich, commanding them, that they should cause twentie and foure of their Barons (for so their Burgesses, or townesmen, and the citizens of London likewise, were wont to be termed) to appeare. **1613** SHAKS. *Hen. VIII*, IV. i. 48 They that beare The Cloath of Honour ouer her, are foure Barons Of the Cinque-Ports. **1641** *Harl. Misc.* (Malh.) V. 49 They choose the knights and citizens, and burgesses, or barons, for so the citizens were anciently called; and the cinque-ports retain that name to this day. **1702** *Lond. Gaz.* No. 3804/1 Then the Queen.. under a Canopy born by twelve Barons of the Cinque-Ports. **1753** CHAMBERS *Cycl. Supp.* s.v., Barons of the cinque ports, are members of the house of commons elected by the five ports, two for each port. **1861** *Times* 29 Aug., 'Baron' in London and in the Cinque Ports was but another name for 'freeman.'

4. Title of the judges of the Court of Exchequer (the president being the ***Chief Baron***). (As to origin of this, see quot. 1751.)

[**1130** *Pipe Roll 31 Hen. I*, Barones Scaccarii.] **1377** LANGL. *P. Pl.* B. III. 319 Al shal be but one Courte, and one baroun be iustice. **1502** ARNOLD *Chron.* 41 The Tresourer and Barnes and other Ministers of the cheker. **1556** *Chron. Grey Friars* (1852) 71 Theys ware the commyshoners,—the lorde cheffe barne, doctor Olyver, &c. **1751** CHAMBERS *Cycl.* s.v., Barons of the exchequer.. are called *Barons*, because Barons of the realm were used to be employed in that office. **1827** HALLAM *Const. Hist.* (1876) II. xi. 360 The barons of the exchequer.. were to issue process. **1884** *Oliver and Boyd's Almanac* 541 IRELAND.. Her Majesty's Court of Appeal, the Lord Chancellor, the Lord Chief Justice.. the Lord Chief Baron of the Exchequer.

5. *Law* and *Her.* (conjoined with *feme, femme*): Husband.

[**1292** BRITTON II. iii. §6 Ne femmes espouses sauntz lour barouns.] **1594** PARSONS *Confer. Success.* II. iv. 92 If a baron match with a femme that is an inheretrix. **1611** GWILLIM *Heraldry* V. i. 254 The bearing of the Armes of the Femme by the Baron after issue receiued by her. **1678** *Lond. Gaz.* No. 1332/4 Baron and Feme in the first six coats quartered. **1845** STEPHEN *Laws of Eng.* II. 238 Husband and wife, or, as most of our elder law books call them, baron and feme. **1862** BURTON *Bk. Hunter* II. 132 Baron and feme we call husband and wife, and coverture we term marriage.

6. As a foreign title (giving no rank or privileges in Britain).

e.g. Baron Rothschild, Baron de Worms.

‖**7.** In foreign use applied in respect or honour to any man, also to Christ and the saints.

a **1300** *Cursor M.* 16876 Ioseph, þat god barune. **1534** LD. BERNERS *Gold. Bk. M. Aurel.* (1546) C v, Comode Calcedonien, an auncient baron whiche expounded to hym Homer. **1867** LONGF. *Dante's Parad.* xxv. 17 Look, look! behold the Baron [St. James of Compostella], for whom below Galicia is frequented.

8. ***Baron of Beef*** [of unknown origin; possibly a distinct word]: a joint consisting of two sirloins left uncut at the backbone.

1755 in JOHNSON (quoted from some earlier Dict.), *Baron of Beef* is when the two sirloins are not cut asunder, but joined together by the end of the backbone. **1822** KITCHINER *Cook's Orac.* Introd., The Baron of Beef was another favorite and substantial support of Old English Hospitality. *a* **1859** L. HUNT *Rob. Hood* IV. xvi, A bishop was a baron of beef With cut and come again. **1864** *Times* 24 Dec., On Thursday the Royal 'baron of beef' was roasted, under the superintendence of Mr. Godfrey, the Queen's cook.

9. *Comb.* **baron-bailie** (*Sc.*), a bailie or magistrate appointed by the lord-superior in a burgh of barony. Hence **baron-bailie-court, baron-court**, the court of justice held by a baron in his barony. (See also COURT-BARON.)

1753 *Stewart's Trial* App. 145, I intend.. to hold a Baron-balie-court on the estate of Ardshiel. **1813** N. CARLISLE *Topogr. Dict. Scot.* II, The Baron-Baillie Court of Macleod, the Chief, is the only Court of Justice in the Parish. **1818** SCOTT *Hrt. Midl.* xxvii, There was a Baron Court to be held at Loanhead that day, and.. he was acquainted with the baron-bailie.

baron, obs. form of BARN, BAIRN.

†**baronady.** *Obs.* [f. BARON: the origin of the suffix does not appear.]

1. The dignity or rank of baron.

1586 FERNE *Blaz. Gentrie* Ep. Ded., Some that were honored with the dignity of Baronady.

2. The body of barons collectively.

1587 FLEMING *Contn. Holinshed* III. 1365/1 How stoutlie the kings & the baronadie of England.. haue so repelled the popes vsurpations.

baronage ('bærənɪdʒ). Forms: 3-6 **barnage**, 4 **barunage, barunnage**, 6 **barnag, barronage**, 4- **baronage**. [ME. *barnage*, a. OF. *barnage, bernage*:—L. type **bārōnāticum*, f. *barōn-em*, but actually latinized in Middle Ages *barnagium, baronagium*, whence *baronage* and mod.F. *baronnage*.]

1. The body of barons collectively; the great vassals of the Crown; the nobles, lords, peerage.

a **1300** *Floriz & Bl.* 639 After his barnage he haþ isend. *a* **1300** *Cursor M.* 4649 Al þat barunage, less and mare. *Ibid.* 8016 Bath to þe and to þi barnage. *c* **1400** *Rom. Rose* 5815 The baronage to councel went. *c* **1420** *Chron. Vilod.* 269 With all hurre faderes holle barnage. **1535** STEWART *Cron. Scot.* II. 86 All oure barnage into bandone brocht. **1589** WARNER *Alb. Eng.* V. xxv. (1597) 123 Ciuill warres betwixt the King and Barronage. **1649** SELDEN *Laws of Eng.* I. lviii. (1739) 109 The Judges in this Court were the Baronage of England. **1738** *Hist. Crt. Excheq.* i. 5 The greatest Part of the Baronage was summoned to Parliament. **1855** MACAULAY *Hist. Eng.* IV. 317 That authority which had belonged to the baronage of England ever since the foundation of the monarchy. **1876** GREEN *Short Hist.* ii. §4 (1882) 71 The most turbulent baronage in Christendom.

b. *fig.* applied to: The angels.

1340 *Ayenb.* 58 Beuore god and al þe baronage of heuene.

c. *ellipt.* A list of the barons; a book containing such a list with historical and other particulars; a 'Peerage.'

†**2.** The domain of a baron; a barony. *Obs.*

1475 *Bk. Noblesse* (1860) 55 The governaunce of.. a roiaume, dukedom, erledom, barnage, or seignourie. **1480** CAXTON *Chron. Eng.* cii. 84 The saxons helden the Countees, baronages, lordshippes.. in maner as the britons byfore tyme had compaced hem.

3. The dignity or rank of a baron.

1614 SELDEN *Titles Hon.* (1614) 290 All Dignities aboue Baron is included in the Baronage. **1642** W. BIRD *Mag. Hon.* 94 The dignity of Baronage unto them descended by women.

†**4.** The relation of a baron to his lord superior; homage. *Obs.*

1671 F. PHILIPPS *Reg. Necess.* 436 By the Bond of his homage or Baronage to do all things as his Baron.. to be his Liege-man, and more extraordinary Subject.

†**5.** (see quot.) *Obs.*

1678 PHILLIPS, *Baronage*, a Tax, or Subsidy of Aid, to be levied for the King out the Precincts of Baronies.

baroness ('bærənɪs). Forms: 5 **barnesse, baronys, -es, -esse, baronnesse**, 6- **baroness**. [a. OF. *barnesse, -onnesse*, in med.L. *baronissa*: see BARON and -ESS.] **a.** The wife of a baron. **b.** A lady holding a baronial title 'in her own right.'

c **1420** *Chron. Vilod.* 116 Bothe erlys and barnesse and ladyes clere. *c* **1420** in Wright *Voc.* 194/2 *Baronissa*, baronys. **1483** CAXTON *G. de la Tour* I v b, The example of a baronnesse or wyf of a baron. **1529** *Act 21 Hen. VIII*, xiii. §28 Any Duchess, Marquess, Countess, Viscountess, or Baroness. **1695** *Lond. Gaz.* No. 3059/1 Assistants of the Chief Mourner were two Dutchesses, twelve Countesses, and four Baronesses. **1822** BYRON *Werner* IV. i. 65 He is to espouse the gentle Baroness. **1884** *Harper's Mag.* July 260/2 A baroness in her own right.

baronet ('bærənɪt), *sb.* Forms: 4 **baronete,** 5–6 **-ette,** 6 **barronett,** 5– **baronet.** [dim. of BARON: see -ET[1].]

†**1.** *orig.* A word meaning *young, little,* or *lesser baron,* found as a title from the 14th c. According to Spenser (*State of Ireland*) originally applied to gentlemen, not barons by tenure, summoned to the House of Lords by Edward III; perhaps to the heirs of barons summoned by writ in their fathers' life-time. Applied in Ireland to the holder of a small barony. Often used as synonymous with BANNERET. *Obs.*

a **1400** *Chester Pl.* 172 All that heare be sette, Barrones, burges and baronete. *c* **1460** *Launfal* 56 No nother man was yn halle ysette, But he wer prelat, other baronette. *c* **1475** in Wright *Voc.* 262 *Barunculus,* baronet. **1523** LD. BERNERS *Froiss.* I. liii. 75 He departed fro Gaunt with vii. erles of his contrey, viii. prelates, xxviii. baronettes [F. *vingt-huit bannerets*], ii. C. knyghtes. **1596** SPENSER *State Irel.* (J.) The which barrons, they say, were not afterwards lordes but only barronetts, as sundrye of them doe yet retayne the name. **1617** MORYSON *Itin.* III. III. iii. 157 Thomastowne, and the ancient City Rheban, now a poore Village with a Castle, yet of old giuing the title of Baronet. **1662** FULLER *Worthies* I. 111 Ancient Baronets..promiscuously blended with Bannerets, (Sir Ralph Fane in a Patent passed unto him, is expressly term'd a Baronet).

2. *now,* A titled order, the lowest that is hereditary, ranking next below a baron, having precedence of all orders of knighthood, except that of the Garter. A baronet is a commoner, the principle of the order being 'to give rank, precedence, and title without privilege.'

They consist of ***Baronets of England*** (now of *Great Britain*) instituted in 1611, to raise money for the settlement of Ulster by the fees paid for the dignity; ***Baronets of Scotland*** (or of *Nova Scotia*) instituted 1625 for the encouragement of the planting and settling of Nova Scotia; ***Baronets of Ireland*** instituted 1619. Of the two latter there have been no new creations since 1707 and 1801 respectively.

1614 SELDEN *Titles Hon.* 355 Baronet became a new erected distinct Title vnder our present Soueraigne. **1702** J. CHAMBERLAYNE *St. Gt. Brit.* I. III. iv. (1743) 169 The next degree to Barons, are Baronets, which is the lowest degree of Honour that is Hereditary. **1751** CHAMBERS *Cycl.* s.v., Both a baronet and his eldest son, being of full age, may claim knighthood. **1785** BURKE *Nab. Arcot's Debts* Wks. IV. 195 The prosecutor of the worthy baronet. **1826** DISRAELI *Viv. Grey* II. xii. 58 Baronets with blood older than the creation. **1855** MACAULAY *Hist. Eng.* xix. (L.) A decided majority of.. rustic baronets and squires.

3. ***baronet's hand***: the 'bloody hand,' or hand gules in a field argent (the arms of Ulster), granted by James I to English baronets to be borne on a canton or in an escutcheon on their shield, in allusion to the purpose for which the order was instituted.

1710 *Lond. Gaz.* No. 4654/3 Two Salts, Ermine and Baronets Hand, 1 Saucepan.

baronet ('bærənɛt), *v.* Pa. t. and pple. **-eted.** [f. prec. sb.; cf. *to knight.*] *trans.* To raise to the rank of baronet. (Mostly in *passive.*)

a **1733** NORTH *Exam.* III. vii. ¶73 He had deserved to have been Baronetted. **1819** SOUTHEY *Lett.* (1856) III. 116, I have long expected that Scott would be baronetted. **1872** M. COLLINS *Two Plunges* III. viii. 210 The unfortunate gentlemen whom I notice as being knighted or baroneted.

baronetage ('bærənɪtɪdʒ). [f. BARONET *sb.* + -AGE: cf. *baronage.*]

1. The rank of baronet.

1760 T. HUTCHINSON *Hist. Col. Mass.* i. (1765) 128 He obtained also a grant of a baronettage of Nova-Scotia. **1818** *Blackw. Mag.* III. 711 Baronetages have been conferred on them.

2. The order of baronets, the body of baronets collectively.

1876 *Echo* 6 Dec. 1/6 This family is of great antiquity, and in point of precedence the second in the baronetage. **1882** *Standard* 30 Dec. 2/4 In the Baronetage the following deaths have taken place.

b. A list of the order of baronets; a book giving such a list with historical and other particulars.

1720 A. COLLINS (*title-p.*) The Baronettage of England, being an Historical and Genealogical Account of Baronets. *c* **1815** MISS AUSTEN *Persuas.* (1833) I. i. 215 Sir Walter Elliot..for his own amusement, never took up any book but the Baronetage. (*Titles of Annuals*) Burke's Peerage and Baronetage; Debrett's Baronetage with Knightage.

baronetcy ('bærənɪtsɪ). [f. as prec. + -CY.] A baronet's position or rank; a baronet's patent.

1812 *Examiner* 23 Nov. 745/1 The advancement of the Proprietor..to a Baronetcy. **1845** DISRAELI *Sybil* (1863) 87 A baronetcy has become the distinction of the middle class ..some of our tradesmen; brewers, or people of that class. **1879** BURKE *Peerage and Bar.* Pref. Note, The false assumption of baronetcies still continues.

baroneted ('bærəˌnɛtɪd), *ppl. a.* Raised to the rank of baronet.

1873 *Echo* 14 Oct. 4/3 The baroneted chief magistrate.

baronetess ('bærənɪˌtɛs). *rare.* [f. BARONET + -ESS.] The wife of a baronet.

1652 BROME *Damoiselle* I. ii, My Daughter here, that was, But now a Barronetesse in Reversion. **1878** F. WILLIAMS *Midl. Railw.* 453 The ghost of one Lady Bolles, a 'baronetess,' the only one ever made. [A sense due only to popular error.]

'baronethood. [f. as prec. + -HOOD.] The degree or rank of baronet; baronetcy.

1869 *Pall Mall. G.* 18 Dec. 2 What is necessary to become a knight..How may a baronethood be achieved?

baro'netical, *a.* [f. as prec. + -ICAL.] Of or pertaining to baronets.

1863 BURKE *Viciss. Fam.* III. 5 The old Baronetical family of Piers. **1883** *Illust. Lond. News,* A scion of the baronetical family of Mostyn of Falacre.

baronetize ('bærənɪtaɪz), *v.* [f. BARONET + -IZE.] *trans.* To confer a baronetcy on, make a baronet. Also *transf.*

1860 MEREDITH *Evan Harrington* xiv. 164 *Third* son! Don't commit yourself there. We dare not baronetize him. **1892** T. G. HAKE *Mem. 80 Years* lxv. 276 We have no 'Sir Barry' nowadays; premiers do not build houses, so that they do not baronetize architecture. **1967** K. GILES *Death & Mr. Prettyman* i. 32 The late Sir Ebenezer had been a jerry builder..whom Lloyd George had baronetized for war services.

baronetship ('bærənɪt-ʃɪp). = BARONETCY.

1661 MORGAN *Sph. Gentry* IV. ii. 37 John Newton..on whom the Baronetship is entailed.

baronial (bə'rəʊnɪəl), *a.* [f. BARONY + -AL[1].] Of or pertaining to a baron or the barons; befitting the rank of a baron.

1767 LD. LYTTELTON *Hist. Hen. II.* Introd. (T.) The policy to which he subjected other baronial possessions. **1837** HOWITT *Rur. Life* I. iii. (1862) 20 Some splendid baronial Castle, as Warwick, Alnwick, or Raby. **1863** COX *Inst. Eng. Govt.* I. vii. 63 The bishops of the new sees..never had any estate by baronial tenure.

baronian (bə'rəʊnɪən), *a.* [f. BARON(Y + -IAN.] = BARONIAL *a.*

1656 PRYNNE *Fund. Rights of Eng. Freemen* 31 The particulars whereof would amount to many Baronian Tomes, if at large recorded. **1905** *Daily Chron.* 14 June 4/7 The castle is built of granite, in the Scotch Baronian style.

'baronism. *rare.* [f. BARON *sb.* + -ISM.] The baronial system, feudalism.

1884 *Harper's Mag.* Aug. 422/2 The spirit of Norman baronism..and the spirit of Anglo-Saxon freedom.

'baronist. *rare.* [see -IST; cf. *royalist.*] An adherent of the Barons' party.

1611 SPEED *Hist. Gt. Brit.,* A faithlesse Baronist.

'baronize, *v. rare.* [see -IZE.] *trans.* To make or create (any one) a baron.

1611 BARREY *Ram Alley* III. in Dodsley *O.P.* V. 469 Didst thou not swear thou shouldst be baroniz'd? [cf. 439, I stand in hope To be created baron.]

‖**baronnette** (bærəʊ'nɛt). [mod.F., dim. of *baronne* baroness.] A little baroness, a baron's daughter; sometimes used for the wife of a baronet.

1861 TROLLOPE *Barchester T.* 290 A leash of baronets with their baronnettes.

baronry ('bærənrɪ). ? *Obs.* Forms: 5 **barunrie,** 6 **-onrie, barronry,** 5– **baronry.** [f. BARON + -RY; cf. late OF. *baronnerie,* in same senses.]

1. The domain of a baron; a barony.

c **1449** PECOCK *Repr.* III. xviii. 400 Lordschipis of barunries. **1483** *Cath. Angl.* 22/1 Baronry (*v.r.* Barony), *baronia.* ? **1530** *Dyal. betw. Gent. & Husb.* 136 (D.) Many noble baronries & erldomes, With esquyres landes & knightes fees. **1607** HIERON *Wks.* I. 102 When a great man carries the name of his baronry. **1736** J. M'URE *Hist. Glasgow* (1830) 182 Minister of the baronry church of Glasgow.

2. The rank or dignity of baron.

? *a* **1600** *Earles Chester* 43 in Furniv. *Percy Folio* I. 274 Robert fitz Norman..in whose heyre[s] that Barronry succession had 226 yeeres. **1648** PRYNNE *Plea for Lords* C, By vertue of their Peerage, Baronries, and Offices.

3. The body of barons; the barons collectively.

1653 A. WILSON *Jas. I,* 187 Gentlemen, who had procured those Titles, to perch above the English Baronry.

'baronship. [see -SHIP.] The office or position of a baron; *e.g.* of Baron of the Exchequer.

1874 *Daily News* 17 Feb. 3/6 The Chief Baronship of the Court of Exchequer.

barony ('bærənɪ). Forms: 3–7 **baronie,** 4 **barnye,** 4–5 **baronye,** 5– **barony.** [a. OF. *baronie*:—late L. **baronia*: see BARON and -Y. Cf. BARNÉ.]

1. The domain of a baron: **a.** *strictly.*

1297 R. GLOUC. 479 He ȝef him & is eirs the noble baronie. **1340** *Ayenb.* 38 þet..nimeþ þe cites, þe casteles, þe londes, þe baronyes. **1470–85** MALORY *Arthur* (1816) II. 413 King Arthur gave unto every each of them a barony of lands. **1614** SELDEN *Titles Hon.* 274 Lands and Mannors..of sufficient reuenue and qualitie to make what was accounted a Baronie, which was xiii. Knights Fees, and a Third part. **1649** MILTON *Eikon.* iv. Wks. (1851) 364 The People, that drove the Bishops out of their Baronies. **1860** FORSTER *Grand Remonstr.* 29 A baron claimed his barony not as a lord..but as a proprietor. **1876** FREEMAN *Norm. Conq.* V. xxiv. 417 To say that the Bishops sit in Parliament simply because they hold baronies runs counter to all the facts of our history.

b. In Ireland: A division of a county; see quot.

1596 SPENSER *State Irel.* (T.) That in every county or barony they should keep another able schoolmaster. **1607** DAVIES *1st Let. Earl Salisb.* (1787) 229 The county of Monaghan was divided into five baronies. **1672** PETTY *Pol. Anat.* (1691) 326 In Ireland..an head constable for each barony or hundred, being 252. **1752** CARTE *Hist. Eng.* III. 577 Baronies, into which the Irish counties are divided as the English are into hundreds. **1873** *Gen. Rep. Census Eng.* IV. 181 The Baronies appear to have been formed successively on the submission of the Irish chiefs..the territory of each constituting a barony.

c. In Scotland: A large freehold estate or manor, even though the proprietor is a simple commoner.

1843 *Oliver & Boyd's Almanac* 473 Incorporated Trades of the Barony of Calton [Edinburgh]. **1854** H. MILLER *Sch. & Schm.* v. 97 The proprietor of the Barony, who lived at a distance, and had no dwelling upon the land. *Mod.* The best farm in the whole barony.

†**2.** The body of barons collectively, the baronage. *Obs.* (Cf. BARNÉ.)

1297 R. GLOUC. 535 The Erl of Gloucetre Richard deide tho, Tho was the baronie wel in the more wo. *c* **1300** *Beket* 1105 The King and al his Baronie: and his Bischops echon. *c* **1450** *Merlin* vi. 106 Alle the baronye come to the mynster. **1596** DRAYTON *Leg.* iii. 445 The bold Barony.

3. The rank or dignity of baron; the office of Baron of the Exchequer; baronship.

1788 H. WALPOLE *Remin.* vii. 52 A barony, a red riband, and a good place for her brother. **1868** *Daily News* 6 July, The lowest order in the English peerage—a barony. **1885** *Law Times* 14 Mar. 347/2 The abolition of the Chief Justiceship of the Common Pleas, and the Chief Barony.

4. The tenure by which a baron held of his superior; military or other 'honourable' tenure.

1863 COX *Inst. Eng. Govt.* I. vii. 63 William the Conqueror changed the spiritual tenure of frankalmoign or free alms.. into the feudal tenure by barony.

baroque (bə'rəʊk), *a.* and *sb.* [a. F. *baroque* adj., ad. Pg. *barroco,* Sp. *barrueco,* rough or imperfect pearl; of uncertain origin.

In earlier Sp., Minsheu 1623 has '*berruca, berruga* a wart' (evidently L. *verruca*), also '*berrueco* a hillocke, a wart,' '*berrocál* a place full of hillocks'; mod. Pg. has besides *barroco* 'rough or Scotch pearl,' *barroca* 'a gutter made by a water-flood' Vieyra, 'uneven stony ground' (Diez), which native etymologists refer to Arab. *burāq,* pl. of *burqah* 'hard earth mixed with stones, pebbly place' (Freytag). Diez has also suggested confusion of the ending with *roca, rocca* rock: the forms in *o, ue,* cannot come directly from L. *verrūca.* Littré's suggestion that the word is identical with the logical term *baroko* seems to rest on no historical evidence; yet form-association with that may have influenced the later Eng. and Fr. use.]

A. *adj.* Irregularly shaped; whimsical, grotesque, odd. ('Originally a jeweller's term, soon much extended in sense.' Brachet.) Applied *spec.* to a florid style of architectural decoration which arose in Italy in the late Renaissance and became prevalent in Europe during the 18th century. Also *absol.* as *sb.* and *transf.* in reference to other arts.

This term and *rococo* are not infrequently used without distinction for styles of ornament characterized by profusion, oddity of combinations, or abnormal features generally.

1765 H. FUSELI tr *Winkelmann's Refl. Painting & Sculpt. of Greeks* 122 This style in decorations got the epithet of *Barroque* taste, derived from a word signifying pearls and teeth of unequal size. **1846** *Athenæum* 17 Jan. 58/2 Sometimes *baroque,* Mr. Browning is never ignoble: pushing versification to the extremity of all rational allowances, and sometimes beyond it, with a hardihood of rhythm and cadence little short of Hudibrastic. **1851** SIR F. PALGRAVE *Norm. & Eng.* I. Introd. 44 Which rendered every name and thing connected with the mediæval times baroque or absurd. **1867** HOWELLS *Ital. Journ.* 77 The building..coldly classic or frantically baroque. **1877** *Baedeker's Central Italy & Rome* (ed. 5) p. lix, The authors of the degenerated Renaissance known as Baroque were really Vignola (1507–73) and Fontana's nephew Carlo Maderna (1556–1639)... An undoubted vigour in the disposition of detail, a feeling for vastness and pomp, together with an internal decoration which spared neither colour nor costly material to secure an effect of dazzling splendour: such are the distinguishing attributes of the Baroque style. **1882** A. B. HOPE *Brandreths* I. i. 3 Studded with baroque pearls. **1921** B. F. FLETCHER *Hist. Archit.* (ed. 6) I. 546 In the fullness of time the Renaissance..passed into the Baroque, which at the beginning of the seventeenth century gave expression once again to the human side in architecture, for it was a spontaneous breaking away from orthodoxy in plan, design, and treatment. **1928** *Times Lit. Suppl.* 15 Mar. 188/2 French-Canadian art..is being recognized..as a baroque style which is other than the European baroques. **1938** W. S. MAUGHAM *Summing Up* 28 The sonorous periods and the baroque massiveness of Jacobean language. **1938** *Mod. Lang. Notes* Oct. 547 The period of literature..described as 'baroque' ends about 1690, when German baroque architecture..is beginning to develop. **1949** *Times Lit. Suppl.* 10 June 376/4 The word 'baroque'..has come to be accepted as a convenient portmanteau term which covers the music composed between 1580 and 1750 and the plastic arts of an era which begins and ends slightly earlier. **1953** O. DE MOURGUES (*title*) Metaphysical, Baroque and Précieux Poetry. **1953** J. N. SUMMERSON *Archit. Brit. 1530 to 1830* III. 125 (*heading*) Wren and the Baroque (1660–1710). *Ibid.* xvii. 172 At Blenheim the English Baroque culminates. *Ibid.* 178 Its spirit is the emotional spirit of English Baroque, and it was that which touched Burlington's antipathies. **1954** L. D. ETTLINGER in *Listener* 2 Dec. 954/1 The robustness of the Baroque gives way [in the 18th cent.] to the gentler graces of Rococo. **1957** T. S. ELIOT *On Poetry & Poets* 167 The conjunction of Christian and classical imagery[in *Lycidas*] is in accord with a baroque taste which did not please the eighteenth century.

B. *sb.* Grotesque or whimsical ornamentation.

1879 BARING-GOULD *Germany* II. 358 French baroque was too much under Palladian influence to be other than formal.

baroreceptor (ˌbærəʊrɪˈseptə(r)). *Physiol.* [f. Gr. βαρό-ς weight + RECEPTOR.] = BAROCEPTOR.

1951 *Jrnl. Physiol.* CXIII. 450 The carotid sinus nerve is a mixed afferent nerve containing afferents from the baroreceptors of the carotid sinus. **1955** *Sci. News* XXXV. 81 Preliminary investigations have not proved that this plexus can function as a baroreceptor, i.e. that it is sensitive to changes in pressure and capable of transmitting such information.

baroscope (ˈbærəskəʊp). [f. Gr. βάρο-ς weight + -σκοπος -observing, -observer.]

† **1.** An instrument for indicating variations in the density of the atmosphere; a kind of barometer.

(The Statical Baroscope or Barometer of Boyle consisted of a large glass bubble exactly balanced by a small brass weight; increased density of the atmosphere giving greater support to the bubble, but not sensibly affecting the brass weight, the rise or fall of the former corresponded to that of the mercury in a barometer.)

1665 *Phil. Trans.* I. 31 A Baroscope, or an Instrument to shew all the Minute Variations in the Pressure of the Air. **1675** *Phil. Trans.* X. 490 That useful instrument the Baroscope, telling the changes of the weather beforehand. **1751** CHAMBERS *Cycl.* s.v. *Barometer*, The baroscope..in strictness, being a machine that barely shews an alteration in the weight of the atmosphere..To measure how much that difference is..is the business of the barometer.

2. An instrument designed, when placed under the air-pump, to show that bodies in air lose as much weight as that of the air they displace.

1881 in *Syd. Soc. Lex.*

baroscopic (bærəʊˈskɒpɪk), *a.* [f. prec. + -IC.] Pertaining to or indicated by the baroscope. **baroˈscopical** *a.* = prec.

1665–6 *Phil. Trans.* I. 182 That some Inquisitive men would make Baroscopical Observations. **1847** in CRAIG.

† **ˈbaroˈselenite.** *Min. Obs.* [f. BAR-YTES + SELENITE; see quot.] Native sulphate of barium; now called BARITE or BARYTES.

1786 *Phil. Trans.* LXXVI. 130 The solution of acetous baro-selinite (that is, ponderous earth dissolved in distilled vinegar). **1811** PINKERTON *Petral.* II. 138 Mr. Kirwan calls this kind of barytes, *baroselenite*; because it resembles selenite, or gypsum crystallised in plates.

barostat (ˈbærəʊstæt). [f. Gr. βάρο-ς weight + -STAT.] An automatic apparatus for regulating pressure; *spec.* a device that controls the pressure of fuel.

1929 F. DANIELS et al. *Exper. Phys. Chem.* xviii. 301 The Bureau of Mines has developed a barostat for use in vacuum distillations. **1946** *Jrnl. R. Aeronaut. Soc.* I. 363/2 Failures of fuel pumps, barostats and throttle valves were still far too common. **1951** *Engineering* 30 Mar. 368/1 A barostat-controlled timing device automatically opens the pilot's parachute. **1956** *Flight* 8 June 696/2 The pilot is automatically released from his seat after three seconds, whereupon the barostat in his parachute pack will ensure free fall down to 15,000 feet before the rip-cord is pulled by a spring.

barotaxis (bærəʊˈtæksɪs). *Physiol.* [a. G. (M. Verworn, *Allgemeine Physiologie* (1894)), f. Gr. βάρο-ς weight + τάξις arrangement.] 'Stimulation of living matter by change of the pressure relations under which it exists' (Dorland).

1899 F. S. LEE tr. *Verworn's Gen. Physiol.* v. 440. **1901** CALKINS *Protozoa* 300 A general result of mechanical stimulation is a motor response followed by the tendency to turn away from the source, and the general reaction, whether positive or negative, since it deals with the question of pressure in some form or other, is called *barotaxis* (Verworn). **1912** E. A. MINCHIN *Introd. Study of Protozoa* x. 202 We can distinguish..Chemotaxis, or reactions to chemical stimuli..Barotaxis, or reactions to mechanical stimuli.

barotaxy (ˈbærəʊtæksɪ). *Physiol.* [f. as prec. + -Y[3].] = prec.

1906 M. HARTOG in *Cambr. Nat. Hist.* I. 20 Most living beings are able to maintain their level in water by floating or crawling against gravity, and they react in virtue of the same power against centrifugal force. This mode of irritability is termed (negative) 'geotaxy' or 'barotaxy'.

barothermograph (ˌbærəʊˈθɜːməʊgrɑːf, -æ-). *Meteorol.* [f. BARO(GRAPH + THERMOGRAPH.] (See quots.)

1896 *Monthly Weather Rev.* Sept. 323/2 Early in August [1895] a baro-thermograph..was constructed and observations begun with the new instrument. **1911** R. M. PIERCE *Dict. Aviation* 42 *Barothermograph*, an apparatus for recording simultaneously the pressure and the temperature of the atmosfere, often used on kites and sounding-balloons; a combination of a barograf and thermograf. **1923** GLAZEBROOK *Dict. Appl. Physics* III. 192/2 *Barothermograph*, a self-recording instrument which records the temperature as a function of the pressure.

Barotse (bəˈrɒtsiː). The name of a negroid race inhabiting the region of the Upper Zambezi basin in southern Africa, and of the language spoken by them.

Barotse represents the pronunciation of the name in former times by the inhabitants of Basutoland and is now replaced in local official usage by *Balozi*, the language being called *Silozi*. *Barotse* and *Balozi* are based upon the same root pronounced differently by different people. (M. Guthrie, private letter, 1959.)

1851 LIVINGSTONE *Let.* 1 Oct. (1940) 151 We proceeded..to see the Sesheke or river of the Barotse. **1857** —— *Trav.* iv. 87 The black men referred to were the Barotse, or, as they term themselves, Baloiána. **1888** *Encycl. Brit.* XXIV. 828/1 Language..Zambesi Group..Ba-Rotse. **1910** *Ibid.* III. 424/2 Barotse..is also applied to contiguous subject tribes, Barotseland being the country over which the Barotse paramount chief exercises authority. **1936** P. M. CLARK *Autobiogr. Old Drifter* ix. 127 At this time I knew nothing of the Barotse language, but got along with some of the natives who could talk what was called Kitchen Kaffir.

barouche (bəˈruːʃ). [ad. dial. Ger. *barutsche* (also *birutsche*), ad. Sp. *barrocho* or It. *baroccio*, properly *biroccio* 'chariot,' orig. 'two-wheeled car,' f. L. *birotus* 'two-wheeled,' perhaps assimilated in its ending to *carroccio* 'chariot' (Diez). The Eng. *barouche* assumes, in spelling and pronunciation, a French form, but no such word exists in F. (exc. as taken from Eng.)]

a. A four-wheeled carriage with a half-head behind which can be raised or let down at pleasure, having a seat in front for the driver, and seats inside for two couples to sit facing each other.

1801 E. FREMANTLE *Diary* 27 Sept. in *Wynne Diaries* (1940) III. 63 Drove out with Ly. Westmoreland in her Baroutsch. [**1805** MRS. R. TRENCH *Rem.* (1862) 172, I saw a birutsche today, which the baroness has bought for 150 louis. It..has no resemblance to an English carriage.] **1805** *Naval Chron.* XIV. 284 The Duke of Sussex arrived in his barouche. **1811** JANE AUSTEN *Sense & Sens.* I. iii. 32 It would have quieted her ambition to see him driving a barouche. **1813** *Examiner* 29 Mar. 198/2 Escorted to our Exchange in a barouche and six. **1854** THACKERAY *Newcomes* I. 62 Great dowager barouches roll along emblazoned with coronets.

b. *attrib.* and *Comb.*

1805 C. WILMOT *Let.* 31 Aug. in Londonderry & Hyde *Russ. Jrnls.* (1934) II. 178 My 2 protectors..ride on the Barooch seat. **1807** C. SEDLEY (*title*) The barouche-driver and his wife: a tale for haut ton. **1815** MISS AUSTEN *Emma* (1870) II. xiv. 233 Their barouche-landau..holds four perfectly. **1820** G. COLMAN (Jun.) *X.Y.Z.* I. i, I went in a Brutus wig, and a barouche great-coat. **1960** CUNNINGTON & BEARD *Dict. Eng. Costume* 11/1 *Barouche coat.* 1809. A ¾-length close-fitting outdoor coat, with round bosom and full sleeves; fastened down the front with barrel-snaps and a buckled girdle round the waist.

barouchet (ˈbæruːʃeɪ). Also **barouchette.** [f. prec. + -ET[1]; as if of French origin.] A kind of light barouche.

1807 C. L. BIRCH *Brit. Pat. 3063*, An Improvement in the Construction of the Roofs and Upper Quarters of Barouches, Barouchets, Curricles, and other Carriages. **1816** PEACOCK *Headlong Hall* xi. 144 Every chariot, coach, barouche and barouchette..was in motion. **1852** J. W. CARLYLE *Let.* 5 Aug. (1883) II. 170 A gentleman who was preparing to start in a barouchette with two horses.

[**barowe**, *triturare.* Levins *Manip.* (1570)/181.]

bar-post: see BAR *sb.*[1] 30.

barque (bɑːk). Variant of BARK *sb.*[2]

barquentine, bark- (ˈbɑːkəntiːn). Also 7 **-enteen**, 9 **-antine**. [f. BARK *sb.*[2] on the analogy of BRIGANTINE; or perh. an assimilated form of Sp. *bergantine* 'small ship, brigandine' (Minsheu).]

A small bark; *spec.* in mod. use: A vessel somewhat similar to a bark, having the fore-mast square-rigged, and the main- and mizen-masts fore-and-aft-rigged.

1693 *Col. Rec. Penn.* I. 379 Having Sailled from Barbadoes in the barkenteen Ann. **1867** SMYTH *Sailor's Wd.-bk.*, *Barkantine* or *Barquantine*, a name applied on the great lakes of North America to a vessel, etc. **1881** *Leeds Merc.* 5 Feb. 2/6 Landed..from the barquentine Girl of Devon.

† **barr**, *v. Obs.* [variant of BARY *v.* (= F. *barrier*, L. *barrīre*).] *intr.* To utter the peculiar cry of an elephant. Hence BARRING *vbl. sb.*

1653 URQUHART *Rabelais* III. xiii. (1737) II. 303 The bawling of mastiffs..barring of elephants. *Ibid.* note, An elephant, which out of reverence for the pope his master would barr and bend the knee.

barr, obs. form of BAR.

barrable (ˈbɑːrəb(ə)l), *a.* [f. BAR *v.* + -ABLE.] Capable of being barred or legally stayed.

1788 J. POWELL *Devises* (1827) II. 576 The legacies..being barrable by a recovery. **1875** POSTE *Gaius* III. 406 An action might be brought, but was barrable by an exception pleading the senatusconsult.

barracado, obs. form of BARRICADO.

† **ˈbarracan.** *Obs.* (exc. as alien.) Also 9 **baracan.** [a. F. *barracan*, *baragant* (Cotgr.), mod. *bouracan* (= Pr. *barracan*, It. *baracane*, Sp. *barragan*, Pg. *barregana*), a. Arab. *barrakān*, or *burrukān* (Dozy), camlet, a cloak of camlet, f. Pers. *barak* 'a blanket or garment of camel's hair.']

A fabric: orig. coarse camlet; still in Spain 'a sort of water-proof cloth of coarse wool or goat's hair,' also 'the name of a coarse black woollen garment still used in Morocco' (Marsh). Vaguely employed by European writers (see Du Cange *barracanus*): in some passages taken as 'a fine cloth of silk or other delicate material.' See also BARRAGAN.

1638 *Lanc. Wills* III. 206 My petticoate of barracan. **1821** BYRON *Juan* III. lxx, The striped white gauze baracan that bound her.

† **barrace** (ˈbærəs). *Obs.* exc. *Hist.* Forms: 4–6 **barres, -as,** 5 **-ais, -eys,** (6 **barrowis**), 5–9 **barrace.** [a. OF. *barras*, f. *barre* bar.]

1. A barrier or outwork in front of a fortress.

c **1375** BARBOUR *Bruce* IV. 96 Ysche thai wald And bargane at the barras [*v.r.* barrais] hald. **1380** *Sir Ferumb.* 4679 þanne come þe Sarzinz out And defendede þe barres al about. *c* **1470** HENRY *Wallace* IX. 830 Off hewyn temyr in haist he gert thaim tak..and a stark barres mak. **1483** *Cath. Angl.* 23 A Barras, *antemurale.* **1490** CAXTON *Eneydos* xxxv. 124 Rounde aboute this place he dyd make diches and barreys for to defende himselfe.

2. The bar of a tribunal; = BAR *sb.*[1] 22. *rare.*

1499 *Plumpton Corr.* 142 This day was new barresses made in Westmynster hall, and thether was brought Therle of Warwek, and arrened.

3. A hindrance, obstruction, delay. *rare.*

1480 CAXTON *Ovid's Met.* XIII. iv, But I, whyche wel knowe this barras and whilis, toke w[t] me armes for squyres.

4. The enclosure within which knightly encounters took place; the lists.

1513 DOUGLAS *Æneis* XII. xiv. 10 Bot we debait suld this barres wythin, With wapynnis kene. **1536** BELLENDENE *Cron. Scot.* (1821) II. 261 Quhen thir thevis war enterit in barras, quhare thay suld have fouchtin. **1562** A. SCOTT *New Y. Gift to Quene*, With scheild and speir To fecht in barrowis. **1808** JAMIESON s.v., We still speak of 'a cock in a barrace,' in allusion to a cock-pit. **1828** SCOTT *F.M. Perth* xiii, Will justify this cartel in knightly weapons within the barrace.

5. Hence (perh. confused with BARRAT): Hostility, contention, strife.

c **1470** HENRY *Wallace* II. 238 Me think we suld in barrat [*v.r.* barrace] mak thaim bow. **1603** *Philotus* cxliii, Is this ane plesant godlie lyfe, To be in barrace, sturt and stryfe.

barrack (ˈbærək), *sb.*[1] Forms: 7–8 **barraque,** 7 **barack,** 8– **barrack.** [a. F. *baraque*, ad. It. *baracca* or Sp. *barraca* 'a souldier's tent, or a booth, or such like thing made of the sayle of a shippe, or such like stuffe' (Minsheu 1617). Of uncertain origin: Diez thinks from *barra* bar, comparing, for the form, *trab-acca* from *trab-s* beam. Others have tried to find an Arabic or Celtic source. Marsh has shown that the word occurs early in Sp. and Catalan.

1249 *Ord.* in *Privilegia Valentiæ* in Marsh *Wedgwood* s.v., Concedimus vobis..habentibus barraquas sive patua aut loca determinata ad edificandum, etc. *a* **1276** *Conq. Valencia* ibid., Barraques de tapits e vanoues. **1611** ESCOLANO *Hist. Valencia* /271 Barracas y choças de pescadores.]

1. a. A temporary hut or cabin; *e.g.* for the use of soldiers during a siege, etc. Still in *north. dial.*

1686 *Lond. Gaz.* No. 2107/2 The Houses ruined..are not yet rebuilt, so that greatest part of the Garison is still lodged in Barraques. **1706** PHILLIPS, *Barrack* or *Barraque*, a Hut like a little Cottage for Soldiers to lodge in a Camp, when they have no tents. **1729** SWIFT *Grand Quest.* Wks. 1755 IV. I. 103 To dispose of it to the best bidder, For a barrack or malt-house. **1781** GIBBON *Decl. & F.* III. lvi. 367 He lodged in a miserable hut or barrack. **1854** H. MILLER *Sch. & Schm.* (1858) 192 These barracks or bothies are almost always of the most miserable description.

b. 'A straw-thatched roof supported by four posts, capable of being raised or lowered at pleasure, under which hay is kept.' Bartlett *Dict. Amer.* 1848.

2. A set of buildings erected or used as a place of lodgement or residence for troops.

a. usually in *pl.* (collective), sometimes improperly treated as a *sing.*

1697 *Lond. Gaz.* No. 3314/3 An Estimate of the Charge of Building a Cittadel at Limericke; and of Baracks to be made for the Soldiers. **1760** WESLEY in *Jrnl.* 21 July (1827) III. 11, I preached near the barracks. **1879** JENKINSON *Guide I. Wight* 43 Barracks were also erected, and the place was considered of military importance. **1884** *Harper's Mag.* Nov. 813/1 The college building had been seized for a barracks.

b. sometimes in *sing.*

1698 *Par. Reg. Drypool, Hull*, 21 Dec., [Baptism of] Jane, Daughter of Hugh Scot, Gentleman, Officer in the Barwick. **1699** *Ibid.* 2 Nov., Officer at the Berwick. **1774** T. WARTON *Hist. Eng. Poetry* lxii. (1840) III. 404 He..lived to see his cathedral converted into a barrack. **1845** DISRAELI *Sybil* (1853) 27 His own idea of a profession being limited to a barrack in a London park.

c. *transf.*

1883 EARL CAIRNS in *Chr. Commw.* 834/3 The children were not massed together in great barracks, but were broken up into small detachments.

d. (*sing.* or *pl.*). A large plain building or range of buildings, tenements, or flats in which a number of people are housed; also, any strikingly plain-looking building suggestive of a military barracks. Also *attrib.* as ***barrack-flat***.

1862 MRS. GASKELL *Let.* 23 July (1966) 926 We went to the Hotel de Sévigné, her old town house,.. an immense barrack of an old half-fortified house. **1880** TROLLOPE *Duke's Children* III. xix. 215 'What a nice little room..' said Isabel. 'It's a beastly great barrack,' said Silverbridge. **1886** *Contemp. Rev.* Sept. 329 The railway has come close under the walls of the *château*, while an ugly barrack has sprung up on the other side. **1909** *Westm. Gaz.* 20 Oct. 1/3 A feature of German housing which reformers desire to abolish: that is, of the many-storied barrack-flat system. **1922** JOYCE *Ulysses* 750, I dont like being alone in this big barracks of a place. **1956** M. DUGGAN *Immanuel's Land* 108 The secret drink, I've heard it said, of old Ignatz, back at the barracks.

e. *spec.* The regular quarters of the Salvation Army.

1887 W. BOOTH in A. R. Wiggins *Hist. Salvation Army* (1964) IV. v. 189 No barracks are.. to be let or used for Political Meetings of any kind. **1907** G. B. SHAW *Maj. Barbara* II. 224 She's gone to Canning Town, to our barracks there.

3. *attrib.*, as in ***barrack-field***, ***-life***, ***-like*** (or ***barracks-like***), ***-room*** (also *attrib.*), ***-shed***, ***-wing***, ***-yard***; **barrack-master**, an officer who superintends soldiers' barracks; whence ***barrack-master general***, an appointment abolished in 1806; **barrack-rat** (see quot.); **barrack-room lawyer** *slang* (orig. *Mil.*), a layman who claims special knowledge of rules, regulations, or the law; a pompously argumentative person; **barrack school**, a disparaging term formerly applied to a large district school for poor-law children; **barrack-square**, the square near military barracks, where drill, parades, etc., take place; also *fig.*, = strictness, rigorous training; also *attrib.*

1769 J. WESLEY *Jrnl.* 13 July (1916) V. 328, I was driven to the barrack-field, where were twice as many as the hall could have contained. **1854** H. MILLER *Sch. & Schm.* (1858) 186 Somewhat dismayed by this specimen of barrack-life. **1915** R. LANKESTER *Divers. of Naturalist* 164 The latter barrack-like edifices. **1951** S. SPENDER *World within World* 221 Albacete was a barracks-like town in a dull plain. **1715** ADDISON *Let.* 9 Mar. (1941) 313 The Barrack-Master of Waterford.. may not be thought proper to be continued in that Station. *a* **1745** SWIFT *Lett.* (R.) An Irishman, who pretended to be barrack-master-general of Ireland. **1844** *Regul. & Ord. Army* 233 Barrack-Masters being expressly enjoined.. to confine the issues of Bedding, Furniture, Utensils, and Stores to such only as, etc. **1936** F. RICHARDS *Old Soldier Sahib* viii. 160 Children born in Barracks were referred to as 'barrack-rats'. **1777** in *New Hampshire Hist. Soc. Coll.* VII. 68 That.. he leave the paying for Barrack room.. to a special Committee. **1787** W. DYOTT *Diary* 9 July (1907) I. 30 We were not able to get into our barrack-rooms. **1844** *Regul. & Ord. Army* 236 The Officer of the Day is to visit the Barrack-Rooms to see that they are properly cleaned. **1892** KIPLING *(title)* Barrack-room ballads and other verses. **1945** A. J. P. TAYLOR *Course German Hist.* 100 Roon had the typical barrack-room mentality. **1943** 'RAFF' & 'ARMSTRONG' *Nice Types* 77 The Barrack-Room Lawyer has an ancient copy of King's Regulations in his locker. **1970** *Times* 12 May 25/2 Reuther set about winkling out lazy.. trade unionists.. barrack-room lawyers, [etc.]. **1985** *Financial Times* 1 Aug. 39/1 A line of policy has to be drawn.. to guard against the barrack-room lawyer who seeks to draw out the dispute and involve the courts on technicalities. **1894** E. HART in *Brit. Med. Jrnl.* 21 Apr. 879/2 The system of pauper district schools organised on the 'barrack' principle should be mended or ended as soon as possible. *Ibid.* 28 Apr. 928 Poor Law Barrack Schools. **1902** *Encycl. Brit.* XXXI. 835/1 Adverse criticism.. in 1874.. has been directed against these large, or, as they are invidiously called, barrack schools. **1749** in J. S. MCLENNAN *Louisbourg* (1918) 410 Two Barrack Sheds of hundred feet long each. **1932** *Statesman* (Calcutta) 21 July, Our cricket.. needs a bit of the barrack square. **1958** S. RACE in P. Gammond *Decca Bk. of Jazz* x. 124 The Goodman band was the first to combine barrack-square precision with solo freedom. **1901** KIPLING *Kim* vi. 143 Spreading his cloth in the shade of a deserted barrack-wing. **1760** J. WESLEY *Jrnl.* 28 June (1913) IV. 395 The colonel.. gave me the liberty of preaching in the barrack-yard. **1863** KINGLAKE *Crimea* II. 436 Here on the bloody slope of Alma no less than in the barrack-yard at home.

barrack, *sb.*[2] *Austral.* and *N.Z.* [f. BARRACK *v.*[2]] An act, or the action, of barracking.

c **1890** D. MCK. WRIGHT in A. E. Woodhouse *N.Z. Farm & Station Verse* (1950) 33 There's the 'barrack' at the table and the clever things are said. **1931** V. PALMER *Separate Lives* 13 They received him with shouts and good-natured barrack, as if he were one of the crowd. **1948** —— *Golconda* viii. 60 His flood of good-humoured barrack made the newcomers feel at home. **1949** P. NEWTON *High Country Days* 46 The other four, full of noisy barrack, were playing pitch and toss with a set of old horse shoes.

barrack ('bærək), *v.*[1] [f. BARRACK *sb.*[1]]

1. *trans.* To provide barracks for; to locate in barracks.

1701 LUTTRELL *Brief Rel.* V. 101 Prince Eugene has demanded.. 30,000 planks for barracking his troops. **1872** *Echo* 1 Oct. 4 When men are not barracked, when military service implies.. nothing but home defence.

2. *intr.* To lodge in barracks.

1834 H. MILLER *Scenes & Leg.* xxxii. (1857) 478 A small recruiting party barracked in one of the neighbouring lanes.

barrack ('bærək), *v.*[2] [app. orig. Australian (? alteration of BORAK), but E.D.D. cites *barrack* 'to brag, to be boastful of one's fighting powers', *barracker* 'a braggart', and *barracking* 'bragging, boastfulness' from northern Ireland.] *intr.* To shout jocular or derisive remarks or words of advice as partisans against a person, esp. a person, or side collectively, engaged in a contest. Also, with *for*, to support (a player, speaker, etc.) (esp. by shouting). (Said of a section of the crowd of spectators, orig. Australian.) Also *transf.* **b.** *trans.* To shout in this way at (a player, speaker, etc.). Hence **'barracking** *vbl. sb.* and *ppl. a.*; also **'barracker** *sb.*, one who barracks.

1885 in Baker *Austral. Lang.* (1945) xvii. 309 Barracking. **1889** *Cricket* 99 Junior clubs [in Sydney] have their armies of what are known as 'barrackers', who follow and howl for their side. **1890** FARMER *Slang, Barracking* (Australian), banter, chaff. **1890** *Melbourne Punch* 14 Aug. 106/3 To use a football phrase, they all to a man 'barrack' for the British Lion. **1893** *The Age* 27 June 6/6 (Morris), People were afraid to go to them [*sc.* football matches] on account of the conduct of the crowd of 'barrackers'. *Ibid.*, The 'barracking' that was carried on at football matches. **1895** *Westm. Gaz.* 1 Mar. 5/1 A spontaneous burst of cheering and 'barracking', with loud cries of 'Bravo, Stoddart!' were heard. **1900** H. LAWSON *On Track* 89, I was too shy to go in where there was a boy wanted and barrack for myself properly. **1901** *Westm. Gaz.* 19 Aug. 6/2 The crowd had absolutely no right.. to 'barrack' the players by yelling in concert now and again, at a critical moment. **1904** WARNER *How we recovered Ashes* 73 Hayward and myself had to undergo some 'barracking' for playing slowly. *Ibid.* 167 They will grow up into the type of man who 'barracked' Crockett so disgracefully at Sydney. **1911** E. M. CLOWES *On the Wallaby* iii. 47 It seems as if I was 'barracking' for Australia as against England. **1926** *Chambers's Jrnl.* 543/2 Only once.. was a querulous barracking voice raised. **1934** A. E. MULGAN *Spur of Morning* 87 'Varsity barrackers gave up hope. **1943** *Coast to Coast 1942* 165 Dingo kept his pipe in his mouth all evening, not saying a word till even Ward barracked him. **1955** *Glasgow Herald* 25 July, It has helped to correct the poor impression he has of the supporters of Scottish Rugby, who never barrack. **1963** *Times* 18 Feb. 20/4 It was a hot day but the heat did not deter the barrackers as England struggled for runs. *Ibid.* 11 May 5/1 When Miss Truman led 4–1 in the first set, the crowd began to barrack every point she scored and to encourage the Italian girl with prolonged cheering.

barraclade ('bærəkleɪd). [f. Du. *baar-e* bare, napless + *kleed* cloth.] 'A home-made woollen blanket without nap.' Bartlett *Dict. Amer.* 1848.

barracoat, var. *barrow-coat*: see BARROW *sb.*[4]

barracoon (bærə'kuːn). [a. Sp. *barracon* (?), augmentative f. *barraca*: see BARRACK *sb.*[1] and -OON.] A rough barrack, set of sheds, or enclosure, in which negro-slaves (originally), convicts, etc., are temporarily detained. Also *fig.*

1851 T. PARKER *Wks.* VII. 290 The chain.. visible on the necks of the judges as they entered the Bastile of Boston—the Barracoon of Boston! **1861** *Du Chaillu's Equat. Afr.* xi. 141, I made a visit to the barracoons, or slave-pens. **1862** MERIVALE *Rom. Emp.* (1865) VIII. lxviii. 358 The empire became no more than an ergastulum or barracoon on a vast scale.

barracuda, -coota, -couta (bærə'kuːdə, -'uːtə). Also 7 **-coutha**, 8 **bara-**. [Amer. Sp. *barracuda*.] A large and voracious fish (*Sphyræna barracuda*) of the Perch family, from six to ten feet in length, found in the seas of the West Indies. Also, a similar fish found in Australian and New Zealand waters (*Thyrsites atun*). In S. Afr. the same fish is called the SNOEK.

1678 PHILLIPS, *Barracoutha.* **1734** MORTIMER in *Phil. Trans.* XXXVIII. 315 The Barracuda. The Flesh of this Fish is very unwholsome. **1772** COOK *Voy.* (1790) I. 155 Breams, barracootas, gurnard. **1830** MARRYAT *King's Own* xiii, With the.. rapidity of a barracouta. **1839** J. HEBERLEY *Autobiogr.* (MS.) 81 This is a piece of red wood with a nail driven through it and bent round in the shape of a hook commonly called a Barracoota hook. **1845** J. DEANS *Lett.* (1939) 94 Baricouta are also to be got in great abundance and are very easily caught. **1874** A. BATHGATE *Colonial Experiences* iii. 27 The barracouta (*thyrsites atun*), a rather coarse fish,.. a great favourite with boarding-house keepers. **1880** W. SENIOR *Trav. & Trout in Antipodes* 295 The barracuda is.. well known throughout the colonies. **1885** LADY BRASSEY *In Trades* 331 The Barracuda is.. sometimes.. good to eat and of excellent flavour, and at others malignantly poisonous. **1897** W. SAVILLE-KENT *Naturalist in Australia* 170 The well-known Barracouta of the Adelaide, Melbourne, Sydney and Hobart markets. **1960** DOOGUE & MORELAND *N.Z. Sea Anglers' Guide* 262 There are four kinds of snake-mackerel in New Zealand waters of which the barracouta is best known.

||**barrad** ('bærəd). [a. Ir. *baireud*, *bairread*, ad. F. *barrette*: see BARRET.] (See quot.)

1834 PLANCHÉ *Brit. Costume* 371 The barrad, or Irish conical cap. **1862** BROWNE *Campion Alice* 19 With the tall barrad or conical cap upon their heads.

'barragan, -on. [a. Sp. *barragan*: see BARRACAN, of which this is a modern revival, in the Spanish form, for trade purposes.] (See quots.) Also *attrib.*

1677 W. CUNNINGHAM *Diary* 12 Feb. (1887) 89, 11 ells Barragon to be a cloak. **1735** *London Even. Post* 25–27 Nov. 3/1 In his Walk [the missing man] stoops in his Shoulders, about 24 or 25 Years of Age, had on a light Barragon Coat and short brown Wigg. **1787** G. WHITE *Selborne* v. 14 Barragons, a genteel corded stuff, much in vogue at that time for summer wear. **1840** *L'pool Jrnl.* 4 July 1/2 A great Stock of Fustians, in Beaverteens, Moleskins, Barragans. **1854** *Poultry Chron.* I. 114 On that barragon sleeve a human dew-drop glistened.

barrage ('bærɑːʒ, -ɪdʒ, formerly 'bɑːrɪdʒ), *sb.* [a. F. *barrage*, f. *barre* BAR *sb.*[1]: see -AGE.] **1. a.** The action of barring; the formation of an artificial bar in a river or watercourse, to increase the depth of water; the artificial bar thus formed, *esp.* those in the Nile.

1859 W. GREGORY *Egypt in* 1855–6 I. 64 Useless barrages that obstruct, and do not benefit. **1865** *Daily Tel.* 8 Dec. 5/1 The execution of the barrage of the Nile. **1868** J. MACGREGOR *Voy. Alone* 88 The vast locks, barrages, quays.

b. In modern military use: a barrier of continuous artillery or machine-gun fire concentrated in a given area, used to prevent the advance or retreat of enemy troops, to protect troops advancing against the enemy, to repulse attacks by aircraft, and for destructive purposes; ***creeping*** or ***moving barrage***, a curtain of fire moving before and directed from behind advancing troops. More explicitly ***barrage fire***.

1916 H. W. YOXALL *Let.* 22 Sept. in *Fashion of Life* (1966) iv. 32 The Bosche barrage was almost as good as ours. **1917** *Times* 11 July 5/5 The German barrage fire on the trenches, though it lasted so short a time, was of extreme severity. *Ibid.* 26 Sept. 7/6 The barrage was effective in keeping the raiders at a great height. **1918** 'BOYD CABLE' *Air Men o' War* ix. 118 Next instant he plunged at, into, and through the barrage, his machine rocking and pitching and rolling in the turmoil of shell-torn air. **1922** *Encycl. Brit.* XXX. 250/1 This breakdown of communications.. led to the general introduction of the 'creeping barrage' (French *barrage roulant*, German *Feuerwalze*). Briefly, it is a screen of shells bursting on and close to the ground, which is moved forward across the country by short leaps according to a pre-determined time-table. **1938** *Times* 7 Sept. 9/1 Aeroplanes, balloons, guns, and searchlights, and the barrage itself had their part to play in the air defences of London.

c. *transf.* and *fig.*

1917 W. OWEN *Let.* 25 May (1967) 464 You too have walked slowly through many barrages.. from resisting Life. **1918** *Daily Chron.* 20 Dec. (Weekley), Field-Marshal Sir Douglas Haig passed into London through a creeping barrage of cheers. **1920** W. J. LOCKE *House of Baltazar* xxiv. 300 If the barrage of silence is maintained. **1927** M. DIVER *But Yesterday* xxvii. 301 All that barrage about his health. **1942** E. COLBY *Army Talk* 20 The word 'Barrage'.. also gets into slang, in the service.. to describe a flood of conversation purposely put up to deceive and divert. **1958** F. C. AVIS *Boxing Ref. Dict.* 8 *Barrage*, a succession of fast and hard punches by one boxer against another. **1964** *Observer* 5 Jan. 2/5 The barrage of official statements.

d. In *Sport*: a heat for the selection of contestants. Also, the deciding jump-off, run-off, etc., in the event of a draw.

1955 *Times* 23 July 3/2 Twelve competitors out of a representative international field qualified for the first barrage for the puissance jumping. **1956** *Times* 1 Dec. 10/1 Miss G. Sheen, successful in the final barrage of the women's individual foils at Melbourne yesterday. **1963** BLOODGOOD & SANTINI *Horseman's Dict.* 16 *Barrage*, jump-off in a horse-show.

2. barrage balloon, a captive balloon forming part of a balloon barrage. Cf. *balloon barrage* s.v. BALLOON *sb.*[1] 10.

1923 *Aviation* 25 June 690/2 The employment of barrage balloons.. permits the realization of economy in the distribution of 'active means' of anti-aircraft defense. **1925** *Sci. Amer.* July 61/1 The Barrage Balloon.. is designed to ascend to a great height, trailing fine steel wires extending to the ground and wrecking any hostile airplane. **1943** *Roof over Britain* 5 The 'plane had struck a barrage balloon cable.

Hence **barrage** *v. trans.*, to put a barrage upon; *intr.* to put down a barrage. Also *fig.*

a **1917** E. A. MACKINTOSH (1918) *War, the Liberator* 124 The artillery will barrage at x. 20. **1918** 'BOYD CABLE' *Air Men o' War* xvii. 230 The only bit of the whole line they managed to barrage properly. **1960** *New Left Rev.* May–June 64/1 She.. barraged *me* with questions.

barragouin: see BARAGOUIN.

barramundi (ˌbærə'mʌndɪ). Also **burramundi**, **-munda**. [Aboriginal.] The native name in Australia for any of various freshwater fish (see quots. 1880, 1898).

1873 TROLLOPE *Australia* I. xi. 189 There is a fish too at Rockhampton called the Burra Mundi,—I hope I spell the name rightly,—which is very commendable. **1880** GÜNTHER *Stud. Fishes* 357 Two species, *C[eratodus] forsteri* and *C. miolepis*, are known from fresh waters of Queensland... The aborigines [call it] 'Barramunda', a name which they appear to apply also to other large-scaled freshwater fishes, as the Osteoglossum leichardti. **1898** MORRIS *Austral Eng.* 67/2 *Burramundi* or *Barramunda*.. is also incorrectly applied by the colonists to the large tidal perch of the Fitzroy River, Queensland, *Lates calcarifer*, Günth., a widely distributed fish in the East Indies. **1909** WEBSTER, Barramundi. **1930** E. R. B. GRIBBLE *Forty Yrs. with Aborigines* xvi. 165 John left at once,.. returning in the evening with a fine barramundi. **1938** *Bulletin* (Sydney) 6 Dec. 21/2 The waters teem with barramundi (king of Australian fishes).

||**barranca** (bə'ræŋkə). Also **barranco**. [Sp., used in U.S.] A deep ravine with precipitous sides.

a **1691** BOYLE *Hist. Air* (1692) xix. 178 The Canary-Birds.. breed in the Barrancos of Gills, which the Water has fretted away in the Mountains. **1816** C. SMITH *Jrnl.* 9 Apr. in J. K. Tuckey *Narr. Exped. R. Zaire* (1818) 245 Another barranco was winding its course down to *Publico grande.* **1829** W. IRVING *Granada* I. xii. 112 A barranco, or deep rocky valley. *Ibid.* II. lxxvii. 226 Threads of water.. tinkling down the bottoms of the barrancas or ravines. 1850 PRESCOTT *Mexico* I. 399 Over a deep barranca, or ravine, they crossed. 1939 G. GREENE *Lawless Roads* viii. 213 The nearly dry barranca where the women did their washing.

barrand, -ant, obs. forms of BARREN.

barrandite ('bærəndaɪt). *Min.* [Named (in 1867) after Barrande, a Bohemian geologist: see -ITE.] A phosphate of alumina and iron occurring in spheroidal concretions at Cerhovic in Bohemia.

1868 DANA *Min.* 574.

† **'barras**[1]. *Obs.* 'A coarse linen fabric originally imported from Holland.' *Drapers' Dict.*

1640 *Charter Lond.* in Beck *Drapers' Dict.* 13 Dutch Barras. 1714 *Lond. Gaz.* No. 5240/3 Buckrams, Barras and Silesia Neckcloths.

‖ **barras**[2] (ba'rɑː, 'bærəs). [Fr., f. *barre* BAR *sb.*[1], from its appearance on the tree.] The resin which exudes from wounds made in the bark of fir-trees.

1847 in CRAIG.

barras, obs. form of BARRACE.

† **'barrat.** *Obs.* Forms: 3-5 baret, 4 -ete, 4-5 -ette, -ett, -at, 5 -ate, -eyt, barret, -ette, 5-6 barrat. [a. OF. *barat* (nom. *baras*) masc. (= It. *baratto*, OSp. *barato*, Pr. *barat*), also OF. *barate* fem. (= OSp., Cat., Pr. *barata*) 'deceit, fraud, confusion, trouble, embarrassment.' Of doubtful origin: the final *-at* of OF., and It. *-atto*, indicate an original *a* in position, as *-att-*, *-apt-* (Godef. has a 14th c. spelling *barapt*). The original sense in Romanic seems to have been 'traffic, commerce, dealing' (P. Meyer). Diez, Scheler, and E. Müller favour a possible derivation from Gr. πράττειν 'to practise, do business, deal,' as to which see their works. Chevallet and Stokes compare OIr. *mrath*, later *brath*, OBreton *brat*, later *brad*, Welsh *brad* 'betrayal, treachery,' as the possible source of the Fr. and thence of the other Romanic forms. Sense 3 cannot be separated from ON. *barátta* 'fight, contest, strife, (in deriv.) trouble,' which appears to have concurrently or independently influenced the Eng. word.]

1. Deception, fraud, fraudulent dealing.

[1292 BRITTON IV. iii. §3 Par extorsioun..par barat et par contek.] 1340 *Ayenb.* 39 Barat, ualshedes and alle gyles. *c* 1400 MAUNDEV. xxvii. 272 Thei sette not be no Barettes.. Cawteles, Disceytes. 1485 CAXTON *Chas. Gt.* 231 Doon in good entent and equyte and without barat. 1503 *Sheph. Kal.* xlii, A Person with a short neck, is full of fraude, [of] barate, of deception.

2. Trouble, distress, sorrow, grief, pain.

c 1230 *Ancr. R.* 414 'Marthe, Marthe,' cweð he, 'þu ert ine muchele baret.' *c* 1325 *Metr. Hom.* 124 Baret sal he thol and wa. *c* 1400 *Epiph.* (Turnb. 1843) 1727 Then saw he hym in gret bareyt And in a fyr to the navylle y-seytt. 1552 LYNDESAY *Dreme* 851 Quho sall beir of our barrat the blame?

3. Contention, strife, quarrel, fighting.

c 1300 *Beket* 703 The King him makede wroth ynouȝ: that so ofte in baret was. 1330 R. BRUNNE *Chron.* 99 Whan þis barette was ent. *c* 1340 *Gaw. & Gr. Knt.* 21 Bolde breden þer-inne, baret þat lofden. 1496 *Dives & Paup.* (W. de W.) IX. xiv. 366 Whiche in fyght & barett lese theyr eyen, theyr feet, theyr hondes.

† **'barrat,** *v.* *Obs. rare*[−1]. [? f. BARRAT *sb.* (in sense 3), or perh. f. BARRATOR; but cf. OF. *barater*, OSp., Pg., Cat., Pr. *baratar*, It. *barattare* to exchange, to cheat, deceive (after sense 1 of the *sb.*).] To quarrel, strive, brawl. Hence **barrating** *vbl. sb.*

1600 PORY *Leo Africa* III. 134 To see how they will barret and scould one at another. 1635 F. WHITE *Sabbath* Ep. Ded. 7 Senators..with their barking, barrating, and libelling, haue brought..their venerable calling into much contempt.

'barrateen, -ine. ? *Obs.* Also bara-. Some kind of woven fabric.

1689 *Lond. Gaz.* No. 2438/4 A New black Barratine Mantua and Petticoat. 1745 *Lond. Mag.* 403 Baratees [*sic*], and other Francfort Commodities. 1761 *Brit. Mag.* II. 117 Thick barateen curtains were close drawn round the bed.

barrator, -er ('bærətə(r)). Forms: 5-6 baratour, 5-8 barretor, 5 baratoure, -atowre, -atur, -itur, -iter, barratoure, 6 baratter, -ater, -ator, -ettour, -etour, barratur, 6-7 barretour, 6-8 -eter, 7-8 -etter, 7-9 -ettor, 6- barrator, -er. [a. AF. *baratour = OF. barateor, -eeur (= It. *barattatore*, Pr. *baratador*) fraudulent dealer, cheat, trickster, f. *barat*: see BARRAT *v.* Notwithstanding the derivation of the form from OF., the sense of 'fighter, quarreller' (see BARRAT *sb.* 3) is much more prominent in this word; the most usual sense, III. intimately blends the two ideas.]

I. [from AF. *baratour*.] One who deals fraudulently in his business or office.

1. A person who buys or sells ecclesiastical preferment, a simoniac or simonist (*obs.*); one who buys or sells offices of state.

1427 *Acts Jas. I* (Scot.) §106 (1597) The King forbiddis, that onie of his lieges send onie expenses till ony barratour, that is now out-with the Realme. 1867 LONGF. *Dante's Inf.* XXI. 41 *note*, A Barrator, in Dante's use of the word, is..one who sells justice, office, or employment. Benvenuto says.. Bontura was an arch-barrator.

2. A judge who takes bribes.

1864 WEBSTER cites BURRILL. 1867 [see prec.] 1884 J. SIBBALD *Dante's Inf.* XXII. 52 *note*, The barrators took toll of the administration of justice.

3. A ship's master who commits BARRATRY (3).

1847 in CRAIG.

II. [from BARRAT *sb.* 3, ON. *barátta*.]

† 4. One who fights; *esp.* a hired bully. *Obs.*

a 1400 *Sir Perc.* 263 Kay the bolde baratour. 1460 CAPGRAVE *Chron.* 264 The Kyng..sent into Chestirschire for baretores..that thei schuld com and have the kepying of his body. 1577 HOLINSHED *Chron.* II. 538 Such barretors as used to take monie to beat any man, and againe would not sticke to take monie of him whom they had so beaten, to beat him that first hired them to beat the other. 1583 STANYHURST *Æneis* I. (Arb.) 33 Hee sees with baretours Troy wals inuironed.

† 5. A quarrelsome person; one given to brawling and riot; a rowdy. *Obs.*

c 1440 *Promp. Parv.* 23 Baratowre, *pugnax*, *rixosus*, *jurgosus*. *a* 1450 *Knt. de la Tour* xxxvii. 53 Theues, usureres, bariters, ouerthwarteres. 1502 ARNOLD *Chron.* 90 Yf ther be ony comon ryator, barratur, or ony comon nyght walker wythout light. 1662 FULLER *Worthies* II. 199 Wild Barretters who delight in brawls and blows. 1714 SCROGGS *Courts-leet* 9 All common Barretors, Scolds, and other Breakers of the Peace.

fig. (of winds). 1583 STANYHURST *Æneis* I. (Arb.) 22 Dare ye loa, curst baretours..Too raise such raks iaks on seas?

III. (Combining II. and I.)

6. *Law* and *gen.* One who vexatiously raises, or incites to, litigation; a mover or maintainer of law-suits; one who from maliciousness, or for the sake of gain, raises discord between neighbours.

The action of a barrator consists, says Coke (*On Litt.* 368) '(1) in disturbance of the Peace; (2) in taking or keeping of possessions of Lands in controversie, not only by force, but also by subtiltie and a deceit, and most commonly in suppression of truth and right; (3) by false inuentions, and sowing of calumniations, rumors, and reports, etc.'

c 1430 LYDG. *Bochas* I. xii. (1554) 26 a, Simples which that cannot vary May neuer accord with a baratour. *c* 1440 *Promp. Parv.* 115 Debate maker, or baratour, *incentor*. 1591 LAMBARDE *Arch.* (1635) 188 No Sheriffe or Steward..shall suffer any Barettor, or maintainer of Quarrels, in their Countrie Courts, or other Courts. 1642 FULLER *Holy & Prof. St.* II. xiii. 183 A Barreter is a horseleach that onely sucks the corrupted bloud of the law. He trades onely in tricks and quirks. 1770 LANGHORNE *Plutarch* (1879) II. 800/1 Those public barreters, who..make it their business to form impeachments. 1809 TOMLINS *Law Dict.* s.v., A common solicitor, who solicits suits, is a common barretor. 1855 MACAULAY *Fredk. Gt.* 80 The true wisdom of the great powers was to attack, not each other, but this common barrator.

† 7. *transf.* of things. *Obs.*

1624 BP. MOUNTAGU *Gagg* 146 'Mine' and 'thine' are the common barretters of the world. 1691 TRYON *Wisdom's Dict.* 89 Intemperance..is the Common Barreter that disquiets private Families.

'barrator,ship. [see -SHIP.] = BARRATRY.

1884 J. SIBBALD *Dante's Inf.* XXII. 52 As servant next to Thiebault, righteous King, I set myself to ply barratorship.

† **'barratous,** *a.* *Obs.* In 5 baraytous, -atous, 6 -atows. [a. OF. *barateus*, f. *barat*: see BARRAT *sb.* and -OUS.] Contentious, quarrelsome.

1430 LYDG. *Chron. Troy* II. xv, To his seruantes ful inpacient, And baraytous where that so euer he went. 1496 *Dives & Paup.* (W. de W.) II. xiii. 123 Yf the lorde be fell cruell and baratous. 1523 SKELTON *Garl. Laurel* 673 Preservative..Ageynst all baratows broisiours. 1592 G. HARVEY *Pierces Super.* 97 The world is too-full of litigious, and barratous pennes.

† **'barratress.** *Obs. rare.*[−1] In 6 bara-. [a. OF. *barateresse*, fem. of *barateeur*, BARRATOR: see -ESS.] A female fighter, amazon, virago.

1583 STANYHURST *Æneis* I. (Arb.) 34 A baratresse, daring with men, thogh a mayd, to be buckling.

† **'barratring,** *ppl. a.* *Obs. rare.*[−1] [cf. BARRATR-Y, and BARRAT *v.*] Practising barratry.

1716 M. DAVIES *Ath. Brit.* (1716) *Crit. Hist.* 18 Such as are but Barretring and Champetring Sollicitors in Learning.

barratrous ('bærətrəs), *a.* [f. BARRATR-Y + -OUS.] In *Marine Law*: Of the nature of barratry, fraudulent. **'barratrously** *adv.*, by barratry.

1842 SIR J. PARK *Syst. Mar. Insur.* I. v. 189 Where a ship and cargo was barratrously taken out of her course..by the barratrous act of the crew. 1848 ARNOULD *Mar. Insur.* (1866) II. III. ii. 713 No act can be barratrous to which the owners have..been consenting parties. 1883 *Law Rep.* Appeal VIII. 394 A barratrously caused seizure.

barratry ('bærətrɪ). Forms: 5-7 barratrie, 7 baratrie, 7-8 barretry, 8 baratry, 6- barratry. [a. OF. *baraterie*, *barterie* (= Pr. *barataria*), f. *barat*: see BARRAT and -ERY, -RY.]

1. The purchase or sale of ecclesiastical preferment, or of offices of state.

1427 *Acts Jas. I* (Scot.) §106 (1597) That na Clerkes.. passe out of the Realme, bot gif he..mak faith..that he do no barratrie. 1567 *Acts Jas. VI* (1597) §2 That nane of our said Soveraines subjects..desire title or richt of the said Bishop of Rome..to ony thing within this Realme, vnder the paines of Barratrie. *a* 1639 SPOTTISWOOD *Hist. Ch. Scot.* v. (1677) 270 Against whom the sentence of Barratry had been pronounced. 1705 HICKERINGILL *Priest-cr.* I. (1721) 63 Twenty four Articles to prove Barretry..against me. 1867 LONGF. *Dante's Inf.* XXII. 52, I set me to practise barratry.

2. (*Sc. Law.*) The acceptance of bribes by a judge.

1773 ERSKINE *Inst. Laws Scot.* (1838) 1091 Corruption of Judges, *Crimen repetundarum*, Baratry, Theftbote.

3. *Marine Law.* Fraud, or gross and criminal negligence, on the part of the master or mariners of a ship, to the prejudice of the owners, and without their consent; *e.g.* dishonestly sinking, deserting, or running away with the ship, or embezzling the cargo.

(The risk of *barratry* is usually excluded in bills of lading from the liabilities of the shipowner to the shipper or consignee of goods, and is undertaken by underwriters in policies of marine insurance.)

1622 MALYNES *Anc. Law-Merch.* 155 Barratrie of the Master and Mariners can hardly be auoided, but by a prouident care to know them. 1755 MAGENS *Insurances* I. 75 The Insurers were obliged to answer for the Barretry of the Master. 1865 J. LEES *Laws Brit. Ship.* (ed. 9) 140 Barratry ..includes whatever is a cheat, or fraud, or fraudulent act of the captain or crew to the injury of the owner.

4. The offence of habitually exciting quarrels, or moving or maintaining law-suits; vexatious persistence in, or incitement to, litigation.

1645 *Ord. Lords & Com. Sacram.* 6 Legally attainted of Barretry. *a* 1670 HACKET *Abp. Williams* II. (1693) 171 Inhibiting the Corinthians very sharply for their..common Barretry, in going to Law one with another. 1768 BLACKSTONE *Comm.* IV. 133 Common barretry is the offence of frequently exciting and stirring up suits and quarrels between his majesty's subjects. 1835 *Penny Cycl.* III. 495/2 A single act cannot amount to barratry.

barre (bɑː(r)). [F., lit. 'bar'.] 1. *Mus.* = CAPO TASTO; also, the placing of the forefinger of the left hand across the finger-board to act as a capo tasto. So ‖ **barré** (bɑːreɪ) *a.* [*ppl. a.* of F. *barrer* to bar], (of a chord) played with all strings stopped in this way.

1876 STAINER & BARRETT *Dict. Mus. terms* 51/1 *Barré*. 1900 GROVE *Dict. Mus.* I. 135/1 'Barre' designates the false nut made by placing the first finger of the left hand across the whole of the strings at certain lengths from the bridge to effect transposition. 1927 *Melody Maker* Aug. 756/3 Remember the most-used chord (the common chord) root position on the 'G' [banjo] is merely a barre, whilst it is a big stretch on the tenor [banjo]. 1934 S. R. NELSON *All about Jazz* ii. 55 Placing the index finger across the entire fingerboard in what is known as a 'barré' position. 1965 *Melody Maker* 10 July 12/4 Girls with small hands can play barre chords on a normal Spanish guitar.

2. *Dancing.* (See BAR *sb.*[1] 13 d.)

barre, obsolete form of BAR.

barred (bɑːd), *ppl. a.*; also 5 barrid, 6-7 bard(e. [f. BAR *v.* and *sb.*[1] + -ED.]

I. 1. Secured, enclosed, or shut with bars.

1593 SHAKS. *Rich. II*, I. i. 180 A ten times barr'd vp chest. 1611 BIBLE *Song. Sol.* iv. 12 A garden inclosed [*marg.* barred] is my sister. 1820 SCOTT *Abbot* xix, The close-barred portal. 1862 THORNBURY *Turner* II. 228 Turner was notoriously a barred-up man, a man who would come to the threshold of his mind..but would by no means open the door.

II. Having, or furnished with, a bar or bars.

2. *generally*.

a 1571 JEWEL *Serm. bef. Queen* (1583) TheÆgyptians had mighty chariots, straked and barred with yron. 1712 STEELE *Spect.* No. 474 ¶2 Five-barred gates. 1825 SCOTT *Talism.* i, His barred helmet of steel.

3. Ornamented with bars (see BAR *sb.*[1] 4); striped, streaked. *spec.* in *Zool.* names (see quots.); also *Comb.*, as ***barred-breasted*** adj.

c 1340 *Gaw. & Gr. Knt.* 159 Silk bordes, barred ful ryche. *c* 1386 CHAUCER *Miller T.* 49 A seint she wered barred all of silk. 1387 TREVISA *Higden* Rolls Ser. VI. 297 Clerks dede awey barred gurdelles. 1459 *Test. Ebor.* (1855) II. 235 Meam..Cristenynge-gyrdill barred throgh-oute. 1552 *Eng. Ch. Furniture* (1866) 221 One of black velvet and an other of barde silke. 1572 BOSSEWELL *Armorie* II. 31 b, Armes may in diuerse wise be Barred, and the firste maner is playne and streyghte. 1797 BEWICK *Birds* I. 9 The feathers on the thighs are..pure white; those of the tail are barred. 1809 SHAW *Gen. Zool.* VII. I. 113 Barred-Breasted Buzzard. Falco lineatus. 1811 WILSON *Amer. Ornith.* IV. 61 Barred Owl, *Strix nebulosa*,..is frequently observed flying during day. 1885 SWAINSON *Prov. Names Birds* 98 Lesser spotted woodpecker (*Dendrocopus minor*). Also called Little wood pie (Hants). Barred woodpecker. 1961 R. SOUTH *Moths of Brit. Isles* (ed. 4) II. 147 The Barred Carpet (*Perizoma taeniata* Steph.). *Ibid.* 150 The Barred Rivulet (*Perizoma bifaciata* Haw.). *Ibid.* 168 The Barred Straw (*Lygris pyraliata* Schiff.).

4. Of harbours: Obstructed by a BAR *sb.*[1] 15.

1552 T. BARNABE in Ellis *Orig. Lett.* II. II. 198 In all France be barde havens. 1647 FULLER *Gd. Th. in Worse T.* (1841) 132 Barred havens, choked up with the envious sands. 1796 MORSE *Amer. Geog.* I. 427 Its decline is attributed to a barred harbour and shoal rivers. 1858 *Merc. Mar. Mag.* V. 48 The river forms a barred harbour.

† 5. ***barred dice*** (cf. BAR *sb.*[1] 21): see quot. *Obs.*

1532 *Dice Play* (1850) 24 Lo, here..a well-favoured die, that seemeth good and square, yet is the forehead longer on the cater & tray than any other way..Such be also called bard cater tres, because, commonly, the longer end will, of his own sway, draw downwards, and turn up to the eye sice, sinke, deuis or ace. **1604** DEKKER *Honest Wh.* Wks. 1873 II. 145 She suffred your tongue, like a bard Cater tra, to runne all this while.

6. *Mus.* Marked off by bars: see BAR *sb.*[1] 16.

1883 SIR H. OAKELEY *Bible Psalter* Pref. 6 To hesitate.. just before the barred or strict time commences.

¶ For BARD *ppl. a.* = BARDED.

1612 DRAYTON *Polyolb.* xii. 206 Armed cap-à-pie upon their barred horse.

barrel ('bærəl), *sb.* Forms: 4 **barayl**, 4–5 **barele**, 4–6 **-ell(e**, 4–7 **-el**, 5 **barylle**, 5–6 **barrelle**, 6 **beryll**, 6–7 **barrell**, 7– **barrel**. [a. F. *baril* (12th c. in Littrè) = Pr., Pg., Sp. *barril*, It. *barile*, med.L. *barile*, *barillus*, *baurilis* (9th c.); cf. also *barrale* 'a cask, a measure of liquids' Du Cange: of unknown origin; Diez thinks possibly a deriv. of *barra*, BAR *sb.*[1] The Celtic words (Welsh *baril*, Gael. *baraill*, Ir. *bairile*, Manx *barrel*) sometimes cited as the source, are all from English.]

I. A cask.

1. a. A cylindrical wooden vessel, generally bulging in the middle and of greater length than breadth, formed of curved staves bound together by hoops, and having flat ends or heads; a cask.

c **1305** *Judas* 23 in *E.E.P.* (1862) 107 He seȝe a barayl.. þer inne hi dude þis liþer child: and amidde þe see hit caste. **1485** CAXTON *Chas. Gt.* 60 Two barylles.. ful of bawme. **1591** SHAKS. *1 Hen. VI*, v. iv. 57 Place barrelles of pitch vpon the fatall stake. **1604** T. WRIGHT *Passions* v. 226 Diogenes.. satte in his philosophicall barrell. **1724** SWIFT *Drapier's Lett.* Wks. 1841 II. 2 This Wood.. sends over a great many barrels of those halfpence to Cork. **1855** MACAULAY *Hist. Eng.* III. 401 A barrel of Colchester oysters, his favourite dainties.

b. With various substantives defining its specific use, as *beer-*, *brandy-*, *fire-*, *herring-*, *sugar-*, *tar-*, *thunder-*, *treacle-barrel*.

1753 CHAMBERS *Cycl. Supp.*, *Fire Barrels* are casks of divers capacities, filled with bombs, grenados, etc... These are sometimes also called thundering barrels. **1815** SCOTT *Guy M.* xlviii, If they burn the Custom-house.. we'll lunt like a tar-barrel a' thegither. **1818** —— *Rob Roy* xxvii, He wadna, for a' the herring-barrels in Glasgow. **1837** CARLYLE *Fr. Rev.* I. ii. I. 9 Their pasteboard coulisses, thunder-barrels, their kettles, fiddles. *Ibid.* III. i. III. 146 Groceries enough: sugar-barrels rolled forth into the street. **1841** MARRYAT *Poacher* xxiii, The beer barrel being empty.

c. In slang phr. *over a barrel* [app. in allusion to the state of a person placed over a barrel to clear his lungs of water after being rescued from drowning], helpless, in someone's power. Chiefly *U.S.*

1939 R. CHANDLER *Big Sleep* xxx. 270 We keep a file on unidentified bullets nowadays. Some day you might use that gun again. Then you'd be over a barrel. **1945** L. MCCLUNG *Stream runs Fast* xv. 129 You sure have me over a barrel. You caught me red-handed. **1963** N. FREELING *Because of Cats* xi. 175 If he's been fool enough to get himself over a barrel, that's his business.

2. Used as a measure of capacity both for liquids and dry goods, varying with the commodity.

1379 *MS. Records Grocers' Comp.* 28a, Reseyns corences i barell. **1382** WYCLIF *Luke* xvi. 6 An hundrid barelis of oyle. **1502** ARNOLD *Chron.* (1811) 246 The barell of soep, xxx galones. The barell of aell, xxxii galones. The barell of beer, xxxvi galones. **1672** PETTY *Pol. Anat.* (1691) 21 Corn was then at 50*s.* per Barrel. **1712** *Act 10 Anne* in *Lond. Gaz.* No. 5012/1 A Barrel of Soap is to contain 256 pound. **1749** REYNARDSON in *Phil. Trans.* XLVI. 57, 36 Gallons.. were to be reckoned as a Barrel of Beer, and 32 such Gallons a Barrel of Ale. **1862** F. GRIFFITHS *Artill. Man.* 92 Whole Barrels [of gunpowder] contain 100 lb.

3. a. By metonymy: The contents of a barrel; intoxicating liquor. Cf. 'the bottle.'

c **1300** *K. Alis.* 28 For they no haveth no joye.. Bote in the gutte, and the barell. **1798** W. HUTTON *Fam. Hutton* 104 When in liquor he was good-natured. His children knew his weak side, and omitted to ask a favour till the barrel worked.

b. (in *U.S. political slang*): Money for use in a political campaign, *esp.* for corrupt purposes.

1884 *Boston* (*Mass.*) *Herald* 18 Sept., There is a plenty of evidence that the head of Mr. Lodge's barrel has already been knocked in. **1884** *Savannah News* Aug., It would be much better for General Butler if he would turn one of his barrels over to the Democratic campaign committee.

†**4.** *abst.* Brand, quality, sort. See HERRING.

1542 UDALL *Erasm. Apoph.* 165b, Twoo feloes beeyng lyke flagicious, and neither barell better hearyng, accused either other. **1579** GOSSON *Sch. Abuse* 32 Therefore of both barrelles, I judge Cookes and Painters the better hearing. **1659** GAUDEN *Tears Ch.* 245 (D.) There meanest comrades, which are of the same bran and barrell with themselves. **1789** H. WALPOLE *Corr.* (1820) IV. 490 (D.) A committee of those Amazons stopped the Duke of Orleans, who, to use their style, I believe is not a barrel the better herring.

II. Things cylindrical or shaped like a barrel.

5. a. A revolving cylinder or drum, round which a chain or rope is wound, in various machines and appliances; *e.g.* that of a capstan, jack, wheel, windlass. *Hence* **b.** the cylindrical box, containing the main-spring of a watch, round which the chain is wound. **c.** the revolving cylinder of a musical box, barrel-organ, etc., in which are fixed the pins that strike the keys. **d.** A cylindrical button used in conjunction with a loop of braid as an ornamental fastening of a coat.

a. *c* **1500** *Cocke Lorelles B.* 12 Some pulde at the beryll.. Some howysed the mayne sayle. **1611** COTGR., The barrell of a windlesse, *Moulinet.* **1753** CHAMBERS *Cycl. Supp.*, *Barrel* of a jack is the cylindrical part whereon the line is wound. **1769** FALCONER *Dict. Marine* (1789), *Drosse*.. the tiller-rope.. wound about the barrel of a ship's wheel. *c* **1850** *Rudim. Nav.* (Weale) 94 *Barrel*, the main piece of a capstan or steering-wheel.

b. **1591** in *Mod. Lang. Rev.* (1951) XLVI. 323 For peisinge ye spindle of ye howre wheele & ii newe bushes for ye barrell of ye same wheele. **1753** CHAMBERS *Cycl. Supp.*, *Barrel* of a clock is a cylindrical part, about which the string is wound. **1884** F. BRITTEN *Watch & Clockm.* 31 [A] Barrel hook.. [is] a pin in the barrel to which the mainspring is attached; Barrel Hollow.. [is] the sink cut in the top plate of a watch to give freedom to the barrel; Barrel Cover.. [is] a lid that snaps into a rebate in the barrel.

c. **1659** LEAK *Water-wks.* 32 Make the Musical Barrel to turn.. and the Pins that are put upon the said Barrel, shall touch the keys. **1876** EMERSON *Ess.* Ser. II. ii. 98 The revolving barrel of the music-box.

d. **1898** *Daily News* 12 Nov. 6/3 Frogs and barrels are adapted to the otherwise plain red coats. **1900** *Ibid.* 29 Dec. 6/6 The fronts are fitted out with braided frogs and barrels.

6. a. A (usually hollow) cylinder forming part of various objects; *esp.* **b.** one forming the trunk or body, *e.g.* of a pump, engine-boiler, bell, feather.

a. **1727** BRADLEY *Fam. Dict.*, *Curry-Comb*.. consists of these Parts, 1. The Barrel or Back of the Comb. **1874** BOUTELL *Arms & Arm.* ix. 173 The barrel (*fusée*), which is the hilt itself, adapted to be grasped by the hand. **1881** RAYMOND *Mining Gloss.*, *Barrel*, a piece of small pipe inserted in the end of a cartridge to carry the *squib* to the powder.

b. **1659** LEAK *Water-wks.* 17 If the Water be not high enough between the top of the Barrel and the Bucket. **1836** TODD *Cycl. Anat. & Phys.* I. 350/1 All feathers are composed of a quill or barrel. **1872** ELLACOMBE *Bells of Ch.* i. 4 The various parts of a bell may be described as the body or barrel, etc. **1882** *Law Rep.* Appeal IX. 429 The trunk or barrel of the tree. **1884** *Leis. Ho.* Sept. 533/2 Three lengths of cylinder, firmly riveted together, form what is called the barrel of the boiler [of a locomotive engine].

c. *slang.* (A nickname for) a corpulent person.

1909 LD. HARCOURT in *Daily Chron.* 16 July 1/5 When that measure reached the House of Lords it was met with a barricade of barrels insufficiently disguised in robes and coronets. **1959** I. & P. OPIE *Lore & Lang. Schoolch.* ix. 168 The unfortunate fat boy.. is known as:.. barrel, barrel-belly, [etc.].

7. The metal tube of a gun, through which the bullet or shot is discharged. Hence in *single-barrel*, *double-barrel*, etc., of the whole weapon.

a **1648** DIGBY (J.) Take the barrel of a long gun perfectly bored. **1705** *Lond. Gaz.* No. 4140/3 We also took 10 Pieces of Cannon, 8 whereof were treble Barrels. **1858** W. ELLIS *Vis. Madagascar* iv. 96 The long tin barrel of a painted gun.

8. The belly and loins of a horse, ox, etc.

1703 *Lond. Gaz.* No. 3948/4 A dun Gelding.. with a round Barrel. **1855** SINGLETON *Virgil* I. 151 Lofty is his neck, And elegant his head, his barrel short. **1880** BRET HARTE *Jeff. Briggs* ii, His legs clasping the barrel of his horse.

9. *Phys.* The cavity of the ear situated within the membrane of the tympanum.

1706 in PHILLIPS.

10. *Comb.* **a.** objective, as *barrel-forger*, *-maker*; **b.** attrib. (simply), as *barrel-barricade*, *-board*, *-form*, *-frame*, *-head*; (= packed in barrels), as *barrel-butter*, *-figs*, *-soap*; **c.** similative, as *barrel-belly*, *-bodied*, *-churn*, *-shaped*. See also 5c.

1837 CARLYLE *Fr. Rev.* v. v. I. 225 Cram the earth in *barrel-barricades. **1561** T. NORTON *Calvin's Inst.* Pref., The ydell and *barrell bealies of monkes. **1565** *Act 8 Eliz.* ix. §2 Coopers might have bought a Thousand of *Barrel-boards for twelve Shillings. **1894** M. DYAN *All in Man's Keeping* I. xiv. 219 Nipper, fat, puffing, and *barrel-bodied. **1743** ELLIS *Mod. Husb.* May 101 When the Cream is ready, carefully strain it.. into the *Barrel Churn. **1805** R. W. DICKSON *Pract. Agric.* I. pl. XXII, The improved barrel-churn with wheel. **1853** Barrel-churn [see DASHER 2]. **1853** 'A LADY' *Facts: Experiences Rec. Colonist N.Z.* iv. 34 The second churn for the larger quantity had better be a barrel churn fixed on a stand. **1620** VENNER *Via Recta* vii. 116 Dry or *barrell Figs. **1720** *Lond. Gaz.* No. 5873/4 William Thomas, late of White-Chappel, *Barrel Forger. **1874** PARKER *Ill. Goth. Archit.* I. iii. 80 The earliest Norman Vaults are.. of the *barrel form. **1856** KANE *Arct. Exp.* I. xxix. 386 A magnificent hut of *barrel-frames. **1883** *Glasg. Weekly Her.* 1 Sept. 4/2 Herring fishery.. finds profitable labour for.. *barrelmakers. **1869** NICHOLSON *Zool.* (1880) xxiv. 241 A free-swimming, *barrel-shaped ciliated body. **1710** *Lond. Gaz.* No. 4674/7 English *Barrel Soap for 48*s.* a Barrel.

11. Special combinations: **barrel-amalgamation** (see quot.); **barrel-bellied**, **-stomached** *a.*, having a well-rounded belly; **barrel-bird**, dial. name of the long-tailed tit; **barrel bolt**, a bolt made to slide into a barrel-shaped socket; **barrel-bulk**, a measure used in estimating capacity (*e.g.* of a vessel for freight) equal to five cubic feet; **barrel cactus**, the genus *Echinocactus*; **barrel-campaign** (in *U.S.*), a political contest in which bribery is lavishly employed; **barrel-chair** *U.S.*, an upholstered chair having a back shaped like a barrel; **barrel-chest** (see quot. 1907); so *barrel-chested* adj.; **barrel distortion** *Opt.* (see quot. 1953); **barrel-drain**, a cylindrical brick drain; **barrel-fever**, disease produced by immoderate drinking; **barrel-fish**, the black rudder-fish, *Lirus perciformis*, found off the U.S. coast; **barrelful**, as much as a barrel will hold; **barrel-head**, (either) flat end of a barrel; **barrel-like** *a.*, resembling a barrel; **barrel-pen**, one with a split cylindrical shank, which can be fitted on a wooden holder; **barrel-plating** (see quot.); **barrel roll**, an aeronautical feat in which an aeroplane makes a complete revolution about the longitudinal axis; so as *v. intr.*, to make a barrel-roll; **barrel-scraping** *vbl. sb.*, the action or result of 'scraping the barrel' (see SCRAPE *v.*); so *barrel-scraper*; *barrel-scraping* ppl. a.; **barrel-sewer** (cf. *barrel-drain*); **barrel shop** *U.S.*, a low-class drinking-saloon; **barrel-vault**, one with a simple semi-cylindrical roof, whence *barrel-vaulted*; **barrel winding** *Electr.*, an armature winding in which the end connections lie flat upon a cylindrical surface; **barrel-work** (see quot.). See also BARREL-ORGAN.

1881 RAYMOND *Mining Gloss.*, **Barrel-amalgamation*, the amalgamation of silver ores by revolution in wooden barrels with quicksilver, etc. **1697** DRYDEN *Virg. Georg.* III. 126 The Colt, that for a Stallion is design'd.. Sharp-headed, *Barrel-belly'd. **1856** J. GRANT *Bl. Dragoon* xli, His barrel-bellied charger. **1865** *Cornh. Mag.* July 36 The rustic.. call[s] the long-tailed tit.. the *'barrel-bird,' from its making a long moss and lichen-woven nest. **1909** WEBSTER, *Barrel bolt. **1911** *Encycl. Brit.* XV. 482/2 Among locks and fastenings the ordinary barrel or tower bolt needs no description. **1930** *Engineering* 2 May 564/2 Turned barrel bolts were used for connecting the brackets to the post webs. **1720** J. STEUART *Letter-Book* 22 Aug. (1915) 122 If William Binie Desires two *barell bulk home, let him have it. **1853** *Harper's Mag.* VI. 581/2 Freights from Detroit to Lake Superior ports are usually $1 the barrel bulk. **1881** *Amer. Naturalist* XV. 984 The 'nigger-head' or '*barrel' cactus. **1884** *Boston* (*Mass.*) *Jrnl.* 1 Nov. 1 We are accustomed to *'barrel' campaigns here. Nobody supposes this district to be Democratic, but the Democrats depend upon carrying it with money. **1850** A. J. DOWNING *Arch. Country Ho.* (1853) xii. 414 Another of the cheapest and simplest seats for a cottage is the **barrel-chair*. **1947** *Downtown Shop. News* (Chicago) 10 Feb. 15 (D.A.), Curved back barrel chairs foster that new look in fine furniture. **1907** GOULD *Practitioner's Med. Dict.* 267/2 **Barrel-chest*, a peculiar formation of the chest observed in cases of long-standing emphysema of the lungs. **1961** WEBSTER, *Barrel-chested. **1961** J. HELLER *Catch-22* (1962) xxi. 212 The wing commander was a blunt, chunky, barrel-chested man in his early fifties. **1889** *Barrel distortion [see VIEW *sb.* 19b]. **1903** BECK & ANDREWS *Photogr. Lenses* iii. 73 These two types of distortion found in single lenses are known as 'barrel' and 'pin-cushion' distortion. **1929** G. H. GLIDDON *Opt. Replica Human Eye* 21 At 20 degrees a trace of barrel distortion developed. **1937** A. T. WITTS *Television Cycl.* 16 *Barrel Distortion*, the type of distortion produced by defective optical systems that causes a square image to have rounded (convex) sides, similar to the form of a barrel. **1953** AMOS & BIRKINSHAW *Television Engin.* I. ix. 187 When distortion is present, the image of a rectangular object has sides which curve inwards (pincushion distortion) or outwards (barrel distortion), depending whether the magnification increases or decreases with distance from the centre of the image field. **1823** P. NICHOLSON *Pract. Build. Price-bk.* 117 The contents of gun-*barrel drains. **1884** GOODE et al. *Nat. Hist. Useful Aquatic Anim.* I. 334 This fish is also called by the fishermen 'Log-fish' and '*Barrel-fish'. **1885** J. S. KINGSLEY *Stand. Nat. Hist.* (1888) III. 191 The fishermen call them barrel-fish, though the most usual name is rudder-fish. **1936** J. T. JENKINS *Fishes Brit. Is.* (ed. 2) 71 The barrel-fish.. secretes itself in floating barrels or boxes. **1386** CHAUCER *Wife's Prol.* 301 Thus saistow, *olde barel ful of lies. **1436** *Pol. Poems* (1859) II. 169 To drinke a barelle fulle Of gode berkyne. **1865** *Rtldg's. Mag. Boys* Nov. 680 Another barrel-full of air is removed. **1840** CARLYLE *Heroes* vi. 352 Who cannot do without standing on *barrel-heads, to spout. **1911** *Handbk. Electro-Plating, Polishing* (ed. 4) 58 The Mechanical Plating of small articles in a barrel, revolving in a solution of the metal to be deposited, has reached a stage where developments in *Barrel Plating can be looked forward to. **1927** in *Amer. Speech* (1930) V. 210 She looped, *barrel-rolled, tail-spinned.. and then swooped some. **1932** AUDEN *Orators* II. 69 Went into a barrel roll at 8000 ft. and never came out. **1959** *Observer* 11 Jan. 18/6 A makeweight in a volume of *barrel-scrapings. *Ibid.* 15 Feb. 21/6 These over-edited, barrel-scraping volumes. *Ibid.* 15 Mar. 20/8 As for the Sunday-night offerings [on television], they were both barrel-scrapers. **1961** *Guardian* 22 June 8/7 The significance which critical barrel-scraping has bestowed on him. **1904** *N.Y. Tribune* 12 Oct. 1 A poisonous substitute for whiskey sold in the low '*barrel shops' along Tenth Avenue. **1884** *Littell's Living Age* No. 2077, 90 Your.. *barrel-stomached.. Chinese porker. **1849** FREEMAN *Archit.* 252 *Barrel-vaults prevail throughout the.. building. **1825** *Ann. Reg. 1824* 276*/2 Three large connected chambers, all *barrel-vaulted. **1851** TURNER *Dom. Archit.* I. vi. 214 The passage.. is barrel vaulted. **1902** *Encycl. Brit.* XXVII. 583/2 For multipolar armatures with two or more layers of inductors, 'surface' or '**barrel*' winding is now extensively used. **1881** RAYMOND *Mining Gloss.*, **Barrel-work* (Lake Sup.), native copper occurring in pieces of a size to be sorted out by hand in sufficient purity for smelting without mechanical concentration.

barrel ('bærəl), *v.* [f. prec. sb.]

1. a. *trans.* To put, pack, store up, or stow away, in a barrel or barrels.

1466 *Mann. & Househ. Exp.* 210 My mastyr sent to the kervelle iij. oxsen barellede. *c* **1525** MORE *De Quat. Nouiss.* 74/1 Iseland loueth no butter till it bee long barrelled. **1624** DONNE *Devotions* 43 (T.) That perverse man, that barrelled himself in a tub. **1769** FALCONER *Dict. Marine* (1789) *Caqueurs*, sailors appointed to cure and barrel the herring.

1865 CARLYLE *Fredk. Gt.* III. VIII. v. 34 Show him how.. the beer [is] drawn off, barrelled.

b. often emphasized with *up*. Cf. BARRELET. **1631** SPEED *Prosp. World* 30 Much provision.. barrelled vp for longer keeping. **1796** MRS. GLASSE *Cookery* xxii. 347 Barrel it up, with two or three spoonfuls of good yeast.

2. *gen.* To store up.

1589 *Pappe w. Hatchet* B ij, If Martin haue not barrelde vp all rakehell words. **1649** MILTON *Eikon.* XVI. Wks. (1851) 456 All benefit and use of Scripture, as to public prayer, should be deny'd us, except what was barreld up in a Common-praier Book. **1746** HERVEY *Medit.* (1818) 101 The tendrils of the cucumber.. barrel up for his use, the most cooling juices of the soil.

3. *to barrel off*: to transfer into barrels.

1756 J. LLOYD in W. Thompson *R.N. Advoc.* (1757) 50 These.. Grotts were barrell'd off.

4. *intr.* To move or travel quickly, *esp.* in a motor vehicle. Freq. with advb. (phr.). Also *fig. slang* (orig. and chiefly *U.S.*).

1930 *Amer. Speech* V. 305 *Barrel*, make haste or hurry, or cause to make haste. Used especially of vehicles. 'They went bareling up the hill for dinner.' **1943** *Yank* 3 Dec. 9 We dove for that, sweating bullets as I barreled over Shimushu at 800 feet full throttle. **1957** *New Yorker* 2 Nov. 47/1 He thought nothing of barrelling down to Munich at eighty miles an hour. *a* **1963** J. LUSBY in 'B. James' *Austral. Short Stories* (1963) 237 A Hurri was plunging abreast of me, barrelling. **1966** M. WOODHOUSE *Tree Frog* xxv. 192, I heard him barrelling by on my starboard. **1971** *Daily Colonist* (Victoria, B.C.) 20 June 31/5 Gravel trucks 'barrelling' through a residential area are worrying the parents of children. **1984** *Bulletin* (Sydney) 23 Oct. 165/1 Deng Xiaoping barreled on down the capitalist road last week—but he might be headed for a collision. **1985** *Truck & Driver* June 43/2 For lap after lap he tried, coming faster out of Clark Curve on the outside, and barreling along Brabham straight.

barrelage ('bærəlɪdʒ). [f. BARREL *sb.* + -AGE.] The total amount of any commodity, especially beer, as measured by barrels in a specified period; output estimated in barrels.

1890 *Certificate of valuation of Breweries*, The barrelage for the same period was, for the year 1888/9.. 312,292 bls. **1893** *Star* 10 Jan. 3/5 The increase in barrelage since the company was formed in 1887 amounted to 42,400. **1917** *Times* 26 Feb. 9/6 It is.. impossible for us to guarantee the food of this country without making a very much deeper cut into the barrelage of the country. **1960** *Economist* 9 July 123/1 Not enough barrelage in prospect is the reason given for the lack of development in the hotel industry.

†'**barrelet.** *Obs.* Also 7 barellet. [f. BARREL *sb.* + -ET[1].: cf. BARILLET.] A little barrel or cask.

1611 COTGR., *Hambour*, a kind of barrelet or firkin. **1699** EVELYN *Acetaria* (1729) 176 Range them in the Jarr or Barellet with Herbs and Spice.

†,**barrel-'ferrer, -ar, -or.** *Obs.* [f. BARREL + OF. *ferriere* a long-necked bottle or jar carried on journeys.] A vessel (either cask, jar, or leather bottle) in which water or wine was carried on horseback on a journey or military expedition.

1375 BARBOUR *Bruce* xv. 39 The Barell-ferraris [*v.r.* feris, ferrars] that war thar Cumrayd thame fast that rydand war. *c* **1425** WYNTOUN *Cron.* VIII. xxxviii. 53 Ane [hors] a payr of Coil Crelis bare.. Þe toþir Barrell ferraris twa, Full of wattyr. *c* **1440** *Morte Arth.* 2715 Barelle ferrers they brochede and broghte theme the wyne. **1480** CAXTON *Chron. Eng.* ccv. 186 They lete fylle v. barel ferrors [ed. 1520 barelles ferrours] with siluer.

barrel-house. orig. *U.S.* [f. BARREL *sb.* 1.]

1. A low-class drinking saloon, often incorporating a lodging-house or brothel.

1883 G. W. PECK *Peck's Bad Boy* 120 After I had put a few things in his brandy he concluded it was cheaper to buy it, and he is now patronizing a barrel-house. **1888** *Missouri Republican* 11 Feb. (Farmer), The West-side police are still arresting barrel-house loafers. **1934** J. A. & A. LOMAX *Amer. Ballads* (1960) p. xxxi, Jazz reigns happily and completely in the barrel-house regions. **1950** A. LOMAX *Mr. Jelly Roll* (1952) 79 Any musician who wasn't too proud to earn a dollar in a barrelhouse.

2. *attrib.*, passing into *adj.* Designating an unrestrained type of jazz such as is played in barrel-houses, characterized by a forceful rhythm. Also *absol.*

1926 H. O. OSGOOD *So this is Jazz* 99 Trumpets and trombones.. in that semi-muffled voice aptly described by the term 'barrel-house tone'. **1937** *Amer. Speech* XII. 182/1 The barrelhouse style is very African. **1938** *Manch. Guardian Weekly* 2 Sept. 188/3 It may start 'barrelhouse' (free improvisation), blending into 'screwball' (fast free improvisation). **1958** P. GAMMOND *Decca Bk. Jazz* xv. 181 Barrel-house retains a close allegiance with ragtime.

barrelled, -eled ('bærəld), *ppl. a.* [f. BARREL + -ED.]

1. Packed or stored in barrels; stowed away or enclosed in a barrel.

1494 *Act 11 Hen. VII*, xxiii, No Merchant.. should sell.. any barrelled Fish, except, etc. **1563** *Wills & Inv. N.C.* (1835) 210, Item, xxvii stone of barreled butter. **1603** DAVIES *Microcosm.* (1875) 83 The barrell'd Cynick hee. **1727** SWIFT *Modest Prop.* Wks. 1755 II. II. 66 Our exportation of barreled beef. **1842** GWILT *Archit.* §2259 Barrelled bolts are those in which the whole length of the bolt is enclosed in a continued cylindrical barrel.

fig. **1599** MARSTON *Sco. Villanie* I. iv. 188 Retayling others wit long barrelled, To glib some great mans eares.

2. Shaped like a barrel.

1853 KANE *Grinnell Exp.* xlv. (1856) 414 A great barreled arch went back into a cavern.

3. Having a barrel or barrels; chiefly in *comb.*, as ***round-, long-, single-, double-barrelled.*** Cf. BARREL *sb.* 8, 9.

1704 *Lond. Gaz.* No. 3984/4 A dark Mouse colour'd Mare, round Barrell'd. **1711** *Ibid.* No. 4888/4 Large limb'd, but small barrell'd. **1818** SCOTT *Rob Roy* xxx, The.. long-barrelled guns of several mountaineers. **1883** ROE in *Harper's Mag.* Dec. 45/2 A double-barrelled shot-gun.

barrelling, -eling ('bærəlɪŋ), *vbl. sb.* [f. BARREL *v.* + -ING[1].] The action or process of packing or storing in barrels.

1570 *Act 13 Eliz.* xi. §3 Uprightness and Truth in the Barrelling of such Fish. **1753** CHAMBERS *Cycl. Supp.* s.v., Barrelling of herring imports the cutting off their heads.

barrel-organ ('bærəl,ɔːgən). [f. BARREL *sb.* 6 c.] A musical instrument of the organ type, the keys of which are mechanically acted on by a revolving barrel or cylinder studded with metal pins. Also extended to similar instruments not of the organ type but producing the notes by means of metal tongues which are struck by pins fixed in the barrel. The tone resembles that of a piano; hence they are distinguished as 'piano organs'. (Occas. *attrib.*) Hence **barrel-organ** *v. intr.*, to play a barrel-organ; **barrel-organist**, one who plays such an instrument.

1772 A. WALKER *Specification of Patent* No. 1020 The Celestina.. is also made to be played by a pricked barrel, as the hand or barrel organ. **1796** *Month. Rev.* XX. 400 A barrel-organ.. would do the business much more to his satisfaction than the fingers of a man of genius. **1842** DICKENS *Amer. Notes* I. vi. 209, I remember [seeing in New York].. one barrel-organ and a dancing-monkey. **1866** HOWELLS *Venet. Life* ii. 28 Habitually came a barrel-organist and ground before the barracks. **1870** LOWELL *Among my Bks.* II. (1873) 326 The barrel-organ style which had been reigning. **1871** LE FANU *Checkmate* II. xiii. 128 The guitarring, singing, barrel-organing,.. all make a curious and merry Babel. **1928** *Times* 27 Dec. 15/7 Those who have barrel-organed in a hard December. **1938** *Oxf. Compan. Mus.* 554/1 The application of the colloquial term 'Barrel Organ' to this instrument [the street piano] is evidently due to mere association of ideas at the time it became popular.

Barremian (bə'reɪmɪən), *a. Geol.* Also -ien. [f. F. *Barrême*, canton in department of Basses-Alpes, France + -IAN.] = URGONIAN *a.*

1903 GEIKIE *Text-bk. Geol.* (ed. 4) 1197 The abandonment of the term Urgonian and the adoption in its place of 'Barremien'. **1914** *Brit. Mus. Return* 210 The Barremian Beds of Sandown Bay, I. of Wight. **1963** D. W. & E. E. HUMPHRIES tr. *Termier's Erosion & Sedimentation* i. 30 In the Cretaceous, from the Barremian-Aptian to the Lower Senonian, the widespread transgression which led to a uniform marine fauna also favored the development of forests.

barren ('bærən), *a.* and *sb.* Forms: 3 barain, -aigne, 4 barein, -en, 4–5 bareine, -eyn(e, 5 -ane, 4–6 ayn(e, barreyne, -ayne, (5 berhayn), 6 baraine, (barune, baryn), barreine, -ayn, (*Sc.* barrane, -and, -ant), 6–7 barraine, 6– barren. Compared *barrener, -est.* [a. OF. **barain*, *brahain, brehaing*, in fem. *baraine, baraigne, barhaine, barahaine, braaigne, brahaigne, brehaigne*, of uncertain origin and original form: assuming this to be *barain*, Diez suggests derivation from *bar* 'man, male' (L. type **bārāneus*), as if 'male-like, not producing offspring, sterile,' which suits the sense well; but there seems to be good reason for taking *brahain* as the original type, whence *bréhain*, and *barhain*, *barain*; the latter was the Anglo-Norman form. (The Breton *bréchagn* is certainly from Fr.: Thurneysen.)]

A. *adj.* **I.** Literal senses. Oppos. to *fertile.*

1. Of a woman: Bearing no children; without issue, childless.

c **1200** *Trin. Coll. Hom.* 133 Þe wimman was barrage [? barraigne], swo þat heo ne mihte for unkinde hauen no child. *c* **1230** *Ancr. R.* 158 Al were he, þuruh miracle, of barain iboren. *a* **1300** *Cursor M.* 16655 Þe baraigne blisced sal man call. *c* **1340** *Ibid.* (Fairf.) 2600 Sare.. sayde til abraham.. I am baren [*Cotton* geld]. *Ibid.* (Trin.) 12257 Þe bareyn [*Cotton* vnfruitand] shal hir fruyt fynde. **1483** CAXTON *G. de la Tour* F. vij b, Fenenna scorned.. Anna and called her berhayn. **1536** BELLENDENE *Cron. Scot.* Prol., The barrant wyfe Appeiris yung. **1590** SHAKS. *Mids. N.* I. i. 72 In shady Cloister mew'd, To liue a barren sister all your life. **1751** JORTIN *Serm.* (1771) I. ii. 22 His wife Sarah being barren.

2. a. Of animals: Not bearing, not pregnant at the usual season.

c **1340** *Gaw. & Gr. Knt.* 1320 To hunt.. at hyndez barayne. *c* **1400** *Ywaine & Gaw.* 2027 Sone he met a barayn da. **1653** WALTON *Angler* 84 So there be some barren Trouts, that are good in Winter. **1725** POPE *Odyss.* x. 622 A barren cow, the stateliest of the isle. **1882** *Somerset Co. Gaz.* 18 Mar. (*Advt.*), Cow and calf, barreners, barren heifers.

b. Of male animals: Sterile, castrated.

1617 MINSHEU *Ductor* 872 A boare hogge made a barren hogge.. a libd or gelded hogge, *porcus castratus*.

3. Of trees or plants: Without fruit or seed. (Sometimes specifically, as in ***Barren Strawberry***, a strawberry-like plant bearing only a dry seed.)

c **1386** CHAUCER *Knts. T.* 1119 Knotty knarry bareyn trees olde. **1580** HOLLYBAND *Treas. Fr. Tong, Aveneron*, barren oates. **1597** GERARD *Herbal* cxxviii §3. 397 Barren Welde hath a thicke wooddie roote. **1776** ADAM SMITH *W.N.* I. I. xi. 256 Rise in the real price of barren timber, in consequence of the improvement of land. **1861** MISS PRATT *Flower Pl.* I. 9 Flowers.. which have stamens only, are said to be barren. **1878** B. TAYLOR *Deukalion* I. ii. 23 The barren bough hung apples to the sun.

4. a. Of land: Producing little or no vegetation; not fertile, sterile, unproductive, bare. So of mines, etc.

1377 LANGL. *P. Pl.* B. XVIII. 106 Ne no lond tylye But al bareyne be. *c* **1420** *Pallad. on Husb.* I. 169 In bareine lande to sette or foster vynes. **1513** DOUGLAS *Æneis* VII. Prol. 41 Bewtie wes lost, and barrand schew the landis. **1551** TURNER *Herbal* (1568) F ij a, Gotes bearde in barune places hath but a short stalke. **1614** RALEIGH *Hist. World* II. 349 Land.. exceeding stony and barraine. **1776** ADAM SMITH *W.N.* I. I. xi. 249 The most fertile mine then known may be more barren than any that was wrought before the discovery of America. **1848** MILL *Pol. Econ.* II. ii. §5 One of the barrennest soils in the world.

b. ***Barren Grounds***, the district lying between Hudson Bay and Mackenzie River in Canada, used attrib. in ***Barren-Ground bear*** (see quots.); ***Barren-Ground caribou, reindeer***, any of the several varieties of reindeer found in the Barren Grounds and Greenland, esp. *Rangifer arcticus* and *R. grœnlandicus*.

1691 KELSEY in Doughty & Martin *Papers* 23 Aug. (1929) 13 Now yᵉ manner of their hunting these Beast on yᵉ Barren ground is.. they surround them. **1781** *Cumberland House Jrnls.* (1952) 226 The Indians lying Dead about the Barren Ground like rotten sheep. **1825** J. RICHARDSON in *Parry's Jrnl. 2nd Voy.* App. 329 The *cetrariæ, cornicularia*, and *cenomyces*, which clothe the barren-grounds like a carpet. *Footnote*, The Barren Grounds ('Hi lichene obsiti campi quos Terram Damnatam diceret peregrinus', Flor. Lapp., p. 374). **1829** —— *Fauna Bor.-Amer.* I. 23, I have given this one the *ad interim* name of Barren-ground Bear, until its difference from, or identity with, the *Ursus arctos* of Linnæus be fully established. *Ibid.* 241 Cervus tarandus var. α, arctica. Barren Ground Caribou. **1836** R. KING *Narr. Journey Arctic Ocean* I. vi. 149 The barren-ground reindeer, or *caribou*.. is of small size compared to the other deer. **1877** *Encycl. Brit.* VII. 25/1 The Barren Ground Caribou, and the Woodland Caribou. **1897** LYDEKKER in *Proc. Zool. Soc.* 425 *Ursus arctus Richardsoni*—Barren-Ground Bear... This Bear.. differs from the Grizzly in the shorter skull.

5. Void of vital germs.

1871 TYNDALL *Fragm. Sc.* II. xiii. 333 An infusion found to be barren by six months' exposure to moteless air.

II. Figurative senses.

6. Bare of intellectual wealth, destitute of attraction or interest, poor, meagre, jejune, arid, dry.

1387 TREVISA *Higden* Rolls Ser. I. 11, I.. dradde, after so noble spekers.. to putte forþ my bareyn speche. **1430** LYDG. *Chron. Troy* I. v, Thy wyt was to barrayne. **1549** OLDE *Erasm. Par. Eph.* Prol. E ij, The kynges maiesties playne Englyshe subiectes vnderstande none other but theyr owne natiue barayne tongue. **1598** BARRET *Theor. Warres* Pref. 5 Discourses.. not so barraine, but you may reape some good fruit from them. **1782** V. KNOX *Ess.* (1819) I. xlvii. 260 The barrenest periods of English literature. **1846** GROTE *Greece* I. iv. (1862) I. 79 A list of barren names fills up the interval.

7. Unproductive of results; fruitless, unprofitable.

1549 COVERDALE *Erasm. Par. 1 Cor.* xv. 10, I suffered not hys grace in me to be either idle or baraine. **1665** BOYLE *Occas. Refl.* (1675) Pref. 12 Who may chance to have either Barrenner Fancy's, or more unpractis'd Pens, than even I had. **1681** DRYDEN *Abs. & Achit.* 297 Barren Praise.. that Gaudy Flow'r, Fair only to the sight. **1753** CHAMBERS *Cycl. Supp.* s.v., Barren money is used, in the civil law, for that which is not put out to interest. **1779** J. MOORE *View Soc. Fr.* (1789) I. viii. 55 They could shed a few barren tears at a tragedy. **1877** MOZLEY *Univ. Serm.* i. 12 A barren and unrepaid attachment, a wasted affection.

8. Of persons: Mentally unproductive; unresponsive, dull, yielding no mental fruit.

1590 SHAKS. *Mids. N.* III. ii. 13 The shallowest thick-skin of that barren sort. **1602** —— *Haml.* III. ii. 46 Will themselues laugh, to set on some quantitie of barren Spectators to laugh too. **1779** JOHNSON *L.P.*, *Phillips* Wks. II. 291 He was in company silent and barren. **1866** CARLYLE *Remin.* (1881) I. 324 The stupidest and barrenest of living mortals.

9. *Const.* in all prec. senses with *of*.

c **1375** WYCLIF *Serm.* Sel. Wks. 1869 II. 278 Þou.. þat art barayne of goostly children. **1413** LYDG. *Pylgr. Sowle* IV. xx, Of ioye am I barayne. **1547** BOORDE *Introd. Knowl.* 198 These countreys be baryn of wine and corne. **1633** BP. HALL *Hard Texts* 374 Have I been barren of my favours to you? **1710** STEELE *Tatler* No. 196 ⁋5 Hearts barren of Kindness. **1856** FROUDE *Hist. Eng.* (1858) I. ii. 154 The league with France.. had been barren of results.

III. *Comb.* in parasynthetic deriv., as ***barren-brained, -spirited, -witted, -wombed***; and complemental, as ***barren-beaten.***

1597 DRAYTON *Mortimer.* 117 Renewe this wearie barren-wombed earth. **1601** SHAKS. *Jul. C.* IV. i. 36 A barren spirited Fellow. **1798** SOUTHEY *Lett.* (1856) I. 58 A barren-brained blockhead. **1859** TENNYSON *Elaine* 161 He left the barren-beaten thoroughfare. **1870** EMERSON *Soc. & Solit.* ix. 187 What a barren-witted pate is mine!

B. *sb.* [the adj. used *absol.*]

†**1.** A barren woman or animal. *Obs.*

[Cf. **1230** and **1340** in A I.] *c* **1420** *Anturs Arth.* iv, Vndur boes thay byde.. To beker at the barrens.

†**2.** Specific term for a drove of mules. *Obs.*

1486 *Bk. St. Albans* F vj a, A Baren of Mulis.

3. A tract of barren land; *spec.* applied in N. America to: **a.** elevated plains on which grow small trees and shrubs, but no timber, classed as ***oak-barrens***, ***pine-barrens***, etc., according to the trees growing on them; also *attrib.* as **barrens oak** (see quot. 1832); **b.** in Kentucky, to certain really fertile tracts in the carboniferous limestone formation; **c.** in Nova Scotia and New Brunswick (see quot. 1879).

1784 T. JEFFERSON in Sparks *Corr. Amer. Rev.* (1853) IV. 63 A mountainous barren which can never be inhabited. **1832** D. J. BROWNE *Sylva Amer.* 269 In New Jersey and Pennsylvania it [*sc.* the Black Jack Oak] is called Barrens Oak. **1850** LYELL *2nd Visit U.S.* II. 12, I had sometimes to put up with rough quarters in the pine-barrens. **1859** KINGSLEY *Life* II. 100 (D.) To have the sewage conveyed.. to fertilize the barrens of Surrey and Berkshire. **1877** J. ALLEN *Amer. Bison* 460 The so-called Barrens of Kentucky, the southward extension of the Wabash prairies. **1879** LD. DUNRAVEN in *19th Cent.* July 54 A barren.. means in Nova Scotia and New Brunswick an open marshy space in the forest, sometimes so soft as to be almost impassable, at other times composed of good solid hard peat.

† **'barren,** *v. Obs.* Also 6 **barrain -ayn.** [f. prec. adj.] To make barren, unfruitful, or sterile; to exhaust or impoverish (land); = BARRENIZE.

1581 A. ANDRESON *Serm. Paules Crosse* 69 So to barren the soyle rounde aboute them. **1593** NASHE *Christ's T.* (1613) 160 Barrayning their wombes by drugges. **1649** BLITH *Eng. Improv. Impr.* ii. (1653) 13 And this I charge as a great prejudice, and may be as a barrenning the land. **1725** BRADLEY *Fam. Dict.* s.v. *Stock Gilly*, They may be set again in the same Earth, after.. mixing Sand therewith to Barren it.

barrener ('bærənə(r)). [f. as prec. + -ER.] A cow not in calf for the year.

1882 [see BARREN *a.* 2].

† **'barrenhood.** *Obs.* Forms: 4 **bareynheed,** 5 **baraynhede.** [f. as prec. + -HOOD.] = BARRENNESS.

c **1380** WYCLIF *Sel. Wks.* (1871) III. 13 My Lorde.. was sory for my bareynheed. **1496** *Dives & Paup.* (W. de W.) I. xxv. 61/2 Wydowehede and baraynhede shall come to the bothe in one daye.

† **'barrenize,** *v. Obs.* [f. as prec. + -IZE; cf. *fertilize.*] To make barren or sterile; = BARREN *v.*

1649 BLITH *Eng. Improv. Impr.* (1653) 187 Not to barrennize Land, but to better or fatten it. **1725** BRADLEY *Fam. Dict., Sainfoin*.. does considerably meliorate and not barrenize the land on which it grows.

barrenly ('bærənlɪ), *adv.* [f. as prec. + -LY[2].] In a barren manner; without offspring, produce, or result; meagrely, scantily.

1552 HULOET, Barrenlye, *steriliter.* **1562** J. HEYWOOD *Prov. & Epigr.* (1867) 50 Though your pasture looke barreinly. *c* **1600** SHAKS. *Sonn.* xi, Let those whom nature hath not made for store.. barrenly perish. **1625** USSHER *Answ. Jesuit* 472 Yet haue they onely barrenly adorned this temporall life. **1877** BLACKIE *Wise Men* 36 Barrenly increase Mere itch of knowledge.

barrenness ('bærənnɪs). Forms: 4 **barynes,** 4–5 **bareynes(se,** 5 **-ines, -aynesse,** 6 **barenes, barraynesse, -ennis, -ennes,** 7 **-ennesse, -eness,** 7– **barrenness.** [f. as prec. + -NESS.]

1. Incapacity for child-bearing; sterility as regards offspring. The opposite of *fertility.*

1382 WYCLIF *Isa.* xlvii. 9 Comen shal to thee.. bareynesse and widewehed. *a* **1400** *Cov. Myst.* 75 My barynes he may amend. **1526** TINDALE *Rom.* iv. 19 Nor yet considered he.. the barenes of Sara. **1615** BP. HALL *Contempl. N.T.* I. i, Among the Jewes, barrennesse was.. a reproach. **1856** FROUDE *Hist. Eng.* II. 141 Providence had not pronounced against the marriage by a sentence of barrenness.

2. Unproductiveness or sterility of the earth; *hence*, dearth, scarcity, famine.

1388 WYCLIF *Gen.* xxvi. 1 Hungur roos on the lond aftir thilke bareynesse. **1480** CAXTON *Chron. Eng.* ccxxxi. 247 For defaute of rayne ther was grete barines of corn. **1590** SHAKS. *Com. Err.* III. ii. 123 Where Scotland? *Dro.* I found it by the barrennesse, hard in the palme of the hand. **1611** BIBLE *Ps.* cvii. 34 A fruitfull land into barrennesse. **1866** J. MURPHY *Comm. Ex.* xvi. 4 The very barrenness of the wilderness gave way to the bountiful hand of the Lord.

3. *fig.* Unproductiveness; *hence*, poverty of supply, lack of fullness or copiousness, bareness, scantiness, meagreness, poverty.

1586 THYNNE in *Animadv.* Introd. 70 Carping at my barrennes in writing, because I omit manie thinges. *a* **1617** HIERON *Wks.* II. 337 Such a generall barrennesse in mens hearts.. that they know not what to say vpon such occasions. *a* **1797** H. WALPOLE *Mem. Geo. II* (1847) I. iv. 94 Great hesitation in his elocution, and a barrenness of expression. **1879** FROUDE *Cæsar* xvii. 286 The barrenness of practical results.

4. Lack of intellectual capacity; mental poverty, slowness, dullness.

1552 HULOET, Barrennes properlye of capacitie, *segnities.* **1599** THYNNE *Animadv.* 2 The barrennesse of my feble skyll. **1750** JOHNSON *Rambl.* No. 19 ⁋8 The barrenness of his fellow students forced him.. into other company. **1837** WHEWELL *Hist. Induct. Sc.* (1857) I. 238 The prevalent feebleness and barrenness of intellect.

5. 'Aridity, want of emotion or sensibility.' J.

a **1667** JER. TAYLOR (J.) The greatest saints sometimes are fervent and sometimes feel a barrenness of devotion.

† **'barrenty.** *Obs.* In 4–5 **bareynte.** [a. OF. *barainete*, (also *brehennete*, *brehaignete*), f. *baraine*: see BARREN *a.* and -TY: cf. *sovereignty.*] = prec.

1382 WYCLIF *Gen.* xxvi. 1 Thilk bareynte that felle in the daies of Abraham. —— *2 Kings* ii. 21 There schal be no more in hem deth ne bareynte. *c* **1440** *Promp. Parv.* 24 Bareynte, *sterilitas.*

barrenwort ('bærənwɜːt). *Herb.* [f. BARREN *a.* + WORT.] English name of the genus *Epimedium*, esp. of *Epimedium alpinum* (N.O. *Berberidaceæ*), a low plant, with creeping rhizomes and long-stalked tri-ternate leaves.

1597 GERARD *Herbal* cxxiii. 389, I have thought good to call it Barren woort in English.. bicause.. being drunke it is an enimie to conception. **1769** SIR J. HILL *Fam. Herbal* (1789) 78 Barren-wort.. grows in woods, and has beautiful purple and yellow flowers. **1882** *Garden* 22 Apr. 284/1 When well grown these Barrenworts are very fine plants.

barrer ('bɑːrə(r)). [f. BAR *v.* + -ER[1].] One who bars.

1865 J. D. HARDY in *Athenæum* No. 1981. 501/2 Sends prompt word to the barrers-out.

barrer(e, obs. form of BARRIER.

‖ **barrera** (ba'rera). [Sp., barricade, barrier: see BARRIER.] A barrier, *spec.* that encircling a bull-ring; also the row of seats nearest to it.

1924 HEMINGWAY *In our Time* 22 He [*sc.* a horse] cantered jerkily along the barrera. **1926** —— *Sun also Rises* xiv. 155 Carpenters replaced weakened or cracked planks in the barrera. *Ibid.* xv. 167, I had taken six seats.. three of them were barreras, the first row at the ringside. **1932** —— *Death in Afternoon* iii. 35 A red wooden fence a little over four feet high.. called a barrera.

barres, -ez, obs. ff. BARRACE; obs. pl. of BAR *sb.*[1]

† **'barret**[1]. *Obs. rare.*[−1] [f. BAR *sb.*[1] + -ET[1]; cf. F. *barrette.*] A little bar.

1577 HOLINSHED *Chron.* III. 1256/2 The field of ten barrets silver and azure.

barret[2] ('bærɪt). Also 9 **baret, barrette.** [a. F. *barrette* (= Pr. *barreta*, *berreta*, It. *berretta*, Sp. *birreta*): see BIRETTA.] A little flat cap; esp. the BIRETTA, worn by Roman Catholic clerics.

1828 SCOTT *F.M. Perth* ii, The steel caps, barrets, and plumes, of squires, archers, and men-at-arms. **1845** E. HOLMES *Mozart* 66 The Cardinal taking his baret from his head. **1870** DISRAELI *Lothair* viii. 32 Waving, as he spoke.. his pink barrette. **1880** J. HAWTHORNE *E. Quentin* I. 159 A kind of scarlet barret-cap surmounted the heavy black coil of her hair.

barret, var. BARRAT, *Obs.*, strife, distress.

barrette (bə'rɛt). Also **barette.** [a. F. *barrette*, dim. of *barre* BAR *sb.*[1]] **1.** The crossbar of a fencing foil or the hilt of a rapier.

1909 *Cent. Dict.* Suppl.

2. A bar for supporting a woman's back hair; also, a hair-ornament.

1901 *Daily Colonist* (Victoria, B.C.) 10 Oct. 5/6 Shell Hair Barrettes, each 10 c. **1908** *Westm. Gaz.* 29 Feb. 13/2 The front part of the barette forms a bandeau. **1908** *Ladies' Field* 4 Apr. 197/1 The favourite [hair-ornament] seems to be Greek barrettes over hair combed low. **1952** M. MCCARTHY *Groves of Academe* (1953) ii. 21 [Girls with] jewelled barrettes in their new-washed hair.

barretter (bə'rɛtə(r)). *Electr.* [Said to be alt. of OF. *barateor* BARRATOR, exchanger.] **a.** An early device for detecting radio waves by means of the change in resistance in a metal filament. **b.** A modern adaptation used to stabilize an electrical current.

1903 R. A. FESSENDEN *U.S. Pat. 727,331*, The hot-wire receiver described.. which has been termed a 'barretter'. **1905** *Trans. Internat. Electr. Congress* III. 417 The device selected [as a detector for wireless reception].. was the 'solid barretter'... This consists of a minute loop of very fine platinum wire or filament. **1923** [see *hot wire* s.v. HOT *a.*]. **1935** *Wireless World* 15 Nov. 522/1 A barretter is a device in which the resistance varies according to the current. **1940** *Chambers's Techn. Dict.* 77/2 *Barretter*, an iron wire resistance mounted in a glass bulb containing hydrogen, and having a temperature coefficient so arranged that the variation of resistance produced ensures that the current in the circuit to which it is connected remains constant over a wide range of voltage. **1942** *Electronic Engin.* XV. 36 The filament heating of the master oscillator is stabilised by a barretter which also contributes to frequency stability. **1943** *Ibid.* 384 The barretter tube, which although fundamentally a current stabiliser does not actually regulate the voltage.

barricade (bærɪ'keɪd). Also 8 **barrocade.** [a. F. *barricade*, or assimilation of the earlier BARRICADO to the F. form.]

1. An obstruction hastily erected across a path or street to stop an enemy's advance; = BARRICADO 1.

1642 S. HARCOURT in *Macm. Mag.* XLV. 290 They had cast upp a travers or barricade. **1670** COTTON *Espernon* I. II. 72 All the world has heard of the Barricades of Paris. **1816** SCOTT *Old Mort.* 182 They.. forced the barricade, killing and wounding several of the defenders. **1850** TENNYSON *In Mem.* cxxvii, Tho' thrice again The red fool-fury of the Seine Should pile her barricades with dead.

2. *transf.* and *fig.* Any barrier blocking up or obstructing passage.

a **1735** DERHAM (J.) There must be such a barricade, as would greatly annoy or absolutely stop the currents of the atmosphere. **1742** MIDDLETON *Cicero* I. III. 201 He had broken through that barricade of Nobility. **1853** KANE *Grinnell Exp.* xxxiii. (1856) 285 A uniform curve.. abutted on each side by a barricade of rubbish.

3. *Naut.* = BARRICADO 4.

1769 FALCONER *Dict. Marine* s.v. *Abaft*, The barricade stands abaft the main-mast. **1867** in SMYTH *Sailor's Word-bk.*

4. *Comb.*, as ***barricade-work.***

1867 *Times* 29 Aug., The hands that were so ready at barricade-work have forgot their cunning.

barri'cade, *v.* [f. prec., or a. F. *barricade-r.*]

1. *trans.* To block (a passage) with a barricade.

1592 *No-body & Some-b.* (1878) 328 Man the Court gates, barricade al the streets. **1649** CROMWELL *Lett.* (Carl.) lxxx, Having burnt the gates, which our men barricaded up with stones. **1776** C. LEE in Sparks *Corr. Amer. Rev.* I. 159 To barricade all the streets. **1875** BRYCE *Holy Rom. Emp.* xvi. 287 Frederick barricaded the bridge over the Tiber.

b. *transf.* and *fig.* To block, bar, obstruct, render impassable.

a **1677** MANTON in Spurgeon *Treas. Dav.* Ps. cxix. 77 The way is barricaded and shut up by our sins. **1714** GAY *Trivia* III. 30 And the mixt hurry barricades the Street. **1718** J. CHAMBERLAYNE *Relig. Philos.* I. xiii. §16 To stop the Way.. and barricade it against Flies. **1883** FROUDE *Short Stud.* IV. II. iv. 208 The folios in the library bore marks of having been used to barricade the windows.

2. To shut in or defend with or as with a barricade. *lit.* and *fig.*

1657 *Deuine Louer* 98 Barricade mee with these Bulwarkes against myne enemyes. **1790** BEATSON *Nav. & Mil. Mem.* I. 310 The revolters barricaded themselves in some streets. **1802** PALEY *Nat. Theol.* viii. (1819) 102 To barricade the joint on both sides by a continuation of.. the bone over it. **1885** *Standard* 11 Apr. 4/8 The settlers are barricaded in the railway station.

barri'caded, *ppl. a.* [f. prec. + -ED.] Obstructed, closed, or defended, by a barricade.

1603 FLORIO *Montaigne* (1634) 349 Baricaded and armed houses. **1701** *Lond. Gaz.* No. 3759/7 Our Men found the Streets.. Barricaded.

barri'cader. [f. as prec. + -ER[1].] One who barricades.

1880 J. COLQUHOUN *Moor & Loch* I. 129 This was not difficult, as the barricaders in front would give me the signal.

barri'cading, *vbl. sb.* [f. as prec. + -ING[1].] **a.** A blocking or defending with a barricade.

1697 *C'tess D' Aunoy's Trav.* (1706) 125 She caused the Key to be taken out of the Door, and that to be bolted. I enquired the Reason of this Barricading. **1837** CARLYLE *Fr. Rev.* VII. x. I. 341 Barricading serves not: fly fast.

b. *concr.* A barricade or the materials of a barricade.

1890 J. WATSON *Conf. Poacher* 159 Quietly as we could, we undid the barricading. **1910** *Westm. Gaz.* 24 Jan. 8/1 Some of the barricading was thrown among the crowd.

barri'cading, *ppl. a.* [f. as prec. + -ING[2].] That constructs barricades.

1880 CARLYLE *Latter-d. Pamph.* Wks. VIII. 19, I will become a nomadic Chactaw rather, a barricading Sansculotte.

barricado (bærɪ'keɪdəʊ), *sb.* Forms: 6–7 **barracado, baricado,** (7 **baracadowe,** 8 **barricadoe),** 6– **barricado.** *Pl.* **-oes, -os.** [ad. F. *barricade* or Sp. *barricada* (see -ADO), f. F. *barrique* or Sp. *barrica* a cask, the first street *barricades* in Paris being composed of casks filled with earth, paving stones, etc. (Littré: cf. quots. 1590–98, 1602, 1743). Now usually BARRICADE in ordinary prose.]

1. A hastily formed rampart of barrels, wagons, timber, stones, household furniture, or any other materials readily available, thrown up to obstruct the advance of an enemy.

1590 *Foxe's A. & M.* (1684) III. 934 Soon after the day of the Barricadoes [*la journée des barricades*, in Paris, 1588] the Judges of Chastellat adjudged them to be hanged. **1598** FLORIO, *Baricata, Barricada*, a baricado or fortification with barels, timber and earth. **1602** WARNER *Alb. Eng.* x. lviii. 257 Till the Barricados Feast, when Guize vn-vizard was. **1603** HOLLAND *Plutarch's Mor.* 160 He fortified himselfe, not with barres and barricadoes. **1627** SIR R. COTTON in Rushw. *Hist. Coll.* I. 467 To block them up by Land, and.. to make a Barracado cross the Channel. **1670** COTTON *Espernon* III. XI. 541 Making great Barricado's upon all the Avenues. **1743** TINDAL *Rapin's Hist. Eng.* XVII. (1757) VII. 513 The barricadoes of Paris (*note*, What occasioned this name was, that the streets were blocked with *Barriques*, i.e. Hogsheads). **1854** J. STEPHENS *Centr. Amer.* (1854) 252 A barricado constructed with trunks of trees.

2. *transf.* and *fig.* Any barrier or obstruction to passage.

1611 SHAKS. *Wint. T.* I. ii. 204 No Barricado for a Belly. **1656** HOBBES *Liberty, etc.* (1841) 394 As if the needle.. were free to point either towards the north or towards the south, because there is not a barricado in its way to hinder it. **1693** LUTTRELL *Brief Rel.* III. 156 Many were drowned in the river, which proved a barricado to the French.

† 3. A natural frontier or boundary line. *Obs.*

1644 MILTON *Jus. Pop.* 50 Few Nations have prospered when their pride had transported them beyond their native Barricado's.

4. *Naut.*; see quots. Now usually BARRICADE.
1675 TEONGE *Diary* (1825) 52 Wee are fortifying our longe-boate with baracadowes. **1769** FALCONER *Dict. Marine* (1789), *Barricadoe*, a strong wooden rail, supported by..stanchions, and extending, as a fence, across the foremost part of the quarter-deck. **1804** NELSON in Nicolas *Disp.* (1846) VI. 282 If her barricado could be nearly all taken away she would be much better for the service.

barricado (bærɪ'keɪdəʊ), *v.* Forms: 7 baricado, -acado, barricadoe, -ocado, 6- barricado. [f. prec. sb.]

1. *trans.* To close or block (a passage) with (or as with) a barricade. (Formerly often with *up.*)
1611 CORYAT *Crudities* 16 Another..with..cart and horse barricadoed, and stopped the passage of the gate. *a* **1649** DRUMM. OF HAWTH. *Jas. V.* Wks. (1711) 88 Barricado'd some lanes with carts and other impediments. **1682** BUNYAN *Holy War* 117 They shut up Ear-gate, they barricado'd it up. **1755** SMOLLETT *Quix.* IV. 134 Barricado the streets with woolpacks! **1796** MORSE *Amer. Geog.* I. 139 Vast shoals of ice which barricadoed that part of the coast.

2. To fortify or defend (a place) with or as with barricades. Also *fig.*
1601 SHAKS. *All's Well* I. i. 123 Man is enemie to virginitie, how may we barricado it against him? **1678** TEONGE *Diary* (1825) 260 Wee..baracado our quarter deck with an old cable, to keepe off small shott. **1836** MARRYAT *Midsh. Easy* (1863) 221 The house was barricadoed as well as circumstances would permit. **1857** *Fraser's Mag.* LVI. 276 The birds had not only barricadoed the nest, but the bush itself.

3. *trans.* and *refl.* To enclose (a person) with a barricade; to shut up, bar in securely. *lit.* and *fig.*
1598 E. GILPIN *Skial.* (1878) 36 Be Barricadode in the peoples loue. **1633** T. STAFFORD *Pac. Hib.* viii. (1821) 569 They barricadoed themselves with barrells of earth. **1652** L. S. *People's Liberty* xiii. 34 They are so baracadoed by the Law of God against all opposition. **1719** DE FOE *Crusoe* 46, I barricado'd myself round with the chests. **1816** SCOTT *Old Mort.* (1830–2) II. xxvi. 270 [They] barricadoed themselves in the centre of the city.

4. To shut up, debar, preclude *from. lit.* and *fig.*
1611 SPEED *Hist. Gt. Brit.* IX. xii. 88 As if he meant to barricado them from flying. **1635** BRATHWAIT *Arcad. Pr.* II. 58 Which barrocadoed mine eare from inclining to any ones opinion but mine owne.

barri'cadoed, *ppl. a.* [f. prec. + -ED.] Closed or defended with a barricade. *lit.* and *fig.*
1611 HEYWOOD *Gold. Age* II. i. Wks. 1874 III. 24 The Iron bar'd dores..The Barricadoed gates. **1682** N. O. *Boileau's Lutrin* IV. 166 Could never pierce their Barricado'd Ears. *a* **1711** KEN *Edmund* Wks. 1721 II. 300 A Surcoat reaching to his Knees he wore, With Scales of Steel all barricado'd o're. **1809** W. IRVING *Knickerb.* VII. xi. (1849) 839 They found the castle strongly barricadoed.

barrico (bə'riːkəʊ). Pl. -oes. [ad. Sp. *barrica* cask, barrel, keg, ? f. *barra* bar; cf. BARECA.] A keg, a small cask or barrel.
1607 *Relat. Disc. River* in *Capt. Smith's Wks.* Introd. 54 There issued out of the hart of the tree the quantity of two barricoes of liquor. **1626** SMITH *Accid. Yng. Seamen* 5 The Cowper is..to staue or repaire the buckets, Baricoes, Cans. **1840** MARRYAT *Poor Jack* x, We had..only a barrico of water.

barrier ('bærɪə(r)), *sb.* Forms: 4 barer, 4–5 barrere, 4–6 barrer, 5 barreere, barryȝer, 5–6 barryer, 6 baryer, -ier, -iar, 6- barrier. [ME. *barrere*, a. AF. *barrere*, OF. *barrière* (= Pr., It. *barriera*, Sp., med.L. *barrera*):—late L. *barrāria*, f. *barra* BAR. Subsequently influenced by continental Fr. spelling.]

1. *gen.* A fence or material obstruction of any kind erected (or serving) to bar the advance of persons or things, or to prevent access to a place.

a. *orig.* A palisade or stockade erected to bar the way of an enemy, or defend a gate or passage; an external defence.
c **1325** *E.E. Allit. P.* B. 1239 He brek þe bareres as bylyue, & þe burȝ after. *c* **1380** *Sir Ferumb.* 4668 Enfachoun ys to þe ȝeate y-come..And at þe barers he hym sette. *c* **1425** WYNTOUN *Cron.* IX. vii. 70 At þe Barreris he faucht sa welle. *c* **1430** LYDG. *Stor. Thebes* III. (R.) Barbicans and bulwerkes ..Barreres, chaines, and ditches. *c* **1440** *Promp. Parv.* 24 Barrere, or barreere (*v.r.* barryȝer), *barraria, barrus.* **1490** CAXTON *Eneydos* lv. 152 Camilla and Mesapus rode all armed..vnto the barryers. **1523** LD. BERNERS *Froiss.* I. xxxviii. 52 He cast hymselfe bytwene the barrers and the gate. **1721** *Lond. Gaz.* No. 5928/6 The outer Barrier of that Place.
fig. **1713** YOUNG *Last Day* III. 124 Who burst the barriers of my peaceful grave?

b. *transf.* A fortress or fortified town which commands the entrance into a country; a 'bulwark.'
1600 HOLLAND *Livy* IX. xxxii. 337 b, Which cittie [Sutrium]..was (as a man would say) the verie Barriers [*claustra*] of all Hetruria. **1709** [cf. c]. **1716–8** LADY MONTAGUE *Lett.* I. xxvii. 86 Belgrade was formerly the barrier of Hungary.

†c. A fortified frontier; a frontier generally; *spec.* a name formerly given to a district which commanded the frontier of the Netherlands. *Obs.*
1709 ADDISON *Tatler* No. 20 ¶10 The Dutch are to have for their Barriers, Newport, Berg, St. Vinox..Lille. **1713** *Lond. Gaz.* No. 5180/2 The Frontier-Places of the Dutch-Barrier. **1775** ADAIR *Amer. Ind.* 463 Without allowing them any militia, even on their barriers. **1835** *Penny Cycl.* III. 502 The Treaty of the Barrier is an instance of a similar species of political adjustment.

d. A fence, or railing, to prevent access to any reserved place.
1570 B. GOOGE *Pop. Kingd.* IV. (1880) 51 b, With tapers all the people come, and at the barriers stay, Where downe upon their knees they fall, and night and day they pray. *Mod.* Strong barriers were erected at each end of the street.

e. Applied to the *carcer* or starting-place in the ancient race-course.
1600 HOLLAND *Livy* VIII. xx. 295 The Barriers [*carceres*], from whence the horses and their chariots are let forth. **1656** COWLEY *Pind. Odes* Wks. 1710 I. 203 How swiftly [has he] run, And born the Noble Prize away, Whilst other Youths yet at the Barrier stay? **1880** LEWIS & SHORT *Lat. Dict.*, *Carcer*..the barrier or starting-place in the race-course.

f. In continental towns: The gate at which custom duties are collected.
1825 T. JEFFERSON *Autobiog.* I. 86 The oppressions of the tithes..the gabelles, the farms and the barriers. [*a* **1847** MRS. SHERWOOD *Lady of Manor* I. iv. 96 Versailles is distant about ten miles from the barriere of Paris.]
attrib. **1804** *Edin. Rev.* IV. 47 The barrier duties.

g. *Coal-mining.* 'A breadth of coal left against an adjoining royalty, for security against casualty arising from water or foul air.'
1851 *Coal-tr. Terms Northumbld. & Durh.* 6 Barriers are left of various thicknesses..varying..from 10 to 50 yards.

2. a. *spec.* in *pl.* The palisades enclosing the ground where a tournament, tilting, or other martial contest or exhibition was held; the lists. Also, a low railing or fence running down the centre of the lists on opposite sides of which, and in opposite directions the combatants rode, reaching their lances across.
1581 J. BELL *Haddon's Answ. Osor.* 79 To challenge me unto the Barriers. *Ibid.* 82 One champion is taken from the Barriers. **1817** SCOTT *Ivanhoe* viii, At length the barriers were opened, and five knights advanced slowly into the area.

†b. Hence, the expression *to fight at barriers*, and *Barriers* as the name of a martial exercise in 15th and 16th centuries. *Obs.* exc. *Hist.*
1494 FABYAN an. 1546 (R.) Chalengours..at tilt, barriers and turney. **1532** *Act 24 Hen. VIII*, xiii, Iustes, tourneis, barriers..or other marcial feates. **1583** GOLDING *Calvin on Deut.* xii. 67 Like the Game of the Barriers wherein he that winneth today looseth tomorrow. **1608** MIDDLETON *Fam. Love* III. vi. Wks. II. 159 To see my gallants play at barriers with scourge-sticks. **1616** BULLOKAR, *Barriers*, a war-like exercise of men fighting together with short swords, and within some appointed compasse. **1625** FLETCHER *Noble Gentl.* II. i. 32 You shall not see a mask or Barriers Or tilting or a solemn christning. **1625** BACON *Masques, Ess.* (Arb.) 540 For Iusts, and Tourneys, and Barriers; The Glories of them, are chiefly in the chariots, wherein the Challengers make their Entry. **1636** RANDOLPH in *Ann. Dubrensia* (1877) 19 What is the Barriers, but a Courtly way Of our more doune-right sport, the Cudgell-play? **1650** BP. HALL *Balm of Gilead* 104 [He] puts him upon Tiltings, and Barriers, and publique Duels. **1839** KEIGHTLEY *Hist. Eng.* I. 445 He frequently fought at barriers.
fig. **1622** WITHER in Farr's *S.P.* (1848) 219 These long-gowned warriers, Who play at Westminster, unarm'd, at barriers. *a* **1680** BUTLER *Rem.* (1759) I. 220 As he, who fought at Barriers with Salmasius Engag'd with nothing but his Stile and Phrases.

3. a. Any natural obstacle which stops or obstructs passage, defends from foes, prevents access, or produces separation; a separating boundary-line.
1703 MAUNDRELL *Journ. Jerus.* (1732) 32 In order to pass this Barrier, we turned up on the left hand. *a* **1744** POPE (J.) An ocean flows, Around our realm, a barrier from the foes. **1747** in *Col. Rec. Penn.* V. 153 The Colonies of New Jersey and Pennsylvania will have but a very thin Barrier between them. *c* **1854** STANLEY *Sinai & Pal.* iii. (1858) 174 This plain was encompassed with a barrier of heights. **1855** PRESCOTT *Philip II*, I. II. vi. 207 No mountain barrier lay between France and Flanders.

b. The mass of ice which fringes the Antarctic coast, occas. spec. *the Barrier.*
1847 J. C. ROSS *Voy. Discovery & Research* I. viii. 222 Some of the numerous fragments of the barrier that were about us. **1905** R. F. SCOTT *Voy. 'Discovery'* I. v. 168 The barrier edge, in shadow, looked like a narrowing black ribbon. **1930** *Discovery* Mar. 91/1 Flat fields of snow-ice, strictly speaking neither land-ice nor sea-ice, which, under the name of 'barriers' fringe almost the whole circumference of the continent.

c. *Physics.* The region of high potential energy through which a charged particle must pass on leaving or entering a nucleus; also *attrib.*
1929 RUTHERFORD in *Proc. R. Soc.* A. CXXIII. 378 The nucleus, supposed spherical in shape, is thus surrounded by a very high potential barrier. **1938** R. W. LAWSON tr. *Hevesy & Paneth's Man. Radioactivity* (ed. 2) ix. 98 The nucleus is thus protected by a barrier at an exceedingly high potential. **1955** J. A. WHEELER in W. Pauli *Niels Bohr* 166 Odd nuclei have a higher barrier against fission than corresponding even nuclei. *Ibid.* 167 The barrier penetration exponent is roughly proportional to the barrier height. **1962** SIMPSON & RICHARDS *Junction Transistors* ii. 23 Because electrons flowing from *n*- to *p*-type material or holes flowing from *p*- to *n*-type material require excess energy to mount the potential step, the latter is sometimes called the 'barrier'.

4. a. Anything immaterial that stops advance hostile or friendly, that defends from attack, prevents intercourse or union, or keeps separate and apart.
1702 POPE *Thebais* 20 Fix, O Muse! the barrier of thy song at Œdipus. **1715** BURNET *Own Time* an. 1685 (R.) The tests stood as a barrier to defend us from popery. **1742** YOUNG *Nt. Th.* III. 733 A good man, and an angel! these between How thin the barrier? **1776** GIBBON *Decl. & F.* I. 60 Every barrier of the Roman constitution had been levelled by the vast ambition of the dictator. **1797** GODWIN *Enquirer* II. xii. 480 He..erects a barrier between himself and his reader. **1832** HT. MARTINEAU *Ireland* 128 The barrier which they believed to separate the rich and the poor in Ireland. **1855** MOTLEY *Dutch Rep.* II. ii. (1866) 138 All history shows how feeble are barriers of paper or lambskin..against the torrent of..despotism. **1883** GILMOUR *Mongols* xvii. 207 Felt to be barriers to the acceptance of Christianity.

b. Freq. with defining word; ***sound barrier*** (see SOUND *sb.*[3]).
1923 *Internat. Jrnl. Psycho-analysis* Oct. 495 (*sub-heading*) The Incest Barrier. **1957** *Ann. Reg. 1956* 346 Problems of producing aircraft for still higher speeds, with special attention for the next main obstacle—the heat barrier. **1958** F. KENYON *Our Bible & Anc. MSS.* (ed. 5) i. 36 They [*sc.* the Dead Sea Scrolls]..enable us..to 'penetrate the Massoretic barrier' by centuries.

5. *attrib.* and *Comb.*, as in ***barrier fen, -like, -net.*** Also **barrier-act** (see quot.); **barrier cream,** a protective cream for the skin; **barrier-gate,** a heavy gate closing the opening through a barrier; **barrier layer** in *Physics*, an electrical layer lying between two different metals or between a metal and a semiconductor; also *attrib.*; **barrier-pillar, barrier-reef** (see quots.); **barrier-treaty,** a treaty fixing the frontier of a country, esp. the 'Treaty of the Barriers' between Germany, Great Britain, and Holland, signed at Antwerp 15 November 1715.
1868 CHAMBERS *Encycl.* I. 712 *Barrier Act..an act of the General Assembly of the Church of Scotland, 8th January 1697, intended as a barrier against innovations, and a hindrance to hasty legislation. **1950** *N.Y. Times* 16 Apr. E9/5 A British chemical firm protects workers who handle dyestuffs, chemicals, explosives, oils, acids, alkalis and grease by means of '*barrier creams'. The cream is spread over the hands until an invisible 'glove' is formed. **1958** *Sunday Times* 20 July 16/5 A reputable barrier cream against sunburn. **1855** SINGLETON *Virgil* I. 215 To cross the *barrier fen. **1833** MARRYAT *P. Simple* (1863) 159 When we had crossed the moat, we found a *barrier-gate locked. **1934** *Physical Rev.* XLVI. 1051 A *barrier layer photo-cell.. consists of a closed conducting circuit which comprises a semi-conductor forming a link in a metallic circuit. **1944** C. E. K. MEES *Theory of Photographic Process* xvii. 663 Numerous densitometers consist..merely of a light source, a barrier layer cell, and a microammeter. **1948** R. C. WALKER *Photoelectr. Cells in Indust.* i. 35 The rectifier type of light sensitive cell, often referred to by alternative names such as barrier layer, blocking layer, or self-generative cells. **1845** DARWIN *Voy. Nat.* xx, There is a simplicity in the *barrier-like beach. **1884** D. WATT in S. Dawson *Handbk. Canada* 279 The *barrier-nets and weirs of pale-faces. **1881** RAYMOND *Mining Gloss.*, **Barrier-pillars*, pillars of coal, larger than ordinary, left at intervals to prevent too extensive crushing when the ground comes to be *robbed.* **1805** FLINDERS in *Phil. Trans.* XCVI. 252 Amongst the *barrier reefs. **1853** DE LA BECHE *Geol. Observ.* xi. 181 The Great Barrier Reef, extending off the east coast of Australia for about 1100 miles, with a mean breadth of about 30 miles. **1877** GREEN *Phys. Geol.* iv. §3. 136 A mighty wall of coral rock, separated from the land by a deep and broad channel, and bounded on the seaward side by a face almost vertical and of enormous height. Such a reef is called a Barrier reef. **1712** LUTTRELL *Brief Rel.* VI. 719 The *barrier treaty made by the lord Townsend with the states general. **1804** GEO. III. in G. Rose *Diaries* (1860) II. 177 He..considered the Barrier Treaty as..a very effectual one..for preserving the balance of power in Europe.

barrier ('bærɪə(r)), *v.* [f. prec. sb.] To close or shut with a barrier. Commonly with *off, in.*
1776 C. LEE in Sparks *Corr. Amer. Rev.* (1853) I. 153, I shall barrier the principal streets. **1869** *Daily News* 2 July, A space was barriered off by ropes. **1879** F. MALLESON in *Lett. Clergy* 51 The mountain tarn barriered in by its stupendous crags.

'barriered, *ppl. a.* [f. prec. + -ED[1].] Furnished with or confined by a barrier or barriers.
1846 RUSKIN *Mod. Paint.* I. II. I. vii. §5. 76 A weak, rippling, bound and barriered water.

†**'barriket.** *Obs.* Also barriquet. [dim. f. BARRICO, or F. *barrique* cask. (The French would be *barriquette.*)] A small cask, a firkin.
1611 COTGR., *Barrot*, a ferkin or barriket. *Fillette*, a firkin, barriquet, small wine vessell.

barrikin ('bærɪkɪn). = BARAGOUIN.
1851 MAYHEW *London Lab.* I. 15/1 The high words in a tragedy we calls jaw-breakers, and say we can't tumble to that barrikin.

barring ('bɑːrɪŋ), *vbl. sb.* [f. BAR *v.* + -ING[1].] The action of the vb. BAR: a. Fastening up, in, or out, with a bar or bars. b. Exclusion, prohibition. c. Marking or ornamentation with bars. Also *attrib.*
c **1386** CHAUCER *Pers. T.* ¶343 The cost of embrowdynge the degise, endentynge, barrynge..and semblable wast of clooth. **1440** *Promp. Parv.* 24 Barrynge of dorys, *repagulacio.* Barrynge of harneys, *stipacio.* **1638** *Penit. Conf.* iii. (1657) 32 The exclusion and barring of haynous offenders from the assembly of Christians. **1875** POSTE *Gaius* III. 448 The barring of any subsequent suit. **1922** R. C. PUNNETT *Mendelism* (ed. 6) ix. 88 The cock in a pure breeding strain of Plymouth Rocks is homozygous for the barring factor. **1961** BANNERMAN *Birds Brit. Isles* IX. 2 The breast is also russet in colour, merging into black barring on the abdomen.

d. *barring-out*: a mode of schoolboy rebellion, when they shut the schoolroom or house against the master, and refuse to admit him until their demands are conceded.

1728 SWIFT *Jrnl. Mod. Lady* Wks. 1755 III. II. 194 Not school-boys at a barring-out Rais'd ever such incessant rout. **1847** TENNYSON *Princ.* Concl. 66 Revolts, republics, revolutions, most No graver than a schoolboys' barring-out. **1876** GRANT *Burgh. Sch. Scot.* II. v. 188 Another barring-out in the high School of Edinburgh, ended more tragically.

e. *attrib.*, as in ***barring engine***: small auxiliary engine for starting large mill engines; so called from the employment of a crow-bar to move a fly-wheel round for a portion of a revolution, and assist in setting the engine going.

1885 *Engineer* 22 May New Patent Barring Engine.

f. The division of music into bars: see BAR *sb.*[1] 16.

1874 CHAPPELL *Hist. Mus.* I. viii. 166 When bars were first introduced, they were mere measures of time, therefore old barring is not to be followed implicitly. **1920** *Times Lit. Suppl.* 6 Aug. 493/3 Latter-day music..shuns symmetrical barring and full closes. **1959** D. COOKE *Lang. Mus.* iv. 187 The same key, tempo, dynamics, phrasing, and barring.

'barring, *ppl. a.* [f. as prec. + -ING[2].] Fastening up, in, or out; restraining, prohibitive.

1567 DRANT *Horace' Ars P.* A. v, Vnbearded youth, at last rid from the Tutors barring charge.

barring ('bɑːrɪŋ), *prep.* [absolute use of pr. pple. of BAR *v.* 8: cf. similar use of *saving*, *excepting*; also *notwithstanding*, *pending*, *during*.] Excluding from consideration, leaving out of account, omitting, excepting, except.

1481–90 *Howard Househ. Bks.* 283, vj^xx. yardes, barin one pese, of lynnen cloth. **1656** H. MORE *Antid. Ath.* III. ix. (1712) 169 It is allow'd..to a Christian, barring the wrong done to Religion, to make use of the help and advice of the Devil. **1762** tr. *Duhamel's Husb.* I. viii. 38 Barring it's being so near the stable. **1793** GOUVR. MORRIS in Sparks *Life & Writ.* (1832) II. 281 That immense army (barring accidents) will be completed. **1845** DE QUINCEY *Coleridge* Wks. XII. 86 Nobody else, barring the author, knew.

barring, *vbl. sb. Obs.* cry of elephant: see BARR.

‖**Barring'tonia.** *Bot.* [named after the Hon. D. Barrington.] A genus of flowering trees, found in parts of India, Australia, America, and Africa.

1871 MATEER *Travancore* 100 The Barringtonia, with its pendulous racemes of lovely pink tassels.

barrio ('bærɪəʊ). Chiefly *N. Amer.* [a. Sp. *barrio* district, suburb.] **1.** A ward or quarter of a city or town in Spain or a Spanish-speaking country; in some Spanish-speaking countries, a rural settlement. Also *attrib.*

1841 BORROW *Zincali* I. I. xii. 199 The quarters (barrios) where they now live with the denomination of Gitános. **1892** E. J. PAYNE *Hist. Amer.* I. II. 482 Tezcatlipoca..was considered to be the tutelary god of Huitznahuac, one of the six quarters or *barrios* of which this pueblo was composed. **1899** A. LAST tr. *P. F. X. Baranera's Handbk. Philippine Islands* 45 Each town, or township, is divided into wards or *barrios*, the headsman of which is called *cabeza de barangay*. **1934** W. STARKIE *Spanish Raggle-Taggle* xxxv. 436, I found myself in the *barrio de Tetuan*, the guest of my Gypsy friends. **1963** *New Yorker* 8 June 145 All the barrios have their own elected councils..each headed by a barrio lieutenant. **1972** *N.Y. Times* 1 June 18/8 On Monday, most of the Protestants of a tiny Puerto Rican barrio 20 miles outside San Juan gathered for a gay send-off for their pastor and seven friends. **1985** *Sunday Times* 13 Jan. 8/4 When he gets back home..his supporters will hear about the barrio Jorge Dimitrov, an exceedingly poor neighbourhood in Managua which he was taken to see.

2. A Spanish-speaking district in a U.S. city or town, esp. a poor neighbourhood populated by immigrants. Also *attrib.*

1939 *Time* 13 Mar. 78/2 At 110th Street, Manhattan's.. Fifth Avenue..plunges into a new world—the teeming, Spanish-speaking slums, or barrio, of Lower Harlem. **1954** J. H. BURMA *Spanish-speaking Groups* iii. 88 Always in the Southwest and commonly throughout the rest of the United States, the Mexican lives in a segregated section of town. He calls it the *barrio* or the *colonia*. **1969** L. KENNEDY *Very Lovely People* i. 100 I've been living in a *barrio*.... Oh, those *barrio* people are sweet. **1971** *Daily Colonist* (Victoria, B.C.) 2 Feb. 3/7 An overnight curfew brought calm to the East Los Angeles Mexican-American barrio Monday. **1978** *Guardian Weekly* 30 Apr. 17/3 The Mexican-American sections of Phoenix are organized into 16 barrios—or neighbourhoods. **1985** G. PALEY *Later Same Day* 84 I'd never fool around with a Spanish guy. They all have tough ladies back in the barrio.

barrister ('bærɪstə(r)). Forms: 6–7 **barester**, 6–8 **barrester**, 7 **barraster**, 7– **barrister**. [f. BAR *sb.*[1] (or F. *barre* or med.L. *barra*): the rest of the word is obscure, being formerly written *-ester*, *-aster*, but now *-ister*, perh. after words like *chorister*, *sophister*, but there is no trace of an earlier **barrist*, like *chorist*, *sophist*; Spelman cities 16th c. L. *barrasterius* (probably formed from the Eng.).]

A student of the law, who, having been called to the bar, has the privilege of practising as advocate in the superior courts of law. The formal title is ***barrister-at-law***; the equivalent designation in Scotland is *advocate*.

The name originated in the ancient internal arrangements of the Inns of Court: see quot. 1545 infra, and BAR *sb.* 24. But by 1600, it was currently associated with the bar of the courts of justice, at which utter-barristers had before that date secured the right to plead, formerly possessed only by sergeants and apprentices-at-law.

c **1545** T. DENTON, N. BACON, and R. CARY, *Return to Hen. VIII. of State of Inns of Court* (in Waterhouse *Comment. on Fortescue* 1663, 544) The whole company and fellowship of learners is divided..into three..degrees:.. *Benchers*, or as they call them in some of the houses, *Readers*, *Utter-Barresters*, and *Inner-Barresters*..Utter-Barresters are such, that for their learning and continuance, are called by the Readers to plead and argue in the said house doubtful cases and questions..and are called *Utter-Barresters* for that they, when they argue the said Motes, sit uttermost on the formes which are called the Barr, and this degree is the chiefest..in the house, next the Benchers. All the residue of learners are called *Inner-Barresters*, which are the youngest men. *c* **1570** *Pride & Lowl.* (1841) 70 Therefore beseech I.. Barresters, or how so ye be termed, To Judgen it after your wisdome. **1603** HOLLAND *Plutarch's Mor.* 167 Expert Advocates or Barristers..to plead for us. *a* **1613** OVERBURY *A Wife* (1638) 176 The velvet breeches he was first made Barester in. **1616** BULLOKAR, *Barrester*, he that is allowed to plead causes at the barre. *a* **1674** CLARENDON *Hist. Reb.* I. III. 158 William Pryn, a Barrester of Lincoln's-Inn. **1722** T. WOOD *Inst. Laws Eng.* (1763) 465 A Barrister (heretofore called an Apprentice of the Law) is a counsellor learned in the Law..admitted to plead without the Bar. **1725** *Lond. Gaz.* No. 6380/14 Joshua Ireland..Barrister at Law. **1768** BLACKSTONE *Comm.* III. 26 Of advocates, or counsel, there are two species or degrees; barristers, and serjeants. **1836** HOR. SMITH *Tin Trump.* (1876) 52 All briefless barristers will please to consider themselves excepted.

b. ***inner, utter, vacation barrister*** (all obs.): see quot. and cf. quot. *c* 1545 above; ***revising barrister***: one appointed to revise the lists of persons qualified to vote for Members of Parliament.

a **1547** in Dugdale *Orig. Jurid.* (1671) 148 The Masters commens are ferder divided into three Companies; that is to say, no Utter-Barristers, Utter-Barristers, and Benchers. **1584** *Wills & Inv. N.C.* (1860) 105 So longe as he remayneth at th'ins of courte, vntyll he be utter barester. **1607** COWELL *Interpr.* s.v. *Utter-Barristers*, A barrister newly called is to attend the six next long Vacations the Exercise of the House ..and is therefore for those three years called a Vacation Barrister. And they are called utter Barristers, *i.* Pleaders without the Bar to distinguish them from Benchers..who are sometimes admitted to plead within the Bar. **1835** *Penny Cycl.* III. 503 Students of the law under the degree of utter barristers, took their places nearer to the centre of the hall and farther from the bar, and from this manner of distribution appear to have been called inner barristers.

barrister, obs. f. BALUSTER, BANISTER.

1662 FULLER *Worthies* III. 11 A leaden Tarras, with Railes, and Barristers. **1662** GERBIER *Princ.* (1665) 15 To spare charges of Rails, Barresters and Pedestals. **1663** —— *Counsel* 69 All Barristers at one penny an inch.

barristerial (bærɪ'stɪərɪəl), *a.* [f. prec. after *ministerial*.] Of or pertaining to a barrister.

1839 *Blackw. Mag.* XLVI. 32 The youthful aspirant for barristerial honours. **1864** KINGSLEY *What does Newman mean?* 41 Great literary, and even barristerial ability.

'barristership. [f. BARRISTER + -SHIP.] The position of a barrister.

1839 *Blackw. Mag.* XLVI. 32 Barristers..eat their tedious way to a..revising barristership. **1864** *Spectator* 1421 Here..is a writer thrusting his barristership on our notice.

barri'stration. *nonce-wd.* [f. after *ministration*, *registration*.] The action of a barrister.

1837 SYD. SMITH *Let. Singleton* Wks. 1859 II. 284/1 The one thing wanting to sublunary happiness—the great principle of Commission, and six years' Barristration.

barristress ('bærɪstrɪs). Also **-eress.** [f. BARRISTER + -ESS.] A woman barrister.

1898 *Fortn. Rev.* LXIV. 127 The modern barristress. **1899** *Westm. Gaz.* 8 June 1/2 Barristeress-at-law.

barrow ('bærəʊ), *sb.*[1] Forms: 1 **biorȝ**, 1–3 **beorȝ**, 1–2 **beorh**, 2 **beoruh**, 3 **berhȝ**, **borew**, 4 **berȝ**, **bergh**, **beruȝ**, **beruh**, **berw**, (**borw**, **borȝ**, **borgh**, **burgh**), 6 **barow**, (7 **barrough**), 6– **barrow**. See also BARGH, BURROW. [Com. Teut.: OE. *beorȝ* (:—*berg*) = OS., OHG. *berg*, MDu. *berch*, Ger., Du. *berg*, Goth. **bairgs*:—OTeut. **bergo-z*, all masc.; cf. ON. *berg* and *bjarg* (neut.) 'rock.' Cogn. with OSlav. *brĕgŭ* mountain, height, OIr. *brigh* mountain, Skr. *b'rhant*, Zend *barezant* high:—Aryan **bhergh* height. In Eng. literature, the word went out of use before 1400, but was preserved, in special senses, in the north. dial. *bargh*, *barf*, and south-western *barrow*; the latter has since been taken back into archæological and general use from the 'barrows' of Salisbury Plain, etc.]

†**1.** A mountain, mount, hill, or hillock. (Applied, as the date becomes later, to lower eminences.)

c **885** K. ÆLFRED *Oros.* I. i. §12 þa beorȝas þe mon hæt Alpis. *c* **1000** *Ags. Gosp.* Luke iii. 5 Ælc munt and beorh byþ ȝenyðerod. *c* **1150** in Wright *Voc.* 92 Hul *uel* beoruh. **1205** LAY. 12311 Vnder ane berhȝe. *Ibid.* 20854 Segges vnder beorȝen [**1250** borewe] mid hornen, mid hunden. **1340** *Gaw. & Gr. Knt.* 2172 A balȝ berȝ, bi a bonke. **1393** LANGL. *P. Pl.* C. VIII. 227 Thenne shalt þou blenche at a bergh [*v.r.* berwe, borw, borȝ, borgh], ber-no-fals-wytnesse. **1578** LYTE *Dodoens* 36 Sterrewurte groweth vpon small hillockes, barrowes, or knappes. **1662** FULLER *Worthies* I. 212 Planted on a little Barrough within Randome-shot of the Enemy.

2. Still in local use: **a.** in the southwest, forming part of the name of hills, as Cadon Barrow in Cornwall, Trentishoe Barrow in North Devon, Bull Barrow in Dorset; **b.** in the north, usually a long low hill, as Barrow near Derwentwater, Whitbarrow in North Lancashire: see BARGH.

3. A mound of earth or stones erected in early times over a grave; a grave-mound, a tumulus. Also *attrib.* as **barrow-wight** (see quot. 1891); so ***barrow-wightish*** adj. (*nonce*).

c **1000** ÆLFRIC *Joshua* vii. 26 (Bosw.) Worhton mid stánum ánne steápne beorh him ofer. *c* **1000** *Sax. Leechd.* I. 124 Ðeos wyrt..bið cenned abutan byrȝenne, & on beorȝum. **1576** LAMBARDE *Peramb. Kent* (1826) 392 These hillocks, in the West Countrie (where is no small store of the like) are called Barowes..which signifieth Sepulchres. **1656** J. CHALONER in D. King *Vale Royall* IV. 10 Those round hills, which in the Plains of Wiltshire are..by the Inhabitants termed Barrowes, like as in the Midland parts of England they call them Lowes, commonly and truly held to be the Sepulchres of the Danes. **1772** PENNANT *Tours Scot.* (1774) 185 A plain, on which are five earthen tumuli, or barrows. **1836** THIRLWALL *Greece* II. xiv. 244 Another barrow was consecrated to the Platæans and the slaves. **1851** D. WILSON *Preh. Ann.* (1863) I. 65 Sir Richard Colt Hoare ..adopted a subdivision, which embraces fourteen different kinds of barrows, classified according to their shape. **1860** TENNYSON *Tithonus* 71 Grassy barrows of the happier dead. **1877** GREENWELL & ROLLESTON (*title*) British Barrows; a record of the examination of sepulchral mounds. **1891** A. LANG *Ess. in Little* 146 In the graves where treasures were hoarded the Barrowwights dwelt, ghosts that were sentinels over the gold. **1954** TOLKIEN *Fellowship of Ring* I. viii. 151 The dreadful spells of the Barrow-wights about which whispered tales spoke. *Ibid.* xi. 197 It has a—well, rather a barrow-wightish look.

4. *dial.* A mound or heap.

1869 BLACKMORE *Lorna D.* iii. 18 John lay on the ground by a barrow of heather. **1881** RAYMOND *Mining Gloss.*, *Barrow* (Cornw.), a heap of *attle* or rubbish.

barrow ('bærəʊ), *sb.*[2] *Obs.* exc. *dial.* Forms: 1 **bearȝ**, **bearh**, **berȝ**, 3 **baru**, 4 **bareȝ**, 5 **barowe**, 6 **barrowe**, 6– **barrow**. [Common Teut.: OE. *bearȝ* (:—*barg*) = Fris. *baerg*, MDu. *barch*, Du. *barg*, OHG. *barug*, *barh*, MHG. *barc* (*barg-es*), Ger. *barch*, ON. *börgr*:—OTeut. **bargu-z* or *bargwo-z*; not known beyond Teutonic.]

1. A castrated boar; a swine. Still *dial.*

a **1000** *Riddles* (Grein) xli. 106 Fættra þonne amæsted swín, bearȝ bellende on bóc-wuda. *c* **950** *Lindisf. Gosp.* Matt. vii. 6 Ne sendas ȝe mere-grotta iurre before berȝ [*Rushw.* swinum]. *a* **1250** *Owl & Night.* 408 He wie of bore wurchen bareȝ [*v.r.* bareh]. **1297** R. GLOUC. 207 [He] hadde an vatte baru ynome. **1398** TREVISA *Barth. De P.R.* XVIII. lxxxvii. (1495) 836 Amonge the tame swyne the males be callyd boores and barowes. **1577** B. GOOGE *Husb.* (1586) 122 b, Take..of Barrowes grease very olde two poundes. **1725** BRADLEY *Fam. Dict.* s.v. *Mange*, Anoint them with stale Barrows-Lard. **1741** *Compl. Fam.-Piece* III. 498 Better to keep all Boars and Sows, and no Barrows. **1864** CAPERN *Devon Provinc.*, *Barrow*, a castrated boar.

b. In later times commonly ***barrow-hog***, ***-pig***.

1547 RECORDE *Judic. Ur.* 61 b, Tame barrow-hogs. **1599** A. M. tr. *Gabelhouer's Bk. Physic* 252/2 Take the greace of a little redde Barrowe Pigge. **1693** W. ROBERTSON *Phraseol. Gen.* 732 A barrow-hog, *porcus castratus*. *Mod. Kent. Dial.*, I bought two open sows and one barrow pig. [In most of the dialect glossaries.]

†**2.** A badger. *Obs. rare.* (? mispr. for *bauson*).

1552 HULOET, Badger, barrow, brocke, or graye beaste.

3. *Comb.*, **barrow-flick**, the fatty membrane covering the kidneys of a hog; **barrow-guttlings**, pig's chitterlings; intestines, bowels.

1575 TURBERV. *Falconrie* 363 An unguent made of Barrowe flicke. **1611** L. BARREY *Ram Alley* IV. in Dodsl. *O.P.* (1780) V. 484 My barrow-guttlings grumble And would have food. **1725** BRADLEY *Fam. Dict.* s.v. *Mange*, Take a Pound of Barrow-flick.

barrow ('bærəʊ), *sb.*[3] Forms: 4 **barewe**, 5 **barwe**, **barow**, 5–6 **barowe**, 6 **barrowe**, 5– **barrow**. [ME. *barewe* points to an OE. **bearwe*, *barwe*, OTeut. **barwâ-* or *barwôn-*, a derivative of *ber-an* to BEAR: cf. the MHG. *bere* hand-barrow, *rade-ber(e*, now in Thuringian dial. *rade-berre*, wheel-barrow (Lexer I. 127, II. 333 '*Cenovectorium*, radeber': cf. quot. 1483 in sense 2 below):—OTeut. *barjâ-*. Cf. also ON. *barar* pl.:—OTeut. **barâ-*; and with long vowel OE. *bǽr*:—WGer. **bârâ-*, OTeut. **bêrâ-*, BIER.]

1. A utensil for the carrying of a load by two or more men; a stretcher, a bier; *spec.* a flat rectangular frame of transverse bars, having shafts or 'trams' before and behind, by which it is carried; sometimes with four legs to raise it from the ground. Now more usually called *hand-barrow* to distinguish it from the *wheel-barrow*: see next.

c **1300** *Beket* 899 Theȝ ich scholde beo thider ibore in barewe other in bere. *c* **1450** HENRYSON *Mouse & Frog*, For thou war better beir of stane the barrow. **1535** COVERDALE *Acts* v. 15 They brought out the sycke..and layed them vpon beddes and barowes. **1632** SHERWOOD s.v., A hand barrow, *civiere*..*à bras*. A necke-barrow, *civiere à col*. **1669** WORLIDGE *Syst. Agric.* (1681) 322 Barrow, is of two sorts; either a Hand-barrow, or a Wheel-barrow. **1837** CARLYLE

Fr. Rev. VII. v. III. 379 The wounded..defile in handbarrows.

2. a. A modification of the preceding, having one small wheel inserted between the front shafts, so that it can be pushed by a single man, the body or frame being usually converted into a kind of shallow open box; more fully called *wheel-barrow*. **b.** Also, in London and its vicinity, a small two-wheeled cart similarly pushed by the shafts, a hand-cart, or 'costermonger's barrow.'

a **1420** OCCLEVE *De Reg. Princ.* 983 Lade a carte or fille a barwe. **1436** *Pol. Poems* (1859) II. 169 Halfe here shippes.. wyth barowes are laden. *c* **1440** *Promp. Parv.* 105 Crowde wythe a barow, *cinevecto*. **1483** *Cath. Angl.* 22 A Barrow, *cenovectorium*. **1552** HULOET, Barrowe for to carye out dunge or filthe, *cœnouectorium*. **1768** GOLDSM. *Good Nat. Man* II. i. (1780) 42 He had scarce talents to be groom-porter to an orange barrow. **1816** SOUTHEY *Poet's Pilgr.* I. 26 Carts, barrows, coaches, hurry from all sides. **1837** CARLYLE *Fr. Rev.* I. xi. II. 70 Setting down his own barrow, he snatches the Abbé's; trundles it fast, like an infected thing. **1837** WHITTOCK *Bk. Trades* (1842) 17 He has to wheel it [bread] in a barrow round to the customers.

c. The contents of a barrow, a barrowful.

1598 SHAKS. *Merry W.* III. v. 4 To be carried in a Basket like a barrow of butchers Offall.

3. *Salt-making.* A conical basket into which the wet salt is put to drain.

1686 PLOT *Staffordsh.* 94 Which [the corned salt] they put into wicker baskets they call Barrows, made in a Conical form. *a* **1728** KENNETT *MS. Lansd.* 1033 (Halliw.) At Nantwich and Droitwich, the conical baskets wherein they put the salt to..drain..are called barrows. A barrow contained about six pecks.

4. *Comb.*, as *barrow-maker*; **barrow boy**, a coster-monger; †**barrow-bunter, -man, -woman**, one employed in wheeling a barrow; **barrowful**, the quantity that fills a barrow; **barrow-tram**, the shaft of a barrow; **barrow-way** (*Mining*), see quot.

1939 J. WORBY *Spiv's Progress* viii. 72, I then gave him a brief I had got from one of the *barrow boys to take him back to Manchester. **1949** *Hansard Commons* CDLXVII. 2970 A lesson might be learnt from that humble member of the trading community, the barrow boy. **1771** SMOLLETT *Humphr. Cl.* (1815) 145, I saw a dirty *barrow-bunter in the street. *c* **1485** *Digby Myst.* (1882) II. 97 A *barowfull..of horsdowng. **1881** MISS BRADDON *Asph.* xxvii, To buy a *barrowful of red and orange pots and pans. **1468** *Medulla Gram.* in *Cath. Angl.* 22 *Vecticularius*, a *barwe-maker. ?*c* **1650** LD. HERRIES in Calderwood *Hist. Kirk* (1843) II. 417 *note*, He scorned to be a *barrowman. **1822** HOGG *3 Perils of Man* II. 326 Old masons are the best *barrowmen. *a* **1550** *Christis Kirke* 166 Than followit feymen rycht onaffeird, Bet on with *barrow trammis. **1657** COLVIL *Whigs Supplic.* (1751) 19 His arms were stiff like *barrow-trams. **1815** SCOTT *Guy M.* xlvi, Ye black *barrow-tram o' the kirk. **1851** *Coal-tr. Terms Northumbld. & Durh.* 7, *Barrow-way, the way along which the barrow-men put the corves or tubs of coals..laid with tram-plates or bridge-rails. *c* **1475** in Wright *Voc.* 268 *Psraannia*, a *barowwoman. **1818** HAN. MORE *Betty Brown, Tales* (1830) II. 289 A *barrow-woman ..is as much her own mistress on Sundays as a duchess.

barrow ('bærəʊ), *sb.*^{4} Also (*north. dial.*) barrie, barry. [? connected with OE. *beorȝan* to protect, cover.] (Also in *comb.*, **barrow-coat.**) A long sleeveless flannel garment for infants.

1878 HALLIWELL, *Barricoat*, a child's coat; a word in use in the Northumbrian dialect. **1884** *Cassell's Mag.* Apr. 303/1 (*Baby clothing*), The barrow-coats are best made of real Welsh flannel.

barrow ('bærəʊ), *v.*^{1} [f. BARROW *sb.*^{3}] To wheel or transport in a barrow; cf. *to cart.*

1674 RAY *Allom Work Whitby* 139 When it is sufficiently burned they barrow it into a pit. **1862** BORROW *Wild Wales* III. 84 Barrowing stones on a Welsh road.

barrow ('bærəʊ), *v.*^{2} *Austral.* and *N.Z.* [Etym. unkn.; ? cf. Gaelic *bearradh*, shearing, clipping.] (See quot. 1933.) Hence **barrowing** *vbl. sb.*; **barrowman**^{2}, one who barrows; also **barrower**.

1933 L. ACLAND in *Press* (N.Z.) 16 Sept. 15/7 *Barrow*, to shear or partly shear a sheep for a shearer. 'No barrowing allowed on the board' was at one time a rule which the Shearers' Union got into the award. **1940** E. C. STUDHOLME *Te Waimate* (1954) I. xv. 129 There were always a certain number of'barrowmen' and 'learners' on the board. [*footnote*] Friends of the shearers who came on to the board for a chat and..shore a few sheep for their pals. **1949** P. NEWTON *High Country Days* v. 54 The wool rollers and fleece pickers..tried their hand at shearing, a practice known as 'barrowing'. **1959** H. P. TRITTON *Time means Tucker* 26/1, I spent most of the afternoon watching and 'barrowing'; that is, finishing-off. **1965** J. S. GUNN *Terminol. Shearing Ind.* I. 6 *Barrowing*, a term to describe the action of a shed-hand or other learner who finishes off a sheep for a shearer after the bell has gone for the end of the run. *Ibid.*, Barrowers could cause considerable union trouble because they delay the other shedhands who have to clean up after the last sheep shorn in a run. Thus an accepted rule in most sheds to-day is 'no barrowing on the board'.

'Barrowist. *Hist.* One who followed, or held the tenets of, Henry Barrowe, one of the founders of Independency or Congregationalism, executed along with John Greenwood, in 1593, for nonconformity to the Church of England. (Barrowe has been by some identified with *Martin Marprelate.*)

1589 *Pasquils Ret.* 20 There neuer yet wanted..Brownist, Barowist, Martinist, Anabaptist. **1645** PAGITT *Heresiogr.* (1661) 87 The second sort of separatists may be called Barrowists..who say that the Church of England is Sodom, Babylon, and Ægypt. **1884** G. HUNTINGTON in *Chicago Advance* 11 Dec., The Barrowist party in New England.

barrulet ('bærjʊlɪt). *Her.* Also **-ette.** [dim. of **barrule*, assumed dim. of F. *barre*, or BAR *sb.*^{1}.] The fourth part of a *bar*, the half of a *closet*.

1562 LEIGH *Armorie* 67 b, The field is sanguin, a Barrulet, Or. **1766** PORNY *Heraldry* (1787) 74 The Closet which contains the half of the Bar, and the Barrulet which is the half of the Closet. **1883** BURKE *Peerage* 1167 Or, two barrulets az. between three wolves' heads erased.

'barrulety, *a. Her.* [f. prec. + -Y.] = BARRULY. [In mod. Dicts.]

barruly ('bærjʊlɪ), *a. Her.*; also 6 **-ley, -lye,** 9 **-lée.** [ad. AF. *barrulée*, f. **barrule*: see BARRULET.] (A field) Crossed by barrulets or small bars.

1562 LEIGH *Armorie* (1597) 49 He beareth of ten barruley, Argent and Azure. **1864** BOUTELL *Heraldry Hist. & Pop.* xv. 188 The paternal shield..was simply barruly (the bars *sans nombre*) arg., and az. *Ibid.* xv. 224 The points barrulée argent and azure.

barry ('bɑːrɪ), *a. Her.* [a. F. *barré* barred, f. *barrer* to BAR.] (A field) Divided horizontally into a number of equal parts by bars of two colours arranged alternately.

1486 *Bk. St. Albans, Her.* D. vij, He berith barri of siluer and sable. **1572** BOSSEWELL *Armorie* II. 31 b, The blazon.. how they differ from playne armes barrie. [See quotation for BENDY.] **1864** BOUTELL *Heraldry Hist. & Pop.* xv. 211 This shield of De Grey with the barry field.

barry-'bendy *a.*, divided into both bars and bends, with colours alternating. **barry-'nebuly** *a.*, barry, but with the lines bounding the bars made wavy. **barry-'pily** *a.*, divided into a number of equal 'piles' or wedge-shaped pieces, horizontally arranged, and alternately coloured.

1611 GWILLIM *Heraldry* v. iii. (1660) 369, iv. 371.

Barsac, barsac ('bɑːsæk). Also †**barasack, barsack.** [a. F. (see below).] A sweet white wine from the district of Barsac, department of Gironde, France.

1728 J. STEUART *Letter-Bk.* 21 Dec. (1915) 302 A Tun of Barasack white wine in hogsheads. **1820** *Blackw. Mag.* VIII. 44 To lawyers I would give the sharp *Bar-sac*. **1827** *Mirror of Lit.* II. 164/1 Elephants don't drink barsack. **1845** *Tait's Mag.* XII. 698 Barsac, champagne, hock, and claret. **1951** *Good Housek. Home Encycl.* 360/2 Such white wines as Sauternes, Graves and Barsac.

†**barse.** *Obs.* exc. *dial.* [Common Teut.: OE. *bærs, bears* (:—*bars*) = MDu. *bars*, Du. *baars*, MHG. *bars*, Ger. *barsch*, f. root **bars-, bors-*, whence OHG. *burst*, OE. *byrst*, Sc. *birse* 'bristle.'] Name of a species of fish: the original form of the word subsequently corrupted to BASE, and BASS(E); still retained in some dialects.

c **1000** ÆLFRIC *Gloss* in Wülcker /180 *Lupus, uel scardo*, bærs. *c* **1050** *Ags. Voc.* ibid. /293 *Lypus*, bærs. **1753** CHAMBERS *Cycl. Supp.*, *Barse*, in ichthyology, an English name for the common pearch. **1860** H. RILEY *Liber Custum.* Gloss., *Barcius*, a perch, which in Cumberland and Westmoreland is still known as *barse*.

barselette, -slett, var. BERCELET, *Obs.*, hound.

barst(e, obs. pa. t. of BURST *v.*

barstness, dial. f. BURST(EN)NESS, *Obs.*, rupture.

Bart., an abbreviation of the title BARONET, commonly written after the name of one who holds that rank, to supplement the prefixed *Sir*, also given to a Knight; *e.g.* Sir Wilfrid Lawson, Bart.

a **1771** T. MARTIN *Hist. Thetford* (1779) xxii. 285 The rev. Sir John Cullum, bart. of Hardwicke. **1793** W. B. STEVENS *Jrnl.* 14 Mar. (1965) 72 Dined at Foremark—the Bart delighted with the carnage of the French. **1813** THOMPSON in *Examiner* 26 Apr. 270/2 When he saw *Bart.* against a man's name, he thought it stood for 'bartered.' **1887** W. S. GILBERT *Ruddigore* (1963) I. 104 When I'm a bad Bart, I will tell taradiddles! **1906** 'Q' *Mayor of Troy* xiv. 188 But if you ask me what was peculiar about the man, he was called Bart. —Sir Samuel Brooks Bart. **1958** B. HAMILTON *Too much of Water* iii. 46 We've really got a frightfully distinguished company on board. There's the Bart of course.

†**barta'vel.** *Obs. rare*$^{-1}$. [a. F. *bartavelle*, a name given, according to Lavallée, on account of the bird's monotonous note, f. med.L. *bartavella* for *vertevella* (cf. Pr. *bartaveo*) windlass, f. *vertĕre* to turn.] The Red Partridge.

1773 BARRINGTON in *Phil. Trans.* LXIII. 273 *note*, Buffon contends that the περδιξ of Aristotle does not mean the common partridge, but the bartavel. [**1819** in REES *Cycl.* s.v. *Tetrao*, The bartavelle of Buffon..the Greek or great red partridge of Willughby.]

Bartelemy, a. F. *Barthélemy* BARTHOLOMEW.

bartender ('bɑː,tɛndə(r)). orig. *U.S.* Also **bar-tender.** [f. BAR *sb.*^{1} + TENDER *sb.*^{1}] **a.** A keeper or manager of a refreshment bar. **b.** A bar-attendant or barman.

1836 *Franklin Repository* (Chambersburg, Pa.) 5 Apr. 3/3 My bar-tender..has become a drunkard according to the course of trade. **1864** G. A. SALA in *Daily Tel.* 21 Nov., The bar-tender is a person of great gravity of countenance. **1876** J. HARTLEY *Seets i' Lundun* iv. 53 Aw axed th' bar-tender if he'd onny. **1883** [see TENDER *sb.*^{1} 2]. **1884** *Fortn. Rev.* Mar. 389 A bar-tender in..this low groggery. **1961** *Spectator* 11 Aug. 199 A dish-washer and part-time bartender. **1968** *Globe & Mail* (Toronto) 17 Feb. 51 (Advt.), Bartender, for dining lounge.

barter ('bɑːtə(r)), *v.* [App. a derivative formation from *barat*, BARRAT *v.*; cf. sense of F. *barater* 'to cheat, cousen..to trucke, scourse, barter, exchange' (Cotgr.), in Godefroy = 'troquer, échanger' under date 1373, It. *barattare* 'to barter, trucke, chop and change one thing for another' (Florio 1598), Sp. *baratar* 'to sell cheape, or deceive.' With the final -ER, cf. *batter, falter, stutter*; but an intermediate form **barat-er* connecting *barat* and *barter* has not been found.]

1. *trans.* To give (a commodity) in exchange for something taken as of equivalent value; distinguished from *purchase* and *sell*, which imply that money is given for the commodity. ***to barter away***: to dispose of by barter; cf. also 2. Const. *for* (*with* obs.) a thing, (*with* a person.

c **1440** *Promp. Parv.* 25 Bartryn or changyn, or chafare oone thynge for a othere, *cambio*. **1530** PALSGR. 444/1 It is a comen feate of marchauntes to barter [*trocquer*] ware for ware. **1590** SHAKS. *1 Hen. VI*, I. iv. 31 But with a baser man of Arms by farre, Once, in contempt, they would haue barter'd me. **1669** GALE *Crt. Gentiles* I. I. iv. 23 They, by frequent Commerce..barter and exchange commodities, each with other. *a* **1704** LOCKE (J.) He also bartered away plums that would have rotted in a week, for nuts that would last good..a whole year. **1796** COLERIDGE *Answ. Melanch. Let.* Wks. I. 87 Barter for food the jewels of his crown. **1833** HT. MARTINEAU *Charmed Sea* iv. 44 Those who have little merchandise to barter away.

2. *fig.* **a.** To exchange.

1602 WARNER *Alb. Eng.* IX. xlix. (1612) 226 Such hearts to barter blowes. **1664** H. MORE *Myst. Iniq.* v. 12 They have.. bartered away one great evil for several others. **1848** KINGSLEY *Saint's Trag.* III. i. 18, I but barter Less grief for greater.

b. To part with for a consideration, usually a mercenary or unworthy one; to bargain away.

1664 *Decay Chr. Piety* (J.) They will barter away their time. **1764** GOLDSM. *Trav.* 305 E'en liberty itself is barter'd here. **1862** (18 Dec.) BRIGHT *Amer., Sp.* (1876) 110 Writers of eminence and honour who will not barter human rights for the patronage of the great. **1863** W. PHILLIPS *Speeches* iii. 49 The greatest hour of the age was bartered away.

3. *intr.* To trade by exchange of commodities.

1485 in Arnold *Chron.* (1811) 229 To selle, barter, and occupye in our sayd landis and lordships. **1635** QUARLES *Emblems* II. v. (1718) 83 With thy bastard bullion thou hast barter'd for wares of price. **1865** LIVINGSTONE *Zambesi* xix. 391 We did not see much evidence of a wish to barter.

barter ('bɑːtə(r)), *sb.* [f. prec. vb.]

1. The act or practice of trafficking by exchange of commodities; truck.

1592 WEST *Symbol.* B j. §26 The putting of such thinges in fellowship or barter. **1677** YARRANTON *Eng. Improv.* 186 In the way of barter, the Pin-Makers may have..Bacon from Shrewsbury for Pins. **1796** BURKE *Regic. Peace* Wks. VIII. 334 Differences arising from the spirit of huckstering and barter. **1857** LIVINGSTONE *Trav.* xx. 407 Salt..and calico are the common medium of barter.

2. *fig.* Exchange, interchange.

1819 SCOTT *Ivanhoe* xxxii, I will exchange no more cuffs with thee, having been a loser by the barter. **1844** KINGLAKE *Eothen* ii. (1878) 24 We made our sullen way through the darkness with scarcely one barter of words.

3. Goods to be bartered or traded in by exchange.

1740 FELTON (J.) Ladies that change plate for china: for which the laudable traffick of old clothes is much the fairest barter. **1800** STUART in *Wellesley Disp.* 577 Piece goods and grain may be made barter for any quantity of coffee.

4. *Arith.* The computation of the quantity or value of one commodity, to be given for a known quantity and value of another; the 'rule' or method of computing this.

barterable ('bɑːtərəb(ə)l), *a.* [f. BARTER *v.* + -ABLE.] Capable of being bartered; suitable for trading by exchange.

1852 MUNDY *Antipodes* (ed. 2) II. 234 They found it a barterable commodity. **1890** H. M. STANLEY *Darkest Africa* I. vii. 155 Trifles..were easily barterable for sugar-cane.

barterer ('bɑːtərə(r)). [f. BARTER *v.* + -ER.] One who barters; a petty or mercenary trafficker.

1611 COTGR., *Permutateur*, a barterer, exchanger. **1624** F. WHITE *Repl. Fisher* 564 The onely or principall Key-bearer, and Barterer of this Treasurie. **1794** COLERIDGE *Relig. Musings* vii, Soul-hardened barterers of human blood. **1837** W. WARE *Lett. fr. Palmyra* xiii. (1860) 306 A community of money-makers, hucksters, and barterers.

'bartering, *vbl. sb.* [f. as prec. + -ING^1.] Trading or trafficking by exchange of commodities.

c **1440** *Promp. Parv.* 25 Bartrynge, or changynge of chafyre, *cambium*. **1485** *Act 1 Hen. VII*, viii, The said Sale or Barterings of them. **1674** *Ch. & Crt. Rome* 7 Shall the bartering for Masses..be laid aside? **1851** MAYHEW *Lond. Labour* 324 The crockery-ware and glass-sellers..are peculiar from their principle of bartering.

†**'bartery.** *Obs.* Also 6 bartry, 7 bartrie, -terie. [f. BARTER + -Y. Cf. BARRATRY, and It. *baratteria* 'bartring or chaffring one thing for another' (Florio 1611).]

1. Traffic by exchange, barter; = prec.
1570 *Act 13 Eliz.* vii. §1 Using..the Trade of Merchandize by way of Bargaining, Exchange, Rechange, Bartry. **1662** FULLER *Worthies* IV. 8 By the bartery or change of Wares and Commodities.

2. Wares for barter or exchange.
a **1638** MEDE *Wks.* I. xi. 45 They permitted a Market of Oxen and Sheep, Doves and other bartery.

bartes, Sc. var. BRETASCE, -ACHE; cf. BARTIZAN.

†**barth.** *Obs.* exc. *dial.* [Origin unknown. Welsh *barth* 'floor' does not explain the sense. Wedgwood suggests derivation from OE. *beorȝan* 'to protect, shelter,' but no instance is known of the required OE. derivative **beorhþ*. See BERTH *sb.*] A warm sheltered place for cattle and sheep.
1573 TUSSER *Husb.* (1878) 73 Warme barth giue lams. *Ibid.* 62 In tempest..Warme barth, vnder hedge, is a sucker to beast. **1674** RAY *S. & E. Countr. Wds.* 58 *Barth*, a warm place or pasture for calves or lambs. [So **1727** BRADLEY *Fam. Dict.*]

Barthian ('bɑːtɪən), *a.* and *sb.* [f. name of Karl *Barth*, Swiss theologian (1886–1968) + -IAN.] **A.** *adj.* Of, pertaining to, or characteristic of Barth, or his writings. **B.** *sb.* A follower of Barth. Hence **'Barthianism**, the substance of Barthian theology.
1929 E. BRUNNER *Theology of Crisis* iv. 87 The 'Barthian theology' had as its origin the teaching of men like Blumhardt, Ragaz, and Kutter. **1931** J. MCCONNACHIE *Significance of K.B.* ii. 60 He [*sc.* Barth] says ruefully that he is punished for the success of his books by the existence of regular 'Barthians'. **1934** *Times Lit. Suppl.* 25 Oct. 724/2 The main currents in German Protestant theology..with particular attention to Barthianism. **1939** V. A. DEMANT *Religious Prospect* viii. 200 In their [*sc.* Hegel's and Luther's] following we have liberal modernism on the one hand and the Barthian school on the other. **1945** *Mind* LIV. 183 What ..are moral philosophers to make of the Barthian distinction between moral sin and religious sin?

Bartholomean (bɑrˌθɒləʊ'miːən), *a.* [f. L. *Bartholomæ-us*, Gr. Βαρθολομαῖ-ος + -AN.] Of or pertaining to Bartholomew or Bartholomew's-day.
1645 HOWELL *Dodona's Gr.* 49 The Trinacrian Vespers, and Bartholomean Massacre, were nothing to this.

Bartholomew (bɑː'θɒləmjuː). Also 6 Bartelmewe, -tylmew, -tilmew, 7 -tholmew, -thlomew; and, after F. *Barthélemy*, 7- **Bartlemy** ('bɑːt(ə)lmɪ), 7 **Bartelemy**, 8 **Bart'lemy**. [partly ad. L. *Bartholomæus*, Gr. Βαρθολομαῖος; partly a. F. *Barthélemy*.]

a. Name of one of the twelve apostles, the festival in whose honour is held on the 24th of August (***Bartholomew-day, -tide***). **b.** On this day, in 1572, took place the great massacre of the Protestants in France. **c.** On the same day, in 1662, the penalties of the English Act of Uniformity (***Bartholomew Act***) came into force. **d.** At the same time of year, a fair was held annually from 1133 to 1855, at West Smithfield (***Bartholomew Fair***); whence the name was applied to articles sold at it, e.g. ***Bartholomew-baby*** or ***-puppet*** (a doll), ***-beef***, ***(-boar)-pig***, ***-ware***; see also quot. 1777.
a. 1552-3 *Inv. Ch. Goods Staffordsh.* 61, ij challeses were stolne owte of the churche abowt Bartelmewe tyde. *c* **1626** *Dick of Devon* IV. i. *in Old Pl.* (1883) II. 59 What a buzzing you make, as if you were a fly at Bartholomew-tyde at a Butcher's stall. **1678** *Trial Coleman* 80 Where was you the last Bartholomew day? **1854** THACKERAY *Newcomes* I. 253 It being the Bartlemytide vacation.
b. 1646 BUCK *Rich. III*, 63 A glimpse like that Bartholomew in France..All such slaughters from thence call'd Bartelemies..in a perpetuall Stigma of that Butchery.
c. 1711 B. SACHEVERELL *Sachev. agst. Sachev.* 15 Being silenc'd by the Bartholomew-Act, he retir'd to Stalbridge.
d. 1597 SHAKS. *2 Hen. IV*, II. iv. 250 Thou whorson little tydie Bartholmew Bore-pigge. **1614** B. JONSON *Bartholomew Fair* I. vi. (N.) For the very calling it a Bartholomew pig, and to eat it so, is a spice of idolatry. *c* **1645** HOWELL *Lett.* (1650) I. 2 Freighted with mere Bartholomew ware, with trite and trivial phrases only. **1660** HEXHAM *Dutch Dict.*, *Geroockt vleesch*, smoaked meate, or Bartholomew beefe. **1668** R. LESTRANGE *Vis. Quev.* (1708) 30 Rolling their Eyes (like a Bartlemy-Puppet, without so much as moving the Head). **1670** BROOKS *Wks.* (1867) VI. 51 Men..were dressed up like fantastical antics, and women like Bartholomew-babies. **1711** SHAFTESB. *Charac.* (1737) I. 28 A choice droll or puppet-show at Bart'lemy-fair. **1777** HOWARD *Prisons Eng.* (1780) 177 There are four floors [in the Fleet]..besides the cellar-floor, called Bartholomew-Fair.

bartizan (bɑːtɪ'zæn). [In no dictionary before 1800; not in Todd 1818, nor Craig 1847. Apparently first used by Sir Walter Scott, and due to a misconception of a 17th c. illiterate Sc. spelling, *bertisene*, for *bertising*, i.e. *bretising*, BRATTICING, f. *bretasce* (BRATTICE), a. OF. *bretesche*, 'battlemented parapet, originally of wood and temporary.' *Bartizan* is thus merely a spurious 'modern antique,' which had no existence in the times to which it is attributed.]

A battlemented parapet at the top of a castle or church; *esp.* an over-hanging battlemented turret projecting from an angle at the top of a tower, etc.
[*c* **1375** WYCLIF *Sel. Wks.* (1869) I. 191 þe hiȝest part of his tour is briteysing of charite. **1483** *Cath. Angl.* 43/1 Bretasynge, *propugnaculum*. **1651** *Rec. Pittenweem* in *Statist. Acc.* IV. 376 (JAM.) That the morn afternoon the town's colours be put upon the bertisene of the steeple.] **1808** SCOTT *Marm.* VI. ii, Its varying circle did combine Bulwark, and bartisan, and line. **1814** —— *Wav.* xiii, A bartizan, or projecting gallery, before the windows of her parlour. **1859** TURNER *Dom. Archit.* III. iv. 146 Small stone closets, called Bartizans or machicoulis, are thrown out on corbels immediately over the doorway.
attrib. **1801** SCOTT *Eve of St. John* 127 He mounted the narrow stair, To the bartizan seat. [See also the *Introd.*]
fig. **1821** JOANNA BAILLIE *Met. Leg. Lady J.B.* Concl. 15 Bartizan of braided locks.

barti'zaned, *ppl. a.* [f. prec. + -ED[2].] Furnished with a bartizan or bartizans.
1818 SCOTT *Hrt. Midl.* xxvi, A half-circular turret, battlemented, or, to use the appropriate phrase, bartizan'd on the top. **1834** H. MILLER *Scenes & Leg.* vi. (1857) 79 A small court..bartisaned and turreted.

Bartlemy: see BARTHOLOMEW.

†**'Bartolist.** *Obs.* [f. *Bartolo*, name of an eminent Italian lawyer born 1313 + -IST.] A student of Bartolo; one skilled in the law.
1602 DANIEL *Ep. Sir T. Egerton* xiii, These great Italian Bartolists Called in of purpose to explain the law.

barton[1] ('bɑːtən). Forms: 1 bere-tun, 7 barten, berton, 7–9 *dial.* barken, 6- barton. [OE. *bęre-tún* barley-enclosure, courtyard, farmstead, etc., f. *bęre* barley (see BEAR *sb.*[2]) + *tún* enclosure: see TOWN. Cf. BARN, OE. *bere-ærn*.]

†**1.** A threshing-floor. *Obs.*; only in OE.
c **950** *Lindisf. Gosp.* Matt. iii. 12 Ðerh clænsade bere-tun [Vulg. *aream*] his.

2. A farm-yard. (The regular modern sense.)
1552 HULOET, Barton or place enclosed where husbandry is vsed, *cohors.* **1674** RAY *S. & E. Countr. Wds.* 58 A Barken or (as they use it in Sussex) Barton: a yard of a house, a backside. **1721** BAILEY, *Barton*..a Backside, Fold-yard or Out-house. **1816** SOUTHEY *Poet's Pilgr.* III. 41 Spacious bartons clean, well-wall'd around, Where all the wealth of rural life was found.
attrib. **1787** WINTER *Syst. Husb.* 59 Stale urine and barton draining, are greatly preferable to dung. **1862** BARNES *Rhymes Dorset Dial.* I. 79 Flop Down into barken pon'.

3. A demesne farm; the demesne lands of a manor, not let out to tenants, but retained for the lord's own use.
[*a* **1243** *Monast. Angl.* II. 887 (Du Cange), Et in Bertonia mea de Cadeham unum locum ad construendam aliam grangiam. **1393** *Rot. 17 Rich. II* (Spelman), Gulielmus le Scrope..habet Castrum, villam et bertonam de Marlebergh.] **1587** FLEMING *Contn. Holinshed* III. 303/2 He also did..purchase the lordship and house of Clist Sachisfield, and..did inlarge the Barton thereof, by gaining of Cornish wood. **1602** CAREW *Cornwall* 36 a, That part of the demaines, which appertaineth to the Lord's dwelling house, they call his *Barten*, or *Berton*. **1724** *Lond. Gaz.* No. 6253/3 The Barton of Tregarrick..contains 80 Acres of..good Land, 150 Acres of good Arable, etc. **1813** VANCOUVER *Agric. Devon* 253 A fine grove of Scotch and silver fir on the barton of Bridestow.
attrib. *c* **1630** RISDON *Surv. Devon* §91 The barton tenants [cf. BARTONER]. **1708** *Lond. Gaz.* No. 4412/3 The Barton-House of Kentaberry.

†**4.** An enclosure for poultry, a pen. *Obs.*
1552 HULOET, Inclusure called a barton to feade fowles in, *chors.* **1756** NUGENT *Montesquieu's Spir. Laws* (1758) II. XXXI. xviii. 452 The eggs of the bartons of his demesnes. **1783** AINSWORTH *Lat. Dict.* (Morell), A barton for poultry, *gallinarium*.

†**5.** Used to translate L. *cavædium*: The inner court of a Roman house. *Obs.*
1519 HORMAN *Vulg.* 138 Moche of the showre felle into the louer: but moche more into the barton [L. *cauedium*].

Barton[2] ('bɑːtən). The name of a district near Lymington, Hampshire, applied *attrib.* to deposits of a division of the Eocene period in Britain. Hence **Bar'tonian** *a.*, pertaining to or resembling the deposits at Barton.
1847 J. PRESTWICH in *Q. Jrnl. Geol. Soc.* III. 357 Having thus associated the London clay with the Barton beds..the organic remains..were taken as belonging to one and the same deposit. **1893** GEIKIE *Textbk. Geol.* (ed. 3) VI. iv. 980 In..the northern Apennines Professor Sacco regards as Eocene a mass of strata..which he subdivides as follows:—Bartonian. 100 metres [etc.]. **1902** A. J. JUKES-BROWNE *Stratigr. Geol.* xvi. 487 The Calcaire Grossier of the Paris Basin is succeeded by a group of sands... The upper part corresponds to our Barton Sands..containing Bartonian fossils. **1957** *Encycl. Brit.* VIII. 632/2 Overlying these in the Bartonian stage are the Barton clay and sands.

'bartoner. [f. prec. + -ER[1].] (See quot.)
1832 BOUCHER s.v. *Barton*, The persons who took care of, and managed such reserved lands were called *bertonarii*, i.e. bartoners, or husbandmen.

bartram, obs. form of BERTRAM, q.v.

‖**Bartsia** ('bɑːtsɪə). *Bot.* [named by Linnæus after Bartsch of Königsberg.] A genus of *Scrophulariaceæ*. *B. Odontites* is a wayside weed in Britain, with dull purple flowers and purplish stem.
1753 in CHAMBERS *Cycl. Supp.* **1861** S. THOMSON *Wild Flowers* III. (ed. 4) 246 The dull-looking bartsia, with its.. conspicuous bracteas. **1863** BARING-GOULD *Iceland* 190 The rich purple flowers of Alpine bartsia.

barukhzy (bæ'ruːkzɪ). [ad. *Bārakzi*, name of an Afghan people.] The Afghan hound.
1895 *Daily News* 11 Dec. 2/1 An Afghan Barukhzy hound. **1927** *Daily Tel.* 17 May 15/6 Every sort of dog—from the barukhzy of Cabul..to my lady's Pekingese.

Barum = Barnstaple (Devon). Used *attrib.*
1899 *Westm. Gaz.* 6 Mar. 9/2 They presented to 'Barumites in London' one of the choicest production of the Royal Barum ware pottery.

barune, baruot, obs. ff. BARREN, BAREFOOT.

barvel, -ell ('bɑːvəl). [? phonetic corruption of *barm-fell* leather apron: see BARM *sb.*[1] 3.] A kind of leather apron.
1878 HALLIWELL, *Barvel*, a short leathern apron worn by washerwomen; a slabbering bib. *Kent.* **1883** *Chamb. Jrnl.* 271 The man..dressed in a petticoat barvel is cutting away the fish. **1883** *Fisheries Exhib. Catal.* 217 Petticoat Barvell. Barvell or Apron..Common Barvell.

barwood ('bɑːwʊd). [prob. so named from its being sent over in bars; cf. *logwood*.] A red wood imported from the Gaboon and adjacent parts of Africa, used chiefly for dyeing purposes, and also for ramrods and violin bows. It is the produce of the *Baphita nitida*.
1788 CLARKSON *Impol. Slave Tr.* 7 The first African woods, that were known to be objects of commercial importance, were Camwood and Barwood. **1861** *Du Chaillu's Equat. Afr.* x. 121 The bar-wood of commerce is the heart or main part of the trunk.

†**'bary,** *v.* *Obs. rare*[−1]. [a. OF. *bari-er*, later *barrier*:—L. *barrī-re*, f. *barrus* elephant; cf. BARR *v.*] *intr.* To utter the peculiar cry of an elephant.
1594 *2nd Rep. Faustus* in Thoms *E.E. Pr. Rom.* (1858) III. 399 His meekness turned into rage, and began to rise and bary, and stamp.

barya, var. BARIA, obs. name for BARYTA.

barycentric (bærɪ'sɛntrɪk), *a.* [f. Gr. βαρύ-ς heavy + κέντρ-ον centre + -IC.] Of or pertaining to the centre of gravity.

baryon ('bærɪɒn). *Nucl. Physics.* [f. Gr. βαρύ-ς heavy + *-on* of ELECTRON[2].]

Any hyperon other than the proton or neutron. Also *attrib.*
1953 *Prog. Theor. Physics* X 457 It seems practical to have a collective name for these particles and other which possibly may still be discovered... It is proposed to use the fitting name 'baryon' for this purpose. **1958** *Physical Rev.* CXII. 640/1 It is at this stage that we first explicitly meet S and N, the baryon number. **1959** *Sci. News* LII. 99 Nucleons and hyperons, or baryons as they are called collectively. **1967** *New Scientist* 22 June 724/1 Mesons could be composed of a quark plus an antiquark, baryons of three quarks.

Hence **bary'onic** *a.*, of or pertaining to a baryon or baryons; consisting of baryons.
1959 *Bull. Inst. Physics* X. 140/1 The current solution is to ascribe to both the proton and the neutron a baryonic charge ..which is always conserved. **1963** S. TOLANSKY *Introd. Atomic Physics* (ed. 5) xxiii. 396 By postulating the conservation of this baryonic number in a closed system then we see that annihilation of protons by electrons is prevented. **1974** *Physics Bull.* Dec. 579/1 The baryonic matter in the nucleus. **1982** *New Scientist* 9 Sept. 689/3 Matter as we know it (baryonic matter, dominated by neutrons and protons) may make up less than 10 per cent of the gravitational mass of the Universe.

baryphony (bə'rɪfənɪ). *Med.* [f. Gr. βαρύ-ς heavy, deep + φωνή voice.] Difficulty of speech.

barysphere ('bærɪsfɪə(r)). [f. Gr. βαρύ-ς heavy + σφαῖρα SPHERE *sb.*] The internal substance of the earth enclosed by the lithosphere.
1901 *Science* 15 Nov. 747 It was argued by Posepny that the ores came from the barysphere. **1926** *Encycl. Brit.* New Suppl. II. 172 The bulk of the earth consists of a nickel-iron mass, the barysphere, which is enclosed by a rocky crust, the lithosphere.

†**'baryt.** *Chem. Obs.* [a. F. *baryte*, ad. mod.L. *barytēs*: see BARYTES.] = next.
1794 PEARSON in *Phil. Trans.* LXXXIV. 395 Nitrate and muriate of baryt. **1809** —— *ibid.* XCIX. 327 Precipitation with muriate of baryt.

baryta (bə'raɪtə). *Chem.* Also (obs.) **barita.** [f. next: see quot. Cf. also BARIA.] **a.** The protoxide of barium; an alkaline earth distinguished by its great weight.
1809 YOUNG in *Phil. Trans.* XCIX. 151 Phosphate of barita. *Ibid.* 154 *Barytes*, as a single Greek word, means weight..but as the name of a stone, accented on the second syllable, it must be written *barites*; and the pure earth may properly be called *barita*. **1812** SIR H. DAVY *Chem. Philos.* 338 Witherite, or carbonate of baryta.

attrib. **1877** W. THOMSON *Voy. Challenger* I. i. 26 Baryta-water of known strength.

b. Special Comb. **baryta paper**, paper coated with an emulsion of barium sulphate; **baryta white** = permanent white (see PERMANENT *a.* 1 d).

1900 *Photogr. Ann.* 235 *Baryta Paper*, (Faced Paper).. Fine paper, faced with an emulsion of barium sulphate, rendered partly insoluble by chrome alum. **1954** *Spalding & Hodge's Paper Terminol.* 13 *Baryta Paper*, a form of metallic paper on which marks can be made with a metal point or stylus... It..is used in certain types of automatic recording apparatus. **1885** *Encycl. Brit.* XIX. 86/2 *Baryta White*..is prepared by grinding to a fine powder the pure white native sulphate of baryta (heavy spar). **1886** H. C. STANDAGE *Artists' Man. Pigments* i. 1 *Baryta White* (also known as Constant or Permanent White).

barytes (bəˈraɪtiːz). *Chem.* [mod. f. Gr. βαρύς heavy (in reference to its great weight), partly assimilated to names of minerals in -ITES, Gr. -ίτης (whence some early chemists preferred *barites*: see prec.). Cf. mod.F. *baryte*, and *trachyte*.]

†**1.** = BARYTA. (Occas. *attrib.*) *Obs.*

1791 HAMILTON *Berthollet's Dyeing* I. I. I. v. 86 Solutions of lime..[and] barytes, are not decomposed. **1802** CHEVENIX in *Phil. Trans.* XCII. 341 No precipitate took place from a mixture of barytes-water and strontia-water. **1854** F. BAKEWELL *Geol.* 32 A lining of sulphate of barytes.

2. Native sulphate of barium, heavy spar, BARITE.

1789 A. CRAWFORD in *Med. Comm.* II. 301 The medicinal properties of the Muriated Barytes. **1822** IMISON *Sc. & Art* II. 90 Barytes is used as a white paint, under the name of permanent white. **1878** LAWRENCE *Cotta's Rocks Class.* 41 Barytes seldom occurs as an independent rock.

barytic (bəˈrɪtɪk), *a. Chem.* [f. prec. + -IC.] Of, pertaining to, or containing baryta or barium.

1789 A. CRAWFORD in *Med. Comm.* II. 349 The purity of the barytic salt. **1831** T. P. JONES *Convers. Chem.* xvii. 176 Barytic water..a solution of baryta in water, is kept as a test by the chemist.

barytine, barytite, synonyms of BARITE.

baryto- (bəˈraɪtəʊ), comb. form of BARYTA, as in **baryto-ˈcalcite**, a carbonate of barium and calcium. **baryto-ceˈlestite**, a sulphate of barium and strontium. Both found as native minerals.

barytone (ˈbærɪtəʊn), *a.* and *sb. Gr. Gram.* [ad. Gr. βαρύτονος: see BARITONE *sb.* and *a.*] **a.** *adj.* Not having the acute accent on the last syllable. **b.** *sb.* A baritone word.

1828 WALKER *Dict.* Introd. 65 The tendency to the barytone pronunciation in the noun [*prophecy*] and the oxytone in the verb [*prophesy*]. **1863** *Rudim. Grk. Lang. Edin. Acad.* 184 Words unaccented on the last syllable are called barytone. **1881** CHANDLER *Grk. Accent.* §905 When words are combined in a sentence..oxytones become barytone, except before a colon, a full stop, etc.

barytone, variant of BARITONE.

†**ˈbarytoˌnize**, *v. Obs. rare*⁻¹. [? f. BARITONE *sb.* + -IZE; but cf. F. '*baritonner* to wag, or dangle, vp and downe' (Cotgr.).]

1653 URQUHART *Rabelais* I. vii, [Gargantua] would loll and rock himself in the cradle..monocordising with his Fingers and barytonising with his Tail.

baryum, obs. form of BARIUM.

bas, obs. form of BASE *a.*

basal (ˈbeɪsəl), *a.* (*sb.*) [f. BASE *sb.* + -AL[1].]

A. *adj.* **1.** Pertaining to, situated at, or forming the base. In *Bot.* Situated at the base of the ovary. ***basal plane*** and ***cleavage*** in *Crystallog.*: one parallel to the lateral or horizontal axis.

1828 KIRBY & SP. *Entomol.* III. xxxii. 330 The elytra have a basal gibbosity. **1845** DARWIN *Voy. Nat.* xii. (1879) 254 Geologising the basal parts of the Andes. **1870** HOOKER *Stud. Flora* 314 Amaranthaceæ ..ovules..basal.

2. *fig.* Fundamental.

1865 BUSHNELL *Vicar. Sacr.* III. v. (1868) 330 A much deeper and more nearly basal office. **1883** H. DRUMMOND *Nat. Law in Spir. W.* 378 Classification should rest on the most basal characteristics. **1918** F. WOOD-JONES *Probl. Man's Ancestry* 34 A being, whose body is replete with features of basal mammalian simplicity. **1963** *Publishers' Weekly* 2 Sept. 44/2 To what extent are available paperback books adequate as compared with basal readers and early reading textbooks.

3. *Comb.*, **basal anæsthesia**, administration of a light but long-acting anæsthetic which may be supplemented when necessary during an operation by a deeper short-acting anæsthetic; so ***basal anæsthetic***; **basal area**, (*a*) the area situated at or forming the base; spec. in *Ecol.* (see quot. 1962); (*b*) *Forestry*, the area of the cross-section of a tree at a height of 4·5 feet above the ground, or the sum of such areas; **basal complex** *Geol.* = *basement complex*; **basal conglomerate** *Geol.*, a conglomerate forming the lowest of a particular series of strata; **basal cover** *Ecol.* = *basal area* (*a*); **basal ganglion**, a ganglion situated at the base of the cerebrum (*Cent. Dict.* 1889); esp. in *pl.* **basal ganglia**, the thalamus, lentiform, and caudate nuclei considered as a group; **basal granule**, a granule found at the base of a flagellum or cilium in certain protozoa; **basal metabolism**, the metabolism of an organism in a fasting and resting state; so ***basal metabolic rate*** (see quots.); **basal narcosis** (see quots.); cf. *basal anæsthesia*; **basal-nerved**, *a.*, 'with nerves all springing from the base of the leaf' (Gray *Bot. Text-bk*); **basal rot** *Hort.* (see quot. 1954).

1934 H. W. FEATHERSTONE in *Brit. Med. Jrnl.* 24 Feb. 322/2 The pioneer work in basal anaesthesia. *Ibid.* 326/1 Basal anaesthetics are a boon to patients. **1610** W. FOLKINGHAM *Art of Survey* II. viii. 62 Multiply the Basall Area by 6. **1895** W. SCHLICH *Man. Forestry* III. i. 46 The sample tree should show a basal area which corresponds exactly to the mean section of the class. **1938** J. R. CARPENTER *Ecol. Gloss.* 39 *Basal area*, (1)..The sum of the basal areas of trees in a forest stand is the basal area of the stand. (2)..Ground cover, basal cover. **1962** H. HANSON *Dict. Ecol.* 43 *Basal Area*..the surface of the soil actually covered or occupied by a plant, especially the basal part, as compared to the full spread of the herbage. **1897** Basal complex [see BASEMENT 1]. **1900** *Geol. Mag.* VII. 564 On the western shore of Ullswater..a good section has recently been exposed of the basal conglomerates variously ascribed to the Old Red or lowermost Carboniferous age. **1923** J. T. SARVIS *U.S. Dept. Agric. Bull.* MCLXX. 20 Basal cover, as used here, means the extent of ground surface actually covered by plants after the foliage has been removed by grazing or clipping. **1913** *Cunningham's Text-bk. Anat.* (ed. 4) 637 (*heading*) Basal Ganglia of the Cerebral Hemisphere. **1945** *New Biol.* I. 82 Deep seated primitive components of the brain which include..the basal ganglia. **1920** I. F. & W. D. HENDERSON *Dict. Scientific Terms* 28/2 Basal granule. **1951** *New Biol.* XI. 114 Beneath the pellicle [of paramecium] the cilia connect with small round bodies known as basal granules or kinetosomes. **1922** *Jrnl. Amer. Med. Assoc.* LXXVIII. 1887/2 (*title*) Correlation of Basal Metabolic Rate with Pulse Rate and Pulse Pressure. Extreme deviations from the normal basal metabolic rate are accompanied by..alterations in other functions. **1951** M. ABERCROMBIE et al. *Dict. Biol.* 138 In man, basal metabolic rate (B.M.R.) is expressed as the output of Calories per square metre of body surface per hour. **1952** *New Biol.* XIII. 64 The standard index of the latter [i.e. the metabolism of the body] being the 'basal metabolic rate' (B.M.R.), which is essentially the rate at which oxygen is consumed by the body when it is in a resting condition. **1914** *Jrnl. Biol. Chem.* XIX. 239 (*title*) Basal metabolism and creatinin elimination. **1920** *Lancet* 7 Aug. 289/2 Basal metabolism—i.e., the metabolism of the individual during complete muscular repose, where a period of twelve hours had been allowed to elapse since taking the last meal. **1963** M. MCCARTHY *Group* xiii. 303 The result of her basal metabolism [test] seemed to have restored her natural optimism. **1935** *Brit. Jrnl. Anaesthesia* XIII. 15 This preliminary narcosis, or basal narcosis as it has been called. **1938** *Encycl. Brit. Bk. of Year* 39/1 'Basal narcosis'..means the giving, at various times before the anaesthetic itself, of a sedative or hypnotic drug, which will reinforce the action of the gas. **1896** *Daily News* 15 Apr. 715 Dr. Crawford [spoke] on basal rot. **1950** *N.Z. Jrnl. Agric.* Feb. 176/2 The lily is subject to certain diseases; the most common are leaf spot.. and basal rot (*fusarium*). **1954** A. G. L. HELLYER *Encycl. Garden Work* 18/1 *Basal rot*, a name rather loosely applied to several quite distinct diseases which all attack bulbs, causing a decay of the base of the bulb... The decay is caused by fungal attack.

B. as *sb.* A basal part; *spec.* one of the basal plates encircling the stem of the crinoids.

1620 W. FOLKINGHAM *Brachigraphy* sig. A 6ᵛ, The third are Basals, falling from the Head of the Line, and landing below the Foot. **1877** HUXLEY *Anat. Inv. An.* ix. 589 The basals coalescing into the rosette are hidden by the first radials. **1881** *Nature* 4 Aug. 305 Those species of Pentacrinus in which the basals form a complete ring.

ˈbasally, *adv.* [f. prec. + -LY[2].] As a base or basis, fundamentally.

1882 J. STIRLING *Text-bk. Kant* 208 The first condition, that..must..basally underlie objects, so far as form is concerned..in the mind.

basalt (bəˈsɔːlt, ˈbæsɒlt). *Min.* [ad. L. *basaltes*, (originally an African word, Pliny), long used in Eng. unchanged.]

1. A kind of trap rock; a greenish- or brownish-black rock, igneous in origin, of compact texture and considerable hardness, composed of augite or hornblende containing titaniferous magnetic iron and crystals of feldspar (labradorite), often lying in columnar strata, as at the Giant's Causeway in Ireland, and Fingal's Cave in the Hebrides. (Pliny's *basaltes* was probably a variety of Syenite.)

1601 HOLLAND *Pliny* XXXVI. vii. §11 The Ægyptians also found in Æthyopia another kind of Marble which they call Basaltes, resembling yron as well in colour as hardnes. **1694** MOLYNEUX *Giants Causeway* in *Phil. Trans.* XVIII. 181 Our Irish Basaltes is composed of Columns. **1789** MRS. PIOZZI *Journ. France* II. 364 Its composition seemed black basalt. **1813** SIR H. DAVY *Agric. Chem.* iv. 195 Basalt or whinstone. **1837** W. IRVING *Capt. Bonneville* (1849) 317 Prismoids of basaltes, rising to the height of fifty or sixty feet. **1845** DARWIN *Voy. Nat.* ix. (1852) 180 The Basalt is only Lava, which has flowed beneath the sea.

b. *attrib.* and in *comb.*, as in ***basalt rock***, ***-building***.

1769 RASPE in *Phil. Trans.* LXI. 580 Our basalt rocks differ from those of the Giant's Causeway. **1873** TRISTRAM *Moab* ix. 174 The basalt-building inhabitants.

2. A black porcelain invented by Wedgwood.

1832 G. PORTER *Porcelain* 17 Basaltes, or black ware..was a black porcelainous biscuit, having nearly the same properties as the natural stone.

basaltic (bəˈsɔːltɪk), *a.* [f. prec. + -IC.] Of, consisting of, of the nature of, or resembling basalt.

1772 PENNANT *Tours Scot.* (1774) 161 Basaltic, a term I apply to the jointed columns, resembling those of the giants causeway. **1813** SIR H. DAVY *Agric. Chem.* (1814) 201 Fine red Earth..immediately above decomposing basalt..may be denominated basaltic soil. **1843** J. PORTLOCK *Geol.* 149 Eruptions of basaltic lava.

basaltiform (bəˈsɔːltɪfɔːm), *a.* [f. as prec. + -(I)FORM.] Having the form of basalt.

1791 BEDDOES in *Phil. Trans.* LXXXI. 51 Basaltiform colonnades of granite. **1876** PAGE *Advd. Text-bk. Geol.* xix. 377 The basaltiform structure of the carboniferous traps.

†**baˈsaltin(e**. *Min. Obs.* [f. as prec.] A kind of basaltic hornblende, classed by Dana as an aluminous variety of Pyroxene; a crystal of this mineral.

1794 KIRWAN *Min.* I. 219 Basaltine. Basaltic Hornblende, or Crystallized Hornblende, of Werner. **1811** PINKERTON *Petral.* I. 9 The trap of the Swedes, with a fine grain, is here called basaltin.

basaltine (bəˈsɔːltɪn), *a.* ? *Obs.* [f. BASALT + -INE.] = BASALTIC.

1774 STRANGE in *Phil. Trans.* LXV. 14 The profusion of basaltine phænomena in..Auvergne. **1796** MORSE *Amer. Geog.* II. 12 Basaltine pillars are very common in Iceland.

basaltoid (bəˈsɔːltɔɪd), *a.* [f. BASALT + -OID.] = BASALTIFORM.

[In mod. Dicts.]

basan, bazan (ˈbæzən). Also 8 **bazin**. [a. F. *basane*, (Cotgr. *bazane*, Palsgr. *basanne*), prob. ad. Pr. **bazana*, a. Sp. *badana* (med.L. *bedana*), ad. Arab. *biṭānah*, lining, 'inside'; see also the Eng. corruption BASIL *sb.*[3], BAZIL.] Sheep-skin tanned in oak- or larch-bark; distinguished from *roan*, which is tanned in sumach.

1714 *Fr. Bk. of Rates* 153 Cloth made of Hemp, Fustians, or Bazins. **1851** TURNER *Dom. Archit.* II. iii. 126 The prepared sheepskin called bazan. **1865** HANNETT *Bibliopegia* (ed. 6) 104 The cover is of black basin, the back full gilt.

basanite (ˈbæsənaɪt). *Min.* [ad. L. *basanītes* (*lapis*), in Pliny, f. Gr. βάσανος touchstone, test.] A velvet-black siliceous variety of quartz, used on account of its blackness and hardness for testing the purity of precious metals, by means of the mark left after rubbing the metal upon it.

[**1753** CHAMBERS *Cycl. Supp.*, *Basanites*..the touchstone used for trying gold.] **1794** KIRWAN *Min.* I. 307 Basanite. Lydian stone of Werner. Black Jasper of some. **1850** *Müller's Anc. Art* §403 Statue of the Nile..of basanite.

basar, obs. form of BAZAAR.

‖**bas bleu** (bɑːblø). *Obs.* [French rendering of Eng. BLUE-STOCKING, q.v.] A 'blue-stocking,' a literary lady. Hence **bas-ˈbleuism**.

? **1786** HAN. MORE *Bas bleu* Wks. I. 13 Or how Aspasia's parties shone, The first *Bas-bleu* at Athens known. **1788** H. WALPOLE *Let.* 12 July (1961) XXXI. 271 You have gratified my self-love so amply in your '*Bas Bleu*'. **1808** *Miss Talbot's Lett.* Introd. 15 The appellation which the company that assembled at her [Mrs. Vesey's] house acquired of the *Bas bleu*. **1812** *Dramatic Censor for 1811* 360 Lady Bab Blue is a literary woman of fashion, and a vestige of the Bas bleu club. **1821** BYRON *Juan* IV. cxii. (*MS. reading*), By measuring the *intensity of blue*; I'll back a a London *bas* against Peru. **1842** *Times* 2 Sept. 2/6 The aristocratic *bas-bleus* are at present very much devoted to the abolition of slavery. **1871** J. C. YOUNG *Mem. C.M. Young* I. v. 200 They are utterly devoid of pedantry, or Bas-Bleu-ism, or any other ism.

†**ˈbascaud** *Obs.* Used to english L. *bascauda*, instead of adopting the doubtful translation BASKET.

1647 R. STAPYLTON *Juvenal* 231 From British Picts the barbarous bascaud came.

bascaudal (bæˈskɔːdəl), *a.* [f. L. *bascauda*, taken as meaning BASKET + -AL[1].] Of or pertaining to a basket or basket-work.

1870 *Archæol.* XLIII. 367 (D.) In a cup..deeper than usual, the bascaudal character was confined to the upper part.

baschar, -at, obs. forms of BASHAW, PASHA.

‖**bas chevalier** (bɑʃəvalje). [F. *bas* low, *chevalier* knight.] 'Low or Inferiour Knights, by bare Tenure of a Military Fee, as distinguished from Bannerets and Baronets.' Phillips 1706; whence in mod. Dicts.

(Founded on an erroneous derivation of BACHELOR.)

bascinet, variant of BASINET.

Bascology (bɑːˈskɒlədʒɪ, -æ-). Also **Bask-**. [f. *Basc-*, used as comb. f. BASQUE + -OLOGY.] The study of the Basques and their language. **Baˈsco logist**, a student of, or one versed in Bascology.

1896 *Academy* 18 July 52/2 This Bascologist is incorrect. **1901** E. S. DODGSON in *N. & Q.* 9th Ser. VIII. 377/2 The following complementary details concerning the book..will be of interest to Baskologists. **1903** *Ibid.* XI. 355/2 Mr. Hutchinson has done good service to Bascology.

†'**Bascuence.** *Obs.* The Basque language.

c **1645** HOWELL *Lett.* v. (1650) 164, I have bin shewn for Irish and Bascuence Imperfect rules couchd in an Accidence. **1696** PHILLIPS, *Bascuence*, the language of a Country of Spain called Biscay.

basculation (bæskjuːˈleɪʃən). *Surg.* [mod. f. F. *basculer* to see-saw, f. *bascule*; see next and -ATION.] A term applied to the movement by which retroversion of the uterus is remedied.

1881 in *Syd. Soc. Lex.*

bascule (ˈbæskjuːl). [a. F. *bascule*, formerly *bacule* a see-saw, f. *battre* to beat, bump, or *bas* low, down + *cul* the posteriors.] An apparatus acting on the principle of the lever or pulley, whereby one end is raised when the other is depressed; *esp.* in **bascule-bridge**, a kind of drawbridge, balanced by a counterpoise which rises or falls, usually into a prepared pit, as the bridge is lowered or raised.

1678 *Phil. Trans.* XII. 1007 At the Extremity of this Bascule is ty'd a Cord which passes through the Pully. **1883** *Pall Mall G.* 11 Sept. 11/2 A weighing machine on the bascule principle. **1884** *Daily News* 29 Oct. 5/3 A 'bascule' or lifting bridge..would be more speedily opened than a swing bridge..Steamboats and small craft generally would not require the opening of the bascule.

base (ˈbeɪs), *sb.*[1] Forms: 4–7 **basse**, 4–6 **baas**, 4 **bas, bays**, 7 **bass**, 4– **base**. [a. F. *base* (12th c. in Littré):—L. *bas-is*, a Gr. *βάσις* a stepping, also that on which one steps or stands, pedestal, base, f. *βα-* 'walk, go.' The ME. spellings *bas, baas, basse*, indicate confusion with BASE *a.*, which, in Fr., is distinct in origin and pronunciation.]

I. The lowest or supporting part.

* *generally.*

1. The bottom of any object, when considered as its support, or as that on which it stands or rests.

c **1325** *E.E. Allit. P.* A. 999 Isaper hyȝt þe fyrst gemme þat I on þe fyrst basse con wale. *c* **1391** CHAUCER *Astrol.* II. §41 b, þe baas of þe tour. *Ibid.* §43 a, To knowe þe heyȝte of þynges, ȝif þou mayst nat come to þe bas of a þyng. *c* **1440** *Promp. Parv.* 20 Bace, or fundament, *basis.* **1483** *Cath. Angl.* 23 Base (*v.r.* Bays), *basis.* **1599** SHAKS. *Hen. V*, III. i. 13 As doth a galled Rocke O'erhang and iutty his confounded Base. **1613** HEYWOOD *Silv. Age* II. i. Wks. 1874 III. 120 Let all yon starry structure from his basses Shrinke to the earth. **1759** JOHNSON *Rasselas* xxx. (1787) 88 When they came to the great pyramid they were astonished at the extent of the base. **1862** STANLEY *Jew. Ch.* (1877) I. ix. 182 From the Jabbok up to the base of Hermon. **1866** TATE *Brit. Mollusks* iv. 149 At the bases of the trees.

2. a. *fig.* Fundamental principle, foundation, groundwork.

c **1500** *Blowbol's Test.* in Halliw. *Nugæ P.* 2 Phisike.. Whiche men callen baas naturall. **1581** LAMBARDE *Eiren.* IV. v. (1588) 505 Enditements..be the chiefe base and groundworke whereupon the whole Triall is afterward to be built. **1646** SIR T. BROWNE *Pseud. Ep.* I. x. (1686) 28 Hereby he undermineth the Base of Religion. **1738** WESLEY *Psalms* xxxvi, Nor Earth can shake, nor Hell remove The Base of thine eternal Love. **1879** GREEN *Read. Eng. Hist.* xx. 100 Henry's charter..was at once welcomed as a base for the needed reforms.

†**b.** Ground of action or attitude. *Obs.*

1601 SHAKS. *Twel. N.* V. i. 78 Anthonio [is]..on base and ground enough Orsino's enemie. *a* **1628** F. GREVILLE in Farr's *S.P.* (1845) I. 112 That man..nothing yet done amisse And so in him no base of this defection, Should fall from God.

c. A notional structure or entity conceived of as underlying some system of activity or operations; the resources, etc., on which something draws or depends for its operation. Usu. with preceding sb., as *customer base, power base*, (and in technical application) *database, knowledge base*, etc.

1959, etc. [see *power base* s.v. POWER *sb.*[1] 18 a]. **1967** [see DATABASE 1]. **1967** B. SHOEMAKER *Vocational—Technical Educ. Rep.* (ED 072) 189 31 Large cities..normally have sufficient tax base and student base to provide for a comprehensive vocational education program. **1971** [see *knowledge base* s.v. KNOWLEDGE *sb.* 16]. **1975** *Facts on File* 18 Oct. 759 The exodus of middle- and upper-income persons and industrial establishments would..further erode the city's shrinking tax base. **1977** *Economist* 13 Aug. 65/3 After its customer base, IBM's biggest asset is that $1 billion annual R&D budget. **1979** *Sci. Amer.* Aug. 1 (Advt.), With CADD, you are creating, and have available for recall, an easily accessed base of geometrically accurate data. **1984** *Which Micro?* Dec. 19/1 A well built computer with a large software base to draw upon.

** *specifically* and *technically.*

3. *Arch.* **a.** The part of a column, consisting of the plinth and various mouldings, between the bottom of the shaft and top of the pedestal, or, if there is no pedestal, between the shaft and the pavement.

c **1325** *E.E. Allit P.* B. 1278 þe bases of þe bryȝt postes. *c* **1400** *Destr. Troy* v. 1652 Pight into pilers prudly to shewe The bases and bourdurs all of bright perle. **1563** SHUTE *Archit.* C j b, Vpon the which Base shalbe set Scapus, or the body of the pillor. **1643** BURROUGHES *Exp. Hosea* ii. (1652) 174 God many times raises up golden pillars upon leaden Bases. **1734** *Builder's Dict.* s.v., The Corinthian Base has two Tores, two Scotia's, and two Astragals. **1868** FREEMAN *Norm. Conq.* II. x. 514 Of Eadward's minster nothing is left save a few bases of pillars.

b. The plinth and mouldings which form the slightly projecting part at the bottom of the wall of a room. **c.** The lowest course of masonry in a building.

1823 P. NICHOLSON *Pract. Build.* 165 Bases and Surbases for Rooms.

4. A pedestal.

c **1440** BIBLE (Wyclif) *Ex.* xxxi. 9 (MS. I) The greet.. lauatorie with his baas [**1388** foundement]. **1463** *Bury Wills* (1850) 19 That the ymage of oure lady..be set vp..with the baas redy therto. **1614** RALEIGH *Hist. World* II. 292 These shee mounted on two great Bases or Pedestals of the same Metall. **1835** THIRLWALL *Greece* I. vii. 258 The base of his statue..bore an inscription.

†**5.** A socket. *Obs.*

c **1325** [cf. 5]. **1380** *Sir Ferumb.* 1329 þe raftres..And þe bases þat hem bere. **1648** LIGHTFOOT *Glean. Ex.* 49 Each Pillar was fastned in a base of brasse.

6. In mechanical arts: **a.** in *Printing*, The bottom or footing of letters. **b.** in *Gunnery*, The protuberant rear-portion of a cannon, between the knob of the cascabel and the base-ring.

1676 MOXON *Print. Lett.* 6 Capital I is all Stem, except the Base and Topping. **1626–1862** [see 20].

c. *Electr.* One of the three electrodes of a transistor. Also *attrib.*

1948 *Physical Rev.* LXXIV. 230/1 The transistor.. consists of three electrodes... The third is a large area low resistance contact on the base. **1957** *Encycl. Brit.* XXII. 404/1 In a typical transistor,..the charge carriers are.. controlled by a signal between the emitter and a control electrode (base). **1959** *Electronic Engin.* XXXI. 331 The base current of the transistor under test is changed in steps.

7. *Bot.* and *Zool.* That extremity of a part or organ by which it is attached to the trunk; *e.g.* the part of a leaf adjoining the leaf-stalk, of a pericarp adjoining the peduncle, of a thumb adjoining the hand.

1831 R. KNOX *Cloquet's Anat.* 435 Its base is continuous with the tentorium cerebelli. **1866** *Treas. Bot.* 121 A five-parted calyx..with glands at its base.

8. *Her.* The lower part of a shield; *spec.* the width of a 'bar' (or fifth part of the shield's height) parted off from the bottom by a horizontal line.

1611 GWILLIM *Heraldry* III. vii. 105 He beareth Or, on a Mount in Base a peare tree fructed. **1706** PHILLIPS, *Base*.. in Heraldry, the lowest part of an escutcheon, consisting of the Dexter, Middle, and Sinister Base-points.

9. a. *Geom.* That line or surface of a plane or solid figure on which it stands, or is considered to stand, Thus:—of a triangle, any one side in respect of the other two; of a cone or pyramid, the circle or polygon remote from its apex; of a cylinder or prism, the lower of the two circles or equal polygons which form its ends.

1570 BILLINGSLEY *Euclid* I. def. 29 In comparison of any two sides of a triangle, the third is called a base. **1571** DIGGES *Pantom.* IV. def. 22 Any one of the Figures wherewith these solides be enuironed, is called the base of that solide. **1660** BARROW *Euclid.* I. v, The angles at the base of an isosceles triangle are equal. **1817** R. JAMESON *Charac. Min.* 104 Terminal planes are the smallest planes that bound the greatest extent. In the prism they form the bases. **1831** BREWSTER *Optics* ii. 17 A cone of rays, whose base is the circular mirror.

†**b.** ***distinct base*** in *Optics*: focal distance. *Obs.*

1706 in PHILLIPS. **1727–51** CHAMBERS *Cycl.*, *Distinct base* ..is that distance, from the pole of a convex glass, in which objects, beheld through it, appear distinct, and well defined.

10. *Fortification.* The imaginary line which connects the salient angle of two adjacent bastions.

1721 in BAILEY.

II. The main or most important element or ingredient, looked upon as its fundamental part.

11. a. *generally.*

1471 RIPLEY *Comp. Alch.* in Ashm. (1652) Ep. 112 Our Base principally, Wherof doth spring both Whyte and Red naturally. **1696** PHILLIPS, *Base*..the principal Ingredient in a prescription. **1810** HENRY *Elem. Chem.* (1826) I. 627 A strong presumption that alumina is a metallic oxide; but its base, aluminum, has not been yet obtained.

b. *Cosmetics.* A substance used as a foundation.

1932 *Woman's Pictorial* 23 Apr. 8/2 Use a pure vanishing cream..for the powder base. **1950** J. EMERALD *Photographic Make-Up* IV. 115 It should be applied to the surface of the features..over an invisible make-up base.

12. *Dyeing.* A substance used as a mordant, by which colours are fixed in the material dyed.

1791 HAMILTON *Berthollet's Dyeing* II. II. ii. 121 Its colouring particles are fixed by a base. **1875** URE *Dict. Arts* II. 168 The fixation of iron oxide and several other bases depends on the same change within the pores or fibre.

13. *Mod. Chem.* The electropositive compound body, whether metallic oxide (sulphide, selenide), hydrate, or alkaloid, which enters into combination with an acid to form a salt; the correlative of ACID, including, but having wider meaning than, ALKALI.

1810 HENRY *Elem. Chem.* (1826) II. 51 Arsenites..may be formed by simply boiling the arsenious acid with the respective bases. **1855** BAIN *Senses & Int.* II. ii. §1 In salts the taste is determined more by the base than by the acid. **1871** ROSCOE *Elem. Chem.* 427 *Vegeto-alkaloids*..a series of bodies containing carbon, hydrogen, oxygen, and nitrogen, which act as bases, and are found in certain plants.

14. *Gram.* The form of a word to which suffixes are attached; the theme.

1845 *Proc. Philol. Soc.* I. 28 The *p* is indicatory, signifying that, for the radical vowel of the base, a Guna letter or diphthong is to be substituted. **1848** *Ibid.* III. 58 This being the characteristic of the case itself, has of course nothing to do with the base of the word. **1875** WHITNEY *Life Lang.* iv. 71 In the Scythian languages, it is the final vowel of the base which assimilates that of the following suffixes. *Ibid.* x. 207 The derivative theme or base.

III. That from which a commencement of action or reckoning is made, regarded as a fundamental starting-point.

15. a. The line or limit from which the start is made in a race, or which serves as a goal for the finish. **b.** The fixed line or 'goal' across which players endeavour to strike the ball in such games as hockey. **c.** The fixed points or stations round which the striker at rounders has to run, and at any of which he is allowed to stay; esp. in *Baseball*, each of the four stations at the angles of the 'diamond', all of which the batsman has to touch in succession in order to score a run. Phr. ***base on balls***, an advance to first base allowed to the batsman when the pitcher has delivered four balls outside the strike zone.

1695 BLACKMORE *Pr. Arth.* IX. 358 While round the Base the wanton Coursers play, Th' ambitious Riders in just Scales they weigh. **1812** W. TENNANT *Anster F.* III. lvi, His toils are o'er, and he has gained the base. **1845** in *Appleton's Ann. Cycl.* (1886) X. 77/2 No ace or base can be made on a foul strike. **1868** CHADWICK *Game Base Ball* 34 He has also to look sharp after a base runner, when he is trying to run to second base. **1874** —— *Base Ball Manual* 92 The bases must be four in number, and they must be placed and securely fastened upon each corner of a square whose sides are respectively thirty yards... The first, second, and third bases shall be canvas bags, painted white, and filled with some soft material; the home base shall consist of white marble or stone. **1875** 'STONEHENGE' *Brit. Sports* III. I. iv. §1 If while running between the bases he is hit by the ball, he is put out. **1886** [see HOME *sb.*[1] B. 4]. **1891** N. CRANE *Baseball* x. 79 *Base on balls.* When a batsman is awarded first base by the umpire on 'four balls' called on the pitcher, the batsman is said to 'take his base on balls'.

d. *fig.*, in various expressions in *U.S. slang*, as ***off one's base***, wildly mistaken, crazy, mad; ***to get to first base***: to achieve the first step towards one's objective.

1882 G. W. PECK *Peck's Sunshine* 42 The Boston lady held up her hands in holy horror, and was going to explain..how she was off her base. **1888** 'MARK TWAIN' in *Century Mag.* Jan. 463 It's about the gaudiest thing in the book, if you boom it right along and don't get left on a base. **1907** M. C. HARRIS *Tents of Wickedness* III. iii. 251 Mrs. Butterbeans was so off her base about it, it was ludicrous. **1938** F. SCOTT FITZGERALD *Let.* May (1964) 31, I thought I'd read Italian to read Dante and didn't get to first base. **1962** WODEHOUSE *Service with Smile* x. 157 She gives you the feeling that you'll never get to first base with her.

16. a. *Mil.* The line or place upon which the general of an army relies as a stronghold and magazine, and from which the operations of a campaign are conducted. Also *transf.* to other operations.

1860 GEN. P. THOMPSON *Audi Alt.* III. cxxii. 68 The theory of the base. A leading point in it, being that you must not pass a fortification, by reason of the effects its garrison would have on you if you left it in your rear. **1863** KINGLAKE *Crimea* II. 193 The territory on which these resources are spread is called the 'base of operations.'

b. Similarly, an air or naval station.

1896 *19th Cent.* Mar. 461 Tactical considerations demand a strong naval base, which we already possess in Gibraltar and Malta. **1909** R. P. HEARN *Aerial Warfare* x. 134 (*caption*) Airship base. **1914** *War Illustr.* 5 Dec. 384 Three Englishmen..on November 23rd..made a bomb attack on the Zeppelin workshops... Two..adventurers succeeded in flying back to their base. **1940** *Economist* 7 Sept. 299/1 The leasing to the United States of air and naval bases in British possessions in America. **1947** AUDEN *Age of Anxiety* (1948) I. 19 While we hurried on to our home bases.

17. *Surv.* A line on the earth's surface or in space, of which the exact length and position are accurately determined, and which is used as a base (sense 9) for trigonometrical observations and computations.

1834 MRS. SOMERVILLE *Connex. Phys. Sc.* vi. 54 Measuring 500 feet of a base in Ireland. *Ibid.* (1849) Introd. 2 Use the globe he inhabits as a base wherewith to measure the magnitude and distance of the sun and planets.

18. *Math.* The number from which, as a definite starting-point, a system of numeration or logarithms proceeds.

1874 TODHUNTER *Trigon.* x. 93 Suppose $a^x = n$, then x is called the logarithm of n to the base a..e.g. $3^4 = 81$; thus 4 is the logarithm of 81 to the base 3. *Mod.* The base of our system of numeration is 10.

IV. *Comb.* and *Attrib.*

19. General relations: **a.** appositive (= forming a base), as ***base-colour, -line, -plate, -squadron, -unit***; in sense 16, ***base camp, censor, port, ship, wallah***. **b.** attrib. (= belonging to, or situated at, the base), as ***base-course, -moulding*** (see 5 b), ***-shoot, -table***.

a. 1832 *Regul. Instr. Cavalry* III. 46 The Base Squadron, Troop, or Division, is the one upon which a Formation is made. **1871** C. Davies *Metr. Syst.* II. 41 That the metre is too large for a base-unit. **1879** Harlan *Eyesight* v. 61 Red, yellow, and blue were formerly considered the base colors. **1879** *Cassell's Tech. Educ.* IV. 243/1 At the back of the base-plate is a small stud. **1898** *Daily News* 27 May 7/5 The boats will be used as base camps. **1900** *Blackw. Mag.* Sept. 442/1 If.. the senior officer commanding the Channel Squadron.. brings his fleet into one of its natural base-ports. **1915** *Daily Express* 12 Nov. 5/3 It had been resealed in the customary way with the printed label showing that it had been 'Examined by Base Censor'. **1919** W. Deeping *Second Youth* xxix. 251 This Base-wallah of a doctor. **1928** *Daily Express* 13 June 1 It was sent by wireless to the expedition's baseship. **1937** *Discovery* Dec. 376/1 He.. established a base-camp where supplies could be concentrated before he advanced. **1962** P. Purser *Peregrination 22* xv. 69 Some of the chaps are going to cross an ice-cap... Not me.. Strictly a base-wallah.

b. **1845** *Gloss. Goth. Archit.* I. 47 Base-moulding, Base-table.. a projecting moulding or band of mouldings near the bottom of a wall. **1879** Sir G. Scott *Lect. Archit.* II. 82 The walls were further relieved by projecting base-courses. **1882** *Garden* 11 Mar. 169/1 When all the base shoots are neatly tied down.

20. a. Special combinations: **baseboard**, a board situated at or forming the base; *spec.* (chiefly U.S.) a skirting-board; **baseboard heating**, heating of a room by means of heat supplied to the skirting-boards; **base box** = *basis box* (basis III); **base-burner**, a furnace or stove in which the fuel is supplied to the fire automatically from a hopper as the lower stratum is consumed; **base hospital** *Mil.*, a hospital at some place distant from the area of active operations; **base level**, *spec.* in *Phys. Geogr.* (see quots.); hence **base-levelled** *ppl. a.*, brought to base level; **base-line** (see quot. and cf. 16, 17); also in *Perspective*, the common section of a picture and the geometrical plane, and in *Gunnery*, a line traced round a cannon at the rear of the vent; also *fig.*; cf. also quot. 1802; **base-load** (see load *sb.*); **base-point**, in *Her.*, the middle point of the base (see 8); **base rate** (see quot.); **base-ring**, (*a*) a moulding on the breech of a cannon between the base and the first reinforce; (*b*) a projecting circular base; applied *attrib.* to a type of late Bronze Age pottery from Cyprus; †**base-square** (see quot.).

1854 O. S. Fowler *Home for All* 159 After mop or *base-boards are nailed on.. fill in between these boards.. with stone or mortar. **1899** *Nature* 15 June 149/2 The author conceived the idea of using on a base-board a rotary disc to represent a crank-shaft. **1935** A. Squire *Sing Sing Doctor* xiv. 210 A broad baseboard curves inward on either side [of the electric chair] to form a single wide center leg. **1943** *Electronic Engin.* XV. 390 The chassis is fixed vertically to a wooden baseboard so that the components are easily accessible. **1958** M. L. Hall *Newnes Complete Amat. Photogr.* iii. 42 The scale is engraved on the base-board of the camera. **1954** *Archit. Rev.* CXVI. 343 One last variety is skirting panel heating, which is used extensively in America where it is known as '*baseboard' heating. **1925** A. H. Mundey *Tin & Tin Industry* 95 There was hot-rolled a total of 213,940 *base boxes. **1956** Base box [see *basis box* s.v. basis III]. **1895** *Daily News* 29 Apr. 5/3 It was intended to divide the '*Base Hospital' among several of the larger stations within easy reach of the frontier. **1895** *Westm. Gaz.* 30 Dec. 5/1 There are no dangerous cases of illness at the base hospital. **1875** J. W. Powell *Explor. Colorado River* II. xii. 203 We may consider the level of the sea to be a grand *base level, below which the dry lands cannot be eroded. **1939** Bailey & Weir *Introd. Geol.* xxxii. 188 Sea-level is often called the base level of stream erosion, although rivers do cut a little below sea-level. **1949** W. G. Moore *Dict. Geogr.*, The permanent base-level is the level of the sea; a lake provides a temporary base-level, but the sediment deposited in it by the stream destroys its effect. **1925** J. Joly *Surface-Hist. Earth* v. 81 The *base-levelled stumps of Archaean mountains cover two millions of square miles in Canada. *Ibid.* vii. 114 The base-levelled remains of pre-Cambrian mountains or of the ancestral Rockies. **1750** M. Mackenzie *Orcades* 3/1 The Direction of this *Base-line having been exactly taken with a Magnetic Needle, from each of its Extremities, with a good Theodelite, the Angles were observed, contained between the Base and visual rays connecting the Beacons. **1785** Roy *Surveying* in *Phil. Trans.* LXXV. 406 It was seen that the computed base-line.. would fall.. little short of the hypothenusal distance. **1802** C. James *Mil. Dict.*, *Base-line*, the line on which troops in column move, the first division that marches into the alignement forms the base line, which each successive division prolongs. **1810** *Ibid.*, *Base-line* also signifies the line on which all the magazines and means of supply of an army are established, and from whence the lines of operation proceed. **1830** E. Campbell *Dict. Mil. Sc.*, *Base-line*, in Military Tactics, signifies the line on which all Magazines and means of Supply of an Army are established. **1902** *Daily Chron.* 25 July 3/3 A definite base-line from which the future progress of Irish industry can be measured. **1961** *Lancet* 29 July 227/2 The distribution of sensitivities found in various parts of the country served as a baseline. **1605** Camden *Rem.* (1637) 225 John of Clarence bare.. a Floure-de-lis Or in *Base-Point. **1923** J. D. Hackett *Labor Terms* in *Management Engineering* May, **Base Rate*, the ordinary day rate of wages guaranteed, in scientific management, whether the standard task is accomplished or not. **1626** Capt. Smith *Accid. Yng. Seamen* 32 Her carnooze or *base ring at her britch. **1862** F. Griffiths *Artill. Man.* 53 The Length of a gun is ascertained by measuring it from the rear of the *base ring to the face of the muzzle. **1899** Myres & Ohnefalsch-Richter *Catal. Cyprus Museum* 16 With the exception of a few late and distinct fabrics, the vessels have no foot or base-ring to enable them to stand upright. *Ibid.* 37 *Base-Ring Ware*.. is confined to the later Bronze Age, and does not appear much before the Mykenaean vases. **1905** H. B. Walters *Hist. Anc. Pottery* I. vi. 242 Base-ring ware.. is marked off from other Bronze-Age types by its flat-ringed base in all cases. **1949** W. F. Albright *Archæol. Palestine* v. 99 Base-ring ware from Cyprus.. died out rapidly after the beginning of the thirteenth century. **1598** Barret *Theor. Warres* IV. i. 95 The Base square, is the battell [*i.e.* battalion] which containeth almost thrise, or 3 times more in breadth then in depth.

b. In *Baseball*, as ***base-bag***, ***-player***, ***-playing***, ***-stealer***, ***-stealing*** (cf. steal *v.*[1] 5 g); **base hit**, a hit from which the ball cannot be fielded in time to prevent the batsman from reaching his base; **base-line** (*a*) the line, three feet wide, marked on the turf from base to base of a baseball field; (*b*) the line at each end of a lawn-tennis court, also *attrib.*, as ***base-line game***, ***driver***; hence **base-liner**, one who drives from the base-line, also a base-line drive; **base-runner**, in *Baseball*, the player who, having made a fair hit or in other contingencies specified in the rules, is running the bases; so ***base running*** vbl. sb.

1864 *Wilkes' Spirit of Times* 10 Dec. 229/1 The player shall not be declared out if he maintains his position with any part of his person on the place where the base-bag belongs. **1867** Chadwick *Beadle's Dime Base Ball Player* 10 The rule makes the base-bag the base, not the post to which it is fastened. **1874** —— *Base Ball Manual* 83 All ordinary errors, such as dropped flyballs, bad muffs, wild throws, and failures on the part of base players to hold balls thrown to them—all count in preventing base hits being made. **1867** *Ball Players' Chron.* 4 July 5/1 Foul balls are those striking the ground or a player back of the base lines. **1875** *Encycl. Brit.* III. 406/2 [*Base ball*] The position of the bases and base lines may be likened to a 90 feet square shaped diamond. **1875** 'Stonehenge' *Brit. Rural Sports* 690/1 (*Lawn tennis*) The player who wins choice of courts serves; *i.e.* delivers the ball, standing with one foot outside the base line. **1878** *Laws of Lawn-tennis* 7 At each end of the Court, parallel with the net, and at a distance of 39 ft. from it, are drawn Base-Lines. **1905** *Westm. Gaz.* 29 June 5/2 Unsurpassed as a base-line driver. **1929** W. E. Collinson *Spoken Eng.* 90 You'd better stand clear of the base-line or you may foot-fault. **1903** *Westm. Gaz.* 27 July 10/2 Ritchie displayed remarkable activity and resource in getting back most of his opponent's lightning 'base-liners'. **1867** Chadwick *Base Ball Player's Bk.* 23 A base player taking a ball from a fielder. **1868** —— *Game of Base Ball* 34 We now come to base playing, and we propose to show that each position has its peculiar points of play. **1867** —— *Beadle's Dime Base Ball Player* 129 The base-runner ceased to be forced to leave the base. **1875** *Encycl. Brit.* III. 407/1 Directly a striker has fairly struck a fair ball he becomes a base-runner. **1867** *Ball Players' Chron.* 6 June 4/2 Prohibiting base running on called balls. **1886** Chadwick (*title*) The Art of Batting and Base Running. **1896** —— *Spalding's Base Ball Guide* 88 We have made up a record of the most successful base-stealers of the twelve League clubs who have a record of total stolen bases for at least three seasons. **1912** Mathewson *Pitching in a Pinch* 272 Merkle.. is a great base stealer because he has acquired the knack of 'getting away'. **1886** *Chicago Tribune* 14 May 3/3 The fifth inning was characterized by a cheeky bit of base-stealing by Dalrymple. **1917** Mathewson *Sec. Base Sloan* xi. 145 He got to first and gave a very pretty exhibition of base-stealing a moment later.

c. *Chem.* **base exchange**, a reaction in which atoms of one chemical base in a compound substance are replaced by those of another; also *attrib.* (Also called cation *exchange*.) So **base-exchanger**, a substance capable of such a reaction; ***base-exchanging*** adj.; **base-rich** *a.*, rich in basic ions.

1922 *Chem. Abstr.* 3042 (*title*) Base exchange in silicates. I. Exchange of alkalies and ammonia in.. permutite. **1930** *Discovery* Oct. 340/1 Work on the base-exchange (zeolite) method of water-softening was.. described. **1949** P. C. Carman *Chem. Constit. & Prop. Engin. Materials* xiii. 385 A potassium-kaolinite can be prepared by base-exchange and shows no reluctance to exchange K^+ for other cations. **1943** *Thorpe's Dict. Appl. Chem.* VI. 218/1 Processes involving base-exchangers include water-softening, total demineralising of water, purification of sugar juices, [etc.]. **1917** *Chem. Abstr.* 80 Base-exchanging substances, such as Na zeolites. **1958** *New Biol.* XXVI. 91 Fen peat formed under conditions which are base-rich (i.e. containing relatively substantial concentrations of cations such as those of calcium, magnesium, potassium and sodium) and alkaline. **1959** A. R. Clapham et al. *Excursion Flora Brit. Isles* 328 Base-rich water.

base (beɪs), *sb.*[2] Also prisoner's base: in 5 bace, 6 baase. [either a specific use of base *sb.*[1] III., or a phonetic corruption of *bars* (cf. bar *sb.*[1], and base *sb.*[5],[6]); if the latter is the real origin, the former accounts equally well for the sense.] A popular game among boys; it is played by two sides, who occupy contiguous 'bases' or 'homes'; any player running out from his 'base' is chased by one of the opposite side, and, if caught, made a prisoner.

c **1440** *Promp. Parv.* 20/2 Bace, pleye.. *barri, barrorum, dantur ludi puerorum.* **1558** Phaër *Æneid* v. Oj, Thys kind of pastime fyrst, and custome boyes to learne at Baase, Ascanius.. dyd bryng in place. **1611** Shaks. *Cymb.* v. iii. 20 Lads more like to run The Country base, then to commit such slaughter. **1653** Greaves *Seraglio* 80 The Jeeret [is] a kind of running at base on horsback. **1880** *Boy's Own Bk.* 27 Prisoners' Base is a capital game for cold weather.

†**b.** ***to bid base***: to challenge to a chase in this game; *gen.* to challenge. Hence ***base-bidding*** adj.

1548 Udall, etc. *Erasm. Par. Luke* iv. 1 (R.) The spirite of wickednesse.. biddeth bace, and begynneth firste with hym, of whom he was to be subdued. **1592** Shaks. *Ven. & Ad.* li, To bid the wind a base he now prepares. **1593** Nashe *Christ's T.* (1613) 69 Sportiue Base-bidding Roundelayes. **1641** Milton *Animadv.* Wks. (1851) 202, I shall not intend this hot season to bid you the base through the wide, and dusty Champaine of the Councels.

†**base** (beɪs), *sb.*[3] *Obs.* exc. *Hist.* Also 6–7 **baise**, 7 **bass**. [app. an Eng. application of base *sb.*[1] 'bottom, lower part' to these articles of dress.]

I. *sing.*

1. ? The housing of a horse.

1548 Hall *Chron. Hen. VIII*, an. 1 (R.) The basses and bardes of their horse were grene sattyn. *Ibid.* an. 2 (R.) Their basses and trappers of clothe of gold, euery of them his name embroudered on hys basse and trapper. **1577** Holinshed *Chron.* III. 825/1 The king had a base and a trapper of purple velvet. **1667** Milton *P.L.* IX. 36 Caparisons and steeds; Bases and tinsel Trappings.

II. pl. *bases* (cf. *skirts*).

2. A plaited skirt, of cloth, velvet, or rich brocade, appended to the doublet, and reaching from the waist to the knee, common in the Tudor period; also an imitation of this in mailed armour.

1580 Sidney *Arcadia* III. 285 His bases which he ware so long as they came almost to his ankle. **1596** Spenser *F.Q.* v. v. 20 An apron white, Instead of curiets and bases fit for fight. **1602** Warner *Alb. Eng.* XII. lxix. (1612) 291 The Taishes, Cushies, and the Graues, Staffe, Pensell, Baises. **1639** J. Aston *Iter Boreale* Add. MS. B.M. 28566 f. 25 b, A paire of bases of Plad and stockings of yᵉ same. **1821** Scott *Kenilw.* xxxix, His bases and the foot-cloth of his hobbyhorse dropping water.

3. The skirt of a woman's outer petticoat or robe.

1591 Harington *Orl. Fur.* XXXII. xlvii, The collour of her bases was almost Like to the falling whitish leaves. **1672** Jordan *Lond. Tri.* in Heath *Grocer's Comp.* (1869) 496 A short Petticoat or Bases of Silver, fringed with Gold. **1697** *C'tess D'Aunoy's Trav.* (1706) 125 She had Basses all of Flowers of Point de Spain in Silk and Gold.

4. An apron.

c **1605** Marston (in Webster), Bakers in their linen bases. **1663** Butler *Hud.* I. ii. 769 [The butcher] With gauntlet blue and bases white.

†**base**, *sb.*[4] *Mus. Obs.* Also 5–6 **bace**. The regular form up to the present century of the word now spelt bass *sb.*[5], q.v.

? *a* **1450** *Songs & Carols* (1847) 67 Whan.. bulles of the see syng a good bace. **1629** Milton *Ode Nativ.* 130 The base of Heaven's deep organ. **1728** Pope *Dunc.* II. 225 Whose hoarse heroic base Drowns the loud clarion of the braying Ass. **1835** *Penny Cycl.* s.v. *Base* in *music*, This word is frequently written *bass*, but the etymology, and more especially the pronunciation, are decidedly in favour of the orthography here adopted, which is sanctioned by Dr. Johnson and other high authorities.

†**base**, *sb.*[5] *Obs.* exc. *dial.* Also 5–6 **bace**. [phonetic corruption of OE. *bærs*, barse, now bass.] Earlier and dial. form of bass *sb.*[1], a fish.

c **1440** *Promp. Parv.* 20/2 Bace, fysche. *c* **1460** J. Russell *Bk. Nurture* in *Babees Bk.* (1878) 167 Carpe, base, mylet, or trowt. **1513** *Bk. Kerving* ibid. 281 Base, molet, roche, perche. **1611** Cotgr., *Bar*, the fish called a Base. **1620** Venner *Via Recta* iv. 74 The Base is in goodnesse of iuyce inferiour to the Mullet. **1724** De Foe, etc. *Tour Gt. Brit.* (1769) III. 341 One Draught of Base had equalled a Cart-load. **1851** *Cumbld. Gloss.*, *Base*, a perch.

†**base**, *sb.*[6] *Obs.* 6–7; also 6 **bass**. [app. a corruption (cf. prec.) of F. *barce*, *berche* (both in Cotgr.), in same sense.] The smallest kind of cannon used in the 16–17th centuries; see quot.

1544 in Lodge *Illustr. Brit. Hist.* (1838) I. 105 Bastard culverins.. besides other small field pieces, falcons, and bases. **1587** Fleming *Contn. Holinshed* III. 1021/1 Their ordinance, namelie basses and slings. **1611** Cotgr., *Berche*, the peece of ordnance called a Base. **1623** Minsheu, *Esmirel*, a kind of artillery, to the bignes of an harquebus de croc called a base. **1692** in *Capt. Smith's Seaman's Gram.* II. vii. 96 Base.. Diameter of bore 1·25 in., weight 200 lb., weight of shot 0·5 lb.

attrib. **1599** Hakluyt *Voy.* II. II. 20 We let fall our grapnel almost a base shot off the shoare.

base (beɪs), *a.* Forms: 4–7 **bass**, 5 **baas**, (*Sc.* **baisse**), bas, 5–7 **basse**, 6–7 **bace**, 5– **base**. [a. F. *bas*, fem. *basse*, cogn. with Pr. *bas*, It. *basso*:—late L. *bassus*, explained by Isidore, as 'thick, fat,' by Papias as 'short, low'; found in cl. L. as a family cognomen. For the remoter etymology some suggest a Celtic source; others, including Diez, refer to Gr. *βάσσων*, compar. of *βαθύς* deep.]

A. I. Literal senses.

1. Low absolutely; of small height. *arch.*

1393 Gower *Conf.* I. 98 Her nase bass, her browes high. **1596** Spenser *F.Q.* I. v. 31 An entraunce, darke and bace.. Descends to hell. **1605** Shaks. *Lucr.* 664 The cedar stoops not to the base shrubs foot. **1863** Kinglake *Crimea* (1876) I. iii. 56 A crowd of monks with base foreheads.

b. In *Bot.* denoting lowly growth; e.g. *Base Broom, Base Rocket.*

1578 Lyte *Dodoens* 667 Of base Broome or Woodwaren.. called in Latine, *Genista humilis*: in Italian *Cerretta*: that is, lowe and base Broome. **1863** Prior *Plant-n.* 15 Base-rocket, from its rocket-like leaves, and lowly growth.

†2. Low comparatively; below its usual height.

1525 LD. BERNERS *Froiss.* II. xcix. [xcv.] 291 They founde the ryuer in suche a poynt, that in xxx. yeres before it was not so base. *Ibid.* cii. [xcviii.] 297 In wynter.. the ryuers are but base and lowe.

†3. Occupying a low position, low-lying; of lower situation than neighbouring parts. *Obs.* Cf. BASE-COURT.

c **1440** *Promp. Parv.* 20 Bace chambyr, *camera bassa.* **1509** HAWES *Past. Pleas.* XXXVIII. iii, Alofte the basse toure foure ymages stode. **1561** HOLLYBUSH *Hom. Apoth.* 33b, When the basse or last gut issueth or is swollen. **1593** SHAKS. *Richard II*, II. iv. 20, I see thy Glory, like a shooting Starre, Fall to the base Earth from the Firmament. **1644** Z. BOYD *Zion's Flowers* (1855) App. 8/1 The base valleyes enjoy a calm in a gentle gale. **1851** TURNER *Dom. Archit.* I. i. 6 To construct a base-chamber with a fireplace.

†**b.** *esp.* geographically or topographically. *Obs.*

1475 *Bk. Noblesse* 45 He wanne.. base Normandie. **1578** LYTE *Dodoens* 5 The base Almaignes do call it 'alsene.' **1601** HOLLAND *Pliny* II. 210 Base Egypt watered.. with Nilus. *a* **1628** F. GREVILLE *Sidney* (1652) 226 They took the base Towne.. even to the gates of the High Towne.

4. Of sounds: Low, not loud; deep, BASS.

c **1450** *Merlin* xxviii. 572 He seide in bas voice: I am Monevall. *c* **1500** *Partenay* 945 Ful gret mynstracy; Bothe hye and bas instrumentes sondry. **1596** SPENSER *F.Q.* III. ii. 50 Sad words with hollow voice and bace, Shee to the virgin sayd. **1833** BREWSTER *Nat. Magic* ix. 230 His ears were insensible to all sounds below F, marked by the base cliff.

†**5.** Deep-coloured, dark. Also *adverbially. Obs.*

1533 ELYOT *Cast. Helth* (1541) 87 Urine base redde, lyke to bole armenake. **1586** COGAN *Haven Health* i. (1636) 8 That [urine] which is well colored not too high or base. [**1588** SHAKS. *Tit. A.* IV. ii. 72 Is black so base a hue?]

II. Figurative senses.

6. Low in the social scale, of lowly condition, plebeian; belonging to the 'lower orders.' *arch.*

1490 CAXTON *Eneydos* xi. 42 They whiche ben borne of basse parentage. *c* **1500** *Partenay* 523 If any you demaunde, hie other bas, Of your said lord. **1534** MORE *On the Passion* Wks. 1289/2 To the keeping of hym from synne.. a more base estate was better. **1602** FULBECKE *Pandectes* 47 Hauing singled the most noble, did kill the baser prisoners. **1741–3** WESLEY *Jrnl.* (1749) 42 Many of the baser people would fain have interrupted.

†**b.** *to bring base*: to bring low. *Obs.*

c **1430** LYDG. *Bochas* v. xi. (1554) 130b, The noblesse of Grece was brought baas. *a* **1528** SKELTON *Image Hypocr.* III. 430 This were a hevy case To se you brought so base To play without a place. **1550** *Scot. Poems 16th C.* (1801) II. 195 Quhen say weill at sumtimes sall be brought base, Do weill sall triumph in euery place.

7. Illegitimate, bastard. ? *Obs.* exc. in BASE-BORN.

1570–87 HOLINSHED *Scot. Chron.* (1806) II. 430 His base brother, Robert Maxwell. **1601** F. GODWIN *Bps. Eng.* 189 In his youth he was wantonly giuen, and gate a base daughter. **1695** KENNETT *Par. Antiq.* ix. 124 Jeffery the Kings base son. **1755** in *Wesley's Wks.* (1872) III. 342 Their wretched Minister told them.. that 'John Wesley was expelled the College for a base child.'

8. Low in natural rank, or in the scale of creation.

1534 MORE *On the Passion* Wks. 1324/1 A thing of more base nature then was the thing that was wont to be sacrificed to forefigure it. **1600** SHAKS. *A.Y.L.* III. ii. 69 Ciuet is of a baser birth then Tarre, the verie vncleanly fluxe of a Cat. **1680** H. MORE *Apocal. Apoc.* 127 The Wafer may happen to be eaten by base Vermine, such as Rats. **1775** HARRIS *Philos. Arrangem.* (1841) 369 Providence has given to every animal, however base.. a consciousness of this want [of food]. **1853** KINGSLEY *Hypatia* iv. 43 She might sacrifice the base body, and ennoble the soul by the self-sacrifice.

9. Low in the moral scale; without dignity of sentiment; reprehensibly cowardly or selfish, despicably mean; opposed to *high-minded*: **a.** of persons.

1593 SHAKS. *3 Hen. VI*, I. i. 178 Base, fearefull, and despayring Henry. **1675** DRYDEN *Aurengz.* I. i. 248 Hast thou been never base? Did Love ne'er bend Thy frailer Virtue, to betray thy Friend? **1771** *Junius Lett.* xlix. 253, I .. call you the meanest and basest fellow in the kingdom. **1849** MACAULAY *Hist. Eng.* II. 98 He offered Rochester a simple choice, to pronounce the Bishop guilty, or to quit the Treasury. Rochester was base enough to yield.

b. of actions, habits, thoughts, etc.

a **1535** MORE *Wks.* 361 (R.) Such a base foule fleshly liuing. **1583** STANYHURST *Æneis* I. (Arb.) 24 On with a fresh courradge, and bace thoghts fearful abandon. **1614** RALEIGH *Hist. World* v. vi. §6 II. 642 A most base piece of flatterie. **1780** BURKE *Let. T. Burgh* Wks. IX. 250 A market-overt for legalizing a base traffick of Votes and Pensions. **1852** MCCULLOCH *Taxation* I. iv. 121 Their most upright decisions may be.. ascribed to the basest motives.

10. Befitting an inferior person or thing; degraded or degrading, unworthy, menial.

1594 T. B. *La Primaud. Fr. Acad.* II, The guttes and other partes of baser seruice. **1602** SHAKS. *Ham.* v. i. 223 To what base vses we may returne Horatio. **1603** KNOLLES *Hist. Turks* (1621) 106 Better fitted for merchandize and other base occupations than for Chivalrie. **1685** BAXTER *Paraphr. N.T.* Luke xv. 15 Foolish sinners will submit to the basest servitude, and be attendants of swine.

11. *Law.* Servile, as opposed to *free.* ***base tenure, estate,*** or ***fee***: *orig.* tenure, not by 'free' or military service, but by ***base service***, such as a 'villain' owed to his lord; *later*, since this was tenure at the mere will of the lord, applied to such tenure in fee simple as may determine on the fulfilment of a contingent qualification or limitation. So ***base-tenant.*** See also BASE-COURT.

1523 FITZHERB. *Surv.* 14 These maner of copye holders haue an estate of enherytaunce, after the custome of the maner, yet haue they no franke tenement.. and therfore they be called tenantes of base tenure. **1607** COWELL *Interpr.* s.v., Base tenants be they which do to their lords villeinous service. **1741** T. ROBINSON *Gavelkind* v. 45 As well to free Socage as base. **1768** BLACKSTONE *Comm.* II. 61 Base services.. as to plough the lord's land, to make his hedges. **1849** MACAULAY *Hist. Eng.* II. 589 English liberty would thenceforth be held by a base tenure. It would be, not, as heretofore, an immemorial inheritance. **1876** DIGBY *Real Prop.* iv. §3. 189 An estate in fee which was thus liable to be defeated was called in later times a base fee.

†**12.** Of price: Low, cheap. *Obs. rare.*

1599 HAKLUYT *Voy.* II. 164 As base prices as is possible. *Ibid.* 239 They.. sell them at most vile and base prices.

13. Of inferior quality; mean, paltry, common, poor, shabby.

1561 T. NORTON *Calvin's Inst.* III. 274 He may yet sustaine his body with bacer foode. **1576** LAMBARDE *Peramb. Kent* (1826) 157 This old house.. may now seeme but a base Barn in your eie. **1607** ROWLANDS *Diog. Lanth.* 5 Base is thy attyre, as thrid-bare in thy apparel as my Gowne. **1785** COWPER *Task* I. 50 The rest.. content With base materials, sat on well-tann'd hides. **1849** RUSKIN *Sev. Lamps* vi. §18. 180 The cheapest and basest imitation which can escape detection.

b. Of language: Not classical, debased.

1549 OLDE *Erasm. Par. Thess.* Ded., A translacion of basse kinde of thenglishe phrase. **1591** SPENSER *M. Hubberd* 44 Base is the style, and matter meane withall. *a* **1661** FULLER (in Webster), Base Latin. *Mod.* 'Of very base Latinity.'

14. Of comparatively little value, worthless. ***base metals***: those not classed as ***noble*** or ***precious***.

1607 SHAKS. *Timon* III. iii. 6 They haue all bin touch'd, and found Base-Mettle. **1613** SIR H. FINCH *Law* (1636) 23 A base Myne where there is Ore, shall be the Kings for the worthinesse of the Ore. **1684** *Contemp. State Man* II. i. (1699) 133 All Temporal things are in themselves little and bass. **1702** ADDISON *Dial. Medals* iii. 145 Coins.. made of your baser sorts of metal. **1881** RAYMOND *Mining Gloss.*, *Base metals.* See *Noble metals.*

15. Alloyed with less valuable metal; debased, counterfeit.

a **1528** SKELTON *Vox Populi* VIII. vi. 9 The coyne yt is so scante.. But even as much to base. **1611** COTGR. s.v. *Argent*, Silver.. twelue grains baser than *Argent le Roy.* **1725** SWIFT *Wood the Ironm.* Wks. 1755 IV. I. 66 They search'd his pockets on the place, And found his copper all was base. **1855** MACAULAY *Hist. Eng.* III. 215 Persons who refused the base money were arrested.

16. *Comb.* **a.** *adverbially* with pa. pple., as in ***base-begged, -begot, -bred***, BASE-BORN; also ***base-like*** adj., seeming base. **b.** parasynthetic deriv., as ***base-hearted, -mettled, -spirited, -witted***, BASE-MINDED; and deriv. from these, as ***base-heartedly, base-spiritedness.***

a. **1579** SPENSER *Sheph. Cal.* To Bk., If that any aske thy name, Say, thou wert base-begot. **1600** *Gowrie's Conspir.* in *Harl. Misc.* (1793) 190 Recountred a base-like fellow, vnknowne to him. **1609** DANIEL *Civ. War* (1717) II. 22 Prolongs this not long base-begg'd Breath. **1616** *Pasquil & Kath.* IV. 120 Whose verie eyes will blaze His base-bred spirit.

b. **1547** LATIMER *Serm. & Rem.* (1845) 422 Every silly soul and base-witted man. *a* **1683** OLDHAM *Wks. & Rem.* (1685) 10 To rein, and curb base-mettled Hereticks. **1748** RICHARDSON *Clarissa* (1811) VII. lxxxi. 338 His generous confessions taken for a mark of base-spiritedness. **1843** CARLYLE *Past & Pr.* 391 Thy stupidities and grovelling baseheartedness.

B. quasi-*adv.*; cf. 'high and low'; OF. *en haut et en bas* completely. See also A 6.

c **1500** *Partenay* 927 Ther fair chapel.. Wel apparailled it was, hie and bas.

C. *absol.* quasi-*sb.* Cf. BAST *sb.*[2]

†**1.** Bastard. *Obs.*

1591 *Troub. Raigne K. John* (1611) 18 Base to a King addes title of more State, Than Knights begotten, though legitimate. **1602** *Parish Reg. Roxwell, Essex* 8 June, Agnes, the base of Maudlin Wonner. **1624** *Ibid.* 18 July, Richardus, the base of Dominici Godstret.

†**2.** Bastardy. *Obs.* (? error for *bast.*)

1611 SPEED *Hist. Gt. B.* IX. xviii, Children.. begot in base.

†**base,** *v.*[1] *Obs.*; Also 4–5 besse, 6 baisse, baas. [partly aphetic f. ABASE *v.*; partly a. F. *baisse-r* (= Pr. *baissar*:—late L. *bassā-re*, f. *bassus*: see BASE *a.*), whence the frequent 16th c. form *baisse.*]

1. To lower; to bring, cast, or lay down.

c **1375** BARBOUR *Bruce* IV. 94 Sum best, sum woundyt, sum als slayne. **1580** NORTH *Plutarch* (1676) 343 They could not once base their Pikes, nor fight. **1592** WYRLEY *Armorie* 50 Sir Eustace.. Did baisse his gleaue. **1600** HOLLAND *Livy* XLV. xix. 1213 To base at the feet of.. his conquerour, the crowne.. which he came unjustly by.

2. To lower in rank, condition, or character; to debase, humble, depose, degrade.

1538 POLE in Strype *Eccl. Mem.* I. ii. lxxxiii. 217 Long continuance in other studies, that baseth the mind. **1559** *Myrr. Mag.*, *Warwick* xii, That plaaste and baaste his soverayne so oft. **1626** BRETON *Fantasticks* (1857) 323 Love .. weakneth strength, and baseth Honour.

3. To lessen in amount or value, depreciate; to debase (metals).

1581 W. STAFFORD *Exam. Compl.* ii. (1876) 49 By basing the estimacion of wooll and felles. *a* **1626** BACON (J.) Metals, which we cannot base.

base (beɪs), *v.*[2]; in 6 bace. [f. BASE *sb.*[1]]

1. *trans.* To make, lay, or form a foundation for.

1587 *Myrr. Mag.*, *Brennus* xl, By bloudshed they doe founde, bace, builde, and prop their state. **1809** J. BARLOW *Columb.* IV. 514 Long toils.. Must base the fabric of so vast a throne. **1878** G. MACDONALD *Phantastes* vi. 94 Great roots based the tree-columns.

2. To place *on* or *upon* a foundation or logical basis; to found, establish securely, secure. (So mod.F. *baser.*)

1841 MYERS *Cath. Th.* IV. §12. 247 The foundations on which any moral judgement.. can be based. **1868** ROGERS *Pol. Econ.* iv. 46 These [bank-]notes were based on gold. **1878** HOPPS *Princ. Relig.* iii. 13 Upon this great truth of His eternal goodness and mercy we base all our hopes.

†**base,** *v.*[3] *Obs. rare.* [f. BASE *sb.*[2]] *intr.* To run at, or as at, prisoner's base.

1589 WARNER *Alb. Eng.* Prose Addit. (1612) 341 With Bacing on foote and on horsbacke, a sport lately vsed of our English youthes. **1614** CHAPMAN *Odyss.* x. 527 Yong heiffers.. all so spritely given.. about Bace by the dams.

baseball ('beɪsbɔːl). Also **base-ball.** [f. BASE *sb.*[1] 15.] **a.** The national field-game of the United States, a more elaborate variety of the English 'rounders,' played by two sides of nine each; so called from the 'bases' or bounds (usually four in number) which mark the circuit to be taken by each player of the in-side after striking the ball. Also, the ball used in the game.

c **1815** MISS AUSTEN *Northang. Ab.* i. (1848) 3 It was not very wonderful that Catherine.. should prefer cricket, base ball.. to books. **1870** EMERSON *Soc. & Solit.* x. 209 Amiable boys, who had never encountered any rougher play than a base-ball match. **1883** *Harper's Mag.* Dec. 106/2 An oval ball.. a little larger than a base-ball.

b. *attrib.*, as ***baseball club, field, game, player.***

1855 (*title*) Atlantic Base Ball Club, Jamaica, N.Y. (D.A.E.). **1857** in Chadwick *Base Ball Manual* (1874) 7 The National Association of Base Ball Players. **1860** CHADWICK (*title*) Beadle's Dime Base Ball Player comprising [etc.]. **1874** —— *Base Ball Manual* 9 A base ball field. **1886** *Baltimore Amer.* in *Boston Jrnl.* 21 July 2/3 (D.A.E.), Any respectable base ball game can attract from 2000 to 7000. **1911** H. HARRISON *Queed* xviii. 225 On the following Saturday,.. he took Miss Weyland to another base-ball game.

Hence **'baseballer, -ballist.**

1868 (*title*) New England Base Ballist. A weekly journal. **1886** *Congress. Rec.* 2 Apr. 3043/2 [He is well known] as a baseballist among constitutional lawyers, and a constitutional lawyer among baseballists. **1888** *Battle Creek Jrnl.* 12 Dec., Western Base Ballers. **1896** KNOWLES & MORTON *Baseball* 79 He.. at once became a London baseballer.

base-born ('beɪsbɔːn), *a.* [f. BASE *a.* 6,7,16.]

A. 1. Of low or humble birth, plebeian.

1593 SHAKS. *2 Hen. VI*, IV. viii. 49 Better ten-thousand base-born Cades miscarry. **1741** RICHARDSON *Pamela* (1824) I. 95 That a gentleman of your rank in life should stoop.. to the base-born Pamela. **1845** DISRAELI *Sybil* (1863) 153 Very often the baseborn change their liveries for coronets.

2. *fig.* Of base origin or nature.

1591 SPENSER *Teares Muses* 392 Such high conceipt of that celestiall fire, The base-born brood of Blindnes cannot gesse. **1852** TUPPER *Prov. Philos.* 179 A base-born mirth, springing out of carelessness and folly

3. Illegitimate, born out of wedlock.

1645 FEATLY *Dippers Dipt* 51 (T.) Neither doth holy imply no bastard; for some holy men have been base-born. **1851** KINGSLEY *Yeast* xi. 203 Our daughters with base-born babies Have wandered away in their shame.

B. quasi-*sb.* One of humble or illegitimate birth.

1605 *Parish Reg. Romford, Essex* 11 Aug., George, the base-borne of one of my Ladye Coke's servants. **1879** E. ARNOLD *Lt. Asia* 195 Huts where the base-born dwelt.

base-burner. *U.S.* (See BASE *sb.*[1] 20 and quots.)

a **1877** KNIGHT *Dict. Mech.* I. 242/1. **1877** BARTLETT *Dict. Amer.* (ed. 4) 32 *Base-burner*, a sheet-iron stove for burning anthracite coal, which is only fed at the top, while the fire is confined to the base, or lower part of the stove. **1893** 'O. THANET' *Stories Western Town* 34 We got to keep a fire in the base-burner good, all night, or the plants will freeze. **1908** S. E. WHITE *Riverman* xxi. 188 When the very cold weather came and they had to light the base-burner stove. *Ibid.* 189 He shook down the base-burner vigorously. **1922** TITUS '*Timber*' ii. 28 A gaunt man.. was putting wood in the base burner.

So **base-burning** *a.*, applied to a furnace or stove.

a **1877** KNIGHT *Dict. Mech.* I. 242/1.

base-court ('beɪskɔət). Also 5–6 **basse-courte,** 7–9 **bass-court.** [f. BASE *a.* 3 + COURT; in sense 1 directly from 15th c. F. *basse-court* (OF. *basse-cort, -curt,* mod.F. *basse-cour*).]

1. The lower or outer court of a castle or mansion, occupied by the servants; the court in the rear of a farm-house, containing the out-buildings.

1491 CAXTON *Four Sons* iii. (1885) 98 Reynawde.. sawe that the basse-courte of the castell brenned. **1575** CHURCHYARD *Chippes* (1817) 83 Thei laye under the rampire of the base courte, and slue sondrie of our souldiours. **1616** SURFL. & MARKH. *Countr. Farm* 38 [The farmer's wife] is tyed to matters within the House and base Court. **1759** B. MARTIN *Nat. Hist. Eng.* I. 212 Bass-Courts for Officers and

Servants. **1821** Scott *Kenilw.* xxv, The large base-court or outer-yard of the noble Castle.

2. An inferior court of justice, one that is not a court of record; *e.g.* a court baron.

1542-3 *Act. 34-5 Hen. VIII*, xxvii. §82 The returne of a write of false iudgement, out of a base court, before the sayde Iustices. **1757** Burke *Abridgm. Eng. Hist.* Wks. X. 438 The original manner of granting feudal property, and something like it is still practised in our base-courts.

† **based,** *ppl. a.*[1] *Obs.* Also 6 **baissed.** [f. BASE *v.*[1] + -ED. Cf. F. *baissé*.] Lowered.

1592 Wyrley *Armorie* 103 With baissed launce the knights approch amaine.

based (beɪst), *ppl. a.*[2] [f. BASE *sb.*[1] + -ED[2].] Having or standing on a base, esp. in comb., as ***broad-based***; *spec.* in *Crystallog.* (see quot.).

1610 Shaks. *Temp.* v. i. 46 The strong bass'd promontorie Haue I made shake. **1817** R. Jameson *Charac. Min.* 197 Based, when the primitive form is either a double pyramid, or a rhomboid, in which the summits are intercepted by planes perpendicular to the axis, which take the place of terminal planes. Based sulphur..is a double four-sided pyramid, truncated on the extremities.

† **based,** *ppl. a.*[3] *Obs.* In 6 **bassed.** [f. BASE *sb.*[3] + -ED[2].] Wearing or furnished with 'bases.'

1548 Hall *Chron. Hen. VIII*, an. 6 (R.) The Duke of Burbones bende was apparelled and bassed in lawny veluet. **1577** Holinshed *Chron.* III. 834/1 Bassed in tawnie velvet.

based (beɪst), *pa. pple.* [f. BASE *sb.*[1] 16 + -ED[2].] Established as a base.

1925 E. F. Norton *Fight for Everest 1924* 57 No. 1 party was to..remain based there for the purpose of getting the next camp on to the North Col.

Hence in Comb. with preceding sbs.

1927 *Daily Tel.* 22 Mar. 10/7 Limiting the number of shore-based aircraft..in commission. **1933** *Bulletin* (Glasgow) 21 Sept. 18/4 The flying boats..have the assistance of land-based aircraft. **1935** Carrier-based [see CARRIER 7]. **1943** in *Amer. Speech* (1945) XX. 142 Mediterranean-based. **1944** *Ibid.*, Russia-based. **1965** *Listener* 10 June 857/2, I..doubt whether ten years from now this 'science-based' or technological university will be very different from any other.

† **base-dance.** *Obs.* [a. F. *basse dance.*] A term formerly applied to dances in slow time (*e.g.* the minuet), which consist of gliding motions and stately posing, the feet being but little raised from the ground.

1509 Hawes *Past. Pleas.* xvi. xlvi, Musyke..Dyvers base daunces moost swetely dyd playe. **1521** in *Laneham's Let.* (1871) Pref. 160 For to daunce ony bace daunce there behoueth .iiii. paces..syngle, double: repryse, & braule. **1549** *Compl. Scot.* vi. 66 Base dansis, pauans, galȝardis.

Basedow's disease: see BRONCHOCELE.

† **basel.** *Obs.* The alleged name according to Holinshed (and copyists down to the present day) of certain pieces of money abrogated by Henry II., of which numismatists have no knowledge. (Prob. Holinshed's error for *baseling*, in sense of 'base piece': cf. *silverling*, etc.)

1577 Holinshed *Chron.* III. 67/1 The same yeare [1158] also the King altered his coine, abrogating certeine peeces called basels. [*Marg. note* in Rolls ed. Matt. Paris I. 309 from one MS. 'Moneta tunc reprobata *Baseling* dicebatur.']

† **'baselard.** *Obs.* Forms: 4-6 **baselarde, baslard(e,** 5 **basulard,** 6 **baslaerd bazelarde,** 7 **basiliard,** 4-8 **baselard.** [a. AF. *baselard(e* (Act 12 Richard II), OF. *basalart* (med.L. *bassilardus*); perh. from same source as OF. *baselaire, bazelaire, badelaire*, probably a derivative of late L. *badile, badillus* a bill-hook (P. Meyer); the *z* (*s*) for *d* being of Provençal origin. In *baselard* the suffix is evidently -ARD augmentative.] A species of dagger or hanger, usually worn at the girdle.

1377 Langl. *P. Pl.* B. iii. 303 Alle þat bereþ baslarde, brode swerde or launce. **1450** Myrc 48 Baselard ny bawdryke were thou non. **1460** Capgrave *Chron.* 125 Sodeynly with a scharp basulard he smet the Kyng among the boweles. *c* **1500** in *Ripon Ch. Acts* 303 Cum gladiis vocatis hyngers vel baselardys. **1598** Stow *Surv.* xxiv. (1603) 221 Drew his basiliard. **1602** in Southey's *Comm.-pl. Bk.* Ser. ii. (1849) 338 Two baslaerd swords, the blades to be one yard and half a quarter of length. **1788** *New Lond. Mag.* 150 The Mayor, drawing his baselard, grievously wounded Wat [Tyler] in the neck.

baseless ('beɪslɪs), *a.* [f. BASE *sb.*[1] + -LESS.] Without base or foundation, groundless.

1610 Shaks. *Temp.* iv. i. 151 The baselesse fabricke of this vision. **1815** Southey *Roderick* xvii. 181 A baseless faith. **1876** Green *Short Hist.* v. §6 (1882) 261 No claim could have been more utterly baseless.

b. in reference to military tactics; cf. BASE *sb.*[1] 16.

1862 Helps *Organiz. Daily Life* 79 Occasionally, baseless operations have effected great results in war.

'baselessness. [f. prec. + -NESS.] The quality of being baseless; groundlessness.

1850 Whipple *Ess. & Rev.* I. 315 To show the baselessness of the objections to his writings. **1864** Pusey *Daniel* 395 The baselessness of the imputation.

† **'baseling.** *Obs. rare*$^{-1}$. [f. BASE *a.* + -LING; cf. BASEL.] A base creature.

1618 *Barnevelt's Apol.* Biiij, They should bee ranked in the number of double-harted baselings

‖ **Basella** (bə'sɛlə). [mod.L., ? dim. of L. *basis* base.] A genus of climbing plants (N.O. *Chenopodiaceæ*), with smooth fleshy leaves, known as the Malabar Nightshade.

1761 Miller *Gard. Kal.* (1775) 24 Plants in the Green-House [in January]..Basella in fruit. **1830** Lindley *Nat. Syst. Bot.* 167 Some of these are used as potherbs; as Basella, Spinage.

basely ('beɪslɪ), *adv.* [f. BASE *a.* + -LY[2].]

† **1.** In a low position, low down. *Obs.*

c **1500** *Partenay* 1216 Sauyng þat on ey had he more basly Then þat other.

† **2.** In a low tone, softly, quietly. *Obs.*

1562 J. Heywood *Prov. & Epigr.* (1867) 216 Talke thou basely, talke thou boldely. **1577** Dee *Relat. Spir.* i. (1659) 365, I hear..a whistling very basely.

3. In humble rank of life; illegitimately. ? *Obs.*

1583 Stanyhurst *Æneis* ii. (Arb.) 61 Baselye Neoptolemus was borne. **1631** Gouge *God's Arrows* iii. ii. 185 Commonly such as are basely borne..are of ill disposition.

4. With contemptible cowardice, treachery, or meanness; dishonourably, disingenuously.

? *c* **1550** *Robin Hood* (Ritson) ix. 92 Beshrew thy heart, said Little John, Thou basely dost begin. **1656** Cowley *Davideis* ii. Wks. 1710 I. 342 Some basely die, and some more basely yield. **1872** Yeats *Growth Comm.* 122 The King of Portugal basely betrayed Colombus.

† **5.** At small value or esteem, meanly; cheaply.

1584 Powel *Lloyd's Cambria* 210 Sonnes were not baselie esteemd. **1620** Venner *Via Recta* iii. 52 Them that desire to look big, and to liue basely. **1651** Wittie tr. *Primrose's Pop. Err.* iv. 197 Those of Galens method..they basely account of, and contemne.

baseman ('beɪsmən). [f. BASE *sb.*[1] 15 c + MAN *sb.*[1]] Each of the fielders who stand near the first, second, and third bases in baseball.

1857 *Spirit of Times* 28 Nov. 196/1 Logan, as third base, is..probably the best baseman on the club. **1874** Chadwick *Base Ball Manual* 13 The positions in the field are as follows:—Catcher, pitcher, first baseman, second baseman, third baseman, short-stop, left fielder, centre fielder, and right fielder. **1917** Mathewson *Sec. Base Sloan* xi. 145 A dexterous hook-slide that kept him far out of reach of the baseman's sweep. **1968** *Washington Post* 4 July C1/7 The Yankee second baseman charged Mike Epstein's slow hopper up the middle.

basement ('beɪsmənt). Also 8 **bassment.** [f. BASE *sb.*[1] or *v.*[2] + -MENT; cf. F. *soubassement.*]

1. The lowest or fundamental portion of a structure. ***basement-membrane***: a fine transparent layer lying between the epithelium and the fibrovascular layer of mucous membranes. ***basement complex*** *Geol.* (see quot. 1961).

1793 Smeaton *Edystone L.* Cont. 7 Establishing a solid Basement of Wood. **1843** J. Portlock *Geol.* 97 The..augitic rock which forms the basement of the promontory. **1847** Todd *Cycl. Anat. & Phys.* III. 751/1 The cell-germs contained in this basement-membrane. **1897** W. B. Scott *Introd. Geol.* iv. xxi. 358 The Archaean includes the most ancient rocks, often spoken of as the 'basement, or basal complex'. **1940** R. A. Daly *Strength & Struct. of Earth* i. 17 The average density of the Basement (Archean) Complex of each continent. **1961** Challinor *Dict. Geol.* 19/1 *Basement complex*, a regional mass of Archaean metamorphic crystalline rocks (gneisses and schists) and igneous intrusions on which lie veneers of obviously sedimentary rocks (of ages from the later Pre-Cambrian onwards)...'Fundamental complex' may be said to be synonymous, and 'Archaean' is an equivalent name.

2. *fig.* Groundwork; *attrib.* = fundamental.

1818 Hallam *Mid. Ages* ii. i, That Great Charter, the basement, at least, if not the foundation of our free constitution. **1829** I. Taylor *Enthus.* iii. (1867) 55 This belief constitutes the basement-principle of all religion.

3. a. *spec.* The lowest storey (not a cellar) of a building, esp. when sunk below the general ground level.

1730 A. Gordon *Maffei's Amphith.* 389 There is a small Basement..under the lower Pilasters. **1823** Scott in *Lockhart* (1839) VII. 204 The under or sunk story—basement the learned call it.

b. *attrib.*

1766 Entick *Lond.* IV. 360 The bassment story is very massy. **1865** Dickens *Mut. Fr.* iv. 22 Down stairs to a little basement front door. **1917** T. S. Eliot *Prufrock & other Observations* 31 They are rattling breakfast plates in basement kitchens. **1939** —— *Old Possum's Pract. Cats* 29 A small basement flat. **1962** J. G. Bennett *Witness* xv. 178 My wife and I had found a small basement flat in Bayswater. **1966** *Listener* 3 Feb. 176/2 A despondent servant-girl from the country in each basement kitchen.

4. The action of basing; the state of being based; cf. *debasement*.

1836 G. Faber *An Inquiry, etc.* 579 Evinced by its actual basement upon the unhallowed principle, that nations, as such, ought, etc.

'base-'minded, *a.* [f. BASE *a.* 9, 16.] Having a base mind; = BASE *a.* 9. Hence **base-mindedly** = BASELY 4; **base-mindedness** = BASENESS 4.

1586 Q. Eliz. in Ellis *Orig. Lett.* i. 225 III. 23, I am not so baceminded that feare of any livinge..prince shoulde make me afrayde. **1614** Selden *Titles Hon.* 62 Base-minded Jewes, with acclamations, affirmed Herod Agrippa..a Deitie. **1792** *Chron.* in *Ann. Reg.* 4/1 To deter base-minded persons from such shocking enormities.

b. 1599 Sandys *Europæ Spec.* (1632) 160 A timorous base mindednesse and abjectnesse. **1627** Bp. Hall *Heav. vpon Earth* iv. 76 To whom repentance seems base-mindednesse.

basence, obs. form of BEZANT.

baseness ('beɪsnɪs). [f. BASE *a.* + -NESS.]

† **1.** Lowness or feebleness in sound; deepness in tone. *Obs.*; cf. BASSNESS.

1609 Bible (Douay) *Eccles.* xii. 4 The baseness of the grinders voice. **1626** Bacon *Sylva* §184 The Baseness or Trebleness of Tones.

2. Low birth or rank, lowly or mean estate, lowliness; a trait or characteristic of low rank (*obs.*).

1552 Huloet, Basenes of bloude or ignobilitie. **1563** *Homilies* ii. xxi. i. (1859) 554 As the Majesty of heavenly things may by the basenesse of earthly things be shadowed. **1602** Shaks. *Ham.* v. ii. 34, I once did hold it..A basenesse to write faire. **1615** T. Adams *Christ's Star* Wks. 1871 II. 7 God did ever so strangely qualify the baseness of Christ. **1850** Tennyson *In Mem.* lx, He mixing with his proper sphere, She finds the baseness of her lot.

† **3.** Illegitimacy of birth, bastardy. *Obs.*

1605 Shaks. *Lear* i. ii. 10 Why brand they vs With Base? With basenes, Bastardie?

4. Moral turpitude, reprehensible cowardice or selfishness, contemptible meanness; an act or trait of this character.

1598 Shaks. *Merry W.* ii. ii. 21 You stand vpon your honor..thou vnconfinable baseness? **1639** Fuller *Holy War* v. xv. (1840) 269 Soldiers count it baseness to be thrifty of their own healths. **1767** *Junius Lett.* iii. 18, I acquit him of the baseness of selling Commissions. **1858** Gen. P. Thompson *Audi Alt.* I. lxxii. 240 Having no basenesses of his own to prosecute, and therefore under no temptation to pander to the basenesses of other people.

5. Inferior or debased quality.

1577 Harrison *England* ii. vi. (1877) 159 As she seeth cause by the goodnesse or basenesse of the hops. **1581** W. Stafford *Exam. Compl.* i. (1876) 28 That basenesse of our English Coyne. *a* **1745** Swift (J.) We alledged..the baseness of his metal. **1851** Ruskin *Stones Ven.* I. i. 49 The world is so widely encumbered with forgeries and basenesses.

basenet, -ette, variant of BASINET.

basenji (bə'sɛndʒɪ). [Bantu.] An African breed of smallish hunting dog, native to the inner Congo regions, which rarely barks.

1933 O. Burn in *Field* 4 Nov. 1157/1 Three years ago I imported to England five Baseiyis—the smooth-coated chestnut dog of terrier size used by the native chiefs for hunting antelope etc. on the Congo plateaux. **1935** *Ibid.* 18 May 1251/1 Basentis don't bark! **1937** *Daily Herald* 11 Feb. 3/6 The Basenjis—the most puzzled dogs in the show [*sc.* Crufts']. They cannot bark, and could not understand all the other noisy dogs... They come from the Congo, are used for hunting by Central African tribes, and are believed to descend from dogs depicted on old Egyptian tombs. **1938, 1957** [see BARKLESS *a.*[2]].

† **'baser.** *Obs.* Also 4 **basare.** [Etymol. unknown.] An executioner.

c **1375** ? Barbour *St. Cristofore* 598 Syne to þe basare sade in hy: Stryk of myne hede, bruthyre dere. —— *St. Jacobus* 239 Fra þe baser sancte James gat A pot with vattir.

† **'basery.** *Obs. rare*$^{-1}$. [f. BASE *a.* + -RY.] Base dealing, dishonourable practice.

1637 Brian *Pisse-proph.* i. (1679) 2 They will hardly acknowledge their errours, and relinquish this basery.

baset, basetry: see BASSADE.

† **bash,** *v.*[1] Forms: 4 **baise-n, bayse-n,** 4-6 **basshe-n,** 5 **basche, baysche,** 6 **bashe,** 6-7 **bash.** *North.* 4 **baise,** 6 **base.** [Aphetic form of ABASH *v.*]

1. *trans.* To destroy the confidence or self-possession of; to daunt, dismay, discomfit; to disconcert, put out of countenance, abash.

c **1375** (MS. *c* **1440**) *Morte Arth.* 2857 Bees noghte baiste of ȝone boyes, ne of paire bryghte wedis! *c* **1480** *Kyng & Hermit* 442 in Hazl. *E.P.P.* (1864) 30 Thoff I be here in pore clothing, I am no bayschyd for to bryng Gestys two or thre. **1515** *Scot. Field* 179 in *Chetham Misc.* II, Because they bashed them at Berwick, that boldeth them the more. **1594** Carew *Tasso* (1881) 104 He made Semblant, as nought him could dismay or bash.

2. *intr.* **a.** To be daunted or dismayed; to quail, lose confidence; to be confounded.

c **1340** *Gaw. & Gr. Knt.* 376 He baldly hym bydez, he bayst neuer þe helder. **1382** Wyclif *Josh.* ii. 11 Oure herte basshede, ne spiryt bood in us. *c* **1450** Lonelich *Grail* xxxvii. 244 Grettere tempestes..where offen they bascheden. **1580** North *Plutarch* (1676) 38 Alcander..strake out one of his eyes..Yet for all this Lycurgus never bashed.

b. To be put out of countenance; to shrink back for shame, to be ashamed or abashed. Const. *inf.*, *at*.

c **1460** Russell *Bk. Nurture* in *Babees Bk.* (1868) 161 With salt & wyne serue ye hym þe same, boldly & not to basshe. **1554** Philpot *Exam. & Writ.* (1842) 303 Their corrupt faces bash not to deny the eternal Son of God. **1589** Greene *Tullies Loue* Wks. 1882 VII. 115 Like Diana when shee basht at Acteons presence. **1606** Holland *Sueton.* 148 He bashed not to kisse him even in the open Theater. **1610** —— *Camden's Brit.* (1637) 309 Bash not, but deigne (I pray) to be my Soveraigne Ladie deere.

bash (bæʃ), *v.*[2] [Chiefly northern; perhaps from Scand.; cf. Sw. *basa* to baste, whip, flog, lash, Da. *baske* to beat, strike, cudgel. But possibly onomatopoetic, with the *b* of *beat*, *bang*, and the termination of *dash*, *gash*, *gnash*, *hash*, *lash*, *pash*, *smash*, etc.]

1. To strike with a heavy blow that tends to beat or smash in the surface struck: **a.** *trans.* Also ***to bash up*** (the edge or point of an instrument).

1790 A. WILSON *Pack* Wks. 26 Fir'd wi' indignance I turn'd round, And basht wi' mony a fung The Pack, that day. **1834** M. SCOTT *Cruise Midge* (1863) 200 The callant has.. bashed my neb as saft as pap. **1882** *Pall Mall G.* 24 Apr. 2/2 A proposition to 'smash' or 'bash' in the tall hats aforesaid.

b. *refl.* (of a hen beating her wings in the dust.)

1641 BEST *Farm Bks.* (1856) 110 The henne.. will alsoe bashe her in the dust, and so oftentimes crush them to death.

c. *absol.* or *intr.* (with *at.*)

1833 M. SCOTT *Tom Cringle* xi. (1859) 255 The gun is loaded. The negro continued to bash at it with all his might.

d. *to bash up*, to beat (someone) repeatedly; to thrash or batter. Cf. *to beat up* s.v. BEAT *v.*[1] 40 f. *colloq.*

1954 WILLANS & SEARLE *How to be Topp* iv. 48 Give him a helping hand and do not bash him up. **1959** I. & P. OPIE *Lore & Lang. Schoolch.* x. 195 'Hand it over—or else',—'I'll bash you up' (the most usual suggestion). **1963** *Daily Tel.* 30 Aug. 19/3 Discussing intimidation, the lawyer says: 'How would you advise a wretched statutory tenant who is threatened he will be "bashed up" by a rough-looking individual on the staircase one night?' **1974** *Age* (Melbourne) 12 Oct. 12/2 *I'll get Rourky to bash you up.* I'll ask Colin O'Rourke to hit you in return for dosh.

2. The verb-stem is used adverbially with other verbs. Cf. BANG *v.*[1] 8.

1833 M. SCOTT *Tom Cringle* xviii. (1859) 511 A fine preserved Pine Apple flew bash on Isaac Shingle's sharp snout.

3. In colloq. phr. ***to bash on***, to persevere; to pursue a course of action regardless of difficulties, criticism, etc. (In quot. 1950 as attrib. phr.)

1950 *Leader Mag.* 4 Mar. 15/3 Even on a muddy, badly surfaced ground, the bash-on spirit of the riders and the keenness of the supporters is thrilling. **1965** R. SHECKLEY *Game of X* (1966) xxii. 155, I didn't like the sound of that; but.. there was nothing to do but bash on. **1986** *Financial Times* 11 Aug. 4/6 Over charities, the Government 'bashed on with something that would have turned charity tax law upside down,' he said.

bash (bæʃ), *v.*[3] *local.* 'To fill with rubbish the spaces from which the coal has been worked away' (Gresley *Gloss. Coal-m.* 1883). Hence **'bashing** *vbl. sb.*

1905 *Daily Chron.* 26 June 6/5 A 'bashing'—a barricade of coal and rubbish.

bash, *sb.* [f. BASH *v.*[2]; cf. Sw. *bas* whipping, beating, Da. *bask* stripe, blow.] **1.** A heavy blow that beats or smashes in a surface (orig. *Sc.*). Now in *gen.* use, a heavy blow.

1805 J. NICOL *Poems* I. 36 (JAM.) An' gae her a desperate bash on The chafts. *c* **1817** HOGG *Tales* I. 17 (JAM.) Then, giving two or three bashes on the face, he left me. **1949** C. FRY *Lady's not for Burning* 86 If he wants to fight me, let him come out in the garden. Whatever happens I shall have one bash at him. **1959** *Listener* 8 Jan. 77/1 A weak, wan lad.. escaped with no worse than a bash and a hang-over.

2. In various slang uses: (i) an attempt, esp. in ***to have a bash*** (*at*); (ii) a good time; a spree; a party (see quot. 1948, *Amer. Speech*) *U.S.*; phr. ***on the bash***, on a drinking bout (app. *Sc.* and *N.Z.*); also (examples are U.K.), soliciting as a prostitute (quots. 1936 and 1959[1]); (iii) in *Jazz*, a 'jam session' (only *U.S.*?).

1901 G. DOUGLAS *House with Green Shutters* xxi. 222 Let us go out and do a bash! **1919** J. BUCHAN *Mr. Standfast* viii. 167 Ye ken what a man's like when he's been on the bash. **1924** *Kelso Chron.* 12 Sept. 2/8 The village tailor.. had an unfortunate weakness for getting terribly 'on the bash' perhaps twice a year. **1936** J. CURTIS *Gilt Kid* ii. 23 Most of the time she's on the bash round the flash bars. **1948** *Amer. Speech* XXIII. 219 One could store or *stash* food for a big *bash*. This involved eating two or three days' rations at one time. **1948** D. BALLANTYNE in *Landfall* II. 111 He figured what he spent on beer weeknights would total no more than what most jokers spent on their Saturday bashes. **1948** PARTRIDGE *Dict. Forces' Slang 1939–45* 11 *Have a bash at*, to make an attempt. **1949** L. FEATHER *Inside Be-Bop* vi. 42 One jazz concert promoter, who in previous years had presented nothing but Dixieland bashes. **1950** *Home* (U.S.) 2 Apr. 8 (Wentworth & Flexner), Some of these bashes were impromptu at 4 in the morning by trumpet players. **1950** C. MACINNES *To Victors the Spoils* I. 135 He's decided to have a bash at tightening up the discipline. **1957** J. BRAINE *Room at Top* xxiii. 192 I'll have a bash just the same. **1957** I. MURDOCH *Sandcastle* iii. 38 Come on.. have a bash. You can translate the first word anyway. **1959** *Streetwalker* iii. 58 From the hours you keep.. I'd say you were on the bash. **1959** M. SHADBOLT *New Zealanders* 156 Jack and I went on the bash every Saturday... Drink all day and pay a visit to the local house at night. **1959** *Times* 26 May 12/6 Tried some anti-rust oil? Worth a bash. **1961** A. BERKMAN *Singers' Gloss. Show Business* 7 *Bash*, a ball; party.

basha ('bæʃə). [Assamese.] A hut made of bamboo with a thatched roof.

1921 *Blackw. Mag.* Feb. 257/1, I was awakened by my servant entering the basha with the tea-tray. **1947** 'N. SHUTE' *Chequer Board* v. 107 They drove on around the house to a small bashah made of bamboo, palm leaf matting, and palm thatch. **1956** W. SLIM *Defeat into Victory* vii. 143 The troops lived in tents or *bashas*, the bamboo huts, thatched with leaves. *Ibid.* xiii. 287 There were now orderly *basha* camps, hutted hospitals. **1969** *Sunday Mail Mag.* (Brisbane) 18 May 1/3 At his 'basha'.. he has a radio with a 700-mile range by his bed.

†**ba'shalic(k.** *Obs.* Also 7 -ique, 8 bassalick. [a. Turkish *bāshālik*, *pāshālik* jurisdiction of a *pāshā*: see next.] Earlier form of PASHALIK, the district under the jurisdiction of a pasha.

1682 WHELER *Journ. Greece* III. 238 It.. remaineth yet a Bashalique, although of late governed by a Deputy. **1703** MAUNDRELL *Journ. Jerus.* (1726) 5 A Woody Mountainous Country, which ends the Bashalick of Aleppo.

bashaw (bə'ʃɔː). Forms: 6 bassawe, -shawe, -cha, (bassat, basso), 6–7 bassi, 6–8 bassa, basha, 7 bashawe, bassaw, -shaw, -char, bacha, 9 bashe, 7– bashaw. [a. Turkish *bāshā*, variant of *pāshā*, prob. f. *bāsh* head, the Old Turkish not distinguishing *p* and *b* (Prof. Rieu): see PASHA. The earliest English form came indirectly through med.L. and It. *bassa* (later It. *bascià*); other spellings represent 16–17th c. F. *bachat*, mod.F. *bacha*, *pacha*.]

1. a. The earlier form of the Turkish title PASHA.

1534 MORE *Comf. agst. Trib.* III. Wks. 1218/2 His Bassawes.. surmount verye farre aboue any christen estate. **1548** HALL *Chron.* (1809) 771 The Turke loste foure score 1000 men as one of his Bassates did afterwarde confesse. **1601** R. JOHNSON *Kingd. & Commw.* 49 The Bassas.. as it were Harpies, sucke the verye bloud of the people. **1602** WARNER *Alb. Eng.* x. lvii. 252 His Bands of Janizaries.. He out of these his Captaines, and his Bassies doth elect. **1678** BUTLER *Hud.* III. III. 306 Or else their Sultan-Populaces Still strangle all their routed Bassa's. **1693** *Mem. Teckely* IV. 15 He created Vizier Ismal Bacha. **1695** MOTTEUX *St. Olon's Morocco* 31 A Captain, to whom they give the Title of Baschar. **1743** FIELDING *J. Wild* III. vii. (1762) 322 He addressed me with all the insolence of a basha to a Circassian slave. **1860** MOTLEY *Netherl.* (1868) I. iii. 79, I will offer service to one of the Turk's bashaws.

b. ***bashaw of two*** or ***three tails***: one of lower or higher rank, as indicated by the number of horse-tails borne on his standard.

1753 HANWAY *Trav.* (1762) II. XIII. ii. 295 He was appointed basha of three tails. **1798** WOLCOTT (P. Pindar) *Tales of Hoy* Wks. 1812 IV. 422 He would fly to Constantinople, hang up a bashaw of three tails.

2. *fig.* A grandee; a haughty, imperious man.

1593 NASHE *Christ's T.* (1613) 85 The diuels chiefe Basso, Ambition. *a* **1670** HACKET *Abp. Williams* I. 82 In every society of men there will be some Bashawes, who presume that there are many rules of law from which they should be exempted. **1794** GODWIN *Cal. Williams* 16 The young men .. looked up to this insolent bashaw with timid respect. **1872** GEO. ELIOT *Middlem.* liii. (1873) 185 You've taken to being a nob, buying land, being a country bashaw!

3. Local name for a very large catfish of the species *Pylodictis olivaris*; the mud cat. *U.S.*

1888 G. B. GOODE *Amer. Fishes* 378 *Leptops olivaris*, the 'Mud Cat', 'Yellow Cat', 'Goujon', or 'Bashaw' is found in all the large rivers of the West and South. **1923** *Public Opinion* 12 Oct. 357/3 A good-sized fish, itself Carnivorous, called a basha.

ba'shawism. [see -ISM.] The imperiousness or haughty tyranny of a bashaw.

1839 LADY LYTTON *Cheveley* II. v. 146 Exercising a truly manly degree of embryo bashawism over his younger sister.

ba'shawship. [f. as prec. + -SHIP.] **a.** The jurisdiction or office of a bashaw. **b.** *fig.* Dignity or demeanour of a bashaw.

1687 *Lond. Gaz.* No. 2252/6 To be paid yearly during his Bassawship. **1701** GREW *Cosm. Sacra* IV. vi. §15 (L.) At this day it [Egypt] is no better than a bashawship, under the Grand Signior. **1882** H. MERIVALE *Faucit of B.* I. I. xiv. 237 Mr. Fairfield's angry airs of Bashawship.

†**bashed,** *ppl. a.*[1] *Obs.* [f. BASH *v.*[1] + -ED.] Abashed, disconcerted, dismayed.

c **1440** [see next]. **1553** BRENDE *Q. Curtius* 156 (R.) Ceballinus with a bashed countenance.. reported all those thinges. **1594** CAREW *Tasso* (1881) 94 Sometimes her basht eye seemes by shame controld.

bashed (bæʃt), *ppl. a.*[2] [f. BASH *v.*[2] + -ED[1].] Having the surface beaten or smashed in.

1830 J. WILSON *Noct. Ambr.* xxv. in *Wks.* (1856) III. 16 Like a heap o' bashed and birzed paddocks. **1898** *Westm. Gaz.* 31 Mar. 7/2 A bashed mask.

†**'bashedness.** *Obs.* [f. BASHED *ppl. a.*[1] + -NESS.] Abashment, bashfulness.

c **1440** *Partonope* 6000 What for shame and basshednes.

basher[1] ('bæʃə(r)). [f. BASH *v.*[2] + -ER[1].] **1.** One who gives, or strikes with, a smashing blow; *spec.* a pugilist.

1882 *Daily Tel.* 16 Dec. 2/6 The professed 'basher'. **1886** *World* 11 Aug. 8 This bruiser of the police court, this basher of a little foreign Jew. **1888** J. GREENWOOD *Policeman's Lantern* 35 (*title*) The Man-Basher. *Ibid.* 44 'Does that mean for simply knocking him down?'.. 'It means whatever you mean,' returned the professional 'basher'..; 'it wont make no odds to me, when I'm once set about him.' **1927** *Daily Tel.* 11 Oct. 12/6 He fights as if he enjoys fighting; and there is much of a basher in him.

2. *Services' slang* (see quot. 1943). Also, more generally, a man, often with defining word. Cf. BIBLE-*basher*.

1942 F. RHODES *Let.* in Partridge *Dict. Slang* (1961) II. 991/1 *Buster* or *basher* is very common for mechanics, as in *compass basher*, *instrument basher*. **1943** HUNT & PRINGLE *Service Slang* 13 *Bashers*, instructors in physical training. **1945** *Gen* 30 June 51/2 One of the cookhouse bashers that came off at five. **1946** E. H. PARTRIDGE in Raymond & Langton *Slipstream* 62 The term basher, as in clock basher, stores basher.. now means no more than fellow, chap, man.

basher[2] ('bæʃə(r)). *slang.* [Perh. same as prec.] A straw hat, a boater.

1901 *Westm. Gaz.* 9 Aug. 8/1 They parade in the grounds of the Exhibition with well-cut clothes and straw 'bashers'. **1933** *Bulletin* (Glasgow) 11 July 5/5, I am inclined to think that there are certain kinds of clothes that do not blend with a 'basher'.

bashful ('bæʃfʊl), *a.* [f. BASH *v.*[1] + -FUL; cf. also ABASH *sb.*, though *-ful* is occasionally added to vbs., as in *mournful*, *assistful*.]

†**1.** Wanting in self-possession, daunted, dismayed. *Obs.*

1552 HULOET Bashfull or amased, *attonitus.* *a* **1674** CLARENDON *Hist. Reb.* II. VI. 15 Those Forces would.. by their success give much courage to his bashful Army. **1709** STEELE *Tatler* No. 39 ¶7 [Duelling was] as great an Impediment to Advancement in the Service, as being bashful in Time of Action.

2. Of persons: Shrinking from publicity, shamefaced, shy. Sometimes used in a good or neutral sense = Sensitively modest in demeanour; sometimes depreciatively = Excessively self-conscious, embarrassed and ill at ease in society, 'sheepish.'

1548 UDALL, etc. *Erasm. Par. John* xii. 12 (R.) These folke beyng very desirous to see Jesus.. yet they were bashefull. **1570** ASCHAM *Scholem.* (1863) 42 If a yong jentleman.. be bashefull, and will soon blushe, they call him a babishe and ill brought up thyng. **1624** CAPT. SMITH *Virginia* I. 3 His wife and children.. were.. well fauored and very bashful. **1764** GOLDSM. *Trav.* 21 Or press the bashful stranger to his food. **1781** COWPER *Convers.* 347, I pity bashful men. **1810** SCOTT *Lady of L.* II. xxiv, Like Summer rose, The bashful maiden's cheek appeared.

3. Of things, actions, etc.: Characterizing or characterized by extreme sensitiveness or modesty.

1595 SPENSER *Wks.* (Grosart) IV. 122 His face with bashfull blood did flame. **1610** SHAKS. *Temp.* III. i. 81 Hence bashfull cunning, And prompt me plaine and holy innocence. *a* **1711** KEN *Hymnotheo* Wks. 1721 III. 313 Naked they walk'd, but had no bashful sense. **1816** SOUTHEY *Poet's Pilgr.* Proem 10 With impulse shy of bashful tenderness, Soliciting again the wish'd caress.

†**4.** Exciting a feeling of shame. *Obs.*

1559 *Mirr. Mag.* 59 (T.) A woman yet must blush when bashful is the case, Though truth bid tell the story as it fell.

'bashfully, *adv.* [f. prec. + -LY[2].]

†**1.** Without self-possession; with misgiving or dismay. *Obs.*

1552 HULOET, Bashfullye or in amase, *attonite.* **1675** HOBBES *Odyssey* (1677) 382 He went not to the battle bashfully.

2. In a shy or shamefaced manner; cf. BASHFUL 2.

1552 HULOET, Bashfullye or wyth shamefastnes, *pudibunde.* **1651** DAVENANT *Gondib.* II. vi. (R.) Here the check'd Sun his universal face Stops bashfully, and will no entrance make. **1832** HT. MARTINEAU *Ella of Gar.* vi. 70 Angus looked down as bashfully as if he had never seen the world.

'bashfulness. [f. as prec. + -NESS.]

†**1.** *bashfulness of*: a timid or reverential shrinking back from (something). *Obs.*

1534 WHITTINTON *Tullyes Offyces* I. (1540) 42 One parte of honesty.. in the which is a basshfulnes of dishonesty. **1674** N. FAIRFAX *Bulk & Selv.* To Rdr., Led by such a clue of understanding, and softened by such a bashfulness of knowledge, that we may be wise and awful both in one.

2. The quality of being BASHFUL (see sense 2).

1539 TAVERNER *Erasm. Prov.* (1552) 26 Cast awaye bashfulness where nede constrayneth. **1590** SHAKS. *Mids. N.* III. ii. 286 Haue you no modesty, no maiden shame, No touch of bashfulnesse? **1603** JAS. I. in Ellis *Orig. Lett.* I. 244 III. 80 Awaye with chyldishe bashefullnes. **1792** MARY WOLLSTONECR. *Rights Wom.* vii. 275 Modesty is the graceful calm virtue of maturity; bashfulness, the charm of vivacious youth. **1814** SCOTT *Wav.* xlii, An air of bashfulness, which was in reality the effect of want of habitual intercourse with the world.

‖**Bashi-Bazouk** (ˌbæʃɪbə'zuːk). [mod.Turk.; lit. 'one whose head is turned.']

1. A mercenary soldier belonging to the skirmishing or irregular troops of the Turkish army; notorious for their lawlessness, plundering, and savage brutality. Hence **Bashi-Ba'zoukery**, Bashi-Bazouks collectively, their habits, etc.

1859 *Blackw. Mag.* Mar. 302/1 The Bashi-Bazouks bolted, and dashing in amongst the Turkish regulars, put them to the rout too. **1861** MISS BEAUFORT *Egypt. Sepul.* II. xvii. 60 Bashi-Bazouk, the generic name given to any of the Arabs of this country who attached themselves to the government and fought for pay. **1884** *Pall Mall G.* 1 Mar. 1/2 His government was a system of Bashi-Bazoukery plus slave-raiding.. The Bashi-Bazoukery from Brunei ceased to trouble the tribes.

2. *fig.* An 'irregular,' a skirmisher.
1855 WYNTER *Cur. Civiliz.* II. 404 The Bashi-Bazouks of private establishments. **1861** SALA *Tw. round Clock* 33 Hard-working boys are these juvenile Bashi-Bazouks of the newspaper trade.

bashing ('bæʃɪŋ), *vbl. sb.* [f. BASH *v.*² + -ING¹.]
1. The action of striking so as to dint, bruise, or crush; an instance of this.
1733 W. ELLIS *Chiltern & Vale Farm.* 45 Its hard and crusty Surface, so made by the Weights and Bashings of the heavy Rains. **1921** *Public Opinion* 21 Jan. 62/2 One would have expected to find a studious cultivation of more scientific methods of bashing. **1956** E. GRIERSON *Second Man* ix. 201 Street brawling—what the Aussies call 'Bashing'. **1958** J. CANNAN *And be a Villain* iii. 49 The first murder, other than slum-area bashings, that had occurred.
2. a. A flogging (with the cat-o'-nine-tails).
1877 W. H. THOMSON *Five Years' Penal Servitude* iii. 157 There were the evidences of former floggings, or 'bashings', as the prisoners call them. **1898** *Daily News* 23 Feb. 3/5, I got a bashing as well.—What do you mean by that?—Oh, I had the 'cat'.
b. *transf.* and *fig.*
1948 PARTRIDGE *Dict. Forces' Slang* 11 *Take, get, a bashing*, to suffer heavy losses. **1959** *Listener* 29 Jan. 219/1 In their 1911 bashing of Mr. Lloyd George the profession far excelled their efforts of 1948.
3. Used in *Services' slang* to denote any arduous task.
1940 *Daily Mail* 7 Sept. 3/8 Here are some current military phrases, interpreted:..'Spud-bashing'—Potato peeling. **1942** *Horizon* VI. 114 C.B. for a cert. Scrubbing, or mebbe a spot of spud bashing. **1943** WARD-JACKSON *Piece of Cake* 56 *Square bashing*, marching, drilling or walking. **1946** G. KERSH *Clean, Bright & Slightly Oiled* i. 3 Poor old Gerald done fourteen drills that week, plus a nice basinful of spud-bashing.

† **'bashless**, *a. Obs.* [f. BASH *v.*¹ + -LESS; cf. *bashful*.] Unabashed, shameless, unblushing, bold.
1578 SIDNEY *Lady of May* Wks. (1674) 619 (D.) 'Com on, master school-master, bee not so bashless.' **1597** BRETON *Abr. Amor. Devises* (1879) 4 (D.) Blush now, you bashles dames, that vaunt of beautie rare.

bashlik ('bæʃlɪk). Also **bashluik, beshlik**, etc. [ad. Russ. *bashlýk*.] A kind of hood with long side-pieces worn by Russians in inclement weather as a protective covering for the head. Also *transf.*, a light covering for the head, worn by women in the U.S. (*Cent. Dict.*).
1881 A. LESLIE tr. *Nordenskiöld's Voy. of Vega* I. x. 477, I had bought the baschliks in St. Petersburg. **1882** O'DONOVAN *Merv Oasis* I. iv. 74 Hanging between the shoulders, and knotted around the neck, is the *bashlik*, or hood, worn during bad weather. **1885** A. FORBES *Souvenirs of some Continents* 330 The flames danced..on the sombre hoods of beshliks. **1904** *Daily Chron.* 28 Mar. 3/1 The bashluik, or hood, worn to protect the ears.

† **'bashment.** *Obs.* In 4 **bays-**. [Aphetic form of ABASHMENT.] Confusion from surprise or sudden check; discomfiture, shame.
c **1325** *E.E. Allit. P.* A. 174 Bot baysment gef myn hert a brunt. **1519** HORMAN *Vulg.* 48 A mannis mynde is neuer more vnstable than in soden chauncis, and soden bashement. **1610** HOLLAND *Camden's Brit.* (1637) 86 Where to controll lesse feare it was, lesse bashment to displease.

† **bash-rag.** *Obs. rare*⁻¹. ? Ragamuffin.
c **1600** J. DAVIES *Extasie* 95 (D.) Wilt loose thy roiall sole prerogatiue, To make vngrateful base Bash-rags to thriue!

† **bashron(e.** *Obs.* 'A kettle.' Halliwell.
1660 *Act 12 Chas. II*, iv. Sched., Batterie, Bashrons, or Kettles, the hundred weight, ix*l*.

bashyle: see BASYLE.

basi- ('beɪsɪ), combining form of BASE, BASIS, forming the first element of many adjs. in *Phys.*, in sense of 'pertaining to, situated at, or forming, the base of'; e.g. **basibranchial, -cranial, -facial, -hyal, -occipital, -radial, -rostral, -sphenoid(al, -temporal, -vertebral**, pertaining to, situated at, or forming, the base or posterior part of, the branchial arch (in fishes), the skull, the face, the hyoid bone, the occiput, the ray or *radius*, the beak, the sphenoid bone, the temples, the vertebræ. These are often used *ellipt.*; e.g. the ***basihyal*** (bone).
1872 MIVART *Anat.* 477 The branchial arches are attached to a..series of pieces termed basi-branchials. **1866** HUXLEY *Preh. Rem. Caithn.* 99 The basi-cranial line is from the anterior margin of the *foramen magnum* to the fronto-nasal suture. **1863** —— *Man's Place Nat.* iii. 149 The basifacial axis..drawn through the axis of the face, between the bones called ethmoid and vomer. **1849–52** TODD *Cycl. Anat. & Phys.* IV. 1145/2 The basi-hyal is generally elongated proportionately to the shape of the tongue. *Ibid.* 1322/1 The fissure that..separates the basi-occipital bone from the exoccipitals. **1880** CARPENTER in *Jrnl. Linn. Soc.* XV. 208 The basiradial suture is an obtuse angle. **1837** MACGILLIVRAY *Hist. Brit. Birds* III. 643 Its basirostral bristles. **1870** ROLLESTON *Anim. Life* 17 The junction of the basisphenoid to the basioccipital. *Ibid.* The basitemporals form a second floor to the cranium. **1849–52** TODD *Cycl. Anat. & Phys.* IV. 1410/1 The basi-vertebral veins.

basial ('beɪzɪəl), *a.*¹ [f. L. *bāsi-um* kiss + -AL¹.] Of or pertaining to kissing, osculatory.
Mod. The basial salutation.

† **'basial**, *a.*² *Obs.* [f. L. *basi-s* BASE + -AL¹.] = BASAL.
1836–9 TODD *Cycl. Anat. & Phys.* II. 622/1 The basial part of the heart. **1842** E. WILSON *Anat. Vade M.* 489 The ..Basial band, passes directly backwards through the septum.

basiate ('beɪzɪeɪt), *v.* ? *Obs.* [f. L. *bāsiāt-* ppl. stem of *bāsiāre*, f. *bāsium* kiss.] To kiss.
1623 in COCKERAM.

basiation (beɪzɪ'eɪʃən). [ad. L. *bāsiātiōn-em*, f. *bāsiāre*; see prec. and -ATION.] Kissing.
1879 G. MEREDITH *Egoist* I. 85 Love that..seems to the scoffing world to go slinking into basiation's obscurity.

basic ('beɪsɪk), *a.* (and *sb.*¹) [f. BASE *sb.*¹ + -IC.]
A. *adj.* **1. a.** Of, pertaining to, or forming a base; fundamental, essential: *spec.* in *Arch.*, and in *Chem.* Also applied *spec.* to an industry which plays a major role in the national economy.
1842 W. GROVE *Corr. Phys. Forces* 146 The amount of heat produced is determined by the basic ingredient. **1849** RUSKIN *Sev. Lamps* v. 141 Its capital resting..on its basic plinth. **1869** ROSCOE *Elem. Chem.* 67 Basic oxides or bases act upon acids to form salts. **1884** *Harper's Mag.* Apr. 770/2 This is Miss Hill's basic principle. **1928** *Rep. Liberal Industr. Inquiry* i. 12 The great basic exporting industries of Great Britain—coal, metallurgy and textiles—have been in a bad way. **1929** *Times* 25 May 9/4 The industry [*sc.* shipbuilding]..still had the highest percentage of unemployment of any of the basic industries in the country. **1940** *R. Comm. on Distrib. Industr. Pop.* (*Cmd.* 6153) iii. 28 The industries which, for the purposes of exchange, send their products to places outside the area in which they are situated, may be termed 'basic' industries.
b. That is or constitutes a standard minimum amount in a scale of remuneration or the like. Also *ellipt.* as *sb.*
1922 *Encycl. Brit.* XXXI. 392/1 When trade unions fix the length of the working day, they mean the basic work-day, with a higher rate of pay for overtime. **1923** J. D. HACKETT in *Management Engineering* May, *Basic Eight-Hour Day*, that period of time for which a specific wage rate is paid, beyond which a higher rate, generally 'time and a half', is paid. **1939** *Times* 25 Oct. 5/2 The next issue of basic petrol ration books will be made for a period beginning November 23. **1940** *Ibid.* 27 Feb. 5/6 At any time the unit of the basic petrol ration may be made smaller. **1948** *Observer* 11 Apr., The right way to check abuses of E and S petrol would be to confine it strictly to essential needs, leaving basic to fulfil its supposed purpose of allowing all motorists some pleasure trips. **1949** *Ann. Reg.* *1948* 447 The 'basic allowance' of foreign currency for tourists outside the sterling area was restored. **1958** A. HACKNEY *Private Life* viii. 78 There's a job in Stores and Packing. Hundred and eighty-nine shillings basic.
c. *Gram.* Of or belonging to the base or theme of a word. See BASE *sb.*¹ 14.
1885 A. S. COOK tr. *Sievers' O.E. Gram.* §86. 38 The development of the basic vowel into a diphthong.
d. Applied to a limited, 'essential' vocabulary in any language; spec. **Basic English**, a variety of the English language, comprising a select vocabulary of 850 words, invented by C. K. Ogden, of Cambridge, and intended for use as a medium of international communication; also ellipt. *Basic*.
1929 C. K. OGDEN in *Psyche* IX. III. 4 It is the continuous approximation of East and West, as a result of the analytic character of Chinese and English..which makes this particular [Panoptic] form of English *basic* for the whole world. Many special captions or trade-marks for the system have been suggested, but *Basic* = British American Scientific International Commercial (English)—is for the time being as good as any. *Ibid.* 97 (*title*) Translation into Basic English. **1930** C. K. OGDEN (*title*) Basic English. **1931** *Routledge Autumn Books*, Basic English is a system in which 850 English words do all the work of over 20,000, and so give to everyone a second or international language which will take as little of the learner's time as possible. **1933** *Discovery* Sept. 280/1 Science itself..might go forward with greatly increased efficiency if the language barrier were removed by the adoption of Basic for Abstracts and Congresses. **1933** H. G. WELLS *Shape of Things to Come* v. §7. 419 It was more difficult to train English speakers to restrict themselves to the forms and words selected than to teach outsiders the whole of Basic. **1935** *N. & Q.* CLXIX. 145/2 The Swedish Anglic and our own Basic English. **1944** H. G. WELLS *'42 to '44* 141 'Basic' English, Russian or Italian is the minimum vocabulary necessary to talk understandably in any of these tongues. **1965** *New Statesman* 2 July 20/2 The tale is told in a Basic American style to represent the rudimentary nature of his mind.
e. *spec.* in *Philos.* Applied to a statement, proposition, etc. (see quots.).
1933 *Proc. Arist. Soc.* XXXIII. 80 The facts upon which all facts which are the immediate reference of a true proposition are based..may..be called basic facts. **1936** *Mind* XLV. 273 A basic proposition is one which asserts that an object has a particular property or that a particular relation holds between two objects, e.g. 'this is red', 'this is earlier than that'. **1937** A. J. AYER in *Proc. Arist. Soc.* XXXVII. 138 Propositions which need not wait upon other propositions for the determination of their truth or falsehood, but are such that they can be directly confronted with the given facts..I propose to call basic propositions. **1939** *Mind* XLVIII. 485 (*title*) On the class of 'basic' sentences. **1959** K. R. POPPER *Logic Sci. Discovery* §7 p. 43 What I call a 'basic statement' or a 'basic proposition' is a statement which can serve as a premise in an empirical falsification; in brief, a statement of a singular fact. **1961** *Proc. Arist. Soc.* LXI. 180 We must..treat some concepts as not requiring reduction to others; these I shall call *basic concepts*.
f. *basic box*, see *basis box* (BASIS III).

1914 J. H. JONES *Tinplate Industry* 141 Orders are often given for the equivalent of a specific number of basic boxes, for example, 10,000 boxes of 20/14.
2. Having the base in excess. **a.** *Chem.* (A salt) Having the amount of the base atomically greater than that of the acid, or exceeding in proportion that of the related neutral salt. **b.** *Min.* (An igneous rock) Having little silica in proportion to the amount of lime, potash, magnesia, etc. present.
1854 SCOFFERN in *Orr's Circ. Sc.* Chem. 400 The class of subsalts is now generally termed basic salts, because the base predominates. **1876** tr. *Wagner's Gen. Pathol.* 319 Neutral or basic phosphates of the alkalies. **1877** GREEN *Phys. Geol.* ii. §5. 47 The Poorly Silicated or Basic rocks.
c. Applied to an improved 'Bessemer' process of steel-manufacture, in which phosphorus is eliminated from the pig-iron by the use of non-silicious materials (*e.g.* limestone, dolomite, magnesia) for the lining of the converters, and for introduction in the course of the 'blow'; hence also applied to the steel thus produced, etc. ***basic refractory***, a refractory material with a high content of basic oxides.
1880 ROBERTS *Introd. Lect. Metallurgy* 20 The practical application of basic linings in the Bessemer converter. **1883** *Birmghm. Weekly Post* 18 Aug. 8/2 Basic steel and ingot iron, made from phosphoric pig. **1917** R. MOLDENKE *Princ. Iron Founding* viii. 277 The iron foundry has so far had but little to do with basic refractories. **1944** GREGORY & SIMONS *Steel Manuf.* (ed. 3) xxi. 164 For this reason silica bricks cannot be used, and therefore magnesite, dolomite or other basic refractories have to be employed.
d. ***basic slag***, slag from the basic or Bessemer process of steel manufacture, used as a fertilizer when finely ground.
1888 *Chambers's Jrnl.* 28 July 478/2 The value of basic slag as a manure. **1920** *Conquest* Aug. 487/2 Owing to the cattle grazing..phosphates and lime are withdrawn from the soil, but a dressing of basic slag..replaces this loss.
e. ***basic dye***, a dye consisting of salts of bases containing aromatic amino- and substituted amino-groups.
1891 [see MORDANT *sb.* 3 c]. **1905** CAIN & THORPE *Synth. Dyestuffs & Intermed. Prod.* vii. 35 Wool takes up the basic dyes in a very uniform manner without the aid of any addition to the dye bath. **1952** J. R. BAKER in G. H. Bourne *Cytol. & Cell Physiol.* (ed. 2) i. 2 When no further structure can be discovered in unstained cells, the effect of dyes of small toxicity should be tried. Many basic dyes are suitable.
See also MONOBASIC, BIBASIC, TRIBASIC.
B. *sb.* Usu. *pl.* **a.** The essential or elementary aspects of a situation, subject, etc.; fundamentals; primary requirements.
1934 E. McD. GALE (*title*) Basics of the Chinese Civilization; a Topical Survey in Outline. **1961** *Newsweek* 14 Aug. 45/2 The appeal of Mantle and Maris in 1961 comes down to one basic: the home run. **1965** *Times Lit. Suppl.* 25 Nov. 1062/3 Let us refer to basics again—to dialogue. **1969** *Engineer* 19 June 32 The computer is not a monster but a powerful ally. B. K. Cooper reviews the basics and explains the principal uses of this misunderstood machine. **1971** *Hi-Fi Sound* Feb. 25 A transcription unit with much more than 'the basics' for enthusiasts who don't require extreme sophistication of design. **1984** *Times* 25 July 5/2 People in northern Niger are going short of food and other basics. **1985** M. GEE *Light Years* lii. 340 Basics for Christmas, dammit. Turkey? Chickens?
b. *back to* (*the*) *basics*: a catch-phrase applied (freq. *attrib.*) to a movement or enthusiasm for a return to the fundamental principles in education, etc., or to policies reflecting this. orig. *U.S.*
1975 *N.Y. Times* 9 Mar. 1 The style and tone of the churches have undergone a major adustment.., gradually turning toward a 'back-to-basics' approach. **1977** *National Observer* (U.S.) 8 Jan. 3/1 The current 'back to basics' movement, the campaign to give the highest priority to the teaching of the fundamentals of reading, writing, and arithmetic. **1978** *Today's Educ.* Feb.–Mar. 34/1 No matter how it is described, this back-to-the-basics issue is attracting more and more legislative and public interest. **1983** *Times* 23 July 13/1 Brown Shipley is launching a back-to-basics savings plan linked to term life assurance. **1985** *Toronto Life* Sept. 15/1 The public areas show a back-to-basics thinking.

BASIC ('beɪsɪk), *sb.*² *Computing.* Also **Basic**. [Acronym of *B*eginners' *A*ll-purpose *S*ymbolic *I*nstruction *C*ode.] A high-level programming language originally developed as a general-purpose language similar to English and easy to learn, and now widely used with personal computers.
Invented by J. G. Kemeny and T. E. Kurtz.
1964 *BASIC Instruction Man.* (Dartmouth College Computation Center) 4 An instruction in BASIC consists of three parts, an instruction number, an operation, and an operand. *Ibid.*, The last instruction in any BASIC program is 'END'. **1967** KEMENY & KURTZ *BASIC Programming* i. 3/1 It is possible to write a tremendous variety of simple programs with very few different types of BASIC statement. **1973** C. W. GEAR *Introd. Computer Sci.* ii. 74 In practice, programs are written in one of a number of languages, such as FORTRAN, PL/1, ALGOL, BASIC, or COBOL. **1974** W. W. PETERSON *Introd. Programming Languages* i. 13 Although BASIC was designed for time-sharing use,..the language itself is also well-suited for conventional batch use. **1979** *Sci. Amer.* Dec. 34/3 Basic is a simple-to-learn high-level computer language related to the Sanskrit of computer tongues, Fortran. **1984** *Which Micro?* Dec. 1 (Advt.), There are different kinds of BASIC and, like languages, some are

easier to understand than others. **1985** *Personal Computer World* Feb. 150/1 You can return to Basic by entering R.

basically (ˈbeɪsɪkəlɪ), *adv.* [f. BASIC *a.*: see -ICALLY.] As a basic or fundamental principle, condition, matter, etc.; essentially; fundamentally.

1903 *Academy* 11 Apr. 364/1 Accent..though usual, is not invariable, not basically indispensable. **1905** CHESTERTON *Heretics* 270 The basically democratic quality which belongs to a hereditary despotism. **1927** *Observer* 20 May 17/7 The author's thesis that airship navigation is basically impracticable.

basicerite (beɪˈsɪsəraɪt). *Anim. Phys.* [f. Gr. βάσι-ς base + κέρ-ας horn, antenna + -ITE.] The second segment of the antenna of an Arthropod, reckoning from the head.

1877 HUXLEY *Anat. Inv. An.* vi. 314 A basicerite, to the outer portion of which a flattened plate..is articulated.

basichromatin (ˌbeɪsɪˈkrəʊmətɪn). *Biol.* [G. (M. Heidenhain 1894, in *Arch. f. Mikrosk. Anatomie* XLIII. 543), f. Gr. βάσι-ς base + CHROMATIN.] Chromatin that stains readily with a basic dye; basophilic chromatin.

1902 E. B. WILSON *Cell in Devel. & Inheritance* (ed. 2) i. 38 Heidenhain..distinguishes..*lanthanin*- or *oxychromatin*-granules from the *basichromatin*-granules of the chromatic network. *Ibid.* 438 *Basichromatin*,..that portion of the nuclear network stained by basic tar-colours. **1903** J. B. FARMER in E. R. Lankester *Treatise Zool.* I. II. 13 In addition to the true nuclein chromatin there have been described other inclusions within the linin known as..oxy- or basi-chromatin, which appear to be related to the nuclein series. **1952** R. J. LUDFORD in G. H. Bourne *Cytol. & Cell Physiol.* (ed. 2) ix. 398 Lucas has sought to correlate the degree of association between basichromatin and virus bodies with the cellular specificity of the viruses.

basicity (beɪˈsɪsɪtɪ). *Chem.* [f. BASIC *a.* + -ITY.]

1. The power of combining with bases possessed by an acid, dependent on the number of atoms of hydrogen replaceable by a metal which are contained in it; thus nitric acid (HNO_3) is monobasic, phosphoric acid (H_3PO_4) is tribasic.

1849 *Liebig & Kopp's Rep. Progr. Chem.* I. 469 The capacity of saturation or the basicity B of a compound. **1883** MUIR *Heroes of Sc.* V. 23 Graham..added to science the conception of acids of different basicity.

2. (See quot.)

1888 J. G. HORNER *Lockwood's Dict. Terms Mech. Engin., Basicity.* Refers to the proportion of metallic oxide present in, and the absence of silicon from a furnace lining, a cinder, flux, or slag. The fettling of a puddling furnace depends for its efficacy on its basic character.

basidiospore (bəˈsɪdɪəʊspɔə(r)). *Bot.* [f. next + SPORE.] A spore borne at the extremity of a basidium. Hence **basidiˈosporous** *a.*

1859 TODD *Cycl. Anat. & Phys.* V. 232/1 The basidiospore is distinguished from all the other acrogenous forms. *Ibid.* 224/2 Basidiosporous Fungi.

‖**basidium** (bəˈsɪdɪəm). [mod.L., f. Gr. βάσις, base + -ιδιον dim. ending.] Name given to the cells of the fructification in some fungi, which form the 'gills,' and bear the spores.

1858 CARPENTER *Veg. Phys.* §778 The spores are arranged on this hymenium in clusters of four, each group being attached to the points of a small body, rounded below, which is called the basidium. **1861** H. MACMILLAN *Footn. Page Nat.* 214 Each of the gills..is found to consist of a number of elongated cells called basidia.

basifier (ˈbeɪsɪfaɪə(r)). [f. BASIFY + -ER[1].] That which basifies.

1847 in CRAIG.

basifixed (ˈbeɪsɪfɪkst), *a. Bot.* [f. L. *basi-s* BASE + FIXED.] Attached by the base or lower end.

1870 HOOKER *Stud. Flora* 85 Genista..Anthers..long and basifixed.

basifugal (beɪˈsɪfjuːgəl), *a. Bot.* [f. L. *basi-s* BASE *sb.*[1] + *-fug-us* fleeing + -AL[1].] Tending away from the base. ***basifugal growth***: that which begins at the apex (of a leaf, etc.), and proceeds in a direction away from the base. **baˈsifugally**, *adv.*, in a basifugal manner.

1875 BENNETT & DYER *Sachs' Bot.* 138 Two extreme cases may therefore be distinguished in leaves..the predominantly basifugal or apical, and the predominantly basal growth. **1882** VINES *Sachs' Bot.* 170 Lateral members usually arise on their common axial structure in acropetal or basifugal order. *Ibid.* 448 The leaves grow..basifugally.

basify (ˈbeɪsɪfaɪ), *v.* [f. L. *basi-s* BASE *sb.*[1] + -FY.] 'To convert into a salifiable base.' Craig.

‖**basigynium** (beɪsɪˈdʒɪnɪəm). *Bot.* [mod.L., f. Gr. βασι-ς base + γυν-ή female + -IUM, repr. Gr. dim. -ιον.] The pedicel or stalk bearing the ovary.

1880 GRAY *Bot. Text-bk.* 398 *Basigynium*, synonym of Carpophore or Thecaphore.

basil[1] (ˈbæzɪl). *Herb.* Forms: 5 (*basilicon*), basile, 6 basyle, -yll, bazil, bassel, 6–7 basill, 6– basil. [a. OF. *basile*, ad. L. *basilica*, f. *basiliscus* BASILISK: the Gr. name of the plant was βασιλικὸν 'royal,' whence the botanical specific name *basilicum*, perhaps because the herb was used 'in some royal unguent, bath, or medicine' (Prior). In Lat. this seems to have been confused with *basiliscus*, on the supposition that it was an antidote to the basilisk's venom: in OF., *basile, basilicoq, basilique*, and in mod.F., *basilic* are applied both to the serpent and the plant.]

1. Popular name of a genus (*Ocymum*, N.O. *Labiatæ*) of aromatic, shrubby plants, with flowers arranged in whorled racemes, widely dispersed in tropical and sub-tropical countries. The best-known species are the culinary herbs, Common or Sweet Basil (*O. basilicum*) and Bush or Lesser Basil (*O. minimum*), the leaves of which are used for seasoning soups and made dishes.

[*c* **1420** *Pallad. on Husb.* II. 201 Basilicon, radish and rucul stronge.] **1481** CAXTON *Tulle of Old Age*, Violettys, rosemarynes, majorons, gylofres, basiles. **1562** TURNER *Herbal* II. 66 a, Basil..is good for the stryking of a se dragon. **1573** TUSSER *Husb.* xlii. (1878) 95 Bassel, fine and busht, sowe in May. **1586** COGAN *Haven Health* xxxvi. (1612) 50 A certaine Italian, by often smelling to Basill, had a Scorpion bred in his braine. **1627** H. BURTON *Baiting Pope's Bull* Ep. Ded. 26 Basil (the Embleme of the Throne established by mercy) which being gently stroked on the hand, yeelds a pleasant smell, but crushed hard vpon it, vnsauory. **1725** BRADLEY *Fam. Dict.* s.v. *Sallet*, Basil imparts a grateful Flavour if not too strong. **1861** DELAMER *Kitch. Gard.* 122 Sweet basil..is, as its name imports, one of the royalties among sweet herbs.

2. Used as a book-name for other plants: e.g. Wild Basil (*Calamintha Acinos*, Lyte, *C. Clinopodium*, Benth.), Field or Cow Basil (*Saponaria Vaccaria*, Lyte); also Basil-balm, -thyme (*Calamintha Acinos*).

1578 LYTE *Dodoens* 239 Wilde Basill hath square hearie stemmes, beset with small leaues, much lyke to the leaues of Bushe Basill. *Ibid.* 241 Of Vaccaria, or Cow Basill. **1597** GERARD *Herball* II. ccxxiii. 675 The wilde Basil or Acynos. **1640** PARKINSON *Theat. Bot.* 19 Basil-thyme..because the smell thereof is so excellent, that it is fit for a king's house.

†ˈ**basil**[2]. *Obs. rare*[−1]. In 6 bassil. [a. OF. *basile* BASILISK: see prec.]

1. = BASILISK 3.

c **1565** R. LINDSAY *Chron. Scot.* (1728) 108 She bare many cannons..with three great bassils.

†**2.** An 'iron' or fetter fastened round the ankle of a prisoner. *Obs.* (Perhaps a distinct word.)

1592 GREENE *Art Conny Catch.* II. 31 Clap a strong paire of bolts on his heeles, and a basill of 28. pound weight. **1755** *Mem. Capt. P. Drake* I. xiii. 106 One of my Irons taken off ..only one of the Bassils, which did not weigh above two Pounds out of thirty. **1865** SALA in *N. & Q.* Ser. III. VIII. 369/2 The iron ring or fetter which English convicts were wont to wear round one ankle was called a Basil.

basil[3], **bazil** (ˈbæzɪl). [App. an Eng. corruption of Fr. *basane*: see BASAN.] Sheepskin tanned in bark; distinguished from *roan*, which is tanned in sumach. Often *attrib.*

1674 GUIDOTT *Observ. Bath.* in *Harl. Misc.* (Malh.) IV. 130 The water happened..to fall upon a Bazil-skin I sometimes use. **1697** *Lond. Gaz.* No. 3285/4 All Tanners, Bazil Tanners, Curriers. **1755** JOHNSON, *Basil*, the skin of a sheep tanned. This is I believe more properly written *basen.* **1794** W. FELTON *Carriages* (1801) I. 215 An inferior leather ..called bazil leather..tears almost like paper. **1854** MAYHEW *Lond. Labour* III. 419 (Hoppe) Each sleeper has for covering a large basil such as cobblers use for aprons.

basil, *sb.*[4] and *v.* corrupt form of BEZEL.

basilar (ˈbæsɪlə(r)), *a.* Also 6 basylare. [ad. mod.L. *basilāris*, irreg. f. *basis*: see BASE *sb.*[1]] **a.** Of, pertaining to, or situated at the base, *esp.* at that of the skull. ***basilar membrane***, spec. the membrane in the cochlea that bears the organ of Corti.

1541 R. COPLAND *Guydon's Quest. Cyrurg.*, The .vij. bone is the bone basylare..that closeth and susteyneth all the sayd bones ouer the rofe. **1782** A. MONRO *Anat. Bones & Nerves* 77 Made concave for the reception..of the basilar artery. **1840** G. ELLIS *Anat.* 17 The basilar artery..lies on the basilar process of the occipital bone. **1867** QUAIN *Elem. Anat.* (ed. 7) II. ii. 760 Cochlea..At its inner angle is a structure named limbus laminæ spiralis, and in its interior, resting on the basilar membrane, is the organ of Corti. **1934** *Brit. Jrnl. Psychol.* Oct. 137 The analysis of sound stimuli at the basilar membrane cannot possibly provide a basis for the psychological experience[of hearing].

b. Of or belonging to a low moral nature or condition.

1884 H. W. BEECHER in *Chr. World Pulpit* XXV. 235/2 Rousing men and lifting them out of the basilar into this higher spiritual condition. **1899** *Westm. Gaz.* 9 June 2/1 He makes evident the disgust of his own higher nature for the past excesses of his basilar passions.

basilary (ˈbæsɪlərɪ), *a.* [ad. F. *basilaire* (16th c.), ad. mod.L. *basilāris*: see prec. and -ARY[2].] = prec.

1800 CARLISLE in *Phil. Trans.* XCI. 144 The basilary artery. **1874** M. COOKE *Fungi* 22 Upon the hymenium of Agarics..elongated cells, called by Corda basilary cells.

†**basilean.** *Obs. rare*[−1]. [f. Gr. βασιλε-ύς king + -AN.] A Royalist.

c **1645** HOWELL *Lett.* iv. (1726) 23 (D.) If any intemperate Basilean take exceptions thereat.

basilect (ˈbæsɪlɛkt). *Linguistics.* [f. BASI- + -LECT.] In a post-creole community, the social dialect that is most closely related to the creole and furthest removed from the standard language; also, the least prestigious or 'lowest' variety of any language. Cf. ACROLECT, MESOLECT.

1965, etc. [see -LECT]. **1977** [see ACROLECT]. **1982** R. QUIRK *Style & Communication in Eng. Lang.* iii. 44 Nuclear English can carry no such stigma as that frequently perceived..in relation to basilect forms of English.

Hence **basiˈlectal** *a.*, of, pertaining to, or characteristic of the basilect.

1977 *Language* LIII. 334 The major social motives account for these classes of variation: (a) pressure to avoid basilectal forms, [etc.]. **1982** *English World-Wide* III. I. 56 There is no equivalent of the mesolectal or basilectal speech styles found, for example, in Singapore. **1985** *Amer. Speech* LX. 45 The language impresses the reader as basilectal through and through.

basileiˈolatry. *nonce-wd.* [f. Gr. βασίλειο-ς of the king + λατρεία worship.] King-worship.

1872 *Sacristy* II. 10 *note*, At Westminster the established religion is Basileiolatry.

Basilian (bəˈzɪlɪən), *a.* [f. L. *Basilius*, St. Basil the Great + -AN.] Of or pertaining to St. Basil or to the order of monks and nuns following his monastic rule.

1780 A. BUTLER *Lives Saints* (ed. 2) VII. 344 A..convent of Basilian monks. **1848** DE LIANCOURT & MANNING *Pius IX* II. ii. 59 The Basilian nuns of Minsk. **1890** *Athenæum* 8 Feb. 182/2 The Basilian monk and savant Father Cozza. **1923** L. PULLAN *Relig. since Reform.* App. 278 In it there were seven Greek Basilian monasteries in the fifteenth century.

basilic (bəˈsɪlɪk), *a.* Forms: 6 **basylyc**, 7–8 **basilick(e**, 8– **basilic**. [a. F. *basilique* (16th c.), ad. L. *basilicus*, a. Gr. βασιλικός royal, kingly, f. βασιλεύς king.]

1. Kingly, royal, sovereign. ? *Obs. rare.*

1728 EARBERY tr. *Burnet's St. Dead* I. 13 In this world we see nothing except God's basilick justice.

2. *Phys.* Specific epithet of the large vein of the arm starting from the elbow and discharging into the axillary vein. [So called from its supposed great importance; the right and left basilic veins were formerly thought to be in direct communication with the liver and spleen respectively.]

1541 R. COPLAND *Guydon's Quest. Cyrurg.*, That party that was deuyded vnder the arme pyttes that goeth in to the inwarde party in descending appereth within the bought of the elbowe, and is called Basylyc. *a* **1670** HACKET *Abp. Williams* I. (1692) 88 As if he had prick'd the Court in the Basilick or Liver-vein. **1849–52** TODD *Cycl. Anat. & Phys.* IV. 1407/1 The basilic vein..ascends along the inner margin of the biceps muscle.

basilic (ˈbæsɪlɪk), *sb. arch.* [a. F. *basilique*, ad. L. *basilica*.]

1. = BASILICA 1.

1727–51 CHAMBERS *Cycl.*, *Basilic* or *Basilica.* **1811** J. MILNER *Eccl. Archit. Eng.* ii. 12 The emperors gave up their palaces and courts of justice, called Basilics, for the service of religion.

2. = BASILICA 2.

1703 *Lond. Gaz.* No. 3891/2 Considerable Damage to the Basilick, or Great Church of St. Peter. **1753** CHAMBERS *Cycl. Supp.*, *Basilics* were also little chapels built by the antient Franks over the tombs of their great men. **1840** LD. HOUGHTON in *Blackw. Mag.* XLVII. 29 Oh! never in high Roman basilic, Prime dome of art, or elder Lateran.

basilica (bəˈsɪlɪkə). Pl. **-as**, *rarely* **-æ**. Also 6 (transliterated Greek) **basilike**, 8 **basilika**. [a. L. *basilica*, Gr. βασιλική (sc. οἰκία, στοά), fem. of adjs. *basilicus*, βασιλικός, royal, f. βασιλεύς king.]

1. *Anc. Hist.* Literally and originally, a royal palace; thence, a large oblong building or hall, with double colonnades and a semicircular apse at the end, used for a court of justice and place of public assembly.

1541 ELYOT *Image Govt.* (1556) 66 A *Basilike*, or place where civile controversies were herde and judged. **1741** MIDDLETON *Cicero* I. VI. 468 A Basilica also or grand hall. **1852** CONYBEARE & H. *St. Paul* (1862) II. xxvii. 500 The basilicas were buildings of great size, so that a vast multitude of spectators was always present at any trial which excited public interest.

2. A building of the preceding type, used for Christian worship. Originally, a hall of justice handed over by Roman emperors and consecrated for religious use; thence applied to other early churches built on the same plan, and improperly to churches generally. In Rome applied spec. to the seven principal churches founded by Constantine.

1563 *Homilies* II. ii. III. (1859) 256 Called Basilicæ, eyther for that the Greeks used to call all great and goodly places Basilicas, or for that the high and everlasting King..was served in them. **1725** tr. *Dupin's Eccl. Hist. 17th C.* I. v. 99 There were some Churches..which were not dedicated to any Saint, but had only in general the Name of a Basilika.

1851 RUSKIN *Stones Ven.* I. i. §27 An imitation in wood of the Christian Roman churches or basilicas. **1852** MISS YONGE *Cameos* (1877) III. xxx. 303 Sending a deputation to do penance at the seven basilicæ. **1874** PARKER *Illust. Goth. Archit.* II. 276 The application of the name of Basilica to the small burial-chapels in the Catacombs is a mistake.

†**3.** The basilic vein: see BASILIC *a.* 2. *Obs.*

1625 HART *Anat. Ur.* II. viii. 105 The basilica or liver veine. **1751** CHAMBERS *Cycl.* s.v., The basilica is one of the veins used in bleeding in the arm.

4. (*neut. pl*) = BASILICS, q.v.

basilical (bəˈsɪlɪkəl), *a.*[1] [f. Gr. βασιλικ-ός + -AL[1].]

1. Kingly, royal, regal.

1652 URQUHART *Jewel* Wks. (1834) 277 Basilical rule or any other temporal soveraignty. **1885** T. KERSLAKE *Liberty Hist. Research* 5 Up wells this basilical word 'must.'

†**2.** = BASILIC *a.* 2. *Obs.*

1649 HOWELL *Lett.* (1650) III. 40 How England will thrive now that she is let bloud in the basilicall veine. **1686** PLOT *Staffordsh.* 290 Upon squeesing her Arm he forced thence from about the Basilical vein..a pins point.

baˈsilical, *a.*[2] [f. BASILICA + -AL[1].] = next.

1613 T. GODWIN *Rom. Antiq.* (1658) 10 Many men..were wont to walk under those basilical buildings. **1881** G. SCOTT *Ch. Archit.* Pref., The basilical church of Lyminge.

basilican (bəˈsɪlɪkən), *a.* [ad. med.L. *basilicān-us*, f. *basilica*: see prec. and -AN.] Of, pertaining to, or resembling a basilica. **baˈsilicanism,** adherence to the basilican type of church.

1797 HOLCROFT *Stolberg's Trav.* II. l. 228 It is built in the basilican manner. **1879** BARING-GOULD *Germany* II. 345 But the basilican churches were not always adaptations of this sort. **1861** A. B. HOPE *Eng. Cathedr. 19th C.* vi. 179 In very many Italian monastic churches..basilicanism has as it were been caricatured.

basilicate (bəˈsɪlɪkət), *a.* [f. BASILICA + -ATE[2].] Shaped like a basilica; basilican.

1882 S. BUTLER *Alps & Sanct.* xxv. 357 A fine old basilicate Church.

†**basilicock.** *Obs.* Forms: 4 baselycoc, 4–5 -cok, basilicok, -iskoc, 5 basylicock, -ycok, 6 basilicock. [a. OF. *basilicoc*, *-ecoc* (nom. sing. and acc. pl. *basilicos*), f. *basilic*:—L. *basiliscus* BASILISK + *-oc* = It. *-occo*, usually augmentative, sometimes diminutive. Here perhaps associated with *coq* cock: cf. *cockatrice*.] = BASILISK I.

1340 *Ayenb.* 28 Þanne is he [the envious] of þe kende of þe baselycoc, uor no grenhede ne may yleste beuore hym. *c* **1386** CHAUCER *Pers. T.* ¶778 That sleeth right as the Basilicok [*v.r.* Baselycok] sleeth folk by the venym of his sighte. **1481** CAXTON *Myrr.* II. vi. 77 Basylicocks [have]..the heed lyke a cocke and body of a serpent. **1583** STUBBES *Anat. Abus.* (1877) 109 Like a Cockatrise, or Basilicock, which slay or kill men with the poison of their sighte.

‖**baˈsilicon, -um.** [L. *basilicum*, Gr. βασιλικόν (sc. φάρμακον drug, plaster), neut. of adj. *basilicus*, βασιλικός, royal.] Name given to several ointments supposed to possess 'sovereign' virtues.

1541 R. COPLAND *Guydon's Formul.* Tj, The fourth fourme is the great basilicon that is praysed ouer all, and is called tetrafarmacum. **1659** CULPEPPER *Pharm. Lond.* 298 Basilicon, the greater. Take of white Wax, Pine Rozin, Heifers suet, etc. **1762** STERNE *Tr. Shandy* V. xxvii. 96 He had stepped down for lint and basilicon. **1782** SCHOTTE in *Phil. Trans.* LXXIII. 88 A pledget of basilicum was put over it.

¶ See also BASIL *sb.*[1]

basilics (bəˈsɪlɪks), *sb. pl.* [ad. L. *basilica* (also used in Eng.), a. Gr. βασιλικά, neut. pl. of adj. βασιλικός.] A digest of the laws of Justinian and other emperors, translated from Latin into Greek by command of the emperors Basil and Leo, and constituting the code of the Eastern empire.

[**1652** NEEDHAM *Selden's Mare Cl.* 96 Which is manifest enough, not onely in the Basilica..but also by the Decrees established by the Emperor Leo.] **1751** CHAMBERS *Cycl.* s.v., The basilics comprehend the institutes, digests, code and novels, and some edicts of Justinian. **1771** RAPER in *Phil. Trans.* LXI. 513 A scholiast on the Basilics tells us.

Basilidian (bæsɪˈlɪdɪən), *a.* and *sb.* [f. L. *Basilid-es*, Gr. Βασιλίδ-ης + -IAN.]

A. *adj.* Of, pertaining to, or derived from, Basilides, an Alexandrian Gnostic of the 2nd century. **B.** *sb.* One of his disciples or followers.

1586 T. ROGERS 39 *Art.* (1607) 118 Some utterly cast off all grace, virtue, and godliness, as did the Basilidians. **1860** T. BALFOUR *Typ. Charact. Nat.* 120 The Basilideans believed that Simon the Cyrenian was crucified in the room of Christ. **1877** W. JONES *Finger-ring L.* 113 The Gnostic or Basilidian gems, evidently used for magical purposes.

basiˈliscan, *a. rare.* [f. L. *basilisc-us* BASILISK + -AN.] Pertaining to a basilisk.

c **1600** *Timon* IV. iii. (1842) 65 With my basilican eies May I kill all I see.

basiˈliscine, *a. rare.* [f. as prec. + -INE[1].] = prec.

1855 KINGSLEY *Westw. Ho* (1861) 79 Our fair Oriana, and the slaughter which her basiliscine eyes have caused.

basilisco: see next.

basilisk (ˈbæzɪlɪsk, ˈbæs-). Forms: α. 4– basilisk; 5–7 basiliske, 6 (basseliskie), 6–7 basilisque, 7 -isck, basalisk, 8 basilisc. β. (unchanged L.) 4–7 basiliscus, 6 (basilicus). γ. (from Fr.) 5 basilique, basylyque, 6 -ike. δ. (from Sp.) 7 basilisco, -sko. See also BASILICOCK. [ad. L. *basiliscus*, a. Gr. βασιλίσκος a kinglet, a kind of serpent, the golden-crested wren, dim. of βασιλεύς king: see -ISK. The Latin form was occas. used unchanged from 14th to 17th c.; Caxton, in 15th c., introduced forms after Fr. *basilique*, now *basilic*; and in 17th c., *basilisco*, *-sko*, after Sp., occur.]

1. A fabulous reptile, also called a *cockatrice*, alleged to be hatched by a serpent from a cock's egg; ancient authors stated that its hissing drove away all other serpents, and that its breath, and even its look, was fatal. [So called, says Pliny, from a spot, resembling a crown, on its head; mediæval authors furnished it with 'a certain combe or coronet.']

α. *a* **1300** *E.E. Psalter* xci. 13 Oure aspide and basilisk saltou ga. *c* **1400** MAUNDEV. xxviii. 285 Thei slen him anon with the beholdynge, as dothe the Basilisk. **1599** PORTER *Angry Wom. Abingd.* (1841) 121 O, that it were the basseliskies fell eye, To poyson thee! **1611** SHAKS. *Wint. T.* I. ii. 389 Make me not sighted like the Basilisque. **1657** *Phys. Dict.*, Basilisk..kills a man with its very sight (as some say) but by its breath infallibly: it's about a foot long, with a black and yellow skin, and fiery red eyes. **1712** POPE *Messiah* 82 The smiling infant in his hand shall take The crested basilisk and speckled snake. **1847** LD. LINDSAY *Chr. Art* I. Introd. 147 The abbot..cried, 'Lord, either I must die, or this basilisk!' And instantly the basilisk died.

β. **1387** TREVISA *Higden* Rolls Ser. I. 159 Basiliscus is kyng of serpentes þat wiþ smyl and siȝt sleeþ beestes. **1536** LATIMER *2nd Serm. bef. Convoc.* i. 45 To do hurt, more than either aspis or basiliscus. **1609** BIBLE (Douay) *Isa.* xxx. 6 The viper, and the flying basiliscus.

γ. **1491** CAXTON *Vitas Patr.* (W. de W.) II. 218 a/2 He founde in his waye a grete serpente basylyque. **1530** PALSGR. 196/2 Basylike serpent, *basilisque*.

δ. **1655** JENNINGS *Elise* 57 He loses his countenance at the aspect of the Basilisco, whose sight kills him.

2. *fig.* Often *attrib.*

α. **1549** CHEKE *Hurt Sedit.* (1641) 42 But what is a loyterer? A sucker of Honie..a Basiliske of the Commonwealth. *a* **1789** BURNEY *Hist. Mus.* I. viii. 123 Satire..becomes a basilisk in the hands of a man..who employs it to blast the reputation of another. **1831** CARLYLE *Sart. Res.* II. vi, That Basilisk-glance of the barouche-and-four.

γ. **1475** CAXTON *Jason* 45 Certes madame youre eyen basilique haue hurte me unto the deth.

3. *transf.* A large cannon, generally made of brass, and throwing a shot of about 200 pounds weight. (Other pieces of ordnance of the time were named from venomous reptiles; e.g. *culverin*, *serpentine*, *slang*, etc. Cf. Shaks. *Hen. V*, v. ii. 17.)

α. **1577** HARRISON *England* II. xvi. (1877) 281 Basiliske [weigheth] 9000 pounds, eight inches and three quarters within the mouth. **1586** MARLOWE *1st Pt. Tamburl.* IV. i, The basilisks, That, roaring, shake Damascus turrets down! **1613** PURCHAS *Pilgr.* I. v. vii. 408 Great Brazen Ordinance, ..whereof foure Basiliskes were drawne (such was their weight) by so many hundred yokes of Oxen. **1861** MISS BEAUFORT *Egypt. Sepul.* II. xxiv. 328 Stone shot lying about, some of the latter thrown by basilisks.

β. **1549** EDW. VI. *Lit. Rem.* (1858) 250 The pecis of new conquest, and 2 basilicus, 2 demy canons, etc.

δ. **1627** CAPT. SMITH *Seaman's Gram.* xiv. 70 A Basilisco. Height [= bore] in Inches, 5. Weight in Pounds, 4000. Shot, Pounds, 15½. Powder, Pounds, 10. **1644** in Rushw. *Hist. Coll.* III. II. 701 The Rebels Train of Artillery.. amongst which was the great Basilisco of Dover.

4. *Zool.* A small American lizard of the family *Iguanidæ*, having on the top of its head a hollow crest which can be inflated at will.

1813 SHELLEY *Q. Mab* VIII. 86 The green and golden basilisk. **1847** CARPENTER *Zool.* §495 The Mitred Basilisk is an inhabitant of Guiana, Martinique, etc... It swims with great address by means of the lateral motions of its finny tail.

†**5.** *Ornith.* Obs. name of the Golden-crested Wren or Kinglet (*Regulus cristatus*). (So in Gr.)

β. **1753** CHAMBERS *Cycl. Supp.*, *Basiliscus.*

†**6.** *Astr.* Obs. name of the star Regulus, in Leo.

1551 RECORDE *Cast. Knowl.* (1556) 266 The Basilyske or Kyngely starre. **1727–51** in CHAMBERS *Cycl.*

7. *Comb.* **basilisco-proof,** *a.*, proof against eyes, even those of a basilisk; unabashed, shameless.

1649 *Lanc. Tracts Civ. War* (1844) 236 Though your brows be Basilisco-proof, yet you could be content I should end this language.

basiˈliskian, *a.* [f. prec. + -IAN.] Of or pertaining to a basilisk; basiliscan.

1828 J. WILSON in *Blackw. Mag.* XXIII. 783 That.. fascinating and basiliskian glare of gorgeous and rhetorical embellishment.

basin (ˈbeɪs(ə)n), *sb.* Forms: 3 bascin, bacin, 4–5 bacine, bacyn(e, bassyn(e, -eyn, 4–6 basyn, 5 basson, bassyng, -ien, bacen, 6 bayseyn, bassine, basing, baiseing, 6–7 basen, 8 bassin, 6– bason, 5– basin. [ME. *bacin*, *bascin*, a. OF. *bacin* (12th c. in Littré), mod. *bassin* (= Picard *bachin*, Pr., Sp. *bacin*, It. *bacino*):—late L. *bachīnus*, *bacchīnus*; in Greg. of Tours, 6th c., 'vulgo' *bacchīnon*; supposed by some to be for *baccīnus*, *-um*, and to be a derivative of *bacca* 'vas aquārium' Isidore. Thence also OHG. *becchin*, mod.G. *becken*, Du. *bekken*. The med.L. had *bacīnus*, *bassīnus* from the mod. langs. The ulterior source is unknown: the Celtic *bacc-* 'hook, crook,' to which Diez and others have referred it, has no derivative with any approach to the sense of 'basin': see Thurneysen.]

I. A hollow circular vessel.

1. a. A circular vessel of greater width than depth, with sloping or curving sides, used for holding water and other liquids, especially for washing purposes. ***barber's basin***: see BARBER *sb.* 3.

c **1220** *St. Marher.* 9 His twa ehnen..brad as bascins. *c* **1330** *Florice & Bl.* 550 Water and cloth and bacyn For to wasschen his hondes in. *c* **1400** *Destr. Troy* VII. 3169 Bassons of bright gold. **1486** *Bk. St. Albans* B v a, Put it in a bassien of brasse. **1513–75** *Diurn. Occurr.* (1833) 103 The basing and the lawar. **1596** SHAKS. *Tam. Shrew* II. i. 350 Basons and ewers, to laue her dainty hands. **1616** R. C. *Times' Whis.* IV. 1613 Faire water in a basen. **1726** GAY *Fables* I. xxi. 23 His pole with pewter basons hung. **1794** G. ADAMS *Nat. & Exp. Philos.* I. iii. 70 A barometer..immersed in a bason of mercury. *c* **1845** LANE *Arab. Nts.* (Rtldg.) 290 The slave brought a basin and water; the prince then washed himself.

b. The quantity held by a basin; a basinful.

1834 HT. MARTINEAU *Farrers* vii. 127 [She] made a basin of tea. *Mod.* A basin of soup on a cold day.

2. A similar circular dish for any purpose.

1525 LD. BERNERS *Froiss.* II. cxvi. (R.) His bedde was wont to be chafed with a bason of hote coles. *a* **1704** T. BROWN *Sat. Antients* (1730) I. 14 Satura Lanx was properly a bason filled with all sorts of fruit. **1777** J. RICHARDSON *Dissert. East. Nations* 26 Four large basons filled with gold and silver. **1662** *Bk. Com. Prayer* Commun., Shall receive the Alms for the Poor..in a decent bason.

3. The scale-dish of a balance.

1413 LYDG. *Pylgr. Sowle* I. xvi. (1859) 18 Lete hym put it in the ryȝt bacyn of the balaunce. **1727–51** CHAMBERS *Cycl.*, *Basons* of a Balance. **1833** J. HOLLAND *Manuf. Metal* II. 292 The boards or basins are suspended by means of hooks to the ends of the beam.

†**4.** *pl.* Hollow metal dishes clashed together to produce sound; ? cymbals. The beating of metal basins was formerly part of the mocking accompaniment when infamous persons were condemned to be publicly carted. *Obs.*

c **1302** *Pol. Songs* (1839) 189 The Flemmysche.. Agynneth to clynken huere basyns of bras. *c* **1374** CHAUCER *Boeth.* IV. vi. 133 Forto rescowe þe moone [in eclipses] þei betyn hire basines wiþ þikke strokes. **1604** DEKKER *Honest Wh.* Wks. 1873 II. 181 Why before her does the Bason ring? **1609** B. JONSON *Sil. Wom.* III. v. (N.) Let there be no bawd carted that year, to employ a bason of his.

5. *spec.* **a.** A concave tool used by glass-grinders in the manufacture of convex glasses.

1727–51 CHAMBERS *Cycl.* s.v., Various kinds of basons, of copper, iron, etc...some deeper, others shallower, according to the focus of the glasses that are to be ground.

†**6.** The hollow part of a plate or dish. *Obs.*

1662 PEPYS *Diary* 21 July, Silver dishes and plates..in the edges and basins of which was placed..gold medals.

7. A helmet; a BASINET. *Obs.*

c **1300** *K. Alis.* 2333 So he tok his basyn, That hit clevyd into the chyn. *c* **1325** *Coeur de L.* 2557 Some he hytte on the bacyn, That he cleff hym to the chyn.

†**8.** *Phys.* **a.** The pelvis; **b.** A funnel-shaped cavity situated between the anterior ventricles of the brain. *Obs.*

1727–51 in CHAMBERS *Cycl.* **1760** BRADY in *Phil. Trans.* LI. 660 A bone found in the pelvis or bason of a man. **1771** J. S. *Le Dran's Observ. Surg.* Dict. C c b, The Pelvis, or Bason of the Kidnies.

II. A hollow depression, natural or artificial.

9. A hollow receptacle, natural or artificial, containing water. *spec.* a submarine hollow or cavity.

1712 BLACKMORE (J.) And from its ample basin cast the main. **1764** HARMER *Observ.* x. viii. 327 Their waters being conveyed by acqueducts into two very large basons. **18..** WORDSW. *Idle Sheph. Boys*, And in a basin black and small Receives a lofty waterfall. **1867** LADY HERBERT *Cradle L.* viii. 213 Inland basins of rain-water. **1881** J. F. WILLIAMS *Geogr. Oceans* III. i. 142 The eastern and north-western basins have average depths of 2,500 and 3,000 fathoms respectively. **1904** A. KNOX *Gloss. Geogr. & Topogr. Terms* 37 *Basin*,..used, in sub-oceanic relief, for a depression of approximately round form.

10. a. A dock constructed in a tidal river or harbour, in which by means of flood-gates the water is kept at a constant level, used for ships discharging or lading cargo, or when laid up.

1709 *Lond. Gaz.* No. 4510/5 A great Fleet of Merchant Ships..have contracted with the Officers of his Majesty's Customs to open their way into the great Basin of this City. **1815** WELLINGTON in Gurw. *Disp.* XII. 265 A wet dock or basin of considerable size and depth may be considered nessesary for the trade of Antwerp.

b. Part of a river or canal widened and furnished with wharfs for the lading and unlading of barges.

1837 WHITTOCK *Bk. Trades* (1842) 203 Basins are formed near towns to which the canal has a communication.

11. A land-locked harbour; a bay.

1725 POPE *Odyss.* VI. 315 The spacious basins arching rocks enclose. **1781** GIBBON *Decl. & F.* II. xxxi. 191 The largest vessels securely rode at anchor within three deep and capacious basons. **1855** MACAULAY *Hist. Eng.* IV. 226 His army..was encamped round the basin of La Hogue. **1866** THOREAU *Yankee in Can.* ii. 20 The harbor of Quebec..a basin two miles across.

12. *Phys. Geog.* The tract of country drained by a river and its tributaries, or which drains into a particular lake or sea.

[**1792** A. YOUNG *Trav. France* 289 Modern French geographers..have divided the kingdom into what they call *bassins*..into several great plains, through which flow the principal rivers.] **1804** C. B. BROWN tr. *Volney's View of Soil & Climate U.S.A.* 67 Their basins, the vallies which supply them, are of a greater elevation. **1830** LYELL *Princ. Geol.* I. 434 The hydrographical basin of the Thames. **1860** MAURY *Phys. Geog. Sea* v. §270 The basin of the Amazon is usually computed at 1,512,000 square miles. *Ibid.* xii. §534 The basin of the Dead Sea..and the other inland basins of Asia.

13. *gen.* A circular or oval valley or hollow.

c **1854** STANLEY *Sinai & Pal.* v. 243 The traveller finds himself in a wide basin, encircled by hills. **1860** TYNDALL *Glac.* I. §23. 166 The basin had been scooped by glaciers.

14. *Geol.* A circumscribed formation in which the strata dip inward from all sides to the centre; the stratified deposit, especially of coal, lying in such a depression.

1821 *Abridgem. R. Turner's Arts. & Sc.* 230 What is called a coal-field, or district, or sometimes a coal-basin. **1850** LYELL *Princ. Geol.* Gloss. 776 Basin of Paris, Basin of London. Deposits lying in a hollow or trough, formed of older rocks. **1877** GREEN *Phys. Geol.* ix. §3. 347 If the beds dip everywhere towards a centre, they..form a basin.

15. *Hort.* The depression at the apex of a pomaceous fruit, in which is situated the calyx or eye.

1909 in *Cent. Dict.* Suppl.

III. *Comb.*, chiefly attrib., as ***basin-pan, -sign, -stand***; also ***basin-like, -shaped***, adj.; **basinful**, the content of a basin; also *transf.* an excessive amount, (more than) enough (*slang*); **basin irrigation** (see quot. 1961); **basin-wide** *a.*, as wide as a basin (cf. *saucer-eyed*).

1799 G. SMITH *Laborat.* I. 434 Take two *basonfuls of river sand. **1935** G. INGRAM *Cockney Cavalcade* 136 My mother's had a 'basinful', if anyone has, I can tell you. **1957** 'J. WYNDHAM' *Midwich Cuckoos* iii. 24 That there Miss Ogle ain't 'alf goin' to cop 'erself a basinful of 'Er Majesty's displeasure over this little lot. **1960** *News Chron.* 27 June 4/8 I've had a basinful of bowler-hat and furled-umbrella parts. **1903** *Westm. Gaz.* 29 Sept. 1/3 The old *basin irrigation will be transformed into a perennial system. **1961** L. D. STAMP *Gloss. Geogr. Terms* 54/2 *Basin irrigation*: the type of irrigation associated especially with the Nile in Egypt and the Sudan whereby flood waters are led off into specially prepared 'basins' which vary in size from a few dozen acres to many square miles. The basins are separated from one another by earth banks. **1836–9** TODD *Cycl. Anat. & Phys.* II. 134/2 A horny *basin-like cavity. **1462** *Test. Ebor.* (1855) II. 261 Wirt-pannes, *basyn-pan. **1859** TODD *Cycl. Anat. & Phys.* V. 146/2 The pelvis offers a *basin-shaped structure. **1613** ROWLANDS *Spy-Knaues* B iij b, First to my Barber, at his *Bason signe. **1842** T. MARTIN in *Fraser's Mag.* Dec., Ducking and diving into the *basin-stand. **1591** SPENSER *M. Hubberd* 670 Then gan the Courtiers..stare on him, with big lookes *basen wide.

basined ('beɪs(ə)nd), *ppl. a.* Also 8–9 **basoned**. [f. prec. + -ED[2].] Placed or contained in a basin.

1742 YOUNG *Nt. Th.* IX. 918 Thy basined rivers, and imprisoned seas. **1809** J. BARLOW *Columb.* I. 651 Bason'd high, on earth's broad bosom gay, The bright Superior silvers down the day.

basinerved ('beɪsɪ,nɜːvd), *a. Bot.* [f. L. *basi-s* BASE *sb.*[1] + NERVED; cf. F. *basinerve.*] Of leaves: Having the ribs all springing from the base.

1866 in *Treas. Bot.*

basinet, basnet ('bæsɪnɪt, 'bæsnɪt). *Obs.* exc. *Hist.* Forms: 3–9 **basnet**, 4–9 **bacinet, basenet**, 9 **basinet, bassinet, bascinet**; also 4 **basinett**, 4–6 **basenett(e**, 5 **bacenett, basnite, -nette**, 4–5 **basynet, bacynet, -ette**, 5–7 **bassenet**. [a. OF. *bacinet, bassiné, bassinet* (= Sp. *bacinete*, It. *bacinetto*, med.L. *basinetum, bacinetum*), dim. of *bacin* BASIN: see -ET[1].]

A small, light, steel headpiece, in shape somewhat globular, terminating in a point raised slightly above the head, and closed in front with a ventail or visor; when used in action without the ventail, as was frequently the case in England, the great 'helm,' resting on the shoulders, was worn over it.

c **1300** *K. Alis.* 2234 Helm and basnet..The scharpe sweord carf bothe. *c* **1380** *Sir Ferumb.* 5577 þorw helm, & coyphe, & bacynet, þe swerd goþ forþ. **1391** *Test. Ebor.* (1836) I. 151 Unum melius basenett cum ventayll. *c* **1440** *Morte Arth.* 906 A bacenett burneschte of sylver. **1523** LD. BERNERS *Froiss.* I. lx. 81 Such a stroke..that their basenettes were clouen. **1581** T. NEWTON *Seneca's Thebais* 51 On head thy Basnet tye. **1611** GWILLIM *Heraldry* IV. xv. 234 Their bassenets or sculles. **1808** SCOTT *Marm.* VI. xxi, My basnet to a prentice cap, Lord Surrey's o'er the Till! **1843** LYTTON *Last Bar.* I. ix, Thou talkest of bassinets and hauberks. **1856** R. VAUGHAN *Mystics* (1860) I. 154 Sir Rudolf's new bascinet with the beaked ventaille. **1874** BOUTELL *Arms & Arm.* viii. 127 The basinet was considered to be incomplete without..a mail defence for the neck and shoulders, called the *camail*. **1875** STUBBS *Const. Hist.* II. xvii. 543 *note*, Aketons, bacinets, gauntlets.

fig. **1496** *Dives & Paup.* (W. de W.) VIII. viii. 332 The amyt betokeneth the basynet of helthe, that is hope of the lyfe that is to come.

See also BASSINET, BASSINATE.

†**'basineted**, *ppl. a. Obs.* [f. prec. + -ED[2].] Furnished with, or as if with, a basinet.

1596 FITZ-GEFFREY *Sir F. Drake* (1881) 24 Even as the Larke..Mounteth her basinetted head on high.

†**'basing**, *sb. Obs. rare*[−1]. [f. BASE *sb.*[1] + -ING.] Foundation, base.

c **1325** *E.E. Allit. P.* A. 991 Bantelez..on basyng boun.

†**'basing**, *vbl. sb. Obs.* [f. BASE *v.*[1] + -ING[1].] The action of BASE *v.*[1]; abasing, debasement.

1581 W. STAFFORD *Exam. Compl.* ii. (1876) 55 The basing or rather the corrupting of our coyne & treasure.

basioccipital (,beɪsɪɒk'sɪpɪtəl), *a.* and *sb.* [f. L. *basi-s* base + OCCIPITAL *a.*] Pertaining or belonging to the base of the occiput or the basilar part of the occipital bone. Also as *sb.*

1853 in MAYNE *Expos. Lex.* **1878** T. DUNMAN *Gloss. Biol., Anat. Terms* 15 *Basioccipital*, a bone of the skull which in Human Anatomy is represented by the basilar process of the occipital bone. **1933** *Jrnl. R. Anthrop. Inst.* LX. 20 The Calotte..is made up by the bones of the calvaria deprived of the basioccipital, the ethmoid and the basal parts of the sphenoid and temporal bones.

basion ('beɪsɪən). *Anat.* [mod.L., f. Gr. βάσι-ς BASE *sb.*[1]] The middle of the anterior border of the occipital foramen.

1878 BARTLEY tr. *Topinard's Anthrop.* 234.

basiophthalmite (,beɪsɪɒf'θælmaɪt). *Anim. Phys.* [f. Gr. βασι-ς base + ὀφθαλμ-ός eye + -ITE.] The lowest joint of the eye-stalk of Crustacea.

1877 HUXLEY *Anat. Inv. An.* vi. 315 The peduncles of the eye..are composed of..a small proximal basiophthalmite, and a larger terminal podophthalmite.

basipetal (beɪ'sɪpɪtəl), *a. Bot.* [f. L. *basi-s* base + *-pet-us* seeking + -AL[1].] 'Developing from the apex towards the base' (Gray *Bot. Text-bk.* 1880). Hence **ba'sipetally** *adv.*

1869 *Student* II. 13 The well ascertained basipetal formation of many foliary parts. **1882** VINES *Sachs' Bot.* 171 Lateral members..arranged in basipetal order. **1939** *Nature* 18 Mar. 486/2 There is no suggestion that this procambial activity contributes basipetally to an enlargement of the vascular system. **1946** *Ibid.* 23 Nov. 737/2 The supposed basipetal development of the leaf traces.

basipodite (beɪ'sɪpədaɪt). *Anim. Phys.* [f. Gr. βάσι-ς base + ποδ- (πούς) foot + -ITE.] The second segment of the leg of an Arthropod.

1870 ROLLESTON *Anim. Life* 94 The second joint is known as the basipodite. **1877** HUXLEY *Anat. Inv. An.* vi. 309 The proximal one..is the coxopodite, the next, small and conical, is the basipodite.

basis ('beɪsɪs). Pl. **bases**. [a. L. *basis*, a. Gr. βάσις: see BASE *sb.*[1]]

I. Literal senses. (Now rarely used: see BASE.)

1. *gen.* The bottom of anything, considered as the part on which it rests or is supported; the foundation, base, foot. *arch.*

1571 DIGGES *Pantom.* I. xxx. I iij, The distance of the ship from the basis or foote of the cliffe. **1610** SHAKS. *Temp.* II. i. 120 Th'shore; that ore his waue-worne basis bowed As stooping to releeue him. **1656** H. MORE *Antid. Ath.* I. iv. (1712) 143 The basis of the Cedar. **1718** POPE *Iliad* VII. 545 Whose rage can make The solid earth's eternal basis shake! **1837** CARLYLE *Fr. Rev.* IV. iv. III. 155 Triumphal Arches: at the basis of the first of which, we descry, etc.

†**2.** The base of a pillar; = BASE *sb.*[1] 5.

[**1532** MORE *Confut. Barnes* VIII. Wks. 742/2 The grounde or foote of the piller called in laten *basis*.] **1677** HALE *Prim. Orig. Man.* I. ii. 64 His Feet, the Basis of the Pillar of his Body. *a* **1719** ADDISON (J.) Observing an English inscription upon the basis, we read it over several times.

†**3.** A pedestal. *Obs.*

1601 SHAKS. *Jul. C.* III. i. 115 Cæsar..That now on Pompeyes Basis lye[s] along, No worthier then the dust. **1686** AGLIONBY *Paint. Illustr.* 367 The Basis likewise is a Balusted of Granite-Stone.

4. *Bot.* and *Zool.* That part of an organ by which it is attached to its support; = BASE *sb.*[1] 7. Now only in specific use: see quots. 1870.

1615 CROOKE *Body of Man* 467 A Pine-apple, broade and round in the Basis. **1664** POWER *Exp. Philos.* I. 40 The obtuse Tip of this Capsula..shoots itself into the basis of the Liver. **1753** CHAMBERS *Cycl. Supp.* s.v. *Antholyza*, The upper lip [of the flower]..near its basis has two short jaggs. **1870** NICHOLSON *Zool.* (1880) 289 A shelly or membranous plate closes the lower aperture of the [Acorn-] shell, and is termed the 'basis.' **1870** ROLLESTON *Anim. Life* 94 The second joint is known as the 'basipodite,' or 'basis.'

†**5.** A geometrical base: = BASE *sb.*[1] 9.

1571 DIGGES *Pantom.* I. vi. C iij b, That subtendente side, or basis. **1661** BOYLE *Examen* (1682) 95 A Pyramide..whose Basis is part of the surface of the Atmosphere. **1748** HARTLEY *Observ. Man* I. iii.§1 ⁋ 80 The Angles at the Basis of an Isosceles Triangle.

†**6.** Each of the boards of a pair of bellows. *Obs.*

1669 BOYLE *Cont. New Exp.* I. (1682) 129 Another pair of Tite Bellows made with a very light Clack in the lower Basis. *Ibid.* I. 109 The Orifice of the Vent in the basis.

II. Transferred and figurative senses.

7. The main constituent, fundamental ingredient.

1601 HOLLAND *Pliny* Gloss., *Basis* in a compound medicine is that drug or simple which is predominant. **1665** *Phil. Trans.* I. 117 Salt, the Basis of all Natural Productions. **1712** tr. *Pomet's Hist. Drugs* I. 179 Several People make it the Basis of the Liquorice juice. **1867** J. HOGG *Microsc.* I. iii. 225 Colouring-solutions should be always prepared with glycerine..as a basis.

8. That by or on which anything immaterial is supported or sustained; a foundation, support

1605 SHAKS. *Macb.* IV. iii. 32 Great Tyrrany, lay thou thy basis sure. **1686** W. DE BRITAINE *Hum. Prud.* 126 The love of the Subject is the most sure Basis of the Princes Greatness. **1718** *Free-thinker* No. 75. 142 Integrity is the Basis of all Human Prudence. **1860** TYNDALL *Glac.* II. §3. 243 This speculation..rested upon a basis of conjecture.

9. That on which anything is reared, constructed, or established, and by which its constitution or operation is determined; groundwork, footing: **a.** a thing material.

1668 HALE *Pref. Rolle's Abridgm.* 9 This Book will be the Basis of such a Common-place Book. **1808** MIDDLETON *Grk. Article* (ed. 3) I. 485 The critical possessor of the basis filled its margin with glosses and readings.

b. a thing immaterial; a principle, a fact.

1601 SHAKS. *Twel. N.* III. ii. 36 Build me thy fortunes vpon the basis of valour. **1622** MALYNES *Anc. Law-Merch.* 423 Where the Basis of Exchange..is made vpon our twentie shillings sterling. **1852** MCCULLOCH *Taxation* II. vi. 254 Assessing licence duties on such inapplicable bases. **1871** R. W. DALE *Commandm.* vi. 151 If Moses had to regulate our legislation in reference to railway accidents, he would put it on altogether a new basis. **1876** GREEN *Short Hist.* iv. §4 (1882) 190 Among the German races society rested on the basis of the family.

c. a set of principles laid down or agreed upon as the ground of negotiation, argument, or action.

1796 BURKE *Regic. Peace* Wks. VIII. 334 We had gained a great point in getting this basis admitted..a basis of mutual compensation. **1855** (7 June) BRIGHT *Russia, Sp.* (1876) 253 It is necessary therefore to have a basis for our discussion. **1880** MCCARTHY *Own Times* III. xxxvi. 129 A basis of legislation was at last agreed upon.

10. The tract of country from, and in connexion with, which military or other operations are conducted; = BASE *sb.*[1] 16. *lit.* and *fig.*

1833 HT. MARTINEAU *Cinnamon & P.* vii. 124 Colonies are not advantageous to the mother-country as the basis of a peculiar trade. **1865** M. ARNOLD *Ess. Crit.* vii. 219 [Joubert's] soul had, for its basis of operations, hardly any body at all. **1865** *Times* 2 Jan., To make Canada..the basis of operations against the Northern States.

III. *attrib.*, as in ***basis-structure, -tissue***. **basis box**, also *basic box*, the unit of area in the tinplate industry (see quot. 1956); **basis wine**, a fermented liquor obtained chiefly from raisins or concentrated must and used as the basis or main constituent in the manufacture of various wines.

1926 *Jrnl. Iron & Steel Inst.* CXIII. 602 There are two gas-fired furnaces each with a capacity of about 30 tons, or 600 basis boxes per charge. **1956** W. E. HOARE *Tinplate Handbk.* (ed. 3) iv. 13 The unit of area used by the tinplate industries is the basis box or base box, originally defined as 112 sheets each 20 in. × 14 in. **1958** A. D. MERRIMAN *Dict. Metallurgy* 16/1 The weight may vary from 55 to 275 lb. per basis box, but is usually between 100 and 150 lb. **1839–47** TODD *Cycl. Anat. & Phys.* III. 727/1 The basis-substance is..destitute of fibres. *Ibid.* IV. 878/1 These 'dental tubuli'..subdivide rapidly in the hard basis-tissue. **1905** A. CHAMBERLAIN in *Hansard* 10 Apr. CXLIV. 1049 Wine manufactured..partly from imported grape must, more largely from currants and raisins..known to the trade as 'basis' wine. **1905** *Daily Chron.* 21 Dec. 6/3 Fraudulent wines, containing what was called 'basis' wine.

basiscopic (beɪsɪ'skɒpɪk), *a. Bot.* [f. Gr. βάσι-ς base + -σκοπ-ος viewing + -IC.] Looking or turned towards the base.

1882 VINES *Sachs' Bot.* 450 Each of these halves is divided..into an acroscopic and a basiscopic portion.

basisolute (beɪ'sɪsəʊljuːt), *a. Bot.* [f. L. *basi-s* base + *solūtus* unbound, free.] Of leaves: Prolonged at the base below the point of origin.

1847 in CRAIG. **1866** *Treas. Bot.*, *Basisolute*, a term applied to leaves which, like those of *Sedum* and *Echeveria*, are extended downwards below their true origin.

bask (bɑːsk, -æ-), *v.* Also 4–6 **baske**. [app. for earlier **bathask*, a. ON. *baðask*, in later Icel. *baðast* to bathe oneself, refl. of *baða* to bathe. (With loss of *th* cf. *or* from *other*, *sou' west*, etc.)]

†**1.** *intr.* (also *refl.*, and with pa. pple. quasi-*trans.*) To bathe, especially in warm water or liquid, and so *transf.* to be suffused with, or swim in, blood, etc. *Obs.*

1393 GOWER *Conf.* I. 290 The child lay bathend in her blood..And for the blood was hote and warme He basketh him about therinne. **1430** LYDG. *Chron. Troy* v. xxxvii, Seynge his brother baskynge in his bloud. *c* **1525** SKELTON *Replyc.* Wks. I. 209 Basked and baththed in their wylde burblyng..blode. **1530** PALSGR. 444/1, I baske, I bathe in water or any lycour, *Je baigne* (Lydgate).

2. *trans.* To expose to a flood of warmth, to suffuse with genial warmth. (Cf. *to bathe in sunshine.*) Chiefly *refl.*; = 3.

1600 SHAKS. *A.Y.L.* II. vii. 15 A foole, Who laid him downe, and bask'd him in the Sun. **1632** MILTON *Allegro*

110 The lubbar fiend.. Basks at the fire his hairy strength. **1678** WYCHERLEY *Pl.-Dealer* I. i. 3 To go.. and bask himself on the sunny side of the Globe. **1691** RAY *Creation* I. (1704) 163 Other Birds bask themselves in the Dust. **1725** POPE *Odyss.* IV. 542 The seer.. Basks on the breezy shore.. His oozy limbs.

3. *intr.* To expose oneself to, or disport oneself in, an ambient flood of genial warmth, as in the sunshine, the rays of a fire; to lie enjoying the heat which radiates upon one.

1697 DRYDEN *Virg. Georg.* III. 473 Where basking in the Sun-shine they may lye. **1718** POPE *Iliad* III. 198 Antenor.. Lean'd on the walls, and bask'd before the sun. **1819** S. ROGERS *Hum. Life* 15 Basking in the chimney's ample blaze. **1841** BORROW *Zincali* I. iv. 1. 76 The swarthy children basked naked in the sun. **1873** G. DAVIES *Mount. & Mere* xiv. 109 A large pike was basking over the weeds.

b. *fig.* of the 'sunshine' of love, favour, prosperity.

1647 COWLEY *Mistr., Change* i, Love in her Sunny eyes does basking play. **1791** BURKE *Let. Memb. Assembly* Wks. VI. 27 Basking in the sunshine of unmerited fortune. **1867** FREEMAN *Norm. Conq.* (1876) I. v. 382 Traitors basking in the royal smiles.

bask (bɑːsk, -æ-), *sb. rare.* [f. prec. vb.] **a.** A 'bath' or suffusion of genial warmth.

1790 T. WILKINSON *Memoirs* I. 239 However, that bask of sunshine did not last. **1847** STODDART *Angler's Compan.* 308 Pike.. when on the bask, or in sunning humour, distribute themselves along the margin.. of floating weeds. **1876** MRS. WHITNEY *Sights & Ins.* II. xxxvi. 654 A perfect bask of sunshine lying over it.

b. *fig.* The 'sunshine' or 'warmth' (of favour, popularity, etc.).

1762 H. WALPOLE in Vertue *Anecdotes of Painting* I. p. ix, Milton and Fontaine did not write in the bask of court-favour. **1779** —— *Let.* 16 Sept. (1904) 26 Lord Temple.. had grown up in the bask of Lord Chatham's glory.

†**bask**, *a. Obs.* or *dial.* Forms: 3 beʒʒsc, 4–5 baisk(e, 4–6 **bask**. [a. ON. *beisk* bitter, acrid; hence the etymological form is *baisk*.] Bitter, acrid, ungrateful or irritating to the senses.

c **1200** ORMIN 6698 Itt iss full bitterr & full beʒʒsc. ?*c* **1300** *MS. Cott. Faust.* B. vi. f. 123b, The froite.. is soure And baiske and bittere of odoure. *c* **1380** WYCLIF *Sel. Wks.* (1871) III. 42 Pride and coveitise.. ben bask or bittir synnes. *a* **1550** CLAPPERTON *Wa Worth Maryage*, Of boure-bourding baith bask and bair. **1808** JAMIESON s.v., 'A bask day,' a day distinguished by drought with a withering wind (*Dumfriesshire*).

†**baske**, *v. Obs.* [A variant of BASH *v.*[2], a. Da. *baske.*] To strike with a bruising blow.

1642 ROGERS *Naaman* 369 Temptations, crosses, discouragements, which many others are basked withall. *Ibid.* 443 Many things.. which buffet and baske it shrewdly.

basker ('bɑːskə(r), -æ-). One who basks.

1856 N. SENIOR *Convers. Egypt* II. 130, I think that the baskers have been about one-third.

Baskerville ('bæskəvɪl). The name of John *Baskerville* (1706–75), type-founder and printer, applied to types of his founding re-cut.

1802 C. WILMOT *Let.* 28 Nov. in T. U. Sadleir *Irish Peer* (1920) 121 Lady Mount Cashell bought a good many books from Bodini (*sic*)... His type surpasses Baskerville. **1828** E. FRY in T. B. Reed *Old Eng. Letter Foundries* (1887) xv. 310 The Baskerville and Caslon imitations.. were laid by for ever. **1887** T. B. REED *Ibid.* xv. 299 The complete series of Romans, cut after the Baskerville models. **1922** D. B. UPDIKE *Printing Types* II. xvii. 107 The slight touch of over-delicacy which the Baskerville letter possessed. **1928** R. B. MCKERROW *Introd. Bibliogr.* 302 The rather weak and grey descendants of Caslon plus Baskerville.

basket ('bɑːskɪt, -æ-), *sb.* Forms: 3– **basket**; also 4–5 baskett(e, 5 -att, -yt, 6 baszkett(e, basquette, 7 basquet. [Origin not ascertained: not in Teutonic or Romanic; found in Eng. since 13th c.

Basket has been conjecturally identified with L. *bascauda*, used by Juvenal and Martial; by the latter (xiv. 99) given as British, 'Barbara de pictis veni bascauda Britannis, Sed me jam mavult dicere Roma suam.' But the senses anciently assigned to *bascauda* of *washing tub* or *tray* 'vasa ubi calices lavabantur, cacabus,' or *brazen vessel* 'conchæ æreæ, genera vasorum' Papias (see Du Cange), do not favour this identification. The word is unknown in Old Irish or Welsh (*basgawd* is a figment invented to suggest *bascauda*), and the mod. Celtic words, Welsh *basged*, Corn. *basced*, Ir. *basceid*, Gael. *bascaid*, cannot phonetically be descended from an original *bascauda*, but seem to be simply adopted from Eng. (Prof. Rhys). At present, therefore, there is no evidence to connect *basket* with *bascauda*, or to refer it to a Celtic origin.]

A. 1. a. A vessel of wickerwork, made of plaited osiers, cane, rushes, bast, or other materials.

a **1300** W. DE BIBLESW. in Wright *Voc.* 158 *Un corbel*, a litel basket. *c* **1386** CHAUCER *Pard. Prol.* 117, I wil do no labour with myn hondes, Ne make basketis and lyve therby. **1398** TREVISA *Barth. De P.R.* IX. xvii. (1495) 357 A gardyner gaderynge grapes in a baskette. **1535** COVERDALE *2 Kings* x. 7 They.. slewe them.. and layed their heades in baszkettes. **1598** SHAKS. *Merry W.* III. iii. 137 Looke, heere is a basket.. he may creepe in heere. **1656** COWLEY *Davideis* II. (1669) 61 With gilded basquets in their hands. **1725** POPE *Odyss.* IX. 293 High in wicker-baskets heaped. **1863** STANLEY *Jew. Ch.* v. 104 His mother placed him in a small boat or basket of papyrus.

b. with sb. defining the purpose, as ***alms-basket, bread-basket, clothes-basket, eel-basket, work-basket.***

1851 KINGSLEY *Yeast* iii. 43 A high weir, with all its appendages of bucks and hatchways, and eel-baskets. **1863** MISS WHATELY *Ragged Life Egypt* vii. 50 A work-basket was stocked. **1868** H. LEE *B. Godfrey* i. 2 Everywhere.. hung.. clothes-baskets, work-baskets, toy-baskets, market-baskets.

c. taken as the type of daily provisions; also, of alms formerly in special reference to the alms-basket on which poor prisoners in the public gaols were mainly dependent for their sustenance; hence ***to go to the basket***: i.e. to prison.

1535 COVERDALE *Deut.* xxviii. 5 Blessed shal be thy baszkett, & thy stoare. **1632** MASS. & FIELD *Fatal Dowry* v. i, *Pontalier* [to Liladam, who is in custody for debt], Go to the basket, and repent. **1679** *Trials of White, etc.* 75 He was in the Marshalsey, and lived a poor mean life, and all the time fed upon the Basket. *c* **1700** *Gentl. Instruc.* (1732) 6 (D.) God be praised! I am not brought to the basket though I had rather live on charity than rapine. **1705** HICKERINGILL *Priest-Cr.* II. ii. 16 Living, as Prisoners in Ludgate, of the Basket. **1866** NEALE *Seq. & Hymns* 80 Helpless, hopeless, if Thou spare not, Of their basket and their store.

d. phrases. ***to pin the basket***: to conclude the matter (*obs.*). ***to be left in the basket***: to remain unchosen, or to the last (like the worst apples, etc.). ***the pick of the basket***: i.e. of the lot or number.

a **1659** OSBORN *Observ. Turks* Pref. (1673) 4 Steer contrary to the current of Antiquity, imagined only by idle Dunces, to have pinned the Basket. *a* **1704** T. BROWN *Sat. Fr. King* Wks. 1730 I. 61 Thus far in jest; but now to pin the basket, May'st thou to England come. **1756** W. YOUNG *Lat. Dict.* s.v. *Pin*, To pin the basket.. *concludo, conficio, finio.* **1847** BARHAM *Ingol. Leg., House-warm.* (D.) And all other suitors are 'left in the basket.' **1874** *Bell's Life* 26 Dec., The pick of the basket, a compact young greyhound.

e. In *Basketball*, the structure which forms the goal, consisting of a metal hoop from which is suspended a circular net, open at the bottom (but orig. a fruit basket: see quot. 1892); hence, a goal scored by shooting the ball through the net.

1892 J. NAISMITH in *Triangle* 15 Jan. 145 The baskets [are] hung up, one at each end... The goals are a couple of baskets.. about fifteen inches in diameter. **1893**, etc. [see HOOP *sb.*[1] 8 c]. **1907** T. H. SMITH *Basket Ball Guide* 31 He.. always succeeded in outscoring his opponent at least to the extent of two baskets to one. **1922** MATHER & MITCHELL *Basket Ball* 48 A team that carries the ball up the floor and then misses an easy basket has needlessly given the opponents a chance to control the ball. **1948** *Daily Ardmoreite* (Ardmore, Okla.) 21 Mar. 15/2 They broke through the Lions' loosening defenses for five straight baskets. **1969** *Eugene* (Oregon) *Register-Guard.* 3 Dec. D1 (*heading*) Oregon's Bill Drozdiak drives for Wichita State basket. **1975** *New Yorker* 7 Apr. 92/3 It was impossible for his man to stay with him as he came tearing towards the basket. **1985** *Cincinnati Enquirer* 18 Oct. D8/1 He takes refuge from the chaos of his home by shooting baskets in a neighbor's driveway.

f. *fig.* A group, category; a range. *spec.* in *Econ.*, an agreed range of currencies, goods, etc., whose combined values can be used as a basis for calculating an average or comparative value; *esp.* in phr. ***basket of currencies.***

1916 H. WALPOLE *Dark Forest* II. i. 211 Semyonov at this time flung Nikitin, Andrew Vasslievitch, Trenchard and myself into one basket. We were all 'crazy romantics'. **1959** *Times* 9 Mar. (Suppl. Britain's Food) p. i/4 The types of goods on sale are continually changing: so also is the way in which housewives choose to spend their money on this changing basket of available commodities. **1962** *Economist* 26 May 799/1 Might various categories of exports be grouped in comparable 'baskets'. **1973** *Times* 31 July 17/7 An agreed 'basket' of goods which will enable the purchasing powers of the various currencies.. to be.. compared. **1974** *Times* 19 Jan. 17/3 The Group of 20 agreed that for an interim period, the base of valuation for special drawing rights should be a 'basket' of currencies. **1974** *Bank of England Q. Bull.* Sept. 282 The value of the SDR was based upon the value of a group of major currencies in specified proportions. This came to be referred to as the 'standard basket'. **1977** J. PAXTON *Dict. European Econ. Community* 269 The E.U.A. is a composite basket of fixed amounts of currencies of the nine member states... To establish the value of the composite basket in any given currency.. the going market exchange rates are used. **1978** *Times* 6 Oct. 25/8 The Belgian compromise.. incorporates a weighted basket of currencies which could be used to determine if any of the currencies in the system are deviating from the norm. **1985** *Observer* 27 Jan. 19/4 One possible solution.. is to change OPEC's reference point from the marker crude to a weighted average price reflecting a basket of different qualities.

2. a. The quantity which fills a basket, a basketful; used as a measure of uncertain amount.

1631 in *Rec. Mass. Bay* (1853) I. 92 Plastowe shall (for stealing 4 basketts of corne from the Indians) returne them 8 basketts againe. **1725** BRADLEY *Fam. Dict.*, *Basket*.. of Medlars, two Bushels; Assa-fœtida, 20 to 50 lib. Weight. **1855** MACAULAY *Hist. Eng.* xvi, A basket of the first cherries.. was accepted.. by the king. **1867** F. FRANCIS *Angling* xii. (1880) 456, I killed baskets of white trout. **1908** *Westm. Gaz.* 26 Sept. 8/2 Scotland trout-fishing remains open.. and some nice baskets are being made. **1965** A. MACLEOD *Blessed above Women* vii. 80 'The fishing's pretty good here, I believe?'.. 'I've certainly been lucky in getting good baskets.'

b. Phr. ***a basket of chips***, used allusively in comparisons. Chiefly *U.S.*

1788 GROSE *Dict. Vulgar T.* (ed. 2), *Basket*.. He grins like a basket of chips; a saying of one who is on the broad grin. **1819** MOORE *Tom Crib's Mem. Congress* 25 On which the whole Populace flash'd the white grin Like a basket of chips. **1827** *Massachusetts Spy* 28 Nov. (Th.), The Yankee will say of a young lady, 'She is a real pretty girl, but she is as homely as a basket of chips.' **1892** *Congress. Rec.* Mar. 2367/1 My ticket was handed to me at once and the seller looked as pleasant as a basket of chips. **1938** *Amer. Speech* XIII. 74/1 As illustrations of the type of expression familiar to me in Ohio, I may list.. 'polite as a basket of chips'.

3. A wickerwork protection for the hand on a sword-stick, in the form of a small basket; *ellipt.* a basket-hilt sword or stick.

1773 GOLDSM. *Stoops to Conq.* IV. *Tony*, I'll fight you both, one after the other—with baskets. **1833** *Regul. Instr. Cavalry* I. 171 This exercise should.. be tried with.. sticks with baskets.

†**4.** A head-dress of wickerwork, or of basket shape. *Obs.*

1555 *Fardle Facions* II. x. 219 Their maried Women weare on their headdes, fine wickre Basquettes of a foote and a haulf long. **1606** *Choice Chance, etc.* (1881) 33 This youth in a basket, with a face of Brasse.

5. a. The overhanging back compartment on the outside of a stage-coach. *arch.*

1773 GOLDSM. *Stoops to Conq.* v. (1780) 249 It has shook me worse than the basket of a stage-coach. **1827** MACAULAY *Clergym. Trip Camb.* in *Misc.* (1865) 374 There were parsons in hood and in basket; There were parsons below and above. **1840** MARRYAT *Poor Jack* xi, Long stages, with a basket to hold six behind.

b. A *colloq.* name for a part of the auditorium of a theatre. (See quots.) *Obs.*

1812 *Dramatic Censor 1811* 99 There shall not be the nuisance called a *basket*, which is the constant rendezvous of tumult and profligacy. **1812** G. WYATT *Design for Theatre* ii. 13 The deep recess of Boxes, commonly called ' the Basket' (which has generally been permitted to extend to a great depth at the back of the circle), as well as the public Saloon.. have been entirely excluded. *Ibid.* 14 This.. does not include the deep chasm of 'the basket', which reached still farther backwards, to an extent of nearly 15 feet. **1815** L. SIMOND *Jrnl. Tour Gt. Brit.* I. 104 The pit of Covent-Garden is nearly square.. certain back boxes, called the basket, may hold one hundred and eighty people at 7s. **1831** *Examiner* 390/1 A sort of black hole (we believe called the basket at the back of the front boxes, in which all the raff of the house have place).

6. *Mil.* A gabion.

1753 CHAMBERS *Cycl. Supp.* s.v., At sieges, they make use of a small basket filled with earth, and ranged on the top of the parapet.

7. A part of the hinder leg of the bee, adapted to carry pollen.

1861 HULME *Moquin-Tandon* II. III. 208 The leg [of the Bee] is dilated, and forms a triangular cavity on its inner surface, which is known as the 'basket.'

8. The vase of a Corinthian capital, with its foliage, etc. Gwilt.

1753 in CHAMBERS *Cycl. Supp.*

9. A wickerwork or wire screen used in hat-making.

10. *Aeronaut.* A structure suspended from the envelope of a balloon to carry passengers, ballast, etc.

1783 FRANKLIN *Let.* 8 Oct. (1907) IX. 106 The Basket [of the Montgolfier balloon] contain'd a Sheep, a Duck & a Cock. **1784** *London Chron.* LVI. 219/2 The balloon being filled.. he seated himself in the basket. **1909** *Flight* 29 May 310/2 Thanks to Mr. Brewer's insisting on the envelope being immediately over the basket in the course of its swayings during the trying of the lift of the balloon, we were able to carry easily two more bags of ballast. **1910** R. FERRIS *How it Flies* i. 16 In its usual form [the balloon] is spherical, with a car or basket suspended below it.

11. Euphem. alteration of *bastard* (esp. in sense A. 1 c). *slang.*

1936 N. COWARD *Still Life* iii. 73 Come on, Johnnie—don't argue with the poor little basket. **1958** 'J. GILLESPIE' *Disobedience* i. 10 He's a nice old basket really.

B. *Comb.* and *Attrib.*

1. General relations: **a.** objective with vbl. or agent-noun or pr. pple., as ***basket-bearer, -bearing, -carrier, -maker, -making, -seller***; **b.** attrib. of material (= formed as a basket, or of basket-work), as ***basket-balcony, -bonnet, -box, -car, -carriage, -fire, -grate, -net, -trap, -ware***; **basket-bodied** *a.*, having a wicker body; **c.** attrib. of purpose (= used for baskets or basket-making), as ***basket-osier, -twine***; **d.** attrib. of origin (= carried in a basket), as ***basket-alms, -dole.***

1660 EARL ROSCOM. *Poems* (1780) 53 With *basket-alms scarce kept alive. **1866** HOWELLS *Venet. Life* xv. 223 The hideous *basket-balcony over the main door. **1530** PALSGR. 196/2 *Basketbearer, *hochqueteur.* **1831** CARLYLE *Sart. Res.* II. i, The mysterious *Basket-bearing stranger. **1903** *Daily Chron.* 19 Oct. 3/2 The wax-headed *basket-bodied lady in a draper's window. **1908** *Ibid.* 25 Aug. 7/3 The slender-wheeled basket-bodied chairs. **1824** MISS MITFORD *Village* Ser. I. (1863) 51 The pockets are almost full, and so is the *basket-bonnet. **1881** MISS YONGE *Lads & Lasses of L.* iii. 133 A porter.. with a large foreign *basket-box on his shoulders. **1922** JOYCE *Ulysses* 699 Roadster cycle with side *basketcar attached. **1962** *Times* 26 Oct. Suppl. p. xiv/4 The basket-car weigh-bridge. **1870** MISS BRIDGMAN *R. Lynne* II. viii. 161 The little *basket carriage. **1849** GROTE *Greece* II. xxx. VI. 150 One of the Kanêphoræ or *basket-carriers. **1618** HOLYDAY *Juvenal* 4 A *basket-doal at the outmost door to wait. **1932** G. BOTTOMLEY *Bower of Wandel* in *Lyric Plays* 64 (*stage direction*) An arras-hung interior is seen, lit by a *basket-fire. **1889** *Cent. Dict.* I. 468/2 *Basket grate. **1942** CARY *To be Pilgrim* xxiv. 51 Lucy's room.. still has the iron basket grate. **1603** *Patient Grissil* 6 I'll hamper somebody if I die because I am a *basket-maker. **1721** AMHERST *Terræ Fil.* x. 47 To teach the art and mystery of *basket-making.

1652 STERRY *Eng. Deliv. North. Presb.* 12 *Basket-nets laid in those Wyers, to catch Lampries. *c* **1500** *Cocke Lorelles B.* 5 Jacke *basket seler. **1866** LIVINGSTONE *Jrnl.* v. (1873) I. 123 Hunting with a dog and *basket-trap. **1833** TENNYSON *Poems* 82 Piles of flavorous fruits, in *basket-twine Of gold, up-heapèd. **1858** W. ELLIS *Vis. Madagascar* iii. 61 *Basket-ware, cooper's work.

2. Special combinations: **basket-beagle**, a small dog used to hunt a basket-hare; **basket-boat**, a boat of basket-work; in India, a circular basket of 10 or 12 ft. diameter, covered with skins; **basket-button**, a metal button with a basket-pattern on it, instead of crest or arms; **basket case** *slang* (orig. *U.S.*), (*a*) a person (esp. a soldier) who has lost all four limbs; (*b*) *transf.*, one who is emotionally or mentally unable to cope; something that is no longer functional, *esp.* a country that is unable to pay its debts or to feed its people; **basket cell**, a nerve cell having a basket-like network of fibrils; **basket chair**, one made of wickerwork, a wicker chair; **basket clause** *N. Amer.*, a clause of a general or comprehensive nature; **basket-clerk** (see quot.); **basket coil, winding** *Electr.* (see quots.); **basket-darning**, darning in which the threads cross each other above and below, like simple wickerwork; **basket dinner, lunch, picnic** *U.S.*, one for which the provisions are brought in a basket; **basket fern** *dial.* = male fern (MALE *a.* 2 b); **basket-fish**, a star-fish of the genus *Astrophyton*, with five rays divided into a number of curled filaments; **basket-hare**, one turned out of a basket to be coursed (cf. *bag-fox*); **basket-justice** (see quot.); **Basket Maker** *Archæol.*, a member of an ancient culture in south-western U.S. preceding the Pueblo culture and characterized by basket-work; also applied *attrib.* to this culture or period; **basket mat** (see MAT *sb.*[1]); **basket meal**, a meal served (as in a public house) in a small basket rather than on a plate; **basket-meeting** *U.S.* (see quots.); **basket-osier**, the *Salix Forbyana*; **basket-plant**, an orchid of the genus *Stanhopea*, often grown in baskets through which the flowers protrude; **basket-salt**, that made from salt-springs, of finer quality than ordinary salt, so called from the vessels in which the brine is evaporated; **basket-scrambler**, one who scrambles for the dole from a basket, *i.e.* who lives on charity; **basket-shell**, a bivalve mollusc, esp. of the genus *Corbula*, having valves of unequal size; **basket-stick**, a fencing-stick with a wickerwork protection for the hand; **basket-stitch** (cf. *basket-darning*); **basket-stones**, fossil fragments of the stems of *Crinoidea*; **basket sugar** (see quot.); **basket weave**, a style of weave in which the pattern resembles basket-work (Webster, 1911); a fabric woven in this pattern; **basket-woman**, one who carries goods for sale in a basket; **basket-work**, structure composed of interlaced osiers, twigs, etc., or so carved as to resemble it.

1824 SCOTT *St. Ronan's* i. 19 (D.) Grey-headed sportsmen, who had sunk from fox-hounds to *basket-beagles and coursing. **1801** WELLINGTON in Gurw. *Disp.* I. 357 Communication.. kept up by means of the common *Basket boats. **1858** BEVERIDGE *Hist. India* II. v. viii. 522 Crossing in basket-boats at Trichinopoly. **1836** DICKENS *Sk. Boz* (1877) 173 In a blue coat and bright *basket buttons. **1919** *U.S. Official Bull.* (U.S. Comm. on Public Information) 28 Mar. 1/1 The Surgeon General of the Army .. denies.. that there is any foundation for the stories that have been circulated.. of the existence of '*basket cases' in our hospitals. **1944** *Yank* 12 May 17 Maj. Gen. Norman T. Kirk, Surgeon General, says there is nothing to rumors of so-called 'basket cases'— cases of men with both legs and both arms amputated. **1967** *Saturday Rev.* (U.S.) 25 Mar. 30/3 Kwame Nkrumah should not be written off as a political basket case. **1972** *Observer* 24 Sept. 36/6 The 'hero', a legless, armless, faceless 1914–18 basket-case. **1973** *Ibid.* 15 Apr. 6/2 The real basket cases of European agriculture are the Italians and the Bavarians. **1978** S. BRILL *Teamsters* vi. 227 He was a basket case because of Spilotro. A totally broken man, crying and whimpering. **1978** M. PUZO *Fools Die* xxiv. 275 'Hunchbacks are not as good as anybody else?' I asked... 'No.. nor are people with one eye, basket cases and.. chickenshit guys.' **1982** *Newsweek* 11 Jan. 21/2 On a continent that is full of economic basket cases, the small, landlocked nation is virtually debt free. **1901** *Gray's Anat.* (ed. 15) viii. 671 [Cells] of the inner layer run for some distance horizontally.. giving off at intervals collaterals, which pass.. towards the cell-bodies of Purkinje's corpuscles, around which they become enlarged, and ramify like a basket. Hence these cells of the inner layer are named **basket-cells*. **1910** *Encycl. Brit.* IV. 395/1 The.. *basket-cells* .. have a rounded body giving off many branching dendrons. *a* **1631** DONNE *Elegies* in *Poems* (1912) I. 79 When he swolne, and pamper'd with great fare, Sits downe, and snorts, cag'd in his *basket chaire. *a* **1782** E. PARKMAN *Diary* 298, 1 great chair 3/- Six lath basket chairs 24/-. **1896** MRS. CAFFYN *Quaker Grandmother* 20 He sank into a well-cushioned basket-chair. **1883** *Congress. Rec.* Feb. 2580/1 This *basket-clause seems to be a sort of Prophetic fine-comb with us. **1897** *Ibid.* Mar. 367/2 If we strike.. [an item] from the dutiable list, we transfer it to the 'basket clause' at 25 per cent. **1968** *Globe & Mail* (Toronto) 13 Feb. B 4/6 The basket clause permits trust companies to invest up to 15 per cent of capital. **1653** MILTON *Hirelings* Wks (1851) 376 The Clergy had thir Portions given them in Baskets, and were thence call'd *sportularii*, *basket-clerks. **1923** *Daily Mail* 28 Apr. 5 Those compact multilayer coils called '*basket', 'pancake', or 'honeycomb' coils. **1960** H. CARTER *Dict. Electronics* 25 *Basket coil*, an inductor consisting of a self-supporting spiral winding, adjacent turns being disposed in criss-cross fashion to minimize self-capacitance. **1884** *Harper's Mag.* Aug. 346/2 Ordinary *basket darning. **1892** *Illinois Kentuckian* (Lexington) Dec. 88/3 (D.A.), This is a noted place for picnics where pies and cake and *basket dinners prevail. **1883** W. H. COPE *Gloss. Hampsh. Words & Phr.* 5 *Basket Fern. **1945** E. STEP *Wayside & Woodl. Ferns* (ed. 2) 76 There are several other names [for the male fern] in use locally, such as Basket-fern in Cornwall and Hampshire. **1753** CHAMBERS *Cycl. Supp.*, **Basket-fish*.. a name given by the English in North America to a very remarkable fish, sometimes caught in the seas thereabout. *a* **1698** HOWARD *Committee* IV. (D.) As if we had brought a *basket-hare to be set down and hunted. **1860** WYNTER *Curios. Civiliz.* 493 The *basket justices were so called because they allowed themselves to be bought over by presents of game. **1905** *Springfield Weekly Republ.* 11 Aug. 14 At noon a bountiful *basket lunch was served under the trees in the park. **1897** *Harper's Mag.* June 61/1 Over the head a small flat basket, and a great finely woven basket over all—such was their burial fashion... The Wetherills [i.e. R. Wetherill and brothers] soon recognized the ethnological importance of their discovery, and have provisionally named the people who buried in these older graves the '*Basket-Makers'. **1904** A. J. BURDICK *Mystic Mid-Region, Deserts of Southwest* 92 The basket-makers of that time had all the skill that is known to their descendants to-day. **1938** *Southwestern Lore* June 5 (D.A.), We now place the beginning of the Basket Maker II period as about the opening of the Christian Era and its end about 400 A.D., with the Basket Maker III period lasting up to 700 A.D. **1948** A. L. KROEBER *Anthropology* (ed. 2) xviii. 806 The Basket Maker and Pueblo cultures are continuous in character as well as in time... The.. sequence begins with Basket Maker II, stage I having been left for an as yet undiscovered culture which was inferred as earlier. **1976** *Leicester Mercury* 16 July 1/1 (Advt.), *Basket meals available every evening. **1981** R. LEWIS *Seek for Justice* v. 148 The main floor itself was packed with small tables where men and women sat, beer glasses and basket meals in front of them. **1859** BARTLETT *Dict. Amer.* (ed. 2), **Basket-meeting*, in the West, a sort of pic-nic, generally with some religious 'exercises'. **1872** SCHELE DE VERE *Americanisms* 191 A corn-husking is announced.. and the neighbors from far and near assemble, each bringing his provisions in a basket. From the latter feature these pic-nics derive their names of Basket-meetings. **1882** in G. FOREMAN *Last Trek of Indians* (1946) 198 This year witnessed a good, old-fashioned *basket picnic. **1904** *Boston Herald* 22 Aug. 6 A long political speech in the open air.. at a basket picnic meeting in Ohio. **1865** *Trans. Ill. Agric. Soc.* V, The *stanhopea sigrina* (or *basket plant) is exceedingly rare and fragrant. **1753** CHAMBERS *Cycl. Supp.* s.v., *Basket salt.. is.. made from the water of our salt springs in Cheshire. **1769** ELLIS in *Phil. Trans.* LIX. 148 Grains of salt.. about the size of the finest basket salt. **1647** R. STAPYLTON *Juvenal* 40 With fine young fencers, *basquet-scramblers, thus It pleas'd vaine Otho to distinguish us. **1713** J. PETIVER *Aquat. Anim. Amboinæ* 1/2 *Cassis rubra*.. Red *Basket-shell. **1945** E. STEP *Shell Life* IX. 150 The Basket-shells (*Corbula*), though a large genus, are represented in this country by a single species, the Common Basket-shell (*C. gibba*). *Ibid.* 151 There are.. other Basket-shells beside those of the genus *Corbula*.. the Pointed Basket-shell (*Neæra cuspidata*). *Ibid.* 152 The Short Basket-shell (*N. abbreviata*)... The Fine-ribbed Basket-shell (*N. costellata*). **1833** *Regul. Instr. Cavalry* I. 66 The files being prepared with masks and *basket-sticks. **1883** *Daily News* 12 July 3/5 Embroidered in raised gold, worked in *basket stitch on white satin. **1851** RICHARDSON *Geol.* ii. 24 Variously termed.. cheesestones, *basketstones, caskstones. **1902** *Encycl. Brit.* XXXIII. 45/1 In certain districts, notably in the Straits Settlements.. it [*sc.* syrup] is slowly boiled up in open double-bottom pans... The sugar thus produced.. forms a species of small-grained concrete. It is called '*Basket Sugar'... In the Straits Settlements the 'Basket Sugar' factories are of considerable importance. **1925** *New Yorker* 4 Apr. 22/2 His attached silk collar, which he wore plain with *basket-weave tie. **1940** *Chambers's Techn. Dict.* 80/1 *Basket weave*, woollen fabrics of hopsack or mat-weave, with a basket effect. **1960** *Times* 21 Jan. 14/4 Fabrics were interesting in texture, including basket-weave woollens. **1694** LUTTRELL *Brief Rel.* III. 403 Having gott armes, brought them the day before by *basket women. **1837** MARRYAT *Dog-Fiend* ix, The basket-women flitted about displaying their stores. **1769** FALCONER *Dict. Marine* (1789), *Dame-jeanne*, a.. large bottle.. covered with *basket-work. **1867** LADY HERBERT *Cradle L.* iv. 123 Its venerable pillars and beautiful basket-work capitals. **1910** H. M. HOBART *Dict. Electrical Engin.*, *Winding*, **Basket*, more often known as the chain type of winding.., in which the coils belonging to the three separate phases are laid out in two ranges, the centre of one coil or set of coils being occupied by the side or sides of the adjacent coil or coils on opposite sides.

basket (ˈbɑːskɪt, -æ-), *v.* [f. prec. sb.; cf. *to bag*.]

1. To put into a basket; also *fig.*

1583 STANYHURST *Æneid* I. (Arb.) 27 Maunchets sum in pantrie doe basket. **1650** FULLER *Pisgah* III. vi. 370 Christ commanded the fragments.. to be basketed up. **1785** COWPER *Task* II. 667 Basket up the family of plagues. **1867** F. FRANCIS *Angling* viii. (1880) 297 A grayling.. is scarcely so easy to basket.

2. To hang up in a basket; also *fig.*

1778 KIPPIS *Biog. Brit.* I. 240 *note*, He.. would suffer himself to be banged and basketted for refusing a challenge. **1822** T. MITCHELL *Aristoph.* II. 37, I see you're basketed so high, That you look down upon the gods.

3. To throw into the waste-paper basket; also *fig.* to reject as unsuitable.

1867 *Daily Tel.* Mar., The meeting of Opposition members had a good deal to do with its being 'basketed.' **1883** PROCTOR in *Knowledge* 6 July 13/2 Your handwriting will cause our.. sub-editor to 'basket' your communications rather summarily.

ˈbasket-ˌball. Also **basketball**. A game played indoors or out of doors with a large inflated ball, which is thrown from player to player, the object being to score by casting it into one's opponents' goal, a basket fixed ten feet above the ground at each end of the field of play.

1892 J. NAISMITH in *Triangle* (U.S.) Jan. 144 (*heading*) Basket Ball. We present to our readers a new game of ball. **1893** *Birkenhead News* 9 Dec. 7/5 Interesting Basket-Ball Match. **1898** *Daily News* 8 June 5/2 Vassar, Syracuse, Cornell, Wellesley, and Rosemary Hall have each their teams of girl basket-ball players. **1901** *Westm. Gaz.* 1 May 7/1 A game of 'basket ball', played by ten over-heated and dishevelled ladies in—bloomers! **1926** *Encycl. Brit.* New Suppl. I. 337/2 Basketball has become the national indoor game of the United States.

baskeˈteer. *nonce-wd.* A passenger in the basket of a stage-coach.

1866 *Cornh. Mag.* XIII. 346 Seldom is there wanting a sufficient quorum of grave 'basketeers.'

ˈbasketful. [see -FUL.] As much as fills a basket; also *fig.*

1574 R. SCOT *Hop Gard.* 49 Laye downe Basketfull by Basketfull till the bedde be all couered. *a* **1656** BP. HALL in Spurgeon *Treas. Dav.* Ps. xlvi. 8 Whole basketfuls of heads .. presented to Jehu. **1841** GEN. THOMPSON *Exerc.* (1842) VI. 34 We are to pay the expenses of a basketfull of disgraceful wars.

ˈbasket-ˌhilt. [f. BASKET *sb.* 3.] A hilt provided with a defence for the swordsman's hand, consisting of narrow plates of steel curved into the shape of basket.

1663 BUTLER *Hud.* I. i. 353 With basket-hilt, that would hold broth, And serve for fight and dinner both. **1708** W. KING *Cookery* (1807) 81 Their beef, they often in their murrions stew'd, And in their basket-hilts their bev'rage brew'd. **1820** SCOTT *Monast.* xiv, My father's broad-sword with its great rusty basket-hilt.

b. *attrib.* = next.

c **1550** *Rob. Hood* (Ritson) iii. 41 Then Robin got on his basket-hilt sword. **1597** SHAKS. *2 Hen. IV*, II. iv. 141 You Basket-hilt stale Iuggler, you! **1711** STEELE *Spect.* No. 109 ¶4 His Viol hangs by his Basket-hilt sword.

ˈbasket-ˌhilted, *ppl. a.* [f. prec. + -ED.[2]] Of swords: Having a basket-hilt. Of persons: Wearing a basket-hilted sword.

1600 ROWLANDS *Let. Humours Blood* v. 72 Basket hilted Sword. *a* **1659** CLEVELAND *Count. Com. Man* (1677) 99 A good Basket-hilted Yeoman. **1854** F. CATHERWOOD *Trav. Centr. Amer.* 100 Don Clementino.. swung a large basket-hilted sword through a strap in the saddle.

ˈbasketing. [cf. *matting*.] Basket-work.

1623 FAVINE *Theat. Hon.* II. xiii. 223 This same Chariot was couered with Basketting Wicker. **1830** GALT *Lawrie T.* VIII. iii. (1849) 366 The thickly interwoven basketing of the arborous vaults above us.

basketry (ˈbɑːskɪtrɪ, -æ-). [see -RY; cf. *pottery*.]

a. Basket-work, basket-ware.

1851 *Art Jrnl.* Sept. 231 Matting and basketry in all their branches. **1883** BURTON & CAMERON *Gold Coast* I. iv. 95 Basketry, and.. wicker chairs.

b. The art or craft of basket-making.

1893 K. SANBORN *Truthful Woman S. Calif.* viii. 104 The art of basketry is rapidly deteriorating [among Indians]. **1905** *Daily Chron.* 24 May 3/5 The Red Indians of America had their own particular craft of basketry. **1957** *Encycl. Brit.* III. 180/2 No satisfactory automatic basket-weaving machinery was perfected. True basketry, therefore, remains a handicraft.

basking (ˈbɑːskɪŋ, -æ-), *vbl. sb.*[1] [f. BASK *v.*] The action of exposing oneself to genial warmth. Also *attrib.*, as in *basking-hole*.

1856 KANE *Arct. Exp.* II. xiii. 134 Until the seals begin to form their basking-holes.

†**ˈbasking,** *vbl. sb.*[2] *Obs.* [f. BASKE *v.* + -ING[1].] Beating, flagellation; also *fig.*

1642 ROGERS *Naaman* 137 Full of tedious accusations, and baskings of herselfe.

ˈbasking, *ppl. a.* [f. BASK *v.* + -ING[2].]

1. That basks or suns himself.

1742 YOUNG *Nt. Th.* III. 19 Take Phœbus to yourselves, ye basking bards! **1870** MORRIS *Earthly Par.* II. III. 303 The basking pike's abode.

2. basking-shark: the largest species of shark (*Selachus maximus*), called also Sun-fish and Sail-fish, found in the Northern Seas: see quot. 1802.

1769 PENNANT *Zool.* III. 78. **1802** BINGLEY *Anim. Biog.* (1813) III. 97 The basking shark has derived its name from its propensity to lie on the surface of the water, as if to bask itself in the sun. **1860** GOSSE *Rom. Nat. Hist.* 149 The huge basking-shark of six-and-thirty feet.

Baskish, var. BASQUISH.

†**ˈbaskle.** *Obs.* [a. OF. *Basclois* 'a name given indifferently to all foreign peoples' (Roquefort) = med.L. *Basculi*, *Basculones*, brigands or raiders from Vasconia: see BASQUE.] A Basque.

1330 R. BRUNNE *Chron.* 242 Fote folk inouh of baskles & Gascouns.. þorghe mountayn & more þe baskles ȝe[de].

'Baskonize, *v. trans.* To turn into Basque.
1904 *N. & Q.* 10th Ser. I. 18/2 Castilian *voz* = voice would be baskonized by *boz*.

baslard(e, basme, obs. ff. BASELARD, BALM.

basmati (bæz'mɑːtiː, ‖'basmǝti). Also 9 **bas(s)mut(t)ee; bhasmatti**, and with capital initial. [a. Hindi *bāsmatī*, lit. 'fragrant'.] In full ***basmati rice***: a superior variety of Indian rice, characteristically light and fragrant when cooked.
1845 H. M. ELLIOT *Suppl. Gloss. Indian Terms* 46 *Basmutee*, a fragrant kind of rice and millet. **1888** W. H. DAWE *Wife's Help to Indian Cookery* xxi. 50 Rice is largely used by Europeans in India... The Bassmuttee and the Cheenee-sukur are the best qualities for table use. **1932** M. R. ANAND *Curries* 77 Take a breakfastcupful of good (Patna or Basmati) rice. **1968** *Punch* 6 Mar. 349 They could have had lobster or salami, some excellent steak, some bean sprouts, bhasmatti rice, ortaniques, coconuts, and much else. **1969** *Daily Nation* (Nairobi) 7 Nov. 3/5 Kenya ceased to import *basmati* rice a year ago and all that traders are getting now is a very small quantity of second class paddy rice. **1973** M. JAFFREY *Invitation to Indian Cooking* 230 This rice is grown in the foothills of the Himalayas... The best *basmati* is aged before it is cooked—and it is cooked only by the rich because it is also very expensive. **1986** *Cambridge* (Mass.) *Chron.* 27 Feb. 2A/3 Our waiter also brought us a generous plate of delicate Basmati (yellow) rice that nearly melted upon contact, if you can believe rice would do such a thing.

bas mitzvah, var. BAT MITZVAH.

basmutee, obs. var. BASMATI.

basnat, -et, -ette, -ite, variants of BASINET.

bason ('beɪs(ǝ)n), *sb. Hat-making.* [Origin doubtful; taken by some as a specific use of BASIN (of which *bason* was a common spelling), but evidence of this is wanting.] A bench with a plate of iron or stone flag fitted in it, and a little fire underneath, on which (before the introduction of machinery) the first part of the felting process was performed.
1727-51 CHAMBERS *Cycl.* s.v., The hatters have also *basons* for the brims of hats, usually of lead, having an aperture in the middle. **1837** WHITTOCK *Bk. Trades* (1842) 294 'Basoning' follows next in making the coarser kind of hat; the bason being a piece of cast-iron, or mixed metal, on which the felt is drawn.

'bason, *v.* [f. prec.] To harden the felt on the bason in hat-making. Hence **basoned** *ppl. a.*, **basoning** *vbl. sb.*
1727-51 CHAMBERS *Cycl.* s.v. *Hat*, The basoned hat being first dipt in the kettle. **1837** [see prec.] **1875** URE *Dict. Arts* II. 784 Till the hat is basoned or rendered tolerably firm. **1885** (A hat-maker writes) 'Basoning' is the first part of the felting process for making hats from sheep's wool or a mixture of sheep's wool and rabbit's fur.

bason, variant of BASIN.

basophil ('beɪsǝfɪl), *a.* and *sb. Biol.* Also **-phile** (-faɪl). [f. Gr. βάσι-ς BASE *sb.*[1] + φίλος loving: see -PHIL, -PHILE.] **A.** *adj.* Applied to a cell or other structure having an affinity for basic substances; that stains readily with a basic dye. **B.** *sb.* A cell, etc., of this nature. Hence **baso'philic**, **ba'sophilous** *adjs.*
1890 BILLINGS *Med. Dict.*, *Basophile*, staining well with basic aniline dyes. **1894** GOULD *Dict. Med.*, *Basophilic*.., combining readily with bases; stainable by means of basic dyes. *Basophilous*.., stained by basic rather than by acid dyes (applied to certain cells and tissue-elements). **1898** *Allbutt's Syst. Med.* V. 402 The further division of the latter [*sc.* the granular form of white blood-corpuscles] into basophil and oxyphil. **1900** DORLAND *Med. Dict.*, *Basophil*, a basophilic element. **1907** *Practitioner* Sept. 455 The nuclei of all these varieties of colourless blood corpuscles are basophil, which means that they have a strong affinity for basic aniline dyes such as methylene blue. **1908** *Ibid.* Dec. 839 The red corpuscles of those affected by lead poisoning are basophilic. **1932** FULLER & CONARD tr. *Braun-Blanquet's Plant Sociol.* xiii. 311 Those basophiles which cannot endure high concentration of salts. *Ibid.* 314 In cool, humid climates the development of vegetation becomes essentially a struggle of the acidophilous against the neutrophilous and basophilous species. **1962** *Lancet* 27 Jan. 206/2 In the early stages of the production pathway, the lymphocytes are large and possess an intensely basophilic cytoplasm. **1966** *Lancet* 31 Dec. 1457/1 Mast cells in the rabbit exist mainly in its blood as the mast leucocytes, or basophils.

basophilia (beɪsǝ'fɪlɪǝ). Also **ba'sophily**. [f. as prec.: see -IA[1].] **a.** A tendency to stain readily with a basic dye. **b.** A condition of the blood marked by the formation and accumulation of an excess of basophil cells.
1905 J. H. DRYSDALE in *Allbutt's Syst. Med.* I. I. 669 (*title*) Granular Basophilia (Degeneration) of the Red Cells. **1946** *Nature* 27 July 120/2 Normal grain showed a gradual increase in the size of the nucleolus..accompanied by a rapid decrease in the basophily of the cytoplasm. **1960** L. PICKEN *Organiz. of Cells* v. 182 A cytochemical consequence of this presence of nucleic acids is the long familiar basophilia (affinity for basic dyes) of the cytoplasm of embryonic and other actively growing cells. **1962** *Lancet* 27 Jan. 206/2 A cell with a large faintly staining nucleus and pale cytoplasm, with hardly any basophilia.

Basque (bɑːsk, -æ-), *sb.* and *a.* [a. F. *Basque*:—late L. *Vasco* an inhabitant of Vasconia, the country upon the slopes of the western Pyrenees.]
A. *sb.* [Senses 3 and 4 may have some connexion with Basque dress and habits, but may also be of distinct origin.]
1. A native of Biscay; name of the ancient race inhabiting both slopes of the western Pyrenees, adjacent to the Bay of Biscay, who speak a language of non-Aryan origin.
1835 *Penny Cycl.* III. 543/1 In the middle ages the Basques were notorious for their propensity to brigandage. **1878** *N. Amer. Rev.* CXXVI. 368 Representing the Basques as the special descendants of the ancient Iberians.
2. The language of this race, of which there are many distinct dialects and sub-dialects.
1860 *All Y. Round* No. 68. 420 The Basque and Béarnais along the Western Pyrenees. **1878** *N. Amer. Rev.* 368 He studied the Basque in order to verify these conclusions.
†**3.** A dish of minced mutton, mixed with bread-crumbs, eggs, anchovies, wine, lemon-peel, etc., and baked in the 'caul of a leg of veal.' *Obs.*
1769 MRS. RAFFALD *Eng. Housekpr.* (1778) 107 A Basque of Mutton.
4. The continuation, formerly of a doublet or waistcoat, now only of a lady's bodice, slightly below the waist, forming a kind of short skirt. Sometimes used of the bodice thus extended.
[**1611** COTGR., *Basque de pourpoint*, the skirt of a doublet.] **1860** *Rutledge* 75 Putting my hands in the pockets of my Basque. **1884** *Harper's Mag.* Oct. 788/1 A brown over-skirt and basque of an obsolete cut. **1885** *Globe* 31 Jan. 7/4 The bodice, with basques cut open in front.
B. *adj.* Of or pertaining to the Basques. ***Basque beret, cap***, a soft, close-fitting cap resembling that worn by Basque peasants.
1817 FRERE *Whistlecraft* in *Byron's Wks.* (1846) 144/2 Many a lay Asturian, or Armoric, Irish, Basque. **1835** *Penny Cycl.* III. 543/2 The Basque nation is certainly the first that settled in the Spanish peninsula. **1926** HEMINGWAY *Fiesta* (1927) xiii. 154 Brett was wearing a Basque beret. **1928** GALSWORTHY *Swan Song* II. v. 146 Everything now depended on the Basque cap. If women took to them, shingling would stay. **1941** KOESTLER *Scum of Earth* 132 He wore a strange sort of Basque beret.

basqued (bɑːskt, -æ-), *ppl. a.* [f. prec. sb. + -ED[2].] Furnished with a BASQUE (sense 4).
1870 *Daily News* 20 Dec., His long basqued waistcoat. **1885** *Globe* 31 Jan. 7/4 With basqued bodice, an under basque of velvet..is fashionable.

basqueless ('bɑːsklɪs, -æ-), *a.* [f. BASQUE *sb.* + -LESS.] Without a basque (BASQUE *sb.* 4).
1895 *Daily News* 3 Sept. 6/3 A tight-fitting coat.., basqueless in front and at the sides, but with a full one at the back. **1909** *Daily Chron.* 8 Dec. 9/2 A basqueless blouse.

basquine (bɑː'skiːn, -æ-). [a. F. *basquine*, Sp. *basquiña*, f. *basque*; see BASQUED *ppl. a.*] A rich outer petticoat worn by Basque and Spanish women.
1819 BYRON *Juan* II. cxx, While wave Around them..The basquina and the mantilla. **1873** MRS. WHITNEY *Other Girls* xv. 149 In the street they contented themselves with their plain basquines.

'Basquish, *a.* and *sb.* Also **Baskish**. [f. BASQUE + -ISH[1].] Basque (language).
1612 SHELTON *Quix.* I. i. 8 (T.) He said in bad Spanish, and worse Basquish, Get thee away. *a* **1682** SIR T. BROWNE *Tracts* 136 (T.) Their words were Basquish or Cantabrian. **1706** J. STEVENS *Sp. & Eng. Dict.* Pref., This Basquish is so different from all the other European Languages. *Ibid.*, *Arriugurriáca*, it signifies red Stones in the Basquish Language. **1904** E. S. DODGSON (*title*) A Synopsis..of..Forms of the Verb..as found in the Baskish New Testament..printed in 1571. **1918** *Trans. Scott. Eccles. Soc.* 229 They..spoke a language probably akin to the Baskish.

bas-relief, bass-relief (ˌbɑːsrɪ'liːf, -æ-, ˌbɑː-rɪ'liːf). Forms: 7–8 **basse relieve, base relief, bas-relieve**, 8–9 **bass-relief, bas-relief**. [a. F. *bas-relief*, ad. It. *basso-rilievo*, low RELIEF. Cf. BASSO-RELIEVO.]
1. Low relief; sculpture or carved work in which the figures project less than one half of their true proportions from the surface on which they are carved.
1696 PHILLIPS, *Base Relief*..emboss'd work. **1706** *Basso Relievo.* Bass or Low Relief..when the work is low, flat, or but a little raised. *a* **1711** KEN *Hymnotheo* Wks. 1721 III. 192 Upon the Frontispiece..In bas-relieve the Story was impress'd, Of Lazarus and Dives. **1755** JOHNSON, *Bass-relief.* **1843** PRESCOTT *Mexico* iv. i. (1864) 205 Two statues of that monarch..cut in bas-relief in the porphyry.
attrib. **1884** *Harper's Mag.* Feb. 350/1 The lithic forms must give place to a more bass-relief treatment.
2. *concr.* A sculpture or carving in low relief.
1667 OLDENBURG in *Phil. Trans.* II. 420 Excellent Pictures and Basse Relieves. **1762** H. WALPOLE *Vertue's Anecd. Paint.* (1786) II. 58 The basrelief..of James I. on horseback. **1858** HAWTHORNE *Fr. & It. Jrnls.* I. 196 Bas-reliefs the figures of which almost step and struggle out of the marble.

bass, basse (bæs), *sb.*[1] Forms: 5 **bace**, 6 **bas**, 6–7 **base**, 7–9 **basse**, 9 **bass**. [A phonetic corruption of BARSE, OE. *bærs*, another form of which was BASE *sb.*[5]]
1. The Common Perch (*Perca fluviatilis*), or an allied freshwater species.
[See BARSE, BASE *sb.*[5]]. *c* **1440** *Promp. Parv.* 20 Bace, fysche. **1586** COGAN *Haven Health* (1636) 164 Roch, Loch, Base, Smelt, are very wholesome fishes. **1801** GOUVR. MORRIS in Sparks *Life & Writ.* (1832) III. 140 Trout and perch, called by the Dutch name of *barsch*, or *bass.* **1866** *Intell. Observ.* No. 56. 101 Sticklebacks, perches, basses.
b. ***black bass***: a fish of the Perch family (*Perca huro*) found in Lake Huron.
1840 *Penny Cycl.* XVII. 432/1 The Black Bass.. one of best-flavoured fishes of that lake. **1881** *Harper's Mag.* Sept. 511 The much-prized black bass.
2. A voracious marine fish (*Labrax lupus*) of the Perch family, common in European seas; called also Sea-wolf and Sea-dace. Also an allied species (Sea-bass) caught on the coasts of North America.
1530 PALSGR. 196/1 Bace, fysshe, *ung bar.* **1602** CAREW *Cornwall* 106 b, Sucking Millet, swallowing Basse. **1611** COTGR., *Lubin*, a base, or sea wolfe. **1624** CAPT. SMITH *Virginia* vi. 237 There hath beene taken one thousand Bases at a draught. **1769** PENNANT *Zool.* III. 213 The basse is a strong, active, and voracious fish. **1852** KINGSLEY *Andromeda* 394 Chasing the bass and the mullet.

bass (bɑːs, -æ-), *sb.*[2] Also 7 **basse**. [phonetic corruption of BAST *sb.*[1]]
1. a. *strictly.* The inner bark of the lime or linden; sometimes applied loosely to any similar fibre, *e.g.* split rushes or straw.
1691 WORLIDGE *Cider* 54 Fit it aptly to the Stock, and bind it on with..Basse. **1769** FALCONER *Dict. Marine* (1789), *Bass*..is a sort of long straw or rushes. **1825** R. WARD *Tremaine* I. xxix. 231 A soft bit of wood..bound with bass to the stem.
b. *attrib.*, as in ***bass-mat***.
1727 BRADLEY *Fam. Dict.* s.v. *Cabbage*, Wrap..Bass-mat, etc. about the Roots. **1837** CARLYLE *Fr. Rev.* III. VII. iii. 368 Straw rope shoes and cloaks of bass-mat.
c. A fibre obtained from the leaf-bases or leaf-stalks of certain palms, used in the manufacture of brushes, ropes, etc.; also the palm from which this fibre is obtained. Also Comb.: **bass-broom** (cf. BAST *sb.*[1] 1 b).
1881 *Instr. Census Clerks* (1885) 79 Bass Broom Maker. **1883** *Cassell's Fam. Mag.* 222/1 The coarse familiar bass-brooms. **1891** *Kew Bulletin* Jan. 3 (*heading*) Extract of Minute by the Governor of Lagos on the Bass fibre of the Bamboo palm (*Raphia vinifera*). *Ibid.*, The 'African Bass' is ..a stiff and wiry fibre, varying in colour from dark brown to light red. **1895** *Army & Navy Co-op. Soc. Price List* p. xx, Bass Brooms. *Ibid.* 182 Bass Heads... Handles for Bass, each extra, 0/2. **1902** HANNAN *Textile Fibres Commerce* 145 Bass, Monkey, or Grass, Leopoldinia Piassava or Para Piassava.
2. The name given elliptically to various articles made of this or similar material; *e.g.* a mat, a hassock, a flat plaited bag or flexible basket.
1706 PHILLIPS, *Bass* or *Hassock*, a kind of Cushion made of Straw, such as are us'd to kneel upon in Churches. *Basse*, a Collar for Cart-horses, made of Straw, Sedge, Rushes, etc., whence the *Bass* for kneeling in Churches. **1837** HOWITT *Rur. Life* VI. xiii. (1862) 552 Carrying home a bass brimful of vegetables. **1861** RAMSAY *Remin.* v. 118 You hear him..wipe his feet upon the bass.
3. *Building.* 'A short trough for holding mortar, when tiling the roof; it is hung to the lath.' Nicholson *Practical Builder* 1823.

†**bass**, *sb.*[3] *Obs.* Also 5–6 **basse**, 6 **bas**. [prob. f. BASS *v.*[1]: cf. L. *bāsium*, Pr. *bais*, It. *bacio*, Sp. *beso*, kiss. The OF. equivalent **bais* is not found, and its Eng. repr. would be *beace* (cf. OF. *pais*, Eng. *peace*). Cf. also BUSS.] A kiss.
c **1450** *Crt. Love* cxiv, If the basse ben full there is delight. *a* **1529** SKELTON *My Darling dere* 9 With ba, ba, ba, and bas, bas, bas, She cheryshed hym both cheke and chyn. **1570** *Play Wit & Sc.* (1848) 13 Nay, Syr, as for basses, From hence none passes But as in grage Of mary-age.

bass (bɑːs, -æ-), *sb.*[4] [? for *bas-* or *base-coal*, as in *base coin.*] A miners' term for shale stained dark by vegetable matter. Cf. BAT *sb.*[2] 11.
1686 PLOT *Staffordsh.* 131 Bass or freestone above, and Ironston, or earth, below. **1861** E. HULL *Coal-fields Gt. Brit.* 54 Some of the shales are so highly carbonaceous as to be nearly black, and form impure coal called 'bass.'

bass (beɪs), *a.* and *sb.*[5] Forms: 5–6 **bas**, 6 **bace**, *Sc.* **bays**, 6–7 **basse**, 6–9 **base**, 7– **bass**. [ME. *bas*, *base* (see BASE *a.*) in specific senses in Music; now spelt *bass* after It. *basso*, but still pronounced as *base*. (Pope rimed *base* and *ass.*)]
A. *adj.*
†**1.** Low in sound, barely audible, soft. *Obs.*
c **1450** *Merlin* xxviii. 572 He seide in bas voice, 'I am Monewall.' **1513** DOUGLAS *Æneis* IX. vi. 28 With ane bays voce thus Nisus spak agane.
2. Deep-sounding, low in the musical scale.
1533 ELYOT *Cast. Helth* (1541) 51 Let him..begyne to synge lowder and lowder, but styl in a base voice. **1613** BP. HALL *Serm.* v. 66 The trumpets..sounded basest and dolefullest at the last. **1626** BACON *Sylva* §173 All base notes, or very treble notes, give an asper sound. **1866** TYNDALL *Glac.* II. §i. 226 Boys are chosen..to produce the shrill notes; men are chosen to produce the bass notes.

3. a. [partly attrib. use of sb.] Of, pertaining to, or suited to, the lowest part in harmonized musical composition.

bass voice: that ranging from E♭ below the bass stave to F above it. *bass clef*: the F clef, now placed on the fourth line from the bottom of the bass stave, formerly sometimes on the third, and earlier on the fifth.

1552 HULOET, Base synger, *succentor*. **1597** MORLEY *Introd. Mus.* 86 Base descant is that kinde of descanting where your sight of taking and vsing your cordes must be vnder the plainsong. **1880** in GROVE *Dict. Mus.* I. 149/1 A bass voice is too..deficient in sweetness for single songs.

b. Hence prefixed, sometimes with hyphen, to names of musical instruments or their strings, to indicate that they are of the lowest pitch. For ***bass clarinet, sax, tuba***, see the sbs.

1590 [see BASS-VIOL]. **1596** SHAKS. *1 Hen. IV*, II. iv. 6, I haue sounded the verie base string of humility. **1674** PLAYFORD *Skill Mus.* II. 112 The Bass or fourth string is called G sol re ut. **1804** W. BENTLEY *Diary* (1911) III. 68 The instrument Music..consisted of the Bass Drum, Bassoon, Clarinet & flute. **1856** tr. *Berlioz' Instrument.* 152 The sound of the bass trombone is majestic. **1863** HAWTHORNE *Old Home* I. 248 Rain-drops..pattering on the bass-drum. **1880** in GROVE *Dict. Mus.* I. 150/2 The Bass-flute requires a great deal of breath. **1884** G. W. CABLE *Dr. Sevier* II. liv. 171 The soft boom of a bass-drum.

B. *sb.* [By some erroneously taken as derived from BASE *sb.*[1], foundation, with which it has etymologically no connexion.]

1. a. The lowest part in harmonized musical composition; the deepest male voice, or lowest tones of a musical instrument, which sing or sound this part. Cf. A. 3.

?*a* **1450** *Songs & Carols* (Wright) 67 Whan..bulles of the see syng a good bace. **1535** STEWART *Cron. Scot.* I. 432 Mony trumpet into sindrie tune, Sum in bas and sum in alt abone. **1597** MORLEY *Introd. Mus.* 3 The Basse or lowest part. **165.** PEPYS *Diary* (1879) IV. 32 One of my new tunes that I have got Dr. Childe to set me a base to. **1674** PLAYFORD *Skill Mus.* I. xi. 49 The Bass for the Theorbo. **1706** A. BEDFORD *Temple Mus.* viii. 163 The Base usually closing in the Fifth above the Key. **1849** MARRYAT *Valerie* vi, The milkmaid's falsetto, and the dustman's bass.

b. *fig.*

1532 MORE *Confut. Tindale* Wks. 405/2 Hys false translacion with their farther false construccion, they thoughte shoulde be the basse and the tenour, whereuppon they woulde synge the trouble, with muche false descant. **1649** JER. TAYLOR *Gt. Exemp.* III. Add. xv. 103 The goodman knew Christ's voice to be a low base of humility. **1870** M. CONWAY *Earthw. Pilgr.* vi. 94 Above the bass of Commerce is the clear tenor of Fraternity.

2. One who sings the bass part.

1591 SPENSER *Tears of Muses* 28 The..streames..were..taught to beare A Bases part amongst their consorts. **1611** SHAKS. *Wint. T.* IV. iii. 45 Song-men..most of them Meanes and Bases. **1880** in GROVE *Dict. Mus.* I. 148/2 The employment of basses and barytons in principal characters on the operatic stage.

3. The bass string of a musical instrument.

1562 J. HEYWOOD *Prov. & Epigr.* (1867) 186 Which string in all the harpe wouldst thou styll harpe on. Not the base. *a* **1649** DRUMM. OF HAWTH. *Poems* Wks. (1711) 5/2 Sound hoarse, sad lute..Sad treble weep; and you, dull basses, show Your masters sorrow in a doleful strain. *a* **1700** DRYDEN (J.) At thy well-sharpen'd thumb..The trebles squeak for fear, the bases roar.

4. a. A BASS-VIOL.

1702 *Lond. Gaz.* No. 3819/8 For two Violins and a Bass. **1794** WOLCOTT (P. Pindar) *Rowl. for Oliver* Wks. II. 66 Watkyn..forbore his bass to seize.

b. A double-bass.

1927 *Melody Maker* Sept. 926/3 The bass, being a rhythm instrument, must conform to the rhythm set by the rhythm section. **1962** *Oxf. Mail* 22 June 5/5 The rules allow competitors to use bass and drum accompaniment.

5. ***thorough-bass*** (ellipt. *bass*): the bass part written with figures beneath it which indicate concisely but vaguely the kind of harmony to be played with it. Hence *formerly*, An accompaniment for harpsichord or organ; *now*, The theory or science of harmony. See also DOUBLE-BASS.

1674 PLAYFORD *Skill Mus.* I. xi. 36 The Thorough-bass of Songs or Ayres. **1685** EVELYN *Mem.* (1857) II. 223 She had an excellent voice, to which she played a thorough-bass on the harpsichord. **1706** in *Lond. Gaz.* No. 4249/3 With a Thorough-Bass to each Song. **1868** OUSELEY *Harmony* iii. (1875) 29 Thorough-bass-figuring..is a kind of musical short-hand.

Bass (bæs), *sb.*[6] [Proper name: see below.] Bass's ale or beer, the 'India Pale Ale' or 'Bitter Beer' manufactured by Messrs. Bass & Co. of Burton-on-Trent. Also with *a* and *pl.*, a bottle of Bass.

1849 *Illustr. Lond. News* 26 May 336 The consumption of Bass..is beyond belief. **1850** THACKERAY *Pendennis* II. v. 42 Many a day I've drunk a dozen of Bass at Calcutta. **1909** *Daily Chron.* 3 Feb. 4/6 The first signs of returning vitality given by the Prince was to ask feebly for a bottle of 'Bass'. **1953** DYLAN THOMAS *Let.* 24 Aug. (1966) 412 Oh, to bask unasked in a Bass cask.

†**bass**, *v.*[1] *Obs.*; also 5-6 **basse**. [cf. F. *baise-r*, *baisier* (11th c. in Littré):—L. *bāsiā-re* to kiss; cf. BASIATE.] *trans.* and *absol.* To kiss.

c **1500** *Bk. Mayd Emlyn* 26 One that yonge was, That coude ofte her basse. **1530** *Calisto & Mel.* in Hazl. *Dodsl.* I. 74 Thus they kiss and bass. **1562** J. HEYWOOD *Prov. & Epigr.* (1867) 57 He must nedes basse hir. **1570** in LEVINS.

bass, *v.*[2] *nonce-wd.*; in 7 **base**. [f. BASS *sb.*[5]] To utter or proclaim with bass voice or sound.

1610 SHAKS. *Temp.* III. iii. 99 The Thunder (That deepe and dreadful Organ-Pipe)..did base my Trespasse.

bass, obs. form of BASE *sb.*, *a.*, *v.*

bassa, -awe, obs. forms of BASHAW.

†**'bassade.** *Obs.* Also 5 **basset**. Shortened form of AMBASSADE. So **'bassatour**, ambassador; **'basetry**, ambassadry.

c **1400** *Sowdone Bab.* 995 He sente oute his bassatoures. **1458** *Paston Lett.* 317 I. 428 Ye Basset of Burgoyne schall come to Calleys. **1462** *Ibid.* 452 II. 104 Ther came the Quene of Skoots..in basetry to my seyd Lord of Werwek. *c* **1532** LD. BERNERS *Huon* cxxvii. 466 A bysshop of Grece who was come thether in bassade.

Bassalia (bə'seɪlɪə). *Zoogeogr.* [mod.L., f. late L. *bassus* deep, BASE *a.* + Gr. ἁλία assembly, with allusion to ἅλς sea.] The region of the deep sea. Hence **Bassalian** (bə'seɪlɪən), *a.*, of, pertaining to, or found in this region.

1884 *Science* 23 May 621/1 A special realm, which has been called 'Bassalia' or the 'Bassalian realm'. **1885** T. GILL in *Rep. Nat. Acad. Sci. Washington 1884* 6 On the Ichthyological Peculiarities of the Bassalian Realm.

bassarid ('bæsərɪd). [ad. L. *Bassarid-*, *Bassaris*, a. Gr. βασσαρίς a Thracian bacchanal, lit. a fox, prob. from their dress, made of fox-skins (βασσάρα a fox).] A Thracian bacchanal; a bacchante.

1865 SWINBURNE *Atalanta* 108 And Pan by noon and Bacchus by night,..fills with delight The Mænad and the Bassarid. **1871** —— *Songs before Sunrise* 5 Hills that hid The blood-feasts of the Bassarid. **1948** R. GRAVES *Coll. Poems* 239 Her Bassarids now bed With the ignoble usurer. **1949** E. POUND *Pisan Cantos* lxxix. 77 Shake the castagnettes of the bassarids.

bass-bar ('beɪsbɑː(r)). *Mus.* [f. BASS *sb.*[5]] An oblong piece of wood fixed lengthwise within the belly of various musical instruments of the violin type, to strengthen it against the pressure of the left foot of the bridge.

1838 *Penny Mag.* 30 June, The bar of harmony or bass-bar, was placed under the middle of the instrument. **1848** J. BISHOP tr. *Otto's Violin* iv. 30 The same difficulty in bringing out the tone arises if the bass-bar is placed too far inwards, instead of being more under the foot of the bridge.

bass-court, var. BASE-COURT.

basse, bassel: see BASS *sb.*[1], BASIL.

‖**basse danse** (bas dɑ̃ːs). Also **basse dance**. [Fr., lit. 'low dance'.] A court dance in duple or triple time which originated in France in the 15th century; = BASE-DANCE. Also *attrib.*

1789 BURNEY *Hist. Mus.* III. 263 John D'Etrée..published four books of *Danseries*... The editor of these books tells us, that they contained..*ballets, voltes, basses dances,..allemandes.* Printed at Paris, 1564. **1899** STAINER in *Musical Times* 1 July 461/2 The 'basse danse', as it was termed in French, was so named by way of contrast to the 'danse par haut' or 'danse sautée'. **1927** *Daily Tel.* 30 Aug. 10/6 There was the Basse Dance, queen of measures in the fifteenth century. **1954** GROVE *Dict. Mus.* (ed. 5) III. 821/1 Ortiz's first example is a well-known *basse-danse* tenor.

†**basselan.** *Obs.* Some kind of fabric.

1453 in Heath *Grocers' Comp.* (1869) 422 Coton, Cyprus or basselan.

bassemain, obs. variant of BAISEMAIN.

†**'bassen**, *a. Obs. rare*—[1]. In 6 **bassyn**. [? f. BASS *sb.*[2] + -EN[1].] Made of bass or bast.

1513 DOUGLAS *Æneis* II. v. (iv.) 66 About the nek knyt mony bassyn raip [L. *stuppea vincula*].

bassen'd, obs. form of BAUSONED.

bassenet, -inet, variants of BASINET.

†**'basser.** *Obs.* [f. BASS *v.*[1] + -ER[1].] A kisser.

1552 HULOET, Basser or kysser, *basiator*.

basset ('bæsɪt), *sb.*[1] [a. F. *basset* 'a terrier, or earthing beagle' (Cotgr.), orig. adj., dim. of *basse* low; see BASE *a.*] A short-legged dog used in unearthing foxes and badgers. Freq. *attrib.* in ***basset-hound***.

1616 SURFL. & MARKH. *Countr. Farm* 700 Couple vp all the old earth dogs, and after let loose the young ones, incouraging them to take the earth, and crying vnto them, Creepe into them basset, creep into them. **1883** *Illustr. Sporting & Dram. News* 23 June 371/2 The last new club is 'The Basset-hound Club', its objects being to promote the breeding of pure Basset-hounds d'Artois, rough and smooth. **1885** *Daily News* 2 May 3/5 Pictures of harriers and bassets. **1928** *Morning Post* 20 Oct. 6/1 Basset Hounds—those wholly delightful miniatures of the classic Bloodhound.

basset ('bæsɪt), *sb.*[2] Also 7-8 **bassett(e** (bə'sɛt). [(a. F. *bassette*), ad. It. *bassetta*, f. *bassetto* somewhat low, dim. of *basso* low; see BASE *a.*] An obsolete game at cards, resembling Faro, first played at Venice. Hence ***basset-table***.

1645 EVELYN *Mem.* (1857) I. 211 We went to the Chetto de San Felice, to see the noblemen..at Basset, a game at cards which is much used. **1705** VANBURGH *Confed.* I. ii, Advised her to set up a basset-table. **1716** POPE *Basset-t.* 85 Poems (1785) 16 Look upon Bassette, you who reason boast; And see if reason must not there be lost. *a* **1718** ROWE *R. Convert* Prol. 8 Not to forget Your Piquet Parties, and your dear Basset. **1849** MACAULAY *Hist. Eng.* I. 347 Gamblers playing deep at basset.

basset ('bæsɪt), *sb.*[3] *Geol.* [etymol. uncertain; ? from F. *basset* 'a low stoole' (Cotgr.); see BASSET *sb.*[1]] The edge of a geological stratum showing at the surface of the ground; an outcrop.

1686 PLOT *Staffordsh.* 131 To what points soever the rise and dip direct their course, the row, side basset or streek, lyes quite contrary. **1830** *Edin. Encycl.* III. 396 The regular basset or outcrop of the Bedford limestone.

attrib. **1791** E. DARWIN *Econ. Veg.* II. *notes*, A basset coal-mine at Woolarton in Nottinghamshire. **1851** CLARKE in *Jrnl. R. Agric. Soc.* XII. I. 264 The oolite range..presenting a lofty baset-edge to the west.

basset ('bæsɪt), *v.*[1] [f. BASSET *sb.*[2]] In phrase ***to basset away***: to play away at basset.

c **1700** *Gentl. Instruc.* (1732) 492 (D.) He had bassetted away his money and good humour.

basset ('bæsɪt), *v.*[2] *Geol.* [f. BASSET *sb.*[3]] Of strata: To crop out at the surface.

1783 WEDGEWOOD in *Phil. Trans.* LXXIII. 284, I collected some of this earth, which bassetted out..near Winster. **1843** J. PORTLOCK *Geol.* 98 The strata of the chalk basset, therefore, to the north.

‖**basse-taille** (bastɑːj). [Fr. *basse*, fem. of *bas* low (see BASE *a.*) + *taille* cut.] (See quots.)

1899 H. CUNYNGHAME *Art-Enamelling upon Metals* i. 12 Gold was also used for champlevé work... The later style of this is called 'basse-taille', and consists in carving out a subject in a thick plate of gold in low relief. **1956** G. TAYLOR *Silver* i. 17 *Bassetaille* is a rather more sophisticated form of enamelling in which the ground is decorated with engraving. **1962** *Internat. Art Treasures Exhib.* (*V. & A. Museum*) 45/2 A Louis XV gold eye-glass case..the exterior decorated in coloured 'basse taille enamels' with diamond push-piece.

basset-horn ('bæsɪthɔːn). *Mus.* [translation of F. *cor de bassette*, It. *corno di bassetto*; see BASSETTO.] A tenor clarinet, of somewhat greater compass than the ordinary clarinet.

1835 in *Penny Cycl.* **1880** in GROVE *Dict. Mus.* I. 151/1 Mendelssohn..two concert-pieces for clarinet and bassethorn.

basseting ('bæsɪtɪŋ), *vbl. sb. Geol.* [f. BASSET *v.*[2] + -ING[1].] The outcrop or cropping out of strata at the surface of the ground.

1686 PLOT *Staffordsh.* 129 This basseting, and diping of coal. **1861** W. WALLACE *Depos. Lead Ore*, A steep escarpment..is formed by the basseting of the Scar Limestone.

‖**bassette** (ba'sɛt), ‖**bassetto** (bas'setto). *Mus.* [Fr. *bassette*, ad. It. *bassetto*, dim. of *basso*; see BASE *a.*, BASS *a.*] A small bass-viol.

1847 CRAIG, *Bassette*. **1864** WEBSTER, *Bassetto*.

'bass-horn. *Mus.* [see BASS *a.* 3 b.] A modification of the bassoon, much deeper in its tones.

1859 WORCESTER cites BUCHANAN.

‖**Bassia** ('bæsɪə). *Bot.* [mod.L.; named after Fernando Bassi, an Italian botanist of last century.] A genus of tropical or subtropical trees (N.O. *Sapotaceæ*), from the seeds of which a butter-like oil is pressed. Hence **'Bassic** *a.*

1863 WATTS *Dict. Chem.* I. 519 Bassic Acid is identical in composition and properties with stearic acid. *c* **1865** LETHEBY in *Circ. Sc.* I. 95/1 The solid fats obtained from three species of *Bassia* indigenous to India.

bassil, obs. form of BASIL *sb.*[2]

bassin, -on, -yn, obs. forms of BASIN.

†**'bassinat(e.** *Sc. Obs.* [? f. *bassinet*, BASINET, helmet.] A kind of fish; ? a porpoise.

1536 BELLENDEN *Cron. Scot.* (1821) II. 179 Fische..the tane half of thame above the watter, na thing different fra the figour of man: callit, by the pepil, Bassinatis. Thir fische hes blak skinnis hingand on thair bodyis, with quhilk, sum time, thay covir thair heid. **1570** HOLINSHED *Scot. Chron.* (1806) I. 272 Fishes..called Bassinates.

bassine (bæ'siːn). [f. BASS *sb.*[2] + -INE[4].] A fibre obtained from the leaf-bases of the palmyra *Borassus flabellifer*, used in the manufacture of brooms, ropes, etc. Also *attrib.*, as ***bassine broom***.

1902 HANNAN *Textile Fibres Commerce* 149 Bassine or Palmyra Fibre. **1923** *Daily Mail* 16 June 10 Best Hair broom, bassine broom [etc.]. **1969** *Sunday Mail* (Brisbane) 26 Jan. 25 Bassine yard broom.

bassinet. Also 9 **bassinett(e**. [a. F. *bassinet*, diminutive of *bassin* BASIN; see BASINET.]

1. ('bæsɪnɪt.) Variant of BASINET.

†**2.** *Herb.* Name given to species of Ranunculus and Geranium, and to the Marsh Marigold. *Obs.*

1578 LYTE *Dodoens* 32 The Braue Bassinet, or Marshe Marigolde. *Ibid.* 47 Bassinet Geranium or Crowfoote. **1629** PARKINSON *Parad.* (1656) 230 Some [Geraniums] are called in many places of England Bassinets. **1727** BRADLEY *Fam. Dict.* s.v. *Bassinets*, The yellow Bassinet grows usually upon a small Stalk.

3. (ˌbæsɪˈnɛt.) An oblong wickerwork basket, with a hood over one end, used as a cradle for babies. *Also*, a form of child's perambulator of the same shape.

1854 THACKERAY *Newcomes* II. 122 The cradle or what I believe is called the bassinet of Master Pendennis. **1862** *Macm. Mag.* July 258 A row of bassinetts..indicated possibilities of sleep. *a* **1878** P'CESS ALICE *Mem.* 85 Victoria sleeps in the bassinet, which is done up with chintz.

attrib. **1883** *Daily News* 18 Sept. 8/3 Very handsome Bassinette Perambulator..fitted with..brass-jointed hood.

†**ˈbassing**, *vbl. sb.* [f. BASS *v.*[1]] Kissing.

1552 HULOET, Bassynge, *basiatio.* **1562** J. HEYWOOD *Prov. & Epigr.* (1867) 65 Our lord blys me From bassyng of beastes.

bassist (ˈbeɪsɪst). [See -IST.] **1.** = BASS *sb.*[5] 2.

1870 WESSELY *Germ. Dict.*, *Bass-sänger*, bassist. **1883** *Pall Mall G.* 28 Nov. 4/1 One swears he is the prince of double-bassists, the other that he can sing like Sims Reeves.

2. One who plays a bass instrument, spec. a double-bass (see BASS *sb.*[5] 4 b).

1909 in *Cent. Dict.* Suppl. **1955** *Jazzbook 1955* 15 Within the ranks of this band he met up with tenor saxist Chu Berry, trombonist Tyree Glenn, bassist Milton Hinton. **1956** S. TRAILL *Play that Music* 13 He..was offered the part of principal bassist to the Los Angeles Symphony Orchestra.

bassman (ˈbeɪsmæn). orig. *U.S.* [f. BASS *sb.*[5] + MAN *sb.*[1]] One who plays the double-bass.

1952 B. ULANOV *Hist. Jazz in Amer.* (1958) xix. 241 The best bassman jazz has ever known. **1958** K. GOODWIN in P. Gammond *Decca Bk. of Jazz* xiii. 154 One of the most important bassmen..is Monty Budwig.

bassmuttee, obs. var. BASMATI.

bassness (ˈbeɪsnɪs). [f. BASS *a.* + -NESS.] Bass quality or depth (of sounds).

1880 LANIER *Sci. Eng. Verse* i. 28 The pitch of sounds, i.e. their bassness or trebleness.

‖**basso** (ˈbasso), *a.* and *sb. Mus.* [It.:—late L. *bassus*: see BASE *a.*] = BASS *a.* 3, *sb.*[5] 1, 2.

1817 BYRON *Beppo* xxxii, Soprano, basso, even the contra-alto, Wish'd him five fathom under the Rialto. **1883** *Harper's Mag.* Mar. 554/1 The minor basso part..was given to Kindermann.

Hence, **basso-buffo** (-ˈbuffo) [It., = comic bass], a bass singer who plays the comic part in opera; **basso cantante** (-kanˈtante) [It., lit. 'singing bass'], a male voice of fine quality and power of expression in the upper register of the bass range; also, a singer having such a voice; **basso continuo**, thorough-bass (see BASS *sb.*[5] 5); **basso ostinato** (-ostiˈnato) [It., lit. ' persistent bass'], a musical structure in which a figure is repeated successively throughout a work, with or without variation, usually in the bass part; ground-bass (cf. GROUND *sb.* 6 c, 18 a); also *transf.*; **basso-ripieno** (cf. *alto-ripieno*), a bass part used only occasionally in a grand chorus.

1909 in *Cent. Dict.* Suppl., Basso-buffo. **1960** *Times* 15 July 16/3 Mr. Forbes Robinson..may seem an unlikely *basso buffo.* **1876** STAINER & BARRETT *Dict. Mus. Terms* 52/1 Basso cantante. **1889** G. B. SHAW in *Star* 11 Oct. 2/3 He was by no means the deep, powerful *basso cantante* his brother Edouard now is. **1916** —— in *Nation* 6 May 158/1 A good rough *basso cantante.* **1963** *Times* 28 Feb. 16/2 Voice that seemed most like a *basso cantante.* **1876** STAINER & BARRETT *Dict. Mus. Terms* 211/1 The connecting link between one form of the falso-bordone and the basso ostinato. **1935** A. GALSWORTHY in J. Galsworthy *End of Chapter* Foreward p. v, This is not by any means the whole of the plan, or story, but is a sort of *basso ostinato* to it.

bassock. App. by confusion for HASSOCK.

1706 PHILLIPS and **1708** KERSEY have 'Bass or Hassock' [see BASS *sb.*[2] 2]. **1721** BAILEY brackets *Bass* and *Hassock.* **1736** BAILEY, and following edd., bracket *Bass* and *Bassock.*

bassoon (bəˈsuːn). *Mus.* [ad. F. *basson*, augmentative f. *bas, basse* BASS *sb.*[5]; or perhaps *bas son* deep sound (Littré).]

1. A wooden double-reed instrument, with a compass of about three octaves, used as a bass to the oboe, having a pipe eight feet in length, so arranged in parts (whence the Italian name *fagotto*) that the whole instrument measures only four feet.

1727–51 CHAMBERS *Cycl.* s.v., A good bassoon is said to be worth four or five hundred pistoles. **1778** JOHNSON in *Boswell* III. 39 In a different language it [poetry] may be the same tune, but it has not the same tone. Homer plays it on a bassoon; Pope on a flagelet. **1798** COLERIDGE *Anc. Mar.* I. viii, The wedding-guest here beat his breast, For he heard the loud bassoon. **1855** O. W. HOLMES *Poems* 148 As if a broken fife should strive To drown a cracked bassoon. **1880** in GROVE *Dict. Mus.* I. 152/1 Handel's scores contain few bassoon parts.

2. a. An organ-stop of a quality of tone similar to that of the bassoon. **b.** A series of reeds of similar tone in a harmonium, etc.

bassoonist (bəˈsuːnɪst). [f. prec. + -IST.] A performer on the bassoon.

1865 *Spohr's Autobiog.* I. 67, I received assistance from.. the Basso[o]nist Barnbeck.

‖**basso-profondo**, usually **-profundo** (ˈbassoproˈfondo). *Mus.* [It., = deep bass.] A deep bass voice, having a compass of about two octaves above the D below the bass stave; also, a singer having a voice of this compass. Also *attrib.*

1860 THACKERAY *Round. Papers* (1863) 34 Why not a singing artist? Why not a basso-profondo? **1909** *Daily Chron.* 19 Jan. 4/4 The basso-profondo thunderer of the church choir. **1924** *N. & Q.* 22 Mar. 221/1, I heard a song sung by a *basso profundo*, once a professional. **1965** G. MCINNES *Road to Gundagai* xi. 195, I..had to be.. prompted..in the basso profundo of an over zealous Latin teacher.

‖**ˈbasso-reliˈevo, riliˈevo.** Pl. -os. Also 8 basse-, bas-relievo. [ad. It. *basso-rilievo* (ˈbasso riˈljevo) low relief.] = BAS-RELIEF, q.v.

a **1666** EVELYN *Diary* 19 Nov. an. 1644 (1955) II. 259 A deepe basso-relievo, a l'antique. **1676** F. VERNON in *Phil. Trans.* I. 578 About the Cornice..is a basso relievo of men on horseback. **1780** SIR J. REYNOLDS *Disc.* x. (1842) 179 A single group in basso-relievo. *Ibid.* (1876) 17 In bas-relievos it is totally different. **1850** MRS. JAMESON *Leg. Monast. Ord.* (1863) 282 The fine series of basso-relievos on the walls of the chapel. **1930** R. CAMPBELL *Poems* 15 We know the veld ..This basso-relievo of a land. **1960** R. LISTER *Decorative Cast Ironwork Gt. Brit.* iv. 83 Giving some firebacks the appearance of borders from title pages translated into basso-relievo.

bassorin (ˈbæsərɪn). [f. *Bassor-a* gum + -IN.] An inodorous, colourless, translucent substance, found in Bassora and other gums, insoluble but swelling to a gelatinous state in water.

1830 LINDLEY *Nat. Syst. Bot.* 265 The nutritive substance called Salep..consists almost entirely of a chemical principle called Bassorin.

bass-relief: variant spelling of BAS-RELIEF.

‖**ˈbassus.** *Obs.* [L. *bassus* low.] = BASS *sb.*[5]

1598 SYLVESTER *Du Bartas* (1608) 73 Lift me above Parnassus, With your loud Trebbles help my lowly bassus.

bass-viol (beɪsˈvaɪəl). [see BASS *a.* 3 b and VIOL.] A stringed instrument for playing the bass part in concerted music; a violoncello.

1590 SHAKS. *Com. Err.* IV. iii. 23 Went like a Base-Viole in a case of leather. **1638** J. KIRKE *Sev. Champions* III. i, The resined stick of a base viol. **1709** ADDISON *Tatler* No. 153 ¶7 Your Bass-Viol, which grumbles in the Bottom of the Consort. **1861** HUGHES *Tom Brown Oxf.* II. ii. 29 Carrying a great bass-viol bigger than himself.

bass-wood (ˈbɑːswʊd, -æ-). [f. BASS *sb.*[2] + WOOD.] The American Lime or Linden (*Tilia americana*); the wood of this tree. Also *attrib.*

1670 *Rowley Rec.* (1894) 210 The Northwest Angle is a basswood tree. **1728** *Rec. Early Hist. Boston* 25 June (1883) VIII. 222 We are of Opinion That no..Black ash, Basswood, or Ceder Shall be Corded up. **1824** W. IRVING *Braceb. Hall* II. 271 A man is never a man till he can..sleep under a tree and live on bass-wood leaves. **1855** LONGF. *Hiaw.* x. 153 Gave them drink in bowls of bass-wood.

bast (bɑːst, -æ-), *sb.*[1] Also 6–7 baste. [Common Teut.: OE. *bæst* is cogn. with MHG., mod.G., MDu., Du. *bast* (masc.), Goth. **bastus* not found, also ON., Da., Sw. *bast* (neuter), all in same sense. Ulterior deriv. unknown: not related to *bind* (Kluge). See also the corrupted form BASS *sb.*[2]]

1. a. The inner bark of the lime or linden, which, cut into strips and coarsely plaited, is sold as 'Russia matting'; also applied generally to flexible fibrous barks, and other similar materials (cf. BASS *sb.*[2]), and in *Physiological Botany* to all fibres of the same cellular structure.

a **800** *Corpus Gl.* (Sweet *O.E.T.* 101), *Tilio*, baest. [*c* **1000** ÆLFRIC *Judg.* xiii. 15 Hiȝ ða hine ȝebundon mid twám bæstenum rápum.] *c* **1400** *Destr. Troy* XI. 4773 Till all was bare as a bast. **1523** FITZHERB. *Husb.* §136 Bastes or pyllynge of wythy or elme. **1599** HAKLUYT *Voy.* II. 178 Ropes of bast. **1693** W. ROBERTSON *Phraseol. Gen.* 213 Baste or the bark of twigs, *spartum.* **1872** *Q. Rev.* CXXXII. 221 They make paper of the fine white bast or skin which lies between the wood and the bark. **1881** BLACKMORE *Christowell* iii, With ..a trail of bast around her neck.

b. *attrib.*, as in **bast-broom** (cf. BASS *sb.*[2] 1 c), **-cell, -fibre, -mat, -tree.**

c **1425** in Wülcker *Voc.* /647, *Tilia*, baste-tre. **1577** HARRISON *Descr. Brit.* iii, They bind the planks togither verie artificiallie with bast ropes. **1660** *Act 12 Chas. II.* iv. Sched., Bast or straw-hats knotted. **1837** CARLYLE *Fr. Rev.* (1872) III. v. vi. 201 They skewer a bast mat round their shoulders. **1867** *Ure's Dict. Arts* (ed. 6) I. 282 *Bass* or *Bast.* .. The name is also used for the bark or tough fibres of the flax and hemp plants of which Bast brooms are made. **1877** *Design & Work* 11 Aug. 235/2, I have been making some bast brooms. **1880** GRAY *Bot. Text-bk.* 398 Bast-cells..give to the kinds of inner bark that largely contain them their strength and toughness.

2. A rope, mat, etc. made of bast; cf. BASS *sb.*[2]

?*c* **1450** *MS. Lincoln* A i. 17 f. 127 (Halliw.) Ȝe salle take a stalworthe baste, And bynde my handes byhynd me faste.

†**bast**, *sb.*[2] and *a. Obs.* Also 5 baste, baaste. [a. OF. *bast* (mod. *bât* = Pr. *bast*, med.L. *bastum*) pack-saddle (used as a bed by muleteers in the inns), in phr. *fils* (*homme*, etc.) *de bast*, lit. 'pack-saddle child,' as opposed to a child of the marriage-bed; thus forming a tersely allusive epithet for illegitimate offspring; cf. BASTARD, BANTLING.]

A. *sb.* Bastardy. (In phr.: *on, in, a, o, of bast.*)

1297 R. GLOUC. 516 Gentil man was inou, thei he were a bast ibore. *c* **1330** *Arth. & Merl.* 7643, Bast Ywain he was y-hote, For he was bigeten o bast. *c* **1430** LYDG. *Bochas* III. xxvi. (1554) 97 b, Hys brethren in bast an hundred and fiftene. *c* **1440** *Promp. Parv.* 26 Baaste, not wedlocke, *bastardia.* **1494** FABYAN VI. ccii. 212 Arnolde, Sone of bast of Lothayr.

B. *adj.* [the sb. used *attrib.*: *bast son* = son of bast. *fils de bast.*] Bastard, illegitimate.

c **1330** [see prec.] **1387** TREVISA *Higden* Rolls Ser. VII. 27 Þe erle his bast sone. **1494** FABYAN VII. ccxix. 240 Willyam duke of Normandye.. bast sone of Robert. **1572** *Scholehouse Wom.* 324 in Hazl. *E.P.P.* IV. 117 The childe I warrant shalbe bast.

†**bast**, *sb.*[3] *Obs.* Erroneous form of BASS *sb.*[1], a kind of fish [due to use of *bass* for *bast* in other words.]

1709 T. ROBINSON *Nat. Hist. Westmld.*, The fish bred in Bassenthwait water are basts. **1759** *MS. at Urswick*, Perch or basts brought from Dalton Tarn.

bast, *sb.*[4] [Persian.] Sanctuary, refuge, asylum. So **ˈbasti**, a refugee.

1856 M. L. SHEIL *Glimpses Life & Manners in Persia* x. 165 An extraordinary device adopted by the moollas..for restoring the right of bast, or sanctuary, to its ancient vigour. **1894** SAFAR NAMEH *Persian Pict.* 32 Across the gateways a chain is drawn, denoting that the garden is Bast—sanctuary —and into these the European may not go. **1923** *Blackw. Mag.* Jan. 49/1 In Persia the system of 'bast', or asylum, was the only means whereby the oppressed could do something to right..his grievances. *Ibid.* 49/2 The refusal of bast to any one with a legitimate grievance would be an affront to public opinion. *Ibid.* 56/1 The Bastis had not come to the Consulate by my invitation.

bast, obs. form of BOAST.

‖**basta** (ˈbasta). *int. Obs.* [a. It. (also Sp.) *basta* enough.] Enough! no more! no matter!

1596 SHAKS. *Tam. Shr.* I. i. 203 Basta, content thee: for I haue it full. **1632** BROME *Crt. Beggar* IV. i, And for thy meanes (basta) let me alone. **1819** SCOTT *Ivanhoe* II. iii. 40 If he will not consent—basta—I can but go away home.

bastailye, obs. form of BASTILLE.

bastan(n)ado, obs. form of BASTINADO.

†**ˈbastant**, *a. Obs.* [a. F. *bastant*, It., Sp. *bastante*, pr. pple. of *bastare* to suffice; see prec. and -ANT.] Sufficient, able, capable.

1637 MONRO *Exped.* v. i. 80 (JAM.) His Majestie..not being bastant to resist the enemy, retired. **1652** URQUHART *Jewel* Wks. (1834) 194 Each language borrows from another ..nor is the perfectest..without being beholden to another, in all things enuncible, bastant to afford instruction.

bastard (ˈbɑːstəd, -æ-), *sb.* and *a.* Also 5–6 bastarde, (7 basterˈd). [a. OF. *bastard*, mod. *bâtard* (= Pr. *bastard*, It., Sp., Pg. *bastardo*) = *fils de bast*, 'pack-saddle child,' f. *bast* (see BAST *sb.*[2]) + the pejorative suffix -ARD. Cf. BANTLING.]

A. *sb.*

1. a. One begotten and born out of wedlock; an illegitimate or natural child.

By the civil and canon laws, a child born out of wedlock is legitimated by the subsequent marriage of his parents; but by the law of England, retained in some of the United States, a child to be legitimate must at least be born after the marriage of the parents. ***bastard eigne*** or ***elder***: the bastard son of a man who afterwards marries the mother, and has a legitimate son; the latter is called in legal phrase *mulier puisne* or *younger.*

1297 R. GLOUC. 295 Of þulke blode Wyllam bastard com. **1362** LANGL. *P. Pl.* A. VIII. 76 Bringeþ forþ Barnes þat Bastardes beon holden. *c* **1450** *Merlin* vii. 112 Thei wolde neuer haue no bastarde to theire kynge. **1528** PERKINS *Prof. Bk.* i. §49 A bastard eigne who is mulier in the spirituall law. **1601** SHAKS. *All's Well* II. iii. 100 Sure they are bastards to the English, the French nere got em. **1662** FULLER *Worthies* I. 322 He confuted their Etymology who deduced *Bastard* from the Dutch words *boes* and *art*, that is an abject Nature, and verifyed their deduction deriving it from *besteaerd*, that is the best disposition. **1764** BURN *Just. Peace* s.v., The word *bastard* seemeth to have been brought unto us by the Saxons; and to be compounded of *base*, vile or ignoble, and *start*, or *steort* signifying a rise or original. **1868** FREEMAN *Norm. Conq.* II. viii. 210 Spiritual preferments..for cadets or bastards of the royal house.

b. Also **bastaard.** [Afrikaans *bastaard* (now *baster*).] A person of mixed breed; a Griqua. *S. Afr.*

1790 E. HELME tr. *Le Vaillant's Travels into Africa* II. viii. 163, I mean to speak of the natural children which have sprung from an intercourse of the Whites with the female Hottentots, or between these same women and the negroes. They are commonly known at the Cape under the appellation of Bastards. **1806** J. BARROW *Voy. to Cochinchina* 377 They came..to a second horde of Bastaards and Bosjesmans. **1814** W. BROWN *Hist. Propag. Christianity* II. ix. 425 The term *Bastard* applied to a Hottentot, does not mean that he is illegitimate, but merely that he is of mixed breed. **1866** J. LEYLAND *Adv. Far Interior S. Afr.* ii. 32 The Griquas or Bastards. **1900** A. H. KEANE *Boer States* vi. 85 Many are in fact 'Bastaards', that is to say, Hottentot-Dutch half breeds.

c. Used vulgarly as a term of abuse for a man or boy, and, with weakened force, as the equivalent of 'fellow', 'chap'; also trivially for 'thing', esp. something bad or annoying.

1830 SCATCHERD *Hist. Morley* 339 *Bastard*, a term of reproach for a mischievous or worthless boy. **1833** C. LAMB *Let.* 27 Apr. (1935) III. 367 We have had a sick child, who sleeping, or not sleeping, next me with a pasteboard partition between, killed my sleep. The little bastard is gone. **1917** J. MASEFIELD *Old Front Line* iv. 58 For all their bloody talk the bastards couldn't bring it down. **1919** H. CRANE *Let.* 22 Nov. (1965) 24 —— is a poor ignorant bastard of some kind. **1927** T. WOLFE *Lett.* (1956) 118 Joe, you old bastard, how the hell are you! **1931** R. ALDINGTON *Colonel's Daughter* i. 56 The smug bastards who declare that all is for the best in this best of all possible worlds. **1936** J. CURTIS *Gilt Kid* ii. 18 What's Wandsworth like? Proper bastard, I suppose. **1937** J. A. LEE *Civilian into Soldier* i. 29 'He's a bastard.' Guy used the term not for its dictionary meaning, but because among New Zealanders no term expressed greater contempt. **1938** J. MASEFIELD *Dead Ned* 233 It's a bastard being in quad with no blunt. **1940** H. G. WELLS *Babes in Darkling Wood* I. iv. 104 Serve the cocky little bastard right. **1942** T. RATTIGAN *Flare Path* III. 164 Johnny, you old bastard! Are you all right? **1960** *Observer* 18 Dec. 10/3 Australians pride themselves on their imperviousness to excitement. The phrase 'she's a bastard' is usually regarded as adequate for most dramas from four-year droughts to bush fires. **1961** J. MACLAREN-ROSS *Doomsday Book* II. i. 108 This bastard of a bump on the back of my head. **1968** K. WEATHERLY *Roo Shooter* 23 'You're not a bad bastard, Hunter,' he said, 'in spite of your lousy cooking.'

2. *fig.*

1583 FULKE *Defence* iv, He pronounceth the Epistle of James..to be a bastard. **1642** FULLER *Holy & Prof. St.* III. xxiii. 215 Fame being a bastard or *filia populi*, 'tis very hard to find her father. **1785** BURKE *Nab. Arcots' Debts* Wks. IV. 319 Six great chopping bastards [Reports of Committee of Secrecy], each as lusty as an infant Hercules.

3. a. A mongrel, an animal of inferior breed. ? *Obs.*

1601 HOLLAND *Pliny* I. 191 The lesser sort of [elephants], which they call Bastards. **1602** *Ret. fr. Parnass.* II. v. 30 Small Ladies puppies, Caches and Bastards.

†**4.** A sweet kind of Spanish wine, resembling muscadel in flavour; sometimes applied to any kind of sweetened wine. *Obs.* exc. *Hist.* (See B. 7.)

1399 [ROGERS *Agric. & Prices* (1866) I. xxv. 619 The fellows of Merton purchase..some bastard in 1399.] *c* **1460** J. RUSSELL *Bk. Nurture* in *Babees Bk.* 125 The namys of swete wynes y wold þat ye them knewe..Bastard, Tyre, Oȝey, etc. *a* **1536** TINDALE *Exp. Matt.* Wks. II. 97 With basta[r]do, muscadell, and ipocrass. **1596** SHAKS. *1 Hen. IV*, II. iv. 30 Anon, Anon sir, Score a Pint of Bastard in the Halfe Moone. **1616** SURFL. & MARKH. *Countr. Farm* 642 Bastards..seeme to me to be so called, because they are oftentimes adulterated and falsified with honey. **1631** HEYWOOD *Maid of West* III. Wks. 1874 II. 301 Ile furnish you with bastard white or brown. **1869** BLACKMORE *Lorna D.* xiv. 85 He..called for a little mulled bastard.

†**5.** A kind of cloth, ? of inferior or mixed quality, or unusual make or size. *Obs.*

1483 *Act 1 Rich. III*, viii. §18 Woollen Cloths called Bastards. **1523** *Act 14–15 Hen. VIII*, i, White brode wollen clothes with Crumpil listes, other wise called bastardes.

†**6.** A kind of war-vessel, a variety of galley.

1506 GUYLFORD *Pylgr.* 7 An .c. galyes, grete bastardes and sotell. **1599** HAKLUYT *Voy.* II. I. 78 Gallies, as well bastards as subtill mahonnets.

†**7.** A species of cannon, also called *bastard culverin*. Cf. BASTARD *a.* 6. *Obs.*

[**1549** *Compl. Scotl.* vi. 41 (1872) Mak reddy ȝour cannons, culuerene moyens, culuerene bastardis, falcons, saikyrs.] **1670** COTTON *Espernon* I. IV. 149 Thirty brass Pieces, of which fourteen were Royal Culverines, or Bastards. **1753** CHAMBERS *Cycl. Supp.* s.v., The long bastards..are either common or uncommon. To the common kind belong the double culverin extraordinary, etc.

8. A large sail used in the Mediterranean when there is little wind. (So F. *bâtard.*)

1753 in CHAMBERS *Cycl. Supp.* **1867** SMYTH *Sailor's Word-bk.*, *Bastard*, a fair-weather square sail..occasionally used for an awning.

9. A particular size of paper. ? *Obs.*

1712 *Act 10 Anne* in *Lond. Gaz.* No. 5018/3 Paper called .. bastard or double Copy. **1774** BURKE *Amer. Tax.* Wks. II. 374 The duties on..blue royal, or bastard, or fool's-cap.

10. *Sugar-refining.* **a.** An impure coarse brown sugar, made from the refuse syrup of previous boilings. **b.** A large mould into which sugar is drained. (So F. *bâtard.*)

1859 in WORCESTER. **1864** in WEBSTER.

11. = BASTARDA.

1928 S. MORISON *German Incunabula in Brit. Mus.* 10 The Bastards are scripts answering to the need for a speedy letter appropriate for the copying of books or documents of minor value or importance. *Ibid.* The Bastard of the 36-line Indulgence.

12. *Comb.*, as *bastard-bearing*, *-bellied*, *-like*.

1594 T. B. *La Primaud. Fr. Acad.* II. 423 Whereby the warlike vertues..of their subjects become degenerate and bastardlike. **1633** FORD *'Tis Pity* IV. iii. (1839) 40 Thy corrupted bastard-bearing womb! **1640** BROME *Sparag. Gard.* IV. iv. 183 Though she prov'd bastard-bellyed, I will owne her.

B. *adj.* [At first not separable from the sb.: so in Fr.]

1. Born out of wedlock, illegitimate.

1297 R. GLOUC. 412 He was Wyllammes sone bastard. *c* **1386** CHAUCER *Monkes T.* 388 Thy bastard brother made the to fle. **1597** SHAKS. *2 Hen. IV*, II. iv. 307 Ha? a Bastard Sonne of the Kings? **1729** SWIFT *Wks.* (1841) II. 100 That horrid practice of women murdering their bastard children. **1844** LD. BROUGHAM *Brit. Const.* xiv. (1862) 202 The marriage..void, and the issue counterfeit or bastard.

2. a. Mongrel, hybrid, of inferior breed. ? *Obs.*

1398 TREVISA *Barth. De P.R.* XVIII. lxxxiii. (1495) 834 The perde..gendreth wyth the lyennesse: of that bastarde generacion comith leopardus. **1607** TOPSELL *Four-f. Beasts* 161 Their lesser Elephants (which they call bastard Elephants). **1641** HINDE *J. Bruen* vii. 27 To beget and bring forth mules, a bastard brood.

b. In South Africa: of or pertaining to a person of mixed breed. Cf. sense A. 1 b above.

1792 E. RIOU tr. *Van Reenen's Jrnl. Journey from Cape of Good Hope* 28 A village of *bastaard* Christians, who were descended from people shipwrecked on that coast... The Cape people..call all those Hottentots, bastaard Hottentots, whose race has been intermixed with the slaves brought from the East Indies, [etc.].

3. a. *fig.* Illegitimate, unrecognized, unauthorized.

1558 KNOX *First Blast* (Arb.) 48 Who soeuer receiueth of a woman, office or authoritie, are adulterous and bastard officers before God. **1622** BACON *Hen. VII*, 66 Usurie..is the Bastard use of Money. **1711** SHAFTESB. *Charac.* (1737) III. 67 After speaking of prophetical enthusiasm, and establishing..a legitimate and a bastard-sort. **1843** GLADSTONE *Gleanings* V. i. 38 The bastard sense..strives to eject what he firmly holds to be legitimate.

b. *bastard branch* or *slip*: a shoot or sucker springing of its own accord from the root of a tree, or where not wanted. Often *fig.* = BASTARD *sb.*

1398 TREVISA *Barth. De P.R.* XVII. clxxix. (1495) 720 Vitulamen is that bastarde plante other braunche..that spryngeth oute of the rote of the vyne or elles where in the vyne . and not out of the knottes. *c* **1525** MORE *Wks.* (1557) 60/2 Bastard slippes shal neuer take depe roote. **1622** BACON *Hen. VII*, 86 The Kingdome of Naples, beeing now in the possession of a Bastardslip of Arragon. **1768** BLACKSTONE *Comm.* IV. 409 From this root has sprung a bastard slip, known by the name of the game law. **1852** TUPPER *Proverb. Philos.* 293 Grey-headed men, the bastard slips of science, Go for light to glow-worms.

4. *fig.* Not genuine; counterfeit, spurious; debased, adulterated, corrupt.

1552 HULOET, Bastarde hande, letter, or wrytynge, *Litera adulterina.* **1635** QUARLES *Emblems* II. v. (1718) 83 With thy bastard bullion thou hast barter'd for wares of price. *a* **1639** W. WHATELEY *Prototypes* I. xix. (1640) 194 Favourable dealing with a man..for a faire sister, or kinswomans sake, is a kinde of bastard curtesie. **1796** MORSE *Amer. Geog.* II. 314 The Swisses speak a bastard French. **1826** DISRAELI *Viv. Grey* II. iv. 36 That bastard, but picturesque style of architecture, called the Italian Gothic.

5. Having the appearance of, somewhat resembling; an inferior or less proper kind of; esp. in scientific nomenclature applied to things resembling, but not identical with, the species which legitimately bear the name. **a.** *generally.*

1530 PALSGR. 196/2 Bastarde floure, *folle farine.* **1601** HOLLAND *Pliny* I. 99 Foure more [mouths of the Nile], which they themselues call bastard mouthes. **1670** H. STUBBE *Plus Ultra Reduced* 145 A florid red, but paler than blood..resembling a bastard-scarlet. **1691** RAY *Creation* I. (1704) 106 Bastard Diamonds. **1844** H. HUTCHINSON *Pract. Drainage* 153 A portion of which is strong clay, and more of which is of the description requiring Bastard Draining.

b. *esp.* in *Bot.*, often forming the specific name of a plant; see *Bastard* ALKANET, BALM, PIMPERNEL, SAFFRON, TOADFLAX, etc.

1578 LYTE *Dodoens* 42 Of the false and Bastard Rewbarbes, there are at yᵉ least foure or fiue kindes. **1671** SALMON *Syn. Med.* III. xxii. 432 Sison, bastard Stone-parsley. **1779** FORREST *Voy. N. Guinea* 130 A grove of bastard pine trees, called by Malays, Arrow. **1865** GOSSE *Land & Sea* (1874) 385 The beautiful spotted bastard-balm ..spangling the hedge with its large white flowers.

c. in *Zool.*, *Phys.*, etc. *bastard-wing*, a set of three or four quill-like feathers placed at a small joint in the middle of a bird's wing, taken as the analogue of the thumb in mammals.

1594 T. B. *La Primaud. Fr. Acad.* II. 46 The lower part of the ribs are commonly called the false ribbes, or bastard ribbes. **1678** RAY *Willughby's Ornith.* 307 The Lapwing or Bastard Plover. **1772** FORSTER in *Phil. Trans.* LXII. 420 The Alula, or bastard wing, is black. **1799** G. SMITH *Laborat.* II. 298 Alder-fly, withy-fly, or bastard-caddis. **1859** DARWIN *Orig. Spec.* xiv. (1878) 397 The 'bastard-wing' may safely be considered as a rudimentary digit.

d. in *Medicine.*

1625 HART *Anat. Ur.* II. v. 79, I was surprised with a bastard Tertian ague. **1728** NICHOLLS in *Phil. Trans.* XXXV. 442 Some Resemblance of the Aneurysm; for which Reason it is by some Chirurgeons term'd a Bastard-Aneurysm. **1881** *Syd. Soc. Lex.* s.v., Bastard Measles, the *Roseola epidemica.*

e. in *Geology* and *Mineralogy.*

1695 *Voy. Eng. Merch.* in *Misc. Cur.* (1708) III. 127 Covered with an Arch of Bastard Marble. **1839** MURCHISON *Silur. Syst.* I. xxxi. 415 A bastard limestone charged with encrinites. **1851** *Coal-tr. Terms Northumbld. & Durh.* 7 *Bastard Whin*, very hard post or sandstone, but not so flinty as to be called whin.

6. Of abnormal shape or irregular (*esp.* unusually large) size; *spec.* applied: †**a.** *Mil.* to swords, guns, etc.; †**b.** to ships (cf. A 6); **c.** to a file intermediate between the coarse and fine 'cuts'; **d.** in *Printing*, to (*a*) a fount of type cast on a smaller or larger body than that to which it usually belongs, (*b*) an abbreviated or half-title on the page preceding the full title-page of a book.

a. 1418 *E.E. Wills* (1882) 30, I bequethe to Symond Wrenchin..my Bastard Swerd. **1598** BARRET *Theor. Warres* IV. i. 95 The Bastard square, is the battell which conteineth almost twise so many men in front, as in flanke. **1627** CAPT. SMITH *Seaman's Gram.* xiv. 69 Bastard-muskets, Coliuers. **1753** CHAMBERS *Cycl. Supp.* s.v., The ordinary bastard culverin carries a ball of eight pounds.

b. 1667 *Lond. Gaz.* No. 220/2 The Bastard Gally that lies ready to sail. **1693** *Ibid.* No. 2878/2 One Bastard Galley on which the Doge is embarked.

c. 1677 MOXON *Mech. Exerc.* (1703) 15 The Bastard-tooth'd file is to take out of your work, the deep cuts..the Rough-file made; the Fine-tooth'd file is to take out the cuts ..the Bastard-file made. **1884** F. BRITTEN *Watch & Clockm.* 32 Bastard Cut..a file between rough and smooth.

e. Of the Gothic script known as *bastard* (sense A. 11) or *bastarda.*

1888 J. H. HESSELS in *Encycl. Brit.* XXIII. 694/1 Bastard Italian or bastard Roman was introduced in 1454 at Mainz in the 31-line and 30-line indulgence.

7. Applied as a specific epithet:

a. to wine (cf. A. 4).

1436 *Pol. Poems* (1859) II. 160 Raysyns, wyne bastarde, and dates. **1598** *Epulario* B.ij, Bastard wine, that is, wine sod with new wine, called Must. **1616** SURFL. & MARKH. *Countr. Farm* 635 Mungrell or bastard vvines, vvhich.. haue neither manifest sweetnesse nor manifest astriction.

b. to sugar (cf. A. 10).

1833 B. SILLIMAN *Man. Sugar Cane* 93 The language of the sugar refiners appears to be tolerably uniform, in applying the term bastard sugar to that which is formed from the first dripping of the lump. **1863** *Act 26 Vict.* xxii. Sched. A, Bastard or Refined Sugar unstoved. **1877** BURROUGHS *Taxation* 551 Bastard sugar is the residuum..of clayed sugars.

8. *bastard trenching* in *Hort.* (see quots.). Hence (as a back-formation) *bastard-trench* v. trans.

1842 LOUDON *Suburban Hort.* II. iii. 230 'Double digging' is in horticulture what subsoil ploughing is in agriculture; the surface soil is kept on the surface, but the bottom of the trench is dug over as the work proceeds... By many this is called 'bastard trenching'. **1909** *Daily Chron.* 23 Oct. 3/5 The best method is to dig out the surface soil..and to carry it to the far end of the bed, to work the manure into the lower soil now exposed..and cover it with the upper soil of the next yard; and so on down the bed, filling the last hole with the soil taken from the first. This is known as 'bastard-trenching'. **1923** W. DEEPING *Secret Sanctuary* x. 104 Stretton set himself to bastard-trench a quarter of an acre. **1933** *Jrnl. R. Hort. Soc.* LVIII. 98, I invariably endeavour to bastard trench all the ground to be occupied by chrysanthemums.

†'**bastard**, *v.* *Obs.* [f. prec. sb.; cf. 16th c. F. *abastardir*, Sp. *abastardar*, It. *abbastardire*, *bastardire*, Eng. ABASTARD.]

1. *trans.* To declare or stigmatize as a bastard; to render illegitimate, BASTARDIZE. Also *fig.*

1549 CHALONER tr. *Erasm. Moriæ Enc.* Pijb, They do binde Christ in certaine money lawes of theyr owne, and with wrested gloses..doe bastard him. **1589** WARNER *Alb. Eng.* VI. xxx. (1597) 149 He bastards Cupid, and..Venus did chaife. *a* **1658** CLEVELAND *To Earl Newcastle* Gen. Poems (1677) 147 To Bastard her present Issue.

2. *intr.* To beget a bastard.

‖**bastarda** (bəˈstɑːdə). [It., f. *bastardo* (see BASTARD *sb.*).] A Gothic script used in France and Germany during the 14th and 15th centuries.

1934 A. F. JOHNSON *Type Design* i. 6 For..theological texts a less formal and rounded letter was used.., for works in the vernacular, a still less formal and cursive hand known as Bastarda. *Ibid.* 31 The French 'lettre bâtarde' then passed out of use..but in Germany the Bastarda has remained the national type. **1963** *Times* 7 Feb. 16/4 Illustrated manuscripts..with Gothic bastarda script.

†'**bastarded**, *ppl. a.* *Obs.* [f. BASTARD *v.* + -ED.] Tainted with bastardy, illegitimate; unfathered.

1579 TOMSON *Calvin's Serm. Tim.* 681/1 That their race be a good race and not bastarded. *a* **1603** T. CARTWRIGHT *Confut. Rhem. N.T.* (1618) 403 [It] is confessed to be the authours owne, and not bastarded.

†'**bastardice, -ise.** *Obs.* [a. F. *bastardise* (16th c. in Littré), mod. *bâtardise*, f. *bâtard* BASTARD.] Bastardy, illegitimacy; falsity.

1579 TOMSON *Calvin's Serm. Tim.* 1030/1 This is such a bastardise, as the diuell hath brought into the worlde. **1600** CHAPMAN *Iliad* III. 319 With bastardice brand all their future race. **1611** SPEED *Hist. Gt. Brit.* VII. cxxv. 271 Affecting the Crown, vpon..supposed bastardise of Arthur.

†'**bastarding**, *vbl. sb.* *Obs.* [f. BASTARD *v.* + -ING[1].] **a.** The action of declaring (a child) illegitimate. **b.** The begetting of a bastard.

1563 GRAFTON *Chron. Rich. III*, an. 3, Putting in oblivion the bastardyng of her daugters. **1633** FORD *Love's Sacr.* V. i. (1811) 436 Thy bastarding the issues of a prince. **1677** OTWAY *Cheats of Sc.* II. i. (1736) 78 They'll..tell all your Fornications, Bastardings, and Commutings.

bastardism (ˈbɑːstədɪz(ə)m, -æ-). ? *Obs.* [f. BASTARD *sb.* + -ISM.] The condition of a bastard, illegitimacy, BASTARDY.

1589 *Almond for P.* 38 Is Christ descended of bastardisme or no, as you gaue out in the pulpyt. **1753** *Scots Mag.* Oct. 489/1 We ought to remove..the incapacities of bastardism.

bastardization (ˌbɑːstədaɪˈzeɪʃən, -æ-). [f. next; see -ATION.] The declaring or rendering bastard.

1818 W. TAYLOR in *Monthly Rev.* LXXXVII. 534 The illegitimation, or bastardization, of the children of Edward IV. **1838** *Blackw. Mag.* XLIII. 763 Declaring wedlock to be a mere civil engagement..to the bastardization, one may almost say, of society.

bastardize (ˈbɑːstədaɪz, -æ-), *v.* Also 7 bastardise. [f. BASTARD + -IZE: cf. F. *abastardir, -iss-*, Eng. ABASTARDIZE, and BASTARD *v.*]

1. *trans.* To declare or stigmatize as bastard.
1611 COTGR., *Abastardir*, to bastardise. **1631** W. SALTONSTALL *Pict. Loq.* E ij b, His ielous thoughts are ready to bastardize his Children. **1768** BLACKSTONE *Comm.* I. 435 To annul the marriage and bastardize the issue. **1827** HALLAM *Const. Hist.* (1876) I. i. 34 To bastardize the princess Mary.
fig. **1656** TRAPP *Comm. Matt.* xxv. 45 Moabites were bastardized and banished the beauty of holiness.

†**2.** To beget bastard issue. *Obs. rare.*
1605 SHAKS. *Lear* I. ii. 144 Had the maidenliest Starre in the Firmament twinkled on my bastardizing.

3. To make degenerate, deteriorate, debase.
1587 HARMAR tr. *Beza's Serm.* 142 (T.) The ground articles and points of true religion..[may] be in divers sorts ..disguised and bastardized. **1601** CORNWALLYES *Seneca*, Feare..bastardizeth their natures, and corrupts them. **1779** *Phil. Trans.* LXIX. 239 Defect of the season..keeps back and bastardizes the one sort.

4. *intr.* To become degenerate, to deteriorate.
1878 SEELEY *Stein* I. 249 Lets his army..lie idle in garrison service, where it rusts and bastardises.

ˈbastardized, *ppl. a.* Rendered or declared illegitimate; debased, degenerate.
1611 COTGR., *Abastardi*..sophisticated, bastardized. **1859** DARWIN *Orig. Spec.* ix. (1873) 247 Bastardised and deteriorated offspring. **1871** —— *Desc. Man* I. ii. 62 Abbreviated and bastardised languages.

†**ˈbastardliness.** *Obs. rare.* [f. next + -NESS.] Bastardly or illegitimate quality.
1656 TRAPP *Comm. 2 Cor.* viii. 8 Legitimateness opposed to bastardliness. **1660** HEXHAM *Dutch Dict., Bastaerdye*, bastardlinesse.

†**ˈbastardly,** *a. Obs.* Also 6 basterlie, basterdly, 6–7 bastardlye. [f. BASTARD *sb.* + -LY[1].]

1. Of bastard sort: mongrel, base-born.
1552 HULOET, Bastardlye, as not after the ryght sort begotten, *spurius.* **1555** BALE in Strype *Eccl. Mem.* III. App. xxxix. 108 Our unnatural and bastardly brethren. **1586** J. HOOKER *Girald. Irel.* in *Holinsh.* II. 141/1 His sonnes, that basterlie brood. **1597** SHAKS. *2 Hen. IV*, II. i. 55 Wilt thou? wilt thou? thou bastardly rogue. **1640** J. DYKE *Rt. Receiv. Christ* 44 A bastardly fruit, upon which shee cannot looke without blushing. **1749** FIELDING *Tom Jones* (1775) III. 63 Married to a poor bastardly vagabond. **1785** GROSE *Dict. Vulg. Tongue*, Bastardly Gullion, a bastard's bastard.

2. Unlicensed, unauthorized; counterfeit, spurious.
1586 FERNE *Blaz. Gentrie* 56 Our bastardly and apochryphate poets. **1626** DONNE *21 Serm.* 208 Apocryphall and Bastardly Canons which they father upon the Apostles. *a* **1679** T. GOODWIN Wks. (1864) VIII. 51 It is..a bastardly spurious mercy that is in creatures.

3. = BASTARD *a.* 5.
1607 TOPSELL *Serpents* 638 Others..are without a sting, as counterfeit and bastardly Bees. **1610** BARROUGH *Meth. Physick* IV. viii. (1639) 234 A Bastardly Tertian is caused, when choler is mixed..with fleame.

4. Degenerate, debased, corrupt.
1587 GOLDING *De Mornay* xvii. 273 Such an vnkindly and Bastardly Nature, that not euen the best of vs haue any whit of our former nature..sauing onely shame. **1669** W. SIMPSON *Hydrol. Chym.* 71 The bastardly fermentation of the blood.

†**ˈbastardry.** *Obs.* [f. as prec. + -RY; or ? error for BASTARDY.]
1483 *Cath. Angl.* 23/1 Bastardrye, *bastardia.*

†**ˈbastardry,** *v. Obs.* [? f. prec.] = BASTARDIZE.
1644 HEYLIN *Stumbling-block* in *Hist. & Misc. Tracts* (1681) 725 To bastardry his daughter Mary in favour of the Lady Elizabeth.

bastardy (ˈbɑːstədɪ, -æ-). [a. AF. and OF. *bastardie*, f. *bastard*; see -Y.]

1. The condition of a bastard, illegitimate birth.
[**1292** BRITTON I. v. §4 De bastardie et de bigamie]. **1486** *Bk. St. Albans, Her.* E viij, His faderis armys he may bere with sych a staffe as is sayd afore: in signe of his bastardy. **1594** SHAKS. *Rich. III*, III. v. 75 Inferre the Bastardie of Edwards Children. **1655** FULLER *Ch.-Hist.* I. 31 No Crosse-barre of Bastardy..can bolt Grace out of that Heart, wherein God will have to enter. **1820** BYRON *Mar. Fal.* v. iii. 72 Shall bear about their bastardy in triumph To the third spurious generation. **1868** ROGERS *Pol. Econ.* viii. 70 Bastardy laws..put the maintenance of an illegitimate child on its putative parent.

2. Begetting of bastards, fornication.
1577 NORTHBROOKE *Dicing* (1843) 175 It is the storehouse and nurserie of bastardie. **1642** ROGERS *Naaman* 303 Over-throwing the foundation of the family, by such bastardy. **1839** CARLYLE *Chartism* iii. 121 Any law..which has become a bounty on unthrift..bastardy and beer-drinking.

3. *fig.* in prec. senses.
1601 SHAKS. *Jul. C.* II. i. 138 When euery drop of blood.. Is guilty of a seuerall Bastardie, If, etc. **1678** CUDWORTH *Intell. Syst.* I. iv. §18. 34 No signs of Spuriousness or Bastardy [being] discovered in them.

†**4.** Bastards collectively, bastard brood. *Obs.*
1599 MARSTON *Sco. Villanie* III. xi. 228 Which still he hugs, and luls as tenderly As cuckold Tisus his wifes bastardie.

5. *attrib.*, as ***bastardy law***; **bastardy order**, an order made by a magistrate for the support of an illegitimate child by the putative father.
1867 *Law Rep. Queen's Bench* II. 468 In *Slater's Case* it was held that an original bastardy order could not be annulled by a subsequent order. **1872** *Act 35 & 36 Vict.* c. 65 An Act to amend the Bastardy Laws. **1880** *Act 43 & 44 Vict.* c. 32 §2 This Act may be cited as the Bastardy Orders Act, 1880. **1912** G. STONE *Quest. National Insur.* 100 Will the fact that the mother..is receiving maternity benefit make any difference to the amount of the bastardy order?

baste (beɪst), *sb.*[1] *Card-playing.* Also **bast.** A variant of BEAST, of which it retains the former pronunciation, the spelling being altered to suit.
1850 *Hand-bk. of Games* (Bohn) 226 Bast is a penalty incurred by not winning when you stand your game, or by renouncing. *Ibid.* 243 A baste off the board is always paid out of the pool.

†**baste,** *sb.*[2] *Her. Obs.* App. corruption of BASE *sb.*[1] 8; cf. BAST *sb.*[3]
1562 LEIGH *Armorie* (1579) 80 He beareth partie per bast barre erased, Argent, and Vert. **1586** FERNE *Blaz. Gentrie* 177 You haue seene in one coate..both a cheefe and a baste.

baste (beɪst), *v.*[1] Also 6 **baest,** 6–7 **bast.** [a. OF. *bastir* (mod. *bâtir*), cogn. with Sp. *bastear*, *embastar*, It. *imbastire* 'to stuffe, to quilt..to baste as taylers doe' (Florio); separated by Littré and others from *bâtir* to build, with which it is identical in form, and referred to OHG. *bestan* to patch, MHG. *besten* to lace, tie, f. *bast* BAST *sb.*[1]; but Diez thinks it sufficiently accounted for by 'put together, join,' dialectal senses of It. and Romanic *bastire* to build, construct.]

trans. To sew together loosely: *hence* †**a.** To stitch through (the folds of a doublet, contents of a bag or cushion), so as to keep them in place, to quilt (*obs.*); **b.** in mod. use, To sew or 'tack' together with long loose stitches the parts of (a piece of work), in order to hold them in place for the time. **c.** *transf.* or *fig.*
a. *c* **1440** *Rom. Rose* 104 With a threde bastyng my slevis. *c* **1440** *Promp. Parv.* 26 Bastyn clothys, *subsuo, sutulo.* **1530** PALSGR. 442 This dublet was not well basted at the first, and that maketh it to wrinkle thus: *ce pourpoynt nestoyt pas bien basty.* **1599** A. M. tr. *Gabelhouer's Bk. Physick* 178/2 Replenishe therwith a little bagge..baest least the herbes fall together on a heape. **1611** COTGR., *Glacer*..to flesh-bast; or stitch downe the lyning of a garment, thereby to keep it from sagging.
b. **1589** R. HARVEY *Pl. Perc.* (1590) 25 This patch here placd, the which I bast: And sow so fast. **1883** *Chr. Globe* 13 Sept. 819/2 A doll's dress that has been cut and basted by 'a real dressmaker.'
c. **1540** RAYNALD *Birth Man* I. ii. (1634) 19 The very skin and it being both basted together, by a great number of small fibres. **1599** SHAKS. *Much Ado* I. i. 289 The body of your discourse is sometime guarded with fragments, and the guardes are but slightly basted on neither. **1816** SCOTT *Old Mort.* Concl., You have..basted up your first story very hastily and clumsily.

baste (beɪst), *v.*[2] Forms: 6 **baast** (*pa. pple.*), 6–7 **bast,** 6– **baste.** [Origin unknown: it has been conjectured to be a transferred sense of the next, with idea of 'stroking' (Wedgwood), which is not favoured by the relative dates of the two words, or to be from Romanic *bastire* (see BASTE *v.*[1]), with general sense of 'prepare'; but nothing like the special sense occurs in Romanic.]

1. To moisten (a roasting joint, etc.) by the application of melted fat, gravy, or other liquid, so as to keep it from burning, and improve its flavour.
1509 BARCLAY *Shyp of Folys* I. 100 The fat pygge is baast, the lene cony is brent. **1598** *Epulario* C j b, Let it rost sokingly, basting it oft with the foresaid sauce. **1653** WALTON *Angler* 159 Let him be..often basted with claret wine. **1741** *Compl. Fam. Piece* I. ii. 126 Tie your Lobsters to the Spit alive, baste them with Water and Salt. **1853** SOYER *Pantropheon* 163 Baste it with its own gravy.

b. *transf.* or *fig.*
1575 TURBERV. *Venerie* 61 That I the wine should taste.. and so my throte I baste. **1598** E. GILPIN *Skial.* (1878) 50 See how he basts himselfe in his owne greace. **1606** SHAKS. *Tr. & Cr.* II. iii. 195 That bastes his arrogance with his owne seame. **1883** GILMOUR *Mongols* xxiv. 297 Some white flour scones basted in butter.

†**2.** To perfuse as with a liniment. *Obs.*
1570 LEVINS *Manip.* /36 Baste, *linire.* **1727** BRADLEY *Fam. Dict.* s.v. *Fleas*, Put to your water two ounces of Staves-acre ..and..baste your dog therewith. **1735** OLDYS *Raleigh* (R.) Having had their naked bodies basted or dropped over with burning bacon.

3. In *Candle-making*: see BASTING *vbl. sb.*[2] 2.

4. To mark (sheep) with tar. 'North.' (Halliwell.)
[**1590** GREENE *Mourn. Garm.* (1616) 2 The prime of his yeeres was in the flowre, and youth sate and basted him *Calendes* in his forehead]. (Cf. BUIST.)

baste (beɪst), *v.*[3] Forms: 6 (*pa. pple.*) **baste, basit,** (*pa. t.*) **baist;** 6–7 **bast,** 6– **baste.** [Of uncertain origin, not known before 16th c.; the early instances being all in pa. t. or pa. pple. *basit, baste, baist*, might be from a present *bas, base*, to be compared with Sw. *basa* 'to baste, whip, beat, flog.' With *baste*, if it was the original form, cf. Icel. *beysta, beyrsta* 'to bruise, thrash, flog,' Sw. *bösta* 'to thump'; but the vowels do not agree with the Eng. Possibly, after all, a figurative use of the preceding: cf. *anoint* in sense of *thrash.*]

trans. To beat soundly, thrash, cudgel.
1533 BELLENDEN *Livy* III. (1822) 223 He departit weil basit, and defuleyeit of his clething. ? *a* **1550** *Rob. Hood* (Ritson) iii. 102 He paid good Robin back and side, And baist him up and down. *Ibid.* 364 Their bones were baste so sore. **1596** COLSE *Penelope* (1880) 172 Would not sticke to baste your bones. **1660** PEPYS *Diary* 1 Dec., I took a broom, and basted her, till she cried extremely. **1704** STEELE *Lying Louer* IV. ii. 43 I'll have the Rascal well basted for his insolence. **1801** STRUTT *Sports & Past.* IV. iv. §8 Baste the bear [a kind of game]. **1847** BARHAM *Ingol. Leg.* (1877) 13 Would now and then seize..A stick..And baste her lord and master most confoundedly.
fig. **1797** WOLCOTT (P. Pindar) *Livery Lond.* Wks 1812 III. 443 Basted by saucy Verse and Prose..Like Bears by ruffian Bull-dogs baited.

baste (beɪst), *v.*[4] *Card-playing.* Also **bast.** [f. BASTE *sb.*[1]] A modern variant of to BEAST (retaining the former pronunciation).
1850 *Hand-Bk of Games* (Bohn) 231 He who renounces is basted as often as detected. **1878** H. H. GIBBS *Ombre* 27 *note*, Quadrille-players call it a Baste or being Basted, not from any idea connected with Baste or being beaten, but by corruption from the word Beaste.

bastel(e, obs. form of BASTILLE.

bastel-house (ˈbæstəlhaʊs). Also **bastle-.** [f. *bastel*, var. of BASTILE + HOUSE.] A fortified house, usually having the lower floors arched over.
1544 *Exped. Scotl.* in Arb. *Garner* I. 125 Divers bastel and fortified houses. **1849** *Mem. Kirkaldy Gr.* xxi. 242 The Potterrow Port, an arch between two bastel houses. **1884** *Programme Archæol. Inst. Newcastle*, The Mediæval Castles, Towers, and Bastle-houses in Northumberland.

basten (ˈbæstən), *a.* [OE. *bæsten*: see BAST *sb.*[1] and -EN[1].] Made of bast.
c **1000** ÆLFRIC *Judg.* xv. 13 Híȝ ðá hine ȝebundon mid twám bæstenum rápum. **1677** PLOT *Oxfordsh.* 263 The.. small leav'd Lime or Linden tree..called Bast; whence the ropes are also called Basten ropes. **1693** W. ROBERTSON *Phraseol. Gen.* 213 A Basten rope, *funis sparteus.*

baster[1] (ˈbeɪstə(r)). [f. BASTE *v.*[1] + -ER[1].] One who bastes (with thread); cf. BASTE *v.*[1]
1883 *Standard* 6 Nov. 2/2 A garment is manipulated by the cutter, the baster, the machinist.

ˈbaster[2] (in 16th c. basteter). [f. BASTE *v.*[2]] One who bastes meat.
1525 *Churchw. Acc. Heybridge* (Nichols 1797) 181 To she that turned the spitt, 8*d.*; to the Basteter, 4*d.*

baster[3] (ˈbeɪstə(r)). [f. BASTE *v.*[3] + -ER[1].] He who or that which bastes or thrashes; *hence*, a stick or cudgel; *also*, a heavy blow.
1726 W. WAGSTAFFE *Misc. Wks.* 48 (L.) Jack took up the poker, and gave me such a baster upon my head. **1770** in Smith's *Bk. Rainy Day* (1861) 14 A fellow riding a hog, brandishing a birch broom by way of a baster.

basterly, obs. form of BASTARDLY.

‖**bastide** (ˈbɑːstɪd, -æ-, baˈstid). [a. OF. *bastide*, ad. Pr. *bastida* 'building,' sb. from fem. pa. pple. of *bastir* to build: cf. -ADA, -ADE.]

†**1. a.** A bastel-house or fortlet. **b.** A temporary hut or tower erected for besieging purposes. Cf. BASTILLE. *Obs.* exc. *Hist.*
1523 LD. BERNERS *Froiss.* I. xxvi. 39 They fortified the bastyde of Rosebourge, and made it a strong Castel. **1577** HOLINSHED *Chron.* II. 640 He came before the strong towne of Calis..and erected bastides betweene the towne and the river. **1858** MORRIS *G. Teste-Noire* 138 Therefore we set our bastides round the tower That Geffray held.

‖**2.** A country-house in southern France.
1721 *Lond. Gaz.* No. 6073/2 The Bastides and Farm-Houses in that Neighbourhood. **1837** CARLYLE *Fr. Rev.* II. VI. ii. 332 White glittering bastides that crown the hill.

bastille, -ile (bɑːˈstiːl, -æ-, ˈbɑːstɪl, -æ-), *sb.* Forms: 4 **bastele,** 4–5 **-el,** 5 **-yle, -elle, -yll,** 5–6 **ylle,** 6 **-il, -ell,** (*Sc.* **bastillie, -alyie, -ailyei**), 7 **bastill,** 8– **bastille,** 4–**bastile.** [a. F. *bastille* (15th c. in Littré):——late L. *bastīlia*, pl. of *bastīle*, f. *bastire* to build (cf. *sedīle, sedīlia*, f. *sedēre*). In mod.Eng. refashioned after Fr.; the regular form from ME. *bastel(e* would be *bastle.*]

1. A tower or bastion of a castle; a fortified tower; a small fortress.
c **1340** *Gaw. & Gr. Knt.* 799 Bastel rouez, þat blenked ful quyte. *c* **1430** LYDG. *Bochas* II. xvii. (1554) 56 a, Square bastiles and bulwarkes to make. **1494** FABYAN VII. 516 Y[e] prouoste..went to dyner vnto ye bastyle of Seynt Denys. **1536** BELLENDEN *Cron. Scot.* (1821) I. 182 To repair the said wall in all partis, with touris and bastailyeis. **1664** BUTLER *Hud.* I. II. Argt., Conveys him to enchanted Castle, There shuts him fast in Wooden Bastile. **1853** G. JOHNSTON *Nat. Hist. E. Borders* I. 144 Ruins of bastiles and castles.

2. *spec.* in siege operations: **a.** A wooden tower on wheels for the protection of the besieging troops. **b.** One of a series of huts, surrounded by entrenchments, provided for their accommodation.
c **1325** *E.E. Allit. P.* B. 1187 At vch brugge a berfray on basteles wyse. **1430** LYDG. *Chron. Troy* II. xviii, Sette their bastyles and their hurdeys eke Rounde about to the harde wall. **1489** CAXTON *Faytes of A.* II. xxxiv, Thys bastylle

muste be aduironned with hirdels aboute and dawbed thykke with erthe and clay therupon, and it may be sette vpon wheles. **1523** LD. BERNERS *Froiss.* I. ccccxxix. 754 And so lodged in Calays..in bastylles that they made dayly. **1600** HOLLAND *Livy* XXII. lx. 471 Good no where, neither in battaile nor in bastill [*castris*]. **1750** CARTE *Hist. Eng.* II. 717 A bastille or small wooden fort was erected on the land side. **1839** KEIGHTLEY *Hist. Eng.* I. 352 Bastilles, or huts defended by intrenchments were constructed round the city.

fig. *c* **1430** LYDG. *Bochas* (1554) 67 b Oblivion, Hath a bastyll of foryetfulnes To stop the passage.

3. Name of the prison-fortress built in Paris in the 14th century, and destroyed in 1789.

1561 R. NORVELL (*title*) The Meroure of an Christian, composed..during the tyme of his captiuetie at Paris, in the Bastillie. **1783** COWPER *Task* v. 383 Her[France's] house of bondage..the Bastille. **1837** CARLYLE *Fr. Rev.* IV. iii. I. 162 That rock-fortress, Tyranny's stronghold, which they name Bastille, or Building, as if there were no other building.

4. By extension: A prison.

1790 BURKE *Fr. Rev.* Wks. V. 143 One of the old palaces of Paris, now converted into a Bastile for kings. **1861** SALA *Tw. round Clock* 58 Pentonville's frowning bastille. **1884** *Ransom City* (Dakota) *Paper* 9 Feb., Fined $25, and ten days in the bastile, for selling liquor to the Indians.

bastille, -ile (bɑːˈstiːl, -æ-, ˈbɑːstɪl, -æ-), *v.*; also 5 bastyle. [a. OF. *bastille-r* (also *bateillier*), f. *bastille*; see prec. In sense 2 formed on the Eng. sb.]

†1. To fortify (a castle). *Obs.*

1480 CAXTON *Ovid's Met.* XI. v, Laomedon..redyed hym for to bastyle & edefy the new Troye. *c* **1500** *Partenay* 1134 When thys castell was bastiled fair.

2. To confine in a bastille; to imprison.

1742 YOUNG *Nt. Th.* IX. 1058 Instead of forging chains for foreigners, Bastile thy Tutor. *a* **1798** MARY WOLLSTONECR. *Wks.* II. 34 Marriage had bastilled me for life. **1863** W. PHILLIPS *Speeches* xix. 422 One thousand men..are 'bastiled' by an authority as despotic as that of Louis.

baˈstillion. *Obs.* or *Hist.* Forms: 6–7 **bastilion**, 7 **bastillon**, 6–9 **bastillion**. [a. OF. *bastillon*, *-illion*, dim. of *bastille*; see prec.] A small fortress or castle; a fortified tower.

1549 THOMAS *Hist. Italy* 101 Buildyng of fortresses and bastilions about Petabubula. **1603** KNOLLES *Hist. Turks* (1621) 82 They gained one of the greatest bastillions..of the citie, called the Angels tower. **1825** SOUTHEY in *Q. Rev.* XXXII. 385 An assult was made..upon a bastillion by the gate of Codalonga.

†**ˈbastiment.** *Obs.* Also 8 **bastimento**. [partly ad. Sp. *bastimiento* 'fortification, victuall, furniture' (Minsheu), partly a. F. *bastiment* (mod. *bâtiment* 'building, ship'; both f. Romanic *bastire* to put together, build, prepare.]

1. Military supplies, stores, provisions.

1598 BARRET *Theor. Warres* v. iii. 133 To prouide all Bastiments, prouision, and other necessarie things. **1622** F. MARKHAM *Bks. Warre* III. x. 5 All his prouisions..of Bastiments or other necessaries.

2. A building, a wall.

1679 *Trials White & Jesuits* 61 He is a Mason, and..built a Bastyment there by direction from Sir John Warner.

3. A ship, a vessel; cf. Fr. *bâtiment*.

1740 GLOVER *Hosier's Ghost* vii. in *Pol. Ball.* (1860) II. 261 Then the bastimentos never Had our foul dishonour seen, Nor the sea the sad receiver Of this gallant train had been.

bastinade, -onade (bæstɪˈneɪd, -əˈneɪd), *sb. arch.* [In 17th c., *bastonade*, a. F. *bastonnade* (ad. Sp. *bastonada* or It. *bastonata*, taking place of OF. *bastonée*: see -ADE); or Eng. adaptation of *bastonado*, after Fr.: see BASTINADO.] = BASTINADO *sb.* 1–3.

1660 *Plea for Mon.* in *Harl. Misc.* I. 17 We have learned quietly to take the bastonade. *c* **1700** *Gentl. Instruc.* (1732) 351 (D.) They would..submit to a bastinade rather than occasion bloodshed. **1813** J. HOBHOUSE *Journ.* 297 Offenders, whom he may punish with the bastinade. **1878** LADY HERBERT tr. *Hübner's Ramble* III. ii. 487 Sure of their bastinade and sure also of their taels.

bastiˈnade, -oˈnade (see prec.), *v. arch.* [f. prec. sb.] To thrash or thwack with a stick, *esp.* on the soles of the feet; to BASTINADO.

1601 R. JOHNSON *Kingd. & Commw.* 59 The euening following he is well bastinaded. **1753** HANWAY *Trav.* (1762) I. III. xxxviii. 174 The shah..ordered the executioners to bastonade him to death. **1828** *Blackw. Mag.* XXIII. 828 Away with him..bow-string him, bastinade him.

bastiˈnaded, *ppl. a. arch.* [f. prec. + -ED.] Thrashed, beaten, *esp.* on the soles of the feet.

a **1711** KEN *Hymnotheo* Wks. 1721 III. 134 The starv'd bastinaded Slave in Chains.

bastiˈnading, *vbl. sb.* = BASTINADOING.

1748 ANSON *Voy.* III. ix 388 Such a sum of money would ..have enticed a Chinese to have undergone a dozen bastinadings. **1859** LANE *Arab. Nts.* I. 273 *note*, On Bastinading.

bastinado (bæstɪˈneɪdəʊ), *sb.* Forms: 6– **bastinado**; also 6 **bastannado, -anado,** 7 **-onada,** 7–8 **onado**. [a. Sp. *bastonada* (= It. *bastonata*, OF. *bastonnée*) a caning or cudgelling, f. *baston* stick, staff, cudgel. For termination see -ADO[2]: the unaccented *o* in the second syllable has fluctuated from the first as *ă*, *ŏ*, *ĭ*, tending to settle down under the closest vowel *i*.]

1. A blow with a stick or cudgel; a whack or thwack; *esp.* one upon the soles of the feet. *arch.*

1577 HOLINSHED *Chron.* III. 897/1 Leading him..with buffets and bastanadoes into the borough. **1592** GREENE *Art Conny Catch.* 25 As many bastinadoes as thy bones will beare. **1598** HAKLUYT *Voy.* II. 203 Beaten with so many bastonadoes vpon the soles of their feete. **1625** *Modell of Wit* 41 b, Lifting up the Cudgell, he gave him therewith halfe a score good bastinadoes. **1849** W. IRVING *Mahomed & Succ.* xiii. (1853) 58 Let him who drinks wine..receive twenty bastinadoes on the soles of his feet.

2. A beating with a stick; a cudgelling. *arch.*

1594 T. B. *La Primaud. Fr. Acad.* II. 717 If a Romane soldior..went out of his ranke..he had the bastannado. *a* **1600** BURLEIGH *Adv. Q. Eliz.* in *Harl. Misc.* (1809) II. 277 No man loves one the better for giving him the bastinado, though with never so little a cudgel. **1828** SCOTT *F.M. Perth* xvi, Must I show thee that thou art a captive, by giving thee incontinently the bastinado?

fig. **1595** SHAKS. *John* II. 463 He giues the bastinado with his tongue.

3. *spec.* An Eastern method of corporal punishment, by beating with a stick the soles of the culprit's feet.

1726 AYLIFFE *Parerg.* 46 Remitted the punishment of Death..and in lieu thereof introduced the Bastinado. **1884** BROWNING *Ferishtah's F.* 133 To cool his heels Uncarpeted, or warm them—likelier still—With bastinado.

4. A stick, staff, rod, cudgel, truncheon.

1598 HAKLUYT *Voy.* I. 55 He receiueth an hundreth blowes on the backe with a bastinado, layd on by a tall fellow. **1624** CAPT. SMITH *Virginia* II. 36 Having a Bastinado..made of reeds bound together. **1878** WAKE *Evol. Morality* II. 128 Her paramour receiving a thousand blows of the bastinado.

bastiˈnado, *v.* Also 8 -onado. [f. prec. sb.]

1. To beat with a stick; to thrash, thwack. *arch.*

1614 [see next]. **1633** MARMYON *Fine Comp.* iv. 5 A gentleman that I bastinadoed the other day. **1728** MORGAN *Algiers* II. iv. 273 Cruelly bastonadoed on the Shoulders, Buttocks, Belly, and Feet. **1775** ADAIR *Amer. Ind.* 156 He bastinadoed the young sinner severely, with a thick whip.

2. *spec.* To beat or cane on the soles of the feet.

1688 *Lond. Gaz.* No. 2318/3 Were put on the Rack, or Bastinadoed. **1855** MACAULAY *Hist. Eng.* III. 547 The Sallee rover, who threatened to bastinado a Christian captive to death.

bastiˈnadoing, *vbl. sb.* [f. prec. + -ING[1].] The action of the vb. BASTINADO; cudgelling, thrashing (*spec.* on the soles of the feet).

1614 SELDEN *Titles Hon.* 63 The punishment for periury was inflicted, that was *Fustigatio*..bastinadoing. **1879** A. FORBES in *Daily News* 25 Mar. 5/7 He is treated to a vehement bastinadoing.

basting (ˈbeɪstɪŋ), *vbl. sb.*[1] [f. BASTE *v.*[1]]

1. Sewing with large loose stitches; quilting (*obs.*), 'tacking'; also *attrib.*, as in *basting-thread*.

1530 PALSGR. 196/2 Bastyng of clothe, *bastiment.* **1860** R. COBBOLD *Pict. Chinese* 146 When the scissors..have done their work of cutting the material..the next process.. answers to our basting. **1870** *Daily News* 4 Apr., Waistcoats without buttons, coats disfigured by basting threads.

†2. Something basted or quilted on; a lining or trimming. *Obs.*

c **1525** SKELTON *Agst. Garnesche* 200 The flesche bastyng of hys cote was sewyd with slendyr thred. **1592** NASHE *P. Penilesse* 12 a, Blisterd with light sarcenet bastings.

ˈbasting, *vbl. sb.*[2] [f. BASTE *v.*[2] + -ING[1].]

1. The action of moistening a roasting joint with melted butter, gravy, etc.; also *fig.* and *attrib.*

1530 PALSGR. 196/2 Bastyng of meate, *bastiment.* **1550** CROWLEY *Epigr.* 365 The tonge must have bastynge, it will the better wagge. **1822** KITCHINER *Cook's Orac.* 187 Put a little bit of butter into your basting-ladle.

b. The material used for this purpose.

1615 MARKHAM *Eng. Housew.* (1660) 69 To know the best bastings for meat, which is sweet Butter, sweet Oyl, etc.

2. *Candle-making.* The process of pouring melted wax from a ladle over the wicks.

c **1865** LETHEBY in *Circ. Sc.* I. 94/1 The operations of basting and rolling are repeated as often as necessary. **1879** G. GLADSTONE in *Cassell's Techn. Educ.* II. 75/2 Wax candles are..made by another process, which is termed basting.

ˈbasting, *vbl. sb.*[3] [f. BASTE *v.*[3] + -ING[1].] A cudgelling, beating, thrashing. (In 'a dry basting' there is a humorous reference to the preceding.)

1590 SHAKS. *Com. Err.* II. ii. 64 Lest it make you chollericke, and purchase me another drie basting. **1720** SWIFT *Irish Feast* Misc. (1735) V. 16 What Stabs and what Cuts..What Bastings and Kicks! **1833** MARRYAT *P. Simple* (1863) 64 A good basting..was a sovereign remedy for sea-sickness.

bastion (ˈbæstɪən). [a. F. *bastion*, 16th c., ad. It. *bastione*, f. *bastire* to build, construct, late L. or common Romanic, of uncertain origin; generally referred to the same root as *baston*, *baton*.]

1. A projecting part of a fortification, consisting of an earthwork, faced with brick or stone, or of a mass of masonry, in the form of an irregular pentagon, having its base in the main line, or at an angle, of the fortification; its 'flanks' are the two sides which spring from the base, and are shorter than the 'faces' or two sides which meet in the acute 'salient angle.'

cut bastion: one with its salient angle cut off and replaced by an inward angle. ***detached bastion***: one constructed apart from the fortification, also called a LUNETTE. ***double bastion***: two bastions, one placed inside the other. ***empty bastion***: one in which the interior surface is lower than the rampart. ***flat bastion***: one placed in front of a 'curtain.' ***Full*** or ***solid bastion***: one in which the interior surface is level with the rampart. ***tower bastion***: a tower built like a bastion and provided with casemates.

1598 BARRET *Theor. Warres* v. iii. 135 Baskets to cary earth to the bastion. **1693** *Mem. Ct. Teckely* I. 14 This small City, flanked with five good Bastions. **1703** MAUNDRELL *Journ. Jerus.* (1732) 54 Bastions faced with hewn stone. **1812** WELLINGTON in Gurw. *Disp.* IX. 27 To breach the face of Bastion at the south east angle of the fort. **1851** RUSKIN *Stones Ven.* I. v. 58 Sharp as the frontal angle of a bastion.

2. *transf.* and *fig.* Rampart, fortification, defence.

1679 *Est. Test.* 27 The frontier and Bastion of the Protestant Religion. **1781** COWPER *Convers.* 688 They build each other up..As bastions set point-blank against God's will. **1858** LONGF. *Ladder St. Aug.* ix, The distant mountains, that uprear Their solid bastions to the skies.

bastion, variant of BASTON *sb.*, a staff.

ˈbastioned, *ppl. a.* [f. prec. + -ED[2].] Furnished with or defended by a bastion or bastions.

1817 MOORE *Lalla R., Veiled Proph.* 111, If tower and battlement And bastion'd wall be not less hard to win. **1875** *Hist. Civ. War Amer.* I. 457 Closed at the gorge by a bastioned curtain with a lunette.

bastionet (ˈbæstɪəˌnɛt). [f. BASTION + -ET[1].] A small bastion.

1871 TYNDALL *Fragm. Sc.* I. vi. 207 On Tuesday..I was early at the bastionet.

bastite (ˈbæstaɪt). *Min.* [f. *Baste* in the Harz Mountains, where first found + -ITE.] A bronze-or greenish-coloured impure foliated serpentine; also called *Schiller-spar*.

1837–68 DANA *Min.* 409. **1879** RUTLEY *Stud. Rocks* x. 120 Enstatite becomes altered to schiller-spar or bastite.

bastle-house, modern variant of BASTEL-HOUSE.

bastnäsite (ˈbæstneɪsaɪt). *Min.* [a. F. *bastnaesite* (1841), f. the place-name *Bastnäs*, Sweden, its locality: see -ITE[1] 2 b.] A fluocarbonate of cerium, occurring in small embedded masses, with a greasy lustre and wax-yellow colour.

1872 G. J. BRUSH in *Dana's Syst. Min.* (ed. 5) App. **1914** *Brit. Mus. Return* 229 Crystals of betafite, bastnasite, columbite [etc.]. **1967** *New Scientist* 3 Aug. 253/1 All the europium obtained in Britain is extracted from an ore known as bastnaesite, imported from deposits at Mountain Pass, California.

basto (ˈbɑːstəʊ, -æ-). [a. Sp. *basto*, in same sense, the whole suit of Clubs being also called *Bastos*, and the ace being *el Basto* par excellence; in It. *Bastone*: cf. *baston* club, staff.] The ace of clubs in quadrille and ombre.

1675 COTTON *Compl. Gamester* (1680) 70 The Malillio or black Deuce, the Basto or Ace of Clubs. **1714** POPE *Rape Lock* III. 53 Him basto follow'd, but his fate more hard, Gain'd but one trump and one plebeian card. **1861** *Macm. Mag.* Dec. 130 The ace of clubs..is always ranked as the third best trump card, and is called Basto.

†**baston.** *Obs.* or (in sense 6) *arch.* Forms: 4 **bastun**, 4–8 **baston**, 6 **bastoun**, **bastion**, 6–7 **bastone**, 7 (**bastome**). [a. OF. *baston* (mod.F. *bâton*), cogn. with Sp. *baston*, Pg. *bastão*, It. *bastone*, pointing to a late L. **bastōn-em*, of unknown origin: Diez suggests a connexion with Gr. βαστάζ-ειν to lift, carry. Replaced in 17th c. by BATOON, and now by BATON *sb.*; another form is BATTEN.]

1. A staff or stick used as a weapon or a staff of office; a cudgel, club, bat, truncheon; = BATON *sb.* 1, BATOON 1.

a **1300** *Cursor M.* 15827 Wit þair bastons [*v.r.* bastunes; staues] bete þai him. **1485** CAXTON *Chas. Gt.* (1880) 182 Florypes..took a baston in her honde. **1577** HOLINSHED *Chron.* III. 1226/1 His baston (a staffe of an ell long made taper wise tipt with horne). **1598** BARRET *Theor. Warres* IV. i. 102 Armed but lightly, with a short baston or trunchion in his hand. **1598** STOW *Surv.* (transl. Fitzstephen) xi. (1603) 93 The schollers of euery schoole haue their ball or bastion in their hands. **1693** W. ROBERTSON *Phraseol. Gen.* 213 A Baston, or batoon, *fustis, baculus.* **1756** NUGENT *Montesquieu's Spir. Laws* (1758) II. XXVIII. xx. 271 In process of time none but bondmen fought with the baston.

2. A stanza, or verse. (Transl. of *staff*, *stave*.)

a **1300** *Cursor M.* 14923 Es resun þat wee vr rime rune, And set fra nu langer bastune [*v.r.* bastoun] . *c* **1308** in *Rel. Ant.* II. 175 The clerk that this baston wrowȝte. *Ibid.* 176 Nis this bastun wel i-piȝte, Euch word him sitte a-riȝte. **1330** R. BRUNNE *Chron.* Pref. 99 If it were made in ryme couwee..outhere in couwee or in baston.

3. *Her.* = BATON *sb.* 3.

1592 WYRLEY *Armorie* 79 Thimperiall egle..In siluer, gulie baston ouer all. **1622** PEACHAM *Compl. Gentl.* III.

(1634) 144 A baston .. must not touch the Scotcheon at both the ends. **1660** WATERHOUSE *Arms and Arm.* 112 That were .. a baston of Allay to that Gentleman who should extenuate the merit of Military Grandees.

4. *Card-playing.* A club. Cf. BASTO.

1593 MUNDAY *Def. Contraries* 49 The inuenter of the Italian Cardes .. put the Deniers or monyes, and the Bastons or clubs in combate togither.

5. *Old Law.* Title of 'one of the Warden of the Fleet's men, who attends the king's courts with a red staff, for taking such to ward as are committed by the court; and likewise attends on such prisoners as are suffered to go at large by licence.' Chambers *Cycl.* 1727–51. (Cf. *tip-staff, gold-stick-in-waiting*, etc.) Hence, to go out of prison ***by baston***, to remain in prison ***without baston***.

1366 *Act 1 Rich. II.* xii, [Whereas diuers people be .. suffered to goe at large by the Warden of the prison] alefoitz sanz as-cun maynpris avec une baston de Flete [sometimes without any maineprise with a baston of the Fleet .. It is ordained and assented, that .. no Warden of the Fleet shall suffer any prisoner] aler hors de prisone par maynpris, baill ne par baston [to go out of prison by mainprise, baile, nor by baston.] **1562** *Act 5 Eliz.* xxiii. §8 The same Party .. shall remain in the Prison .. without Bail, Baston or Mainprize. **1619** DALTON *Countr. Just.* cvi. (1630) 273 If the officer shall suffer his prisoners to go abroad for a time, by baile or baston. **1671** F. PHILLIPS *Reg. Necess.* 475 Committed to the Tower of London, there to remain one year without bayle, baston or Mainprize.

6. *Arch.* A round moulding at the base of a column, a torus. [So *bâton* in mod.F.]

1751 CHAMBERS *Cycl., Baston* or *Batoon* .. a mould in the base of a column, otherwise called a tore. **1847** in CRAIG.

†**'baston,** *v. Obs.* [f. prec. sb.; cf. OF. *bastonner* (mod.F. *bâtonner*); and see BATON *v.*] To beat with a staff or cudgel. Hence **bastoned** *ppl. a.*

1593 DEE *Diary* 43 And that I wold try on the fleysh of him, or b(u)y a bastoned gown of him.

bastonade, -ado, obs. ff. BASTINADO.

†**'bastonate,** *v. Obs. rare*⁻¹. [formed after Romanic vb. (It. *bastonāre*, Sp. *bastonar*, OF. *bastoner*) + -ATE: cf. It. pa. pple. *bastonato*.] = prec.

1604 T. WRIGHT *Passions* v. §4. 285 The very Cudgell wherewith a Cavalero is bastonated.

†**bastonet.** *Obs.* [a. OF. *bastonet* (mod. *bâtonnet*) lit. 'little stick,' dim. of *baston* stick, BATON *sb.*] A kind of bit: see the quot.

1611 COTGR., *Bastonnet* .. the bastonet of a bridle. **1617** MARKHAM *Caval.* II. 59, I haue seen some horsmen vse that bytt which we call the Bastonet or Jeiue bytt, which is made with round buttons or great rough ringes.

bastonite ('bæstənaɪt). *Min.* [f. *Bastoigne*, in Luxembourg, where it was discovered + -ITE.] Mica in large plicated plates of greenish-brown colour; a variety of LEPIDOMELANE. (Dana.)

bastose ('bæstəʊs). *Chem.* [f. BAST *sb.*[1] + -OSE[1].] = *Lignocellulose* (see LIGNO-). Also *attrib.*

1882 CROSS & BEVAN in *Jrnl. Chem. Soc.* XLI. 102 We propose to give the name of *Bastose* to this transition modification of cellulose, at the same time observing that as there are many celluloses, so there would be necessarily corresponding forms of bastose. **1902** HANNAN *Textile Fibres* 17 The blending of the bastose and plumose fibres to make one complete yarn is not feasible to begin with.

basular, -ylare, obs. forms of BASILAR *a.*

basulard, variant of BASELARD a dagger.

Basuto (bə'suːtəʊ). A member of a S. African people of the Bantu stock. Also *attrib.* or *adj.*

1835 A. SMITH *Diary* 7 Dec. (1939) I. 163 A Basutu said the hamerkop gives rain. **1837** F. OWEN *Diary* (1926) 64 Sintuala chief of the Mantitees or Basutoos. *Ibid.* 70 The *Boers* in conjunction with the Busutoos had made another attack on him. **1842** R. MOFFAT *Missionary Labours S. Afr.* xv. 242 The Basuto country, once the theatre of plunder and bloodshed, is now studded with missionary stations. **1876** *Encycl. Brit.* V. 47/1 The Basutos, sometimes called Mountain Bechwanas, the fragments of several broken tribes of the Bechwana Kaffres. **1878** P. GILLMORE *Great Thirst Land* 268 My poor little Basuto pony, the last of my Natal stud, has died of horsesickness. **1892** WIDDICOMBE *14 Yrs. Basutoland* ii. 20 The Basuto Christians in communion with the English Church are called *Machurche*. **1926** *Blackw. Mag.* June 826/1 He is a Basuto. **1958** *Yr. Bk. & Guide S. Afr.* 205 The once-famous Basuto pony has deteriorated, but steps are being taken to rehabilitate the breed.

basyl(e ('beɪsɪl, 'bæsɪl). *Chem.* [f. Gr. βάσ-ις base + -YL, Gr. ὕλη, *hyle*, wood, substance. (Webster has also *bashyle*.)] A metal or other electro-positive constituent of a compound; a body that unites with oxygen to form a *base*.

1863 WATTS *Dict. Chem., Basyl*, Graham's name for the metal or other electropositive constituent of a salt. *a* **1866** G. WILSON *Inorg. Chem.* (ed. 3) §1130 A base, may be constructed of a metal and oxygen, and in such circumstances a metal is known as a basyle .. Other substances than metals, however, may be basyles and form bases.

basylous ('beɪsɪləs, 'bæs-), *a. Chem.* [f. prec. + -OUS.] Pertaining to, or of the nature of, a basyl.

1881 WILLIAMSON in *Nature* XXIV. 414 Such primary compounds were classified .. into electro-positive or basylous and electro-negative or chlorous compounds.

basyn, -et, obs. forms of BASIN, BASINET.

bat (bæt), *sb.*[1] Forms: α. 3 ? **balke**, 4–6 **bakke, backe**, 5–6 **bake, bak, back**; β. 6–7 **batte**, 6–8 **batt**, 6– **bat**. [The mod. *bat*, found *c* 1575, takes the place of ME. *bakke*, apparently from Scand.; cf. Da. *aften-bakke* 'evening-bat,' ODa. *nath-bakkæ*, OSw. (Ihre) *natt-backa* 'night-bat.' Swedish dial. have also *natt-batta. natt-blacka*: with the latter cf. Icel. *leðr-blaka* 'bat,' lit. 'leather-flutterer,' f. *blaka* 'to flap, wave, flutter with wings,' whence it has been suggested that *bakke, backa* have lost an *l*; but as the *l* does not appear in the OSw. and ODa. forms above, this is very unlikely. The med.L. *blatta, blacta, batta*, glossed 'lucifuga, vespertilio, vledermus' (Diefenbach *Suppl. to Du Cange*) = cl. L. *blatta* 'an insect that shuns the light' (*blattæ lucifugæ*, Vergil) 'cockroach, moth,' is distinct in origin, but may have influenced the English change to *bat*; evidence is wanting. *Back-* in comb., *backie-bird, bawkie-bird* still survive in north Eng. and Sc.]

1. a. An animal, a member of the Mammalian order *Cheiroptera*, and especially of the family *Vespertilionidæ*; consisting of mouse-like quadrupeds (whence the names *Rere-mouse, Flitter-mouse*), having the fingers extended to support a thin membrane which stretches from the side of the neck by the toes of both pairs of feet to the tail, and forms a kind of wing, with which they fly with a peculiar quivering motion; hence they were formerly classed as birds. They are all nocturnal, retiring by day to dark recesses, to which habits there are many references in literature.

Of about 17 species found in Britain the best-known are the Common Bat or Pipistrelle (*Vespertilio Pipistrellus*) and the Long-eared Bat (*Plecotus auritus*); of the much larger foreign species, the most noted are the Vampires.

α. *a* **1300** W. DE BIBLESW. in Wright *Voc.* 164 Balke, *chaufe-soriz en mesoun*. *c* **1340** *Alex. & Dind.* 723 Bringen her a nihte-bird . a bakke . or an oule. **1388** WYCLIF *Isa.* ii. 20 Moldewarpis and backis, *ether rere myis*. [**1535** COVERDALE, Molles and Backes; **1590** *Genev.* .. To the mowles and to the backes; **1611** Moules and battes.] **1414** BRAMPTON *Penit. Ps.* lxxx. 31 A backe, that flyith be nyȝt. *c* **1440** *Promp. Parv.* 21 Bakke (*v.r.* bak), flyinge best (*v.r.* fleynge byrde), *vespertilio*. **1483** *Cath. Angl.* 18 A Bakke, *blata, vespertilio*. **1496** *Dives & Paup.* (W. de W.) III. viii. 144 Lyke oules & backes whiche hate the daye & loue the nyght. *a* **1500** in Wülcker *Voc.* /761 *Hic vespertilio, hec lucifuga*, a bake. **1509** FISHER *Wks.* I. (1876) 87 More louynge derkenes than lyght, lyke vnto a beest called a backe. **1513** DOUGLAS *Æneis* XIII. Prol. 33 Vpgois the bak wyth hir pelit ledderyn flycht. **1552** HULOET, Reremowse, or backe whiche flyeth in the darcke, *nycteris*. *c* **1554** CROKE *Ps.* (1844) 20 The backe or owle, That lurketh yn an olde house syde. **1607** *Schol. Disc. agst. Antichr.* II. vi 71 To cast them to the Moules and to the backes. [**1808** JAMIESON s.v. Bak, The modern name in Sc. is *backie-bird*. **1863** *Prov. Danby, Back-bearaway*, the bat, or rere mouse.]

β. **1580** HOLLYBAND *Treas. Fr. Tong., Chauvesouris*, a Backe, some call it a Bat. **1596** SPENSER *F.Q.* II. xii. 36 The lether-winged batt, dayes enimy. **1604** DRAYTON *Owle* 502 The blacke-ey'd Bat (the Watch-Man of the Night). **1605** SHAKS. *Macb.* III. ii. 40 Ere the Bat hath flowne His Cloyster'd flight. **1725** POPE *Odyss.* XII. 513 So to the beam the bat tenacious clings, And pendant round it clasps his leathern wings. **1768** PENNANT *Zool.* I. 114 The irregular, uncertain and jerking motion of the bat in the air. **1770** GOLDSM. *Des. Vill.* 350 Silent bats in drowsy clusters cling. **1791** BOSWELL *Johnson* (1831) IV. 209 The curious formation of a bat, a mouse with wings. **1807** CRABBE *Par. Reg.* I. Wks. 1834 II. 156 Bats on their webby wings in darkness move. **1847** CARPENTER *Zool.* §165, *Cheiroptera*; the animals of this Order, all of them commonly known as Bats. **1852** D. MOIR *Ruins Seton Chapel* v, The twilight-loving bat, on leathern wing. **1870** MORRIS *Earthly Par.* I. I. 112 Now the shrill bats were upon the wing.

b. Colloq. phr. (*to have*) ***bats in the belfry***: (to be) crazy or eccentric. Similarly (rare) ***to take the bats***. Hence ***bats*** = BATTY *a.*, used esp. as adj. complement.

c **1901** G. W. PECK *Peck's Red-Headed Boy* 82 They all thought a crazy man with bats in his belfry had got loose. **1907** A. BIERCE in *Cosmopolitan Mag.* July 335/2 He was especially charmed with the phrase 'bats in the belfry', and would indubitably substitute it for 'possessed of a devil', the Scriptural diagnosis of insanity. **1919** F. HURST *Humoresque* viii. 314 'Are you bats?' she said. **1927** A. E. W. MASON *No other Tiger* xix. 197 'On this sort of expedition!' Phyllis Harmer exclaimed, looking at Strickland as if he was a natural. 'Dear man, you've got bats in the belfry.' **1927** *Chambers's Jrnl.* 740/2 Have you taken the 'bats' or what? **1928** *Blackw. Mag.* Jan. 17/2 The sahib had bats in his belfry, and must be humoured. **1938** E. BOWEN *Death of Heart* II. vi. 285 You're completely bats. **1948** *Daily Express* 8 Oct. 2/5 The Secret Life of Walter Mitty .. was written by James Thurber, whose bats viewpoint on life can be summed up by a story about him.

c. Slang phr. (*to go*) ***like a bat out of hell***, (to go) very quickly.

1921 J. DOS PASSOS *Three Soldiers* (1922) II. ii. 67 We went like a bat out of hell along a good state road. **1925** FRASER & GIBBONS *Soldier & Sailor Words* 19 *To go like a bat out of hell*, to go at extreme high speed (Air Force). **1939** I. BAIRD *Waste Heritage*, iv. 52 When it started to move I hared off an' picked out my car an' beat it like a bat out of hell. **1961** I. FLEMING *Thunderball* viii. 87 The motor cyclist .. had gone like a bat out of hell towards Baker Street.

2. *Comb.* **a.** *sbs.*, as ***bat-flight, -flying***, whence ***bat-flying time***, dusk; **bat-light** *poet.*, darkness or gloom; **bat-shell**, a species of volute; **bat-tick**, an insect parasitical on bats. **b.** *adjs.*, as **bat-blind**, blind as a bat in the sunlight; **bat-like**, like a bat, or like that of a bat, also *adv.* after the manner of a bat; **bat-wing, bats-wing** (also **bat's-wing**), shaped like the wing of a bat, applied *spec.* to a laterally spreading flame from a gas-jet, and the burner producing it; also applied to that part of the human face which surrounds the eyes and nose, and to a long sleeve having a deep armhole and fitting closely at the cuff (Webster, 1934). Also in many parasynthetic derivatives, as **bat-eared**, having ears like those of a bat; **bat-eyed**, having bat's eyes; **bat-minded**, mentally blind; **bat-winged**, having bat's wings; also *fig.*; whence deriv. sbs., as **bat-mindedness**, etc.

1609 J. DAVIES *Holy Rood* 13 (D.) O *Bat-blind Fooles, doe ye infatuate That Wisdome? **1834** M. SCOTT *Cruise Midge* (1859) 503 If you are not bat-blind it will evince to you that, etc. **1903** *Daily Chron.* 25 May 5/2 Several of the *bat-eared French bull-dogs. **1638** SANDERSON *Serm.* II. 118 One, to be cat-eyed outward .. another, to be *bat-eyed inward; in not perceiving .. a beam in a man's own eye. **1927** *Glasgow Herald* 24 Oct. 10 A recumbent area of, say, six feet in diameter would be sufficient for the most bat-eyed foozler. **1927** E. WALLACE *Feathered Serpent* xviii. 226 I'd had a couple of drinks that night, and naturally I was a bit bat-eyed. **1818** SCOTT *Hrt. Midl.* xvii, I hae sat on the grave frae *bat-fleeing time till cock-crow. **1934** T. S. ELIOT *Rock* ii. 84 The twilight over stagnant pools at *batflight. **1871** G. M. HOPKINS *Let.* 2 Aug. (1935) 27, I live in *bat-light and shoot at a venture. **1946** C. FRY *Firstborn* 10, I was out before daybreak. It's a good marksman who hunts by batlight. *a* **1711** KEN *Edmund* Wks. 1721 II. 90 His *Bat-like Wings he to full stretch expands. **1785–95** WOLCOTT (P. Pindar) *Lousiad* II. Wks. I. 230 Conscience .. That, bat-like, winks by day and wakes by night. **1858** SEARS *Athan.* II. xii. 249 Bat-like fallacies. **1878** B. TAYLOR *Deukalion* I. iv. 34 Bat-like cries, thin, impotent of sound. **1869** *Echo* 23 Jan., There is enough .. *bat-mindedness in the world to give Rome a fair chance. **1838** *Penny Cycl.* XI. 88/2 The burners are of many different forms.... The *batswing is a thin sheet of gas produced by its passing through a fine saw-cut in a hollow globe. **1846** HOLTZAPFFEL *Turning* II. 753 The gas-burners designated as *bat's-wing burners* have a narrow slit through which the gas issues: these are cut .. by thin circular saws. **1869** *Daily News* 18 June, The common batswing burner .. is of about the same illuminating power as the fishtails. **1872** *Young Englishwoman* Oct. 547/1 The batswing skirt is made in all colours.... The best is seamless; the second .. in seams .. [is] cheaper than the seamless batswing. **1904** *Daily Chron.* 23 Aug. 8/1 In the red straw hat there are batswing bows. **1908** *Practitioner* Jan. 22 The bat's-wing area of the face. **1852** T. HARRIS *Insects New Eng.* 501 A remarkable group of insects, which seems to connect the flies with the true ticks and spiders. Such are sheep-ticks and *bat-ticks. **1823** *Local & Pers. Acts* I. 128 Any Light or Lights, or Argand, Cockspur, *Batwing or any other Kind of Burner. **1872** H. MACMILLAN *True Vine* vii. 296 The leaves of the bat-wing passion-flower. **1959** *Guardian* 28 Aug. 3/5 The new Balenciaga coat has very wide batwing armholes. **1961** *Harper's Bazaar* June 22/2 Loosely-fitting top with batwing sleeves. **1847** LD. LINDSAY *Chr. Art.* I. 84 The triple-headed, *bat-winged, horned and hoofed monster of the later middle ages. **1911** FLETCHER & KIPLING *Hist. England* i. 9, I remember the bat-winged lizard birds. **1923** D. H. LAWRENCE *Birds, Beasts & Flowers* 76 Bat-winged heart of man.

bat (bæt), *sb.*[2] Forms: 3 (*dat. sing.*) **botte**, (*pl.*) **botten**, 3–5 **bottes**, 3–6 **battes**; 5–6 **batte**, 6–8 **batt**, 4– **bat**. [As the nom. sing. does not occur in 13th c., it is uncertain whether it was *bat* or *batte*, and thus whether it was an adoption of OF. *batte* (partly identical in sense, referred by Littré to *battre* to beat), or represented an OE. **bat* (fem.)'fustis,' alleged by Somner, from an unknown source. The forms in Layamon rather favour the latter; but in any case some of the senses are from F. *batte*. The supposed OE. **bat* is by some referred to a Celtic origin; cf. Ir. and Gael. *bat, bata* staff, cudgel. The development and relations of the senses are obscure: some of them appear to be from the verb, and some may be immediately due to onomatopœia, from the sound of a solid, slightly dull, blow: cf. *pat*. Thus there may be two or three originally distinct words, though no longer satisfactorily separable.]

I. A stick or stout piece of wood.

1. A stick, a club, a staff for support and defence. (In 1387 applied to a crosier.) *arch.* Still *dial.* (Kent, Sussex, etc.) = staff, walking-stick.

1205 LAY. 21593 Þa botten [**1250** battes] heo up heouen. *c* **1230** *Ancr. R.* 366 Us forto buruwen from þes deofles botte. *c* **1300** *K. Alis.* 78 And made heom fyghte with battes. *c* **1320** *Syr Bevis* 391 He nemeth is bat and forth a goth. **1387** TREVISA *Higden* Rolls Ser. I. 381 Forto swere vppon eny of þilke belles and gold battes. *c* **1440** *Promp. Parv.* 26 Batte, staffe, *fustis*. *c* **1440** *Gesta Rom.* 179 As to a thef ye come oute, with swerdes & battes to take me. **1494** FABYAN VII. 596 This was clepyd of the comon people the parlyament of battes . . for proclamacyons were made, yt men shulde leue theyr swerdes & . . the people toke great battes & stauys. **1555** *Fardle Facions* App. 327 Let there bee giuen vnto hym by the commune Sergeaunt of the batte .xxxix. stripes with a waster. **1591** SPENSER *M. Hubberd* 217 A handsome bat he held, On which he leaned. **1607** SHAKS. *Cor.* I. i. 165 Make you ready your stiffe bats and clubs. **1655** GOUGE *Comm. Heb.* xi. 35 *Τύμπανον* . . signifieth a 'bat,' or a 'staff.' **1687** DRYDEN *Hind & P.* III. 631 He headed all the rabble of a town, And finish'd 'em with bats. **1822** SCOTT *Nigel* xxi, I have given up . . my bat for a sword. **1875** STUBBS *Const. Hist.* III. xviii. 103 Called . . the parliament of bats or bludgeons.

†**2.** ? A balk of timber. *batt's end* apparently = mast-head. *Obs.* or *dial.*

1577 B. GOOGE *Heresbach's Husb.* (1586) 42 Though the corne be laide upon Battes in the floores. *a* **1618** RALEIGH *Royal Navy* 4 Necessaries belonging to shipping, even from the Batts end to the very Kilson of a Ship. **1686** PLOT *Staffordsh.* 211 Neat Timber, a fift part (which is sufficient in such large batts) . . allow'd for the wast of rind, chipps, etc.

3. a. The wooden implement with rounded handle and flattened blade used to strike or 'bat' the ball in cricket. (The most common mod. sense.)

1706 PHILLIPS, *Bat* . . a kind of Club to strike a Ball with, at the Play call'd Cricket. [So in BAILEY 1731, etc.] **1770** J. LOVE *Cricket* 3 He weighs the well-turned Bat's experienc'd Force. **1807** CRABBE *Village* I. 336 The bat, the wicket, were his labours all. **1850** in *Cricket. Man.* 100 Pilch scored sixty-one, and brought out his bat.

b. short for *batter, batsman.*

1756 *Connoisseur* 5 Aug. 796 His greatest excellence is cricket-playing, in which he is reckoned as good a bat as either of the Bennets. **1859** *All Y. Round* No. 13. 306 McJug . . one of our best bats, went to the wicket first.

c. Hence the phrase, ***off his own bat***, in reference to the score made by a player's own hits; *fig.* solely by his own exertions, by himself. Also †***bat's end***, a local term for 'point' (see POINT *sb.*[1] B. 11 a) (*Obs.*); ***with the bat***, in batting; as a batsman; ***from*** or ***off the bat***: of runs scored from actual hits (opp. 'extras'); ***to carry one's bat***: see CARRY *v.* 53 c.

1742 in H. T. Waghorn *Cricket Scores* (1899) 29 The bets on the Slendon man's head that he got 40 notches off his own bat were lost. **1786** *County Mag.* Nov. 171 These two things then you next must do, Place one at middle wick't, at batt's end two. **1832** *P. Egan's Bk. Sports* 345/2 Pilch . . showed great capabilities, both in the field and with the bat. **1845** SYD. SMITH *Fragm. Irish Ch.* Wks. II. 340/1 He had no revenues but what he got off his own bat. **1859** *All Y. Round* No. 13. 305 One of our adversaries scored 70 off his own bat. **1862** *Baily's Mag.* Aug. 83 Out of the 204 runs scored from the bat by Oxford, 90 . . were contributed by Mr. Mitchell. **1863** *Lillywhite's Cricket Scores* III. 97 Hodgson got more runs in his one innings than Rochdale did in their twenty-two innings *off the bat.* **1865** *Fraser's Mag.* Nov. 667 It is a mistake . . to suppose that Lord Palmerston did everything off his own bat after 1834. **1887** F. GALE *Game Cricket* 45 Seventy years ago . . He played as substitute for an absent mate and was placed at 'bat's-end', as point was always called. **1939** T. S. ELIOT *Old Possum's Pract. Cats* 30 All his Inventions are off his own bat.

d. In baseball, the implement used to strike the ball or the act of using it; esp. in phrases ***at bat, hot*** (or ***right***) ***off the bat, to*** (***the***) ***bat***; also *fig. N. Amer.*

1856 *Spirit of Times* (N.Y.) 6 Dec. 229/1 The bat or club [used in baseball] is of hickory or ash, about 3 feet long, tapering . . and round. **1868** *Iowa State Reporter* (Des Moines) 21 Oct. 2/4 The penny was flipped to see who should go first to the bat. **1875** *Chicago Tribune* 18 Aug. 5/6 The fine play of the home nine . . both in the field and at the bat. **1881** *Sun-beam* (Terre-Haute, Ind.) June 5/1 Picking up a base-ball bat. **1884** E. W. NYE *Baled Hay* 52 Common decency ought to govern conversation without its being necessary to hire an umpire to announce who is at bat. **1888** *Outing* (U.S.) May 118/2 Ferguson . . sent the Cincinnatis to the bat. **1888** 'M. TWAIN' *Meisterschaft* 459 Whoever may ask us a Meisterschaft question shall get a Meisterschaft answer—and hot from the bat! **1889** —— *Conn. Yankee* xi. 516 Step to the bat, it's your innings. **1914** *Maclean's Mag.* Feb. 135/2 Get one that chums-up with your spirit right off the bat, natural like. **1955** *New Yorker* 21 May 76/3 You can tell right off the bat that they're wicked, because they keep eating grapes indolently.

e. In the game of two-up (see quot. 1945).

1917 *N.Z.E.F. Chrons.* 16 May 137/2 The big brown paw that held the 'bat' Was trembling like a leaf. **1945** BAKER *Austral. Lang.* ix. 176 The small piece of board upon which the two pennies are rested for spinning is called the *kip, stick, bat* or *kiley.*

f. Usu. in pl., the objects resembling table-tennis bats used to guide aircraft landing (e.g. on a ship's deck). Hence used *colloq.* as a name for one who signals with these bats; = BATSMAN 2.

1943 *Fleet Air Arm* (Min. of Information) v. 32 (*caption*) The Deck-Landing Control Officer guides the Seafire pilot in with his 'bats'. **1943** T. HORSLEY *Find, Fix & Strike* v. 45 The control officer 'bats', which are now fitted with small electric bulbs, are clearly seen against the background of 'glim' lights. *Ibid.* x. 80 (*caption*) The 'Bats' Officer, in charge of the landing, is about to give the pilot the signal to cut his engine. **1948** PARTRIDGE *Dict. Forces' Slang 1939–45* 12 *Bats*, the Ward-room name for the Deck Landing Officer on an aircraft carrier.

4. The 'sword of wood' or light lath wand of Harlequin in pantomimes. [Directly from F. '*batte*, sabre de bois d'arlequin' (Littré).]

1859 *Illustr. Lond. News* 8 Jan., Harlequin's wonder-working bat.

5. *dial.* (Kent, etc.): The wooden handle or stick of an implement, *e.g.* of a scythe.

6. *dial.* (*Herefordsh.* etc.): A wooden implement for breaking clods of earth. [So F. *batte.*]

II. A lump, a piece of certain substances; a mass, dull-sounding, or formed by beating.

†**7.** A lump, piece, bit. *Obs.* in general sense.

c **1340** *Alexander* (Stev.) 4166 Quare flaggis of the fell snawe · fell fra þe heuen . . a-brade . . as battis ere of wolle. **1393** LANGL. *P. Pl.* C. XIX. 92 Þe of heuene . . bad hit be [of] a bat of erþe · a man and a mayde.

8. a. *esp.* A piece of a brick having one end entire.

1519 HORMAN *Vulg.* 240 b, Battz and great rubbrysshe . . to fyll vp in the myddell of the wall. **1667** PRIMATT *City & C. Build.* 50 Let him get his foundation cleared, and his Bricks and Bats laid up. **1677** MOXON *Mech. Exerc.* (1703) 261 Lay a three quarter Bat at the Quine in the stretching course. [See BRICKBAT.]

b. *Pottery.* (*a*) = STILT *sb.* 4 f; (*b*) a piece of unfired clay (see quot. 1825[2]).

1825 J. NICHOLSON *Operat. Mechanic* 273 Pieces of clay, called stilts, pins, bats [etc.] are put to keep them apart. *Ibid.* 466 The piece is then laid on a flat surface of board, or plaster, and the workman with a heavy lump of clay, with a level under-surface, adapted for holding in the hand, beats the clay to the thinness the vessel is intended to form. These pieces of clay are technically called *bats.* **1961** M. JONES *Potbank* viii. 30 A tool . . comes down to press the lump out into a . . pancake. The maker puts the clay—now called a bat—in the mould.

9. A kind of sun-dried brick.

1816 SOUTHEY in *Q. Rev.* XV. 214 Preparing bats,—a sort of bricks made of clay and straw, well beaten together, 18 inches long, 12 wide, 4 deep, not burnt, but dried in the sun.

10. A brick-shaped peat.

1846 CLARKE in *Jrnl. R. Agric. Soc.* VII. II. 517 The dried 'peat bats,' or brick-shaped turf, used for fuel.

11. Shale interstratified between seams of coal, iron-ore, etc. Cf. BASS *sb.*[4]

1686 PLOT *Staffordsh.* 132 Substances call'd partings . . of consistence between an earth and a coal, or soft bat. **1712** H. BELLERS in *Phil. Trans.* XXVII. 543 Those Substances, which divide the Strata of Coals and Iron Oars from each other, are called Bats by the Miners. **1839** MURCHISON *Silur. Syst.* I. xxxv. 474 Black 'bat,' a dull, compact, bituminous shale, which sounds under the hammer like wood.

12. A felted mass of fur, or of hair and wool in hat-making: often spelt BATT.

1836 *Scenes Commerce* 195 The whole mass . . is called a batt; a second batt is added to it; and by dint of pressure . . the two batts become one. **1837** WHITTOCK *Bk. Trades* (1842) 294 A batt is quantity sufficient for making half the thickness of one hat. **1875** URE *Dict. Arts* II. 784 The bat or *capade* thus formed is rendered compact by pressing it down with the *hardening* skin.

13. A sheet of cotton wadding used for filling quilts; batting.

III. A stroke.

14. a. A firm blow as with a staff or club. Cf. BAT *v.*

a **1400** *Cov. Myst.* 296 That xal be asayd be this batte, What thou, Ihesus? ho ȝaff the that? **1535** STEWART *Cron. Scot.* II. 432 Sum gat ane bat that breissit all thair bonis. **1566** DRANT *Horace' Sat.* I. i. A ij, The souldyer that doth deale the battes and makes his foes to flye. **1674** P. WHALLEY *Establ. Relig.* 22 To have a Batt at the Pope with the Butt end of a Dominican. **1864** ATKINSON *Whitby Gloss.* s.v. *Bat*, 'It gets more bats than bites,' said of the dog that gets more blows than food.

b. A movement of the eyelids (see BAT *v.*[2] 2).

1932 E. CALDWELL *Tobacco Road* iv. 41 Almost as quickly as the bat of an eye. **1941** 'M. HOME' *Place of Little Birds* ii. 21 He didn't show by the bat of an eyelid that you were a friend. **1948** C. FRY *Thor, with Angels* 7 We were at the boy in the bat of an eye.

15. *dial.* and *slang.* Beat, rate of stroke or speed, pace; in *Sc. dial.* rate, manner, style.

1808 JAMIESON s.v., [Getting on] about the auld bat. **1824** *Craven Dial.* 49 There com by me, at a feaful girt bat, a par o'shay and four. **1877** PEACOCK *Manley* (*Linc.*) *Gloss.* s.v., They do go at a strange bat on them railroads. **1880** *Daily Tel.* 11 Mar., Going off at a lively bat of 34 . . the boat travelled at a good pace. **1888** 'R. BOLDREWOOD' *Robb. under Arms* I. xxi. 293 We could hear a horse coming along at a pretty good bat. *Ibid.* II. xvi. 247 A cove comes tearing up full batt. **1949** 'J. TEY' *Brat Farrar* xv. 138 [The horse] took Felix under an oak, going an awful bat. **1961** J. WELCOME *Beware of Midnight* ii. 20 We turned on to the main . . road and started going a hell of a bat across the Cotswolds.

IV. *Comb.*, as **bat-ball**, a ball to be struck with a bat; **batboy** *Baseball*, a youth employed to look after the bats and other equipment of a baseball team; **batman**, one who carries a bludgeon, a clubman; **bat-willow**, a species of willow from which cricket bats are made. Also BAT-FOWL, -ER, -ING. See also CRICKET-BAT *willow.*

1876 EMERSON *Ess.* Ser. I. x. 241 Moons are no more bounds to spiritual power than bat-balls. **1914** *N.Y. Tribune* 5 Oct. 10/1 Everybody connected with the Boston team, from Jim Gaffney, president and chief owner, down to the bat boy, has been pulling in the same direction. **1976** *National Observer* (U.S.) 12 June 14/1 Still several weeks shy of 22, Randolph looks more like a bat boy than a big-deal Yankee. **1833** *Extracts as to Administ. Poor Laws* 26 The batmen, so called from the provincial term of bat, for a bludgeon which they use. **1907** *Kew Bulletin* No. 8. 311 The supplies of the best 'Bat Willow' have become seriously limited. **1910** *Westm. Gaz.* 6 Apr. 4/2 The fast growing bat-willow . . a first-cross between two common varieties of willow . . appeared in Norfolk about 1700. It is still chiefly obtained from East Anglia.

‖**bat, bât** (bɑː, bɑːt, bæt), *sb.*[3] [a. F. *bât* pack-saddle, OF. *bast*:—late L. *bastum*, perhaps connected with Gr. *βαστ-άζειν* to bear.]

1. A pack-saddle. Only in *comb.*, as **bat-needle**, a packing-needle (*obs.*); **bât-horse** (F. *cheval de bât*), a sumpter-beast, a horse which carries the baggage of military officers, during a campaign; as **bât-mule**. See also BATMAN.

1393 LANGL. *P. Pl.* C. VII. 218 To brochen hem with a batte-nelde · and bond hem to-gederes. **1578** *Richmond Wills* (1853) 279 Batt nedles, ij *s.* **1787** T. JEFFERSON *Writ.* (1859) II. 137 Putting my baggage into portable form for my bat-mule. **1863** KINGLAKE *Crimea* II. 144 It was found necessary to dispense with the bât horses of the army. **1879** *Pall Mall Budg.* 17 Oct. 20 A new pack-saddle for bat mules or horses has been invented by an officer of the French military train.

2. In ***bat-money***: An allowance for carrying baggage in the field. Sometimes confused with BATTA *sb.*[1]

1793 PITT in G. Rose *Diaries* (1860) I. 127 He shall have directions about the bât and forage money. **1808** WELLINGTON in Gurw. *Disp.* IV. 82, I should make an issue of bât and forage money to the Officers. **1813** SIR R. WILSON *Pr. Diary* II. 279 Lord Castlereagh also notes that my income will be suitably augmented by a bât and forage allowance.

bat, *sb.*[4] *slang* (orig. *U.S.*). Also **batt.** [Of obscure origin: cf. BATTER *sb.*[4]] A spree or binge.

1848 DURIVAGE & BURNHAM *Stray Subj.* 102 (Th.), Zenas had been on 'a bat' during the night previous. **1869** W. T. WASHBURN *Fair Harvard* 69 (Th.), I went to a 'bat' in S.'s room, and we smoked and drank till three. **1891** *Harper's Mag.* Oct. 778/1 He had been on a bat, and all on earth that ailed him was that spree. **1901** *House Party* 188 We defied the Head and went off on the meekest and stupidest little bat you ever saw. **1942** E. WAUGH *Put out more Flags* iii. §4. 187 Why don't you switch to rum? It's much better for you. . . When did you start on this bat?

bat (bat), *sb.*[5] [Hindi, = speech, language, word.] ***the bat***: the colloquial speech of a foreign country; chiefly in phr. ***to sling the bat.***

1887 KIPLING *3 Musketeers* in *Plain Tales* (1888) 62 T' *Sahib* doesn't speak t' *bat.* **1889** —— *Barrack-r. Ballads* (1892) 67 An' ow they would admire for to hear us sling the *bat.* **1919** *War Terms* in *Athenæum* 8 Aug. 729/1 A variant for 'sling the bat' (speak the lingo) is 'spin the bat'. **1924** *Glasgow Herald* 14 Apr. 10 He continued eagerly . . 'that in the bat of the Arab "Shmallock" and "Amenak" mean "left" and "right".'

bat (bæt), *v.*[1] [f. BAT *sb.*[2]; cf. also F. *batt-re* to beat.]

1. *trans.* To strike with, or as with, a bat; to cudgel, thrash, beat.

c **1440** *Promp. Parv.* 26 Battyn, or betyn wyth stavys (*v.r.* battis), *fustigo, baculo.* **1570** LEVINS *Manip.* 37 To batte, beate, *fustigare, tundere.* **1606** HOLLAND *Sueton.* 116 Mariners, who with their sprits, poles, and oares . . beate and batt their carkasses. **1859** REEVE *Brittany* 49 Women vehemently batting heaps of wet linen at the lavatories.

2. a. To strike or hit a ball with a bat, so as to drive it away, esp. in *Cricket.* Also *absol.* and *fig.*

1745 in H. T. Waghorn *Cricket Scores* (1899) 36 The girls bowled, batted, ran, and catched . . as well as most men could do in that game. **1773** *Gentl. Mag.* XLIII. 451 To bat and bowl with might and main. **1859** BARNES *Rhymes Dorset Dial.* II. 14 Well here . . 'S a ball for you if you can bat it. **1884** *Manch. Exam.* 16 May 5 The Notts team was batting all day against Sussex. **1959** *Observer* 18 Jan. 19/2 The healer, who went in to bat last, was lured into the last ditch of philosophical idealism. **1961** *Listener* 2 Nov. 737/3 Two contributors, finally, bat for Christianity.

b. ***to bat on a sticky wicket***: see STICKY *a.*[2]

†**3.** To fasten by beating. *Obs.*

1793 SMEATON *Edystone L.* §302 By batting them closely to the stone underneath, by the gentle blows of a small hammer. *Ibid.* The leaden cap . . that I had carefully batted to the stone.

4. To go or move; to wander, to potter. Usu. with advb. extension, *along, around, away*, etc. Chiefly *dial.* and *U.S.*

a **1898** *Old Radicals & Young Reformers* 13 (E.D.D.), Heaw they staret when they seed Billy battin away across a fielt. **1907** W. D. HOWELLS *Let.* 3 Oct. in *Mark Twain—Howells Lett.* (1960) II. 826 [She] was in England . . batting round with two other girls, and having a great time. **1926** *S.P.E. Tract* XXIV. 119 *Bat round*, have a good time, go from place to place (in quest of pleasure). 'We've been batting round all evening.' **1929** E. RICE *Street Scene* (1930) I, I want 'em [*sc.* the kids] home, instead o' battin' around the streets. **1938** *Reader's Digest* Mar. 13/2 A Department Sanitation truck was batting along as fast as it could go. **1959** *Encounter* Aug. 30/2 So I batted along, and I tried to make conversation with the kiddo. **1959** I. & P. OPIE *Lore & Lang. Schoolchildren* x. 192 Expressions inviting a person's departure . . bat off, beat it, [etc.].

bat, *v.*[2] [A variant of BATE *v.*[1]; in sense 2 perh. of BATE *v.*[2]]

1. *intr.* To bate or flutter as a hawk.

1615 LATHAM *Falconry* (1633) Gloss., Batting, or to bat is when a Hawke fluttereth with her wings either from the pearch or the mans fist, striuing as it were to flie away.

2. *trans.* (orig. *dial.* and in U.S.) ***to bat the eyes***: to move the eyelids quickly, to wink. Also freq. in colloq. phr. (normally in negative form), ***not to bat an eye, eyelid***, etc. (i) not to sleep a wink; (ii) to betray no emotion (orig. *U.S.*). Also *intr.*

In quot. 1950 the phr. means contextually 'I didn't open my eyes (*i.e.* I slept heavily)'.

1838 HOLLOWAY *Prov. Dict.* 9/1 *Bat*, to wink.. *Derby.* **1846** J. J. HOOPER *Adv. Simon Suggs* xii. 143, I didn't say nuthin, but jist batted my eye at old Chamblin. **1847–78** HALLIWELL, *Bat*, to wink. *Derbysh.* **1879** MISS JACKSON *Shropsh. Word-bk.*, *Bat*, to wink, or rather to move the eyelids up and down quickly. **1883** *American* VI. 237 To bat the eyes, meaning to wink, when we desire to express the rapidity of the action. **1883** J. HARRIS in *Century Mag.* May 146 You hol' your head high; don't you bat your eyes to please none of 'em. **1889** 'CRADDOCK' *Broomsedge Cove* xii. 208 If my patient can't sleep, not a soul in the house shall bat an eye all night. **1904** *Sun* (N.Y.) 7 Aug. 1 The Judge would say: 'That's interesting.. I hadn't heard of it.' But, as they say out West, 'he wouldn't bat an eye'. **1910** 'O. HENRY' *Whirligigs* viii. 113 I've stood by you without batting an eye in earthquakes, fire and flood. **1930** *English Jrnl.* XIX. 607 We do want the facts, and we are willing to look them straight in the eye without batting a lash. **1950** J. CANNAN *Murder Incl.* vi. 109, I was tired.. and I never batted an eyelid until Beatrice brought in my breakfast. **1959** *News Chron.* 14 July 4/6 [Japan] slipped from.. past to.. present without, you might say, batting an eyelid.

bat, obs. f. BATH *sb.*³ a Heb. measure.

bat: see BATZ, a German coin.

bat(e, obs. form of BOAT.

† **'batable**, *a. Obs.* Also 7 bateable, 7–8 battable. [Shortened form of DEBATABLE; cf. BATE *sb.*¹] Debatable, disputed; used esp. of the 'debatable ground' on the Scottish border.

1453 in Rymer *Fœdera* (1710) XI. 337 The Batable Landes in the Westmarch. **1531–2** *Act 23 Hen. VIII*, xvi, The batable grounde betwene England and Scotland. **1610** HOLLAND *Camden's Brit.* I. 782 Called Batable ground, as one would say *Litigious*, because the English and the Scottish have litigiously contended about it. **1751** CHAMBERS *Cycl.*, *Battable ground.* [In mod. Dicts.]

batable, variant of BATTABLE *a.*¹ *Obs.* fertile.

batail(e, -ailler, -ailling, -aillous, obs. forms of BATTLE, -ER, -ING, BATTAILOUS.

Batak ('bætək), *a.* and *sb.*¹ Also Battak. = BATTA³.

1811 W. MARSDEN *Hist. Sumatra* (ed. 3) 365 By many regarded as having the strongest claims to originality, is the nation of the *Battas* (properly *Batak*), whose remarkable dissimilitude to the other inhabitants.. renders it necessary that.. attention should be paid to their description. **1875** *Encycl. Brit.* III. 442/2 (*heading*) Batta or Batak language. *Ibid.* 443/1 The Batak literature consists chiefly in books on witchcraft, [etc.]. **1933** BLOOMFIELD *Language* xviii. 310 The eight normal types of correspondence will appear sufficiently if we consider three languages: Tagalog.., Javanese, and Batak (on the island of Sumatra). **1957** *Encycl. Brit.* XXI. 550/2 The Batak inhabit the mountainous region about Lake Toba and a part of the east coast [of Sumatra]. **1958** A. TOYNBEE *East to West* xviii. 54, I was told.. that the Batak Church has more theological students in training than are to be found in all the Anglican theological colleges in Britain.

Batak (bə'tɑːk), *sb.*² [Native name.] (A member of) a people on the island of Palawan, Philippines.

1904 W. A. REED in *Ethnol. Survey Pubns. Manila* II. I. 22 The Taghanua and Batak of Paragua... The Taghanua.. can not be classed with the Negritos... The Batak who inhabit the territory from the Bay of Ulugan north to Caruray and Barbacan may be so classed, although they are by no means of pure blood. **1905** E. Y. MILLER *Ibid.* III. 183 The peculiar primitive people known as Bataks are to be found in the mountains in the interior of Palawan. **1957** *Encycl. Brit.* III. 198/2 *Batak*.. Short statured and brown to dark skinned they appear to be a composite of Negrito and Malayan type elements.

† **batand**, *pr. pple.* used *advb. Obs.* Also bata(u)nt, baitand. [a. OF. *batant*, pr. pple. of *bat-re* to beat, in phrase *venir batant* to come with haste; in form *batand*, assimilated to native pples. in -AND¹, q.v.] Hastening, in haste.

1330 R. BRUNNE *Chron.* 149 Batand fro Cezile com him a messengere. *Ibid.* 307 So com þe erle Marschalle baitand to London.

‖ **batardeau** (batar'do). Also 8 batter-. [Fr.: formerly *bastardeau*, considered by Littré and Scheler to be a dim. of *bastard* 'a dike,' of doubtful origin: see Littré. (The idea that the termination is *d'eau* 'of water' is not entertained by French scholars.)] **a.** A coffer-dam. **b.** A wall built across the moat or ditch surrounding a fortification.

1767 DUCAREL *Anglo-Norm. Antiq.* 36 Laying the foundations of such piers under water.. by means of a Batterdeaux. **1830** E. CAMPBELL *Dict. Mil. Sc.* 62 The Enemy may be greatly annoyed by means of certain works called Batard'eaux. **1862** F. GRIFFITHS *Artill. Man.* 262 A *Batardeau* is a solid piece of masonry, 7 or 8 feet thick, crossing the whole breadth of the ditch opposite the flanked angles of the bastions. It retains the water in those parts of the ditch which require to be inundated.

† **batardier.** *Obs.* [a. F. *batardière*, f. *bâtard* bastard, 'because the plants are there only bastards, awaiting their definitive family' (Littré).] A plantation of young grafted trees intended to be transplanted into gardens.

1725 BRADLEY *Fam. Dict.*, *Batardier*, a Place in a Garden, whose Soil should be good, etc., in order to plant Fruit-Trees there.

batata (bə'tɑːtə, bə'teɪtə). [a. Sp. and Pg. *batata*, from a native American language; according to Peter Martyr and Navagerio, 1526, the native name in Haiti. (Hence, transferred to a different plant, *potato*.)]

A plant (*Batatas edulis*, N.O. *Convolvulaceæ*) having an edible tuberous root, called also Spanish or Sweet Potato, a native of the West Indies, whence it was introduced into Spain early in the 16th c.

1577 FRAMPTON *Joyf. Newes* 104 The Batatas.. a common frute in those countries.. a victaill of much substaunce. **1613** PURCHAS *Pilgr.* v. xiv. 516 The islands of Moratay.. where Battata-roots is their bread. **1832** *Veg. Subst. Food* 126 The plant carried to Ireland by Captain Hawkins, in 1565, was the Spanish batata, or sweet potato. **1866** LIVINGSTONE *Jrnl.* I. iii. 73 Batatas and maize were often planted.

bataunt, var. BATAND, *Obs.* hastening, eager.

¶ Misused by Chatterton (and J. M. Neale).

a **1770** CHATTERTON *Sir C. Bawdin* 276 Behynde theyre backes syx mynstrelles came, Who tun'd the strunge bataunt.

† **batauntly**, *adv. Obs.* In 4 -liche. [f. prec. + -LY².] Hastily, pressingly, eagerly.

1393 LANGL. *P. Pl.* C. XVII. 56 Batauntliche, as beggers don · and boldeliche he craueþ. [**1677** COLES, *Batauntly*, boldly. *Obs.* (Hence in Kersey, Bailey, etc.) *a* **1768** CHATTERTON *Ælla* 826 Yette woulde I battentlie assuage mie fyre.]

Batavia (bə'teɪvɪə). [Former name of Djakarta, capital of Indonesia.] A kind of shot silk material. Also *attrib.*

1907 *Daily Chron.* 10 June 8/1 A new shot silk, known as 'Batavia'... Smart little coats carried out in this Batavia silk look particularly well. **1909** *Cent. Dict.* Suppl. s.v. *Weave*, *Batavia weave*, a kind of twilled armure weave made on four harnesses.

Batavian (bə'teɪvɪən), *a.* and *sb.* [f. L. *Batavia*, f. *Batavi* an ancient people who dwelt on the island Betawe, between the Rhine and the Waal, in part of what is now Holland. See -AN.]

A. *adj.* **a.** Of or pertaining to the ancient Batavi: see above. **b.** Pertaining to Holland or to the Dutch.

1796 MORSE *Amer. Geog.* II. 339 First year of Batavian liberty. **1859** MACAULAY *Hist. Eng.* V. 141 The peculiarity of the Batavian polity threw some difficulties in his way. **1876** BANCROFT *Hist. U.S.* I. iv. 100 He had fought for the independence of the Batavian republic.

B. *sb. pl.* **a.** The ancient Batavi: see above. **b.** The Dutch or Netherlanders (*rare*).

1598 GREENWEY *Tacitus' Ann.* iv. (1622) 266 The Batavians.. inhabit an Ilande of the River of Rhene. **1876** BANCROFT *Hist. U.S.* II. xxii. 24 There would be no war but on water, the home of the Batavians.

batayle, -ynge, etc., obs. ff. BATTLE, etc.

bat-ball: see BAT *sb.*¹

batch (bætʃ), *sb.*¹ Forms: 5 **bahche**, 5–6 **bache, batche**, 7 **bach**, 6– **batch**. [ME. *bache, bacche*, repr. an unrecorded OE. **bæcce*, f. *bacan* to BAKE: cf. *wake, watch, make, match, speak, speech.*]

† **1.** The process of baking. *Obs.*

1440 *Promp. Parv.* 21 Bahche, or bakynge (*v.r.* batche), *pistura.* **1551** T. WILSON *Logike* 42 b, Except the baker doe his part also in the batch.

2. a. *concr.* A baking; the quantity of bread produced at one baking.

1461–83 *Ord. R. Househ.* 70 He shall trulye delyver into the bredehouse.. the whole numbyr of his bache. **1530** PALSGR. 197/1 Batche of bredde—*fournée de pain.* *a* **1656** BP. HALL *Rem. Wks.* (1660) 186 They had no leisure to make up their bach. **1760** T. HUTCHINSON *Hist. Col. Mass.* i. (1765) 23 The last batch was in the oven. **1856** KANE *Arct. Exp.* II. xix. 192 We.. baked a large batch of bread.

fig. **1606** SHAKS. *Tr. & Cr.* v. i. 5 Thou crusty batch of Nature, what's the newes?

† **b.** *ellipt.* The bread itself: cf. *bread of life. Obs.*

1648 EARL WESTMLD. *Otia Sacra* (1879) 92 Those blest With the True batch of Life may ever rest So satisfi'd.

† **3.** *fig.* and *transf.* The sort of 'lot' to which a thing belongs by origin (as loaves do to their own batch). *Obs.*

1598 B. JONSON *Ev. Man in Hum.* I. ii. (1616) 9 One is a Rimer Sir, o' your owne batch. **1641** MILTON *Ch. Discip.* II. Wks. (1851) 42 This worthy Motto, No Bishop, no King is of the same batch, and infanted out of the same feares. **1705** HICKERINGILL *Priest-cr.* (1721) I. 47 All sorts of Priest-craft are of one *Leven* and one *Batch.*

4. a. The quantity of flour or dough to be used for one baking. **b.** The quantity of corn sent at one time to the mill to be ground. *dial.*

1549 COVERDALE *Erasm. Par. 1 Cor.* vi. 6 A lytle leauen sowreth the whole batche, wherwith it is myngled. **1570** LEVINS *Manip.* 38 A batche, *fermentum.* **1579** LANGHAM *Gard. Health* (1633) 90 Bake a loafe of wheat meale as it cometh from the mill in the midst of the batch. **1796** W. MARSHALL *Midl. Count.* II. Gloss., *Batch*, a grist; a quantity of corn sent to mill. **1859** *Autobiog. Beggar-boy* 65 To bring the farmers' *batches* to be ground, and take them home when made into meal.

5. *transf.* A quantity produced at one operation, *e.g.* a brewing; a lot. *arch.*

1713 *Lond. & Country Brew.* I. (1742) 31 You are welcome to a good Batch of my October [Beer]. **1878** MISS BRADDON *Open Verd.* I. i. 13 That last batch of soup was excellent.

6. a. A quantity of anything coming at a time, an instalment. **b.** A number of things or persons introduced, put, or treated together; a set.

a. 1833 MARRYAT *P. Simple* (1863) 85, I have just received a batch of prize-money. **1840** HOOD *Up Rhine* 58, I am not going to favour you with a batch of politics. **1881** RAYMOND *Mining Gloss.*, *Batch* (Cornw.), the quantity of ore sent to the surface by a *pare* of men.

b. [**1598**; cf. 4.] **1632** MASSINGER *City Mad.* IV. i, A whole batch, sir, Almost of the same leaven. **1793** LD. AUCKLAND *Corr.* III. 75 A new batch of visitors, who are coming for the day. **1845** DISRAELI *Sybil* (1863) 39 A baronet of the earliest batch. **1863** KINGLAKE *Crimea* (1876) I. xiv. 297 Shot by platoons and in batches. **1872** BLACK *Adv. Phaeton* xxxi. 413 The batch of letters awaiting us in Edinburgh.

c. The quantity of stricks or bundles of jute laid out at one time for treatment. (Cf. BATCH *v.* 1.)

1880 *Encycl. Brit.* XIII. 803/1 These batches [of jute], which generally contained from 4 to 5 tons each, were allowed to lie from twenty-four to forty-eight hours. **1893** W. LEGGATT *Jute Spinning* 21 The batch put down for ordinary hessian warps should be composed of six bales.

d. *Calico-printing* and *Dyeing.* The mass of material collected in 'batching' (cf. BATCH *v.* 2). Also *attrib.*

1911 TROTMAN & THORP *Princ. Bleaching and Finishing Cotton* xxviii. 304 The chief use of the machine is to transfer cloth from the lap to the batch form. *Ibid.*, The bearings of the batch roller work in vertical slides under the pressure of springs or weights, and can be raised and held with a pawl to unroll a part of the batch for detailed inspection.

e. *Glass-making* = FRIT *sb.*² 1.

a **1877** KNIGHT *Dict. Mech.* I. 246/1 *Batch*,.. the frit of a glass-maker compounded and sifted for use, ready for the glass-pot or crucible. **1933** *Antiquity* VII. 420 Glass workers use the term 'batch' to denote the raw ingredients of the glass before fusing.

7. *attrib.*, as in ***batch-bread, -flour.*** Also in various combinations denoting a machine or process that treats a batch of material (esp. as opposed to a continuous process).

1862 *Lond. Rev.* 16 Aug. 140 Baking rolls and fancy bread, taking the batch-bread out of the oven. **1878** HALLIWELL s.v., Coarse flour is sometimes called *batch* flour. **1940** *Chambers's Techn. Dict.* 80/2 *Batch furnace*, a furnace in which the charge is placed and heated to the requisite temperature, subsequently being withdrawn... Distinguished from continuous furnace. **1954** *Economist* 20 Feb. 537/2 Strenuous attempts to convert their batch processes to the continuous processes which have so much lower labour costs. **1955** J. G. DAVIS *Dict. Dairying* (ed. 2) 136 Batch pasteurisation is a satisfactory and economical method for small factories. **1957** *Economist* 16 Nov. 621/1 Glass for spectacles.. has to be of very precise physical qualities... Until recently this has meant making it in a form of batch process known as the pot roast method. **1957** *Ibid.* 23 Nov. 645 Continuous batch testing with the latest scientific equipment. **1958** A. HACKNEY *Private Life* vii. 65 Num-nums and Chokers are still in batch production, but the Bumper Bars themselves are in continuous-flow production.

batch, *sb.*² [? a variant of BACK *sb.*²] A vessel used in brewing.

1697 *View Penal Laws* 21 By which any Beer.. may be conveyed into or out of such Tun, Batch or Float.

batch, mod. dial. form of BACHE.

batch (bætʃ), *v.* [f. BATCH *sb.*¹] **1.** *trans.* To treat (bundles of raw fibre of jute, wool, etc.) in batches for various purposes. Hence **'batching** *vbl. sb.*, the action or process by which this is done; also *attrib.* Also **'batcher**, an operative who does this.

1880 *Chemical News* XLII. 77/2 The fibres are matted together by a resinous constituent, and in order to fit them for the operations of combing they are subjected to the preliminary treatment of 'batching'. This consists in moistening the fibre with a mixture of oil, [etc.]. **1880** *Encycl. Brit.* XIII. 802/2 (Jute) Batching or Softening. **1881** *Instr. Census Clerks* (1885) 71 Jute preparing: Preparer. Batcher. **1882** P. SHARP *Flax, Tow, & Jute Spinning* 158 In this system the jute is batched in the same way as tow. **1893** W. LEGGATT *Jute Spinning* 19 The batchers.. break up the large streaks or heads into streaks of about two pounds each. *Ibid.*, The jute warehouse, which will be seen from a reference to the ground plan to adjoin the batching house. **1921** MACKINNON *Social & Industr. Hist. Scot.* II. 115 This is done in the 'batching room', where the raw material is sprinkled with oil and water. **1921** *Dict. Occup. Terms* (1927) §398 Batcher (flax and hemp); (i) arranges different qualities of tow in layers to facilitate mixing of tow for carder; (ii) applies water and oil to opened out hemp, to soften fibre and to prevent it from 'licking up' during.. carding. **1943** J. S. HUXLEY *TVA* 23 From the quarry the rock was carried to the crusher, thence to the screening plant, the batching plant and concrete mixers. **1950** *Engineering* 20 Jan. 81/3 In the batching process, the quantities of cement and.. aggregate are best measured by weight. **1952** *Electronic Engin.* XXIV. 205 Electronics can accurately control a mechanical batching device.

2. *Calico-printing* and *Dyeing*. To collect into a 'batch' or mass. Hence **'batching** *vbl. sb.* (also *attrib.*).

1876 *Encycl. Brit.* IV. 685/2 In printing, the white calico is batched at C, and the cloth D passes inwards over tension rails. **1911** H. R. CARTER *Bleaching, Dyeing of Flax*, etc. 90 The cloth..is..'batched' on to a larger roller, upon which it is removed for subsequent processes—washing, drying, &c. **1911** TROTMAN & THORP *Princ. Bleaching & Finishing Cotton* xxviii. 304 When wound up, the bearings of the batching roller are racked up and the roll unwound or removed. *Ibid.*, The winding-on frame, or canroy, is a frame with tensioning staves, rollers, and scrimp rails, and batching tackle.

batch, var. BACH *sb.* 2, BACH *v.*

batchelor, -ry, obs. ff. BACHELOR, -RY, etc.

batchy ('bætʃɪ), *a. slang.* = BATTY *a.*; dotty.

1898 F. T. BULLEN *Cruise of Cachalot* v. 39 They [*sc.* two of the crew] had gone quite 'batchy' with fright. **1931** *Punch* 14 Oct. 402 Anyone who continues to keep a car in London these days in preference to a horse is batchy. **1960** J. STROUD *Shorn Lamb* xii. 140 Perhaps Egbert's all right and we're all a bit batchy?

bate (beɪt), *v.*[1] Also 6–7 baite, bayte, 7–9 bait. [a. OF. *batre* (mod. *battre*):—late L. *batĕre*, *battĕre*, for cl. L. *batuĕre*. In sense 1 partly also a shortened form of DEBATE *v.*]

†**1.** To contend, fight, strive, with blows or arguments. Const. *on*. *Obs.*

a **1300** *Cursor M.* 5913 And for he wil þus bate [*Trin. MS.* debate] on me, I sal him drenkil in þe se. *c* **1400** *Destr. Troy* XIV. 5914 Durst no buerne on hym bate for his bold dedis. *c* **1440** *Promp. Parv.* 26/2 Batyn, or make debate, *Iurgor*.

2. *Falconry.* To beat the wings impatiently and flutter away from the fist or perch. (Fr. *se battre*: cf. ABATE *v.*[1] 18.)

1398 TREVISA *Barth. De P.R.* XII. iii. (1495) 412 That she bate not to ofte fro his honde. **1486** *Bk. St. Alban's, Hawking* A vj, Holde faste at all timys and specially whan she batith. **1596** SHAKS. *Tam. Shrew* IV. i. 99 These kites, That baite, and beate, and will not be obedient. **1631** *Celestina* I. 3 The Gyrfalcon bated, and I came in to set him on the pearch. **1828** SEBRIGHT *Observ. Hawking* 14 In the field the hood prevents them from baiting. *Ibid.* 48 Which assists the hawk in regaining the perch when he has baited off.

b. *fig.* To flutter, struggle; to be restless or impatient. *Obs.*

1592 SHAKS. *Rom. & Jul.* III. ii. 14 Come, civil night.. Hood my vnman'd blood, bayting in my Cheekes. **1673** DRYDEN *Assignation* I. i, You are eager, and baiting to be gone. **1682** SIR T. BROWNE *Chr. Mor.* (1756) 106 It's now somewhat late to bait after things before us.

c. with some sense of BATE *v.*[2] combined: To flutter downwards. Also *to bate the wings*.

1590 GREENE *Never too late* (1600) 93, I haue soared with the Hobby, I shall bate with the Bunting. **1641** MILTON *Ch. Discip.* I. Wks. (1851) 2 Till the Soule by this meanes of over-bodying herselfe..bated her wing apace downeward.

bate (beɪt), *v.*[2] Forms: 4– bate; (4 bawt), 6–7 bayte, baite. [aphetic form of ABATE *v.*[1]]

†**1.** *trans.* To beat down or away; *fig.* to put an end to. *Obs.*

c **1300** *K. Alis.* 7496 Thow batest wrong, and hauntest ryght. **1330** R. BRUNNE *Chron.* 87 Bated was þe strife. *Ibid.* 338 And bate alle oþer outrage. *c* **1430** *Hymns to Virg.* (1867) 57 þe deuelis boost þus gan he bate. **1601** HOLLAND *Pliny* II. 521 Bate the earth from about the roots of Oliues.

†**b.** *intr.* To come to an end, cease. *Obs.*

c **1325** *E.E. Allit. P.* B. 440 þe rayn..batede as fast.

2. *trans.* To lower, let down; *fig.* to cast down, humble, depress, deject. (With quot. 1834 cf. 6.)

c **1380** *Sir Ferumb.* 749 ȝut stod he strong & stif..& ne batedede noȝt is mod. **1523** FITZHERB. *Husb.* §153 Myght bere it though he lost and bate nat his countenaunce. **1530** PALSGR. 443/1, I bayte myne eares (Lydgate), I applye them to herken a thynge, *Je embats*. **1834** S. ROGERS *Inscript. Strathfieldsaye*, On he went, Bating nor heart, nor hope.

†**b.** *to bate of, from*: to bring down or remove from; to deprive of. *Obs.*

1399 LANGL. *Rich. Redeless* II. 13 Ffor mowtynge.. bawtid ȝoure bestis of here bolde chere. **1642** ROGERS *Naaman* 869 Who will baite their children and servants from their diligence.

†**c.** *intr.* To become dejected or depressed. *Obs.*

1608 TOURNEUR *Rev. Trag.* II. ii. 54, I bate in courage now. **1678** DRYDEN *Dram. Wks.* IV. 192 His Heroe..Bates of his Mettle; and scarce Rants at all.

3. *trans.* To beat back or blunt the edge of. *lit.* and *fig.* (Perhaps in fig. use combined with some idea of BAIT *v.*[1] II., as if 'to satisfy the hunger of.')

1535 COVERDALE *Jer.* xlvi. 10 The swearde shal deuoure, it shal be satisfied and bated [**1611** made drunke] in their bloude. **1588** SHAKS. *L.L.L.* I. i. 6 Which shall bate his sythes keene edge. **1649** JER. TAYLOR *Gt. Exemp.* III. xv. 85 Caiaphas..to baite his envy, was furiously determined Jesus should die. **1827** F. COOPER *Prairie* I. iii. 43 And now I have bated your curiosity.

†**4.** *trans.* To lower in amount, weight, estimation, to reduce. *Obs.*

c **1460** *Pol. Poems* (1859) II. 286 Theyre..wages be batyd. **1596** SHAKS. *Merch. V.* III. iii. 32 These greefes and losses haue so bated mee. **1607** —— *Timon* III. iii. 26 Who bates mine Honor, shall not know my Coyne. **1691** LOCKE *Money* Wks. 1727, II. 34 He must bate the Labourer's Wages.

†**b.** *intr.* To decrease in amount, weight, estimation. *Obs.*

a **1541** WYATT *Poet. Wks.* (1861), How that my wealth doth bate. **1596** SHAKS. *1 Hen. IV*, III. iii. 2 Doe I not bate? doe I not dwindle?

5. *trans.* To lessen in force or intensity; to mitigate, moderate, assuage, diminish. Now chiefly in phr. *to bate one's breath*: to restrain one's breathing, and make it soft and gentle.

a **1300** *Cursor M.* 10942 And dow þai þar-fore murnand were, þai batid it mekil wid þair chere. **1398** TREVISA *Barth.* XIII. xxi. (1495) 452 Takyth fro us the beemes of the sonne and batyth heete therof. *a* **1650** CRASHAW *Poems* (1858) 117 And with some daring drug, Bait the disease. *a* **1653** G. DANIEL *Idyll* v. 105 Let's sift the World; and bate yᵗ Proverbe's force. **1859** GEO. ELIOT *A. Bede* 41 To his dying day he bated his breath a little when he told the story.

b. *intr.* To fall off in force or intensity. (Cf. 6.)

1860 TYNDALL *Glac.* I. §3. 29 His cheerfulness and energy did not bate a jot.

6. *trans.* To strike off or take away (a part *of*); to deduct, subtract.

c **1440** *Promp. Parv.* 26/2 Batyn or abaten of weyte or mesure, *subtraho*. **1543** RECORDE *Gr. Arts* 120 b, Then 8.. from 3 cannot be, therefore do they bate it from a hygher roume. **1602** *Life T. Cromwell* II. iii. 92, I will not bate a penny. **1720** OZELL *Vertot's Rom. Rep.* I. IV. 202 Neither of the Parties wou'd bate any thing of its Pretensions. **1809** W. IRVING *Knickerb.* (1861) 120 I'd not bate one nail's breadth of the honest truth.

b. with obj. (orig. *dative*) of the person, etc.

1597 SHAKS. *2 Hen. IV*, Epil., Bate me some, and I will pay you some. **1633** G. HERBERT *Ch. Porch* xlv. in *Temple* 10 Do not bate The place its honour. **1712** ADDISON *Spect.* No. 488 ¶2 They offered..to bate him the article of bread and butter in the tea-table account. **1867** PARKMAN *Jesuits N. Amer.* viii. (1875) 91 Brébeuf would bate them nothing.

c. *ellipt.* To deprive (a person) *of*; also *dial.* to deduct part of the wages of.

1823 BYRON *Juan* XIII. xcviii, Must let slip no occasion, Nor bate (abate) their hearers of an inch. **1854** MRS. GASKELL *North & S.* xvi, 'Their business [being] to bate us down to clemming point.' **1865** Harland's *Lanc. Lyrics* 242 He winna' 'bate' me when He sees Aw 've done as weel 's aw could. Aw 'se get my wage.

d. *to bate an ace*: see ACE *sb.* 3 b. *bate me an ace, quoth Bolton*: an obsolete expression of incredulity.

1570 R. EDWARDS *Damon & P.* in Hazl. *Dodsl.* IV. 77 Nay, there bate an ace (quod Bolton). *c* **1600** DAY *Begg-Bednell Gr.* (1881) 110 Bate me an ace of that, qd. Bolton.

†**7.** To omit, leave out of count, except. *Obs.*

a **1611** BEAUM. & FL. *Maids Trag.* I. i, Bate me the King ..He lyes that saies it. **1647** R. STAPYLTON *Juvenal* 183 For, bate reward, who will at vertue aime? **1679** DRYDEN *Œdipus* III. i, Bate but his Years, You are his Picture. **1704** SWIFT *T. Tub* (1768) I. 117 If you will bate him but the circumstances of method and style.

†**8.** *to bate of*: **a.** to make an abatement or deduction from, or lessening of. *Obs.*

1625 B. JONSON *Stapl. News* III. iv, And yet not pay the use; Bate of the use? I am mad with this times manners. **1628** EARL *Microcosm.* vi. 14 A good conceit or two bates of such a man, and makes a sensible weakning in him. **1642** R. CARPENTER *Experience* II. iv. 179 The dearest friends would bate of their love.

b. to be deficient in.

1633 T. ADAMS *Exp. 2 Pet.* ii. 2 Suppose the example bates of multitude, and is supplied with magnitude.

bate (beɪt), *v.*[3] *Tanning.* [immediate source doubtful; cf. Sw. *beta* to tan, G. *beiszen* to steep in lye, to macerate, also to BAIT *v.*[1] (with which it is cognate).] To steep in bate: see BATE *sb.*[5]

1875 URE *Dict. Arts* III. 89 The liming and bating, or the unhairing and cleansing. **1879** JAMIESON, *Bait*, to steep skins in a ley made of hens' or pigeons' dung, for the purpose of reducing them to a proper softness.

†**bate**, *sb.*[1] *Obs.* Forms: 4–7 **bate**; also 4–5 **bat**, 5 **batte**, 6 **baate**, **bayte**. [f. BATE *v.*[1]; or directly shortened from DEBATE *sb.*]

1. Contention, strife, discord.

a **1300** *Cursor M.* 9684 Bituix mi sisteris es þe bate [*Cotton MS.* debat]. *a* **1400** *Cov. Myst.* (1841) 12 Cryst that lovyd not stryff nor bat. **1569** SPENSER *Sonnets* viii, Ciuile bate Made me the spoile and bootie of the world. **1690** SHADWELL *Am. Bigot* I. i, I'll breed no bate nor division between young people.

b. *at (the) bate*: at strife, contending, fighting.

a **1500** *E.E. Misc.* (1855) 64 Thowth men be now at the batte, They may be frendys anodyre day. **1509** HAWES *Past. Pleas.* xx. v, Was never man yet surely at the bayte Wyth Sapyence, but that he dyd repent. **1623** SIR J. STRADLING in Farr's *S.P.* 233 A man within himself may be at bate.

2. *Comb.*, as *bate-breeding*, *-maker*, *-making*.

1533 MORE *Debell. Salem* Wks. 963/1 Hys bate making booke. *a* **1564** BECON *Christ & Antichr.* (1844) 517 Antichrist is our disturber, bate-maker and destroyer. **1592** SHAKS. *Ven. & Ad.* cx, This sour informer, this bate-breeding spy. **1646** *Vox Populi* Pref., And our Peace-preachers turnes our Bate-makers.

¶ With the following cf. BAIT *sb.*[1] III, BATE *v.*[1] 2.

c **1340** *Gaw. & Gr. Knt.* 1461 þen, braynwod for bate on burnez he [the boar] rasez. **1627** FELTHAM *Resolves* II. xi. Wks. 181 The Bates and Flutterings of a Conscience within.

bate (beɪt), *sb.*[2] *Obs.* or *dial.* [f. BATE *v.*[2]]

†**1.** Depression, lowering: cf. ABATE *sb.* 1. *Obs.*

1686 GOAD *Celest. Bod.* I. iii. 9 The difformity of the parts of the Earth..of Hault or Bate.

2. Deduction, diminution, abatement: cf. ABATE *sb.* 3. Still in *north. dial.*, esp. in *comb.*

c **1450** in *Babees Bk.* (1868) 329 Withoute bate or betyng be hit distribute..to powre men. **1845** DISRAELI *Sybil* (1863) 72 You're never paid wages, but there's a bate ticket. **1851** *Coal-tr. Terms Northumbld.*, *Batework*, short work.

†**3.** That which is deducted or remains over. *Obs.*

1798 *Ann. Reg.* 35/2 The bate or surplus of the chain remained suspended.

†**bate**, *sb.*[3] *Obs. rare.* [ad. Gr. *βάτος*, ad. Heb. *bath*.] = BATH *sb.*[3]

1548 UDALL, etc. *Erasm. Par. Luke* xvi. 6 An hundred bates of oyle.

bate (beɪt), *sb.*[4] *Obs.* exc. in *north. dial.* [Origin unknown.] The grain of wood or stone.

1664 POWER *Exp. Philos.* III. 159 Finding the grain and bait of the stone to lye fit for their Tranation. **1692** RAY *Disc.* II. v. (1732) 231 The Bate or Texture of the wood. **1746** ARDERON in *Phil. Trans.* XLIV. 185, I sawed seven Pieces cross the Bate or Grain. **1879** JAMIESON, *Bait*, the grain of wood or stone. Aberd.

bate (beɪt), *sb.*[5] *Tanning.* [immediate source doubtful; cf. Sw. *beta* 'maceration, soaking, lime-pit, corrosive,' G. *beisze* 'maceration, steeping,' f. *beiszen* to cause to bite, BAIT *v.*[1] See BATE *v.*[3]] An alkaline lye which neutralizes the effect of the previous application of lime, and makes the hides supple; a vat containing it; the process of steeping in it.

1804 *Hull Advertiser* 30 June 2/3 A Tan-Yard, containing ..Securing-tubs, and Bates. **1875** URE *Dict. Arts* III. 89 The bate consists in steeping the haired hides in a solution of pigeons' dung. **1879** JAMIESON, *Bait*, the ley in which skins are put.

bate, *sb.*[6] See BAIT *sb.*[2]

bate, variant of BAIT; obs. form of BOAT.

batea (bæ'tiːə). *U.S. mining.* [a. Sp. *batea* tray, trough.] A shallow wooden vessel used in the washing of ores in California and Mexico.

1864 S. MOWRY *Arizona & Sonora* 44 In the rubbish which was thrown out of the old mine a comfortable subsistence is gained by washing in bateas [ed. 1859, battas]. **1874** RAYMOND *Sixth Rep. Mines* 315 In these they wash the gravel and earth, by means of wooden bowls or Bateas. **1897** *Engineering Mag.* XVI. 51 Wooden bateas about eighteen inches in diameter (probably used to carry the ore out of the mine).

‖**bateau** (bato). Also, less correctly, **batteau**. Pl. **bateaux** (batoːz). [Fr.:—OF. *batel* 'boat,' cogn. w. Sp. *batel*, It. *battello*, dim. of *batto*; cf. med.L. *batellus*, *batus*, *battus*, prob. from Teut., and ON. *bátr*, OE. *bát*, Eng. BOAT.] **1.** A light river boat; esp. the long tapering boats with flat bottoms used by the French Canadians. ***bateau-bridge***: a floating bridge supported by bateaux. Cf. BATTOE.

1711 in *N.J. Archives* (1882) IV. 137 If you have not engaged Sloops for Albany they may go from hence in Bateaux. *Ibid.* 318, I pressed all the carpenters in the place ..for the dispatch of these batteaux. **1759** *Hist. Eur.* in *Ann. Reg.* 44/2 Dangerous to venture his troops..upon the water in open batteaux. **1823** F. COOPER *Pioneer* xxiii, The batteau shot into the circle of light. **1848** THOREAU *Maine Woods* i. (1864) 4 The making of batteaux is quite a business here. **1884** *Century Mag.* Apr. 826 The bateau which was to carry Mr. Lincoln. **1905** G. E. COLE *Early Oregon* i. 12 The batteau which was to bring our luggage would not be there for several hours. **1947** *Amer. Dial. Soc. Pubn.* VIII. 34 *Bateau*: In southern Virginia this is not a small boat but a flat-bottomed freight boat.

2. *attrib.* and *Comb.*, as **bateau-mouche**, a boat which takes sightseers on the Seine in Paris; **bateau (neck-) line**, in *Dressmaking*, a décolletage having a bow-shaped curve from shoulder to shoulder; hence ***bateau-necked*** adj.; cf. *boat neck(-line)*.

1903 H. JAMES *Ambassadors* XII. xxxiv. 434 An hour with his present friend on a *bateau-mouche*. **1923** *Daily Mail* 20 Feb. 14 The bateau neck-line... This décolletage still retains its popularity. *Ibid.* 1 Mar. 15 The bateau line is still seen on smart gowns. **1938** W. S. MAUGHAM *Summing Up* 19, I used to go down with him every Sunday by the Seine on a *bateau-mouche*. **1959** *Times* 31 July 8/4 A simple bodice often bateau-necked. **1961** *Guardian* 30 Mar. 9/3 The very latest knitted jumpers have..bateau necklines.

bated ('beɪtɪd), *ppl. a.* [f. BATE *v.*[2] + -ED.] Lowered or lessened in position, amount, force, estimation, etc.; esp. in *bated breath*: breathing subdued or restrained under the influence of awe, terror, or other emotion.

1596 SHAKS. *Merch. V.* I. iii. 125 With bated breath, and whispring humblenesse. *a* **1637** B. JONSON *Masques* (1692) 335 The longing Bridegroom, in the Porch, Shews you again the bated Torch. **1854** MRS. GASKELL *North & S.* xvi, Take the bated wage, and be thankful. **1872** FREEMAN *Norm. Conq.* (1876) IV. xxi. 632 It was whispered with bated breath that the vengeance for the blood of Waltheof had begun.

†**'bateful**, *a. Obs.* [f. BATE *sb.*[1] + -FUL.] Full of strife, quarrelsome, contentious.

a **1588** SIDNEY (J.) And taught his sheep her sheep in food to thwart; Which soon as it did bateful question frame, etc.

1582 STANYHURST *Conceites* (Arb.) 138 Thee surlye God angerd.. too wrath towns bat'ful on eggeth.

†**'bateless**, *a. Obs.* [f. BATE *v.*[2] 3 + -LESS.] **1.** That cannot be 'bated' or blunted; unalterably keen.

1593 SHAKS. *Lucr.* ii, Haply that name of chaste unhappily set This bateless edge on his keen appetite. **1595** MARKHAM *Sir R. Grinuile* cv, Sets a batelesse edge, grownd by his word Vpon their blunt harts.

2. Unabating.

1886 *Harper's Mag.* May 884 From heaven of heavens above God speaketh with bateless breath.

bateleur ('bat(ə)lœːr). [Fr., = mountebank, juggler.] In full ***bateleur eagle***: a short-tailed African and Arabian eagle, *Terathopius* (*Helotarsus*) *ecaudatus*. Cf. BERGHAAN, DASSIE-VANGER 1.

1864 J. A. GRANT *Walk across Africa* 306 The largest birds were the Batteleur eagle and the Buceros. *a* **1867** K. J. ANDERSSON *Notes Birds Damara Land* (1872) 10 Helotarsus ecaudatus.. Rufous-backed Bateleur eagle. **1895** LYDEKKER *R. Nat. Hist.* IV. 211 The handsomely coloured bird known as the bateleur eagle.. differs from the sea-eagles.. by the extreme shortness of its tail. **1940** V. POHL *Bushveld Adventures* xi. 233 A couple of bateleur eagles that were circling round a spot. **1955** K. A. THOMPSON *Great House* iii. 106 The trousered bateleurs.

batell, -elment, obs. ff. BATTLE, -MENT.

†**batelle.** *Obs.* Also 6–7 battle. [a. OF. *batel*: see BATEAU.] A small boat, a skiff.

1330 R. BRUNNE *Chron.* 241 Vnder þam alle sank, bothe batelle and barge. *c* **1440** *Morte Arth.* (Roxb.) 103 With his batelle one brede, by tha blythe stremes. **1720** *Stow's Survey* (Strype 1754) I. II. x. 486/1 The lesser boat called a Battle [temp. Edw. III].

batelur, obs. form of BATTLER.

batement. ? *Obs.* exc. *Hist.* [aphetic form of ABATEMENT[1].] **a.** Reduction, lessening, diminution.

1677 MOXON *Mech. Exerc.* (1703) 157 Instead of asking how much was cut off such a piece of Stuff, Carpenters ask what Batement that piece of Stuff had.

b. ***batement light*** [LIGHT *sb.* 10], an upper window or opening with a sloping or curved sill, i.e. abated or cut off at the low end to accommodate the curve of an arch, etc.

1445 in J. A. NICHOLS *Descr. Beauchamp Chapel* (1838) 29 In the est windowe be vij lights.. also sixe bat[t]ments lights, every light conteininge ij foote. **1844** R. WILLIS *Archit. Nomencl. Mid. Ages* iv. 51 They are lights with the lower corner cut off, or, in the language of workmen, they are lights with a *batement*.. hence the term 'batement lights'. **1901** R. STURGIS *Dict. Archit. & Building* 238/2 *Batement light*, in English Gothic traceried windows, a peculiar form of light, or subdivision of a window; one comprised between two mullions, and having a curved or inclined bottom caused by the arched heads of other lights below.

bater ('beɪtə(r)). *Falconry.* [f. BATE *v.*[1] 2 + -ER[1].] A hawk that bates.

1575 TURBERV. *Falconrie* 32 Great Baters and therefore not very greedy of meate.

Batesian ('beɪtsɪən), *a.* [f. the name of H. W. *Bates* (1825–92), English naturalist: see -IAN.] **Batesian mimicry** *Zool.*, a form of mimicry in which an edible species is protected by its resemblance to one which is avoided by predators. So ***Batesian mimic***, the species which is so protected.

1896 E. B. POULTON *Darwin* xxv. 214 Many cases which have been up to the present explained under the theory of true (Batesian) mimicry are now believed to come under that which we owe to F. Müller. **1899** D. SHARP in *Cambr. Nat. Hist.* VI. vi. 339 The comparatively simple, hypothetical explanation, originally promulgated by Bates, is sometimes called Batesian mimicry; while the 'inedible association' hypothesis is termed Müllerian mimicry. **1933** *Discovery* Nov. 357/2 The cuckoo's egg, a clear instance of Batesian mimicry deceiving the selective-agents, i.e., the foster-parents. **1951** *New Biol.* X. 73 Müllerian and Batesian mimics may be involved together in nature in a complex mimetic association.

batesme, obs. form of BAPTISM.

batey ('beɪtɪ), *a.* var. *baity* adj. s.v. BAIT *sb.*[2].

1946 B. MARSHALL *G. Brown's Schooldays* 66 You'll make me batey if you say rotten caddish things like that. **1954** P. H. JOHNSON *Impossible Marriage* 11 I'd better roll the damned thing in or Mater will be batey.

bat-fowl ('bætˌfaʊl), *v.* [app. f. BAT *sb.*[2] + FOWL *v.*, as if to go a fowling with bats or clubs. Perhaps afterwards associated with BAT the nocturnal animal.]

1. To catch birds at night by dazing them with a light, and knocking them down or netting them.

c **1440** *Promp. Parv.* 26 Batfowlyn (*v.r.* or go to take birdes in the nyght), *aucubaculo.* **1538** LELAND *Itin.* VII. 143 There they bat Fowle, and kil many Birdes. **1611** COTGR., *Breller*, to batfowle; to catch birds by batfowling.

2. (See BAT-FOWLING *vbl. sb.*)

'bat-ˌfowler. [f. prec. + -ER[1].]

1. One who practises bat-fowling.

c **1440** *Promp. Parv.* 26 Battfowlere, *aucubaculator.* **1530** PALSGR. 197/1 Batfouler, a taker of byrdes, *pipevr.* **1770** G. WHITE *Hist. Selborne* xxvii. 78 The bat-fowlers.. take many red-wings in the hedges.

†**2.** *slang.* A swindler, a sharper who makes victims of the simple or credulous. *Obs.*

1602 ROWLANDS *Greene's Cony-catchers* 16 Gentlemen Bat-fowlers in comparison of the common rablement of Cut-purses and pickpockets.

'bat-ˌfowling, *vbl. sb.* [f. as prec. + -ING[1].]

1. The catching of birds by night when at roost.

c **1440** *Promp. Parv.* 26 Batte fowlynge, *aucubaculatus.* **1530** PALSGR. 197/1 Batfoulyng, *la pipée.* **1610** SHAKS. *Temp.* II. i. 185 We vvould so, and then go a Bat-fowling. **1727** BRADLEY *Fam. Dict.* s.v. *Bird*, Bat fowling.. may be used with nets or without. **1873** BROWNING *Red Cott. Night-C.* 1405 Bat-fowling is all fair with birds at roost; The lantern and the clapnet suit the hedge.

fig. *a* **1670** HACKET *Abp. Williams* II. (1692) 66 They that go a batt-fowling in the dark, to seek matter of crimination.

†**2.** *slang.* Swindling, victimizing the simple. *Obs.*

1602 ROWLANDS *Greene's Cony-catchers* 8 As for Coni-catching, they cleape it Batfowling, the wine the Strap, and the cards the Limetwigs. **1608** DEKKER *Belman Lond.* Wks. 1885 III. 131 Sometimes likewise this Card-cheating.. is called Batt fowling, and then y[e] Setter is the Beater.

†**'batful**, *a. Obs.* [f. *bat-* (see BATTEN *v.*) + -FUL; a favourite word of Drayton's.] = BATTABLE.

1549 THOMAS *Hist. Italy* 1 Fertile fieldes, pleasaunt hilles, batfull pastures, &c. **1607** J. DAVIES *Summa Tot.* (1875) 26 The Beggers Belly is the batful'st ground That we can sow in. **1612** DRAYTON *Poly-olb.* x. 159 That Brooke whose course so batfull makes her mould.

bath (bɑːθ, -æ-), *sb.*[1] Forms: 1–2 **bæþ**, 2–3 **beð**, 3 **beaþ**, 3–6 **baþe**, 3–7 **bathe**, 2– **bath**. [Common Teutonic: OE. *bæð* = OS. *bað*, OHG. *bad*, *pad*, mod.G. *bad*, ON. *bað* (not recorded in Gothic):—OTeut. **batho-(m)*, neut. Prob. f. OTeut. verbal base **bajo-* to foment (cf. OHG. *pâwan*, *pâan*, mod.G. *bähen*), cogn. with L. *fovēre*; the idea of 'heat' being originally prominent in *bath*: cf. STEW. The technical senses show a parallel transition from the heating bath of chemistry to the merely steeping or washing bath of photography.]

I. The action of bathing; the state of being bathed.

1. The action of bathing or immersing the body, or a part of it, in water or other liquid. (Used playfully of accidental or involuntary immersion.)

Preceded by words indicating differences in the mode of application, or the part of the body subjected to it: thus, ***douche-, hip-, plunge-, shower-, sitz-, sponge-bath.*** Phrase, ***to take a bath.***

c **1000** *Sax. Leechd.* II. 244 Bæþ him eȝleð swiðost æfter mete. **1398** TREVISA *Barth. De P.R.* III. xxiv. (1495) 74 A bathe in cold water. **1711** F. FULLER *Med. Gymn.* Pref., A Warm Bath is.. suppos'd.. to be only a kind of a last Resort. **1837** DICKENS *Pickw.* xxxvi, He had imprudently taken a bath at too high a temperature. **1851** KINGSLEY *Yeast* iv. 75 Well, my man.. how are you after your cold-bath? You are the heaviest fish I ever landed. *Mod.* The dripping trees gave us a gratuitous shower-bath.

†**2.** The immersion or washing of baptism. *Obs.*

c **885** K. ÆLFRED *Oros.* VI. xxxiv. §4 Hu hi hine bædan rihtes ȝeleafan, and fullwihtes bæþes. *c* **1175** *Lamb. Hom.* 23 Al swa clenliche swa crist ha þe bitahte on þas fulhtes beðe. *c* **1200** ORMIN 18044 Þurrh shriffte & þurrh dædbotess baþþ, & ec þurrh beȝȝske tæress.

3. By extension: The action of immersing the body in, or surrounding it with, any medium, such as vapour, hot air, mud, to produce effects analogous to those of bathing.

1771 J. S. *Le Dran's Observ. Surg.* 294 The last Remedy he used was dry Baths.. performed with Spirit of Wine.

4. The state of being suffused with a liquid, as perspiration.

1598 SHAKS. *Merry W.* III. v. 120 And in the height of this Bath.. to be throwne into the Thames. **1714** MANDEVILLE *Fab. Bees* (1725) I. 271 His head all over in a bath of sweat. **1783** AINSWORTH *Lat. Dict.* (Morell) 1, To be all in a bath, *sudore diffluere.*

5. *fig.* **bath of blood**: carnage. (Ger. *blutbad.*)

1882 FARRAR *Early Chr.* II. 207 Once more began the bath of blood for the hapless race.

II. The liquid or element in which one bathes.

6. A quantity of water or other liquid prepared for bathing.

Preceded by attrib. words indicating differences in the nature or temperature of the liquid used: thus, ***hot, warm, tepid, cold, salt, fresh-water bath.***

c **885** K. ÆLFRED *Bæda* IV. xix, On hátum baðum. *a* **1000** CYNEWULF *Juliana* (Grein) 581 Bæþ háte wéoll. *a* **1200** *Moral Ode* 218 His baþ scal bon wallinde [*v.r.* in *E.E.P.* 29 His beað scal beo wallinde pich]. **1340** HAMPOLE *Pr. Consc.* 7481 A bathe of water, nouther hate ne cald. *c* **1440** *Gesta Rom.* i. 2 Be nakid, and go into a baþ þat I shalle make for the. **1526** *Pilgr. Perf.* (W. de W. 1531) 135 To some.. ye hote forneys of fyre hath ben moche pleasaunt, as a temperate bathe. **1607** SHAKS. *Cor.* I. vi. 63 Conducted to a gentle Bath, And Balms applyed to you. **1647** W. BROWNE *Polex.* II. 263 They put him into a bathe of fresh water. **1709** STEELE *Tatler* No. 80 ¶5 To rise the next Morning and plunge into the Cold Bath. **1866** KINGSLEY *Herew.* xviii. 227 Countess, your bath is ready.

†**7.** The water of baptism. *Obs.*

971 *Blickl. Hom.* 27þe he of þam fulwihtes bæþe eode. *c* **1230** *Ancr. R.* 396 þreo beðes he greiðede to his deore leofmon uorto wasshen hire in ham.. þet erest beð is fuluht. **1548** CRANMER *Catech.* 212 The water of Baptisme, which Paule calleth the bathe of regeneration.

†**8.** A spring of water (chiefly hot or impregnated with minerals) suitable for bathing. *Obs.*

864 *Cod. Dipl.* 290 Æt þam hátum baðum. **1297** R. GLOUC. 7 þat water of Baþe.. þat euer ys yliche hot.. Suche baþes þer beþ fele in þe clos & in þe stret. *c* **1400** MAUNDEV. viii. 88 In that Bathe was wont to come Watre fro Paradys. **1519** *Four Elem.* in Hazl. *Dodsl.* I. 6 The cause of the baths of water in the earth, which be perpetually hot. **1605** CAMDEN *Rem.* 1 That I may say nothing of healthfull Bathes. *a* **1711** KEN *Prayers for Baths* Wks. (1838) 449 Look on the bath, as a very admirable and propitious work of Divine Providence.

9. a. Any particular liquid or mixture of liquids applied to the body to produce a certain remedial effect; a wash or lotion wherewith to bathe the whole or any part of the body, or to immerse animals, or objects of any kind, in order to expose them to its effects. Cf. 16, 17.

1542–3 *Act 34–5 Hen. VIII*, viii. §3 To.. minister.. to anie outwarde sore.. herbes, oyntmentes, bathes, pultes and emplasters. **1607** TOPSELL *Four-f. Beasts* 295 To bath his legs with this bath. **1610** MARKHAM *Masterp.* II. lxxxii, Make a bathe or pultus thereof, and lay it to the sicke member. *Mod.* One of the best baths for sheep now in use.

b. In the hydropathic treatment of disease, any yielding medium, as water (natural or medicated), mud, sand, etc., in which the body is bathed or immersed, or with which it is sprayed or showered: for examples see DOUCHE-*bath*, MUD-*bath*, NEEDLE-*bath*, SAND-BATH 2, SHOWER-BATH, TURKISH *bath*.

10. *fig.* and *transf.* Any enveloping or surrounding medium, producing effects analogous to those of bathing.

c **1386** CHAUCER *Wife's T.* 397 His herte bathid in a bath of blisse. **1605** SHAKS. *Macb.* II. ii. 38 Sleepe.. The death of each dayes Life, sore Labors Bath. **1871** SMILES *Charac.* iii. (1876) 73 Enjoying a bath of sunshine. **1878** B. TAYLOR *Deukalion* II. v. 84 Bath of dazzling Day, Take these spent limbs, revive the old Titan blood.

III. A receptacle, apartment, or place for bathing.

11. A vessel or receptacle intended to contain water for the purpose of bathing. (Cf. 17.)

1607 SHAKS. *Timon* IV. iii. 86 Season the slaues for Tubbes and Bathes. **1635** R. BOLTON *Comf. Affl. Consc.* i. 355 It is nothing to swimme in a warme Bath. **1790** COWPER *Odyss.* XVII. 104 And plung'd his feet into a polish'd bath. *Mod.* Baths for sale or hire. To run the water out of the bath.

12. An apartment arranged for bathing, or a building containing a series of such apartments; (the latter usually *pl.*). Now esp. a room where one may bathe, a bathroom.

In Britain chiefly used as an advertising term for *bathroom*; in somewhat more general use in N. Amer.

1591 SPENSER *Ruines Rome* xxvii, These walls, these arcks, these baths, these temples hie. **1636** HEALEY *Epictetus' Man.* xxxi. 39 You cannot builde it a schoole, an Exchange, or a Bathe. **1757** BURKE *Abridgm. Eng. Hist.* Wks. X. 218 A fondness for baths, for gardens, for grand houses. **1844** *Mem. Babylon. P'cess.* II. 30 At the principal bath in Beyroot. **1879** *Boy's Own P.* 118/2 The Autumn swimming fête was held at the Lambeth Baths. **1922** S. LEWIS *Babbitt* x. 141, I think I can let you have a room with bath. **1939** O. LANCASTER *Homes Sweet Homes* 66 Three bed, two bath, a kitchen and all the usual offices. **1953** G. V. CAREY *Amer. into Eng.* 34 *Bath*, sometimes denotes in American (scarcely ever in English) 'bathroom': 'He went into the bath for a shower.' 'In the bath there was no shower but only a bathtub.' **1967** R. RAINE *Wreath for America* vii. 55 You've got a room booked for me, a single room with bath. **1968** *Globe & Mail* (Toronto) 3 Feb. 43/8 (Advt.), Don Mills townhouse, 3 bedrooms, 1½ baths.

13. A place for undergoing medical treatment by bathing and similar remedial agencies; a town resorted to for the sake of such treatment, *e.g. Matlock Bath.* Usually in pl. Cf. BATH[2] 1.

1562 TURNER *Baths* 1 Of the bathe of Baeth.. The bath of England is.. in a city called in Latin Bathonia, and Baeth in Englishe, of the bathes y[t] are in it. **1572** J. JONES (*title*) The Bathes of Bathes Ayde. **1670** COTTON *Espernon* III. x. 487 At liberty to go as far as the Frontier to the Baths at Banieres. **1739** HUXHAM *Fevers* iii. (1750) 30 Sent him to use the Waters at the Bath. **1864** TENNYSON *Aylmer's F.* 27 His wife a faded beauty of the Baths.

IV. Transferred uses in science and the arts.

†**14.** (*St.*) ***Mary's Bath*** in *Alch.*, etc.: see BAIN-MARIE. *Obs.*

c **1470** *Bk. Quintessence* 13 Putte by .vij. daies to encorpere wel as tofore in þe bath of marien. **1610** B. JONSON *Alch.* II. i, F. is come over the helm too, I thank my maker, in S. Mary's bath. **1632** SHERWOOD, Maries Bath, *Bain de Marie.*

15. *Chem.* (See quot. 1846.)

1599 A. M. *Gabelhouer's Bk. Physick* 54 Bath it 3 dayes after other, euery day in a water bath. **1709** G. WILSON *Chym.* Expl. 3rd Table, The Sand Bath of the digesting Furnace. *Ibid.* 8th Table, The moist Bath of the Athanor. **1846** G. WRIGHT *Cream Sci. Knowl.* 37 Bath in Chemistry, is a contrivance for producing a steady heat at high temperature, or at a temperature not exceeding that of boiling water. In the former, the substance to be heated is placed in a vessel immersed in sand, and this is called a sand-bath; in the latter water is employed instead, and this is called a water-bath, or balneum Mariæ.

16. a. *Dyeing*, A preparation of colouring liquid in which the dyer immerses his cloth, etc.

1791 HAMILTON *Berthollet's Dyeing* I. I. I. i. 19 Each of them he dyed separately in a cochineal bath.

b. *spec.* in *dung-bath*: see DUNG *sb.* 5 c; ***long bath***, a dilute bath in which chemical action is comparatively slow; ***short bath***, a concentrated bath; ***single bath***, one in which the whole operation is completed; ***standing bath***, one that is used continuously; ***white bath***: see WHITE *a.* 11 e.

17. *Photography*, A solution in which photographic plates or prints are immersed, for the purposes of 'sensitizing,' fixing, toning, washing, etc.; the vessel in which the solution is contained.

1861 *Photogr. News Alm.* in *Circ. Sc.* 160/1 A thirty-five grain nitrate bath..is the best sensitising solution. *c* **1865** J. WYLDE in *Circ. Sc.* I. 148/2 The choice of a 'bath'..for rendering a coated plate sensitive, has been a subject of great discussion amongst photographers. **1869** *Eng. Mech.* 17 Dec. 335/1 It varies with the strength of the..albumenising ..bath. **1879** *Cassell's Techn. Educ.* II. 65 For the sensitising of the late, a glass or porcelain bath will be required. **1882** ABNEY *Instr. Photogr.* 109 The ordinary negative bath is used.

18. *Metallurgy*, 'A mass of molten material in a furnace.' Raymond *Mining Gloss.* 1881.

V. An order of knighthood.

19. a. Order of the Bath: a high order of British knighthood. (So called from the bath which preceded installation.)

1603 KNOLLES *Hist. Turks* Ep. Ded., My most especial good friend Sir Peter Manwood Knight of the Bath. **1614** SELDEN *Titles Hon.* 359 Those of the Bath were anciently mongst the old Franks. [See the whole passage.] **1747** LIND *Lett. Navy* (1757) I. 45 To wear..a star as the knights of the Bath do. **1835** *Penny Cycl.* IV. 24/2 The re-modelling of the Order of the Bath was dated January 2, 1815.

b. Short for: *Bath King of Arms*, the herald or marshal of the order.

1725 *Lond. Gaz.* No. 6382/4 Bath King of Arms then made his Reverences. Bath then delivered the Collar of the Order.

VI. *Attrib.* and *Comb.*, as ***bath-bed***, ***-brush***, ***-cloth***, †***-fat*** (= sense 11), ***-gown***, ***-keeper***, ***-mat***, ***-night***, ***oil***, ***-powder***, ***-sponge***, ***-stove***, ***-time***, ***-towel***, ***-tub***, , ***-waste***, ***-water***; ***bath-loving*** adj., etc. **bath cubes, essence, salts**, toilet preparations for softening or perfuming bath-water; **bath house**, a building equipped with facilities for bathing, occas. public baths; *U.S.*, a place where one may change into beach clothes at the seaside, etc.; **bath-robe** orig. *U.S.*, a dressing-gown, esp. one made of towelling; **bath-sheet**, a large bath-towel; **bath-towel**, a large towel; hence ***bath-towelling***; **bath-tub gin**, a concoction of spirits simulating gin (orig. used to designate illicitly manufactured liquor); **bath vat** (now *poet.*) = sense 11; cf. *bath-fat* above.

1894 *Daily News* 8 Oct. 7/1 The appliances for treatment of special diseases, such as bath beds for typhoid. **1895** *Montgomery Ward Catal.* 103/2 Combined Bath and Flesh Brushes..for wet or dry use. **1900** H. LAWSON *On Track* 72 In the other hand she carried her tooth-brush and bath-brush, and soap. **1618** R. HOLYDAY *Juvenal* 42 They fold the bath-cloaths. **1959** A. WESKER *Roots* II. ii. 53 These bath cubes smell beautiful. **1911** BEERBOHM *Zuleika D.* xxi. 302 Eau de Violettes was the bath-essence that Zuleika always had. **1954** E. JENKINS *Tortoise & Hare* viii. 75 The bland scent of expensive soap and bath essence. **1536** BELLENDEN *Cron. Scot.* (1821) II. 267 The third sonne, Johne Stewart, was..slane in the Cannongait, in ane baith fatt. **1909** *Westm. Gaz.* 19 Aug. 5/3 The dressing-and bath-gowns. **1705** *Lond. Gaz.* No. 4139/7 The Bath House at Buxton. **1882** H. LANSDELL *Siberia* I. 192 Out-houses, such as kitchen-house and bath-house. **1800** W. BENTLEY *Diary* (1907) II. 399, I bathed in the river this evening, and the Bath House was opened for the first time. **1851** C. CIST *Cincinnati* 167 There are several public bath houses. **1591** PERCIVALL *Sp. Dict.*, *Bañador*, a bathe keeper. **1895** *Army & Navy Co-op. Soc. Price List* 190 Felt Bath Mats. **1927** M. DE LA ROCHE *Jalna* vii. 82 She stepped dripping on to the thick bath mat. **1921** D. H. LAWRENCE *Phoenix* (1936) 15 It was Saturday night—bath-night. **1925** W. DE LA MARE *Broomsticks* 367 Even though it was 'bath-night' on Saturday. **1962** *Guardian* 5 Dec. 6/4 'Arpège' Bath Oil, 43*s.* 6*d.*, will do 30 baths. **1968** K. BIRD *Smash Glass Image* iii. 43 My array of bath oils and talcum powder. **1907** *Yesterday's Shopping* (1969) 536/2 Parma violet bath powder and water softener. **1923** W. A. POUCHER *Perfumes & Cosmetics* 327 Bath Powders are generally..highly perfumed. **1940** N. MARSH *Surfeit of Lampreys* (1941) viii. 115 Her round face shone and she smelt of bath powder. **1902** *Sears Catal.* (ed. 112) 846/2 Fine Terry Cloth Bath Robe with Hood. **1924** A. D. SEDGWICK *Little French Girl* II. v. 139 One undressed in one's room and ran out over the cliff-top in *espadrilles* and bath-robe. **1907** *Yesterday's Shopping* (1969) 536/1 Bath Salts (Fragrant)..will instantly soften the hardest water. **1920** A. HUXLEY *Limbo* 236 A very hot bath with lots of verbena bath-salts. **1930** J. B. PRIESTLEY *Angel Pavement* viii. 411 My worthy employeress's terribly expensive bath salts. **1899** *Westm. Gaz.* 3 Jan. 3/2 The bath-sheets..seem to become masses of vibrating silver. **1912** E. M. DELL *Way of Eagle* (1927) lvi. 221 He stepped from the tent, clad loosely in a bath-sheet. **1967** *Guardian* 5 Sept. 4/6 Enormous great bath towels..as big as the bath sheets in Swiss hotels. **1889** *Cent. Dict.* I. 474/3 Bath sponge. **1927** HALDANE & HUXLEY *Animal Biol.* xii. 266 Our bath-sponges ..are colonial, composed of a large number of sponge-bodies aggregated together. **1591** G. FLETCHER *Russe Commw.* (1836) 147 Made lyke the Germane bathstoaves. **1907** A. BENNETT *Grim Smile Five T.* 40 He isn't used to you at bath-time. **1863** DICKENS *Uncommercial Traveller* in *All the Year Round* 24 Oct. 206/1 A piece of sculptured drapery resembling the effigy of Titbull's bath-towel. **1903** *Town & Country* 24 Jan. 2/1 There's..a bath room with hot and cold water, soap, and *real* bath towels. **1880** Bath towelling [see TOWELLING 1]. **1926** 'R. CROMPTON' *Wm.—the Conqueror* iv. 65 Henry's was made of bath towelling and was rather conspicuous in design. **1869** 'MARK TWAIN' *Innoc. Abroad* xix. 187 They were going to put all three of us in one bath-tub. **1884** *Century Mag.* Dec. 266/2 English earthenware bath-tubs. **1930** C. BEATON *Diary* Dec. in *Wandering Years* (1961) 196 Five-star scotch or bathtub gin. **1967** *Boston Sunday Herald* 26 Mar. IV. 1/1 Marijuana has become the Bathtub Gin of the 1960s. **1874** SWINBURNE *Bothwell* II. xviii. 216 A cover for his bath-vat. **1887** MORRIS *Odyssey* VIII. 456 He gat him up out of the bath-vat. **1936** *Discovery* Aug. 244/1 The trunk sprang from near the cement bath-waste channel... A large, shining drop of water splashed from the bath waste pipe. **1958** BETJEMAN *Coll. Poems* 142 All the bells of all the churches Sounded in the bath-waste running out into the frosty air. *a* **1350** *S. Eng. Legendary* (E.E.T.S., 1956) I. 46 A uat þer stod of *baþ water [*a* **1325** of baþ]. **1891** *Babyhood* VII. 143/2 After the baby is three months old, the temperature of the bath water should be gradually reduced..until 80 degrees is reached. **1922, 1957** [see BABY *sb.* A. 1 e]. **1978** E. GUNDREY *Simple Plumbing* 51 To siphon bathwater out to re-use for household cleaning.. two people are needed.

Bath (bɑːθ, -æ-), *sb.*[2] [The same word as the prec. originally used in dat. pl. in a defining phrase, thus, *Cod. Dipl.* 290 (an. 864) 'in illa famosa urbe ðæt is æt ðæm hátum baðum' (in that famous town that is at the hot baths), 193 (an. 808) 'in civitate æt Baðun' (in the city at the Baths), whence as an indecl. sb. *Baðum*, *Baðun*, *Baðon* (latinized *Bathonia*), *Baðan*, *Baðanceaster* (see Bosworth); in 13th c. reduced to *Baþen*, *Baþe*, *Bathe*: in 17th c. *Bath*, in 18th c. sometimes with renewed reference to its spa, *the Bath* (or allusively *the Baths*).]

1. a. A well-known city in the west of England, so called from its hot springs.

973 *O.E. Chron.*, On ðære ealdan byriȝ Acemannes ceastre, éac hi, oðre worde, beornas Baðan nemnað. **1130** *Ibid.* Godefreith of Bathe. **1297** [see prec. 8]. **1562** [see prec. 13]. **1624** MASSINGER *Parl. Love* II. iii, The far-famed English Bath, or German Spa. **1711** ADDISON *Spect.* No. 179 ¶7 An Under-Citizen of the Bath. **1727** R. NEWTON *Expl. Univ. Educ. reduced* 13 To take Oxford and Blenheim in his Way to the Bath. **1759** H. WALPOLE *Let. H. Mann* 25 Sept., I am going to the Bath, with more opinion of..the change of air, than of the waters. (Cf. BATH[1] 13.)

b. As a place of consignment for a person one does not wish to see again, in the phrase ***to go to Bath***, chiefly used imperatively.

1837 BARHAM in *Ingol. Leg.* (1840) Ser. I. 83 'Go to Bath!' Said the Baron. **1858** THACKERAY *Virgin.* I. xvi. 127 She may go to Bath, or she may go to Jericho, for me. **1908** *Daily Chron.* 27 Oct. 6/6 A later use of the expression was 'Go to Bath and get your head shaved'.

2. a. *attrib.* of natural or artificial productions of the city, or of objects connected with it: e.g. *Bath water(s)*, etc. **b.** Used as a specific description in ***Bath-bun***, ***-chap***, ***-fagot***, ***-ring***, etc. **c. Bath asparagus**, a variety of Star of Bethlehem (*Ornithogalum pyrenaicum*) with edible shoots; **Bath-brick**, a preparation of calcareous earth moulded in form of a brick, made at Bridgwater; used for cleaning polished metal; **Bath-chair**, a large chair on wheels for invalids (both this and the preceding item are often written without a capital B); **Bath-coating**, a material formerly fashionable for male attire; **Bath coup**, a method of play in whist or bridge in which a player, who holds the ace, knave and another card of the same suit, refrains from taking his adversary's king; **Bath Guide**, a popular 'Society' poem of the 18th c., sometimes taken as a type of such verse; **Bath-metal**, an alloy, consisting of 3 or 4 oz. of zinc to one pound of copper (Ure); **Bath Oliver**, an unsweetened biscuit said to have been invented by William Oliver (1695–1764), a physician of Bath; formerly simply *Oliver*; **Bath oolite**, **Bath-stone**, a building stone quarried from the oolite formation near Bath; **Bath-post**, a sort of letter-paper; **Bath White (butterfly)**, a rare European pierid butterfly, *Pontia daplidice*, having the under side of the hind wing of a greenish colour spotted with white.

1791 COLLINSON *Hist. Somerset* I. p. xx, Wood Star of Bethlehem or *Bath Asparagus... The young shoots of it are eaten by the common people as asparagus. **1959** A. R. CLAPHAM et al. *Excursion Flora Brit. Isles* 445 Very locally abundant in woods and scrub. Bath Asparagus. **1837** CARLYLE *Fr. Rev.* VII. i. I. 300 Scanty ill-baked loaves, more like baked *Bath bricks. **1801** JANE AUSTEN *Let.* 3 Jan. (1952) 101 Disordering my Stomach with *Bath bunns. **1863** KINGSLEY *Water-Bab.* iv. 177 And found that the moon was just the shape of a Bath bun. **1769** MRS. RAFFALD *Eng. Housekpr.* (1778) 271 To make *Bath Cakes. **1823** M. WILMOT *Let.* 30 Apr. (1935) 188 My dearest Mother, do you not make use of a *Bath Chair? **1847** M. EDGEWORTH *Tour Connemara* (1950) 109 She cannot walk now beside Honora's Bath chair. **1860** VENABLES *I. Wight* 121 Bath chairs are always waiting the arrival of the steamers. **1873** MISS BRADDON *Str. & Pilgr.* III. xviii. 389 She..was brought here in a bath-chair. **1829** MARRYAT *F. Mildmay* xvi, A *Bath chair-man. **1791** J. LACKINGTON *Mem. Let.* xix. (D.) One [great-coat] made of *Bath-coating. **1875** 'STONEHENGE' *Brit. Sports* I. I. ix. §3. 123 A waistcoat of Bath-coating or shag. **1897** R. F. FOSTER *Complete Hoyle* 613 *Bath Coup, holding up Ace Jack on a King led by an adversary. **1899** W. M. BUTLER *Whist Reference Book* 51/1 *The Bath Coup.* A strategic play at whist which originated at Bath, England, in the time of Hoyle. The fourth hand, holding ace, jack, and others, refuses to take a king when it is led. **1936** E. CULBERTSON *Contr. Bridge Complete* xl. 456 The Bath Coup gains time by causing the opponents to waste an entry before they can establish their suit. **1711** ADDISON *Spect.* No. 3 ¶7 Little piles of notched sticks, bound up together in bundles like *Bath faggots. **1824** MISS MITFORD *Village* Ser. I. (1863) 92 [He] bepommelled it through three pages of *Bath-guide verses. **1714** *Boston News-Let.* 7 June 2/2 A blew Coat..with wrought *Bath metal Buttons. **1738** J. WESLEY *Let.* 1 Dec. (1931) I. 276 Could not you purchase for me half a dozen Bath-metal tea-spoons? **1750** *Phil. Trans.* XLVI. 586 Platina..like Bath-metal, or cast Iron, brittle. **1958** A. D. MERRIMAN *Dict. Metallurgy* 16/1 *Bath metal*, a silvery-white copper-zinc alloy which at one time was favoured for cheap table-ware. Approximate composition: Zn 45%, Cu 55%. **1878** *Official Guide & Album Cunard Steamship Co.* 156/1 *Bath Oliver. **1900** in Ware *Passing Eng.* (1909) 21/1 'Bobs' fights on 'Bath Olivers'. **1915** A. D. GILLESPIE *Let.* 14 June in *Lett. from Flanders* (1916) 320 The sausages [bombs] are rather like a Bath Oliver biscuit tin—only not quite so big—full of old nails and rusty scrap-iron. **1928** COMPTON MACKENZIE *Extremes Meet* 123 We had a periscope scare about five hours out from Malta... This time it was a Bath Oliver biscuit tin. **1837** DICKENS in *Bentley's Misc.* I. 53 Four sides of closely-written, gilt-edged, hot-pressed *Bath post letter paper. **1845** *Ainsworth's Mag.* VII. 26 They beheld their father..repiling the quires of Bath post. *c* **1865** J. WYLDE in *Circ. Sc.* I. 153/2 The plain Bath or satin post may be employed. **1771** SMOLLETT *Humph. Cl.* I. 118, I send you two dozen of *Bath rings... I don't know how you will approve of the mottoes. **1785** *Archæol.* VII. 104 (D.) A lock of hair which was so perfectly strong that I had it woven into Bath rings. **1833** LYELL *Princ. Geol.* III. 232 At Vichy, the oolite resembles our *Bath stone in appearance. **1673** J. LOCKE *Let.* 14 Feb. in Fox Bourne *Life* (1876) I. 317 You may possibly bring home with you a new use of our *Bath waters. **1693** E. CLARKE *Let.* 2 Aug. in Rand *Locke & Clarke* (1927) 379 Whether advisable to drink the Bath water, if she be desirous of it, whilst she is with child. *Ibid.*, Frequently asks if the Bath waters may not be drank here at home with good success. **1723** *Lond. Gaz.* 6127/3 The Mayor..having appointed Carew Davis..Pumper of all the Bath-waters. **1836** *Scenes Commerce* 162 The Bath water is hot. **1795** W. LEWIN *Insects Gt. Britain* 62 *Bath White. Daplidice. *Linnæus*. This is a rare butterfly in England..named the Bath white, from a piece of needle work, executed at Bath, by a young lady, from a specimen of this insect, said to be taken near that place. **1832** J. RENNIE *Consp. Butterfl. & M.* Index, Bath White B. **1885** KANE *European Butterflies* 9 *Pieris Daplidice* L. The Bath White.

bath (bæθ), *sb.*[3] Forms: (4 batus), 6 bat, batte, 6– bath. [a. Heb. *bath*: the earlier forms represented L. *batus*, Gr. *βάτος* of the Vulgate and Septuagint.] A Hebrew liquid-measure, containing about six and a half gallons.

1398 TREVISA *Barth. De P.R.* XIX. cxxviii. (1495) 932 Batus is in fletynge thynges as cours, and Ephi in drye thynges. **1535** COVERDALE *Ezek.* xlv. 14 The oyle shal be measured with the Bat..Ten Battes make one Homer. **1581** MARBECK *Bk. of Notes* 99 Bath & Epha seeme to be both one measure. **1611** BIBLE *Isa.* v. 10 Ten acres of Vineyard shall yeeld one Bath. **1623** COCKERAM, *Bath*, ten pottles in liquor.

bath (bɑːθ, -æ-), *v.* [f. BATH *sb.*[1]; cf. to *shoe*, *tub*, *pot*, etc.; distinct from *bathe*; but the inflected forms, except *baths*, coincide in spelling, though not in pronunc., with the corresponding forms of *bathe*, and therefore are avoided in writing; *batht* and *bath-ing*, with a hyphen, have however been employed. In some early instances, *bath* may probably be only a variant spelling of *bathe*.]

trans. To subject to a bath; to wash or immerse in a bath. Differing from *bathe* in having a more distinct reference to sense 11 of BATH *sb.*[1], and in being always literal.

[**1483** *Cath. Angl.* 24 To bath or bathe, *balneare*. *c* **1485** *Digby Myst.* (1882) IV. 296 A bath of þi blude to bath mans saule in. **1616** R. C. *Times' Whis.* (1871) 116 That fountaine rather Where faire Diana with her nymphs doth bath her?] **1660** EVELYN *Mem.* (1857) I. 366 To London and saw the bath-ing..of the Knights of the Bath. **1876** G. MACDONALD *T. Wingfield*, He batht himself. *Mod.* The nurse who dresses and baths the younger children.

bathe (beɪð), *v.* Forms: 1 baðian, beðian, 2–4 baðien, beþien, baþe(n, beðe(n, 4 bathie, -ey, 5–6 bath, 5– bathe. [Common Teutonic: OE. *baðian*, also *bęðian* = ON. *baða*, OHG. *badôn*, *bathôn*, mod. G. *baden*, Du. *baden*:—OTeut. *baþ-ôn*, f. *baþo-(m)* BATH *sb.*[1] The difference of vowel and consonant between *bathe* and *bath* (beɪð, bɑːθ, -æ-) has been developed since the OE. period, through the additional syllable and open vowel of *ba-ðian*; cf. *grass*, *graze*, *staff*, *stave*.]

I. *trans.* (Now mostly reflexive or passive.)

1. To immerse, as in a bath: **a.** *lit.* To immerse (the body, or any part of it) in water or other liquid, for the sake of some effect (*e.g.* health, warmth, cleansing) promoted by the action of the liquid.

a 1200 *Moral Ode* 245 þer is bernunde pich hore saule to baþien inne. 1398 TREVISA *Barth. de P.R.* VI. ix. (1495) 195 The moder batheth the chylde. *c* 1400 MAUNDEV. x. 112 Gabrielles welle, where our Lord was wont to bathe him. 1611 BIBLE *Lev.* xv. 5 [He] shall wash his clothes, and bathe himselfe in water. 1667 MILTON *P.L.* VII. 437 Others on Silver Lakes and Rivers, Bath'd Thir downie Brest. 1796 MORSE *Amer. Geog.* I. 205 He has the convenience of sometimes bathing himself.

b. To immerse in other elements or substances, *e.g.* sand, fire.

c 1386 CHAUCER *Nonne Pr. T.* 447 Faire in the sond, to bathe hir merily, Lith Pertelot.. Agayn the sonne. 1612 DRAYTON *Poly-olb.* Frontisp., The Norman Leopards bath'd in Gules. 1849 ROBERTSON *Serm.* Ser. I. i. (1866) 16 The later martyr bathes his fingers in the flames.

c. To plunge, or dip, without reference to the action of the liquid.

a 1325 *E.E. Allit. P.* C. 211 [Jonah says] Berez me to þe borde, & baþeþes me þer-oute. 1583 STANYHURST *Æneis* III. (Arb.) 82 In flud Trinacrian thy great oars must deeplye be bathed.

2. To apply water or other liquid to anything so as to wet it all over, or moisten it copiously; to lave, perfuse, suffuse, wet, moisten: **a.** *literally.*

c 1000 *Sax. Leechd.* II. 206 Ðonne is sio beðianne mid hatan wætre. *c* 1250 *Gen. & Ex.* 2447 First .ix. niȝt ðe liches beðen, And smeren. 1526 *Pilgr. Perf.* (W. de W. 1531) 140 We come to the gates.. all bathed in rayne and frosen with yce. 1593 SHAKS. *3 Hen. VI*, II. ii. 169 Till we haue.. bath'd thy growing, with our heated bloods. 1652 CULPEPPER *Eng. Physic.* 6 To bath the place grieved.. for the Inflammation. 1877 CHAVASSE *Adv. to Mother* §290 Well bathe the eye with vinegar and water.

b. said of the action of a river or the sea upon the adjacent banks or land.

1591 SPENSER *Bellay's Vis.* ix, A water, whose out gushing flood Ran bathing all the creakie shore aflot. 1697 *C'tess D'Aunoy's Trav.* (1706) 52 The River which passes under it bathes a meadow. 1776 GIBBON *Decl. & F.* I. xix. 537 The river bathed the foot of the walls. 1872 BAGEHOT *Physics & Pol.* 85 Groups of islands.. bathed by the same oceans.

c. said of the action of tears, perspiration, or any secretion, in flowing over and wetting the body or its parts.

1578 T. N. tr. *Conq. W. India* 32 His eyes toward heaven, and his face bathed with teares. 1718 POPE *Iliad* XXIII. 18 Tears bathe their arms, and tears the sands bedew. 1746 HERVEY *Medit.* (1818) 166 The laborer, bathed in sweat, drops the scythe. 1790 BURKE *Fr. Rev.* Wks. V. 89 Bathing in tears.. thousands of worthy men and worthy families. 1875 DARWIN *Insectiv. Pl.* vi. 87 When bathed in the secretion.

d. (Inverted construction.)

1611 SHAKS. *Cymb.* I. vi. 100 Had I this cheeke To bathe my lips vpon.

3. The phrase '*to bathe in blood*' includes and often blends 1 and 2, and is generally used *fig.* to express the great quantity of blood shed.

c 1300 *K. Alis.* 2708 Mony pencel god, Quyk, y-bathed in heorte blod. *c* 1325 *E.E. Allit. P.* B. 1248 þay.. Baþed barnes in blod & her brayn spylled. *c* 1380 *Sir Ferumb.* 3100 Ro[land].. baþede is swerd in hure blod. *c* 1590 GREENE *Fr. Bacon* viii. 79, I will bathe my poniard in the bosom of an Earl. 1601 SHAKS. *Jul. C.* III. i. 106 Let vs bathe our hands in Cæsars blood Vp to the Elbowes. 1647 W. BROWNE *Polex.* II. 306 A tyrant which took pleasure in bathing himselfe in humane blood. 1836 THIRLWALL *Greece* II. xvi. 377 His plan.. would have bathed Sparta in blood.

4. a. To suffuse, envelope, or encompass, like the air or the sunshine.

1816 J. WILSON *City of Plague* II. ii. 136 A stream of sunshine bathing The bright moss-roses. 1853 KINGSLEY *Hypatia* xiii. 164 Heavenly glory seemed to bathe her from head to foot. 1853 KANE *Grinnell Exp.* xxxi. (1856) 272 The Bay of Baffin, bathed in foggy darkness. 1878 HUXLEY *Physiogr.* 88 An ocean of air bathing the entire earth.

b. said of mental influences.

1526 SKELTON *Magnyf.* 1490 Bathyd with blysse, embraced with comfort. 1535 COVERDALE *Isa.* lxiii. 6 And thus haue I troden downe the people in my wrath, and bathed them in my displeasure. 1857 EMERSON *Poems* 8 The babe.. Lies bathed in joy.

II. *intr.* (from *reflexive* use of 1.)

5. a. *lit.* To take a bath, to plunge or immerse oneself in water or other liquid, so as to enjoy its influence; in earlier usage also, to lie or remain so immersed, to bask.

c 1200 *Moral Ode* (245) in *E.E.P.* (1862) 29 Pich þat eure wealð · þat sculle baþien inne þo þe ladde vuel lif. *c* 1275 *Death* in *O.E. Misc.* 180 In ful a bitter bað bathien ich schal naked. 1398 TREVISA *Barth. De P. R.* III. xxiv. (1495) 73 They that bathen temperatly in hote water. 1667 MILTON *P.L.* II. 660 Vex'd Scylla, bathing in the Sea. 1765 COWPER *Lett.* 24 June, It is a noble stream to bathe in. 1862 STANLEY *Jew. Ch.* v. (1875) 89 The princess came down.. to bathe in the sacred river.

b. in various transferred and figurative senses: see the transitive uses above, 3-4.

1576 LD. VAUX in *Parad. Dainty Dev.*, He most of all doth bathe in bliss. 1590 MARLOWE *2nd Pt. Tamburl.* II. iii, Now lie the Christians bathing in their bloods. 1656 TRAPP *Comm. Mark* i. 35 Shall Christians be bathing in their beds on their Lord's day? *c* 1720 S. WESLEY *Eupolis* 40 The feathered souls, that swim the air, And bathe in liquid ether there. 1855 F. W. FABER *Growth in Holiness* xi. 169 Youth.. bathing in devotional sweetness.

bathe (beɪð), *sb.* [f. prec. vb.] An act of bathing (in the intr. sense of *bathe*).

Of modern origin, and used instead of BATH *sb.*[1], sense 1, to exclude the suggestion of other senses.

1831 SOUTHEY *Lett.* (1856) IV. 230 A two hours' walk, and a bathe in the Greta. 1861 *Sat. Rev.* 30 Nov. 565 A mountain stream in which the happy party took every day their morning bathe.

batheable ('beɪðəb(ə)l), *a.* [f. BATHE *v.* + -ABLE.] Able to be bathed; suitable for bathing in.

1831 MRS. KEMBLE *Rec. Girlhood* III. 90 It [the sea] was not expected to be batheable till eleven.

bather ('beɪðə(r)). [f. BATHE *v.* + -ER[1].]

†**1.** A bath-keeper, or attendant at a bath. *Obs.*

1636 HEALEY *Theophrast.* 40 Turning to the Bather or Bath-keeper, saith, Sir, now I thanke you for nothing. 1813 J. HOBHOUSE *Journ.* 537 The appearance of the bathers.. is most disgusting; and it requires some practice to bear patiently the kneading of your limbs, etc.

2. One who takes a bath.

1716-8 LADY MONTAGUE *Lett.* I. xxix. 94 What degree of warmth the bathers please to have. *c* 1854 STANLEY *Sinai & Pal.* vii. (1858) 315 Most of the bathers keep within the shelter of the bank.

3. *pl.* Bathing trunks; a bathing suit. esp. *Austral.*

1945 BAKER *Austral. Lang.* ix. 183 Swimming costumes are known variously as *togs, bathers.* 1957 'N. SHUTE' *On Beach* 3 You join us there for a swim. I could take the trailer and your bathers. 1965 J. R. STOW *Merry-go-round in Sea* i. 23 His mother sat by the water, on a red towel, in blue bathers. 1966 *Southerly* XXVI. 175 The girl wore a blouse over her bathers. 1968 N. MARSH *Clutch of Constables* viii. 204 It was nothing, really... I'm a Sydneysider, don't forget, and I *was* in my bathers.

bathetic (bə'θɛtɪk), *a.* [A mod. word, formed irregularly from *bathos*, on the assumed analogy of *pathetic* (which is not derived from *pathos*); cf. also BATHOTIC.] Characterized by bathos; 'sinking' rhetorically, or in literary style; absol. ***the bathetic*** = BATHOS. (A favourite word of reviewers.)

a 1834 COLERIDGE in *Rem.* (1836) II. 163 Even Warburton would scarcely have made so deep a plunge into the bathetic. 1866 *Lond. Rev.* 15 Sept. 289/1 The bathetic of our women novelists. 1879 O'CONNOR *Beaconsfield* 189 His bathetic and impotent epic. 1884 *Inquirer* 21 June 390/1 Verbose when they should have been concise, bathetic when they wanted to be pathetic.

bathinette (,bɑːθɪ'nɛt, -æ-). *U.S.* Also **-et**. [Proprietary name.] A small bath used in bathing infants.

1936 *Sears, Roebuck Catal.* (ed. 173) 173 Genuine bathinette... Dupont rubber coated fabric tub. 1938 *Capital* (Topeka, Kan.) 25 Nov. 3 (Advt.), Genuine baby bathinette. 1954 F. G. PATTON *Good Morning, Miss Dove* (1955) 5 Stop at the Burnhams' and pick up the bathinet they're lending us. 1963 M. MCCARTHY *Group* xiv. 326 She did not possess a baby scales or a bathinet. He was bathed in the wash-basin.

bathing ('beɪðɪŋ), *vbl. sb.* [f. BATHE *v.* + -ING[1].]

1. a. The exposing of oneself or others to the free action of water, etc. by immersion or suffusion.

1541 COPLAND *Galyen's Terap.* 2 A iv, Moderate it with bathynge, and wetynge in temperate water. 1778 MISS BURNEY *Evelina* in *Casquet Lit.* V. 311/2, I always hated bathing. 1788 G. SANDEMAN in *Med. Comm.* II. 277 She used sea bathing. 1809 LD. MALMESBURY in G. Rose *Diaries* (1860) II. 355 Remaining a week for the purpose of bathing.

b. The conditions under which bathing can be carried on at a watering-place, etc. (including the quality of the water, the character of the beach, accessibility, and the like).

c 1830 F. COGHLAN *Coast Compan.* 37 The prospects are fine, and the walks and rides excellent; and the bathing is remarkably good. 1877 *Seaside Watering Places* xxiv. 46 The bathing is excellent and especially safe. 1881 *Dict. Watering Places* 108 The sands and bathing [at Westward Ho!] are good, machines and tents abundant.

2. *attrib.* or in *comb.*, *as* ***bathing beach, -box, -cabin, -cap, -costume, -drawers, -dress, -gown, -house, -hut, -machine, -place, -robe, -room, -season, -shed, -suit, trunks, -tub, -woman***, etc.

1926 *Daily Colonist* (Victoria, B.C.) 2 July 5/3 The lure of the bathing beach and wooded lane. 1943 J. S. HUXLEY *TVA* ix. 63 There are bathing beaches, a wading pool for children, and a diving tower. 1883 *Harper's Mag.* Feb. 336/2 'Bathing-boxes' (as the sea-side cottages are called) perched about on the.. hill-sides. 1905 W. J. LOCKE *Morals M. Ordeyne* xii. 145 Below the terrace are the bathing-cabins. 1968 L. DURRELL *Tunc* ii. 51 The cubicles of the girls, somewhat like a row of bathing cabins. 1867 *Belgravia* III. 355 A bathing-cap is *de rigueur.* 1937 J. LAVER *Taste & Fashion* xvi. 220 In 1919.. the bathing cap has made its appearance.. not yet made of rubber. 1830 F. TROLLOPE *Domestic Manners Amer.* (1960) 273 Her petticoat, the most important part of her bathing costume, dropped off. 1839 DICKENS *Tugg's at Ramsgate* in *Sk. Boz* 369 One of the young ladies.. in her bathing costume. 1928 H. WILLIAMSON *Pathway* xii. 275 'We came without bathing costumes.' 'Bathing *suits*,' Ronnie corrected him, with a self-assured air. 'Only board-school boys say *costumes*.' 1940 GRAVES & HODGE *Long Week-end* viii. 122 The conjunction of a negro band with white girls in bathing costumes. 1893 Bathing-drawers [see DRAWERS]. 1931 W. DE LA MARE *Seven Short Stories* 109 In one of the huge 'stores' in search of bathing-drawers. 1774 J. SCHAW *Jrnl. Lady of Quality* (1921) i. 69 When we are to leave the cabin in our bathing dress, all the people quit the deck. 1859 *All Y. Round* No. 19. 447 Coloured bathing-dresses, towels, and other apparatus. 1598 FLORIO *Worlde of Wordes* 36/2 *Bagno*, a bathe, a baine, or bathing house. 1695 in LADY G. BAILLIE *Household Bk.* (1911) 3 For bathing in Rees bathing hows. 1754 in *N. & Q.* (1865) VIII. 178 Notice is hereby Given, That the Bathing-House in this Place [*sc.* Portsmouth] will be finished and fit for Use, by about the 10th Day of May. 1835 J. H. INGRAHAM *South-West* I. xvi. 174 The long white bathing-houses, which stretched along the south side of the pier. 1838 F. A. KEMBLE *Let.* 10 Aug. in *Records of Later Life* (1882) I. 158 There are two little stationary bathing-huts. 1922 A. HUXLEY *Mortal Coils* 180 Running up towards his bathing hut. 1771 SMOLLETT *Humph. Cl.* (1815) 214 Bathing machines are ranged along the beach. 1860 C. A. COLLINS *Eye-Witness* ii. 15 Four bathing-machine boys. 1906 *Westm. Gaz.* 26 July 10/1 A writer in *T.P.'s Weekly* states, that the first bathing-machine was seen at Margate.. in 1750. 1646 SIR T. BROWNE *Pseud. Ep.* 309 The Balnearies or bathing places.. hee exposeth unto the Summer setting. 1810 in *Risdon's Surv. Devon* 431 The town is frequented.. as a bathing place. 1625 BACON *Gardens, Ess.* (Arb.) 561 The other Kinde of Fountaine, which we may call a Bathing Poole. 1924 A. D. SEDGWICK *Little French Girl* II. ix. 168 When they came to the rock where, with safety, the bathing-robes might be deposited. *a* 1700 EVELYN *Diary* 10 Sept. an. 1677 (1955) IV. 118 There are bathing roomes, Elaboratorie, Dispensatorie, what not. *c* 1702 C. FIENNES *Journeys* (1947) 100 A batheing roome, the walls all with blew and white marble.. the bath is one entire marble. *a* 1828 D. WORDSWORTH *Tour Continent* in *Jrnls.* (1941) II. 270 The commencement of the bathing-season. 1932 N. PALMER *Talking it Over* 139 A few large bathing-sheds tucked against the cliffs. 1873 *Young Englishwoman* June 280/2 Very pretty cases for holding the complete bathing suit are easily made of American cloth. 1881 MARSHALL *Through Amer.* (1882) 398 There had appeared in the *Salt Lake Daily Tribune*, in the morning, the following announcement: 'Bathing Suits to order in six hours.' 1906 *Daily Chron.* 18 Aug. 4/6 The 'Bathing Suit Dance' is the latest idea.. at American summer resorts. 1922 JOYCE *Ulysses* 723 If all women were her sort down on bathingsuits and lownecks. 1895 *Montgomery Ward Catal.* 488/2 Knee Tights.. also make good bathing trunks. 1956 F. CASTLE *Violent Hours* (1966) x. 98 He wore bathing trunks, wet and clinging. 1583 PLAT *Diuerse New Exper.* (1594) 94 The room would be close wherein you place your bathing-tub. 1633 MASSINGER *Guardian* II. iv, The Silver Bathing Tub. 1841 CATLIN *N. Amer. Indians* I. 97 A crib or basket, much in the shape of a bathing-tub. 1789 F. BURNEY *Diary* 30 June (1842) V. 33 Even the bathing-women had it [*sc.* 'God save the King'] in large coarse girdles round their waists. *a* 1845 HOOD *Storm at Hastings* xxvi, No bathing woman waded —none would dare.

'**bathing**, *ppl. a.* [f. BATHE *v.* + -ING[2].]

1. That bathes.

1884 *Pall Mall G.* 29 July 4/2 Bathing boys grow up clean men.

2. ***bathing beauty, belle***, an attractive woman in a bathing suit, used esp. of one taking part in a beauty contest; also *attrib.* and *transf.*

1920 B. LEVY in *Stage Year Bk.* 69 It would be hard to throw a stone.. upon the American Vaudeville stage without hitting what the eight-sheets describe as 'California Bathing Beauties'. 1926 A. HUXLEY *Jesting Pilate* IV. 266 Mack Sennett Bathing Beauties by the hundred. 1946 J. IRVING *Royal Navalese* 28 *Bathing Beauty*, strawberry- or raspberry-flavoured pink blancmange. 1967 MCLUHAN *Medium is Massage* 18 Today's television child is attuned to 'adult' news—inflation, rioting, war,.. bathing beauties. 1924 P. MACDONALD *Rasp* v. 57 Minister murdered by Bathing Belle. 1928 *Oxford Poetry* 39 The others all Were giggling blond bathingbelles. 1948 'J. TEY' *Franchise Affair* xv. 162 Coloured publications with bathing-belle covers.

bathless ('bɑːθlɪs, -æ-), *a.* [f. BATH *sb.*[1] + -LESS.] Without a bath or baths; not having had a bath. Hence '**bathlessness**, bathless condition.

1889 *Century Mag.* Aug. 503/2 A bathless, breakfastless Mexican smokes his cigarette. 1907 *Daily Chron.* 14 Oct. 4/4 A crowd who have worked for a hot week, bathless. 1909 *Cornhill Mag.* Aug. 230 About the fact—of the bathlessness of the Pickwickians—we may infer that there is no doubt whatever. 1963 *Guardian* 13 Feb. 8/4 Birmingham is.. preparing to mount a broad-fronted attack on bathlessness.. 30,000 to 50,000 homes lack bathrooms.

bathmic ('bæθmɪk), *a.* [f. Gr. βαθμός: see BATHMISM + -IC.] Of or pertaining to bathmism; exhibiting or caused by bathmism as a form of evolution.

1872 in COPE *Origin of Fittest* (1887) i. 26 It is a nice point of phylogeny (or the science of genealogy) to ascertain whether adaptive or strictly 'bathmic' (or embryonic grade) characters came first in time in a given group. 1879 *Ibid.* (1887) vi. 229, I compared the transmission of bathmic force to that of the phenomenon of combustion. 1905 G. A. REID *Princ. Heredity* i. 12 The Bathmic [doctrine of racial change], which attributes it to an 'inherent adaptive growth-force'.

bathmism ('bæθmɪz(ə)m). [f. Gr. βαθμός step, threshold (f. root of βαίνειν to walk, step) + -ISM.] A term invented by E. D. Cope to denote a supposed form of chemical force which is active in the processes of growth.

1871 in Cope *Origin of Fittest* (1887) v. 205 The Vital forces are (nerve-force) Neurism, (growth-force) Bathmism, and (thought-force) Phrenism. 1904 G. S. HALL *Adolescence* II. x. 90 It is the age of bathmism, or most rapid variation.

batholith ('bæθəʊlɪθ). *Geol.* Also **batholite, bathylith.** [a. G. *batholith* (Suess 1892, *Das Antlitz der Erde* I. 219), f. Gr. βάθο-ς depth + -LITH.] A large dome-shaped mass of intrusive igneous rock without a visible foundation. Hence ,**batho'lithic** *a.*

1903 R. A. DALY in *Amer. Jrnl. Sci.* XV. 270 'Batholiths'.. characteristically occur in regions of great structural complexity. 1904 SOLLAS tr. *Suess's Face of Earth* I. I. iv. 168 The magma simply filled the space.. forming a cake of rock or true *batholite.* **1905** CHAMBERLIN & SALISBURY *Geol.* I. 477 Great masses of irregular or undetermined forms.. are called *bathyliths.* **1906** *Ibid.* II. 131 The Archean batholiths. **1912** R. A. DALY *Geol. N. Amer. Cordillera* II. 726 The batholithic axes may have indefinite relations to axes of earlier and later crustal deformation. **1937** WOOLDRIDGE & MORGAN *Physical Basis Geogr.* viii. 106 The larger bodies of intrusive rock. These are the so-called bathyliths. **1960** L. D. STAMP *Britain's Struct.* (ed. 5) ix. 80 The great igneous bosses or batholiths of plutonic rock.. stand up as hill masses.

bathometer (bəˈθɒmɪtə(r)). [f. Gr. βάθο-ς depth + μέτρον measure.] A spring balance of peculiar construction for ascertaining the depth of water without actually measuring the sounding line.
1875 J. PRESTWICH in *Phil. Trans.* CLXV. 616 Obtained, by means of his bathometer.. the low readings given.

Baˈthonian, *a.* [f. *Bathonia*, latinized name of the city of Bath, in England + -AN; cf. *Oxonian.*]
1. Of or pertaining to the city of Bath.
1766 ANSTEY *Horace' Ode* II. i. (1808) 189 Whose genius guides, whose counsel guards The labours of Bathonian bards.
2. *Geol.* [ad. F. *bathonien* (J. J. D'O. D'Halloy *Précis El. Géol.* (1843) 471.] Denoting a subdivision of the Jurassic, of which the formations at Bath are typical.
1858 *Q. Jrnl. Geol. Soc.* XIV. 100 The Oolitic rocks.. may be thus tabulated.. Portland Oolite [is] Portlandian... Cornbrash, Forest Marble, Bradford Clay, Great Oolite, Stones-field Slate, Fuller's Earth [are] Bathonian. **1903** GEIKIE *Text-bk. Geol.* (ed. 4) 1140 The Great Oolite (Bathonian), between Dorset and Somerset on the west and Oxfordshire on the east. **1914** *Brit. Mus. Return* 201 Ophiuroidea from.. the Bathonian of Ardèche. **1960** L. D. STAMP *Britain's Struct.* (ed. 5) xii. 133 The Inferior Oolite or Bajocian beds are represented.. by limestones, the succeeding Great Oolite or Bathonian by deltaic deposits of coarse sand.

bat-horse: see BAT *sb.*[3]

bathos (ˈbeɪθɒs). [a. Gr. βάθος depth. First made Eng. in sense 2 by Pope's treatise, the title being a parody on Longinus's περὶ ὕψους; subseq. in the more etymological sense 1.]
1. Depth; lowest phase, bottom.
[**1638** SANDERSON *Serm.* II. 101 There is such a height, and depth, and length, and breadth in that love; such a βάθος in every dimension of it.] **1758** JOHNSON *Idler* No. 79 ¶7 Declining.. to the very bathos of insipidity. **1840** MARRYAT *Olla Podr.* (Rtldg.) 276, I am at the very bathos of stupidity.
2. *Rhet.* Ludicrous descent from the elevated to the commonplace in writing or speech; anticlimax.
1727 POPE *Bathos* 71 While a plain and direct road is paved to their ὕψος, or sublime; no track has been yet chalked out to arrive at our βάθος, or profund. **1787** J. ANDREWS *Anecdotes* s.v. *Bathos*, Had Ovid introduced this supper of Niobé between the death of her children and her own metamorphosis into stone, he would have furnished us, with a compleat instance of the Bathos. **1875** McLAREN *Serm.* Ser. II. xii. 211 It is as absurd bathos as to say, the essentials of a judge are integrity, learning, and an ermine robe!
3. Hence *gen.* A 'come-down' in one's career.
1814 T. JEFFERSON *Writ.* (1830) IV. 240 How meanly has he closed his inflated career! What a sample of the bathos will his history present! **1841** MARRYAT *Poacher* xxviii, It was rather a bathos.. to sink from a gentleman's son to an under usher.

baˈthotic, *a.* [f. Gr. βάθος, on superficial analogy; cf. *chaos, chaotic.*] = BATHETIC. Also *absol.*
1863 *Temple Bar* VII. 193 The appearance of this bathotic ebullition. **1874** E. S. NADAL in *Scribner's Monthly* VII. 486/1 The cadencies of this bathotic expression rolled among the arches of the cathedral. **1903** A. MCNEILL *Egreg. Eng.* 35 In England the bathotic has always had the majority in its grip. *Ibid.* 36 On that stop—the bathotic stop—the English journalist makes a point of playing. **1952** R. CAMPBELL *Lorca* 49 The gipsy.. comes right down with a bathotic lapse at the end.

bathroom. [BATH *sb.*[1]] A room containing a bath and often other toilet facilities. Hence also euphem. for a lavatory.
1780 COXE *Russ. Disc.* 99 An empty Russian dwelling, and near it a bath-room. **1888** BARRIE *When a Man's Single* xv. 242 What are politics when the pipes in the bathroom burst? **1934** J. O'HARA *Appointment in Samarra* (1935) iv. 108 Julian wanted to go to the bathroom after the dinner party stood up, and on his way to the men's locker room he had to pass Mrs. Gorman's table. **1946** 'J. TEY' *Miss Pym Disposes* ii. 9 It would show on the bathroom scales at the end of the week, but who cared? **1956** A. HUXLEY *Adonis & Alphabet* 260 The Prince of Venosa could never go to the bathroom (*cacare non poterat*) unless he had first been flogged. **1960** *Times* 14 Sept. 12/7 It is necessary [in U.S.A.].. to realize just what a rest room or bathroom is. I did find it odd.. when told that a small day school.. had a bathroom on every floor. **1962** J. BRAINE *Life at Top* xiii. 144 The bathroom cabinet crammed with eau-de-Cologne and talcum and bath salts. **1967** *House & Garden* June 88/4 Bathroom scales.. with magnified reading panel, 56*s.* 9*d.* **1968** *Listener* 22 Feb. 228/2 An unfortunate amount of the humour in other light British programmes tends to centre around the bathroom.

bathukolpian (bæθjuːˈkɒlpɪən), *a. rare.* [f. Gr. βαθύκολπ-ος (f. βαθύς deep + κόλπος breast, bosom) + -IAN.] Deep-bosomed. **bathukolpic** (-ˈkɒlpɪk), *a.* [see -IC] = prec.
1825 *Blackw. Mag.* XVII. 222 Our bathukolpian attendant. **1872** M. COLLINS *Pr. Clarice* I. i. 8 A colossal red-haired maiden of twenty, bathukolpic.

Bathurst burr (ˈbæθɜːst ˈbɜː(r)). [f. *Bathurst*, a town in N.S. Wales, Australia + BUR *sb.*] A plant of the genus *Xanthium*, found esp. in Australia.
1855 W. HOWITT *Land, Labour & Gold* I. 261 The Bathurst bur (*Xanthium spinosum*), a plant with long triple spines like the barberry, and burs which are ruinous to the wool of sheep. **1904** 'S. RUDD' *Sandy's Selection* 4 The remaining hundred and fifty-six were under scrub, prickly-pear, wallaby-bush and Bathurst burr. **1921** H. GUTHRIE-SMITH *Tutira* xxx. 291 A dense crop of.. Bathurst burr. **1926** J. DOONE *Timely Tips* Gloss., *Bathurst Burr*, a spiny, bean-shaped pod which grows on a weed and is notorious for attaching itself to the wool of passing sheep. **1934** *Bulletin* (Sydney) 12 Dec. 25/1 He 'ad whiskers all over him and they was as stiff as the spines on a Bathurst burr. **1967** *Southerly* XXVII. 199 Weeds flourished, wait-a-whiles, bull-burrs, wild blackberries, Bathurst burrs.

bathy- (ˈbæθɪ), comb. form of Gr. βαθύς deep, as in BATHYMETRIC *a.*: **ˌbathyæsˈthesia**, muscle sensation produced by muscular movement (Dorland, *Med. Dict.* 1901); **ˈbathyal** *a.* [-AL[1]], pertaining to the zone between the continental shelf and the abyssal zone (see quots.); **bathyˈcolpian** *a.*, a more normal form of BATHUKOLPIAN *a.*; **ˌbathylimˈnetic** [Gr. λίμνη pool], pertaining to or inhabiting the depths of freshwater lakes (Webster, Suppl. 1902); **ˈbathylite** [-LITE], = BATHOLITH; **baˈthymeter** = BATHOMETER (Cent. Dict. 1889); **ˌbathyoro-ˈgraphic, -ˈgraphical** *adjs.*, applied to representations of the contours of the surface of the earth and of the sea-bed; so **ˌbathyoroˈgraphically** *adv.*; **ˌbathypeˈlagic** *a.*, pertaining to or inhabiting the intermediate depths of the sea (opp. *abyssal, pelagic*); **ˌbathy ˈthermograph**, an instrument which records automatically the temperature of water at various depths; so **ˌbathythermoˈgraphic** *a.*, pertaining or relating to a bathythermograph or its recordings.
1926 W. H. TWENHOFEL *Treat. Sedimentation* vii. 612 The bathyal environment of the sea bottom is that portion between 100 and 1000 fathoms. *Ibid.* 613 The same processes noted in connection with the neritic environment are operative in the waters and sediments of the bathyal, but probably with less intensity. **1944** A. HOLMES *Princ. Physical. Geol.* II. xv. 314 The muds, etc., of the continental slope, and of similar depths around oceanic islands, belong to the *bathyal* zone; while the oozes of the deep ocean floor belong to the *abyssal* zone. **1961** CHALLINOR *Dict. Geol.* 19/2 *Bathyal*, applied to the moderately deep seas beyond the continental shelf and down to an indefinite depth, various authorities taking 6,000 ft., 10,000 ft. &c., but approximately to the limit of the accumulation of the terrigenous deposits, beyond which are the abyssal depths. **1858** O. W. HOLMES *Aut. Breakf.-t.* (1859) iv. 66 The bathycolpian Herè.. sent down Iris. **1902** *Encycl. Brit.* XXVI. 528/2 The Rocky Mountains.. comprise, however, in their central parts.. great masses of granite that have welled up as 'bathylites' along the axis of elevation. **1938** *Geogr. Jrnl.* XCI. 475 A new bathy-orographic map of the sea. **1911** *Bartholomew's Physical Atlas* V. pl. 1 Note to bathy-orographical map. *Ibid.* pl. 1 Bathy-orographical configuration. **1932** *Nelson's World Gaz.* 543/1 A *bathyorographical* map shows depths of the oceans and heights of the land. **1921** *Times Lit. Suppl.* 6 Oct. 646/3 This map of the Pacific, on Mollweide's homolographic projection, is bathyorographically coloured in shades of blue and brown. **1909** WEBSTER Bathypelagic. **1912** MURRAY & HJORT *Depths of Ocean* ix. 563 We shall.. simply use the term 'bathypelagic' to denote those animals that live deep in the intermediate layers. **1936** J. T. JENKINS *Fishes Brit. Is.* (ed. 2) 249 They [sc. *Argentina sphyræna*] are also bathypelagic, that is, found floating at intermediate depths and not at or near the surface. **1958** *New Biol.* XXV. 125 Other deep sea anglers [*i.e.* fish] are.. bathypelagic, living well above the bottom. **1938** A. F. SPILHAUS in *Jrnl. Marine Res.* I. 97 Measurements with the bathythermograph were carried out hourly.. and remarkably sudden discontinuities in the thermocline and inversions of the thermocline were revealed. *Ibid.*, The bathythermograph records were traced directly on to this diagram from photographic enlargements of the original traces. **1947** *Sci. News* IV. 84 The bathythermograph.. scratches a temperature depth record on a smoked glass slide as it sinks almost vertically on a thin wire running very freely from a small winch. **1952** *Jane's Fighting Ships 1951–52* 109 *New Liskeard*.. is now used for Bathythermographic duties at Halifax.

bathybial (bəˈθɪbɪəl), *a.* [f. BATHYBIUS + -AL.] Of or pertaining to bathybius or the depths at which it is found; belonging to or living in the deepest parts of the sea. So **baˈthybian, baˈthybic** *adjs.*
1876 *Encycl. Brit.* XXI. 774/2 [Sharks] known to belong to the bathybial fauna. **1881** *Arc. Cruise of Corwin* 14 (Cent. Dict.), The use of the dredge resulted in finding the usual bathybian forms. **1891** G. W. FIELD tr. *Haeckel's Planktonic Studies* in *Rep. U.S. Fish. Comm.* XVII. 582 The deepest part of this zonary fauna forms the bathybic plankton. **1898** *Athenæum* 4 June 729/3 Bathybial and pelagic life.

‖**bathybius** (bəˈθɪbɪəs). *Zool.* [mod.L., f. Gr. βαθύς deep + -βιος living, f. βίος life.] A name given by Prof. Huxley to a gelatinous substance found at the bottom of the Atlantic Ocean, and at first supposed to be a formless mass of living protoplasm, but now regarded as an inorganic precipitate.
1868 HUXLEY in *Q. Jrnl. Microsc. Sc.* 211, I propose to confer upon this new 'Moner' the generic name of *Bathybius.* **1875** DAWSON *Dawn of Life* iv. 66 The Bathybius ..may possibly be merely the pulpy sarcode of sponges. **1884** *Sat. Rev.* 14 June 770/2 Below the ooze, and bathybius, and so forth, in the Salaminian bay.

bathymetric (bæθɪˈmɛtrɪk), *a.* [f. Gr. βαθύ-ς deep + μετρικός of measuring; cf. BATHOMETER.] Of or pertaining to the measurement of depth, *spec.* to the vertical range of distribution of plants and animals in the sea.
1862 T. COBBOLD in *Intell. Observ.* No. 1. 27 Their bathymetric position.. will also accord with that of the infested creatures. **1880** *Jrnl. Linn. Soc.* XV. 88 Their bathymetric limits are not absolutely constant.

bathyˈmetrical, *a.* [f. as prec. + -AL[1].] = prec.
1861 GEIKIE *E. Forbes* x. 299 This bathymetrical principle of classification was also applied.. to the Ægean.

bathyˈmetrically, *adv.* [f. prec. + -LY[2].] In bathymetrical manner; as regards bathymetry.
c **1880** *Geog. Distrib. Anim.* in *Libr. Univ. Knowl.*, Life extends bathymetrically (to use Prof. Forbes's word) much further than was formerly supposed.

bathymetry (bəˈθɪmɪtrɪ). [f. Gr. βαθύ-ς deep + -μετρια measurement.] The art or science of measuring depths (in the sea).
1864 in WEBSTER.

bathyscaph(e (ˈbæθɪskæf). [a. Fr. *bathyscaphe* (A. Piccard), f. Gr. βαθύ-ς (BATHY-) + σκάφος ship.] The name given by the Swiss scientist Professor Auguste Piccard to his deep-sea diving vessel; also applied gen. to other similar vessels. (See quots.)
1947 *Time* 18 Aug. 38/1 Last week 63-year-old Scientist Piccard told the North American Newspaper Alliance about the 'bathyscaphe'.. his submarine balloon which will descend into the sea suspended from a.. 'gas bag' full of lightweight gasoline. **1953** J. Y. COUSTEAU *Silent World* ix. 87 The elderly scientific extremist [Auguste Piccard] had designed the *Bathyscaphe* ('Depth-craft') a decade before and, after the delay of a world war, it had been built by a brilliant Belgian physicist, Dr. Max Cosyns. *Ibid.* 89 The *Bathyscaphe* was to navigate twenty-five times as deep as conventional submarines. **1958** *New Scientist* 17 Apr. 31/3 The bathyscaph is an untethered and self-contained craft.. capable of diving to the deep sea bed and rising again by its own devices. **1959** *Sunday Times* 5 Apr. 7/4 (*caption*) The bathyscaphe Trieste in which.. United States scientists are to explore the ocean depths of the Pacific.

bathysphere (ˈbæθɪsfɪə(r)). [f. Gr. βαθύ-ς (BATHY-) + SPHERE.] A spherical diving apparatus for deep-sea observation.
1930 W. BEEBE in *Bull. N.Y. Zool. Soc.* XXXIII. 203/1 When I was writing the name of a deep-sea fish—*Bathytroctes*—the appropriateness of the Greek prefix occurred to me: I coined the word *Bathysphere*, and the name has stuck. **1931** *New Statesman* 21 Mar. 142/1 They crossed the yellow beam of the search-light from the bathysphere. **1947** *Sci. News* V. 67 'Bathyspheres'—closed diving chambers maintained at normal atmospheric pressure—.. are provided with a tripod-type base to give stability, and the job of the occupant is to chart the variation in the strength of gravity, when he is moved from one position to another over the sea bed.

†**ˈbatie-bum, -bummil.** *Sc. Obs.* An inactive helpless fellow; a useless bungler.
a **1550** *Christis Kirke Gr.* 131 He muddlit thame doun lyk ony myss, He wes na baity bummil. **1572** A. ARBUTHNOT *Mis. Pure Scolar*, Bot thane am I comptit ane batie-bum, And all men thinks a play me till injure.

batik (ˈbætɪk, bəˈtiːk). Also **battik.** [Javanese, lit. 'painted'.] **1.** The Javanese art and method (introduced into England by way of Holland) of executing designs on textiles by covering the material with wax in a pattern, dyeing the parts left exposed, and then removing the wax, the process being repeated when more than one dye is used. Also, (a garment made of) a fabric dyed in this way; the kind of pattern, consisting of a medley of colours, characteristic of this art.
1880 *Encycl. Brit.* XIII. 604/2 Another mode is to cover with melted wax or damar the part of the cloth not intended to receive the dye... The 'battiks', as the cloths thus treated are called, are in request by the wealthier classes. **1906** *Daily Chron.* 26 Jan. 4/6 Java is the home of Batik, which is a kind of colour-printing on fabrics. **1922** *Daily Mail* 8 Aug. 3/3 Exact in detail, faultless in design, brilliant in colour, good batik is a joy. **1924** *Times Lit. Suppl.* 20 Nov. 777/1 'Batik' is a Javanese word, and the art was originally practised in Java, whence the Dutch brought it to Europe over three hundred years ago. **1936** J. DOS PASSOS *Big Money* 428 Ladies in flowing batiks. **1958** *Times* 13 Aug. 12/5 Real wax batiks are now being sold to meet the demand for gay summer frocks.
2. *attrib.* passing into *adj.* Executed by the art or method of batik; of, or ornamented with, batik work; hence, loosely, characterized by a fantastic colour-pattern.
1914 *Studio* 14 Mar. 154/2 Examples of embroidery and batik work. *Ibid.* 155/1 Batik Shawl. **1920** *Brit. Mus. Return* 64 A piece of batik cloth, dyed with Chinese designs, from

Java. **1920** S. LEWIS *Main St.* xvii. 215 An arty arrangement of batik scarfs and heavy tables. **1923** *Advt.* (Nonesuch Press) in *Times Lit. Suppl.* 27 Sept. 627 [Volumes] bound in quarter-vellum with batik sides. **1927** *Punch* 20 Apr. 424/3 He removed his horn-rims and began polishing them vigorously, producing for the purpose a large silk handkerchief of chaste design. There is nothing batik about Edward. **1967** *Spectator* 14 July 53/2 'Digs' from Hampstead to Earls Court are littered with batik-patterned fabrics.

Hence **'bat(t)iking** *vbl. sb.*, the production of batik work.

1880 *Encycl. Brit.* XIII. 604/2 A more rapid process of battiking by means of hand stamps has begun to be employed both by native and Chinese workers.

batilde, obs. form of BATTLED, embattled.

bating ('beɪtɪŋ), *vbl. sb.*[1] [f. BATE *v.*[1] 2 + -ING[1].] The action of beating the wings, and (*spec.* in *Falconry*) fluttering off the fist or perch.

1456 *Bk. St. Albans* A vj, It is calde batyng for she batith with hir selfe most oftyn causeless. **1614** RALEIGH *Hist. World* I. 175 The crying of Crowes, and bating of Ducks foreshew raine. **1783** AINSWORTH *Lat. Dict.* (Morell) 1, The bating of a hawk, *alarum plausus*.

bating ('beɪtɪŋ), *vbl. sb.*[2] [f. BATE *v.*[2] 6 + -ING[1].] Lessening, abatement.

1628 EARLE *Microcosm.* xxxix. 86 This bating shall in conclusion take away all he granted.

bating ('beɪtɪŋ), *ppl. a.* [f. BATE *v.*[1] 2 + -ING[2].] Beating the wings impatiently, fluttering.

1587 GASCOIGNE *Herbes* 138 The hooded hawke.. fast tied, yet beats hir baiting wing.

bating ('beɪtɪŋ), *prep.* Also 6 **baiting**. [absolute use of pr. pple. of BATE *v.*[2] 7; cf. similar use of *barring*, *excepting*.] Abating, leaving out of account, excepting, except. †*bating of*: less than.

1568 C. WATSON *Polyb.* 73 b, Another tyme [they fought] with few baiting of seven hundreth. **1647** R. STAPYLTON *Juvenal* ii. 182 Nobler then.. all that from the scaffolds saw the sport He made, not bating him that paid him for't. **1721** *Wodrow Corr.* (1843) II. 594 Bating this, I know nothing to the youth's disadvantage. **1817** BYRON *Beppo* v, For, bating Covent Garden, I can hit on No place that's call'd 'Piazza' in Great Britain. **1859** MACAULAY *Jrnl.* 16 Dec. in G. O. Trevelyan *Life & Lett.* (1959) xv. 684 Bating the irregularity of the pulse, I suffered all that I suffered.. in 1852.

batiste (bəˈtiːst). Also 7 **baptist**. [a. F. *batiste* = *Baptiste*, according to Littré and Scheler from the alleged original maker, Baptiste of Cambray; according to others, from its use in wiping the heads of children after baptism.]

The French word for *cambric*; applied, in commerce, to a fine light fabric of the same texture, but differently finished, and made of cotton as well as of linen. Often *attrib.*

1697 *C'tess D'Aunoy's Trav.* (1706) 155 A sort of a Gown made of their Baptist Cloth very fine. **1863** B. TAYLOR *H. Thurston* xviii. 240 Wiped her eyes with a very small batiste handkerchief. **1880** MISS BRADDON *Asph.* I. vi. 188 A graceful, gracious figure in a pale yellow batiste gown.

batle, batled, batling: see BATTLE, etc.

batle, -er, obs. ff. BATTEL, -ER (at Oxford).

†**'batler**, *Obs. rare*[−1]. in mod. edd. of Shakspere **batlet**. [f. BATTLE *v.*[4] + -ER[1]; or ? dim. f. BAT *sb.*[2] + -LET.] Probably, a 'beetle' for battling clothes: see BATTLE *v.*[4]

1600 SHAKS. *A.Y.L.* II. iv. 49 And I remember the kissing of her batler. [**1865** *Reader* 29 Apr. 481/3, I lately picked up in an old house in Yorkshire a 'batlet,' such as Touchstone kissed when in love.]

'batling, *dial. rare*[−1]. [f. BAT *sb.*[2] 1 + -LING.] A small stick, a fagot. (Halliwell.)

1864 MAR. CHARLESWORTH *Eng. Yeomen* 52 Tell 'em to bring in a batling, and make up the fire.

batling, obs. form of BATTLING.

‖**batman**[1] ('bætmən). Also 6–7 **bateman**. [Turkish (Chaghatai) *bātmān*, (Osmanli) *baṭmān*, *baṭman*. a weight equal to the Pers. *man*, the Anglo-Indian *maund*.] An oriental weight varying greatly in value according to the locality.

1599 HAKLUYT *Voy.* II. 247 Euery bateman here [i.e. Babylon] maketh 7 pound and 5 ounces English waight. **1616** PURCHAS *Pilgr.* (1864) 38 A Batman is fiue and fiftie pound weight English. **1740** THOMPSON & HOGG in Hanway *Trav.* (1762) I. IV. iii. 242 Their weights [at Khiva] are the great batman, equal to eighteen lb. russian, and the lesser batman, nine and a quarter. **1852** MCCULLOCH *Dict. Comm.* 391 [At Constantinople] 6 okes [*i.e.* about 16 lbs.] = 1 batman.

batman[2] ('bætmən, 'bɑːmən). [f. BÂT *sb.* + MAN.] A man in charge of a bat-horse and its load; a military servant of a cavalry officer. Now generally, an officer's servant.

1755 in S. M. HAMILTON *Lett. to Washington* I. 96 They have taken.. another man who was batman to Doct. Craik. **1809** WELLINGTON in Gurw. *Disp.* V. 198 The care of the Camp Kettles is not only the business of the Bâtman of the company, but of all the Bâtmen of the regiment. **1844** *Regul. & Ord. Army* 271 A Bât Man is allowed to the Surgeon for the care of the horse carrying the Instruments. **1855** W. SARGENT *Braddock's Exp.* 206 The English loss was.. a waggoner, three bat-men, and a horse. **1941** *Aeronautics* Oct. 60/3 R.A.F. officers in the future are to have the services of members of the W.A.A.F. for duties which have been carried out hitherto by batmen. **1955** *Times* 18 Aug. 5/1 Men employed as outside batmen in the married quarters were expected to clean and polish the houses, clean windows, cut lawns, fetch coal, and run errands. **1966** *Times* 9 July 9/7 Command Orders say a batman must now be dignified as an 'orderly'.

¶ See also BAT *sb.*[2]

Bat Mitzvah (bat'mɪtsva). *Judaism.* Also with lower-case initials and **bas** (bas) **'mitzvah**, etc. [Heb., lit. 'daughter of commandment'; after BAR-MITZVAH.] **a.** A Jewish girl who has reached the age of twelve, regarded as the age of religious majority. **b.** The ceremony held in celebration of this occasion. Cf. BAR-MITZVAH.

1950 *Liberal Judaism* Dec. 54/1 They also conduct Bar Mitsvo services for their boys at thirteen, and more than ½ conduct Bat Mitsvo services for the girls. **1952** *Synagogue Rev.* Mar. 223/1 A *bar mitsvah* and *bat mitsvah* class meets on Wednesdays at 5 p.m. **1952** *Amer. Jewish Yearbk.* 156 Half of the congregations permit girls to be bas mitzvah. **1959** D. D. RUNES *Conc. Dict. Judaism* 31/2 Non-orthodox synagogues have a Bat Mitzvah ceremony for girls. **1962** *New Jewish Encycl.* 43/1 All branches of Judaism oppose the cessation of Jewish education after Bar Mitzvah is reached. Some congregations have instituted a corresponding ceremony for girls called Bat (Bas) Mitzvah. **1969** S. B. FREEHOF *Current Reform Responsa* 70 His daughter was Bat Mitzvah at the age of twelve. **1977** *Washington Post* 3 Dec. B10/6 He.. prepared young people for bar and bat mitzvahs. **1980** *N.Y. Times* 11 Sept. A19/3 Before my bas mitzvah a new building opened, with the 12 Tribes of Israel in dark blue glass, and a Hebrew school wing. **1985** *Ibid.* 9 May A31/1 A young Jewish woman who recently had had her bat mitzvah. **1986** J. TELUSHKIN *Unorthodox Murder Rabbi Moss* i. 6, I joined for my daughter's sake. Jessica is in the congregation's *bar-* and *bat-mitzvah* class.

batning, obs. form of BATTENING.

batologist (bə'tɒlədʒɪst). [f. Gr. βάτο-ς bramble + *-ologist*: see -OLOGY.] One who makes a botanical study of the genus *Rubus*, esp. the blackberry bramble. So **ba'tology**; **bato'logical** *a.*

1889 in *Cent. Dict.* **1897** G. C. DRUCE *Flora Berks.* 187 Boar's Hill, that very interesting locality to the batologist. **1899** HANBURY & MARSHALL *Flora of Kent* 109 Our leading English batologist.

baton ('bætən, ‖batɔ̃), *sb.* Forms: 6– **batton**, 7– **baton**. [a. mod.F. *bâton*:—OF. *baston*, whence the earlier Eng. BASTON. *Baton* appeared first in 16th c. in Sc. writers: the usual Eng. form during 17th and 18th c. was BATOON, but 'baton' was occasionally used in sense 2, and has now all but supplanted *batoon*.]

†**1. a.** A staff or stick used as a weapon, sometimes also of iron or iron-tipped; a club, cudgel, or truncheon; = BASTON 1. *Obs.* in general sense, in which also BATOON was the form always used during 17th and 18th c.

1548 *Compl. Scot.* 28 The father takkis ane batton or sum othir sterk vappin to puneise his sonne. **1596** SPENSER *F.Q.* VI. vii. 46 The Villaine.. with his yron batton which he bore Let drive at him. **1609** SKENE *Reg. Maj.* 142 Gif any.. mutilates ane other with ane batton. **1829** SCOTT *Anne of G.* i, If you use your baton, he rewards you with the stab of a knife.

b. A staff or stick generally; a walking-stick (after French use).

1801 STRUTT *Sports & Past.* II. iii. 98 A small batton or stump set up. **1860** TYNDALL *Glac.* I. §11. 79 Driving.. the spikes of our batons into the slope above our feet.

c. *transf.* Of bread: a long loaf; also, a thin short stick.

1857 GEO. ELIOT *Amos Barton* ii. in *Blackw. Mag.* LXXXI. 11/1 Chubby, who is making a round O of her mouth to receive a bit of papa's 'baton'. **1901** *Westm. Gaz.* 22 Apr. 7/2 The crowd consumed.. 17,000 batons. **1959** M. STEEN *Tower* I. v. 76 A *bâton* of French bread and some cheese.

d. *pl.* [See note at CLUB *sb.* 8.] One of the four suits (equivalent to Clubs) in packs of playing-cards used in Italy and Spanish-speaking countries, and in tarot packs.

[**1816**], **1848**, etc. [see SWORD *sb.* 1 e]. **1892** M. K. VAN RENSSELAER *Devil's Picture Bks.* 82 Francis Fibbia.. had obtained as the inventor of Tarocchino.. the privilege of placing his own arms on the Queen of Batons. **1930** C. P. HARGRAVE *Hist. Playing Cards* viii. 235 (*caption*) Hombre cards in which the suit signs of swords and batons interlace in the Italian manner. *Ibid.* 245 The King of batons bears a round escutcheon. **1964** A. WYKES *Gambling* vii. The earliest known Tarot pack.. had four suits: Cups (or Chalices), Swords, Money, and Batons (or Clubs).

2. a. A staff or truncheon carried as the symbol of office, command, or authority; a staff of office; *e.g.* a Marshal's baton, that carried by engine-drivers on a single line of railway, and the truncheon of a constable. Formerly also BATOON (2). Also *attrib.* esp. in ***baton charge***, a charge made by police constables with drawn truncheons; hence (hyphened) as *v. trans.* and *intr.* Also ***baton round***, a rubber or plastic bullet (as fired from a ***baton gun***).

1590 J. BUREL *Entry of Queen*, With battons blank into thair hands. **1662** J. BARGRAVE *Pope Alex. VII* (1867) 116 Æsculapius.. in a long robe, with his baton or knotty staff in his hand. **1690** *Lond. Gaz.* No. 2527/3 His High-Steward and Chamberlain, having gilt Batons in their Hands. **1813** SCOTT *Trierm.* II. xxvii, The weighty baton of command. **1813** WELLINGTON in Gurw. *Disp.* X. 452 Marshal Jourdan's Bâton of a Marshal of France. **1864** BURTON *Scot Abr.* I. i. 39 Buchan got the baton of High Constable. **1890** *Rev. of Reviews* Nov. 489/1 As police officer, having headed a bâton charge upon them. **1900** *Westm. Gaz.* 12 Nov. 5/1 There a large force of police was gathered, and, a baton charge taking place, several people were badly injured. **1906** *Daily Chron.* 2 Nov. 7/6 Bleeding.. from stick and baton wounds. **1968** *Hong Kong Rep. 1967* i. 12 On July 8.. the police post was attacked and.. the police opened fire with gas and wooden 'baton' projectiles. **1972** *Times* 11 Aug. 1/1 An Army officer emphasized tonight that the PVC bullet would not replace the rubber baton round. **1973** D. BARZILAY *Brit. Army in Ulster* (1978) I. 73/2 The rubber bullet was developed from an idea used in the Hong Kong riots when wooden bullets were fired from the baton gun. **1976** *Guardian Weekly* 14 Nov. 2/3 A police car stopped in the road.. and a policeman jumped out and baton-charged a boy of nine or ten. **1977** *Times* 4 Apr. 1/6 The police and troops baton-charged, and running battles with the demonstrators took place over a wide area. **1985** *Ibid.* 8 Oct. 2/5 Weighing 4.75 oz and composed of solid PVC, the bullet, known officially as a baton round, is fired by a special launcher. **1986** *Financial Times* 31 Jan. 2/4 In one incident several hundred women were baton-charged by Spanish riot police who also fired rubber bullets and tear gas. **1986** *Daily Tel.* 25 Sept. 3/2 In the great majority of instances the discharge of a baton round when a riot is taking place does not cause serious injury or death.

b. *Athletics.* The short stick or rod passed from one runner to another in a relay race.

1920 *Isis* 13 Oct. 2/2 Ten yards is allotted each side of the starting line in which to pass the baton to the next competitor. **1927** W. DEEPING *Kitty* xxiv, You snatched the baton from the failing hand of the past. **1958** *Times* 25 Aug. 4/1 The British sprint relay teams won their silver medals through immaculate baton changing.

3. *Her.* An ordinary, in breadth the fourth part of a BEND, not extending to the extremities of an escutcheon, but broken off short at each end, so as to have the figure of a truncheon; used by French heralds as a difference or mark of consanguinity, but in English coats of arms only in the form of the ***baton sinister***, the badge of bastardy. (Popularly called *bar sinister*.) Formerly BASTON (3), *batune*, BATTOON (3).

1816 SCOTT *Antiq.* xxiii, Here is the baton-sinister, the mark of illegitimacy, extended diagonally through both coats upon the shield. **1864** BOUTELL *Heraldry Hist. & Pop.* xxviii. 438 The eldest son of this Earl removed his father's baton from his arms.

4. *Music.* The light stick or wand used by a musical conductor for beating time. (From mod.Fr., and often pronounced as French.) Also in the phr. ***under the baton of***, under the conductorship of, conducted by.

1785 C. BURNEY in *Mus. Performances in Westm. Abbey 1784* 14 So numerous a band moving in such exact measure, without.. a *Coryphæus* to beat the time, either with a roll of paper, or a noisy *baton*. **1829** *Morning Post* 27 May 3/2 Mr. Mendlessohn conducted his Sinfonia with a *baton*, as is customary in Germany, France, etc. **1867** *Athenæum* 6 Apr., The introduction of the bâton in England. **1877** G. B. SHAW in *Hornet* 27 June 330/2 Its [*sc.* the opera's] new aspect under the *bâton* of Signor Vianesi. *Ibid.* 1 Aug. 378/2 He is the only chief under whose baton orchestras display good training. **1880** GROVE *Dict. Mus.* I. 82 There.. 1820, Spohr appeared.. when a baton was used for perhaps the first time at an English concert. **1884** *Yorksh. Post* 30 Apr., It was Costa, who founded in England the order of conductor, and who introduced the wand as *baton* in lieu of the fiddlestick. **1962** *Observer* 15 July 22/3 The work was played by another British orchestra under the composer's baton.

5. See BATTEN.

baton ('bætən), *v.* Also 6 **battoun(e**. [f. prec. sb.] To strike with a baton or truncheon; formerly, to cudgel: see the earlier form BATOON *v.*

c **1580** MONTGOMERIE *To R. Hudson*, They battouned her quhill that thay saw her bluid. **1820** SCOTT *Abbot* iv, That this young esquire shall poniard the servants, as well as switch and baton them. **1885** *Times* 17 Apr. 6/4 If they did not leave peaceably, they would be batoned by the police.

batoned ('bætənd), *ppl. a.* Also 7 **battoned**. [f. prec. + -ED.] Furnished or armed with, or bearing, a baton; in *Her.* marked with, or bearing, the baton of bastardy.

1691 *Lond. Gaz.* No. 2682/4 A Coat quartered with the Arms of the Crown battoned. **1883** W. C. SMITH *N. Country Folk* 156 Gibbets, and soldiers, and batoned police.

batonless ('bætənlɪs), *a.* [f. BATON *sb.* + -LESS.] Without a baton.

1885 *Blackw. Mag.* May 73/1 The batonless chiefs, the disinherited princes of the Irish name. **1906** *Daily Chron.* 7 May 4/5 Batonless conductor. **1909** *Westm. Gaz.* 22 Oct. 5/2 M. Safonoff conducted, and the chorus-singers seemed a little bewildered by his batonless movements.

‖**bâtonné** (batɔne). *Philately.* [Fr., pa. pple. of *bâtonner* to beat with a stick, f. *bâton* stick.] (See quot. 1897.)

1892 R. B. EARÉE *Album Weeds* (ed. 2) p. ix. **1897** O. FIRTH *Postage Stamps* 15 The thin laid paper commonly called 'foreign note' is known in the stamp world as *batonné*; if it be plain between the lines for writing on, it is known as 'wove *bâtonné*'; if filled with the usual lines, 'laid *bâtonné*'. *Ibid.* 16 The local Mexican stamps of Guadalajara.. are to be found printed upon these *bâtonné* and *quadrillé* papers of various colours. **1928** *Stanley Gibbons' Catal. Stamps, Foreign Countries* 12.

‖**bâtonnier** (batɔnje). [Fr., = 'staff-bearer', f. *bâton* staff.] The title of the doyen of the Bar of Paris and of Quebec.

1907 *Westm. Gaz.* 26 Nov. 10/1 It is from circumstances connected with St. Catherine's festivals that the 'bâtonnier' of the Paris Bar derives his curious designation. **1918** E. CLARKE *Story of my Life* xxviii. 368, I was entertained at dinner by the Quebec Bar; Mr. Donald MacMaster, the batonnier, presided. **1921** *Q. Rev.* Jan. 23 The riding in which he [*sc.* Sir W. Laurier] had practised as a lawyer; in which he achieved the only prize in his profession that ever fell to him—election as batonnier by the Bar of the county.

batoon (bəˈtuːn), *sb. arch.* Forms: 6 **batune**, 6–7 **battune** (sense 3), 7 **battoune**, 7–8 **battoone**, 7– **battoon, batoon**. [17th c. ad. F. *baton*, of which it retained the accent: see -OON. Now almost superseded by BATON *sb.*, which follows the French spelling.]

1. A stout staff or stick used as a weapon, a cudgel, club, truncheon; = BASTON 1, BATON *sb.* 1.

a **1625** FLETCH. & MASS. *Elder Bro.* v. i, My sword forc'd from me.. Get me a battoon. **1632** CHAPM. & SHIRLEY *Ball* IV. ii, I'll cullice thee With a batoon. **1664** BUTLER *Hud.* II. ii. 719 Although his Shoulders with Batoon Be claw'd and cudgel'd to some tune. **1719** D'URFEY *Pills* (1872) III. 321 Often he fought with huge Battoon. **1801** STRUTT *Sports & Past.* III. vii. 238 The bowls.. are driven with a battoon, or mace. **1860** *All Y. Round* No. 71. 491 Winterfield, though he escaped the batoon, was ordered to leave his shop.

2. A staff of office; = BATON *sb.* 2.

1658 BROME *Covent Gard.* III. i, The Lord and the Lowne, Must move by the motion of the Leaders Battoon. *a* **1693** ASHMOLE *Antiq. Berks* (1723) III. 60 In his right hand is a Battoon, as a General. **1704** LUTTRELL *Brief Rel.* V. 427 A battoon set with diamonds, sent him from the French King. **1807** ROBINSON *Archæol. Græca* I. xiv. 65 The Areopagites .. held in their hands, as a mark of their authority, a sort of batoon made in the form of a sceptre.

3. *Her.* = BASTON 3, BATON *sb.* 3, which is the form now used. (In 16–17th c. usually written *batune.*)

1562 LEIGH *Armorie* (1597) 64 b, The bastard shal beare the fourth part of this [Bende Sinyster] which must bee called a batune sinister. **1611** COTGR., *Cottice*, a Cottice or Battune. **1611** GWILLIM *Heraldry* II. v. 52 Batune is derived from the French word *Baston*.. This is the proper and most vsuall note of Illegitimation, perhaps for the affinitie betwixt *Baston* and Bastards; or else for that Bastards lost the priuilege of Freemen, and so were subject to the seruile stroke. **1662** FULLER *Worthies* II. 299 Over all a Batune dexter-ways Argent. **1725** BRADLEY *Fam. Dict.*, *Battoone*, the fourth Part of a Bend Sinister.

4. *Arch.* = BASTON 6 (q.v.), BATON *sb.* 5, BATTEN.

1819 P. NICHOLSON *Dict. Archit.* I. 57 Bastion or Batoon; see Torus. **1852** *Archit. Publ. Soc. Dict.* I. 45 Baton, Batoon, or Battoon.. a name given to the torus between the listel or fillet and the plinth, in the base commonly assigned to the Roman Doric order.

batoon (bəˈtuːn), *v. arch.* [f. prec. sb.] To beat or strike with a batoon, to thrash with a stick, to cudgel. (See BATON *v.*)

1683 *Roxb. Bal.* (1885) 336 Payton batoon'd him for calling him Rogue. **1818** SCOTT *Br. Lamm.* xvi, If you do not depart.. I will batoon you to death. **1863** SALA *Capt. Dang.* I. iv. 102, I would batoon you to a mummy.

‖**Batrachia** (bəˈtreɪkɪə), *sb. pl. Zool.* [prop. *batrachīa*, mod.L., a. Gr. βατράχεια (sc. ζῷα animals), neut. pl. of βατράχειος, adj. f. βάτραχος frog.] **a.** One of Brongniart's four orders of Reptiles, including frogs, toads, newts, salamanders, etc., which have no ribs, and a soft scaleless skin, and breathe by means of gills during the early part, or whole, of their existence. **b.** By modern zoologists restricted to an order of the class Amphibia, containing those animals only, as frogs and toads, which subsequently discard the gills and tail of their larval state. (The sing. is supplied by BATRACHIAN.)

1847 CARPENTER *Zool.* §514 In the Proteidæ, or perennibranchiate Batrachia, the gills remain during the whole of life. **1881** MIVART in *Nature* No. 615. 337 Efts of all kinds, with all frogs and toads.. form the class Batrachia.

baˈtrachian, *a.* and *sb.* [f. prec. + -AN.]

A. *adj.* Of or pertaining to the Batrachia, *esp.* frogs and toads.

1834 SIR C. BELL *Hand* 156 In the batrachian orders, the ribs are wanting. **1858** O. W. HOLMES *Aut. Breakf. T.* 84 The batrachian hymns from the neighbouring swamp.

B. *sb.* An animal of the order Batrachia.

1838 *Penny Cycl.* X. 487/1 Anurous or Tailless Batrachians, having no tails except in their young state. **1848** H. MILLER *First Impr.* xii. (1857) 190 The footprints of some betailed batrachian.

batrachiate (bəˈtreɪkɪeɪt), *a.* and *sb.* [f. BATRACHIA + -ATE[2].] = BATRACHIAN.

1902 *Encycl. Brit.* XXVIII. 139/2 In the batrachiate Amphibia, Héron Royer succeeded in 1883 in rearing.. a few hybrids.

batrachite (ˈbætrəkaɪt). [ad. L. *batrachītes* a., Gr. βατραχίτης (λίθος), f. Gr. βάτραχ-ος frog; see -ITE.] **a.** A stone or gem resembling a frog in colour. **b.** A fossil batrachian.

[**1727** CHAMBERS *Cycl.*, *Batrachites*, a kind of gem, found in Egypt.] **1837–68** DANA *Min.* 256 s.v. *Monticellite*, Batrachite is found in small masses containing black spinel, at Mt. Rinzoni in the Tyrol. **1847** in CRAIG.

'batracho-, combining form of Gr. βάτραχο-ς frog; whence **batrachomyomachy** (ˌbætrə ˌkəʊmaɪˈɒməkɪ) [ad. Gr. βατραχομυομαχία, f. βάτραχο-ς + μυ-ς mouse + -μαχια fighting.] The battle of the frogs and mice, a mock heroic poem, possibly of the Homeric age. **batrachophagous** (bætrəˈkɒfəgəs), *a.* [Gr. -φαγ -ος eating + -OUS.] Frog-eating. **ˌbatrachoˈphobia** [Gr. -φοβία fear.] Dread of or aversion to frogs, toads, newts, etc.

1825 SOUTHEY *Q. Rev.* XXXI. 385 Delivered the remnant of the race from their batrachophagous oppressors. **1863** G. KEARLEY *Links in Chain* viii. 162 The batrachophobia is at length giving way.. for the Aquarium has made it manifest that the Water Newts.. are perfectly harmless little creatures.

batrachoid (ˈbætrəkɔɪd), *a.* [f. Gr. βάτραχο-ς frog + -ειδής like (cf. Gr. βατραχώδης); see -OID.] Resembling a frog, frog-like.

1825 SOUTHEY in *Q. Rev.* XXXI. 384 Compared with all other batrachoid colonies.. the frogs of Cintra are the.. nobles of the species. **1854** OWEN in *Orr's Circ. Sc.* Org. Nat. I. 187 The most batrachoid of fishes.

bats, batts *sb. pl.*, Sc. form of *bots*, *botts* (see BOT).

batsman (ˈbætsmən). [f. *bat's* (BAT *sb.*[2]) + -MAN.]

1. a. One who handles the bat at cricket. ***batsman's wicket***, a cricket pitch more favourable to the batsman than to the bowler.

1756 *Gentl. Mag.* XXVI. 489 The wary batsman watches o'er the game. **1830** MISS MITFORD *Village* Ser. IV. (1863) 147 The best batsman in the county. **1851** PYCROFT *Cricket Field* (1859) 225 With fast bowling and good batsmen. **1876** *Baily's Mag.* June 415 Much.. will depend on.. whether it is a batsman's or a bowler's wicket on the day of the match. **1927** G. A. TERRILL *Out in Glare* v. 84 It would be a dumbfounding disgrace.. if wickets went on falling in this way—on this 'batsman's wicket'.

b. *U.S.* One who wields the bat in baseball.

1856 *Spirit of Times* (N.Y.) 6 Dec. 229/1 He who strikes it [*sc.* a fast ball by Stevens] fairly must be a fine batsman.

2. A man who signals an aircraft with a pair of bats. Cf. BAT *sb.*[2] 3 f.

1943 *Fleet Air Arm* (Ministry of Information) iv. 30/1 The Deck-Landing Control Officer is known as 'the Batsman'—from the implements with which he signals to the pilots. **1949** *Aeronautics* July 35 When a pilot is high the batsman stands with the bats above his shoulders.

batsmanship (ˈbætsmænʃɪp). [f. BATSMAN + -SHIP.] The batsman's art; the art of batting at cricket; batting performance.

1907 *Westm. Gaz.* 30 May 10/1 The Rev. F. H. Gillingham.. has done splendid service for Essex by his vigorous batsmanship. **1912** C. B. FRY (*title*) Cricket: batsmanship.

†**ˈbatsome**, *a. Obs. rare*[−1]. [f. *bat-* (see BATTEN *v.*) + -SOME: cf. *batful.*] = BATTABLE.

1555 BONNER *Necess. Doctr.* L i, He had planted them in a batsome and frutefull countrey.

batt, variant of BAT *sb.*[2] 12. A felted mass of hair and wool in hat-making.

‖**batta** (ˈbætə), *sb.*[1] *Anglo-Ind.* [a. Indo-Portuguese *bata*, prob. ad. Canarese *bhatta* rice in the husk (also called by Europeans *batty*), which became, first with the Portuguese, a term for 'maintenance,' 'allowance for maintenance' (Col. Yule).] *orig.* Subsistence money (given to soldiers in the field, witnesses, prisoners, etc.). Hence, extra pay given to East Indian regiments when on a campaign, and *spec.* An extra allowance, which grew in time to be a constant addition to the pay of officers serving in India.

[**1548** *Ordenadas de Dio* (i.e. *Diu*) in S. BOTELHO, *Tombo*, 233 E pera dous ffarazes, dous pardaos a anbos por mês, e quoatro tanguas pera bata. (*Called in a later entry* mantimento.)] **1680** *Fort St. George Consultations* (1872) Feb. 10 The peons were.. fined each one month's pay, and to repay the money paid them for *Battee.* **1707** in J. T. Wheeler *Madras in O.T.* II. 63 (Y.) That they would allow Batta or subsistence money to all that should desert us. **1800** WELLINGTON in Gurw. *Disp.* I. 69 The government intend to put the troops in this country on half batta. **1835** *Penny Cycl.* IV. 39/2 The half batta of a lieutenant colonel is 304 rupees per month. **1883** *Standard* 22 Jan. 5/6 The question of batta for the troops employed in Egypt has been.. under consideration.

‖**batta** (ˈbætə), *sb.*[2] *Anglo-Ind.* [a. Urdu *baṭṭā*, Bengali *bāṭṭā*.] In Indian Banking, agio or difference in exchange; discount on coins not current, or of short weight. (Col. Yule.)

1680 *Ft. St. George Consultations* (1872) 17 Payment or receipt of *Batta* or *Vatum* upon the exchange of Pollicat for Madras pagodas prohibited. **1760** *Fort William Consultations* June 30 All siccas of a lower date.. are bought and sold at a certain discount called *batta*, which rises and falls like the price of other goods. **1810** T. WILLIAMSON *E. Ind. Vade-mec.* I. 203 (Y.) He immediately tells master that the batta, *i.e.* the exchange, is altered.

Batta (ˈbætə), *a.* and *sb.*[3] [Native name.] **A.** *adj.* Of or pertaining to a people of the northern part of Sumatra. **B.** *sb.* A member of this people or its language. Cf. BATAK *a.* and *sb.*[1]

1779 C. MILLER in *Phil. Trans. R. Soc. 1778* LXVIII. 162 In the Batta country, immediately under the line, I have seen it [*i.e.* thermometer] frequently at six A.M. as low as 61°. *Ibid.* 165 The country.. is well inhabited by a people called Battas, who differ from all the other inhabitants of Sumatra in language, manners, and customs. **1783** W. MARSDEN *Hist. Sumatra* 165 The principal internal languages of Sumatra, are the Rejang and the Batta. *Ibid.* 296 The *Battas* are in their persons rather below the stature of the *Malay*, and their complexions are fairer. *Ibid.* 300 Human flesh is eaten .. on the island of Sumatra, by the *Batta* people. **1860** MAYNE REID *Odd People* 408 Ptolemy.. may have referred to Sumatra and its Battas—who *are* cannibals beyond a doubt. **1875** [see BATAK *a.* and *sb.*[1]]. **1890** FRAZER *Golden Bough* I. i. 28 During a tempest the inhabitants of a Batta village in Sumatra have been seen to rush from their houses armed with sword and lance.

†**ˈbattable**, *a. Obs.* Also 6–7 **batable**. [f. *bat-* (see BATTEN *v.*) + -ABLE.] Of pasture-land: Good for the sustenance of flocks and herds; feeding, fattening; fertile in pasture.

1570–87 HOLINSHED *Scot. Chron.* (1806) I. 8 There is good grasse and verie batable for their heards. **1589** FLEMING *Virg. Georg.* II. 27 What ground also is battable, or fat and lustie soile. **1621** BURTON *Anat. Mel.* Democr. 53 a, Massinissa made many inward parts of Barbary.. fruitfull and battable by this meanes. **1641** HEYLIN *Help to Hist.* (1680) 491 Grounds as battable and rich for the feeding of cattle.

†**battable**, *a.*[2] *Obs.* [a. OF. *batable*, *battable*, f. *batt-re* to beat; see -ABLE.] Of metals: That may be hammered or beaten out, malleable.

1601 HOLLAND *Pliny* II. 505 The other sort of copper.. yeeldeth to the hammer and will be drawne out, whereupon some call it Ductile, *i.* battable. [**1611** COTGR., *Batable*, beatable.]

†**battailant**, *a.* and *sb. Obs.* In 6 **batteilant**, 7 **-ellant**. [a. F. *bataillant*, pr. pple. of *batailler* to BATTLE.]

A. *adj.* Engaged in battle, combatant.

1591 SPENSER *Vis. World's Van.* 101 An Elephant.. That on his backe did beare (as batteilant) A gilden towre.

B. *sb.* One who does battle; a combatant.

1620 SHELTON *Quix.* I. III. ii. 125 Those Battellants that fought so eagerly.. had slain him.

battaile, obs. form of BATTLE.

†**baˈttaillerous**, *a. Obs.* [a. OF. *bataillerous*, *-eux*, f. *batailleur* BATTLER[1]; see -OUS.] Fond of fighting, warlike, bellicose.

c **1480** CAXTON *Ovid's Met.* XI. xviii, A man of grete puyssance ffyers, corageous, batayllerous, and full of prowesse.

battailous (ˈbætɪləs), *a. arch.* Forms: 4 **batelouse, -ailous, -aillous, -ayllous**, 5 **-ellous**, 5–6 **battelous**, 6– **-aylous**, 7 **-ellous, -alouse**, 6–9 **-ailous**, (8 **battlous**). [a. OF. *bataillos* (*-eus*), f. *bataille* BATTLE: see -OUS.] Fond of fighting, ready for battle; warlike, bellicose, pugnacious.

c **1380** WYCLIF *Sel. Wks.* (1871) III. 165 Bothe mon and beestis ben pure batelouse. **1393** GOWER *Conf.* III. 118 Mighty Mars the batailous. **1483** CAXTON *Cato* E vi. b, The hors is a beest fyghtyng and batayllous. **1592** WYRLEY *Armorie* 44 With battelous axe in fist. **1596** SPENSER *F.Q.* I. v. 2 In sunbright armes, and battailous array. **1667** MILTON *P.L.* VI. 81 A fierie Region stretcht In battailous aspect. **1760** BEATTIE *Pigm. & Cranes* 126 In battailous array display'd. **1876** LOWELL *Among my Bks.* II. 241 The silent thunders of their battailous armaments.

battailyng, obs. form of BATTLING.

battalia (bəˈtɑːljə). *arch.* or *Obs.* Forms: 7– **battalia**; also 7 **batalia -allia -alio, battailia, -alio, -aglio**. [late 16th century a. It. *battaglia* or ? Sp. *batalla* (in same sense). The forms *battaglio*, *-alio*, etc. are examples of a tendency then common to turn It. and Sp. final *-a* into *-o*; see -ADO[2]. Cf. BATTLE, of which this is a doublet.]

1. *Mil.* Order of battle, battle array; disposition or arrangement of troops (or naval forces) for action. (Usually with prep. *in*, *into.*)

1613 CHAPMAN *Bussy d'Amb.* Plays 1873 II. 138, I haue made all his Troopes and Companies Aduance, and put themselues randg'd in Battailia. **1629** tr. *Herodian* (1635) 403 Having marched in battalia over all the plaine. **1645** SLINGSBY *Diary* (1836) 137 They had drawn out in Battalio upon yᵉ side of Nasby hill. **1650** R. STAPYLTON *Strada's Low-C. Warres* IX. 46 The ships on both sides put in Battalia. **1719** DE FOE *Crusoe* (1869) 479 An Army might enter in Battalia. **1858** CARLYLE *Fredk. Gt.* XIX. vii. (1865) VIII. 235 Friedrich draws out in battalia.

b. *fig.* **1645** *Sacr. Decretal* 4 Draw up all your Instruments of torture and torment in Battalio. **1798** W. HUTTON *Autobiog.* 27 Marshalling, in battalia, fifty bright guineas.

†**2.** A large body of men in battle array, a marshalled force or host, whether constituting the whole of an army, or one of its great

divisions or battalions; = BATTLE *sb.* 8. *Obs.* (cf. BATTALION 1).

1594 SHAKS. *Rich. III*, v. iii. 11 *Nor.* Six or seuen thousand is their vtmost power. *K. Rich.* Why, our Battalia trebbles that account. **1639** SALTMARSHE *Pract. Policie* 136 If your forces bee divided and your troopes scattered into severall battalios. **1659** GAUDEN *Tears of Ch.* 366 (D.) The Pope's main Battaglio. **1677** HALE *Prim. Orig. Man.* I. i. 6 The Rules and Exercise of Architecture, Fortifications, and ordering of Battalia's. **1684** CHARNOCK *Attrib. God* (1834) II. 500 The general of an army appoints the station of every regiment in a battalia. **1750** CARTE *Hist. Eng.* II. 412 A great army..marching towards them in three battalias.

b. *fig.*; cf. 'host.'

1653 J. HALL *Paradoxes* 75 The Sunne, the Moone, and all the glorious battalia of heaven. **1668** CHILD *Disc. Trade* (1698) 44 The gentleman brings up his battalia.

c. (*short for* 'main battalia'): The main body of an army, as distinguished from the wings.

1645 *Sacr. Decretal* 14 Wee quickly plac'd Jockey in the right wing, Sir John in the left wing, and Old Nick in the Battalia. **1805** GIFFORD *Massinger's Picture* II. i. (1840) 260.

†**3.** The summons or call to form into line. *Obs.*

1625 MARKHAM *Souldiers Accid.* 16 The Drum doth beat ..a Call, a March..a Battalia, a Charge.

ba'ttalia pie. Forms: 7–8 **beatille, beatilla, beatilia,** 9 **battalia.** [ad. F. *béatilles* 'titbits, as cocks' combs, sweetbreads, etc. in a pie'; also in convents applied to small pieces of needlework (as pincushions,'samplers' embroidered with sacred subjects) worked by nuns. The latter is the original sense; Cotgr. has the intermediate 'trinkets or vaine toyes, wherewith finicall people decke themselues; trifles, nifles, odde attires'; whence 'trifles' in cookery. Du Cange gives med.L. *beatillæ*, which he regards as formed from the Fr.; but its existence in early conventual L. seems proved by Sp. *beatilla* 'a sort of thin fine linen.' The original sense was evidently 'small blessed articles,' the form being dim. of L. *beātus*. The corruption to *battalia* is due to 'popular etymology.']

1664 EVELYN *Sylva* (1776) 169 We here use Chesnuts in stewed meats and Beatille pies. *Ibid.* 272 Other ingredients in Beatilla-pies. **1672** ASHMOLE *Inst. Ord. Garter* 605 The Supper for the Soveraign..First Course, 1. Ducklings boyled..19. Beatilia pye. **1706** PHILLIPS, *Beatilles*, certain Tit-bits, as Cocks-combs, Goose-gibbets, Ghizzards, Livers, and other Appurtenances of Fowls, to be put into Pies, Pottages, etc. **1837** DISRAELI *Venetia* I. iv. (1871) 15 That masterpiece of the culinary art, a grand battalia pie.

battalion (bəˈtælıən). Forms: 6 **bataillon,** 6–7 **battailon, -aillion,** 7 **-allion, -alian** 7– **battalion.** [a. F. *battaillon*, 16th c. ad. It. *battaglione*, augm. or dim. of *battaglia* BATTLE; cf. Sp. *batallon* 'a pettie battell or army.' (Cf. BATTALIA.)]

1. *gen.* **a.** A large body of men in battle array; one of the large divisions of an army.

1589 IVE *Du Bellay's Instr. Warres* 73, I will goe range the ten bands in one whole Batailon. **1598** BARRET *Theor. Warres* III. i. 33 Deuiding them [Companies] into so many parts or battaillions. **1652** C. STAPYLTON *Herodian* XVII. 146 His Army..he divideth into three Battalians. **1658** LENNARD tr. *Charron's Wisd.* III. iii. §31 (1670) 373 The distribution of the Troops, into Battalions, Regiments, Ensigns. **1697** POTTER *Antiq. Greece* III. vi. (1715) 61 The Roman Battalions..were still call'd Legiones. **1868** KIRK *Chas. Bold* III. v. ii. 377 The army was broken up into eight battalions and a reserve.

†**b.** The main body of an army. (= BATTLE 9.)

[**1628** WITHER *Brit. Rememb.* I. 403 The maine Battalion was both rang'd and led By that slye Prince.] **1653** HOLCROFT *Procopius* I. 14 Compast by the Enemy..who staid it not, but gallopt home to the Batallion. **1656** BLOUNT *Glossogr.*, *Battalion*, the main battle.

c. In, or with allusion to, the saying: *God* (or *Providence*) ***is on the side of the big battalions.***

[**1702** E. BOURSAULT *Lettres Nouvelles* 356 La Reine-Mere dit un jour au Maréchal de la Ferté..les Ennemis sont plus forts que nous..mais nous avons le bon droit pour nous... *Madame*, lui répondit-il, *ne vous y fiez pas: j'ay toûjours vû Dieu du coté des gros Bataillons.*] **1842** [see PROVIDENCE *sb.* 4 a]. **1862** T. HUGHES *Struggle Kansas* 363 'Providence is on the side of the strongest battalions' is a saying..much believed in here. **1914** G. B. SHAW in *New Statesman* 14 Nov. Suppl., A Militarist is a person who believes that.. Providence is on the side of the big battalions. **1944** BLUNDEN *Shells by Stream* 37 Four hundred thousand men there lay, The Big Battalions blessed the day.

2. *spec.* A body of infantry (or engineers) composed of several companies, and forming part of a regiment. (The number of battalions in a regiment varies greatly in different countries, and even in the British Army at the present time.)

1708 *Lond. Gaz.* No. 4467/4 Each regiment is to consist of two Battalions, and each Battalion of 1000 Men. **1810** WELLINGTON in Gurw. *Disp.* VI. 81 An army composed of divisions, brigades, regiments, and battalions. **1877** *Field Exerc. Infantry* 148 A Battalion in line may advance or retire in fours from the right or left of Companies.

3. *transf.* and *fig.* (from 1.)

1603 FLORIO *Montaigne* II. xii. (1632) 267 [The Tunnyfish] alwaies frame their shole of a cubike figure..a solide, close and welranged battailon.

ba'ttalion, *v. rare.* [f. prec. sb.] To form into a battalion.

1865 *Daily Tel.* 18 Apr. 2 The fine body of volunteers.. with whom are battalioned one or two companies raised in the..London Docks.

battalioned (bəˈtælıənd), *ppl. a.* [f. prec. + -ED.] Formed into a battalion or battalions.

1809 J. BARLOW *Columb.* VII. 731 Battalion'd infantry and squadron'd horse.

battalogize, erron. form of BATTOLOGIZE.

battalyng, obs. form of BATTLING.

†**'battard.** *Sc. Obs.* Also 6 **battart, -irt, batter.** [a. OF. *bastard*, pronounced *bâtard* (in same sense), perhaps confused in Scotl. with *batter* vb.] = BASTARD, or *culverin bastard*, a small cannon. Similarly *battard-falcon*, a kind of cannon.

1513–75 *Diurn. Occurr.* (1833) 124 Foure cannonis, twa gross culveringis, and ane battart. *c* **1565** R. LINDSAY *Hist. Scot.* (1728) 108 Small artillery, that is to say, myand and battert-falcon. **1566** *Inventories* 166 (JAM.) Item, tua pair of irne calmes for moyan and battard. *c* **1570** BANNATYNE *Jrnl.* 126 (JAM.) Item, tuo batteris monted for the wallis.

batte, obs. form of BAT and BATZ.

†**batte,** *a. Obs. rare*—[1]. [Mätzner compares BAT *sb.*[2] in sense of 'speed.'] ? Hasty, in a hurry.

c **1420** *Liber Cocorum* 22 With porke thou sethe tho henne fatte, Grynde brede and peper and be not batte.

batteau, var. BATEAU. Cf. BATTOE.

batteilant, -ellant, variant of BATTAILANT *a.*

battel (ˈbæt(ə)l), *sb.* As a separate word only in pl. battels; also 4 ? **batails,** 8 **battles,** 9 **battells.** [Of uncertain origin: in 16th c. L. *batilli, battilli*; in the Laudian Statutes *batellæ*. The etymology of this, with its associated vb., and deriv. *batteler*, has been the subject of abundant conjecture. Much depends on the original sense at Oxford: if this was 'food, provisions,' it is natural to connect it with BATTLE *v.*[3] to feed, receive nourishment; cf. esp. BATTLING *vbl. sb.*[3], explained by Sherwood (1632) as '*vivres, manger, morche.*' But conclusive evidence that *battels* had this sense is wanting, while already before 1600 it had that of 'debita,' *sums due* to the college for provisions, etc. The verb however appears to have been sometimes used for 'to take or receive provisions,' i.e. from the college buttery, which brings us close to the senses of BATTLE *v.*[3] 'to feed, take nourishment.' Cf. also the Eton use, and Winchester *battlings*. On the other hand, sense 3 of the vb. (if the same word) suggests the idea of contributing to a common fund or stock: compare the terms 'commons' and 'commoner.' See BATTELER.

Taking 'accounts' or 'score' as the original sense, some have conjectured *battel* to be a dimin. of BAT. *sb.*[2] or of F. *batte*, with sense of 'little staff or stick,' whence perhaps 'tally-stick.' But nothing appears in med.L., OF., or Eng., to support this conjecture. Reference to Du. *betaalen*, G. *bezahlen* 'to pay,' or to the possibility of *batilli* arising out of a misreading of *bacilli* 'little sticks,' do not fall within the limits of scientific etymology.]

†**1.** See quot. (Perhaps a distinct word.) *Obs.*

c **1400** *Apol. Loll.* 76 To cry þis day..aȝennis þe multitude of lawis of þe kirk..aȝen batails, aȝen reseruacouns, aȝen furst frutis, & oþer spolingis of goodis of þe kirk.

2. In Univ. of Oxford: **a.** College accounts for board and provisions supplied from the kitchen and buttery. **b.** In looser use: The whole college accounts for board and lodgings, rates, tuition, and contribution to various funds, as 'My last term's battels came to £40.' Also *attrib.*, as *battel-bills.*

The word has apparently undergone progressive extensions of application, owing partly to changes in the internal economy of the colleges. Some Oxford men of a previous generation state that it was understood by them to apply to the buttery accounts alone, or even to the provisions ordered from the buttery, as distinct from the 'commons' supplied from the kitchen: but this latter use is disavowed by others. See the quotations, and cf. those under BATTEL *v.* and BATTELER, which bear that *battels* applied in 17–18th c. to provisions supplied to members of the college individually at their own order and cost, i.e. to *battelers*, who had no commons, but were charged their 'battels' only, and to *commoners* as extras ' above the ordinary stint of their appointed commons': but whether the *battels* were originally the provisions themselves, or the sums due on account of them, must at present be left undecided.

[**1557** *Reg. Exeter Coll.* 41 Ad solvendum debita seu batillos sociorum. **1636** *Corpus Statut. Oxon.* II. §4 Diligenti examinatione habita tam libri Batellarum quam Obsonatoris cujuslibet Collegii et Aulæ.] **1706** HEARNE *Remarks & Coll.* (1885) I. 220 For sometime kept a name in yᵉ Buttery Book; at wᶜʰ time Dr. Charlett was sponsor for discharge of his Battles. **1792** *Gentl. Mag.* Aug. 716 The word *battel*, which ..signifies to account, and *battels* the College accounts in general. **1842** ARNOLD in *Life & Corr.* (1844) II. x. 305 Their authority might be exerted to compel payment to tradesmen with nearly the same regularity as they exact their own battells. **1861** HUGHES *Tom Brown Oxf.* in *Macm. Mag.* IV. 61 The dinners and wines are charged in their battel bills. **1882** *Spectator* 18 Mar. 352 Receipts..in respect of battels, room rent and tuition fees.

3. Elsewhere: (see quots.).

1798 H. TOOKE *Purley* 390 Battel, a term used at Eton for the small portion of food which, in addition to the College allowance, the Collegers receive from their Dames. **1851** *Cumbrld. Gloss.*, *Battles*, commons or board. [*a* **1883** TROLLOPE *Autobiogr.* (1883) I. 13 Every boy had a shilling a week pocket-money, which we called battels [This is an error of the author: the Winchester term is *battlings*], and which was advanced to us out of the pocket of the second master.]

'battel, *v.* Also 6–9 **battle.** [See prec., and next, and cf. BATTLE *v.*[3]]

1. In the University of Oxford: To have a kitchen and buttery account in college; to be supplied with provisions from the buttery. (For earlier use see quotations, and cf. the sb. above.)

1570 LEVINS *Manip.* /38 Battle commons, *sumere.* **1632** SHERWOOD, Battle (as schollers doe in Oxford), *estre debteur au College pour ses vivres.* **1678** PHILLIPS (App.), *Battle*, in the University of Oxford is taken for to run on to Exceedings above the ordinary stint of the appointed Commons. **1721** BAILEY, *Battle* (in the University of Oxford) is to take up Provision in the College-Book. *a* **1733** NORTH *Lives* I. 300 He kept a table there, and his family were allowed to battle in the butteries. **1791–1824** D'ISRAELI *Cur. Lit.* (1866) II. 168 To battle is to be nourished, a term still retained at the University of Oxford. **1884** *Regul. Merton College*, Undergraduates who live in lodgings are charged terminally, if they battel in College, £2 5*s.* 6*d.*

†**2.** (?) To put into a common fund or stock. *Obs.*

1600 HEYWOOD *If you know not* Wks. 1874 I. 243 And you be a true subject, you'll battle with vs your faggot [towards making a bonfire]. **1606** DEKKER *Sev. Sins* III. (Arb.) 26 [He] slips into a Tauerne, where either alone, or with some other that battles their money together, they plye themselues with penny pots.

battel, obs. form of BATTLE.

'batteler. *Obs.* exc. *Hist.* Also 6–9 **battler,** 7 **batler.** [f. BATTEL *v.* + -ER[1].] *lit.* One who battels in college; formerly, a rank or order of students at Oxford below Commoners.

1604 MIDDLETON *Black Bk.* Wks. V. 544 Pierce Pennyless, exceeding poor scholar, that hath made clean shoes in both universities, and been a pitiful battler all thy lifetime. **1691** WOOD *Ath. Oxon* I./277 Thomas Floyd.. became a Batler or Commoner of New Inn in the beginning of 1589. **1715** *Mem. J. Radcliffe* 4 Resided as a *Battler*, a Condition of Life there, between a Commoner and a Servitor. **1736** BAILEY, *Batteler* (in an University), a Student that battles or goes on Score for his Diet. **1744** SALMON *Pres. State of Univ.* I. 423 Undergraduates consisting of Noblemen, Gentlemen-Commoners, Commoners, Scholars of the Foundation, Exhibitioners, Battlers and Servitors..The Commoners I presume are so called from their commoning together, and having a certain Portion of Meat and Drink provided for them, denominated Commons..The Battlers are entitled to no Commons, but purchase their Meat and Drink of the Cook and Butler, unless they serve a Fellow or Gentleman Commoner, and then they may have the Dishes, which come from their Tables..Of these Battlers, some are Servitors, who attend the Bachelors and Commoners in the Hall, for which they have an Allowance. **1814** CHALMERS *Hist. Univ. Oxf.* II. 238 In 1665 he was admitted a Batteler of University College. **1824** HEBER *Jer. Taylor* I. 24 John entered..in the year 1613, as battler, or poor scholar, of Merton College.

‖**battement** (batmɑ̃). *Dancing.* [Fr., lit. 'beating'.] A rhythmic movement of one leg or foot (see quot. 1830). Hence ***grand battement, b. tendu***, etc. Cf. BEAT *sb.*[1] 1 b.

1830 R. BARTON tr. *Blasis's Code Terpsichore* II. 100 *Battements* consist of the motions of one leg in the air, whilst the other supports the body. They are of three kinds, viz., *grands battements, petits battements*, and *battements* on the instep. **1869** W. S. GILBERT *'Bab' Ballads* 93 The Bishop buckled to his task With *battements*, cuts, and *pas de basque*. **1917** FIRBANK *Caprice* xi. 95 A dance all fearless somersaults and quivering *battements*. **1952** KERSLEY & SINCLAIR *Dict. Ballet Terms* 27 *Battements tendus*..in which one leg slides out along the floor until the foot is fully pointed..and then steadily closes again. **1953** *Ballet Ann.* VII. 66/1 The soloists in the centre and the *corps* on the three sides doing simple *battements tendus.*

batten (ˈbæt(ə)n), *sb.*[1]. Also 7 **battin, -oun, -une,** 8 **-on.** [A variant of BATON *sb.*, which in technical use preserved the earlier pronunciation, while *batoon* came in for the more general sense.]

1. a. *Carp.* and *Build.* A piece of squared timber, not more than 7 inches broad and 2½ inches thick, used for flooring, and as a support for laths, etc.; a scantling. (The length may be anything over 6 feet; shorter pieces are known as ***batten-ends.***)

1658 *Jrnl.* in I. Mather *Remark. Provid.* (1856) 52 The battens next the chimney..were broken. **1743** *Lond. & Countr. Brew.* III. 179 Three Sides in four of its..second Floor should be built with wooden Battons about three Inches broad, and two thick. **1835** *Penny Cycl.* s.v., Battens are never, and deals are always, above seven inches wide.

b. *spec.* A strip of wood carrying gas or electric lamps; esp. *Theatr.*, one carrying a series of lamps for lighting a stage; also, such a bar used for supporting scenery, curtains, etc. Also *attrib.*, as ***batten (lamp-)holder***, a lamp-holder fitted with a support which enables it to be screwed on to a flat surface.

1881 [see *ground-row*, GROUND *sb.* 18 a]. **1899** *Army & Navy Auxiliary C.S.L. Catal.* 384 Batten lampholders. For use on low ceilings, such as lavatories, &c. **1902** *Daily Chron.* 19 July 6/1 That electric light 'battens' should be substituted for gas. **1920** F. HAMILTON *Days bef. Yest.* vi. 160 Thin screens of coloured silk over the gas-battens in the flies. **1921** G. B. SHAW in *Times Lit. Suppl.* 17 Mar. 178/2 Take your ambers out of your number one batten. **1926** J. A. FLEMING *Electr. Educator* I. 138/1 The Batten Holder.. is just a simpler..form of backplate holder. **1933** P. GODFREY *Back-Stage* i. 16 The sky-cloth..leaps to dazzling life as the 'floods' and 'battens' throw their massed beams upon its surface. **1967** *Times Rev. Industry* Feb. 41/3 In smaller factories management will often 'put in batten fittings without reflectors'.

2. *spec.* A bar or strip (orig. as in sense 1) nailed or glued across a door or anything composed of parallel boards, to hold these together, give strength, or prevent warping; a ledge, a clamp.

1663 GERBIER *Counsel* 94 Shutters..framed within with Battens. **1667** PRIMATT *City & C. Builder* 64 A good firm door of board..with handsome ledges or battouns for ornament. **1794** W. FELTON *Carriages* (1801) I. 21 The battens made of wood or thin iron plates, which cross the boards. **1859** TIMBS & GULLICK *Painting* 217 The best contrivance to preserve wood flat and sound is to strengthen the back with battens, or ledges.

3. *Naut.* A narrow strip of wood nailed to various parts of the masts and spars to preserve them from chafing; a similar strip used to fasten down the edges of the tarpaulin fixed over the hatchways to keep out the water in bad weather; also, a wooden bar (in place of a cleat) from which hammocks are slung.

1769 FALCONER *Dict. Marine* (1789) s.v., The battens serve to confine the edges of the tarpaulings down to the sides of the hatches. **1840** MARRYAT *Poor Jack* i, We were permitted to..hoist her..up again to the battens. **1840** R. DANA *Bef. Mast* iii. 5 This chafing gear consists of.. roundings, battens, and service of all kinds. *Ibid.* xxix. 98 We took the battens from the hatches, and opened the ship.

4. *Comb.*, as **batten-door**, a door formed of narrow boards, held together by 'battens' or cross-pieces nailed to them. Cf. BATTENED.

batten ('bæt(ə)n), *sb.*[2] [a corruption of F. *battant* (of same meaning).] A movable bar or arm in a silk-loom which strikes in or closes the weft.

1831 G. PORTER *Silk Manuf.* 216 This batten is suspended by its bar from the upper framing of the loom. **1863** *Morn. Star* 1 Jan. 6 The superior machinery containing numerous battens for making elaborate and also cheap figured goods.

'batten, *sb.*[3] *dial.* A bundle of straw consisting of two or more sheaves.

(In most of the northern and midland dial. glossaries.)

†batten, *a. Obs.* [Cf. next.] = BATTLE *a.*

1627 SPEED *Eng. Abridged* x. §3 Which [earth] by a sea-weed..and certaine kinde of fruitfull Sea-sand, they make so ranke and batten, as is vncredible.

batten ('bæt(ə)n), *v.*[1] [First found in end of 16th c., but may have been in dialectal use before; app. a. ON. *batna* to improve, get better, recover, f. *bati* advantage, improvement, amelioration; cogn. w. Goth. *gabatnan* 'to be advantaged, to be bettered, to profit,' a neuter-passive form derived from ***batan, bôt, batans** 'to be useful, to profit, to boot.' Cf. also Du. *baten* to avail, yield profit, *baat* profit, gain, advantage, benefit, and see Grimm s.v. *batten*. A cogn. *bat* in sense of 'profit, advantage, improvement,' although not known as a separate word in Eng., is implied in the derivatives *batt-able, bat-ful, batt-le* adj. With all the senses cf. BATTLE *v.*[3]]

1. *intr.* To grow better or improve in condition; *esp.* (of animals) to improve in bodily condition by feeding, to feed to advantage, thrive, grow fat.

1591 LYLY *Endym.* III. iii. 39 No, let him batten, when his tongue Once goes, a cat is not worse strung. **1614** B. JONSON *Barth. Fair* II. iii. (1631) 21 It makes her fat you see. Shee battens with it. **1648** HERRICK *Hesper.* (1869) 214 We eate our own, and batten more, Because we feed on no man's score. **1684** DRYDEN in *Southerne's Disappoint.* Prol. 53 Our women batten well on their good Nature. **1687** —— *Hind & P.* I. 390 Th' etherial pastures with so fair a flock..bat'ning on their food.

b. To feed gluttonously *on*, glut oneself; to gloat or revel *in*. (With indirect passive, *to be battened on*, in mod. writers.)

1602 SHAKS. *Ham.* III. iv. 67 Could you on this faire Mountaine leaue to feed, And batten on this Moor? **1693** W. ROBERTSON *Phraseol. Gen.* 215 To batten in's own dung, *fimo volutari*. **1789** WOLCOTT (P. Pindar) *Subj. Painters* Wks. 1812 II. 210 Dainty mud..In which they had been battening. **1830** TENNYSON *Poems* 130 Battening upon huge seaworms in his sleep. **1833** MRS. BROWNING *Prometh. Bd.* Poems (1850) I. 187 The strong carnivorous eagle shall.. batten deep Upon thy dusky liver. **1879** DIXON *Brit. Cyprus* viii. 78 A skeleton battened on by kites and crows.

c. *fig.* To thrive, grow fat, prosper (*esp.* in a bad sense, at the expense or to the detriment of another); to gratify a morbid mental craving.

1605 B. JONSON *Volpone* in Campbell's *Spec.* III. 185 And with these thoughts so battens, as if fate Would be as easily cheated on, as he. **1641** J. JACKSON *True Evang. T.* I. 56 That religion should batten with blood. **1837** CARLYLE *Fr. Rev.* (1872) II. III. ii. 91 Battening vampyre-like on a People next door to starvation. **1870** EMERSON *Soc. & Solit.* x. 220 Melancholy sceptics with a taste for carrion, who batten on the hideous facts in history,—persecutions, inquisitions.

2. To grow fertile (as soil); to grow rank (as a plant).

1855 SINGLETON *Virgil* I. 104 That twice should batten with our blood Emathia and Hæmus' spacious plains. **1859** HOLLAND *Gold F.* xxiv. 283 A potato—a bloated tuber that battens in the muck of other times.

†3. *trans.* To improve, feed to advantage, fatten up. *Obs.* (The pa. pple. *battened*, belonged orig. to the intr. sense; cf. *well-grown, well-read*, etc.)

[**1611** COTGR. s.v. *Advenu*, *Vne fille bien advenuë*, well growne..well batned, or batled.] **1637** MILTON *Lycidas* 29 We drove a-field..Battening our flocks with the fresh dews of night. **1643** BURROUGHES *Exp. Hosea* ii. (1852) 172 They did batten themselves and suck out the Egyptian manners and customs. **1790** COWPER *Iliad* xxii. 107 As some fell serpent..batten'd with herbs Of baneful juice to fury.

†4. To fertilize (soil). *Obs. rare.*

1611 SPEED *Theat. Gt. Brit.* xxxv. 69/1 Others [rivers] doe so batten the ground that the meadowes even in the midst of winter grow greene.

batten ('bæt(ə)n), *v.*[2] [f. BATTEN *sb.*[1]]

1. To furnish or strengthen with battens.

1775 FALCH *Day's Diving Vess.* 26 These windlasses being battened and holed for common handspikes. **1794** W. FELTON *Carriages* (1801) I. 17 Deal boardings firmly battened on the inside. **1881** *Mechanic* §1651 The wall must be battened.

2. (chiefly *Naut.*) ***to batten down***: to fasten down with battens; see BATTEN *sb.*[1]

1823 J. BADCOCK *Dom. Amusem.* 53 The severity of the climate having compelled them to batten down and caulk their abiding place. *c* **1860** H. STUART *Seaman's Catech.* 72 It is sometimes necessary in bad weather to put on the gratings and nail tarpaulings over them: this is called 'battening down.' **1883** *Chamb. Jrnl.* 20 Batten down the hatches—quick, men.

Battenberg ('bætənbɜːg). Also (*erron.*) -burg. The name of a town in Germany, used *attrib.* to designate a kind of oblong cake, usu. of two colours (with square cross-section showing alternating blocks of colour) and covered with almond paste. (See also quot. 1912.) Also *fig.*

The town of Battenberg is the seat of the family which became known in Britain as Mountbatten. The Battenberg/Mountbatten connection by marriage with the British Royal Family may help to account for the name: see quot. 1981.

1903 LEWIS & BROMLEY *Bk. Cakes* 60 *Battenburg Cake*... Take a good Genoese mixing... Colour one portion red and leave another plain... When cold, cut from the Genoese nine bars... Place them together with colours alternating... Roll the cake up in the [almond] paste. **1912** *Cassell's New Dict. Cookery* 43/2 *Battenburg cake.* Crush four ounces of almonds with one egg..then put twelve ounces of sugar with twelve yolks of eggs into a pan. Beat..add..almonds, ..currants..and..eight ounces of flour... Mix slowly, putting in the ten whites of eggs... Finish with six ounces of good melted butter. **1935** *1500 New Econ. Cookery Recipes* (Success Publishing Co.) (ed. 4) 204 Battenberg cake: Genoese pastry, cochineal, almond paste, apricot jam. **1948** *Good Housek. Cookery Bk.* 564 Battenberg cake... Put half the mixture into one of the tins, colour the other half pink and put in the second tin. **1969** *Harrod's Summer Food News* 8/1 Battenberg Roll. Pink and white genoese squares covered with almond paste. Each 6/-. **1977** *Economist* 29 Jan. 77/1 Volume one of this year's public spending white paper..is a quarter of a slice of Battenberg cake without any marzipan. It gives summary figures without many details. **1981** *N.Y. Times* 30 Sept. C20/4 The tea, with its cucumber and watercress sandwiches, Battenberg cake (a favorite of Queen Victoria), [etc.].

'battened, *ppl. a.*[1] [f. BATTEN *v.*[1] + -ED.] Nourished, fed, fattened.

1791 COWPER *Odyss.* XII. 309 His well-batten'd flocks.

'battened, *ppl. a.*[2] [f. BATTEN *sb.*[1], *v.*[2] + -ED.]

a. Formed of battens. **b.** Furnished, lined, or strengthened with battens.

1663 GERBIER *Counsel* 68 Doores glued and Battined at nine shillings. **1677** MOXON *Mech. Exerc.* (1703) 153 In a Battend-door..they use Cross-Garnets. *c* **1850** *Rudim. Nav.* 130 The louvered or battened parts of ships' wells.

'battener. [f. BATTEN *v.*[1] + -ER[1].] One who battens (*on, upon*).

a **1849** POE *Wks.* (1864) III. 542 A fetid battener upon the garbage of thought.

battening ('bæt(ə)nɪŋ) *sb.* [f. BATTEN *sb.* + -ING[1].] The application or addition of battens; a structure formed with battens.

1794 W. FELTON *Carriages* (1801) I. 17 The other inside work is battening, blocking, and gluing. **1796** W. MARSHALL *Yorksh.* (ed. 2) I. 194 Fence Walls.—Battoning, in the Norfolk manner, is unknown. **1834** *Brit. Husbandry* I. 89 Palings, battenings, and other fences. **1880** HOWELLS *Undisc. Country* I. 29 'Mr. Hatch, will you put up the battening?' Hatch made haste to darken the windows completely with some light wooden sheathings prepared for the purpose.

battening ('bæt(ə)nɪŋ), *ppl. a.* [f. BATTEN *v.*[1]]

1. *intr.* Feeding to advantage, or with a relish; growing fat.

1593 DRAYTON *Eclog.* ix. 70 Their batning Flocks on grassy Leaes to hold. **1714** GAY *Sheph. Week* Friday 156 Battening hogs roll in the sinking mire. **1765** BEATTIE *Judgm. Paris* lxxxii, Battening Avarice mocks his tuneless lyre.

2. *trans.* Fattening; fertilizing.

1612 DRAYTON *Poly-olb.* xii. 206 Twixt Trent and batning Dove. **1708** J. PHILIPS *Cyder* I. 34 The Meadows here, with bat'ning ooze enrich'd.

battentlie: see BATAUNTLY.

batter ('bætə(r)), *v.*[1] Also 4-6 **bater(e.** [f. the stem *bat-* 'beat,' as in OF. *bat-re*, Eng. BAT *v.*, BAT *sb.*[2], with freq. suffix -ER; cf. *stutter, patter.*]

I. Main senses.

1. *trans.* (and *absol.*) To strike with repeated blows of an instrument or weapon, or with frequent missiles; to beat continuously and violently so as to bruise or shatter. (Also with complemental *about, down, in.*)

c **1325** *E.E. Allit. P.* B. 1416 Symbales & sonetez sware the noyse & bougounz busch batered so þikke. **1377** LANGL. *P. Pl.* B. III. 198, I batered hem on þe bakke. **1591** GARRARD *Art Warre* 204 The drums ought to be ready to batter their caisses. **1610** SHAKS. *Temp.* III. ii. 98 Or with a logge Batter his skull. **1641** WILKINS *Math. Mag.* I. xvii. (1648) 122 These would he presently batter in pieces with great stones. **1727** SWIFT *Gulliver* IV. xii. 341 Battering the warriors' faces into mummy. **1801** HUNTINGTON *Bank of Faith* 136 They had so battered me about. **1873** BURTON *Hist. Scot.* V. lix. 325 Carrying in a wooden beam, as if to batter in a door.

†b. To beat out (metal); ? to inlay. *Obs. rare.*

c **1380** *Sir Ferumb.* 896 Ys scheld þat was wyþ golde y-batrid: & eke wyþ ire y-bounde.

2. *Mil.* To operate against (walls, fortifications, etc.) with artillery, or in ancient times with the battering ram, with the purpose (and result) of breaking down or demolishing them; to bombard. Often with *down*.

1570 LEVINS *Manip.* /77 To batter walles, *demoliri muros*. **1583** STANYHURST *Æneis* I. (Arb.) 18 Which would thee Tyrian turrets quite batter a sunder. **1606** SHAKS. *Tr. & Cr.* I. iii. 206 The Ramme that batters downe the wall. **1762** HUME *Hist. Eng.* (1806) IV. lx. 498 Having led the army without delay to Wexford, he began to batter the town. **1803** WELLINGTON in Gurw. *Disp.* II. 289, I shall be able to begin to batter to-morrow morning. **1876** GREEN *Short Hist.* vii. §8 (1882) 436 The castles which had hitherto sheltered rebellion were battered into ruins.

3. *transf.* and *fig.* To subject (persons, opinions, etc.) to heavy, crushing, or persistent attack.

1578 FENTON *Guicciard.* (1618) 30 So that the Florentines by this meanes should remaine battered. **1605** SHAKS. *Macb.* IV. iii. 178 The Tyrant ha's not batter'd at their peace? **1670** G. H. *Hist. Cardinals* II. I. 107 Every Fryer..battering the ears of their Protectors with informations of their Rogueries. *a* **1733** NORTH *Exam.* I. ii. ¶174 But none batter'd it more than the Earl of Shaftsbury, who said it was absolutely impossible to be true. **1873** BROWNING *Red Cott. Night-c.* 1177 What foe would dare approach? Historic Doubt? Ay, were there some half-knowledge to attack! Batter doubt's best, sheer ignorance will beat.

4. To bruise, beat out of shape, or indent by blows or rough usage; in *Printing*, to deface the surface of type.

1697 EVELYN *Numism.* i. 8 Type and Form of one single Stamp..being greatly batter'd and impaired. **1840** HOOD *Up Rhine* 44 The beautiful brass pail..look how it's all bruised and battered! **1856** KANE *Arct. Exp.* II. xvi. 169 Boats..well battered by exposure to ice and storm.

†5. *intr.* **a.** To become crushed, dinted, or defaced with blows. **b.** To yield to beating, to be malleable. *Obs.*

1589 BP. ANDREWES *Serm.* II. 10 All our cups would batter with the fall. **1677** MOXON *Mech. Exerc.* (1703) 8 Iron ..if it be too cold..will not batter under the Hammer.

6. *Comb.*, with attrib. sense, as **batter-head**, the part of the drum beaten.

1704 *Athen. Orac.* III. 423 in Southey *Comm.-Pl. Bk.* Ser. II. (1849) 657 They [the drums] received several small shot in the batter heads.

II. (From BATTER *sb.*[1])

†7. *trans.* To beat into a paste or batter, to mix by beating. *Obs.*

1585 LLOYD *Treas. Health* I vj, Masticke baterid with whyte of an egge and vineger. **1622** MABBE *Aleman's Guzman d' Alf.* II. 334 With a fewe egges battered together, and seasoned with a little pepper.

†8. *Sc.* To paste, to fix (as with paste); to cover with things stuck on. *Obs.*

1624 A. H. *Paper-Persec.* in J. Davies *Papers Compl.* Wks. 1876-8 II. 81 To behold the wals Batter'd with weekely Newes. **1650** ROW *Hist. Kirk* (1842) 72 Who mutilated and did ryue out many leaues of the Register, and did batter others together. **1756** MRS. CALDERWOOD *Jrnl.* (1884) 86 This church is battered as full of escutchions as the wall can hold. *Ibid.* 105 A certain sort of mutch they wear..close battered to their faces.

batter ('bætə(r)), *v.*[2] *Arch.* [Of doubtful origin: hardly connected with preceding; can it be related to F. *abattre* to beat down, throw down?]

1. *intr.* Of walls, etc.: To incline from the perpendicular, so as to have a receding slope.

1546 LANGLEY *Pol. Verg. De Invent.* III. x. 77 a, Dædalus ..first inuented the plomline, whereby the Euenes of the Squares bee tried whether they batter or hang ouer. **1677** MOXON *Mech. Exerc.* (1703) 157 The side..of a Wall..that bulges from its bottom or Foundation, is said to Batter, or hang over the Foundation. **1793** RENNIE in Smiles *Engineers* II. 208 Made five feet thick at the base next to the bridge, and four feet thick at the top, battering one-fifth of their height in a curvilinear form. **1845** *Gloss. Gothic Archit.* I. 48 Wharf walls, and walls built to support embankments and fortifications, generally batter.

2. *trans.* 'To give (a wall) in building it, an inclination inwards.' Jamieson.

1398 TREVISA *Barth. De P.R.* xv. xxii. (1495) 497 A toure in Babilon..whyche conteynyth at heyghte two lewges batryd in brede. [The sense is here doubtful].

batter ('bætə(r)), *sb.*[1] Forms: 5 bater(e, -our, -owre, -ure, 6 battre, 7– batter. [prob. f. BATTER *v.*[1]; cf. however OF. *bature, -eure* action of beating, also metal beaten into thin leaf.]

I. Materials beaten or battered.

1. a. A mixture of two or more ingredients beaten up with a liquid for culinary purposes.

c **1420** *Liber Cocorum* (1862) 26 Of almond mylke and amydone, Make bater. *a* **1500** *Recipes* in *Babees Bk.* (1868) 53 Make bature of floure, ale, peper & saferon, with oper spices. **1615** MARKHAM *Eng. Housew.* (1660) 56 Taking the Apples and Batter out together with a spoon. **1796** MRS. GLASSE *Cookery* viii. 140 Dip the oysters in a batter. **1879** BEERBOHM *Patagonia* xi. 171 The batter must be stirred well, or else it will stick to the sides.

b. *Sc.* Flour and water made into 'paste'; *transf.* that which is pasted upon walls, etc. (*obs.*)

[*c* **1440** *Promp. Parv.* 27 Batowre of flowre and mele wyth water (*v.r.* batour), *mola.* **1530** PALSGR. 197/1 Batter of floure, *paste.*] **1624** A. H. Paper-Persec. in J. Davies *Papers Compl.* Wks. 1878 II 81 To see such Batter euerie weeke besmeare Each publike post, and Church dore. **1831** CARLYLE *Sart. Res.* I. vii, Multiple ruffs of cloth, pasted together with batter.

c. *attrib.*, as in ***batter-cake, pan, pudding***.

1769 MRS. RAFFALD *Eng. Housekpr.* (1778) 167 Batter and rice puddings [require] a quick oven. **1830** F. TROLLOPE in *Dom. Manners Amer.* (1960) 427 Waffles. Batter cakes. **1833** in *Maryland Hist. Mag.* (1918) XIII. 319 Hot muffins and corn batter cakes. **1853** KANE *Grinnell Exp.* xxxiv. (1856) 306 Flattened it out like a batter-cake.

2. *transf.* A thick paste of any kind, of the consistency of cook's batter; liquid mud.

1601 HOLLAND *Pliny* II. 555 The batter or lome that goeth to the making of [bricks]. **1884** LD. COLERIDGE in *Law Times Rep.* 19 July 635/1 They had swept mud in a state of batter to the side of a road by means of 'squeegees.'

†**3.** = BATTERY 14. *Obs.*

1567 *Wills & Inv. N.C.* (1835) 278 One batter kettill, and a brasse chaffer.

II. The action or result of battering.

4. A heavy bruising blow. *rare.*

1823 GALT *Entail* I. xxviii. 245 Such a thundering batter on the ribs, that he fell reeling from the shock.

5. A cannonade of heavy ordnance against a fortress.

1859 in WORCESTER.

6. *Printing.* A bruise on the face of printing type or stereotype plate. (Cf. BATTER *v.*[1] 4.)

1824 J. JOHNSON *Typogr.* II. xxii. 659 The pressmen never observe a batter (unless it be very glaring), because they would be stopped in their progress. **1880** *Printing Times* 15 May 102/2 Defective letters or batters may thus be easily detected.

ˈ**batter**, *sb.*[2] [f. BATTER *v.*[2]] The slope of a wall, terrace, or bank, from the perpendicular; a receding slope, etc.

1743 BP. MAXWELL *Sel. Trans.* 193 (JAM.) When the kill is formed to four and a half feet high.., the second batter begins. **1823** P. NICHOLSON *Pract. Build.* 329 Batter, the leaning part of the upper part of the face of a wall which so inclines as to make the plumb-line fall within the base. **1884** *Scotsman* 10 Apr. 6/2 These brick piers are all erected with a 'batter' of 1 in 36—which means that they are to that extent broader at the base than at the top.

b. ***batter-rule***, an instrument consisting of a plumb-line and a triangular frame, one side of which makes a given angle with the line, used for setting a wall, etc. at the proper slope or batter.

1847 in CRAIG.

batter ('bætə(r)), *sb.*[3] [f. BAT *v.*[1] + -ER[1].] One who bats; *esp.* the player who uses the bat in the game of cricket.

1773 J. DUNCOMBE *Surry Triumphant* st. xxxiii, in R. Freeman *Kentish Poets* (1821) II. 368 At last, Sir Horace took the field, A batter of great might. **1824** MISS MITFORD *Village* Ser. I. (1863) 174 Such mutual compliments from man to man—bowler to batter, batter to bowler. **1854** WARTER *Old Squires* v. 48 The old Squire..had been a good batter in his day.

ˈ**batter**, *sb.*[4] *slang.* [Of obscure origin: cf. BAT *sb.*[4]] A spree, debauch, esp. in phr. ***on the batter***. (See also quot. 1890.)

1839 A. RODGER in *Whistle-Binkie* Ser. II. 17 My hat was smash'd..Ae night when on the batter. **1856** *Knickerbocker* XLVIII. 502 Ellis had..just returned from a prolonged batter in Paris. **1865** *N. & Q.* Ser. III. VIII. 369/2 It was among working-men that I first heard 'on the batter' employed as an equivalent for going 'on the spree'. **1890** FARMER *Slang* I. 143/2 *To go on the batter, i.e.*, to walk the streets for purposes of prostitution. **1899** R. WHITEING *No. 5 John St.* xxi. 214 D'ye call that goin' on the batter?.. I call it goin' out with the governiss. **1957** J. OSBORNE *Entertainer* v. 35 Have you been on the batter, you old gubbins! **1966** A. PRIOR *Operators* iii. 25 The mothers and sisters on the batter —any man on the streets.

batter: see BATTARD.

batterable ('bætərəb(ə)l), *a.* [f. BATTER *v*[1] + -ABLE.] That can be battered or bruised by beating.

1611 COTGR., *Batable*, beatable, batterable. **1623** FAVINE *Theat. Hon.* II. xiii. 265 A strong Citie for Warre, without Suburb, not batter-able.

†ˈ**batterdasher.** *Obs. rare*[−1]. [? f. BATTER + DASHER or ? (from F. *d' acier*) of steel.] A weapon of offence.

1696 AUBREY *Misc.* (1857) 215 (D.) The skreens were garnished with corslets and helmets, gaping with open mouth, with coats of mail, laces, pikes, halberts, brown bills, batter-dashers, bucklers.

batterdeau, obs. form of BATARDEAU.

battered ('bætəd), *ppl. a.* [f. BATTER *v.*[1] + -ED.]

a. Bruised and shattered by repeated blows; worn and defaced by rough or hard usage, the chances of time, etc. Often *fig.*

1592 SHAKS. *Ven. & Ad.* 104 Over my altars hath he hung his lance, His batter'd shield. **1680** *Lond. Gaz.* No. 1538/4 A Brown Bay Nag..his Feet somewhat battered. **1700** MAUNDRELL *Journ. Jerus.* (1721) T'iijb, Old batter'd Horses. **1765** TUCKER *Lt. Nat.* II. 57 The battered rake.. has exhausted all his health. **1809** J. BARLOW *Columb.* II. 336 And pours destruction o'er its batter'd walls. **1840** DICKENS *Old C. Shop* liii. (1848) 240 The sexton's spade gets worn and battered.

b. battered baby, an infant exhibiting symptoms (the ***battered baby syndrome***) resulting from repeated injuries inflicted upon it over a period; **battered wife, woman**, a woman who has been repeatedly injured or otherwise ill-treated by her partner.

[**1962** C. H. KEMPE et al. in *Jrnl. Amer. Med. Assoc.* 7 July 17/1 The battered-child syndrome is a term used by us to characterize a clinical condition in young children who have received serious physical abuse, generally from a parent or foster parent.] **1963** *Brit. Med. Jrnl.* 21 Dec. 1558 (*heading*) Multiple epiphysial injuries in babies ('*battered baby' syndrome). *Ibid.* 1560/1 The *x*-ray changes in the 'battered baby' are..like those often described in infantile scurvy. **1973** *Nursing Times* 14 June 777/1 Erin Pizzey is always hot under the collar about the lack of help a *battered wife can get. **1980** LD. DENNING *Due Process of Law* VII. iv. 224 By a short Act entitled the Domestic Violence Act 1976 it [*sc.* Parliament] enabled the County Courts to grant injunctions to protect a 'battered wife' even though the house was in the husband's sole name. **1973** *Times* 14 June 2/4 A voluntarily run centre that shelters *battered women and their children seeking refuge from brutality by the man of the household is preparing a report. **1976** *Spare Rib* Oct. 22/4 The only refuge for battered women in the area is threatened with closure. **1985** *Rep. Cases Supreme Court New Jersey* XCVII. 187 The central issue before us is whether expert testimony about the battered-woman's syndrome is admissable to help establish a claim of self-defense in a homicide case.

batterer ('bætərə(r)). [f. as prec. + -ER[1].] One who batters; a vigorous assailant, a bruiser.

1611 COTGR., *Fracasseur*, a crasher, violent breaker, batterer. *a* **1619** DANIEL *Coll. Hist. Eng.* (1626) 169 Batterers hyred to beate men. **1656** *Artif. Handsom.* 185 Batterers or demolishers of stately and elegant buildings. **1823** *Blackw. Mag.* XIV. 512 A jolly batterer, who never looked for a soft word when he could get a hard one.

†**batterfang** ('bætəfæŋ), *v. Obs.* or *dial.* [? f. BATTER *v.*[1] + FANG a claw.] Explained in glossaries as: To assail with fists and nails, to beat and beclaw; but in use apparently = BATTER *v.*[1] 1.

1630 J. TAYLOR (Water P.) *Wks.* II. 191/2 The poore man was so batterfanged and belabour'd with tongue mettle, that he was weary of his life. **1716** T. WARD *Eng. Ref.* 124 The Pastor lays on lusty Bangs, Whitehead the Pastor Batterfangs. **1864** ATKINSON *Whitby Gloss.*, *Batterfang'd*, beaten and beclawed, as a termagant will fight with her fists and nails. **1877** in E. Peacock *Manley* (*Linc.*) *Gloss.* s.v., He'd been a soldger in th' Roosian war, an' came home strangely batterfanged about.

‖**batterie** (batri). [Fr., see BATTERY.]

1. *Dancing.* A movement in which the dancer's feet or calves are beaten together during a leap.

1712 J. WEAVER *Hist. Dancing* vii. 163 Notwithstanding there are some Steps peculiarly adapted to this Sort of Dancing, viz. Capers, and Cross-Capers of all kinds; Piruottes [*sic*], Batteries, and indeed almost all Steps from the Ground. **1949** *Ballet Ann.* III. 54 *Temps de batterie*, or beaten steps. *Ibid.* 116/2 Articulate and well-arched feet that helped to give a brilliant display of *petite batterie.* **1950** *Ibid.* IV. 131/1 One of the best classical dancers, with a *batterie* unequalled for brilliance. **1952** KERSLEY & SINCLAIR *Dict. Ballet Terms* 17 *Batterie*,..this word added to the name of a step does not imply any alteration in the basic movement, but that the dancer beats his calves together.. and possibly also changes the position of his legs while doing so.

2. ***batterie de cuisine*** (see BATTERY 12).

1773 H. WALPOLE *Let.* 26 Oct. (1857) VI. 1 Unless he carries his *batterie de cuisine*, cook and camp equipage, I doubt he must eat the game raw. **1819** [see BATTERY 12]. **1906** I. BEETON *Househ. Managem.* lxii. 1654 *Batterie de cuisine*, complete set of cooking utensils and apparatus. **1934** 'A. BRIDGE' *Ginger Griffin* vii. 84 Some different and highly burnished article of her *batterie de cuisine.*

3. = BATTERY 17.

1934 S. R. NELSON *All about Jazz* ii. 50 The drummer was banging away at his *batterie*!

battering ('bætərɪŋ), *vbl. sb.* [f. BATTER *v.*[1]]

1. The action of beating with successive blows, *esp.* in *Mil.* of attacking a fortification with cannon or other engines. Also *fig.*

1542 UDALL *Erasm. Apoph.* 220a, His manier of battreyng. **1647** W. BROWNE *Polex.* II. 180 The Turkes.. after two daies battering, wonne it [the palace] by force. **1678** CUDWORTH *Intell. Syst.* I. i. §43 A most Effectual Engine..for the battering of all their Atheistical Structure down about their Ears. **1862** THACKERAY *Philip* I. 89 Amidst enthusiastic battering of glasses.

2. The result of this action; bruising or defacement caused by successive blows.

1558 PHAËR *Æneid* in Webbe *Eng. Poetrie* (1870) 50 Helmets, skulles, with battrings marrd. **1591** PERCIVALL *Sp. Dict.*, *Desabollar*, to beate out the batterings in a peece of armor or plate.

3. *attrib.* **a.** in ancient warfare, **battering-engine**, an engine constructed for breaking down walls; so ***battering-machine***, BATTERING-RAM. **b.** in modern warfare, **battering-train**, a number of cannon specially intended for siege purposes; so ***battering-artillery, -cannon, -gun, -piece***. **c. battering-charge**, the full charge of powder for a cannon.

a. 1774 COLLYER *Hist. Eng.* II. 84 He assaulted the castle ..with battering engines. **1852** GROTE *Greece* II. lxxxi. X. 560 He distributed his army into two parts, each provided with battering machines.

b. 1577 HOLINSHED *Chron.* III. 875/1 They raised their siege, cheeflie bicause they had no great battering peeces to ouerthrow the walles. **1697** *Lond. Gaz.* No. 3319/2 Having ordered a Train of Battering Artillery to be provided. **1753** HANWAY *Trav.* I. VII. xcvii. 452 Ten pieces of large brass battering Cannon. **1810** WELLINGTON in Gurw. *Disp.* V. 593 They are bringing a Battering Train into Spain from France.

c. 1868 *Morn. Star* 17 June, A charge of 100lb. is now considered the full battering charge. **1885** *Pall Mall G.* 13 Apr. 2/1 With a full battering charge (900lb. of powder).

battering ('bætərɪŋ), *ppl. a.*[1] Also 6 batring. [f. as prec. + -ING[2].] That batters or violently assails with blows.

1587 GASCOIGNE *Flowers, Hearbs, etc.* 290 Such batring tiro this pamph[l]et here bewraies. **1791** COWPER *Iliad* v. 38 Town-battering Mars! **1871** FARRAR *Witn. Hist.* iii. 102 The battering violence of his impassioned rhetoric.

ˈ**battering**, *ppl. a.*[2] *Arch.* [f. BATTER *v.*[2] + -ING[2].] Leaning away from the perpendicular, with an inward or receding slope.

1589 IVE *Fortif.* 25 The rampier must be raised, scarping, battering, or comming in, for euery one foot of height, one foot of scarpe. **1823** P. NICHOLSON *Pract. Build.* 339 The.. Battering surface, whence all projectures arise.

battering-ram. [f. BATTERING *vbl. sb.* + RAM. Cf. L. *aries* ram, battering-ram.]

1. An ancient military engine employed for battering down walls, consisting of a beam of wood, with a mass of iron at one end, sometimes in the form of a ram's head; (also *fig.*).

1611 BIBLE *Ezek.* iv. 2 Set battering rams against it round about [cf. COVERDALE *Ezek.* xxi. 22 Batell-rammes]. **1776** GIBBON *Decl. & F.* I. xiv. 330 The battering-rams had shaken the walls in several places. **1818** BENTHAM *Ch. Eng.* 55 In the hands of Lancaster..the Bible..worked as a battering-ram against the Established Church. **1840** THIRLWALL *Greece* VII. lix. 344 Battering-rams, each 150 feet long.

2. *transf.* A blacksmith's hammer suspended and worked horizontally.

1864 in WEBSTER.

Battersea ('bætəsi:). The name of a district of London, used to designate articles ornamented with a decorative enamel produced at York House, Battersea, in the 18th century.

1869 LADY C. SCHREIBER *Jrnl.* (1911) I. 2 One or two pieces of Battersea enamel. *Ibid.* 16 A pair of Battersea enamel candlesticks. *Ibid.* 27 Battersea needlecase with birds in pink. **1924** A. E. W. MASON *House of Arrow* xiii. 153 Pen-tray, candlestick, sand-castor and all were of the pink Battersea enamel. **1949** A. CHRISTIE *Crooked House* x. 74 A small Battersea enamel box.

battert: see BATTARD.

battery ('bætərɪ). Forms: 6 batterye, battrie, -tre(e, batery, 6–7 battry(e, -erie, 6– battery. [a. F. *batterie* (13th c.) 'beating, battering, a group of cannon', etc. (= Pr. *bataria*, Sp. *batería*, It. *batteria*), f. *battre* to beat: see -ERY.]

I. 1. The action of beating or battering.

a. An assailing with blows: *spec.* in *Law*, an unlawful attack upon another by beating or wounding, including technically the slightest touching of another's person or clothes in a menacing manner.

1531 ELYOT *Gov.* III. i. (1557) 142 Intermedlynge sometyme is vyolent as batrye, open murder. **1601** SHAKS. *Twel. N.* IV. i. 36 Ile haue an action of Battery against him. **1752** FIELDING *Amelia* I. ii. Wks. 1784 VIII. 160 Charged with a battery by a much stouter man than himself. **1868** G. DUFF *Pol. Surv.* 127 Murder, to say nothing of assault and battery, has been..an everyday matter.

†**b.** A mark of beating; a wound or bruise. *Obs.*

1592 SHAKS. *Ven. & Ad.* 426 For where a heart is hard they make no battery. **1639** *City-Match* I. iv. in Hazl. *Dodsl.*

XIII. 218 Lets feel: No batteries in thy head, to signify Th' art a constable.

†2. The beating of drums; sometimes a particular kind of drum-beat, perhaps that giving the signal for an assault. *Obs.*

1591 GARRARD *Art Warre* 118 The most fit and apt time ..ought to be shewed by..stroke or batterie of drums to the footemen. **1625** MARKHAM *Souldiers Accid.*, The Drum doth beat..a call, a march, a troope, a battalia, a charge, a retrait, a batterie, a reliefe.

†3. **a.** A succession of heavy blows inflicted upon the walls of a city or fortress by means of artillery; bombardment. ***to plant battery***: to prepare for such an attack. ***to lay battery to***: to carry it into execution. ***to change one's battery***: to change the direction of attack. *Obs.* exc. *fig.*

1548 HALL *Chron. Hen. VIII.* an. 13 (R.) The battery of the walles discorages vs not. **1587** TURBERV. *Trag. T.* (1837) 47 Planting battrie to my fort. **1603** KNOLLES *Hist. Turkes* (1638) 304 He laid battery to the wal four daies. **1667** MILTON *P.L.* XI. 656 By Batterie, Scale, and Mine, Assaulting. **1732** LEDIARD *Sethos* II. IX. 275 The most violent battery would have weaken'd their walls.

b. *transf.* or *fig.*

1562 VERON (*title*) A Strong Battery against the Idolatrous Inuocation of the Dead Saintes. **1640** LD. DIGBY *Parl. Sp.* 9 Nov. 4 Mischiefs which have..layed battery either to our Estates or Consciences. **1655** FULLER *Ch. Hist.* I. §6 The scaling of the swelling Surges, and constant Battery of the Tide. **1865** GROTE *Plato* I. xix. 559 Plato..changes his battery, and says something against these enemies.

†**c.** ***battery piece*** or ***piece of battery***: a siege gun.

1570 SIR R. CONSTABLE in Lodge *Illustr. Brit. Hist.* (1838) I. 509 With three battery pieces..went to the siege of Hume. **1648** *Petit. Eastern Ass.* 18 Was it ill done to fill the Tower with..great pieces of Battery?

II. The apparatus used in battering or beating.

4. a. A number of pieces of artillery placed in juxtaposition for combined action; in Military use, the smallest division of artillery for tactical purposes (corresponding to a *company* of infantry).

Technically, including also the artillerymen who work the guns, the drivers, and horses. In ***horse batteries***, the gunners are carried partly on the carriages and partly on horses, in ***field batteries*** wholly on the carriages; ***garrison batteries*** are bodies of artillerymen serving heavy guns in forts or coast batteries.

1555 *Fardle Facions* II. xi. 246 To plante bateries, make Ladders, and suche other thinges necessarie for the siege. **1732** LEDIARD *Sethos* II. VIII. 163 He will begin to work his batteries. **1803** WELLINGTON in Gurw. *Disp.* II. 286 You will have a breaching battery of two 18 pounders and one 12 pounder. **1861** *Man. Artill. Exerc.* 102 The centre battery halts when the rear battery wheels to the left.

b. *fig.*, esp. in phr. ***to turn any one's battery against himself***.

1581 J. BELL *Haddon's Answ. Osor.* 82b, Three wordes onely may suffice to overthrow the whole Battrye of these three Invectives. **1771** SMOLLETT *Humph. Cl.* (1815) 183 The fellow who accused him has had his own battery turned upon himself. **1823** LAMB *Elia* Ser. I. xxviii. (1865) 231 You think he has exhausted his battery of looks.

c. In baseball, applied to the pitcher and catcher (orig. used of the pitcher alone). Also *attrib. U.S.*

1867 *Ball Players' Chron.* 6 June 2/2 He soon resumed his position, once more facing the battery of Lovett. **1886** CHADWICK *Art of Pitching* 8 The 'battery' of a club's team, that is the pitcher and catcher. **1897** *Daily News* 29 July 9/2 So good was the fielding and battery work..that no scoring took place. **1967** *Boston Sunday Herald* 14 May II. 5/1 Pitcher Ed McGrath went the distance and battery mate, Tony Carderelli, drove in four runs in the Boston State victory.

5. a. The platform or fortified work, on or within which artillery is mounted (sometimes including the guns or mortars there mounted).

1590 MARLOWE *2nd Pt. Tamburl.* III. iii, The bringing of our ordnance..into the battery. **1688** *Lond. Gaz.* No. 2378/3 We had finished a Battery of three Mortars. **1769** FALCONER *Dict. Marine* (1789) Hh2b, Those on the lower battery are 32 pounders. **1810** WELLINGTON in Gurw. *Disp.* VI. 346 The batteries and works erecting at Cadiz. **1836** MARRYAT *Midsh. Easy* xxx, She continued her destructive fire..from the main-deck battery.

b. *transf.* or *fig.*

1581 J. BELL *Haddon's Answ. Osor.*, Before you had raysed your Battrye agaynst Luther. **1684** T. BURNET *Th. Earth* 89 These [burning] mountains are as so many batteries, planted by Providence in several parts of the earth. **1692** BENTLEY *Boyle Lect.* iv. 111 The Towers and Batteries that the Atheists have raised against Heaven.

c. An oblong box or boat submerged to the brim, used in wild-fowl shooting; = SINK *sb.*[1] 12 a. Also *attrib.*, as ***battery-gunner, -shooting***. *U.S.*

a **1841** W. HAWES *Sporting Scenes* (1842) I. 198 A machine, or battery, is a wooden box of the necessary dimensions to let a man lie down upon his back, just tightly fitting enough to let him rise again. **1859** [see SINK *sb.*[1] 12 a]. **1866** *Game Laws Va.* in *Fur, Fin & Feather* (1872) 144 Any person shooting or using a skiff, box or battery while hunting wild fowl. **1874** J. W. LONG *Wild-Fowl Shooting* 71, I shall describe that in reference to battery-shooting. **1875** *Fur, Fin & Feather* 120 But this is nothing to the numbers slain by the battery; and we have known one battery to kill over three hundred fowl in a tide. *Ibid.* 122 The battery gunner..has a great advantage over the fowler who shoots from the shore.

6. Phrases and locutions. ***battery-wagon***: one in which are carried tools and materials for repair of the battery. ***cross batteries***: two batteries playing upon the same point from different directions. ***enfilading battery***: one which sweeps the whole line attacked. ***floating battery***: a heavily armed and armoured vessel intended for bombarding fortresses. ***in battery***: (a gun) projecting in readiness for firing through an embrasure or over a parapet. ***masked battery***: one screened from the enemy's view by natural or artificial obstacles. ***out of*** or ***from battery***: (a gun) withdrawn for the purpose of loading.

1813 WELLINGTON in Gurw. *Disp.* X. 487 On what days did you disembark the artillery?.. On what days did you put them in battery? **1837** CARLYLE *Fr. Rev.* II. v. I. 57 Wondrous leather-roofed Floating-batteries..give gallant summons; to which..Gibraltar answers Plutonically. **1861** GEN. P. THOMPSON *Audi Alt.* III. clxxvii. 214 Do not go probing for 'masked batteries' to run your heads against.

7. *Mining.* The set of stamps, usually five in number, that work in one 'mortar' of a stamp-mill.

1853 *Harper's Mag.* VI. 578/2 Openings in this opposite each cover or battery of stamps. **1872** 'MARK TWAIN' *Roughing It* in *Writings* (1900) VII. xxxvi. 278 These [six rods] rose and fell, one after the other,..in an iron box called a 'battery'... One of us stood by the battery all day long. **1881** S. JENNINGS *Vis. Wynaad* viii. 69 Eight batteries of five gravitation stamps each. **1884** *Century Mag.* XXVII. 923 Batteries, where the quartz is pounded into white mud.

8. *Dyeing.* (See quots.)

1737 MILLER *Gard. Dict.* s.v. *Anil*, The second [vat] is called the Battery..It is in the second that they agitate and beat this Water impregnated and loaded with the Salts of the plant [Indigo]. **1815** *Encycl. Brit.* X. 287/2 A battery, consisting of a kettle, containing water slightly acidulated with sulphuric acid.

III. (from 4) A combination of simple instruments, usually to produce a compound instrument of increased power; applied originally with a reference to the *discharge* of electricity from such a combination.

9. *Electr.* An apparatus consisting of a number of Leyden jars so connected that they may be charged and discharged simultaneously.

1748 FRANKLIN *Lett.* Wks. 1840 V. 202 An electrical battery, consisting of eleven panes of large sash-glass, armed with thin leaden plates. **1822** IMISON *Sc. & Art* I. 340 When a number of Jars are thus connected it is called a battery. *fig.* **1831** CARLYLE *Sart. Res.* III. 339 Till your whole vital Electricity..is cut into two isolated portions of Positive and Negative (of Money and of Hunger); and stands there bottled up in two World-Batteries!

10. a. *Galvanism.* An apparatus consisting of a series of cells, each containing the essentials for producing voltaic electricity, connected together. Also used of any such apparatus for producing voltaic electricity, whether of one cell or more.

1801 SIR H. DAVY in *Phil. Trans.* XCI. 400 The third and most powerful class of Galvanic batteries..is formed, when metallic substances, oxidable in acids..are connected, as plates, with oxidating fluids. **1812** —— *Chem. Philos.* 162 Zinc, copper, and nitric acid form a powerful battery. *c* **1865** J. WYLDE in *Circ. Sc.* I. 190/1 No arrangement equals Grove's platina battery.

b. *attrib.* and *Comb.*, as ***battery-receiver, -set, -unit; battery-operated, -powered*** adjs.

1930 *Wireless World* 11 June 601/1 Few battery-operated portables consume more than the economical limit of 10 mA. **1964** T. L. KINSEY *Audio-Typing & Electric Typewriters* iii. 16 Battery-operated machines are also available. **1957** *BBC Handbk.* 52 Small self-contained battery-powered tape recorders. **1928** *Wireless World* 5 Dec. 754/3 A battery-receiver unit... The H.T. battery can therefore be adapted to serve as the actual receiver, by incorporating in it the necessary coupling unit. **1930** *Ibid.* 16 July 71/3 (*heading*) An Ambitious Battery Set. **1933** *Boy's Mag.* XLVII. 135/2 The Class 'B' valve..is of great importance to users of battery sets. **1939** *War Illustr.* 9 Dec. p. ii/3 This trade, which consists in selling torches that are loaded with worn-out battery-units from wireless sets. **1958** M. L. HALL et al. *Newnes Compl. Amat. Photogr.* x. 112 A flashgun consists of a socket to hold the flashbulb, a case to contain the battery unit and a reflector.

11. *Optics.* A combined series of lenses or prisms.

1867–77 CHAMBERS *Astron.*, An eye-piece..intermediate between the 1st and 2nd of the 'battery.' **1879** WARREN *Astron.* iii. 49 The best instruments pass the beam of light through a series of prisms called a battery.

12. Apparatus for preparing or serving meals. Also *batterie de cuisine* (see BATTERIE 2).

1819 REES *Cycl.* s.v. *Battery*, Some make battery for the kitchen, *batterie de cuisine*, comprehend all utensils for the service of the kitchen, whether of iron, brass, copper, or other matters. **1883** G. BOUGHTON in *Harper's Mag.* Apr. 695/1 Our tea battery came in. **1884** —— *ibid.* Aug. 334/2 The feasting batteries of the..guilds.

13. a. Used *gen.* for a collection of similar pieces of apparatus grouped together as a set (see quots.).

1885 [see TACHE *sb.*[3] 1]. **1911** D. S. HULFISH *Cycl. Motion-Pict. Work* II. 137 The remaining proportion of light may be supplied by lighting a partial battery of lamps. **1920** *Sci. Amer.* 2 Oct. 346 (*caption*) A battery of projectors and a stereopticon machine in the operator's booth of a leading motion-picture theatre. **1931** *Economist* 25 Apr. 888/2 There are batteries of forty looms each. **1958** *Engineering* 18 Apr. 509/1 When the Coal Board took over there were 45 ovens..in two batteries of 15 and 30.

b. A series of psychological or clinical tests.

1921 *Mem. Nat. Acad. Sci.* XV. II. ii. 316 If a test correlated almost perfectly with some other test in the battery, it could be omitted without loss. **1928** K. J. HOLZINGER *Statist. Methods in Educ.* xv. 310 The writers..eliminate certain tests..and thus obtain a shorter and possibly as good a test with unweighted items as with the whole battery. **1930** —— *Statist. Resumé Spearman Two-Factor Theory* 42 Two arithmetic tests or two opposite tests should not be used in a given battery. **1940** *Brit. Jrnl. Psychol.* Apr. 358 This is the estimated reliability of the battery formed by the straight sum of its constituent tests. **1961** *Lancet* 26 Aug. 487/1, I also heartily endorse his call for a refinement in the constituent subtests of psychological batteries.

c. A series of hutches, cages, or nesting-boxes in which laying hens are confined for intensive laying or poultry reared and fattened. Later extended to denote accommodation for fattening cattle; freq. *attrib.*, as ***battery hen, system***.

1931 G. W. WRENTMORE *Battery System of Poultry Keeping* 27 The system is best carried out with birds that have been in Batteries from the start. *Ibid.*, The battery is commenced at a temperature of 90–94 degrees and gradually lowered to a temperature of about 65 degrees as the size of the chicks increases. **1938** *Reader's Digest* Mar. 93/1 The smallest complete battery..fills a 14-by-20-foot space. **1940** N. MITFORD *Pigeon Pie* ix. 138 Those raising hens on the battery system. **1953** A. WATKYN *For Better, For Worse* II. i, It ain't right to ask 'uman beings to live like Battery Hens. **1958** *Observer* 19 Oct. 17/4 They [*sc.* geese] defy horrible human plans to mass-produce in battery and deep scratch **1960** *Farmer & Stockbreeder* 16 Feb. 78/1 We are going to hear more of battery beef. **1960** *News Chron.* 8 June 4/4 The broiler battery..may be good business, but is..revolting. **1961** *Guardian* 17 May 3/5 It was doubtful if..battery eggs were less nutritious than other eggs.

IV. 14. Metal, or articles of metal, especially of brass or copper, wrought by hammering.

1502 ARNOLD *Chron.* (1811) 74 Batery for the bale, xij*d.* **1577** *Wills & Inv. N.C.* (1860) 414, ij panes of battrye weyinge xv*lb.* **1742** H. HINES *Specif. Patent* No. 462 Raising copper battery cold in common battery mills. **1812** J. SMYTH *Pract. Customs* 107 Black Latten..and Battery.. This last is known by the dint of the mill-hammers upon the kettles.

attrib. **1592** *Wills & Inv. N.C.* (1860) 252 Kettell of battre mettell. **1802** REES *Cycl.* s.v., Battery-works include pots, saucepans, kettles..which though cast at first, are to be afterwards hammered or beaten into form. **1885** *Birmhm. Directory*, The Birmingham Battery and Metal Company.

V. [Cf. OF. *baterie* 'sorte de rempart' (Godefroy); ? an extension of 5; or can it be related to BATTER *v.*[2]?]

15. An embankment.

1799 J. ROBERTSON *Agric. Perth.* 276 A battery of stone, to join another island to the main land. **1862** SMILES *Engineers* III. 156 The expense of cuts and batteries (since called cuttings and embankments) on the different..lines.

16. *Mining.* **a.** A bulkhead of timber. **b.** The plank closing the bottom of a coal-chute. Raymond *Mining Gloss.* 1881.

17. [F. *batterie*; cf. BATTERIE 3.] The percussion section of an orchestra.

1926 WHITEMAN & MCBRIDE *Jazz* ix. 197 The battery of an orchestra includes so many instruments... Perhaps the most important instruments of the battery are the timpani or kettle drums. **1955** R. BLESH *Shining Trumpets* (ed. 3) ii. 30 A part of the rhythm is kept separate in drum battery. **1960** *Times* 23 June 17/3 A percussion player..proceeded to exploit a battery including cowbells and finger-cymbals.

battil, obs. f. BATTEL, BATTLE.

batting ('bætɪŋ), *vbl. sb.* [f. BAT *v.*[1], *sb.*[2]]

1. The action of using or striking with a bat: †**a.** formerly in washing or smoothing linen (*attrib.* in ***batting-staff, -log***, etc.).

1611 COTGR., *Batoir*, a Launderesses batting staffe. **1798** W. HUTTON *Fam. Hutton* 98 A girl of fifteen..lading water into her pail, while standing upon her batting-lag.

b. in *Cricket* and *Baseball*. Also *attrib.*, as ***batting average, glove***.

1773 *Gentl. Mag.* XLIII. 451 The hay may rue, that is unhous'd, The batting of that day. **1856** *Househ. Words* 2 Feb. 59/2 Some tubular batting-gloves. **1867** *Ball Players' Chron.* 12 Dec. 5/3 The best players are those making the best batting and fielding average. **1870** [see AVERAGE *sb.*[2] 6 b]. **1882** *Daily Tel.* 27 May, Messrs. Thornton and Schultz opened the batting for the Gentlemen. **1910** *Westm. Gaz.* 14 Apr. 7/4 Cricketers will have to pay a trifle more for batting-gloves and bat handles.

c. Beating out the impurities from raw cotton, an operation now superseded by use of 'opening' and 'scutching' machines.

1819 *Pantologia*, *Batting Machine*..for beating and cleaning cotton. **1835** Ure *Philos. Manuf.* 311 Batting cotton by hand..seems by far the hardest work in a factory..and is somewhat similar to threshing corn.

2. *concr.* Cotton fibre prepared in sheets for quilts or bed-covers; cf. BAT *sb.*[2] 13.

1875 H. WOOD *Therap.* (1879) 645 For some purposes a stronger batting..is prepared. **1883** *Century Mag.* Oct. 819/2 Filtered through six layers of cotton batting.

battish ('bætɪʃ), *a.* [f. BAT *sb.*[1] + -ISH[1].] Befitting a bat, bat-like.

c **1700** *Gentl. Instruc.* (1732) 1 Why Men should dote on Shades, and range in Obscurity..a battish Humour.

†'**battism.** *Obs. rare*$^{-1}$. [f. Gr. *Βάττος* stammerer (see BATTOLOGICAL) + -ISM.] Tautological repetition; = BATTOLOGY.

1617 COLLINS *Def. Bp. Ely* I. v. 198 The frequencie of repeating it, to which his Battismes..and his abhominable Crambes giue the only occasion.

battle ('bæt(ə)l), *sb.* Forms: 3-6 **batayle**, 4-6 **bataile, -ayl, -ail**, 4 **bateil, -al**, 4-5 **bataill(e, batel(e**, 5 **batayll(e, -aill, -eyl, -eil, -elle, -ill**, (*Sc.*) **battalʒe**, 5-6 **batel(e, battayle, battal(l**, 5-7 **batell, battell**, 6 **batyl, battaille, -ayl(l**, (*Sc.*) **battal**, 6-7 **battail(e, batle**, 6-9 **battel**, 6- **battle.** [ME. *batayle, -aile, -aille*, a. OF. *bataille* (= It. *battaglia*, Sp. *batalla*):—vulgar L. *battālia*, corruption of late L. *battuālia*, neut. pl. of adj. **battuālis*, f. late L. *battu-ĕre* to beat (perh. of Celtic origin). *Battuālia* is mentioned by the grammarian Adamantius or Martyrius (Keil *Gram. Lat.* vii. 178) as a neut. pl. meaning 'exercitationes militum vel gladiatorum': Cassiodorius (Keil *ibid.*), reproducing the passage, adds, 'quæ vulgo *battālia* dicuntur.' Like *murālia, mirabilia, biblia*, and many other neuter plurals, *battālia* came to be used as a feminine sing. in Romanic.]

I. A fight, fighting.

1. a. A hostile engagement or encounter between opposing forces on land or sea; a combat, a fight.

1297 R. GLOUC. 369 Þere, as þe batayle was, an abbey he let rere..Þat ys ycluped in Engelond, abbey of þe batayle. *c* **1386** CHAUCER *Prol.* 61 At mortal batailles [bataylis] hadde he been fiftene. **1477** EARL RIVERS (Caxton) *Dictes* 64 A man that fled venquisshed from a bataille. **1526** *Pilgr. Perf.* (W. de W. 1531) 4 The victory in many great batayles. **1535** COVERDALE *1 Chron.* xxi. Cont., Of certaine batels which Dauid winneth. **1559** BP. SCOT in Strype *Ann. Ref.* I. App. vii. 18 Our king..shall fyght our battailles for us. **1605** CAMDEN *Rem.* (1637) 49 The sea-battell at Actium. **1642** PR. RUPERT *Declar.* 3 In a battell, where two Armies fight. **1728** NEWTON *Chronol. Amended* Introd. 7 Before the Battel of Thermopylæ. **1808** SCOTT *Marm.* VI. xxvi, Wide raged the battle on the plain.

b. With various qualifying attributes:

close battle, a naval battle at 'close quarters,' in which the ships engage each other side by side. ***pitched battle***, a battle which has been planned, and of which the ground has been chosen beforehand, by both sides. ***plain battle***, 'open field,' fair fight. ***general's battle***, a battle in which the issue turns mainly upon the skill of the general, as contrasted with a ***soldier's battle***, in which the main element is the courage and energy of the soldier.

1529 RASTELL *Pastyme* (1811) 64 He slew, in playne battayl, Grosius, kynge of Wandalys. **1596** SHAKS. *Tam. Shr.* I. ii. 206 Haue I not in a pitched battell heard Loud larums? **1840** NAPIER *Penins. War* VI. XXII. iv. 269 It [Passage of the Bidassoa] was a general's not a soldier's battle. Wellington had with overmastering combinations overwhelmed each point of attack. **1850** E. WARBURTON *Cresc. & Cross* I. 36 The signal for 'close battle' flew from his mast head. **1851** CREASY *Decis. Battles* (1864) 187 To encounter Varus's army in a pitched battle.

2. a. A fight between two persons, a single combat, a duel. ***trial by battle***: the legal decision of a dispute by the issue of a single combat.

a **1300** *Cursor M.* 3463 Bituix vn-born a batel blind. *c* **1430** LYDG. *Bochas* II. xxix. (1554) 65 b, Romains By singuler batayle had wonne the victory. *c* **1440** *Promp. Parv.* 26 Batayle, *pugna, duellum.* **1556** *Chron. Grey Friars* (1852) 12 A gret batle rose betwene Roberte Glocitre & Arthur Ormesby in Smythfelde. **1593** SHAKS. *Rich. II*, I. i. 92, I say, and will in battaile proue..That, etc. **1641** *Termes de la Ley* 39 Battaile is an ancient triall in our Law, which the Defendant in appeale of murder, robbery, or felony, may chuse. **1641** in Rushw. *Hist. Coll.* III. (1692) I. 356 The House afterwards Ordered a Bill to be brought in to take away Tryal by Battel. **1819** REES *Cycl.* s.v. *Battle*, The last trial by battel that was waged in the court of common pleas at Westminster..was in 1571.

b. An encounter between two animals, especially when set to fight to provide sport. Hence ***battle-cock***, a fighting cock.

1605 VERSTEGAN *Dec. Intell.* viii. (1628) 284 Beasts of battaile, as is..the beare. **1606** SHAKS. *Ant. & Cl.* II. iii. 36 His Cocks do winne the Battaile, still of mine. **1611** MARKHAM *Countr. Content.* I. xix, The breeding of these Cocks for the battail, is much differing from those of the dung-hill. **1704** *Lond. Gaz.* No. 4005/4 There will be..a Cock Match..for 6 Guineas a Battel.

3. battle royal, a fight in which several combatants engage (*spec.* applied to a cock-fight of this character); a general engagement; a 'free' fight; hence *fig.* a general squabble.

1672 J. HOWARD *All Mistaken* I. (D.) Hist—now for a battle-royal. **1687** DRYDEN *Hind. & P.* II. 248 Though Luther, Zuinglius, Calvin, holy chiefs Have made a battel Royal of beliefs. **1804** NELSON in Nicolas *Disp.* VI. 178 We may as well have a Battle Royal, Line-of-Battle Ships opposed to Ships of the Line, and Frigates to Frigates. **1860** GEN. P. THOMPSON *Audi Alt.* III. ci. 1 Cockerels crow across a ditch, till they get up a battle-royal.

4. (In certain phrases): The favourable issue of a combat, victory (cf. *game, match, race*). ***to give the battle***: to grant victory. ***to have the battle***: to be victorious. ***it is half the battle***: (said of anything which contributes largely to success).

c **1400** *Ywaine & Gaw.* 1003 Whether is the better?..He that has the bataile. **1611** BIBLE *Eccles.* ix. 11 The race is not to the swift nor the battle to the strong. **1849** MARRYAT *Valerie* ii, Youth..is more than half the battle.

5. (Without article or pl.): Fighting, actual hostilities, conflict between enemies, war.

a **1300** *Cursor M.* 6970 Whenne þat þei to bataile ȝede. **1375** BARBOUR *Bruce* I. 105 Durst nane of Walis in bataill ride. *c* **1400** *Destr. Troy* IV. 1216 Pollux..Brusshit into batell & moche bale wroght. *c* **1430** *Life St. Kath.* (1884) 61 The tyraunt Maxence went in batayle aȝenst the Emperour Constantyne. **1535** COVERDALE *Josh.* ii. 19 They wanne them all with battayll. **1596** SPENSER *F.Q.* II. i. 27 His steede ..did cruell battell breath. **1676** HOBBES *Iliad* I. 238 Two ages he in battel honour gain'd. **1872** RUSKIN *Fors Clav.* xiv. II. 8 The best men still go out to battle.

†6. A continued state of hostilities between two or more armed forces, a war. *Obs.*

1382 WYCLIF *Wisd.* xiv. 22 In gret bataile [**1611** war] or vnkunnyng liuende. **1387** TREVISA *Higden* Rolls Ser. IV. 153 Þe bataille þat heet bellum Sociale. **1542** UDALL *Erasm. Apoph.* 262 b, Sylla..made civile battail with Marius. **1557** PAYNELL *Barclay's Jugurth.* Bj, The Romayns had thre notable and famous batayls agaynste the Carthaginences.

7. *fig.* Strife, conflict, contest, struggle for victory.

c **1375** WYCLIF *Serm.* Sel. Wks. 1871 II. 250 Batailis and stryvyngis in plee shulden be forsaken of Cristene men. *c* **1485** *Digby Myst.* (1882) IV. 1118 His gret bataile He had on crosse of tree. **1535** COVERDALE *Ps.* lv. 21 Their mouthes are softer then butter and yet haue they batell in their mynde. **1704** SWIFT *Batt. Bks.* (1711) 215 The Battel between the antient and modern Books. **1863** STANLEY *Jew. Ch.* xi. 246 Round this famous prayer was fought a battle of words. **1864** KINGSLEY *Lett.* (1878) II. 197 It is curious to watch the battle between the two waters, quite unmixed, owing to their different specific gravity.

II. Battle array, an army or battalion in array.

8. a. A body or line of troops in battle array, whether composing an entire army, or one of its main divisions; = BATTALION. *arch.* (since *c* 1700).

1330 R. BRUNNE *Chron.* 276, I se an oste..comand bi batailes ten. *c* **1350** *Will. Palerne* 3562 Alle his burnes bliue in x batailes he sett. *c* **1400** *Destr. Troy* VI. 2133 Gird furthe into grese with a gret batell. **1480** CAXTON *Chron. Eng.* ccxxvii. 234 Kyng Edward in a felde fast by crescy hauyng iij batayls countred and met with philip of valoys hauyng with hym iiij bataylles. **1560** WHITEHORNE *Art Warre* (1573) 21 b, A Macedonicall Fallange, was no other wise then is now a days a battaile of Swizzers. **1596** SHAKS. *1 Hen. IV*, IV. i. 129 What may the Kings whole Battaile reach vnto? **1598** BARRET *Theor. Warres* III. i. 32 Whereof we frame our battels or battaillions. **1664** S. CLARKE *Tamerlane* 8 He divided his Army into three main Battels. **1697** POTTER *Antiq. Greece* III. vi. 58 Their Phalanx is..a square Battail of Pike-men. *a* **1718** ROWE *Lucan* (1807) 141 The joining battles shout. **1814** SCOTT *Ld. Isles* VI. x, In battles four beneath their eye, The forces of King Robert lie.

b. *fig.* A martial array, a line.

1592 SHAKS. *Ven. & Ad.* civ, On his [the boar's] bow-back he hath a battle set Of bristly pikes.

†9. (More fully called 'great' or 'main battle'): The main body of an army or naval force, as distinguished from the van and rear, or from the wings; = BATTALIA 2 c, BATTALION 1 b. *Obs.*

1489 CAXTON *Faytes of A.* I. xxiii. 71 After the fyrst batayll that men calle the forwarde commeth the grete bataylle. **1594** SHAKS. *Rich. III*, V. iii. 299 They thus directed, we will follow In the maine Battell. **1655** FULLER *Ch.-Hist.* VIII. §36 IV. 171 He suffered Wyat his Van and main Battell..to march undisturbed..to Charing Chrosse. **1548** W. PATTEN *Exped. Scot.* in Arb. *Garner* III. 82 Our three Battles kept order in pace..The Foreward, foremost; the Battle, in the midst; and the Rereward, hindermost. *a* **1618** RALEIGH *Invent. Shipping* 30 A Vanguard..of these hoyes..with a Battaile of 400 other warlike ships, and a Reare of thirty. **1655** LESTRANGE *Chas. I*, 112 So terrible a shock, as..disordered both Battail and Rere. **1868** KIRK *Chas. Bold* III. v. iii. 436 The artillery..was divided between the vanguard and the 'battle,' or main body.

†10. Battle array; = BATTALIA 1. *Obs.*

1570-87 HOLINSHED *Scot. Chron.* (1806) I. 200 Seeing the enemies readie ranged in battel. **1596** SIR F. VERE *Comm.* 37 He should march on roundly to the enemy where they stood in battel.

III. Phrases (chiefly in sense 1).

11. In obvious phrases, as ***to have, keep, make, smite, strike, battle*** (all obs.); ***to bid*** (obs.), ***offer, refuse, accept, take*** (arch.) ***battle***; ***to join battle***; also, ***to do battle***, to fight; ***to give battle***, to attack, engage; ***to pitch a battle*** (cf. ***pitched battle*** in 1 b).

1297 R. GLOUC. 514 Hii mette hom atte laste..at Lincolne ..& smite there an bataile. *a* **1300** *Cursor M.* 471 Aȝeyn him ȝaf he batail grym. **1460** in *Pol. Rel. & L. Poems* (1866) 185 Þe world biddiþ me bataile blijf. **1475** CAXTON *Jason* 76 They had batayll togeder. **1470-85** MALORY *Arthur* I. iii, His enemies..did a great battle upon his men. **1495** *Act 11 Hen. VII*, lxiii. Pream., Divers..rered Warre, and made Bataill ayenst him. **1513** BRADSHAW *St. Werburge* (1848) 181 William Conquerour Pight a stronge batell. **1542** UDALL *Erasm. Apoph.* 336 a, The battail was kept in Cherronea. **1577** NORTHBROOKE *Dicing* (1843) 64 To make battel vpon the Sabboth day. **1593** SHAKS. *3 Hen. VI*, V. iv. 66 Here pitch our Battaile, hence we will not budge. **1599** —— *Hen. V*, II. iv. 54 When Cressy Battell fatally was strucke. **1611** BIBLE *Gen.* XIV. 8 They joyned battell with them, in the vale of Siddim. **1656** H. MORE *Antid. Ath.* II. viii. 117 He did bid battel to the very fiercest of them. **1697** DRYDEN *Virg. Georg.* II. 382 Before the Battel joins. **1723** DE FOE *Mem. Cavalier* (1840) 125 Shall we give battle to the imperialists or not? **1847** MAXWELL *Vict. Brit. Armies* 270 He advanced with sixty thousand men, determined to offer battle. **1851** CREASY *Decis. Battles* (1864) 48 Miltiades immediately joined battle and gained the victory *Ibid.* 149 He should abstain from giving or taking battle. **1855** KINGSLEY *Westw. Ho!* xxxi. (1878) 496 The Spaniard had refused battle. **1881** R. STEVENSON *Virg. Puerisque* 85 We must strive and do battle for the truth.

12. ***line of battle***: the position of troops drawn up in battle array in their usual order; the line or arrangement formed by ships of war in an engagement. Hence ***line-of-battle ship***, a ship of sufficient size to take part in a main attack; formerly, one of 74 guns and upward; also irreg. ***line of battleship***.

1695 ADDISON *King* Misc. Wks. 1726 I. 11 Spain's numerous Fleet..Cou'd scarce a longer Line of battel boast. **1705** *Admiralty Sec. In-Lett.* 5249 (P.R.O.), The capital ships and line-of-battle ships are often laid up in the winter. **1710** *Lond. Gaz.* No. 4700/1 Eighteen Men of War, all of the Line of Battel. **1769** FALCONER *Dict. Marine* (1789) A a, In the line, or order of battle, all the ships..are close-hauled. **1800** NELSON in A. Duncan *Nelson* (1806) 121, I saw the Alexander in chase of a line of battle ship. **1842** WELLINGTON in Gurw. *Disp.* X. 516 The army..made up in the form of what is called 'a line of battle.' **1863** *Cornh. Mag.* Feb. *Life Man-of-War*, The typical vessel—the two-decker line-of-battle ship, say of eighty guns. **1894** *Times* (weekly ed.) 19 Jan. 50/1 A heavily armoured line-of-battleship. **1899** R. ROUTLEDGE *Discov. & Invent. 19th Cent.* (ed. 13) 167 Before the close of 1894, the British navy possessed no fewer than eight of the largest armoured line of battle-ships.

IV. *Combinations.*

13. General relations: **a.** instrumental with pa. pple., as ***battle-grimed, -hardened, -scarred, -slain, -spent*** (exhausted with fighting), ***-tried, -weary, -writhen*** (twisted in struggle) adjs.; **b.** attrib. with sb., as ***battle-day, -din, fleet, -front, -hymn, -line, -order, -painter, -picture, -place, -practice*** (also *attrib.*), ***-rank, -shout, -smoke, -song, -training, -zone***, and poetical combinations without limit.

1701 *Lond. Gaz.* 3694/4 Mr. Alexander van Gaalon, the Battel-Painter. **1814** BYRON *Lara* II. xi, The battle-day They could encounter as a veteran may. **1814** SCOTT *Ld. of Isles* IV. xxx, To wreak thy wrongs in battle-line. **1831** CARLYLE *Sart. Res.* III. viii, The steel Host, that yelled in fierce battle-shouts at Issus and Arbela. **1859** TENNYSON *Elaine* 808 Battle-writhen arms and mighty hands. **1862** [J. W. HOWE] in *Atlantic Monthly* Feb. 145 *Battle Hymn of the Republic.* Mine eyes have seen the glory of the coming of the Lord: [etc.]. **1865** O. W. HOLMES *To Gen. Grant*, Our leaders battle-scarred. **1870** BRYANT *Iliad* I. IV. 12 The battle-din was loud. **1877** TENNYSON *Harold* III. i. 87 A ghostly horn Blowing continually, and faint battle-hymns. **1897** *Trans. Inst. Naval Archit.* XXXVIII. 50 These two ships form still part of the German battle fleet. **1898** KIPLING *Fleet in Being* ii. 17 That a cruiser at 7.30 that morning had reported to the Battle Fleet..'Enemy to the Westward'. **1899** R. MEINERTZHAGEN *Army Diary* 1 July (1960) 15 The hopelessly out-of-date battle-training of my battalion. **1900** *Blackw. Mag.* Dec. 931/2 No amount of battle-smoke can hide the red stain of pure unadulterated murder. **1902** *Westm. Gaz.* 6 Jan. 4/3 So long as our battle-fleet is able to keep the seas. **1905** L. BINYON *Penthesilea* 38 So now the battle-weary Greeks prepared their meal. **1905** *Westm. Gaz.* 20 June 2/2 Battle-practice has for 1905 been ordered on more regular and practical lines than hitherto. **1907** *Daily Chron.* 14 Oct. 4/4 Winchelsea sees battle-grimed French and Spaniards scale her walls. **1909** *Westm. Gaz.* 18 Jan. 3/1 These men fought in the ranks of battle-tried battalions. *Ibid.* 9 Feb. 1/2 Mr. Solano, the inventor of the new system of battle-practice targets, which has received the approval of the War Office. **1914** *Scotsman* 6 Oct. 4/1 The latest news from the two great battle-fronts affords no ground for dissatisfaction. **1931** *Times Lit. Suppl.* 21 May 399/3 Soult..decided to make the main defence in the rear line, turning this into the 'battle zone', as it was called in France in 1918. **1937** KOESTLER *Span. Testament* iv. 82 Every town along the enemy's line of retreat and all the areas behind the enemy lines are to be considered as battle zones. **1940** W. TEMPLE *Thoughts in War-time* vii. 43 If we pray as Christ taught us to pray, we pray in perfect unity on both sides of the battle-front. **1944** *Ann. Reg. 1943* 19 In training the most notable innovation had been the introduction of realistic battle training. **1945** *Finito! Po Valley Campaign* 31 Exhausted, battle-weary crews. **1949** KOESTLER *Promise & Fulf.* III. i. 299 The battle-hardened workers of the Soviet Union. **1949** E. POUND *Pisan Cantos* lxxx. 88 Following the Battle Hymn of the Republic.

14. Special combinations: **battle array**, formerly **battle-ray**, the order of troops arranged for battle; **battle bowler** *slang* = TIN HAT 1; **battle-cry**, a war-cry, a slogan; **battle-field, -ground**, the field or ground on which a battle is fought; **battle-lantern**, a lantern used on a ship; formerly one placed at each gun to light up the deck during a night engagement, a fighting-lantern; **battle-piece**, a painting of a battle, a poetical or rhetorical passage describing a battle; **†battle-ram**, a battering-ram; **battle-school**, a military establishment providing training under conditions resembling those of battle; **battle-stead** (*arch.*), place of battle; **battle-twig** *dial.* [corruption of *beetle-wig*; cf. BEETLE *sb.*^{2}, EARWIG *sb.*], an earwig; see also quot. 1942; **battle-wag(g)on** *slang* (orig. *U.S.*), (*a*) a battleship; (*b*) (see quot. 1926); (*c*) an armed or armoured vehicle; **battle-word**, war-cry; **† battle-wright**, a warrior; **battle-wise** *adv.*, in manner or order of battle.

1552 HULOET, *Battayle arraye, in fourme or order of battayle, *turmatim.* *c* **1600** *Rob. Hood* (Ritson) xii. 66 The King is into Finsbury field Marching in battle-ray. **1618** BOLTON *Florus* (1636) 234 Athenio..puts them under Banners into battelray. **1840** THIRLWALL *Greece* VII. lviii. 285 The two armies were drawn up in battle-array. **1925** FRASER & GIBBONS *Soldier & Sailor Words* 19 *Battle-bowler. **1940** N. MITFORD *Pigeon Pie* iv. 75 She lunched alone at the Ritz yesterday in a black wig, a battle bowler and her silver foxes. **1814** Scott *Ld. of Isles* vi. xxxii, He shouted loud his *battle-cry, 'Saint James for Argentine!' **1879** *Pall Mall Budg.* 12 Sept. 8 The noisy battle-cries that are put into their mouths. **1812** Byron *Ch. Har.* ii. lxxxix, The *Battle-field, where Persia's victim horde First bow'd. **1820** Scott *Abbot* xxii, The French and English have..made Scotland the battle-field on which to fight out their own ancient quarrel. **1865** Mill *Exam. Hamilton* 154 The question of an external world is the great *battle-ground of metaphysics. **1830** J. F. Cooper *Water Witch* III. vii. 206 Lifting a lighted *battle-lantern to his face, he saw that he slept. **1938** Masefield *Dead Ned* 235 He had a battle-lantern with him, a ship's lamp with a strong reflector. **1711** Shaftesb. *Charac.* (1737) III. 379 Representations of the human passions; as we see even in *battel-pieces. **1867** Freeman *Norm. Conq.* I. v. 271 Verses which echo the true ring of the battle-pieces of Homer. **1535** Coverdale *Ezek.* xxi. 22 To crie out Alarum, to set *batell-rammes agaynst the gates. **1942** *Hutchinson's Pict. Hist. War* 18 Mar.–9 June 219 Attack is the spirit of the *battle school. **1375** Barbour *Bruce* xiv. 301 [Thai] levit in the *battell-stede Weill mony of thar gud men ded. **1787** Grose *Prov. Gloss.*, *Battle-twig, an earwig. Derb. **1885** Tennyson *Tiresias*, etc. 111 'Twur as bad as a battle-twig 'ere i' my oän blue chaumber to me. **1929** D. H. Lawrence *Pansies* 144 There isn't a damn thing in 'em..they haven't the spunk of a battle-twig. **1942** *Archit. Rev.* XCII. 154/2 He has needles of several sizes and of two different types: the small 'battletwig' (i.e. earwig) needle for tiny work, the regular netting needle for string and rope nets. **1926** *Amer. Speech* I. 650/2 **Battle wagon*, an iron coal car. **1927** *Ibid.* III. 452 *Battle wagon*, warship. **1938** *Newsweek* 14 Nov. 11/2 The Navy had sent out bids.. for three new 35,000-ton battlewagons. **1945** *Penguin New Writing* XXIII. 10 But the battle-wagon—her great guns swing up in a silent arc. **1949** F. Maclean *Eastern Appr.* ii. ii. 200 The 'battlewagon'..was a new, cut-down Ford station waggon... It was fitted with mountings for two machine guns in front and two behind. **1559** *Myrr. for Mag.*, *Jack Cade* ix. 6 And *battayle wyse to cum to blackeheth playne. **1622** Mabbe *Aleman's Guzman d' Alf.* ii. 333 Wee did presently battell-wise cast our selues into a Wing. **1814** Scott *Ld. of Isles* vi. xxvii, Sinks, Argentine, thy *battle-word. *a* **1300** *Cursor M.* 7495 Yon es a stalworth *batail wright.

battle, variant of battel *sb.*

battle, battel ('bæt(ə)l), *a.* *Obs.* exc. *dial.* Forms: 6–7 **battill, battell, batle, battle,** 6 **batel(l,** 7 **battel,** 8–9 *Sc.* **baittle, bettle.** [For the etymology and mutual relations of this and the cognate battle *v.*³, data are wanting; according to present evidence, the adj. appears earliest, being found in Scotch in 1513. Its form and sense agree with a derivation from **bat*, representing ON. *bati* 'improvement, getting better,' Du. *baat* 'improvement, advantage, profiting, profit,' referred to under batten *v.*¹; with suffix as in *brittle, bruckle, fickle, newfangle*, and OE. *etol, drincol, wittol*. This would give as the primary sense 'given, tending, or fitted, to improve, better, fatten, etc.' All the related words have a smack of Northern origin: '*battle* or *baittle grass*' is still common in south of Scotland.

The non-occurrence of *bat*, while its presumed derivatives, *battle, battable, batful, batsome*, are so frequent in 16–17th c., is a difficulty; as is also the fact that *batt-le, batt-able* point to a verbal rather than a substantive base, and yet can hardly have been formed on *batt-en*.]

1. Of grass or pasture: Improving or nutritious to sheep and cattle; feeding, nourishing, fattening.

1513 Douglas *Æneis* vi. x. 25 With battill gers, fresche erbis and grene suardis. **1533** Bellenden *Livy* i. (1822) 13 To refresche thaim with the battell gers thairof. **1641** Best *Farm. Bks.* (1856) 28 A battle, sweete, moist, and (as wee say) a naturall grasse, and doth the sheepe much good. **1822** Scott *Pirate* III. 182 (Jam.) We turn heather into greensward, and the poor yarpha into baittle grass-land. *Mod.* (*Roxburghshire*), Hillsides covered with fine baittle grass.

2. Hence, of soil or land: Rich, fertile, productive, fruitful (properly in pasture, but sometimes generally).

c **1540** Brinklow *Complaynt* iv. B. v b, Ye most batell and frutefull grownd in Ingland. **1563** Hyll *Art Garden.* (1593) 6 A fruitfull profitable, and a batle ground. **1601** Holland *Pliny* I. 472 The soile is exceeding battill and fat. **1610** —— *Camden's Brit.* ii. 102 A plenteous and battle country for feeding and raising of cattell. **1609** Butler *Fem. Mon.* i. (1623) Bj, There is no ground..whether it be battle or barren. **1693** W. Robertson *Phraseol. Gen.* 214 Battel or fruitful, *fertilis.* **1807** Hogg *Mount. Bard* 124 (Jam.) On Ettrick's baittle haughs.

battle ('bæt(ə)l), *v.*¹ Forms: 4 **bataille, -ale,** 4–5 **-ail,** 5 **-aylle, -el(l, -ol, -il,** 6 **-ayle, battaile,** 7– **battle.** [a. F. *bataille-r* (12th c. in Littré) to fight, f. *bataille* battle.]

1. *intr.* To fight, to engage in war. (Now rare in literal sense, in which *fight* is usual.)

1330 R. Brunne *Chron.* 252 In þinkeng of alle þis, þe batailed in þe se. *c* **1374** Chaucer *Boeth.* i. iv. 18 Whom þei han seyn alwey batailen and defenden goode men. *c* **1400** *Destr. Troy* iii. 945 These balefull brether batell so longe. **1483** Caxton *Gold. Leg.* 430/1 This..fader bataylled and foughte ageynst the heretykes. **1593** Shaks. *3 Hen. VI*, ii. v. 74 Whiles Lyons Warre, and bataile for their Dennes. **1704** Rowe *Ulysses* Prol. 8 To seek Renown And Battel for a Harlot at Troy Town. **1831** Carlyle *Sart. Res.* ii. viii, To ..battle with innumerable wolves.

b. *fig.* To contend, maintain a (usually defensive) struggle, e.g. *with* or *against* pestilence, bigotry, the waves, etc.

1502 *Ord. Crysten Men* (W. de W. 1506) i. vii. 75 To resist and batayle in this present lyfe. **1729** Swift *Libel Delany* Wks. 1755 IV. i. 99 His virtues battling with his place. **1820** Scott *Abbot* viii, A lively brook, which battled with every stone that interrupted its passage. **1876** Green *Short Hist.* 713 Walpole battled stubbornly against the cry of war.

c. (with indefinite object) *to battle it* (lit. and fig.).

1714 Addison *Spect.* No. 556 ⁋9, I was battling it across the Table with a young Templar. **1821** Byron *Sardan.* v. i. 60 They battle it beyond the wall. **1885** Browning *Ferishtah's F.* 141 So we battled it like men.

†**2.** *trans.* and *refl.* To put into battle array, form into battalions, embattle. *Obs.*

1330 R. Brunne *Chron.* 170 Þan cried Richard on hie, 'Now batale vs belyue.' *c* **1430** *Syr Gener.* 7822 Thei batailed hem in ranges fiftene.

3. *trans.* To give battle to, fight against, assail in battle. Also *fig.*

c **1399** *Pol. Poems* (1859) II. 9 Cristes feith is every dal assailed..and batailed. **1590** Greene *Orl. Fur.* (1599) 31 To battaile him that scornes to iniure thee. **1765** Tucker *Lt. Nat.* I. 39 The work..of battling the opinions of others. **1852** Dickinson in *Jrnl. R. Agric. Soc.* XIII. ii. 257 The calves are suffered to battle each other in loose sheds.

4. Phrases.

1794 Southey *Bot. Bay Eclog.* iii, Every step that he takes he must battle his way. **1875** B. Taylor *Faust* ii. iii. II. 103 Here a lesson grand was battled to the end.

†'**battle**, *v.*² *Obs.* Forms: 4 **batayle, -aile,** 5 **battaile,** 7 **battel:** see battled *ppl. a.*² [a. OF. *bataillie-r, -eillie-r* (= Pr. *batalhar*) to furnish with *batailles* 'battlements,' temporary or movable turrets of wood, etc. erected upon walls when besieged; formally the same word as *bataille* battle, though the sense-development is not clear. Later OF. had also in same sense *batillier, bastillier*, either a distinct formation on *bastille* (see bastille), or refashioned after this word, which eventually displaced *bataillier*, so that mod.F. has only *bastiller*: in Eng. on the other hand the word followed the phonetic course of *battle*. See also battlement.]

trans. To fortify or furnish with battlements. (Usually in passive: cf. battled *ppl. a.*²)

c **1340** *Cursor M.* (Trin.) 9902 Þis castel..of loue and grace..is..batailed aboute al wiþ sele. *c* **1375** Barbour *Bruce* ii. 221 Perth..then wes wallyt all about With feile towris rycht hey battaillyt. *c* **1618** Fletcher *Woman's Prize* iii. ii. 110 Ile have it batteld too.

†**battle, battel** ('bæt(ə)l), *v.*³ *Obs.* Forms: 6 **battill, battell,** 7 **batle,** 7, 9 **battel,** 6– **battle.** [See battle *a.*, of which this appears to be a derivative, and cf. the synonymous batt-en *v.*¹.

(As we cannot be quite sure whether the pr. pple. in the earliest instances is *trans.* 'feeding,' or *intr.* 'thriving, flourishing,' the order of development is uncertain. If derived from the adj., we should expect the earliest sense to be 'to render pasture or land *battle*, to fertilize.')]

I. *transitive.*

†**1.** To nourish cattle, as a rich pasture does; to feed or nourish (men or beasts). *Obs.*

1548 Udall *Erasm. Par. Luke* Pref. 3 The fatte batleyng yearth of the Paraphrase. **1617** Collins *Def. Bp. Ely* i. ii. 120 As they may wish wel to the childe, that are not particularly put in trust to battle it, or to giue it suck. **1653** A. Wilson *Jas. I*, 43 A Courtier from his infancie, Batteld by Art, and industrie. **1655** Mouff. & Benn. *Health's Improv.* 190 Snails..towards winter, having..batled themselves fat with sleep. **1662** Fuller *Worthies* i. 229 [see battling *ppl. a.*² 1].

†**2.** To render (soil) fertile and productive. *Obs.*

1611 Cotgr., *Engraisser un champ*, to battle it, or make it fertile. **1662** Fuller *Worthies* (1840) I. 399 Ashes are a marvellous improvement to battle barren ground. *Ibid.* iii. 40 Dove..is the Nilus of Staffordshire, much battling the Meadowes thereof.

II. *intransitive.*

†**3.** Of men and animals: To grow fat, to thrive.

1575 Turberv. *Venerie.* 189 The badgerd battles much with slepe and is a verie fat beast. **1601** Holland *Pliny* ix. xxxi, In autumne and spring they battle and wax fat. **1656** Trapp *Comm. 1 Pet.* ii. 2 Like the changeling Luther mentioneth, ever sucking, never batling. **1699** Coles, *Battle*, as cattle turned into rank ground, *impascor, vescor*.. *Battle* [get flesh] *pinguesco.* **1721** Bailey, *Battle*, to feed as Cattle do; to grow fat.

†**4.** To become fertile and fruitful. *Obs.*

1576 Foxe *A. & M.* To Rdr. ⁋ij b, These with fatnes of their bloud dyd cause it [fieldes of the church] to battell and fructifie. **1578** *Chr. Prayers* in *Priv. Prayers Q. Eliz.* (1851) 516 That the good seed..battle, as in good ground, and bring forth plentiful fruit.

†**battle.** *v.*⁴ *Obs.* [? freq. of bat *v.*¹, or var. of beetle; cf. batting and batler.] *trans.* To beat (clothes) with a wooden beetle during the process of washing, or in order to smooth them after they are dried. See also battling *vbl. sb.*⁴

1570 Levins *Manip.* 38 To battle clothes, *excutere.*

battle, variant of batelle.

†**battleage.** *Obs.* [Of uncertain etymology and meaning.]

1526 *Ord. R. Househ.* 195 Grindeing of Wheate, Messurage, Carridge, and Battleage of Wheat, Bread, and Meale.

battle-axe, -ax, ('bæt(ə)l,æks). (The spelling with *-ax* is now chiefly *U.S.*)

1. A kind of axe used as a weapon of war in the Middle Ages.

c **1380** in Tytler *Hist. Scot.* (1864) I. 367 Bow, and spier, And battle-axe, their fechting gear. **1437** *Test. Ebor.* (1855) II. 70 Unam loricam de optimis, et optimum batelax. **1546** *Lanc. Wills* II. 27 Also my batell axe wth all other harnishe belongyng to my bodie. **1588** Shaks. *Tit. A.* iii. i. 169 Rear'd aloft the bloody Battle axe. **1762** Hume *Hist. Eng.* II. (1803) xiv. 238 Cleft his adversary to the chin with a battle-ax. **1850** Prescott *Peru* II. 213 Long lances and battle-axes edged with copper.

2. A halberd or bill carried by guards.

1709 *Lond. Gaz.* No. 4536/2 His Excellency proceeded to the Castle, attended by the Privy-Council, with the Guard of Battel-Axes. **1714** *Ibid.* No. 5282/6 The Company of Foot-Guards armed with Battel-axes.

3. *Archæol.* A type of prehistoric stone weapon; hence applied *attrib.* to a neolithic culture characterized by this weapon.

1859 *Proc. Soc. Antiq. Scotl. 1856–7* II. 306 Stone Hammer or Battle Axe, formed of fine-grained mica schist. **1880** Dawkins *Early Man* x. 390 A bronze battle-axe fifteen inches in length and seven pounds in weight. **1925** Childe *Dawn Europ. Civiliz.* xii. 198 The most conspicuous weapons, the battle-axes and hammer-axes..go back to the copper age and prove the dominance of the battle-axe element in the population. **1928** C. Dawson *Age of Gods* xii. 268 The Battle-axe Culture. *Ibid.* 270 The Battle-axe People. **1931** *Jrnl. R. Anthrop. Inst.* LXI. 345 The process of assimilation was accelerated in Sweden and replaced in the East Baltic regions by intrusions of the battle-axe folk... Battle-axes and even battle-axe graves in the dwelling-places are the proofs of their advent. **1950** H. L. Lorimer *Homer & Monum.* i. 6 The Battle-axe culture commonly regarded as Indo-European.

4. *fig.* A formidable or domineering woman. orig. *U.S. slang*, now *colloq.*

1896 Ade *Artie* ix. 81 Say, there was a battle-ax if ever you see one. She had a face on her that'd fade flowers. **1938** 'E. Queen' *Four of Hearts* i. ii. 25 These old female battle-axes don't feaze me. **1957** C. Brooke-Rose *Languages of Love* 8 Do I look like a female novelist? I thought they were all battle-axes. **1959** *Punch* 21 Jan. 135/3 Though slim as an arrow A girl can wax In the course of time To a battle-axe.

'**battle-'cruiser.** A heavily armoured cruiser or cruiser-battleship (see battleship b).

1911 *Times* 22 Nov. 6/3 In order to distinguish the armoured cruisers of earlier dates from those of the 'Invincible' and later types the latter vessels are to be.. classified as battle cruisers. **1914** *Daily Express* 9 Sept. 1/2 The Nuremberg, a German cruiser, is said to be flying from a British battle cruiser. **1946** *Jane's Fighting Ships 1944–45* 432 The repair and refit of this battle-cruiser.

battled ('bæt(ə)ld), *ppl. a.*¹ [f. battle *v.*¹ + -ed.]

1. Ranged in battle-array; disposed in battalions.

1592 Wyrley *Armorie* 46 He sommoned braue Dukes, stout Earles and Lordes In batteled armes before him to appeere. **1841** Orderson *Creol.* xviii. 213 She could not.. stay the 'battled pestilence.'

2. *poet.* Fought, contested.

1810 Scott *Lady of L.* i. xxxi, Soldier rest! Thy warfare o'er, Dream of battled fields no more.

battled ('bæt(ə)ld), *ppl. a.*² *Obs.* exc. *poet.* Forms: 4 **batayld, -ailed, -ayled,** (*Sc.*) **battalit,** 4–5 **baytayled,** (*Sc.*) **battailyt,** 5 **batild,** 6 **batteled, -eld,** (*Sc.*) **battelit,** 7 **batled,** 7– **battled.** [f. battle *v.*² + -ed: cf. OF. *bataillié* now *bastillé*.]

1. Fortified with battlements; embattled.

c **1325** *E.E. Allit. P.* B 1183 For þe borȝ watz so bygge baytayled alofte. *c* **1400** *Rom. Rose* 4162 Lest ony tyme it were assayled, Ful wel aboute it was batayled. **1600** Fairfax *Tasso* xiii. xlviii. 244 Built like a batled wall. **1810** Scott *Lady of L.* v. xxix, The castle's battled verge. **1830** Tennyson *Dream Fair Wom.* 220 The valleys of grape-loaded vines that glow Beneath the battled tower.

†**2.** *transf.* Having an edge or outline shaped like a battlement; crenelated. *Obs.*

c **1386** Chaucer *Nonne Pr. T.* 40 His comb was redder than the fyn coral, And batayld, as it were a castel wal. [**1405** *Test. Ebor.* (1836) I. 318 Unum gobellum..cum operculo battellato. **1422** (?) *Ibid.* I. 404, j. murreus..cum ligacione batilde.]

†**battled** ('bæt(ə)ld), *ppl. a.*³ *Obs.* Also 7 **batled, battilled.** [f. battle *v.*³ + -ed.] Of animals: Nourished, fed up, fattened. Of pasture, land; Fertilized, manured. (Commonly *well-battled*.)

1611 Cotgr., *Vne fille bien advenuë*, well proeued, well growne..well batned, or batled. **1616** Surfl. & Markh. *Countr. Farm* 212 Well manured and batled ground. *Ibid.* 311 In a free and well battilled ground.

battledore ('bæt(ə)ldɔə(r)), *sb.* Forms: 5 **batyldoure, -dore, batylledore, (batyndore, badildore), batildure,** 6 **-dore, batil(l)dore, batteldore,** 7 **battledoore,** 6–9 **battledoor,** 6– **battledore.** [Perh. ad. Pr. *batedor* 'beater'; cf. Sp. *batidor* applied to instruments as well as to persons, f. *batir* to beat; Minsheu gives a Sp. *batador*, with the meaning of a beetle used in washing. But historical connexion with these Romanic words is not proved, and the date offers difficulties. If we refer the first part to BATTLE *v.*[4], or to BAT, the *-dore* remains without satisfactory explanation.]

1. A beetle or wooden 'bat' used in washing, also (when made cylindrical) for smoothing out or 'mangling' linen clothes; *hence* also applied to similarly shaped instruments, *e.g.* the paddle of a canoe, a utensil for inserting loaves into an oven, or glass-ware into the kiln, etc.

c **1440** *Promp. Parv.* 27 Batyldoure, or wasshynge betylle, *feretorium.* *c* **1450** in Wülcker *Voc.* /582 *Feritorium*, batyndore. *Ibid.* /601 *Pecten*, batyndore. **1483** *Cath. Angl.* 17 Badildore, batildure, *pecten.* *c* **1555** HARPSFIELD *Divorce Hen. VIII* (1878) 276[She] all to beat her yokemate with a wash-beetle or battledore. **1617** F. MORISON *Itin.* I. 11 Boats of a hollow tree, driuen..by battledores. **1655** *Queen's Clos. Open.* 222 (D.) Rowl them [the gumbals] with battledores into long pieces, and tie them up in knots, and so dry them. **1822** J. PLATTS *Bk. Curios.* 579 A Laundress..turning the clothes up and down with her hand and battledore. **1883** *Knowledge* 22 June 371/2 The loaves are inserted..by means of a flat battledore with a long handle, called a 'peel.'

2. An instrument like a small racket used in playing with a shuttlecock.

1598 FLORIO, *Poletta*, a scoope or batledore to play at tenis with. **1690** LOCKE *Educ.* Wks. 1812 IX. 126 Play-things..as tops, gigs, battledores. **1836–7** DICKENS *Sk. Boz* (1850) 274/2 The shuttlecocks fluttered from the little deal battledores.

b. The game played with this by two persons who strike the shuttlecock to and from each other.

1719 D'URFEY *Pills* (1872) II. 303 Have you seen Battledore play, Where the Shuttlecock flys to and fro one? **1782** COWPER *Let. to Hill* 7 Dec., I..have been playing at battledore and shuttle-cock. **1794** SCOTT in *Lockhart* (1839) I. 311, I hope they are improved at the battledore.

fig. **1879** LOWELL *Orient. Apol.* Poet. Wks. 363 So they two played at wordy battledore.

†**3.** (more fully *battledore-book*): A horn-book; so called from its usual shape. Hence *battledore boy*, an abecedarian. *Obs.* or *dial.*

1693 W. ROBERTSON *Phraseol. Gen.* 215 A battledore book, or Horn-book: *Abecedarium. Ibid.* A Battledore boy or Horn-book-boy. **1697** G. KEITH *2nd Narr. Turner's Hall* 9 G. H. Has Printed..a Battle-dore to teach them to speak true English. **1877** E. PEACOCK *Manley* (*Linc.*) *Gloss.*, *Battledoor*, a piece of cardboard on which was printed the A.B.C., the Lord's prayer, and a few short syllables, employed as a substitute for the horn-book. They were in use here, in dames' schools, thirty years ago. 'He doesn't knaw his A.B.C. fra a battledoor' perhaps refers to this. **1884** MRS. BANKS *In his own Hand* xx, Behold the lad with battledore or book before him.

4. battledore barley: a species of cultivated barley (*Hordeum zeocriton*) with short broad ears, also called *Sprat barley*.

1848 MILBURN in *Jrnl. R. Agric. Soc.* IX. II. 506 The variety of barley usually sown is Chevalier..the 'battledore,' an old variety, is nearly extinct.

5. Phrases. *not to know a B from a battledore* (arch.): to be utterly illiterate; *to say B* (or *Bo!*) *to a battledore* (obs.): to open one's mouth in speech (cf. *to say Bo! to a goose*); hence, *battledore* is alliteratively used along with *B* in various locutions.

1553–87 FOXE *A. & M.* II. 474 He knew not a B from a battledore nor ever a letter of the book. **1592** NASHE *P. Penilesse* 30 b, Now you talke of a Bee, Ile tell you a tale of a Battle-dore. **1599** ——*Lent. Stuffe* Wks. 1885 V. 197 Euery man can say Bee to a Battledore, and write in prayse of Vertue. **1621** BP. MOUNTAGU *Diatribæ* 118 The Clergy of this time were..not able to say bo to a battledore. **1630** J. TAYLOR (Water P.) *Wks.* II. 43/1 Critticks..That of a B. will make a Battledore. **1877** [see 3]. **1884** BLACK *Jud. Shaks.* xxi, Fools that scarce know a B from a battledoor.

'battledore, *v.* [f. prec. sb. (in sense 2).] To drive, toss or fly to and fro.

1858 BUSHNELL *Serm. New Life* 181 Battle-dooring always in opinions and dogmas. **1864** *Daily Tel.* 9 Apr., Honest men were not to be battledored and shuttlecocked thus between names and names.

battle-dress. [f. BATTLE *sb.* + DRESS *sb.* 2.] A soldier's normal 'undress' khaki uniform, consisting essentially of a tunic and trousers. Also *attrib.* and *transf.*

1938 *Times* 1 June 7/3 The experimental 'battle-dress' is being tried on a large scale this year. **1940** *Hutchinson's Pict. Hist. War* 14 Feb.–9 Apr. 93 The men have discarded their kilts for the more suitable battle dress. **1963** *Guardian* 29 Jan. 7/7 A plain, natural shantung dress has a matching battledress top.

†**battleful,** *a.* *Obs.* *rare*$^{-1}$. [f. BATTLE *sb.*[1] + -FUL.] Full of strife or conflict; contentious.

c **1449** PECOCK *Repr.* 348 To seke aftir the surer to him weies than aftir the hardir and the bateilfuller weies.

battlement ('bæt(ə)lmənt), *sb.* Forms: 4–5 **batelment,** 5 **-eillement,** 5–6 **-ilment, -illement, -ylment(e, battilment,** 6– **battlement.** [ME. *bateill-, batayle-, batelment*, a. OF. **bataille-*, **bateillement*. f. *batailler* (= Pr. *batalhar*). OF. had also (later) *batillement*, f. *ba(s)tillier*, whence Caxton's *batillement*: as to the relation of the two forms see BATTLE *v.*[2]]

An indented parapet at the top of a wall, at first used only in fortified buildings for purposes of defence against assailants, but afterwards in the architectural decoration of ecclesiastical and other edifices. The raised parts are called *cops* or *merlons*, the indentations *embrasures* or *crenelles*.

c **1325** *E.E. Allit. P.* B. 1459 Enbaned vnder batelment with bantelles quoynt. **1443** *Test. Ebor.* (1855) II. 89 Ad facturam unius batilment super ecclesiam predictam. **1475** CAXTON *Jason* 100 b, Som ran to the creneaulx or batillements of the walles. **1593** SHAKS. *Rich. II*, III. iii. 52 This Castle's tatter'd Battlements. **1611** BIBLE *Deut.* xxii. 8 When thou buildest a new house, then thou shalt make a battlement for thy roofe. **1762** H. WALPOLE *Vertue's Anecd. Paint.* (1786) I. 169 The battlements of all the said chapels and porches. **1814** SCOTT *Wav.* lxiii, The battlements above the gates were broken and thrown down.

b. *loosely* for 'embattled roof.'

1595 SHAKS. *John* II. i. 375 These scroyles of Anjou.. stand securely on their battlements. **1677** MOXON *Mech. Exerc.* (1703) 157 *Battlement*, a flat Roof or Platform to walk on. But Battlements are more properly Walls build about the Platform to inclose it. **1803** BRISTED *Ped. Tour* II. 470 Presently appeared, upon the battlements above, some female forms, arrayed in white.

c. *transf.* A crenelated brim on cups, etc. **d.** *fig.* The towering summits of the mountains, the roof of the heavens.

1444 *Test. Ebor.* (1855) II. 98 Unam peciam [cup] coopertam cum batelment deauratam. *c* **1530** in Gutch *Coll. Cur.* II. 327 A standing Cuppe withe a Cover and Batilments of silvar. **1667** MILTON *P.L.* I. 742 Thrown by angry Jove Sheer o're the Chrystal Battlements **1860** TYNDALL *Glac.* I. §16. 112 The torn battlements of the mountain.

e. *Comb.*, as *battlement-wise* adv.

1616 SURFL. & MARKH. *Countr. Farm* 512 A smooth board, six or seuen ynches square, and cut battlement-wise at each end.

'battlement, *v.* [f. prec. sb.] To furnish or decorate with battlements.

1603 [see next]. **1884** *Pall Mall G.* 18 July 11/2 It is proposed to..battlement the top of the wall.

battlemented, *ppl. a.* [f. prec. sb. or vb.] Furnished with or surmounted by battlements.

1603 FLORIO *Montaigne* II. xii. (1632) 336 The walls or battlements of an high tower or steeple, if they be battlemented. **1826** SCOTT *Woodstock* (1832) 179 A battlemented portal. **1873** G. DAVIES *Mount. & Mere* xxiv. 213 Lurid flames seem springing from above the battlemented rocks.

†**battleness.** *Obs.* [f. BATTLE *a.* + -NESS.] The quality of being 'battle,' fertility.

1598 FLORIO, *Vbertà*, fertilitie, fruitfulnes, battlenes.

'battleplane. [f. BATTLE *sb.* + PLANE *sb.*[3], after *battleship*.] An aeroplane designed for use in warfare, carrying a gun or guns, bombs, etc.

[**1915** *Daily Express* 15 Oct. 4/3 The French Government has now no objection to the world at large knowing that battle-aeroplanes of large size are being built in France.] *Ibid.* 16 Dec. 4/5 Genuine battleplanes were first heard of officially in the German communiqués. **1917** 'CONTACT' *Airman's Outings* 180 The Fokkers were satisfactorily dealt with by the de Haviland and the F.E. 'battleplane', as the newspapers of the period delighted to call it. **1917** *Observer* 11 Mar. 10/3 The effort of each side is bent on producing not giant battleplanes but faster and better climbing small craft.

battler[1] ('bætlə(r)). Forms: 3 **batelur,** 5 **batailler,** 9 **battler.** [ME. *batelur*, a. OF. *batailleor, -eur*, agent-noun f. *bataillier* to BATTLE; also ME. *batailler*, a. OF. *bataillier*, f. *bataille* BATTLE. In mod. Eng. perh. directly f. BATTLE *v.*] **1.** One who battles or fights; a warrior, a fighter.

c **1300** *K. Alis.* 1433 He wan of that lond the honor, And mony noble batelur. **1489** CAXTON *Faytes of A.* I. x. 28 The right worthy and preu batailler Cena the romain. **1862** *Q. Rev.* Apr. 410 Rough battlers with the world.

2. a. *spec.* A swagman (cf. SWAG *sb.* 12 (b). *Austral.*

1900 H. LAWSON *Over Sliprails* 6 We're only 'battlers', and me and my mate, pickin' up crumbs by the wayside. **1928** *Bulletin* (Sydney) 15 Feb. 21/1 Last time the poor old battler jus' struggled to our place. **1961** 'J. DANVERS' *Living came First* vii. 116 'Nice bloke, Marty,' added the swagman .., 'always got a crust for a battler, an' a kind word.'

b. Used in Australia and New Zealand in various other senses and shades of meaning (see quots.), esp. a person struggling against odds. Cf. quot. 1862 under sense 1.

1898 *Bulletin* (Sydney) 17 Dec. (*Red Page*), A *bludger* is about the lowest grade of human thing, and is a brothel bully... A *battler* is the feminine. **1941** K. TENNANT *Battlers* xvi. 165 They were a new sort of people, the travellers; and he belonged to them... He was a 'battler'... They would still have a job on their hands clearing out the battlers; men and women who could face a desert and live off the country, travelling in small mobs. **1943** J. A. W. BENNETT in *Amer. Speech* XVIII. 88 [In N.Z.] a *toiler* or *battler* is a hard, conscientious worker—both are used with a shade of condescension. **1943** BAKER *Dict. Austral. Slang* (ed. 3) 9 *Battler*, a small-time hawker; a hard-up horse trainer struggling along in the game; a broken-down punter who still continues betting;..anyone who struggles for existence. **1962** *Listener* 18 Jan. 128/1 Ditchburn is another Australian, a 'battler' as we say, a man who knows what he wants. **1964** D. HORNE *Lucky Country*: Australia 25 Australians love a 'battler', an underdog who is fighting the top dog, although their veneration for him is likely to pass if he comes out from under.

†**'battler**[2]. *Obs. rare.* Also 7 **batteller.** [f. BATTLE *v*[4] + -ER[1].]

1. One who beats with a 'bat' or 'battledore.'

1662 FULLER *Worthies* IV. 49 Capping anciently set fifteen distinct Callings on work..9. Dyers. 10. Battellers. 11. Shearers. **1720** *Stow's Surv.* (Strype 1754) II. v. xvi. 318/1 Carders, spinners, knitters..dyers, Battlers, shearers.

2. A small bat to play at ball with.

?*c* **1650** HALLIWELL refers to HOWELL.

3. A utensil for battling clothes. [see BATLER.]

battler[3], var. BATTELER (at Oxford).

battleship ('bæt(ə)lʃɪp). orig. *U.S.* [Shortening of *line-of-battle ship*: see BATTLE *sb.* 12.] A line-of-battle ship; a warship of the largest and most heavily armoured class.

1794 D. HUMPHREYS *Poem on Industry* 20 The dock equips, With batt'ries black and strong, the battleships. **1834** GLASCOCK *Naval Sk. Bk.* I. 185 A bluff weather-beaten captain of a battle ship. *Ibid.* 235 A battle-ship's bowsprit. **1845** R. FORD *Handbk. Trav. Spain* I. III. 363 Like the spars of a storm-wrecked battle-ship. **1884** *Marine Engineer* 1 Apr. 4/2 The very heavily-armed battle-ship. **1959** *Chambers's Encycl.* II. 162/1 The battleship has been the basic unit in all navies.

b. ***cruiser-battleship*** or ***battleship cruiser***: a battleship of the type designed for speed, less heavily armoured than a ship of the line.

1909 *Whitaker's Alm.* 681/2 Modern vessels of this class are no longer, save in official phraseology, 'armoured cruisers', but 'cruiser-battleships', or 'cruiser-Dreadnoughts'. **1909** *Westm. Gaz.* 18 Mar. 7/2 Armoured cruisers, or 'battleship cruisers', as they have been popularly termed.

c. *attrib.* and *Comb.* **battleship grey** (or **gray**), a slightly bluish grey colour often used in painting battleships.

1834 GLASCOCK *Naval Sk. Bk.* I. 154 To ascertain 'the difference 'twixt the rigging and palaver of a methody parson, and the togs and talk of a reg'lar-built battle-ship preacher'. **1901** *Westm. Gaz.* 8 Aug. 6/1 To choose his own time and place for the battleship action. **1904** *Ibid.* 11 Feb. 8/2 The battleship strength of the Russians at Port Arthur. **1908** *Ibid.* 11 Feb. 3/3 When the Dreadnought appeared battleship building in foreign yards paused. **1908** *Daily Chron.* 21 Aug. 1/7 The American battleship fleet. **1916** *Daily Colonist* (Victoria, B.C.) 1 July 12/3 The colors include battleship grey. **1938** L. MACNEICE *Earth Compels* 54 Nights with stars or closely interleaved with battleship grey or plum.

battlesome ('bæt(ə)lsəm), *a.*[1] *rare.* [f. as BATTLER[3] + -SOME.] Given to fighting, quarrelsome.

1877 *Daily News* 10 Nov. 6/1 To be strong, France needs not be battlesome. **1888** *Harper's Mag.* Apr. 690 Of battlesome wit..the author has so much of his own that he has given some to all of his characters.

†**'battlesome,** *a.*[2] *Obs. rare.* [f. BATTLE *v.*[3] + -SOME.] Nutritious.

1627 J. CARTER *Plaine & Comp. Expos.* 23 The most foysonable and battlesome word, and Ordinances of God.

battle-worthy ('bæt(ə)l,wɜːðɪ), *a.* [f. BATTLE *sb.* + -WORTHY; after *seaworthy*.] Fit for use in battle. Hence **'battle-,worthiness.**

1889 MUNDELLA in *Hansard* CCCXXXIII. 119 Really good,..battle-worthy swords. **1892** *Pall Mall G.* 13 Sept. 2/2 If the ship is not battle-worthy, the best thing is to sell her or break her up at once. **1904** *Times* (weekly ed.) 1 Jan. 7/1 Battle-worthiness—a..compendious term, including all the essential qualities required of a vessel intended to fight in line. **1940** *Illustr. London News* CXCVI. 840/1 What the Germans did was to concentrate all their tanks which were still battle-worthy on one or two roads. **1943** *Jane's All World's Aircraft* p. iii/2 Experience played no small part in making the..aeroplanes and aero-engines battle-worthy.

battling ('bætlɪŋ), *vbl. sb.*[1] [f. BATTLE *v.*[1].] The action of the vb. BATTLE; fighting, conflict.

c **1300** *K. Alis.* 100 Nyne and twenty ryche kynges, To make on him bataylynges. **1860** FROUDE *Hist. Eng.* VI. 361 After forty years of battling with the stormy waters. **1878** P. BAYNE *Purit. Rev.* i. 10 The United Kingdom is now what the battlings of the seventeenth century made it.

attrib. **1856** KANE *Arc. Exp.* II. xxix. 289 The familiar localities of the whalers' battling-ground.

†**'battling,** *vbl. sb.*[2] *Obs.* Forms: 4–5 **battaillyng,** 4–6 **-alyng,** 5 **batayling,** 6 **bateling, -elyng, -elling, battalling, -alyng, -elyng,** 7 **battling.** [f. BATTLE *v.*[2] + -ING[1].]

1. The furnishing with battlements, embattling.

1506 in *MS. Reg. Test. Ebor.* VI. 173 [Robt. Drayton.. leaves 30*s.*] to the edificacion of a new rooff wt batelling of the church. **1527** *Lanc. & Chesh. Wills* (1854) 5, I giff to the batelyng of the church of Northen xxxiijs. iiij*d.*

2. *concr.* Battlement work, battlements.

1375 BARBOUR *Bruce* IV. 136 That batalyng [*v.r.* battaillyng], withouten dout, Saffit thair liffis. **1430** LYDG. *Chron. Troy* II. xi, To reyse a wall With batayling and crestes marciall. **1540** *Coventry Acc.* in T. Sharp *Dissert.* (1825) 19 For mendyng the bateling yn the toppe of the pagent, viij*d.* **1620** SHELTON *Quix.* IV. xi. II. 140 Two foot broad of a Plank on the Battlings.

†**battling, batteling,** *vbl. sb.*[3] *Obs.* Also 7 **batling.** [f. BATTLE *v.*[3] + -ING[1].]

1. The action or process of causing to grow or thrive; nourishing, feeding; fertilizing, manuring of land. **b.** *intr.* A growing fat or thriving.

1616 SURFL. & MARKH. *Countr. Farm* 218 You shall helpe it [the earth] by such manner of batteling as hath beene spoken of. **1650** FULLER *Pisgah* II. viii. 177 A jolly dame no doubt, as appears by the well-battling of the plump boy. *Ibid.* II. x. 217 The well batling of the Giants bred in Philistia..attests the fertility of their soil.

2. That which 'battles' or nourishes; feeding, food: **a.** that which nourishes animals; food, victuals; **b.** that which fertilizes land; manure.

1601 HOLLAND *Pliny* I. 508 The fruit it selfe of the earth is a batling to the earth. **1611** COTGR., *Morche*, food, victualls, cheere, batling. **1616** SURFL. & MARKH. *Countr. Farm* 371 Anie other sort of dung or batling. **1632** SHERWOOD, Battling, *vivres, manger, morche.*

ˈ**battling,** *vbl. sb.*[4] *Obs.* exc. *dial.* [f. BATTLE *v.*[4] + -ING[1].] The action of beating with a 'bat,' battler, battledore, etc.; in quot. *attrib.* ***battling-bench, -board, -stick.***

1519 HORMAN *Vulg.* 239b, Fet IIII. battyllyng roddis [*rudiculas*] to beate this wolle. **1846** J. J. HOOPER *Taking Census* in *adv. Simon Suggs* etc. (1851) II. 183 John Green's sister..goes to her battlin bench. **1848** —— *Ride with Old Kit Kuncker* in *Widow Rugby's Husb.* etc. (1851) 96 What a devil of a paddlin' the old woman gin him with the battlin'-stick. **1878** HALLIWELL *Dict.*, *Battling-stone*, a large smooth-faced stone..by the side of a stream, on which washerwomen beat their linen to clean it. *North.* **1887** *Harper's Mag.* July 272/1 The splay legged battling-boards fastened themselves into the earth under the blows of the bats.

battling (ˈbætlɪŋ), *ppl. a.*[1] [f. BATTLE *v.*[1] + -ING[2].] Fighting, engaged in conflict; combative.

1787 J. WOLCOTT (P. Pindar) *Ode upon O.* Wks. 1794 I. 421 The mighty battl'ing Broughtons and the Slacks. **1834** R. MUDIE *Brit. Birds* (1841) II. 51 The gold-finch..is somewhat of a battling bird. **1840** CARLYLE *Heroes* iv. (1858) 236 The much-enduring, hard-worn, ever-battling man.

†ˈ**battling,** *ppl. a.*[2] *Obs.* Also 7 **batling.** [f. BATTLE *v.*[3] + -ING[2].]

(As manure *battled* pasture, or made it *battle*, and as *battling* pasture *battled* the cattle that fed or *battled* on it, it is in some cases not possible to be sure whether 'fertile' or 'fertilizing' is the notion intended.)

1. Nourishing or fattening to cattle; *hence*, fertile, productive, fruitful.

1548 [see BATTLE *v.*[3] 1.] **1565** GOLDING *Ovid's Met.* VII. (1593) 164 [It] tooke roote And thriving in the battling soyle in burgeons foorth did shoote. *c* **1590** GREENE *Fr. Bacon* ix. 4 The battling pastures lade [*v.r.* laid] with kine. **1662** FULLER *Worthies* (1840) I. 365 The fair pasture nigh Haddon..so incredibly battling of cattle.

2. *gen.* Nourishing, making to grow or thrive; fertilizing to soil; nutritious to man.

1555 *Fardle Facions* II. viii. 164 The battling breathe of the gentle Weast winde. **1565** GOLDING *Ovids's Met.* XV. (1593) 359 Udders full of batling milke. **1610** HOLLAND *Camden's Brit.* I. 556 A batling fruitfull slugh, or humour.

battlous: see BATTAILOUS *a.*

ˈ**battoe,** freq. U.S. var. of BATEAU, BATTEAU. *Obs.*

1711 *Boston News-Let.* 23–30 July 2/1 All our Battoes are finished. **1770** WASHINGTON *Diaries* (1925) I. 381 Got the Battoe, and the two Boats round to the Mill with Stone. **1801** *Austin Papers* (1924) I. 72 Passed a Battoe in from New Orleans.

Hence **battoe man, battoeing** *vbl. sb.*

1756 in *Doc. Hist. N.Y. State* (1849) I. 477 Upwards of 500 Battoe Men were sent different Ways into the Woods. **1760** in *Essex Inst. Hist. Coll.* XX. 199 This Day ye Battoue men marched off. *Ibid.*, To Day there was a Draught out of our Company for battowing from fort Miller to fort Edward.

battological (bætəˈlɒdʒɪkəl), *a.* [f. Gr. *βαττολόγος* a stammerer, one who repeats himself needlessly + -ICAL. The Gr. word is f. the personal name *Βάττος* (see the story in Herodotus, IV. 155) + *-λογος* speaking, speaker.] Given to battology.

1863 C. READE *Hard Cash* II. xiv. 200 The battological author.

battologist (bæˈtɒlədʒɪst). [f. as prec. + -IST.] One who needlessly repeats the same thing.

1653 GAUDEN *Hierasp.* 384 What perfect Battologists they are; what circles they make..in their Prayings.

battologize (-lədʒaɪz), *v.*; also 8 **-ise.** [f. as prec. + -IZE; cf. Gr. *βαττολογέ-ειν*.]

1. *trans.* To keep repeating (a word or phrase).

1634 SIR T. HERBERT *Trav.* (1677) 191 Battologizing the names *Allough Whoddaw* and *Mohumet* very often.

2. *intr.* To repeat words or phrases with needless iteration; to multiply words.

1712 SIR P. KING *Const. Prim. Ch.* I. ii. (1713) 37 When we pray, let us not battologise. *a* **1716** BLACKALL *Wks.* 1723 I. 480 Do not Battologize in your prayers, says Our Saviour.

battology (bæˈtɒlədʒɪ). Also 7 **-logie, -logee.** [ad. Gr. *βαττολογία* vain repetition, n. of quality f. *βαττολόγος*: see BATTOLOGICAL.] A needless and tiresome repetition in speaking or writing.

a **1603** T. CARTWRIGHT *Confut. Rhem. N.T.* (1618) 142 The Marginall notes..are meere Battologies of loathsome repetitions. **1765** TUCKER *Lt. Nat.* II. 440 We are warned against the battology or vain repetitions of the heathens. **1818** SOUTHEY in *Q. Rev.* XIX. 96 Away then with..the battology of statistics.

batton, -oon(e, -oun(e: see BATON, -OON.

‖**battue** (baty). Also 9 **battu.** [F. (= Pr. *batuda*, It. *battuta*, L. type *batūta*) 'a beating, a beat-up,' sb. formed on fem. pa. ppl. of *battre* to beat. (Analogous to those in -ATA, -ADE.)]

1. The driving of game from cover (by beating the bushes, etc. in which they lodge) to a point where a number of sportsmen wait to shoot them.

1816 *Gentl. Mag.* LXXXVI. I. 414 The keen Sportsman ..and a favoured few, on a set day, have the Grand Battu. **1860** *All Y. Round* No. 71. 485 A battue is a contrivance for killing the largest quantity of game in the smallest time, with the least amount of trouble, by a small select party.

attrib. **1849** COBDEN *Speeches* 52 That modern innovation of battue shooting, which was not known in 1790.

2. *transf.* **a.** A beat up, a thorough search. **b.** Wholesale slaughter, *esp.* of unresisting crowds.

1854 CDL. WISEMAN *Fabiola* I. viii. 43 Ordered a grand general battue through every part of the house where Syra had been. **1864** BURTON *Scot Abr.* I. iv. 162 The great battue of St. Bartholomew's Day.

3. The game thus driven from cover.

1849 in SMART.

‖**batture** (‖batyr, bəˈtjʊə(r)). [a. F. *batture* bottom of a sandy or rocky shallow.] A river- or sea-bed elevated to the surface. Also *attrib.*

1856 OLMSTED *Slave States* 464 The great capability of our batture lands for the production of rice. **1860** J. KENNEDY *W. Wirt* I. xix. 292 Constructed certain works upon the beach, or batture, as it was called.

‖**battuta** (batˈtuːta). *Mus.* [It. n. of action f. *battere* to beat: cf. BATTUE.] The beating of time.

1819 in *Pantologia*. **1880** GROVE *Dict. Mus.* s.v.,'A batuta,' like 'a tempo,' means a return to the strict beat.

batty (ˈbætɪ), *a.* Also 7 **battie.** [f. BAT *sb.*[1] + -Y[1].]

1. Of or belonging to a bat, bat-like.

1590 SHAKS. *Mids. N.* III. ii. 365 Sleepe With leaden legs, and Battie-wings doth creepe. **1883** E. H. A. *Tribes on Frontier* 69 The fruit-bat or flying-fox..would not be a bat at all but for..a strong batty smell.

2. 'Balmy', 'dotty'. (Cf. BAT *sb.*[1] 1 b.) *colloq.* or *slang.*

1903 A. L. KLEBERG *Slang Fables from Afar* iii. 23 She.. acted so queer..that he decided she was Batty. **1917** J. FARNOL *Definite Object* iii. 32, I mean, is 'e batty? **1926** *British Weekly* 25 Nov. 242/3 He's a bit batty every now and anon. **1934** R. MACAULAY *Going Abroad* vii. 57 He'd go batty with rage.

batune, obs. f. BATOON, BATON, esp. in *Her.*

batus: see BATH *sb.*[3]

†ˈ**batwell,** *a. Obs. rare*[−1]. [f. *bat-* (see BATTEN *v.*[1]) + WELL.] = BATFUL, BATTLE *a.*

1534 WHITTINTON *Tullyes Offices* I. (1540) 22 Groundes that be batwell..brynge moche more fruyte than they receyved.

batwing: see BAT *sb.*[1]

ˈ**batwoman** [after BATMAN[2].] A member of one of the women's auxiliary services performing the duties of a batman.

1941 *Aeronautics* Oct. 60/3 R.A.F. officers in future are to have the services of members of the W.A.A.F. for duties which have been carried out hitherto by batmen. These 'batwomen' are being trained in Service methods. **1944** 'N. SHUTE' *Pastoral* i. 4 The W.A.A.F. batwoman found him sitting so when she brought in his tea.

batyl alcohol (ˈbætɪl ˈælkəhɒl). [ad. G. *batyl-alkohol* (M. Tsujimoto and Y. Toyama 1922, in *Chem. Umschau* XXIX. 36/1), f. mod.L. *Batis* genus of fishes (Gr. *βατ-ίς* flat fish) + -YL.] A colourless crystalline alcohol, $C_{21}H_{44}O_3$, found in many shark and ray liver oils.

1922 *Chem. Abstr.* 1513 The formula $C_{20}H_{42}O_3$ was selected to represent this satd. alc. and the name *batyl alcohol* given to it. **1955** *Sci. News Let.* 19 Feb. 121/3 Batyl alcohol promises to become a prized material for possible protection against atomic radiation.

‖**batz** (bæts). Also 7 **batte,** 8 **bat.** [Ger. *batz*, *batze*; prob. taken as a plural, *bats*, whence as sing. *bat.* 17–18th c.] A small coin worth four kreuzers in Switzerland and South Germany; originally having as device the bear of Berne, where it was first coined.

1625 tr. *Gonsalvio's Sp. Inquis.* 73 Halfe a riall..is as much as a dutch batte, and is worth..3 pence sterling. **1753** CHAMBERS *Cycl. Supp.*, *Bat*, in commerce, a small base silver coin, current in divers parts of Germany and Switzerland at different prices. **1753** HANWAY *Trav.* (1762) I. VII. xciv. 434 The currency of such a coin as their bats and driers must be detrimental. **1756** NUGENT *Gr. Tour* II. 283 In Franconia, you meet with batzes, eighteen of which make a dollar.

bau-: for forms so beginning see also BAW-.

baubee, -bie, variants of BAWBEE.

baubish, ? for BABISH *a.*

a **1641** BP. MOUNTAGU *Acts & Mon.* (1642) 219 It is as baubish a discourse as the former.

bauble (ˈbɔːb(ə)l). For forms see the senses. [Probably two original words are here blended: (1) OF. *babel*, also *baubel* 'child's toy, trinket, plaything'; whence also the dim. *baubelet* (Littré, s.v. *babiole*), *beubelet* (Godef.), adopted in Eng. at a very early date as BEAUBELET, q.v. The etymology of the F. is uncertain: it is very doubtful whether it can be connected with mod.F. *babiole* in same sense, which Littré thinks derived from a root *bab-*, appearing in L. *babulus* babbler, fool, It. *babbeo*, *babbano* silly, Pr. *babau* fool, and perh. in Eng. *baby*. (2) ME. *babyll*, *babulle*, *bable*, translated *librilla*, is evidently connected with '*bablyn* to waver or oscillate, *librillare*,' '*babelynge* wavering, *oscillatio*, *librillacio*'; see BABBLE *v.* 5, BABBLING *vbl. sb.* 3, which has been suggested to be a frequentative derivative of *bab* or BOB *v.* It must, in any case, be distinct from the OF. word. But the 'fool's bauble' (see sense 4) may, so far as evidence goes, be from either, according as it was named from its shape or its purpose, or may blend the two notions; it has certainly been associated phonetically and in idea with the 'toy' senses, and has probably coloured the later use of these, in which 'childish' and 'foolish' are united.

If sense 1 has no connexion with the 'fool's bauble,' it would be better treated as a distinct word under main-form BABLE.]

†**1.** An instrument consisting of a stick with a mass of lead fixed or suspended at one end, used for weighing, and apparently for other purposes. Forms: **babyll(e, babulle,** 5–6 **bable.** *Obs.*

The *Catholicon* explains *Pegma*,'baculus cum massa plumbi in summitate pendente, et, ut dicit Cornutus, tali baculo scenici ludebant.' The *Ortus Voc.* explains *Librilla*, 'instrumentum librandi, idem est percutiendi lapides in castra, i. *mangonus*, a bable, or a dogge malyote.' It is not easy to say in which of these senses *pegma* and *librilla* corresponded to 'bable.'

c **1440** *Promp. Parv.* 20 Babulle or bable (*v.r.* babyll) *librilla*, *pegma*. *c* **1475** in Wright *Voc.* 263/2 *Babrilla* [? *Librilla*], dong [? dog] babylle. **1483** *Cath. Angl.* 17 Babylle, *pigma*. **1570** LEVINS *Manip.* /124 Bable, *pegma*.

†**2.** A child's plaything or toy. (Now *obs.*, except as coloured by 3, 4). Forms: 4 **babel,** 5 **babulle,** 6 **babyl, babell,** 6–7 **bable,** 7–8 **bawble,** 7– **bauble** (first in Shaks. Folio 1623).

c **1460** J. RUSSELL *Bk. Nurture* in *Babees Bk.* (1868) 117 He þat no good can..He shalle neuer y-thryve, þerfore take to hym a babulle. *c* **1525** SKELTON *Replyc.* 175 Marked in your cradels To beare fagottes for babyls. **1590** NASHE *Pasquils Apol.* 12 To beguile my argument as women do their children..when they giue them a bable to play withall. **1611** COTGR., *Poupée*, a babie; a puppet or bable. **1652** *Sectary Dissect.* 24 Give the childe his bable before he cry. **1791** COWPER *Yardly Oak* 17 Thou wast a bauble once, a cup and ball, Which babes might play with. **1814** SOUTHEY *Roderick* XIX. 70 The little hand which there Played with the bauble.

3. A showy trinket or ornament such as would please a child, a piece of finery of little worth, a pretty trifle, a gewgaw. Forms as in 2.

c **1320** *Pol. Songs* 335 Nu nis no squier of pris..But if that he bere a babel and a long berd. **1581** J. BELL *Haddon's Answ. Osor.* 41 b, To abandone images out of Churches..to finde no want of any such paynted bables. **1584** R. W. *Three Ladies Lond.* in Hazl. *Dodsl.* VI. 276 Amber, jet, coral, crystal, and every such bable That is slight, pretty, and pleasant. **1596** SHAKS. *Tam. Shrew* IV. iii. 82 Paltrie cap..a bauble, a silken pie. **1621** BURTON *Anat. Mel.* II. iii. II (1651) 315 Coats of armes..and such like bables. **1740** H. WALPOLE *Corr.* I. 69 A little box of bawbles that I have bought for presents. **1740-61** MRS. DELANY *Life & Corr.* (1861) III. 386, I send you enclosed what I am sure you will value above a Bath bauble,—the picture of a friend. **1802** MAR. EDGEWORTH *Moral T.* (1816) I. iv. 18 Forester looked upon a watch as a useless bauble. **1803** BRISTED *Pedest. Tour* I. 393 We treat women as if they were pretty idiots, little baubles. **1843** LYTTON *Last Bar.* I. iii, The knight's baubles become the aldermans badges.

4. A baton or stick, surmounted by a fantastically carved head with asses' ears, carried by the Court Fool or jester of former days as a mock emblem of office. Forms: 4 **babulle,** 5–6 **babel, babyll,** 6–7 **bable,** 7– **bauble,** (first in Shaks. Folio 1623).

?*c* **1370** *K. Robt. Cysille* 161 in Hazl. *E.P.P.* I. 275 Thou art a fole, seyde the aungelle,..Thy babulle schalle be thy dygnyté. **1393** GOWER *Conf.* III. 224 The Kinges fole.. That with his babel plaide. **1509** BARCLAY *Shyp of Folys* (1874) I. 89 Such is a fole and well worthy a babyll. **1588** SHAKS. *Tit. A.* v. i. 79 An Ideot holds his Bauble for a God. **1611** COTGR. s.v. *Fol*, If all fooles bables bore, wood would be very deere. **1821** SCOTT *Kenilw.* xxv, The licensed jester ..brandished his bauble.

b. *allusively.*

1653 S. MEWCE in *Hatton Corr.* (1878) [Cromwell] then comanded that bable to bee taken awaye. *a* **1676**

WHITELOCKE *Mem.* (Bute MS.), He bid one of his soldiers take away that fooles bable, the Mace.

†**c.** ***to deserve the bauble; to give (a person) the bauble***: to make a fool of, befool. *Obs.*

1599 *Broughton's Lett.* v. 17 Not sparing the holy fathers of the Church..but giuing some the bable..befooling the penner of the *Creede.* **1606** DAY *Ile of Guls* (1881) 107 If in any thing your wits deserue the bable, tis in that.

5. In various transf. or fig. senses (from 2, 3, coloured by 4): **a.** A childish or foolish matter or affair; a piece of childish foolery.

1579 FULKE *Heskins's Parl.* 456 Their *Agnus Dei*, their graines of the Trinitie, and such other gaudes and bables. **1583** GOLDING *Calvin on Deut.* cci. 628 A sort of pelting babies or ceremonies. **1613** WITHER *Sat. Vanity* in Southey *Comm.-pl. Bk.* Ser. II. (1849) 302 If the salt fall towards them at table, Or any such like superstitious bable, Their mirth is spoil'd. **1671** *True Non-Conf.* Pref., To apologize for the seriousnesse that I have used in confuting such a trifling bable. **1838** MACAULAY in Trevelyan *Life* (1876) II. i. 29 The Right Honourable before my name is a bauble.

†**b.** *fig.* A childish or foolish person, a silly trifler. *Obs.* (In quot. 1606 perh. = *babbler.*)

a **1606** SIR J. MELVIL *Diary* 37, I perceivit at annes yat I was bot an ignorant babble. **1604** SHAKS. *Oth.* IV. i. 140 Thither comes the Bauble, and falls me thus about my neck. **1728** MORGAN *Algiers* I. Pref. 17 Nor can I bring [the Coxcomb] in without an apology for interrupting my worthy Audience with a Bauble of his Nothingness.

†**c.** 'A mere toy'; applied to a machine, etc., considered too small or weak for actual work. *Obs.*

1611 SHAKS. *Cymb.* III. i. 27 His Shipping (Poore ignorant Baubles)..Like Egge-shels mou'd vpon their Surges. **1615** J. TAYLOR (Water P.) *Seiges of Jerus.* in Farr *S.P.* (1848) 303 Jehovah with a puff was able To make ambitious Babel but a bable. **1748** ANSON *Voy.* II. iv. 168 It was impossible such a bawble as that could pass round Cape Horn.

d. A thing or article of no value, a paltry piece of rubbish.

1634 J. TAYLOR (Water P.) *Gt. Eater Kent* 12 The Spanish potato he holds as a bable, and the Italian figge he esteemes as poyson. **1685** TEMPLE *Gardening* Wks. 1731 I. 184 Of Figs..the White, the Blue, and the Tawny: The last is very small, bears ill, and I think but a Bawble. **1871** MACDUFF *Mem. Patmos* xiv. 195 Are all earthly joys, and honours, and pleasures a bauble, compared with..the splendours of immortality?

6. *attrib.* = 'toy-,' as in ***bauble boat, coach***, etc.

1606 SHAKS. *Tr. & Cr.* I. iii. 35 How many shallow bauble Boates dare saile vpon her patient brest. **1790** COWPER *Mothers's Pict.* 50 Delighted with my bauble coach. **1873** BROWNING *Red Cott. Night-c.* 706 Yonder bauble world Of silvered glass.

7. *Comb.* **bauble-bearer**, a court-fool or jester. (The quot. may mean *babble-bearer* story teller.)

1535 LYNDESAY *Sat. Three Estates* 2607 Thir babil-beirers and thir bairds.

†**'bauble,** *v. Obs.* [f. prec. sb.] *intr.* To trifle.

1608 ARMIN *Nest Ninn.* (1880) 50 That musically fret their time in idle baubling.

†**'baublery.** *Obs.* In 6 bablerie, babelerie, babelry. [f. as prec. + -RY.] Childish foolery, trifling business. See also BABBLERY, BABERY, BABOONERY, all liable to contact of form and sense.

1583 STUBBES *Anat. Abus.* (1877) 81 These new toyes..fond deuyces and childish babelries (new fashions I should say). *Ibid.* (1595) M ij b, Papers, wherein is painted some babelerie or other of imagerie worke, and these they call my Lord of Misrule's badges. [See also BABBLERY.]

†**baubling** ('bɔːblɪŋ), *a. Obs.* [f. BAUBLE *sb.* or ? *v.* + -ING.] Trifling, contemptible, paltry.

1601 SHAKS. *Twel. N.* V. i. 57 A bawbling Vessell was he Captaine of. **1849** DE QUINCEY *Mail-Coach* in *Blackw. Mag.* LXVI. 496 But a baubling schooner.

baubyn, obs. form of BABOON.

bauch, baugh (bɑːx, bɑːf), *a. Sc.* [perh. a. ON. *bágr*, uneasy, poor, hard up; cf. also *bagr*, awkward, clumsy.] Weak, poor, pithless, without substance or stamina; 'indifferent,' 'sorry,' 'shaky.' Hence **bauchly** *adv.*, **bauchness.**

a **1560** ROLLAND *Crt. Venus* IV. 355 Thocht he and I throw play fell in bawch pleid. *a* **1603** SIR J. MELVIL *Diary* 37 He fond me bauche in the latin toung. **1728** RAMSAY *Gent. Sheph.* Poems (1844) 41 Without estate A youth, though sprung frae kings, looks bauch and blate. **1866** *N. Brit. Daily Mail* 9 Mar., Though the ice was rather baugh. **1723** MᶜWARD *Contend. Faith* 155 (JAM.) How bluntly and bauchly soever the matter be handled.

¶ The north. Eng. dial. form is *baff*, as in ***baff week***, 'hard-up week.'

1885 *Weekly Times* 21 Aug. 9/2 The workers in collieries receive their pay once a fortnight, and call the intervening no-pay week 'baff-week.' The expression 'as long as a baff-week' has become proverbial among them.

bauchill, Sc. var. BACUL, staff, crosier.

1535 STEWART *Cron. Scotl.* II. 468 On buke and bauchill so oft is mensworne.

bauchle, bachle ('bɑːx(ə)l). *Sc.* [Etymol. unknown; ? connected with BAUCH.]

1. An old shoe used as a slipper, or worn down at the heel, which causes the wearer to shamble.

1787 W. TAYLOR *Scots Poems* 4 (JAM.) Thro' my auld bachle peep'd my muckle tae. **1868** G. MACDONALD *R. Falconer* II. 33 My sins are jist like muckle bauchles upo' my feet, and winna lat me [come].

2. A shambler, a ne'er-do-well.

1829 HOGG *Sheph. Cal.* II. 195 He'll be but a bauchle in this world and a backsitter in the neist.

†**bauchle, bachle,** *v. Sc. Obs.* [? f. BAUCH = 'to treat as bauch': apparently the original or one of the sources of BAFFLE.] *trans.* To subject to disgrace or ignominy, treat with contumely, vilify; = BAFFLE 1, 2; also *absol.*

c **1470** HENRY *Wallace* VIII. 723 He..Rapreiffit Eduuard ..off this thing, Bawchillyt his seyll, blew out on that fals king, as a tyrand. **1496** *Seal of Cause for Hammermen* (JAM.) In bachlying of the Hammyrmenis work..and dishonouring of our said burgh. *c* **1550** SIR J. BALFOUR *Practicks* (JAM.) He at ane inconvenient time bauchlit and reprovit.

bauckie-bird: see BAWKIE-BIRD.

baucyne, baud, obs. ff. BAUSON, BAWD.

baud (bəʊd, bɔːd). *Telegr.* and *Computing.* [From the name of J. M. E. *Baudot* (1845–1903), a French engineer, who invented a telegraph printing system (*Baudot code, system*).] **1.** The unit of speed of telegraphic code transmission, the number of bauds being the reciprocal of the duration in seconds of the unit interval. (Freq. used in *sing.* with pl. sense.)

Often equivalent to 1 bit per second.

[**1929** *Documents de la deuxième réunion du comité consultatif international des communications télégraphiques à Berlin 1929* 115 L'avis que la vitesse de transmission soit exprimée par l'inverse de la valeur de l'intervalle élémentaire mesurée en secondes; que la vitesse de transmission d'un intervalle par seconde soit appelée baud, pour honorer la mémoire du grand télégraphiste Emile Baudot.] **1932** *P.O. Electr. Engin. Jrnl.* XXV. 262/2 It has been proposed to use the duration of the 'unit' element to define the speed of transmission of successive signals. According to this suggestion the speed is defined as N 'Bauds' where the duration of the unit element is equal to 1/N seconds. **1934** A. T. STARR *Electr. Circuits & Wave Filters* xii. 345 The most usual telegraph system of to-day is the Baudot code... The speed of the system is said to be (1/τ') bauds: thus if the duration of an element is 1/60 sec., the speed is 60 bauds. **1954** *Electronic Engin.* XXVI. 228/1 For speeds up to 120 bauds twelve channels..are normally grouped together. **1961** *Flight* LXXX. 428/1 Of particular interest..is the use of..land lines to achieve high information rates of up to 3,600 bauds. **1969** J. MARTIN *Telecommunications & Computer* xi. 204 The term 'bauds' is sometimes taken to mean 'bits per second'. While this is true with many lines because they use two-state signaling, it is not true in general. **1977** *Sci. Amer.* Oct. 16/1 (Advt.), It receives computer instructions at any of eight speeds from 75 to 2400 baud, half or full duplex. **1984** *Which Micro?* Dec. 26 (Advt.), The MSX system can load and save data onto cassette at 1200 or 2400 baud.

2. Special Comb.: **baud rate**, a rate of transmission expressed in bauds.

1968 *Bell Syst. Techn. Jrnl.* XLVII. 1691 When the *baud rate 1/*T* increases from zero, the bit rate *R* first increases and then decreases. **1983** JORDAN & CHURCHILL *Communications & Networking for IBM PC* iv. 63 The baud rate being used by the Personal Computer during transmission has to match the baud rate of the receiving computer for data to be communicated properly.

baud(e, obs. form of BAWD.

†**baude,** *a. Obs. rare*⁻¹. [a. OF. *baud* gay, sprightly, a. OLG. *bald* bold, lively.] Joyous, gay.

c **1400** *Rom. Rose* 5677 And many a ribaude is mery and baude That swynkith, and berith..Many a burthen.

baudekin, baudkin ('bɔːdɪkɪn, 'bɔːdkɪn). *Obs.* exc. *Hist.* Forms: 4–9 **baudekyn, baudekin,** 5–9 **baudkin,** 6–9 **bawdkin;** also 4 **baudekine,** 4–6 **bawdekyn(e,** 5 **bawdkyne, bawedekyn,** 5–6 **bawdekin,** 6 **baudkyn, bawdikyn, bawdkyn,** 7 **bodkin.** [a. OF. *baudekin, -quin:*—med.L. *baldakinus, -ekinus* (= It. *baldacchino*), f. *Baldacco*, It. form of *Bagdad*; see BALDACHIN.]

A rich embroidered stuff, originally made with warp of gold thread and woof of silk; *later*, with wider application, rich brocade, rich shot silk. Sometimes, more fully, ***cloth of baud(e)kin.***

c **1300** *K. Alis.* 759 He dude his temple al by-honge With bawdekyn, brod and longe. *c* **1320** *Seuyn Sag.* (W.) 2744 Th' emperour was browt abedde, With riche baudekines i-spredde. **1440** *Lincolnsh. Ch. Furn.* (1866) 182 A vesment of baudekyn yᵉ ground black with grene Werk. **1525** LD. BERNERS *Froiss.* II. clvii. [cliii.] 429 Aparelled in gownes of one sute of clothe of Baudkyn, grene and crymosyn. **1536** *Regist.* in *Antiq. Sarisb.* (1771) 197 Ten Chesibles of white Bawdkin, with leaves and hearts of Gold. **1552** HULOET, Bawdkyn or Tynsel clothe. **1610** HOLLAND *Camden's Brit.* I. 174 Arraied in cloth of gold of the most pretious and costly Bawdkin. **1624** HEYWOOD *Gunaik.* V. 241 Women apparrelled in cloth of bodkin. **1861** H. AINSWORTH *Constable of T.* 43 Her dress was of gold bawdkin.

attrib. *c* **1440** *Promp. Parv.* 27 Bawdekyn clothe, *olosericus.* **1609** HOLLAND *Amm. Marcel.* XIV. *note*, Surcoat of scarlet, likewise of bawdkin work. **1843** LYTTON *Last Bar.* II. ii. 124 The baudekin stripes (blue and gold) of her tunic attested her royalty.

baudelaire, variant of BADELAR, a dagger.

Baudelairean, -ian (bəʊdə'lɛərɪən), *a.* Also occas. **-ien.** [f. the name of Charles *Baudelaire* (1821–67), French poet and critic + -IAN.] Of, or pertaining to, or characteristic of Charles Baudelaire or his poetry. Hence as *sb.*, an admirer or imitator of Baudelaire's work; also **Baude'lairianism.**

1899 'G. F. MONKSHOOD' *R. Kipling* 181 'Love-o'-Woman', a Baudelairean study of physical passion, disease and Death. **1909** *Daily Chron.* 30 Aug. 3/3 The little Baudelairiens who have an itch to seem Satanic. **1921** *Glasgow Herald* 9 Apr. 6 The moral aspect of Baudelairianism. **1962** A. HUXLEY *Island* iii. 20 In a Baudelairian sort of way it's rather beautiful. **1967** *Listener* 27 July 109/2 André Gide, who was a great Baudelairean.

†**'baudery.** *Obs.* Also **-erie, -rie, -ry.** [a. OF. *bauderie* gayety, jollity, f. *baud*: see BAUDE and -RY.] Gayety, jollity, mirth.

c **1386** CHAUCER *Knts. T.* 1068 Beautee and youthe, bauderie, richesse.

baudery, -erie, -ry, obs. form of BAWDRY.

baudric, -derick, obs. forms of BALDRIC.

baudrons ('bɔːdrənz). *Sc.* Forms: 5–9 **badrans,** 6 **bawdrones,** 7 **batrons,** 8 **baudrins,** 6–9 **bawdrons,** 8– **baudrons** (*mod. dial.* **badrans, bauthrans**). [Origin uncertain: perh. Celtic; cf. Ir. *beadrac̈* frolicsome, *beadrad̈* playing, joking, fondness (O'Reilly), Scotch Gaelic *beadrach* a playful girl, *beadradh* a fondling, flattering, caressing (Macleod and Dewar). Cf. also BAD *sb.*] Scotch name for the cat (like 'reynard' for the fox).

c **1450** HENRYSON *Two Mice* (*Mor. Fab.* 13), Badrans [*other edd.* bawdrons, -ones] the uthir be the back has hint. **1657** COLVIL *Whigs Supplic.* (1751) 151 Batrons for grief of scorched members, Doth fall..a mewing. **1794** BURNS *Wks.* IV. 327 Auld baudrons by the ingle sits, An' wi' her loof her face a-washin. **1816** SCOTT *Antiq.* ix, He had a beard too, and whiskers..as long as baudrons'.

bauer, obs. form of BEAVER (of helmet).

bauera ('baʊərə). [mod.L., f. the name of Franz and Ferdinand *Bauer*, botanical draughtsmen.] The Tasmanian name for a shrub of the species *Bauera rubioides*, one of the three Australasian species of the family Saxifragaceæ. Also *attrib.*

1835 *Ross's Hobart Town Alm.* 70 *Bauera rubiæfolia.* Madder leaved Bauera. **1888** R. M. JOHNSTON *Geol. Tasmania* Introd. 6 The Bauera scrub..is a tiny, beautiful shrub. **1891** [see ROSE *sb.* 2 b]. **1927** *Chambers's Jrnl.* May 345/1 An impenetrable thicket of bauera.

†**'baufrey.** *Obs. rare.* [perh. identical with BELFRY, OF. *bercfrit*; the sense of a framework of wooden beams may have passed into that of a single beam in such a framework.] (See quot.)

[**1676** FÉLIBIEN *Princ. Archit.* 492 Befray ou Befroy, c'est la charpenterie qui soutient les cloches dans une tour.] **1639** HORN & ROB. *Gate Lang. Unl.* xlix. §545 The tiles, gutter-tiles or slates, on rafters..baufries and spars. **1693** W. ROBERTSON *Phraseol. Gen.* 216 A baufrey, *lignum, trabs.* **1830** R. STUART *Dict. Archit.*, Baufrey, an old word for beam.

‖**bauge** (boːʒ). [mod.Fr. (in Littré).] A drugget manufactured at Bauge in Burgundy of stout thread and coarse wool.

1847 in CRAIG.

†**'bauger,** *a. Obs. rare*⁻¹. [Of uncertain origin: cf. F. *baugeart* 'a scowndrell, a scurvie or beastly companion' (Cotgr.), f. *bauge* mud, filth; it might also be a form of the national name *Bulgar, Bolgar, Bugar*, used as a term of reproach in the Middle Ages.] Barbarous (or ? vile, beastly).

1544 BALE *Sir J. Oldcastell* in *Harl. Misc.* (Malh.) I. 273 Then brought he forth another bill..that he redde also in his bauger Latyne.

†**baugh, baw,** *v. Obs.* [Imitative of the sound: cf. BOW-WOW.] To bark, as a dog.

1576 FLEMING tr. *Caius' Dogs* in Arb. *Garner* III. 255 Bawing and wawing at the moon. **1639** HORN & ROB. *Gate Lang. Unl.* xv. §187 If you smite him, he yelpeth..and baughs.

Bauhaus ('baʊhaʊs). [Ger., lit. 'architecture house', f. *bau* building (*bauen* to build) + *haus* house.] The name of a school of design founded in Weimar, Germany, in 1919 by Walter Gropius (1883–1969); used for the principles or traditions characteristic of the Bauhaus.

1923 H. G. SCHEFFAUER in *Freeman* 5 Dec. 304 The Staatliche Bauhaus of Weimar represents one of the most interesting and significant enterprises in the vivifying of modern arts and crafts. **1932** D. M. HOFFMANN tr. *Moholy-Nagy's New Vision* i. 18 The Bauhaus became in Germany the focussing point of the new creative forces accepting the challenge of the time and technical progress. *Ibid.*, Systematic work toward 'standardized production' did not, however, form the first step in Bauhaus instruction. **1935** P. M. SHAND tr. *Gropius' New Architecture & the Bauhaus* 37 The *Bauhaus* represented a school of thought which believes that the difference between industry and handicraft is due..to subdivision of labour in the one and undivided control by a single workman in the other. **1958** *Times* 11 Oct. 7/6 The contemporary Russian style [of architecture], which is a blend of Bauhaus and post-Waterloo station grandiose.

bauhinia (bəʊˈhɪnɪə). [mod.L. (Linnæus 1737), named after Jean (1541–1613) and Gaspard (1560–1624) *Bauhin.*] A plant of the genus *Bauhinia* (family Leguminosæ) of which there are many tropical species. Also *attrib.*

1790 J. BRUCE *Trav. Source of Nile* V. App. 59 Mr. Jussieu says this bauhinia is by Mr. Bruce taken for an acacia. **1833** *Penny Cycl.* I. 447/1 (*America*) Bauhinias..cling round the trees like enormous cables. **1849** C. STURT *Narr. Exped. C. Australia* I. 359 The Bauhinia here grew to the height of 16 to 20 feet. **1887** MOLONEY *Forestry W. Africa* 187 Plaintain and Bauhinia fibres. **1922** *Chambers's Jrnl.* Dec. 859/2 Trees ..with a good deal of Bauhinia creeper all over. **1934** *Bulletin* (Sydney) 27 June 24/1 Scattered cabbage-gum, kurrajong, bauhinia and other fodder trees. **1967** 'A. CORDELL' *Bright Cantonese* xiii. 150 The bauhinia trees were etched in darkness against a round China moon.

bauk, baul(e, obs. ff. BALK, BALL, BAWL.

bauld, dial. form of BOLD.

baulk, variant of BALK, *esp.* in billiards.

baulme, baum(e, obs. forms of BALM.

† **ˈbaultering,** *ppl. a. Obs.* [f. BALTER *v.* + -ING².] Moving unwieldily, floundering.

a **1704** T. BROWN *Sat. Wom.* Wks. 1730 I. 55 Days.. never free From baultering impotence and jealousy.

Baumé (ˈbəʊmeɪ). Also erron. **Beaumé**. The name of a French chemist, Antoine *Baumé* (1728–1804), the inventor, in 1768, of a hydrometer, of which the scale is uniformly graduated. Used in the possessive, also *attrib.* and *ellipt.*, to denote the scale introduced by him.

1844 G. FOWNES *Man. Chem.* 545 Hydrometer Tables. Comparison of the degrees of Baumé's Hydrometer, with the real specific gravities. *a* **1877** KNIGHT *Dict. Mech.* II 1153/2 The following table shows the specific gravity corresponding to different degrees of Beaumé. **1877** *Proc. Amer. Chem. Soc.* I. II. 11 The degree Beaumé..is equal to the fractional part of the number expressing the corresponding specific gravity. *Ibid.* 13, I have adopted an even scale of which 1°.805 is equal to 1°, Beaumé. *Ibid.*, The coarse Beaumé areometer..is commonly used in the arts. **1884** *Mem. Nat. Acad. Sci.* III. 63 The degrees on the Baumé scale are entirely arbitrary, and bear no obvious relation to the specific gravity of the liquid. **1886** *Harper's Mag.* Jan. 248/1 All that is below 60° B. (Baumé, standard of density)..is turned into a tank for kerosene distillates. **1951** *Good Housek. Home Encycl.* 486/1 If a hydrometer is available, test the strength of the syrup, which should register 25° Beaumé or 37° Balling.

baum marten (ˈbaʊm ˌmɑːtən). [Partial tr. G. *baummarder*, f. *baum* tree (see BEAM *sb.*¹) + *marder*, MARTER¹, marten.] The pine marten or its fur.

1879 *Encycl. Brit.* IX. 838/2 *Baum Marten*,..Found in Europe and Asia, of fine overhair, but woolly fur, of a brownish colour, approaching that of the American marten. **1906** *Westm. Gaz.* 3 Nov. 31/1 There are many kinds of sable, the Russian, Canadian, the baum-marten, and the stone-marten. **1909** *Daily Chron.* 23 Feb. 7/3 The Hudson Bay sables and the dyed baum marten. **1954** *Economist* 20 Feb. 567/1 Sable and ermine..silver and blue fox, baum marten and squirrel.

bauour, obs. form of BEAVER.

† **bause,** *v. Obs. rare.* [? f. L. *bāsiāre* to kiss.] 'To kiss' (is Halliwell's explanation); but cf. BAWZE.

1607 MARSTON *What you w.* II. i, My spaniell slept, whilst I bausd leaves..por'd on the old print Of titled wordes.

bauson (ˈbɔːsən). *arch.* Forms: 4–6 **bausen**, 4–7 **bawson**, 4– **bauson**; also 4 **baucyne**, **bawcyn**, 5 **bawsone**, **-ym**, (**bawstone**, **bauston**), 6 **bauzon**, **bawsym**, (**balstone**), 7 **boson**, 8 **bawsin**, (**boreson**). [ME. *bausen*, a. OF. *bausen*, *bauzan*, see next word, the animal taking its name from the white mark on its face: cf. *bauson-faced*. See BADGER *sb.*² for the etymological parallel of F. *blaireau* badger, from Flem. *blaer*, Du. *blaar* white spot on the forehead. (But in Fr., *bausen*, etc., has never been applied to the badger, and its being so used in Eng. implies a much earlier use of the adj. than we have evidence of.)]

A. *sb.* A badger; see BADGER *sb.*²

c **1325** *E.E. Allit. P.* B. 392 Bukkez, bausenez, & bulez to þe bonkkez hyȝed. *c* **1350** *Will. Palerne* 2299 Bores boles and baucynes. **1387** TREVISA *Higden* Rolls Ser. I. 327 White beres, bausons, and brokkes. **1496** *Dives & Paup.* VI. xiv. 256 Taxus..is a brok or a bawsym in Englysshe. **1587** M. GROVE *Poems* (1878) 67 The wilie subtile foxe The balstone or [*printed* on] the grey doth chase and beate from cliuie rocks. **1593** DRAYTON *Eclog.* iv. 176 His Mittens were of Bauzons skin. **1741** *Compl. Fam.-Piece* II. i. 298 A Badger is known by several Names, as a Gray, a Brock, a Boreson or Bauson. **1783** AINSWORTH *Lat. Dict.* (Morell) I, A bawsin, *melis.*

b. applied contemptuously to persons, fat (like the badger before winter), or pertinacious.

1607 *Lingua* V. xvi. in Hazl. *Dodsl.* IX. 452 Peace, you fat bawson, peace. **1862** H. AINSWORTH *Constable of T.* 131 Know, ye incredulous bawsons, that I am now one of the royal household.

B. *adj.* = BAUSONED. Hence **bauson-faced**.

1587 *Wills & Inv. N.C.* (1860) 288 One stud mare of colour bawson sored. **1829** SCOTT *Hrt. Midl.* xxviii, Ye might try it on the bauson-faced year-auld quey.

ˈ**bausond,** *a. Obs.* or *dial.* Forms: 4 **bausand**, 6 **bawsonde**, 6–8 **bawsand**, 8 **bawsint**, **baws'nt**, 8–9 **bassen'd**, 9 **bauson'd**. [a. OF. *bausant*, *-ssant*, *-sent*, *-cent*, *balcent*, also *bauchant*, *baulchant*, and (without final *t*) *bauzan*, *-sen*, *-sain*, *-çain*, black and white spotted, piebald, a word of doubtful form and etymology, but of which the forms without *-t* correspond to Pr. *bausan*, It. *balzano*, white spotted (Baretti), white-footed (Minsheu), whence also mod.F. *balzan* 'black or bay (horse) with white feet' (Littré). The word appears also in med.L. as *bausendus*, *bausennus*, *bauchantus*, from Fr. In view of the It. and Pr., the OF. forms in *-nt* are not easy to account for, but they seem to be the source of the ME. *bausand*, though later spelling assimilates the word to ppl. adjs. in *-ed*, as if formed on *bawson*.

(For the ulterior etymology there is nothing satisfactory. Conjectures may be seen in Boehmer *De colorum nominibus equinorum* in *Roman. Studien* vol. I; in Diez, who referred *balzano* to *balza* 'border, fringe'; and in Devic (Littré, *Suppl.*) who has pointed out the striking identity of meaning between *bausant* and Arab. *ablaq*, fem. *balqā*; but notwithstanding this, the forms of the Arabic and Romanic words cannot (at present at least) be phonetically reconciled.)]

Of animals: Having white spots on a black or bay ground; *esp.* (in modern use) having a white patch on the forehead, or a white stripe down the face.

c **1320** *Durham Wills* (1835) I. 19 Quidam equus bausand. **1513** DOUGLAS *Æneis* v. x. 40 A hors of Trace dapill gray.. With bawsand face. **1549** *Wills & Inv. N.C.* (1835) 131 A bawsonde curtall nagge. **1786** BURNS *Twa Dogs* 31 A faithful tyke..His honest sonsie baws'nt face. **1807–10** TANNAHILL *Poems* (1846) 12 Bauson'd Crummock's broken frae the sta'. **1837** SCOTT in *Lockhart* (1839) I. 93 A bow of Kye and a bassen'd (brindled) bull.

baustrott, var. of BAWDSTROT.

bauude, obs. form of BAWD.

bauxite (ˈbɔːksaɪt) *Min.* Also 9 **beauxite** (ˈbəʊzaɪt). [F. *bauxite* (1821), f. *Baux* or *Beaux*, near Arles in France, where found + -ITE.] A hydrous oxide of alumina and iron, used in the manufacture of aluminium.

1861 H. SAINTE-CLAIRE DEVILLE in *Chem. News* 9 Nov. 241/1 This substance, obtained from Baux, near Arles, consisted of small round grains buried in a perfectly crystallised pure limestone... I then recognised it as the mineral to which M. Berthier gave the name of Bauxite. It is a hydrate of alumina which M. Dufrénoy has ranked with gibsite, or rather diaspore. **1868** DANA *Min.* 175 The purest beauxite..is called aluminum ore. **1872** *Jrnl. Chem. Soc.* XXV. 467 Bauxite from the Wochein (Austria). **1873** in *Proc. Amer. Phil. Soc.* XIII. 373 The presence of grains of corundum in the beauxite. **1883** *Ibid.* XLIV. 397 The practical value of bauxite depends on the high amount of alumina in proportion to the silica. **1922** *Blackw. Mag.* July 18/2 A pink vein of bauxite ore. **1940** *Geogr. Jrnl.* XCVI. 45 The supply of aluminium is also dependent upon external sources for the bauxite and cryolite from which it is extracted.

‖**bavardage** (bavarˈdaʒ). [Fr., f. *bavard-er* to chatter, f. *bavard* talkative, f. *bave* saliva, drivel.] Idle talk, prattle, chattering.

1835 LYTTON *Rienzi* II. v. 133 Replying only by monosyllables to the gay bavardage of the Knight. **1882** *Q. Rev., Jacobin Conq.* 152 They were browbeat, contradicted, told to cease their bavardage.

Bavarian (bəˈvɛərɪən), *a.* [f. *Bavaria* + -AN.] Of or belonging to Bavaria; also in special collocations (see quots.).

1638 *Invasions of Germanie* §10 On the Bavarian, and Imperialists-side, slaine some 250. **1700** RYCAUT *Turkish Hist.* III. 201/1 The Bavarian Troops approaching towards Pesth, enter'd it without any opposition. **1815** *Wynne Diaries* 14 Sept. (1940) III. 382 We found the Inn occupied by Bavarian Officers. **1880** WEBSTER Suppl. s.v. *Cream*, *Bavarian cream*, a preparation of gelatine, milk, cream, and eggs, flavored, and eaten cold. **1892** T. F. GARRETT *Encycl. Cookery* I. 9/2 Almond Bavaroise, or Bavarian Cream. *Ibid.* 87/2 *Bavarian beer*... The average beer brewed is not of a very high alcoholic character, and is said to obtain some of its characteristic flavour from the pitch used to line the casks. *Ibid.*, *Bavarian creams*, a great variety of these are to be found under the name of Bavaroises. **1893** *Ibid.* II. 385/2 Bavarian Sauce. **1893** E. KNECHT et al. *Man. Dyeing* 479 Diphenylamine-blue. $C_{37}H_{30}N_3$.Cl. Bavarian Blue..gives a finer blue shade than..any other blue. **1934** PRIEBSCH & COLLINSON *German Lang.* vii. 327 The Bavarian-Austrian group includes the dialects of Old Bavaria with a southern set of dialects. **1968** *Globe & Mail* (Toronto) 17 Feb. 43/1 *Happy Valley* (Walkerton)—Excellent with three inches new on packed base of 6 inches. T-bar, Bavarian lift.

bavaroise (bavarˈwɑːz). Also **bavarois**. [Fr.] A cream dessert containing gelatine and whipped cream, and served cold.

1846 A. SOYER *Gastronomic Regenerator* 529 Bavaroise aux Fraises. **1868** E. ACTON *Mod. Cookery* (rev. ed.) xxiii. 478 By mingling the cream..the preparation becomes what is called *un Fromage Bavarois*, or Bavarian cream, sometimes simply, *une Bavaroise*. **1877** E. S. DALLAS *Kettner's Book of Table* 56 Bavarois—Bavarian cheese. Boil as much of the best milk as will half fill the mould... Sugar it, and add whatever flavour may be chosen... Mix in..yolks of eggs... Being cool, it is to be mixed well with..whipt cream, poured ..into a mould..and given over to the ice-box. **1892** [see BAVARIAN *a.*]. **1964** *Observer* 11 Dec. 34/5 *Bavaroise* is just a Crême Bavaroise in a mould. **1968** *Woman* 7 Dec. 26/1 This wonderful sweet [*sc.* charlotte russe] filled with a rich bavaroise mixture.

† ˈ**bavaroy.** *Obs.* Also 8 **baˈvary**. [prob. ad. F. *bavarois* Bavarian (Todd).] A kind of cloak or surtout; sometimes *fig.*

1714 GAY *Trivia* I. 53 Let the loop'd Bavaroy the fop embrace. **1788** PICKEN *Poems* 90 (JAM.) Dinna use to hide yer sin Hypocrisy's Bavary.

bavian, bavier(e, obs. form of BABION, BEAVER.

bavin (ˈbævɪn), *sb.* Forms: 6 **bauine**, 6–7 **bauen**, **-in**, 7 **baven**, **-yn**, 7–8 **bavine**, 6– **bavin**. [Derivation unknown; among sources which have been suggested are OF. *baffe* a bundle; also Gael. *baban*, *babhaid*, tassel, cluster.]

1. A bundle of brushwood or light underwood, such as is used in bakers' ovens, differing from a fagot in being bound with only one withe or band instead of two; in *Mil.* a fascine.

1528 in T. Whitaker *Hist. Craven* (1812) 303 Item, for 40 load of cutwood & bavins. **1580** LYLY *Euphues* (Arb.) 331 Bavins be knowen by their bands. **1603** H. CROSSE *Vertues Commw.* (1878) 133 Which like a bauin giueth goodly blaze ..but is soone out. **1629** *S'hertogenbosh* 39 The Enemies did nothing else but fill the ditches with wet Bauins of trees. **1776** T. BOWDEN *Farm. Direct.* 11 All hay ricks should be bottomed with faggots and bavins. *a* **1848** MARRYAT *R. Reefer* xiii, The bavins of furze..shall be sold.

fig. **1593** NASHE *Christ's T.* (1613) 144 Adding more Bauines vnto it of lasciuious embolstrings. **1605** CHAPMAN *Eastw. Hoe* A iij, If he out-last not a hundred such crackling Bauins as thou art.

b. *collect. sing.* Brushwood, firewood.

1577 TUSSER *Husb.* (1878) 133 In stacking of bauen.. make vnder thy bauen a houell for hogs. **1664** EVELYN *Sylva* 48 [They] be profitable for the Oven, and make good Bavin.

c. *attrib.*, as in ***bavin-band***, ***-stack***; **bavin wits**, wits bavin-like in quick and short-lived blaze.

1596 SHAKS. 1 *Hen. IV*, III. ii. 61 Shallow Iesters, and rash Bauin Wits, Soone kindled and soone burnt. **1725** BRADLEY *Fam. Dict.*, *Birch*..is of use for Bavin bands. **1762** tr. *Duhamel's Husb.* I. viii. 21 The bottom of bavine-stacks.

2. *Min.* Impure limestone. (? a different word).

1839 MURCHISON *Silur. Syst.* I. xxxvi. 484 These concretions..are called 'bavin,' the shale associated with them being termed 'rotch.'

† ˈ**bavin,** *v. Obs.* [f. prec. sb.] *trans.* To bind up into bavins.

1664 EVELYN *Sylva* (1776) 538 Kid or Bavin them (the underwood)..to preserve them from rotting. **1685** COTTON *Montaigne* II. 516 They saw [him] ingeniously bavin up a burthen of brushwood.

bavour, obs. form of BEAVER.

baw-, for forms so beginning, see also BAU-.

baw, *int.* ? *Obs.* Also 4 **bawe**. [a natural expression of disgust, probably at first directed against tastes or smells; cf. *bah!*] Ejaculation of disgust, aversion, or contempt.

1377 LANGL. *P. Pl.* B. XI. 135 ȝee! baw for bokes! quod one. **1393** *Ibid.* XXII. 398 ȝe, bawe! quap a brewere, ich wol nat beo rueled. **1768** GOLDSM. *Good N. Man* IV. ii, Baw! damn me, but I'll fight you both.

† **bawaty, bowety.** *Obs.*—⁰ 'Linsey-wolsey.' Ray *North Country Wds.* 1691.

bawbee (bɔːˈbiː). *Sc.* Forms: 6 **bawbie**, **babie**, 7 **babee**, **baubie**, **baubye**, **baubee**, 7– **bawbee**. [Of doubtful origin: it has been conjecturally identified with *baby* (with which it was sometimes identical in form in 16th c.), derived from *basse-pièce* (phonetically impossible), and *bas billon* 'base bullion' or mixed metal, and from the name of a contemporary mint-master, the laird of Sillebawby.

(The last conjecture is on the whole probable, and is strengthened by the similar origin of the name of the ATCHISON, and perhaps of the BODLE. The laird of *Sillebawby* (notwithstanding his designation, and its suggestion of *Siller bawbee*) was a real person: on 7 Sept. 1541, Kirkcaldy of Grange, the Treasurer, accounted for amounts 'in argento receptis a Jacobo Atzinsone, et Alexandro Orok de Sillebawby respective' (Cochran-Patrick I. 60). There is only wanting some direct proof of the abbreviation of *Sillebawby* to *bawby*. The idle surmise that the first issue bore the head of, or was issued by, an infant king, is disposed of by the preliminary fact that 'bawbeis' were first issued in 1541–2 *near the close* of the reign of James V, and *bore no head*; moreover there exists no Scottish coin bearing a baby head. Beside the fatal phonetic objection to *basse pièce*, *bas billon*, there is not the slightest indication that the *bawbeis* were ever so called, and coins of billon, or base metal, had been too common for a century and a half in Scotland to make them a novelty in 1541.)]

A Scotch coin of base silver equivalent originally to three, and afterwards to six, pennies of Scotch money, about a halfpenny of

English coin; *hence*, in modern use, a halfpenny, a 'copper.'

1542 *Hopetoun MS.* (in Cochran-Patrick, *Coinage of Scotl.* 96) The said James [Atcheson] being commandet to worke bawbeis he altogether refusit.. First thair wes cunyeit of bawbeis of iii d. fyne xvj in the ounce. The cause of thir bawbeis cunyeing was the warres that schortlie begowde betuixt ws and Ingland. **1544** *Ibid.* 97 The maist pairt of the saidis bawbeis were coinyeit of clippit soussis quhilkis than were proclamit in France for bullion, and send heer to be conuertit in bawbeis. *a* **1572** KNOX *Hist. Ref.* 151 (JAM.) With us thare did not remane the valow of a Babie. **1573** *Let.* in Tytler *Hist. Scot.* (1864) III. 361 A piece of their coin called a bawbee.. which is in value English one penny and a quarter. **1623** COCKERAM, *Baubee*, a farthing. **1635** BRERETON *Trav.* (1844) 188 Baubyes 2 to one penny English or 12 Scottish. **1732** DE FOE, &c. *Tour Gt. Brit.* (1769) IV. 253 Boys and girls.. sold.. us near a Mutchkin for a baubee. **1862** *Macm. Mag.* Oct. 502 Proposing to solicit a bawbee from a party of strangers.

bawble, obs. form of BAUBLE.

bawcock (ˈbɔːkɒk). [a. F. *beau coq* 'fine cock,' for *bewcock* (cf. *bawshere*).] A colloquial or burlesque term of endearment: = Fine fellow, good fellow.

1599 SHAKS. *Hen. V.* III. ii. 25 Good Bawcock bate thy Rage. *Ibid.* IV. i. 44 The King's a Bawcock, and a Heart of Gold. **1862** H. AINSWORTH *Constable of T.* 131 One of the gamesome little bawcock's jests.

bawd (bɔːd), *sb.*[1] Forms: 4–5 **bauude**, 4–7 **baude**, 4–6 **bawde**, 6 **bawed**, 6–7 **baud**, 6– **bawd**. [Of uncertain origin: the original sense shows no approach to that of OF. *baud*, *baude*, 'bold, lively, gay, merry' (see BAUDE), to which it has often been referred: even allowing that 'gay' might have passed into the sense of 'wanton, licentious, personally unchaste,' no trace of such sense appears either in ME. or Fr.; nor is the Fr. word found as a sb. The earliest instance yet found occurs in *Piers Plowman*, 1362, where one MS. reads BAWDSTROT. *Bawd* may not improbably be an abbreviation of that word, which is found in Fr. a century earlier.]

One employed in pandering to sexual debauchery; a procurer or procuress; *orig.* in a more general sense, and in the majority of passages masculine, a 'go-between,' a pander; since *c* 1700 only feminine, and applied to a procuress, or a woman keeping a place of prostitution.

1362 LANGL. *P. Pl.* A. III. 42 And eke be þi Bawde, and Bere wel þin ernde. [*One MS. has* bawdstrot; *texts B, C,* bedeman, bedman (messenger).] *c* **1374** CHAUCER *Troylus* II. 304 For me were lever, that ye, and I, and he, Were hangid, than I [*i.e.* Pandarus] sholde be his bawde. **1386** —— *Frere's T.* 54 He was A theef, and eek a somnour, and a baude [*v.r.* bawde]. *c* **1440** *Promp. Parv.* 27 Bawde, *leno.* **1483** CAXTON *Gold. Leg.* 83/1 Thenne Vago his bawde wente in to his preuy chambre. **1541** *Act 33 Hen. VIII*, xxi. §1 That baude the lady Jane Rochford, by whose meanes Culpeper came thither. **1642** ROGERS *Namaan* 303 Bauds and Pandars to their Masters. **1706** PHILLIPS, *Bawd*, a leud Woman that makes it her Business to debauch others for Gain; a Procuress. **1771** SMOLLETT *Humph. Cl.* (1815) 222 Where she stuck like a bawd in the pillory. **1842** LONGF. *Sp. Stud.* I. i, A vile, shameless bawd, Whose craft was to deceive the young and fair.

b. *fig.* He who or that which panders to any evil design or vicious practice.

1607 HIERON *Wks.* I. 185 The mercy of God.. is made.. a Baude to all manner of vngodlinesse. **1688** LD. DELAMERE *Wks.* 12 Ignorant Ambitious Clergy, who in hopes of preferment have turned Bawds to Arbitrary Power. **1785** BURKE *Nab. Arcot's Debts* Wks. IV. 285 Their affected purity.. becomes pander and bawd to the unbridled debauchery and licentious lewdness of usury and extortion.

†**bawd** (bɔːd), *sb.*[2] *dial.* [Perh. the same word as *badde*, BAD *sb.*, a cat, or a contraction of *baudrons*, or otherwise related to the latter; cf. the Eng. use of *puss*, and the Sc. use of *malkin*, for both hare and cat.] A hare.

[**1592** SHAKS. *Rom. & Jul.* II. iv. 13 *Mercutio.* A baud, a baud, a baud. So ho. *Romeo.* What hast thou found? *Mer.* No Hare sir, vnlesse a Hare sir in a Lenten pie, etc.] **1785** *Poems in Buchan Dial.* 23, I saw you rin awa' like bawds. ('This is the common name for a hare, Aberd. Used in the same sense, Roxb.' Jamieson. Also in Fife.)

†**bawd**, *v.*[1] *Obs.* In 6 **baud**. [cf. BAWDY *a.*[1]] *trans.* To befoul or dirty.

c **1529** SKELTON *El. Rum.* 90 Dyrt, That baudeth her skirt.

bawd (bɔːd), *v.*[2] *arch.* or *Obs.* Also 7 **baud**. [f. BAWD *sb.*[1]] *intr.* To pander; also *fig.*

1651 J. C[LEVELAND] *Poems* 39 To whose viler ends Your pow'r hath bauded. **1712** STEELE *Spect.* No. 266 ⁋2 Lucippe.. bawds at the same time for the whole Court.

†**ˈbawdefy**, *v.* *Obs. rare*⁻¹. [? f. F. *baude* (see BAUDE) + -FY.] ? To make gay, deck.

1562 LEIGH *Armory*, His coate.. was of cloth garded with a burgunian garde of bare velvet, well bawdefied on the halfe placard and squalioted in the fore quarters.

bawdekin, -eryke, obs. ff. BAUDEKIN, BALDRIC.

bawdily (ˈbɔːdɪlɪ), *adv.* [f. BAWDY *a.*[2] + -LY[2].] In a bawdy manner, lasciviously.

1628 EARLE *Microcosm.* lxii. 134 He talks loud and baudily. **1630** J. TAYLOR (Water P.) *Wks.* II. 95 She can speake and write Amorously, Fainedly.. Purposely, Bawdily.

ˈbawdiness. [f. BAWDY *a.* + -NESS.] †**a.** Dirtiness; dirt, filth. *Obs.* **b.** Lewdness, obscenity.

1552 HULOET, Bawdines or filthines vpon clothes or other thynge, *squallido, squalliditas.* **1731** in BAILEY II.

ˈbawding, *vbl. sb. arch.* or *Obs.* [f. BAWD *v.*[2] + -ING[1].] The practice of a bawd.

1676 SHADWELL *Virtuoso* IV. *Wks.* I. 381 Their very art of.. adorning women is implicit bawding. **1688** E. RAVENSCROFT *Lond. Cuckolds* 27 Formerly stil'd Bawding and Pimping.. it is now a modish piece of service only.

†**ˈbawdish**, *a.* *Obs. rare*⁻¹. In 6 **bawdische**. [f. BAWD *sb.*[1] + -ISH[1].] Obscene, filthy.

1572 A. ARBUTHNOT *Mis. Pure Scolar* ix, To bawdische bourdis yet man I oft gif ear.

bawdkin, variant of BAUDEKIN.

bawdle, obs. form of BODLE, Scotch coin.

bawˈdreaminy. *nonce-wd.* Bawdry.

1608 MIDDLETON *Trick to Catch* III. ii, Thou cavernesed quean of foolery, knavery, and bawdreaminy.

†**ˈbawdress.** *Obs.* [formed, as if on a masc. *bawder*, from BAWD *v.*[2]] A woman bawd.

1569 J. SANFORD *Agrippa's Van. Artes* 97 b, A perfecte and absolute bawde and bawdresse.

bawdrick, variant form of BALDRIC.

bawdry[1] (ˈbɔːdrɪ). *arch.* Forms: 4–8 **bawdery**, 4–7 **baudery**, 5 **baudre**, 6 **baudrey**, **baudrye**, **bawdrye**, (**baudeir**,) **bauderie**, **baudrie**, 6–7 **baudry**, **bawdrie**, 7–8 **bawdry**. [f. BAWD *sb.*[1] + -RY; the sense does not agree with F. *bauderie*, which means simply 'boldness, liveliness.']

1. The practice of a bawd; the business of providing opportunities for sexual immorality.

c **1374** CHAUCER *Troylus* III. 348 Me thoght.. I shold wene hit were a bawdery. **1447–8** SHILLINGFORD *Lett.* (1871) 104 Yif any such mysrule and bawdery bee within the saide taverne. **1569** J. SANFORD *Agrippa's Van. Artes* 97 Bawdrie is the arte of assaultinge and makinge common an others chastitie. **1634** T. JOHNSON *Parey's Chirurg.* XXIV. xlii. (1678) 571 The most filthy and infamous Arts of Baudery. **1726** AYLIFFE *Parerg.* 42 Bawdry.. is a wicked Practice of procuring and bringing Whores and Rogues together.

†**2.** *gen.* Unchastity, fornication. *Obs.*

1460 in *Pol. Rel. & L. Poems* (1866) 97 And he be getten in bawdre. **1600** SHAKS. *A.Y.L.* III. iii. 99 We must be married, or we must liue in baudrey. **1651** WELDON *Crt. Jas. I.* 7 For the bringing this bawdery to a marriage.

3. Lewdness in speech or writing; lewd, obscene, or filthy talk, etc.

1589 *Pappe w. Hatchet* (1844) 23 If Martin speake broad bawdrie. **1611** SHAKS. *Wint. T.* IV. iv. 194 He has the prettiest Loue-songs for Maids, so without bawdrie. **1711** STEELE *Spect.* No. 51 ⁋2 No one ever writ Bawdry for any other Reason but Dearth of Invention. **1792** A. YOUNG *Trav. France* 135 A voluble garniture of bawdry or nonsense.

b. *attrib.* = BAWDY *a.*[2]

1763 CHURCHILL *Duellist* III Poems II. 36 Bawl'd bawdry songs to a Psalm Tune.

†**4.** Material filth; dirt, defilement. Cf. BAWDY *a.*[1] *Obs.*

1648 HERRICK *Hesper.* 141 (D.) And have our roofe.. And seeling free From that cheape candle baudery.

†**bawdry**[2]. *Obs.* [? f. BAUDE gay.] Finery.

a **1529** SKELTON *Agst. Garnische* 40 Crimson velvet for your bawdry. **1693** W. ROBERTSON *Phraseol. Gen.* 216 Bawdry, *i.e.* bravery.. *lautitia vestium.*

bawdry[3], obs. form of BALDRIC.

a **1697** AUBREY in D'Israeli *Cur. Lit.* (1866) 293 They wore about their necks a great horn.. in a string or bawdry.

bawdship (ˈbɔːdʃɪp). [f. BAWD *sb.*[1] + -SHIP; cf. *lordship*.] The position or personality of a bawd. (Used as a mock style of address.)

1633 FORD *Broken H.* II. i. (1811) 256 One word with your old bawdship. **1676** SHADWELL *Virtuoso* IV. Wks. 1720 I. 384 I'll maul your bawdship.

†**ˈbawdstrot.** *Obs.* Forms: 4 **baudstrot**, 5 **bawdstrot(t**, **baustrott**, **balde- baldystrot**, **bawstrop**. [Identical with OF. *baudetrot*: Godefroy, s.v., quotes 'pronuba, *baudetrot*,' from a Latin-French glossary of 13th c. This, with the Eng. forms, indicates an earlier OF. *baldestrot*, *baudestrot*, the first element of which appears to be *bald*, *baud* 'bold, forward, lively, gay' (see BAUDE); the second suggests the Teutonic *strutt*, STRUT. (Cant names have been frequent for the class of persons in question.) This is probably the full word from which *bawd* was shortened; the form *bawstrop* seems to be the origin of the word BRONSTROPS, a procuress, which is frequent in Middleton's comedies.] A BAWD, male or female; a pander, a procuress.

1362 LANGL. *P. Pl.* A. III. 42 (MS. H.), I [a Confessor] schal asoyle þe [Meede þe Mayden] my-self And eke be þi bawdstrot [*v.r.* bawde] and bere wel þin ernde Among Clerkes and knihtes. *c* **1450** in Wülcker *Voc.* /693 *Leno*, baustrott. *Ibid.* /695 *Pronuba*, bawdstrott. *c* **1475** in Wright *Voc.* 269/1 *Pronuba*, bawstrop. **1483** *Cath. Angl.* 18 Baldestrot (*v.r.* Baldystrot), *pronubus, pronuba.*

†**ˈbawdy**, *a.* *Obs.* Forms: 4–5 **baudy**, 5–6 **bawdy**, 6 **baudye**, 7 **bawdy**. [Derivation unknown. Skeat compares W. *bawaidd* dirty, f. *baw* mud. The F. *boue* 'mud' is probably of same origin.] Soiled, dirty, filthy.

1377 LANGL. *P. Pl.* B. v. 197 A tauny tabarde.. Al totorne and baudy, and ful of lys crepynge. *c* **1430** LYDG. *Bochas* IX. xxxiv. (1554) 214 b, He.. in the kechen laye Among the pottes with baudy coate. **1527** WHITTINTON *Vulg.* 28 b, Holde thy bawdy handes fro my boke.. My handes be as clene as thyne. **1621** BURTON *Anat. Mel.* II. iii. III. (1651) 323 Slovenly cooks, that.. never wash their bawdy hands.

b. *fig.* of language: Vile, abominable, barbarous.

1519 HORMAN *Vulg.* 90 b, Them that wyll nat come out of theyr baudy latyn [*qui barbariem nunquam exuunt*].

bawdy (ˈbɔːdɪ), *a.*[2] Forms: 6 **bawdye**, **bawdie**, 6–7 **baudie**, **baudy**, 6– **bawdy**.) [f. BAWD *sb.* + -Y. Probably often associated in sense with prec.]

1. Of, pertaining to, or befitting a bawd; lewd, obscene, unchaste. (Usually applied to language.)

1513 BRADSHAW *St. Werburge* (1848) 209 Baudy balades full of.. wanton wylde gestis. **1616** R. C. *Times' Whis.* v. 2137 The chamber wher you lay your head With baudie pictures round about doe spread. *c* **1765** BURKE *On Drama* Wks. X. 158 Listening to a bawdy story from his host.

2. *absol.* quasi-*sb.*, esp. in phr. *to talk bawdy* (where perh. orig. adverbial): Lewd, obscene language, lewdness, obscenity.

1656 SANDERSON *Serm.* (1689) 16 To drink, talk bawdy, swear and stare. **1698** VANBRUGH *Æsop* Prol., No rape, no bawdy, no intrigue, no beau. **1702** DE FOE *More Reform.* 787 Eternal Bawdy fills up every Song. **1760** STERNE *Tr. Shandy* 220 How can that unconscionable coachman talk so much bawdy to that lean horse.

3. *Comb.* **bawdy-basket**, a hawker of indecent literature; **bawdy-house**, a brothel.

1552 HULOET, Bawdye house or house of bawdrye.. *summœnium.* **1567** HARMAN *Caveat* 65 These Bawdy baskets be.. women, and go with baskets.. where in they have laces, pynnes, nedles. **1785** GROSE *Dict. Vulg. Tongue*, *Bawdy Basket*, the twenty-third rank of canters, who carry pins, tape, ballads and obscene books to sell. **1882** *Ev. Man's Own Lawyer* 390 The keeping a bawdy house is a common nuisance.

†**ˈbawdy**, *v.* *Obs.* Also 6 **baudy**. [f. BAWDY *a.*[1]] To make dirty or filthy, to befoul, defile.

1398 TREVISA *Barth. De P.R.* XVIII. lxxxvii. (1495) 836 The swyne.. walowyth in dyrte.. and bawdyeth hymself therwyth. **1530** PALSGR. 444/2 He hath baudyed his sleves on this facyon.

bawe, obs. form of BOW *sb.*

bawhorse, obs. form (after anglicized pronunciation of F. *bât*) of *bât-horse*; see BAT *sb.*[3]

bawk, obs. form of BALK.

bawke. *dial.* [? dial. variant of BACK *sb.*[2]] A large bucket used in mines for raising coal, etc.

1880 *Times* 13 Dec. 10/2 That both cages should be removed and that the large bawke or bucket.. used instead.

†**ˈbawker.** *Obs.* [? for BALKER[1].] (See quot.)

1592 GREENE *Art Conny Catch.* II. 7 The Bawkers, for so the common hanters of the Ally are tearmed.. come to bowle, as though rather they did it for sport then gaines.

bawkie, var. of BAUKIE, bat.

bawl (bɔːl), *v.* Forms: 6 **baull**, **bool**, 6–7 **ball**, **baule**, 6–8 **baul**, 5– **bawl**. [Found only from 15th c. Prob. ad. med L. *baulā-re* to bark as a dog, 'latrare, et est proprie canum' (Du Cange); also in an 11th or 12th c. list of cries of animals 'canum latrare, seu baulare, vulpium gannire,' etc. The Promp. Parv. has 'baffyn as houndys, *baulo*, *baffo*, *latro*,' and the earliest English instances refer to dogs. But cf. Icel. *baula*, Sw. *böla* to low like a cow, pointing to an ON. vb. **baula*. f. *baula* a cow. In any case, originally applied to the voice of animals; hence more or less vituperative as applied to human utterance.]

†**1.** *intr.* To bark or howl as a dog, to give mouth or tongue as an animal.

[*c* **1440** *Promp. Parv.* 20 Baffynge or bawlynge of howndys, *baulatus, baffatus.*] **1563** BECON *New Catech.* (1844) 390 Singing-men.. in churches.. may roar, bool, bleat, yell, grunt. **1556** J. HEYWOOD *Sp. & Flie* xxxv, At my blunte behauour barke ye or ball ye. **1621** BURTON *Anat. Mel.* I. iii. I. ii. (1651) 183 A barking dog that alwayes bawls, but seldome bites. **1675** HOBBES *Odyss.* (1677) 166 The other three [dogs] ran bawling forth. **1753** [see BAWLING *vbl. sb.*]

2. a. *gen.* To shout at the top of one's voice, with a loud, full, protracted sound; to cry loudly and roughly, to bellow. Often emphasized by *out*.

1570 LEVINS *Manip.* /12 Baull, to cry, *vociferare.* **1583** STANYHURST *Æneis* II. (Arb.) 67, I belcht owt blasphemye bawling. **1622** HEYLYN *Cosmogr.* III. (1682) 104 The cryers kept a bauling in the steeples..for the people to come to Church. **1782** COWPER *Gilpin* 104 And ev'ry soul cried out, well done, As loud as he could bawl. **1872** THACKERAY *Christm. Bks.* 8, I heard him bawling out to Gregory in the passage.

b. Const. *against, at, for.*

1618 HOLYDAY *Juvenal* 240 We baul, More for our gold, then for a funeral. **1708** SWIFT *Abol. Chr.* Wks. 1755 II. I. 88 To bawl one day in seven against the lawfulness of those methods. **1863** KINGSLEY *Water-Bab.* vii. 267 They all bawled at her at once.

3. a. *trans.* To utter with bawling; to shout at the top of one's voice. (Often with *out.*)

1597 SHAKS. *2 Hen. IV.* II. ii. 27 Those that bawl out the ruins of thy linen. **1709** STEELE & SWIFT *Tatler* No. 66 ¶1 To bawl out, My Beloved; and the Words Grace! Regeneration! Sanctification! **1836** MARRYAT *Japhet* lxvi, Bawling out his ditty. **1850** THACKERAY *Pendennis* xxvii. 257, 'I will fling you out of window'..bawled out Mr. Pen.

b. To 'cry' for sale, as a hawker.

a **1745** SWIFT (J.), It grieved me when I saw labours which had cost so much, bawled about by common hawkers.

c. With *out*: To reprove or reprimand loudly or severely. orig. *U.S.* Also *ball out* (see BALL *v.*[5]).

1908 R. BEACH *Barrier* xvii. 270 If you'll go back on your word like this you'll 'bawl me out' before the priest. **1917** MATHEWSON *Sec. Base Sloan* xv. 203 You'll get bawled out when you pull a boner. *Ibid.* xviii. 239 Wayne thought that the manager's 'bawling out' that forenoon had done good. **1922** H. L. FOSTER *Adv. Trop. Tramp* ix. 119 In private Griffis bawled me out for my rashness. **1933** *New Statesman* 18 Mar. 331/2 All the *plats du jour* were 'off' and we bawled out the head waiter. **1942** L. A. G. STRONG *Unpractised Heart* xii. 82 He bawled him out. Gave him such a tongue lashing as the louse will remember to his dying day.

Hence **bawl-out** *sb.* a reprimand. *U.S.*

1926 J. BLACK *You can't Win* vi. 70, I..don't want to.. give myself a bawl-out in front of the woman.

bawl (bɔːl), *sb.* [f. prec. vb.] A shout at the top of one's voice, a loud prolonged rough cry.

1792 WOLCOTT (P. Pindar) *Acad. Ode* Wks. 1812 II. 509 Proud of a loud, clear, melancholy bawl.

bawle, obs. form of BALL *sb.*[1]

bawler (ˈbɔːlə(r)). [f. BAWL *v.* + -ER[1].] One who bawls; sometimes applied contemptuously to a declamatory preacher.

1656 S. H. *Gold. Law* 73 One hath thrown Baal's Altar, what's this to the Bawlers? **1758** JORTIN *Erasm.* 140 When you meet with one of these bawlers, let him rave..till he hath made himselfe hoarse. **1882** BESANT *All Sorts* I. xii. 259 Listening, as most bawlers discover, is not conviction.

bawley (ˈbɔːlɪ). *local.* Also **bauley, baully.** [Of obscure origin.] A fishing-smack peculiar to the coasts of Essex and Kent. Also *attrib.*, as *bawley-boat.*

1887 PARISH & SHAW *Dict. Kentish Dial.* 9 *Bawley*, a small fishing smack used on the coasts of Kent and Essex, about the mouth of the Thames and Medway. **1888** *Sat. Rev.* 24 Mar. 349 A little creek where barges and bawley-boats can ride. **1895** RYE *Gloss. E. Anglia, Bauley Boats*, Harwich fishing-smacks. **1921** *Spectator* 7 May 589/1 Leigh-on-Sea is the producer of the bawley, a type of craft which has a loose-footed mainsail, but would otherwise be called a cutter. **1948** H. BENHAM *Last Strongholds of Sail* xxiii. 194 They are comely little bawleys, well kept, power-driven, and obviously prosperous.

bawling (ˈbɔːlɪŋ), *vbl. sb.* [f. BAWL *v.* + -ING[1].]

†**1.** The howling or yelping of dogs, wolves, etc.; *spec.* in *Hunting* (see quot. 1753). *Obs.*

c **1440** *Promp. Parv.* [see BAWL *v.* 1]. **1555** *Fardle Facions* II. x. 213 Their [Tartares'] singyng is like the bawlynge of Woulues. **1635** WITHER *Lord's Prayer* 129 The bawlings and snarlings of Dogs. **1753** CHAMBERS *Cycl. Supp.*, *Bawling*, among hunters, is spoke of the dogs, when they are too busy to find the scent good.

2. Shouting at the top of one's voice, loud vehement outcry, vociferation.

1629 GAULE *Pract. The.* 239 The Rancour and Bawlings of Fiends and Wretches. **1722** WOLLASTON *Relig. Nat.* ix. 208 Propagating..senseless opinions with bawling and fury. **1865** LIVINGSTONE *Zambesi* xix. 366 But talking and bawling did not put them out of breath.

attrib. **1882** *19th Cent.* No. 69. 749 They were in the bawling stage of beer. **1884** *Graphic* 23 Aug. 190/2 To row within bawling distance.

bawling (ˈbɔːlɪŋ), *ppl. a.* [f. BAWL *v.* + -ING[2].]

†**1.** Of dogs, etc.: Howling, yelping; *spec.* in *Hunting*, giving tongue too loudly (cf. prec.). *Obs.*

1594 T. B. *La Primaud. Fr. Acad.* II. 510 A barking and bawling dogge. **1669** WORLIDGE *Syst. Agric.* (1681) 228 Small bawling Curs are the surest Watchers.

2. Shouting at the top of one's voice; making loud noise or outcry, vociferating.

1603 KNOLLES *Hist. Turks.* (1621) 830 Their barbarous bawling instruments. **1697** DRYDEN *Virg. Georg.* II. 719 Nor heard, at bawling Bars, corrupted Law. **1850** MRS. STOWE *Uncle Tom's C.* xxxi. 286, I have none o' yer bawling, praying, singing niggers on my place.

bawm(e, obs. form of BALM.

bawn (bɔːn). Also 6 **baon, banne,** 7–8 **baune,** 9 **bane.** [ad. Ir. *bábhun* (O'Clery), of unknown derivation.]

1. A fortified enclosure, enceinte, or circumvallation; the fortified court or outwork of a castle.

1537 *St. Papers Hen. VIII*, II. 441 Our Englishe men assauted the diges and baon of the castell. **1586** J. HOOKER *Girald. Irel.* in *Holinsh.* II. 167/1 This castell..and the bannes about it. **1596** SPENSER *State Irel.* 502 b, These.. square bawns which you see so strongly trenched and thrown up. **1736** CARTE *Ormonde* II. 6 Defects in the walls of the outward Bawne..rendered it assaultable. **1827** HALLAM *Const. Hist.* III. 506 in *N. & Q.* 1850 Ser. I. I. 440/1 Those who received 2000 acres were bound..to build a castle and bawn or strong court yard: the second class..to build a stone house with a bawn; the third class a bawn only.

2. A cattlefold.

1850 *N. & Q.* Ser. I. II. 60/2 The word *bawn* or *bane*..is still applied in the south of Ireland to the..place for milking the cows of a farm..Before the practice of housing cattle became general, every country gentleman's house had its bawn. **1882** *Whitehall Rev.* No. 21. 6/1 A large castle..with a bawn attached to preserve their cattle at night.

bawne, variant of BALNE. *Obs.*, bath.

bawneen, bauneen (ˈbɔːniːn). [ad. Irish *báinín* undyed flannel, f. *bán* (*báin-*) white.] In Ireland: a sleeved waistcoat made from undyed flannel worn by farm-labourers. Also *attrib.*; **bawneen yarn,** a coarse light fawn unwashed knitting-wool.

1910 *Month* CXV. 66 The last rays of the setting sun fell slanting, lighting up the white bauneen of the turf cutters. **1919** YEATS *Two Plays for Dancers* 2 He seems an Aran fisher, for he wears The flannel bawneen and the cow-hide shoe. **1958** *Observer* 19 Jan. 11/2 Tweed car-coats will be lined in firm handknits, some in the 'bawneen' yarn which washes so magnificently. **1967** N. FITZGERALD *Affairs of Death* x. 164, I bought cigars, a bawneen sweater and..a cuddly toy.

†ˈ**bawrel, ˈbawret.** *Obs.* [Of unknown origin: some compare It. '*barletta* a tree falcon, a hobby'; the Corpus Gloss. has '*bariulus* reagufinc,' some kind of finch. Cf. also BAWTERE.]

According to 18th c. dictionaries, the female and male respectively of a kind of hawk; see quot.

1706 PHILLIPS, *Bawrel*, a kind Hawk, that for Size and Shape, is somewhat like the Lanner, but has a longer Body and Sails. **1727** BRADLEY *Fam. Dict.* s.v. *Hawk*, [The] Bawrel [has] her Bawret. **1755** in JOHNSON, and mod. dicts.

bawshere, obs. form of BEAU SIRE

bawsint, bawson, -stone, var. BAUSON, -OND.

†ˈ**bawtere.** *Obs. rare*⁻¹. [? an error for *vawtere*, VULTURE; or by transposition of letters for BAWRET.] (See quot.)

1486 *Bk. St. Albans* D iij b, Theys haukes belong to an Emproure..an Egle, a Bawtere, a Melowne.

bawty, -tie (ˈbɔːtɪ). *Sc.* [cf. F. *baud* white hound (Cotgr. s.v. *Souillard*).] Scotch titular name for a dog, esp. a large one; also for a hare.

c **1536** LYNDESAY (*title*) Complaint..of the Kingis auld Hound callit Bagsche, directit to Bawte, the Kingis best belouit Dog. *Ibid.* 21 For Bawte now..lyis on the kingis nycht goun. **1728** RAMSAY *Gent. Sheph.* II. ii. *Poems* (1844) 60 The devil's..Appearing sometimes like a black-horned cow, Aft-times like bawty. *Sc. Proverb*, Bourd not wi' bawtie lest he bite you.

†ˈ**baw-ˈwaw.** *Obs.* [imitative of the sound; cf. BAUGH and BOW-WOW.]

1. The barking of a dog.

1576 LAMBARDE *Peramb. Kent.* (1826) 233 A Dogs barking that soundeth nothing els—but Baw waw waw.

2. An exclamation of contempt.

1599 NASHE *Lent. Stuffe* 59 Bawwaw, quoth Bagshaw. ? *c* **1600** *Distr. Emperor* V. iii. in *Old Pl.* (1884) III. 247 Baw, waw, waw! Sir, trouble not your selfe.

b. *attrib.* quasi-*adj.* Vainly or contemptibly noisy.

1570 LEVINS *Manip.* 45 Bawwawe spoken of one, that talketh to no purpose. **1583** STANYHURST *Æneis* IV. (Arb.) 108 Ne on baw-vaw tromperye descant.

baw-ways, bawways (ˈbɔːweɪz), *adv.* and quasi-*adj.* *Anglo-Irish.* [Origin of first element uncertain; cf. Sc. *baw(w)aw* side-glance of contempt or scorn. For the formation cf. *edgeways, endways*, etc.] Crookedly; leaning awkwardly, leaning to one side; sideways.

1907 J. JOYCE *Let.* 1 Mar. (1966) II. 218 Scholz's five crown cloak hung bawways on me. **1922** —— *Ulysses* 297 Little Alf was knocked bawways. **1944** *Béaloideas* XIV. 164 [South-West Dublin Glossary] *Baw-ways* (aw as in *bawl*). Crooked or leaning to one side. 'That hay-reek is badly built; it's all baw-ways.' **1947** *Ibid.* XVII. 264 [North-County Dublin Glossary] *Baw-ways.* Crooked. Awkwardly. He did it *baw-ways* = wrong.

†**bawze,** *v. Obs. rare*⁻¹. [Of doubtful origin and use. Hardly likely to be related to Du. *bassen* to bark (pret. *bies* in MDu.), considered by Franck to be a modern onomatopœia, as it is found in no other Teut. lang.] To exclaim, shout.

1677 LITTLETON *Lat. Dict.*, To bawze, *exclamare, intonare.*

†ˈ**baxter.** *Obs.* or *dial.* Forms: 1 **bæcestre, -istre, -ystre,** 2–3 **bakestre,** 4–5 **bakestir, bacstare,** 5 **baxstere, backstare,** 6–7 **backster, baxster,** 7 **bakster,** 5– **baxter.** [OE. *bæcestre*, fem. of *bæcere*, f. *bacan* to BAKE: see -STER. A true feminine in origin, and used of women as late as 16th c.; but already in OE. used also of men (see *Gen.* xl. 1, of a eunuch), and in ME. used of both sexes, as the Vocabularies expressly show; in later use only masculine, being the regular northern, and esp. Sc, equivalent of *baker*, in which use it still lingers dialectally. In 16th c. a new feminine BACKSTR-ESS was formed upon it; cf. *songstress, seamstress.*] A baker: **a.** applied to women.

1390 *Test. Ebor.* (1836) I. 143 Lego Matildæ bakestir j. goune. *c* **1425** *Gloss.* in Wright *Voc.* 194 *Hic* [? hec] *pandoxatrix*, bacstare. *c* **1450** *Ibid.* 215 *Hec pistrix*, a baxter. *a* **1550** *Thersytes* in *Four Old Plays* (1848) 81 The backster of Balockburye with her baking pele.

b. without distinction of sex. Apparently not used in southern English after 1400.

c **1000** ÆLFRIC *Gen.* xl. 1, 2 Twegen afyryde men..Egypta cynges byrle and his bæcistre..his byrlas oþer his bæcestran. *c* **1150** *Gloss.* in Wright *Voc.* 93 Pistor, bakestre, **1377** LANGL. *P. Pl.* B. Prol. 218 Baxsteres & brewesteres, and bocheres manye. **1460** CAPGR. *Chron.* 55 Plauctus..was compelled for to dwel with a baxter. *c* **1550** J. BALFOUR *Practicks* (1754) 15 The Baxter, for his fie, fiue pundis. **1753** *Scots Mag.* Apr. 206/1 Mr. Robert Bartleman, baxter. **1818** SCOTT *Hrt. Midl.* vi. *note*, One in appearance a baxter, *i.e.* a baker's lad, handed her out of her chair.

Baxterian (bækˈstɪərɪən), *a.* and *sb.* [f. BAXTER + -IAN.] **A.** *adj.* Of or pertaining to Richard Baxter, the eminent Puritan divine, or his doctrines. **B.** *sb.* One who holds Baxter's tenets. **Baxˈterianism,** Baxter's doctrines, one special point of which was the amalgamation of the Arminian doctrine of free grace with the Calvinistic doctrine of election.

1835 in *Penny Cycl.* IV. 62/1. **1839** SIR J. STEPHEN *Eccl. Biogr.* 44 Baxter was opposed to every sect, and belonged to none. He can be properly described only as a Baxterian.

baxtone, dial. form of BAKESTONE.

bay (beɪ), *sb.*[1] Also 4–7 **baye, baie.** [a. OF. *baie* (= Pr. *baga*):—L. *bāca* berry.

In OE. *begbeam* occurs in the OE. Gospels, and in a glossary of the 11th c. (Wülcker /450) as a rendering of *mōrārius*; the glossarist adds that *mōra* is a name for 'berries' generally, whence *beg* appears to be = berry. In the 11th c. it might perhaps already be adopted from Fr.; but the Corpus Glossary of the 8th c. (Wülcker /8) has also 'baccinia (= vaccinia) *beger*' which suggests that this (elsewhere *begir*) might be an archaic plural of an original *-is, -os* stem, and that *beg* was a native word. Its ME. repr. would be *bey, bay*; but the extant *bay* appears to be from French.]

†**1. a.** A berry, a small fruit, esp. used of that of the laurel or bay-tree: see 2. *Obs.*

1398 TREVISA *Barth. De P.R.* XVII. xlviii, The frute of lauri tre ben clepid baies. **1483** *Cath. Angl.* 17 Bay; *bacca, est fructus lauri & oliue.* **1601** HOLLAND *Pliny* I. 452 The Baies or berries that it [the roiall Lawrel] beareth are nothing sharp biting..in tast. **1616** SURFL. & MARKH. *Countr. Farm* 290 The bayes, or berries of myrtle-tree. **1661** LOVELL *Hist. Anim. & Min.* 245 Drunk with the Oile of Bayes in black Wine. **1866** *Treas. Bot.* 664 From the fruit is expressed a butter-like substance known as oil of Bays.

†**b.** A small ball, a globule. *Obs. rare.*

c **1420** *Pallad. on Husb.* II. 198 Take a bay of gootes dounge, And with a nal..make it holowe.

2. a. Short for *Bay-tree* or *Bay Laurel*, English name of the *Laurus nobilis* (called also Sweet Bay), a fine tree, with deep-green leaves and a profusion of dark-purple berries; also applied to other laurels (*e.g.* the Red Bay of S. America), and in America to *Magnolia glauca* (White Bay).

1530 PALSGR. 914/3 The bay tre, *laurier.* **1535** COVERDALE *Ps.* xxxvii. 35, I my self haue sene the vngodly..florishinge like a grene baye tre. **1684** I. MATHER *Remark. Provid.* iv. 93 Philosophers told him the lightning could not hurt the bay-tree. **1866** *Treas. Bot.* 664/1 The Bay Laurel is a native of the south of Europe.

1557 Tottell's *Misc.* (Arb.) 264 When other frutes and flowers decay, The bay yet growes full grene. **1794** MARTYN *Rousseau's Bot.* xix. 262 The true Bay is known by its lance-shaped, veiny evergreen leaves. **1855** KINGSLEY *Heroes* II. iv. Slopes of oak..arbutus, and fragrant bay.

b. A piece of low, marshy ground producing large numbers of Bay-trees. Bartlett *Dict. Amer.* 1848.

1795 F. ASBURY *Journal* (1821) II. 285 This country [*sc.* S. Carolina] abounds with bays, swamps, and drains. **1845** W. G. SIMMS *Wigwam & Cabin* 17 He wandered along the edges of a dense bay or swamp-bottom. **1884** *Harper's Mag.* Mar. 60l/1 Swamps and 'bay' (the word applied in Florida to slough and water-grass meadows).

3. Usually in *pl.* Leaves or sprigs of this tree, *esp.* as woven into a wreath or garland to reward a conqueror or poet; hence *fig.* the fame and repute attained by these.

1564 HAWARD *Eutropius* VII. 75 When he had subdued the Sarmatianes, he ware but a garland of baies only. *c* **15**—

GREENE *Fr. Bacon* iv. 64 A poet's garland made of bays. **1647** *Churchw. Acc. St. Margaret's Westm.* (Nichols 1797) 53 Rosemarie and baies, that was stuck about the Church at Christmas. **1656** COWLEY *Misc.* (1669) 8 The gain of Civil wars will not allow Bay to the Conquerors Brow. **1730** THOMSON *Autumn* 666 For virtuous Young and thee they twine the bay. *a* **1764** LLOYD *Author's Apol.* Poet. Wks. 1774 I. 7, I seek to blast no scholar's bays.

4. *Comb.* and *Attrib.*: **a.** attrib., as ***bay-bow*** (= bough), ***-branch***, ***-leaf***, ***-tree*** (see 2 a), ***-wood***; **b.** instrumental and similative, as ***bay-crowned***, ***-leaved***. Also **bay-cherry**, the Cherry-laurel (*Cerasus Laurocerasus*); **bay-gall** *U.S.* (*a*) = BAY *sb.*² 4 b; (*b*) *Bot.*, the red bay (see RED *a.* 17 d); **bay-rum**, an aromatic liquid, used by perfumers, obtained by distilling rum in which bay-leaves have been steeped; **bay-swamp** *U.S.* = BAY *sb.*² 4 b.

1607 *Schol. Disc. agst. Antichr.* I. iii. 157 They doe not set lights and *bay bowes at their dores. **1579** SPENSER *Sheph. Cal.* Apr. 104 Bene they not *Bay branches, which they doe beare? **1665–76** RAY *Flora* 14 The *Bay-Cherry is a stately evergreen tree. **1638–48** G. DANIEL *Eclog.* iv. Song 3 Wouldst thow still *Bay-crowned Sitt? **1775** ROMANS *Florida* 15 Swamps, marshes, and *bay, or cypress galls. **1861** A. WOOD *Class-bk. Botany* 620 Red Bay.. Bay Galls.. Wood of a fine rose-color, once used in cabinet-work. **1872** SCHELE DE VERE *Americanisms* 440 Bay-Galls are large, gloomy, almost impenetrable swamps in Florida, full of deer, bear, and catamount. **1636** HEALEY *Theophrast.* 59 Bearing a *bay leafe in his mouth. **1855** BROWNING *Protus* Poet. Wks. I. 297 Half-emperors and quarter-emperors, Each with his bay-leaf fillet. **1883** *Harper's Mag.* Jan. 199 Pepper-woods, whose leaves smell of *bay-rum. **1840** *Knickerbocker* XVI. 34 Perfumed 'as to our locks' with the *bay-rum or fragrant cologne. **1859** BARTLETT *Dict. Amer.* (ed. 2) 25 *Bay Rum*.. is chiefly used for the purposes of the toilet. **1741** in *Colonial Rec. Georgia* (1908) IV. Suppl. 237 The Land in these parts, setting aside the Pine-Barren, and some *Bay-swamps,.. with proper cultivation, will yield a reasonable Increase. **1832** D. J. BROWNE *Sylva Amer.* 164 These spots are entirely covered with the loblolly bay, and are called Bay Swamps.

bay (beɪ), *sb.*² Also 5–7 **baye.** [a. F. *baie*:—late L. *baia*, in Isidore, *c* 640. (Isidore illustrates his derivation of *portus* from *portare* by the analogy of *baia* from *bajulare.* He does not consider *baia* a modern word; but says it made its genitive in *-as*, like *familia.* It may thus be an old word in popular Latin.) The meaning of the Fr. word (which the Eng. follows) may have been modified by confusion with *baee, bee*, on L. type **badāta* an opening (see BAY *sb.*³). The two have certainly been associated in English; see esp. 2–4, where the senses of recess and projection appear.

Derivation from *badare*, to be open (see BAY *sb.*³) is disproved by It. *baja*, unless this is borrowed from some other Romanic language, as Sp. or Fr.]

1. An indentation of the sea into the land with a wide opening.

1385 TREVISA *Higden* (1865) I. 57 In that grete mouthe and baye, beth ilondes Calchos, Patmos, and others. **1436** *Pol. Poems* II. (1859) 186 Ffor they have havenesse grete and godely bayes Sure, wyde, and depe. **1596** SHAKS. *Merch. V.* II. vi. 15 The skarfed barke puts from her natiue bay. **1600** —— *A.Y.L.* IV. i. 211 My affection hath an vnknowne bottome, like the Bay of Portugall. **1685** R. BURTON *Eng. Emp. Amer.* ii. 54 A fair Sandy Bay or Beach, which the Sea washeth on one side. **1719** DE FOE *Crusoe* I. 50 We might happen into some Bay or Gulph. **1875** MACKAY *Mod. Geog.* 24 Bay of Biscay, noted for its heavy seas and dangerous navigation.

fig. **1601** CORNWALLYES *Ess.* xix, Yet did I once touch at the baye of Armes. **1633** G. HERBERT *Sunday* i. in *Temple* 66 The couch of time; care's balm and bay.

†**2.** An indentation or rounded projection of the land into the sea. *Obs.*

[Perhaps a distinct word, f. BEY *v.* to bend; cf. BAYING.]

1611 COTGR., *Surgidoire*, a road, gulfe, or bosome, of the sea.. sometimes also the opposite, a Promontorie, Cape, or Bay of land entering into the sea.

3. An indentation, recess in a range of hills, etc.

1853 G. JOHNSTON *Nat. Hist. E. Bord.* I. 9 The hills.. stand out generally well-defined by bays and vales, which run in about their bases.

4. An arm of a prairie extending into, and partly surrounded by, woods.

1850 W. COLTON *Three Years Calif.* 370 Still, in some of its bays, the evidences of fertility exist. **1874** B. F. TAYLOR *World on Wheels* 17 In the bottom of a bay of land bounded.. by wooded hills.

5. *Comb.*, mostly attrib., as ***bay-head***, ***-man***, ***-side***. Also **bay-bird** *U.S.*, a shore-bird that frequents the bays and estuaries of the Atlantic coast; **bay-craft** *U.S.*, a vessel or vessels used in the navigation of bays; **bay-duck**, dial. (east English) name of the Sheldrake (*Tadorna vulpanser*); **bay-floe, -ice**, new-formed ice, such as first appears in sheltered water; **bay-like** *a.*, resembling a bay; **bay-snipe** *U.S.* = *bay-bird*; **Bay State**, popular name in U.S. for the State of Massachusetts, originally the Colony of Massachusetts Bay; hence ***Bay Stater***; **bay-vessel** *U.S.* = *bay-craft*; **bay whaling**, a method of whaling in the shore waters of Australia and New Zealand using land-based stations; formerly called *shore whaling*; hence **bay whaler**, a boat used in bay whaling; **bay whale**, a whale that frequents bays, spec. the Southern Right Whale (*Balæna australis*).

1889 *Cent. Dict.* *Bay-birds. **1725** in *New Eng. Quarterly* (1929) II. 660 We met a Ship which they took and burnt then sending away what Prisoners they thought fit in a *Bay Craft. **1835** C. J. LATROBE *Rambler in N. Amer.* II. vi. 102 Many a settler loads his small bay-craft with planks and shingles in the spring of the year. **1856** KANE *Arct. Exp.* I. xxvi. 342 The big *bay-floe. **1818** SCORESBY in *Ann. Reg. 1817* 534/2 This is termed *bay-ice. **1853** KANE *Grinnell Exp.* xv. (1856) 109 The 'young,' or as it is called by the whalers, the 'bay ice.' **1874** DISRAELI in Buckle *Life* (1920) V. ix. 354 The waters glittering in the *bay-like coast. **1897** M. KINGSLEY *W. Africa* 130 The great forest sweeping away in a bay-like curve. **1779** *Hist. Eur.* in *Ann. Reg.* (1781) 211/2 The *Bay-men on the Musquito and bay of Honduras shores. **1883** BURTON & CAMERON *Gold Coast* I. i. 16 The shallow brown waters of the *Bayside. **1856** *Spirit of Times* 6 Sept. 9/1 *Bay Snipe shooting is at its acme, and can be enjoyed everywhere on Long Island. **1875** *Fur, Fin & Feather* 121 It is also a capital place for bay-snipe shooting in summer. **1789** S. DAVIS *Jrnl.* 1 Sept. in *Proc. Mass. Hist. Soc. 1869* (1871) XI. 14 The style of building varies somewhat from that of the *Bay State, as they term Massachusetts. **1837** R. M. BIRD *Nick of Woods* I. 132 He was from the Down-East country; a representative of the Bay State. **1845** *St. Louis Reveille* 14 May 2/4 The inhabitants of.. Massachusetts [are called] Bay Staters. **1856** LOWELL *Biglow P.* 37, I love our own Bay-State. **1789** *Maryland Jrnl.* 24 Feb. (Th.), I will exchange a small *Bay Vessel for a large one, and give the difference. **1850** H. T. CHEEVER *Whaleman's Adv.* vi. 79 *Bay whaling, which destroys the cows about the time of calving. **1853** G. B. EARP *New Zealand* vii. 95 [The] whale fishery [was] carried on chiefly on the coasts of the northern and middle island by means of boats—a method technically called 'bay-whaling', these animals frequenting the coasts in great numbers during the breeding season. **1905** W. B. *Where White Man Treads* 36 The lawless pakeha bay-whaler. *Ibid.* 75 An old-time bay whaling station consisted.. of at least two boats. **1913** R. MCNAB *Old Whaling Days* i. 6 During the following month—November—the remaining bay whalers returned to Sydney. **1933** F. D. OMMANEY *Whaling in N.Z.* in *Discovery Rep.* VII. 243 Much of the Right whale industry was carried on by the method known as 'bay whaling'. This branch of the fishery derived its name from the Right whales' habit of entering shallow bays and inlets of the coast for the purpose of.. calving. **1947** A. H. CLARK in H. Belshaw *New Zealand* 32 Fur seals and bay whales (i.e., the right whales) which once frequented the island are now virtually extinct.

bay (beɪ), *sb.*³ Forms: 6 **baie**, 6–7 **baye**, 4– **bay.** [a. F. *baie*, OF. *baée* (L. type *badāta*), f. *bayer*, OF. *baer, béer* to gape, stand open = Pr. and It. *badare*, as to which see Diez. See prec.]

1. An opening in a wall; *esp.* the space between two columns.

c **1325** *E.E. Allit. P.* B. 1392 Heȝe houses withinne þe halle to hit med, So brod bilde in a bay, þat blonkes moȝt renne. *c* **1400** *Sowdone Bab.* 940, O Thow rede Marz.. That in the trende baye hase made thy trone. **1849** FREEMAN *Archit.* 371 The division into bays by a marked vertical line seems everywhere rigidly preserved. **1870** F. WILSON *Ch. Lindisf.* 102 The last two bays of the nave.. are unoccupied. **1884** *Manch. W. Times* 11 Oct. 5/6 The replacing of the tracery of the cloisters.. proceeding bay by bay.

2. 'The division of a barn or other building, generally from fifteen to twenty feet in breadth,' Gwilt. (See the dialect Glossaries.) Applied to a house, it appears to be the space lying under one gable, or included between two party-walls.

1557 *Richmond Wills* (1853) 101 Ij bayes of rye, bye est. xxxqu. xvb. **1577** HOLINS. *Chron.* III. 1198/2 Two and fortie baies of houses. **1603** SHAKS. *Meas. for M.* II. i. 255 Ile rent the fairest house in it after three pence a Bay. **1616** SURFL. & MARKH. *Countr. Farm* 18 One of the sides of your Barne, all along for the space of three Bayes, shall serue to put your Rie and Wheat in. **1725** BRADLEY *Fam. Dict.*, *Bay*, a rural Word used to signify the Bigness of a Barn; for if a Barn consists of a Floor and two Heads, wherein they lay Corn, they say a barn of two Bays. **1759** *Ann. Reg.* 127/2 Ten bay of Buildings.

3. Applications of the idea of 'recess': e.g. ***horse-bay***, the stall for a horse; ***sick-bay***, part of the fore-part of a ship's main-deck, used as a hospital (see also SICK *a.* 10 a); ***bomb bay***: see BOMB *sb.* 6.

1582 *Wills & Inv. N.C.* (1860) II. 47 Iij swalles for a horse baye 8*d.* **1851** *Art. Jrnl. Hist. Gt. Exhib.* 20/1 The crowding of the bays of the galleries. **1863** *Man-of-War* in *Cornh. Mag.* Feb., Their 'sick-bay' probably does not differ from any hospital ward. **1867** SMYTH *Sailor's Word-bk.*, *Bay*, the fore part of a ship between decks before the bitts. **1885** *Pall Mall G.* 31 Mar. 6/1 The 'bays' between the gun stations.. afford shelter to the gunners.

4. Applications of 'intervening space,' usually receding, as *bay* in plastering, of joists, of roofing.

1823 P. NICHOLSON *Pract. Build.* 384 *Bay*, a strip or rib of plaster between screeds, for regulating the floating rule. **1842** GWILT *Archit.* (1875) 1193 *Bay of joists*, the joisting between two binding joists, or between two girders, when binding joists are not used. *Bay of roofing*, the small rafters and their supporting purlins between two principal rafters.

5. a. An internal recess formed by causing a wall to project outwardly beyond the general line, for the reception of a window or other feature.

1428–1741 [see BAY-WINDOW]. **1805** REPTON *Landsc. Gard.* 178 Large recesses or bays, sometimes called bowre windows, and now bow windows. **1855** MERIVALE *Rom. Emp.* (1865) VI. xlviii. 60 Projecting the bay of the tribune from the flat wall of the basilica. **1877** E. WALFORD *Our Gt. Fam.* I. 76 A substantial brick house, the front diversified by two bays.

b. *Mil.* A section of a trench in which the line is modified in order to allow more space for passing.

1916 'BOYD CABLE' *Action Front* 73 The trenches.. with bays and niches cut deep in the side to permit the passing of anyone meeting a line of pack-burdened men in the shoulder-wide alley-way. *a* **1917** E. A. MACKINTOSH *War, the Liberator* (1918) 154 'Don't put it in so high up, boys,' he said. 'They'll see it and knock this bay to hell.'

6. A side or subordinate line of railway at a station; also *attrib.* in **bay-line**, a line at the side of, and terminating in, a railway station.

1906 *Westm. Gaz.* 20 Sept. 7/1 A bay line out of Grantham Station crosses some of the roads. **1907** *Ibid.* 10 June 9/1 The passenger station has not been interfered with, except in No. 1 bay-line. **1939** A. CHRISTIE *Murder is Easy* i. 13 A train.. came slowly puffing in and deposited itself in a modest bay.

7. A series of racks in a telephone exchange on which equipment is mounted.

1906 J. POOLE *Pract. Telephone Handbk.* (ed. 3) xxi. 291 The incoming and outgoing junction and other.. lines are also accommodated on the arrester frame, special bays being reserved for them. **1920** *Post Office Electr. Engin. Jrnl.* Jan. 205 The apparatus is placed on the various bays of the racks.

bay (beɪ), *sb.*⁴ Also 4 **baie**, 5 **baye.** [Two different words seem to be here inextricably confused. Originally, the phrase *to hold at bay* seems ad. OF. *tenir a bay* (Godefroy) = It. *tenere a bada*, where *bay, bada*, means the state of suspense, expectation, or unfulfilled desire, indicated by the open mouth (late L. *badare* to open the mouth); but *to stand at bay, be brought to bay*, correspond to mod.F. *être aux abois*, meaning to be at close quarters with the barking dogs, and *bay* is here aphetically formed from ABAY, a. OF. *abai* barking. See BAY *v.*¹ In the phrase *at a bay*, some early quotations may read *at abay.*]

I. Barking or baying.

1. The deep prolonged barking of a dog when pursuing or attacking.

1530 PALSGR. 196/2 Bay of houndes, *aboyement de chiens.* **1588** SHAKS. *Tit. A.* II. ii. 3 Vncouple heere, and let vs make a bay, And wake the Emperour. **1784** COWPER *Task* I. 230 The bay of curs. **1810** SCOTT *Lady of L.* I. i, The deep-mouthed bloodhounds' heavy bay. **1849** C. BRONTË *Shirley* xv. 230 Formidable-looking dogs.. all bristle and bay.

2. *esp.* The chorus of barking raised by hounds in immediate conflict with a hunted animal; *hence*, the final encounter between hounds and the prey they have chased.

c **1300** *K. Alis.* 200 Of liouns chas, of beore baityng, And bay of bor. *a* **1400** *Cov. Myst.* 180 Tyl a beggere blede be bestys baye. **1575** TURBERV. *Venerie* 125 That there are Bayes in the water and bayes on the lande. **1876** WHYTE-MELVILLE *Katerfelto* xxiii. 261 Soon would burst on his ear that loud and welcome chorus called the 'bay.'

†**b.** *transf.* applied to the singing of birds. *Obs.*

1513 DOUGLAS *Æneis* XII. Prol. 232 Dame naturis menstralis.. Thayr blyssfull bay entonyng euery art.

II. Most commonly, and often figuratively, in hunting phrases relating to the position of a hunted animal when, unable to flee farther, it turns, faces the hounds, and defends itself at close quarters.

3. Of the position of the hunted animal: ***to stand, be*** (***abide*** obs.) ***at bay, turn to bay***; and of the relative action of the hounds: ***to hold*** or ***have at bay, bring*** or ***drive to bay, make a bay at*** (obs.)

c **1314** *Guy Warw.* 245 He stod at a bay, And werd him while that he may. *c* **1350** *Will. Palerne* 35 He gan to berke on þat barn and to baie it hold. **1530** PALSGR. 586/2 Yonder stagge is almoste yelden, I here the houndes holde hym at a beye, *je os les chiens laboyer*, or *le tenyr a laboy.* **1579** TOMSON *Calvin's Serm. Tim.* 309/1 He shall be sette uppon on all sides, they make a bay at him, they will bite him, if it bee possible. **1593** SHAKS. *Rich. II*, II. iii. 128 To rowze his Wrongs, and chase them to the bay. **1611** COTGR., s.v. *Acculé*.. the wild Bore, which, brought vnto a bay, sets him on his Gammons, and.. is forced to defende himselfe against both dogs, and men. **1735** SOMERVILLE *Chase* III. 535 He stands at Bay against yon knotty Trunk. **1879** FROUDE *Cæsar* xxiv. 422 To fight to the last and die at bay.

b. *fig.* In phr. ***at a*** or ***to the bay***: at or to close quarters; in great straits, in distress, at or to one's last extremity. Cf. F. *aux abois.*

1596 SPENSER *State Irel.* 510 a, All former purposes were blanked, the governor at a bay, and, etc. **1599** *Pass. Pilgr.* xi, Ah! that I had my lady at this bay, to kiss and clip me till I run away. **1642** ROGERS *Naaman* 17 Shall God haue us at so great a bay as he hath, and shall we wax carelesse. **1682** DRYDEN *Medal, Epistle*, In utter Despair of your own Satyr, make me Satyrize myself. Some of you have been driven to this Bay already.

4. Of the effective action of the hunted animal: ***to hold*** or ***keep at*** (***a***) ***bay*** (the assailing hounds); ***to give the bay to*** (obs.); and (rarely) of the corresponding position of the hounds: ***to be at bay.***

c **1532** LD. BERNERS *Huon* (1883) 395 As the wyld bore doth kepe a baye agaynst the mastyues and bayynge houndes. **1553–87** FOXE *A. & M.* III. 239 Whereat the Chancellor was much offended: but Bradford still kept him at the bay. **1577** FENTON *Guicciard.* I. (1599) 35 With his industry..he had giuen the bay to his aduersaries. **1592** SHAKS. *Ven. & Ad.* 973 She hears the hounds are at a bay. **1697** DRYDEN *Virg. Georg.* III 620 Thy faithful Dogs..who ..hold at Bay The Mountain Robbers. **1711** F. FULLER *Med. Gymn.* Pref., By Riding..keep Death as it were at a Bay. **1858** FROUDE *Hist. Eng.* III. xiv. 256 The spoils of the church furnished the arms by which the Pope..could be held at bay.

bay (beɪ), *sb.*[5] Also 7 **baye**. [A word of doubtful standing and origin: it may be questioned whether senses 1 and 2 are really connected, and whether the word in the *Promp. Parv.* is not BAY *sb.*[4], but sense 2 does not fall easily under any other of the words spelt *bay*. For the etymology, the ON. *bág-r* 'opposition,' has been compared, with its derived vb. *bægja* 'to push back, hinder'; the latter might be the direct source of the related BAY *v.*[4], if we could assume the sb. to have been taken from the vb. But if, as seems more likely, the vb. is from the sb., the origin of the latter has still to be discovered.]

†**1.** 'Obstacle.' *Obs.*

c **1440** *Promp. Parv.* 21 Bay, or withstondynge, *obstaculum.*

2. An embankment or dam to retain water, or divert its course into a mill stream, etc.

1581 LAMBARDE *Eiren.* IV. iv. (1588) 421 If any persons.. have bene assembled..to cut downe any houses, Barnes, Milles, or Bayes. **1604** *Fr. Bacon's Proph.* 507 in Hazl. *E.P.P.* IV. 286 The Ducke must have a Bay, the Hawke must have a stone. **1607** COWELL *Interpr.*, Baye..is a pond head made vp of a great heith, to keep in a great quantitie or store of water. **1632** SHERWOOD, Bay of plankes, to breake the force of water, *moile.* **1879** JEFFERIES *Wild Life S.C.* 126 A strong bay or dam crosses..[the brook], forcing the water into a pond for the cattle.

bay (beɪ), *sb.*[6] Also 7 (in *comb.*) be-. [short for *bay-antler*, earlier *be-* or *bes-antlier*, f. OF. *bes* twice, second, secondary + ANTLER.] The second branch of a stag's horn, formerly also called the *sur-antlier*, being next above the 'antler' proper, or (as it is now called) brow-antler.

[**1611** COTGR, *Surandoillier*, the beankler or second branch of a Deere's head.] **1863** KINGSLEY *Water-Bab.* ii. 67 You may..know..what his rights mean, if he has them, brow, bay, tray, and points. **1884** JEFFERIES *Red Deer* iv. 69 This is a full horn; brow, bay, tray, and three on top, or six points a side. *Ibid.* 71 The ancient terms..next the *bez-antlier*, now the bay.

†**bay** ('beɪ), *sb.*[7] *Obs.* exc. *Hist.* Also 7 **baye**. [a. F. *baie*, or its Du. repr. *baai*, f. F. *bai*, *baie*, the colour BAY: see BAIZE.]

1. Baize; originally a fabric of a finer lighter texture than now, the manufacture of which was introduced into England in the 16th c. by fugitives from France and the Netherlands. Usually in the pl., whence the modern corruption BAIZE, q.v.

1581 *Act 23 Eliz.* ix. §1. Pennestones, Bays, Cottons, Hose-Yarn..and other Things. **1648** in Rushw. *Hist. Coll.* IV. II. 1152 In making of Bays and Says. **1660** *Act 12 Chas. II.* xxii, None shall weave in Colchester any bay known by the names of *four-and-fifties, sixties*..but within two days after weaving shall carry it to the Dutch Bay Hall to be viewed. **1713** *Guardian* No. 170 (1756) II. 344 Colchester bays, Exeter serges. **1727-51** CHAMBERS *Cycl.*, *Bay* is also a sort of woollen stuff, made chiefly in Colchester, where there is a hall, called the Dutch Bay-hall.

2. *Comb.*, as ***bay-maker, -making, -market, -trade, -yarn***; **bay-hall** a hall in Colchester used as an exchange by traders in this commodity.

1684 *Lond. Gaz.* No. 1988/3 The Moot-Hall and Bay-Hall hung with the same. **1708** *Lond. Gaz.* No. 4501/4 Zacheus Skingsley of Colchester..Baymaker. **1753** *Scots Mag.* Nov. 538/1 Woollen or bay yarn. **1858** *People's Hist. Gt. Brit.* 104 The Protestants..fled many to this country bringing with them the art of Bay and say making.

bay, *sb.*[8] [Of uncertain origin and sense: cf. BECK.]

1593 PEELE *Edward I* 381 (D). Friar, I am at beck and bay, And at thy commandment to sing and say.

bay (beɪ), *a.*[1] (and *sb.*[1]) Also 5-6 **baye**, 6-7 **baie**. [a. F. *bai* bay-coloured:—L. *badius*, mentioned by Varro in a list of colours appropriate to horses.]

1. A reddish brown colour; **a.** generally used of horses, and taken to include various shades. Hence qualified as ***bright-bay, light-bay, blood-bay, golden-bay.***

c **1374** CHAUCER *Troylus* I. 1072 His stede bay. **1420** *E.E. Wills* (1882) 53 A bay hors þat was Gerards my son. **1460** *Lybeaus Disc.* 462 An stedes baye brown. **1551** T. WILSON *Logike* 79 All horses bee not of one colour, but..some baye, some daple. **1622** PEACHAM *Compl. Gentl.* I. xxiv. (1634) 85 A Bay or a Chesnut Colour, of all others it is most to be commended in Horses. **1671** *Lond. Gaz.* No. 636/4 Stoln.. a Bay Ball Nag. **1715** ADDISON *Drummer* v. i. concl., I have a horse..a bay gelding. **1823** LOCKHART *Vow of Reduan* xi. in *Sp. Ball.*, He spurred his bright bay mare. **1860** J. BROWN *Horæ Subs.*, *My Father's Mem.*, His little blood bay horse.

b. rarely used otherwise.

1653 URQUHART *Rabelais* I. xii. (1694) I. 45 He made him also change his colour of Hair..from Bay, Brown, to Sorrel ..gingioline. **1839** LADY LYTTON *Cheveley* II. v. 143 Mrs. Tymmons had been a blonde, and consequently had subsided into a bay wig.

2. as *sb.*, *ellipt.* for 'bay horse.'

1535 STEWART *Cron. Scot.* II. 187 Occa..Vpoun ane bay out of the feild him bair. ? *a* **1600** *Came you not fr. N.* in Furniv. *Percy Folio* I. 253 Met yee not my true loue ryding on a bony bay. **1774** J. BRYANT *Mythol.* I. 327 The horse was of a Palm colour, which is a bright red. We call such horses bays. **1781** COWPER *Retirem.* 392 Lolls at his ease behind four handsome bays. **1884** *Times* 27 Feb. 7/6 The compact, black-legged bays of Essex.

b. *The Bays*: see quots.

1837 R. CANNON *Hist. Records Brit. Army, Second Dragoon Guards* 64 About this period [*sc.* 1767] the regiment was mounted on Bay Horses; and as the other regiments of heavy cavalry were mounted on black horses (except the Scots Greys) the Queen's Dragoon Guards were commonly styled the Queen's Bays. **1878** R. TRIMEN *Regiments Brit. Army* 14 Second Dragoon Guards... Being mounted on bay horses about 1767 caused it to be called the 'Queens Bays'. .. It is now commonly called 'the Bays'.

3. *Comb.*, as ***bay-brown, -coloured.***

1591 PERCIVALL *Sp. Dict.*, *Vayo*, baye coloured. **1616** SURFL. & MARKH. *Countr. Farm* 675 The baie coloured ones haue the second place for goodnesse. **1852** T. HARRIS *Insects New Eng.* 85 [An insect] of a light bay-brown color, with the head and antennæ darker.

bay (beɪ), *v.*[1] Also 5-6 **baye**. [Partly a. OF. *baye-r*, more frequently occurring in the deriv. *abayer* (see Littré s.v. *aboyer*; cf. It. *bajare*, *abbajare* to bark) of uncertain origin; but influenced in later Eng. use by BAY *sb.*[4], in phrases 'at bay, to bay,' so that the two notions were even more inextricably blended than in the sb.

(Diez's reference of *abayer* to L. **ad-baubāre* 'to bark at' is now rejected; recently it has been proposed to connect it with *badāre*, in which case both words would ultimately be from the same source.)]

1. To bark, properly applied to the deep voice of a large dog, as a hound or mastiff. Const. *on*, *at* (with *indirect passive* 'to be bayed at').

c **1340** *Gaw. & Gr. Knt.* 1142 Braches bayed þerfore & breme noyse maked. **1486** *Bk. St. Albans* E viij, They. houndes all Bayen and cryen. **1530** PALSGR. 442/2 This hounde bayeth at somwhat: *ce chien aboye a quelque choses* **1596** SPENSER *F.Q.* I. v. 30 The wakefull dogs did never cease to bay. *a* **1771** GRAY *Poems* (1775) 50 Hoarse he bays with hideous din. **1805** SCOTT *Last. Minstr.* I. vi, They watch to hear the blood hound baying.

†**b.** (said of other animals.) *Obs.*

c **1450** HOLLAND *Houlat*, Sum bird will bay at my beke, and sum will me byte.

2. *fig.* Applied (depreciatively) to the noise of human assailants.

1399 LANGL. *Rich. Redeless* III. 235 And alle þe berdles burnes bayed on him euere. **1583** STUBBES *Anat. Abus.* Pref. 18 Zoilvs crew, Who'le dayly at thee bay. **1606** SHAKS. *Tr. & Cr.* II. iii. 99 What moves Ajax thus to bay at him?

3. *trans.* To bark at, to assail with barking.

c **1420** *Avow. Arth.* vii, The raches comun reuynyng him by And bayet him fulle boldely. **1596** DRAYTON *Leg.* iii. 669 Some againe did bay me, As hungrie Wolves at Passengers doe howle. **1601** SHAKS. *Jul. C.* IV. iii. 27, I had rather be a dog, and bay the moon, Than such a Roman. *c* **1800** K. WHITE *Clift Gr.* 166 The deep-mouth'd mastiff bays the troubled night. **1866** HOWELLS *Venet. Life* (1883) I. iv. 75 Sleepless youths who there melodiously bayed the moon in chorus.

b. *fig.* of persons.

1796-7 COLERIDGE *Poems* (1862) 34 Though superstition and her wolfish brood Bay his mild radiance. **1839** BAILEY *Festus* v. (1848) 36 Millions..bay a mind Which drives the darkness out of them, like hounds.

4. To give forth, utter, or express by baying.

1591 SPENSER *Virg. Gnat* xliv, Cerberus, whose many mouthes doo bay And barke out flames. **1856** KANE *Arct. Exp.* I. xxii. 279 These faithful servants generally bayed their full-mouth welcome from afar off.

5. To pursue with barking like a pack of hounds; to drive to bay with barking.

1590 SHAKS. *Mids. N.* IV. i. 118 In a wood of Creete they bayed the Beare With hounds of Sparta. **1597** —— *2 Hen. IV.* I. iii. 80 He leaves his backe vnarm'd, the French, and Welch Baying him at the heeles. **1661** HICKERINGILL *Jamaica* 17 The whole Herd making homewards so soon as ever the Doggs do Bay them. **1845** DARWIN *Voy. Nat.* vii. (1879) 136 The jaguar is killed by the aid of dogs baying and driving him up a tree.

6. To bring to bay, hold at bay. (The notion of barking disappears.)

1575 TURBERV. *Bk. Venerie* 239 We tree and baye both Martern and wild Catte. **1601** SHAKS. *Jul. C.* IV. i. 49 We are at the stake, And bayed about with many Enemies. **1713** *Guardian* No. 125 (1756) II. 164 He taught to turn the hare, to bay the deer. **1795** SOUTHEY *Joan of Arc* VI. 96 The men of Orleans, Long by their foemen bay'd.

bay (beɪ), *v.*[2] [A later deriv. of the sb. in the expression 'at bay,' due to the ambiguity with which that was said both of the pursued and of the pursuing animal: see BAY *sb.*[4]]

1. *intr.* To turn to bay, stand at bay.

1649 G. DANIEL *Trinarch.*, *Rich II*, civ, They knew Hee Bay'd to their Destruction. **1774** GOLDSM. *Nat. Hist.* (1862) I. II. v. 325 When a stag turns his head against the hounds, he is said to bay.

2. *trans.* To stand at bay against. *rare.*

1848 G. RUXTON in *Blackw. Mag.* LXIII. 719 Baying his enemies like the hunted deer.

†**bay**, *v.*[3] *Obs. rare*$^{-1}$. [a. OF. *baye-r*, *bée-r* to gape, seek with open mouth:—late L. *badāre* to gape, be open.] To seek with open mouth, as the young of animals for the dugs.

1580 HOLLYBAND *Treas. Fr. Tong.*, *Bayer á la mamelle*, to seeke or baye for the dugge.

bay (beɪ), *v.*[4] [Immediately connected with BAY *sb.*[5], but whether as its source or derivative does not appear; the latter is more likely. Supposing the vb. to be the source, it has been conjecturally derived from ON. *bægjan* 'to push back, hinder'; it might also be referred to 'hold at bay' in some of its uses (see BAY *sb.*[4]): or even to BAY *sb.*[2] or [3] in some of their applications.] *trans.* To obstruct, dam (water): often with *up*, *back.*

1598 SYLVESTER *Du Bartas* I. ii. (1641) 18/2 He, whose pow'rfull hand Bay'd-up the Red-Sea with a double Wall. **1635** CARPENTER *Geog. Del.* II. x. 177 By baying vp the Riuers into certaine Artificiall Channells. **1883** SIR A. HOBHOUSE *Law Rep.* IX. Appeal 177 The defendants' barrier has been found to bay back the water to a maximum depth of twenty-two inches.

†**bay(e**, *v.*[5] *Obs. rare*$^{-1}$. [app. a pseudo-archaism; cf. the similar use of EMBAY in same work I. vii. 3.] ? To bathe, immerse.

1596 SPENSER *F.Q.* I. vii. 3 He..bayes His sweatie fore-head in the breathing wind.

bay, *v.*[6] [f. BAY *sb.*[2]] *intr.* To spread *out* in a bay-like form.

1906 'A. HOPE' *Sophy of Kravonia* viii, The town was no more than one long street, which bayed out at the farther end into a market-place.

‖**bayadère** (bɑːjə'dɛər, -'dɪə(r)). Also 6 **balliadera**, 8 **balliadere**, 9 **bayadeer**. [F. *bayadère*, ad. Pg. *bailadeira* female dancer; cf. *bailar* to dance. The earlier forms were taken directly from the Portuguese.] **1.** A Hindoo dancing girl: the French name, occasionally used by English writers.

1598 W. PHILLIPS *Linschoten's Trav.* 74 (Y.) The heathenish whore called Balliadera, who is a dancer. **1794** E. MOOR *Narrat. Little's Det.* 356 (Y.) The name of balliadere, we never heard applied to the dancing girls. **1826** HEBER *Journ. India* (1828) II. xxviii. 282 The southern Bayadêre, who differ considerably from the nâch girls of northern India. **1835** *Penny Cycl.* IV. 62/2 The little arts and manners which form the accomplished bayadeer. **1859** SALA *Tw. round Clock* (1861) 240 A gay audience shouting applause to mimes and jesters and painted bayadères.

2. Any textile fabric having stripes running across the material. Also *attrib.* or as *adj.*, defining a material striped in this way.

1856 *Illustr. London News* 27 Dec. 653/1 Bayadere skirts. **1879** *Cassell's Fam. Mag.* Apr. 312/1 Pompadour silks with Bayadère stripes beneath the bunches of flowers are somewhat new. **1960** *Guardian* 22 Apr. 8/4 Exquisite evening shoes of glazed Bayadere material.

bayard ('beɪəd), *a.* and *sb.*[1] *arch.* Forms: 4-7 **bayard**, 5 **beyard**, 5-7 **bayarde**, 6 **bayart**, **baierd**, **baiarde**, 6-7 **baiard**, **bayerd**. [a. OF. *baiard*, *-art*, *bayard* bay-coloured, f. *bai*: see BAY *a.*[1] and -ARD.]

1. Bay coloured; *absol.* a bay horse.

1330 R. BRUNNE *Chron.* 272 Sir Edward..Opon his stede bayard first he wan þe dike. **1464** *Mann. & Househ. Exp.* 184, I bowete of Roberd Bernard the Konstabelschepe of Bramborou, and he ad of me ther fore my bayard Kreseuer. **1623** MINSHEU *Sp. Gram.* 6, Bays, which is vsed in good authors for Bay coloured or Bayard. **1868** D. EVANS 4 *Bks. Wales* I. 520 Saddle thou the bayard with the long bound.

2. Proper name of the bright-bay-coloured magic steed given by Charlemagne to Renaud (or Rinaldo), one of the four sons of Aimon, famous in mediæval romance; *whence* **a.** Formerly used as a kind of mock-heroic allusive name for any horse; cf. the occasional use of *Rosinante, Bucephalus, Pegasus.*

c **1374** CHAUCER *Troylus* I. 218 As proud Bayard gynnyth for to skippe Out of the wey. *c* **1400** *Beryn* 3184 A man to seruesabill Ledith offt beyard from his own stabill. *c* **1489** CAXTON *Four Sonnes Aymon* i. (1884) 31 Thenne mounted Reynawde on horsebacke vpon Bayarde. **1575** CHURCHYARD *Chippes* (1817) 147 But he that holdes..the horses rain, When steede bolts out, calles bayard back again.

b. ***bayard's bun***: a kind of bread given to horses. ***bayard of ten toes***: the human feet, 'shanks' mare, nag, or pony'; also called *horse of ten toes.*

c **1520** SKELTON *Agst. Comely Coystrowne* 8 A swete sugar loaf and sowre bayardys bun. **1616** BRETON *Good & Badde* 35 The walke of the wofull and his Horse, Bayard of ten-toes.

c. Alluded to in many phrases and proverbial sayings, the origin of which was in later times forgotten, and 'Bayard' as the type of blindness or blind recklessness.

c **1325** *E.E. Allit. P.* B. 886 Þay blustered as blynde as bayard watz euer. **1393** GOWER *Conf.* III. 44 But as Bayard the blinde stede..He goth there no man will him bidde. **1401** *Pol. Poems* (1859) II. 53 Thou, as blynde Bayarde, berkest at the mone. **1532** MORE *Confut. Tindale* Wks. 500/1 Bee bolde vpon it lyke blynde bayarde. **1609** BRETON *Poste w. Packet*, Who is so blind as Bold Bayarde. **1625** *Gonsalvio's Sp. Inquis.* 168 As blind & yet as bold as Bayard. *c* **1630** JACKSON *Creed* IV. Wks. III. 33 As..boldly as blind bayard rusheth into the battle. **1674** N. FAIRFAX *Bulk & Selv.* 157 Bayard must ever be as bold as blind.

3. *Hence*: One blind to the light of knowledge, who has the self-confidence of ignorance.

a **1529** SKELTON *Agst. Garnesche* Wks. I. 123 Bolde bayarde, ye are to blynde. **1579** TOMSON *Calvin's Serm. Tim.* 65/2 Them that shall walke negligently, and like blinde bayardes. **1645** MILTON *Colast.* Wks. (1851) 368 Being a bayard, who never had the soul to know, what conversing means. *a* **1677** BARROW *Serm.* (1686) III. 487 The bold and blind Bayards (who usually out of self-conceit are so exceedingly confident of their election and salvation).

† **'bayard,** *sb.*² *Obs.* [a. F. *bayard, baiart*, in same sense: cf. BAIARDOUR.] A kind of hand-barrow used for heavy loads; also *fig.*

1642 ROGERS *Naaman* 30 When they are laid upon his bayard, and when he hath them upon the hip. *Ibid.* 35 Surely he is faine to lay men upon the bayard.

† **bayardism.** *Obs.* [f. BAYARD *sb.*¹ + -ISM.] Ignorant presumption.

1624 BP. MOUNTAGU *New Gagg* 89 Grosse Bayardismes in so insolent a Bard.

† **'bayardly,** *a. Obs.* [f. BAYARD *sb.*¹ + -LY¹.] Bayard-like; characterized by the blindness and self-confidence of ignorance.

1636 GOODMAN *Wint. Even. Confer.* III. 20 Religion is.. not a formal and bayardly round of duties. **1656** *Artif. Handsom.* 143 A blind credulity, a bayardly confidence. **1659** GAUDEN *Tears Ch.* 118 The bayardly blindness of common people.. neither able nor willing to discern.

† **'bayardly,** *adv. Obs.* [f. as prec. + -LY².] Blindly, with blind self-confidence.

1624 H. MASON *Art of Lying* iv. 67 Some ignorant Iesuite: (for none else can be imagined to be so Bayardly bold).

bayberry ('beɪˌbɛrɪ). [f. BAY *sb.*¹ 2]

1. The fruit of the bay-tree.

1578 LYTE *Dodoens* 688 Called in Latine *Lauri baccæ*, in English Bay berries. **1747** *Gentl. Mag.* XVII. 409 Take of aniseed.. bay-berries, myrrh.. of each half an ounce.

2. In U.S., the fruit of the Wax-myrtle (*Myrica cerifera*), and the plant itself, an American shrub that bears a berry covered with a wax-like coating.

1687 in *Manchester* (Mass.) *Rec.* 32 The sd. tree being near Vincsons baiberry medow. **1769** *Massachusetts Gaz.* 21 Dec., Advt. (Th.), Bayberry-wax candles. **1792** J. BELKNAP *New Hampsh.* III. 123 The bay berry (*myrica cerifera*), the leaves of which yield an agreeable perfume, and the fruit a delicate green wax, which is made into candles. **1860** BARTLETT *Dict. Amer.* s.v., The berries when boiled in water yield a fragrant green wax, known as bayberry tallow, used for making candles, etc. **1878** R. THOMPSON *Gard. Assist.* (Moore) 657/1 *Myrica cerifera*, candleberry, bay-berry, or wax-myrtle.—Very near the sweet-gale.

3. In Jamaica, the fruit of the 'Bayberry Tree,' *Eugenia acris*, a species of Pimento.

1756 P. BROWNE *Jamaica* 247 The Bayberry Tree.. The berries resemble our cloves, both in form and flavour.

bayche, baye, obs. ff. BEACH, BO, both.

† **bayed,** *a.*¹ *Obs.* Also 5 bayde. [f. BAY *a.*¹ + -ED; or ad. L. *badius.*] Bay-coloured.

c **1440** *Promp. Parv.* 21 Bayyd, as a horse (*v.r.* bay), *badius.* **1483** *Cath. Angl.* 17 Bayde [with no Latin equivalent].

† **bayed,** *ppl. a.*² *Obs.* [? short for EMBAYED.] Surrounded, enclosed.

1577 HOLINSHED *Chron.* II. 11/1 The territorie baied and perclosed within the river. **1583** STANYHURST *Æneis* III. (Arb.) 74 A plentiful Island.. roundlye bayed.. With Mycone, and eke with Giarus, two famosed Islands.

bayed (beɪd), *ppl. a.*³ [f. BAY *v.*⁴ + -ED]. Dammed.

a **1618** SYLVESTER *Lawe* 694 (D.) He smot the sea with his dead-liuing rod: The sea obayed, as bay'd. **1879** JEFFERIES *Wild Life in S.C.* 64 It [the brook] swells sufficiently, if bayed up properly, to drive a mill.

bayed (beɪd), *ppl. a.*⁴ [f. BAY *sb.*³ + -ED.] Having a bay, formed as a bay or recess.

a **1848** MARRYAT *R. Reefer* lxvi. 258 The bayed windows. **1851** HELPS *Comp. Solit.* vii. (1874) 130 A window, in a bayed recess.

Bayer ('baɪə(r)). [From the name of the inventor, K. J. *Bayer*, a German metallurgist.] **Bayer process**: a process for the production of aluminium from bauxite.

1910 *Metall. & Chem. Engin.* Aug. 498/1 Two processes are used in France to produce alumina from bauxite. The Bayer process is used at Gardanne, where the ore is attacked under pressure with caustic soda solution. **1911** *Ibid.* Mar. 147/1 The alumina is purified from the bauxite by the Bayer process—solution in caustic soda and precipitation therefrom. **1949** P. C. CARMAN *Chem. Const. & Prop. Engin. Materials* vii. 229 To get pure Al_2O_3, the Bayer process is used, in which bauxite is treated with 45% NaOH heated to 100 p.s.i. **1956** *Nature* 10 Mar. 462/2 The purification of the mineral by the Bayer process.

Bayer 205 ('baɪə(r)). [G. *205 Bayer* (L. Haendel and K. W. Joetten 1920, in *Berliner Klin. Wochenschr.* 30 Aug. 821/1), f. the name of F. Bayer & Co., a German chemical firm.] A synthetic trypanocidal drug, $C_{51}H_{34}N_6Na_6O_{23}S_6$.

1922 *Chem. Abstr.* XVI. 3128 Chemotherapeutic experiments with 'Bayer 205', a new trypanocidal agent of special activity. **1933** *Discovery* Apr. 116/1 In sleeping sickness drugs like arsenic and 'Bayer 205' are relatively effective.

baygne, bayne, obs. forms of BAIN.

baying ('beɪɪŋ), *vbl. sb.*¹ [f. BAY *v.*¹ + -ING¹.] The continued deep barking of a large dog.

1611 COTGR., *Abbay*, a barking, or baying of dogs. **1814** SCOTT *Wav.* xxiv, The baying of the dogs was soon added to the chorus.

baying ('beɪɪŋ), *vbl. sb.*² [f. BAY *a.*¹ + -ING .] The imparting of a bay colour.

1634 in H. Walpole *Vertue's Anecd. Paint.* (1786) II. 212 For baying and colouring the whole number of the oares for the row barge.

baying ('beɪɪŋ), *ppl. a.*¹ [f. BAY *v.*¹ + -ING².] That bays; deep-barking.

c **1532** LD. BERNERS *Huon* (1883) 395 The mastyues and bayynge houndes. **1791** COWPER *Iliad* III. 29 Baying hounds Disturb not him.

† **'baying,** *ppl. a.*² *Obs.* [f. BAY *sb.*² or ³; cf. BEY *v.* to bow.] Curving, receding.

1538 LELAND *Itin.* III. 75 From Bridport to the North West Point of the Chisil renning from Portland thither about a Mile.. Shore somewhat baying.

bayish ('beɪɪʃ), *a. rare.* [f. BAY *a.* + -ISH¹.] Somewhat bay, inclining to bay (in colour).

1697 *Lond. Gaz.* No. 3289/4 A Bayish dun Horse.

bayl, bayle, bayll, obs. ff. BAIL, BALE, BAILEY.

baylable, obs. form of BAILABLE q.v.

‖ **bayle, baylo,** obs. variants of BAILO.

1703 *Lond. Gaz.* No. 3891/2 To go in the Quality of Bayle or Ambassador.. to the Ottoman Porte. *Ibid.* No. 3903/2 This Republick's Baylo or Ambassador.. to the.. Porte.

baylet ('beɪlɪt). [f. BAY *sb.*²] A little bay.

1826 *Blackw. Mag.* XX. 426 Headland bold, And silver-sanded baylet. **1876** R. BURTON *Gorilla L.* II. 265 Off this baylet are three rocky islets.

bayliary, bayllive, etc.: see BAILIERY, BAILIFF.

bay-man, bayman¹. [BAY *sb.*² 5.] **1.** A resident beside a bay (usu. some specific bay); one accustomed to navigating a bay. *U.S. Hist.*, an inhabitant or native of Massachusetts Bay.

1641 in *New Plymouth Colony Records* II. 23 That clause .. which concerned the boundes from Narragansetts Bay to .. Pockanockett, in regard the Bay men would haue had Sicquncke from us. **18..** *Shore Birds* 43 (Cent. D.), When the birds are traveling with the wind, or as baymen call it, a 'free wind'. **1904** *N.Y. Even. Post* 11 June, Somers P'int, as the baymen call it, is one of several very attractive summer resorts that have grown up about the bay in recent years.

†**2.** A mahogany-cutter of the Bay of Honduras. *Obs.*

1715 *Boston News-Let.* 10 Oct. 2/2 Huntingdon and.. Holder.. report that 250 of the Bay-Men.. were designed to Campeche, to burn the Shipping there. **1781** *Ann. Reg.* 1780 *211/2 The baymen on the Musquito and bay of Honduras shores, (as the logwood cutters are called). *a* **1821** C. BIDDLE *Autobiogr.* (1884) i. 17 The baymen at this time would frequently sell their wood to two or three different captains.

bayman². *U.S.* [BAY *sb.*³ 3.] A sick-bay nurse.

1888 CHURCHWARD *'Blackbirding'* 25, I stole a beautiful knife from the sick bayman's locker. **1891** H. PATTERSON *Naut. Dict.* 346 Bayman, a hospital nurse.

bayne, -ly, variant of BAIN, -LY; obs. f. BANE.

bayne = both: see BO.

bayness ('beɪnɪs). [f. BAY *a.*¹ + -NESS.] The quality of being bay-coloured.

1570 LEVIN *Manip.* 90 Also many other that end in *nesse*, derived of adiectiues.. as of bay, *baynesse.* **1610** MARKHAM *Masterp.* I. lxvi. 140 Baynesse turnes to dunnesse.

baynyd (*Promp. Parv.*): see BAINED.

bayonet ('beɪənɛt), *sb.* Also 7 baggonet, 7–8 bagonet, 8 bagnet. all still in vulgar use. [a. F. *baïonnette*, in Cotgr. *bayonnette*, of uncertain origin. Diez, Littré, Scheler, favour the usual derivation from the name of the city *Bayonne*, the weapon being supposed to have been either first made or first used there; the former notion is strengthened by a statement of Des Accords (*a* 1583) that people spoke of *bayonnettes de Bayonne* 'Bayonne bayonets,' as of 'Toulouse scissors,' etc. But it is possible that the word may be a dim. of OF. *bayon, baion* 'arrow or shaft of a cross-bow,' from which Cotgr. still has *bayonnier* 'an old word' = *arbalestier*: the Sp. *bayona* sheath, and It. *bajonetta* 'little joker' (a possible appellation for a dagger), have also been suggested as the source.

(See Notes on the Origin and History of the Bayonet; by Mr. Akerman, read to the Soc. of Antiquaries, May 1860.)]

‖ **1.** A short flat dagger. *Obs.*

[**1611** COTGR., *Bayonnette*, a kind of small flat pocket-dagger, furnished with kniues; or a great knife to hang at the girdle, like a dagger.] **1692** *Lond. Gaz.* No. 2742/2 Skeyns, Baggonets, and all other Arms. **1707** *Ibid.* No. 4389/1 (Venice), That no persons.. shall presume to wear the Bayonet, or Sword, on pain of being sent to the Gallies.

2. a. A stabbing instrument of steel, which may be fixed to the muzzle of a musket or rifle; originally its handle was inserted in the mouth of the gun, but it is now secured by a circular band clasping the barrel. See also SWORD-BAYONET.

[**1672** CHAS. II *Warrant* 2 Apr. in Carter *Curiosities of War* (1860) 239 The souldiers of the several troopes aforesaid are.. also to have and to carry one bayonet or great knive.] **1704** *Lond. Gaz.* No. 4044/3 Our Granadiers, after .. two or three Vollies.. put their Bayonets in the Muzzles of their Pieces. *a* **1774** FERGUSSON *Leith Races, Poems* (1845) 32 On guns your bagnets thraw. **1817** J. SCOTT *Paris Revisit.* 130 The soldier.. was about to plunge his bayonet into the breast of the unfortunate Frenchman.

b. *abst.* Military force.

1774 BURKE *Amer. Tax.* Wks. II. 373 You are obeyed soley from respect to the bayonet. **1879** D. HILL *Bryant* 112 He visited Paris, then.. under the rule of the bayonet.

3. *pl.* Soldiers armed with bayonets.

1780 BURKE *Let. Merlott* Wks. IX. 259 On the demand of 40,000 Irish bayonets. *c* **1880** GRANT *Hist. India* I. li. 261/1 Colonel Pearse's column.. returned.. reduced from 5000 to 2000 bayonets.

4. *transf.* or *fig.* **a.** generally.

1883 G. ALLEN in *Knowledge* 8 June 337/1 In wild barley the entire inflorescence bristles.. with stiff bayonets.

b. *Mech.* A pin which plays in and out of a hole, and serves to engage and disengage portions of machinery, a clutch.

1798 in *Specif. Patent* No. 2228 (*Sellars' Spin. Mach.*). **1864** in WEBSTER.

5. *Spanish Bayonet*: A species of *Yucca*, a liliaceous plant, with a crown of linear-lanceolate leaves, found in the south of North America.

1865 PARKMAN *Huguenots* vii. (1875) 109 Hacking their way through thickets of the Yucca, or Spanish bayonet. **1882** W. BISHOP in *Harper's Mag.* Dec. 47/1 In the door-yards are the Mexican aloe and the Spanish bayonet.

6. *attrib.*, as in *bayonet-belt, -charge, -sheath, -thrust, -wound*; also **bayonet cap**, a cap on an electric light bulb for insertion in a bayonet socket; **bayonet-capped** *a.*, fitted with a cap for fastening in a socket as a bayonet joint; **bayonet catch**, the spring catch by which a bayonet is secured to a rifle; **bayonet-clutch**, a clutch with two prongs for engaging and disengaging machinery; **bayonet grass**, a popular name for a New Zealand umbelliferous plant of the genus *Aciphylla*; **bayonet-joint**, one in which the two parts are so interlocked that they cannot be separated by a simple longitudinal movement; **bayonet-socket**, a socket with which a bayonet-capped fitting engages.

1812 WELLINGTON in Gurw. *Disp.* IX. 603 There are in the stores at Lisbon Bayonet belts for infantry. **1877** BRYANT *Country's Call* i, The rifle and the bayonet-blade For arms like yours were fitter now. **1914** S. C. BATSTONE *Electric Light Fitting* vii. 136 In Fig. 142 the finished lamps are shown, No. 1 with what is known as the 'bayonet cap', B.C. **1943** *Electronic Engin.* XVI. 247 The activated electrodes at either end are connected to a two-pin bayonet cap. **1904** *Daily Chron.* 18 June 2/6 Bayonet-capped [electric] lamps. **1901** 'LINESMAN' *Words Eyewitness* (1902) 317 They have struck as true and hard as any, right up to the bayonet-catch. **1868** W. L. LINDSAY *Contrib. N.Z. Bot.* xii. 49 *Aciphylla*.. The larger species are familiar to the settler as 'Spear-grass', or 'Bayonette-grass'.. in allusion to their very rigid, strong, poniard-like, sharp-pointed leaves. **1899** T. KIRK *Students' Flora N.Z.* 207 Bayonet-grass. **1946** *Jrnl. Polynesian Soc.* LV. 158 *Taramea*.. spear-grass, bayonet-grass, spaniard: a hill and mountain plant from whose spiny blades the Maori by heat and torsion extracted a valued scent. **1870** *Eng. Mech.* 4 Feb. 501/3 A lens, which is adapted to the apparatus by a bayonet-joint. **1817** J. SCOTT *Paris Revisit.* 215 Bayonet sheaths, bits of caps, and the rags of clothes, covered the ground. **1892** F. C. ALLSOP *Pract. Electric-Light Fitting* vi. 75 The.. lamp.. is used with the bayonet socket holders, which is certainly the most convenient and efficient method of making connection between lamp and conducting wires. **1955** *Times* 13 July 4/1 The rod.. was then removed by a turn of a bayonet socket.

bayonet ('beɪənɛt), *v.* [f. prec. sb.]

1. *trans.* To stab or pierce with a bayonet.

c **1700** *Gentl. Instruc.* 535 (D.), I came not into the world to be cannonaded or *bagonetted* out of it. **1858** BEVERIDGE *Hist. Ind.* III. VII. iii. 85 The Arabs within were bayoneted.

2. To drive at the point of the bayonet; to coerce or compel as by military force.

1790 BURKE *Fr. Rev.* 325 You send troops to sabre and to bayonet us into a submission. **1863** *Commonwealth* (Boston) 18 Feb. 65 It has been bayoneted up to it by the pressure of outside public opinion.

bayoneted ('beɪəˌnɛtɪd), *ppl. a.* [f. BAYONET *sb.* + -ED.] Armed or provided with a bayonet.

1815 *Edin. Rev.* XXV. 532 Guarded by a bayonetted soldiery against a bludgeoned mob. **1856** OLMSTED *Slave States* 20 A bright bayonetted firelock.

bayoneteer (ˌbeɪənɪ'tɪə(r)). *nonce-wd.* [f. BAYONET *sb.* + -EER¹.] A soldier armed with the bayonet.

1848 THACKERAY *Cornh. to Cairo* iv. 33 Knights shout their war cries and jovial Irish bayoneteers hurrah.

bayoneting (ˈbeɪənɛtɪŋ), *vbl. sb.* [f. BAYONET *v.* + -ING[1].] Stabbing with a bayonet.
1885 *Pall Mall G.* 10 Feb. 10/2 The bayoneting of a soldier at Woolwich.

bayou (ˈbaɪuː). Also byo, bayoue, bayeau, *pl.* bayoux. [Amer. Fr., f. Choctaw *bayuk*.] The name given (chiefly in the southern States of N. America) to the marshy off-shoots and overflowings of lakes and rivers.
1766 H. GORDON in N. D. Mereness *Travels Amer. Col.* (1916) 484 We left New Orleans.. and lay that night in the Bayoue. **1808** ASHE *Trav. Amer.* xl. 323 Below the Red River, five miles, is one of the most dangerous bayeaus on the Mississippi. **1814** BRACKENRIDGE *Views Louisiana* 162 On some of these bayoux the land is sufficiently high to admit of settlements. **1818** COBBETT *Resid. U.S.* (1822) 273 Johnson's Ferry, a place where a Bayou (Boyau) of the Wabash is crossed. This Bayou is a run out of the main river, round a flat portion of land. **1834** CROCKETT *Narr. Life* vi. 53 A small byo, cross which there was a log. **1847** LONGF. *Ev.* II. iii. 51 How have you nowhere encountered my Gabriel's boat on the bayous? **1872** *Amer. Naturalist* VI. 725 A peculiar feature of the bottom lands of the western and southern rivers, locally termed bayous. **1901** S. E. WHITE *Westerners* xiii. 93 In a word the broad sea of the wilderness has shrunken to bayous and bays.
attrib. **1850** H. C. LEWIS *Louisiana Swamp Doctor* 161, I saw the dust up the bayou road shaken up by a half-naked negro. **1886** *Harper's Mag.* Aug. 483/1 The following bayou version of one of the negro folk-lore stories.

Bayreuth (ˈbaɪrɔɪt). The name of a Bavarian town in which festivals of the music of Richard Wagner have been held since 1876 in a theatre specially built for the production of his operas. Also *attrib.* and *ellipt.* Hence **Bay'reuthian**, pertaining to or characteristic of Bayreuth. **Bay'reuther**, an inhabitant of Bayreuth.
1876 *All Year Round* 23 Sept. 39/2 The Bayreuth Performances. There has probably never been an event in.. the history of music which has caused so much excitement as the recent first performances, at Bayreuth,.. of Richard Wagner's.. 'Der Ring des Nibelungen'. **1876** *Nation* 7 Sept. 148/1 Dazzling spectacles, in an opera-house.., were not strange to the eyes of the Bayreuthers. **1885** G. B. SHAW *How to become Musical Critic* (1960) 101 Singers of Bayreuth music-dramas. **1889** *Ibid.* 151 As to the peculiar merits of the Bayreuth mode of performance, they are simply the direct results of scrupulous reverence for Wagner. **1896** *Ibid.* 243 And this, if you please, is Bayreuthian fidelity to 'The Meister'. **1896** —— *Our Theatres in Nineties* (1932) II. 67 We could build it [*sc.* the Stage Festival Playhouse] for ourselves better and cheaper than the Bayreuthers built it for Wagner. **1959** *Listener* 29 Jan. 216/1 The error, common in the past, against which Bayreuth now ensures the spectator is that of believing that Wagner used Teutonic myth and medieval legend simply as a vehicle for crude theories of German nationalism.

bayrn, bayt, bayz, etc.: see BAI-.

bay-salt (ˈbeɪˌsɒlt). Forms: 5–6 baye-, 7 bai-, base-, 6– bay-salt. [prob. f. BAY *sb.*[2]
Many explanations have been offered. A derivation from *Bayonne* dates from 1633; but if salt was really imported into England from that place, it would seem more probable that *bay-salt* meant 'salt from the Bay (of Biscay)'; cf. '*Cape* wines,' etc. The conjecture that it means salt procured from bays (of the sea) indefinitely, seems less probable, for it would have been more obvious, in this case, to say '*sea*-salt.' There seems to be no good authority for the statement that the Cheshire brine-pools are called *bays*, nor would this explain why one kind of salt should bear the name of *bay-salt* more than another.]
Salt, obtained in large crystals by slow evaporation; originally, from sea-water by the sun's heat.
1465 *Mann. & Househ. Exp.* 201 Item, for di. a bz. of baye salt ij.*d.* ob. **1559** *Wills & Inv. N.C.* (1835) 184 In the Salt Garner. Halffe a weye of baye salte. **1612** WOODALL *Surg. Mate* Wks. (1653) 207 Bay or Sea salt, dried meerely from salt Sea water by the heat of the Sunne. **1633** C. BUTLER *Eng. Gram.* Index, Bai Salt, salt of Bayonne in France. **1654** GAYTON *Fest. Notes* III. iii. 80 Train oyle, dead wine, Base-salt. **1708** *Lond. Gaz.* No. 4486/3 Her Lading, consisting of French Bay Salt. **1866** ROGERS *Agric. & Prices* I. xix. 456 Great or gross salt was no doubt the larger crystals known now as bay salt.

baysche, bayse, -ment, obs. f. BASH, -MENT.

'bay-stone. [? corruption of BASE-STONE: cf. *base* for *bay* in prec.] A stone laid on the surface of the ground as part of the foundation of a slight building.
1845 WILLIAMS in *Jrnl. R. Agric. Soc.* VI. I. 45 The tenant has the right to remove.. any buildings put up by himself on 'bay stones,' where the buildings do not enter into the ground.

'Bayswater 'Captain. *slang.* [f. *Bayswater*, a residential part of London: cf. *dry-land sailor.*]
1880 *Daily News* 2/4 Several persons used to frequent the club who did not apppear to have any ostensible means of living, but were known as 'Spongers' or 'Bayswater Captains.'

bayt(e, obs. form of BAIT and BEAT *sb.*[2]

baythe, var. BAITHE *v. Obs.* to grant.

bay-window (ˈbeɪˈwɪndəʊ). [f. BAY *sb.*[3] + WINDOW.] 'A window forming a bay or recess in a room, and projecting outwards from the wall, either in a rectangular, polygonal, or semicircular form; often called a *bow*-window.' Parker *Concise Gloss. Archit.*
1428 in Heath *Grocers' Comp.* (1869) 6 In the baye wyndowe of the chambre. **1562** J. HEYWOOD *Prov. & Epigr.* (1867) 204 All Newgate wyndowes bay wyndowes they bee. **1601** SHAKS. *Twel. N.* v. ii. 40 Why it hath bay Windowes transparant as baricadoes. **1741** RICHARDSON *Pamela* (1824) I. 233 The old bay-windows he will have preserved. **1861** DICKENS *Gt. Expect.* iii. 105 Three stories of bow-window (not *bay-window*, which is another thing).
Hence **bay-windowed,** having bay-windows.
1836 T. HOOK *G. Gurney* III. vi. 331 In the bay windowed drawing-room. **1881** MISS BRADDON *Asph.* II. 137 An airy bay-windowed drawing room. **1883** AGNES CRANE in *Leis. H.* 481/2 The 'bay-windowed' city of San Francisco.

'baywood (ˈbeɪwʊd). Mahogany from the Bay of Campeachy and its vicinity.
1869 *Eng. Mech.* 24 Dec. 370/2 Drawers of baywood.

bazaar, bazar (bəˈzɑː(r)). Forms: 6 **bazare, -arro,** 7 **bussar, buzzar(r, bazarr, -are,** 7–8 **basar,** 7–9 **bazar,** 8 **-aard,** 9 **bazaar.** [Ult. a. Pers. *bāzār* market. It has been adopted in Hindustani and Turkish, and seems to have come into English use first from the latter, through Italian.]
1. a. An Oriental market-place or permanent market, usually consisting of ranges of shops or stalls, where all kinds of merchandise are offered for sale.
[*c* **1340** BALDUCCI PEGOLOTTI *Merc. Handbk.* gives *Bazarra* as Genoese word for 'market-place' (Y.).] **1599** HAKLUYT *Voy.* II. I. 214 A faire place or towne, and in it a faire Bazarro for marchants. **1616** PURCHAS *Pilgr.* (1864) 58 A great Basar or Market of Brazen wares. *c* **1650** R. BACON *Mirza* 5 A giddy stream of people.. Powring themselves from all parts to the Buzzarr. **1702** W. J. *Bruyn's Voy. Levant* ix. 33 Several Bazaards or publick Markets. **1815** MOORE *Lalla R.* Introd., The bazaars.. were all covered with the richest tapestry. **1863** M. WHATELY *Ragged Life Egypt* iv. 25 Then we dive into a dark little street.. it is the shoe-bazaar.
b. A market in an Oriental camp.
1803 WELLINGTON in *Disp.* 392 The enemy.. were completely defeated, with the loss of all their bazars. **1882** C. FRANCIS *Med. Temp. Jrnl.* No. 52. 148 Country liquor is too readily obtainable from the bazaar even though the sale of it to soldiers is strictly prohibited.
2. A fancy fair in imitation of the Eastern bazaar; *esp.* a sale of useful and ornamental articles, in behalf of some charitable or religious object. Also used of a shop, or arcade of shops, displaying an assortment of fancy goods (see quot. 1889).
1807 SOUTHEY *Lett. from England* I. vii. 82 My way.. took me through a place called Exeter Change, which is precisely a *Bazar*, a sort of street under cover, or large long room, with a row of shops on either hand, and a thoroughfare between them; the shops being furnished with such articles as might .. remind a passenger of his wants. **1816** *Soho Bazaar.* **1829** SOUTHEY *Sir T. More* II. 216 No Vanity Fair opened in aid of the funds, under the title of a Ladies' *Bazaar*. **1835** *Penny Cycl.* IV. 76/1 Paternoster-row with its books, Monmouth-street with its shoes.. are more properly bazaars than the miscellaneous shops assembled under cover, which are in London designated by the name. **1849** MACAULAY *Hist. Eng.* I. 346 Milliners, toymen, and jewellers came down from London, and opened a bazaar under the trees. **1876** *World* No. 106. 16 A bazaar is the clergyman's recognised ultimate hope when he wants to enlarge his school. **1888** E. BELLAMY *Looking Backward* (1889) v. 42 The great city bazaar crushed its country rivals with branch stores. **1889** *Cent. Dict.* s.v., Marts bearing the name of bazaars, for the sale of miscellaneous articles, chiefly fancy goods, are now to be found in most European and American cities. **1930** *Economist* 3 May 1008/2 A preliminary statement issued by this progressive company of bazaar proprietors reports excellent results for the year ended March 31, 1930.

bazan, -in, bazar, see BASAN, BEZOAR.

†**baze,** *v. Obs.* or *dial.* Also baize. [App. identical with Du. *bazen, verbazen* to astonish, stupefy; but its late appearance in Eng. (or Sc.) is not explained. Cf. also obs. Ger. *basen* (in Grimm) to rave.] To stupefy, frighten, alarm.
1603 *Philotus* cxlviii, As with a Bogill bazed. **1807** J. STAGG *Poems* 39 Guod neebor's ne'er be baz'd, I'll undertake the wark. **1808** *Cumb. Ball.* lxxv. 172 Tom Ridley was aw baized wi' drinkin.

bazil, obs. form of BASIL, and BEZEL *sb.*

bazoo (bəˈzuː). *U.S. slang.* [Origin unknown; cf. Du. *bazuin* trumpet.] = KAZOO; also *transf.*, mouth.
1877 BARTLETT *Dict. Amer.* (ed. 4) 49 *Blowin' his bazoo*, gasconade; braggadocio. Tennessee. **1884** E. W. NYE *Baled Hay* 237 People.. listen to the silvery tinkle of his bazoo. **1888** W. WHITMAN *November Boughs* 407 Among the far-west newspapers, have been, or are,.. *The Bazoo*, of Missouri. **1909** WEBSTER, *Bazoo*, a kind of wind instrument; also, the mouth. **1928** *Collier's* 18 Aug. 34/3 After the orators have been braying away on their bazoos, futilely naming obscure statesmen for Vice President. **1932** J. T. FARRELL *Young Lonigan* (1936) iii. 53 His mother was always blowing off her bazoo about him being her blue-eyed baby. **1948** *Sat. Even. Post* 24 Apr. 173/2 Shut yer big bazoo!

bazooka (bəˈzuːkə). orig. *U.S.* [app. f. prec.]
1. (See quot. 1935.)
1935 *Newsweek* 14 Dec. 29/2 Burns peps up his lengthy yarns with periodic outbursts on his own invention, the bazooka, a trombone-like instrument confected of two gas-pipes and a whisky funnel. **1945** *N. & Q.* 19 May 215/2 Each broadcast Mr. Burns renders a bazooka solo. **1956** R. NETTEL *Seven Centuries Pop. Song* xiv. 229 During the troubles of 1926 a group of miners.. formed themselves into a band. The instruments they used were called in the musical trade 'kazoos' and by the miners themselves 'bazoukas'.
2. A tubular anti-tank rocket-launcher.
1943 *War Illustr.* 15 Oct. 297 (*caption*) American anti-tank rocket thrower.., known as the 'bazooka'. **1944** *Britannica Bk. of Year* 769/2 *Bazooka*, a firearm, consisting of a metal tube slightly over 50 inches long and under 3 inches in diameter. **1945** *N. & Q.* 10 Mar. 106/2 The world's fastest fighting plane.. carries six bazooka tubes.

bazoom (bəˈzuːm). *slang* (orig. *U.S.*). Also bozoom. [Joc. alteration of BOSOM *sb.*] *pl.* A woman's breasts.
1955 J. LATIMER *Sinners & Shrouds* xiv. 123 'Do I have to diagram it?' She straightened up, swaying a little. 'Muffins. Biscuits. Cantaloupes. Bazooms. Knockers. McGuffeys.' **1959** N. MAILER *Advts. for Myself* 161 'Which girl was it now?' he asks a second time. 'Oh, you know, the hysteric.. the one who was parading her bazooms in your face.' **1973** *Observer* 7 Oct. 38/6 A brand new pair of mildly boosted counterfeit bazooms... Piping at the fascinated Whicker over her dummy Bristols. **1978** *Washington Post* 20 Jan. D4/1 She can do it with very small bozooms. Titism has taken over this country. This girl single-handed may make bozooms a thing of the past. **1980** *Brit. Jrnl. Photogr.* 9 May 447/1 Daddy says tits. Daddy says knockers and jugs and bazooms and dingleberries and jujubes. And then he laughs and goes 'wuff! wuff!' **1983** E. LEONARD *LaBrava* xii. 114 Another case of Bio-Energetic Breast Cream.. for South Beach bazooms.

bazouki, see BOUZOUKI.

DOMI MINA
NVS TIO
ILLV MEA